PETERSON'S
GRADUATE PROGRAMS
IN THE
HUMANITIES, ARTS &
SOCIAL SCIENCES

2010

About Peterson's

To succeed on your lifelong educational journey, you will need accurate, dependable, and practical tools and resources. That is why Peterson's is everywhere education happens. Because whenever and however you need education content delivered, you can rely on Peterson's to provide the information, know-how, and guidance to help you reach your goals. Tools to match the right students with the right school. It's here. Personalized resources and expert guidance. It's here. Comprehensive and dependable education content—delivered whenever and however you need it. It's all here.

For more information, contact Peterson's, 2000 Lenox Drive, Lawrenceville, NJ 08648; 800-338-3282; or find us on the World Wide Web at www.petersons.com/about.

© 2010 Peterson's, a Nelnet company

Previous editions © 1966, 1967, 1968, 1969, 1970, 1971, 1972, 1973, 1974, 1975, 1976, 1977, 1978, 1979, 1980, 1981, 1982, 1983, 1984, 1985, 1986, 1987, 1988, 1989, 1990, 1991, 1992, 1993, 1994, 1995, 1996, 1997, 1998, 1999, 2000, 2001, 2002, 2003, 2004, 2005, 2006, 2007, 2008, 2009

Stephen Clemente, President; Bernadette Webster, Director of Publishing; Jill C. Schwartz, Editor; Ken Britschge, Research Project Manager; Courtney Foust, Amy L. Weber, Research Associates; Phyllis Johnson, Programmer; Ray Golaszewski, Manufacturing Manager; Linda M. Williams, Composition Manager; Justin Freid, Janet Garwo, Mimi Kaufman, Karen Mount, Danielle Vreeland, Shannon White, Client Relations Representatives

ISSN 1097-1076
ISBN-13: 978-0-7689-2709-2
ISBN-10: 0-7689-2709-9

Printed in the United States of America

10 9 8 7 6 5 4 3 2 1   12 11 10

Forty-fourth Edition

By producing this book on recycled paper (40% post consumer waste) 145 trees were saved.

CONTENTS

A Note from the Peterson's Editors   vii

THE GRADUATE ADVISER

The Admissions Process   3

Financial Support   5

Accreditation and Accrediting Agencies   9

How to Use These Guides   13

**DIRECTORY OF INSTITUTIONS WITH
PROGRAMS IN HUMANITIES, ARTS &
SOCIAL SCIENCES**

**Directory of Institutions and Their
Offerings**   19

**ACADEMIC AND PROFESSIONAL
PROGRAMS IN ARTS AND
ARCHITECTURE**

Section 1: Applied Arts and Design   91
Program Directories
    Applied Arts and Design—General   92
    Computer Art and Design   96
    Graphic Design   99
    Illustration   102
    Industrial Design   103
    Interior Design   104
    Medical Illustration   107
    Photography   107
    Textile Design   112
Close-Ups   115

Section 2: Architecture   133
Program Directories
    Architectural History   134
    Architecture   134
    Building Science   141
    Environmental Design   142
    Historic Preservation   142
    Landscape Architecture   145
    Lighting Design   148
    Urban Design   148
Close-Ups   151

Section 3: Art and Art History   163
Program Directories
    Art/Fine Arts   164

Art History   181
Arts Administration   189
Art Therapy   191
Decorative Arts   193
Museum Studies   193
Close-Ups   199

**Section 4: Comparative and
Interdisciplinary Arts**   235
Program Directory
    Comparative and Interdisciplinary
    Arts   236

Section 5: Film, Television, and Video   237
Program Directories
    Film, Television, and Video
    Production   238
    Film, Television, and Video Theory
    and Criticism   243

Section 6: Performing Arts   245
Program Directories
    Dance   246
    Music   248
    Theater   271
    Therapies—Dance, Drama, and Music   283
Close-Ups   285

**ACADEMIC AND PROFESSIONAL
PROGRAMS IN THE HUMANITIES**

Section 7: History   297
Program Directories
    History   298
    History of Medicine   321
    History of Science and Technology   321
    Medieval and Renaissance Studies   323
    Public History   325
Close-Ups   329

Section 8: Humanities   335
Program Directories
    Humanities   336
    Liberal Studies   339
Close-Ups   347

Section 9: Language and Literature   353
Program Directories
    Asian Languages   354
    Celtic Languages   356
    Chinese   356

Classics 357
Comparative Literature 361
English 366
French 394
German 403
Italian 409
Japanese 412
Near and Middle Eastern Languages 413
Portuguese 414
Romance Languages 416
Russian 418
Scandinavian Languages 419
Slavic Languages 420
Spanish 422
Close-Ups 435

Section 10: Linguistic Studies 451
Program Directories
Linguistics 452
Translation and Interpretation 460
Close-Up 463

Section 11: Philosophy and Ethics 465
Program Directories
Ethics 466
Philosophy 468
Close-Up 479

Section 12: Religious Studies 481
Program Directories
Missions and Missiology 482
Pastoral Ministry and Counseling 485
Religion 497
Theology 508
Close-Ups 529

Section 13: Writing 535
Program Directories
Technical Writing 536
Writing 537
Close-Ups 551

ACADEMIC AND PROFESSIONAL PROGRAMS IN INTERDISCIPLINARY STUDIES

Section 14: Interdisciplinary Studies 563
Program Directory
Interdisciplinary Studies 564
Close-Ups 573

ACADEMIC AND PROFESSIONAL PROGRAMS IN THE SOCIAL SCIENCES

Section 15: Area and Cultural Studies 579
Program Directories
African-American Studies 580
African Studies 581

American Indian/Native American
Studies 583
American Studies 584
Asian-American Studies 588
Asian Studies 588
Canadian Studies 593
Cultural Studies 594
East European and Russian Studies 596
Ethnic Studies 598
Folklore 598
Gender Studies 599
Hispanic Studies 600
Holocaust Studies 602
Jewish Studies 602
Latin American Studies 604
Near and Middle Eastern Studies 608
Northern Studies 611
Pacific Area/Pacific Rim Studies 611
Western European Studies 611
Women's Studies 613
Close-Ups 619

Section 16: Communication and Media 627
Program Directories
Communication—General 628
Arts Journalism 646
Broadcast Journalism 646
Corporate and Organizational
Communication 646
Health Communication 651
Internet and Interactive Multimedia 652
Journalism 654
Mass Communication 659
Media Studies 664
Publishing 669
Rhetoric 670
Speech and Interpersonal
Communication 674
Technical Communication 678
Close-Ups 681

Section 17: Conflict Resolution and Mediation/Peace Studies 711
Program Directory
Conflict Resolution and Mediation/
Peace Studies 712

Section 18: Criminology and Forensics 717
Program Directories
Criminal Justice and Criminology 718
Forensic Sciences 736
Close-Ups 739

Section 19: Economics 745
Program Directories
   Agricultural Economics and
     Agribusiness 746
   Applied Economics 750
   Economic Development 752
   Economics 755
   International Economics 773
   Mineral Economics 773
Close-Ups 775

Section 20: Family and Consumer Sciences 785
Program Directories
   Family and Consumer
     Sciences-General 786
   Child and Family Studies 789
   Child Development 796
   Clothing and Textiles 798
   Consumer Economics 800
   Gerontology 802

Section 21: Geography 809
Program Directories
   Geographic Information Systems 810
   Geography 813

Section 22: Military and Defense Studies 823
Program Directories
   Military and Defense Studies 824
   National Security 825
Close-Ups 827

**Section 23: Political Science and
International Affairs** 831
Program Directories
   International Affairs 832
   International Development 841
   International Trade Policy 843
   Political Science 844
Close-Ups 861

Section 24: Psychology and Counseling 885
Program Directories
   Psychology—General 887
   Addictions/Substance Abuse
     Counseling 922
   Clinical Psychology 925
   Cognitive Sciences 944
   Counseling Psychology 948
   Developmental Psychology 970
   Experimental Psychology 974
   Forensic Psychology 980
   Genetic Counseling 982
   Health Psychology 982
   Human Development 985

   Industrial and Organizational
     Psychology 992
   Marriage and Family Therapy 1001
   Psychoanalysis and Psychotherapy 1011
   Rehabilitation Counseling 1012
   School Psychology 1017
   Social Psychology 1034
   Sport Psychology 1044
   Thanatology 1046
   Transpersonal and Humanistic
     Psychology 1046
Cross-Discipline Announcement 1047
Close-Ups 1049

**Section 25: Public, Regional, and
Industrial Affairs** 1155
Program Directories
   Disability Studies 1156
   Emergency Management 1156
   Homeland Security 1158
   Industrial and Labor Relations 1160
   Philanthropic Studies 1162
   Public Administration 1163
   Public Affairs 1185
   Public Policy 1188
   Rural Planning and Studies 1197
   Sustainable Development 1198
   Urban and Regional Planning 1200
   Urban Studies 1208
Close-Ups 1211

Section 26: Social Sciences 1245
Program Directory
   Social Sciences 1246
Close-Up 1251

**Section 27: Sociology, Anthropology, and
Archaeology** 1253
Program Directories
   Anthropology 1254
   Applied Social Research 1264
   Archaeology 1265
   Biological Anthropology 1268
   Demography and Population Studies 1268
   Rural Sociology 1269
   Sociology 1270
   Survey Methodology 1286
Close-Ups 1287

APPENDIXES

Institutional Changes Since the
2009 Edition   1299

Abbreviations Used in the Guides   1301

INDEXES

Close-Ups and Announcements   1323

Directories and Subject Areas in
Other Books in This Series   1326

Directories and Subject Areas in
This Book   1333

A Note from the Peterson's Editors

The six volumes of Peterson's *Graduate and Professional Programs*, the only annually updated reference work of its kind, provide wide-ranging information on the graduate and professional programs offered by accredited colleges and universities in the United States, U.S. territories, and Canada and by those institutions outside the United States that are accredited by U.S. accrediting bodies. More than 44,000 individual academic and professional programs at more than 2,200 institutions are listed. Peterson's *Graduate and Professional Programs* have been used for more than forty years by prospective graduate and professional students, placement counselors, faculty advisers, and all others interested in postbaccalaureate education.

Graduate & Professional Programs: An Overview contains information on institutions as a whole, while the other books in the series are devoted to specific academic and professional fields:

Graduate Programs in the Humanities, Arts & Social Sciences
Graduate Programs in the Biological Sciences
Graduate Programs in the Physical Sciences, Mathematics, Agricultural Sciences, the Environment & Natural Resources
Graduate Programs in Engineering & Applied Sciences
Graduate Programs in Business, Education, Health, Information Studies, Law & Social Work

The books may be used individually or as a set. For example, if you have chosen a field of study but do not know what institution you want to attend or if you have a college or university in mind but have not chosen an academic field of study, it is best to begin with the Overview guide.

Graduate & Professional Programs: An Overview presents several directories to help you identify programs of study that might interest you; you can then research those programs further in the other books in the series by using the Directory of Graduate and Professional Programs by Field, which lists 500 fields and gives the names of those institutions that offer graduate degree programs in each.

For geographical or financial reasons, you may be interested in attending a particular institution and will want to know what it has to offer. You should turn to the Directory of Institutions and Their Offerings, which lists the degree programs available at each institution. As in the Directory of Graduate and Professional Programs by Field, the level of degrees offered is also indicated.

All books in the series include advice on graduate education, including topics such as admissions tests, financial aid, and accreditation. **The Graduate Adviser** includes two essays and information about accreditation. The first essay, "The Admissions Process," discusses general admission requirements, admission tests, factors to consider when selecting a graduate school or program, when and how to apply, and how admission decisions are made. Special information for international students and tips for minority students are also included. The second essay, "Financial Support," is an overview of the broad range of support available at the graduate level. Fellowships, scholarships, and grants; assistantships and internships; federal and private loan programs, as well as Federal Work-Study; and the GI bill are detailed. This essay concludes with advice on applying for need-based financial aid. "Accreditation and Accrediting Agencies" gives information on accreditation and its purpose and lists institutional accrediting agencies first and then specialized accrediting agencies relevant to each volume's specific fields of study.

With information on more than 44,000 graduate programs in 500 disciplines, Peterson's *Graduate and Professional Programs* give you all the information you need about the programs that are of interest to you in three formats: **Profiles** (capsule summaries of basic information), **Announcements** and **Displays** (information that an institution or program wants to emphasize, written by administrators), and **Close-Ups** (also written by administrators, with more expansive information than the **Profiles**, emphasizing different aspects of the programs). By using these various formats of program information, coupled with **Appendixes** and **Indexes** covering directories and subject areas for all six books, you will find that these guides provide the most comprehensive, accurate, and up-to-date graduate study information available.

Peterson's publishes a full line of resources with information you need to guide you through the graduate admissions process. Peterson's publications can be found at your local bookstore or library—or visit us on the Web at www.petersons.com.

Colleges and universities will be pleased to know that Peterson's helped you in your selection. Admissions staff members are more than happy to answer questions, address specific problems, and help in any way they can. The editors at Peterson's wish you great success in your graduate program search!

THE GRADUATE ADVISER

The Admissions Process

Generalizations about graduate admissions practices are not always helpful because each institution has its own set of guidelines and procedures. Nevertheless, some broad statements can be made about the admissions process that may help you plan your strategy.

Factors Involved in Selecting a Graduate School or Program

Selecting a graduate school and a specific program of study is a complex matter. Quality of the faculty; program and course offerings; the nature, size, and location of the institution; admission requirements; cost; and the availability of financial assistance are among the many factors that affect one's choice of institution. Other considerations are job placement and achievements of the program's graduates and the institution's resources, such as libraries, laboratories, and computer facilities. If you are to make the best possible choice, you need to learn as much as you can about the schools and programs you are considering before you apply.

The following steps may help you narrow your choices.

- Talk to alumni of the programs or institutions you are considering to get their impressions of how well they were prepared for work in their fields of study.
- Remember that graduate school requirements change, so be sure to get the most up-to-date information possible.
- Talk to department faculty members and the graduate adviser at your undergraduate institution. They often have information about programs of study at other institutions.
- Visit the Web sites of the graduate schools in which you are interested to request a graduate catalog. Contact the department chair in your chosen field of study for additional information about the department and the field.
- Visit as many campuses as possible. Call ahead for an appointment with the graduate adviser in your field of interest and be sure to check out the facilities and talk to students.

General Requirements

Graduate schools and departments have requirements that applicants for admission must meet. Typically, these requirements include undergraduate transcripts (which provide information about undergraduate grade point average and course work applied toward a major), admission test scores, and letters of recommendation. Most graduate programs also ask for an essay or personal statement that describes your personal reasons for seeking graduate study. In some fields, such as art and music, portfolios or auditions may be required in addition to other evidence of talent. Some institutions require that the applicant have an undergraduate degree in the same subject as the intended graduate major.

Most institutions evaluate each applicant on the basis of the applicant's total record, and the weight accorded any given factor varies widely from institution to institution and from program to program.

The Application Process

You should begin the application process at least one year before you expect to begin your graduate study. Find out the application deadline for each institution (many are provided in the **Profile** section of this guide). Go to the institution's Web site and find out if you can apply online. If not, request a paper application form. Fill out this form thoroughly and neatly. Assume that the school needs all the information it is requesting and that the admissions officer will be sensitive to the neatness and overall quality of what you submit. Do not supply more information than the school requires.

The institution may ask at least one question that will require a three- or four-paragraph answer. Compose your response on the assumption that the admissions officer is interested in both what you think and how you express yourself. Keep your statement brief and to the point, but, at the same time, include all pertinent information about your past experiences and your educational goals. Individual statements vary greatly in style and content, which helps admissions officers differentiate among applicants. Many graduate departments give considerable weight to the statement in making their admissions decisions, so be sure to take the time to prepare a thoughtful and concise statement.

If recommendations are a part of the admissions requirements, carefully choose the individuals you ask to write them. It is generally best to ask current or former professors to write the recommendations, provided they are able to attest to your intellectual ability and motivation for doing the work required of a graduate student. It is advisable to provide stamped, preaddressed envelopes to people being asked to submit recommendations on your behalf.

Completed applications, including references, transcripts, and admission test scores, should be received at the institution by the specified date.

Be advised that institutions do not usually make admissions decisions until all materials have been received. Enclose a self-addressed postcard with your application, requesting confirmation of receipt. Allow at least 10 days for the return of the postcard before making further inquiries.

If you plan to apply for financial support, it is imperative that you file your application early.

ADMISSION TESTS

The major testing program used in graduate admissions is the Graduate Record Examinations (GRE) testing program, sponsored by the GRE Board and administered by Educational Testing Service, Princeton, New Jersey.

The Graduate Record Examinations testing program consists of a General Test and eight Subject Tests. The General Test measures critical thinking, verbal reasoning, quantitative reasoning, and analytical writing skills. It is offered as an Internet-based test (iBT) in the United States, Canada, and many other countries.

The typical computer-based General Test consists of one 30-minute verbal reasoning section, one 45-minute quantitative reasoning sections, one 45-minute issue analysis (writing) section, and one 30-minute argument analysis (writing) section. In addition, an unidentified verbal or quantitative section that doesn't count toward a score may be included and an identified research section that is not scored may also be included.

The Subject Tests measure achievement and assume undergraduate majors or extensive background in the following eight disciplines:

- Biochemistry, Cell and Molecular Biology
- Biology
- Chemistry
- Computer Science
- Literature in English
- Mathematics
- Physics
- Psychology

The Subject Tests are available three times per year as paper-based administrations around the world. Testing time is approximately 2 hours and 50 minutes. You can obtain more information about the GRE by visiting the ETS Web site at www.ets.org or consulting the *GRE Information and Registration Bulletin*. The *Bulletin* can be obtained at many undergraduate colleges. You can also download it from the ETS Web site or obtain it by contacting Graduate Record Examinations, Educational Testing Service, PO Box 6000, Princeton, NJ 08541-6000; phone: 1-609-771-7670.

If you expect to apply for admission to a program that requires any of the GRE tests, you should select a test date well in advance of the application deadline. Scores on the computer-based General Test are reported within ten to fifteen days; scores on the paper-based Subject Tests are reported within six weeks.

Another testing program, the Miller Analogies Test (MAT), is administered at more than 500 Controlled Testing Centers, licensed by Harcourt Assessment, Inc., in the United States, Canada, and other countries. The MAT computer-based test is now available. Testing time is 60 minutes. The test consists of 120 partial analogies. You can obtain the *Candidate Information Booklet,* which contains a list of test centers and instructions for taking the test, from http://www.milleranalogies.com or by calling 1-800-622-3231.

Check the specific requirements of the programs to which you are applying.

How Admission Decisions Are Made

The program you apply to is directly involved in the admissions process. Although the final decision is usually made by the graduate dean (or an associate) or the faculty admissions committee, recommendations from faculty members in your intended field are important. At some institutions, an interview is incorporated into the decision process.

A Special Note for International Students

In addition to the steps already described, there are some special considerations for international students who intend to apply for graduate study in the United States. All graduate schools require an indication of competence in English. The purpose of the Test of English as a Foreign Language (TOEFL) is to evaluate the English proficiency of people who are nonnative speakers of English and want to study at colleges and universities where English is the language of instruction. The TOEFL is administered by Educational Testing Service (ETS) under the general direction of a policy board established by the College Board and the Graduate Record Examinations Board.

The TOEFL iBT assesses the four basic language skills: listening, reading, writing, and speaking. It was administered for the first time in September 2005, and ETS continues to introduce the TOEFL iBT in selected cities. The Internet-based test is administered at secure, official test centers. The testing time is approximately 4 hours. Because the TOEFL iBT includes a speaking section, the Test of Spoken English (TSE) is no longer needed.

The TOEFL is also offered in the paper-based format in areas of the world where Internet-based testing is not available. The paper-based TOEFL consists of three sections—listening comprehension, structure and written expression, and reading comprehension. The testing time is approximately 3 hours. The Test of Written English (TWE) is also given. The TWE is a 30-minute essay that measures the examinee's ability to compose in English. Examinees receive a TWE score separate from their TOEFL score. The *Information Bulletin* contains information on local fees and registration procedures.

Additional information and registration materials are available from TOEFL Services, Educational Testing Service, P.O. Box 6151, Princeton, New Jersey 08541-6151. Telephone: 1-609-771-7100. Web site: www.toefl.org.

International students should apply especially early because of the number of steps required to complete the admissions process. Furthermore, many United States graduate schools have a limited number of spaces for international students, and many more students apply than the schools can accommodate.

International students may find financial assistance from institutions very limited. The U.S. government requires international applicants to submit a certification of support, which is a statement attesting to the applicant's financial resources. In addition, international students *must* have health insurance coverage.

Tips for Minority Students

Indicators of a university's values in terms of diversity are found both in its recruitment programs and its resources directed to student success. Important questions: Does the institution vigorously recruit minorities for its graduate programs? Is there funding available to help with the costs associated with visiting the school? Are minorities represented in the institution's brochures or Web site or on their faculty rolls? What campus-based resources or services (including assistance in locating housing or career counseling and placement) are available? Is funding available to members of underrepresented groups?

At the program level, it is particularly important for minority students to investigate the "climate" of a program under consideration. How many minority students are enrolled and how many have graduated? What opportunities are there to work with diverse faculty and mentors whose research interests match yours? How are conflicts resolved or concerns addressed? How interested are faculty in building strong and supportive relations with students? "Climate" concerns should be addressed by posing questions to various individuals, including faculty members, current students, and alumni.

Information is also available through various organizations, such as the Hispanic Association of Colleges & Universities (HACU), and publications such as *Diverse Issues in Higher Education* and *Hispanic Outlook* magazine. There are also books devoted to this topic, such as *The Multicultural Student's Guide to Colleges* by Robert Mitchell.

Financial Support

The range of financial support at the graduate level is very broad. The following descriptions will give you a general idea of what you might expect and what will be expected of you as a financial support recipient.

Fellowships, Scholarships, and Grants

These are usually outright awards of a few hundred to many thousands of dollars with no service to the institution required in return. Fellowships and scholarships are usually awarded on the basis of merit and are highly competitive. Grants are made on the basis of financial need or special talent in a field of study. Many fellowships, scholarships, and grants not only cover tuition, fees, and supplies but also include stipends for living expenses with allowances for dependents. However, the terms of each should be examined because some do not permit recipients to supplement their income with outside work. Fellowships, scholarships, and grants may vary in the number of years for which they are awarded.

In addition to the availability of these funds at the university or program level, many excellent fellowship programs are available at the national level and may be applied for before and during enrollment in a graduate program. A listing of many of these programs can be found at the Council of Graduate Schools' Web site: http://www. cgsnet.org. There is a wealth of information in the "Programs" and "Awards" sections.

Assistantships and Internships

Many graduate students receive financial support through assistantships, particularly involving teaching or research duties. It is important to recognize that such appointments should not be viewed simply as employment relationships but rather should constitute an integral and important part of a student's graduate education. As such, the appointments should be accompanied by strong faculty mentoring and increasingly responsible apprenticeship experiences. The specific nature of these appointments in a given program should be considered in selecting that graduate program.

TEACHING ASSISTANTSHIPS

These usually provide a salary and full or partial tuition remission and may also provide health benefits. Unlike fellowships, scholarships, and grants, which require no service to the institution, teaching assistantships require recipients to provide the institution with a specific amount of undergraduate teaching, ideally related to the student's field of study. Some teaching assistants are limited to grading papers, compiling bibliographies, taking notes, or monitoring laboratories. At some graduate schools, teaching assistants must carry lighter course loads than regular full-time students.

RESEARCH ASSISTANTSHIPS

These are very similar to teaching assistantships in the manner in which financial assistance is provided. The difference is that recipients are given basic research assignments in their disciplines rather than teaching responsibilities. The work required is normally related to the student's field of study; in most instances, the assistantship supports the student's thesis or dissertation research.

ADMINISTRATIVE INTERNSHIPS

These are similar to assistantships in application of financial assistance funds, but the student is given an assignment on a part-time basis, usually as a special assistant with one of the university's administrative offices. The assignment may not necessarily be directly related to the recipient's discipline.

RESIDENCE HALL AND COUNSELING ASSISTANTSHIPS

These assistantships are frequently assigned to graduate students in psychology, counseling, and social work, but they may be offered to students in other disciplines, especially if the student has worked in this capacity during his or her undergraduate years. Duties can vary from being available in a dean's office for a specific number of hours for consultation with undergraduates to living in campus residences and being responsible for both counseling and administrative tasks or advising student activity groups. Residence hall assistantships often include a room and board allowance and, in some cases, tuition assistance and stipends. Contact the Housing and Student Life Office for more information.

Health Insurance

The availability and affordability of health insurance is an important issue and one that should be considered in an applicant's choice of institution and program. While often included with assistantships and fellowships, this is not always the case and, even if provided, the benefits may be limited. It is important to note that the U.S. government requires international students to have health insurance.

The GI Bill

This provides financial assistance for students who are veterans of the United States armed forces. If you are a veteran, contact your local Veterans Administration office to determine your eligibility and to get full details about benefits. There are a number of programs that offer educational benefits to current military enlistees. Some states have tuition assistance programs for members of the National Guard. Contact the VA office at the college for more information.

Federal Work-Study Program (FWS)

Employment is another way some students finance their graduate studies. The federally funded Federal Work-Study Program provides eligible students with employment opportunities, usually in public and private nonprofit organizations. Federal funds pay up to 75 percent of the wages, with the remainder paid by the employing agency. FWS is available to graduate students who demonstrate financial need. Not all schools have these funds, and some only award them to undergraduates. Each school sets its application deadline and work-study earnings limits. Wages vary and are related to the type of work done. You must file the Free Application for Federal Student Aid (FAFSA) to be eligible for this program.

Loans

Many graduate students borrow to finance their graduate programs when other sources of assistance (which do not have to be repaid) prove insufficient. You should always read and understand the terms of any loan program before submitting your application.

FEDERAL LOANS

Federal Stafford Loans. The Federal Stafford Loan Program offers government-sponsored, low-interest loans to students through a private lender such as a bank, credit union, or savings and loan association.

There are two components of the Federal Stafford Loan program. Under the *subsidized* component of the program, the federal government pays the interest on the loan while you are enrolled in graduate school on at least a half-time basis during the six-month grace period after you drop below half-time enrollment, as well as during any period of deferment. Under the *unsubsidized* component of the program, you pay the interest on the loan from the day proceeds are issued. Eligibility for the federal subsidy is based on demonstrated financial need as determined by the financial aid office from the information you provide on the FAFSA. A cosigner is not required, since the loan is not based on creditworthiness.

Although *unsubsidized* Federal Stafford Loans may not be as desirable as *subsidized* Federal Stafford Loans from the student's perspective, they are a useful source of support for those who may not qualify for the subsidized loans or who need additional financial assistance.

Graduate students may borrow up to $20,500 per year through the Stafford Loan Program, up to a cumulative maximum of $138,500, including undergraduate borrowing. This may include up to $8500 in *subsidized* Stafford Loans annually, depending on eligibility, up to a cumulative maximum of $65,500, including undergraduate borrowing. The amount of the loan borrowed through the *unsubsidized* Stafford Program equals the total amount of the loan (as much as $20,500) minus your eligibility for a *subsidized* Stafford Loan (as much as $8500). You may borrow up to the cost of attendance at the school in which you are enrolled or will attend, minus estimated financial assistance from other federal, state, and private sources, up to a maximum of $20,500.

Stafford Loans made on or after July 1, 2006, carry a fixed interest rate of 6.8% both for in-school and in-repayment borrowers.

Two fees may be deducted from the loan proceeds upon disbursement: a Federal Default Fee of 1 percent, which is deposited in an insurance pool to ensure repayment to the lender if the borrower defaults, and a federally mandated 0.5 percent origination fee, for loans made after July 1, 2009, which is used to offset the administrative cost of the Federal Stafford Loan Program. A few lenders may offer reduced-fee or "zero fee" loans. The origination fees are scheduled to be eliminated by July 1, 2010.

Under the *subsidized* Federal Stafford Loan Program, repayment begins six months after your last date of enrollment on at least a half-time basis. Under the *unsubsidized* program, repayment of interest begins within thirty days from disbursement of the loan proceeds, and repayment of the principal begins six months after your last enrollment on at least a half-time basis. Some borrowers may choose to defer interest payments while they are in school. The accrued interest is added to the loan balance when the borrower begins repayment. There are several repayment options.

Federal Direct Loans. Some schools participate in the Department of Education's William D. Ford Direct Loan Program instead of the Federal Stafford Loan Program. The two programs are essentially the same except that with the Direct Loans, schools themselves provide the loans with funds from the federal government. Terms and interest rates are virtually the same except that there are a few additional repayment options with Federal Direct Loans.

Federal Perkins Loans. The Federal Perkins Loan is available to students demonstrating financial need and is administered directly by the school. Not all schools have these funds, and some may award them to undergraduates only. Eligibility is determined from the information you provide on the FAFSA. The school will notify you of your eligibility.

Eligible graduate students may borrow up to $6000 per year, up to a maximum of $40,000, including undergraduate borrowing (even if your previous Perkins Loans have been repaid). The interest rate for Federal Perkins Loans is 5 percent, and no interest accrues while you remain in school at least half-time. There are no guarantee, loan, or disbursement fees. Repayment begins nine months after your last date of enrollment on at least a half-time basis and may extend over a maximum of ten years with no prepayment penalty.

Federal Graduate PLUS Loans. Effective July 1, 2006, graduate and professional students are eligible for Graduate PLUS loans. This program allows students to borrow up to the cost of attendance, less any other aid received. These loans have a fixed interest rate of 8.5% (7.9% for the Federal Direct PLUS), and interest begins to accrue at the time of disbursement. The PLUS loans do involve a credit check; a PLUS borrower may obtain a loan with a cosigner if his or her credit is not good enough. Grad PLUS loans may be deferred while a student in school and for the six months following a drop below half-time enrollment. For more information, contact your FFELP lender or your college financial aid office.

Deferring Your Federal Loan Repayments. If you borrowed under the Federal Stafford Loan Program, Federal Direct Loan Program, or the Federal Perkins Loan Program for previous undergraduate or graduate study, your repayments may be deferred when you return to graduate school, depending on when you borrowed and under which program.

There are other deferment options available if you are temporarily unable to repay your loan. Information about these deferments is provided at your entrance and exit interviews. If you believe you are eligible for a deferment of your loan repayments, you must contact your lender to request a deferment form. The deferment must be filed prior to the time your repayment is due, and it must be refiled when it expires if you remain eligible for deferment at that time.

SUPPLEMENTAL (PRIVATE) LOANS

Many lending institutions offer supplemental loan programs and other financing plans, such as the ones described here, to students seeking additional assistance in meeting their education expenses. Some loan programs target all types of graduate students; others are designed specifically for business, law, or medical students. In addition, you can use private loans not specifically designed for education to help finance your graduate degree.

If you are considering borrowing through a supplemental or private loan program, you should carefully consider the terms and be sure to "read the fine print." Check with the program sponsor for the most current terms that will be applicable to the amounts you intend to borrow for graduate study. Most supplemental loan programs for graduate study offer unsubsidized, credit-based loans. In general, a credit-ready borrower is one who has a satisfactory credit history or no credit history at all. A creditworthy borrower generally must pass a credit test to be eligible to borrow or act as a cosigner for the loan funds.

Many supplemental loan programs have minimum and maximum annual loan limits. Some offer amounts equal to the cost of attendance minus any other aid you will receive for graduate study. If you are planning to borrow for several years of graduate study, consider whether there is a cumulative or aggregate limit on the amount you may borrow. Often this cumulative or aggregate limit will include any amounts you borrowed and have not repaid for undergraduate or previous graduate study.

The combination of the annual interest rate, loan fees, and the repayment terms you choose will determine how much you will repay over time. Compare these features in combination before you decide which loan program to use. Some loans offer interest rates that are adjusted monthly, some quarterly, some annually. Some offer interest rates that are lower during the in-school, grace, and deferment periods and then increase when you begin repayment. Some programs include a loan "origination" fee, which is usually deducted from the principal amount you receive when the loan is disbursed and must be repaid along with the interest and other principal when you graduate, withdraw from school, or drop below half-time study. Sometimes the loan fees are reduced if you borrow with a qualified cosigner. Some programs allow you to defer interest and/or principal payments while you are enrolled in graduate school. Many programs allow you to capitalize your interest payments; the interest due on your loan is added to the outstanding balance of your loan, so you don't have to repay immediately, but this increases the amount you owe. Other programs allow you to pay the interest as you go, which reduces the amount you later have to repay.

Some examples of supplemental programs follow. The private loan market is very competitive, and your financial aid office can help you evaluate these and other programs.

CitiAssist® Graduate Loans. Offered by Citibank, these loans help graduate students fill the gap between the financial aid they receive and the money they need for school. Note that there is a one-time minimum loan amount of $1,000. No minimum loan amount is required on subsequent CitiAssist loans. Visit www.studentloan.com for more loan information from Citibank.

Chase Select℠ Private Student Loans. Offered by Chase, these loans are subject to credit approval, receipt of a completed and signed Application/Promissory Note, verification of application information including enrollment at a participating school, and verification that the requested loan amount does not exceed the student's actual cost of attendance. For more information, visit www.chasestudentloans.com.

Graduate Access Loans. Sponsored by the Access Group, this is for graduate students enrolled at least half-time. The Web site is www.accessgroup.com.

Smart Option Student Loans. Sponsored by Sallie Mae, this loan program is for graduate students who are enrolled at least half-time. Visit www.salliemae.com for more information.

Applying for Need-Based Financial Aid

Schools that award federal and institutional financial assistance based on need will require you to complete the FAFSA and, in some cases, an institutional financial aid application.

If you are applying for federal student assistance, you **must** complete the FAFSA. A service of the U.S. Department of Education, it is free to all applicants. Most applicants apply online at www.fafsa. ed.gov. Paper applications are available at the financial aid office of your local college.

After your FAFSA information has been processed, you will receive a Student Aid Report (SAR). If you provided an e-mail address on the FAFSA, this will be sent to you electronically; otherwise, it will be mailed to your home address.

Follow the instructions on the SAR if you need to correct information reported on your original application. If your situation changes after you file your FAFSA, contact your financial aid officer to discuss amending your information. You can also appeal your financial aid award if you have extenuating circumstances.

If you would like more information on federal student financial aid, visit the FAFSA Web site or download the most recent version of *Funding Education Beyond High School: The Guide to Federal Student Aid* at http://studentaid.ed.gov/students/publications/student_guide/index.html. This guide is also available in Spanish.

The U.S. Department of Education also has a toll-free number for questions concerning federal student aid programs. The number is 1-800-4-FED AID (1-800-433-3243). If you are hearing impaired, call toll-free, 1-800-730-8913.

Summary

Remember that these are generalized statements about financial assistance at the graduate level. Because each institution allots its aid differently, you should communicate directly with the school and the specific department of interest to you. It is not unusual, for example, to find that an endowment vested within a specific department supports one or more fellowships. You may fit its requirements and specifications precisely.

Accreditation and Accrediting Agencies

Colleges and universities in the United States, and their individual academic and professional programs, are accredited by nongovernmental agencies concerned with monitoring the quality of education in this country. Agencies with both regional and national jurisdictions grant accreditation to institutions as a whole, while specialized bodies acting on a nationwide basis—often national professional associations—grant accreditation to departments and programs in specific fields.

Institutional and specialized accrediting agencies share the same basic concerns: the purpose an academic unit—whether university or program—has set for itself and how well it fulfills that purpose, the adequacy of its financial and other resources, the quality of its academic offerings, and the level of services it provides. Agencies that grant institutional accreditation take a broader view, of course, and examine university-wide or college-wide services with which a specialized agency may not concern itself.

Both types of agencies follow the same general procedures when considering an application for accreditation. The academic unit prepares a self-evaluation, focusing on the concerns mentioned above and usually including an assessment of both its strengths and weaknesses; a team of representatives of the accrediting body reviews this evaluation, visits the campus, and makes its own report; and finally, the accrediting body makes a decision on the application. Often, even when accreditation is granted, the agency makes a recommendation regarding how the institution or program can improve. All institutions and programs are also reviewed every few years to determine whether they continue to meet established standards; if they do not, they may lose their accreditation.

Accrediting agencies themselves are reviewed and evaluated periodically by the U.S. Department of Education and the Council for Higher Education Accreditation (CHEA). Recognized agencies adhere to certain standards and practices, and their authority in matters of accreditation is widely accepted in the educational community.

This does not mean, however, that accreditation is a simple matter, either for schools wishing to become accredited or for students deciding where to apply. Indeed, in certain fields the very meaning and methods of accreditation are the subject of a good deal of debate. For their part, those applying to graduate school should be aware of the safeguards provided by regional accreditation, especially in terms of degree acceptance and institutional longevity. Beyond this, applicants should understand the role that specialized accreditation plays in their field, as this varies considerably from one discipline to another. In certain professional fields, it is necessary to have graduated from a program that is accredited in order to be eligible for a license to practice, and in some fields the federal government also makes this a hiring requirement. In other disciplines, however, accreditation is not as essential, and there can be excellent programs that are not accredited. In fact, some programs choose not to seek accreditation, although most do.

Institutions and programs that present themselves for accreditation are sometimes granted the status of candidate for accreditation, or what is known as "preaccreditation." This may happen, for example, when an academic unit is too new to have met all the requirements for accreditation. Such status signifies initial recognition and indicates that the school or program in question is working to fulfill all requirements; it does not, however, guarantee that accreditation will be granted.

Institutional Accrediting Agencies—Regional

MIDDLE STATES ASSOCIATION OF COLLEGES AND SCHOOLS
Accredits institutions in Delaware, District of Columbia, Maryland, New Jersey, New York, Pennsylvania, Puerto Rico, and the Virgin Islands.
Jean Avnet Morse, President
Middle States Commission on Higher Education
3624 Market Street, Second Floor Annex
Philadelphia, Pennsylvania 19104
Phone: 267-284-5000
Fax: 215-662-5501
E-mail: info@msche.org
Web: www.msche.org

NEW ENGLAND ASSOCIATION OF SCHOOLS AND COLLEGES
Accredits institutions in Connecticut, Maine, Massachusetts, New Hampshire, Rhode Island, and Vermont.
Barbara E. Brittingham, Director
Commission on Institutions of Higher Education
209 Burlington Road, Suite 201
Bedford, Massachusetts 01730-1433
Phone: 781-271-0022
Fax: 781-271-0950
E-mail: CIHE@neasc.org
Web: www.neasc.org

NORTH CENTRAL ASSOCIATION OF COLLEGES AND SCHOOLS
Accredits institutions in Arizona, Arkansas, Colorado, Illinois, Indiana, Iowa, Kansas, Michigan, Minnesota, Missouri, Nebraska, New Mexico, North Dakota, Ohio, Oklahoma, South Dakota, West Virginia, Wisconsin, and Wyoming.
Sylvia Manning, President
The Higher Learning Commission
30 North LaSalle Street, Suite 2400
Chicago, Illinois 60602
Phone: 312-263-0456
Fax: 312-263-7462
E-mail: smanning@hlcommission.org
Web: www.ncahigherlearningcommission.org

NORTHWEST COMMISSION ON COLLEGES AND UNIVERSITIES
Accredits institutions in Alaska, Idaho, Montana, Nevada, Oregon, Utah, and Washington.
Sandra E. Elman, President
8060 165th Avenue, NE, Suite 100
Redmond, Washington 98052
Phone: 425-558-4224
Fax: 425-376-0596
E-mail: selman@nwccu.org
Web: www.nwccu.org

SOUTHERN ASSOCIATION OF COLLEGES AND SCHOOLS
Accredits institutions in Alabama, Florida, Georgia, Kentucky, Louisiana, Mississippi, North Carolina, South Carolina, Tennessee, Texas, and Virginia.
Belle S. Wheelan, President
Commission on Colleges
1866 Southern Lane
Decatur, Georgia 30033-4097
Phone: 404-679-4512
Fax: 404-679-4528
E-mail: bwheelan@sacscoc.org
Web: www.sacsoc.org

WESTERN ASSOCIATION OF SCHOOLS AND COLLEGES
Accredits institutions in California, Guam, and Hawaii.
Ralph A. Wolff, President and Executive Director
Accrediting Commission for Senior Colleges and Universities
985 Atlantic Avenue, Suite 100
Alameda, California 94501
Phone: 510-748-9001
Fax: 510-748-9797
E-mail: wascsr@wascsenior.org
Web: www.wascweb.org

Institutional Accrediting Agencies—Other

ACCREDITING COUNCIL FOR INDEPENDENT COLLEGES AND SCHOOLS
Albert C. Gray, Ph.D., Executive Director and CEO
750 First Street, NE, Suite 980
Washington, DC 20002-4242
Phone: 202-336-6780
Fax: 202-842-2593
E-mail: info@acics.org
Web: www.acics.org

DISTANCE EDUCATION AND TRAINING COUNCIL (DETC)
Accrediting Commission
Michael P. Lambert, Executive Director
1601 18th Street, NW, Suite 2
Washington, DC 20009
Phone: 202-234-5100
Fax: 202-332-1386
E-mail: detc@detc.org
Web: www.detc.org

Specialized Accrediting Agencies

[Only *Graduate & Professional Programs: An Overview* of *Peterson's Graduate and Professional Programs* Series includes the complete list of specialized accrediting groups recognized by the U.S. Department of Education and the Council on Higher Education Accreditation (CHEA). The list in this book is abridged.]

ART AND DESIGN
Samuel Hope, Executive Director
Karen P. Moynahan, Associate Director
National Association of Schools of Art and Design (NASAD)
Commission on Accreditation
11250 Roger Bacon Drive, Suite 21
Reston, Virginia 20190-5243
Phone: 703-437-0700
Fax: 703-437-6312
E-mail: info@arts-accredit.org
Web: www.arts-accredit.org

CLINICAL PASTORAL EDUCATION
Teresa E. Snorton, Executive Director
Accreditation Commission
Association for Clinical Pastoral Education, Inc.
1549 Claremont Road, Suite 103
Decatur, Georgia 30033-4611
Phone: 404-320-1472
Fax: 404-320-0849
E-mail: acpe@acpe.edu
Web: www.acpe.edu

DANCE
Samuel Hope, Executive Director
Karen P. Moynahan, Associate Director
National Association of Schools of Dance (NASD)
Commission on Accreditation
11250 Roger Bacon Drive, Suite 21
Reston, Virginia 20190-5248
Phone: 703-437-0700
Fax: 703-437-6312
E-mail: info@arts-accredit.org
Web: www.arts-accredit.org

DIETETICS
Ulric K. Chung, Ph.D., Senior Director
American Dietetic Association
Commission on Accreditation for Dietetics Education (CADE-ADA)
120 South Riverside Plaza, Suite 2000
Chicago, Illinois 60606-6995
Phone: 800-877-1600
Fax: 312-899-4817
E-mail: cade@eatright.org
Web: www.eatright.org/cade

INTERIOR DESIGN
Holly Mattson, Executive Director
Council for Interior Design Accreditation
206 Grandview Avenue, Suite 350
Grand Rapids, Michigan 49503
Phone: 616-458-0400
Fax: 616-458-0460
E-mail: info@accredit-id.org
Web: www.accredit-id.org

JOURNALISM AND MASS COMMUNICATIONS
Susanne Shaw, Executive Director
Accrediting Council on Education in Journalism and Mass Communications (ACEJMC)
School of Journalism
Stauffer-Flint Hall
University of Kansas
1435 Jayhawk Boulevard
Lawrence, Kansas 66045-7575
Phone: 785-864-3986
Fax: 785-864-5225
E-mail: sshaw@ku.edu
Web: www2.ku.edu/~acejmc

LANDSCAPE ARCHITECTURE
Ronald C. Leighton, Executive Director
Landscape Architectural Accreditation Board
American Society of Landscape Architects
636 Eye Street, NW
Washington, DC 20001-3736
Phone: 202-898-2444
Fax: 202-898-1185
E-mail: info@asla.org
Web: www.asla.org

MARRIAGE AND FAMILY THERAPY
Jeff S. Harmon, Director of Accreditation Services
Commission on Accreditation for Marriage and Family Therapy Education
American Association for Marriage and Family Therapy
112 South Alfred Street
Alexandria, Virginia 22314-3061
Phone: 703-838-9808
Fax: 703-838-9805
E-mail: coamfle@aamft.org
Web: www.aamft.org

MEDICAL ILLUSTRATION
Commission on Accreditation of Allied Health Education Programs (CAAHEP)
Kathleen Megivern, Executive Director
1361 Park Street
Clearwater, Florida 33756
Phone: 727-210-2350
Fax: 727-210-2354
E-mail: mail@caahep.org
Web: www.caahep.org

MUSIC
Samuel Hope, Executive Director
Karen P. Moynahan, Associate Director
National Association of Schools of Music (NASM)
Commission on Accreditation
11250 Roger Bacon Drive, Suite 21
Reston, Virginia 20190-5248
Phone: 703-437-0700
Fax: 703-437-6312
E-mail: info@arts-accredit.org
Web: www.arts-accredit.org

PLANNING
Shonagh Merits, Executive Director
American Institute of Certified Planners/Association of Collegiate Schools of Planning/American Planning Association
Planning Accreditation Board (PAB)

122 South Michigan Avenue, Suite 1600
Chicago, Illinois 60603
Phone: 312-334-1271
Fax: 312-334-1273
E-mail: pab@planning.org
Web: www.planningaccreditationboard.org

PSYCHOLOGY AND COUNSELING
Susan Zlotlow, Executive Director
Office of Program Consultation and Accreditation
American Psychological Association
750 First Street, NE
Washington, DC 20002-4242
Phone: 202-336-5979
Fax: 202-336-5978
E-mail: apaaccred@apa.org
Web: www.apa.org/ed/accreditation

Carol L. Bobby, Executive Director
Council for Accreditation of Counseling and Related Educational
Programs (CACREP)
1001 North Fairfax Street, Suite 510
Alexandria, Virginia 22314
Phone: 703-535-5990
Fax: 703-739-6209
E-mail: cacrep@cacrep.org
Web: www.cacrep.org

PUBLIC AFFAIRS AND ADMINISTRATION
Crystal Calarusse, Executive Director
Commission on Peer Review and Accreditation
National Association of Schools of Public Affairs and Administration
1120 G Street, NW, Suite 730
Washington, DC 20005
Phone: 202-628-8965
Fax: 202-626-4978
E-mail: calarusse@naspaa.org
Web: www.naspaa.org

SPEECH-LANGUAGE PATHOLOGY AND AUDIOLOGY
Patrima L. Tice, Director of Accreditation
American Speech-Language-Hearing Association
2200 Research Boulevard
Rockville, Maryland 20850-3289
Phone: 301-897-5700
Fax: 301-296-8750
E-mail: ptice@asha.org
Web: www.asha.org/about/credentialing/accreditation

TECHNOLOGY
Elise Scanlon, Executive Director
Accrediting Commission of Career Schools and Colleges of
Technology
2101 Wilson Boulevard, Suite 302
Arlington, Virginia 22201
Phone: 703-247-4212
Fax: 703-247-4533
E-mail: escanlon@accsct.org
Web: www.accsct.org

THEATER
Samuel Hope, Executive Director
Karen P. Moynahan, Associate Director
National Association of Schools of Theatre
Commission on Accreditation
11250 Roger Bacon Drive, Suite 21
Reston, Virginia 20190
Phone: 703-437-0700
Fax: 703-437-6312
E-mail: info@arts-accredit.org
Web: www.arts-accredit.org

THEOLOGY
Bernard Fryshman, Executive Vice President
Association of Advanced Rabbinical and Talmudic Schools (AARTS)
Accreditation Commission
11 Broadway, Suite 405
New York, New York 10004
Phone: 212-363-1991
Fax: 212-533-5335

Daniel O. Aleshire, Executive Director
Association of Theological Schools in the United States and Canada
(ATS)
Commission on Accrediting
10 Summit Park Drive
Pittsburgh, Pennsylvania 15275-1103
Phone: 412-788-6505
Fax: 412-788-6510
E-mail: ats@ats.edu
Web: www.ats.edu

Russell Guy Fitzgerald, Executive Director
Transnational Association of Christian Colleges and Schools
(TRACS)
Accreditation Commission
P.O. Box 328
Forest, Virginia 24551
Phone: 434-525-9539
Fax: 434-525-9538
E-mail: info@tracs.org
Web: www.tracs.org S:
ditorial≥radProgs-Humanitiesâccredit-Grad2.txt

How to Use These Guides

As you identify the particular programs and institutions that interest you, you can use both the *Graduate & Professional Programs: An Overview* volume and the specialized volumes in the series:

- *Graduate Programs in the Physical Sciences, Mathematics, Agricultural Sciences, the Environment & Natural Resources*
- *Graduate Programs in Engineering & Applied Sciences*
- *Graduate Programs the Humanities, Arts & Social Sciences*
- *Graduate Programs in the Biological Sciences*
- *Graduate Programs in Business, Education, Health, Information Studies, Law & Social Work*

to obtain detailed information. Each of the specialized volumes in the series is divided into sections that contain one or more directories devoted to programs in a particular field. If you do not find a directory devoted to your field of interest in a specific volume, consult "Directories and Subject Areas" (located at the end of each volume). After you have identified the correct volume, consult the "Directories and Subject Areas in This Book" index, which shows (as does the more general directory) what directories cover subjects not specifically named in a directory or section title.

Each of the specialized volumes in the series has a number of general directories. These directories have entries for the largest unit at an institution granting graduate degrees in that field. For example, the general Engineering and Applied Sciences directory in the *Graduate Programs in Engineering & Applied Sciences* volume consists of Profiles for colleges, schools, and departments of engineering and applied sciences.

General directories are followed by other directories, or sections, that give more detailed information about programs in particular areas of the general field that has been covered. The general Engineering and Applied Sciences directory, in the previous example, is followed by nineteen sections with directories in specific areas of engineering, such as Chemical Engineering, Industrial/Management Engineering, and Mechanical Engineering.

Because of the broad nature of many fields, any system of organization is bound to involve a certain amount of overlap. Environmental studies, for example, is a field whose various aspects are studied in several types of departments and schools. Readers interested in such studies will find information on relevant programs in the *Graduate Programs in the Biological Sciences* volume under Ecology and Environmental Biology; in the *Graduate Programs in the Physical Sciences, Mathematics, Agricultural Sciences, the Environment & Natural Resources* volume under Environmental Management and Policy and Natural Resources; in the *Graduate Programs in Engineering & Applied Sciences* volume under Energy Management and Policy and Environmental Engineering; and in the *Graduate Programs in Business, Education, Health, Information Studies, Law & Social Work* volume under Environmental and Occupational Health. To help you find all of the programs of interest to you, the introduction to each section within the specialized volumes includes, if applicable, a paragraph suggesting other sections and directories with information on related areas of study.

Directory of Institutions with Programs in the Humanities, Arts & Social Sciences

This directory lists institutions in alphabetical order and includes beneath each name the academic fields in which each institution offers graduate programs. The degree level in each field is also indicated, provided that the institution has supplied that information in response to Peterson's Annual Survey of Graduate and Professional Institutions. An M indicates that a master's degree program is offered; a D indicates that a doctoral degree program is offered; a P indicates that the first professional degree is offered; an O signifies that other advanced degrees (e.g., certificates or specialist degrees) are offered; and an *

(asterisk) indicates that a **Close-Up** and/or **Announcement** or **Display** is located in this volume. See the index, "Close-Ups and Announcements," for the specific page number.

Profiles of Academic and Professional Programs in the Specialized Volumes

Each section of **Profiles** has a table of contents that lists the Program Directories, **Announcements** or **Displays**, and **Close-Ups**. Program Directories consist of the **Profiles** of programs in the relevant fields, with **Announcements** following if programs have chosen to include them. **Cross-Discipline Announcements**, if any programs have chosen to submit such entries, and **Close-Ups**, which are more individualized statements, again if programs have chosen to submit them, are also listed.

The **Profiles** found in the 500 directories in the specialized volumes provide basic data about the graduate units in capsule form for quick reference. To make these directories as useful as possible, **Profiles** are generally listed for an institution's smallest academic unit within a subject area. In other words, if an institution has a College of Liberal Arts that administers many related programs, the **Profile** for the individual program (e.g., Program in History), not the entire College, appears in the directory.

There are some programs that do not fit into any current directory and are not given individual **Profiles**. The directory structure is reviewed annually in order to keep this number to a minimum and to accommodate major trends in graduate education.

The following outline describes the **Profile** information found in the guides and explains how best to use that information. Any item that does not apply to or was not provided by a graduate unit is omitted from its listing. The format of the **Profiles** is constant, making it easy to compare one institution with another and one program with another.

Identifying Information. The institution's name, in boldface type, is followed by a complete listing of the administrative structure for that field of study. (For example, University of Akron, Buchtel College of Arts and Sciences, Department of Theoretical and Applied Mathematics, Program in Mathematics.) The last unit listed is the one to which all information in the **Profile** pertains. The institution's city, state, and zip code follow.

Offerings. Each field of study offered by the unit is listed with all postbaccalaureate degrees awarded. Degrees that are not preceded by a specific concentration are awarded in the general field listed in the unit name. Frequently, fields of study are broken down into subspecializations, and those appear following the degrees awarded; for example, "Offerings in secondary education (M.Ed.), including English education, mathematics education, science education." Students enrolled in the M.Ed. program would be able to specialize in any of the three fields mentioned.

Professional Accreditation. Some **Profiles** indicate whether a program is professionally accredited. Because it is possible for a program to receive or lose professional accreditation at any time, students entering fields in which accreditation is important to a career should verify the status of programs by contacting either the chairperson or the appropriate accrediting association.

Jointly Offered Degrees. Explanatory statements concerning programs that are offered in cooperation with other institutions are included in the list of degrees offered. This occurs most commonly on a regional basis (for example, two state universities offering a cooperative Ph.D. in special education) or where the specialized nature of the institutions encourages joint efforts (a J.D./M.B.A. offered by a law school at an institution with no formal business programs and an institution with a business school but lacking a law school). Only programs that are truly cooperative are listed; those involving only limited course work at another institution are not. Interested students should contact the heads of such units for further information.

Part-Time and Evening/Weekend Programs. When information regarding the availability of part-time or evening/weekend study appears in the **Profile**, it means that students are able to earn a degree exclusively through such study.

Postbaccalaureate Distance Learning Degrees. A postbaccalaureate distance learning degree program signifies that course requirements can be fulfilled with minimal or no on-campus study.

Faculty. Figures on the number of faculty members actively involved with graduate students through teaching or research are separated into full-and part-time as well as men and women whenever the information has been supplied.

Students. Figures for the number of students enrolled in graduate and professional programs pertain to the semester of highest enrollment from the 2008–09 academic year. These figures are broken down into full-and part-time and men and women whenever the data have been supplied. Information on the number of matriculated students enrolled in the unit who are members of a minority group or are international students appears here. The average age of the matriculated students is followed by the number of applicants, the percentage accepted, and the number enrolled for fall 2008.

Degrees Awarded. The number of degrees awarded in the calendar year is listed. Many doctoral programs offer a terminal master's degree if students leave the program after completing only part of the requirements for a doctoral degree; that is indicated here. All degrees are classified into one of four types: master's, doctoral, first professional, and other advanced degrees. A unit may award one or several degrees at a given level; however, the data are only collected by type and may therefore represent several different degree programs.

Degree Requirements. The information in this section is also broken down by type of degree, and all information for a degree level pertains to all degrees of that type unless otherwise specified. Degree requirements are collected in a simplified form to provide some very basic information on the nature of the program and on foreign language, thesis or dissertation, comprehensive exam, and registration requirements. Many units also provide a short list of additional requirements, such as fieldwork or an internship. For complete information on graduation requirements, contact the graduate school or program directly.

Entrance Requirements. Entrance requirements are broken down into the four degree levels of master's, doctoral, first professional, and other advanced degrees. Within each level, information may be provided in two basic categories: entrance exams and other requirements. The entrance exams are identified by the standard acronyms used by the testing agencies, unless they are not well known. Other entrance requirements are quite varied, but they often contain an undergraduate or graduate grade point average (GPA). Unless otherwise stated, the GPA is calculated on a 4.0 scale and is listed as a minimum required for admission. Additional exam requirements/recommendations for international students may be listed here. Application deadlines for domestic and international students, the application fee, and whether electronic applications are accepted may be listed here. Note that the deadline should be used for reference only; these dates are subject to change, and students interested in applying should always contact the graduate unit directly about application procedures and deadlines.

Expenses. The typical cost of study for the 2008–09 academic year is given in two basic categories: tuition and fees. Cost of study may be quite complex at a graduate institution. There are often sliding scales for part-time study, a different cost for first-year students, and other variables that make it impossible to completely cover the cost of study for each graduate program. To provide the most usable information, figures are given for full-time study for a full year where available and for part-time study in terms of a per-unit rate (per credit, per semester hour, etc.). Occasionally, variances may be noted in tuition and fees for reasons such as the type of program, whether courses are taken during the day or evening, whether courses are at the master's or doctoral level, or other institution-specific reasons. Expenses are usually subject to change; for exact costs at any given time, contact your chosen schools and programs directly. Keep in mind that the tuition of Canadian institutions is usually given in Canadian dollars.

Financial Support. This section contains data on the number of awards administered by the institution and given to graduate students during the 2008–09 academic year. The first figure given represents the total number of students receiving financial support enrolled in that unit. If the unit has provided information on graduate appointments, these are broken down into three major categories: fellowships give money to graduate students to cover the cost of study and living expenses and are not based on a work obligation or research commitment, research assistantships provide stipends to graduate students for assistance in a formal research project with a faculty member, and teaching assistantships provide stipends to graduate students for teaching or for assisting faculty members in teaching undergraduate classes. Within each category, figures are given for the total number of awards, the average yearly amount per award, and whether full or partial tuition reimbursements are awarded. In addition to graduate appointments, the availability of several other financial aid sources is covered in this section. Tuition waivers are routinely part of a graduate appointment, but units sometimes waive part or all of a student's tuition even if a graduate appointment is not available. Federal Work-Study is made available to students who demonstrate need and meet the federal guidelines; this form of aid normally includes 10 or more hours of work per week in an office of the institution. Institutionally sponsored loans are low-interest loans available to graduate students to cover both educational and living expenses. Career-related internships or fieldwork offer money to students who are participating in a formal off-campus research project or practicum. Grants, scholarships, traineeships, unspecified assistantships, and other awards may also be noted. The availability of financial support to part-time students is also indicated here.

Some programs list the financial aid application deadline and the forms that need to be completed for students to be eligible for financial awards. There are two forms: FAFSA, the Free Application for Federal Student Aid, which is required for federal aid, and the CSS PROFILE®.

Faculty Research. Each unit has the opportunity to list several keyword phrases describing the current research involving faculty members and graduate students. Space limitations prevent the unit from listing complete information on all research programs. The total expenditure for funded research from the previous academic year may also be included.

Unit Head and Application Contact. The head of the graduate program for each unit is listed with academic title and telephone and fax numbers and e-mail address if available. In addition to the unit head, many graduate programs list a separate contact for application and admission information, which follows the listing for the unit head. If no unit head or application contact is given, you should contact the overall institution for information on graduate admissions.

Announcements, Displays, and Close-Ups

The **Announcements** or **Displays** and **Close-Ups** are supplementary insertions submitted by deans, chairs, and other administrators who wish to offer an additional, more individualized statement to readers. A number of graduate school and program administrators have attached **Announcements** to the end of their **Profile** listings or a **Display** ad near the **Profile** listing. In them you will find information that an institution or program wants to emphasize. The **Close-Ups** are by their very nature more expansive and flexible than the **Profiles**, and the administrators who have written them may emphasize different aspects of their programs. All of the **Close-Ups** are organized in the same way (with the exception of a few that describe research and training opportunities instead of degree programs), and in each one you will find information on the same basic topics, such as programs of study, research facilities, tuition and fees, financial aid, and application procedures. If an institution or program has submitted a **Close-Up**, a boldface cross-reference appears below its **Profile**. As with the **Announcements** and **Displays**, all of the **Close-Ups** in the guides have been submitted by choice; the absence of an **Announcement, Display,** or **Close-Up** does not reflect any type of editorial judgment on the part of Peterson's, and their presence in the guides should not be taken as an indication of status, quality, or approval. Statements regarding a university's objectives and accomplishments are a reflection of its own beliefs and are not the opinions of the Peterson's editors.

Cross-Discipline Announcements

In addition to the regular directories that present **Profiles** of programs in each field of study, many sections in the specialized volumes contain special notices under the heading **Cross-Discipline Announcements**. Appearing at the end of many **Profile** sections, these **Cross-Discipline Announcements** inform you about programs that you may find of interest described in a different section. A biochemistry department, for example, may place a notice under **Cross-Discipline Announcements** in the Chemistry section of the *Graduate Programs in the Physical Sciences, Mathematics, Agricultural Sciences, the Environment & Natural Resources* volume to alert chemistry students to that course of study. **Cross-Discipline Announcements**, also written by administrators to highlight their programs, will be helpful to you not only in finding out about programs in fields related to your own but also in locating departments that are actively recruiting students with a specific undergraduate major.

Appendixes

This section contains two appendixes. The first, "Institutional Changes Since the 2009 Edition," lists institutions that have closed, moved, merged, or changed their name or status since the last edition of the guides. The second, "Abbreviations Used in the Guides," gives abbreviations of degree names, along with what those abbreviations stand for. These appendixes are identical in all six volumes of *Peterson's Graduate and Professional Programs*.

Indexes

There are three indexes presented here. The first index, "Close-Ups and Announcements," gives page references for all programs that have chosen to place **Close-Ups, Announcements,** and **Displays** in this volume. It is arranged alphabetically by institution; within institutions, the arrangement is alphabetical by subject area. It is not an index to all programs in the book's directories of **Profiles**; readers must refer to the directories themselves for **Profile** information on programs that have not submitted the additional, more individualized statements. The second index, "Directories and Subject Areas in Other Books in This Series", gives book references for the directories in the specialized volumes and also includes cross-references for subject area names not used in the directory structure, for example, "Computing Technology (see Computer Science)." The third index, "Directories and Subject Areas in This Book," gives page references for the directories in this volume and cross-references for subject area names not used in this volume's directory structure.

Data Collection Procedures

The information published in the directories and **Profiles** of all the books is collected through Peterson's Annual Survey of Graduate and Professional Institutions. The survey is sent each spring to more than 2,200 institutions offering postbaccalaureate degree programs, including accredited institutions in the United States, U.S. territories, and Canada and those institutions outside the United States that are accredited by U.S. accrediting bodies. Deans and other administrators complete these surveys, providing information on programs in the 500 academic and professional fields covered in the guides as well as overall institutional information. While every effort has been made to ensure the accuracy and completeness of the data, information is sometimes unavailable or changes occur after publication deadlines. All usable information received in time for publication has been included. The omission of any particular item from a directory or **Profile** signifies either that the item is not applicable to the institution or program or that information was not available. **Profiles** of programs scheduled to begin during the 2009–10 academic year cannot, obviously, include statistics on enrollment or, in many cases, the number of faculty members. If no usable data were submitted by an institution, its name, address, and program name appear in order to indicate the availability of graduate work.

Criteria for Inclusion in This Guide

To be included in this guide, an institution must have full accreditation or be a candidate for accreditation (preaccreditation) status by an institutional or specialized accrediting body recognized by the U.S. Department of Education or the Council for Higher Education Accreditation (CHEA). Institutional accrediting bodies, which review each institution as a whole, include the six regional associations of schools and colleges (Middle States, New England, North Central, Northwest, Southern, and Western), each of which is responsible for a specified portion of the United States and its territories. Other institutional accrediting bodies are national in scope and accredit specific kinds of institutions (e.g., Bible colleges, independent colleges, and rabbinical and Talmudic schools). Program registration by the New York State Board of Regents is considered to be the equivalent of institutional accreditation, since the board requires that all programs offered by an institution meet its standards before recognition is granted. A Canadian institution must be chartered and authorized to grant degrees by the provincial government, affiliated with a chartered institution, or accredited by a recognized U.S. accrediting body. This guide also includes institutions outside the United States that are accredited by these U.S. accrediting bodies. There are recognized specialized or professional accrediting bodies in more than fifty different fields, each of which is authorized to accredit institutions or specific programs in its particular field. For specialized institutions that offer programs in one field only, we designate this to be the equivalent of institutional accreditation. A full explanation of the accrediting process and complete information on recognized institutional (regional and national) and specialized accrediting bodies can be found online at www.chea.org or at www.ed.gov/admins/finaid/accred/index.html.

DIRECTORY OF INSTITUTIONS WITH PROGRAMS IN HUMANITIES, ARTS & SOCIAL SCIENCES

ABILENE CHRISTIAN UNIVERSITY

Clinical Psychology	M
Communication—General	M
Conflict Resolution and Mediation/Peace Studies	M,O
Counseling Psychology	M
English	M
Gerontology	M,O
Liberal Studies	M
Marriage and Family Therapy	M
Missions and Missiology	M
Pastoral Ministry and Counseling	M,D
Psychology—General	M
Rhetoric	M
School Psychology	M
Theology	P,M
Writing	M

ACADEMY OF ART UNIVERSITY

Applied Arts and Design—General	M
Architecture	M
Art/Fine Arts	M
Clothing and Textiles	M
Computer Art and Design	M
Film, Television, and Video Production	M
Graphic Design	M
Illustration	M
Industrial Design	M
Interior Design	M
Internet and Interactive Multimedia	M
Photography	M
Textile Design	M

ACADIA UNIVERSITY

Clinical Psychology	M
English	M
Geographic Information Systems	M
Political Science	M
Psychology—General	M
Sociology	M
Theology	P,M,D

ADAMS STATE COLLEGE

Art/Fine Arts	M
History	M

ADELPHI UNIVERSITY

Art/Fine Arts	M*
Clinical Psychology	D
Counseling Psychology	M
Emergency Management	O
Gerontology	M,O
Psychology—General	M,D*
Public Administration	O
School Psychology	M
Writing	M*

ADLER GRADUATE SCHOOL

Counseling Psychology	M,O
Industrial and Organizational Psychology	M,O
Marriage and Family Therapy	M,O
Psychoanalysis and Psychotherapy	M,O

ADLER SCHOOL OF PROFESSIONAL PSYCHOLOGY

Addictions/Substance Abuse Counseling	M,D,O
Art Therapy	M,D,O
Clinical Psychology	M,D,O
Counseling Psychology	M,D,O
Gerontology	M,D,O
Industrial and Organizational Psychology	M,D,O
Marriage and Family Therapy	M,D,O
Psychology—General	M,D,O*

ALABAMA AGRICULTURAL AND MECHANICAL UNIVERSITY

Agricultural Economics and Agribusiness	M
Clinical Psychology	M,O
Counseling Psychology	M,O
Family and Consumer Sciences-General	M,D
Music	M
Psychology—General	M,O
School Psychology	M,O
Urban and Regional Planning	M

ALABAMA STATE UNIVERSITY

Music	M

ALASKA PACIFIC UNIVERSITY

Counseling Psychology	M
Interdisciplinary Studies	M
Liberal Studies	M

ALBANY STATE UNIVERSITY

Criminal Justice and Criminology	M
Economic Development	M
Economics	M
Public Administration	M
Public Policy	M

ALBERTUS MAGNUS COLLEGE

Art Therapy	M
Liberal Studies	M

ALCORN STATE UNIVERSITY

Agricultural Economics and Agribusiness	M

ALFRED UNIVERSITY

Applied Arts and Design—General	M
Art/Fine Arts	M,D
Computer Art and Design	M
Internet and Interactive Multimedia	M
School Psychology	M,D,O*

ALLIANCE THEOLOGICAL SEMINARY

Missions and Missiology	P,M
Pastoral Ministry and Counseling	P,M
Theology	P,M

ALLIANT INTERNATIONAL UNIVERSITY–FRESNO

Clinical Psychology	D*
Forensic Psychology	D*
Industrial and Organizational Psychology	M,D
Psychology—General	D

ALLIANT INTERNATIONAL UNIVERSITY–IRVINE

Forensic Sciences	D*
Marriage and Family Therapy	M,D*
School Psychology	M,D,O

ALLIANT INTERNATIONAL UNIVERSITY–LOS ANGELES

Addictions/Substance Abuse Counseling	M
Clinical Psychology	D*
Forensic Psychology	D*
Gerontology	M
Industrial and Organizational Psychology	M,D
Marriage and Family Therapy	M*
Psychology—General	M,D
School Psychology	M,D,O

ALLIANT INTERNATIONAL UNIVERSITY–MÉXICO CITY

Counseling Psychology	M
International Affairs	M

ALLIANT INTERNATIONAL UNIVERSITY–SACRAMENTO

Clinical Psychology	D*
Forensic Psychology	D*
Industrial and Organizational Psychology	D
Marriage and Family Therapy	M*
Psychology—General	M,D

ALLIANT INTERNATIONAL UNIVERSITY–SAN DIEGO

Clinical Psychology	M,D*
Forensic Psychology	D*
Industrial and Organizational Psychology	M,D
International Affairs	M
Marriage and Family Therapy	M,D*
Psychology—General	M,D
School Psychology	M,D,O

ALLIANT INTERNATIONAL UNIVERSITY–SAN FRANCISCO

Clinical Psychology	D,O*
Industrial and Organizational Psychology	M,D
Psychology—General	M,D,O
School Psychology	M,D,O

ALVERNIA UNIVERSITY

Liberal Studies	M
Social Psychology	M

AMBERTON UNIVERSITY

Counseling Psychology	M
Interdisciplinary Studies	M

AMBROSE UNIVERSITY COLLEGE

Cultural Studies	P,M,O
Missions and Missiology	P,M,O
Pastoral Ministry and Counseling	P,M,O
Theology	P,M,O

AMERICAN BAPTIST SEMINARY OF THE WEST

Pastoral Ministry and Counseling	P,M
Theology	P,M

AMERICAN CONSERVATORY THEATER

Theater	M,O

AMERICAN FILM INSTITUTE CONSERVATORY

Film, Television, and Video Production	M

AMERICAN GRADUATE SCHOOL OF INTERNATIONAL RELATIONS AND DIPLOMACY

International Affairs	M,D

AMERICAN INTERCONTINENTAL UNIVERSITY ONLINE

Industrial and Organizational Psychology	M

AMERICAN INTERNATIONAL COLLEGE

Child Development	M,D,O
Clinical Psychology	M
Forensic Psychology	M
Psychology—General	M,D
Public Administration	M

AMERICAN JEWISH UNIVERSITY

Jewish Studies	M
Theology	M

AMERICAN PUBLIC UNIVERSITY SYSTEM

Conflict Resolution and Mediation/Peace Studies	M
Criminal Justice and Criminology	M

Emergency Management	M
History	M
Homeland Security	M
Humanities	M
International Affairs	M
Military and Defense Studies	M
National Security	M
Political Science	M
Public Administration	M

AMERICAN UNIVERSITY

American Studies	M,D,O
Anthropology	M,D,O
Applied Economics	M,D,O
Applied Social Research	M,O
Art History	M
Art/Fine Arts	M
Arts Administration	M,O
Broadcast Journalism	M
Clinical Psychology	D
Communication— General	M*
Comparative Literature	M
Conflict Resolution and Mediation/Peace Studies	M,D,O
Criminal Justice and Criminology	M,D
Cultural Studies	M,D,O
Economics	M,D,O
Ethics	M,D,O
Experimental Psychology	M
Film, Television, and Video Production	M
French	O
History	M,D
Interdisciplinary Studies	M
International Affairs	M,D,O*
International Development	M,D,O
Journalism	M
Latin American Studies	M,O
Mass Communication	M,D,O
Media Studies	M
Philosophy	M
Political Science	M,D,O
Psychology—General	D
Public Administration	M,D,O
Public Affairs	M
Public Policy	M
Russian	O
Social Psychology	M
Sociology	M,O
Spanish	M,O
Sustainable Development	M,D,O
Translation and Interpretation	M,O
Western European Studies	M,D,O
Writing	M

THE AMERICAN UNIVERSITY IN CAIRO

Anthropology	M
Broadcast Journalism	M
Communication— General	M
Comparative Literature	M
Demography and Population Studies	M
Economics	M
English	M
Gender Studies	M,O

Journalism	M
Mass Communication	M
Near and Middle Eastern Languages	M,O
Near and Middle Eastern Studies	M,O
Political Science	M
Public Administration	M,O
Public Policy	M,O
Sociology	M
Women's Studies	M,O

THE AMERICAN UNIVERSITY OF ATHENS

Corporate and Organizational Communication	M
Political Science	M

AMERICAN UNIVERSITY OF BEIRUT

Agricultural Economics and Agribusiness	M
Anthropology	M
Archaeology	M
Economics	M
English	M
Health Psychology	M
History	M
Near and Middle Eastern Languages	M
Near and Middle Eastern Studies	M
Philosophy	M
Political Science	M
Psychology—General	M
Public Administration	M
Sociology	M
Urban and Regional Planning	M,D
Urban Design	M,D

THE AMERICAN UNIVERSITY OF PARIS

Communication— General	M
Conflict Resolution and Mediation/Peace Studies	M
International Affairs	M
Near and Middle Eastern Studies	M
Public Administration	M

AMERICAN UNIVERSITY OF PUERTO RICO

Art History	M
Criminal Justice and Criminology	M

AMERICAN UNIVERSITY OF SHARJAH

Public Administration	M
Translation and Interpretation	M
Urban and Regional Planning	M

AMRIDGE UNIVERSITY

Counseling Psychology	P,M,D
Marriage and Family Therapy	P,M,D
Pastoral Ministry and Counseling	P,M,D

Religion	P,M,D
Theology	P,M,D

ANDERSON UNIVERSITY (IN)

Missions and Missiology	P,M,D
Theology	P,M,D

ANDERSON UNIVERSITY (SC)

Criminal Justice and Criminology	M
Pastoral Ministry and Counseling	M

ANDOVER NEWTON THEOLOGICAL SCHOOL

Theology	P,M,D

ANDREW JACKSON UNIVERSITY

Criminal Justice and Criminology	M
Public Administration	M

ANDREWS UNIVERSITY

Architecture	M
Communication— General	M
Counseling Psychology	D
Developmental Psychology	M,D
Economics	M
English	M
History	M
International Development	M
Music	M
Pastoral Ministry and Counseling	P,M,D,O
Psychology—General	M,D,O
School Psychology	M,O
Social Psychology	M
Theology	P,M,D,O

ANGELO STATE UNIVERSITY

Communication— General	M
Counseling Psychology	M
English	M
History	M
Industrial and Organizational Psychology	M
Interdisciplinary Studies	M
Journalism	M
Psychology—General	M
Public Administration	M

ANNA MARIA COLLEGE

Art/Fine Arts	M,O
Counseling Psychology	M
Criminal Justice and Criminology	M
Emergency Management	M,O
Pastoral Ministry and Counseling	M
Public Administration	M

ANTIOCH UNIVERSITY LOS ANGELES

Clinical Psychology	M
Psychology—General	M
Writing	M,O

ANTIOCH UNIVERSITY MCGREGOR

Art/Fine Arts	M
Comparative Literature	M
Conflict Resolution and Mediation/Peace Studies	M
Counseling Psychology	M
Film, Television, and Video Production	M
Liberal Studies	M
Psychology—General	M
Theater	M
Writing	M

ANTIOCH UNIVERSITY NEW ENGLAND

Clinical Psychology	M,D
Counseling Psychology	M
Interdisciplinary Studies	M
Marriage and Family Therapy	M,D*
Psychology—General	M,D,O
Therapies—Dance, Drama, and Music	M

ANTIOCH UNIVERSITY SANTA BARBARA

Clinical Psychology	D
Psychology—General	M

ANTIOCH UNIVERSITY SEATTLE

Corporate and Organizational Communication	M
Industrial and Organizational Psychology	M
Psychology—General	M,D

APEX SCHOOL OF THEOLOGY

Theology	P,M

APPALACHIAN STATE UNIVERSITY

American Studies	M
Child Development	M
Clinical Psychology	M,O
Criminal Justice and Criminology	M
Cultural Studies	M
English	M
Experimental Psychology	M,O
Family and Consumer Sciences-General	M
Geographic Information Systems	M
Geography	M
Gerontology	M
Health Psychology	M,O
History	M
Industrial and Organizational Psychology	M,O
International Affairs	M
Marriage and Family Therapy	M
Music	M
Political Science	M
Psychology—General	M,O
Public Administration	M
Public History	M
Romance Languages	M

School Psychology	M
Social Psychology	M
Sustainable Development	M
Therapies—Dance, Drama, and Music	M

AQUINAS INSTITUTE OF THEOLOGY

Pastoral Ministry and Counseling	P,M,D,O
Theology	P,M,D,O

ARCADIA UNIVERSITY

Child Development	M,D,O
Conflict Resolution and Mediation/Peace Studies	M
English	M
Forensic Sciences	M
Genetic Counseling	M
Humanities	M
International Affairs	M
Psychology—General	M,D,O
School Psychology	M
Social Psychology	M
Theater	M,D,O

ARGOSY UNIVERSITY, ATLANTA

Clinical Psychology	M,D,O
Health Psychology	M,D,O
Marriage and Family Therapy	M,D,O
Psychology—General	M,D,O*
Social Psychology	M,D,O

ARGOSY UNIVERSITY, CHICAGO

Clinical Psychology	M,D*
Counseling Psychology	D
Forensic Psychology	D
Health Psychology	D
Human Development	D
Marriage and Family Therapy	D
Psychoanalysis and Psychotherapy	D
Psychology—General	M,D
Social Psychology	M,D

ARGOSY UNIVERSITY, DALLAS

Clinical Psychology	M,D*
Psychology—General	M,D
Social Psychology	M

ARGOSY UNIVERSITY, DENVER

Clinical Psychology	M,D
Counseling Psychology	M,D
Forensic Psychology	M,D
Marriage and Family Therapy	M,D
Psychology—General	M,D
Social Psychology	M,D*

ARGOSY UNIVERSITY, HAWAI'I

Addictions/Substance Abuse Counseling	O
Clinical Psychology	M,D,O
Counseling Psychology	D
Marriage and Family Therapy	M
Psychology—General	M,D,O*
School Psychology	M

ARGOSY UNIVERSITY, INLAND EMPIRE

Clinical Psychology	M,D
Counseling Psychology	M,D*
Forensic Psychology	M,D
Marriage and Family Therapy	M,D
Psychology—General	M,D

ARGOSY UNIVERSITY, LOS ANGELES

Clinical Psychology	M,D*
Counseling Psychology	M,D
Marriage and Family Therapy	M
Psychology—General	M,D

ARGOSY UNIVERSITY, NASHVILLE

Counseling Psychology	M,D*
Psychology—General	M,D

ARGOSY UNIVERSITY, ORANGE COUNTY

Clinical Psychology	M,D
Counseling Psychology	M,D
Forensic Psychology	M
Marriage and Family Therapy	M,D
Psychology—General	M,D,O*
Public Administration	M,D,O
Sport Psychology	M

ARGOSY UNIVERSITY, PHOENIX

Clinical Psychology	M,D
Counseling Psychology	M
Forensic Psychology	M
Psychology—General	M,D*
School Psychology	M,D
Sport Psychology	M,D

ARGOSY UNIVERSITY, SALT LAKE CITY

Counseling Psychology	M,D
Marriage and Family Therapy	M,D
Psychology—General	M,D*

ARGOSY UNIVERSITY, SAN DIEGO

Clinical Psychology	M,D
Counseling Psychology	M,D*
Marriage and Family Therapy	M,D
Psychology—General	M,D

ARGOSY UNIVERSITY, SAN FRANCISCO BAY AREA

Clinical Psychology	M,D
Counseling Psychology	M,D
Forensic Psychology	M
Psychology—General	M,D*

ARGOSY UNIVERSITY, SARASOTA

Counseling Psychology	M,D,O
Forensic Psychology	M,D,O
Marriage and Family Therapy	M,D,O

Pastoral Ministry and Counseling	M,D,O
Psychology—General	M,D,O*
School Psychology	M,D,O
Social Psychology	M,D,O

ARGOSY UNIVERSITY, SCHAUMBURG

Clinical Psychology	M,D,O*
Counseling Psychology	M,D,O
Forensic Psychology	M,D,O
Health Psychology	M,D,O
Marriage and Family Therapy	M,D,O
Psychology—General	M,D,O
Social Psychology	M,D,O

ARGOSY UNIVERSITY, SEATTLE

Clinical Psychology	M,D,O*
Counseling Psychology	M,D
Psychology—General	M,D,O

ARGOSY UNIVERSITY, TAMPA

Clinical Psychology	M,D
Counseling Psychology	M,D
Marriage and Family Therapy	M,D
Psychology—General	M,D*
Public Administration	M,D

ARGOSY UNIVERSITY, TWIN CITIES

Clinical Psychology	M,D,O
Forensic Psychology	M,D,O
Health Psychology	M,D,O
Marriage and Family Therapy	M,D,O
Psychology—General	M,D,O*

ARGOSY UNIVERSITY, WASHINGTON DC

Clinical Psychology	M,D*
Counseling Psychology	M,D
Forensic Psychology	M,D
Health Psychology	M,D
Marriage and Family Therapy	M,D
Psychology—General	M,D
Social Psychology	M,D

ARIZONA STATE UNIVERSITY

Agricultural Economics and Agribusiness	M,D
Anthropology	M,D
Applied Arts and Design—General	M
Architectural History	D
Architecture	M
Art/Fine Arts	M,D
Building Science	M
Child and Family Studies	M,D
Chinese	M
Clinical Psychology	D
Cognitive Sciences	D
Communication—General	M,D
Comparative Literature	M,D
Computer Art and Design	M
Counseling Psychology	D
Cultural Studies	M
Dance	M

Developmental Psychology	D
Economics	M,D
English	M,D
Environmental Design	D
Film, Television, and Video Production	M
French	M
Gender Studies	D
Geographic Information Systems	M,D
Geography	M,D
German	M
History	M,D
Human Development	M,D
Industrial Design	M
Interior Design	M
Japanese	M
Landscape Architecture	M
Latin American Studies	M,D
Linguistics	M,D
Marriage and Family Therapy	M,D
Media Studies	M
Museum Studies	M,D
Music	M,D
Philosophy	M,D
Political Science	M,D
Psychology—General	D
Public Affairs	M,D
Public History	M,D
Public Policy	P,M
Religion	M,D
Social Psychology	D
Social Sciences	M,D
Sociology	M,D
Spanish	M,D
Speech and Interpersonal Communication	M,D
Sustainable Development	M,D
Theater	M,D
Therapies—Dance, Drama, and Music	M,D
Urban and Regional Planning	M,D
Urban Design	M
Writing	M

ARIZONA STATE UNIVERSITY AT THE DOWNTOWN PHOENIX CAMPUS

Journalism	M
Mass Communication	M

ARIZONA STATE UNIVERSITY AT THE POLYTECHNIC CAMPUS

Agricultural Economics and Agribusiness	M
Psychology—General	M

ARIZONA STATE UNIVERSITY AT THE WEST CAMPUS

Communication—General	M
Criminal Justice and Criminology	M,D
Gerontology	M,O
Interdisciplinary Studies	M

ARKANSAS STATE UNIVERSITY

Art/Fine Arts	M

---

*M—master's degree; P—first professional degree; D—doctorate; O—other advanced degree; *—Close-Up and/or Announcement or Display*

Communication—	
General	M,O
Criminal Justice and	
Criminology	M,O
English	M,O
Gerontology	M,D,O
Historic Preservation	M,D
History	M,O
Journalism	M
Media Studies	M
Music	M,O
Political Science	M,O
Public Administration	M,O
Rehabilitation	
Counseling	M,O
School Psychology	M,O
Sociology	M,O
Speech and	
Interpersonal	
Communication	M,O
Theater	M,O

ARKANSAS TECH UNIVERSITY

Art/Fine Arts	M
Communication—	
General	M
Emergency	
Management	M
English	M
History	M
Homeland Security	M
Journalism	M
Social Sciences	M
Spanish	M

ARMSTRONG ATLANTIC STATE UNIVERSITY

Criminal Justice and	
Criminology	M
History	M
Liberal Studies	M

ART CENTER COLLEGE OF DESIGN

Applied Arts and	
Design—General	M*
Art/Fine Arts	M
Computer Art and	
Design	M
Environmental Design	M
Film, Television, and	
Video Production	M
Industrial Design	M

THE ART INSTITUTE OF BOSTON AT LESLEY UNIVERSITY

Art/Fine Arts	M*

THE ART INSTITUTE OF CALIFORNIA–SAN FRANCISCO

Art/Fine Arts	M
Film, Television, and	
Video Production	M

ASBURY COLLEGE

English	M,O
French	M,O
Spanish	M,O
Writing	M,O

ASBURY THEOLOGICAL SEMINARY

Missions and Missiology	M,D,O
Pastoral Ministry and	
Counseling	M,D,O
Theology	M,D,O

ASHLAND THEOLOGICAL SEMINARY

History	P,M,D,O
Pastoral Ministry and	
Counseling	P,M,D,O
Theology	P,M,D,O

ASHLAND UNIVERSITY

History	M
Political Science	M
Writing	M

ASSEMBLIES OF GOD THEOLOGICAL SEMINARY

Cultural Studies	P,M,D
Missions and Missiology	P,M,D
Pastoral Ministry and	
Counseling	P,M,D
Theology	P,M,D
Women's Studies	P,M,D

ASSOCIATED MENNONITE BIBLICAL SEMINARY

Conflict Resolution and	
Mediation/Peace	
Studies	P,M,O
Missions and Missiology	P,M,O
Theology	P,M,O

ASSUMPTION COLLEGE

Child and Family	
Studies	M,O
Counseling Psychology	M,O
Economics	M,O
Psychology—General	M,O
Rehabilitation	
Counseling	M,O
School Psychology	M,O

ATHABASCA UNIVERSITY

Art Therapy	M,O
Counseling Psychology	M,O
Cultural Studies	M
Interdisciplinary Studies	M
International	
Development	M
Psychology—General	M,O

THE ATHENAEUM OF OHIO

Pastoral Ministry and	
Counseling	P,M,O
Theology	P,M,O

ATLANTIC COLLEGE

Graphic Design	M

ATLANTIC SCHOOL OF THEOLOGY

Theology	P,M,O

ATLANTIC UNIVERSITY

Art/Fine Arts	M

Transpersonal and	
Humanistic Psychology	M

A.T. STILL UNIVERSITY OF HEALTH SCIENCES

Gerontology	M,D

AUBURN UNIVERSITY

Agricultural Economics	
and Agribusiness	M,D
Applied Economics	M,D
Architecture	M
Building Science	M
Child and Family	
Studies	M,D
Clothing and Textiles	M
Communication—	
General	M
Counseling Psychology	M,D,O
Economics	M
English	M,D*
Experimental	
Psychology	M,D
Geography	M
History	M,D
Human Development	M,D
Industrial and	
Organizational	
Psychology	M,D
Industrial Design	M
Landscape Architecture	M
Mass Communication	M
Political Science	M,D
Psychology—General	M,D
Public Administration	M,D*
Rehabilitation	
Counseling	M,D
Rural Sociology	M
School Psychology	M,D,O
Social Psychology	M,D,O
Sociology	M
Spanish	M
Urban and Regional	
Planning	M

AUBURN UNIVERSITY MONTGOMERY

Criminal Justice and	
Criminology	M
Liberal Studies	M
Political Science	M,D
Psychology—General	M
Public Administration	M,D

AUGUSTA STATE UNIVERSITY

Political Science	M
Psychology—General	M

AUSTIN COLLEGE

Theater	M

AUSTIN GRADUATE SCHOOL OF THEOLOGY

Theology	M

AUSTIN PEAY STATE UNIVERSITY

Communication—	
General	M
English	M
Military and Defense	
Studies	M

Music	M
Psychology—General	M

AUSTIN PRESBYTERIAN THEOLOGICAL SEMINARY

Pastoral Ministry and	
Counseling	P,M,D
Theology	P,M,D

AVE MARIA UNIVERSITY

Pastoral Ministry and	
Counseling	M,D
Theology	M,D

AVILA UNIVERSITY

Counseling Psychology	M
Psychology—General	M

AZUSA PACIFIC UNIVERSITY

Art/Fine Arts	M
Clinical Psychology	M,D
Ethics	M
Marriage and Family	
Therapy	M,D
Music	M
Pastoral Ministry and	
Counseling	P,M
Psychology—General	M,D
Religion	M
School Psychology	M
Theology	M,D

BABEL UNIVERSITY SCHOOL OF TRANSLATION

Translation and	
Interpretation	M

BAKER UNIVERSITY

Conflict Resolution and	
Mediation/Peace	
Studies	M
Liberal Studies	M

BAKKE GRADUATE UNIVERSITY

Pastoral Ministry and	
Counseling	M,D

BALL STATE UNIVERSITY

Anthropology	M
Architecture	M
Art/Fine Arts	M
Clinical Psychology	M
Cognitive Sciences	M
Communication—	
General	M
Counseling Psychology	M,D
English	M,D
Family and Consumer	
Sciences-General	M
Gerontology	M
Historic Preservation	M
History	M
Journalism	M
Landscape Architecture	M
Linguistics	D
Political Science	M
Psychology—General	M
Public Administration	M
Rhetoric	M
School Psychology	M,D,O
Social Psychology	M
Social Sciences	M
Sociology	M

Speech and Interpersonal Communication	M
Urban and Regional Planning	M*
Urban Design	M
Writing	M,D

BALTIMORE HEBREW UNIVERSITY

Jewish Studies	M,D

BANGOR THEOLOGICAL SEMINARY

Theology	P,M,D

BANK STREET COLLEGE OF EDUCATION

Child and Family Studies	M
Museum Studies	M

BAPTIST BIBLE COLLEGE

Cultural Studies	P,M
Pastoral Ministry and Counseling	P,M
Theology	P,M

BAPTIST BIBLE COLLEGE OF PENNSYLVANIA

Missions and Missiology	P,M,D
Pastoral Ministry and Counseling	P,M,D
Religion	P,M,D
Theology	P,M,D

BAPTIST MISSIONARY ASSOCIATION THEOLOGICAL SEMINARY

Theology	P,M

BAPTIST THEOLOGICAL SEMINARY AT RICHMOND

Music	P,D
Pastoral Ministry and Counseling	P,D
Theology	P,D

BARD COLLEGE

Art History	M,D
Art/Fine Arts	M
Decorative Arts	M,D
Museum Studies	M
Music	M
Photography	M

BARD GRADUATE CENTER FOR STUDIES IN THE DECORATIVE ARTS, DESIGN, AND CULTURE

Art History	M,D*
Decorative Arts	M,D

BARRY UNIVERSITY

Art/Fine Arts	M
Clinical Psychology	M,O
Communication— General	M,O

Corporate and Organizational Communication	M,O
Liberal Studies	M
Marriage and Family Therapy	M,O
Pastoral Ministry and Counseling	M,D
Photography	M
Psychology—General	M,O*
Public Administration	M
Rehabilitation Counseling	M,O
School Psychology	M,O
Sport Psychology	M
Theology	M,D

BASTYR UNIVERSITY

Health Psychology	M

BAYAMÓN CENTRAL UNIVERSITY

Criminal Justice and Criminology	M
Psychology—General	M
Rehabilitation Counseling	M

BAYLOR UNIVERSITY

American Studies	M
Clinical Psychology	M,D
Communication— General	M
Economics	M
English	M,D
History	M
Interdisciplinary Studies	M,D
International Affairs	M,D
Journalism	M
Museum Studies	M
Music	M
Philosophy	M,D
Political Science	M,D
Psychology—General	M,D
Public Administration	M,D
Public Policy	M,D
Religion	M,D
Sociology	M,D
Spanish	M
Theater	M
Theology	P,M,D

BEACON UNIVERSITY

Pastoral Ministry and Counseling	P,M
Theology	P,M

BELHAVEN COLLEGE (MS)

Public Administration	M

BELLARMINE UNIVERSITY

Communication— General	M
Religion	M

BELLEVUE UNIVERSITY

Criminal Justice and Criminology	M,D
Public Administration	M,D

BELMONT UNIVERSITY

English	M
Music	M
Writing	M

BEMIDJI STATE UNIVERSITY

Counseling Psychology	M
English	M

BENEDICTINE UNIVERSITY

Clinical Psychology	M
Emergency Management	M

BENNINGTON COLLEGE

Dance	M
English	M
French	M
Music	M
Spanish	M
Writing	M

BERNARD M. BARUCH COLLEGE OF THE CITY UNIVERSITY OF NEW YORK

Corporate and Organizational Communication	M
Economics	M
Industrial and Labor Relations	M
Industrial and Organizational Psychology	M,D,O
Public Administration	M

BETHANY THEOLOGICAL SEMINARY

Conflict Resolution and Mediation/Peace Studies	P,M,O
Pastoral Ministry and Counseling	P,M,O
Religion	P,M,O
Theology	P,M,O

BETHANY UNIVERSITY

Clinical Psychology	M

BETH BENJAMIN ACADEMY OF CONNECTICUT

Theology	

BETHEL COLLEGE (IN)

Pastoral Ministry and Counseling	M
Theology	M

BETHEL SEMINARY

Marriage and Family Therapy	P,M,D,O
Missions and Missiology	P,M,D,O
Pastoral Ministry and Counseling	P,M,D,O
Theology	P,M,D,O

BETHEL UNIVERSITY

Communication— General	M,O

Counseling Psychology	M,O
Gerontology	M

BETHESDA CHRISTIAN UNIVERSITY

Music	P,M
Religion	P,M
Theology	P,M

BETH HAMEDRASH SHAAREI YOSHER INSTITUTE

Theology	

BETH HATALMUD RABBINICAL COLLEGE

Theology	

BETH MEDRASH GOVOHA

Theology	

BETHUNE-COOKMAN UNIVERSITY

Theology	M

BEULAH HEIGHTS UNIVERSITY

Religion	M

BEXLEY HALL EPISCOPAL SEMINARY

Theology	P,M

BIBLICAL THEOLOGICAL SEMINARY

Missions and Missiology	P,M,D,O
Pastoral Ministry and Counseling	P,M,D,O
Theology	P,M,D,O

BIOLA UNIVERSITY

Cultural Studies	M,D,O
Ethics	P,M,D
Linguistics	M,D,O
Missions and Missiology	M,D,O
Psychology—General	M,D
Religion	P,M,D
Theology	P,M,D

BIRMINGHAM-SOUTHERN COLLEGE

Music	M
Public Administration	M

BLESSED JOHN XXIII NATIONAL SEMINARY

Theology	P

BOB JONES UNIVERSITY

Art/Fine Arts	P,M,D,O
English	P,M,D,O
Film, Television, and Video Production	P,M,D,O
Graphic Design	P,M,D,O
History	P,M,D,O
Illustration	P,M,D,O
Journalism	P,M,D,O
Media Studies	P,M,D,O
Music	P,M,D,O

*M—master's degree; P—first professional degree; D—doctorate; O—other advanced degree; *—Close-Up and / or Announcement or Display*

Pastoral Ministry and Counseling	P,M,D,O
Religion	P,M,D,O
Rhetoric	P,M,D,O
Speech and Interpersonal Communication	P,M,D,O
Theater	P,M,D,O
Theology	P,M,D,O

BOISE STATE UNIVERSITY

Art/Fine Arts	M
Communication—General	M
Criminal Justice and Criminology	M
English	M
History	M
Interdisciplinary Studies	M
Music	M
Public Administration	M
Public Policy	M
Technical Communication	M
Writing	M

BORICUA COLLEGE

Latin American Studies	M

BOSTON ARCHITECTURAL COLLEGE

Architecture	M
Interior Design	M

BOSTON COLLEGE

Classics	M
Counseling Psychology	M,D
Developmental Psychology	M,D
East European and Russian Studies	M
Economics	D
English	M,D
French	M,D*
History	M,D
Italian	M,D
Linguistics	M
Pastoral Ministry and Counseling	P,M,D,O
Philosophy	M,D
Political Science	M,D
Psychology—General	M,D
Russian	M
Slavic Languages	M
Sociology	M,D
Spanish	M,D
Theology	P,M,D,O
Western European Studies	M,D

THE BOSTON CONSERVATORY

Music	M,O
Theater	M

BOSTON GRADUATE SCHOOL OF PSYCHOANALYSIS

Counseling Psychology	M
Psychoanalysis and Psychotherapy	M,D,O
Psychology—General	M

BOSTON UNIVERSITY

African Studies	M,O

African-American Studies	M
American Studies	D
Anthropology	M,D
Archaeology	M,D
Art History	M,D,O
Art/Fine Arts	M
Arts Administration	M,O
Broadcast Journalism	M
Classics	M,D
Cognitive Sciences	M,D
Communication—General	M*
Counseling Psychology	M,D
Criminal Justice and Criminology	M
Economic Development	M
Economics	M,D
English	M,D
Film, Television, and Video Production	M
Film, Television, and Video Theory and Criticism	M
Forensic Sciences	M
French	M,D
Geographic Information Systems	M,D
Geography	M,D
Graphic Design	M
Health Communication	M
Historic Preservation	M
History	M,D
Human Development	M,D,O
Interdisciplinary Studies	M
International Affairs	M,D,O
Journalism	M
Liberal Studies	M
Linguistics	M,D
Mass Communication	M
Media Studies	M
Museum Studies	M,D,O
Music	M,D,O
Philosophy	M,D
Political Science	M,D
Psychology—General	M,D
Public Administration	M,O
Religion	M,D
Romance Languages	M,D
Sociology	M,D
Spanish	M,D
Theater	M,O
Theology	P,M,D
Urban and Regional Planning	M
Urban Studies	M
Writing	M,D

BOWIE STATE UNIVERSITY

Corporate and Organizational Communication	M,O
Counseling Psychology	M
English	M
Public Administration	M

BOWLING GREEN STATE UNIVERSITY

American Studies	M,D
Applied Arts and Design—General	M
Art History	M
Art/Fine Arts	M
Child and Family Studies	M
Clinical Psychology	M,D

Communication—General	M,D
Computer Art and Design	M
Counseling Psychology	M
Criminal Justice and Criminology	M
Demography and Population Studies	M
Developmental Psychology	M,D
Economics	M
English	M,D
Experimental Psychology	M,D
Family and Consumer Sciences-General	M
Film, Television, and Video Production	M,D
French	M
German	M
Graphic Design	M
History	M,D
Human Development	M
Industrial and Organizational Psychology	M,D
Interdisciplinary Studies	M,D
Music	M,D
Philosophy	M,D
Political Science	M
Psychology—General	M,D
Public Administration	M
Rehabilitation Counseling	M
Rhetoric	M,D
School Psychology	M,O
Social Psychology	M,D
Sociology	M,D
Spanish	M
Speech and Interpersonal Communication	M,D
Technical Communication	M,D
Theater	M,D
Writing	M,D

BRADLEY UNIVERSITY

Applied Arts and Design—General	M
Art/Fine Arts	M
Comparative and Interdisciplinary Arts	M
English	M
Human Development	M
Illustration	M
Liberal Studies	M
Photography	M

BRANDEIS UNIVERSITY

American Studies	M,D
Anthropology	M,D
Art/Fine Arts	O
Child and Family Studies	M,D
Classics	O
Cognitive Sciences	M,D
Communication—General	O
Conflict Resolution and Mediation/Peace Studies	M
Cultural Studies	M
Developmental Psychology	M,D
Disability Studies	D

Economics	M,D
English	M,D
Genetic Counseling	M
History	M,D
International Affairs	M,D
International Development	M
Jewish Studies	M,D
Linguistics	M
Music	M,D
Near and Middle Eastern Languages	M,D
Near and Middle Eastern Studies	M,D
Political Science	M,D
Psychology—General	M
Public Policy	M
Social Psychology	M,D
Sociology	M,D
Sustainable Development	M
Theater	M
Women's Studies	M

BRANDON UNIVERSITY

Music	M
Rural Planning and Studies	M,O

BRENAU UNIVERSITY

Interior Design	M
Psychology—General	M

BRIDGEWATER STATE COLLEGE

Criminal Justice and Criminology	M
English	M
Psychology—General	M
Public Administration	M

BRIERCREST SEMINARY

Marriage and Family Therapy	M
Missions and Missiology	M
Pastoral Ministry and Counseling	P,M
Religion	P,M
Theology	P,M

BRIGHAM YOUNG UNIVERSITY

Anthropology	M
Art History	M
Art/Fine Arts	M
Child and Family Studies	M,D
Clinical Psychology	M,D
Communication—General	M
Comparative and Interdisciplinary Arts	M
Comparative Literature	M
Counseling Psychology	M,D,O
English	M
Film, Television, and Video Production	M
French	M
Geography	M
German	M
Human Development	M,D
Humanities	M
Industrial Design	M
Linguistics	M,O
Marriage and Family Therapy	M,D

Mass Communication	M
Music	M
Political Science	M
Portuguese	M
Psychology—General	M,D
Public Administration	M
Public Policy	M
School Psychology	M,D,O
Social Psychology	M,D
Sociology	M
Spanish	M
Theater	M

BRITISH AMERICAN COLLEGE LONDON

International Affairs	M

BROCK UNIVERSITY

Child and Family Studies	M
Classics	M
Comparative Literature	M
Cultural Studies	M
Disability Studies	M,O
Economics	M
English	M
Geography	M
History	M
Human Development	M,D
International Affairs	M
Philosophy	M
Political Science	M
Psychology—General	M,D
Public Administration	M
Social Psychology	M,D

BROOKLYN COLLEGE OF THE CITY UNIVERSITY OF NEW YORK

Art History	M,D
Art/Fine Arts	M,D
Counseling Psychology	M,D,O
Economics	M
English	M,D
Experimental Psychology	M,D
Film, Television, and Video Production	M
French	M,D
History	M,D
Industrial and Organizational Psychology	M
International Affairs	M,D
Internet and Interactive Multimedia	M,O
Jewish Studies	M
Liberal Studies	M
Music	M,D,O
Photography	M,D
Political Science	M,D
Psychology—General	M,D
Public Policy	M,D
School Psychology	M,O
Social Psychology	M,D
Sociology	M,D
Spanish	M,D
Speech and Interpersonal Communication	M,D
Thanatology	M
Theater	M,D
Urban Studies	M,D
Writing	M

BROOKS INSTITUTE

Photography	M

BROWN UNIVERSITY

American Studies	M,D
Anthropology	M,D
Archaeology	M,D
Art History	M,D
Classics	M,D
Cognitive Sciences	M,D
Comparative Literature	D
Developmental Psychology	D
East European and Russian Studies	M,D
Economics	D
English	M,D
French	D
German	D
Hispanic Studies	M,D
History	M,D
Italian	D
Jewish Studies	D
Latin American Studies	M,D
Linguistics	M,D
Museum Studies	M,D
Music	D
Philosophy	M,D
Political Science	D
Psychology—General	D
Public Policy	M
Religion	D
Russian	M,D
Slavic Languages	M,D
Social Psychology	D
Sociology	M,D
Theater	M,D
Western European Studies	M,D
Writing	M

BRYN ATHYN COLLEGE OF THE NEW CHURCH

Religion	P,M
Theology	P,M

BRYN MAWR COLLEGE

Archaeology	M,D*
Art History	M,D*
Classics	M,D*
Clinical Psychology	D
Developmental Psychology	D
French	M,D
Psychology—General	D
Russian	M,D

BUCKNELL UNIVERSITY

English	M
Psychology—General	M
School Psychology	M

BUFFALO STATE COLLEGE, STATE UNIVERSITY OF NEW YORK

Applied Economics	M
Criminal Justice and Criminology	M
Economics	M
English	M
Historic Preservation	M,O
History	M
Interdisciplinary Studies	M

BUTLER UNIVERSITY

English	M
History	M
Music	M

CALDWELL COLLEGE

Art Therapy	M
Counseling Psychology	M
Pastoral Ministry and Counseling	M
Psychology—General	M

CALIFORNIA BAPTIST UNIVERSITY

Counseling Psychology	M
English	M
Forensic Psychology	M
Music	M
Pastoral Ministry and Counseling	M
Public Administration	M
School Psychology	M

CALIFORNIA COAST UNIVERSITY

Psychology—General	M

CALIFORNIA COLLEGE OF THE ARTS

Applied Arts and Design—General	M
Architecture	M
Art/Fine Arts	M*
Film, Television, and Video Production	M
Film, Television, and Video Theory and Criticism	M
Museum Studies	M
Photography	M
Textile Design	M
Writing	M

CALIFORNIA INSTITUTE OF INTEGRAL STUDIES

Anthropology	M,D
Art Therapy	M,D
Asian Studies	M,D
Clinical Psychology	M,D
Counseling Psychology	M,D
Health Psychology	M,D
Humanities	M,D*
Philosophy	M,D
Psychology—General	M,D*
Religion	M,D
Social Psychology	M,D
Theology	M,D
Therapies—Dance, Drama, and Music	M,D
Women's Studies	M,D

CALIFORNIA INSTITUTE OF TECHNOLOGY

Economics	M,D
Political Science	M,D
Social Sciences	M,D

CALIFORNIA INSTITUTE OF THE ARTS

Applied Arts and Design—General	M,O

[California Institute of the Arts continued]

Art/Fine Arts	M,O
Dance	M,O
Film, Television, and Video Production	M,O
Graphic Design	M,O
Music	M,O
Photography	M,O
Theater	M,O
Writing	M,O

CALIFORNIA LUTHERAN UNIVERSITY

Clinical Psychology	M
Marriage and Family Therapy	M
Psychology—General	M
Public Administration	M
Public Policy	M

CALIFORNIA POLYTECHNIC STATE UNIVERSITY, SAN LUIS OBISPO

Agricultural Economics and Agribusiness	M
Architecture	M
English	M
History	M
Political Science	M
Psychology—General	M
Urban and Regional Planning	M

CALIFORNIA STATE POLYTECHNIC UNIVERSITY, POMONA

Architecture	M
Economics	M
English	M
History	M
Landscape Architecture	M
Psychology—General	M
Public Administration	M
Urban and Regional Planning	M

CALIFORNIA STATE UNIVERSITY, BAKERSFIELD

Anthropology	M
Counseling Psychology	M
English	M
History	M
Interdisciplinary Studies	M
Psychology—General	M
Public Administration	M
Sociology	M
Spanish	M

CALIFORNIA STATE UNIVERSITY, CHICO

Anthropology	M
Art History	M
Art/Fine Arts	M
Communication—General	M
English	M
Geography	M
History	M
Interdisciplinary Studies	M
Marriage and Family Therapy	M
Museum Studies	M
Music	M
Political Science	M

*M—master's degree; P—first professional degree; D—doctorate; O—other advanced degree; *—Close-Up and / or Announcement or Display*

Psychology—General	M
Public Administration	M
Rural Planning and Studies	M
Social Sciences	M
Urban and Regional Planning	M

CALIFORNIA STATE UNIVERSITY, DOMINGUEZ HILLS

Applied Social Research	M,O
Clinical Psychology	M
Conflict Resolution and Mediation/Peace Studies	M
English	M,O
Humanities	M
Marriage and Family Therapy	M
Psychology—General	M
Public Administration	M
Rhetoric	M,O
Sociology	M,O

CALIFORNIA STATE UNIVERSITY, EAST BAY

Anthropology	M
Communication— General	M
Economics	M
English	M
Geography	M
History	M
Interdisciplinary Studies	M,O
Internet and Interactive Multimedia	M
Music	M
Public Administration	M
Sociology	M

CALIFORNIA STATE UNIVERSITY, FRESNO

Applied Arts and Design—General	M
Art/Fine Arts	M
Communication— General	M
Criminal Justice and Criminology	M
English	M
Family and Consumer Sciences-General	M
History	M
International Affairs	M
Journalism	M
Linguistics	M
Marriage and Family Therapy	M
Mass Communication	M
Music	M
Psychology—General	M
Public Administration	M
Rehabilitation Counseling	M
Spanish	M
Sport Psychology	M
Writing	M

CALIFORNIA STATE UNIVERSITY, FULLERTON

American Studies	M
Anthropology	M
Applied Arts and Design—General	M
Art History	M
Art/Fine Arts	M

Clinical Psychology	M
Communication— General	M
Comparative Literature	M
Dance	M
Economics	M
English	M
Film, Television, and Video Production	M
French	M
Geography	M
German	M
Gerontology	M
History	M
Journalism	M
Linguistics	M
Media Studies	M
Music	M
Photography	M
Political Science	M
Psychology—General	M
Public Administration	M
Social Psychology	M
Sociology	M
Spanish	M
Speech and Interpersonal Communication	M
Theater	M

CALIFORNIA STATE UNIVERSITY, LONG BEACH

African Studies	M
American Studies	M
Anthropology	M
Art History	M
Art/Fine Arts	M
Asian Studies	M,O
Asian-American Studies	M,O
Communication— General	M
Consumer Economics	M
Criminal Justice and Criminology	M
Dance	M
Economics	M
Emergency Management	M
English	M
Family and Consumer Sciences-General	M
French	M
Geography	M
German	M
Gerontology	M
History	M
Interdisciplinary Studies	M
Latin American Studies	M
Linguistics	M
Marriage and Family Therapy	M
Medieval and Renaissance Studies	M
Music	M
Near and Middle Eastern Studies	M
Philosophy	M
Political Science	M
Psychology—General	M
Public Administration	M
Public Policy	M
Religion	M
Spanish	M
Sport Psychology	M
Theater	M
Western European Studies	M
Writing	M

CALIFORNIA STATE UNIVERSITY, LOS ANGELES

Anthropology	M
Applied Arts and Design—General	M
Art History	M
Art Therapy	M
Art/Fine Arts	M
Child and Family Studies	M
Child Development	M
Communication— General	M
Criminal Justice and Criminology	M
Economics	M
English	M
Film, Television, and Video Production	M
French	M
Geography	M
Graphic Design	M
Hispanic Studies	M
History	M
Latin American Studies	M
Music	M
Philosophy	M
Photography	M
Political Science	M
Psychology—General	M
Public Administration	M
Rehabilitation Counseling	M,D
School Psychology	M,D
Sociology	M
Spanish	M
Speech and Interpersonal Communication	M
Textile Design	M
Theater	M

CALIFORNIA STATE UNIVERSITY, MONTEREY BAY

Interdisciplinary Studies	M
Public Policy	M

CALIFORNIA STATE UNIVERSITY, NORTHRIDGE

Anthropology	M
Archaeology	M
Art History	M
Art/Fine Arts	M
Clinical Psychology	M
Communication— General	M
Comparative Literature	M
English	M
Experimental Psychology	M
Family and Consumer Sciences-General	M
Film, Television, and Video Production	M
Geography	M
Hispanic Studies	M
History	M
Interdisciplinary Studies	M
Journalism	M
Linguistics	M
Marriage and Family Therapy	M
Mass Communication	M
Music	M
Political Science	M

Psychology—General	M
Public Administration	M
Rhetoric	M
School Psychology	M
Sociology	M
Spanish	M
Speech and Interpersonal Communication	M
Theater	M
Writing	M

CALIFORNIA STATE UNIVERSITY, SACRAMENTO

Anthropology	M
Art/Fine Arts	M
Communication— General	M
Counseling Psychology	M
Criminal Justice and Criminology	M
Dance	M
English	M
French	M
German	M
International Affairs	M
Liberal Studies	M
Music	M
Political Science	M
Psychology—General	M
Public Administration	M
Public History	M
Public Policy	M
School Psychology	M
Sociology	M
Spanish	M
Theater	M
Writing	M

CALIFORNIA STATE UNIVERSITY, SAN BERNARDINO

Art/Fine Arts	M
Child Development	M
Clinical Psychology	M
Communication— General	M
Corporate and Organizational Communication	M
Counseling Psychology	M
Criminal Justice and Criminology	M
English	M
Experimental Psychology	M
Human Development	M
Industrial and Organizational Psychology	M
Interdisciplinary Studies	M
National Security	M
Psychology—General	M
Public Administration	M
Rehabilitation Counseling	M
Social Sciences	M
Spanish	M
Theater	M
Writing	M

CALIFORNIA STATE UNIVERSITY, SAN MARCOS

English	M
Psychology—General	M
Sociology	M

Spanish	M
Writing	M

CALIFORNIA STATE UNIVERSITY, STANISLAUS

Art/Fine Arts	O
Child Development	M,O
Criminal Justice and Criminology	M
English	M,O
Genetic Counseling	M
Gerontology	O
History	M
Interdisciplinary Studies	M
International Affairs	M
Psychology—General	M,O
Public Administration	M
Rhetoric	M,O
Sustainable Development	M
Writing	M,O

CALIFORNIA UNIVERSITY OF PENNSYLVANIA

Criminal Justice and Criminology	M
School Psychology	M
Social Sciences	M
Sport Psychology	M

CALUMET COLLEGE OF SAINT JOSEPH

Criminal Justice and Criminology	M

CALVARY BIBLE COLLEGE AND THEOLOGICAL SEMINARY

Pastoral Ministry and Counseling	P,M
Theology	P,M

CALVIN THEOLOGICAL SEMINARY

Missions and Missiology	P,M,D
Theology	P,M,D

CAMBRIDGE COLLEGE

Addictions/Substance Abuse Counseling	M,O
Conflict Resolution and Mediation/Peace Studies	M
Counseling Psychology	M,O
Forensic Psychology	M,O
Interdisciplinary Studies	M,D,O
Marriage and Family Therapy	M,O
Psychology—General	M,O

CAMERON UNIVERSITY

Psychology—General	M

CAMPBELLSVILLE UNIVERSITY

Music	M
Social Sciences	M
Theology	M

CAMPBELL UNIVERSITY

Interdisciplinary Studies	M
Theology	P,M,D

CANADIAN SOUTHERN BAPTIST SEMINARY

Theology	P,M

CANISIUS COLLEGE

Corporate and Organizational Communication	M
School Psychology	M
Social Psychology	M

CAPE BRETON UNIVERSITY

Economic Development	M

CAPELLA UNIVERSITY

Addictions/Substance Abuse Counseling	M,D,O
Child and Family Studies	M,D,O
Clinical Psychology	M,D,O
Counseling Psychology	M,D,O
Criminal Justice and Criminology	M,D,O
Emergency Management	M,D
Gerontology	M,D
Industrial and Organizational Psychology	M,D,O
Marriage and Family Therapy	M,D,O
Psychology—General	M,D,O
Public Administration	M,D
School Psychology	M,D,O
Sport Psychology	M,D,O

CAPITAL BIBLE SEMINARY

Pastoral Ministry and Counseling	P,M,O
Theology	P,M,O

CAPITAL UNIVERSITY

Music	M

CARDINAL STRITCH UNIVERSITY

Applied Arts and Design—General	M
Clinical Psychology	M
Graphic Design	M
History	M
Liberal Studies	M
Music	M
Pastoral Ministry and Counseling	M
Psychology—General	M
Religion	M

CAREY THEOLOGICAL COLLEGE

Theology	M,D

CARIBBEAN UNIVERSITY

Art History	M,D
Criminal Justice and Criminology	M,D
Museum Studies	M,D

CARLETON UNIVERSITY

Anthropology	M
Architecture	M
Art History	M
Canadian Studies	M,D
Cognitive Sciences	D
Communication—General	M,D
Comparative Literature	D
Conflict Resolution and Mediation/Peace Studies	M,O
East European and Russian Studies	M,O
Economics	M,D
English	M,D
Film, Television, and Video Production	M
French	M
Geography	M,D
History	M,D
Industrial Design	M
International Affairs	M,D
Journalism	M,D
Linguistics	M
Music	M
Philosophy	M
Political Science	M,D
Psychology—General	M,D
Public Administration	M,D
Public Policy	M,D
Sociology	M,D
Western European Studies	M,O

CARLOS ALBIZU UNIVERSITY

Clinical Psychology	M,D
Industrial and Organizational Psychology	M,D
Psychology—General	M,D

CARLOS ALBIZU UNIVERSITY, MIAMI CAMPUS

Clinical Psychology	M,D
Counseling Psychology	M,D
Industrial and Organizational Psychology	M,D
Marriage and Family Therapy	M,D
Psychology—General	M,D
School Psychology	M,D

CARLOW UNIVERSITY

Counseling Psychology	M
Humanities	M
Writing	M

CARNEGIE MELLON UNIVERSITY

African Studies	M,D
African-American Studies	M,D
Applied Arts and Design—General	D
Architecture	M,D
Art/Fine Arts	M
Arts Administration	M
Building Science	M,D
Cognitive Sciences	D
Communication—General	M,D
Comparative Literature	M,D
Computer Art and Design	M,D

Corporate and Organizational Communication

Corporate and Organizational Communication	M
Criminal Justice and Criminology	M
Cultural Studies	M,D
Developmental Psychology	D
Economics	D
English	M,D
Film, Television, and Video Production	M
Gender Studies	M,D
History of Science and Technology	M,D
History	M,D
Industrial and Labor Relations	M,D
Linguistics	D
Media Studies	M
Music	M
Philosophy	M,D
Psychology—General	D
Public Administration	M
Public Policy	M,D
Publishing	M
Rhetoric	M,D
Social Psychology	D
Social Sciences	D
Technical Writing	M
Theater	M
Urban Design	M,D
Writing	M*

CASE WESTERN RESERVE UNIVERSITY

Anthropology	M,D
Art History	M,D
Clinical Psychology	D
Cognitive Sciences	M
Comparative Literature	M,D
Dance	M
Economics	M
English	M,D
Experimental Psychology	D
French	M
Genetic Counseling	M
Gerontology	M,D,O
History	M,D
Industrial and Labor Relations	M
Linguistics	M
Museum Studies	M,D
Music	M,D
Political Science	M,D
Psychology—General	D
Sociology	D
Theater	M

CASTLETON STATE COLLEGE

Forensic Psychology	M
Psychology—General	M

THE CATHOLIC DISTANCE UNIVERSITY

Theology	M

CATHOLIC THEOLOGICAL UNION AT CHICAGO

Missions and Missiology	P,M,D,O
Pastoral Ministry and Counseling	P,M,D,O
Theology	P,M,D,O

*M—master's degree; P—first professional degree; D—doctorate; O—other advanced degree; *—Close-Up and/or Announcement or Display*

THE CATHOLIC UNIVERSITY OF AMERICA

American Studies	M,D
Anthropology	M
Architecture	M
Classics	M,D
Clinical Psychology	M,D
Comparative Literature	M
Computer Art and Design	M
Cultural Studies	M
Economics	M
English	M,D
Experimental Psychology	M,D
History	M,D
International Affairs	M,D
Medieval and Renaissance Studies	M,D,O
Music	M,D,O
Near and Middle Eastern Languages	M,D
Near and Middle Eastern Studies	M,D
Pastoral Ministry and Counseling	P,M,D,O
Philosophy	M,D,O
Political Science	M,D
Psychology—General	M,D
Religion	P,M,D,O
Rhetoric	M,D
Sociology	M
Spanish	M,D
Theater	M
Theology	P,M,D,O
Urban and Regional Planning	M
Urban Design	M
Western European Studies	M,D

CEDAR CREST COLLEGE

Forensic Sciences	M

CENTENARY COLLEGE

Counseling Psychology	M

CENTRAL BAPTIST THEOLOGICAL SEMINARY

Missions and Missiology	P,M,O
Theology	P,M,O

CENTRAL BAPTIST THEOLOGICAL SEMINARY OF VIRGINIA BEACH

Theology	P,M

CENTRAL CONNECTICUT STATE UNIVERSITY

Communication—General	M,O
Corporate and Organizational Communication	M,O
Criminal Justice and Criminology	M
English	M,O
French	M,O
Geography	M
Health Psychology	M
History	M,O
International Affairs	M

Italian	M,O
Marriage and Family Therapy	M,O
Psychology—General	M
Rehabilitation Counseling	M,O
School Psychology	M,O
Social Psychology	M
Spanish	M,O

CENTRAL EUROPEAN UNIVERSITY

Anthropology	M,D
Economics	M,D
Gender Studies	M,D
History	M,D
Humanities	M,D*
International Affairs	M,D
Medieval and Renaissance Studies	M,D
Philosophy	M,D
Political Science	M,D
Public Policy	M,D
Social Sciences	M,D
Sociology	M,D

CENTRAL MICHIGAN UNIVERSITY

American Indian/Native American Studies	M
American Studies	M,D,O
Child and Family Studies	M,O
Clinical Psychology	M,D
Clothing and Textiles	M,O
Communication—General	M
Corporate and Organizational Communication	M,O
Counseling Psychology	M,D,O
Cultural Studies	M
Economics	M
English	M
Experimental Psychology	M,D
Family and Consumer Sciences-General	M,O
Film, Television, and Video Production	M
Film, Television, and Video Theory and Criticism	M
Gender Studies	M
History	M,D,O
Human Development	M,O
Humanities	M
Industrial and Organizational Psychology	M,D
International Affairs	M,O
Mass Communication	M
Media Studies	M
Music	M
Political Science	M,O
Psychology—General	M,D,O
Public Administration	M,O
School Psychology	D,O
Spanish	M
Speech and Interpersonal Communication	M
Western European Studies	M,D,O
Writing	M

CENTRAL WASHINGTON UNIVERSITY

Art/Fine Arts	M
Child and Family Studies	M
Counseling Psychology	M
English	M
Experimental Psychology	M
Family and Consumer Sciences-General	M
History	M
Interdisciplinary Studies	M
Music	M
Psychology—General	M
School Psychology	M
Theater	M

CENTRAL YESHIVA TOMCHEI TMIMIM-LUBAVITCH

Theology	

CENTRO DE ESTUDIOS AVANZADOS DE PUERTO RICO Y EL CARIBE

History	M,D
Latin American Studies	M,D

CHAMINADE UNIVERSITY OF HONOLULU

Conflict Resolution and Mediation/Peace Studies	M
Counseling Psychology	M
Criminal Justice and Criminology	M,O
Forensic Sciences	M
Homeland Security	M,O
Pastoral Ministry and Counseling	M
Theology	M

CHAPMAN UNIVERSITY

Cultural Studies	D
Disability Studies	D
Economics	P,M
English	M
Film, Television, and Video Production	M
Health Communication	M
International Affairs	M
Marriage and Family Therapy	M
School Psychology	M,D,O
Writing	M

CHARLESTON SOUTHERN UNIVERSITY

Criminal Justice and Criminology	M

CHATHAM UNIVERSITY

Computer Art and Design	M
Counseling Psychology	M,D
Developmental Psychology	M,D
Film, Television, and Video Production	M
Health Psychology	M,D

Industrial and Organizational Psychology	M,D
Interior Design	M
Landscape Architecture	M
Marriage and Family Therapy	M,D
Sport Psychology	M,D
Writing	M

CHESTNUT HILL COLLEGE

Clinical Psychology	M,D,O
Counseling Psychology	M,O
Gerontology	M,O
Psychology—General	M,D,O
Religion	M,O

CHEYNEY UNIVERSITY OF PENNSYLVANIA

Public Administration	M

THE CHICAGO SCHOOL OF PROFESSIONAL PSYCHOLOGY

Clinical Psychology	M,D,O
Counseling Psychology	M,D,O
Forensic Psychology	M
Industrial and Organizational Psychology	M,D
Marriage and Family Therapy	M,D
Psychology—General	M,D,O
School Psychology	O
Social Psychology	M,D

CHICAGO STATE UNIVERSITY

Criminal Justice and Criminology	M
Economic Development	M
English	M
Geography	M
History	M
Writing	M

CHICAGO THEOLOGICAL SEMINARY

Ethics	P,M,D
Pastoral Ministry and Counseling	P,M,D
Religion	P,M,D
Theology	P,M,D

CHRISTENDOM COLLEGE

Theology	M

CHRISTIAN BROTHERS UNIVERSITY

Religion	M

CHRISTIAN THEOLOGICAL SEMINARY

Marriage and Family Therapy	P,M,D
Pastoral Ministry and Counseling	P,M,D
Religion	P,M,D
Theology	P,M,D

CHRISTIE'S EDUCATION

Art History	M
Museum Studies	M

CHRISTOPHER NEWPORT UNIVERSITY

History	M
Theater	M

CHRIST THE KING SEMINARY

Pastoral Ministry and Counseling	P,M,O
Theology	P,M,O

CHURCH DIVINITY SCHOOL OF THE PACIFIC

Theology	P,M,D,O

CHURCH OF GOD THEOLOGICAL SEMINARY

Pastoral Ministry and Counseling	P,M,D
Theology	P,M,D

CINCINNATI CHRISTIAN UNIVERSITY

Pastoral Ministry and Counseling	M
Religion	P,M
Theology	P,M

THE CITADEL, THE MILITARY COLLEGE OF SOUTH CAROLINA

English	M
History	M
Psychology—General	M
School Psychology	M,O
Social Sciences	M

CITY COLLEGE OF THE CITY UNIVERSITY OF NEW YORK

Architecture	M
Art History	M
Art/Fine Arts	M
Clinical Psychology	M,D
Counseling Psychology	M
Economics	M
English	M
Experimental Psychology	M,D
Graphic Design	M
History	M
International Affairs	M
Landscape Architecture	M,O
Media Studies	M
Museum Studies	M
Music	M
Psychology—General	M,D
Sociology	M
Spanish	M
Urban Design	M
Writing	M

CITY UNIVERSITY OF SEATTLE

Counseling Psychology	M
School Psychology	M,O

CLAREMONT GRADUATE UNIVERSITY

African Studies	M,D,O
American Studies	M,D,O
Art/Fine Arts	M
Arts Administration	M
Cognitive Sciences	M,D,O
Comparative Literature	M,D
Computer Art and Design	M
Cultural Studies	M,D,O
Developmental Psychology	M,D,O
Economic Development	M,D,O
Economics	M,D,O
English	M,D
Ethics	M,D
Film, Television, and Video Theory and Criticism	M,D
Health Psychology	M,D,O
History	M,D,O
Human Development	M,D,O
Humanities	M,D,O
Industrial and Organizational Psychology	M,D,O
International Affairs	M,D
International Economics	M,D,O
Media Studies	M,D,O
Museum Studies	M,D,O
Music	M,D
Philosophy	M,D
Photography	M
Political Science	M,D
Psychology—General	M,D,O
Public Policy	M,D,O
Religion	M,D
Social Psychology	M,D,O
Theology	M,D
Western European Studies	M,D,O
Women's Studies	M,D
Writing	M,D

CLAREMONT SCHOOL OF THEOLOGY

Pastoral Ministry and Counseling	D
Religion	M,D
Theology	P,M,D

CLARION UNIVERSITY OF PENNSYLVANIA

Communication— General	M
English	M

CLARK ATLANTA UNIVERSITY

African-American Studies	M,D
Criminal Justice and Criminology	M
Economics	M
English	M,D
History	M,D
Political Science	M,D
Public Administration	M
Romance Languages	M,D
Sociology	M
Women's Studies	M,D

CLARK UNIVERSITY

American Studies	D
Clinical Psychology	D
Communication— General	M

Developmental Psychology	D
Economics	D
English	M
Geographic Information Systems	M
Geography	M,D
History	M,D,O
Holocaust Studies	D
International Development	M
Liberal Studies	M
Psychology—General	D
Public Administration	M,O
Social Psychology	D
Sustainable Development	M
Urban and Regional Planning	M

CLAYTON STATE UNIVERSITY

Liberal Studies	M

CLEMSON UNIVERSITY

Applied Economics	M,D
Architecture	M
Art/Fine Arts	M
Communication— General	M,D
Computer Art and Design	M
Economics	M,D
English	M,D
Environmental Design	D
Historic Preservation	M
History	M
Human Development	M
Industrial and Organizational Psychology	D
Landscape Architecture	M
Psychology—General	M,D
Public Administration	M,D
Public Policy	M,D
Rhetoric	D
Sociology	M
Urban and Regional Planning	M
Writing	M

CLEVELAND INSTITUTE OF MUSIC

Music	M,D,O

CLEVELAND STATE UNIVERSITY

Addictions/Substance Abuse Counseling	M,O
Art History	M
Art/Fine Arts	M
Clinical Psychology	M,D,O
Communication— General	M,O
Counseling Psychology	M,D,O
Economic Development	M,D,O
Economics	M,D,O
English	M
Experimental Psychology	M,D,O
French	M
Geographic Information Systems	M,D,O
Gerontology	M,D,O
Health Communication	M,O

History	M
Industrial and Labor Relations	P,M
Industrial and Organizational Psychology	M,D,O
Latin American Studies	M
Linguistics	M
Museum Studies	M,D
Music	M
Philosophy	M,O
Psychology—General	M,D,O
Public Administration	M,O
School Psychology	M,D,O
Sociology	M
Spanish	M
Sport Psychology	M
Urban and Regional Planning	M,O
Urban Design	M,O
Urban Studies	M,D,O
Writing	M

COLGATE ROCHESTER CROZER DIVINITY SCHOOL

Theology	P,M,D,O

THE COLLEGE AT BROCKPORT, STATE UNIVERSITY OF NEW YORK

Art/Fine Arts	M
Communication— General	M
Counseling Psychology	M,O
Dance	M
English	M
History	M
Liberal Studies	M
Psychology—General	M
Public Administration	M

COLLÈGE DOMINICAIN DE PHILOSOPHIE ET DE THÉOLOGIE

Pastoral Ministry and Counseling	M
Philosophy	M,D
Theology	M,D,O

COLLEGE OF CHARLESTON

Arts Administration	M,O
Communication— General	M
Corporate and Organizational Communication	O
English	M
Historic Preservation	M
History	M
Public Administration	M
Translation and Interpretation	O

COLLEGE OF EMMANUEL AND ST. CHAD

Theology	P,M

COLLEGE OF MOUNT ST. JOSEPH

Pastoral Ministry and Counseling	M
Theology	M

*M—master's degree; P—first professional degree; D—doctorate; O—other advanced degree; *—Close-Up and/or Announcement or Display*

Peterson's Graduate Programs in the Humanities, Arts & Social Sciences 2010

graduateschools.petersons.com

29

THE COLLEGE OF NEW JERSEY

Addictions/Substance Abuse Counseling	M,O
English	M
Marriage and Family Therapy	O
Spanish	M

THE COLLEGE OF NEW ROCHELLE

Art Therapy	M
Art/Fine Arts	M
Communication— General	M,O
Counseling Psychology	M,O
Gerontology	M,O
Graphic Design	M
School Psychology	M
Social Psychology	M

COLLEGE OF NOTRE DAME OF MARYLAND

Communication— General	M
Liberal Studies	M

COLLEGE OF SAINT ELIZABETH

Counseling Psychology	M,O
Forensic Psychology	M,O
Psychology—General	M,O
Theology	M

COLLEGE OF ST. JOSEPH

Addictions/Substance Abuse Counseling	M
Clinical Psychology	M
Counseling Psychology	M
Psychology—General	M
School Psychology	M
Social Psychology	M

THE COLLEGE OF SAINT ROSE

English	M
History	M
Mass Communication	M
Music	M
Political Science	M
School Psychology	M,O

COLLEGE OF STATEN ISLAND OF THE CITY UNIVERSITY OF NEW YORK

Counseling Psychology	M
English	M
Film, Television, and Video Theory and Criticism	M
History	M
Liberal Studies	M
Media Studies	M

COLLEGE OF THE HUMANITIES AND SCIENCES, HARRISON MIDDLETON UNIVERSITY

Comparative Literature	M,D
Humanities	M,D
Interdisciplinary Studies	M,D
Philosophy	M,D
Religion	M,D
Social Sciences	M,D

THE COLLEGE OF WILLIAM AND MARY

Addictions/Substance Abuse Counseling	M,D
American Studies	M,D
Anthropology	M,D
History	M,D
Marriage and Family Therapy	M,D
Psychology—General	M,D
Public Policy	M
School Psychology	M,O

COLLÈGE UNIVERSITAIRE DE SAINT-BONIFACE

Canadian Studies	M

COLORADO CHRISTIAN UNIVERSITY

Counseling Psychology	M

COLORADO SCHOOL OF MINES

International Affairs	M,O
Mineral Economics	M,D

COLORADO STATE UNIVERSITY

Agricultural Economics and Agribusiness	M,D
Anthropology	M
Art/Fine Arts	M
Child and Family Studies	M
Consumer Economics	M
Economics	M,D
History	M
Human Development	M
Mass Communication	M,D
Music	M
Philosophy	M
Political Science	M,D
Psychology—General	M,D
Sociology	M,D
Speech and Interpersonal Communication	M
Technical Communication	M,D
Technical Writing	M,D
Writing	M

COLORADO TECHNICAL UNIVERSITY COLORADO SPRINGS

Conflict Resolution and Mediation/Peace Studies	M,D
Criminal Justice and Criminology	M

COLORADO TECHNICAL UNIVERSITY DENVER

Conflict Resolution and Mediation/Peace Studies	M
Criminal Justice and Criminology	M

COLORADO TECHNICAL UNIVERSITY SIOUX FALLS

Criminal Justice and Criminology	M

COLUMBIA COLLEGE (MO)

Criminal Justice and Criminology	M

COLUMBIA COLLEGE (SC)

Conflict Resolution and Mediation/Peace Studies	M,O

COLUMBIA COLLEGE CHICAGO

Architecture	M
Arts Administration	M
Comparative and Interdisciplinary Arts	M
Film, Television, and Video Production	M
Interior Design	M
Journalism	M
Media Studies	M
Photography	M
Therapies—Dance, Drama, and Music	M,O
Writing	M

COLUMBIA INTERNATIONAL UNIVERSITY

Cultural Studies	P,M,D,O
Missions and Missiology	P,M,D,O
Pastoral Ministry and Counseling	P,M,D,O
Theology	P,M,D,O

COLUMBIA SOUTHERN UNIVERSITY

Criminal Justice and Criminology	M

COLUMBIA THEOLOGICAL SEMINARY

Theology	P,M,D

COLUMBIA UNION COLLEGE

Religion	M

COLUMBIA UNIVERSITY

African Studies	O
African-American Studies	M
American Studies	M
Anthropology	M,D
Archaeology	M,D
Architecture	M,D
Art History	M,D
Art/Fine Arts	M
Asian Languages	M,D
Asian Studies	M,D,O
Classics	M,D
Communication— General	M,D
Comparative Literature	M,D
Conflict Resolution and Mediation/Peace Studies	M
Corporate and Organizational Communication	M
East European and Russian Studies	M,O
Economics	M,D
English	M,D
Environmental Design	M
Experimental Psychology	M,D

Film, Television, and Video Production	M
French	M,D
German	M,D
Historic Preservation	M,O
History	M,D
Interdisciplinary Studies	M
International Affairs	M*
Italian	M,D
Jewish Studies	M,D
Journalism	M,D*
Landscape Architecture	M
Latin American Studies	M,O
Liberal Studies	M
Medieval and Renaissance Studies	M
Music	M,D
Near and Middle Eastern Languages	M,D
Near and Middle Eastern Studies	M,D,O
Philosophy	M,D
Photography	M
Political Science	M,D
Psychology—General	M,D
Public Administration	M
Public Policy	M
Religion	M,D
Romance Languages	M,D
Russian	M,D
Slavic Languages	M,D
Social Psychology	M,D
Social Sciences	M
Sociology	M,D
Spanish	M,D
Sustainable Development	M,D
Theater	M,D*
Urban and Regional Planning	M,D
Western European Studies	M,O
Writing	M

COLUMBUS STATE UNIVERSITY

Counseling Psychology	M,O
Criminal Justice and Criminology	M
Public Administration	M

CONCORDIA LUTHERAN SEMINARY

Theology	P,O

CONCORDIA SEMINARY

Theology	P,M,D,O

CONCORDIA THEOLOGICAL SEMINARY

Theology	P,M,D

CONCORDIA UNIVERSITY (CA)

International Affairs	M
Theology	M

CONCORDIA UNIVERSITY (CANADA)

Anthropology	M
Applied Arts and Design—General	O
Art History	M,D
Art Therapy	M
Art/Fine Arts	M

Child and Family Studies	M
Clinical Psychology	M,D,O
Communication— General	M,D,O
Computer Art and Design	O
Economic Development	O
Economics	M,D,O
English	M
Film, Television, and Video Production	M
Film, Television, and Video Theory and Criticism	M
French	M,O
Geography	M,D,O
History	M,D
Humanities	D
Internet and Interactive Multimedia	M,O
Jewish Studies	M
Journalism	O
Linguistics	M,D,O
Media Studies	M,D,O
Music	O
Philosophy	M
Political Science	M,D
Psychology—General	M,D
Public Administration	M,D
Public Affairs	O
Public Policy	M,D
Religion	M,D
Rural Planning and Studies	M,D,O
Sociology	M
Theology	M
Translation and Interpretation	M,O
Urban and Regional Planning	O
Urban Studies	M,O
Writing	M

CONCORDIA UNIVERSITY CHICAGO

Counseling Psychology	M
Gerontology	M
Liberal Studies	M
Music	M
Psychology—General	M
Religion	M

CONCORDIA UNIVERSITY, NEBRASKA

Pastoral Ministry and Counseling	M

CONCORDIA UNIVERSITY, ST. PAUL

Child and Family Studies	M,O
Criminal Justice and Criminology	M
Pastoral Ministry and Counseling	M,O
Theology	M,O

CONCORDIA UNIVERSITY WISCONSIN

Child and Family Studies	M

Corporate and Organizational Communication	M
Counseling Psychology	M
Music	M
Psychology—General	M
Public Administration	M

CONNECTICUT COLLEGE

Psychology—General	M

CONSERVATORIO DE MUSICA

Music	O

CONVERSE COLLEGE

English	M
History	M
Liberal Studies	M
Marriage and Family Therapy	O
Music	M
Political Science	M

CONWAY SCHOOL OF LANDSCAPE DESIGN

Landscape Architecture	M

COOPER UNION FOR THE ADVANCEMENT OF SCIENCE AND ART

Architecture	M

COPPIN STATE UNIVERSITY

Addictions/Substance Abuse Counseling	M
Criminal Justice and Criminology	M
Rehabilitation Counseling	M

CORCORAN COLLEGE OF ART AND DESIGN

Decorative Arts	M
Interior Design	M

CORNELL UNIVERSITY

African Studies	M,D
African-American Studies	M,D
Agricultural Economics and Agribusiness	M,D
American Studies	M,D
Anthropology	D
Applied Economics	D
Archaeology	M,D
Architectural History	M,D
Architecture	M,D
Art History	D
Art/Fine Arts	M
Asian Languages	M,D
Asian Studies	M,D
Building Science	M,D
Child and Family Studies	D
Chinese	M,D
Classics	D
Clothing and Textiles	M,D
Cognitive Sciences	D
Communication— General	M,D
Comparative Literature	D

Computer Art and Design	M,D
Conflict Resolution and Mediation/Peace Studies	M,D
Consumer Economics	M,D
Cultural Studies	M,D
Demography and Population Studies	M,D
Developmental Psychology	D
East European and Russian Studies	M,D
Economic Development	M,D
Economics	M,D
English	M,D
Environmental Design	M
Ethnic Studies	M,D
Experimental Psychology	D
Family and Consumer Sciences-General	M,D
French	D
Gender Studies	M,D
German	M,D
Historic Preservation	M,D
History of Science and Technology	M,D
History	M,D
Human Development	D
Industrial and Labor Relations	M,D*
Interior Design	M
International Affairs	D
International Development	M
Italian	D
Japanese	M,D
Jewish Studies	M,D
Landscape Architecture	M
Latin American Studies	M,D
Linguistics	M,D
Medieval and Renaissance Studies	M,D
Music	M,D
Near and Middle Eastern Studies	M,D
Philosophy	D
Photography	M
Political Science	D
Psychology—General	D
Public Affairs	M*
Public Policy	M,D
Religion	D
Romance Languages	M,D
Rural Planning and Studies	M
Rural Sociology	M,D
Scandinavian Languages	M,D
Slavic Languages	M,D
Social Psychology	M,D
Sociology	M,D
Spanish	D
Textile Design	M,D
Theater	D
Urban and Regional Planning	M,D
Urban Design	M,D
Western European Studies	M,D
Women's Studies	M,D
Writing	M,D

COVENANT THEOLOGICAL SEMINARY

Theology	P,M,D,O

CRANBROOK ACADEMY OF ART

Applied Arts and Design—General	M
Architecture	M
Art/Fine Arts	M*
Graphic Design	M
Photography	M
Textile Design	M

CREIGHTON UNIVERSITY

Conflict Resolution and Mediation/Peace Studies	M,O
English	M
International Affairs	M
Liberal Studies	M
Theology	M

THE CRISWELL COLLEGE

Jewish Studies	P,M
Pastoral Ministry and Counseling	P,M
Theology	P,M

CROWN COLLEGE

Theology	M

CUMBERLAND UNIVERSITY

Public Administration	M

CUNY GRADUATE SCHOOL OF JOURNALISM

Journalism	M*

CURRY COLLEGE

Criminal Justice and Criminology	M

THE CURTIS INSTITUTE OF MUSIC

Music	M

DALHOUSIE UNIVERSITY

Anthropology	M,D
Architecture	M
Classics	M,D
Clinical Psychology	M,D
Economics	M,D
English	M,D
French	M,D
German	M
History	M,D
Interdisciplinary Studies	D
International Development	M
Music	M
Philosophy	M,D
Political Science	M,D
Psychology—General	M,D
Public Administration	M,O
Rural Planning and Studies	M
Sociology	M,D
Urban and Regional Planning	M

*M—master's degree; P—first professional degree; D—doctorate; O—other advanced degree; *—Close-Up and/or Announcement or Display*

DALLAS BAPTIST UNIVERSITY

Conflict Resolution and Mediation/Peace Studies	M
Corporate and Organizational Communication	M
Counseling Psychology	M
Criminal Justice and Criminology	M
Experimental Psychology	M
Interdisciplinary Studies	M
Liberal Studies	M
Missions and Missiology	M
Pastoral Ministry and Counseling	M

DALLAS THEOLOGICAL SEMINARY

Media Studies	M,D,O
Missions and Missiology	M,D,O
Pastoral Ministry and Counseling	M,D,O
Theology	M,D,O

DARKEI NOAM RABBINICAL COLLEGE

Theology	

DARTMOUTH COLLEGE

Cognitive Sciences	D
Comparative Literature	M
Liberal Studies	M*
Music	M
Psychology—General	D

DEFIANCE COLLEGE

Criminal Justice and Criminology	M

DELAWARE STATE UNIVERSITY

Historic Preservation	M

DELAWARE VALLEY COLLEGE

Agricultural Economics and Agribusiness	M

DELL'ARTE SCHOOL OF PHYSICAL THEATRE

Theater	M

DELTA STATE UNIVERSITY

Criminal Justice and Criminology	M
Urban and Regional Planning	M

DENVER SEMINARY

Marriage and Family Therapy	P,M,D,O
Pastoral Ministry and Counseling	P,M,D,O
Religion	P,M,D,O
Theology	P,M,D,O

DEPAUL UNIVERSITY

Clinical Psychology	M,D
Communication— General	M

Computer Art and Design	M,D
Corporate and Organizational Communication	M
Economics	M
English	M
Experimental Psychology	M,D
History	M
Human Development	M,D
Industrial and Organizational Psychology	M,D
Interdisciplinary Studies	M
Internet and Interactive Multimedia	M,D
Journalism	M
Media Studies	M
Music	M,O
Philosophy	M,D
Psychology—General	M,D
Public Administration	M,O
Public Affairs	M,O
Public Policy	M,O
Publishing	M
Social Psychology	M,D
Sociology	M
Theater	M
Urban and Regional Planning	M,O
Writing	M

DESALES UNIVERSITY

Criminal Justice and Criminology	M

DEVRY UNIVERSITY

Communication— General	M
Public Administration	M

DIGITAL MEDIA ARTS COLLEGE

Computer Art and Design	M
Graphic Design	M
Media Studies	M

DOMINICAN HOUSE OF STUDIES, PONTIFICAL FACULTY OF THE IMMACULATE CONCEPTION

Theology	P,M,O

DOMINICAN SCHOOL OF PHILOSOPHY AND THEOLOGY

Philosophy	M
Theology	P,O

DOMINICAN UNIVERSITY OF CALIFORNIA

Counseling Psychology	M
Gerontology	M
Humanities	M
Marriage and Family Therapy	M
Sustainable Development	M

DOWLING COLLEGE

Human Development	M,D,O
Liberal Studies	M

DRAKE UNIVERSITY

American Studies	M
Art/Fine Arts	M
Communication— General	M
History	M
Journalism	M
Public Administration	M
Rehabilitation Counseling	M
Sociology	M
Speech and Interpersonal Communication	M
Theater	M

DREW UNIVERSITY

English	M,D
Ethics	M,D
History	M,D
Holocaust Studies	M,D,O
Humanities	M,D,O
Interdisciplinary Studies	M,D,O
Near and Middle Eastern Studies	M,D
Religion	M,D
Theology	P,M,D,O
Women's Studies	M

DREXEL UNIVERSITY

Applied Arts and Design—General	M
Art Therapy	M,O
Arts Administration	M
Clinical Psychology	D
Communication— General	M
Computer Art and Design	M
Corporate and Organizational Communication	M
Economics	M,D,O
Emergency Management	M
Film, Television, and Video Production	M
Forensic Psychology	D
Health Psychology	D
History of Science and Technology	M
Interior Design	M
Journalism	M
Marriage and Family Therapy	M,D
Mass Communication	M
Media Studies	M
Psychology—General	M,D
Publishing	M
Technical Communication	M
Technical Writing	M
Textile Design	M
Therapies—Dance, Drama, and Music	M,O

DRURY UNIVERSITY

Art/Fine Arts	M
Communication— General	M
Criminal Justice and Criminology	M

DUKE UNIVERSITY

Anthropology	D

Art History	D
Art/Fine Arts	D
Asian Studies	M,O
Biological Anthropology	D
Classics	D
Clinical Psychology	D
Cognitive Sciences	D
Comparative Literature	D
Developmental Psychology	D
Economics	M,D
English	D
Experimental Psychology	D
French	D
German	D
Health Psychology	D
History of Medicine	
History	M,D
Human Development	D
Humanities	M
International Development	M,O
Latin American Studies	M,D,O
Liberal Studies	M
Medieval and Renaissance Studies	O
Music	M,D
Philosophy	M,D
Political Science	M,D
Psychology—General	D
Public Policy	M,D,O
Religion	M,D
Slavic Languages	M
Sociology	M,D
Spanish	D
Theology	P,M,D
Women's Studies	O

DUQUESNE UNIVERSITY

Clinical Psychology	D
Communication— General	M,D
Conflict Resolution and Mediation/Peace Studies	M,O
English	M,D
Ethics	M
Forensic Sciences	M
History	M
Internet and Interactive Multimedia	M,O
Liberal Studies	M
Museum Studies	M
Music	M,O
Philosophy	M,D
Psychology—General	D
Public Administration	M,O
Public Policy	M,O
Rhetoric	M,D
School Psychology	M,D,O
Theology	M,D

EARLHAM SCHOOL OF RELIGION

Religion	P,M
Theology	P,M

EAST CAROLINA UNIVERSITY

Addictions/Substance Abuse Counseling	M
American Studies	M
Anthropology	M
Art/Fine Arts	M
Child and Family Studies	M

Child Development	M
Clinical Psychology	M
Criminal Justice and Criminology	M
Economics	M
English	M
Geography	M
Health Communication	M
Health Psychology	D
History	M
International Affairs	M
Marriage and Family Therapy	M
Music	M
Political Science	M
Psychology—General	M
Public Administration	M
Rehabilitation Counseling	M
School Psychology	M
Sociology	M
Therapies—Dance, Drama, and Music	M
Western European Studies	M

EAST CENTRAL UNIVERSITY

Criminal Justice and Criminology	M
Psychology—General	M
Rehabilitation Counseling	M

EASTERN ILLINOIS UNIVERSITY

Art/Fine Arts	M
Clinical Psychology	M,O
Consumer Economics	M
Economics	M
English	M
Family and Consumer Sciences-General	M
Gerontology	M
History	M
Music	M
Political Science	M
Psychology—General	M,O
Public History	M
School Psychology	M,O
Speech and Interpersonal Communication	M

EASTERN KENTUCKY UNIVERSITY

Clinical Psychology	M,O
Criminal Justice and Criminology	M
English	M
History	M
Industrial and Organizational Psychology	M,O
Music	M
Political Science	M
Psychology—General	M,O
Public Administration	M
School Psychology	M,O
Urban and Regional Planning	M
Writing	M

EASTERN MENNONITE UNIVERSITY

Conflict Resolution and Mediation/Peace Studies	M,O
Pastoral Ministry and Counseling	P,M,O
Religion	P,M,O
Theology	P,M,O

EASTERN MICHIGAN UNIVERSITY

Addictions/Substance Abuse Counseling	M,O
African-American Studies	O
American Studies	M,O
Applied Economics	M
Art/Fine Arts	M
Arts Administration	M
Child and Family Studies	M,O
Clinical Psychology	M,D
Clothing and Textiles	M
Communication— General	M
Criminal Justice and Criminology	M,O
Cultural Studies	M
Economic Development	M
Economics	M
English	M,O
French	M,O
Gender Studies	M
Geographic Information Systems	M,O
Geography	M,O
German	M,O
Gerontology	M,O
Hispanic Studies	M,O
Historic Preservation	M,O
History	M,O
Interior Design	M
International Economics	M
Japanese	M,O
Linguistics	M
Music	M
Political Science	M
Psychology—General	M,D
Public Administration	M,O
Public Policy	M,O
Social Psychology	M,O
Social Sciences	M,O
Sociology	M
Spanish	M,O
Technical Communication	M,O
Theater	M
Urban and Regional Planning	M,O
Women's Studies	M
Writing	M,O

EASTERN NAZARENE COLLEGE

Counseling Psychology	M
Marriage and Family Therapy	M

EASTERN NEW MEXICO UNIVERSITY

Anthropology	M

Communication— General	M
English	M

EASTERN UNIVERSITY

Counseling Psychology	M,O
Economic Development	M
International Development	M
Marriage and Family Therapy	D
Missions and Missiology	D
Pastoral Ministry and Counseling	D
School Psychology	M,O
Social Psychology	M,O
Theology	P,M,D
Urban and Regional Planning	M
Urban Studies	M

EASTERN VIRGINIA MEDICAL SCHOOL

Art Therapy	M
Clinical Psychology	D

EASTERN WASHINGTON UNIVERSITY

Clinical Psychology	M
Communication— General	M
Counseling Psychology	M
English	M
Experimental Psychology	M
History	M
Interdisciplinary Studies	M
Music	M
Psychology—General	M
Public Administration	M
Rhetoric	M
School Psychology	M
Sport Psychology	M
Technical Communication	M
Urban and Regional Planning	M
Writing	M

EAST STROUDSBURG UNIVERSITY OF PENNSYLVANIA

History	M
Political Science	M

EAST TENNESSEE STATE UNIVERSITY

Art History	M
Art/Fine Arts	M
Clinical Psychology	M
Communication— General	M
Computer Art and Design	M
Criminal Justice and Criminology	M
Economic Development	M
Economics	M
English	M
Gerontology	M,O
History	M
Human Development	M

Liberal Studies	M
Marriage and Family Therapy	M
Psychology—General	M
Sociology	M
Urban and Regional Planning	M
Urban Studies	M

ECUMENICAL THEOLOGICAL SEMINARY

Pastoral Ministry and Counseling	D
Theology	P

EDEN THEOLOGICAL SEMINARY

Theology	P,M,D

EDGEWOOD COLLEGE

Marriage and Family Therapy	M
Religion	M

EDINBORO UNIVERSITY OF PENNSYLVANIA

Art/Fine Arts	M
Clinical Psychology	M
Communication— General	M
Media Studies	M
Psychology—General	M
Rehabilitation Counseling	M,O
School Psychology	M,O
Social Sciences	M

ELMHURST COLLEGE

English	M
Industrial and Organizational Psychology	M

ELMS COLLEGE

Religion	M

ELON UNIVERSITY

Internet and Interactive Multimedia	M

EMERSON COLLEGE

Broadcast Journalism	M
Communication— General	M
Corporate and Organizational Communication	M
Health Communication	M
Journalism	M
Media Studies	M
Publishing	M
Theater	M
Writing	M

EMILY CARR INSTITUTE OF ART + DESIGN

Applied Arts and Design—General	M
Art/Fine Arts	M

---

*M—master's degree; P—first professional degree; D—doctorate; O—other advanced degree; *—Close-Up and / or Announcement or Display*

Computer Art and
Design — M

EMMANUEL SCHOOL OF RELIGION

Missions and Missiology — P,M,D
Pastoral Ministry and
Counseling — P,M,D
Religion — P,M,D
Theology — P,M,D

EMORY & HENRY COLLEGE

American Studies — M
History — M

EMORY UNIVERSITY

Anthropology — D
Art History — D
Clinical Psychology — D
Cognitive Sciences — D
Comparative Literature — D,O
Developmental
Psychology — D
Economics — D
English — D,O
Film, Television, and
Video Theory and
Criticism — M,D,O
French — D,O
Gerontology — M
History — D
Interdisciplinary Studies — D
Jewish Studies — M
Music — M
Near and Middle
Eastern Studies — D,O
Philosophy — D,O
Political Science — D
Portuguese — D,O
Psychology—General — D
Religion — D,O
Sociology — M,D*
Spanish — D,O
Theology — P,M,D
Women's Studies — D,O

EMPORIA STATE UNIVERSITY

Art Therapy — M
Clinical Psychology — M
Counseling Psychology — M
English — M
History — M
Industrial and
Organizational
Psychology — M
Music — M
Psychology—General — M
Rehabilitation
Counseling — M
School Psychology — M,O

EPISCOPAL DIVINITY SCHOOL

Theology — P,M,D,O

ERIKSON INSTITUTE

Child Development — M
Developmental
Psychology — M,O
Human Development — M,O

ERSKINE THEOLOGICAL SEMINARY

Theology — P,M,D

EVANGELICAL SEMINARY OF PUERTO RICO

Theology — P,M,D

EVANGELICAL THEOLOGICAL SEMINARY

Marriage and Family
Therapy — P,M,O
Pastoral Ministry and
Counseling — P,M,O
Religion — P,M,O
Theology — P,M,O

EVANGEL UNIVERSITY

Clinical Psychology — M
Counseling Psychology — M
Psychology—General — M
School Psychology — M

EVEREST UNIVERSITY

Criminal Justice and
Criminology — M

EVEREST UNIVERSITY

Criminal Justice and
Criminology — M

EVEREST UNIVERSITY

Criminal Justice and
Criminology — M

EVEREST UNIVERSITY

Criminal Justice and
Criminology — M

THE EVERGREEN STATE COLLEGE

Public Administration — M

EXCELSIOR COLLEGE

Liberal Studies — M

FAIRFIELD UNIVERSITY

American Studies — M
Communication—
General — M
Industrial and
Organizational
Psychology — M,O
Marriage and Family
Therapy — M
Psychology—General — M,O
School Psychology — M,O
Writing — M

FAIRLEIGH DICKINSON UNIVERSITY, COLLEGE AT FLORHAM

Corporate and
Organizational
Communication — M
Counseling Psychology — M
Industrial and
Organizational
Psychology — M
Psychology—General — M,O
Public Administration — M
Writing — M

FAIRLEIGH DICKINSON UNIVERSITY, METROPOLITAN CAMPUS

Art/Fine Arts — M
Clinical Psychology — M,D*
Communication—
General — M
Comparative Literature — M
English — M
Experimental
Psychology — M,O
Forensic Psychology — M
History — M
Homeland Security — M
International Affairs — M
Media Studies — M
Political Science — M
Psychology—General — M,D,O
Public Administration — M,O
School Psychology — M,D

FAIRMONT STATE UNIVERSITY

Criminal Justice and
Criminology — M

FAITH BAPTIST BIBLE COLLEGE AND THEOLOGICAL SEMINARY

Pastoral Ministry and
Counseling — P,M
Religion — P,M
Theology — P,M

FAITH EVANGELICAL LUTHERAN SEMINARY

Theology — P,M,D

FASHION INSTITUTE OF TECHNOLOGY

Applied Arts and
Design—General — M*
Art History — M
Arts Administration — M
Clothing and Textiles — M
Illustration — M
Museum Studies — M

FAYETTEVILLE STATE UNIVERSITY

Criminal Justice and
Criminology — M
English — M
History — M
Political Science — M
Psychology—General — M
Sociology — M

FELICIAN COLLEGE

Counseling Psychology — M*

FERRIS STATE UNIVERSITY

Applied Arts and
Design—General — M
Art/Fine Arts — M
Criminal Justice and
Criminology — M

FIELDING GRADUATE UNIVERSITY

Clinical Psychology — M,D,O
Human Development — M,D,O

Psychology—General — M,D,O*

FISK UNIVERSITY

Clinical Psychology — M
Psychology—General — M

FITCHBURG STATE COLLEGE

Communication—
General — M,O
Counseling Psychology — M,O
Criminal Justice and
Criminology — M
English — M,O
History — M,O
Interdisciplinary Studies — O
Marriage and Family
Therapy — M,O
Technical Writing — M,O

FIVE TOWNS COLLEGE

Music — M,D

FLORIDA AGRICULTURAL AND MECHANICAL UNIVERSITY

African-American
Studies — M
Agricultural Economics
and Agribusiness — M
Architecture — M
Criminal Justice and
Criminology — M
Economics — M
History — M
International Affairs — M
Journalism — M
Landscape Architecture — M
Political Science — M
Psychology—General — M
Public Administration — M
School Psychology — M
Social Psychology — M
Social Sciences — M
Sociology — M

FLORIDA ATLANTIC UNIVERSITY

Anthropology — M
Applied Arts and
Design—General — M
Art/Fine Arts — M
Communication—
General — M,O
Comparative and
Interdisciplinary Arts — D
Comparative Literature — M
Computer Art and
Design — M
Counseling Psychology — M,D,O
Criminal Justice and
Criminology — M
Economic Development — M,O
Economics — M
English — M
Environmental Design — M,O
Film, Television, and
Video Production — M,O
Film, Television, and
Video Theory and
Criticism — M,O
French — M
Geography — M
Graphic Design — M
History — M,O
Journalism — M,O
Liberal Studies — M

Linguistics	M
Marriage and Family Therapy	M,D,O
Music	M
Political Science	M
Psychology—General	M,D
Public Administration	M,D
Rehabilitation Counseling	M,D,O
Sociology	M
Spanish	M
Sustainable Development	M,O
Theater	M
Urban and Regional Planning	M,O
Women's Studies	M,O
Writing	M

FLORIDA GULF COAST UNIVERSITY

Criminal Justice and Criminology	M
English	M
Forensic Sciences	M
History	M
Interdisciplinary Studies	M
Public Administration	M

FLORIDA INSTITUTE OF TECHNOLOGY

Clinical Psychology	M,D
Communication—General	M
Industrial and Organizational Psychology	M,D
Psychology—General	M,D*
Public Administration	M

FLORIDA INTERNATIONAL UNIVERSITY

African Studies	M
Architecture	M
Art/Fine Arts	M
Asian Studies	M
Conflict Resolution and Mediation/Peace Studies	O
Counseling Psychology	M
Criminal Justice and Criminology	M
Developmental Psychology	M,D
Economics	M,D
English	M
Forensic Sciences	M,D
History	M,D
Interior Design	M
International Affairs	M,D
Landscape Architecture	M
Latin American Studies	M
Liberal Studies	M
Linguistics	M
Mass Communication	M
Music	M
Political Science	M,D
Psychology—General	M,D
Public Administration	M,D
Rehabilitation Counseling	M
Religion	M
School Psychology	M,O
Sociology	M,D

Spanish	M,D
Writing	M

FLORIDA STATE UNIVERSITY

American Studies	M,O
Anthropology	M,D
Archaeology	M,D
Art History	M,D,O
Art/Fine Arts	M
Arts Administration	M,D
Asian Studies	M
Child and Family Studies	M,D
Classics	M,D
Clinical Psychology	D
Cognitive Sciences	D
Communication—General	M,D
Corporate and Organizational Communication	M,D
Counseling Psychology	M,D,O
Criminal Justice and Criminology	M,D
Dance	M
Demography and Population Studies	M,O
Developmental Psychology	D
East European and Russian Studies	M
Economics	M,D
English	M,D
Family and Consumer Sciences-General	M,D
Film, Television, and Video Production	M
French	M,D
Geographic Information Systems	M,D
Geography	M,D
German	M
History	M,D
Humanities	M,D,O
Interior Design	M
International Affairs	M
Italian	M
Marriage and Family Therapy	M,D
Mass Communication	M,D
Media Studies	M,D
Museum Studies	M,D,O
Music	M,D
Philosophy	M,D
Political Science	M,D
Psychology—General	M,D
Public Administration	M,D,O
Public History	M,D
Public Policy	M,D,O
Rehabilitation Counseling	M,D,O
Religion	M,D
Rhetoric	M,D
School Psychology	M,O
Slavic Languages	M
Social Psychology	D
Sociology	M,D
Spanish	M,D
Speech and Interpersonal Communication	M,D
Sport Psychology	M,D,O
Theater	M,D
Therapies—Dance, Drama, and Music	M,D

Urban and Regional Planning	M,D
Writing	M,D

FONTBONNE UNIVERSITY

Art/Fine Arts	M
Family and Consumer Sciences-General	M
Theater	M

FORDHAM UNIVERSITY

Classics	M,D
Clinical Psychology	D
Communication—General	M
Corporate and Organizational Communication	M
Counseling Psychology	M,D,O
Developmental Psychology	D
Economic Development	M,O
Economics	M,D,O
English	M,D
Ethics	O
History	M,D
International Affairs	M,O
International Development	M,O*
International Economics	M,O
Latin American Studies	M,O
Liberal Studies	M
Mass Communication	M
Media Studies	M
Medieval and Renaissance Studies	M,O
Pastoral Ministry and Counseling	M,D,O
Philosophy	M,D
Political Science	M
Psychology—General	D
Religion	M,D,O
School Psychology	M,D,O
Sociology	M,D
Theology	M,D
Urban Studies	M

FORT HAYS STATE UNIVERSITY

Art/Fine Arts	M
Communication—General	M
English	M
Geography	M
History	M
Liberal Studies	M
Psychology—General	M,O
School Psychology	O

FORT VALLEY STATE UNIVERSITY

Counseling Psychology	M
Rehabilitation Counseling	M

FRAMINGHAM STATE COLLEGE

Art/Fine Arts	M
Psychology—General	M
Public Administration	M
Spanish	M

FRANCISCAN SCHOOL OF THEOLOGY

Theology	P,M

FRANCISCAN UNIVERSITY OF STEUBENVILLE

Counseling Psychology	M
Philosophy	M
Theology	M

FRANCIS MARION UNIVERSITY

Clinical Psychology	M
Psychology—General	M
School Psychology	M
Social Psychology	M

FRANKLIN PIERCE UNIVERSITY

Interdisciplinary Studies	M,D,O

FRANKLIN UNIVERSITY

Corporate and Organizational Communication	M

FRANK LLOYD WRIGHT SCHOOL OF ARCHITECTURE

Architecture	M

FREDERICK S. PARDEE RAND GRADUATE SCHOOL

Public Policy	D

FREED-HARDEMAN UNIVERSITY

Ethics	M
Pastoral Ministry and Counseling	M
Theology	P,M

FRESNO PACIFIC UNIVERSITY

Conflict Resolution and Mediation/Peace Studies	M
Interdisciplinary Studies	M
School Psychology	M

FRIENDS UNIVERSITY

Marriage and Family Therapy	M
Theology	M

FROSTBURG STATE UNIVERSITY

Counseling Psychology	M
Interdisciplinary Studies	M
Psychology—General	M

FULLER THEOLOGICAL SEMINARY

Clinical Psychology	D
Marriage and Family Therapy	M,O
Missions and Missiology	P,M,D
Music	P,M,D
Pastoral Ministry and Counseling	P,M,D
Psychology—General	M,D,O
Theology	P,M,D

FULL SAIL UNIVERSITY

Internet and Interactive Multimedia	M
Media Studies	M

*M—master's degree; P—first professional degree; D—doctorate; O—other advanced degree; *—Close-Up and/or Announcement or Display*

GALLAUDET UNIVERSITY

Clinical Psychology	D
Counseling Psychology	M
Developmental Psychology	M,O
Linguistics	M,D
Psychology—General	M,D,O
School Psychology	M,O

GANNON UNIVERSITY

Counseling Psychology	D
English	M
Gerontology	O
Pastoral Ministry and Counseling	M,O
Public Administration	M,O

GARDNER-WEBB UNIVERSITY

Counseling Psychology	M
English	M
Missions and Missiology	P,D
Pastoral Ministry and Counseling	P,D
Psychology—General	M
School Psychology	M
Theology	P,D

GARRETT-EVANGELICAL THEOLOGICAL SEMINARY

Music	P,M,D
Pastoral Ministry and Counseling	P,M,D
Theology	P,M,D

GENERAL THEOLOGICAL SEMINARY

Pastoral Ministry and Counseling	P,M,D,O
Religion	P,M,D,O
Theology	P,M,D,O

GENEVA COLLEGE

Counseling Psychology	M
Marriage and Family Therapy	M
Psychology—General	M

GEORGE FOX UNIVERSITY

Clinical Psychology	M,D*
Counseling Psychology	M,O
Marriage and Family Therapy	M,O
Missions and Missiology	P,M,D,O
Pastoral Ministry and Counseling	P,M,D,O
Psychology—General	M,D
Religion	P,M,D,O
School Psychology	M,O
Theology	P,M,D,O

GEORGE MASON UNIVERSITY

Anthropology	M
Art History	M
Arts Administration	M
Clinical Psychology	M,D
Communication— General	M,D
Conflict Resolution and Mediation/Peace Studies	M,D
Criminal Justice and Criminology	
Cultural Studies	D*
Dance	M
Developmental Psychology	M,D
Economics	M,D,O
English	M,O
Film, Television, and Video Production	M
Folklore	M
Forensic Sciences	M,D,O
Geographic Information Systems	M,D,O
Geography	M
Graphic Design	M
History	M,D,O
Homeland Security	M,D
Industrial and Organizational Psychology	M,D
Interdisciplinary Studies	M
International Affairs	M
Linguistics	M,O
Music	M,O
Philosophy	
Political Science	M,D
Psychology—General	M,D
Public Affairs	M,D
Public Policy	M,D*
Religion	M
School Psychology	M
Social Sciences	M,D,O
Sociology	M
Women's Studies	M
Writing	M

GEORGETOWN UNIVERSITY

American Studies	M,D
Communication— General	M
Comparative Literature	M,D
Conflict Resolution and Mediation/Peace Studies	M
East European and Russian Studies	M
Economic Development	D
Economics	D
English	M
Ethics	M,D
German	M,D
History	M,D
Humanities	M,D
Industrial and Labor Relations	D
Interdisciplinary Studies	M,D
International Affairs	P,M,D
Internet and Interactive Multimedia	M
Journalism	M,D
Latin American Studies	M
Liberal Studies	M,D
Linguistics	M,D,O
Media Studies	M,D
Medieval and Renaissance Studies	M,D
Near and Middle Eastern Languages	M,D
Near and Middle Eastern Studies	M,D,O
Philosophy	M,D
Political Science	M,D
Psychology—General	D
Public Policy	M,D
Religion	M,D
Spanish	M,D
Theology	D
Western European Studies	M

THE GEORGE WASHINGTON UNIVERSITY

American Studies	M,D
Anthropology	M,D
Art History	M
Art Therapy	M
Art/Fine Arts	M
Asian Studies	M
Clinical Psychology	D
Cognitive Sciences	D
Communication— General	M
Criminal Justice and Criminology	M
East European and Russian Studies	M
Economics	M,D
Emergency Management	M,D,O
English	M,D
Folklore	M,D
Forensic Sciences	M
Geography	M
Health Communication	M
Health Psychology	D
Historic Preservation	M
History	M,D
Human Development	M
Industrial and Organizational Psychology	M,D
Interior Design	M
International Affairs	M
International Development	M
International Trade Policy	M
Latin American Studies	M
Mass Communication	M
Military and Defense Studies	M
Museum Studies	M,O
Near and Middle Eastern Studies	M
Philosophy	M,D
Photography	M
Political Science	M,D
Psychology—General	D
Public Administration	M,D
Public Affairs	M
Public Policy	M,D
Publishing	M
Rehabilitation Counseling	M
Religion	M
Social Psychology	M,D
Sociology	M
Theater	M
Western European Studies	M
Women's Studies	M,D,O

GEORGIA COLLEGE & STATE UNIVERSITY

Criminal Justice and Criminology	M
English	M
History	M
Public Administration	M
Public Affairs	M
Therapies—Dance, Drama, and Music	M
Writing	M

GEORGIA INSTITUTE OF TECHNOLOGY

Architecture	M,D
Building Science	M,D
Computer Art and Design	M,D
Economic Development	M,D
Economics	M
Experimental Psychology	M,D
Geographic Information Systems	M,D
History of Science and Technology	M,D
Industrial and Organizational Psychology	M,D
International Affairs	M,D
Internet and Interactive Multimedia	M,D
Psychology—General	M,D
Public Policy	M,D
Urban and Regional Planning	M,D
Urban Design	M,D

GEORGIAN COURT UNIVERSITY

Counseling Psychology	M,O
Pastoral Ministry and Counseling	M,O
Theology	M,O

GEORGIA SOUTHERN UNIVERSITY

Applied Economics	M
Art/Fine Arts	M
English	M
History	M
Music	M
Psychology—General	M,D
Public Administration	M
School Psychology	M,O
Sociology	M
Spanish	M

GEORGIA STATE UNIVERSITY

Anthropology	M
Art History	M
Art/Fine Arts	M
Communication— General	M,D
Counseling Psychology	M,D,O
Criminal Justice and Criminology	M,D
Economic Development	M,D,O
Economics	M,D
Emergency Management	M,D,O
English	M,D
Film, Television, and Video Production	M,D
French	M,O
Geographic Information Systems	O
Geography	M
German	M,O
Gerontology	M
Historic Preservation	M,O
History	M,D
Latin American Studies	M,D,O
Linguistics	M,D
Mass Communication	M,D
Music	M
Philosophy	M
Photography	M,D
Political Science	M,D
Psychology—General	M,D
Public Administration	M
Public Policy	D

Rehabilitation Counseling	M
Religion	M
Rhetoric	M,D
School Psychology	M,D,O
Sociology	M,D
Spanish	M,O
Speech and Interpersonal Communication	M,D
Translation and Interpretation	O
Urban and Regional Planning	M,D,O
Urban Studies	M
Women's Studies	M
Writing	M,D

GLOBAL UNIVERSITY

Missions and Missiology	P,M
Theology	P,M

GODDARD COLLEGE

Comparative and Interdisciplinary Arts	M
Counseling Psychology	M
Industrial and Organizational Psychology	M
Interdisciplinary Studies	M
Writing	M

GOLDEN GATE BAPTIST THEOLOGICAL SEMINARY

Pastoral Ministry and Counseling	P,M,D,O
Theology	P,M,D,O

GOLDEN GATE UNIVERSITY

Psychology—General	M,D,O

GONZAGA UNIVERSITY

Communication— General	M
Counseling Psychology	M
Pastoral Ministry and Counseling	M
Philosophy	M
Religion	M

GORDON-CONWELL THEOLOGICAL SEMINARY

Archaeology	P,M,D
Missions and Missiology	P,M,D
Pastoral Ministry and Counseling	P,M,D
Religion	P,M,D
Theology	P,M,D

GOUCHER COLLEGE

Arts Administration	M
Historic Preservation	M
Writing	M

GOVERNORS STATE UNIVERSITY

Addictions/Substance Abuse Counseling	M
Art/Fine Arts	M
Communication— General	M

Counseling Psychology	M
English	M
Media Studies	M
Political Science	M
Psychology—General	M
Public Administration	M

GRACE COLLEGE

Counseling Psychology	M

GRACELAND UNIVERSITY (IA)

Pastoral Ministry and Counseling	M
Religion	M

GRACE THEOLOGICAL SEMINARY

Cultural Studies	P,M,D,O
Missions and Missiology	P,M,D,O
Pastoral Ministry and Counseling	P,M,D,O
Theology	P,M,D,O

GRACE UNIVERSITY

Counseling Psychology	M
Pastoral Ministry and Counseling	M
Theology	M

GRADUATE INSTITUTE OF APPLIED LINGUISTICS

Linguistics	M,O

GRADUATE SCHOOL AND UNIVERSITY CENTER OF THE CITY UNIVERSITY OF NEW YORK

Anthropology	D
Archaeology	D
Architectural History	D
Art History	D
Classics	M,D
Clinical Psychology	D
Cognitive Sciences	D
Comparative Literature	M,D
Criminal Justice and Criminology	D
Developmental Psychology	D
Economics	D
English	D
Experimental Psychology	D
French	D
German	M,D
History	D
Industrial and Organizational Psychology	D
Interdisciplinary Studies	M,D
Italian	M,D
Liberal Studies	M
Linguistics	M,D
Medieval and Renaissance Studies	M,D
Music	D
Philosophy	M,D
Political Science	M,D
Psychology—General	D
Public Policy	M,D
Social Psychology	D
Sociology	D

Spanish	D
Theater	D
Urban Studies	M,D
Women's Studies	M,D

GRADUATE THEOLOGICAL UNION

Art History	M,D,O
Cultural Studies	M,D,O
Ethics	M,D,O
Jewish Studies	M,D,O
Religion	M,D,O
Social Sciences	M,D,O
Theology	M,D,O
Women's Studies	M,D,O

GRAMBLING STATE UNIVERSITY

Criminal Justice and Criminology	M
English	M,D
Mass Communication	M
Political Science	M
Public Administration	M

GRAND CANYON UNIVERSITY

Addictions/Substance Abuse Counseling	M

GRAND RAPIDS THEOLOGICAL SEMINARY OF CORNERSTONE UNIVERSITY

Missions and Missiology	P,M
Pastoral Ministry and Counseling	P,M
Religion	P,M
Theology	P,M

GRAND VALLEY STATE UNIVERSITY

Communication— General	M
Criminal Justice and Criminology	M
English	M
Public Administration	M
School Psychology	M

GRATZ COLLEGE

Holocaust Studies	M,O
Jewish Studies	M,O
Music	M,O

GREENVILLE COLLEGE

Pastoral Ministry and Counseling	M

HAMLINE UNIVERSITY

Liberal Studies	M,O
Public Administration	M,D

HAMPTON UNIVERSITY

Pastoral Ministry and Counseling	M

HARDING UNIVERSITY

Counseling Psychology	M
Marriage and Family Therapy	M

Pastoral Ministry and Counseling	M

HARDING UNIVERSITY GRADUATE SCHOOL OF RELIGION

Pastoral Ministry and Counseling	P,M,D
Religion	P,M,D
Theology	P,M,D

HARDIN-SIMMONS UNIVERSITY

English	M
History	M
Marriage and Family Therapy	M
Music	M
Pastoral Ministry and Counseling	M
Psychology—General	M
Religion	M
Theology	P,M

HARTFORD SEMINARY

Pastoral Ministry and Counseling	M,D,O
Religion	M,D,O
Theology	M,D,O

HARVARD UNIVERSITY

African Studies	D
African-American Studies	D
American Studies	D
Anthropology	M,D
Archaeology	M,D
Architectural History	D
Architecture	M,D
Art History	D
Asian Languages	M,D
Asian Studies	M,D
Celtic Languages	D
Chinese	D
Classics	D
Cognitive Sciences	M,D
Communication— General	M,O
Comparative Literature	D
Demography and Population Studies	M,D
Developmental Psychology	D
East European and Russian Studies	M
Economics	D
English	M,D,O
Experimental Psychology	D
French	M,D
German	D
History of Science and Technology	M,D
History	D
Human Development	M,D
International Affairs	P,D
International Development	M
Italian	M,D
Japanese	D
Jewish Studies	M,D
Journalism	M,O
Landscape Architecture	M,D
Liberal Studies	M,O
Linguistics	D

Medieval and Renaissance Studies	D
Museum Studies	M,O
Music	M,D
Near and Middle Eastern Languages	M,D
Near and Middle Eastern Studies	M,D
Philosophy	M,D
Political Science	M,D
Portuguese	M,D
Psychology—General	D
Public Administration	M
Public Policy	M,D
Religion	D
Russian	D
Scandinavian Languages	D
Slavic Languages	D
Social Psychology	D
Sociology	D
Spanish	M,D
Technical Communication	M
Theology	P,M,D
Urban and Regional Planning	M,D
Urban Design	M

HAWAI'I PACIFIC UNIVERSITY

Communication—General	M*
Economics	M
Military and Defense Studies	M*
Sustainable Development	M*

HAZELDEN GRADUATE SCHOOL OF ADDICTION STUDIES

Addictions/Substance Abuse Counseling	M,O

HEBREW COLLEGE

Jewish Studies	M,O
Music	M,O
Theology	M

HEBREW THEOLOGICAL COLLEGE

Theology	O

HEBREW UNION COLLEGE–JEWISH INSTITUTE OF RELIGION (CA)

Jewish Studies	M,D
Theology	P

HEBREW UNION COLLEGE–JEWISH INSTITUTE OF RELIGION (NY)

Jewish Studies	M
Music	M
Near and Middle Eastern Languages	D
Theology	P,D

HEBREW UNION COLLEGE–JEWISH INSTITUTE OF RELIGION (OH)

Jewish Studies	P,M,D

Near and Middle Eastern Studies	M,D
Religion	M,D
Theology	P

HEC MONTREAL

Applied Economics	M
Arts Administration	O
Corporate and Organizational Communication	O
Sustainable Development	O

HEIDELBERG UNIVERSITY

Counseling Psychology	M

HENDERSON STATE UNIVERSITY

Liberal Studies	M
Social Psychology	M

HERITAGE BAPTIST COLLEGE AND HERITAGE THEOLOGICAL SEMINARY

Pastoral Ministry and Counseling	P,M,D,O
Theology	P,M,D,O

HERITAGE CHRISTIAN UNIVERSITY

Classics	M
Pastoral Ministry and Counseling	M
Religion	M

HERITAGE UNIVERSITY

English	M

HIGH POINT UNIVERSITY

History	M

HILLSDALE FREE WILL BAPTIST COLLEGE

Pastoral Ministry and Counseling	M

HODGES UNIVERSITY

Criminal Justice and Criminology	M
Interdisciplinary Studies	M
Psychology—General	M
Public Administration	M

HOFSTRA UNIVERSITY

Applied Social Research	M
Art Therapy	M
Art/Fine Arts	M
Clinical Psychology	M,D
Communication—General	M
Comparative Literature	M
Counseling Psychology	M,O
English	M
Film, Television, and Video Production	M
French	M
German	M
Gerontology	M,O
Human Development	M,D,O
Humanities	M

Industrial and Organizational Psychology	M,D
Interdisciplinary Studies	M
Journalism	M
Linguistics	M,D,O
Marriage and Family Therapy	M
Music	M
Psychology—General	M,D,O
Rehabilitation Counseling	M,O
Rhetoric	M
Russian	M
School Psychology	M,D,O
Social Psychology	M,D,O
Sociology	M
Spanish	M
Speech and Interpersonal Communication	M
Writing	M

HOLLINS UNIVERSITY

Art/Fine Arts	M,O
Dance	M
English	M
Film, Television, and Video Production	M
Film, Television, and Video Theory and Criticism	M
Humanities	M,O
Interdisciplinary Studies	M,O
Liberal Studies	M,O
Music	M,O
Social Sciences	M,O
Theater	M
Writing	M

HOLMES INSTITUTE

Pastoral Ministry and Counseling	M

HOLY APOSTLES COLLEGE AND SEMINARY

Theology	P,M,O

HOLY CROSS GREEK ORTHODOX SCHOOL OF THEOLOGY

Theology	P,M

HOLY FAMILY UNIVERSITY

Counseling Psychology	M
Criminal Justice and Criminology	M

HOLY NAMES UNIVERSITY

Counseling Psychology	M,O
Forensic Psychology	M,O
Music	M,O
Pastoral Ministry and Counseling	M,O
Religion	M,O

HOOD COLLEGE

Art/Fine Arts	M,O
Human Development	M,O
Humanities	M
Psychology—General	M,O
Public Administration	M
Thanatology	M,O

HOOD THEOLOGICAL SEMINARY

Theology	P,M,D

HOPE INTERNATIONAL UNIVERSITY

International Development	M
Marriage and Family Therapy	M
Missions and Missiology	M
Music	M
Religion	M

HOUGHTON COLLEGE

Music	M

HOUSTON BAPTIST UNIVERSITY

Counseling Psychology	M
Liberal Studies	M
Pastoral Ministry and Counseling	M
Psychology—General	M
Theology	M

HOUSTON GRADUATE SCHOOL OF THEOLOGY

Pastoral Ministry and Counseling	P,M,D
Theology	P,M,D

HOWARD UNIVERSITY

African Studies	M,D
Applied Arts and Design—General	M
Art History	M
Art/Fine Arts	M
Clinical Psychology	M,D
Communication—General	M,D
Corporate and Organizational Communication	M,D
Counseling Psychology	M,D,O
Developmental Psychology	M,D
Economics	M,D
English	M,D
Experimental Psychology	M,D
Film, Television, and Video Production	M
French	M
History	M,D
Human Development	M
Mass Communication	M,D
Media Studies	M,D
Music	M
Philosophy	M
Photography	M
Political Science	M,D
Psychology—General	M,D
Public Administration	M
School Psychology	M,D,O
Social Psychology	M,D
Sociology	M,D
Spanish	M
Theology	P,M,D

HULT INTERNATIONAL BUSINESS SCHOOL

Conflict Resolution and Mediation/Peace Studies	M
International Affairs	M
National Security	M
Political Science	M

HUMBOLDT STATE UNIVERSITY

Counseling Psychology	M
English	M
Film, Television, and Video Production	M
Psychology—General	M
School Psychology	M
Social Sciences	M
Sociology	M
Theater	M

HUNTER COLLEGE OF THE CITY UNIVERSITY OF NEW YORK

Anthropology	M
Applied Social Research	M
Art History	M
Art/Fine Arts	M
Classics	M
Cognitive Sciences	M
Economics	M
English	M
French	M
Geographic Information Systems	M,O
Geography	M,O
History	M
Italian	M
Media Studies	M
Music	M
Psychology—General	M
Rehabilitation Counseling	M
Romance Languages	M
Social Psychology	M
Sociology	M
Spanish	M
Theater	M
Urban and Regional Planning	M
Urban Studies	M
Writing	M

HUNTINGTON UNIVERSITY

Pastoral Ministry and Counseling	M

HUSSON UNIVERSITY

Counseling Psychology	M
Criminal Justice and Criminology	M

IDAHO STATE UNIVERSITY

Anthropology	M
Art/Fine Arts	M
Clinical Psychology	D
Counseling Psychology	M,D,O
English	M,D,O
Geographic Information Systems	M,O
History	M
Interdisciplinary Studies	M

Marriage and Family Therapy	M,D,O
Political Science	M,D
Psychology—General	M,D
Public Administration	M
Rhetoric	M
School Psychology	M,D,O
Sociology	M
Speech and Interpersonal Communication	M
Theater	M

ILIFF SCHOOL OF THEOLOGY

Pastoral Ministry and Counseling	P,M,D
Religion	P,M,D
Theology	P,M,D

ILLINOIS INSTITUTE OF TECHNOLOGY

Applied Arts and Design—General	M,D*
Architecture	M,D
Clinical Psychology	M,D
Communication—General	M,D
Corporate and Organizational Communication	M
Industrial and Organizational Psychology	M,D
Landscape Architecture	M,D
Psychology—General	M,D
Public Administration	M
Rehabilitation Counseling	M,D
Technical Writing	M,D

ILLINOIS STATE UNIVERSITY

Agricultural Economics and Agribusiness	M
Archaeology	M
Art History	M
Art/Fine Arts	M
Clinical Psychology	M,D,O
Communication—General	M
Counseling Psychology	M,D,O
Criminal Justice and Criminology	M
Developmental Psychology	M,D,O
Economics	M
English	M,D
Experimental Psychology	M,D,O
Family and Consumer Sciences-General	M
French	M
German	M
Graphic Design	M
History	M
Industrial and Organizational Psychology	M,D,O
Music	M
Photography	M
Political Science	M
Psychology—General	M,D,O
School Psychology	D,O
Sociology	M

Spanish	M
Textile Design	M
Theater	M
Writing	M

IMMACULATA UNIVERSITY

Clinical Psychology	M,D,O
Counseling Psychology	M,D,O
Psychology—General	M,D,O
School Psychology	M,D,O
Therapies—Dance, Drama, and Music	M

INDIANA STATE UNIVERSITY

Art/Fine Arts	M
Clinical Psychology	M,D
Communication—General	M
Comparative Literature	M
Consumer Economics	M
Counseling Psychology	M,D,O
Criminal Justice and Criminology	M
English	M
Family and Consumer Sciences-General	M
Geography	M,D
Graphic Design	M
History	M
Linguistics	M,O
Media Studies	M
Music	M
Photography	M
Political Science	M
Psychology—General	M,D
Public Administration	M
School Psychology	M,D,O
Writing	M

INDIANA UNIVERSITY BLOOMINGTON

African Studies	M
African-American Studies	M
Anthropology	M,D
Art History	M,D
Art/Fine Arts	M,D
Asian Languages	M,D
Asian Studies	M,D
Child and Family Studies	M,D
Chinese	M,D
Classics	M,D
Cognitive Sciences	M,D
Communication—General	M,D*
Comparative Literature	M,D
Computer Art and Design	M,D
Counseling Psychology	M,D,O
Criminal Justice and Criminology	M,D
Developmental Psychology	M,D
East European and Russian Studies	M,O
Economics	M,D
English	M,D
Film, Television, and Video Theory and Criticism	M,D
Folklore	M,D
French	M,D

Gender Studies	D
Geography	M,D
German	M,D
History of Science and Technology	M,D
History	M,D
Human Development	M,D
Italian	M,D
Japanese	M,D
Journalism	M,D
Latin American Studies	M
Linguistics	M,D
Mass Communication	M,D
Media Studies	M,D
Medieval and Renaissance Studies	M,D
Music	M,D,O
Near and Middle Eastern Languages	M,D
Philosophy	M,D
Political Science	M,D
Portuguese	M,D
Psychology—General	M,D
Public Administration	M,D,O
Public Affairs	M,D,O*
Public Policy	M,D,O
Religion	M,D
Rhetoric	M,D
School Psychology	M,D,O
Slavic Languages	M,D
Social Psychology	M,D
Social Sciences	P,M,D,O
Sociology	M,D
Spanish	M,D
Speech and Interpersonal Communication	M,D
Theater	M,D
Western European Studies	M
Writing	M,D

INDIANA UNIVERSITY KOKOMO

Liberal Studies	M
Public Administration	M,O

INDIANA UNIVERSITY NORTHWEST

Criminal Justice and Criminology	M,O
Public Administration	M,O
Public Affairs	M,O

INDIANA UNIVERSITY OF PENNSYLVANIA

Art/Fine Arts	M
Clinical Psychology	D
Communication—General	M,D
Criminal Justice and Criminology	M,D
Emergency Management	M
English	M,D
Geography	M
History	M
Industrial and Labor Relations	M
Linguistics	M,D
Media Studies	M,D
Music	M
Political Science	M
Psychology—General	M,D

*M—master's degree; P—first professional degree; D—doctorate; O—other advanced degree; *—Close-Up and/or Announcement or Display*

Peterson's Graduate Programs in the Humanities, Arts & Social Sciences 2010

graduateschools.petersons.com **39**

Public Affairs	M
Rhetoric	M,D
School Psychology	D,O
Sociology	M
Writing	M,D

INDIANA UNIVERSITY–PURDUE UNIVERSITY FORT WAYNE

Communication—	
General	M
English	M,O
Liberal Studies	M
Public Affairs	M,O
Sociology	M

INDIANA UNIVERSITY–PURDUE UNIVERSITY INDIANAPOLIS

Addictions/Substance	
Abuse Counseling	M,D
Applied Arts and	
Design—General	M
Art/Fine Arts	M
Child and Family	
Studies	M
Clinical Psychology	M,D
Criminal Justice and	
Criminology	M
Economics	M
English	M
Gender Studies	M
Geographic Information	
Systems	M,O
History	M
Industrial and	
Organizational	
Psychology	M
Internet and Interactive	
Multimedia	M,D
Liberal Studies	M,D,O
Museum Studies	M,O
Music	M
Philanthropic Studies	M,D
Philosophy	M,O
Political Science	M,O
Psychology—General	M,D
Public Administration	M
Public Affairs	M*
Public History	M
Public Policy	M
Rehabilitation	
Counseling	M,D
Sociology	M

INDIANA UNIVERSITY SOUTH BEND

English	M
Liberal Studies	M
Music	M
Psychology—General	M
Public Administration	M,O
Public Affairs	M,O

INDIANA UNIVERSITY SOUTHEAST

Liberal Studies	M

INDIANA WESLEYAN UNIVERSITY

Addictions/Substance	
Abuse Counseling	M
Counseling Psychology	M

Marriage and Family	
Therapy	M
Pastoral Ministry and	
Counseling	M
Social Psychology	M
Theology	P,M

INSTITUTE FOR CHRISTIAN STUDIES

Philosophy	M,D
Political Science	M,D
Theology	M,D

INSTITUTE OF PUBLIC ADMINISTRATION

Public Administration	M,O

INSTITUTE OF TRANSPERSONAL PSYCHOLOGY

Clinical Psychology	M,D
Counseling Psychology	M,D
Psychology—General	M,D,O
Transpersonal and	
Humanistic Psychology	M,D,O
Women's Studies	M,D

THE INSTITUTE OF WORLD POLITICS

Military and Defense	
Studies	M,O
National Security	M,O
Political Science	M,O*
Public Affairs	M,O
Public Policy	M,O

INSTITUTO CENTROAMERICANO DE ADMINISTRACIÓN DE EMPRESAS

Agricultural Economics	
and Agribusiness	M
Economics	M
Sustainable	
Development	M

INSTITUTO TECNOLÓGICO DE SANTO DOMINGO

Linguistics	M
Psychology—General	M

INSTITUTO TECNOLÓGICO Y DE ESTUDIOS SUPERIORES DE MONTERREY, CAMPUS CENTRAL DE VERACRUZ

Humanities	M

INSTITUTO TECNOLÓGICO Y DE ESTUDIOS SUPERIORES DE MONTERREY, CAMPUS CIUDAD DE MÉXICO

Economics	M,D
Humanities	M,D

INSTITUTO TECNOLÓGICO Y DE ESTUDIOS SUPERIORES DE MONTERREY, CAMPUS CIUDAD JUÁREZ

Humanities	M
Public Administration	M

INSTITUTO TECNOLÓGICO Y DE ESTUDIOS SUPERIORES DE MONTERREY, CAMPUS CIUDAD OBREGÓN

Communication—	
General	M
International Affairs	M

INSTITUTO TECNOLÓGICO Y DE ESTUDIOS SUPERIORES DE MONTERREY, CAMPUS ESTADO DE MÉXICO

Architecture	M,D
Humanities	M,D

INSTITUTO TECNOLÓGICO Y DE ESTUDIOS SUPERIORES DE MONTERREY, CAMPUS IRAPUATO

Architecture	M,D
Humanities	M,D

INSTITUTO TECNOLÓGICO Y DE ESTUDIOS SUPERIORES DE MONTERREY, CAMPUS MONTERREY

Communication—	
General	M,D

INTER AMERICAN UNIVERSITY OF PUERTO RICO, AGUADILLA CAMPUS

Counseling Psychology	M
Criminal Justice and	
Criminology	M

INTER AMERICAN UNIVERSITY OF PUERTO RICO, METROPOLITAN CAMPUS

Criminal Justice and	
Criminology	M
English	M
History	M
Industrial and Labor	
Relations	M,D
Industrial and	
Organizational	
Psychology	M,D
Pastoral Ministry and	
Counseling	D
Psychology—General	M,D
School Psychology	M,D
Spanish	M
Theology	D

INTER AMERICAN UNIVERSITY OF PUERTO RICO, PONCE CAMPUS

Criminal Justice and	
Criminology	M
Spanish	M

INTER AMERICAN UNIVERSITY OF PUERTO RICO, SAN GERMÁN CAMPUS

Art/Fine Arts	M
Counseling Psychology	M,D
Industrial and Labor	
Relations	M,D
Photography	M

Psychology—General	M,D
School Psychology	M,D

INTERDENOMINATIONAL THEOLOGICAL CENTER

Theology	P,M,D

INTERNATIONAL BAPTIST COLLEGE

Pastoral Ministry and	
Counseling	M,D
Theology	M

INTERNATIONAL TECHNOLOGICAL UNIVERSITY

Computer Art and	
Design	M

INTERNATIONAL UNIVERSITY IN GENEVA

Communication—	
General	M
Media Studies	M

IONA COLLEGE

Counseling Psychology	M
Criminal Justice and	
Criminology	M
English	M
Experimental	
Psychology	M
History	M
Industrial and	
Organizational	
Psychology	M
Italian	M
Journalism	M
Marriage and Family	
Therapy	M,O
Mass Communication	M
Pastoral Ministry and	
Counseling	M,O
Psychology—General	M
School Psychology	M
Spanish	M

IOWA STATE UNIVERSITY OF SCIENCE AND TECHNOLOGY

Agricultural Economics	
and Agribusiness	M,D
Anthropology	M
Applied Arts and	
Design—General	M
Architecture	M
Child and Family	
Studies	M,D
Clothing and Textiles	M,D
Cognitive Sciences	D
Consumer Economics	M,D
Corporate and	
Organizational	
Communication	M,D
Counseling Psychology	D
Economics	M,D
English	M,D
Family and Consumer	
Sciences-General	M
Graphic Design	M
History of Science and	
Technology	M,D
History	M,D
Human Development	M,D
Interdisciplinary Studies	M
Interior Design	M
Journalism	M

Landscape Architecture M
Mass Communication M
Political Science M
Psychology—General D
Public Administration M
Rhetoric M,D
Rural Planning and
  Studies M,D
Rural Sociology M,D
Social Psychology D
Sociology M,D
Sustainable
  Development M,D
Urban and Regional
  Planning M

ITHACA COLLEGE

Communication—
  General M
Music M

JACKSON STATE UNIVERSITY

Clinical Psychology D
Criminal Justice and
  Criminology M
English M
History M
Mass Communication M
Political Science M
Psychology—General D
Public Administration M,D
Public Affairs M
Public Policy M,D
Rehabilitation
  Counseling M,O
Sociology M
Urban and Regional
  Planning M

JACKSONVILLE STATE UNIVERSITY

Criminal Justice and
  Criminology M
Emergency
  Management M
English M
History M
Liberal Studies M
Music M
Political Science M
Psychology—General M

JAMES MADISON UNIVERSITY

Art History M
Art/Fine Arts M
Clinical Psychology D
Counseling Psychology M,O
English M
History M
Music D
Photography M
Political Science M
Psychology—General M,D,O
Public Administration M
School Psychology M,D,O
Technical Writing M
Textile Design M

JESUIT SCHOOL OF THEOLOGY AT BERKELEY

Theology P,M,D,O

THE JEWISH THEOLOGICAL SEMINARY

Jewish Studies M,D
Music M
Religion M,D*
Theology M,D,O*

JEWISH UNIVERSITY OF AMERICA

Jewish Studies P,D
Pastoral Ministry and
  Counseling M,D

JOHN BROWN UNIVERSITY

Marriage and Family
  Therapy M
Pastoral Ministry and
  Counseling M

JOHN CARROLL UNIVERSITY

Corporate and
  Organizational
  Communication M
Counseling Psychology M,O
English M
History M
Humanities M
Religion M

JOHN F. KENNEDY UNIVERSITY

Art/Fine Arts M
Comparative and
  Interdisciplinary Arts M
Counseling Psychology M
Health Psychology M
Industrial and
  Organizational
  Psychology M,O
Interdisciplinary Studies M
Museum Studies M,O
Psychology—General M,D,O
Sport Psychology M
Transpersonal and
  Humanistic Psychology M

JOHN JAY COLLEGE OF CRIMINAL JUSTICE OF THE CITY UNIVERSITY OF NEW YORK

Criminal Justice and
  Criminology M,D
Forensic Psychology M,D
Forensic Sciences M,D
Public Administration M
Public Policy M,D

THE JOHNS HOPKINS UNIVERSITY

Addictions/Substance
  Abuse Counseling M,D,O
African Studies M,D,O
Anthropology D
Applied Economics M
Art History M
Asian Studies M,D,O
Canadian Studies M,D,O
Classics D
Clinical Psychology M,D
Cognitive Sciences D
Communication—
  General M
Comparative Literature D

Conflict Resolution and
  Mediation/Peace
  Studies M,D,O
Criminal Justice and
  Criminology M
Demography and
  Population Studies M,D
East European and
  Russian Studies M,D,O
Economics D
Emergency
  Management M,O
English D
French D
Genetic Counseling M,D
Geography M,D
German D
History of Science and
  Technology M,D
History D
Homeland Security M,O
International Affairs M,D,O
International
  Development M,D,O
Italian D
Latin American Studies M,D,O
Liberal Studies M,O
Medical Illustration M
Military and Defense
  Studies M
Museum Studies M
Music M,D,O
Near and Middle
  Eastern Studies M,D,O
Pastoral Ministry and
  Counseling M,O
Philosophy M,D
Political Science M,D,O
Psychology—General D
Public Policy M*
Romance Languages D
Social Sciences M,D
Sociology D
Spanish D
Technical Writing M
Western European
  Studies M,D,O
Writing M

JOHNSON BIBLE COLLEGE

Marriage and Family
  Therapy M
Theology M

JOHNSON STATE COLLEGE

Art/Fine Arts M

JOINT MILITARY INTELLIGENCE COLLEGE

Military and Defense
  Studies M

JONES INTERNATIONAL UNIVERSITY

Conflict Resolution and
  Mediation/Peace
  Studies M
Corporate and
  Organizational
  Communication M

THE JUDGE ADVOCATE GENERAL'S SCHOOL, U.S. ARMY

Military and Defense
  Studies M

JUDSON UNIVERSITY

Architecture M

THE JUILLIARD SCHOOL

Music M,D,O

KANSAS STATE UNIVERSITY

Agricultural Economics
  and Agribusiness M,D
Architecture M
Art/Fine Arts M
Child and Family
  Studies M,D
Clothing and Textiles M,D
Communication—
  General M
Economics M,D
English M
Family and Consumer
  Sciences-General M,D
French M
Geography M,D
German M
History M,D
Human Development D
International Affairs M
Landscape Architecture M
Marriage and Family
  Therapy D
Mass Communication M
Music M
National Security M,D
Political Science M
Psychology—General M,D
Public Administration M
Rhetoric M
Sociology M,D
Spanish M
Speech and
  Interpersonal
  Communication M
Theater M
Urban and Regional
  Planning M

KAPLAN UNIVERSITY–DAVENPORT CAMPUS

Criminal Justice and
  Criminology M
Political Science M,O

KEAN UNIVERSITY

Addictions/Substance
  Abuse Counseling M
Art/Fine Arts M
Clinical Psychology D
Communication—
  General M
Counseling Psychology M
Criminal Justice and
  Criminology M
Graphic Design M
Holocaust Studies M
Industrial and
  Organizational
  Psychology M
Liberal Studies M

*M—master's degree; P—first professional degree; D—doctorate; O—other advanced degree; *—Close-Up and / or Announcement or Display*

Marriage and Family Therapy	O
Political Science	M
Psychology—General	M
Public Administration	M
School Psychology	D,O
Sociology	M
Spanish	M

KEHILATH YAKOV RABBINICAL SEMINARY

Theology	

KEISER UNIVERSITY

Criminal Justice and Criminology	M

KENNESAW STATE UNIVERSITY

Conflict Resolution and Mediation/Peace Studies	M
Public Administration	M
Writing	M

KENRICK-GLENNON SEMINARY

Theology	P,M

KENT STATE UNIVERSITY

Anthropology	M
Architecture	M,O
Art History	M
Art/Fine Arts	M
Biological Anthropology	D
Classics	M,D
Clinical Psychology	M,D
Communication— General	M,D
Comparative Literature	M,D
Counseling Psychology	M
Criminal Justice and Criminology	M
Economics	M
English	M,D
Experimental Psychology	M,D
Family and Consumer Sciences-General	M
French	M,D
Geography	M,D
German	M,D
Gerontology	M
Graphic Design	M
Historic Preservation	M,O
History	M,D
Human Development	M,D
Illustration	M
Japanese	M,D
Journalism	M
Liberal Studies	M
Mass Communication	M
Music	M,D
Philosophy	M
Political Science	M,D
Psychology—General	M,D
Public Administration	M
Public Policy	M,D
Rehabilitation Counseling	M,O
Rhetoric	M,D
Russian	M,D
School Psychology	M,D,O
Sociology	M,D
Spanish	M,D
Textile Design	M
Theater	M

Translation and Interpretation	M,D
Urban Design	M,O
Writing	M,D

KENTUCKY CHRISTIAN UNIVERSITY

Religion	M
Theology	M

KENTUCKY STATE UNIVERSITY

International Affairs	M
Public Administration	M

KEUKA COLLEGE

Criminal Justice and Criminology	M

KNOX COLLEGE

Theology	P,M,D

KNOX THEOLOGICAL SEMINARY

Missions and Missiology	M
Pastoral Ministry and Counseling	D
Religion	M
Theology	P,M,O

KOL YAAKOV TORAH CENTER

Theology	O

KUTZTOWN UNIVERSITY OF PENNSYLVANIA

Counseling Psychology	M
English	M
Marriage and Family Therapy	M
Media Studies	M
Public Administration	M

LABORATORY INSTITUTE OF MERCHANDISING

Textile Design	M

LAGUNA COLLEGE OF ART & DESIGN

Art/Fine Arts	M

LAKE FOREST COLLEGE

Liberal Studies	M

LAKEHEAD UNIVERSITY

Clinical Psychology	M,D
Economics	M
English	M
Experimental Psychology	M,D
Gerontology	M,D
History	M
Psychology—General	M,D
Sociology	M
Women's Studies	M,D

LAKELAND COLLEGE

Theology	M

LAMAR UNIVERSITY

Applied Arts and Design—General	M
Art History	M
Art/Fine Arts	M
Clinical Psychology	M
Criminal Justice and Criminology	M
English	M
Family and Consumer Sciences-General	M,O
History	M
Industrial and Organizational Psychology	M
Music	M
Photography	M
Political Science	M
Psychology—General	M
Public Administration	M
Social Psychology	M
Theater	M

LANCASTER BIBLE COLLEGE

Pastoral Ministry and Counseling	M
Theology	M

LANCASTER THEOLOGICAL SEMINARY

Theology	P,M,D,O

LANGSTON UNIVERSITY

Rehabilitation Counseling	M

LA SALLE UNIVERSITY

Clinical Psychology	M,D
Corporate and Organizational Communication	M
Counseling Psychology	M
East European and Russian Studies	M
Hispanic Studies	M
History	M
Latin American Studies	M
Marriage and Family Therapy	D
Pastoral Ministry and Counseling	M
Psychology—General	D
Rehabilitation Counseling	D
Religion	M
Theology	M

LASELL COLLEGE

Communication— General	M,O
Corporate and Organizational Communication	M,O

LA SIERRA UNIVERSITY

Communication— General	M
English	M
Pastoral Ministry and Counseling	P,M
Religion	P,M
School Psychology	M,O
Writing	M

LAURA AND ALVIN SIEGAL COLLEGE OF JUDAIC STUDIES

Holocaust Studies	M
Humanities	M
Jewish Studies	M

LAURENTIAN UNIVERSITY

Applied Social Research	M
Experimental Psychology	M
History	M
Human Development	M
Humanities	M
Psychology—General	M
Sociology	M
Technical Writing	O

LAWRENCE TECHNOLOGICAL UNIVERSITY

Architecture	M
Interior Design	M
Technical Communication	M

LEADERSHIP INSTITUTE OF SEATTLE

Counseling Psychology	M
Psychology—General	M

LEBANESE AMERICAN UNIVERSITY

International Affairs	M

LEE UNIVERSITY

Counseling Psychology	M
Music	M
Religion	M
Theology	M

LEHIGH UNIVERSITY

American Studies	M
Counseling Psychology	M,D,O
Economics	M,D
English	M,D
History	M,D
Human Development	M,D
Political Science	M
Psychology—General	M,D
School Psychology	M,D,O
Sociology	M

LEHMAN COLLEGE OF THE CITY UNIVERSITY OF NEW YORK

Art/Fine Arts	M
English	M
History	M
Spanish	M

LENOIR-RHYNE UNIVERSITY

School Psychology	M
Social Psychology	M

LESLEY UNIVERSITY

Art Therapy	M,D,O*
Art/Fine Arts	M*
Clinical Psychology	M,D,O
Counseling Psychology	M*
Health Psychology	M
Interdisciplinary Studies	M
International Affairs	M,O

Psychology—General	M,D,O
School Psychology	M
Social Psychology	M,D,O
Sustainable Development	M
Therapies—Dance, Drama, and Music	M,D,O
Urban and Regional Planning	M
Women's Studies	M
Writing	M*

LEWIS & CLARK COLLEGE

Addictions/Substance Abuse Counseling	M
Counseling Psychology	M,O
Cultural Studies	M,O
Marriage and Family Therapy	M
Psychology—General	M,O
School Psychology	M,O
Social Psychology	M

LEWIS UNIVERSITY

Counseling Psychology	M
Criminal Justice and Criminology	M
Public Administration	M

LEXINGTON THEOLOGICAL SEMINARY

Theology	P,M,D

LIBERTY UNIVERSITY

Communication—General	M
Counseling Psychology	M,D
Pastoral Ministry and Counseling	M,D
Religion	P,M,D
Theology	P,M,D

LINCOLN CHRISTIAN SEMINARY

Pastoral Ministry and Counseling	P,M,D
Theology	P,M,D

LINCOLN UNIVERSITY (MO)

Criminal Justice and Criminology	M
History	M
Political Science	M
Public Administration	M
Public Policy	M
Social Sciences	M
Sociology	M

LINDENWOOD UNIVERSITY

American Studies	M
Art/Fine Arts	M
Communication—General	M,O
Counseling Psychology	M,D,O
Criminal Justice and Criminology	M,O
Gerontology	M,O
Public Administration	M
School Psychology	M,D,O
Theater	M
Writing	M,O

LINDSEY WILSON COLLEGE

Counseling Psychology	M
Human Development	M

LIPSCOMB UNIVERSITY

Conflict Resolution and Mediation/Peace Studies	M,O
Counseling Psychology	M,O
Psychology—General	M,O
Religion	P,M
Theology	P,M

LOCK HAVEN UNIVERSITY OF PENNSYLVANIA

Liberal Studies	M

LOGOS EVANGELICAL SEMINARY

Theology	P,M,D

LOMA LINDA UNIVERSITY

Child and Family Studies	M,D,O
Pastoral Ministry and Counseling	M,O
Psychology—General	D
Religion	M

LONG ISLAND UNIVERSITY AT RIVERHEAD

Homeland Security	M,O

LONG ISLAND UNIVERSITY, BRENTWOOD CAMPUS

Counseling Psychology	M
Criminal Justice and Criminology	M

LONG ISLAND UNIVERSITY, BROOKLYN CAMPUS

Clinical Psychology	D
Comparative Literature	M
Computer Art and Design	M
Economics	M
English	M
History	M,O
International Affairs	M,O
Political Science	M
Psychology—General	M,D
Public Administration	M
School Psychology	M
Social Sciences	M,O
Urban Studies	M
Writing	M

LONG ISLAND UNIVERSITY, C.W. POST CAMPUS

Art Therapy	M
Art/Fine Arts	M
Clinical Psychology	D
Computer Art and Design	M
Criminal Justice and Criminology	M
English	M
Gerontology	M,O
History	M
Interdisciplinary Studies	M
International Affairs	M
Internet and Interactive Multimedia	M
Music	M
Political Science	M
Psychology—General	M,D
Public Administration	M,O
Social Sciences	M
Spanish	M
Theater	M

LONG ISLAND UNIVERSITY, ROCKLAND GRADUATE CAMPUS

Counseling Psychology	M
Gerontology	M,O
Public Administration	M,O

LONG ISLAND UNIVERSITY, WESTCHESTER GRADUATE CAMPUS

Counseling Psychology	M
School Psychology	M

LONGWOOD UNIVERSITY

Criminal Justice and Criminology	M
English	M
Writing	M

LONGY SCHOOL OF MUSIC

Music	M,O

LORAS COLLEGE

Pastoral Ministry and Counseling	M
Psychology—General	M
Theology	M

LOUISIANA STATE UNIVERSITY AND AGRICULTURAL AND MECHANICAL COLLEGE

Agricultural Economics and Agribusiness	M,D
Anthropology	M,D
Applied Arts and Design—General	M
Architecture	M
Art History	M
Art/Fine Arts	M
Clinical Psychology	M,D
Cognitive Sciences	M,D
Communication—General	M,D
Comparative Literature	M,D
Developmental Psychology	M,D
Economics	M,D
English	M,D
Family and Consumer Sciences-General	M,D
French	M,D
Geography	M,D
Graphic Design	M
Hispanic Studies	M
History	M,D
Industrial and Organizational Psychology	M,D
Landscape Architecture	M
Liberal Studies	M
Linguistics	M,D

Mass Communication	M,D
Media Studies	M,D
Music	M,D
Philosophy	M
Photography	M
Political Science	M,D
Psychology—General	M,D
Public Administration	M,D
School Psychology	M,D
Sociology	M,D
Theater	M,D
Writing	M,D

LOUISIANA STATE UNIVERSITY HEALTH SCIENCES CENTER

Rehabilitation Counseling	M

LOUISIANA STATE UNIVERSITY IN SHREVEPORT

Counseling Psychology	M
Liberal Studies	M
School Psychology	O

LOUISIANA TECH UNIVERSITY

Applied Arts and Design—General	M
Art/Fine Arts	M
Counseling Psychology	M,D
Economics	M,D
English	M
Family and Consumer Sciences-General	M
Graphic Design	M
History	M
Industrial and Organizational Psychology	M,D
Interior Design	M
Photography	M
Psychology—General	M,D
Speech and Interpersonal Communication	M

LOUISVILLE PRESBYTERIAN THEOLOGICAL SEMINARY

Religion	P,M,D
Theology	P,M,D

LOYOLA MARYMOUNT UNIVERSITY

English	M
Film, Television, and Video Production	M
Marriage and Family Therapy	M
Pastoral Ministry and Counseling	M
Philosophy	M
Theology	M
Writing	M

LOYOLA UNIVERSITY CHICAGO

Clinical Psychology	M,D
Cognitive Sciences	M
Corporate and Organizational Communication	M
Counseling Psychology	D
Criminal Justice and Criminology	M

M—master's degree; P—first professional degree; D—doctorate; O—other advanced degree; *—Close-Up and/or Announcement or Display

Developmental Psychology	M,D
English	M,D
History	M,D
Industrial and Labor Relations	M
Pastoral Ministry and Counseling	M,O
Philosophy	M,D
Political Science	M,D
Psychology—General	M,D
Public History	M,D
Public Policy	M,D
Religion	P,M,O
School Psychology	M,D,O
Social Psychology	M,D
Sociology	M,D
Spanish	M
Theology	P,M,D,O

LOYOLA UNIVERSITY MARYLAND

Clinical Psychology	M,D,O
Counseling Psychology	M,O
Liberal Studies	M
Pastoral Ministry and Counseling	M,D,O
Psychology—General	M,D,O*

LOYOLA UNIVERSITY NEW ORLEANS

Criminal Justice and Criminology	M
Music	M
Theology	M,O
Therapies—Dance, Drama, and Music	M

LUBBOCK CHRISTIAN UNIVERSITY

Theology	M

LUTHERAN SCHOOL OF THEOLOGY AT CHICAGO

Pastoral Ministry and Counseling	P,M,D
Theology	P,M,D

LUTHERAN THEOLOGICAL SEMINARY

Ethics	P,M,D
Pastoral Ministry and Counseling	P,M,D
Religion	P,M,D
Theology	P,M,D

LUTHERAN THEOLOGICAL SEMINARY AT GETTYSBURG

Pastoral Ministry and Counseling	P,M,D
Religion	P,M,D
Theology	P,M,D

THE LUTHERAN THEOLOGICAL SEMINARY AT PHILADELPHIA

Pastoral Ministry and Counseling	P,M,D,O
Religion	P,M,D,O
Theology	P,M,D,O

LUTHERAN THEOLOGICAL SOUTHERN SEMINARY

Theology	P,M,D

LUTHER RICE UNIVERSITY

Missions and Missiology	P,M,D
Pastoral Ministry and Counseling	P,M,D
Theology	P,M,D

LUTHER SEMINARY

Theology	P,M,D

LYNCHBURG COLLEGE

English	M
History	M
Music	M
Social Psychology	M

LYNN UNIVERSITY

Criminal Justice and Criminology	M,O
Emergency Management	M,O
Mass Communication	M,D
Media Studies	M,D
Music	M,O
Psychology—General	M,O

MACHZIKEI HADATH RABBINICAL COLLEGE

Theology	O

MADONNA UNIVERSITY

Clinical Psychology	M
Criminal Justice and Criminology	M
Liberal Studies	M
Pastoral Ministry and Counseling	M
Psychology—General	M
Theology	M

MAHARISHI UNIVERSITY OF MANAGEMENT

Asian Studies	M,D

MAINE COLLEGE OF ART

Art/Fine Arts	M

MALONE UNIVERSITY

Pastoral Ministry and Counseling	M
Theology	M

MANHATTAN SCHOOL OF MUSIC

Music	M,D,O

MANHATTANVILLE COLLEGE

Corporate and Organizational Communication	M
Liberal Studies	M
Writing	M

MANSFIELD UNIVERSITY OF PENNSYLVANIA

Music	M

MAPLE SPRINGS BAPTIST BIBLE COLLEGE AND SEMINARY

Pastoral Ministry and Counseling	P,M,D,O
Theology	P,M,D,O

MARANATHA BAPTIST BIBLE COLLEGE

Cultural Studies	M
Pastoral Ministry and Counseling	M
Theology	M

MARIETTA COLLEGE

Corporate and Organizational Communication	M
Psychology—General	M

MARIST COLLEGE

Corporate and Organizational Communication	M
Counseling Psychology	M,O
Psychology—General	M,O
Public Administration	M
School Psychology	M,O

MARLBORO COLLEGE

Internet and Interactive Multimedia	M

MARQUETTE UNIVERSITY

Clinical Psychology	M,D
Communication—General	M
Economics	M
English	M,D
Ethics	M,D
Health Communication	M
History	M,D
Interdisciplinary Studies	D
International Affairs	M
Journalism	M
Mass Communication	M
Media Studies	M
Medieval and Renaissance Studies	M,D
Philosophy	M,D
Political Science	M
Psychology—General	M,D
Public Administration	M
Spanish	M
Speech and Interpersonal Communication	M
Theology	M,D

MARSHALL UNIVERSITY

Art/Fine Arts	M
Classics	M
Clinical Psychology	M,D
Communication—General	M
Criminal Justice and Criminology	M
English	M
Family and Consumer Sciences-General	M
Geography	M
History	M
Humanities	M

Industrial and Organizational Psychology	M,D
Journalism	M
Mass Communication	M
Music	M
Political Science	M
Psychology—General	M,D
School Psychology	O
Sociology	M
Spanish	M

MARS HILL GRADUATE SCHOOL

Counseling Psychology	M
Religion	M
Theology	M

MARTIN UNIVERSITY

Pastoral Ministry and Counseling	M
Psychology—General	M
Social Psychology	M

MARY BALDWIN COLLEGE

English	M
Theater	M

MARYGROVE COLLEGE

English	M
Translation and Interpretation	O

MARYLAND INSTITUTE COLLEGE OF ART

Art/Fine Arts	M,O
Computer Art and Design	M
Graphic Design	M
Photography	M

MARYLHURST UNIVERSITY

Art Therapy	M,O
Counseling Psychology	M,O
Interdisciplinary Studies	M
Theology	P,M

MARYMOUNT UNIVERSITY

Counseling Psychology	M,O
English	M
Forensic Psychology	M
Humanities	M
Interior Design	M
Pastoral Ministry and Counseling	M,O
Social Psychology	

MARYVILLE UNIVERSITY OF SAINT LOUIS

Addictions/Substance Abuse Counseling	M
Marriage and Family Therapy	M
Rehabilitation Counseling	M
Therapies—Dance, Drama, and Music	M

MARYWOOD UNIVERSITY

Addictions/Substance Abuse Counseling	M
Architecture	M

Art Therapy	M,O
Art/Fine Arts	M
Clinical Psychology	M,D
Communication—	
General	M,O
Corporate and	
Organizational	
Communication	M,O
Counseling Psychology	M
Criminal Justice and	
Criminology	M
Film, Television, and	
Video Production	M,O
Gerontology	M,O
Graphic Design	M
Health Communication	M,O
Human Development	D
Illustration	M
Interdisciplinary Studies	M,O
Interior Design	M
Media Studies	M,O
Photography	M
Psychology—General	M
Public Administration	M
School Psychology	M,O
Textile Design	M
Therapies—Dance,	
Drama, and Music	M,O

MASSACHUSETTS COLLEGE OF ART AND DESIGN

Applied Arts and	
Design—General	M
Architecture	M
Art/Fine Arts	M
Film, Television, and	
Video Production	M
Photography	M
Textile Design	M
Theater	M

MASSACHUSETTS INSTITUTE OF TECHNOLOGY

Archaeology	M,D,O
Architectural History	M,D
Architecture	M,D
Art History	M,D
Cognitive Sciences	D
Economics	M,D
History of Science and	
Technology	D
Humanities	M
Linguistics	D
Media Studies	M,D
Philosophy	D
Political Science	M,D
Social Sciences	D
Technical Writing	M
Urban and Regional	
Planning	M,D
Urban Studies	M,D
Writing	M

MASSACHUSETTS MARITIME ACADEMY

Emergency	
Management	M

MASSACHUSETTS SCHOOL OF PROFESSIONAL PSYCHOLOGY

Clinical Psychology	M,D,O
Counseling Psychology	M,D,O
Forensic Psychology	M,D,O

Industrial and	
Organizational	
Psychology	M,D,O
Psychology—General	M,D,O
School Psychology	M,D,O

THE MASTER'S COLLEGE AND SEMINARY

Pastoral Ministry and	
Counseling	P,M,D
Theology	P,M,D

MCCORMICK THEOLOGICAL SEMINARY

Pastoral Ministry and	
Counseling	P,M,D,O
Theology	P,M,D,O

MCDANIEL COLLEGE

Liberal Studies	M

MCGILL UNIVERSITY

Agricultural Economics	
and Agribusiness	M
Anthropology	M,D
Architecture	M,D,O
Art History	M,D
Asian Studies	M,D
Clinical Psychology	M,D
Communication—	
General	M,D
Counseling Psychology	M,D,O
Developmental	
Psychology	M,D,O
Economics	M,D
English	M,D
Experimental	
Psychology	M,D
Forensic Sciences	M,D,O
French	M,D
Genetic Counseling	M,D
Geography	M,D
German	M,D
Hispanic Studies	M,D
History of Medicine	M,D
History	M,D
International	
Development	M,D,O
Italian	M,D
Jewish Studies	M
Linguistics	M,D
Music	M,D
Near and Middle	
Eastern Studies	M,D,O
Philosophy	M,D
Political Science	M,D
Psychology—General	M,D
Religion	M,D
Russian	M,D
School Psychology	M,D,O
Sociology	M,D,O
Theology	M,D
Urban and Regional	
Planning	M,D

MCKENDREE UNIVERSITY

Counseling Psychology	M

MCMASTER UNIVERSITY

Anthropology	M,D
Classics	M,D
Cultural Studies	M,D
Economics	M,D

English	M,D
French	M
Geography	M,D
History	M,D
Industrial and Labor	
Relations	M
International Affairs	M,D
Pastoral Ministry and	
Counseling	P,M,D,O
Philosophy	M,D
Political Science	M,D
Psychology—General	M,D
Public Administration	M,D
Public Affairs	M,D
Public Policy	M,D
Religion	M,D
Sociology	M,D
Theology	P,M,D,O

MCNEESE STATE UNIVERSITY

Addictions/Substance	
Abuse Counseling	M
Counseling Psychology	M
English	M
Experimental	
Psychology	M
Psychology—General	M
School Psychology	M
Writing	M

MEADVILLE LOMBARD THEOLOGICAL SCHOOL

Pastoral Ministry and	
Counseling	P,M,D
Theology	P,M,D

MEDAILLE COLLEGE

Counseling Psychology	M
Psychology—General	M

MEDICAL COLLEGE OF GEORGIA

Medical Illustration	M

MEMORIAL UNIVERSITY OF NEWFOUNDLAND

Anthropology	M,D
Archaeology	M,D
Classics	M
Economics	M
English	M,D
Experimental	
Psychology	M,D
Folklore	M,D
French	M
Gender Studies	M,D
Geography	M,D
German	M
History	M,D
Humanities	M
Industrial and Labor	
Relations	M
Linguistics	M,D
Music	M,D
Philosophy	M
Political Science	M
Psychology—General	M,D
Religion	M
Social Psychology	M,D
Sociology	M,D
Sport Psychology	M
Women's Studies	M

MEMPHIS COLLEGE OF ART

Applied Arts and	
Design—General	M
Art/Fine Arts	M*
Computer Art and	
Design	M
Photography	M

MEMPHIS THEOLOGICAL SEMINARY

Theology	P,M,D

MENNONITE BRETHREN BIBLICAL SEMINARY

Marriage and Family	
Therapy	M,O
Missions and Missiology	M
Pastoral Ministry and	
Counseling	M
Theology	P,M

MERCER UNIVERSITY

Music	M
Theology	P,M,D

MERCY COLLEGE

Addictions/Substance	
Abuse Counseling	M,O
Counseling Psychology	M,O
English	M
Marriage and Family	
Therapy	M
Psychology—General	M
School Psychology	M

MERCYHURST COLLEGE

Biological Anthropology	M
Criminal Justice and	
Criminology	M,O
Forensic Sciences	M

MEREDITH COLLEGE

Music	M

MESIVTA OF EASTERN PARKWAY–YESHIVA ZICHRON MEILECH

Theology	

MESIVTA TIFERETH JERUSALEM OF AMERICA

Theology	

MESIVTA TORAH VODAATH RABBINICAL SEMINARY

Theology	

METHODIST THEOLOGICAL SCHOOL IN OHIO

Theology	P,M,D

METHODIST UNIVERSITY

Criminal Justice and	
Criminology	M

*M—master's degree; P—first professional degree; D—doctorate; O—other advanced degree; *—Close-Up and/or Announcement or Display*

METROPOLITAN COLLEGE OF NEW YORK

Corporate and Organizational Communication	M
Media Studies	M
Public Administration	M

METROPOLITAN STATE UNIVERSITY

Liberal Studies	M
Psychology—General	M
Public Administration	M,O
Technical Writing	M

MIAMI INTERNATIONAL UNIVERSITY OF ART & DESIGN

Art/Fine Arts	M
Computer Art and Design	M
Film, Television, and Video Production	M
Graphic Design	M*
Interior Design	M

MIAMI UNIVERSITY

Architecture	M
Art/Fine Arts	M*
Child and Family Studies	M
Clinical Psychology	D
Communication— General	M
Economics	M
English	M,D
Experimental Psychology	D
French	M
Geography	M
Gerontology	M
History	M,D
Mass Communication	M
Music	M
Philosophy	M
Political Science	M,D
Psychology—General	D
Religion	M
Rhetoric	M,D
School Psychology	M,O
Social Psychology	D
Spanish	M
Speech and Interpersonal Communication	M
Technical Writing	M
Theater	M
Writing	M,D

MICHIGAN SCHOOL OF PROFESSIONAL PSYCHOLOGY

Clinical Psychology	M,D
Psychology—General	M,D
Transpersonal and Humanistic Psychology	M,D

MICHIGAN STATE UNIVERSITY

African Studies	M,D
African-American Studies	M,D
Agricultural Economics and Agribusiness	M,D
American Studies	M,D
Anthropology	M,D
Art/Fine Arts	M

Child and Family Studies	M,D
Child Development	M,D
Communication— General	M,D
Criminal Justice and Criminology	M,D*
Economics	M,D
English	M,D
Environmental Design	M,D
Forensic Sciences	M,D
French	M,D
Geography	M,D
German	M,D
Health Communication	M
Hispanic Studies	M,D
History	M,D
Humanities	M
Industrial and Labor Relations	M,D
Interior Design	M,D
International Affairs	M
Journalism	M
Latin American Studies	D
Linguistics	M,D
Marriage and Family Therapy	M,D
Media Studies	M,D
Music	M,D
Philosophy	M,D
Political Science	M,D
Portuguese	M,D
Psychology—General	M,D
Rehabilitation Counseling	M,D,O
Rhetoric	M,D
Romance Languages	M,D
School Psychology	M,D,O
Social Sciences	M
Sociology	M,D
Spanish	M,D
Theater	M
Therapies—Dance, Drama, and Music	M,D
Urban and Regional Planning	M,D
Writing	M,D

MICHIGAN TECHNOLOGICAL UNIVERSITY

Archaeology	M,D
Historic Preservation	D
Mineral Economics	M
Rhetoric	M,D
Sustainable Development	O
Technical Communication	M,D

MICHIGAN THEOLOGICAL SEMINARY

Counseling Psychology	P,M,O
Religion	P,M,O
Theology	P,M,O

MID-AMERICA BAPTIST THEOLOGICAL SEMINARY

Theology	P,M,D

MID-AMERICA BAPTIST THEOLOGICAL SEMINARY NORTHEAST BRANCH

Theology	P

MIDAMERICA NAZARENE UNIVERSITY

Counseling Psychology	M,O

MID-AMERICA REFORMED SEMINARY

Theology	P,M

MIDDLEBURY COLLEGE

Chinese	M
English	M
French	M,D
German	M,D
Italian	M,D
Russian	M,D
Spanish	M,D

MIDDLE TENNESSEE STATE UNIVERSITY

Child and Family Studies	M
Child Development	M
Criminal Justice and Criminology	M
Economics	M,D
English	M,D
Gerontology	O
History	M
Industrial and Organizational Psychology	M,O
Mass Communication	M
Music	M
Psychology—General	M
Public History	D
School Psychology	M,O
Sociology	M

MIDWESTERN BAPTIST THEOLOGICAL SEMINARY

Archaeology	P,M,D,O
Linguistics	P,M,D,O
Missions and Missiology	P,M,D,O
Music	P,M,D,O
Pastoral Ministry and Counseling	P,M,D,O
Religion	P,M,D,O
Theology	P,M,D,O

MIDWESTERN STATE UNIVERSITY

Criminal Justice and Criminology	M
English	M
History	M
Political Science	M
Psychology—General	M
Public Administration	M

MIDWESTERN UNIVERSITY, DOWNERS GROVE CAMPUS

Clinical Psychology	M,D*

MIDWESTERN UNIVERSITY, GLENDALE CAMPUS

Clinical Psychology	D

MIDWEST UNIVERSITY

Theology	P,M,D

MILLERSVILLE UNIVERSITY OF PENNSYLVANIA

Clinical Psychology	M
Emergency Management	M
English	M
French	M
German	M
History	M
Psychology—General	M
School Psychology	M
Spanish	M

MILLS COLLEGE

Art/Fine Arts	M
Dance	M
English	M
Illustration	M
Interdisciplinary Studies	M,O
Music	M
Photography	M
Public Policy	M
Writing	M

MINNEAPOLIS COLLEGE OF ART AND DESIGN

Applied Arts and Design—General	M
Art/Fine Arts	M,O
Computer Art and Design	O
Film, Television, and Video Production	M
Graphic Design	M
Illustration	M
Photography	M
Sustainable Development	O

MINNESOTA STATE UNIVERSITY MANKATO

Anthropology	M
Art/Fine Arts	M
Clinical Psychology	M,D
English	M,O
Ethnic Studies	M
French	M
Geography	M
Gerontology	M,O
History	M
Industrial and Organizational Psychology	M,D
Interdisciplinary Studies	M
Marriage and Family Therapy	M,D,O
Music	M
Psychology—General	M,D
Public Administration	M
Rehabilitation Counseling	M
School Psychology	M,D
Social Psychology	M,D,O
Sociology	M
Spanish	M
Speech and Interpersonal Communication	M
Technical Communication	M,O
Theater	M
Urban and Regional Planning	M,O
Urban Studies	M,O
Women's Studies	M,O
Writing	M,O

MINNESOTA STATE UNIVERSITY MOORHEAD

Liberal Studies	M
Public Administration	M
School Psychology	M,O
Writing	M

MINOT STATE UNIVERSITY

Criminal Justice and Criminology	M
School Psychology	O

MIRRER YESHIVA

Theology	

MISSISSIPPI COLLEGE

Art/Fine Arts	M
Communication— General	M
Corporate and Organizational Communication	M
Counseling Psychology	M,O
Criminal Justice and Criminology	M,O
English	M
History	M,O
Liberal Studies	M
Marriage and Family Therapy	M,O
Music	M
Political Science	M,O
Social Sciences	M,O

MISSISSIPPI STATE UNIVERSITY

Agricultural Economics and Agribusiness	M
American Studies	M,D
Anthropology	M
Applied Economics	M,D
Architecture	M
Clinical Psychology	M,D
Cognitive Sciences	M,D
Computer Art and Design	M
Economics	M,D
English	M
Experimental Psychology	M,D
French	M
German	M
History	M,D
Landscape Architecture	M
Political Science	M,D
Psychology—General	M,D
Public Administration	M,D
Public Policy	M,D
School Psychology	M,D,O
Sociology	M,D
Spanish	M
Western European Studies	M,D

MISSISSIPPI VALLEY STATE UNIVERSITY

Criminal Justice and Criminology	M

MISSOURI BAPTIST UNIVERSITY

Pastoral Ministry and Counseling	M,O

MISSOURI SOUTHERN STATE UNIVERSITY

Criminal Justice and Criminology	M

MISSOURI STATE UNIVERSITY

Art/Fine Arts	M
Child and Family Studies	M
Clinical Psychology	M
Communication— General	M
Criminal Justice and Criminology	M
English	M
Experimental Psychology	M
Family and Consumer Sciences-General	M
French	M
Geography	M
German	M
History	M
Industrial and Organizational Psychology	M
Interior Design	M
International Affairs	M*
Military and Defense Studies	M
Music	M
Political Science	M
Psychology—General	M
Public Administration	M
Religion	M
Social Psychology	M
Spanish	M
Textile Design	M
Theater	M
Urban and Regional Planning	M

MONMOUTH UNIVERSITY

Addictions/Substance Abuse Counseling	M,O
Communication— General	M,O
Corporate and Organizational Communication	M,O
Counseling Psychology	M,O
Criminal Justice and Criminology	M,O
English	M
History	M
Liberal Studies	M
Media Studies	M,O
Psychology—General	M,O
Public Policy	M

MONTANA STATE UNIVERSITY

Agricultural Economics and Agribusiness	M
American Indian/Native American Studies	M
American Studies	M,D
Applied Economics	M
Architecture	M
Art/Fine Arts	M
English	M
Film, Television, and Video Production	M
History	M,D
Human Development	M

Psychology—General	M
Public Administration	M

MONTANA STATE UNIVERSITY– BILLINGS

Communication— General	M
Interdisciplinary Studies	M
Psychology—General	M
Public Administration	M
Rehabilitation Counseling	M

MONTANA TECH OF THE UNIVERSITY OF MONTANA

Interdisciplinary Studies	M
Technical Communication	M

MONTCLAIR STATE UNIVERSITY

Addictions/Substance Abuse Counseling	M,D,O
Art History	M,O
Art/Fine Arts	M,O
Arts Administration	M
Clinical Psychology	M,O
Communication— General	M
Conflict Resolution and Mediation/Peace Studies	M,O
Corporate and Organizational Communication	M
Counseling Psychology	M,D,O
Economics	M
English	M,O
French	M,O
Geographic Information Systems	M,D,O
History	M,O
Industrial and Organizational Psychology	M,O
Italian	M,O
Linguistics	M,O
Marriage and Family Therapy	M,O
Music	M,O
Philosophy	M,D,O
Psychology—General	M,O
School Psychology	M,O
Social Psychology	M,D,O
Social Sciences	M,O
Sociology	M
Spanish	M,O
Speech and Interpersonal Communication	M
Theater	M
Therapies—Dance, Drama, and Music	M,O
Translation and Interpretation	M,O

MONTEREY INSTITUTE OF INTERNATIONAL STUDIES

International Affairs	M*
International Trade Policy	M
Public Administration	M
Translation and Interpretation	M*

MOODY BIBLE INSTITUTE

Pastoral Ministry and Counseling	P,M,O
Theology	P,M,O
Urban Studies	P,M,O

MORAVIAN THEOLOGICAL SEMINARY

Theology	P,M

MOREHEAD STATE UNIVERSITY

Art/Fine Arts	M
Clinical Psychology	M
Communication— General	M
Counseling Psychology	M
Criminal Justice and Criminology	M
English	M
Experimental Psychology	M
Gerontology	M
Music	M
Psychology—General	M
Public Administration	M
Sociology	M

MORGAN STATE UNIVERSITY

African-American Studies	M,D
Architecture	M
Economics	M
English	M,D
History	M,D
International Affairs	M
Landscape Architecture	M
Music	M
Psychology—General	M,D
Sociology	M
Urban and Regional Planning	M

MOUNTAIN STATE UNIVERSITY

Criminal Justice and Criminology	M
Interdisciplinary Studies	M*

MOUNT ALOYSIUS COLLEGE

Criminal Justice and Criminology	M
Psychology—General	M

MOUNT ANGEL SEMINARY

Theology	P,M

MOUNT HOLYOKE COLLEGE

Psychology—General	M

MOUNT MARTY COLLEGE

Pastoral Ministry and Counseling	M

MOUNT MARY COLLEGE

Art Therapy	M
English	M

MOUNT ST. MARY'S COLLEGE

Counseling Psychology	M

*M—master's degree; P—first professional degree; D—doctorate; O—other advanced degree; *—Close-Up and/or Announcement or Display*

Humanities	M
Religion	M

MOUNT ST. MARY'S UNIVERSITY

Theology	P,M

MOUNT SAINT VINCENT UNIVERSITY

Child and Family Studies	M
Gerontology	M
School Psychology	M
Women's Studies	M

MOUNT SINAI SCHOOL OF MEDICINE OF NEW YORK UNIVERSITY

Genetic Counseling	M;D

MOUNT VERNON NAZARENE UNIVERSITY

Theology	M

MURRAY STATE UNIVERSITY

Clinical Psychology	M
Corporate and Organizational Communication	M
Economics	M
English	M
History	M
Mass Communication	M
Music	M
Psychology—General	M
Public Affairs	M
Writing	M

NAROPA UNIVERSITY

Art Therapy	M
Asian Languages	M
Clinical Psychology	M
Counseling Psychology	M
Psychoanalysis and Psychotherapy	M
Religion	M
Social Psychology	M
Theater	M
Theology	P
Therapies—Dance, Drama, and Music	M
Transpersonal and Humanistic Psychology	M*
Writing	M

NASHOTAH HOUSE

Theology	P,M,O

NATIONAL DEFENSE UNIVERSITY

Conflict Resolution and Mediation/Peace Studies	M
Homeland Security	M
Military and Defense Studies	M
National Security	M

NATIONAL-LOUIS UNIVERSITY

Addictions/Substance Abuse Counseling	M,O
Gerontology	M,O
Health Psychology	M,O
Human Development	M,D,O
Industrial and Organizational Psychology	M,O
Psychology—General	M,O
School Psychology	M,D,O
Social Psychology	M,O
Writing	M

NATIONAL THEATRE CONSERVATORY

Theater	M,O

NATIONAL UNIVERSITY

Art/Fine Arts	M
Communication— General	M
Computer Art and Design	M
Conflict Resolution and Mediation/Peace Studies	M
Corporate and Organizational Communication	M
Counseling Psychology	M
Criminal Justice and Criminology	M
Economics	M
English	M
Forensic Sciences	M
History	M
Homeland Security	M
Humanities	M
Internet and Interactive Multimedia	M
Media Studies	M
Psychology—General	M
Public Administration	M
School Psychology	M
Writing	M

NATIONAL UNIVERSITY OF SINGAPORE

Public Administration	M,D
Public Affairs	M,D
Public Policy	M,D

NAVAL POSTGRADUATE SCHOOL

International Affairs	M
Military and Defense Studies	M,D
National Security	M
Political Science	M

NAVAL WAR COLLEGE

National Security	M

NAZARENE THEOLOGICAL SEMINARY

Missions and Missiology	P,M,D
Theology	P,M,D

NAZARETH COLLEGE OF ROCHESTER

Art Therapy	M
Liberal Studies	M
Therapies—Dance, Drama, and Music	M

NEBRASKA WESLEYAN UNIVERSITY

Forensic Sciences	M
History	M

NER ISRAEL RABBINICAL COLLEGE

Theology	M,D,O

NER ISRAEL YESHIVA COLLEGE OF TORONTO

Theology	

NEUMANN UNIVERSITY

Pastoral Ministry and Counseling	M,O

NEW BRUNSWICK THEOLOGICAL SEMINARY

Pastoral Ministry and Counseling	D
Theology	P,M,D

NEW ENGLAND COLLEGE

Counseling Psychology	M
Public Policy	M
Writing	M

NEW ENGLAND CONSERVATORY OF MUSIC

Music	M,D,O

NEW JERSEY CITY UNIVERSITY

Art/Fine Arts	M
Counseling Psychology	M
Criminal Justice and Criminology	M
Music	M
Psychology—General	M,O
School Psychology	M,O
Urban Studies	M

NEW JERSEY INSTITUTE OF TECHNOLOGY

Architecture	M
Emergency Management	M,D
History	M
Technical Communication	M
Urban Studies	D

NEW LIFE THEOLOGICAL SEMINARY

Religion	M

NEWMAN THEOLOGICAL COLLEGE

Theology	P,M

NEW MEXICO HIGHLANDS UNIVERSITY

American Studies	M
Anthropology	M
Clinical Psychology	M
English	M
Internet and Interactive Multimedia	M
Media Studies	M
Psychology—General	M
Public Affairs	M
Rhetoric	M
School Psychology	M
Sociology	M
Writing	M

NEW MEXICO STATE UNIVERSITY

Agricultural Economics and Agribusiness	M,D
Anthropology	M
Applied Arts and Design—General	M
Art History	M
Art/Fine Arts	M
Communication— General	M
Corporate and Organizational Communication	M,D
Counseling Psychology	M,D,O
Criminal Justice and Criminology	M
Economic Development	M,D
Economics	M,D
English	M,D
Family and Consumer Sciences-General	M
Geography	M
History	M
Interdisciplinary Studies	M,D
Music	M
Photography	M
Political Science	M
Psychology—General	M,D
Rhetoric	M,D
School Psychology	M,D,O
Sociology	M
Spanish	M
Writing	M,D

NEW ORLEANS BAPTIST THEOLOGICAL SEMINARY

Music	M,D
Pastoral Ministry and Counseling	P,M,D
Theology	P,M,D

THE NEW SCHOOL: A UNIVERSITY

Anthropology	M,D
Applied Arts and Design—General	M
Applied Social Research	M,D
Architecture	M*
Art/Fine Arts	M*
Clinical Psychology	M,D
Communication— General	M*
Computer Art and Design	M*
Decorative Arts	M*
Economics	M,D
History	M,D
Interior Design	M*
International Affairs	M*
International Development	M
Liberal Studies	M
Lighting Design	M*
Mass Communication	M
Media Studies	M
Music	M,O
Philosophy	M,D
Photography	M*

Political Science	M,D
Psychology—General	M,D
Public Policy	D*
Social Sciences	M,D*
Sociology	M,D
Theater	M*
Urban Studies	M*
Writing	M*

NEWSCHOOL OF ARCHITECTURE & DESIGN

Architecture	M

NEW YORK ACADEMY OF ART

Art/Fine Arts	M

NEW YORK FILM ACADEMY

Film, Television, and Video Production	M

NEW YORK INSTITUTE OF TECHNOLOGY

Architecture	M
Communication—General	M
Counseling Psychology	M
Human Development	M
Industrial and Labor Relations	M,O
Urban Design	M

NEW YORK MEDICAL COLLEGE

Disability Studies	M

NEW YORK SCHOOL OF INTERIOR DESIGN

Interior Design	M*

NEW YORK STUDIO SCHOOL OF DRAWING, PAINTING AND SCULPTURE

Art/Fine Arts	M,O

NEW YORK THEOLOGICAL SEMINARY

Theology	P,M,D

NEW YORK UNIVERSITY

African Studies	M,D,O
American Studies	M,D
Anthropology	M,D
Applied Arts and Design—General	M
Applied Economics	M,D,O
Archaeology	M,D
Art History	M,D
Art Therapy	M
Art/Fine Arts	M,D
Arts Administration	M
Asian Studies	M,D
Classics	M,D,O
Cognitive Sciences	M,D,O
Communication—General	M,D
Comparative Literature	M,D
Computer Art and Design	M
Corporate and Organizational Communication	M

Counseling Psychology	M,D,O
Cultural Studies	M,D,O
Dance	M,D
Developmental Psychology	M,D
Economics	M,D,O
English	M,D
Film, Television, and Video Production	M
Film, Television, and Video Theory and Criticism	M,D
French	M,D,O
German	M,D
Graphic Design	M
Historic Preservation	M
History	M,D,O
Human Development	M,D,O
Humanities	M,O
Industrial and Organizational Psychology	M,D,O
Interdisciplinary Studies	M*
International Affairs	M,D,O
Internet and Interactive Multimedia	M
Italian	M,D
Jewish Studies	M,D,O
Journalism	M,D,O
Latin American Studies	M,O
Linguistics	M,D
Media Studies	M,D
Museum Studies	M,D,O
Music	M,D,O
Near and Middle Eastern Studies	M,D,O
Philosophy	M,D
Political Science	M,D
Portuguese	M,D
Psychoanalysis and Psychotherapy	M,D,O
Psychology—General	M,D,O
Public Administration	M,D,O*
Public History	M,D,O
Publishing	M
Religion	M,O
Romance Languages	M,D
Russian	M
School Psychology	M,D
Slavic Languages	M
Social Psychology	M,D,O
Social Sciences	M,O
Sociology	M,D
Spanish	M,D
Speech and Interpersonal Communication	M,D
Theater	M,D,O
Therapies—Dance, Drama, and Music	M,D
Urban and Regional Planning	M,O
Western European Studies	M
Writing	M

NIAGARA UNIVERSITY

Criminal Justice and Criminology	M
Interdisciplinary Studies	M
School Psychology	M,O

NICHOLLS STATE UNIVERSITY

Counseling Psychology	M,O
School Psychology	M,O

NICHOLS COLLEGE

Criminal Justice and Criminology	M

THE NIGERIAN BAPTIST THEOLOGICAL SEMINARY

Music	P,M,D,O
Pastoral Ministry and Counseling	P,M,D,O
Theology	P,M,D,O

NORFOLK STATE UNIVERSITY

Art/Fine Arts	M
Clinical Psychology	M
Communication—General	M
Criminal Justice and Criminology	M
Media Studies	M
Music	M
Psychology—General	M,D
Social Psychology	M
Sociology	M
Urban Studies	M

NORTH CAROLINA AGRICULTURAL AND TECHNICAL STATE UNIVERSITY

African-American Studies	M
Agricultural Economics and Agribusiness	M
Applied Economics	M
English	M
Rehabilitation Counseling	M,D

NORTH CAROLINA CENTRAL UNIVERSITY

Criminal Justice and Criminology	M
English	M
Family and Consumer Sciences-General	M
History	M
Music	M
Psychology—General	M
Public Administration	M
Social Psychology	M
Sociology	M

NORTH CAROLINA STATE UNIVERSITY

Agricultural Economics and Agribusiness	M
Anthropology	M
Applied Arts and Design—General	M,D
Architecture	M
Clothing and Textiles	D
Communication—General	M
Computer Art and Design	D
Developmental Psychology	D
Economics	M,D
English	M
Experimental Psychology	D
French	M
Geographic Information Systems	M,D

Graphic Design	M
History	M
Industrial and Organizational Psychology	D
Industrial Design	M
International Affairs	M
Landscape Architecture	M
Liberal Studies	M
Psychology—General	D
Public Administration	M,D
Public History	M
Rhetoric	D
School Psychology	D
Social Psychology	M
Sociology	M,D
Spanish	M
Technical Communication	M
Writing	M

NORTH CENTRAL COLLEGE

Liberal Studies	M

NORTHCENTRAL UNIVERSITY

Psychology—General	M,D,O

NORTH DAKOTA STATE UNIVERSITY

Agricultural Economics and Agribusiness	M
Child and Family Studies	M,D
Child Development	M,D
Clinical Psychology	M,D
Cognitive Sciences	M,D
Communication—General	M,D
Consumer Economics	M,D
Criminal Justice and Criminology	M,D
Emergency Management	M,D
English	M
Family and Consumer Sciences-General	M
Gerontology	M,D
Health Psychology	M,D
History	M,D
Human Development	D
Marriage and Family Therapy	M,D
Mass Communication	M,D
Music	M,D
Psychology—General	M,D
Social Psychology	M,D
Social Sciences	M,D
Sociology	M,D
Speech and Interpersonal Communication	M,D

NORTHEASTERN ILLINOIS UNIVERSITY

English	M
Geography	M
Gerontology	M
History	M
Linguistics	M
Music	M
Political Science	M
Speech and Interpersonal Communication	M
Writing	M

---

*M—master's degree; P—first professional degree; D—doctorate; O—other advanced degree; *—Close-Up and/or Announcement or Display*

NORTHEASTERN SEMINARY AT ROBERTS WESLEYAN COLLEGE

Theology	P,M,D

NORTHEASTERN STATE UNIVERSITY

American Studies	M
Communication—General	M
Counseling Psychology	M
Criminal Justice and Criminology	M
English	M
Psychology—General	M

NORTHEASTERN UNIVERSITY

Applied Economics	M,D
Architecture	M
Counseling Psychology	M,D,O
Criminal Justice and Criminology	M,D
Economics	M,D
English	M,D,O
Experimental Psychology	M,D
History	M,D
International Affairs	M,D,O
Journalism	M
Political Science	M,D,O
Psychology—General	M,D,O
Public Administration	M,O
Public Affairs	M,D,O
Public History	M,D
Public Policy	M,D
Rehabilitation Counseling	M
School Psychology	M,D,O
Sociology	M,D
Speech and Interpersonal Communication	D
Urban Studies	M,O

NORTHERN ARIZONA UNIVERSITY

Anthropology	M
Archaeology	M
Clinical Psychology	M
Communication—General	M
Counseling Psychology	D
Criminal Justice and Criminology	M,O
English	M
Geographic Information Systems	M,O
Geography	M,O
Health Psychology	M
History	M,D
Liberal Studies	M
Linguistics	M,D,O
Music	M
Political Science	M,D,O
Psychology—General	M
Public Administration	M,D,O
School Psychology	M,D
Social Psychology	M
Sociology	M
Sustainable Development	M
Technical Writing	M
Writing	M

NORTHERN BAPTIST THEOLOGICAL SEMINARY

Missions and Missiology	P,M,D
Pastoral Ministry and Counseling	P,M,D
Theology	P,M,D

NORTHERN ILLINOIS UNIVERSITY

Anthropology	M
Art/Fine Arts	M
Child and Family Studies	M
Communication—General	M
Dance	M
Economics	M,D
English	M,D
French	M
Geography	M
History	M,D
Music	M,O
Philosophy	M
Political Science	M,D
Psychology—General	M,D
Public Administration	M
Romance Languages	M
Sociology	M
Spanish	M
Theater	M

NORTHERN KENTUCKY UNIVERSITY

Communication—General	M
English	M,O
Health Psychology	M,O
Industrial and Organizational Psychology	M,O
Liberal Studies	M,O
Public Administration	M,O
Social Psychology	M,O

NORTHERN MICHIGAN UNIVERSITY

Criminal Justice and Criminology	M
English	M
Psychology—General	M
Public Administration	M
Writing	M

NORTH GEORGIA COLLEGE & STATE UNIVERSITY

Public Administration	M
Social Psychology	M

NORTH GREENVILLE UNIVERSITY

Pastoral Ministry and Counseling	M

NORTH PARK THEOLOGICAL SEMINARY

Pastoral Ministry and Counseling	M,O
Theology	P,M,D

NORTHWEST BAPTIST SEMINARY

Theology	P,M,D,O

NORTHWESTERN OKLAHOMA STATE UNIVERSITY

Counseling Psychology	M

NORTHWESTERN STATE UNIVERSITY OF LOUISIANA

Archaeology	M
Art/Fine Arts	M
Clinical Psychology	M
English	M
Historic Preservation	M
Music	M
Psychology—General	M

NORTHWESTERN UNIVERSITY

African Studies	O
Anthropology	D
Art History	D
Art/Fine Arts	M*
Broadcast Journalism	M
Clinical Psychology	D
Cognitive Sciences	D
Communication—General	M,D
Comparative Literature	M,D,O
Corporate and Organizational Communication	M
Counseling Psychology	M
Economics	M,D
English	M,D*
Film, Television, and Video Production	M,D
French	D,O
Gender Studies	
Genetic Counseling	M
German	D
History	D
Human Development	D
International Affairs	P,M,O
Italian	D,O
Journalism	M
Liberal Studies	M
Linguistics	M,D
Marriage and Family Therapy	M
Media Studies	M,D
Music	M,D,O
Philosophy	D
Political Science	M,D
Psychology—General	D*
Public Policy	D*
Publishing	M
Slavic Languages	D
Social Psychology	D
Social Sciences	M,O
Sociology	D
Speech and Interpersonal Communication	M,D
Theater	M,D
Writing	M

NORTHWEST MISSOURI STATE UNIVERSITY

Agricultural Economics and Agribusiness	M
English	M
Geographic Information Systems	M,O
Geography	M,O
History	M
Psychology—General	M

NORTHWEST NAZARENE UNIVERSITY

Marriage and Family Therapy	M
Missions and Missiology	P,M
Pastoral Ministry and Counseling	P,M
Religion	P,M
School Psychology	M
Social Psychology	M

NORTHWEST UNIVERSITY

Counseling Psychology	M
Psychology—General	M

NORWICH UNIVERSITY

Conflict Resolution and Mediation/Peace Studies	M
Criminal Justice and Criminology	M
International Affairs	M
Military and Defense Studies	M
Public Administration	M

NOTRE DAME COLLEGE (OH)

Pastoral Ministry and Counseling	M,O

NOTRE DAME DE NAMUR UNIVERSITY

Art Therapy	M
Clinical Psychology	M
English	M,O
Gerontology	M,O
Marriage and Family Therapy	M
Music	M
Psychology—General	M,O
Public Administration	M
Public Affairs	M

NOTRE DAME SEMINARY

Theology	P,M

NOVA SOUTHEASTERN UNIVERSITY

Child and Family Studies	M,D
Clinical Psychology	D,O
Conflict Resolution and Mediation/Peace Studies	M,D
Counseling Psychology	M
Criminal Justice and Criminology	M*
Humanities	M,O
Interdisciplinary Studies	M,O
Marriage and Family Therapy	M,D,O
Psychology—General	M,D,O
Public Administration	M
School Psychology	O
Social Sciences	M,O
Spanish	M,O

NSCAD UNIVERSITY

Applied Arts and Design—General	M
Art/Fine Arts	M

NYACK COLLEGE

Social Sciences	M

OAKLAND CITY UNIVERSITY

Theology	P,D

OAKLAND UNIVERSITY

Counseling Psychology	M,D,O
Economics	O
English	M
History	M
Liberal Studies	M
Linguistics	M,O
Music	M,D
Public Administration	M

OAKWOOD UNIVERSITY

Pastoral Ministry and Counseling	M

OBERLIN COLLEGE

Music	M,O

OBLATE SCHOOL OF THEOLOGY

Pastoral Ministry and Counseling	P,M,D,O
Religion	P,M,D,O
Theology	P,M,D,O

OCCIDENTAL COLLEGE

Liberal Studies	M

OHIO DOMINICAN UNIVERSITY

Liberal Studies	M
Theology	M

THE OHIO STATE UNIVERSITY

African Studies	M
African-American Studies	M
Agricultural Economics and Agribusiness	M,D
Anthropology	M,D
Architecture	M
Art History	M,D
Art/Fine Arts	M
Arts Administration	M
Asian Languages	M,D
Child and Family Studies	M,D
Chinese	M,D
Classics	M,D
Clinical Psychology	M,D
Clothing and Textiles	M,D
Cognitive Sciences	M,D
Communication— General	M,D
Consumer Economics	M,D
Dance	D
Developmental Psychology	M,D
East European and Russian Studies	M
Economics	M,D
English	M,D
Family and Consumer Sciences-General	M

Film, Television, and Video Theory and Criticism	M
French	M,D
Geography	M,D
German	M,D
History	M,D
Human Development	M,D
Industrial and Labor Relations	M,D
Industrial Design	M
Interdisciplinary Studies	M,D
Interior Design	M
Italian	M,D
Japanese	M,D
Journalism	M
Landscape Architecture	M
Linguistics	M,D
Music	M,D
Near and Middle Eastern Languages	M,D
Philosophy	M,D
Photography	M
Political Science	M,D
Portuguese	M,D
Psychology—General	M,D
Public Affairs	M,D
Rural Sociology	M,D
Slavic Languages	M,D
Social Psychology	M,D
Sociology	M,D
Spanish	M,D
Theater	M,D
Urban and Regional Planning	M,D
Women's Studies	M,D

OHIO UNIVERSITY

African Studies	M
Applied Economics	M
Art History	M
Art/Fine Arts	M
Asian Studies	M
Child and Family Studies	M
Child Development	M
Clinical Psychology	D
Communication— General	M,D
Comparative and Interdisciplinary Arts	D
Economics	M
English	M,D
Experimental Psychology	D
Family and Consumer Sciences-General	M
Film, Television, and Video Production	M
Film, Television, and Video Theory and Criticism	M
French	M
Geography	M
Graphic Design	M
History	M,D
Industrial and Organizational Psychology	D
International Affairs	M
International Development	M
Journalism	M,D
Latin American Studies	M
Linguistics	M

Media Studies	M,D
Music	M,O
Philosophy	M
Photography	M
Political Science	M
Psychology—General	D
Public Administration	M
Rehabilitation Counseling	M,D
Social Sciences	M
Sociology	M
Spanish	M
Speech and Interpersonal Communication	D
Theater	M
Therapies—Dance, Drama, and Music	M,O

OHR HAMEIR THEOLOGICAL SEMINARY

Theology	

OKLAHOMA CHRISTIAN UNIVERSITY

Pastoral Ministry and Counseling	P,M
Theology	P,M

OKLAHOMA CITY UNIVERSITY

Art/Fine Arts	M
Comparative Literature	M
Corporate and Organizational Communication	M
Criminal Justice and Criminology	M
Dance	M
Liberal Studies	M
Mass Communication	M
Music	M
Philosophy	M
Religion	M
Theater	M
Writing	M

OKLAHOMA STATE UNIVERSITY

Agricultural Economics and Agribusiness	M,D
Applied Arts and Design—General	M,D
Child and Family Studies	M,D
Clinical Psychology	M,D
Clothing and Textiles	M,D
Consumer Economics	M,D
Economics	M,D
Emergency Management	M,D
English	M,D
Family and Consumer Sciences-General	M,D
Geography	M,D
History	M,D
Human Development	M,D
Landscape Architecture	M,D
Mass Communication	M
Music	M
Philosophy	M
Political Science	M,D
Psychology—General	M,D
Sociology	M,D

Theater	M
Writing	M,D

OKLAHOMA STATE UNIVERSITY CENTER FOR HEALTH SCIENCES

Forensic Psychology	M,O
Forensic Sciences	M,O

OLD DOMINION UNIVERSITY

Applied Economics	M
Clinical Psychology	D
Conflict Resolution and Mediation/Peace Studies	M,D
Criminal Justice and Criminology	D
Economics	M
English	M,D
Experimental Psychology	D
History	M
Humanities	M
Industrial and Organizational Psychology	D
International Affairs	M,D
Linguistics	M
Psychology—General	M,D
Public Administration	M,D
Sociology	M
Urban Studies	D
Women's Studies	M,D
Writing	M

OLIVET NAZARENE UNIVERSITY

Religion	M
Theology	M

ORAL ROBERTS UNIVERSITY

Marriage and Family Therapy	P,M,D
Missions and Missiology	P,M,D
Near and Middle Eastern Languages	P,M,D
Pastoral Ministry and Counseling	P,M,D
Theology	P,M,D

OREGON HEALTH & SCIENCE UNIVERSITY

Gerontology	M,O

OREGON STATE UNIVERSITY

Agricultural Economics and Agribusiness	M,D
Anthropology	M
Child and Family Studies	M,D
Clothing and Textiles	M,D
Economics	M,D
English	M
Family and Consumer Sciences-General	M
Geography	M,D
Gerontology	M
History	M,D
Human Development	M,D
Interdisciplinary Studies	M
Philosophy	

*M—master's degree; P—first professional degree; D—doctorate; O—other advanced degree; *—Close-Up and/or Announcement or Display*

OREGON STATE UNIVERSITY–CASCADES

School Psychology	M
Social Psychology	M

OTIS COLLEGE OF ART AND DESIGN

Art/Fine Arts	M
Graphic Design	M
Photography	M
Writing	M

OTTAWA UNIVERSITY

Art Therapy	M
Counseling Psychology	M
Marriage and Family Therapy	M
Pastoral Ministry and Counseling	M
School Psychology	M

OUR LADY OF HOLY CROSS COLLEGE

Marriage and Family Therapy	M

OUR LADY OF THE LAKE UNIVERSITY OF SAN ANTONIO

Communication— General	M
Counseling Psychology	M,D
English	M
Human Development	M
Marriage and Family Therapy	M,D
Psychology—General	M,D
School Psychology	M,D
Writing	M

OXFORD GRADUATE SCHOOL

Child and Family Studies	M,D
Religion	M,D

PACE UNIVERSITY

Addictions/Substance Abuse Counseling	M
Clinical Psychology	D
Economics	M
Forensic Sciences	M
Psychology—General	M,D
Public Administration	M
Publishing	M
School Psychology	M
Theater	M

PACIFICA GRADUATE INSTITUTE

Clinical Psychology	M,D
Counseling Psychology	M,D
Psychology—General	M,D

PACIFIC LUTHERAN THEOLOGICAL SEMINARY

Theology	P,M,D,O

PACIFIC LUTHERAN UNIVERSITY

Marriage and Family Therapy	M
Writing	M

PACIFIC OAKS COLLEGE

Human Development	M
Marriage and Family Therapy	M

PACIFIC SCHOOL OF RELIGION

Religion	P,M,D,O
Theology	P,M,D,O

PACIFIC UNIVERSITY

Psychology—General	M,D

PALM BEACH ATLANTIC UNIVERSITY

Addictions/Substance Abuse Counseling	M
Counseling Psychology	M
Marriage and Family Therapy	M

PALO ALTO UNIVERSITY

Clinical Psychology	D*
Psychology—General	M,D*

PARK UNIVERSITY

Emergency Management	M
Public Administration	M
Public Affairs	M

PAYNE THEOLOGICAL SEMINARY

Theology	P

PENN STATE HARRISBURG

American Studies	M
Clinical Psychology	M,D
Criminal Justice and Criminology	M,D
Humanities	M
Psychology—General	M,D
Public Administration	M,D
Social Psychology	M,D

PENN STATE UNIVERSITY PARK

Agricultural Economics and Agribusiness	M,D
Anthropology	M,D
Architecture	M
Art History	M,D
Art/Fine Arts	M,D
Child and Family Studies	M,D
Clinical Psychology	M,D
Cognitive Sciences	M,D
Communication— General	M,D
Comparative Literature	M,D
Counseling Psychology	M,D
Criminal Justice and Criminology	M,D
Developmental Psychology	M,D
Economics	M,D
English	M,D
French	M,D
Geography	M,D
German	M,D
History	M,D
Human Development	M,D
Industrial and Labor Relations	M
Industrial and Organizational Psychology	M,D
Landscape Architecture	M
Mass Communication	M,D
Music	M,D
Philosophy	M,D
Photography	M,D
Political Science	M,D
Psychology—General	M,D
Rural Sociology	M,D
Russian	M,D
School Psychology	M,D
Social Psychology	M,D
Sociology	M,D
Spanish	M,D
Theater	M
Writing	M,D

PENNSYLVANIA ACADEMY OF THE FINE ARTS

Art/Fine Arts	M,O

PEPPERDINE UNIVERSITY

Clinical Psychology	M,D
Marriage and Family Therapy	M,D
Psychology—General	M,D

PEPPERDINE UNIVERSITY

American Studies	M
Clinical Psychology	M
Communication— General	M
Conflict Resolution and Mediation/Peace Studies	M
Economics	M
History	M
Humanities	M
International Affairs	M
Political Science	M
Psychology—General	M
Public Administration	M
Public Policy	M
Religion	P,M

PERU STATE COLLEGE

Economics	M

PHILADELPHIA BIBLICAL UNIVERSITY

Pastoral Ministry and Counseling	M
Theology	P,M

PHILADELPHIA COLLEGE OF OSTEOPATHIC MEDICINE

Clinical Psychology	M,D,O
Counseling Psychology	M,D,O
Forensic Sciences	M
Health Psychology	M,D,O
Industrial and Organizational Psychology	M,D,O
Psychology—General	M,D,O*
School Psychology	M,D,O

PHILADELPHIA UNIVERSITY

Architecture	M
Clothing and Textiles	M
Computer Art and Design	M
Emergency Management	M
Sustainable Development	M
Textile Design	M

PHILLIPS GRADUATE INSTITUTE

Clinical Psychology	D
Marriage and Family Therapy	M,D

PHILLIPS THEOLOGICAL SEMINARY

Ethics	P,M,D
Missions and Missiology	P,M,D
Music	P,M,D
Pastoral Ministry and Counseling	D
Theology	P,M,D

PIEDMONT BAPTIST COLLEGE AND GRADUATE SCHOOL

Theology	M,D

PITTSBURGH THEOLOGICAL SEMINARY

Theology	P,M,D

PITTSBURG STATE UNIVERSITY

Art/Fine Arts	M
Communication— General	M
English	M
Graphic Design	M,O
History	M
Music	M
Psychology—General	M
School Psychology	O
Social Psychology	M
Theater	M

POINT LOMA NAZARENE UNIVERSITY

Religion	M

POINT PARK UNIVERSITY

Communication— General	M*
Criminal Justice and Criminology	M
Journalism	M
Mass Communication	M
Music	M
Theater	M

POLYTECHNIC INSTITUTE OF NYU

Communication— General	O
Criminal Justice and Criminology	M,D,O
Film, Television, and Video Production	O
History of Science and Technology	M
Humanities	M,O
Internet and Interactive Multimedia	M,O
Journalism	M
Psychology—General	M

Technical Communication	O
Technical Writing	M

PONCE SCHOOL OF MEDICINE

Clinical Psychology	D

PONTIFICAL CATHOLIC UNIVERSITY OF PUERTO RICO

Clinical Psychology	M,D
Criminal Justice and Criminology	M
Hispanic Studies	M,O
History	M
Industrial and Organizational Psychology	M,D
Psychology—General	M,D
Public Administration	M
Rehabilitation Counseling	M
Spanish	M,O
Theology	P

PONTIFICAL COLLEGE JOSEPHINUM

Theology	P,M

PONTIFICIA UNIVERSIDAD CATOLICA MADRE Y MAESTRA

Architecture	M
Criminal Justice and Criminology	M
Industrial and Labor Relations	M
Interior Design	M

PORTLAND STATE UNIVERSITY

Anthropology	M,D,O
Applied Economics	M,D
Applied Social Research	M,D
Art/Fine Arts	M
Conflict Resolution and Mediation/Peace Studies	M
Criminal Justice and Criminology	M,D
Economics	M,D,O
English	M
French	M
Geography	M,D
German	M
Gerontology	O
History	M
Japanese	M
Music	M
Political Science	M,D
Psychology—General	M,D,O
Public Administration	M,D
Sociology	M,D,O
Spanish	M
Speech and Interpersonal Communication	M,O
Theater	M
Urban and Regional Planning	M
Urban Studies	M,D

PRAIRIE VIEW A&M UNIVERSITY

Agricultural Economics and Agribusiness	M
Architecture	M

Clinical Psychology	M,D
English	M
Family and Consumer Sciences-General	M
Forensic Psychology	M,D
Sociology	M
Urban Design	M

PRATT INSTITUTE

Applied Arts and Design—General	M,O
Architecture	M*
Art History	M
Art Therapy	M
Art/Fine Arts	M*
Arts Administration	M
Graphic Design	M
Historic Preservation	M
Industrial Design	M
Interior Design	M
Internet and Interactive Multimedia	M
Photography	M
Therapies—Dance, Drama, and Music	M
Urban and Regional Planning	M
Urban Design	M

PRESCOTT COLLEGE

Art Therapy	M
Counseling Psychology	M
Health Psychology	M
Humanities	M
Psychoanalysis and Psychotherapy	M

PRINCETON THEOLOGICAL SEMINARY

Religion	P,M,D
Theology	P,M,D

PRINCETON UNIVERSITY

Anthropology	D
Archaeology	D
Architecture	M,D
Asian Studies	D
Classics	D
Comparative Literature	D
Demography and Population Studies	D,O
Economics	D,O
English	D
French	D
German	D
History of Science and Technology	D
History	D
International Affairs	M,D
Music	D
Near and Middle Eastern Studies	M,D
Philosophy	D
Political Science	D
Portuguese	D
Psychology—General	D
Public Affairs	M,D,O
Public Policy	M,D
Religion	D
Russian	D
Slavic Languages	D
Sociology	D,O
Spanish	D

THE PROTESTANT EPISCOPAL THEOLOGICAL SEMINARY IN VIRGINIA

Theology	P,M,D

PROVIDENCE COLLEGE

American Studies	M
Economics	M
History	M
Religion	M
Theology	M

PROVIDENCE COLLEGE AND THEOLOGICAL SEMINARY

Counseling Psychology	P,M,D,O
Missions and Missiology	P,M,D,O
Pastoral Ministry and Counseling	P,M,D,O
Theology	P,M,D,O

PURCHASE COLLEGE, STATE UNIVERSITY OF NEW YORK

Art History	M
Art/Fine Arts	M
Dance	M
Music	M
Theater	M

PURDUE UNIVERSITY

Agricultural Economics and Agribusiness	M,D
American Studies	M,D
Anthropology	M,D
Applied Arts and Design—General	M
Art/Fine Arts	M
Child and Family Studies	M,D
Child Development	M,D
Clothing and Textiles	M,D
Communication—General	M,D
Comparative Literature	M,D
Consumer Economics	M,D
Economics	D
English	M,D
Family and Consumer Sciences-General	M,D
French	M,D
German	M,D
History	M,D
Human Development	M,D
Linguistics	M,D
Marriage and Family Therapy	M,D
Philosophy	M,D
Political Science	M,D
Psychology—General	D
Sociology	M,D
Spanish	M,D
Sport Psychology	M,D
Theater	M
Writing	M,D

PURDUE UNIVERSITY CALUMET

Communication—General	M
Counseling Psychology	M
English	M
History	M
Marriage and Family Therapy	M
School Psychology	M

QUEENS COLLEGE OF THE CITY UNIVERSITY OF NEW YORK

Art History	M
Art/Fine Arts	M
Clinical Psychology	M
English	M
Family and Consumer Sciences-General	M
French	M
History	M
Italian	M
Liberal Studies	M
Linguistics	M
Music	M
Psychology—General	M
Romance Languages	M
School Psychology	M,O
Social Sciences	M
Sociology	M
Spanish	M
Urban Studies	M
Writing	M

QUEEN'S UNIVERSITY AT KINGSTON

Canadian Studies	M,D
Classics	M
Clinical Psychology	M,D
Cognitive Sciences	M,D
Communication—General	M,D
Developmental Psychology	M,D
English	M,D
French	M,D
Gender Studies	M,D
Geography	M,D
German	M,D
Hispanic Studies	M
Industrial and Labor Relations	M
International Affairs	M,D
Philosophy	M,D
Political Science	M,D
Psychology—General	M,D
Public Policy	M
Religion	M
Social Psychology	M,D
Sociology	M,D
Spanish	M
Sport Psychology	M,D
Theology	P,M,O
Urban and Regional Planning	M
Women's Studies	M,D

QUEENS UNIVERSITY OF CHARLOTTE

Corporate and Organizational Communication	M
Writing	M

QUINCY UNIVERSITY

Theology	M

QUINNIPIAC UNIVERSITY

Communication—General	M*
Internet and Interactive Multimedia	M
Journalism	M

*M—master's degree; P—first professional degree; D—doctorate; O—other advanced degree; *—Close-Up and/or Announcement or Display*

RABBI ISAAC ELCHANAN THEOLOGICAL SEMINARY

Theology	O

RABBINICAL ACADEMY MESIVTA RABBI CHAIM BERLIN

Theology	O

RABBINICAL COLLEGE BETH SHRAGA

Theology	

RABBINICAL COLLEGE BOBOVER YESHIVA B'NEI ZION

Theology	

RABBINICAL COLLEGE CH'SAN SOFER

Theology	

RABBINICAL COLLEGE OF LONG ISLAND

Theology	

RABBINICAL SEMINARY M'KOR CHAIM

Theology	

RABBINICAL SEMINARY OF AMERICA

Theology	

RADFORD UNIVERSITY

Art/Fine Arts	M
Clinical Psychology	M,D,O
Corporate and Organizational Communication	M
Counseling Psychology	M,D,O
Criminal Justice and Criminology	M
English	M
Experimental Psychology	M,D,O
Industrial and Organizational Psychology	M,D,O
Music	M
Psychology—General	M,D,O
School Psychology	M,D,O
Therapies—Dance, Drama, and Music	M

RAMAPO COLLEGE OF NEW JERSEY

Liberal Studies	M

RECONSTRUCTIONIST RABBINICAL COLLEGE

Theology	P,M,D,O

REED COLLEGE

Liberal Studies	M

REFORMED PRESBYTERIAN THEOLOGICAL SEMINARY

Theology	P,M,D

REFORMED THEOLOGICAL SEMINARY–CHARLOTTE CAMPUS

Pastoral Ministry and Counseling	P,M,D
Religion	P,M,D
Theology	P,M,D

REFORMED THEOLOGICAL SEMINARY–JACKSON CAMPUS

Marriage and Family Therapy	P,M,D,O
Missions and Missiology	P,M,D,O
Pastoral Ministry and Counseling	P,M,D,O
Theology	P,M,D,O

REFORMED THEOLOGICAL SEMINARY–ORLANDO CAMPUS

Pastoral Ministry and Counseling	P,M,D
Theology	P,M,D

REFORMED THEOLOGICAL SEMINARY–WASHINGTON D.C.

Religion	P,M
Theology	P,M

REGENT COLLEGE

Theology	P,M,O

REGENT UNIVERSITY

Clinical Psychology	M,D,O
Communication— General	M,D
Computer Art and Design	M,D
Counseling Psychology	M,D,O
Economics	M
Film, Television, and Video Production	M,D
Homeland Security	M
International Economics	M
Journalism	M,D
Missions and Missiology	P,M,D
Near and Middle Eastern Studies	M
Pastoral Ministry and Counseling	P,M,D
Political Science	M
Public Administration	M
Public Policy	M
Social Psychology	M,D,O
Theater	M,D
Theology	P,M,D

REGIS COLLEGE (CANADA)

Pastoral Ministry and Counseling	P,M,D,O
Theology	P,M,D,O

REGIS COLLEGE (MA)

Corporate and Organizational Communication	M
Public Administration	M,O
Public Policy	M,O

REGIS UNIVERSITY

Art/Fine Arts	M,O
Arts Administration	M,O

Communication— General	M,O
Conflict Resolution and Mediation/Peace Studies	M,O
Counseling Psychology	M,O
Criminal Justice and Criminology	M,O
Interdisciplinary Studies	M,O
Marriage and Family Therapy	M,O
Music	M,O
Psychology—General	M,O
Social Psychology	M,O
Social Sciences	M,O
Technical Writing	M,O

REINHARDT COLLEGE

Music	M

RENSSELAER POLYTECHNIC INSTITUTE

Architecture	M,D
Art/Fine Arts	M,D
Cognitive Sciences	D
Communication— General	M,D
Computer Art and Design	M,D
Economics	M
Historic Preservation	M
History of Science and Technology	M,D
Interdisciplinary Studies	M,D
Lighting Design	M
Rhetoric	M,D
Speech and Interpersonal Communication	M,D
Technical Communication	M

RHODE ISLAND COLLEGE

Art/Fine Arts	M
Arts Administration	M
English	M
History	M
Psychology—General	M
Public Administration	M
Theater	M
Writing	M

RHODE ISLAND SCHOOL OF DESIGN

Applied Arts and Design—General	M
Architecture	M
Art/Fine Arts	M
Computer Art and Design	M
Graphic Design	M
Industrial Design	M
Interior Design	M
Landscape Architecture	M
Photography	M
Textile Design	M

RICE UNIVERSITY

Anthropology	M,D
Architecture	M,D
Cognitive Sciences	M,D
Economics	M,D
English	M,D
French	M,D
History	M,D

Industrial and Organizational Psychology	M,D
Linguistics	M,D
Music	M,D
Philosophy	M,D
Political Science	M,D
Psychology—General	M,D
Religion	D
Spanish	M
Urban Design	M,D

THE RICHARD STOCKTON COLLEGE OF NEW JERSEY

Criminal Justice and Criminology	M
Holocaust Studies	M

RICHMOND, THE AMERICAN INTERNATIONAL UNIVERSITY IN LONDON

Art History	M

RICHMONT GRADUATE UNIVERSITY

Counseling Psychology	M
Marriage and Family Therapy	M
Psychology—General	M

RIDER UNIVERSITY

French	O
German	O
School Psychology	O
Spanish	O

RIVIER COLLEGE

Counseling Psychology	M,O
English	M
Writing	M

ROBERT MORRIS UNIVERSITY

Internet and Interactive Multimedia	M,D

ROBERTS WESLEYAN COLLEGE

Child and Family Studies	M
Pastoral Ministry and Counseling	M
School Psychology	M

ROCHESTER INSTITUTE OF TECHNOLOGY

Art/Fine Arts	M
Communication— General	M
Computer Art and Design	M
Film, Television, and Video Production	M
Gerontology	O
Graphic Design	M
Industrial Design	M
Interdisciplinary Studies	M
Internet and Interactive Multimedia	M,O
Media Studies	M
Medical Illustration	M
Photography	M
Psychology—General	M

Public Policy	M
School Psychology	M,O
Sustainable Development	D
Technical Communication	O

ROGER WILLIAMS UNIVERSITY

Architecture	M
Criminal Justice and Criminology	M*
Forensic Psychology	M*
Public Administration	M*

ROLLINS COLLEGE

Liberal Studies	M

ROOSEVELT UNIVERSITY

Anthropology	M
Applied Economics	M
Clinical Psychology	M,D
Communication— General	M
Corporate and Organizational Communication	M
Economics	M
English	M
Gender Studies	M,O
History	M
Industrial and Organizational Psychology	M
Journalism	M
Music	M,O
Political Science	M
Psychology—General	D
Public Administration	M
Sociology	M
Spanish	M
Theater	M
Women's Studies	M,O
Writing	M

ROSALIND FRANKLIN UNIVERSITY OF MEDICINE AND SCIENCE

Clinical Psychology	M,D
Interdisciplinary Studies	D
Psychology—General	M,D

ROSEMONT COLLEGE

Counseling Psychology	M
English	M
Publishing	M
Writing	M

ROWAN UNIVERSITY

Counseling Psychology	M
Criminal Justice and Criminology	M
Music	M
Psychology—General	M
School Psychology	M,O
Theater	M
Writing	M

ROYAL MILITARY COLLEGE OF CANADA

Military and Defense Studies	M,D

ROYAL ROADS UNIVERSITY

Conflict Resolution and Mediation/Peace Studies	M,O
Emergency Management	M,O

RUTGERS, THE STATE UNIVERSITY OF NEW JERSEY, CAMDEN

Child Development	M,D
Criminal Justice and Criminology	M
English	M
History	M
International Affairs	M
International Development	M
Liberal Studies	M
Psychology—General	M
Public Administration	M
Public History	M
Public Policy	M
Writing	M

RUTGERS, THE STATE UNIVERSITY OF NEW JERSEY, NEWARK

American Studies	M,D
Cognitive Sciences	D*
Criminal Justice and Criminology	D
Economics	M
English	M
History	M
International Affairs	M,D
Liberal Studies	M
Music	M
Political Science	M
Psychology—General	D
Public Administration	M,D
Public Policy	M,D
Social Psychology	D
Urban Studies	M,D
Writing	M

RUTGERS, THE STATE UNIVERSITY OF NEW JERSEY, NEW BRUNSWICK

African Studies	D
African-American Studies	D
Agricultural Economics and Agribusiness	M
Anthropology	M,D
Applied Arts and Design—General	M
Art History	M,D,O
Art/Fine Arts	M
Asian Studies	D
Classics	M,D
Clinical Psychology	M,D
Cognitive Sciences	D
Communication— General	D
Comparative Literature	M,D
Counseling Psychology	M
Economics	M,D
English	D
French	M,D
Gender Studies	M,D
Geography	M,D
German	M,D
Health Psychology	D

Historic Preservation	M,D,O
History of Medicine	D
History of Science and Technology	D
History	D
Industrial and Labor Relations	M,D*
Industrial and Organizational Psychology	M,D
Interdisciplinary Studies	D
International Affairs	D
Italian	M,D
Linguistics	D
Medieval and Renaissance Studies	D
Music	M,D,O
Philosophy	D
Political Science	D
Psychology—General	M,D
Public Policy	M,D
School Psychology	M,D
Social Psychology	D
Sociology	M,D
Spanish	M,D
Theater	M
Translation and Interpretation	M,D
Urban and Regional Planning	M,D
Women's Studies	M,D
Writing	M

RYERSON UNIVERSITY

Arts Administration	M

SACRED HEART MAJOR SEMINARY

Pastoral Ministry and Counseling	P,M
Theology	P,M

SACRED HEART SCHOOL OF THEOLOGY

Theology	P,M

SACRED HEART UNIVERSITY

Criminal Justice and Criminology	M
Gerontology	M
Internet and Interactive Multimedia	M,O
Religion	M

SAGE GRADUATE SCHOOL

Child and Family Studies	M
Criminal Justice and Criminology	M,O
Forensic Psychology	M,O
Gerontology	M,O
Psychology—General	M,O
Public Administration	M
Social Psychology	M
Sociology	M,O

SAGINAW VALLEY STATE UNIVERSITY

Communication— General	M
Media Studies	M
Public Administration	M

ST. AMBROSE UNIVERSITY

Criminal Justice and Criminology	M
Pastoral Ministry and Counseling	M

ST. ANDREW'S COLLEGE IN WINNIPEG

Theology	P

ST. AUGUSTINE'S SEMINARY OF TORONTO

Pastoral Ministry and Counseling	P,M,O
Theology	P,M,O

SAINT BERNARD'S SCHOOL OF THEOLOGY AND MINISTRY

Pastoral Ministry and Counseling	P,M,O
Theology	P,M,O

ST. BONAVENTURE UNIVERSITY

Counseling Psychology	M,O
English	M
Theology	M,O

ST. CATHERINE UNIVERSITY

Theology	M

ST. CHARLES BORROMEO SEMINARY, OVERBROOK

Religion	M
Theology	P,M

ST. CLOUD STATE UNIVERSITY

Applied Economics	M
Archaeology	M
Child and Family Studies	M
Criminal Justice and Criminology	M
Economics	M
English	M
Geography	M
Gerontology	M
Historic Preservation	M
History	M
Industrial and Organizational Psychology	M
Marriage and Family Therapy	M
Mass Communication	M
Music	M
Psychology—General	M
Rehabilitation Counseling	M
Social Psychology	M

ST. EDWARD'S UNIVERSITY

Computer Art and Design	M
Conflict Resolution and Mediation/Peace Studies	M,O
Counseling Psychology	M,O
Ethics	M
Humanities	M,O
Liberal Studies	M,O

M—master's degree; P—first professional degree; D—doctorate; O—other advanced degree; *—Close-Up and / or Announcement or Display

Public Administration	M,O
Social Sciences	M,O

SAINT FRANCIS SEMINARY

Pastoral Ministry and Counseling	P,M
Theology	P,M

ST. FRANCIS XAVIER UNIVERSITY

Cultural Studies	M

ST. JOHN FISHER COLLEGE

Counseling Psychology	M
International Affairs	M

ST. JOHN'S COLLEGE (MD)

Liberal Studies	M

ST. JOHN'S COLLEGE (NM)

Asian Languages	M
Asian Studies	M
Liberal Studies	M

ST. JOHN'S SEMINARY (CA)

Pastoral Ministry and Counseling	P,M
Theology	P,M

SAINT JOHN'S SEMINARY (MA)

Religion	P,M
Theology	P,M

SAINT JOHN'S UNIVERSITY (MN)

Music	P,M
Pastoral Ministry and Counseling	P,M
Theology	P,M

ST. JOHN'S UNIVERSITY (NY)

African Studies	M,O
Asian Studies	M,O
Clinical Psychology	D
Communication—General	M,D,O
Criminal Justice and Criminology	M
English	M,D
Experimental Psychology	M
History	M,D
Liberal Studies	M
Pastoral Ministry and Counseling	P,M,O
Philosophy	M
Political Science	M,O
Psychology—General	M,D
Rehabilitation Counseling	M,D,O
School Psychology	M,D
Sociology	M
Spanish	M,O
Theater	M,D,O
Theology	P,M,O

SAINT JOSEPH COLLEGE

Child and Family Studies	M
Counseling Psychology	M
Gerontology	M,O
Human Development	M,O

Marriage and Family Therapy	M
Social Psychology	M

SAINT JOSEPH'S COLLEGE

Music	M,O

ST. JOSEPH'S SEMINARY

Theology	P,M

SAINT JOSEPH'S UNIVERSITY

Criminal Justice and Criminology	M,O
Gerontology	M,O
Homeland Security	M,O
Industrial and Organizational Psychology	M,O
Psychology—General	M,O
Writing	M

ST. LAWRENCE UNIVERSITY

Human Development	M,O

SAINT LEO UNIVERSITY

Criminal Justice and Criminology	M
Pastoral Ministry and Counseling	M

SAINT LOUIS UNIVERSITY

American Studies	M,D
Clinical Psychology	M,D
Communication—General	M
English	M,D
Experimental Psychology	M,D
French	M
Geographic Information Systems	M,D,O
History	M,D
Human Development	M,D,O
Industrial and Organizational Psychology	M,D
Marriage and Family Therapy	M,D,O
Philosophy	M,D
Political Science	M
Psychology—General	M,D
Public Administration	M,D,O
Public Policy	M,D,O
Spanish	M
Theology	M,D
Urban Studies	M,D,O

SAINT LOUIS UNIVERSITY–MADRID CAMPUS

English	M
Spanish	M*

SAINT MARTIN'S UNIVERSITY

Counseling Psychology	M
Social Psychology	M

SAINT MARY-OF-THE-WOODS COLLEGE

Art Therapy	M,O
Pastoral Ministry and Counseling	M,O
Theology	M,O

Therapies—Dance, Drama, and Music	M

SAINT MARY'S COLLEGE OF CALIFORNIA

Liberal Studies	M
Marriage and Family Therapy	M
Writing	M

SAINT MARY SEMINARY AND GRADUATE SCHOOL OF THEOLOGY

Theology	P,M,D

ST. MARY'S SEMINARY AND UNIVERSITY

Theology	P,M,D,O*

SAINT MARY'S UNIVERSITY (CANADA)

Canadian Studies	M
Criminal Justice and Criminology	M
History	M
Industrial and Organizational Psychology	M,D
International Development	M
Philosophy	M
Psychology—General	M,D
Women's Studies	M

ST. MARY'S UNIVERSITY (UNITED STATES)

Addictions/Substance Abuse Counseling	M,D,O
Clinical Psychology	M
Communication—General	M
Counseling Psychology	M
English	M
Industrial and Organizational Psychology	M
International Affairs	M
Marriage and Family Therapy	M,D
Pastoral Ministry and Counseling	M
Political Science	M
Psychology—General	M
Public Administration	M
Social Psychology	M
Theology	M

SAINT MARY'S UNIVERSITY OF MINNESOTA

Arts Administration	M
Counseling Psychology	M
Geographic Information Systems	M,O
Human Development	M
Marriage and Family Therapy	M,O
Pastoral Ministry and Counseling	M,O
Philanthropic Studies	M

SAINT MEINRAD SCHOOL OF THEOLOGY

Theology	P,M

SAINT MICHAEL'S COLLEGE

Clinical Psychology	M
Theology	M,O

ST. NORBERT COLLEGE

Liberal Studies	M
Theology	M

ST. PATRICK'S SEMINARY & UNIVERSITY

Theology	P,M

SAINT PAUL SCHOOL OF THEOLOGY

Theology	P,M,D

SAINT PAUL UNIVERSITY

Conflict Resolution and Mediation/Peace Studies	M
Counseling Psychology	M
Marriage and Family Therapy	M
Missions and Missiology	M
Pastoral Ministry and Counseling	M,D,O
Theology	M,D,O

ST. PETERSBURG THEOLOGICAL SEMINARY

Jewish Studies	P,M,D
Pastoral Ministry and Counseling	P,M,D
Theology	P,M,D

ST. PETER'S SEMINARY

Theology	P,M

SAINTS CYRIL AND METHODIUS SEMINARY

Pastoral Ministry and Counseling	P,M
Theology	P,M

ST. STEPHEN'S COLLEGE

Pastoral Ministry and Counseling	M,D
Theology	M,D

ST. THOMAS UNIVERSITY

Arts Administration	M
Communication—General	M,D,O
Counseling Psychology	M
Criminal Justice and Criminology	M,O
Film, Television, and Video Production	M
Hispanic Studies	M,O
Marriage and Family Therapy	M,O
Pastoral Ministry and Counseling	M,D,O
Public Administration	M,O
Theology	M,D,O

ST. TIKHON'S ORTHODOX THEOLOGICAL SEMINARY

Theology	P

SAINT VINCENT DE PAUL REGIONAL SEMINARY

Theology	P,M

SAINT VINCENT SEMINARY

Theology	P,M

ST. VLADIMIR'S ORTHODOX THEOLOGICAL SEMINARY

Music	P,M,D
Theology	P,M,D

SAINT XAVIER UNIVERSITY

Counseling Psychology	M,O
English	M,O
Psychology—General	M,O
Writing	M,O

SALEM STATE COLLEGE

Counseling Psychology	M
Criminal Justice and Criminology	M
English	M
Geography	M
History	M
Psychology—General	M
Spanish	M

SALISBURY UNIVERSITY

English	M
Geographic Information Systems	M
History	M
Public Administration	M
Writing	M

SALVE REGINA UNIVERSITY

Art Therapy	M,O
Counseling Psychology	M,O
Criminal Justice and Criminology	M
Homeland Security	M,O
Humanities	M,D,O
International Affairs	M,O
Rehabilitation Counseling	M,O

SAMFORD UNIVERSITY

Music	M
Theology	P,M,D

SAM HOUSTON STATE UNIVERSITY

Clinical Psychology	M,D
Criminal Justice and Criminology	M,D
Dance	M
English	M
Family and Consumer Sciences-General	M
Forensic Sciences	M,D
History	M
Humanities	M,D
Music	M
Political Science	M
Psychology—General	M,D
Public Administration	M
Sociology	M

SAN DIEGO STATE UNIVERSITY

Anthropology	M
Applied Arts and Design—General	M
Art History	M
Art/Fine Arts	M
Asian Studies	M
Child and Family Studies	M
Child Development	M
Clinical Psychology	M,D
Communication— General	M
Criminal Justice and Criminology	M
Economics	M
Emergency Management	M,D
English	M
Environmental Design	M
Film, Television, and Video Production	M
Geography	M,D
Gerontology	M
Graphic Design	M
Health Psychology	M,D
History	M
Industrial and Organizational Psychology	M,D
Interdisciplinary Studies	M
Interior Design	M
Internet and Interactive Multimedia	M
Latin American Studies	M
Liberal Studies	M
Linguistics	M,O
Media Studies	M
Music	M
Philosophy	M
Political Science	M
Psychology—General	M,D
Public Administration	M
Rehabilitation Counseling	M
Rhetoric	M
Romance Languages	M
School Psychology	M
Sociology	M
Spanish	M
Theater	M
Urban and Regional Planning	M
Western European Studies	M
Women's Studies	M
Writing	M

SAN FRANCISCO ART INSTITUTE

Applied Arts and Design—General	M,O
Art History	M
Art/Fine Arts	M,O*
Film, Television, and Video Production	M,O
Museum Studies	M
Photography	M,O
Urban Studies	M

SAN FRANCISCO CONSERVATORY OF MUSIC

Music	M

SAN FRANCISCO STATE UNIVERSITY

Anthropology	M
Art History	M
Art/Fine Arts	M
Asian-American Studies	M
Chinese	M
Classics	M
Comparative Literature	M
Counseling Psychology	M
Cultural Studies	M
Economics	M
English	M,O
Ethnic Studies	M
Family and Consumer Sciences-General	M
Film, Television, and Video Production	M
Film, Television, and Video Theory and Criticism	M
French	M
Geography	M
German	M
Gerontology	M
History	M
Humanities	M
Industrial Design	M
International Affairs	M
Italian	M
Japanese	M
Linguistics	M
Marriage and Family Therapy	M
Media Studies	M
Museum Studies	M
Music	M
Philosophy	M,O
Political Science	M
Psychology—General	M
Public Administration	M
Public Policy	M
Rehabilitation Counseling	M
Spanish	M
Speech and Interpersonal Communication	M
Theater	M
Women's Studies	M
Writing	M

SAN FRANCISCO THEOLOGICAL SEMINARY

Theology	P,M,D

SAN JOSE STATE UNIVERSITY

Anthropology	M
Applied Arts and Design—General	M
Applied Economics	M
Art History	M
Art/Fine Arts	M
Child and Family Studies	M
Clinical Psychology	M
Communication— General	M
Comparative Literature	M,O
Computer Art and Design	M
Criminal Justice and Criminology	M
Economics	M
English	M,O

SANTA CLARA UNIVERSITY

Counseling Psychology	M
Music	M
Pastoral Ministry and Counseling	M
Religion	M

SARAH LAWRENCE COLLEGE

Child Development	M
Dance	M*
Genetic Counseling	M
History	M
Interdisciplinary Studies	M
Theater	M
Women's Studies	M*
Writing	M

Experimental Psychology — M
Film, Television, and Video Production — M
French — M
Geographic Information Systems — M,O
Geography — M,O
Gerontology — M,O
Hispanic Studies — M
History — M
Industrial and Organizational Psychology — M
Interdisciplinary Studies — M
Linguistics — M,O
Mass Communication — M
Music — M
Philosophy — M,O
Photography — M
Psychology—General — M
Public Administration — M
Sociology — M
Spanish — M
Speech and Interpersonal Communication — M
Theater — M
Urban and Regional Planning — M,O
Writing — M,O

SAVANNAH COLLEGE OF ART AND DESIGN

Applied Arts and Design—General	M
Architectural History	M
Architecture	M
Art History	M
Art/Fine Arts	M*
Arts Administration	M
Computer Art and Design	M
Film, Television, and Video Production	M
Film, Television, and Video Theory and Criticism	M
Graphic Design	M
Historic Preservation	M
Illustration	M
Industrial Design	M
Interior Design	M
Internet and Interactive Multimedia	M
Media Studies	M
Music	M
Photography	M

*M—master's degree; P—first professional degree; D—doctorate; O—other advanced degree; *—Close-Up and/or Announcement or Display*

Textile Design	M
Theater	M
Urban Design	M
Writing	M

SAVANNAH STATE UNIVERSITY

Public Administration	M
Urban Studies	M

SAYBROOK GRADUATE SCHOOL AND RESEARCH CENTER

Clinical Psychology	M,D
Health Psychology	M,D
Marriage and Family Therapy	M,D
Psychology—General	M,D
Transpersonal and Humanistic Psychology	M,D

SCHILLER INTERNATIONAL UNIVERSITY

International Affairs	M

SCHILLER INTERNATIONAL UNIVERSITY (UNITED KINGDOM)

Corporate and Organizational Communication	M
International Affairs	M

SCHOOL OF ADVANCED AIR AND SPACE STUDIES

Military and Defense Studies	M

THE SCHOOL OF PROFESSIONAL PSYCHOLOGY AT FOREST INSTITUTE

Clinical Psychology	M,D,O
Counseling Psychology	M,D,O
Marriage and Family Therapy	M,D,O
Psychology—General	M,D,O

SCHOOL OF THE ART INSTITUTE OF CHICAGO

Applied Arts and Design—General	M
Architecture	M
Art History	M,O
Art Therapy	M
Art/Fine Arts	M*
Arts Administration	M
Arts Journalism	M
Film, Television, and Video Production	M
Graphic Design	M
Historic Preservation	M
Interior Design	M
Journalism	M
Music	M
Photography	M
Textile Design	M,O
Writing	M,O

SCHOOL OF THE MUSEUM OF FINE ARTS, BOSTON

Art/Fine Arts	M

SCHOOL OF VISUAL ARTS

Applied Arts and Design—General	M
Art Therapy	M
Art/Fine Arts	M
Computer Art and Design	M
Film, Television, and Video Production	M
Illustration	M
Internet and Interactive Multimedia	M
Photography	M

SEABURY-WESTERN THEOLOGICAL SEMINARY

Music	P,M,D,O
Theology	P,M,D,O

SEATTLE PACIFIC UNIVERSITY

Clinical Psychology	D
Industrial and Organizational Psychology	M,D
Marriage and Family Therapy	M,O
Writing	M

SEATTLE UNIVERSITY

Criminal Justice and Criminology	M
Pastoral Ministry and Counseling	M
Psychology—General	M
Public Administration	M
School Psychology	M,O
Theology	P,M,O
Transpersonal and Humanistic Psychology	M

SEMINARY OF THE IMMACULATE CONCEPTION

Pastoral Ministry and Counseling	P,M,D,O
Theology	P,M,D,O

SEMINARY OF THE SOUTHWEST

Pastoral Ministry and Counseling	P,M,O
Religion	P,M,O
Theology	P,M,O

SETON HALL UNIVERSITY

Art/Fine Arts	M
Asian Languages	M
Asian Studies	M*
Chinese	M
Communication—General	M
Corporate and Organizational Communication	M*
Counseling Psychology	M,D
English	M*
Experimental Psychology	M*
History	M*
Holocaust Studies	M
International Affairs	M*
Jewish Studies	M
Marriage and Family Therapy	M,D,O
Museum Studies	M*
Pastoral Ministry and Counseling	P,M
Psychology—General	M,D,O
Public Administration	M,O
Public Policy	M,O*
Religion	M*
School Psychology	O
Speech and Interpersonal Communication	M
Theology	P,M
Writing	M

SETON HILL UNIVERSITY

Art Therapy	M,O
Holocaust Studies	O
Marriage and Family Therapy	M
Writing	M

SEWANEE: THE UNIVERSITY OF THE SOUTH

English	M
Theology	P,M,D
Writing	M

SHASTA BIBLE COLLEGE

Pastoral Ministry and Counseling	M

SHAW UNIVERSITY

Theology	P,M

SHENANDOAH UNIVERSITY

Arts Administration	M,D,O
Dance	M,D,O
Music	M,D,O
Public Administration	M,D,O
Therapies—Dance, Drama, and Music	M,D,O

SHIPPENSBURG UNIVERSITY OF PENNSYLVANIA

Addictions/Substance Abuse Counseling	M,O
Communication—General	M
Counseling Psychology	M,O
Criminal Justice and Criminology	M
Geography	M
Gerontology	M,O
History	M,O
Marriage and Family Therapy	M,O
Psychology—General	M
Public Administration	M
Public History	M,O
Social Psychology	M,O
Sociology	M

SH'OR YOSHUV RABBINICAL COLLEGE

Theology	M

SIMMONS COLLEGE

Corporate and Organizational Communication	M
Cultural Studies	M
English	M
Gender Studies	M

Public History
Spanish	M

SIMON FRASER UNIVERSITY

Anthropology	M,D
Archaeology	M,D
Communication—General	M,D
Comparative and Interdisciplinary Arts	M
Criminal Justice and Criminology	M,D
Economics	M,D
English	M,D
French	M,D
Geography	M,D
Gerontology	M,D
History	M,D
Internet and Interactive Multimedia	M,D
Latin American Studies	M
Liberal Studies	M
Linguistics	M,D
Philosophy	M,D
Political Science	M,D
Psychology—General	M,D
Public Policy	M
Publishing	M
Sociology	M,D
Urban Studies	M,O
Women's Studies	M,D

SIMPSON UNIVERSITY

Cultural Studies	P,M
Missions and Missiology	P,M
Pastoral Ministry and Counseling	P,M
Religion	P,M

SIOUX FALLS SEMINARY

Marriage and Family Therapy	M
Pastoral Ministry and Counseling	P,M
Religion	M
Theology	M,D,O

SIT GRADUATE INSTITUTE

Conflict Resolution and Mediation/Peace Studies	M
International Affairs	M
Near and Middle Eastern Studies	M
Sustainable Development	M

SKIDMORE COLLEGE

Liberal Studies	M

SLIPPERY ROCK UNIVERSITY OF PENNSYLVANIA

English	M
History	M
Music	M
Sustainable Development	M
Writing	M

SMITH COLLEGE

Dance	M
French	M

History	M
Theater	M

SOJOURNER-DOUGLASS COLLEGE

Public Administration	M

SONOMA STATE UNIVERSITY

Anthropology	M
Counseling Psychology	M
English	M
History	M
Interdisciplinary Studies	M
Marriage and Family Therapy	M
Political Science	M
Public Administration	M
Public History	M
Writing	M

SOUTH CAROLINA STATE UNIVERSITY

Agricultural Economics and Agribusiness	M
Child and Family Studies	M
Family and Consumer Sciences-General	M
Rehabilitation Counseling	M

SOUTH DAKOTA STATE UNIVERSITY

Clothing and Textiles	M
Communication—General	M
Economics	M
English	M
Family and Consumer Sciences-General	M
Geography	M
Human Development	M
Interior Design	M
Journalism	M
Rural Sociology	M,D

SOUTHEASTERN BAPTIST THEOLOGICAL SEMINARY

Ethics	P,M,D
Missions and Missiology	P,M,D
Music	P,M,D
Philosophy	P,M,D
Psychology—General	P,M,D
Theology	P,M,D
Women's Studies	P,M,D

SOUTHEASTERN LOUISIANA UNIVERSITY

Communication—General	M
English	M
History	M
Music	M
Psychology—General	M
Sociology	M

SOUTHEASTERN OKLAHOMA STATE UNIVERSITY

Social Psychology	M

SOUTHEASTERN UNIVERSITY

Public Administration	M

SOUTHEAST MISSOURI STATE UNIVERSITY

Counseling Psychology	M,O
Criminal Justice and Criminology	M
English	M
Forensic Sciences	M
History	M
Public Administration	M
School Psychology	M,O

SOUTHERN ADVENTIST UNIVERSITY

Counseling Psychology	M
Missions and Missiology	M
Psychology—General	M
Religion	M
Theology	M

SOUTHERN ARKANSAS UNIVERSITY–MAGNOLIA

Counseling Psychology	M
Public Administration	M

SOUTHERN BAPTIST THEOLOGICAL SEMINARY

Missions and Missiology	P,M,D
Music	P,M,D
Pastoral Ministry and Counseling	P,M,D
Philosophy	P,M,D
Religion	P,M,D
Theology	P,M,D

SOUTHERN CALIFORNIA INSTITUTE OF ARCHITECTURE

Architecture	M

SOUTHERN CALIFORNIA SEMINARY

Counseling Psychology	P,M,D
Psychology—General	P,M,D
Religion	P,M,D
Theology	P,M,D

SOUTHERN CONNECTICUT STATE UNIVERSITY

English	M
History	M
Marriage and Family Therapy	M
Political Science	M
Psychology—General	M
School Psychology	M,O
Sociology	M
Sport Psychology	M
Urban Studies	M
Women's Studies	M

SOUTHERN EVANGELICAL SEMINARY

Jewish Studies	M,D,O
Missions and Missiology	P,M,O
Near and Middle Eastern Studies	M,D,O
Pastoral Ministry and Counseling	P,M,O
Philosophy	M,D,O
Religion	P,M,D,O
Theology	P,M,D,O

SOUTHERN ILLINOIS UNIVERSITY CARBONDALE

Agricultural Economics and Agribusiness	M
Anthropology	M,D*
Applied Arts and Design—General	M*
Architecture	M
Art/Fine Arts	M
Clinical Psychology	M,D
Communication—General	M,D*
Counseling Psychology	M,D
Criminal Justice and Criminology	M
Cultural Studies	M
Economics	M,D*
English	M,D*
Experimental Psychology	M,D
Geography	M,D
History	M,D*
Human Development	M,D
Journalism	D
Linguistics	M
Mass Communication	M*
Media Studies	M
Music	M
Philosophy	M,D*
Political Science	M,D*
Psychology—General	M,D*
Public Administration	M
Rehabilitation Counseling	M,D*
Rhetoric	M,D
Sociology	M,D*
Speech and Interpersonal Communication	M,D*
Theater	M,D*
Writing	M*

SOUTHERN ILLINOIS UNIVERSITY EDWARDSVILLE

Art Therapy	M
Art/Fine Arts	M
Clinical Psychology	M
Corporate and Organizational Communication	O
Economics	M
English	M,O
Geography	M
History	M
Industrial and Organizational Psychology	M
Mass Communication	M
Media Studies	O
Museum Studies	O
Music	M
Psychology—General	M,O
Public Administration	M
School Psychology	O
Sociology	M
Speech and Interpersonal Communication	M
Writing	M

SOUTHERN METHODIST UNIVERSITY

Anthropology	M,D
Applied Economics	M,D
Art History	M
Art/Fine Arts	M
Arts Administration	
Clinical Psychology	D
Communication—General	M
Conflict Resolution and Mediation/Peace Studies	M,O
Dance	M
Economics	M,D
English	M,D
Film, Television, and Video Production	M
History	M,D
Medieval and Renaissance Studies	M
Music	M,O
Photography	M
Psychology—General	D
Religion	M,D
Theater	M
Theology	P,M,D

SOUTHERN NAZARENE UNIVERSITY

Counseling Psychology	M
Marriage and Family Therapy	M
Psychology—General	M
Religion	M
Theology	M

SOUTHERN NEW HAMPSHIRE UNIVERSITY

Addictions/Substance Abuse Counseling	M,O
Child Development	M,O
Clinical Psychology	M,O
Economic Development	M,D
Psychology—General	M,O
Public Policy	M,D
Writing	M,O

SOUTHERN OREGON UNIVERSITY

Music	M
Psychology—General	M
Social Sciences	M

SOUTHERN POLYTECHNIC STATE UNIVERSITY

Communication—General	M,O
Corporate and Organizational Communication	M,O
Graphic Design	M,O
Internet and Interactive Multimedia	M,O
Technical Communication	M,O

SOUTHERN UNIVERSITY AND AGRICULTURAL AND MECHANICAL COLLEGE

Criminal Justice and Criminology	M
History	M
Mass Communication	M
Political Science	M
Psychology—General	M
Public Administration	M
Public Policy	D

*M—master's degree; P—first professional degree; D—doctorate; O—other advanced degree; *—Close-Up and/or Announcement or Display*

Rehabilitation
  Counseling   M
Social Sciences   M

SOUTHERN UTAH UNIVERSITY

Arts Administration   M
Communication—
  General   M
Forensic Sciences   M
Public Administration   M

SOUTHERN WESLEYAN UNIVERSITY

Pastoral Ministry and
  Counseling   M

SOUTH UNIVERSITY (AL)

Counseling Psychology   M*

SOUTH UNIVERSITY (FL)

Counseling Psychology   M*

SOUTH UNIVERSITY (GA)

Counseling Psychology   M*

SOUTH UNIVERSITY (SC)

Counseling Psychology   M*

SOUTHWESTERN ASSEMBLIES OF GOD UNIVERSITY

Counseling Psychology   M
History   M
Missions and Missiology   P,M
Pastoral Ministry and
  Counseling   P,M
Religion   P,M
Theology   P,M

SOUTHWESTERN BAPTIST THEOLOGICAL SEMINARY

Music   M,D,O
Theology   P,M,D,O

SOUTHWESTERN CHRISTIAN UNIVERSITY

Missions and Missiology   M
Pastoral Ministry and
  Counseling   M

SOUTHWESTERN COLLEGE (KS)

Criminal Justice and
  Criminology   M
Pastoral Ministry and
  Counseling   M

SOUTHWESTERN COLLEGE (NM)

Art Therapy   M
Counseling Psychology   M,O*
Health Psychology   O
Psychology—General   O
Social Psychology   O
Thanatology   M,O

SOUTHWESTERN OKLAHOMA STATE UNIVERSITY

Music   M
School Psychology   M

SPALDING UNIVERSITY

Clinical Psychology   M,D
Communication—
  General   M
Corporate and
  Organizational
  Communication   M
Psychology—General   M,D
Writing   M

SPERTUS INSTITUTE OF JEWISH STUDIES

Jewish Studies   M,D

SPRING ARBOR UNIVERSITY

Child and Family
  Studies   M
Communication—
  General   M
Counseling Psychology   M
Pastoral Ministry and
  Counseling   M
Theology   M

SPRINGFIELD COLLEGE

Addictions/Substance
  Abuse Counseling   M
Art Therapy   M,O
Counseling Psychology   M,O
Industrial and
  Organizational
  Psychology   M,O
Marriage and Family
  Therapy   M,O
Rehabilitation
  Counseling   M
Social Psychology   M
Sport Psychology   M,D,O

SPRING HILL COLLEGE

Liberal Studies   M
Theology   M

STANFORD UNIVERSITY

Anthropology   M,D
Art/Fine Arts   M,D
Asian Studies   M
Child and Family
  Studies   D
Chinese   M,D
Classics   M,D
Communication—
  General   M,D
Comparative Literature   D
Counseling Psychology   D
Developmental
  Psychology   D
East European and
  Russian Studies   M
Economics   D
English   M,D
French   M,D
German   M,D
History   M,D
Humanities   M
Interdisciplinary Studies   M,D
International Affairs   M

Italian   M,D
Japanese   M,D
Journalism   M,D
Linguistics   M,D
Music   M,D
Philosophy   M,D
Political Science   M,D
Psychology—General   D
Religion   M,D
Russian   M,D
Slavic Languages   M,D
Sociology   D
Spanish   M,D
Theater   D

STARR KING SCHOOL FOR THE MINISTRY

Theology   P

STATE UNIVERSITY OF NEW YORK AT BINGHAMTON

Anthropology   M,D
Art History   M,D*
Clinical Psychology   M,D
Cognitive Sciences   M,D
Comparative Literature   M,D
Cultural Studies   M,D
Economics   M,D
English   M,D
French   M
Geography   M
History   M,D
Italian   M
Music   M
Philosophy   M,D
Political Science   M,D
Psychology—General   M,D
Public Administration   M
Public Policy   M,D
Sociology   M,D
Spanish   M,O
Theater   M
Translation and
  Interpretation   M,O

STATE UNIVERSITY OF NEW YORK AT FREDONIA

English   M
Interdisciplinary Studies   M
Music   M

STATE UNIVERSITY OF NEW YORK AT NEW PALTZ

Art/Fine Arts   M
Counseling Psychology   M
English   M
Interdisciplinary Studies   M
Music   M
Psychology—General   M
Therapies—Dance,
  Drama, and Music   M

STATE UNIVERSITY OF NEW YORK AT OSWEGO

Art/Fine Arts   M
Child and Family
  Studies   M
Consumer Economics   M
Counseling Psychology   M,O
English   M
History   M
School Psychology   M,O

STATE UNIVERSITY OF NEW YORK AT PLATTSBURGH

Liberal Studies   M
Psychology—General   M,O
School Psychology   M,O

STATE UNIVERSITY OF NEW YORK COLLEGE AT CORTLAND

American Studies   O
English   M
History   M

STATE UNIVERSITY OF NEW YORK COLLEGE AT ONEONTA

Family and Consumer
  Sciences-General   M
Museum Studies   M

STATE UNIVERSITY OF NEW YORK COLLEGE AT POTSDAM

Communication—
  General   M
English   M
Music   M

STATE UNIVERSITY OF NEW YORK COLLEGE OF ENVIRONMENTAL SCIENCE AND FORESTRY

Communication—
  General   M,D
Landscape Architecture   M
Urban and Regional
  Planning   M,D
Urban Design   M

STATE UNIVERSITY OF NEW YORK EMPIRE STATE COLLEGE

Industrial and Labor
  Relations   M
Liberal Studies   M
Public Policy   M

STATE UNIVERSITY OF NEW YORK INSTITUTE OF TECHNOLOGY

Sociology   M

STEPHEN F. AUSTIN STATE UNIVERSITY

Applied Arts and
  Design—General   M
Art/Fine Arts   M
Communication—
  General   M
English   M
Family and Consumer
  Sciences-General   M
History   M
Interdisciplinary Studies   M
Mass Communication   M
Music   M
Psychology—General   M
Public Administration   M
School Psychology   M

STEPHENS COLLEGE

Counseling Psychology   M

Marriage and Family Therapy	M

STETSON UNIVERSITY

English	M
Marriage and Family Therapy	M

STEVENS INSTITUTE OF TECHNOLOGY

Communication— General	M,D,O
Computer Art and Design	M,D,O
Corporate and Organizational Communication	O
Internet and Interactive Multimedia	M,D,O

STEVENSON UNIVERSITY

Forensic Sciences	M

STONY BROOK UNIVERSITY, STATE UNIVERSITY OF NEW YORK

Addictions/Substance Abuse Counseling	M
African Studies	M
Anthropology	M,D
Art History	M,D
Art/Fine Arts	M
Clinical Psychology	D
Comparative Literature	M,D
Cultural Studies	M,D
Economics	M,D
English	M,D,O
Experimental Psychology	D
French	M
Health Psychology	D
Hispanic Studies	M,D
History	M,D
Italian	M
Liberal Studies	M,O
Linguistics	M,D
Music	M,D
Philosophy	M,D
Political Science	M,D
Psychology—General	D
Public Policy	M,D
Romance Languages	M
Social Psychology	D
Social Sciences	M,O
Sociology	M,D
Theater	M
Writing	M

STRAYER UNIVERSITY

Public Administration	M

SUFFOLK UNIVERSITY

Applied Arts and Design—General	M
Clinical Psychology	D
Communication— General	M
Corporate and Organizational Communication	M
Counseling Psychology	M,O
Criminal Justice and Criminology	M

Economics	M,D*
Ethics	M
Graphic Design	M
Interior Design	M
Political Science	M,O
Psychology—General	D
Public Administration	M,O
Public Policy	M
Women's Studies	M

SULLIVAN UNIVERSITY

Conflict Resolution and Mediation/Peace Studies	P,M

SUL ROSS STATE UNIVERSITY

Applied Arts and Design—General	M
Art History	M
Art/Fine Arts	M
Criminal Justice and Criminology	M
English	M
History	M
Political Science	M
Psychology—General	M
Public Administration	M
Textile Design	M

SYRACUSE UNIVERSITY

African Studies	M
African-American Studies	M
Anthropology	M,D
Applied Arts and Design—General	M
Architecture	M
Art History	M
Art/Fine Arts	M
Arts Journalism	M
Broadcast Journalism	M
Child and Family Studies	M,D
Clinical Psychology	D
Communication— General	M,D*
Computer Art and Design	M
Conflict Resolution and Mediation/Peace Studies	
Disability Studies	O
Economics	M,D
English	M,D
Experimental Psychology	D
Film, Television, and Video Production	M
Film, Television, and Video Theory and Criticism	M
Forensic Sciences	M
French	M
Geography	M,D
History	M,D
Illustration	M
International Affairs	M
Journalism	M
Linguistics	M
Marriage and Family Therapy	M,D
Mass Communication	M,D
Media Studies	M
Museum Studies	M
Music	M

Philosophy	M,D
Photography	M
Political Science	M,D
Public Administration	M,D,O
Rehabilitation Counseling	M
Religion	M,D
Rhetoric	M,D
School Psychology	M,D,O
Social Psychology	M,D
Social Sciences	M,D
Sociology	M,D
Spanish	M
Textile Design	M
Writing	M,D

TALMUDIC COLLEGE OF FLORIDA

Theology	M,D

TARLETON STATE UNIVERSITY

Counseling Psychology	M,O
Criminal Justice and Criminology	M
Economics	M
English	M
History	M
Liberal Studies	M
Political Science	M
School Psychology	M,O

TAYLOR COLLEGE AND SEMINARY

Cultural Studies	P,M,O
Missions and Missiology	P,M,O
Theology	P,M,O

TAYLOR UNIVERSITY

Religion	M

TEACHERS COLLEGE, COLUMBIA UNIVERSITY

Anthropology	M,D
Arts Administration	M
Clinical Psychology	D
Communication— General	M,D
Counseling Psychology	M,D
Developmental Psychology	M,D
Economics	M,D
History	M,D
Industrial and Organizational Psychology	M,D
Interdisciplinary Studies	M,D
Linguistics	M,D
Political Science	M,D
School Psychology	M,D
Social Psychology	M,D
Sociology	M,D

TELSHE YESHIVA–CHICAGO

Jewish Studies	O

TEMPLE BAPTIST SEMINARY

Archaeology	P,M,D
Religion	P,M,D
Theology	P,M,D

TEMPLE UNIVERSITY

African-American Studies	M,D
Anthropology	D
Art History	M,D*
Art/Fine Arts	M
Arts Administration	M,D
Clinical Psychology	D
Cognitive Sciences	D
Communication— General	M,D
Corporate and Organizational Communication	M,D
Counseling Psychology	M,D
Criminal Justice and Criminology	M,D
Dance	M,D
Developmental Psychology	D
Economics	M,D
English	M,D
Film, Television, and Video Production	M
Geography	M
Graphic Design	M
History	M,D
Industrial and Organizational Psychology	M
Journalism	M
Liberal Studies	M
Linguistics	M
Mass Communication	D
Media Studies	M,D
Music	M,D
Philosophy	M,D
Photography	M
Political Science	M,D
Psychology—General	D
Religion	M,D
School Psychology	M,D
Social Psychology	D
Sociology	M,D
Spanish	M,D
Textile Design	M
Theater	M
Therapies—Dance, Drama, and Music	M,D
Urban and Regional Planning	M
Urban Studies	M
Writing	M

TENNESSEE STATE UNIVERSITY

Counseling Psychology	M,D
Criminal Justice and Criminology	M
English	M
Family and Consumer Sciences-General	M
Psychology—General	M,D
Public Administration	M,D
School Psychology	M,D

TENNESSEE TECHNOLOGICAL UNIVERSITY

English	M

TEXAS A&M INTERNATIONAL UNIVERSITY

Counseling Psychology	M
Criminal Justice and Criminology	M
English	M,D

*M—master's degree; P—first professional degree; D—doctorate; O—other advanced degree; *—Close-Up and/or Announcement or Display*

Hispanic Studies — M,D
History — M
Political Science — M
Psychology—General — M
Public Administration — M
Social Sciences — M
Sociology — M
Spanish — M,D

TEXAS A&M UNIVERSITY

Agricultural Economics
  and Agribusiness — M,D
Anthropology — M,D
Architecture — M,D
Clinical Psychology — M,D
Cognitive Sciences — M,D
Communication—
  General — M,D
Counseling Psychology — M,D
Developmental
  Psychology — M,D
Economics — M,D
English — M,D
Geography — M,D
History — M,D
Homeland Security — M,O
Human Development — M,D
Industrial and
  Organizational
  Psychology — M,D
International Affairs — M,O
International
  Development — M,O
Landscape Architecture — M,D
National Security — M,O
Philosophy — M,D
Political Science — M,D
Psychology—General — M,D
Public Administration — M,O
Public Affairs — M,O
Public Policy — M,O
School Psychology — M,D
Social Psychology — M,D
Sociology — M,D*
Spanish — M,D
Urban and Regional
  Planning — M,D

TEXAS A&M UNIVERSITY–COMMERCE

Art History — M
Art/Fine Arts — M
Cognitive Sciences — M,D
Counseling Psychology — M,D
Economics — M
English — M,D
History — M
Music — M
Psychology—General — M,D
Social Sciences — M
Sociology — M
Spanish — M,D
Speech and
  Interpersonal
  Communication — M
Theater — M

TEXAS A&M UNIVERSITY–CORPUS CHRISTI

Art/Fine Arts — M
English — M
History — M
Psychology—General — M
Public Administration — M

TEXAS A&M UNIVERSITY–KINGSVILLE

Agricultural Economics
  and Agribusiness — M
Art/Fine Arts — M
English — M
Family and Consumer
  Sciences-General — M
Gerontology — M
History — M
Political Science — M
Psychology—General — M
Sociology — M
Spanish — M

TEXAS A&M UNIVERSITY–TEXARKANA

Counseling Psychology — M
English — M
History — M
Interdisciplinary Studies — M
Psychology—General — M

TEXAS CHRISTIAN UNIVERSITY

Art History — M
Art/Fine Arts — M
English — M,D
History — M,D
Journalism — M
Liberal Studies — M
Music — M,O
Psychology—General — M,D
Speech and
  Interpersonal
  Communication — M

TEXAS SOUTHERN UNIVERSITY

Art/Fine Arts — M
Communication—
  General — M
Criminal Justice and
  Criminology — M,D
English — M
Family and Consumer
  Sciences-General — M
History — M
Music — M
Psychology—General — M
Public Administration — M
Sociology — M
Urban and Regional
  Planning — M,D

TEXAS STATE UNIVERSITY–SAN MARCOS

Anthropology — M
Child and Family
  Studies — M
Communication—
  General — M
Computer Art and
  Design — M
Criminal Justice and
  Criminology — M
English — M
Geographic Information
  Systems — M,D
Geography — M,D
Graphic Design — M
Health Psychology — M
History — M
Interdisciplinary Studies — M
International Affairs — M

Mass Communication — M
Music — M
Political Science — M
Psychology—General — M
Public Administration — M
Rhetoric — M
School Psychology — M
Sociology — M
Spanish — M
Technical
  Communication — M
Theater — M
Writing — M

TEXAS TECH UNIVERSITY

Agricultural Economics
  and Agribusiness — M,D
Anthropology — M
Applied Economics — M,D
Architecture — M
Art/Fine Arts — M,D
Child and Family
  Studies — M,D
Classics — M
Clinical Psychology — M,D
Communication—
  General — M
Consumer Economics — M,D
Counseling Psychology — M,D
Dance — M,D
Economics — M,D
English — M,D
Environmental Design — M,D
Experimental
  Psychology — M,D
Family and Consumer
  Sciences-General — M,D
French — M
German — M
Gerontology — M,D
Historic Preservation — M
History — M,D
Human Development — M,D
Humanities — M,D
Interdisciplinary Studies — M
Interior Design — M,D
Landscape Architecture — M
Linguistics — M
Marriage and Family
  Therapy — M,D
Mass Communication — M,D
Museum Studies — M
Music — M,D
Philosophy — M
Political Science — M,D
Psychology—General — M,D
Public Administration — M,D
Rhetoric — M,D
Romance Languages — M,D
Sociology — M
Spanish — M,D
Technical Writing — M,D
Theater — M,D

TEXAS TECH UNIVERSITY HEALTH SCIENCES CENTER

Rehabilitation
  Counseling — M

TEXAS WESLEYAN UNIVERSITY

Counseling Psychology — M

TEXAS WOMAN'S UNIVERSITY

Art/Fine Arts — M

Child and Family
  Studies — M,D
Child Development — M,D
Counseling Psychology — M,D,O
Dance — M,D
English — M,D
History — M
Marriage and Family
  Therapy — M,D
Music — M
Political Science — M
Psychology—General — M,D,O
Rhetoric — M,D
School Psychology — M,D,O
Sociology — M,D
Theater — M
Women's Studies — M

THOMAS EDISON STATE COLLEGE

Homeland Security — M,O
Liberal Studies — M
Public Administration — O

THOMAS JEFFERSON UNIVERSITY

Marriage and Family
  Therapy — M

THOMAS UNIVERSITY

Rehabilitation
  Counseling — M
Social Psychology — M

TIFFIN UNIVERSITY

Criminal Justice and
  Criminology — M
Forensic Psychology — M
Homeland Security — M
Humanities — M

TORONTO SCHOOL OF THEOLOGY

Theology — P,M,D

TOURO COLLEGE

Jewish Studies — M

TOWSON UNIVERSITY

Art/Fine Arts — M
Child and Family
  Studies — O
Clinical Psychology — M
Communication—
  General — M,O
Corporate and
  Organizational
  Communication — M
Counseling Psychology — O
Forensic Sciences — M
Geography — M
Gerontology — M,O
Homeland Security — M,O
Humanities — M
Internet and Interactive
  Multimedia — D,O
Liberal Studies — M
Music — M
School Psychology — O
Social Sciences — M
Theater — M

Women's Studies	M,O
Writing	M

TRENT UNIVERSITY

American Indian/Native American Studies	M,D
Anthropology	M
Canadian Studies	M,D
Cultural Studies	D
Geography	M,D

TREVECCA NAZARENE UNIVERSITY

Counseling Psychology	M
Marriage and Family Therapy	M
Psychology—General	M,D
Religion	M
Theology	M

TRINE UNIVERSITY

Criminal Justice and Criminology	M

TRINITY BAPTIST COLLEGE

Pastoral Ministry and Counseling	M

TRINITY COLLEGE

American Studies	M
Economics	M
English	M
Public Policy	M

TRINITY EPISCOPAL SCHOOL FOR MINISTRY

Missions and Missiology	P,M,D,O
Pastoral Ministry and Counseling	P,M,D,O
Religion	P,M,D,O
Theology	P,M,D,O

TRINITY INTERNATIONAL UNIVERSITY

Archaeology	P,M,D,O
Communication—General	M
Counseling Psychology	P,M,D,O
Missions and Missiology	P,M,D,O
Pastoral Ministry and Counseling	P,M,D,O
Theology	P,M,D,O

TRINITY INTERNATIONAL UNIVERSITY, SOUTH FLORIDA CAMPUS

Counseling Psychology	M
Religion	M,O

TRINITY LUTHERAN SEMINARY

Music	P,M
Theology	P,M

TRINITY UNIVERSITY

School Psychology	M

TRINITY (WASHINGTON) UNIVERSITY

Communication—General	M
National Security	M

TRINITY WESTERN UNIVERSITY

Counseling Psychology	M
English	M
History	M
Humanities	M
Interdisciplinary Studies	M
Linguistics	M
Pastoral Ministry and Counseling	P,M,D
Philosophy	M
Theology	P,M,D

TROPICAL AGRICULTURE RESEARCH AND HIGHER EDUCATION CENTER

Agricultural Economics and Agribusiness	M,D

TROY UNIVERSITY

Art/Fine Arts	M
Clinical Psychology	M
Communication—General	M
Criminal Justice and Criminology	M
International Affairs	M
Public Administration	M
Rehabilitation Counseling	M,O
School Psychology	M

TRUMAN STATE UNIVERSITY

English	M
Music	M

TUFTS UNIVERSITY

Archaeology	M
Art History	M
Art/Fine Arts	M
Child and Family Studies	M,D,O
Child Development	M,D,O*
Classics	M
Conflict Resolution and Mediation/Peace Studies	M,D
Dance	M,D
Developmental Psychology	M,D,O
Economics	M
English	M,D
Family and Consumer Sciences-General	M,D,O
French	M
German	M
Health Communication	M
History	M,D
International Affairs	M,D*
International Development	M,D
Museum Studies	O
Music	M
Philosophy	M
Psychology—General	M,D

Public Administration	O
Public Policy	M*
School Psychology	M,O
Theater	M,D
Urban and Regional Planning	M
Urban Studies	M

TUI UNIVERSITY

Conflict Resolution and Mediation/Peace Studies	M,D
Criminal Justice and Criminology	M,D
Emergency Management	M,D,O
Public Administration	M,D

TULANE UNIVERSITY

Anthropology	M,D
Architecture	M
Art History	M
Art/Fine Arts	M
Classics	M
Dance	M
Economics	M,D
English	M,D
French	M,D
Health Communication	M
History	M,D
Interdisciplinary Studies	D
International Development	M,D
Latin American Studies	M,D
Liberal Studies	M
Music	M
Philosophy	M,D
Political Science	M,D
Portuguese	M,D
Psychology—General	M,D
Sociology	M,D
Spanish	M,D
Theater	M

TUSKEGEE UNIVERSITY

Agricultural Economics and Agribusiness	M

TYNDALE UNIVERSITY COLLEGE & SEMINARY

Missions and Missiology	P,M,O
Pastoral Ministry and Counseling	P,M,O
Theology	P,M,O

UNIFICATION THEOLOGICAL SEMINARY

Theology	P,M,D

UNIFORMED SERVICES UNIVERSITY OF THE HEALTH SCIENCES

Clinical Psychology	D
History of Medicine	M
History of Science and Technology	M,D
Psychology—General	D

UNION COLLEGE (KY)

Clinical Psychology	M
Counseling Psychology	M

Psychology—General	M
School Psychology	M

UNION INSTITUTE & UNIVERSITY

Clinical Psychology	D
Counseling Psychology	M
Cultural Studies	M
History	M
Interdisciplinary Studies	M,D
Psychology—General	M
Writing	M

UNION THEOLOGICAL SEMINARY AND PRESBYTERIAN SCHOOL OF CHRISTIAN EDUCATION

Theology	P,M,D

UNION THEOLOGICAL SEMINARY IN THE CITY OF NEW YORK

Theology	P,M,D

UNION UNIVERSITY

Cultural Studies	M
Pastoral Ministry and Counseling	M,D
Religion	M,D

UNITED STATES ARMY COMMAND AND GENERAL STAFF COLLEGE

Military and Defense Studies	M

UNITED STATES INTERNATIONAL UNIVERSITY

Counseling Psychology	M
International Affairs	M

UNITED TALMUDICAL SEMINARY

Theology

UNITED THEOLOGICAL SEMINARY

Theology	P,M,D

UNITED THEOLOGICAL SEMINARY OF THE TWIN CITIES

Art/Fine Arts	P,M,D,O
Asian Studies	P,M,D,O
Conflict Resolution and Mediation/Peace Studies	P,M,D,O
Ethnic Studies	P,M,D,O
Pastoral Ministry and Counseling	P,M,D,O
Religion	P,M,D,O
Theology	P,M,D,O
Women's Studies	P,M,D,O

UNIVERSIDAD ADVENTISTA DE LAS ANTILLAS

History	M
Spanish	M

*M—master's degree; P—first professional degree; D—doctorate; O—other advanced degree; *—Close-Up and/or Announcement or Display*

UNIVERSIDAD AUTONOMA DE GUADALAJARA

Architecture	M,D
Corporate and Organizational Communication	M,D
Internet and Interactive Multimedia	M,D
Philosophy	M,D
Spanish	M,D
Translation and Interpretation	M,D

UNIVERSIDAD CENTRAL DEL CARIBE

Addictions/Substance Abuse Counseling	M

UNIVERSIDAD CENTRAL DEL ESTE

Public Policy	M,D

UNIVERSIDAD DE IBEROAMERICA

Clinical Psychology	P,M
Forensic Psychology	P,M

UNIVERSIDAD DE LAS AMERICAS, A.C.

International Affairs	M
Marriage and Family Therapy	M
Psychology—General	M

UNIVERSIDAD DE LAS AMÉRICAS–PUEBLA

American Studies	M
Anthropology	M
Archaeology	M
Computer Art and Design	M
Economics	M
English	M
Linguistics	M
Psychology—General	M

UNIVERSIDAD DEL ESTE

Agricultural Economics and Agribusiness	M
Criminal Justice and Criminology	M
Public Policy	M

UNIVERSIDAD DEL TURABO

Art/Fine Arts	M
Arts Administration	M
Counseling Psychology	M
Criminal Justice and Criminology	M
Forensic Sciences	M
School Psychology	M

UNIVERSIDAD NACIONAL PEDRO HENRIQUEZ URENA

Architecture	P,M,D
Economics	P,M,D
Historic Preservation	P,M,D
Humanities	P,M,D
International Affairs	P,M,D
Public Administration	P,M,D
Social Sciences	P,M,D

UNIVERSITÉ DE MONCTON

Economics	M
French	M,D
History	M
Public Administration	M

UNIVERSITÉ DE MONTRÉAL

Anthropology	M,D
Art History	M,D
Communication— General	M,D,O
Comparative Literature	M,D
Criminal Justice and Criminology	M,D
Demography and Population Studies	M,D
Developmental Psychology	M,D,O
Economics	M,D
Emergency Management	O
English	M,D
Environmental Design	M,D,O
Film, Television, and Video Theory and Criticism	M,D
French	M,D
Geography	M,D,O
German	M
Gerontology	O
Hispanic Studies	M,D
History	M,D
Industrial and Labor Relations	M,D,O
Linguistics	M,D,O
Museum Studies	M
Music	M,D,O
Philosophy	M,D
Political Science	M,D
Psychology—General	M,D
Rehabilitation Counseling	O
Sociology	M,D
Spanish	M
Theology	M,D,O
Translation and Interpretation	M,D,O

UNIVERSITÉ DE SHERBROOKE

Canadian Studies	M,D
Comparative Literature	M,D
Conflict Resolution and Mediation/Peace Studies	P,M,D,O
Economics	M
Ethics	M,D,O
French	M,D
Geography	M,D
Gerontology	M
History	M
Linguistics	M,D
Philosophy	M,D,O
Psychology—General	M
Religion	M,D,O
Theater	M,D
Theology	M,D,O

UNIVERSITÉ DU QUÉBEC À CHICOUTIMI

Art/Fine Arts	M
Canadian Studies	M
Comparative Literature	M
Ethics	O
French	O
Linguistics	M
Theology	M

UNIVERSITÉ DU QUÉBEC À MONTRÉAL

Art History	M,D
Art/Fine Arts	M
Communication— General	M,D
Comparative Literature	M,D
Dance	M
Economics	M,D
Geographic Information Systems	O
Geography	M
History	M,D
Linguistics	M,D
Museum Studies	M
Philosophy	M,D
Political Science	M,D
Psychology—General	D
Public Administration	M
Religion	M,D
Sociology	M,D
Urban Studies	M,D

UNIVERSITÉ DU QUÉBEC À RIMOUSKI

Comparative Literature	M,D
Ethics	M,O
Social Psychology	M
Urban and Regional Planning	M,D,O

UNIVERSITÉ DU QUÉBEC À TROIS-RIVIÈRES

Communication— General	M,O
Comparative Literature	M
Industrial and Labor Relations	O
Philosophy	M,D
Psychology—General	D,O

UNIVERSITÉ DU QUÉBEC, ÉCOLE NATIONALE D'ADMINISTRATION PUBLIQUE

Public Administration	D,O
Urban Studies	M

UNIVERSITÉ DU QUÉBEC EN OUTAOUAIS

Industrial and Labor Relations	M,D,O
Urban and Regional Planning	M

UNIVERSITÉ DU QUÉBEC, INSTITUT NATIONAL DE LA RECHERCHE SCIENTIFIQUE

Demography and Population Studies	M,D
Urban Studies	M,D

UNIVERSITÉ LAVAL

Agricultural Economics and Agribusiness	M
Anthropology	M,D
Archaeology	M,D
Architecture	M
Art History	M,D
Art/Fine Arts	M
Clinical Psychology	D
Comparative Literature	M,D
Consumer Economics	O
Economics	M,D

English	M,D
Ethics	O
Ethnic Studies	M,D
Film, Television, and Video Theory and Criticism	M,D
Geographic Information Systems	M,O
Geography	M,D
Gerontology	O
Graphic Design	M
History	M,D
Industrial and Labor Relations	M,D
International Affairs	M,D
Journalism	O
Linguistics	M,D
Mass Communication	M,D
Museum Studies	O
Music	M,D
Philosophy	M,D
Political Science	M,D
Psychology—General	D
Religion	M,D
Rural Planning and Studies	O
Social Psychology	D
Sociology	M,D
Spanish	M,D
Theater	M,D
Theology	M,D
Translation and Interpretation	M,O
Urban and Regional Planning	M,D
Women's Studies	O

UNIVERSITY AT ALBANY, STATE UNIVERSITY OF NEW YORK

African Studies	M
African-American Studies	M
Anthropology	M,D
Art/Fine Arts	M
Clinical Psychology	M,D,O
Communication— General	M,D
Counseling Psychology	M,D,O
Criminal Justice and Criminology	M,D
Demography and Population Studies	M,D,O
Economics	M,D,O
English	M,D
Experimental Psychology	M,D,O
Forensic Sciences	M,D
French	M,D
Geographic Information Systems	M,O
Geography	M,O
History	M,D,O
Industrial and Organizational Psychology	M,D,O
Italian	M
Latin American Studies	M,O
Liberal Studies	M
Philosophy	M,D
Political Science	M,D
Psychology—General	M,D,O
Public Administration	M,D,O
Public History	M,D,O
Public Policy	M,D,O

Rehabilitation Counseling	M
Russian	M,O
School Psychology	M,D,O
Social Psychology	M,D,O
Sociology	M,D,O
Spanish	M,D
Theater	M
Translation and Interpretation	M,O
Urban and Regional Planning	M
Urban Studies	M,D,O
Women's Studies	M,D

UNIVERSITY AT BUFFALO, THE STATE UNIVERSITY OF NEW YORK

American Studies	M,D
Anthropology	M,D
Architecture	M
Art History	M,O
Art/Fine Arts	M,O
Classics	M,D
Clinical Psychology	M,D
Cognitive Sciences	M,D
Communication— General	M,D
Comparative Literature	M,D
Counseling Psychology	M,D,O
Economics	M,D,O
English	M,D
French	M,D
Geographic Information Systems	M,D,O
Geography	M,D,O
History	M,D
Japanese	M,D,O
Linguistics	M,D
Media Studies	M,O
Museum Studies	M,O
Music	M,D
Philosophy	M,D
Political Science	M,D
Psychology—General	M,D
Rehabilitation Counseling	M,D,O
Romance Languages	M,D
School Psychology	M,D,O
Social Psychology	M,D
Sociology	M,D
Spanish	M,D
Urban and Regional Planning	M
Urban Design	M

UNIVERSITY OF ADVANCING TECHNOLOGY

Internet and Interactive Multimedia	M

THE UNIVERSITY OF AKRON

Arts Administration	M
Child and Family Studies	M
Child Development	M
Clothing and Textiles	M
Cognitive Sciences	M,D
Communication— General	M
Counseling Psychology	M,D
Economics	M
English	M
Family and Consumer Sciences-General	M

Geographic Information Systems	M
Geography	M
History	M,D
Industrial and Organizational Psychology	M,D
Marriage and Family Therapy	M
Music	M
Political Science	M
Psychology—General	M,D
Public Administration	M
School Psychology	M
Sociology	M,D
Spanish	M
Theater	M
Urban and Regional Planning	M
Urban Studies	M,D
Writing	M

THE UNIVERSITY OF ALABAMA

American Studies	M
Anthropology	M,D
Art History	M
Art/Fine Arts	M
Child and Family Studies	M
Clinical Psychology	D
Clothing and Textiles	M
Communication— General	M,D
Consumer Economics	M
Criminal Justice and Criminology	M
Economics	M,D
English	M,D
Experimental Psychology	D
Family and Consumer Sciences-General	M,D
Film, Television, and Video Production	M
French	M,D
Geography	M
German	M,D
History	M,D
Human Development	M
Interior Design	M
Journalism	M
Mass Communication	D
Media Studies	M
Music	M,D
Photography	M
Political Science	M,D
Psychology—General	D
Public Administration	M,D
Rhetoric	M,D
Romance Languages	M,D
Spanish	M,D
Speech and Interpersonal Communication	M
Theater	M
Women's Studies	M
Writing	M,D

THE UNIVERSITY OF ALABAMA AT BIRMINGHAM

Anthropology	M
Art History	M
Communication— General	M
Criminal Justice and Criminology	M

English	M
Forensic Sciences	M
History	M
Psychology—General	M,D
Public Administration	M
Sociology	M,D

THE UNIVERSITY OF ALABAMA IN HUNTSVILLE

Criminal Justice and Criminology	O
English	M,O
History	M
Interdisciplinary Studies	M,D,O
Psychology—General	M
Public Affairs	M
Technical Writing	M,O

UNIVERSITY OF ALASKA ANCHORAGE

Anthropology	M
Clinical Psychology	M,D
English	M
Interdisciplinary Studies	M
Psychology—General	M,D
Public Administration	M
Social Psychology	M,D
Writing	M

UNIVERSITY OF ALASKA FAIRBANKS

Anthropology	M,D
Art/Fine Arts	M
Clinical Psychology	D
Communication— General	M
Computer Art and Design	M
Corporate and Organizational Communication	M
Criminal Justice and Criminology	M
Cultural Studies	M
Economics	M
English	M
History	M
Interdisciplinary Studies	M,D
Linguistics	M
Music	M
Northern Studies	M
Photography	M
Psychology—General	D
Rural Planning and Studies	M
Social Psychology	M,D
Writing	M

UNIVERSITY OF ALASKA SOUTHEAST

Public Administration	M

UNIVERSITY OF ALBERTA

Agricultural Economics and Agribusiness	M,D
Anthropology	M,D
Applied Arts and Design—General	M
Archaeology	M,D
Art History	M
Art/Fine Arts	M
Asian Studies	M
Chinese	M

Classics	M,D
Clothing and Textiles	M,D
Communication— General	M
Counseling Psychology	M,D
Criminal Justice and Criminology	M,D
Demography and Population Studies	M,D
East European and Russian Studies	M,D
Economics	M,D
English	M,D
Family and Consumer Sciences-General	M,D
Folklore	M,D
French	M,D
German	M,D
Hispanic Studies	M,D
History	M,D
Industrial and Labor Relations	D
Italian	M,D
Japanese	M
Linguistics	M,D
Music	M,D
Philosophy	M,D
Political Science	M,D
Psychology—General	M,D
Rural Sociology	M,D
School Psychology	M,D
Slavic Languages	M,D
Sociology	M,D
Theater	M

THE UNIVERSITY OF ARIZONA

Agricultural Economics and Agribusiness	M
American Indian/Native American Studies	M,D
Anthropology	M,D
Architecture	M
Art History	M,D
Art/Fine Arts	M
Asian Studies	M,D
Child and Family Studies	M,D
Classics	M
Communication— General	M,D
Consumer Economics	M,D
Economics	M,D
English	M,D
Family and Consumer Sciences-General	M,D
French	M,D
Geography	M,D
German	M,D
History	M,D
Human Development	M,D
Interdisciplinary Studies	M,D
Landscape Architecture	M
Latin American Studies	M
Linguistics	M,D
Media Studies	M
Music	M,D
Near and Middle Eastern Studies	M,D
Philosophy	M,D
Political Science	M,D
Psychology—General	D
Public Administration	M,D
Public Policy	M,D
Rehabilitation Counseling	
Rhetoric	M,D
Russian	M

*M—master's degree; P—first professional degree; D—doctorate; O—other advanced degree; *—Close-Up and/or Announcement or Display*

Sociology	M,D
Spanish	M,D
Theater	M
Urban and Regional Planning	
Women's Studies	M,D
Writing	M

UNIVERSITY OF ARKANSAS

Agricultural Economics and Agribusiness	M
Anthropology	M,D
Art/Fine Arts	M
Communication—General	M
Comparative Literature	M,D
Economics	M,D
English	M,D
Family and Consumer Sciences-General	M
French	M
Geography	M
German	M
History	M,D
Interdisciplinary Studies	M,D
Journalism	M
Music	M
Philosophy	M,D
Political Science	M
Psychology—General	M,D
Public Administration	M
Public Policy	D
Rehabilitation Counseling	M,D
Sociology	M
Spanish	M
Theater	M
Translation and Interpretation	M
Writing	M

UNIVERSITY OF ARKANSAS AT LITTLE ROCK

Art History	M
Art/Fine Arts	M
Conflict Resolution and Mediation/Peace Studies	O
Criminal Justice and Criminology	M
Gerontology	O
Journalism	M
Liberal Studies	M
Marriage and Family Therapy	O
Mass Communication	M
Psychology—General	M
Public Administration	M
Public Affairs	M,O
Public History	M
Rehabilitation Counseling	M,O
Rhetoric	M
Speech and Interpersonal Communication	M
Technical Writing	M
Writing	M

UNIVERSITY OF ARKANSAS AT PINE BLUFF

Addictions/Substance Abuse Counseling	M

UNIVERSITY OF ARKANSAS FOR MEDICAL SCIENCES

Genetic Counseling	M

UNIVERSITY OF BALTIMORE

Applied Arts and Design—General	M
Computer Art and Design	M,D
Conflict Resolution and Mediation/Peace Studies	M
Counseling Psychology	M
Criminal Justice and Criminology	M
Ethics	M
Graphic Design	M,D
Industrial and Organizational Psychology	M
Psychology—General	M
Public Administration	M,D
Publishing	M
Writing	M

UNIVERSITY OF BRIDGEPORT

Conflict Resolution and Mediation/Peace Studies	M
International Affairs	M

THE UNIVERSITY OF BRITISH COLUMBIA

Agricultural Economics and Agribusiness	M
Anthropology	M,D
Archaeology	M,D
Architecture	M
Art History	M,D,O
Art/Fine Arts	M,D,O
Asian Studies	M,D
Classics	M,D
Clinical Psychology	M,D
Cognitive Sciences	M,D
Counseling Psychology	M,D,O
Developmental Psychology	M,D
East European and Russian Studies	M,D
Economics	M,D
English	M,D
Film, Television, and Video Production	M,O
Film, Television, and Video Theory and Criticism	M,O
Forensic Psychology	M,D
French	M,D
Genetic Counseling	M
Geography	M,D
German	M,D
Health Psychology	M,D
Hispanic Studies	M,D
History	M,D
Human Development	M,D,O
International Affairs	M
Journalism	M
Landscape Architecture	M
Linguistics	M,D
Museum Studies	M,D,O
Music	M,D
Philosophy	M,D
Political Science	M,D
Psychology—General	M,D
Public History	M,D
Religion	M,D

School Psychology	M,D,O
Social Psychology	M,D
Sociology	M,D
Theater	M,D
Urban and Regional Planning	M,D
Western European Studies	M
Writing	M,O

UNIVERSITY OF CALGARY

Anthropology	M,D
Archaeology	M,D
Architecture	M,D
Art/Fine Arts	M
Classics	M,D
Clinical Psychology	M,D
Communication—General	M,D
Counseling Psychology	M,D
Economics	M,D
English	M,D
Environmental Design	M,D
Geography	M,D
German	M
History	M,D
Human Development	M,D
Linguistics	M,D
Military and Defense Studies	M,D
Music	M,D
Philosophy	M,D
Political Science	M,D
Psychology—General	M,D
Religion	M,D
School Psychology	M,D
Sociology	M,D
Theater	M

UNIVERSITY OF CALIFORNIA, BERKELEY

African-American Studies	D
Agricultural Economics and Agribusiness	D
Anthropology	D
Applied Arts and Design—General	M
Archaeology	M,D
Architectural History	M,D
Architecture	M,D
Art History	D
Art/Fine Arts	M
Asian Languages	M,D
Asian Studies	M,D
Building Science	M,D
Chinese	D
Classics	M,D
Comparative Literature	D
Demography and Population Studies	M,D
Economics	D
English	D
Environmental Design	M
Ethnic Studies	D
Folklore	M
French	D
Geography	D
German	D
Hispanic Studies	D
History of Science and Technology	D
History	M,D
Human Development	D
Industrial and Labor Relations	D
International Affairs	M

Italian	D
Japanese	D
Jewish Studies	D
Journalism	M
Landscape Architecture	M
Latin American Studies	M
Linguistics	D
Music	D
Near and Middle Eastern Studies	M,D
Philosophy	D
Political Science	D
Psychology—General	D
Public Policy	M,D
Religion	D
Rhetoric	D
Romance Languages	D
Russian	D
Scandinavian Languages	D
School Psychology	
Slavic Languages	D
Sociology	M,D
Spanish	D
Theater	D
Urban and Regional Planning	M,D
Urban Design	M,D

UNIVERSITY OF CALIFORNIA, DAVIS

Agricultural Economics and Agribusiness	M,D
American Indian/Native American Studies	M,D
Anthropology	M,D
Art History	M*
Art/Fine Arts	M
Child Development	M
Clothing and Textiles	M
Communication—General	M
Comparative Literature	D
Cultural Studies	M,D
Economics	M,D
English	M,D
Forensic Sciences	M
French	D
Geography	M,D
German	M,D
History	M,D
Human Development	D
Linguistics	M,D
Music	M,D
Philosophy	M,D
Political Science	M,D
Psychology—General	D
Sociology	M,D
Spanish	M,D
Textile Design	M
Theater	M
Urban and Regional Planning	M
Writing	M,D

UNIVERSITY OF CALIFORNIA, IRVINE

Anthropology	M,D
Art History	M,D
Art/Fine Arts	M
Asian Languages	M,D
Chinese	M,D
Classics	M,D
Comparative Literature	M,D
Criminal Justice and Criminology	M,D
Dance	M

Demography and Population Studies	M
Economics	M,D
English	M,D
French	M,D
Genetic Counseling	M
German	M,D
History	M,D
Japanese	M,D
Music	M
Philosophy	M,D
Political Science	D
Psychology—General	D
Social Sciences	M,D
Sociology	M,D
Spanish	M,D
Theater	M,D
Urban and Regional Planning	M,D
Urban Studies	M,D
Writing	M

UNIVERSITY OF CALIFORNIA, LOS ANGELES

African Studies	M
African-American Studies	M
American Indian/Native American Studies	M
Anthropology	M,D
Applied Arts and Design—General	M
Applied Social Research	M,D
Archaeology	M,D
Architecture	M,D
Art History	M,D
Art/Fine Arts	M
Asian Languages	M,D
Asian Studies	M,D
Asian-American Studies	M
Classics	M,D
Comparative Literature	M,D
Dance	M,D
Economics	M,D
English	M,D
Film, Television, and Video Production	M,D,O
French	M,D
Geography	M,D
German	M,D
Hispanic Studies	D
History	M,D
Italian	M,D
Latin American Studies	M
Linguistics	M,D
Music	M,D
Near and Middle Eastern Languages	M,D
Near and Middle Eastern Studies	M,D
Philosophy	M,D
Political Science	M,D
Portuguese	M
Psychology—General	M,D
Public Policy	M
Scandinavian Languages	M
Slavic Languages	M,D
Sociology	M,D
Spanish	M
Theater	M,D
Urban and Regional Planning	M,D
Urban Design	M,D
Women's Studies	M,D

UNIVERSITY OF CALIFORNIA, RIVERSIDE

Anthropology	M,D
Art History	M
Art/Fine Arts	M
Asian Studies	M
Classics	D
Comparative Literature	M,D
Dance	M,D
Economics	M,D*
English	M,D
Ethnic Studies	D
Hispanic Studies	M,D
Historic Preservation	M,D
History	M,D
Museum Studies	M,D
Music	M,D
Philosophy	M,D
Political Science	M,D
Psychology—General	M,D
School Psychology	M,D
Sociology	M,D
Spanish	M,D
Writing	M

UNIVERSITY OF CALIFORNIA, SAN DIEGO

Anthropology	D
Art/Fine Arts	M,D
Clinical Psychology	D
Cognitive Sciences	D
Communication—General	M,D
Comparative Literature	M,D
Economics	M,D
English	M
Ethnic Studies	M,D
French	M
German	M
History of Science and Technology	M,D
History	M,D
International Affairs	M,D*
Jewish Studies	M,D
Latin American Studies	M
Linguistics	D
Music	M,D
Pacific Area/Pacific Rim Studies	M,D*
Philosophy	D
Political Science	M,D
Psychology—General	D
Sociology	D
Spanish	M
Theater	M,D

UNIVERSITY OF CALIFORNIA, SAN FRANCISCO

Anthropology	D
History of Science and Technology	M,D
Sociology	D

UNIVERSITY OF CALIFORNIA, SANTA BARBARA

Agricultural Economics and Agribusiness	M,D
Anthropology	M,D
Archaeology	M,D
Art History	D
Art/Fine Arts	M,D
Asian Languages	M,D
Asian Studies	M,D

Child and Family Studies	M,D
Classics	M,D
Clinical Psychology	M,D
Cognitive Sciences	M,D
Communication—General	D
Comparative Literature	D
Counseling Psychology	M,D
Developmental Psychology	M,D
Economics	M,D
English	D
Film, Television, and Video Production	D
French	M,D
Geography	M,D
German	M,D
Hispanic Studies	M,D
History	D
Human Development	D
International Affairs	M,D
Latin American Studies	M,D
Linguistics	M,D
Media Studies	M,D
Medieval and Renaissance Studies	M,D
Music	M,D
Philosophy	D
Political Science	M,D
Portuguese	M,D
Psychology—General	M,D
Religion	M,D
School Psychology	M,D
Sociology	D
Spanish	M,D
Speech and Interpersonal Communication	D
Theater	M,D
Women's Studies	M,D

UNIVERSITY OF CALIFORNIA, SANTA CRUZ

Anthropology	D
Applied Economics	M
Archaeology	D
Art/Fine Arts	M
Communication—General	O
Comparative Literature	M,D
Computer Art and Design	M
Economics	D
English	M,D
History	M,D
Humanities	D
Illustration	O
International Affairs	D
Linguistics	M,D
Music	M,D
Philosophy	M,D
Political Science	D
Psychology—General	D
Social Sciences	D
Sociology	D
Technical Writing	O
Theater	O
Writing	M

UNIVERSITY OF CENTRAL ARKANSAS

Computer Art and Design	M
Counseling Psychology	M
Economic Development	M

Economics	M
English	M
Family and Consumer Sciences-General	M
Film, Television, and Video Production	M
Geographic Information Systems	M,O
Geography	M,O
History	M
Music	M
Psychology—General	M,D
School Psychology	M,D
Social Psychology	M

UNIVERSITY OF CENTRAL FLORIDA

Addictions/Substance Abuse Counseling	M,O
Anthropology	M
Art/Fine Arts	M
Child and Family Studies	M,O
Clinical Psychology	M,D
Communication—General	M
Computer Art and Design	M
Corporate and Organizational Communication	M
Criminal Justice and Criminology	M,O
Economics	M,D
Emergency Management	M,O
English	M
Experimental Psychology	M,D
Film, Television, and Video Production	M
Forensic Sciences	M,D,O
Gerontology	M,O
History	M
Homeland Security	M,O
Industrial and Organizational Psychology	M,D
Interdisciplinary Studies	M
International Affairs	M
Internet and Interactive Multimedia	M
Latin American Studies	M,D,O
Marriage and Family Therapy	M,O
Mass Communication	M
Music	M
Political Science	M
Psychology—General	M,D
Public Administration	M,O
Public Affairs	D
Public History	M
School Psychology	O
Sociology	M,D,O
Spanish	M
Speech and Interpersonal Communication	M
Technical Writing	M,D,O
Theater	M
Urban and Regional Planning	M,O
Writing	M

---

*M—master's degree; P—first professional degree; D—doctorate; O—other advanced degree; *—Close-Up and/or Announcement or Display*

UNIVERSITY OF CENTRAL MISSOURI

Communication— General	M
Criminal Justice and Criminology	M,O
English	M
Gerontology	M
History	M
Mass Communication	M
Music	M
Psychology—General	M
Sociology	M
Speech and Interpersonal Communication	M
Theater	M

UNIVERSITY OF CENTRAL OKLAHOMA

Addictions/Substance Abuse Counseling	M
American Studies	M
Applied Arts and Design—General	M
Counseling Psychology	M
Criminal Justice and Criminology	M
English	M
Family and Consumer Sciences-General	M
Gerontology	M
History	M
Human Development	M
Interior Design	M
International Affairs	M
Museum Studies	M
Music	M
Political Science	M
Psychology—General	M
Urban Studies	M
Writing	M

UNIVERSITY OF CHICAGO

Anthropology	M,D
Archaeology	M,D
Art History	M,D
Art/Fine Arts	M
Asian Languages	M,D
Asian Studies	M,D
Classics	M,D
Comparative Literature	M,D
Economics	D
English	M,D
Film, Television, and Video Theory and Criticism	M,D
French	M,D
German	M,D
History	D
Human Development	D
Humanities	M
Interdisciplinary Studies	D
International Affairs	M
Italian	M,D
Latin American Studies	M
Linguistics	M,D
Media Studies	M,D
Music	M,D
Near and Middle Eastern Languages	M,D
Near and Middle Eastern Studies	M,D
Philosophy	M,D
Political Science	D
Psychology—General	D
Public Policy	M,D

Religion	P,M,D
Romance Languages	M,D
Slavic Languages	M,D
Social Sciences	M,D
Sociology	D
Spanish	M,D
Theology	P,M,D

UNIVERSITY OF CINCINNATI

Anthropology	M
Applied Arts and Design—General	M
Architecture	M
Art History	M
Art/Fine Arts	M
Arts Administration	M,D
Classics	M,D
Clinical Psychology	D
Communication— General	M
Criminal Justice and Criminology	M,D
Economics	M
English	M,D
Experimental Psychology	D
French	M,D
Genetic Counseling	M
Geography	M,D
German	M,D
Graphic Design	M
History	M,D
Industrial and Labor Relations	M
Industrial Design	M
Interdisciplinary Studies	D
Interior Design	M
Music	M,D,O
Philosophy	M,D
Political Science	M,D
Psychology—General	D
Romance Languages	M,D
School Psychology	D,O
Sociology	M,D
Spanish	M,D
Textile Design	M
Theater	M,D
Urban and Regional Planning	M
Women's Studies	M,O

UNIVERSITY OF COLORADO AT BOULDER

Anthropology	M,D
Art History	M
Art/Fine Arts	M
Asian Studies	M,D
Chinese	M,D
Classics	M,D
Communication— General	M,D
Comparative Literature	M,D
Dance	M,D
Economics	M,D
English	M,D
French	M,D
Geography	M,D
German	M
History	M,D
International Affairs	M,D
Japanese	M,D
Journalism	M,D
Linguistics	M,D
Mass Communication	M,D
Media Studies	D
Medieval and Renaissance Studies	M,D

Museum Studies	M
Music	M,D
Philosophy	M,D
Photography	M
Political Science	M,D
Psychology—General	M,D
Public Policy	M,D
Religion	M
Sociology	D
Spanish	M,D
Theater	M,D
Writing	M,D

UNIVERSITY OF COLORADO AT COLORADO SPRINGS

Communication— General	M
Criminal Justice and Criminology	M
Geography	M
History	M
Psychology—General	M,D
Public Administration	M
Public Affairs	M
Sociology	M

UNIVERSITY OF COLORADO DENVER

Anthropology	M
Architecture	M
Clinical Psychology	D
Communication— General	M
Counseling Psychology	M
Criminal Justice and Criminology	M
Economics	M
English	M,O
Genetic Counseling	M
Geographic Information Systems	M,D
Health Psychology	D
History	M
Humanities	M
Landscape Architecture	M
Linguistics	M,O
Music	M
Political Science	M
Psychology—General	D
Public Administration	M
Public Affairs	D
Social Sciences	M
Sociology	M
Spanish	M
Technical Communication	M
Urban and Regional Planning	M,D
Urban Design	M

UNIVERSITY OF CONNECTICUT

African Studies	M
Agricultural Economics and Agribusiness	M,D
Anthropology	M,D
Art History	M
Art/Fine Arts	M
Child and Family Studies	M,D,O
Clinical Psychology	M,D,O
Cognitive Sciences	M,D,O
Communication— General	M,D
Comparative Literature	M,D

UNIVERSITY OF COLORADO AT COLORADO SPRINGS

(listed above)

Corporate and Organizational Communication	M,D
Counseling Psychology	M,D,O
Developmental Psychology	M,D,O
Economics	M,D
English	M,D
Experimental Psychology	M,D,O
French	M,D
Geographic Information Systems	M,D,O
Geography	M,D,O
German	M,D
Health Psychology	M,D,O
History	M,D
Homeland Security	M
Human Development	M,D,O
Industrial and Organizational Psychology	M,D,O
International Affairs	M
Italian	M,D
Jewish Studies	M
Latin American Studies	M
Linguistics	M,D
Medieval and Renaissance Studies	M,D
Music	M,D,O
Philosophy	M,D
Political Science	M,D
Psychology—General	M,D,O
Public Administration	M,O
School Psychology	M,D,O
Social Psychology	M,D,O
Sociology	M,D
Spanish	M,D
Sustainable Development	M
Theater	M
Western European Studies	M

UNIVERSITY OF DALLAS

American Studies	M
Art/Fine Arts	M
Comparative Literature	D
English	M
Humanities	M
Pastoral Ministry and Counseling	M
Philosophy	M,D
Political Science	M,D
Psychology—General	M
Theology	M

UNIVERSITY OF DAYTON

Clinical Psychology	M
Communication— General	M
English	M
Human Development	M,O
Pastoral Ministry and Counseling	M,D
Psychology—General	M
Public Administration	M
School Psychology	M,O
Social Psychology	M,O
Theology	M,D

UNIVERSITY OF DELAWARE

Agricultural Economics and Agribusiness	M
American Studies	M
Applied Arts and Design—General	M

Art History	M,D
Art/Fine Arts	M
Child and Family Studies	M,D
Clinical Psychology	D
Cognitive Sciences	D
Communication—General	M
Criminal Justice and Criminology	M,D
Economics	M,D
English	M,D
French	M
Geography	M,D
German	M
Historic Preservation	M,D
History of Science and Technology	M,D
History	M,D
Human Development	M,D
International Affairs	M,D
Liberal Studies	M
Linguistics	M,D
Music	M
Political Science	M,D
Psychology—General	D
Public Administration	M*
Public Policy	M,D
School Psychology	M,D,O
Social Psychology	D
Sociology	M,D
Spanish	M
Theater	M
Urban Studies	M,D

UNIVERSITY OF DENVER

Anthropology	M
Art History	M
Art/Fine Arts	M
Child and Family Studies	M,D,O
Clinical Psychology	M,D
Communication—General	M,D,O*
Computer Art and Design	M
Conflict Resolution and Mediation/Peace Studies	M
Counseling Psychology	M,D,O
Criminal Justice and Criminology	M,O
Economics	M
English	M,D
Film, Television, and Video Production	M
Geographic Information Systems	M,O
Geography	M,D
International Affairs	M,D
Liberal Studies	M,O
Mass Communication	M
Media Studies	M
Museum Studies	M
Music	M,O
Psychology—General	M,D
Public Policy	M
Religion	M,D
School Psychology	M,D,O
Speech and Interpersonal Communication	M,D
Theology	D
Translation and Interpretation	M,O

UNIVERSITY OF DETROIT MERCY

Addictions/Substance Abuse Counseling	M,O
Clinical Psychology	M,D
Criminal Justice and Criminology	M
Industrial and Organizational Psychology	M
Liberal Studies	M
Military and Defense Studies	M
Psychology—General	M,D,O
Religion	M
School Psychology	O

UNIVERSITY OF DUBUQUE

Communication—General	M
Theology	P,M,D

UNIVERSITY OF EVANSVILLE

Public Administration	M

THE UNIVERSITY OF FINDLAY

Liberal Studies	M
Public Administration	M

UNIVERSITY OF FLORIDA

African Studies	O
Agricultural Economics and Agribusiness	M,D
Anthropology	M,D
Architecture	M,D
Art History	M,D
Art/Fine Arts	M,D
Arts Administration	M
Building Science	M,D
Classics	M,D
Clinical Psychology	D
Cognitive Sciences	M,D
Communication—General	M,D
Computer Art and Design	M,D
Counseling Psychology	M,D
Criminal Justice and Criminology	M,D
Developmental Psychology	M,D
Economics	M,D
English	M,D
Family and Consumer Sciences-General	M
Forensic Sciences	M,O
French	M,D
Gender Studies	M,O
Geography	M,D
German	M,D
Graphic Design	M,D
Health Communication	M,D,O
Health Psychology	D
History	M,D
Interior Design	M,D
International Affairs	M
International Development	M,D,O
Internet and Interactive Multimedia	M,D
Journalism	M
Landscape Architecture	M,D
Latin American Studies	M,O
Linguistics	M,D,O

Marriage and Family Therapy	M,D,O
Mass Communication	M,D
Media Studies	M
Museum Studies	M,D
Music	M,D
Philosophy	M,D
Photography	M,D
Political Science	M,D,O
Psychology—General	M,D
Public Affairs	M,D,O
Rehabilitation Counseling	M
Religion	M,D
School Psychology	M,D,O
Social Psychology	M,D
Social Sciences	M
Sociology	M,D
Spanish	M,D
Sport Psychology	M,D
Theater	M
Urban and Regional Planning	M,D
Women's Studies	M,O
Writing	M,D

UNIVERSITY OF GEORGIA

Agricultural Economics and Agribusiness	M,D
Anthropology	M,D
Applied Economics	M,D
Archaeology	M,D
Art History	M
Art/Fine Arts	M
Child and Family Studies	M,D,O
Classics	M
Clothing and Textiles	M,D
Communication—General	M,D
Comparative Literature	M,D
Consumer Economics	M,D
Economics	M,D
English	M,D
Environmental Design	M
Family and Consumer Sciences-General	M,D
French	M
Geography	M,D
German	M
Gerontology	O
Historic Preservation	M
History	M,D
Interior Design	M,D
Internet and Interactive Multimedia	M
Journalism	M,D
Landscape Architecture	M
Linguistics	M,D
Mass Communication	M,D
Music	M,D
Philosophy	M,D
Political Science	M,D
Psychology—General	M,D
Public Administration	M,D
Public Policy	M,D
Religion	M
Romance Languages	M,D
Sociology	M,D
Spanish	M
Speech and Interpersonal Communication	M,D
Sustainable Development	M,D
Theater	M,D
Women's Studies	O

Writing	M,D

UNIVERSITY OF GREAT FALLS

Addictions/Substance Abuse Counseling	O
Counseling Psychology	M
Criminal Justice and Criminology	M

UNIVERSITY OF GUAM

Art/Fine Arts	M
English	M
Graphic Design	M
Pacific Area/Pacific Rim Studies	M
Public Administration	M

UNIVERSITY OF GUELPH

Agricultural Economics and Agribusiness	M,D
Anthropology	M,D
Art/Fine Arts	M
Child and Family Studies	M,D
Clinical Psychology	M,D
Cognitive Sciences	M,D
Comparative Literature	D
Consumer Economics	M
Criminal Justice and Criminology	M,D
Demography and Population Studies	M,D
Economics	M,D
English	M
French	M
Geography	M,D
History	M,D
Human Development	M,D
Industrial and Organizational Psychology	M,D
International Development	M,D
Landscape Architecture	M
Marriage and Family Therapy	M,D
Medieval and Renaissance Studies	D
Philosophy	M,D
Political Science	M
Psychology—General	M,D
Public Administration	M
Public Policy	M
Rural Planning and Studies	M,D
Social Psychology	M,D
Sociology	M,D
Theater	M
Western European Studies	M

UNIVERSITY OF HARTFORD

Architecture	M
Art/Fine Arts	M
Clinical Psychology	M,D
Communication—General	M
Experimental Psychology	M
Music	M,D,O
Psychology—General	M,D
School Psychology	M

*M—master's degree; P—first professional degree; D—doctorate; O—other advanced degree; *—Close-Up and/or Announcement or Display*

UNIVERSITY OF HAWAII AT MANOA

American Studies	M,D,O
Anthropology	M,D
Architecture	D
Art History	M
Art/Fine Arts	M
Asian Languages	M,D
Asian Studies	O
Chinese	M,D,O
Clinical Psychology	M,D,O
Communication— General	M
Conflict Resolution and Mediation/Peace Studies	O
Cultural Studies	O
Dance	M,D
Demography and Population Studies	O
Disability Studies	O
Economics	M,D
Emergency Management	O
English	M,D
French	M
Geography	M,D,O
Historic Preservation	O
History	M,D
International Affairs	O
Japanese	M,D,O
Linguistics	M,D
Museum Studies	O
Music	M,D
Pacific Area/Pacific Rim Studies	M,O
Philosophy	M,D
Political Science	M,D
Psychology—General	M,D,O
Public Administration	M,O
Public Policy	O
Religion	M
Social Psychology	M,D,O
Sociology	M,D,O
Spanish	M
Speech and Interpersonal Communication	M
Theater	M,D*
Urban and Regional Planning	M,D,O
Women's Studies	O

UNIVERSITY OF HOUSTON

Anthropology	M
Architecture	M
Art/Fine Arts	M
Clinical Psychology	M,D
Communication— General	M
Counseling Psychology	M,D
Economics	M,D
English	M,D
Family and Consumer Sciences-General	M
French	M,D
History	M,D
Human Development	M
Industrial and Organizational Psychology	M,D
Interior Design	M
Linguistics	M,D
Mass Communication	M
Music	M,D
Philosophy	M
Photography	M
Political Science	M,D

Psychology—General	M,D
Public History	M,D
Social Psychology	M,D
Sociology	M
Spanish	M,D
Speech and Interpersonal Communication	M
Theater	M
Writing	M,D

UNIVERSITY OF HOUSTON–CLEAR LAKE

Clinical Psychology	M
Criminal Justice and Criminology	M
Cultural Studies	M
English	M
History	M
Humanities	M
Marriage and Family Therapy	M
Psychology—General	M
School Psychology	M
Sociology	M

UNIVERSITY OF HOUSTON–DOWNTOWN

Criminal Justice and Criminology	M
English	M
Technical Communication	M
Writing	M

UNIVERSITY OF HOUSTON–VICTORIA

Counseling Psychology	M
Economic Development	M
Interdisciplinary Studies	M
Psychology—General	M
School Psychology	M

UNIVERSITY OF IDAHO

Agricultural Economics and Agribusiness	M
Anthropology	M
Applied Arts and Design—General	M
Applied Economics	M
Architecture	M
Art/Fine Arts	M
Consumer Economics	M
English	M
Geography	M,D
History	M,D
Interdisciplinary Studies	M
Landscape Architecture	M
Music	M
Political Science	M,D
Psychology—General	M
Public Administration	M
Public Affairs	M,D
School Psychology	O
Social Sciences	M
Theater	M
Urban and Regional Planning	M
Writing	M

UNIVERSITY OF ILLINOIS AT CHICAGO

Anthropology	M,D
Architecture	M
Art History	M,D

Art/Fine Arts	M
Communication— General	M,D
Criminal Justice and Criminology	M,D
Disability Studies	M,D
Economics	M,D
English	M,D
Forensic Sciences	M
French	M
Geography	M
German	M,D
Graphic Design	M
Hispanic Studies	M,D
History	M,D
Human Development	M,D
Industrial Design	M
Linguistics	M
Medical Illustration	M
Philosophy	M,D
Photography	M
Political Science	M,D
Psychology—General	D
Public Administration	M,D
Sociology	M,D
Spanish	M,D
Urban and Regional Planning	M,D
Writing	M,D

UNIVERSITY OF ILLINOIS AT SPRINGFIELD

Addictions/Substance Abuse Counseling	M
Child and Family Studies	M
Communication— General	M
English	M
Gerontology	M
History	M
Human Development	M
Interdisciplinary Studies	M
Journalism	M
Political Science	M
Public Administration	M,D
Public History	M
Social Sciences	M

UNIVERSITY OF ILLINOIS AT URBANA–CHAMPAIGN

African Studies	M
Agricultural Economics and Agribusiness	M,D
Anthropology	M,D
Applied Arts and Design—General	M,D
Architecture	M,D
Art History	M,D
Art/Fine Arts	M
Asian Languages	M,D
Asian Studies	M,D
Classics	M,D
Communication— General	M,D
Comparative Literature	M,D
Consumer Economics	M,D
Dance	M
East European and Russian Studies	M
Economics	M,D*
English	M,D
French	M,D
Geography	M,D
German	M,D
Graphic Design	M
History	M,D

Human Development	M,D
Industrial and Labor Relations	M,D
Industrial Design	M
Italian	M,D
Journalism	M
Landscape Architecture	M,D
Latin American Studies	M
Linguistics	M,D
Media Studies	D
Music	M,D,O
Philosophy	M,D
Photography	M
Political Science	M,D
Portuguese	M,D
Psychology—General	M,D
Slavic Languages	M,D
Sociology	M,D
Spanish	M,D
Theater	M,D
Urban and Regional Planning	M,D
Writing	M,D

UNIVERSITY OF INDIANAPOLIS

Art/Fine Arts	M
Clinical Psychology	M,D
Counseling Psychology	M,D
English	M
Gerontology	M,O
History	M
International Affairs	M
Psychology—General	M,D
Sociology	M

THE UNIVERSITY OF IOWA

African-American Studies	M
American Studies	M,D
Anthropology	M,D
Art History	M,D
Art/Fine Arts	M
Asian Studies	M
Classics	M,D
Communication— General	M,D
Comparative Literature	M,D
Counseling Psychology	M,D,O
Dance	M
Economics	D
English	M,D
Film, Television, and Video Production	M
Film, Television, and Video Theory and Criticism	M,D
French	M,D
Geography	M,D
German	M,D
History	M,D
Journalism	M
Linguistics	M,D
Mass Communication	M,D
Media Studies	M,D
Music	M,D
Philosophy	M,D
Political Science	M,D
Psychology—General	M,D,O
Rehabilitation Counseling	M,D
Religion	M,D
Rhetoric	M,D
School Psychology	M,D,O
Sociology	M,D
Spanish	M,D
Sport Psychology	M,D
Theater	M

Translation and Interpretation	M
Urban and Regional Planning	M
Women's Studies	D
Writing	M,D

THE UNIVERSITY OF KANSAS

African Studies	M,O
African-American Studies	M,O
American Indian/Native American Studies	M
American Studies	M,D
Anthropology	M,D
Applied Arts and Design—General	M
Architecture	M,D,O
Art History	M,D
Art/Fine Arts	M
Asian Languages	M
Asian Studies	M
Classics	M
Clinical Psychology	M,D
Cognitive Sciences	M,D
Communication—General	M,D
Computer Art and Design	M
Counseling Psychology	M,D
Developmental Psychology	M,D
East European and Russian Studies	M
Economics	M,D
English	M,D
Film, Television, and Video Theory and Criticism	M,D
French	M,D
Geography	M,D
German	M,D
Gerontology	M,D,O
History	M,D
Interdisciplinary Studies	M,D
International Affairs	M
Journalism	M
Latin American Studies	M,O
Linguistics	M,D
Museum Studies	M,O
Music	M,D
Near and Middle Eastern Studies	M
Philosophy	M,D
Political Science	M,D
Psychology—General	M,D
Public Administration	M,D
Religion	M
School Psychology	D,O
Slavic Languages	M,D
Social Sciences	M,D
Sociology	M,D
Spanish	M,D
Theater	M,D
Therapies—Dance, Drama, and Music	M
Urban and Regional Planning	M
Writing	M,D

UNIVERSITY OF KENTUCKY

Agricultural Economics and Agribusiness	M,D
Anthropology	M,D
Applied Arts and Design—General	M

Architecture	M
Art History	M
Art/Fine Arts	M
Child and Family Studies	M,D
Classics	M
Clinical Psychology	M,D
Clothing and Textiles	M
Communication—General	M,D
Counseling Psychology	M,D,O
Economics	M,D
English	M,D
Experimental Psychology	M,D
French	M
Geography	M,D
German	M
Gerontology	D
Hispanic Studies	M,D
Historic Preservation	M
History	M,D
Interior Design	M
International Affairs	M
Music	M,D
Philosophy	M,D
Political Science	M,D
Psychology—General	M,D
Public Administration	M,D
Rehabilitation Counseling	M,D
School Psychology	M,D,O
Sociology	M,D
Theater	M

UNIVERSITY OF LA VERNE

Child and Family Studies	M
Child Development	M
Clinical Psychology	D
Counseling Psychology	M
Gerontology	M,O
Marriage and Family Therapy	M
Psychology—General	M,D
Public Administration	M,D,O
Social Psychology	D

UNIVERSITY OF LETHBRIDGE

Addictions/Substance Abuse Counseling	M,D
American Indian/Native American Studies	M,D
Anthropology	M,D
Archaeology	M,D
Art/Fine Arts	M,D
Canadian Studies	M,D
Counseling Psychology	M,D
Economics	M,D
English	M,D
French	M,D
Geographic Information Systems	M,D
Geography	M,D
German	M,D
History	M,D
Media Studies	M,D
Music	M,D
Philosophy	M,D
Political Science	M,D
Psychology—General	M,D
Religion	M,D
Sociology	M,D
Spanish	M,D
Urban Studies	M,D

UNIVERSITY OF LOUISIANA AT LAFAYETTE

American Studies	D
Cognitive Sciences	D
Communication—General	M
English	M,D
Family and Consumer Sciences-General	M
Folklore	M,D
French	M,D
History	M
Mass Communication	M
Music	M
Psychology—General	M
Rehabilitation Counseling	M
Rhetoric	M,D
Writing	M,D

UNIVERSITY OF LOUISIANA AT MONROE

Addictions/Substance Abuse Counseling	M
Communication—General	M
Criminal Justice and Criminology	M
English	M
Experimental Psychology	M
Gerontology	M,O
History	M
Marriage and Family Therapy	M,D
Music	M
Psychology—General	M,O
School Psychology	M,O

UNIVERSITY OF LOUISVILLE

Addictions/Substance Abuse Counseling	M,D,O
African Studies	M
African-American Studies	M
Art History	M,D
Art/Fine Arts	M
Clinical Psychology	M,D
Criminal Justice and Criminology	M
English	M,D
Experimental Psychology	D
French	M
Gerontology	M,D,O
History	M
Humanities	M,D
Interdisciplinary Studies	M
Marriage and Family Therapy	M,D,O
Museum Studies	M,D
Music	M,D
Philosophy	M
Political Science	M
Psychology—General	M,D
Public Administration	M
Public Affairs	D
Public Policy	M
Rhetoric	M,D
Sociology	M
Spanish	M
Theater	M
Urban and Regional Planning	M
Urban Studies	D

Women's Studies	M,O
Writing	M

UNIVERSITY OF MAINE

Agricultural Economics and Agribusiness	M
Clinical Psychology	M,D
Communication—General	M
Developmental Psychology	M,D
Economics	M
English	M
Experimental Psychology	M,D
French	M
History	M,D
Human Development	M
Interdisciplinary Studies	D
Liberal Studies	M
Music	M
Psychology—General	M,D
Public Administration	M,D*
Social Psychology	M,D

UNIVERSITY OF MANAGEMENT AND TECHNOLOGY

Criminal Justice and Criminology	M
Public Administration	M,O

UNIVERSITY OF MANITOBA

Agricultural Economics and Agribusiness	M,D
American Indian/Native American Studies	M
Anthropology	M,D
Architecture	M
Canadian Studies	M
Child and Family Studies	M
Classics	M
Clinical Psychology	M,D
Clothing and Textiles	M
Disability Studies	M
Economics	M,D
English	M,D
Family and Consumer Sciences-General	M
French	M,D
Geography	M,D
German	M
History	M,D
Interdisciplinary Studies	M,D
Interior Design	M
Landscape Architecture	M
Linguistics	M,D
Museum Studies	M,D
Music	M
Northern Studies	M
Philosophy	M
Political Science	M
Psychology—General	M,D
Public Administration	M
Religion	M,D
School Psychology	M,D
Slavic Languages	M
Sociology	M,D
Urban and Regional Planning	M

UNIVERSITY OF MARY

Addictions/Substance Abuse Counseling	M

---

*M—master's degree; P—first professional degree; D—doctorate; O—other advanced degree; *—Close-Up and/or Announcement or Display*

School Psychology	M
Social Psychology	M

UNIVERSITY OF MARY HARDIN-BAYLOR

Counseling Psychology	M
Marriage and Family Therapy	M
Psychology—General	M
School Psychology	M
Social Psychology	M

UNIVERSITY OF MARYLAND, BALTIMORE

Gerontology	D

UNIVERSITY OF MARYLAND, BALTIMORE COUNTY

Art/Fine Arts	M
Cognitive Sciences	D
Communication—General	M
Developmental Psychology	D
Economics	M
Geographic Information Systems	M,O
Geography	M,D
Gerontology	D
History	M
Industrial and Organizational Psychology	M,D
Linguistics	M
Music	O
Psychology—General	M,D
Public Policy	M,D
Social Sciences	D
Sociology	M,O
Women's Studies	O

UNIVERSITY OF MARYLAND, COLLEGE PARK

Agricultural Economics and Agribusiness	M,D
American Studies	M,D
Anthropology	M
Architecture	M
Art History	M,D
Art/Fine Arts	M
Broadcast Journalism	M,D
Child and Family Studies	M,D
Classics	M
Clinical Psychology	M,D
Cognitive Sciences	D
Communication—General	M,D
Comparative Literature	M,D
Counseling Psychology	M,D,O
Criminal Justice and Criminology	M,D
Dance	M
Developmental Psychology	M,D
Economics	M,D
English	M,D
Experimental Psychology	M,D
Family and Consumer Sciences-General	M,D
French	M,D
Geography	M,D
German	M,D
Historic Preservation	M,O

History	M,D
Human Development	M,D
Industrial and Organizational Psychology	M,D
Interdisciplinary Studies	D
Japanese	M,D
Jewish Studies	M
Journalism	M,D
Linguistics	M,D
Marriage and Family Therapy	M,D
Media Studies	M,D
Music	M,D
Near and Middle Eastern Languages	M,O
Philosophy	M,D
Political Science	D
Portuguese	M,D
Psychology—General	M,D
Public Administration	M
Public Policy	M,D
Rehabilitation Counseling	M,D,O
School Psychology	M,D,O
Social Psychology	M,D
Sociology	M,D
Spanish	M,D
Speech and Interpersonal Communication	M,D
Survey Methodology	M,D
Sustainable Development	M
Theater	M,D
Urban and Regional Planning	M,D
Women's Studies	M,D
Writing	M,D

UNIVERSITY OF MARYLAND EASTERN SHORE

Criminal Justice and Criminology	M
Rehabilitation Counseling	M

UNIVERSITY OF MASSACHUSETTS AMHERST

African-American Studies	M,D
Agricultural Economics and Agribusiness	M,D
Anthropology	M,D
Architecture	M
Art History	M
Art/Fine Arts	M
Child and Family Studies	M,D,O
Chinese	M
Classics	M
Clinical Psychology	M,D
Cognitive Sciences	M,D
Communication—General	M,D
Comparative Literature	M,D
Conflict Resolution and Mediation/Peace Studies	M,D
Developmental Psychology	M,D
Economics	M,D
English	M,D
French	M,D
Geography	M
German	M,D

History of Science and Technology	M,D
History	M,D
Industrial and Labor Relations	M
Interior Design	M
Italian	M
Japanese	M
Landscape Architecture	M
Linguistics	M,D
Music	M,D
Philosophy	M,D
Political Science	M,D
Portuguese	M,D
Psychology—General	M,D
Public Administration	M
Public History	M,D
Public Policy	M
Scandinavian Languages	M,D
School Psychology	D
Social Psychology	M,D
Sociology	M,D
Spanish	M,D
Theater	M
Urban and Regional Planning	M,D
Writing	M,D

UNIVERSITY OF MASSACHUSETTS BOSTON

American Studies	M
Archaeology	M
Clinical Psychology	D
Conflict Resolution and Mediation/Peace Studies	M,O
Counseling Psychology	M,O
English	M
Forensic Psychology	M,O
Gerontology	M,D,O
History	M
Linguistics	M
Marriage and Family Therapy	M,O
Political Science	M,D,O
Public Affairs	M
Public History	M
Public Policy	D
Rehabilitation Counseling	M,O
School Psychology	M,O
Sociology	M
Women's Studies	M,D,O

UNIVERSITY OF MASSACHUSETTS DARTMOUTH

Applied Arts and Design—General	M
Art/Fine Arts	M,O
Clinical Psychology	M,O
Computer Art and Design	M
Graphic Design	M
Illustration	M
Latin American Studies	M,D
Photography	M
Portuguese	M,D
Psychology—General	M,O
Public Policy	M,O
Textile Design	M,O
Writing	M,O

UNIVERSITY OF MASSACHUSETTS LOWELL

Criminal Justice and Criminology	M
Economic Development	M,O
Economics	M,O
Music	M
Psychology—General	M
Social Psychology	M
Sociology	M,O
Sustainable Development	M,D,O

UNIVERSITY OF MEDICINE AND DENTISTRY OF NEW JERSEY

Counseling Psychology	M,D,O
Interdisciplinary Studies	M,D
Rehabilitation Counseling	M,D

UNIVERSITY OF MEMPHIS

Anthropology	M
Archaeology	M,O
Architecture	M
Art History	M,O
Art/Fine Arts	M,O
Clinical Psychology	M,D
Communication—General	M,D
Counseling Psychology	M,D
Criminal Justice and Criminology	M
Economics	M,D
English	M,D,O
Experimental Psychology	M,D
Family and Consumer Sciences-General	M
Film, Television, and Video Production	M,D
French	M
Graphic Design	M,O
History	M,D
Interior Design	M,O
Journalism	M
Liberal Studies	M
Music	M,D
Philosophy	M,D
Photography	M,O
Political Science	M
Psychology—General	M,D
Rehabilitation Counseling	M,D
School Psychology	M,D
Sociology	M
Spanish	M
Theater	M
Urban and Regional Planning	M
Writing	M,D,O

UNIVERSITY OF MIAMI

Architecture	M*
Art History	M
Art/Fine Arts	M
Broadcast Journalism	M,D
Clinical Psychology	M,D
Communication—General	M,D
Counseling Psychology	D
Developmental Psychology	M,D
Economic Development	M,D
Economics	M,D
English	M,D

Film, Television, and Video Production	M,D
Film, Television, and Video Theory and Criticism	M,D
French	D
Geography	M
Graphic Design	M
History	M,D
International Affairs	M,D
International Economics	M,D
Internet and Interactive Multimedia	M
Journalism	M,D
Latin American Studies	M
Liberal Studies	M
Marriage and Family Therapy	M,O
Music	M,D,O
Philosophy	M,D
Photography	M
Political Science	M
Psychology—General	M,D
Romance Languages	D
Sociology	M,D
Spanish	M,D
Therapies—Dance, Drama, and Music	M,D,O
Urban Design	M
Writing	M,D

UNIVERSITY OF MICHIGAN

American Studies	M,D
Anthropology	D
Applied Arts and Design—General	M
Applied Economics	M
Archaeology	M
Architecture	M,D
Art History	D
Art/Fine Arts	M
Asian Languages	M,D
Asian Studies	M,D,O
Classics	M,D,O
Clinical Psychology	D
Communication—General	D
Comparative Literature	D
Dance	M
Developmental Psychology	D
East European and Russian Studies	M,O
Economics	M,D
English	M,D,O
Experimental Psychology	D
Film, Television, and Video Theory and Criticism	D,O
French	D
German	M,D
History	D,O
Jewish Studies	M,O
Landscape Architecture	M,D
Linguistics	D
Mass Communication	D
Media Studies	M
Medieval and Renaissance Studies	O
Music	M,D,O
Near and Middle Eastern Languages	M,D
Near and Middle Eastern Studies	M,D
Philosophy	M,D
Political Science	M,D

Psychology—General	D,O
Public Policy	M,D
Romance Languages	D
Russian	M,D
Slavic Languages	M,D
Social Psychology	D
Social Sciences	D
Sociology	D,O
Spanish	D
Survey Methodology	M,D,O
Sustainable Development	M,D
Theater	M,D
Urban and Regional Planning	M,D,O
Urban Design	M
Women's Studies	D,O
Writing	M

UNIVERSITY OF MICHIGAN–DEARBORN

Clinical Psychology	M
Health Psychology	M
Liberal Studies	M
Public Administration	M,O
Public Policy	M

UNIVERSITY OF MICHIGAN–FLINT

American Studies	M
English	M
Public Administration	M
Social Sciences	M

UNIVERSITY OF MINNESOTA, DULUTH

Anthropology	M
Art/Fine Arts	M
Criminal Justice and Criminology	M
English	M
Graphic Design	M
Liberal Studies	M
Music	M
Sociology	M

UNIVERSITY OF MINNESOTA, TWIN CITIES CAMPUS

American Studies	D
Anthropology	M,D
Applied Arts and Design—General	M,D,O
Applied Economics	M,D
Archaeology	M,D
Architecture	M
Art History	M,D
Art/Fine Arts	M
Asian Languages	D
Asian Studies	D
Child and Family Studies	M,D
Child Development	M,D
Classics	M,D
Clinical Psychology	D
Clothing and Textiles	M,D,O
Cognitive Sciences	D
Communication—General	M,D,O
Comparative Literature	D
Counseling Psychology	D
Cultural Studies	D
Dance	M,D
Economic Development	M
Economics	D

English	M,D
French	M,D
Genetic Counseling	M,D
Geographic Information Systems	M
Geography	M,D
German	M,D
History of Medicine	M,D
History of Science and Technology	M,D
History	M,D
Industrial and Labor Relations	M,D
Industrial and Organizational Psychology	D
Interdisciplinary Studies	D
Interior Design	M,D,O
Landscape Architecture	M
Linguistics	M,D
Marriage and Family Therapy	M,D
Mass Communication	M,D
Medieval and Renaissance Studies	M,D
Music	M,D
Philosophy	M,D
Political Science	D
Portuguese	M,D
Psychology—General	D
Public Affairs	M
Public Policy	M
Religion	M,D
Scandinavian Languages	M,D
School Psychology	M,D,O
Social Psychology	D
Sociology	M,D
Spanish	M,D
Textile Design	M,D,O
Theater	M,D
Urban and Regional Planning	M
Women's Studies	D

UNIVERSITY OF MISSISSIPPI

American Studies	M
Anthropology	M
Art History	M
Art/Fine Arts	M
Classics	M
Clinical Psychology	M,D
Economics	M,D
English	M,D
Experimental Psychology	M,D
Family and Consumer Sciences-General	M
French	M
German	M
History	M,D
Journalism	M
Music	M,D
Philosophy	M
Political Science	M,D
Psychology—General	M,D
Sociology	M
Spanish	M

UNIVERSITY OF MISSOURI–COLUMBIA

Agricultural Economics and Agribusiness	M,D
Anthropology	M,D
Archaeology	M,D
Architecture	M

Art History	M,D
Art/Fine Arts	M
Child and Family Studies	M,D
Classics	M,D
Clothing and Textiles	M
Communication—General	M,D
Comparative Literature	M,D
Computer Art and Design	M
Conflict Resolution and Mediation/Peace Studies	M
Consumer Economics	M
Counseling Psychology	M,D,O
Economics	M,D
English	M,D
Environmental Design	M
Family and Consumer Sciences-General	M,D
French	M,D
Geography	M
German	M
History	M,D
Human Development	M,D
Journalism	M,D
Music	M
Philosophy	M,D
Political Science	M,D
Psychology—General	M,D
Public Affairs	M
Religion	M
Romance Languages	M,D
Rural Sociology	M,D
School Psychology	M,D,O
Sociology	M,D
Spanish	M,D
Theater	M,D

UNIVERSITY OF MISSOURI–KANSAS CITY

Art History	M,D
Art/Fine Arts	M,D
Clinical Psychology	M,D
Counseling Psychology	M,D,O
Criminal Justice and Criminology	M
Economics	M,D
English	M,D
History	M,D
Interdisciplinary Studies	D
Music	M,D
Political Science	M,D
Psychology—General	M,D
Public Administration	M,D
Public Affairs	M,D
Romance Languages	M
Social Psychology	M,D
Sociology	M,D
Theater	M

UNIVERSITY OF MISSOURI–ST. LOUIS

Clinical Psychology	M,D,O
Communication—General	M
Conflict Resolution and Mediation/Peace Studies	M
Criminal Justice and Criminology	M,D
Economics	M,O
English	M,O
Gerontology	M,O

*M—master's degree; P—first professional degree; D—doctorate; O—other advanced degree; *—Close-Up and/or Announcement or Display*

Industrial and Organizational Psychology	M,D,O
Linguistics	M,O
Museum Studies	M,O
Philosophy	M
Political Science	M,D
Psychology—General	M,D,O
Public Administration	M,D,O
Public Policy	M,D,O
School Psychology	D,O
Social Psychology	M,D,O
Sociology	M
Writing	M,O

UNIVERSITY OF MOBILE

Marriage and Family Therapy	M
Religion	M
Theology	M

THE UNIVERSITY OF MONTANA

Anthropology	M,D
Art/Fine Arts	M
Clinical Psychology	M,D,O
Communication— General	M
Counseling Psychology	M,D,O
Criminal Justice and Criminology	M
Developmental Psychology	M,D,O
Economics	M
English	M
Experimental Psychology	M,D,O
French	M
Geographic Information Systems	M
Geography	M
German	M
History	M,D
Interdisciplinary Studies	M,D
Jewish Studies	M
Journalism	M
Linguistics	M,D
Music	M
Philosophy	M
Political Science	M
Psychology—General	M,D,O
Public Administration	M
Rural Planning and Studies	M
Rural Sociology	M
School Psychology	M,D,O
Sociology	M
Spanish	M
Theater	M
Writing	M

UNIVERSITY OF MONTEVALLO

English	M
Marriage and Family Therapy	M
Social Psychology	M

UNIVERSITY OF NEBRASKA AT KEARNEY

English	M
History	M
School Psychology	M,O
Writing	M

UNIVERSITY OF NEBRASKA AT OMAHA

Communication— General	M
Criminal Justice and Criminology	M,D
Developmental Psychology	M,D,O
Economics	M
English	M,O
Geography	M,O
Gerontology	M,O
History	M
Industrial and Organizational Psychology	M,D,O
Music	M
Political Science	M
Psychology—General	M,D,O
Public Administration	M,D,O
School Psychology	M,D,O
Technical Communication	M,O
Theater	M
Writing	M,O

UNIVERSITY OF NEBRASKA–LINCOLN

Anthropology	M
Archaeology	M,D
Architecture	M,D
Art History	M
Art/Fine Arts	M
Child Development	M,D
Classics	M
Clinical Psychology	M,D
Cognitive Sciences	M,D,O
Communication— General	M,D
Comparative Literature	M,D
Corporate and Organizational Communication	M,D
Counseling Psychology	M,D,O
Developmental Psychology	M,D,O
Economics	M,D
English	M,D
Family and Consumer Sciences-General	M,D
French	M,D
Geography	M,D
German	M,D
Gerontology	M,D
History	M,D
Human Development	M,D,O
Interior Design	M,D
Journalism	M
Marriage and Family Therapy	M,D
Mass Communication	M
Music	M,D
Philosophy	M,D
Psychology—General	M,D
Public Policy	M,D,O
Rhetoric	M,D
School Psychology	M,D,O
Social Psychology	M,D
Sociology	M,D
Spanish	M,D
Speech and Interpersonal Communication	M,D
Survey Methodology	M,D
Theater	M
Urban and Regional Planning	M,D
Writing	M,D

UNIVERSITY OF NEVADA, LAS VEGAS

Addictions/Substance Abuse Counseling	M,O
Anthropology	M,D
Architecture	M
Art/Fine Arts	M
Communication— General	M
Criminal Justice and Criminology	M
Economics	M
Emergency Management	M,D,O
English	M,D
Ethics	M
Film, Television, and Video Production	M
Forensic Sciences	M,O
Hispanic Studies	M,O
History	M,D
Journalism	M
Marriage and Family Therapy	M,O
Media Studies	M
Music	M,D
Political Science	M,D
Psychology—General	D
Public Administration	M,D,O
Public Affairs	M,D,O
Public Policy	M
Rehabilitation Counseling	M,O
Sociology	M,D
Spanish	M,O
Theater	M
Translation and Interpretation	M,O
Women's Studies	O
Writing	M,D

UNIVERSITY OF NEVADA, RENO

Agricultural Economics and Agribusiness	M,D
Anthropology	M,D
Applied Economics	M,D
Art/Fine Arts	M
Child and Family Studies	M
Clinical Psychology	M,D
Cognitive Sciences	M,D
Criminal Justice and Criminology	M
Economics	M
English	M,D
French	M
Geography	M,D
German	M
History	M,D
Human Development	M
Journalism	M
Music	M
Philosophy	M
Political Science	M,D
Psychology—General	M,D
Public Administration	M
Social Psychology	D
Sociology	M
Spanish	M
Speech and Interpersonal Communication	M
Western European Studies	D

UNIVERSITY OF NEW BRUNSWICK FREDERICTON

Anthropology	M
Applied Economics	M
Classics	M
Conflict Resolution and Mediation/Peace Studies	M
Economics	M
English	M,D
History	M,D
Interdisciplinary Studies	M,D
Philosophy	M
Political Science	M
Psychology—General	M,D
Public Administration	M
Public Policy	M
Sociology	M,D
Sustainable Development	M

UNIVERSITY OF NEW BRUNSWICK SAINT JOHN

Clinical Psychology	M,D
Experimental Psychology	M,D
Psychology—General	M,D

UNIVERSITY OF NEW ENGLAND

Addictions/Substance Abuse Counseling	M,O
Gerontology	M,O

UNIVERSITY OF NEW HAMPSHIRE

Art/Fine Arts	M
Child and Family Studies	M
Comparative Literature	M,D
Economics	M,D*
English	M,D
History	M,D
Liberal Studies	M
Linguistics	M,D
Marriage and Family Therapy	M
Museum Studies	M,D
Music	M
Political Science	M
Psychology—General	D
Public Administration	M,O
Sociology	M,D
Spanish	M
Writing	M,D

UNIVERSITY OF NEW HAVEN

Criminal Justice and Criminology	M
Forensic Sciences	M
Industrial and Labor Relations	M
Industrial and Organizational Psychology	M,O*
National Security	M*
Public Administration	M
Social Psychology	M,O

UNIVERSITY OF NEW MEXICO

American Studies	M,D
Anthropology	M,D
Architecture	M
Art History	M,D
Art/Fine Arts	M

Child and Family Studies	M,D
Clinical Psychology	M,D
Communication— General	M,D
Comparative Literature	M,D
Criminal Justice and Criminology	M
Dance	M
Economics	M
English	M,D
French	M,D
Geography	M
German	M,D
Historic Preservation	O
History	M,D
Landscape Architecture	M
Latin American Studies	M,D
Linguistics	M,D
Music	M
Philosophy	M,D
Political Science	M,D
Portuguese	M,D
Psychology—General	M,D
Public Administration	M
Sociology	M,D
Spanish	M,D
Theater	M
Urban and Regional Planning	M
Urban Design	O
Women's Studies	O
Writing	M,D

UNIVERSITY OF NEW ORLEANS

Art/Fine Arts	M
Arts Administration	M
Economics	D
English	M
Film, Television, and Video Production	M
Geography	M
History	M
Music	M
Political Science	M,D
Psychology—General	M,D
Public Administration	M
Romance Languages	M
Sociology	M
Theater	M
Urban and Regional Planning	M
Urban Studies	M,D

UNIVERSITY OF NORTH ALABAMA

Criminal Justice and Criminology	M
English	M
History	M

THE UNIVERSITY OF NORTH CAROLINA AT ASHEVILLE

Liberal Studies	M

THE UNIVERSITY OF NORTH CAROLINA AT CHAPEL HILL

Anthropology	M,D
Archaeology	M,D
Art History	M,D
Art/Fine Arts	M
Classics	M,D
Clinical Psychology	D
Cognitive Sciences	D

Communication— General	M,D
Comparative Literature	M,D
Developmental Psychology	D
East European and Russian Studies	M
Economics	M,D
English	M,D
Experimental Psychology	D
Folklore	M
French	M,D
Geography	M,D
German	M,D
History	M,D
Italian	M,D
Latin American Studies	M,D,O
Linguistics	M,D
Mass Communication	M,D
Music	M,D
Philosophy	M,D
Political Science	M,D
Portuguese	M,D
Psychology—General	D
Public Administration	M
Public Policy	D
Rehabilitation Counseling	M,D
Religion	M,D
Romance Languages	M,D
Russian	M,D
School Psychology	M,D
Slavic Languages	M,D
Social Psychology	D
Sociology	M,D
Spanish	M,D
Theater	M
Urban and Regional Planning	M,D

THE UNIVERSITY OF NORTH CAROLINA AT CHARLOTTE

Architecture	M
Child Development	M,D
Clinical Psychology	M
Communication— General	M
Criminal Justice and Criminology	M
Dance	M
Economics	M
English	M
Geography	M,D
Gerontology	M
Health Psychology	D
History	M
Industrial and Organizational Psychology	M,D
Latin American Studies	M
Liberal Studies	M
Psychology—General	M,D
Public Administration	M
Public Policy	D
Religion	M
Social Psychology	M
Sociology	M
Spanish	M
Theater	M

THE UNIVERSITY OF NORTH CAROLINA AT GREENSBORO

Applied Economics	M
Architecture	M,O
Art/Fine Arts	M

Child and Family Studies	M,D
Classics	M
Clinical Psychology	M,D
Cognitive Sciences	M,D
Communication— General	M
Conflict Resolution and Mediation/Peace Studies	M,O
Counseling Psychology	M,D,O
Criminal Justice and Criminology	M
Dance	M
Developmental Psychology	M,D
Economic Development	M,D,O
Economics	D
English	M,D
Family and Consumer Sciences-General	M,D,O
Film, Television, and Video Production	M
French	M
Gender Studies	M,O
Genetic Counseling	M
Geographic Information Systems	M,D,O
Geography	M,D,O
Gerontology	M,O
Hispanic Studies	M,O
Historic Preservation	M,O
History	M,D,O
Human Development	M,D
Interior Design	M,O
Liberal Studies	M
Marriage and Family Therapy	M,D,O
Media Studies	M
Museum Studies	M,D,O
Music	M,D
Political Science	M,O
Psychology—General	M,D
Public Affairs	M,O
Rhetoric	M,D
School Psychology	M,D,O
Social Psychology	M,D
Sociology	M
Spanish	M,O
Technical Writing	M,D,O
Textile Design	M,D
Theater	M
Women's Studies	M,D,O
Writing	M

THE UNIVERSITY OF NORTH CAROLINA AT PEMBROKE

Public Administration	M

UNIVERSITY OF NORTH CAROLINA SCHOOL OF THE ARTS

Film, Television, and Video Production	M
Music	M
Theater	M

THE UNIVERSITY OF NORTH CAROLINA WILMINGTON

Criminal Justice and Criminology	M
English	M
Gerontology	M
Hispanic Studies	M,O
History	M

Liberal Studies	M
Psychology—General	M
Public Administration	M
Sociology	M
Writing	M

UNIVERSITY OF NORTH DAKOTA

Applied Economics	M
Art/Fine Arts	M
Clinical Psychology	M,D
Communication— General	M,D
Counseling Psychology	M
Criminal Justice and Criminology	D
English	M,D
Experimental Psychology	M,D
Forensic Psychology	M,D
Geography	M
History	M,D
Linguistics	M
Music	M,D
Psychology—General	M,D
Public Administration	M
Sociology	M
Theater	M

UNIVERSITY OF NORTHERN BRITISH COLUMBIA

Disability Studies	M,D,O
Gender Studies	M,D,O
History	M,D,O
Interdisciplinary Studies	M,D,O
International Affairs	M,D,O
Political Science	M,D,O
Psychology—General	M,D,O

UNIVERSITY OF NORTHERN COLORADO

Art/Fine Arts	M
Communication— General	M
Counseling Psychology	D
English	M
Gerontology	M
History	M
Music	M,D
Psychology—General	M,D
Rehabilitation Counseling	M,D
School Psychology	D,O
Sociology	M
Spanish	M

UNIVERSITY OF NORTHERN IOWA

Art/Fine Arts	M
Communication— General	M
Criminal Justice and Criminology	M
English	M
French	M
Gender Studies	M
Geography	M
German	M
History	M
Music	M
Political Science	M
Psychology—General	M
Public Policy	M
School Psychology	M,O

*M—master's degree; P—first professional degree; D—doctorate; O—other advanced degree; *—Close-Up and/or Announcement or Display*

Social Sciences	M
Sociology	M
Spanish	M
Women's Studies	M

UNIVERSITY OF NORTHERN VIRGINIA

Public Administration	M,D

UNIVERSITY OF NORTH FLORIDA

Counseling Psychology	M
Criminal Justice and Criminology	M
English	M
Ethics	M,O
Gerontology	M,O
History	M
Philosophy	M,O
Psychology—General	M
Public Administration	M
Rehabilitation Counseling	M,O
Sociology	M
Writing	M

UNIVERSITY OF NORTH TEXAS

Anthropology	M
Applied Arts and Design—General	M
Applied Economics	M
Art History	M
Art/Fine Arts	M
Child and Family Studies	M
Clinical Psychology	M,D
Clothing and Textiles	M
Communication— General	M
Counseling Psychology	M,D
Criminal Justice and Criminology	M
Economics	M
English	M,D
Experimental Psychology	M,D
Film, Television, and Video Production	M
French	M
Geography	M
Gerontology	M,D,O
Health Psychology	M,D
History	M,D
Human Development	M
Industrial and Labor Relations	M
Interdisciplinary Studies	M
Journalism	M,O
Linguistics	M,D
Music	M,D
Philosophy	M,D
Political Science	M,D
Psychology—General	M,D
Public Administration	M,D
Rehabilitation Counseling	M
Religion	M,D
School Psychology	M
Sociology	M,D
Spanish	M
Technical Writing	M,D
Writing	M,D

UNIVERSITY OF NORTH TEXAS HEALTH SCIENCE CENTER AT FORT WORTH

Forensic Sciences	M,D

UNIVERSITY OF NOTRE DAME

Applied Arts and Design—General	M
Architecture	M
Art History	M
Art/Fine Arts	M
Cognitive Sciences	D
Comparative Literature	D
Conflict Resolution and Mediation/Peace Studies	M,D
Counseling Psychology	D
Developmental Psychology	D
Economics	M,D
English	M,D
French	M
Graphic Design	M
History of Science and Technology	M,D
History	M,D
Industrial Design	M
Italian	M
Latin American Studies	M
Medieval and Renaissance Studies	M,D
Philosophy	D
Photography	M
Political Science	D
Psychology—General	D
Religion	M
Romance Languages	M
Sociology	D
Spanish	M
Theology	P,M,D
Writing	M

UNIVERSITY OF OKLAHOMA

American Indian/Native American Studies	M
Anthropology	M,D
Applied Arts and Design—General	M
Architecture	M
Art History	M
Art/Fine Arts	M
Communication— General	M,D
Counseling Psychology	D
Dance	M
Economics	M,D
English	M,D
Film, Television, and Video Production	M
French	M,D
Geography	M,D
German	M
History of Science and Technology	M,D
History	M,D
Interdisciplinary Studies	M,D
International Affairs	M
Journalism	M
Landscape Architecture	M
Liberal Studies	M
Mass Communication	M
Museum Studies	M
Music	M,D
Philosophy	M,D
Photography	M

Political Science	M,D
Psychology—General	M,D
Public Administration	M
School Psychology	M,D
Social Psychology	M
Sociology	M,D
Spanish	M,D
Theater	M
Urban and Regional Planning	M
Writing	M

UNIVERSITY OF OKLAHOMA HEALTH SCIENCES CENTER

Genetic Counseling	M

UNIVERSITY OF OREGON

Anthropology	M,D
Architecture	M,D
Art History	M,D
Art/Fine Arts	M
Arts Administration	M*
Asian Languages	M,D
Asian Studies	M
Chinese	M,D
Classics	M
Clinical Psychology	D
Cognitive Sciences	M,D
Communication— General	M,D
Comparative Literature	M,D
Dance	M
Developmental Psychology	M,D
Economics	M,D
English	M,D
Folklore	M
French	M
Geography	M,D
German	M,D
Historic Preservation	M
History	M,D
Interdisciplinary Studies	M
Interior Design	M
International Affairs	M
Italian	M
Japanese	M,D
Journalism	M,D
Landscape Architecture	M
Linguistics	M,D
Music	M,D
Philosophy	M,D
Political Science	M,D
Psychology—General	M,D
Public Policy	M
Romance Languages	M,D
Russian	M
Social Psychology	M,D
Sociology	M,D
Spanish	M
Theater	M,D
Urban and Regional Planning	M
Writing	M

UNIVERSITY OF OTTAWA

Anthropology	M
Canadian Studies	D
Classics	M,D
Communication— General	M
Criminal Justice and Criminology	M,D
Economics	M,D
English	M,D

French	M,D
Geography	M,D
History	M,D
Interdisciplinary Studies	D,O
International Development	M
Linguistics	M,D
Music	M,O
Philosophy	M,D
Political Science	M,D
Psychology—General	D
Public Administration	D,O
Religion	M,D
Sociology	M
Spanish	M,D
Theater	M
Translation and Interpretation	M,D
Women's Studies	M

UNIVERSITY OF PENNSYLVANIA

Anthropology	M,D
Applied Economics	D
Archaeology	M,D
Architecture	M,D,O*
Art History	M,D
Art/Fine Arts	M
Asian Studies	M,D
Classics	M,D
Clinical Psychology	D
Communication— General	D
Comparative Literature	M,D
Computer Art and Design	M
Counseling Psychology	M
Criminal Justice and Criminology	M,D
Demography and Population Studies	M,D
Economics	M,D
English	M,D
Ethics	M,D
French	M,D
German	M,D
Historic Preservation	M,O
History of Science and Technology	M,D
History	M,D
Human Development	M,D
International Affairs	M
Italian	M,D
Landscape Architecture	M,O
Liberal Studies	M
Linguistics	M,D
Music	M,D
Near and Middle Eastern Studies	M,D
Philosophy	M,D
Political Science	M,D
Psychology—General	D
Public Administration	M*
Public Policy	M,D
Religion	D
Romance Languages	M,D
School Psychology	D
Social Psychology	D
Sociology	M,D
Spanish	M,D
Urban and Regional Planning	M,D,O
Urban Design	D
Writing	M,D

UNIVERSITY OF PHOENIX

Criminal Justice and Criminology	M
Gerontology	M
Marriage and Family Therapy	M
Psychology—General	M
Public Administration	M
Social Psychology	M

UNIVERSITY OF PHOENIX–ATLANTA CAMPUS

Criminal Justice and Criminology	M
Public Administration	M

UNIVERSITY OF PHOENIX–AUGUSTA CAMPUS

Criminal Justice and Criminology	M
Public Administration	M

UNIVERSITY OF PHOENIX–AUSTIN CAMPUS

Criminal Justice and Criminology	M
Psychology—General	M
Public Administration	M

UNIVERSITY OF PHOENIX–BAY AREA CAMPUS

Criminal Justice and Criminology	M
Marriage and Family Therapy	M
Public Administration	M

UNIVERSITY OF PHOENIX–BIRMINGHAM CAMPUS

Criminal Justice and Criminology	M
Gerontology	M
Psychology—General	M
Public Administration	M

UNIVERSITY OF PHOENIX–CENTRAL FLORIDA CAMPUS

Public Administration	M

UNIVERSITY OF PHOENIX–CENTRAL VALLEY CAMPUS

Gerontology	M
Marriage and Family Therapy	M
Public Administration	M

UNIVERSITY OF PHOENIX–CHATTANOOGA CAMPUS

Criminal Justice and Criminology	M
Gerontology	M
Psychology—General	M
Public Administration	M

UNIVERSITY OF PHOENIX–CHEYENNE CAMPUS

Criminal Justice and Criminology	M
Psychology—General	M
Public Administration	M

UNIVERSITY OF PHOENIX–CINCINNATI CAMPUS

Criminal Justice and Criminology	M
Psychology—General	M
Public Administration	M

UNIVERSITY OF PHOENIX–CLEVELAND CAMPUS

Criminal Justice and Criminology	M
Psychology—General	M
Public Administration	M

UNIVERSITY OF PHOENIX–COLUMBUS GEORGIA CAMPUS

Criminal Justice and Criminology	M
Public Administration	M

UNIVERSITY OF PHOENIX–COLUMBUS OHIO CAMPUS

Criminal Justice and Criminology	M
Psychology—General	M
Public Administration	M

UNIVERSITY OF PHOENIX–DALLAS CAMPUS

Criminal Justice and Criminology	M
Psychology—General	M
Public Administration	M

UNIVERSITY OF PHOENIX–DENVER CAMPUS

Criminal Justice and Criminology	M
Marriage and Family Therapy	M
Psychology—General	M
Public Administration	M
School Psychology	M
Social Psychology	M

UNIVERSITY OF PHOENIX–DES MOINES CAMPUS

Criminal Justice and Criminology	M
Public Administration	M

UNIVERSITY OF PHOENIX–EASTERN WASHINGTON CAMPUS

Public Administration	M

UNIVERSITY OF PHOENIX–HARRISBURG CAMPUS

Criminal Justice and Criminology	M
Psychology—General	M
Public Administration	M

UNIVERSITY OF PHOENIX–HAWAII CAMPUS

Criminal Justice and Criminology	M
Gerontology	M

Marriage and Family Therapy	M
Psychology—General	M
Public Administration	M
Social Psychology	M

UNIVERSITY OF PHOENIX–HOUSTON CAMPUS

Criminal Justice and Criminology	M
Psychology—General	M
Public Administration	M

UNIVERSITY OF PHOENIX–IDAHO CAMPUS

Criminal Justice and Criminology	M
Psychology—General	M
Public Administration	M

UNIVERSITY OF PHOENIX–INDIANAPOLIS CAMPUS

Criminal Justice and Criminology	M
Psychology—General	M
Public Administration	M

UNIVERSITY OF PHOENIX–JERSEY CITY CAMPUS

Criminal Justice and Criminology	M
Psychology—General	M
Public Administration	M

UNIVERSITY OF PHOENIX–KANSAS CITY CAMPUS

Criminal Justice and Criminology	M
Public Administration	M
Social Psychology	M

UNIVERSITY OF PHOENIX–LAS VEGAS CAMPUS

Counseling Psychology	M
Criminal Justice and Criminology	M
Marriage and Family Therapy	M
Psychology—General	M
Public Administration	M
School Psychology	M

UNIVERSITY OF PHOENIX–LOUISIANA CAMPUS

Criminal Justice and Criminology	M
Psychology—General	M
Public Administration	M

UNIVERSITY OF PHOENIX–MADISON CAMPUS

Internet and Interactive Multimedia	M
Public Administration	M

UNIVERSITY OF PHOENIX–MARYLAND CAMPUS

Criminal Justice and Criminology	M

Psychology—General	M
Public Administration	M

UNIVERSITY OF PHOENIX–MEMPHIS CAMPUS

Criminal Justice and Criminology	M
Public Administration	M

UNIVERSITY OF PHOENIX–METRO DETROIT CAMPUS

Criminal Justice and Criminology	M

UNIVERSITY OF PHOENIX–MINNEAPOLIS/ST. LOUIS PARK CAMPUS

Public Administration	M
Social Psychology	M

UNIVERSITY OF PHOENIX–NEW MEXICO CAMPUS

Criminal Justice and Criminology	M
Marriage and Family Therapy	M
Psychology—General	M

UNIVERSITY OF PHOENIX–NORTHERN NEVADA CAMPUS

Criminal Justice and Criminology	M
Marriage and Family Therapy	M
Psychology—General	M
Public Administration	M
School Psychology	M

UNIVERSITY OF PHOENIX–NORTHERN VIRGINIA CAMPUS

Criminal Justice and Criminology	M
Public Administration	M

UNIVERSITY OF PHOENIX–NORTH FLORIDA CAMPUS

Public Administration	M

UNIVERSITY OF PHOENIX–NORTHWEST ARKANSAS CAMPUS

Criminal Justice and Criminology	M
Public Administration	M

UNIVERSITY OF PHOENIX–OKLAHOMA CITY CAMPUS

Criminal Justice and Criminology	M
Psychology—General	M

UNIVERSITY OF PHOENIX–OMAHA CAMPUS

Criminal Justice and Criminology	M
Public Administration	M

M—master's degree; P—first professional degree; D—doctorate; O—other advanced degree; *—Close-Up and/or Announcement or Display

UNIVERSITY OF PHOENIX–OREGON CAMPUS

Criminal Justice and Criminology	M
Psychology—General	M
Public Administration	M

UNIVERSITY OF PHOENIX–PHILADELPHIA CAMPUS

Criminal Justice and Criminology	M
Psychology—General	M
Public Administration	M

UNIVERSITY OF PHOENIX–PHOENIX CAMPUS

Gerontology	M,O
Marriage and Family Therapy	M,O
Psychology—General	M,O
Social Psychology	M,O

UNIVERSITY OF PHOENIX–PITTSBURGH CAMPUS

Criminal Justice and Criminology	M
Psychology—General	M
Public Administration	M

UNIVERSITY OF PHOENIX–PUERTO RICO CAMPUS

Counseling Psychology	M
Marriage and Family Therapy	M
School Psychology	M

UNIVERSITY OF PHOENIX–RENTON LEARNING CENTER

Criminal Justice and Criminology	M
Public Administration	M

UNIVERSITY OF PHOENIX–RICHMOND CAMPUS

Criminal Justice and Criminology	M
Psychology—General	M
Public Administration	M

UNIVERSITY OF PHOENIX–SACRAMENTO VALLEY CAMPUS

Counseling Psychology	M
Criminal Justice and Criminology	M
Marriage and Family Therapy	M
Psychology—General	M
Public Administration	M

UNIVERSITY OF PHOENIX–ST. LOUIS CAMPUS

Criminal Justice and Criminology	M
Public Administration	M

UNIVERSITY OF PHOENIX–SAN ANTONIO CAMPUS

Criminal Justice and Criminology	M

Psychology—General	M
Public Administration	M

UNIVERSITY OF PHOENIX–SAN DIEGO CAMPUS

Criminal Justice and Criminology	M
Marriage and Family Therapy	M
Public Administration	M

UNIVERSITY OF PHOENIX–SAVANNAH CAMPUS

Criminal Justice and Criminology	M
Public Administration	M

UNIVERSITY OF PHOENIX–SOUTHERN ARIZONA CAMPUS

Criminal Justice and Criminology	M,O
Marriage and Family Therapy	M,O
Psychology—General	M,O

UNIVERSITY OF PHOENIX–SOUTHERN CALIFORNIA CAMPUS

Criminal Justice and Criminology	M,O
Marriage and Family Therapy	M,O
Psychology—General	M,O
Public Administration	M

UNIVERSITY OF PHOENIX–SOUTHERN COLORADO CAMPUS

Criminal Justice and Criminology	M
Gerontology	M
Marriage and Family Therapy	M
Psychology—General	M
Public Administration	M
School Psychology	M,O
Social Psychology	M

UNIVERSITY OF PHOENIX–SOUTH FLORIDA CAMPUS

Public Administration	M

UNIVERSITY OF PHOENIX–SPRINGFIELD CAMPUS

Criminal Justice and Criminology	M
Public Administration	M

UNIVERSITY OF PHOENIX–TULSA CAMPUS

Criminal Justice and Criminology	M
Psychology—General	M

UNIVERSITY OF PHOENIX–UTAH CAMPUS

Counseling Psychology	M
School Psychology	M

UNIVERSITY OF PHOENIX–WEST FLORIDA CAMPUS

Public Administration	M

UNIVERSITY OF PHOENIX–WISCONSIN CAMPUS

Public Administration	M

UNIVERSITY OF PITTSBURGH

African Studies	O
Anthropology	M,D
Architectural History	M,D
Art History	M,D
Asian Studies	M,O
Classics	M,D
Cognitive Sciences	D
Communication—General	M,D
Conflict Resolution and Mediation/Peace Studies	M
Criminal Justice and Criminology	D
Cultural Studies	M,D
Developmental Psychology	M,D
Disability Studies	O
East European and Russian Studies	O
Economics	M,D
Emergency Management	M,D,O
English	M,D*
French	M,D
Genetic Counseling	M
Geographic Information Systems	M,D
German	M,D
Gerontology	M,D,O
Hispanic Studies	M,D
History of Science and Technology	M,D
History	M,D
Interdisciplinary Studies	D
International Affairs	M,D,O
International Development	M,O
Italian	M
Latin American Studies	O
Linguistics	M,D
Military and Defense Studies	M
Music	M,D
National Security	M
Philosophy	M,D
Political Science	M,D
Psychology—General	M,D
Public Administration	M,D,O*
Public Policy	M,D,O
Rehabilitation Counseling	M
Religion	M,D
Slavic Languages	M,D
Sociology	M,D
Spanish	M,D
Theater	M,D
Urban and Regional Planning	M,O
Western European Studies	O
Women's Studies	O
Writing	M,D

UNIVERSITY OF PORTLAND

Communication—General	M

Corporate and Organizational Communication	M
Music	M
Pastoral Ministry and Counseling	M
Theater	M

UNIVERSITY OF PRINCE EDWARD ISLAND

Geography	M

UNIVERSITY OF PUERTO RICO, MAYAGÜEZ CAMPUS

Agricultural Economics and Agribusiness	M
English	M
Hispanic Studies	M

UNIVERSITY OF PUERTO RICO, MEDICAL SCIENCES CAMPUS

Demography and Population Studies	M
Gerontology	M,O

UNIVERSITY OF PUERTO RICO, RÍO PIEDRAS

Architecture	M
Clinical Psychology	M,D
Comparative Literature	M
Economics	M
English	M,D
Family and Consumer Sciences-General	M
Hispanic Studies	M,D
History	M,D
Industrial and Organizational Psychology	M,D
Linguistics	M
Mass Communication	M
Philosophy	M
Psychology—General	M,D
Public Administration	M
Rehabilitation Counseling	M
Sociology	M
Translation and Interpretation	M,O
Urban and Regional Planning	M

UNIVERSITY OF PUGET SOUND

Counseling Psychology	M
Pastoral Ministry and Counseling	M

UNIVERSITY OF REDLANDS

Geographic Information Systems	M
Music	M

UNIVERSITY OF REGINA

American Indian/Native American Studies	M
Anthropology	M
Art/Fine Arts	M
Canadian Studies	M,D
Clinical Psychology	M,D
Criminal Justice and Criminology	M
Economics	M,D,O
English	M,D

Experimental	
Psychology	M,D
French	M
Geography	M,D
Gerontology	M
History	M,D
Linguistics	M
Music	M,D
Philosophy	M
Political Science	M
Psychology—General	M,D
Public Administration	M,D,O
Public Policy	M,D,O
Religion	M,D
Social Sciences	M,D
Sociology	M,D
Women's Studies	M

UNIVERSITY OF RHODE ISLAND

Child and Family	
Studies	M
Clinical Psychology	M,D
Clothing and Textiles	M
Communication—	
General	M
Counseling Psychology	M
Economics	M,D
English	M,D
Forensic Sciences	M,D,O
Gerontology	M,D
History	M
Industrial and Labor	
Relations	M
International Affairs	M,O
Music	M
Political Science	M,O
Psychology—General	D
Public Administration	M,O
Public Policy	M,O
School Psychology	M,D
Spanish	M
Sport Psychology	M,D

UNIVERSITY OF ROCHESTER

Art History	M,D
Art/Fine Arts	M,D*
Clinical Psychology	M,D
Cognitive Sciences	M,D
Developmental	
Psychology	M,D
Economics	M,D
English	M,D
History	M,D
Marriage and Family	
Therapy	M
Music	M,D
Philosophy	M,D
Political Science	M,D
Psychology—General	M,D
Social Psychology	M,D

UNIVERSITY OF SAINT FRANCIS (IN)

Art/Fine Arts	M
Counseling Psychology	M
Pastoral Ministry and	
Counseling	M
Psychology—General	M

UNIVERSITY OF SAINT MARY

Psychology—General	M

UNIVERSITY OF SAINT MARY OF THE LAKE–MUNDELEIN SEMINARY

Theology	P,M,D,O

UNIVERSITY OF ST. MICHAEL'S COLLEGE

Jewish Studies	P,M,D,O
Pastoral Ministry and	
Counseling	P,M,D,O
Theology	P,M,D,O

UNIVERSITY OF ST. THOMAS (MN)

Art History	M
Corporate and	
Organizational	
Communication	M
Counseling Psychology	M,D,O
English	M*
Human Development	M,D,O
Marriage and Family	
Therapy	M,D,O
Pastoral Ministry and	
Counseling	M
Psychology—General	M,D,O
Religion	M
Theology	P,M

UNIVERSITY OF ST. THOMAS (TX)

Liberal Studies	M
Philosophy	M,D
Theology	P,M

UNIVERSITY OF SAN DIEGO

Conflict Resolution and	
Mediation/Peace	
Studies	M
Counseling Psychology	M
History	M
International Affairs	M
Marriage and Family	
Therapy	M
Theater	M

UNIVERSITY OF SAN FRANCISCO

Asian Studies	M
Counseling Psychology	M,D
Economic Development	M
Economics	M
International Affairs	M
International	
Development	M
International Economics	M
Internet and Interactive	
Multimedia	M
Marriage and Family	
Therapy	M,D
Pacific Area/Pacific Rim	
Studies	M
Public Administration	M
Theology	M
Writing	M

UNIVERSITY OF SASKATCHEWAN

Agricultural Economics	
and Agribusiness	M,D
Anthropology	M
Archaeology	M,D

Art/Fine Arts	M
Canadian Studies	M,D
East European and	
Russian Studies	M
Economics	M
English	M,D
French	M
Gender Studies	M,D
Geography	M,D
German	M
History	M,D
Industrial and Labor	
Relations	M
Music	M
Philosophy	M
Political Science	M
Psychology—General	M,D
Religion	M
Sociology	M,D
Theater	M
Women's Studies	M,D

THE UNIVERSITY OF SCRANTON

Counseling Psychology	M,O
History	M
Rehabilitation	
Counseling	M
Social Psychology	M
Theology	M

UNIVERSITY OF SOUTH AFRICA

Anthropology	M,D
Archaeology	M,D
Art History	M,D
Classics	M,D
Clinical Psychology	M,D
Communication—	
General	M,D
Counseling Psychology	M,D
Criminal Justice and	
Criminology	M,D
Economics	M,D
English	M,D
Ethics	M,D
Family and Consumer	
Sciences-General	M,D
French	M,D
Geography	M,D
German	M,D
History	M,D
Human Development	M,D
Industrial and	
Organizational	
Psychology	M,D
Italian	M,D
Linguistics	M,D
Missions and Missiology	M,D
Music	M,D
Near and Middle	
Eastern Languages	M,D
Near and Middle	
Eastern Studies	M,D
Pastoral Ministry and	
Counseling	M,D
Philosophy	M,D
Political Science	M,D
Portuguese	M,D
Psychology—General	M,D
Public Administration	M,D
Religion	M,D
Romance Languages	M,D
Russian	M,D
Sociology	M,D
Spanish	M,D
Theology	M,D

UNIVERSITY OF SOUTH ALABAMA

Communication—	
General	M
English	M
Gerontology	O
History	M
Psychology—General	M
Public Administration	M
Rehabilitation	
Counseling	M,D
School Psychology	M,D
Sociology	M

UNIVERSITY OF SOUTH CAROLINA

Anthropology	M,D
Art History	M
Art/Fine Arts	M
Clinical Psychology	M,D
Comparative Literature	M,D
Consumer Economics	M
Criminal Justice and	
Criminology	M,D
Economics	M,D
English	M,D
Experimental	
Psychology	M,D
French	M,D
Genetic Counseling	M
Geography	M,D
German	M,D
Gerontology	O
Historic Preservation	M,O
History	M,D,O
International Affairs	M,D
Journalism	M,D
Linguistics	M,D,O
Media Studies	M
Museum Studies	M,O
Music	M,D,O
Philosophy	M,D
Political Science	M,D
Psychology—General	M,D
Public Administration	M
Public History	M,O
Rehabilitation	
Counseling	M,O
Religion	M
School Psychology	D
Social Psychology	M,D
Sociology	M,D
Spanish	M,D
Speech and	
Interpersonal	
Communication	M,D
Theater	M,D
Women's Studies	O
Writing	M,D

UNIVERSITY OF SOUTH CAROLINA AIKEN

Clinical Psychology	M

THE UNIVERSITY OF SOUTH DAKOTA

Art/Fine Arts	M
Clinical Psychology	M,D
Communication—	
General	M
English	M,D
History	M
Interdisciplinary Studies	M
Music	M

*M—master's degree; P—first professional degree; D—doctorate; O—other advanced degree; *—Close-Up and / or Announcement or Display*

Political Science	M,D
Psychology—General	M,D
Public Administration	M,D
Theater	M

UNIVERSITY OF SOUTHERN CALIFORNIA

American Studies	D
Architecture	M
Art History	M,D,O
Art/Fine Arts	M,D,O
Arts Administration	M
Asian Languages	M,D
Asian Studies	M,D
Broadcast Journalism	M
Building Science	M
Classics	M,D
Communication—General	M,D*
Comparative Literature	M,D
Corporate and Organizational Communication	M,D
Counseling Psychology	M
Economic Development	M,D
Economics	M,D
English	M,D
Film, Television, and Video Production	M
Film, Television, and Video Theory and Criticism	M,D
French	M,D
Geographic Information Systems	M,D,O
Geography	M,D,O
Gerontology	M,D,O
Health Communication	M
Historic Preservation	M
History	D
International Affairs	M,D
Internet and Interactive Multimedia	M,D
Journalism	M
Landscape Architecture	M
Linguistics	D
Marriage and Family Therapy	M
Mass Communication	M,D
Media Studies	M,D
Music	M,D,O
Philosophy	M,D
Political Science	M,D
Psychology—General	M,D,O
Public Administration	M,D,O
Public Policy	M
Religion	M,D
Slavic Languages	M,D
Sociology	D
Speech and Interpersonal Communication	M,D
Theater	M*
Urban and Regional Planning	M,D
Writing	M,D

UNIVERSITY OF SOUTHERN INDIANA

Liberal Studies	M
Public Administration	M

UNIVERSITY OF SOUTHERN MAINE

American Studies	M
Music	M

Public Policy	M,D,O
School Psychology	M,D,O
Urban and Regional Planning	M,O
Writing	M

UNIVERSITY OF SOUTHERN MISSISSIPPI

Anthropology	M
Child and Family Studies	M
Clinical Psychology	M,D
Counseling Psychology	M,D
Criminal Justice and Criminology	M,D
Economic Development	M,D
Economics	M,D
English	M,D
Experimental Psychology	M,D
Geography	M,D
History	M,D
International Affairs	M,D
International Development	M,D
Marriage and Family Therapy	M
Mass Communication	M,D
Music	M,D
Philosophy	M
Political Science	M,D
Psychology—General	M,D
School Psychology	M,D
Speech and Interpersonal Communication	M,D
Theater	M

UNIVERSITY OF SOUTH FLORIDA

African Studies	M
American Studies	M
Anthropology	M,D
Architecture	M
Art History	M
Art/Fine Arts	M
Classics	M
Clinical Psychology	M,D
Cognitive Sciences	M,D
Communication—General	M,D
Criminal Justice and Criminology	M,D
Economics	M,D
English	M,D
French	M
Geography	M,D
Gerontology	M,D
History	M,D
Industrial and Organizational Psychology	M,D
International Affairs	M,D
Latin American Studies	M,D,O
Liberal Studies	M
Linguistics	M
Mass Communication	M
Music	M,D
Philosophy	M,D
Political Science	M,D
Psychology—General	M,D
Public Administration	M
Rehabilitation Counseling	M
Religion	M
School Psychology	M,D,O
Sociology	M,D

Spanish	M
Women's Studies	M

THE UNIVERSITY OF TAMPA

Economics	M

THE UNIVERSITY OF TENNESSEE

Anthropology	M,D
Archaeology	M,D
Architecture	M
Art/Fine Arts	M
Child and Family Studies	M,D
Clinical Psychology	M,D
Clothing and Textiles	M,D
Communication—General	M,D
Consumer Economics	M,D
Counseling Psychology	M,D
Criminal Justice and Criminology	M,D
Economics	M,D
English	M,D
Experimental Psychology	M,D
Family and Consumer Sciences-General	D
French	M,D
Geography	M,D
German	M,D
Gerontology	M
Graphic Design	M
History	M,D
Industrial and Organizational Psychology	D
Italian	D
Journalism	M,D
Landscape Architecture	M
Linguistics	D
Media Studies	M,D
Music	M
Philosophy	M,D
Photography	M
Political Science	M,D
Portuguese	D
Psychology—General	M,D
Public Administration	M
Rehabilitation Counseling	M,D
Religion	M,D
Russian	D
School Psychology	M,D,O
Sociology	M,D
Spanish	M,D
Speech and Interpersonal Communication	M,D
Theater	M

THE UNIVERSITY OF TENNESSEE AT CHATTANOOGA

Criminal Justice and Criminology	M
English	M
Experimental Psychology	M
Industrial and Organizational Psychology	M
Music	M
Psychology—General	M
Public Administration	M,O
School Psychology	O

THE UNIVERSITY OF TENNESSEE AT MARTIN

Child and Family Studies	M
Child Development	M
Family and Consumer Sciences-General	M
Social Psychology	M

THE UNIVERSITY OF TEXAS AT ARLINGTON

Anthropology	M
Architecture	M
Art/Fine Arts	M
Communication—General	M
Criminal Justice and Criminology	M
Economics	M
English	M,D
Experimental Psychology	M,D
French	M
Health Psychology	M,D
History	M,D
Humanities	M
Industrial and Organizational Psychology	M,D
Interdisciplinary Studies	M
Landscape Architecture	M
Linguistics	M,D
Music	M
Political Science	M
Psychology—General	M,D
Public Administration	M
Public Affairs	D
Sociology	M
Spanish	M
Urban and Regional Planning	M

THE UNIVERSITY OF TEXAS AT AUSTIN

African Studies	M,D
American Studies	M,D
Anthropology	M,D
Applied Arts and Design—General	M
Archaeology	M,D
Architectural History	M,D
Architecture	M,D
Art History	M,D
Art/Fine Arts	M
Asian Languages	M,D
Asian Studies	M,D
Child and Family Studies	M,D
Child Development	M,D
Classics	M,D
Cognitive Sciences	M,D
Communication—General	M,D
Comparative Literature	M,D
Counseling Psychology	M,D
Dance	M,D
East European and Russian Studies	M
Economics	M,D
English	M,D
Family and Consumer Sciences-General	M,D
Film, Television, and Video Production	M,D
Folklore	M,D
French	M,D
Geography	M,D

German	M,D
Hispanic Studies	M
Historic Preservation	M,D
History	M,D
Human Development	M,D
Italian	M,D
Journalism	M,D
Landscape Architecture	M,D
Latin American Studies	M,D
Linguistics	M,D
Media Studies	M,D
Mineral Economics	M
Music	M,D
Near and Middle Eastern Languages	M,D
Near and Middle Eastern Studies	M,D
Philosophy	D
Political Science	D
Portuguese	M,D
Psychology—General	D
Public Affairs	M,D
Public History	M,D
Public Policy	M,D
Romance Languages	M,D
School Psychology	M,D
Slavic Languages	M,D
Sociology	M,D
Spanish	M,D
Sport Psychology	M,D
Theater	M,D
Urban and Regional Planning	M,D
Urban Design	M,D
Writing	M,D

THE UNIVERSITY OF TEXAS AT BROWNSVILLE

English	M
History	M
Interdisciplinary Studies	M
Political Science	M
Psychology—General	M
Public Administration	M
Public Policy	M
Spanish	M

THE UNIVERSITY OF TEXAS AT DALLAS

Child and Family Studies	M,D
Cognitive Sciences	M,D
Communication— General	M,D
Comparative Literature	M,D
Criminal Justice and Criminology	M,D
Economics	M,D*
Geographic Information Systems	M,D
Humanities	M,D
Interdisciplinary Studies	M
Political Science	M,D
Psychology—General	M,D
Public Affairs	M,D
Public Policy	M,D
Sociology	M

THE UNIVERSITY OF TEXAS AT EL PASO

Art/Fine Arts	M
Clinical Psychology	M,D
Communication— General	M
Economics	M

English	M,D
Experimental Psychology	M,D
History	M,D
Interdisciplinary Studies	M
Linguistics	M
Military and Defense Studies	M
Music	M
National Security	M
Political Science	M
Psychology—General	M,D
Public Administration	M
Public Policy	M
Rhetoric	M,D
Sociology	M
Spanish	M
Writing	M,D

THE UNIVERSITY OF TEXAS AT SAN ANTONIO

Anthropology	M,D
Architecture	M,O
Art History	M
Art/Fine Arts	M
Communication— General	M
Criminal Justice and Criminology	M
Cultural Studies	M,D
Demography and Population Studies	D
Economics	M
English	M,D,O
Historic Preservation	M,O
History	M
Interdisciplinary Studies	M
Music	M,O
Political Science	M
Psychology—General	M
Public Administration	M
Sociology	M
Spanish	M,O
Translation and Interpretation	M,O
Urban and Regional Planning	M,O
Writing	M,D,O

THE UNIVERSITY OF TEXAS AT TYLER

Art History	M
Art/Fine Arts	M
Clinical Psychology	M
Communication— General	M
Counseling Psychology	M
Criminal Justice and Criminology	M
English	M
History	M
Interdisciplinary Studies	M
Marriage and Family Therapy	M
Political Science	M
Psychology—General	M
Public Administration	M
School Psychology	M
Social Sciences	M
Sociology	M

THE UNIVERSITY OF TEXAS HEALTH SCIENCE CENTER AT HOUSTON

Genetic Counseling	M

THE UNIVERSITY OF TEXAS MEDICAL BRANCH

Humanities	M,D

THE UNIVERSITY OF TEXAS OF THE PERMIAN BASIN

Clinical Psychology	M
Criminal Justice and Criminology	M
English	M
Experimental Psychology	M
History	M
Political Science	M
Psychology—General	M
Spanish	M

THE UNIVERSITY OF TEXAS–PAN AMERICAN

Art/Fine Arts	M
Clinical Psychology	M
Communication— General	M
Criminal Justice and Criminology	M
Economics	D
English	M
Experimental Psychology	M
History	M
Interdisciplinary Studies	M
Music	M
Psychology—General	M
Public Administration	M
Rehabilitation Counseling	M
School Psychology	M
Sociology	M
Spanish	M
Theater	M

THE UNIVERSITY OF TEXAS SOUTHWESTERN MEDICAL CENTER AT DALLAS

Clinical Psychology	D
Medical Illustration	M
Rehabilitation Counseling	M

THE UNIVERSITY OF THE ARTS

Art/Fine Arts	M*
Industrial Design	M
Museum Studies	M
Music	M

UNIVERSITY OF THE DISTRICT OF COLUMBIA

Clinical Psychology	M
Counseling Psychology	M
English	M
Public Administration	M

UNIVERSITY OF THE FRASER VALLEY

Criminal Justice and Criminology	M

UNIVERSITY OF THE INCARNATE WORD

Communication— General	M,O

Interdisciplinary Studies	M
Religion	M

UNIVERSITY OF THE PACIFIC

Communication— General	M
Criminal Justice and Criminology	P,M,D
International Affairs	P,M,D
Music	M
Psychology—General	M
Public Policy	P,M,D
School Psychology	M,D,O
Therapies—Dance, Drama, and Music	M

UNIVERSITY OF THE SACRED HEART

Communication— General	M
Conflict Resolution and Mediation/Peace Studies	M
Cultural Studies	M
Film, Television, and Video Production	M
Writing	M

UNIVERSITY OF THE SCIENCES IN PHILADELPHIA

Health Psychology	M
Technical Writing	M,O

UNIVERSITY OF THE VIRGIN ISLANDS

Public Administration	M

UNIVERSITY OF THE WEST

Religion	M,D

THE UNIVERSITY OF TOLEDO

Clinical Psychology	M,D
Cognitive Sciences	M,D
Communication— General	O
Criminal Justice and Criminology	M,O
Economics	M
English	M,O
Experimental Psychology	M,D
French	M
Geographic Information Systems	M,O
Geography	M,O
German	M
Gerontology	O
History	M,D
Homeland Security	M,O
Liberal Studies	M
Music	M
Philosophy	M
Political Science	M
Psychology—General	M,D
Public Administration	M,O
School Psychology	M,D,O
Social Psychology	M,D,O
Sociology	M
Spanish	M
Urban and Regional Planning	M,O
Writing	M,O

*M—master's degree; P—first professional degree; D—doctorate; O—other advanced degree; *—Close-Up and/or Announcement or Display*

UNIVERSITY OF TORONTO

Anthropology	M,D
Architecture	M
Art History	M,D
Art/Fine Arts	M,D
Asian Studies	M,D
Classics	M,D
Comparative Literature	M,D
Criminal Justice and Criminology	M,D
East European and Russian Studies	M
Economics	M,D
English	M,D
French	M,D
Genetic Counseling	M,D
Geography	M,D
German	M,D
History of Science and Technology	M,D
History	M,D
Industrial and Labor Relations	M,D
Italian	M,D
Linguistics	M,D
Medieval and Renaissance Studies	M,D
Museum Studies	M,D
Music	M,D
Near and Middle Eastern Studies	M,D
Philosophy	M,D
Political Science	M,D
Portuguese	M,D
Psychology—General	M,D
Religion	M,D
Slavic Languages	M,D
Sociology	M,D
Spanish	M,D
Theater	M,D
Urban and Regional Planning	M,D
Urban Design	M,D

UNIVERSITY OF TRINITY COLLEGE

Music	P,M,D,O
Pastoral Ministry and Counseling	P,M,D,O
Theology	P,M,D,O

UNIVERSITY OF TULSA

Anthropology	M
Art/Fine Arts	M
Clinical Psychology	M,D
English	M,D
History	M
Industrial and Organizational Psychology	M,D
Psychology—General	M,D

UNIVERSITY OF UTAH

American Studies	M,D
Anthropology	M,D
Architecture	M
Art History	M
Art/Fine Arts	M
Asian Studies	M
Child and Family Studies	M
Clinical Psychology	D
Communication—General	M,D
Comparative Literature	M,D
Consumer Economics	M

Counseling Psychology	M,D
Dance	M
Economics	M,D
English	M,D
Film, Television, and Video Production	M
French	M,D
Geography	M,D
German	M,D
Gerontology	M,O
Graphic Design	M
History	M,D
International Affairs	M
Linguistics	M,D
Music	M,D
Near and Middle Eastern Languages	M,D
Near and Middle Eastern Studies	M,D
Philosophy	M,D
Photography	M
Political Science	M,D
Psychology—General	D
Public Administration	M,O
Public Policy	M
Rhetoric	M,D
School Psychology	M,D
Sociology	M,D
Spanish	M,D
Urban and Regional Planning	M
Writing	M

UNIVERSITY OF VERMONT

Agricultural Economics and Agribusiness	M
Applied Economics	M
Classics	M
Clinical Psychology	D
Communication—General	M
Counseling Psychology	M
English	M
French	M
German	M
Historic Preservation	M
History	M
Psychology—General	D
Public Administration	M

UNIVERSITY OF VICTORIA

Anthropology	M
Art History	M,D
Art/Fine Arts	M
Asian Studies	M
Child and Family Studies	M,D
Classics	M,D
Clinical Psychology	M,D
Computer Art and Design	M
Conflict Resolution and Mediation/Peace Studies	M,D
Counseling Psychology	M,D
Developmental Psychology	M,D
Economics	M,D
English	M,D
Experimental Psychology	M,D
Film, Television, and Video Production	M
French	M
Geography	M,D
German	M
Hispanic Studies	M

History	M,D
Human Development	M,D
Italian	M
Linguistics	M,D
Music	M,D
Pacific Area/Pacific Rim Studies	M
Philosophy	M
Photography	M
Political Science	M,D
Psychology—General	M,D
Public Administration	M,D
Social Psychology	M,D
Sociology	M,D
Theater	M
Writing	M

UNIVERSITY OF VIRGINIA

Anthropology	M,D
Archaeology	M,D
Architectural History	M,D
Architecture	M
Art History	M,D
Asian Studies	M
Classics	M,D
Clinical Psychology	M,D,O
Economics	M,D
English	M,D,O
French	M,D
German	M,D
History	M,D
Interdisciplinary Studies	M,D
International Affairs	M,D
Italian	M
Landscape Architecture	M
Linguistics	M
Music	M,D
Philosophy	M,D
Political Science	M,D
Psychology—General	M,D
Public Policy	M
Religion	M,D
Romance Languages	M,D
School Psychology	M,D,O
Slavic Languages	M,D
Sociology	M,D
Spanish	M,D
Theater	M
Urban and Regional Planning	M,O
Writing	M

UNIVERSITY OF WASHINGTON

Anthropology	M,D
Applied Arts and Design—General	M
Architecture	M,D,O
Art History	M,D
Art/Fine Arts	M
Asian Languages	M,D
Asian Studies	M,D
Chinese	M,D
Classics	M,D
Clinical Psychology	D
Cognitive Sciences	D
Communication—General	M,D
Comparative Literature	M,D
Dance	M
Developmental Psychology	D
East European and Russian Studies	M
Economics	D
English	M,D
French	M,D
Geography	M,D

German	M,D
Hispanic Studies	M
Historic Preservation	O
History	M,D
Human Development	M,D
Industrial Design	M
International Affairs	M
Italian	M,D
Japanese	M,D
Landscape Architecture	M
Lighting Design	M,D,O
Linguistics	M,D
Museum Studies	M
Music	M,D
Near and Middle Eastern Studies	M,D
Philosophy	M,D
Photography	M
Political Science	M,D
Portuguese	M
Psychology—General	D
Public Administration	M,D
Public Affairs	M,D
Public Policy	M,D
Religion	M,D
Romance Languages	M,D
Russian	M,D
Scandinavian Languages	M,D
School Psychology	M,D
Slavic Languages	M,D
Social Psychology	D
Sociology	M,D
Spanish	M
Sustainable Development	P,M,D
Technical Communication	M,D
Theater	M,D
Urban and Regional Planning	M,D
Urban Design	M,D,O
Women's Studies	D
Writing	M,D

UNIVERSITY OF WASHINGTON, BOTHELL

Public Policy	M

UNIVERSITY OF WASHINGTON, TACOMA

Interdisciplinary Studies	M

UNIVERSITY OF WATERLOO

Anthropology	M
Architecture	M
Art/Fine Arts	M
Economic Development	M
Economics	M,D
English	M,D
French	M,D
Geography	M,D
German	M,D
History	M,D
International Affairs	M,D
Near and Middle Eastern Studies	M
Philosophy	M,D
Political Science	M,D
Psychology—General	M,D
Public Affairs	M
Religion	M,D
Russian	M,D
Sociology	M,D
Technical Writing	M,D

Urban and Regional Planning	M,D

THE UNIVERSITY OF WESTERN ONTARIO

Anthropology	M,D
Classics	M
Comparative Literature	M,D
Counseling Psychology	M
Economics	M,D
English	M,D
French	M,D
Geography	M,D
History	M,D
Interdisciplinary Studies	M,D
Journalism	M
Media Studies	M,D
Music	M,D
Philosophy	M,D
Political Science	M,D
Psychology—General	M,D
Sociology	M,D
Spanish	M,D
Sustainable Development	M,D

UNIVERSITY OF WEST FLORIDA

Anthropology	M
Archaeology	M
Communication—General	M
Counseling Psychology	M
Criminal Justice and Criminology	M
English	M
Historic Preservation	M
History	M
Humanities	M
Industrial and Organizational Psychology	M
Political Science	M
Psychology—General	M
Public Administration	M
Public History	M
Writing	M

UNIVERSITY OF WEST GEORGIA

Criminal Justice and Criminology	M
English	M
Geographic Information Systems	O
History	M
Museum Studies	O
Music	M
Psychology—General	M,D
Public Administration	M,O
Rural Planning and Studies	M
Sociology	M

UNIVERSITY OF WINDSOR

Art/Fine Arts	M
Clinical Psychology	M,D
Communication—General	
Criminal Justice and Criminology	M,D
Economics	M
English	M
History	M
Philosophy	M
Political Science	M

Psychology—General	M,D
Social Psychology	M,D
Sociology	M,D
Writing	M

THE UNIVERSITY OF WINNIPEG

History	M
Marriage and Family Therapy	P,M,O
Public Administration	M
Religion	M
Theology	P,M,O

UNIVERSITY OF WISCONSIN–EAU CLAIRE

English	M
History	M
Psychology—General	M,O
School Psychology	M,O

UNIVERSITY OF WISCONSIN–LA CROSSE

Psychology—General	M,O
School Psychology	M,O

UNIVERSITY OF WISCONSIN–MADISON

African Studies	M,D
African-American Studies	M
Agricultural Economics and Agribusiness	M,D
American Studies	M,D
Anthropology	D
Applied Arts and Design—General	M,D
Applied Economics	M,D
Archaeology	D
Art History	M,D
Art/Fine Arts	M
Arts Administration	M
Asian Languages	M,D
Asian Studies	M,D
Child and Family Studies	M,D
Chinese	M,D
Classics	M,D
Clinical Psychology	D
Cognitive Sciences	D
Communication—General	M,D
Comparative Literature	M,D
Consumer Economics	M,D
Counseling Psychology	D
Developmental Psychology	D
Economics	D
English	M,D
Family and Consumer Sciences-General	M,D
Film, Television, and Video Theory and Criticism	M,D
Folklore	M,D
French	M,D,O
Genetic Counseling	M
Geographic Information Systems	M,D,O
Geography	M,D,O
German	M,D
History of Science and Technology	M,D
History	M,D
Human Development	M,D

Italian	M,D
Japanese	M,D
Jewish Studies	M,D
Journalism	M,D
Landscape Architecture	M
Latin American Studies	M,D
Linguistics	M,D
Mass Communication	M,D
Media Studies	M,D
Music	M,D
Near and Middle Eastern Languages	M,D
Near and Middle Eastern Studies	M,D
Philosophy	M,D
Political Science	D
Portuguese	M,D
Psychology—General	D
Public Affairs	M
Rehabilitation Counseling	M,D
Rhetoric	M,D
Rural Sociology	M,D
Scandinavian Languages	M,D
Slavic Languages	M,D
Social Psychology	D
Social Sciences	D
Sociology	M,D
Spanish	M,D
Speech and Interpersonal Communication	M,D
Sustainable Development	M
Theater	M,D
Urban and Regional Planning	M,D
Women's Studies	M,D
Writing	M,D

UNIVERSITY OF WISCONSIN–MILWAUKEE

African Studies	D
Anthropology	M,D,O
Architecture	M,D,O
Art History	M,O
Art/Fine Arts	M
Classics	M,O
Clinical Psychology	M,D
Communication—General	M,D,O
Comparative Literature	M,D,O
Conflict Resolution and Mediation/Peace Studies	M,O
Counseling Psychology	M,D
Criminal Justice and Criminology	M
Dance	M
Developmental Psychology	M,D
Economics	M,D
English	M,D,O
Film, Television, and Video Production	M
French	M,O
Geographic Information Systems	M,O
Geography	M,D
German	M,O
Gerontology	M,D,O
Historic Preservation	M,D,O
History	M,D
Industrial and Labor Relations	M,O
Interdisciplinary Studies	D

Italian	M,O
Jewish Studies	M,O
Liberal Studies	M
Linguistics	M,D,O
Marriage and Family Therapy	M,D,O
Media Studies	M,O
Museum Studies	M,D,O
Music	M,D,O
Philosophy	M
Political Science	M,D
Psychology—General	M,D
Public Administration	M
Rhetoric	M,D,O
School Psychology	D,O
Slavic Languages	M,O
Social Psychology	M,D
Sociology	M
Spanish	M,O
Theater	M
Translation and Interpretation	M,O
Urban and Regional Planning	M,O
Urban Studies	M,D
Writing	M,D,O

UNIVERSITY OF WISCONSIN–OSHKOSH

English	M
Experimental Psychology	M
Industrial and Organizational Psychology	M
Psychology—General	M
Public Administration	M

UNIVERSITY OF WISCONSIN–PLATTEVILLE

Criminal Justice and Criminology	M

UNIVERSITY OF WISCONSIN–RIVER FALLS

Art/Fine Arts	M
School Psychology	M,O

UNIVERSITY OF WISCONSIN–STEVENS POINT

Communication—General	M
Corporate and Organizational Communication	M
English	M
Family and Consumer Sciences-General	M
History	M
Human Development	M
Mass Communication	M
Speech and Interpersonal Communication	M

UNIVERSITY OF WISCONSIN–STOUT

Child and Family Studies	M
Counseling Psychology	M
Human Development	M
Marriage and Family Therapy	M

M—master's degree; P—first professional degree; D—doctorate; O—other advanced degree; *—Close-Up and/or Announcement or Display

Psychology—General M
Rehabilitation
  Counseling M
School Psychology M,O

UNIVERSITY OF WISCONSIN–SUPERIOR
Art History M
Art Therapy M
Art/Fine Arts M
Arts Administration M
Communication—
  General M
Mass Communication M
Social Psychology M
Speech and
  Interpersonal
  Communication M
Theater M

UNIVERSITY OF WISCONSIN–WHITEWATER
Communication—
  General M
Corporate and
  Organizational
  Communication M
Mass Communication M
Psychology—General M,O
School Psychology M,O
Social Psychology M

UNIVERSITY OF WYOMING
Agricultural Economics
  and Agribusiness M
American Studies M
Anthropology M,D
Applied Economics M
Child Development M
Communication—
  General M
Consumer Economics M
Economics M,D
English M
French M
Geography M
German M
History M
International Affairs M
Music M
Philosophy M
Political Science M
Psychology—General M,D
Public Administration M
Rural Planning and
  Studies M
Sociology M
Spanish M
Writing M

UPPER IOWA UNIVERSITY
Criminal Justice and
  Criminology M
Homeland Security M
Public Administration M

URSULINE COLLEGE
Art Therapy M
Historic Preservation M
Liberal Studies M
Theology M

UTAH STATE UNIVERSITY
American Studies M

Applied Economics M
Art/Fine Arts M
Child and Family
  Studies M,D
Clinical Psychology M,D
Communication—
  General M
Consumer Economics M
Counseling Psychology M,D
Disability Studies M,D,O
Economics M,D
English M
Family and Consumer
  Sciences-General M,D
Folklore M
Geography M,D
History M
Human Development M,D
Interior Design M
Landscape Architecture M
Marriage and Family
  Therapy M,D
Political Science M
Psychology—General M,D
Rehabilitation
  Counseling M
School Psychology M,D
Sociology M,D
Theater M
Urban and Regional
  Planning M,D
Writing M

UTICA COLLEGE
Criminal Justice and
  Criminology M
Liberal Studies M

VALDOSTA STATE UNIVERSITY
Clinical Psychology M,O
Counseling Psychology M,O
Criminal Justice and
  Criminology M
English M
History M
Industrial and
  Organizational
  Psychology M,O
Marriage and Family
  Therapy M
Psychology—General M,O
School Psychology M,O
Sociology M

VALPARAISO UNIVERSITY
Asian Studies M
Clinical Psychology M,O
Counseling Psychology M,O
English M,O
Ethics M,O
Gerontology M,O
History M,O
Liberal Studies M,O
Psychology—General M,O
School Psychology
Theology M,O

VANCOUVER SCHOOL OF THEOLOGY
Theology P,M,O

VANDERBILT UNIVERSITY
Anthropology M,D
Child and Family
  Studies M

Classics M
Economic Development M,D
Economics P,M,D
English M,D
French M,D
German M,D
History M,D
Human Development M
Latin American Studies M
Liberal Studies M
Philosophy M,D
Political Science M,D
Portuguese M,D
Psychology—General M,D
Public Policy M,D
Religion M,D
Sociology M,D
Spanish M,D
Theology P,M
Urban and Regional
  Planning M
Writing M

VANGUARD UNIVERSITY OF SOUTHERN CALIFORNIA
Clinical Psychology M
Religion M
Theology M

VICTORIA UNIVERSITY
Theology P,M,D,O

VILLANOVA UNIVERSITY
Communication—
  General M
Criminal Justice and
  Criminology M
English M*
Hispanic Studies M
History M*
Humanities M
Liberal Studies M
Philosophy D
Political Science M*
Psychology—General M*
Public Administration M
Theater M
Theology M

VIRGINIA COLLEGE AT BIRMINGHAM
Criminal Justice and
  Criminology M

VIRGINIA COMMONWEALTH UNIVERSITY
Applied Arts and
  Design—General M
Applied Social Research M,O
Architectural History M,D
Art History M,D
Art/Fine Arts M,D
Clinical Psychology D
Communication—
  General D
Counseling Psychology M,D,O
Criminal Justice and
  Criminology M,O
Economics M
Emergency
  Management M,O
English M
Forensic Sciences M
Gender Studies O

Geographic Information
  Systems O
Gerontology M,D,O
Historic Preservation O
History M,D
Homeland Security M,O
Humanities M,D,O
Interdisciplinary Studies M
Interior Design M
Internet and Interactive
  Multimedia M
Journalism M
Mass Communication M
Media Studies D
Museum Studies M,D
Music M
Photography M
Political Science M,D,O
Psychology—General D
Public Administration M,O
Public Affairs M,D,O
Public Policy D
Rehabilitation
  Counseling M,O
Rhetoric M
Sociology M
Theater M
Urban and Regional
  Planning M,O
Writing M

VIRGINIA POLYTECHNIC INSTITUTE AND STATE UNIVERSITY
Agricultural Economics
  and Agribusiness M,D
Applied Arts and
  Design—General M,D
Applied Economics M,D
Architecture M,D
Arts Administration M
Child and Family
  Studies M,D
Child Development M,D
Clinical Psychology M,D
Clothing and Textiles M,D
Communication—
  General M
Consumer Economics M,D
Developmental
  Psychology M,D
Economic Development M,D
Economics M,D
English M,D
Environmental Design D
Geography M,D
Gerontology M,D
History of Science and
  Technology M,D
History M
Human Development M,D
Industrial and
  Organizational
  Psychology M,D
Interdisciplinary Studies M,D,O
Interior Design M,D
International Affairs M,D
International
  Development M,D
International Economics M,D
Landscape Architecture M,D
Marriage and Family
  Therapy M,D
Philosophy M
Political Science M
Psychology—General M,D
Public Administration M,D,O
Public Affairs M,D

Public Policy M,D,O
Rural Planning and
  Studies M,D
Sociology M,D
Theater M
Urban and Regional
  Planning M,D
Urban Studies M,D

VIRGINIA STATE UNIVERSITY

Clinical Psychology M,D
Economics M
English M
Health Psychology M,D
History M
Interdisciplinary Studies M
Psychology—General M,D

VIRGINIA UNION UNIVERSITY

Theology P,D

VIRGINIA UNIVERSITY OF LYNCHBURG

Religion P

WAKE FOREST UNIVERSITY

Communication—
  General M
English M
Liberal Studies M
Psychology—General M
Religion M
Speech and
  Interpersonal
  Communication M

WALDEN UNIVERSITY

Child and Family
  Studies M,D
Clinical Psychology M,D,O
Conflict Resolution and
  Mediation/Peace
  Studies M,D,O
Counseling Psychology M,D,O
Criminal Justice and
  Criminology M,D,O
Developmental
  Psychology M,D,O
Forensic Psychology M,D,O
Health Psychology M,D,O
Homeland Security M,D,O
Industrial and
  Organizational
  Psychology M,D,O
International Affairs M,D,O
Psychology—General M,D,O
Public Administration M,D,O
Public Policy M,D,O
School Psychology M,D,O
Social Psychology M,D,O
Sustainable
  Development M,D,O

WALLA WALLA UNIVERSITY

Counseling Psychology M

WALSH COLLEGE OF ACCOUNTANCY AND BUSINESS ADMINISTRATION

Economics M

WALSH UNIVERSITY

Counseling Psychology M
Theology M

WARNER PACIFIC COLLEGE

Ethics M
Pastoral Ministry and
  Counseling M
Religion M
Theology M

WARREN WILSON COLLEGE

Writing M

WARTBURG THEOLOGICAL SEMINARY

Theology P,M

WASHBURN UNIVERSITY

Clinical Psychology M
Criminal Justice and
  Criminology M
Liberal Studies M
Psychology—General M

WASHINGTON COLLEGE

English M
History M
Psychology—General M

WASHINGTON STATE UNIVERSITY

Agricultural Economics
  and Agribusiness M,D,O
American Studies M,D
Anthropology M,D
Applied Economics M,D,O
Archaeology M,D
Architecture M
Art/Fine Arts M
Asian Studies M,D
Clinical Psychology M,D
Clothing and Textiles M,D
Communication—
  General M,D
Computer Art and
  Design M
Corporate and
  Organizational
  Communication M,D
Counseling Psychology M,D,O
Criminal Justice and
  Criminology M,D
Cultural Studies M,D
Demography and
  Population Studies M,D
Economics M,D,O
English M,D
Ethnic Studies M,D
Experimental
  Psychology M,D
Health Communication M,D
History M,D
Human Development M
Interdisciplinary Studies D
Interior Design M,D
International Affairs M,D
Landscape Architecture M,D
Media Studies M,D
Music M
Philosophy M
Photography M

Political Science M,D
Psychology—General M,D
Public History M,D
Public Policy M,D
School Psychology M,D,O
Social Psychology M,D
Sociology M,D
Spanish M
Western European
  Studies M,D
Women's Studies M,D

WASHINGTON STATE UNIVERSITY SPOKANE

Architecture M,D
Criminal Justice and
  Criminology M,D
Interior Design M,D
Landscape Architecture M,D

WASHINGTON STATE UNIVERSITY VANCOUVER

History M
Public Affairs M

WASHINGTON THEOLOGICAL UNION

Theology P,M,D

WASHINGTON UNIVERSITY IN ST. LOUIS

Anthropology D
Archaeology M,D
Architecture M*
Art History M,D
Art/Fine Arts M
Asian Languages M,D
Asian Studies M*
Chinese M,D
Classics M
Clinical Psychology D
Comparative Literature M,D
Economics D*
English M,D
Experimental
  Psychology D
French M,D
German M,D
History M,D
Japanese M,D
Music M,D
Philosophy M,D
Political Science M,D
Psychology—General D
Public Policy M
Romance Languages M,D
Social Psychology D
Spanish M,D
Speech and
  Interpersonal
  Communication M,D
Urban Design M
Writing M

WAYLAND BAPTIST UNIVERSITY

Counseling Psychology M
Criminal Justice and
  Criminology M
Homeland Security M
Interdisciplinary Studies M
Pastoral Ministry and
  Counseling M

Public Administration M
Religion M

WAYNESBURG UNIVERSITY

Counseling Psychology M,D

WAYNE STATE COLLEGE

Communication—
  General M

WAYNE STATE UNIVERSITY

Addictions/Substance
  Abuse Counseling O
Anthropology M,D
Applied Arts and
  Design—General M
Art History M
Art/Fine Arts M
Child and Family
  Studies O
Classics M
Clinical Psychology M,D,O
Cognitive Sciences M,D
Communication—
  General M,D
Comparative Literature M
Conflict Resolution and
  Mediation/Peace
  Studies M,O
Corporate and
  Organizational
  Communication M,D
Criminal Justice and
  Criminology M
Developmental
  Psychology M,D
Economic Development O
Economics M,D,O
English M,D
French M
Geography M
German M,D
Gerontology O
History M,D
Human Development M
Industrial and Labor
  Relations M
Industrial and
  Organizational
  Psychology M,D
Italian M
Linguistics M
Media Studies M,D
Music M,O
Near and Middle
  Eastern Studies M
Philosophy M,D
Political Science M,D
Psychology—General M,D
Public Administration M
Rehabilitation
  Counseling M,D,O
Russian M,D
School Psychology M,D,O
Sociology M,D
Spanish M
Speech and
  Interpersonal
  Communication M,D
Theater M,D
Urban and Regional
  Planning M
Writing M,D

*M—master's degree; P—first professional degree; D—doctorate; O—other advanced degree; *—Close-Up and/or Announcement or Display*

WEBBER INTERNATIONAL UNIVERSITY

Criminal Justice and Criminology	M

WEBER STATE UNIVERSITY

English	M

WEBSTER UNIVERSITY

Art/Fine Arts	M
Arts Administration	M
Communication—General	M
Corporate and Organizational Communication	M
Counseling Psychology	M
Criminal Justice and Criminology	M,D
Gerontology	M
International Affairs	M
Media Studies	M
Music	M
Public Administration	M,D

WESLEYAN UNIVERSITY

Liberal Studies	M,O
Music	M,D
Psychology—General	M

WESLEY BIBLICAL SEMINARY

Marriage and Family Therapy	P,M
Missions and Missiology	P,M
Pastoral Ministry and Counseling	P,M
Theology	P,M

WESLEY THEOLOGICAL SEMINARY

Theology	P,M,D

WEST CHESTER UNIVERSITY OF PENNSYLVANIA

Anthropology	M,O
Classics	M,O
Clinical Psychology	M,O
Communication—General	M
Criminal Justice and Criminology	M
Economics	M
Emergency Management	M,O
English	M,O
Ethics	M,O
French	M,O
Geographic Information Systems	M,O
Geography	M,O
German	M,O
Gerontology	M,O
Health Psychology	M,O
History	M,O
Holocaust Studies	M,O
Industrial and Organizational Psychology	M,O
Music	M,O
Philosophy	M,O
Political Science	M,O
Psychology—General	M,O
Public Administration	M,O
Public Affairs	M,O
Sociology	M,O
Spanish	M,O
Urban and Regional Planning	M,O
Women's Studies	M,O

WESTERN CAROLINA UNIVERSITY

Applied Arts and Design—General	M
Art/Fine Arts	M
English	M
History	M
Music	M
Psychology—General	M
Public Affairs	M
School Psychology	M
Social Psychology	M

WESTERN CONNECTICUT STATE UNIVERSITY

Art/Fine Arts	M
Criminal Justice and Criminology	M
English	M
History	M
Illustration	M
Social Psychology	M
Writing	M

WESTERN ILLINOIS UNIVERSITY

Clinical Psychology	M,O
Communication—General	M
Criminal Justice and Criminology	M,O
Economics	M,O
English	M,O
Geographic Information Systems	M,O
Geography	M,O
Graphic Design	M,O
History	M
Internet and Interactive Multimedia	M,O
Liberal Studies	M
Museum Studies	M
Music	M
Political Science	M,O
Psychology—General	M,O
Public Administration	M,O
School Psychology	M,O
Social Psychology	M,O
Sociology	M
Sustainable Development	M,O
Theater	M

WESTERN INTERNATIONAL UNIVERSITY

Public Administration	M

WESTERN KENTUCKY UNIVERSITY

Anthropology	M
Communication—General	M
Comparative Literature	M
English	M
Geography	M
History	M
Interdisciplinary Studies	M
Political Science	M

WESTERN MICHIGAN UNIVERSITY

Anthropology	M
Applied Arts and Design—General	M
Applied Economics	M,D
Clinical Psychology	M,D
Communication—General	M
Corporate and Organizational Communication	M
Counseling Psychology	M,D
Economics	M,D
English	M,D
Experimental Psychology	M,D
Family and Consumer Sciences-General	M
Geography	M
Graphic Design	M
History	M,D
Industrial and Organizational Psychology	M,D
Marriage and Family Therapy	M,D
Medieval and Renaissance Studies	M
Music	M
Philosophy	M
Political Science	M,D
Psychology—General	M,D
Public Administration	M,D,O
Public Affairs	M,D,O
Rehabilitation Counseling	M
Religion	M
Sociology	M,D
Spanish	M,D
Therapies—Dance, Drama, and Music	M
Writing	M,D

WESTERN NEW ENGLAND COLLEGE

Psychology—General	D

WESTERN NEW MEXICO UNIVERSITY

Interdisciplinary Studies	M
School Psychology	M

WESTERN OREGON UNIVERSITY

Criminal Justice and Criminology	M
Music	M
Rehabilitation Counseling	M

WESTERN SEMINARY

Missions and Missiology	M,O
Pastoral Ministry and Counseling	P,M,D,O
Religion	M,O
Theology	M,O
Women's Studies	M,O

WESTERN SEMINARY– SACRAMENTO CAMPUS

Marriage and Family Therapy	P,M
Pastoral Ministry and Counseling	P,M
Theology	P,M

WESTERN SEMINARY– SAN JOSE CAMPUS

Marriage and Family Therapy	P,M
Pastoral Ministry and Counseling	P,M
Theology	P,M

WESTERN THEOLOGICAL SEMINARY

Theology	P,M,D

WESTERN WASHINGTON UNIVERSITY

Anthropology	M
Counseling Psychology	M
English	M
Experimental Psychology	M
Geography	M
History	M
Music	M
Political Science	M
Psychology—General	M
Rehabilitation Counseling	M

WESTFIELD STATE COLLEGE

Counseling Psychology	M
Criminal Justice and Criminology	M
English	M
History	M
Psychology—General	M

WESTMINSTER CHOIR COLLEGE OF RIDER UNIVERSITY

Music	M

WESTMINSTER COLLEGE (UT)

Communication—General	M
Counseling Psychology	M
Writing	M

WESTMINSTER SEMINARY CALIFORNIA

Religion	P,M
Theology	P,M

WESTMINSTER THEOLOGICAL SEMINARY

Missions and Missiology	P,M,D,O
Pastoral Ministry and Counseling	P,M,D,O
Religion	P,M,D,O
Theology	P,M,D,O

WEST TEXAS A&M UNIVERSITY

Agricultural Economics and Agribusiness	M

Art/Fine Arts	M
Communication—	
General	M
Criminal Justice and	
Criminology	M
Economics	M
English	M
History	M
Interdisciplinary Studies	M
Music	M
Political Science	M
Psychology—General	M

WEST VIRGINIA STATE UNIVERSITY

Media Studies	M

WEST VIRGINIA UNIVERSITY

African Studies	M,D
African-American Studies	M,D
Agricultural Economics and Agribusiness	M
American Studies	M,D
Applied Social Research	M
Art History	M
Art/Fine Arts	M
Asian Studies	M,D
Child and Family Studies	M
Clinical Psychology	M,D
Communication—	
General	M,D
Corporate and Organizational Communication	M,D
Counseling Psychology	D
Developmental Psychology	M,D
Economic Development	M,D
Economics	M,D
English	M,D
Forensic Sciences	M,D
French	M
Geographic Information Systems	M,D
Geography	M,D
Graphic Design	M
History of Science and Technology	M,D
History	M,D
Human Development	M,D
Industrial and Labor Relations	M
International Affairs	M,D
International Economics	M,D
Journalism	M
Latin American Studies	M,D
Liberal Studies	M
Linguistics	M
Music	M,D
Political Science	M,D
Psychology—General	M,D
Public Administration	M
Public Policy	M,D
Rehabilitation Counseling	M
Sociology	M
Spanish	M
Sport Psychology	M,D
Sustainable Development	D
Theater	M
Urban and Regional Planning	M,D
Writing	M

WHEATON COLLEGE

American Studies	M
Archaeology	M
Clinical Psychology	M,D
Cultural Studies	M,O
Missions and Missiology	M,O
Pastoral Ministry and Counseling	M,D
Psychology—General	M,D
Religion	M
Theology	M,D

WHEELOCK COLLEGE

Child and Family Studies	M
Human Development	M

WHITTIER COLLEGE

Child Development	M

WICHITA STATE UNIVERSITY

Anthropology	M
Art/Fine Arts	M
Clinical Psychology	M,D
Communication—	
General	M
Criminal Justice and Criminology	M
Economics	M
English	M
Gerontology	M
History	M
Liberal Studies	M
Music	M
Political Science	M
Psychology—General	M,D
Public Administration	M
School Psychology	M,D,O
Social Psychology	M,D
Sociology	M
Spanish	M
Writing	M

WIDENER UNIVERSITY

Clinical Psychology	D*
Criminal Justice and Criminology	M
Liberal Studies	M
Psychology—General	
Public Administration	M

WILFRID LAURIER UNIVERSITY

Archaeology	M
Classics	M
Cognitive Sciences	M,D
Communication—	
General	M
Cultural Studies	M
Developmental Psychology	M,D
Economics	M
English	M,D
Ethics	P,M,D,O
Film, Television, and Video Theory and Criticism	M,D
Geography	M,D
History	M,D
International Affairs	M,D
Pastoral Ministry and Counseling	P,M,D,O
Philosophy	M
Political Science	M

Psychology—General	M,D
Public Policy	M
Religion	M,D
Social Psychology	M,D
Sociology	M
Theology	P,M,D,O
Therapies—Dance, Drama, and Music	M

WILKES UNIVERSITY

Writing	M

WILLAMETTE UNIVERSITY

Public Administration	M

WILLIAM CAREY UNIVERSITY

Counseling Psychology	M
Psychology—General	M

WILLIAM PATERSON UNIVERSITY OF NEW JERSEY

Art/Fine Arts	M
Clinical Psychology	M
Communication—	
General	M
Counseling Psychology	M
English	M
History	M
Media Studies	M
Music	M
Public Policy	M
Sociology	M

WILLIAMS COLLEGE

Art History	M

WILLIAM WOODS UNIVERSITY

Agricultural Economics and Agribusiness	M,O

WILMINGTON UNIVERSITY

Criminal Justice and Criminology	M
Gerontology	M
Homeland Security	M
Internet and Interactive Multimedia	M
Public Administration	M
Social Psychology	M

WINEBRENNER THEOLOGICAL SEMINARY

Theology	P,M,D

WINONA STATE UNIVERSITY

English	M

WINSTON-SALEM STATE UNIVERSITY

Rehabilitation Counseling	M

WINTHROP UNIVERSITY

Art/Fine Arts	M
Arts Administration	M
English	M
History	M
Liberal Studies	M
Music	M

Psychology—General	M,O
Spanish	M

WISCONSIN SCHOOL OF PROFESSIONAL PSYCHOLOGY

Clinical Psychology	M,D
Psychology—General	M,D

WOODBURY UNIVERSITY

Architecture	M

WORCESTER POLYTECHNIC INSTITUTE

Interdisciplinary Studies	M,D,O
Social Sciences	M,D,O

WORCESTER STATE COLLEGE

History	M
School Psychology	M,O
Spanish	M

WRIGHT INSTITUTE

Clinical Psychology	D
Counseling Psychology	M
Psychology—General	D

WRIGHT STATE UNIVERSITY

Applied Economics	M
Clinical Psychology	D
Criminal Justice and Criminology	M
Economics	M
English	M
History	M
Humanities	M
Industrial and Organizational Psychology	M,D
Interdisciplinary Studies	M
Music	M
Psychology—General	M,D
Public Administration	M
Rehabilitation Counseling	M
Rhetoric	M
Urban Studies	M
Writing	M

WYCLIFFE COLLEGE

Religion	P,M,D,O
Theology	P,M,D,O

XAVIER UNIVERSITY

Clinical Psychology	M,D
Criminal Justice and Criminology	M
English	M
Experimental Psychology	M,D
Industrial and Organizational Psychology	M,D
Psychology—General	M,D
Theology	M

XAVIER UNIVERSITY OF LOUISIANA

Pastoral Ministry and Counseling	M
Theology	M

*M—master's degree; P—first professional degree; D—doctorate; O—other advanced degree; *—Close-Up and/or Announcement or Display*

YALE UNIVERSITY

African Studies	M
African-American Studies	D
American Studies	D
Anthropology	M,D
Applied Arts and Design—General	M
Archaeology	M,D
Architecture	M
Art History	D
Art/Fine Arts	M
Asian Languages	D
Asian Studies	M
Classics	M,D
Clinical Psychology	D
Cognitive Sciences	D
Comparative Literature	D
Developmental Psychology	D
East European and Russian Studies	M,D
Economic Development	M
Economics	M,D
English	M,D
Environmental Design	M
Film, Television, and Video Theory and Criticism	D
French	M,D
German	D
Graphic Design	M
History of Medicine	M,D
History of Science and Technology	M,D
History	M,D
International Affairs	M
International Economics	M
Italian	D
Latin American Studies	D
Linguistics	D
Medieval and Renaissance Studies	M,D
Music	M,D,O
Near and Middle Eastern Languages	M,D
Near and Middle Eastern Studies	M,D
Philosophy	D
Photography	M
Political Science	D
Portuguese	D
Psychology—General	D
Religion	D
Russian	D
Slavic Languages	D
Social Psychology	D
Social Sciences	M,D
Sociology	D
Spanish	D
Theater	M,D,O
Theology	P,M

YESHIVA BETH MOSHE

Theology	O

YESHIVA KARLIN STOLIN RABBINICAL INSTITUTE

Theology	O

YESHIVA OF NITRA RABBINICAL COLLEGE

Theology	

YESHIVA SHAAR HATORAH TALMUDIC RESEARCH INSTITUTE

Theology	

YESHIVATH ZICHRON MOSHE

Theology	O

YESHIVA TORAS CHAIM TALMUDICAL SEMINARY

Theology	

YESHIVA UNIVERSITY

Clinical Psychology	D
Counseling Psychology	M
Health Psychology	D
Jewish Studies	M,D
Psychology—General	M,D
School Psychology	D

YORK UNIVERSITY

Anthropology	M,D
Applied Arts and Design—General	M
Art History	M,D
Art/Fine Arts	M,D
Communication—General	M,D
Dance	M
Disability Studies	M,D
Economics	M,D
Emergency Management	M
English	M,D
Film, Television, and Video Production	M,D
French	M
Geography	M,D
History	M,D
Humanities	M,D
Industrial and Labor Relations	M,D
Interdisciplinary Studies	M
International Affairs	M
Linguistics	M,D
Music	M,D
Philosophy	M,D
Political Science	M,D
Psychology—General	M,D
Public Administration	M,D
Public Affairs	M
Public Policy	M
Social Sciences	M
Sociology	M,D
Theater	M,D
Translation and Interpretation	M
Women's Studies	M,D

YOUNGSTOWN STATE UNIVERSITY

Counseling Psychology	M
Criminal Justice and Criminology	M
Economics	M
English	M
History	M
Music	M
Psychology—General	M
School Psychology	M

ACADEMIC AND PROFESSIONAL
PROGRAMS IN ARTS AND ARCHITECTURE

Section 1
Applied Arts and Design

This section contains a directory of institutions offering graduate work in applied arts and design, followed by in-depth entries submitted by institutions that chose to prepare detailed program descriptions. Additional information about programs listed in the directory but not augmented by an in-depth entry may be obtained by writing directly to the dean of a graduate school or chair of a department at the address given in the directory.

For programs offering related work, see also in this book *Architecture* and *Art and Art History.* In another guide in this series: **Graduate Programs in Business, Education, Health, Information Studies, Law & Social Work**

See *Advertising and Public Relations*

CONTENTS

Program Directories

Applied Arts and Design—General	92
Computer Art and Design	96
Graphic Design	99
Illustration	102
Industrial Design	103
Interior Design	104
Medical Illustration	107
Photography	107
Textile Design	112

Close-Ups

Art Center College of Design	115
Fashion Institute of Technology	117
Illinois Institute of Technology	119
Miami International University of Art & Design	121
The New School: A University	
Design and Technology	123
Interior Design	125
Photography	127
New York School of Interior Design	129
Southern Illinois University Carbondale	131

See also:

California College of the Arts—Art, Architecture, Design, and Writing	207
Columbia University—Film, Theater Arts, Visual Arts, and Writing	285
Cranbrook Academy of Art—Fine Arts and Architecture	209
Memphis College of Art—Studio Practice and Art Education	213
The New School: A University—Lighting Design	153
Pratt Institute—Art and Design	219
San Francisco Art Institute—Fine Arts	221
Savannah College of Art and Design—Art and Design	223
School of the Art Institute of Chicago—Graduate Studies in Art	225
Syracuse University—Public Communications	705
The University of the Arts—Graduate Studies	233

Applied Arts and Design—General

Academy of Art University, Graduate Program, School of Advertising, San Francisco, CA 94105-3410. Offers MFA. Part-time programs available. Postbaccalaureate distance learning degree programs offered (no on-campus study). *Faculty:* 4 full-time (2 women), 22 part-time/adjunct (3 women). *Students:* 161 full-time (88 women), 58 part-time (39 women); includes 16 African Americans, 15 Asian Americans or Pacific Islanders, 11 Hispanic Americans, 83 international. Average age 28. 73 applicants. In 2008, 29 master's awarded. *Degree requirements:* For master's, thesis, final review. *Entrance requirements:* For master's, minimum GPA of 3.0, portfolio. *Application deadline:* For fall admission, 9/7 for domestic and international students; for spring admission, 2/2 for domestic and international students. Applications are processed on a rolling basis. Application fee: $100 ($500 for international students). Electronic applications accepted. *Expenses:* Tuition: Full-time $18,400; part-time $770 per term. Tuition and fees vary according to program. *Financial support:* Fellowships, career-related internships or fieldwork and Federal Work-Study available. Support available to part-time students. Financial award application deadline: 8/10; financial award applicants required to submit FAFSA. *Unit head:* Melinda Mettler, Director, 800-544-ARTS, E-mail: mmettler@academyart.edu. *Application contact:* 800-544-ARTS, Fax: 415-263-4130, E-mail: info@academyart.edu.

Alfred University, Graduate School, New York State College of Ceramics, School of Art and Design, Alfred, NY 14802-1205. Offers ceramic art (MFA); electronic integrated arts (MFA); glass art (MFA); sculpture (MFA). *Accreditation:* NASAD. *Degree requirements:* For master's, exhibit. *Entrance requirements:* For master's, portfolio. Additional exam requirements/recommendations for international students: Required—TOEFL (minimum score 550 paper-based; 213 computer-based; 80 iBT), IELTS (minimum score 6). Electronic applications accepted. *Faculty research:* Ceramic sculpture, functional ceramics, wood, mixed media, hot and cold glass.

Arizona State University, Graduate College, College of Design, Program in Design, Tempe, AZ 85287. Offers arts/media/engineering (MSD); healthcare and healing environments (MSD); industrial design (MSD); interaction design (MSD); interior design (MSD); new product innovation (MSD); visual communication design (MSD). *Accreditation:* NASAD. *Degree requirements:* For master's, thesis optional. *Entrance requirements:* For master's, GRE General Test, design portfolio.

Art Center College of Design, Graduate Division, Pasadena, CA 91103-1999. Offers MFA, MS. *Accreditation:* NASAD. *Degree requirements:* For master's, thesis, studio project. *Entrance requirements:* For master's, portfolio. Additional exam requirements/recommendations for international students: Required—TOEFL (minimum score 100 iBT). *Faculty research:* Computer graphics, automobile aerodynamics.

See Close-Up on page 115.

Bowling Green State University, Graduate College, College of Arts and Sciences, School of Art, Bowling Green, OH 43403. Offers 2-D studio art (MA, MFA); 3-D studio art (MA, MFA); art education (MA); art history (MA); computer art (MA); design (MFA); digital arts (MFA); graphics (MFA). *Accreditation:* NASAD. Part-time programs available. *Degree requirements:* For master's, thesis or alternative, final exhibit (MFA). *Entrance requirements:* For master's, GRE General Test (MA), slide portfolio (15-20 slides). Additional exam requirements/recommendations for international students: Required—TOEFL. Electronic applications accepted. *Faculty research:* Computer animation and virtual reality, Spanish still-life painting from 1600 to 1800, art and psychotherapy, Japanese wood-firing techniques in ceramics, non-toxic printmaking technologies.

Bradley University, Graduate School, Slane College of Communications and Fine Arts, Department of Art, Peoria, IL 61625-0002. Offers ceramics (MA, MFA); drawing/illustration (MA, MFA); interdisciplinary art (MA, MFA); painting (MA, MFA); photography (MA, MFA); printmaking (MA, MFA); sculpture (MA, MFA); visual communication and design (MA, MFA). *Accreditation:* NASAD. Part-time programs available. *Degree requirements:* For master's, comprehensive exam, thesis, final exhibit. *Entrance requirements:* For master's, portfolio, 2 letters of recommendation. Additional exam requirements/recommendations for international students: Required—TOEFL (minimum score 550 paper-based; 213 computer-based; 79 iBT).

California College of the Arts, Graduate Programs, Program in Design, San Francisco, CA 94107. Offers MFA. *Degree requirements:* For master's, thesis, exhibit. *Entrance requirements:* For master's, appropriate bachelor's degree, portfolio, resumé, letters of recommendation. Additional exam requirements/recommendations for international students: Required—TOEFL (minimum score 600 paper-based; 250 computer-based). Electronic applications accepted.

See Close-Up on page 207.

California College of the Arts, Graduate Programs, Program in Design Strategy, San Francisco, CA 94107. Offers MBA.

California Institute of the Arts, School of Art, Valencia, CA 91355-2340. Offers art (MFA, Adv C); graphic design (MFA, Adv C); photography (MFA, Adv C). *Accreditation:* NASAD (one or more programs are accredited). *Degree requirements:* For master's, final project. *Entrance requirements:* For master's, portfolio. Additional exam requirements/recommendations for international students: Required—TOEFL. Electronic applications accepted.

California State University, Fresno, Division of Graduate Studies, College of Arts and Humanities, Department of Art and Design, Fresno, CA 93740-8027. Offers art (MA). Part-time and evening/weekend programs available. *Degree requirements:* For master's, thesis or alternative. *Entrance requirements:* For master's, GRE General Test, minimum GPA of 3.0, portfolio. Additional exam requirements/recommendations for international students: Required—TOEFL. Electronic applications accepted. *Faculty research:* Art history, graphic design, studio art.

California State University, Fullerton, Graduate Studies, College of the Arts, Department of Art, Fullerton, CA 92834-9480. Offers art (MA, MFA), including ceramics (MFA), crafts, creative photography (MFA), design (MFA), drawing and painting, printmaking (MFA), sculpture; art history (MA); design (MA). *Accreditation:* NASAD (one or more programs are accredited). Part-time programs available. *Students:* 56 full-time (33 women), 29 part-time (15 women); includes 24 minority (2 African Americans, 1 American Indian/Alaska Native, 11 Asian Americans or Pacific Islanders, 10 Hispanic Americans), 7 international. Average age 34. 74 applicants, 34% accepted, 20 enrolled. In 2008, 28 master's awarded. *Degree requirements:* For master's, project or thesis. *Entrance requirements:* For master's, minimum GPA of 2.5 in last 60 units of course work, portfolio. Application fee: $55. Tuition and fees vary according to degree level. *Financial support:* Career-related internships or fieldwork, Federal Work-Study, institutionally sponsored loans, and scholarships/grants available. Support available to part-time students. Financial award application deadline: 3/1. *Unit head:* Larry Johnson, Chair, 657-278-3471. *Application contact:* Al Ching, Adviser, 657-278-3471.

California State University, Los Angeles, Graduate Studies, College of Arts and Letters, Department of Art, Los Angeles, CA 90032-8530. Offers art (MA), including art education, art history, art therapy, ceramics, metals, and textiles, design (MA, MFA), painting, sculpture, and graphic arts, photography; fine arts (MFA), including crafts, design (MA, MFA), studio arts. *Accreditation:* NASAD (one or more programs are accredited). Part-time and evening/weekend programs available. *Faculty:* 16 full-time (6 women). *Students:* 23 full-time (14 women), 52 part-time (37 women); includes 29 minority (2 African Americans, 3 American Indian/Alaska Native, 7 Asian Americans or Pacific Islanders, 17 Hispanic Americans), 4 international. Average age 38. 30 applicants, 100% accepted, 14 enrolled. In 2008, 15 master's awarded. *Degree requirements:* For master's, comprehensive exam, project or thesis. *Entrance requirements:* For master's, portfolio. Additional exam requirements/recommendations for international students: Required—TOEFL (minimum score 500 paper-based; 173 computer-based). *Application deadline:* For fall admission, 6/15 for domestic students, 5/1 for international students; for winter admission, 11/1 for domestic students, 9/1 for international students; for spring admission, 2/1 for domestic students, 10/1 for international students. Applications are processed on a rolling basis. Application fee: $55. Electronic applications accepted. *Expenses:* Tuition, nonresident: part-time $226 per credit. Required fees: $4019. *Financial support:* Federal Work-Study available. Support available to part-time students. Financial award application deadline: 3/1. *Faculty research:* The artist and the book, conceptual art, ceramic processes, computer graphics, architectural graphics. *Unit head:* Dr. Robert Martin, Chair, 323-343-4010, Fax: 323-343-4045, E-mail: rjmartin@calstatela.edu. *Application contact:* Dr. Jose L. Galvan, Dean of Graduate Studies, 323-343-3820, Fax: 323-343-5653, E-mail: jgalvan@cslanet.calstatela.edu.

Cardinal Stritch University, College of Arts and Sciences, Department of Art, Milwaukee, WI 53217-3985. Offers visual studies (MA). Part-time and evening/weekend programs available. *Degree requirements:* For master's, thesis, portfolio, exhibit. *Entrance requirements:* For master's, minimum GPA of 2.75; 3 letters of recommendation.

Carnegie Mellon University, College of Fine Arts, School of Design, Program in Design, Pittsburgh, PA 15213-3891. Offers PhD. *Accreditation:* NASAD. *Degree requirements:* For doctorate, one foreign language, comprehensive exam, thesis/dissertation. *Entrance requirements:* For doctorate, GRE, portfolio of relevant work. Additional exam requirements/recommendations for international students: Required—TOEFL (minimum score 600 paper-based; 250 computer-based). *Faculty research:* Design theory, typography and information design, new product development, organizational behavior, interaction design.

Concordia University, School of Graduate Studies, Faculty of Fine Arts, Department of Design and Computation Arts, Montréal, QC H3G 1M8, Canada. Offers digital technologies in design art practice (Certificate).

Cranbrook Academy of Art, Graduate School, Program in Fine Arts, Bloomfield Hills, MI 48303-0801. Offers ceramics (MFA); design (MFA), including graphic design; fiber arts (MFA); metalsmithing (MFA); painting (MFA); photography (MFA); printmaking (MFA); sculpture (MFA). *Accreditation:* NASAD. *Degree requirements:* For master's, thesis, exhibit. *Entrance requirements:* Additional exam requirements/recommendations for international students: Required—TOEFL (minimum score 550 paper-based; 213 computer-based).

See Close-Up on page 209.

Drexel University, College of Media Arts and Design, Philadelphia, PA 19104-2875. Offers design (MS), including digital media, fashion design, interior design, television management; media arts (MS); performing arts (MS), including arts administration; MS/MBA. *Accreditation:* NASAD. Part-time and evening/weekend programs available. *Entrance requirements:* For master's, interview. Additional exam requirements/recommendations for international students: Required—TOEFL. Electronic applications accepted. *Expenses:* Contact institution.

Emily Carr Institute of Art + Design, Program in Applied Arts, Vancouver, BC V6H 3R9, Canada. Offers design (MAA); media arts (MAA); visual arts (MAA). *Degree requirements:* For master's, internship. *Entrance requirements:* For master's, minimum overall GPA of 3.0, visual portfolio, 3 letters of recommendation. Additional exam requirements/recommendations for international students: Required—TOEFL (minimum score 570 paper-based; 230 computer-based; 84 iBT), IELTS (minimum score 6.5), Michigan English language Assessment Battery (minimum score of 81). Electronic applications accepted.

Fashion Institute of Technology, School of Graduate Studies, New York, NY 10001-5992. Offers MA, MPS. *Accreditation:* NASAD. Part-time and evening/weekend programs available. *Degree requirements:* For master's, one foreign language, thesis, internship. *Entrance requirements:* For master's, GRE or GMAT, portfolio, letters of recommendation, resumé, transcripts. Additional exam requirements/recommendations for international students: Required—TOEFL (minimum score 550 paper-based; 213 computer-based). Electronic applications accepted. *Faculty research:* Fashion history, material conservation, international marketing and global sourcing, sustainable economic development, luxury braiding in China.

See Close-Up on page 117.

Ferris State University, Kendall College of Art and Design, Big Rapids, MI 49307. Offers MFA. *Accreditation:* NASAD. Part-time programs available. *Degree requirements:* For master's, thesis, seminars. *Entrance requirements:* For master's, portfolio, 3 letters of recommendation, curriculum vitae. Additional exam requirements/recommendations for international students: Required—TOEFL (minimum score 500 paper-based; 173 computer-based; 61 iBT).

Florida Atlantic University, Dorothy F. Schmidt College of Arts and Letters, Department of Visual Arts and Art History, Boca Raton, FL 33431-0991. Offers art education (MAT); ceramics (MFA); computer art (MFA); graphic design (MFA); painting (MFA). *Faculty:* 23 full-time (12 women), 17 part-time/adjunct (11 women). *Students:* 15 full-time (10 women), 7 part-time (5 women); includes 6 minority (1 African American, 5 Hispanic Americans), 3 international. Average age 31. 30 applicants, 20% accepted, 3 enrolled. In 2008, 8 master's awarded. *Degree requirements:* For master's, one foreign language, project. *Entrance requirements:* For master's, GRE General Test, minimum GPA of 3.0 during last 60 hours of course work, slide portfolio. *Application deadline:* For fall admission, 2/21 for domestic and international students; for spring admission, 10/1 for domestic and international students. Application fee: $30. Electronic applications accepted. *Expenses:* Tuition, state resident: full-time $4867; part-time $270.40 per credit hour. Tuition, nonresident: full-time $16,486; part-time $915.87 per credit hour. *Financial support:* Research assistantships with full tuition reimbursements, teaching assistantships with full tuition reimbursements, career-related internships or fieldwork, Federal Work-Study, and institutionally sponsored loans available. Financial award applicants required to submit FAFSA. *Faculty research:* Painting, ceramics (traditional and non-traditional), installation, video and interactive sculpture. *Unit head:* Dr. Linda Johnson, Chair, 561-297-3870, Fax: 561-297-3078, E-mail: ljohnson@fau.edu. *Application contact:* James A Novak, Associate Professor/Graduate Coordinator/Advisor, 561-297-2430, Fax: 561-297-3078, E-mail: jnovak@fau.edu.

Howard University, Graduate School, Division of Fine Arts, Department of Art, Program in Fine Arts, Washington, DC 20059-0002. Offers 3D reality (sculpture and ceramics) (MFA); design (MFA); electronic studio (MFA); painting (MFA); photography (MFA). *Accreditation:* NASAD. *Degree requirements:* For master's, comprehensive exam, thesis, exhibit. *Entrance requirements:* For master's, minimum GPA of 3.0, portfolio.

Illinois Institute of Technology, Graduate College, Institute of Design, Chicago, IL 60616-3793. Offers M Des, MSDM, PhD. *Faculty:* 10 full-time (1 woman), 11 part-time/adjunct (1 woman). *Students:* 115 full-time (70 women), 30 part-time (11 women); includes 28 minority (2 African Americans, 23 Asian Americans or Pacific Islanders, 3 Hispanic Americans), 45 international. Average age 31. 183 applicants, 64% accepted, 51 enrolled. In 2008, 56 master's, 1 doctorate awarded. Terminal master's awarded for partial completion of doctoral program. *Degree requirements:* For master's, comprehensive exam; for doctorate, 2 foreign languages, comprehensive exam, thesis/dissertation. *Entrance requirements:* For master's, GRE General Test or GMAT; for doctorate, GRE General Test, master's degree in design, portfolio (MSDM degree). Additional exam requirements/recommendations for international students: Required—TOEFL (minimum score 600 paper-based; 250 computer-based; 100 iBT). *Application deadline:* For fall admission, 2/15 priority date for domestic students, 2/15 for international students; for spring admission, 10/15 priority date for domestic students, 10/15 for international students. Application fee: $75. *Financial support:* In 2008–09, fellowships (averaging $5,400 per year), research assistantships (averaging $10,000 per year), teaching assistantships (averaging $10,000 per year) were awarded; career-related internships or fieldwork, Federal Work-Study, institutionally sponsored loans, scholarships/grants, health care benefits, and unspecified assistantships also available. Support available to part-time students. Financial award applicants required to submit FAFSA. *Faculty research:* Design planning, human-centered design, new product definition, interactive systems, context-sensitive design. *Unit head:* Rachel Williams Smothers, Director of Admissions and Retention, 312-808-4900, Fax: 312-808-4901, E-mail: rachels@iit.edu. *Application contact:* Rachel Williams Smothers, Director of Admissions and Retention, 312-808-4900, Fax: 312-808-4901, E-mail: rachels@iit.edu.

See Close-Up on page 119.

Indiana University–Purdue University Indianapolis, Herron School of Art and Design, Indianapolis, IN 46202-2896. Offers art education (MAE); furniture design (MFA); printmaking (MFA); sculpture (MFA); visual communication (MFA). *Accreditation:* NASAD. Part-time and evening/weekend programs available. *Entrance requirements:* For master's, portfolio, 44 hours of course work in art history and studio art. Electronic applications accepted.

Iowa State University of Science and Technology, Graduate College, College of Design, Department of Art and Design, Ames, IA 50011. Offers art and design (MA); graphic design (MFA); integrated visual arts (MFA); interior design (MFA). Part-time programs available. *Faculty:* 34 full-time (20 women), 2 part-time/adjunct (both women). *Students:* 27 full-time (19 women), 23 part-time (17 women); includes 2 minority (1 African American, 1 Asian American or Pacific Islander), 16 international. 40 applicants, 65% accepted, 18 enrolled. In 2008, 11 master's awarded. *Degree requirements:* For master's, thesis (for some programs). *Entrance requirements:* For master's, GRE General Test, resumé, supplemental departmental form. Additional exam requirements/recommendations for international students: Required—TOEFL (minimum score 550 paper-based; 79 iBT), IELTS (6.5) or TOEFL. *Application deadline:* For fall admission, 5/1 priority date for domestic and international students. Applications are processed on a rolling basis. Application fee: $30 ($70 for international students). Electronic applications accepted. *Expenses:* Tuition, area resident: Full-time $6446; part-time $359 per credit. Tuition, state resident: full-time $6446; part-time $359 per credit. Tuition, nonresident: full-time $17,330; part-time $963 per credit. Required fees: $790; $249.25 per semester. Tuition and fees vary according to course load and program. *Financial support:* In 2008–09, 22 research assistantships with full and partial tuition reimbursements (averaging $14,130 per year), 1 teaching assistantship with full and partial tuition reimbursement (averaging $14,130 per year) were awarded; career-related internships or fieldwork, Federal Work-Study, institutionally sponsored loans, and tuition waivers (partial) also available. Support available to part-time students. Financial award application deadline: 2/15; financial award applicants required to submit FAFSA. *Faculty research:* Computer applications, fire safety, human factors in design, art and design education, fine arts, craft design. *Unit head:* Roger Baer, Chair, 515-294-6724, Fax: 515-294-2725, E-mail: artdn@iastate.edu. *Application contact:* Roger Baer, Chair, 515-294-6724, Fax: 515-294-2725, E-mail: artdn@iastate.edu.

Lamar University, College of Graduate Studies, College of Fine Arts and Communication, Department of Art, Beaumont, TX 77710. Offers art history (MA); photography (MA); studio art (MA); visual design (MA). Part-time and evening/weekend programs available. *Faculty:* 7 full-time (3 women). *Students:* 1 (woman) full-time. Average age 45. 2 applicants, 0% accepted. In 2008, 2 master's awarded. *Degree requirements:* For master's, thesis. *Entrance requirements:* For master's, GRE General Test, minimum GPA of 2.5 in last 60 hours of undergraduate course work. Additional exam requirements/recommendations for international students: Required—TOEFL. *Application deadline:* For fall admission, 8/1 priority date for domestic students; for spring admission, 12/1 for domestic students. Applications are processed on a rolling basis. Application fee: $25 ($50 for international students). *Expenses:* Tuition, state resident: full-time $5000; part-time $195 per credit. Tuition, nonresident: full-time $12,376; part-time $476 per credit. Required fees: $1570. *Financial support:* Fellowships, career-related internships or fieldwork, Federal Work-Study, and scholarships/grants available. Financial award application deadline: 4/1. *Faculty research:* Nineteenth century academic paintings, metal casting, pigment color stability, computer-modified photography, manipulated photography. *Unit head:* Donna M. Meeks, Chair, 409-880-8141, Fax: 409-880-1799, E-mail: meeksdm@lub002.lamar.edu. *Application contact:* Debbie Piper, Coordinator of Graduate Admissions, 409-880-8356, Fax: 409-880-8414, E-mail: gradmissions@hal.lamar.edu.

Louisiana State University and Agricultural and Mechanical College, Graduate School, College of Art and Design, Baton Rouge, LA 70803. Offers M Arch, MA, MFA, MLA. *Accreditation:* ASLA (one or more programs are accredited); NASAD (one or more programs are accredited). Part-time programs available. *Degree requirements:* For master's, thesis. *Entrance requirements:* For master's, GRE General Test, minimum GPA of 3.0. Additional exam requirements/recommendations for international students: Required—TOEFL (minimum score 550 paper-based; 213 computer-based; 79 iBT). Electronic applications accepted. *Faculty research:* Creative studio work, site design, computer applications, historic preservation, energy conservation.

Louisiana Tech University, Graduate School, College of Liberal Arts, School of Art, Ruston, LA 71272. Offers art and graphic design (MFA); photography (MFA); studio art (MFA). *Accreditation:* NASAD. Part-time programs available. *Degree requirements:* For master's, exhibit. *Entrance requirements:* For master's, GRE General Test, portfolio.

Massachusetts College of Art and Design, Graduate Programs, Program in Fine Arts, Boston, MA 02115-5882. Offers ceramics (MFA); design (MFA); fibers (MFA); film (MFA); glass (MFA); media and performing arts (MFA); metals (MFA); painting (MFA); photography (MFA); printmaking (MFA); sculpture (MFA). *Accreditation:* NASAD. *Faculty:* 10 full-time (5 women), 8 part-time/adjunct (6 women). *Students:* 83 full-time (53 women), 17 part-time (10 women); includes 8 minority (1 American Indian/Alaska Native, 4 Asian Americans or Pacific Islanders, 3 Hispanic Americans), 15 international. Average age 34. 295 applicants, 24% accepted, 40 enrolled. In 2008, 37 master's awarded. *Degree requirements:* For master's, thesis, exhibit. *Entrance requirements:* For master's, 12 units of course work in art history, portfolio, resumé, college transcripts, statement of purpose, letters of reference, interview. Additional exam requirements/recommendations for international students: Required—TOEFL (minimum score 563 paper-based; 223 computer-based; 85 iBT); Recommended—IELTS (minimum score 6.5). *Application deadline:* For fall admission, 1/15 for domestic and international students; for spring admission, 11/1 for domestic students. Application fee: $75. *Expenses:* Tuition, area resident: Full-time $17,100; part-time $570 per credit. Tuition and fees vary according to program. *Financial support:* In 2008–09, 50 research assistantships (averaging $2,000 per year), 30 teaching assistantships (averaging $2,000 per year) were awarded; career-related internships or fieldwork, Federal Work-Study, and clerical/technical assistantships also available. Support available to part-time students. Financial award application deadline: 5/1; financial award applicants required to submit FAFSA. *Unit head:* George Creamer, Director, 617-879-7163, Fax: 617-879-7171, E-mail: creamer@massart.edu. *Application contact:* George Creamer, Director, 617-879-7163.

Memphis College of Art, Graduate Programs, Memphis, TN 38104-2764. Offers art education (MA, MAT); computer arts (MFA); studio art (MFA), including painting, photography, printmaking, sculpture. *Accreditation:* NASAD. Part-time programs available. *Faculty:* 25 full-time (13 women), 4 part-time/adjunct (2 women). *Students:* 19 full-time (10 women), 62 part-time (41 women); includes 18 minority (15 African Americans, 1 Asian American or Pacific Islander, 2 Hispanic Americans). Average age 29. 74 applicants, 59% accepted, 24 enrolled. In 2008, 4 master's awarded. *Degree requirements:* For master's, thesis. *Entrance requirements:* For master's, portfolio, interview, resumé. Additional exam requirements/recommendations for international students: Required—TOEFL (minimum score 525 paper-based; 195 computer-based). *Application deadline:* For fall admission, 3/1 priority date for domestic and international students; for spring admission, 11/1 priority date for domestic and international students. Application fee: $50. Electronic applications accepted. *Expenses:* Tuition: Full-time $22,000; part-time $958 per credit hour. Required fees: $560; $280 per semester. Tuition and fees vary according to program. *Financial support:* In 2008–09, 5 teaching assistantships with partial tuition reimbursements (averaging $2,000 per year) were awarded; career-related internships or fieldwork, Federal Work-Study, institutionally sponsored loans, scholarships/grants, tuition waivers (partial), unspecified assistantships, and merit awards also available. Support available to part-time students. Financial award application deadline: 8/1; financial award applicants required to submit FAFSA. *Unit head:* Ken Strickland, Vice President for Academic Affairs, 901-272-5100, Fax: 901-272-5104, E-mail: info@mca.edu. *Application contact:* Annette James Moore, Director of Admissions, 800-727-1088, Fax: 901-272-5158, E-mail: info@mca.edu.

See Close-Up on page 213.

Minneapolis College of Art and Design, Program in Visual Studies, Minneapolis, MN 55404-4347. Offers animation (MFA); comic art (MFA); drawing (MFA); filmmaking (MFA); fine arts (MFA); furniture design (MFA); graphic design (MFA); illustration (MFA); interactive media (MFA); painting (MFA); photography (MFA); printmaking (MFA); sculpture (MFA). *Accreditation:* NASAD. Part-time programs available. *Faculty:* 23 full-time (7 women), 9 part-time/adjunct (4 women). *Students:* 40 full-time (21 women), 1 (woman) part-time; includes 1 minority (American Indian/Alaska Native). Average age 27. 172 applicants, 24% accepted, 15 enrolled. In 2008, 7 master's awarded. *Degree requirements:* For master's, thesis, thesis exhibit. *Entrance requirements:* For master's, portfolio, resumé, 3 letters of recommendation, personal statement. Additional exam requirements/recommendations for international students: Required—TOEFL (minimum score 550 paper-based; 213 computer-based; 79 iBT). *Application deadline:* For fall admission, 1/15 for domestic and international students. Application fee: $50. Electronic applications accepted. *Expenses:* Tuition: Full-time $28,400; part-time $813 per credit. *Financial support:* In 2008–09, 23 students received support, including 15 teaching assistantships (averaging $6,000 per year); career-related internships or fieldwork, Federal Work-Study, scholarships/grants, and unspecified assistantships also available. Support available to part-time students. Financial award application deadline: 3/15; financial award applicants required to submit FAFSA. *Faculty research:* Visual arts. *Unit head:* Carole Fisher, Graduate Director, 612-874-3629, E-mail: carole_fisher@mcad.edu. *Application contact:* William Mullen, Vice President of Enrollment Management, 612-874-3762, Fax: 612-874-3701, E-mail: william_mullen@mcad.edu.

New Mexico State University, Graduate School, College of Arts and Sciences, Department of Art, Las Cruces, NM 88003-8001. Offers art history (MA); ceramics (MA, MFA); design (MA, MFA); drawing (MFA); metals (MA, MFA); painting (MFA); photography (MFA); printmaking (MA, MFA); sculpture (MA, MFA). *Faculty:* 12 full-time (7 women), 2 part-time/adjunct (1 woman). *Students:* 31 full-time (14 women), 3 part-time (all women); includes 8 minority (1 American Indian/Alaska Native, 7 Hispanic Americans), 1 international. Average age 33. 30 applicants, 40% accepted, 9 enrolled. In 2008, 7 master's awarded. *Degree requirements:* For master's, comprehensive exam (for some programs), thesis, thesis exhibit. *Entrance requirements:* For master's, portfolio, 10-page paper (art history). *Application deadline:* For fall admission, 2/15 for domestic students; for winter admission, 10/15 for domestic students; for spring admission, 7/15 for domestic students. Application fee: $30 ($50 for international students). Electronic applications accepted. *Expenses:* Tuition, area resident: Full-time $3890; part-time $212.85 per credit. Tuition, state resident: full-time $3890; part-time $212.85 per credit. Tuition, nonresident: full-time $13,916; part-time $630.55 per credit. Required fees: $1218; $609 per semester. *Financial support:* In 2008–09, 33 students received support, including 29 teaching assistantships (averaging $9,807 per year); research assistantships, Federal Work-Study and health care benefits also available. Support available to part-time students. Financial award application deadline: 3/1; financial award applicants required to submit FAFSA. *Faculty research:* Painting, graphic design, sculpture, printmaking, drawing, ceramics, photo, jewelry. *Unit head:* Spencer D. Fidler, Head, 575-646-1705, Fax: 575-646-8036, E-mail: sfidler@nmsu.edu. *Application contact:* Elena Luna, Coordinator, 575-646-3498, Fax: 575-646-7721, E-mail: rosluna@nmsu.edu.

The New School: A University, Parsons The New School for Design, New York, NY 10003. Offers M Arch, MA, MFA. *Accreditation:* NASAD (one or more programs are accredited). *Faculty:* 47 full-time (18 women), 182 part-time/adjunct (66 women). *Students:* 344 full-time (215 women), 82 part-time (69 women); includes 65 minority (11 African Americans, 1 American Indian/Alaska Native, 42 Asian Americans or Pacific Islanders, 11 Hispanic Americans), 114 international. Average age 28. 1,068 applicants, 47% accepted, 177 enrolled. In 2008, 152 master's awarded. *Entrance requirements:* Additional exam requirements/recommendations for international students: Required—TOEFL (minimum score 580 paper-based; 237 computer-based; 93 iBT). *Application deadline:* For fall admission, 3/1 priority date for domestic students. Applications are processed on a rolling basis. Application fee: $50. *Expenses:* Tuition: Full-time $27,144; part-time $1508 per credit. Required fees: $355 per semester. *Financial support:* Fellowships with partial tuition reimbursements, research assistantships with partial tuition reimbursements, teaching assistantships with partial tuition reimbursements, Federal Work-Study, scholarships/grants, and tuition waivers (partial) available. Financial award application deadline: 3/1; financial award applicants required to submit FAFSA. *Unit head:* Dean. *Application contact:* David Norris, Director of Admissions, 212-229-8989, Fax: 212-229-8975, E-mail: norrisd@newschool.edu.

New York University, Tisch School of the Arts Asia, Singapore, NY 248923, Singapore. Offers animation and digital arts (MFA); dramatic writing (MFA); film production (MFA). *Entrance requirements:* Additional exam requirements/recommendations for international students: Required—TOEFL (minimum score 610 paper-based; 250 computer-based; 105 iBT). Electronic applications accepted.

New York University, Tisch School of the Arts, Department of Design for Stage and Film, New York, NY 10012-1019. Offers MFA. *Degree requirements:* For master's, thesis. *Entrance requirements:* For master's, interview, portfolio. Additional exam requirements/recommendations for international students: Required—TOEFL (minimum score 620 paper-based; 260 computer-based; 105 iBT), IELTS. Electronic applications accepted.

North Carolina State University, Graduate School, College of Design, Program in Art and Design, Raleigh, NC 27695. Offers MAD. *Degree requirements:* For master's, thesis optional. Electronic applications accepted.

North Carolina State University, Graduate School, College of Design, Program in Design, Raleigh, NC 27695. Offers PhD. *Degree requirements:* For doctorate, thesis/dissertation. *Entrance requirements:* For doctorate, GRE. Electronic applications accepted. *Faculty research:* Design and cognition, children's environments, community design, ecological design, sustainable communities and urban spatial development.

NSCAD University, Program in Fine Arts, Halifax, NS B3J 3J6, Canada. Offers craft (MFA); design (M Des); fine and media arts (MFA). *Degree requirements:* For master's, thesis, exhibit. *Entrance requirements:* For master's, portfolio, at least 5 art history classes. Additional exam requirements/recommendations for international students: Required—Michigan English Language Assessment Battery (minimum score: 80), CanTEST (minimum score: 4.5), CAEL (minimum score: 70); Recommended—TOEFL (minimum score 575 paper-based; 233 computer-based; 90 iBT), IELTS (minimum score 6.5).

Oklahoma State University, College of Human Environmental Sciences, Department of Design, Housing and Merchandising, Stillwater, OK 74078. Offers MS, PhD. Postbaccalaureate distance learning degree programs offered. *Faculty:* 19 full-time (15 women), 3 part-time/adjunct (all women). *Students:* 13 full-time (8 women), 23 part-time (21 women); includes 3 minority (1 African American, 2 Asian Americans or Pacific Islanders), 17 international. Average age 31. 15 applicants, 67% accepted, 6 enrolled. In 2008, 8 master's awarded. *Degree requirements:* For master's, thesis (for some programs); for doctorate, comprehensive exam, thesis/dissertation. *Entrance requirements:* For master's and doctorate, GRE or GMAT. Additional exam requirements/recommendations for international students: Required—TOEFL. *Application deadline:* For fall admission, 3/1 priority date for international students; for spring admission, 8/1 priority date for international students. Applications are processed on a rolling basis. Application fee: $40 ($75 for international students). Electronic applications accepted. *Expenses:*

Applied Arts and Design—General

Oklahoma State University (continued)

Tuition, state resident: full-time $3716.40; part-time $154.85 per credit hour. Tuition, nonresident: full-time $14,448; part-time $602 per credit hour. Required fees: $1772.40; $73.85 per credit hour. One-time fee: $50. Tuition and fees vary according to course load and campus/location. *Financial support:* In 2008–09, 18 research assistantships (averaging $10,775 per year), 8 teaching assistantships (averaging $11,595 per year) were awarded; career-related internships or fieldwork, Federal Work-Study, scholarships/grants, health care benefits, tuition waivers (partial), and unspecified assistantships also available. Support available to part-time students. Financial award application deadline: 3/1; financial award applicants required to submit FAFSA. *Faculty research:* Environmental sciences design, housing and merchandising, creativity and physical environment; product development, production and evaluation; experimental learning and critical thinking, technology strategies and assessment, customer expectation and satisfaction. *Unit head:* Dr. Randall Russ, Interim Head, 405-744-5049, Fax: 405-744-6910. *Application contact:* Dr. Gordon Emslie, Dean, 405-744-6368, Fax: 405-744-0355, E-mail: grad_i@okstate.edu.

Pratt Institute, School of Art and Design, Brooklyn, NY 11205-3899. Offers MFA, MID, MPS, MS, Adv C, MS/MFA, MS/MS. *Accreditation:* NASAD (one or more programs are accredited). Part-time programs available. *Faculty:* 41 full-time (17 women), 200 part-time/adjunct (99 women). *Students:* 937 full-time (713 women), 53 part-time (43 women); includes 142 minority (40 African Americans, 3 American Indian/Alaska Native, 60 Asian Americans or Pacific Islanders, 39 Hispanic Americans), 331 international. Average age 28. 1,553 applicants, 44% accepted, 334 enrolled. In 2008, 381 master's awarded. *Degree requirements:* For master's, thesis. *Entrance requirements:* Additional exam requirements/recommendations for international students: Required—TOEFL (minimum score 550 paper-based; 213 computer-based). *Application deadline:* For fall admission, 2/1 for domestic and international students; for spring admission, 10/1 for domestic and international students. Application fee: $50 ($90 for international students). Electronic applications accepted. *Expenses:* Tuition: Full-time $20,412; part-time $1134 per credit. Required fees: $1190; $1190 per year. *Financial support:* Career-related internships or fieldwork, Federal Work-Study, institutionally sponsored loans, scholarships/grants, health care benefits, and unspecified assistantships available. Support available to part-time students. Financial award application deadline: 2/1; financial award applicants required to submit FAFSA. *Faculty research:* Painting, sculpture, and printmaking; package, interior, and communications design; art therapy; graphic and industrial design; four-dimensional design. *Unit head:* Concetta Stewart, Chairperson. *Application contact:* Young Hah, Director of Graduate Admissions, 718-636-3683, Fax: 718-399-4242, E-mail: yhah@pratt.edu.

See Close-Up on page 219.

Purdue University, Graduate School, College of Liberal Arts, Department of Visual and Performing Arts, West Lafayette, IN 47907. Offers art and design (MA); theatre (MA, MFA). *Accreditation:* NASAD; NAST. Part-time programs available. *Degree requirements:* For master's, terminal exhibit, project, or thesis. *Entrance requirements:* Additional exam requirements/recommendations for international students: Required—TOEFL. Electronic applications accepted. *Faculty research:* Design, fine arts, photography, acting, directing, theatre technology.

Rhode Island School of Design, Graduate Studies, Providence, RI 02903-2784. Offers M Arch, MA, MAT, MFA, MIA, MID, MLA. *Accreditation:* NASAD (one or more programs are accredited). *Degree requirements:* For master's, thesis, exhibit. *Entrance requirements:* For master's, portfolio, 3 letters of recommendation. Additional exam requirements/recommendations for international students: Required—TOEFL (minimum score 580 paper-based; 237 computer-based), IELTS (minimum score 6.5). Electronic applications accepted. *Faculty research:* Ceramics, glass, graphic design, sculpture, jewelry/metalsmithing, photography, painting, industrial design, architecture.

Rutgers, The State University of New Jersey, New Brunswick, Mason Gross School of the Arts, Department of Theater Arts, Piscataway, NJ 08854-8097. Offers acting (MFA); design (MFA); directing (MFA); playwriting (MFA); stage management (MFA). *Degree requirements:* For master's, thesis (for some programs), performance project. *Entrance requirements:* For master's, audition, interview, portfolio. Electronic applications accepted. *Faculty research:* Faculty of working professional.

San Diego State University, Graduate and Research Affairs, College of Professional Studies and Fine Arts, School of Art, Design and Art History, San Diego, CA 92182. Offers art history (MA); studio arts (MA, MFA), including applied design, environmental design, graphic design, interior design, painting and printmaking, sculpture. *Accreditation:* NASAD (one or more programs are accredited). *Degree requirements:* For master's, variable foreign language requirement, thesis. *Entrance requirements:* For master's, GRE General Test, bachelor's degree in related field, slide portfolio, typed slide information sheet, 2 letters of recommendation. Additional exam requirements/recommendations for international students: Required—TOEFL. Electronic applications accepted.

San Francisco Art Institute, Graduate Program, Department of Design and Technology, San Francisco, CA 94133. Offers MFA, Certificate. Part-time programs available. *Degree requirements:* For master's and Certificate, oral reviews. *Entrance requirements:* For master's and Certificate, portfolio. Additional exam requirements/recommendations for international students: Required—TOEFL (minimum score 580 paper-based; 237 computer-based). Electronic applications accepted.

San Jose State University, Graduate Studies and Research, College of Humanities and the Arts, School of Art and Design, San Jose, CA 95192-0001. Offers art education (MA); art history (MA); digital media (MFA); digital media in art history and education (MA); photography (MFA); pictorial arts (MFA); spatial arts (MFA). *Accreditation:* NASAD (one or more programs are accredited). *Entrance requirements:* For master's, GRE. Electronic applications accepted.

Savannah College of Art and Design, Graduate School, Savannah, GA 31402-3146. Offers advertising design (MA, MFA); animation (MA, MFA); architectural history (MA, MFA); architecture (M Arch); art history (MA, MFA); arts administration (MA); broadcast design (MA, MFA); cinema studies (MA); commercial photography (MA); digital photography (MA); documentary photography (MA); fashion (MA, MFA); fibers (MA, MFA); film and television (MA, MFA); furniture design (MA, MFA); graphic design (MA, MFA); historic preservation (MA, MFA); illustration (MA, MFA); illustration design (MA); industrial design (MA, MFA); interactive design and game development (MA, MFA); interior design (MA, MFA); metals and jewelry (MA, MFA); painting (MA, MFA); performing arts (MA, MFA); photography (MA, MFA); printmaking (MA, MFA); production design (MA, MFA); professional education (MA); professional writing (MFA); sculpture (MA, MFA); sequential art (MA, MFA); sound design (MA, MFA); urban design and development (MA); visual effects (MA, MFA). Part-time programs available. Postbaccalaureate distance learning degree programs offered (no on-campus study). *Degree requirements:* For master's, thesis, internship. *Entrance requirements:* For master's, interview, 3 letters of recommendation. Additional exam requirements/recommendations for international students: Required—TOEFL (minimum score 500 paper-based; 133 computer-based). Electronic applications accepted. *Expenses:* Tuition: Full-time $28,215; part-time $3135 per course. One-time fee: $500. *Faculty research:* Urban planning for diverse communities, photovoltaics-powered environmental control, computer-aided design and virtual reality, multimedia design.

See Close-Up on page 223.

School of the Art Institute of Chicago, Graduate Division, Department of Architecture, Interior Architecture, and Designed Objects, Program in Designed Objects, Chicago, IL 60603-3103. Offers M Des. *Entrance requirements:* Additional exam requirements/recommendations for international students: Required—TOEFL, IELTS.

See Close-Up on page 225.

School of the Art Institute of Chicago, Graduate Division, Department of Architecture, Interior Architecture, and Designed Objects, Program in Design for Emerging Technologies, Chicago, IL 60603-3103. Offers MFA. *Entrance requirements:* Additional exam requirements/recommendations for international students: Required—TOEFL, IELTS.

See Close-Up on page 225.

School of the Art Institute of Chicago, Graduate Division, Department of Architecture, Interior Architecture, and Designed Objects, Program in Interior Architecture, Chicago, IL 60603-3103. Offers M Arc. *Entrance requirements:* Additional exam requirements/recommendations for international students: Required—TOEFL, IELTS.

See Close-Up on page 225.

School of Visual Arts, Graduate Programs, Design Department, New York, NY 10010-3994. Offers MFA. *Accreditation:* NASAD. *Degree requirements:* For master's, final review, project or thesis. *Entrance requirements:* For master's, portfolio. Additional exam requirements/recommendations for international students: Required—TOEFL (minimum score 550 paper-based; 213 computer-based; 79 iBT). Electronic applications accepted. *Expenses:* Contact institution.

School of Visual Arts, Graduate Programs, Program in Design Criticism, New York, NY 10010-3994. Offers MFA.

Southern Illinois University Carbondale, Graduate School, College of Liberal Arts, School of Art and Design, Carbondale, IL 62901-4701. Offers ceramics (MFA); drawing (MFA); fiber/weaving (MFA); glass (MFA); jewelry (MFA); metalsmithing/blacksmithing (MFA); painting (MFA); printmaking (MFA); sculpture (MFA). *Accreditation:* NASAD. *Degree requirements:* For master's, thesis or alternative. *Entrance requirements:* For master's, minimum GPA of 2.7, portfolio, slides. Additional exam requirements/recommendations for international students: Required—TOEFL. *Faculty research:* Prints/woodcuts, foundry, watercolor.

See Close-Up on page 131.

Stephen F. Austin State University, Graduate School, College of Fine Arts, School of Art, Nacogdoches, TX 75962. Offers art (MA); design (MFA); drawing (MFA); painting (MFA); sculpture (MFA). *Accreditation:* NASAD. Part-time programs available. *Degree requirements:* For master's, comprehensive exam, thesis, exhibit. *Entrance requirements:* For master's, GRE General Test, portfolio. Additional exam requirements/recommendations for international students: Required—TOEFL. *Faculty research:* Printmaking, jewelry, photography, ceramics, art history.

Suffolk University, New England School of Art and Design, Boston, MA 02108-2770. Offers graphic design (MA); interior design (MA). *Accreditation:* CIDA; NASAD. Part-time and evening/weekend programs available. *Entrance requirements:* For master's, art portfolio, interview, statement of professional goals, official transcripts, 2 letters of recommendation, resumé. Additional exam requirements/recommendations for international students: Required—TOEFL (minimum score 550 paper-based; 213 computer-based; 80 iBT). Electronic applications accepted. *Expenses:* Contact institution. *Faculty research:* Adaptive re-use of historical structures, universal design, American architecture history, interior design to reduce inefficiency, meditation SPA.

Sul Ross State University, School of Arts and Sciences, Department of Fine Arts and Communication, Alpine, TX 79832. Offers art education (M Ed); art history (M Ed); studio art (M Ed), including ceramics, design, drawing, jewelry, painting, printmaking, sculpture, weaving. Part-time programs available. *Degree requirements:* For master's, oral or written exam. *Entrance requirements:* For master's, GRE General Test, minimum GPA of 2.5 in last 60 hours of undergraduate work. *Faculty research:* Ceramic sculpture, watercolor, wood sculpture, rock art.

Syracuse University, Graduate School, College of Visual and Performing Arts, Program in Art Video, Syracuse, NY 13244. Offers MFA. *Accreditation:* NASAD. Part-time programs available. Postbaccalaureate distance learning degree programs offered (no on-campus study). *Degree requirements:* For master's, thesis or alternative. *Entrance requirements:* For master's, portfolio. Additional exam requirements/recommendations for international students: Required—TOEFL. Electronic applications accepted.

University of Alberta, Faculty of Graduate Studies and Research, Department of Art and Design, Edmonton, AB T6G 2E1, Canada. Offers drawing (MFA); history of art, design, and visual culture (MA); industrial design (M Des); painting (MFA); printmaking (MFA); sculpture (MFA); visual communication design (M Des). *Degree requirements:* For master's, thesis. *Entrance requirements:* For master's, portfolio (MFA and MDES). Additional exam requirements/recommendations for international students: Required—TOEFL (minimum score 550 paper-based; 213 computer-based).

University of Baltimore, Graduate School, The Yale Gordon College of Liberal Arts, Program in Integrated Design, Baltimore, MD 21201-5779. Offers MFA. Part-time and evening/weekend programs available. *Faculty:* 6 full-time (3 women), 10 part-time/adjunct (6 women). *Students:* 13 full-time (8 women), 17 part-time (8 women); includes 1 minority (African American), 3 international. Average age 34. 37 applicants, 65% accepted, 21 enrolled. In 2008, 12 master's awarded. *Entrance requirements:* Additional exam requirements/recommendations for international students: Required—TOEFL (minimum score 550 paper-based; 213 computer-based). *Application deadline:* For fall admission, 7/15 for domestic students; for spring admission, 12/15 for domestic students. Applications are processed on a rolling basis. Application fee: $30. Electronic applications accepted. *Expenses:* Contact institution. *Financial support:* In 2008–09, 2 fellowships with full tuition reimbursements (averaging $15,000 per year) were awarded. Financial award application deadline: 4/1; financial award applicants required to submit FAFSA. *Faculty research:* Information and graphics design, economics, hypermedia communications. *Unit head:* Dr. Edwin Gold, Co-Director, 410-837-6022, E-mail: egold@ubalt.edu. *Application contact:* Kevin Nies, Assistant Director, Office of Graduate Admission, 410-837-6565, E-mail: knies@ubalt.edu.

University of California, Berkeley, Graduate Division, College of Environmental Design, Department of Architecture, Program in Design, Berkeley, CA 94720-1500. Offers MA. *Degree requirements:* For master's, thesis. *Entrance requirements:* For master's, GRE General Test, minimum GPA of 3.0, portfolio, 3 letters of recommendation. Additional exam requirements/recommendations for international students: Required—TOEFL.

University of California, Los Angeles, Graduate Division, School of the Arts and Architecture, Department of Design/Media Arts, Los Angeles, CA 90095. Offers MFA. *Degree requirements:* For master's, comprehensive exam. *Entrance requirements:* For master's, portfolio, 20 slides and/or videotape, minimum GPA of 3.0. Additional exam requirements/recommendations for international students: Required—TOEFL. Electronic applications accepted. *Expenses:* Tuition, nonresident: full-time $14,694. Required fees: $9669.50. Full-time tuition and fees vary according to course load, degree level, program and student level.

University of Central Oklahoma, College of Graduate Studies and Research, College of Arts, Media, and Design, Department of Design and Interior Design, Edmond, OK 73034-5209. Offers MFA. Part-time programs available. Postbaccalaureate distance learning degree programs offered (minimal on-campus study). *Entrance requirements:* Additional exam requirements/recommendations for international students: Required—TOEFL (minimum score 550 paper-based; 213 computer-based). Electronic applications accepted.

University of Cincinnati, Graduate School, College of Design, Architecture, Art, and Planning, School of Design, Cincinnati, OH 45221. Offers fashion design (M Des); graphic design (M Des); industrial design (M Des); interaction design (M Des); product development (M Des). *Accreditation:* NASAD. *Degree requirements:* For master's, thesis. *Entrance requirements:* For master's, undergraduate degree in design or related field, 2 years of work experience in design or related field. Additional exam requirements/recommendations for international students: Required—TOEFL. Electronic applications accepted. *Faculty research:* Design theory, interdisciplinary design topics.

University of Delaware, College of Arts and Sciences, Department of Art, Newark, DE 19716. Offers MA, MFA. *Degree requirements:* For master's, exposition paper final exhibition. *Entrance requirements:* For master's, portfolio of creative work. Electronic applications accepted. *Faculty research:* Painting, printmaking, ceramics, photography, sculpture.

University of Idaho, College of Graduate Studies, College of Art and Architecture, Department of Art and Design, Moscow, ID 83844-2282. Offers art (MAT, MFA). *Accreditation:* NASAD. *Faculty:* 7 full-time. *Students:* 14 full-time, 9 part-time. Average age 33. In 2008, 6 master's awarded. *Degree requirements:* For master's, thesis (for some programs). *Entrance requirements:* For master's, minimum GPA of 2.8. *Application deadline:* For fall admission, 8/1 for domestic students; for spring admission, 12/15 for domestic students. Application fee: $55 ($60 for international students). *Expenses:* Tuition, nonresident: full-time $10,080; part-time $336 per credit. Required fees: $5212; $267 per credit. Tuition and fees vary according to program. *Financial support:* Research assistantships, teaching assistantships available. Financial award application deadline: 2/15. *Faculty research:* Information design. *Unit head:* William Woolston, Chair, 208-885-7837. *Application contact:* William Woolston, Chair, 208-885-7837.

University of Illinois at Urbana–Champaign, Graduate College, College of Fine and Applied Arts, School of Art and Design, Champaign, IL 61820. Offers Ed M, MA, MFA, PhD. *Accreditation:* NASAD. *Faculty:* 46 full-time (21 women), 5 part-time/adjunct (1 woman). *Students:* 89 full-time (62 women), 18 part-time (14 women); includes 11 minority (1 African American, 1 American Indian/Alaska Native, 7 Asian Americans or Pacific Islanders, 2 Hispanic Americans), 25 international. 190 applicants, 15% accepted, 27 enrolled. In 2008, 18 master's, 5 doctorates awarded. *Entrance requirements:* For master's, minimum GPA of 3.0. *Application deadline:* Applications are processed on a rolling basis. Application fee: $60 ($75 for international students). Electronic applications accepted. *Financial support:* In 2008–09, 25 fellowships, 26 research assistantships, 61 teaching assistantships were awarded; tuition waivers (full and partial) also available. *Unit head:* Nan Goggin, Interim Director, 217-333-0855, Fax: 217-244-7688, E-mail: goggin@illinois.edu. *Application contact:* Marsha Biddle, Assistant to the Associate Director, 217-333-0642, Fax: 217-244-7688, E-mail: mbiddle@uiuc.edu.

The University of Kansas, Graduate Studies, School of Architecture, Design, and Planning, Department of Design, Program in Design, Lawrence, KS 66045. Offers MA, MFA. *Faculty:* 29. *Students:* 17 full-time (8 women), 1 (woman) part-time. Average age 31. 30 applicants, 40% accepted, 9 enrolled. In 2008, 7 master's awarded. *Degree requirements:* For master's, thesis, gallery exhibition, oral exam. *Entrance requirements:* For master's, portfolio, 3 letters of recommendation, minimum GPA of 3.0, statement of design philosophy. Additional exam requirements/recommendations for international students: Required—TOEFL (minimum score 570 paper-based; 230 computer-based), IELTS. *Application deadline:* For fall admission, 2/1 for domestic and international students; for spring admission, 10/15 for domestic students. Application fee: $55 ($60 for international students). Electronic applications accepted. *Expenses:* Tuition, area resident: Full-time $6122; part-time $255.10 per credit hour. Tuition, state resident: full-time $6122; part-time $255.10 per credit hour. Tuition, nonresident: full-time $14,629; part-time $609.55 per credit hour. Required fees: $847; $70.56 per credit hour. Tuition and fees vary according to course load and program. *Financial support:* Fellowships, teaching assistantships with full tuition reimbursements, Federal Work-Study, scholarships/grants, and unspecified assistantships available. Financial award application deadline: 2/1; financial award applicants required to submit FAFSA. *Faculty research:* Ceramics, metalsmithing and jewelry, textiles, scenography. *Unit head:* Prof. Gregory Thomas, Chairperson, 785-864-4401. *Application contact:* Gina Westergard, Director, 785-864-4401, Fax: 785-864-4404, E-mail: ginaw@ku.edu.

University of Kentucky, Graduate School, College of Design, Lexington, KY 40506-0032. Offers M Arch, MAIDM, MHP, MSIDM. *Entrance requirements:* For master's, GRE, minimum GPA of 2.75. Additional exam requirements/recommendations for international students: Required—TOEFL (minimum score 550 paper-based; 213 computer-based). Electronic applications accepted.

University of Massachusetts Dartmouth, Graduate School, College of Visual and Performing Arts, Program in Visual Design, North Dartmouth, MA 02747-2300. Offers digital media (MFA); graphic design (MFA); illustration (MFA); photography (MFA); typography (MFA). *Accreditation:* NASAD. *Faculty:* 17 full-time (8 women), 6 part-time/adjunct (2 women). *Students:* 6 full-time (5 women), 1 (woman) part-time, 1 international. Average age 40. 15 applicants, 27% accepted, 2 enrolled. In 2008, 4 master's awarded. *Degree requirements:* For master's, visual thesis. *Entrance requirements:* For master's, portfolio, interview, minimum GPA of 3.0, 3 letters of recommendation. Additional exam requirements/recommendations for international students: Required—TOEFL (minimum score 500 paper-based). *Application deadline:* For fall admission, 3/1 priority date for domestic students, 1/1 priority date for international students. Applications are processed on a rolling basis. Application fee: $40 ($60 for international students). Electronic applications accepted. *Expenses:* Tuition, state resident: full-time $2071; part-time $86.29 per credit. Tuition, nonresident: full-time $8099; part-time $337.46 per credit. Required fees: $7946. Tuition and fees vary according to class time, course load and reciprocity agreements. *Financial support:* In 2008–09, 1 research assistantship with full tuition reimbursement (averaging $3,940 per year), 4 teaching assistantships with full tuition reimbursements (averaging $3,500 per year) were awarded; Federal Work-Study and unspecified assistantships also available. Support available to part-time students. Financial award application deadline: 3/1; financial award applicants required to submit FAFSA. *Unit head:* Memory Hollowy, Director, 508-999-8554, E-mail: mholloway@umassd.edu. *Application contact:* Elan Turcotte-Shamski, Graduate Admissions Officer, 508-999-8604, Fax: 508-999-8183, E-mail: graduate@umassd.edu.

University of Michigan, Horace H. Rackham School of Graduate Studies, School of Art and Design, Ann Arbor, MI 48109. Offers art and design (MFA). *Accreditation:* NASAD. *Degree requirements:* For master's, thesis, exhibit (MFA), slide lecture. *Entrance requirements:* For master's, portfolio. Additional exam requirements/recommendations for international students: Required—TOEFL, IELTS. Electronic applications accepted. *Faculty research:* Creative expression, commercial design, preparation for teaching.

University of Minnesota, Twin Cities Campus, Graduate School, College of Design, Department of Design, Housing, and Apparel, Minneapolis, MN 55455-0213. Offers apparel (MA, MS, PhD); design communication (MA, MS, PhD); housing studies (MA, MS, PhD, Postbaccalaureate Certificate); interactive design (MFA); interior design (MA, MS, PhD). Part-time programs available. *Degree requirements:* For master's and Postbaccalaureate Certificate, comprehensive exam, thesis (for some programs); for doctorate, comprehensive exam, thesis/dissertation. *Entrance requirements:* For master's, GRE General Test, minimum GPA of 3.0 (preferred), portfolio, 3 letters of recommendation; for doctorate, GRE General Test, minimum GPA of 3.0 (preferred), portfolio, 3 letters of recommendation, writing sample; for Postbaccalaureate Certificate, GRE General Test, minimum GPA of 3.0 (preferred). Additional exam requirements/recommendations for international students: Required—TOEFL (minimum score 550 paper-based; 213 computer-based; 79 iBT). Electronic applications accepted. *Faculty research:* Housing policy and community development; consumer behavior; interactive design; design history; social, cultural, and behavioral issues related to designed environments.

University of North Texas, Robert B. Toulouse School of Graduate Studies, College of Visual Arts and Design, Department of Design, Denton, TX 76203. Offers MFA. *Accreditation:* NASAD. *Degree requirements:* For master's, problem or thesis. *Entrance requirements:* Additional exam requirements/recommendations for international students: Required—proof of English language proficiency; Recommended—TOEFL (minimum score 550 paper-based; 213 computer-based). *Faculty research:* Color, lighting, sustainable design, hand sewing techniques, ethics.

University of Notre Dame, Graduate School, College of Arts and Letters, Division of Humanities, Department of Art, Art History, and Design, Notre Dame, IN 46556. Offers art history (MA); design (MFA), including graphic design, industrial design; studio art (MFA), including ceramics, painting, photography, printmaking, sculpture. *Accreditation:* NASAD. *Faculty:* 19 full-time (6 women), 3 part-time/adjunct (1 woman). *Students:* 23 full-time (12 women); includes 2 minority (both Hispanic Americans), 1 international. 83 applicants, 18% accepted, 10 enrolled. In 2008, 11 master's awarded. *Degree requirements:* For master's, comprehensive exam (for some programs), thesis. *Entrance requirements:* For master's, GRE General Test, minimum GPA of 3.0. Additional exam requirements/recommendations for international students: Required—TOEFL (minimum score 600 paper-based; 250 computer-based; 80 iBT). *Application deadline:* For fall admission, 2/1 priority date for domestic and international students. Application fee: $50. Electronic applications accepted. *Financial support:* In 2008–09, 20 students received support; fellowships with full tuition reimbursements available, research assistantships with full tuition reimbursements available, teaching assistantships with full tuition reimbursements available, scholarships/grants, tuition waivers (full), and unspecified assistantships available. Financial award application deadline: 2/1. *Faculty research:* Studio art practice in ceramics, printing, photography, printmaking and sculpture, graphic design and industrial design, digital imaging in design and photography, Renaissance and American art history, contemporary art theory and criticism. *Unit head:* Prof. Martina Lopez, Director of Graduate Studies, 574-631-7652, E-mail: art.1@nd.edu. *Application contact:* Dr. Barbara Turpin, Director of Graduate Admissions, 574-631-7706, Fax: 574-631-4183.

University of Oklahoma, Graduate College, College of Fine Arts, School of Drama, Norman, OK 73019. Offers acting (MFA); design (MFA); directing (MFA); drama (MA). *Accreditation:* NAST. *Faculty:* 8 full-time (4 women), 1 (woman) part-time/adjunct. *Students:* 12 full-time (7 women); includes 1 minority (Asian American or Pacific Islander), 3 international. 3 applicants, 100% accepted, 3 enrolled. In 2008, 6 master's awarded. *Degree requirements:* For master's, comprehensive exam, thesis (MA), departmental qualifying exam. *Entrance requirements:* For master's, BA with 36 hours in drama, auditions. Additional exam requirements/recommendations for international students: Required—TOEFL (minimum score 550 paper-based; 213 computer-based). *Application deadline:* For fall admission, 6/1 for domestic students, 4/1 for international students; for spring admission, 11/1 for domestic students, 9/1 for international students. Applications are processed on a rolling basis. Application fee: $40 ($90 for international students). Electronic applications accepted. *Expenses:* Tuition, state resident: full-time $3744; part-time $156 per credit hour. Tuition, nonresident: full-time $13,577; part-time $565.70 per credit hour. Required fees: $2415.40; $90.10 per credit hour. *Financial support:* In 2008–09, 5 students received support, including 5 research assistantships with partial tuition reimbursements available (averaging $9,586 per year), 7 teaching assistantships with partial tuition reimbursements available (averaging $9,586 per year); unspecified assistantships also available. Financial award application deadline: 4/7; financial award applicants required to submit FAFSA. *Faculty research:* Directing, costume design, lighting design, dramalurgy. *Unit head:* Dr. Tom Orr, Director, 405-325-4021, Fax: 405-325-0400, E-mail: thorr@ou.edu. *Application contact:* Dr. Judith Pender, Graduate Liaison, 405-325-5319, Fax: 405-325-0400, E-mail: jmpender@ou.edu.

The University of Texas at Austin, Graduate School, College of Fine Arts, Department of Art and Art History, Program in Design, Austin, TX 78712-1111. Offers MFA. *Accreditation:* NASAD. *Degree requirements:* For master's, thesis, oral exam, exhibition. *Entrance requirements:* For master's, minimum GPA of 3.0, portfolio. Electronic applications accepted.

University of Washington, Graduate School, College of Arts and Sciences, School of Art, Division of Design, Seattle, WA 98195. Offers industrial design (MFA); visual communication design (MFA).

University of Wisconsin–Madison, Graduate School, School of Human Ecology, Program in Design Studies, Madison, WI 53706-1380. Offers MFA, MS, PhD. *Degree requirements:* For master's, thesis (for some programs); for doctorate, comprehensive exam, thesis/dissertation. *Entrance requirements:* For master's, portfolio, scholarly paper, 3 letters of recommendation from faculty; for doctorate, letters of recommendation, scholarly paper. Additional exam requirements/recommendations for international students: Required—TOEFL (minimum score 580 paper-based; 237 computer-based). *Faculty research:* Feng shui, material culture, behavior and environment, use of pattern to enhance environment, design visualization.

Virginia Commonwealth University, Graduate School, School of the Arts, Department of Graphic Design, Richmond, VA 23284-9005. Offers design/visual communications (MFA); interior environment (MFA); photography and film (MFA). *Accreditation:* NASAD. *Degree requirements:* For master's, thesis, exhibition. *Entrance requirements:* For master's, portfolio. *Faculty research:* Film, photography, interior environments, visual communication.

Virginia Polytechnic Institute and State University, Graduate School, College of Architecture and Urban Studies, School of Architecture and Design, Blacksburg, VA 24061. Offers architecture (M Arch, MS); architecture design research (PhD). *Accreditation:* NASAD. *Entrance requirements:* For master's, GRE General Test. Additional exam requirements/recommendations for international students: Required—TOEFL (minimum score 550 paper-based; 213 computer-based). Electronic applications accepted. *Faculty research:* Computer applications in design, building technology, architectural design theory, solar/passive energy design, building assembly.

Wayne State University, College of Fine, Performing and Communication Arts, Department of Art and Art History, Program in Design and Merchandising, Detroit, MI 48202. Offers MA. *Degree requirements:* For master's, one foreign language. *Entrance requirements:* Additional exam requirements/recommendations for international students: Required—TOEFL (minimum score 550 paper-based; 213 computer-based); Recommended—TWE (minimum score 6). Electronic applications accepted.

Western Carolina University, Graduate School, College of Fine and Performing Arts, School of Art and Design, Cullowhee, NC 28723. Offers MFA. Part-time programs available. *Degree requirements:* For master's, thesis. *Entrance requirements:* For master's, GRE, appropriate undergraduate, portfolio, letters of recommendation. Additional exam requirements/recommendations for international students: Required—TOEFL (minimum score 550 paper-based; 270 computer-based; 79 iBT). *Faculty research:* Art and society, visual literacy, vernacular cultural studies and oral history, environments for aging, health and leisure.

Western Michigan University, Graduate College, College of Fine Arts, Gwen Frostic School of Art, Kalamazoo, MI 49008-5202. Offers art education (MA); studio design (MFA). *Accreditation:* NASAD (one or more programs are accredited). *Degree requirements:* For master's, thesis or alternative.

Yale University, School of Art, New Haven, CT 06520. Offers graphic design (MFA); painting/printmaking (MFA); photography (MFA); sculpture (MFA). *Degree requirements:* For master's, thesis (for some programs). *Entrance requirements:* Additional exam requirements/recommendations for international students: Required—TOEFL (minimum score 550 paper-based; 250 computer-based; 100 iBT). *Expenses:* Contact institution.

York University, Faculty of Graduate Studies, Faculty of Fine Arts, Program in Design, Toronto, ON M3J 1P3, Canada. Offers M Des. Electronic applications accepted.

Computer Art and Design

Academy of Art University, Graduate Program, School of Web Design and New Media, San Francisco, CA 94105-3410. Offers MFA. Part-time and evening/weekend programs available. *Faculty:* 3 full-time (2 women), 11 part-time/adjunct (4 women). *Students:* 181 full-time (104 women), 129 part-time (76 women); includes 66 minority (18 African Americans, 31 Asian Americans or Pacific Islanders, 17 Hispanic Americans), 112 international. Average age 31. 81 applicants. In 2008, 30 master's awarded. *Degree requirements:* For master's, thesis, final review. *Entrance requirements:* For master's, portfolio. *Application deadline:* For fall admission, 9/7 for domestic and international students; for spring admission, 2/2 for domestic students, 9/2 for international students. Applications are processed on a rolling basis. Application fee: $100 ($500 for international students). Electronic applications accepted. *Expenses:* Tuition: Full-time $18,400; part-time $770 per term. Tuition and fees vary according to program. *Financial support:* Career-related internships or fieldwork and Federal Work-Study available. Support available to part-time students. Financial award application deadline: 8/10; financial award applicants required to submit FAFSA. *Unit head:* Lourdes Livingston, Director, 800-544-ARTS, E-mail: info@academyart.edu. *Application contact:* 800-544-ARTS, Fax: 415-263-4130, E-mail: info@academyart.edu.

Alfred University, Graduate School, New York State College of Ceramics, School of Art and Design, Alfred, NY 14802-1205. Offers ceramic art (MFA); electronic integrated arts (MFA); glass art (MFA); sculpture (MFA). *Accreditation:* NASAD. *Degree requirements:* For master's, exhibit. *Entrance requirements:* For master's, portfolio. Additional exam requirements/recommendations for international students: Required—TOEFL (minimum score 550 paper-based; 213 computer-based; 80 iBT), IELTS (minimum score 6). Electronic applications accepted. *Faculty research:* Ceramic sculpture, functional ceramics, wood, mixed media, hot and cold glass.

Arizona State University, Graduate College, College of Design, Program in Design, Tempe, AZ 85287. Offers arts/media/engineering (MSD); healthcare and healing environments (MSD); industrial design (MSD); interaction design (MSD); interior design (MSD); new product innovation (MSD); visual communication design (MSD). *Accreditation:* NASAD. *Degree requirements:* For master's, thesis optional. *Entrance requirements:* For master's, GRE General Test, design portfolio.

Art Center College of Design, Graduate Division, Department of Media Design, Pasadena, CA 91103-1999. Offers MFA. *Accreditation:* NASAD. *Degree requirements:* For master's, thesis, studio project. *Entrance requirements:* For master's, portfolio. Additional exam requirements/recommendations for international students: Required—TOEFL (minimum score 600 paper-based; 250 computer-based; 100 iBT).

See Close-Up on page 115.

Bowling Green State University, Graduate College, College of Arts and Sciences, School of Art, Bowling Green, OH 43403. Offers 2-D studio art (MA, MFA); 3-D studio art (MA, MFA); art education (MA); art history (MA); computer art (MA); design (MFA); digital arts (MFA); graphics (MFA). *Accreditation:* NASAD. Part-time programs available. *Degree requirements:* For master's, thesis or alternative, final exhibit (MFA). *Entrance requirements:* For master's, GRE General Test (MA), slide portfolio (15-20 slides). Additional exam requirements/recommendations for international students: Required—TOEFL. Electronic applications accepted. *Faculty research:* Computer animation and virtual reality, Spanish still-life painting from 1600 to 1800, art and psychotherapy, Japanese wood-firing techniques in ceramics, non-toxic printmaking technologies.

Carnegie Mellon University, College of Fine Arts, School of Design, Program in Interaction Design, Pittsburgh, PA 15213-3891. Offers M Des, PhD. Part-time programs available. *Degree requirements:* For master's, thesis. *Entrance requirements:* For master's, GRE, portfolio of relevant work. Additional exam requirements/recommendations for international students: Required—TOEFL (minimum score 600 paper-based; 250 computer-based). *Faculty research:* Interaction and emotion, visual interface design, robotics, visualization and diagramming, design theory.

The Catholic University of America, School of Architecture and Planning, Washington, DC 20064. Offers M Arch, M Arch Studies. Part-time programs available. *Degree requirements:* For master's, thesis. *Entrance requirements:* For master's, minimum GPA of 2.7, portfolio, 3 letters of recommendation. Additional exam requirements/recommendations for international students: Required—TOEFL (minimum score 500 paper-based; 173 computer-based). Electronic applications accepted. *Expenses:* Contact institution. *Faculty research:* Architectural history, sacred architecture, computers, technology, urban design, preservation.

Chatham University, Program in Film and Digital Technology, Pittsburgh, PA 15232-2826. Offers emerging media (MFA). Part-time and evening/weekend programs available. *Students:* 9 full-time (6 women), 2 part-time (0 women). Average age 35. 16 applicants, 88% accepted, 10 enrolled. *Degree requirements:* For master's, thesis, capstone project. *Entrance requirements:* Additional exam requirements/recommendations for international students: Required—TOEFL (minimum score 600 paper-based; 250 computer-based; 100 iBT), IELTS (minimum score 6.5), TWE. *Application deadline:* For fall admission, 7/1 priority date for domestic students, 6/1 priority date for international students; for spring admission, 12/1 priority date for domestic students, 11/1 priority date for international students. Applications are processed on a rolling basis. Application fee: $45. Electronic applications accepted. *Expenses:* Tuition: Part-time $686 per credit. Tuition and fees vary according to program. *Financial support:* Applicants required to submit FAFSA. *Unit head:* Dr. Prajna Parasher, Director, 412-365-1182, E-mail: parasher@chatham.edu. *Application contact:* Dory Perry, Associate Director of Graduate Admissions, 412-365-2758, Fax: 412-365-1609, E-mail: gradadmissions@chatham.edu.

Claremont Graduate University, Graduate Programs, School of Arts and Humanities, Department of Art, Claremont, CA 91711. Offers digital media (MA, MFA); drawing (MA, MFA); installation (MA, MFA); new genre (MA, MFA); painting (MA, MFA); performance (MA, MFA); photography (MA, MFA); sculpture (MA, MFA). Part-time programs available. *Faculty:* 4 full-time (1 woman), 1 (woman) part-time/adjunct. *Students:* 62 full-time (34 women); includes 12 minority (3 African Americans, 4 Asian Americans or Pacific Islanders, 5 Hispanic Americans), 4 international. Average age 32. In 2008, 29 master's awarded. *Degree requirements:* For master's, final project show. *Entrance requirements:* For master's, BA in art or BFA, slide review. Additional exam requirements/recommendations for international students: Required—TOEFL (minimum score 550 paper-based; 213 computer-based; 80 iBT). *Application deadline:* For fall admission, 2/1 priority date for domestic students. Applications are processed on a rolling basis. Application fee: $60. Electronic applications accepted. *Expenses:* Contact institution. *Financial support:* Fellowships, research assistantships, teaching assistantships, Federal Work-Study, institutionally sponsored loans, and scholarships/grants available. Support available to part-time students. Financial award application deadline: 2/15; financial award applicants required to submit FAFSA. *Faculty research:* Acoustic sculpture, feminization of abstraction, installation sculpture. *Unit head:* David Pagel, Chair, 909-607-2479, Fax: 909-607-1276, E-mail: david.pagel@cgu.edu. *Application contact:* Pat Evans, Program Administrator, 909-607-9292, Fax: 909-607-1276, E-mail: patricia.evans@cgu.edu.

Clemson University, Graduate School, College of Architecture, Arts, and Humanities, Department of Art, Program in Digital Production Arts, Clemson, SC 29634. Offers MFA. *Students:* 16 full-time (5 women), 6 part-time (0 women); includes 4 minority (3 African Americans, 1 Asian American or Pacific Islander), 4 international. Average age 28. 12 applicants, 83% accepted, 8 enrolled. In 2008, 1 master's awarded. *Degree requirements:* For master's, thesis. *Entrance requirements:* For master's, GRE General Test, portfolio. Additional exam requirements/recommendations for international students: Required—TOEFL. *Application deadline:* For fall admission, 4/15 for domestic and international students; for spring admission, 9/15 for international students. Application fee: $55. Full-time tuition and fees vary according to

program. *Financial support:* Fellowships, research assistantships available. *Unit head:* Dr. Michael Vatalaro, Chair, 864-656-3881, E-mail: vatalam@clemson.edu. *Application contact:* Timothy A Davis, Coordinator, 864-656-3891, Fax: 864-656-0204, E-mail: tadavis@cs.clemson.edu.

Concordia University, School of Graduate Studies, Faculty of Fine Arts, Department of Design and Computation Arts, Montréal, QC H3G 1M8, Canada. Offers digital technologies in design art practice (Certificate).

Cornell University, Graduate School, Graduate Fields of Architecture, Art and Planning, Field of Architecture, Ithaca, NY 14853-0001. Offers architectural design (M Arch); architectural science (MS); building technology and environmental science (MS); computer graphics (MS); history of architecture (MA, PhD); history of urban development (MA, PhD); theory and criticism of architecture (M Arch); urban design (M Arch). *Faculty:* 28 full-time (6 women). *Students:* 93 full-time (40 women); includes 13 minority (2 African Americans, 6 Asian Americans or Pacific Islanders, 5 Hispanic Americans), 36 international. Average age 29. 488 applicants, 18% accepted, 53 enrolled. In 2008, 6 master's awarded. *Degree requirements:* For master's, one foreign language, thesis (MA, MS); for doctorate, 2 foreign languages, comprehensive exam, thesis/dissertation. *Entrance requirements:* For master's, GRE General Test, 5-year bachelor's degree in architecture, portfolio (M Arch), 3 letters of recommendation; for doctorate, GRE General Test, 3 letters of recommendation. Additional exam requirements/recommendations for international students: Required—TOEFL (minimum score 600 paper-based; 250 computer-based; 77 iBT). *Application deadline:* For fall admission, 1/15 priority date for domestic students. Application fee: $70. Electronic applications accepted. *Expenses:* Tuition: Full-time $29,500. Required fees: $70. Full-time tuition and fees vary according to degree level, program and student level. *Financial support:* In 2008–09, 16 students received support, including 8 fellowships with full tuition reimbursements available, 1 research assistantship with full tuition reimbursement available, 7 teaching assistantships with full tuition reimbursements available; institutionally sponsored loans, scholarships/grants, health care benefits, tuition waivers (full and partial), and unspecified assistantships also available. Financial award applicants required to submit FAFSA. *Faculty research:* Architectural design and urban design, theory and criticism of architecture, computer graphics, building technology and environmental science, history of architecture and history of urban-development. *Unit head:* Director of Graduate Studies, 607-255-6701, Fax: 607-255-0291. *Application contact:* Graduate Field Assistant, 607-255-6701, Fax: 607-255-0291, E-mail: cuarch@cornell.edu.

DePaul University, College of Computing and Digital Media, Chicago, IL 60604. Offers business information technology (MS); computational finance (MS); computer game development (MS); computer graphics and motion technology (MS); computer science (MS, PhD); computer, information and network security (MS), including applied technology; digital cinema (MFA, MS), including information technology project management (MS); e-commerce technology (MS); human-computer interaction (MS); information systems (MS); information technology (MA); information technology project management (MS); software engineering (MS); telecommunications systems (MS); JD/MS. Part-time and evening/weekend programs available. Post-baccalaureate distance learning degree programs offered (no on-campus study). *Faculty:* 76 full-time (15 women), 182 part-time/adjunct (43 women). *Students:* 966 full-time (254 women), 932 part-time (217 women); includes 429 minority (194 African Americans, 3 American Indian/Alaska Native, 149 Asian Americans or Pacific Islanders, 83 Hispanic Americans), 395 international. Average age 31. 930 applicants, 73% accepted, 319 enrolled. In 2008, 444 master's, 4 doctorates awarded. *Degree requirements:* For master's, thesis (for some programs); for doctorate, comprehensive exam, thesis/dissertation. *Entrance requirements:* For master's, GRE or GMAT (MS in computational finance), bachelor's degree; for doctorate, GRE, master's degree in computer science. Additional exam requirements/recommendations for international students: Required—TOEFL (minimum score 550 paper-based; 213 computer-based), IELTS (minimum score 6.5). *Application deadline:* For fall admission, 8/15 priority date for domestic students, 6/1 priority date for international students; for winter admission, 2/15 priority date for domestic students, 9/15 priority date for international students; for spring admission, 3/1 priority date for domestic students, 12/15 priority date for international students. Applications are processed on a rolling basis. Application fee: $25. Electronic applications accepted. *Expenses:* Contact institution. *Financial support:* In 2008–09, 69 students received support, including 2 fellowships with full tuition reimbursements available (averaging $18,000 per year), 75 teaching assistantships with full and partial tuition reimbursements available (averaging $5,780 per year); research assistantships, Federal Work-Study, scholarships/grants, tuition waivers (full and partial), and unspecified assistantships also available. Support available to part-time students. Financial award application deadline: 4/30; financial award applicants required to submit FAFSA. *Faculty research:* Bioinformatics, visual computing, graphics and animation, high performance and scientific computing, databases. Total annual research expenditures: $790,000. *Unit head:* Dr. David Miller, Dean, 312-362-8381, Fax: 312-362-5185. *Application contact:* Dr. Liz Friedman, Assistant Dean of Student Services, 312-362-8714, Fax: 312-362-5327, E-mail: efriedm2@cdm.depaul.edu.

Digital Media Arts College, Graduate Programs, Boca Raton, FL 33431. Offers graphic design (MFA); special FX animation (MFA).

Drexel University, College of Media Arts and Design, Department of Design, Philadelphia, PA 19104-2875. Offers digital media (MS); fashion design (MS); interior design (MS); television management (MS); MS/MBA. *Degree requirements:* For master's, thesis. *Entrance requirements:* For master's, interview. Additional exam requirements/recommendations for international students: Required—TOEFL. Electronic applications accepted.

East Tennessee State University, School of Graduate Studies, College of Business and Technology, Department of Technology and Geomatics, Johnson City, TN 37614. Offers digital media (MS); engineering technology (MS); industrial arts/technology education (MS). Part-time programs available. *Degree requirements:* For master's, thesis or alternative, final oral exam. *Entrance requirements:* For master's, bachelor's degree in technical or related area, minimum GPA of 3.0. Additional exam requirements/recommendations for international students: Required—TOEFL (minimum score 550 paper-based; 213 computer-based). *Faculty research:* Computer-integrated manufacturing, technology education, CAD/CAM, organizational change.

Emily Carr Institute of Art + Design, Program in Digital Media, Vancouver, BC V5T 1E1, Canada. Offers MDM. *Degree requirements:* For master's, internship. *Entrance requirements:* For master's, portfolio, minimum undergraduate B+ average, 3 reference letters. Additional exam requirements/recommendations for international students: Required—TOEFL (minimum score 86 iBT). Electronic applications accepted.

Florida Atlantic University, Dorothy F. Schmidt College of Arts and Letters, Department of Visual Arts and Art History, Boca Raton, FL 33431-0991. Offers art education (MAT); ceramics (MFA); computer art (MFA); graphic design (MFA); painting (MFA). *Faculty:* 23 full-time (12 women), 17 part-time/adjunct (11 women). *Students:* 15 full-time (10 women), 7 part-time (5 women); includes 6 minority (1 African American, 5 Hispanic Americans), 3 international. Average age 31. 30 applicants, 20% accepted, 3 enrolled. In 2008, 8 master's awarded. *Degree requirements:* For master's, one foreign language, project. *Entrance requirements:* For master's, GRE General Test, minimum GPA of 3.0 during last 60 hours of course work, slide portfolio. *Application deadline:* For fall admission, 2/21 for domestic and international students; for spring admission, 10/1 for domestic and international students. Application fee: $30. Electronic applications accepted. *Expenses:* Tuition, state resident: full-time $4867; part-time $270.40 per credit hour. Tuition, nonresident: full-time $16,486; part-time $915.87 per credit hour. *Financial support:* Research assistantships with full tuition reimbursements, teaching assistantships with full tuition reimbursements, career-related internships or fieldwork, Federal Work-Study, and institutionally sponsored loans available. Financial award applicants required to submit FAFSA. *Faculty research:* Painting, ceramics (traditional and non-traditional), installation, video and interactive sculpture. *Unit head:* Dr. Linda Johnson, Chair, 561-297-3870, Fax: 561-297-3078, E-mail: ljohnson@fau.edu. *Application contact:* James A Novak, Associate Professor/Graduate Coordinator/Advisor, 561-297-2430, Fax: 561-297-3078, E-mail: jnovak@fau.edu.

Georgia Institute of Technology, Graduate Studies and Research, Ivan Allen College of Policy and International Affairs, School of Literature, Communication and Culture, Atlanta, GA 30332-0001. Offers digital media (MS, PhD); human computer interaction (MSHCI). *Degree requirements:* For master's, thesis or alternative. *Entrance requirements:* Additional exam requirements/recommendations for international students: Required—TOEFL. Electronic applications accepted. *Faculty research:* New media studies.

Indiana University Bloomington, School of Informatics, Bloomington, IN 47408. Offers bioinformatics (MS); chemical informatics (MS); computer science (MS, PhD); health informatics (MS); human computer interaction (MS); informatics (PhD); laboratory informatics (MS); media arts and science (MS); music informatics (MS); security informatics (MS); MS/PhD. PhD offered through University Graduate School. Part-time programs available. Postbaccalaureate distance learning degree programs offered (no on-campus study). *Faculty:* 63 full-time (12 women). *Students:* 317 full-time (78 women), 30 part-time (9 women); includes 14 minority (4 African Americans, 8 Asian Americans or Pacific Islanders, 2 Hispanic Americans), 213 international. Average age 28. 680 applicants, 62% accepted, 176 enrolled. In 2008, 77 master's, 10 doctorates awarded. Terminal master's awarded for partial completion of doctoral program. *Degree requirements:* For master's, thesis optional; for doctorate, comprehensive exam, thesis/dissertation, oral and written exams. *Entrance requirements:* For master's and doctorate, GRE, letters of reference. Additional exam requirements/recommendations for international students: Required—TOEFL. *Application deadline:* For fall admission, 1/15 for domestic students, 12/1 for international students. Application fee: $50 ($60 for international students). Electronic applications accepted. *Expenses:* Tuition, area resident: Part-time $291.97 per credit hour. Tuition, state resident: part-time $291.97 per credit hour. Tuition, nonresident: part-time $850.33 per credit hour. Required fees: $110 per semester. Tuition and fees vary according to course load and program. *Financial support:* In 2008–09, 2 fellowships with full and partial tuition reimbursements (averaging $20,000 per year), 41 research assistantships (averaging $14,000 per year), 84 teaching assistantships (averaging $13,000 per year) were awarded; Federal Work-Study, institutionally sponsored loans, scholarships/grants, health care benefits, tuition waivers (full and partial), and unspecified assistantships also available. Support available to part-time students. Total annual research expenditures: $2 million. *Unit head:* Dr. David Leake, Associate Dean for Graduate Studies, 812-855-9756, E-mail: leake@cs.indiana.edu. *Application contact:* Rachel Lawmaster, Manager of Graduate Admissions and Graduate Studies, 812-856-3622, Fax: 812-856-3825, E-mail: raclee@indiana.edu.

International Technological University, Program in Digital Arts, Santa Clara, CA 95050. Offers MA.

Long Island University, Brooklyn Campus, Richard L. Conolly College of Liberal Arts and Sciences, Department of Media Arts, Brooklyn, NY 11201-8423. Offers MA. Part-time and evening/weekend programs available. *Degree requirements:* For master's, integrated thesis project. *Entrance requirements:* For master's, 2 letters of recommendation. Additional exam requirements/recommendations for international students: Required—TOEFL (minimum score 500 paper-based; 173 computer-based). *Faculty research:* Film noir, art and photography, new media/new aesthetic.

Long Island University, C.W. Post Campus, School of Visual and Performing Arts, Department of Theatre, Film, Dance and Arts Management, Brookville, NY 11548-1300. Offers interactive multimedia (MA); theatre (MA). Part-time and evening/weekend programs available. *Degree requirements:* For master's, thesis. *Entrance requirements:* For master's, placement exam. Electronic applications accepted. *Faculty research:* Playwriting, intercultural dance and theatre, translation, Suzuki, set and costume design.

Maryland Institute College of Art, Graduate Studies, Program in Digital Arts, Baltimore, MD 21217. Offers MA. *Degree requirements:* For master's, thesis, exhibit. *Entrance requirements:* For master's, portfolio, 40 studio credits, 6 credits in art history. Additional exam requirements/recommendations for international students: Required—TOEFL (minimum score 550 paper-based; 213 computer-based).

Memphis College of Art, Graduate Programs, Memphis, TN 38104-2764. Offers art education (MA, MAT); computer arts (MFA); studio art (MFA), including painting, photography, printmaking, sculpture. *Accreditation:* NASAD. Part-time programs available. *Faculty:* 25 full-time (13 women), 4 part-time/adjunct (2 women). *Students:* 19 full-time (10 women), 62 part-time (41 women); includes 18 minority (15 African Americans, 1 Asian American or Pacific Islander, 2 Hispanic Americans). Average age 29. 74 applicants, 59% accepted, 24 enrolled. In 2008, 4 master's awarded. *Degree requirements:* For master's, thesis. *Entrance requirements:* For master's, portfolio, interview, resumé. Additional exam requirements/recommendations for international students: Required—TOEFL (minimum score 525 paper-based; 195 computer-based). *Application deadline:* For fall admission, 3/1 priority date for domestic and international students; for spring admission, 11/1 priority date for domestic and international students. Application fee: $50. Electronic applications accepted. *Expenses:* Tuition: Full-time $22,000; part-time $958 per credit hour. Required fees: $560; $280 per semester. Tuition and fees vary according to program. *Financial support:* In 2008–09, 5 teaching assistantships with partial tuition reimbursements (averaging $2,000 per year) were awarded; career-related internships or fieldwork, Federal Work-Study, institutionally sponsored loans, scholarships/grants, tuition waivers (partial), unspecified assistantships, and merit awards also available. Support available to part-time students. Financial award application deadline: 8/1; financial award applicants required to submit FAFSA. *Unit head:* Ken Strickland, Vice President for Academic Affairs, 901-272-5100, Fax: 901-272-5104, E-mail: info@mca.edu. *Application contact:* Annette James Moore, Director of Admissions, 800-727-1088, Fax: 901-272-5158, E-mail: info@mca.edu.

See Close-Up on page 213.

Miami International University of Art & Design, Program in Computer Animation, Miami, FL 33132-1418. Offers MFA. Postbaccalaureate distance learning degree programs offered.

See Close-Up on page 121.

Minneapolis College of Art and Design, Program in Arts, Minneapolis, MN 55404-4347. Offers design (Certificate); fine arts (Certificate); media (Certificate); sustainable design (Certificate). Part-time programs available. Postbaccalaureate distance learning degree programs offered. *Faculty:* 23 full-time (7 women), 9 part-time/adjunct (4 women). *Students:* 32 full-time (15 women), 31 part-time (18 women); includes 5 minority (2 African Americans, 1 American Indian/Alaska Native, 2 Hispanic Americans), 4 international. Average age 24. 172 applicants, 27% accepted, 19 enrolled. In 2008, 15 Certificates awarded. *Degree requirements:* For Certificate, final project. *Entrance requirements:* For degree, resumé, portfolio, letter of recommendation. Additional exam requirements/recommendations for international students: Required—TOEFL (minimum score 550 paper-based; 213 computer-based; 79 iBT). *Application deadline:* For fall admission, 1/15 for domestic and international students. Application fee: $50. Electronic applications accepted. *Expenses:* Tuition: Full-time $28,400; part-time $813 per credit. *Financial support:* Career-related internships or fieldwork and scholarships/grants available. Financial award application deadline: 3/15; financial award applicants required to submit FAFSA. *Faculty research:* Visual arts. *Unit head:* Carole Fisher, Graduate Director, 612-874-3629, E-mail: carole_fisher@mcad.edu. *Application contact:* William Mullen, Vice President, Enrollment Management, 612-874-3762, Fax: 612-874-3701, E-mail: william_mullen@mcad.edu.

Mississippi State University, College of Architecture, Art and Design, Mississippi State, MS 39762. Offers MFA, MS. *Accreditation:* NASAD. *Degree requirements:* For master's, comprehensive exam, thesis, final written and oral exam. *Entrance requirements:* For master's, GRE General Test, portfolio, minimum GPA of 3.0. Additional exam requirements/recommendations for international students: Required—TOEFL. Electronic applications accepted. *Faculty research:* Digital art in architecture, process change and management, multi-media databases, 3-D modeling and animation, virtual archaeology.

National University, Academic Affairs, School of Media and Communication, Department of Media, La Jolla, CA 92037-1011. Offers digital cinema (MFA); educational and instructional technology (MS); video game production and design (MFA). Part-time and evening/weekend programs available. Postbaccalaureate distance learning degree programs offered (no on-campus study). *Faculty:* 9 full-time (3 women), 61 part-time/adjunct (20 women). *Students:* 70 full-time (26 women), 141 part-time (62 women); includes 64 minority (28 African Americans, 1 American Indian/Alaska Native, 10 Asian Americans or Pacific Islanders, 25 Hispanic Americans). Average age 39. 118 applicants, 100% accepted, 118 enrolled. In 2008, 58 master's awarded. *Degree requirements:* For master's, thesis. *Entrance requirements:* For master's, interview, minimum GPA of 2.5. Additional exam requirements/recommendations for international students: Required—TOEFL (minimum score 550 paper-based; 213 computer-based; 79 iBT), IELTS (minimum score 6). *Application deadline:* Applications are processed on a rolling basis. Application fee: $60 ($65 for international students). Electronic applications accepted. *Expenses:* Tuition: Full-time $8694; part-time $322 per credit hour. Tuition and fees vary according to course load. *Financial support:* Career-related internships or fieldwork, institutionally sponsored loans, scholarships/grants, and tuition waivers (partial) available. Support available to part-time students. Financial award application deadline: 6/30; financial award applicants required to submit FAFSA. *Unit head:* Dr. Timothy Langdell, Department Chair, 310-662-2149, Fax: 858-309-3450, E-mail: tlangdell@nu.edu. *Application contact:* Dominick Giovanniello, Associate Regional Dean—San Diego, 800-NAT-UNIV, Fax: 858-541-7792, E-mail: dgiovann@nu.edu.

The New School: A University, Parsons The New School for Design, Program in Design and Technology, New York, NY 10011. Offers MFA. *Accreditation:* NASAD. *Faculty:* 10 full-time (7 women), 40 part-time/adjunct (11 women). *Students:* 147 full-time (83 women), 6 part-time (5 women); includes 34 minority (4 African Americans, 24 Asian Americans or Pacific Islanders, 6 Hispanic Americans), 59 international. Average age 27. In 2008, 54 master's awarded. *Entrance requirements:* For master's, portfolio. Additional exam requirements/recommendations for international students: Required—TOEFL (minimum score 580 paper-based; 237 computer-based; 93 iBT). *Application deadline:* For fall admission, 2/1 priority date for domestic students. Applications are processed on a rolling basis. Application fee: $50. *Expenses:* Tuition: Full-time $27,144; part-time $1508 per credit. Required fees: $355 per semester. *Financial support:* Fellowships with partial tuition reimbursements, research assistantships with partial tuition reimbursements, teaching assistantships with partial tuition reimbursements, Federal Work-Study and scholarships/grants available. Financial award application deadline: 3/1; financial award applicants required to submit FAFSA. *Unit head:* Colleen Macklin, Chair, 212-229-8908 Ext. 4097, E-mail: macklinc@newschool.edu. *Application contact:* Anthony Padilla, Director of Admissions, 212-229-8989 Ext. 4023, Fax: 212-229-8975, E-mail: padillaa@newschool.edu.

See Close-Up on page 123.

New York University, School of Continuing and Professional Studies, Center for Advanced Digital Applications, New York, NY 10012-1019. Offers digital imaging and design (MS). *Degree requirements:* For master's, comprehensive exam, thesis. *Entrance requirements:* For master's, GRE or GMAT (recommended), portfolio, 2 letters of recommendation, resumé, essay. Additional exam requirements/recommendations for international students: Required—TOEFL (minimum score 600 paper-based; 250 computer-based; 100 iBT), TWE. Electronic applications accepted.

New York University, School of Continuing and Professional Studies, Division for Media Industry Studies and Design, Program in Graphic Communications Management and Technology, New York, NY 10012-1019. Offers MA. Part-time and evening/weekend programs available. *Degree requirements:* For master's, project. *Entrance requirements:* For master's, GRE General Test or GMAT (for recent graduates), resumé, 2 letters of recommendation, work experience, essay. Additional exam requirements/recommendations for international students: Required—TOEFL (minimum score 600 paper-based; 250 computer-based; 100 iBT), TWE. Electronic applications accepted. *Faculty research:* Production operations management and marketing, human resources and quality management.

New York University, Tisch School of the Arts Asia, Singapore, NY 248923, Singapore. Offers animation and digital arts (MFA); dramatic writing (MFA); film production (MFA). *Entrance requirements:* Additional exam requirements/recommendations for international students: Required—TOEFL (minimum score 610 paper-based; 250 computer-based; 105 iBT). Electronic applications accepted.

North Carolina State University, Graduate School, College of Humanities and Social Sciences, Program in Communication, Rhetoric, and Digital Media, Raleigh, NC 27695. Offers PhD.

Philadelphia University, School of Design and Media, Program in Digital Design, Philadelphia, PA 19144-5497. Offers MS. *Accreditation:* NASAD. *Entrance requirements:* For master's, portfolio. Additional exam requirements/recommendations for international students: Required—TOEFL (minimum score 550 paper-based; 213 computer-based; 79 iBT). Electronic applications accepted.

Regent University, Graduate School, School of Communication and the Arts, Virginia Beach, VA 23464-9800. Offers acting (MFA); acting and directing (MFA); cinema arts/television arts (MA); communication (MA, PhD); digital media (MA); directing for cinema/TV (MA); journalism (MA); producing for cinema/TV (MA); script and screenwriting (MFA); theatre (MA). Part-time programs available. Postbaccalaureate distance learning degree programs offered (minimal on-campus study). *Faculty:* 26 full-time (3 women), 15 part-time/adjunct (3 women). *Students:* 136 full-time (77 women), 163 part-time (90 women); includes 83 minority (59 African Americans, 3 American Indian/Alaska Native, 5 Asian Americans or Pacific Islanders, 16 Hispanic Americans), 15 international. Average age 32. 230 applicants, 63% accepted, 102 enrolled. In 2008, 53 master's, 16 doctorates awarded. *Degree requirements:* For master's, thesis or alternative; for doctorate, thesis/dissertation. *Entrance requirements:* For master's, GRE General Test or MAT, minimum undergraduate GPA of 3.0, writing sample, computer literacy survey, recommendation, resumé, interview, audition (MFA programs); for doctorate, GRE General Test, minimum graduate GPA of 3.0, writing sample, computer literacy survey, recommendation, interview, transcripts. Additional exam requirements/recommendations for international students: Required—TOEFL (minimum score 577 paper-based; 233 computer-based). *Application deadline:* For fall admission, 3/1 priority date for domestic students; for spring admission, 10/1 priority date for domestic students. Applications are processed on a rolling basis. Application fee: $50. Electronic applications accepted. *Expenses:* Contact institution. *Financial support:* Fellowships with full and partial tuition reimbursements, career-related internships or fieldwork, scholarships/grants, tuition waivers (full and partial), and unspecified assistantships available. Support available to part-time students. Financial award application deadline: 9/1; financial award applicants required to submit FAFSA. *Faculty research:* Southern gospel music, education and entertainment, celebrities and the media, journalism and ethics, C. S. Lewis. *Unit head:* Michael Patrick, Dean, 757-352-4970, Fax: 757-352-4279, E-mail: michpat@regent.edu. *Application contact:* Matthew Chadwick, Director of Admissions, 800-373-5504, Fax: 757-352-4381, E-mail: admissions@regent.edu.

Rensselaer Polytechnic Institute, Graduate School, School of Humanities and Social Sciences, Department of the Arts, Program in Electronic Arts, Troy, NY 12180-3590. Offers MFA, PhD. *Degree requirements:* For master's, thesis, thesis in the form of a large-scale creative project; for doctorate, comprehensive exam, thesis/dissertation, dissertation or creative project and dissertation text. *Entrance requirements:* For master's, portfolio; for doctorate, portfolio, writing sample, evidence of research-based creative orientation. Additional exam requirements/

Computer Art and Design

Rensselaer Polytechnic Institute (continued)
recommendations for international students: Required—TOEFL (minimum score 570 paper-based; 230 computer-based; 88 iBT). Electronic applications accepted. *Faculty research:* Computer music, video art, Net art, interactivity, bio art.

Rhode Island School of Design, Graduate Studies, Program in Digital Media, Providence, RI 02903-2784. Offers MFA. *Entrance requirements:* Additional exam requirements/recommendations for international students: Required—TOEFL (minimum score 580 paper-based; 237 computer-based), IELTS (minimum score 6.5).

Rochester Institute of Technology, Graduate Enrollment Services, College of Imaging Arts and Sciences, School of Design, Program in Computer Graphics Design, Rochester, NY 14623-5603. Offers MFA. *Accreditation:* NASAD. *Degree requirements:* For master's, thesis. *Entrance requirements:* For master's, portfolio, minimum GPA of 3.0. Additional exam requirements/recommendations for international students: Required—TOEFL.

St. Edward's University, School of Management and Business, Area of Digital Media Management, Austin, TX 78704. Offers MBA. *Students:* 23 full-time (11 women); includes 6 minority (1 African American, 5 Hispanic Americans). Average age 26. 28 applicants, 54% accepted, 12 enrolled. In 2008, 12 master's awarded. *Entrance requirements:* For master's, GRE or GMAT, interview, 2 letters of recommendation, minimum GPA of 3.0 in last 60 hours of course work. Additional exam requirements/recommendations for international students: Required—TOEFL (minimum score 550 paper-based; 213 computer-based; 79 iBT). *Application deadline:* For fall admission, 2/15 priority date for domestic and international students. Applications are processed on a rolling basis. Application fee: $45 ($50 for international students). Electronic applications accepted. *Expenses:* Contact institution. *Financial support:* In 2008–09, 1 student received support. Scholarships/grants available. *Unit head:* Russell Rains, Director, 512-428-1220, Fax: 512-448-8492, E-mail: russellr@stedwards.edu. *Application contact:* Kay L. Arnold, Assistant Director of Admissions, 512-233-1661, Fax: 512-428-1032, E-mail: kayla@stedwards.edu.

San Jose State University, Graduate Studies and Research, College of Humanities and the Arts, School of Art and Design, San Jose, CA 95192-0001. Offers art education (MA); art history (MA); digital media (MFA); digital media in art history and education (MA); photography (MFA); pictorial arts (MFA); spatial arts (MFA). *Accreditation:* NASAD (one or more programs are accredited). *Entrance requirements:* For master's, GRE. Electronic applications accepted.

Savannah College of Art and Design, Graduate School, Program in Animation, Savannah, GA 31402-3146. Offers MA, MFA. Part-time programs available. *Degree requirements:* For master's, thesis, internships. *Entrance requirements:* For master's, interview, portfolio. Additional exam requirements/recommendations for international students: Required—TOEFL (minimum score 450 paper-based; 133 computer-based). Electronic applications accepted. *Expenses:* Tuition: Full-time $28,215; part-time $3135 per course. One-time fee: $500.

Savannah College of Art and Design, Graduate School, Program in Broadcast Design, Savannah, GA 31402-3146. Offers MA, MFA. Part-time programs available. *Degree requirements:* For master's, thesis, internships. *Entrance requirements:* For master's, interview, portfolio. Additional exam requirements/recommendations for international students: Required—TOEFL (minimum score 450 paper-based; 133 computer-based). Electronic applications accepted. *Expenses:* Tuition: Full-time $28,215; part-time $3135 per course. One-time fee: $500.

Savannah College of Art and Design, Graduate School, Program in Digital Photography, Savannah, GA 31402-3146. Offers MA. Part-time programs available. *Degree requirements:* For master's, thesis. *Entrance requirements:* For master's, interview, portfolio. Additional exam requirements/recommendations for international students: Required—TOEFL (minimum score 450 paper-based; 133 computer-based). Electronic applications accepted. *Expenses:* Tuition: Full-time $28,215; part-time $3135 per course. One-time fee: $500.

Savannah College of Art and Design, Graduate School, Program in Interactive Design and Game Development, Savannah, GA 31402-3146. Offers MA, MFA. Part-time programs available. *Degree requirements:* For master's, thesis, internships. *Entrance requirements:* For master's, interview, portfolio. Additional exam requirements/recommendations for international students: Required—TOEFL (minimum score 450 paper-based; 133 computer-based). Electronic applications accepted. *Expenses:* Tuition: Full-time $28,215; part-time $3135 per course. One-time fee: $500.

School of Visual Arts, Graduate Programs, Computer Art Department, New York, NY 10010-3994. Offers MFA. *Accreditation:* NASAD. *Degree requirements:* For master's, final review, project or thesis. *Entrance requirements:* For master's, portfolio. Additional exam requirements/recommendations for international students: Required—TOEFL (minimum score 550 paper-based; 213 computer-based; 79 iBT). Electronic applications accepted.

Stevens Institute of Technology, Graduate School, Charles V. Schaefer Jr. School of Engineering, Department of Computer Science, Hoboken, NJ 07030. Offers computer graphics (Certificate); computer science (MS, PhD); computer systems (Certificate); database management systems (Certificate); distributed systems (Certificate); elements of computer science (Certificate); enterprise computing (Certificate); enterprise security and information assurance (Certificate); health informatics (Certificate); multimedia experience and management (Certificate); networks and systems administration (Certificate); security and privacy (Certificate); service oriented computing (Certificate); software design (Certificate); theoretical computer science (Certificate). Part-time and evening/weekend programs available. Terminal master's awarded for partial completion of doctoral program. *Degree requirements:* For master's, thesis optional; for doctorate, variable foreign language requirement, comprehensive exam, thesis/dissertation. *Entrance requirements:* For master's and doctorate, GRE, minimum GPA of 3.0. Additional exam requirements/recommendations for international students: Required—TOEFL. Electronic applications accepted. *Faculty research:* Semantics, reliability theory, programming language, cyber security.

Syracuse University, Graduate School, College of Visual and Performing Arts, Program in Computer Art, Syracuse, NY 13244. Offers MFA.

Texas State University–San Marcos, Graduate School, College of Fine Arts and Communication, Department of Art and Design, Program in Communication Design, San Marcos, TX 78666. Offers MFA. *Entrance requirements:* For master's, 2.75 GPA on last 60 hours of undergrad work, 20 work portfolio. Additional exam requirements/recommendations for international students: Required—TOEFL (minimum score 550 paper-based; 213 computer-based). Electronic applications accepted.

Universidad de las Américas–Puebla, Division of Graduate Studies, School of Humanities, Program in Information Design, Puebla, Mexico. Offers MA. Part-time and evening/weekend programs available. *Degree requirements:* For master's, one foreign language, thesis. *Entrance requirements:* Additional exam requirements/recommendations for international students: Required—TOEFL. *Faculty research:* Typography, project development, organizational image.

University of Alaska Fairbanks, College of Liberal Arts, Department of Art, Fairbanks, AK 99775-5640. Offers art (MFA); ceramics (MFA); computer art (MFA); drawing (MFA); Native arts (MFA); painting (MFA); photography (MFA); printmaking (MFA); sculpture (MFA). Part-time programs available. *Faculty:* 7 full-time (2 women), 6 part-time/adjunct (4 women). *Students:* 7 full-time (2 women), 1 (woman) part-time; includes 1 minority (American Indian/Alaska Native). Average age 33. 14 applicants, 29% accepted, 3 enrolled. In 2008, 6 master's awarded. *Degree requirements:* For master's, comprehensive exam, thesis, oral exam, oral defense. *Entrance requirements:* For master's, portfolio. Additional exam requirements/recommendations for international students: Required—TOEFL (minimum score 550 paper-based; 213 computer-based; 80 iBT). *Application deadline:* For fall admission, 6/1 for domestic students, 3/1 for international students; for spring admission, 10/15 for domestic students, 9/1 for international students. Applications are processed on a rolling basis. Application fee: $60. Electronic applications accepted. *Expenses:* Tuition, area resident: Full-time $5418; part-time $301 per credit. Tuition, state resident: full-time $5418; part-time $301 per credit. Tuition, nonresident: full-time $11,070; part-time $615 per credit. Required fees: $849; $25 per credit. $78 per semester. Tuition and fees vary according to course load and reciprocity agreements. *Financial support:* In 2008–09, 1 fellowship (averaging $13,500 per year), 4 teaching assistantships (averaging $12,058 per year) were awarded; research assistantships, Federal Work-Study, scholarships/grants, health care benefits, and unspecified assistantships also available. Support available to part-time students. Financial award application deadline: 7/1; financial award applicants required to submit FAFSA. *Faculty research:* Computer art, survey of arts in Alaska, found object art, visualization and animation, painting from the wilderness. *Unit head:* Todd Sherman, Chair, 907-474-7530, Fax: 907-474-5853, E-mail: fyart@uaf.edu. *Application contact:* Todd Sherman, Chair, 907-474-7530, Fax: 907-474-5853, E-mail: fyart@uaf.edu.

University of Baltimore, Graduate School, The Yale Gordon College of Liberal Arts, School of Information Arts and Technologies, Baltimore, MD 21201-5779. Offers communications design (DCD); human-computer interaction (MS); interaction design and information technology (MS). Part-time and evening/weekend programs available. *Faculty:* 6 full-time (3 women), 10 part-time/adjunct (6 women). *Students:* 8 full-time (4 women), 30 part-time (17 women); includes 8 minority (6 African Americans, 1 Asian American or Pacific Islander, 1 Hispanic American), 2 international. Average age 33. 18 applicants, 28% accepted, 4 enrolled. In 2008, 2 master's awarded. *Entrance requirements:* For master's, GRE or MAT, minimum undergraduate GPA of 3.0. Additional exam requirements/recommendations for international students: Required—TOEFL (minimum score 550 paper-based; 213 computer-based). *Application deadline:* For fall admission, 8/1 for domestic students, 6/1 for international students. Application fee: $30. *Expenses:* Tuition, state resident: part-time $568 per credit. Tuition, nonresident: part-time $824 per credit. Required fees: $250 per semester. *Unit head:* Dr. Kathryn Summers, Director, MS in Interaction Design and Information Architecture, 410-837-6207, E-mail: ksummers@ubalt.edu. *Application contact:* Kevin Nies, Assistant Director, Office of Graduate Admission, 410-837-6565, E-mail: Knies@ubalt.edu.

University of California, Santa Cruz, Division of Graduate Studies, Division of the Arts, Program in Digital Arts and New Media, Santa Cruz, CA 95064. Offers MFA. *Entrance requirements:* Additional exam requirements/recommendations for international students: Required—TOEFL; Recommended—IELTS. Electronic applications accepted.

University of Central Arkansas, Graduate School, College of Fine Arts and Communication, Program in Digital Filmmaking, Conway, AR 72035-0001. Offers MFA. *Accreditation:* NASAD. *Degree requirements:* For master's, thesis. *Entrance requirements:* For master's, GRE General Test, minimum GPA of 2.7. Additional exam requirements/recommendations for international students: Required—TOEFL (minimum score 550 paper-based; 213 computer-based).

University of Central Florida, College of Arts and Humanities, Department of Art, Orlando, FL 32816. Offers studio art and the computer (MFA). *Faculty:* 24 full-time (5 women), 6 part-time/adjunct (2 women). *Students:* 21 full-time (13 women); includes 4 minority (2 African Americans, 1 Asian American or Pacific Islander, 1 Hispanic American). In 2008, 8 master's awarded. Application fee: $30. *Expenses:* Tuition, area resident: Full-time $6816; part-time $284 per credit. Tuition, state resident: full-time $6816; part-time $1076 per credit. Tuition, nonresident: full-time $25,824. Required fees: $216; $9 per credit. *Financial support:* In 2008–09, 1 fellowship (averaging $10,000 per year), 7 research assistantships (averaging $4,000 per year), 5 teaching assistantships (averaging $4,400 per year) were awarded. *Unit head:* Mark Price, Chair, 407-823-2676, Fax: 407-823-6470, E-mail: maprice@mail.ucf.edu. *Application contact:* Mark Price, Chair, 407-823-2676, Fax: 407-823-6470, E-mail: maprice@mail.ucf.edu.

University of Central Florida, College of Arts and Humanities, Division of Film and Digital Media, Orlando, FL 32816. Offers entrepreneurial digital cinema (MFA); interactive entertainment (MS); visual language and interactive media (MA, MFA). *Faculty:* 28 full-time (10 women), 7 part-time/adjunct (3 women). *Students:* 72 full-time (13 women), 42 part-time (6 women); includes 28 minority (10 African Americans, 2 Asian Americans or Pacific Islanders, 16 Hispanic Americans), 6 international. In 2008, 59 master's awarded. *Expenses:* Tuition, area resident: Full-time $6816; part-time $284 per credit. Tuition, state resident: full-time $6816; part-time $1076 per credit. Tuition, nonresident: full-time $25,824. Required fees: $216; $9 per credit. *Financial support:* In 2008–09, 2 fellowships (averaging $10,000 per year), 2 research assistantships (averaging $5,480 per year), 13 teaching assistantships (averaging $7,100 per year) were awarded. *Unit head:* Dr. Jose Maunez-Cuadra, Interim Chair, 407-823-6100, E-mail: jmaunez@mail.ucf.edu. *Application contact:* Dr. Jose Maunez-Cuadra, Interim Chair, 407-823-6100, E-mail: jmaunez@mail.ucf.edu.

University of Denver, Division of Arts, Humanities and Social Sciences, School of Art and Art History, Denver, CO 80208. Offers art history (MA); art history/museum studies (MA); electronic media arts and design (MFA). *Accreditation:* NASAD. Part-time programs available. *Faculty:* 15 full-time (11 women), 6 part-time/adjunct (2 women). *Students:* 15 full-time (12 women), 10 part-time (all women); includes 2 minority (1 Asian American or Pacific Islander, 1 Hispanic American), 1 international. Average age 29. In 2008, 11 master's awarded. *Degree requirements:* For master's, one foreign language, research paper. *Entrance requirements:* For master's, GRE. Additional exam requirements/recommendations for international students: Required—TOEFL. *Application deadline:* Applications are processed on a rolling basis. Application fee: $50. Electronic applications accepted. *Financial support:* Career-related internships or fieldwork, Federal Work-Study, institutionally sponsored loans, and scholarships/grants available. Support available to part-time students. Financial award application deadline: 3/1; financial award applicants required to submit FAFSA. *Faculty research:* Images of women in alchemical manuscripts and books, Giovanni Benedetto, Salvatore Castiglione. *Unit head:* Dr. Annette Stott, Director, 303-871-2846. *Application contact:* Dr. Annabeth Headrick, Graduate Advisor, 303-871-3574, E-mail: saah-interest@du.edu.

University of Florida, Graduate School, College of Engineering and College of Liberal Arts and Sciences, Department of Computer and Information Science and Engineering, Gainesville, FL 32611. Offers computer engineering (ME, MS, PhD); computer science (MS); digital arts and sciences (MS). Part-time programs available. *Degree requirements:* For master's, thesis (for some programs); for doctorate, thesis/dissertation. *Entrance requirements:* For master's and doctorate, GRE General Test, minimum GPA of 3.0. Additional exam requirements/recommendations for international students: Required—TOEFL (minimum score 550 paper-based; 213 computer-based). Electronic applications accepted. *Faculty research:* Artificial intelligence, networks security, distributed computing, parallel processing system, vision and visualization, database systems.

University of Florida, Graduate School, College of Fine Arts, School of Art and Art History, Gainesville, FL 32611. Offers art (MFA), including ceramics, creative photography, drawing, electronic intermedia, graphic design, painting, printmaking, sculpture; art education (MA); art history (MA, PhD); digital arts and sciences (MA); museology (museum studies) (MA). *Accreditation:* NASAD. *Degree requirements:* For master's, variable foreign language requirement, project or thesis (MFA). *Entrance requirements:* For master's, portfolio (MFA), writing sample (MA), GRE General Test or minimum GPA of 3.0. Additional exam requirements/recommendations for international students: Required—TOEFL (minimum score 550 paper-based; 213 computer-based). Electronic applications accepted. *Faculty research:* Studio production, art historical studies of style context.

The University of Kansas, Graduate Studies, School of Architecture, Design, and Planning, Department of Design, Lawrence, KS 66045. Offers design (MA, MFA); design management (MA); interaction design (MA). *Accreditation:* NASAD (one or more programs are accredited). *Faculty:* 13. *Students:* 3 full-time (1 woman), 6 part-time (3 women). Average age 32. 7 applicants, 71% accepted, 5 enrolled. *Degree requirements:* For master's, thesis. *Entrance requirements:* For master's, portfolio, 3 letters of recommendation, minimum GPA of 3.0.

Additional exam requirements/recommendations for international students: Required—TOEFL, IELTS. *Application deadline:* For fall admission, 2/1 for domestic and international students; for spring admission, 10/15 for domestic students. Application fee: $45 ($55 for international students). Electronic applications accepted. *Expenses:* Tuition, area resident: Full-time $6122; part-time $255.10 per credit hour. Tuition, state resident: full-time $6122; part-time $255.10 per credit hour. Tuition, nonresident: full-time $14,629; part-time $609.55 per credit hour. Required fees: $847; $70.56 per credit hour. Tuition and fees vary according to course load and program. *Financial support:* Fellowships, teaching assistantships with full and partial tuition reimbursements, Federal Work-Study, scholarships/grants, and unspecified assistantships available. Financial award application deadline: 2/1; financial award applicants required to submit FAFSA. *Faculty research:* Interaction design, design management, photography, graphic design, industrial design. *Unit head:* Prof. Gregory Thomas, Chairperson, 785-864-4401. *Application contact:* Prof. Gregory Thomas, Chairperson, 785-864-4401.

University of Massachusetts Dartmouth, Graduate School, College of Visual and Performing Arts, Program in Visual Design, North Dartmouth, MA 02747-2300. Offers digital media (MFA); graphic design (MFA); illustration (MFA); photography (MFA); typography (MFA). *Accreditation:* NASAD. *Faculty:* 17 full-time (8 women), 6 part-time/adjunct (2 women). *Students:* 6 full-time (5 women), 1 (woman) part-time, 1 international. Average age 40. 15 applicants, 27% accepted, 2 enrolled. In 2008, 4 master's awarded. *Degree requirements:* For master's, visual thesis. *Entrance requirements:* For master's, portfolio, interview, minimum GPA of 3.0, 3 letters of recommendation. Additional exam requirements/recommendations for international students: Required—TOEFL (minimum score 500 paper-based). *Application deadline:* For fall admission, 3/1 priority date for domestic students, 1/1 priority date for international students. Applications are processed on a rolling basis. Application fee: $40 ($60 for international students). Electronic applications accepted. *Expenses:* Tuition, state resident: full-time $2071; part-time $86.29 per credit. Tuition, nonresident: full-time $8099; part-time $337.46 per credit. Required fees: $7946. Tuition and fees vary according to class time, course load and reciprocity agreements. *Financial support:* In 2008–09, 1 research assistantship with full tuition reimbursement (averaging $3,940 per year), 4 teaching assistantships with full tuition reimbursements (averaging $3,500 per year) were awarded; Federal Work-Study and unspecified assistantships also available. Support available to part-time students. Financial award application deadline: 3/1; financial award applicants required to submit FAFSA. *Unit head:* Memory Hollowy, Director, 508-999-8554, E-mail: mholloway@umassd.edu. *Application contact:* Elan Turcotte-Shamski, Graduate Admissions Officer, 508-999-8604, Fax: 508-999-8183, E-mail: graduate@umassd.edu.

University of Missouri–Columbia, Graduate School, College of Human Environmental Science, Department of Architectural Studies, Columbia, MO 65211. Offers design with digital media (MA, MS); environmental design (MS). *Faculty:* 7 full-time (2 women). *Students:* 7 full-time (all women), 27 part-time (17 women); includes 2 minority (both African Americans), 9 international. Average age 37. 16 applicants, 44% accepted, 3 enrolled. In 2008, 2 master's awarded. *Entrance requirements:* For master's, GRE General Test, minimum GPA of 3.0. Additional exam requirements/recommendations for international students: Required—TOEFL (minimum score 500 paper-based; 173 computer-based; 61 iBT). *Application deadline:* For fall admission, 4/1 priority date for domestic students; for winter admission, 10/1 priority date for domestic students; for spring admission, 4/1 priority date for domestic students. Applications are processed on a rolling basis. Application fee: $45 ($60 for international students). *Financial support:* Research assistantships, teaching assistantships, institutionally sponsored loans available. *Unit head:* Dr. Ruth Brent Tofle, Department Chair, E-mail: brentr@missouri.edu. *Application contact:* Charles-Ryan Duncan, 573-882-7224, E-mail: duncancd@missouri.edu.

University of Pennsylvania, School of Engineering and Applied Science, Computer Graphics and Game Technology Program, Philadelphia, PA 19104. Offers MSE.

University of Victoria, Faculty of Graduate Studies, Faculty of Fine Arts, Department of Visual Arts, Victoria, BC V8W 2Y2, Canada. Offers digital multimedia (MFA); drawing (MFA); painting (MFA); photography (MFA); sculpture (MFA); video (MFA). *Degree requirements:* For master's, exhibit, oral exam. *Entrance requirements:* For master's, portfolio, BFA. Additional exam requirements/recommendations for international students: Required—TOEFL (minimum score 575 paper-based; 233 computer-based), IELTS (minimum score 7). Electronic applications accepted.

Washington State University, Graduate School, College of Liberal Arts, Department of Fine Arts, Pullman, WA 99164. Offers ceramics (MFA); digital media (MFA); drawing (MFA); painting (MFA); photography (MFA); print making (MFA); sculpture (MFA). *Degree requirements:* For master's, comprehensive exam (for some programs), thesis, exhibit, oral exam. *Entrance requirements:* For master's, GRE, minimum GPA of 3.0, portfolio, 3 letters of recommendation. Additional exam requirements/recommendations for international students: Required—TOEFL (minimum score 550 paper-based; 213 computer-based). Electronic applications accepted. *Faculty research:* Polynesian art, museum representation, number theory.

Graphic Design

Academy of Art University, Graduate Program, School of Graphic Design, San Francisco, CA 94105-3410. Offers MFA. *Accreditation:* NASAD. Part-time programs available. Post-baccalaureate distance learning degree programs offered (no on-campus study). *Faculty:* 6 full-time (1 woman), 22 part-time/adjunct (10 women). *Students:* 168 full-time (115 women), 134 part-time (94 women); includes 51 minority (15 African Americans, 1 American Indian/Alaska Native, 23 Asian Americans or Pacific Islanders, 12 Hispanic Americans), 107 international. Average age 29. 109 applicants. In 2008, 18 master's awarded. *Degree requirements:* For master's, final review. *Entrance requirements:* For master's, minimum GPA of 3.0, portfolio. *Application deadline:* For fall admission, 9/7 for domestic and international students; for spring admission, 2/2 for domestic and international students. Applications are processed on a rolling basis. Application fee: $100 ($500 for international students). Electronic applications accepted. *Expenses:* Tuition: Full-time $18,400; part-time $770 per term. Tuition and fees vary according to program. *Financial support:* Career-related internships or fieldwork and Federal Work-Study available. Support available to part-time students. Financial award application deadline: 8/10; financial award applicants required to submit FAFSA. *Unit head:* Phil Hamlett, Director, 800-544-ARTS, Fax: 415-263-4124. *Application contact:* Prospective Student Services, 800-544-ARTS, Fax: 415-263-4130, E-mail: info@academyart.edu.

Atlantic College, Program in Graphic Arts, Guaynabo, PR 00970. Offers digital graphic design (MA, MGD). Part-time programs available. *Degree requirements:* For master's, thesis. *Entrance requirements:* For master's, minimum GPA of 3.0, 2 letters of recommendation, portfolio, interview. *Faculty research:* Digital design, technology.

Bob Jones University, Graduate Programs, Greenville, SC 29614. Offers accountancy (MS); Bible (MA); Bible translation (MA); Biblical studies (Certificate); broadcast management (MS); business administration (MBA); church history (MA, PhD); church ministries (MA); church music (MM); cinema and video production (MA); counseling (MS); curriculum and instruction (Ed D); divinity (M Div); dramatic production (MA); educational leadership (MS, Ed D, Ed S); elementary education (M Ed, MAT); English (M Ed, MA, MAT); fine arts (MA); graphic design (MA); history (M Ed, MA); illustration (MA); interpretative speech (MA); mathematics (M Ed, MAT); medical missions (Certificate); ministry (MM, D Min); multi-categorical special education (M Ed, MAT); music (M Ed); New Testament interpretation (PhD); Old Testament interpretation (PhD); orchestral instrument performance (MM); organ performance (MM); pastoral studies (MA); personnel services (MS, Ed S); piano pedagogy (MM); piano performance (MM); platform arts (MA); radio and television broadcasting (MS); rhetoric and public address (MA); secondary education (M Ed); studio art (MA); teaching Bible (MA); theology (MA, PhD); voice performance (MM); youth ministries (MA); M Div/MM.

Boston University, College of Fine Arts, School of Visual Arts, Program in Graphic Design, Boston, MA 02215. Offers MFA. *Entrance requirements:* For master's, portfolio. Additional exam requirements/recommendations for international students: Required—TOEFL.

Bowling Green State University, Graduate College, College of Arts and Sciences, School of Art, Bowling Green, OH 43403. Offers 2-D studio art (MA, MFA); 3-D studio art (MA, MFA); art education (MA); art history (MA); computer art (MA); design (MFA); digital arts (MFA); graphics (MFA). *Accreditation:* NASAD. Part-time programs available. *Degree requirements:* For master's, thesis or alternative, final exhibit (MFA). *Entrance requirements:* For master's, GRE General Test (MA), slide portfolio (15-20 slides). Additional exam requirements/recommendations for international students: Required—TOEFL. Electronic applications accepted. *Faculty research:* Computer animation and virtual reality, Spanish still-life painting from 1600 to 1800, art and psychotherapy, Japanese wood-firing techniques in ceramics, non-toxic printmaking technologies.

California Institute of the Arts, School of Art, Valencia, CA 91355-2340. Offers art (MFA, Adv C); graphic design (MFA, Adv C); photography (MFA, Adv C). *Accreditation:* NASAD (one or more programs are accredited). *Degree requirements:* For master's, final project. *Entrance requirements:* For master's, portfolio. Additional exam requirements/recommendations for international students: Required—TOEFL. Electronic applications accepted.

California State University, Los Angeles, Graduate Studies, College of Arts and Letters, Department of Art, Los Angeles, CA 90032-8530. Offers art (MA), including art education, art history, art therapy, ceramics, metals, and textiles, design (MA, MFA), painting, sculpture, and graphic arts, photography; fine arts (MFA), including crafts, design (MA, MFA), studio arts. *Accreditation:* NASAD (one or more programs are accredited). Part-time and evening/weekend programs available. *Faculty:* 16 full-time (6 women). *Students:* 23 full-time (14 women), 52 part-time (37 women); includes 29 minority (2 African Americans, 3 American Indian/Alaska Native, 7 Asian Americans or Pacific Islanders, 17 Hispanic Americans), 4 international. Average age 38. 30 applicants, 100% accepted, 14 enrolled. In 2008, 15 master's awarded. *Degree requirements:* For master's, comprehensive exam, project or thesis. *Entrance*

requirements: For master's, portfolio. Additional exam requirements/recommendations for international students: Required—TOEFL (minimum score 500 paper-based; 173 computer-based). *Application deadline:* For fall admission, 6/15 for domestic students, 5/1 for international students; for winter admission, 11/1 for domestic students, 9/1 for international students; for spring admission, 2/1 for domestic students, 10/1 for international students. Applications are processed on a rolling basis. Application fee: $55. Electronic applications accepted. *Expenses:* Tuition, nonresident: part-time $226 per credit. Required fees: $4019. *Financial support:* Federal Work-Study available. Support available to part-time students. Financial award application deadline: 3/1. *Faculty research:* The artist and the book, conceptual art, ceramic processes, computer graphics, architectural graphics. *Unit head:* Dr. Robert Martin, Chair, 323-343-4010, Fax: 323-343-4045, E-mail: rjmartin@calstatela.edu. *Application contact:* Dr. Jose L. Galvan, Dean of Graduate Studies, 323-343-3820, Fax: 323-343-5653, E-mail: jgalvan@cslanet.calstatela.edu.

Cardinal Stritch University, College of Arts and Sciences, Department of Art, Milwaukee, WI 53217-3985. Offers visual studies (MA). Part-time and evening/weekend programs available. *Degree requirements:* For master's, thesis, portfolio, exhibit. *Entrance requirements:* For master's, minimum GPA of 2.75; 3 letters of recommendation.

City College of the City University of New York, Graduate School, College of Liberal Arts and Science, Division of the Humanities and Arts, Department of Art, Program in Fine Arts, New York, NY 10031-9198. Offers advertising design (MFA); ceramic design (MFA); painting (MFA); printmaking (MFA); sculpture (MFA); wood and metal design (MFA). *Degree requirements:* For master's, thesis exhibit. *Entrance requirements:* For master's, 20 slide portfolio. Additional exam requirements/recommendations for international students: Required—TOEFL (minimum score 575 paper-based; 233 computer-based).

The College of New Rochelle, Graduate School, Division of Art and Communication Studies, Program in Studio Art, New Rochelle, NY 10805-2308. Offers MS. Part-time and evening/weekend programs available. *Degree requirements:* For master's, apprenticeship. *Entrance requirements:* For master's, portfolio, 36 credits of course work in studio art. *Faculty research:* Experimental computer graphics.

Cranbrook Academy of Art, Graduate School, Program in Fine Arts, Bloomfield Hills, MI 48303-0801. Offers ceramics (MFA); design (MFA), including graphic design; fiber arts (MFA); metalsmithing (MFA); painting (MFA); photography (MFA); printmaking (MFA); sculpture (MFA). *Accreditation:* NASAD. *Degree requirements:* For master's, thesis, exhibit. *Entrance requirements:* Additional exam requirements/recommendations for international students: Required—TOEFL (minimum score 550 paper-based; 213 computer-based).

See Close-Up on page 209.

Digital Media Arts College, Graduate Programs, Boca Raton, FL 33431. Offers graphic design (MFA); special FX animation (MFA).

Florida Atlantic University, Dorothy F. Schmidt College of Arts and Letters, Department of Visual Arts and Art History, Boca Raton, FL 33431-0991. Offers art education (MAT); ceramics (MFA); computer art (MFA); graphic design (MFA); painting (MFA). *Faculty:* 23 full-time (12 women), 17 part-time/adjunct (11 women). *Students:* 15 full-time (10 women), 7 part-time (5 women); includes 6 minority (1 African American, 5 Hispanic Americans), 3 international. Average age 31. 30 applicants, 20% accepted, 3 enrolled. In 2008, 8 master's awarded. *Degree requirements:* For master's, one foreign language, project. *Entrance requirements:* For master's, GRE General Test, minimum GPA of 3.0 during last 60 hours of course work, slide portfolio. *Application deadline:* For fall admission, 2/21 for domestic and international students; for spring admission, 10/1 for domestic and international students. Application fee: $30. Electronic applications accepted. *Expenses:* Tuition, state resident: full-time $4867; part-time $270.40 per credit hour. Tuition, nonresident: full-time $16,486; part-time $915.87 per credit hour. *Financial support:* Research assistantships with full tuition reimbursements, teaching assistantships with full tuition reimbursements, career-related internships or fieldwork, Federal Work-Study, and institutionally sponsored loans available. Financial award applicants required to submit FAFSA. *Faculty research:* Painting, ceramics (traditional and non-traditional), installation, video and interactive sculpture. *Unit head:* Dr. Linda Johnson, Chair, 561-297-3870, Fax: 561-297-3078, E-mail: ljohnson@fau.edu. *Application contact:* James A Novak, Associate Professor/Graduate Coordinator/Advisor, 561-297-2430, Fax: 561-297-3078, E-mail: jnovak@fau.edu.

George Mason University, College of Visual and Performing Arts, Program in Visual Technologies, Fairfax, VA 22030. Offers art and visual technology (MA, MFA); art education

Graphic Design

George Mason University (continued)

(MAT). *Degree requirements:* For master's, thesis, apprenticeship in business. *Entrance requirements:* For master's, GRE General Test, minimum GPA of 3.0 in last 60 hours of course work, portfolio. Electronic applications accepted.

Illinois State University, Graduate School, College of Fine Arts, School of Art, Normal, IL 61790-2200. Offers art history (MA, MS); ceramics (MFA, MS); drawing (MFA, MS); fibers (MFA, MS); glass (MFA, MS); graphic design (MFA, MS); metals (MFA, MS); painting (MFA, MS); photography (MFA, MS); printmaking (MFA, MS); sculpture (MFA, MS). *Accreditation:* NASAD (one or more programs are accredited). *Degree requirements:* For master's, thesis or alternative, internship. *Entrance requirements:* For master's, portfolio, sample of scholarly writing. *Faculty research:* General operations support: Normal Editions Workshop for FY2007.

Indiana State University, School of Graduate Studies, College of Arts and Sciences, Department of Art, Terre Haute, IN 47809-1401. Offers ceramics (MA, MFA); drawing (MA, MFA); graphic design (MA, MFA); painting (MA, MFA); photography (MA, MFA); printmaking (MA, MFA); sculpture (MA, MFA). *Accreditation:* NASAD (one or more programs are accredited). Part-time programs available. *Degree requirements:* For master's, thesis or alternative, departmental qualifying exam. *Entrance requirements:* For master's, portfolio. Additional exam requirements/recommendations for international students: Required—TOEFL (minimum score 550 paper-based).

Iowa State University of Science and Technology, Graduate College, College of Design, Department of Art and Design, Ames, IA 50011. Offers art and design (MA); graphic design (MFA); integrated visual arts (MFA); interior design (MFA). Part-time programs available. *Faculty:* 34 full-time (20 women), 2 part-time/adjunct (both women). *Students:* 27 full-time (19 women), 23 part-time (17 women); includes 2 minority (1 African American, 1 Asian American or Pacific Islander), 16 international. 40 applicants, 65% accepted, 18 enrolled. In 2008, 11 master's awarded. *Degree requirements:* For master's, thesis (for some programs). *Entrance requirements:* For master's, GRE General Test, resumé, supplemental departmental form. Additional exam requirements/recommendations for international students: Required—TOEFL (minimum score 550 paper-based; 79 iBT), IELTS (6.5) or TOEFL. *Application deadline:* For fall admission, 5/1 priority date for domestic and international students. Applications are processed on a rolling basis. Application fee: $30 ($70 for international students). Electronic applications accepted. *Expenses:* Tuition, area resident: Full-time $6446; part-time $359 per credit. Tuition, state resident: full-time $6446; part-time $359 per credit. Tuition, nonresident: full-time $17,330; part-time $963 per credit. Required fees: $790; $249.25 per semester. Tuition and fees vary according to course load and program. *Financial support:* In 2008–09, 22 research assistantships with full and partial tuition reimbursements (averaging $14,130 per year), 1 teaching assistantship with full and partial tuition reimbursement (averaging $14,130 per year) were awarded; career-related internships or fieldwork, Federal Work-Study, institutionally sponsored loans, and tuition waivers (partial) also available. Support available to part-time students. Financial award application deadline: 2/15; financial award applicants required to submit FAFSA. *Faculty research:* Computer applications, fire safety, human factors in design, art and design education, fine arts, craft design. *Unit head:* Roger Baer, Chair, 515-294-6724, Fax: 515-294-2725, E-mail: artdn@iastate.edu. *Application contact:* Roger Baer, Chair, 515-294-6724, Fax: 515-294-2725, E-mail: artdn@iastate.edu.

Kean University, School of Visual and Performing Arts, Program in Graphic Communication Technology Management, Union, NJ 07083. Offers MS. Part-time and evening/weekend programs available. *Faculty:* 14 full-time (4 women). *Students:* 8 full-time (6 women), 16 part-time (8 women); includes 4 African Americans, 1 Asian American or Pacific Islander, 3 Hispanic Americans, 2 international. Average age 34. 10 applicants, 100% accepted, 8 enrolled. In 2008, 20 master's awarded. *Degree requirements:* For master's, research. *Entrance requirements:* For master's, minimum GPA of 3.0, 2 letters of recommendation, departmental interview. *Application deadline:* For fall admission, 5/1 for domestic students; for spring admission, 11/1 for domestic students. Application fee: $60 ($150 for international students). Electronic applications accepted. *Expenses:* Tuition, state resident: full-time $10,128; part-time $422 per credit. Tuition, nonresident: full-time $13,728; part-time $572 per credit. Required fees: $2570; $107 per credit. Part-time tuition and fees vary according to course load, degree level and program. *Financial support:* In 2008–09, 3 research assistantships with full tuition reimbursements (averaging $3,217 per year) were awarded; unspecified assistantships also available. *Unit head:* Dr. Cyril Nwako, Program Coordinator, 908-737-3530, E-mail: cnwako@kean.edu. *Application contact:* Steven Koch, Pre-Admissions Coordinator, 908-737-4723, Fax: 908-737-5965, E-mail: grad-adm@kean.edu.

Kent State University, College of Communication and Information, School of Visual Communication Design, Kent, OH 44242-0001. Offers MA, MFA. *Accreditation:* NASAD. Part-time programs available. *Degree requirements:* For master's, thesis, portfolios. *Entrance requirements:* For master's, portfolio (studio majors), minimum GPA of 2.75, GPA of 3.0 in major. *Faculty research:* Graphic design.

Louisiana State University and Agricultural and Mechanical College, Graduate School, College of Art and Design, School of Art, Program in Studio Art, Baton Rouge, LA 70803. Offers ceramics (MFA); graphic design (MFA); painting and drawing (MFA); photography (MFA); printmaking (MFA); sculpture (MFA). *Accreditation:* NASAD. *Degree requirements:* For master's, thesis. *Entrance requirements:* For master's, minimum GPA of 3.0. Additional exam requirements/recommendations for international students: Required—TOEFL (minimum score 550 paper-based; 213 computer-based; 79 iBT). Electronic applications accepted.

Louisiana Tech University, Graduate School, College of Liberal Arts, School of Art, Ruston, LA 71272. Offers art and graphic design (MFA); photography (MFA); studio art (MFA). *Accreditation:* NASAD. Part-time programs available. *Degree requirements:* For master's, exhibit. *Entrance requirements:* For master's, GRE General Test, portfolio.

Maryland Institute College of Art, Graduate Studies, Program in Graphic Design, Baltimore, MD 21217. Offers MFA. *Degree requirements:* For master's, thesis, exhibit. *Entrance requirements:* For master's, 40 credits in studio art, 6 credits in art history, portfolio. Additional exam requirements/recommendations for international students: Required—TOEFL (minimum score 550 paper-based; 213 computer-based).

Marywood University, Academic Affairs, Insalaco College of Creative Arts and Management, Art Department, Program in Studio Art, Scranton, PA 18509-1598. Offers advertising design (MA); ceramics (MA); clay (MA); graphic design (MA); illustration (MA); interior architecture (MA); painting (MA); photography (MA); printmaking (MA); sculpture (MA); weaving (MA). *Accreditation:* NASAD. Part-time and evening/weekend programs available. *Degree requirements:* For master's, comprehensive exam, thesis or alternative. *Entrance requirements:* For master's, portfolio. Additional exam requirements/recommendations for international students: Required—TOEFL (minimum score 550 paper-based; 213 computer-based). Electronic applications accepted. *Faculty research:* Texture and line in clay, cast bronze sculpture, color theories, book art and illustration, sculptural form.

Marywood University, Academic Affairs, Insalaco College of Creative Arts and Management, Art Department, Program in Visual Arts, Scranton, PA 18509-1598. Offers advertising design (MFA); clay (MFA); fibers (MFA); graphic design (MFA); illustration (MFA); metals (MFA); painting (MFA); photography (MFA); printmaking (MFA). *Accreditation:* NASAD. Part-time and evening/weekend programs available. *Degree requirements:* For master's, thesis or alternative, exhibit. *Entrance requirements:* For master's, portfolio. Additional exam requirements/recommendations for international students: Required—TOEFL (minimum score 550 paper-based; 213 computer-based). Electronic applications accepted. *Expenses:* Contact institution. *Faculty research:* Mariology, exploration of visual imagery, explorations involving drawing on the loom, clay as sculptural medium, oil paintings.

Miami International University of Art & Design, Program in Graphic Design, Miami, FL 33132-1418. Offers MFA. Postbaccalaureate distance learning degree programs offered.

See Close-Up on page 121.

Minneapolis College of Art and Design, Program in Visual Studies, Minneapolis, MN 55404-4347. Offers animation (MFA); comic art (MFA); drawing (MFA); filmmaking (MFA); fine arts (MFA); furniture design (MFA); graphic design (MFA); illustration (MFA); interactive media (MFA); painting (MFA); photography (MFA); printmaking (MFA); sculpture (MFA). *Accreditation:* NASAD. Part-time programs available. *Faculty:* 23 full-time (7 women), 9 part-time/adjunct (4 women). *Students:* 40 full-time (21 women), 1 (woman) part-time; includes 1 minority (American Indian/Alaska Native). Average age 27. 172 applicants, 24% accepted, 15 enrolled. In 2008, 7 master's awarded. *Degree requirements:* For master's, thesis, thesis exhibit. *Entrance requirements:* For master's, portfolio, resumé, 3 letters of recommendation, personal statement. Additional exam requirements/recommendations for international students: Required—TOEFL (minimum score 550 paper-based; 213 computer-based; 79 iBT). *Application deadline:* For fall admission, 1/15 for domestic and international students. Application fee: $50. Electronic applications accepted. *Expenses:* Tuition: Full-time $28,400; part-time $813 per credit. *Financial support:* In 2008–09, 23 students received support, including 15 teaching assistantships (averaging $6,000 per year); career-related internships or fieldwork, Federal Work-Study, scholarships/grants, and unspecified assistantships also available. Support available to part-time students. Financial award application deadline: 3/15; financial award applicants required to submit FAFSA. *Faculty research:* Visual arts. *Unit head:* Carole Fisher, Graduate Director, 612-874-3629, E-mail: carole_fisher@mcad.edu. *Application contact:* William Mullen, Vice President of Enrollment Management, 612-874-3762, Fax: 612-874-3701, E-mail: william_mullen@mcad.edu.

New York University, School of Continuing and Professional Studies, Division for Media Industry Studies and Design, Program in Graphic Communications Management and Technology, New York, NY 10012-1019. Offers MA. Part-time and evening/weekend programs available. *Degree requirements:* For master's, project. *Entrance requirements:* For master's, GRE General Test or GMAT (for recent graduates), resumé, 2 letters of recommendation, work experience, essay. Additional exam requirements/recommendations for international students: Required—TOEFL (minimum score 600 paper-based; 250 computer-based; 100 iBT), TWE. Electronic applications accepted. *Faculty research:* Production operations management and marketing, human resources and quality management.

North Carolina State University, Graduate School, College of Design, Department of Graphic Design, Raleigh, NC 27695. Offers MGD. *Accreditation:* NASAD. *Degree requirements:* For master's, thesis optional, oral exam. *Entrance requirements:* For master's, GRE General Test, portfolio. Electronic applications accepted. *Faculty research:* Typography, graphic design, interaction design, design and cognition, design and culture.

Ohio University, Graduate College, College of Fine Arts, School of Art, Athens, OH 45701-2979. Offers art history (MA); ceramics (MFA); graphic design (MFA); painting (MFA); photography (MFA); printmaking (MFA); sculpture (MFA). Part-time programs available. *Degree requirements:* For master's, thesis. *Entrance requirements:* For master's, portfolio. Additional exam requirements/recommendations for international students: Required—TOEFL. *Faculty research:* Vapor fired ceramics, video installation, art theory, digital photography, mixed and interdisciplinary media work.

Otis College of Art and Design, Program in Graphic Design, Los Angeles, CA 90045-9785. Offers MFA. *Faculty:* 3. *Students:* 7 full-time (5 women); includes 2 African Americans, 4 Asian Americans or Pacific Islanders. 38 applicants, 24% accepted, 7 enrolled. *Entrance requirements:* Additional exam requirements/recommendations for international students: Required—TOEFL (minimum score 600 paper-based; 250 computer-based). *Application deadline:* For fall admission, 2/15 for domestic and international students. Electronic applications accepted. *Expenses:* Tuition: Full-time $30,464. Required fees: $700. *Unit head:* Kali Nikitas, Chair, Graduate Studies: Graphic Design, 310-665-6820, Fax: 310-665-6843, E-mail: jhayes@otis.edu. *Application contact:* Information Contact, 310-665-6820, Fax: 310-665-6821, E-mail: admissions@otis.edu.

Pittsburg State University, Graduate School, College of Technology, Departments of Graphics and Imaging Technologies and Technology Management, Pittsburg, KS 66762. Offers human resource development (MS); industrial education (Ed S); technology (MS), including printing management. *Degree requirements:* For master's, thesis or alternative.

Pratt Institute, School of Art and Design, Program in Communications Design, New York, NY 10011. Offers MS. *Accreditation:* NASAD. Part-time programs available. *Faculty:* 5 full-time (2 women), 33 part-time/adjunct (9 women). *Students:* 196 full-time (150 women), 18 part-time (14 women); includes 33 minority (12 African Americans, 16 Asian Americans or Pacific Islanders, 5 Hispanic Americans), 132 international. Average age 27. 195 applicants, 61% accepted, 65 enrolled. In 2008, 106 master's awarded. *Degree requirements:* For master's, thesis. *Entrance requirements:* For master's, portfolio, bachelor's degree, transcripts, letters of recommendation, statement. Additional exam requirements/recommendations for international students: Required—TOEFL (minimum score 550 paper-based; 213 computer-based). *Application deadline:* For fall admission, 2/1 for domestic and international students; for spring admission, 10/1 for domestic and international students. Application fee: $50 ($90 for international students). Electronic applications accepted. *Expenses:* Tuition: Full-time $20,412; part-time $1134 per credit. Required fees: $1190; $1190 per year. *Financial support:* Career-related internships or fieldwork, Federal Work-Study, institutionally sponsored loans, scholarships/grants, and unspecified assistantships available. Support available to part-time students. Financial award application deadline: 2/1; financial award applicants required to submit FAFSA. *Faculty research:* Graphics, film, photography, media presentations, computer graphics for community service organizations. *Unit head:* Jeffrey Bellantoni, Chairperson, 212-647-7573, E-mail: jbell189@pratt.edu. *Application contact:* Young Hah, Director of Graduate Admissions, 718-636-3683, Fax: 718-399-4242, E-mail: yhah@pratt.edu.

See Close-Up on page 219.

Pratt Institute, School of Art and Design, Program in Digital Arts, Brooklyn, NY 11205-3899. Offers digital arts (MFA); MS/MFA. *Accreditation:* NASAD. Part-time programs available. *Faculty:* 6 full-time (1 woman), 17 part-time/adjunct (8 women). *Students:* 73 full-time (37 women); includes 8 minority (2 African Americans, 3 Asian Americans or Pacific Islanders, 3 Hispanic Americans), 37 international. Average age 29. 124 applicants, 28% accepted, 15 enrolled. In 2008, 10 master's awarded. *Degree requirements:* For master's, thesis, exhibit. *Entrance requirements:* For master's, portfolio or video tape, bachelor's degree, transcripts, letters of recommendation, statement. Additional exam requirements/recommendations for international students: Required—TOEFL (minimum score 550 paper-based; 213 computer-based). *Application deadline:* For fall admission, 2/1 for domestic and international students; for spring admission, 10/1 for domestic and international students. Applications are processed on a rolling basis. Application fee: $50 ($90 for international students). Electronic applications accepted. *Expenses:* Tuition: Full-time $20,412; part-time $1134 per credit. Required fees: $1190; $1190 per year. *Financial support:* Career-related internships or fieldwork, Federal Work-Study, institutionally sponsored loans, scholarships/grants, health care benefits, and unspecified assistantships available. Support available to part-time students. Financial award application deadline: 2/1; financial award applicants required to submit FAFSA. *Unit head:* Peter Patchen, Chair, 718-636-3693, E-mail: ppatchen@pratt.edu. *Application contact:* Young Hah, Director of Graduate Admissions, 718-636-3683, Fax: 718-399-4242, E-mail: yhah@pratt.edu.

See Close-Up on page 219.

Rhode Island School of Design, Graduate Studies, Division of Architecture and Design, Department of Graphic Design, Providence, RI 02903-2784. Offers MFA. *Accreditation:* NASAD.

Degree requirements: For master's, thesis, exhibit. *Entrance requirements:* For master's, portfolio, 3 letters of recommendation. Additional exam requirements/recommendations for international students: Required—TOEFL (minimum score 580 paper-based; 237 computer-based), IELTS (minimum score 6.5).

Rochester Institute of Technology, Graduate Enrollment Services, College of Imaging Arts and Sciences, School of Design, Program in Computer Graphics Design, Rochester, NY 14623-5603. Offers MFA. *Accreditation:* NASAD. *Degree requirements:* For master's, thesis. *Entrance requirements:* For master's, portfolio, minimum GPA of 3.0. Additional exam requirements/recommendations for international students: Required—TOEFL.

Rochester Institute of Technology, Graduate Enrollment Services, College of Imaging Arts and Sciences, School of Design, Program in Graphic Design, Rochester, NY 14623-5603. Offers MFA. *Accreditation:* NASAD. *Degree requirements:* For master's, thesis (for some programs). *Entrance requirements:* For master's, portfolio, minimum GPA of 3.0. Additional exam requirements/recommendations for international students: Required—TOEFL.

Rochester Institute of Technology, Graduate Enrollment Services, College of Imaging Arts and Sciences, School of Print Media, Program in Print Media, Rochester, NY 14623-5603. Offers MS. *Entrance requirements:* For master's, minimum GPA of 3.0. Additional exam requirements/recommendations for international students: Required—TOEFL (minimum score 550 paper-based; 213 computer-based; 79 iBT).

San Diego State University, Graduate and Research Affairs, College of Professional Studies and Fine Arts, School of Art, Design and Art History, San Diego, CA 92182. Offers art history (MA); studio arts (MA, MFA), including applied design, environmental design, graphic design, interior design, painting and printmaking, sculpture. *Accreditation:* NASAD (one or more programs are accredited). *Degree requirements:* For master's, variable foreign language requirement, thesis. *Entrance requirements:* For master's, GRE General Test, bachelor's degree in related field, slide portfolio, typed slide information sheet, 2 letters of recommendation. Additional exam requirements/recommendations for international students: Required—TOEFL. Electronic applications accepted.

Savannah College of Art and Design, Graduate School, Program in Advertising Design, Savannah, GA 31402-3146. Offers MA, MFA. Part-time programs available. *Degree requirements:* For master's, thesis, internships. *Entrance requirements:* For master's, interview, portfolio. Additional exam requirements/recommendations for international students: Required—TOEFL (minimum score 450 paper-based; 133 computer-based). Electronic applications accepted. *Expenses:* Tuition: Full-time $28,215; part-time $3135 per course. One-time fee: $500.

Savannah College of Art and Design, Graduate School, Program in Graphic Design, Savannah, GA 31402-3146. Offers MA, MFA. Part-time programs available. *Degree requirements:* For master's, thesis, exhibit, internships. *Entrance requirements:* For master's, interview, portfolio. Additional exam requirements/recommendations for international students: Required—TOEFL (minimum score 450 paper-based; 133 computer-based). Electronic applications accepted. *Expenses:* Tuition: Full-time $28,215; part-time $3135 per course. One-time fee: $500.

See Close-Up on page 223.

School of the Art Institute of Chicago, Graduate Division, Department of Visual Communication, Chicago, IL 60603-3103. Offers MFA. *Entrance requirements:* Additional exam requirements/recommendations for international students: Required—TOEFL, IELTS.

See Close-Up on page 225.

Southern Polytechnic State University, School of Arts and Sciences, Department of English, Technical Communication, and Media Arts, Marietta, GA 30060-2896. Offers communications management (Graduate Certificate); content development (Graduate Certificate); information design and communication (MS); instructional design (Graduate Certificate); technical and professional communication (Graduate Certificate); visual communication and graphics (Graduate Certificate). Part-time and evening/weekend programs available. Postbaccalaureate distance learning degree programs offered (minimal on-campus study). *Faculty:* 4 full-time (3 women), 1 part-time/adjunct. *Students:* 5 full-time (4 women), 38 part-time (25 women); includes 13 minority (12 African Americans, 1 Hispanic American), 3 international. Average age 38. 38 applicants, 68% accepted, 23 enrolled. In 2008, 10 master's awarded. *Degree requirements:* For master's, thesis optional, 36 hours completed through thesis option (6 hours), internship option (6 hours) or advanced coursework option (6 hours); for Graduate Certificate, thesis optional, 18 hours completed through thesis option (6 hours), internship option (6 hours) or advanced coursework option (6 hours). *Entrance requirements:* For master's, GRE, statement of purpose, writing sample, professional recommendations, proctored essay; for Graduate Certificate, statement of purpose, writing sample, professional recommendations, proctored essay. Additional exam requirements/recommendations for international students: Required—TOEFL (minimum score 550 paper-based; 213 computer-based; 79 iBT), IELTS (minimum score 6.5). *Application deadline:* For fall admission, 5/1 priority date for domestic students, 7/1 priority date for international students; for spring admission, 9/1 priority date for domestic students, 11/1 priority date for international students. Applications are processed on a rolling basis. Application fee: $20. Electronic applications accepted. *Expenses:* Tuition, area resident: Full-time $2752; part-time $172 per semester hour. Tuition, state resident: full-time $2752; part-time $172 per semester hour. Tuition, nonresident: full-time $10,992; part-time $687 per semester hour. Required fees: $365 per semester. *Financial support:* In 2008–09, 14 students received support, including 1 research assistantship with full tuition reimbursement available (averaging $4,000 per year); career-related internships or fieldwork, Federal Work-Study, scholarships/grants, and unspecified assistantships also available. Support available to part-time students. Financial award application deadline: 5/1; financial award applicants required to submit FAFSA. *Faculty research:* Usability, user-centered design, instructional design, information architecture, information design. *Unit head:* Dr. Mark Nunes, Chair, 678-915-7202, Fax: 678-915-7425, E-mail: mnunes@spsu.edu. *Application contact:* Nikki Palamiotis, Director of Graduate Studies, 678-915-4276, Fax: 678-915-7292, E-mail: npalamio@spsu.edu.

Suffolk University, New England School of Art and Design, Program in Graphic Design, Boston, MA 02108-2770. Offers MA. *Entrance requirements:* For master's, portfolio, interview, statement of professional goals, official transcripts, 2 letters of recommendation, resumé. *Expenses:* Tuition: Full-time $31,550; part-time $1052 per credit. Required fees: $10 per year. Tuition and fees vary according to program.

Temple University, Graduate School, Tyler School of Art, Department of Graphic Arts and Design, Philadelphia, PA 19122-6096. Offers graphic and interactive design (MFA); photography (MFA); printmaking (MFA). *Accreditation:* NASAD. *Degree requirements:* For master's, essay, exhibit. *Entrance requirements:* For master's, minimum GPA of 3.0; slide portfolio, 40 credits in studio art; 12 credits in art history. Additional exam requirements/recommendations for international students: Required—TOEFL (minimum score 550 paper-based; 213 computer-based; 79 iBT). Electronic applications accepted.

Texas State University–San Marcos, Graduate School, College of Fine Arts and Communication, Department of Art and Design, Program in Communication Design, San Marcos, TX 78666. Offers MFA. *Entrance requirements:* For master's, 2.75 GPA on last 60 hours of undergrad work, 20 work portfolio. Additional exam requirements/recommendations for international students: Required—TOEFL (minimum score 550 paper-based; 213 computer-based). Electronic applications accepted.

Université Laval, Faculty of Architecture, Planning and Visual Arts, School of Visual Arts, Programs in Visual Arts, Québec, QC G1K 7P4, Canada. Offers graphic design and multimedia (MA); visual arts (MA). *Degree requirements:* For master's, thesis (for some programs). *Entrance requirements:* For master's, technical exam, interview, mastery of pertinent software, knowledge of French. Electronic applications accepted.

University of Baltimore, Graduate School, The Yale Gordon College of Liberal Arts, Program in Publications Design, Baltimore, MD 21201-5779. Offers MA. Part-time and evening/weekend programs available. *Faculty:* 6 full-time (3 women), 10 part-time/adjunct (6 women). *Students:* 30 full-time (20 women), 135 part-time (107 women); includes 46 minority (35 African Americans, 6 Asian Americans or Pacific Islanders, 5 Hispanic Americans), 5 international. Average age 30. 79 applicants, 62% accepted, 43 enrolled. In 2008, 39 master's awarded. *Degree requirements:* For master's, seminar project. *Entrance requirements:* For master's, minimum GPA of 3.0, portfolio, interview. Additional exam requirements/recommendations for international students: Required—TOEFL (minimum score 550 paper-based; 213 computer-based). *Application deadline:* For fall admission, 8/1 priority date for domestic students, 6/1 for international students; for spring admission, 12/15 for domestic students, 11/1 for international students. Applications are processed on a rolling basis. Application fee: $30. Electronic applications accepted. *Expenses:* Tuition, state resident: part-time $568 per credit. Tuition, nonresident: part-time $824 per credit. Required fees: $250 per semester. *Financial support:* In 2008–09, 9 research assistantships were awarded; fellowships, career-related internships or fieldwork and Federal Work-Study also available. Support available to part-time students. Financial award application deadline: 4/1; financial award applicants required to submit FAFSA. *Faculty research:* Communication theory, graphic design, media technology. *Unit head:* Dr. Stephanie Gibson, Director, Main Publications Design, 410-837-6050, E-mail: sgibson@ubalt.edu. *Application contact:* Kevin Nies, Assistant Director, Office of Graduate Admission, 410-837-6565, E-mail: knies@ubalt.edu.

University of Baltimore, Graduate School, The Yale Gordon College of Liberal Arts, School of Information Arts and Technologies, Doctoral Program in Communications Design, Baltimore, MD 21201-5779. Offers DCD. Part-time and evening/weekend programs available. *Students:* 2 full-time (1 woman), 15 part-time (11 women); includes 3 minority (2 African Americans, 1 Asian American or Pacific Islander), 1 international. Average age 38. 14 applicants, 21% accepted, 2 enrolled. In 2008, 1 doctorate awarded. *Entrance requirements:* For doctorate, minimum GPA of 3.2, previous graduate study in related discipline, portfolio, resumé. *Application deadline:* For fall admission, 3/31 for domestic and international students. Application fee: $30. Electronic applications accepted. *Expenses:* Tuition, state resident: part-time $568 per credit. Tuition, nonresident: part-time $824 per credit. Required fees: $250 per semester. *Financial support:* Application deadline: 3/10; *Unit head:* Dr. Stuart Moulthrop, Director, 410-837-6022, Fax: 410-837-6029, E-mail: jcrooks@ubalt.edu. *Application contact:* Kevin Nies, Assistant Director, Office of Graduate Admission, 410-837-6565, E-mail: knies@ubalt.edu.

University of Cincinnati, Graduate School, College of Design, Architecture, Art, and Planning, School of Design, Cincinnati, OH 45221. Offers fashion design (M Des); graphic design (M Des); industrial design (M Des); interaction design (M Des); product development (M Des). *Accreditation:* NASAD. *Degree requirements:* For master's, thesis. *Entrance requirements:* For master's, undergraduate degree in design or related field, 2 years of work experience in design or related field. Additional exam requirements/recommendations for international students: Required—TOEFL. Electronic applications accepted. *Faculty research:* Design theory, interdisciplinary design topics.

University of Florida, Graduate School, College of Fine Arts, School of Art and Art History, Gainesville, FL 32611. Offers art (MFA), including ceramics, creative photography, drawing, electronic intermedia, graphic design, painting, printmaking, sculpture; art education (MA); art history (MA, PhD); digital arts and sciences (MA); museology (museum studies) (MA). *Accreditation:* NASAD. *Degree requirements:* For master's, variable foreign language requirement, project or thesis (MFA). *Entrance requirements:* For master's, portfolio (MFA), writing sample (MA), GRE General Test or minimum GPA of 3.0. Additional exam requirements/recommendations for international students: Required—TOEFL (minimum score 550 paper-based; 213 computer-based). Electronic applications accepted. *Faculty research:* Studio production, art historical studies of style context.

University of Guam, Office of Graduate Studies, College of Liberal Arts and Social Sciences, Division of Fine Arts, Mangilao, GU 96923. Offers ceramics (MA); graphics (MA); painting (MA). *Degree requirements:* For master's, thesis or alternative, exhibit, final oral exam. *Entrance requirements:* For master's, GRE General Test, portfolio. Additional exam requirements/recommendations for international students: Required—TOEFL.

University of Illinois at Chicago, Graduate College, College of Architecture and Art, School of Art and Design, Chicago, IL 60607-7128. Offers electronic visualization (MFA); film animation (MFA); graphic design (MFA); industrial design (MFA); photography (MFA); studio arts (MFA). *Accreditation:* NASAD. *Degree requirements:* For master's, thesis, exhibit. *Entrance requirements:* For master's, MAT, portfolio. Additional exam requirements/recommendations for international students: Required—TOEFL. Electronic applications accepted.

University of Illinois at Urbana–Champaign, Graduate College, College of Fine and Applied Arts, School of Art and Design, Program in Design and Media, Champaign, IL 61820. Offers graphic design (MFA); industrial design (MFA). *Accreditation:* NASAD. *Students:* 18 full-time (11 women), 2 part-time (0 women); includes 2 minority (both Asian Americans or Pacific Islanders), 9 international. 78 applicants, 6% accepted, 5 enrolled. In 2008, 4 master's awarded. *Entrance requirements:* For master's, minimum GPA of 3.0. Additional exam requirements/recommendations for international students: Required—TOEFL (minimum score 550 paper-based; 213 computer-based; 79 iBT). *Application deadline:* Applications are processed on a rolling basis. Application fee: $60 ($75 for international students). Electronic applications accepted. *Financial support:* Fellowships, research assistantships, teaching assistantships, tuition waivers (full and partial) available. *Unit head:* Nan Goggin, Interim Director, 217-333-9327, Fax: 217-244-7688, E-mail: goggin@illinois.edu. *Application contact:* Marsha Biddle, Assistant to the Associate Director, 217-333-0642, Fax: 217-244-7688, E-mail: mbiddle@illinois.edu.

University of Massachusetts Dartmouth, Graduate School, College of Visual and Performing Arts, Program in Visual Design, North Dartmouth, MA 02747-2300. Offers digital media (MFA); graphic design (MFA); illustration (MFA); photography (MFA); typography (MFA). *Accreditation:* NASAD. *Faculty:* 17 full-time (8 women), 6 part-time/adjunct (2 women). *Students:* 6 full-time (5 women), 1 (woman) part-time, 1 international. Average age 40. 15 applicants, 27% accepted, 2 enrolled. In 2008, 4 master's awarded. *Degree requirements:* For master's, visual thesis. *Entrance requirements:* For master's, portfolio, interview, minimum GPA of 3.0, 3 letters of recommendation. Additional exam requirements/recommendations for international students: Required—TOEFL (minimum score 500 paper-based). *Application deadline:* For fall admission, 3/1 priority date for domestic students, 1/1 priority date for international students. Applications are processed on a rolling basis. Application fee: $40 ($60 for international students). Electronic applications accepted. *Expenses:* Tuition, state resident: full-time $2071; part-time $86.29 per credit. Tuition, nonresident: full-time $8099; part-time $337.46 per credit. Required fees: $7946. Tuition and fees vary according to class time, course load and reciprocity agreements. *Financial support:* In 2008–09, 1 research assistantship with full tuition reimbursement (averaging $3,940 per year), 4 teaching assistantships with full tuition reimbursements (averaging $3,500 per year) were awarded; Federal Work-Study and unspecified assistantships also available. Support available to part-time students. Financial award application deadline: 3/1; financial award applicants required to submit FAFSA. *Unit head:* Memory Hollowy, Director, 508-999-8554, E-mail: mholloway@umassd.edu. *Application contact:* Elan Turcotte-Shamski, Graduate Admissions Officer, 508-999-8604, Fax: 508-999-8183, E-mail: graduate@umassd.edu.

University of Memphis, Graduate School, College of Communication and Fine Arts, Department of Art, Memphis, TN 38152. Offers art (Graduate Certificate); art history (MA), including Egyptian art and archaeology, general art history; ceramics (MFA); graphic design (MFA); interior design (MFA); painting (MFA); printmaking/photography (MFA); sculpture (MFA). *Accreditation:* NASAD (one or more programs are accredited). *Faculty:* 21 full-time (7 women), 1 (woman) part-time/adjunct. *Students:* 41 full-time (28 women), 3 part-time (all women); includes 6 African Americans, 1 Asian American or Pacific Islander, 1 international. Average age 28. 45 applicants, 73% accepted, 12 enrolled. In 2008, 15 master's, 3 other advanced

Graphic Design

University of Memphis (continued)
degrees awarded. *Degree requirements:* For master's, 2 foreign languages, comprehensive exam, thesis. *Entrance requirements:* For master's, GRE General Test or MAT, portfolio (MFA). *Application deadline:* For fall admission, 8/1 for domestic students; for spring admission, 12/1 for domestic students. Applications are processed on a rolling basis. Application fee: $35 ($60 for international students). *Expenses:* Tuition, area resident: Full-time $6242; part-time $330 per credit hour. Tuition, state resident: full-time $6242; part-time $330 per credit hour. Tuition, nonresident: full-time $17,828; part-time $815 per credit hour. Required fees: $1156. *Financial support:* Research assistantships with full tuition reimbursements, teaching assistantships with full tuition reimbursements available. Financial award applicants required to submit FAFSA. *Faculty research:* Online collaborative learning, advanced art history studies, electronic publishing/design, studio arts, architectural studies. *Unit head:* Prof. Richard Lou, Chair, 901-678-2216, Fax: 901-678-2735, E-mail: gmyatt@memphis.edu. *Application contact:* Greely Myat, Graduate Studies Coordinator, 901-678-2650.

University of Miami, Graduate School, College of Arts and Sciences, Department of Art and Art History, Coral Gables, FL 33124. Offers art history (MA); ceramics/glass (MFA); graphic design/multimedia (MFA); painting (MFA); photography/digital imaging (MFA); printmaking (MFA); sculpture (MFA). Part-time programs available. *Degree requirements:* For master's, variable foreign language requirement, thesis, exhibit (MFA), comprehensive exam (MA). *Entrance requirements:* For master's, GRE General Test (MA), research paper (MA), slide portfolio (MFA), artist statement (MFA). Additional exam requirements/recommendations for international students: Required—TOEFL. Electronic applications accepted. *Faculty research:* Installation art, public art.

University of Minnesota, Duluth, Graduate School, School of Fine Arts, Department of Art and Design, Duluth, MN 55812-2496. Offers graphic design (MFA). Part-time programs available. *Degree requirements:* For master's, final exhibit, project, supporting paper. *Entrance requirements:* For master's, minimum GPA of 3.0, writing sample, slide portfolio. Additional exam requirements/recommendations for international students: Required—TOEFL (minimum score 550 paper-based; 213 computer-based). *Faculty research:* Motion graphics, graphic design history, interactive design, typography, education.

University of Notre Dame, Graduate School, College of Arts and Letters, Division of Humanities, Department of Art, Art History, and Design, Notre Dame, IN 46556. Offers art history (MA); design (MFA), including graphic design, industrial design; studio art (MFA), including ceramics, painting, photography, printmaking, sculpture. *Accreditation:* NASAD. *Faculty:* 19 full-time (6 women), 3 part-time/adjunct (1 woman). *Students:* 23 full-time (12 women); includes 2 minority (both Hispanic Americans), 1 international. 83 applicants, 18% accepted, 10 enrolled. In 2008, 11 master's awarded. *Degree requirements:* For master's, comprehensive exam (for some programs), thesis. *Entrance requirements:* For master's, GRE General Test, minimum GPA of 3.0. Additional exam requirements/recommendations for international students: Required—TOEFL (minimum score 600 paper-based; 250 computer-based; 80 iBT). *Application deadline:* For fall admission, 2/1 priority date for domestic and international students. Application fee: $50. Electronic applications accepted. *Financial support:* In 2008–09, 20 students received support; fellowships with full tuition reimbursements available, research assistantships with full tuition reimbursements available, teaching assistantships with full tuition reimbursements available, scholarships/grants, tuition waivers (full), and unspecified assistantships available. Financial award application deadline: 2/1. *Faculty research:* Studio art practice in ceramics, printing, photography, printmaking and sculpture, graphic design and industrial design, digital imaging in design and photography, Renaissance and American art history, contemporary art theory and criticism. *Unit head:* Prof. Martina Lopez, Director of Graduate Studies, 574-631-7652, E-mail: art.1@nd.edu. *Application contact:* Dr. Barbara Turpin, Director of Graduate Admissions, 574-631-7706, Fax: 574-631-4183.

The University of Tennessee, Graduate School, College of Arts and Sciences, School of Art, Knoxville, TN 37996. Offers ceramics (MFA); drawing (MFA); graphic design (MFA); inter-area studies (MFA); media arts (MFA); painting (MFA); printmaking (MFA); sculpture (MFA); watercolor (MFA). *Accreditation:* NASAD. *Degree requirements:* For master's, thesis or alternative, exhibit. *Entrance requirements:* For master's, portfolio, minimum GPA of 2.7. Additional exam requirements/recommendations for international students: Required—TOEFL. Electronic applications accepted. *Expenses:* Tuition, area resident: Part-time $348 per credit hour. Tuition, state resident: full-time $6262. Tuition, nonresident: full-time $18,920; part-time $1052 per credit hour. Required fees: $812; $36 per credit hour. Tuition and fees vary according to program.

University of Utah, The Graduate School, College of Fine Arts, Department of Art and Art History, Salt Lake City, UT 84112-1107. Offers art history (MA); ceramics (MFA); community-based art education (MFA); drawing (MFA); graphic design (MFA); painting (MFA); photography/digital imaging (MFA); printmaking (MFA); sculpture/intermedia (MFA). *Degree requirements:* For master's, variable foreign language requirement, comprehensive exam (for some programs), thesis or alternative, exhibit (MFA), final project paper. *Entrance requirements:* For master's, CD portfolio (MFA), resumé, letters of recommendation. Additional exam requirements/recommendations for international students: Required—TOEFL (minimum score 575 paper-based; 183 computer-based; 75 iBT). Electronic applications accepted. *Faculty research:* Intermedia, digital arts, installation, traditional media, Asian art, medieval arts.

Western Illinois University, School of Graduate Studies, College of Education and Human Services, Department of Instructional Design and Technology, Macomb, IL 61455-1390. Offers distance learning (Certificate); graphic applications (Certificate); instructional design and technology (MS); multimedia (Certificate); technology integration in education (Certificate); training development (Certificate). Part-time programs available. Postbaccalaureate distance learning degree programs offered (no on-campus study). *Students:* 22 full-time (11 women), 61 part-time (42 women); includes 8 minority (7 African Americans, 1 Hispanic American), 5 international. Average age 38. 22 applicants, 82% accepted. In 2008, 31 master's, 4 other advanced degrees awarded. *Degree requirements:* For master's, thesis or alternative. *Entrance requirements:* Additional exam requirements/recommendations for international students: Required—TOEFL (minimum score 550 paper-based; 213 computer-based; 80 iBT). *Application deadline:* Applications are processed on a rolling basis. Application fee: $30. Electronic applications accepted. *Expenses:* Tuition, state resident: full-time $5696; part-time $237.34 per credit hour. Tuition, nonresident: full-time $11,392; part-time $474.68 per credit hour. Required fees: $1453; $60.55 per credit hour. *Financial support:* In 2008–09, 13 students received support, including 11 research assistantships with full tuition reimbursements available (averaging $7,040 per year), 2 teaching assistantships with full tuition reimbursements available (averaging $8,120 per year). Financial award applicants required to submit FAFSA. *Unit head:* Dr. Hoyet Hemphill, Chairperson, 309-298-1952. *Application contact:* Evelyn Hoing, Assistant Director of Graduate Studies, 309-298-1806, Fax: 309-298-2345, E-mail: grad-office@wiu.edu.

Western Michigan University, Graduate College, College of Fine Arts, Gwen Frostic School of Art, Kalamazoo, MI 49008-5202. Offers art education (MA); studio design (MFA). *Accreditation:* NASAD (one or more programs are accredited). *Degree requirements:* For master's, thesis or alternative.

West Virginia University, College of Creative Arts, Division of Art and Design, Morgantown, WV 26506. Offers art education (MA); art history (MA); ceramics (MFA); graphic design (MFA); painting (MFA); printmaking (MFA); sculpture (MFA); studio art (MA). *Accreditation:* NASAD. *Degree requirements:* For master's, thesis, exhibit. *Entrance requirements:* For master's, minimum GPA of 2.75, portfolio. Additional exam requirements/recommendations for international students: Required—TOEFL. *Expenses:* Contact institution. *Faculty research:* Medieval art history.

Yale University, School of Art, New Haven, CT 06520. Offers graphic design (MFA); painting/printmaking (MFA); photography (MFA); sculpture (MFA). *Degree requirements:* For master's, thesis (for some programs). *Entrance requirements:* Additional exam requirements/recommendations for international students: Required—TOEFL (minimum score 550 paper-based; 250 computer-based; 100 iBT). *Expenses:* Contact institution.

Illustration

Academy of Art University, Graduate Program, School of Illustration, San Francisco, CA 94105-3410. Offers MFA. *Accreditation:* NASAD. Part-time programs available. Post-baccalaureate distance learning degree programs offered (no on-campus study). *Faculty:* 8 full-time (1 woman), 16 part-time/adjunct (5 women). *Students:* 117 full-time (63 women), 84 part-time (49 women); includes 29 minority (8 African Americans, 1 American Indian/Alaska Native, 12 Asian Americans or Pacific Islanders, 8 Hispanic Americans), 44 international. Average age 31. 61 applicants. In 2008, 11 master's awarded. *Degree requirements:* For master's, final review. *Entrance requirements:* For master's, minimum GPA of 3.0, portfolio. *Application deadline:* For fall admission, 9/7 for domestic and international students; for spring admission, 2/2 for domestic and international students. Applications are processed on a rolling basis. Application fee: $100 ($500 for international students). Electronic applications accepted. *Expenses:* Tuition: Full-time $18,400; part-time $770 per term. Tuition and fees vary according to program. *Financial support:* Career-related internships or fieldwork and Federal Work-Study available. Support available to part-time students. Financial award application deadline: 8/10; financial award applicants required to submit FAFSA. *Unit head:* William Maughan, Director, 800-544-ARTS, Fax: 415-263-4124, E-mail: info@academyart.edu. *Application contact:* Prospective Student Services, 800-544-ARTS, Fax: 415-263-4130, E-mail: info@academyart.edu.

Bob Jones University, Graduate Programs, Greenville, SC 29614. Offers accountancy (MS); Bible (MA); Bible translation (MA); Biblical studies (Certificate); broadcast management (MS); business administration (MBA); church history (MA, PhD); church ministries (MA); church music (MM); cinema and video production (MA); counseling (MS); curriculum and instruction (Ed D); divinity (M Div); dramatic production (MA); educational leadership (MS, Ed D, Ed S); elementary education (M Ed, MAT); English (M Ed, MA, MAT); fine arts (MA); graphic design (MA); history (M Ed, MA); illustration (MA); interpretative speech (MA); mathematics (M Ed, MAT); medical missions (Certificate); ministry (MM, D Min); multi-categorical special education (M Ed, MAT); music (M Ed); New Testament interpretation (PhD); Old Testament interpretation (PhD); orchestral instrument performance (MM); organ performance (MM); pastoral studies (MA); personnel services (MS, Ed S); piano pedagogy (MM); piano performance (MM); platform arts (MA); radio and television broadcasting (MS); rhetoric and public address (MA); secondary education (M Ed); studio art (MA); teaching Bible (MA); theology (MA, PhD); voice performance (MM); youth ministries (MA); M Div/MM.

Bradley University, Graduate School, Slane College of Communications and Fine Arts, Department of Art, Peoria, IL 61625-0002. Offers ceramics (MA, MFA); drawing/illustration (MA, MFA); interdisciplinary art (MA, MFA); painting (MA, MFA); photography (MA, MFA); printmaking (MA, MFA); sculpture (MA, MFA); visual communication and design (MA, MFA). *Accreditation:* NASAD. Part-time programs available. *Degree requirements:* For master's, comprehensive exam, thesis, final exhibit. *Entrance requirements:* For master's, portfolio, 2 letters of recommendation. Additional exam requirements/recommendations for international students: Required—TOEFL (minimum score 550 paper-based; 213 computer-based; 79 iBT).

Fashion Institute of Technology, School of Graduate Studies, Program in Illustration, New York, NY 10001-5992. Offers MA. *Entrance requirements:* Additional exam requirements/recommendations for international students: Required—TOEFL (minimum score 550 paper-based; 213 computer-based). Electronic applications accepted.

Kent State University, College of Communication and Information, School of Visual Communication Design, Kent, OH 44242-0001. Offers MA, MFA. *Accreditation:* NASAD. Part-time programs available. *Degree requirements:* For master's, thesis, portfolios. *Entrance requirements:* For master's, portfolio (studio majors), minimum GPA of 2.75, GPA of 3.0 in major. *Faculty research:* Graphic design.

Marywood University, Academic Affairs, Insalaco College of Creative Arts and Management, Art Department, Program in Studio Art, Scranton, PA 18509-1598. Offers advertising design (MA); ceramics (MA); clay (MA); graphic design (MA); illustration (MA); interior architecture (MA); painting (MA); photography (MA); printmaking (MA); sculpture (MA); weaving (MA). *Accreditation:* NASAD. Part-time and evening/weekend programs available. *Degree requirements:* For master's, comprehensive exam, thesis or alternative. *Entrance requirements:* For master's, portfolio. Additional exam requirements/recommendations for international students: Required—TOEFL (minimum score 550 paper-based; 213 computer-based). Electronic applications accepted. *Faculty research:* Texture and line in clay, cast bronze sculpture, color theories, book art and illustration, sculptural form.

Marywood University, Academic Affairs, Insalaco College of Creative Arts and Management, Art Department, Program in Visual Arts, Scranton, PA 18509-1598. Offers advertising design (MFA); clay (MFA); fibers (MFA); graphic design (MFA); illustration (MFA); metals (MFA); painting (MFA); photography (MFA); printmaking (MFA). *Accreditation:* NASAD. Part-time and evening/weekend programs available. *Degree requirements:* For master's, thesis or alternative, exhibit. *Entrance requirements:* For master's, portfolio. Additional exam requirements/recommendations for international students: Required—TOEFL (minimum score 550 paper-based; 213 computer-based). Electronic applications accepted. *Expenses:* Contact institution. *Faculty research:* Mariology, exploration of visual imagery, explorations involving drawing on the loom, clay as sculptural medium, oil paintings.

Mills College, Graduate Studies, Department of English, Oakland, CA 94613-1000. Offers book art and creative writing (MFA); creative writing, poetry (MFA); creative writing, prose (MFA); English and American literature (MA). Part-time programs available. *Faculty:* 9 full-time (7 women), 24 part-time/adjunct (20 women). *Students:* 94 full-time (67 women), 7 part-time (6 women); includes 29 minority (13 African Americans, 8 Asian Americans or Pacific Islanders, 8 Hispanic Americans). Average age 30. 154 applicants, 86% accepted, 50 enrolled. In 2008, 37 master's awarded. *Degree requirements:* For master's, comprehensive exam, thesis. *Entrance requirements:* For master's, manuscript, writing sample. Additional exam requirements/recommendations for international students: Required—TOEFL. *Application deadline:* For fall admission, 2/1 priority date for domestic students; for spring admission, 11/1 for domestic students. Applications are processed on a rolling basis. Application fee: $50. Electronic applications accepted. *Expenses:* Tuition: Full-time $25,072; part-time $6272 per course. Required fees: $880. *Financial support:* In 2008–09, 86 students received support, including 83 fellowships (averaging $6,994 per year), 28 teaching assistantships with partial tuition reimbursements available (averaging $2,430 per year); scholarships/grants also available. Support available to part-time students. Financial award application deadline: 2/1; financial award applicants required to submit FAFSA. *Faculty research:* Creative writing, African-American literature, Victorian women writers, theories of sexuality, Shakespeare. *Unit head:* Dr. Cynthia Scheinberg, Chair, 510-430-2213, E-mail: cyns@mills.edu. *Application contact:* Marika Benko, Graduate Admission Specialist, 510-430-3309, Fax: 510-430-2159, E-mail: grad-studies@mills.edu.

Minneapolis College of Art and Design, Program in Visual Studies, Minneapolis, MN 55404-4347. Offers animation (MFA); comic art (MFA); drawing (MFA); filmmaking (MFA); fine arts (MFA); furniture design (MFA); graphic design (MFA); illustration (MFA); interactive media (MFA); painting (MFA); photography (MFA); printmaking (MFA); sculpture (MFA). *Accreditation:* NASAD. Part-time programs available. *Faculty:* 23 full-time (7 women), 9 part-time/adjunct (4 women). *Students:* 40 full-time (21 women), 1 (woman) part-time; includes 1 minority (American Indian/Alaska Native). Average age 27. 172 applicants, 24% accepted, 15 enrolled. In 2008, 7 master's awarded. *Degree requirements:* For master's, thesis, thesis exhibit. *Entrance requirements:* For master's, portfolio, resumé, 3 letters of recommendation, personal statement. Additional exam requirements/recommendations for international students: Required—TOEFL (minimum score 550 paper-based; 213 computer-based; 79 iBT). *Application deadline:* For fall admission, 1/15 for domestic and international students. Application fee: $50. Electronic applications accepted. *Expenses:* Tuition: Full-time $28,400; part-time $813 per credit. *Financial support:* In 2008–09, 23 students received support, including 15 teaching assistantships (averaging $6,000 per year); career-related internships or fieldwork, Federal Work-Study, scholarships/grants, and unspecified assistantships also available. Support available to part-time students. Financial award application deadline: 3/15; financial award applicants required to submit FAFSA. *Faculty research:* Visual arts. *Unit head:* Carole Fisher, Graduate Director, 612-874-3629, E-mail: carole_fisher@mcad.edu. *Application contact:* William Mullen, Vice President of Enrollment Management, 612-874-3762, Fax: 612-874-3701, E-mail: william_mullen@mcad.edu.

Savannah College of Art and Design, Graduate School, Program in Illustration, Savannah, GA 31402-3146. Offers MA, MFA. Part-time programs available. *Degree requirements:* For master's, thesis, exhibit, internships. *Entrance requirements:* For master's, interview, portfolio. Additional exam requirements/recommendations for international students: Required—TOEFL (minimum score 450 paper-based; 133 computer-based). Electronic applications accepted. *Expenses:* Tuition: Full-time $28,215; part-time $3135 per course. One-time fee: $500.

See Close-Up on page 223.

Savannah College of Art and Design, Graduate School, Program in Illustration Design, Savannah, GA 31402-3146. Offers MA. Part-time programs available. *Degree requirements:* For master's, thesis. *Entrance requirements:* For master's, interview, portfolio. Additional exam requirements/recommendations for international students: Required—TOEFL (minimum score 450 paper-based; 133 computer-based). Electronic applications accepted. *Expenses:* Tuition: Full-time $28,215; part-time $3135 per course. One-time fee: $500.

Savannah College of Art and Design, Graduate School, Program in Sequential Art, Savannah, GA 31402-3146. Offers MA, MFA. Part-time programs available. *Degree requirements:* For master's, thesis, exhibit, internships. *Entrance requirements:* For master's, interview, portfolio. Additional exam requirements/recommendations for international students: Required—TOEFL (minimum score 450 paper-based; 133 computer-based). Electronic applications accepted. *Expenses:* Tuition: Full-time $28,215; part-time $3135 per course. One-time fee: $500.

See Close-Up on page 223.

School of Visual Arts, Graduate Programs, Illustration Department, New York, NY 10010-3994. Offers MFA. *Accreditation:* NASAD. *Degree requirements:* For master's, final review, project or thesis. *Entrance requirements:* For master's, portfolio. Additional exam requirements/recommendations for international students: Required—TOEFL (minimum score 550 paper-based; 213 computer-based; 79 iBT). Electronic applications accepted.

Syracuse University, Graduate School, College of Visual and Performing Arts, Program in Illustration, Syracuse, NY 13244. Offers MFA.

University of California, Santa Cruz, Division of Graduate Studies, Division of Physical and Biological Sciences, Program in Science Communication, Santa Cruz, CA 95064. Offers science illustration (Certificate); science writing (Certificate). *Entrance requirements:* For degree, GRE General Test, GRE Subject Test, bachelor's degree in science. Electronic applications accepted.

University of Massachusetts Dartmouth, Graduate School, College of Visual and Performing Arts, Program in Visual Design, North Dartmouth, MA 02747-2300. Offers digital media (MFA); graphic design (MFA); illustration (MFA); photography (MFA); typography (MFA). *Accreditation:* NASAD. *Faculty:* 17 full-time (8 women), 6 part-time/adjunct (2 women). *Students:* 6 full-time (5 women), 1 (woman) part-time, 1 international. Average age 40. 15 applicants, 27% accepted, 2 enrolled. In 2008, 4 master's awarded. *Degree requirements:* For master's, visual thesis. *Entrance requirements:* For master's, portfolio, interview, minimum GPA of 3.0, 3 letters of recommendation. Additional exam requirements/recommendations for international students: Required—TOEFL (minimum score 500 paper-based). *Application deadline:* For fall admission, 3/1 priority date for domestic students, 1/1 priority date for international students. Applications are processed on a rolling basis. Application fee: $40 ($60 for international students). Electronic applications accepted. *Expenses:* Tuition, state resident: full-time $2071; part-time $86.29 per credit. Tuition, nonresident: full-time $8099; part-time $337.46 per credit. Required fees: $7946. Tuition and fees vary according to class time, course load and reciprocity agreements. *Financial support:* In 2008–09, 1 research assistantship with full tuition reimbursement (averaging $3,940 per year), 4 teaching assistantships with full tuition reimbursements (averaging $3,500 per year) were awarded; Federal Work-Study and unspecified assistantships also available. Support available to part-time students. Financial award application deadline: 3/1; financial award applicants required to submit FAFSA. *Unit head:* Memory Hollowy, Director, 508-999-8554, E-mail: mholloway@umassd.edu. *Application contact:* Elan Turcotte-Shamski, Graduate Admissions Officer, 508-999-8604, Fax: 508-999-8183, E-mail: graduate@umassd.edu.

Western Connecticut State University, Division of Graduate Studies, School of Visual and Performing Arts, Department of Art, Danbury, CT 06810-6885. Offers illustration (MFA); painting (MFA). Part-time programs available. *Faculty:* 4 full-time (1 woman). *Students:* 22 full-time (14 women); includes 4 minority (1 African American, 1 Asian American or Pacific Islander, 2 Hispanic Americans). Average age 31. 19 applicants, 79% accepted, 12 enrolled. In 2008, 7 master's awarded. *Degree requirements:* For master's, individual exhibition of artwork, review of student's progress prior to admission to final semester, completion of program in 6 years with minimum cumulative GPA of 3.0. *Entrance requirements:* For master's, portfolio review, minimum GPA of 2.5. *Application deadline:* For fall admission, 8/5 priority date for domestic students; for spring admission, 1/5 priority date for domestic students. Application fee: $50. *Expenses:* Tuition, state resident: full-time $4377; part-time $363 per credit. Tuition, nonresident: full-time $12,195; part-time $363 per credit. Required fees: $3574; $60 per credit. Part-time tuition and fees vary according to degree level and program. *Financial support:* Career-related internships or fieldwork available. Support available to part-time students. Financial award application deadline: 5/1; financial award applicants required to submit FAFSA. *Unit head:* Margaret Grimes, Graduate Co-Coordinator, 203-837-8402, Fax: 203-837-8945, E-mail: grimesm@wcsu.edu. *Application contact:* Chris Shankle, Associate Director of Graduate Studies, 203-837-9005, Fax: 203-837-8326, E-mail: shanklec@wcsu.edu.

Industrial Design

Academy of Art University, Graduate Program, School of Industrial Design, San Francisco, CA 94105-3410. Offers MFA. Part-time programs available. Postbaccalaureate distance learning degree programs offered (no on-campus study). *Faculty:* 4 full-time (0 women), 12 part-time/adjunct (1 woman). *Students:* 103 full-time (36 women), 15 part-time (5 women); includes 2 African Americans, 10 Asian Americans or Pacific Islanders, 1 Hispanic American, 84 international. Average age 28. 62 applicants. In 2008, 7 master's awarded. *Degree requirements:* For master's, final review. *Entrance requirements:* For master's, portfolio. *Application deadline:* For fall admission, 9/7 for domestic and international students; for spring admission, 2/2 for domestic and international students. Applications are processed on a rolling basis. Application fee: $100 ($500 for international students). Electronic applications accepted. *Expenses:* Tuition: Full-time $18,400; part-time $770 per term. Tuition and fees vary according to program. *Financial support:* Career-related internships or fieldwork and Federal Work-Study available. Support available to part-time students. Financial award application deadline: 8/10; financial award applicants required to submit FAFSA. *Unit head:* Mark Bolick, Director, 800-544-ARTS, Fax: 415-263-4130, E-mail: info@academyart.edu. *Application contact:* 800-544-ARTS, Fax: 415-263-4130, E-mail: info@academyart.edu.

Arizona State University, Graduate College, College of Design, Program in Design, Tempe, AZ 85287. Offers arts/media/engineering (MSD); healthcare and healing environments (MSD); industrial design (MSD); interaction design (MSD); interior design (MSD); new product innovation (MSD); visual communication design (MSD). *Accreditation:* NASAD. *Degree requirements:* For master's, thesis optional. *Entrance requirements:* For master's, GRE General Test, design portfolio.

Art Center College of Design, Graduate Division, Industrial Design Department, Pasadena, CA 91103-1999. Offers environmental design (MS); product design (MS). *Accreditation:* NASAD. *Degree requirements:* For master's, thesis, studio project. *Entrance requirements:* For master's, portfolio. Additional exam requirements/recommendations for international students: Required—TOEFL (minimum score 600 paper-based; 250 computer-based; 100 iBT).

See Close-Up on page 115.

Auburn University, Graduate School, College of Architecture, Design, and Construction, Department of Industrial Design, Auburn University, AL 36849. Offers MID. *Accreditation:* NASAD. Part-time programs available. *Faculty:* 16 full-time (3 women). *Students:* 12 full-time (5 women), 9 part-time (3 women); includes 4 minority (3 African Americans, 1 Asian American or Pacific Islander), 1 international. Average age 27. 25 applicants, 40% accepted, 5 enrolled. In 2008, 7 master's awarded. *Entrance requirements:* For master's, GRE General Test. *Application deadline:* For fall admission, 9/1 for domestic students; for spring admission, 3/1 for domestic students. Applications are processed on a rolling basis. Application fee: $25 ($50 for international students). Electronic applications accepted. *Expenses:* Tuition, area resident: Full-time $5880; part-time $243 per credit hour. Tuition, state resident: full-time $5880; part-time $243 per credit hour. Tuition, nonresident: full-time $17,640; part-time $729 per credit hour. International tuition: $17,846 full-time. Required fees: $620. Tuition and fees vary according to program and reciprocity agreements. *Financial support:* Federal Work-Study available. Support available to part-time students. Financial award application deadline: 3/15. *Faculty research:* Design of space living facilities, color use in business communications. *Unit head:* Clark E. Lundell, Head, 334-844-2364. *Application contact:* Dr. George Flowers, Dean of the Graduate School, 334-844-2125.

Brigham Young University, Graduate Studies, Ira A. Fulton College of Engineering and Technology, School of Technology, Provo, UT 84602-1001. Offers construction management (MS); information technology (MS); manufacturing systems (MS); technology and engineering education (MS). *Faculty:* 25 full-time (0 women). *Students:* 35 full-time (4 women), 6 part-time (1 woman). Average age 25. 6 applicants, 83% accepted, 4 enrolled. In 2008, 11 master's awarded. *Degree requirements:* For master's, thesis. *Entrance requirements:* For master's, GRE General Test, GMAT (construction management), minimum GPA of 3.0 in last 60 hours of course work. Additional exam requirements/recommendations for international students: Required—TOEFL (minimum score 580 paper-based; 237 computer-based; 85 iBT). *Application deadline:* For fall admission, 2/15 for domestic and international students; for winter admission, 9/15 for domestic and international students. Application fee: $50. Electronic applications accepted. *Expenses:* Tuition: Full-time $5160; part-time $287 per credit hour. Tuition and fees vary according to program and student's religious affiliation. *Financial support:* In 2008–09, 34 students received support, including 5 research assistantships (averaging $2,530 per year), 10 teaching assistantships (averaging $3,600 per year); fellowships, career-related internships or fieldwork also available. Financial award application deadline: 3/15. *Faculty research:* Real time process control in IT, electronic physical design, processing and non-linear systems, networking, computerized systems in CM. Total annual research expenditures: $52,110. *Unit head:* Val D. Hawks, Director, 801-422-6300, Fax: 801-422-0490, E-mail: hawksv@byu.edu. *Application contact:* Ronald E. Terry, Graduate Coordinator, 801-422-4297, Fax: 801-422-0490, E-mail: ralowe@byu.edu.

Carleton University, Faculty of Graduate Studies, Faculty of Engineering and Design, School of Industrial Design, Ottawa, ON K1S 5B6, Canada. Offers M Des. *Degree requirements:* For master's, thesis optional. *Entrance requirements:* For master's, honors degree. Additional exam requirements/recommendations for international students: Required—TOEFL.

North Carolina State University, Graduate School, College of Design, Department of Industrial Design, Raleigh, NC 27695. Offers MID. *Accreditation:* NASAD. Part-time programs available. *Degree requirements:* For master's, thesis optional, oral exam, project. *Entrance requirements:* For master's, GRE General Test (recommended), portfolio. Electronic applications accepted. *Faculty research:* Computer graphics, ergonomics, product design.

The Ohio State University, Graduate School, College of the Arts, Department of Industrial, Interior, and Visual Communication Design, Columbus, OH 43210. Offers MA, MFA. *Accreditation:* NASAD. Part-time programs available. *Degree requirements:* For master's, project or thesis. *Entrance requirements:* For master's, bachelor's degree in interior space, graphics, product design, or related field. Additional exam requirements/recommendations for international students: Recommended—TOEFL (minimum score 600 paper-based; 250 computer-based). Electronic applications accepted.

Pratt Institute, School of Art and Design, Program in Industrial Design, Brooklyn, NY 11205-3899. Offers MID. *Accreditation:* NASAD. Part-time programs available. *Faculty:* 6 full-time (1 woman), 26 part-time/adjunct (8 women). *Students:* 73 full-time (44 women), 4 part-time (3 women); includes 10 minority (2 African Americans, 1 American Indian/Alaska Native, 6 Asian Americans or Pacific Islanders, 1 Hispanic American), 13 international. Average age 29. 190 applicants, 26% accepted, 22 enrolled. In 2008, 31 master's awarded. *Degree requirements:* For master's, thesis. *Entrance requirements:* For master's, portfolio, bachelor's degree,

Industrial Design

Pratt Institute (continued)

transcripts, letters of recommendation, statement. Additional exam requirements/recommendations for international students: Required—TOEFL (minimum score 550 paper-based; 213 computer-based). *Application deadline:* For fall admission, 2/1 for domestic and international students; for spring admission, 10/1 for domestic and international students. Application fee: $50 ($90 for international students). Electronic applications accepted. *Expenses:* Tuition: Full-time $20,412; part-time $1134 per credit. Required fees: $1190; $1190 per year. *Financial support:* Career-related internships or fieldwork, Federal Work-Study, institutionally sponsored loans, scholarships/grants, health care benefits, and unspecified assistantships available. Support available to part-time students. Financial award application deadline: 2/1; financial award applicants required to submit FAFSA. *Faculty research:* Universal design, design ethics, sustainability in design. *Unit head:* Matthew Burger, Chairperson, 718-636-3520, Fax: 718-636-3553, E-mail: mburger@pratt.edu. *Application contact:* Young Hah, Director of Graduate Admissions, 718-636-3683, Fax: 718-399-4242, E-mail: yhah@pratt.edu.

See Close-Up on page 219.

Pratt Institute, School of Art and Design, Program in Package Design, New York, NY 10011. Offers MS. *Accreditation:* NASAD. Part-time programs available. *Faculty:* 5 full-time (2 women), 33 part-time/adjunct (9 women). *Students:* 29 full-time (25 women), 2 part-time (1 woman); includes 5 minority (3 Asian Americans or Pacific Islanders, 2 Hispanic Americans), 18 international. Average age 27. 17 applicants, 88% accepted, 9 enrolled. In 2008, 10 master's awarded. *Degree requirements:* For master's, thesis. *Entrance requirements:* For master's, portfolio, bachelor's degree, transcripts, letters of recommendation, statement. Additional exam requirements/recommendations for international students: Required—TOEFL (minimum score 550 paper-based; 213 computer-based). *Application deadline:* For fall admission, 2/1 for domestic and international students; for spring admission, 10/1 for domestic and international students. Application fee: $50 ($90 for international students). Electronic applications accepted. *Expenses:* Tuition: Full-time $20,412; part-time $1134 per credit. Required fees: $1190; $1190 per year. *Financial support:* Career-related internships or fieldwork, Federal Work-Study, institutionally sponsored loans, scholarships/grants, health care benefits, and unspecified assistantships available. Support available to part-time students. Financial award application deadline: 2/1; financial award applicants required to submit FAFSA. *Unit head:* Jeffrey Bellantoni, Chairperson, 212-647-7573, E-mail: jbell189@pratt.edu. *Application contact:* Young Hah, Director of Graduate Admissions, 718-636-3683, Fax: 718-399-4242, E-mail: yhah@pratt.edu.

See Close-Up on page 219.

Rhode Island School of Design, Graduate Studies, Division of Architecture and Design, Department of Industrial Design, Providence, RI 02903-2784. Offers MID. *Accreditation:* NASAD. *Degree requirements:* For master's, thesis, exhibit. *Entrance requirements:* For master's, portfolio, 3 letters of recommendation. Additional exam requirements/recommendations for international students: Required—TOEFL (minimum score 580 paper-based; 237 computer-based), IELTS (minimum score 6.5).

Rochester Institute of Technology, Graduate Enrollment Services, College of Imaging Arts and Sciences, School of Design, Program in Industrial Design, Rochester, NY 14623-5603. Offers MFA. *Accreditation:* NASAD. *Degree requirements:* For master's, thesis (for some programs). *Entrance requirements:* For master's, portfolio, minimum GPA of 3.0. Additional exam requirements/recommendations for international students: Required—TOEFL.

San Francisco State University, Division of Graduate Studies, College of Creative Arts, Department of Design and Industry, San Francisco, CA 94132-1722. Offers industrial arts (MA).

Savannah College of Art and Design, Graduate School, Program in Industrial Design, Savannah, GA 31402-3146. Offers MA, MFA. Part-time programs available. *Degree requirements:* For master's, thesis, exhibit, internships. *Entrance requirements:* For master's, interview, portfolio. Additional exam requirements/recommendations for international students: Required—TOEFL (minimum score 450 paper-based; 133 computer-based). Electronic applications accepted. *Expenses:* Tuition: Full-time $28,215; part-time $3135 per course. One-time fee: $500.

See Close-Up on page 223.

University of Cincinnati, Graduate School, College of Design, Architecture, Art, and Planning, School of Design, Cincinnati, OH 45221. Offers fashion design (M Des); graphic design (M Des); industrial design (M Des); interaction design (M Des); product development (M Des). *Accreditation:* NASAD. *Degree requirements:* For master's, thesis. *Entrance requirements:* For master's, undergraduate degree in design or related field, 2 years of work experience in design or related field. Additional exam requirements/recommendations for international students: Required—TOEFL. Electronic applications accepted. *Faculty research:* Design theory, interdisciplinary design topics.

University of Illinois at Chicago, Graduate College, College of Architecture and Art, School of Art and Design, Chicago, IL 60607-7128. Offers electronic visualization (MFA); film animation (MFA); graphic design (MFA); industrial design (MFA); photography (MFA); studio arts (MFA). *Accreditation:* NASAD. *Degree requirements:* For master's, thesis, exhibit. *Entrance requirements:* For master's, MAT, portfolio. Additional exam requirements/recommendations for international students: Required—TOEFL. Electronic applications accepted.

University of Illinois at Urbana–Champaign, Graduate College, College of Fine and Applied Arts, School of Art and Design, Program in Design and Media, Champaign, IL 61820. Offers graphic design (MFA); industrial design (MFA). *Accreditation:* NASAD. *Students:* 18 full-time (11 women), 2 part-time (0 women); includes 2 minority (both Asian Americans or Pacific Islanders), 9 international. 78 applicants, 6% accepted, 5 enrolled. In 2008, 4 master's awarded. *Entrance requirements:* For master's, minimum GPA of 3.0. Additional exam requirements/recommendations for international students: Required—TOEFL (minimum score 550 paper-based; 213 computer-based; 79 iBT). *Application deadline:* Applications are processed on a rolling basis. Application fee: $60 ($75 for international students). Electronic applications accepted. *Financial support:* Fellowships, research assistantships, teaching assistantships, tuition waivers (full and partial) available. *Unit head:* Nan Goggin, Interim Director, 217-333-9327, Fax: 217-244-7688, E-mail: goggin@illinois.edu. *Application contact:* Marsha Biddle, Assistant to the Associate Director, 217-333-0642, Fax: 217-244-7688, E-mail: mbiddle@illinois.edu.

University of Notre Dame, Graduate School, College of Arts and Letters, Division of Humanities, Department of Art, Art History, and Design, Notre Dame, IN 46556. Offers art history (MA); design (MFA), including graphic design, industrial design; studio art (MFA), including ceramics, painting, photography, printmaking, sculpture. *Accreditation:* NASAD. *Faculty:* 19 full-time (6 women), 3 part-time/adjunct (1 woman). *Students:* 23 full-time (12 women); includes 2 minority (both Hispanic Americans), 1 international. 83 applicants, 18% accepted, 10 enrolled. In 2008, 11 master's awarded. *Degree requirements:* For master's, comprehensive exam (for some programs), thesis. *Entrance requirements:* For master's, GRE General Test, minimum GPA of 3.0. Additional exam requirements/recommendations for international students: Required—TOEFL (minimum score 600 paper-based; 250 computer-based; 80 iBT). *Application deadline:* For fall admission, 2/1 priority date for domestic and international students. Application fee: $50. Electronic applications accepted. *Financial support:* In 2008–09, 20 students received support; fellowships with full tuition reimbursements available, research assistantships with full tuition reimbursements available, teaching assistantships with full tuition reimbursements available, scholarships/grants, tuition waivers (full), and unspecified assistantships available. Financial award application deadline: 2/1. *Faculty research:* Studio art practice in ceramics, printing, photography, printmaking and sculpture, graphic design and industrial design, digital imaging in design and photography, Renaissance and American art history, contemporary art theory and criticism. *Unit head:* Prof. Martina Lopez, Director of Graduate Studies, 574-631-7652, E-mail: art.1@nd.edu. *Application contact:* Dr. Barbara Turpin, Director of Graduate Admissions, 574-631-7706, Fax: 574-631-4183.

The University of the Arts, College of Art and Design, Department of Industrial Design, Philadelphia, PA 19102-4944. Offers MID. *Accreditation:* NASAD. *Degree requirements:* For master's, thesis. *Entrance requirements:* For master's, portfolio. Additional exam requirements/recommendations for international students: Required—TOEFL (minimum score 550 paper-based; 213 computer-based).

See Close-Up on page 233.

University of Washington, Graduate School, College of Arts and Sciences, School of Art, Division of Design, Seattle, WA 98195. Offers industrial design (MFA); visual communication design (MFA).

Interior Design

Academy of Art University, Graduate Program, School of Interior Architecture and Design, San Francisco, CA 94105-3410. Offers MFA. Part-time programs available. Postbaccalaureate distance learning degree programs offered (no on-campus study). *Faculty:* 4 full-time (3 women), 24 part-time/adjunct (7 women). *Students:* 100 full-time (77 women), 76 part-time (62 women); includes 23 minority (9 African Americans, 8 Asian Americans or Pacific Islanders, 6 Hispanic Americans), 63 international. Average age 31. 75 applicants. In 2008, 13 master's awarded. *Degree requirements:* For master's, final review. *Entrance requirements:* For master's, portfolio. *Application deadline:* For fall admission, 9/7 for domestic and international students; for spring admission, 2/2 for domestic and international students. Applications are processed on a rolling basis. Application fee: $100 ($500 for international students). Electronic applications accepted. *Expenses:* Tuition: Full-time $18,400; part-time $770 per term. Tuition and fees vary according to program. *Financial support:* Career-related internships or fieldwork and Federal Work-Study available. Support available to part-time students. Financial award application deadline: 8/10; financial award applicants required to submit FAFSA. *Unit head:* Marlene Farrell, Director, 800-544-ARTS, Fax: 415-263-4130, E-mail: info@academyart.edu. *Application contact:* 800-544-ARTS, Fax: 415-263-4130, E-mail: info@academyart.edu.

Arizona State University, Graduate College, College of Design, Program in Design, Tempe, AZ 85287. Offers arts/media/engineering (MSD); healthcare and healing environments (MSD); industrial design (MSD); interaction design (MSD); interior design (MSD); new product innovation (MSD); visual communication design (MSD). *Accreditation:* NASAD. *Degree requirements:* For master's, thesis optional. *Entrance requirements:* For master's, GRE General Test, design portfolio.

Boston Architectural College, Graduate Programs, Boston, MA 02115-2795. Offers architecture (M Arch); interior design (MID). *Accreditation:* CIDA. *Degree requirements:* For master's, thesis. *Entrance requirements:* For master's, portfolio (recommended). Electronic applications accepted.

Brenau University, Graduate Programs, School of Fine Arts and Humanities, Gainesville, GA 30501. Offers interior design (MID). Part-time programs available. *Faculty:* 5 full-time (4 women), 1 (woman) part-time/adjunct. *Students:* 6 full-time (all women). Average age 29. 77 applicants, 65% accepted, 20 enrolled. *Degree requirements:* For master's, thesis, internship. *Entrance requirements:* For master's, portfolio review, minimum GPA of 3.0. Additional exam requirements/recommendations for international students: Required—TOEFL (minimum score 500 paper-based). *Application deadline:* Applications are processed on a rolling basis. Application fee: $35. Electronic applications accepted. Tuition and fees vary according to course load, campus/location and program. *Unit head:* Dr. Andrea Birch, Dean, E-mail: abirch@brenau.edu. *Application contact:* Michelle Leavell, Admissions Coordinator, 770-538-4390, Fax: 770-538-4701, E-mail: mleavell@brenau.edu.

Chatham University, Program in Interior Architecture, Pittsburgh, PA 15232-2826. Offers MIA, MSIA. Part-time and evening/weekend programs available. Postbaccalaureate distance learning degree programs offered (no on-campus study). *Students:* 24 full-time (20 women), 9 part-time (8 women). Average age 34. 25 applicants, 80% accepted, 11 enrolled. In 2008, 6 master's awarded. *Entrance requirements:* Additional exam requirements/recommendations for international students: Required—TOEFL (minimum score 600 paper-based; 250 computer-based; 100 iBT), IELTS (minimum score 6.5), TWE. *Application deadline:* For fall admission, 7/1 priority date for domestic students, 6/1 priority date for international students; for spring admission, 12/1 priority date for domestic students, 11/1 priority date for international students. Applications are processed on a rolling basis. Application fee: $45. Electronic applications accepted. *Expenses:* Tuition: Part-time $686 per credit. Tuition and fees vary according to program. *Financial support:* Applicants required to submit FAFSA. *Faculty research:* Sustainability. *Unit head:* Prof. Lori Anthony, Director, 412-365-2977, E-mail: lanthony@chatham.edu. *Application contact:* Michael May, Director of Graduate Admissions, 412-365-1141, Fax: 412-365-1609, E-mail: gradadmissions@chatham.edu.

Columbia College Chicago, Graduate School, Program in Interior Design, Chicago, IL 60605-1996. Offers MFA. *Students:* 16 full-time (12 women), 6 part-time (all women); includes 4 minority (2 African Americans, 2 Hispanic Americans), 5 international. Average age 28. 24 applicants, 13 enrolled. In 2008, 5 master's awarded. *Degree requirements:* For master's, thesis. *Entrance requirements:* For master's, minimum GPA of 3.0, portfolio. Additional exam requirements/recommendations for international students: Required—TOEFL (minimum score 550 paper-based; 213 computer-based). *Application deadline:* For fall admission, 3/1 for domestic and international students. Application fee: $55. Electronic applications accepted. *Expenses:* Tuition: Full-time $15,992; part-time $633 per credit hour. *Financial support:* Career-related internships or fieldwork, Federal Work-Study, and scholarships/grants available. Support available to part-time students. Financial award application deadline: 8/13; financial award applicants required to submit FAFSA. *Unit head:* Jay Wolke, Chairperson of Art and Design, 312-369-6968, Fax: 312-369-8009, E-mail: jwolke@colum.edu. *Application contact:* Keith Cleveland, Office of Provost/Senior Vice President, 312-369-7261, Fax: 312-369-8022, E-mail: kcleveland@colum.edu.

Corcoran College of Art and Design, Graduate Programs, Washington, DC 20006-4804. Offers art education (MAT); history of decorative arts (MA); interior design (MA). *Accreditation:* NASAD. Part-time programs available. *Entrance requirements:* Additional exam requirements/recommendations for international students: Required—TOEFL.

Cornell University, Graduate School, Graduate Fields of Human Ecology, Field of Design and Environmental Analysis, Ithaca, NY 14853-0001. Offers applied research in human-environment relations (MS); facilities planning and management (MS); housing and design (MS); human factors and ergonomics (MS); human-environment relations (MS); interior design (MA, MPS). *Faculty:* 14 full-time (6 women). *Students:* 22 full-time (20 women); includes 5 minority (1 American Indian/Alaska Native, 2 Asian Americans or Pacific Islanders, 2 Hispanic Americans), 4 international. Average age 27. 39 applicants, 56% accepted, 11 enrolled. In 2008, 12 master's awarded. *Degree requirements:* For master's, thesis. *Entrance requirements:* For master's, GRE General Test, portfolio or slides of recent work; bachelor's degree in interior design, architecture or related design discipline; 2 letters of recommendation. Additional exam requirements/recommendations for international students: Required—TOEFL (minimum score 600 paper-based; 250 computer-based; 105 iBT). *Application deadline:* For fall admission, 2/1 priority date for domestic students. Application fee: $70. Electronic applications accepted. *Expenses:* Tuition: Full-time $29,500. Required fees: $70. Full-time tuition and fees vary according to degree level, program and student level. *Financial support:* In 2008–09, 13 students received support, including 2 fellowships with full tuition reimbursements available, 11 teaching assistantships with full tuition reimbursements available; research assistantships with full tuition reimbursements available, institutionally sponsored loans, scholarships/grants, health care benefits, tuition waivers (full and partial), and unspecified assistantships also available. Financial award applicants required to submit FAFSA. *Faculty research:* Facility planning and management, environmental psychology, housing, interior design, ergonomics and human factors. *Unit head:* Director of Graduate Studies, 607-255-2168, Fax: 607-255-0305. *Application contact:* Graduate Field Assistant, 607-255-2168, Fax: 607-255-0305, E-mail: deagrad@cornell.edu.

Drexel University, College of Media Arts and Design, Philadelphia, PA 19104-2875. Offers design (MS), including digital media, fashion design, interior design, television management; media arts (MS); performing arts (MS), including arts administration; MS/MBA. *Accreditation:* NASAD. Part-time and evening/weekend programs available. *Entrance requirements:* For master's, interview. Additional exam requirements/recommendations for international students: Required—TOEFL. Electronic applications accepted. *Expenses:* Contact institution.

Drexel University, College of Media Arts and Design, Department of Design, Program in Interior Design, Philadelphia, PA 19104-2875. Offers MS. *Accreditation:* NASAD. *Degree requirements:* For master's, thesis. *Entrance requirements:* For master's, interview. Additional exam requirements/recommendations for international students: Required—TOEFL. Electronic applications accepted. *Faculty research:* History of commercial interiors, hospice spaces, environmental sculpture, painting.

Eastern Michigan University, Graduate School, College of Technology, School of Engineering Technology, Program in Interior Design, Ypsilanti, MI 48197. Offers MS. Part-time and evening/weekend programs available. Postbaccalaureate distance learning degree programs offered (minimal on-campus study). *Entrance requirements:* Additional exam requirements/recommendations for international students: Required—TOEFL.

Florida International University, College of Architecture and the Arts, School of Architecture, Interior Design Program, Miami, FL 33199. Offers MID. *Entrance requirements:* For master's, minimum GPA of 3.0 (upper level coursework). Additional exam requirements/recommendations for international students: Required—TOEFL (minimum score 550 paper-based; 213 computer-based). Electronic applications accepted.

Florida State University, Graduate Studies, College of Visual Arts, Theatre and Dance, Department of Interior Design, Tallahassee, FL 32306. Offers MA, MFA, MS. *Accreditation:* NASAD (one or more programs are accredited). *Degree requirements:* For master's, thesis or alternative. *Entrance requirements:* For master's, GRE General Test, minimum GPA of 3.0 during previous 2 years. Additional exam requirements/recommendations for international students: Required—TOEFL (minimum score 550 paper-based). Electronic applications accepted. *Faculty research:* Graphics techniques, history of interiors, technical proficiencies, computer-aided design and drafting, historic restoration.

The George Washington University, Columbian College of Arts and Sciences, Department of Fine Arts and Art History, Program in Interior Design, Washington, DC 20052. Offers MFA. *Students:* 25 full-time (22 women), 21 part-time (20 women); includes 10 minority (4 African Americans, 4 Asian Americans or Pacific Islanders, 2 Hispanic Americans), 2 international. Average age 29. 33 applicants, 58% accepted, 9 enrolled. *Entrance requirements:* Additional exam requirements/recommendations for international students: Required—TOEFL (minimum score 550 paper-based; 213 computer-based; 80 iBT). *Application deadline:* For fall admission, 3/1 for domestic students, 1/15 for international students; for spring admission, 10/1 for domestic students, 9/1 for international students. *Financial support:* Application deadline: 1/15. *Unit head:* Thomas K Brown, Chair, 202-994-9067, E-mail: thbrown@gwu.edu. *Application contact:* Information Contact, 202-994-6085, Fax: 202-994-8657, E-mail: art@gwu.edu.

Iowa State University of Science and Technology, Graduate College, College of Design, Department of Art and Design, Ames, IA 50011. Offers art and design (MA); graphic design (MFA); integrated visual arts (MFA); interior design (MFA). Part-time programs available. *Faculty:* 34 full-time (20 women), 2 part-time/adjunct (both women). *Students:* 27 full-time (19 women), 23 part-time (17 women); includes 2 minority (1 African American, 1 Asian American or Pacific Islander), 16 international. 40 applicants, 65% accepted, 18 enrolled. In 2008, 11 master's awarded. *Degree requirements:* For master's, thesis (for some programs). *Entrance requirements:* For master's, GRE General Test, resumé, supplemental departmental form. Additional exam requirements/recommendations for international students: Required—TOEFL (minimum score 550 paper-based; 79 iBT), IELTS (6.5) or TOEFL. *Application deadline:* For fall admission, 5/1 priority date for domestic and international students. Applications are processed on a rolling basis. Application fee: $30 ($70 for international students). Electronic applications accepted. *Expenses:* Tuition, area resident: Full-time $6446; part-time $359 per credit. Tuition, state resident: full-time $6446; part-time $359 per credit. Tuition, nonresident: full-time $17,330; part-time $963 per credit. Required fees: $790; $249.25 per semester. Tuition and fees vary according to course load and program. *Financial support:* In 2008–09, 22 research assistantships with full and partial tuition reimbursements (averaging $14,130 per year), 1 teaching assistantship with full and partial tuition reimbursement (averaging $14,130 per year) were awarded; career-related internships or fieldwork, Federal Work-Study, institutionally sponsored loans, and tuition waivers (partial) also available. Support available to part-time students. Financial award application deadline: 2/15; financial award applicants required to submit FAFSA. *Faculty research:* Computer applications, fire safety, human factors in design, art and design education, fine arts, craft design. *Unit head:* Roger Baer, Chair, 515-294-6724, Fax: 515-294-2725, E-mail: artdn@iastate.edu. *Application contact:* Roger Baer, Chair, 515-294-6724, Fax: 515-294-2725, E-mail: artdn@iastate.edu.

Lawrence Technological University, College of Architecture and Design, Southfield, MI 48075-1058. Offers architecture (M Arch); interior design (MID). *Accreditation:* NASAD. Part-time and evening/weekend programs available. *Faculty:* 9 full-time (2 women), 12 part-time/adjunct (3 women). *Students:* 17 full-time (12 women), 105 part-time (44 women); includes 19 minority (8 African Americans, 1 American Indian/Alaska Native, 6 Asian Americans or Pacific Islanders, 4 Hispanic Americans), 13 international. Average age 30. 66 applicants, 83% accepted, 17 enrolled. In 2008, 36 master's awarded. *Degree requirements:* For master's, thesis. *Entrance requirements:* For master's, portfolio. Additional exam requirements/recommendations for international students: Required—TOEFL (minimum score 550 paper-based; 213 computer-based; 79 iBT). *Application deadline:* For fall admission, 2/1 priority date for domestic students, 2/1 for international students; for winter admission, 11/1 priority date for domestic students, 11/1 for international students; for spring admission, 2/1 priority date for domestic students, 2/1 for international students. Applications are processed on a rolling basis. Application fee: $50. Electronic applications accepted. *Expenses:* Tuition: Part-time $763 per credit hour. Required fees: $115 per semester. Tuition and fees vary according to course level, degree level, campus/location and program. *Financial support:* In 2008–09, 105 students received support. Federal Work-Study available. Financial award application deadline: 4/1; financial award applicants required to submit FAFSA. *Unit head:* Glen LeRoy, Dean, 248-204-2800, Fax: 248-204-2900, E-mail: archdean@ltu.edu. *Application contact:* Jane Rohrback, Director of Admissions, 248-204-3160, Fax: 248-204-3188, E-mail: admissions@ltu.edu.

Louisiana Tech University, Graduate School, College of Liberal Arts, School of Architecture, Ruston, LA 71272. Offers interior design (MFA). *Entrance requirements:* For master's, GRE General Test.

Marymount University, School of Arts and Sciences, Program in Interior Design, Arlington, VA 22207-4299. Offers MA. *Accreditation:* CIDA. Part-time and evening/weekend programs available. *Faculty:* 5 full-time (4 women), 2 part-time/adjunct (1 woman). *Students:* 25 full-time (all women), 32 part-time (30 women); includes 15 minority (8 African Americans, 3 Asian Americans or Pacific Islanders, 4 Hispanic Americans), 1 international. Average age 33. 21 applicants, 100% accepted, 14 enrolled. In 2008, 18 master's awarded. *Degree requirements:* For master's, thesis or alternative. *Entrance requirements:* For master's, GRE, National Council for Interior Design Qualification (NCIDQ) exam, or National Council of Architectural Registration Boards (NCARB) Architectural Registration Exam, 2 letters of recommendation, interview, resumé, personal statement, portfolio. Additional exam requirements/recommendations for international students: Required—TOEFL (minimum score 600 paper-based; 250 computer-based; 100 iBT). *Application deadline:* For fall admission, 6/24 for domestic students, 7/1 for international students; for spring admission, 11/11 for domestic students, 10/15 for international students. Applications are processed on a rolling basis. Application fee: $40. Electronic applications accepted. *Expenses:* Tuition: Full-time $12,420; part-time $690 per credit hour. Required fees: $126; $7 per credit hour. Tuition and fees vary according to degree level. *Financial support:* In 2008–09, 34 students received support; research assistantships with partial tuition reimbursements available, career-related internships or fieldwork, Federal Work-Study, scholarships/grants, and unspecified assistantships available. Support available to part-time students. Financial award applicants required to submit FAFSA. *Unit head:* Robin Wagner, Assistant Chair and Director of Graduate Studies in Interior Design, 703-526-6819, Fax: 703-284-3859, E-mail: robin.wagner@marymount.edu. *Application contact:* Francesca Reed, Director, Graduate Admissions, 703-284-5901, Fax: 703-527-3815, E-mail: grad.admissions@marymount.edu.

Marywood University, Academic Affairs, Insalaco College of Creative Arts and Management, Art Department, Program in Studio Art, Scranton, PA 18509-1598. Offers advertising design (MA); ceramics (MA); clay (MA); graphic design (MA); illustration (MA); interior architecture (MA); painting (MA); photography (MA); printmaking (MA); sculpture (MA); weaving (MA). *Accreditation:* NASAD. Part-time and evening/weekend programs available. *Degree requirements:* For master's, comprehensive exam, thesis or alternative. *Entrance requirements:* For master's, portfolio. Additional exam requirements/recommendations for international students: Required—TOEFL (minimum score 550 paper-based; 213 computer-based). Electronic applications accepted. *Faculty research:* Texture and line in clay, cast bronze sculpture, color theories, book art and illustration, sculptural form.

Miami International University of Art & Design, Program in Interior Design, Miami, FL 33132-1418. Offers MFA.

See Close-Up on page 121.

Michigan State University, The Graduate School, College of Agriculture and Natural Resources and College of Social Science, School of Planning, Design and Construction, East Lansing, MI 48824. Offers construction management (MS, PhD); environmental design (MA); interior design and facilities management (MA); international planning studies (MIPS); urban and regional planning (MURP). *Degree requirements:* For master's, thesis or alternative. *Entrance requirements:* Additional exam requirements/recommendations for international students: Required—TOEFL. Electronic applications accepted.

Missouri State University, Graduate College, College of Natural and Applied Sciences, Department of Fashion and Interior Design, Springfield, MO 65804-0094. Offers secondary education (MS Ed), including consumer sciences. Part-time programs available. *Faculty:* 2 full-time (both women), 1 (woman) part-time/adjunct. *Students:* 1 (woman) part-time. Average age 46. 1 applicant, 100% accepted, 0 enrolled. *Degree requirements:* For master's, comprehensive exam, thesis or alternative. *Entrance requirements:* For master's, GRE (MNAS), 9-12 teaching certification (MS Ed), minimum GPA of 3.0 (MNAS). Additional exam requirements/recommendations for international students: Required—TOEFL (minimum score 550 paper-based; 213 computer-based; 79 iBT). *Application deadline:* For fall admission, 7/20 priority date for domestic students, 5/1 for international students; for spring admission, 12/20 priority date for domestic students, 9/1 for international students. Applications are processed on a rolling basis. Application fee: $35 ($50 for international students). Electronic applications accepted. *Expenses:* Tuition, state resident: full-time $3852; part-time $214 per credit hour. Tuition, nonresident: full-time $7524; part-time $418 per credit hour. Required fees: $230 per semester. Tuition and fees vary according to course level and course load. *Financial support:* Career-related internships or fieldwork, Federal Work-Study, institutionally sponsored loans, scholarships/grants, and unspecified assistantships available. Financial award application deadline: 3/31; financial award applicants required to submit FAFSA. *Unit head:* Dr. Jeannie Ireland, Head, 417-836-5497, Fax: 417-836-4341, E-mail: jeannieireland@missouristate.edu. *Application contact:* Eric Eckert, Coordinator of Graduate Admissions and Recruitment, 417-836-5331, Fax: 417-836-6888, E-mail: ericeckert@missouristate.edu.

The New School: A University, Parsons The New School for Design, Program in Interior Design, New York, NY 10011. Offers MFA. *Degree requirements:* For master's, thesis. *Expenses:* Tuition: Full-time $27,144; part-time $1508 per credit. Required fees: $355 per semester. *Unit head:* Tim Marshall, Dean, 212-229-8950 Ext. 4201, E-mail: marshalt@newschool.edu. *Application contact:* Anthony Padilla, Director of Admissions, 212-229-8989 Ext. 4023, Fax: 212-229-8975, E-mail: padillaa@newschool.edu.

See Close-Up on page 125.

The New School: A University, Parsons The New School for Design, Program in Lighting Design, New York, NY 10011. Offers MFA. *Accreditation:* NASAD. *Faculty:* 1 full-time (0 women), 13 part-time/adjunct (6 women). *Students:* 38 full-time (25 women); includes 3 minority (all Asian Americans or Pacific Islanders), 21 international. Average age 28. In 2008, 14 master's awarded. *Entrance requirements:* For master's, portfolio. Additional exam requirements/recommendations for international students: Required—TOEFL (minimum score 580 paper-based; 237 computer-based; 93 iBT). *Application deadline:* For fall admission, 2/1 priority date for domestic students. Applications are processed on a rolling basis. Application fee: $50. *Expenses:* Tuition: Full-time $27,144; part-time $1508 per credit. Required fees: $355 per semester. *Financial support:* Federal Work-Study, scholarships/grants, and tuition waivers (partial) available. Financial award application deadline: 3/1; financial award applicants required to submit FAFSA. *Unit head:* Kent Kleinman, Chair, 212-229-8955 Ext. 2953, E-mail: kleinmak@newschool.edu. *Application contact:* Anthony Padilla, Director of Admissions, 212-229-8989 Ext. 4023, Fax: 212-229-8975, E-mail: padillaa@newschool.edu.

See Close-Up on page 153.

New York School of Interior Design, Program in Interior Design, New York, NY 10021-5110. Offers MFA. *Accreditation:* NASAD. *Faculty:* 9 part-time/adjunct (5 women). *Students:* 16 full-time (13 women); includes 9 minority (1 African American, 7 Asian Americans or Pacific Islanders, 1 Hispanic American), 1 international. Average age 25. 86 applicants, 24% accepted, 8 enrolled. In 2008, 6 master's awarded. *Degree requirements:* For master's, thesis. *Entrance requirements:* For master's, portfolio, undergraduate degree in interior design or closely related field. Additional exam requirements/recommendations for international students: Required—TOEFL (minimum score 550 paper-based; 213 computer-based; 79 iBT). *Application deadline:* For fall admission, 3/1 priority date for domestic and international students. Applications are processed on a rolling basis. Application fee: $50 ($75 for international students). Electronic applications accepted. *Expenses:* Tuition: Full-time $21,750. One-time fee: $75 full-time.

Interior Design

New York School of Interior Design (continued)

Financial support: In 2008–09, 6 students received support, including 6 fellowships (averaging $10,000 per year); career-related internships or fieldwork, Federal Work-Study, institutionally sponsored loans, and scholarships/grants also available. Financial award application deadline: 5/1; financial award applicants required to submit FAFSA. *Faculty research:* History, theory, aesthetics, sociology, and green design; landscape, lighting, furniture, product, and set design. *Unit head:* Scott Ageloff, Dean, 212-472-1500 Ext. 301, Fax: 212-288-6577, E-mail: sageloff@nysid.edu. *Application contact:* David T. Sprouls, Director of Admissions, 212-472-1500 Ext. 202, Fax: 212-472-1867, E-mail: dsprouls@nysid.edu.

See Close-Up on page 129.

The Ohio State University, Graduate School, College of the Arts, Department of Industrial, Interior, and Visual Communication Design, Columbus, OH 43210. Offers MA, MFA. *Accreditation:* NASAD. Part-time programs available. *Degree requirements:* For master's, project or thesis. *Entrance requirements:* For master's, bachelor's degree in interior space, graphics, product design, or related field. Additional exam requirements/recommendations for international students: Recommended—TOEFL (minimum score 600 paper-based; 250 computer-based). Electronic applications accepted.

Pontificia Universidad Catolica Madre y Maestra, Graduate School, Santiago, Dominican Republic. Offers administration (M Adm); architecture of interiors (M Arch); architecture of tourist lodgings (M Arch); banking and financial management (M Mgmt); civil law (LL M); construction administration (ME); corporate business law (LL M); criminal procedure law (LL M); environmental engineering (ME, MEE); finance (M Mgmt); human resources (EMBA); international business (M Mgmt); labor law and Social Security (LL M); logistics management (ME); marketing (M Mgmt); renewable energy (ME). *Entrance requirements:* For master's, curriculum vitae, interview.

Pratt Institute, School of Art and Design, Program in Interior Design, Brooklyn, NY 11205-3899. Offers MS. *Accreditation:* NASAD. Part-time programs available. *Faculty:* 4 full-time (1 woman), 27 part-time/adjunct (10 women). *Students:* 155 full-time (130 women), 8 part-time (7 women); includes 29 minority (5 African Americans, 1 American Indian/Alaska Native, 13 Asian Americans or Pacific Islanders, 10 Hispanic Americans), 52 international. Average age 28. 232 applicants, 56% accepted, 60 enrolled. In 2008, 56 master's awarded. *Degree requirements:* For master's, thesis. *Entrance requirements:* For master's, portfolio, bachelor's degree, transcripts, letters of recommendation, statement. Additional exam requirements/recommendations for international students: Required—TOEFL (minimum score 575 paper-based; 232 computer-based). *Application deadline:* For fall admission, 2/1 for domestic and international students; for spring admission, 10/1 for domestic and international students. Application fee: $50 ($90 for international students). Electronic applications accepted. *Expenses:* Tuition: Full-time $20,412; part-time $1134 per credit. Required fees: $1190; $1190 per year. *Financial support:* Career-related internships or fieldwork, Federal Work-Study, institutionally sponsored loans, scholarships/grants, health care benefits, and unspecified assistantships available. Support available to part-time students. Financial award application deadline: 2/1; financial award applicants required to submit FAFSA. *Unit head:* Anita Cooney, Chairperson, 718-636-3630, Fax: 718-636-3553, E-mail: acooney@pratt.edu. *Application contact:* Young Hah, Director of Graduate Admissions, 718-636-3683, Fax: 718-399-4242, E-mail: yhah@pratt.edu.

See Close-Up on page 219.

Rhode Island School of Design, Graduate Studies, Division of Architecture and Design, Department of Interior Architecture, Providence, RI 02903-2784. Offers MIA. *Degree requirements:* For master's, thesis, exhibit. *Entrance requirements:* For master's, portfolio, 3 letters of recommendation. Additional exam requirements/recommendations for international students: Required—TOEFL (minimum score 580 paper-based; 237 computer-based), IELTS (minimum score 6.5).

San Diego State University, Graduate and Research Affairs, College of Professional Studies and Fine Arts, School of Art, Design and Art History, San Diego, CA 92182. Offers art history (MA); studio arts (MA, MFA), including applied design, environmental design, graphic design, interior design, painting and printmaking, sculpture. *Accreditation:* NASAD (one or more programs are accredited). *Degree requirements:* For master's, variable foreign language requirement, thesis. *Entrance requirements:* For master's, GRE General Test, bachelor's degree in related field, slide portfolio, typed slide information sheet, 2 letters of recommendation. Additional exam requirements/recommendations for international students: Required—TOEFL. Electronic applications accepted.

Savannah College of Art and Design, Graduate School, Program in Interior Design, Savannah, GA 31402-3146. Offers MA, MFA. Part-time programs available. *Degree requirements:* For master's, thesis, internship. *Entrance requirements:* For master's, interview, portfolio. Additional exam requirements/recommendations for international students: Required—TOEFL (minimum score 450 paper-based; 133 computer-based). Electronic applications accepted. *Expenses:* Tuition: Full-time $28,215; part-time $3135 per course. One-time fee: $500.

See Close-Up on page 223.

School of the Art Institute of Chicago, Graduate Division, Department of Architecture, Interior Architecture, and Designed Objects, Chicago, IL 60603-3103. Offers architecture (M Arc); design for emerging technologies (MFA); designed objects (M Des); interior architecture (M Arc). *Entrance requirements:* Additional exam requirements/recommendations for international students: Required—TOEFL, IELTS.

See Close-Up on page 225.

South Dakota State University, Graduate School, College of Family and Consumer Sciences, Department of Apparel Merchandising and Interior Design, Brookings, SD 57007. Offers MFCS. Part-time and evening/weekend programs available. Postbaccalaureate distance learning degree programs offered. *Faculty:* 4 full-time (all women). *Students:* 3 part-time (all women). *Entrance requirements:* Additional exam requirements/recommendations for international students: Required—TOEFL (minimum score 550 paper-based; 213 computer-based; 79 iBT). *Application deadline:* For fall admission, 4/15 for international students; for spring admission, 8/15 for international students. Application fee: $35. *Faculty research:* Rural internet shopping, professional development in apparel merchandising, gender, aesthetics. *Unit head:* Prof. Jane E. Hegland, Department Head, 605-688-5196, Fax: 605-688-5578, E-mail: jane.hegland@sdstate.edu. *Application contact:* The Graduate School, 605-688-4181, E-mail: sdsu_gradschool@sdstate.edu.

Suffolk University, New England School of Art and Design, Program in Interior Design, Boston, MA 02108-2770. Offers MA. *Entrance requirements:* For master's, statement of professional goals, official transcripts, 2 letters of recommendation, resumé. *Expenses:* Tuition: Full-time $31,550; part-time $1052 per credit. Required fees: $10 per year. Tuition and fees vary according to program.

Texas Tech University, Graduate School, College of Human Sciences, Department of Design, Lubbock, TX 79409. Offers interior and environmental design (MS, PhD). *Faculty:* 4 full-time (2 women). *Students:* 10 full-time (8 women), 8 part-time (6 women); includes 3 minority (2 Asian Americans or Pacific Islanders, 1 Hispanic American), 3 international. Average age 33. 23 applicants, 87% accepted, 9 enrolled. In 2008, 4 master's, 1 doctorate awarded. *Degree requirements:* For master's, thesis or alternative; for doctorate, thesis/dissertation. *Entrance requirements:* For master's and doctorate, GRE. Application fee: $50 ($60 for international students). *Expenses:* Tuition, area resident: Part-time $194 per credit hour. Tuition, state resident: full-time $4648; part-time $194 per credit hour. Tuition, nonresident: full-time $11,392; part-time $475 per credit hour. Required fees: $2206; $69 per credit hour. $389 per semester. *Financial support:* In 2008–09, 24 students received support; research assistantships, teaching

assistantships available. Financial award application deadline: 4/15. *Faculty research:* Meanings in the built environment, influence of technology on pedagogic environments, interior design components, computer usage in interior design, design and evaluation of physical environments for the elderly and physically and mentally challenged. Total annual research expenditures: $43,671. *Unit head:* Dr. Cherif M. Amor, Interim Chair, 806-742-3050, Fax: 806-742-1639, E-mail: cherif.amor@ttu.edu. *Application contact:* Dr. JoAnn Shroyer, Graduate Programs Director, 806-742-3050 Ext. 228, Fax: 806-742-1639, E-mail: joann.shroyer@ttu.edu.

The University of Alabama, Graduate School, College of Human Environmental Sciences, Department of Clothing, Textiles, and Interior Design, Tuscaloosa, AL 35487. Offers MSHES. *Faculty:* 4 full-time (all women). In 2008, 1 master's awarded. *Degree requirements:* For master's, comprehensive exam, thesis optional. *Entrance requirements:* For master's, GRE General Test or MAT, minimum GPA of 3.0. *Application deadline:* For fall admission, 7/6 for domestic students. Applications are processed on a rolling basis. Application fee: $30. *Expenses:* Tuition, area resident: Full-time $6400. Tuition, state resident: full-time $6400. Tuition, nonresident: full-time $18,000. *Financial support:* In 2008–09, 1 research assistantship with full tuition reimbursement (averaging $8,100 per year), 2 teaching assistantships with full tuition reimbursements (averaging $8,100 per year) were awarded; fellowships, career-related internships or fieldwork, Federal Work-Study, and scholarships/grants also available. Financial award application deadline: 3/15. *Faculty research:* Archeological textiles, textile science, material culture, social psychology, international trade. *Unit head:* Dr. Carolyn Callis, Chair and Associate Professor, 205-348-6176, Fax: 205-348-0022, E-mail: ccallis@ches.ua.edu. *Application contact:* Dr. Carolyn Callis, Chair and Associate Professor, 205-348-6176, Fax: 205-348-0022, E-mail: ccallis@ches.ua.edu.

University of Central Oklahoma, College of Graduate Studies and Research, College of Arts, Media, and Design, Department of Design and Interior Design, Edmond, OK 73034-5209. Offers MFA. Part-time programs available. Postbaccalaureate distance learning degree programs offered (minimal on-campus study). *Entrance requirements:* Additional exam requirements/recommendations for international students: Required—TOEFL (minimum score 550 paper-based; 213 computer-based). Electronic applications accepted.

University of Central Oklahoma, College of Graduate Studies and Research, College of Education, Department of Human Environmental Sciences, Edmond, OK 73034-5209. Offers family and child studies (MS); family and consumer science education (MS); interior design (MS); nutrition-food management (MS). Part-time programs available. *Entrance requirements:* Additional exam requirements/recommendations for international students: Required—TOEFL (minimum score 550 paper-based; 213 computer-based). Electronic applications accepted. *Faculty research:* Dietetics and food science.

University of Cincinnati, Graduate School, College of Design, Architecture, Art, and Planning, School of Architecture and Interior Design, Cincinnati, OH 45221. Offers architecture (M Arch). *Accreditation:* NASAD. *Degree requirements:* For master's, one foreign language, thesis. *Entrance requirements:* Additional exam requirements/recommendations for international students: Required—TOEFL. *Faculty research:* Theory and history of architecture.

University of Florida, Graduate School, College of Design, Construction and Planning, Department of Interior Design, Gainesville, FL 32611. Offers MID, PhD. *Entrance requirements:* For master's, GRE General Test, minimum GPA of 3.0. Additional exam requirements/recommendations for international students: Required—TOEFL.

University of Georgia, Graduate School, College of Family and Consumer Sciences, Department of Textiles, Merchandising, and Interiors, Athens, GA 30602. Offers historic costume and textiles (MS); merchandising/international trade (MS); textile analysis (PhD); textile chemical processes (PhD); textile products and standards (PhD); textile science (MS). *Degree requirements:* For master's, thesis; for doctorate, thesis/dissertation. *Entrance requirements:* For master's and doctorate, GRE General Test. Electronic applications accepted.

University of Houston, College of Liberal Arts and Social Sciences, Department of Art, Houston, TX 77204. Offers interior design (MA); painting (MA); photography (MA); sculpture (MA); MFA/MA. *Faculty:* 13 full-time (6 women), 9 part-time/adjunct (8 women). *Students:* 35 full-time (19 women); includes 5 minority (1 Asian American or Pacific Islander, 4 Hispanic Americans), 2 international. Average age 31. 30 applicants, 43% accepted, 10 enrolled. In 2008, 12 master's awarded. *Degree requirements:* For master's, comprehensive exam, visual thesis. *Entrance requirements:* For master's, GRE General Test, portfolio. *Application deadline:* For fall admission, 2/28 for domestic students; for spring admission, 10/30 for domestic students. Application fee: $25 ($100 for international students). *Expenses:* Tuition, state resident: full-time $5164; part-time $287 per credit. Tuition, nonresident: full-time $10,222; part-time $568 per credit. *Financial support:* In 2008–09, 31 teaching assistantships with full tuition reimbursements (averaging $10,600 per year) were awarded; career-related internships or fieldwork, Federal Work-Study, institutionally sponsored loans, scholarships/grants, health care benefits, and unspecified assistantships also available. Support available to part-time students. Financial award application deadline: 3/10. *Faculty research:* Alternative art projects. *Unit head:* Dr. John Reed, Chairperson, 713-743-3001, Fax: 713-743-2823, E-mail: jreed@uh.edu. *Application contact:* Dr. John Reed, Chairperson, 713-743-3001, Fax: 713-743-2823, E-mail: jreed@uh.edu.

University of Kentucky, Graduate School, College of Design, Program in Interior Design, Merchandising, and Textiles, Lexington, KY 40506-0032. Offers MAIDM, MSIDM. *Degree requirements:* For master's, comprehensive exam, thesis optional. *Entrance requirements:* For master's, GRE General Test, minimum undergraduate GPA of 2.75. Additional exam requirements/recommendations for international students: Required—TOEFL (minimum score 550 paper-based; 213 computer-based). Electronic applications accepted. *Faculty research:* Interior design, apparel merchandising, textile evaluation, creativity in design, social-psychological aspects of dress and interiors.

University of Manitoba, Faculty of Graduate Studies, Faculty of Architecture, Department of Interior Design, Winnipeg, MB R3T 2N2, Canada. Offers MID. *Accreditation:* CIDA.

University of Massachusetts Amherst, Graduate School, College of Humanities and Fine Arts, Department of Art, Programs in Architecture, Amherst, MA 01003. Offers architecture and design (M Arch); interior design (MS). Part-time programs available. *Degree requirements:* For master's, thesis or alternative. *Entrance requirements:* For master's, GRE General Test (M Arch), portfolio. Additional exam requirements/recommendations for international students: Required—TOEFL (minimum score 550 paper-based; 213 computer-based; 79 iBT), IELTS (minimum score 6.5). Electronic applications accepted. *Expenses:* Tuition, area resident: Full-time $2640. Tuition, nonresident: full-time $9936. One-time fee: $332 full-time. Tuition and fees vary according to course load.

University of Memphis, Graduate School, College of Communication and Fine Arts, Department of Art, Memphis, TN 38152. Offers art (Graduate Certificate); art history (MA), including Egyptian art and archaeology, general art history; ceramics (MFA); graphic design (MFA); interior design (MFA); painting (MFA); printmaking/photography (MFA); sculpture (MFA). *Accreditation:* NASAD (one or more programs are accredited). *Faculty:* 21 full-time (7 women), 1 (woman) part-time/adjunct. *Students:* 41 full-time (28 women), 3 part-time (all women); includes 6 African Americans, 1 Asian American or Pacific Islander, 1 international. Average age 28. 45 applicants, 73% accepted, 12 enrolled. In 2008, 15 master's, 3 other advanced degrees awarded. *Degree requirements:* For master's, 2 foreign languages, comprehensive exam, thesis. *Entrance requirements:* For master's, GRE General Test or MAT, portfolio (MFA). *Application deadline:* For fall admission, 8/1 for domestic students; for spring admission, 12/1 for domestic students. Applications are processed on a rolling basis. Application fee: $35 ($60 for international students). *Expenses:* Tuition, area resident: Full-time $6242; part-time $330 per credit hour. Tuition, state resident: full-time $6242; part-time $330 per credit hour. Tuition, nonresident: full-time $17,828; part-time $815 per credit hour. Required fees: $1156. *Financial support:* Research assistantships with full tuition reimbursements, teaching assistantships with full tuition reimbursements available. Financial award applicants required to submit FAFSA. *Faculty research:* Online collaborative learning, advanced art history studies, electronic publishing/design, studio arts, architectural studies. *Unit head:* Prof. Richard Lou, Chair, 901-678-2216, Fax: 901-678-2735, E-mail: gmyatt@memphis.edu. *Application contact:* Greely Myat, Graduate Studies Coordinator, 901-678-2650.

University of Minnesota, Twin Cities Campus, Graduate School, College of Design, Department of Design, Housing, and Apparel, Minneapolis, MN 55455-0213. Offers apparel (MA, MS, PhD); design communication (MA, MS, PhD); housing studies (MA, MS, PhD, Postbaccalaureate Certificate); interactive design (MFA); interior design (MA, MS, PhD). Part-time programs available. *Degree requirements:* For master's and Postbaccalaureate Certificate, comprehensive exam, thesis (for some programs); for doctorate, comprehensive exam, thesis/dissertation. *Entrance requirements:* For master's, GRE General Test, minimum GPA of 3.0 (preferred), portfolio, 3 letters of recommendation; for doctorate, GRE General Test, minimum GPA of 3.0 (preferred), portfolio, 3 letters of recommendation, writing sample; for Postbaccalaureate Certificate, GRE General Test, minimum GPA of 3.0 (preferred). Additional exam requirements/recommendations for international students: Required—TOEFL (minimum score 550 paper-based; 213 computer-based; 79 iBT). Electronic applications accepted. *Faculty research:* Housing policy and community development; consumer behavior; interactive design; design history; social, cultural, and behavioral issues related to designed environments.

University of Nebraska–Lincoln, Graduate College, College of Architecture, Department of Architecture, Lincoln, NE 68588. Offers architecture (M Arch, MS, PhD); interior design (MS); M Arch/MBA; M Arch/MCRP. *Faculty:* 14 full-time (2 women). *Students:* 67 full-time (24 women), 8 part-time (5 women); includes 5 minority (1 African American, 1 American Indian/Alaska Native, 2 Asian Americans or Pacific Islanders, 1 Hispanic American), 2 international. In 2008, 2 master's awarded. *Entrance requirements:* Additional exam requirements/recommendations for international students: Required—TOEFL. *Application deadline:* For fall admission, 2/1 for domestic and international students. Application fee: $40. Electronic applications accepted. *Expenses:* Tuition, state resident: full-time $4275; part-time $237.50 per credit hour. Tuition, nonresident: full-time $11,525; part-time $640.25 per credit hour. Required fees: $1068; $10.35 per credit hour. $440.70 per semester. Tuition and fees vary according to course load and program. *Financial support:* Fellowships, research assistantships, teaching assistantships available. Financial award application deadline: 2/15. *Unit head:* F. Duncan Case, Graduate Committee Chair, 402-472-9233, Fax: 402-472-3806. *Application contact:* Ginny Gross, Director of Graduate Admissions, 402-472-2878, Fax: 402-472-0589, E-mail: grad_admissions@unl.edu.

The University of North Carolina at Greensboro, Graduate School, School of Human Environmental Sciences, Department of Interior Architecture, Greensboro, NC 27412-5001. Offers historic preservation (Certificate); interior architecture (MS); museum studies (Certificate). *Degree requirements:* For master's, thesis. *Entrance requirements:* For master's, GRE General Test or MAT, bachelor's degree in interior design, interview, portfolio. Additional exam requirements/recommendations for international students: Required—TOEFL. Electronic applications accepted.

University of Oregon, Graduate School, School of Architecture and Allied Arts, Department of Architecture, Eugene, OR 97403. Offers architecture (M Arch); interior architecture (MI Arch). *Accreditation:* CIDA. *Degree requirements:* For master's, thesis (for some programs). *Entrance*

requirements: For master's, GRE General Test. Additional exam requirements/recommendations for international students: Required—TOEFL. *Faculty research:* Innovation in housing design and design production, climate responsive design, passive heating and cooling, computer software development for design applications, vernacular architecture.

Utah State University, School of Graduate Studies, College of Humanities, Arts and Social Sciences, Program in Interior Design, Logan, UT 84322. Offers MS. Part-time programs available. Postbaccalaureate distance learning degree programs offered. *Entrance requirements:* For master's, GRE General Test, MAT, minimum GPA of 3.0. Additional exam requirements/recommendations for international students: Required—TOEFL.

Virginia Commonwealth University, Graduate School, School of the Arts, Department of Graphic Design, Richmond, VA 23284-9005. Offers design/visual communications (MFA); interior environment (MFA); photography and film (MFA). *Accreditation:* NASAD. *Degree requirements:* For master's, thesis, exhibition. *Entrance requirements:* For master's, portfolio. *Faculty research:* Film, photography, interior environments, visual communication.

Virginia Polytechnic Institute and State University, Graduate School, College of Liberal Arts and Human Sciences, Department of Apparel, Housing, and Resource Management, Blacksburg, VA 24061. Offers apparel business and economics (MS, PhD); apparel product design and analysis (MS, PhD); apparel quality analysis (MS, PhD); consumer studies (MS, PhD); family financial management (MS, PhD); household equipment (MS, PhD); housing (MS, PhD); interior design (MS, PhD); resource management (MS, PhD). *Degree requirements:* For master's, thesis; for doctorate, thesis/dissertation. *Entrance requirements:* For master's and doctorate, GRE General Test. Additional exam requirements/recommendations for international students: Required—TOEFL (minimum score 550 paper-based; 213 computer-based). Electronic applications accepted. *Faculty research:* Housing for elderly, affordable housing, household time use, phosphate laundry study, economic well-living.

Washington State University, Graduate School, College of Agricultural, Human, and Natural Resource Sciences, Department of Apparel, Merchandising, Design, and Textiles, Pullman, WA 99164. Offers apparel, merchandising, design and textiles (MA); interdisciplinary (PhD); interior design (MA). *Degree requirements:* For master's, comprehensive exam (for some programs), thesis, oral exam; for doctorate, comprehensive exam, thesis/dissertation. *Entrance requirements:* For master's, GRE, minimum GPA of 3.0, 3 writing samples, 3 letters of recommendation, portfolio. Additional exam requirements/recommendations for international students: Required—TOEFL. Electronic applications accepted. *Faculty research:* Product development, design theory, cultural diversity, computer design accessibility.

Washington State University Spokane, Graduate Programs, Interdisciplinary Design Institute, Spokane, WA 99210-1495. Offers architecture (M Arch, MS); design (Dr DES); interior design (MA); landscape architecture (MS). Part-time programs available. *Degree requirements:* For master's, comprehensive exam (for some programs), thesis (for some programs); for doctorate, comprehensive exam, thesis/dissertation. *Entrance requirements:* For master's, minimum GPA of 3.0, portfolio of design work, 3 letters of recommendation (M Arch); for doctorate, minimum graduate GPA of 3.5. Additional exam requirements/recommendations for international students: Required—TOEFL (minimum score 550 paper-based; 213 computer-based). *Faculty research:* Environment-behavior relationships, land use and environmental planning, urban space as interior design, art and architectural aesthetics.

Medical Illustration

The Johns Hopkins University, School of Medicine, Graduate Programs in Medicine, Department of Art as Applied to Medicine, Baltimore, MD 21218-2699. Offers medical and biological illustration (MA). *Accreditation:* ARCMI. *Degree requirements:* For master's, thesis. Electronic applications accepted. *Faculty research:* 3D modeling, instructional design, microreconstruction, visualization, digital media.

Medical College of Georgia, School of Graduate Studies, Program in Medical Illustration, Augusta, GA 30912-1500. Offers MS. *Accreditation:* ARCMI. *Faculty:* 2 full-time (0 women), 2 part-time/adjunct (0 women). *Students:* 17 full-time (9 women), 2 part-time (1 woman); includes 1 minority (African American), 1 international. Average age 28. 18 applicants, 56% accepted, 8 enrolled. In 2008, 8 master's awarded. *Degree requirements:* For master's, thesis or alternative, project. *Entrance requirements:* For master's, GRE General Test, portfolio. Additional exam requirements/recommendations for international students: Required—TOEFL (minimum score 550 paper-based; 213 computer-based; 79 iBT). *Application deadline:* For fall admission, 1/31 for domestic and international students. Application fee: $30. Electronic applications accepted. *Financial support:* In 2008–09, 11 students received support. Federal Work-Study and institutionally sponsored loans available. Support available to part-time students. Financial award application deadline: 5/31; financial award applicants required to submit FAFSA. *Faculty research:* Digital visual communication modalities, information science education, Southwestern Native American art pedagogy, medical illustration pedagogy, public health/visual education. *Unit head:* Dr. Shelley Mishoe, Dean and Professor, 706-721-2621, Fax: 706-721-7312, E-mail: smishoe@mail.mcg.edu. *Application contact:* Dr. Steven Harrison, Chair, Associate Professor and Graduate Program Director, 706-721-3266, E-mail: sharriso@mcg.edu.

Rochester Institute of Technology, Graduate Enrollment Services, College of Imaging Arts and Sciences, School of Art, Program in Medical Illustration, Rochester, NY 14623-5603.

Offers MFA. *Degree requirements:* For master's, thesis. *Entrance requirements:* For master's, portfolio, 3.0 GPA. Additional exam requirements/recommendations for international students: Required—TOEFL (minimum score 550 paper-based; 213 computer-based; 79 iBT).

University of Illinois at Chicago, Graduate College, College of Applied Health Sciences, Program in Biomedical Visualization, Chicago, IL 60607-7128. Offers MS. *Accreditation:* ARCMI. *Degree requirements:* For master's, thesis. *Entrance requirements:* For master's, GRE General Test, minimum GPA of 2.75. Additional exam requirements/recommendations for international students: Required—TOEFL. Electronic applications accepted. *Expenses:* Contact institution. *Faculty research:* Medical illustration, graphics, reconstruction, anatomical modeling.

The University of Texas Southwestern Medical Center at Dallas, Southwestern Graduate School of Biomedical Sciences, Division of Applied Science, Biomedical Communications Program, Dallas, TX 75390. Offers MA. *Accreditation:* ARCMI. *Students:* 11 full-time (7 women), 5 part-time (3 women); includes 5 minority (2 Asian Americans or Pacific Islanders, 3 Hispanic Americans), 1 international. Average age 26. 21 applicants, 33% accepted, 4 enrolled. In 2008, 6 master's awarded. *Degree requirements:* For master's, thesis. *Entrance requirements:* For master's, GRE General Test, minimum GPA of 3.0. *Application deadline:* For spring admission, 9/1 priority date for domestic students. Applications are processed on a rolling basis. Application fee: $0. Electronic applications accepted. *Expenses:* Tuition, state resident: full-time $3600. Tuition, nonresident: full-time $10,344. Required fees: $763. *Financial support:* In 2008–09, 4 teaching assistantships were awarded; career-related internships or fieldwork and institutionally sponsored loans also available. Financial award application deadline: 3/1; financial award applicants required to submit FAFSA. *Faculty research:* Breast self-examination to indigent populations. *Unit head:* Lewis E. Calver, Chair, 214-648-4699, Fax: 214-648-5353, E-mail: lcalve@mednet.swmed.edu. *Application contact:* Sonja Shryer, Education Coordinator, 214-648-4634, Fax: 214-648-5353, E-mail: marcelle.hanson@utsouthwestern.edu.

Photography

Academy of Art University, Graduate Program, School of Photography, San Francisco, CA 94105-3410. Offers MFA. *Accreditation:* NASAD. Part-time programs available. Postbaccalaureate distance learning degree programs offered (no on-campus study). *Faculty:* 9 full-time (4 women), 30 part-time/adjunct (7 women). *Students:* 143 full-time (80 women), 147 part-time (76 women); includes 47 minority (13 African Americans, 2 American Indian/Alaska Native, 19 Asian Americans or Pacific Islanders, 13 Hispanic Americans), 39 international. Average age 34. 72 applicants. In 2008, 25 master's awarded. *Degree requirements:* For master's, final review. *Entrance requirements:* For master's, portfolio. *Application deadline:* For fall admission, 9/7 for domestic and international students; for spring admission, 2/2 for domestic and international students. Applications are processed on a rolling basis. Application fee: $100 ($500 for international students). Electronic applications accepted. *Expenses:* Tuition: Full-time $18,400; part-time $770 per term. Tuition and fees vary according to program. *Financial support:* Career-related internships or fieldwork and Federal Work-Study available. Support available to part-time students. Financial award application deadline: 8/10; financial award applicants required to submit FAFSA. *Unit head:* William Musgrove, Director, 800-544-

ARTS, E-mail: info@academyart.edu. *Application contact:* 800-544-ARTS, Fax: 415-263-4130, E-mail: info@academyart.edu.

Bard College, International Center of Photography, Annandale-on-Hudson, NY 12504. Offers advanced photographic studies (MFA).

Barry University, School of Arts and Sciences, Department of Fine Arts, Miami Shores, FL 33161-6695. Offers photography (MA, MFA). *Degree requirements:* For master's, thesis (for some programs). *Entrance requirements:* For master's, GRE General Test, minimum GPA of 3.0. Electronic applications accepted. *Faculty research:* Inclusion education, exceptional education, art-based assessments.

Bradley University, Graduate School, Slane College of Communications and Fine Arts, Department of Art, Peoria, IL 61625-0002. Offers ceramics (MA, MFA); drawing/illustration (MA, MFA); interdisciplinary art (MA, MFA); painting (MA, MFA); photography (MA, MFA); printmaking (MA, MFA); sculpture (MA, MFA); visual communication and design (MA, MFA).

Photography

Bradley University (continued)

Accreditation: NASAD. Part-time programs available. *Degree requirements:* For master's, comprehensive exam, thesis, final exhibit. *Entrance requirements:* For master's, portfolio, 2 letters of recommendation. Additional exam requirements/recommendations for international students: Required—TOEFL (minimum score 550 paper-based; 213 computer-based; 79 iBT).

Brooklyn College of the City University of New York, Division of Graduate Studies, Department of Art, Brooklyn, NY 11210-2889. Offers art history (MA, PhD); digital art (MFA); drawing and painting (MFA); photography (MFA); printmaking (MFA); sculpture (MFA). The department offers courses at Brooklyn College that are creditable toward the CUNY doctoral degree; MFA programs—Fall admissions only, application deadline 2/1. Part-time programs available. *Students:* 24 full-time (7 women), 13 part-time (12 women); includes 4 minority (1 African American, 1 Asian American or Pacific Islander, 2 Hispanic Americans), 1 international. Average age 30. 102 applicants, 48% accepted, 20 enrolled. In 2008, 15 master's awarded. *Degree requirements:* For master's, thesis. *Entrance requirements:* For master's, bachelor's degree in art, portfolio, 2 letters of recommendation. Additional exam requirements/recommendations for international students: Required—TOEFL (minimum score 500 paper-based; 173 computer-based; 61 iBT). *Application deadline:* For fall admission, 2/1 priority date for domestic students, 2/1 for international students; for spring admission, 11/1 priority date for domestic students, 10/1 for international students. Applications are processed on a rolling basis. Application fee: $125. Electronic applications accepted. *Expenses:* Tuition, state resident: full-time $7360; part-time $310 per credit hour. Tuition, nonresident: full-time $13,800; part-time $575 per credit hour. *Financial support:* Career-related internships or fieldwork, Federal Work-Study, institutionally sponsored loans, scholarships/grants, and painting awards available. Support available to part-time students. Financial award application deadline: 5/1; financial award applicants required to submit FAFSA. *Unit head:* Dr. Michael Mallory, Chairperson, 718-951-5181, E-mail: mmallory@brooklyn.cuny.edu. *Application contact:* Hernan Sierra, Graduate Admissions Coordinator, 718-951-4536, Fax: 718-951-4506, E-mail: grads@brooklyn.cuny.edu.

Brooks Institute, Graduate Program in Professional Photography, Santa Barbara, CA 93101. Offers MFA. Evening/weekend programs available. *Degree requirements:* For master's, thesis. *Entrance requirements:* For master's, portfolio review testing procedure (written exam), minimum GPA of 3.0, 3 letters of recommendation, official college transcripts. Additional exam requirements/recommendations for international students: Required—TOEFL (minimum score 580 paper-based; 237 computer-based). Electronic applications accepted.

California College of the Arts, Graduate Programs, Programs in Fine Art, San Francisco, CA 94107. Offers ceramics (MFA); film/video/performance (MFA); glass (MFA); jewelry/metal arts (MFA); painting/drawing (MFA); photography (MFA); printmaking (MFA); sculpture (MFA); textiles (MFA); wood/furniture (MFA). *Accreditation:* NASAD. *Degree requirements:* For master's, thesis, exhibit. *Entrance requirements:* For master's, appropriate bachelor's degree, portfolio. Additional exam requirements/recommendations for international students: Required—TOEFL (minimum score 600 paper-based; 250 computer-based). Electronic applications accepted.

California Institute of the Arts, School of Art, Valencia, CA 91355-2340. Offers art (MFA, Adv C); graphic design (MFA, Adv C); photography (MFA, Adv C). *Accreditation:* NASAD (one or more programs are accredited). *Degree requirements:* For master's, final project. *Entrance requirements:* For master's, portfolio. Additional exam requirements/recommendations for international students: Required—TOEFL. Electronic applications accepted.

California State University, Fullerton, Graduate Studies, College of the Arts, Department of Art, Fullerton, CA 92834-9480. Offers art (MA, MFA), including ceramics (MFA), crafts, creative photography (MFA), design (MFA), drawing and painting, printmaking (MFA), sculpture; art history (MA); design (MA). *Accreditation:* NASAD (one or more programs are accredited). Part-time programs available. *Students:* 56 full-time (33 women), 29 part-time (15 women); includes 24 minority (2 African Americans, 1 American Indian/Alaska Native, 11 Asian Americans or Pacific Islanders, 10 Hispanic Americans), 7 international. Average age 34. 74 applicants, 34% accepted, 20 enrolled. In 2008, 28 master's awarded. *Degree requirements:* For master's, project or thesis. *Entrance requirements:* For master's, minimum GPA of 2.5 in last 60 units of course work, portfolio. Application fee: $55. Tuition and fees vary according to degree level. *Financial support:* Career-related internships or fieldwork, Federal Work-Study, institutionally sponsored loans, and scholarships/grants available. Support available to part-time students. Financial award application deadline: 3/1. *Unit head:* Larry Johnson, Chair, 657-278-3471. *Application contact:* Al Ching, Adviser, 657-278-3471.

California State University, Los Angeles, Graduate Studies, College of Arts and Letters, Department of Art, Los Angeles, CA 90032-8530. Offers art (MA), including art education, art history, art therapy, ceramics, metals, and textiles, design (MA, MFA), painting, sculpture, and graphic arts, photography; fine arts (MFA), including crafts, design (MA, MFA), studio arts. *Accreditation:* NASAD (one or more programs are accredited). Part-time and evening/weekend programs available. *Faculty:* 16 full-time (6 women). *Students:* 23 full-time (14 women), 52 part-time (37 women); includes 29 minority (2 African Americans, 3 American Indian/Alaska Native, 7 Asian Americans or Pacific Islanders, 17 Hispanic Americans), 4 international. Average age 38. 30 applicants, 100% accepted, 14 enrolled. In 2008, 15 master's awarded. *Degree requirements:* For master's, comprehensive exam, project or thesis. *Entrance requirements:* For master's, portfolio. Additional exam requirements/recommendations for international students: Required—TOEFL (minimum score 500 paper-based; 173 computer-based). *Application deadline:* For fall admission, 6/15 for domestic students, 5/1 for international students; for winter admission, 11/1 for domestic students, 9/1 for international students; for spring admission, 2/1 for domestic students, 10/1 for international students. Applications are processed on a rolling basis. Application fee: $55. Electronic applications accepted. *Expenses:* Tuition, nonresident: part-time $226 per credit. Required fees: $4019. *Financial support:* Federal Work-Study available. Support available to part-time students. Financial award application deadline: 3/1. *Faculty research:* The artist and the book, conceptual art, ceramic processes, computer graphics, architectural graphics. *Unit head:* Dr. Robert Martin, Chair, 323-343-4010, Fax: 323-343-4045, E-mail: rjmartin@calstatela.edu. *Application contact:* Dr. Jose L. Galvan, Dean of Graduate Studies, 323-343-3820, Fax: 323-343-5653, E-mail: jgalvan@cslanet.calstatela.edu.

Claremont Graduate University, Graduate Programs, School of Arts and Humanities, Department of Art, Claremont, CA 91711. Offers digital media (MA, MFA); drawing (MA, MFA); installation (MA, MFA); new genre (MA, MFA); painting (MA, MFA); performance (MA, MFA); photography (MA, MFA); sculpture (MA, MFA). Part-time programs available. *Faculty:* 4 full-time (1 woman), 1 (woman) part-time/adjunct. *Students:* 62 full-time (34 women); includes 12 minority (3 African Americans, 4 Asian Americans or Pacific Islanders, 5 Hispanic Americans), 4 international. Average age 32. In 2008, 29 master's awarded. *Degree requirements:* For master's, final project show. *Entrance requirements:* For master's, BA in art or BFA, slide review. Additional exam requirements/recommendations for international students: Required—TOEFL (minimum score 550 paper-based; 213 computer-based; 80 iBT). *Application deadline:* For fall admission, 2/1 priority date for domestic students. Applications are processed on a rolling basis. Application fee: $60. Electronic applications accepted. *Expenses:* Contact institution. *Financial support:* Fellowships, research assistantships, teaching assistantships, Federal Work-Study, institutionally sponsored loans, and scholarships/grants available. Support available to part-time students. Financial award application deadline: 2/15; financial award applicants required to submit FAFSA. *Faculty research:* Acoustic sculpture, feminization of abstraction, installation sculpture. *Unit head:* David Pagel, Chair, 909-607-2479, Fax: 909-607-1276, E-mail: david.pagel@cgu.edu. *Application contact:* Pat Evans, Program Administrator, 909-607-9292, Fax: 909-607-1276, E-mail: patricia.evans@cgu.edu.

Columbia College Chicago, Graduate School, Department of Photography, Chicago, IL 60605-1996. Offers MA, MFA. *Students:* 19 full-time (15 women), 5 part-time (2 women); includes 1 minority (Asian American or Pacific Islander). Average age 27. 73 applicants, 8 enrolled. In 2008, 8 master's awarded. *Degree requirements:* For master's, thesis, project. *Entrance requirements:* For master's, minimum GPA of 3.0, portfolio. Additional exam requirements/recommendations for international students: Required—TOEFL (minimum score 550 paper-based; 213 computer-based). *Application deadline:* For fall admission, 2/2 for domestic and international students. Application fee: $55. Electronic applications accepted. *Expenses:* Tuition: Full-time $15,992; part-time $633 per credit hour. *Financial support:* Fellowships, Federal Work-Study and scholarships/grants available. Support available to part-time students. Financial award application deadline: 8/13; financial award applicants required to submit FAFSA. *Unit head:* Bob Thall, Chairperson, 312-369-7328, E-mail: bthall@colum.edu. *Application contact:* Keith Cleveland, 312-369-7261, Fax: 312-369-8022, E-mail: kcleveland@colum.edu.

Columbia University, School of the Arts, Visual Arts Division, New York, NY 10027. Offers new genres (MFA); painting (MFA); photography (MFA); printmaking (MFA); sculpture (MFA). *Degree requirements:* For master's, thesis. *Entrance requirements:* For master's, 3 letters of recommendation, portfolio, personal statement, resumé, official transcript. Additional exam requirements/recommendations for international students: Required—TOEFL (minimum score 600 paper-based; 250 computer-based; 100 iBT). Electronic applications accepted.

See Close-Up on page 285.

Cornell University, Graduate School, Graduate Fields of Architecture, Art and Planning, Field of Art, Ithaca, NY 14853-0001. Offers creative visual arts (MFA), including painting, photography, printmaking, sculpture. *Faculty:* 20 full-time (7 women). *Students:* 10 full-time (3 women). Average age 30. 107 applicants, 7% accepted, 4 enrolled. In 2008, 6 master's awarded. *Degree requirements:* For master's, thesis, exhibit. *Entrance requirements:* For master's, slide portfolio of 10-20 slides, 3 letters of recommendation, resumé. Additional exam requirements/recommendations for international students: Required—TOEFL (minimum score 550 paper-based; 213 computer-based; 77 iBT). *Application deadline:* For fall admission, 2/15 for domestic students. Application fee: $70. Electronic applications accepted. *Expenses:* Tuition: Full-time $29,500. Required fees: $70. Full-time tuition and fees vary according to degree level, program and student level. *Financial support:* In 2008–09, 10 students received support, including 10 teaching assistantships with full tuition reimbursements available; fellowships with full tuition reimbursements available, research assistantships with full tuition reimbursements available, institutionally sponsored loans, scholarships/grants, health care benefits, tuition waivers (full and partial), and unspecified assistantships also available. Financial award applicants required to submit FAFSA. *Faculty research:* Painting, sculpture, photography, printmaking. *Unit head:* Director of Graduate Studies, 607-255-6730, Fax: 607-255-3462. *Application contact:* Graduate Field Assistant, 607-255-6730, Fax: 607-255-3462, E-mail: artinfo@cornell.edu.

Cranbrook Academy of Art, Graduate School, Program in Fine Arts, Bloomfield Hills, MI 48303-0801. Offers ceramics (MFA); design (MFA), including graphic design; fiber arts (MFA); metalsmithing (MFA); painting (MFA); photography (MFA); printmaking (MFA); sculpture (MFA). *Accreditation:* NASAD. *Degree requirements:* For master's, thesis, exhibit. *Entrance requirements:* Additional exam requirements/recommendations for international students: Required—TOEFL (minimum score 550 paper-based; 213 computer-based).

See Close-Up on page 209.

The George Washington University, Columbian College of Arts and Sciences, Department of Fine Arts and Art History, Washington, DC 20052. Offers art history (MA), including art history, museum training; ceramics (MFA); drawing/painting (MFA); interior design (MFA); new media (MFA); photography (MFA); sculpture (MFA). *Accreditation:* CIDA. Part-time and evening/weekend programs available. *Faculty:* 16 full-time (7 women), 31 part-time/adjunct (19 women). *Students:* 49 full-time (44 women), 37 part-time (34 women); includes 16 minority (4 African Americans, 6 Asian Americans or Pacific Islanders, 6 Hispanic Americans), 2 international. Average age 28. 204 applicants, 49% accepted, 63 enrolled. In 2008, 39 master's awarded. *Entrance requirements:* For master's, GRE General Test, bachelor's degree in field, minimum GPA of 3.0. Additional exam requirements/recommendations for international students: Required—TOEFL (minimum score 550 paper-based; 213 computer-based; 80 iBT). *Application deadline:* For fall admission, 3/1 priority date for domestic students, 1/15 priority date for international students; for spring admission, 10/1 priority date for domestic students, 9/1 priority date for international students. Applications are processed on a rolling basis. Application fee: $60. Electronic applications accepted. *Financial support:* In 2008–09, 12 students received support; fellowships, teaching assistantships, career-related internships or fieldwork, Federal Work-Study, and tuition waivers available. Financial award application deadline: 1/15. *Unit head:* Thomas K. Brown, Chair, 202-994-9067, E-mail: thbrown@gwu.edu. *Application contact:* Information Contact, 202-994-6085, Fax: 202-994-8657, E-mail: art@gwu.edu.

Georgia State University, College of Arts and Sciences, Department of Communication, Atlanta, GA 30303-3083. Offers film/video/digital imaging (MA); human communication and social influence (MA); mass communication (MA); moving image studies (PhD); public communication (PhD). Part-time programs available. *Degree requirements:* For master's, one foreign language, thesis or alternative; for doctorate, comprehensive exam, thesis/dissertation. *Entrance requirements:* For master's and doctorate, GRE General Test. Additional exam requirements/recommendations for international students: Required—TOEFL (minimum score 80 computer-based). Electronic applications accepted. *Faculty research:* Critical/cultural studies, rhetoric studies, film/media studies, mass communications/journalism, audience studies.

Howard University, Graduate School, Division of Fine Arts, Department of Art, Program in Fine Arts, Washington, DC 20059-0002. Offers 3D reality (sculpture and ceramics) (MFA); design (MFA); electronic studio (MFA); painting (MFA); photography (MFA). *Accreditation:* NASAD. *Degree requirements:* For master's, comprehensive exam, thesis, exhibit. *Entrance requirements:* For master's, minimum GPA of 3.0, portfolio.

Illinois State University, Graduate School, College of Fine Arts, School of Art, Normal, IL 61790-2200. Offers art history (MA, MS); ceramics (MFA, MS); drawing (MFA, MS); fibers (MFA, MS); glass (MFA, MS); graphic design (MFA, MS); metals (MFA, MS); painting (MFA, MS); photography (MFA, MS); printmaking (MFA, MS); sculpture (MFA, MS). *Accreditation:* NASAD (one or more programs are accredited). *Degree requirements:* For master's, thesis or alternative, internship. *Entrance requirements:* For master's, portfolio, sample of scholarly writing. *Faculty research:* General operations support: Normal Editions Workshop for FY2007.

Indiana State University, School of Graduate Studies, College of Arts and Sciences, Department of Art, Terre Haute, IN 47809-1401. Offers ceramics (MA, MFA); drawing (MA, MFA); graphic design (MA, MFA); painting (MA, MFA); photography (MA, MFA); printmaking (MA, MFA); sculpture (MA, MFA). *Accreditation:* NASAD (one or more programs are accredited). Part-time programs available. *Degree requirements:* For master's, thesis or alternative, departmental qualifying exam. *Entrance requirements:* For master's, portfolio. Additional exam requirements/recommendations for international students: Required—TOEFL (minimum score 550 paper-based).

Inter American University of Puerto Rico, San Germán Campus, Graduate Studies Center, Program in Fine Arts, San Germán, PR 00683-5008. Offers art (MFA); ceramics (MFA); drawing (MFA); engraving (MFA); painting (MFA); photography (MFA); sculpture (MFA). *Degree requirements:* For master's, comprehensive exam, thesis. *Entrance requirements:* For master's, GRE General Test or EXADEP, minimum GPA of 3.0.

James Madison University, The Graduate School, College of Visual and Performing Arts, School of Art and Art History, Harrisonburg, VA 22807. Offers art education (MA); art history (MA); ceramics (MFA); drawing/painting (MFA); metal/jewelry (MFA); photography (MFA); printmaking (MFA); sculpture (MFA); studio art (MA); weaving/fibers (MFA). *Accreditation:* NASAD. Part-time programs available. *Faculty:* 13 full-time (8 women). *Students:* 7 full-time (5 women), 1 part-time (0 women); includes 2 minority (1 African American, 1 Asian American or Pacific Islander). Average age 27. In 2008, 3 master's awarded. *Degree requirements:* For master's, thesis (for some programs). *Entrance requirements:* For master's, GRE General Test, language exam in French or German, portfolio, 3 letters of recommendation, research paper. Additional exam requirements/recommendations for international students: Required—TOEFL. *Application deadline:* For fall admission, 2/15 priority date for domestic students, 2/15 for international students; for spring admission, 10/15 priority date for domestic students, 10/15 for international students. Applications are processed on a rolling basis. Application fee: $55. Electronic applications accepted. *Expenses:* Tuition, area resident: Full-time $7008; part-time $292 per credit hour. Tuition, state resident: full-time $7008; part-time $292 per credit hour. Tuition, nonresident: full-time $20,352; part-time $848 per credit hour. *Financial support:* In 2008–09, 8 students received support, including 3 teaching assistantships with full tuition reimbursements available (averaging $8,664 per year); Federal Work-Study and 3 graduate assistantships ($7,382) also available. Financial award application deadline: 3/1; financial award applicants required to submit FAFSA. *Unit head:* Leslie M. Bellavance, Academic Unit Head, 540-568-6216. *Application contact:* Lynette M. Bible, Director of Graduate Admissions, 540-568-6395, Fax: 540-568-7860, E-mail: biblelm@jmu.edu.

Lamar University, College of Graduate Studies, College of Fine Arts and Communication, Department of Art, Beaumont, TX 77710. Offers art history (MA); photography (MA); studio art (MA); visual design (MA). Part-time and evening/weekend programs available. *Faculty:* 7 full-time (3 women). *Students:* 1 (woman) full-time. Average age 45. 2 applicants, 0% accepted. In 2008, 2 master's awarded. *Degree requirements:* For master's, thesis. *Entrance requirements:* For master's, GRE General Test, minimum GPA of 2.5 in last 60 hours of undergraduate course work. Additional exam requirements/recommendations for international students: Required—TOEFL. *Application deadline:* For fall admission, 8/1 priority date for domestic students; for spring admission, 12/1 for domestic students. Applications are processed on a rolling basis. Application fee: $25 ($50 for international students). *Expenses:* Tuition, state resident: full-time $5000; part-time $195 per credit. Tuition, nonresident: full-time $12,376; part-time $476 per credit. Required fees: $1570. *Financial support:* Fellowships, career-related internships or fieldwork, Federal Work-Study, and scholarships/grants available. Financial award application deadline: 4/1. *Faculty research:* Nineteenth century academic paintings, metal casting, pigment color stability, computer-modified photography, manipulated photography. *Unit head:* Donna M. Meeks, Chair, 409-880-8141, Fax: 409-880-1799, E-mail: meeksdm@lub002.lamar.edu. *Application contact:* Debbie Piper, Coordinator of Graduate Admissions, 409-880-8356, Fax: 409-880-8414, E-mail: gradmissions@hal.lamar.edu.

Louisiana State University and Agricultural and Mechanical College, Graduate School, College of Art and Design, School of Art, Program in Studio Art, Baton Rouge, LA 70803. Offers ceramics (MFA); graphic design (MFA); painting and drawing (MFA); photography (MFA); printmaking (MFA); sculpture (MFA). *Accreditation:* NASAD. *Degree requirements:* For master's, thesis. *Entrance requirements:* For master's, minimum GPA of 3.0. Additional exam requirements/recommendations for international students: Required—TOEFL (minimum score 550 paper-based; 213 computer-based; 79 iBT). Electronic applications accepted.

Louisiana Tech University, Graduate School, College of Liberal Arts, School of Art, Ruston, LA 71272. Offers art and graphic design (MFA); photography (MFA); studio art (MFA). *Accreditation:* NASAD. Part-time programs available. *Degree requirements:* For master's, exhibit. *Entrance requirements:* For master's, GRE General Test, portfolio.

Maryland Institute College of Art, Graduate Studies, Program in Photography and Digital Imaging, Baltimore, MD 21217. Offers MFA. *Accreditation:* NASAD. *Degree requirements:* For master's, thesis, exhibit. *Entrance requirements:* For master's, portfolio, 40 studio credits, 6 credits in art history. Additional exam requirements/recommendations for international students: Required—TOEFL (minimum score 550 paper-based; 213 computer-based).

Marywood University, Academic Affairs, Insalaco College of Creative Arts and Management, Art Department, Program in Studio Art, Scranton, PA 18509-1598. Offers advertising design (MA); ceramics (MA); clay (MA); graphic design (MA); illustration (MA); interior architecture (MA); painting (MA); photography (MA); printmaking (MA); sculpture (MA); weaving (MA). *Accreditation:* NASAD. Part-time and evening/weekend programs available. *Degree requirements:* For master's, comprehensive exam, thesis or alternative. *Entrance requirements:* For master's, portfolio. Additional exam requirements/recommendations for international students: Required—TOEFL (minimum score 550 paper-based; 213 computer-based). Electronic applications accepted. *Faculty research:* Texture and line in clay, cast bronze sculpture, color theories, book art and illustration, sculptural form.

Marywood University, Academic Affairs, Insalaco College of Creative Arts and Management, Art Department, Program in Visual Arts, Scranton, PA 18509-1598. Offers advertising design (MFA); clay (MFA); fibers (MFA); graphic design (MFA); illustration (MFA); metals (MFA); painting (MFA); photography (MFA); printmaking (MFA). *Accreditation:* NASAD. Part-time and evening/weekend programs available. *Degree requirements:* For master's, thesis or alternative, exhibit. *Entrance requirements:* For master's, portfolio. Additional exam requirements/recommendations for international students: Required—TOEFL (minimum score 550 paper-based; 213 computer-based). Electronic applications accepted. *Expenses:* Contact institution. *Faculty research:* Mariology, exploration of visual imagery, explorations involving drawing on the loom, clay as sculptural medium, oil paintings.

Massachusetts College of Art and Design, Graduate Programs, Program in Fine Arts, Boston, MA 02115-5882. Offers ceramics (MFA); design (MFA); fibers (MFA); film (MFA); glass (MFA); media and performing arts (MFA); metals (MFA); painting (MFA); photography (MFA); printmaking (MFA); sculpture (MFA). *Accreditation:* NASAD. *Faculty:* 10 full-time (5 women), 8 part-time/adjunct (6 women). *Students:* 83 full-time (53 women), 17 part-time (10 women); includes 8 minority (1 American Indian/Alaska Native, 4 Asian Americans or Pacific Islanders, 3 Hispanic Americans), 15 international. Average age 34. 295 applicants, 24% accepted, 40 enrolled. In 2008, 37 master's awarded. *Degree requirements:* For master's, thesis, exhibit. *Entrance requirements:* For master's, 12 units of course work in art history, portfolio, resumé, college transcripts, statement of purpose, letters of reference, interview. Additional exam requirements/recommendations for international students: Required—TOEFL (minimum score 563 paper-based; 223 computer-based; 85 iBT); Recommended—IELTS (minimum score 6.5). *Application deadline:* For fall admission, 1/15 for domestic and international students; for spring admission, 11/1 for domestic students. Application fee: $75. *Expenses:* Tuition, area resident: Full-time $17,100; part-time $570 per credit. Tuition and fees vary according to program. *Financial support:* In 2008–09, 50 research assistantships (averaging $2,000 per year), 30 teaching assistantships (averaging $2,000 per year) were awarded; career-related internships or fieldwork, Federal Work-Study, and clerical/technical assistantships also available. Support available to part-time students. Financial award application deadline: 5/1; financial award applicants required to submit FAFSA. *Unit head:* George Creamer, Director, 617-879-7163, Fax: 617-879-7171, E-mail: creamer@massart.edu. *Application contact:* George Creamer, Director, 617-879-7163.

Memphis College of Art, Graduate Programs, Program in Studio Art, Memphis, TN 38104-2764. Offers painting (MFA); photography (MFA); printmaking (MFA); sculpture (MFA). *Accreditation:* NASAD. Part-time programs available. *Faculty:* 11 full-time (5 women), 2 part-time/adjunct (1 woman). *Students:* 18 full-time (9 women); includes 2 minority (both African Americans). Average age 29. 49 applicants, 55% accepted, 9 enrolled. In 2008, 4 master's awarded. *Degree requirements:* For master's, thesis, exhibition. *Entrance requirements:* For master's, portfolio, interview, resumé. Additional exam requirements/recommendations for international students: Required—TOEFL (minimum score 525 paper-based; 195 computer-based). *Application deadline:* For fall admission, 3/1 priority date for domestic and international students; for spring admission, 11/1 priority date for domestic and international students. Application fee: $50. Electronic applications accepted. *Expenses:* Tuition: Full-time $22,000; part-time $958 per credit hour. Required fees: $560; $280 per semester. Tuition and fees vary according to program. *Financial support:* In 2008–09, 11 students received support, including 2 teaching assistantships (averaging $2,000 per year); career-related internships or fieldwork, Federal Work-Study, institutionally sponsored loans, scholarships/grants, tuition waivers (partial), unspecified assistantships, and merit awards also available. Support available to part-time students. Financial award application deadline: 8/1; financial award applicants required to submit FAFSA. *Unit head:* Howard Paine, Graduate Program Director, 901-272-5100, Fax: 901-272-5158, E-mail: hpaine@mca.edu. *Application contact:* Annette James Moore, Director of Admissions, 800-727-1088, Fax: 901-272-5158, E-mail: info@mca.edu.

See Close-Up on page 213.

Mills College, Graduate Studies, Department of Art, Oakland, CA 94613-1000. Offers ceramics (MFA); intermedia (MFA); painting (MFA); photography (MFA); sculpture (MFA). *Faculty:* 7 full-time (6 women), 11 part-time/adjunct (7 women). *Students:* 22 full-time (10 women). Average age 30. 85 applicants, 29% accepted, 12 enrolled. In 2008, 12 master's awarded. *Degree requirements:* For master's, thesis or alternative, exhibit. *Entrance requirements:* Additional exam requirements/recommendations for international students: Required—TOEFL. *Application deadline:* For fall admission, 2/1 for domestic students; for spring admission, 11/1 for domestic students. Application fee: $50. *Expenses:* Contact institution. *Financial support:* In 2008–09, 12 students received support, including 7 fellowships (averaging $2,086 per year), 12 teaching assistantships with partial tuition reimbursements available (averaging $13,783 per year); scholarships/grants and unspecified assistantships also available. Financial award application deadline: 2/1; financial award applicants required to submit FAFSA. *Faculty research:* Contemporary Chinese/American art, Asian art, performance art, feminist theory, installation. *Unit head:* Ron Nagle, Chairperson, 510-430-3142, Fax: 510-430-3314. *Application contact:* Marika Benko, Graduate Admission Specialist, 510-430-3309, Fax: 510-430-2159, E-mail: grad-studies@mills.edu.

Minneapolis College of Art and Design, Program in Visual Studies, Minneapolis, MN 55404-4347. Offers animation (MFA); comic art (MFA); drawing (MFA); filmmaking (MFA); fine arts (MFA); furniture design (MFA); graphic design (MFA); illustration (MFA); interactive media (MFA); painting (MFA); photography (MFA); printmaking (MFA); sculpture (MFA). *Accreditation:* NASAD. Part-time programs available. *Faculty:* 23 full-time (7 women), 9 part-time/adjunct (4 women). *Students:* 40 full-time (21 women), 1 (woman) part-time; includes 1 minority (American Indian/Alaska Native). Average age 27. 172 applicants, 24% accepted, 15 enrolled. In 2008, 7 master's awarded. *Degree requirements:* For master's, thesis, thesis exhibit. *Entrance requirements:* For master's, portfolio, resumé, 3 letters of recommendation, personal statement. Additional exam requirements/recommendations for international students: Required—TOEFL (minimum score 550 paper-based; 213 computer-based; 79 iBT). *Application deadline:* For fall admission, 1/15 for domestic and international students. Application fee: $50. Electronic applications accepted. *Expenses:* Tuition: Full-time $28,400; part-time $813 per credit. *Financial support:* In 2008–09, 23 students received support, including 15 teaching assistantships (averaging $6,000 per year); career-related internships or fieldwork, Federal Work-Study, scholarships/grants, and unspecified assistantships also available. Support available to part-time students. Financial award application deadline: 3/15; financial award applicants required to submit FAFSA. *Faculty research:* Visual arts. *Unit head:* Carole Fisher, Graduate Director, 612-874-3629, E-mail: carole_fisher@mcad.edu. *Application contact:* William Mullen, Vice President of Enrollment Management, 612-874-3762, Fax: 612-874-3701, E-mail: william_mullen@mcad.edu.

New Mexico State University, Graduate School, College of Arts and Sciences, Department of Art, Las Cruces, NM 88003-8001. Offers art history (MA); ceramics (MA, MFA); design (MA, MFA); drawing (MFA); metals (MA, MFA); painting (MFA); photography (MFA); printmaking (MA, MFA); sculpture (MA, MFA). *Faculty:* 12 full-time (7 women), 2 part-time/adjunct (1 woman). *Students:* 31 full-time (14 women), 3 part-time (all women); includes 8 minority (1 American Indian/Alaska Native, 7 Hispanic Americans), 1 international. Average age 33. 30 applicants, 40% accepted, 9 enrolled. In 2008, 7 master's awarded. *Degree requirements:* For master's, comprehensive exam (for some programs), thesis, thesis exhibit. *Entrance requirements:* For master's, portfolio, 10-page paper (art history). *Application deadline:* For fall admission, 2/15 for domestic students; for winter admission, 10/15 for domestic students; for spring admission, 7/15 for domestic students. Application fee: $30 ($50 for international students). Electronic applications accepted. *Expenses:* Tuition, area resident: Full-time $3890; part-time $212.85 per credit. Tuition, state resident: full-time $3890; part-time $212.85 per credit. Tuition, nonresident: full-time $13,916; part-time $630.55 per credit. Required fees: $1218; $609 per semester. *Financial support:* In 2008–09, 33 students received support, including 29 teaching assistantships (averaging $9,807 per year); research assistantships, Federal Work-Study and health care benefits also available. Support available to part-time students. Financial award application deadline: 3/1; financial award applicants required to submit FAFSA. *Faculty research:* Painting, graphic design, sculpture, printmaking, drawing, ceramics, photo, jewelry. *Unit head:* Spencer D. Fidler, Head, 575-646-1705, Fax: 575-646-8036, E-mail: sfidler@nmsu.edu. *Application contact:* Elena Luna, Coordinator, 575-646-3498, Fax: 575-646-7721, E-mail: rosluna@nmsu.edu.

The New School: A University, Parsons The New School for Design, Program in Photography, New York, NY 10011. Offers MFA. *Faculty:* 6 full-time (2 women), 4 part-time/adjunct (0 women). *Students:* 8 full-time (6 women), 25 part-time (17 women); includes 2 minority (1 African American, 1 Asian American or Pacific Islander), 8 international. Average age 27. In 2008, 14 master's awarded. *Entrance requirements:* Additional exam requirements/recommendations for international students: Required—TOEFL (minimum score 580 paper-based; 237 computer-based; 93 iBT). *Application deadline:* For fall admission, 2/1 priority date for domestic students. Applications are processed on a rolling basis. Application fee: $50. *Expenses:* Tuition: Full-time $27,144; part-time $1508 per credit. Required fees: $355 per semester. *Financial support:* Federal Work-Study, scholarships/grants, and tuition waivers (partial) available. Financial award application deadline: 3/1. *Unit head:* Michelle Bogre, Chair, 212-229-8923 Ext. 4239, E-mail: bogrem@newschool.edu. *Application contact:* Anthony Padilla, Director of Admissions, 212-229-8989 Ext. 4023, Fax: 212-229-8975, E-mail: padillaa@newschool.edu.

See Close-Up on page 127.

The Ohio State University, Graduate School, College of the Arts, Department of Photography and Cinema, Columbus, OH 43210. Offers MA. Electronic applications accepted.

Ohio University, Graduate College, College of Fine Arts, School of Art, Athens, OH 45701-2979. Offers art history (MA); ceramics (MFA); graphic design (MFA); painting (MFA); photography (MFA); printmaking (MFA); sculpture (MFA). Part-time programs available. *Degree requirements:* For master's, thesis. *Entrance requirements:* For master's, portfolio. Additional exam requirements/recommendations for international students: Required—TOEFL. *Faculty research:* Vapor fired ceramics, video installation, art theory, digital photography, mixed and interdisciplinary media work.

Ohio University, Graduate College, Scripps College of Communication, School of Visual Communication, Athens, OH 45701-2979. Offers MA. *Accreditation:* NASAD. *Entrance requirements:* For master's, minimum GPA of 2.5, portfolio. Additional exam requirements/recommendations for international students: Required—TOEFL (minimum score 600 paper-based; 250 computer-based). Electronic applications accepted. *Faculty research:* Photographic communication (photojournalism, multimedia, and documentary), photographic illustration (product, editorial, architectural), multimedia (planning and design), media management.

Otis College of Art and Design, Program in Fine Arts, Los Angeles, CA 90045-9785. Offers new genres (MFA); painting (MFA); photography (MFA); sculpture (MFA). *Accreditation:* NASAD. *Faculty:* 1 (woman) full-time, 8 part-time/adjunct (3 women). *Students:* 17 full-time (8 women); includes 6 minority (1 African American, 1 American Indian/Alaska Native, 2 Asian Americans or Pacific Islanders, 2 Hispanic Americans), 1 international. Average age 32. 129 applicants, 21% accepted, 8 enrolled. In 2008, 12 master's awarded. *Degree requirements:* For master's, thesis. *Entrance requirements:* For master's, portfolio. Additional exam requirements/recommendations for international students: Required—TOEFL (minimum score 600 paper-based; 250 computer-based). *Application deadline:* For fall admission, 2/15 for domestic and

Photography

Otis College of Art and Design (continued)
international students. Application fee: $50. Electronic applications accepted. *Expenses:* Tuition: Full-time $30,464. Required fees: $700. *Financial support:* Career-related internships or fieldwork, Federal Work-Study, scholarships/grants, and tuition waivers (partial) available. Financial award applicants required to submit FAFSA. *Unit head:* Roy Dowell, Chair, 310-665-6893, Fax: 310-665-6998, E-mail: grads@otis.edu. *Application contact:* Information Contact, 310-665-6820, Fax: 310-665-6821, E-mail: admissions@otis.edu.

Penn State University Park, Graduate School, College of Arts and Architecture, School of Visual Arts, State College, University Park, PA 16802-1503. Offers art (MFA), including ceramics, drawing/painting, photography, printmaking, sculpture; art education (M Ed, MS, PhD). *Accreditation:* NASAD.

Pratt Institute, School of Art and Design, Program in Fine Arts, Brooklyn, NY 11205-3899. Offers new forms (MFA); painting and drawing (MFA); photography (MFA); printmaking (MFA); sculpture (MFA). *Accreditation:* NASAD. Part-time programs available. *Faculty:* 8 full-time (2 women), 30 part-time/adjunct (15 women). *Students:* 140 full-time (90 women), 5 part-time (4 women); includes 16 minority (3 African Americans, 8 Asian Americans or Pacific Islanders, 5 Hispanic Americans), 43 international. Average age 29. 282 applicants, 49% accepted, 56 enrolled. In 2008, 69 master's awarded. *Degree requirements:* For master's, thesis, exhibit. *Entrance requirements:* For master's, portfolio, bachelor's degree, transcripts, letters of recommendation. Additional exam requirements/recommendations for international students: Required—TOEFL (minimum score 550 paper-based; 213 computer-based). *Application deadline:* For fall admission, 2/1 for domestic and international students; for spring admission, 10/1 for domestic and international students. Application fee: $50 ($90 for international students). Electronic applications accepted. *Expenses:* Tuition: Full-time $20,412; part-time $1134 per credit. Required fees: $1190; $1190 per year. *Financial support:* Career-related internships or fieldwork, Federal Work-Study, institutionally sponsored loans, scholarships/grants, health care benefits, and unspecified assistantships available. Support available to part-time students. Financial award application deadline: 2/1; financial award applicants required to submit FAFSA. *Unit head:* Donna Moran, Chairperson, 718-636-3602, E-mail: dmoran@pratt.edu. *Application contact:* Young Hah, Director of Graduate Admissions, 718-636-3683, Fax: 718-399-4242, E-mail: yhah@pratt.edu.

See Close-Up on page 219.

Rhode Island School of Design, Graduate Studies, Division of Fine Arts, Department of Photography, Providence, RI 02903-2784. Offers MFA. *Accreditation:* NASAD. *Degree requirements:* For master's, thesis, exhibit. *Entrance requirements:* For master's, portfolio, 3 letters of recommendation. Additional exam requirements/recommendations for international students: Required—TOEFL (minimum score 580 paper-based; 237 computer-based), IELTS (minimum score 6.5).

Rochester Institute of Technology, Graduate Enrollment Services, College of Imaging Arts and Sciences, School of Photographic Arts and Sciences, Program in Imaging Arts, Rochester, NY 14623-5603. Offers MFA. *Accreditation:* NASAD. *Degree requirements:* For master's, thesis, exhibit. *Entrance requirements:* For master's, portfolio, minimum GPA of 3.0. Additional exam requirements/recommendations for international students: Required—TOEFL (minimum score 550 paper-based; 213 computer-based; 79 iBT).

San Francisco Art Institute, Graduate Program, Department of Photography, San Francisco, CA 94133. Offers MFA, Certificate. *Accreditation:* NASAD. Part-time programs available. *Degree requirements:* For master's and Certificate, oral reviews. *Entrance requirements:* For master's and Certificate, portfolio. Additional exam requirements/recommendations for international students: Required—TOEFL (minimum score 580 paper-based; 237 computer-based). Electronic applications accepted.

See Close-Up on page 221.

San Jose State University, Graduate Studies and Research, College of Humanities and the Arts, School of Art and Design, San Jose, CA 95192-0001. Offers art education (MA); art history (MA); digital media (MFA); digital media in art history and education (MA); photography (MFA); pictorial arts (MFA); spatial arts (MFA). *Accreditation:* NASAD (one or more programs are accredited). *Entrance requirements:* For master's, GRE. Electronic applications accepted.

Savannah College of Art and Design, Graduate School, Program in Commercial Photography, Savannah, GA 31402-3146. Offers MA. Part-time programs available. *Degree requirements:* For master's, thesis. *Entrance requirements:* For master's, interview, portfolio. Additional exam requirements/recommendations for international students: Required—TOEFL (minimum score 450 paper-based; 133 computer-based). Electronic applications accepted. *Expenses:* Tuition: Full-time $28,215; part-time $3135 per course. One-time fee: $500.

Savannah College of Art and Design, Graduate School, Program in Digital Photography, Savannah, GA 31402-3146. Offers MA. Part-time programs available. *Degree requirements:* For master's, thesis. *Entrance requirements:* For master's, interview, portfolio. Additional exam requirements/recommendations for international students: Required—TOEFL (minimum score 450 paper-based; 133 computer-based). Electronic applications accepted. *Expenses:* Tuition: Full-time $28,215; part-time $3135 per course. One-time fee: $500.

Savannah College of Art and Design, Graduate School, Program in Documentary Photography, Savannah, GA 31402-3146. Offers MA. Part-time programs available. *Degree requirements:* For master's, thesis. *Entrance requirements:* For master's, interview, portfolio. Additional exam requirements/recommendations for international students: Required—TOEFL (minimum score 450 paper-based; 133 computer-based). Electronic applications accepted. *Expenses:* Tuition: Full-time $28,215; part-time $3135 per course. One-time fee: $500.

Savannah College of Art and Design, Graduate School, Program in Photography, Savannah, GA 31402-3146. Offers MA, MFA. Part-time programs available. *Degree requirements:* For master's, thesis, exhibit, internships. *Entrance requirements:* For master's, interview, portfolio. Additional exam requirements/recommendations for international students: Required—TOEFL (minimum score 450 paper-based; 133 computer-based). Electronic applications accepted. *Expenses:* Tuition: Full-time $28,215; part-time $3135 per course. One-time fee: $500.

See Close-Up on page 223.

School of the Art Institute of Chicago, Graduate Division, Department of Photography, Chicago, IL 60603-3103. Offers MFA. *Accreditation:* NASAD. *Entrance requirements:* Additional exam requirements/recommendations for international students: Required—TOEFL.

See Close-Up on page 225.

School of Visual Arts, Graduate Programs, Digital Photography Department, New York, NY 10010-3994. Offers MPS. *Degree requirements:* For master's, thesis or project. *Entrance requirements:* For master's, portfolio. Additional exam requirements/recommendations for international students: Required—TOEFL (minimum score 550 paper-based; 213 computer-based; 79 iBT). Electronic applications accepted.

School of Visual Arts, Graduate Programs, Program in Photography, Video and Related Media, New York, NY 10010-3994. Offers MFA. *Accreditation:* NASAD. *Degree requirements:* For master's, final review, project or thesis. *Entrance requirements:* For master's, portfolio. Additional exam requirements/recommendations for international students: Required—TOEFL (minimum score 550 paper-based; 213 computer-based; 79 iBT). Electronic applications accepted.

Southern Methodist University, Meadows School of the Arts, Division of Art, Dallas, TX 75275. Offers studio art (MFA), including ceramics, drawing, painting, photography, printmaking, sculpture. *Accreditation:* NASAD. *Faculty:* 11 full-time (3 women), 6 part-time/adjunct (3 women). *Students:* 8 full-time (4 women), 1 international. Average age 31. 35 applicants, 20% accepted, 6 enrolled. In 2008, 4 master's awarded. *Degree requirements:* For master's, thesis or alternative, exhibit. *Entrance requirements:* For master's, BFA or equivalent, letters of recommendation, portfolio. Additional exam requirements/recommendations for international students: Required—TOEFL (minimum score 550 paper-based; 213 computer-based; 80 iBT). *Application deadline:* For fall admission, 2/15 for domestic and international students. Application fee: $75. *Financial support:* In 2008–09, 5 fellowships (averaging $32,914 per year), 5 teaching assistantships (averaging $3,000 per year) were awarded; scholarships/grants and unspecified assistantships also available. Financial award application deadline: 3/1; financial award applicants required to submit FAFSA. *Faculty research:* American stoneware, Southwestern furniture traditions, photographic apparatus and techniques, American ceramists, architecture. Total annual research expenditures: $20,000. *Unit head:* James W. Sullivan, Chair, 214-768-2489, E-mail: jsulliva@smu.edu. *Application contact:* Jean Cherry, Director of Graduate Admissions and Records, 214-768-3765, Fax: 214-768-3272, E-mail: jcherry@smu.edu.

Syracuse University, Graduate School, College of Visual and Performing Arts, Program in Art Photography, Syracuse, NY 13244. Offers MFA. *Accreditation:* NASAD. Part-time programs available. *Degree requirements:* For master's, thesis or alternative. *Entrance requirements:* For master's, portfolio. Additional exam requirements/recommendations for international students: Required—TOEFL. Electronic applications accepted.

Syracuse University, Graduate School, S. I. Newhouse School of Public Communications, Program in Photography, Syracuse, NY 13244. Offers MS. *Degree requirements:* For master's, thesis optional, special project. *Entrance requirements:* For master's, GRE General Test, portfolio. Additional exam requirements/recommendations for international students: Required—TOEFL (minimum score 600 paper-based; 250 computer-based). Electronic applications accepted.

See Close-Up on page 705.

Temple University, Graduate School, Tyler School of Art, Department of Graphic Arts and Design, Philadelphia, PA 19122-6096. Offers graphic and interactive design (MFA); photography (MFA); printmaking (MFA). *Accreditation:* NASAD. *Degree requirements:* For master's, essay, exhibit. *Entrance requirements:* For master's, minimum GPA of 3.0; slide portfolio, 40 credits in studio art; 12 credits in art history. Additional exam requirements/recommendations for international students: Required—TOEFL (minimum score 550 paper-based; 213 computer-based; 79 iBT). Electronic applications accepted.

The University of Alabama, Graduate School, College of Arts and Sciences, Department of Art, Tuscaloosa, AL 35487. Offers art history (MA); studio art (MA, MFA), including ceramics, painting, photography, printmaking, sculpture. *Accreditation:* NASAD. Part-time programs available. *Faculty:* 15 full-time (8 women). *Students:* 16 full-time (8 women), 4 part-time (all women), 1 international. Average age 31. 17 applicants, 41% accepted, 6 enrolled. In 2008, 9 master's awarded. *Degree requirements:* For master's, one foreign language, comprehensive exam (for some programs), thesis (for some programs), oral exam, thesis statement, exhibit (studio art), thesis (art history). *Entrance requirements:* For master's, GRE General Test or MAT (art history), minimum GPA of 3.0, BFA or equivalent (studio art). Additional exam requirements/recommendations for international students: Required—TOEFL (minimum score 550 paper-based; 213 computer-based). *Application deadline:* For fall admission, 3/15 for domestic and international students; for spring admission, 10/15 for domestic and international students. Applications are processed on a rolling basis. Application fee: $30. Electronic applications accepted. *Expenses:* Tuition, area resident: Full-time $6400. Tuition, state resident: full-time $6400. Tuition, nonresident: full-time $18,000. *Financial support:* In 2008–09, 2 fellowships with full tuition reimbursements (averaging $14,000 per year), 13 teaching assistantships with full and partial tuition reimbursements (averaging $9,206 per year) were awarded; career-related internships or fieldwork, institutionally sponsored loans, scholarships/grants, and unspecified assistantships also available. Financial award application deadline: 7/14. *Faculty research:* Nineteenth century American art history, Chinese art history, baroque art history, twentieth century art history, Asian art history. *Unit head:* William T. Dooley, Chairperson, 205-348-1890, Fax: 205-348-0287, E-mail: wtdooley@bama.ua.edu. *Application contact:* Craig R. Wedderspoon, Graduate Coordinator, 205-348-1898, Fax: 205-348-0287, E-mail: cwedders@bama.edu.

University of Alaska Fairbanks, College of Liberal Arts, Department of Art, Fairbanks, AK 99775-5640. Offers art (MFA); ceramics (MFA); computer art (MFA); drawing (MFA); Native arts (MFA); painting (MFA); photography (MFA); printmaking (MFA); sculpture (MFA). Part-time programs available. *Faculty:* 7 full-time (2 women), 6 part-time/adjunct (4 women). *Students:* 7 full-time (2 women), 1 (woman) part-time; includes 1 minority (American Indian/Alaska Native). Average age 33. 14 applicants, 29% accepted, 3 enrolled. In 2008, 6 master's awarded. *Degree requirements:* For master's, comprehensive exam, thesis, oral exam, oral defense. *Entrance requirements:* For master's, portfolio. Additional exam requirements/recommendations for international students: Required—TOEFL (minimum score 550 paper-based; 213 computer-based; 80 iBT). *Application deadline:* For fall admission, 6/1 for domestic students, 3/1 for international students; for spring admission, 10/15 for domestic students, 9/1 for international students. Applications are processed on a rolling basis. Application fee: $60. Electronic applications accepted. *Expenses:* Tuition, area resident: Full-time $5418; part-time $301 per credit. Tuition, state resident: full-time $5418; part-time $301 per credit. Tuition, nonresident: full-time $11,070; part-time $615 per credit. Required fees: $849; $25 per credit. $78 per semester. Tuition and fees vary according to course load and reciprocity agreements. *Financial support:* In 2008–09, 1 fellowship (averaging $13,500 per year), 4 teaching assistantships (averaging $12,058 per year) were awarded; research assistantships, Federal Work-Study, scholarships/grants, health care benefits, and unspecified assistantships also available. Support available to part-time students. Financial award application deadline: 7/1; financial award applicants required to submit FAFSA. *Faculty research:* Computer art, survey of arts in Alaska, found object art, visualization and animation, painting from the wilderness. *Unit head:* Todd Sherman, Chair, 907-474-7530, Fax: 907-474-5853, E-mail: fyart@uaf.edu. *Application contact:* Todd Sherman, Chair, 907-474-7530, Fax: 907-474-5853, E-mail: fyart@uaf.edu.

University of Colorado at Boulder, Graduate School, College of Arts and Sciences, Department of Art and Art History, Boulder, CO 80309. Offers art history (MA), including 19th century art, contemporary art criticism, early 20th century art, Russian and Soviet art; ceramics (MFA); drawing (MFA); painting (MFA); photography and media arts (MFA); printmaking (MFA); sculpture (MFA). *Degree requirements:* For master's, variable foreign language requirement, comprehensive exam, thesis (for some programs). *Entrance requirements:* For master's, GRE General Test, minimum undergraduate GPA of 3.0, portfolio. *Faculty research:* Drawing, painting, ceramics, sculpture, photography and media arts, printmaking (MFA); history-Russian and Soviet art, Early 20th Century art, contemporary art criticism, 19th Century art (MA).

University of Florida, Graduate School, College of Fine Arts, School of Art and Art History, Gainesville, FL 32611. Offers art (MFA), including ceramics, creative photography, drawing, electronic intermedia, graphic design, painting, printmaking, sculpture; art education (MA); art history (MA, PhD); digital arts and sciences (MA); museology (museum studies) (MA). *Accreditation:* NASAD. *Degree requirements:* For master's, variable foreign language requirement, project or thesis (MFA). *Entrance requirements:* For master's, portfolio (MFA), writing sample (MA), GRE General Test or minimum GPA of 3.0. Additional exam requirements/recommendations for international students: Required—TOEFL (minimum score 550 paper-based; 213 computer-based). Electronic applications accepted. *Faculty research:* Studio production, art historical studies of style context.

University of Houston, College of Liberal Arts and Social Sciences, Department of Art, Houston, TX 77204. Offers interior design (MA); painting (MA); photography (MA); sculpture (MA); MFA/MA. *Faculty:* 13 full-time (6 women), 9 part-time/adjunct (8 women). *Students:* 35 full-time (19 women); includes 5 minority (1 Asian American or Pacific Islander, 4 Hispanic Americans), 2 international. Average age 31. 30 applicants, 43% accepted, 10 enrolled. In

2008, 12 master's awarded. *Degree requirements:* For master's, comprehensive exam, visual thesis. *Entrance requirements:* For master's, GRE General Test, portfolio. *Application deadline:* For fall admission, 2/28 for domestic students; for spring admission, 10/30 for domestic students. Application fee: $25 ($100 for international students). *Expenses:* Tuition, state resident: full-time $5164; part-time $287 per credit. Tuition, nonresident: full-time $10,222; part-time $568 per credit. *Financial support:* In 2008–09, 31 teaching assistantships with full tuition reimbursements (averaging $10,600 per year) were awarded; career-related internships or fieldwork, Federal Work-Study, institutionally sponsored loans, scholarships/grants, health care benefits, and unspecified assistantships also available. Support available to part-time students. Financial award application deadline: 3/10. *Faculty research:* Alternative art projects. *Unit head:* Dr. John Reed, Chairperson, 713-743-3001, Fax: 713-743-2823, E-mail: jreed@uh.edu. *Application contact:* Dr. John Reed, Chairperson, 713-743-3001, Fax: 713-743-2823, E-mail: jreed@uh.edu.

University of Illinois at Chicago, Graduate College, College of Architecture and Art, School of Art and Design, Chicago, IL 60607-7128. Offers electronic visualization (MFA); film animation (MFA); graphic design (MFA); industrial design (MFA); photography (MFA); studio arts (MFA). *Accreditation:* NASAD. *Degree requirements:* For master's, thesis, exhibit. *Entrance requirements:* For master's, MAT, portfolio. Additional exam requirements/recommendations for international students: Required—TOEFL. Electronic applications accepted.

University of Illinois at Urbana–Champaign, Graduate College, College of Fine and Applied Arts, School of Art and Design, Program in Studio Arts, Champaign, IL 61820. Offers art and design (MFA); crafts (MFA); metals (MFA); painting (MFA); photography (MFA); sculpture (MFA). *Accreditation:* NASAD. *Students:* 17 full-time (9 women), 3 part-time (all women); includes 3 minority (1 American Indian/Alaska Native, 1 Asian American or Pacific Islander, 1 Hispanic American), 5 international. 52 applicants, 13% accepted, 6 enrolled. In 2008, 4 master's awarded. *Entrance requirements:* For master's, minimum GPA of 3.0. Additional exam requirements/recommendations for international students: Required—TOEFL (minimum score 550 paper-based; 213 computer-based; 79 iBT). *Application deadline:* Applications are processed on a rolling basis. Application fee: $60 ($75 for international students). Electronic applications accepted. *Financial support:* Fellowships, research assistantships, teaching assistantships, tuition waivers (full and partial) available. *Unit head:* Alan Mette, Chair, 217-244-7496, Fax: 217-244-7688, E-mail: amette@illinois.edu. *Application contact:* Marsha Biddle, Assistant to the Associate Director, 217-333-0642, Fax: 217-244-7688, E-mail: mbiddle@illinois.edu.

University of Massachusetts Dartmouth, Graduate School, College of Visual and Performing Arts, Program in Visual Design, North Dartmouth, MA 02747-2300. Offers digital media (MFA); graphic design (MFA); illustration (MFA); photography (MFA); typography (MFA). *Accreditation:* NASAD. *Faculty:* 17 full-time (8 women), 6 part-time/adjunct (2 women). *Students:* 6 full-time (5 women), 1 (woman) part-time, 1 international. Average age 40. 15 applicants, 27% accepted, 2 enrolled. In 2008, 4 master's awarded. *Degree requirements:* For master's, visual thesis. *Entrance requirements:* For master's, portfolio, interview, minimum GPA of 3.0, 3 letters of recommendation. Additional exam requirements/recommendations for international students: Required—TOEFL (minimum score 500 paper-based). *Application deadline:* For fall admission, 3/1 priority date for domestic students, 1/1 priority date for international students. Applications are processed on a rolling basis. Application fee: $40 ($60 for international students). Electronic applications accepted. *Expenses:* Tuition, state resident: full-time $2071; part-time $86.29 per credit. Tuition, nonresident: full-time $8099; part-time $337.46 per credit. Required fees: $7946. Tuition and fees vary according to class time, course load and reciprocity agreements. *Financial support:* In 2008–09, 1 research assistantship with full tuition reimbursement (averaging $3,940 per year), 4 teaching assistantships with full tuition reimbursements (averaging $3,500 per year) were awarded; Federal Work-Study and unspecified assistantships also available. Support available to part-time students. Financial award application deadline: 3/1; financial award applicants required to submit FAFSA. *Unit head:* Memory Hollowy, Director, 508-999-8554, E-mail: mholloway@umassd.edu. *Application contact:* Elan Turcotte-Shamski, Graduate Admissions Officer, 508-999-8604, Fax: 508-999-8183, E-mail: graduate@umassd.edu.

University of Memphis, Graduate School, College of Communication and Fine Arts, Department of Art, Memphis, TN 38152. Offers art (Graduate Certificate); art history (MA), including Egyptian art and archaeology, general art history; ceramics (MFA); graphic design (MFA); interior design (MFA); painting (MFA); printmaking/photography (MFA); sculpture (MFA). *Accreditation:* NASAD (one or more programs are accredited). *Faculty:* 21 full-time (7 women), 1 (woman) part-time/adjunct. *Students:* 41 full-time (28 women), 3 part-time (all women); includes 6 African Americans, 1 Asian American or Pacific Islander, 1 international. Average age 28. 45 applicants, 73% accepted, 12 enrolled. In 2008, 15 master's, 3 other advanced degrees awarded. *Degree requirements:* For master's, 2 foreign languages, comprehensive exam, thesis. *Entrance requirements:* For master's, GRE General Test or MAT, portfolio (MFA). *Application deadline:* For fall admission, 8/1 for domestic students; for spring admission, 12/1 for domestic students. Applications are processed on a rolling basis. Application fee: $35 ($60 for international students). *Expenses:* Tuition, area resident: Full-time $6242; part-time $330 per credit hour. Tuition, state resident: full-time $6242; part-time $330 per credit hour. Tuition, nonresident: full-time $17,828; part-time $815 per credit hour. Required fees: $1156. *Financial support:* Research assistantships with full tuition reimbursements, teaching assistantships with full tuition reimbursements available. Financial award applicants required to submit FAFSA. *Faculty research:* Online collaborative learning, advanced art history studies, electronic publishing/design, studio arts, architectural studies. *Unit head:* Prof. Richard Lou, Chair, 901-678-2216, Fax: 901-678-2735, E-mail: gmyatt@memphis.edu. *Application contact:* Greely Myat, Graduate Studies Coordinator, 901-678-2650.

University of Miami, Graduate School, College of Arts and Sciences, Department of Art and Art History, Coral Gables, FL 33124. Offers art history (MA); ceramics/glass (MFA); graphic design/multimedia (MFA); painting (MFA); photography/digital imaging (MFA); printmaking (MFA); sculpture (MFA). Part-time programs available. *Degree requirements:* For master's, variable foreign language requirement, thesis, exhibit (MFA), comprehensive exam (MA). *Entrance requirements:* For master's, GRE General Test (MA), research paper (MA), slide portfolio (MFA), artist statement (MFA). Additional exam requirements/recommendations for international students: Required—TOEFL. Electronic applications accepted. *Faculty research:* Installation art, public art.

University of Notre Dame, Graduate School, College of Arts and Letters, Division of Humanities, Department of Art, Art History, and Design, Notre Dame, IN 46556. Offers art history (MA); design (MFA), including graphic design, industrial design; studio art (MFA), including ceramics, painting, photography, printmaking, sculpture. *Accreditation:* NASAD. *Faculty:* 19 full-time (6 women), 3 part-time/adjunct (1 woman). *Students:* 23 full-time (12 women); includes 2 minority (both Hispanic Americans), 1 international. 83 applicants, 18% accepted, 10 enrolled. In 2008, 11 master's awarded. *Degree requirements:* For master's, comprehensive exam (for some programs), thesis. *Entrance requirements:* For master's, GRE General Test, minimum GPA of 3.0. Additional exam requirements/recommendations for international students: Required—TOEFL (minimum score 600 paper-based; 250 computer-based; 80 iBT). *Application deadline:* For fall admission, 2/1 priority date for domestic and international students. Application fee: $50. Electronic applications accepted. *Financial support:* In 2008–09, 20 students received support; fellowships with full tuition reimbursements available, research assistantships with full tuition reimbursements available, teaching assistantships with full tuition reimbursements available, scholarships/grants, tuition waivers (full), and unspecified assistantships available. Financial award application deadline: 2/1. *Faculty research:* Studio art practice in ceramics, printing, photography, printmaking and sculpture, graphic design and industrial design, digital imaging in design and photography, Renaissance and American art history, contemporary art theory and criticism. *Unit head:* Prof. Martina Lopez, Director of Graduate Studies, 574-631-7652, E-mail: art.1@nd.edu. *Application contact:* Dr. Barbara Turpin, Director of Graduate Admissions, 574-631-7706, Fax: 574-631-4183.

University of Oklahoma, Graduate College, College of Fine Arts, School of Art and Art History, Norman, OK 73019. Offers art (MA, MFA); art history (MA, MFA); ceramics (MFA); film and video (MFA); painting (MFA); photography (MFA); printmaking (MFA); visual communications (MFA). *Faculty:* 27 full-time (10 women), 2 part-time/adjunct (0 women). *Students:* 20 full-time (13 women), 12 part-time (10 women); includes 6 minority (2 African Americans, 4 American Indian/Alaska Native), 3 international. 28 applicants, 39% accepted, 9 enrolled. In 2008, 8 master's awarded. *Degree requirements:* For master's, thesis (MA), exhibit (MFA), departmental qualifying exam. *Entrance requirements:* For master's, GRE General Test (MA), bachelor's degree in art (MFA) or art history (MA), minimum GPA of 3.0 in last 60 undergraduate hours, 3 letters of recommendation, written research paper. Additional exam requirements/recommendations for international students: Required—TOEFL (minimum score 550 paper-based; 213 computer-based). *Application deadline:* For fall admission, 2/1 priority date for domestic students, 2/1 for international students; for spring admission, 10/1 for domestic and international students. Applications are processed on a rolling basis. Application fee: $40 ($90 for international students). Electronic applications accepted. *Expenses:* Tuition, state resident: full-time $3744; part-time $156 per credit hour. Tuition, nonresident: full-time $13,577; part-time $565.70 per credit hour. Required fees: $2415.40; $90.10 per credit hour. *Financial support:* In 2008–09, 16 students received support, including 14 research assistantships with partial tuition reimbursements available (averaging $10,014 per year), 4 teaching assistantships with partial tuition reimbursements available (averaging $9,586 per year); career-related internships or fieldwork, Federal Work-Study, institutionally sponsored loans, scholarships/grants, health care benefits, tuition waivers (partial), and unspecified assistantships also available. Support available to part-time students. Financial award application deadline: 4/7; financial award applicants required to submit FAFSA. *Faculty research:* Native American art history and art of the American West, contemporary and figurative sculpture, painting and print making, graphic design, media. Total annual research expenditures: $29,536. *Unit head:* Mary Jo Watson, Director, 405-325-2691, Fax: 405-325-1668, E-mail: mjwatson@ou.edu. *Application contact:* Jonathan Hils, Graduate Liaison, 405-325-2691, Fax: 405-325-1668, E-mail: hils@ou.edu.

The University of Tennessee, Graduate School, College of Arts and Sciences, School of Art, Knoxville, TN 37996. Offers ceramics (MFA); drawing (MFA); graphic design (MFA); inter-area studies (MFA); media arts (MFA); painting (MFA); printmaking (MFA); sculpture (MFA); watercolor (MFA). *Accreditation:* NASAD. *Degree requirements:* For master's, thesis or alternative, exhibit. *Entrance requirements:* For master's, portfolio, minimum GPA of 2.7. Additional exam requirements/recommendations for international students: Required—TOEFL. Electronic applications accepted. *Expenses:* Tuition, area resident: Part-time $348 per credit hour. Tuition, state resident: full-time $6262. Tuition, nonresident: full-time $18,920; part-time $1052 per credit hour. Required fees: $812; $36 per credit hour. Tuition and fees vary according to program.

University of Utah, The Graduate School, College of Fine Arts, Department of Art and Art History, Salt Lake City, UT 84112-1107. Offers art history (MA); ceramics (MFA); community-based art education (MFA); drawing (MFA); graphic design (MFA); painting (MFA); photography/digital imaging (MFA); printmaking (MFA); sculpture/intermedia (MFA). *Degree requirements:* For master's, variable foreign language requirement, comprehensive exam (for some programs), thesis or alternative, exhibit (MFA), final project paper. *Entrance requirements:* For master's, CD portfolio (MFA), resumé, letters of recommendation. Additional exam requirements/recommendations for international students: Required—TOEFL (minimum score 575 paper-based; 183 computer-based; 75 iBT). Electronic applications accepted. *Faculty research:* Intermedia, digital arts, installation, traditional media, Asian art, medieval arts.

University of Victoria, Faculty of Graduate Studies, Faculty of Fine Arts, Department of Visual Arts, Victoria, BC V8W 2Y2, Canada. Offers digital multimedia (MFA); drawing (MFA); painting (MFA); photography (MFA); sculpture (MFA); video (MFA). *Degree requirements:* For master's, exhibit, oral exam. *Entrance requirements:* For master's, portfolio, BFA. Additional exam requirements/recommendations for international students: Required—TOEFL (minimum score 575 paper-based; 233 computer-based), IELTS (minimum score 7). Electronic applications accepted.

University of Washington, Graduate School, College of Arts and Sciences, School of Art, Division of Art, Seattle, WA 98195. Offers painting and drawing (MFA); photography (MFA). *Degree requirements:* For master's, thesis, exhibit. *Entrance requirements:* For master's, BFA or equivalent academic work in art, 20 slide portfolio. Additional exam requirements/recommendations for international students: Required—TOEFL. Electronic applications accepted.

Virginia Commonwealth University, Graduate School, School of the Arts, Department of Graphic Design, Richmond, VA 23284-9005. Offers design/visual communications (MFA); interior environment (MFA); photography and film (MFA). *Accreditation:* NASAD. *Degree requirements:* For master's, thesis, exhibition. *Entrance requirements:* For master's, portfolio. *Faculty research:* Film, photography, interior environments, visual communication.

Washington State University, Graduate School, College of Liberal Arts, Department of Fine Arts, Pullman, WA 99164. Offers ceramics (MFA); digital media (MFA); drawing (MFA); painting (MFA); photography (MFA); print making (MFA); sculpture (MFA). *Degree requirements:* For master's, comprehensive exam (for some programs), thesis, exhibit, oral exam. *Entrance requirements:* For master's, GRE, minimum GPA of 3.0, portfolio, 3 letters of recommendation. Additional exam requirements/recommendations for international students: Required—TOEFL (minimum score 550 paper-based; 213 computer-based). Electronic applications accepted. *Faculty research:* Polynesian art, museum representation, number theory.

Yale University, School of Art, New Haven, CT 06520. Offers graphic design (MFA); painting/printmaking (MFA); photography (MFA); sculpture (MFA). *Degree requirements:* For master's, thesis (for some programs). *Entrance requirements:* Additional exam requirements/recommendations for international students: Required—TOEFL (minimum score 550 paper-based; 250 computer-based; 100 iBT). *Expenses:* Contact institution.

Textile Design

Academy of Art University, Graduate Program, School of Fashion, San Francisco, CA 94105-3410. Offers fashion design (MFA); fashion merchandising (MFA); fashion textiles (MFA); knitwear (MFA). Part-time programs available. Postbaccalaureate distance learning degree programs offered (no on-campus study). *Faculty:* 16 full-time (12 women), 32 part-time/adjunct (22 women). *Students:* 353 full-time (313 women), 130 part-time (119 women); includes 95 minority (36 African Americans, 2 American Indian/Alaska Native, 39 Asian Americans or Pacific Islanders, 18 Hispanic Americans), 225 international. Average age 28. 179 applicants. In 2008, 48 master's awarded. *Degree requirements:* For master's, thesis, final review. *Entrance requirements:* For master's, minimum GPA of 3.0, portfolio. *Application deadline:* For fall admission, 9/7 for domestic and international students; for spring admission, 2/2 for domestic and international students. Applications are processed on a rolling basis. Application fee: $100 ($500 for international students). Electronic applications accepted. *Expenses:* Tuition: Full-time $18,400; part-time $770 per term. Tuition and fees vary according to program. *Financial support:* Career-related internships or fieldwork and Federal Work-Study available. Support available to part-time students. Financial award application deadline: 8/10; financial award applicants required to submit FAFSA. *Unit head:* Simon Ungless, Director, 800-544-ARTS, Fax: 415-296-2089, E-mail: info@academyart.edu. *Application contact:* Prospective Student Services, 800-544-ARTS, Fax: 415-263-4130, E-mail: info@academyart.edu.

California College of the Arts, Graduate Programs, Programs in Fine Art, San Francisco, CA 94107. Offers ceramics (MFA); film/video/performance (MFA); glass (MFA); jewelry/metal arts (MFA); painting/drawing (MFA); photography (MFA); printmaking (MFA); sculpture (MFA); textiles (MFA); wood/furniture (MFA). *Accreditation:* NASAD. *Degree requirements:* For master's, thesis, exhibit. *Entrance requirements:* For master's, appropriate bachelor's degree, portfolio. Additional exam requirements/recommendations for international students: Required—TOEFL (minimum score 600 paper-based; 250 computer-based). Electronic applications accepted.

California State University, Los Angeles, Graduate Studies, College of Arts and Letters, Department of Art, Los Angeles, CA 90032-8530. Offers art (MA), including art education, art history, art therapy, ceramics, metals, and textiles, design (MA, MFA), painting, sculpture, and graphic arts, photography; fine arts (MFA), including crafts, design (MA, MFA), studio arts. *Accreditation:* NASAD (one or more programs are accredited). Part-time and evening/weekend programs available. *Faculty:* 16 full-time (6 women). *Students:* 23 full-time (14 women), 52 part-time (37 women); includes 29 minority (2 African Americans, 3 American Indian/Alaska Native, 7 Asian Americans or Pacific Islanders, 17 Hispanic Americans), 4 international. Average age 38. 30 applicants, 100% accepted, 14 enrolled. In 2008, 15 master's awarded. *Degree requirements:* For master's, comprehensive exam, project or thesis. *Entrance requirements:* For master's, portfolio. Additional exam requirements/recommendations for international students: Required—TOEFL (minimum score 500 paper-based; 173 computer-based). *Application deadline:* For fall admission, 6/15 for domestic students, 5/1 for international students; for winter admission, 11/1 for domestic students, 9/1 for international students; for spring admission, 2/1 for domestic students, 10/1 for international students. Applications are processed on a rolling basis. Application fee: $55. Electronic applications accepted. *Expenses:* Tuition, nonresident: part-time $226 per credit. Required fees: $4019. *Financial support:* Federal Work-Study available. Support available to part-time students. Financial award application deadline: 3/1. *Faculty research:* The artist and the book, conceptual art, ceramic processes, computer graphics, architectural graphics. *Unit head:* Dr. Robert Martin, Chair, 323-343-4010, Fax: 323-343-4045, E-mail: rjmartin@calstatela.edu. *Application contact:* Dr. Jose L. Galvan, Dean of Graduate Studies, 323-343-3820, Fax: 323-343-5653, E-mail: jgalvan@cslanet.calstatela.edu.

Cornell University, Graduate School, Graduate Fields of Human Ecology, Field of Textiles, Ithaca, NY 14853-0001. Offers apparel design (MA, MPS); fiber science (MS, PhD); polymer science (MS, PhD); textile science (MS, PhD). *Faculty:* 17 full-time (7 women). *Students:* 20 full-time (14 women); includes 2 minority (1 African American, 1 Hispanic American), 12 international. Average age 30. 33 applicants, 15% accepted, 4 enrolled. In 2008, 4 master's, 3 doctorates awarded. *Degree requirements:* For master's, thesis (MA, MS), project paper (MPS); for doctorate, comprehensive exam, thesis/dissertation. *Entrance requirements:* For master's, GRE General Test, 2 letters of recommendation, portfolio (functional apparel design); for doctorate, GRE General Test, 2 letters of recommendation. Additional exam requirements/recommendations for international students: Required—TOEFL (minimum score 600 paper-based; 250 computer-based; 77 iBT). *Application deadline:* For fall admission, 3/1 for domestic students; for spring admission, 10/1 for domestic students. Application fee: $70. Electronic applications accepted. *Expenses:* Tuition: Full-time $29,500. Required fees: $70. Full-time tuition and fees vary according to degree level, program and student level. *Financial support:* In 2008–09, 19 students received support, including 2 fellowships with full tuition reimbursements available, 12 research assistantships with full tuition reimbursements available, 5 teaching assistantships with full tuition reimbursements available; institutionally sponsored loans, scholarships/grants, health care benefits, tuition waivers (full and partial), and unspecified assistantships also available. Financial award applicants required to submit FAFSA. *Faculty research:* Apparel design, consumption, mass customization, 3-D body scanning. *Unit head:* Director of Graduate Studies, 607-255-3151, Fax: 607-255-1093. *Application contact:* Graduate Field Assistant, 607-255-3151, Fax: 607-255-1093, E-mail: textiles_grad@cornell.edu.

Cranbrook Academy of Art, Graduate School, Program in Fine Arts, Bloomfield Hills, MI 48303-0801. Offers ceramics (MFA); design (MFA), including graphic design; fiber arts (MFA); metalsmithing (MFA); painting (MFA); photography (MFA); printmaking (MFA); sculpture (MFA). *Accreditation:* NASAD. *Degree requirements:* For master's, thesis, exhibit. *Entrance requirements:* Additional exam requirements/recommendations for international students: Required—TOEFL (minimum score 550 paper-based; 213 computer-based).

See Close-Up on page 209.

Drexel University, College of Media Arts and Design, Philadelphia, PA 19104-2875. Offers design (MS), including digital media, fashion design, interior design, television management; media arts (MS); performing arts (MS), including arts administration; MS/MBA. *Accreditation:* NASAD. Part-time and evening/weekend programs available. *Entrance requirements:* For master's, interview. Additional exam requirements/recommendations for international students: Required—TOEFL. Electronic applications accepted. *Expenses:* Contact institution.

Drexel University, College of Media Arts and Design, Department of Design, Program in Fashion Design, Philadelphia, PA 19104-2875. Offers MS. *Accreditation:* NASAD. *Degree requirements:* For master's, thesis, portfolio review. *Entrance requirements:* For master's, interview. Additional exam requirements/recommendations for international students: Required—TOEFL. Electronic applications accepted.

Illinois State University, Graduate School, College of Fine Arts, School of Art, Normal, IL 61790-2200. Offers art history (MA, MS); ceramics (MFA, MS); drawing (MFA, MS); fibers (MFA, MS); glass (MFA, MS); graphic design (MFA, MS); metals (MFA, MS); painting (MFA, MS); photography (MFA, MS); printmaking (MFA, MS); sculpture (MFA, MS). *Accreditation:* NASAD (one or more programs are accredited). *Degree requirements:* For master's, thesis or alternative, internship. *Entrance requirements:* For master's, portfolio, sample of scholarly writing. *Faculty research:* General operations support: Normal Editions Workshop for FY2007.

James Madison University, The Graduate School, College of Visual and Performing Arts, School of Art and Art History, Harrisonburg, VA 22807. Offers art education (MA); art history (MA); ceramics (MFA); drawing/painting (MFA); metal/jewelry (MFA); photography (MFA); printmaking (MFA); sculpture (MFA); studio art (MA); weaving/fibers (MFA). *Accreditation:* NASAD. Part-time programs available. *Faculty:* 13 full-time (8 women). *Students:* 7 full-time (5 women), 1 part-time (0 women); includes 2 minority (1 African American, 1 Asian American or Pacific Islander). Average age 27. In 2008, 3 master's awarded. *Degree requirements:* For

master's, thesis (for some programs). *Entrance requirements:* For master's, GRE General Test, language exam in French or German, portfolio, 3 letters of recommendation, research paper. Additional exam requirements/recommendations for international students: Required—TOEFL. *Application deadline:* For fall admission, 2/15 priority date for domestic students, 2/15 for international students; for spring admission, 10/15 priority date for domestic students, 10/15 for international students. Applications are processed on a rolling basis. Application fee: $55. Electronic applications accepted. *Expenses:* Tuition, area resident: Full-time $7008; part-time $292 per credit hour. Tuition, state resident: full-time $7008; part-time $292 per credit hour. Tuition, nonresident: full-time $20,352; part-time $848 per credit hour. *Financial support:* In 2008–09, 8 students received support, including 3 teaching assistantships with full tuition reimbursements available (averaging $8,664 per year); Federal Work-Study and 3 graduate assistantships ($7,382) also available. Financial award application deadline: 3/1; financial award applicants required to submit FAFSA. *Unit head:* Leslie M. Bellavance, Academic Unit Head, 540-568-6216. *Application contact:* Lynette M. Bible, Director of Graduate Admissions, 540-568-6395, Fax: 540-568-7860, E-mail: biblelm@jmu.edu.

Kent State University, College of the Arts, School of Art, Kent, OH 44242-0001. Offers art education (MA); art history (MA); crafts (MA, MFA), including ceramics (MA), glass, jewelry/metals, textiles/art; fine art (MA, MFA), including drawing/painting, printmaking, sculpture. *Accreditation:* NASAD (one or more programs are accredited). *Degree requirements:* For master's, one foreign language, thesis. *Entrance requirements:* For master's, undergraduate degree in proposed area of study (for fine arts and crafts programs); minimum overall GPA of 2.75 (3.0 for art major); 3 letters of recommendation; portfolio (15-20 slides for MA, 20-25 for MFA), brief autobiographical statement (MFA). Additional exam requirements/recommendations for international students: Required—TOEFL. Electronic applications accepted.

Laboratory Institute of Merchandising, MBA Program, New York, NY 10022-5268. Offers entrepreneurship (MBA); fashion management (MBA).

Marywood University, Academic Affairs, Insalaco College of Creative Arts and Management, Art Department, Program in Studio Art, Scranton, PA 18509-1598. Offers advertising design (MA); ceramics (MA); clay (MA); graphic design (MA); illustration (MA); interior architecture (MA); painting (MA); photography (MA); printmaking (MA); sculpture (MA); weaving (MA). *Accreditation:* NASAD. Part-time and evening/weekend programs available. *Degree requirements:* For master's, comprehensive exam, thesis or alternative. *Entrance requirements:* For master's, portfolio. Additional exam requirements/recommendations for international students: Required—TOEFL (minimum score 550 paper-based; 213 computer-based). Electronic applications accepted. *Faculty research:* Texture and line in clay, cast bronze sculpture, color theories, book art and illustration, sculptural form.

Marywood University, Academic Affairs, Insalaco College of Creative Arts and Management, Art Department, Program in Visual Arts, Scranton, PA 18509-1598. Offers advertising design (MFA); clay (MFA); fibers (MFA); graphic design (MFA); illustration (MFA); metals (MFA); painting (MFA); photography (MFA); printmaking (MFA). *Accreditation:* NASAD. Part-time and evening/weekend programs available. *Degree requirements:* For master's, thesis or alternative, exhibit. *Entrance requirements:* For master's, portfolio. Additional exam requirements/recommendations for international students: Required—TOEFL (minimum score 550 paper-based; 213 computer-based). Electronic applications accepted. *Expenses:* Contact institution. *Faculty research:* Mariology, exploration of visual imagery, explorations involving drawing on the loom, clay as sculptural medium, oil paintings.

Massachusetts College of Art and Design, Graduate Programs, Program in Fine Arts, Boston, MA 02115-5882. Offers ceramics (MFA); design (MFA); fibers (MFA); film (MFA); glass (MFA); media and performing arts (MFA); metals (MFA); painting (MFA); photography (MFA); printmaking (MFA); sculpture (MFA). *Accreditation:* NASAD. *Faculty:* 10 full-time (5 women), 8 part-time/adjunct (6 women). *Students:* 83 full-time (53 women), 17 part-time (10 women); includes 8 minority (1 American Indian/Alaska Native, 4 Asian Americans or Pacific Islanders, 3 Hispanic Americans), 15 international. Average age 34. 295 applicants, 24% accepted, 40 enrolled. In 2008, 37 master's awarded. *Degree requirements:* For master's, thesis, exhibit. *Entrance requirements:* For master's, 12 units of course work in art history, portfolio, resumé, college transcripts, statement of purpose, letters of reference, interview. Additional exam requirements/recommendations for international students: Required—TOEFL (minimum score 563 paper-based; 223 computer-based; 85 iBT); Recommended—IELTS (minimum score 6.5). *Application deadline:* For fall admission, 1/15 for domestic and international students; for spring admission, 11/1 for domestic students. Application fee: $75. *Expenses:* Tuition, area resident: Full-time $17,100; part-time $570 per credit. Tuition and fees vary according to program. *Financial support:* In 2008–09, 50 research assistantships (averaging $2,000 per year), 30 teaching assistantships (averaging $2,000 per year) were awarded; career-related internships or fieldwork, Federal Work-Study, and clerical/technical assistantships also available. Support available to part-time students. Financial award application deadline: 5/1; financial award applicants required to submit FAFSA. *Unit head:* George Creamer, Director, 617-879-7163, Fax: 617-879-7171, E-mail: creamer@massart.edu. *Application contact:* George Creamer, Director, 617-879-7163.

Missouri State University, Graduate College, College of Natural and Applied Sciences, Department of Fashion and Interior Design, Springfield, MO 65804-0094. Offers secondary education (MS Ed), including consumer sciences. Part-time programs available. *Faculty:* 2 full-time (both women), 1 (woman) part-time/adjunct. *Students:* 1 (woman) part-time. Average age 46. 1 applicant, 100% accepted, 0 enrolled. *Degree requirements:* For master's, comprehensive exam, thesis or alternative. *Entrance requirements:* For master's, GRE (MNAS), 9-12 teaching certification (MS Ed), minimum GPA of 3.0 (MNAS). Additional exam requirements/recommendations for international students: Required—TOEFL (minimum score 550 paper-based; 213 computer-based; 79 iBT). *Application deadline:* For fall admission, 7/20 priority date for domestic students, 5/1 for international students; for spring admission, 12/20 priority date for domestic students, 9/1 for international students. Applications are processed on a rolling basis. Application fee: $35 ($50 for international students). Electronic applications accepted. *Expenses:* Tuition, state resident: full-time $3852; part-time $214 per credit hour. Tuition, nonresident: full-time $7524; part-time $418 per credit hour. Required fees: $230 per semester. Tuition and fees vary according to course level and course load. *Financial support:* Career-related internships or fieldwork, Federal Work-Study, institutionally sponsored loans, scholarships/grants, and unspecified assistantships available. Financial award application deadline: 3/31; financial award applicants required to submit FAFSA. *Unit head:* Dr. Jeannie Ireland, Head, 417-836-5497, Fax: 417-836-4341, E-mail: jeannieireland@missouristate.edu. *Application contact:* Eric Eckert, Coordinator of Graduate Admissions and Recruitment, 417-836-5331, Fax: 417-836-6888, E-mail: ericeckert@missouristate.edu.

Philadelphia University, School of Engineering and Textiles, Program in Textile Design, Philadelphia, PA 19144-5497. Offers MS. *Accreditation:* NASAD. Part-time programs available. *Entrance requirements:* For master's, GRE or MAT, minimum GPA of 2.8. Additional exam requirements/recommendations for international students: Required—TOEFL (minimum score 550 paper-based; 213 computer-based; 79 iBT). Electronic applications accepted.

Rhode Island School of Design, Graduate Studies, Division of Fine Arts, Department of Textiles, Providence, RI 02903-2784. Offers MFA. *Accreditation:* NASAD. *Degree requirements:* For master's, thesis, exhibit. *Entrance requirements:* For master's, portfolio, 3 letters of recommendation. Additional exam requirements/recommendations for international students: Required—TOEFL (minimum score 580 paper-based; 237 computer-based), IELTS (minimum score 6.5).

Savannah College of Art and Design, Graduate School, Program in Fashion, Savannah, GA 31402-3146. Offers MA, MFA. Part-time programs available. *Degree requirements:* For master's, thesis, internship. *Entrance requirements:* For master's, interview, portfolio. Additional exam requirements/recommendations for international students: Required—TOEFL (minimum score 450 paper-based; 133 computer-based). Electronic applications accepted. *Expenses:* Tuition: Full-time $28,215; part-time $3135 per course. One-time fee: $500.

See Close-Up on page 223.

Savannah College of Art and Design, Graduate School, Program in Fibers, Savannah, GA 31402-3146. Offers MA, MFA. Part-time programs available. *Degree requirements:* For master's, thesis, internship. *Entrance requirements:* For master's, interview, portfolio. Additional exam requirements/recommendations for international students: Required—TOEFL (minimum score 450 paper-based; 133 computer-based). Electronic applications accepted. *Expenses:* Tuition: Full-time $28,215; part-time $3135 per course. One-time fee: $500.

See Close-Up on page 223.

School of the Art Institute of Chicago, Graduate Division, Program in Fashion, Body, and Garment, Chicago, IL 60603-3103. Offers M Des, Certificate.

See Close-Up on page 225.

Sul Ross State University, School of Arts and Sciences, Department of Fine Arts and Communication, Alpine, TX 79832. Offers art education (M Ed); art history (M Ed); studio art (M Ed), including ceramics, design, drawing, jewelry, painting, printmaking, sculpture, weaving. Part-time programs available. *Degree requirements:* For master's, oral or written exam. *Entrance requirements:* For master's, GRE General Test, minimum GPA of 2.5 in last 60 hours of undergraduate work. *Faculty research:* Ceramic sculpture, watercolor, wood sculpture, rock art.

Syracuse University, Graduate School, College of Visual and Performing Arts, Program in Fiber Arts/Material Studies, Syracuse, NY 13244. Offers MFA.

Temple University, Graduate School, Tyler School of Art, Department of Crafts, Philadelphia, PA 19122-6096. Offers ceramics/glass (MFA); fibers and fabric design (MFA); metals/jewelry/CAD-CAM (MFA). *Accreditation:* NASAD. *Degree requirements:* For master's, essay, exhibit. *Entrance requirements:* For master's, minimum GPA of 3.0, slide portfolio, 40 credits in studio art, 12 credits in art history. Additional exam requirements/recommendations for international students: Required—TOEFL (minimum score 550 paper-based; 213 computer-based; 79 iBT). Electronic applications accepted.

University of California, Davis, Graduate Studies, Program in Textile Arts and Costume Design, Davis, CA 95616. Offers MFA. *Degree requirements:* For master's, presentation of an individual project/body of work. *Entrance requirements:* For master's, minimum GPA of 3.0, portfolio. Additional exam requirements/recommendations for international students: Required—TOEFL (minimum score 550 paper-based; 213 computer-based). Electronic applications accepted. *Faculty research:* Historic ethnographic and contemporary costume and textile design, computer-aided design.

University of Cincinnati, Graduate School, College of Design, Architecture, Art, and Planning, School of Design, Cincinnati, OH 45221. Offers fashion design (M Des); graphic design (M Des); industrial design (M Des); interaction design (M Des); product development (M Des). *Accreditation:* NASAD. *Degree requirements:* For master's, thesis. *Entrance requirements:* For master's, undergraduate degree in design or related field, 2 years of work experience in design or related field. Additional exam requirements/recommendations for international students:

Required—TOEFL. Electronic applications accepted. *Faculty research:* Design theory, interdisciplinary design topics.

University of Massachusetts Dartmouth, Graduate School, College of Visual and Performing Arts, Program in Artisanry, North Dartmouth, MA 02747-2300. Offers ceramics (MFA, Postbaccalaureate Certificate); fibers (MFA); fibers/textiles (Postbaccalaureate Certificate); jewelry/metals (MFA, Postbaccalaureate Certificate); wood/furniture design (MFA, Postbaccalaureate Certificate). *Accreditation:* NASAD. *Faculty:* 6 full-time (3 women), 2 part-time/adjunct (1 woman). *Students:* 15 full-time (11 women), 15 part-time (6 women); includes 3 minority (all Asian Americans or Pacific Islanders), 4 international. Average age 31. 40 applicants, 68% accepted, 9 enrolled. In 2008, 5 master's awarded. *Degree requirements:* For master's, thesis, visual thesis. *Entrance requirements:* For master's, portfolio, interview, minimum GPA of 3.0, 3 letters of recommendation. Additional exam requirements/recommendations for international students: Required—TOEFL (minimum score 500 paper-based). *Application deadline:* For fall admission, 3/1 for domestic students, 1/1 for international students. Applications are processed on a rolling basis. Application fee: $40 ($60 for international students). Electronic applications accepted. *Expenses:* Tuition, state resident: full-time $2071; part-time $86.29 per credit. Tuition, nonresident: full-time $8099; part-time $337.46 per credit. Required fees: $7946. Tuition and fees vary according to class time, course load and reciprocity agreements. *Financial support:* In 2008–09, 1 research assistantship with full tuition reimbursement (averaging $3,940 per year), 16 teaching assistantships with full tuition reimbursements (averaging $3,500 per year) were awarded; Federal Work-Study and unspecified assistantships also available. Support available to part-time students. Financial award application deadline: 3/1; financial award applicants required to submit FAFSA. *Faculty research:* Historic European tapestry, computerized weaving. *Unit head:* Memory Holloway, Director, 508-999-8010, E-mail: mholloway@umassd.edu. *Application contact:* Elan Turcotte-Shamski, Graduate Admissions Officer, 508-999-8604, Fax: 508-999-8183, E-mail: graduate@umassd.edu.

University of Minnesota, Twin Cities Campus, Graduate School, College of Design, Department of Design, Housing, and Apparel, Minneapolis, MN 55455-0213. Offers apparel (MA, MS, PhD); design communication (MA, MS, PhD); housing studies (MA, MS, PhD, Postbaccalaureate Certificate); interactive design (MFA); interior design (MA, MS, PhD). Part-time programs available. *Degree requirements:* For master's and Postbaccalaureate Certificate, comprehensive exam, thesis (for some programs); for doctorate, comprehensive exam, thesis/dissertation. *Entrance requirements:* For master's, GRE General Test, minimum GPA of 3.0 (preferred), portfolio, 3 letters of recommendation; for doctorate, GRE General Test, minimum GPA of 3.0 (preferred), portfolio, 3 letters of recommendation, writing sample; for Postbaccalaureate Certificate, GRE General Test, minimum GPA of 3.0 (preferred). Additional exam requirements/recommendations for international students: Required—TOEFL (minimum score 550 paper-based; 213 computer-based; 79 iBT). Electronic applications accepted. *Faculty research:* Housing policy and community development; consumer behavior; interactive design; design history; social, cultural, and behavioral issues related to designed environments.

The University of North Carolina at Greensboro, Graduate School, School of Human Environmental Sciences, Department of Consumer, Apparel, and Retail Studies, Greensboro, NC 27412-5001. Offers MS, PhD. *Degree requirements:* For master's, one foreign language; for doctorate, one foreign language, thesis/dissertation. *Entrance requirements:* For master's and doctorate, GRE General Test. Additional exam requirements/recommendations for international students: Required—TOEFL. Electronic applications accepted. *Faculty research:* Impact of phosphate removal, protective clothing for pesticide workers, fabric hand: subjective and objective measurements.

ArtCenter

ART CENTER COLLEGE OF DESIGN

Programs of Study
Art Center's graduate programs provide a framework in which students can pursue advanced studies in media design, broadcast cinema (film), art, and industrial design. The graduate programs enable students to broaden their practical, conceptual, and analytical skills by providing a balance between professional and theoretical approaches to art and design practice.

Every program has its own graduate seminar, which brings artists, designers, and critics to the campus regularly. Each program's curriculum allows students to follow their own interests and direction, yet is designed to ensure that every student covers comprehensive course material and receives critical feedback. In addition to regular meetings with graduate faculty members, students benefit from interaction with visiting artists and designers.

Broadcast cinema, Art Center's M.F.A. program for filmmakers, is focused on the creation of works for existing, emerging, and future forms of broadcast and theatrical distribution. The traditional term "broadcast" represents the College's exploration of the vast potential of satellite distribution and "cinema" represents innovation in visual aesthetics and content. Early development of each student's individual creative identity is a priority. Students may choose to specialize in any creative leadership roles in filmmaking. The program encourages students to explore new content, forms, and methods of storytelling.

The M.F.A. program in media design is for students who are interested in exploring the future of communication in an information-saturated, media-driven world. This interdisciplinary program encourages innovation and experimentation, theoretical research, the development of technological sophistication, and individual creativity. Students work in state-of-the-art facilities under the direction of a diverse faculty of accomplished designers, technology specialists, theorists, and thought leaders, and meet regularly with visiting artists, scholars, and entrepreneurs.

An M.S. degree is offered in industrial design. This graduate program encourages students with a background in product or environmental design to expand their knowledge and expertise while emphasizing experimentation, innovation, and multidisciplinary research. Particular emphasis is placed on broadening students' intellectual grasp of design issues, using digital and written media for communication, and realizing the full potential of the creative process. The first year of the program is spent in a joint multidisciplinary project. Students work closely with a distinguished core faculty and with many visiting specialists.

The M.F.A. program in art brings together students and a varied faculty composed of internationally known artists. The size of the program—about 35 students and 7 graduate advisers—allows for intensive one-on-one dialogue while offering sufficient diversity to generate critical exchange and controversy. The program emphasizes both making and theorizing the art object and provides studios for independent work as well as classes in theory and technique.

Research Facilities
The James Lemont Fogg Memorial Library contains 92,000 volumes of books and periodicals, and 9,000 videotapes and DVDs of rare features, animation, documentaries, advertising, computer graphics, and instructional programs. A photo reference collection contains more than 90,000 pictures. The Rare Book Room houses limited and signed editions, portfolios, and other materials. Subscriptions are maintained for more than 400 magazines, and online subscriptions provide access to thousands of magazine articles and images. A CD-ROM workstation can be used to view a collection of more than 350 interactive CD-ROMs. Occidental College's library of more than 1 million volumes serves as another resource for Art Center students.

Art Center maintains state-of-the-art studios and shops, including a rapid-modeling machine that creates three-dimensional prototype models. Archetype Press, a 3,000-square-foot facility, houses fourteen presses and 2,400 drawers of rare type from American and European foundries. Students have access to a wide range of interactive multimedia and digital resources for exploring and refining their ideas, including sixty Silicon Graphics workstations, 140 Apple Macintosh computers, twelve Compaq Professional NT workstations, and the latest design software available.

In addition, the Wind Tunnel facility at Art Center's South Campus includes the New Ecology of Things (N.E.T.) research lab, dedicated to exploring a future world of interactive networked technologies. The lab includes a collection of experimental media and technologies, including custom hardware and software created by the media design faculty.

Financial Aid
Graduate students may apply for scholarships by meeting priority deadlines. Scholarships are awarded by a graduate scholarship committee. Candidates must demonstrate financial need and present an exceptional portfolio of work for scholarship consideration. Grants and loans, including the California Graduate Fellowship and FFELP Loan Program, are available. Teaching assistantships are also available.

Cost of Study
The cost of tuition for 2009 is $16,423 per fifteen-week semester.

Living and Housing Costs
The College does not currently maintain dormitories. A wide variety of housing is available in Pasadena and neighboring communities. The average cost of rent and food per semester is approximately $5000.

Student Group
Approximately 130 graduate students, of whom 60 percent are men and 40 percent are women, are enrolled in the College.

Student Outcomes
Most students pursue careers as practicing artists and designers within their professions.

Location
Art Center is located in Pasadena, California, a residential community near Los Angeles. With two campuses, one in a striking glass and steel facility on the hillsides of Pasadena and the other near old town Pasadena, the College is a short distance from greater Los Angeles. Students benefit from their proximity to art galleries, advertising and design agencies, and the entertainment industry.

The College
A private, nonprofit institution, Art Center College of Design was founded in 1930 with the purpose of educating students for distinguished careers in the visual arts professions. The total enrollment, including undergraduates, is 1,600. Eighteen percent of students are international and represent forty-seven different countries. The College is accredited by WASC and NASAD.

Applying
Applicants for the broadcast cinema and art programs may apply for entry in any of the three scheduled terms each year: fall, spring, or summer. Applications are accepted on a rolling admissions basis, with consideration given as long as space is available in a class. Spaces in some graduate programs are extremely limited and may require application a number of semesters in advance. Media design and industrial design applicants may apply only for the fall semester, and the application deadline for these programs is February 1. Graduate programs are normally six semesters in length. However, the media design and broadcast cinema programs offer two- and three-year options. Applicants may consult the Admissions Office about the status of any entering class.

Correspondence and Information
Admissions Office
Art Center College of Design
1700 Lida Street
Pasadena, California 91103
Phone: 626-396-2373
Fax: 626-795-0578
E-mail: admissions@artcenter.edu
Web site: http://www.artcenter.edu

Art Center College of Design

THE FACULTY

The faculty members are core faculty advisers for graduate programs. Graduate students have access to a wide variety of classes and additional faculty members at Art Center.

Media Design Program

Anne Burdick, Chair; M.F.A., California Institute of the Arts. Designer, writer, editor. Work is included in the Museum of Modern Art in New York and the San Francisco Museum of Modern Art. Publications include *eye, I.D., Idea, Adobe Think Tank,* and *Emigre* magazines. Awards include the Leipzig Award (Most Beautiful Book in the World), AIGA 50 Books/50 Covers, I.D. Interactive Design Annual, Webby Award, ACD 100, and others. Projects include electronic corpora and text-dictionaries with the Austrian Academy of Sciences, experimental fiction at the Walker Art Center's Gallery 9, and books of literary/media criticism by authors such as Marshall McLuhan and N. Katherine Hayles. Burdick has been the design editor of *Electronic Book Review* since 1995.

Elise Co, M.S., MIT. Co is a media artist and founding partner of Aeolab, a design and technology consulting firm in Los Angeles. She is a former Assistant Professor of New Media at the Hochschule für Gestaltung und Kunst in Basel, Switzerland, where she taught courses in interaction design and physical computing. Her work has been shown internationally, including at the Museum of Modern Art, New York, SIGGRAPH, IMRF Tokyo, Cooper Union, and the New York Art Directors Club. She was recently selected as an Artist in Residence for Extending Creativity in Digital Media at the Anderson Ranch Art Center in Snowmass, Colorado.

Sean Donahue, M.F.A., Art Center College of Design. Principal of ResearchCenteredDesign, a Los Angeles–based design practice. His practice consists of professional commissions, self-initiated research, design advocacy, education and publishing. Donahue has lectured and published internationally at RISD, RCA, and North Carolina State University, where he was also the 2004 Designer-in-Residence. Published research: the University of Cambridge, Princeton Architectural Press, MIT Press, and *I.D.* magazine.

Tim Durfee, M.Arch., Yale. He is a partner of the Los Angeles firm of Durfee I Regn which has created—in collaboration with other designers—award-winning exhibitions for LACMA, the Hammer, Huntington Library, Pacific Design Center, UCLA, the Indianapolis Museum of Art, the International Center for Photography in New York, and a permanent exhibition for Target Corporation's headquarters in Minneapolis. He also collaborates with artists, including Ultraworld at the Centre Pompidou's L'ARC in Paris with Doug Aitken in 2005. He has developed interface prototypes and production designs for SF MOMA and LAUNCH and an award-winning Web site for LACMA.

Ben Hooker, M.A., B.Sc., Royal College of Art (London). Collaborates with architects, industrial designers, and computer scientists working in the field of human-computer interaction, resulting in computer-generated data landscapes merging with real, physical spaces. He is also a member of the Visiting Faculty at Intel's Research Lab in Berkeley. Clients include Shona Kitchen; San Jose International Airport, and projects for Vitra Design Museum and Art Center College of Design.

Lisa Krohn, M.F.A., Cranbrook Academy of Art. Krohn is the creative director and lead designer at Krohn Design. Clients have included Herman Miller, Walt Disney Imagineering, Alessi, and the San Diego Children's Museum. Lisa's products and furniture are in the collections of the San Francisco and New York Museums of Modern Art and the Cooper-Hewitt National Design Museum. She received a Fulbright fellowship to Italy to work with renowned designer Mario Bellini. She has received numerous design accolades including grand prize in the Forma Finlandia competition, the Brooklyn Museum's Young Designer award, an NEA Design Arts grant, the Daimler-Chrylsler award for Innovation in Design and the prestigious Rome Prize.

Norman Klein is a cultural critic, a historian of the urban condition as well as a theorist of the media that permeate these conditions. He is also an accomplished novelist. His books include *Freud in Coney Island, The Vatican to Vegas: The History of Special Effects,* and *The History of Forgetting: Los Angeles and the Erasure of Memory.* He is also the author of the data/cinematic novel, *Bleeding Through Layers of Los Angeles, 1920–86* a DVD-ROM with book in collaboration with USC's Labyrinth Project.

Philip Van Allen, B.A., California, Santa Cruz. Interaction designer/producer/technologist for experimental information and entertainment systems with a research focus on interactive objects and spaces, productive interaction (productiveinteraction.com) and interactive audio. Background in music recording and software development. Principal: Commotion New Media. Clients: Infiniti, George P. Johnson, Interval Research, Philips, Yahoo/Launch Media, Virgin Interactive Entertainment, Art Center College of Design, Nestlé, U2, The Germs. Teacher: ACCD, Santa Monica College, McGill University. Interactive art collaborations: Yoko Ono, Kim Abeles. Exhibitions: Nucleus Gallery, SIGGRAPH Virtual Lounge. Publications: Founded mid-nineties magazine ArtCommotion.com, DIS 2004 ACM conference proceedings, USC Annenberg Online Journalism Review.

Industrial Design Program

Andrew Ogden, Chair; B.S., Art Center College of Design. Vice president and executive designer, Walt Disney Imagineering; designer, Honda R&D North America.

Mark Andersen, B.S., Art Center College of Design. Designer; founder/owner, ZoomOutDesign. Clients: Zaca Inc. and BioControl Inc. Exhibitions: *Brewery Art Walk 2005–06,* Los Angeles. Awards: IDSA silver for Zaca SpaceCab, IDSA bronze for Hycore Biomedical accuPINCH, and honorable mention, "Why Design?", Art Center faculty grant for 3-D digital modeling research.

Katherine Bennett, B.S.I.D., Philadelphia College of Art. Design research, product development, information architecture, strategic planning. Clients: Johnson Controls International, Avery Dennison. Formerly with Donald Chadwick Associates, Hauser, Saul Bass, Henry Dreyfuss Associates. Projects: contract and residential furniture, consumer products, equipment and instrumentation, communications. Publications (periodicals): *Los Angeles Times, Innovation, Modern Photography.*

Richard Keyes, B.F.A., Art Center College of Design. Owner, Keyes Design; former designer, Steven Jacobs, Fulton & Green, the Graphics Studio. Clients: Warner Brothers Records, Atlantic Richfield, Guess? Jeans, Convergent Technologies, His Holiness the Dalai Lama, Empire Berol (color consulting), Homebody, Los Angeles Housing Department, Parson's Engineering (design consultant). Former instructor: California State University, Los Angeles; Los Angeles Valley College; UCLA Extension.

Steven Montgomery, B.A., Michigan State. Industrial designer; principal, BioDesign, specializing in medical and consumer product design; former project manager for S. G. Hauser Associates, Inc.; designer, Huck & Studer Design, KMH Associates. Clients: Johnson & Johnson, Baxter Healthcare Corporation, Becton Dickinson, Omron Healthcare, Cepheid, Panasonic, Technicolor, Boeing/Teague, Bissell, Thomson Electronics, Reebok, Acer, Whirlpool, Hyundai, Honda R&D, Goldstar, Caterpillar, DaimlerChrysler, Nokia, Microsoft, Disney. Awards: IDSA.

Geoff Wardle, M.Des., Royal College of Art (London). Corporate design experience: British Leyland, Chrysler Europe, Saab, Ford Asia Pacific. Design consultant: Tatra, Czech Republic; TVS-Suzuki, India. Former chair of Transportation Design, Art Center Europe.

Broadcast Cinema Program

Robert W. Peterson, Chair; B.F.A., Art Center College of Design. Director/Director of Photography. Production design, visual effects design, commercials, music videos, documentary films, television, theater. Clients: 20th Century Fox, Paramount, Columbia, Universal, United Artists. Awards: Clio, Belding, Council for Advancement of Secondary Education, New York Film Festival.

Jean-Pierre Geuens, Ph.D., USC. Professor of Cinema, Los Angeles City College. Author: *Film Production Theory.* Publications: *Film Quarterly, Film Criticism, Spectator, LA/CA Journal.*

John Hartzog, Ph.D., USC. Director, Learning Resource Center, California State University, Northridge. Publications: *Film Quarterly, Magill Cinema Annual, Academe.*

Victoria Hochberg, B.A., Antioch College. Fulbright Fellowship. Writer/director: feature films, television, documentaries, music videos. Television: *Sex and the City, Ghost Whisperer, Kitchen Confidential, Reaper.* Feature writer: *The Love of Good Women,* performed with the San Francisco Mime Troupe, Pantomime Theatre of New York. Awards: two Emmy awards for writing and directing, four nominations and two Directors Guild of America awards, Writers Guild of America Award nomination. Member: National Board of the Directors Guild of America, including the Special Projects and Creative Rights Committees.

Ron Osborn, B.F.A., Art Center College of Design. Television producer/writer; feature writer television: executive producer/writer/director, *She Spies;* supervising producer/writer, *The West Wing;* executive producer/writer, *Cupid;* executive producer/writer/creator, *Duckman;* executive producer/writer, *Moonlighting;* executive story editor, *Night Court;* story editor, *Mork and Mindy;* features writer, *Meet Joe Black, Radioland Murders, Just My Luck* (rewrite), *The Flintstones* (rewrite), *The Hard Way* (rewrite). Awards: multiple Emmy nominations, Cable Ace Awards, Best Animated Show (Duckman), Banff International TV Festival.

Eric Sherman, B.A., Yale. Director, cinematographer, producer: *Pep Squad, Mystic Nights & Pirate Fights, After Freedom.* President, Film Transform. Author: *The Director's Event, Directing The Film, Frame by Frame, Selling Your Film, Home Entertainment–The Ultimate Movie Marketplace.* Publications: *Moviemaker.* Awards: Montreal Film Festival, Audience Award, Methodfest *(After Freedom),* New York, Bilbao, Columbus Film Festivals, Peabody Broadcasting Award. Member: Board of Trustees, American Cinematheque; Board of Directors, Film Forum.

Fine Art Program

Jeremy Gilbert-Rolfe, Chair; M.F.A., Florida State. Paintings exhibited nationally and internationally since 1971. Major publications include *Immanence and Contradiction: Recent Essays on the Artistic Device* and *Beyond Piety: Critical Essays on the Visual Arts, 1986–1993.* Recipient, John Simon Guggenheim Memorial Fellowship and the Frank Jewett Mather Award for distinction in art or architectural criticism.

Lita Albuquerque, B.A., UCLA. In the 1970s and 1980s, Albuquerque was a seminal part of the California Light and Space movement and a pioneer in Process Art, Environmental Art, and Earth Art. In recent years, she completed an installation on the pyramids in Egypt called Sol Star. She is currently preparing for a global project at the North and South Poles.

Walead Beshty, M.F.A., Yale. Exhibitions: Hirschhorn Museum, Washington D.C.; Museum of Modern Art, New York; The Tate Britain, U.K.; Armand Hammer Museum of Art, Los Angeles; Whitney Museum of American Art, New York; Wallspace, New York. Faculty: Art Institute of Chicago, Bard College, Roski Graduate School of Fine Arts–UCLA, CalArts.

Stan Douglas, M.F.A., Emily Carr Institute. Exhibitions: Vancouver Art Gallery; Waterloo Art Gallery, Ontario; Joslyn Art Museum, Omaha; The Art Institute of Chicago; Institute of Contemporary Arts, London; Galerie Nationale du Jeu de Paume, Paris. Faculty: Professor of Photography and Digital Media, Universität der Künste, Berlin, 2004–06.

Patricia E. Podesta, M.F.A., Claremont. Artist, production designer of feature films, *Bobby, Memento, Nowhere, Splendor, The Chumbscrubber.* Exhibitions: the Museum of Modern Art, the Rotterdame Film Festival, the American Film Institute, the Pacific Film Archives, LACMA, UCLA Hammer Museum. Awards: the National Endowment for the Arts 1985, 1987, 1989; Art Matters, Inc., 1987, 1989; the Western States Regional Media Award; the James Phelen Award in Film.

Diana Maria Thater, M.F.A., Art Center College of Design. Exhibitions: Dia Center for the Arts, the Museum of Modern Art, the Saint Louis Art Museum, the Renaissance Society at the University of Chicago, Walker Center for the Arts, Portland Art Museum, Vienna Secession, the Basel Kunsthalle, and the Salzburger Kunstverein, among many others. Grants: NEA and the Etants-Donnes Foundation, Guggenheim Fellowship, 2005–06.

Annette Weisser, M.A., Academy of Media Arts (Cologne). Solo exhibitions include *Annette Weisser/Ingo Vetter: Works 1996–2006,* Westphalian State Museum of Art and Culture, Munster (2006); *NameGame,* Hall for Art, Luneburg (2003); *NameGame,* platform ev, Berlin and Forum Citypark, , Graz (2002); *What counts is to absorb all the antitheses at once, rather than resolving them,* Bethany Arthouse, Berlin (1998); *Tableau,* Current Art Society, Munster (1998).

FIT

FASHION INSTITUTE OF TECHNOLOGY

State University of New York

School of Graduate Studies

Programs of Study

The Fashion Institute of Technology (FIT), a State University of New York (SUNY) college of art and design, business, and technology, is home to a rich mix of innovative achievers, creative thinkers, and industry pioneers. FIT fosters interdisciplinary initiatives, advances study and research, and provides access to an international network of professionals. With selective admissions and a reputation for excellence, FIT offers its diverse student body access to world-class faculty, dynamic and relevant curricula, and a superior education at an affordable cost. It offers six programs of graduate study leading to the Master of Arts (M.A.) and Master of Professional Studies (M.P.S.) degrees. The programs in Art Market: Principles and Practices; Exhibition Design; Fashion and Textile Studies: History, Theory, Museum Practice; and Illustration lead to the M.A. degree. The M.P.S. degree programs are Cosmetics and Fragrance Marketing and Management and Global Fashion Management. The School of Graduate Studies is also home to the Center for Executive Education, which offers advanced management programs for senior management in fashion retailing, marketing, or manufacturing.

Art Market: Principles and Practices is a 48-credit, full- or part-time M.A. program preparing students for careers in the business, collection, and exhibition of art. The curriculum includes art history, writing for the art market, gallery design and operation, business practices, computer technology for the art world, marketing, valuation and appraisal, exhibition theory, and art law and professional ethics. Students in the program are required to complete a relevant internship and to research and write a master's qualifying paper. Graduating students must also complete a practicum in which they assemble a group show from concept to execution at a New York City gallery. Their spring 2009 show, *The Ghosts of Coleridge,* invited viewers to suspend their disbelief and see that the extraordinary is often right before their eyes.

Cosmetics and Fragrance Marketing and Management is a 36-credit, part-time M.P.S. program providing industry professionals with high-level management skills and an interdisciplinary, global perspective. The curriculum is designed to encompass three skill sets that leaders in the cosmetics and fragrance industries have identified as crucial to managerial success: core business skills such as management, corporate finance, international business, and management communication; marketing skills such as advanced marketing theory, marketing communications, and market research and strategy; and technical and creative competencies such as cosmetics and fragrance product knowledge, retail and creative management, and an intellectual foundation in beauty and fashion culture. A global component sends students abroad for an intensive week of meetings with industry leaders in major overseas markets. The program culminates in a capstone seminar, in which student teams undertake marketing and management challenges reflecting current business trends and practices and present their solutions to a panel of faculty and industry experts.

The 36-credit, full-time Exhibition Design M.A. program prepares students for careers in the exhibition design and visual display production industry. The studio-driven, one-year course of study focuses on the designer's role within the exhibition team, with emphasis on the development of both design and fabrication skills. Studio projects—such as museum and gallery design, traveling exhibits, and corporate collections—are linked to graphic, lighting, and presentation courses. All graduating students complete an independent, theme-driven design project. Students are also required to complete a related internship.

The 48-credit, full- or part-time Fashion and Textile Studies: History, Theory, Museum Practice M.A. program prepares students for professional curatorial, conservation, education, and other scholarly careers that focus on historic clothing, accessories, textiles, and related materials. The curriculum incorporates conservation skills, current collections management methods, exhibition techniques, art historical methodologies, material culture studies, and gender studies and utilizes the resources of The Museum at FIT, one of the world's largest collections of clothing, textiles, and accessories. Students may elect either a conservation or curatorial emphasis; they may also select up to two independent study courses with an appropriate focus on their chosen specialization. All students are required to complete an internship in the field, write a master's qualifying paper based on original research, and take an active role in a yearlong course culminating in a professional exhibition. Their spring 2009 exhibition, *Muriel King: Artist of Fashion,* examined the designer's contribution to American fashion.

Global Fashion Management is a 36-credit, full-time M.P.S. program offered in collaboration with Hong Kong Polytechnic University in Hong Kong and the Institut Français de la Mode in Paris, preparing current fashion executives for senior managerial positions. The course of study is completed in a three-semester period and includes one intensive seminar course taught in each of the three participating institutions. The curriculum includes courses in production management and the supply chain, global marketing and fashion brand management, current technologies in the fashion industry, international team management, international culture and business, challenges to profitability, and politics and world trade.

The 37-credit, part-time, evening and weekend Illustration M.A. program is designed for working professionals seeking advanced study to further develop their skills as master illustrators. The program focuses on high-level techniques, new media applications, and illustration business practices. The curriculum encompasses digital and traditional studio methods, entrepreneurial research and writing, and opportunities in new and emerging markets. A faculty of noted, active professionals; assignments mirroring marketplace demands and specifications; regular guest lecturers; and off-campus visits maximize student exposure to New York City's art and design world. Students complete a capstone project and an independently researched and written master's thesis.

Research Facilities

The School of Graduate Studies is primarily located in the campus's Shirley Goodman Resource Center, which also houses the Gladys Marcus Library and The Museum at FIT. School of Graduate Studies facilities include conference rooms; a fully equipped conservation laboratory; a multipurpose laboratory for conservation projects and the dressing of mannequins; specialized storage facilities for costume and textile materials; a graduate student lounge with computer and printer access; a graduate student library reading room with computers, reference materials, and copies of past classes' qualifying and thesis papers; specialized wireless classrooms; and classrooms equipped with model stands, easels, and drafting tables.

The Gladys Marcus Library houses a collection of print, nonprint, multimedia, and digital resources comprising more than 300,000 volumes. Specialized holdings include industry reference materials, manufacturers' catalogues, original fashion sketches and scrapbooks, portfolios of plates, photographs, and sample books. The FIT Digital Library provides access to over 90 searchable online databases, including journals, images, books, and research reports.

The Museum at FIT houses one of the world's most important collections of clothing and textiles and is the only museum in New York City dedicated to the art of fashion. The permanent collection encompasses more than 50,000 garments and accessories dating from the eighteenth century, with particular strength in twentieth-century fashion, as well as 30,000 textiles, 300,000 textile swatches, and 1,500 sample books. Award-winning exhibitions, lectures, and symposia inform and inspire nearly 100,000 visitors each year. Recent exhibitions include *Arbiters of Style: Women at the Forefront of Fashion, Gothic: Dark Glamour,* and *Seduction.*

Financial Aid

FIT directly administers its institutional grants and scholarships. Federal funding administered by the college may include Federal Supplemental Educational Opportunity Grants, Federal Perkins Loans, federally subsidized and unsubsidized loans for students and parents, and the Federal Work-Study Program. New York State residents who meet state guidelines for eligibility may also receive Educational Opportunity Program funds. Priority for institutionally administered funds is given to students enrolled and designated as full-time.

Cost of Study

Tuition for New York State residents is $4099 per semester, or $342 per credit. Out-of-state residents' tuition is $6486 per semester, or $541 per credit. Tuition and fees are subject to change at the discretion of FIT's Board of Trustees. Additional expenses—for class materials, textbooks, and travel—may apply and vary per program.

Living and Housing Costs

Residence facilities are available to graduate students. Traditional residence hall accommodations (including meal plan) cost from $5438.50 to $5593.50 per semester. Apartment-style housing options (not including meal plan) cost from $4465 to $8325 per semester.

Student Group

Enrollment in the School of Graduate Studies is approximately 200 students per academic year, allowing considerable individualized advisement. Students come to FIT from throughout the country and around the world.

Student Outcomes

Art Market: Principles and Practices graduates find employment as art gallery directors, public art program directors, art consultants for private and corporate collections, art foundation administrators, museum marketing and development directors, independent curators, auction house department heads, and artists' representatives. Students in the Cosmetics and Fragrance Marketing and Management and Global Fashion Management programs maintain full-time employment in the industry while working toward their degree, which provides the basis for advancement to positions of upper-level managerial responsibility. Graduates of the Exhibition Design program find employment with architectural and exhibition design firms, museums, historic trusts, and special-events companies. Graduates of the Fashion and Textile Studies: History, Theory, Museum Practice program find positions as museum curators, research specialists, collections managers and registrars, historic house directors, museum educators, independent exhibition curators, corporate curators, fashion and textile historians, costume and textile conservators, auction house department specialists and researchers, vintage clothing and textile dealers, and consultants. Students in the Illustration program graduate with the skills needed to succeed as freelance and in-house illustrators for advertising agencies, design firms, magazines, online media, and publishing houses.

Location

FIT is connected to New York City, to students, and to careers. Located in Manhattan's Chelsea neighborhood, it places students at the heart of the advertising, visual arts, fashion, business, and communications industries. Students gain unparalleled exposure to their field through guest lectures, field trips, internships, and sponsored competitions. The college's location provides convenient access to major museums, galleries, and auction houses located throughout the city. Dining, entertainment, and shopping options are within walking distance. Within easy access of New York City's public transportation system, the campus is near subway, bus, and commuter rail lines.

Applying

Applicants to all School of Graduate Studies programs must hold a baccalaureate degree in an appropriate major from an accredited college or university, with a cumulative GPA of 3.0 or higher. International students from non-English-speaking countries are required to submit minimum TOEFL scores of 550 on the written test, 213 on the computer test, or 79 on the Internet test. Students applying to the Art Market: Principles and Practices; Fashion and Textile Studies: History, Theory, Museum Practice; and Global Fashion Management programs must submit GRE scores. Each major has additional, specialized prerequisites for admission; for detailed information, students should visit the School of Graduate Studies on FIT's Web site.

Domestic and international students use the same application when seeking admission. The deadline for completed applications with transcripts and supplemental materials is February 15 for Art Market: Principles and Practices; Exhibition Design; Fashion and Textile Studies: History, Theory, Museum Practice; Illustration; and Global Fashion Management. The deadline for Cosmetics and Fragrance Marketing and Management is March 15. After the deadline dates, applicants are considered on a rolling admissions basis. Candidates may apply online at http://www.fitnyc.edu/gradstudies.

Correspondence and Information

Dr. Steven Zucker, Dean
School of Graduate Studies
Room E315
Fashion Institute of Technology
Seventh Avenue at 27th Street
New York, New York 10001-5992

Phone: 212-217-4300
Fax: 212-217-4301
E-mail: gradinfo@fitnyc.edu
Web site: http://www.fitnyc.edu/gradstudies

Fashion Institute of Technology

THE FACULTY

Dean
Steven Zucker, Ph.D., CUNY Graduate Center.

Art Market: Principles and Practices
Katherine Jánszky Michaelsen, Associate Chairperson; Ph.D., Columbia.
Catherine Hannah Behrend, M.A., M.B.A., NYU; Certificate in Executive Education, INSEAD (France).
Ágnes Berecz, Ph.D., Paris (Sorbonne).
Eric Feinblatt, B.A., SUNY Empire State College.
Christine Helm, M.A., M.Ed., Columbia Teachers College.
John Lee, A.B., Vassar.
Sheri L. Pasquarella, Stony Brook, SUNY, and Columbia (Reid Hall).
Rose Polidoro, B.S., New Haven.
Lucille A. Roussin, Ph.D., Columbia; J.D., Yeshiva.
Martha Schwendener, M.A., Texas at Austin.
Beth Miller Servetar, M.F.A., Bennington.
Gayle M. Skluzacek, B.A., Barat.
Steven Zucker, Ph.D., CUNY Graduate Center.

Cosmetics and Fragrance Marketing and Management
Stephen Kanlian, Associate Chairperson; M.A., Durham (England); M.P.A., Pennsylvania.
Bruce Abramson, M.P.S., Fashion Institute of Technology; M.B.A., Fordham.
Jean Broom, M.S.W., Minnesota; M.M., Northwestern.
Dorothy C. Foster, J.D., Fordham.
Kenneth Freeman, M.B.A., Harvard.
Judy Galloway, A.B., Mary Baldwin.
Bradley Horowitz, M.B.A., Fordham.
Guillermo Jimenez, J.D., Berkeley.
Janice Levine, M.P.S., Fashion Institute of Technology.
Mary C. Manning, Institute of Marketing (England) and Kingston Upon Thames (England).
Mark Polson, M.P.S., Fashion Institute of Technology.
Cynthia Strite, Ph.D. candidate, Columbia Teachers College.
Mary Tumolo, former Vice President, Promotional Marketing, Lancôme, L'Oreal USA.
Pamela Vaile, M.B.A., Pace.
Karen Young, B.A., Denver.

Exhibition Design
Brenda Cowan, Associate Chairperson; M.S.Ed., Bank Street College of Education.
Norman Bleckner, B.I.D., Pratt.
Robin Drake, B.S., Pratt.
John Katimaris, M.F.A., Parsons; RA, AIA, IES, IIDA.
Lucian J. Leone, B.I.D., Pratt.
Ran Lerner, M.I.D., Domus Academy (Italy).
Scott Lundberg, M.I.D., Pratt.

Karl Matsuda, Certificate in Art, Cooper Union.
John Newman, M.A., Parsons; IES.
Michael Stiller, B.A., Bard.
Michele Y. T. Washington, M.S., Pratt.

Fashion and Textile Studies: History, Theory, Museum Practice
Denyse Montegut, Associate Chairperson; Ph.D. candidate, Delaware.
June Burns Bové, M.A., NYU.
Maria Ann Conelli, Ph.D., Columbia.
Nancy Deihl, M.A., NYU.
Marlene Eidelheit, M.A., Fashion Institute of Technology.
Judith Eisenberg, M.A., Wichita State.
Lourdes M. Font, Ph.D., NYU.
Joanne Dolan Ingersoll, M.A., Fashion Institute of Technology.
Désirée Koslin, M.F.A., CUNY, City College; Ph.D., NYU.
Diane Maglio, M.A., Fashion Institute of Technology.
Patricia E. Mears, M.A., Fashion Institute of Technology.
Maya Naunton, M.A. candidate, Conservation Certificate, NYU.
Denise Stone, M.A., Fashion Institute of Technology.

Global Fashion Management
Pamela Ellsworth, Associate Chairperson; M.P.S., Fashion Institute of Technology.
Praveen K. Chaudhry, Ph.D., Philadelphia University.
Thomas Claire, M.A., Brown; M.B.A., Columbia.
Virginia Cutchin, M.B.A., CUNY, Baruch.
Naomi Daremblum, Ph.D., NYU.
Kenneth Freeman, M.B.A., Harvard.
Guillermo Jimenez, J.D., Berkeley.
John Mincarelli, M.A., NYU.
Jeanette Nostra, B.S., Goddard.
Christine S. Pomeranz, M.B.A., NYU.

Illustration
Melanie Reim, Associate Chairperson; M.F.A., Syracuse.
Salvatore Catalano, B.A., SUNY Empire State College.
Vincent DiFate, M.A., Syracuse.
Dennis Dittrich, M.F.A., Syracuse.
Michael Hyde, M.F.A., Columbia; Ph.D., NYU.
Amy Lemmon, Ph.D., Cincinnati.
William Low, M.A., Syracuse.
Daniel Pelavin, M.F.A., Cranbrook Academy of Art.
Cheryl Phelps, B.F.A., Memphis College of Art.
Stanley Solomon, Ph.D., NYU.
Ed Soyka, B.F.A., Regents.
Nancy Stahl, Arizona.
Murray Tinkelman, Cooper Union.

The faculty members listed above constitute a partial listing. Guest lecturers are not included.

IIT Institute of Design

ILLINOIS INSTITUTE OF TECHNOLOGY

Institute of Design

Programs of Study

Founded in 1937 as the New Bauhaus, the Institute of Design (ID) at Illinois Institute of Technology (IIT) is distinguished by its insistence on user-centeredness; its development of rigorous, verifiable methods; and its emphasis on placing design at the center of the development process. ID is one of the few graduate programs in design that welcomes applicants with no formal design training. Going beyond the traditional role of design as styling or execution of an existing idea, ID's mission is to develop, teach, and promote design methods that lead to more humane technology by helping innovation professionals better decide what to make. ID's methods are about understanding user needs as a platform for creating new offerings that bring meaningful value to people and businesses. They are about using design to reframe problems in unique ways, make sense of complex information, explore alternatives quickly and effectively, and visualize and communicate compelling solutions. As a result of their training, ID graduates are recognized worldwide as highly skilled leaders for creative teams of many kinds, with the tools to discover and solve a wide range of problems and deliver breakthrough innovations.

ID offers four programs of study. The Master of Design (M.Des.) degree is for those who wish to achieve mastery in the application of advanced design theories and processes. This two-year, full-time, 54-credit-hour program offers a variety of options for concentration in areas such as communication design, product and environment design, interaction, complex systems, strategic design planning, visualization, and user-centered research. In addition to experienced designers, students may enter this program with no formal design training by completing a one-year foundation program of introductory courses providing prerequisite skills and experience.

The Master of Design/Master of Business Administration (M.Des./M.B.A.) dual-degree program is offered jointly with the IIT Stuart School of Business. It provides a way to attain both degrees in a shortened period of time. Experienced designers can complete both degrees in two years plus one quarter of full-time study, including summer sessions. Students without design training who take the foundation sequence can complete both degrees in three years plus one quarter.

The Master of Design Methods (M.D.M.) is a two-semester (or a part-time four- or six-semester) professional master's degree for exceptional midcareer designers, managers, engineers, and other leaders of innovation, focusing exclusively on advanced methods and frameworks for leading innovation and strategy teams. It concentrates on the design theories and methods developed and taught at the Institute of Design, in areas such as user observation and research, prototyping, interaction design, visualization, and strategic design planning. The M.D.M. is open to both designers and nondesigners, provided they have demonstrated leadership experience. The Doctor of Philosophy (Ph.D.) degree is for those who wish to conduct fundamental research to extend the body of knowledge about design theory and process. The Ph.D. program requires a minimum of 84 credit hours beyond the master's degree. A master's degree in design is prerequisite to enrollment in the Ph.D. program. For those without a design degree, the master's degree can be obtained at ID before admission to the Ph.D. program.

Research Facilities

Research at the Institute of Design is supported by a networked computing system that enables students to digitize and manipulate photographic images, analyze problems, model forms, create interactive multimedia and individualized publications, and develop new systems and tools. Equipment includes Silicon Graphics, Sun, and Apple computers and a wide range of peripherals.

Financial Aid

Limited graduate fellowships are available on a competitive basis. International students frequently obtain special scholarships from their governments or from international sources, e.g., Fulbright, LASPAU for South America, INLAKS Foundation UK for India, and others.

Cost of Study

The M.Des. and Ph.D. programs are full-time only. Graduate tuition in these programs for 2009–10 is $36,316 per academic year. The M.D.M. program may be completed on a part-time basis; the total tuition for the M.D.M. is $43,976 for the 30-credit-hour program. The thesis fee for the Ph.D. is $150. Books and studio materials cost approximately $850 per semester. Mandatory health insurance costs approximately $900 per year.

Living and Housing Costs

Rooms in Graduate Hall (based on double occupancy) range from $5566 to $6632 per year. There are also 356 apartments in four high-rise apartment buildings on the campus. Units range from efficiencies to three bedrooms, and rents, including all utilities except telephone and cable television, range from $579 to $1145 per month. Various meal plans are available at additional costs. Most students live off campus, as ID is located in downtown Chicago. Prospective students should contact Graduate Admissions by e-mail for more details.

Student Group

The Institute of Design is a focused community of very creative and highly motivated students. Graduate enrollment is about 150 students. Typically, half of the graduate students have been professional designers and half come from other disciplines. About 60 percent are from the United States, and the rest are from countries in the Americas, Europe, and Asia. Fifty percent are women.

Student Outcomes

Graduates typically work in design and planning consultancies such as Cheskin, Design Continuum, Doblin, IDEO, Smart Design, and Sapient or in corporations such as Hewlett-Packard, Microsoft, Motorola, Pitney Bowes, Philips, Sony, Steelcase, and Whirlpool.

Location

Chicago, one of the world's largest cities, has more than 7 million people in its metropolitan area. Located on the western shores of Lake Michigan, it is an international center of business, one of the world's largest inland ports, and an air and rail transportation hub. Chicago offers students an exceptional variety of educational, cultural, and recreational opportunities. The city is known for its architecture, sports teams, music and comedy clubs, museums, and symphony orchestra.

The Institute

Since its founding, the Institute of Design has attracted students and faculty members from around the world—people who have eagerly experimented with new media and have developed important new processes, concepts, and theories. Laszlo Moholy-Nagy, a master of the influential German Bauhaus school of design, brought Bauhaus principles to Chicago in 1937 and founded the New Bauhaus, which was later renamed the Institute of Design. In 1949, the school merged with Illinois Institute of Technology. IIT offers programs in engineering and science, architecture, business, technical communication, psychology, and law.

Applying

Students may be admitted to graduate study at the beginning of the regular semester, either fall or spring. Completed applications and supporting documents should be received by February 15 for fall enrollment or September 15 for spring enrollment. Under no circumstances are international applications considered after the stated deadlines. Applications for graduate fellowships should be submitted at the time of application for admission.

Applicants must hold a baccalaureate degree from an accredited educational institution. A portfolio is required of all applicants with a background in design or the visual arts. Regardless of previous degrees, students may be required to complete some prerequisite design courses before beginning their degree requirements. Applicants without design degrees are encouraged to apply. They are first required to complete a sequence of prerequisite courses and other appropriate background work, which normally takes two additional semesters.

Applicants with undergraduate degrees in disciplines other than design, all applicants to the Ph.D. program, and international applicants must submit GRE scores. Applicants from non-English-speaking countries must submit TOEFL scores, unless a college-level degree has been obtained from a U.S. institution prior to admission to ID.

Correspondence and Information

Graduate Admissions
Institute of Design
Illinois Institute of Technology
350 North LaSalle Street
Chicago, Illinois 60654

Phone: 312-595-4900
Fax: 312-595-4901
E-mail: design@id.iit.edu
Web site: http://www.id.iit.edu

Illinois Institute of Technology

THE FACULTY

Jeremy Alexis, Assistant Professor and Assistant Dean; M.Des., IIT.
Dale Fahnstrom, Professor; M.F.A., Illinois.
Judith Gregory, Assistant Professor; Ph.D., California, San Diego.
John Grimes, Professor and Associate Director; M.S., IIT.
Vijay Kumar, Associate Professor; M.S., IIT.
Tom MacTavish, Visiting Associate Professor; M.A., Iowa; M.A., Michigan.
Anijo Mathew, Assistant Professor; M.Des.S. Harvard.
Charles Owen, Distinguished Professor; M.S., IIT.
Keiichi Sato, Professor; M.S., Osaka Institute of Technology (Japan); M.S., IIT.
Martin Thaler, Visiting Associate Professor; M.F.A., Royal College of Art.
Patrick Whitney, Steelcase/Robert C. Pew Professor and Director; M.F.A., Cranbrook Academy of Art.

Adjunct Faculty

Ken Douros, Motorola.
Kim Erwin, Designer and Writer.
Ronald Gordon, Ron Gordon Photographic Services.
Tomoko Ichikawa, Information Designer.
Megan Fath, Conifer Research.
Ben Jacobson, Conifer Research.
Mark Jones, IDEO.
Larry Keeley, Doblin.
John Paul Kusz, IIT Stuart School of Business.
Peter Laundy, Doblin.
Mathew Mayfield, Motorola.
Thomas McLeish, IIT College of Architecture.
Todd McCullough, Doblin.
Tim McKeown, Motorola.
Peter Pfanner, Motorola.
John Pipino, Doblin.
Russ Rosenzweig, Round Table Group.
Jeffrey Tull, Doblin
Bill Verplank, Stanford.
Denis Weil, McDonald's Corporation.
Michael Winnick, gravitytank.
Robert Zolna, gravitytank.

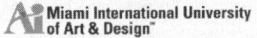

MIAMI INTERNATIONAL UNIVERSITY OF ART & DESIGN
Master's Programs

Programs of Study	Miami International University of Art & Design offers Master of Fine Arts degrees in film, graphic design, interior design, and visual arts.
	Many of the programs require students to take a course in teaching methodologies, enabling them to learn the language of the industry. In addition, students discover techniques that help them to communicate within an area of expertise. Aesthetics, planning, research, and writing are also important elements in rounding out the educational experience.
	Most degrees require six quarters of study, for a total of 90 credits. Course work varies by program, and the detailed curriculum may be viewed online at http://www.artinstitutes.edu/miami.
Research Facilities	Miami International University of Art & Design is located within a 60,000-square-foot academic and administration building. The facility includes industry-related equipment, a painting and sculpture studio, a production facility, and an editing facility. There are also interior design and fashion resource rooms.
Financial Aid	Financial aid is available to those who qualify. Students who require financial assistance to attend Miami International University of Art & Design must first submit a Free Application for Federal Student Aid (FAFSA) and then meet with a financial aid officer to determine the amount of aid needed and the types of aid available. Aid comes in the form of Federal Pell Grants, Federal Supplemental Educational Opportunity Grants (FSEOG), Florida Postsecondary Student Assistance Grants, and Florida Bright Futures Scholarships. Federal Perkins Loans, Federal PLUS Program awards, and Federal Stafford Student Loans may also be an option for students. Part-time employment is available, or students may apply for a number of scholarships, including those offered to international students. Scholarships award partial or full tuition, and deadlines and eligibility requirements vary.
Cost of Study	Tuition and other fees vary by graduate program and are due in full prior to matriculation for each quarter of study.
Living and Housing Costs	Students should contact the University for information on housing options and living expenses.
Student Group	Individuals enrolled in graduate programs at Miami International University of Art & Design come from a variety of backgrounds. Students (graduate and undergraduate) at the school are from out of state and across America; many also come from other countries.
Student Outcomes	The University works to foster the students' desire to maintain high levels of professionalism in their chosen careers. Special emphasis is placed on helping students to reach their personal, academic, and career goals. As part of this objective, the Office of Career Services works with students throughout their education and after graduation, offering career assessment and planning, job search assistance, and networking opportunities.
Location	Miami is a culturally rich region that celebrates events year-round, including the African-American Heritage Festival, Haitian Heritage Week, the Viva Mexico Celebration, the Israel Independence Celebration, and Asian Cultural Week. The city is home to professional sports teams, and residents enjoy the sandy beaches, international cuisine, local clubs, the historic Art Deco District, Coral Gables, and Key Biscayne. The Florida Keys, Disney World, and the Bahamas are all just a short trip away.
The University	Students are creative, competitive, and open to new ideas. The University's faculty consists of full-time and part-time professors, many of whom have advanced degrees and professional experience in their respective fields.
	Student clubs and organizations include the American Institute of Graphic Arts (AIGA), American Society of Interior Designers (ASID), International Student Club, and Student Council.
	Miami International University of Art & Design and its branch campuses, The Art Institute of Jacksonville and The Art Institute of Tampa, are accredited by the Commission on Colleges of the Southern Association of Colleges and Schools to award the master's, bachelor's, and associate degrees. Contact the Commission on Colleges at 1866 Southern Lane, Decatur, Georgia 30033-4097 or call 404-679-4500 for questions about the accreditation of Miami International University of Art & Design.
Applying	Applicants are interviewed, either in person or by telephone, to explore their background and interest in program offerings. Each applicant's transcript and essay are evaluated by the Admissions Acceptance Committee, which reserves the right to request additional records of accomplishment in core academic courses. There is a $50 application fee.
	International students' transcripts must be prepared in English or include a complete and official English translation. Proof of English language proficiency or enrollment in the school's English as a second language (ESL) course is required for all prospective international students.
	To obtain an application, make arrangements for an interview, or tour the school, prospective students should contact the University at the address listed in this description.
Correspondence and Information	Miami International University of Art & Design 1501 Biscayne Boulevard, Suite 100 Miami, Florida 33132-1418 Phone: 305-428-5700 800-225-9023 (toll-free) Fax: 305-374-5933 Web site: http://www.artinstitutes.edu/miami

Miami International University of Art & Design

THE FACULTY AND THEIR RESEARCH

At Miami International University of Art & Design, students find an experienced faculty focused on providing students with the skills needed for the marketplace. Many faculty members are researchers and practitioners in their fields, who bring their experience into the classroom. These members are qualified to prepare students to face the challenges of the real world. The faculty members of the school are committed to the personal and professional development of their students.

The Art Institute of Atlanta®, GA; The Art Institute of California[SM]–Inland Empire; The Art Institute of California[SM]–Los Angeles; The Art Institute of California[SM]–Orange County; The Art Institute of California[SM]–San Diego; The Art Institute of California[SM]–San Francisco; The Art Institute of Charleston[SM], SC, A branch of The Art Institute of Atlanta, GA; The Art Institute of Charlotte®, NC; The Art Institute of Colorado® (Denver); The Art Institute of Dallas®, TX; The Art Institute of Fort Lauderdale®, FL; The Art Institute of Houston®, TX; The Art Institute of Indianapolis[SM], IN*; The Art Institute of Jacksonville[SM], A branch of Miami International University of Art & Design, FL; The Art Institute of Las Vegas®, NV; The Art Institute of New York City®, NY; The Art Institute of Ohio[SM]–Cincinnati**; The Art Institute of Philadelphia®, PA; The Art Institute of Phoenix®, AZ; The Art Institute of Pittsburgh® PA; The Art Institute of Portland®, OR; The Art Institute of Seattle®, WA; The Art Institute of Tampa[SM], FL, A branch of Miami International University of Art & Design; The Art Institute of Tennessee[SM]–Nashville, A branch of The Art Institute of Atlanta, GA; The Art Institute of Vancouver[SM], BC (Burnaby location, Downtown location, Dubrulle Culinary Arts location); The Art Institute of Washington® (Arlington, VA), A branch of The Art Institute of Atlanta, GA; The Art Institute Online[SM], A division of The Art Institute of Pittsburgh, PA; The Art Institutes International Minnesota[SM] (Minneapolis); Bradley Academy for the Visual Arts[SM] (York, PA); California Design College[SM] (Wilshire Boulevard, Los Angeles); The Illinois Institute of Art®–Chicago; The Illinois Institute of Art®–Schaumburg; Miami International University of Art & Design[SM], FL; The New England Institute of Art[SM] (Boston, MA).

*The Art Institute of Indianapolis is licensed by the Indiana Commission on Proprietary Education, 302 West Washington Street, Room E201, Indianapolis, IN 46204, AC-0080.

**The Art Institute of Ohio–Cincinnati, 8845 Governors Hill Drive, Suite 100, Cincinnati, OH 45249-3317, Reg. #04-01-1698B.

THE NEW SCHOOL: A UNIVERSITY

Parsons The New School for Design
Program in Design and Technology

Program of Study

Parsons' 64-credit M.F.A. in Design and Technology program is an intense and rigorous program in which students explore the design implications of emerging technologies and the evolving connections between technology, design, and the human experience. The curriculum integrates critical discourse, theory, experimentation, and hands-on production, with an emphasis on critique in areas including multimedia, physical computing, animation, and broadcast design. Students complete individual and collaborative studio projects that demonstrate aesthetic and intellectual refinement as well as technical mastery. The program and its curriculum are closely linked to the real world, and students are actively engaged in effecting or responding to social change through their design projects.

Whether students are interested in the commercial world, academia, or fine arts, they graduate with far more than an expanded technology skill set; they bring the creative, intellectual, and philosophical ability to shape the future in meaningful ways. Students are expected to achieve advanced academic and professional levels in both design theory and practice, as demonstrated by the Thesis Project and Document. The thesis is the systematic study of a design question that requires students to identify an idea and area of study, research its major assumptions and precedents, explain the significance of the undertaking, set forth the process and method for proposing solutions, create prototypes, and offer a conclusion through the production of a body of work. The finished project demonstrates originality and experimentation, critical and independent thinking, appropriate organization and format, and thorough documentation.

Digital Boot Camp is a four-week summer course designed to enable students who may not be well versed in visual and interactive Web design and development to enter the fall semester with confidence, so they can focus on the conceptual and pragmatic concerns of the design process. Two primary areas are addressed in Boot Camp: Web development and interactive design. Some students are required to complete Boot Camp as a condition of their acceptance into the program. Students in Boot Camp earn 3 academic credits, applicable toward the 64 credits required for graduation.

Research Facilities

Collaboration Studios (or Collab Studios) team students with industry partners to undertake real-world projects. Many Collab Studios are dedicated to applied design research areas in the Parsons Design Lab, with cross-disciplinary teams formed from the various design disciplines at Parsons. Students have access to every lab on campus. Computing facilities are comprehensive and cutting edge. The Knowledge Union—the primary working environment of M.F.A. Design and Technology students—consists of state-of-the-art technology spread over four floors. Six hundred networked workstations include all relevant platforms. Servers support work ranging from traditional print output to online projects using webcasting and secure transaction technology.

Specialty work, whether audio/video production, MIDI, recording, or physical computing installation, takes place in the Design and Technology Lab. Portable production equipment, including digital still, video, and audio equipment, is readily available. Digital projectors, surround sound, and active white boards feed into equipment racks that enable presentation of all media types. M.F.A. Design and Technology students who wish to work from home have full access to the University network over the Internet and can take advantage of the University network and full Internet 2 connectivity while on campus.

Financial Aid

Graduate students are automatically considered for scholarship funds upon acceptance into the program. Scholarship recipients are notified of their award by either their program or a Student Financial Services award letter soon after being admitted. Graduate students should contact their academic department early in the admissions process for separate applications for institutional awards, such as assistantships. U.S. citizens and permanent residents applying for financial aid outside the University should file the Free Application for Federal Student Aid (FAFSA) by March 1. More information can be found at the Student Financial Services Web site at http://www.newschool.edu/studentservices/financialaid/.

Cost of Study

In 2009–10 full-time students will pay $18,060 in tuition and $145 in fees per term. Additional fees may apply.

Living and Housing Costs

The University offers on-campus housing, University-run apartments, and assistance in finding housing off campus. The cost of housing, food, transportation, books, and living expenses in New York City averages $17,000 annually. For more information, interested students should visit http://www.newschool.edu/studentservices.html.

Student Group

There are 148 students in the program, 143 of whom are full-time. This includes 81 women, 30 students who are members of minority groups, and 64 international students.

Location

Parsons The New School for Design is located in Greenwich Village, at the heart of New York's vibrant architecture and design communities. In addition to using the neighborhoods, city streets, and wireless networks as laboratories for experimentation, students collaborate with an array of corporate, governmental, educational, nonprofit, and arts organizations to ensure a working environment that is both technically current and socially relevant.

The University and The School

Parsons is part of The New School, a leading university in New York City offering some of the nation's most distinguished programs in design, liberal arts, management and policy, and the performing arts, leading to seventy graduate and undergraduate degrees. More information can be found at http://www.newschool.edu/degreeprograms. Parsons and The New School are fully accredited by the Commission on Higher Education of the Middle States Association of Colleges and Schools.

Applying

A Bachelor of Arts, a Bachelor of Fine Arts, or an equivalent international degree is required. Applicants are not required to have a degree in design or computer programming knowledge. Students must submit the completed application, the $50 application fee, a resume, a statement of interest, official copies of all college transcripts, two letters of recommendation, and a portfolio submitted in one of the following formats: CD-ROM, DVD, videotape, slides, or URLs for Web-based work. The portfolio must include an inventory list and clear run instructions. In addition, international students must submit TOEFL scores—a minimum of 580 on the written test or 237 on the computerized version. The application deadline is February 1.

Correspondence and Information

Master of Fine Arts in Design and Technology Program
Parsons The New School for Design
2 West 13th Street, 10th Floor
New York, New York 10011
Phone: 212-229-8908
Fax: 212-229-5941
E-mail: office@parsons.edu
Web site: http://www.newschool.edu/parsons
http://dt.parsons.edu

The New School: A University

THE FACULTY AND THEIR RESEARCH

Complete faculty biographies can be found at http://dt.parsons.edu/faculty.html.

Joao Amorim. Animation, including 3-D; design.

Cory Arcangel.

J. Z. Barrell. Commercial/industrial audio production (TV/radio/Internet), music production, narrative editing, teaching, composition.

John Blackford.

Mitchell Butler, Animation Director. Character and story, 3-D animation, 2-D Flash animation.

Louisa Campbell. Children's television, theater, and film.

David Carroll, Multimedia Director, Second Thought. Macromedia Flash MX design technology, inclusive of its commercial, academic, and artistic contexts, with a special interest in the possibilities of intersections and hybridized forms.

Adam Chapman, Award-winning artist. Writing, design.

James Dean Conklin. Animation, design.

Anthony Deen, Vice President of Design, CDI Group. Synchronization of design and technology.

Sharon Denning. Interactive media.

Andrea Dezso, Artist, award-winning graphic designer and typographer, illustrator, educator, and writer.

Nicole DiDio.

Nicholas Fortugno. Role playing, live action, game culture.

Morry Galonoy, Principal, Litchinut. Relative impact of technology on society and society on technology, with particular interest in global communications and culture.

Yury Gitman. New media art, broadcast design, wireless development.

Joshua Goldberg, Artist and programmer. Multimedia sampling and live video performance.

Rachel Johnson.

David Kanter. Web site and interactive development.

Christopher Kirwan, Principal, Urban Technologies.

Alison Lewis, Interactive digital design artist, engineer, and educator.

Colleen Macklin, Department Chair, Design and Technology. Digital art, interactive design emphasizing social interaction and collaboration.

Jonathan Marcus.

Nino Mendolia. Digitally manipulated 2-D and 3-D elements.

Robert Milazzo. Film directing, screenwriting, performance.

Katherine Moriwaki. How the disciplines of architecture, product design, and fashion converge with technological advances to form new modalities of expression.

Barbara Morris. Product design and development, writing.

Karen Nourse, Filmmaker.

Stephanie Owens, Cofounder and COO, Oddcast. Relationship between materiality and representation.

Nina Paley. Animation.

Igor Pusenjak. Experimental connections between the virtual and the physical using different materials and technologies.

Chris Romero, Design Partner, Oscillation Digital Design Studio. Interfaces between humans and computers.

Evan Roth. Artistic uses of technology in popular culture and the urban environment.

Katie Salen, Director, Design and Technology, Graduate Studies. Connections between game design, interactivity, and play.

Jun Sassa. 2-D and 3-D animation.

Anezka Sebek. Animation, all aspects of time-based work.

Sabine Seymour, Founder, Moondial, Inc. Next-generation wearables and the intertwining of aesthetics and function.

Mark Stafford, Coordinator, Critical Studies and Writing. Psychoanalysis, fiction and nonfiction.

Michael Sweet, Composer and sound designer.

Marko Tandefelt. Interface and concept design, 3-D/VR, physical computing art for public spaces, audiovisual interactive instrument design.

Tom Toth.

Sven Travis. Interactive media.

Michael Waldron, Creative Director, Nailgun. Broadcast design.

Loretta Wolozin. Multimedia for young children's literacy.

Marina Zurkow, Flash computer animator. Interactive design.

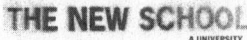

THE NEW SCHOOL: A UNIVERSITY

Parsons The New School for Design
M.F.A. in Interior Design

Program of Study

Parsons launched the nation's first interior design program in 1906. Parsons The New School for Design's new M.F.A. in Interior Design program (MFA ID), launching in 2009 (pending New York State approval), builds on this leadership to offer a program based on a scholarly, research-oriented curriculum. Graduates will be educated to play transformative roles in the profession and to become the teachers of the next generation of practitioners.

The discipline of interiors is situated between many specialties, including architecture, product design, and engineering. Housed in the only integrated school of interior design, lighting design, product design, and architecture nationally, students are offered an unparalleled depth and intimacy of exposure, preparing them for this multifaceted discipline.

Three foci distinguish the program: the history and theory of the interior; materials, including an emphasis on sustainable practices, fabrication processes, and digital technologies; and interior design as a material and social practice.

Interior designers are now commonly expected to incorporate sustainable design practices and enhanced building performance into their work. They have at their disposable new technologies and materials for modifying spatial relationships and functions within building envelopes, and they are facing new client types and user groups as a consequence of social change and shifts in population demographics. With Parsons' strong emphasis on the social impact of design, the program is uniquely qualified to confront these modern challenges.

Research Facilities

Interior design students share an open studio space across two floors in a loft building with graduate students in architecture and lighting design, which encourages dialogues across disciplines. Support for course work is provided through a computer lab, giving access to a multitude of software programs specific to the profession, along with large-format plotters. Wireless digital technology is accessible from the design studios, where students are given semester-long dedicated work spaces.

A lighting lab and fabrication shop are located within the School, and a metal fabrication shop is housed within the building, encouraging students to interact with the Fine Arts Department on upper floors. The Interior Design program is additionally supported by the Donghia Materials Library and Study Center, generously donated by the late interior designer Angelo Donghia. The library is curated to reflect sustainable and emerging materials and used as a resource for core courses. The program is additionally supported by The New School's Library Consortium.

Financial Aid

The Angelo Donghia Graduate Scholarship program provides merit-based scholarships to M.F.A. ID students. These generous and prestigious scholarships offer full-tuition funding for the duration of the two-year MFA ID program. The Jamie Drake Graduate Scholarship program provides merit-based scholarships to MFA ID students. This prestigious scholarship offers a $10,000 tuition award for the first year of the two-year MFA ID program.

Cost of Study

Parsons' M.F.A. in Interior Design program is scheduled to launch in fall 2009. In 2008–09, tuition for Parsons M.F.A. programs (except photography) was $17,280 per term. University fees were $140.

Living and Housing Costs

For the nine-month academic year, transportation and living expenses for a single student are estimated at $15,000.

Student Group

Parsons plans to enroll approximately 12 students in its M.F.A. in Interior Design program.

Location

Parsons is located in Greenwich Village in New York City.

The University and The School

Parsons is part of The New School, which was founded in New York City in 1919 as a bastion of intellectual and artistic freedom. Today, The New School is a leading urban university containing some of the nation's most respected programs in design, liberal arts, the performing arts, professional management and urban policy, and social and political science. Students from across the country and around the world attend The New School's diverse programs, enjoying small class sizes, superior resources, and a renowned faculty of artists, scholars, and professionals who practice what they teach. The New School's founding mission was to create a place where global peace and justice were more than theoretical ideals. To this day, New School students participate in programs that strive for academic excellence, technical mastery, innovation, and engaged world citizenship.

Applying

Applicants must have an undergraduate degree before entering the graduate program. Applicants outside of design-based disciplines are encouraged to apply but should be prepared to take the Parsons Summer Studies in Architecture program to establish design and drawing foundations prior to the start of the first semester of the M.F.A. program. Admissions for the M.F.A. in Interior Design program are handled directly by the School of Constructed Environments at Parsons. For admissions information, students should e-mail aidladmission@newschool.edu.

Correspondence and Information

School of Constructed Environments
Product, Lighting, Architecture, and Interior Design
Parsons The New School for Design
25 East 13th Street, 2nd Floor
New York, New York 10003
Phone: 212-229-8955
Fax: 212-229-8937
E-mail: sce@newschool.edu
Web site: http://www2.parsons.edu/sce/mfaid/index.php

The New School: A University

THE FACULTY AND THEIR RESEARCH

To learn more about the following Parsons' Interior Design faculty members, students should visit http://www.newschool.edu.mfaid.

Matthew Baird
Daniel Barber
Jeremy Barbour
Katherine Chia
Charles Davis
Douglas Fanning
Jean M. Gardner
Anita Jorgensen
Robert Kirkbride
Barbara Lewandowska
Brian McGrath
Joanna Merwood
Michael Morris
Jonsara Ruth
Ioanna Theocharopoulou
Timothy Ventimiglia
Lois Weinthal
Alan Wexler
Peter Wheelwright
Anthony Whitfield
Alfred Zollinger

THE NEW SCHOOL: A UNIVERSITY

Parsons The New School for Design
Program in Photography

Program of Study

The M.F.A. in Photography program at Parsons The New School for Design functions as a twenty-first-century atelier and think tank. Students are encouraged to develop individual vision in a collaborative environment and explore related technologies focusing on the relationship between concept and production. The goal of the program is to educate students about the expanding and evolving creative position of the photographer today, specifically in relation to emerging imaging technologies and new media. This program grounds students in both the evolving language of photography and the technology driving that evolution. Graduates are prepared to define the future of photography and its creative role within contemporary culture, either as scholars or as practicing artists.

Departing from the traditional semester format, the M.F.A. in Photography program is a twenty-six-month, 64-credit program that blends practice and theory. The curriculum consists of technical and academic studies as well as significant studio work. Students earn credits through summer residencies and by utilizing the latest distributed-learning technologies. Participants complete requirements during three consecutive eight-week intensive summer sessions in residence at Parsons and engage in independent study and online learning during the fall/spring terms. The fall/spring semesters culminate in five-day intensive residencies in January and June.

Required courses are Graduate Studio, Graduate Seminars I–III, Independent Studio I–IV, Wired Studio, Think Tank, Thesis and Exhibition, and Cyber-Community Conference (CCC). In Graduate Studio, students explore a personal direction in their studio. In Graduate Seminars I–III, students utilize the artistic and intellectual wealth of the city to explore contemporary issues in art and photography. Independent Studio I–IV continues the personal studio work initiated in Graduate Studio. Wired Studio is a skills acquisition course designed to introduce participants to new photographic technologies and working methods. Think Tank brings into focus the impact of new technologies on working methods and production and how they are viewed. Thesis and Exhibition prepares students for their thesis exhibitions through close work with their advisory and graduate committees. Through asynchronous and live discussion groups and critique space, with guest lecturers and critics, CCC facilitates a free and creative exchange despite geographic boundaries.

Research Facilities

The Adam and Sophie Gimbel Library of Art and Design includes books on art and design, special collections, and several hundred rare books. The library also contains a collection of mounted plates, slides, and periodicals on the history and the latest developments in fine arts and design. The Gimbel Library has begun development of a digital image collection that will enable online access to images from Parsons' slide collection. The Angelo Donghia Materials Library and Study Center, funded by the Angelo Donghia Foundation, includes a library, a gallery, a computer lab, and a lecture hall. The library allows students and faculty members to review and check out state-of-the-art resources, putting the latest and most exclusive materials at their fingertips.

Financial Aid

Graduate students are automatically considered for scholarship funds upon acceptance into the program. Scholarship recipients are notified of their award by either their program or a Student Financial Services award letter soon after being admitted. Graduate students should contact their academic department early in the admissions process for separate applications for institutional awards, such as assistantships. U.S. citizens and permanent residents applying for financial aid outside the University should file the Free Application for Federal Student Aid (FAFSA) by March 1. More information can be found at the Student Financial Services Web site at http://www.newschool.edu/studentservices/financialaid/.

Cost of Study

In 2009–10, full-time students pay $1131 per credit in tuition and $145 in fees per term. Additional fees may apply.

Living and Housing Costs

The University offers on-campus housing, University-run apartments, and assistance in finding housing off campus. The cost of housing, food, transportation, books, and living expenses in New York City averages $17,000 annually. For more information, interested students should visit http://www.newschool.edu/studentservices.html.

Student Group

Of the 29 students in the program, 6 are full-time, 17 are women, and 6 are international. Students in the M.F.A. in Photography program come from varied backgrounds, which adds to the diversity of visions and styles within the program.

Location

Parsons' main campus is located downtown in Greenwich Village, a historic neighborhood with a style and atmosphere found nowhere else in New York City. The Village is home to design and art studios, galleries, shops, and restaurants as well as avant-garde artists, musicians, and writers.

With rich cultural resources, international sophistication, and cutting-edge attitude, New York City is a vibrant environment that has inspired and challenged artists and designers throughout its history. New York is home to more than eighty museums, including the Metropolitan Museum of Art, the Museum of Modern Art, and Cooper-Hewitt, National Design Museum. To Parsons faculty, the city is an extension of the classroom and is incorporated into the basic fabric of the curriculum.

The University and The School

Parsons is part of The New School, a leading university in New York City offering some of the nation's most distinguished programs in design, liberal arts, management and policy, and the performing arts, leading to seventy graduate and undergraduate degrees. Learn more at http://www.newschool.edu/degreeprograms. Parsons and The New School are fully accredited by the Commission on Higher Education of the Middle States Association of Colleges and Schools.

Applying

Applicants should have undergraduate or graduate degrees in photography, video, or other related media. Those whose bachelor's or graduate degrees are in an unrelated discipline should have considerable experience working in the field. Students must submit the completed application, the $50 application fee, a resume, a statement of interest, official copies of all college transcripts, two letters of recommendation, and a portfolio consisting of twenty examples of current work submitted as slides or on disk, CD, or videotape. An interview may be requested. International students must submit TOEFL scores—a minimum of 580 on the written test or 237 on the computerized version. The application deadline is February 1.

Correspondence and Information

Master of Fine Arts in Photography Program
Parsons The New School for Design
72 Fifth Avenue
New York, New York 10011
Phone: 212-229-8923
Fax: 212-229-5619
E-mail: mfaphoto@newschool.edu
Web site: http://www.newschool.edu/parsons
http://www.parsons.newschool.edu/photography

The New School: A University

THE FACULTY AND THEIR RESEARCH

Complete faculty biographies are available at the Web site, http://www.parsons.newschool.edu/faculty_and_staff/directory.aspx.

Adam Ames, Photographer and Video Installation Artist; M.F.A., School of Visual Arts.
Anthony Aziz, Artist and Photographer; M.F.A., San Francisco Art Institute. Digital imaging.
Woody Batts. New media, relationship between technology and design.
Michelle Bogre, Photographer; B.J., Missouri.
Andrew Bordwin, B.A., NYU. Photography, video installation.
Martha H. Burgess, Photographer, Installation, and New Media Artist; M.F.A., Yale.
Sean Callahan, Photographer.
Sammy A. Cucher, Photographer; M.F.A., San Francisco Art Institute. Digitally based images.
Simone Douglas, Photographer and Designer.
Jenny Gage, Artist; M.F.A., Yale.
Thyrza Nichols Goodeve, Author.
Charles LaBelle.
Jonathan Lipkin, Photographer and Author. Relationship between art, culture, and technology.
Cay Sophie Rabinowitz, Senior Editor, *Parkett.*
James L. Ramer, Photographer and Installation Artist; M.F.A., Memphis College of Art.
Mark Stafford, Editor, Allworth Press, and Psychoanalyst; M.F.A., Edinburgh.
Jeff Weiss, Fine Artist and Photographer; B.S., Michigan.

Visiting Lecturers
Reverend Ethan Acres, Multidisciplinary Artist.
Shimon Attie, Photographer.
Ellen Birell, Multidisciplinary Artist.
Slater Bradley, Photographer.
Nathan Carter, Artist.
Daniel Conogar, Photographer.
Tim Davis, Photographer.
Stephanie Diamond, Photographer.
Ollivier Dyens, Artist, Essayist, and Poet.
Elliot Erwitt, Photographer.
Allan Frame, Writer, Photographer, and Director.
Anna Gaskell, Photographer.
Anthony Goicolea, Artist and Photographer.
Neil Goldberg, Photographer.
Dan Graham, Multidisciplinary Artist.
Sharon Harper, Photographer.
David Alan Harvey, Writer and Photographer.
Craig Kalpakjian, Photographer.
Eve Andre Larame, Installation Artist.
Glen Luchford, Photographer.
Joseph Maida, Fine Artist, Photographer, and Video Artist.
Joel Meyerowitz, Author and Photographer.
Antoni Muntadas, Media Artist.
Alix Pearlstein, Multidisciplinary Artist.
John Salvest, Artist.
Gary Scheider, Photographer.
Erik Schmidt, Multimedia Artist.
Carolee Schneemann, Photographer.
Collier Schorr, Photographer.
Laurie Simmons, Photographer.
Karina Aguilera Skvirsky, Photographer and Video Artist.
Larry Sulton, Photographer.
Javier Tellez, Photographer and Video Artist.
Catherine Wagner, Artist and Photographer.
Charlie White, Photographer.
Wendel White, Photographer.
Melanie Wiora, Photographer.

New York
School
of Interior
Design
founded 1916

NEW YORK SCHOOL OF INTERIOR DESIGN

Master of Fine Arts in Interior Design

Program of Study

The Master of Fine Arts (M.F.A.) at the New York School of Interior Design is a postprofessional degree that is of particular interest to graduates of various design programs and to practitioners in interior design, architecture, and other related disciplines who wish to pursue advanced study. The M.F.A. in interior design program focuses on advanced studio and academic research in history, theory, and methods as they relate to an interdisciplinary approach to interiors and design. The M.F.A. curriculum is composed of 60 credits of study and is formulated to expand understanding of different design disciplines, with special emphasis on their interdependence.

There are four components of the program: a core design studio sequence, specialty studios, lectures and seminars, and electives. Students may earn up to 3 elective credits in a supervised internship arranged by the college. The core design studio sequence consists of a series of experiences of increasing complexity that culminate in the thesis studio. The thesis (11 credits) is required as a culminating project and consists of 3 credits of directed research followed by an 8-credit individually mentored studio project. Each student must demonstrate originality, research and design skill, and creative capacity to resolve advanced problems in design. The thesis is presented to a graduate faculty jury for evaluation.

Research Facilities

The library, with more than 10,000 books, periodicals, and indexes, covers every aspect of international art, design, decorative arts, architecture, professional practice, and related subjects and houses a materials collection of current trade catalogs and manufacturers' samples. There is access to the Internet and other electronic resources. New York School of Interior Design (NYSID) is part of a cooperative arrangement with prominent New York City universities that gives students and faculty members reciprocal access to over 2.6 million volumes. NYSID is also a member of the Metropolitan New York Library Council (METRO), a consortium of more than 300 regional libraries.

Financial Aid

NYSID offers a limited number of merit-based graduate fellowships. These fellowships are awarded in the amount of $5000 to $10,000 per academic year and are renewable in the second year on the basis of demonstrated continuing need and maintenance of good academic standing. Students may also qualify for financial assistance in the form of federal, state, private loan, and grant programs. For further information, applicants should contact the NYSID Financial Aid Administrator.

Cost of Study

Tuition for students in the graduating class of 2010 is $10,875 per semester for a total of 60 credits over four semesters.

Living and Housing Costs

NYSID's charge for room only is approximately $15,600 for the nine-month academic year. Transportation and living expenses vary but may be $3000 for a single student.

Student Group

The New York School of Interior Design enrolls up to 20 students in its master's degree program each year.

Student Outcomes

NYSID offers current students and graduates active career placement services, including individual counseling on writing a resume and preparing a portfolio. Recent placements have included such prominent residential and contract design firms as Clodagh Architectural Design, Aero Studios Ltd., John Saladino, Gensler & Associates, Skidmore Owings & Merrill, and The Rockwell Group.

Location

The New York School of Interior Design is located in Manhattan's Upper East Side Historic District. NYSID's campus is within easy walking distance of some of New York City's finest museums, showrooms, antiques shops, and auction houses.

The School

Founded in 1916, the New York School of Interior Design is the only private, nonprofit college in New York City that specializes solely in interior design. Chartered by the Board of Regents of the University of the State of New York in 1924, the New York School of Interior Design is authorized by the Board of Regents to confer the degrees of Associate in Applied Science (A.A.S.), Bachelor of Fine Arts (CIDA-accredited B.F.A.), and Master of Fine Arts (M.F.A.). NYSID is an accredited institutional member of the National Association of Schools of Art and Design (NASAD).

Applying

This postprofessional program is designed primarily for students who have earned professional-level degrees in interior design, architecture, environmental design, or a closely related field. Each applicant must submit a portfolio of a minimum of fifteen pieces of design work that demonstrate an ability to pursue advanced study in design. A personal interview is recommended for all applicants. Students are not required to take the Graduate Record Examinations, but a minimum score of 550 (paper-based), 213 (computer-based), or 79–80 (Internet-based) on the TOEFL is required of all international students whose language of education was not English. The preferred submission deadline is March 15. The application fee is $50 for U.S. applicants and $75 for international applicants.

Correspondence and Information

Office of Graduate Admissions
New York School of Interior Design
170 East 70th Street
New York, New York 10021

Phone: 212-472-1500 Ext. 204
E-mail: admissions@nysid.edu
Web site: http://www.nysid.edu

New York School of Interior Design

THE FACULTY

Scott Ageloff, Dean, NYSID; M.Arch., Yale; IDEC, ASID, AIA. Educator, interior designer, and architect. Certified by NCIDQ and the State of New York. Principal, Ageloff & Associates.

Peter Brandt, B.Arch., MIT. Architect, interior designer, and author. Certified by NCIDQ. Former Vice President and Managing Principal, Gensler and Associates. Principal, Brandt Design Associates.

Debra Bryant, M.F.A., Syracuse. Set designer. Production designer, CBS Evening News.

Renee Estacio, B.S.Arch., Santo Tomas (Philippines). Furniture and interior designer.

Donna Goodman, M.Arch., Columbia; AIA. Registered architect. Exhibitions and research funded by the Graham Foundation, the New York State Council of the Arts, and the J. M. Kaplan Fund.

Tobias Holler, M.Arch., Pratt. LEED-Accredited Professional; licensed architect in New York State; AIA; Associate, Cook + Fox Architects.

Eileen Imber, M.U.P., CUNY Graduate Center; M.S., CUNY, Brooklyn; ASLA, President, 1 Land Design landscape architecture.

Barbara A. Lowenthal, M.Arch., Princeton. Registered architect. Principal, Barbara Lowenthal.

Kim Plaskon Nadel, M.S., Pratt; NCIDQ. LEED-Accredited Professional. President, NICHE Design.

John Otis, M.S., Massachusetts; IDSA. Interior, exhibit, furniture, and product designer. Director, Object Inc.

Matthew Postal, Ph.D., CUNY Graduate Center. Architectural historian.

Ann L. Schiffers, M.F.A., Parsons. Architectural lighting designer. Principal, Ann Schiffers Lighting Design.

Gregory Stanford, B.Arch., Syracuse. Interior designer and architect. Senior Designer, The Rockwell Group.

Edwin J. Zawadski, M. Arch., Yale. Principal, In Situ Design.

SOUTHERN ILLINOIS UNIVERSITY CARBONDALE

School of Art and Design

Programs of Study

In its graduate studio programs, the School of Art and Design strives to maintain a vital, creative environment in which developing artists with strong motivation develop a clear, mature, and professional focus. The core of the program involves frequent, sustained contact with professional faculty members and fellow students. Work is supported and extended through formal studio courses and studies in the history of art as well as through access to the many resources and possibilities available at a large, multipurpose university.

The School of Art and Design has a very robust graduate assistantship program. Assistantships are awarded on a competitive basis. These assistantships are allocated based on the students' abilities to carry out a specific position with a high degree of efficiency, effectiveness, and professionalism. Every attempt is made to provide all graduate students with an assistantship, but it is the students' responsibility to seek out those assistantships for which they are most qualified.

The faculty members select promising national and international candidates; provide them with a professional studio environment; and encourage self-discipline, high standards, and productivity. A high level of creative inquiry is developed through peer exchange. A variety of career goals are addressed, ranging from preparation for an academic career to sustaining oneself as an independent artist. The School of Art and Design encourages diversity and dialogue and favors no single style or ideology. The School also recognizes the importance of addressing art issues from a global perspective, which Southern Illinois University Carbondale fosters in part through the multinational composition of its graduate student community. A solo thesis exhibition documents the graduate's experience.

M.F.A. candidates, as well as other interested graduate students, are eligible to enroll in the certificate program in art history. A modest amount of additional course work in art history can significantly enhance graduates' academic knowledge, skills, and employment prospects.

Research Facilities

The School of Art and Design is housed mainly in five buildings spread across the campus. The most central building is the Allyn Building, which contains the administrative offices, art history and art education offices, printmaking facilities, and classrooms dedicated to painting, drawing, art history, and art education. The industrial wing of Pulliam Hall houses ceramics, metals, blacksmithing, and glass programs, areas that have all recently been renovated. The former Good Luck Glove Factory was thoroughly rehabbed in the early 1990s and recently renovated to accommodate the Foundations Program. The Glove Factory is also the location of the Surplus Gallery, a large, urban-style gallery space suitable for a broad range of traditional exhibitions and experimental installations. Pulliam and "The Glove" provide excellent individual studios for M.F.A. students and faculty members. Additional buildings around the campus house more studio facilities for glass, small metals, and sculpture, including a sculpture foundry.

Financial Aid

Quarter-time and half-time teaching research assistantships and fellowships are a source of financial support for most students. Assistantships and fellowships come with full tuition waivers. Students who are accepted into the graduate program are automatically considered for assistantships and, whenever possible, are placed in positions that reflect their studio strengths. Assistantships are awarded on merit and according to programmatic needs. The School recommends that applicants with undergraduate GPAs of 3.5 and above include recent GRE scores with their applications so they may be considered for competitive campuswide fellowships. Special financial assistance, for first-year students only, is available through the Master's Fellowship, the Graduate Dean's Fellowship, and ICEOP and PROMPT Fellowships for members of minority groups and women. Applications are available on request.

Cost of Study

In-state graduate tuition is $328 per credit hour in 2009–10. Out-of-state tuition is 2.5 times the in-state tuition rate ($820 per credit hour). Graduate students with at least a 25 percent appointment as a graduate assistant receive a tuition scholarship. Fees vary from $589.03 (1 credit hour) to $1557.50 (12 credit hours). Students with a graduate assistantship receive a 50 percent reduction in the primary care medical fee. New graduate students from Arkansas, Indiana, Kentucky, Missouri, and Tennessee qualify for the alternate tuition rate, which is equivalent to the in-state graduate tuition rate.

Living and Housing Costs

For married couples, students with families, and single graduate students, the University has 690 efficiency and one-, two-, three-, and four-bedroom apartments that rent for $499 to $720 per month in 2009–10. Residence halls for single graduate students are also available, as are accessible residence hall rooms and apartments for students with disabilities.

Location

The School of Art and Design at Southern Illinois University Carbondale is located in Carbondale, a small city approximately 60 miles north of the southern tip of Illinois. Students from northern Illinois find Amtrak (train) and Interstate Route 57 the fastest and most direct routes. Students also have access to Williamson County Airport, on Route 13 east of Carbondale. Carbondale is about 110 miles (a 2-hour drive) southeast of Lambert–St. Louis International Airport, St. Louis, Missouri, and 330 miles (a 6-hour drive) south of Chicago, Illinois.

The University and The School

Founded in 1869, Southern Illinois University is currently home to more than 20,000 students, including 4,000 graduate and professional students. In keeping with the state's master plan, and with a commitment to enhance its Carnegie II Research status, the University's objective is to provide a comprehensive educational program meeting as many individual student needs as possible. The University comprises a faculty and the facilities to offer general and professional training ranging from two-year associate degree to doctoral programs. The School of Art and Design has sustained a strong national reputation for many years, with a stable graduate enrollment of about 50 students—one third of whom graduate each year with an M.F.A. degree.

Applying

Applicants are evaluated and selected by the faculty members of the specific studio discipline to which they apply. The portfolio should include a statement of intent, fifteen to twenty slides of recent work, transcripts, and three letters of recommendation. GRE scores are necessary only for students interested in applying for fellowships and are not necessary for all other forms of financial aid. The School affirmatively seeks to attract to its faculty, staff, and student body qualified individuals of diverse backgrounds.

Correspondence and Information

Jerry Monteith, Head of Graduate Studies
School of Art and Design
Southern Illinois University Carbondale
Carbondale, Illinois 62901-4301
Phone: 618-453-4313
Web site: http://www.artanddesign.siuc.edu/home.html

Southern Illinois University Carbondale

THE FACULTY

Najjar Abdul-Musawwir, Associate Professor; M.F.A., Southern Illinois Carbondale, 1997. Drawing, painting, core curriculum. (E-mail: mekka@siu.edu)

Steve Belletire, Professor; B.F.A., Illinois at Urbana-Champaign, 1971. Industrial design. (E-mail: sbell@siu.edu)

Barbara Bickel, Assistant Professor; Ph.D., British Columbia, 2008. Art education. (E-mail: bickel@siu.edu)

Pattie Chalmers, Assistant Professor; M.F.A., Minnesota, 2001. Ceramics.

Peter Chametzky, Associate Professor and Director; Ph.D., CUNY, 1991. Art history. (E-mail: pchamet@siu.edu)

Harris Deller, Professor; M.F.A., Cranbrook Academy of Art, 1973. Ceramics. (E-mail: ga4252@siu.edu)

Elina Gertsman, Assistant Professor; Ph.D., Boston University, 2004. Art history. (E-mail: gertsman@siu.edu)

Carma Gorman, Associate Professor; Ph.D., Berkeley, 1998. Art history. (E-mail: cgorman@siu.edu)

Sally Gradle, Assistant Professor; Ed.D., Illinois at Urbana-Champaign, 2004. Art education. (E-mail: gradle@siu.edu)

Sun Kyoung Kim, Assistant Professor; M.F.A., Illinois at Urbana-Champaign, 2008. Metalsmithing, jewelry. (E-mail: sunkim@siu.edu)

Jiyong Lee, Assistant Professor; M.F.A., RIT, 2000. Glass. (E-mail: jiyong@siu.edu)

Alex Lopez, Assistant Professor; M.F.A., Alfred, 1998. Foundations/sculpture. (E-mail: alxlpz@siu.edu)

Robert Lopez, Assistant Professor; M.F.A., Illinois at Urbana-Champaign, 2000. Industrial design. (E-mail:roblopez@siu.edu)

Jerry Monteith, Professor; M.F.A., Cranbrook Academy of Art, 1978. Sculpture. (E-mail: monteith@siu.edu)

Erin Palmer, Associate Professor; M.F.A., Yale, 1993. Drawing, painting. (Contact: Art Office, 618-453-4315)

Mark Pease, Assistant Professor; M.F.A., Pennsylvania, 2003. Digital media. (E-mail: markpease@siu.edu)

Aaron Scott, Assistant Professor; M.F.A., Purdue, 2008. Industrial design. (E-mail: aaronsiu@siu.edu)

Xuhong Shang, Professor; M.F.A., Temple, 1992. Painting. (E-mail: xuhong@siu.edu)

Edward Shay, Emeritus Professor; M.F.A., Illinois at Urbana-Champaign, 1971. Painting, printmaking, drawing. (E-mail: shay@siu.edu)

Stacey Sloboda, Assistant Professor; Ph.D., UCLA, 2004. Art history. (E-mail: sloboda@siu.edu)

Rick Smith, Associate Professor; M.F.A., Southern Illinois Carbondale, 1992. Metalsmithing, blacksmithing. (E-mail: rshotforged@gmail.com)

Kay Zivkovich, Professor and Assistant Director; M.F.A., 1973, M.Ed., 1979, Southern Illinois Carbondale. Communication design. (E-mail: kmpzivko@siu.edu)

Section 2
Architecture

This section contains a directory of institutions offering graduate work in architecture, followed by in-depth entries submitted by institutions that chose to prepare detailed program descriptions. Additional information about programs listed in the directory but not augmented by an in-depth entry may be obtained by writing directly to the dean of a graduate school or chair of a department at the address given in the directory.

For programs offering related work, see also in this book *Applied Arts and Design, Art and Art History,* and *Public, Regional, and Industrial Affairs. In another guide in this series:*

Graduate Programs in Engineering & Applied Sciences

See *Architectural Engineering* and *Civil and Environmental Engineering*

CONTENTS

Program Directories

Architectural History   134
Architecture   134
Building Science   141
Environmental Design   142
Historic Preservation   142
Landscape Architecture   145
Lighting Design   148
Urban Design   148

Close-Ups
The New School: A University
  Architecture   151
  Lighting Design   153
Pratt Institute   155
University of Miami   157
University of Pennsylvania   159
Washington University in St. Louis   161

  See also:
Art Center College of Design—Design   115
Cranbrook Academy of Art—Fine Arts and
  Architecture   209
Savannah College of Art and Design—Art and
  Design   223
School of the Art Institute of Chicago—Graduate
  Studies in Art   225
University of Delaware—Urban Affairs and Public
  Policy   1239

Architectural History

Arizona State University, Graduate College, College of Design, Program in Environmental Design and Planning, Tempe, AZ 85287. Offers design (PhD); history, theory, and criticism (PhD); planning (PhD). *Degree requirements:* For doctorate, thesis/dissertation.

Cornell University, Graduate School, Graduate Fields of Architecture, Art and Planning, Field of Architecture, Ithaca, NY 14853-0001. Offers architectural design (M Arch); architectural science (MS); building technology and environmental science (MS); computer graphics (MS); history of architecture (MA, PhD); history of urban development (MA, PhD); theory and criticism of architecture (M Arch); urban design (M Arch). *Faculty:* 28 full-time (6 women). *Students:* 93 full-time (40 women); includes 13 minority (2 African Americans, 6 Asian Americans or Pacific Islanders, 5 Hispanic Americans), 36 international. Average age 29. 488 applicants, 18% accepted, 53 enrolled. In 2008, 6 master's awarded. *Degree requirements:* For master's, one foreign language, thesis (MA, MS); for doctorate, 2 foreign languages, comprehensive exam, thesis/dissertation. *Entrance requirements:* For master's, GRE General Test, 5-year bachelor's degree in architecture, portfolio (M Arch), 3 letters of recommendation; for doctorate, GRE General Test, 3 letters of recommendation. Additional exam requirements/recommendations for international students: Required—TOEFL (minimum score 600 paper-based; 250 computer-based; 77 iBT). *Application deadline:* For fall admission, 1/15 priority date for domestic students. Application fee: $70. Electronic applications accepted. *Expenses:* Tuition: Full-time $29,500. Required fees: $70. Full-time tuition and fees vary according to degree level, program and student level. *Financial support:* In 2008–09, 16 students received support, including 8 fellowships with full tuition reimbursements available, 1 research assistantship with full tuition reimbursement available, 7 teaching assistantships with full tuition reimbursements available; institutionally sponsored loans, scholarships/grants, health care benefits, tuition waivers (full and partial), and unspecified assistantships also available. Financial award applicants required to submit FAFSA. *Faculty research:* Architectural design and urban design, theory and criticism of architecture, computer graphics, building technology and environmental science, history of architecture and history of urban-development. *Unit head:* Director of Graduate Studies, 607-255-6701, Fax: 607-255-0291. *Application contact:* Graduate Field Assistant, 607-255-6701, Fax: 607-255-0291, E-mail: cuarch@cornell.edu.

Graduate School and University Center of the City University of New York, Graduate Studies, Program in Art History, New York, NY 10016-4039. Offers architecture (PhD); graphic arts (PhD); painting (PhD); photography (PhD); sculpture (PhD). *Degree requirements:* For doctorate, 2 foreign languages, thesis/dissertation. *Entrance requirements:* For doctorate, GRE General Test. Additional exam requirements/recommendations for international students: Required—TOEFL. Electronic applications accepted.

Harvard University, Graduate School of Arts and Sciences, Department of History of Art and Architecture, Cambridge, MA 02138. Offers ancient art (PhD); ancient Near Eastern art (PhD); baroque art (PhD); Byzantine art (PhD); classical art (PhD); Indian art (PhD); Islamic art (PhD); Japanese and Chinese art (PhD); medieval art (PhD); modern art (PhD); Renaissance and modern architecture (PhD); Renaissance art (PhD). *Degree requirements:* For doctorate, variable foreign language requirement, thesis/dissertation, general exams; reading exams in French, German, and Italian. *Entrance requirements:* For doctorate, GRE General Test. Additional exam requirements/recommendations for international students: Required—TOEFL. *Expenses:* Tuition: Full-time $32,556. Required fees: $1426. Full-time tuition and fees vary according to program and student level.

Massachusetts Institute of Technology, School of Architecture and Planning, Department of Architecture, Cambridge, MA 02139-4307. Offers architecture (M Arch, PhD), including building technology (PhD), design and computation (PhD), history and theory of architecture (PhD), history and theory of art (PhD); architecture studies (SM Arch S); visual studies (SM Vis S, SMBT); M Arch/MCP; M Arch/SMRED; SM Arch S/MCP; SM Arch S/SMRED. *Degree requirements:* For master's, thesis; for doctorate, comprehensive exam, thesis/dissertation. *Entrance requirements:* For master's, GRE General Test (for some programs), portfolio (for some programs); for doctorate, GRE General Test (for some programs). Additional exam requirements/recommendations for international students: Required—TOEFL. Electronic applications accepted.

Savannah College of Art and Design, Graduate School, Program in Architectural History, Savannah, GA 31402-3146. Offers MA, MFA. Part-time programs available. *Degree requirements:* For master's, one foreign language, thesis, internship. *Entrance requirements:* For master's, interview, research paper. Additional exam requirements/recommendations for international students: Required—TOEFL (minimum score 450 paper-based; 133 computer-based). Electronic applications accepted. *Expenses:* Tuition: Full-time $28,215; part-time $3135 per course. One-time fee: $500.

See Close-Up on page 223.

University of California, Berkeley, Graduate Division, College of Environmental Design, Department of Architecture, Berkeley, CA 94720-1500. Offers architecture (M Arch); building science (MS, PhD); building structures, construction and materials (MS, PhD); design (MA); design theories, methods, and practices (MS, PhD); environmental design in developing countries (MS, PhD); history of architecture and urbanism (MS, PhD); social and cultural processes in architecture and urbanism (MS, PhD); M Arch/MCP; M Arch/MS; MLA/M Arch. *Degree requirements:* For master's, thesis; for doctorate, thesis/dissertation, qualifying exam. *Entrance requirements:* For master's and doctorate, GRE General Test, minimum GPA of 3.0, 3 letters of recommendation. Additional exam requirements/recommendations for international students: Required—TOEFL. Electronic applications accepted.

University of Pittsburgh, School of Arts and Sciences, Department of History of Art and Architecture, Pittsburgh, PA 15260. Offers MA, PhD. Part-time programs available. Terminal master's awarded for partial completion of doctoral program. *Degree requirements:* For master's, one foreign language, thesis; for doctorate, 2 foreign languages, comprehensive exam, thesis/dissertation. *Entrance requirements:* For doctorate, GRE General Test, 3 letters of recommendation, writing sample, personal statement, foreign language questionnaire. Additional exam requirements/recommendations for international students: Required—TOEFL. Electronic applications accepted. *Faculty research:* Asian, medieval, Renaissance/baroque, modern art and architecture, contemporary.

The University of Texas at Austin, Graduate School, School of Architecture, Austin, TX 78712-1111. Offers architecture (M Arch); community and regional planning (MSCRP, PhD); historic preservation (MS); history of architecture (MA, PhD); landscape architecture (MLA); urban design (MSUD); JD/MSCRP; MSCRP/MA; MSCRP/PhD. *Degree requirements:* For doctorate, thesis/dissertation. *Entrance requirements:* For master's and doctorate, GRE General Test. Additional exam requirements/recommendations for international students: Required—TOEFL (minimum score 550 paper-based; 213 computer-based). Electronic applications accepted.

University of Virginia, College and Graduate School of Arts and Sciences, McIntire Department of Art, Charlottesville, VA 22904-4130. Offers classical art and archaeology (MA, PhD); history of art and architecture (MA, PhD). *Degree requirements:* For master's, one foreign language, thesis, defense; for doctorate, 2 foreign languages, comprehensive exam, thesis/dissertation, defense. *Entrance requirements:* For master's and doctorate, GRE General Test, writing sample. Additional exam requirements/recommendations for international students: Recommended—TOEFL (minimum score 600 paper-based; 250 computer-based; 90 iBT), IELTS (minimum score 7). Electronic applications accepted. *Expenses:* Tuition, area resident: Full-time $10,452. Tuition, state resident: full-time $10,452. Tuition, nonresident: full-time $20,010. Required fees: $2176. Part-time tuition and fees vary according to course load and program. *Faculty research:* Classical art, renaissance art and architecture, American material culture.

University of Virginia, School of Architecture, Department of Architectural History, Charlottesville, VA 22903. Offers M Arch H, PhD. *Faculty:* 7 full-time (3 women). *Students:* 25 full-time (20 women), 1 part-time (0 women), 2 international. Average age 31. 32 applicants, 78% accepted, 12 enrolled. In 2008, 11 master's awarded. *Degree requirements:* For master's, one foreign language, thesis. *Entrance requirements:* For master's, GRE General Test, 3 letters of recommendation; essay. Additional exam requirements/recommendations for international students: Required—TOEFL (minimum score 600 paper-based; 250 computer-based; 90 iBT). *Application deadline:* For fall admission, 1/5 for domestic and international students. Applications are processed on a rolling basis. Application fee: $60. Electronic applications accepted. *Expenses:* Tuition, area resident: Full-time $10,452. Tuition, state resident: full-time $10,452. Tuition; nonresident: full-time $20,010. Required fees: $2176. Part-time tuition and fees vary according to course load and program. *Financial support:* Career-related internships or fieldwork, Federal Work-Study, and institutionally sponsored loans available. Financial award applicants required to submit FAFSA. *Faculty research:* Urban form, nineteenth and twentieth century American architecture. *Unit head:* Louis Nelson, Chair, 434-924-1428, Fax: 434-982-2678, E-mail: lnelson@virginia.edu. *Application contact:* Graduate Admissions Officer, 434-924-6442, E-mail: arch-admissions@virginia.edu.

Virginia Commonwealth University, Graduate School, School of the Arts, Department of Art History, Richmond, VA 23284-9005. Offers architectural history (MA); art history (MA, PhD); historical studies (MA); museum studies (MA). *Accreditation:* NASAD. *Degree requirements:* For master's, thesis; for doctorate, comprehensive exam, thesis/dissertation. *Entrance requirements:* For master's and doctorate, GRE General Test. *Faculty research:* Modern, nineteenth century, Renaissance, American, and Medieval art.

Architecture

Academy of Art University, Graduate Program, School of Architecture, San Francisco, CA 94105-3410. Offers M Arch. Part-time programs available. *Faculty:* 2 full-time (1 woman), 14 part-time/adjunct (5 women). *Students:* 64 full-time (35 women), 10 part-time (5 women); includes 2 African Americans, 5 Asian Americans or Pacific Islanders, 2 Hispanic Americans, 40 international. Average age 29. 51 applicants. In 2008, 8 master's awarded. *Degree requirements:* For master's, final review. *Entrance requirements:* For master's, portfolio, bachelor's degree in architecture or related field. *Application deadline:* For fall admission, 9/7 for domestic and international students; for spring admission, 2/2 for domestic and international students. Applications are processed on a rolling basis. Application fee: $100 ($500 for international students). Electronic applications accepted. *Expenses:* Tuition: Full-time $18,400; part-time $770 per term. Tuition and fees vary according to program. *Financial support:* Career-related internships or fieldwork and Federal Work-Study available. Support available to part-time students. Financial award application deadline: 8/10; financial award applicants required to submit FAFSA. *Unit head:* Alberto Bertoli, Director, 800-544-ARTS, E-mail: info@academyart.edu. *Application contact:* Prospective Students Services, 800-544-ARTS, Fax: 415-263-4131, E-mail: info@academyart.edu.

Andrews University, School of Graduate Studies, Division of Architecture, Berrien Springs, MI 49104. Offers M Arch. *Faculty:* 8 full-time (2 women), 1 part-time/adjunct (0 women). *Students:* 25 full-time (6 women), 1 (woman) part-time; includes 10 minority (3 African Americans, 1 Asian American or Pacific Islander, 6 Hispanic Americans), 3 international. Average age 24. 34 applicants, 68% accepted, 18 enrolled. In 2008, 29 master's awarded. *Entrance requirements:* For master's, GRE. Additional exam requirements/recommendations for international students: Required—TOEFL (minimum score 550 paper-based). Application fee: $40. *Expenses:* Tuition: Full-time $18,360; part-time $765 per credit hour. Required fees: $476; $765 per credit hour. $238 per semester. Tuition and fees vary according to degree level. *Unit head:* Carey Carscallen, Director, 269-471-6003. *Application contact:* Carolyn Hurst, Supervisor of Graduate Admission, 800-253-2874, Fax: 269-471-6321, E-mail: graduate@andrews.edu.

Arizona State University, Graduate College, College of Design, School of Architecture and Landscape Architecture, Tempe, AZ 85287. Offers architecture (M Arch); building design (MS);

landscape architecture (MLA); urban design (MUD); MA/MBA. *Degree requirements:* For master's, thesis optional. *Entrance requirements:* For master's, GRE General Test, design portfolio.

Auburn University, Graduate School, College of Architecture, Design, and Construction, Auburn University, AL 36849. Offers MBS, MCP, MDB, MID, MLA, MPA/MCP. Part-time programs available. *Faculty:* 62 full-time (10 women), 4 part-time/adjunct (1 woman). *Students:* 98 full-time (33 women), 14 part-time (5 women); includes 9 minority (5 African Americans, 2 Asian Americans or Pacific Islanders, 2 Hispanic Americans), 10 international. Average age 27. 76 applicants, 54% accepted, 21 enrolled. In 2008, 60 master's awarded. *Entrance requirements:* For master's, GRE General Test. *Application deadline:* For fall admission, 7/7 for domestic students; for spring admission, 11/24 for domestic students. Applications are processed on a rolling basis. Application fee: $25 ($50 for international students). Electronic applications accepted. *Expenses:* Contact institution. *Financial support:* Fellowships, Federal Work-Study available. Support available to part-time students. Financial award application deadline: 3/15. *Unit head:* Prof. Dan D. Bennett, Dean, 334-844-4524. *Application contact:* Dr. George Flowers, Dean of the Graduate School, 334-844-2125.

Ball State University, Graduate School, College of Architecture and Planning, Department of Architecture, Program in Architecture, Muncie, IN 47306-1099. Offers M Arch. *Degree requirements:* For master's, thesis. *Entrance requirements:* For master's, minimum undergraduate B average, portfolio, writing sample.

Boston Architectural College, Graduate Programs, Boston, MA 02115-2795. Offers architecture (M Arch); interior design (MID). *Accreditation:* CIDA. *Degree requirements:* For master's, thesis. *Entrance requirements:* For master's, portfolio (recommended). Electronic applications accepted.

California College of the Arts, Graduate Programs, Program in Architecture, San Francisco, CA 94107. Offers M Arch. *Degree requirements:* For master's, thesis. *Entrance requirements:* For master's, appropriate bachelor's degree, portfolio, resumé, minimum 2 letters of recommendation. Additional exam requirements/recommendations for international students: Required—TOEFL (minimum score 600 paper-based; 250 computer-based).

California Polytechnic State University, San Luis Obispo, College of Architecture and Environmental Design, Department of Architecture, San Luis Obispo, CA 93407. Offers MS. Part-time programs available. *Faculty:* 6 full-time (0 women), 1 (woman) part-time/adjunct. *Students:* 13 full-time (4 women), 8 part-time (5 women); includes 6 minority (4 Asian Americans or Pacific Islanders, 2 Hispanic Americans). Average age 30. 23 applicants, 65% accepted, 9 enrolled. *Degree requirements:* For master's, thesis. *Entrance requirements:* For master's, GRE, minimum GPA of 3.0, 2 letters of recommendation. Additional exam requirements/recommendations for international students: Required—TOEFL (minimum score 550 paper-based; 213 computer-based), IELTS (minimum score 6), Either TOEFL or IELTS is acceptable. *Application deadline:* For fall admission, 7/1 for domestic students, 11/30 for international students; for winter admission, 11/1 for domestic students, 6/30 for international students. Applications are processed on a rolling basis. Application fee: $55. Electronic applications accepted. *Expenses:* Tuition, nonresident: full-time $10,170; part-time $226 per unit. Required fees: $5751; $1265 per quarter. *Financial support:* Research assistantships, teaching assistantships, Federal Work-Study and institutionally sponsored loans available. Support available to part-time students. Financial award application deadline: 3/2; financial award applicants required to submit FAFSA. *Faculty research:* Computer assisted design, decision support systems, building science, facilities management. Total annual research expenditures: $2.4 million. *Unit head:* Dr. Jens Pohl, Graduate Coordinator, 805-756-2841, Fax: 805-756-1500, E-mail: jpohl@calpoly.edu. *Application contact:* Dr. James Maraviglia, Assistant Vice President for Admissions, Recruitment and Financial Aid, 805-756-2311, Fax: 805-756-5400, E-mail: admissions@calpoly.edu.

California State Polytechnic University, Pomona, Academic Affairs, College of Environmental Design, Program in Architecture, Pomona, CA 91768-2557. Offers M Arch. Part-time programs available. *Students:* 59 full-time (34 women), 7 part-time (3 women); includes 20 minority (1 African American, 15 Asian Americans or Pacific Islanders, 4 Hispanic Americans), 3 international. Average age 29. 136 applicants, 20% accepted, 12 enrolled. In 2008, 14 master's awarded. *Degree requirements:* For master's, thesis or alternative. *Application deadline:* For fall admission, 5/1 for domestic students; for winter admission, 10/15 priority date for domestic students; for spring admission, 1/20 priority date for domestic students. Applications are processed on a rolling basis. Application fee: $55. Electronic applications accepted. *Expenses:* Tuition, nonresident: full-time $7232; part-time $226 per credit. Required fees: $4272. One-time fee: $2694 part-time. Tuition and fees vary according to course load. *Financial support:* Career-related internships or fieldwork, Federal Work-Study, and institutionally sponsored loans available. Support available to part-time students. Financial award application deadline: 3/2; financial award applicants required to submit FAFSA. *Unit head:* Kip Dickson, Graduate Coordinator, 909-869-2682, Fax: 909-869-4331, E-mail: kadickson@csupomona.edu. *Application contact:* Scott J. Duncan, Director, Admissions, 909-869-3258, Fax: 909-869-4529, E-mail: sjduncan@csupomona.edu.

Carleton University, Faculty of Graduate Studies, Faculty of Engineering and Design, School of Architecture, Ottawa, ON K1S 5B6, Canada. Offers design studies (M Arch). *Degree requirements:* For master's, thesis. *Entrance requirements:* For master's, honors degree. Additional exam requirements/recommendations for international students: Required—TOEFL. *Faculty research:* Theoretical issues in architecture and culture, cultural diversity, architecture and technoscientific culture.

Carnegie Mellon University, College of Fine Arts, School of Architecture, Pittsburgh, PA 15213-3891. Offers architectural engineering construction management (M Sc); architecture (MSA); architecture, engineering, and construction management (PhD); building performance and diagnostics (M Sc, PhD); computational design (M Sc, PhD); sustainable design (M Sc); urban design (M Sc). Terminal master's awarded for partial completion of doctoral program. *Degree requirements:* For doctorate, thesis/dissertation. *Entrance requirements:* For master's and doctorate, GRE General Test. Additional exam requirements/recommendations for international students: Required—TOEFL.

The Catholic University of America, School of Architecture and Planning, Washington, DC 20064. Offers M Arch, M Arch Studies. Part-time programs available. *Degree requirements:* For master's, thesis. *Entrance requirements:* For master's, minimum GPA of 2.7, portfolio, 3 letters of recommendation. Additional exam requirements/recommendations for international students: Required—TOEFL (minimum score 500 paper-based; 173 computer-based). Electronic applications accepted. *Expenses:* Contact institution. *Faculty research:* Architectural history, sacred architecture, computers, technology, urban design, preservation.

City College of the City University of New York, Graduate School, School of Architecture and Environmental Studies, Program in Architecture, New York, NY 10031-9198. Offers M Arch. *Entrance requirements:* For master's, GRE. Additional exam requirements/recommendations for international students: Required—TOEFL (minimum score 550 paper-based; 213 computer-based).

Clemson University, Graduate School, College of Architecture, Arts, and Humanities, Department of Architecture, Clemson, SC 29634. Offers M Arch, MS. *Faculty:* 19 full-time (5 women), 6 part-time/adjunct (2 women). *Students:* 48 full-time (24 women), 3 part-time (2 women); includes 8 minority (2 African Americans, 1 American Indian/Alaska Native, 5 Asian Americans or Pacific Islanders), 3 international. Average age 27. 149 applicants, 38% accepted, 24 enrolled. In 2008, 25 master's awarded. *Degree requirements:* For master's, thesis. *Entrance requirements:* For master's, GRE General Test, portfolio. Additional exam requirements/recommendations for international students: Required—TOEFL, IELTS. *Application deadline:* For fall admission, 2/1 for domestic students, 4/15 for international students; for spring admission, 9/15 for international students. Application fee: $55. Electronic applications accepted. Full-time tuition and fees vary according to program. *Financial support:* In 2008–09, 13 fellowships (averaging $1,315 per year), 16 research assistantships (averaging $3,931 per year), 18 teaching assistantships (averaging $3,144 per year) were awarded; unspecified assistantships also available. Financial award application deadline: 2/15; financial award applicants required to submit FAFSA. *Faculty research:* Color and computers, light energy, theory and philosophy, architecture for education, architecture for health. Total annual research expenditures: $318,911. *Unit head:* Dr. Jose Caban, Chair, 864-656-3898, Fax: 864-656-0204, E-mail: jcaban@clemson.edu. *Application contact:* Michelle McLane, Student Services, 864-656-3938, Fax: 864-656-1810, E-mail: wking@clemson.edu.

Columbia College Chicago, Graduate School, Program in Architectural Studies, Chicago, IL 60605-1996. Offers MFA. Part-time programs available. *Students:* 1 full-time (0 women), 1 (woman) part-time. Average age 35. 7 applicants, 1 enrolled. In 2008, 1 master's awarded. *Degree requirements:* For master's, thesis. *Entrance requirements:* For master's, minimum GPA of 3.0, portfolio. Additional exam requirements/recommendations for international students: Required—TOEFL (minimum score 550 paper-based; 213 computer-based). *Application deadline:* For fall admission, 3/1 for domestic and international students. Application fee: $55. Electronic applications accepted. *Expenses:* Tuition: Full-time $15,992; part-time $633 per credit hour. *Financial support:* Career-related internships or fieldwork, Federal Work-Study, and scholarships/grants available. Support available to part-time students. Financial award application deadline: 8/13; financial award applicants required to submit FAFSA. *Unit head:* Jay Wolke, Head, 312-369-6968, Fax: 312-336-8009, E-mail: jwolke@colum.edu. *Application contact:* Keith Cleveland, Office of Provost/Senior Vice President, 312-369-7261, Fax: 312-369-8022, E-mail: kcleveland@colum.edu.

Columbia University, Graduate School of Architecture, Planning, and Preservation, Program in Advanced Architectural Design, New York, NY 10027. Offers MS. *Entrance requirements:* For master's, GRE General Test.

Columbia University, Graduate School of Architecture, Planning, and Preservation, Program in Architecture, New York, NY 10027. Offers M Arch, PhD, M Arch/MS. PhD offered through the Graduate School of Arts and Science. *Degree requirements:* For master's, thesis optional. *Entrance requirements:* For master's, GRE General Test.

Cooper Union for the Advancement of Science and Art, Irwin S. Chanin School of Architecture, New York, NY 10003-7120. Offers M Arch II. *Degree requirements:* For master's, thesis. *Entrance requirements:* For master's, GRE, 1 year of work experience, 3 letters of recommendation, resumé or curriculum vitae, essay, portfolio, interview. Additional exam requirements/recommendations for international students: Required—TOEFL. *Application deadline:* For fall admission, 2/1 for domestic students. Application fee: $65. *Expenses:* Tuition: Full-time $35,000. Required fees: $1600. *Unit head:* Anthony Vidler, Dean. *Application contact:* Student Contact, 212-353-4120, E-mail: admissions@cooper.edu.

Cornell University, Graduate School, Graduate Fields of Architecture, Art and Planning, Field of Architecture, Ithaca, NY 14853-0001. Offers architectural design (M Arch); architectural science (MS); building technology and environmental science (MS); computer graphics (MS); history of architecture (MA, PhD); history of urban development (MA, PhD); theory and criticism of architecture (M Arch); urban design (M Arch). *Faculty:* 28 full-time (6 women). *Students:* 93 full-time (40 women); includes 13 minority (2 African Americans, 6 Asian Americans or Pacific Islanders, 5 Hispanic Americans), 36 international. Average age 29. 488 applicants, 18% accepted, 53 enrolled. In 2008, 6 master's awarded. *Degree requirements:* For master's, one foreign language, thesis (MA, MS); for doctorate, 2 foreign languages, comprehensive exam, thesis/dissertation. *Entrance requirements:* For master's, GRE General Test, 5-year bachelor's degree in architecture, portfolio (M Arch), 3 letters of recommendation; for doctorate, GRE General Test, 3 letters of recommendation. Additional exam requirements/recommendations for international students: Required—TOEFL (minimum score 600 paper-based; 250 computer-based; 77 iBT). *Application deadline:* For fall admission, 1/15 priority date for domestic students. Application fee: $70. Electronic applications accepted. *Expenses:* Tuition: Full-time $29,500. Required fees: $70. Full-time tuition and fees vary according to degree level, program and student level. *Financial support:* In 2008–09, 16 students received support, including 8 fellowships with full tuition reimbursements available, 1 research assistantship with full tuition reimbursement available, 7 teaching assistantships with full tuition reimbursements available; institutionally sponsored loans, scholarships/grants, health care benefits, tuition waivers (full and partial), and unspecified assistantships also available. Financial award applicants required to submit FAFSA. *Faculty research:* Architectural design and urban design, theory and criticism of architecture, computer graphics, building technology and environmental science, history of architecture and history of urban-development. *Unit head:* Director of Graduate Studies, 607-255-6701, Fax: 607-255-0291. *Application contact:* Graduate Field Assistant, 607-255-6701, Fax: 607-255-0291, E-mail: cuarch@cornell.edu.

Cranbrook Academy of Art, Graduate School, Program in Architecture, Bloomfield Hills, MI 48303-0801. Offers M Arch. *Degree requirements:* For master's, thesis, exhibit. *Entrance requirements:* Additional exam requirements/recommendations for international students: Required—TOEFL (minimum score 550 paper-based; 213 computer-based).

See Close-Up on page 209.

Dalhousie University, Faculty of Architecture and Planning, Halifax, NS B3J 2X4, Canada. Offers M Arch, M Eng, M Plan, MEDS, MPS. *Degree requirements:* For master's, thesis. *Entrance requirements:* Additional exam requirements/recommendations for international students: Required—TOEFL, IELTS, 1 of 5 approved tests: TOEFL, IELTS, CANTEST, CAEL, Michigan English Language Assessment Battery. *Application deadline:* For fall admission, 6/1 priority date for domestic students, 4/1 priority date for international students; for winter admission, 11/15 priority date for domestic students, 8/31 priority date for international students; for spring admission, 2/28 priority date for domestic students, 12/31 priority date for international students. Applications are processed on a rolling basis. Application fee: $70. Electronic applications accepted. *Financial support:* Career-related internships or fieldwork and scholarships/grants available. *Unit head:* Christine Macy, Dean, 902-494-3973, Fax: 902-423-6672, E-mail: Christine.Macy@dal.ca. *Application contact:* Bev Nightingale, Graduate Secretary, 902-494-3973, Fax: 902-423-6672, E-mail: grad.arch@dal.ca.

Florida Agricultural and Mechanical University, Division of Graduate Studies, Research, and Continuing Education, School of Architecture, Tallahassee, FL 32307-3200. Offers architectural studies (MS Arch); architecture (professional) (M Arch); landscape architecture (MLA). Part-time programs available. *Degree requirements:* For master's, thesis. *Entrance requirements:* For master's, GRE General Test, minimum GPA of 3.0, portfolio. Additional exam requirements/recommendations for international students: Required—TOEFL (minimum score 550 paper-based). *Faculty research:* Environmental technology, post-occupancy evaluation, building economics, design methods, computer-aided design.

Florida International University, College of Architecture and the Arts, Miami, FL 33199. Offers M Arch, MFA, MID, MLA, MM, MS. *Accreditation:* ASLA. Part-time and evening/weekend programs available. *Degree requirements:* For master's, thesis. *Entrance requirements:* For master's, minimum GPA of 3.0 (upper level coursework). Additional exam requirements/recommendations for international students: Required—TOEFL (minimum score 550 paper-based; 213 computer-based). Electronic applications accepted.

Florida International University, College of Architecture and the Arts, School of Architecture, Architecture Program, Miami, FL 33199. Offers M Arch. Part-time and evening/weekend programs available. *Entrance requirements:* For master's, minimum GPA of 3.0 (upper level coursework). Additional exam requirements/recommendations for international students: Required—TOEFL (minimum score 550 paper-based; 213 computer-based). Electronic applications accepted.

Frank Lloyd Wright School of Architecture, Graduate Program, Scottsdale, AZ 85261-4430. Offers M Arch. Summer session held in Spring Green, WI. *Degree requirements:* For master's, thesis or alternative. *Entrance requirements:* For master's, interviews, portfolio. Additional exam requirements/recommendations for international students: Required—TOEFL.

Georgia Institute of Technology, Graduate Studies and Research, College of Architecture, City and Regional Planning Program, Atlanta, GA 30332-0001. Offers city and regional planning (PhD); economic development (MCRP); environmental planning and management (MCRP); geographic information systems (MCRP); land and community development (MCRP); land use planning (MCRP); transportation (MCRP); urban design (MCRP); MCP/MSCE. *Accreditation:* ACSP. *Degree requirements:* For master's, thesis, internship. *Entrance requirements:* For master's, GRE General Test, minimum GPA of 2.7. Additional exam requirements/recommendations for international students: Required—TOEFL. Electronic applications accepted.

Georgia Institute of Technology, Graduate Studies and Research, College of Architecture, Doctoral Program in Architecture, Atlanta, GA 30332-0001. Offers PhD. Part-time programs available. Postbaccalaureate distance learning degree programs offered. *Degree requirements:* For doctorate, comprehensive exam, thesis/dissertation. *Entrance requirements:* For doctorate, GRE General Test. Additional exam requirements/recommendations for international students: Required—TOEFL (minimum score 600 paper-based; 250 computer-based). Electronic applications accepted.

Georgia Institute of Technology, Graduate Studies and Research, College of Architecture, Master's Program in Architecture, Atlanta, GA 30332-0001. Offers M Arch, MS, M Arch/MCRP. Part-time programs available. *Degree requirements:* For master's, thesis or alternative. *Entrance requirements:* For master's, GRE General Test. Additional exam requirements/recommendations for international students: Required—TOEFL (minimum score 600 paper-based; 250 computer-based). Electronic applications accepted.

Georgia Institute of Technology, Graduate Studies and Research, College of Architecture, Program in Building Construction, Atlanta, GA 30332-0001. Offers building construction (PhD); integrated facility management (MS); integrated project delivery systems (MS); residential construction development (MS). Part-time and evening/weekend programs available. *Entrance requirements:* For master's and doctorate, GRE or GMAT. Additional exam requirements/recommendations for international students: Required—TOEFL (minimum score 550 paper-

Architecture

Georgia Institute of Technology (continued)

based; 213 computer-based). Electronic applications accepted. *Faculty research:* Design-build, mold, indoor air quality, real estate.

Harvard University, Graduate School of Arts and Sciences, Committee on Architecture, Landscape Architecture, and Urban Planning, Cambridge, MA 02138. Offers architecture (PhD); landscape architecture (PhD); urban planning (PhD). *Degree requirements:* For doctorate, one foreign language, thesis/dissertation, oral exam. *Entrance requirements:* For doctorate, GRE General Test. Additional exam requirements/recommendations for international students: Required—TOEFL. *Expenses:* Tuition: Full-time $32,556. Required fees: $1426. Full-time tuition and fees vary according to program and student level.

Harvard University, Graduate School of Design, Department of Architecture, Cambridge, MA 02138. Offers M Arch. *Degree requirements:* For master's, thesis (for some programs). *Entrance requirements:* For master's, GRE General Test. Additional exam requirements/recommendations for international students: Required—TOEFL (minimum score 600 paper-based; 250 computer-based; 100 iBT). Electronic applications accepted. *Expenses:* Tuition: Full-time $32,556. Required fees: $1426. Full-time tuition and fees vary according to program and student level.

Harvard University, Graduate School of Design, Program in Design, Cambridge, MA 02138. Offers Dr DES. *Entrance requirements:* For doctorate, GRE General Test. Additional exam requirements/recommendations for international students: Required—TOEFL (minimum score 600 paper-based; 250 computer-based; 100 iBT). Electronic applications accepted. *Expenses:* Tuition: Full-time $32,556. Required fees: $1426. Full-time tuition and fees vary according to program and student level.

Harvard University, Graduate School of Design, Program in Design Studies, Cambridge, MA 02138. Offers M Des S. *Entrance requirements:* For master's, GRE General Test. Additional exam requirements/recommendations for international students: Required—TOEFL (minimum score 600 paper-based; 250 computer-based; 100 iBT). Electronic applications accepted. *Expenses:* Tuition: Full-time $32,556. Required fees: $1426. Full-time tuition and fees vary according to program and student level.

Illinois Institute of Technology, Graduate College, College of Architecture, Chicago, IL 60616-3793. Offers architecture (M Ar, PhD); integrated building delivery (M IBD); landscape architecture (MLA). Part-time programs available. *Faculty:* 40 full-time (5 women), 55 part-time/adjunct (15 women). *Students:* 202 full-time (85 women), 27 part-time (11 women); includes 19 minority (2 African Americans, 6 Asian Americans or Pacific Islanders, 11 Hispanic Americans), 96 international. Average age 28. 427 applicants, 78% accepted, 105 enrolled. In 2008, 54 master's, 2 doctorates awarded. *Degree requirements:* For master's, comprehensive exam (for some programs), thesis (for some programs); for doctorate, comprehensive exam, thesis/dissertation. *Entrance requirements:* For master's, GRE General Test, minimum GPA of 3.0, portfolio, 3 letters of recommendation; for doctorate, GRE General Test, minimum GPA of 3.0, portfolio. Additional exam requirements/recommendations for international students: Required—TOEFL (minimum score 550 paper-based; 213 computer-based; 80 iBT). *Application deadline:* For fall admission, 1/15 for domestic and international students. Applications are processed on a rolling basis. Application fee: $40. Electronic applications accepted. *Financial support:* In 2008–09, 125 teaching assistantships (averaging $4,000 per year) were awarded; fellowships, career-related internships or fieldwork, Federal Work-Study, institutionally sponsored loans, scholarships/grants, and health care benefits also available. Support available to part-time students. Financial award applicants required to submit FAFSA. *Faculty research:* Sustainability and environmental design, comprehensive tall building design, innovative materials technology, advanced structural systems, digital design methods. *Unit head:* Donna V. Robertson, John and Jeanne Rowe Chair, 312-567-3230, Fax: 312-567-5820, E-mail: robertson@iit.edu. *Application contact:* Sarah Pariseau, Coordinator for Academic Affairs, 312-567-3231, Fax: 312-567-5820.

Instituto Tecnológico y de Estudios Superiores de Monterrey, Campus Estado de México, Professional and Graduate Division, Estado de Mexico, Mexico. Offers administration of information technologies (MITA); architecture (M Arch); business administration (GMBA, MBA); computer sciences (MCS, PhD); education (M Ed); educational institution administration (MAD); educational technology and innovation (PhD); electronic commerce (MEC); environmental systems (MS); finance (MAF); humanistic studies (MHS); information sciences and knowledge management (MISKM); information systems (MS); manufacturing systems (MS); marketing (MEM); quality systems and productivity (MS); science and materials engineering (PhD); telecommunications management (MTM). Part-time programs available. Postbaccalaureate distance learning degree programs offered (minimal on-campus study). *Degree requirements:* For master's, one foreign language, thesis (for some programs); for doctorate, one foreign language, thesis/dissertation. *Entrance requirements:* For master's, E-PAEP 500, interview; for doctorate, E-PAEP 500, research proposal. Additional exam requirements/recommendations for international students: Required—TOEFL (minimum score 550 paper-based). *Faculty research:* Surface treatments by plasmas, mechanical properties, robotics, graphical computing, mechatronics security protocols.

Instituto Tecnológico y de Estudios Superiores de Monterrey, Campus Irapuato, Graduate Programs, Irapuato, Mexico. Offers administration (MBA); administration of information technology (MAIT); administration of telecommunications (MAT); architecture (M Arch); computer science (MCS); education (M Ed); educational administration (MEA); educational innovation and technology (DEIT); educational technology (MET); electronic commerce (MBA); environmental administration and planning (MEAP); environmental systems (MES); finances (MBA); humanistic studies (MHS); international management for Latin American executives (MIMLAE); library and information science (MLIS); manufacturing quality management (MMQM); marketing research (MBA).

Iowa State University of Science and Technology, Graduate College, College of Design, Department of Architecture, Ames, IA 50011. Offers architectural studies (MSAS); architecture (M Arch); M Arch/MBA; M Arch/MCRP; M Arch/MS. *Faculty:* 25 full-time (8 women), 2 part-time/adjunct (1 woman). *Students:* 28 full-time (13 women), 12 part-time (5 women); includes 1 minority (Hispanic American), 5 international. 59 applicants, 58% accepted, 21 enrolled. In 2008, 19 master's awarded. *Degree requirements:* For master's, thesis (for some programs). *Entrance requirements:* For master's, GRE General Test, portfolio, letters of reference. Additional exam requirements/recommendations for international students: Required—TOEFL (minimum score 600 paper-based; 79 iBT), IELTS (6.5) or TOEFL. *Application deadline:* For fall admission, 1/1 priority date for domestic and international students. Applications are processed on a rolling basis. Application fee: $30 ($70 for international students). Electronic applications accepted. *Expenses:* Tuition, area resident: Full-time $6446; part-time $359 per credit. Tuition, state resident: full-time $6446; part-time $359 per credit. Tuition, nonresident: full-time $17,330; part-time $963 per credit. Required fees: $790; $249.25 per semester. Tuition and fees vary according to course load and program. *Financial support:* In 2008–09, 30 students received support, including 1 research assistantship with full and partial tuition reimbursement available (averaging $12,978 per year), 25 teaching assistantships with tuition reimbursements available (averaging $14,130 per year); career-related internships or fieldwork, Federal Work-Study, institutionally sponsored loans, tuition waivers (partial), and unspecified assistantships also available. Support available to part-time students. Financial award application deadline: 2/1; financial award applicants required to submit FAFSA. *Faculty research:* Computer-aided architectural design, social dimensions of urban architecture, designing for the elderly, energy utilization in buildings, architectural theory. *Unit head:* Dr. Calvin F. Lewis, Chair, 515-294-2665, Fax: 515-294-1440, E-mail: calewis@iastate.edu. *Application contact:* Dr. Marwan Ghandour, Director of Graduate Education, 515-294-3543, E-mail: jejonas@iastate.edu.

Judson University, Graduate Programs, Elgin, IL 60123-1498. Offers architecture (M Arch); literacy (M Ed); organizational leadership (MA); teaching (M Ed). Part-time and evening/weekend programs available. Postbaccalaureate distance learning degree programs offered (no on-campus study). *Degree requirements:* For master's, comprehensive exam (for some programs), thesis. *Entrance requirements:* For master's, essays, interviews.

Kansas State University, Graduate School, College of Architecture, Planning and Design, Department of Architecture, Manhattan, KS 66506. Offers M Arch. Part-time programs available. *Faculty:* 19 full-time (3 women), 1 (woman) part-time/adjunct. *Students:* 115 full-time (40 women), 11 part-time (2 women); includes 8 minority (2 African Americans, 1 American Indian/Alaska Native, 1 Asian American or Pacific Islander, 4 Hispanic Americans), 11 international. Average age 23. 98 applicants, 85% accepted, 80 enrolled. In 2008, 60 master's awarded. *Degree requirements:* For master's, thesis optional, residency. *Entrance requirements:* For master's, portfolio, minimum GPA of 3.0. Additional exam requirements/recommendations for international students: Required—TOEFL (minimum score 600 paper-based). *Application deadline:* For fall admission, 2/1 for domestic students; for spring admission, 10/1 for domestic students. Application fee: $70 ($80 for international students). *Expenses:* Tuition, area resident: Full-time $6466; part-time $269.40 per credit hour. Tuition, state resident: full-time $6466; part-time $269.40 per credit hour. Tuition, nonresident: full-time $14,874; part-time $619.75 per credit hour. Required fees: $673; $23.40 per credit hour. Tuition and fees vary according to campus/location. *Financial support:* In 2008–09, 5 teaching assistantships with full tuition reimbursements (averaging $10,863 per year) were awarded; research assistantships, institutionally sponsored loans and scholarships/grants also available. Support available to part-time students. Financial award application deadline: 3/1; financial award applicants required to submit FAFSA. *Faculty research:* Design theory, environment behavior and place studies, ecological and sustainable design. Total annual research expenditures: $77,632. *Unit head:* Peter Magyar, Head, 785-532-5953, Fax: 785-532-6722, E-mail: pmagyar@ksu.edu. *Application contact:* Todd Gabbard, Director, 785-532-1129, Fax: 785-532-6722, E-mail: rtodd@ksu.edu.

Kent State University, College of Architecture and Environmental Design, Kent, OH 44242-0001. Offers architecture (M Arch); preservation architecture (Certificate); urban design (M Arch, MUD, Certificate). Part-time programs available. *Degree requirements:* For master's, thesis optional. *Entrance requirements:* For master's, GRE, portfolio, minimum GPA of 2.75, 3 letters of reference, resumé, undergraduate architecture degree. Additional exam requirements/recommendations for international students: Required—TOEFL (minimum score 550 paper-based). Electronic applications accepted. *Faculty research:* History and theory, building technology, landscape architecture and urbanism, urbanism, sustainable development.

Lawrence Technological University, College of Architecture and Design, Southfield, MI 48075-1058. Offers architecture (M Arch); interior design (MID). *Accreditation:* NASAD. Part-time and evening/weekend programs available. *Faculty:* 9 full-time (2 women), 12 part-time/adjunct (3 women). *Students:* 17 full-time (12 women), 105 part-time (44 women); includes 19 minority (8 African Americans, 1 American Indian/Alaska Native, 6 Asian Americans or Pacific Islanders, 4 Hispanic Americans), 13 international. Average age 30. 66 applicants, 83% accepted, 17 enrolled. In 2008, 36 master's awarded. *Degree requirements:* For master's, thesis. *Entrance requirements:* For master's, portfolio. Additional exam requirements/recommendations for international students: Required—TOEFL (minimum score 550 paper-based; 213 computer-based; 79 iBT). *Application deadline:* For fall admission, 2/1 priority date for domestic students, 2/1 for international students; for winter admission, 11/1 priority date for domestic students, 11/1 for international students; for spring admission, 2/1 priority date for domestic students, 2/1 for international students. Applications are processed on a rolling basis. Application fee: $50. Electronic applications accepted. *Expenses:* Tuition: Part-time $763 per credit hour. Required fees: $115 per semester. Tuition and fees vary according to course level, degree level, campus/location and program. *Financial support:* In 2008–09, 105 students received support. Federal Work-Study available. Financial award application deadline: 4/1; financial award applicants required to submit FAFSA. *Unit head:* Glen LeRoy, Dean, 248-204-2800, Fax: 248-204-2900, E-mail: archdean@ltu.edu. *Application contact:* Jane Rohrback, Director of Admissions, 248-204-3160, Fax: 248-204-3188, E-mail: admissions@ltu.edu.

Louisiana State University and Agricultural and Mechanical College, Graduate School, College of Art and Design, School of Architecture, Baton Rouge, LA 70803. Offers M Arch. Part-time programs available. *Degree requirements:* For master's, thesis. *Entrance requirements:* For master's, GRE General Test, minimum GPA of 3.0. Additional exam requirements/recommendations for international students: Required—TOEFL (minimum score 550 paper-based; 213 computer-based; 79 iBT). Electronic applications accepted. *Faculty research:* Architectural design, history of architecture, sustainable design, digital fabrication, community design.

Marywood University, Academic Affairs, School of Architecture, Scranton, PA 18509-1598. Offers M Arch.

Massachusetts College of Art and Design, Graduate Programs, Program in Architecture, Boston, MA 02115-5882. Offers MA. Part-time programs available. *Degree requirements:* For master's, comprehensive exam, thesis (for some programs). *Entrance requirements:* For master's, portfolio, resumé, college transcripts, statement of purpose, letters of reference, interview. Additional exam requirements/recommendations for international students: Required—TOEFL (minimum score 563 paper-based; 223 computer-based; 85 iBT); Recommended—IELTS (minimum score 6.5). *Application deadline:* For fall admission, 1/15 for domestic and international students. Applications are processed on a rolling basis. Application fee: $75. Electronic applications accepted. *Expenses:* Contact institution. *Financial support:* Application deadline: 3/1; *Unit head:* George Creamer, Director, 617-879-7163, Fax: 617-879-7171, E-mail: creamer@massart.edu. *Application contact:* George Creamer, Director, 617-879-7163.

Massachusetts Institute of Technology, School of Architecture and Planning, Department of Architecture, Cambridge, MA 02139-4307. Offers architecture (M Arch, PhD), including building technology (PhD), design and computation (PhD), history and theory of architecture (PhD), history and theory of art (PhD); architecture studies (SM Arch S); visual studies (SM Vis S, SMBT); M Arch/MCP; M Arch/SMRED; SM Arch S/MCP; SM Arch S/SMRED. *Degree requirements:* For master's, thesis; for doctorate, comprehensive exam, thesis/dissertation. *Entrance requirements:* For master's, GRE General Test (for some programs), portfolio (for some programs); for doctorate, GRE General Test (for some programs). Additional exam requirements/recommendations for international students: Required—TOEFL. Electronic applications accepted.

McGill University, Faculty of Graduate and Postdoctoral Studies, Faculty of Engineering, School of Architecture, Montréal, QC H3A 2T5, Canada. Offers affordable homes (M Arch II, Diploma); architectural history and theory (M Arch II); architecture (PhD); domestic environment (M Arch II); domestic environments (Diploma); minimum cost housing in developing countries (M Arch II, Diploma); professional architecture (M Arch I).

Miami University, Graduate School, School of Fine Arts, Department of Architecture, Oxford, OH 45056. Offers M Arch. *Degree requirements:* For master's, thesis, final exam. *Entrance requirements:* For master's, portfolio, minimum undergraduate GPA of 3.0 during previous 2 years or 3.0 overall. Additional exam requirements/recommendations for international students: Required—TOEFL (minimum score 550 paper-based; 213 computer-based), TWE (minimum score 4).

Mississippi State University, College of Architecture, Art and Design, Mississippi State, MS 39762. Offers MFA, MS. *Accreditation:* NASAD. *Degree requirements:* For master's, comprehensive exam, thesis, final written and oral exam. *Entrance requirements:* For master's, GRE General Test, portfolio, minimum GPA of 3.0. Additional exam requirements/recommendations for international students: Required—TOEFL. Electronic applications accepted. *Faculty research:* Digital art in architecture, process change and management, multi-media databases, 3-D modeling and animation, virtual archaeology.

Montana State University, College of Graduate Studies, College of Arts and Architecture, Department of Architecture, Bozeman, MT 59717. Offers M Arch. Part-time programs available. *Degree requirements:* For master's, comprehensive exam. *Entrance requirements:* For master's, GRE General Test. Additional exam requirements/recommendations for international students:

Required—TOEFL (minimum score 550 paper-based; 213 computer-based). Electronic applications accepted. *Faculty research:* Sustainability, design.

Morgan State University, School of Graduate Studies, Institute of Architecture and Planning, Program in Architecture, Baltimore, MD 21251. Offers M Arch. *Degree requirements:* For master's, thesis. *Entrance requirements:* Additional exam requirements/recommendations for international students: Required—TOEFL (minimum score 550 paper-based; 213 computer-based).

New Jersey Institute of Technology, Office of Graduate Studies, School of Architecture, Program in Architecture, Newark, NJ 07102. Offers M Arch, MS, M Arch/MIP, M Arch/MS. Part-time and evening/weekend programs available. *Students:* 65 full-time (34 women), 13 part-time (4 women); includes 17 minority (6 African Americans, 6 Asian Americans or Pacific Islanders, 5 Hispanic Americans), 14 international. Average age 28. 112 applicants, 60% accepted, 23 enrolled. In 2008, 33 master's awarded. *Degree requirements:* For master's, thesis (for some programs). *Entrance requirements:* For master's, GRE General Test, minimum GPA of 3.0. Additional exam requirements/recommendations for international students: Required—TOEFL (minimum score 550 paper-based; 213 computer-based; 79 iBT). *Application deadline:* For fall admission, 6/5 priority date for domestic students, 4/1 for international students; for spring admission, 11/15 for domestic and international students. Applications are processed on a rolling basis. Application fee: $60. Electronic applications accepted. *Expenses:* Tuition, area resident: Full-time $13,780; part-time $750 per credit. Tuition, state resident: full-time $13,780; part-time $750 per credit. Tuition, nonresident: full-time $19,580; part-time $1033 per credit. Required fees: $1956; $197 per credit. *Financial support:* Fellowships with full and partial tuition reimbursements, research assistantships with full and partial tuition reimbursements, teaching assistantships with full and partial tuition reimbursements, career-related internships or fieldwork, Federal Work-Study, institutionally sponsored loans, and unspecified assistantships available. Financial award application deadline: 3/15. *Faculty research:* Management of new technologies, information systems management, operations management systems, marketing management, human resource management. *Unit head:* Anthony Schuman, Director, 973-596-6370, E-mail: anthony.w.schuman@njit.edu. *Application contact:* Kathryn Kelly, Director of Admissions, 973-596-3300, Fax: 973-596-3461, E-mail: admissions@njit.edu.

New Jersey Institute of Technology, Office of Graduate Studies, School of Architecture, Program in Infrastructure Planning, Newark, NJ 07102. Offers MIP. Part-time and evening/weekend programs available. *Students:* 5 full-time (4 women), 5 part-time (1 woman); includes 2 minority (both Asian Americans or Pacific Islanders), 3 international. Average age 35. 20 applicants, 60% accepted, 5 enrolled. In 2008, 5 master's awarded. *Degree requirements:* For master's, thesis (for some programs). *Entrance requirements:* For master's, GRE General Test, minimum GPA of 3.0. Additional exam requirements/recommendations for international students: Required—TOEFL (minimum score 550 paper-based; 213 computer-based; 79 iBT). *Application deadline:* For fall admission, 6/5 priority date for domestic students, 4/1 for international students; for spring admission, 11/15 for domestic and international students. Applications are processed on a rolling basis. Application fee: $60. Electronic applications accepted. *Expenses:* Tuition, area resident: Full-time $13,780; part-time $750 per credit. Tuition, state resident: full-time $13,780; part-time $750 per credit. Tuition, nonresident: full-time $19,580; part-time $1033 per credit. Required fees: $1956; $197 per credit. *Financial support:* Fellowships with full and partial tuition reimbursements, research assistantships with full and partial tuition reimbursements, teaching assistantships with full and partial tuition reimbursements, career-related internships or fieldwork, Federal Work-Study, institutionally sponsored loans, and unspecified assistantships available. Financial award application deadline: 3/15. *Unit head:* Antonio P. De Sousa Santos, Director, 973-596-3029, Fax: 973-596-3073, E-mail: antonio.de_sousa_santos@njit.edu. *Application contact:* Kathryn Kelly, Director of Admissions, 973-596-3300, Fax: 973-596-3461, E-mail: admissions@njit.edu.

The New School: A University, Parsons The New School for Design, Program in Architecture, New York, NY 10011. Offers M Arch. *Faculty:* 7 full-time (1 woman), 26 part-time/adjunct (10 women). *Students:* 55 full-time (28 women), 2 part-time (1 woman); includes 9 minority (2 African Americans, 3 Asian Americans or Pacific Islanders, 4 Hispanic Americans), 8 international. Average age 26. In 2008, 22 master's awarded. *Degree requirements:* For master's, thesis or alternative. *Entrance requirements:* For master's, GRE General Test, portfolio. Additional exam requirements/recommendations for international students: Required—TOEFL (minimum score 580 paper-based; 237 computer-based; 93 iBT). *Application deadline:* For fall admission, 2/1 priority date for domestic students. Applications are processed on a rolling basis. Application fee: $50. *Expenses:* Tuition: Full-time $27,144; part-time $1508 per credit. Required fees: $355 per semester. *Financial support:* Federal Work-Study, scholarships/grants, and tuition waivers (partial) available. Financial award application deadline: 3/1; financial award applicants required to submit FAFSA. *Unit head:* David Lewis, Director, 212-229-8955 Ext. 2915, E-mail: lewisd@newschool.edu. *Application contact:* Anthony Padilla, Director of Admissions, 212-229-8989 Ext. 4023, Fax: 212-229-8975, E-mail: padillaa@newschool.edu.

See Close-Up on page 151.

NewSchool of Architecture & Design, Program in Architecture, San Diego, CA 92101-6634. Offers M Arch, MS. Part-time and evening/weekend programs available. *Degree requirements:* For master's, thesis. *Entrance requirements:* For master's, portfolio, interview. *Faculty research:* Urban studies, regional studies, environmental design, structures, cross-cultural studies.

New York Institute of Technology, Graduate Division, School of Architecture and Design, Old Westbury, NY 11568-8000. Offers urban and regional design (M Arch). Part-time programs available. *Students:* 11 full-time (8 women), 4 part-time (1 woman); includes 2 minority (1 Asian American or Pacific Islander, 1 Hispanic American), 10 international. Average age 31. In 2008, 5 master's awarded. *Degree requirements:* For master's, thesis. *Entrance requirements:* For master's, minimum QPA of 2.85, portfolio. Additional exam requirements/recommendations for international students: Required—TOEFL (minimum score 550 paper-based; 213 computer-based). *Application deadline:* For fall admission, 7/1 priority date for domestic students; for spring admission, 12/1 priority date for domestic students. Applications are processed on a rolling basis. Application fee: $50. Electronic applications accepted. *Expenses:* Tuition: Part-time $783 per credit. *Financial support:* Research assistantships with partial tuition reimbursements, institutionally sponsored loans and tuition waivers (full and partial) available. Support available to part-time students. Financial award applicants required to submit FAFSA. *Faculty research:* Affordable housing, urban modeling and simulation, transport systems and infrastructure, relationships of policy and form. *Unit head:* Judith DiMaio, Dean, 516-686-7594, Fax: 516-686-7921, E-mail: jdimaio@nyit.edu. *Application contact:* Dr. Jacquelyn Nealon, Vice President for Enrollment Services, 516-686-7925, Fax: 516-686-7597, E-mail: jnealon@nyit.edu.

North Carolina State University, Graduate School, College of Design, School of Architecture, Raleigh, NC 27695. Offers M Arch. *Degree requirements:* For master's, thesis optional, oral exam, project. *Entrance requirements:* For master's, GRE General Test, portfolio. Electronic applications accepted. *Faculty research:* Architectural design, architectural history and theory, construction materials, sustainable design.

Northeastern University, School of Architecture, Boston, MA 02115-5096. Offers M Arch. *Entrance requirements:* Additional exam requirements/recommendations for international students: Required—TOEFL or IELTS. Electronic applications accepted.

The Ohio State University, Graduate School, College of Engineering, Austin E. Knowlton School of Architecture, Program in Architecture, Columbus, OH 43210. Offers M Arch, MAS. *Degree requirements:* For master's, thesis optional. *Entrance requirements:* For master's, GRE General Test. Additional exam requirements/recommendations for international students: Required—TOEFL (minimum score 600 paper-based; 250 computer-based). Electronic applications accepted.

Penn State University Park, Graduate School, College of Arts and Architecture, Department of Architecture, State College, University Park, PA 16802-1503. Offers M Arch.

Philadelphia University, School of Architecture, Philadelphia, PA 19144-5497. Offers MS.

Pontificia Universidad Catolica Madre y Maestra, Graduate School, Santiago, Dominican Republic. Offers administration (M Adm); architecture of interiors (M Arch); architecture of tourist lodgings (M Arch); banking and financial management (M Mgmt); civil law (LL M); construction administration (ME); corporate business law (LL M); criminal procedure law (LL M); environmental engineering (ME, MEE); finance (M Mgmt); human resources (EMBA); international business (M Mgmt); labor law and Social Security (LL M); logistics management (ME); marketing (M Mgmt); renewable energy (ME). *Entrance requirements:* For master's, curriculum vitae, interview.

Prairie View A&M University, School of Architecture, Prairie View, TX 77446-0519. Offers architecture (M Arch); community development (MCD). Part-time and evening/weekend programs available. *Entrance requirements:* For master's, GRE General Test, portfolio (M Arch). Additional exam requirements/recommendations for international students: Required—TOEFL (minimum score 550 paper-based). Electronic applications accepted. *Faculty research:* Community management, sustainable design.

Pratt Institute, School of Architecture, Program in Architecture, Brooklyn, NY 11205-3899. Offers architecture (first-professional) (M Arch); architecture (post-professional) (MS Arch). Part-time programs available. *Faculty:* 10 full-time (3 women), 47 part-time/adjunct (18 women). *Students:* 176 full-time (84 women), 1 (woman) part-time; includes 32 minority (3 African Americans, 16 Asian Americans or Pacific Islanders, 13 Hispanic Americans), 49 international. Average age 26. 567 applicants, 51% accepted, 90 enrolled. In 2008, 63 master's awarded. *Degree requirements:* For master's, thesis. *Entrance requirements:* For master's, B Arch, portfolio, transcripts, letters of recommendation, statement. Additional exam requirements/recommendations for international students: Required—TOEFL (minimum score 550 paper-based; 213 computer-based). *Application deadline:* For fall admission, 2/1 for domestic and international students; for spring admission, 10/1 for domestic and international students. Application fee: $50 ($90 for international students). Electronic applications accepted. *Expenses:* Tuition: Full-time $20,412; part-time $1134 per credit. Required fees: $1190; $1190 per year. *Financial support:* Career-related internships or fieldwork, Federal Work-Study, institutionally sponsored loans, scholarships/grants, health care benefits, and unspecified assistantships available. Support available to part-time students. Financial award application deadline: 2/1; financial award applicants required to submit FAFSA. *Faculty research:* Design theory, advanced structural systems, urban investigations. *Unit head:* William J. Mac Donald, Chairperson, 718-636-4308, E-mail: wmacdona@pratt.edu. *Application contact:* Young Hah, Director of Graduate Admissions, 718-636-3683, Fax: 718-399-4242, E-mail: yhah@pratt.edu.

See Close-Up on page 155.

Princeton University, Graduate School, School of Architecture, Princeton, NJ 08544-1019. Offers M Arch, PhD. Terminal master's awarded for partial completion of doctoral program. *Degree requirements:* For master's, thesis; for doctorate, 2 foreign languages, comprehensive exam, thesis/dissertation. *Entrance requirements:* For master's, GRE General Test, design portfolio, math, 2 semesters of physics, and art/architecture survey; for doctorate, GRE General Test, samples of written work. Additional exam requirements/recommendations for international students: Required—TOEFL (minimum score 600 paper-based; 260 computer-based). Electronic applications accepted. *Faculty research:* Design, urban studies, landscape architecture, media and information technologies in architecture.

Rensselaer Polytechnic Institute, Graduate School, School of Architecture, Troy, NY 12180-3590. Offers architectural science (MS, PhD); architecture (M Arch); building conservation (MS); lighting (MS). Part-time programs available. Terminal master's awarded for partial completion of doctoral program. *Degree requirements:* For master's, thesis (for some programs); for doctorate, comprehensive exam (for some programs), thesis/dissertation. *Entrance requirements:* For master's and doctorate, GRE, portfolio, letters of recommendation, resumé. Additional exam requirements/recommendations for international students: Required—TOEFL (minimum score 570 paper-based; 230 computer-based), IELTS (minimum score 7). Electronic applications accepted. *Faculty research:* Architectural design, architectural acoustics, lighting performance, built ecologies, materials.

Rhode Island School of Design, Graduate Studies, Division of Architecture and Design, Department of Architecture, Providence, RI 02903-2784. Offers M Arch. *Degree requirements:* For master's, thesis, exhibit. *Entrance requirements:* For master's, portfolio, 3 letters of recommendation. Additional exam requirements/recommendations for international students: Required—TOEFL (minimum score 580 paper-based; 237 computer-based), IELTS (minimum score 6.5).

Rice University, Graduate Programs, School of Architecture, Houston, TX 77251-1892. Offers architecture (M Arch, D Arch); urban design (M Arch UD). *Degree requirements:* For master's, thesis; for doctorate, thesis/dissertation. *Entrance requirements:* For master's and doctorate, GRE General Test, minimum GPA of 3.0. Additional exam requirements/recommendations for international students: Required—TOEFL (minimum score 650 paper-based; 250 computer-based; 90 iBT).

Roger Williams University, School of Architecture, Art and Historic Preservation, Bristol, RI 02809. Offers architecture (M Arch). Students often begin 5-6 year dual degree sequence as undergraduates. *Faculty:* 9 full-time (1 woman), 2 part-time/adjunct (1 woman). *Students:* 53 full-time (16 women), 8 part-time (2 women); includes 1 minority (Hispanic American), 2 international. Average age 23. 38 applicants, 87% accepted, 31 enrolled. In 2008, 5 master's awarded. *Degree requirements:* For master's, thesis. *Entrance requirements:* For master's, portfolio, statement, transcripts, 2 letters of recommendation. Additional exam requirements/recommendations for international students: Recommended—IELTS. *Application deadline:* For fall admission, 3/1 priority date for domestic students. Application fee: $50. Electronic applications accepted. *Expenses:* Contact institution. *Financial support:* In 2008–09, 61 students received support. Application deadline: 6/15; *Unit head:* Dean Stephen White, Dean, 401-254-3607, E-mail: swhite@rwu.edu. *Application contact:* Lori Vales, Graduate Admission Coordinator, 401-254-6600, Fax: 401-254-3557, E-mail: gradadmit@rwu.edu.

Savannah College of Art and Design, Graduate School, Program in Architecture, Savannah, GA 31402-3146. Offers M Arch. Part-time programs available. *Degree requirements:* For master's, thesis, internship. *Entrance requirements:* For master's, interview, portfolio. Additional exam requirements/recommendations for international students: Required—TOEFL (minimum score 450 paper-based; 133 computer-based). Electronic applications accepted. *Expenses:* Tuition: Full-time $28,215; part-time $3135 per course. One-time fee: $500. *Faculty research:* Computer-aided design, photovoltaics-powered environmental control.

See Close-Up on page 223.

School of the Art Institute of Chicago, Graduate Division, Department of Architecture, Interior Architecture, and Designed Objects, Chicago, IL 60603-3103. Offers architecture (M Arc); design for emerging technologies (MFA); designed objects (M Des); interior architecture (M Arc). *Entrance requirements:* Additional exam requirements/recommendations for international students: Required—TOEFL, IELTS.

See Close-Up on page 225.

Southern California Institute of Architecture, Graduate Program in Architecture, Los Angeles, CA 90013. Offers M Arch. *Degree requirements:* For master's, thesis, final project. *Entrance requirements:* For master's, GRE General Test, portfolio of architectural and creative work, letters of recommendation. *Faculty research:* Architectural theory.

Architecture

Southern Illinois University Carbondale, Graduate School, College of Applied Science, School of Architecture, Carbondale, IL 62901-4701. Offers M Arch.

Syracuse University, Graduate School, School of Architecture, Syracuse, NY 13244. Offers M Arch I, M Arch II. *Degree requirements:* For master's, thesis. *Entrance requirements:* For master's, GRE General Test, interview, portfolio. Additional exam requirements/recommendations for international students: Required—TOEFL. Electronic applications accepted. *Faculty research:* Urban design, urban mapping, building systems, landscape, theory.

Texas A&M University, College of Architecture, Department of Architecture, College Station, TX 77843. Offers architecture (M Arch, MS Arch, PhD); visualization science (MS). *Faculty:* 36. *Students:* 131 full-time (63 women), 24 part-time (10 women); includes 18 minority (2 African Americans, 1 American Indian/Alaska Native, 8 Asian Americans or Pacific Islanders, 7 Hispanic Americans), 66 international. Average age 24. In 2008, 40 master's, 4 doctorates awarded. *Degree requirements:* For master's, comprehensive exam, thesis; for doctorate, comprehensive exam, thesis/dissertation. *Entrance requirements:* For master's, GRE General Test, portfolio, letters of recommendation; for doctorate, GRE General Test. Additional exam requirements/recommendations for international students: Required—TOEFL. *Application deadline:* For fall admission, 1/15 priority date for domestic and international students. Applications are processed on a rolling basis. Application fee: $50 ($75 for international students). Electronic applications accepted. *Expenses:* Tuition, area resident: Full-time $3838.50. Tuition, state resident: full-time $3838.50. Tuition, nonresident: full-time $8897. Required fees: $2359.60. *Financial support:* Fellowships, research assistantships, teaching assistantships, career-related internships or fieldwork, Federal Work-Study, institutionally sponsored loans, and scholarships/grants available. Financial award application deadline: 1/15; financial award applicants required to submit FAFSA. *Faculty research:* Energy optimization, architecture pedagogy, environment and behavior. *Unit head:* Glen Mills, Head, 979-845-1015, Fax: 979-862-1571, E-mail: gmills@archmail.tamu.edu. *Application contact:* 979-845-6582, Fax: 979-862-7119, E-mail: gradoff@archone.tamu.edu.

Texas Tech University, Graduate School, College of Architecture, Post-Professional Program in Architecture, Lubbock, TX 79409. Offers MS. Part-time programs available. *Students:* 4 full-time (1 woman), 5 part-time (3 women), 5 international. Average age 28. 22 applicants, 27% accepted, 1 enrolled. In 2008, 1 master's awarded. *Degree requirements:* For master's, thesis. *Entrance requirements:* For master's, GRE General Test, portfolio. Additional exam requirements/recommendations for international students: Required—TOEFL (minimum score 550 paper-based; 213 computer-based). *Application deadline:* For fall admission, 3/1 priority date for domestic students; for spring admission, 11/1 priority date for domestic students. Applications are processed on a rolling basis. Application fee: $50 ($60 for international students). Electronic applications accepted. *Expenses:* Tuition, area resident: Part-time $194 per credit hour. Tuition, state resident: full-time $4648; part-time $194 per credit hour. Tuition, nonresident: full-time $11,392; part-time $475 per credit hour. Required fees: $2206; $69 per credit hour. $389 per semester. *Financial support:* Research assistantships with partial tuition reimbursements, teaching assistantships with partial tuition reimbursements, career-related internships or fieldwork, Federal Work-Study, and institutionally sponsored loans available. Support available to part-time students. Financial award application deadline: 4/15; financial award applicants required to submit FAFSA. *Faculty research:* Historic preservation, visualization, community development and design, sustainable architecture, international architecture. *Unit head:* Glenn Eugene Hill, Associate Dean of Research and Post-Professional Graduate Studies, 806-742-3136, Fax: 806-742-2855, E-mail: glenn.hill@ttu.edu. *Application contact:* Jess Schwintz, Academic Program Assistant, 806-742-3136 Ext. 272, Fax: 806-742-2855, E-mail: jess.schwintz@ttu.edu.

Texas Tech University, Graduate School, College of Architecture, Professional Program in Architecture, Lubbock, TX 79409. Offers M Arch, M Arch/MBA. Part-time programs available. *Students:* 99 full-time (27 women), 10 part-time (1 woman); includes 21 minority (1 American Indian/Alaska Native, 4 Asian Americans or Pacific Islanders, 16 Hispanic Americans). Average age 25. 53 applicants, 81% accepted, 32 enrolled. In 2008, 43 master's awarded. *Degree requirements:* For master's, thesis. *Entrance requirements:* For master's, GRE General Test, portfolio. Additional exam requirements/recommendations for international students: Required—TOEFL (minimum score 550 paper-based; 213 computer-based). *Application deadline:* For fall admission, 3/1 priority date for international students; for spring admission, 11/1 priority date for international students. Applications are processed on a rolling basis. Application fee: $50 ($60 for international students). Electronic applications accepted. *Expenses:* Tuition, area resident: Part-time $194 per credit hour. Tuition, state resident: full-time $4648; part-time $194 per credit hour. Tuition, nonresident: full-time $11,392; part-time $475 per credit hour. Required fees: $2206; $69 per credit hour. $389 per semester. *Financial support:* Research assistantships with partial tuition reimbursements, teaching assistantships with partial tuition reimbursements, career-related internships or fieldwork, Federal Work-Study, and institutionally sponsored loans available. Support available to part-time students. Financial award application deadline: 4/15; financial award applicants required to submit FAFSA. *Faculty research:* Historical preservation; visualization; community design; digital design and construction; healthcare facilities. *Unit head:* Michael Peters, Associate Dean for Academics, 806-742-3136, Fax: 806-742-2855, E-mail: architecture.programs@ttu.edu. *Application contact:* Lori Rodriguez, Academic Program Assistant, 806-742-3136 Ext. 247, Fax: 806-742-2855, E-mail: lori.rodriguez@ttu.edu.

Tulane University, School of Architecture, New Orleans, LA 70118-5669. Offers M Arch, MPS. Part-time programs available. *Degree requirements:* For master's, thesis. *Entrance requirements:* For master's, GRE, portfolio. Additional exam requirements/recommendations for international students: Required—TOEFL. *Expenses:* Contact institution. *Faculty research:* Design topics, preservation and environmental conservation, architecture and human health, computing.

Universidad Autonoma de Guadalajara, Graduate Programs, Guadalajara, Mexico. Offers advertising and corporate communications (MA); architecture (M Arch); business (MBA); computational science (MCC); education (Ed M, Ed D); English-Spanish translation (MA); fiscal law (MA); international business (MIB); international corporate law (LL M); internet technologies (MS); labor health (MS); manufacturing systems (MMS); market research (MBA); philosophy (MA, PhD); quality systems (MQS); renewable energy (MS); teaching mathematics (MA).

Universidad Nacional Pedro Henriquez Urena, Graduate School, Santo Domingo, Dominican Republic. Offers accounting and auditing (M Acct); animal production (M Agr); business administration (MBA, PhD); Caribbean tropical architecture (M Arch); conservation of monuments and cultural goods (M Arch); economics (M Econ); education (PhD); environmental engineering (MEE); horticulture (M Agr); hospital administration (PhD); humanities (PhD); international relations (MPS); management of natural resources (MNRM); project management (M Man, MPM); public administration (MPS); sanitary engineering (ME); social science (PhD); veterinary medicine (DVM).

Université Laval, Faculty of Architecture, Planning and Visual Arts, School of Architecture, Program in Architecture, Québec, QC G1K 7P4, Canada. Offers M Arch, M Sc. Part-time programs available. *Degree requirements:* For master's, thesis (for some programs). *Entrance requirements:* For master's, mastery of software (CAO), knowledge of French and English. Electronic applications accepted.

University at Buffalo, the State University of New York, Graduate School, School of Architecture and Planning, Department of Architecture, Buffalo, NY 14260. Offers M Arch, M Arch/MBA, M Arch/MFA, M Arch/MUP. Part-time programs available. *Degree requirements:* For master's, thesis or alternative, project. *Entrance requirements:* For master's, GRE, portfolio. Additional exam requirements/recommendations for international students: Required—TOEFL (minimum score 550 paper-based; 213 computer-based). Electronic applications accepted. *Faculty research:* Inclusive design, landscape and environment, theory and design, urban design, virtual architecture.

The University of Arizona, Graduate College, College of Architecture and Landscape Architecture, School of Architecture, Tucson, AZ 85721. Offers M Arch.

The University of British Columbia, Faculty of Graduate Studies, Faculty of Applied Science, School of Architecture and Landscape Architecture, Vancouver, BC V6T 1Z1, Canada. Offers architecture (M Arch, MASA); landscape architecture (MASLA, MLA). *Degree requirements:* For master's, thesis. *Entrance requirements:* For master's, portfolio, resumé, 3 reference letters. Additional exam requirements/recommendations for international students: Required—TOEFL (minimum score 600 paper-based; 250 computer-based; 100 iBT). Electronic applications accepted. *Expenses:* Contact institution. *Faculty research:* Energy and resource use of buildings, advanced design research, urban design and community activism, advanced research in computer applications, cultural studies.

University of Calgary, Faculty of Graduate Studies, Faculty of Environmental Design, Calgary, AB T2N 1N4, Canada. Offers architecture (M Arch); environmental design (M Env Des, PhD). *Degree requirements:* For master's, thesis; for doctorate, thesis/dissertation. *Entrance requirements:* For master's, minimum GPA of 3.0; for doctorate, minimum GPA of 3.5. Additional exam requirements/recommendations for international students: Required—TOEFL (minimum score 550 paper-based; 213 computer-based). *Faculty research:* Sustainable development in architecture, planning and product design, energy and environment, impact assessment, ecotourism.

University of California, Berkeley, Graduate Division, College of Environmental Design, Department of Architecture, Berkeley, CA 94720-1500. Offers architecture (M Arch); building science (MS, PhD); building structures, construction and materials (MS, PhD); design (MA); design theories, methods, and practices (MS, PhD); environmental design in developing countries (MS, PhD); history of architecture and urbanism (MS, PhD); social and cultural processes in architecture and urbanism (MS, PhD); M Arch/MCP; M Arch/MS; MLA/M Arch. *Degree requirements:* For master's, thesis; for doctorate, thesis/dissertation, qualifying exam. *Entrance requirements:* For master's and doctorate, GRE General Test, minimum GPA of 3.0, 3 letters of recommendation. Additional exam requirements/recommendations for international students: Required—TOEFL. Electronic applications accepted.

University of California, Los Angeles, Graduate Division, School of the Arts and Architecture, Department of Architecture and Urban Design, Los Angeles, CA 90095. Offers M Arch, MA, PhD. *Degree requirements:* For master's, thesis or alternative, comprehensive exam or design project; for doctorate, 2 foreign languages, thesis/dissertation, oral and written qualifying exams. *Entrance requirements:* For master's and doctorate, GRE General Test, portfolio. Additional exam requirements/recommendations for international students: Required—TOEFL. Electronic applications accepted. *Expenses:* Tuition, nonresident: full-time $14,694. Required fees: $9669.50. Full-time tuition and fees vary according to course load, degree level, program and student level. *Faculty research:* Urban poverty and low wage labor markets; environmental planning and politics; international political economy; physical planning, urban design, planning history; housing and land development; transportation and land use; critical urban and regional studies.

University of Cincinnati, Graduate School, College of Design, Architecture, Art, and Planning, School of Architecture and Interior Design, Cincinnati, OH 45221. Offers architecture (M Arch). *Accreditation:* NASAD. *Degree requirements:* For master's, one foreign language, thesis. *Entrance requirements:* Additional exam requirements/recommendations for international students: Required—TOEFL. *Faculty research:* Theory and history of architecture.

University of Colorado Denver, College of Architecture and Planning, Program in Architecture, Denver, CO 80217-3364. Offers M Arch. Part-time programs available. *Degree requirements:* For master's, thesis optional. *Entrance requirements:* For master's, GRE or minimum GPA of 3.0, portfolio, course work in trigonometry and physics. Additional exam requirements/recommendations for international students: Required—TOEFL (minimum score 550 paper-based; 213 computer-based). *Faculty research:* Architectural design; history, theory, and criticism of architecture; regional and environmental issues; sustainability; intervention and transformation in the urban and rural landscape.

University of Florida, Graduate School, College of Design, Construction and Planning, Doctoral Program in Design, Construction and Planning, Gainesville, FL 32611. Offers PhD. *Degree requirements:* For doctorate, thesis/dissertation. *Entrance requirements:* For doctorate, GRE General Test, minimum GPA of 3.2. Additional exam requirements/recommendations for international students: Required—TOEFL. Electronic applications accepted. *Faculty research:* Architecture, building construction, urban and regional planning.

University of Florida, Graduate School, College of Design, Construction and Planning, School of Architecture, Gainesville, FL 32611. Offers M Arch, MSAS, PhD.

University of Hartford, College of Engineering, Technology and Architecture, Program in Architecture, West Hartford, CT 06117-1599. Offers M Arch. *Entrance requirements:* For master's, 3 letters of recommendation, portfolio. Additional exam requirements/recommendations for international students: Required—TOEFL (minimum score 550 paper-based; 213 computer-based).

University of Hawaii at Manoa, School of Architecture, Honolulu, HI 96822. Offers D Arch. *Faculty research:* Housing, future cities, environmental studies, preservation, professional practice.

University of Houston, College of Architecture, Houston, TX 77204-4431. Offers M Arch, MS. *Faculty:* 16 full-time (3 women), 16 part-time/adjunct (1 woman). *Students:* 60 full-time (34 women), 10 part-time (3 women); includes 17 minority (2 African Americans, 8 Asian Americans or Pacific Islanders, 7 Hispanic Americans), 10 international. Average age 28. 97 applicants, 57% accepted, 24 enrolled. In 2008, 32 master's awarded. *Entrance requirements:* For master's, GRE General Test, portfolio. Additional exam requirements/recommendations for international students: Required—TOEFL. *Application deadline:* For fall admission, 2/1 priority date for domestic students; for spring admission, 10/1 for domestic students. Applications are processed on a rolling basis. Application fee: $10 ($75 for international students). *Expenses:* Tuition, state resident: full-time $5164; part-time $287 per credit. Tuition, nonresident: full-time $10,222; part-time $568 per credit. *Financial support:* In 2008–09, 1 fellowship with full tuition reimbursement (averaging $9,900 per year), 1 research assistantship with full tuition reimbursement (averaging $9,900 per year), 2 teaching assistantships with full tuition reimbursements (averaging $9,900 per year) were awarded; career-related internships or fieldwork, Federal Work-Study, institutionally sponsored loans, scholarships/grants, health care benefits, and unspecified assistantships also available. Support available to part-time students. Financial award application deadline: 2/1. *Faculty research:* Extraterrestrial habitation, computer applications, methods and materials of construction, historic preservation, simulation, architectural design, urban design. *Unit head:* Joseph Mashburn, Dean, 713-743-2400, Fax: 713-743-2358, E-mail: mashburn@uh.edu. *Application contact:* Thomas M. Colbert, Director of Graduate Studies, 713-743-2380, Fax: 713-743-2358, E-mail: colbert@bayou.uh.edu.

University of Idaho, College of Graduate Studies, College of Art and Architecture, Department of Architecture and Interior Design, Moscow, ID 83844-2282. Offers M Arch, MA, MS. *Faculty:* 9 full-time, 2 part-time/adjunct. *Students:* 52 full-time, 4 part-time. Average age 28. In 2008, 53 master's awarded. *Entrance requirements:* For master's, minimum GPA of 2.8. *Application deadline:* For fall admission, 8/1 for domestic students; for spring admission, 12/15 for domestic students. Application fee: $55 ($60 for international students). *Expenses:* Tuition, nonresident: full-time $10,080; part-time $336 per credit. Required fees: $5212; $267 per credit. Tuition and fees vary according to program. *Financial support:* Research assistantships, teaching assistantships available. Financial award application deadline: 2/15. *Faculty research:* Sustainable interior environments, multi-hazard design, environmental technologies for sustainable architectural design. *Unit head:* Wendy McClure, Chair, 208-885-6473. *Application contact:* Wendy McClure, Chair, 208-885-6473.

University of Illinois at Chicago, Graduate College, College of Architecture and Art, School of Architecture, Chicago, IL 60607-7128. Offers architecture (M Arch, MS Arch); architecture in health design (MS Arch). *Entrance requirements:* For master's, GRE General Test, portfolio, minimum GPA of 3.0. Additional exam requirements/recommendations for international students: Required—TOEFL. Electronic applications accepted. *Faculty research:* Housing values, elderly housing, design theory, deconstructivism.

University of Illinois at Urbana–Champaign, Graduate College, College of Fine and Applied Arts, School of Architecture, Champaign, IL 61820. Offers architectural studies (MS); architecture (M Arch, PhD); M Arch/MBA; M Arch/MS; M Arch/MUP; MCS/M Arch; MRP/JD. *Faculty:* 34 full-time (6 women), 6 part-time/adjunct (0 women). *Students:* 193 full-time (74 women), 3 part-time (0 women); includes 21 minority (4 African Americans, 1 American Indian/Alaska Native, 14 Asian Americans or Pacific Islanders, 2 Hispanic Americans), 39 international. 387 applicants, 25% accepted, 88 enrolled. In 2008, 99 master's, 2 doctorates awarded. *Entrance requirements:* For master's, minimum GPA of 3.0; portfolio; for doctorate, GRE, minimum GPA of 3.0; portfolio. Additional exam requirements/recommendations for international students: Required—TOEFL (minimum score 590 paper-based; 243 computer-based; 96 iBT), IELTS (minimum score 6.5), TOEFL or IELTS. *Application deadline:* Applications are processed on a rolling basis. Application fee: $60 ($75 for international students). Electronic applications accepted. *Financial support:* In 2008–09, 25 fellowships, 21 research assistantships, 44 teaching assistantships were awarded; tuition waivers (full and partial) also available. *Unit head:* David Chasco, Director, 217-333-1331, Fax: 217-244-8866, E-mail: dchasco@illinois.edu. *Application contact:* Molly Blixen, Office Support Specialist, 217-244-4723, Fax: 217-244-8866, E-mail: mhelgese@illinois.edu.

The University of Kansas, Graduate Studies, School of Architecture, Design, and Planning, Program in Architecture, Lawrence, KS 66045. Offers architecture (PhD); facility management (AC); management option (M Arch); professional track (M Arch); M Arch/MBA; M Arch/MUP. *Faculty:* 20 full-time (5 women). *Students:* 96 full-time (43 women), 18 part-time (8 women); includes 13 minority (5 African Americans, 5 Asian Americans or Pacific Islanders, 3 Hispanic Americans), 6 international. Average age 27. 101 applicants, 54% accepted, 20 enrolled. In 2008, 65 master's awarded. Terminal master's awarded for partial completion of doctoral program. *Degree requirements:* For master's, thesis or alternative, 7 semesters of design studio, 1 summer abroad; for doctorate, comprehensive exam, thesis/dissertation. *Entrance requirements:* For master's, portfolio, minimum GPA of 3.0; for doctorate, GRE, portfolio. Additional exam requirements/recommendations for international students: Required—TOEFL. *Application deadline:* For fall admission, 3/1 priority date for domestic and international students; for spring admission, 11/1 priority date for domestic and international students. Applications are processed on a rolling basis. Application fee: $45 ($55 for international students). Electronic applications accepted. *Expenses:* Tuition, area resident: Full-time $6122; part-time $255.10 per credit hour. Tuition, state resident: full-time $6122; part-time $255.10 per credit hour. Tuition, nonresident: full-time $14,629; part-time $609.55 per credit hour. Required fees: $847; $70.56 per credit hour. Tuition and fees vary according to course load and program. *Financial support:* Fellowships, research assistantships with partial tuition reimbursements, teaching assistantships with full and partial tuition reimbursements, scholarships/grants, health care benefits, and unspecified assistantships available. Financial award application deadline: 2/1; financial award applicants required to submit FAFSA. *Faculty research:* Design build, sustainability, emergent technology, healthy places, urban design. *Unit head:* Prof. Keith Diaz Moore, Chair, 785-864-5088, Fax: 785-864-5185, E-mail: archku@ku.edu. *Application contact:* Gera Elliott, Admissions Coordinator, 785-864-3167, Fax: 785-864-5185, E-mail: archku@ku.edu.

University of Kentucky, Graduate School, College of Design, School of Architecture, Lexington, KY 40506-0032. Offers M Arch. *Degree requirements:* For master's, comprehensive exam. *Entrance requirements:* For master's, GRE General Test, minimum undergraduate GPA of 2.75. Additional exam requirements/recommendations for international students: Required—TOEFL (minimum score 550 paper-based; 213 computer-based). Electronic applications accepted.

University of Manitoba, Faculty of Graduate Studies, Faculty of Architecture, Department of Architecture, Winnipeg, MB R3T 2N2, Canada. Offers M Arch. *Degree requirements:* For master's, thesis or alternative.

University of Maryland, College Park, Graduate Studies, School of Architecture, Planning and Preservation, Program in Architecture, College Park, MD 20742. Offers M Arch, M Arch/MCP. Part-time and evening/weekend programs available. *Entrance requirements:* For master's, GRE General Test, portfolio, minimum GPA of 3.0, letters of recommendation. Additional exam requirements/recommendations for international students: Required—TOEFL. Electronic applications accepted. *Faculty research:* Design, history, theory.

University of Massachusetts Amherst, Graduate School, College of Humanities and Fine Arts, Department of Art, Programs in Architecture, Amherst, MA 01003. Offers architecture and design (M Arch); interior design (MS). Part-time programs available. *Degree requirements:* For master's, thesis or alternative. *Entrance requirements:* For master's, GRE General Test (M Arch), portfolio. Additional exam requirements/recommendations for international students: Required—TOEFL (minimum score 550 paper-based; 213 computer-based; 79 iBT), IELTS (minimum score 6.5). Electronic applications accepted. *Expenses:* Tuition, area resident: Full-time $2640. Tuition, nonresident: full-time $9936. One-time fee: $332 full-time. Tuition and fees vary according to course load.

University of Memphis, Graduate School, College of Communication and Fine Arts, Department of Architecture, Memphis, TN 38152. Offers M Arch. *Faculty:* 4 full-time (1 woman). *Students:* 4 full-time (3 women); includes 1 African American, 1 American Indian/Alaska Native, 2 international. Average age 31. 3 applicants, 100% accepted, 3 enrolled. *Expenses:* Tuition, area resident: Full-time $6242; part-time $330 per credit hour. Tuition, state resident: full-time $6242; part-time $330 per credit hour. Tuition, nonresident: full-time $17,828; part-time $815 per credit hour. Required fees: $1156. *Financial support:* Applicants required to submit FAFSA. *Unit head:* Dr. Michael D. Hagge, Chair, 901-678-2724, Fax: 901-678-1755, E-mail: mdhagge@memphis.edu. *Application contact:* Sherry Brian, Coordinator of Graduate Studies, 901-678-3302, Fax: 901-678-1755.

University of Miami, Graduate School, School of Architecture, Coral Gables, FL 33124. Offers architecture (M Arch); suburb and town design (M Arch). *Entrance requirements:* For master's, GRE General Test, minimum GPA of 3.0, portfolio. Additional exam requirements/recommendations for international students: Required—TOEFL. Electronic applications accepted. *Faculty research:* Housing, town planning, retrofit.

See Close-Up on page 157.

University of Michigan, A. Alfred Taubman College of Architecture and Urban Planning, Doctoral Program in Architecture, Ann Arbor, MI 48109. Offers M Sc, PhD. Offered through the Horace H. Rackham School of Graduate Studies. Terminal master's awarded for partial completion of doctoral program. *Degree requirements:* For master's, thesis, research project; for doctorate, comprehensive exam, thesis/dissertation, oral defense of dissertation, preliminary exam, practicum. *Entrance requirements:* For master's and doctorate, GRE General Test. Additional exam requirements/recommendations for international students: Required—TOEFL (minimum score 560 paper-based; 220 computer-based; 84 iBT). Electronic applications accepted. *Expenses:* Contact institution. *Faculty research:* Environment and behavior, environmental technology, history-theory, design process and methods.

University of Michigan, A. Alfred Taubman College of Architecture and Urban Planning, Program in Architecture, Ann Arbor, MI 48109. Offers M Arch, M Sc, M Arch/M Eng, M Arch/MSE, M Arch/MUP, MBA/M Arch. *Entrance requirements:* For master's, GRE. Additional exam requirements/recommendations for international students: Required—TOEFL (minimum score 600 paper-based; 250 computer-based; 100 iBT). Electronic applications accepted. *Expenses:* Contact institution.

University of Minnesota, Twin Cities Campus, Graduate School, College of Design, School of Architecture, Minneapolis, MN 55455-0213. Offers architecture (M Arch); sustainable design (MS). First professional and post-professional tracks available in M Arch program. *Degree requirements:* For master's, thesis (for some programs). *Entrance requirements:* For master's, GRE General Test, suggested GPA of 3.0, portfolio. Additional exam requirements/recommendations for international students: Required—TOEFL (minimum score 550 paper-based; 213 computer-based; 79 iBT). *Expenses:* Contact institution. *Faculty research:* History, daylighting, computer-aided design, sustainable design, structures.

University of Missouri–Columbia, Graduate School, College of Human Environmental Science, Department of Architectural Studies, Columbia, MO 65211. Offers design with digital media (MA, MS); environmental design (MS). *Faculty:* 7 full-time (2 women). *Students:* 7 full-time (all women), 27 part-time (17 women); includes 2 minority (both African Americans), 9 international. Average age 37. 16 applicants, 44% accepted, 3 enrolled. In 2008, 2 master's awarded. *Entrance requirements:* For master's, GRE General Test, minimum GPA of 3.0. Additional exam requirements/recommendations for international students: Required—TOEFL (minimum score 500 paper-based; 173 computer-based; 61 iBT). *Application deadline:* For fall admission, 4/1 priority date for domestic students; for winter admission, 10/1 priority date for domestic students; for spring admission, 4/1 priority date for domestic students. Applications are processed on a rolling basis. Application fee: $45 ($60 for international students). *Financial support:* Research assistantships, teaching assistantships, institutionally sponsored loans available. *Unit head:* Dr. Ruth Brent Tofle, Department Chair, E-mail: brentr@missouri.edu. *Application contact:* Charles-Ryan Duncan, 573-882-7224, E-mail: duncancd@missouri.edu.

University of Nebraska–Lincoln, Graduate College, College of Architecture, Department of Architecture, Graduate Program in Architecture, Lincoln, NE 68588. Offers MS, PhD. *Students:* 2 full-time (1 woman), 5 part-time (all women); includes 1 minority (African American). In 2008, 2 master's awarded. *Degree requirements:* For master's, comprehensive exam, thesis. *Entrance requirements:* For master's, GRE General Test. Additional exam requirements/recommendations for international students: Required—TOEFL (minimum score 550 paper-based; 213 computer-based). *Application deadline:* For fall admission, 2/1 for domestic and international students. Application fee: $40. Electronic applications accepted. *Expenses:* Tuition, state resident: full-time $4275; part-time $237.50 per credit hour. Tuition, nonresident: full-time $11,525; part-time $640.25 per credit hour. Required fees: $1068; $10.35 per credit hour. $440.70 per semester. Tuition and fees vary according to course load and program. *Financial support:* Fellowships, research assistantships, teaching assistantships, Federal Work-Study and health care benefits available. Support available to part-time students. Financial award application deadline: 2/15. *Faculty research:* Housing, environmental design, architectural history, sustainable design, rural architecture. *Application contact:* Ginny Gross, Director of Graduate Admissions, 402-472-2878, Fax: 402-472-0589, E-mail: grad_admissions@unl.edu.

University of Nebraska–Lincoln, Graduate College, College of Architecture, Department of Architecture, Professional Program in Architecture, Lincoln, NE 68588. Offers M Arch, M Arch/MBA, M Arch/MCRP. *Students:* 65 full-time (23 women), 3 part-time (0 women); includes 4 minority (1 American Indian/Alaska Native, 2 Asian Americans or Pacific Islanders, 1 Hispanic American), 2 international. *Entrance requirements:* For master's, GRE General Test. Additional exam requirements/recommendations for international students: Required—TOEFL. *Application deadline:* For fall admission, 2/1 for domestic and international students. Application fee: $40. *Expenses:* Tuition, state resident: full-time $4275; part-time $237.50 per credit hour. Tuition, nonresident: full-time $11,525; part-time $640.25 per credit hour. Required fees: $1068; $10.35 per credit hour. $440.70 per semester. Tuition and fees vary according to course load and program. *Financial support:* Fellowships, research assistantships, teaching assistantships, health care benefits available. Financial award application deadline: 2/15. *Faculty research:* Housing, environmental design, architectural history, sustainable design, rural architecture. *Application contact:* Ginny Gross, Director of Graduate Admissions, 402-472-2878, Fax: 402-472-0589, E-mail: grad_admissions@unl.edu.

University of Nevada, Las Vegas, Graduate College, College of Fine Arts, School of Architecture, Las Vegas, NV 89154. Offers M Arch. Part-time programs available. *Faculty:* 10 full-time (1 woman), 3 part-time/adjunct (0 women). *Students:* 28 full-time (11 women), 11 part-time (4 women); includes 9 minority (1 American Indian/Alaska Native, 2 Asian Americans or Pacific Islanders, 6 Hispanic Americans), 3 international. Average age 30. 61 applicants, 48% accepted, 17 enrolled. In 2008, 11 master's awarded. *Degree requirements:* For master's, thesis (for some programs), professional project. *Entrance requirements:* For master's, GRE General Test (minimum score: 410 Verbal/430 Quantitative). Additional exam requirements/recommendations for international students: Required—TOEFL (minimum score 550 paper-based; 213 computer-based; 80 iBT), IELTS (minimum score 7). *Application deadline:* For fall admission, 2/1 priority date for domestic and international students. Applications are processed on a rolling basis. Application fee: $60 ($75 for international students). Electronic applications accepted. *Expenses:* Tuition, state resident: full-time $1414; part-time $198 per credit. Tuition, nonresident: full-time $12,509; part-time $415.75 per credit. International tuition: $14,249 full-time. Required fees: $4 per credit. $252 per semester. Tuition and fees vary according to course load. *Financial support:* In 2008–09, 11 students received support, including 6 research assistantships with partial tuition reimbursements available (averaging $12,500 per year), 5 teaching assistantships with partial tuition reimbursements available (averaging $12,500 per year); institutionally sponsored loans, scholarships/grants, health care benefits, and unspecified assistantships also available. Financial award application deadline: 3/1. *Faculty research:* Passive solar architecture and solar water distillation, urban design frameworks involving applications of IT tools to address issues of sustainable urban life, creative processes considered as leadership in project development, architecture of George Barber, design guidelines for educational facilities. *Unit head:* Dr. Attila Lawrence, Chair/Professor, 702-895-3031, Fax: 702-895-1119, E-mail: attila.lawrence@unlv.edu. *Application contact:* Graduate College Admissions Evaluator, 702-895-3320, Fax: 702-895-4180, E-mail: gradcollege@unlv.edu.

University of New Mexico, Graduate School, School of Architecture and Planning, Program in Architecture, Albuquerque, NM 87131-2039. Offers M Arch. *Degree requirements:* For master's, thesis (for some programs), graduate review. *Entrance requirements:* For master's, experience in field. Additional exam requirements/recommendations for international students: Required—TOEFL (minimum score 550 paper-based; 213 computer-based). *Faculty research:* Professional practice, design theory, sustainable environments, architecture and children, environment and behavior.

The University of North Carolina at Charlotte, Graduate School, College of Arts and Architecture, Charlotte, NC 28223-0001. Offers M Arch. *Faculty:* 46 full-time (16 women), 2 part-time/adjunct (both women). *Students:* 63 full-time (43 women), 4 part-time (3 women); includes 12 minority (6 African Americans, 5 Asian Americans or Pacific Islanders, 1 Hispanic American). Average age 27. 83 applicants, 61% accepted, 26 enrolled. In 2008, 17 master's awarded. *Degree requirements:* For master's, project or thesis. *Entrance requirements:* For master's, GRE General Test or MAT, resumé, portfolio. Additional exam requirements/recommendations for international students: Required—TOEFL (minimum score 557 paper-based; 220 computer-based). *Application deadline:* For fall admission, 2/15 for domestic students, 1/31 for international students. Application fee: $55. Electronic applications accepted. *Expenses:* Tuition, area resident: Full-time $2919; part-time $122 per credit hour. Tuition, state resident: full-time $2919; part-time $122 per credit hour. Tuition, nonresident: full-time $13,126; part-time $547 per credit hour. Required fees: $1779; $91 per credit hour. Tuition and fees vary according to program. *Financial support:* In 2008–09, 10 research assistantships (averaging

Architecture

The University of North Carolina at Charlotte (continued)
$7,925 per year), 20 teaching assistantships (averaging $6,620 per year) were awarded; career-related internships or fieldwork, Federal Work-Study, institutionally sponsored loans, scholarships/grants, unspecified assistantships, and 2 administrative assistantships ($9,032 average) also available. Support available to part-time students. Financial award application deadline: 4/1; financial award applicants required to submit FAFSA. *Faculty research:* Daylighting and energy control, urban design, history and theory, construction techniques. *Unit head:* Kenneth A. Lambla, Dean, 704-687-4841, Fax: 704-687-3353, E-mail: kalambla@email. uncc.edu. *Application contact:* Kathy B. Giddings, Director of Graduate Admissions, 704-687-3366, Fax: 704-687-3279, E-mail: agidding@uncc.edu.

The University of North Carolina at Greensboro, Graduate School, School of Human Environmental Sciences, Department of Interior Architecture, Greensboro, NC 27412-5001. Offers historic preservation (Certificate); interior architecture (MS); museum studies (Certificate). *Degree requirements:* For master's, thesis. *Entrance requirements:* For master's, GRE General Test or MAT, bachelor's degree in interior design, interview, portfolio. Additional exam requirements/recommendations for international students: Required—TOEFL. Electronic applications accepted.

University of Notre Dame, Graduate School, School of Architecture, Notre Dame, IN 46556. Offers architectural design and urbanism (M ADU); architecture (M Arch). *Faculty:* 20 full-time (2 women), 1 part-time/adjunct (0 women). *Students:* 46 full-time (17 women); includes 3 minority (1 African American, 2 Asian Americans or Pacific Islanders), 4 international. 84 applicants, 30% accepted, 16 enrolled. In 2008, 9 master's awarded. *Degree requirements:* For master's, thesis or alternative. *Entrance requirements:* For master's, GRE General Test, portfolio. Additional exam requirements/recommendations for international students: Required—TOEFL (minimum score 600 paper-based; 250 computer-based; 80 iBT). *Application deadline:* For fall admission, 2/1 priority date for domestic and international students. Application fee: $50. Electronic applications accepted. *Financial support:* Fellowships with full tuition reimbursements, research assistantships, teaching assistantships, institutionally sponsored loans and tuition waivers (full) available. Financial award application deadline: 2/1. *Faculty research:* Architectural theory, urban design, classical and traditional architecture and urbanism. *Unit head:* Prof. Philip Bess, Director of Graduate Studies, 574-631-2312. *Application contact:* Dr. Barbara Turpin, Director of Graduate Admissions, 574-631-7706, Fax: 574-631-4183.

University of Oklahoma, Graduate College, College of Architecture, Division of Architecture, Norman, OK 73019-0390. Offers M Arch. Part-time programs available. *Faculty:* 31 full-time (7 women), 1 (woman) part-time/adjunct. *Students:* 15 full-time (7 women), 12 part-time (2 women); includes 3 minority (1 African American, 1 American Indian/Alaska Native, 1 Asian American or Pacific Islander), 9 international. 23 applicants, 57% accepted, 7 enrolled. In 2008, 7 master's awarded. *Degree requirements:* For master's, thesis or alternative, portfolio, project. *Entrance requirements:* For master's, GRE General Test, portfolio. Additional exam requirements/recommendations for international students: Required—TOEFL (minimum score 550 paper-based; 213 computer-based). *Application deadline:* For fall admission, 4/1 for domestic and international students; for spring admission, 11/1 for domestic students, 9/1 for international students. Applications are processed on a rolling basis. Application fee: $40 ($90 for international students). Electronic applications accepted. *Expenses:* Tuition, state resident: full-time $3744; part-time $156 per credit hour. Tuition, nonresident: full-time $13,577; part-time $565.70 per credit hour. Required fees: $2415.40; $90.10 per credit hour. *Financial support:* In 2008–09, 7 students received support, including 5 teaching assistantships with partial tuition reimbursements available (averaging $9,586 per year); career-related internships or fieldwork, Federal Work-Study, scholarships/grants, tuition waivers (partial), and unspecified assistantships also available. Support available to part-time students. Financial award applicants required to submit FAFSA. *Faculty research:* Sustainability, regionalism, facilities management. Total annual research expenditures: $632,143. *Unit head:* Nickolas L. Harm, Interim Director, 405-325-2444, Fax: 405-325-7558, E-mail: nharm@ou.edu. *Application contact:* Terry Patterson, Professor/Graduate Liaison, 405-325-3869, Fax: 405-325-7558, E-mail: tpatterson@ou.edu.

University of Oklahoma, Graduate College, College of Architecture, Division of Construction Science, Norman, OK 73019-0390. Offers MS. Part-time and evening/weekend programs available. *Students:* 8 full-time (2 women), 20 part-time (3 women); includes 3 minority (1 African American, 1 American Indian/Alaska Native, 1 Hispanic American), 5 international. 19 applicants, 95% accepted, 13 enrolled. In 2008, 13 master's awarded. *Degree requirements:* For master's, thesis or alternative, portfolio, project. *Entrance requirements:* For master's, GRE General Test, portfolio. Additional exam requirements/recommendations for international students: Required—TOEFL (minimum score 600 paper-based; 250 computer-based). *Application deadline:* For fall admission, 4/1 for domestic and international students; for spring admission, 11/1 for domestic students, 9/1 for international students. Applications are processed on a rolling basis. Application fee: $40 ($90 for international students). Electronic applications accepted. *Expenses:* Tuition, state resident: full-time $3744; part-time $156 per credit hour. Tuition, nonresident: full-time $13,577; part-time $565.70 per credit hour. Required fees: $2415.40; $90.10 per credit hour. *Financial support:* In 2008–09, 10 students received support, including 2 research assistantships with partial tuition reimbursements available (averaging $11,543 per year), 2 teaching assistantships with partial tuition reimbursements available (averaging $9,586 per year); career-related internships or fieldwork, scholarships/grants, tuition waivers (partial), and unspecified assistantships also available. Support available to part-time students. Financial award applicants required to submit FAFSA. *Faculty research:* Online education, highway construction, lean construction, Hispanic construction worker design/safety, online instructional design. *Unit head:* Kenneth Robson, Director, 405-325-2444, Fax: 405-325-7558, E-mail: krobson@ou.edu. *Application contact:* Richard C. Ryan, Professor, 405-325-3976, Fax: 405-325-7558, E-mail: rryan@ou.edu.

University of Oregon, Graduate School, School of Architecture and Allied Arts, Department of Architecture, Eugene, OR 97403. Offers architecture (M Arch); interior architecture (MI Arch). *Accreditation:* CIDA. *Degree requirements:* For master's, thesis (for some programs). *Entrance requirements:* For master's, GRE General Test. Additional exam requirements/recommendations for international students: Required—TOEFL. *Faculty research:* Innovation in housing design and design production, climate responsive design, passive heating and cooling, computer software development for design applications, vernacular architecture.

University of Pennsylvania, School of Design, Graduate Group in Architecture, Philadelphia, PA 19104. Offers architecture (PhD); real estate design and development (PhD); urban design (PhD). Part-time programs available. *Degree requirements:* For doctorate, 2 foreign languages, comprehensive exam, thesis/dissertation, qualifying exam, final exam. *Entrance requirements:* For doctorate, GRE General Test, B Arch, M Arch, portfolio, writing sample. Additional exam requirements/recommendations for international students: Required—TOEFL. *Faculty research:* Theory, history, technology, representation, visualization, landscape, urban design, historic preservation.

See Close-Up on page 159.

University of Pennsylvania, School of Design, Master of Architecture Program, Philadelphia, PA 19104. Offers architecture (M Arch); real estate design and development (Certificate); urban design (Certificate). *Degree requirements:* For master's, thesis (for some programs). *Entrance requirements:* For master's and Certificate, GRE, portfolio. Additional exam requirements/recommendations for international students: Required—TOEFL. *Faculty research:* Computer modeling, metropolitan and regional urbanism, contemporary architectural theory structure and technology.

See Close-Up on page 159.

University of Puerto Rico, Río Piedras, School of Architecture, San Juan, PR 00931-3300. Offers M Arch. Part-time programs available. *Degree requirements:* For master's, comprehensive

exam, thesis, design project. *Entrance requirements:* For master's, PAEG or GRE, bachelor's degree in architecture, interview, minimum GPA of 3.0, portfolio, 2 letters of recommendation.

University of Southern California, Graduate School, School of Architecture, Program in Architecture, Los Angeles, CA 90089. Offers M Arch. *Entrance requirements:* For master's, GRE General Test.

University of Southern California, Graduate School, School of Architecture, Program in Historic Preservation, Los Angeles, CA 90089. Offers MHP. Part-time programs available. *Entrance requirements:* For master's, GRE.

University of South Florida, Graduate School, College of The Arts, School of Architecture and Community Design, Tampa, FL 33620-9951. Offers M Arch. *Faculty:* 8 full-time (1 woman), 9 part-time/adjunct (4 women). *Students:* 73 full-time (31 women), 43 part-time (17 women); includes 34 minority (7 African Americans, 2 American Indian/Alaska Native, 5 Asian Americans or Pacific Islanders, 20 Hispanic Americans), 3 international. Average age 30. 83 applicants, 39% accepted, 21 enrolled. In 2008, 35 master's awarded. *Degree requirements:* For master's, comprehensive exam, thesis. *Entrance requirements:* For master's, GRE General Test, minimum GPA of 3.0 in last 60 hours of coursework. Additional exam requirements/recommendations for international students: Required—TOEFL (minimum score 550 paper-based; 213 computer-based). *Application deadline:* For fall admission, 2/1 priority date for domestic students, 1/2 for international students. Applications are processed on a rolling basis. Application fee: $30. Electronic applications accepted. *Expenses:* Tuition, state resident: full-time $2624.40; part-time $291.60 per credit hour. Tuition, nonresident: full-time $7822; part-time $869.13 per credit hour. *Financial support:* Career-related internships or fieldwork, scholarships/grants, and unspecified assistantships available. *Faculty research:* Community design, sustainability, portable classrooms. Total annual research expenditures: $31,358. *Unit head:* Daniel Powers, Program Director, 813-974-6018, Fax: 813-974-2557, E-mail: powers@arch.usf.edu. *Application contact:* Mary Hayward, Program Director, 813-974-6003, Fax: 813-974-2557, E-mail: hayward@arch.usf.edu.

The University of Tennessee, Graduate School, College of Architecture and Design, Program in Architecture, Knoxville, TN 37996. Offers architecture (professional) (M Arch); architecture (research) (M Arch). *Degree requirements:* For master's, thesis. *Entrance requirements:* For master's, GRE General Test, completed application form, transcripts of undergraduate and/or graduate work, minimum GPA of 3.0, 3 letters of recommendation, samples of portfolio work (highly recommended for professional track). Additional exam requirements/recommendations for international students: Required—TOEFL (minimum score 550 paper-based). *Expenses:* Tuition, area resident: Part-time $348 per credit hour. Tuition, state resident: full-time $6262. Tuition, nonresident: full-time $18,920; part-time $1052 per credit hour. Required fees: $812; $36 per credit hour. Tuition and fees vary according to program.

The University of Texas at Arlington, Graduate School, School of Architecture, Program in Architecture, Arlington, TX 76019. Offers M Arch, M Arch/MCRP. *Students:* 112 full-time (38 women), 32 part-time (15 women); includes 38 minority (5 African Americans, 11 Asian Americans or Pacific Islanders, 22 Hispanic Americans), 13 international. 145 applicants, 66% accepted, 64 enrolled. In 2008, 44 master's awarded. *Entrance requirements:* For master's, GRE General Test (minimum score of 1000 for Verbal and Quantitative), minimum GPA of 3.0, portfolio, 3 letters of recommendation. Additional exam requirements/recommendations for international students: Required—TOEFL (minimum score 550 paper-based; 213 computer-based). *Application deadline:* For fall admission, 6/6 for domestic students, 4/4 for international students; for spring admission, 10/17 for domestic students, 9/5 for international students. Applications are processed on a rolling basis. Application fee: $35 ($60 for international students). Electronic applications accepted. *Expenses:* Tuition, area resident: Full-time $6500. Tuition, state resident: full-time $6500. Tuition, nonresident: full-time $11,558. *Financial support:* In 2008–09, 12 research assistantships with full and partial tuition reimbursements (averaging $4,824 per year), 16 teaching assistantships with full and partial tuition reimbursements (averaging $4,824 per year) were awarded; career-related internships or fieldwork, scholarships/grants, and unspecified assistantships also available. Financial award application deadline: 6/1; financial award applicants required to submit FAFSA. *Unit head:* Donald Gatzke, Director, 817-272-2801, Fax: 817-272-5098, E-mail: gatzke@uta.edu. *Application contact:* David Jones, Associate Dean, 817-272-2801, Fax: 817-272-5098, E-mail: djonesarch@uta.edu.

The University of Texas at Austin, Graduate School, School of Architecture, Austin, TX 78712-1111. Offers architecture (M Arch); community and regional planning (MSCRP, PhD); historic preservation (MS); history of architecture (MA, PhD); landscape architecture (MLA); urban design (MSUD); JD/MSCRP; MSCRP/MA; MSCRP/PhD. *Degree requirements:* For doctorate, thesis/dissertation. *Entrance requirements:* For master's and doctorate, GRE General Test. Additional exam requirements/recommendations for international students: Required—TOEFL (minimum score 550 paper-based; 213 computer-based). Electronic applications accepted.

The University of Texas at San Antonio, College of Architecture, San Antonio, TX 78249-0617. Offers architecture (M Arch, MS Arch); historical preservation (Graduate Certificate); urban and regional planning (Graduate Certificate). *Degree requirements:* For master's, comprehensive exam, thesis. *Entrance requirements:* For master's, GRE General Test, minimum GPA of 3.0 in last 60 hours and in all architecture courses. Additional exam requirements/recommendations for international students: Required—TOEFL (minimum score 500 paper-based; 173 computer-based). Electronic applications accepted.

University of Toronto, School of Graduate Studies, Social Sciences Division, Faculty of Architecture, Landscape and Design, Toronto, ON M5S 1A1, Canada. Offers M Arch, MLA, MUD. *Accreditation:* ASLA. *Entrance requirements:* For master's, minimum B average; 3 letters of reference; resumé; 3 writing samples; 5 samples of design work, drawing, or work in a related field. Additional exam requirements/recommendations for international students: Required—TOEFL (minimum score 580 paper-based; 237 computer-based), TWE (minimum score 5), Michigan English Language Assessment Battery (minimum score: 85), IELTS (minimum score: 7) or COPE (minimum score: 4). *Expenses:* Contact institution.

University of Utah, The Graduate School, College of Architecture and Planning, Salt Lake City, UT 84112-1107. Offers architectural studies (M Arch, MS); urban planning (MUP); M Arch/MBA. Part-time programs available. *Degree requirements:* For master's, thesis (for some programs), comprehensive project. *Entrance requirements:* For master's, minimum undergraduate GPA of 3.0. Additional exam requirements/recommendations for international students: Required—TOEFL (minimum score 500 paper-based; 173 computer-based). Electronic applications accepted. *Expenses:* Contact institution. *Faculty research:* History, design, acoustics, photography, structures, architecture of American West, architectural communication and representation, impact of technology.

University of Virginia, School of Architecture, Department of Architecture and Landscape Architecture, Charlottesville, VA 22903. Offers architecture (M Arch); landscape architecture (M Land Arch). *Faculty:* 25 full-time (10 women), 1 (woman) part-time/adjunct. *Students:* 105 full-time (67 women); includes 10 minority (2 African Americans, 6 Asian Americans or Pacific Islanders, 2 Hispanic Americans), 5 international. Average age 28. 549 applicants, 20% accepted, 28 enrolled. In 2008, 40 master's awarded. *Entrance requirements:* For master's, GRE General Test, 3 letters of recommendation, portfolio, essay. Additional exam requirements/recommendations for international students: Required—TOEFL (minimum score 600 paper-based; 250 computer-based; 90 iBT). *Application deadline:* For fall admission, 1/5 for domestic and international students. Applications are processed on a rolling basis. Application fee: $60. Electronic applications accepted. *Expenses:* Tuition, area resident: Full-time $10,452. Tuition, state resident: full-time $10,452. Tuition, nonresident: full-time $20,010. Required fees: $2176. Part-time tuition and fees vary according to course load and program. *Financial support:* Career-related internships or fieldwork, Federal Work-Study, and institutionally sponsored loans available. Financial award applicants required to submit FAFSA. *Unit head:* Craig

Barton, Chair, 434-924-1493, Fax: 434-982-2678, E-mail: ceb8x@virginia.edu. *Application contact:* Graduate Admissions Officer, 434-924-6442, E-mail: arch-admissions@virginia.edu.

University of Washington, Graduate School, College of Architecture and Urban Planning, Department of Architecture, Seattle, WA 98195. Offers architecture (M Arch, MS); built environment (PhD); design computing (Certificate); design firm leadership and management (Certificate); historic preservation (Certificate); lighting (Certificate); urban design (Certificate). *Degree requirements:* For master's, thesis. *Entrance requirements:* For master's, GRE General Test, minimum GPA of 3.0, portfolio, 3 letters of recommendation. Additional exam requirements/recommendations for international students: Required—TOEFL. *Faculty research:* Lighting, materials, computing theory, media, culture, environment.

University of Waterloo, Graduate Studies, Faculty of Engineering, School of Architecture, Waterloo, ON N2L 3G1, Canada. Offers M Arch. Part-time programs available. *Degree requirements:* For master's, thesis. *Entrance requirements:* For master's, bachelor's degree in pre-professional architecture. Electronic applications accepted.

University of Wisconsin–Milwaukee, Graduate School, School of Architecture and Urban Planning, Department of Architecture, Milwaukee, WI 53201-0413. Offers architecture (PhD); preservation studies (Certificate); M Arch/MUP. *Faculty:* 27 full-time (4 women). *Students:* 150 full-time (48 women), 11 part-time (7 women); includes 16 minority (4 African Americans, 1 American Indian/Alaska Native, 5 Asian Americans or Pacific Islanders, 6 Hispanic Americans), 13 international. Average age 28. 128 applicants, 62% accepted, 34 enrolled. In 2008, 22 master's, 3 doctorates awarded. *Degree requirements:* For master's, comprehensive exam, thesis; for doctorate, comprehensive exam, thesis/dissertation. *Entrance requirements:* For master's, GRE General Test, portfolio. Additional exam requirements/recommendations for international students: Required—TOEFL (minimum score 600 paper-based; 250 computer-based; 100 iBT), IELTS (minimum score 7). *Application deadline:* For fall admission, 1/1 priority date for domestic students; for spring admission, 9/1 for domestic students. Applications are processed on a rolling basis. Application fee: $45 ($75 for international students). *Expenses:* Tuition, area resident: Full-time $7320; part-time $165 per credit. Tuition, state resident: Full-time $7320; part-time $165 per credit. Tuition, nonresident: full-time $17,840; part-time $714 per credit. Tuition and fees vary according to campus/location, program and reciprocity agreements. *Financial support:* In 2008–09, 19 teaching assistantships were awarded; career-related internships or fieldwork and unspecified assistantships also available. Support available to part-time students. Financial award application deadline: 4/15. Total annual research expenditures: $150,000. *Unit head:* Joan Simuncak, Representative, 414-229-4015, Fax: 414-229-6976, E-mail: joanarch@uwm.edu. *Application contact:* Brian Schermer, General Information Contact, 414-229-3815, Fax: 414-229-6967, E-mail: bscherm@uwm.edu.

Virginia Polytechnic Institute and State University, Graduate School, College of Architecture and Urban Studies, School of Architecture and Design, Blacksburg, VA 24061. Offers architecture (M Arch, MS); architecture design research (PhD). *Accreditation:* NASAD. *Entrance requirements:*

For master's, GRE General Test. Additional exam requirements/recommendations for international students: Required—TOEFL (minimum score 550 paper-based; 213 computer-based). Electronic applications accepted. *Faculty research:* Computer applications in design, building technology, architectural design theory, solar/passive energy design, building assembly.

Washington State University, Graduate School, College of Engineering and Architecture, School of Architecture and Construction Management, Pullman, WA 99164. Offers architecture (M Arch); architecture design theory (MS). *Degree requirements:* For master's, comprehensive exam (for some programs), thesis, oral exam. *Entrance requirements:* For master's, GRE General Test, minimum GPA of 3.0, 3 letters of recommendation. Additional exam requirements/recommendations for international students: Required—TOEFL. *Faculty research:* Cultural, technological, and environmental design.

Washington State University Spokane, Graduate Programs, Interdisciplinary Design Institute, Spokane, WA 99210-1495. Offers architecture (M Arch, MS); design (Dr DES); interior design (MA); landscape architecture (MS). Part-time programs available. *Degree requirements:* For master's, comprehensive exam (for some programs), thesis (for some programs); for doctorate, comprehensive exam, thesis/dissertation. *Entrance requirements:* For master's, minimum GPA of 3.0, portfolio of design work, 3 letters of recommendation (M Arch); for doctorate, minimum graduate GPA of 3.5. Additional exam requirements/recommendations for international students: Required—TOEFL (minimum score 550 paper-based; 213 computer-based). *Faculty research:* Environment-behavior relationships, land use and environmental planning, urban space as interior design, art and architectural aesthetics.

Washington University in St. Louis, Sam Fox School of Design and Visual Arts, Graduate School of Architecture and Urban Design, Program in Architecture, St. Louis, MO 63130-4899. Offers M Arch, M Arch/MBA, M Arch/MCM, M Arch/MSW, M Arch/MUD. *Degree requirements:* For master's, final project. *Entrance requirements:* For master's, GRE General Test, portfolio. Additional exam requirements/recommendations for international students: Required—TOEFL (minimum score 550 paper-based; 213 computer-based; 80 iBT), TWE. *Faculty research:* Urban design development issues.

See Close-Up on page 161.

Woodbury University, School of Architecture, Burbank, CA 91504-1099. Offers real estate development (M Arch). *Degree requirements:* For master's, thesis. *Entrance requirements:* For master's, 3 letters of recommendation, portfolio. Additional exam requirements/recommendations for international students: Required—TOEFL (minimum score 550 paper-based; 213 computer-based), IELTS (minimum score 7). *Expenses:* Contact institution.

Yale University, School of Architecture, New Haven, CT 06520. Offers M Arch, M Env Des, MEM, M Arch/M Env Des, M Arch/MBA. *Entrance requirements:* For master's, GRE General Test, design portfolio. Additional exam requirements/recommendations for international students: Required—TOEFL. *Expenses:* Contact institution.

Building Science

Arizona State University, Graduate College, College of Design, School of Architecture and Landscape Architecture, Tempe, AZ 85287. Offers architecture (M Arch); building design (MS); landscape architecture (MLA); urban design (MUD); MA/MBA. *Degree requirements:* For master's, thesis optional. *Entrance requirements:* For master's, GRE General Test, design portfolio.

Auburn University, Graduate School, College of Architecture, Design, and Construction, Department of Building Science, Auburn University, AL 36849. Offers building science (MBS); construction management (MBS). *Faculty:* 20 full-time (1 woman), 1 part-time/adjunct (0 women). *Students:* 22 full-time (4 women), 1 part-time (0 women); includes 1 minority (Asian American or Pacific Islander), 1 international. Average age 26. 13 applicants, 46% accepted, 4 enrolled. In 2008, 10 master's awarded. *Entrance requirements:* For master's, GRE General Test. *Application deadline:* For fall admission, 7/17 for domestic students; for spring admission, 11/24 for domestic students. Applications are processed on a rolling basis. Application fee: $25 ($50 for international students). Electronic applications accepted. *Expenses:* Tuition, area resident: Full-time $5880; part-time $243 per credit hour. Tuition, state resident: full-time $5880; part-time $243 per credit hour. Tuition, nonresident: full-time $17,640; part-time $729 per credit hour. International tuition: $17,846 full-time. Required fees: $620. Tuition and fees vary according to program and reciprocity agreements. *Financial support:* Application deadline: 3/15. *Unit head:* John D. Murphy, Head, 334-844-4518. *Application contact:* Dr. George Flowers, Dean of the Graduate School, 334-844-2125.

Auburn University, Graduate School, College of Architecture, Design, and Construction, Program in Design-Build, Auburn University, AL 36849. Offers MDB. *Faculty:* 10 full-time (1 woman). *Students:* 11 full-time (5 women); includes 1 African American. Average age 26. In 2008, 1 master's awarded. *Expenses:* Tuition, area resident: Full-time $5880; part-time $243 per credit hour. Tuition, state resident: full-time $5880; part-time $243 per credit hour. Tuition, nonresident: full-time $17,640; part-time $729 per credit hour. International tuition: $17,846 full-time. Required fees: $620. Tuition and fees vary according to program and reciprocity agreements. *Unit head:* Dan D. Bennett, Dean, 334-844-4524. *Application contact:* Dr. George Flowers, Dean of the Graduate School, 334-844-2125.

Carnegie Mellon University, College of Fine Arts, School of Architecture, Pittsburgh, PA 15213-3891. Offers architectural engineering construction management (M Sc); architecture (MSA); architecture, engineering, and construction management (PhD); building performance and diagnostics (M Sc, PhD); computational design (M Sc, PhD); sustainable design (M Sc); urban design (M Sc). Terminal master's awarded for partial completion of doctoral program. *Degree requirements:* For doctorate, thesis/dissertation. *Entrance requirements:* For master's and doctorate, GRE General Test. Additional exam requirements/recommendations for international students: Required—TOEFL.

Cornell University, Graduate School, Graduate Fields of Architecture, Art and Planning, Field of Architecture, Ithaca, NY 14853-0001. Offers architectural design (M Arch); architectural science (MS); building technology and environmental science (MS); computer graphics (MS); history of architecture (MA, PhD); history of urban development (MA, PhD); theory and criticism of architecture (M Arch); urban design (M Arch). *Faculty:* 28 full-time (6 women). *Students:* 93 full-time (40 women); includes 13 minority (2 African Americans, 6 Asian Americans or Pacific Islanders, 5 Hispanic Americans), 36 international. Average age 29. 488 applicants, 18% accepted, 53 enrolled. In 2008, 6 master's awarded. *Degree requirements:* For master's, one foreign language, thesis (MA, MS); for doctorate, 2 foreign languages, comprehensive exam, thesis/dissertation. *Entrance requirements:* For master's, GRE General Test, 5-year bachelor's degree in architecture, portfolio (M Arch), 3 letters of recommendation; for doctorate, GRE General Test, 3 letters of recommendation. Additional exam requirements/recommendations for international students: Required—TOEFL (minimum score 600 paper-based; 250 computer-based; 77 iBT). *Application deadline:* For fall admission, 1/15 priority date for domestic students. Application fee: $70. Electronic applications accepted. *Expenses:* Tuition: Full-time $29,500. Required fees: $70. Full-time tuition and fees vary according to degree level, program and student level. *Financial support:* In 2008–09, 16 students received support, including 8 fellowships with full tuition reimbursements available, 1 research assistantship with full tuition reimbursement available, 7 teaching assistantships with full tuition reimbursements available; institutionally sponsored loans, scholarships/grants, health care benefits, tuition waivers (full and partial), and unspecified assistantships also available. Financial award applicants required to submit FAFSA. *Faculty research:* Architectural design and urban design, theory and criticism of architecture, computer graphics, building technology and environmental science, history of architecture and history of urban-development. *Unit head:* Director of Graduate Studies, 607-255-6701, Fax: 607-255-0291. *Application contact:* Graduate Field Assistant, 607-255-6701, Fax: 607-255-0291, E-mail: cuarch@cornell.edu.

Georgia Institute of Technology, Graduate Studies and Research, College of Architecture, Program in Building Construction, Atlanta, GA 30332-0001. Offers building construction (PhD); integrated facility management (MS); integrated project delivery systems (MS); residential construction development (MS). Part-time and evening/weekend programs available. *Entrance requirements:* For master's and doctorate, GRE or GMAT. Additional exam requirements/recommendations for international students: Required—TOEFL (minimum score 550 paper-based; 213 computer-based). Electronic applications accepted. *Faculty research:* Design-build, mold, indoor air quality, real estate.

University of California, Berkeley, Graduate Division, College of Environmental Design, Department of Architecture, Berkeley, CA 94720-1500. Offers architecture (M Arch); building science (MS, PhD); building structures, construction and materials (MS, PhD); design (MA); design theories, methods, and practices (MS, PhD); environmental design in developing countries (MS, PhD); history of architecture and urbanism (MS, PhD); social and cultural processes in architecture and urbanism (MS, PhD); M Arch/MCP; M Arch/MS; MLA/M Arch. *Degree requirements:* For master's, thesis; for doctorate, thesis/dissertation, qualifying exam. *Entrance requirements:* For master's and doctorate, GRE General Test, minimum GPA of 3.0, 3 letters of recommendation. Additional exam requirements/recommendations for international students: Required—TOEFL. Electronic applications accepted.

University of Florida, Graduate School, College of Design, Construction and Planning, M. E. Rinker, Sr. School of Building Construction, Gainesville, FL 32611. Offers MBC, MICM, MSBC, PhD. Part-time programs available. *Degree requirements:* For master's, thesis. *Entrance requirements:* For master's, GRE General Test, minimum GPA of 3.0. Additional exam requirements/recommendations for international students: Required—TOEFL. Electronic applications accepted. *Faculty research:* Safety, affordable housing, construction management, environmental issues, sustainable construction.

University of Southern California, Graduate School, School of Architecture, Program in Building Science, Los Angeles, CA 90089. Offers MBS. Part-time programs available. *Entrance requirements:* For master's, GRE General Test.

University of Southern California, Graduate School, School of Architecture, Program in Historic Preservation, Los Angeles, CA 90089. Offers MHP. Part-time programs available. *Entrance requirements:* For master's, GRE.

Environmental Design

Arizona State University, Graduate College, College of Design, Program in Environmental Design and Planning, Tempe, AZ 85287. Offers design (PhD); history, theory, and criticism (PhD); planning (PhD). *Degree requirements:* For doctorate, thesis/dissertation.

Art Center College of Design, Graduate Division, Industrial Design Department, Pasadena, CA 91103-1999. Offers environmental design (MS); product design (MS). *Accreditation:* NASAD. *Degree requirements:* For master's, thesis, studio project. *Entrance requirements:* For master's, portfolio. Additional exam requirements/recommendations for international students: Required—TOEFL (minimum score 600 paper-based; 250 computer-based; 100 iBT).

See Close-Up on page 115.

Clemson University, Graduate School, College of Architecture, Arts, and Humanities, Department of Planning and Landscape Architecture, Program in Environmental Design and Planning, Clemson, SC 29634. Offers PhD. *Students:* 15 full-time (2 women), 4 part-time (1 woman); includes 1 minority (African American), 5 international. Average age 37. 17 applicants, 47% accepted, 6 enrolled. *Entrance requirements:* For doctorate, GRE. Additional exam requirements/recommendations for international students: Required—TOEFL. *Application deadline:* For fall admission, 4/15 for international students; for spring admission, 9/15 for international students. Applications are processed on a rolling basis. Application fee: $55. Full-time tuition and fees vary according to program. *Unit head:* Roger Liska, Interim Director, 864-656-3878, E-mail: riggor@clemson.edu. *Application contact:* Mickey Lauria, Concentration Coordinator, 864-656-0520, E-mail: mlauria@clemson.edu.

Columbia University, School of Continuing Education, Program in Landscape Design, New York, NY 10027. Offers MS. Part-time programs available. *Degree requirements:* For master's, 36 credits. *Entrance requirements:* For master's, BA/BS with minimum GPA of 3.0. Additional exam requirements/recommendations for international students: Required—American Language Program (ALP) placement test.

Cornell University, Graduate School, Graduate Fields of Human Ecology, Field of Design and Environmental Analysis, Ithaca, NY 14853-0001. Offers applied research in human-environment relations (MS); facilities planning and management (MS); housing and design (MS); human factors and ergonomics (MS); human-environment relations (MS); interior design (MA, MPS). *Faculty:* 14 full-time (6 women). *Students:* 22 full-time (20 women); includes 5 minority (1 American Indian/Alaska Native, 2 Asian Americans or Pacific Islanders, 2 Hispanic Americans), 4 international. Average age 27. 39 applicants, 56% accepted, 11 enrolled. In 2008, 12 master's awarded. *Degree requirements:* For master's, thesis. *Entrance requirements:* For master's, GRE General Test, portfolio or slides of recent work; bachelor's degree in interior design, architecture or related design discipline; 2 letters of recommendation. Additional exam requirements/recommendations for international students: Required—TOEFL (minimum score 600 paper-based; 250 computer-based; 105 iBT). *Application deadline:* For fall admission, 2/1 priority date for domestic students. Application fee: $70. Electronic applications accepted. *Expenses:* Tuition: Full-time $29,500. Required fees: $70. Full-time tuition and fees vary according to degree level, program and student level. *Financial support:* In 2008–09, 13 students received support, including 2 fellowships with full tuition reimbursements available, 11 teaching assistantships with full tuition reimbursements available; research assistantships with full tuition reimbursements available, institutionally sponsored loans, scholarships/grants, health care benefits, tuition waivers (full and partial), and unspecified assistantships also available. Financial award applicants required to submit FAFSA. *Faculty research:* Facility planning and management, environmental psychology, housing, interior design, ergonomics and human factors. *Unit head:* Director of Graduate Studies, 607-255-2168, Fax: 607-255-0305. *Application contact:* Graduate Field Assistant, 607-255-2168, Fax: 607-255-0305, E-mail: deagrad@cornell.edu.

Florida Atlantic University, College of Architecture, Urban and Public Affairs, School of Urban and Regional Planning, Boca Raton, FL 33431-0991. Offers economic development and tourism (Certificate); environmental planning (Certificate); sustainable community planning (Certificate); urban and regional planning (MURP); visual planning technology (Certificate). *Accreditation:* ACSP. Part-time and evening/weekend programs available. *Faculty:* 8 full-time (6 women), 1 (woman) part-time/adjunct. *Students:* 21 full-time (12 women), 11 part-time (5 women); includes 15 minority (5 African Americans, 10 Hispanic Americans), 1 international. Average age 33. 47 applicants, 47% accepted, 8 enrolled. In 2008, 12 master's awarded. *Entrance requirements:* For master's, GRE General Test, minimum GPA of 3.0. Additional exam requirements/recommendations for international students: Required—TOEFL. *Application deadline:* For fall admission, 7/1 priority date for domestic students, 2/15 for international students; for spring admission, 11/1 priority date for domestic students, 7/15 for international students. Applications are processed on a rolling basis. Application fee: $30. *Expenses:* Tuition, state resident: full-time $4867; part-time $270.40 per credit hour. Tuition, nonresident: full-time $16,486; part-time $915.87 per credit hour. *Financial support:* Fellowships with full tuition reimbursements, research assistantships, career-related internships or fieldwork, Federal Work-Study, institutionally sponsored loans, and tuition waivers (partial) available. Financial award application deadline: 4/1. *Faculty research:* Growth management, urban design, computer applications/geographical information systems, environmental planning. *Unit head:* Dr. Jaap Vos, Chair, 954-762-5653, Fax: 954-762-5673, E-mail: jvos@fau.edu. *Application contact:* Dr. Jaap Vos, Chair, 954-762-5653, Fax: 954-762-5673, E-mail: jvos@fau.edu.

Michigan State University, The Graduate School, College of Agriculture and Natural Resources and College of Social Science, School of Planning, Design and Construction, East Lansing, MI 48824. Offers construction management (MS, PhD); environmental design (MA); interior design and facilities management (MA); international planning studies (MIPS); urban and regional planning (MURP). *Degree requirements:* For master's, thesis or alternative. *Entrance requirements:* Additional exam requirements/recommendations for international students: Required—TOEFL. Electronic applications accepted.

San Diego State University, Graduate and Research Affairs, College of Professional Studies and Fine Arts, School of Art, Design and Art History, San Diego, CA 92182. Offers art history (MA); studio arts (MA, MFA), including applied design, environmental design, graphic design, interior design, painting and printmaking, sculpture. *Accreditation:* NASAD (one or more programs are accredited). *Degree requirements:* For master's, variable foreign language requirement, thesis. *Entrance requirements:* For master's, GRE General Test, bachelor's degree in related field, slide portfolio, typed slide information sheet, 2 letters of recommendation. Additional exam requirements/recommendations for international students: Required—TOEFL. Electronic applications accepted.

Texas Tech University, Graduate School, College of Human Sciences, Department of Design, Lubbock, TX 79409. Offers interior and environmental design (MS, PhD). *Faculty:* 4 full-time (2 women). *Students:* 10 full-time (8 women), 8 part-time (6 women); includes 3 minority (2 Asian Americans or Pacific Islanders, 1 Hispanic American), 3 international. Average age 33. 23 applicants, 87% accepted, 9 enrolled. In 2008, 4 master's, 1 doctorate awarded. *Degree requirements:* For master's, thesis or alternative; for doctorate, thesis/dissertation. *Entrance requirements:* For master's and doctorate, GRE. Application fee: $50 ($60 for international students). *Expenses:* Tuition, area resident: Part-time $194 per credit hour. Tuition, state resident: full-time $4648; part-time $194 per credit hour. Tuition, nonresident: full-time $11,392; part-time $475 per credit hour. Required fees: $2206; $69 per credit hour. $389 per semester. *Financial support:* In 2008–09, 24 students received support; research assistantships, teaching assistantships available. Financial award application deadline: 4/15. *Faculty research:* Meanings in the built environment, influence of technology on pedagogic environments, interior design components, computer usage in interior design, design and evaluation of physical environments for the elderly and physically and mentally challenged. Total annual research expenditures: $43,671. *Unit head:* Dr. Cherif M. Amor, Interim Chair, 806-742-3050, Fax: 806-742-1639, E-mail: cherif.amor@ttu.edu. *Application contact:* Dr. JoAnn Shroyer, Graduate Programs Director, 806-742-3050 Ext. 228, Fax: 806-742-1639, E-mail: joann.shroyer@ttu.edu.

Université de Montréal, Faculty of Environmental Design and Planning, Montréal, QC H3C 3J7, Canada. Offers M Sc A, M Urb, PhD, DESS. *Accreditation:* ACSP. *Faculty:* 39 full-time (11 women), 27 part-time/adjunct (7 women). *Students:* 279 full-time (148 women), 179 part-time (100 women). 484 applicants, 36% accepted, 150 enrolled. In 2008, 122 master's, 8 doctorates, 15 other advanced degrees awarded. *Degree requirements:* For doctorate, thesis/dissertation, general exam. *Application deadline:* For fall admission, 2/1 priority date for domestic students; for winter admission, 11/1 priority date for domestic students; for spring admission, 2/1 priority date for domestic students. Application fee: $100. Electronic applications accepted. *Expenses:* Contact institution. *Faculty research:* Wayfinding, environmental evaluation, housing studies, urban design, urban and regional planning. *Unit head:* Giovanni de Paoli, Dean, 514-343-6001, Fax: 514-343-2183, E-mail: giovanni.de.paoli@umontreal.ca. *Application contact:* Tilu Poldma, Associate Dean Graduate Studies, 514-343-2125, Fax: 514-343-2183, E-mail: tilu.poldma@umontreal.ca.

University of Calgary, Faculty of Graduate Studies, Faculty of Environmental Design, Calgary, AB T2N 1N4, Canada. Offers architecture (M Arch); environmental design (M Env Des, PhD). *Degree requirements:* For master's, thesis; for doctorate, thesis/dissertation. *Entrance requirements:* For master's, minimum GPA of 3.0; for doctorate, minimum GPA of 3.5. Additional exam requirements/recommendations for international students: Required—TOEFL (minimum score 550 paper-based; 213 computer-based). *Faculty research:* Sustainable development in architecture, planning and product design, energy and environment, impact assessment, ecotourism.

University of California, Berkeley, Graduate Division, College of Environmental Design, Department of Architecture, Program in Design, Berkeley, CA 94720-1500. Offers MA. *Degree requirements:* For master's, thesis. *Entrance requirements:* For master's, GRE General Test, minimum GPA of 3.0, portfolio, 3 letters of recommendation. Additional exam requirements/recommendations for international students: Required—TOEFL.

University of California, Berkeley, Graduate Division, College of Environmental Design, Department of Landscape Architecture and Environmental Planning, Program in Landscape Architecture, Berkeley, CA 94720-1500. Offers environmental planning (MLA); landscape design and site planning (MLA); urban and community design (MLA); MLA/M Arch; MLA/MCP. *Accreditation:* ASLA. *Degree requirements:* For master's, professional project or thesis. *Entrance requirements:* For master's, GRE General Test, minimum GPA of 3.0, portfolio, 3 letters of recommendation.

University of Georgia, Graduate School, College of Environment and Design, Athens, GA 30602. Offers MHP, MLA.

University of Missouri–Columbia, Graduate School, College of Human Environmental Science, Department of Architectural Studies, Columbia, MO 65211. Offers design with digital media (MA, MS); environmental design (MS). *Faculty:* 7 full-time (2 women). *Students:* 7 full-time (all women), 27 part-time (17 women); includes 2 minority (both African Americans), 9 international. Average age 37. 16 applicants, 44% accepted, 3 enrolled. In 2008, 2 master's awarded. *Entrance requirements:* For master's, GRE General Test, minimum GPA of 3.0. Additional exam requirements/recommendations for international students: Required—TOEFL (minimum score 500 paper-based; 173 computer-based; 61 iBT). *Application deadline:* For fall admission, 4/1 priority date for domestic students; for winter admission, 10/1 priority date for domestic students; for spring admission, 4/1 priority date for domestic students. Applications are processed on a rolling basis. Application fee: $45 ($60 for international students). *Financial support:* Research assistantships, teaching assistantships, institutionally sponsored loans available. *Unit head:* Dr. Ruth Brent Tofle, Department Chair, E-mail: brentr@missouri.edu. *Application contact:* Charles-Ryan Duncan, 573-882-7224, E-mail: duncancd@missouri.edu.

Virginia Polytechnic Institute and State University, Graduate School, College of Architecture and Urban Studies, Program in Environmental Design and Planning, Blacksburg, VA 24061. Offers PhD. *Entrance requirements:* For doctorate, GRE General Test. Additional exam requirements/recommendations for international students: Required—TOEFL (minimum score 550 paper-based; 213 computer-based). Electronic applications accepted. *Faculty research:* Urban studies, architecture, landscape planning.

Yale University, School of Architecture, New Haven, CT 06520. Offers M Arch, M Env Des, MEM, M Arch/M Env Des, M Arch/MBA. *Entrance requirements:* For master's, GRE General Test, design portfolio. Additional exam requirements/recommendations for international students: Required—TOEFL. *Expenses:* Contact institution.

Historic Preservation

Arkansas State University, Graduate School, College of Humanities and Social Sciences, Heritage Studies Program, Jonesboro, State University, AR 72467. Offers MA, PhD. Part-time programs available. *Faculty:* 2 full-time (1 woman), 2 part-time/adjunct (1 woman). *Students:* 15 full-time (11 women), 28 part-time (15 women); includes 8 minority (all African Americans), 3 international. Average age 41. 7 applicants, 71% accepted, 3 enrolled. In 2008, 3 master's awarded. *Degree requirements:* For master's, comprehensive exam, thesis or alternative; for doctorate, comprehensive exam, thesis/dissertation. *Entrance requirements:* For master's, GRE, MAT or GMAT, appropriate bachelor's degree, letters of reference, official transcript; for doctorate, GRE, MAT, or GMAT, appropriate master's degree, interview, letters of reference, official transcript, letter of interest, writing sample. Additional exam requirements/ recommendations for international students: Required—TOEFL (minimum score 550 paper-based; 213 computer-based; 79 iBT), IELTS (minimum score 6). *Application deadline:* Applications are processed on a rolling basis. Application fee: $50. Electronic applications accepted. *Expenses:* Tuition, state resident: full-time $3744; part-time $208 per credit hour. Tuition, nonresident: full-time $9540; part-time $530 per credit hour. International tuition: $7938 full-time. Required fees: $896; $47 per credit hour. $25 per term. One-time fee: $50. Tuition and fees vary according to course load and program. *Financial support:* In 2008–09, 14 students received support; fellowships, teaching assistantships, career-related internships or fieldwork, scholarships/grants; tuition waivers (partial), and unspecified assistantships available. Financial award application deadline: 7/1; financial award applicants required to submit FAFSA.

Unit head: Dr. Clyde Milner, Director, 870-972-3509, Fax: 870-972-3207, E-mail: cmilner@astate.edu. *Application contact:* Dr. Andrew Sustich, Dean of the Graduate School, 870-972-3029, Fax: 870-972-3857, E-mail: sustich@astate.edu.

Ball State University, Graduate School, College of Architecture and Planning, Department of Architecture, Program in Historic Preservation, Muncie, IN 47306-1099. Offers M Arch, MS. *Degree requirements:* For master's, thesis. *Entrance requirements:* For master's, minimum undergraduate B average, portfolio, writing sample.

Boston University, Graduate School of Arts and Sciences, Program in Preservation Studies, Boston, MA 02215. Offers MA, JD/MA. *Degree requirements:* For master's, one foreign language, thesis or alternative, internship. *Entrance requirements:* For master's, GRE General Test, scholarly writing sample, 3 letters of recommendation. Additional exam requirements/recommendations for international students: Required—TOEFL (minimum score 550 paper-based; 213 computer-based).

Buffalo State College, State University of New York, Graduate Studies and Research, Faculty of Arts and Humanities, Department of Art Conservation, Buffalo, NY 14222-1095. Offers art conservation (CAS); conservation of historic works and art works (MA). *Degree requirements:* For master's, final oral exam; for CAS, internship. *Entrance requirements:* For master's, GRE General Test, minimum GPA of 2.8. Additional exam requirements/recommendations for international students: Required—TOEFL (minimum score 550 paper-based; 213 computer-based). *Faculty research:* Mechanics of deterioration of art, conservation of materials.

Clemson University, Graduate School, College of Architecture, Arts, and Humanities, Department of Planning and Landscape Architecture, Program in Historic Preservation, Clemson, SC 29634. Offers MS. *Students:* 21 full-time (17 women), 2 part-time (both women); includes 1 minority (Hispanic American). Average age 25. 23 applicants, 17% accepted, 3 enrolled. In 2008, 9 master's awarded. *Entrance requirements:* For master's, GRE General Test. *Application deadline:* For fall admission, 4/15 for international students; for spring admission, 9/15 for international students. Application fee: $55. Full-time tuition and fees vary according to program. *Unit head:* Ashley Robbins, Interim Director of the Graduate Program in Historic Preservation, 864-937-9596, E-mail: arobbin@CLEMSON.EDU. *Application contact:* Dr. Terry Farris, Coordinator, 864-656-3903, Fax: 864-656-0204, E-mail: jfarris@clemson.edu.

College of Charleston, Graduate School, School of the Arts, Program in Historic Preservation, Charleston, SC 29424-0001. Offers MS. *Faculty:* 7 full-time (1 woman). *Students:* 10 full-time (8 women). Average age 26. *Entrance requirements:* For master's, GRE. Additional exam requirements/recommendations for international students: Required—TOEFL. Electronic applications accepted. *Expenses:* Tuition, area resident: Full-time $6624; part-time $368 per credit hour. Tuition, state resident: full-time $6624; part-time $368 per credit hour. Tuition, nonresident: full-time $16,074; part-time $893 per credit hour. Required fees: $30; $30 per course. One-time fee: $45. *Financial support:* Scholarships/grants available. Financial award applicants required to submit FAFSA. *Unit head:* Dr. Robert Russell, Director, 843-953-6352, E-mail: russellr@cofc.edu. *Application contact:* Susan Hallatt, Director of Graduate Admissions, 843-953-5614, Fax: 843-953-1434, E-mail: hallatts@cofc.edu.

Columbia University, Graduate School of Architecture, Planning, and Preservation, Program in Historic Preservation, New York, NY 10027. Offers MS, Certificate, M Arch/MS, MS/MS. *Degree requirements:* For master's, thesis. *Entrance requirements:* For master's, GRE General Test.

Cornell University, Graduate School, Graduate Fields of Architecture, Art and Planning, Field of City and Regional Planning, Ithaca, NY 14853-0001. Offers city and regional planning (MRP, PhD); environmental planning and design (MRP, PhD); historic preservation planning (MA); international development planning (MRP, PhD); planning theory and systems analysis (MRP, PhD); regional economics and development planning (MRP, PhD); regional science (MRP, PhD); social and health systems planning (MRP, PhD); urban and regional theory (MRP, PhD); urban planning history (MRP, PhD). *Accreditation:* ACSP (one or more programs are accredited). *Faculty:* 27 full-time (10 women). *Students:* 113 full-time (71 women); includes 13 minority (3 African Americans, 6 Asian Americans or Pacific Islanders, 4 Hispanic Americans), 26 international. Average age 30. 268 applicants, 47% accepted, 46 enrolled. In 2008, 23 master's, 5 doctorates awarded. *Degree requirements:* For master's, thesis (MA); for doctorate, comprehensive exam, thesis/dissertation. *Entrance requirements:* For master's and doctorate, GRE General Test, 2 letters of recommendation. Additional exam requirements/recommendations for international students: Required—TOEFL (minimum score 600 paper-based; 250 computer-based; 77 iBT). *Application deadline:* For fall admission, 1/10 for domestic students. Application fee: $70. Electronic applications accepted. *Expenses:* Tuition: Full-time $29,500. Required fees: $70. Full-time tuition and fees vary according to degree level, program and student level. *Financial support:* In 2008–09, 24 students received support, including 9 fellowships with full tuition reimbursements available, 5 research assistantships with full tuition reimbursements available, 10 teaching assistantships with full tuition reimbursements available; institutionally sponsored loans, scholarships/grants, health care benefits, tuition waivers (full and partial), and unspecified assistantships also available. Financial award applicants required to submit FAFSA. *Faculty research:* Land use planning, economic development, international development, historic preservation, community development. *Unit head:* Director of Graduate Studies, 607-255-6848, Fax: 607-255-1971. *Application contact:* Graduate Field Assistant, 607-255-6848, Fax: 607-255-1971, E-mail: crp_admissions@cornell.edu.

Delaware State University, Graduate Programs, Department of History, Philosophy and Political Sciences, Dover, DE 19901-2277. Offers historic preservation (MA). *Entrance requirements:* Additional exam requirements/recommendations for international students: Required—TOEFL (minimum score 550 paper-based). Electronic applications accepted.

Eastern Michigan University, Graduate School, College of Arts and Sciences, Department of Geography and Geology, Program in Historic Preservation, Ypsilanti, MI 48197. Offers heritage interpretation and tourism (MS); historic preservation (MS, Graduate Certificate). Part-time and evening/weekend programs available. Postbaccalaureate distance learning degree programs offered (minimal on-campus study). *Entrance requirements:* Additional exam requirements/recommendations for international students: Required—TOEFL.

The George Washington University, Columbian College of Arts and Sciences, Department of American Studies, Concentration in Historic Preservation, Washington, DC 20052. Offers MA. Evening/weekend programs available. In 2008, 4 master's awarded. *Degree requirements:* For master's, comprehensive exam, thesis. *Entrance requirements:* For master's, GRE General Test, minimum GPA of 3.0. *Application deadline:* For fall admission, 4/1 priority date for domestic and international students; for spring admission, 10/1 priority date for domestic and international students. Application fee: $60. *Financial support:* Fellowships, teaching assistantships, career-related internships or fieldwork, Federal Work-Study, and institutionally sponsored loans available. Financial award application deadline: 2/1. *Unit head:* Richard Longstreth, Director, 202-994-6070. *Application contact:* Information Contact, 202-994-6070, Fax: 202-994-8651, E-mail: amst@gwu.edu.

Georgia State University, College of Arts and Sciences, Department of History, Program in Heritage Preservation, Atlanta, GA 30303-3083. Offers MHP, Certificate. Part-time and evening/weekend programs available. *Degree requirements:* For master's, exam, internship or thesis. *Entrance requirements:* For master's, GRE General Test, minimum GPA of 3.0. Additional exam requirements/recommendations for international students: Required—TOEFL. Electronic applications accepted. *Faculty research:* Historic preservation, local history, public history, museum studies.

Goucher College, Historic Preservation Program, Baltimore, MD 21204-2794. Offers MA. Part-time and evening/weekend programs available. Postbaccalaureate distance learning degree programs offered (minimal on-campus study). *Degree requirements:* For master's, thesis.

Entrance requirements: For master's, 2 years of post-baccalaureate work or volunteer experience. *Expenses:* Contact institution.

Kent State University, College of Architecture and Environmental Design, Kent, OH 44242-0001. Offers architecture (M Arch); preservation architecture (Certificate); urban design (M Arch, MUD, Certificate). Part-time programs available. *Degree requirements:* For master's, thesis optional. *Entrance requirements:* For master's, GRE, portfolio, minimum GPA of 2.75, 3 letters of reference, resumé, undergraduate architecture degree. Additional exam requirements/recommendations for international students: Required—TOEFL (minimum score 550 paper-based). Electronic applications accepted. *Faculty research:* History and theory, building technology, landscape architecture and urbanism, urbanism, sustainable development.

Michigan Technological University, Graduate School, College of Sciences and Arts, Department of Social Sciences, Program in Industrial Heritage and Archeology, Houghton, MI 49931-1295. Offers PhD. Part-time programs available. *Degree requirements:* For doctorate, comprehensive exam, thesis/dissertation. *Entrance requirements:* Additional exam requirements/recommendations for international students: Required—TOEFL (minimum score 550 paper-based; 213 computer-based). Electronic applications accepted.

New York University, Graduate School of Arts and Science, Institute of Fine Arts, Program in Conservation Training, New York, NY 10012-1019. Offers MA/Diploma.

Northwestern State University of Louisiana, Graduate Studies and Research, Program in Heritage Resources, Natchitoches, LA 71497. Offers MA. *Faculty:* 5 full-time (3 women). *Students:* 18 full-time (9 women), 1 (woman) part-time; includes 1 minority (American Indian/Alaska Native). Average age 34. 10 applicants, 100% accepted, 10 enrolled. In 2008, 5 master's awarded. *Degree requirements:* For master's, comprehensive exam, thesis or alternative. *Entrance requirements:* For master's, GRE General Test, minimum undergraduate GPA of 2.5. *Unit head:* Dr. Elizabeth Guin, Head, 318-357-4057, Fax: 318-357-6153, E-mail: guine@nsula.edu. *Application contact:* Dr. Steven G. Horton, Associate Provost/Dean, Graduate Studies, Research, and Information Systems, 318-357-5851, Fax: 318-357-5019, E-mail: grad_school@nsula.edu.

Pratt Institute, School of Architecture, Program in Historic Preservation, New York, NY 10011. Offers MS. Part-time programs available. *Faculty:* 4 part-time/adjunct (1 woman). *Students:* 17 full-time (13 women), 5 part-time (4 women); includes 3 minority (all African Americans), 5 international. Average age 27. 42 applicants, 88% accepted, 12 enrolled. In 2008, 9 master's awarded. *Entrance requirements:* For master's, writing sample, bachelor's degree, transcripts, letters of recommendation, statement, portfolio. Additional exam requirements/recommendations for international students: Required—TOEFL (minimum score 550 paper-based; 213 computer-based). *Application deadline:* For fall admission, 2/1 for domestic and international students; for spring admission, 10/1 for domestic and international students. Application fee: $50 ($90 for international students). Electronic applications accepted. *Expenses:* Tuition: Full-time $20,412; part-time $1134 per credit. Required fees: $1190; $1190 per year. *Financial support:* Career-related internships or fieldwork, Federal Work-Study, institutionally sponsored loans, scholarships/grants, health care benefits, and unspecified assistantships available. Support available to part-time students. Financial award application deadline: 2/1; financial award applicants required to submit FAFSA. *Unit head:* Eric Allison, Coordinator, 212-647-7532, E-mail: eallison@pratt.edu. *Application contact:* Young Hah, Director of Graduate Admissions, 718-636-3683, Fax: 718-399-4242, E-mail: yhah@pratt.edu.

See Close-Up on page 155.

Rensselaer Polytechnic Institute, Graduate School, School of Architecture, Program in Building Conservation, Troy, NY 12180-3590. Offers MS. Part-time and evening/weekend programs available. *Degree requirements:* For master's, thesis (for some programs). *Entrance requirements:* For master's, resumé, letters of recommendation. Additional exam requirements/recommendations for international students: Required—TOEFL (minimum score 570 paper-based; 230 computer-based), IELTS (minimum score 7). Electronic applications accepted. *Expenses:* Contact institution. *Faculty research:* Building conservation, 20th century American architecture, historic structure and technology, preservation theory, historical archaeology.

Rutgers, The State University of New Jersey, New Brunswick, Graduate School, Program in Art History, Piscataway, NJ 08854-8097. Offers art history (MA, PhD); curatorial studies (Certificate); historic preservation (Certificate). Part-time programs available. Terminal master's awarded for partial completion of doctoral program. *Degree requirements:* For master's, one foreign language, comprehensive exam; for doctorate, 2 foreign languages, comprehensive exam, thesis/dissertation. *Entrance requirements:* For master's and doctorate, GRE General Test, writing sample. Additional exam requirements/recommendations for international students: Required—TOEFL (minimum score 550 paper-based; 213 computer-based). Electronic applications accepted. *Faculty research:* Ancient and medieval art and architecture; Renaissance and Baroque art and architecture; modern and contemporary art and architecture; Italian studies; the arts of Asia, Africa, and the Americas.

St. Cloud State University, School of Graduate Studies, College of Social Sciences, Program in Cultural Resource Management Archeology, St. Cloud, MN 56301-4498. Offers MS. *Entrance requirements:* For master's, GRE General Test, minimum 2.75 GPA. Additional exam requirements/recommendations for international students: Required—Michigan English Language Assessment Battery; Recommended—TOEFL (minimum score 550 paper-based; 213 computer-based).

Savannah College of Art and Design, Graduate School, Program in Historic Preservation, Savannah, GA 31402-3146. Offers MA, MFA. Part-time programs available. *Degree requirements:* For master's, thesis, internship. *Entrance requirements:* For master's, interview, research paper. Additional exam requirements/recommendations for international students: Required—TOEFL (minimum score 450 paper-based; 133 computer-based). Electronic applications accepted. *Expenses:* Tuition: Full-time $28,215; part-time $3135 per course. One-time fee: $500.

See Close-Up on page 223.

School of the Art Institute of Chicago, Graduate Division, Program in Historic Preservation, Chicago, IL 60603-3103. Offers MSHP. *Entrance requirements:* Additional exam requirements/recommendations for international students: Required—TOEFL, IELTS.

See Close-Up on page 225.

Texas Tech University, Graduate School, Program in Museum Science and Heritage Management, Lubbock, TX 79409. Offers heritage management (MS); museum science (MA). Part-time programs available. *Faculty:* 6 full-time (3 women). *Students:* 30 full-time (27 women), 9 part-time (8 women); includes 3 minority (all Hispanic Americans). Average age 28. 25 applicants, 76% accepted, 13 enrolled. In 2008, 8 master's awarded. *Degree requirements:* For master's, thesis. *Entrance requirements:* For master's, GRE General Test. Additional exam requirements/recommendations for international students: Required—TOEFL (minimum score 550 paper-based; 213 computer-based). *Application deadline:* For fall admission, 3/1 priority date for international students; for spring admission, 11/1 priority date for international students. Applications are processed on a rolling basis. Application fee: $50 ($60 for international students). Electronic applications accepted. *Expenses:* Tuition, area resident: Part-time $194 per credit hour. Tuition, state resident: full-time $4648; part-time $194 per credit hour. Tuition, nonresident: full-time $11,392; part-time $475 per credit hour. Required fees: $2206; $69 per credit hour. $389 per semester. *Financial support:* In 2008–09, 34 students received support, including 7 research assistantships with partial tuition reimbursements available (averaging $10,018 per year), 2 teaching assistantships with partial tuition reimbursements available (averaging $7,479 per year); career-related internships or fieldwork, Federal Work-Study, and institutionally sponsored loans also available. Support available to part-time students. Financial award application deadline: 4/15; financial award applicants required to submit FAFSA. *Faculty*

Historic Preservation

Texas Tech University (continued)
research: Lubbock Lake Landmark anthropology, regional American fine art, regional ethnology, anthropology of the southern plains, natural science research. Total annual research expenditures: $248,030. *Unit head:* Gary F. Edson, Chair, 806-742-2442, Fax: 806-742-1136, E-mail: gary.edson@ttu.edu. *Application contact:* Claudia Cory, Assistant to the Director, 806-742-2442 Ext. 222, Fax: 806-742-1136, E-mail: claudia.cory@ttu.edu.

Universidad Nacional Pedro Henriquez Urena, Graduate School, Santo Domingo, Dominican Republic. Offers accounting and auditing (M Acct); animal production (M Agr); business administration (MBA, PhD); Caribbean tropical architecture (M Arch); conservation of monuments and cultural goods (M Arch); economics (M Econ); education (PhD); environmental engineering (MEE); horticulture (M Agr); hospital administration (PhD); humanities (PhD); international relations (MPS); management of natural resources (MNRM); project management (M Man, MPM); public administration (MPS); sanitary engineering (ME); social science (PhD); veterinary medicine (DVM).

University of California, Riverside, Graduate Division, Department of History, Riverside, CA 92521-0102. Offers archival management (MA); historic preservation (MA); history (MA, PhD); museum curatorship (MA). Part-time programs available. Terminal master's awarded for partial completion of doctoral program. *Degree requirements:* For master's, one foreign language, comprehensive exam, internship report and oral exams, or thesis; for doctorate, 2 foreign languages, thesis/dissertation, qualifying exams, teaching experience. *Entrance requirements:* For master's, GRE General Test, minimum GPA of 3.2; for doctorate, GRE General Test, MA in history, minimum GPA of 3.2. Additional exam requirements/recommendations for international students: Required—TOEFL (minimum score 550 paper-based; 213 computer-based; 80 iBT). Electronic applications accepted. *Expenses:* Tuition, nonresident: full-time $4898. Required fees: $10,362. *Faculty research:* Native American history, United States, public history, Russia, Europe.

University of Delaware, College of Arts and Sciences, Program in Art Conservation, Newark, DE 19716. Offers practicing art conservation (MS). *Degree requirements:* For master's, internship, portfolio, oral exam, oral presentation. *Entrance requirements:* For master's, GRE General Test, course work in chemistry, art history/anthropology and studio art; minimum of 400 hours of conservation experience. Electronic applications accepted. *Faculty research:* Emergency response cleaning techniques, degradation process, art history, artists, materials, techniques of preservation and treatment.

University of Delaware, College of Human Services, Education and Public Policy, Center for Energy and Environmental Policy, Program in Urban Affairs and Public Policy, Newark, DE 19716. Offers community development and nonprofit leadership (MA); energy and environmental policy (MA); governance, planning and management (PhD); historic preservation (MA); social and urban policy (PhD); technology, environment and society (PhD). Part-time programs available. Terminal master's awarded for partial completion of doctoral program. *Degree requirements:* For master's, analytical paper or thesis; for doctorate, thesis/dissertation. *Entrance requirements:* For master's, GRE General Test, minimum GPA of 3.0; for doctorate, GRE General Test, minimum GPA of 3.5. Additional exam requirements/recommendations for international students: Required—TOEFL. Electronic applications accepted. *Faculty research:* Political economy; social policy analysis; technology and society; historic preservation; urban policy.

See Close-Up on page 1239.

University of Georgia, Graduate School, College of Environment and Design, School of Environmental Design, Program in Historic Preservation, Athens, GA 30602. Offers MHP. *Degree requirements:* For master's, thesis. *Entrance requirements:* For master's, GRE General Test. Electronic applications accepted.

University of Hawaii at Manoa, Graduate Division, Colleges of Arts and Sciences, College of Arts and Humanities, Department of American Studies, Program in Historic Preservation, Honolulu, HI 96822. Offers Graduate Certificate. Part-time programs available. *Entrance requirements:* Additional exam requirements/recommendations for international students: Required—TOEFL (minimum score 600 paper-based; 250 computer-based; 100 iBT), IELTS (minimum score 7).

University of Kentucky, Graduate School, College of Design, Department of Historic Preservation, Lexington, KY 40506-0032. Offers MHP. *Degree requirements:* For master's, comprehensive exam. *Entrance requirements:* For master's, GRE General Test, minimum undergraduate GPA of 2.75. Additional exam requirements/recommendations for international students: Required—TOEFL (minimum score 550 paper-based; 213 computer-based). Electronic applications accepted.

University of Maryland, College Park, Graduate Studies, School of Architecture, Planning and Preservation, Program in Historic Preservation, College Park, MD 20742. Offers MHP, Certificate. *Degree requirements:* For Certificate, thesis. *Entrance requirements:* For master's, GRE, minimum GPA of 3.0, 3 letters of recommendation, writing sample. Additional exam requirements/recommendations for international students: Required—TOEFL. Electronic applications accepted.

University of New Mexico, Graduate School, School of Architecture and Planning, Program in Historic Preservation and Regionalism, Albuquerque, NM 87131-2039. Offers Graduate Certificate. Part-time and evening/weekend programs available.

The University of North Carolina at Greensboro, Graduate School, School of Human Environmental Sciences, Department of Interior Architecture, Greensboro, NC 27412-5001. Offers historic preservation (Certificate); interior architecture (MS); museum studies (Certificate). *Degree requirements:* For master's, thesis. *Entrance requirements:* For master's, GRE General Test or MAT, bachelor's degree in interior design, interview, portfolio. Additional exam requirements/recommendations for international students: Required—TOEFL. Electronic applications accepted.

University of Oregon, Graduate School, School of Architecture and Allied Arts, Program in Historic Preservation, Eugene, OR 97403. Offers MS. *Degree requirements:* For master's, thesis, internship. *Entrance requirements:* For master's, participation in Pacific Northwest Field School. Additional exam requirements/recommendations for international students: Required—TOEFL. *Faculty research:* Vernacular architecture, Native American architecture, masonry structure and details, wood construction systems, cultural landscapes.

University of Pennsylvania, School of Design, Graduate Group in Historic Preservation, Philadelphia, PA 19104. Offers conservation and heritage management (Certificate); historic conservation (Certificate); historic preservation (MS). Part-time programs available. *Degree requirements:* For master's, thesis. *Entrance requirements:* For master's, GRE. Additional exam requirements/recommendations for international students: Required—TOEFL. *Faculty research:* Historic building technology, architectural conservation, architectural theory, preservation in the Third World.

See Close-Up on page 159.

University of South Carolina, The Graduate School, College of Arts and Sciences, Department of History, Program in Public History, Columbia, SC 29208. Offers archives (MA); historic preservation (MA); museum (MA); museum management (Certificate); MLIS/MA. *Degree requirements:* For master's, one foreign language, thesis, internship. *Entrance requirements:* For master's, GRE General Test, writing sample. Additional exam requirements/recommendations for international students: Required—TOEFL. Electronic applications accepted. *Faculty research:* Museum studies, historic preservation, archives administration.

University of Southern California, Graduate School, School of Architecture, Program in Historic Preservation, Los Angeles, CA 90089. Offers MHP. Part-time programs available. *Entrance requirements:* For master's, GRE.

The University of Texas at Austin, Graduate School, School of Architecture, Austin, TX 78712-1111. Offers architecture (M Arch); community and regional planning (MSCRP, PhD); historic preservation (MS); history of architecture (MA, PhD); landscape architecture (MLA); urban design (MSUD); JD/MSCRP; MSCRP/MA; MSCRP/PhD. *Degree requirements:* For doctorate, thesis/dissertation. *Entrance requirements:* For master's and doctorate, GRE General Test. Additional exam requirements/recommendations for international students: Required—TOEFL (minimum score 550 paper-based; 213 computer-based). Electronic applications accepted.

The University of Texas at San Antonio, College of Architecture, San Antonio, TX 78249-0617. Offers architecture (M Arch, MS Arch); historical preservation (Graduate Certificate); urban and regional planning (Graduate Certificate). *Degree requirements:* For master's, comprehensive exam, thesis. *Entrance requirements:* For master's, GRE General Test, minimum GPA of 3.0 in last 60 hours and in all architecture courses. Additional exam requirements/recommendations for international students: Required—TOEFL (minimum score 500 paper-based; 173 computer-based). Electronic applications accepted.

University of Vermont, Graduate College, College of Arts and Sciences, Program in Historic Preservation, Burlington, VT 05405. Offers MS. *Students:* 24 (15 women). 36 applicants, 69% accepted, 9 enrolled. In 2008, 14 master's awarded. *Entrance requirements:* For master's, GRE General Test, sample project or equivalent. Additional exam requirements/recommendations for international students: Required—TOEFL (minimum score 550 paper-based; 213 computer-based; 80 iBT). *Application deadline:* For fall admission, 3/1 for domestic students. Application fee: $40. Electronic applications accepted. *Expenses:* Tuition, state resident: part-time $488 per credit. Tuition, nonresident: part-time $1232 per credit. *Financial support:* Fellowships, teaching assistantships available. Financial award application deadline: 3/1. *Faculty research:* Architectural environment. *Unit head:* T. Visser, Director, 802-656-3180. *Application contact:* T. Visser, Director, 802-656-3180.

University of Washington, Graduate School, College of Architecture and Urban Planning, Interdisciplinary Program in Historic Preservation, Seattle, WA 98195. Offers Certificate. Offered in cooperation with the Departments of Architecture, Landscape Architecture, and Urban Design and Planning. Part-time programs available. Electronic applications accepted. *Faculty research:* History of the built environment, historic preservation planning, vernacular architecture, ethnic and gender issues in preservation, restoration.

University of West Florida, College of Arts and Sciences: Arts, Department of History, Pensacola, FL 32514-5750. Offers historic preservation (MA); history (MA); public history (MA). Part-time and evening/weekend programs available. *Faculty:* 6 full-time (1 woman), 1 part-time/adjunct (0 women). *Students:* 11 full-time (4 women), 28 part-time (12 women); includes 2 minority (1 African American, 1 Hispanic American). Average age 34. 29 applicants, 69% accepted, 13 enrolled. In 2008, 11 master's awarded. *Degree requirements:* For master's, thesis or alternative. *Entrance requirements:* For master's, GRE General Test, minimum GPA of 3.0, minimum 15 hours of upper-level history courses. Additional exam requirements/recommendations for international students: Required—TOEFL (minimum score 550 paper-based; 213 computer-based). *Application deadline:* For fall admission, 6/1 for domestic students, 5/15 for international students; for spring admission, 11/1 for domestic students, 10/1 for international students. Applications are processed on a rolling basis. Application fee: $30. *Expenses:* Tuition, state resident: full-time $6095; part-time $253.97 per credit hour. Tuition, nonresident: full-time $21,919; part-time $913.31 per credit hour. *Financial support:* In 2008–09, 3 research assistantships with partial tuition reimbursements (averaging $5,640 per year) were awarded; fellowships, teaching assistantships with partial tuition reimbursements, Federal Work-Study, institutionally sponsored loans, scholarships/grants, and unspecified assistantships also available. Financial award application deadline: 4/15; financial award applicants required to submit FAFSA. *Unit head:* Dr. John J. Clune, Chairperson, 850-474-2680. *Application contact:* Terry McCray, Assistant Director of Graduate Admissions, 850-473-7718, Fax: 850-473-7714, E-mail: gradadmissions@uwf.edu.

University of Wisconsin–Milwaukee, Graduate School, School of Architecture and Urban Planning, Department of Architecture, Milwaukee, WI 53201-0413. Offers architecture (PhD); preservation studies (Certificate); M Arch/MUP. *Faculty:* 27 full-time (4 women). *Students:* 150 full-time (48 women), 11 part-time (7 women); includes 16 minority (4 African Americans, 1 American Indian/Alaska Native, 5 Asian Americans or Pacific Islanders, 6 Hispanic Americans), 13 international. Average age 28. 128 applicants, 62% accepted, 34 enrolled. In 2008, 22 master's, 3 doctorates awarded. *Degree requirements:* For master's, comprehensive exam, thesis; for doctorate, comprehensive exam, thesis/dissertation. *Entrance requirements:* For master's, GRE General Test, portfolio. Additional exam requirements/recommendations for international students: Required—TOEFL (minimum score 600 paper-based; 250 computer-based; 100 iBT), IELTS (minimum score 7). *Application deadline:* For fall admission, 1/1 priority date for domestic students; for spring admission, 9/1 for domestic students. Applications are processed on a rolling basis. Application fee: $45 ($75 for international students). *Expenses:* Tuition, area resident: Full-time $7320; part-time $165 per credit. Tuition, state resident: full-time $7320; part-time $165 per credit. Tuition, nonresident: full-time $17,840; part-time $714 per credit. Tuition and fees vary according to campus/location, program and reciprocity agreements. *Financial support:* In 2008–09, 19 teaching assistantships were awarded; career-related internships or fieldwork and unspecified assistantships also available. Support available to part-time students. Financial award application deadline: 4/15. Total annual research expenditures: $150,000. *Unit head:* Joan Simuncak, Representative, 414-229-4015, Fax: 414-229-6976, E-mail: joanarch@uwm.edu. *Application contact:* Brian Schermer, General Information Contact, 414-229-3815, Fax: 414-229-6967, E-mail: bscherm@uwm.edu.

Ursuline College, School of Graduate Studies, Program in Historic Preservation, Pepper Pike, OH 44124-4398. Offers MA. Part-time programs available. *Students:* 1 (woman) full-time, 5 part-time (4 women). Average age 34. 6 applicants, 67% accepted, 3 enrolled. *Degree requirements:* For master's, thesis. *Entrance requirements:* For master's, minimum undergraduate GPA of 3.0. Additional exam requirements/recommendations for international students: Required—TOEFL (minimum score 500 paper-based; 173 computer-based). *Application deadline:* For fall admission, 8/1 priority date for domestic students. Applications are processed on a rolling basis. Application fee: $25. *Expenses:* Tuition: Full-time $13,590; part-time $775 per credit hour. Required fees: $220; $70 per semester. *Financial support:* In 2008–09, 4 students received support. Federal Work-Study available. Financial award application deadline: 3/1. *Unit head:* Bari Stith, 440-646-8135. *Application contact:* Lauren Anderson, Secretary, 440-646-8119, Fax: 440-684-6088, E-mail: gradsch@ursuline.edu.

Virginia Commonwealth University, Graduate School, College of Humanities and Sciences, Wilder School of Government and Public Affairs, Department of Urban Studies and Planning, Program in Historic Preservation Planning, Richmond, VA 23284-9005. Offers Certificate.

Landscape Architecture

Arizona State University, Graduate College, College of Design, School of Architecture and Landscape Architecture, Tempe, AZ 85287. Offers architecture (M Arch); building design (MS); landscape architecture (MLA); urban design (MUD); MA/MBA. *Degree requirements:* For master's, thesis optional. *Entrance requirements:* For master's, GRE General Test, design portfolio.

Auburn University, Graduate School, College of Architecture, Design, and Construction, Program in Landscape Architecture, Auburn University, AL 36849. Offers MLA. *Accreditation:* ASLA. *Faculty:* 26 full-time (6 women), 3 part-time/adjunct (1 woman). *Students:* 31 full-time (9 women), 1 part-time (0 women); includes 1 minority (Hispanic American), 6 international. Average age 27. 22 applicants, 50% accepted, 6 enrolled. In 2008, 16 master's awarded. *Entrance requirements:* For master's, 3 letters of recommendation. *Expenses:* Tuition, area resident: Full-time $5880; part-time $243 per credit hour. Tuition, state resident: full-time $5880; part-time $243 per credit hour. Tuition, nonresident: full-time $17,640; part-time $729 per credit hour. International tuition: $17,846 full-time. Required fees: $620. Tuition and fees vary according to program and reciprocity agreements. *Unit head:* Charlene Lebleu, Chair, 334-844-4516. *Application contact:* Dr. George Flowers, Dean of the Graduate School, 334-844-2125.

Ball State University, Graduate School, College of Architecture and Planning, Department of Landscape Architecture, Muncie, IN 47306-1099. Offers MLA. *Accreditation:* ASLA. *Degree requirements:* For master's, thesis. *Entrance requirements:* For master's, writing sample.

California State Polytechnic University, Pomona, Academic Affairs, College of Environmental Design, Program in Landscape Architecture, Pomona, CA 91768-2557. Offers M Land Arch. *Accreditation:* ASLA. Part-time programs available. *Students:* 47 full-time (26 women), 11 part-time (2 women); includes 13 minority (1 American Indian/Alaska Native, 12 Asian Americans or Pacific Islanders), 1 international. Average age 32. 72 applicants, 4% accepted, 2 enrolled. In 2008, 9 master's awarded. *Degree requirements:* For master's, thesis or alternative. *Application deadline:* For fall admission, 5/1 priority date for domestic students; for winter admission, 10/15 priority date for domestic students; for spring admission, 1/20 priority date for domestic students. Applications are processed on a rolling basis. Application fee: $55. Electronic applications accepted. *Expenses:* Tuition, nonresident: full-time $7232; part-time $226 per credit. Required fees: $4272. One-time fee: $2694 part-time. Tuition and fees vary according to course load. *Financial support:* Career-related internships or fieldwork, Federal Work-Study, and institutionally sponsored loans available. Support available to part-time students. Financial award application deadline: 3/2; financial award applicants required to submit FAFSA. *Unit head:* Joan H. Woodward, Graduate Coordinator, 909-869-2715, Fax: 909-869-4460, E-mail: lagradprog@csupomona.edu. *Application contact:* Scott J. Duncan, Director, Admissions, 909-869-3258, Fax: 909-869-4529, E-mail: sjduncan@csupomona.edu.

Chatham University, Program in Landscape Architecture, Pittsburgh, PA 15232-2826. Offers landscape architecture (ML Arch); landscape studies (MA). Part-time and evening/weekend programs available. *Students:* 14 full-time (9 women), 19 part-time (12 women). Average age 35. 26 applicants, 65% accepted, 10 enrolled. In 2008, 6 master's awarded. *Degree requirements:* For master's, thesis, capstone project. *Entrance requirements:* Additional exam requirements/recommendations for international students: Required—TOEFL (minimum score 600 paper-based; 250 computer-based; 100 iBT), IELTS (minimum score 6.5), TWE. *Application deadline:* For fall admission, 7/1 priority date for domestic students, 6/1 priority date for international students; for spring admission, 12/1 priority date for domestic students, 11/1 priority date for international students. Applications are processed on a rolling basis. Application fee: $45. Electronic applications accepted. *Expenses:* Tuition: Part-time $686 per credit. Tuition and fees vary according to program. *Financial support:* Career-related internships or fieldwork available. Financial award applicants required to submit FAFSA. *Faculty research:* Sustainability. *Unit head:* Prof. Lisa Kunst Vavaro, Director, 412-365-1882, E-mail: lvavro@chatham.edu. *Application contact:* Michael May, Director of Graduate Admissions, 412-365-1825, Fax: 412-365-1609, E-mail: gradadmissions@chatham.edu.

City College of the City University of New York, Graduate School, School of Architecture and Environmental Studies, New York, NY 10031-9198. Offers architecture (M Arch, PD); landscape architecture (PD); urban design (MUP). Part-time programs available. *Degree requirements:* For master's, thesis. *Entrance requirements:* For master's, portfolio, professional degree in architecture or equivalent. Additional exam requirements/recommendations for international students: Required—TOEFL (minimum score 550 paper-based; 213 computer-based).

Clemson University, Graduate School, College of Architecture, Arts, and Humanities, Department of Planning and Landscape Architecture, Program in Landscape Architecture, Clemson, SC 29634. Offers MLA. *Students:* 35 full-time (14 women), 4 part-time (all women); includes 2 minority (1 African American, 1 Hispanic American), 4 international. Average age 31. 17 applicants, 47% accepted, 6 enrolled. In 2008, 7 master's awarded. *Entrance requirements:* Additional exam requirements/recommendations for international students: Required—TOEFL. *Application deadline:* For fall admission, 4/15 for international students; for spring admission, 9/15 for international students. Application fee: $55. Full-time tuition and fees vary according to program. *Unit head:* Umit Yilmaz, Director of Landscape Architecture, 864-656-7349, Fax: 864-656-7519, E-mail: uyilmaz@clemson.edu. *Application contact:* Dr. Terry Farris, Coordinator, 864-656-3903, Fax: 864-656-0204, E-mail: jfarris@clemson.edu.

Columbia University, School of Continuing Education, Program in Landscape Design, New York, NY 10027. Offers MS. Part-time programs available. *Degree requirements:* For master's, 36 credits. *Entrance requirements:* For master's, BA/BS with minimum GPA of 3.0. Additional exam requirements/recommendations for international students: Required—American Language Program (ALP) placement test.

Conway School of Landscape Design, Graduate Program in Landscape Design, Conway, MA 01341-0179. Offers landscape design/environmental planning (MA). *Degree requirements:* For master's, projects. *Faculty research:* Restoration of native plant communities; integration of humanities, environment, and design.

Cornell University, Graduate School, Graduate Fields of Agriculture and Life Sciences and Graduate Fields of Architecture, Art and Planning, Field of Landscape Architecture, Ithaca, NY 14853-0001. Offers MLA. *Accreditation:* ASLA. *Faculty:* 19 full-time (5 women). *Students:* 45 full-time (19 women); includes 5 minority (1 American Indian/Alaska Native, 2 Asian Americans or Pacific Islanders, 2 Hispanic Americans), 6 international. Average age 31. 110 applicants, 36% accepted, 21 enrolled. In 2008, 9 master's awarded. *Degree requirements:* For master's, project or thesis. *Entrance requirements:* For master's, GRE General Test (recommended), portfolio, 2 letters of recommendation. Additional exam requirements/recommendations for international students: Required—TOEFL (minimum score 550 paper-based; 213 computer-based; 77 iBT). *Application deadline:* For fall admission, 2/15 priority date for domestic students. Applications are processed on a rolling basis. Application fee: $70. Electronic applications accepted. *Expenses:* Tuition: Full-time $29,500. Required fees: $70. Full-time tuition and fees vary according to degree level, program and student level. *Financial support:* In 2008–09, 11 students received support, including 1 research assistantship with full tuition reimbursement available, 10 teaching assistantships with full tuition reimbursements available; fellowships with full tuition reimbursements available, institutionally sponsored loans, scholarships/grants, health care benefits, tuition waivers (full and partial), and unspecified assistantships also available. Financial award applicants required to submit FAFSA. *Faculty research:* Urban horticulture and landscape design, urban design research, cultural landscape history, women in landscape architecture, landscape design language, Japanese landscape architecture. *Unit head:* Director of Graduate Studies, 607-254-9552. *Application contact:* Graduate School Application Requests, Caldwell Hall, 607-254-9552, E-mail: lafield@cornell.edu.

Florida Agricultural and Mechanical University, Division of Graduate Studies, Research, and Continuing Education, School of Architecture, Tallahassee, FL 32307-3200. Offers architectural studies (MS Arch); architecture (professional) (M Arch); landscape architecture (MLA). Part-time programs available. *Degree requirements:* For master's, thesis. *Entrance requirements:* For master's, GRE General Test, minimum GPA of 3.0, portfolio. Additional exam requirements/recommendations for international students: Required—TOEFL (minimum score 550 paper-based). *Faculty research:* Environmental technology, post-occupancy evaluation, building economics, design methods, computer-aided design.

Florida International University, College of Architecture and the Arts, School of Architecture, Landscape Architecture Program, Miami, FL 33199. Offers MLA. *Entrance requirements:* For master's, minimum GPA of 3.0 (upper level coursework). Additional exam requirements/recommendations for international students: Required—TOEFL (minimum score 550 paper-based; 213 computer-based). Electronic applications accepted.

Harvard University, Graduate School of Arts and Sciences, Committee on Architecture, Landscape Architecture, and Urban Planning, Cambridge, MA 02138. Offers architecture (PhD); landscape architecture (PhD); urban planning (PhD). *Degree requirements:* For doctorate, one foreign language, thesis/dissertation, oral exam. *Entrance requirements:* For doctorate, GRE General Test. Additional exam requirements/recommendations for international students: Required—TOEFL. *Expenses:* Tuition: Full-time $32,556. Required fees: $1426. Full-time tuition and fees vary according to program and student level.

Harvard University, Graduate School of Design, Department of Landscape Architecture, Cambridge, MA 02138. Offers MLA. *Accreditation:* ASLA. *Entrance requirements:* For master's, GRE General Test. Additional exam requirements/recommendations for international students: Required—TOEFL (minimum score 600 paper-based; 250 computer-based; 100 iBT). Electronic applications accepted. *Expenses:* Tuition: Full-time $32,556. Required fees: $1426. Full-time tuition and fees vary according to program and student level.

Illinois Institute of Technology, Graduate College, College of Architecture, Chicago, IL 60616-3793. Offers architecture (M Ar, PhD); integrated building delivery (M IBD); landscape architecture (MLA). Part-time programs available. *Faculty:* 40 full-time (5 women), 55 part-time/adjunct (15 women). *Students:* 202 full-time (85 women), 27 part-time (11 women); includes 19 minority (2 African Americans, 6 Asian Americans or Pacific Islanders, 11 Hispanic Americans), 96 international. Average age 28. 427 applicants, 78% accepted, 105 enrolled. In 2008, 54 master's, 2 doctorates awarded. *Degree requirements:* For master's, comprehensive exam (for some programs), thesis (for some programs); for doctorate, comprehensive exam, thesis/dissertation. *Entrance requirements:* For master's, GRE General Test, minimum GPA of 3.0, portfolio, 3 letters of recommendation; for doctorate, GRE General Test, minimum GPA of 3.0, portfolio. Additional exam requirements/recommendations for international students: Required—TOEFL (minimum score 550 paper-based; 213 computer-based; 80 iBT). *Application deadline:* For fall admission, 1/15 for domestic and international students. Applications are processed on a rolling basis. Application fee: $40. Electronic applications accepted. *Financial support:* In 2008–09, 125 teaching assistantships (averaging $4,000 per year) were awarded; fellowships, career-related internships or fieldwork, Federal Work-Study, institutionally sponsored loans, scholarships/grants, and health care benefits also available. Support available to part-time students. Financial award applicants required to submit FAFSA. *Faculty research:* Sustainability and environmental design, comprehensive tall building design, innovative materials technology, advanced structural systems, digital design methods. *Unit head:* Donna V. Robertson, John and Jeanne Rowe Chair, 312-567-3230, Fax: 312-567-5820, E-mail: robertson@iit.edu. *Application contact:* Sarah Pariseau, Coordinator for Academic Affairs, 312-567-3231, Fax: 312-567-5820.

Iowa State University of Science and Technology, Graduate College, College of Design, Department of Landscape Architecture, Ames, IA 50011. Offers MLA, MCRP/MLA. Part-time programs available. *Faculty:* 12 full-time (4 women), 1 part-time/adjunct (0 women). *Students:* 7 full-time (4 women), 1 (woman) part-time; includes 1 minority (African American), 1 international. 12 applicants, 33% accepted, 3 enrolled. In 2008, 4 master's awarded. *Degree requirements:* For master's, thesis. *Entrance requirements:* For master's, GRE (highly recommended), portfolio. Additional exam requirements/recommendations for international students: Required—TOEFL (minimum score 600 paper-based; 79 iBT), IELTS (6.5) or TOEFL. *Application deadline:* For fall admission, 2/1 priority date for domestic and international students. Applications are processed on a rolling basis. Application fee: $30 ($70 for international students). Electronic applications accepted. *Expenses:* Tuition, area resident: Full-time $6446; part-time $359 per credit. Tuition, state resident: full-time $6446; part-time $359 per credit. Tuition, nonresident: full-time $17,330; part-time $963 per credit. Required fees: $790; $249.25 per semester. Tuition and fees vary according to course load and program. *Financial support:* In 2008–09, 4 research assistantships with full and partial tuition reimbursements (averaging $12,978 per year), 1 teaching assistantship with full and partial tuition reimbursement (averaging $14,130 per year) were awarded; career-related internships or fieldwork, Federal Work-Study, institutionally sponsored loans, tuition waivers (partial), and unspecified assistantships also available. Support available to part-time students. Financial award application deadline: 2/15; financial award applicants required to submit FAFSA. *Faculty research:* Landscape ecology, geographic information systems, landscape perception, historic preservation, resource management, design. Total annual research expenditures: $1.2 million. *Unit head:* Dr. Douglas Johnston, Chair, 515-294-6942, Fax: 515-294-2348, E-mail: landarch@iastate.edu. *Application contact:* Dr. Paul F. Anderson, Director of Graduate Education, 515-294-8958, E-mail: landarch@iastate.edu.

Kansas State University, Graduate School, College of Architecture, Planning and Design, Department of Landscape Architecture and Regional and Community Planning, Manhattan, KS 66506. Offers MLA. *Accreditation:* ASLA. Part-time programs available. *Faculty:* 13 full-time (4 women), 4 part-time/adjunct (0 women). *Students:* 75 full-time (33 women), 21 part-time (15 women); includes 5 minority (1 African American, 1 American Indian/Alaska Native, 2 Asian Americans or Pacific Islanders, 1 Hispanic American), 6 international. Average age 27. 45 applicants, 89% accepted, 37 enrolled. In 2008, 7 master's awarded. *Degree requirements:* For master's, thesis, residency, oral exam. *Entrance requirements:* For master's, portfolio. Additional exam requirements/recommendations for international students: Required—TOEFL (minimum score 600 paper-based). *Application deadline:* For fall admission, 2/1 priority date for domestic and international students; for spring admission, 10/1 priority date for domestic students, 8/1 priority date for international students. Applications are processed on a rolling basis. Application fee: $70 ($80 for international students). Electronic applications accepted. *Expenses:* Tuition, area resident: Full-time $6466; part-time $269.40 per credit hour. Tuition, state resident: full-time $6466; part-time $269.40 per credit hour. Tuition, nonresident: full-time $14,874; part-time $619.75 per credit hour. Required fees: $673; $23.40 per credit hour. Tuition and fees vary according to campus/location. *Financial support:* In 2008–09, 1 research assistantship (averaging $8,500 per year), 13 teaching assistantships with full tuition reimbursements (averaging $8,205 per year) were awarded; fellowships, career-related internships or fieldwork, Federal Work-Study, institutionally sponsored loans, and scholarships/grants also available. Support available to part-time students. Financial award application deadline: 3/15; financial award applicants required to submit FAFSA. *Faculty research:* Community planning and design, design and planning theory, geospatial technology infrastructure, watershed restoration, landscape ecology. Total annual research expenditures: $17,414. *Unit head:* Dr. Dan Donelin, Head, 785-532-5961, Fax: 785-532-6722, E-mail: dandon@ksu.edu. *Application contact:* Jody Fronce, Application Contact, 785-532-5961, Fax: 785-532-6722, E-mail: la-rcp@ksu.edu.

Louisiana State University and Agricultural and Mechanical College, Graduate School, College of Art and Design, School of Landscape Architecture, Baton Rouge, LA 70803. Offers

Landscape Architecture

Louisiana State University and Agricultural and Mechanical College (continued)

MLA. *Accreditation:* ASLA. *Degree requirements:* For master's, thesis. *Entrance requirements:* For master's, GRE General Test, minimum GPA of 3.0. Additional exam requirements/recommendations for international students: Required—TOEFL (minimum score 550 paper-based; 213 computer-based). Electronic applications accepted. *Faculty research:* Digital representation, cultural landscapes, urban infrastructure, community design.

Mississippi State University, College of Agriculture and Life Sciences, Department of Landscape Architecture, Mississippi State, MS 39762. Offers MLA. Part-time programs available. *Degree requirements:* For master's, thesis. *Entrance requirements:* For master's, minimum GPA of 2.8. Additional exam requirements/recommendations for international students: Required—TOEFL (minimum score 600 paper-based). Electronic applications accepted. *Faculty research:* Natchez Trace Fuel Buildup.

Morgan State University, School of Graduate Studies, Institute of Architecture and Planning, Program in Landscape Architecture, Baltimore, MD 21251. Offers MLA, MSLA. *Accreditation:* ASLA. *Degree requirements:* For master's, thesis. *Entrance requirements:* Additional exam requirements/recommendations for international students: Required—TOEFL (minimum score 550 paper-based; 213 computer-based). *Faculty research:* Philosophy and design, urban design, design history and theory, computer-aided design and community design.

North Carolina State University, Graduate School, College of Design, Department of Landscape Architecture, Raleigh, NC 27695. Offers MLA. *Accreditation:* ASLA. *Degree requirements:* For master's, thesis optional, oral exam, project. *Entrance requirements:* For master's, GRE General Test (recommended), portfolio. Electronic applications accepted. *Faculty research:* Community development and co-operative engagement, landscape planning and design.

The Ohio State University, Graduate School, College of Engineering, Austin E. Knowlton School of Architecture, Program in Landscape Architecture, Columbus, OH 43210. Offers M Land Arch. *Accreditation:* ASLA. *Degree requirements:* For master's, thesis or alternative. *Entrance requirements:* For master's, GRE General Test. Additional exam requirements/recommendations for international students: Required—TOEFL (minimum score 600 paper-based; 250 computer-based). Electronic applications accepted.

Oklahoma State University, College of Agricultural Science and Natural Resources, Department of Horticulture and Landscape Architecture, Stillwater, OK 74078. Offers crop science (PhD); environmental science (PhD); food science (PhD); horticulture (M Ag, MS); plant science (PhD). *Faculty:* 21 full-time (2 women), 2 part-time/adjunct (0 women). *Students:* 12 part-time (6 women); includes 1 minority (African American), 6 international. Average age 31. 7 applicants, 43% accepted, 3 enrolled. *Degree requirements:* For master's, thesis (for some programs); for doctorate, comprehensive exam, thesis/dissertation. *Entrance requirements:* For master's and doctorate, GRE or GMAT. Additional exam requirements/recommendations for international students: Required—TOEFL. *Application deadline:* For fall admission, 3/1 priority date for international students; for spring admission, 8/1 priority date for international students. Applications are processed on a rolling basis. Application fee: $40 ($75 for international students). Electronic applications accepted. *Expenses:* Tuition, state resident: full-time $3716.40; part-time $154.85 per credit hour. Tuition, nonresident: full-time $14,448; part-time $602 per credit hour. Required fees: $1772.40; $73.85 per credit hour. One-time fee: $50. Tuition and fees vary according to course load and campus/location. *Financial support:* In 2008–09, 11 research assistantships (averaging $16,091 per year), 1 teaching assistantship (averaging $14,400 per year) were awarded; career-related internships or fieldwork, Federal Work-Study, scholarships/grants, health care benefits, tuition waivers (partial), and unspecified assistantships also available. Support available to part-time students. Financial award application deadline: 3/1; financial award applicants required to submit FAFSA. *Faculty research:* Stress and postharvest physiology; water utilization and runoff; IPM systems and nursery, turf, floriculture, vegetable, net and fruit produces and natural resources, food extraction, and processing; public garden management. *Unit head:* Dr. Dale Maronek, Head, 405-744-5414, Fax: 405-744-9709. *Application contact:* Dr. Gordon Emslie, Dean, 405-744-6368, Fax: 405-744-0355, E-mail: grad_i@okstate.edu.

Penn State University Park, Graduate School, College of Arts and Architecture, Department of Landscape Architecture, State College, University Park, PA 16802-1503. Offers MLA.

Rhode Island School of Design, Graduate Studies, Division of Architecture and Design, Department of Landscape Architecture, Providence, RI 02903-2784. Offers MLA. *Accreditation:* ASLA. *Degree requirements:* For master's, thesis, exhibit. *Entrance requirements:* For master's, portfolio, 3 letters of recommendation. Additional exam requirements/recommendations for international students: Required—TOEFL (minimum score 580 paper-based; 237 computer-based), IELTS (minimum score 6.5).

State University of New York College of Environmental Science and Forestry, Department of Landscape Architecture, Syracuse, NY 13210-2779. Offers community design and planning (MLA, MS); cultural landscape studies and conservation (MLA, MS); landscape and urban ecology (MLA, MS). *Accreditation:* ASLA (one or more programs are accredited). *Degree requirements:* For master's, comprehensive exam (for some programs), thesis (for some programs). *Entrance requirements:* For master's, GRE General Test, minimum GPA of 3.0. Additional exam requirements/recommendations for international students: Required—TOEFL (paper-based 550, computer-based 213, iBT 80) or IELTS (6) or STEP Aiken (Grade 1). *Faculty research:* Site analysis and design, city and regional planning, community environments.

Texas A&M University, College of Architecture, Department of Landscape Architecture and Urban Planning, College Station, TX 77843. Offers land development (MSLD); landscape architecture (MLA); urban and regional science (PhD); urban planning (MUP). *Accreditation:* ACSP (one or more programs are accredited); ASLA (one or more programs are accredited). *Faculty:* 27. *Students:* 137 full-time (51 women), 27 part-time (9 women); includes 13 minority (4 African Americans, 2 Asian Americans or Pacific Islanders, 7 Hispanic Americans), 87 international. Average age 31. In 2008, 36 master's, 4 doctorates awarded. Terminal master's awarded for partial completion of doctoral program. *Degree requirements:* For master's, thesis optional, professional internship; for doctorate, comprehensive exam, thesis/dissertation, methods statistics seminar. *Entrance requirements:* For master's, GMAT or GRE General Test, portfolio (MLA), minimum GPA of 3.0; for doctorate, GMAT or GRE General Test. Additional exam requirements/recommendations for international students: Required—TOEFL. *Application deadline:* For fall admission, 2/1 priority date for domestic students; for spring admission, 8/1 for domestic students. Applications are processed on a rolling basis. Application fee: $50 ($75 for international students). Electronic applications accepted. *Expenses:* Tuition, area resident: Full-time $3838.50. Tuition, state resident: full-time $3838.50. Tuition, nonresident: full-time $8897. Required fees: $2359.60. *Financial support:* In 2008–09, fellowships with tuition reimbursements (averaging $1,000 per year), research assistantships with partial tuition reimbursements (averaging $8,100 per year), teaching assistantships with partial tuition reimbursements (averaging $11,250 per year) were awarded; career-related internships or fieldwork, institutionally sponsored loans, and scholarships/grants also available. Financial award application deadline: 4/1; financial award applicants required to submit FAFSA. *Faculty research:* Erosion control/water quality, geographic information systems/spatial information technology, transport hazards, international sustainable development. *Unit head:* Dr. Forester Ndubisi, Head, 979-845-1019, Fax: 979-862-1784, E-mail: ndubis@tamu.edu. *Application contact:* Marie Prihoda, Graduate Office, 979-845-6582, Fax: 979-845-4491.

Texas Tech University, Graduate School, College of Agricultural Sciences and Natural Resources, Department of Landscape Architecture, Lubbock, TX 79409. Offers MLA. *Accreditation:* ASLA. Part-time programs available. *Faculty:* 6 full-time (1 woman). *Students:* 7 full-time (2 women), 7 part-time (4 women), 3 international. Average age 31. 14 applicants, 50% accepted, 3 enrolled. In 2008, 1 master's awarded. *Entrance requirements:* For master's, GRE General Test. Additional exam requirements/recommendations for international students: Required—TOEFL (minimum score 550 paper-based; 213 computer-based). *Application deadline:* For fall admission, 3/1 priority date for international students; for spring admission, 11/1 priority date for international students. Applications are processed on a rolling basis. Application fee: $50 ($60 for international students). Electronic applications accepted. *Expenses:* Tuition, area resident: Part-time $194 per credit hour. Tuition, state resident: full-time $4648; part-time $194 per credit hour. Tuition, nonresident: full-time $11,392; part-time $475 per credit hour. Required fees: $2206; $69 per credit hour. $389 per semester. *Financial support:* In 2008–09, 9 students received support; research assistantships with partial tuition reimbursements available, teaching assistantships with partial tuition reimbursements available, Federal Work-Study and institutionally sponsored loans available. Support available to part-time students. Financial award application deadline: 4/15; financial award applicants required to submit FAFSA. *Faculty research:* Computer-aided design, environmental planning and design, therapeutic landscapes, geographic information systems in planning, creative problem solving, site planning. *Unit head:* Alon Kvashny, Chair, 806-742-2894, Fax: 806-742-0770, E-mail: alon.kvashny@ttu.edu. *Application contact:* John C. Billing, Graduate Coordinator, 806-742-2858, Fax: 806-742-0770, E-mail: john.billing@ttu.edu.

The University of Arizona, Graduate College, College of Architecture and Landscape Architecture, School of Landscape Architecture, Tucson, AZ 85721. Offers ML Arch. *Accreditation:* ASLA. *Degree requirements:* For master's, thesis. *Entrance requirements:* For master's, GRE General Test, minimum GPA of 3.2, 3 letters of reference, statement of intent, portfolio. Additional exam requirements/recommendations for international students: Required—TOEFL (minimum score 600 paper-based). Electronic applications accepted. *Faculty research:* Children's environments, cultural landscapes, arid lands plant communities, geographic information systems and science (GS), computer-aided drafting and design (CAD).

The University of British Columbia, Faculty of Graduate Studies, Faculty of Applied Science, School of Architecture and Landscape Architecture, Programs in Landscape Architecture, Vancouver, BC V6T 1Z1, Canada. Offers MASLA, MLA. *Accreditation:* ASLA (one or more programs are accredited). *Degree requirements:* For master's, comprehensive exam or thesis. *Entrance requirements:* For master's, portfolio. Additional exam requirements/recommendations for international students: Required—TOEFL (minimum score 560 paper-based; 220 computer-based). Electronic applications accepted. *Faculty research:* Landscape design, urban-rural interface, urban ecology, sustainable development, collaborative planning and community forestry.

University of California, Berkeley, Graduate Division, College of Environmental Design, Department of Landscape Architecture and Environmental Planning, Program in Landscape Architecture, Berkeley, CA 94720-1500. Offers environmental planning (MLA); landscape design and site planning (MLA); urban and community design (MLA); MLA/M Arch; MLA/MCP. *Accreditation:* ASLA. *Degree requirements:* For master's, professional project or thesis. *Entrance requirements:* For master's, GRE General Test, minimum GPA of 3.0, portfolio, 3 letters of recommendation.

University of Colorado Denver, College of Architecture and Planning, Program in Landscape Architecture, Denver, CO 80217-3364. Offers MLA. *Accreditation:* ASLA. Part-time programs available. *Degree requirements:* For master's, thesis optional. *Entrance requirements:* For master's, GRE or minimum GPA of 3.0, portfolio. Additional exam requirements/recommendations for international students: Required—TOEFL (minimum score 550 paper-based; 213 computer-based). *Faculty research:* Landscape architectural design theory and process, urban design, advanced landscape technologies, landscape planning.

University of Florida, Graduate School, College of Design, Construction and Planning, Department of Landscape Architecture, Gainesville, FL 32611. Offers MLA, PhD. *Accreditation:* ASLA. Part-time programs available. *Degree requirements:* For master's, thesis, internship. *Entrance requirements:* For master's, GRE General Test, minimum GPA of 3.0. Electronic applications accepted. *Faculty research:* Landscape reclamation, community development, landscape ethics, land-use planning, international conservation.

University of Georgia, Graduate School, College of Environment and Design, School of Environmental Design, Program in Landscape Architecture, Athens, GA 30602. Offers MLA. *Accreditation:* ASLA. *Degree requirements:* For master's, thesis. *Entrance requirements:* For master's, GRE General Test. Additional exam requirements/recommendations for international students: Required—TOEFL. Electronic applications accepted. *Expenses:* Contact institution.

University of Guelph, Graduate Program Services, Ontario Agricultural College, School of Environmental Design and Rural Development, Landscape Architecture Program, Guelph, ON N1G 2W1, Canada. Offers MLA. *Accreditation:* ASLA. *Degree requirements:* For master's, thesis. *Entrance requirements:* For master's, minimum B- average during previous 2 years of honors degree, portfolio and questionnaire. Additional exam requirements/recommendations for international students: Required—TOEFL (minimum score 600 paper-based; 250 computer-based; 89 iBT), IELTS (minimum score 7), Canadian Academic Language Assessment, Michigan English Language Assessment Battery. Electronic applications accepted. *Faculty research:* Land planning, human factors in design, landscape assessment (biophysical and cultural), landscape ecology and restoration, community design.

University of Idaho, College of Graduate Studies, College of Art and Architecture, Department of Landscape Architecture, Moscow, ID 83844-2282. Offers MS. *Faculty:* 3 full-time. *Students:* 6 full-time, 2 part-time. Average age 35. In 2008, 4 master's awarded. Application fee: $55 ($60 for international students). *Expenses:* Tuition, nonresident: full-time $10,080; part-time $336 per credit. Required fees: $5212; $267 per credit. Tuition and fees vary according to program. *Unit head:* Stephen R. Drown, Chair, 208-885-7902, E-mail: larch@uidaho.edu. *Application contact:* Stephen R. Drown, Chair, 208-885-7902, E-mail: larch@uidaho.edu.

University of Illinois at Urbana–Champaign, Graduate College, College of Fine and Applied Arts, Department of Landscape Architecture, Champaign, IL 61820. Offers MLA, PhD, MLA/MUP. *Accreditation:* ASLA. *Faculty:* 11 full-time (5 women). *Students:* 40 full-time (25 women), 4 part-time (1 woman); includes 1 minority (African American), 13 international. 79 applicants, 44% accepted, 17 enrolled. In 2008, 11 master's, 1 doctorate awarded. *Entrance requirements:* For master's, GRE, minimum GPA of 3.0; portfolio; for doctorate, GRE, minimum GPA of 3.0. Additional exam requirements/recommendations for international students: Required—TOEFL (minimum score 570 paper-based; 230 computer-based; 89 iBT). *Application deadline:* Applications are processed on a rolling basis. Application fee: $60 ($75 for international students). Electronic applications accepted. *Financial support:* In 2008–09, 6 fellowships, 12 research assistantships, 20 teaching assistantships were awarded; tuition waivers (full and partial) also available. *Unit head:* Margaret Elen Deming, Head, 217-333-0176, Fax: 217-244-4568, E-mail: medeming@illinois.edu. *Application contact:* Connie Coleman, Administrative Secretary, 214-244-1699, Fax: 214-244-4568, E-mail: cjcolema@illinois.edu.

University of Manitoba, Faculty of Graduate Studies, Faculty of Architecture, Department of Landscape Architecture, Winnipeg, MB R3T 2N2, Canada. Offers M Land Arch. *Accreditation:* ASLA. *Degree requirements:* For master's, thesis or alternative.

University of Massachusetts Amherst, Graduate School, College of Natural Resources and the Environment, Department of Landscape Architecture and Regional Planning, Program in Landscape Architecture, Amherst, MA 01003. Offers MLA, MLA/MRP. *Accreditation:* ASLA. Part-time programs available. *Degree requirements:* For master's, thesis or alternative. *Entrance requirements:* For master's, GRE General Test, portfolio. Additional exam requirements/recommendations for international students: Required—TOEFL (minimum score 550 paper-based; 213 computer-based; 79 iBT), IELTS (minimum score 6.5). Electronic applications accepted. *Expenses:* Tuition, area resident: Full-time $2640. Tuition, nonresident: full-time $9936. One-time fee: $332 full-time. Tuition and fees vary according to course load.

University of Massachusetts Amherst, Graduate School, College of Natural Resources and the Environment, Department of Landscape Architecture and Regional Planning, Program in Landscape Architecture and Regional Planning, Amherst, MA 01003. Offers MLA/MRP. *Accreditation:* ACSP; ASLA. Part-time programs available. *Entrance requirements:* Additional exam requirements/recommendations for international students: Required—TOEFL (minimum score 550 paper-based; 213 computer-based; 79 iBT), IELTS (minimum score 6.5). Electronic applications accepted. *Expenses:* Tuition, area resident: Full-time $2640. Tuition, nonresident: full-time $9936. One-time fee: $332 full-time. Tuition and fees vary according to course load.

University of Michigan, School of Natural Resources and Environment, Program in Landscape Architecture, Ann Arbor, MI 48109. Offers MLA, PhD, MLA/M Arch, MLA/MBA, MLA/MUP. Offered through the Horace H. Rackham School of Graduate Studies. *Accreditation:* ASLA (one or more programs are accredited). *Degree requirements:* For master's, thesis, practicum or group project; for doctorate, comprehensive exam, thesis/dissertation, oral defense of dissertation, preliminary exam. *Entrance requirements:* For master's, GRE General Test; for doctorate, GRE General Test, master's degree, portfolio. Additional exam requirements/recommendations for international students: Required—TOEFL (minimum score 560 paper-based; 220 computer-based; 84 iBT), TOEFL (paper-based 560, computer-based 220) or IELTS (6.5). *Faculty research:* Historic landscape documentation, ADA and landscape architecture, landscape perception, sustainable design, ecological design.

University of Minnesota, Twin Cities Campus, Graduate School, College of Design, Department of Landscape Architecture, Minneapolis, MN 55455-0213. Offers MLA, MS. *Accreditation:* ASLA (one or more programs are accredited). *Degree requirements:* For master's, thesis (MS). *Entrance requirements:* For master's, GRE General Test (MS), suggested GPA of 3.0. Additional exam requirements/recommendations for international students: Required—TOEFL (minimum score 550 paper-based; 213 computer-based; 79 iBT). Electronic applications accepted. *Expenses:* Contact institution. *Faculty research:* Landscape history, landscape ecology, urban design, sustainable design, public art/space.

University of New Mexico, Graduate School, School of Architecture and Planning, Program in Landscape Architecture, Albuquerque, NM 87131-2039. Offers MLA. *Accreditation:* ASLA. Part-time programs available. *Degree requirements:* For master's, thesis optional, portfolio review, thesis studio. *Entrance requirements:* For master's, minimum GPA of 3.0. Additional exam requirements/recommendations for international students: Required—TOEFL. *Expenses:* Contact institution. *Faculty research:* Cultural landscape studies, arid landscape studies, urban design and sustainability, landscape and infrastructure.

University of Oklahoma, Graduate College, College of Architecture, Division of Landscape Architecture, Norman, OK 73019-0390. Offers MLA, MRCP/MLA. *Accreditation:* ASLA. Part-time programs available. *Faculty:* 1 full-time (0 women). *Students:* 12 full-time (5 women), 2 part-time (1 woman); includes 1 minority (Hispanic American), 1 international. 10 applicants, 90% accepted, 3 enrolled. In 2008, 5 master's awarded. *Degree requirements:* For master's, comprehensive exam, portfolio, project. *Entrance requirements:* For master's, GRE General Test, portfolio. Additional exam requirements/recommendations for international students: Required—TOEFL (minimum score 550 paper-based; 213 computer-based). *Application deadline:* For fall admission, 4/1 for domestic and international students; for spring admission, 11/1 for domestic students, 9/1 for international students. Applications are processed on a rolling basis. Application fee: $40 ($90 for international students). Electronic applications accepted. *Expenses:* Tuition, state resident: full-time $3744; part-time $156 per credit hour. Tuition, nonresident: full-time $13,577; part-time $565.70 per credit hour. Required fees: $2415.40; $90.10 per credit hour. *Financial support:* In 2008–09, 11 students received support, including 2 research assistantships with partial tuition reimbursements available (averaging $9,586 per year); career-related internships or fieldwork, Federal Work-Study, institutionally sponsored loans, scholarships/grants, and unspecified assistantships also available. Financial award applicants required to submit FAFSA. *Faculty research:* Sustainable urban design; greenways; community based design and planning; site design and site planning; meaning in built environments. *Unit head:* Thomas Schurch, Director, 405-325-2444, Fax: 405-325-7558, E-mail: schurch@ou.edu. *Application contact:* Thomas Schurch, Director, 405-325-2444, Fax: 405-325-7558, E-mail: schurch@ou.edu.

University of Oregon, Graduate School, School of Architecture and Allied Arts, Department of Landscape Architecture, Eugene, OR 97403. Offers MLA. *Accreditation:* ASLA. *Degree requirements:* For master's, thesis or alternative, project. *Entrance requirements:* For master's, portfolio. Additional exam requirements/recommendations for international students: Required—TOEFL. *Faculty research:* Design, landscape planning analysis, history and theory, computer applications.

University of Pennsylvania, School of Design, Program in Landscape Architecture and Regional Planning, Philadelphia, PA 19104. Offers landscape architecture and regional planning (MLA); landscape studies (Certificate). *Accreditation:* ASLA (one or more programs are accredited). Part-time programs available. *Degree requirements:* For master's, thesis optional. *Entrance requirements:* For master's, GRE, portfolio. Additional exam requirements/recommendations for international students: Required—TOEFL. *Faculty research:* Early landscape architecture, natural distribution through landslides, urban gardens, landscape registration, watershed studies.

See Close-Up on page 159.

University of Southern California, Graduate School, School of Architecture, Program in Historic Preservation, Los Angeles, CA 90089. Offers MHP. Part-time programs available. *Entrance requirements:* For master's, GRE.

University of Southern California, Graduate School, School of Architecture, Program in Landscape Architecture, Los Angeles, CA 90089. Offers ML Arch. *Entrance requirements:* For master's, GRE General Test. *Faculty research:* Urban landscapes, plant ecology, city and urban planning.

The University of Tennessee, Graduate School, College of Architecture and Design, Program in Landscape Architecture, Knoxville, TN 37996. Offers landscape architecture (MLA); landscape architecture (research) (MA, MS). *Degree requirements:* For master's, oral exam, project and thesis optional (MLA); oral exam and thesis (MA, MS). *Entrance requirements:* For master's, GRE General Test, completed application form, transcripts of undergraduate and/or graduate work, minimum GPA of 3.0, 3 letters of recommendation, samples of portfolio work. Additional exam requirements/recommendations for international students: Required—TOEFL (minimum score 550 paper-based). *Expenses:* Tuition, area resident: Part-time $348 per credit hour. Tuition, state resident: full-time $6262. Tuition, nonresident: full-time $18,920; part-time $1052 per credit hour. Required fees: $812; $36 per credit hour. Tuition and fees vary according to program.

The University of Texas at Arlington, Graduate School, School of Architecture, Program in Landscape Architecture, Arlington, TX 76019. Offers MLA. *Accreditation:* ASLA. Part-time and evening/weekend programs available. *Students:* 21 full-time (15 women), 8 part-time (2 women); includes 2 minority (1 African American, 1 Hispanic American), 5 international. In 2008, 5 master's awarded. *Degree requirements:* For master's, thesis. *Entrance requirements:* For master's, GRE General Test, minimum GPA of 3.0, portfolio. Additional exam requirements/recommendations for international students: Required—TOEFL (minimum score 550 paper-based; 213 computer-based). *Application deadline:* For fall admission, 6/16 for domestic students. Applications are processed on a rolling basis. Application fee: $35 ($50 for international students). *Expenses:* Tuition, area resident: Full-time $6500. Tuition, state resident: full-time $6500. Tuition, nonresident: full-time $11,558. *Financial support:* In 2008–09, 1 research assistantship with partial tuition reimbursement (averaging $4,824 per year), 2 teaching assistantships with partial tuition reimbursements (averaging $4,824 per year) were awarded; fellowships, career-related internships or fieldwork and tuition waivers (partial) also available. Financial award application deadline: 6/1; financial award applicants required to submit FAFSA. *Unit head:* Dr. Pat D. Taylor, Program Director, 817-272-2801, Fax: 817-272-5098, E-mail: pdt@uta.edu. *Application contact:* David Jones, Associate Dean, 817-272-2801, Fax: 817-272-5098, E-mail: djonesarch@uta.edu.

The University of Texas at Austin, Graduate School, School of Architecture, Austin, TX 78712-1111. Offers architecture (M Arch); community and regional planning (MSCRP, PhD); historic preservation (MS); history of architecture (MA, PhD); landscape architecture (MLA); urban design (MSUD); JD/MSCRP; MSCRP/MA; MSCRP/PhD. *Degree requirements:* For doctorate, thesis/dissertation. *Entrance requirements:* For master's and doctorate, GRE General Test. Additional exam requirements/recommendations for international students: Required—TOEFL (minimum score 550 paper-based; 213 computer-based). Electronic applications accepted.

University of Virginia, School of Architecture, Department of Architecture and Landscape Architecture, Program in Landscape Architecture, Charlottesville, VA 22903. Offers M Land Arch. *Accreditation:* ASLA. *Faculty:* 25 full-time (10 women), 1 (woman) part-time/adjunct. *Students:* 40 full-time (31 women), 4 international. Average age 29. 119 applicants, 25% accepted, 9 enrolled. In 2008, 10 master's awarded. *Entrance requirements:* For master's, GRE General Test, 3 letters of recommendation; portfolio; essay. Additional exam requirements/recommendations for international students: Required—TOEFL (minimum score 600 paper-based; 250 computer-based; 90 iBT). *Application deadline:* For fall admission, 1/16 for domestic and international students. Applications are processed on a rolling basis. Application fee: $60. Electronic applications accepted. *Expenses:* Tuition, area resident: Full-time $10,452. Tuition, state resident: full-time $10,452. Tuition, nonresident: full-time $20,010. Required fees: $2176. Part-time tuition and fees vary according to course load and program. *Financial support:* Applicants required to submit FAFSA. *Faculty research:* History of landscape architecture. *Unit head:* Kristina Hill, Director, Landscape Architecture, 434-924-1493, Fax: 434-982-2678, E-mail: kzhill@virginia.edu. *Application contact:* Graduate Admissions Officer, 434-924-6442, Fax: 434-982-2678, E-mail: arch-admissions@virginia.edu.

University of Washington, Graduate School, College of Architecture and Urban Planning, Department of Landscape Architecture, Seattle, WA 98195. Offers MLA. *Accreditation:* ASLA. *Degree requirements:* For master's, thesis. *Entrance requirements:* For master's, GRE, minimum GPA of 3.0. Additional exam requirements/recommendations for international students: Required—TOEFL. *Faculty research:* Cultural landscape, history of gardens, urban stream restoration, campus master planning, urban ecology.

University of Wisconsin–Madison, Graduate School, College of Agricultural and Life Sciences, Department of Landscape Architecture, Madison, WI 53076. Offers MA, MS. Part-time programs available. *Degree requirements:* For master's, thesis. *Entrance requirements:* For master's, GRE (recommended), samples of creative work. Additional exam requirements/recommendations for international students: Required—TOEFL (minimum score 580 paper-based; 237 computer-based). Electronic applications accepted. *Faculty research:* Urban/landscape ecology, land restoration, cultural resource preservation, community design, conservation design.

Utah State University, School of Graduate Studies, College of Humanities, Arts and Social Sciences, Department of Landscape Architecture and Environmental Planning, Logan, UT 84322. Offers bioregional planning (MS); landscape architecture (MLA). *Accreditation:* ASLA (one or more programs are accredited). *Degree requirements:* For master's, thesis. *Entrance requirements:* For master's, GRE General Test, minimum GPA of 3.0. Additional exam requirements/recommendations for international students: Required—TOEFL. *Faculty research:* Visual resource management, planning for wildlife, agricultural land preservation, watershed planning, community planning and design.

Virginia Polytechnic Institute and State University, Graduate School, College of Architecture and Urban Studies, Department of Landscape Architecture, Blacksburg, VA 24061. Offers MLA. *Accreditation:* ASLA. *Entrance requirements:* For master's, GRE. Additional exam requirements/recommendations for international students: Required—TOEFL (minimum score 550 paper-based; 213 computer-based). Electronic applications accepted. *Faculty research:* Land planning issues in rural areas, landscape perception and visual management theory, universal design, accessibility, ecological and cultural processes.

Virginia Polytechnic Institute and State University, Graduate School, College of Architecture and Urban Studies, School of Public and International Affairs, Blacksburg, VA 24061. Offers environmental planning and policy (MURP); government and international affairs (MPIA); housing, community and economic development (MURP); international development planning (MURP); land use and physical planning (MURP); planning, governance and globalization (PhD), including environmental planning and landscape analysis, physical planning and urban design, public and international affairs, urban and environmental design and planning; urban and regional planning (MURP). *Accreditation:* ACSP. *Entrance requirements:* Additional exam requirements/recommendations for international students: Required—TOEFL (minimum score 550 paper-based; 213 computer-based). Electronic applications accepted. *Faculty research:* Design theory, environmental planning, town planning, transportation planning.

Washington State University, Graduate School, College of Agricultural, Human, and Natural Resource Sciences, Department of Horticulture and Landscape Architecture, Pullman, WA 99164. Offers horticulture (MS, PhD); landscape architecture (MSLA). Part-time programs available. *Degree requirements:* For master's, comprehensive exam (for some programs), thesis (for some programs), oral exam; for doctorate, comprehensive exam, thesis/dissertation, oral exam, written exam. *Entrance requirements:* For master's and doctorate, GRE General Test, GRE Subject Test, minimum GPA of 3.0, 3 letters of recommendation. Additional exam requirements/recommendations for international students: Required—TOEFL (minimum score 550 paper-based). Electronic applications accepted. *Faculty research:* Post-harvest physiology, genetics/plant breeding, molecular biology.

Washington State University Spokane, Graduate Programs, Interdisciplinary Design Institute, Spokane, WA 99210-1495. Offers architecture (M Arch, MS); design (Dr DES); interior design (MA); landscape architecture (MS). Part-time programs available. *Degree requirements:* For master's, comprehensive exam (for some programs), thesis (for some programs); for doctorate, comprehensive exam, thesis/dissertation. *Entrance requirements:* For master's, minimum GPA of 3.0, portfolio of design work, 3 letters of recommendation (M Arch); for doctorate, minimum graduate GPA of 3.5. Additional exam requirements/recommendations for international students: Required—TOEFL (minimum score 550 paper-based; 213 computer-based). *Faculty research:* Environment-behavior relationships, land use and environmental planning, urban space as interior design, art and architectural aesthetics.

Lighting Design

The New School: A University, Parsons The New School for Design, Program in Lighting Design, New York, NY 10011. Offers MFA. *Accreditation:* NASAD. *Faculty:* 1 full-time (0 women), 13 part-time/adjunct (6 women). *Students:* 38 full-time (25 women); includes 3 minority (all Asian Americans or Pacific Islanders), 21 international. Average age 28. In 2008, 14 master's awarded. *Entrance requirements:* For master's, portfolio. Additional exam requirements/recommendations for international students: Required—TOEFL (minimum score 580 paper-based; 237 computer-based; 93 iBT). *Application deadline:* For fall admission, 2/1 priority date for domestic students. Applications are processed on a rolling basis. Application fee: $50. *Expenses:* Tuition: Full-time $27,144; part-time $1508 per credit. Required fees: $355 per semester. *Financial support:* Federal Work-Study, scholarships/grants, and tuition waivers (partial) available. Financial award application deadline: 3/1; financial award applicants required to submit FAFSA. *Unit head:* Kent Kleinman, Chair, 212-229-8955 Ext. 2953, E-mail: kleinmak@newschool.edu. *Application contact:* Anthony Padilla, Director of Admissions, 212-229-8989 Ext. 4023, Fax: 212-229-8975, E-mail: padillaa@newschool.edu.

See Close-Up on page 153.

Rensselaer Polytechnic Institute, Graduate School, School of Architecture, Program in Lighting, Troy, NY 12180-3590. Offers MS. Part-time programs available. Terminal master's awarded for partial completion of doctoral program. *Degree requirements:* For master's, comprehensive exam (for some programs), thesis. *Entrance requirements:* For master's, GRE General Test, letters of recommendation, resumé, portfolio or sample of research writing. Additional exam requirements/recommendations for international students: Required—TOEFL (minimum score 570 paper-based; 230 computer-based), IELTS (minimum score 7). Electronic applications accepted. *Faculty research:* Energy-efficient lighting, lighting product development, lighting design demonstration, daylighting, transportation lighting.

University of Washington, Graduate School, College of Architecture and Urban Planning, Department of Architecture, Seattle, WA 98195. Offers architecture (M Arch, MS); built environment (PhD); design computing (Certificate); design firm leadership and management (Certificate); historic preservation (Certificate); lighting (Certificate); urban design (Certificate). *Degree requirements:* For master's, thesis. *Entrance requirements:* For master's, GRE General Test, minimum GPA of 3.0, portfolio, 3 letters of recommendation. Additional exam requirements/recommendations for international students: Required—TOEFL. *Faculty research:* Lighting, materials, computing theory, media, culture, environment.

Urban Design

American University of Beirut, Graduate Programs, Faculty of Engineering and Architecture, Beirut, Lebanon. Offers civil engineering (ME, PhD); electrical and computer engineering (ME, PhD); engineering management (MEM); environmental and water resources (ME); environmental and water resources engineering (PhD); environmental technology (MSES); mechanical engineering (ME, PhD); urban design (MUD); urban planning and policy (MUP). Part-time programs available. *Degree requirements:* For master's, one foreign language, comprehensive exam, thesis (for some programs); for doctorate, one foreign language, comprehensive exam, thesis/dissertation, publications. *Entrance requirements:* For master's, letters of recommendation; for doctorate, letters of recommendation, master's degree, transcripts, curriculum vitae, interview. Additional exam requirements/recommendations for international students: Required—TOEFL (minimum score 600 paper-based; 250 computer-based; 100 iBT), IELTS (minimum score 7.5). Electronic applications accepted.

Arizona State University, Graduate College, College of Design, School of Architecture and Landscape Architecture, Tempe, AZ 85287. Offers architecture (M Arch); building design (MS); landscape architecture (MLA); urban design (MUD); MA/MBA. *Degree requirements:* For master's, thesis optional. *Entrance requirements:* For master's, GRE General Test, design portfolio.

Ball State University, Graduate School, College of Architecture and Planning, Department of Architecture, Program in Urban Design, Muncie, IN 47306-1099. Offers MUD.

Carnegie Mellon University, College of Fine Arts, School of Architecture, Pittsburgh, PA 15213-3891. Offers architectural engineering construction management (M Sc); architecture (MSA); architecture, engineering, and construction management (PhD); building performance and diagnostics (M Sc, PhD); computational design (M Sc, PhD); sustainable design (M Sc); urban design (M Sc). Terminal master's awarded for partial completion of doctoral program. *Degree requirements:* For doctorate, thesis/dissertation. *Entrance requirements:* For master's and doctorate, GRE General Test. Additional exam requirements/recommendations for international students: Required—TOEFL.

The Catholic University of America, School of Architecture and Planning, Washington, DC 20064. Offers M Arch, M Arch Studies. Part-time programs available. *Degree requirements:* For master's, thesis. *Entrance requirements:* For master's, minimum GPA of 2.7, portfolio, 3 letters of recommendation. Additional exam requirements/recommendations for international students: Required—TOEFL (minimum score 500 paper-based; 173 computer-based). Electronic applications accepted. *Expenses:* Contact institution. *Faculty research:* Architectural history, sacred architecture, computers, technology, urban design, preservation.

City College of the City University of New York, Graduate School, School of Architecture and Environmental Studies, Program in Urban Design, New York, NY 10031-9198. Offers MUP. Part-time programs available. *Degree requirements:* For master's, thesis. *Entrance requirements:* For master's, portfolio, professional degree in architecture or equivalent. Additional exam requirements/recommendations for international students: Required—TOEFL (minimum score 550 paper-based; 213 computer-based). *Faculty research:* Real estate, planning, law.

Cleveland State University, College of Graduate Studies, Maxine Goodman Levin College of Urban Affairs, Program in Urban Planning, Design, and Development, Cleveland, OH 44115. Offers geographic information systems (Certificate); local and urban management (Certificate); urban economic development (Certificate); urban planning, design, and development (MUPDD); urban real estate development and finance (Certificate); JD/MUPDD. *Accreditation:* ACSP. Part-time and evening/weekend programs available. *Faculty:* 26 full-time (10 women), 12 part-time/adjunct (5 women). *Students:* 37 full-time (17 women), 41 part-time (21 women); includes 13 minority (9 African Americans, 1 American Indian/Alaska Native, 3 Hispanic Americans), 10 international. Average age 38. 63 applicants, 63% accepted, 21 enrolled. In 2008, 24 master's, 9 Certificates awarded. *Degree requirements:* For master's, project or thesis. *Entrance requirements:* For master's, GRE General Test (minimum score: verbal and quantitative 50th percentile, analytical writing 4.0), minimum GPA of 3.0. Additional exam requirements/recommendations for international students: Required—TOEFL (minimum score 525 paper-based; 197 computer-based; 65 iBT). *Application deadline:* For fall admission, 7/15 priority date for domestic students, 5/15 for international students; for spring admission, 11/1 for international students. Applications are processed on a rolling basis. Application fee: $30. Electronic applications accepted. *Financial support:* In 2008–09, 15 students received support, including 10 research assistantships with full and partial tuition reimbursements available (averaging $6,960 per year), 5 teaching assistantships with full and partial tuition reimbursements available (averaging $6,960 per year); career-related internships or fieldwork, Federal Work-Study, tuition waivers (full and partial), and unspecified assistantships also available. Support available to part-time students. Financial award application deadline: 3/1. *Faculty research:* Housing and neighborhood development, urban housing policy, environmental sustainability, economic development. *Unit head:* Dr. W. Dennis Keating, Director, 216-687-2298, Fax: 216-687-2013, E-mail: w.keating@csuohio.edu. *Application contact:* Graduate Program Coordinator, 216-523-7522, Fax: 216-687-5398, E-mail: urbanprograms@csuohio.edu.

Cornell University, Graduate School, Graduate Fields of Architecture, Art and Planning, Field of Architecture, Ithaca, NY 14853-0001. Offers architectural design (M Arch); architectural science (MS); building technology and environmental science (MS); computer graphics (MS); history of architecture (MA, PhD); history of urban development (MA, PhD); theory and criticism of architecture (M Arch); urban design (M Arch). *Faculty:* 28 full-time (6 women). *Students:* 93 full-time (40 women); includes 13 minority (2 African Americans, 6 Asian Americans or Pacific Islanders, 5 Hispanic Americans), 36 international. Average age 29. 488 applicants, 18% accepted, 53 enrolled. In 2008, 6 master's awarded. *Degree requirements:* For master's, one foreign language, thesis (MA, MS); for doctorate, 2 foreign languages, comprehensive exam, thesis/dissertation. *Entrance requirements:* For master's, GRE General Test, 5-year bachelor's degree in architecture, portfolio (M Arch), 3 letters of recommendation; for doctorate, GRE General Test, 3 letters of recommendation. Additional exam requirements/recommendations for international students: Required—TOEFL (minimum score 600 paper-based; 250 computer-based; 77 iBT). *Application deadline:* For fall admission, 1/15 priority date for domestic students. Application fee: $70. Electronic applications accepted. *Expenses:* Tuition: $29,500. Required fees: $70. Full-time tuition and fees vary according to degree level, program and student level. *Financial support:* In 2008–09, 16 students received support, including 8 fellowships with full tuition reimbursements available, 1 research assistantship with full tuition reimbursement available, 7 teaching assistantships with full tuition reimbursements available; institutionally sponsored loans, scholarships/grants, health care benefits, tuition waivers (full and partial), and unspecified assistantships also available. Financial award applicants required to submit FAFSA. *Faculty research:* Architectural design and urban design, theory and criticism of architecture, computer graphics, building technology and environmental science, history of architecture and history of urban-development. *Unit head:* Director of Graduate Studies, 607-255-6701, Fax: 607-255-0291. *Application contact:* Graduate Field Assistant, 607-255-6701, Fax: 607-255-0291, E-mail: cuarch@cornell.edu.

Georgia Institute of Technology, Graduate Studies and Research, College of Architecture, City and Regional Planning Program, Atlanta, GA 30332-0001. Offers city and regional planning (PhD); economic development (MCRP); environmental planning and management (MCRP); geographic information systems (MCRP); land and community development (MCRP); land use planning (MCRP); transportation (MCRP); urban design (MCRP); MCP/MSCE. *Accreditation:* ACSP. *Degree requirements:* For master's, thesis, internship. *Entrance requirements:* For master's, GRE General Test, minimum GPA of 2.7. Additional exam requirements/recommendations for international students: Required—TOEFL. Electronic applications accepted.

Harvard University, Graduate School of Design, Department of Urban Planning and Design, Cambridge, MA 02138. Offers urban planning (MUP); urban planning and design (MAUD, MLAUD). *Accreditation:* ACSP (one or more programs are accredited). *Entrance requirements:* For master's, GRE General Test. Additional exam requirements/recommendations for international students: Required—TOEFL (minimum score 600 paper-based; 250 computer-based; 100 iBT). Electronic applications accepted. *Expenses:* Tuition: Full-time $32,556. Required fees: $1426. Full-time tuition and fees vary according to program and student level.

Kent State University, College of Architecture and Environmental Design, Kent, OH 44242-0001. Offers architecture (M Arch); preservation architecture (Certificate); urban design (M Arch, MUD, Certificate). Part-time programs available. *Degree requirements:* For master's, thesis optional. *Entrance requirements:* For master's, GRE, portfolio, minimum GPA of 2.75, 3 letters of reference, resumé, undergraduate architecture degree. Additional exam requirements/recommendations for international students: Required—TOEFL (minimum score 550 paper-based). Electronic applications accepted. *Faculty research:* History and theory, building technology, landscape architecture and urbanism, urbanism, sustainable development.

New York Institute of Technology, Graduate Division, School of Architecture and Design, Old Westbury, NY 11568-8000. Offers urban and regional design (M Arch). Part-time programs available. *Students:* 11 full-time (8 women), 4 part-time (1 woman); includes 2 minority (1 Asian American or Pacific Islander, 1 Hispanic American), 10 international. Average age 31. In 2008, 5 master's awarded. *Degree requirements:* For master's, thesis. *Entrance requirements:* For master's, minimum QPA of 2.85, portfolio. Additional exam requirements/recommendations for international students: Required—TOEFL (minimum score 550 paper-based; 213 computer-based). *Application deadline:* For fall admission, 7/1 priority date for domestic students; for spring admission, 12/1 priority date for domestic students. Applications are processed on a rolling basis. Application fee: $50. Electronic applications accepted. *Expenses:* Tuition: Part-time $783 per credit. *Financial support:* Research assistantships with partial tuition reimbursements, institutionally sponsored loans and tuition waivers (full and partial) available. Support available to part-time students. Financial award applicants required to submit FAFSA. *Faculty research:* Affordable housing, urban modeling and simulation, transport systems and infrastructure, relationships of policy and form. *Unit head:* Judith DiMaio, Dean, 516-686-7594, Fax: 516-686-7921, E-mail: jdimaio@nyit.edu. *Application contact:* Dr. Jacquelyn Nealon, Vice President for Enrollment Services, 516-686-7925, Fax: 516-686-7597, E-mail: jnealon@nyit.edu.

Prairie View A&M University, School of Architecture, Prairie View, TX 77446-0519. Offers architecture (M Arch); community development (MCD). Part-time and evening/weekend programs available. *Entrance requirements:* For master's, GRE General Test, portfolio (M Arch). Additional exam requirements/recommendations for international students: Required—TOEFL (minimum score 550 paper-based). Electronic applications accepted. *Faculty research:* Community management, sustainable design.

Pratt Institute, School of Architecture, Program in Architecture and Urban Design, Brooklyn, NY 11205-3899. Offers architecture and urban design (post-profession) (MS). Part-time programs available. *Faculty:* 4 part-time/adjunct (2 women). *Students:* 9 full-time (6 women); includes 2 minority (both Asian Americans or Pacific Islanders), 7 international. Average age 24. 44 applicants, 57% accepted, 7 enrolled. In 2008, 6 master's awarded. *Degree requirements:* For master's, thesis. *Entrance requirements:* For master's, portfolio, bachelor's degree, transcripts, letters of recommendation, statement. Additional exam requirements/recommendations for international students: Required—TOEFL (minimum score 550 paper-based; 213 computer-based). *Application deadline:* For fall admission, 2/1 for domestic and international students; for spring admission, 10/1 for domestic and international students. Applications are processed on a rolling basis. Application fee: $50 ($90 for international students). Electronic applications accepted. *Expenses:* Tuition: Full-time $20,412; part-time $1134 per credit. Required fees:

$1190; $1190 per year. *Financial support:* Career-related internships or fieldwork, Federal Work-Study, institutionally sponsored loans, scholarships/grants, health care benefits, and unspecified assistantships available. Support available to part-time students. Financial award application deadline: 2/1; financial award applicants required to submit FAFSA. *Faculty research:* Urban development process; historical, social, and economic implications of planning. *Unit head:* William J. Mac Donald, Chairperson, 718-399-4357, E-mail: wmacdona@pratt.edu. *Application contact:* Young Hah, Director of Graduate Admissions, 718-636-3683, Fax: 718-399-4242, E-mail: yhah@pratt.edu.

See Close-Up on page 155.

Rice University, Graduate Programs, School of Architecture, Houston, TX 77251-1892. Offers architecture (M Arch, D Arch); urban design (M Arch UD). *Degree requirements:* For master's, thesis; for doctorate, thesis/dissertation. *Entrance requirements:* For master's and doctorate, GRE General Test, minimum GPA of 3.0. Additional exam requirements/recommendations for international students: Required—TOEFL (minimum score 650 paper-based; 250 computer-based; 90 iBT).

Savannah College of Art and Design, Graduate School, Program in Urban Design and Development, Savannah, GA 31402-3146. Offers MA. Part-time programs available. *Degree requirements:* For master's, thesis. *Entrance requirements:* For master's, interview, portfolio. Additional exam requirements/recommendations for international students: Required—TOEFL (minimum score 450 paper-based; 133 computer-based). *Expenses:* Tuition: Full-time $28,215; part-time $3135 per course. One-time fee: $500.

State University of New York College of Environmental Science and Forestry, Department of Landscape Architecture, Syracuse, NY 13210-2779. Offers community design and planning (MLA, MS); cultural landscape studies and conservation (MLA, MS); landscape and urban ecology (MLA, MS). *Accreditation:* ASLA (one or more programs are accredited). *Degree requirements:* For master's, comprehensive exam (for some programs), thesis (for some programs). *Entrance requirements:* For master's, GRE General Test, minimum GPA of 3.0. Additional exam requirements/recommendations for international students: Required—TOEFL (paper-based 550, computer-based 213, iBT 80) or IELTS (6) or STEP Aiken (Grade 1). *Faculty research:* Site analysis and design, city and regional planning, community environments.

University at Buffalo, the State University of New York, Graduate School, School of Architecture and Planning, Department of Urban and Regional Planning, Buffalo, NY 14260. Offers planning (MUP); JD/MUP; M Arch/MUP. *Accreditation:* ACSP. Part-time programs available. *Degree requirements:* For master's, thesis or alternative, project. *Entrance requirements:* For master's, minimum GPA of 3.0. Additional exam requirements/recommendations for international students: Required—TOEFL (minimum score 550 paper-based; 213 computer-based; 79 iBT), IELTS (minimum score 6.5). Electronic applications accepted. *Faculty research:* International planning development, economic development, governance, information technology and geographic information systems in planning, environmental planning and policy.

University of California, Berkeley, Graduate Division, College of Environmental Design, Department of Architecture, Berkeley, CA 94720-1500. Offers architecture (M Arch); building science (MS, PhD); building structures, construction and materials (MS, PhD); design (MA); design theories, methods, and practices (MS, PhD); environmental design in developing countries (MS, PhD); history of architecture and urbanism (MS, PhD); social and cultural processes in architecture and urbanism (MS, PhD); M Arch/MCP; M Arch/MS; MLA/M Arch. *Degree requirements:* For master's, thesis; for doctorate, thesis/dissertation, qualifying exam. *Entrance requirements:* For master's and doctorate, GRE General Test, minimum GPA of 3.0, 3 letters of recommendation. Additional exam requirements/recommendations for international students: Required—TOEFL. Electronic applications accepted.

University of California, Berkeley, Graduate Division, College of Environmental Design, Department of Landscape Architecture and Environmental Planning, Program in Landscape Architecture, Berkeley, CA 94720-1500. Offers environmental planning (MLA); landscape design and site planning (MLA); urban and community design (MLA); MLA/M Arch; MLA/MCP. *Accreditation:* ASLA. *Degree requirements:* For master's, professional project or thesis. *Entrance requirements:* For master's, GRE General Test, minimum GPA of 3.0, portfolio, 3 letters of recommendation.

University of California, Berkeley, Graduate Division, College of Environmental Design, Department of Landscape Architecture and Environmental Planning, Program in Urban Design, Berkeley, CA 94720-1500. Offers MUD. *Degree requirements:* For master's, professional project or thesis. *Entrance requirements:* For master's, GRE General Test, minimum GPA of 3.0, portfolio, 3 letters of recommendation.

University of California, Los Angeles, Graduate Division, School of the Arts and Architecture, Department of Architecture and Urban Design, Los Angeles, CA 90095. Offers M Arch, MA, PhD. *Degree requirements:* For master's, thesis or alternative, comprehensive exam or design project; for doctorate, 2 foreign languages, thesis/dissertation, oral and written qualifying exams. *Entrance requirements:* For master's and doctorate, GRE General Test, portfolio. Additional exam requirements/recommendations for international students: Required—TOEFL. Electronic applications accepted. *Expenses:* Tuition, nonresident: full-time $14,694. Required fees: $9669.50. Full-time tuition and fees vary according to course load, degree level, program

and student level. *Faculty research:* Urban poverty and low wage labor markets; environmental planning and politics; international political economy; physical planning, urban design, planning history; housing and land development; transportation and land use; critical urban and regional studies.

University of Colorado Denver, College of Architecture and Planning, Program in Urban Design, Denver, CO 80217-3364. Offers MUD. Part-time programs available. *Degree requirements:* For master's, thesis optional. *Entrance requirements:* For master's, BA in architecture, minimum GPA of 3.0, portfolio. Additional exam requirements/recommendations for international students: Required—TOEFL (minimum score 550 paper-based; 213 computer-based). *Faculty research:* Architecture of the city, architectural experimentation and exploration, composition and decomposition, intervention and transformation in the urban and rural landscape.

University of Miami, Graduate School, School of Architecture, Program in Suburb and Town Design, Coral Gables, FL 33124. Offers M Arch. *Entrance requirements:* For master's, GRE General Test, minimum GPA of 3.0, portfolio. Additional exam requirements/recommendations for international students: Required—TOEFL. Electronic applications accepted.

University of Michigan, A. Alfred Taubman College of Architecture and Urban Planning, Program in Urban Design, Ann Arbor, MI 48109. Offers MUD. *Entrance requirements:* For master's, GRE General Test, 5-year bachelor of architecture or M Arch or bachelor of landscape architecture or master of landscape architecture or MUP, portfolio. Additional exam requirements/recommendations for international students: Required—TOEFL (minimum score 560 paper-based; 220 computer-based; 84 iBT). *Expenses:* Contact institution.

University of New Mexico, Graduate School, School of Architecture and Planning, Program in Town Design, Albuquerque, NM 87131-2039. Offers Graduate Certificate.

University of Pennsylvania, School of Design, Graduate Group in Architecture, Philadelphia, PA 19104. Offers architecture (PhD); real estate design and development (PhD); urban design (PhD). Part-time programs available. *Degree requirements:* For doctorate, 2 foreign languages, comprehensive exam, thesis/dissertation, qualifying exam, final exam. *Entrance requirements:* For doctorate, GRE General Test, B Arch, M Arch, portfolio, writing sample. Additional exam requirements/recommendations for international students: Required—TOEFL. *Faculty research:* Theory, history, technology, representation, visualization, landscape, urban design, historic preservation.

See Close-Up on page 159.

The University of Texas at Austin, Graduate School, School of Architecture, Austin, TX 78712-1111. Offers architecture (M Arch); community and regional planning (MSCRP, PhD); historic preservation (MS); history of architecture (MA, PhD); landscape architecture (MLA); urban design (MSUD); JD/MSCRP; MSCRP/MA; MSCRP/PhD. *Degree requirements:* For doctorate, thesis/dissertation. *Entrance requirements:* For master's and doctorate, GRE General Test. Additional exam requirements/recommendations for international students: Required—TOEFL (minimum score 550 paper-based; 213 computer-based). Electronic applications accepted.

University of Toronto, School of Graduate Studies, Social Sciences Division, Department of Geography, Toronto, ON M5S 1A1, Canada. Offers geography (M Sc, MA, PhD); planning (M.Sc Pl); urban design studies (MUD). Part-time programs available. *Degree requirements:* For master's, thesis optional; for doctorate, thesis/dissertation. *Entrance requirements:* For master's, bachelor's degree or equivalent in geography or a closely related field, minimum B+ average in each of 2 final years of degree, 3 letters of reference; for doctorate, master of geography degree, minimum A–average.

University of Washington, Graduate School, College of Architecture and Urban Planning, Department of Urban Design and Planning, Seattle, WA 98195. Offers strategic planning for critical infrastructures (MSCPI); urban design and planning (PhD); urban planning (MUP). *Accreditation:* ACSP (one or more programs are accredited). *Degree requirements:* For master's, thesis or alternative; for doctorate, thesis/dissertation. *Entrance requirements:* For master's and doctorate, GRE General Test, minimum GPA of 3.0. Additional exam requirements/recommendations for international students: Required—TOEFL. *Faculty research:* Land-use and growth management, urban form and travel behavior, geographic information systems/remote sensing, historic preservation, urban ecology and environmental planning.

University of Washington, Graduate School, College of Architecture and Urban Planning, Interdisciplinary Program in Urban Design, Seattle, WA 98195. Offers Certificate. Electronic applications accepted. *Faculty research:* Urban design process; urban form; place theory; place analysis; race, class, and gender in community design.

Washington University in St. Louis, Sam Fox School of Design and Visual Arts, Graduate School of Architecture and Urban Design, Program in Urban Design, St. Louis, MO 63130-4899. Offers MUD, M Arch/MUD, MUD/MSW. *Entrance requirements:* For master's, GRE General Test, portfolio. Additional exam requirements/recommendations for international students: Required—TOEFL (minimum score 600 paper-based; 250 computer-based; 100 iBT), TWE. *Faculty research:* Urban design development issues: city revitalization, sustainability and suburbanization; urban history and visualization of urban form.

See Close-Up on page 161.

THE NEW SCHOOL: A UNIVERSITY

Parsons The New School for Design
Program in Architecture

Program of Study

The Department of Architecture, Interior Design, and Lighting offers an NAAB-accredited professional Master of Architecture (M.Arch.) degree. The program emphasizes the study of architecture as a material and cultural practice. It places particular emphasis on the creative role of architects and fosters the task of translating the everyday into extraordinary works of architectural invention. Using the urban environment of New York as a laboratory, the department's rigorous curriculum integrates courses in studio work, history, theory, and technology to investigate the capacity of architecture to shape social interaction in space; the relationship between space, the body, and sensory perception; the integration of material construction and speculative design; the impact of digital technologies and new media on design; and the ecology of technological and natural systems.

The Design Workshop focuses on materiality, detail, and form/space-making in their capacity to reflect and direct social practice. This unique "design-build" studio option is offered in the spring semester of the second year. Students explore the architectural design process from concept to actual construction over six months. The program's small size, atelier atmosphere, and urban environment create an intimate setting where students work closely with a faculty of distinguished professional architects, historians, and theorists drawn from New York's international design community. The department publishes a journal, *Scapes*, that focuses on global, metropolitan, and departmental perspectives on architecture. Students may enroll on a full-time basis only; classes are held Monday through Friday.

Students who already hold a B.Arch. First Professional Degree or an international equivalent typically enroll in the 1½-year postprofessional degree program (54 credits). This program offers a flexible course of study that allows students to custom-design course work to suit their academic interests.

Students with a four-year undergraduate degree in a nonarchitecture major pursue the three-year (106 credits) course of study leading to a First Professional Degree. Prior to entry into this program, students must take college-level courses in calculus, physics, and the history of architecture. It is also required that students without a design background prepare by taking the Parsons Summer Intensive Studio in Architectural Drawing and Modeling or an equivalent course elsewhere.

An M.Arch./M.F.A. dual degree in architecture and lighting design is also available.

Research Facilities

The heart of the architecture program is the large, open studio loft where students develop design projects in interaction with faculty members and peers. The 5,000-square-foot space is supported by wireless digital technology, which allows for direct printing and plotting from students' desks to the adjacent twenty-five-station computer laboratories. A curated material library and staffed model shop are also located next to the studio. Use of the fabrication shops in the Department of Fine Arts, located above the studio, is encouraged and promotes important exchanges with M.F.A. graduate students. The department's facilities are augmented by an extensive collection of books, periodicals, and slides housed at the Adam and Sophie Gimbel Library of Art and Design. In addition, a consortium membership gives Parsons students access to the libraries of The Cooper Union and New York University.

The Angelo Donghia Materials Library and Study Center, funded by the Angelo Donghia Foundation, includes a library, gallery, computer lab, and lecture hall. The library allows students and faculty members to review and check out state-of-the-art resources, putting the latest and most exclusive materials at their fingertips. Regular exhibitions at the gallery—run by a full-time curator—are open to the public, creating an open forum and dialogue with the larger interior design community.

Financial Aid

Graduate students are automatically considered for scholarship funds upon admission into the program. Scholarship recipients are notified of their award by either their program or a Student Financial Services award letter soon after being admitted. Graduate students should contact their academic department early in the admissions process for separate applications for institutional awards, such as assistantships. U.S. citizens and permanent residents applying for financial aid outside the University should file the Free Application for Federal Student Aid (FAFSA) by March 1. More information can be found at the Student Financial Services Web site at http://www.newschool.edu/studentservices/financialaid/.

Cost of Study

In 2009–10 full-time students pay $18,060 in tuition and $145 in fees per term. Additional fees may apply.

Living and Housing Costs

The University offers on-campus housing, University-run apartments, and assistance in finding housing off campus. The cost of housing, food, transportation, books, and living expenses in New York City averages $17,000 annually. For more information, interested students should visit http://www.newschool.edu/studentservices.html.

Student Group

There are 65 students, 31 of whom are women. Of the total, 13 students are members of minority groups and 7 are international.

Location

Parsons The New School for Design, located in Greenwich Village, is fortunate to be situated at the very crossroads of New York's vibrant architecture and design communities. Its location in the city provides students with some of their greatest resources. Students are encouraged to take advantage of the museums, performance venues, and other cultural institutions that are only a walk or subway ride away.

The University and The School

Parsons is part of The New School, a leading university in New York City offering some of the nation's most distinguished programs in design, liberal arts, management and policy, and the performing arts, leading to seventy graduate and undergraduate degrees. More information can be found at http://www.newschool.edu/degreeprograms. Parsons and The New School are fully accredited by the Commission on Higher Education of the Middle States Association of Colleges and Schools.

Applying

Students must submit the completed application, the $50 application fee, a resume, GRE general test scores, a statement of interest, official copies of all college transcripts, two letters of recommendation, and a portfolio that does not exceed 9 inches by 12 inches. The portfolio may include drawings and photographs of architectural projects and should include examples of other artwork. Slides, films, and videos will not be viewed. International students must also submit TOEFL scores—a minimum of 580 on the written test or 237 on the computerized version. The .application deadline is February 1.

Correspondence and Information

Master of Architecture Program
Parsons The New School for Design
66 Fifth Avenue
New York, New York 10011
Phone: 212-229-8955
Fax: 212-229-8937
E-mail: aidl@newschool.edu
Web site: http://www.newschool.edu/parsons
      http://www2.parsons.edu/architecture/aidl/march.html

The New School: A University

THE FACULTY AND THEIR RESEARCH

Complete faculty biographies can be found at http://www2.parsons.edu/architecture/aidl/march/marchfaculty.html

Kimberly Ackert, Architect and Principal, Ackert Architecture; B.Arch., Caltech.
Matthew Baird, Principal, Matthew Baird Design; M.Arch., Columbia.
Sunil Bald, Partner, studioSUMO; M.Arch., Columbia.
Stella Betts, Partner, Leven Betts Studio; M.Arch., Harvard.
Laura Briggs, Director, B.F.A., Architecture and Design; Partner, BriggsKnowles Architecture and Design; M.Arch., Columbia.
Eric Bunge, Principal, nARCHITECTS; M.Arch. II, Harvard.
Dilip da Cunha, Principal, Mathur/da Cunha; Ph.D., Berkeley.
Natalie Fizer, Principal, Fizer/Forley Design; M.Arch., Princeton.
Carlo Frugiuele, Partner, Urban Office Architecture; M.Des., Columbia.
Jean Gardner, Architecture and Landscape Historian; M.A., Columbia.
James Garrison, Principal, Garrison Siegel Architects; B.Arch., Syracuse.
Douglas Gauthier, Partner, SYSTEMarchitects; M.Arch., Columbia.
Ed Keller, Co-Founder, a/Um Studio; M.Arch., Columbia.
Silvia Kolbowski, Multimedia Artist; B.S., CUNY, Hunter.
James Koster, Principal, James Koster Architects; M.Arch., Princeton.
David J. Lewis, Director, M.Arch. Program; M.Arch., Princeton.
Harriet Markis, Structural Engineer and Partner, Dunne & Markis Consulting Structural Engineers; M.Eng., Cornell; PE.
Jonathan Marvel, Principal, Rogers/Marvel Architects; M.Arch., Harvard.
Michael McGough, Vice President, Laszlo Bodak Engineer; B.S.M.E., Columbia; PC.
Brian McGrath, Architect; M.Arch., Princeton.
Joanna Merwood-Salisbury, Associate Chair and Editor, *Scapes;* Ph.D., Princeton.
Luc Nadal, Architect and Scholar; Ph.D., Columbia.
Greg Otto, Senior Engineer, Buro Happold Consulting Engineers; MIT.
Mitchell B. Owen, Partner, Consolidated Design Studios, Ltd.; M.Arch., M.A., Princeton.
David Piscuskas, Partner, 1100 Architect; M.Arch., UCLA.
Derek Porter, Director, M.F.A., Lighting and Design; Principal, Derek Porter Studio; B.F.A., Kansas City Art Institute.
Gundula Proksch, Principal, TAAN Transatlantic Architectural Network; M.Arch., Cornell.
Mark Rakatansky, Principal, Mark Rakatansky Studio; M.Arch., Berkeley.
Juergen Riehm, Partner, 1100 Architect; Diploma in Architecture, Fachhochschule Rheinland-Pfalz (Germany).
Robert Rogers, Principal, Rogers/Marvel Architects; M.Des., Harvard.
Chris Sharples, Principal, Sharples Holden Pasquarelli; M.Arch., Columbia.
William Sharples, Principal, Sharples Holden Pasquarelli; M.Arch., Columbia.
Henry Smith-Miller, Partner, Smith-Miller+Hawkinson Architects; M.Arch., Pennsylvania.
Calvin Tsao, Partner, Tsao & McKowan; M.Arch., Harvard.
Timothy Ventimiglia, Associate/Project Director, Ralph Appelbaum Associates; M.Arch., Cornell.
Perry Winston, Senior Architect, Pratt Planning and Architectural Collaborative; M.Arch., Rice.

THE NEW SCHOOL: A UNIVERSITY

Parsons The New School for Design
Program in Lighting Design

Program of Study

Lighting design is integral to architecture, interior design, product design, theater, and many other disciplines. Offered by Parsons' School of Constructed Environments (which also includes architecture, product design, and interior design), the M.F.A. in Lighting Design program provides a strong interdisciplinary education in the intellectual, aesthetic, and technical aspects of lighting design. This degree program has the distinction of being the first in the field of architectural lighting, as well as the only graduate lighting program focused primarily on design and social practice. The curriculum, which recognizes that human physiology and psychology are central to an understanding of light as a design medium, offers a broad and rigorous study in the design, history, practice, and theory of light and lighting. Students come into close contact with other graduate architecture and interior design students. Distinguished faculty members serve as mentors, and the large, supportive professional community in New York City supplements Parsons' formal studies with numerous programs and lectures in which students are always encouraged to participate.

The program is a two-year (four-semester) full-time course of study. A minimum of 64 credits of required courses are necessary to graduate. This total includes 52 credits of lighting-specific study, 3 credits in the history of architecture, and 9 credits of interdisciplinary departmental electives that include students from the programs in architecture and interior design. Six elective courses (up to a total of 19 credits per semester) are allowed and encouraged, but only three (one from each concentration) are required for the degree.

A dual degree in Architecture and lighting design (M.Arch./M.F.A.) is also available

Research Facilities

Lighting design students work in an open studio alongside graduate architecture and interior design students. A lighting resource library and a lighting laboratory are adjacent to the studio. All the resources of the School of Constructed Environment are available to lighting students, including a large materials library and model shop located next to the second-floor architecture studio and the Donghia Materials Center on the third floor. Use of the fabrication shops in the Department of Fine Arts located above the studio is encouraged and promotes important exchanges with other M.F.A. students. The studio is equipped with wireless digital technology; students also have access to computer labs on both departmental floors and the University's computer centers nearby. Participation in the department's lecture series and exhibitions further the dialogue among lighting, architecture, and interior design.

Financial Aid

Graduate students are automatically considered for scholarship funds upon acceptance into the program. Scholarship recipients are notified of their award by either their program or a Student Financial Services award letter soon after being admitted. Graduate students should contact their academic department early in the admissions process for separate applications for institutional awards, such as assistantships. U.S. citizens and permanent residents applying for financial aid outside the University should file the Free Application for Federal Student Aid (FAFSA) by March 1. More information can be found at the Student Financial Services Web site at http://www.newschool.edu/studentservices/financialaid/.

Cost of Study

In 2009–10, full-time students pay $18,060 in tuition and $145 in fees per term. Additional fees may apply.

Living and Housing Costs

The University offers on-campus housing, University-run apartments, and assistance in finding housing off campus. The cost of housing, food, transportation, books, and living expenses in New York City averages $17,000 annually. For more information, interested students should visit http://www.newschool.edu/studentservices.html.

Student Group

There are 43 students, including 33 women, 4 students who are members of minority groups, and 26 international students. All of the students in the program attend full-time.

Student Outcomes

Graduates of the program have varied career choices and may fill an important role either as architectural lighting designers in private practice or as lighting specialists within architecture and interior design firms. Some graduates choose to concentrate in theatrical and/or exhibition lighting, while others become research professionals in companies designing lighting-related equipment.

Location

Parsons The New School for Design, located in Greenwich Village, is fortunate to be situated at the crossroads of New York's vibrant architecture and design communities. Its location in the city provides students with some of their greatest resources. Students are encouraged to take advantage of the museums, performance venues, and other cultural institutions that are only a walk or subway ride away.

The University and The School

Parsons is part of The New School, a leading university in New York City offering some of the nation's most distinguished programs in design, liberal arts, the performing arts, and social and political science, leading to seventy graduate and undergraduate degrees. Learn more at http://www.newschool.edu/degreeprograms. Parsons and The New School are fully accredited by the Commission on Higher Education of the Middle States Association of Colleges and Schools.

Applying

All applicants must have an undergraduate or graduate degree, preferably in architecture, environmental design, interior design, engineering, or theater arts. Applicants whose bachelor's degrees are in unrelated disciplines should have experience working in these fields. Students must submit the completed application, the $50 application fee, a resume, a statement of interest, official copies of all college transcripts, two letters of recommendation, GRE and general test scores, and a portfolio that does not exceed 9 inches by 12 inches. The portfolio may include drawings and photographs of projects and should include samples of other artwork. In addition, international students must submit TOEFL scores—a minimum of 580 on the written test or 237 on the computerized version. The application deadline is February 1.

Correspondence and Information

Master of Fine Arts in Lighting Design Program
Parsons The New School for Design
72 Fifth Avenue
New York,, New York 10011
Phone: 212-229-8955
Fax: 212-229-8937
E-mail: aidl@newschool.edu
Web site: http://www.newschool.edu/parsons
http://www2.parsons.edu/architecture/aidl/lighting.html

The New School: A University

THE FACULTY

Complete faculty biographies can be found at http://www2.parsons.edu/architecture/aidl/mfaltd/lightingfaculty.html.

Kimberly Ackert, Architect and Principal, Ackert Architecture; B.Arch., Caltech.
James R. Brogan, Architect and Senior Associate Principal, Kohn Pedersen Fox, AIA; B.Arch., Pratt.
Jim Conti, Lighting Designer; M.F.A., Ohio State.
Jessica Corr, Product Designer and Founding Member, Collaborative; B.F.A., Parsons.
Jean Gardner, Art Historian, Author, and Co-founder, Environment '90; M.A., Columbia.
Stephen Horner, Senior Designer, Tillet Lighting Design, Inc.; M.F.A., Parsons.
Nelson Jenkins, Founder, Lumen Architecture; B.F.A., B.Arch., Rhode Island School of Design.
John Katimaris, Architect and Principal, Katimaris + Associates; M.F.A., Parsons.
Jungsoo Kim, Senior Associate, Brandston Partnership, Inc.; M.F.A., Ewha Women's (Korea); M.A., NYU; M.F.A., Parsons.
Pamela Z. Kladzyk, Art Historian and Artist; Ph.D., Catholic University (Lublin).
Chou Lien, Partner, Brandston Partnership, Inc.; M.F.A., SUNY at Buffalo; M.S., Pratt.
Mark Loeffler, Lighting and Sustainable Design Consultant, RETEC Group; M.F.A., Parsons.
Margaret Maile, Ph.D. candidate, Bard Graduate Center.
Paul Marantz, Principal, Fisher Marantz Stone.
Joanna Merwood-Salisbury, Director of Public Programs, Department of Architecture, Interior Design, and Lighting; Scholar of Architectural History and Theory; Ph.D., Princeton.
Enrique Peiniger, Co-founder, Office for Visual Interaction, Inc.; M.Arch., Berlin Technical.
Derek Porter, Director, M.F.A. Lighting Design Program and Principal, Derek Porter Studio; B.F.A., Kansas City Art Institute.
Robert Prouse, Partner, Brandston Partnership, Inc.; M.Arch., Colorado.
Caroline Razook, Designer, Rogers Marvel Architecture; M.Arch., Parsons.
Nathalie Rozot, Consultant, L'Observatoire International.
Leni Schwendinger, Leni Schwendinger Light Projects Ltd.
Christine Sciulli. Video installation, lighting consultant.
Amy Sharp.
Joel R. Siegel, Lighting Engineer and Vice President of Marketing and Sales, Edison Price Lighting; B.A., CUNY, City College.
David S. Singer, Principal, Arc Light Design; M.Arch., Washington (St. Louis).
Jean Sundin, Co-founder, Office for Visual Interaction, Inc.; B.F.A., Virginia Commonwealth.
Matthew Tanteri, Lighting Designer, Tanteri + Associates; M.F.A., Parsons.
Thomas Thompson, Principal, Thompson + Sears, LLC; B.A.E., Penn State.
Linnaea Tillett, Lighting Designer; Ph.D., CUNY.
Attila Uysal, Principal, Susan Brady Lighting Design; M.A., Pratt.
Alexa Griffith Winton, Design Historian; M.A., Bard Graduate Center.
James Yorgey, Technical Applications Manager, Lutron Electronics Company; B.S., Penn State.

PRATT INSTITUTE

School of Architecture

Programs of Study

The School of Architecture is dedicated to maintaining the connection between design theory and practice and to extending the range of knowledge necessary to an understanding of the built environment. The diversity of programs within the School and the accessibility of other programs within the Institute enable students to pursue a wide range of interests. Students can take electives in fine arts, film, digital arts, industrial design, furniture design, interior design, and photography as well as electives in advanced architectural theory, design, technology, and management. The School has many internationally recognized faculty members who bring to the graduate programs a strong theoretical base and the high standards of their professional work. The programs are distinguished by strong studio cultures and creative approaches to architectural design. Many special courses are offered in contemporary theoretical and critical issues, advanced computing and media, building technology, architectural history, and experimental structures. The electronic laboratory is a fifty-station PC-based facility that offers instruction in a wide variety of two-dimensional and three-dimensional design programs. Students are exposed to the professional world through optional internship programs that place them in outstanding New York architectural offices, public agencies, and nonprofit design institutions, giving them firsthand work experience and credit towards their degree.

The School of Architecture offers at total of seven graduate programs. There are two graduate architecture programs: the first professional accredited Master of Architecture (M.Arch.) and the postprofessional Master of Architecture (M.S.Arch.). There are also five Master of Science programs: architecture and urban design, city and regional planning, environmental systems management, facilities management, and historic preservation.

The three-year M.Arch. is designed for students holding a four-year undergraduate program in any field, including architecture. Graduate courses and seminars are designed to familiarize students with all aspects of the discipline and practice of architecture. Design studios at Pratt find many of their coordinates within the rich territory of New York City. However, the program also reaches into areas worldwide and into other frames, such as global marketplaces, digital worlds, and historical, theoretical, and political networks. This program is fully accredited by NAAB. Students with a B.S. in architecture or other nonprofessional degree should apply for this M.Arch. program. The postprofessional M.S.Arch. program is for those who hold an accredited architecture degree or the equivalent. The program takes approximately three semesters to complete. Students with significant professional experience can also apply for work credit, which reduces total credit-hour requirements. The postprofessional M.S.Arch. allows intensive theoretical and technical engagement of architecture and the city and stresses research and experimentation concentrating on the relations between architecture and other urban forms, scales, and forces. Research is conducted primarily within the analytic and synthetic content of the design studio and culminates in a required thesis.

The Master of Science in architecture and urban design program is intended for students who are interested in careers that enhance the growth and development of the built urban environments, the context for an urban laboratory. The 33-credit program requires 17 hours of design studio and research, with the balance of the credits in required courses in urban history, theory, infrastructure, and implementation and electives in law, transportation, housing, and preservation. The program is open to those with professional undergraduate degrees in architecture.

The three programs offered by the Graduate Center for Planning and the Environment (GCPE)—the M.S. in city and regional planning (CRP), the M.S. in environmental systems management (ESM), and the M.S. in historic preservation—emphasize planning and preservation practice rooted in the principles of sustainability, equity, and public participation.

The curricula are designed to build the professional skills and knowledge of students who desire to affect the built, natural, and social environments of the nation's cities and communities in positive ways. CRP and EMS courses are offered in the evenings, enabling students to work full-time. The city and regional planning program offers specializations in community development, environmental planning, physical planning, and preservation planning. The CRP program requires the completion of 60 credits, including the thesis or the Demonstration of Professional Competence course. The EMS program requires 40 credits of course work.

Students with undergraduate degrees in architecture and engineering may have up to 9 credits waived in either the CRP or EMS program. GCPE's newest program is a two-year graduate program leading to the M.S. in historic preservation. The program, designed primarily for full-time students and based at the Manhattan campus, is a 44-credit sequence of courses that provides studies in community planning, history, interpretation, design, policy, and regulatory practice.

Recognizing that today's field of preservation requires more than curatorial management, the program fosters the knowledge preservationists must have in order to participate in policy-making to revitalize urban areas, suburban communities, and rural landscapes. With its urban focus, the program emphasizes hands-on work and makes extensive use of New York City's rich resources.

All three graduate programs in the GCPE maintain strong ties with Pratt's architecture and design programs and with the Pratt Center for Community Development, an innovative center for the practice of planning, design, and policy work that focuses on increasing quality of life and affecting social change in New York City's diverse communities.

The M.S. in facilities management program prepares individuals to assume leadership roles in corporations, institutions, and government. The degree requires the completion of 45 credits of course work and the 5-credit Demonstration of Professional Competence course, for a total of 50 credits. Students entering the program with prior professional experience or graduate work in related fields may be eligible for advanced standing; up to 12 credits may be waived. The facilities management program is offered at the Pratt Manhattan Center on an evening schedule, allowing maximum flexibility to combine full-time work with study and research.

Research Facilities

The Pratt Library has grown with the Institute to house one of the finest collections of reference material on art, design, and architecture. Recently remodeled and expanded to accommodate its growing collection, the library contains 186,589 bound volumes, serial backfiles, and other material, including government documents; 251,603 audiovisual materials; and 3,996 microforms and subscribes to 925 periodicals.

Pratt maintains numerous studios, shops, and technical facilities for work in all media, as well as state-of-the-art computer facilities. Pratt also has extensive gallery space for the exhibition of works by the student body, alumni, faculty members, and well-known architects and designers.

Financial Aid

Financial aid is offered through a variety of programs funded by the institution and the federal and state governments. These include Federal Perkins Loan and Federal Work-Study programs, the Tuition Assistance Program of New York State, and Pratt loans and student help. Graduate scholarships are awarded to entering students on a competitive basis. Fellowships and assistantships are awarded on a competitive basis to continuing students in all departments. Special alumni-sponsored fellowships are also available.

Cost of Study

Graduate tuition for 2008–09 was $27,216 per year (24 credits, $1134 per credit). Student fees were $1190 per semester. The cost of books and supplies varies widely, depending on the program in which the student is enrolled.

Living and Housing Costs

Campus housing continues to be expanded to meet student needs and is available for single students on a first-come, first-served basis. Housing costs average $15,294 per academic year. There is a plentiful supply of moderately priced rentals in the immediate area and in adjacent neighborhoods for married students seeking housing as well as for those students choosing to reside off campus.

Student Group

There are more than 248 students enrolled in Pratt's School of Architecture graduate programs; 53 percent are women. They come from all parts of the United States and the world. The graduate programs are noted for an exceptional placement ratio, with more than 85 percent of the graduating students finding employment before graduation.

Location

Pratt Institute is located in the Clinton Hill section of Brooklyn, on a 25-acre park-like campus. Pratt's Manhattan campus houses the Institute's graduate arts and cultural management, communications design, design management, facilities management, historic preservation, and library and information science programs as well as offering courses in architecture, city and regional planning, creative arts therapy, and urban design.

The Institute

A private, nonsectarian institute of higher education, Pratt Institute was founded in 1887 by the industrialist and philanthropist Charles Pratt. Today, Pratt educates 3,066 undergraduates and 1,602 graduate students for careers in art and design, architecture, and library and information science.

Applying

The application deadline is January 15. Early submission of applications, together with all necessary credentials, is highly desirable. For the applicant who intends to file for merit-based scholarships, applications and all supporting documents need to be received no later than January 15 for the fall semester and October 1 for the spring semester. All application materials must be received by January 5, or the application may not be considered. Materials should be submitted in one package that includes the three letters of recommendation in sealed envelopes with the reference's signature across the flap.

Correspondence and Information

Graduate Admissions Office
Pratt Institute
200 Willoughby Avenue
Brooklyn, New York 11205
Phone: 718-636-3514
     800-331-0834 (toll-free outside New York State)
Fax: 718-399-4242
E-mail: admissions@pratt.edu
Web site: http://www.pratt.edu

Pratt Institute

THE FACULTY

Thomas Hanrahan, Dean; M.Arch., Harvard; AIA, NCARB.

Architecture
William MacDonald, Professor and Chair; M.S., Columbia.
Philip Parker, Assistant Chair; M.Arch., Yale.
Gilland Akos, Visiting Assistant Professor.
Phillip Anzalone, Visiting Assistant Professor; M.Arch., Columbia.
Ezra Ardolino, Adjunct Assistant Professor.
Alexandra Barker, Adjunct Assistant Professor; M.Arch., Harvard.
Stephanie Bayard, Adjunct Assistant Professor; M.A., Columbia.
Karen Brandt, Visiting Professor; M.Arch., Harvard.
Dan Bucsescu, Adjunct Professor.
Theodore Calvin, Visiting Professor; M.S., Columbia.
Amber Chapin, Visiting Assistant Professor.
Manuel DeLanda, Adjunct Professor; B.F.A., School of Visual Arts.
Livio Dimitriu, Adjunct Professor.
Jeremy Edmiston, Adjunct Assistant Professor; M.S., Columbia.
Giuiano Fiorenzoli, Professor; M.A.S., MIT; M.Arch., Florence (Italy).
Erik Ghenoiu, Visiting Assistant Professor.
Jose Gonzalez, Visiting Assistant Professor.
Lara Guerra, Visiting Instructor.
Matthew Herman, Visiting Assistant Professor.
Michael Hollander, Visiting Associate Professor; M.Arch.
Alicia Imperiale, Visiting Assistant Professor; Ph.D. candidate, Princeton.
Catherine Ingraham, Professor, Ph.D.
Hina Jamelle, Visiting Assistant Professor.
Robert Kearns, Visiting Assistant Professor.
Michael Kennedy, Visiting Instructor.
Nico Kienzl, Visiting Instructor; D.Des., Harvard.
Karel Klein, Adjunct Associate Professor; M.Arch., Columbia.
Kevin Kleyla, Visiting Assistant Professor.
Carisima Koenig, Visiting Instructor.
M. Ferda Kolatan, Visiting Assistant Professor.
Craig Konyk, Adjunct Associate Professor.
Sameer Kumar, Adjunct Assistant Professor; M.Arch.
David Lallemant, Adjunct Assistant Professor; B.S.
Thomas Leeser, Adjunct Associate Professor.
Peter Macapia, Adjunct Assistant Professor; Ph.D., Columbia.
Radhi Majmuder, Visiting Assistant Professor.
Alexandru Marin, Adjunct Assistant Professor.
Natalia Martinez, Adjunct Instructor.
Katherine Mearns, Visiting Assistant Professor.
Tali Mejicovsky, Visiting Instructor; B.S., B.A., Pennsylvania.
Robert Mezquiti, Visiting Instructor; M.Arch.
Nilay Oza, Visiting Assistant Professor; M.S.Arch., MIT.
David Ruy, Adjunct Associate Professor; M.Arch., Columbia.
Maria Sieira, Adjunct Instructor; M.Arch., Pennsylvania.
Henry Smith-Miller, Adjunct Professor; M.Arch., Pennsylvania.
Jeremy Snyder, Visiting Assistant Professor.
Nathaniel Stanton, Adjunct Associate Professor.
Michael Szivos, Visiting Assistant Professor.
Jeffrey Taras, Visiting Instructor; M.Arch., Columbia.
Meredith Tenhoor, Visiting Instructor; Ph.D. candidate, Princeton.
Kenneth Tracy, Visiting Assistant Professor.
Maria Ludovica Tramontin, Adjunct Assistant Professor; Ph.D., Cagliari (Italy).
Jason Vigneri-Beane, Adjunct Assistant Professor; M.Arch., Iowa State.
Aaron White, Visiting Instructor; M.Arch., Pratt.
J. Christopher Whitelaw, Visiting Instructor; M.Arch., Columbia.
Lebbeus Woods, Adjunct Professor.

Urban Design
William MacDonald, Professor and Chair; M.S., Columbia.
Meta Brunzema, Adjunct Assistant Professor; M.Arch., Columbia.
Franklin Lee, Visiting Instructor; M.S., Columbia.
Elliot Maltby, Adjunct Associate Professor; M.L.A., Berkeley.
Victoria Marshall, Adjunct Associate Professor; M.L.A., Pennsylvania.
Brian McGrath, Adjunct Associate Professor; M.Arch., Princeton.
Anne Save de Beaurecueil, Visiting Instructor; B.Arch., Caltech.
Roland Snooks, Adjunct Assistant Professor; M.S., Columbia.

Planning and the Environment (City and Regional Planning and Environmental Systems Management)
Catherine Herman, Chair; M.S.CRP, Pratt.
Eric Allison, Adjunct Associate Professor and Coordinator; Ph.D., Columbia.

Moshe Adler, Visiting Associate Professor; Ph.D., UCLA.
Robert Alpern, Visiting Associate Professor; I.L.B., Yale.
Erica Avrami, Visiting Instructor; Ph.D. candidate, Rutgers.
Jennifer Becker, Visiting Assistant Professor; M.S.CRP, Pratt.
Christine Benedict, Visiting Instructor; B.Arch., Cooper Union.
Viren Brahmbhatt, Visiting Assistant Professor; M.S.
Carlton Brown, Visiting Instructor; B.A., Princeton.
Darryl Cabbagestalk, Visiting Assistant Professor; J.D., Pace.
Erick Carcamo, Visiting Assistant Professor.
Robert Chapman, Visiting Associate Professor.
Ramon Cruz, Visiting Assistant Professor.
Resa A. Dimino, Visiting Instructor; B.A., Dickinson.
Rayna Erlich, Visiting Instructor.
Stefanie Feldman, Visiting Assistant Professor; M.S., NJIT.
Patricia Fisher-Olsen, Visiting Assistant Professor.
Roland Gebhardt, Visiting Assistant Professor; M.A., Hamburg (Germany).
Henry Gifford, Visiting Instructor.
Steven Hammer, Visiting Assistant Professor; Ph.D., London School of Economics and Political Science.
Eva Hanhardt, Adjunct Assistant Professor; M.U.P., NYU.
Larissa Justine Heilner, Visiting Assistant Professor; M.L.A., Pennsylvania.
Jeanne Houck, Visiting Assistant Professor; Ph.D., NYU.
Edward Kaufman, Adjunct Associate Professor.
Tanushri Kumar, Visiting Assistant Professor.
Brad Lander, Visiting Assistant Professor; M.S.CRP, Pratt.
Frank Lang, Visiting Assistant Professor.
Floyd Lapp, Visiting Associate Professor; Ph.D., NYU.
Paul Mankiewicz, Visiting Associate Professor; Ph.D., CUNY.
Jonathan Martin, Visiting Assistant Professor; Ph.D., Cornell.
Jane McNamara, Visiting Assistant Professor.
William Menking, Professor; M.S., London; M.S.CRP, Pratt.
Norman Mintz, Visiting Associate Professor.
Gita Nandan, Visiting Assistant Professor; M.Arch., Berkeley.
Theodore Prudon, Adjunct Associate Professor.
Marci Reaven-Tanis, Visiting Assistant Professor; Ph.D. candidate, NYU.
Steven Romalewski, Visiting Assistant Professor; M.S., Columbia.
Ariella Rosenberg, Visiting Assistant Professor; M.S., MIT.
Ron Shiffman, Professor; M.S.CRP, Pratt.
Mi Shih, Visiting Instructor.
Anika Singh, Visiting Assistant Professor; J.D., NYU.
Mathy Stanislaus, Visiting Assistant Professor; J.D., IIT.
Ira Stern, Visiting Assistant Professor; M.S.CRP, Pratt.
Gelvin Stevenson, Visiting Associate Professor; Ph.D., Washington (St. Louis).
Samara Swanston, Visiting Assistant Professor; J.D., St. John's (New York).
Val Washington, Visiting Assistant Professor; J.D., Albany Law.
Vicki Weiner, Adjunct Associate Professor; M.S., Columbia.
Joseph Weisbord, Visiting Assistant Professor; M.S.CRP, Pratt.
Edward Perry Winston, Visiting Assistant Professor; M.Arch., Rice.
Kevin Wolfe, Visiting Assistant Professor; M.Arch., Columbia.
Ayse Yonder, Associate Professor; Ph.D., Berkeley.
Catherine Zidar, Visiting Assistant Professor; M.S.CRP, Pratt.

Historic Preservation
William MacDonald, Chair; M.S., Columbia.
Eric Allison, Adjunct Associate Professor and Coordinator; Ph.D., Columbia.
Erica Avrami, Visiting Assistant Professor; Ph.D. candidate, Rutgers.
Ned Kaufman, Adjunct Associate Professor; Ph.D., Yale.
Jane McNamara, Visiting Assistant Professor; M.A., NYU.
Marci Reaven-Tanis, Visiting Assistant Professor; Ph.D. candidate, NYU.
Theodore Prudon, Visiting Associate Professor; Ph.D., Columbia.
Vicki Weiner, Visiting Assistant Professor; M.S., Columbia.
Kevin Wolfe, Visiting Assistant Professor; M.Arch., Columbia.

Facilities Management and Construction Management
Harriet Markis, Assistant Professor and Chair; M. Engr., Cornell.
William Henry, Visiting Assistant Professor; B.A., NYU.
Keith Keppler, Visiting Assistant Professor; M.B.A., USC.
Stephen Lograsso, Visiting Assistant Professor; B.S., NYIT.
Mary J. Matthews, Professor; M.S., Boston College.
Martin J. McManus, Visiting Assistant Professor; B.B.A., Pace.
Russell Olson, Visiting Assistant Professor; M.S., Pratt.
John E. Osborn, Visiting Associate Professor; J.D., South Carolina.
Edward D. Re Jr., Adjunct Associate Professor; M.S., Pratt.

UNIVERSITY OF MIAMI

School of Architecture

Programs of Study

The School of Architecture offers both professional and postprofessional graduate programs. The Professional Master of Architecture degree has two tracks, one for students with preprofessional degrees in architecture and one for students with degrees outside of architecture. Candidates with a preprofessional architecture degree typically pursue the two-year track of concentrated study. Students with degrees in other disciplines follow a program of 3½ years' duration.

The postprofessional Master of Architecture in Suburb and Town Design program has attracted international recognition for its efforts to develop guiding principles for the building of communities. Designed for students already holding a professional degree, the one-calendar-year curriculum includes special opportunities to work directly with municipalities, civic and neighborhood groups, and other governmental agencies and prepares students to be effective designers and advocates for both private and public development and public-sector redevelopment enterprises.

The Master of Real Estate Development and Urbanism (MRED+U) is an interdisciplinary one-year graduate program that blends the fundamentals of real estate development with livable community planning and design. The Master of Real Estate Development and Urbanism draws on the combined interdisciplinary strengths of the School of Architecture, an international leader in urbanism and livable community design; the School of Business Administration, named the number 1 business school in Florida by the *Wall Street Journal* and the number 5 business school in the nation by *Hispanic Business;* the School of Law, which offers an LL.M. degree in real property; the College of Engineering, with strong civil, architectural, and environmental engineering programs; and the Urban Studies Program, directed by faculty members from the College of Arts and Science.

The MRED+U program is administered by the School of Architecture, which is led by Dean Elizabeth Plater-Zyberk. The University of Miami's School of Architecture was ranked number 1 in the nation for the study of New Urbanism in a survey conducted by *New Urban News* and was awarded the John Nolen Medal for Contributions to Urbanism in Florida in 2007. The MRED+U program is designed to provide students with the tools and practical experiences needed to compete in the fast-paced and changing world of urban real estate development. Students benefit from the program's location in the heart of one of the world's most exciting and dynamic real estate markets and from leading experts, entrepreneurs, and business leaders in the real estate industry. Course topics include cutting-edge practice in real estate finance, market analysis, real estate law, land-use policies and codes, project management, public-private partnerships, the development process, sustainable development, and entrepreneurship. The MRED+U prepares real estate industry professionals who are capable of tapping the power of the market to deliver compact, walkable, mixed-use development that offers a high quality of life for diverse populations to live, work, and carry out their daily activities in attractive, sustainable neighborhoods and communities.

Research Facilities

The architecture library includes books, journals, magazines, and an archive of maps and drawings. Computer terminals provide access to the catalogs of the University's main library and other research libraries in South Florida. The University's Richter Library has specialized collections in government publications and Floridiana and a growing archive of New Urbanism. CD-ROM databases and other extensive databases are available. In addition to the conventional software, the School's computer laboratory has advanced programs in computer-aided design, imaging, animation, and geographical information systems. Opportunities for research are available through the School's Center for Urban and Community Design, which offers the opportunity for graduate students to work with faculty members on issues critical to the region.

Financial Aid

The University of Miami provides financial assistance in the form of fellowships, tuition scholarships, assistantships in research or instruction, loans, and student employment for full-time graduate students.

To be considered for these sources of financial aid, applicants must have all academic credentials, letters of recommendation, and examination scores in prior to February 1. Decisions on applications are announced in March and April. The normal workload of the assistantship is 10–12 hours per week during the academic year. Assistantship stipends vary depending upon the field of work.

Cost of Study

The cost per credit hour for the 2008–09 academic year was $1424, with additional fees of $328.

Living and Housing Costs

The Department of Residence Halls provides limited accommodations for full-time graduate students. Graduate students live in single or up to four-bedroom units in the University's newest residential community, University Village. For 2008–09, monthly rental rates range from $1522 to $6955. Annual rates range from $10,080 to $16,692. Housing is not available for married students or families. The University maintains off-campus listings.

Student Group

Students in the graduate degree program come from various humanities, art, and science backgrounds. Approximately half of the students are women, and there are numerous international students. Overall, the majority of graduate students receive financial aid in the form of tuition scholarships, graduate assistantships, or both.

Student Outcomes

Miami alumni are sought after by employers. Recent graduates can be found working in renowned architecture and planning firms across the country and internationally as well as with real estate development companies and municipal government. Many open their own professional practice.

Location

The main campus of the University of Miami is situated in Coral Gables, one of America's notable garden cities. There are links by Metrorail to downtown Miami. The campus is less than 3 miles from Biscayne Bay and Miami Beach.

The University and The School

George Merrick, the visionary founder of Coral Gables, inspired the founding of the architecture program in the early 1920s when he encouraged the association of the planners and designers of the new community with the newly formed University of Miami. That initial association of architects, planners, landscape architects, and artists—working within the context of an emerging region—remains a hallmark of the School.

Today, the School of Architecture reaches beyond the region to a worldwide network of professional contacts, affiliations, and alumni. These associations generate numerous opportunities for collaborative studies, exchange programs, summer internships, and career placement upon graduation.

Applying

Applications submitted to the School of Architecture Office of Graduate Admissions by March 1 receive the highest consideration. Requests for assistantships or scholarships should be submitted at the same time. To be admitted to the graduate programs, an applicant is required to hold a baccalaureate degree from an accredited institution. The academic record should be outstanding. Prior to admission, an applicant is required to present scores from the verbal and quantitative sections of the Graduate Record Examinations (GRE). The application fee is $65 for mailed-in forms and $55 for online submissions.

Correspondence and Information

Teofilo Victoria
Director of Graduate Studies
School of Architecture
University of Miami
P.O. Box 249178
Coral Gables, Florida 33124

Phone: 305-284-3731
Fax: 305-284-6879

University of Miami

THE FACULTY AND THEIR RESEARCH

Roberto M. Behar, Associate Professor in Practice; Diploma in Architecture, National University of Rosario (Argentina). Design, theory.
Charles C. Bohl, Associate Professor; Ph.D., North Carolina at Chapel Hill. Real estate development, community building.
Jacob Brillhart, Lecturer; M.S.A.A.D., Columbia; M.Arch., Tulane. Design, graphics.
Rocco Ceo, Professor; M.Arch., Harvard. Design, graphics.
Sonia Chao, Research Associate Professor; M.Arch., Columbia. Design, community building.
Jaime Correa, Associate Professor in Practice; M.A.U.D., M.C.P., Pennsylvania. Urban design, town planning, theory.
Adib Cure, Lecturer; M.Arch., Harvard. Design, building systems.
David Fix, Research Assistant Professor; M.Arch., Yale. Design, technology.
Jose Gelabert-Navia, Professor; M.F.A., Cornell. Design, graphics, history of architecture.
Gary C. Greenan, Professor; M.C.R.P., Catholic University. Design, landscape architecture.
Carmen Guerrero, Research Associate Professor; M.Arch., Cornell. Design, history of architecture.
Denis Hector, Associate Professor and Associate Dean; M.S., Pennsylvania. Design, structures, technology.
Jorge L. Hernandez, Professor; M.Arch., Virginia. Historic preservation, design, theory, graphics.
Jan Hochstim, Professor; M.A., Miami (Florida). Design, history of architecture.
Richard John, Assistant Professor; M.Phil., Warburg. History of architecture and urbanism.
Jean-François Lejeune, Professor; Diploma in Engineering and Architecture, Liege (Belgium). Design, theory, history of cities.
Joanna Lee Lombard, Professor; M.Arch., Harvard. Design, environmental studies, history of landscape.
Tomas L. Lopez-Gottardi, Professor and Director of Undergraduate Studies; M.A.U.D., M.C.P., Pennsylvania. Design, theory.
Catherine Lynn, Visiting Assistant Professor; Ph.D., Yale. Historic preservation.
Frank Martinez, Associate Professor; M.Arch., Princeton. Design, methods, graphics.
Joseph Middlebrooks, Professor; M.Arch., M.C.P., Yale. Design, professional practice.
Aristides J. Millas, Associate Professor; M.Arch., Harvard. Design, history of architecture.
Nicholas N. Patricios, Professor; Ph.D., University College, London. Urban planning, behavioral studies.
Carie Ann Penabad, Assistant Professor; M.Arch., Harvard. Design, graphics.
Elizabeth Plater-Zyberk, Distinguished Professor and Dean; M.Arch., Yale. Design, urban design.
Allan Schulman, Research Assistant Professor; M.Arch., Miami (Florida). Design, historic preservation, housing.
Vincent Scully, Distinguished Visiting Professor; Ph.D., Yale. History of architecture.
Thomas Alton Spain, Professor; M.Des., Harvard. Design, visual studies.
Jorge Trelles, Lecturer; M.Arch., Cornell. Design.
Luis Trelles, Assistant Professor; M.Arch., Cornell. Design, technology.
Teofilo Victoria, Associate Professor and Director of Graduate Studies; M.Arch., Columbia. Design, theory.
Katherine Wheeler, Assistant Professor, Ph.D., MIT. History of architecture, graphics.

UNIVERSITY OF PENNSYLVANIA

School of Design

Programs of Study

For men and women who wish to study design and planning within a rich, cross-disciplinary context, the University of Pennsylvania's School of Design offers exceptional opportunities. Founded more than 100 years ago, the School is known throughout the world for its exceptional mix of programs and for fostering seminal thought about the way we shape and are shaped by the natural and man-made environment.

The School offers professional master's degrees in fine arts, architecture, landscape architecture, city planning, urban spatial analytics, and historic preservation. Great emphasis is placed on interdisciplinary study, and a series of both dual-degree options and certificates is offered to enable students to take their creative and intellectual study and research in-depth across conventional departmental or program boundaries. Collaborative studios and cooperative programming with Penn's Wharton School and the School of Arts and Sciences provide students with opportunities to interact with the multiple disciplines they are likely to encounter later on in professional practice. To Ph.D. candidates, the graduate groups in architecture and city and regional planning offer advanced training for teaching and research.

Research Facilities

The Architectural Archives of the University of Pennsylvania preserve the works of more than 200 designers from the eighteenth century to the present and include the Louis I. Kahn Collection. The Architectural Conservation Laboratory of the graduate program in historic preservation is devoted to advanced training and research in the conservation of the built environment. The PennDesign Computing Center supports a variety of computing activities, including CAD, GIS, and urban simulation modeling, as well as database, spreadsheet, and word processing applications. The Fabrication Center includes both conventional and computer-driven equipment. The University of Pennsylvania library is a composite of fourteen campus libraries of which the Jerome and Anne Fisher Fine Arts Library is one, as well as the Perkins Rare Architectural Book Collection and the Slide Collection.

Financial Aid

The School of Design provides its students with assistance in planning for and securing adequate financing for graduate school. New students apply for fellowships and scholarships at the time of application to their chosen department. Diversity scholarships are available.

Cost of Study

The tuition and general fee for full-time graduate students in the School of Design is $38,590 for the 2009–10 academic year. This includes a general fee of $2074. The 2009–10 nine-month budget is estimated at $61,340, which included tuition and fees, room, board, and all other expenses.

Living and Housing Costs

There are several residential options offering both apartment and suite living arrangements for single and married students as well as students with families. Many graduate students live off campus, where housing is available at varying costs that begin at approximately $450 per month.

Student Group

The student body is drawn from all over the United States, from many other countries, and from a variety of undergraduate disciplines. There is an enrollment of approximately 575 full-time students. An active PennDesign Student Council and a University Graduate and Professional Student Association provide the opportunity for interaction among the departments and the twelve schools of the University.

Location

Philadelphia was founded more than 300 years ago and is famous for its historic significance. It is today the nation's sixth-largest city, the home to major cultural institutions, and a vibrant mosaic of many cultures. Philadelphia and the surrounding region act as a laboratory for PennDesign students and faculty members.

The University and The School

Founded in 1740 by Benjamin Franklin, the University of Pennsylvania is composed of twelve graduate, professional, and undergraduate schools. The guiding philosophy of "one university" connotes the spirit of cooperation unifying the diverse intellectual and social activities of the University. PennDesign students are encouraged to take advantage of courses offered by the other graduate and professional schools through electives and audits.

Applying

Applicants to each degree program in the School of Design must submit an online application form, application fee, three letters of recommendation, official transcripts, and GRE scores. In addition, there are specific requirements for portfolios, or written statements by individual departments. The application fee is $70. The application deadline is January 2 for the Ph.D. and M.S. programs, January 6 for the Master of Architecture program, and February 1 for all other programs.

Correspondence and Information

Office of Admissions
School of Design
110 Meyerson Hall
University of Pennsylvania
Philadelphia, Pennsylvania 19104-6311

Phone: 215-898-6520
Fax: 215-573-3927
E-mail: admissions@design.upenn.edu
Web site: http://www.design.upenn.edu

University of Pennsylvania

THE FACULTY AND THEIR RESEARCH

Architecture
Tony Atkin, M.Arch., Adjunct Associate Professor. Cultural and architectural design.
Cecil Balmond, M.Sc., Paul Philippe Cret Practice Professor of Architecture. Structural engineering, design.
William Braham, Ph.D., Associate Professor and Interim Chair. Design and building systems, lighting, color.
Winka Dubbeldam, M.Arch., Practice Professor. Design practice.
Homa Farjadi, M.Arch., Practice Professor. Design practice.
Richard Farley, M.Arch., Adjunct Associate Professor. Structures, architecture practice.
Annette Fierro, M.Arch., Associate Professor. Construction technology, design.
Helene Furján, Ph.D., Assistant Professor. History and theory.
Gary A. Hack, Ph.D., Professor. Urban design and physical planning.
Stephen Kieran, M.Arch., Adjunct Professor. Building systems, design.
David Leatherbarrow, Ph.D., Professor. History and theory of architecture.
Ali Malkawi, Ph.D., Professor. Energy systems and design.
Peter McCleary, D.I.C., Emeritus Professor. Philosophy and history of architectural technology.
Detlef Mertins, Ph.D., Professor. History and theory.
Enrique Norten, M.Arch., Practice Professor. Design.
Ali Rahim, M.Arch., Associate Professor. Design theory and digital media.
Witold Rybczynski, M.Arch., Meyerson Professor of Urbanism. Design history and theory.
Marilyn Jordan Taylor, M.Arch., Dean and Paley Professor. Urban design and planning.
James Timberlake, M.Arch., Adjunct Professor. Building systems, design.
Cathrine Veikos, M.Arch., Assistant Professor. Digital methods and design.
Marion Weiss, M.Arch., Professor. Design, drawing, urbanism.
Richard Wesley, M.Arch., Adjunct Associate Professor and Undergraduate Chair. Design, theory.

City and Regional Planning
Jonathan Barnett, M.Arch., Practice Professor of City and Regional Planning. Physical planning and urban design.
Eugenie L. Birch, Ph.D., Nussdorf Professor of Urban Research and Education. History of planning, inner-city revitalization, international planning.
Thomas L. Daniels, Ph.D., Professor of Urban Research. Growth management, watershed protection, farmland preservation.
Gary A. Hack, Ph.D., Professor. Urban design and physical planning.
Amy Hillier, Ph.D., Assistant Professor. Geographic information systems.
John Landis, Ph.D., Crossways Professor and Chair. Growth management, transportation and land use, planning history.
Michael Larice, Ph.D., Associate Professor. Community and regional planning.
Harris Steinberg, M.Arch., Adjunct Assistant Professor. Professional practice.
Marilyn Jordan Taylor, M.Arch., Dean and Paley Professor. Urban design and planning.
Domenic Vitiello, Ph.D., Assistant Professor. Urban studies.
Rachel Weinberger, Ph.D., Assistant Professor. Transportation and land use.
Robert Yaro, M.C.P., Practice Professor. Regional planning and growth strategies.

Fine Arts
Terry Adkins, M.F.A., M.S., Professor. Sculpture.
Sharka Brod Hyland, M.F.A., Adjunct Assistant Professor. Graphic design, digital imaging.
Susana Jacobson, M.F.A., Adjunct Associate Professor. Painting.
John Moore, M.F.A., Professor Emeritus. Painting.
Joshua Mosley, M.F.A., Associate Professor and Interim Chair. Digital animation.
Julie Schneider, M.F.A., Adjunct Associate Professor. Drawing and painting.
Jackie Tileston, M.F.A., Associate Professor. Painting.

Historic Preservation
David De Long, Ph.D., Emeritus Professor. Historic preservation, history and theory of architecture.
Michael Henry, M.S., Adjunct Professor. Building pathology and diagnostics.
Randall Mason, Ph.D., Associate Professor and Chair. Preservation planning, cultural policy, site management.
Frank Matero, M.S., Professor and Director, Architecture Conservation Laboratory. Building and conservation technology.
John Milner, B.Arch., Adjunct Professor. Restoration and adaptive reuse of historic buildings, design of new buildings.

Landscape Architecture and Regional Planning
Anita Berrizbeitia, M.L.A., Associate Professor. Design theory.
James Corner, M.L.A., Professor and Chair. Landscape urbanism.
John Dixon Hunt, Ph.D., Professor Emeritus. Landscape history and theory.
Peter Latz, M.A., Adjunct Professor. Landscape remediation.
Anuradha Mathur, M.L.A., Associate Professor. Landscape design and theory.
Karen M'Closkey, M.L.A., Assistant Professor. Landscape design and theory.
Cora Olgyay, M.L.A., Adjunct Assistant Professor. Landscape materials.
Laurie Olin, B.Arch., Practice Professor. Design practice.
Christopher Reed, M.L.A. Adjunct Associate Professor. Design practice, ecological design.
Lucinda Sanders, M.L.A., Adjunct Associate Professor. Design practice.
C. Dana Tomlin, Ph.D., Professor. Geographic information systems.

WASHINGTON UNIVERSITY IN ST. LOUIS

Sam Fox School of Design & Visual Arts
Graduate School of Architecture & Urban Design

Programs of Study

Washington University's graduate programs in architecture and urban design provide students with rigorous design skills, challenging intellectual inquiry, and thorough professional development. Within an environment known for academic excellence and innovation, Master of Architecture (M.Arch.) and Master of Urban Design (M.U.D.) degrees are offered along with opportunities for international study and interdisciplinary work with other divisions of the University. Dual graduate degrees are also available with the John M. Olin School of Business, the George Warren Brown School of Social Work, and the School of Engineering and Applied Science.

The Master of Architecture program leads to an NAAB–accredited first professional degree and is open to those who already hold baccalaureate degrees in architecture as well as in other fields. The program focuses on the synthetic activity of design and on the critical role of architects in society and culture. The aim is to educate expressive, skillful designers prepared to act as thoughtful, effective members of the profession and practice of architecture. Depending on an applicant's prior experiences and academic qualifications, this course of study may be completed in 2 to 3½ years.

The Master of Urban Design (M.U.D.) program focuses on contemporary urban issues through a unique blend of architectural, landscape, and planning perspectives. The one-year postprofessional program combines course work with research design studios and a summer practicum. The program provides training for professional architects and landscape architects who wish to further their knowledge base and become conversant in the contemporary metropolitan issues faced in practice.

The postprofessional Master of Architecture program is open to those who already hold NAAB–accredited professional degrees. This highly independent and self-directed program offers opportunities for advanced design work and research to qualified and motivated individuals.

The Graduate School's faculty members offer expertise in history and theory, building technology, landscape and environmental design, digital media, urban design, and professional practice. The skills of the resident faculty members are augmented by the School's long-distinguished Visiting Faculty Program that attracts designers, lecturers, and critics from around the world. Graduate-level international semesters are offered in Barcelona, Buenos Aires, and Helsinki.

Research Facilities

The Kenneth and Nancy Kranzberg Art and Architecture Library contains a collection of more than 105,000 volumes in all formats and is part of the larger campus library system with holdings of more than 3 million volumes and facilities for research in the humanities, social sciences, engineering, and mathematics. Other resources available to architecture students include diverse and distributed computer and media technologies as well as fully equipped metal and woodworking shops.

Financial Aid

Financial aid for the 2007–08 academic year was offered to 100 percent of the financial aid applicants and to 93 percent of the total graduate enrollment. Awards are based on academic excellence and financial need. Aid is available in the form of scholarships and loans (federally, state, and/or locally financed). Highly qualified students are considered for a full-tuition scholarship and the partial-tuition Danforth Scholarship that is offered by the University, as well as for teaching and research assistantships. An Asian Student Scholarship Fund is also available.

Cost of Study

Tuition for the 2008–09 academic year was $36,200.

Living and Housing Costs

St. Louis is considered among the ten most livable areas in the United States, and its residents enjoy a pleasant environment and an extremely modest cost of living. Most graduate students live off campus in large and affordable apartments that are plentiful and convenient to the School of Architecture. The University's estimate of living expenses for the nine-month academic year, including room and board, books and supplies, clothing, recreation, incidentals, and medical insurance, is $17,833.

Student Group

The School currently has an enrollment of 230 graduate and 204 undergraduate students. These students come from all over the world, with 15 percent from countries other than the United States. Approximately 47 percent of the entering students have a baccalaureate degree with a major in architecture; the remaining 53 percent of graduate students come with varied backgrounds, including math, history, art, music, business, and psychology. Women make up 45 percent of the graduate class. The student-faculty ratio is approximately 10:1.

Student Outcomes

Most graduates pursue design careers in architecture, while others choose to concentrate in teaching, development, construction, business, social work, development, and government work related to architecture. Students receive career planning and placement support from a career specialist on the School's staff. Graduates are employed in all geographic areas of the U.S. and in many international markets.

Location

Washington University is located in metropolitan St. Louis, which lies in the heart of the American Midwest at the confluence of the Mississippi and Missouri Rivers. The location provides a unique design laboratory in both urban issues and the regional landscape. St. Louis and the surrounding region possess a rich and varied architectural heritage, from the Cahokia Mounds to Louis Sullivan's Wainwright Building to Eero Saarinen's Gateway Arch to Tadao Ando's Pulitzer Foundation for the Arts. Culturally, the city offers a world-renowned symphony, diverse visual arts institutions, a range of theater companies, and successful professional sports teams.

The University and The School

Established in 1853, Washington University is an independent major university characterized by academic excellence in many fields at the undergraduate and graduate levels. Graduate and professional programs in architecture, law, business, medicine, and social work are nationally recognized. The Graduate School of Architecture & Urban Design, part of the Sam Fox School of Design & Visual Arts, is housed in Givens and Steinberg Halls, which sit on the eastern edge of a historic, tree-lined campus plan that is adjacent to remarkable residential areas and one of the country's largest urban parks. The nearby Mildred Lane Kemper Museum, designed by Fumihiko Maki for the Sam Fox School, was dedicated in October 2006, greatly expanding the resources available to students in architecture and art.

Applying

Applicants to all graduate programs must submit a online application form (found on the Web site), as well as transcript(s) of undergraduate work, three letters of recommendation (submitted online), and GRE scores by February 1. All applicants must also submit a portfolio showing examples of visual material. M.Arch 3 candidates are advised to include in their portfolio creative design efforts such as drawing, sculpture, or other efforts in the visual arts to demonstrate a potential for further creative accomplishment. Applicants to all other graduate programs must include architectural design work; however, other types of artistic endeavors are also welcome. For nonnative English speakers, a minimum TOEFL score of 550 on the paper-based test, 213 on the computer-based test, or 80 on the Internet-based test is required for admission.

Correspondence and Information

Office of Graduate Admissions
Graduate School of Architecture & Urban Design
Campus Box 1079
Washington University in St. Louis
One Brookings Drive
St. Louis, Missouri 63130
Phone: 314-935-6227
      800-295-6227 (toll-free in the continental U.S.)
Fax: 314-935-7656
E-mail: wuarch@architecture.wustl.edu
Web site: http://www.arch.wustl.edu

Washington University in St. Louis

THE FACULTY AND THEIR RESEARCH

Carmon Colangelo, Dean of the Sam Fox School of Design & Visual Arts; M.F.A., Louisiana State. Administration. Collaboration within community of architects and artists.

Peter MacKeith, Associate Dean of the Sam Fox School of Design & Visual Arts and Associate Professor of Architecture; M.Arch., Yale. Design. Scandinavian architecture, concepts and principles of architecture.

Bruce Lindsey, Dean of the College of Architecture and Graduate School of Architecture & Urban Design; M.Arch., Yale. Design, sustainable architecture, collaboration of architecture and the arts.

Jeffrey Berk, Affiliate Associate Professor (Buenos Aires); M.Arch., Buenos Aires. Design studio.

Randy Burkett, Lecturer; B.Arch.Eng., Penn State. Architectural lighting.

Gerardo Caballaro, Affiliate Associate Professor (Buenos Aires); M.Arch., Washington (St. Louis). Design studio.

Gustavo Cardon, Affiliate Associate Professor (Buenos Aires); M.Arch., Miami (Florida). Design studio.

Gia Daskalakis, Associate Professor; B.Arch., B.F.A., Rhode Island School of Design. Design studio and theory courses. Intersection of architecture, urbanism, and landscape architecture; study of early twentieth-century avant-garde phenomenon.

Kathryn Dean, Professor and Director of Graduate Programs; M.Arch., Oregon. Housing and design.

Paul Donnelly, Professor; M.S., Columbia. Design studio. Building systems, structures and construction technology, technology transfer.

Iain Fraser, Professor and Director of Undergraduate Studies; M.Arch., Washington (St. Louis). Design studio. Design methods, architecture and urban typology.

Gay Goldman-Lorberbaum, Affiliate Associate Professor; M.Arch, Washington (St. Louis). Fundamental design.

Esley Hamilton, Affiliate Assistant Professor; M.S., Wisconsin. Historic preservation/urban design.

Robert Hansman, Associate Professor; B.F.A., Kansas. Graphics, drawing and painting.

John Hoal, Associate Professor and Chair, Urban Design Program; Ph.D., Washington (St. Louis). Design studio and theories of urban design and urban planning. City and land use revitalization.

Philip Holden, Affiliate Associate Professor; M.Arch., Washington (St. Louis). Design studio.

Richard Janis, Affiliate Associate Professor; M.Arch, M.S., Washington (St. Louis). Mechanical systems.

George Johannes, Affiliate Assistant Professor; M.Arch., Washington (St. Louis). Professional practice.

Sung Ho Kim, Assistant Professor; S.M.Arch.S., MIT. Design studio, digital technology. Research using newly emerging digital media and mechanical/material procedures.

Stephen Leet, Associate Professor; B.Arch., Kentucky. Design studio. Exhibit design and curation, modern American and Italian architecture and industrial design, photography.

Zeuler Lima, Assistant Professor; M.S., São Paolo (Brazil). Design studio and history-theory, Modernism and post-World War II architecture and urbanism.

Jenny Lovell, Assistant Professor; Dip.Arch., Bartlett School (London). Design and environmental systems.

Adrian Luchini, Professor and Co-Director, Graduate Program; M.Arch., Harvard. Design and theory. Relationship between architectural theory and practice, international architecture.

Paula Lupkin, Assistant Professor; Ph.D., Pennsylvania. Architectural history. Modern American architecture and urbanism, social reform and modernism as it relates to architecture.

Jen Maigret, Assistant Professor; M.Arch., Michigan. Design/architecture as a component within broader environmental and social ecologies.

Roy Manttari, Affiliate Assistant Professor (Helsinki); M.S.Arch., Helsinki. Design studio.

Igor Marjanovic, Assistant Professor; M.Arch., Illinois at Chicago. Design studio and architectural theory. History of design pedagogy.

Robert McCarter, Professor; M.Arch., Columbia. Design studio, history and theory.

Eric Mumford, Associate Professor and Director, Master of Urban Design Program; Ph.D., Princeton. Architectural history and urbanism. American urban design education, global considerations of urban design practice.

Michael Repovich, Affiliate Assistant Professor; B.Arch., Kansas State. Construction technology, sustainable architecture.

Carl B. Safe, Professor; M.E.D., Yale. Design studio. Principles of humane design, design/build studios, furniture design.

James J. Scott, Lecturer; J.D., St. Louis. Professional practice.

Phillip Shinn, Affiliate Assistant Professor; B.S., Princeton. Structures.

William Wischmeyer, Affiliate Associate Professor; M.Arch., Washington (St. Louis). Design studio.

Heather Woofter, Assistant Professor; M.Arch., Harvard. Design studio. Investigation of measured drawing and spatial procedures using emerging technologies.

Visiting Faculty

Dennis Crompton, Ruth and Norman Moore Visiting Professor; Dip.Arch., Manchester (U.K.). Design.

David Dowell, Visiting Assistant Professor; M.Arch., Berkeley. Design.

Patricia Heyda, Visiting Assistant Professor; M.Arch., Harvard. Design and urban issues.

Eric Hoffman, Visiting Assistant Professor; M.Arch., Washington (St. Louis). Design.

Donald Koster, Weese Fellow Visiting Assistant Professor; M.Arch., Washington (St. Louis). Design studio and representation.

Jonathan Marvel, Ruth and Norman Moore Visiting Professor; M.Arch., Harvard. Design.

Jodi Polzin, Visiting Assistant Professor; M.Arch., Columbia. Design studio and representation. Explorations of cities and representations of place.

Rob Rogers, Ruth and Norman Moore Visiting Professor; M.Des. Harvard. Design.

Lawrence Scarpa, Ruth and Norman Moore Visiting Professor; M.Arch, Florida. Design.

Section 3
Art and Art History

This section contains a directory of institutions offering graduate work in art and art history, followed by in-depth entries submitted by institutions that chose to prepare detailed program descriptions. Additional information about programs listed in the directory but not augmented by an in-depth entry may be obtained by writing directly to the dean of a graduate school or chair of a department at the address given in the directory.

For programs offering related work, see also in this book *Applied Arts and Design; Architecture; Area and Cultural Studies; Film, Television, and Video; Performing Arts;* and *Sociology, Anthropology, and Archaeology.* In another guide in this series: ***Graduate Programs in Business, Education, Health, Information Studies, Law & Social Work***

See *Subject Areas (Art Education)*

CONTENTS

Program Directories

Art/Fine Arts	164
Art History	181
Arts Administration	189
Art Therapy	191
Decorative Arts	193
Museum Studies	193

Announcements and Displays

Miami University	170
Northwestern University	171
Savannah College of Art and Design	173
State University of New York at Binghamton	184
University of California, Davis	185
University of Oregon	190

Close-Ups

Adelphi University	199
The Art Institute of Boston at Lesley University	201
Bard Graduate Center for Studies in the Decorative Arts, Design, and Culture	203
Bryn Mawr College	205
California College of the Arts	207
Cranbrook Academy of Art	209
Lesley University	
Expressive Therapies	211
Visual Arts	201
Memphis College of Art	213
The New School: A University	
Fine Arts	215
History of Decorative Arts and Design	217
Pratt Institute	219
San Francisco Art Institute	221
Savannah College of Art and Design	223
School of the Art Institute of Chicago	225
Seton Hall University	227
Temple University	229
University of Rochester	231
The University of the Arts	233

See also:

Adler School of Professional Psychology— Psychology	1051
Art Center College of Design—Design	115
California Institute of Integral Studies—Psychology	1105
Columbia University—Film, Theater Arts, Visual Arts, and Writing	285
Fashion Institute of Technology—Graduate Studies	117
Miami International University of Art & Design—Art and Design	121
Naropa University—Graduate Studies	1121
Southern Illinois University Carbondale—Art and Design	131
University of Pennsylvania—Design	159

Art/Fine Arts

Academy of Art University, Graduate Program, School of Fine Art, San Francisco, CA 94105-3410. Offers figurative painting (MFA); non-figurative painting (MFA); printmaking (MFA); sculpture (MFA). *Accreditation:* NASAD. Part-time programs available. Postbaccalaureate distance learning degree programs offered (no on-campus study). *Faculty:* 14 full-time (9 women), 32 part-time/adjunct (12 women). *Students:* 135 full-time (86 women), 167 part-time (123 women); includes 52 minority (13 African Americans, 1 American Indian/Alaska Native, 23 Asian Americans or Pacific Islanders, 15 Hispanic Americans), 43 international. Average age 38. 88 applicants. In 2008, 36 master's awarded. *Degree requirements:* For master's, final review. *Entrance requirements:* For master's, minimum GPA of 3.0, portfolio. *Application deadline:* For fall admission, 9/7 for domestic and international students; for spring admission, 2/2 for domestic and international students. Applications are processed on a rolling basis. Application fee: $100 ($500 for international students). Electronic applications accepted. *Expenses:* Tuition: Full-time $18,400; part-time $770 per term. Tuition and fees vary according to program. *Financial support:* Career-related internships or fieldwork and Federal Work-Study available. Support available to part-time students. Financial award application deadline: 8/10; financial award applicants required to submit FAFSA. *Unit head:* William Maughan, Director, 800-544-ARTS, Fax: 415-263-4124, E-mail: info@academyart.edu. *Application contact:* Prospective Student Services, 800-544-ARTS, Fax: 415-263-4130, E-mail: info@academyart.edu.

Adams State College, The Graduate School, Department of Art, Alamosa, CO 81102. Offers MA. Part-time programs available. *Degree requirements:* For master's, thesis, departmental qualifying exam. *Entrance requirements:* For master's, GRE General Test or MAT, minimum undergraduate GPA of 2.75.

Adelphi University, Graduate School of Arts and Sciences, Department of Art and Art History, Garden City, NY 11530-0701. Offers MA. Part-time programs available. *Students:* 13 part-time (11 women); includes 1 minority (Hispanic American), 1 international. Average age 34. In 2008, 10 master's awarded. *Degree requirements:* For master's, art exhibit. *Entrance requirements:* For master's, portfolio, 2 letters of recommendation. Additional exam requirements/recommendations for international students: Required—TOEFL (minimum score 550 paper-based; 213 computer-based; 80 iBT). *Application deadline:* For fall admission, 5/1 for international students; for spring admission, 12/1 for international students. Applications are processed on a rolling basis. Application fee: $50. Electronic applications accepted. *Expenses:* Tuition: Full-time $25,700; part-time $775 per credit hour. Required fees: $500. Tuition and fees vary according to course load, degree level, campus/location, program and student level. *Financial support:* Research assistantships with full and partial tuition reimbursements, career-related internships or fieldwork, Federal Work-Study, institutionally sponsored loans, and unspecified assistantships available. Financial award application deadline: 2/15; financial award applicants required to submit FAFSA. *Unit head:* David Hornung, Chairperson, 516-877-4458, E-mail: hornung@adelphi.edu. *Application contact:* Christine Murphy, Director of Admissions, 516-877-3050, Fax: 516-877-3039, E-mail: graduateadmissions@adelphi.edu.

See Close-Up on page 199.

Alfred University, Graduate School, New York State College of Ceramics, School of Art and Design, Alfred, NY 14802-1205. Offers ceramic art (MFA); electronic integrated arts (MFA); glass art (MFA); sculpture (MFA). *Accreditation:* NASAD. *Degree requirements:* For master's, exhibit. *Entrance requirements:* For master's, portfolio. Additional exam requirements/recommendations for international students: Required—TOEFL (minimum score 550 paper-based; 213 computer-based; 80 iBT), IELTS (minimum score 6). Electronic applications accepted. *Faculty research:* Ceramic sculpture, functional ceramics, wood, mixed media, hot and cold glass.

Alfred University, Graduate School, New York State College of Ceramics, School of Engineering, Alfred, NY 14802-1205. Offers biomedical materials engineering science (MS); ceramic engineering (MS); ceramics (PhD); electrical engineering (MS); glass science (MS, PhD); materials science and engineering (MS, PhD); mechanical engineering (MS). *Degree requirements:* For master's, thesis; for doctorate, thesis/dissertation. *Entrance requirements:* Additional exam requirements/recommendations for international students: Required—TOEFL (minimum score 590 paper-based; 243 computer-based). Electronic applications accepted. *Expenses:* Contact institution. *Faculty research:* Fine-particle technology, x-ray diffraction, superconductivity, electronic materials.

American University, College of Arts and Sciences, Department of Art, Programs in Painting, Sculpture and Printmaking, Washington, DC 20016-8004. Offers MFA. *Students:* 21 full-time (15 women); includes 3 minority (1 Asian American or Pacific Islander, 2 Hispanic Americans), 1 international. Average age 28. 31 applicants, 52% accepted, 12 enrolled. In 2008, 12 master's awarded. *Degree requirements:* For master's, comprehensive exam, thesis. *Entrance requirements:* For master's, GRE, portfolio. *Application deadline:* For fall admission, 1/15 priority date for domestic students. Application fee: $80. *Expenses:* Tuition: Full-time $21,204; part-time $1178 per credit hour. Required fees: $380. Part-time tuition and fees vary according to course load and program. *Financial support:* Teaching assistantships with tuition reimbursements, career-related internships or fieldwork, Federal Work-Study, and institutionally sponsored loans available. Support available to part-time students. Financial award application deadline: 1/15. *Faculty research:* Drawing. *Unit head:* Luis Silva, Chair, 202-885-1682, Fax: 202-885-1132. *Application contact:* Glenna K. Haynie, Administrative Coordinator, 202-885-1671.

Anna Maria College, Graduate Division, Program in Education, Paxton, MA 01612. Offers early childhood education (M Ed); education (CAGS); elementary education (M Ed); English language arts (M Ed); visual arts (M Ed). Part-time and evening/weekend programs available. *Faculty:* 4 full-time (all women), 8 part-time/adjunct (6 women). *Students:* 1 (woman) full-time, 85 part-time (84 women); includes 2 minority (1 Asian American or Pacific Islander, 1 Hispanic American). Average age 33. In 2008, 30 master's, 2 CAGSs awarded. *Entrance requirements:* For master's, bachelor's degree in liberal arts or sciences, minimum GPA of 3.0. Additional exam requirements/recommendations for international students: Required—TOEFL (minimum score 500 paper-based). *Application deadline:* For fall admission, 3/1 priority date for domestic and international students; for spring admission, 11/1 priority date for domestic and international students. Applications are processed on a rolling basis. Application fee: $40. Electronic applications accepted. *Expenses:* Tuition: Part-time $1400 per course. *Financial support:* Applicants required to submit FAFSA. *Unit head:* Christine Holmes, Director, 508-849-3418, Fax: 508-849-3343, E-mail: cholmes@annamaria.edu. *Application contact:* Dennis Braun, Director, Graduate Studies and Continuing Education, 508-849-3293, Fax: 508-819-3362, E-mail: dbraun@annamaria.edu.

Anna Maria College, Graduate Division, Program in Visual Arts, Paxton, MA 01612. Offers art and visual art (MA); teacher of visual art (M Ed). Part-time and evening/weekend programs available. *Faculty:* 1 (woman) full-time, 1 (woman) part-time/adjunct. *Students:* 3 part-time (all women). Average age 45. In 2008, 1 master's awarded. *Degree requirements:* For master's, thesis. *Entrance requirements:* For master's, minimum GPA of 2.7, undergraduate major in art, portfolio. Additional exam requirements/recommendations for international students: Required—TOEFL (minimum score 500 paper-based). *Application deadline:* For fall admission, 3/1 priority date for domestic and international students; for spring admission, 11/1 priority date for domestic and international students. Applications are processed on a rolling basis. Application fee: $40. Electronic applications accepted. *Expenses:* Tuition: Part-time $1400 per course. *Unit head:* Dennis Braun, Director, Graduate Studies and Continuing Education, 508-849-3293, Fax: 508-819-3362, E-mail: dbraun@annamaria.edu. *Application contact:* Janet LaPointe, Admissions Coordinator, Graduate and Continuing Education, 508-849-3234, Fax: 508-819-3362, E-mail: jlapointe@annamaria.edu.

Antioch University McGregor, Graduate Programs, Individualized Liberal and Professional Studies Program, Yellow Springs, OH 45387-1609. Offers liberal and professional studies (MA), including counseling, creative writing, education, film studies, liberal studies, management, modern literature, psychology, theatre, visual arts. Part-time and evening/weekend programs available. Postbaccalaureate distance learning degree programs offered (minimal on-campus study). *Degree requirements:* For master's, thesis or alternative. *Entrance requirements:* For master's, resumé, 2 letters of reference. Electronic applications accepted. *Expenses:* Contact institution.

Arizona State University, Graduate College, Herberger College of the Arts, School of Art, Tempe, AZ 85287. Offers MA, MFA, PhD.

Arkansas State University, Graduate School, College of Fine Arts, Department of Art, Jonesboro, State University, AR 72467. Offers MA. *Accreditation:* NASAD. Part-time programs available. *Faculty:* 9 full-time (4 women). *Students:* 3 full-time (0 women), 3 part-time (2 women). Average age 36. 9 applicants, 56% accepted, 3 enrolled. In 2008, 2 master's awarded. *Degree requirements:* For master's, comprehensive exam, thesis. *Entrance requirements:* For master's, GRE General Test or MAT, portfolio, appropriate bachelor's degree, letters of reference, official transcript, writing sample. Additional exam requirements/recommendations for international students: Required—TOEFL (minimum score 550 paper-based; 213 computer-based; 79 iBT), IELTS (minimum score 6). *Application deadline:* Applications are processed on a rolling basis. Application fee: $30 ($40 for international students). Electronic applications accepted. *Expenses:* Tuition, state resident: full-time $3744; part-time $208 per credit hour. Tuition, nonresident: full-time $9540; part-time $530 per credit hour. International tuition: $7938 full-time. Required fees: $896; $47 per credit hour. $25 per term. One-time fee: $50. Tuition and fees vary according to course load and program. *Financial support:* In 2008–09, 3 students received support; teaching assistantships, career-related internships or fieldwork, scholarships/grants, and unspecified assistantships available. Financial award application deadline: 7/1; financial award applicants required to submit FAFSA. *Faculty research:* Art and visual psychology, digital photography, graphic design, modern art, painting-reverse on plexiglass. *Unit head:* Curtis Steele, Chair, 870-972-3050, Fax: 870-972-3932, E-mail: csteele@astate.edu. *Application contact:* Dr. Andrew Sustich, Dean of the Graduate School, 870-972-3029, Fax: 870-972-3857, E-mail: sustich@astate.edu.

Arkansas Tech University, Graduate School, School of Liberal and Fine Arts, Russellville, AR 72801. Offers communication (MLA); English (M Ed, MA); fine arts (MLA); history (MA); multi-media journalism (MA); social science (MLA); social studies (M Ed); Spanish (MA, MLA); teaching English as a second language (MA, MLA). Part-time programs available. *Students:* 40 full-time (31 women), 81 part-time (60 women); includes 10 minority (3 African Americans, 2 American Indian/Alaska Native, 2 Asian Americans or Pacific Islanders, 3 Hispanic Americans), 19 international. Average age 33. In 2008, 70 master's awarded. *Degree requirements:* For master's, project. *Entrance requirements:* For master's, GRE General Test or MAT. Additional exam requirements/recommendations for international students: Required—TOEFL (minimum score 500 paper-based; 173 computer-based; 61 iBT). *Application deadline:* For fall admission, 3/1 priority date for domestic students, 5/1 priority date for international students; for winter admission, 10/1 priority date for international students; for spring admission, 10/1 priority date for domestic and international students. Applications are processed on a rolling basis. Application fee: $0 ($30 for international students). Electronic applications accepted. *Expenses:* Tuition, state resident: full-time $1575; part-time $175 per credit hour. Tuition, nonresident: full-time $3150; part-time $350 per credit hour. Tuition and fees vary according to course load. *Financial support:* In 2008–09, teaching assistantships with full tuition reimbursements (averaging $4,000 per year); career-related internships or fieldwork, Federal Work-Study, scholarships/grants, health care benefits, and unspecified assistantships also available. Support available to part-time students. Financial award application deadline: 4/15; financial award applicants required to submit FAFSA. *Unit head:* Dr. Georgena Duncan, Dean, 479-968-0266, Fax: 479-968-0275, E-mail: georgena.duncan@atu.edu. *Application contact:* Dr. Eldon G. Clary, Dean of Graduate School, 479-968-0398, Fax: 479-964-0542, E-mail: graduate.school@atu.edu.

Art Center College of Design, Graduate Division, Fine Arts Department, Pasadena, CA 91103-1999. Offers MFA. *Accreditation:* NASAD. *Degree requirements:* For master's, thesis, studio project. *Entrance requirements:* For master's, portfolio. Additional exam requirements/recommendations for international students: Required—TOEFL (minimum score 600 paper-based; 250 computer-based; 100 iBT).

See Close-Up on page 115.

The Art Institute of Boston at Lesley University, Program in Visual Arts, Boston, MA 02215-2598. Offers MFA. *Accreditation:* NASAD.

See Close-Up on page 201.

The Art Institute of California–San Francisco, Master of Fine Arts Program, San Francisco, CA 94102-4908. Offers computer animation (MFA).

Atlantic University, Program in Visionary Art and Consciousness, Virginia Beach, VA 23451-2061. Offers MFA. Part-time and evening/weekend programs available. Postbaccalaureate distance learning degree programs offered (no on-campus study). *Faculty:* 2 part-time/adjunct (1 woman). *Degree requirements:* For master's, thesis. *Entrance requirements:* For master's, BFA or BA or BS in studio art with 40 studio credits or more. Additional exam requirements/recommendations for international students: Required—TOEFL (minimum score 550 paper-based; 213 computer-based). *Application deadline:* For fall admission, 3/31 for domestic and international students. Application fee: $50. *Expenses:* Contact institution. *Unit head:* Kevin J. Todeschi, Chief Executive Officer, 757-631-8101, Fax: 757-631-8096, E-mail: info@atlanticuniv.edu. *Application contact:* R. Gregory Deming, Director of Admissions, 757-631-8101, Fax: 757-631-8096, E-mail: admissions@atlanticuniv.edu.

Azusa Pacific University, College of Liberal Arts and Sciences, Program in Fine Arts in Visual Art, Azusa, CA 91702-7000. Offers MFA.

Ball State University, Graduate School, College of Fine Arts, Department of Art, Muncie, IN 47306-1099. Offers art (MA); art education (MA, MAE). *Accreditation:* NASAD.

Bard College, Milton Avery Graduate School of the Arts, Annandale-on-Hudson, NY 12504. Offers MFA. *Degree requirements:* For master's, thesis, project, 8-week summer residency, independent study. *Entrance requirements:* For master's, interview, portfolio, 2 letters of recommendation, personal statement, history of work in the arts. Additional exam requirements/recommendations for international students: Required—TOEFL (minimum score 550 paper-based; 213 computer-based). Electronic applications accepted. *Faculty research:* Original work in painting, writing, sculpture, photography, video/film, sound/music.

Barry University, School of Arts and Sciences, Department of Fine Arts, Miami Shores, FL 33161-6695. Offers photography (MA, MFA). *Degree requirements:* For master's, thesis (for some programs). *Entrance requirements:* For master's, GRE General Test, minimum GPA of 3.0. Electronic applications accepted. *Faculty research:* Inclusion education, exceptional education, art-based assessments.

Bob Jones University, Graduate Programs, Greenville, SC 29614. Offers accountancy (MS); Bible (MA); Bible translation (MA); Biblical studies (Certificate); broadcast management (MS); business administration (MBA); church history (MA, PhD); church ministries (MA); church music (MM); cinema and video production (MA); counseling (MS); curriculum and instruction (Ed D); divinity (M Div); dramatic production (MA); educational leadership (MS, Ed D, Ed S); elementary education (M Ed, MAT); English (M Ed, MA, MAT); fine arts (MA); graphic design (MA); history (M Ed, MA); illustration (MA); interpretative speech (MA); mathematics (M Ed,

MAT); medical missions (Certificate); ministry (MM, D Min); multi-categorical special education (M Ed, MAT); music (M Ed); New Testament interpretation (PhD); Old Testament interpretation (PhD); orchestral instrument performance (MM); organ performance (MM); pastoral studies (MA); personnel services (MS, Ed S); piano pedagogy (MM); piano performance (MM); platform arts (MA); radio and television broadcasting (MS); rhetoric and public address (MA); secondary education (M Ed); studio art (MA); teaching Bible (MA); theology (MA, PhD); voice performance (MM); youth ministries (MA); M Div/MM.

Boise State University, Graduate College, College of Arts and Sciences, Department of Art, Program in Visual Arts, Boise, ID 83725-0399. Offers MFA. *Accreditation:* NASAD. Part-time programs available. *Degree requirements:* For master's, thesis. *Entrance requirements:* For master's, minimum GPA of 3.0, portfolio. Additional exam requirements/recommendations for international students: Required—TOEFL (minimum score 587 paper-based; 240 computer-based). Electronic applications accepted.

Boston University, College of Fine Arts, School of Visual Arts, Boston, MA 02215. Offers art education (MFA); graphic design (MFA); painting (MFA); sculpture (MFA); studio teaching (MFA). *Entrance requirements:* For master's, portfolio. Additional exam requirements/recommendations for international students: Required—TOEFL.

Bowling Green State University, Graduate College, College of Arts and Sciences, School of Art, Bowling Green, OH 43403. Offers 2-D studio art (MA, MFA); 3-D studio art (MA, MFA); art education (MA); art history (MA); computer art (MA); design (MFA); digital arts (MFA); graphics (MFA). *Accreditation:* NASAD. Part-time programs available. *Degree requirements:* For master's, thesis or alternative, final exhibit (MFA). *Entrance requirements:* For master's, GRE General Test (MA), slide portfolio (15-20 slides). Additional exam requirements/recommendations for international students: Required—TOEFL. Electronic applications accepted. *Faculty research:* Computer animation and virtual reality, Spanish still-life painting from 1600 to 1800, art and psychotherapy, Japanese wood-firing techniques in ceramics, non-toxic printmaking technologies.

Bradley University, Graduate School, Slane College of Communications and Fine Arts, Department of Art, Peoria, IL 61625-0002. Offers ceramics (MA, MFA); drawing/illustration (MA, MFA); interdisciplinary art (MA, MFA); painting (MA, MFA); photography (MA, MFA); printmaking (MA, MFA); sculpture (MA, MFA); visual communication and design (MA, MFA). *Accreditation:* NASAD. Part-time programs available. *Degree requirements:* For master's, comprehensive exam, thesis, final exhibit. *Entrance requirements:* For master's, portfolio, 2 letters of recommendation. Additional exam requirements/recommendations for international students: Required—TOEFL (minimum score 550 paper-based; 213 computer-based; 79 iBT).

Brandeis University, Graduate School of Arts and Sciences, Program in Studio Art, Waltham, MA 02454-9110. Offers Certificate. *Degree requirements:* For Certificate, thesis, exhibit of work. *Entrance requirements:* For degree, resumé, sample of work, studio work, letters of recommendation. Additional exam requirements/recommendations for international students: Required—TOEFL (minimum score 600 paper-based; 250 computer-based; 100 iBT), IELTS (minimum score 7). Electronic applications accepted. *Expenses:* Contact institution. *Faculty research:* Painting, sculpture, three-dimensional design, printmaking, drawing.

Brigham Young University, Graduate Studies, College of Fine Arts and Communications, Department of Visual Arts, Provo, UT 84602-6414. Offers art education (MA); art history (MA); studio art (MFA). Art education applications accepted biennially. *Accreditation:* NASAD. *Faculty:* 22 full-time (7 women), 2 part-time/adjunct (1 woman). *Students:* 32 full-time (23 women); includes 5 minority (all Asian Americans or Pacific Islanders). Average age 26. 19 applicants, 47% accepted, 7 enrolled. In 2008, 16 master's awarded. *Degree requirements:* For master's, 2 foreign languages, thesis (art history), selected project (MFA), curriculum project (art education). *Entrance requirements:* For master's, GRE (art history), minimum GPA of 3.0 (MFA, MA in art education), 3.3 (MA in art history), portfolio in slide form (MFA), writing samples (MA in art education, art history). Additional exam requirements/recommendations for international students: Required—TOEFL (minimum score 500 paper-based). *Application deadline:* For fall admission, 2/1 for domestic and international students. Application fee: $50. Electronic applications accepted. *Expenses:* Tuition: Full-time $5160; part-time $287 per credit hour. Tuition and fees vary according to program and student's religious affiliation. *Financial support:* In 2008–09, 30 students received support; research assistantships, teaching assistantships with partial tuition reimbursements available, scholarships/grants and tuition waivers (partial) available. Financial award application deadline: 2/1. *Faculty research:* Methodology-standards-assessment, Medieval architecture, classical/Islamic eighteenth- and nineteenth-century art, Netherlandish art, contemporary art. Total annual research expenditures: $83,932. *Unit head:* Prof. Linda A. Reynolds, Chair, 801-422-4429, Fax: 801-422-0695, E-mail: sullivan@byu.edu. *Application contact:* Sharon Lyn Heelis, Secretary, 801-422-4429, Fax: 801-422-0695, E-mail: sharon_heelis@byu.edu.

Brooklyn College of the City University of New York, Division of Graduate Studies, Department of Art, Brooklyn, NY 11210-2889. Offers art history (MA, PhD); digital art (MFA); drawing and painting (MFA); photography (MFA); printmaking (MFA); sculpture (MFA). The department offers courses at Brooklyn College that are creditable toward the CUNY doctoral degree; MFA programs—Fall admissions only, application deadline 2/1. Part-time programs available. *Students:* 24 full-time (7 women), 13 part-time (12 women); includes 4 minority (1 African American, 1 Asian American or Pacific Islander, 2 Hispanic Americans), 1 international. Average age 30. 102 applicants, 48% accepted, 20 enrolled. In 2008, 15 master's awarded. *Degree requirements:* For master's, thesis. *Entrance requirements:* For master's, bachelor's degree in art, portfolio, 2 letters of recommendation. Additional exam requirements/recommendations for international students: Required—TOEFL (minimum score 500 paper-based; 173 computer-based; 61 iBT). *Application deadline:* For fall admission, 2/1 priority date for domestic students, 2/1 for international students; for spring admission, 11/1 priority date for domestic students, 10/1 for international students. Applications are processed on a rolling basis. Application fee: $125. Electronic applications accepted. *Expenses:* Tuition, state resident: full-time $7360; part-time $310 per credit hour. Tuition, nonresident: full-time $13,800; part-time $575 per credit hour. *Financial support:* Career-related internships or fieldwork, Federal Work-Study, institutionally sponsored loans, scholarships/grants, and painting awards available. Support available to part-time students. Financial award application deadline: 5/1; financial award applicants required to submit FAFSA. *Unit head:* Dr. Michael Mallory, Chairperson, 718-951-5181, E-mail: mmallory@brooklyn.cuny.edu. *Application contact:* Hernan Sierra, Graduate Admissions Coordinator, 718-951-4536, Fax: 718-951-4506, E-mail: grads@brooklyn.cuny.edu.

California College of the Arts, Graduate Programs, Program in Visual and Critical Studies, San Francisco, CA 94107. Offers MA. *Degree requirements:* For master's, thesis, exhibit. *Entrance requirements:* For master's, appropriate bachelor's degree, portfolio. Additional exam requirements/recommendations for international students: Required—TOEFL (minimum score 600 paper-based; 250 computer-based). Electronic applications accepted.

See Close-Up on page 207.

California College of the Arts, Graduate Programs, Programs in Fine Art, San Francisco, CA 94107. Offers ceramics (MFA); film/video/performance (MFA); glass (MFA); jewelry/metal arts (MFA); painting/drawing (MFA); photography (MFA); printmaking (MFA); sculpture (MFA); textiles (MFA); wood/furniture (MFA). *Accreditation:* NASAD. *Degree requirements:* For master's, thesis, exhibit. *Entrance requirements:* For master's, appropriate bachelor's degree, portfolio. Additional exam requirements/recommendations for international students: Required—TOEFL (minimum score 600 paper-based; 250 computer-based). Electronic applications accepted.

California Institute of the Arts, School of Art, Valencia, CA 91355-2340. Offers art (MFA, Adv C); graphic design (MFA, Adv C); photography (MFA, Adv C). *Accreditation:* NASAD (one or more programs are accredited). *Degree requirements:* For master's, final project. *Entrance requirements:* For master's, portfolio. Additional exam requirements/recommendations for international students: Required—TOEFL. Electronic applications accepted.

California State University, Chico, Graduate School, College of Humanities and Fine Arts, Department of Art and Art History, Program in Fine Arts, Chico, CA 95929-0722. Offers MFA. *Accreditation:* NASAD. *Degree requirements:* For master's, thesis or alternative. *Entrance requirements:* For master's, Two letters of recommendation, statement of purpose, department application. Additional exam requirements/recommendations for international students: Required—TOEFL (minimum score 550 paper-based; 213 computer-based; 80 iBT), IELTS (minimum score 6.5). Electronic applications accepted.

California State University, Fresno, Division of Graduate Studies, College of Arts and Humanities, Department of Art and Design, Fresno, CA 93740-8027. Offers art (MA). Part-time and evening/weekend programs available. *Degree requirements:* For master's, thesis or alternative. *Entrance requirements:* For master's, GRE General Test, minimum GPA of 3.0, portfolio. Additional exam requirements/recommendations for international students: Required—TOEFL. Electronic applications accepted. *Faculty research:* Art history, graphic design, studio art.

California State University, Fullerton, Graduate Studies, College of the Arts, Department of Art, Fullerton, CA 92834-9480. Offers art (MA, MFA), including ceramics (MFA), crafts, creative photography (MFA), design (MFA), drawing and painting, printmaking (MFA), sculpture; art history (MA); design (MA). *Accreditation:* NASAD (one or more programs are accredited). Part-time programs available. *Students:* 56 full-time (33 women), 29 part-time (15 women); includes 24 minority (2 African Americans, 1 American Indian/Alaska Native, 11 Asian Americans or Pacific Islanders, 10 Hispanic Americans), 7 international. Average age 34. 74 applicants, 34% accepted, 20 enrolled. In 2008, 28 master's awarded. *Degree requirements:* For master's, project or thesis. *Entrance requirements:* For master's, minimum GPA of 2.5 in last 60 units of course work, portfolio. Application fee: $55. Tuition and fees vary according to degree level. *Financial support:* Career-related internships or fieldwork, Federal Work-Study, institutionally sponsored loans, and scholarships/grants available. Support available to part-time students. Financial award application deadline: 3/1. *Unit head:* Larry Johnson, Chair, 657-278-3471. *Application contact:* Al Ching, Adviser, 657-278-3471.

California State University, Long Beach, Graduate Studies, College of the Arts, Department of Art, Long Beach, CA 90840. Offers art education (MA); art history (MFA); studio art (MA). *Accreditation:* NASAD. Part-time programs available. *Faculty:* 36 full-time (17 women), 8 part-time/adjunct (5 women). *Students:* 76 full-time (47 women), 39 part-time (29 women); includes 28 minority (2 American Indian/Alaska Native, 10 Asian Americans or Pacific Islanders, 16 Hispanic Americans), 3 international. Average age 37. 183 applicants, 37% accepted, 43 enrolled. *Degree requirements:* For master's, thesis (for some programs). *Entrance requirements:* For master's, minimum GPA of 3.0 in last 60 hours. *Application deadline:* For fall admission, 7/1 for domestic students; for spring admission, 12/1 for domestic students. Applications are processed on a rolling basis. Application fee: $55. Electronic applications accepted. *Expenses:* Tuition, nonresident: full-time $11,160; part-time $372 per unit. Required fees: $4100; $1261 per semester. *Financial support:* Federal Work-Study, institutionally sponsored loans, and scholarships/grants available. Financial award application deadline: 3/2. *Unit head:* Prof. David A Hadlock, Chair, 562-985-4376, Fax: 562-985-1650, E-mail: dhadlock@csulb.edu. *Application contact:* Prof. Christopher Miles, Graduate Advisor, 562-985-4376, Fax: 562-985-1650, E-mail: cmiles@csulb.edu.

California State University, Los Angeles, Graduate Studies, College of Arts and Letters, Department of Art, Los Angeles, CA 90032-8530. Offers art (MA), including art education, art history, art therapy, ceramics, metals, and textiles, design (MA, MFA), painting, sculpture, and graphic arts, photography; fine arts (MFA), including crafts, design (MA, MFA), studio arts. *Accreditation:* NASAD (one or more programs are accredited). Part-time and evening/weekend programs available. *Faculty:* 16 full-time (6 women). *Students:* 23 full-time (14 women), 52 part-time (37 women); includes 29 minority (2 African Americans, 3 American Indian/Alaska Native, 7 Asian Americans or Pacific Islanders, 17 Hispanic Americans), 4 international. Average age 38. 30 applicants, 100% accepted, 14 enrolled. In 2008, 15 master's awarded. *Degree requirements:* For master's, comprehensive exam, project or thesis. *Entrance requirements:* For master's, portfolio. Additional exam requirements/recommendations for international students: Required—TOEFL (minimum score 500 paper-based; 173 computer-based). *Application deadline:* For fall admission, 6/15 for domestic students, 5/1 for international students; for winter admission, 11/1 for domestic students, 9/1 for international students; for spring admission, 2/1 for domestic students, 10/1 for international students. Applications are processed on a rolling basis. Application fee: $55. Electronic applications accepted. *Expenses:* Tuition, nonresident: part-time $226 per credit. Required fees: $4019. *Financial support:* Federal Work-Study available. Support available to part-time students. Financial award application deadline: 3/1. *Faculty research:* The artist and the book, conceptual art, ceramic processes, computer graphics, architectural graphics. *Unit head:* Dr. Robert Martin, Chair, 323-343-4010, Fax: 323-343-4045, E-mail: rjmartin@calstatela.edu. *Application contact:* Dr. Jose L. Galvan, Dean of Graduate Studies, 323-343-3820, Fax: 323-343-5653, E-mail: jgalvan@cslanet.calstatela.edu.

California State University, Northridge, Graduate Studies, College of Arts, Media, and Communication, Department of Art, Northridge, CA 91330. Offers art education (MA); art history (MA); studio art (MA, MFA); visual communications (MA, MFA). *Accreditation:* NASAD. *Faculty:* 22 full-time (12 women), 48 part-time/adjunct (18 women). *Students:* 24 full-time (16 women), 36 part-time (25 women); includes 4 Asian Americans or Pacific Islanders, 5 Hispanic Americans, 4 international. Average age 37. 73 applicants, 33% accepted, 17 enrolled. In 2008, 11 master's awarded. *Application deadline:* For fall admission, 11/30 for domestic students. Application fee: $55. *Financial support:* Application deadline: 3/1. *Unit head:* Prof. Edward Alfano, Chair, 818-677-2242, E-mail: art.dept@csun.edu. *Application contact:* Prof. Edward Alfano, Chair, 818-677-2242, E-mail: art.dept@csun.edu.

California State University, Sacramento, Graduate Studies, College of Arts and Letters, Department of Art, Sacramento, CA 95819-6048. Offers studio art (MA). *Accreditation:* NASAD. Part-time programs available. *Degree requirements:* For master's, thesis or alternative, departmental qualifying exam, writing proficiency exam. *Entrance requirements:* For master's, minimum GPA of 3.0 during previous 2 years. Additional exam requirements/recommendations for international students: Required—TOEFL. Electronic applications accepted.

California State University, San Bernardino, Graduate Studies, College of Arts and Letters, Department of Art, San Bernardino, CA 92407-2397. Offers MA. *Accreditation:* NASAD. *Faculty:* 5 full-time (2 women). *Students:* 4 full-time (2 women), 5 part-time (2 women); includes 3 minority (1 African American, 1 Asian American or Pacific Islander, 1 Hispanic American). Average age 34. 21 applicants, 38% accepted, 6 enrolled. In 2008, 2 master's awarded. *Entrance requirements:* Additional exam requirements/recommendations for international students: Required—TOEFL. *Application deadline:* For fall admission, 8/31 priority date for domestic students. Application fee: $55. *Expenses:* Tuition, area resident: Full-time $1252; part-time $726 per quarter. Required fees: $334 per quarter. Tuition and fees vary according to degree level and student level. *Unit head:* Dr. Thomas McGovern, Chair, 909-537-7267, Fax: 909-537-7068. *Application contact:* Olivia Rosas, Director of Admissions, 909-537-7577, Fax: 909-537-7034, E-mail: orosas@csusb.edu.

California State University, Stanislaus, College of the Arts, Department of Art, Turlock, CA 95382. Offers printmaking (Certificate). *Accreditation:* NASAD. Part-time programs available. *Degree requirements:* For Certificate, portfolio submission, exhibition participation. *Entrance requirements:* For degree, BA—Arts, 2.50 GPA, portfolio evaluation, 3 letters of reference, personal statement. Electronic applications accepted.

Carnegie Mellon University, College of Fine Arts, School of Art, Pittsburgh, PA 15213-3891. Offers MFA. *Accreditation:* NASAD. *Degree requirements:* For master's, thesis, exhibit. *Entrance requirements:* For master's, portfolio. Additional exam requirements/recommendations for international students: Required—TOEFL.

Art/Fine Arts

Central Washington University, Graduate Studies, Research and Continuing Education, College of Arts and Humanities, Department of Art, Ellensburg, WA 98926. Offers MA, MFA. *Degree requirements:* For master's, thesis or alternative. *Entrance requirements:* For master's, minimum GPA of 3.0, portfolio. Additional exam requirements/recommendations for international students: Required—TOEFL (minimum score 550 paper-based; 213 computer-based; 79 iBT). Electronic applications accepted.

City College of the City University of New York, Graduate School, College of Liberal Arts and Science, Division of the Humanities and Arts, Department of Art, Program in Fine Arts, New York, NY 10031-9198. Offers advertising design (MFA); ceramic design (MFA); painting (MFA); printmaking (MFA); sculpture (MFA); wood and metal design (MFA). *Degree requirements:* For master's, thesis exhibit. *Entrance requirements:* For master's, 20 slide portfolio. Additional exam requirements/recommendations for international students: Required—TOEFL (minimum score 575 paper-based; 233 computer-based).

Claremont Graduate University, Graduate Programs, School of Arts and Humanities, Department of Art, Claremont, CA 91711. Offers digital media (MA, MFA); drawing (MA, MFA); installation (MA, MFA); new genre (MA, MFA); painting (MA, MFA); performance (MA, MFA); photography (MA, MFA); sculpture (MA, MFA). Part-time programs available. *Faculty:* 4 full-time (1 woman), 1 (woman) part-time/adjunct. *Students:* 62 full-time (34 women); includes 12 minority (3 African Americans, 4 Asian Americans or Pacific Islanders, 5 Hispanic Americans), 4 international. Average age 32. In 2008, 29 master's awarded. *Degree requirements:* For master's, final project show. *Entrance requirements:* For master's, BA in art or BFA, slide review. Additional exam requirements/recommendations for international students: Required—TOEFL (minimum score 550 paper-based; 213 computer-based; 80 iBT). *Application deadline:* For fall admission, 2/1 priority date for domestic students. Applications are processed on a rolling basis. Application fee: $60. Electronic applications accepted. *Expenses:* Contact institution. *Financial support:* Fellowships, research assistantships, teaching assistantships, Federal Work-Study, institutionally sponsored loans, and scholarships/grants available. Support available to part-time students. Financial award application deadline: 2/15; financial award applicants required to submit FAFSA. *Faculty research:* Acoustic sculpture, feminization of abstraction, installation sculpture. *Unit head:* David Pagel, Chair, 909-607-2479, Fax: 909-607-1276, E-mail: david.pagel@cgu.edu. *Application contact:* Pat Evans, Program Administrator, 909-607-9292, Fax: 909-607-1276, E-mail: patricia.evans@cgu.edu.

Clemson University, Graduate School, College of Architecture, Arts, and Humanities, Department of Art, Program in Visual Arts, Clemson, SC 29634. Offers MFA. *Accreditation:* NASAD. *Students:* 20 full-time (9 women); includes 1 minority (Hispanic American). Average age 31. 33 applicants, 42% accepted, 10 enrolled. In 2008, 5 master's awarded. *Entrance requirements:* For master's, GRE General Test. Additional exam requirements/recommendations for international students: Required—TOEFL. *Application deadline:* For fall admission, 4/15 for international students; for spring admission, 9/15 for international students. Application fee: $50. Full-time tuition and fees vary according to program. *Unit head:* Dave Detrick, Coordinator, 864-656-3890, Fax: 864-656-0204, E-mail: ddavid@clemson.edu. *Application contact:* Dave Detrick, Coordinator, 864-656-3890, Fax: 864-656-0204, E-mail: ddavid@clemson.edu.

Cleveland State University, College of Graduate Studies, College of Liberal Arts and Social Sciences, Department of Art, Cleveland, OH 44115. Offers art education (M Ed); art history (MA). *Faculty:* 12 full-time (7 women), 9 part-time/adjunct (6 women). *Students:* 1 (woman) full-time, 4 part-time (all women). In 2008, 2 master's awarded. *Unit head:* Howie Smith, Chair, 212-523-7546, E-mail: art.chair@csuohio.edu. *Application contact:* Dr. Giannina Pianalto, Director of Graduate Admissions, 216-687-5599, Fax: 216-687-5400, E-mail: g.pianalto@csuohio.edu.

The College at Brockport, State University of New York, School of Arts and Performance, Visual Studies Workshop, Brockport, NY 14420-2997. Offers visual studies (MFA). *Degree requirements:* For master's, thesis or alternative, internship, final project. *Entrance requirements:* For master's, portfolio, letters of recommendation, minimum GPA of 3.0. Additional exam requirements/recommendations for international students: Required—TOEFL (minimum score 550 paper-based; 213 computer-based; 79 iBT). *Faculty research:* Photography, film, video, digital media, artists' books.

The College of New Rochelle, Graduate School, Division of Art and Communication Studies, Program in Studio Art, New Rochelle, NY 10805-2308. Offers MS. Part-time and evening/weekend programs available. *Degree requirements:* For master's, apprenticeship. *Entrance requirements:* For master's, portfolio, 36 credits of course work in studio art. *Faculty research:* Experimental computer graphics.

Colorado State University, Graduate School, College of Liberal Arts, Department of Art, Fort Collins, CO 80523-1779. Offers MFA. *Faculty:* 23 full-time (11 women), 2 part-time/adjunct (0 women). *Students:* 19 full-time (13 women), 3 part-time (all women); includes 1 minority (Asian American or Pacific Islander), 1 international. Average age 30. 67 applicants, 9% accepted, 4 enrolled. In 2008, 6 master's awarded. *Degree requirements:* For master's, comprehensive exam (for some programs), thesis (for some programs), exhibition. *Entrance requirements:* For master's, portfolio, statement of purpose, letters of recommendation, department application. Additional exam requirements/recommendations for international students: Required—TOEFL. *Application deadline:* For fall admission, 2/1 priority date for domestic students; for spring admission, 10/15 priority date for domestic students. Applications are processed on a rolling basis. Application fee: $50. Electronic applications accepted. *Expenses:* Contact institution. *Financial support:* In 2008–09, 8 students received support, including 8 teaching assistantships with tuition reimbursements available (averaging $9,248 per year); fellowships, research assistantships, Federal Work-Study, institutionally sponsored loans, scholarships/grants, health care benefits, and unspecified assistantships also available. Support available to part-time students. Financial award application deadline: 3/1; financial award applicants required to submit FAFSA. *Faculty research:* African art history, bronze castings, etching/lithography, pre-Columbian art history, contemporary crafts. Total annual research expenditures: $9,570. *Unit head:* Gary W. Voss, Chair, 970-491-5192, E-mail: gary.voss@colostate.edu. *Application contact:* Tom Lundberg, Graduate Coordinator, 970-491-5734, E-mail: thomas.lundberg@colostate.edu.

Columbia University, School of the Arts, Visual Arts Division, New York, NY 10027. Offers new genres (MFA); painting (MFA); photography (MFA); printmaking (MFA); sculpture (MFA). *Degree requirements:* For master's, thesis. *Entrance requirements:* For master's, 3 letters of recommendation, portfolio, personal statement, resumé, official transcript. Additional exam requirements/recommendations for international students: Required—TOEFL (minimum score 600 paper-based; 250 computer-based; 100 iBT). Electronic applications accepted.

See Close-Up on page 285.

Concordia University, School of Graduate Studies, Faculty of Fine Arts, Department of Studio Arts, Montréal, QC H3G 1M8, Canada. Offers studio arts (MFA), including film production, open media, painting, photography, print media, sculpture, ceramics and fibers. *Degree requirements:* For master's, thesis or alternative. *Entrance requirements:* For master's, portfolio.

Cornell University, Graduate School, Graduate Fields of Architecture, Art and Planning, Field of Art, Ithaca, NY 14853-0001. Offers creative visual arts (MFA), including painting, photography, printmaking, sculpture. *Faculty:* 20 full-time (7 women). *Students:* 10 full-time (3 women). Average age 30. 107 applicants, 7% accepted, 4 enrolled. In 2008, 6 master's awarded. *Degree requirements:* For master's, thesis, exhibit. *Entrance requirements:* For master's, slide portfolio of 10-20 slides, 3 letters of recommendation, resumé. Additional exam requirements/recommendations for international students: Required—TOEFL (minimum score 550 paper-based; 213 computer-based; 77 iBT). *Application deadline:* For fall admission, 2/15 for domestic students. Application fee: $70. Electronic applications accepted. *Expenses:* Tuition: Full-time $29,500. Required fees: $70. Full-time tuition and fees vary according to degree level, program and student level. *Financial support:* In 2008–09, 10 students received support, including 10 teaching assistantships with full tuition reimbursements available; fellowships with full tuition reimbursements available, research assistantships with full tuition reimbursements available, institutionally sponsored loans, scholarships/grants, health care benefits, tuition waivers (full and partial), and unspecified assistantships also available. Financial award applicants required to submit FAFSA. *Faculty research:* Painting, sculpture, photography, printmaking. *Unit head:* Director of Graduate Studies, 607-255-6730, Fax: 607-255-3462. *Application contact:* Graduate Field Assistant, 607-255-6730, Fax: 607-255-3462, E-mail: artinfo@cornell.edu.

Cranbrook Academy of Art, Graduate School, Program in Fine Arts, Bloomfield Hills, MI 48303-0801. Offers ceramics (MFA); design (MFA), including graphic design; fiber arts (MFA); metalsmithing (MFA); painting (MFA); photography (MFA); printmaking (MFA); sculpture (MFA). *Accreditation:* NASAD. *Degree requirements:* For master's, thesis, exhibit. *Entrance requirements:* Additional exam requirements/recommendations for international students: Required—TOEFL (minimum score 550 paper-based; 213 computer-based).

See Close-Up on page 209.

Drake University, School of Education, Department of Teaching and Learning, Program in Secondary Education, Des Moines, IA 50311-4516. Offers art (MAT); biology (MAT); business (MAT); chemistry (MAT); English (MAT); general science (MAT); history-American (MAT); history-world (MAT); journalism (MAT); mathematics (MAT); physical science (MAT); physics (MAT); sociology (MAT); speech (MAT); speech communication (MAT); theatre (MAT). Part-time programs available. *Degree requirements:* For master's, comprehensive exam, thesis (for some programs), internships (for some programs). *Entrance requirements:* For master's, GRE General Test, MAT, or Drake Writing Assessment, resumé, 2 letters of recommendation. Additional exam requirements/recommendations for international students: Required—TOEFL (minimum score 550 paper-based; 213 computer-based). Electronic applications accepted. *Faculty research:* Counseling and rehabilitation, behavioral supports, inquiry-based science methods, teacher quality enhancement.

Drury University, Program in Studio Art and Theory, Springfield, MO 65802. Offers MA. *Entrance requirements:* For master's, GRE or MAT. Additional exam requirements/recommendations for international students: Required—TOEFL. Electronic applications accepted.

Duke University, Graduate School, Department of Art, Art History and Visual Studies, Durham, NC 27708-0764. Offers PhD. *Degree requirements:* For doctorate, thesis/dissertation. *Entrance requirements:* For doctorate, GRE General Test. Additional exam requirements/recommendations for international students: Required—TOEFL (minimum score 550 paper-based; 213 computer-based; 83 iBT), IELTS (minimum score 7). Electronic applications accepted.

East Carolina University, Graduate School, College of Fine Arts and Communication, School of Art and Design, Greenville, NC 27858-4353. Offers MA, MA Ed, MFA. *Accreditation:* NASAD (one or more programs are accredited). Part-time and evening/weekend programs available. *Degree requirements:* For master's, comprehensive exam, thesis (for some programs). *Entrance requirements:* For master's, GRE General Test or MAT, portfolio. Additional exam requirements/recommendations for international students: Required—TOEFL.

Eastern Illinois University, Graduate School, College of Arts and Humanities, Department of Art, Charleston, IL 61920-3099. Offers art (MA); art education (MA). *Accreditation:* NASAD. *Degree requirements:* For master's, thesis or alternative, portfolio.

Eastern Michigan University, Graduate School, College of Arts and Sciences, Department of Art, Ypsilanti, MI 48197. Offers art (MA); art education (MA); studio art (MA, MFA). Part-time and evening/weekend programs available. Postbaccalaureate distance learning degree programs offered (minimal on-campus study). *Entrance requirements:* Additional exam requirements/recommendations for international students: Required—TOEFL.

East Tennessee State University, School of Graduate Studies, College of Arts and Sciences, Department of Art and Design, Johnson City, TN 37614. Offers art education (MA); art history (MA); studio art (MA, MFA). *Accreditation:* NASAD. *Degree requirements:* For master's, thesis, exhibit, oral exam (MFA). *Entrance requirements:* For master's, GRE General Test, portfolio (MFA), bachelor's degree in art, minimum GPA of 3.0. Additional exam requirements/recommendations for international students: Required—TOEFL (minimum score 550 paper-based; 213 computer-based). *Faculty research:* History of sculpture, art and senior citizens, encaustic paintings, digital media in art history.

Edinboro University of Pennsylvania, Graduate Studies and Research, School of Liberal Arts, Department of Art, Edinboro, PA 16444. Offers art (MA); fine arts (MFA), including ceramics, jewelry/metalsmithing, painting, printmaking, sculpture. *Accreditation:* NASAD. Evening/weekend programs available. *Faculty:* 10 full-time (2 women). *Students:* 19 full-time (9 women); includes 1 minority (Asian American or Pacific Islander). Average age 29. In 2008, 10 master's awarded. *Degree requirements:* For master's, comprehensive exam, thesis or alternative, competency exam, exhibit, portfolio. *Entrance requirements:* For master's, GRE or MAT, interview, minimum QPA of 2.5, portfolio. *Application deadline:* Applications are processed on a rolling basis. Application fee: $30. Electronic applications accepted. *Expenses:* Tuition, state resident: full-time $6430; part-time $357 per credit. Tuition, nonresident: full-time $8038; part-time $572 per credit. International tuition: $15,171.58 full-time. Required fees: $2113; $60 per credit. Tuition and fees vary according to course load. *Financial support:* In 2008–09, 13 research assistantships with full and partial tuition reimbursements (averaging $3,850 per year) were awarded; Federal Work-Study, scholarships/grants, and unspecified assistantships also available. Financial award application deadline: 2/15; financial award applicants required to submit FAFSA. *Unit head:* Prof. John Lysak, Program Head, 814-732-2271, E-mail: jlysak@edinboro.edu. *Application contact:* Prof. John Lysak, Program Head, 814-732-2271, E-mail: jlysak@edinboro.edu.

Emily Carr Institute of Art + Design, Program in Applied Arts, Vancouver, BC V6H 3R9, Canada. Offers design (MAA); media arts (MAA); visual arts (MAA). *Degree requirements:* For master's, internship. *Entrance requirements:* For master's, minimum overall GPA of 3.0, visual portfolio, 3 letters of recommendation. Additional exam requirements/recommendations for international students: Required—TOEFL (minimum score 570 paper-based; 230 computer-based; 84 iBT), IELTS (minimum score 6.5), Michigan English language Assessment Battery (minimum score of 81). Electronic applications accepted.

Fairleigh Dickinson University, Metropolitan Campus, University College: Arts, Sciences, and Professional Studies, School of Art and Media Studies, Teaneck, NJ 07666-1914. Offers MA. *Students:* 6 full-time (5 women), 12 part-time (7 women), 5 international. Average age 31. 15 applicants, 67% accepted, 7 enrolled. In 2008, 4 master's awarded. *Application deadline:* Applications are processed on a rolling basis. Application fee: $40. *Application contact:* Susan Brooman, University Director of Graduate Admissions, 201-692-2554, Fax: 201-692-2560, E-mail: globaleducation@fdu.edu.

Ferris State University, Kendall College of Art and Design, Big Rapids, MI 49307. Offers MFA. *Accreditation:* NASAD. Part-time programs available. *Degree requirements:* For master's, thesis, seminars. *Entrance requirements:* For master's, portfolio, 3 letters of recommendation, curriculum vitae. Additional exam requirements/recommendations for international students: Required—TOEFL (minimum score 500 paper-based; 173 computer-based; 61 iBT).

Florida Atlantic University, Dorothy F. Schmidt College of Arts and Letters, Department of Visual Arts and Art History, Boca Raton, FL 33431-0991. Offers art education (MAT); ceramics (MFA); computer art (MFA); graphic design (MFA); painting (MFA). *Faculty:* 23 full-time (12 women), 17 part-time/adjunct (11 women). *Students:* 15 full-time (10 women), 7 part-time (5 women); includes 6 minority (1 African American, 5 Hispanic Americans), 3 international. Average age 31. 30 applicants, 20% accepted, 3 enrolled. In 2008, 8 master's awarded. *Degree requirements:* For master's, one foreign language, project. *Entrance requirements:* For master's, GRE General Test, minimum GPA of 3.0 during last 60 hours of course work, slide portfolio. *Application deadline:* For fall admission, 2/21 for domestic and international students; for spring admission, 10/1 for domestic and international students. Application fee: $30.

Electronic applications accepted. *Expenses:* Tuition, state resident: full-time $4867; part-time $270.40 per credit hour. Tuition, nonresident: full-time $16,486; part-time $915.87 per credit hour. *Financial support:* Research assistantships with full tuition reimbursements, teaching assistantships with full tuition reimbursements, career-related internships or fieldwork, Federal Work-Study, and institutionally sponsored loans available. Financial award applicants required to submit FAFSA. *Faculty research:* Painting, ceramics (traditional and non-traditional), installation, video and interactive sculpture. *Unit head:* Dr. Linda Johnson, Chair, 561-297-3870, Fax: 561-297-3078, E-mail: ljohnson@fau.edu. *Application contact:* James A Novak, Associate Professor/Graduate Coordinator/Advisor, 561-297-2430, Fax: 561-297-3078, E-mail: jnovak@fau.edu.

Florida International University, College of Architecture and the Arts, School of Art and Art History, Miami, FL 33199. Offers visual arts (MFA). *Accreditation:* NASAD. *Entrance requirements:* For master's, minimum GPA of 3.0 (upper level coursework), 3 letters of recommendation, 20 slides of creative work. Additional exam requirements/recommendations for international students: Required—TOEFL (minimum score 550 paper-based; 213 computer-based). Electronic applications accepted.

Florida State University, Graduate Studies, College of Visual Arts, Theatre and Dance, Department of Art, Tallahassee, FL 32306. Offers studio art (MFA). *Accreditation:* NASAD. *Degree requirements:* For master's, thesis, exhibit. *Entrance requirements:* For master's, portfolio, minimum GPA of 3.0. Additional exam requirements/recommendations for international students: Required—TOEFL (minimum score 550 paper-based). Electronic applications accepted. *Faculty research:* Photography, painting, sculpture, printmaking, ceramics.

Fontbonne University, Graduate Programs, Department of Fine Arts, St. Louis, MO 63105-3098. Offers art (MA); fine arts (MFA); theater education (MA). Part-time and evening/weekend programs available. *Faculty:* 5 full-time (1 woman), 4 part-time/adjunct (all women). *Students:* 13 full-time (7 women), 5 part-time (2 women); includes 2 minority (1 African American, 1 Asian American or Pacific Islander), 2 international. Average age 35. In 2008, 15 master's awarded. *Degree requirements:* For master's, thesis exhibit (MFA). *Entrance requirements:* For master's, minimum GPA of 3.0, portfolio. *Application deadline:* For fall admission, 8/1 priority date for domestic students. Applications are processed on a rolling basis. Application fee: $25. *Expenses:* Tuition: Part-time $540 per credit hour. Required fees: $270 per year. *Financial support:* In 2008–09, teaching assistantships (averaging $2,500 per year). Support available to part-time students. Financial award application deadline: 4/1; financial award applicants required to submit FAFSA. *Unit head:* Catherine Connor-Talasek, Chairperson, 314-889-1431, Fax: 314-889-4545, E-mail: cconnor@fontbonne.edu. *Application contact:* Catherine Connor-Talasek, Chairperson, 314-889-1431, Fax: 314-889-4545, E-mail: cconnor@fontbonne.edu.

Fort Hays State University, Graduate School, College of Arts and Sciences, Department of Art, Hays, KS 67601-4099. Offers studio art (MFA). Part-time programs available. *Degree requirements:* For master's, comprehensive exam, thesis. *Entrance requirements:* For master's, slides. Additional exam requirements/recommendations for international students: Required—TOEFL (minimum score 550 paper-based; 213 computer-based; 79 iBT). Electronic applications accepted. *Faculty research:* Migration art of Germanic tribes, iconographic and stylistic development, graphic design, photography, lithography.

Framingham State College, Division of Graduate and Continuing Education, Program in Art, Framingham, MA 01701-9101. Offers M Ed.

The George Washington University, Columbian College of Arts and Sciences, Department of Fine Arts and Art History, Washington, DC 20052. Offers art history (MA), including art history, museum training; ceramics (MFA); drawing/painting (MFA); interior design (MFA); new media (MFA); photography (MFA); sculpture (MFA). *Accreditation:* CIDA. Part-time and evening/weekend programs available. *Faculty:* 16 full-time (7 women), 31 part-time/adjunct (19 women). *Students:* 49 full-time (44 women), 37 part-time (34 women); includes 16 minority (4 African Americans, 6 Asian Americans or Pacific Islanders, 6 Hispanic Americans), 2 international. Average age 28. 204 applicants, 49% accepted, 63 enrolled. In 2008, 39 master's awarded. *Entrance requirements:* For master's, GRE General Test, bachelor's degree in field, minimum GPA of 3.0. Additional exam requirements/recommendations for international students: Required—TOEFL (minimum score 550 paper-based; 213 computer-based; 80 iBT). *Application deadline:* For fall admission, 3/1 priority date for domestic students, 1/15 priority date for international students; for spring admission, 10/1 priority date for domestic students, 9/1 priority date for international students. Applications are processed on a rolling basis. Application fee: $60. Electronic applications accepted. *Financial support:* In 2008–09, 12 students received support; fellowships, teaching assistantships, career-related internships or fieldwork, Federal Work-Study, and tuition waivers available. Financial award application deadline: 1/15. *Unit head:* Thomas K. Brown, Chair, 202-994-9067, E-mail: thbrown@gwu.edu. *Application contact:* Information Contact, 202-994-6085, Fax: 202-994-8657, E-mail: art@gwu.edu.

Georgia Southern University, Jack N. Averitt College of Graduate Studies, College of Liberal Arts and Social Sciences, Department of Art, Statesboro, GA 30460. Offers fine arts (MFA). *Accreditation:* NASAD. Part-time programs available. *Students:* 13 full-time (7 women), 3 part-time (all women); includes 2 minority (1 African American, 1 Hispanic American), 2 international. Average age 32. 8 applicants, 88% accepted, 5 enrolled. In 2008, 2 master's awarded. *Degree requirements:* For master's, thesis. *Entrance requirements:* For master's, minimum GPA of 2.5, 18 semester hours of course work in studio art, 9 semester hours of course work in art history, portfolio, letters of reference. Additional exam requirements/recommendations for international students: Required—TOEFL (minimum score 550 paper-based; 213 computer-based). *Application deadline:* For fall admission, 3/1 priority date for domestic and international students; for spring admission, 10/1 priority date for domestic students, 10/1 for international students. Applications are processed on a rolling basis. Application fee: $50. Electronic applications accepted. *Expenses:* Tuition, area resident: Full-time $3840; part-time $160 per semester hour. Tuition, state resident: full-time $3840; part-time $160 per semester hour. Tuition, nonresident: full-time $15,336; part-time $639 per semester hour. Required fees: $1152. *Financial support:* In 2008–09, 15 students received support, including research assistantships with partial tuition reimbursements available (averaging $6,850 per year), teaching assistantships with partial tuition reimbursements available (averaging $6,850 per year); career-related internships or fieldwork, Federal Work-Study, scholarships/grants, tuition waivers (partial), and unspecified assistantships also available. Support available to part-time students. Financial award application deadline: 4/15; financial award applicants required to submit FAFSA. *Faculty research:* International design trends, folk art, cultural diversity in art education and art appreciation, public sculpture, studio arts. *Unit head:* Patricia Carter, Chair, 912-478-5358, Fax: 912-478-5104, E-mail: pwcarter@georgiasouthern.edu. *Application contact:* 912-478-5384, Fax: 912-478-0740, E-mail: gradadmissions@georgiasouthern.edu.

Georgia State University, College of Arts and Sciences, Ernest G. Welch School of Art and Design, Program in Studio Art, Atlanta, GA 30303-3083. Offers MFA. *Accreditation:* NASAD. *Degree requirements:* For master's, thesis, exhibit, presentations, screening. *Entrance requirements:* For master's, portfolio. Additional exam requirements/recommendations for international students: Required—TOEFL (minimum score 550 paper-based; 213 computer-based). Electronic applications accepted. *Faculty research:* Photography, drawing/painting, printmaking, sculpture, ceramics.

Governors State University, College of Arts and Sciences, Program in Art, University Park, IL 60466-0975. Offers MA. Part-time and evening/weekend programs available. *Degree requirements:* For master's, thesis or alternative. *Entrance requirements:* For master's, portfolio, bachelor's degree in humanities. *Faculty research:* Historical study of art of selected ethnic groups of southwestern Zaire.

Hofstra University, School of Education, Health, and Human Services, Department of Curriculum and Teaching, Program in Fine Arts Education, Hempstead, NY 11549. Offers MA,

MS Ed. Part-time and evening/weekend programs available. *Students:* 15 full-time (14 women), 14 part-time (13 women); includes 1 minority (African American). Average age 29. 17 applicants, 88% accepted, 7 enrolled. In 2008, 16 master's awarded. *Degree requirements:* For master's, one foreign language, thesis or alternative, teaching portfolio. *Entrance requirements:* For master's, 2 letters of recommendation, portfolio, teacher certification (MA), essay. Additional exam requirements/recommendations for international students: Required—TOEFL (minimum score 550 paper-based; 213 computer-based; 80 iBT). *Application deadline:* Applications are processed on a rolling basis. Application fee: $60. Electronic applications accepted. *Expenses:* Tuition: Full-time $15,300; part-time $850 per credit. Required fees: $970; $165 per term. Tuition and fees vary according to program. *Financial support:* In 2008–09, 20 students received support, including 1 fellowship with full and partial tuition reimbursement available (averaging $2,500 per year); research assistantships with full and partial tuition reimbursements available, career-related internships or fieldwork, Federal Work-Study, institutionally sponsored loans, scholarships/grants, tuition waivers (full and partial), and unspecified assistantships also available. Support available to part-time students. Financial award applicants required to submit FAFSA. *Faculty research:* Art education and interdisciplinary curricula, teacher/artist role in identity issues, early childhood art education, marginalization of the arts in education, gender issues. *Unit head:* Dr. Susan G. Zwirn, Director, 516-463-4976, Fax: 516-463-6196, E-mail: catsgz@hofstra.edu. *Application contact:* Carol Drummer, Dean of Graduate Admissions, 516-463-4876, Fax: 516-463-4664, E-mail: gradstudent@hofstra.edu.

Hollins University, Graduate Programs, Program in Liberal Studies, Roanoke, VA 24020-1603. Offers humanities (MALS); interdisciplinary studies (MALS); justice and legal studies (MALS); liberal studies (CAS); social science (MALS); visual and performing arts (MALS). Part-time and evening/weekend programs available. *Faculty:* 6 full-time (1 woman), 7 part-time/adjunct (4 women). *Students:* 20 full-time (17 women), 78 part-time (56 women); includes 14 minority (13 African Americans, 1 Hispanic American), 1 international. Average age 39. 33 applicants, 85% accepted, 23 enrolled. In 2008, 42 master's awarded. *Degree requirements:* For master's, thesis. *Entrance requirements:* For master's, letters of recommendation, interview. Additional exam requirements/recommendations for international students: Required—TOEFL (minimum score 550 paper-based; 213 computer-based; 79 iBT). *Application deadline:* For fall admission, 7/1 priority date for domestic and international students; for spring admission, 12/10 priority date for domestic and international students. Applications are processed on a rolling basis. Application fee: $40. Electronic applications accepted. *Expenses:* Tuition: Full-time $26,720; part-time $590 per credit hour. Required fees: $280. *Financial support:* In 2008–09, 53 students received support, including 2 fellowships (averaging $1,189 per year); Federal Work-Study and scholarships/grants also available. Support available to part-time students. Financial award application deadline: 7/15; financial award applicants required to submit FAFSA. *Faculty research:* Elderly blacks, film, feminist economics, US voting patterns, Wagner, diversity. *Unit head:* Dr. Edward A. Lynch, Director, 540-362-6475, Fax: 540-362-6288, E-mail: elynch@hollins.edu. *Application contact:* Cathy S. Koon, Manager of Graduate Services, 540-362-6326, Fax: 540-362-6288, E-mail: ckoon@hollins.edu.

Hood College, Graduate School, Program in Ceramic Arts, Frederick, MD 21701-8575. Offers ceramic arts (Certificate); ceramics (MFA). Part-time and evening/weekend programs available. *Faculty:* 1 (woman) full-time, 5 part-time/adjunct (all women). *Students:* 1 (woman) full-time, 24 part-time (21 women). Average age 38. 11 applicants, 100% accepted, 5 enrolled. In 2008, 6 other advanced degrees awarded. *Degree requirements:* For master's, comprehensive exam. *Entrance requirements:* For master's, minimum GPA of 2.75; for Certificate, portfolio. Additional exam requirements/recommendations for international students: Required—TOEFL (minimum score 575 paper-based; 231 computer-based; 89 iBT). *Application deadline:* For fall admission, 7/15 for domestic and international students; for spring admission, 12/15 for domestic and international students. Applications are processed on a rolling basis. Application fee: $35. Electronic applications accepted. *Expenses:* Tuition: Full-time $6480. Required fees: $100; $50 per semester. *Financial support:* Applicants required to submit FAFSA. *Unit head:* Joyce Michaud, Director, 301-696-3526, E-mail: jmichaud@hood.edu. *Application contact:* Dr. Allen P. Flora, Dean of Graduate School, 301-696-3811, Fax: 301-696-3597, E-mail: gofurther@hood.edu.

Howard University, Graduate School, Division of Fine Arts, Department of Art, Program in Fine Arts, Washington, DC 20059-0002. Offers 3D reality (sculpture and ceramics) (MFA); design (MFA); electronic studio (MFA); painting (MFA); photography (MFA). *Accreditation:* NASAD. *Degree requirements:* For master's, comprehensive exam, thesis, exhibit. *Entrance requirements:* For master's, minimum GPA of 3.0, portfolio.

Hunter College of the City University of New York, Graduate School, School of Arts and Sciences, Department of Art, Program in Studio Art, New York, NY 10021-5085. Offers fine arts (MFA). Part-time and evening/weekend programs available. *Faculty:* 16 full-time (5 women), 1 part-time/adjunct (0 women). *Students:* 4 full-time (all women), 121 part-time (63 women); includes 10 minority (1 American Indian/Alaska Native, 3 Asian Americans or Pacific Islanders, 6 Hispanic Americans). Average age 30. 636 applicants, 6% accepted, 19 enrolled. In 2008, 47 master's awarded. *Degree requirements:* For master's, exhibit, project. *Entrance requirements:* For master's, minimum of 24 credits of course work in studio art and 9 credits of course work in art history, portfolio. Additional exam requirements/recommendations for international students: Required—TOEFL. *Application deadline:* For fall admission, 2/1 for domestic students; for spring admission, 10/1 for domestic students. Application fee: $125. *Financial support:* Career-related internships or fieldwork, Federal Work-Study, scholarships/grants, and tuition waivers (partial) available. Support available to part-time students. Financial award application deadline: 4/15. *Faculty research:* Color theory, public printmaking and environmental commissions in painting and sculpture, graphics, ceramics, contemporary film and video. *Unit head:* Joel Carreiro, Graduate Adviser, 212-650-3398, E-mail: grad.arthistoryadvisor@hunter.cuny.edu. *Application contact:* William Zlata, Director for Graduate Admissions, 212-772-4482, Fax: 212-650-3336, E-mail: admissions@hunter.cuny.edu.

Idaho State University, Office of Graduate Studies, College of Arts and Sciences, Department of Art and Pre-Architecture, Pocatello, ID 83209. Offers art (MFA). Part-time programs available. *Faculty:* 4 full-time (0 women). *Students:* 7 full-time (2 women), 7 part-time (2 women); includes 1 minority (Hispanic American). Average age 41. In 2008, 2 master's awarded. *Degree requirements:* For master's, comprehensive exam, thesis, exhibit. *Entrance requirements:* For master's, GRE General Test, GMAT or MAT, minimum GPA of 3.0 in all upper division classes, portfolio of work, 3 letters of recommendation. Additional exam requirements/recommendations for international students: Required—TOEFL (minimum score 550 paper-based; 213 computer-based; 80 iBT). *Application deadline:* For fall admission, 3/15 for domestic and international students; for spring admission, 10/15 for domestic and international students. Applications are processed on a rolling basis. Application fee: $55. Electronic applications accepted. *Expenses:* Tuition, area resident: Full-time $3114; part-time $276 per credit hour. Tuition, state resident: full-time $3114; part-time $276 per credit hour. Tuition, nonresident: full-time $12,318; part-time $404 per credit hour. Required fees: $2360. Tuition and fees vary according to course load and reciprocity agreements. *Financial support:* In 2008–09, 3 teaching assistantships with full and partial tuition reimbursements (averaging $9,401 per year) were awarded; Federal Work-Study, institutionally sponsored loans, scholarships/grants, traineeships, health care benefits, tuition waivers (full and partial), and unspecified assistantships also available. Support available to part-time students. Financial award application deadline: 1/1; financial award applicants required to submit FAFSA. *Faculty research:* Computerized weaving, anodizing refractory metals, viscosity printing, neon, ceramic shell casting. *Unit head:* Rudy Kovacs, Chair, 208-282-2488, Fax: 208-282-4741, E-mail: kovarudo@isu.edu. *Application contact:* Ellen Combs, Graduate School Technical Records Specialist, 208-282-2150, Fax: 208-282-4847, E-mail: combelle@isu.edu.

Illinois State University, Graduate School, College of Fine Arts, Program in Arts Technology, Normal, IL 61790-2200. Offers MS. *Accreditation:* NASAD. *Degree requirements:* For master's, thesis or alternative.

Art/Fine Arts

Illinois State University, Graduate School, College of Fine Arts, School of Art, Normal, IL 61790-2200. Offers art history (MA, MS); ceramics (MFA, MS); drawing (MFA, MS); fibers (MFA, MS); glass (MFA, MS); graphic design (MFA, MS); metals (MFA, MS); painting (MFA, MS); photography (MFA, MS); printmaking (MFA, MS); sculpture (MFA, MS). *Accreditation:* NASAD (one or more programs are accredited). *Degree requirements:* For master's, thesis or alternative, internship. *Entrance requirements:* For master's, portfolio, sample of scholarly writing. *Faculty research:* General operations support: Normal Editions Workshop for FY2007.

Indiana State University, School of Graduate Studies, College of Arts and Sciences, Department of Art, Terre Haute, IN 47809-1401. Offers ceramics (MA, MFA); drawing (MA, MFA); graphic design (MA, MFA); painting (MA, MFA); photography (MA, MFA); printmaking (MA, MFA); sculpture (MA, MFA). *Accreditation:* NASAD (one or more programs are accredited). Part-time programs available. *Degree requirements:* For master's, thesis or alternative, departmental qualifying exam. *Entrance requirements:* For master's, portfolio. Additional exam requirements/recommendations for international students: Required—TOEFL (minimum score 550 paper-based).

Indiana University Bloomington, University Graduate School, College of Arts and Sciences, Henry Radford Hope School of Fine Arts, Bloomington, IN 47405-7000. Offers MA, MFA, PhD. *Accreditation:* NASAD (one or more programs are accredited). *Faculty:* 17 full-time (10 women). *Students:* 122 full-time (82 women), 21 part-time (15 women); includes 8 minority (1 African American, 1 American Indian/Alaska Native, 4 Asian Americans or Pacific Islanders, 2 Hispanic Americans), 12 international. Average age 30. 301 applicants, 34% accepted, 50 enrolled. In 2008, 33 master's, 5 doctorates awarded. *Degree requirements:* For doctorate, 2 foreign languages, thesis/dissertation. *Entrance requirements:* For master's, portfolio (MFA); for doctorate, minimum GPA of 3.0. Additional exam requirements/recommendations for international students: Required—TOEFL. *Application deadline:* For fall admission, 1/15 priority date for domestic students, 12/15 for international students; for spring admission, 9/1 for domestic and international students. Applications are processed on a rolling basis. Application fee: $50 ($60 for international students). *Expenses:* Tuition, area resident: Part-time $291.97 per credit hour. Tuition, state resident: part-time $291.97 per credit hour. Tuition, nonresident: part-time $850.33 per credit hour. Required fees: $110 per semester. Tuition and fees vary according to course load and program. *Financial support:* Fellowships with tuition reimbursements, research assistantships with tuition reimbursements, teaching assistantships with tuition reimbursements, career-related internships or fieldwork, Federal Work-Study, scholarships/grants, tuition waivers (full and partial), and stipends available. Financial award application deadline: 2/15. *Faculty research:* Infrared reflectography, Italian Renaissance painters, hand papermaking, British Romantic landscape painting, late nineteenth century American art. *Unit head:* Paul Brown, Director, 812-855-7498. *Application contact:* Brad Wicklund, Graduate Services Coordinator, 812-855-7766, E-mail: bwicklun@indiana.edu.

Indiana University of Pennsylvania, School of Graduate Studies and Research, College of Fine Arts, Department of Art, Program in Art, Indiana, PA 15705-1087. Offers MA, MFA. *Accreditation:* NASAD. Part-time programs available. *Faculty:* 10 full-time (5 women). *Students:* 15 full-time (7 women), 10 part-time (6 women); includes 1 minority (Asian American or Pacific Islander), 4 international. Average age 29. 26 applicants, 50% accepted, 9 enrolled. In 2008, 2 master's awarded. *Degree requirements:* For master's, thesis optional. *Entrance requirements:* For master's, 3 letters of recommendation, portfolio. Additional exam requirements/recommendations for international students: Required—TOEFL. *Application deadline:* For fall admission, 7/1 priority date for domestic students; for spring admission, 11/1 for domestic students. Applications are processed on a rolling basis. Application fee: $30. *Expenses:* Tuition, area resident: Full-time $6430; part-time $357 per credit. Tuition, nonresident: full-time $10,288; part-time $572 per credit. Required fees: $1547.50; $107 per credit. $283 per year. *Financial support:* In 2008–09, 11 research assistantships with full and partial tuition reimbursements (averaging $4,451 per year) were awarded; fellowships, career-related internships or fieldwork and Federal Work-Study also available. Support available to part-time students. Financial award application deadline: 3/15; financial award applicants required to submit FAFSA. *Unit head:* Dr. James Nestor, 724-357-2593, E-mail: nestor@iup.edu. *Application contact:* Dr. James Nestor, Graduate Coordinator, 724-357-2593, E-mail: nestor@iup.edu.

Indiana University–Purdue University Indianapolis, Herron School of Art and Design, Indianapolis, IN 46202-2896. Offers art education (MAE); furniture design (MFA); printmaking (MFA); sculpture (MFA); visual communication (MFA). *Accreditation:* NASAD. Part-time and evening/weekend programs available. *Entrance requirements:* For master's, portfolio, 44 hours of course work in art history and studio art. Electronic applications accepted.

Inter American University of Puerto Rico, San Germán Campus, Graduate Studies Center, Program in Fine Arts, San Germán, PR 00683-5008. Offers art (MFA); ceramics (MFA); drawing (MFA); engraving (MFA); painting (MFA); photography (MFA); sculpture (MFA). *Degree requirements:* For master's, comprehensive exam, thesis. *Entrance requirements:* For master's, GRE General Test or EXADEP, minimum GPA of 3.0.

James Madison University, The Graduate School, College of Visual and Performing Arts, School of Art and Art History, Harrisonburg, VA 22807. Offers art education (MA); art history (MA); ceramics (MFA); drawing/painting (MFA); metal/jewelry (MFA); photography (MFA); printmaking (MFA); sculpture (MFA); studio art (MA); weaving/fibers (MFA). *Accreditation:* NASAD. Part-time programs available. *Faculty:* 13 full-time (8 women). *Students:* 7 full-time (5 women), 1 part-time (0 women); includes 2 minority (1 African American, 1 Asian American or Pacific Islander). Average age 27. In 2008, 3 master's awarded. *Degree requirements:* For master's, thesis (for some programs). *Entrance requirements:* For master's, GRE General Test, language exam in French or German, portfolio, 3 letters of recommendation, research paper. Additional exam requirements/recommendations for international students: Required—TOEFL. *Application deadline:* For fall admission, 2/15 priority date for domestic students, 2/15 for international students; for spring admission, 10/15 priority date for domestic students, 10/15 for international students. Applications are processed on a rolling basis. Application fee: $55. Electronic applications accepted. *Expenses:* Tuition, area resident: Full-time $7008; part-time $292 per credit hour. Tuition, state resident: full-time $7008; part-time $292 per credit hour. Tuition, nonresident: full-time $20,352; part-time $848 per credit hour. *Financial support:* In 2008–09, 8 students received support, including 3 teaching assistantships with full tuition reimbursements available (averaging $8,664 per year); Federal Work-Study and 3 graduate assistantships ($7,382) also available. Financial award application deadline: 3/1; financial award applicants required to submit FAFSA. *Unit head:* Leslie M. Bellavance, Academic Unit Head, 540-568-6216. *Application contact:* Lynette M. Bible, Director of Graduate Admissions, 540-568-6395, Fax: 540-568-7860, E-mail: biblelm@jmu.edu.

John F. Kennedy University, Graduate School of Holistic Studies, Department of Arts and Consciousness, Program in Studio Arts, Pleasant Hill, CA 94523-4817. Offers MFA. Part-time and evening/weekend programs available. *Degree requirements:* For master's, thesis or alternative. *Entrance requirements:* For master's, interview, portfolio. Additional exam requirements/recommendations for international students: Required—TOEFL. *Expenses:* Contact institution.

Johnson State College, Program in Studio Arts, Johnson, VT 05656-9405. Offers drawing (MFA); mixed media (MFA); painting (MFA); sculpture (MFA). Part-time programs available. Postbaccalaureate distance learning degree programs offered (minimal on-campus study). *Entrance requirements:* For master's, portfolio. Additional exam requirements/recommendations for international students: Required—TOEFL. *Expenses:* Contact institution.

Kansas State University, Graduate School, College of Arts and Sciences, Department of Art, Manhattan, KS 66506. Offers MFA. *Accreditation:* NASAD. Part-time programs available. *Faculty:* 13 full-time (5 women), 1 part-time/adjunct (0 women). *Students:* 16 full-time (10 women), 1 (woman) part-time; includes 1 minority (African American), 2 international. Average age 31. 21 applicants, 19% accepted, 3 enrolled. In 2008, 8 master's awarded. *Degree requirements:* For master's, thesis, gallery exhibit. *Entrance requirements:* For master's, slides of artistic work, portfolio. Additional exam requirements/recommendations for international students: Required—TOEFL (minimum score 550 paper-based; 213 computer-based). *Application deadline:* For fall admission, 2/15 for domestic students, 2/1 for international students; for winter admission, 12/1 for international students; for spring admission, 10/15 for domestic students, 8/1 for international students. Application fee: $30 ($55 for international students). *Expenses:* Tuition, area resident: Full-time $6466; part-time $269.40 per credit hour. Tuition, state resident: full-time $6466; part-time $269.40 per credit hour. Tuition, nonresident: full-time $14,874; part-time $619.75 per credit hour. Required fees: $673; $23.40 per credit hour. Tuition and fees vary according to campus/location. *Financial support:* In 2008–09, 14 teaching assistantships with full tuition reimbursements (averaging $8,893 per year) were awarded; research assistantships, career-related internships or fieldwork, Federal Work-Study, institutionally sponsored loans, and scholarships/grants also available. Support available to part-time students. Financial award application deadline: 3/1; financial award applicants required to submit FAFSA. *Faculty research:* Drawing, painting, sculpture, metalsmithing, visual communication. *Unit head:* Gerry Craig, Head, 785-532-6605, Fax: 785-532-0334, E-mail: gkcraig@ksu.edu. *Application contact:* Elliot Pujol, Director, 785-532-6605, Fax: 785-532-0334, E-mail: hepujol@ksu.edu.

Kean University, School of Visual and Performing Arts, Union, NJ 07083. Offers MA, MS. Part-time and evening/weekend programs available. *Faculty:* 28 full-time (9 women). *Students:* 27 full-time (21 women), 66 part-time (40 women); includes 21 minority (10 African Americans, 2 Asian Americans or Pacific Islanders, 9 Hispanic Americans), 3 international. Average age 36. 23 applicants, 96% accepted, 19 enrolled. In 2008, 47 master's awarded. *Degree requirements:* For master's, comprehensive exam (for some programs), thesis (for some programs). *Entrance requirements:* For master's, minimum GPA of 3.0, 3 letters of recommendation, portfolio. *Application deadline:* For fall admission, 5/1 for domestic students; for spring admission, 11/1 for domestic students. Application fee: $60 ($150 for international students). Electronic applications accepted. *Expenses:* Tuition, state resident: full-time $10,128; part-time $422 per credit. Tuition, nonresident: full-time $13,728; part-time $572 per credit. Required fees: $2570; $107 per credit. Part-time tuition and fees vary according to course load, degree level and program. *Financial support:* In 2008–09, 12 research assistantships with full tuition reimbursements (averaging $3,217 per year) were awarded; unspecified assistantships also available. *Unit head:* Dr. Holly Logue, Dean, 908-737-4376, Fax: 908-737-4377, E-mail: hlogue@kean.edu. *Application contact:* Steven Koch, Pre-Admissions Coordinator, 908-737-4723, Fax: 908-737-5965, E-mail: grad-adm@kean.edu.

Kent State University, College of the Arts, School of Art, Kent, OH 44242-0001. Offers art education (MA); art history (MA); crafts (MA, MFA), including ceramics (MA), glass, jewelry/metals, textiles/art; fine art (MA, MFA), including drawing/painting, printmaking, sculpture. *Accreditation:* NASAD (one or more programs are accredited). *Degree requirements:* For master's, one foreign language, thesis. *Entrance requirements:* For master's, undergraduate degree in proposed area of study (for fine arts and crafts programs); minimum overall GPA of 2.75 (3.0 for art major); 3 letters of recommendation; portfolio (15-20 slides for MA, 20-25 for MFA), brief autobiographical statement (MFA). Additional exam requirements/recommendations for international students: Required—TOEFL. Electronic applications accepted.

Laguna College of Art & Design, Graduate Program, Laguna Beach, CA 92651-1136. Offers painting (MFA). *Entrance requirements:* For master's, BA with a studio concentration or BFA; minimum GPA of 3.0 in studio subjects; portfolio; resumé. Additional exam requirements/recommendations for international students: Required—TOEFL (minimum score 550 paper-based). Electronic applications accepted.

Lamar University, College of Graduate Studies, College of Fine Arts and Communication, Department of Art, Beaumont, TX 77710. Offers art history (MA); photography (MA); studio art (MA); visual design (MA). Part-time and evening/weekend programs available. *Faculty:* 7 full-time (3 women). *Students:* 1 (woman) full-time. Average age 45. 2 applicants, 0% accepted. In 2008, 2 master's awarded. *Degree requirements:* For master's, thesis. *Entrance requirements:* For master's, GRE General Test, minimum GPA of 2.5 in last 60 hours of undergraduate course work. Additional exam requirements/recommendations for international students: Required—TOEFL. *Application deadline:* For fall admission, 8/1 priority date for domestic students; for spring admission, 12/1 for domestic students. Applications are processed on a rolling basis. Application fee: $25 ($50 for international students). *Expenses:* Tuition, state resident: full-time $5000; part-time $195 per credit. Tuition, nonresident: full-time $12,376; part-time $476 per credit. Required fees: $1570. *Financial support:* Fellowships, career-related internships or fieldwork, Federal Work-Study, and scholarships/grants available. Financial award application deadline: 4/1. *Faculty research:* Nineteenth century academic paintings, metal casting, pigment color stability, computer-modified photography, manipulated photography. *Unit head:* Donna M. Meeks, Chair, 409-880-8141, Fax: 409-880-1799, E-mail: meeksdm@lub002.lamar.edu. *Application contact:* Debbie Piper, Coordinator of Graduate Admissions, 409-880-8356, Fax: 409-880-8414, E-mail: gradmissions@hal.lamar.edu.

Lehman College of the City University of New York, Division of Arts and Humanities, Department of Art, Bronx, NY 10468-1589. Offers MA, MFA. Part-time and evening/weekend programs available. *Entrance requirements:* For master's, 33 undergraduate credits in art, interview, portfolio. *Faculty research:* Graphic art, modern and contemporary art, sculpture, primitive and pre-Columbian art, medieval art.

Lesley University, Graduate School of Arts and Social Sciences, Program in Visual Arts, Cambridge, MA 02138-2790. Offers MFA. Postbaccalaureate distance learning degree programs offered. *Entrance requirements:* For master's, portfolio. Additional exam requirements/recommendations for international students: Required—TOEFL (minimum score 550 paper-based; 213 computer-based; 80 iBT). *Expenses:* Contact institution.

See Close-Up on page 201.

Lindenwood University, Graduate Programs, School of Fine and Performing Arts, St. Charles, MO 63301-1695. Offers arts management (MA); communication arts (MA); studio art (MA, MFA); theatre (MA, MFA). Part-time programs available. *Faculty:* 21 full-time (10 women). *Students:* 28 full-time (18 women), 27 part-time (21 women); includes 8 minority (all African Americans), 7 international. Average age 35. In 2008, 16 master's awarded. *Degree requirements:* For master's, thesis (for some programs). *Entrance requirements:* For master's, audition or interview, minimum GPA of 3.0, official transcripts, submission of portfolio, essay, letter of recommendation. Additional exam requirements/recommendations for international students: Required—TOEFL (minimum score 550 paper-based; 213 computer-based; 80 iBT). *Application deadline:* For fall admission, 8/30 priority date for domestic and international students; for spring admission, 12/30 priority date for domestic and international students. Applications are processed on a rolling basis. Application fee: $30 ($100 for international students). Electronic applications accepted. *Expenses:* Tuition: Full-time $12,700; part-time $360 per credit hour. *Financial support:* Career-related internships or fieldwork, institutionally sponsored loans, tuition waivers (partial), and unspecified assistantships available. Financial award application deadline: 6/30; financial award applicants required to submit FAFSA. *Unit head:* Donnell Walsh, Dean of Fine Arts, 636-949-4853, Fax: 636-949-4910, E-mail: dwalsh@lindenwood.edu. *Application contact:* Brett Barger, Dean of Evening Admissions and Extension Campuses, 636-949-4934, Fax: 636-949-4109, E-mail: adultadmissions@lindenwood.edu.

Long Island University, C.W. Post Campus, School of Visual and Performing Arts, Department of Art, Brookville, NY 11548-1300. Offers art (MA); art education (MS); clinical art therapy (MA); fine art and design (MFA). Part-time and evening/weekend programs available. *Degree requirements:* For master's, thesis. Electronic applications accepted. *Faculty research:* Painting, sculpture, installation, computers, video.

Louisiana State University and Agricultural and Mechanical College, Graduate School, College of Art and Design, School of Art, Program in Studio Art, Baton Rouge, LA 70803. Offers ceramics (MFA); graphic design (MFA); painting and drawing (MFA); photography

(MFA); printmaking (MFA); sculpture (MFA). *Accreditation:* NASAD. *Degree requirements:* For master's, thesis. *Entrance requirements:* For master's, minimum GPA of 3.0. Additional exam requirements/recommendations for international students: Required—TOEFL (minimum score 550 paper-based; 213 computer-based; 79 iBT). Electronic applications accepted.

Louisiana Tech University, Graduate School, College of Liberal Arts, School of Art, Ruston, LA 71272. Offers art and graphic design (MFA); photography (MFA); studio art (MFA). *Accreditation:* NASAD. Part-time programs available. *Degree requirements:* For master's, exhibit. *Entrance requirements:* For master's, GRE General Test, portfolio.

Maine College of Art, Program in Studio Arts, Portland, ME 04101. Offers MFA. *Accreditation:* NASAD. *Degree requirements:* For master's, thesis. *Entrance requirements:* Additional exam requirements/recommendations for international students: Required—TOEFL (minimum score 550 paper-based; 213 computer-based). Electronic applications accepted.

Marshall University, Academic Affairs Division, College of Fine Arts, Department of Art, Huntington, WV 25755. Offers MA. Evening/weekend programs available. *Degree requirements:* For master's, thesis optional. *Entrance requirements:* For master's, GRE General Test, portfolio.

Maryland Institute College of Art, Graduate Studies, Fine Arts Post Baccalaureate Certificate Program, Baltimore, MD 21217. Offers Certificate. Part-time programs available. *Degree requirements:* For Certificate, thesis. *Entrance requirements:* For degree, portfolio, 40 studio credits, 6 credits in art history. Additional exam requirements/recommendations for international students: Required—TOEFL (minimum score 550 paper-based; 213 computer-based).

Maryland Institute College of Art, Graduate Studies, Hoffberger School of Painting, Baltimore, MD 21217. Offers MFA. *Accreditation:* NASAD. *Degree requirements:* For master's, thesis, exhibit. *Entrance requirements:* For master's, portfolio, 40 studio credits, 6 credits in art history. Additional exam requirements/recommendations for international students: Required—TOEFL (minimum score 550 paper-based; 213 computer-based).

Maryland Institute College of Art, Graduate Studies, Mount Royal School of Art, Baltimore, MD 21217. Offers painting (MFA). *Degree requirements:* For master's, thesis, exhibit. *Entrance requirements:* For master's, 40 credits in studio art, 6 credits in art history, portfolio. Additional exam requirements/recommendations for international students: Required—TOEFL (minimum score 550 paper-based; 213 computer-based).

Maryland Institute College of Art, Graduate Studies, Program in Community Arts, Baltimore, MD 21217. Offers MA. Part-time programs available. *Degree requirements:* For master's, thesis. *Entrance requirements:* For master's, portfolio, professional certification (BFA), 40 studio credits, 6 credits in art history. Additional exam requirements/recommendations for international students: Required—TOEFL (minimum score 550 paper-based; 213 computer-based).

Maryland Institute College of Art, Graduate Studies, Program in Studio Art, Baltimore, MD 21217. Offers MFA. Offered during summer only. Part-time programs available. *Degree requirements:* For master's, thesis. *Entrance requirements:* For master's, portfolio, professional certification (BFA), 40 studio credits, 6 credits in art history. Additional exam requirements/recommendations for international students: Required—TOEFL (minimum score 550 paper-based; 213 computer-based).

Maryland Institute College of Art, Graduate Studies, Rinehart School of Sculpture, Baltimore, MD 21217. Offers MFA. *Accreditation:* NASAD. *Degree requirements:* For master's, thesis, exhibit. *Entrance requirements:* For master's, portfolio, 40 studio credits, 6 credits in art history. Additional exam requirements/recommendations for international students: Required—TOEFL (minimum score 550 paper-based; 213 computer-based).

Marywood University, Academic Affairs, Insalaco College of Creative Arts and Management, Art Department, Program in Studio Art, Scranton, PA 18509-1598. Offers advertising design (MA); ceramics (MA); clay (MA); graphic design (MA); illustration (MA); interior architecture (MA); painting (MA); photography (MA); printmaking (MA); sculpture (MA); weaving (MA). *Accreditation:* NASAD. Part-time and evening/weekend programs available. *Degree requirements:* For master's, comprehensive exam, thesis or alternative. *Entrance requirements:* For master's, portfolio. Additional exam requirements/recommendations for international students: Required—TOEFL (minimum score 550 paper-based; 213 computer-based). Electronic applications accepted. *Faculty research:* Texture and line in clay, cast bronze sculpture, color theories, book art and illustration, sculptural form.

Marywood University, Academic Affairs, Insalaco College of Creative Arts and Management, Art Department, Program in Visual Arts, Scranton, PA 18509-1598. Offers advertising design (MFA); clay (MFA); fibers (MFA); graphic design (MFA); illustration (MFA); metals (MFA); painting (MFA); photography (MFA); printmaking (MFA). *Accreditation:* NASAD. Part-time and evening/weekend programs available. *Degree requirements:* For master's, thesis or alternative, exhibit. *Entrance requirements:* For master's, portfolio. Additional exam requirements/recommendations for international students: Required—TOEFL (minimum score 550 paper-based; 213 computer-based). Electronic applications accepted. *Expenses:* Contact institution. *Faculty research:* Mariology, exploration of visual imagery, explorations involving drawing on the loom, clay as sculptural medium, oil paintings.

Massachusetts College of Art and Design, Graduate Programs, Program in Fine Arts, Boston, MA 02115-5882. Offers ceramics (MFA); design (MFA); fibers (MFA); film (MFA); glass (MFA); media and performing arts (MFA); metals (MFA); painting (MFA); photography (MFA); printmaking (MFA); sculpture (MFA). *Accreditation:* NASAD. *Faculty:* 10 full-time (5 women), 8 part-time/adjunct (6 women). *Students:* 83 full-time (53 women), 17 part-time (10 women); includes 8 minority (1 American Indian/Alaska Native, 4 Asian Americans or Pacific Islanders, 3 Hispanic Americans), 15 international. Average age 34. 295 applicants, 24% accepted, 40 enrolled. In 2008, 37 master's awarded. *Degree requirements:* For master's, thesis, exhibit. *Entrance requirements:* For master's, 12 units of course work in art history, portfolio, resumé, college transcripts, statement of purpose, letters of reference, interview. Additional exam requirements/recommendations for international students: Required—TOEFL (minimum score 563 paper-based; 223 computer-based; 85 iBT); Recommended—IELTS (minimum score 6.5). *Application deadline:* For fall admission, 1/15 for domestic and international students; for spring admission, 11/1 for domestic students. Application fee: $75. *Expenses:* Tuition, area resident: Full-time $17,100; part-time $570 per credit. Tuition and fees vary according to program. *Financial support:* In 2008–09, 50 research assistantships (averaging $2,000 per year), 30 teaching assistantships (averaging $2,000 per year) were awarded; career-related internships or fieldwork, Federal Work-Study, and clerical/technical assistantships also available. Support available to part-time students. Financial award application deadline: 5/1; financial award applicants required to submit FAFSA. *Unit head:* George Creamer, Director, 617-879-7163, Fax: 617-879-7171, E-mail: creamer@massart.edu. *Application contact:* George Creamer, Director, 617-879-7163.

Memphis College of Art, Graduate Programs, Program in Studio Art, Memphis, TN 38104-2764. Offers painting (MFA); photography (MFA); printmaking (MFA); sculpture (MFA). *Accreditation:* NASAD. Part-time programs available. *Faculty:* 11 full-time (5 women), 2 part-time/adjunct (1 woman). *Students:* 18 full-time (9 women); includes 2 minority (both African Americans). Average age 29. 49 applicants, 55% accepted, 9 enrolled. In 2008, 4 master's awarded. *Degree requirements:* For master's, thesis, exhibition. *Entrance requirements:* For master's, portfolio, interview, resumé. Additional exam requirements/recommendations for international students: Required—TOEFL (minimum score 525 paper-based; 195 computer-based). *Application deadline:* For fall admission, 3/1 priority date for domestic and international students; for spring admission, 11/1 priority date for domestic and international students. Application fee: $50. Electronic applications accepted. *Expenses:* Tuition: Full-time $22,000; part-time $958 per credit hour. Required fees: $560; $280 per semester. Tuition and fees vary according to program. *Financial support:* In 2008–09, 11 students received support, including 2 teaching assistantships (averaging $2,000 per year); career-related internships or fieldwork, Federal Work-Study, institutionally sponsored loans, scholarships/grants, tuition waivers (partial), unspecified assistantships, and merit awards also available. Support available to part-time students. Financial award application deadline: 8/1; financial award applicants required to submit FAFSA. *Unit head:* Howard Paine, Graduate Program Director, 901-272-5100, Fax: 901-272-5158, E-mail: hpaine@mca.edu. *Application contact:* Annette James Moore, Director of Admissions, 800-727-1088, Fax: 901-272-5158, E-mail: info@mca.edu.

See Close-Up on page 213.

Miami International University of Art & Design, Program in Visual Arts, Miami, FL 33132-1418. Offers MFA. Postbaccalaureate distance learning degree programs offered.

See Close-Up on page 121.

Miami University, Graduate School, School of Fine Arts, Department of Art, Program in Studio Art, Oxford, OH 45056. Offers MFA. *Accreditation:* NASAD. *Degree requirements:* For master's, thesis, final project. *Entrance requirements:* For master's, portfolio, minimum undergraduate GPA of 3.0 during previous 2 years or 2.75 overall.

See Display on page 170.

Michigan State University, The Graduate School, College of Arts and Letters, Department of Art and Art History, East Lansing, MI 48824. Offers studio art (MFA). *Entrance requirements:* For master's, minimum GPA of 3.0, portfolio, resumé. Additional exam requirements/recommendations for international students: Required—TOEFL, Michigan State University ELT (85), Michigan ELAB (83). Electronic applications accepted.

Mills College, Graduate Studies, Department of Art, Oakland, CA 94613-1000. Offers ceramics (MFA); intermedia (MFA); painting (MFA); photography (MFA); sculpture (MFA). *Faculty:* 7 full-time (6 women), 11 part-time/adjunct (7 women). *Students:* 22 full-time (10 women). Average age 30. 85 applicants, 29% accepted, 12 enrolled. In 2008, 12 master's awarded. *Degree requirements:* For master's, thesis or alternative, exhibit. *Entrance requirements:* Additional exam requirements/recommendations for international students: Required—TOEFL. *Application deadline:* For fall admission, 2/1 for domestic students; for spring admission, 11/1 for domestic students. Application fee: $50. *Expenses:* Contact institution. *Financial support:* In 2008–09, 12 students received support, including 7 fellowships (averaging $2,086 per year), 12 teaching assistantships with partial tuition reimbursements available (averaging $13,783 per year); scholarships/grants and unspecified assistantships also available. Financial award application deadline: 2/1; financial award applicants required to submit FAFSA. *Faculty research:* Contemporary Chinese/American art, Asian art, performance art, feminist theory, installation. *Unit head:* Ron Nagle, Chairperson, 510-430-3142, Fax: 510-430-3314. *Application contact:* Marika Benko, Graduate Admission Specialist, 510-430-3309, Fax: 510-430-2159, E-mail: grad-studies@mills.edu.

Minneapolis College of Art and Design, Program in Arts, Minneapolis, MN 55404-4347. Offers design (Certificate); fine arts (Certificate); media (Certificate); sustainable design (Certificate). Part-time programs available. Postbaccalaureate distance learning degree programs offered. *Faculty:* 23 full-time (7 women), 9 part-time/adjunct (4 women). *Students:* 32 full-time (15 women), 31 part-time (18 women); includes 5 minority (2 African Americans, 1 American Indian/Alaska Native, 2 Hispanic Americans), 4 international. Average age 24. 172 applicants, 27% accepted, 19 enrolled. In 2008, 15 Certificates awarded. *Degree requirements:* For Certificate, final project. *Entrance requirements:* For degree, resumé, portfolio, letter of recommendation. Additional exam requirements/recommendations for international students: Required—TOEFL (minimum score 550 paper-based; 213 computer-based; 79 iBT). *Application deadline:* For fall admission, 1/15 for domestic and international students. Application fee: $50. Electronic applications accepted. *Expenses:* Tuition: Full-time $28,400; part-time $813 per credit. *Financial support:* Career-related internships or fieldwork and scholarships/grants available. Financial award application deadline: 3/15; financial award applicants required to submit FAFSA. *Faculty research:* Visual arts. *Unit head:* Carole Fisher, Graduate Director, 612-874-3629, E-mail: carole_fisher@mcad.edu. *Application contact:* William Mullen, Vice President, Enrollment Management, 612-874-3762, Fax: 612-874-3701, E-mail: william_mullen@mcad.edu.

Minneapolis College of Art and Design, Program in Visual Studies, Minneapolis, MN 55404-4347. Offers animation (MFA); comic art (MFA); drawing (MFA); filmmaking (MFA); fine arts (MFA); furniture design (MFA); graphic design (MFA); illustration (MFA); interactive media (MFA); painting (MFA); photography (MFA); printmaking (MFA); sculpture (MFA). *Accreditation:* NASAD. Part-time programs available. *Faculty:* 23 full-time (7 women), 9 part-time/adjunct (4 women). *Students:* 40 full-time (21 women), 1 (woman) part-time; includes 1 minority (American Indian/Alaska Native). Average age 27. 172 applicants, 24% accepted, 15 enrolled. In 2008, 7 master's awarded. *Degree requirements:* For master's, thesis, thesis exhibit. *Entrance requirements:* For master's, portfolio, resumé, 3 letters of recommendation, personal statement. Additional exam requirements/recommendations for international students: Required—TOEFL (minimum score 550 paper-based; 213 computer-based; 79 iBT). *Application deadline:* For fall admission, 1/15 for domestic and international students. Application fee: $50. Electronic applications accepted. *Expenses:* Tuition: Full-time $28,400; part-time $813 per credit. *Financial support:* In 2008–09, 23 students received support, including 15 teaching assistantships (averaging $6,000 per year); career-related internships or fieldwork, Federal Work-Study, scholarships/grants, and unspecified assistantships also available. Support available to part-time students. Financial award application deadline: 3/15; financial award applicants required to submit FAFSA. *Faculty research:* Visual arts. *Unit head:* Carole Fisher, Graduate Director, 612-874-3629, E-mail: carole_fisher@mcad.edu. *Application contact:* William Mullen, Vice President of Enrollment Management, 612-874-3762, Fax: 612-874-3701, E-mail: william_mullen@mcad.edu.

Minnesota State University Mankato, College of Graduate Studies, College of Arts and Humanities, Department of Art, Mankato, MN 56001. Offers art education (MS); studio art (MA); teaching art (MAT, MT). *Accreditation:* NASAD (one or more programs are accredited). Part-time programs available. *Students:* 4 full-time (1 woman), 6 part-time (4 women). *Degree requirements:* For master's, one foreign language, comprehensive exam, thesis or alternative. *Entrance requirements:* For master's, minimum GPA of 3.0 during previous 2 years, portfolio (MA). Additional exam requirements/recommendations for international students: Required—TOEFL. *Application deadline:* For fall admission, 7/1 priority date for domestic students, 5/1 for international students; for spring admission, 11/1 for domestic students, 10/1 for international students. Applications are processed on a rolling basis. Application fee: $40. Electronic applications accepted. *Financial support:* Research assistantships, teaching assistantships with full tuition reimbursements, unspecified assistantships available. Financial award application deadline: 3/15; financial award applicants required to submit FAFSA. *Faculty research:* Photographic documentation. *Unit head:* James Johnson, Chairperson, 507-389-6412. *Application contact:* 507-389-2321, E-mail: grad@mnsu.edu.

Mississippi College, Graduate School, College of Arts and Sciences, School of Christian Studies and the Arts, Department of Art, Clinton, MS 39058. Offers M Ed, MA, MFA. Part-time and evening/weekend programs available. *Degree requirements:* For master's, one foreign language, comprehensive exam, thesis (for some programs). *Entrance requirements:* For master's, GRE or NTE, minimum GPA of 2.5. Additional exam requirements/recommendations for international students: Recommended—IELTS. Electronic applications accepted.

Missouri State University, Graduate College, College of Arts and Letters, Department of Art and Design, Springfield, MO 65804-0094. Offers secondary education (MS Ed), including art. Part-time programs available. *Faculty:* 8 full-time (3 women). *Students:* 2 part-time (both women). Average age 43. 1 applicant, 100% accepted, 1 enrolled. In 2008, 2 master's awarded. *Entrance requirements:* For master's, minimum GPA of 3.0, 9-12 teaching certification. Additional exam requirements/recommendations for international students: Required—TOEFL (minimum score 550 paper-based; 213 computer-based; 79 iBT). *Application deadline:* For fall

Art/Fine Arts

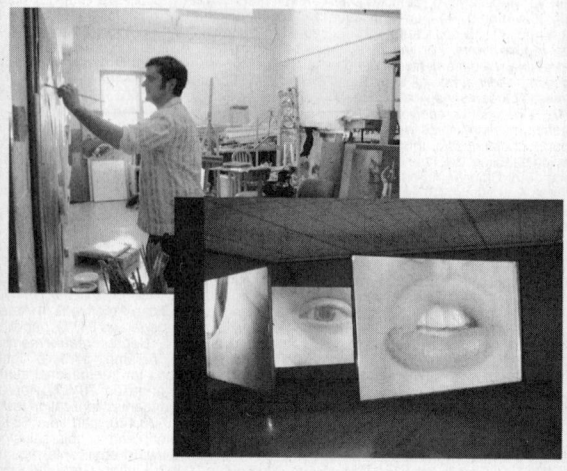
admission, 7/20 priority date for domestic students, 5/1 for international students; for spring admission, 12/20 priority date for domestic students, 9/1 for international students. Applications are processed on a rolling basis. Application fee: $35 ($50 for international students). Electronic applications accepted. *Expenses:* Tuition, state resident: full-time $3852; part-time $214 per credit hour. Tuition, nonresident: full-time $7524; part-time $418 per credit hour. Required fees: $230 per semester. Tuition and fees vary according to course level and course load. *Financial support:* Federal Work-Study and unspecified assistantships available. Financial award applicants required to submit FAFSA. *Unit head:* Wade S. Thompson, Head, 417-836-6055, E-mail: artanddesign@missouristate.edu. *Application contact:* Eric Eckert, Coordinator of Graduate Admissions and Recruitment, 417-836-5331, Fax: 417-386-6888, E-mail: ericeckert@missouristate.edu.

Montana State University, College of Graduate Studies, College of Arts and Architecture, Department of Art, Bozeman, MT 59717. Offers MFA. *Accreditation:* NASAD. Part-time programs available. *Degree requirements:* For master's, comprehensive exam. *Entrance requirements:* For master's, GRE General Test. Additional exam requirements/recommendations for international students: Required—TOEFL (minimum score 550 paper-based; 213 computer-based). Electronic applications accepted. *Faculty research:* Digital animation, printmaking, ceramics, metalsmithing, sculpture.

Montclair State University, The Office of Graduate Admissions and Support Services, School of the Arts, Department of Art and Design, Montclair, NJ 07043-1624. Offers art education (MA, Certificate); art history (MA); studio arts (MA, MFA). *Accreditation:* NASAD (one or more programs are accredited). Part-time and evening/weekend programs available. *Faculty:* 27 full-time (12 women), 68 part-time/adjunct (36 women). *Students:* 28 full-time (18 women), 35 part-time (30 women); includes 6 minority (3 African Americans, 2 Asian Americans or Pacific Islanders, 1 Hispanic American), 5 international. Average age 34. 32 applicants, 69% accepted, 16 enrolled. In 2008, 22 master's awarded. *Degree requirements:* For master's, project. *Entrance requirements:* For master's, GRE General Test or MAT (MA), portfolio, undergraduate degree in fine arts or equivalent, 2 letters of recommendation, teaching certificate (art education). Additional exam requirements/recommendations for international students: Required—TOEFL (minimum score 83 computer-based). *Application deadline:* For fall admission, 2/1 for domestic and international students. Applications are processed on a rolling basis. Application fee: $60. Electronic applications accepted. *Financial support:* In 2008–09, 4 research assistantships with full tuition reimbursements (averaging $7,000 per year) were awarded; Federal Work-Study, scholarships/grants, and unspecified assistantships also available. Support available to part-time students. Financial award application deadline: 3/1; financial award applicants required to submit FAFSA. *Unit head:* Dr. John Luttropp, Chairperson, 973-655-7295. *Application contact:* Dr. Dorothy Heard, Adviser, 973-655-7295, E-mail: heardd@mail.montclair.edu.

Morehead State University, Graduate Programs, Caudill College of Humanities, Department of Art, Morehead, KY 40351. Offers art education (MA); studio art (MA). Part-time and evening/weekend programs available. *Faculty:* 9 full-time (2 women). *Students:* 12 full-time (5 women), 3 part-time (all women); includes 1 minority (African American), 1 international. Average age 30. 8 applicants, 88% accepted, 7 enrolled. In 2008, 3 master's awarded. *Degree requirements:* For master's, comprehensive exam, thesis (for some programs), oral exam. *Entrance requirements:* For master's, GRE General Test, minimum GPA of 3.0 in major, 2.5 overall; portfolio; bachelor's degree in art. Additional exam requirements/recommendations for international students: Required—TOEFL (minimum score 500 paper-based; 173 computer-based). *Application deadline:* For fall admission, 8/1 priority date for domestic and international students; for spring admission, 12/1 priority date for domestic and international students. Applications are processed on a rolling basis. Application fee: $30 ($55 for international students). Electronic applications accepted. *Expenses:* Tuition, area resident: Full-time $6084; part-time $338 per credit hour. Tuition, state resident: full-time $6084; part-time $338 per credit hour. Tuition, nonresident: full-time $15,804; part-time $878 per credit hour. *Financial support:* In 2008–09, 6 teaching assistantships (averaging $6,000 per year) were awarded; career-related internships or fieldwork, Federal Work-Study, and unspecified assistantships also available. Financial award application deadline: 4/1; financial award applicants required to submit FAFSA. *Faculty research:* Computer art, painting, drawing, ceramics, photography. *Unit head:* Robert Franzini, Chair, 606-783-2193, Fax: 606-783-5048, E-mail: r.franzi@moreheadstate.edu. *Application contact:* Michelle Barber, Graduate Admissions Counselor, 606-783-2039, Fax: 606-783-5061, E-mail: m.barber@moreheadstate.edu.

National University, Academic Affairs, College of Letters and Sciences, Department of Art and Humanities, La Jolla, CA 92037-1011. Offers creative writing (MFA); English (MA); history (MA). Part-time and evening/weekend programs available. Postbaccalaureate distance learning degree programs offered (no on-campus study). *Faculty:* 19 full-time (6 women), 180 part-time/adjunct (92 women). *Students:* 208 full-time (153 women), 433 part-time (302 women); includes 137 minority (57 African Americans, 10 American Indian/Alaska Native, 19 Asian Americans or Pacific Islanders, 51 Hispanic Americans). Average age 38. 420 applicants, 100% accepted, 420 enrolled. In 2008, 152 master's awarded. *Degree requirements:* For master's, thesis (for some programs). *Entrance requirements:* For master's, interview, minimum GPA of 2.5. Additional exam requirements/recommendations for international students: Required—TOEFL (minimum score 550 paper-based; 213 computer-based; 79 iBT), IELTS (minimum score 6). *Application deadline:* Applications are processed on a rolling basis. Application fee: $60 ($65 for international students). Electronic applications accepted. *Expenses:* Tuition: Full-time $8694; part-time $322 per credit hour. Tuition and fees vary according to course load. *Financial support:* Career-related internships or fieldwork, institutionally sponsored loans, scholarships/grants, and tuition waivers (partial) available. Support available to part-time students. Financial award application deadline: 6/30; financial award applicants required to submit FAFSA. *Unit head:* Dr. Janet Baker, Chair, 858-642-8472, Fax: 858-642-8715, E-mail: jbaker@nu.edu. *Application contact:* Dominick Giovanniello, Associate Regional Dean—San Diego, 800-NAT-UNIV, Fax: 858-541-7792, E-mail: dgiovann@nu.edu.

New Jersey City University, Graduate Studies and Continuing Education, College of Arts and Sciences, Department of Art, Jersey City, NJ 07305-1597. Offers art (MFA); art education (MA); studio art (MFA). *Accreditation:* NASAD. Evening/weekend programs available. *Degree requirements:* For master's, thesis or alternative, exhibit. *Entrance requirements:* For master's, GRE General Test or MAT, portfolio. Additional exam requirements/recommendations for international students: Required—TOEFL.

New Mexico State University, Graduate School, College of Arts and Sciences, Department of Art, Las Cruces, NM 88003-8001. Offers art history (MA); ceramics (MA, MFA); design (MA, MFA); drawing (MFA); metals (MA, MFA); painting (MFA); photography (MFA); printmaking (MA, MFA); sculpture (MA, MFA). *Faculty:* 12 full-time (7 women), 2 part-time/adjunct (1 woman). *Students:* 31 full-time (14 women), 3 part-time (all women); includes 8 minority (1 American Indian/Alaska Native, 7 Hispanic Americans), 1 international. Average age 33. 30 applicants, 40% accepted, 9 enrolled. In 2008, 7 master's awarded. *Degree requirements:* For master's, comprehensive exam (for some programs), thesis, thesis exhibit. *Entrance requirements:* For master's, portfolio, 10-page paper (art history). *Application deadline:* For fall admission, 2/15 for domestic students; for winter admission, 10/15 for domestic students; for spring admission, 7/15 for domestic students. Application fee: $30 ($50 for international students). Electronic applications accepted. *Expenses:* Tuition, area resident: Full-time $3890; part-time $212.85 per credit. Tuition, state resident: full-time $3890; part-time $212.85 per credit. Tuition, nonresident: full-time $13,916; part-time $630.55 per credit. Required fees: $1218; $609 per semester. *Financial support:* In 2008–09, 33 students received support, including 29 teaching assistantships (averaging $9,807 per year); research assistantships, Federal Work-Study and health care benefits also available. Support available to part-time students. Financial award application deadline: 3/1; financial award applicants required to submit FAFSA. *Faculty research:* Painting, graphic design, sculpture, printmaking, drawing, ceramics, photo, jewelry. *Unit head:* Spencer D. Fidler, Head, 575-646-1705, Fax: 575-646-8036, E-mail: sfidler@nmsu.edu. *Application contact:* Elena Luna, Coordinator, 575-646-3498, Fax: 575-646-7721, E-mail: rosluna@nmsu.edu.

The New School: A University, Parsons The New School for Design, Program in Fine Arts, New York, NY 10011. Offers MFA. *Faculty:* 2 full-time (0 women), 9 part-time/adjunct (4 women). *Students:* 42 full-time (23 women); includes 9 minority (3 African Americans, 1 American Indian/Alaska Native, 5 Asian Americans or Pacific Islanders), 10 international. Average age 27. In 2008, 21 master's awarded. *Entrance requirements:* Additional exam requirements/recommendations for international students: Required—TOEFL (minimum score 580 paper-based; 237 computer-based; 93 iBT). *Application deadline:* For fall admission, 2/1 priority date for domestic students. Applications are processed on a rolling basis. Application fee: $50. *Expenses:* Tuition: Full-time $27,144; part-time $1508 per credit. Required fees: $355 per semester. *Financial support:* Fellowships, Federal Work-Study and scholarships/grants available. Financial award application deadline: 3/1. *Unit head:* Donald Porcaro, Chair, 212-229-8942 Ext. 2960, E-mail: porcarod@newschool.edu. *Application contact:* Anthony Padilla, Director of Admissions, 212-229-8989 Ext. 4023, Fax: 212-229-8975, E-mail: padillaa@newschool.edu.

See Close-Up on page 215.

New York Academy of Art, Program in Figurative Art, New York, NY 10013-2911. Offers MFA. *Degree requirements:* For master's, project. *Entrance requirements:* For master's, slide portfolio. Additional exam requirements/recommendations for international students: Required—TOEFL.

New York Studio School of Drawing, Painting and Sculpture, Certificate Program, New York, NY 10011. Offers studio art (Certificate).

New York Studio School of Drawing, Painting and Sculpture, MFA Program, New York, NY 10011. Offers painting (MFA); sculpture (MFA).

New York University, Graduate School of Arts and Science, Institute of Fine Arts, New York, NY 10012-1019. Offers art history and archaeology (MA, PhD), including architectural studies (PhD), art history and archaeology, classical art and archaeology (PhD), curatorial studies (PhD), East and South Asian art (PhD), Near Eastern art and archaeology (PhD); MA/Diploma; PhD/Certificate. Part-time programs available. Terminal master's awarded for partial completion of doctoral program. *Degree requirements:* For master's, 2 foreign languages, thesis or alternative, 2 qualifying papers; for doctorate, 2 foreign languages, thesis/dissertation. *Entrance requirements:* For master's, GRE General Test; for doctorate, GRE General Test, MA. Additional exam requirements/recommendations for international students: Required—TOEFL.

New York University, Steinhardt School of Culture, Education and Human Development, Department of Art and Art Professions, Program in Studio Art, New York, NY 10012-1019. Offers MA, MFA. Part-time and evening/weekend programs available. *Degree requirements:* For master's, thesis (for some programs). *Entrance requirements:* For master's, portfolio, interview, presentation. Additional exam requirements/recommendations for international students: Required—TOEFL. *Faculty research:* Media and culture, video art and digital media, multimedia works, multiculturalism, critical theory.

New York University, Steinhardt School of Culture, Education and Human Development, Department of Art and Art Professions, Program in Visual Culture, New York, NY 10012-1019. Offers visual culture: costume studies (MA); visual culture: theory (MA, PhD). Part-time and evening/weekend programs available. *Degree requirements:* For master's, thesis (for some programs). *Entrance requirements:* For doctorate, GRE General Test, interview. Additional exam requirements/recommendations for international students: Required—TOEFL. *Faculty research:* Textiles as material culture, contemporary visual culture and globalization, cultural theory.

New York University, Tisch School of the Arts Asia, Singapore, NY 248923, Singapore. Offers animation and digital arts (MFA); dramatic writing (MFA); film production (MFA). *Entrance requirements:* Additional exam requirements/recommendations for international students: Required—TOEFL (minimum score 610 paper-based; 250 computer-based; 105 iBT). Electronic applications accepted.

New York University, Tisch School of the Arts, Program in Arts Politics, New York, NY 10012-1019. Offers MA. *Degree requirements:* For master's, thesis. *Entrance requirements:* For master's, professional resumé, writing sample, statement of purpose. Additional exam requirements/recommendations for international students: Required—TOEFL, IELTS.

Norfolk State University, School of Graduate Studies, School of Liberal Arts, Department of Fine Arts, Norfolk, VA 23504. Offers visual studies (MA, MFA). Part-time programs available. *Degree requirements:* For master's, thesis or alternative. *Entrance requirements:* For master's, portfolio, interview, letters of recommendation. Additional exam requirements/recommendations for international students: Required—TOEFL (minimum score 500 paper-based).

Northern Illinois University, Graduate School, College of Visual and Performing Arts, School of Art, De Kalb, IL 60115-2854. Offers MA, MFA, MS. *Accreditation:* NASAD (one or more programs are accredited). Part-time and evening/weekend programs available. *Degree requirements:* For master's, variable foreign language requirement, comprehensive exam, thesis (for some programs), show or project. *Entrance requirements:* For master's, GRE General Test, minimum GPA of 2.75, portfolio. Additional exam requirements/recommendations for international students: Required—TOEFL (minimum score 550 paper-based; 213 computer-based). Electronic applications accepted. *Faculty research:* Art education, portfolio assessment, central European design history, relationship between modern art and industrialism.

Northwestern State University of Louisiana, Graduate Studies and Research, School of Creative and Performing Arts, Program in Art, Natchitoches, LA 71497. Offers fine and graphic arts (MA). *Accreditation:* NASAD. *Faculty:* 7 full-time (0 women). *Students:* 9 full-time (4 women), 7 part-time (4 women); includes 5 minority (all African Americans). Average age 33. 7 applicants, 100% accepted, 5 enrolled. In 2008, 5 master's awarded. *Degree requirements:* For master's, comprehensive exam, thesis or alternative. *Entrance requirements:* For master's, GRE General Test, minimum undergraduate GPA of 2.5. *Application deadline:* For fall admission, 8/1 priority date for domestic students; for spring admission, 1/10 for domestic students. Applications are processed on a rolling basis. Application fee: $20 ($30 for international students). *Financial support:* Career-related internships or fieldwork and Federal Work-Study available. Support available to part-time students. Financial award application deadline: 7/15. *Unit head:* Dr. Roger Chandler, Head, 318-357-4476, Fax: 318-357-5906, E-mail: chandlerr@nsula.edu. *Application contact:* Dr. Steven G. Horton, Associate Provost/Dean, Graduate Studies, Research, and Information Systems, 318-357-5851, Fax: 318-357-5019, E-mail: grad_school@nsula.edu.

Northwestern University, The Graduate School, Judd A. and Marjorie Weinberg College of Arts and Sciences, Department of Art Theory and Practice, Evanston, IL 60208. Offers visual arts (MFA). Admissions and degrees offered through The Graduate School. *Degree requirements:* For master's, essay, exhibit. *Entrance requirements:* For master's, 20 slides of recent work. Additional exam requirements/recommendations for international students: Required—TOEFL. Electronic applications accepted.

Announcement: Intensive program leading to the Master of Fine Arts. Graduate faculty members include Jeanne Dunning, Kelly Kaczynski, Judy Ledgerwood, Michael Rakowitz, Steve Reinke, and Lane Relyea. Fellowships, assistantships available. Autumn quarter admission is based on outstanding academic record (BA or other), 20 slides of recent work, statement, and recommendations. Visit www.art.northwestern.edu for more information and online application.

NSCAD University, Program in Fine Arts, Halifax, NS B3J 3J6, Canada. Offers craft (MFA); design (M Des); fine and media arts (MFA). *Degree requirements:* For master's, thesis, exhibit. *Entrance requirements:* For master's, portfolio, at least 5 art history classes. Additional exam requirements/recommendations for international students: Required—Michigan English Language Assessment Battery (minimum score: 80), CanTEST (minimum score: 4.5), CAEL (minimum score: 70); Recommended—TOEFL (minimum score 575 paper-based; 233 computer-based; 90 iBT), IELTS (minimum score 6.5).

The Ohio State University, Graduate School, College of the Arts, Department of Art, Columbus, OH 43210. Offers MFA. *Accreditation:* NASAD. *Degree requirements:* For master's, thesis, exhibit, oral exams. *Entrance requirements:* For master's, portfolio. Additional exam requirements/recommendations for international students: Recommended—TOEFL (minimum score 600 paper-based; 250 computer-based). Electronic applications accepted.

Ohio University, Graduate College, College of Fine Arts, School of Art, Athens, OH 45701-2979. Offers art history (MA); ceramics (MFA); graphic design (MFA); painting (MFA); photography (MFA); printmaking (MFA); sculpture (MFA). Part-time programs available. *Degree requirements:* For master's, thesis. *Entrance requirements:* For master's, portfolio. Additional exam requirements/recommendations for international students: Required—TOEFL. *Faculty research:* Vapor fired ceramics, video installation, art theory, digital photography, mixed and interdisciplinary media work.

Oklahoma City University, Petree College of Arts and Sciences, Program in Liberal Arts, Oklahoma City, OK 73106-1402. Offers art (MLA); general studies (MLA); leadership/management (MLA); literature (MLA); mass communications (MLA); philosophy (MLA); writing (MLA). Part-time and evening/weekend programs available. *Degree requirements:* For master's, comprehensive exam, thesis optional. *Entrance requirements:* Additional exam requirements/recommendations for international students: Required—TOEFL.

Otis College of Art and Design, Program in Fine Arts, Los Angeles, CA 90045-9785. Offers new genres (MFA); painting (MFA); photography (MFA); sculpture (MFA). *Accreditation:* NASAD. *Faculty:* 1 (woman) full-time, 8 part-time/adjunct (3 women). *Students:* 17 full-time (8 women); includes 6 minority (1 African American, 1 American Indian/Alaska Native, 2 Asian Americans or Pacific Islanders, 2 Hispanic Americans), 1 international. Average age 32. 129 applicants, 21% accepted, 8 enrolled. In 2008, 12 master's awarded. *Degree requirements:* For master's, thesis. *Entrance requirements:* For master's, portfolio. Additional exam requirements/recommendations for international students: Required—TOEFL (minimum score 600 paper-based; 250 computer-based). *Application deadline:* For fall admission, 2/15 for domestic and international students. Application fee: $50. Electronic applications accepted. *Expenses:* Tuition: Full-time $30,464. Required fees: $700. *Financial support:* Career-related internships or fieldwork, Federal Work-Study, scholarships/grants, and tuition waivers (partial) available. Financial award applicants required to submit FAFSA. *Unit head:* Roy Dowell, Chair, 310-665-6893, Fax: 310-665-6998, E-mail: grads@otis.edu. *Application contact:* Information Contact, 310-665-6820, Fax: 310-665-6821, E-mail: admissions@otis.edu.

Otis College of Art and Design, Program in Public Practice, Los Angeles, CA 90045-9785. Offers MFA. *Faculty:* 7 part-time/adjunct (5 women). *Students:* 11 full-time (10 women); includes 8 minority (3 Asian Americans or Pacific Islanders, 5 Hispanic Americans). 37 applicants, 57% accepted, 11 enrolled. *Entrance requirements:* Additional exam requirements/recommendations for international students: Required—TOEFL (minimum score 600 paper-based; 250 computer-based). *Application deadline:* For fall admission, 2/15 for domestic and international students. Application fee: $50. Electronic applications accepted. *Expenses:* Tuition: Full-time $30,464. Required fees: $700. *Unit head:* Suzanne Lacy, Chair, Graduate Studies: Public Practice, 310-665-6820, Fax: 310-846-2612, E-mail: cvelasco@otis.edu. *Application contact:* Information Contact, 310-665-6820, Fax: 310-665-6821, E-mail: admissions@otis.edu.

Penn State University Park, Graduate School, College of Arts and Architecture, School of Visual Arts, State College, University Park, PA 16802-1503. Offers art (MFA), including ceramics, drawing/painting, photography, printmaking, sculpture; art education (M Ed, MS, PhD). *Accreditation:* NASAD.

Pennsylvania Academy of the Fine Arts, Graduate School, Philadelphia, PA 19102. Offers drawing (MFA, Postbaccalaureate Certificate); painting (MFA, Postbaccalaureate Certificate); printmaking (MFA, Postbaccalaureate Certificate); sculpture (MFA, Postbaccalaureate Certificate). *Accreditation:* NASAD (one or more programs are accredited). *Degree requirements:* For master's, thesis, thesis exhibit. *Entrance requirements:* For master's, 10-20 slides of work and slide list, 3 letters of recommendation. Additional exam requirements/recommendations for international students: Required—TOEFL (minimum score 500 paper-based). Electronic applications accepted.

Pittsburg State University, Graduate School, College of Arts and Sciences, Department of Art, Pittsburg, KS 66762-7512. Offers art education (MA); studio art (MA). *Degree requirements:* For master's, thesis or alternative.

Portland State University, Graduate Studies, School of Fine and Performing Arts, Department of Art, Portland, OR 97207-0751. Offers drawing (MFA); mixed media (MFA); painting (MFA); printmaking (MFA); sculpture (MFA). *Accreditation:* NASAD. *Faculty:* 27 full-time (15 women), 40 part-time/adjunct (26 women). *Students:* 24 full-time (13 women), 1 (woman) part-time; includes 4 minority (3 Asian Americans or Pacific Islanders, 1 Hispanic American), 2 international. Average age 29. 82 applicants, 18% accepted, 12 enrolled. In 2008, 7 master's awarded. *Degree requirements:* For master's, variable foreign language requirement, thesis, exhibit. *Entrance requirements:* For master's, minimum GPA of 3.0 in upper-division course work or 2.75 overall, portfolio, 3 letters of recommendation. Additional exam requirements/recommendations for international students: Required—TOEFL (minimum score 550 paper-based; 213 computer-based). *Application deadline:* For fall admission, 3/1 for domestic and international students. Application fee: $50. *Expenses:* Tuition, area resident: Full-time $8763; part-time $179 per credit hour. Tuition, state resident: full-time $8763; part-time $298 per credit hour. Tuition, nonresident: full-time $12,981; part-time $426 per credit hour. Required fees: $1242. One-time fee: $250. Tuition and fees vary according to course load and program. *Financial support:* Research assistantships with full tuition reimbursements, teaching assistantships with full tuition reimbursements, Federal Work-Study, scholarships/grants, and unspecified assistantships available. Support available to part-time students. Financial award application deadline: 3/1; financial award applicants required to submit FAFSA. *Unit head:* William LePore, Chair, 503-725-3515, Fax: 503-725-4541. *Application contact:* Ellen Wack, Administrative Coordinator, 503-725-8450, Fax: 503-725-4541, E-mail: wacke@pdx.edu.

Pratt Institute, School of Art and Design, Program in Fine Arts, Brooklyn, NY 11205-3899. Offers new forms (MFA); painting and drawing (MFA); photography (MFA); printmaking (MFA); sculpture (MFA). *Accreditation:* NASAD. Part-time programs available. *Faculty:* 8 full-time (2 women), 30 part-time/adjunct (15 women). *Students:* 140 full-time (90 women), 5 part-time (4 women); includes 16 minority (3 African Americans, 8 Asian Americans or Pacific Islanders, 5 Hispanic Americans), 43 international. Average age 29. 282 applicants, 49% accepted, 56 enrolled. In 2008, 69 master's awarded. *Degree requirements:* For master's, thesis, exhibit. *Entrance requirements:* For master's, portfolio, bachelor's degree, transcripts, letters of recommendation. Additional exam requirements/recommendations for international students: Required—TOEFL (minimum score 550 paper-based; 213 computer-based). *Application deadline:* For fall admission, 2/1 for domestic and international students; for spring admission, 10/1 for domestic and international students. Application fee: $50 ($90 for international students). Electronic applications accepted. *Expenses:* Tuition: Full-time $20,412; part-time $1134 per credit. Required fees: $1190; $1190 per year. *Financial support:* Career-related internships or fieldwork, Federal Work-Study, institutionally sponsored loans, scholarships/grants, health care benefits, and unspecified assistantships available. Support available to part-time students. Financial award application deadline: 2/1; financial award applicants required to submit FAFSA. *Unit head:* Donna Moran, Chairperson, 718-636-3602, E-mail: dmoran@pratt.edu. *Application contact:* Young Hah, Director of Graduate Admissions, 718-636-3683, Fax: 718-399-4242, E-mail: yhah@pratt.edu.

See Close-Up on page 219.

Art/Fine Arts

Purchase College, State University of New York, School of Art and Design, Purchase, NY 10577-1400. Offers MFA. *Accreditation:* NASAD. *Students:* 12 full-time (6 women); includes 1 minority (Hispanic American), 1 international. Average age 32. 68 applicants, 10% accepted, 6 enrolled. In 2008, 2 master's awarded. *Degree requirements:* For master's, thesis, exhibit. *Entrance requirements:* For master's, portfolio. *Application deadline:* For fall admission, 3/1 for domestic students. Applications are processed on a rolling basis. Application fee: $50. Electronic applications accepted. *Expenses:* Tuition, area resident: Full-time $6900; part-time $288 per credit. Tuition, state resident: full-time $6900; part-time $288 per credit. Tuition, nonresident: full-time $10,920; part-time $455 per credit. Required fees: $1461; $0.85 per credit. One-time fee: $75 full-time. *Financial support:* Fellowships, teaching assistantships, Federal Work-Study, scholarships/grants, and tuition waivers (partial) available. Support available to part-time students. Financial award application deadline: 3/15; financial award applicants required to submit FAFSA. *Unit head:* Denise Mullen, Dean, 914-251-6750, Fax: 914-251-6793. *Application contact:* Sabrina Johnston, Counselor, 914-251-6479, Fax: 914-251-6314, E-mail: admissn@purchase.edu.

Purdue University, Graduate School, College of Liberal Arts, Department of Visual and Performing Arts, West Lafayette, IN 47907. Offers art and design (MA); theatre (MA, MFA). *Accreditation:* NASAD; NAST. Part-time programs available. *Degree requirements:* For master's, terminal exhibit, project, or thesis. *Entrance requirements:* Additional exam requirements/recommendations for international students: Required—TOEFL. Electronic applications accepted. *Faculty research:* Design, fine arts, photography, acting, directing, theatre technology.

Queens College of the City University of New York, Division of Graduate Studies, Arts and Humanities Division, Department of Art, Program in Fine Arts, Flushing, NY 11367-1597. Offers MFA. *Degree requirements:* For master's, art show. *Entrance requirements:* For master's, minimum GPA of 3.0, portfolio. Additional exam requirements/recommendations for international students: Required—TOEFL.

Radford University, College of Graduate and Professional Studies, College of Visual and Performing Arts, Department of Art, Radford, VA 24142. Offers MFA. Part-time programs available. *Faculty:* 11 full-time (5 women), 4 part-time/adjunct (all women). *Students:* 16 full-time (9 women), 2 part-time (0 women); includes 4 minority (1 African American, 3 Asian Americans or Pacific Islanders), 1 international. Average age 30. 14 applicants, 64% accepted, 5 enrolled. In 2008, 10 master's awarded. *Degree requirements:* For master's, comprehensive exam. *Entrance requirements:* For master's, minimum GPA of 2.75; 2 letters of reference; statement of philosophy; BFA or commensurate collegiate course work; slides of recent work. Additional exam requirements/recommendations for international students: Required—TOEFL (minimum score 550 paper-based; 213 computer-based; 79 iBT). *Application deadline:* For fall admission, 3/15 priority date for domestic students, 12/1 for international students; for spring admission, 10/1 for domestic students, 7/1 for international students. Applications are processed on a rolling basis. Application fee: $40. Electronic applications accepted. *Expenses:* Tuition, area resident: Full-time $4845; part-time $202 per credit. Tuition, state resident: full-time $4845; part-time $202 per credit. Tuition, nonresident: full-time $11,483; part-time $478 per credit. Required fees: $2349; $98 per credit. *Financial support:* In 2008–09, 15 students received support, including 10 research assistantships with partial tuition reimbursements available (averaging $8,000 per year), 2 teaching assistantships with partial tuition reimbursements available (averaging $8,700 per year); fellowships with tuition reimbursements available, career-related internships or fieldwork, Federal Work-Study, institutionally sponsored loans, scholarships/grants, and unspecified assistantships also available. Financial award application deadline: 3/1; financial award applicants required to submit FAFSA. *Unit head:* Dr. Steve S. Arbury, Chair, 540-831-5475, Fax: 540-831-6799, E-mail: sarbury@radford.edu. *Application contact:* Graduate Admissions, 540-831-5431, Fax: 540-831-6061, E-mail: gradcollege@radford.edu.

Regis University, College for Professional Studies, Program in Teacher Education, Denver, CO 80221-1099. Offers adult learning, training, and development (M Ed); curriculum, instruction, and assessment (M Ed); early childhood (M Ed); educational technology (Certificate); elementary (M Ed); ESL (M Ed); fine arts (M Ed), including arts, music; instructional technology (M Ed); professional leadership (M Ed); reading (M Ed); secondary (M Ed); self-designed (M Ed); space studies (M Ed); special education (M Ed); teacher licensure (M Ed). Program also offered in Henderson and Las Vegas (Summerlin), NV. Part-time and evening/weekend programs available. Postbaccalaureate distance learning degree programs offered (no on-campus study). *Degree requirements:* For master's, thesis. *Entrance requirements:* For master's, essays, resumé, minimum GPA of 2.75, criminal background check. Additional exam requirements/recommendations for international students: Required—TOEFL (minimum score 213 computer-based), TWE (minimum score 5). Electronic applications accepted. *Faculty research:* Issues of equity in the middle school classroom, professional learning communities, school reform, socialinguistic and discursive obstacles to student integration, inclusive language arts curriculum.

Rensselaer Polytechnic Institute, Graduate School, School of Humanities and Social Sciences, Department of the Arts, Program in Electronic Arts, Troy, NY 12180-3590. Offers MFA, PhD. *Degree requirements:* For master's, thesis, thesis in the form of a large-scale creative project; for doctorate, comprehensive exam, thesis/dissertation, dissertation or creative project and dissertation text. *Entrance requirements:* For master's, portfolio; for doctorate, portfolio, writing sample, evidence of research-based creative orientation. Additional exam requirements/recommendations for international students: Required—TOEFL (minimum score 570 paper-based; 230 computer-based; 88 iBT). Electronic applications accepted. *Faculty research:* Computer music, video art, Net art, interactivity, bio art.

Rhode Island College, School of Graduate Studies, Faculty of Arts and Sciences, Department of Art, Providence, RI 02908-1991. Offers art education (MA, MAT); media studies (MA). *Accreditation:* NASAD (one or more programs are accredited). Part-time and evening/weekend programs available. *Faculty:* 7 full-time (4 women). *Students:* 2 full-time (0 women), 11 part-time (5 women). Average age 33. In 2008, 10 master's awarded. *Degree requirements:* For master's, thesis. *Entrance requirements:* For master's, GRE General Test or MAT, portfolio (MA), 3 letters of recommendation, interview. Additional exam requirements/recommendations for international students: Recommended—TOEFL (minimum score 550 paper-based; 213 computer-based; 79 iBT). *Application deadline:* For fall admission, 4/1 for domestic students; for spring admission, 11/1 for domestic students. Applications are processed on a rolling basis. Application fee: $50. *Expenses:* Tuition, area resident: Full-time $6816; part-time $284 per credit hour. Tuition, state resident: full-time $6816; part-time $284 per credit hour. Tuition, nonresident: full-time $13,920; part-time $580 per credit hour. Required fees: $454; $16 per credit. $68 per term. *Financial support:* Teaching assistantships with full tuition reimbursements, career-related internships or fieldwork, Federal Work-Study, scholarships/grants, health care benefits, and unspecified assistantships available. Support available to part-time students. Financial award application deadline: 5/15; financial award applicants required to submit FAFSA. *Unit head:* Prof. Nancy Bockbrader, Chair, 401-456-8054. *Application contact:* Graduate Studies, 401-456-8700.

Rhode Island School of Design, Graduate Studies, Division of Fine Arts, Department of Ceramics, Providence, RI 02903-2784. Offers MFA. *Accreditation:* NASAD. *Degree requirements:* For master's, thesis, exhibit. *Entrance requirements:* For master's, portfolio. Additional exam requirements/recommendations for international students: Required—TOEFL (minimum score 580 paper-based; 237 computer-based), IELTS (minimum score 6.5).

Rhode Island School of Design, Graduate Studies, Division of Fine Arts, Department of Glass, Providence, RI 02903-2784. Offers MFA. *Accreditation:* NASAD. *Degree requirements:* For master's, thesis, exhibit. *Entrance requirements:* For master's, portfolio, 3 letters of recommendation. Additional exam requirements/recommendations for international students: Required—TOEFL (minimum score 580 paper-based; 237 computer-based), IELTS (minimum score 6.5).

Rhode Island School of Design, Graduate Studies, Division of Fine Arts, Department of Jewelry and Light Metals, Providence, RI 02903-2784. Offers MFA. *Accreditation:* NASAD. *Degree requirements:* For master's, thesis, exhibit. *Entrance requirements:* For master's, portfolio, 3 letters of recommendation. Additional exam requirements/recommendations for international students: Required—TOEFL (minimum score 580 paper-based; 237 computer-based), IELTS (minimum score 6.5).

Rhode Island School of Design, Graduate Studies, Division of Fine Arts, Department of Painting, Providence, RI 02903-2784. Offers MFA. *Accreditation:* NASAD. *Degree requirements:* For master's, thesis, exhibit. *Entrance requirements:* For master's, portfolio, 3 letters of recommendation. Additional exam requirements/recommendations for international students: Required—TOEFL (minimum score 580 paper-based; 237 computer-based), IELTS (minimum score 6.5).

Rhode Island School of Design, Graduate Studies, Division of Fine Arts, Department of Printmaking, Providence, RI 02903-2784. Offers MFA. *Entrance requirements:* For master's, portfolio, 3 letters of recommendation. Additional exam requirements/recommendations for international students: Required—TOEFL (minimum score 580 paper-based; 237 computer-based), IELTS (minimum score 6.5).

Rhode Island School of Design, Graduate Studies, Division of Fine Arts, Department of Sculpture, Providence, RI 02903-2784. Offers MFA. *Accreditation:* NASAD. *Degree requirements:* For master's, thesis, exhibit. *Entrance requirements:* For master's, portfolio, 3 letters of recommendation. Additional exam requirements/recommendations for international students: Required—TOEFL (minimum score 580 paper-based; 237 computer-based), IELTS (minimum score 6.5).

Rochester Institute of Technology, Graduate Enrollment Services, College of Imaging Arts and Sciences, School for American Crafts, Program in Ceramics, Rochester, NY 14623-5603. Offers MFA. *Accreditation:* NASAD. *Entrance requirements:* For master's, portfolio, 3.0 GPA. Additional exam requirements/recommendations for international students: Required—TOEFL (minimum score 550 paper-based; 230 computer-based; 79 iBT).

Rochester Institute of Technology, Graduate Enrollment Services, College of Imaging Arts and Sciences, School for American Crafts, Program in Glass, Rochester, NY 14623-5603. Offers MFA. *Accreditation:* NASAD. *Entrance requirements:* For master's, portfolio, 3.0 GPA. Additional exam requirements/recommendations for international students: Required—TOEFL (minimum score 550 paper-based; 230 computer-based; 79 iBT).

Rochester Institute of Technology, Graduate Enrollment Services, College of Imaging Arts and Sciences, School for American Crafts, Program in Metal Crafts and Jewelry, Rochester, NY 14623-5603. Offers MFA. *Accreditation:* NASAD. *Entrance requirements:* For master's, portfolio, 3.0 GPA. Additional exam requirements/recommendations for international students: Required—TOEFL (minimum score 550 paper-based; 230 computer-based; 79 iBT).

Rochester Institute of Technology, Graduate Enrollment Services, College of Imaging Arts and Sciences, School for American Crafts, Program in Woodworking and Furniture Design, Rochester, NY 14623-5603. Offers MFA. *Entrance requirements:* For master's, portfolio, 3.0 GPA. Additional exam requirements/recommendations for international students: Required—TOEFL (minimum score 550 paper-based; 213 computer-based; 79 iBT).

Rochester Institute of Technology, Graduate Enrollment Services, College of Imaging Arts and Sciences, School of Art, Program in Fine Arts, Rochester, NY 14623-5603. Offers fine arts studio (MST); painting (MFA); printmaking (MFA). *Accreditation:* NASAD. *Degree requirements:* For master's, thesis (for some programs). *Entrance requirements:* For master's, portfolio, minimum GPA of 3.0. Additional exam requirements/recommendations for international students: Required—TOEFL (minimum score 550 paper-based; 213 computer-based; 79 iBT).

Rutgers, The State University of New Jersey, New Brunswick, Mason Gross School of the Arts, Program in Visual Arts, Piscataway, NJ 08854-8097. Offers drawing (MFA); painting (MFA); sculpture (MFA). *Degree requirements:* For master's, thesis, exhibit. *Entrance requirements:* For master's, portfolio. Additional exam requirements/recommendations for international students: Required—TOEFL (minimum score 550 paper-based; 213 computer-based). Electronic applications accepted. *Faculty research:* Media, painting, sculpture, photography, film.

San Diego State University, Graduate and Research Affairs, College of Professional Studies and Fine Arts, School of Art, Design and Art History, San Diego, CA 92182. Offers art history (MA); studio arts (MA, MFA), including applied design, environmental design, graphic design, interior design, painting and printmaking, sculpture. *Accreditation:* NASAD (one or more programs are accredited). *Degree requirements:* For master's, variable foreign language requirement, thesis. *Entrance requirements:* For master's, GRE General Test, bachelor's degree in related field, slide portfolio, typed slide information sheet, 2 letters of recommendation. Additional exam requirements/recommendations for international students: Required—TOEFL. Electronic applications accepted.

San Francisco Art Institute, Graduate Program, Department of Painting, San Francisco, CA 94133. Offers MFA, Certificate. *Accreditation:* NASAD. Part-time programs available. *Degree requirements:* For master's and Certificate, oral reviews. *Entrance requirements:* For master's and Certificate, portfolio. Additional exam requirements/recommendations for international students: Required—TOEFL (minimum score 580 paper-based; 237 computer-based). Electronic applications accepted.

See Close-Up on page 221.

San Francisco Art Institute, Graduate Program, Department of Printmaking, San Francisco, CA 94133. Offers MFA, Certificate. *Accreditation:* NASAD. Part-time programs available. *Degree requirements:* For master's and Certificate, oral reviews. *Entrance requirements:* For master's and Certificate, portfolio. Additional exam requirements/recommendations for international students: Required—TOEFL (minimum score 580 paper-based; 237 computer-based). Electronic applications accepted.

See Close-Up on page 221.

San Francisco Art Institute, Graduate Program, Department of Sculpture, San Francisco, CA 94133. Offers MFA, Certificate. *Accreditation:* NASAD. Part-time programs available. *Degree requirements:* For master's and Certificate, oral reviews. *Entrance requirements:* For master's and Certificate, portfolio. Additional exam requirements/recommendations for international students: Required—TOEFL (minimum score 580 paper-based; 237 computer-based).

See Close-Up on page 221.

San Francisco State University, Division of Graduate Studies, College of Creative Arts, Department of Art, San Francisco, CA 94132-1722. Offers art (MFA); art history (MA). *Accreditation:* NASAD (one or more programs are accredited).

San Jose State University, Graduate Studies and Research, College of Humanities and the Arts, School of Art and Design, San Jose, CA 95192-0001. Offers art education (MA); art history (MA); digital media (MFA); digital media in art history and education (MA); photography (MFA); pictorial arts (MFA); spatial arts (MFA). *Accreditation:* NASAD (one or more programs are accredited). *Entrance requirements:* For master's, GRE. Electronic applications accepted.

Savannah College of Art and Design, Graduate School, Program in Metals and Jewelry, Savannah, GA 31402-3146. Offers MA, MFA. Part-time programs available. *Degree requirements:* For master's, thesis, internship. *Entrance requirements:* For master's, interview, portfolio. Additional exam requirements/recommendations for international students: Required—TOEFL (minimum score 450 paper-based; 133 computer-based). Electronic applications accepted. *Expenses:* Tuition: Full-time $28,215; part-time $3135 per course. One-time fee: $500.

Savannah College of Art and Design, Graduate School, Program in Painting, Savannah, GA 31402-3146. Offers MA, MFA. Part-time programs available. *Degree requirements:* For master's, thesis, exhibit, internships. *Entrance requirements:* For master's, interview, portfolio. Additional exam requirements/recommendations for international students: Required—TOEFL (minimum score 450 paper-based; 133 computer-based). Electronic applications accepted. *Expenses:* Tuition: Full-time $28,215; part-time $3135 per course. One-time fee: $500.

Announcement: SCAD exists to prepare talented students for professional, creative careers. The university cultivates the unique qualities of each student through interesting curriculum, inspiring locations and environments, and the leadership of involved professors. SCAD offers MA, MArch, MUD, MFA, and MAT degrees in nearly fifty areas of study. Online programs are offered through SCAD-eLearning.

Savannah College of Art and Design, Graduate School, Program in Printmaking, Savannah, GA 31402-3146. Offers MA, MFA. Part-time programs available. *Degree requirements:* For master's, thesis. *Entrance requirements:* For master's, interview, portfolio. Additional exam requirements/recommendations for international students: Required—TOEFL (minimum score 450 paper-based; 133 computer-based). Electronic applications accepted. *Expenses:* Tuition: Full-time $28,215; part-time $3135 per course. One-time fee: $500.

Savannah College of Art and Design, Graduate School, Program in Sculpture, Savannah, GA 31402-3146. Offers MA, MFA. Part-time programs available. *Degree requirements:* For master's, thesis. *Entrance requirements:* For master's, interview, portfolio. Additional exam requirements/recommendations for international students: Required—TOEFL (minimum score 450 paper-based; 133 computer-based). Electronic applications accepted. *Expenses:* Tuition: Full-time $28,215; part-time $3135 per course. One-time fee: $500.

School of the Art Institute of Chicago, Graduate Division, Department of Art and Technology Studies, Chicago, IL 60603-3103. Offers MFA. *Entrance requirements:* Additional exam requirements/recommendations for international students: Required—TOEFL, IELTS. Electronic applications accepted.

See Close-Up on page 225.

School of the Art Institute of Chicago, Graduate Division, Department of Ceramics, Chicago, IL 60603-3103. Offers MFA. *Accreditation:* NASAD. *Entrance requirements:* Additional exam requirements/recommendations for international students: Required—TOEFL, IELTS. Electronic applications accepted.

See Close-Up on page 225.

School of the Art Institute of Chicago, Graduate Division, Department of Fiber and Material Studies, Chicago, IL 60603-3103. Offers MFA. *Accreditation:* NASAD. *Entrance requirements:* Additional exam requirements/recommendations for international students: Required—TOEFL, IELTS.

See Close-Up on page 225.

School of the Art Institute of Chicago, Graduate Division, Department of Painting and Drawing, Chicago, IL 60603-3103. Offers MFA. *Accreditation:* NASAD. *Entrance requirements:* Additional exam requirements/recommendations for international students: Required—TOEFL, IELTS.

See Close-Up on page 225.

School of the Art Institute of Chicago, Graduate Division, Department of Printmaking, Chicago, IL 60603-3103. Offers MFA. *Accreditation:* NASAD. *Entrance requirements:* Additional exam requirements/recommendations for international students: Required—TOEFL, IELTS.

See Close-Up on page 225.

School of the Art Institute of Chicago, Graduate Division, Department of Sculpture, Chicago, IL 60603-3103. Offers MFA. *Accreditation:* NASAD. *Entrance requirements:* Additional exam requirements/recommendations for international students: Required—TOEFL, IELTS.

See Close-Up on page 225.

School of the Art Institute of Chicago, Graduate Division, Program in Visual and Critical Studies, Chicago, IL 60603-3103. Offers MA.

See Close-Up on page 225.

School of the Museum of Fine Arts, Boston, Graduate Program, Boston, MA 02115. Offers MAT, MFA. *Accreditation:* NASAD (one or more programs are accredited). *Degree requirements:* For master's, thesis, exhibition thesis. *Entrance requirements:* For master's, BFA or bachelor's degree in related area, portfolio. Additional exam requirements/recommendations for international students: Required—TOEFL. *Faculty research:* Public art commissions, National Endowment for the Arts grant recipients, international exhibitions.

School of Visual Arts, Graduate Programs, Computer Art Department, New York, NY 10010-3994. Offers MFA. *Accreditation:* NASAD. *Degree requirements:* For master's, final review, project or thesis. *Entrance requirements:* For master's, portfolio. Additional exam requirements/recommendations for international students: Required—TOEFL (minimum score 550 paper-based; 213 computer-based; 79 iBT). Electronic applications accepted.

School of Visual Arts, Graduate Programs, Design Department, New York, NY 10010-3994. Offers MFA. *Accreditation:* NASAD. *Degree requirements:* For master's, final review, project or thesis. *Entrance requirements:* For master's, portfolio. Additional exam requirements/recommendations for international students: Required—TOEFL (minimum score 550 paper-based; 213 computer-based; 79 iBT). Electronic applications accepted. *Expenses:* Contact institution.

School of Visual Arts, Graduate Programs, Fine Arts Department, New York, NY 10010-3994. Offers painting (MFA); printmaking (MFA); sculpture (MFA). *Accreditation:* NASAD. *Degree requirements:* For master's, final review, project or thesis. *Entrance requirements:* For master's, portfolio. Additional exam requirements/recommendations for international students: Required—TOEFL (minimum score 550 paper-based; 213 computer-based; 79 iBT). Electronic applications accepted.

School of Visual Arts, Graduate Programs, Illustration Department, New York, NY 10010-3994. Offers MFA. *Accreditation:* NASAD. *Degree requirements:* For master's, final review, project or thesis. *Entrance requirements:* For master's, portfolio. Additional exam requirements/recommendations for international students: Required—TOEFL (minimum score 550 paper-based; 213 computer-based; 79 iBT). Electronic applications accepted.

School of Visual Arts, Graduate Programs, Program in Photography, Video and Related Media, New York, NY 10010-3994. Offers MFA. *Accreditation:* NASAD. *Degree requirements:* For master's, final review, project or thesis. *Entrance requirements:* For master's, portfolio. Additional exam requirements/recommendations for international students: Required—TOEFL (minimum score 550 paper-based; 213 computer-based; 79 iBT). Electronic applications accepted.

Seton Hall University, College of Arts and Sciences, Department of Art and Music, South Orange, NJ 07079-2697. Offers museum professions (MA). *Accreditation:* NASM. Part-time and evening/weekend programs available. *Degree requirements:* For master's, thesis or alternative. *Entrance requirements:* For master's, GRE General Test, previous course work in art history. Electronic applications accepted. *Faculty research:* History of museums, museum education, theory of museums, nineteenth century art, African-American art, Renaissance art history, museum registration, museum ethics.

See Close-Up on page 227.

Southern Illinois University Carbondale, Graduate School, College of Liberal Arts, School of Art and Design, Carbondale, IL 62901-4701. Offers ceramics (MFA); drawing (MFA); fiber/weaving (MFA); glass (MFA); jewelry (MFA); metalsmithing/blacksmithing (MFA); painting (MFA); printmaking (MFA); sculpture (MFA). *Accreditation:* NASAD. *Degree requirements:* For master's, thesis or alternative. *Entrance requirements:* For master's, minimum GPA of 2.7, portfolio, slides. Additional exam requirements/recommendations for international students: Required—TOEFL. *Faculty research:* Prints/woodcuts, foundry, watercolor.

See Close-Up on page 131.

Southern Illinois University Edwardsville, Graduate Studies and Research, College of Arts and Sciences, Department of Art and Design, Program in Studio Art, Edwardsville, IL 62026-0001. Offers MFA. Part-time programs available. *Students:* 22 full-time (12 women), 2 part-time (both women). Average age 26. 61 applicants, 20% accepted. In 2008, 5 master's awarded. *Degree requirements:* For master's, thesis, exhibition. *Entrance requirements:* For master's, portfolio. Additional exam requirements/recommendations for international students: Required—TOEFL (minimum score 550 paper-based; 213 computer-based; 79 iBT), IELTS (minimum score 6.5). *Application deadline:* For fall admission, 2/1 for domestic and international students. Application fee: $30. Electronic applications accepted. *Expenses:* Tuition, area resident: Full-time $5838. Tuition, nonresident: full-time $14,596. Required fees: $1525. *Financial support:* In 2008–09, 22 teaching assistantships with full tuition reimbursements (averaging $8,064 per year) were awarded; fellowships with full tuition reimbursements, research assistantships with full tuition reimbursements, Federal Work-Study, institutionally sponsored loans, and unspecified assistantships also available. Support available to part-time students. Financial award application deadline: 3/1; financial award applicants required to submit FAFSA. *Unit head:* Dr. Thad Duhigg, Chair, 618-650-3074. *Application contact:* Michelle Robinson, Coordinator for Graduate Recruitment, 618-650-2811, Fax: 618-650-3523, E-mail: michero@siue.edu.

Southern Methodist University, Meadows School of the Arts, Division of Art, Dallas, TX 75275. Offers studio art (MFA), including ceramics, drawing, painting, photography, printmaking, sculpture. *Accreditation:* NASAD. *Faculty:* 11 full-time (3 women), 6 part-time/adjunct (3 women). *Students:* 8 full-time (4 women), 1 international. Average age 31. 35 applicants, 20% accepted, 6 enrolled. In 2008, 4 master's awarded. *Degree requirements:* For master's, thesis or alternative, exhibit. *Entrance requirements:* For master's, BFA or equivalent, letters of recommendation, portfolio. Additional exam requirements/recommendations for international students: Required—TOEFL (minimum score 550 paper-based; 213 computer-based; 80 iBT). *Application deadline:* For fall admission, 2/15 for domestic and international students. Application fee: $75. *Financial support:* In 2008–09, 5 fellowships (averaging $32,914 per year), 5 teaching assistantships (averaging $3,000 per year) were awarded; scholarships/grants and unspecified assistantships also available. Financial award application deadline: 3/1; financial award applicants required to submit FAFSA. *Faculty research:* American stoneware, Southwestern furniture traditions, photographic apparatus and techniques, American ceramists, architecture. Total annual research expenditures: $20,000. *Unit head:* James W. Sullivan, Chair, 214-768-2489, E-mail: jsulliva@smu.edu. *Application contact:* Jean Cherry, Director of Graduate Admissions and Records, 214-768-3765, Fax: 214-768-3272, E-mail: jcherry@smu.edu.

Stanford University, School of Humanities and Sciences, Department of Art and Art History, Stanford, CA 94305-9991. Offers art history (PhD); art practice (MFA); MS/MFA. *Degree requirements:* For master's, thesis (for some programs), faculty reviews; for doctorate, 2 foreign languages, thesis/dissertation. *Entrance requirements:* For master's and doctorate, GRE General Test. Additional exam requirements/recommendations for international students: Required—TOEFL. Electronic applications accepted.

State University of New York at New Paltz, Graduate School, School of Fine and Performing Arts, Department of Fine Arts, New Paltz, NY 12561. Offers ceramics (MFA); interdisciplinary (MA); metal (MFA); painting/drawing (MFA); printmaking (MFA); sculpture (MFA). *Accreditation:* NASAD (one or more programs are accredited). Part-time and evening/weekend programs available. *Faculty:* 22 full-time (16 women), 7 part-time/adjunct (4 women). *Students:* 45 full-time (38 women), 16 part-time (11 women); includes 3 minority (2 Asian Americans or Pacific Islanders, 1 Hispanic American), 8 international. Average age 31. 91 applicants, 34% accepted, 22 enrolled. In 2008, 31 master's awarded. *Degree requirements:* For master's, thesis, portfolio, exhibit (MFA). *Entrance requirements:* For master's, minimum GPA of 3.0, portfolio. Additional exam requirements/recommendations for international students: Required—TOEFL (minimum score 550 paper-based; 213 computer-based; 80 iBT). *Application deadline:* For fall admission, 2/15 for domestic and international students. Applications are processed on a rolling basis. Application fee: $50. Electronic applications accepted. *Financial support:* In 2008–09, 13 students received support, including 3 fellowships (averaging $8,000 per year), 2 research assistantships with partial tuition reimbursements available (averaging $5,000 per year), 8 teaching assistantships with partial tuition reimbursements available (averaging $5,000 per year); Federal Work-Study, institutionally sponsored loans, scholarships/grants, traineeships, tuition waivers (full), and unspecified assistantships also available. Financial award application deadline: 8/11; financial award applicants required to submit FAFSA. *Unit head:* Prof. Myra Mimlitsch-Gray, Chair, 845-257-3833, E-mail: mimlitsm@newpaltz.edu. *Application contact:* Prof. Emily puthoffe@newpaltz.edu, Coordinator, 845-257-3834, E-mail: shiftana@newpaltz.edu.

State University of New York at Oswego, Graduate Studies, College of Arts and Sciences, Department of Art, Oswego, NY 13126. Offers MA. *Accreditation:* NASAD. Part-time programs available. *Degree requirements:* For master's, exhibit, final presentation. *Entrance requirements:* For master's, slides of previous work. Additional exam requirements/recommendations for international students: Required—TOEFL (minimum score 560 paper-based; 220 computer-based). *Faculty research:* Ancient and primitive art, nineteenth century art, medieval art, Renaissance art.

Stephen F. Austin State University, Graduate School, College of Fine Arts, School of Art, Nacogdoches, TX 75962. Offers art (MA); design (MFA); drawing (MFA); painting (MFA); sculpture (MFA). *Accreditation:* NASAD. Part-time programs available. *Degree requirements:* For master's, comprehensive exam, thesis, exhibit. *Entrance requirements:* For master's, GRE General Test, portfolio. Additional exam requirements/recommendations for international students: Required—TOEFL. *Faculty research:* Printmaking, jewelry, photography, ceramics, art history.

Stony Brook University, State University of New York, Graduate School, College of Arts and Sciences, Department of Art, Program in Studio Art, Stony Brook, NY 11794. Offers MFA. *Students:* 15 full-time (11 women); includes 2 minority (1 African American, 1 Hispanic American), 2 international. Average age 32. 21 applicants, 38% accepted. In 2008, 4 master's awarded. *Degree requirements:* For master's, comprehensive exam, thesis, reading knowledge of German, French, or Italian; exhibition. *Entrance requirements:* For master's, GRE General Test, minimum undergraduate GPA of 3.0. Additional exam requirements/recommendations for international students: Required—TOEFL. *Application deadline:* For fall admission, 1/15 priority date for domestic students. Application fee: $60. *Expenses:* Tuition, area resident: Full-time $7880; part-time $328 per credit hour. Tuition, state resident: full-time $7880; part-time $328 per credit hour. Tuition, nonresident: full-time $13,250; part-time $552 per credit hour. Required fees: $848. *Unit head:* Stephanie Dinkins, Director, 631-632-7254, E-mail: sdinkins@ms.cc.sunysb.edu. *Application contact:* Dr. Michele Bogart, Director, 631-632-7270.

Sul Ross State University, School of Arts and Sciences, Department of Fine Arts and Communication, Alpine, TX 79832. Offers art education (M Ed); art history (M Ed); studio art (M Ed), including ceramics, design, drawing, jewelry, painting, printmaking, sculpture, weaving. Part-time programs available. *Degree requirements:* For master's, oral or written exam. *Entrance*

Art/Fine Arts

Sul Ross State University (continued)

requirements: For master's, GRE General Test, minimum GPA of 2.5 in last 60 hours of undergraduate work. *Faculty research:* Ceramic sculpture, watercolor, wood sculpture, rock art.

Syracuse University, Graduate School, College of Visual and Performing Arts, Program in Ceramics, Syracuse, NY 13244. Offers MFA. *Accreditation:* NASAD. Part-time programs available. *Degree requirements:* For master's, thesis or alternative. *Entrance requirements:* For master's, portfolio. Additional exam requirements/recommendations for international students: Required—TOEFL. Electronic applications accepted.

Syracuse University, Graduate School, College of Visual and Performing Arts, Program in Jewelry and Metalsmithing, Syracuse, NY 13244. Offers MFA.

Syracuse University, Graduate School, College of Visual and Performing Arts, Program in Painting, Syracuse, NY 13244. Offers MFA.

Syracuse University, Graduate School, College of Visual and Performing Arts, Program in Printmaking, Syracuse, NY 13244. Offers MFA.

Syracuse University, Graduate School, College of Visual and Performing Arts, Program in Sculpture, Syracuse, NY 13244. Offers MFA.

Temple University, Graduate School, Tyler School of Art, Department of Crafts, Philadelphia, PA 19122-6096. Offers ceramics/glass (MFA); fibers and fabric design (MFA); metals/jewelry/CAD-CAM (MFA). *Accreditation:* NASAD. *Degree requirements:* For master's, essay, exhibit. *Entrance requirements:* For master's, minimum GPA of 3.0, slide portfolio, 40 credits in studio art, 12 credits in art history. Additional exam requirements/recommendations for international students: Required—TOEFL (minimum score 550 paper-based; 213 computer-based; 79 iBT). Electronic applications accepted.

Temple University, Graduate School, Tyler School of Art, Department of Graphic Arts and Design, Philadelphia, PA 19122-6096. Offers graphic and interactive design (MFA); photography (MFA); printmaking (MFA). *Accreditation:* NASAD. *Degree requirements:* For master's, essay, exhibit. *Entrance requirements:* For master's, minimum GPA of 3.0; slide portfolio, 40 credits in studio art; 12 credits in art history. Additional exam requirements/recommendations for international students: Required—TOEFL (minimum score 550 paper-based; 213 computer-based; 79 iBT). Electronic applications accepted.

Temple University, Graduate School, Tyler School of Art, Department of Painting, Drawing, and Sculpture, Philadelphia, PA 19122-6096. Offers painting (MFA); sculpture (MFA). *Accreditation:* NASAD. *Degree requirements:* For master's, essay, exhibit. *Entrance requirements:* For master's, minimum GPA of 3.0, slide portfolio, 40 credits in studio art, 12 credits in art history. Additional exam requirements/recommendations for international students: Required—TOEFL (minimum score 550 paper-based; 213 computer-based; 79 iBT). Electronic applications accepted.

Texas A&M University–Commerce, Graduate School, College of Arts and Sciences, Department of Art, Commerce, TX 75429-3011. Offers art (MA, MS); art history (MA); fine arts (MFA); studio art (MA). Part-time programs available. *Degree requirements:* For master's, comprehensive exam, thesis (for some programs). *Entrance requirements:* For master's, GRE General Test. Electronic applications accepted. *Faculty research:* Use of different art media.

Texas A&M University–Corpus Christi, Graduate Studies and Research, College of Liberal Arts, Program in Studio Arts, Corpus Christi, TX 78412-5503. Offers MA, MFA. Part-time and evening/weekend programs available. *Degree requirements:* For master's, comprehensive exam, thesis (for some programs). *Entrance requirements:* For master's, GRE General Test. Additional exam requirements/recommendations for international students: Required—TOEFL. Electronic applications accepted.

Texas A&M University–Kingsville, College of Graduate Studies, College of Arts and Sciences, Department of Art, Kingsville, TX 78363. Offers MA, MS. Part-time programs available. *Degree requirements:* For master's, comprehensive exam, thesis or alternative. *Entrance requirements:* For master's, GRE General Test, minimum GPA of 3.0. Additional exam requirements/recommendations for international students: Required—TOEFL.

Texas Christian University, College of Fine Arts, Department of Art and Art History, Fort Worth, TX 76129. Offers art history (MA); studio art (MFA). Part-time programs available. *Degree requirements:* For master's, thesis, internship, foreign language exam. *Entrance requirements:* For master's, GRE General Test, writing sample. Additional exam requirements/recommendations for international students: Required—TOEFL. *Application deadline:* For fall admission, 3/15 for domestic students. Applications are processed on a rolling basis. Application fee: $0. *Expenses:* Tuition: Full-time $17,640. *Financial support:* Unspecified assistantships available. Financial award application deadline: 3/1. *Unit head:* Ron Watson, Chairperson, 817-257-7643, E-mail: r.watson@tcu.edu. *Application contact:* Dr. Joseph Butler, Associate Dean, College of Fine Arts, E-mail: j.butler@tcu.edu.

Texas Southern University, Graduate School, College of Liberal Arts and Behavioral Sciences, Department of Fine Arts, Houston, TX 77004-4584. Offers fine arts (MA); music (MA). Part-time programs available. *Faculty:* 2 full-time (1 woman). *Students:* 5 part-time (3 women); all minorities (all African Americans). Average age 33. 2 applicants, 100% accepted, 2 enrolled. *Degree requirements:* For master's, one foreign language, comprehensive exam, recital. *Entrance requirements:* For master's, GRE General Test, minimum GPA of 2.5. Additional exam requirements/recommendations for international students: Required—TOEFL. *Application deadline:* For fall admission, 7/15 priority date for domestic students. Application fee: $50 ($75 for international students). Electronic applications accepted. *Expenses:* Tuition, area resident: Full-time $1912; part-time $96 per credit hour. Tuition, state resident: full-time $1912; part-time $96 per credit hour. Tuition, nonresident: full-time $6302; part-time $343 per credit hour. Required fees: $3542. *Financial support:* Fellowships, teaching assistantships with partial tuition reimbursements, Federal Work-Study, institutionally sponsored loans, scholarships/grants, and unspecified assistantships available. Financial award application deadline: 5/1. *Faculty research:* Music theory, choral music, composition, percussion composition, ethnic musicology. *Unit head:* Dianne F. Jemison-Pollard, Chair, 713-313-7337, Fax: 713-313-1869, E-mail: jemison_dp@tsu.edu. *Application contact:* Dr. Gregory Maddox, Interim Dean of the Graduate School, 713-313-7011 Ext. 4410, Fax: 713-639-1876, E-mail: maddox_gh@tsu.edu.

Texas Tech University, Graduate School, College of Visual and Performing Arts, Fine Arts Doctoral Program, Lubbock, TX 79409. Offers arts (PhD); music (PhD); theatre arts (PhD). *Accreditation:* NAST. *Students:* 50 full-time (22 women), 29 part-time (15 women); includes 9 minority (3 African Americans, 1 American Indian/Alaska Native, 1 Asian American or Pacific Islander, 4 Hispanic Americans), 10 international. Average age 36. 37 applicants, 70% accepted, 16 enrolled. In 2008, 4 doctorates awarded. *Degree requirements:* For doctorate, thesis/dissertation. *Entrance requirements:* For doctorate, GRE General Test. Additional exam requirements/recommendations for international students: Required—TOEFL (minimum score 550 paper-based; 213 computer-based). *Application deadline:* For fall admission, 3/1 priority date for international students; for spring admission, 11/1 priority date for international students. Applications are processed on a rolling basis. Application fee: $50 ($60 for international students). Electronic applications accepted. *Expenses:* Tuition, area resident: Part-time $194 per credit hour. Tuition, state resident: full-time $4648; part-time $194 per credit hour. Tuition, nonresident: full-time $11,392; part-time $475 per credit hour. Required fees: $2206; $69 per credit hour. $389 per semester. *Financial support:* Research assistantships with partial tuition reimbursements, teaching assistantships with partial tuition reimbursements available. Financial award application deadline: 4/15. *Faculty research:* Art criticism and theory, music, aesthetics, theatre arts. *Unit head:* Dr. Brian D. Steele, Director, 806-742-0700, Fax: 806-742-0695, E-mail: brian.steele@ttu.edu. *Application contact:* Dr. Brian D. Steele, Director, 806-742-0700, Fax: 806-742-0695, E-mail: brian.steele@ttu.edu.

Texas Tech University, Graduate School, College of Visual and Performing Arts, School of Art, Lubbock, TX 79409. Offers art (MFA); art education (MAE); fine arts-art (PhD). *Accreditation:* NASAD (one or more programs are accredited). Part-time programs available. *Faculty:* 23 full-time (11 women). *Students:* 40 full-time (16 women), 19 part-time (15 women); includes 6 minority (1 African American, 1 American Indian/Alaska Native, 4 Hispanic Americans), 6 international. Average age 34. 62 applicants, 63% accepted, 20 enrolled. In 2008, 12 master's, 1 doctorate awarded. *Degree requirements:* For master's, thesis (for some programs); for doctorate, thesis/dissertation. *Entrance requirements:* For master's and doctorate, GRE General Test. Additional exam requirements/recommendations for international students: Required—TOEFL (minimum score 550 paper-based; 213 computer-based). *Application deadline:* For fall admission, 3/1 priority date for international students; for spring admission, 11/1 priority date for international students. Applications are processed on a rolling basis. Application fee: $50 ($60 for international students). Electronic applications accepted. *Expenses:* Tuition, area resident: Part-time $194 per credit hour. Tuition, state resident: full-time $4648; part-time $194 per credit hour. Tuition, nonresident: full-time $11,392; part-time $475 per credit hour. Required fees: $2206; $69 per credit hour. $389 per semester. *Financial support:* In 2008–09, 53 students received support, including 37 teaching assistantships with partial tuition reimbursements available (averaging $7,632 per year); research assistantships with partial tuition reimbursements available, career-related internships or fieldwork, Federal Work-Study, and institutionally sponsored loans also available. Support available to part-time students. Financial award application deadline: 4/15; financial award applicants required to submit FAFSA. *Faculty research:* Studio, art history, art education. Total annual research expenditures: $6,655. *Unit head:* Dr. Todd DeVriese, Director, 806-742-3825 Ext. 255, Fax: 806-742-1971, E-mail: todd.devriese@ttu.edu. *Application contact:* Andrew Martin, Graduate Advisor, 806-742-3825 Ext. 228, Fax: 806-742-1971, E-mail: andrew.martin@ttu.edu.

Texas Tech University, Graduate School, College of Visual and Performing Arts, School of Music, Lubbock, TX 79409. Offers composition (MM, DMA); conducting (DMA); fine arts-music (PhD); music (MM Ed); music theory (MM); musicology (MM); pedagogy (MM); performance (MM, DMA); piano pedagogy (DMA). *Accreditation:* NASM. Part-time programs available. *Faculty:* 29 full-time (9 women), 1 part-time/adjunct (0 women). *Students:* 96 full-time (42 women), 29 part-time (14 women); includes 11 minority (3 African Americans, 1 American Indian/Alaska Native, 7 Hispanic Americans), 23 international. Average age 38. 108 applicants, 69% accepted, 34 enrolled. In 2008, 20 master's, 9 doctorates awarded. *Degree requirements:* For master's, thesis or alternative; for doctorate, thesis/dissertation. *Entrance requirements:* For master's and doctorate, GRE General Test. Additional exam requirements/recommendations for international students: Required—TOEFL (minimum score 550 paper-based; 213 computer-based). *Application deadline:* For fall admission, 3/1 priority date for international students; for spring admission, 11/1 priority date for international students. Applications are processed on a rolling basis. Application fee: $50 ($60 for international students). Electronic applications accepted. *Expenses:* Tuition, area resident: Part-time $194 per credit hour. Tuition, state resident: full-time $4648; part-time $194 per credit hour. Tuition, nonresident: full-time $11,392; part-time $475 per credit hour. Required fees: $2206; $69 per credit hour. $389 per semester. *Financial support:* In 2008–09, 96 students received support, including 71 teaching assistantships with partial tuition reimbursements available (averaging $7,591 per year); research assistantships with partial tuition reimbursements available, Federal Work-Study and institutionally sponsored loans also available. Support available to part-time students. Financial award application deadline: 4/15; financial award applicants required to submit FAFSA. *Faculty research:* Strategies for music pedagogy in grades K-12, performance practice of traditional music, role of the woman piano virtuoso, vernacular music center, voice health and culture. *Unit head:* Prof. William Ballenger, Director, 806-742-2270, Fax: 806-742-2294, E-mail: william.ballenger@ttu.edu. *Application contact:* Carin Wanner, Admissions and Scholarship Coordinator, 806-742-2270 Ext. 225, Fax: 806-742-2294, E-mail: melissacarin.wanner@ttu.edu.

Texas Woman's University, Graduate School, College of Arts and Sciences, School of the Arts, Department of Visual Arts, Denton, TX 76201. Offers art (MA, MFA). *Faculty:* 8 full-time (5 women), 2 part-time/adjunct (1 woman). *Students:* 23 full-time (20 women), 26 part-time (24 women); includes 10 minority (2 African Americans, 2 American Indian/Alaska Native, 2 Asian Americans or Pacific Islanders, 4 Hispanic Americans), 2 international. Average age 38. In 2008, 12 master's awarded. *Degree requirements:* For master's, thesis (for some programs), exhibit (MFA), oral exam, thesis or professional paper (MA). *Entrance requirements:* For master's, GRE General Test (MFA), portfolio, interview, curriculum vitae, letter of intent. Additional exam requirements/recommendations for international students: Required—TOEFL (minimum score 550 paper-based; 213 computer-based; 79 iBT). *Application deadline:* For fall admission, 2/15 priority date for domestic students, 4/1 for international students; for spring admission, 10/16 priority date for domestic students, 8/1 for international students. Applications are processed on a rolling basis. Application fee: $30 ($50 for international students). Electronic applications accepted. *Expenses:* Tuition, state resident: full-time $3564; part-time $198 per semester hour. Tuition, nonresident: full-time $8622; part-time $479 per semester hour. Required fees: $1158; $64 per semester hour. Tuition and fees vary according to course load. *Financial support:* In 2008–09, 10 research assistantships (averaging $9,684 per year), 10 teaching assistantships (averaging $9,684 per year) were awarded; career-related internships or fieldwork, Federal Work-Study, institutionally sponsored loans, scholarships/grants, traineeships, health care benefits, and unspecified assistantships also available. Support available to part-time students. Financial award application deadline: 3/1; financial award applicants required to submit FAFSA. *Faculty research:* Art education and electronic technology, film noir, handmade paper, one-of-a-kind art books, women in film. *Unit head:* Gary Washmon, Acting Chair, 940-898-2530, Fax: 940-898-2496, E-mail: gwashmon@twu.edu. *Application contact:* Samuel Wheeler, Assistant Director of Admissions, 940-898-3188, Fax: 940-898-3081, E-mail: wheelersr@twu.edu.

Towson University, College of Graduate Studies and Research, Program in Studio Arts, Towson, MD 21252-0001. Offers MFA. *Degree requirements:* For master's, exam. *Entrance requirements:* For master's, portfolio, minimum GPA of 3.0. Additional exam requirements/recommendations for international students: Required—TOEFL (minimum score 550 paper-based). Electronic applications accepted.

Troy University, Graduate School, College of Communication and Fine Arts, Troy, AL 36082. Offers MS. *Degree requirements:* For master's, comprehensive exam, thesis optional. *Entrance requirements:* For master's, GRE, MAT, or GMAT. Additional exam requirements/recommendations for international students: Required—TOEFL (minimum score 523 paper-based; 200 computer-based).

Tufts University, Graduate School of Arts and Sciences, Department of Art and Art History, Program in Studio Art, Medford, MA 02155. Offers MFA, MA/MFA, MFA/Certificate. *Degree requirements:* For master's, exhibit. *Entrance requirements:* For master's, portfolio. Additional exam requirements/recommendations for international students: Required—TOEFL (minimum score 550 paper-based; 213 computer-based; 80 iBT). Electronic applications accepted.

Tulane University, School of Liberal Arts, Department of Art, New Orleans, LA 70118-5669. Offers art (MFA); art history (MA). *Degree requirements:* For master's, one foreign language, thesis. *Entrance requirements:* For master's, GRE General Test, minimum B average in undergraduate course work. Additional exam requirements/recommendations for international students: Required—TOEFL. Electronic applications accepted.

United Theological Seminary of the Twin Cities, Graduate and Professional Programs, New Brighton, MN 55112-2598. Offers advanced theological studies (Diploma); justice and peace studies (M Div); leadership toward racial justice (MA, Certificate); Methodist studies (M Div, MA); ministry (D Min); ministry renewal and professional development (Certificate); pastoral care and counseling (M Div); religion and theology (MA); theological and religious studies (Certificate); theology and the arts (MA); urban ministry (MARL); women's studies:

religion, theology and ministry (MA). *Accreditation:* ACIPE; ATS. Part-time and evening/weekend programs available. *Faculty:* 10 full-time (6 women), 24 part-time/adjunct (12 women). *Students:* 60 full-time (34 women), 93 part-time (60 women); includes 10 minority (5 African Americans, 1 American Indian/Alaska Native, 3 Asian Americans or Pacific Islanders, 1 Hispanic American), 1 international. Average age 47. 39 applicants, 100% accepted, 32 enrolled. In 2008, 21 first professional degrees, 9 master's awarded. *Degree requirements:* For master's, thesis; for doctorate, comprehensive exam, thesis/dissertation; for M Div, integrative notebook, spiritual chronicle. *Entrance requirements:* For M Div and master's, minimum GPA of 2.75; strong analytical, reflective thinking and writing skills; vocational and academic goals compatible with those of Seminary; for doctorate, M Div or equivalent, minimum GPA of 3.0, 3 years experience in professional ministry; for other advanced degree, BA or equivalent life experience; strong analytical, reflective thinking and writing skills (Certificate); proficiency in English language, previous study of theology at a theological school, recommendation of student's denomination (Diploma). Additional exam requirements/recommendations for international students: Required—TOEFL (minimum score 550 paper-based). *Application deadline:* For fall admission, 7/1 priority date for domestic students, 11/1 priority date for international students; for winter admission, 11/1 priority date for domestic students; for spring admission, 11/15 priority date for domestic students. Applications are processed on a rolling basis. Application fee: $50. *Expenses:* Tuition: Full-time $11,070; part-time $410 per credit hour. Required fees: $295; $135 per term. One-time fee: $25. Tuition and fees vary according to course load, degree level and program. *Financial support:* In 2008–09, 98 students received support. Career-related internships or fieldwork, institutionally sponsored loans, and scholarships/grants available. Support available to part-time students. Financial award application deadline: 5/1; financial award applicants required to submit FAFSA. *Unit head:* Dr. Richard D. Weis, Dean of the Seminary, 651-255-6108 Ext. 108, Fax: 651-633-4315, E-mail: rweis@unitedseminary.edu. *Application contact:* Rev. Glen Herrington-Hall, Director of Admissions, 651-255-6107 Ext. 107, Fax: 651-633-4315, E-mail: gherrington-hall@unitedseminary.edu.

Universidad del Turabo, Graduate Programs, Programs in Education, Program in Teaching of Fine Arts, Gurabo, PR 00778-3030. Offers MFA.

Université du Québec à Chicoutimi, Graduate Programs, Program in Fine Arts, Chicoutimi, QC G7H 2B1, Canada. Offers MA. Part-time programs available. *Degree requirements:* For master's, thesis optional. *Entrance requirements:* For master's, appropriate bachelor's degree, proficiency in French.

Université du Québec à Montréal, Graduate Programs, Program in Fine Arts, Montréal, QC H3C 3P8, Canada. Offers MA. Part-time programs available. *Degree requirements:* For master's, thesis optional. *Entrance requirements:* For master's, appropriate bachelor's degree or equivalent, proficiency in French.

Université Laval, Faculty of Architecture, Planning and Visual Arts, School of Visual Arts, Programs in Visual Arts, Québec, QC G1K 7P4, Canada. Offers graphic design and multimedia (MA); visual arts (MA). *Degree requirements:* For master's, thesis (for some programs). *Entrance requirements:* For master's, technical exam, interview, mastery of pertinent software, knowledge of French. Electronic applications accepted.

University at Albany, State University of New York, College of Arts and Sciences, Department of Art, Albany, NY 12222-0001. Offers MA, MFA. *Degree requirements:* For master's, exhibit. *Entrance requirements:* For master's, portfolio. Additional exam requirements/recommendations for international students: Required—TOEFL (minimum score 550 paper-based; 213 computer-based). *Faculty research:* Art history, sculpture, painting and drawing, photography, digital media.

University at Buffalo, the State University of New York, Graduate School, College of Arts and Sciences, Department of Visual Studies, Buffalo, NY 14260. Offers art (MFA), including fine arts; art history (MA, Certificate), including art history (MA), critical museum studies (Certificate). *Degree requirements:* For master's, thesis.

The University of Alabama, Graduate School, College of Arts and Sciences, Department of Art, Tuscaloosa, AL 35487. Offers art history (MA); studio art (MA, MFA), including ceramics, painting, photography, printmaking, sculpture. *Accreditation:* NASAD. Part-time programs available. *Faculty:* 15 full-time (8 women). *Students:* 16 full-time (8 women), 4 part-time (all women), 1 international. Average age 31. 17 applicants, 41% accepted, 6 enrolled. In 2008, 9 master's awarded. *Degree requirements:* For master's, one foreign language, comprehensive exam (for some programs), thesis (for some programs), oral exam, thesis statement, exhibit (studio art), thesis (art history). *Entrance requirements:* For master's, GRE General Test or MAT (art history), minimum GPA of 3.0, BFA or equivalent (studio art). Additional exam requirements/recommendations for international students: Required—TOEFL (minimum score 550 paper-based; 213 computer-based). *Application deadline:* For fall admission, 3/15 for domestic and international students; for spring admission, 10/15 for domestic and international students. Applications are processed on a rolling basis. Application fee: $30. Electronic applications accepted. *Expenses:* Tuition, area resident: Full-time $6400. Tuition, state resident: full-time $6400. Tuition, nonresident: full-time $18,000. *Financial support:* In 2008–09, 2 fellowships with full tuition reimbursements (averaging $14,000 per year), 13 teaching assistantships with full and partial tuition reimbursements (averaging $9,206 per year) were awarded; career-related internships or fieldwork, institutionally sponsored loans, scholarships/grants, and unspecified assistantships also available. Financial award application deadline: 7/14. *Faculty research:* Nineteenth century American art history, Chinese art history, baroque art history, twentieth century art history, Asian art history. *Unit head:* William T. Dooley, Chairperson, 205-348-1890, Fax: 205-348-0287, E-mail: wtdooley@bama.ua.edu. *Application contact:* Craig R. Wedderspoon, Graduate Coordinator, 205-348-1898, Fax: 205-348-0287, E-mail: cwedders@bama.edu.

University of Alaska Fairbanks, College of Liberal Arts, Department of Art, Fairbanks, AK 99775-5640. Offers art (MFA); ceramics (MFA); computer art (MFA); drawing (MFA); Native arts (MFA); painting (MFA); photography (MFA); printmaking (MFA); sculpture (MFA). Part-time programs available. *Faculty:* 7 full-time (2 women), 6 part-time/adjunct (4 women). *Students:* 7 full-time (2 women), 1 (woman) part-time; includes 1 minority (American Indian/Alaska Native). Average age 33. 14 applicants, 29% accepted, 3 enrolled. In 2008, 6 master's awarded. *Degree requirements:* For master's, comprehensive exam, thesis, oral exam, oral defense. *Entrance requirements:* For master's, portfolio. Additional exam requirements/recommendations for international students: Required—TOEFL (minimum score 550 paper-based; 213 computer-based; 80 iBT). *Application deadline:* For fall admission, 6/1 for domestic students, 3/1 for international students; for spring admission, 10/15 for domestic students, 9/1 for international students. Applications are processed on a rolling basis. Application fee: $60. Electronic applications accepted. *Expenses:* Tuition, area resident: Full-time $5418; part-time $301 per credit. Tuition, state resident: full-time $5418; part-time $301 per credit. Tuition, nonresident: full-time $11,070; part-time $615 per credit. Required fees: $849; $25 per credit. $78 per semester. Tuition and fees vary according to course load and reciprocity agreements. *Financial support:* In 2008–09, 1 fellowship (averaging $13,500 per year), 4 teaching assistantships (averaging $12,058 per year) were awarded; research assistantships, Federal Work-Study, scholarships/grants, health care benefits, and unspecified assistantships also available. Support available to part-time students. Financial award application deadline: 7/1; financial award applicants required to submit FAFSA. *Faculty research:* Computer art, survey of arts in Alaska, found object art, visualization and animation, painting from the wilderness. *Unit head:* Todd Sherman, Chair, 907-474-7530, Fax: 907-474-5853, E-mail: fyart@uaf.edu. *Application contact:* Todd Sherman, Chair, 907-474-7530, Fax: 907-474-5853, E-mail: fyart@uaf.edu.

University of Alberta, Faculty of Graduate Studies and Research, Department of Art and Design, Edmonton, AB T6G 2E1, Canada. Offers drawing (MFA); history of art, design, and visual culture (MA); industrial design (M Des); painting (MFA); printmaking (MFA); sculpture (MFA); visual communication design (M Des). *Degree requirements:* For master's, thesis. *Entrance requirements:* For master's, portfolio (MFA and MDES). Additional exam requirements/recommendations for international students: Required—TOEFL (minimum score 550 paper-based; 213 computer-based).

The University of Arizona, Graduate College, College of Fine Arts, School of Art, Program in Studio Art, Tucson, AZ 85721. Offers MFA. *Accreditation:* NASAD. Part-time programs available. *Degree requirements:* For master's, thesis or alternative. *Entrance requirements:* For master's, portfolio, minimum GPA of 3.0 for last 60 units, 3 letters of recommendation, resumé or curriculum vitae. Additional exam requirements/recommendations for international students: Required—TOEFL (minimum score 550 paper-based). *Faculty research:* Painting, photography and intermedia, sculpture, printmaking, ceramics.

University of Arkansas, Graduate School, J. William Fulbright College of Arts and Sciences, Department of Art, Fayetteville, AR 72701-1201. Offers MFA. *Degree requirements:* For master's, exhibit or thesis.

University of Arkansas at Little Rock, Graduate School, College of Arts, Humanities, and Social Science, Department of Art, Little Rock, AR 72204-1099. Offers art education (MA); art history (MA); studio art (MA). *Accreditation:* NASAD. Part-time programs available. *Degree requirements:* For master's, 4 foreign languages, oral exam, oral defense of thesis or exhibit. *Entrance requirements:* For master's, portfolio review or term paper evaluation, minimum GPA of 2.7.

The University of British Columbia, Faculty of Arts and Faculty of Graduate Studies, Department of Art History, Visual Art, and Theory, Vancouver, BC V6T 1Z1, Canada. Offers art history (MA, PhD, Diploma); critical and curatorial studies (MA); visual art (MFA). Part-time programs available. *Degree requirements:* For master's, one foreign language, thesis, final exhibition (MFA, MA, CCST); for doctorate, 2 foreign languages, comprehensive exam, thesis/dissertation. *Entrance requirements:* For master's, bachelor's degree with minimum B+ average for MFA; for doctorate, master's degree with minimum A- average. Additional exam requirements/recommendations for international students: Required—TOEFL (minimum score 600 paper-based; 250 computer-based). Electronic applications accepted. *Faculty research:* Conceptual art, Asian art, indigenous North American art, post-second war art, eighteenth and nineteenth century art.

University of Calgary, Faculty of Graduate Studies, Faculty of Fine Arts, Department of Art, Calgary, AB T2N 1N4, Canada. Offers MA, MFA. *Degree requirements:* For master's, thesis. *Entrance requirements:* Additional exam requirements/recommendations for international students: Required—TOEFL. *Faculty research:* Painting, sculpture, drawing, photography, printmaking, new media.

University of California, Berkeley, Graduate Division, College of Letters and Science, Department of Art Practice, Berkeley, CA 94720-1500. Offers MFA. *Entrance requirements:* For master's, GRE General Test, minimum GPA of 3.0, sample of work, 3 letters of recommendation. Additional exam requirements/recommendations for international students: Required—TOEFL (minimum score 570 paper-based; 230 computer-based). Electronic applications accepted.

University of California, Davis, Graduate Studies, Program in Art, Davis, CA 95616. Offers MFA. *Degree requirements:* For master's, final exhibit. *Entrance requirements:* For master's, minimum GPA of 3.0, portfolio. Additional exam requirements/recommendations for international students: Required—TOEFL (minimum score 550 paper-based; 213 computer-based). Electronic applications accepted. *Faculty research:* Drawing, painting, photography, video, interactive art.

University of California, Irvine, Office of Graduate Studies, Claire Trevor School of the Arts, Department of Studio Art, Irvine, CA 92697. Offers MFA. *Degree requirements:* For master's, thesis. *Entrance requirements:* For master's, minimum GPA of 3.0. Electronic applications accepted. *Faculty research:* Experimental concepts, processes relevant to contemporary issues.

University of California, Los Angeles, Graduate Division, School of the Arts and Architecture, Department of Art, Los Angeles, CA 90095-1615. Offers MA, MFA. Program is not accepting applications for the MA in Art for 2009-2010. *Degree requirements:* For master's, comprehensive exam. *Entrance requirements:* For master's, 20 slides and/or videotape, minimum GPA of 3.0. Electronic applications accepted. *Expenses:* Tuition, nonresident: full-time $14,694. Required fees: $9669.50. Full-time tuition and fees vary according to course load, degree level, program and student level.

University of California, Riverside, Graduate Division, Program in Visual Arts, Riverside, CA 92521-0102. Offers MFA. *Faculty:* 7 full-time (3 women), 5 part-time/adjunct (4 women). *Students:* 11 full-time (6 women). Average age 25. 36 applicants, 14% accepted, 4 enrolled. In 2008, 3 master's awarded. *Degree requirements:* For master's, thesis. *Entrance requirements:* For master's, portfolio, minimum GPA of 3.2. Additional exam requirements/recommendations for international students: Required—TOEFL (minimum score 550 paper-based; 213 computer-based; 80 iBT). *Application deadline:* 1/5 for domestic and international students. Application fee: $60 ($75 for international students). Electronic applications accepted. *Expenses:* Tuition, nonresident: full-time $4898. Required fees: $10,362. *Financial support:* In 2008–09, 11 students received support, including fellowships with partial tuition reimbursements available (averaging $12,000 per year), teaching assistantships with full tuition reimbursements available (averaging $16,500 per year); career-related internships or fieldwork, institutionally sponsored loans, scholarships/grants, health care benefits, tuition waivers (partial), and unspecified assistantships also available. Financial award application deadline: 1/5; financial award applicants required to submit FAFSA. *Faculty research:* Painting, photography, sculpture, digital art, video. *Unit head:* Jim Isermann, Department Chair, 951-827-4634, Fax: 951-827-2385, E-mail: artdept@uc.redu. *Application contact:* Amir Zaki, Graduate Advisor, 951-827-4634, Fax: 951-827-2385, E-mail: artdept@ucr.edu.

University of California, San Diego, Office of Graduate Studies, Department of Visual Arts, La Jolla, CA 92093. Offers MFA, PhD. *Degree requirements:* For master's, thesis, exhibit, oral exam. Electronic applications accepted. *Faculty research:* Developments within art and art theory.

University of California, Santa Barbara, Graduate Division, College of Letters and Sciences, Division of Humanities and Fine Arts, Department of Art, Santa Barbara, CA 93106-7120. Offers MFA. *Faculty:* 10 full-time (5 women), 11 part-time/adjunct (4 women). *Students:* 12 full-time (7 women). Average age 28. 54 applicants, 20% accepted, 7 enrolled. In 2008, 8 master's awarded. *Entrance requirements:* For master's, 20 slide portfolio, 3 letters of recommendation, statement of purpose, personal achievements/contributions statement, resumé/curriculum vitae, transcripts for post-secondary institutions attended. Additional exam requirements/recommendations for international students: Required—TOEFL (minimum score 550 paper-based; 213 computer-based; 80 iBT), IELTS (minimum score 7), TOEFL or IELTS. *Application deadline:* For fall admission, 1/4 for domestic and international students. Application fee: $70 ($90 for international students). Electronic applications accepted. *Expenses:* Tuition, nonresident: full-time $25,149. Required fees: $10,143. Full-time tuition and fees vary according to campus/location, reciprocity agreements and student level. *Financial support:* In 2008–09, 12 students received support, including 12 fellowships with full and partial tuition reimbursements available (averaging $11,100 per year), 12 teaching assistantships with partial tuition reimbursements available (averaging $7,300 per year); career-related internships or fieldwork, Federal Work-Study, institutionally sponsored loans, scholarships/grants, and health care benefits also available. Financial award application deadline: 1/7; financial award applicants required to submit FAFSA. *Faculty research:* Fine arts, contemporary art practice, visual arts, critical theory, interdisciplinary research. *Unit head:* Prof. Colin Gardner, Chair, 805-893-5694, E-mail: colingardner@cox.net. *Application contact:* Yumi Kinoshita, Staff Graduate Advisor, 805-893-5962, Fax: 805-893-7206, E-mail: ykinoshita@arts.ucsb.edu.

Art/Fine Arts

University of California, Santa Barbara, Graduate Division, College of Letters and Sciences, Division of Humanities and Fine Arts, Department of Media Arts and Technology, Santa Barbara, CA 93106-6065. Offers electronic music and sound design (MA); media arts and technology (PhD); multimedia engineering (MS); visual and spatial arts (MA). *Faculty:* 33 full-time (3 women). *Students:* 29 full-time (3 women). Average age 30. 55 applicants, 33% accepted, 8 enrolled. In 2008, 5 master's awarded. Terminal master's awarded for partial completion of doctoral program. *Degree requirements:* For master's, comprehensive exam, thesis; for doctorate, comprehensive exam, thesis/dissertation. *Entrance requirements:* For master's and doctorate, GRE, portfolios; programming language and calculus-based math (expertise in 1 discipline and experience in another); 3 letters of recommendation; statement of purpose; personal achievements/contributions statement; resumé/curriculum vitae; transcripts for post-secondary institutions attended. Additional exam requirements/recommendations for international students: Required—TOEFL (minimum score 550 paper-based; 213 computer-based; 80 iBT), IELTS (minimum score 7), TOEFL or IELTS. *Application deadline:* For fall admission, 1/15 for domestic and international students. Application fee: $70 ($90 for international students). Electronic applications accepted. *Expenses:* Tuition, nonresident: full-time $25,149. Required fees: $10,143. Full-time tuition and fees vary according to campus/location, reciprocity agreements and student level. *Financial support:* In 2008–09, 23 students received support, including 10 fellowships with full and partial tuition reimbursements available (averaging $4,800 per year), 6 research assistantships with full and partial tuition reimbursements available (averaging $8,300 per year), 18 teaching assistantships with partial tuition reimbursements available (averaging $7,300 per year); career-related internships or fieldwork, Federal Work-Study, institutionally sponsored loans, scholarships/grants, health care benefits, tuition waivers (full and partial), and unspecified assistantships also available. Financial award application deadline: 1/15; financial award applicants required to submit FAFSA. *Faculty research:* Electronic music and sound design: computer music and algorithmic composition, computer generated music, human-computer cooperation in music, design and synthesis of new sounds, sonic diffusion, 3D spatial sound; interactive art: installations, generative and algorithmic art, immersive art environments, computational photography; visualization; transarchitecture, multimedia signal processing, human-computer interaction, multimedia systems. *Unit head:* Prof. Matthew A. Turk, Chair, 805-893-4236, Fax: 805-893-2930, E-mail: mturk@cs.ucsb.edu. *Application contact:* Diane E. Harden, Graduate Program Assistant, 805-893-2887, Fax: 805-893-2930, E-mail: diane@mat.ucsb.edu.

University of California, Santa Cruz, Division of Graduate Studies, Division of the Arts, Program in Digital Arts and New Media, Santa Cruz, CA 95064. Offers MFA. *Entrance requirements:* Additional exam requirements/recommendations for international students: Required—TOEFL; Recommended—IELTS. Electronic applications accepted.

University of Central Florida, College of Arts and Humanities, Department of Art, Orlando, FL 32816. Offers studio art and the computer (MFA). *Faculty:* 24 full-time (5 women), 6 part-time/adjunct (2 women). *Students:* 21 full-time (13 women); includes 4 minority (2 African Americans, 1 Asian American or Pacific Islander, 1 Hispanic American). In 2008, 8 master's awarded. Application fee: $30. *Expenses:* Tuition, area resident: Full-time $6816; part-time $284 per credit. Tuition, state resident: full-time $6816; part-time $1076 per credit. Tuition, nonresident: full-time $25,824. Required fees: $216; $9 per credit. *Financial support:* In 2008–09, 1 fellowship (averaging $10,000 per year), 7 research assistantships (averaging $4,000 per year), 5 teaching assistantships (averaging $4,400 per year) were awarded. *Unit head:* Mark Price, Chair, 407-823-2676, Fax: 407-823-6470, E-mail: maprice@mail.ucf.edu. *Application contact:* Mark Price, Chair, 407-823-2676, Fax: 407-823-6470, E-mail: maprice@mail.ucf.edu.

University of Chicago, Division of the Humanities, Committee on the Visual Arts, Chicago, IL 60637-1513. Offers MFA. *Entrance requirements:* For master's, GRE General Test.

University of Cincinnati, Graduate School, College of Design, Architecture, Art, and Planning, School of Art, Program in Fine Arts, Cincinnati, OH 45221. Offers MFA. *Accreditation:* NASAD. Part-time programs available. *Degree requirements:* For master's, thesis, oral exam. *Entrance requirements:* Additional exam requirements/recommendations for international students: Required—TOEFL. Electronic applications accepted. *Faculty research:* Painting, drawing, ceramics, printmaking, sculpture.

University of Colorado at Boulder, Graduate School, College of Arts and Sciences, Department of Art and Art History, Boulder, CO 80309. Offers art history (MA), including 19th century art, contemporary art criticism, early 20th century art, Russian and Soviet art; ceramics (MFA); drawing (MFA); painting (MFA); photography and media arts (MFA); printmaking (MFA); sculpture (MFA). *Degree requirements:* For master's, variable foreign language requirement, comprehensive exam, thesis (for some programs). *Entrance requirements:* For master's, GRE General Test, minimum undergraduate GPA of 3.0, portfolio. *Faculty research:* Drawing, painting, ceramics, sculpture, photography and media arts, printmaking (MFA); history-Russian and Soviet art, Early 20th Century art, contemporary art criticism, 19th Century art (MA).

University of Connecticut, Graduate School, School of Fine Arts, Department of Art and Art History, Field of Studio Art, Storrs, CT 06269. Offers MFA. *Accreditation:* NASAD. *Entrance requirements:* Additional exam requirements/recommendations for international students: Required—TOEFL (minimum score 550 paper-based; 213 computer-based). Electronic applications accepted.

University of Dallas, Braniff Graduate School of Liberal Arts, Program in Art, Irving, TX 75062-4736. Offers MA, MFA. Part-time programs available. *Degree requirements:* For master's, exhibit, oral exam. *Entrance requirements:* For master's, GRE General Test, portfolio. Additional exam requirements/recommendations for international students: Required—TOEFL (minimum score 550 paper-based; 213 computer-based). *Faculty research:* Ceramics, printmaking, sculpture, art history, religious imagery and architecture.

University of Delaware, College of Arts and Sciences, Department of Art, Newark, DE 19716. Offers MA, MFA. *Degree requirements:* For master's, exposition paper final exhibition. *Entrance requirements:* For master's, portfolio of creative work. Electronic applications accepted. *Faculty research:* Painting, printmaking, ceramics, photography, sculpture.

University of Denver, Division of Arts, Humanities and Social Sciences, School of Art and Art History, Denver, CO 80208. Offers art history (MA); art history/museum studies (MA); electronic media arts and design (MFA). *Accreditation:* NASAD. Part-time programs available. *Faculty:* 15 full-time (11 women), 6 part-time/adjunct (2 women). *Students:* 15 full-time (12 women), 10 part-time (all women); includes 2 minority (1 Asian American or Pacific Islander, 1 Hispanic American), 1 international. Average age 29. In 2008, 11 master's awarded. *Degree requirements:* For master's, one foreign language, research paper. *Entrance requirements:* For master's, GRE. Additional exam requirements/recommendations for international students: Required—TOEFL. *Application deadline:* Applications are processed on a rolling basis. Application fee: $50. Electronic applications accepted. *Financial support:* Career-related internships or fieldwork, Federal Work-Study, institutionally sponsored loans, and scholarships/grants available. Support available to part-time students. Financial award application deadline: 3/1; financial award applicants required to submit FAFSA. *Faculty research:* Images of women in alchemical manuscripts and books, Giovanni Benedetto, Salvatore Castiglione. *Unit head:* Dr. Annette Stott, Director, 303-871-2846. *Application contact:* Dr. Annabeth Headrick, Graduate Advisor, 303-871-3574, E-mail: saah-interest@du.edu.

University of Florida, Graduate School, College of Fine Arts, School of Art and Art History, Gainesville, FL 32611. Offers art (MFA), including ceramics, creative photography, drawing, electronic intermedia, graphic design, painting, printmaking, sculpture; art education (MA); art history (MA, PhD); digital arts and sciences (MA); museology (museum studies) (MA). *Accreditation:* NASAD. *Degree requirements:* For master's, variable foreign language requirement, project or thesis (MFA). *Entrance requirements:* For master's, portfolio (MFA), writing sample (MA), GRE General Test or minimum GPA of 3.0. Additional exam requirements/recommendations for international students: Required—TOEFL (minimum score 550 paper-based; 213 computer-based). Electronic applications accepted. *Faculty research:* Studio production, art historical studies of style context.

University of Georgia, Graduate School, College of Arts and Sciences, Lamar Dodd School of Art, Program in Art, Athens, GA 30602. Offers MFA, PhD. *Accreditation:* NASAD. *Degree requirements:* For doctorate, one foreign language, thesis/dissertation. *Entrance requirements:* For master's and doctorate, GRE General Test. Electronic applications accepted.

University of Guam, Office of Graduate Studies, College of Liberal Arts and Social Sciences, Division of Fine Arts, Mangilao, GU 96923. Offers ceramics (MA); graphics (MA); painting (MA). *Degree requirements:* For master's, thesis or alternative, exhibit, final oral exam. *Entrance requirements:* For master's, GRE General Test, portfolio. Additional exam requirements/recommendations for international students: Required—TOEFL.

University of Guelph, Graduate Program Services, College of Arts, School of Fine Art and Music, Guelph, ON N1G 2W1, Canada. Offers studio art (MFA). *Degree requirements:* For master's, exhibition, support paper, oral defense. *Entrance requirements:* For master's, minimum B- average during previous 2 years of course work. Additional exam requirements/recommendations for international students: Required—TOEFL. Electronic applications accepted. *Faculty research:* Studio practice in painting, sculpture, print, photo, drawing, video.

University of Hartford, Hartford Art School, West Hartford, CT 06117-1599. Offers MFA. *Accreditation:* NASAD. Part-time programs available. *Degree requirements:* For master's, thesis. *Entrance requirements:* For master's, portfolio, 3 letters of recommendation. Additional exam requirements/recommendations for international students: Required—TOEFL (minimum score 550 paper-based; 213 computer-based). Electronic applications accepted. *Expenses:* Contact institution.

University of Hawaii at Manoa, Graduate Division, Colleges of Arts and Sciences, College of Arts and Humanities, Department of Art and Art History, Honolulu, HI 96822. Offers art (MA); art history (MA); visual arts (MFA). Part-time programs available. *Degree requirements:* For master's, thesis optional. *Entrance requirements:* For master's, GRE General Test, BFA, 18 hours of course work in art history. Additional exam requirements/recommendations for international students: Required—TOEFL (minimum score 600 paper-based; 250 computer-based; 100 iBT), IELTS (minimum score 7). *Faculty research:* Painting, sculpture, glass, design, printmaking.

University of Houston, College of Liberal Arts and Social Sciences, Department of Art, Houston, TX 77204. Offers interior design (MA); painting (MA); photography (MA); sculpture (MA); MFA/MA. *Faculty:* 13 full-time (6 women), 9 part-time/adjunct (8 women). *Students:* 35 full-time (19 women); includes 5 minority (1 Asian American or Pacific Islander, 4 Hispanic Americans), 2 international. Average age 31. 30 applicants, 43% accepted, 10 enrolled. In 2008, 12 master's awarded. *Degree requirements:* For master's, comprehensive exam, visual thesis. *Entrance requirements:* For master's, GRE General Test, portfolio. *Application deadline:* For fall admission, 2/28 for domestic students; for spring admission, 10/30 for domestic students. Application fee: $25 ($100 for international students). *Expenses:* Tuition, state resident: full-time $5164; part-time $287 per credit. Tuition, nonresident: full-time $10,222; part-time $568 per credit. *Financial support:* In 2008–09, 31 teaching assistantships with full tuition reimbursements (averaging $10,600 per year) were awarded; career-related internships or fieldwork, Federal Work-Study, institutionally sponsored loans, scholarships/grants, health care benefits, and unspecified assistantships also available. Support available to part-time students. Financial award application deadline: 3/10. *Faculty research:* Alternative art projects. *Unit head:* Dr. John Reed, Chairperson, 713-743-3001, Fax: 713-743-2823, E-mail: jreed@uh.edu. *Application contact:* Dr. John Reed, Chairperson, 713-743-3001, Fax: 713-743-2823, E-mail: jreed@uh.edu.

University of Idaho, College of Graduate Studies, College of Art and Architecture, Department of Art and Design, Moscow, ID 83844-2282. Offers art (MAT, MFA). *Accreditation:* NASAD. *Faculty:* 7 full-time. *Students:* 14 full-time, 9 part-time. Average age 33. In 2008, 6 master's awarded. *Degree requirements:* For master's, thesis (for some programs). *Entrance requirements:* For master's, minimum GPA of 2.8. *Application deadline:* For fall admission, 8/1 for domestic students; for spring admission, 12/15 for domestic students. Application fee: $55 ($60 for international students). *Expenses:* Tuition, nonresident: full-time $10,080; part-time $336 per credit. Required fees: $5212; $267 per credit. Tuition and fees vary according to program. *Financial support:* Research assistantships, teaching assistantships available. Financial award application deadline: 2/15. *Faculty research:* Information design. *Unit head:* William Woolston, Chair, 208-885-7837. *Application contact:* William Woolston, Chair, 208-885-7837.

University of Illinois at Chicago, Graduate College, College of Architecture and Art, School of Art and Design, Chicago, IL 60607-7128. Offers electronic visualization (MFA); film animation (MFA); graphic design (MFA); industrial design (MFA); photography (MFA); studio arts (MFA). *Accreditation:* NASAD. *Degree requirements:* For master's, thesis, exhibit. *Entrance requirements:* For master's, MAT, portfolio. Additional exam requirements/recommendations for international students: Required—TOEFL. Electronic applications accepted.

University of Illinois at Urbana–Champaign, Graduate College, College of Fine and Applied Arts, School of Art and Design, Program in Studio Arts, Champaign, IL 61820. Offers art and design (MFA); crafts (MFA); metals (MFA); painting (MFA); photography (MFA); sculpture (MFA). *Accreditation:* NASAD. *Students:* 17 full-time (9 women), 3 part-time (all women); includes 3 minority (1 American Indian/Alaska Native, 1 Asian American or Pacific Islander, 1 Hispanic American), 5 international. 52 applicants, 13% accepted, 6 enrolled. In 2008, 4 master's awarded. *Entrance requirements:* For master's, minimum GPA of 3.0. Additional exam requirements/recommendations for international students: Required—TOEFL (minimum score 550 paper-based; 213 computer-based; 79 iBT). *Application deadline:* Applications are processed on a rolling basis. Application fee: $60 ($75 for international students). Electronic applications accepted. *Financial support:* Fellowships, research assistantships, teaching assistantships, tuition waivers (full and partial) available. *Unit head:* Alan Mette, Chair, 217-244-7496, Fax: 217-244-7688, E-mail: amette@illinois.edu. *Application contact:* Marsha Biddle, Assistant to the Associate Director, 217-333-0642, Fax: 217-244-7688, E-mail: mbiddle@illinois.edu.

University of Indianapolis, Graduate Programs, College of Arts and Sciences, Department of Art, Indianapolis, IN 46227-3697. Offers MA. *Accreditation:* NASAD. Part-time and evening/weekend programs available. *Faculty:* 3 full-time (1 woman). *Students:* 1 (woman) full-time, 10 part-time (9 women); includes 1 minority (African American), 2 international. Average age 38. *Entrance requirements:* For master's, GRE Subject Test, 3 letters of recommendation, portfolio. Additional exam requirements/recommendations for international students: Required—TOEFL. *Application deadline:* Applications are processed on a rolling basis. Application fee: $30. *Financial support:* Federal Work-Study available. Financial award application deadline: 5/1; financial award applicants required to submit FAFSA. *Unit head:* Dee Schaad, Chair, 317-788-3253, E-mail: dschaad@uindy.edu. *Application contact:* Katherine Fries, 317-788-3253, E-mail: frieskj@uindy.edu.

The University of Iowa, Graduate College, College of Liberal Arts and Sciences, School of Art and Art History, Programs in Art, Iowa City, IA 52242-1316. Offers MA, MFA. *Degree requirements:* For master's, thesis, final exam. *Entrance requirements:* For master's, GRE General Test, portfolio. Additional exam requirements/recommendations for international students: Required—TOEFL (minimum score 550 paper-based; 213 computer-based). Electronic applications accepted. *Faculty research:* Ceramics, painting and drawing, design, printmaking, photography.

The University of Kansas, Graduate Studies, College of Liberal Arts and Sciences, Department of Visual Art, Lawrence, KS 66045. Offers visual art education (MA). *Accreditation:* NASAD. Part-time programs available. *Faculty:* 27. *Students:* 40 full-time (21 women), 10 part-time (8 women); includes 3 minority (1 African American, 2 Hispanic Americans), 1 international. Average age 28. 71 applicants, 38% accepted, 17 enrolled. In 2008, 8 master's awarded. *Degree requirements:* For master's, thesis (for some programs). *Entrance requirements:* For master's, portfolio, minimum GPA of 3.0, 3 letters of recommendation, statement of purpose. Additional exam requirements/recommendations for international students: Required—TOEFL, IELTS. Application fee: $45 ($55 for international students). Electronic applications accepted. *Expenses:* Tuition, area resident: Full-time $6122; part-time $255.10 per credit hour. Tuition, state resident: full-time $6122; part-time $255.10 per credit hour. Tuition, nonresident: full-time $14,629; part-time $609.55 per credit hour. Required fees: $847; $70.56 per credit hour. Tuition and fees vary according to course load and program. *Financial support:* Fellowships, teaching assistantships with full and partial tuition reimbursements, Federal Work-Study, scholarships/grants, and unspecified assistantships available. Financial award application deadline: 2/1; financial award applicants required to submit FAFSA. *Faculty research:* Painting, sculpture, printmaking, mixed media, installation and performance, drawing, museum education, art educator education. *Unit head:* Dawn Marie Guernsey, Chair, 785-864-4401, Fax: 785-864-4404, E-mail: guernsey@ku.edu. *Application contact:* Gina Westergard, Director of Graduate Studies, 785-864-4401, Fax: 785-864-4404, E-mail: ginaw@ku.edu.

The University of Kansas, Graduate Studies, College of Liberal Arts and Sciences, School of the Arts, Program in Visual Arts Education, Lawrence, KS 66045. Offers MA. Part-time programs available. *Faculty:* 29. *Students:* 5 full-time (all women), 3 part-time (all women). Average age 29. 3 applicants, 33% accepted, 1 enrolled. In 2008, 3 master's awarded. *Degree requirements:* For master's, thesis or alternative. *Entrance requirements:* For master's, portfolio, 3 letters of recommendation, minimum GPA of 3.0. Additional exam requirements/recommendations for international students: Required—TOEFL (paper-based 570; computer-based 230) or IELTS (6.5). *Application deadline:* For fall admission, 5/1 for domestic and international students; for spring admission, 10/15 for domestic and international students. Application fee: $55 ($60 for international students). Electronic applications accepted. *Expenses:* Tuition, area resident: Full-time $6122; part-time $255.10 per credit hour. Tuition, state resident: full-time $6122; part-time $255.10 per credit hour. Tuition, nonresident: full-time $14,629; part-time $609.55 per credit hour. Required fees: $847; $70.56 per credit hour. Tuition and fees vary according to course load and program. *Financial support:* Teaching assistantships with full tuition reimbursements, Federal Work-Study, scholarships/grants, and unspecified assistantships available. Financial award application deadline: 5/1. *Faculty research:* Museum education, art educator education. *Unit head:* Prof. Gregory Thomas, Chairperson, 785-864-4401. *Application contact:* Gina Westergard, Director, 785-864-4401, Fax: 785-864-4404, E-mail: ginaw@ku.edu.

University of Kentucky, Graduate School, College of Fine Arts, Program in Art Studio, Lexington, KY 40506-0032. Offers MFA. *Degree requirements:* For master's, comprehensive exam. *Entrance requirements:* For master's, GRE General Test, minimum undergraduate GPA of 2.75. Additional exam requirements/recommendations for international students: Required—TOEFL (minimum score 550 paper-based; 213 computer-based). Electronic applications accepted.

University of Lethbridge, School of Graduate Studies, Lethbridge, AB T1K 3M4, Canada. Offers accounting (MScM); addictions counseling (M Sc); agricultural biotechnology (M Sc); agricultural studies (M Sc, MA); anthropology (MA); archaeology (MA); art (MA); biochemistry (M Sc); biological sciences (M Sc); biomolecular science (PhD); biosystems and biodiversity (PhD); Canadian studies (MA); chemistry (M Sc); computer science (M Sc); computer science and geographical information science (M Sc); counseling psychology (M Ed); dramatic arts (MA); earth, space, and physical science (PhD); economics (MA); educational leadership (M Ed); English (MA); environmental science (M Sc); evolution and behavior (PhD); exercise science (M Sc); finance (MScM); French (MA); French/German (MA); French/Spanish (MA); general education (M Ed); general management (MScM); geography (M Sc, MA); German (MA); health sciences (M Sc, MA); history (MA); human resource management and labour relations (MScM); individualized multidisciplinary (M Sc, MA); information systems (MScM); international management (MScM); kinesiology (M Sc, MA); management (M Sc, MA); marketing (MScM); mathematics (M Sc); music (MA); Native American studies (MA); neuroscience (M Sc, PhD); new media (MA); nursing (M Sc); philosophy (MA); physics (M Sc); policy and strategy (MScM); political science (MA); psychology (M Sc, MA); religious studies (MA); sociology (MA); theoretical and computational science (PhD); urban and regional studies (MA). Part-time and evening/weekend programs available. *Degree requirements:* For doctorate, comprehensive exam, thesis/dissertation. *Entrance requirements:* For master's, GMAT (M Sc in management), bachelor's degree in related field, minimum GPA of 3.0 during previous 20 graded semester courses, 2 years teaching or related experience (M Ed); for doctorate, master's degree, minimum graduate GPA of 3.5. Additional exam requirements/recommendations for international students: Required—TOEFL. *Faculty research:* Movement and brain plasticity, gibberellin physiology, photosynthesis, carbon cycling, molecular properties of main-group ring components.

University of Louisville, Graduate School, College of Arts and Sciences, Department of Fine Arts, Program in Creative Art, Louisville, KY 40292-0001. Offers MA. *Students:* 13 full-time (7 women), 15 part-time (11 women). Average age 36. In 2008, 11 master's awarded. Application fee: $50. *Unit head:* Dr. James T. Grubola, Chair, 502-852-0759, Fax: 502-852-6791, E-mail: grubola@louisville.edu. *Application contact:* Libby Leggett, Director, Graduate Admissions, 502-852-3101, Fax: 502-852-6536, E-mail: gradadm@louisville.edu.

University of Maryland, Baltimore County, Graduate School, College of Arts, Humanities and Social Sciences, Department of Visual Arts, Baltimore, MD 21250. Offers imaging and digital arts (MFA). *Faculty:* 21 full-time (10 women), 1 part-time/adjunct (0 women). *Students:* 16 full-time (7 women), 2 part-time (both women); includes 1 minority (Asian American or Pacific Islander). Average age 32. 20 applicants, 45% accepted, 7 enrolled. In 2008, 5 master's awarded. *Degree requirements:* For master's, thesis, oral defense, thesis exhibition. *Entrance requirements:* For master's, minimum GPA of 3.0. Additional exam requirements/recommendations for international students: Required—TOEFL. *Application deadline:* For fall admission, 2/1 for domestic and international students. Application fee: $45. Electronic applications accepted. *Financial support:* In 2008–09, 14 students received support, including 12 research assistantships with full and partial tuition reimbursements available (averaging $13,800 per year); scholarships/grants and health care benefits also available. Financial award application deadline: 2/1. *Faculty research:* Advanced visual studies, digital imaging and interactive art, studio and computer art, video art. Total annual research expenditures: $22,500. *Unit head:* Prof. Vin Grabill, Chair, 410-455-1656, Fax: 410-455-1053, E-mail: grabill@umbc.edu. *Application contact:* Prof. Steve Bradley, Graduate Program Director, 410-455-2721, Fax: 410-455-1053, E-mail: sbradley@umbc.edu.

University of Maryland, College Park, Graduate Studies, College of Arts and Humanities, Department of Art, College Park, MD 20742. Offers MFA. *Degree requirements:* For master's, thesis, oral defense. *Entrance requirements:* For master's, minimum GPA of 3.0, portfolio, 15 slides, 3 letters of recommendation. Electronic applications accepted. *Faculty research:* Studio art.

University of Massachusetts Amherst, Graduate School, College of Humanities and Fine Arts, Department of Art, Program in Art, Amherst, MA 01003. Offers MA, MFA. Part-time programs available. *Degree requirements:* For master's, thesis (for some programs). *Entrance requirements:* For master's, portfolio. Additional exam requirements/recommendations for international students: Required—TOEFL (minimum score 530 paper-based; 213 computer-based; 79 iBT), IELTS (minimum score 6.5). Electronic applications accepted. *Expenses:* Tuition, area resident: Full-time $2640. Tuition, nonresident: full-time $9936. One-time fee: $332 full-time. Tuition and fees vary according to course load.

University of Massachusetts Dartmouth, Graduate School, College of Visual and Performing Arts, Program in Artisanry, North Dartmouth, MA 02747-2300. Offers ceramics (MFA, Postbaccalaureate Certificate); fibers (MFA); fibers/textiles (Postbaccalaureate Certificate); jewelry/metals (MFA, Postbaccalaureate Certificate); wood/furniture design (MFA, Postbaccalaureate Certificate). *Accreditation:* NASAD. *Faculty:* 6 full-time (3 women), 2 part-time/adjunct (1

woman). *Students:* 15 full-time (11 women), 15 part-time (6 women); includes 3 minority (all Asian Americans or Pacific Islanders), 4 international. Average age 31. 40 applicants, 68% accepted, 9 enrolled. In 2008, 5 master's awarded. *Degree requirements:* For master's, thesis, visual thesis. *Entrance requirements:* For master's, portfolio, interview, minimum GPA of 3.0, 3 letters of recommendation. Additional exam requirements/recommendations for international students: Required—TOEFL (minimum score 500 paper-based). *Application deadline:* For fall admission, 3/1 for domestic students, 1/1 for international students. Applications are processed on a rolling basis. Application fee: $40 ($60 for international students). Electronic applications accepted. *Expenses:* Tuition, state resident: full-time $2071; part-time $86.29 per credit. Tuition, nonresident: full-time $8099; part-time $337.46 per credit. Required fees: $7946. Tuition and fees vary according to class time, course load and reciprocity agreements. *Financial support:* In 2008–09, 1 research assistantship with full tuition reimbursement (averaging $3,940 per year), 16 teaching assistantships with full tuition reimbursements (averaging $3,500 per year) were awarded; Federal Work-Study and unspecified assistantships also available. Support available to part-time students. Financial award application deadline: 3/1; financial award applicants required to submit FAFSA. *Faculty research:* Historic European tapestry, computerized weaving. *Unit head:* Memory Holloway, Director, 508-999-8010, E-mail: mholloway@umassd.edu. *Application contact:* Elan Turcotte-Shamski, Graduate Admissions Officer, 508-999-8604, Fax: 508-999-8183, E-mail: graduate@umassd.edu.

University of Massachusetts Dartmouth, Graduate School, College of Visual and Performing Arts, Program in Fine Arts, North Dartmouth, MA 02747-2300. Offers drawing (MFA); painting (MFA); printmaking (MFA); sculpture (MFA). *Faculty:* 12 full-time (3 women), 6 part-time/adjunct (4 women). *Students:* 13 full-time (9 women), 5 part-time (2 women); includes 1 minority (Hispanic American), 1 international. Average age 30. 24 applicants, 38% accepted, 5 enrolled. In 2008, 5 master's awarded. *Degree requirements:* For master's, visual thesis. *Entrance requirements:* For master's, minimum GPA of 3.0, portfolio, 3 letters of recommendation. Additional exam requirements/recommendations for international students: Required—TOEFL (minimum score 500 paper-based). *Application deadline:* For fall admission, 3/1 priority date for domestic students, 1/1 priority date for international students. Applications are processed on a rolling basis. Application fee: $40 ($60 for international students). Electronic applications accepted. *Expenses:* Tuition, state resident: full-time $2071; part-time $86.29 per credit. Tuition, nonresident: full-time $8099; part-time $337.46 per credit. Required fees: $7946. Tuition and fees vary according to class time, course load and reciprocity agreements. *Financial support:* In 2008–09, 1 research assistantship with full tuition reimbursement (averaging $3,940 per year), 8 teaching assistantships with full tuition reimbursements (averaging $3,500 per year) were awarded; Federal Work-Study and unspecified assistantships also available. Support available to part-time students. Financial award application deadline: 3/1. *Unit head:* Memory Holloway, Director, 508-999-8554, E-mail: mholloway@umassd.edu. *Application contact:* Elan Turcotte-Shamski, Graduate Admissions Officer, 508-999-8604, Fax: 508-999-8183, E-mail: graduate@umassd.edu.

University of Memphis, Graduate School, College of Communication and Fine Arts, Department of Art, Memphis, TN 38152. Offers art (Graduate Certificate); art history (MA), including Egyptian art and archaeology, general art history; ceramics (MFA); graphic design (MFA); interior design (MFA); painting (MFA); printmaking/photography (MFA); sculpture (MFA). *Accreditation:* NASAD (one or more programs are accredited). *Faculty:* 21 full-time (7 women), 1 (woman) part-time/adjunct. *Students:* 41 full-time (28 women), 3 part-time (all women); includes 6 African Americans, 1 Asian American or Pacific Islander, 1 international. Average age 28. 45 applicants, 73% accepted, 12 enrolled. In 2008, 15 master's, 3 other advanced degrees awarded. *Degree requirements:* For master's, 2 foreign languages, comprehensive exam, thesis. *Entrance requirements:* For master's, GRE General Test or MAT, portfolio (MFA). *Application deadline:* For fall admission, 8/1 for domestic students; for spring admission, 12/1 for domestic students. Applications are processed on a rolling basis. Application fee: $35 ($60 for international students). *Expenses:* Tuition, area resident: Full-time $6242; part-time $330 per credit hour. Tuition, state resident: full-time $6242; part-time $330 per credit hour. Tuition, nonresident: full-time $17,828; part-time $815 per credit hour. Required fees: $1156. *Financial support:* Research assistantships with full tuition reimbursements, teaching assistantships with full tuition reimbursements available. Financial award applicants required to submit FAFSA. *Faculty research:* Online collaborative learning, advanced art history studies, electronic publishing/design, studio arts, architectural studies. *Unit head:* Prof. Richard Lou, Chair, 901-678-2216, Fax: 901-678-2735, E-mail: gmyatt@memphis.edu. *Application contact:* Greely Myat, Graduate Studies Coordinator, 901-678-2650.

University of Miami, Graduate School, College of Arts and Sciences, Department of Art and Art History, Coral Gables, FL 33124. Offers art history (MA); ceramics/glass (MFA); graphic design/multimedia (MFA); painting (MFA); photography/digital imaging (MFA); printmaking (MFA); sculpture (MFA). Part-time programs available. *Degree requirements:* For master's, variable foreign language requirement, thesis, exhibit (MFA), comprehensive exam (MA). *Entrance requirements:* For master's, GRE General Test (MA), research paper (MA), slide portfolio (MFA), artist statement (MFA). Additional exam requirements/recommendations for international students: Required—TOEFL. Electronic applications accepted. *Faculty research:* Installation art, public art.

University of Michigan, Horace H. Rackham School of Graduate Studies, School of Art and Design, Ann Arbor, MI 48109. Offers art and design (MFA). *Accreditation:* NASAD. *Degree requirements:* For master's, thesis, exhibit (MFA), slide lecture. *Entrance requirements:* For master's, portfolio. Additional exam requirements/recommendations for international students: Required—TOEFL, IELTS. Electronic applications accepted. *Faculty research:* Creative expression, commercial design, preparation for teaching.

University of Minnesota, Duluth, Graduate School, School of Fine Arts, Department of Art and Design, Duluth, MN 55812-2496. Offers graphic design (MFA). Part-time programs available. *Degree requirements:* For master's, final exhibit, project, supporting paper. *Entrance requirements:* For master's, minimum GPA of 3.0, writing sample, slide portfolio. Additional exam requirements/recommendations for international students: Required—TOEFL (minimum score 550 paper-based; 213 computer-based). *Faculty research:* Motion graphics, graphic design history, interactive design, typography, education.

University of Minnesota, Twin Cities Campus, Graduate School, College of Liberal Arts, Department of Art, Minneapolis, MN 55455-0213. Offers MFA. *Degree requirements:* For master's, oral exam, supporting paper, thesis exhibit. *Entrance requirements:* For master's, portfolio, letters of recommendation, 3.0 GPA. Additional exam requirements/recommendations for international students: Required—TOEFL (minimum score 550 paper-based; 213 computer-based). Electronic applications accepted. *Faculty research:* Photography as code and symbol, sculpture with an emphasis on multimedia, high-fired salt glazed and utilitarian ceramic earthenware, performance and installations contemporary theory, electronic technology and the human body.

University of Mississippi, Graduate School, College of Liberal Arts, Department of Art, Oxford, University, MS 38677. Offers art education (MA); art history (MA); fine arts (MFA). *Accreditation:* NASAD (one or more programs are accredited). Part-time programs available. *Degree requirements:* For master's, thesis (for some programs). *Entrance requirements:* For master's, GRE General Test, minimum GPA of 3.0. Additional exam requirements/recommendations for international students: Required—TOEFL. Electronic applications accepted.

University of Missouri–Columbia, Graduate School, College of Arts and Sciences, Department of Art, Columbia, MO 65211. Offers MFA. *Faculty:* 23 full-time (9 women), 5 part-time/adjunct (4 women). *Students:* 17 full-time (10 women), 4 part-time (2 women); includes 1 minority (Asian American or Pacific Islander), 4 international. Average age 32. 28 applicants, 21% accepted, 5 enrolled. In 2008, 5 master's awarded. *Degree requirements:* For master's, thesis. *Entrance requirements:* For master's, GRE General Test, minimum GPA of 3.0. Additional exam requirements/recommendations for international students: Required—TOEFL (minimum score 530 paper-based; 197 computer-based; 71 iBT), IELTS (minimum score 5.5). *Application*

Art/Fine Arts

University of Missouri–Columbia (continued)
deadline: For fall admission, 2/1 priority date for domestic students; for winter admission, 9/1 for domestic students; for spring admission, 2/1 for domestic students. Applications are processed on a rolling basis. Application fee: $45 ($60 for international students). *Financial support:* Research assistantships, teaching assistantships, institutionally sponsored loans available. *Unit head:* Dr. Lampo Leong, Department Chair, E-mail: leongl@missouri.edu. *Application contact:* Brenda J Warren, 573-882-4037, E-mail: warrenb@missouri.edu.

University of Missouri–Kansas City, College of Arts and Sciences, Department of Art and Art History, Kansas City, MO 64110-2499. Offers art history (MA, PhD); studio art (MA). Part-time programs available. *Faculty:* 11 full-time (5 women), 8 part-time/adjunct (3 women). *Students:* 7 full-time (6 women), 33 part-time (32 women); includes 3 minority (2 African Americans, 1 American Indian/Alaska Native), 2 international. Average age 31. 11 applicants, 100% accepted, 9 enrolled. In 2008, 4 master's awarded. Terminal master's awarded for partial completion of doctoral program. *Degree requirements:* For master's, thesis, qualifying exam; for doctorate, thesis/dissertation, exams. *Entrance requirements:* For master's, good general education in the humanities. Additional exam requirements/recommendations for international students: Required—TOEFL (minimum score 550 paper-based; 213 computer-based; 80 iBT). *Application deadline:* For fall admission, 3/1 priority date for domestic and international students; for spring admission, 10/15 for domestic and international students. Applications are processed on a rolling basis. Application fee: $45 ($50 for international students). Electronic applications accepted. *Expenses:* Tuition, state resident: full-time $5376; part-time $298.70 per credit hour. Tuition, nonresident: full-time $13,882; part-time $771.20 per credit hour. Required fees: $640.28; $34.65 per contact hour. $30 per semester. Tuition and fees vary according to course load and program. *Financial support:* In 2008–09, 6 teaching assistantships with partial tuition reimbursements (averaging $12,600 per year) were awarded; fellowships, research assistantships with partial tuition reimbursements, career-related internships or fieldwork, Federal Work-Study, institutionally sponsored loans, and tuition waivers (full and partial) also available. Support available to part-time students. Financial award application deadline: 3/1; financial award applicants required to submit FAFSA. *Faculty research:* Painting, electronic media, Western and non-Western art history, photography. *Unit head:* Dr. Burton Dunbar, Chair, 816-235-2531, Fax: 816-235-5507, E-mail: dunbarb@umkc.edu. *Application contact:* Dr. Rochelle Ziskin, Associate Professor, 816-235-2991, Fax: 816-235-5507, E-mail: ziskinr@umkc.edu.

The University of Montana, Graduate School, School of Fine Arts, Department of Art, Missoula, MT 59812-0002. Offers fine arts (MA, MFA), including art (MA), art history (MA), ceramics (MFA), integrated arts and education (MA), media arts (MFA), painting and drawing (MFA), photography (MFA), printmaking (MFA), sculpture (MFA). *Accreditation:* NASAD (one or more programs are accredited). *Degree requirements:* For master's, thesis exhibit. *Entrance requirements:* For master's, GRE General Test, portfolio.

The University of Montana, Graduate School, School of Fine Arts, Department of Drama/Dance, Missoula, MT 59812-0002. Offers fine arts (MA, MFA), including acting (MFA), design/technology (MFA), directing (MFA), drama (MA), integrated arts and education (MA), media arts (MFA). *Accreditation:* NAST (one or more programs are accredited). *Degree requirements:* For master's, thesis or alternative. *Entrance requirements:* For master's, GRE General Test, audition, portfolio, production notebook.

University of Nebraska–Lincoln, Graduate College, College of Fine and Performing Arts, Department of Art and Art History, Lincoln, NE 68588. Offers art history (MA); studio art (MFA);). *Accreditation:* NASAD. *Faculty:* 17 full-time (10 women), 2 part-time/adjunct (1 woman). *Students:* 29 full-time (14 women); includes 2 minority (1 African American, 1 Hispanic American), 1 international. Average age 29. In 2008, 9 master's awarded. *Degree requirements:* For master's, thesis. *Entrance requirements:* For master's, slide portfolio. Additional exam requirements/recommendations for international students: Required—TOEFL (minimum score 550 paper-based; 213 computer-based). *Application deadline:* For fall admission, 2/1 for domestic students. Application fee: $40. Electronic applications accepted. *Expenses:* Tuition, state resident: full-time $4275; part-time $237.50 per credit hour. Tuition, nonresident: full-time $11,525; part-time $640.25 per credit hour. Required fees: $1068; $10.35 per credit hour. $440.70 per semester. Tuition and fees vary according to course load and program. *Financial support:* Fellowships, research assistantships, teaching assistantships, Federal Work-Study and health care benefits available. Support available to part-time students. Financial award application deadline: 2/15. *Faculty research:* Classical archaeology, contemporary art, printmaking, photography. *Unit head:* Joseph M. Ruffo, Chair, 402-472-2631. *Application contact:* Ginny Gross, Director of Graduate Admissions, 402-472-2878, Fax: 402-472-0589, E-mail: grad_admissions@unl.edu.

University of Nevada, Las Vegas, Graduate College, College of Fine Arts, Department of Art, Las Vegas, NV 89154-5013. Offers MFA. *Accreditation:* NASAD. Part-time programs available. *Faculty:* 1 full-time (0 women). *Students:* 13 full-time (8 women); includes 1 minority (Hispanic American), 1 international. Average age 32. 34 applicants, 26% accepted, 4 enrolled. In 2008, 3 master's awarded. *Degree requirements:* For master's, comprehensive exam, thesis. *Entrance requirements:* Additional exam requirements/recommendations for international students: Required—TOEFL (minimum score 550 paper-based; 213 computer-based; 80 iBT), IELTS (minimum score 7). *Application deadline:* For fall admission, 2/1 priority date for domestic and international students. Applications are processed on a rolling basis. Application fee: $60 ($75 for international students). Electronic applications accepted. *Expenses:* Tuition, state resident: full-time $1414; part-time $198 per credit. Tuition, nonresident: full-time $12,509; part-time $415.75 per credit. International tuition: $14,249 full-time. Required fees: $4 per credit. $252 per semester. Tuition and fees vary according to course load. *Financial support:* In 2008–09, 13 students received support, including 13 teaching assistantships with partial tuition reimbursements available (averaging $10,000 per year); institutionally sponsored loans, scholarships/grants, health care benefits, and unspecified assistantships also available. Financial award application deadline: 3/1. *Unit head:* Dr. Jeffrey Burden, Chair/Professor, 702-895-3112, Fax: 702-895-4194, E-mail: jeff.burden@unlv.edu. *Application contact:* Graduate College Admissions Evaluator, 702-895-3320, Fax: 702-895-4180, E-mail: gradcollege@unlv.edu.

University of Nevada, Reno, Graduate School, College of Liberal Arts, Department of Fine Arts, Reno, NV 89557. Offers MFA. *Faculty:* 13 full-time (5 women). *Students:* 8 full-time (4 women); includes 1 minority (Hispanic American). Average age 33. 100 applicants, 3% accepted, 3 enrolled. *Degree requirements:* For master's, thesis optional. *Entrance requirements:* For master's, minimum GPA of 2.75. Additional exam requirements/recommendations for international students: Required—TOEFL (minimum score 500 paper-based; 173 computer-based; 61 iBT), IELTS (minimum score 6), TOFEL or IELTS. *Application deadline:* For fall admission, 2/15 priority date for domestic and international students. Application fee: $60 ($95 for international students). Electronic applications accepted. *Expenses:* Tuition, state resident: full-time $1710; part-time $1140 per semester. Tuition, nonresident: full-time $7115. Required fees: $158 per semester. *Financial support:* In 2008–09, 12 teaching assistantships with partial tuition reimbursements (averaging $14,000 per year) were awarded; Federal Work-Study, institutionally sponsored loans, scholarships/grants, health care benefits, and unspecified assistantships also available. Financial award application deadline: 3/1; financial award applicants required to submit FAFSA. *Faculty research:* Ceramics; digital-media; drawing; painting; performance; photography; printmaking; sculpture; video; studio program supported by a strong emphasis in the areas of contemporary art, theory and criticism. *Unit head:* Dr. Tamera Scronce, Head, 775-784-6682, E-mail: tamaras@unr.edu. *Application contact:* Michele Sandberg, Application Contact, 775-784-7026, Fax: 775-784-6064, E-mail: gradschool@unr.edu.

University of New Hampshire, Graduate School, College of Liberal Arts, Program in Painting, Durham, NH 03824. Offers MFA. Part-time programs available. *Faculty:* 12 full-time (4 women). *Students:* 7 full-time (2 women). Average age 29. 17 applicants, 47% accepted, 3 enrolled. In 2008, 4 master's awarded. *Degree requirements:* For master's, thesis or alternative. *Entrance requirements:* For master's, slide portfolio. Additional exam requirements/recommendations for international students: Required—TOEFL (minimum score 550 paper-based; 213 computer-based; 80 iBT). *Application deadline:* For fall admission, 4/1 priority date for domestic students, 4/1 for international students. Applications are processed on a rolling basis. Application fee: $60. Electronic applications accepted. *Expenses:* Tuition, area resident: Full-time $9720; part-time $540 per credit hour. Tuition, nonresident: full-time $23,200; part-time $954 per credit hour. Required fees: $1446; $361.50 per term. *Financial support:* In 2008–09, 7 students received support, including 3 teaching assistantships; fellowships, research assistantships, career-related internships or fieldwork, Federal Work-Study, and scholarships/grants also available. Support available to part-time students. Financial award application deadline: 2/15. *Unit head:* Michael McConnell, Chair, 603-862-3820. *Application contact:* Eileen Wong, Administrative Assistant, 603-862-3820, E-mail: mfa.painting@unh.edu.

University of New Mexico, Graduate School, College of Fine Arts, Department of Art and Art History, Program in Studio Arts, Albuquerque, NM 87131-2039. Offers MFA. Part-time programs available. *Degree requirements:* For master's, comprehensive exam, thesis or alternative, studio reviews, qualifying exams. *Entrance requirements:* Additional exam requirements/recommendations for international students: Required—TOEFL (minimum score 550 paper-based; 213 computer-based). Electronic applications accepted. *Faculty research:* Photography, painting, drawing, printmaking, scuplture & ceramics, electronic arts, land arts.

University of New Orleans, Graduate School, College of Liberal Arts, Department of Fine Arts, New Orleans, LA 70148. Offers MFA. *Accreditation:* NASAD. *Degree requirements:* For master's, thesis. *Entrance requirements:* For master's, GRE General Test, slide review. Additional exam requirements/recommendations for international students: Required—TOEFL (minimum score 550 paper-based; 213 computer-based; 79 iBT). Electronic applications accepted. *Faculty research:* Large-scale painting and sculpture, black-and-white and color photography, computer graphics.

The University of North Carolina at Chapel Hill, Graduate School, College of Arts and Sciences, Department of Art, Studio Art Program, Chapel Hill, NC 27599. Offers MFA. *Degree requirements:* For master's, variable foreign language requirement. *Entrance requirements:* For master's, minimum GPA of 3.0, portfolio. Electronic applications accepted. *Faculty research:* Environmental installation, painting, photography, mixed media, printmaking.

The University of North Carolina at Greensboro, Graduate School, College of Arts and Sciences, Department of Art, Greensboro, NC 27412-5001. Offers studio arts (MFA). *Degree requirements:* For master's, thesis (for some programs). *Entrance requirements:* For master's, GRE General Test, 39 hours of course work in studio art, 15 hours of course work in art history, portfolio. Additional exam requirements/recommendations for international students: Required—TOEFL. Electronic applications accepted.

University of North Dakota, Graduate School, College of Arts and Sciences, Department of Visual Arts, Grand Forks, ND 58202. Offers MFA. *Accreditation:* NASAD. *Degree requirements:* For master's, thesis or alternative, comprehensive evaluation, professional exhibition. *Entrance requirements:* For master's, minimum GPA of 3.0. Additional exam requirements/recommendations for international students: Required—TOEFL (minimum score 550 paper-based; 213 computer-based; 79 iBT), IELTS (minimum score 6.5). Electronic applications accepted. *Faculty research:* Ceramics, drawing, metalsmithing, printmaking, painting.

University of Northern Colorado, Graduate School, College of Performing and Visual Arts, School of Visual Arts, Greeley, CO 80639. Offers visual arts (MA). Part-time programs available. *Faculty:* 5 full-time (3 women). *Students:* 4 full-time (all women), 9 part-time (8 women). Average age 39. 3 applicants, 67% accepted, 1 enrolled. In 2008, 4 master's awarded. *Degree requirements:* For master's, comprehensive exam, thesis. *Entrance requirements:* For master's, GRE General Test, portfolio, 3 letters of recommendation, minimum undergraduate GPA of 3.0. *Application deadline:* Applications are processed on a rolling basis. Application fee: $50 ($60 for international students). Electronic applications accepted. *Expenses:* Tuition, state resident: full-time $4370; part-time $242.75 per credit hour. Tuition, nonresident: full-time $12,366; part-time $687 per credit hour. Required fees: $664.20; $36.90 per credit hour. *Financial support:* In 2008–09, 2 research assistantships (averaging $3,482 per year), 1 teaching assistantship (averaging $11,396 per year) were awarded; fellowships, unspecified assistantships also available. Financial award application deadline: 3/1; financial award applicants required to submit FAFSA. *Unit head:* Dr. Dennis Morimoto, Director, 970-351-2143, Fax: 970-351-2299. *Application contact:* Linda Sisson, Graduate Student Admission Coordinator, 970-351-1807, Fax: 970-351-2371, E-mail: linda.sisson@unco.edu.

University of Northern Iowa, Graduate College, College of Humanities and Fine Arts, Department of Art, Cedar Falls, IA 50614. Offers art (MA); art education (MA). *Accreditation:* NASAD. Part-time and evening/weekend programs available. *Students:* 5 full-time (2 women), 5 part-time (3 women); includes 1 minority (Hispanic American), 2 international. 12 applicants, 8% accepted, 1 enrolled. In 2008, 2 master's awarded. *Degree requirements:* For master's, comprehensive exam (for some programs), thesis or alternative. *Entrance requirements:* For master's, minimum GPA of 3.0, portfolio. Additional exam requirements/recommendations for international students: Required—TOEFL (minimum score 500 paper-based; 180 computer-based; 61 iBT). *Application deadline:* For fall admission, 8/1 priority date for domestic students. Applications are processed on a rolling basis. Application fee: $30 ($50 for international students). Electronic applications accepted. *Expenses:* Tuition, state resident: full-time $6446. Tuition, nonresident: full-time $14,874. Required fees: $852. *Financial support:* Career-related internships or fieldwork, Federal Work-Study, scholarships/grants, and tuition waivers (full and partial) available. Support available to part-time students. Financial award application deadline: 2/1. *Unit head:* Dr. Jeffery Byrd, Acting Head, 319-273-2077, Fax: 319-273-7333, E-mail: jeffery.byrd@uni.edu. *Application contact:* Laurie S. Russell, Record Analyst, 319-273-2623, Fax: 319-273-6792, E-mail: laurie.russell@uni.edu.

University of North Texas, Robert B. Toulouse School of Graduate Studies, College of Visual Arts and Design, Department of Studio Art, Denton, TX 76203. Offers MFA. *Degree requirements:* For master's, MFA exhibition, extended artists statement disk of 20 images from MFA show, MFA committee approval. *Entrance requirements:* For master's, GRE, 2 letters of recommendation, statement of intent, portfolio of 20 works, transcripts. Additional exam requirements/recommendations for international students: Recommended—TOEFL (minimum score 550 paper-based; 213 computer-based). *Faculty research:* Altered terrain, enameling on metal, electrical and mechanical interactivity, interactive animation.

University of Notre Dame, Graduate School, College of Arts and Letters, Division of Humanities, Department of Art, Art History, and Design, Notre Dame, IN 46556. Offers art history (MA); design (MFA), including graphic design, industrial design; studio art (MFA), including ceramics, painting, photography, printmaking, sculpture. *Accreditation:* NASAD. *Faculty:* 19 full-time (6 women), 3 part-time/adjunct (1 woman). *Students:* 23 full-time (12 women); includes 2 minority (both Hispanic Americans), 1 international. 83 applicants, 18% accepted, 10 enrolled. In 2008, 11 master's awarded. *Degree requirements:* For master's, comprehensive exam (for some programs), thesis. *Entrance requirements:* For master's, GRE General Test, minimum GPA of 3.0. Additional exam requirements/recommendations for international students: Required—TOEFL (minimum score 600 paper-based; 250 computer-based; 80 iBT). *Application deadline:* For fall admission, 2/1 priority date for domestic and international students. Application fee: $50. Electronic applications accepted. *Financial support:* In 2008–09, 20 students received support; fellowships with full tuition reimbursements available, research assistantships with full tuition reimbursements available, teaching assistantships with full tuition reimbursements available, scholarships/grants, tuition waivers (full), and unspecified assistantships available. Financial award application deadline: 2/1. *Faculty research:* Studio art practice in ceramics, printing, photography, printmaking and sculpture, graphic design and industrial design, digital imaging in design and photography, Renaissance and American art history, contemporary art theory and criticism. *Unit head:* Prof. Martina Lopez, Director of Graduate Studies, 574-631-

7652, E-mail: art.1@nd.edu. *Application contact:* Dr. Barbara Turpin, Director of Graduate Admissions, 574-631-7706, Fax: 574-631-4183.

University of Oklahoma, Graduate College, College of Fine Arts, School of Art and Art History, Norman, OK 73019. Offers art (MA, MFA); art history (MA, MFA); ceramics (MFA); film and video (MFA); painting (MFA); photography (MFA); printmaking (MFA); visual communications (MFA). *Faculty:* 27 full-time (10 women), 2 part-time/adjunct (0 women). *Students:* 20 full-time (13 women), 12 part-time (10 women); includes 6 minority (2 African Americans, 4 American Indian/Alaska Native), 3 international. 28 applicants, 39% accepted, 9 enrolled. In 2008, 8 master's awarded. *Degree requirements:* For master's, thesis (MA), exhibit (MFA), departmental qualifying exam. *Entrance requirements:* For master's, GRE General Test (MA), bachelor's degree in art (MFA) or art history (MA), minimum GPA of 3.0 in last 60 undergraduate hours, 3 letters of recommendation, written research paper. Additional exam requirements/recommendations for international students: Required—TOEFL (minimum score 550 paper-based; 213 computer-based). *Application deadline:* For fall admission, 2/1 priority date for domestic students, 2/1 for international students; for spring admission, 10/1 for domestic and international students. Applications are processed on a rolling basis. Application fee: $40 ($90 for international students). Electronic applications accepted. *Expenses:* Tuition, state resident: full-time $3744; part-time $156 per credit hour. Tuition, nonresident: full-time $13,577; part-time $565.70 per credit hour. Required fees: $2415.40; $90.10 per credit hour. *Financial support:* In 2008–09, 16 students received support, including 14 research assistantships with partial tuition reimbursements available (averaging $10,014 per year), 4 teaching assistantships with partial tuition reimbursements available (averaging $9,586 per year); career-related internships or fieldwork, Federal Work-Study, institutionally sponsored loans, scholarships/grants, health care benefits, tuition waivers (partial), and unspecified assistantships also available. Support available to part-time students. Financial award application deadline: 4/7; financial award applicants required to submit FAFSA. *Faculty research:* Native American art history and art of the American West, contemporary and figurative sculpture, painting and print making, graphic design, media. Total annual research expenditures: $29,536. *Unit head:* Mary Jo Watson, Director, 405-325-2691, Fax: 405-325-1668, E-mail: mjwatson@ou.edu. *Application contact:* Jonathan Hils, Graduate Liaison, 405-325-2691, Fax: 405-325-1668, E-mail: hils@ou.edu.

University of Oregon, Graduate School, School of Architecture and Allied Arts, Department of Art, Eugene, OR 97403. Offers MFA. *Accreditation:* NASAD. *Degree requirements:* For master's, thesis or alternative. *Entrance requirements:* For master's, BFA or equivalent. Additional exam requirements/recommendations for international students: Required—TOEFL.

University of Pennsylvania, School of Design, Department of Fine Arts, Philadelphia, PA 19104. Offers MFA. *Entrance requirements:* For master's, slide portfolio. Additional exam requirements/recommendations for international students: Required—TOEFL. *Faculty research:* Painting, sculpture, printmaking, combined media.

See Close-Up on page 159.

University of Regina, Faculty of Graduate Studies and Research, Faculty of Fine Arts, Department of Visual Arts, Regina, SK S4S 0A2, Canada. Offers MA, MFA. *Faculty:* 11 full-time (6 women). *Students:* 3 full-time (1 woman), 1 (woman) part-time. Average age 30. 23 applicants, 70% accepted. In 2008, 2 master's awarded. *Degree requirements:* For master's, exhibition, support paper, oral defense. *Entrance requirements:* For master's, 20 slides of recent work, slide list, BFA or the equivalent. Additional exam requirements/recommendations for international students: Required—TOEFL (minimum score 580 paper-based; 237 computer-based; 88 iBT). *Application deadline:* For fall admission, 2/15 for domestic students. Application fee: $85 ($100 for international students). *Financial support:* In 2008–09, 7 students received support, including 2 fellowships (averaging $15,930 per year), 1 research assistantship (averaging $13,720 per year), 1 teaching assistantship (averaging $6,650 per year); scholarships/grants also available. Financial award application deadline: 6/15. *Faculty research:* Painting, sculpture, ceramics, printmaking, intermedia. *Unit head:* Dr. Carmen Robertson, Graduate Program Coordinator, 306-585-2227, Fax: 306-585-5526, E-mail: carmen.robertson@uregina.ca. *Application contact:* Dr. Carmen Robertson, Graduate Program Coordinator, 306-585-2227, Fax: 306-585-5526, E-mail: carmen.robertson@uregina.ca.

University of Rochester, The College, Arts and Sciences, Department of Art and Art History, Rochester, NY 14627-0250. Offers visual and cultural studies (MA, PhD). Terminal master's awarded for partial completion of doctoral program. *Degree requirements:* For master's, thesis optional; for doctorate, one foreign language, thesis/dissertation, qualifying exam. *Entrance requirements:* For master's and doctorate, GRE General Test. Additional exam requirements/recommendations for international students: Required—TOEFL.

See Close-Up on page 231.

University of Saint Francis, Graduate School, Department of Art and Visual Communication, Fort Wayne, IN 46808-3994. Offers fine art (MA). *Accreditation:* NASAD. Part-time and evening/weekend programs available. *Degree requirements:* For master's, thesis, exhibit. *Entrance requirements:* For master's, minimum GPA of 3.0 in art, portfolio.

University of Saskatchewan, College of Graduate Studies and Research, College of Arts and Sciences, Department of Art and Art History, Saskatoon, SK S7N 5A2, Canada. Offers MFA. Part-time programs available. *Degree requirements:* For master's, thesis. *Entrance requirements:* Additional exam requirements/recommendations for international students: Required—TOEFL.

University of South Carolina, The Graduate School, College of Arts and Sciences, Department of Art, Columbia, SC 29208. Offers art education (IMA, MA, MAT); art history (MA); art studio (MA); media arts (MMA); studio art (MFA). *Accreditation:* NASAD. *Degree requirements:* For master's, comprehensive exam (for some programs), thesis (for some programs). *Entrance requirements:* For master's, GRE General Test or MAT, portfolio. Additional exam requirements/recommendations for international students: Required—TOEFL. Electronic applications accepted. *Faculty research:* Script writing, teaching art at the elementary and secondary levels of education, history of art and architecture.

The University of South Dakota, Graduate School, College of Fine Arts, Department of Art, Vermillion, SD 57069-2390. Offers MFA. *Accreditation:* NASAD. *Degree requirements:* For master's, thesis or alternative. *Entrance requirements:* For master's, portfolio, minimum GPA of 2.7. Additional exam requirements/recommendations for international students: Required—TOEFL (minimum score 550 paper-based; 213 computer-based; 79 iBT). Electronic applications accepted.

University of Southern California, Graduate School, College of Letters, Arts and Sciences, Department of Art History, Los Angeles, CA 90089. Offers art history (MA, PhD); visual studies (Certificate). *Degree requirements:* For doctorate, 2 foreign languages, thesis/dissertation. *Entrance requirements:* For doctorate, GRE General Test. *Faculty research:* Art and ideology in the early Roman Empire, gender in Renaissance paintings, religious and scientific images in Northern Renaissance paintings.

University of Southern California, Graduate School, School of Fine Arts, Program in Fine Arts, Los Angeles, CA 90089. Offers MFA. *Degree requirements:* For master's, thesis.

University of South Florida, Graduate School, College of The Arts, School of Art and Art History, Tampa, FL 33620-9951. Offers art history (MA); studio art (MFA). *Accreditation:* NASAD. *Faculty:* 17 full-time (8 women). *Students:* 38 full-time (19 women), 7 part-time (all women); includes 12 minority (2 African Americans, 1 American Indian/Alaska Native, 3 Asian Americans or Pacific Islanders, 6 Hispanic Americans), 1 international. 65 applicants, 28% accepted, 14 enrolled. In 2008, 10 master's awarded. *Degree requirements:* For master's, comprehensive exam, thesis. *Entrance requirements:* For master's, GRE General Test (MA), minimum GPA of 3.0 in last 60 hours of coursework. Additional exam requirements/recommendations for international students: Required—TOEFL (minimum score 550 paper-based; 213 computer-based). *Application deadline:* For fall admission, 1/15 for domestic students, 1/2 for international students. Application fee: $30. *Expenses:* Tuition, state resident: full-time $2624.40; part-time $291.60 per credit hour. Tuition, nonresident: full-time $7822; part-time $869.13 per credit hour. *Financial support:* In 2008–09, 8 fellowships with full tuition reimbursements (averaging $7,640 per year), 34 teaching assistantships with full and partial tuition reimbursements (averaging $4,486 per year) were awarded; career-related internships or fieldwork, Federal Work-Study, scholarships/grants, health care benefits, and unspecified assistantships also available. Financial award application deadline: 2/15. *Faculty research:* Contemporary art and role of the artist, identity strategies, political iconography, art practice and technology, construction of race in art. *Unit head:* Prof. Wallace Wilson, Director, 813-974-2360, Fax: 813-974-9226, E-mail: wilson@arts.usf.edu. *Application contact:* Helena Szepe, Contact Person, 813-974-4531, Fax: 813-974-9226, E-mail: szepe@arts.usf.edu.

The University of Tennessee, Graduate School, College of Arts and Sciences, School of Art, Knoxville, TN 37996. Offers ceramics (MFA); drawing (MFA); graphic design (MFA); inter-area studies (MFA); media arts (MFA); painting (MFA); printmaking (MFA); sculpture (MFA); watercolor (MFA). *Accreditation:* NASAD. *Degree requirements:* For master's, thesis or alternative, exhibit. *Entrance requirements:* For master's, portfolio, minimum GPA of 2.7. Additional exam requirements/recommendations for international students: Required—TOEFL. Electronic applications accepted. *Expenses:* Tuition, area resident: Part-time $348 per credit hour. Tuition, state resident: full-time $6262. Tuition, nonresident: full-time $18,920; part-time $1052 per credit hour. Required fees: $812; $36 per credit hour. Tuition and fees vary according to program.

The University of Texas at Arlington, Graduate School, College of Liberal Arts, Department of Art and Art History, Arlington, TX 76019. Offers MFA. Part-time and evening/weekend programs available. *Faculty:* 10 full-time (3 women). *Students:* 15 full-time (6 women), 1 (woman) part-time; includes 6 minority (1 American Indian/Alaska Native, 1 Asian American or Pacific Islander, 4 Hispanic Americans), 1 international. 24 applicants, 54% accepted, 12 enrolled. *Degree requirements:* For master's, thesis or alternative. *Entrance requirements:* For master's, minimum GPA of 3.0, 3 letters of recommendation, portfolio, resumé. Additional exam requirements/recommendations for international students: Required—TOEFL (minimum score 550 paper-based; 213 computer-based). *Application deadline:* For fall admission, 6/1 for domestic students. Applications are processed on a rolling basis. Electronic applications accepted. *Expenses:* Tuition, area resident: Full-time $6500. Tuition, state resident: full-time $6500. Tuition, nonresident: full-time $11,558. *Financial support:* In 2008–09, 4 fellowships (averaging $2,000 per year), 2 research assistantships (averaging $9,000 per year), 12 teaching assistantships (averaging $10,000 per year) were awarded. Financial award application deadline: 5/1; financial award applicants required to submit FAFSA. *Unit head:* Dr. Robert Hower, Professor, 817-272-2891, E-mail: hower@uta.edu. *Application contact:* Dr. Nancy Palmieri, Associate Professor, 817-272-2891, E-mail: palmieri@uta.edu.

The University of Texas at Austin, Graduate School, College of Fine Arts, Department of Art and Art History, Program in Studio Art, Austin, TX 78712-1111. Offers MFA. *Accreditation:* NASAD. *Degree requirements:* For master's, thesis, oral exam. *Entrance requirements:* For master's, minimum GPA of 3.0, portfolio of 15 slides. Electronic applications accepted. *Faculty research:* Painting, sculpture, transmedia, photography, printmaking.

The University of Texas at El Paso, Graduate School, College of Liberal Arts, Department of Art, El Paso, TX 79968-0001. Offers art education (MA); studio art (MA). Part-time and evening/weekend programs available. *Degree requirements:* For master's, thesis optional. *Entrance requirements:* For master's, minimum GPA of 3.0. Additional exam requirements/recommendations for international students: Required—TOEFL. Electronic applications accepted.

The University of Texas at San Antonio, College of Liberal and Fine Arts, Department of Art and Art History, San Antonio, TX 78249-0617. Offers art history (MA); studio art (MFA). *Accreditation:* NASAD (one or more programs are accredited). *Degree requirements:* For master's, comprehensive exam, thesis. *Entrance requirements:* For master's, GRE General Test, portfolio, minimum GPA of 3.0 in last 60 hours, 3 letters of recommendation. Additional exam requirements/recommendations for international students: Required—TOEFL (minimum score 500 paper-based; 173 computer-based). Electronic applications accepted. *Faculty research:* Wide variety of artistic production in all media, art history and criticism, focusing on American and Hispanic art.

The University of Texas at Tyler, College of Arts and Sciences, Department of Art and Art History, Tyler, TX 75799-0001. Offers MA, MAIS, MFA. *Degree requirements:* For master's, thesis, graduate committee review. *Entrance requirements:* For master's, minimum GPA of 3.0. Additional exam requirements/recommendations for international students: Required—TOEFL (minimum score 79 computer-based). *Faculty research:* Classical myths in contemporary art, social issues in contemporary art, casting methods, Renaissance art.

The University of Texas–Pan American, College of Arts and Humanities, Department of Art, Edinburg, TX 78541-2999. Offers MFA. Part-time programs available. *Degree requirements:* For master's, thesis, thesis show of artwork. *Entrance requirements:* For master's, bachelor's degree in fine arts, portfolio, 3 letters of reference. *Faculty research:* Creative art, ceramics, painting, sculpture, computer art.

The University of the Arts, College of Art and Design, Department of Book Arts/Printmaking, Philadelphia, PA 19102-4944. Offers MFA. *Accreditation:* NASAD. Part-time programs available. *Degree requirements:* For master's, thesis. *Entrance requirements:* For master's, portfolio. Additional exam requirements/recommendations for international students: Required—TOEFL (minimum score 550 paper-based; 213 computer-based).

See Close-Up on page 233.

The University of the Arts, College of Art and Design, Program in Ceramics, Philadelphia, PA 19102-4944. Offers MFA. Offered during summer only. *Accreditation:* NASAD. Part-time programs available. *Degree requirements:* For master's, thesis, summer residency. *Entrance requirements:* For master's, portfolio. Additional exam requirements/recommendations for international students: Required—TOEFL (minimum score 550 paper-based; 213 computer-based). Electronic applications accepted.

See Close-Up on page 233.

The University of the Arts, College of Art and Design, Program in Painting, Philadelphia, PA 19102-4944. Offers MFA. Offered during summer only. *Accreditation:* NASAD. Part-time programs available. *Degree requirements:* For master's, thesis, summer residency. *Entrance requirements:* For master's, portfolio. Additional exam requirements/recommendations for international students: Required—TOEFL (minimum score 550 paper-based; 213 computer-based).

See Close-Up on page 233.

The University of the Arts, College of Art and Design, Program in Sculpture, Philadelphia, PA 19102-4944. Offers MFA. Offered during summer only. *Accreditation:* NASAD. Part-time programs available. *Degree requirements:* For master's, thesis, summer residency. *Entrance requirements:* For master's, portfolio. Additional exam requirements/recommendations for international students: Required—TOEFL (minimum score 550 paper-based; 213 computer-based).

See Close-Up on page 233.

University of Toronto, School of Graduate Studies, Humanities Division, Department of Art, Toronto, ON M5S 1A1, Canada. Offers art history (MA, PhD); visual studies (MVS). Part-time programs available. *Degree requirements:* For master's, 2 foreign languages, language proficiency exams; for doctorate, 2 foreign languages, comprehensive exam, thesis/dissertation. *Entrance requirements:* For master's, coursework in a foreign language, 3 letters of reference, sample research paper, minimum B+ average in senior art history and/or humanities courses;

Art/Fine Arts

University of Toronto (continued)
for doctorate, minimum A– average in senior art history and/or humanities courses, 2 letters of reference, sample research paper.

University of Tulsa, Graduate School, College of Arts and Sciences, Department of Art, Tulsa, OK 74104-3189. Offers MA, MFA, MTA. Part-time programs available. *Faculty:* 10 full-time (5 women), 4 part-time/adjunct (1 woman). *Students:* 10 full-time (4 women), 3 part-time (1 woman); includes 1 minority (American Indian/Alaska Native). Average age 34. 19 applicants, 47% accepted, 7 enrolled. In 2008, 4 master's awarded. *Degree requirements:* For master's, comprehensive exam (for some programs), thesis (for some programs). *Entrance requirements:* For master's, portfolio. Additional exam requirements/recommendations for international students: Required—TOEFL (minimum score 575 paper-based; 231 computer-based; 91 iBT), IELTS (minimum score 6.5). *Application deadline:* Applications are processed on a rolling basis. Application fee: $40. Electronic applications accepted. *Expenses:* Tuition: Full-time $15,408; part-time $899 per credit hour. Required fees: $3.33 per credit hour. One-time fee: $200 full-time. Tuition and fees vary according to course load and program. *Financial support:* In 2008–09, 7 students received support, including 7 teaching assistantships with full and partial tuition reimbursements available (averaging $11,594 per year); fellowships with full tuition reimbursements available, research assistantships with full tuition reimbursements available, career-related internships or fieldwork, Federal Work-Study, scholarships/grants, traineeships, tuition waivers (full and partial), and unspecified assistantships also available. Support available to part-time students. Financial award application deadline: 2/1; financial award applicants required to submit FAFSA. *Faculty research:* Drawing, painting, photography, printmaking, ceramics, graphic design. Total annual research expenditures: $5,500. *Unit head:* Dr. Susan Dixon, Chairperson, 918-631-2740, Fax: 918-631-3423, E-mail: susan-dixon@utulsa.edu. *Application contact:* Prof. Whitney Forsyth, Adviser, 918-631-3700, Fax: 918-631-3423, E-mail: whitney-forsyth@utulsa.edu.

University of Utah, The Graduate School, College of Fine Arts, Department of Art and Art History, Salt Lake City, UT 84112-1107. Offers art history (MA); ceramics (MFA); community-based art education (MFA); drawing (MFA); graphic design (MFA); painting (MFA); photography/digital imaging (MFA); printmaking (MFA); sculpture/intermedia (MFA). *Degree requirements:* For master's, variable foreign language requirement, comprehensive exam (for some programs), thesis or alternative, exhibit (MFA), final project paper. *Entrance requirements:* For master's, CD portfolio (MFA), resumé, letters of recommendation. Additional exam requirements/recommendations for international students: Required—TOEFL (minimum score 575 paper-based; 183 computer-based; 75 iBT). Electronic applications accepted. *Faculty research:* Intermedia, digital arts, installation, traditional media, Asian art, medieval arts.

University of Victoria, Faculty of Graduate Studies, Faculty of Fine Arts, Department of Visual Arts, Victoria, BC V8W 2Y2, Canada. Offers digital multimedia (MFA); drawing (MFA); painting (MFA); photography (MFA); sculpture (MFA); video (MFA). *Degree requirements:* For master's, exhibit, oral exam. *Entrance requirements:* For master's, portfolio, BFA. Additional exam requirements/recommendations for international students: Required—TOEFL (minimum score 575 paper-based; 233 computer-based), IELTS (minimum score 7). Electronic applications accepted.

University of Washington, Graduate School, College of Arts and Sciences, School of Art, Division of Art, Seattle, WA 98195. Offers painting and drawing (MFA); photography (MFA). *Degree requirements:* For master's, thesis, exhibit. *Entrance requirements:* For master's, BFA or equivalent academic work in art, 20 slide portfolio. Additional exam requirements/recommendations for international students: Required—TOEFL. Electronic applications accepted.

University of Waterloo, Graduate Studies, Faculty of Arts, Department of Fine Arts, Waterloo, ON N2L 3G1, Canada. Offers studio art (MFA). *Degree requirements:* For master's, thesis exhibit. *Entrance requirements:* For master's, honors degree, minimum A- average, sample of work. Additional exam requirements/recommendations for international students: Required—TOEFL, TWE. Electronic applications accepted. *Faculty research:* Ceramic sculpture, computer imaging, painting, drawing, contemporary art theory.

University of Windsor, Faculty of Graduate Studies, Faculty of Arts and Social Sciences, School of Visual Arts, Windsor, ON N9B 3P4, Canada. Offers MFA. *Degree requirements:* For master's, thesis. *Entrance requirements:* For master's, minimum B average, portfolio. Additional exam requirements/recommendations for international students: Required—TOEFL (minimum score 560 paper-based; 220 computer-based). Electronic applications accepted.

University of Wisconsin–Madison, Graduate School, School of Education, Department of Art, Madison, WI 53706-1380. Offers art (MA, MFA); art education (MA). *Accreditation:* NASAD. Electronic applications accepted.

University of Wisconsin–Milwaukee, Graduate School, Peck School of the Arts, Department of Art, Milwaukee, WI 53201-0413. Offers art (MA, MFA); art education (MA, MFA, MS). Part-time programs available. *Faculty:* 21 full-time (14 women). *Students:* 20 full-time (12 women), 3 part-time (2 women); includes 1 minority (Asian American or Pacific Islander), 1 international. Average age 32. 52 applicants, 29% accepted, 12 enrolled. In 2008, 12 master's awarded. *Degree requirements:* For master's, comprehensive exam, thesis or alternative. *Entrance requirements:* For master's, portfolio. Additional exam requirements/recommendations for international students: Required—TOEFL (minimum score 550 paper-based; 79 iBT), IELTS (minimum score 6.5). *Application deadline:* For fall admission, 1/1 priority date for domestic students; for spring admission, 9/1 for domestic students. Applications are processed on a rolling basis. Application fee: $45 ($75 for international students). *Expenses:* Tuition, area resident: Full-time $7320; part-time $165 per credit. Tuition, state resident: full-time $7320; part-time $165 per credit. Tuition, nonresident: full-time $17,840; part-time $714 per credit. Tuition and fees vary according to campus/location, program and reciprocity agreements. *Financial support:* In 2008–09, 6 teaching assistantships were awarded; career-related internships or fieldwork and unspecified assistantships also available. Support available to part-time students. Financial award application deadline: 4/15. *Unit head:* Denis Sargent, Representative, 414-229-6053, E-mail: artgrado@uwm.edu. *Application contact:* General Information Contact, 414-229-4982, Fax: 414-229-6967, E-mail: gradschool@uwm.edu.

University of Wisconsin–River Falls, Outreach and Graduate Studies, College of Arts and Science, Program in Fine Arts, River Falls, WI 54022-5001. Offers MSE.

University of Wisconsin–Superior, Graduate Division, Department of Visual Arts, Superior, WI 54880-4500. Offers art education (MA); art history (MA); art therapy (MA); arts administration (MA); studio arts (MA). Part-time programs available. *Degree requirements:* For master's, comprehensive exam, exhibit. *Entrance requirements:* For master's, minimum GPA of 2.75, portfolio.

Utah State University, School of Graduate Studies, College of Humanities, Arts and Social Sciences, Department of Art, Logan, UT 84322. Offers MA, MFA. *Degree requirements:* For master's, thesis, exhibit. *Entrance requirements:* For master's, GRE General Test or MAT, minimum GPA of 3.0, slide portfolio of art. Additional exam requirements/recommendations for international students: Required—TOEFL. *Faculty research:* Painting, drawing, sculpture, ceramics, photography.

Virginia Commonwealth University, Graduate School, College of Humanities and Sciences, School of Mass Communications, Program in Media, Art, and Text, Richmond, VA 23284-9005. Offers PhD. *Entrance requirements:* For doctorate, GRE, MA, MAE, or MFA in appropriate field of study (English, art history, studio art, poetry, mass communications); 3 letters of recommendation.

Virginia Commonwealth University, Graduate School, School of the Arts, Richmond, VA 23284-9005. Offers art education (MAE); art history (MA, PhD), including architectural history (MA), art history, historical studies (MA); museum studies (MA); ceramics (MFA); fibers (MFA);

furniture design (MFA); glassworking (MFA); graphic design (MFA), including design/visual communications, interior environment, photography and film; jewelry/metalworking (MFA); kinetic imaging (MFA); music (MM), including education; painting (MFA); photography and film (MFA); printmaking (MFA); sculpture (MFA); theatre (MFA), including acting, costume design, directing, pedagogy, scene design/technical theater. Part-time programs available. *Entrance requirements:* For doctorate, GRE General Test.

Washington State University, Graduate School, College of Liberal Arts, Department of Fine Arts, Pullman, WA 99164. Offers ceramics (MFA); digital media (MFA); drawing (MFA); painting (MFA); photography (MFA); print making (MFA); sculpture (MFA). *Degree requirements:* For master's, comprehensive exam (for some programs), thesis, exhibit, oral exam. *Entrance requirements:* For master's, GRE, minimum GPA of 3.0, portfolio, 3 letters of recommendation. Additional exam requirements/recommendations for international students: Required—TOEFL (minimum score 550 paper-based; 213 computer-based). Electronic applications accepted. *Faculty research:* Polynesian art, museum representation, number theory.

Washington University in St. Louis, Sam Fox School of Design and Visual Arts, Graduate School of Art, St. Louis, MO 63130-4899. Offers MFA. *Accreditation:* NASAD. *Faculty:* 23 full-time (10 women). *Students:* 46 full-time (27 women); includes 2 minority (1 Asian American or Pacific Islander, 1 Hispanic American), 3 international. Average age 28. 84 applicants, 48% accepted, 19 enrolled. In 2008, 13 master's awarded. *Degree requirements:* For master's, thesis, exhibition. *Entrance requirements:* For master's, portfolio, artist statement, resumé, post-secondary transcripts. Additional exam requirements/recommendations for international students: Required—TOEFL (minimum score 550 paper-based; 213 computer-based; 79 iBT). *Application deadline:* For fall admission, 1/5 for domestic and international students. Application fee: $75. Electronic applications accepted. *Expenses:* Contact institution. *Financial support:* In 2008–09, 45 students received support, including research assistantships with partial tuition reimbursements available (averaging $4,000 per year), teaching assistantships with partial tuition reimbursements available (averaging $4,000 per year); fellowships with partial tuition reimbursements available, Federal Work-Study, institutionally sponsored loans, scholarships/grants, health care benefits, and unspecified assistantships also available. Financial award application deadline: 1/5; financial award applicants required to submit FAFSA. *Faculty research:* New media, design, fine arts. *Unit head:* Dean Franklin 'Buzz' Spector, Dean, 314-935-6500, Fax: 314-935-4862, E-mail: spector@samfox.wustl.edu. *Application contact:* Prof. Patricia Olynyk, Director, Graduate School of Art, 314-935-5884, Fax: 314-935-8413, E-mail: olynyk@samfox.wustl.edu.

Wayne State University, College of Fine, Performing and Communication Arts, Department of Art and Art History, Program in Art, Detroit, MI 48202. Offers MA, MFA. *Degree requirements:* For master's, thesis (MFA). *Entrance requirements:* Additional exam requirements/recommendations for international students: Required—TOEFL (minimum score 550 paper-based; 213 computer-based); Recommended—TWE (minimum score 6). Electronic applications accepted. *Faculty research:* Painting, drawing, computer art.

Webster University, Leigh Gerdine College of Fine Arts, Department of Art, St. Louis, MO 63119-3194. Offers art (MA); arts management and leadership (MFA). *Degree requirements:* For master's, thesis. *Entrance requirements:* For master's, BA or BFA in related field, interview, portfolio.

Western Carolina University, Graduate School, College of Fine and Performing Arts, Cullowhee, NC 28723. Offers MFA, MM. Part-time programs available. *Degree requirements:* For master's, comprehensive exam, thesis optional. *Entrance requirements:* For master's, GRE, appropriate undergraduate, portfolio, letters of recommendation, letter of intent, live audition and/or interview. Additional exam requirements/recommendations for international students: Required—TOEFL (minimum score 550 paper-based; 270 computer-based; 79 iBT). *Faculty research:* Vernacular cultural studies and oral history, sound mixing for television, music technology.

Western Connecticut State University, Division of Graduate Studies, School of Visual and Performing Arts, Department of Art, Danbury, CT 06810-6885. Offers illustration (MFA); painting (MFA). Part-time programs available. *Faculty:* 4 full-time (1 woman). *Students:* 22 full-time (14 women); includes 4 minority (1 African American, 1 Asian American or Pacific Islander, 2 Hispanic Americans). Average age 31. 19 applicants, 79% accepted, 12 enrolled. In 2008, 7 master's awarded. *Degree requirements:* For master's, individual exhibition of artwork, review of student's progress prior to admission to final semester, completion of program in 6 years with minimum cumulative GPA of 3.0. *Entrance requirements:* For master's, portfolio review, minimum GPA of 2.5. *Application deadline:* For fall admission, 8/5 priority date for domestic students; for spring admission, 1/5 priority date for domestic students. Application fee: $50. *Expenses:* Tuition, state resident: full-time $4377; part-time $363 per credit. Tuition, nonresident: full-time $12,195; part-time $363 per credit. Required fees: $3574; $60 per credit. Part-time tuition and fees vary according to degree level and program. *Financial support:* Career-related internships or fieldwork available. Support available to part-time students. Financial award application deadline: 5/1; financial award applicants required to submit FAFSA. *Unit head:* Margaret Grimes, Graduate Co-Coordinator, 203-837-8402, Fax: 203-837-8945, E-mail: grimesm@wcsu.edu. *Application contact:* Chris Shankle, Associate Director of Graduate Studies, 203-837-9005, Fax: 203-837-8326, E-mail: shanklec@wcsu.edu.

West Texas A&M University, College of Fine Arts and Humanities, Department of Art, Communication, and Theater, Program in Art, Canyon, TX 79016-0001. Offers MA. Part-time programs available. *Degree requirements:* For master's, comprehensive exam, thesis optional, exhibit, portfolio review. *Entrance requirements:* For master's, GRE General Test, interview, portfolio. Additional exam requirements/recommendations for international students: Required—TOEFL (minimum score 550 paper-based). Electronic applications accepted. *Faculty research:* Ceramics, graphic design, woodblock prints, art history, aesthetics, glassblowing.

West Texas A&M University, College of Fine Arts and Humanities, Department of Art, Communication, and Theater, Program in Studio Art, Canyon, TX 79016-0001. Offers MFA. Part-time programs available. *Degree requirements:* For master's, comprehensive exam, thesis optional, exhibit, portfolio review, professional paper. *Entrance requirements:* For master's, GRE General Test, interview, portfolio. Additional exam requirements/recommendations for international students: Required—TOEFL (minimum score 550 paper-based). *Faculty research:* Ceramics, printmaking, graphic design, art history, aesthetics, glass blowing.

West Virginia University, College of Creative Arts, Division of Art and Design, Morgantown, WV 26506. Offers art education (MA); art history (MA); ceramics (MFA); graphic design (MFA); painting (MFA); printmaking (MFA); sculpture (MFA); studio art (MA). *Accreditation:* NASAD. *Degree requirements:* For master's, thesis, exhibit. *Entrance requirements:* For master's, minimum GPA of 2.75, portfolio. Additional exam requirements/recommendations for international students: Required—TOEFL. *Expenses:* Contact institution. *Faculty research:* Medieval art history.

Wichita State University, Graduate School, College of Fine Arts, School of Art and Design, Wichita, KS 67260. Offers art education (MA); studio arts (MFA). *Degree requirements:* For master's, project. *Entrance requirements:* For master's, GRE, BAE or BFA, portfolio. Additional exam requirements/recommendations for international students: Required—TOEFL. Electronic applications accepted.

William Paterson University of New Jersey, College of the Arts and Communication, Department of Art, Wayne, NJ 07470-8420. Offers art (MFA); visual arts (MA). *Accreditation:* NASAD. Part-time and evening/weekend programs available. *Degree requirements:* For master's, oral exam, portfolio review, thesis exhibit. *Entrance requirements:* For master's, minimum GPA of 2.75, portfolio, writing sample. Electronic applications accepted.

Winthrop University, College of Visual and Performing Arts, Department of Art, Rock Hill, SC 29733. Offers art (MFA); art administration (MA); art education (MA). *Accreditation:* NASAD.

Part-time programs available. *Degree requirements:* For master's, thesis, documented exhibit, oral exam. *Entrance requirements:* For master's, GRE General Test or MAT, PRAXIS (MA), minimum GPA of 3.0, resumé, slide portfolio, teaching certificate (MA). Electronic applications accepted.

Yale University, School of Art, New Haven, CT 06520. Offers graphic design (MFA); painting/printmaking (MFA); photography (MFA); sculpture (MFA). *Degree requirements:* For master's, thesis (for some programs). *Entrance requirements:* Additional exam requirements/recommendations for international students: Required—TOEFL (minimum score 550 paper-based; 250 computer-based; 100 iBT). *Expenses:* Contact institution.

York University, Faculty of Graduate Studies, Faculty of Fine Arts, Program in Visual Arts, Toronto, ON M3J 1P3, Canada. Offers MFA, PhD. *Degree requirements:* For master's, thesis. *Entrance requirements:* For master's, portfolio. Electronic applications accepted.

Art History

American University, College of Arts and Sciences, Department of Art, Program in Art History, Washington, DC 20016-8004. Offers MA. Part-time programs available. *Students:* 9 full-time (all women), 21 part-time (all women); includes 1 minority (Hispanic American), 1 international. Average age 27. 47 applicants, 51% accepted, 10 enrolled. In 2008, 7 master's awarded. *Degree requirements:* For master's, one foreign language, comprehensive exam, thesis or alternative. *Entrance requirements:* For master's, GRE, 24 hours of undergraduate course work in art history, portfolio. *Application deadline:* For fall admission, 2/1 priority date for domestic students; for spring admission, 10/1 for domestic students. Application fee: $80. *Expenses:* Tuition: Full-time $21,204; part-time $1178 per credit hour. Required fees: $380. Part-time tuition and fees vary according to course load and program. *Financial support:* Fellowships, research assistantships with tuition reimbursements, teaching assistantships with tuition reimbursements, career-related internships or fieldwork, Federal Work-Study, and institutionally sponsored loans available. Support available to part-time students. Financial award application deadline: 1/15. *Faculty research:* Renaissance, twentieth century, American, baroque, rococo. *Unit head:* Luis Silva, Chair, 202-885-1682, Fax: 202-885-1132. *Application contact:* Glenna K. Haynie, Administrative Coordinator, 202-885-1671.

American University of Puerto Rico, Program in Education, Bayamón, PR 00960-2037. Offers art history (M Ed); elementary education (4-6) (M Ed); elementary education (k-3) (M Ed); general science education (M Ed); physical education (k-12) (M Ed); special education at secondary level (transition) (M Ed). *Entrance requirements:* For master's, EXADEP or GRE or MAT, 2 letters of recommendation, minimum GPA of 2.5.

Bard College, Program in History of the Decorative Arts, Design and Culture, Annandale-on-Hudson, NY 12504. Offers MA, PhD. Part-time programs available. *Degree requirements:* For master's, one foreign language, thesis, internship; for doctorate, 2 foreign languages, thesis/dissertation, exams. *Entrance requirements:* For master's, GRE General Test, writing sample, 3 letters of recommendation; for doctorate, GRE General Test, master's thesis or equivalent, 3 letters of recommendation. Additional exam requirements/recommendations for international students: Required—TOEFL. *Expenses:* Contact institution.

Bard Graduate Center for Studies in the Decorative Arts, Design, and Culture, Program in History of the Decorative Arts, Design and Culture, New York, NY 10024-3602. Offers MA, PhD. Bard Graduate Center for Studies in the Decorative Arts is a unit of Bard College. Part-time programs available. *Degree requirements:* For master's, one foreign language, thesis, internship; for doctorate, 2 foreign languages, thesis/dissertation, exams. *Entrance requirements:* For master's, GRE General Test, writing sample, 3 letters of recommendation; for doctorate, GRE General Test, master's thesis or equivalent, 3 letters of recommendation. Additional exam requirements/recommendations for international students: Required—TOEFL. *Faculty research:* English craftsmen, ancient furniture, aesthetics and politics, Art Nouveau jewelry, European sculpture.

See Close-Up on page 203.

Boston University, Graduate School of Arts and Sciences, Department of Art History, Boston, MA 02215. Offers art history (MA, PhD); museum studies (Certificate). Terminal master's awarded for partial completion of doctoral program. *Degree requirements:* For master's, one foreign language, comprehensive exam, thesis; for doctorate, 2 foreign languages, comprehensive exam, thesis/dissertation. *Entrance requirements:* For master's and doctorate, GRE General Test, 3 letters of recommendation; for Certificate, GRE General Test. Additional exam requirements/recommendations for international students: Required—TOEFL (minimum score 600 paper-based; 250 computer-based).

Bowling Green State University, Graduate College, College of Arts and Sciences, School of Art, Bowling Green, OH 43403. Offers 2-D studio art (MA, MFA); 3-D studio art (MA, MFA); art education (MA); art history (MA); computer art (MA); design (MFA); digital arts (MFA); graphics (MFA). *Accreditation:* NASAD. Part-time programs available. *Degree requirements:* For master's, thesis or alternative, final exhibit (MFA). *Entrance requirements:* For master's, GRE General Test (MA), slide portfolio (15-20 slides). Additional exam requirements/recommendations for international students: Required—TOEFL. Electronic applications accepted. *Faculty research:* Computer animation and virtual reality, Spanish still-life painting from 1600 to 1800, art and psychotherapy, Japanese wood-firing techniques in ceramics, non-toxic printmaking technologies.

Brigham Young University, Graduate Studies, College of Fine Arts and Communications, Department of Visual Arts, Provo, UT 84602-6414. Offers art education (MA); art history (MA); studio art (MFA). Art education applications accepted biennially. *Accreditation:* NASAD. *Faculty:* 22 full-time (7 women), 2 part-time/adjunct (1 woman). *Students:* 32 full-time (23 women); includes 5 minority (all Asian Americans or Pacific Islanders). Average age 26. 19 applicants, 47% accepted, 7 enrolled. In 2008, 16 master's awarded. *Degree requirements:* For master's, 2 foreign languages, thesis (art history), selected project (MFA), curriculum project (art education). *Entrance requirements:* For master's, GRE (art history), minimum GPA of 3.0 (MFA, MA in art education), 3.3 (MA in art history), portfolio in slide form (MFA), writing samples (MA in art education, art history). Additional exam requirements/recommendations for international students: Required—TOEFL (minimum score 500 paper-based). *Application deadline:* For fall admission, 2/1 for domestic and international students. Application fee: $50. Electronic applications accepted. *Expenses:* Tuition: Full-time $5160; part-time $287 per credit hour. Tuition and fees vary according to program and student's religious affiliation. *Financial support:* In 2008–09, 30 students received support; research assistantships, teaching assistantships with partial tuition reimbursements available, scholarships/grants and tuition waivers (partial) available. Financial award application deadline: 2/1. *Faculty research:* Methodology-standards-assessment, Medieval architecture, classical/Islamic eighteenth- and nineteenth-century art, Netherlandish art, contemporary art. Total annual research expenditures: $83,932. *Unit head:* Prof. Linda A. Reynolds, Chair, 801-422-4429, Fax: 801-422-0695, E-mail: sullivan@byu.edu. *Application contact:* Sharon Lyn Heelis, Secretary, 801-422-4429, Fax: 801-422-0695, E-mail: sharon_heelis@byu.edu.

Brooklyn College of the City University of New York, Division of Graduate Studies, Department of Art, Program in Art History, Brooklyn, NY 11210-2889. Offers MA, PhD. The department offers courses at Brooklyn College that are creditable toward the CUNY doctoral degree (with permission of the executive officer of the doctoral program). Part-time programs available. *Students:* 12 full-time (11 women); includes 1 minority (African American), 1 international. Average age 31. 27 applicants, 74% accepted, 6 enrolled. In 2008, 4 master's awarded. *Degree requirements:* For master's, one foreign language, thesis or alternative, 2 publishable papers or thesis. *Entrance requirements:* For master's, bachelor's degree in art, minimum GPA of 3.0, portfolio, interview. Additional exam requirements/recommendations for international students: Required—TOEFL (minimum score 500 paper-based; 173 computer-based; 61 iBT). *Application deadline:* For fall admission, 3/1 priority date for domestic students, 2/1 priority date for international students; for spring admission, 11/1 priority date for domestic students, 10/1 priority date for international students. Applications are processed on a rolling basis. Application fee: $125. Electronic applications accepted. *Expenses:* Tuition, state resident: full-time $7360; part-time $310 per credit hour. Tuition, nonresident: full-time $13,800; part-time $575 per credit hour. *Financial support:* Career-related internships or fieldwork, Federal Work-Study, institutionally sponsored loans, and scholarships/grants available. Support available to part-time students. Financial award application deadline: 5/1; financial award applicants required to submit FAFSA. *Faculty research:* Contemporary art, ancient Near East art, northern baroque art, nineteenth-century French art, Italian Renaissance art. *Unit head:* Dr. Mona Hadler, Deputy Chairperson, 718-951-5181, E-mail: mhadler@brooklyn.cuny.edu. *Application contact:* Hernan Sierra, Graduate Admissions Coordinator, 718-951-4536, Fax: 718-951-4506, E-mail: grads@brooklyn.cuny.edu.

Brown University, Graduate School, Department of History of Art and Architecture, Providence, RI 02912. Offers MA, PhD. *Degree requirements:* For master's, 2 foreign languages, thesis; for doctorate, 2 foreign languages, thesis/dissertation, oral exam. *Entrance requirements:* For master's, GRE General Test; for doctorate, GRE General Test, MA with distinction.

Brown University, Graduate School, Joukowsky Institute for Archaeology and the Ancient World, Providence, RI 02912. Offers PhD. *Degree requirements:* For doctorate, thesis/dissertation.

Bryn Mawr College, Graduate School of Arts and Sciences, Department of History of Art, Bryn Mawr, PA 19010-2899. Offers MA, PhD. Part-time programs available. *Degree requirements:* For master's, 2 foreign languages, thesis; for doctorate, 2 foreign languages, comprehensive exam, thesis/dissertation. *Entrance requirements:* For master's and doctorate, GRE General Test. Additional exam requirements/recommendations for international students: Required—TOEFL (minimum score 600 paper-based; 250 computer-based).

See Close-Up on page 205.

California State University, Chico, Graduate School, College of Humanities and Fine Arts, Department of Art and Art History, Program in Art History, Chico, CA 95929-0722. Offers MA. *Accreditation:* NASAD. *Degree requirements:* For master's, thesis or alternative. *Entrance requirements:* For master's, Two letters of recommendation, Statement of Purpose, Department Application. Additional exam requirements/recommendations for international students: Required—TOEFL (minimum score 550 paper-based; 213 computer-based; 80 iBT), IELTS (minimum score 6.5).

California State University, Fullerton, Graduate Studies, College of the Arts, Department of Art, Fullerton, CA 92834-9480. Offers art (MA, MFA), including ceramics (MFA), crafts, creative photography (MFA), design (MFA), drawing and painting, printmaking (MFA), sculpture; art history (MA); design (MA). *Accreditation:* NASAD (one or more programs are accredited). Part-time programs available. *Students:* 56 full-time (33 women), 29 part-time (15 women); includes 24 minority (2 African Americans, 1 American Indian/Alaska Native, 11 Asian Americans or Pacific Islanders, 10 Hispanic Americans), 7 international. Average age 34. 74 applicants, 34% accepted, 20 enrolled. In 2008, 28 master's awarded. *Degree requirements:* For master's, project or thesis. *Entrance requirements:* For master's, minimum GPA of 2.5 in last 60 units of course work, portfolio. Application fee: $55. Tuition and fees vary according to degree level. *Financial support:* Career-related internships or fieldwork, Federal Work-Study, institutionally sponsored loans, and scholarships/grants available. Support available to part-time students. Financial award application deadline: 3/1. *Unit head:* Larry Johnson, Chair, 657-278-3471. *Application contact:* Al Ching, Adviser, 657-278-3471.

California State University, Long Beach, Graduate Studies, College of the Arts, Department of Art, Long Beach, CA 90840. Offers art education (MA); art history (MFA); studio art (MA). *Accreditation:* NASAD. Part-time programs available. *Faculty:* 36 full-time (17 women), 8 part-time/adjunct (5 women). *Students:* 76 full-time (47 women), 39 part-time (29 women); includes 28 minority (2 American Indian/Alaska Native, 10 Asian Americans or Pacific Islanders, 16 Hispanic Americans), 3 international. Average age 37. 183 applicants, 37% accepted, 43 enrolled. *Degree requirements:* For master's, thesis (for some programs). *Entrance requirements:* For master's, minimum GPA of 3.0 in last 60 hours. *Application deadline:* For fall admission, 7/1 for domestic students; for spring admission, 12/1 for domestic students. Applications are processed on a rolling basis. Application fee: $55. Electronic applications accepted. *Expenses:* Tuition, nonresident: full-time $11,160; part-time $372 per unit. Required fees: $4100; $1261 per semester. *Financial support:* Federal Work-Study, institutionally sponsored loans, and scholarships/grants available. Financial award application deadline: 3/2. *Unit head:* Prof. David A Hadlock, Chair, 562-985-4376, Fax: 562-985-1650, E-mail: dhadlock@csulb.edu. *Application contact:* Prof. Christopher Miles, Graduate Advisor, 562-985-4376, Fax: 562-985-1650, E-mail: cmiles@csulb.edu.

California State University, Los Angeles, Graduate Studies, College of Arts and Letters, Department of Art, Los Angeles, CA 90032-8530. Offers art (MA), including art education, art history, art therapy, ceramics, metals, and textiles, design (MA, MFA), painting, sculpture, and graphic arts, photography; fine arts (MFA), including crafts, design (MA, MFA), studio arts. *Accreditation:* NASAD (one or more programs are accredited). Part-time and evening/weekend programs available. *Faculty:* 16 full-time (6 women). *Students:* 23 full-time (14 women), 52 part-time (37 women); includes 29 minority (2 African Americans, 3 American Indian/Alaska Native, 7 Asian Americans or Pacific Islanders, 17 Hispanic Americans), 4 international. Average age 38. 30 applicants, 100% accepted, 14 enrolled. In 2008, 15 master's awarded. *Degree requirements:* For master's, comprehensive exam, project or thesis. *Entrance requirements:* For master's, portfolio. Additional exam requirements/recommendations for international students: Required—TOEFL (minimum score 500 paper-based; 173 computer-based). *Application deadline:* For fall admission, 6/15 for domestic students, 5/1 for international students; for winter admission, 11/1 for domestic students, 9/1 for international students; for spring admission, 2/1 for domestic students, 10/1 for international students. Applications are processed on a rolling basis. Application fee: $55. Electronic applications accepted. *Expenses:* Tuition, nonresident: part-time $226 per credit. Required fees: $4019. *Financial support:* Federal Work-Study available. Support available to part-time students. Financial award application deadline: 3/1. *Faculty research:* The artist and the book, conceptual art, ceramic processes, computer graphics, architectural graphics. *Unit head:* Dr. Robert Martin, Chair, 323-343-4010, Fax: 323-343-4045, E-mail: rjmartin@calstatela.edu. *Application contact:* Dr. Jose L. Galvan, Dean of Graduate Studies, 323-343-3820, Fax: 323-343-5653, E-mail: jgalvan@cslanet.calstatela.edu.

Art History

California State University, Northridge, Graduate Studies, College of Arts, Media, and Communication, Department of Art, Northridge, CA 91330. Offers art education (MA); art history (MA); studio art (MA, MFA); visual communications (MA, MFA). *Accreditation:* NASAD. *Faculty:* 22 full-time (12 women), 48 part-time/adjunct (18 women). *Students:* 24 full-time (16 women), 36 part-time (25 women); includes 4 Asian Americans or Pacific Islanders, 5 Hispanic Americans, 4 international. Average age 37. 73 applicants, 33% accepted, 17 enrolled. In 2008, 11 master's awarded. *Application deadline:* For fall admission, 11/30 for domestic students. Application fee: $55. *Financial support:* Application deadline: 3/1. *Unit head:* Prof. Edward Alfano, Chair, 818-677-2242, E-mail: art.dept@csun.edu. *Application contact:* Prof. Edward Alfano, Chair, 818-677-2242, E-mail: art.dept@csun.edu.

Caribbean University, Graduate School, Bayamón, PR 00960-0493. Offers administration and supervision (MA Ed); criminal justice (MA); curriculum and instruction (MA Ed), including elementary education, English education, history education, mathematics education, primary education, science education, Spanish education; education (PhD); gerontology (MSN); human resources (MBA); museology, archiving and art history (MA Ed); neonatal pediatrics (MSN); physical education (MA Ed); special education (MA Ed). *Entrance requirements:* For master's, interview, minimum GPA of 2.5.

Carleton University, Faculty of Graduate Studies, Faculty of Arts and Social Sciences, School for Studies in Art and Culture, Program in Art History: Art and its Institutions, Ottawa, ON K1S 5B6, Canada. Offers MA. *Degree requirements:* For master's, thesis. *Entrance requirements:* For master's, honors degree.

Case Western Reserve University, School of Graduate Studies, Department of Art History and Art, Program in Art History, Cleveland, OH 44106. Offers MA, PhD. MA, PhD (art history) offered jointly with the Cleveland Museum of Art. Part-time programs available. *Degree requirements:* For master's, one foreign language, thesis or alternative; for doctorate, 2 foreign languages, thesis/dissertation. *Entrance requirements:* For master's, GRE General Test, 2 samples of written work; for doctorate, GRE General Test, 3 samples of written work or MA thesis. Additional exam requirements/recommendations for international students: Required—TOEFL. Electronic applications accepted. *Faculty research:* Greek art and architecture, Northern baroque art, Italian baroque sculpture, abstract expressionism, Indian art, nineteenth-century French art, American and Contemporary art.

Christie's Education, Program in Modern Art, Connoisseurship, and the History of the Art Market, New York, NY 10036. Offers MA. *Degree requirements:* For master's, one foreign language, thesis. *Entrance requirements:* For master's, GRE, writing sample, 3 letters of recommendation, transcripts from all secondary schools and essay statement. Additional exam requirements/recommendations for international students: Required—TOEFL.

City College of the City University of New York, Graduate School, College of Liberal Arts and Science, Division of the Humanities and Arts, Department of Art, Concentrations in Art History and Museum Studies, New York, NY 10031-9198. Offers art history (MA); museum studies (MA). Part-time programs available. *Degree requirements:* For master's, one foreign language, thesis. *Entrance requirements:* For master's, GRE, minimum GPA of 3.0, portfolio, art history paper. Additional exam requirements/recommendations for international students: Required—TOEFL (minimum score 575 paper-based; 233 computer-based). *Faculty research:* Egyptian, Greek, medieval, Romanesque, and Ottoman art.

Cleveland State University, College of Graduate Studies, College of Liberal Arts and Social Sciences, Department of Art, Cleveland, OH 44115. Offers art education (M Ed); art history (MA). *Faculty:* 12 full-time (7 women), 9 part-time/adjunct (6 women). *Students:* 1 (woman) full-time, 4 part-time (all women). In 2008, 2 master's awarded. *Unit head:* Howie Smith, Chair, 212-523-7546, E-mail: art.chair@csuohio.edu. *Application contact:* Dr. Giannina Pianalto, Director of Graduate Admissions, 216-687-5599, Fax: 216-687-5400, E-mail: g.pianalto@csuohio.edu.

Cleveland State University, College of Graduate Studies, College of Liberal Arts and Social Sciences, Department of History, Cleveland, OH 44115. Offers art history (MA); history (MA); museum studies (MA). Part-time and evening/weekend programs available. *Faculty:* 18 full-time (6 women), 10 part-time/adjunct (2 women). *Students:* 14 full-time (8 women), 17 part-time (8 women); includes 4 minority (all African Americans). Average age 34. 39 applicants, 51% accepted, 14 enrolled. In 2008, 20 master's awarded. *Degree requirements:* For master's, thesis optional. *Entrance requirements:* For master's, minimum GPA of 3.0, bachelor's degree in history. Additional exam requirements/recommendations for international students: Required—TOEFL (minimum score 525 paper-based; 197 computer-based). *Application deadline:* For fall admission, 7/15 priority date for domestic students. Applications are processed on a rolling basis. Application fee: $30. Electronic applications accepted. *Financial support:* In 2008–09, 7 students received support, including research assistantships with full tuition reimbursements available (averaging $8,600 per year); career-related internships or fieldwork and unspecified assistantships also available. *Faculty research:* African Diaspora, social history and the city, early modern Europe, local history. *Unit head:* Dr. Elizabeth A. Lehfeldt, Chairperson, 216-687-3920, Fax: 216-687-5592, E-mail: e.lehfeldt@csuohio.edu. *Application contact:* Dr. Robert S. Shelton, Graduate Director, 216-687-3927, E-mail: r.s.shelton@csuohio.edu.

Columbia University, Graduate School of Arts and Sciences, Division of Humanities, Department of Art History and Archaeology, New York, NY 10027. Offers archaeology (M Phil, MA, PhD); art history and archaeology (M Phil, MA, PhD); modern art (MA). *Degree requirements:* For master's, 2 foreign languages, thesis; for doctorate, 3 foreign languages, thesis/dissertation. *Entrance requirements:* For master's and doctorate, GRE General Test. Additional exam requirements/recommendations for international students: Required—TOEFL.

Concordia University, School of Graduate Studies, Faculty of Fine Arts, Department of Art History, Montréal, QC H3G 1M8, Canada. Offers MA, PhD. *Degree requirements:* For master's, one foreign language, thesis. *Entrance requirements:* For master's, BFA or equivalent, minimum B average in major. *Faculty research:* Ancient and modern Canadian art and architecture, Canadian decorative arts, museum studies.

Cornell University, Graduate School, Graduate Fields of Arts and Sciences, Field of History of Art and Archaeology, Ithaca, NY 14853. Offers American art (PhD); ancient art and archaeology (PhD); Asian art (PhD); baroque art (PhD); medieval art (PhD); modern art (PhD); Renaissance art (PhD); Southeast Asian art (PhD); theory and criticism (PhD). *Faculty:* 17 full-time (11 women). *Students:* 23 full-time (19 women); includes 4 minority (1 African American, 2 Asian Americans or Pacific Islanders, 1 Hispanic American), 7 international. Average age 33. 76 applicants, 8% accepted, 4 enrolled. In 2008, 1 doctorate awarded. *Degree requirements:* For doctorate, one foreign language, comprehensive exam, thesis/dissertation, general exams in 3 areas. *Entrance requirements:* For doctorate, GRE General Test, sample of written work, 3 letters of recommendation. Additional exam requirements/recommendations for international students: Required—TOEFL (minimum score 550 paper-based; 213 computer-based; 77 iBT). *Application deadline:* For fall admission, 1/15 for domestic students. Application fee: $70. Electronic applications accepted. *Expenses:* Tuition: Full-time $29,500. Required fees: $70. Full-time tuition and fees vary according to degree level, program and student level. *Financial support:* In 2008–09, 17 students received support, including 10 fellowships with full tuition reimbursements available, 1 research assistantship with full tuition reimbursement available, 6 teaching assistantships with full tuition reimbursements available; institutionally sponsored loans, scholarships/grants, health care benefits, tuition waivers (full and partial), and unspecified assistantships also available. Financial award applicants required to submit FAFSA. *Unit head:* Director of Graduate Studies, 607-255-4905, Fax: 607-255-0566, E-mail: art_history@cornell.edu. *Application contact:* Graduate Field Assistant, 607-255-4905, Fax: 607-255-0566, E-mail: art_history@cornell.edu.

Duke University, Graduate School, Department of Art, Art History and Visual Studies, Durham, NC 27708-0764. Offers PhD. *Degree requirements:* For doctorate, thesis/dissertation. *Entrance requirements:* For doctorate, GRE General Test. Additional exam requirements/recommendations for international students: Required—TOEFL (minimum score 550 paper-based; 213 computer-based; 83 iBT), IELTS (minimum score 7). Electronic applications accepted.

East Tennessee State University, School of Graduate Studies, College of Arts and Sciences, Department of Art and Design, Johnson City, TN 37614. Offers art education (MA); art history (MA); studio art (MA, MFA). *Accreditation:* NASAD. *Degree requirements:* For master's, thesis, exhibit, oral exam (MFA). *Entrance requirements:* For master's, GRE General Test, portfolio (MFA), bachelor's degree in art, minimum GPA of 3.0. Additional exam requirements/recommendations for international students: Required—TOEFL (minimum score 550 paper-based; 213 computer-based). *Faculty research:* History of sculpture, art and senior citizens, encaustic paintings, digital media in art history.

Emory University, Graduate School of Arts and Sciences, Department of Art History, Atlanta, GA 30322-1100. Offers PhD. *Degree requirements:* For doctorate, 2 foreign languages, comprehensive exam, thesis/dissertation, oral exam. *Entrance requirements:* For doctorate, GRE General Test. Electronic applications accepted.

Fashion Institute of Technology, School of Graduate Studies, Program in Art Market: Principles and Practices, New York, NY 10001-5992. Offers MA. *Accreditation:* NASAD. *Degree requirements:* For master's, one foreign language, thesis, internship. *Entrance requirements:* For master's, GRE General Test, previous course work in art history, 4 semesters of a foreign language. Additional exam requirements/recommendations for international students: Required—TOEFL (minimum score 550 paper-based; 213 computer-based). Electronic applications accepted.

See Close-Up on page 117.

Florida State University, Graduate Studies, College of Visual Arts, Theatre and Dance, Department of Art History, Tallahassee, FL 32306. Offers art history (MA, PhD); museum studies (Certificate). *Accreditation:* NASAD. Part-time programs available. Terminal master's awarded for partial completion of doctoral program. *Degree requirements:* For master's, one foreign language, thesis (for some programs), review; for doctorate, 2 foreign languages, comprehensive exam, thesis/dissertation, review. *Entrance requirements:* For master's, GRE General Test, minimum GPA of 3.0; for doctorate, GRE General Test, minimum GPA of 3.5. Additional exam requirements/recommendations for international students: Required—TOEFL. Electronic applications accepted. *Faculty research:* Asian art; modern art and critical theory; non-Western art; medieval, renaissance and baroque art; Pre-Colombian.

George Mason University, College of Humanities and Social Sciences, Department of History and Art History, Program in Art History, Fairfax, VA 22030. Offers MA. *Degree requirements:* For master's, comprehensive exam. *Entrance requirements:* For master's, GRE, resumé, 2 letters of recommendation.

The George Washington University, Columbian College of Arts and Sciences, Department of Fine Arts and Art History, Program in Art History, Washington, DC 20052. Offers art history (MA); museum training (MA). Part-time and evening/weekend programs available. *Faculty:* 4 full-time (1 woman), 2 part-time/adjunct (0 women). *Students:* 15 full-time (all women), 16 part-time (14 women); includes 4 minority (1 Asian American or Pacific Islander, 3 Hispanic Americans). Average age 28. 67 applicants, 46% accepted, 11 enrolled. In 2008, 10 master's awarded. *Degree requirements:* For master's, one foreign language, comprehensive exam, thesis or alternative. *Entrance requirements:* For master's, GRE General Test, bachelor's degree in field, minimum GPA of 3.0. Additional exam requirements/recommendations for international students: Required—TOEFL (minimum score 550 paper-based; 213 computer-based; 80 iBT). *Application deadline:* For fall admission, 3/1 priority date for domestic students, 1/15 priority date for international students; for spring admission, 10/1 priority date for domestic students, 9/1 priority date for international students. Applications are processed on a rolling basis. Application fee: $60. Electronic applications accepted. *Financial support:* In 2008–09, 3 students received support; fellowships, teaching assistantships, career-related internships or fieldwork and Federal Work-Study available. Financial award application deadline: 1/15. *Application contact:* Information Contact, 202-994-6085, Fax: 202-994-8657, E-mail: art@gwu.edu.

Georgia State University, College of Arts and Sciences, Ernest G. Welch School of Art and Design, Program in Art History, Atlanta, GA 30303-3083. Offers MA. *Accreditation:* NASAD. *Degree requirements:* For master's, one foreign language, comprehensive exam, thesis. *Entrance requirements:* For master's, GRE General Test, writing sample. Additional exam requirements/recommendations for international students: Required—TOEFL (minimum score 550 paper-based; 213 computer-based). Electronic applications accepted. *Faculty research:* Latin American art, contemporary art, Egypt/Near East art, African American art, 19th/20th century art.

Graduate School and University Center of the City University of New York, Graduate Studies, Program in Art History, New York, NY 10016-4039. Offers architecture (PhD); graphic arts (PhD); painting (PhD); photography (PhD); sculpture (PhD). *Degree requirements:* For doctorate, 2 foreign languages, thesis/dissertation. *Entrance requirements:* For doctorate, GRE General Test. Additional exam requirements/recommendations for international students: Required—TOEFL. Electronic applications accepted.

Graduate Theological Union, Graduate Programs, Berkeley, CA 94709-1212. Offers art and religion (MA, PhD); biblical languages (MA); biblical studies (Old and New Testament) (MA, PhD, Th D); Buddhist studies (MA); Christian spirituality (MA, PhD); cultural and historical studies of religions (MA, PhD); ethics and social theory (PhD); history (MA, PhD, Th D); homiletics (MA, PhD, Th D); interdisciplinary studies (PhD, Th D); Jewish studies (MA, PhD, Certificate); liturgical studies (MA, PhD, Th D); Near Eastern religions (PhD); Orthodox Christian studies (MA); Orthodox studies (Certificate); religion and psychology (MA, PhD); religion and society/ethics and social theory (MA); systematic and philosophical theology (MA, PhD, Th D); women's studies in religion (Certificate); MA/M Div. *Accreditation:* ATS. Terminal master's awarded for partial completion of doctoral program. *Degree requirements:* For master's, one foreign language, thesis; for doctorate, one foreign language, comprehensive exam, thesis/dissertation. *Entrance requirements:* For master's, GRE General Test; for doctorate, GRE General Test, MA or M Div. Additional exam requirements/recommendations for international students: Required—TOEFL. Electronic applications accepted.

Harvard University, Graduate School of Arts and Sciences, Department of History of Art and Architecture, Cambridge, MA 02138. Offers ancient art (PhD); ancient Near Eastern art (PhD); baroque art (PhD); Byzantine art (PhD); classical art (PhD); Indian art (PhD); Islamic art (PhD); Japanese and Chinese art (PhD); medieval art (PhD); modern art (PhD); Renaissance and modern architecture (PhD); Renaissance art (PhD). *Degree requirements:* For doctorate, variable foreign language requirement, thesis/dissertation, general exams; reading exams in French, German, and Italian. *Entrance requirements:* For doctorate, GRE General Test. Additional exam requirements/recommendations for international students: Required—TOEFL. *Expenses:* Tuition: Full-time $32,556. Required fees: $1426. Full-time tuition and fees vary according to program and student level.

Howard University, Graduate School, Division of Fine Arts, Department of Art, Program in Art History, Washington, DC 20059-0002. Offers art history (MA); history of art and visual culture (MA). *Accreditation:* NASAD. Part-time programs available. *Degree requirements:* For master's, comprehensive exam, thesis. *Entrance requirements:* For master's, GRE General Test, minimum GPA of 3.0, BA in art history or related field, portfolio.

Hunter College of the City University of New York, Graduate School, School of Arts and Sciences, Department of Art, Program in Art History, New York, NY 10021-5085. Offers MA. Part-time and evening/weekend programs available. *Faculty:* 7 full-time (5 women), 4 part-time/adjunct (1 woman). *Students:* 123 part-time (108 women); includes 10 minority (1 African American, 6 Asian Americans or Pacific Islanders, 3 Hispanic Americans). Average age 32. 99

applicants, 68% accepted, 39 enrolled. In 2008, 22 master's awarded. *Degree requirements:* For master's, one foreign language, comprehensive exam, thesis. *Entrance requirements:* For master's, GRE General Test, minimum 12 credits of course work in art history, reading knowledge of a foreign language (Italian, French or German), 2 letters of recommendation. Additional exam requirements/recommendations for international students: Required—TOEFL. *Application deadline:* For fall admission, 3/1 for domestic students; for spring admission, 10/1 for domestic students. Application fee: $125. *Financial support:* Teaching assistantships, career-related internships or fieldwork, Federal Work-Study, scholarships/grants, and tuition waivers (partial) available. Support available to part-time students. Financial award application deadline: 4/15. *Faculty research:* Islamic art, Renaissance and Baroque, Impressionism, critical theory, Modernism. *Unit head:* Dr. Richard Stapleford, Graduate Adviser, 212-650-5052, E-mail: grad.arthisotryadvisor@hunter.cuny.edu. *Application contact:* William Zlata, Director for Graduate Admissions, 212-772-4482, Fax: 212-650-3336, E-mail: admissions@hunter.cuny.edu.

Illinois State University, Graduate School, College of Fine Arts, School of Art, Normal, IL 61790-2200. Offers art history (MA, MS); ceramics (MFA, MS); drawing (MFA, MS); fibers (MFA, MS); glass (MFA, MS); graphic design (MFA, MS); metals (MFA, MS); painting (MFA, MS); photography (MFA, MS); printmaking (MFA, MS); sculpture (MFA, MS). *Accreditation:* NASAD (one or more programs are accredited). *Degree requirements:* For master's, thesis or alternative, internship. *Entrance requirements:* For master's, portfolio, sample of scholarly writing. *Faculty research:* General operations support: Normal Editions Workshop for FY2007.

Indiana University Bloomington, University Graduate School, College of Arts and Sciences, Henry Radford Hope School of Fine Arts, Department of the History of Art, Bloomington, IN 47405-7000. Offers MA, PhD. *Accreditation:* NASAD. *Faculty:* 11 full-time (7 women), 1 (woman) part-time/adjunct. *Students:* 51 full-time (43 women), 11 part-time (9 women); includes 1 minority (African American), 5 international. Average age 31. 73 applicants, 58% accepted, 17 enrolled. In 2008, 6 master's, 5 doctorates awarded. Terminal master's awarded for partial completion of doctoral program. *Degree requirements:* For master's, one foreign language, thesis; for doctorate, 2 foreign languages, comprehensive exam, thesis/dissertation. *Entrance requirements:* For master's, GRE, transcript, writing sample, 3 letters of recommendation; for doctorate, GRE, transcript, writing samples, 3 letters of recommendation. Additional exam requirements/recommendations for international students: Required—TOEFL (minimum score 550 paper-based; 213 computer-based). *Application deadline:* For fall admission, 10/15 for domestic students; for winter admission, 12/1 for international students; for spring admission, 1/15 for domestic students. Application fee: $50 ($60 for international students). Electronic applications accepted. *Expenses:* Tuition, area resident: Part-time $291.97 per credit hour. Tuition, state resident: part-time $291.97 per credit hour. Tuition, nonresident: part-time $850.33 per credit hour. Required fees: $110 per semester. Tuition and fees vary according to course load and program. *Financial support:* Fellowships with full tuition reimbursements, research assistantships with full tuition reimbursements, teaching assistantships with tuition reimbursements, career-related internships or fieldwork and Federal Work-Study available. Financial award application deadline: 2/15. *Faculty research:* Art and social history, consumer culture, feminist art and theory, classical revivals. *Unit head:* Patrick McNaughton, Chair, 812-855-4924, Fax: 812-855-7498, E-mail: mcnaught@indiana.edu. *Application contact:* Fenella Jean Alice Flinn, Administrative Assistant, 812-855-9556, Fax: 812-855-7498, E-mail: fflinn@indiana.edu.

James Madison University, The Graduate School, College of Visual and Performing Arts, School of Art and Art History, Harrisonburg, VA 22807. Offers art education (MA); art history (MA); ceramics (MFA); drawing/painting (MFA); metal/jewelry (MFA); photography (MFA); printmaking (MFA); sculpture (MFA); studio art (MA); weaving/fibers (MFA). *Accreditation:* NASAD. Part-time programs available. *Faculty:* 13 full-time (8 women). *Students:* 7 full-time (5 women), 1 part-time (0 women); includes 2 minority (1 African American, 1 Asian American or Pacific Islander). Average age 27. In 2008, 3 master's awarded. *Degree requirements:* For master's, thesis (for some programs). *Entrance requirements:* For master's, GRE General Test, language exam in French or German, portfolio, 3 letters of recommendation, research paper. Additional exam requirements/recommendations for international students: Required—TOEFL. *Application deadline:* For fall admission, 2/15 priority date for domestic students, 2/15 for international students; for spring admission, 10/15 priority date for domestic students, 10/15 for international students. Applications are processed on a rolling basis. Application fee: $55. Electronic applications accepted. *Expenses:* Tuition, area resident: Full-time $7008; part-time $292 per credit hour. Tuition, state resident: full-time $7008; part-time $292 per credit hour. Tuition, nonresident: full-time $20,352; part-time $848 per credit hour. *Financial support:* In 2008–09, 8 students received support, including 3 teaching assistantships with full tuition reimbursements available (averaging $8,664 per year); Federal Work-Study and 3 graduate assistantships ($7,382) also available. Financial award application deadline: 3/1; financial award applicants required to submit FAFSA. *Unit head:* Leslie M. Bellavance, Academic Unit Head, 540-568-6216. *Application contact:* Lynette M. Bible, Director of Graduate Admissions, 540-568-6395, Fax: 540-568-7860, E-mail: biblelm@jmu.edu.

The Johns Hopkins University, Zanvyl Krieger School of Arts and Sciences, Department of History of Art, Baltimore, MD 21218-2699. Offers MA, PhD. Terminal master's awarded for partial completion of doctoral program. *Degree requirements:* For master's, 2 foreign languages; for doctorate, 2 foreign languages, thesis/dissertation. *Entrance requirements:* For master's and doctorate, GRE General Test. Additional exam requirements/recommendations for international students: Required—TOEFL (minimum score 600 paper-based; 250 computer-based). Electronic applications accepted. *Faculty research:* Modern art, Renaissance art, Medieval art, Roman art.

Kent State University, College of the Arts, School of Art, Kent, OH 44242-0001. Offers art education (MA); art history (MA); crafts (MA, MFA), including ceramics (MA), glass, jewelry/metals, textiles/art; fine art (MA, MFA), including drawing/painting, printmaking, sculpture. *Accreditation:* NASAD (one or more programs are accredited). *Degree requirements:* For master's, one foreign language, thesis. *Entrance requirements:* For master's, undergraduate degree in proposed area of study (for fine arts and crafts programs); minimum overall GPA of 2.75 (3.0 for art major); 3 letters of recommendation; portfolio (15-20 slides for MA, 20-25 for MFA), brief autobiographical statement (MFA). Additional exam requirements/recommendations for international students: Required—TOEFL. Electronic applications accepted.

Lamar University, College of Graduate Studies, College of Fine Arts and Communication, Department of Art, Beaumont, TX 77710. Offers art history (MA); photography (MA); studio art (MA); visual design (MA). Part-time and evening/weekend programs available. *Faculty:* 7 full-time (3 women). *Students:* 1 (woman) full-time. Average age 45. 2 applicants, 0% accepted. In 2008, 2 master's awarded. *Degree requirements:* For master's, thesis. *Entrance requirements:* For master's, GRE General Test, minimum GPA of 2.5 in last 60 hours of undergraduate course work. Additional exam requirements/recommendations for international students: Required—TOEFL. *Application deadline:* For fall admission, 8/1 priority date for domestic students; for spring admission, 12/1 for domestic students. Applications are processed on a rolling basis. Application fee: $25 ($50 for international students). *Expenses:* Tuition, state resident: full-time $5000; part-time $195 per credit. Tuition, nonresident: full-time $12,376; part-time $476 per credit. Required fees: $1570. *Financial support:* Fellowships, career-related internships or fieldwork, Federal Work-Study, and scholarships/grants available. Financial award application deadline: 4/1. *Faculty research:* Nineteenth century academic paintings, metal casting, pigment color stability, computer-modified photography, manipulated photography. *Unit head:* Donna M. Meeks, Chair, 409-880-8141, Fax: 409-880-1799, E-mail: meeksdm@lub002.lamar.edu. *Application contact:* Debbie Piper, Coordinator of Graduate Admissions, 409-880-8356, Fax: 409-880-8414, E-mail: gradmissions@hal.lamar.edu.

Louisiana State University and Agricultural and Mechanical College, Graduate School, College of Art and Design, School of Art, Program in Art History, Baton Rouge, LA 70803. Offers MA. *Accreditation:* NASAD. *Degree requirements:* For master's, one foreign language, thesis. *Entrance requirements:* For master's, GRE General Test, minimum GPA of 3.0. Additional exam requirements/recommendations for international students: Required—TOEFL (minimum score 550 paper-based; 213 computer-based; 79 iBT). Electronic applications accepted. *Faculty research:* Liturgical art, Greco-Roman art, Renaissance prints, American twentieth century art, performance art.

Massachusetts Institute of Technology, School of Architecture and Planning, Department of Architecture, Cambridge, MA 02139-4307. Offers architecture (M Arch, PhD), including building technology (PhD), design and computation (PhD), history and theory of architecture (PhD), history and theory of art (PhD); architecture studies (SM Arch S); visual studies (SM Vis S, SMBT); M Arch/MCP; M Arch/SMRED; SM Arch S/MCP; SM Arch S/SMRED. *Degree requirements:* For master's, thesis; for doctorate, comprehensive exam, thesis/dissertation. *Entrance requirements:* For master's, GRE General Test (for some programs), portfolio (for some programs); for doctorate, GRE General Test (for some programs). Additional exam requirements/recommendations for international students: Required—TOEFL. Electronic applications accepted.

McGill University, Faculty of Graduate and Postdoctoral Studies, Faculty of Arts, Department of Art History and Communication Studies, Montréal, QC H3A 2T5, Canada. Offers MA, PhD.

Montclair State University, The Office of Graduate Admissions and Support Services, School of the Arts, Department of Art and Design, Montclair, NJ 07043-1624. Offers art education (MA, Certificate); art history (MA); studio arts (MA, MFA). *Accreditation:* NASAD (one or more programs are accredited). Part-time and evening/weekend programs available. *Faculty:* 27 full-time (12 women), 68 part-time/adjunct (36 women). *Students:* 28 full-time (18 women), 35 part-time (30 women); includes 6 minority (3 African Americans, 2 Asian Americans or Pacific Islanders, 1 Hispanic American), 5 international. Average age 34. 32 applicants, 69% accepted, 16 enrolled. In 2008, 22 master's awarded. *Degree requirements:* For master's, project. *Entrance requirements:* For master's, GRE General Test or MAT (MA), portfolio, undergraduate degree in fine arts or equivalent, 2 letters of recommendation, teaching certificate (art education). Additional exam requirements/recommendations for international students: Required—TOEFL (minimum score 83 computer-based). *Application deadline:* For fall admission, 2/1 for domestic and international students. Applications are processed on a rolling basis. Application fee: $60. Electronic applications accepted. *Financial support:* In 2008–09, 4 research assistantships with full tuition reimbursements (averaging $7,000 per year) were awarded; Federal Work-Study, scholarships/grants, and unspecified assistantships also available. Support available to part-time students. Financial award application deadline: 3/1; financial award applicants required to submit FAFSA. *Unit head:* Dr. John Luttropp, Chairperson, 973-655-7295. *Application contact:* Dr. Dorothy Heard, Adviser, 973-655-7295, E-mail: heardd@mail.montclair.edu.

New Mexico State University, Graduate School, College of Arts and Sciences, Department of Art, Las Cruces, NM 88003-8001. Offers art history (MA); ceramics (MA, MFA); design (MA, MFA); drawing (MFA); metals (MA, MFA); painting (MFA); photography (MFA); printmaking (MA, MFA); sculpture (MA, MFA). *Faculty:* 12 full-time (7 women), 2 part-time/adjunct (1 woman). *Students:* 31 full-time (14 women), 3 part-time (all women); includes 8 minority (1 American Indian/Alaska Native, 7 Hispanic Americans), 1 international. Average age 33. 30 applicants, 40% accepted, 9 enrolled. In 2008, 7 master's awarded. *Degree requirements:* For master's, comprehensive exam (for some programs), thesis, thesis exhibit. *Entrance requirements:* For master's, portfolio, 10-page paper (art history). *Application deadline:* For fall admission, 2/15 for domestic students; for winter admission, 10/15 for domestic students; for spring admission, 7/15 for domestic students. Application fee: $30 ($50 for international students). Electronic applications accepted. *Expenses:* Tuition, area resident: Full-time $3890; part-time $212.85 per credit. Tuition, state resident: full-time $3890; part-time $212.85 per credit. Tuition, nonresident: full-time $13,916; part-time $630.55 per credit. Required fees: $1218; $609 per semester. *Financial support:* In 2008–09, 33 students received support, including 29 teaching assistantships (averaging $9,807 per year); research assistantships, Federal Work-Study and health care benefits also available. Support available to part-time students. Financial award application deadline: 3/1; financial award applicants required to submit FAFSA. *Faculty research:* Painting, graphic design, sculpture, printmaking, drawing, ceramics, photo, jewelry. *Unit head:* Spencer D. Fidler, Head, 575-646-1705, Fax: 575-646-8036, E-mail: sfidler@nmsu.edu. *Application contact:* Elena Luna, Coordinator, 575-646-3498, Fax: 575-646-7721, E-mail: rosluna@nmsu.edu.

New York University, Graduate School of Arts and Science, Institute of Fine Arts, Program in Art History and Archaeology, New York, NY 10012-1019. Offers architectural studies (PhD); art history and archaeology (MA, PhD); classical art and archaeology (PhD); curatorial studies (PhD); East and South Asian art (PhD); Near Eastern art and archaeology (PhD); MA/Diploma; PhD/Certificate. Part-time programs available. Terminal master's awarded for partial completion of doctoral program. *Degree requirements:* For master's, 2 foreign languages, thesis or alternative, 2 qualifying papers; for doctorate, 2 foreign languages, thesis/dissertation. *Entrance requirements:* For master's, GRE General Test; for doctorate, GRE General Test, MA. Additional exam requirements/recommendations for international students: Required—TOEFL.

Northwestern University, The Graduate School, Judd A. and Marjorie Weinberg College of Arts and Sciences, Department of Art History, Evanston, IL 60208. Offers PhD. Admissions and degrees offered through The Graduate School. *Degree requirements:* For doctorate, 2 foreign languages, comprehensive exam, thesis/dissertation, major and minor field exercises. *Entrance requirements:* For doctorate, GRE General Test. Additional exam requirements/recommendations for international students: Required—TOEFL. Electronic applications accepted. *Faculty research:* Modern American and European art and architecture, prehistoric and ancient art, central Asian art, medieval manuscripts and early printed books, history of museums, art of Western Africa, theory of culture.

The Ohio State University, Graduate School, College of the Arts, Department of History of Art, Columbus, OH 43210. Offers MA, PhD. *Accreditation:* NASAD. *Degree requirements:* For master's, one foreign language, thesis optional; for doctorate, 2 foreign languages, thesis/dissertation. *Entrance requirements:* For master's and doctorate, GRE General Test. Additional exam requirements/recommendations for international students: Recommended—TOEFL (minimum score 600 paper-based; 250 computer-based). Electronic applications accepted. *Faculty research:* Western and Oriental art, African art and archaeology.

Ohio University, Graduate College, College of Fine Arts, School of Art, Athens, OH 45701-2979. Offers art history (MA); ceramics (MFA); graphic design (MFA); painting (MFA); photography (MFA); printmaking (MFA); sculpture (MFA). Part-time programs available. *Degree requirements:* For master's, thesis. *Entrance requirements:* For master's, portfolio. Additional exam requirements/recommendations for international students: Required—TOEFL. *Faculty research:* Vapor fired ceramics, video installation, art theory, digital photography, mixed and interdisciplinary media work.

Penn State University Park, Graduate School, College of Arts and Architecture, Department of Art History, State College, University Park, PA 16802-1503. Offers MA, PhD.

Pratt Institute, School of Art and Design, Program in Art History, Brooklyn, NY 11205-3899. Offers art history (MS); theory and criticism (MS); MS/MFA; MS/MS. *Accreditation:* NASAD. Part-time programs available. *Faculty:* 5 full-time (3 women), 12 part-time/adjunct (7 women). *Students:* 38 full-time (30 women), 4 part-time (3 women); includes 5 minority (3 African Americans, 1 Asian American or Pacific Islander, 1 Hispanic American). Average age 29. 87 applicants, 33% accepted, 11 enrolled. In 2008, 7 master's awarded. *Degree requirements:* For master's, one foreign language, thesis. *Entrance requirements:* For master's, GRE General Test, bachelor's degree, transcripts, letters of recommendation, statement, portfolio. Additional exam requirements/recommendations for international students: Required—TOEFL (minimum score 600 paper-based; 250 computer-based). *Application deadline:* For fall admission, 2/1 for domestic and international students; for spring admission, 10/1 for domestic and international students. Application fee: $50 ($90 for international students). Electronic applications accepted. *Expenses:* Tuition: Full-time $20,412; part-time $1134 per credit. Required fees: $1190; $1190 per year. *Financial support:* Career-related internships or fieldwork, Federal Work-Study,

Art History

Pratt Institute (continued)

institutionally sponsored loans, scholarships/grants, health care benefits, and unspecified assistantships available. Support available to part-time students. Financial award application deadline: 2/1; financial award applicants required to submit CSS PROFILE or FAFSA. *Faculty research:* Conservation techniques, women artists from previous centuries, art of 16th century Veneto, design history, 19th century Germany. *Unit head:* Edward DeCarbo, Chairperson, 718-636-3598, E-mail: edecarbo@pratt.edu. *Application contact:* Young Hah, Director of Graduate Admissions, 718-636-3683, Fax: 718-399-4242, E-mail: yhah@pratt.edu.

See Close-Up on page 219.

Purchase College, State University of New York, Division of Humanities, Purchase, NY 10577-1400. Offers art history (MA). *Accreditation:* NASAD. *Students:* 6 full-time (all women), 12 part-time (11 women); includes 1 minority (Asian American or Pacific Islander), 1 international. Average age 31. 17 applicants, 41% accepted, 3 enrolled. In 2008, 8 master's awarded. *Degree requirements:* For master's, one foreign language, thesis. *Entrance requirements:* For master's, BA or BFA, previous course work in art history. *Application deadline:* For fall admission, 3/15 for domestic students. Application fee: $50. *Expenses:* Tuition, area resident: Full-time $6900; part-time $288 per credit. Tuition, state resident: full-time $6900; part-time $288 per credit. Tuition, nonresident: full-time $10,920; part-time $455 per credit. Required fees: $1461; $0.85 per credit. One-time fee: $75 full-time. *Financial support:* In 2008–09, 1 fellowship (averaging $5,000 per year) was awarded; Federal Work-Study, scholarships/grants, and tuition waivers (partial) also available. Support available to part-time students. Financial award application deadline: 3/15; financial award applicants required to submit FAFSA. *Unit head:* Louise Yelin, Dean, Division of Humanities, 914-251-6000, E-mail: Louise.Yelin@purchase.edu. *Application contact:* Sabrina Johnston, Counselor, 914-251-6479, Fax: 914-251-6314, E-mail: admissn@purchase.edu.

Queens College of the City University of New York, Division of Graduate Studies, Arts and Humanities Division, Department of Art, Program in Art History, Flushing, NY 11367-1597. Offers MA. Part-time and evening/weekend programs available. *Degree requirements:* For master's, 2 foreign languages, thesis, qualifying exam. *Entrance requirements:* For master's, minimum GPA of 3.0. Additional exam requirements/recommendations for international students: Required—TOEFL.

Richmond, The American International University in London, Program in Art History, Richmond, United Kingdom. Offers MA. Part-time programs available. *Faculty:* 1 full-time (0 women), 6 part-time/adjunct (3 women). *Students:* 10 full-time (9 women). Average age 24. 24 applicants, 83% accepted, 8 enrolled. In 2008, 8 master's awarded. *Degree requirements:* For master's, thesis. *Entrance requirements:* For master's, minimum GPA of 3.0. Additional exam requirements/recommendations for international students: Required—TOEFL, IELTS. *Application deadline:* For fall admission, 3/31 priority date for domestic and international students. Application fee: $50. Electronic applications accepted. *Expenses:* Contact institution. *Financial support:* Career-related internships or fieldwork, scholarships/grants, and tuition waivers (partial) available. Support available to part-time students. Financial award application deadline: 6/30; financial award applicants required to submit FAFSA. *Faculty research:* Archaeology of art and representation, contemporary paganisms, nineteenth century modernisms, American twentieth century art, sound media. *Unit head:* Dr. Robert Wallis, Associate Director, 44-208-332-9000, Fax: 44-208-332-1596, E-mail: ma@richmond.ac.uk. *Application contact:* Mark Kopenski, Vice President and Dean of Enrollment, 44-208-332-8252, Fax: 44-208-332-1596, E-mail: ma@richmond.ac.uk.

Rutgers, The State University of New Jersey, New Brunswick, Graduate School, Program in Art History, Piscataway, NJ 08854-8097. Offers art history (MA, PhD); curatorial studies (Certificate); historic preservation (Certificate). Part-time programs available. Terminal master's awarded for partial completion of doctoral program. *Degree requirements:* For master's, one foreign language, comprehensive exam; for doctorate, 2 foreign languages, comprehensive exam, thesis/dissertation. *Entrance requirements:* For master's and doctorate, GRE General Test, writing sample. Additional exam requirements/recommendations for international students: Required—TOEFL (minimum score 550 paper-based; 213 computer-based). Electronic applications accepted. *Faculty research:* Ancient and medieval art and architecture; Renaissance and Baroque art and architecture; modern and contemporary art and architecture; Italian studies; the arts of Asia, Africa, and the Americas.

San Diego State University, Graduate and Research Affairs, College of Professional Studies and Fine Arts, School of Art, Design and Art History, San Diego, CA 92182. Offers art history (MA); studio arts (MA, MFA), including applied design, environmental design, graphic design, interior design, painting and printmaking, sculpture. *Accreditation:* NASAD (one or more programs are accredited). *Degree requirements:* For master's, variable foreign language requirement, thesis. *Entrance requirements:* For master's, GRE General Test, bachelor's degree in related field, slide portfolio, typed slide information sheet, 2 letters of recommendation. Additional exam requirements/recommendations for international students: Required—TOEFL. Electronic applications accepted.

San Francisco Art Institute, Graduate Program, Department of History and Theory of Contemporary Art, San Francisco, CA 94133. Offers MA. *Entrance requirements:* Additional exam requirements/recommendations for international students: Required—TOEFL (minimum score 580 paper-based; 237 computer-based).

San Francisco State University, Division of Graduate Studies, College of Creative Arts, Department of Art, San Francisco, CA 94132-1722. Offers art (MFA); art history (MA). *Accreditation:* NASAD (one or more programs are accredited).

San Jose State University, Graduate Studies and Research, College of Humanities and the Arts, School of Art and Design, San Jose, CA 95192-0001. Offers art education (MA); art history (MA); digital media (MFA); digital media in art history and education (MA); photography (MFA); pictorial arts (MFA); spatial arts (MFA). *Accreditation:* NASAD (one or more programs are accredited). *Entrance requirements:* For master's, GRE. Electronic applications accepted.

Savannah College of Art and Design, Graduate School, Program in Art History, Savannah, GA 31402-3146. Offers MA, MFA. Part-time programs available. *Degree requirements:* For master's, one foreign language, comprehensive exam, thesis, internship. *Entrance requirements:* For master's, art history paper, interview. Additional exam requirements/recommendations for international students: Required—TOEFL (minimum score 550 paper-based; 213 computer-based). Electronic applications accepted. *Expenses:* Tuition: Full-time $28,215; part-time $3135 per course. One-time fee: $500. *Faculty research:* Contemporary art.

See Close-Up on page 223.

School of the Art Institute of Chicago, Graduate Division, Program in Modern Art History, Theory, and Criticism, Chicago, IL 60603-3103. Offers MA, Certificate. *Accreditation:* NASAD. *Entrance requirements:* For master's, GRE. Additional exam requirements/recommendations for international students: Required—TOEFL, IELTS.

See Close-Up on page 225.

Southern Methodist University, Meadows School of the Arts, Division of Art History, Dallas, TX 75275. Offers MA. Part-time and evening/weekend programs available. *Faculty:* 7 full-time (4 women), 2 part-time/adjunct (1 woman). *Students:* 12 full-time (11 women), 8 part-time (7 women); includes 4 minority (1 African American, 3 Hispanic Americans), 2 international. Average age 32. 22 applicants, 59% accepted, 7 enrolled. In 2008, 7 master's awarded. *Degree requirements:* For master's, one foreign language, thesis, translation exam. *Entrance requirements:* For master's, GRE, 12 upper-level hours in art history, sample research paper. Additional exam requirements/recommendations for international students: Required—TOEFL (minimum score 550 paper-based; 213 computer-based; 80 iBT). *Application deadline:* For fall admission, 2/15 priority date for domestic and international students; for spring admission, 11/1 for domestic and international students. Application fee: $75. *Financial support:* In 2008–09, 13 students received support, including 13 teaching assistantships (averaging $3,500 per year); scholarships/grants and unspecified assistantships also available. Financial award application deadline: 3/1; financial award applicants required to submit FAFSA. *Faculty research:* American art, nineteenth and twentieth-century art, classical and Byzantine art, Hispanic art, Mesoamerican art, Renaissance-Baroque. *Unit head:* Randall Griffin, Chair, 214-768-2615, E-mail: randallg@smu.edu. *Application contact:* Jean Cherry, Director of Graduate Admissions and Records, 214-768-3765, Fax: 214-768-3272, E-mail: jcherry@smu.edu.

State University of New York at Binghamton, Graduate School, School of Arts and Sciences, Department of Art History, Binghamton, NY 13902-6000. Offers MA, PhD. *Faculty:* 8 full-time (4 women), 2 part-time/adjunct (0 women). *Students:* 25 full-time (19 women), 14 part-time (10 women); includes 4 minority (2 Asian Americans or Pacific Islanders, 2 Hispanic Americans), 18 international. Average age 34. 28 applicants, 54% accepted, 7 enrolled. In 2008, 2 master's, 1 doctorate awarded. *Degree requirements:* For master's, one foreign language, comprehensive exam, thesis; for doctorate, 2 foreign languages, comprehensive exam, thesis/dissertation, oral exam. *Entrance requirements:* For master's and doctorate, GRE General Test, writing sample. Additional exam requirements/recommendations for international students: Required—TOEFL. *Application deadline:* For fall admission, 1/15 priority date for domestic and international students; for spring admission, 10/1 priority date for domestic and international students. Applications are processed on a rolling basis. Application fee: $60. Electronic applications accepted. *Expenses:* Tuition, area resident: Full-time $6900; part-time $288 per credit. Tuition, state resident: full-time $6900; part-time $288 per credit. Tuition, nonresident: full-time $10,920; part-time $455 per credit. Required fees: $1130. Part-time tuition and fees vary according to course load, program and student level. *Financial support:* In 2008–09, 18 students received support, including 3 fellowships with full tuition reimbursements available (averaging $14,500 per year), 1 research assistantship with full tuition reimbursement available (averaging $14,500 per year), 13 teaching assistantships with full tuition reimbursements available (averaging $14,500 per year); career-related internships or fieldwork, Federal Work-Study, institutionally sponsored loans, scholarships/grants, health care benefits, and unspecified assistantships also available. Financial award application deadline: 2/15; financial award applicants required to submit FAFSA. *Faculty research:* History of art and architecture. *Unit head:* Dr. John Tagg, Professor and Chair, 607-777-2112, Fax: 607-777-4466, E-mail: jtagg@binghamton.edu. *Application contact:* 607-777-2112, Fax: 607-777-4466.

Announcement: Advanced studies and research in history and theory of art and architecture, with distinctive commitment to new theoretical, cross-disciplinary, global, and comparative cultural analyses. Drawing on University interdisciplinary strengths, this very international program develops analytical, theoretical, and professional skills for scholars, curators, educators, and urban and planning professionals.

Stony Brook University, State University of New York, Graduate School, College of Arts and Sciences, Department of Art, Program in Art History and Criticism, Stony Brook, NY 11794. Offers MA, PhD. Part-time programs available. *Students:* 42 full-time (34 women), 4 part-time (2 women); includes 7 minority (2 African Americans, 1 American Indian/Alaska Native, 1 Asian American or Pacific Islander, 3 Hispanic Americans), 7 international. Average age 30. 67 applicants, 43% accepted. In 2008, 7 master's awarded. *Degree requirements:* For master's, comprehensive exam, thesis, reading knowledge of German or French; for doctorate, comprehensive exam, thesis/dissertation, qualifying paper, reading knowledge of German and French, qualifying examination. *Entrance requirements:* For master's, GRE General Test, minimum undergraduate GPA of 3.0; for doctorate, GRE General Test, minimum graduate GPA of 3.0. Additional exam requirements/recommendations for international students: Required—TOEFL (minimum score 550 paper-based; 213 computer-based), IELTS (minimum score 6.5). *Application deadline:* For fall admission, 1/15 for domestic students. Application fee: $60. *Expenses:* Tuition, area resident: Full-time $7880; part-time $328 per credit hour. Tuition, state resident: full-time $7880; part-time $328 per credit hour. Tuition, nonresident: full-time $13,250; part-time $552 per credit hour. Required fees: $848. *Unit head:* Dr. Joseph Monteyne, Director, 631-632-7264, E-mail: jmonteyne@notes.cc.sunysb.edu. *Application contact:* Dr. Michele Bogart, Director, 631-632-7270.

Sul Ross State University, School of Arts and Sciences, Department of Fine Arts and Communication, Alpine, TX 79832. Offers art education (M Ed); art history (M Ed); studio art (M Ed), including ceramics, design, drawing, jewelry, painting, printmaking, sculpture, weaving. Part-time programs available. *Degree requirements:* For master's, oral or written exam. *Entrance requirements:* For master's, GRE General Test, minimum GPA of 2.5 in last 60 hours of undergraduate work. *Faculty research:* Ceramic sculpture, watercolor, wood sculpture, rock art.

Syracuse University, Graduate School, College of Arts and Sciences, Program in Art History, Syracuse, NY 13244. Offers MA. *Degree requirements:* For master's, one foreign language, symposium presentation. *Entrance requirements:* For master's, GRE, research writing sample; second language. Additional exam requirements/recommendations for international students: Required—TOEFL.

Temple University, Graduate School, Tyler School of Art, Department of Art History, Philadelphia, PA 19122-6096. Offers MA, PhD. *Accreditation:* NASAD. Part-time programs available. Terminal master's awarded for partial completion of doctoral program. *Degree requirements:* For master's, 2 foreign languages, thesis, comprehensive slide exam; for doctorate, thesis/dissertation, qualifying exam. *Entrance requirements:* For master's, GRE General Test, minimum GPA of 3.0; for doctorate, MA in art history. Additional exam requirements/recommendations for international students: Required—TOEFL. Electronic applications accepted. *Faculty research:* Aegean, Greek, and Roman art; early Christian art; Medieval art and architecture; Renaissance and baroque painting, sculpture, and architecture; nineteenth and twentieth century painting and sculpture.

See Close-Up on page 229.

Texas A&M University–Commerce, Graduate School, College of Arts and Sciences, Department of Art, Commerce, TX 75429-3011. Offers art (MA, MS); art history (MA); fine arts (MFA); studio art (MA). Part-time programs available. *Degree requirements:* For master's, comprehensive exam, thesis (for some programs). *Entrance requirements:* For master's, GRE General Test. Electronic applications accepted. *Faculty research:* Use of different art media.

Texas Christian University, College of Fine Arts, Department of Art and Art History, Fort Worth, TX 76129. Offers art history (MA); studio art (MFA). Part-time programs available. *Degree requirements:* For master's, thesis, internship, foreign language exam. *Entrance requirements:* For master's, GRE General Test, writing sample. Additional exam requirements/recommendations for international students: Required—TOEFL. *Application deadline:* For fall admission, 3/15 for domestic students. Applications are processed on a rolling basis. Application fee: $0. *Expenses:* Tuition: Full-time $17,640. *Financial support:* Unspecified assistantships available. Financial award application deadline: 3/1. *Unit head:* Ron Watson, Chairperson, 817-257-7643, E-mail: r.watson@tcu.edu. *Application contact:* Dr. Joseph Butler, Associate Dean, College of Fine Arts, E-mail: j.butler@tcu.edu.

Tufts University, Graduate School of Arts and Sciences, Department of Art and Art History, Program in Art History, Medford, MA 02155. Offers MA. Part-time programs available. *Degree requirements:* For master's, one foreign language, thesis (for some programs). *Entrance requirements:* For master's, GRE General Test, previous course work in art history, writing sample. Additional exam requirements/recommendations for international students: Required—TOEFL (minimum score 550 paper-based; 213 computer-based; 80 iBT). Electronic applications accepted.

Tulane University, School of Liberal Arts, Department of Art, Program in Art History, New Orleans, LA 70118-5669. Offers MA. *Degree requirements:* For master's, one foreign language, thesis. *Entrance requirements:* For master's, GRE General Test, minimum B average in undergraduate course work. Additional exam requirements/recommendations for international students: Required—TOEFL. Electronic applications accepted.

Université de Montréal, Faculty of Arts and Sciences, Department of Art History and Film Studies, Montréal, QC H3C 3J7, Canada. Offers art history (MA, PhD); film studies (MA, PhD). *Faculty:* 27 full-time (13 women), 5 part-time/adjunct (1 woman). *Students:* 73 full-time (40 women), 74 part-time (47 women). 90 applicants, 57% accepted, 44 enrolled. In 2008, 23 master's, 3 doctorates awarded. *Degree requirements:* For master's, thesis. *Application deadline:* For fall admission, 2/1 priority date for domestic students; for winter admission, 11/1 priority date for domestic students; for spring admission, 2/1 priority date for domestic students. Application fee: $100. Electronic applications accepted. *Financial support:* Research assistantships, teaching assistantships available. *Faculty research:* Western art from the Middle Ages, classic and modern theory, modern and contemporary art, Canadian art. *Unit head:* Christine Bernier, Director, 514-343-6184, Fax: 514-343-2393, E-mail: christine_bernier@umontreal.ca. *Application contact:* Johanne Lamoureux, Information Contact: Art History, 514-343-5713, E-mail: johanne.lamoureux.2@umontreal.ca.

Université du Québec à Montréal, Graduate Programs, Program in Art Studies, Montréal, QC H3C 3P8, Canada. Offers art history (PhD); art studies (MA); study and practices of the arts (PhD). Part-time programs available. *Degree requirements:* For master's, thesis; for doctorate, thesis/dissertation. *Entrance requirements:* For master's, appropriate bachelor's degree or equivalent, proficiency in French; for doctorate, appropriate master's degree or equivalent, proficiency in French.

Université Laval, Faculty of Letters, Department of History, Programs in Art History, Québec, QC G1K 7P4, Canada. Offers MA, PhD. Terminal master's awarded for partial completion of doctoral program. *Degree requirements:* For master's, thesis; for doctorate, comprehensive exam, thesis/dissertation. *Entrance requirements:* For master's, English test (comprehension of written English), knowledge of French; for doctorate, English test (comprehension of written English), knowledge of French and English, knowledge of a third language. Electronic applications accepted.

University at Buffalo, the State University of New York, Graduate School, College of Arts and Sciences, Department of Visual Studies, Program in Art History, Buffalo, NY 14260. Offers art history (MA); critical museum studies (Certificate). Part-time programs available. *Degree requirements:* For master's, one foreign language, thesis, field exam. *Entrance requirements:* Additional exam requirements/recommendations for international students: Required—TOEFL. Electronic applications accepted. *Faculty research:* Frank Lloyd Wright, non-Western art, Renaissance, Bronze Age Crete, American art.

The University of Alabama, Graduate School, College of Arts and Sciences, Department of Art, Tuscaloosa, AL 35487. Offers art history (MA); studio art (MA, MFA), including ceramics, painting, photography, printmaking, sculpture. *Accreditation:* NASAD. Part-time programs available. *Faculty:* 15 full-time (8 women). *Students:* 16 full-time (8 women), 4 part-time (all women), 1 international. Average age 31. 17 applicants, 41% accepted, 6 enrolled. In 2008, 9 master's awarded. *Degree requirements:* For master's, one foreign language, comprehensive exam (for some programs), thesis (for some programs), oral exam, thesis statement, exhibit (studio art), thesis (art history). *Entrance requirements:* For master's, GRE General Test or MAT (art history), minimum GPA of 3.0, BFA or equivalent (studio art). Additional exam requirements/recommendations for international students: Required—TOEFL (minimum score 550 paper-based; 213 computer-based). *Application deadline:* For fall admission, 3/15 for domestic and international students; for spring admission, 10/15 for domestic and international students. Applications are processed on a rolling basis. Application fee: $30. Electronic applications accepted. *Expenses:* Tuition, area resident: Full-time $6400. Tuition, state resident: full-time $6400. Tuition, nonresident: full-time $18,000. *Financial support:* In 2008–09, 2 fellowships with full tuition reimbursements (averaging $14,000 per year), 13 teaching assistantships with full and partial tuition reimbursements (averaging $9,206 per year) were awarded; career-related internships or fieldwork, institutionally sponsored loans, scholarships/grants, and unspecified assistantships also available. Financial award application deadline: 7/14. *Faculty research:* Nineteenth century American art history, Chinese art history, baroque art history, twentieth century art history, Asian art history. *Unit head:* William T. Dooley, Chairperson, 205-348-1890, Fax: 205-348-0287, E-mail: wtdooley@bama.ua.edu. *Application contact:* Craig R. Wedderspoon, Graduate Coordinator, 205-348-1898, Fax: 205-348-0287, E-mail: cwedders@bama.edu.

The University of Alabama at Birmingham, School of Arts and Humanities, Department of Art and Art History, Birmingham, AL 35294. Offers art history (MA). *Accreditation:* NASAD. *Degree requirements:* For master's, one foreign language, comprehensive exam, thesis optional. *Entrance requirements:* For master's, GRE General Test or MAT, minimum GPA of 2.75. Electronic applications accepted.

University of Alberta, Faculty of Graduate Studies and Research, Department of Art and Design, Edmonton, AB T6G 2E1, Canada. Offers drawing (MFA); history of art, design, and visual culture (MA); industrial design (M Des); painting (MFA); printmaking (MFA); sculpture (MFA); visual communication design (M Des). *Degree requirements:* For master's, thesis. *Entrance requirements:* For master's, portfolio (MFA and MDES). Additional exam requirements/recommendations for international students: Required—TOEFL (minimum score 550 paper-based; 213 computer-based).

The University of Arizona, Graduate College, College of Fine Arts, School of Art, Program in Art History, Tucson, AZ 85721. Offers art history (MA); history and theory of art (PhD). *Accreditation:* NASAD. Part-time programs available. Terminal master's awarded for partial completion of doctoral program. *Degree requirements:* For master's, one foreign language, thesis; for doctorate, 2 foreign languages, comprehensive exam, thesis/dissertation. *Entrance requirements:* For master's, GRE General Test, minimum GPA of 3.0, writing sample, 3 letters of recommendation, statement of purpose, resumé. Additional exam requirements/recommendations for international students: Required—TOEFL (minimum score 550 paper-based; 213 computer-based). *Faculty research:* American art, history of photography, Mexican art, contemporary African art.

University of Arkansas at Little Rock, Graduate School, College of Arts, Humanities, and Social Science, Department of Art, Little Rock, AR 72204-1099. Offers art education (MA); art history (MA); studio art (MA). *Accreditation:* NASAD. Part-time programs available. *Degree requirements:* For master's, 4 foreign languages, oral exam, oral defense of thesis or exhibit. *Entrance requirements:* For master's, portfolio review or term paper evaluation, minimum GPA of 2.7.

The University of British Columbia, Faculty of Arts and Faculty of Graduate Studies, Department of Art History, Visual Art, and Theory, Vancouver, BC V6T 1Z1, Canada. Offers art history (MA, PhD, Diploma); critical and curatorial studies (MA); visual art (MFA). Part-time programs available. *Degree requirements:* For master's, one foreign language, thesis, final exhibition (MFA, MA, CCST); for doctorate, 2 foreign languages, comprehensive exam, thesis/dissertation. *Entrance requirements:* For master's, bachelor's degree with minimum B+ average for MFA; for doctorate, master's degree with minimum A- average. Additional exam requirements/recommendations for international students: Required—TOEFL (minimum score 600 paper-based; 250 computer-based). Electronic applications accepted. *Faculty research:* Conceptual art, Asian art, indigenous North American art, post-second war art, eighteenth and nineteenth century art.

University of California, Berkeley, Graduate Division, College of Letters and Science, Department of History of Art, Berkeley, CA 94720-1500. Offers PhD. *Degree requirements:* For doctorate, 2 foreign languages, thesis/dissertation, qualifying exam. *Entrance requirements:* For doctorate, GRE General Test, minimum GPA of 3.0, 3 letters of recommendation. Additional exam requirements/recommendations for international students: Required—TOEFL. *Faculty research:* Modernism, Italian Renaissance art and architecture, Gothic art and architecture, women artists' representations of the body, the body in ancient Greece.

University of California, Davis, Graduate Studies, Program in Art History, Davis, CA 95616. Offers MA. *Degree requirements:* For master's, thesis. *Entrance requirements:* For master's, GRE, minimum GPA of 3.0, writing sample. Additional exam requirements/recommendations for international students: Required—TOEFL (minimum score 550 paper-based; 213 computer-based). Electronic applications accepted.

Announcement: Master of Arts in the history of art. Special emphasis on the art and architecture of the ancient Mediterranean world, early and modern China, early and modern Islamic world, early and modern Italy, and Europe and America from 1750 to present; critical theory; histories of photography, architecture and urban design, collecting, and museums. Excellent library, nearby museums. Interdisciplinary work encouraged. Applicants from other fields with a strong interest in art history welcome. Gateway degree for museum careers, community college teaching, and top PhD programs.

University of California, Irvine, Office of Graduate Studies, School of Humanities, Department of Art History, Irvine, CA 92697. Offers visual studies (MA, PhD). *Degree requirements:* For doctorate, thesis/dissertation. *Entrance requirements:* For master's, GRE, minimum GPA of 3.0; for doctorate, GRE General Test, writing sample. Additional exam requirements/recommendations for international students: Required—TOEFL (minimum score 550 paper-based; 213 computer-based). Electronic applications accepted. *Faculty research:* Interdisciplinary study and research in art history, critical theory, women's studies, cultural studies, film studies.

University of California, Los Angeles, Graduate Division, College of Letters and Science, Department of Art History, Los Angeles, CA 90095. Offers MA, PhD. *Students:* 64 full-time (54 women); includes 16 minority (2 African Americans, 11 Asian Americans or Pacific Islanders, 3 Hispanic Americans), 6 international. Average age 32. 100 applicants, 16% accepted, 7 enrolled. In 2008, 6 master's, 2 doctorates awarded. Terminal master's awarded for partial completion of doctoral program. *Degree requirements:* For master's, one foreign language, thesis; for doctorate, one foreign language, thesis/dissertation, oral and written qualifying exams. *Entrance requirements:* For master's, Degree objective must be Ph.D; for doctorate, GRE General Test, 2 samples of research writing or thesis, minimum undergraduate GPA of 3.0, 3 letters of recommendation. *Application deadline:* For fall admission, 11/30 for domestic students. Application fee: $60 ($80 for international students). Electronic applications accepted. *Expenses:* Tuition, nonresident: full-time $14,694. Required fees: $9669.50. Full-time tuition and fees vary according to course load, degree level, program and student level. *Financial support:* In 2008–09, 57 fellowships with full and partial tuition reimbursements, 13 research assistantships with full and partial tuition reimbursements, 28 teaching assistantships with full and partial tuition reimbursements were awarded; Federal Work-Study, scholarships/grants, health care benefits, tuition waivers (full and partial), and unspecified assistantships also available. Financial award application deadline: 3/1; financial award applicants required to submit FAFSA. *Unit head:* Dr. Dell Upton, Chair, 310-206-8370. *Application contact:* Departmental Office, 310-825-3480, E-mail: vjohnson@humnet.ucla.edu.

University of California, Riverside, Graduate Division, Department of Art History, Riverside, CA 92521-0102. Offers MA. Part-time programs available. *Faculty:* 8 full-time (4 women), 1 (woman) part-time/adjunct. *Students:* 14 full-time (11 women), 2 part-time (1 woman); includes 1 minority (Asian American or Pacific Islander), 1 international. Average age 32. 22 applicants, 50% accepted, 9 enrolled. In 2008, 7 master's awarded. *Degree requirements:* For master's, one foreign language, thesis. *Entrance requirements:* For master's, GRE General Test, sample of written work, minimum GPA of 3.2. Additional exam requirements/recommendations for international students: Required—TOEFL (minimum score 550 paper-based; 213 computer-based; 80 iBT). *Application deadline:* 1/5 for domestic and international students. Application fee: $60 ($75 for international students). Electronic applications accepted. *Expenses:* Tuition, nonresident: full-time $4898. Required fees: $10,362. *Financial support:* In 2008–09, 16 students received support, including fellowships with full and partial tuition reimbursements available (averaging $12,000 per year), teaching assistantships with full tuition reimbursements available (averaging $16,500 per year); research assistantships with partial tuition reimbursements available, career-related internships or fieldwork, institutionally sponsored loans, scholarships/grants, tuition waivers (full and partial), and readerships also available. Financial award application deadline: 1/5; financial award applicants required to submit FAFSA. *Faculty research:* Ancient, medieval, Renaissance, seventeenth and eighteenth century art; modern European art; contemporary art and theory; modern architecture and urbanism; history of photography. *Unit head:* Dr. Malcolm Baker, Chair, 951-827-4634, Fax: 951-827-2331, E-mail: arthist@ucr.edu. *Application contact:* Dr. Elizabeth Kotz, Graduate Advisor, 951-827-4634, Fax: 951-827-2331, E-mail: arthist@ucr.edu.

University of California, Santa Barbara, Graduate Division, College of Letters and Sciences, Division of Humanities and Fine Arts, Department of History of Art and Architecture, Santa Barbara, CA 93106-7080. Offers PhD, MA/PhD. *Faculty:* 18 full-time (8 women), 2 part-time/adjunct (1 woman). *Students:* 38 full-time (34 women). Average age 30. 71 applicants, 25% accepted, 8 enrolled. In 2008, 2 doctorates awarded. Terminal master's awarded for partial completion of doctoral program. *Degree requirements:* For doctorate, 2 foreign languages, comprehensive exam, thesis/dissertation. *Entrance requirements:* For doctorate, GRE, writing sample, 3 letters of recommendation, statement of purpose, personal achievements/contributions statement, resumé/curriculum vitae, transcripts for post-secondary institutions attended. Additional exam requirements/recommendations for international students: Required—TOEFL (paper: 550, computer: 213, IBT: 80) or IELTS (7). *Application deadline:* For fall admission, 12/15 priority date for domestic and international students. Application fee: $70 ($90 for international students). Electronic applications accepted. *Expenses:* Tuition, nonresident: full-time $25,149. Required fees: $10,143. Full-time tuition and fees vary according to campus/location, reciprocity agreements and student level. *Financial support:* In 2008–09, 36 students received support, including 23 fellowships with full and partial tuition reimbursements available (averaging $10,000 per year), 3 research assistantships with full and partial tuition reimbursements available (averaging $4,800 per year), 28 teaching assistantships with partial tuition reimbursements available (averaging $8,500 per year); career-related internships or fieldwork, Federal Work-Study, institutionally sponsored loans, scholarships/grants, health care benefits, and unspecified assistantships also available. Financial award application deadline: 3/2; financial award applicants required to submit FAFSA. *Faculty research:* Pre-Columbian art, Renaissance-Baroque art, architectural history, Japanese art, ancient-Medieval art. *Unit head:* Prof. Ulrich Keller, Chair, 805-893-8710. *Application contact:* Lesley Fredrickson, Graduate Program Administrator, 805-893-8710, Fax: 805-893-7117, E-mail: gd-arthist@arthistory.ucsb.edu.

University of Chicago, Division of the Humanities, Department of Art History, Chicago, IL 60637-1513. Offers AM, PhD. *Degree requirements:* For master's, variable foreign language requirement, thesis; for doctorate, variable foreign language requirement, thesis/dissertation. *Entrance requirements:* For master's and doctorate, GRE General Test.

University of Cincinnati, Graduate School, College of Design, Architecture, Art, and Planning, School of Art, Program in Art History, Cincinnati, OH 45221. Offers MA. *Accreditation:* NASAD. Part-time programs available. *Degree requirements:* For master's, one foreign language, comprehensive exam, thesis. Electronic applications accepted.

University of Colorado at Boulder, Graduate School, College of Arts and Sciences, Department of Art and Art History, Boulder, CO 80309. Offers art history (MA), including 19th century art, contemporary art criticism, early 20th century art, Russian and Soviet art; ceramics (MFA); drawing (MFA); painting (MFA); photography and media arts (MFA); printmaking (MFA); sculpture (MFA). *Degree requirements:* For master's, variable foreign language requirement, comprehensive exam, thesis (for some programs). *Entrance requirements:* For master's, GRE General Test, minimum undergraduate GPA of 3.0, portfolio. *Faculty research:* Drawing, painting, ceramics,

Art History

University of Colorado at Boulder (continued)
sculpture, photography and media arts, printmaking (MFA); history-Russian and Soviet art, Early 20th Century art, contemporary art criticism, 19th Century art (MA).

University of Connecticut, Graduate School, School of Fine Arts, Department of Art and Art History, Field of Art History, Storrs, CT 06269. Offers MA. *Accreditation:* NASAD. *Degree requirements:* For master's, comprehensive exam. *Entrance requirements:* Additional exam requirements/recommendations for international students: Required—TOEFL (minimum score 550 paper-based; 213 computer-based). Electronic applications accepted.

University of Delaware, College of Arts and Sciences, Department of Art History, Newark, DE 19716. Offers MA, PhD. Part-time programs available. *Degree requirements:* For master's, one foreign language, thesis; for doctorate, 2 foreign languages, comprehensive exam, thesis/dissertation. *Entrance requirements:* For master's and doctorate, GRE General Test, writing sample. Additional exam requirements/recommendations for international students: Required—TOEFL. Electronic applications accepted. *Faculty research:* Art of Europe and the United States, art theory, vernacular architecture, medieval manuscripts, African art and architecture.

University of Denver, Division of Arts, Humanities and Social Sciences, School of Art and Art History, Denver, CO 80208. Offers art history (MA); art history/museum studies (MA); electronic media arts and design (MFA). *Accreditation:* NASAD. Part-time programs available. *Faculty:* 15 full-time (11 women), 6 part-time/adjunct (2 women). *Students:* 15 full-time (12 women), 10 part-time (all women); includes 2 minority (1 Asian American or Pacific Islander, 1 Hispanic American), 1 international. Average age 29. In 2008, 11 master's awarded. *Degree requirements:* For master's, one foreign language, research paper. *Entrance requirements:* For master's, GRE. Additional exam requirements/recommendations for international students: Required—TOEFL. *Application deadline:* Applications are processed on a rolling basis. Application fee: $50. Electronic applications accepted. *Financial support:* Career-related internships or fieldwork, Federal Work-Study, institutionally sponsored loans, and scholarships/grants available. Support available to part-time students. Financial award application deadline: 3/1; financial award applicants required to submit FAFSA. *Faculty research:* Images of women in alchemical manuscripts and books, Giovanni Benedetto, Salvatore Castiglione. *Unit head:* Dr. Annette Stott, Director, 303-871-2846. *Application contact:* Dr. Annabeth Headrick, Graduate Advisor, 303-871-3574, E-mail: saah-interest@du.edu.

University of Florida, Graduate School, College of Fine Arts, School of Art and Art History, Gainesville, FL 32611. Offers art (MFA), including ceramics, creative photography, drawing, electronic intermedia, graphic design, painting, printmaking, sculpture; art education (MA); art history (MA, PhD); digital arts and sciences (MA); museology (museum studies) (MA). *Accreditation:* NASAD. *Degree requirements:* For master's, variable foreign language requirement, project or thesis (MFA). *Entrance requirements:* For master's, portfolio (MFA), writing sample (MA), GRE General Test or minimum GPA of 3.0. Additional exam requirements/recommendations for international students: Required—TOEFL (minimum score 550 paper-based; 213 computer-based). Electronic applications accepted. *Faculty research:* Studio production, art historical studies of style context.

University of Georgia, Graduate School, College of Arts and Sciences, Lamar Dodd School of Art, Program in Art History, Athens, GA 30602. Offers MA. *Accreditation:* NASAD. *Degree requirements:* For master's, one foreign language, thesis. *Entrance requirements:* For master's, GRE General Test. Electronic applications accepted.

University of Hawaii at Manoa, Graduate Division, Colleges of Arts and Sciences, College of Arts and Humanities, Department of Art and Art History, Program in Art History, Honolulu, HI 96822. Offers MA.

University of Illinois at Chicago, Graduate College, College of Architecture and Art, Department of Art History, Chicago, IL 60607-7128. Offers MA, PhD. Part-time and evening/weekend programs available. Terminal master's awarded for partial completion of doctoral program. *Degree requirements:* For master's, one foreign language, thesis or alternative; for doctorate, thesis/dissertation. *Entrance requirements:* For master's, GRE General Test, minimum GPA of 2.75, 3 letters of recommendation; for doctorate, GRE General Test, M.A. in art history or equivalent, minimum GPA of 3.0. Additional exam requirements/recommendations for international students: Required—TOEFL. Electronic applications accepted. *Faculty research:* Modern painting and sculpture, history of architecture, city planning and design, history of photography.

University of Illinois at Urbana–Champaign, Graduate College, College of Fine and Applied Arts, School of Art and Design, Program in Art History, Champaign, IL 61820. Offers MA, PhD. *Accreditation:* NASAD. *Students:* 30 full-time (24 women), 6 part-time (5 women); includes 2 minority (1 Asian American or Pacific Islander, 1 Hispanic American), 6 international. 35 applicants, 17% accepted, 5 enrolled. In 2008, 5 master's, 3 doctorates awarded. *Entrance requirements:* For master's and doctorate, minimum GPA of 3.0. Additional exam requirements/recommendations for international students: Required—TOEFL (minimum score 550 paper-based; 213 computer-based; 79 iBT). *Application deadline:* Applications are processed on a rolling basis. Application fee: $60 ($75 for international students). Electronic applications accepted. *Financial support:* Fellowships, research assistantships, teaching assistantships, tuition waivers (full and partial) available. *Unit head:* Lisa Rosenthal, Chair, 217-265-5236, Fax: 217-244-7688, E-mail: lrosenth@illinois.edu. *Application contact:* Marsha Biddle, Coordinator of Graduate Academic Affairs, 217-333-0642, Fax: 217-244-7688, E-mail: mbiddle@illinois.edu.

The University of Iowa, Graduate College, College of Liberal Arts and Sciences, School of Art and Art History, Program in Art History, Iowa City, IA 52242-1316. Offers MA, PhD. *Degree requirements:* For master's, one foreign language, thesis, exam; for doctorate, 2 foreign languages, comprehensive exam, thesis/dissertation, final exams. *Entrance requirements:* For master's, GRE General Test; for doctorate, GRE General Test, MA in art history. Additional exam requirements/recommendations for international students: Required—TOEFL (minimum score 550 paper-based; 213 computer-based). Electronic applications accepted. *Faculty research:* African, American, ancient, baroque, Medieval, and Renaissance art.

The University of Kansas, Graduate Studies, College of Liberal Arts and Sciences, History of Art Department, Lawrence, KS 66045. Offers MA, PhD. Part-time programs available. *Faculty:* 13. *Students:* 54 full-time (49 women), 6 part-time (4 women); includes 4 minority (all Asian Americans or Pacific Islanders), 14 international. Average age 34. 36 applicants, 56% accepted, 9 enrolled. In 2008, 9 master's, 3 doctorates awarded. Terminal master's awarded for partial completion of doctoral program. *Degree requirements:* For master's, one foreign language, comprehensive exam, thesis optional, 30 credit hours of coursework; for doctorate, 2 foreign languages, comprehensive exam, thesis/dissertation, 1 year full-time enrollment. *Entrance requirements:* For master's, GRE, minimum undergraduate GPA of 3.3, 18 credit hours of art history; for doctorate, GRE, MA in art history or related field. Additional exam requirements/recommendations for international students: Required—TOEFL, TWE (minimum score 4.5). *Application deadline:* For fall admission, 1/1 for domestic and international students; for spring admission, 10/15 for domestic and international students. Application fee: $45 ($55 for international students). Electronic applications accepted. *Expenses:* Tuition, area resident: Full-time $6122; part-time $255.10 per credit hour. Tuition, state resident: full-time $6122; part-time $255.10 per credit hour. Tuition, nonresident: full-time $14,629; part-time $609.55 per credit hour. Required fees: $847; $70.56 per credit hour. Tuition and fees vary according to course load and program. *Financial support:* Fellowships with full tuition reimbursements, research assistantships with partial tuition reimbursements, teaching assistantships with full tuition reimbursements, scholarships/grants and unspecified assistantships available. Financial award application deadline: 1/1. *Faculty research:* American art, history of photography, African art, Asian art, European art, modern art. *Unit head:* Linda Stone-Ferrier, Chair, 785-864-4713, Fax: 785-864-5091, E-mail: lsf@ku.edu. *Application contact:* Karen Brichoux, Graduate Admissions, 785-864-4713, Fax: 785-864-5091, E-mail: arthist@ku.edu.

University of Kentucky, Graduate School, College of Fine Arts, Program in Art History, Lexington, KY 40506-0032. Offers MA. *Degree requirements:* For master's, 2 foreign languages, comprehensive exam, thesis. *Entrance requirements:* For master's, GRE General Test, minimum undergraduate GPA of 2.75. Additional exam requirements/recommendations for international students: Required—TOEFL (minimum score 550 paper-based; 213 computer-based). Electronic applications accepted. *Faculty research:* Northern European prints and drawings, nineteenth century French painting and drawing, Roman sarcophagus sculpture, manuscript illumination, history and theory of photography.

University of Louisville, Graduate School, College of Arts and Sciences, Department of Fine Arts, Program in Art History, Louisville, KY 40292-0001. Offers MA, PhD. *Students:* 8 full-time (7 women), 8 part-time (5 women); includes 2 African Americans, 1 international. Average age 43. In 2008, 1 doctorate awarded. *Degree requirements:* For master's, thesis; for doctorate, thesis/dissertation. *Entrance requirements:* For master's and doctorate, GRE General Test. *Application deadline:* Applications are processed on a rolling basis. Application fee: $50. *Financial support:* Teaching assistantships available. *Unit head:* Dr. James T. Grubola, Chair, 502-852-0759, Fax: 502-852-6791, E-mail: grubola@louisville.edu. *Application contact:* Libby Leggett, Director, Graduate Admissions, 502-852-3101, Fax: 502-852-6536, E-mail: gradadm@louisville.edu.

University of Maryland, College Park, Graduate Studies, College of Arts and Humanities, Department of Art History and Archaeology, College Park, MD 20742. Offers art history (MA, PhD). *Degree requirements:* For master's, one foreign language, thesis, oral exam; for doctorate, 2 foreign languages, thesis/dissertation, oral exam. *Entrance requirements:* For master's, GRE General Test, minimum GPA of 3.0, writing sample, 3 letters of recommendation. Additional exam requirements/recommendations for international students: Required—TOEFL. Electronic applications accepted. *Faculty research:* Western, African, pre-Columbian, American, and East Asian art.

University of Massachusetts Amherst, Graduate School, College of Humanities and Fine Arts, Department of Art, Program in Art History, Amherst, MA 01003. Offers MA. Part-time programs available. *Degree requirements:* For master's, thesis or alternative. *Entrance requirements:* For master's, GRE General Test, 7-20 page writing sample. Additional exam requirements/recommendations for international students: Required—TOEFL (minimum score 550 paper-based; 213 computer-based; 79 iBT), IELTS (minimum score 6.5). Electronic applications accepted. *Expenses:* Tuition, area resident: Full-time $2640. Tuition, nonresident: full-time $9936. One-time fee: $332 full-time. Tuition and fees vary according to course load.

University of Memphis, Graduate School, College of Communication and Fine Arts, Department of Art, Memphis, TN 38152. Offers art (Graduate Certificate); art history (MA), including Egyptian art and archaeology, general art history; ceramics (MFA); graphic design (MFA); interior design (MFA); painting (MFA); printmaking/photography (MFA); sculpture (MFA). *Accreditation:* NASAD (one or more programs are accredited). *Faculty:* 21 full-time (7 women), 1 (woman) part-time/adjunct. *Students:* 41 full-time (28 women), 3 part-time (all women); includes 6 African Americans, 1 Asian American or Pacific Islander, 1 international. Average age 28. 45 applicants, 73% accepted, 12 enrolled. In 2008, 15 master's, 3 other advanced degrees awarded. *Degree requirements:* For master's, 2 foreign languages, comprehensive exam, thesis. *Entrance requirements:* For master's, GRE General Test or MAT, portfolio (MFA). *Application deadline:* For fall admission, 8/1 for domestic students; for spring admission, 12/1 for domestic students. Applications are processed on a rolling basis. Application fee: $35 ($60 for international students). *Expenses:* Tuition, area resident: Full-time $6242; part-time $330 per credit hour. Tuition, state resident: full-time $6242; part-time $330 per credit hour. Tuition, nonresident: full-time $17,828; part-time $815 per credit hour. Required fees: $1156. *Financial support:* Research assistantships with full tuition reimbursements, teaching assistantships with full tuition reimbursements available. Financial award applicants required to submit FAFSA. *Faculty research:* Online collaborative learning, advanced art history studies, electronic publishing/design, studio arts, architectural studies. *Unit head:* Prof. Richard Lou, Chair, 901-678-2216, Fax: 901-678-2735, E-mail: gmyatt@memphis.edu. *Application contact:* Greely Myat, Graduate Studies Coordinator, 901-678-2650.

University of Miami, Graduate School, College of Arts and Sciences, Department of Art and Art History, Coral Gables, FL 33124. Offers art history (MA); ceramics/glass (MFA); graphic design/multimedia (MFA); painting (MFA); photography/digital imaging (MFA); printmaking (MFA); sculpture (MFA). Part-time programs available. *Degree requirements:* For master's, variable foreign language requirement, thesis, exhibit (MFA), comprehensive exam (MA). *Entrance requirements:* For master's, GRE General Test (MA), research paper (MA), slide portfolio (MFA), artist statement (MFA). Additional exam requirements/recommendations for international students: Required—TOEFL. Electronic applications accepted. *Faculty research:* Installation art, public art.

University of Michigan, Horace H. Rackham School of Graduate Studies, College of Literature, Science, and the Arts, Department of History of Art, Ann Arbor, MI 48109. Offers PhD. *Degree requirements:* For doctorate, 2 foreign languages, thesis/dissertation, oral defense of dissertation, preliminary exam. *Entrance requirements:* For doctorate, GRE General Test. Electronic applications accepted. *Faculty research:* Asian, African and African-American, ancient, medieval and Byzantine, early modern, and modern art.

University of Michigan, Horace H. Rackham School of Graduate Studies, College of Literature, Science, and the Arts, Interdepartmental Program in Classical Art and Archaeology, Ann Arbor, MI 48109. Offers PhD. *Degree requirements:* For doctorate, 4 foreign languages, thesis/dissertation, oral defense of dissertation, preliminary exam. *Entrance requirements:* For doctorate, GRE General Test. Additional exam requirements/recommendations for international students: Required—TOEFL (minimum score 560 paper-based; 220 computer-based). Electronic applications accepted.

University of Minnesota, Twin Cities Campus, Graduate School, College of Liberal Arts, Department of Art History, Minneapolis, MN 55455-0213. Offers MA, PhD. *Degree requirements:* For master's, one foreign language, comprehensive exam, thesis; for doctorate, 2 foreign languages, comprehensive exam, thesis/dissertation. *Entrance requirements:* For master's and doctorate, GRE, transcripts, 3 letters of recommendation, writing sample. Additional exam requirements/recommendations for international students: Required—TOEFL. Electronic applications accepted. *Faculty research:* Asian art, ancient art, modern art, contemporary art, early modern.

University of Minnesota, Twin Cities Campus, Graduate School, College of Liberal Arts, Department of Classical and Near Eastern Studies, Minneapolis, MN 55455-0213. Offers ancient and medieval art and archaeology (MA, PhD); classics (MA, PhD); Greek (MA, PhD); Latin (MA, PhD); religions in antiquity (MA). Part-time programs available. Terminal master's awarded for partial completion of doctoral program. *Degree requirements:* For master's, 2 foreign languages, comprehensive exam, thesis or alternative; for doctorate, variable foreign language requirement, comprehensive exam, thesis/dissertation. *Entrance requirements:* For master's and doctorate, GRE, 3 letters of recommendation, department application, writing sample, copies of transcripts, personal statement. Additional exam requirements/recommendations for international students: Required—TOEFL. Electronic applications accepted. *Faculty research:* Greek and Latin literature, archaeology, religions in antiquity, ancient Near East.

University of Mississippi, Graduate School, College of Liberal Arts, Department of Art, Oxford, University, MS 38677. Offers art education (MA); art history (MA); fine arts (MFA). *Accreditation:* NASAD (one or more programs are accredited). Part-time programs available. *Degree requirements:* For master's, thesis (for some programs). *Entrance requirements:* For master's, GRE General Test, minimum GPA of 3.0. Additional exam requirements/recommendations for international students: Required—TOEFL. Electronic applications accepted.

Art History

University of Missouri–Columbia, Graduate School, College of Arts and Sciences, Department of Art History and Archaeology, Columbia, MO 65211. Offers MA, PhD. *Faculty:* 9 full-time (4 women). *Students:* 16 full-time (13 women), 11 part-time (5 women), 2 international. Average age 31. 28 applicants, 21% accepted, 6 enrolled. In 2008, 7 master's, 1 doctorate awarded. Terminal master's awarded for partial completion of doctoral program. *Degree requirements:* For master's, 2 foreign languages, thesis; for doctorate, 2 foreign languages, thesis/dissertation. *Entrance requirements:* For master's and doctorate, GRE General Test, minimum GPA of 3.0. Additional exam requirements/recommendations for international students: Required—TOEFL (minimum score 500 paper-based; 173 computer-based; 61 iBT), IELTS (minimum score 5.5). *Application deadline:* For fall admission, 1/18 priority date for domestic students. Applications are processed on a rolling basis. Application fee: $45 ($60 for international students). *Financial support:* Fellowships, research assistantships, teaching assistantships, institutionally sponsored loans available. *Unit head:* Dr. Anne Rufdloff Stanton, Department Chair, E-mail: stantona@missouri.edu. *Application contact:* Linda Garrison, 573-882-2757, E-mail: garrisonl@missouri.edu.

University of Missouri–Kansas City, College of Arts and Sciences, Department of Art and Art History, Kansas City, MO 64110-2499. Offers art history (MA, PhD); studio art (MA). Part-time programs available. *Faculty:* 11 full-time (5 women), 8 part-time/adjunct (3 women). *Students:* 7 full-time (6 women), 33 part-time (32 women); includes 3 minority (2 African Americans, 1 American Indian/Alaska Native), 2 international. Average age 31. 11 applicants, 100% accepted, 9 enrolled. In 2008, 4 master's awarded. Terminal master's awarded for partial completion of doctoral program. *Degree requirements:* For master's, thesis, qualifying exam; for doctorate, thesis/dissertation, exams. *Entrance requirements:* For master's, good general education in the humanities. Additional exam requirements/recommendations for international students: Required—TOEFL (minimum score 550 paper-based; 213 computer-based; 80 iBT). *Application deadline:* For fall admission, 3/1 priority date for domestic and international students; for spring admission, 10/15 for domestic and international students. Applications are processed on a rolling basis. Application fee: $45 ($50 for international students). Electronic applications accepted. *Expenses:* Tuition, state resident: full-time $5376; part-time $298.70 per credit hour. Tuition, nonresident: full-time $13,882; part-time $771.20 per credit hour. Required fees: $640.28; $34.65 per contact hour. $30 per semester. Tuition and fees vary according to course load and program. *Financial support:* In 2008–09, 6 teaching assistantships with partial tuition reimbursements (averaging $12,600 per year) were awarded; fellowships, research assistantships with partial tuition reimbursements, career-related internships or fieldwork, Federal Work-Study, institutionally sponsored loans, and tuition waivers (full and partial) also available. Support available to part-time students. Financial award application deadline: 3/1; financial award applicants required to submit FAFSA. *Faculty research:* Painting, electronic media, Western and non-Western art history, photography. *Unit head:* Dr. Burton Dunbar, Chair, 816-235-2531, Fax: 816-235-5507, E-mail: dunbarb@umkc.edu. *Application contact:* Dr. Rochelle Ziskin, Associate Professor, 816-235-2991, Fax: 816-235-5507, E-mail: ziskinr@umkc.edu.

University of Nebraska–Lincoln, Graduate College, College of Fine and Performing Arts, Department of Art and Art History, Lincoln, NE 68588. Offers art history (MA); studio art (MFA);). *Accreditation:* NASAD. *Faculty:* 17 full-time (10 women), 2 part-time/adjunct (1 woman). *Students:* 29 full-time (14 women); includes 2 minority (1 African American, 1 Hispanic American), 1 international. Average age 29. In 2008, 9 master's awarded. *Degree requirements:* For master's, thesis. *Entrance requirements:* For master's, slide portfolio. Additional exam requirements/recommendations for international students: Required—TOEFL (minimum score 550 paper-based; 213 computer-based). *Application deadline:* For fall admission, 2/1 for domestic students. Application fee: $40. Electronic applications accepted. *Expenses:* Tuition, state resident: full-time $4275; part-time $237.50 per credit hour. Tuition, nonresident: full-time $11,525; part-time $640.25 per credit hour. Required fees: $1068; $10.35 per credit hour. $440.70 per semester. Tuition and fees vary according to course load and program. *Financial support:* Fellowships, research assistantships, teaching assistantships, Federal Work-Study and health care benefits available. Support available to part-time students. Financial award application deadline: 2/15. *Faculty research:* Classical archaeology, contemporary art, printmaking, photography. *Unit head:* Joseph M. Ruffo, Chair, 402-472-2631. *Application contact:* Ginny Gross, Director of Graduate Admissions, 402-472-2878, Fax: 402-472-0589, E-mail: grad_admissions@unl.edu.

University of New Mexico, Graduate School, College of Fine Arts, Department of Art and Art History, Program in Art History, Albuquerque, NM 87131-2039. Offers MA, PhD. Part-time programs available. *Degree requirements:* For master's, one foreign language, comprehensive exam, thesis, symposium; for doctorate, 2 foreign languages, comprehensive exam, thesis/dissertation, symposium. *Entrance requirements:* Additional exam requirements/recommendations for international students: Required—TOEFL (minimum score 550 paper-based; 213 computer-based). Electronic applications accepted. *Faculty research:* Native American art, modern Latin American art, photographic art, pre-Columbian art, architectural art, American art, Medieval art.

The University of North Carolina at Chapel Hill, Graduate School, College of Arts and Sciences, Department of Art, Program in Art History, Chapel Hill, NC 27599. Offers MA, PhD. *Degree requirements:* For master's, one foreign language, comprehensive exam, thesis; for doctorate, one foreign language, comprehensive exam, thesis/dissertation. *Entrance requirements:* For master's and doctorate, GRE General Test, minimum GPA of 3.0.

University of North Texas, Robert B. Toulouse School of Graduate Studies, College of Visual Arts and Design, Department of Art Education and Art History, Denton, TX 76203. Offers art education (MA, MS); art history (MA). *Degree requirements:* For master's, one foreign language, comprehensive exam (for some programs), thesis (for some programs). *Entrance requirements:* For master's, GRE, writing sample, statement of purpose. Additional exam requirements/recommendations for international students: Required—proof of English language proficiency required for non-native English speakers; Recommended—TOEFL (minimum score 550 paper-based; 213 computer-based). *Faculty research:* Aesthetics, visual culture arts leadership, British art, Latin American art, French art, Indian art.

University of Notre Dame, Graduate School, College of Arts and Letters, Division of Humanities, Department of Art, Art History, and Design, Notre Dame, IN 46556. Offers art history (MA); design (MFA), including graphic design, industrial design; studio art (MFA), including ceramics, painting, photography, printmaking, sculpture. *Accreditation:* NASAD. *Faculty:* 19 full-time (6 women), 3 part-time/adjunct (1 woman). *Students:* 23 full-time (12 women); includes 2 minority (both Hispanic Americans), 1 international. 83 applicants, 18% accepted, 10 enrolled. In 2008, 11 master's awarded. *Degree requirements:* For master's, comprehensive exam (for some programs), thesis. *Entrance requirements:* For master's, GRE General Test, minimum GPA of 3.0. Additional exam requirements/recommendations for international students: Required—TOEFL (minimum score 600 paper-based; 250 computer-based; 80 iBT). *Application deadline:* For fall admission, 2/1 priority date for domestic and international students. Application fee: $50. Electronic applications accepted. *Financial support:* In 2008–09, 20 students received support; fellowships with full tuition reimbursements available, research assistantships with full tuition reimbursements available, teaching assistantships with full tuition reimbursements available, scholarships/grants, tuition waivers (full), and unspecified assistantships available. Financial award application deadline: 2/1. *Faculty research:* Studio art practice in ceramics, printing, photography, printmaking and sculpture, graphic design and industrial design, digital imaging in design and photography, Renaissance and American art history, contemporary art theory and criticism. *Unit head:* Prof. Martina Lopez, Director of Graduate Studies, 574-631-7652, E-mail: art.1@nd.edu. *Application contact:* Dr. Barbara Turpin, Director of Graduate Admissions, 574-631-7706, Fax: 574-631-4183.

University of Oklahoma, Graduate College, College of Fine Arts, School of Art and Art History, Program in Art History, Norman, OK 73019. Offers MA. *Students:* 8 full-time (6 women), 9 part-time (all women); includes 3 minority (all American Indian/Alaska Native), 1 international. 7 applicants, 71% accepted, 4 enrolled. In 2008, 5 master's awarded. Terminal master's awarded for partial completion of doctoral program. *Degree requirements:* For master's, one foreign language, thesis, departmental qualifying exam, reading proficiency in French/German. *Entrance requirements:* For master's, GRE General Test, minimum GPA of 3.0, 18 undergraduate hours in art history, writing sample, 3 letters of recommendation. Additional exam requirements/recommendations for international students: Required—TOEFL (minimum score 550 paper-based; 213 computer-based). *Application deadline:* For fall admission, 2/1 priority date for domestic students, 2/1 for international students; for spring admission, 10/1 for domestic and international students. Applications are processed on a rolling basis. Application fee: $40 ($90 for international students). Electronic applications accepted. *Expenses:* Tuition, state resident: full-time $3744; part-time $156 per credit hour. Tuition, nonresident: full-time $13,577; part-time $565.70 per credit hour. Required fees: $2415.40; $90.10 per credit hour. *Financial support:* In 2008–09, 8 students received support. Career-related internships or fieldwork, institutionally sponsored loans, scholarships/grants, tuition waivers (partial), and unspecified assistantships available. Support available to part-time students. Financial award application deadline: 4/7; financial award applicants required to submit FAFSA. *Faculty research:* American West, Native American art, medieval; Renaissance and Baroque; contemporary art, 19th century art, medieval/Romanesque. *Unit head:* Mary Jo Watson, Director, 405-325-2691, Fax: 405-325-1668, E-mail: mjwatson@ou.edu. *Application contact:* Susan H Caldwell, Assistant Director, MA Program, Professor, 405-325-3252, Fax: 405-325-1668, E-mail: shcaldwell@ou.edu.

University of Oregon, Graduate School, School of Architecture and Allied Arts, Department of Art History, Eugene, OR 97403. Offers MA, PhD. *Degree requirements:* For master's, one foreign language, thesis or alternative; for doctorate, 2 foreign languages, thesis/dissertation. *Entrance requirements:* For master's, GRE General Test, minimum GPA of 3.0; for doctorate, minimum GPA of 3.0. Additional exam requirements/recommendations for international students: Required—TOEFL. *Faculty research:* Scytho-Siberian art, modern Chinese painting, European landscape painting, American architecture, German expressionist graphics.

University of Pennsylvania, School of Arts and Sciences, Graduate Group in the History of Art, Philadelphia, PA 19104. Offers AM, PhD. Terminal master's awarded for partial completion of doctoral program. *Degree requirements:* For master's, 2 foreign languages, thesis; for doctorate, 2 foreign languages, thesis/dissertation. *Entrance requirements:* For master's and doctorate, GRE, language background according to subfield of interest. Additional exam requirements/recommendations for international students: Required—TOEFL. Electronic applications accepted.

University of Pittsburgh, School of Arts and Sciences, Department of History of Art and Architecture, Pittsburgh, PA 15260. Offers MA, PhD. Part-time programs available. Terminal master's awarded for partial completion of doctoral program. *Degree requirements:* For master's, one foreign language, thesis; for doctorate, 2 foreign languages, comprehensive exam, thesis/dissertation. *Entrance requirements:* For doctorate, GRE General Test, 3 letters of recommendation, writing sample, personal statement, foreign language questionnaire. Additional exam requirements/recommendations for international students: Required—TOEFL. Electronic applications accepted. *Faculty research:* Asian, medieval, Renaissance/baroque, modern art and architecture, contemporary.

University of Rochester, The College, Arts and Sciences, Department of Art and Art History, Rochester, NY 14627-0250. Offers visual and cultural studies (MA, PhD). Terminal master's awarded for partial completion of doctoral program. *Degree requirements:* For master's, thesis optional; for doctorate, one foreign language, thesis/dissertation, qualifying exam. *Entrance requirements:* For master's and doctorate, GRE General Test. Additional exam requirements/recommendations for international students: Required—TOEFL.

See Close-Up on page 231.

University of St. Thomas, Graduate Studies, College of Arts and Sciences, Department of Art History, St. Paul, MN 55105-1096. Offers MA. Part-time and evening/weekend programs available. *Degree requirements:* For master's, one foreign language, thesis, oral exam, reading proficiency in one foreign language. *Entrance requirements:* For master's, bachelor's degree in art history or related field; letters of recommendation (3); writing sample. Additional exam requirements/recommendations for international students: Required—TOEFL. *Faculty research:* Pictorial narrative and theory; feminist theory and women's artistic practice; art, ritual, and popular culture; architectural history; modernism.

University of South Africa, College of Human Sciences, Pretoria, South Africa. Offers adult education (M Ed); African languages (MA, PhD); African politics (MA, PhD); Afrikaans (MA, PhD); ancient history (MA, PhD); ancient Near Eastern studies (MA, PhD); anthropology (MA, PhD); applied linguistics (MA); Arabic (MA, PhD); archaeology (MA); art history (MA); Biblical archaeology (MA); Biblical studies (M Th, D Th, PhD); Christian spirituality (M Th, D Th); church history (M Th, D Th); classical studies (MA, PhD); clinical psychology (MA); communication (MA, PhD); comparative education (M Ed, Ed D); consulting psychology (D Admin, D Com, PhD); curriculum studies (M Ed, Ed D); development studies (M Admin, MA, D Admin, PhD); didactics (M Ed, Ed D); education (M Tech); education management (M Ed, Ed D); educational psychology (M Ed); English (MA); environmental education (M Ed); French (MA, PhD); German (MA, PhD); Greek (MA); guidance and counseling (M Ed); health studies (MA, PhD), including health sciences education (MA), health services management (MA), medical and surgical nursing science (critical care general) (MA), midwifery and neonatal nursing science (MA), trauma and emergency care (MA); history (MA, PhD); history of education (Ed D); inclusive education (M Ed, Ed D); information and communications technology policy and regulation (MA); information science (MA, MIS, PhD); international politics (MA, PhD); Islamic studies (MA, PhD); Italian (MA, PhD); Judaica (MA, PhD); linguistics (MA, PhD); mathematical education (M Ed); mathematics education (MA); missiology (M Th, D Th); modern Hebrew (MA, PhD); musicology (MA, MMus, D Mus, PhD); natural science education (M Ed); New Testament (M Th, D Th); Old Testament (D Th); pastoral therapy (M Th, D Th); philosophy (MA); philosophy of education (M Ed, Ed D); politics (MA, PhD); Portuguese (MA, PhD); practical theology (M Th, D Th); psychology (MA, MS, PhD); psychology of education (M Ed, Ed D); public health (MA); religious studies (MA, D Th, PhD); Romance languages (MA); Russian (MA, PhD); Semitic languages (MA, PhD); social behavior studies in HIV/AIDS (MA); social science (mental health) (MA); social science in development studies (MA); social science in psychology (MA); social science in social work (MA); social science in sociology (MA); social work (MSW, DSW, PhD); socio-education (M Ed, Ed D); sociolinguistics (MA); sociology (MA, PhD); Spanish (MA, PhD); systematic theology (M Th, D Th); TESOL (teaching English to speakers of other languages) (MA); theological ethics (M Th, D Th); theory of literature (MA, PhD); urban ministries (D Th); urban ministry (M Th).

University of South Carolina, The Graduate School, College of Arts and Sciences, Department of Art, Program in Art History, Columbia, SC 29208. Offers MA. *Accreditation:* NASAD. Part-time programs available. *Degree requirements:* For master's, one foreign language, comprehensive exam, thesis. *Entrance requirements:* For master's, GRE General Test or MAT, writing sample. Additional exam requirements/recommendations for international students: Required—TOEFL. Electronic applications accepted. *Faculty research:* History of art and architecture.

University of Southern California, Graduate School, College of Letters, Arts and Sciences, Department of Art History, Los Angeles, CA 90089. Offers art history (MA, PhD); visual studies (Certificate). *Degree requirements:* For doctorate, 2 foreign languages, thesis/dissertation. *Entrance requirements:* For doctorate, GRE General Test. *Faculty research:* Art and ideology in the early Roman Empire, gender in Renaissance paintings, religious and scientific images in Northern Renaissance paintings.

University of South Florida, Graduate School, College of The Arts, School of Art and Art History, Tampa, FL 33620-9951. Offers art history (MA); studio art (MFA). *Accreditation:* NASAD. *Faculty:* 17 full-time (8 women). *Students:* 38 full-time (19 women), 7 part-time (all

Art History

University of South Florida (continued)

women); includes 12 minority (2 African Americans, 1 American Indian/Alaska Native, 3 Asian Americans or Pacific Islanders, 6 Hispanic Americans), 1 international. 65 applicants, 28% accepted, 14 enrolled. In 2008, 10 master's awarded. *Degree requirements:* For master's, comprehensive exam, thesis. *Entrance requirements:* For master's, GRE General Test (MA), minimum GPA of 3.0 in last 60 hours of coursework. Additional exam requirements/recommendations for international students: Required—TOEFL (minimum score 550 paper-based; 213 computer-based). *Application deadline:* For fall admission, 1/15 for domestic students, 1/2 for international students. Application fee: $30. *Expenses:* Tuition, state resident: full-time $2624.40; part-time $291.60 per credit hour. Tuition, nonresident: full-time $7822; part-time $869.13 per credit hour. *Financial support:* In 2008–09, 8 fellowships with full tuition reimbursements (averaging $7,640 per year), 34 teaching assistantships with full and partial tuition reimbursements (averaging $4,486 per year) were awarded; career-related internships or fieldwork, Federal Work-Study, scholarships/grants, health care benefits, and unspecified assistantships also available. Financial award application deadline: 2/15. *Faculty research:* Contemporary art and role of the artist, identity strategies, political iconography, art practice and technology, construction of race in art. *Unit head:* Prof. Wallace Wilson, Director, 818-974-2360, Fax: 813-974-9226, E-mail: wilson@arts.usf.edu. *Application contact:* Helena Szepe, Contact Person, 813-974-4531, Fax: 813-974-9226, E-mail: szepe@arts.usf.edu.

The University of Texas at Austin, Graduate School, College of Fine Arts, Department of Art and Art History, Program in Art History, Austin, TX 78712-1111. Offers MA, PhD. *Accreditation:* NASAD. Part-time programs available. *Degree requirements:* For master's, one foreign language, thesis; for doctorate, 2 foreign languages, thesis/dissertation, oral and written qualifying exam. *Entrance requirements:* For master's, GRE General Test, 2 samples of written work; for doctorate, GRE General Test, minimum GPA of 3.0, 2 samples of written work. Electronic applications accepted.

The University of Texas at San Antonio, College of Liberal and Fine Arts, Department of Art and Art History, San Antonio, TX 78249-0617. Offers art history (MA); studio art (MFA). *Accreditation:* NASAD (one or more programs are accredited). *Degree requirements:* For master's, comprehensive exam, thesis. *Entrance requirements:* For master's, GRE General Test, portfolio, minimum GPA of 3.0 in last 60 hours, 3 letters of recommendation. Additional exam requirements/recommendations for international students: Required—TOEFL (minimum score 500 paper-based; 173 computer-based). Electronic applications accepted. *Faculty research:* Wide variety of artistic production in all media, art history and criticism, focusing on American and Hispanic art.

The University of Texas at Tyler, College of Arts and Sciences, Department of Art and Art History, Tyler, TX 75799-0001. Offers MA, MAIS, MFA. *Degree requirements:* For master's, thesis, graduate committee review. *Entrance requirements:* For master's, minimum GPA of 3.0. Additional exam requirements/recommendations for international students: Required—TOEFL (minimum score 79 computer-based). *Faculty research:* Classical myths in contemporary art, social issues in contemporary art, casting methods, Renaissance art.

University of Toronto, School of Graduate Studies, Humanities Division, Department of Art, Toronto, ON M5S 1A1, Canada. Offers art history (MA, PhD); visual studies (MVS). Part-time programs available. *Degree requirements:* For master's, 2 foreign languages, language proficiency exams; for doctorate, 2 foreign languages, comprehensive exam, thesis/dissertation. *Entrance requirements:* For master's, coursework in a foreign language, 3 letters of reference, sample research paper, minimum B+ average in senior art history and/or humanities courses; for doctorate, minimum A– average in senior art history and/or humanities courses, 2 letters of reference, sample research paper.

University of Utah, The Graduate School, College of Fine Arts, Department of Art and Art History, Program in Art History, Salt Lake City, UT 84112-1107. Offers MA. Part-time programs available. *Degree requirements:* For master's, one foreign language, comprehensive exam, thesis, thesis defense. *Entrance requirements:* For master's, curriculum vitae, writing sample, letters of recommendation. Additional exam requirements/recommendations for international students: Required—TOEFL (minimum score 600 paper-based; 173 computer-based). Electronic applications accepted. *Faculty research:* Asian art, medieval art, Baroque art, American art, 20th century art.

University of Victoria, Faculty of Graduate Studies, Faculty of Fine Arts, Department of History in Art, Victoria, BC V8W 2Y2, Canada. Offers MA, PhD. *Degree requirements:* For master's, one foreign language, thesis (for some programs), oral defense; for doctorate, 2 foreign languages, comprehensive exam, thesis/dissertation, oral defense. *Entrance requirements:* For master's, minimum B+ average in undergraduate course work; for doctorate, minimum B+ average in graduate course work. Additional exam requirements/recommendations for international students: Required—TOEFL (minimum score 575 paper-based; 233 computer-based), IELTS (minimum score 7). Electronic applications accepted. *Faculty research:* Europe, Southeast Asia, China and Islamic world, architecture of North America and the Islamic World, film.

University of Virginia, College and Graduate School of Arts and Sciences, McIntire Department of Art, Charlottesville, VA 22904-4130. Offers classical art and archaeology (MA, PhD); history of art and architecture (MA, PhD). *Degree requirements:* For master's, one foreign language, thesis, defense; for doctorate, 2 foreign languages, comprehensive exam, thesis/dissertation, defense. *Entrance requirements:* For master's and doctorate, GRE General Test, writing sample. Additional exam requirements/recommendations for international students: Recommended—TOEFL (minimum score 600 paper-based; 250 computer-based; 90 iBT), IELTS (minimum score 7). Electronic applications accepted. *Expenses:* Tuition, area resident: Full-time $10,452. Tuition, state resident: full-time $10,452. Tuition, nonresident: full-time $20,010. Required fees: $2176. Part-time tuition and fees vary according to course load and program. *Faculty research:* Classical art, renaissance art and architecture, American material culture.

University of Virginia, College and Graduate School of Arts and Sciences, Program in Art and Architectural History, Charlottesville, VA 22903. Offers MA, PhD. *Students:* 54 full-time (40 women); includes 1 minority (African American), 2 international. Average age 31. 52 applicants, 44% accepted, 11 enrolled. In 2008, 2 master's, 2 doctorates awarded. *Degree requirements:* For master's, one foreign language, comprehensive exam, thesis; for doctorate, 2 foreign languages, thesis/dissertation, oral exam. *Entrance requirements:* For master's and doctorate, GRE, 2 letters of recommendation. *Application deadline:* For fall admission, 12/7 for domestic and international students. Applications are processed on a rolling basis. Electronic applications accepted. *Expenses:* Tuition, area resident: Full-time $10,452. Tuition, state resident: full-time $10,452. Tuition, nonresident: full-time $20,010. Required fees: $2176. Part-time tuition and fees vary according to course load and program. *Financial support:* Application deadline: 12/7. *Unit head:* Lawrence O. Goedde, Chair, 434-924-6123, Fax: 434-924-3647, E-mail: artdept@virginia.edu. *Application contact:* Aaron Mills, Associate Dean of Graduate Academic Programs and Research, 434-924-6739, Fax: 434-924-6737, E-mail: grad-a-s@virginia.edu.

University of Washington, Graduate School, College of Arts and Sciences, School of Art, Division of Art History, Seattle, WA 98195. Offers MA, PhD. Terminal master's awarded for partial completion of doctoral program. *Degree requirements:* For master's, 2 foreign languages, practicum or thesis; for doctorate, 2 foreign languages, thesis/dissertation. *Entrance requirements:* For master's, GRE General Test, minimum undergraduate GPA of 3.0, undergraduate major in art history or equivalent; for doctorate, GRE General Test, MA in art history, minimum graduate GPA of 3.0. Additional exam requirements/recommendations for international students: Required—TOEFL (minimum score 580 paper-based; 237 computer-based). Electronic applications accepted. *Faculty research:* European-American (all periods), Japanese, Chinese, African, and Native American art.

University of Wisconsin–Madison, Graduate School, College of Letters and Science, Department of Art History, Madison, WI 53706-1380. Offers MA, PhD. Part-time programs available. Terminal master's awarded for partial completion of doctoral program. *Degree requirements:* For master's, one foreign language; for doctorate, 2 foreign languages, thesis/dissertation. *Entrance requirements:* For master's and doctorate, GRE. Additional exam requirements/recommendations for international students: Required—TOEFL. Electronic applications accepted. *Faculty research:* Twentieth-century, African art, Italian Renaissance, Dutch, material culture.

University of Wisconsin–Milwaukee, Graduate School, College of Letters and Sciences, Department of Art History, Milwaukee, WI 53201-0413. Offers art history (MA); art museum studies (Certificate). Part-time programs available. *Faculty:* 8 full-time (4 women). *Students:* 14 full-time (13 women), 11 part-time (all women); includes 1 minority (African American), 1 international. Average age 28. 21 applicants, 62% accepted, 6 enrolled. In 2008, 14 master's awarded. *Degree requirements:* For master's, one foreign language, comprehensive exam, thesis or alternative. *Entrance requirements:* For master's, GRE. Additional exam requirements/recommendations for international students: Required—TOEFL (minimum score 550 paper-based; 79 iBT), IELTS (minimum score 6.5). *Application deadline:* For fall admission, 1/1 priority date for domestic students; for spring admission, 9/1 for domestic students. Applications are processed on a rolling basis. Application fee: $45 ($75 for international students). *Expenses:* Tuition, area resident: Full-time $7320; part-time $165 per credit. Tuition, state resident: full-time $7320; part-time $165 per credit. Tuition, nonresident: full-time $17,840; part-time $714 per credit. Tuition and fees vary according to campus/location, program and reciprocity agreements. *Financial support:* In 2008–09, 5 teaching assistantships were awarded; fellowships, research assistantships, career-related internships or fieldwork and unspecified assistantships also available. Support available to part-time students. Financial award application deadline: 4/15. Total annual research expenditures: $1,035. *Unit head:* Kenneth Bendiner, Representative, 414-229-5015, Fax: 414-229-2935, E-mail: bendiner@uwm.edu. *Application contact:* General Information Contact, 414-229-4982, Fax: 414-229-6967, E-mail: gradschool@uwm.edu.

University of Wisconsin–Superior, Graduate Division, Department of Visual Arts, Superior, WI 54880-4500. Offers art education (MA); art history (MA); art therapy (MA); arts administration (MA); studio arts (MA). Part-time programs available. *Degree requirements:* For master's, comprehensive exam, exhibit. *Entrance requirements:* For master's, minimum GPA of 2.75, portfolio.

Virginia Commonwealth University, Graduate School, School of the Arts, Department of Art History, Richmond, VA 23284-9005. Offers architectural history (MA); art history (MA, PhD); historical studies (MA); museum studies (MA). *Accreditation:* NASAD. *Degree requirements:* For master's, thesis; for doctorate, comprehensive exam, thesis/dissertation. *Entrance requirements:* For master's and doctorate, GRE General Test. *Faculty research:* Modern, nineteenth century, Renaissance, American, and Medieval art.

Washington University in St. Louis, Graduate School of Arts and Sciences, Department of Art History and Archaeology, St. Louis, MO 63130-4899. Offers art history (MA, PhD); classical archaeology (MA, PhD). *Students:* 23 full-time (19 women); includes 1 minority (Asian American or Pacific Islander), 3 international. 42 applicants, 17% accepted, 4 enrolled. In 2008, 3 master's, 1 doctorate awarded. *Degree requirements:* For doctorate, 2 foreign languages, comprehensive exam, thesis/dissertation. *Entrance requirements:* For master's and doctorate, GRE General Test, sample of written work. *Application deadline:* For fall admission, 12/15 for domestic students. Application fee: $45. Electronic applications accepted. *Financial support:* Fellowships, teaching assistantships, career-related internships or fieldwork, Federal Work-Study, institutionally sponsored loans, and tuition waivers (full and partial) available. Support available to part-time students. Financial award application deadline: 1/15. *Unit head:* Dr. William Wallace, Chairperson, 314-935-5270. *Application contact:* Assistant to the Dean, 314-935-6880, Fax: 314-935-4887.

Wayne State University, College of Fine, Performing and Communication Arts, Department of Art and Art History, Program in Art History, Detroit, MI 48202. Offers MA. *Degree requirements:* For master's, one foreign language. *Entrance requirements:* Additional exam requirements/recommendations for international students: Required—TOEFL (minimum score 550 paper-based; 213 computer-based); Recommended—TWE (minimum score 6). Electronic applications accepted. *Faculty research:* Ancient, medieval, and nineteenth and twentieth century art history; theory and criticism.

West Virginia University, College of Creative Arts, Division of Art and Design, Morgantown, WV 26506. Offers art education (MA); art history (MA); ceramics (MFA); graphic design (MFA); painting (MFA); printmaking (MFA); sculpture (MFA); studio art (MA). *Accreditation:* NASAD. *Degree requirements:* For master's, thesis, exhibit. *Entrance requirements:* For master's, minimum GPA of 2.75, portfolio. Additional exam requirements/recommendations for international students: Required—TOEFL. *Expenses:* Contact institution. *Faculty research:* Medieval art history.

Williams College, Program in the History of Art, Williamstown, MA 01267. Offers MA. Offered jointly with Sterling and Francine Clark Art Institute. Part-time programs available. *Degree requirements:* For master's, 2 foreign languages, symposium paper and lecture. *Entrance requirements:* For master's, GRE General Test. Additional exam requirements/recommendations for international students: Required—TOEFL. Electronic applications accepted.

Yale University, Graduate School of Arts and Sciences, Department of History of Art, New Haven, CT 06520. Offers PhD. *Degree requirements:* For doctorate, 2 foreign languages, thesis/dissertation. *Entrance requirements:* For doctorate, GRE General Test.

York University, Faculty of Graduate Studies, Faculty of Fine Arts, Program in Art History, Toronto, ON M3J 1P3, Canada. Offers MA, PhD. Part-time programs available. *Degree requirements:* For master's, one foreign language, thesis or alternative. Electronic applications accepted.

Arts Administration

American University, College of Arts and Sciences, Department of Performing Arts, Program in Arts Management, Washington, DC 22016-8053. Offers MA, Certificate. Part-time and evening/weekend programs available. *Students:* 37 full-time (31 women), 19 part-time (16 women); includes 7 minority (2 African Americans, 2 Asian Americans or Pacific Islanders, 3 Hispanic Americans), 9 international. Average age 28. In 2008, 14 master's awarded. *Degree requirements:* For master's, comprehensive exam, thesis or alternative. *Entrance requirements:* For master's, GRE, previous course work in theater, dance, music, or related field; minimum GPA of 3.0; for Certificate, bachelor's degree. Additional exam requirements/recommendations for international students: Required—TOEFL. *Application deadline:* For fall admission, 1/15 priority date for domestic students. Application fee: $80. *Expenses:* Tuition: Full-time $21,204; part-time $1178 per credit hour. Required fees: $380. Part-time tuition and fees vary according to course load and program. *Financial support:* Fellowships, teaching assistantships, career-related internships or fieldwork, Federal Work-Study, and institutionally sponsored loans available. Support available to part-time students. Financial award application deadline: 2/1. *Faculty research:* Arts policy, arts education.

Boston University, Metropolitan College (Continuing Education), Program in Arts Administration, Boston, MA 02215. Offers arts administration (MS, Graduate Certificate); fundraising management (Graduate Certificate). Part-time and evening/weekend programs available. *Degree requirements:* For master's, internship. *Entrance requirements:* Additional exam requirements/recommendations for international students: Required—TOEFL (minimum score 590 paper-based; 213 computer-based; 84 iBT), IELTS, TWE, GRE or GMAT. Electronic applications accepted. *Faculty research:* Cultural policy, artists' rights, museum practices, audience development.

Carnegie Mellon University, H. John Heinz III College, Institute for the Management of Creative Enterprises and College of Fine Arts, Program in Arts Management, Pittsburgh, PA 15213-3891. Offers MAM. *Degree requirements:* For master's, internship. *Entrance requirements:* For master's, GMAT or GRE, previous course work in pre-calculus and statistics. Electronic applications accepted.

Claremont Graduate University, Graduate Programs, Program in Arts Management, Claremont, CA 91711-6160. Offers MA. *Students:* 14 full-time (10 women), 3 part-time (all women); includes 4 minority (2 African Americans, 1 Asian American or Pacific Islander, 1 Hispanic American), 1 international. Average age 31. *Entrance requirements:* For master's, GRE General Test. Additional exam requirements/recommendations for international students: Required—TOEFL (minimum score 550 paper-based; 213 computer-based; 80 iBT). *Application deadline:* For fall admission, 2/1 priority date for domestic students. Applications are processed on a rolling basis. Application fee: $60. Electronic applications accepted. *Expenses:* Tuition: Full-time $33,698; part-time $1465 per unit. Required fees: $310; $155 per semester. Tuition and fees vary according to program. *Financial support:* Fellowships, research assistantships, teaching assistantships, Federal Work-Study, institutionally sponsored loans, and scholarships/grants available. Support available to part-time students. Financial award application deadline: 2/15; financial award applicants required to submit FAFSA. *Unit head:* Diana Luna, Program Administrator, 909-607-9109, Fax: 909-621-8330, E-mail: diana.luna@cgu.edu. *Application contact:* Justin Evans, Admissions Coordinator, 909-607-1278, Fax: 909-607-1221, E-mail: justin.evans@cgu.edu.

College of Charleston, Graduate School, School of the Arts, Program in Arts Management, Charleston, SC 29424-0001. Offers MPA, Certificate. Evening/weekend programs available. *Faculty:* 2 full-time (both women), 2 part-time/adjunct (1 woman). *Students:* 1 (woman) part-time. *Entrance requirements:* For degree, minimum GPA of 3.0, writing sample. Additional exam requirements/recommendations for international students: Required—TOEFL. *Application deadline:* For fall admission, 4/1 for domestic students; for spring admission, 11/1 for domestic students. Application fee: $45. *Expenses:* Tuition, area resident: full-time $6624; part-time $368 per credit hour. Tuition, state resident: full-time $6624; part-time $368 per credit hour. Tuition, nonresident: full-time $16,074; part-time $893 per credit hour. Required fees: $30; $30 per course. One-time fee: $45. *Unit head:* Scott Peterson, Director, 843-953-8421, E-mail: petersons@cofc.edu. *Application contact:* Susan Hallatt, Director of Graduate Admissions, 843-953-5614, Fax: 843-953-1434, E-mail: hallatts@cofc.edu.

Columbia College Chicago, Graduate School, Department of Arts, Entertainment and Media Management, Chicago, IL 60605-1996. Offers arts, entertainment and media management (MA), including media management, music business management, performing arts management, visual arts management. Evening/weekend programs available. *Students:* 117 full-time (84 women), 46 part-time (31 women); includes 51 minority (34 African Americans, 1 American Indian/Alaska Native, 4 Asian Americans or Pacific Islanders, 12 Hispanic Americans), 9 international. Average age 27. 247 applicants, 24% accepted, 53 enrolled. In 2008, 52 master's awarded. *Degree requirements:* For master's, thesis, internship. *Entrance requirements:* For master's, self-assessment essay. Additional exam requirements/recommendations for international students: Required—TOEFL (minimum score 550 paper-based; 213 computer-based). *Application deadline:* For fall admission, 2/2 for domestic and international students. Application fee: $55. Electronic applications accepted. *Expenses:* Tuition: Full-time $15,992; part-time $633 per credit hour. *Financial support:* Fellowships, career-related internships or fieldwork, Federal Work-Study, and scholarships/grants available. Support available to part-time students. Financial award application deadline: 8/13; financial award applicants required to submit FAFSA. *Unit head:* Dr. J. Dennis Rich, Chairperson, 312-369-7652, Fax: 312-369-8063, E-mail: drich@colum.edu. *Application contact:* Keith Cleveland, Office of Provost/Senior Vice President, 312-363-7261, Fax: 312-369-8047, E-mail: kcleveland@colum.edu.

Drexel University, College of Media Arts and Design, Department of Performing Arts, Philadelphia, PA 19104-2875. Offers arts administration (MS). *Accreditation:* NASAD. Part-time and evening/weekend programs available. *Degree requirements:* For master's, thesis, internship. *Entrance requirements:* For master's, GRE, interview, minimum GPA of 3.0, previous course work in arts and business. Additional exam requirements/recommendations for international students: Required—TOEFL. Electronic applications accepted. *Faculty research:* Evaluation of art administration structures, funding for the arts, impact of politics in the arts, computer applications.

Eastern Michigan University, Graduate School, College of Arts and Sciences, Department of Communication and Theatre Arts, Program in Arts Administration, Ypsilanti, MI 48197. Offers theatre arts-arts administration (MA). Part-time and evening/weekend programs available. Postbaccalaureate distance learning degree programs offered (minimal on-campus study). *Entrance requirements:* Additional exam requirements/recommendations for international students: Required—TOEFL.

Fashion Institute of Technology, School of Graduate Studies, Program in Art Market: Principles and Practices, New York, NY 10001-5992. Offers MA. *Accreditation:* NASAD. *Degree requirements:* For master's, one foreign language, thesis, internship. *Entrance requirements:* For master's, GRE General Test, previous course work in art history, 4 semesters of a foreign language. Additional exam requirements/recommendations for international students: Required—TOEFL (minimum score 550 paper-based; 213 computer-based). Electronic applications accepted.

See Close-Up on page 117.

Florida State University, Graduate Studies, College of Music, Tallahassee, FL 32306. Offers accompanying (MM); arts administration (MA); choral conducting (MM); composition (MM, DM); ethnomusicology (MM); general music (MA); instrumental accompanying (MM); instrumental conducting (MM); jazz studies (MM); music education (MM Ed, PhD); music theory (MM, PhD); music therapy (MM); musicology (MM, PhD), including ethnomusicology (PhD), historical musicology; opera (MM); performance (MM, DM); piano pedagogy (MM); piano technology (MA); vocal accompanying (MM). *Accreditation:* NASM. *Degree requirements:* For master's, comprehensive exam (for some programs), thesis (for some programs), departmental qualifying exam; for doctorate, comprehensive exam (for some programs), thesis/dissertation, departmental qualifying exam. *Entrance requirements:* For master's and doctorate, audition, GRE General Test or minimum GPA of 3.0. Additional exam requirements/recommendations for international students: Required—TOEFL (minimum score 550 paper-based; 213 computer-based). Electronic applications accepted.

George Mason University, College of Visual and Performing Arts, Program in Arts Management, Fairfax, VA 22030. Offers MA.

Goucher College, Program in Arts Administration, Baltimore, MD 21204-2794. Offers MA. Part-time programs available. Postbaccalaureate distance learning degree programs offered (minimal on-campus study). *Degree requirements:* For master's, internship, major paper. *Entrance requirements:* For master's, 2 years of post-baccalaureate work experience. *Expenses:* Contact institution.

HEC Montreal, School of Business Administration, Diploma Programs in Administration, Program in Management of Cultural Organizations, Montréal, QC H3T 2A7, Canada. Offers Diploma. All courses are given in French. Part-time programs available. *Students:* 37 full-time (27 women), 132 part-time (114 women). 92 applicants, 79% accepted, 55 enrolled. In 2008, 48 Diplomas awarded. *Degree requirements:* For Diploma, one foreign language. *Entrance requirements:* For degree, 2 years of relevant work experience, 2 letters of recommendation. *Application deadline:* For fall admission, 4/15 for domestic and international students; for winter admission, 10/1 for domestic and international students. Application fee: $76 Canadian dollars. Electronic applications accepted. Tuition and fees charges are reported in Canadian dollars. *Expenses:* Tuition, area resident: Part-time $62.27 Canadian dollars per credit. Tuition, state resident: full-time $2241.72 Canadian dollars; part-time $179.28 Canadian dollars per credit. Tuition, nonresident: full-time $6454 Canadian dollars; part-time $419.77 Canadian dollars per credit. International tuition: $15,111.72 Canadian dollars full-time. Required fees: $1218.75 Canadian dollars; $28.25 Canadian dollars per credit. $88 Canadian dollars per term. Tuition and fees vary according to degree level and program. *Financial support:* Scholarships/grants available. *Unit head:* Louise Cote, Director, 514-340-6205, Fax: 514-340-5640, E-mail: louise.cote@hec.ca. *Application contact:* Francine Blais, Administrative Director, 514-340-6112, Fax: 514-340-6411, E-mail: francine.blais@hec.ca.

Montclair State University, The Office of Graduate Admissions and Support Services, School of the Arts, Department of Theatre and Dance, Montclair, NJ 07043-1624. Offers theatre (MA), including arts management, production/stage management, theatre studies. *Accreditation:* NAST. Part-time and evening/weekend programs available. *Faculty:* 15 full-time (8 women), 42 part-time/adjunct (26 women). *Students:* 5 full-time (4 women), 20 part-time (14 women); includes 6 minority (5 African Americans, 1 Hispanic American). Average age 32. 16 applicants, 63% accepted, 7 enrolled. In 2008, 8 master's awarded. *Degree requirements:* For master's, comprehensive exam, thesis or alternative. *Entrance requirements:* For master's, GRE General Test, minimum GPA of 3.0, undergraduate degree or work in theatre, oral interpretation, broadcasting, speech communication or media; 2 letters of recommendation. Additional exam requirements/recommendations for international students: Required—TOEFL (minimum score 83 computer-based). *Application deadline:* For fall admission, 6/1 for international students; for spring admission, 10/1 for international students. Applications are processed on a rolling basis. Application fee: $60. Electronic applications accepted. *Financial support:* In 2008–09, 1 research assistantship with full tuition reimbursement (averaging $7,000 per year) was awarded; Federal Work-Study, scholarships/grants, and unspecified assistantships also available. Support available to part-time students. Financial award application deadline: 3/1; financial award applicants required to submit FAFSA. *Unit head:* Dr. Jane Peterson, Chairperson, 973-655-4217, E-mail: peterson@mail.montclair.edu. *Application contact:* Dr. Jane Peterson, Adviser, 973-655-4109, E-mail: petersonj@mail.montclair.edu.

New York University, Steinhardt School of Culture, Education and Human Development, Department of Art and Art Professions, Program in Visual Arts Administration, New York, NY 10012-1019. Offers for-profit sector (MA); not-for-profit sector (MA). Part-time and evening/weekend programs available. *Degree requirements:* For master's, thesis (for some programs). *Entrance requirements:* For master's, interview. Additional exam requirements/recommendations for international students: Required—TOEFL. *Faculty research:* Corporate philanthropy, contemporary art and culture, public art and urban development, cultural policy, arts advocacy.

New York University, Steinhardt School of Culture, Education and Human Development, Department of Music and Performing Arts Professions, Program in Performing Arts Administration, New York, NY 10012-1019. Offers MA. Part-time and evening/weekend programs available. *Degree requirements:* For master's, thesis (for some programs). *Entrance requirements:* For master's, interview. Additional exam requirements/recommendations for international students: Required—TOEFL. *Faculty research:* Legal dimensions of arts management, global arts management, cultural policy.

New York University, Tisch School of the Arts, Program in Arts Politics, New York, NY 10012-1019. Offers MA. *Degree requirements:* For master's, thesis. *Entrance requirements:* For master's, professional resumé, writing sample, statement of purpose. Additional exam requirements/recommendations for international students: Required—TOEFL, IELTS.

The Ohio State University, Graduate School, College of the Arts, Department of Art Education, Program in Arts Policy and Administration, Columbus, OH 43210. Offers MA. *Degree requirements:* For master's, thesis. *Entrance requirements:* For master's, GRE General Test. Additional exam requirements/recommendations for international students: Required—TOEFL (minimum score 600 paper-based; 250 computer-based). Electronic applications accepted. *Faculty research:* Public policy and advocacy.

Pratt Institute, School of Art and Design, Program in Arts and Cultural Management, New York, NY 10011. Offers MPS. Part-time programs available. *Faculty:* 1 (woman) full-time, 13 part-time/adjunct (9 women). *Students:* 50 full-time (43 women), 4 part-time (all women); includes 11 minority (3 African Americans, 4 Asian Americans or Pacific Islanders, 4 Hispanic Americans), 16 international. Average age 28. 89 applicants, 52% accepted, 27 enrolled. In 2008, 24 master's awarded. *Degree requirements:* For master's, thesis. *Entrance requirements:* For master's, bachelor's degree, transcripts, letters of recommendation, statement, portfolio. Additional exam requirements/recommendations for international students: Required—TOEFL (minimum score 600 paper-based; 250 computer-based). *Application deadline:* For fall admission, 2/1 for domestic and international students; for spring admission, 10/1 for domestic and international students. Application fee: $50 ($90 for international students). Electronic applications accepted. *Expenses:* Tuition: Full-time $20,412; part-time $1134 per credit. Required fees: $1190; $1190 per year. *Financial support:* Career-related internships or fieldwork, Federal Work-Study, institutionally sponsored loans, scholarships/grants, health care benefits, and unspecified assistantships available. Support available to part-time students. Financial award application deadline: 2/1; financial award applicants required to submit FAFSA. *Unit head:* Monica Shay, Director, 212-647-7560, E-mail: mshay@pratt.edu. *Application contact:* Young Hah, Director of Graduate Admissions, 718-636-3683, Fax: 718-399-4242, E-mail: yhah@pratt.edu.

Pratt Institute, School of Art and Design, Program in Design Management, New York, NY 10011. Offers MPS. Part-time programs available. *Faculty:* 2 full-time (both women), 8 part-time/adjunct (4 women). *Students:* 46 full-time (33 women); includes 6 minority (4 African Americans, 2 Asian Americans or Pacific Islanders), 13 international. Average age 30. 98 applicants, 33% accepted, 23 enrolled. In 2008, 23 master's awarded. *Degree requirements:*

Arts Administration

Pratt Institute (continued)

For master's, thesis. *Entrance requirements:* For master's, bachelor's degree, transcripts, letters of recommendation, statement, portfolio. Additional exam requirements/recommendations for international students: Required—TOEFL (minimum score 600 paper-based; 250 computer-based). *Application deadline:* For fall admission, 2/1 for domestic and international students; for spring admission, 10/1 for domestic and international students. Application fee: $50 ($90 for international students). Electronic applications accepted. *Expenses:* Tuition: Full-time $20,412; part-time $1134 per credit. Required fees: $1190; $1190 per year. *Financial support:* Career-related internships or fieldwork, Federal Work-Study, institutionally sponsored loans, scholarships/grants, health care benefits, and unspecified assistantships available. Support available to part-time students. Financial award application deadline: 2/1; financial award applicants required to submit FAFSA. *Unit head:* Mary McBride, Chairperson, 212-647-7538, E-mail: mmcb1033@pratt.edu. *Application contact:* Young Hah, Director of Graduate Admissions, 718-636-3683, Fax: 718-399-4242, E-mail: yhah@pratt.edu.

See Close-Up on page 219.

Regis University, College for Professional Studies, MA Program, Denver, CO 80221-1099. Offers criminology (MA); fine arts administration (Certificate); language and communication (MA); mediation (Certificate); psychology (MA); self-designed major (MA); social justice, peace, and reconciliation (Certificate); social science (MA); technical communication (Certificate). Program also offered in Henderson and Las Vegas (Summerlin), NV. Part-time and evening/weekend programs available. Postbaccalaureate distance learning degree programs offered (minimal on-campus study). *Degree requirements:* For master's, thesis, research project. *Entrance requirements:* For master's, resumé, recommendations, essays. Additional exam requirements/recommendations for international students: Required—TOEFL (minimum score 213 computer-based), TWE (minimum score 5). Electronic applications accepted. *Expenses:* Contact institution. *Faculty research:* Independent/nonresidential graduate study: new methods and models, adult learning and the capstone experience, Goal Setting, behavior of Adult students, Innovative Studies for Community Colleges.

Rhode Island College, School of Graduate Studies, Faculty of Arts and Sciences, Department of Art, Providence, RI 02908-1991. Offers art education (MA, MAT), media studies (MA). *Accreditation:* NASAD (one or more programs are accredited). Part-time and evening/weekend programs available. *Faculty:* 7 full-time (4 women). *Students:* 2 full-time (0 women), 11 part-time (5 women). Average age 33. In 2008, 10 master's awarded. *Degree requirements:* For master's, thesis. *Entrance requirements:* For master's, GRE General Test or MAT, portfolio (MA), 3 letters of recommendation, interview. Additional exam requirements/recommendations for international students: Recommended—TOEFL (minimum score 550 paper-based; 213 computer-based; 79 iBT). *Application deadline:* For fall admission, 4/1 for domestic students; for spring admission, 11/1 for domestic students. Applications are processed on a rolling basis. Application fee: $50. *Expenses:* Tuition, area resident: Full-time $6816; part-time $284 per credit hour. Tuition, state resident: full-time $6816; part-time $284 per credit hour. Tuition, nonresident: full-time $13,920; part-time $580 per credit hour. Required fees: $454; $16 per credit. $68 per term. *Financial support:* Teaching assistantships with full tuition reimbursements, career-related internships or fieldwork, Federal Work-Study, scholarships/grants, health care benefits, and unspecified assistantships available. Support available to part-time students. Financial award application deadline: 5/15; financial award applicants required to submit FAFSA. *Unit head:* Prof. Nancy Bockbrader, Chair, 401-456-8054. *Application contact:* Graduate Studies, 401-456-8700.

Ryerson University, School of Graduate Studies, Program in Photographic Preservation and Collections Management, Toronto, ON M5B 2K3, Canada. Offers MA.

Saint Mary's University of Minnesota, Schools of Graduate and Professional Programs, Graduate School of Business and Technology, Arts and Cultural Management Program, Winona, MN 55987-1399. Offers MA.

St. Thomas University, School of Leadership Studies, Program in Art Management, Miami Gardens, FL 33054-6459. Offers MA.

Savannah College of Art and Design, Graduate School, Program in Arts Administration, Savannah, GA 31402-3146. Offers MA. Part-time programs available. *Degree requirements:* For master's, thesis. *Entrance requirements:* For master's, interview. Additional exam requirements/recommendations for international students: Required—TOEFL (minimum score 450 paper-based; 133 computer-based). *Expenses:* Tuition: Full-time $28,215; part-time $3135 per course. One-time fee: $500.

School of the Art Institute of Chicago, Graduate Division, Program in Arts Administration and Policy, Chicago, IL 60603-3103. Offers MAAAP. *Accreditation:* NASAD. *Degree requirements:* For master's, thesis, telephone interview. *Entrance requirements:* Additional exam requirements/recommendations for international students: Required—TOEFL, IELTS. *Faculty research:* Latin American artists, activist art, community-based art.

See Close-Up on page 225.

Shenandoah University, Shenandoah Conservatory, Winchester, VA 22601-5195. Offers arts administration (MS); church music (MM, Certificate); composition (MM); conducting (MM); dance (MA, MFA, MS); dance accompanying (MM); music (MS); music education (MME, DMA); music therapy (MMT, Certificate); pedagogy (MM, DMA); performance (MM, DMA, Artist Diploma); piano accompanying (MM). *Accreditation:* NASM. Part-time and evening/weekend programs available. *Faculty:* 39 full-time (19 women), 21 part-time/adjunct (9 women). *Students:* 71 full-time (42 women), 150 part-time (80 women); includes 14 minority (9 African Americans, 2 Asian Americans or Pacific Islanders, 3 Hispanic Americans), 32 international. Average age 40. 76 applicants, 96% accepted, 49 enrolled. In 2008, 24 master's, 10 doctorates, 7 other advanced degrees awarded. *Degree requirements:* For master's, comprehensive exam (for some programs), thesis (for some programs), internship (MS), recital (MM), research teaching project or thesis (MME), project (MA); for doctorate, comprehensive exam, thesis/dissertation (for some programs), dissertation or teaching project, recital; for other advanced degree, research project, recital. *Entrance requirements:* For master's, audition, minimum GPA of 2.5, writing sample, resumé; for doctorate, audition, minimum GPA of 3.25, 2 letters of recommendation, writing sample, resumé; for other advanced degree, bachelor or master's degree; minimum GPA of 2.5. Additional exam requirements/recommendations for international students: Required—TOEFL (minimum score 550 paper-based; 213 computer-based), IELTS (minimum score 6.5), Sakae Institute of Study Abroad (SISA): 550. *Application deadline:* Applications are processed on a rolling basis. Application fee: $30. Electronic applications accepted. *Expenses:* Tuition: Full-time $16,900; part-time $670 per credit. *Financial support:* In 2008–09, 154 students received support, including 26 teaching assistantships with partial tuition reimbursements available (averaging $5,870 per year); fellowships, career-related internships or fieldwork, institutionally sponsored loans, scholarships/grants, and unspecified assistantships also available. Support available to part-time students. Financial award application deadline: 3/15; financial award applicants required to submit FAFSA. *Faculty research:* Creative activity, performance practice, music therapy aging, composition, Motown music. Total annual research expenditures: $4,272. *Unit head:* Dr. Laurence A. Kaptain, Dean, 540-665-4600, Fax: 540-665-5402, E-mail: lkaptain@su.edu. *Application contact:* David Anthony, Dean of Admissions, 540-665-4581, Fax: 540-665-4627, E-mail: admit@su.edu.

Southern Methodist University, Meadows School of the Arts, Division of Arts Administration, Dallas, TX 75275. Offers MA/MBA. *Faculty:* 1 (woman) full-time, 1 (woman) part-time/adjunct. *Students:* 24 full-time (21 women); includes 2 minority (1 Asian American or Pacific Islander, 1 Hispanic American), 1 international. Average age 26. 18 applicants, 72% accepted, 7 enrolled. *Entrance requirements:* Additional exam requirements/recommendations for international students: Required—TOEFL (minimum score 600 paper-based; 250 computer-based; 100 iBT). *Application deadline:* For fall admission, 1/15 priority date for domestic and international students. Applications are processed on a rolling basis. Application fee: $75. Electronic applications accepted. *Unit head:* Dr. P. Gregory Warden, Interim Chair, 214-768-3425, E-mail: lhilliar@smu.edu. *Application contact:* Lynette Hilliard, Assistant Director, 214-768-3425, E-mail: ihilliar@smu.edu.

Southern Utah University, College of Performing and Visual Arts, Program in Arts Administration, Cedar City, UT 84720-2498. Offers MFA. *Entrance requirements:* For master's, GRE General Test, interview, 3 letters of recommendation, resumé, minimum GPA of 3.0. Electronic applications accepted.

Teachers College, Columbia University, Graduate Faculty of Education, Department of Arts and Humanities, Program in Arts Administration, New York, NY 10027-6696. Offers MA. *Faculty:* 1 (woman) full-time, 2 part-time/adjunct. *Students:* 50 full-time (38 women), 16 part-time (15 women); includes 13 minority (3 African Americans, 8 Asian Americans or Pacific Islanders, 2 Hispanic Americans), 14 international. Average age 28. 135 applicants, 27% accepted, 27 enrolled. In 2008, 24 master's awarded. *Degree requirements:* For master's, thesis, internship. *Entrance requirements:* For master's, GRE, approximately 3 years of related experience. Additional exam requirements/recommendations for international students: Required—TOEFL. *Application deadline:* For fall admission, 1/15 priority date for domestic students. Application fee: $75. *Expenses:* Tuition: Full-time $26,040; part-time $1085 per credit. Required fees: $720. *Financial support:* Career-related internships or fieldwork, Federal Work-Study, institutionally sponsored loans, tuition waivers (partial), and unspecified assistantships available. Financial award application deadline: 2/1. *Faculty research:* Artists' career development, arts law, American culture, strategic management, international training. *Unit head:* Graeme Sullivan, Chair, 212-678-3799. *Application contact:* Graeme Sullivan, Chair, 212-678-3799.

Temple University, Graduate School, Tyler School of Art, Department of Art History, Philadelphia, PA 19122-6096. Offers MA, PhD. *Accreditation:* NASAD. Part-time programs available. Terminal master's awarded for partial completion of doctoral program. *Degree requirements:* For master's, 2 foreign languages, thesis, comprehensive slide exam; for doctorate, thesis/dissertation, qualifying exam. *Entrance requirements:* For master's, GRE General Test, minimum GPA of 3.0; for doctorate, MA in art history. Additional exam requirements/recommendations for international students: Required—TOEFL. Electronic applications accepted. *Faculty research:* Aegean, Greek, and Roman art; early Christian art; Medieval art and architecture; Renaissance and baroque painting, sculpture, and architecture; nineteenth and twentieth century painting and sculpture.

See Close-Up on page 229.

Universidad del Turabo, Graduate Programs, School of Social Sciences and Humanities, Programs in Public Affairs, Program in Arts Administration, Gurabo, PR 00778-3030. Offers MA.

The University of Akron, Graduate School, College of Fine and Applied Arts, School of Dance, Theatre, and Arts Administration, Program in Arts Administration, Akron, OH 44325. Offers MA. *Accreditation:* NASAD. *Degree requirements:* For master's, thesis optional. *Entrance requirements:* For master's, minimum GPA of 2.75, interview, personal statement. Additional exam requirements/recommendations for international students: Required—TOEFL (minimum score 550 paper-based; 213 computer-based; 79 iBT). Electronic applications accepted.

University of Cincinnati, Graduate School, College-Conservatory of Music, Divisions of Opera, Musical Theater, Drama, and Arts Administration, Cincinnati, OH 45221. Offers arts administration (MA); directing (MFA); theater design and production (MFA); voice and opera (MM, DMA); MBA/MA. *Accreditation:* NAST (one or more programs are accredited). *Degree requirements:* For master's, final project. *Entrance requirements:* For master's, GMAT (MA), audition/interview. Additional exam requirements/recommendations for international students: Required—TOEFL (minimum score 520 paper-based; 190 computer-based). Electronic applications accepted.

University of Florida, Graduate School, Warrington College of Business Administration, Hough Graduate School of Business, Programs in Business Administration, Gainesville, FL 32611. Offers accounting (MBA); arts administration (MBA); business strategy and public policy (MBA); competitive strategy (MBA); decision and information sciences (MBA); electronic commerce (MBA); finance (MBA); general business (MBA); global management (MBA); Graham-Buffett security analysis (MBA); health administration (MBA); human resources management (MBA); international studies (MBA); Latin American business (MBA); management (MBA); marketing (MBA); sports administration (MBA); JD/MBA; MBA/MS; MBA/PhD; MBA/Pharm D; MD/MBA. *Accreditation:* AACSB. Part-time and evening/weekend programs available. Postbaccalaureate distance learning degree programs offered. *Entrance requirements:* For master's, GMAT, minimum GPA of 3.0, interview. Additional exam requirements/recommendations for international students: Required—TOEFL (minimum score 550 paper-based; 213 computer-based). Electronic applications accepted. *Faculty research:* Accounting, finance, insurance, management, real estate and urban analysis marketing.

University of New Orleans, Graduate School, College of Liberal Arts, Program in Arts Administration, New Orleans, LA 70148. Offers MA. Part-time programs available. *Degree requirements:* For master's, internship. *Entrance requirements:* For master's, GMAT, GRE General Test. Additional exam requirements/recommendations for international students: Required—TOEFL (minimum score 550 paper-based; 213 computer-based; 79 iBT). Electronic applications accepted.

University of Oregon, Graduate School, School of Architecture and Allied Arts, Program in Arts and Administration, Eugene, OR 97403-5230. Offers arts management (MA, MS). *Degree requirements:* For master's, summer internship, thesis/project. *Entrance requirements:* For master's, minimum GPA of 3.0; bachelor's degree in history, practice of visual, performing arts or other related degree. Additional exam requirements/recommendations for international students: Required—TOEFL. *Faculty research:* Museum education, arts program evaluation, community arts, information management, arts marketing.

Announcement: The Arts and Administration Program offers a Master of Arts Management, with concentrations in museum studies, community arts, performing arts, and media management. Full-time faculty members address cultural policy, community arts, museum education, events management, administration, evaluation, and aesthetics. Participating faculty members offer courses in information design, artistic administration, and nonprofit management.

University of Southern California, Graduate School, School of Fine Arts, Program in Public Art Studies, Los Angeles, CA 90089. Offers MPAS. *Degree requirements:* For master's, thesis, final project. *Entrance requirements:* For master's, GRE General Test.

University of Wisconsin–Madison, Graduate School, Wisconsin School of Business, Wisconsin Full-Time MBA Program, Madison, WI 53706-1380. Offers applied corporate finance (MBA); applied security analysis (MBA); arts administration (MBA); brand and product management (MBA); entrepreneurial management (MBA); marketing research (MBA); operations and technology management (MBA); real estate (MBA); risk management and insurance (MBA); strategic human resource management (MBA); strategic management in the life and engineering sciences (MBA); supply chain management (MBA). *Degree requirements:* For master's, minimum GPA of 3.0. *Entrance requirements:* For master's, GMAT, bachelors or equivalent degree, 2 years of work experience. Additional exam requirements/recommendations for international students: Required—TOEFL (minimum score 600 paper-based; 250 computer-based; 90 iBT). Electronic applications accepted.

University of Wisconsin–Superior, Graduate Division, Department of Counseling and Psychological Professions, Superior, WI 54880-4500. Offers community counseling (MSE); educational psychology (MSE); elementary school counseling (MSE); human relations (MSE); secondary school counseling (MSE). Part-time and evening/weekend programs available.

Degree requirements: For master's, position paper, practicum. *Entrance requirements:* For master's, California Psychological Inventory, GRE and/or MAT, minimum GPA of 2.75. *Faculty research:* Women and power, intrafamily dynamics.

University of Wisconsin–Superior, Graduate Division, Department of Visual Arts, Superior, WI 54880-4500. Offers art education (MA); art history (MA); art therapy (MA); arts administration (MA); studio arts (MA). Part-time programs available. *Degree requirements:* For master's, comprehensive exam, exhibit. *Entrance requirements:* For master's, minimum GPA of 2.75, portfolio.

Virginia Polytechnic Institute and State University, Graduate School, College of Liberal Arts and Human Sciences, Department of Theatre Arts, Blacksburg, VA 24061. Offers arts administration (MFA); costume design (MFA); lighting design (MFA); property management (MFA); scenic design (MFA); stage management (MFA); technical theatre (MFA). *Accreditation:* NAST. *Entrance requirements:* Additional exam requirements/recommendations for international students: Required—TOEFL (minimum score 550 paper-based; 213 computer-based). Electronic applications accepted.

Webster University, Leigh Gerdine College of Fine Arts, Department of Art, Program in Arts Management and Leadership, St. Louis, MO 63119-3194. Offers MFA. Part-time and evening/weekend programs available. *Degree requirements:* For master's, thesis. *Entrance requirements:* For master's, GRE, BA or BFA in related field, interview.

Winthrop University, College of Visual and Performing Arts, Department of Art, Rock Hill, SC 29733. Offers art (MFA); art administration (MA); art education (MA). *Accreditation:* NASAD. Part-time programs available. *Degree requirements:* For master's, thesis, documented exhibit, oral exam. *Entrance requirements:* For master's, GRE General Test or MAT, PRAXIS (MA), minimum GPA of 3.0, resumé, slide portfolio, teaching certificate (MA). Electronic applications accepted.

Art Therapy

Adler School of Professional Psychology, Programs in Psychology, Chicago, IL 60601-7203. Offers art therapy (Certificate); clinical hypnosis (Certificate); clinical psychology (Psy D); counseling psychology (MACP); counseling psychology/art therapy (MACAT); gerontology (MAGP); marriage and family counseling (MAMFC); marriage and family therapy (Certificate); organizational psychology (MAO); substance abuse counseling (MASAC, Certificate); Psy D/Certificate; Psy D/MACAT; Psy D/MACP; Psy D/MAMFC; Psy D/MASAC. *Accreditation:* APA. Part-time and evening/weekend programs available. Postbaccalaureate distance learning degree programs offered (minimal on-campus study). *Faculty:* 36 full-time (17 women), 45 part-time/adjunct (18 women). *Students:* 514 full-time (404 women), 128 part-time (100 women); includes 147 minority (69 African Americans, 2 American Indian/Alaska Native, 30 Asian Americans or Pacific Islanders, 46 Hispanic Americans), 53 international. Average age 27. 855 applicants, 46% accepted, 195 enrolled. In 2008, 110 master's, 136 doctorates awarded. Terminal master's awarded for partial completion of doctoral program. *Degree requirements:* For master's, thesis or alternative, oral exam, practicum; for doctorate, thesis/dissertation, clinical exam, internship, oral exam, practicum, written qualifying exam. *Entrance requirements:* For master's, 12 semester hours in psychology, minimum GPA of 3.0; for doctorate, 18 semester hours in psychology, minimum GPA of 3.25; for Certificate, appropriate master's or doctoral degree. Additional exam requirements/recommendations for international students: Required—TOEFL (minimum score 550 paper-based; 213 computer-based; 79 iBT). *Application deadline:* For fall admission, 2/15 priority date for domestic students, 12/1 priority date for international students. Applications are processed on a rolling basis. Application fee: $50. Electronic applications accepted. *Expenses:* Tuition: Part-time $850 per credit. Tuition and fees vary according to degree level, campus/location and program. *Financial support:* Career-related internships or fieldwork, Federal Work-Study, scholarships/grants, and tuition waivers (full and partial) available. Support available to part-time students. Financial award application deadline: 5/15; financial award applicants required to submit FAFSA. *Unit head:* Dr. Frank Gruba-McAllister, Vice President of Academic Affairs, 312-201-5900, Fax: 312-207-5917. *Application contact:* Craig A Hines, Director of Admissions, 312-201-5900 Ext. 226, Fax: 312-201-5917, E-mail: chines@adler.edu.

See Close-Up on page 1051.

Albertus Magnus College, Program in Art Therapy, New Haven, CT 06511-1189. Offers MAAT. Part-time and evening/weekend programs available. *Degree requirements:* For master's, thesis. *Entrance requirements:* For master's, interview, writing sample.

Athabasca University, Graduate Centre for Applied Psychology, Athabasca, AB T9S 3A3, Canada. Offers art therapy (MC); career counseling (MC); counseling (Advanced Certificate); counseling psychology (MC); school counseling (MC). *Faculty:* 3 full-time (2 women), 2 part-time/adjunct (0 women). Tuition and fees charges are reported in Canadian dollars. *Expenses:* Tuition, area resident: Full-time $13,255 Canadian dollars; part-time $1205 Canadian dollars per course. Tuition, state resident: full-time $13,255 Canadian dollars; part-time $1205 Canadian dollars per course. Tuition, nonresident: full-time $13,255 Canadian dollars; part-time $1205 Canadian dollars per course. International tuition: $15,455 Canadian dollars full-time. One-time fee: $280 Canadian dollars. *Unit head:* Dr. Sandra Collins, Program Director, 888-611-7121, E-mail: sandrac@athabascau.ca. *Application contact:* Information Contact, 800-788-9041, Fax: 780-675-6437, E-mail: inquire@athabascau.ca.

Caldwell College, Graduate Studies, Program in Counseling Psychology, Caldwell, NJ 07006-6195. Offers art therapy (MA); counseling psychology (MA); school counseling (MA). Part-time and evening/weekend programs available. *Degree requirements:* For master's, comprehensive exam, practicum. *Entrance requirements:* For master's, GRE General Test, minimum GPA of 3.0. Additional exam requirements/recommendations for international students: Required—TOEFL (minimum score 580 paper-based; 237 computer-based). Electronic applications accepted.

California Institute of Integral Studies, Graduate Programs, School of Professional Psychology, San Francisco, CA 94103. Offers clinical psychology (Psy D); community mental health (MA); drama therapy (MA); expressive arts therapy (MA); integral counseling psychology (MA); integral counseling, psychology-weekend (MA); somatic psychology (MA). *Accreditation:* APA. Part-time programs available. *Faculty:* 28 full-time, 59 part-time/adjunct. *Students:* 553 full-time (408 women), 88 part-time (69 women); includes 132 minority (25 African Americans, 3 American Indian/Alaska Native, 57 Asian Americans or Pacific Islanders, 47 Hispanic Americans). Average age 37. 506 applicants, 61% accepted, 181 enrolled. In 2008, 109 master's, 20 doctorates awarded. *Degree requirements:* For master's, comprehensive exam; for doctorate, comprehensive exam, thesis/dissertation. *Entrance requirements:* For master's, minimum GPA of 3.0, letters of recommendation, writing sample; for doctorate, GRE, MA in psychology or social work with appropriate practical experience for advanced standing, or BA with a minimum GPA of 3.1; letters of recommendation; writing sample. Additional exam requirements/recommendations for international students: Required—TOEFL. *Application deadline:* For fall admission, 2/1 priority date for domestic and international students; for spring admission, 10/15 priority date for domestic and international students. Applications are processed on a rolling basis. Application fee: $65. Electronic applications accepted. *Expenses:* Tuition: Part-time $815 per contact hour. Required fees: $270; $135 per semester. Tuition and fees vary according to degree level. *Financial support:* In 2008–09, 496 students received support; research assistantships with tuition reimbursements available, teaching assistantships with tuition reimbursements available, career-related internships or fieldwork, Federal Work-Study, institutionally sponsored loans, scholarships/grants, and tuition waivers (partial) available. Support available to part-time students. Financial award application deadline: 3/15; financial award applicants required to submit FAFSA. *Faculty research:* Somatic psychology, comparative psychology, art therapy, transpersonal psychology, eco-psychology. *Application contact:* David Townes, Senior Admissions Counselor, 415-575-6152, Fax: 415-575-1268, E-mail: dtownes@ciis.edu.

See Close-Up on page 1105.

California State University, Los Angeles, Graduate Studies, College of Arts and Letters, Department of Art, Los Angeles, CA 90032-8530. Offers art (MA), including art education, art history, art therapy, ceramics, metals, and textiles, design (MA, MFA), painting, sculpture, and graphic arts, photography; fine arts (MFA), including crafts, design (MA, MFA), studio arts. *Accreditation:* NASAD (one or more programs are accredited). Part-time and evening/weekend programs available. *Faculty:* 16 full-time (6 women). *Students:* 23 full-time (14 women), 52 part-time (37 women); includes 29 minority (2 African Americans, 3 American Indian/Alaska Native, 7 Asian Americans or Pacific Islanders, 17 Hispanic Americans), 4 international. Average age 38. 30 applicants, 100% accepted, 14 enrolled. In 2008, 15 master's awarded. *Degree requirements:* For master's, comprehensive exam, project or thesis. *Entrance requirements:* For master's, portfolio. Additional exam requirements/recommendations for international students: Required—TOEFL (minimum score 500 paper-based; 173 computer-based). *Application deadline:* For fall admission, 6/15 for domestic students, 5/1 for international students; for winter admission, 11/1 for domestic students, 9/1 for international students; for spring admission, 2/1 for domestic students, 10/1 for international students. Applications are processed on a rolling basis. Application fee: $55. Electronic applications accepted. *Expenses:* Tuition, nonresident: part-time $226 per credit. Required fees: $4019. *Financial support:* Federal Work-Study available. Support available to part-time students. Financial award application deadline: 3/1. *Faculty research:* The artist and the book, conceptual art, ceramic processes, computer graphics, architectural graphics. *Unit head:* Dr. Robert Martin, Chair, 323-343-4010, Fax: 323-343-4045, E-mail: rjmartin@calstatela.edu. *Application contact:* Dr. Jose L. Galvan, Dean of Graduate Studies, 323-343-3820, Fax: 323-343-5653, E-mail: jgalvan@cslanet.calstatela.edu.

The College of New Rochelle, Graduate School, Division of Art and Communication Studies, Program in Art Therapy, New Rochelle, NY 10805-2308. Offers art therapy (MS); art therapy/counseling (MS). Part-time and evening/weekend programs available. *Degree requirements:* For master's, thesis, practicum, fieldwork. *Entrance requirements:* For master's, 12 credits in psychology, 15 credits in studio art, portfolio. *Faculty research:* Phototherapy, assessment and evaluation, developmental stages in art, creativity and mental illness.

Concordia University, School of Graduate Studies, Faculty of Fine Arts, Department of Creative Arts Therapies, Montréal, QC H3G 1M8, Canada. Offers MA.

Drexel University, College of Nursing and Health Professions, Program in Creative Arts in Therapy, Specialization in Art Therapy, Philadelphia, PA 19104-2875. Offers MA, PMC. *Accreditation:* NASAD. *Degree requirements:* For master's, comprehensive exam, thesis. *Entrance requirements:* For master's, GRE General Test or MAT, interview, minimum GPA of 2.75, portfolio. Electronic applications accepted.

Eastern Virginia Medical School, Graduate Art Therapy and Counseling Program, Norfolk, VA 23501-1980. Offers MS. *Faculty:* 3 full-time, 8 part-time/adjunct. *Students:* 25. 32 applicants, 72% accepted, 13 enrolled. In 2008, 10 master's awarded. *Degree requirements:* For master's, comprehensive exam, thesis, internship. *Entrance requirements:* For master's, 12 credit hours in psychology, including abnormal, developmental and personality; 18 credit hours in studio art; face-to-face interview; portfolio (diverse media preferred). *Application deadline:* For fall admission, 1/15 priority date for domestic and international students. Application fee: $60. Electronic applications accepted. *Expenses:* Contact institution. *Faculty research:* Art therapy projective imagery assessment: a collection of children's drawings. *Unit head:* Abby Calisch, Director, 757-446-5895, Fax: 757-446-6179, E-mail: artthrpy@evms.edu. *Application contact:* Kiera Dorsey, Administrative Support Coordinator, 757-446-5895, Fax: 757-446-6179, E-mail: dorseyks@evms.edu.

Emporia State University, School of Graduate Studies, The Teachers College, Department of Psychology, Art Therapy, Rehabilitation and Mental Health Counseling, Program in Art Therapy, Emporia, KS 66801-5087. Offers MS. *Accreditation:* NASAD. Part-time programs available. *Students:* 18 full-time (all women), 2 part-time (both women), 3 international. 10 applicants, 100% accepted, 10 enrolled. In 2008, 7 master's awarded. *Degree requirements:* For master's, comprehensive exam or thesis, internship. *Entrance requirements:* For master's, GRE General Test or MAT, graduate essay exam, appropriate bachelor's degree. Additional exam requirements/recommendations for international students: Required—TOEFL. *Application deadline:* For fall admission, 6/1 for domestic students; for spring admission, 10/1 for domestic students. Applications are processed on a rolling basis. Application fee: $30 ($75 for international students). Electronic applications accepted. *Expenses:* Tuition, area resident: Full-time $3976; part-time $166 per credit hour. Tuition, state resident: full-time $3976; part-time $166 per credit hour. Tuition, nonresident: full-time $12,028; part-time $501 per credit hour. Required fees: $51 per credit hour. Tuition and fees vary according to campus/location. *Financial support:* Career-related internships or fieldwork, Federal Work-Study, institutionally sponsored loans, health care benefits, and unspecified assistantships available. Financial award application deadline: 3/15; financial award applicants required to submit FAFSA. *Unit head:* Dr. Kenneth A. Weaver, Chair, 620-341-5317, E-mail: kweaver@emporia.edu. *Application contact:* Mary Sewell, Admissions Coordinator, 800-950-GRAD, Fax: 620-341-5909, E-mail: msewell@emporia.edu.

The George Washington University, Columbian College of Arts and Sciences, Program in Art Therapy, Washington, DC 20052. Offers MA. *Faculty:* 1 (woman) full-time, 12 part-time/adjunct (11 women). *Students:* 39 full-time (36 women), 12 part-time (11 women); includes 11 minority (3 African Americans, 3 American Indian/Alaska Native, 3 Asian Americans or Pacific Islanders, 2 Hispanic Americans), 4 international. Average age 27. 70 applicants, 43% accepted, 28 enrolled. In 2008, 13 master's awarded. *Degree requirements:* For master's, internship, practicum paper. *Entrance requirements:* For master's, GRE General Test, interview, minimum GPA of 3.0. Additional exam requirements/recommendations for international students: Required—TOEFL (minimum score 550 paper-based; 213 computer-based; 80 iBT). *Application deadline:* For fall admission, 1/1 priority date for domestic students. Application fee: $60. *Financial support:* In 2008–09, 11 students received support; fellowships with partial tuition reimbursements available, career-related internships or fieldwork, Federal Work-Study, institutionally sponsored loans, and tuition waivers available. *Unit head:* Heidi Bardot, Director, 202-994-4148, E-mail: hbardot@gwu.edu. *Application contact:* Information Contact, 202-994-6285, Fax: 202-994-1404, E-mail: artx@gwu.edu.

Hofstra University, School of Education, Health, and Human Services, Department of Counseling, Research, Special Education and Rehabilitation, Program in Creative Arts Therapy, Hempstead, NY 11549. Offers creative arts therapy (MA). Part-time programs available.

Art Therapy

Hofstra University (continued)
Students: 57 full-time (55 women), 22 part-time (21 women); includes 10 minority (2 African Americans, 5 Asian Americans or Pacific Islanders, 3 Hispanic Americans), 13 international. Average age 29. 71 applicants, 72% accepted, 27 enrolled. In 2008, 25 master's awarded. *Degree requirements:* For master's, thesis optional. *Entrance requirements:* For master's, interview, portfolio, 3 letters of recommendation, 12 hours of course work in psychology, 18 hours of course work in studio art, essay. Additional exam requirements/recommendations for international students: Required—TOEFL (minimum score 550 paper-based; 213 computer-based; 80 iBT). *Application deadline:* Applications are processed on a rolling basis. Application fee: $60. Electronic applications accepted. *Expenses:* Tuition: Full-time $15,300; part-time $850 per credit. Required fees: $970; $165 per term. Tuition and fees vary according to program. *Financial support:* In 2008–09, 35 students received support, including 5 fellowships with full and partial tuition reimbursements available (averaging $3,350 per year), 4 research assistantships with full and partial tuition reimbursements available (averaging $14,220 per year); career-related internships or fieldwork, Federal Work-Study, institutionally sponsored loans, scholarships/grants, and tuition waivers (full and partial) also available. Support available to part-time students. Financial award applicants required to submit FAFSA. *Faculty research:* Creativity for non-artists, medical art therapy, play and sand tray therapy, cultural centex. *Unit head:* Margaret E. Carlock-Russo, Director, 516-463-7259, Fax: 516-463-6184, E-mail: Margaret.E.Carlock@hofstra.edu. *Application contact:* Carol Drummer, Dean of Graduate Admissions, 516-463-4876, Fax: 516-463-4664, E-mail: gradstudent@hofstra.edu.

Lesley University, Graduate School of Arts and Social Sciences, Division of Expressive Therapies, Cambridge, MA 02138-2790. Offers art (MA); dance (MA); expressive therapies (MA, PhD, CAGS); music (MA). Terminal master's awarded for partial completion of doctoral program. *Degree requirements:* For master's, internship, practicum; for doctorate, thesis/dissertation. *Entrance requirements:* For master's, art portfolio, performance DVD; for doctorate, GRE or MAT. Additional exam requirements/recommendations for international students: Required—TOEFL (minimum score 550 paper-based; 213 computer-based; 80 iBT). *Expenses:* Tuition: Full-time $13,770; part-time $765 per credit hour. Required fees: $150. Tuition and fees vary according to course load, degree level, campus/location and program.

See Close-Up on page 211.

Long Island University, C.W. Post Campus, School of Visual and Performing Arts, Department of Art, Brookville, NY 11548-1300. Offers art (MA); art education (MS); clinical art therapy (MA); fine art and design (MFA). Part-time and evening/weekend programs available. *Degree requirements:* For master's, thesis. Electronic applications accepted. *Faculty research:* Painting, sculpture, installation, computers, video.

Marylhurst University, Department of Art Therapy Counseling, Marylhurst, OR 97036-0261. Offers art therapy (PGC); art therapy counseling (MA); counseling (PGC). Part-time programs available. *Faculty:* 3 full-time (all women), 4 part-time/adjunct (all women). *Students:* 48 full-time (46 women), 5 part-time (all women); includes 2 minority (1 African American, 1 Asian American or Pacific Islander). Average age 32. 26 applicants, 96% accepted, 21 enrolled. In 2008, 19 master's awarded. *Degree requirements:* For master's, comprehensive exam, practicums. *Entrance requirements:* For master's, MAT, minimum GPA of 3.0, course work in psychology and art, slide portfolio, letters of reference, resumé, autobiography, personal statement, portfolio. Additional exam requirements/recommendations for international students: Required—TOEFL (minimum score 550 paper-based; 213 computer-based; 80 iBT). *Application deadline:* For fall admission, 1/31 priority date for domestic and international students. Applications are processed on a rolling basis. Application fee: $40 ($50 for international students). *Expenses:* Contact institution. *Financial support:* Federal Work-Study and scholarships/grants available. Support available to part-time students. Financial award applicants required to submit FAFSA. *Faculty research:* Scientific approaches to art therapy research, child and adolescent psychotherapy, multicultural counseling. *Unit head:* Christine Turner, Chair, 503-636-8141, Fax: 503-636-9526, E-mail: cturner@marylhurst.edu. *Application contact:* Kathleen Schneff, Admissions Specialist, 800-634-9982 Ext. 3322, Fax: 503-635-6585, E-mail: admissions@marylhurst.edu.

Marywood University, Academic Affairs, Insalaco College of Creative Arts and Management, Art Department, Program in Art Therapy, Scranton, PA 18509-1598. Offers MA, Certificate. *Accreditation:* NASAD. Part-time and evening/weekend programs available. *Degree requirements:* For master's, comprehensive exam, thesis or alternative, internship, practicum. *Entrance requirements:* For master's, portfolio. Additional exam requirements/recommendations for international students: Required—TOEFL (minimum score 550 paper-based; 213 computer-based). Electronic applications accepted. *Faculty research:* Perspectives of leading educators in art therapy, current trends in art education.

Mount Mary College, Graduate Programs, Program in Art Therapy, Milwaukee, WI 53222-4597. Offers MS. Evening/weekend programs available. *Faculty:* 4 full-time (3 women), 6 part-time/adjunct (all women). *Students:* 51 full-time (50 women), 2 part-time (both women); includes 5 minority (3 African Americans, 2 Hispanic Americans). Average age 29. 48 applicants, 60% accepted, 25 enrolled. In 2008, 14 master's awarded. *Degree requirements:* For master's, thesis or alternative, internship. *Entrance requirements:* For master's, minimum GPA of 2.75, portfolio. Additional exam requirements/recommendations for international students: Required—TOEFL (minimum score 500 paper-based; 173 computer-based). *Application deadline:* For fall admission, 3/15 for domestic and international students. Application fee: $35 ($75 for international students). Electronic applications accepted. *Expenses:* Tuition: Part-time $545 per credit. *Financial support:* In 2008–09, 2 students received support. Career-related internships or fieldwork and Federal Work-Study available. Support available to part-time students. Financial award application deadline: 5/1; financial award applicants required to submit FAFSA. *Faculty research:* Art-based research in art therapy, consensus-group supervision, art therapy in public school programs. *Unit head:* Dr. Bruce Moon, Director, 414-256-1215, E-mail: moonb@mtmary.edu. *Application contact:* Dr. Bruce Moon, Director, 414-256-1215, E-mail: moonb@mtmary.edu.

Naropa University, Graduate Programs, Program in Transpersonal Counseling Psychology, Concentration in Art Therapy, Boulder, CO 80302-6697. Offers MA. *Faculty:* 1 (woman) full-time, 11 part-time/adjunct (6 women). *Students:* 28 full-time (24 women), 17 part-time (15 women); includes 5 minority (1 African American, 1 American Indian/Alaska Native, 1 Asian American or Pacific Islander, 2 Hispanic Americans), 2 international. Average age 29. 55 applicants, 44% accepted, 14 enrolled. In 2008, 11 master's awarded. *Degree requirements:* For master's, internships, 180 direct art contact hours of studio-based work. *Entrance requirements:* For master's, portfolio (21 slides), in-person interview, course work in psychology and art, resumé, letter of interest, 3 letters of recommendation. Additional exam requirements/recommendations for international students: Required—TOEFL (minimum score 600 paper-based; 250 computer-based). *Application deadline:* For fall admission, 1/15 priority date for domestic and international students. Applications are processed on a rolling basis. Application fee: $60. Electronic applications accepted. *Expenses:* Tuition: Full-time $14,767; part-time $726 per credit hour. Required fees: $45 per term. *Financial support:* In 2008–09, 27 students received support, including 6 research assistantships with partial tuition reimbursements available (averaging $3,000 per year), 2 teaching assistantships with partial tuition reimbursements available (averaging $3,000 per year); career-related internships or fieldwork, Federal Work-Study, scholarships/grants, health care benefits, tuition waivers (partial), and unspecified assistantships also available. Support available to part-time students. Financial award application deadline: 3/1; financial award applicants required to submit FAFSA. *Unit head:* Michael Franklin, Director, 303-546-3545. *Application contact:* Alice Di Tullio, Admissions Counselor, 303-546-3598, Fax: 303-546-3583, E-mail: aliced@naropa.edu.

See Close-Up on page 1121.

Nazareth College of Rochester, Graduate Studies, Department of Creative Arts Therapy, Program in Art Therapy, Rochester, NY 14618-3790. Offers MS. Part-time programs available. *Entrance requirements:* For master's, minimum GPA of 3.0, portfolio review.

New York University, Steinhardt School of Culture, Education and Human Development, Department of Art and Art Professions, Program in Art Therapy, New York, NY 10012-1019. Offers MA. Part-time and evening/weekend programs available. *Degree requirements:* For master's, thesis (for some programs). *Entrance requirements:* For master's, interview, portfolio. Additional exam requirements/recommendations for international students: Required—TOEFL. *Faculty research:* Art therapy in non-clinical settings, international art therapy.

Notre Dame de Namur University, Division of Academic Affairs, School of Sciences, Department of Art Therapy Psychology, Belmont, CA 94002-1908. Offers MAAT, MAMFT. Part-time programs available. *Faculty:* 2 full-time (1 woman), 8 part-time/adjunct (7 women). *Students:* 38 full-time (all women), 56 part-time (54 women); includes 17 minority (1 African American, 11 Asian Americans or Pacific Islanders, 5 Hispanic Americans). Average age 34. 33 applicants, 94% accepted, 22 enrolled. In 2008, 26 master's awarded. *Degree requirements:* For master's, oral presentation, portfolio. *Entrance requirements:* For master's, interview, minimum GPA of 2.5. Additional exam requirements/recommendations for international students: Required—TOEFL (minimum score 550 paper-based; 213 computer-based; 79 iBT). *Application deadline:* For fall admission, 8/1 priority date for domestic students; for spring admission, 12/1 priority date for domestic students. Applications are processed on a rolling basis. Application fee: $60. Electronic applications accepted. *Expenses:* Tuition: Part-time $699 per unit. Required fees: $3 per unit. $35 per semester. *Financial support:* Career-related internships or fieldwork available. Support available to part-time students. Financial award applicants required to submit FAFSA. *Unit head:* Dr. Richard Carolan, Chair, 650-508-3556, Fax: 650-508-3736. *Application contact:* Candace Hallmark, Assistant Director of Graduate Admissions, 650-508-3592, Fax: 650-508-3426, E-mail: grad.admit@ndnu.edu.

Ottawa University, Graduate Studies-Arizona, Program in Professional Counseling, Ottawa, KS 66067-3399. Offers Christian counseling (MA); expressive arts therapy (MA); marriage and family therapy (MA); treatment of trauma, abuse and deprivation (MA). Programs offered in Mesa, Phoenix, Tempe and West Valley, AZ. Part-time and evening/weekend programs available. Postbaccalaureate distance learning degree programs offered. *Degree requirements:* For master's, comprehensive exam, thesis or alternative, field experience, practicum. *Entrance requirements:* For master's, minimum undergraduate GPA of 3.0; course work in theories of personality, abnormal psychology, and human growth and development. Additional exam requirements/recommendations for international students: Required—TOEFL (minimum score 550 paper-based; 213 computer-based).

Pratt Institute, School of Art and Design, Programs in Creative Arts Therapy, Brooklyn, NY 11205-3899. Offers art therapy and creativity development (MPS); art therapy-special education (MPS); dance/movement therapy (MS). *Accreditation:* NASAD (one or more programs are accredited). Part-time programs available. *Faculty:* 3 full-time (all women), 19 part-time/adjunct (16 women). *Students:* 112 full-time (108 women), 1 (woman) part-time; includes 16 minority (5 African Americans, 3 Asian Americans or Pacific Islanders, 8 Hispanic Americans), 7 international. Average age 29. 196 applicants, 33% accepted, 35 enrolled. In 2008, 32 master's awarded. *Degree requirements:* For master's, thesis. *Entrance requirements:* For master's, bachelor's degree, transcripts, letters of recommendation, statement, portfolio. Additional exam requirements/recommendations for international students: Required—TOEFL (minimum score 600 paper-based; 250 computer-based). *Application deadline:* For fall admission, 2/1 for domestic and international students; for spring admission, 10/1 for domestic and international students. Applications are processed on a rolling basis. Application fee: $50 ($90 for international students). Electronic applications accepted. *Expenses:* Tuition: Full-time $20,412; part-time $1134 per credit. Required fees: $1190; $1190 per year. *Financial support:* Career-related internships or fieldwork, Federal Work-Study, institutionally sponsored loans, scholarships/grants, health care benefits, tuition waivers (full), and unspecified assistantships available. Support available to part-time students. Financial award application deadline: 2/1; financial award applicants required to submit FAFSA. *Faculty research:* Psychology and aesthetic interaction, art therapy and AIDS, art therapy and autism, art diagnosis. *Unit head:* Jean Davis, Chairperson, 718-636-3428, E-mail: jdavis@pratt.edu. *Application contact:* Young Hah, Director of Graduate Admissions, 718-636-3683, Fax: 718-399-4242, E-mail: yhah@pratt.edu.

See Close-Up on page 219.

Prescott College, Graduate Programs, Program in Counseling and Psychology, Prescott, AZ 86301. Offers adventure-based psychotherapy (MA); counseling psychology (MA); ecopsychology (MA); ecotherapy (MA); equine-assisted mental health (MA); expressive arts therapy (MA); somatic psychology (MA); student-directed independent study (MA). Part-time programs available. Postbaccalaureate distance learning degree programs offered (minimal on-campus study). *Faculty:* 43 part-time/adjunct (29 women). *Students:* 74 full-time (66 women), 19 part-time (18 women); includes 9 minority (4 African Americans, 1 American Indian/Alaska Native, 4 Hispanic Americans), 9 international. Average age 37. 54 applicants, 70% accepted, 27 enrolled. In 2008, 29 master's awarded. *Degree requirements:* For master's, thesis, fieldwork or internship, practicum. *Entrance requirements:* For master's, 2 letters of recommendation, resumé, official academic transcripts, personal statement, application form, proposed study plan. Additional exam requirements/recommendations for international students: Required—TOEFL (minimum score 500 paper-based; 173 computer-based). *Application deadline:* For fall admission, 3/15 priority date for domestic and international students; for spring admission, 9/15 priority date for domestic and international students. Applications are processed on a rolling basis. Application fee: $40. Electronic applications accepted. *Expenses:* Tuition: Full-time $13,608; part-time $567 per credit. Required fees: $50 per term. One-time fee: $182. Tuition and fees vary according to degree level. *Financial support:* Career-related internships or fieldwork, Federal Work-Study, and scholarships/grants available. Financial award applicants required to submit FAFSA. *Unit head:* Camille Smith, Chair, Fax: 928-776-5151, E-mail: csmith@prescott.edu. *Application contact:* Kerstin Alicki, Admissions Counselor, 877-350-2102, Fax: 928-776-5242, E-mail: admissions@prescott.edu.

Saint Mary-of-the-Woods College, Program in Art Therapy, Saint Mary-of-the-Woods, IN 47876. Offers MA, Post-Master's Certificate. Part-time and evening/weekend programs available. Postbaccalaureate distance learning degree programs offered (minimal on-campus study). *Degree requirements:* For master's, thesis or project. *Entrance requirements:* For master's, minimum GPA of 2.5; for Post-Master's Certificate, 12 credit hours in abnormal and developmental psychology, 15 credit hours in studio art skills, art portfolio, interview, minimum GPA of 2.5. Electronic applications accepted.

Salve Regina University, Graduate Studies, Holistic Graduate Programs, Newport, RI 02840-4192. Offers expressive and creative arts (CAGS); holistic counseling (MA); holistic leadership (MA, CAGS); mental health (CAGS). Part-time and evening/weekend programs available. *Faculty:* 4 full-time (2 women), 9 part-time/adjunct (6 women). *Students:* 18 full-time (16 women), 90 part-time (81 women); includes 1 minority (American Indian/Alaska Native). Average age 42. 40 applicants, 83% accepted, 30 enrolled. In 2008, 18 master's, 15 other advanced degrees awarded. *Degree requirements:* For master's, internship, project. *Entrance requirements:* For master's, GMAT, GRE General Test, or MAT. Additional exam requirements/recommendations for international students: Required—TOEFL (minimum score 600 paper-based; 250 computer-based; 100 iBT), TOEFL or IELTS. *Application deadline:* For fall admission, 3/15 priority date for domestic and international students; for spring admission, 9/15 priority date for domestic and international students. Applications are processed on a rolling basis. Application fee: $60. Electronic applications accepted. *Expenses:* Tuition: Part-time $395 per credit. Required fees: $40 per term. Tuition and fees vary according to degree level. *Financial support:* Career-related internships or fieldwork and Federal Work-Study available. Support available to part-time students. Financial award application deadline: 3/1; financial award applicants required to submit FAFSA. *Unit head:* Dr. Peter F. Mullen, Director, 401-341-3278, Fax: 401-341-2977, E-mail: mullenp@salve.edu. *Application contact:* Kelly Alverson, Graduate Admissions Counselor, 401-341-2153, Fax: 401-341-2973, E-mail: kelly.alverson@salve.edu.

School of the Art Institute of Chicago, Graduate Division, Program in Art Therapy, Chicago, IL 60603-3103. Offers MAAT. *Accreditation:* NASAD. *Degree requirements:* For master's, thesis, personal interview. *Entrance requirements:* Additional exam requirements/recommendations for international students: Required—TOEFL, IELTS. *Faculty research:* Migrane, ousider art, community-based practice.

See Close-Up on page 225.

School of Visual Arts, Graduate Programs, Art Therapy Department, New York, NY 10010-3994. Offers MPS. *Degree requirements:* For master's, thesis or 750 internship hours. *Entrance requirements:* For master's, portfolio, bachelor's degree with 12 credits in undergraduate psychology including child and abnormal psychology, 18 credits of studio art. Additional exam requirements/recommendations for international students: Required—TOEFL (minimum score 550 paper-based; 213 computer-based; 79 iBT). Electronic applications accepted.

Seton Hill University, Program in Art Therapy, Greensburg, PA 15601. Offers MA, Certificate. Part-time programs available. *Degree requirements:* For master's, thesis or alternative. *Entrance requirements:* For master's, portfolio, 12 undergraduate credits in psychology, 15 undergraduate credits in art, minimum GPA of 3.0. Additional exam requirements/recommendations for international students: Required—TOEFL (minimum score 600 paper-based; 250 computer-based). Electronic applications accepted. *Faculty research:* Art therapy with the deaf, art therapy with children.

Southern Illinois University Edwardsville, Graduate Studies and Research, College of Arts and Sciences, Department of Art and Design, Program in Art Therapy Counseling, Edwardsville, IL 62026-0001. Offers MA. Part-time programs available. *Students:* 18 full-time (17 women), 9 part-time (all women); includes 1 minority (Hispanic American), 1 international. Average age 26. 33 applicants, 39% accepted. In 2008, 4 master's awarded. *Degree requirements:* For master's, thesis or alternative, project. *Entrance requirements:* For master's, MAT, portfolio. Additional exam requirements/recommendations for international students: Required—TOEFL (minimum score 550 paper-based; 213 computer-based; 79 iBT), IELTS (minimum score 6.5). *Application deadline:* For fall admission, 2/1 for domestic and international students. Application fee: $30. Electronic applications accepted. *Expenses:* Tuition, area resident: Full-time $5838. Tuition, nonresident: full-time $14,596. Required fees: $1525. *Financial support:* In 2008–09, 1 fellowship (averaging $8,370 per year), 18 teaching assistantships with full tuition reimbursements (averaging $8,064 per year) were awarded; research assistantships. Financial award application deadline: 3/1; financial award applicants required to submit FAFSA. *Unit head:* Dr. Patricia Klorer, Program Director, 618-650-3183, E-mail: pklorer@siue.edu. *Application contact:* Michelle Robinson, Coordinator of Graduate Recruitment, 618-650-2811, Fax: 618-650-3523, E-mail: michero@siue.edu.

Southwestern College, Program in Art Therapy/Counseling, Santa Fe, NM 87502-4788. Offers MA. Part-time and evening/weekend programs available. *Degree requirements:* For master's, internship. *Entrance requirements:* For master's, resumé, slide portfolio, interview, 3 letters of reference, personal statement of 3 pages.

Springfield College, Graduate Programs, Program in Art Therapy, Springfield, MA 01109-3797. Offers M Ed, MS, CAGS. Part-time programs available. *Faculty:* 2 full-time (1 woman), 9 part-time/adjunct (8 women). *Students:* 25 full-time, 7 part-time. Average age 30. 37 applicants, 81% accepted, 13 enrolled. In 2008, 6 master's, 1 other advanced degree awarded. *Degree requirements:* For master's, research project, final art exhibition. *Entrance requirements:* For master's, portfolio, prerequisite courses required for accreditation. Additional exam requirements/recommendations for international students: Required—TOEFL (minimum score 550 paper-based; 213 computer-based). *Application deadline:* For fall admission, 1/15 for domestic and international students; for winter admission, 11/1 for domestic and international students; for spring admission, 11/1 for domestic and international students. Applications are processed on a rolling basis. Application fee: $50. Electronic applications accepted. *Expenses:* Tuition: Full-time $9132; part-time $761 per semester hour. Required fees: $150. Tuition and fees vary according to course load. *Financial support:* Fellowships with partial tuition reimbursements, teaching assistantships with partial tuition reimbursements, career-related internships or fieldwork, Federal Work-Study, institutionally sponsored loans, and unspecified assistantships available. Financial award application deadline: 3/1; financial award applicants required to submit FAFSA. *Faculty research:* Stage development in art, psychopathology of expression, art history and art therapy. *Unit head:* Dr. Simone Alter-Muri, Director, 413-748-3752, E-mail: saltermuri@spfldcol.edu. *Application contact:* Donald James Shaw, Director of Graduate Admissions, 413-748-3479, Fax: 413-748-3694, E-mail: donald_shaw_jr@spfldcol.edu.

University of Wisconsin–Superior, Graduate Division, Department of Visual Arts, Superior, WI 54880-4500. Offers art education (MA); art history (MA); art therapy (MA); arts administration (MA); studio arts (MA). Part-time programs available. *Degree requirements:* For master's, comprehensive exam, exhibit. *Entrance requirements:* For master's, minimum GPA of 2.75, portfolio.

Ursuline College, School of Graduate Studies, Program in Art Therapy Counseling, Pepper Pike, OH 44124-4398. Offers MA. Part-time programs available. *Faculty:* 4 full-time (all women), 5 part-time/adjunct (4 women). *Students:* 6 full-time (all women), 43 part-time (42 women); includes 3 minority (1 African American, 2 Hispanic Americans). Average age 32. 40 applicants, 65% accepted, 22 enrolled. In 2008, 15 master's awarded. *Degree requirements:* For master's, thesis, 700 hour internship. *Entrance requirements:* For master's, BA in psychology, social sciences, or related field; minimum undergraduate GPA of 3.0; portfolio; work experience with human service agency. Additional exam requirements/recommendations for international students: Required—TOEFL (minimum score 500 paper-based; 173 computer-based). *Application deadline:* For fall admission, 8/1 priority date for domestic students. Applications are processed on a rolling basis. Application fee: $25. *Expenses:* Tuition: Full-time $13,590; part-time $775 per credit hour. Required fees: $220; $70 per semester. *Financial support:* In 2008–09, 57 students received support. Federal Work-Study available. Financial award application deadline: 3/1; financial award applicants required to submit FAFSA. *Faculty research:* Art therapy used with psychiatric and geriatric populations, art therapy used in treatment of chemical dependency, family therapy, child art therapy. *Unit head:* Gale Rule-Hoffman, Director, 440-646-8138, Fax: 440-684-6088. *Application contact:* Lauren Anderson, Secretary, 440-646-8119, Fax: 440-684-6088, E-mail: gradsch@ursuline.edu.

Decorative Arts

Bard College, Program in History of the Decorative Arts, Design and Culture, Annandale-on-Hudson, NY 12504. Offers MA, PhD. Part-time programs available. *Degree requirements:* For master's, one foreign language, thesis, internship; for doctorate, 2 foreign languages, thesis/dissertation, exams. *Entrance requirements:* For master's, GRE General Test, writing sample, 3 letters of recommendation; for doctorate, GRE General Test, master's thesis or equivalent, 3 letters of recommendation. Additional exam requirements/recommendations for international students: Required—TOEFL. *Expenses:* Contact institution.

Bard Graduate Center for Studies in the Decorative Arts, Design, and Culture, Program in History of the Decorative Arts, Design and Culture, New York, NY 10024-3602. Offers MA, PhD. Bard Graduate Center for Studies in the Decorative Arts is a unit of Bard College. Part-time programs available. *Degree requirements:* For master's, one foreign language, thesis, internship; for doctorate, 2 foreign languages, thesis/dissertation, exams. *Entrance requirements:* For master's, GRE General Test, writing sample, 3 letters of recommendation; for doctorate, GRE General Test, master's thesis or equivalent, 3 letters of recommendation. Additional exam requirements/recommendations for international students: Required—TOEFL. *Faculty research:* English craftsmen, ancient furniture, aesthetics and politics, Art Nouveau jewelry, European sculpture.

See Close-Up on page 203.

Corcoran College of Art and Design, Graduate Programs, Washington, DC 20006-4804. Offers art education (MAT); history of decorative arts (MA); interior design (MA). *Accreditation:* NASAD. Part-time programs available. *Entrance requirements:* Additional exam requirements/recommendations for international students: Required—TOEFL.

The New School: A University, Parsons The New School for Design, Program in the History of Decorative Arts, New York, NY 10011. Offers MA. Offered jointly with the Cooper-Hewitt Museum and the Smithsonian Institution. *Accreditation:* NASAD. *Faculty:* 4 full-time (3 women), 13 part-time/adjunct (10 women). *Students:* 54 full-time (50 women), 46 part-time (44 women); includes 8 minority (1 African American, 6 Asian Americans or Pacific Islanders, 1 Hispanic American), 7 international. Average age 33. In 2008, 24 master's awarded. *Degree requirements:* For master's, one foreign language. *Entrance requirements:* For master's, sample of written work. Additional exam requirements/recommendations for international students: Required—TOEFL (minimum score 580 paper-based; 237 computer-based; 93 iBT). *Application deadline:* For fall admission, 2/1 priority date for domestic students. Applications are processed on a rolling basis. Application fee: $50. *Expenses:* Tuition: Full-time $27,144; part-time $1508 per credit. Required fees: $355 per semester. *Financial support:* Fellowships with partial tuition reimbursements, research assistantships with partial tuition reimbursements, teaching assistantships with partial tuition reimbursements, Federal Work-Study, scholarships/grants, tuition waivers (partial), and unspecified assistantships available. Financial award application deadline: 3/1; financial award applicants required to submit FAFSA. *Unit head:* Dr. Sarah E. Lawrence, Director, 212-849-8345, E-mail: lawrences@si.edu. *Application contact:* Anthony Padilla, Director of Admissions, 212-229-8989 Ext. 4023, Fax: 212-229-8975, E-mail: padillaa@newschool.edu.

See Close-Up on page 217.

Museum Studies

Arizona State University, Graduate College, College of Liberal Arts and Sciences, Division of Social Sciences, School of Human Evolution and Social Change, Tempe, AZ 85287. Offers anthropology (PhD); applied mathematics for the life and social sciences (PhD); environmental social science (PhD); museum studies in anthropology (MA); social science and health (PhD). *Degree requirements:* For master's, thesis or alternative; for doctorate, thesis/dissertation. *Entrance requirements:* For master's and doctorate, GRE.

Bank Street College of Education, Graduate School, Department of Curriculum and Instruction, Program in Museum Education, New York, NY 10025. Offers museum education (MS Ed); museum education: elementary education certification (MS Ed); museum education: middle school certification (MS Ed); museum studies (MS Ed). *Students:* 29 full-time (27 women), 22 part-time (19 women); includes 7 minority (1 African American, 2 Asian Americans or Pacific Islanders, 4 Hispanic Americans). Average age 28. 30 applicants, 83% accepted, 16 enrolled. In 2008, 17 master's awarded. *Degree requirements:* For master's, thesis. *Entrance requirements:* For master's, interview. Additional exam requirements/recommendations for international students: Required—TOEFL (minimum score 600 paper-based; 250 computer-based; 100 iBT), IELTS (minimum score 7). *Application deadline:* For fall admission, 3/1 priority date for domestic and international students; for spring admission, 11/1 priority date for domestic and international students. Applications are processed on a rolling basis. Application fee: $50. *Expenses:* Tuition: Full-time $1060; part-time $1060 per credit. Required fees: $250. One-time fee: $600. *Financial support:* Federal Work-Study and scholarships/grants available. Support available to part-time students. Financial award application deadline: 4/15; financial award applicants required to submit FAFSA. *Faculty research:* Equitable access and openness to diversity in museum settings, exhibition display and development, museum/school partnerships. *Unit head:* Nina Jensen, Director, 212-875-4491, Fax: 212-875-4753, E-mail: ninajensen@bankstreet.edu. *Application contact:* Ann Morgan, Director of Graduate Admissions, 212-875-4403, Fax: 212-875-4678, E-mail: amorgan@bankstreet.edu.

Bard College, Center for Curatorial Studies, Annandale-on-Hudson, NY 12504. Offers MA. *Degree requirements:* For master's, thesis, exhibition. *Entrance requirements:* For master's, statement of interest, exhibition review, 3 letters of recommendation. Additional exam requirements/recommendations for international students: Required—TOEFL (minimum score 550 paper-based). Electronic applications accepted. *Expenses:* Contact institution. *Faculty research:* Contemporary art, history of exhibition, curatorial practice.

Baylor University, Graduate School, College of Arts and Sciences, Department of Museum Studies, Waco, TX 76798. Offers MA. *Faculty:* 6 part-time/adjunct (3 women). *Students:* 14 full-time (11 women), 2 part-time (1 woman); includes 2 minority (both American Indian/Alaska Native). 13 applicants, 85% accepted. In 2008, 6 master's awarded. *Degree requirements:* For master's, thesis or alternative. *Entrance requirements:* For master's, GRE General Test. *Application deadline:* For fall admission, 4/30 priority date for domestic students. Applications are processed on a rolling basis. Application fee: $25. Electronic applications accepted. *Financial support:* In 2008–09, 3 research assistantships with partial tuition reimbursements (averaging $7,200 per year) were awarded; career-related internships or fieldwork, Federal Work-Study, institutionally sponsored loans, tuition waivers (full and partial), and unspecified assistantships also available. Support available to part-time students. Financial award application deadline: 6/1; financial award applicants required to submit FAFSA. *Faculty research:* Paleontology/archaeology, preservation. *Unit head:* Dr. Kenneth Hafertepe, Graduate Program

Museum Studies

Baylor University (continued)

Director, 254-710-1233, Fax: 254-710-1173, E-mail: kenneth_hafertepe@baylor.edu. *Application contact:* Marcia Cooper, Administrative Assistant, 254-710-1233, Fax: 254-710-3870, E-mail: marcia_cooper@baylor.edu.

Boston University, Graduate School of Arts and Sciences, Department of Art History, Boston, MA 02215. Offers art history (MA, PhD); museum studies (Certificate). Terminal master's awarded for partial completion of doctoral program. *Degree requirements:* For master's, one foreign language, comprehensive exam, thesis; for doctorate, 2 foreign languages, comprehensive exam, thesis/dissertation. *Entrance requirements:* For master's and doctorate, GRE General Test, 3 letters of recommendation; for Certificate, GRE General Test. Additional exam requirements/recommendations for international students: Required—TOEFL (minimum score 600 paper-based; 250 computer-based).

Brown University, Graduate School, Department of Anthropology, Providence, RI 02912. Offers anthropology (AM, PhD); museum studies (AM). *Degree requirements:* For doctorate, one foreign language, thesis/dissertation, preliminary exam.

California College of the Arts, Graduate Programs, Program in Curatorial Practice, San Francisco, CA 94107. Offers MA. *Entrance requirements:* For master's, appropriate bachelor's degree, portfolio, resumé, letters of recommendation. Additional exam requirements/recommendations for international students: Required—TOEFL (minimum score 600 paper-based; 250 computer-based). Electronic applications accepted.

California State University, Chico, Graduate School, College of Behavioral and Social Sciences, Department of Anthropology, Chico, CA 95929-0400. Offers museum studies (MA). *Degree requirements:* For master's, thesis. *Entrance requirements:* For master's, GRE General Test, statement of purpose, 2 letters of recommendation. Additional exam requirements/recommendations for international students: Required—TOEFL (minimum score 550 paper-based; 213 computer-based; 80 iBT), IELTS (minimum score 6.5). Electronic applications accepted.

Caribbean University, Graduate School, Bayamón, PR 00960-0493. Offers administration and supervision (MA Ed); criminal justice (MA); curriculum and instruction (MA Ed), including elementary education, English education, history education, mathematics education, primary education, science education, Spanish education; education (PhD); gerontology (MSN); human resources (MBA); museology, archiving and art history (MA Ed); neonatal pediatrics (MSN); physical education (MA Ed); special education (MA Ed). *Entrance requirements:* For master's, interview, minimum GPA of 2.5.

Case Western Reserve University, School of Graduate Studies, Department of Art History and Art, Program in Art History and Museum Studies, Cleveland, OH 44106. Offers MA, PhD. Part-time programs available. *Degree requirements:* For master's, one foreign language, thesis or alternative; for doctorate, 2 foreign languages, thesis/dissertation. *Entrance requirements:* For master's, GRE General Test, 2 samples of written work; for doctorate, GRE General Test, 3 samples of written work or MA thesis. Additional exam requirements/recommendations for international students: Required—TOEFL. Electronic applications accepted. *Faculty research:* Greek art and architecture, northern baroque, Italian Renaissance and baroque, abstract expressionism, Indian art, nineteenth-century French art, American and Contemporary art.

Christie's Education, Program in Modern Art, Connoisseurship, and the History of the Art Market, New York, NY 10036. Offers MA. *Degree requirements:* For master's, one foreign language, thesis. *Entrance requirements:* For master's, GRE, writing sample, 3 letters of recommendation, transcripts from all secondary schools and essay statement. Additional exam requirements/recommendations for international students: Required—TOEFL.

City College of the City University of New York, Graduate School, College of Liberal Arts and Science, Division of the Humanities and Arts, Department of Art, Concentrations in Art History and Museum Studies, New York, NY 10031-9198. Offers art history (MA); museum studies (MA). Part-time programs available. *Degree requirements:* For master's, one foreign language, thesis. *Entrance requirements:* For master's, GRE, minimum GPA of 3.0, portfolio, art history paper. Additional exam requirements/recommendations for international students: Required—TOEFL (minimum score 575 paper-based; 233 computer-based). *Faculty research:* Egyptian, Greek, medieval, Romanesque, and Ottoman art.

Claremont Graduate University, Graduate Programs, School of Arts and Humanities, Department of Cultural Studies, Claremont, CA 91711-6160. Offers Africana studies (Certificate); cultural studies (MA, PhD); media studies (MA, PhD); museum studies (MA). Part-time programs available. *Faculty:* 2 full-time (1 woman). *Students:* 57 full-time (41 women), 10 part-time (5 women); includes 21 minority (11 African Americans, 5 Asian Americans or Pacific Islanders, 5 Hispanic Americans), 6 international. Average age 35. In 2008, 8 master's, 2 doctorates awarded. *Entrance requirements:* For master's and doctorate, GRE General Test. Additional exam requirements/recommendations for international students: Required—TOEFL (minimum score 550 paper-based; 213 computer-based; 80 iBT). *Application deadline:* For fall admission, 2/1 priority date for domestic students. Applications are processed on a rolling basis. Application fee: $60. Electronic applications accepted. *Expenses:* Tuition: Full-time $33,698; part-time $1465 per unit. Required fees: $310; $155 per semester. Tuition and fees vary according to program. *Financial support:* Fellowships, research assistantships, Federal Work-Study, institutionally sponsored loans, and scholarships/grants available. Support available to part-time students. Financial award application deadline: 2/15; financial award applicants required to submit FAFSA. *Unit head:* Eve Oishi, Chair, 909-607-7587, E-mail: eve.oishi@cgu.edu. *Application contact:* Justin Evans, Admissions Coordinator, 909-607-1278, Fax: 909-607-1221, E-mail: humanities@cgu.edu.

Cleveland State University, College of Graduate Studies, College of Liberal Arts and Social Sciences, Department of History, Cleveland, OH 44115. Offers art history (MA); history (MA); museum studies (MA). Part-time and evening/weekend programs available. *Faculty:* 18 full-time (6 women), 10 part-time/adjunct (2 women). *Students:* 14 full-time (8 women), 17 part-time (8 women); includes 4 minority (all African Americans). Average age 34. 39 applicants, 51% accepted, 14 enrolled. In 2008, 20 master's awarded. *Degree requirements:* For master's, thesis optional. *Entrance requirements:* For master's, minimum GPA of 3.0, bachelor's degree in history. Additional exam requirements/recommendations for international students: Required—TOEFL (minimum score 525 paper-based; 197 computer-based). *Application deadline:* For fall admission, 7/15 priority date for domestic students. Applications are processed on a rolling basis. Application fee: $30. Electronic applications accepted. *Financial support:* In 2008–09, 7 students received support, including research assistantships with full tuition reimbursements available (averaging $8,600 per year); career-related internships or fieldwork and unspecified assistantships also available. *Faculty research:* African Diaspora, social history and the city, early modern Europe, local history. *Unit head:* Dr. Elizabeth A. Lehfeldt, Chairperson, 216-687-3920, Fax: 216-687-5592, E-mail: e.lehfeldt@csuohio.edu. *Application contact:* Dr. Robert S. Shelton, Graduate Director, 216-687-3927, E-mail: r.s.shelton@csuohio.edu.

Cleveland State University, College of Graduate Studies, College of Science, Department of Biological, Geological, and Environmental Sciences, Cleveland, OH 44115. Offers biology (MS); environmental science (MS); museum studies for natural historians (MS); regulatory biology (PhD); JD/MS. Part-time programs available. *Faculty:* 21 full-time (5 women), 6 part-time/adjunct (3 women). *Students:* 68 full-time (41 women), 31 part-time (13 women); includes 10 minority (4 African Americans, 3 Asian Americans or Pacific Islanders, 3 Hispanic Americans), 39 international. Average age 30. 68 applicants, 43% accepted, 15 enrolled. In 2008, 12 master's, 2 doctorates awarded. Terminal master's awarded for partial completion of doctoral program. *Degree requirements:* For master's, comprehensive exam (for some programs), thesis (for some programs); for doctorate, comprehensive exam, thesis/dissertation. *Entrance requirements:* For master's and doctorate, GRE General Test, 2 letters of recommendation; 1-2 page essay statement of career goals and research interests. Additional exam requirements/recommendations for international students: Required—TOEFL (minimum score 525 paper-based; 197 computer-based). *Application deadline:* For fall admission, 4/1 priority date for domestic and international students; for spring admission, 12/1 priority date for domestic students. Applications are processed on a rolling basis. Application fee: $30. Electronic applications accepted. *Financial support:* In 2008–09, 29 students received support, including research assistantships with full and partial tuition reimbursements available (averaging $16,500 per year), teaching assistantships with full and partial tuition reimbursements available (averaging $16,500 per year); institutionally sponsored loans and unspecified assistantships also available. *Faculty research:* Molecular and cell biology, immunology, urban ecology. *Unit head:* Dr. Jeffrey Dean, Chair, 216-687-2120, Fax: 216-687-6972, E-mail: j.dean@csuohio.edu. *Application contact:* Dr. Jeffrey Dean, Chair, 216-687-2120, Fax: 216-687-6972, E-mail: j.dean@csuohio.edu.

Duquesne University, Graduate School of Liberal Arts, Department of History, Pittsburgh, PA 15282-0001. Offers archival, museum, and editing studies (MA); history (MA). Part-time and evening/weekend programs available. *Faculty:* 6 full-time (1 woman), 3 part-time/adjunct (1 woman). *Students:* 35 full-time (20 women), 8 part-time (5 women). Average age 26. 23 applicants, 96% accepted, 14 enrolled. In 2008, 15 master's awarded. *Degree requirements:* For master's, comprehensive exam (for some programs), thesis optional. *Entrance requirements:* For master's, GRE General Test, writing sample. Additional exam requirements/recommendations for international students: Required—TOEFL. *Application deadline:* For fall admission, 8/15 for domestic students, 5/1 for international students; for spring admission, 11/1 priority date for domestic students. Applications are processed on a rolling basis. Application fee: $50. Electronic applications accepted. *Expenses:* Tuition: Part-time $819 per credit. Required fees: $78 per credit. Tuition and fees vary according to course load. *Financial support:* In 2008–09, 4 research assistantships with full tuition reimbursements (averaging $4,800 per year) were awarded; career-related internships or fieldwork, Federal Work-Study, scholarships/grants, tuition waivers (full and partial), and unspecified assistantships also available. Support available to part-time students. Financial award application deadline: 5/1. *Faculty research:* American studies, immigration history, local social history, applied history, Eastern European history. *Unit head:* Dr. Holly Mayer, Chair, 412-396-6470. *Application contact:* Linda L. Rendulic, Assistant to the Dean, 412-396-6400, Fax: 412-396-5265, E-mail: rendulic@duq.edu.

Fashion Institute of Technology, School of Graduate Studies, Programs in Fashion and Textile Studies: History, Theory, and Museum Practice, New York, NY 10001-5992. Offers MA. *Accreditation:* NASAD. *Degree requirements:* For master's, one foreign language, thesis, internship. *Entrance requirements:* For master's, GRE General Test or GRE Subject Test, previous course work in art history and chemistry, 4 semesters of a foreign language. Additional exam requirements/recommendations for international students: Required—TOEFL (minimum score 550 paper-based; 213 computer-based). Electronic applications accepted.

See Close-Up on page 117.

Florida State University, Graduate Studies, College of Visual Arts, Theatre and Dance, Department of Art History, Tallahassee, FL 32306. Offers art history (MA, PhD); museum studies (Certificate). *Accreditation:* NASAD. Part-time programs available. Terminal master's awarded for partial completion of doctoral program. *Degree requirements:* For master's, one foreign language, thesis (for some programs), review; for doctorate, 2 foreign languages, comprehensive exam, thesis/dissertation, review. *Entrance requirements:* For master's, GRE General Test, minimum GPA of 3.0; for doctorate, GRE General Test, minimum GPA of 3.5. Additional exam requirements/recommendations for international students: Required—TOEFL. Electronic applications accepted. *Faculty research:* Asian art; modern art and critical theory; non-Western art; medieval, renaissance and baroque art; Pre-Colombian.

Florida State University, Graduate Studies, College of Visual Arts, Theatre and Dance, Program in Museum Studies, Tallahassee, FL 32306. Offers Certificate. Part-time programs available. *Degree requirements:* For Certificate, internship. *Entrance requirements:* For degree, GRE, graduate degree or current study towards a graduate degree.

The George Washington University, Columbian College of Arts and Sciences, Department of American Studies, Concentration in Material Culture, Washington, DC 20052. Offers MA. *Degree requirements:* For master's, comprehensive exam, thesis or alternative. *Entrance requirements:* For master's, GRE General Test, minimum GPA of 3.0. Additional exam requirements/recommendations for international students: Required—TOEFL (minimum score 550 paper-based; 213 computer-based). *Application deadline:* For fall admission, 4/1 priority date for domestic and international students; for spring admission, 10/1 priority date for domestic and international students. Application fee: $60. *Financial support:* Fellowships, teaching assistantships available. Financial award application deadline: 2/1. *Application contact:* Information Contact, 202-994-6070, Fax: 202-994-8651, E-mail: amst@gwu.edu.

The George Washington University, Columbian College of Arts and Sciences, Department of Fine Arts and Art History, Washington, DC 20052. Offers art history (MA), including art history, museum training; ceramics (MFA); drawing/painting (MFA); interior design (MFA); new media (MFA); photography (MFA); sculpture (MFA). *Accreditation:* CIDA. Part-time and evening/weekend programs available. *Faculty:* 16 full-time (7 women), 31 part-time/adjunct (19 women). *Students:* 49 full-time (44 women), 37 part-time (34 women); includes 16 minority (4 African Americans, 6 Asian Americans or Pacific Islanders, 6 Hispanic Americans), 2 international. Average age 28. 204 applicants, 49% accepted, 63 enrolled. In 2008, 39 master's awarded. *Entrance requirements:* For master's, GRE General Test, bachelor's degree in field, minimum GPA of 3.0. Additional exam requirements/recommendations for international students: Required—TOEFL (minimum score 550 paper-based; 213 computer-based; 80 iBT). *Application deadline:* For fall admission, 3/1 priority date for domestic students, 1/15 priority date for international students; for spring admission, 10/1 priority date for domestic students, 9/1 priority date for international students. Applications are processed on a rolling basis. Application fee: $60. Electronic applications accepted. *Financial support:* In 2008–09, 12 students received support; fellowships, teaching assistantships, career-related internships or fieldwork, Federal Work-Study, and tuition waivers available. Financial award application deadline: 1/15. *Unit head:* Thomas K. Brown, Chair, 202-994-9067, E-mail: thbrown@gwu.edu. *Application contact:* Information Contact, 202-994-6085, Fax: 202-994-8657, E-mail: art@gwu.edu.

The George Washington University, Columbian College of Arts and Sciences, Department of Fine Arts and Art History, Program in Art History, Concentration in Museum Training, Washington, DC 20052. Offers MA. In 2008, 2 master's awarded. *Degree requirements:* For master's, one foreign language, comprehensive exam, thesis or alternative. *Entrance requirements:* For master's, GRE General Test, bachelor's degree in field, minimum GPA of 3.0. Additional exam requirements/recommendations for international students: Required—TOEFL (minimum score 550 paper-based; 213 computer-based). *Application deadline:* For fall admission, 2/1 priority date for domestic and international students; for spring admission, 10/1 priority date for domestic and international students. Applications are processed on a rolling basis. Application fee: $60. Electronic applications accepted. *Financial support:* Fellowships, teaching assistantships available. Financial award application deadline: 2/1. *Application contact:* Information Contact, 202-994-6085, Fax: 202-994-8657, E-mail: art@gwu.edu.

The George Washington University, Columbian College of Arts and Sciences, Program in Museum Studies, Washington, DC 20052. Offers MA, Certificate. Part-time and evening/weekend programs available. *Faculty:* 2 full-time (both women), 2 part-time/adjunct (both women). *Students:* 58 full-time (52 women), 38 part-time (35 women); includes 10 minority (2 African Americans, 1 Asian American or Pacific Islander, 7 Hispanic Americans), 5 international. Average age 26. 184 applicants, 48% accepted, 37 enrolled. In 2008, 61 master's, 4 other advanced degrees awarded. *Degree requirements:* For master's, comprehensive exam, internship. *Entrance requirements:* For master's, GRE General Test, minimum GPA of 3.0. Additional exam requirements/recommendations for international students: Required—TOEFL (minimum score 550 paper-based; 213 computer-based; 80 iBT). *Application deadline:* For fall admission, 2/1 priority date for domestic students, 1/15 priority date for international students;

for spring admission, 10/15 priority date for domestic students, 9/1 priority date for international students. Applications are processed on a rolling basis. Application fee: $60. Electronic applications accepted. *Financial support:* In 2008–09, 15 students received support; fellowships with tuition reimbursements available, career-related internships or fieldwork, Federal Work-Study, institutionally sponsored loans, and tuition waivers available. Financial award application deadline: 1/15. *Unit head:* Kym S. Rice, Director, 202-994-0165, Fax: 202-994-7034, E-mail: kym@gwu.edu. *Application contact:* Information Contact, 202-994-7030, Fax: 202-994-7034, E-mail: mstd@gwu.edu.

Harvard University, Extension School, Cambridge, MA 02138-3722. Offers applied sciences (CAS); biotechnology (ALM); educational technologies (ALM); educational technology (CET); English for graduate and professional studies (DGP); environmental management (ALM, CEM); information technology (ALM); journalism (ALM); liberal arts (ALM); management (ALM, CM); mathematics for teaching (ALM); museum studies (ALM); premedical studies (Diploma); publication and communication (CPC). Part-time and evening/weekend programs available. *Degree requirements:* For master's, thesis. *Entrance requirements:* For master's, 3 completed graduate courses with grade of B or higher. Additional exam requirements/recommendations for international students: Required—TOEFL (minimum score 600 paper-based; 250 computer-based), TWE (minimum score 5). *Expenses:* Contact institution.

Indiana University–Purdue University Indianapolis, School of Liberal Arts, Department of Museum Studies, Indianapolis, IN 46202. Offers MS, Certificate. *Entrance requirements:* For master's, GRE.

John F. Kennedy University, School of Education and Liberal Arts, Department of Museum Studies, Berkeley, CA 94702. Offers museum studies (MA, Certificate), including administration, collections management, public programming. Part-time programs available. *Degree requirements:* For master's, project. *Entrance requirements:* For master's, interview. Additional exam requirements/recommendations for international students: Required—TOEFL, TWE. *Faculty research:* Emerging museum philosophies, multicultural diversity issues in museums, trends in collections management and preventive conservation, effective programming techniques and application for diverse audiences.

The Johns Hopkins University, Zanvyl Krieger School of Arts and Sciences, Advanced Academic Programs, Program in Museum Studies, Baltimore, MD 21218-2699. Offers MA. Postbaccalaureate distance learning degree programs offered (minimal on-campus study).

New York University, Graduate School of Arts and Science, Department of History, New York, NY 10012-1019. Offers African diaspora (PhD); African history (PhD); archival management and historical editing (Advanced Certificate); Atlantic history (PhD); French studies/history (PhD); Hebrew and Judaic studies/history (PhD); history (MA, PhD), including Europe (PhD), Latin American and the Caribbean (PhD), United States (PhD), women's history (MA); Middle Eastern history (MA); Middle Eastern studies/history (PhD); public history (Advanced Certificate); world history (MA); JD/MA; MA/Advanced Certificate. Part-time programs available. Terminal master's awarded for partial completion of doctoral program. *Degree requirements:* For master's, seminar paper; for doctorate, one foreign language, thesis/dissertation, oral and written exams; for Advanced Certificate, internship. *Entrance requirements:* For master's, GRE General Test, minimum GPA of 3.0, writing sample; for doctorate, GRE. Additional exam requirements/recommendations for international students: Required—TOEFL. *Faculty research:* African, East Asian, Medieval, early modern, and modern European history; U.S. history; African and African diaspora; Latin American history; Atlantic World.

New York University, Graduate School of Arts and Science, Program in Museum Studies, New York, NY 10012-1019. Offers museum studies (MA, Advanced Certificate), including Africana studies (MA), Hebrew and Judaic studies (MA), Latin American and Caribbean studies (MA), Near Eastern studies (MA). Part-time and evening/weekend programs available. *Entrance requirements:* For degree, master's or PhD. *Faculty research:* Modern and contemporary art, history of museums and exhibitions, conservation of cultural materials, museum anthropology, ethnography.

San Francisco Art Institute, Graduate Program, Department of Exhibition and Museum Studies, San Francisco, CA 94133. Offers MA. *Entrance requirements:* Additional exam requirements/recommendations for international students: Required—TOEFL (minimum score 580 paper-based; 237 computer-based). Electronic applications accepted.

San Francisco State University, Division of Graduate Studies, College of Humanities, Museum Studies Program, San Francisco, CA 94132-1722. Offers MA. Part-time programs available.

Seton Hall University, College of Arts and Sciences, Department of Art and Music, South Orange, NJ 07079-2697. Offers museum professions (MA). *Accreditation:* NASM. Part-time and evening/weekend programs available. *Degree requirements:* For master's, thesis or alternative. *Entrance requirements:* For master's, GRE General Test, previous course work in art history. Electronic applications accepted. *Faculty research:* History of museums, museum education, theory of museums, nineteenth century art, African-American art, Renaissance art history, museum registration, museum ethics.

See Close-Up on page 227.

Southern Illinois University Edwardsville, Graduate Studies and Research, College of Arts and Sciences, Department of Historical Studies, Program in Museum Studies, Edwardsville, IL 62026-0001. Offers Postbaccalaureate Certificate. Part-time and evening/weekend programs available. *Students:* 2 part-time (both women). Average age 26. 3 applicants, 67% accepted. In 2008, 3 Postbaccalaureate Certificates awarded. *Entrance requirements:* Additional exam requirements/recommendations for international students: Required—TOEFL (minimum score 550 paper-based; 213 computer-based; 79 iBT), IELTS (minimum score 6.5). *Application deadline:* For fall admission, 7/20 for domestic students, 6/1 for international students; for spring admission, 12/14 for domestic students, 10/1 for international students. Applications are processed on a rolling basis. Application fee: $30. Electronic applications accepted. *Expenses:* Tuition, area resident: Full-time $5838. Tuition, nonresident: full-time $14,596. Required fees: $1525. *Financial support:* Fellowships with full tuition reimbursements, research assistantships with full tuition reimbursements, teaching assistantships with full tuition reimbursements available. Financial award application deadline: 3/1; financial award applicants required to submit FAFSA. *Unit head:* Dr. Laura Fowler Milsk, Director, 618-650-2145, E-mail: lmilsk@siue.edu. *Application contact:* Dr. Laura Fowler Milsk, Director, 618-650-2145, E-mail: lmilsk@siue.edu.

State University of New York College at Oneonta, Graduate Education, Cooperstown Graduate Program in History Museum Studies, Cooperstown, NY 13326. Offers MA. *Students:* 30 full-time (22 women). Average age 25. 45 applicants, 33% accepted, 15 enrolled. In 2008, 16 master's awarded. *Degree requirements:* For master's, research paper or thesis. *Entrance requirements:* For master's, GRE General Test. *Application deadline:* For fall admission, 1/10 for domestic students. Application fee: $50. *Expenses:* Contact institution. *Unit head:* Gretchen Sorin, Director, 607-547-2586, Fax: 607-547-8926, E-mail: sorings@oneonta.edu. *Application contact:* Dean, 607-436-2523, Fax: 607-436-3084, E-mail: gradoffice@oneonta.edu.

Syracuse University, Graduate School, College of Visual and Performing Arts, Program in Museum Studies, Syracuse, NY 13244. Offers MA. *Accreditation:* NASAD. Part-time programs available. *Degree requirements:* For master's, thesis or alternative. *Entrance requirements:* Additional exam requirements/recommendations for international students: Required—TOEFL.

Texas Tech University, Graduate School, Program in Museum Science and Heritage Management, Lubbock, TX 79409. Offers heritage management (MS); museum science (MA). Part-time programs available. *Faculty:* 6 full-time (3 women). *Students:* 30 full-time (27 women), 9 part-time (8 women); includes 3 minority (all Hispanic Americans). Average age 28. 25 applicants, 76% accepted, 13 enrolled. In 2008, 8 master's awarded. *Degree requirements:* For master's, thesis. *Entrance requirements:* For master's, GRE General Test. Additional exam requirements/recommendations for international students: Required—TOEFL (minimum score 550 paper-based; 213 computer-based). *Application deadline:* For fall admission, 3/1 priority date for international students; for spring admission, 11/1 priority date for international students. Applications are processed on a rolling basis. Application fee: $50 ($60 for international students). Electronic applications accepted. *Expenses:* Tuition, area resident: Part-time $194 per credit hour. Tuition, state resident: full-time $4648; part-time $194 per credit hour. Tuition, nonresident: full-time $11,392; part-time $475 per credit hour. Required fees: $2206; $69 per credit hour. $389 per semester. *Financial support:* In 2008–09, 34 students received support, including 7 research assistantships with partial tuition reimbursements available (averaging $10,018 per year), 2 teaching assistantships with partial tuition reimbursements available (averaging $7,479 per year); career-related internships or fieldwork, Federal Work-Study, and institutionally sponsored loans also available. Support available to part-time students. Financial award application deadline: 4/15; financial award applicants required to submit FAFSA. *Faculty research:* Lubbock Lake Landmark anthropology, regional American fine art, regional ethnology, anthropology of the southern plains, natural science research. Total annual research expenditures: $248,030. *Unit head:* Gary F. Edson, Chair, 806-742-2442, Fax: 806-742-1136, E-mail: gary.edson@ttu.edu. *Application contact:* Claudia Cory, Assistant to the Director, 806-742-2442 Ext. 222, Fax: 806-742-1136, E-mail: claudia.cory@ttu.edu.

Tufts University, Graduate School of Arts and Sciences, Graduate Certificate Programs, Museum Studies Program, Medford, MA 02155. Offers Certificate. Part-time and evening/weekend programs available. *Expenses:* Contact institution.

Université de Montréal, Faculty of Arts and Sciences, Program in Museology, Montréal, QC H3C 3J7, Canada. Offers MA. *Students:* 29 full-time (27 women), 39 part-time (34 women). Average age 25. 41 applicants, 59% accepted, 23 enrolled. In 2008, 14 master's awarded. *Application deadline:* For fall admission, 2/1 priority date for domestic students; for winter admission, 11/1 priority date for domestic students; for spring admission, 2/1 priority date for domestic students. Application fee: $100. Electronic applications accepted. *Faculty research:* Museum exhibits, museum education, natural science and museums, new technologies and museums. Total annual research expenditures: $500,000. *Unit head:* ??lise Dubuc, Director, 514-343-7351, Fax: 514-343-7660, E-mail: elise.dubuc@umontreal.ca. *Application contact:* Manon Lebrun, Student Files Management Technician, 514-343-7165, Fax: 514-343-7660, E-mail: manon.lebrun@umontreal.ca.

Université du Québec à Montréal, Graduate Programs, Program in Museology, Montréal, QC H3C 3P8, Canada. Offers MA. Part-time programs available. *Entrance requirements:* For master's, appropriate bachelor's degree or equivalent and proficiency in French.

Université Laval, Faculty of Letters, Department of History, Program in Museology, Québec, QC G1K 7P4, Canada. Offers Diploma. Part-time programs available. *Entrance requirements:* For degree, English exam (comprehension of English), knowledge of French. Electronic applications accepted.

University at Buffalo, the State University of New York, Graduate School, College of Arts and Sciences, Department of Visual Studies, Program in Art History, Buffalo, NY 14260. Offers art history (MA); critical museum studies (Certificate). Part-time programs available. *Degree requirements:* For master's, one foreign language, thesis, field exam. *Entrance requirements:* Additional exam requirements/recommendations for international students: Required—TOEFL. Electronic applications accepted. *Faculty research:* Frank Lloyd Wright, non-Western art, Renaissance, Bronze Age Crete, American art.

The University of British Columbia, Faculty of Arts and Faculty of Graduate Studies, Department of Art History, Visual Art, and Theory, Vancouver, BC V6T 1Z1, Canada. Offers art history (MA, PhD, Diploma); critical and curatorial studies (MA); visual art (MFA). Part-time programs available. *Degree requirements:* For master's, one foreign language, thesis, final exhibition (MFA, MA, CCST); for doctorate, 2 foreign languages, comprehensive exam, thesis/dissertation. *Entrance requirements:* For master's, bachelor's degree with minimum B+ average for MFA; for doctorate, master's degree with minimum A- average. Additional exam requirements/recommendations for international students: Required—TOEFL (minimum score 600 paper-based; 250 computer-based). Electronic applications accepted. *Faculty research:* Conceptual art, Asian art, indigenous North American art, post-second war art, eighteenth and nineteenth century art.

University of California, Riverside, Graduate Division, Department of History, Riverside, CA 92521-0102. Offers archival management (MA); historic preservation (MA); history (MA, PhD); museum curatorship (MA). Part-time programs available. Terminal master's awarded for partial completion of doctoral program. *Degree requirements:* For master's, one foreign language, comprehensive exam, internship report and oral exams, or thesis; for doctorate, 2 foreign languages, thesis/dissertation, qualifying exams, teaching experience. *Entrance requirements:* For master's, GRE General Test, minimum GPA of 3.2; for doctorate, GRE General Test, MA in history, minimum GPA of 3.2. Additional exam requirements/recommendations for international students: Required—TOEFL (minimum score 550 paper-based; 213 computer-based; 80 iBT). Electronic applications accepted. *Expenses:* Tuition, nonresident: full-time $4898. Required fees: $10,362. *Faculty research:* Native American history, United States, public history, Russia, Europe.

University of Central Oklahoma, College of Graduate Studies and Research, College of Liberal Arts, Department of History, Edmond, OK 73034-5209. Offers history (MA); museum studies (MA); social studies teaching (MA); Southwestern studies (MA). Part-time programs available. *Degree requirements:* For master's, thesis optional. *Entrance requirements:* Additional exam requirements/recommendations for international students: Required—TOEFL (minimum score 550 paper-based; 213 computer-based). Electronic applications accepted. *Faculty research:* China, Russia, civil war, American naval logistics.

University of Colorado at Boulder, Graduate School, College of Arts and Sciences, Museum and Field Studies Program, Boulder, CO 80309. Offers MS. *Degree requirements:* For master's, comprehensive exam, thesis or alternative. *Entrance requirements:* For master's, GRE General Test, GRE Subject Test, minimum undergraduate GPA of 3.0.

University of Denver, Division of Arts, Humanities and Social Sciences, School of Art and Art History, Denver, CO 80208. Offers art history (MA); art history/museum studies (MA); electronic media arts and design (MFA). *Accreditation:* NASAD. Part-time programs available. *Faculty:* 15 full-time (11 women), 6 part-time/adjunct (2 women). *Students:* 15 full-time (12 women), 10 part-time (all women); includes 2 minority (1 Asian American or Pacific Islander, 1 Hispanic American), 1 international. Average age 29. In 2008, 11 master's awarded. *Degree requirements:* For master's, one foreign language, research paper. *Entrance requirements:* For master's, GRE. Additional exam requirements/recommendations for international students: Required—TOEFL. *Application deadline:* Applications are processed on a rolling basis. Application fee: $50. Electronic applications accepted. *Financial support:* Career-related internships or fieldwork, Federal Work-Study, institutionally sponsored loans, and scholarships/grants available. Support available to part-time students. Financial award application deadline: 3/1; financial award applicants required to submit FAFSA. *Faculty research:* Images of women in alchemical manuscripts and books, Giovanni Benedetto, Salvatore Castiglione. *Unit head:* Dr. Annette Stott, Director, 303-871-2846. *Application contact:* Dr. Annabeth Headrick, Graduate Advisor, 303-871-3574, E-mail: saah-interest@du.edu.

University of Florida, Graduate School, College of Fine Arts, School of Art and Art History, Gainesville, FL 32611. Offers art (MFA), including ceramics, creative photography, drawing, electronic intermedia, graphic design, painting, printmaking, sculpture; art education (MA); art history (MA, PhD); digital arts and sciences (MA); museology (museum studies) (MA). *Accreditation:* NASAD. *Degree requirements:* For master's, variable foreign language requirement, project or thesis (MFA). *Entrance requirements:* For master's, portfolio (MFA), writing sample (MA), GRE General Test or minimum GPA of 3.0. Additional exam requirements/recommendations for international students: Required—TOEFL (minimum score 550 paper-

Museum Studies

University of Florida (continued)

based; 213 computer-based). Electronic applications accepted. *Faculty research:* Studio production, art historical studies of style context.

University of Hawaii at Manoa, Graduate Division, Colleges of Arts and Sciences, College of Arts and Humanities, Department of American Studies, Program in Museum Studies, Honolulu, HI 96822. Offers Graduate Certificate. Part-time programs available. *Entrance requirements:* Additional exam requirements/recommendations for international students: Required—TOEFL (minimum score 600 paper-based; 250 computer-based; 100 iBT), IELTS (minimum score 7).

The University of Kansas, Graduate Studies, College of Liberal Arts and Sciences, Museum Studies Program, Lawrence, KS 66045-7545. Offers collection conservation (Graduate Certificate); museum studies (MA). Part-time programs available. *Faculty:* 5 full-time (2 women), 4 part-time/adjunct (2 women). *Students:* 24 full-time (21 women), 5 part-time (4 women); includes 1 minority (Asian American or Pacific Islander), 4 international. Average age 30. 46 applicants, 61% accepted, 9 enrolled. In 2008, 12 master's awarded. *Degree requirements:* For master's, comprehensive exam. *Entrance requirements:* For master's, GRE. Additional exam requirements/recommendations for international students: Required—TOEFL. *Application deadline:* For fall admission, 1/1 priority date for domestic and international students; for spring admission, 8/15 priority date for domestic and international students. Applications are processed on a rolling basis. Application fee: $45 ($50 for international students). Electronic applications accepted. *Expenses:* Tuition, area resident: Full-time $6122; part-time $255.10 per credit hour. Tuition, state resident: full-time $6122; part-time $255.10 per credit hour. Tuition, nonresident: full-time $14,629; part-time $609.55 per credit hour. Required fees: $847; $70.56 per credit hour. Tuition and fees vary according to course load and program. *Financial support:* In 2008–09, 2 students received support, including 1 research assistantship with partial tuition reimbursement available. *Faculty research:* Museum history, museum theory, collection studies, museum anthropology, cultural studies. *Unit head:* Dr. Marjorie Swann, Director, 785-864-4543, E-mail: mswann@ku.edu. *Application contact:* Sara Lundberg, Senior Administrative Associate, 785-864-4543, Fax: 785-864-5772, E-mail: saratune@ku.edu.

University of Louisville, Graduate School, College of Arts and Sciences, Department of Fine Arts, Louisville, KY 40292. Offers art history (MA, PhD); creative art (MA); curatorial studies (MA). *Faculty:* 18 full-time (8 women), 3 part-time/adjunct (0 women). *Students:* 21 full-time (14 women), 23 part-time (16 women); includes 2 African Americans, 1 international. Average age 38. 17 applicants, 53% accepted, 9 enrolled. In 2008, 11 master's, 1 doctorate awarded. *Degree requirements:* For master's, thesis; for doctorate, 2 foreign languages, comprehensive exam, thesis/dissertation. *Entrance requirements:* For master's and doctorate, GRE General Test. *Application deadline:* For fall admission, 1/15 for domestic and international students. Applications are processed on a rolling basis. Application fee: $50. *Financial support:* In 2008–09, 4 teaching assistantships with tuition reimbursements (averaging $15,000 per year) were awarded. *Faculty research:* Art history in the periods from ancient to contemporary and various regions, 2D and 3D studio areas, intermedia, curatorial studies. *Unit head:* James T. Grubola, Chair, 502-852-0759, Fax: 502-852-6791, E-mail: grubola@louisville.edu. *Application contact:* Libby Leggett, Director, Graduate Admissions, 502-852-3101, Fax: 502-852-6536, E-mail: gradadm@louisville.edu.

University of Manitoba, Faculty of Graduate Studies, Faculty of Arts, Department of History, Winnipeg, MB R3T 2N2, Canada. Offers archival studies (MA); history (MA, PhD). *Degree requirements:* For master's, thesis; for doctorate, one foreign language, thesis/dissertation.

University of Missouri–St. Louis, College of Arts and Sciences, Department of History, St. Louis, MO 63121. Offers museum studies (MA, Certificate). Part-time and evening/weekend programs available. *Faculty:* 22 full-time (5 women). *Students:* 27 full-time (17 women), 53 part-time (26 women); includes 7 minority (5 African Americans, 2 Hispanic Americans). Average age 32. In 2008, 26 master's awarded. *Degree requirements:* For master's, thesis (for some programs). *Entrance requirements:* For master's, minimum GPA of 2.75, writing sample, supplemental application (museum studies). Additional exam requirements/recommendations for international students: Required—TOEFL (minimum score 550 paper-based; 213 computer-based). *Application deadline:* For fall admission, 7/1 priority date for domestic and international students; for spring admission, 12/1 priority date for domestic and international students. Applications are processed on a rolling basis. Application fee: $35 ($40 for international students). Electronic applications accepted. *Expenses:* Tuition, area resident: Full-time $5377; part-time $298.70 per credit hour. Tuition, nonresident: full-time $13,381; part-time $472.50 per credit hour. Required fees: $4078; $52 per credit hour. *Financial support:* In 2008–09, 1 research assistantship with full and partial tuition reimbursement (averaging $6,000 per year), 5 teaching assistantships with full and partial tuition reimbursements (averaging $6,600 per year) were awarded; career-related internships or fieldwork also available. Financial award applicants required to submit FAFSA. *Faculty research:* U.S., European, East Asian, Latin American, and African history. *Unit head:* Dr. Winston Hsieh, Director of Graduate Studies, 314-516-5681, Fax: 314-516-5415, E-mail: hsiehw@umsl.edu. *Application contact:* 314-516-5458, Fax: 314-516-6996, E-mail: gradadm@umsl.edu.

University of New Hampshire, Graduate School, College of Liberal Arts, Department of History, Durham, NH 03824. Offers history (MA, PhD); museum studies (MA). Part-time programs available. *Faculty:* 24 full-time (13 women). *Students:* 27 full-time (20 women), 22 part-time (13 women); includes 3 minority (2 American Indian/Alaska Native, 1 Asian American or Pacific Islander), 2 international. Average age 35. 93 applicants, 39% accepted, 9 enrolled. In 2008, 8 master's, 1 doctorate awarded. *Degree requirements:* For master's, thesis or alternative; for doctorate, 2 foreign languages, thesis/dissertation. *Entrance requirements:* For master's and doctorate, GRE General Test. Additional exam requirements/recommendations for international students: Required—TOEFL (minimum score 550 paper-based; 213 computer-based; 80 iBT). *Application deadline:* For fall admission, 2/15 priority date for domestic students, 2/15 for international students. Applications are processed on a rolling basis. Application fee: $60. Electronic applications accepted. *Expenses:* Tuition, area resident: Full-time $9720; part-time $540 per credit hour. Tuition, nonresident: full-time $23,200; part-time $954 per credit hour. Required fees: $1446; $361.50 per term. *Financial support:* In 2008–09, 26 students received support, including 4 fellowships, 1 research assistantship, 16 teaching assistantships; career-related internships or fieldwork, Federal Work-Study, scholarships/grants, and tuition waivers (full and partial) also available. Support available to part-time students. Financial award application deadline: 2/15. *Unit head:* Dr. William Harris, Chairperson, 603-862-1764. *Application contact:* Susan Kilday, Administrative Assistant, 603-862-1764, E-mail: history.grad@unh.edu.

The University of North Carolina at Greensboro, Graduate School, College of Arts and Sciences, Department of History, Greensboro, NC 27412-5001. Offers historic preservation (Certificate); history (MA); museum studies (Certificate); U.S. history (PhD). Part-time programs available. *Entrance requirements:* For master's, GRE General Test. Additional exam requirements/recommendations for international students: Required—TOEFL. Electronic applications accepted. *Faculty research:* Simultaneous discovery in science, progressive social reform, Robert Mayer.

The University of North Carolina at Greensboro, Graduate School, School of Human Environmental Sciences, Department of Interior Architecture, Greensboro, NC 27412-5001. Offers historic preservation (Certificate); interior architecture (MS); museum studies (Certificate). *Degree requirements:* For master's, thesis. *Entrance requirements:* For master's, GRE General Test or MAT, bachelor's degree in interior design, interview, portfolio. Additional exam requirements/recommendations for international students: Required—TOEFL. Electronic applications accepted.

University of Oklahoma, Graduate College, College of Liberal Studies, Norman, OK 73019-0390. Offers administrative leadership (MLS); integrated studies (MLS); interprofessional human and health services (MLS); museum studies (MLS). Part-time programs available. Post-baccalaureate distance learning degree programs offered (no on-campus study). *Faculty:* 9 full-time (7 women), 24 part-time/adjunct (15 women). *Students:* 15 full-time (10 women), 328 part-time (178 women); includes 64 minority (39 African Americans, 15 American Indian/Alaska Native, 3 Asian Americans or Pacific Islanders, 7 Hispanic Americans). 96 applicants, 98% accepted, 81 enrolled. In 2008, 71 master's awarded. *Degree requirements:* For master's, thesis, research project, internship. *Entrance requirements:* For master's, minimum GPA of 3.0 in last 60 hours, writing sample. Additional exam requirements/recommendations for international students: Required—TOEFL (minimum score 550 paper-based; 213 computer-based). *Application deadline:* For fall admission, 7/15 priority date for domestic students, 4/1 for international students; for spring admission, 12/1 for domestic students, 9/1 for international students. Applications are processed on a rolling basis. Application fee: $40 ($90 for international students). Electronic applications accepted. *Expenses:* Tuition, state resident: full-time $3744; part-time $156 per credit hour. Tuition, nonresident: full-time $13,577; part-time $565.70 per credit hour. Required fees: $2415.40; $90.10 per credit hour. *Financial support:* In 2008–09, 144 students received support. Career-related internships or fieldwork, scholarships/grants, and tuition waivers (partial) available. Support available to part-time students. Financial award applicants required to submit FAFSA. *Faculty research:* Distance education, adult learning processes, student satisfaction, administrative leadership, organizations, museum studies. *Unit head:* Dr. James Pappas, Dean and Vice President for University Outreach, 405-325-6361, Fax: 405-325-7196, E-mail: jpappas@ou.edu. *Application contact:* Dr. Julie Raadschelders, MA Program Coordinator, 405-325-1061, Fax: 405-325-9632, E-mail: jraadschelders@ou.edu.

University of South Carolina, The Graduate School, College of Arts and Sciences, Department of History, Program in Public History, Columbia, SC 29208. Offers archives (MA); historic preservation (MA); museum (MA); museum management (Certificate); MLIS/MA. *Degree requirements:* For master's, one foreign language, thesis, internship. *Entrance requirements:* For master's, GRE General Test, writing sample. Additional exam requirements/recommendations for international students: Required—TOEFL. Electronic applications accepted. *Faculty research:* Museum studies, historic preservation, archives administration.

The University of the Arts, College of Art and Design, Department of Museum Studies, Philadelphia, PA 19102-4944. Offers museum communication (MA); museum education (MA); museum exhibition planning and design (MFA). *Accreditation:* NASAD. Part-time programs available. *Degree requirements:* For master's, thesis, internship. *Entrance requirements:* For master's, portfolio. Additional exam requirements/recommendations for international students: Required—TOEFL (minimum score 550 paper-based; 213 computer-based).

See Close-Up on page 233.

University of Toronto, School of Graduate Studies, Humanities Division, Department of Art, Toronto, ON M5S 1A1, Canada. Offers art history (MA, PhD); visual studies (MVS). Part-time programs available. *Degree requirements:* For master's, 2 foreign languages, language proficiency exams; for doctorate, 2 foreign languages, comprehensive exam, thesis/dissertation. *Entrance requirements:* For master's, coursework in a foreign language, 3 letters of reference, sample research paper, minimum B+ average in senior art history and/or humanities courses; for doctorate, minimum A– average in senior art history and/or humanities courses, 2 letters of reference, sample research paper.

University of Toronto, School of Graduate Studies, Humanities Division, Program in Museum Studies, Toronto, ON M5S 1A1, Canada. Offers MM St. *Expenses:* Contact institution.

University of Washington, Graduate School, Museology Graduate Program, Seattle, WA 98195. Offers MA. *Degree requirements:* For master's, thesis or alternative. *Entrance requirements:* For master's, GRE General Test, minimum GPA of 3.0. Additional exam requirements/recommendations for international students: Required—TOEFL. Electronic applications accepted. *Expenses:* Contact institution. *Faculty research:* Collection management, conservation, art history, anthropology, administration.

University of West Georgia, Graduate School, College of Arts and Sciences, Department of History, Certificate in Museum Studies Program, Carrollton, GA 30118. Offers Certificate. In 2008, 5 Certificates awarded. *Expenses:* Tuition, state resident: full-time $2844; part-time $158 per semester hour. Tuition, nonresident: full-time $11,340; part-time $630 per semester hour. Required fees: $1120; $41.56 per semester hour. $186 per semester. Tuition and fees vary according to course load. *Unit head:* Dr. Howard Steve Goodson, Interim Chair, 678-839-6042, E-mail: hgoodson@westga.edu. *Application contact:* Dr. Charles W. Clark, Interim Dean, 678-839-6508, E-mail: cclark@westga.edu.

University of Wisconsin–Milwaukee, Graduate School, College of Letters and Sciences, Department of Anthropology, Milwaukee, WI 53201-0413. Offers anthropology (PhD); museum studies (Certificate). *Faculty:* 17 full-time (8 women). *Students:* 50 full-time (32 women), 44 part-time (36 women); includes 9 minority (2 African Americans, 3 American Indian/Alaska Native, 2 Asian Americans or Pacific Islanders, 2 Hispanic Americans), 2 international. Average age 28. 43 applicants, 65% accepted, 17 enrolled. In 2008, 13 master's, 1 doctorate awarded. *Degree requirements:* For master's, thesis or alternative; for doctorate, one foreign language, thesis/dissertation, departmental qualifying exam. *Entrance requirements:* For master's, GRE; for doctorate, GRE, minimum GPA of 3.0, master's degree. Additional exam requirements/recommendations for international students: Required—TOEFL (minimum score 550 paper-based; 79 iBT), IELTS (minimum score 6.5). *Application deadline:* For fall admission, 1/1 priority date for domestic students; for spring admission, 9/1 for domestic students. Applications are processed on a rolling basis. Application fee: $45 ($75 for international students). *Expenses:* Tuition, area resident: Full-time $7320; part-time $165 per credit. Tuition, state resident: full-time $7320; part-time $165 per credit. Tuition, nonresident: full-time $17,840; part-time $714 per credit. Tuition and fees vary according to campus/location, program and reciprocity agreements. *Financial support:* In 2008–09, 15 teaching assistantships were awarded; fellowships, research assistantships, career-related internships or fieldwork and unspecified assistantships also available. Support available to part-time students. Financial award application deadline: 4/15. Total annual research expenditures: $291,663. *Unit head:* J. Patrick Gray, Chair, 414-229-4822, Fax: 414-229-5848, E-mail: jpgray@uwm.edu. *Application contact:* General Information Contact, 414-229-4982, Fax: 414-229-6967, E-mail: gradschool@uwm.edu.

University of Wisconsin–Milwaukee, Graduate School, College of Letters and Sciences, Department of Art History, Milwaukee, WI 53201-0413. Offers art history (MA); art museum studies (Certificate). Part-time programs available. *Faculty:* 8 full-time (4 women). *Students:* 14 full-time (13 women), 11 part-time (all women); includes 1 minority (African American), 1 international. Average age 28. 21 applicants, 62% accepted, 6 enrolled. In 2008, 14 master's awarded. *Degree requirements:* For master's, one foreign language, comprehensive exam, thesis or alternative. *Entrance requirements:* For master's, GRE. Additional exam requirements/recommendations for international students: Required—TOEFL (minimum score 550 paper-based; 79 iBT), IELTS (minimum score 6.5). *Application deadline:* For fall admission, 1/1 priority date for domestic students; for spring admission, 9/1 for domestic students. Applications are processed on a rolling basis. Application fee: $45 ($75 for international students). *Expenses:* Tuition, area resident: Full-time $7320; part-time $165 per credit. Tuition, state resident: full-time $7320; part-time $165 per credit. Tuition, nonresident: full-time $17,840; part-time $714 per credit. Tuition and fees vary according to campus/location, program and reciprocity agreements. *Financial support:* In 2008–09, 5 teaching assistantships were awarded; fellowships, research assistantships, career-related internships or fieldwork and unspecified assistantships also available. Support available to part-time students. Financial award application deadline: 4/15. Total annual research expenditures: $1,035. *Unit head:* Kenneth Bendiner, Representative, 414-229-5015, Fax: 414-229-2935, E-mail: bendiner@uwm.edu. *Application contact:* General Information Contact, 414-229-4982, Fax: 414-229-6967, E-mail: gradschool@uwm.edu.

Virginia Commonwealth University, Graduate School, School of the Arts, Department of Art History, Richmond, VA 23284-9005. Offers architectural history (MA); art history (MA, PhD);

historical studies (MA); museum studies (MA). *Accreditation:* NASAD. *Degree requirements:* For master's, thesis; for doctorate, comprehensive exam, thesis/dissertation. *Entrance requirements:* For master's and doctorate, GRE General Test. *Faculty research:* Modern, nineteenth century, Renaissance, American, and Medieval art.

Western Illinois University, School of Graduate Studies, College of Fine Arts and Communication, Program in Museum Studies, Macomb, IL 61455-1390. Offers MA. *Students:* 4 full-time (3 women), 1 (woman) part-time; includes 1 minority (Hispanic American). Average age 36. 3 applicants, 100% accepted. *Degree requirements:* For master's, minimum GPA of 3.0. *Entrance requirements:* For master's, minimum GPA of 3.0. Additional exam requirements/recommendations for international students: Required—TOEFL (minimum score 600 paper-based; 250 computer-based; 100 iBT). Application fee: $30. *Expenses:* Tuition, state resident: full-time $5696; part-time $237.34 per credit hour. Tuition, nonresident: full-time $11,392; part-time $474.68 per credit hour. Required fees: $1453; $60.55 per credit hour. *Financial support:* In 2008–09, 2 research assistantships with full tuition reimbursements (averaging $7,040 per year) were awarded. *Unit head:* Ann Rowson Love, Director, 309-762-9481 Ext. 266, E-mail: a-rowsonlove@wiu.edu. *Application contact:* Evelyn Hoing, Assistant Director of Graduate Studies, 309-298-1806, Fax: 309-298-2345, E-mail: grad-office@wiu.edu.

ADELPHI UNIVERSITY

College of Arts and Sciences
Program in Fine Arts

Programs of Study

The study of art is the study of making. To make is to create, to interpret, and, finally, to understand one's own vision of the world. To study art and the history of art is to study the very essence of the self and of civilization. The Department of Art and Art History offers a program of study that leads to the Master of Arts degree in studio art. Course requirements total 36 credits. Students generally concentrate in a primary area of studio work (up to 15 credits), supplemented by one or more secondary areas of studio concentration. Concentration areas include ceramics, painting, photography, printmaking, and sculpture. Completion of degree requirements may be undertaken on a part-time basis or by attending summer sessions. Information on these options may be obtained from the department.

The department also offers course options for the Master of Arts degree in art education for those seeking New York State certification for teaching primary and secondary level. Students who successfully complete the program graduate with a Master of Arts degree from the School of Education. Students should consult with the department chair or their graduate faculty adviser to determine the necessary courses to fulfill the degree requirements.

Research Facilities

The University's primary research holdings are at Swirbul Library and include 646,720 volumes (including bound periodicals and government publications), 805,545 items in microformats, 32,353 audiovisual items, 1,738 periodical subscriptions, and access to over 27,000 electronic journal titles. Online access is provided to more than 200 research databases.

Opened in fall 2005, the 18,000-square-foot Fine Arts and Facilities Building greatly expands Adelphi's art studio and classroom space. The one-story building takes advantages of natural light to illuminate two painting studios, a sculpture and ceramics studio, and a printmaking studio. An outdoor courtyard contains kilns and display boxes for student artwork. The department retained its space on the third floor of Blodgett Hall, including its state-of-the-art digital graphics design studio and faculty offices.

Financial Aid

Adelphi University offers a wide variety of federal aid programs, state grants, scholarship and fellowship programs, on- and off-campus employment, and teaching and research assistantships.

Cost of Study

For the 2008–09 academic year, the tuition rate was $830 per credit. University fees ranged from $200 to $400 per semester.

Living and Housing Costs

The University assists single and married students in finding suitable accommodations whenever possible. The cost of living is dependent upon location and the number of rooms rented.

Location

Located in historic Garden City, New York, 45 minutes from Manhattan and 20 minutes from Queens, Adelphi's 75-acre suburban campus is known for the beauty of its landscape and architecture. The campus is a short walk from the Long Island Rail Road and is convenient to New York's major airports and several major highways. Off-campus centers are located in Manhattan, Hauppauge, and Poughkeepsie.

The University and The College

Founded in 1896, Adelphi is a fully accredited, private university with 8,000 undergraduate, graduate, and returning-adult students in the arts and sciences, business, clinical psychology, education, nursing, and social work. Students come from thirty-six states and from forty-seven countries. *The Princeton Review* named Adelphi University a Best College in the Northeastern Region, and *Fiske Guide to Colleges* recognized Adelphi as a "Best Buy" in higher education for two years in a row. The University is the only private institution on Long Island and one of only twenty-six in the nation to earn this recognition.

Mindful of the cultural inheritance of the past, the College of Arts and Sciences encompasses those realms of inquiry that have characterized the modern pursuit of knowledge. The faculty members of the College place a high priority on their students' intellectual development in and out of the classroom and structure programs and opportunities to foster that growth. Students analyze original research or other creative work, develop firsthand facility with creative or research methodologies, undertake collaborative work with peers and mentors, engage in serious internships, and hone communicative skills.

Applying

An applicant must have earned a baccalaureate degree from an accredited four-year college and have developed a portfolio of art work in a representative range of media. A student must submit the completed application form, the $50 application fee, official college transcripts, and two letters of recommendation. A formal portfolio presentation is required of all applicants. All portfolios are reviewed by a faculty committee, and selected applicants are invited to campus for a tour and interview. Portfolios should contain twelve to fifteen examples of recent work.

Correspondence and Information

David Hornung, Department Chair
Blodgett Hall, Room 301
College of Arts and Sciences
Adelphi University
Garden City, New York 11530
Phone: 516-877-4460
Fax: 516-877-4459
E-mail: hornung@adelphi.edu
Web site: http://academics.adelphi.edu/artsci/art/graduate/

Adelphi University

THE FACULTY

Hugh Crean, Professor; Ph.D., CUNY, 1990.
Dale Flashner, Graphic Design Studio Art Director and Senior Adjunct Professor.
Carson Fox, Assistant Professor; M.F.A., Rutgers, 1999.
Geoffrey Grogan, Associate Professor; M.F.A., M.S., Pratt, 1996.
David Hornung, Associate Professor; M.F.A., Wisconsin, 1976.
Jennifer Maloney, Visiting Assistant Professor; M.F.A., CUNY, Brooklyn, 2003.
Thomas McAnulty, Professor; M.F.A., Indiana, 1976.
Kellyann Monaghan, Associate Professor; M.F.A., CUNY, Brooklyn, 2001.
Jean Sorabella, Assistant Professor; Ph.D., Columbia, 2000.

THE ART INSTITUTE OF BOSTON
AT LESLEY UNIVERSITY
M.F.A. in Visual Arts

Programs of Study	The Art Institute of Boston (AIB) at Lesley University offers a low-residency Master of Fine Arts (M.F.A.) in Visual Arts program. It provides the ideal solution for artists, teachers, and professionals in related fields who are seeking professional advancement in the field of visual arts. The M.F.A. in Visual Arts program allows students, with the guidance of a faculty adviser and a studio mentor, to design their own studio and academic plans for each semester. This M.F.A. in Visual Arts program builds on the traditions of collaboration, innovation, and strength in the arts that characterize existing AIB and Lesley programs. It also benefits from the success of Lesley's low-residency model, a longstanding feature of several Lesley programs that meet the diverse needs of adult learners. The M.F.A. in visual arts is a degree that can advance the careers of artists, teachers, or professionals in other art-related fields.

The interdisciplinary focus of the M.F.A. program encourages students to explore the integration of a variety of visual arts media. The M.F.A. in visual arts focuses on developing the tools and expertise to create an individual vision. Students advance their study of art history, culture, and critical thinking through the rigorous academic components of the program while discovering how to situate their own work within a broadly defined contemporary art context. The M.F.A. program broadens the students' knowledge of visual arts as a profession, including relationships with galleries, grant and proposal preparation, post-graduate residencies, public and private collections, and the ongoing development of media and art-making tools.

Over the course of four semesters and five residencies, students learn to devise their own methodology for producing a focused plan of ongoing studio work and research, earning 15 credits per semester. During the intensive residencies, studio work, as outlined in each semester's study-plan contract, is evaluated for credit through critiques with faculty members, visiting artists, and peers. Academic studies are addressed through seminars, lectures, and planning sessions with academic advisers. During the semester, students' work, both academic and studio, is supervised by both a studio mentor and an M.F.A. faculty adviser. Studio components are 48 credits and academic components are 12 credits, for a total of 60 credits.

The M.F.A. in Visual Arts program is fully accredited by both the New England Association of Schools and Colleges (NEASC) and the National Association of Schools of Art and Design (NASAD) and is the only low-residency program based on the two 10-day residencies to be approved by NASAD. Lesley University is licensed by many states' Commission on Higher Education to offer programs in those states.

Research Facilities	The Art Institute of Boston's library maintains a focused collection, specializing in the fields of fine art, art history, illustration, design, and photography. The print collection of more than 10,000 books is focused on modern and contemporary art and design themes. The library has subscriptions to more than 80 current art journals and provides online access to scholarly articles through full-text art databases. Videos and a special collection of artists' books are available.

The library's visual resources collection contains high-quality digital images, which are made available online. The library participates in the ARTstor project, a digital library of nearly one million images in the areas of art, architecture, the humanities, and social sciences.

In addition, Ludcke Library at Lesley University maintains a working collection of books, periodicals, microfilm, microfiche, nonprint materials, and software resources. Through the Fenway Consortium, students can access thirteen other libraries in the Boston-Cambridge area.

Financial Aid	The Lesley University Financial Aid Office assists students as needed in obtaining various types of educational assistance, including Federal Pell Grants, Federal Stafford Student Loans, and Federal Perkins Loans.
Cost of Study	In 2009–10, the tuition for the M.F.A. in Visual Arts program is $7920 per semester. Additional program fees may apply.
Living and Housing Costs	Information on local housing is available upon request.
Student Group	The M.F.A. in Visual Arts program enrollment is approximately 85 students ranging in age from their mid-20s to their 60s. Students come from all fifty states and several other countries.
Location	The Art Institute of Boston at Lesley University occupies a campus in Kenmore Square in Boston. Lesley University occupies a campus between Harvard and Porter Squares in Cambridge. The University is conveniently connected to downtown Boston by public transportation. Numerous historical sites and cultural attractions are easily accessed by train or bus or on foot, including theaters, museums, and concerts.
The University	Lesley University, founded in 1909 as a women's teaching college, continues its commitment to educating undergraduate men and women while also offering undergraduate and graduate programs for men and women in the fields of education, human services, management, the environment, and the arts. Lesley University has successfully pioneered a wide variety of flexible programs for adult learners that share a commitment to quality, innovation, and the integration of theory with practice. Lesley offers degree programs through four schools: Lesley College, The Art Institute of Boston, the Graduate School of Arts and Social Sciences, and the School of Education. The University also supports several centers and hosts a variety of academic and professional conferences and institutes. Lesley programs operate throughout Massachusetts and in twenty-two other states as well as at affiliated international sites.
Applying	Applications for the M.F.A. program should be completed by March 1 for the June residency and September 15 for the January residency. Applications completed after those dates are considered on a space-available basis. Requirements for admission to the M.F.A. program are a bachelor's degree from a regionally accredited college or university as well as a satisfactory grade average, official transcripts of undergraduate work, three letters of recommendation, a written personal statement that describes the applicant's work in relation to contemporary art issues and interests, a portfolio review in the form of twenty images submitted with the application, and a nonrefundable $50 application fee. Applicants seeking a B.A. Waiver should contact the Office of Graduate Admissions. Application materials for the M.F.A. program should be requested from the Office of Graduate Admissions.
Correspondence and Information	Office of Graduate Admissions Lesley University 29 Everett Street Cambridge, Massachusetts 02138-2790 Phone: 617-349-8300 888-LESLEY-U (toll-free) Fax: 617-349-8313 E-mail: info@lesley.edu/ Web site: http://www.aiboston.edu/mfa

The Art Institute of Boston at Lesley University

THE FACULTY AND THEIR RESEARCH

Anthony Apesos is a painter who studied at Vassar College (B.A.), Pennsylvania Academy of Fine Arts (Certificate), and the Milton Avery Graduate School of Fine Arts at Bard College (M.F.A.). Selected one-person shows include the Andrea Marquit Fine Arts, Boston; F.A.N. Gallery, Philadelphia; More Gallery, Philadelphia; Villanova University Art Gallery; and Michael Dunev Gallery, San Francisco. Selected group shows include the Allentown Art Museum, Pennsylvania; Amos Eno Gallery, New York; Artists' Choice Museum, New York; and Philadelphia Sketch Club, Art Alliance, Philadelphia. He was a critic for the *New Art Examiner*. Apesos was chair of the Fine Arts Department at AIB and was the founding director of the AIB M.F.A. in Visual Arts program. He is currently professor in the Fine Arts Department at AIB. Awards include a Kress Travel Fellowship from the University of the Arts, Philadelphia and a grant from the New England Foundation for the Arts.

Cory Arcangel is a Brooklyn-based artist who works with video, installation, music composition, sculpture, print media, the Web, and mathematics. His installation and sculptural work has exhibited internationally in such venues as the Whitney Museum; the Museum of Modern Art, New York; the Migros Museum fur Gegenwartskunst, Zurich; and the Carnegie Museum of Art, Pittsburgh. His projects can be found online at http://www.beigerecords.com/cory.

Jan Avgikos is an art critic and historian based in New York City. She is a contributing editor with *Artforum* international magazine, where she regularly publishes reviews. She is widely published, and her writings appear internationally in magazines, museum catalogs, and anthologies of critical writing. Recent and forthcoming texts include a monograph on Katy Grannan (Aperture Books) and an essay on Roni Horn for the Dia Art Foundation's ongoing series of collected lectures from the Robert Lehman series. Recent and forthcoming catalog essays include Lili Dujourie (for the Palais des Beaux-Arts in Brussels) and Matts Leiderstam (for the Magasin 3 in Stockholm). She is a recipient of the Frank Jewett Mather Award, awarded by the College Art Association for distinction in art criticism. She was a Mellon fellow in graduate studies in art history at Columbia University. Avgikos is an adjunct member of the faculty for the graduate visual arts program at Columbia University, and the graduate visual arts program at NYU. She is also a professor at the School for the Visual Arts in Manhattan. In addition, she lectures regularly for the Dia Art Foundation for contemporary arts and at Sotheby's in its graduate American Art program.

Hannah Barrett is a figurative painter who has exhibited and taught extensively throughout New England. Recent exhibitions include Figuratively Seeing at the Massachusetts College of Art in 2009, and Ambivalent Figuration: People at Samson Projects in 2008. Barrett received an Artadia Award in 2007. Barrett has taught at the Pratt Institute in Brooklyn and the Rhode Island School of Design in Providence. Barrett's work is in the permanent collection of the DeCordova Museum and the Boston Public Library, and can be seen in the Drawing Center Viewing Program and at http://hannahbarrett.net/. Barrett is represented by the Howard Yezerski Gallery in Boston.

Judith Barry is an artist and writer whose work crosses a number of disciplines: performance, installation, sculpture, architecture, photography, and new media. She has exhibited internationally at the Berlin Biennale, Venice Biennale of Art/Architecture, São Paolo Biennale, Nagoya Biennale, Carnegie International, Whitney Biennale, and Australian Biennale. In 2000, she won the Kiesler Prize for Architecture and the Arts. In 2001, she was awarded Best Pavilion at the Cairo Biennale. *Public Fantasy*, a collection of Barry's essays, was published by the ICA in London (1991). Recent publications include *Projections: mise en abyme* (1997) and the catalog for the *Study for the Mirror and Garden in Granada, Spain* (2003). She has taught and lectured extensively in the U.S., Japan, and Europe. Recent full-time teaching positions include the visual arts program in the Department of Architecture at MIT in Boston (2002–2003) and the Merz Akademie in Stuttgart, Germany (2003–2004). A survey of her work originated at Domus Atrium 2002 in Salamanca, Spain, in April 2008 and is traveling to other venues in Europe.

Dike Blair is a painter and sculptor who lives in New York City. He has shown his work in museums and galleries in the United States and abroad for decades, including more than thirty solo exhibitions. His work was included in the 2004 Whitney Biennial and Vanishing Point at the Wexner Art Center in 2005. Blair also writes and was an associate editor of the Paris-based magazine *Purple*. He has contributed articles to a number of magazines including *Art Forum, ArtNews, Bomb, Paper, Art Presse, Parkett*, and *Harper's*. He is an adjunct painting professor at the Rhode Island School of Design. For more information visit: http://www.thing.net/~lilyvac or http://featureinc.com.

Deborah Davidson received her M.F.A. from the School of the Museum of Fine Arts, Tufts University in 1992, and her B.A. from Binghamton University. She currently teaches visual books at AIB and is also part of the core faculty in the M.F.A. program. She was the curator of exhibits and programs for the New Center for Arts and Culture, Boston, for six years. She exhibits widely, including shows at the William Scott Gallery; Plum Gallery, Williamstown; Jane Deering Gallery; Tufts University Art Gallery, Medford; Art Complex, Montserrat College of Art, Beverly; and at GASP. She was the featured artist in the 2005 issue of *Agni*, the Boston University literary magazine. Davidson's work is in many private and public collections, including Yale University; Wellesley College; Boston Public Library; Museum of Fine Arts, Boston; and the Houghton Library, Harvard University. Davidson's curatorial projects include an exhibit at AIB titled Exploding/Exploiting The Book. Most recently, she had a solo exhibition at the Danforth Museum of Art in the spring of 2009.

Andreas Fogarasi is a Vienna-based artist and co-editor of *derive–Magazine for Urban Studies*. Fogarasi's projects pursue and query the mechanisms with which information is transported into public space and how the principles of economic-political agendas are transformed into collective images of desire and possibilities for identification at the same time. A trained architect, his work consists of videos, photography, installation, and publications, combining architectural and typographic research and analysis with spatial interventions. He has participated in several important international exhibitions of contemporary art, such as the 52nd Venice Biennale, 2007 (where his exhibition at the Hungarian Pavilion was awarded the Golden Lion for best national participation); Manifesta 4 in Frankfurt/Main, 2002; and the 6th International Biennale in Gyumri/ Armenia, 2008. Recent exhibitions include solo shows at the Ernst Museum, Budapest; the MAK, Vienna; and Lombard-Freid Projects, New York; as well as group shows at European Kunsthalle, Cologne; Kunstverein Düsseldorf; Centro de Arte Reina Sofia, Madrid; Queensland Art Gallery/Gallery of Modern Art, Brisbane; and Georg Kargl Fine Arts, Vienna.

John Kramer is an artist and graphic designer. His most recent solo exhibition, Interesting and Dull Shapes, at the University Hall Gallery at AIB featured photographs, monotypes, and installation related to the Forest Hills Cemetery. He has also shown digital photography, video, installation work, and monotypes at HallSpace Gallery (Boston), DNA Gallery (Provincetown), film/video festivals (Boston, New York, Los Angeles, and San Francisco), and the "old" ICA Boston. His art and design backgrounds overlap with his interest in the performing arts, for which he has done sets, props, and costumes. He currently runs his own graphic design business, and is on the faculty of AIB's Master of Fine Arts program.

Adam McEwen received his B.F.A. from Oxford University (1984–1987), and continued his studies at the California Institute of the Arts (1989–1991). Through a broad range of media, the artist explores society's perception of human progress and its realities, as demonstrated in his obituaries of living luminaries and his recent chewing gum-dotted paintings that refer to desecrated post-war German landscapes. McEwen has had solo exhibitions at the Nicole Klagsbrun Gallery, New York; Galerie Art: Concept, Paris; and the Jack Hanley Gallery, San Francisco. His work was included in the 2006 Whitney Biennial and is held in the permanent collections of the Solomon M. Guggenheim Museum, the Whitney Museum of American Art, the Aberdeen Art Gallery and Museum, and the Arts Council of Great Britain. McEwen has also curated the recent exhibitions Beneath the Underdog (with Nate Lowman), Gagosian Gallery, New York (2007); Interstate, Nicole Klagsbrun Gallery (2005); and Power, Corruption and Lies (with Neville Wakefield), Roth Horowitz, New York (2004).

Carrie Moyer is a New York-based painter. Her work has been widely exhibited both nationally and internationally, including such venues as PS1/Institute on Contemporary Art; the Palm Beach ICA; Yerba Buena Center for the Arts; the Weatherspoon, Cooper-Hewitt and Tang Museums; Shedhalle (Zurich); Le Magasin (Grenoble); and the Project Centre (Dublin). Moyer was the founder of the public art project Dyke Action Machine! (DAM!). Between 1991 and 2004, DAM!'s culture-jamming campaigns dissected mainstream visual culture by inserting lesbian images into recognizably commercial contexts. Moyer received her B.F.A. from Pratt Institute and her M.F.A. from Bard College. She currently teaches at Yale, Rutgers University, and Pratt Institute.

Michael Newman is Associate Professor in Art History, Theory, and Criticism at the School of the Art Institute of Chicago, and Professor of Art Writing at Goldsmiths College at the University of London. He holds degrees in literature and art history, and a doctorate in philosophy from the Katholeike Universiteit Leuven, Belgium. He has written extensively on contemporary art, including essays on James Coleman, Jeff Wall, Alfred Jensen, Hanne Darboven, and Joëlle Tuerlinckx. He has curated several exhibitions, including Tacita Dean at the Art Gallery of York University, Toronto (2000), on whom his essays have been published by Tate Britain (2001) and Musée d'Art Moderne de la Ville de Paris (2003). His book *Richard Prince: Untitled (couple)* (Afterall and MIT) was published in 2006, and his monograph Jeff Wall: Works and Collected Writings (Poligrafa) was published in June 2007. He is co-editor of *Re-Writing Conceptual Art* (London, Reaktion Books, 1999). In philosophy he has published essays on Kant, Nietzsche, Derrida, Levinas, and Blanchot, and is currently writing a book on the trace.

Oscar Palacio is a Colombian-born, Boston-based photographer. He received his M.F.A. in photography from the Massachusetts College of Art and Design in 1998, and a Bachelor of Architecture from the University of Miami in 1992. His work is included in the permanent collections of the Fogg Art Museum at Harvard University, the Center for Creative Photography at the University of Arizona, MIT List Visual Arts Center, and the Addison Gallery of American Art at Phillips Academy in Andover. His work has been exhibited at Smith College Museum of Art, Julie Saul Gallery, Bonni Benrubi Gallery, Howard Yezerski Gallery, and Elias Fine Art. His work has been reviewed in publications such as the *New Yorker*, the *New York Times*, the *Village Voice*, the *Boston Globe*, *Tema Celeste*, *ArtNexus*, and *Art on Paper*. In 2004 and 2005, he was Edward E. Elson artist-in-residence at the Addison Gallery of American Art, where he had his first solo museum exhibition, Unfamiliar Territory, in the fall of 2005. He is an adjunct professor in Studio Foundation at the Massachusetts College of Art and Design. Recent exhibitions include Are We There Yet? at GASP in Boston and Hyde Park Art Center in Chicago. In August 2008 he was Artist-in-Residence at Light Work, Syracuse University. Visit: http://www.oscarpalacio.net.

Constanze Ruhm is an artist and filmmaker based in Vienna and Berlin. Her films and installations have been exhibited internationally at the Busan Biennale, Korea; 3rd Berlin Biennale; and the Venice Biennale. In 2004, she had a solo exhibition at Kunsthalle, Bern. Recent and upcoming exhibitions include Museo de Arte Reina Sofia, Madrid; Engholm Gallery and Generali Foundation, Vienna; and 57 Berlinale, Berlin. She has curated a number of exhibitions and film screening programs for Künstlerhaus Stuttgart; Secession Vienna; and the Center for Art and Media Technology, Karlsruhe, Germany. She has been a Professor for Film and Video at Merz Academy Stuttgart and currently is Professor for Art and Media at the Academy of Fine Arts in Vienna. Visit: http://www.constanzeruhm.net.

Sunanda K. Sanyal is an art historian originally from India, with an M.F.A. in visual arts (painting and installation) from UCSD (1990), an M.F.A. in art history from Ohio University (1993), and a Ph.D. in art history from Emory University (2000). He is interested in politics of representation and identity, representation and otherness, contemporary artists from former colonies in global discourses, and art pedagogy in nineteenth-century Europe and their colonies. Associate Professor of Art History and Critical Studies at AIB since 1999, Sanyal has chaired panels on contemporary artists of color at various conferences, including those hosted by the College Art Association, the African Studies Association, and the Arts Council of the African Studies Association. In 2008, he produced and directed a documentary film (58 min) titled *A Homecoming Spectacle*, which explores the visual culture of Durga Pujo, an annual religio-cultural festival held in Kolkata, India. Some of Sanyal's publications in art history and criticism include Modernism and Cultural Politics in East Africa: Cecil Todd's Drawings of the Uganda Martyrs, (*African Arts*, spring 2006); Kabiito Richard's Paintings: A Local Reinvention in a Global Perspective, (*African Arts*, summer 2004); The Local and Beyond: Francis Nnaggenda's Sculptural Innovations, (*NKA*, spring/summer, 2003); Transgressing Borders, Shaping an Art History: Rose Kirumira and Makerere's Legacy (*in African Art, Visual Culture and the Museum: Sights/Sites of Creativity and Conflict*, ed. Tobias Doering).

Julia Scher's work focuses on surveillance and the cybersphere. Aiming at the exposure of dangers and ideologies of monitoring systems, Scher creates temporary and transitory web/installation/performance works that explore issues of power, control, and seduction. She has shown in numerous national and international exhibitions. Currently, she is Professor of Media Arts at Kunsthochschule fur Medien (Academy of Media Arts) in Koln, Germany.

Laurel Sparks is an abstract painter who shows at Howard Yezerski Gallery (Boston). Sparks' work has been shown at the Museum of Fine Arts (Boston), DeCordova Museum (Lincoln, Massachusetts), CCS Bard Hessel Museum, Ramapo College, Boston Center for the Arts Mills Gallery, and Gallery at Green Street (Boston). Awards include a Berkshire Taconic Artist Grant, SMFA Alumni Traveling Scholarship, Massachusetts Cultural Council Grant, and an Elaine de Kooning Fellowship. Her work has been reviewed by the *Boston Globe*, *Boston Phoenix*, and *Big RED & Shiny*. Sparks holds a B.F.A. from the School of the Museum of Fine Arts, Boston, and an M.F.A. from Bard College. She currently teaches at the School of the Museum of Fine Arts, Massachusetts College of Art and Design, and the AIB M.F.A. program.

Stuart Steck has worked as both a curator and academic during the past decade. Although he was originally trained in the field of decorative arts, his current interests focus on post-war art and critical theory. He has taught undergraduate and graduate courses at AIB since 1998. In addition to serving on the faculty at AIB, he has also held teaching positions at the Massachusetts Institute of Technology, Brown University, Boston University, and Suffolk University. Most recently, Steck has published essays on Ellsworth Kelly and Sung Ho Kim (forthcoming), with whom he recently collaborated on an architectural project. He is also the producer of the Short Attention Span Digital Video Festival, which showcases the work of students from around the world. Over the years, Steck has received research grants from the Henry Luce Foundation, the Pittsburgh Foundation, and the Boston University Humanities Foundation. Steck received his B.A. in History from Cornell University and his Ph.D. in Art History from Boston University. His dissertation was titled *Veiling the Subject: Ellsworth Kelly and the Discourses of Modernism*.

Oliver Wasow, a photographer, was born in Madison, Wisconsin, in 1960. His work is currently represented by the Kathleen Cullen Gallery in New York City. He has had a number of one-person exhibitions, including shows at the Janet Borden Gallery, the Tom Solomon Gallery in Los Angeles, the South Eastern Center for Contemporary Art in North Carolina, and Galerie De Poche in Paris. His work has also been included in numerous national and international group shows, including such benchmark exhibitions as Image World at the Whitney Museum of Art in New York City, and The Photography of Invention at the National Gallery of Art in Washington, D.C. His photographs are included in a number of private collections and are also represented in various prominent public collections, including the Whitney Museum of Art and the Museum of Modern Art in New York City. Reviews of his work have been featured in most major art publications including, among others, *Art Forum*, *ArtNews*, and the *New York Times*. He has been the recipient of various grants and awards including a Louis Comfort Tiffany Grant in 1999 and, in 2000, his second New York State Council on the Arts Grant.

Deb Todd Wheeler is a sculptor, inventor, and media artist. Her work concerns technology as a mediator for human interaction with the environment. The central focus of her work in the past few years has been to examine the role of science in relation to our human lives through a lens that encompasses the nineteenth century and cutting-edge robotic technologies. Using the vernacular of the nineteenth century, a time when art and science were more closely linked, she investigates alternative avenues for power that reflect our growing concern with sustainability today. In her most recent exhibit, Live Experiments in Human Energy Exchange, she experiments with generators and bicycle power to provide electricity, wind, sound, and motion.

Visiting Artists, Curators, and Critics

Cory Arcangel, Bill Arning, Jan Avgikos, Dike Blair, Nayland Blake, Holly Block, Barbara Bloom, Jurgen Böck, Sarah Charlesworth, Laura Donaldson, Thomas Eggerer, Andreas Fogarasi, Maureen Gallace, Gamaliel R. Herrera, Dana Hoey, Jacqueline Humphries, Wendy Jacob, Byron Kim, Steve Locke, Barbara London, Tony Matelli, Annu Matthew, Marilyn Minter, Rebecca Morris, Michael Newman, Jennifer Pastor, Tom Patti, Alexis Rockman, Barry Schwabsky, Shelburne Thurber, Oliver Wasow, and Wendy White.

BARD GRADUATE CENTER: DECORATIVE ARTS, DESIGN HISTORY, MATERIAL CULTURE

Programs of Study

The Bard Graduate Center (BGC) is a graduate institute affiliated with Bard College committed to the encyclopedic study of things in their historical context, drawing on methodologies and approaches from art and design history, economic history, history of technology, philosophy, anthropology, and archaeology. The project of the school is to study the cultural history of the material world.

Founded in 1993, the BGC offers M.A. and Ph.D. degrees. It is an international study and exhibition center in New York City devoted to the interdisciplinary study of the decorative arts, design history, cultural history, history and theory of museums, Renaissance and early modern studies, cultural geography, American art and culture, Asian Art, the Arts of Antiquity, eighteenth through twentieth century design and European Studies, and the material culture of New York City. Programs are designed to prepare students for careers or career advancement in museums; galleries; auction houses; government agencies; art-related education, research, publishing, and communications; and landscape and historic preservation.

There is hands-on examination of materials and objects and an extensive connection to special programs and exhibition projects with the Metropolitan Museum of Art, the New York Historical Society, the Brooklyn Museum of Art, the American Museum of Natural History, and other major cultural institutions. As part of their studies, all students undertake an internship at one of more than 250 institutions.

A semiannual interdisciplinary journal, *Studies in the Decorative Arts,* is published by the BGC and features scholarly articles about the decorative arts and their interpretation as well as book reviews. Advanced graduate students are invited to submit articles for possible publication.

Research Facilities

The Bard Graduate Center occupies a six-story town house at 18 West 86th Street and a second, newly renovated town house at 38 West 86th Street in Manhattan. The buildings' elegantly appointed rooms provide an aesthetically appropriate setting for the study of the decorative arts. Its facilities include a 40,000-volume research library; a new media research lab; exhibition galleries; classrooms; faculty offices; student lounges; outdoor terraces; symposium spaces; and administrative offices.

Financial Aid

The BGC offers fellowships, scholarships, and a student campus employment program. Aid is awarded on the basis of need and merit. Financial aid applications are due by January 15. About 85 percent of students receive aid.

Cost of Study

The average annual tuition for incoming full-time students in the 2008–09 academic year was $26,730 for M.A. students, based on a cost of $990 per credit. Tuition and fees for Ph.D. students averaged $30,776 for incoming full-time students in the 2008–09 academic year; they vary for subsequent years of doctoral work. Students may contact the Office of Admissions for more detailed and updated fee schedules.

Living and Housing Costs

Bard Hall, located at 410 West 58th Street, provides housing for students, faculty members, and visiting scholars. Nine residential floors offer a variety of furnished studios and one- and two-bedroom suites with kitchens and baths. Apartments are offered year-round. For the 2008–09 academic year, the cost of a studio unit was approximately $13,200, a one-bedroom unit was $15,700, and a two-bedroom unit was $13,000 per student.

Student Group

The Bard Graduate Center accepts approximately 20–25 full-time and a limited number of part-time students into the program annually. Applications are received from many countries and from across the United States. The BGC welcomes students of all ages and backgrounds as well as working professionals.

Location

The Bard Graduate Center is located on the Upper West Side of Manhattan, near Central Park. It is situated in a landmark neighborhood conveniently served by public transportation, with easy access to the innumerable museums, libraries, auction houses, and galleries of metropolitan New York.

The College and The Center

Established by Bard College in 1993, the Bard Graduate Center is one of the many "satellite" institutions that surround the 133-year-old undergraduate liberal arts college. Others include the Jerome Levy Economics Institute of Bard College, the Milton Avery Graduate School of the Arts, and the Center for Curatorial Studies in Art and Contemporary Culture. Other graduate divisions are located in Annandale, New York.

Applying

Students are admitted to the graduate programs annually for fall admission. The application deadline for admission and financial aid is January 15. Applicants to the M.A. program must have a bachelor's degree or the equivalent; applicants to the Ph.D. program are expected to have completed a master's degree in either the decorative arts or a related field. Because of the interdisciplinary nature of the program, there are no limitations on the applicant's prior field of study. Successful applicants, however, will have had some previous study, training, or work experience in the history of art, architecture, archeology, history, the decorative arts, cultural history, or material culture studies.

Applications should include scores on the General Test of the Graduate Record Examinations (GRE), three letters of recommendation, a short resume, a sample of scholarly writing, and a statement of intent describing academic and professional objectives. International candidates must submit TOEFL scores and a Certification of Finances. An interview is required. The application fee for 2009–10 is $65.

Correspondence and Information

Office of Admissions
Bard Graduate Center: Decorative Arts, Design History, Material Culture
18 West 86th Street
New York, New York 10024
Phone: 212-501-3019
Fax: 212-501-3065
E-mail: admissions@bgc.bard.edu
Web site: http://www.bgc.bard.edu

Bard Graduate Center: Decorative Arts, Design History, Material Culture

THE FACULTY AND THEIR RESEARCH

The BGC maintains a distinguished core of full-time faculty members, supplemented by eminent decorative arts scholars visiting from a broad range of national and international museums and institutions of higher learning.

The Bard Graduate Center Faculty

Susan Weber Soros, Iris Horowitz Professor in the History of the Decorative Arts and Director; Ph.D., Royal College of Art. Furniture studies.
Peter N. Miller, Professor and Chair of Academic Programs; Ph.D., Cambridge. European cultural history.
Kenneth Ames, Professor; Ph.D., Pennsylvania. Nineteenth century.
Jeffrey Collins, Professor; Ph.D., Yale. Eighteenth-century European art and culture.
David Jaffee, Professor; Ph.D., Harvard. Landscape history and cultural geography.
Pat Kirkham, Professor; Ph.D., London. Eighteenth-, nineteenth-, and twentieth-century design history and gender studies.
Deborah L. Krohn, Associate Professor; Ph.D., Harvard. Early Modern material culture in southern Europe and museum studies.
François Louis, Associate Professor; Ph.D., Zurich. Art history of Tang and Song China, Chinese goldsmithing.
Michele Majer, Assistant Professor; M.A., NYU. Costume historian.
Andrew Morrall, Professor; Ph.D., Courtauld Institute of Art (England). Fourteenth- to eighteenth-century European arts.
Amy Ogata, Associate Professor; Ph.D., Princeton. Nineteenth- and twentieth-century design history.
Elizabeth Simpson, Professor; Ph.D., Pennsylvania. The arts of the ancient world.
Paul Stirton, Associate Professor; Ph.D. Courtauld Institute of Art (England). Design history.
Catherine Whalen, Assistant Professor; Ph.D., Yale. American material culture and twentieth-century design.

Visiting Faculty

Timothy Benton, M.A., Courtauld Institute of Art (England). Twentieth-century art and architecture.
Thomas Campbell, Ph.D., Courtauld Institute of Art (England). Textile historian.
Ellen Paul Denker, M.A., Delaware. American ceramics.
Stefan Heidemann, Visiting Professor, Ph.D., Free University (Berlin). Islamic art.
Timothy Husband, M.A., Institute of Fine Arts, New York. Medieval decorative arts.
Juliet Kinchin, M.A., Courtauld Institute of Art (England). Twentieth-century architecture and design.
Louis Levine, Ph.D., Pennsylvania. Jewish material culture.
Pamela Long, Ph.D., Maryland. Medieval and Renaissance technology.
Caroline Maniaque, Ph.D., Paris VIII. Architecture and urbanism.
Robert J. Moes, M.A., Michigan. The arts of Japan and Korea.
Kevin L. Stayton, M.Phil., Yale. American decorative arts.
Ittai Weinryb, Ph.D., Johns Hopkins. Medieval material culture.

BRYN MAWR COLLEGE

Graduate School of Arts and Sciences
Department of History of Art

Programs of Study

Bryn Mawr's Department of History of Art offers M.A. and Ph.D. degrees in all areas of Western art history from late antiquity through the present, including film. It is one of three independent departments that comprise the Graduate Group in Archaeology, Classics, and History of Art. The program of study is flexible and can be tailored to the goals and interests of individual students. Faculty members offer seminars on topics related to their current research, including late Gothic painting, Mannerism, seventeenth-century Spain and its colonies, German art criticism and aesthetics, self-portraiture, assemblage, video art, visual art and the Holocaust, and theories of authorship in cinema. Faculty members and students regularly participate in interdisciplinary seminars (GSems) offered by the Graduate Group, which also sponsors internships in Philadelphia area museums. Recent GSems include Public Space, History and Memory, Rome and Its Representation, Vienna 1900, and Death and Beyond. All course work and the M.A. thesis should be completed within two or three years. Ph.D. preliminary examinations should be taken in the fourth or fifth year, followed by the dissertation. For the Ph.D., the average time-to-degree for recent graduates is 8.5 years; over half graduated in 7.5 years or less. Faculty members work closely with students to identify dissertation projects well suited to their strengths and interests. Recent topics include anatomical investigation and the gendered imagination in sixteenth-century Florentine art; Bronzino and the style(s) of Mannerism; Rembrandt's spaces; art and evangelization at Santiago Apóstol at Cuilapan; devotional practice and the art of Velazquez; gesture, costume, and identity in Goya; intersections in the careers of Mary Cassatt and Edgar Degas; Byzantium in Bavaria; Kirchner's "Berlin Style" and its affinities with Bohumil Kubišta; Kandinsky, Marc and the apocalyptic tradition, the painting and writing of Giorgio de Chirico; the nature of representation in the art of Bruce Nauman; Andy Warhol, Robert Gober, Matthew Barney, and the contemporary object of art; modern primitive body art; and art, AIDS, and collective identity; Sophie Calle. Graduates are prepared principally for academic and curatorial careers, but recent Ph.D.s are also employed or self-employed in business and not-for-profit corporations.

Research Facilities

The award-winning Rhys Carpenter Library, inaugurated in 1997, is a specialized library for history of art, archaeology, and classics. Fully wired carrels are reserved there for all graduate students in these fields. In addition to the more than 135,000 volumes in Carpenter Library, the tri-college library consortium of Bryn Mawr, Haverford, and Swarthmore Colleges contains more than 2 million volumes. Bryn Mawr currently subscribes to more than fifty art history journals. Online reference sources include the Bibliography of the History of Art, Art Index, ARTbibliographies Modern, Avery Index, ARTstor, and JSTOR.

Bryn Mawr's art collection numbers more than 25,000 items and is especially strong in works on paper. The College also owns more than 45,000 rare books, including one of the largest collections of incunables in the United States, and more than 13,000 photographs illustrating the development of photography since the mid-nineteenth century.

Financial Aid

Bryn Mawr offers a number of fellowships for full-time study, as well as grants, tuition awards, and summer stipends. Fellowship stipends begin at $17,500, including a summer stipend, and can be guaranteed for multiple years. Special awards include Areté (Excellence) Fellowships with a package of $20,000 plus a health insurance subsidy. Each year, the Department offers four teaching assistantships and one collections assistantship, with a stipend of $14,000 and a health insurance subsidy. For students in the Graduate Group in Archaeology, Classics, and History of Art, additional competitive fellowships and curatorial internships for multidisciplinary study are available, with twelve-month stipends of $20,000 plus a health insurance subsidy. Currently, 81 percent of the students enrolled in the program in history of art receive some form of financial aid.

Cost of Study

Full-time tuition, consisting of six courses per year, is $31,340; part-time tuition is $5290 per course. Units of supervised work cost $845, and the fee for maintaining matriculation (continuing enrollment) is $430 per semester.

Living and Housing Costs

Students live locally or in Philadelphia. Shared apartments can be rented for $600 to $900 per month, studio apartments begin at $800 per month, and food costs are about $200 per month. Other expenses include transportation (about $165 per month if commuting from Philadelphia) and health insurance (approximately $2500 per year for domestic students and approximately $1500 for international students).

Student Group

In 2009–10, there are 28 students enrolled in history of art, 24 women and 4 men. One is international. Seventeen students have progressed to Ph.D. candidacy, 4 are candidates for the M.A., and the remaining are in course work.

Student Outcomes

About half (51 percent) of Ph.D. graduates of the past ten years hold teaching positions at colleges and universities, including Aurora University; Colorado State University; Harvard University; Illinois State University; Maryland Institute College of Art; Rice University; Rochester Institute of Technology; Villanova University; University of Georgia; University of London; University of Minnesota, Duluth; University of Nebraska at Kearney; University of Pittsburgh; University of the South; University of Tennessee, Knoxville; University of Wisconsin–Madison; Touro College; and Ursinus College. Fourteen percent are employed in museums such as the Art Institute of Chicago, Carnegie Museum of Art, Dallas Museum of Art, Figge Art Museum, and the Whitney Museum. Others work in the private sector and for nonprofit organizations.

Location

Bryn Mawr is a suburb of Philadelphia, the fifth-largest city in the U.S. It is well served by rail lines and by bus. Philadelphia is renowned for music, museums, and sports, and it is also a culinary mecca, with restaurants serving many cuisines. The metropolitan area has more than 100 museums and fifty colleges and universities, with a total population of 220,000 students.

The College and The Department

Bryn Mawr is a liberal arts college for women, founded in 1885. It was the first women's college to offer graduate education through the Ph.D. and the first U.S. institution to offer fellowships to women for graduate study. Throughout its history, the College has been committed first and foremost to providing the most rigorous and challenging education to women and, in the Graduate School of Arts and Sciences, also to men. The current enrollment is 1,300 undergraduate students, 150 graduate students in the Graduate School of Arts and Sciences, and about 250 students in the Graduate School of Social Work and Social Research.

The Department of History of Art was founded in 1913 by Georgiana Goddard King, whose courses in Spanish art were the first graduate instruction in that field in the U.S. The graduate program was significantly enlarged by Charles Mitchell (1961–1980). Mitchell established an enduring strength in the Italian Renaissance and the classical tradition that was enhanced by Phyllis Pray Bober (1973–1991), while James Snyder (1964–1989) offered a complementary emphasis on Northern Europe. Collaboration with the program in Growth and Structure of Cities founded by Barbara Miller Lane (1962–1999), created a significant strength in the history of European and American architecture. The diversity of the current Department is due to the maintenance of these traditional specialties in combination with new areas of concentration (contemporary art, film) and rigorous attention to poststructural theory. The weekly colloquiums of the Center for Visual Culture enrich the mix with research presentations by scientists and social scientists as well by specialists in art, literature, and film.

Applying

Application for admission and financial aid should be made on the form available from the Graduate School of Arts and Sciences. Applicants can also download this form from the Graduate School's Web site at http://www.brynmawr.edu/gsas/. The deadline for admission with financial aid is January 4, 2010. Applications for admission without financial aid are accepted until June 30, 2010.

Students admitted to graduate work in history of art typically have reading knowledge of German or French (preferably both) and undergraduate training in art history and/or cognate disciplines in the humanities. Applicants must submit GRE scores; TOEFL scores, if not native speakers of English; a statement of interest, and a recent research paper or critical essay.

Students are encouraged to contact the Department and to visit. The Department's Web site is http://www.brynmawr.edu/hart/.

Correspondence and Information

Lea Miller, Program Assistant
Graduate School of Arts and Sciences
Bryn Mawr College
101 North Merion Avenue
Bryn Mawr, Pennsylvania 19010
Phone: 610-526-5072
Fax: 610-526-5076
E-mail: lrmiller@brynmawr.edu
Web site: http://www.brynmawr.edu/gsas/

Bryn Mawr College

THE FACULTY AND THEIR RESEARCH

David J. Cast, Professor; Ph.D., Columbia, 1970. Renaissance art and criticism, architecture post-1400, twentieth-century British art.

Christiane Hertel, Professor; Ph.D., Tübingen, 1985. German, Austrian, and Netherlandish art and architecture; German intellectual history; aesthetics and art theory.

Homay King, Associate Professor; Ph.D., Berkeley, 2003. American film history; film, feminist, psychoanalytic, and rhetorical theory.

Dale Kinney, Eugenia Chase Guild Professor in the Humanities; Ph.D., NYU, 1975. Late antique and medieval Italian art, medieval architecture, spolia.

Steven Z. Levine, Leslie Clark Professor in the Humanities; Ph.D., Harvard, 1974. Sixteenth- to twentieth-century French painting, psychoanalysis, self-portraiture, visual theory.

Gridley McKim-Smith, Andrew W. Mellon Professor in the Humanities; Ph.D., Harvard, 1974. Seventeenth-century Spanish painting and sculpture, scientific analysis of works of art, costume.

Lisa Saltzman, Professor and Director of the Center for Visual Culture; Ph.D., Harvard, 1994. Post–World War II art and theory, gender and identity, memory and trauma.

Affiliated Faculty

A. A. Donohue, Professor, Department of Classical and Near Eastern Archaeology; Ph.D., NYU, 1984. History and historiography of classical art.

Timothy Harte, Associate Professor, Department of Russian; Ph.D., Harvard, 2001. Russian avant-garde literature and painting, Russian and Soviet film, contemporary Russian culture.

Carola Hein, Associate Professor, Program in Growth and Structure of Cities; Dr.-Ing., Hochschule für bildende Künste (Hamburg), 1995. City planning and design, post–World War II Japan, architecture and planning education.

Madhavi Kale, Professor, Department of History; Ph.D., Pennsylvania, 1992. Postcolonial theory, labor history, Indian cinema.

Imke Meyer, Associate Professor, Department of German; Ph.D., Washington (Seattle), 1993. Modern German and Austrian literature and film, gender and sexuality.

Roberta Ricci, Assistant Professor, Department of Italian; Ph.D., Johns Hopkins, 1998. Medieval and Renaissance literature, philology, Jewish-Italian literature, comparative literature.

CALIFORNIA COLLEGE OF THE ARTS

Programs of Study

California College of the Arts (CCA) offers graduate programs in architecture, curatorial practice, design, design strategy, fine arts, visual and critical studies, and writing. All are two-year programs except architecture, which is a three-year program.

The Master of Architecture (M.Arch.) Program is accredited by the National Architectural Accrediting Board (NAAB). It integrates material, artistic, and critical approaches with the study and practice of architecture, focusing on design and fabrication. This three-year first professional master's degree program is designed for those who have earned a bachelor's degree in another discipline. Advanced standing may be granted to students who have previous education in the field or a B.Arch. degree.

The M.A. Graduate Program in Curatorial Practice offers an expanded perspective on curating contemporary art and culture, exploring the impact of artist-led initiatives and other efforts that take place outside conventional venues. Core faculty members include curators from Bay Area museums and galleries. The program prepares students for careers in museums and galleries, public art, project management, and publishing.

The M.F.A. Graduate Program in Design offers concentrations in communication design, industrial design, and interaction design. It is distinguished by its interdisciplinary nature and its emphasis on research, strategy, entrepreneurship, and futurism. Graduates are prepared to enter the professional design world at the highest levels. In a 2007 issue, *BusinessWeek* magazine named CCA one of the world's best design schools.

The M.B.A. in Design Strategy program, one of the very first of its kind, unites the fields of design, finance, and management. It combines lectures and seminars in organizational development, business strategy, leadership, entrepreneurship, and sustainability with practical studios and sponsored projects. Its unique residency structure—five once-a-month, four-day weekends on campus per semester—accommodates working professionals.

The M.F.A. Graduate Program in Fine Arts is rooted in critically engaged studio practice. Interdisciplinary seminars, critiques, and visiting-artist programs ground students in critical theory and practice while they explore the potential of diverse media. The program explores both the specifics of particular disciplines and the points of interaction and overlap among disciplines. Students may choose to emphasize either studio practice or social practice.

The M.A. Graduate Program in Visual and Critical Studies is intended for students who aspire to write professionally about art, culture, architecture, and design. It emphasizes interdisciplinary and cross-cultural study, historical grounding, and the aesthetic aspects of written communication. Students explore and develop three crucial skills: attentive viewing, the development of analytical perspective, and creative and critical writing. The dual-degree option—an M.A. in visual and critical studies and an M.F.A. in fine arts, writing, or design—is for artists who wish to merge their studio practices with a deep critical understanding of visual culture.

The M.F.A. Program in Writing is for writers in every genre who wish to study in the creative environment of an art college. The program offers traditional workshops but also allows those interested in the large, evolving field of text and image to take courses in performance art, book art, video, film, and multimedia.

Research Facilities

CCA has two main libraries serving the fields of contemporary art, design, and architecture. Their combined collections include some 73,000 volumes, more than 2,000 videos, and 300 current periodical subscriptions. Students have free online access to more than 2,500 electronic journals and reference resources. More than 500,000 digital images are contained in the online ARTstor database. Students in the Visual and Critical Studies and Writing programs also have borrowing privileges at the libraries of the University of California, Berkeley.

CCA offers a wireless network and a wide range of digital technologies on campus. Studios and technological resources are usually accessible 16–24 hours daily. Campus media centers have a wide variety of equipment available for checkout. Thirteen dedicated labs offer a diverse and complete range of software and hardware for print and Web graphics, audio/video editing, animation, 3-D modeling, rapid prototyping, large-format color printing, and laser cutting.

The Graduate Studies Lecture Series features some of the world's most influential and innovative artists, architects, writers, scholars, designers, and curators. Each speaker typically also makes class visits or meets one-on-one with students. The spring 2009 lecturers are Fritjof Capra, Raj Patel, Jürgen Mayer, Trinh T. Minh-ha, Chris Csikszentmihályi, Guillermo Gómez-Peña, Sofía Hernández Chong Cuy, Daniel Alarcón, Shamim M. Momin, J. Morgan Puett, Christine Y. Kim, and Matt Keegan.

The CCA Wattis Institute, located on campus, presents international contemporary art exhibitions and sponsors an impressive array of public artist talks, symposia, and performances.

Financial Aid

Financial assistance is available in the form of merit-based, need-based, and diversity scholarships; grants; teaching assistantships; federal loans; and work-study. Merit and diversity scholarships are awarded by the admissions committee; there is no separate scholarship application. Those who wish to apply for financial aid should complete the Free Application for Federal Student Aid (http://www.fafsa.ed.gov) and visit http://www.cca.edu/financialaid for more information.

Cost of Study

Tuition and fees for full-time study for the 2008–09 school year were $19,754 for the Graduate Program in Visual and Critical Studies and $32,690 for all other graduate programs.

Living and Housing Costs

Graduate students live off campus.

Student Group

In 2008–09, approximately 360 of CCA's 1,700 enrolled students were in the graduate division.

Location

CCA is located in the San Francisco Bay Area, a region known for creative and technological innovation and a thriving art and design community. The San Francisco campus is in the Potrero Hill neighborhood, near the city's design district and the growing Mission Bay neighborhood. It houses all seven graduate programs, a newly completed graduate center, and a graduate writing studio. CCA's 4-acre Oakland campus houses state-of-the-art facilities for ceramics, glass, jewelry, metal arts, photography, printmaking, and textiles.

The College

Founded in 1907, CCA is noted for the interdisciplinarity and breadth of its programs. In addition to its seven graduate programs, it offers twenty undergraduate majors in the areas of fine arts, architecture, design, and writing. Noted faculty members and alumni include the painters Nathan Oliveira and Raymond Saunders; ceramicists Robert Arneson, Viola Frey, and Peter Voulkos; filmmaker Wayne Wang; conceptual artists David Ireland and Dennis Oppenheim; and designers Lucille Tenazas and Michael Vanderbyl.

Applying

Applications for CCA's graduate programs must be received by January 15 for fall admission. Students may apply online or download an application at http://www.cca.edu.

Correspondence and Information

Enrollment Services Office–Graduate Admissions
California College of the Arts
1111 Eighth Street
San Francisco, California 94107-2247
Phone: 415-703-9523
       800-447-1ART (toll-free)
Fax: 415-703-9539
E-mail: graduateprograms@cca.edu
Web site: http://www.cca.edu

California College of the Arts

THE FACULTY

Information about individual faculty members may be found at the College's Web site, http://www.cca.edu.

Juvenal Acosta (Writing)
Cassandra Adams (Architecture)
Opal Palmer Adisa (Writing)
Stephen Ajay (Writing)
Peter Anderson (Architecture)
T. Jason Anderson (Architecture)
Kim Anno (Fine Arts)
Craig Baldwin (Fine Arts)
Tom Barbash (Writing)
John Barone (Architecture)
Mara Baum (Architecture)
Brendan Beazley (Architecture)
Leslie Becker (Design)
Hugh Behm-Steinberg (Writing)
Dodie Bellamy (Writing)
Jeffrey Benningfield (Architecture)
Ila Berman (Architecture)
Michael Bernard (Architecture)
Kory Bieg (Architecture)
Rebekah Bloyd (Writing)
Keith Boadwee (Fine Arts)
Vivian Bobka (Fine Arts)
Michael Bogan (Architecture)
Rebeca Bollinger (Fine Arts)
Carol Buhrmann (Architecture)
Douglas Burnham (Architecture)
Raul Cabra (Design)
Gabrielle Calvocoressi (Writing)
Andre Caradec (Architecture)
Tammy Rae Carland (Fine Arts)
Sydney Carson (Writing)
Julian Carter (Visual and Critical Studies)
Valerie Casey (Design)
Kami Chisholm (Fine Arts, Visual and Critical Studies)
Alan Christ (Architecture)
Susan Ciriclio (Fine Arts)
Brian Conley (Fine Arts)
Lia Cook (Fine Arts)
Sekou Cooke (Architecture)
Benjamin Corotis (Architecture)
Betsy Davids (Writing)
Donna de la Perrière (Writing)
Sergio de la Torre (Fine Arts)
Gregory Di Paolo (Architecture)
Steve Diller (M.B.A. in Design Strategy)
Anthony Discenza (Fine Arts)
Mark Donohue (Architecture)
Susanna Douglas (Architecture)
Beth Dungan (Fine Arts)
Sally Elesby (Fine Arts)
Mona El-Khafif (Architecture)
Carol Elkovich (Fine Arts)

Kota Ezawa (Fine Arts)
Christopher Falliers (Architecture)
Thom Faulders (Architecture)
Maria Fedorchenko (Architecture)
Lisa Findley (Architecture)
Chris Finley (Fine Arts)
Jeanne Finley (Fine Arts)
Karen Fiss (Visual and Critical Studies)
Linda Fleming (Fine Arts)
James Forcier (M.B.A. in Design Strategy)
John Foster (M.B.A. in Design Strategy)
Amy Franceschini (Fine Arts)
Jacqueline Francis (Visual and Critical Studies)
Kathleen Fraser (Writing)
Gloria Frym (Writing)
Linda Geary (Fine Arts)
Jordan Geiger (Architecture)
David Gissen (Architecture)
James Gobel (Fine Arts)
Jim Goldberg (Fine Arts)
Caroline Goodwin (Writing)
Sharon Green (M.B.A. in Design Strategy)
Josh Greene (Fine Arts)
Anthony Grudin (Curatorial Practice, Fine Arts)
Doris Guerrero (Architecture)
Stephen Hartzog (Design)
Glen Helfand (Fine Arts)
Jens Hoffmann (Curatorial Practice)
Steven Skov Holt (Design)
David Huffman (Fine Arts)
Hugh Hynes (Architecture)
Margaret Ikeda (Architecture)
Matthew Iribarne (Writing)
Christian Jankowski (Fine Arts)
Oblio Jenkins (Architecture)
Evan Jones (Architecture)
Jordan Kantor (Fine Arts)
Geoff Kaplan (Design)
David Karam (Design)
Barry Katz (Design)
Lara Kaufman (Architecture)
Kevin Killian (Writing)
Lynn Kirby (Fine Arts)
Andrew Kudless (Architecture)
Genevieve L'Heureux (Architecture)
Amy Larimer (Architecture)
John Laskey (Writing)
Tirza True Latimer (Visual and Critical Studies)
Brenda Laurel (Design)
John Jota Leaños (Fine Arts)

Joseph Lease (Writing)
Steven Leiber (Curatorial Practice, Fine Arts)
Ines Lejarraga (Architecture)
Bruce Levin (Design)
Brendon Levitt (Architecture)
Kenneth Lum (Fine Arts)
Nathan Lynch (Fine Arts)
Sean Madden (Design)
Raimundas Malasauskas (Curatorial Practice, Fine Arts)
Elizabeth Mangini (Fine Arts, Visual and Critical Studies)
Robert Marcial (Architecture)
Ari Marcopoulos (Fine Arts)
Anne N. Marino (Writing)
Leigh Markopoulos (Curatorial Practice)
Christina Marsh (Architecture)
Daria Martin (Fine Arts)
Marina McDougall (Curatorial Practice)
Emily McVarish (Design)
Maria McVarish (Design)
Susannah Meek (Architecture)
Miranda F. Mellis (Writing)
Jeremy Mende (Design)
E. B. Min (Architecture)
Raffi Minasian (M.B.A. in Design Strategy)
Paul Montgomery (Design)
Carol Moukheiber (Architecture)
Ranu Mukherjee (Fine Arts)
Julian Myers (Curatorial Practice)
Scott Nazarian (Design)
Denise Newman (Writing)
James Nisbet (Design)
Margeigh Novotny (Design)
Shaun O'Dell (Fine Arts)
David Ogorzalek (Architecture)
Eric Olsen (Architecture)
Colin Owen (Design)
Miriam Paeslack (Visual and Critical Studies)
Holly Payne (Writing)
Sandra Percival (Curatorial Practice)
Peter Pfau (Architecture)
Aimee Phan (Writing)
Keith Plymale (Architecture)
Maria Porges (Fine Arts)
Renny Pritikin (Curatorial Practice)
Ted Purves (Fine Arts)
Michelle Richmond (Writing)
Katherine Rinne (Architecture)
Lacy Jane Roberts (Fine Arts)
Leslie Carol Roberts (Design, Writing)

Lisa Robertson (Architecture, Fine Arts, Writing)
Clare Robinson (Architecture)
Zack Rogow (Writing)
Rachel Schreiber (Humanities and Sciences)
Neal Schwartz (Architecture)
Mitchell Schwarzer (Visual and Critical Studies)
Craig Scott (Architecture)
Judith Serin (Writing)
Sanjit Sethi (Fine Arts)
Matthew Shears (Writing)
Nathan Shedroff (M.B.A. in Design Strategy)
Linda Sheldon (M.B.A. in Design Strategy)
Kristen Sidell (M.B.A. in Design Strategy)
Brad Simon (M.B.A. in Design Strategy)
Kathrina Simonen (Architecture)
Kristian Simsarian (Design)
Mara Holt Skov (Design)
Mary Snowden (Fine Arts)
Andrew Sparks (Architecture)
Raphael Sperry (Architecture)
Naomi Stanford (M.B.A. in Design Strategy)
Antje Steinmuller (Architecture)
Ryan Stroupe (Architecture)
Larry Sultan (Fine Arts)
Tina Takemoto (Fine Arts, Visual and Critical Studies)
Michael Tauber (Architecture)
Brian Teare (Writing)
Mark Thompson (Fine Arts)
Bruce Tomb (Architecture)
Ignacio Valero (Design, Visual and Critical Studies)
Deborah Valoma (Fine Arts)
Martin Venesky (Design)
Sandra Vivanco (Architecture)
Asher Waldfogel (M.B.A. in Design Strategy)
Ethan Watters (Design)
Megan Werner (Design)
Amanda Williams (Architecture)
Sarah Willmer (Architecture)
Federico Windhausen (Visual and Critical Studies)
Cooley Windsor (Writing)
Bill Wurz (M.B.A. in Design Strategy)
Ben Yalom (Writing)
Linda "L" Yaven (M.B.A. in Design Strategy)
Mario Ybarra Jr. (Fine Arts)
John Zurier (Fine Arts)
Leonardo Zylberberg (Architecture)

2008 MFA Exhibition (photo by Matthew Hughes Boyko).

The new Materials Resource Center contains more than 1,100 samples, from tufts of synthetic fur to futuristic aluminum foam.

All seven graduate programs are housed on CCA's San Francisco campus.

CRANBROOK ACADEMY OF ART

Programs in Fine Arts and Architecture

Programs of Study

Cranbrook Academy of Art, the only independent U.S. art school dedicated solely to graduate study, offers a two-year program for the Master of Fine Arts and Master of Architecture degrees. The Academy provides an intensely challenging and questioning environment for its community of artists. Departments of study are Architecture, Ceramics, Design (both two- and three-dimensional), Fiber, Metalsmithing, Painting, Photography, Print Media, and Sculpture. One artist-in-residence directs each department. There are no formal courses of instruction at the Academy. Students are provided with a studio and the responsibility to define and resolve their own creative projects. The context of work in the studios and academic progress is shaped by reading groups and seminars, regular departmental critiques, research and presentation projects, visiting artists, yearly full reviews by faculty members, and discussions of work on a one-to-one basis with the director and the student's department head. Lectures, symposia on current topics, gallery and museum visits, and field trips also contribute to the ongoing critical dialogue. Described as "a working place for creative art," the Academy is small, which provides an intimate social setting that fosters creative growth and expansive community experiences. Graduate students from around the world choose to study and work at Cranbrook because of its renowned faculty and its superb environment, which was designed in total by Eliel Saarinen. Graduation requirements are the completion of 60 credit hours (four semesters), a degree show mounted in the Cranbrook Art Museum, and the presentation of a written thesis.

All students attend full-time; part-time enrollment is not permitted.

Research Facilities

The Academy Library, which is oriented to the study of fine art, has an extensive rare book collection. The library is linked to six other libraries within the Cranbrook Educational Community to allow simple computer searches for all material within the Cranbrook archives. The library is also linked with other public and private libraries to facilitate interlibrary loans and research without students leaving the campus. The Academy supports a staffed media lab and a fully equipped woodshop and modelshop for fabrication of projects. The Cranbrook Art Museum features exhibits exploring new forms and ideas in the arts, crafts, architecture, and design. The museum conducts educational outreach programs and is the setting for lectures, degree shows, and the student-run Forum Gallery.

Financial Aid

Cranbrook offers competitive need-based aid for U.S. citizens and permanent resident aliens, maximized at approximately one third of tuition. Merit scholarships and department assistantships, ranging from $1000 to $6000, are possible for second-year students. If funds are available, some first-year students may receive merit aid. The Academy participates in the Federal Stafford Student Loan Program and Federal Work-Study Program. Need-based aid is not available for international students. Cranbrook does not offer teaching assistantships or fellowships.

Cost of Study

Fixed costs for 2009–10 are as follows: tuition, $25,958; lab and activity fees, $700; accident and sickness insurance, $705; matriculation fee, $125; dormitory (double), $2390; and dormitory (single), $4190. Estimated additional costs for 2009–10 include the following: supplies, $2000; housing and food, $6970; transportation, $2000; and personal expenses, $2000. Costs are for a nine-month session and are subject to change.

Living and Housing Costs

Single students may need $15,000 for food, housing, and basic expenses. This budget assumes very minimal accommodations and does not reflect an allowance for spouses or dependents. The campus accommodates about 85 dormitory students at a very reasonable cost; there is no housing on campus for couples.

Student Group

The Academy of Art enrolls a maximum of 150 students, averaging 15 per department. Students from minority groups comprise about 6 percent of enrollment and international students up to 20 percent. The median age is 28.

Student Outcomes

The Cranbrook program is one of enrichment, and the Academy does not provide placement or keep statistics on placement. The primary goals for students are enhancing personal expression and expertise in their fields; teaching art, design, and architecture at the college level; and using the advanced credential in business and industry to enhance employment opportunities.

Location

The Academy is located in Bloomfield Hills, an affluent suburb about 25 miles north of Detroit, Michigan. The nearby city of Birmingham offers numerous galleries, restaurants and coffee shops, theaters, and shopping opportunities. Cranbrook is within easy reach of freeways to all areas of Detroit and its environs. A variety of theater, dance, opera, and musical productions, as well as arenas for professional sports, are readily available. Students actively participate in alternative art activities in the Detroit vicinity.

The Academy

The Academy is part of the Cranbrook Educational Community, which also includes an elementary school, two middle schools, and two high schools, along with the Cranbrook Institute of Science and the Cranbrook Art Museum. The Academy is a privately endowed institution devoted to superlative graduate education in the visual and applied arts. The Academy is accredited by the North Central Association and by the National Association of Schools of Art and Design. Cranbrook Educational Community is an Equal Opportunity/Affirmative Action educator and employer.

Applying

Admissions applications are due (postmarked) by February 1 for the following fall term. Applications must be downloaded from the Cranbrook Web site and mailed to the institution as hard copy; as of 2009, online applications are not possible. Financial aid applications, including the required Free Application for Federal Student Aid (FAFSA), must be submitted by February 15. International applicants for whom English is a second language must have a minimum TOEFL score of 213 on the computer-based test or 80 on the Internet-based test. The Academy does not require the GRE. Admission is based primarily and competitively upon the student's portfolio. Interviews are not necessarily required as part of the application process but are encouraged for finalists.

Correspondence and Information

Dean of Admissions
Cranbrook Academy of Art
39221 Woodward Avenue
Bloomfield Hills, Michigan 48304
Phone: 248-645-3300
Fax: 248-645-3591
E-mail: caaadmissions@cranbrook.edu
Web site: http://www.cranbrookart.edu

Cranbrook Academy of Art

THE FACULTY

Director: Reed Kroloff, M.Arch., Texas at Austin, 1986.
Architecture: William Massie, M.Arch., Columbia, 1991.
Ceramics: Anders Ruhwald, M.F.A., Royal College of Art (London), 2005.
Two-Dimensional/Graphic Design: Elliott Earls, M.F.A., Cranbrook Academy of Art, 1993.
Three-Dimensional Design: T. Scott Klinker, M.F.A., Cranbrook Academy of Art, 1996.
Fiber: Mark Newport, M.F.A., Art Institute of Chicago, 1986.
Metalsmithing: Iris Eichenberg, Gerrit Reitveld Academy (Amsterdam), 1994.
Painting: Beverly Fishman, M.F.A., Yale, 1980.
Photography: Liz Cohen, M.F.A., California College of the Arts.
Print Media: Randy Bolton, M.F.A., Ohio State, 1982.
Sculpture: Heather McGill, M.F.A., San Francisco Art Institute, 1984.

Renowned for its architectural beauty, the Cranbrook campus is enhanced by sculptures and fountains by Swedish sculptor Carl Milles.

Students' individual working studios, residences, and resource facilities form a harmonious small community.

LESLEY UNIVERSITY

Programs in Expressive Therapies

LESLEY UNIVERSITY — Let's wake up the world.™

Programs of Study	Expressive therapists integrate the modalities of dance, drama, literature, music, poetry, and the visual arts with the practice of psychotherapy. For more than thirty years, Lesley University's expressive therapies programs have been at the forefront of expressive therapies training, offering degree and certificate programs that enable students to engage in the healing process through the therapeutic use of the arts. Its programs are accredited by the American Art Therapy Association, the American Dance Therapy Association, and the American Music Therapy Association.
	The Master of Arts program is designed for individuals pursuing licensure who wish to practice expressive therapies interventions with a variety of clinical populations. The degree requires 60 credits of course work, a 150-hour practicum, a 300-hour internship during the first year, and a 600-hour internship in a clinical setting. The program can be completed in twenty-four months (including two summer terms) or in three academic years of full-time study. The nonlicensure option, which requires 48 credits of course work and 600 hours of field work, can be completed in two years of full-time study. Specializations in art therapy, dance therapy, and music therapy are available.
	The Ph.D. program prepares students to become skilled educators, practitioners, and supervisors who contribute to scholarly research and practice in the field. During the first phase of study, students complete 24 credits of advanced graduate course work and write a plan identifying an area of doctoral study they wish to pursue. During the second phase, students take 15 credits of electives in their professional concentration, write qualifying papers, and fulfill their professional field service and socio-cultural perspective requirements. During the third phase, students construct dissertation proposals for their doctoral research and write their doctoral dissertations under the supervision of a dissertation committee.
Research Facilities	The Eleanor DeWolfe Ludcke Library houses more than 100,000 titles and 700 print journal subscriptions and offers a growing list of electronic resources. The collections are strong in all curricular areas, with an emphasis on education, psychology, human services, management, and expressive arts therapies. The library is a member of the Fenway Library Consortium and participates in Fenway Libraries Online, which allows library patrons to utilize the resources of all other area libraries.
	The Institute for Body, Mind, and Spirituality was established for the purpose of promoting inquiry, training professionals, conducting research, developing new programs, and providing leadership in the area of mind-body health and education. The Institute draws upon the University's expertise in counseling psychology, expressive therapies, arts, education, and environmental studies to integrate holistic principles and methods into professional practice within a diverse society. The Institute adheres to a transformational approach to education and to the application of the principles of reflective practice.
Financial Aid	The Graduate Assistantship Program offers students the opportunity to assist faculty and staff members in academic activities. Merit-based institutional grants are awarded to students in on-campus programs. Graduate students who are enrolled at least half-time may also be eligible for as much as $18,500 in unsubsidized Stafford loans. Repayment begins six months after the student is no longer enrolled at least half-time. The Federal Work-Study Program offers students the opportunity to earn money through part-time employment. Awards traditionally do not do not exceed $2000 per year. Students who do not apply for work-study may still find part-time work through various University offices.
Cost of Study	In the 2008–09 academic year, graduate tuition was $765 per credit. Other fees include a $30 registration fee per semester and a $295 field experience fee.
Living and Housing Costs	Housing is not available for graduate students on campus. Information about local housing and housing assistance is available upon request from the Residence Life Office of Student Affairs.
Student Group	Students in the program represent a stimulating mix of personal, academic, and career experiences. Students typically range in age from 21 to 65, and several come from other countries. Many have had professional careers as artists and hold advanced degrees in art and other related fields. Others have less background in art but are committed to helping people through creativity. Students who enroll directly from undergraduate programs usually have prior clinical experience.
Student Outcomes	Graduates are prepared to work in a variety of clinical settings, including psychiatric hospitals, community mental health centers, adult day treatment programs, geriatric centers, schools, and clinics. They may work alone or in multidisciplinary teams with other mental health professionals, such as psychiatrists, psychologists, social workers, and mental health counselors.
Location	Lesley University occupies a campus near Harvard Square in Cambridge, an area that benefits from the many advantages of the cities of Boston and Cambridge. The University is connected to downtown Boston by public transportation. Within a 6-mile radius are numerous historical sites and cultural attractions, including theaters, museums, and concerts.
The University	Lesley University, founded in 1909 as a women's teaching college, continues its commitment to educating undergraduates while also offering graduate and Ph.D. programs in the fields of education, environmental studies, human services, counseling and psychology, expressive therapies, and the arts. With today's student in mind, Lesley University has successfully pioneered a wide variety of flexible programs for adult learners that share a commitment to quality, innovation, and the integration of theory with practice.
	Lesley offers degree programs for learners at all levels. The University also supports several centers and hosts a variety of academic and professional conferences and institutes. Lesley programs operate throughout Massachusetts and in twenty-three other states as well as at an affiliated site in Israel.
Applying	Prospective students are required to submit a completed application form, official transcripts from all colleges previously attended, three letters of recommendation, a 3–5 page personal statement describing professional goals, a current resume, and a $50 application fee. Each specialization may have additional application requirements. All applicants are also required to schedule an in-person or telephone interview. An admissions decision is made as soon as all application materials are received.
Correspondence and Information	Office of Graduate and Adult Bachelor's Admissions Lesley University 29 Everett Street Cambridge, Massachusetts 02138-2790 Phone: 617-349-8300 888-LESLEY.U (toll-free) E-mail: info@lesley.edu Web site: http://www.lesley.edu/oncampus/

Lesley University

THE FACULTY AND THEIR RESEARCH

Nancy Beardall, Professor and Dance Therapy Coordinator; Ph.D.

Julia Byers, Professor; Ed.D., Toronto.

Mariagnese Cattaneo, Professor and Director of Field Training; Ph.D., Union (Ohio).

Robyn Flaum Cruz, Associate Professor; Ph.D., Arizona.

Karen Estrella, Assistant Professor and Expressive Therapies Coordinator; M.A., Fielding Institute.

Michele Forinash, Associate Professor, Music Therapy Coordinator, and Ph.D. Program Director; D.A., NYU.

Julia Halevy, Professor and Dean; Dott. Ped., Florence (Italy).

Michaela Kirby, Assistant Professor and Art Therapy Coordinator; Psy.D., Massachusetts School of Professional Psychology.

Mitchell Kossak, Division Director, Instructor, and Academic Coordinator of International Expressive Therapies; M.A., Lesley.

Vivien Marcow-Speiser, Professor; Ph.D., Union Institute.

Martha B. McKenna, Professor and Provost; Ed.D., Columbia.

Shaun McNiff, University Professor; Ph.D., Union (Ohio).

Memphis College of Art

MEMPHIS COLLEGE OF ART

Graduate Programs in Studio Practice and Art Education

Programs of Study	Memphis College of Art is a professional center of art and design education, dedicated to preparing individuals for lives of creating, problem solving, and critical thinking. Small by choice and purpose, MCA is a cultural wellspring of creativity, nurturing and educating artists of all levels since 1936. Located within 340-acre Overton Park, MCA offers state-of-the-art facilities, excellent faculty members, interdisciplinary programs, and cutting-edge exhibitions to the public and those pursuing B.F.A., M.F.A., M.A. in art education, and M.A.T. degrees.
	As a studio-intensive program, the M.F.A. at Memphis College of Art offers a catalytic environment with the goal of developing artistic practices that contribute significantly to contemporary culture. The program offers the opportunity to focus on traditional studio practice, digital technologies, or an interdisciplinary course of study. Areas of study include, but are not limited to, painting, drawing, photography, printmaking, papermaking/book arts, sculpture, digital media, or an individually tailored program of interdisciplinary study. Studio practice is enhanced with course work in issues of history, theory, and criticism. The program consists of structured course work and independent studio practice, with the second year culminating in the M.F.A. thesis exhibition and written thesis document.
	The M.A. in Art Education program is designed for experienced, licensed educators who are ready to further develop their artistic, scholarly, and leadership capabilities in art education. The program explores new approaches to creating, teaching, and researching visual art processes. The M.A.T. in Art Education program is designed for artists committed to the growth and development of others through the exchange of knowledge, but who are not yet certified as teachers. It is a full-time, two-year program that integrates hands-on experience in teaching with in-depth studio preparation; ensuring students are informed by practice, current theory, and research. Upon completion of this program and obtaining passing scores on the required Praxis exams, graduates are eligible for K–12 certification in art in Tennessee and, by reciprocal agreement, most other states.
Research Facilities	Graduate students have full 24-hour access to the Graduate Center, a separate building that supports most of their activities. It includes a conference and seminar room, three dedicated computer labs, individual semiprivate studio spaces, three gallery spaces used throughout the year to exhibit graduate student work, and a separate space that accommodates installation work. Full-time graduate students have studio access during the summer between their two years of study. Available undergraduate facilities in Rust Hall include a 4,400-square-foot shop for woodworking, metalworking, mat cutting, glass cutting, and stretcher and frame construction; large metal, clay, and sculpture studios as well as a separate foundry and welding area for castings and metalwork; printmaking, papermaking, and book arts facilities for lithography, etching, serigraphy, and other print processes; and letterpresses and a bindery, wet room equipped with beaters, a 36-square foot vacuum table, hydraulic press, and pulper. The photo lab includes large- and medium-format work stations, a digital imaging area with digital cameras, slide and transparency scanners, flatbed scanners, high-resolution film printers; a lighting studio with electronic strobe equipment, and facilities for non-silver and alternative photo processes. A large-format digital printing lab for oversized imaging is also available.
Financial Aid	Aid is available for the M.F.A. and M.A.T. programs through renewable scholarships for incoming students, teaching assistantships (in the third semester only), work-study, and Federal Stafford Student Loans and PLUS loans, and merit-based scholarship opportunities are available for second-year students. Students interested in government-based aid are required to complete the Free Application for Federal Student Aid (FAFSA). Applicants should contact the Financial Aid Office or the Admissions Office for forms and information.
Cost of Study	Tuition and fees for the M.F.A. and M.A.T. programs for the 2009–10 academic year are $23,600. This does not include the cost of materials, supplies, books, and fees, which is estimated at $2500. The M.A. in Art Education and Alternative Licensure programs are $455 per credit hour.
Living and Housing Costs	The estimated average cost of food and housing and miscellaneous expenses for the 2009–10 school year is $12,000. There is a large variety of affordable housing available. Student residences conveniently located within walking distance of the campus provide living space for more than 150 students. Suite-style living (single rooms with shared common areas), shared apartments for two, and several single, efficiency apartments are available. The Office of Admissions assists students in locating a place to live and in obtaining roommate referrals.
Student Group	The student body is comprised of students who have demonstrated achievement in their field. Many have pursued careers as fine artists, graphic designers, photographers, professional weavers, surface designers, interior designers, and teachers. There are nearly equal numbers of men and women. The students in the graduate program come from all regions of the United States and from several other countries.
Location	Memphis is a great place for an aspiring artist to study. Known for blues, barbecue, and Elvis, Memphis is also home to Fortune 500 companies, an NBA team, a symphony, an opera company, a theater, a number of colleges and universities, museums, art galleries, and almost 1 million residents. Annual festivals and celebrations are popular with students. The College itself is located in a 342-acre wooded park in midtown Memphis, adjacent to the Memphis Brooks Museum of Art, the Memphis Zoo, and a nine-hole golf course.
The College and The Programs	The College, founded in 1936, is accredited by the National Association of Schools of Art and Design and the Southern Association of Colleges and Schools. All of the College's graduate programs stress independent work toward self-defined career goals relative to the program chosen.
Applying	M.F.A. applications must be submitted by March 1 for the fall semester and November 1 for the spring semester. Graduate Education applications are accepted on a rolling basis. Application requirements include college transcripts, a portfolio with a minimum of fifteen slides (or other appropriate format), a resume, and one letter of recommendation each from a collegiate adviser or instructor and a contemporary. The applicant must also prepare a written statement of not less than 250 words describing his or her reasons for wishing to join the graduate program, life goals, and creative dreams. A personal interview or conference call may be required—a date and time is arranged by the Director of Admissions after all application requirements have been met. Students are accepted for admissions in either the fall or spring semester (or summer for the graduate programs in education), based on space availability. In addition, international students must submit a minimum TOEFL score of 525 (195 on the computer-based test), certified translations of academic records, and an affidavit of support verifying ability to meet projected annual costs.
Correspondence and Information	Office of Admissions, Graduate Programs Memphis College of Art 1930 Poplar Avenue Overton Park Memphis, Tennessee 38104-2764 Phone: 901-272-5151 800-727-1088 (toll-free) Fax: 901-272-5158 E-mail: info@mca.edu Web site: http://www.mca.edu

Memphis College of Art

THE FACULTY

In addition to the regular faculty members listed below, there are guest faculty members and advisers each semester.

Nona Bolin, Professor; M.A., Memphis; M.A., Vanderbilt. Liberal studies.
Fred Burton, Professor; M.F.A., Wichita State; M.A., Kent State. Painting/drawing.
Haley Morris Cafiero, Assistant Professor; M.F.A., Arizona. Photography.
Rob Canfield, Associate Professor; Ph.D., Arizona. Liberal studies.
David Chioffi, Assistant Professor; M.A., Wesleyan. Graphic design.
Ellen Daugherty, Assistant Professor; Ph.D., Virginia. Art history.
Maritza Davila, Professor; M.F.A., Pratt. Printmaking.
Adrian Duran, Assistant Professor; Ph.D., Delaware. Art history.
Tom Lee, Associate Professor; M.F.A., Mississippi. Sculpture.
Susan Maakestad, Associate Professor; M.A., Central Washington; M.F.A., Iowa. Painting.
Remy Miller, Professor; M.F.A., Bowling Green State. Drawing.
Howard Paine, Director of M.F.A. Programs; M.F.A., Washington (St. Louis). Computer arts/design.
Joel Priddy, Assistant Professor; M.F.A., School of Visual Arts. Illustration.
Bill Price, Instructor; M.F.A., Southern Illinois. Sculpture/metals.
James Ramsey, Assistant Professor; Ph.D., Tulane. Art history.
Robert Riseling, Professor; M.A., Northern Iowa; M.F.A., Wisconsin. Painting/drawing.
Meredith Root, Assistant Professor; M.F.A., Wisconsin. Digital media.
Jennifer Sargent, Associate Professor; M.F.A., Arizona State. Surface design.
Cynthia Thompson, Associate Professor; M.F.A., Rutgers. Papermaking/book arts.
Leandra Urrutia, Assistant Professor; M.F.A., Mississippi. Sculpture.
Cathy Wilson, Director of Graduate Programs in Education; M.A.T., Ed.D., Memphis.
Jill Wissmiller, Assistant Professor; M.F.A., Northwestern. Digital media.

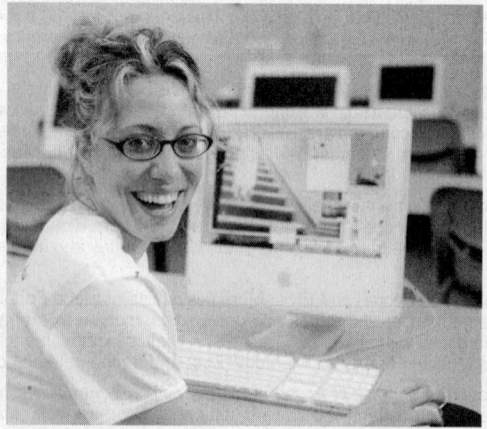

Memphis College of Art offers its students modern computer facilities.

A student at work at Memphis College of Art.

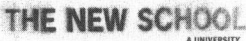

THE NEW SCHOOL: A UNIVERSITY

Parsons The New School for Design
Program in Fine Arts

Program of Study	Students committed to traditional studio practices in painting and sculpture often develop their work in an atmosphere of rigorous formal and intellectual involvement while being exposed to relevant theories and histories. For students interested in pursuing more groundbreaking territories in new media, Parsons' curriculum, faculty, and facilities provide opportunities for further exploration. The Master of Fine Arts is a two-year, 64-credit program for advanced students, offering a comprehensive experience in studio practice, critical studies, and the ever-expanding role of the artist in the contemporary art world. Students benefit from contact with members of the unparalleled artistic community of New York City and the larger university environment. Students have their own studios, work independently, and meet with faculty members for weekly one-on-one tutorials. These extensive individual meetings are augmented by interactions with visiting artists.

All students complete 52 studio credits, which are broken down into two components—graduate fine arts and graduate seminar—and 12 critical studies credits. Students work with each of the 5 core faculty members in a series of rotations. First-year students cycle through all 5 faculty members; second-year students choose 2 faculty members and return to each of them for two 5-week periods. Open sign-up periods and group critiques occur between the rotations. There are approximately 1 to 1½ hours of group discussion each week within the rotations. The balance of the time is spent working in studios with faculty members making one-on-one rounds.

The first-year graduate seminar is meant to expose students to a variety of significant discourses in twentieth- and twenty-first-century art, including the discourses of modernism, postmodernism, feminism, colonialism, and issues of racial representation; commodity culture, including ideas about collecting; and technology and the digital revolution. This is done through selected readings, video and film viewing, and art exhibitions. All of these are discussed in written assignments and in class. The seminar work is interspersed with studio visits. Each student is responsible for one major research paper, written in consultation with an instructor, in addition to small writing assignments that accompany each set of readings.

The second-year graduate seminar is thesis driven. Weekly and bimonthly writing assignments break down the required thesis subjects into smaller elements. Drawing assignments, individual studio visits, and slide lectures on the student's work augment the writing assignments and promote class discussion. At the end of the second year, students present a body of work completed in the program and a written thesis for the final master's review.

Research Facilities	The Adam and Sophie Gimbel Library of Art and Design includes books on art and design, special collections, and several hundred rare books. The library also contains a collection of mounted plates, slides, and periodicals on the history and the latest developments in fine arts and design. The Gimbel Library is developing a digital image collection that enables online access to images from Parsons' slide collection. The Angelo Donghia Materials Library and Study Center, funded by the Angelo Donghia Foundation, includes a library, a gallery, a computer lab, and a lecture hall. The library allows students and faculty members to review and check out state-of-the-art resources, putting the latest and most exclusive materials at their fingertips. A consortium links the libraries of The New School, New York University, and The Cooper Union.
Financial Aid	Graduate students are automatically considered for scholarship funds upon acceptance into the program. Scholarship recipients are notified of their award by either their program or a Student Financial Services award letter soon after being admitted. Graduate students should contact their academic department early in the admissions process for separate applications for institutional awards, such as assistantships. U.S. citizens and permanent residents applying for financial aid outside the University should file the Free Application for Federal Student Aid (FAFSA) by March 1. More information can be found at the Student Financial Services Web site at http://www.newschool.edu/studentservices/financialaid/.
Cost of Study	In 2009–10 full-time students pay $18,060 in tuition and $145 in fees per term. Additional fees may apply.
Living and Housing Costs	The University offers on-campus housing, University-run apartments, and assistance in finding housing off campus. The cost of housing, food, transportation, books, and living expenses in New York City averages $17,000 annually. For more information, interested students should visit http://www.newschool.edu/studentservices.html.
Student Group	There are 44 full-time students, 24 of whom are women. Of the total, 4 students are members of minority groups, and 8 are international students.
Location	Parsons The New School for Design, located in Greenwich Village, is at the heart of New York's vibrant architecture and design communities. Students are encouraged to take advantage of the museums, performance venues, and other cultural institutions that are only a walk or subway ride away.
The University and The School	Parsons is part of The New School, a leading university in New York City offering some of the nation's most distinguished programs in design, liberal arts, management and policy, and the performing arts, leading to seventy graduate and undergraduate degrees. More information can be found at http://www.newschool.edu/degreeprograms. Parsons and The New School are fully accredited by the Commission on Higher Education of the Middle States Association of Colleges and Schools.
Applying	Students must submit the completed application, the $50 application fee, a resume, a statement of interest, official copies of all college transcripts, two letters of recommendation, and a portfolio consisting of twenty images of recent artwork as slides or in CD-ROM format, including an inventory list. DVDs and videotapes are also accepted for installations and performances. An interview may be requested. International students must also submit TOEFL scores—a minimum of 580 on the written test or 237 on the computerized version. The admissions application deadline is February 1.

Correspondence and Information	Donald Porcaro, Chair
	Tom Butter, Director of Fine Arts M.F.A. Program
	Master of Fine Arts Program
	Parsons The New School for Design
	25 East 13th Street, 5th Floor
	New York, New York 10003
	Phone: 212-229-8942
	Fax: 212-741-3485
	E-mail: porcarod@newschool.edu
	       butter@newschool.edu
	Web site: http://www.newschool.edu/parsons
	       http://www.parsons.newschool.edu/finearts/

The New School: A University

THE FACULTY AND THEIR RESEARCH

Jackie Brookner, Environmental Artist and Writer; Ph.D. candidate, Harvard. Collaborates with ecologists and earth scientists on bioremediation/public art projects in the United States and abroad, including commissions near Dresden, Cincinnati, West Palm Beach, and St. Louis. Awards from the New York Foundation for the Arts, the National Endowment for the Arts, the Nancy Gray Foundation for Art in the Environment, and the Trust for Mutual Understanding. Exhibited at the Miro Foundation, Barcelona; the National Civil Rights Museum, Memphis; McKissick Museum, Columbia; Pamela Auchincloss Gallery and Oscarsson-Hood Gallery, New York City. Guest editor of the *ArtJournal* issue, "Art and Ecology."

Tom Butter, M.F.A. Program Director and Artist; Curator, "Delving and Tinkering," E. S. Vandam Gallery, New York; M.F.A., Washington (St. Louis). Taught at Yale, RISD, Tyler School of Art, and Brandeis University. Awards from the New York Foundation for the Arts and the National Endowment for the Arts. Exhibits in New York City since 1981. Published in *Artforum, Art in America, ArtNews,* and the *New York Times.* Selected collections in the Albright Knox Gallery, Buffalo; the Walker Art Center, Minneapolis; the Metropolitan Museum of Art, New York City; and the Pennsylvania Academy of Fine Arts, Philadelphia.

Peter Drake, Artist; B.F.A., Pratt. Solo exhibitions at the Lisa Sette Gallery, Scottsdale, Arizona; Elizabeth Leach Gallery, Portland, Oregon; and the Loew Gallery, Atlanta. Group exhibitions at Surface, Terence Rogers Gallery, Los Angeles; 3M and Fish Tank Gallery, New York City. Taught at New York Academy of Art and Maryland Institute, Baltimore.

Glenn Goldberg, Painter; M.F.A., CUNY, Queens. Awards from the Edward Albee Foundation, the National Endowment for the Arts, and the Guggenheim Fellowship. Selected shows at the Hill Gallery and Charles Cowles Gallery, New York City. Exhibited in the United States and Europe. Selected collections at the Brooklyn Museum; the Museum of Contemporary Art, Los Angeles; the Metropolitan Museum of Art; and the National Gallery of Art, Washington, D.C.

Sharon Loudon, Artist; M.F.A., Yale. Solo exhibitions at the Neuberger Museum of Art; Numark Gallery; Anthony Grant, Inc.; Kemper Museum of Contemporary Art; Urban Institute of Contemporary Arts; Rhona Hoffman Gallery; Dee/Glasoe Gallery; Haines Gallery; and Carnegie Mellon University. Group exhibitions at Berkshire Museum, Wave Hill, Williams Proctor Institute, the Hempel–London, Metaphor Gallery, Krannert Art Museum, and Museum of Art–Athens. Taught at NYU, Massachusetts College of Art, and College of St. Rose, Albany.

Lenore Malen, Artist and Writer; M.A., Pennsylvania. Solo exhibitions at Art in General, Rutgers University, University of Vermont, and Rhode Island School of Design. Group exhibitions at Fischer-Landau Center, Long Island City; and O'Hara Gallery, Bard College. Member of the Art Critics Association. Former executive editor of *Art Journal.* Senior fellow at Terra Foundation. Featured in *Sculpture, Village Voice, Art in America,* and the *New York Times.* Collections at Princeton, the Museum of Modern Art, Brown, Yale, and the New York Public Library.

Alix Pearlstein, Artist; M.F.A., SUNY College at Purchase. Exhibited at Artemis and Greenberg Van Doren Gallery, New York City; Lugar Commum, Lisbon; the Grossman Gallery, School of the Museum of Fine Arts, Boston; the Museum of Contemporary Art, Chicago; and Postmasters Gallery, New York City. Group exhibitions at the Solomon R. Guggenheim Museum, New York City; SMAK, Ghent; Whitney Museum of American Art, New York City; Hirshhorn Museum and Sculpture Garden, Washington, D.C.; Haus der Kunst, Munich; and Museum of Modern Art, New York City.

Bruce Pearson, Artist; B.F.A., San Francisco Art Institute. Solo exhibitions at Ronald Feldman Fine Arts, Gallery of Art Carlsen Center, and the Pierogi Gallery. Group exhibitions at the Galerie Les Filles Du Calvaire (Paris), Rotunda Gallery, Marlborough Gallery, DC Moore Gallery, White Box, Times Square Gallery, Miami Art Museum, Galerie Bernard Jordan (Paris), Robert V. Fullerton Art Museum, Cheryl Pelavin Fine Arts, Colby College Museum of Art, Apex Art, Dee/Glasoe, and the Rose Art Museum at Brandeis University. Public collections at the Karl Ernst Haus Museum (Germany), MoMA, Rose Art Museum, and the Whitney Museum of American Art.

Donald Porcaro, Chair and Artist; M.F.A., Columbia. Distinguished Teaching Award from Parsons The New School for Design. Solo exhibitions at the Kouros Gallery, New York City; Lowe Gallery, Atlanta; Lowe Gallery, Los Angeles; Grounds for Sculpture, Trenton; Nancy Solomon Gallery, Atlanta; and Byron Cohen Gallery, Kansas City. Collections at the Radford University Art Museum, Virginia; CUNY Staten Island; South Bay Center, California; and Rhone-Poulenc Rorer, Inc., Collegeville, Pennsylvania. Large-scale outdoor installations at Socrates Sculpture Park, Long Island City; Ward's Island, New York; and South Beach Sculpture Garden, Staten Island.

Mira Schor, Painter and Writer; M.F.A., California College of the Arts. Participant in Womanhouse Project of the Feminist Art Program, CalArts (1972). Taught at Nova Scotia College of Art and Design; SUNY Purchase, UC Berkeley, RISD, Sarah Lawrence, and the Skowhegan School. Previous co-publisher/co-editor, *M/E/A/N/I/N/G,* a journal of contemporary art issues. Published works include *M/E/A/N/I/N/G: An Anthology of Artists' Writings, Theory, and Criticism; Wet: On Painting, Feminism, and Art Culture,* a collection of essays; *Art Issues;* and *Art Journal.* Solo exhibition at Horodner Romley Gallery. Group exhibitions at the Marianne Boesky Gallery, P.S. 1 Museum, Santa Monica Museum, Neuberger Museum, and the Aldrich Museum. Awards from the NEA, Guggenheim, Pollock-Krasner, Rockefeller Foundation, College Art Association's Frank Jewett Mather Award, and Art Criticism.

Brian Tolle, Artist; M.F.A., Yale. Solo exhibitions at the Shoshana Wayne Gallery, Santa Monica; Schmidt Contemporary Art, St. Louis; and Basilico Fine Arts, New York City. Commissioned piece at the Irish Hunger Memorial, Battery Park City, New York. Group exhibitions at the Whitney Museum of American Art, New York City (2002); and in the Netherlands, Belgium, Italy, Germany, Switzerland, Great Britain, and Korea.

Visiting Critics and Lecturers

Almost 700 adjunct faculty members give Parsons students the unique opportunity to learn from New York's successful working artists and designers. Faculty members and visiting critics are principals in their own design firms, hold key positions in the art and design community, and frequently have their work exhibited and published. Parsons' strong ties to industry bring numerous guest lecturers and critics into forums and classrooms.

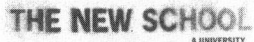

THE NEW SCHOOL: A UNIVERSITY

Parsons The New School for Design
Program in History of Decorative Arts and Design

Program of Study

Parsons The New School for Design offers a two-year Master of Arts (M.A.) in the History of Decorative Arts and Design Program jointly with Cooper-Hewitt, National Design Museum. The degree leads graduates to careers at museums, historic houses, appraisal firms, auction houses, galleries, publishing houses, and universities for decorative arts. The program focuses on the history of European and American decorative arts and design since the Renaissance, offering courses that address issues such as stylistics, techniques, social history, and critical theory. Its unique character is defined by its location within the Cooper-Hewitt—the only museum in the United States devoted exclusively to historical and contemporary design.

The curriculum offers courses in the media of ceramics, costume, furniture, glass, graphic design, metalwork, textiles, and works on paper. These courses go beyond connoisseurship to address a wide range of issues in decorative arts and design, emphasizing object-based teaching using museum collections. Students have the opportunity to work in the Cooper-Hewitt's four curatorial departments—Drawings, Prints, and Graphic Design; Product Design and Decorative Arts; Textiles; and Wall Coverings. Teaching experience is gained through assistantships in the undergraduate program at Parsons. The experience of graduate school in a professional setting facilitates the transition from academic training to career.

The degree is awarded upon completion of 48 credits with a minimum grade point average of 3.0 and the successful completion of the M.A. examination or thesis. Required courses are Proseminar, Survey of Decorative Arts I and II, and either Museology or Theory of Decorative Arts. The student declares a major and minor area of concentration at the completion of 24 credits or, with a 3.5 minimum grade point average, may petition to write an M.A. thesis. An M.A. examination is taken in the student's final semester; students writing a thesis are not required to take the exam. The program is two to three years of full-time study or four years of part-time study.

Research Facilities

Located in the landmark Andrew Carnegie Mansion on Museum Mile, the Cooper-Hewitt has encyclopedic collections of European and American furniture, glass, ceramics, metalwork, architectural and ornamental drawings and prints, textiles, wall coverings, and graphic and industrial design. In addition, the museum has the premier design library in the United States, with a collection of more than 55,000 books and periodicals related to the history of design, as well as extensive holdings of trade catalogs and archives of African American, Latino-Hispanic, and American designers.

The Adam & Sophie Gimbel Library of Art and Design includes books on art and design, special collections, and several hundred rare books. The library also contains a collection of mounted plates, slides, and periodicals, providing information on the history and the latest developments in fine arts and design. The Gimbel Library has begun development of a digital image collection that will enable online access to images from Parsons's slide collection. The Angelo Donghia Materials Library and Study Center, funded by the Angelo Donghia Foundation, includes a library, a gallery, a computer lab, and a lecture hall. The library allows students and faculty members to review and check out state-of-the-art resources, putting the latest and most exclusive materials at their fingertips. A consortium links the libraries of The New School, New York University, and The Cooper Union.

Financial Aid

Graduate students are automatically considered for scholarship funds upon acceptance into the program. Scholarship recipients are notified of their award by either their program or a Student Financial Services award letter soon after being admitted. Graduate students should contact their academic department early in the admissions process for separate applications for institutional awards, such as assistantships. U.S. citizens and permanent residents applying for financial aid outside the University should file the Free Application for Federal Student Aid (FAFSA) by March 1. More information can be found at the Student Financial Services Web site at http://www.newschool.edu/studentservices/financialaid/.

Cost of Study

In 2009–10 full-time students pay $18,060 in tuition and $145 in fees per term. Additional fees may apply.

Living and Housing Costs

The University offers on-campus housing, University-run apartments, and assistance finding housing off campus. The cost of housing, food, transportation, books, and living expenses in New York City averages $17,000 annually. For more information, students should visit http://www.newschool.edu/studentservices.

Student Group

There are 88 students in the program, 51 of whom are full-time, and 82 are women. This includes 13 students who are members of minority groups.

Location

Parsons' main campus is located downtown in Greenwich Village, a historic neighborhood with a style and atmosphere found nowhere else in New York City. The Village is home to design and art studios, galleries, shops, and restaurants as well as avant-garde artists, musicians, and writers.

With rich cultural resources, international sophistication, and cutting-edge attitude, New York City is a vibrant environment that has inspired and challenged artists and designers throughout its history. To Parsons' faculty, the city is an extension of the classroom and is incorporated into the basic fabric of the curriculum. New York is home to more than eighty museums, such as the Metropolitan Museum of Art, Whitney Museum of American Art, and the Museum of Modern Art. Parsons faculty members teach the architecture of the city, the fabric of its populations, and the language of its commercial and private communication.

The University and The School

Parsons is part of The New School, a leading university in New York City offering some of the nation's most distinguished programs in design, liberal arts, management and policy, and the performing arts, leading to seventy graduate and undergraduate degrees. More information can be found at http://www.newschool.edu/degreeprograms. Parsons and The New School are fully accredited by the Commission on Higher Education of the Middle States Association of Colleges and Schools.

Applying

A minimum of 6 credits in American and/or European art history or equivalent experience are required. Students must submit the completed application, the $50 application fee, a resume, a statement of interest, official copies of all college transcripts, and two letters of recommendation—at least one from a faculty member. Applicants who live within 200 miles of New York City are required to be interviewed; those who live farther away are strongly encouraged to make arrangements to be interviewed. In addition, international students must submit TOEFL scores—a minimum of 650 on the written test or 280 on the computerized version. The application deadline is February 1.

Correspondence and Information

Master of History of Decorative Arts and Design Program
Cooper-Hewitt, National Design Museum
2 East 91st Street
New York, New York 10128
Phone: 212-849-8344
Fax: 212-849-8347
E-mail: historyofdecarts@si.edu
Web site: http://www.newschool.edu/parsons
　　　　　http://www.cooperhewitt.org

The New School: A University

THE FACULTY AND THEIR RESEARCH

Complete faculty biographies can be found at: http://www.parsons.edu/faculty_and_staff/directory.aspx.

Donald Albrecht, Independent Curator; B.Arch., IIT. American architecture.

Eric Anderson, Ph.D. candidate, Columbia. Nineteenth-century German architecture and theory of design.

Laura E. Auricchio, Ph.D., Columbia. Eighteenth-century French women artists and contemporary visual culture.

David Brody, Ph.D., Boston University. Material culture, visual culture, and design studies.

Hazel Clark, Chair of Art and Design Studies; Ph.D., Brighton (England). Material artifacts and their relationships to social and cultural contexts; design theory and cultural studies.

Marilyn Cohen, Ph.D., NYU (Institute of Fine Arts). Popular culture.

Elyssa S. da Cruz, Research Associate, Costume Institute at the Metropolitan Museum of Art; M.A., Fashion Institute of Technology. Twentieth-century fashion and accessory design.

Elizabeth De Rosa, Administrator, American Friends of the Attingham Summer School; Ph.D., Columbia. Art nouveau and American and European art glass.

Clive Dilnot, Full-Time Faculty. Fine art, history of art, social philosophy.

Tracy Ehrlich, Ph.D., Columbia. Architecture and landscape design of early modern Italy.

Barry R. Harwood, Curator, Decorative Arts at the Brooklyn Museum; Ph.D., Princeton.

Kristin Herron, Director, Museum Program for the New York State Council on the Arts; M.A., Wintertur Program. Historic house museums.

Sarah E. Lawrence, Director, Master of Arts in the History of Decorative Arts and Design Program; Ph.D., Columbia. Art theory and Renaissance art.

Ulrich Leben, Associate Curator, Furniture of the Rothschild Collection at Waddesdon Manor, Buckinghamshire, Great Britain; Ph.D., Bonn. French and German decorative arts.

Sarah A. Lichtman, Graduate Teaching Fellow and Instructor; Ph.D. candidate, Bard Graduate Center. Interiors, feminist design history, twentieth-century design.

Mary M. Cheek Mills, Manager of School and Docent Programs, Corning Museum of Glass; M.A., Appalachian State. Western glassmaking methods.

Christopher Mount, Director of Exhibitions and Public Programs at Parsons.

Jeffrey Munger, Associate Curator, European Sculpture and Decorative Arts, Metropolitan Museum of Art; M.A., Harvard. European ceramics.

Tessa Murdoch, Deputy Keeper, Victoria and Albert Museum; Ph.D., London. Metalwork, eighteenth- and nineteenth-century English silver.

Anne-Marie Quette, Conférencière at the Musées Nationaux de France and Musée des Arts Décoratifs in Paris. Development of French furniture and interiors.

Ethan Robey, Assistant Director, Master of Arts in the History of Decorative Arts and Design Program; Ph.D., Columbia. American and European nineteenth- and twentieth-century visual culture.

Maria Ruvoldt, Specialist; Ph.D., Columbia. Renaissance art and feminist theory.

Denny Stone, Collections Manager, European Sculpture and Decorative Arts at the Metropolitan Museum of Art; M.A., Fashion Institute of Technology. Jewelry and costume.

Ioanna Theocharopoulou, M.Phil., Columbia. History of modern design.

Deborah Dependahl Waters, Deputy Director, Collections and Exhibitions at the Museum of the City of New York; Ph.D., Delaware. Nineteenth-century British and American silver.

John Wilton-Ely, Professor Emeritus, Hull. Grand Tour's widespread influence on the arts of England; eighteenth-century art, architecture, and decorative arts.

PRATT INSTITUTE
School of Art and Design

Programs of Study

Pratt has been educating professionals for productive careers in the fields of art and design since its founding in 1887. Pratt's School of Art and Design, one of the largest of its kind, offers an outstanding professional art and design education taught by a faculty of working professionals who bring high standards and current practices to the classroom. Faculty members have received more than eighteen Tiffany, Fulbright, and Guggenheim awards as well as other prestigious professional awards. Pratt's graduate industrial and interior design programs were ranked third nationally by *DesignIntelligence* in 2008. *U.S. News and World Report* ranked Pratt's interior design program first in the country; graduate fine art was ranked fifteenth, and industrial design was ranked fourth.

Pratt offers master's degrees in a variety of programs, including Master of Fine Arts in digital arts, history of art and design, or studio arts (new forms–nontraditional investigations, painting and drawing, photography, printmaking, sculpture); Master of Science in art and design education, communication and package design, dance/movement therapy, history of art and design, or interior design; Master of Industrial Design; and Master of Professional Studies in art therapy, art therapy–special education, arts and cultural management, or design management. A postbaccalaureate New York State certification program for the teaching of art in grades pre-K–12 is available for fine arts graduate students. Art therapy majors electing a special education concentration are eligible for provisional New York State teaching certification. Pratt also offers a dual degree in fine arts and library and information science as well as a certificate in museum studies.

Graduates of Pratt's design programs have the competitive edge needed to obtain top administrative and creative positions in design studios, businesses, various industries, and arts organizations; graduates of the digital arts program may also work in interactive media or computer animation. Art and design education graduates are prepared to pursue careers in pre-K–12 schools, museums and cultural institutions, or colleges. Graduates of the creative arts therapy program work in psychiatric, medical rehabilitation, geriatric and family therapy, school, substance abuse, and child-life settings. They also learn to work with a variety of patient populations, including patients with eating disorders and the homeless.

All graduate art and design curricula include supportive course work in the humanities. Students can choose from a wide array of course offerings, including art and design history, comparative literature, philosophy, foreign languages, and social sciences. The graduate programs require the completion of 34 to 68 credits (75 credits for the M.S./M.F.A. dual-degree program) and last from 2 to 3 years, depending on the curriculum and the number of prerequisites that have not been met at the time of admission. For the granting of degrees, all of the graduate programs require the submission of a thesis or a comparable effort. For the M.F.A., an exhibition and supporting corollary statement are required. Candidates for the M.S. and the M.I.D. degrees must present a thesis project that demonstrates a meaningful contribution to design and documents the supportive research that informs all phases of design and construction. For the M.P.S. in art therapy and the M.S. in dance/movement therapy, the thesis project may involve research, an extended case study, the development of a project implementing innovative techniques in therapy, or the opportunity to publish an article. For the M.P.S. in design management, the thesis project is the preparation of a business case study.

Research Facilities

The Pratt Library contains 186,589 bound volumes, serial backfiles, and other material (including government documents); 251,603 audiovisual materials; and 3,996 microforms and subscribes to 925 periodicals.

Pratt maintains numerous studios, shops, and technical facilities for work in all media as well as state-of-the-art computer facilities. Computer graphics labs include state-of-the-art Macintosh, PC/NT, and UNIX operating systems as well as digital video and audio systems. Pratt also has extensive gallery space for exhibitions.

Financial Aid

Financial aid awards are offered through a variety of institutional, state, and federally funded programs. These include the Graduate Scholarships awarded by departments on the basis of merit, Federal Perkins Loan and Federal Work-Study Programs, the Tuition Assistance Program of New York State, and Pratt loans and student help. Assistantships are awarded on a competitive basis to continuing students in all departments. Special alumni-sponsored fellowships are also available.

Cost of Study

Graduate tuition for 2008–09 was $27,216 per year (24 credits, $1134 per credit) and student fees were $1190 per year. The cost of books and supplies varies widely, depending on the program in which the student is enrolled. Updated cost information is available at http://www.pratt.edu/admiss/fees.

Living and Housing Costs

Campus housing continues to be expanded to meet students' needs and is available for single students on a first-come, first-served basis. Housing costs average $15,294 per academic year. Pratt offers limited graduate student housing two blocks away from the campus. There is a plentiful supply of moderately priced rentals in the immediate area and in adjacent neighborhoods for married students seeking housing and for those students choosing to reside off campus.

Student Group

In educating more than four generations of students to be creative, technically skilled, and adaptable professionals, Pratt has gained an international reputation that attracts more than 4,600 undergraduate and graduate students annually from forty-seven states and forty countries.

Location

Pratt Institute's 25-acre, parklike main campus is situated among the turn-of-the-century mansions, Victorian brownstones, and wide, tree-lined boulevards of Clinton Hill, one of Brooklyn's landmark-designated historic neighborhoods. Midtown Manhattan, the heart of New York City, is only 25 minutes away by subway and offers students a vast array of professional, cultural, and recreational opportunities. Pratt also maintains a satellite facility in Manhattan's Chelsea district. Pratt Manhattan houses the Institute's graduate arts and cultural management, communications/packaging design, design management, facilities management, historic preservation, library and information science, and urban design; it also offers Associate of Occupational Studies (A.O.S.) and Associate of Applied Science (A.A.S.) degree programs.

The Institute

A private, nonsectarian institute of higher education, Pratt Institute was founded by the industrialist and philanthropist Charles Pratt. Changing with the needs and requirements of the professional world for which it prepares its graduates, Pratt today educates 3,066 undergraduate and 1,602 graduate students for careers in art and design, architecture, and library and information science.

Applying

The deadline for applications and all supporting materials, including portfolio, is January 5. Applicants should include everything in one package, including recommendations in sealed envelopes with the reference's signature across the flap. Early submission of applications with all necessary credentials is highly desirable. For applicants who intend to file for financial aid, applications and all supporting documents should be received no later than January 5 for the fall semester and October 1 for the spring semester. Applications received after these dates are considered if openings exist in a particular program.

Correspondence and Information

Graduate Admissions Office
Pratt Institute
200 Willoughby Avenue
Brooklyn, New York 11205
Phone: 718-636-3514
     800-331-0834 (toll-free)
Fax: 718-399-4242
E-mail: admissions@pratt.edu
Web site: http://www.pratt.edu
     http://www.pratt.edu/admiss/request (to request information)

Pratt Institute

THE FACULTY

Frank Lind, Dean; M.F.A., Pratt.

Art and Design Education
Amy Brook Snider, Chair; Ph.D., NYU. Lisa Baumwell, Associate Professor; Ph.D. Lisa Capone, Adjunct Instructor; M.F.A. Barbara Danish, Adjunct Associate Professor; Ph.D. Ascha Kells Drake, Visiting Instructor; M.F.A. Sandra Edmonds, Adjunct Assistant Professor; Ph.D. Mary Elmer-Dewitt, Adjunct Instructor; M.S. Leslie Elvin, Visiting Instructor. Shari Fischberg (Lederman), Visiting Professor; Ph.D. Graham Guerra, Visiting Instructor; M.F.A. Miki Iwamura, Visiting Instructor; B.F.A. Heather Lewis, Assistant Professor; Ph.D. Ingrid Menendez, Visiting Instructor; M.F.A. Theodora Skipitares, Assistant Professor; M.F.A. Brynna Tucker, Visiting Instructor; M.S.F. Laurel Voss, Visiting Instructor; M.F.A. Aileen Wilson, Associate Professor; M.A., Ed.M.

Arts and Cultural Management
Monica Shay, Chair; M.P.S., Regis. Sally Block, Visiting Assistant Professor. James Clark, Visiting Assistant Professor. Laurie Cumbo, Visiting Assistant Professor. Eric Dysart, Visiting Assistant Professor. Michele Ferenz, Visiting Assistant Professor; M.A. Young Hah, Visiting Assistant Professor. Radiah Harper, Visiting Assistant Professor; M.S. Susan Haskins, Visiting Assistant Professor; B.A. Erin Hayes, Visiting Assistant Professor. Jeffrey Klein, Visiting Assistant Professor. Bonita Kolb, Visiting Assistant Professor; Ph.D. Sheila McDaniel, Visiting Assistant Professor. Elissa Moorhead, Visiting Assistant Professor. Mario Moorhead, Visiting Assistant Professor. Anthony Patton, Visiting Assistant Professor. Dorothy Ryan, Visiting Assistant Professor; B.A. Susan Schear, Visiting Assistant Professor. Vida Schreibman, Visiting Associate Professor; M.A. Jennifer Scott, Visiting Assistant Professor; M.A. Rachel Selekman, Visiting Assistant Professor. Christopher Shrum, Visiting Assistant Professor; M.A. Misty Stiers, Visiting Assistant Professor. Denise Tahara, Visiting Assistant Professor; Ph.D. Jacqueline Tarry, Visiting Assistant Professor. Yolanda Trincere, Visiting Assistant Professor; Ph.D.

Communications/Packaging Design
Jeff Bellantoni, Chair; B.I.D. James Anderson, Visiting Associate Professor. Chava Ben-Amos, Professor; B.A. Barry Berger, Visiting Assistant Professor. Warren Bernard, Visiting Instructor. Andrew Brenits, Visiting Assistant Professor; M.P.S. Jean Brennan, Adjunct Assistant Professor; M.S. Harry Burnett, Visiting Associate Professor. Antonio Di Spigna, Professor; M.S. Tom Dolle, Adjunct Associate Professor; B.F.A. Kevin Gatta, Professor. Bob Gill, Adjunct Associate Professor. Cheryl Gross, Adjunct Associate Professor; M.S. Graham Hanson, Adjunct Associate Professor; B.F.A. Kristy Hedberg, Visiting Assistant Professor. William Hilson, Adjunct Professor. Milton Kass, Visiting Assistant Professor. Alvin Katz, Visiting Associate Professor. Saima Kazmi, Visiting Instructor. Kimberly Kiser, Visiting Instructor; M.S. Tom Klinkowstein, Adjunct Professor; M.S. Pinar Lacroix, Visiting Instructor. Gusty Lange, Adjunct Associate Professor; M.S. Eunsun Lee, Adjunct Assistant Professor; M.S. Alex Liebergesell, Adjunct Assistant Professor. Marilyn Lyons, Adjunct Associate Professor. Cassandra Tai Marcellini, Visiting Instructor. Scott Menchin, Visiting Associate Professor. Ann Morris, Visiting Assistant Professor; M.A. Eric O'Toole, Adjunct Assistant Professor; B.I.D. Linda Pouder, Visiting Assistant Professor; M.S. Marc Rosen, Visiting Associate Professor. William Schiffmiller, Visiting Assistant Professor; M.P.S. Marc Schneider, Visiting Instructor and Lecturer; M.S. Christie Shin, Visiting Instructor; M.S. Jim Warner, Visiting Assistant Professor. Alisa Zamir, Professor; M.S.

Creative Arts Therapy
Jean Davis, Chair. Josephine Abbenante, Adjunct Assistant Professor. Claudia Bader, Visiting Instructor. Donna Bassin, Visiting Associate Professor. Beate Becker, Adjunct Associate Professor; M.S. Joachim Boenig, Adjunct Assistant Professor. Kimberly Bush, Visiting Instructor; M.F.A. Angela Cooper, Visiting Instructor. Barbara Cooper, Adjunct Associate Professor. Christina Devereaux, Visiting Assistant Professor; M.A. Judith Evans, Visiting Assistant Professor. Alison Gigl-George, Adjunct Assistant Professor. Blair Glaser, Visiting Instructor. Stephanie Gorski, Visiting Instructor; M.P.S. Teresa Haney, Visiting Assistant Professor. Corinna Hiller, Visiting Instructor; M.A. Melissa Klay, Visiting Instructor; Ph.D. Judith Luongo, Adjunct Associate Professor. Julie Miller, Visiting Instructor. .Virginia Reed, Visiting Assistant Professor. Arthur Robbins, Professor. Madeline Rugh, Visiting Associate Professor; Ph.D. Dina Schapiro, Adjunct Instructor. Jean Seibel, Visiting Instructor. Linda Siegel, Assistant Professor. Susan Tortora, Visiting Assistant Professor. Elissa White, Visiting Assistant Professor. Joan Wittig, Assistant Professor; M.S. Robert Wolf, Visiting Assistant Professor. Eva Young, Visiting Instructor.

Design Management
Mary McBride, Chair; Ph.D. Christopher Collette, Adjunct Assistant Professor; M.A. Laurence DeGaetano, Adjunct Assistant Professor; M.B.A. Roger Dunbar, Visiting Professor; Ph.D. Scott Fiaschetti, Visiting Associate Professor. Steven Fuhrmann, Visiting Assistant Professor. Larry Gibbs, Visiting Assistant Professor. Richard Green, Professor; B.S. Francine Martini, Visiting Assistant Professor. Bradley McCallum, Visiting Assistant Professor; M.F.A. Jacqueline McCormack, Adjunct Associate Professor; M.P.S. James Murray, Visiting Assistant Professor; M.P.S. Jo Ann Stonier, Visiting Assistant Professor; J.D. Marvin Waldman, Visiting Assistant Professor; M.B.A.

Digital Arts
Peter Patchen, Chair; M.F.A. Melissa Barrett Lundquist, Assistant Chair; M.F.A. Thomas Bonè, Visiting Assistant Professor. Liubomir Borissov, Associate Professor. Svjetlana Bukvich-Nichols, Visiting Associate Professor. Edward Darino, Adjunct Associate Professor; M.F.A. Marianna Ellenberg, Visiting Instructor. Carla Gurganus (Gannis), Visiting Instructor; M.F.A. Claudia Herbst, Associate Professor; M.F.A. William Kane, Visiting Associate Professor. Sean Kealey, Visiting Instructor. Lara Kohl, Adjunct Assistant Professor; M.F.A. Linda Lauro-Lazin, Adjunct Associate Professor. Peter Mackey, Professor; M.F.A. Natalie Moore, Adjunct Assistant Professor; M.A. Robert O'Neill, Assistant Professor; M.F.A. Michael O'Rourke, Professor; M.F.A. Jo Ann Patel, Visiting Assistant Professor. Gap-Yuel Seo, Visiting Instructor; B.F.A. Jill Song, Visiting Instructor. Sean Sullivan, Adjunct Assistant Professor. Lee Wolland, Visiting Instructor.

Fine Arts
Donna Moran, Chair; M.F.A. Sheila Pepe, Assistant Chair; M.F.A. David Alban, Visiting Assistant Professor; M.F.A. Adam Apostolos, Visiting Instructor. Nicole Awai, Visiting Assistant Professor; M.A. Lisa Bateman, Adjunct Associate Professor; M.F.A. Denise Bergstrom, Visiting Associate Professor. Robert Boyd, Visiting Assistant Professor. Michael Brennan, Adjunct Instructor; M.F.A. Mona Brody, Visiting Assistant Professor; M.F.A. Howard Buchwald, Professor; M.A. Richard Budelis, Associate Professor. Christian Bunce, Visiting Instructor. David Butler, Visiting Assistant Professor; M.F.A. Kirsten Campbell, Visiting Instructor. Anne Carlson, Adjunct Professor. Nanette Carter, Adjunct Assistant Professor; M.F.A. James Costanzo, Adjunct Associate Professor; M.F.A. Peggy Cyphers, Adjunct Professor; M.F.A. Gregory Drasler, Adjunct Assistant Professor; M.F.A. Kelly Driscoll, Assistant Professor; M.F.A. Alexandar Duravcevic, Adjunct Assistant Professor; M.F.A. Ashka Dymel, Visiting Associate Professor. Brad Ewing, Visiting Instructor; M.F.A. Gary Fischer, Visiting Assistant Professor. Allen Frame, Adjunct Associate Professor. Linda Francis, Adjunct Professor; M.A. Matthew Freedman, Visiting Associate Professor. Joseph Fyfe, Visiting Assistant Professor. Anne Gilman, Adjunct Associate Professor; M.F.A. Rupert Goldsworthy, Visiting Assistant Professor. Jonathan Goodman, Adjunct Associate Professor. David Gothard, Visiting Assistant Professor; B.F.A. Nancy Grimes, Adjunct Associate Professor; M.F.A. Graham Guerra, Visiting Instructor; M.F.A. Eric Heist, Visiting Assistant Professor. Gerald Herdman, Adjunct Assistant Professor. Licio Isolani, Professor. Karen Jones, Visiting Assistant Professor. Martine Kaczynski, Adjunct Associate Professor; M.F.A. Shirley Kaneda, Associate Professor; B.F.A. Beth Katleman, Visiting Assistant Professor. Hari Bir Singh Khalsa, Assistant to the Chair. Michael Kirk, Visiting Professor; M.F.A. Julian Kreimer, Visiting Associate Professor. David Lantow, Adjunct Associate Professor. Danielle Laplante, Visiting Assistant Professor. Catherine Lecleire, Adjunct Assistant Professor; M.F.A. Jenny Lee, Adjunct Professor. Patricia Madeja, Adjunct Associate Professor; B.F.A. Schott Malbaurn, Visiting Instructor; M.F.A. Dennis Masback, Adjunct Professor; M.F.A. Naohisa Matsumoto, Visiting Instructor. J. Martin Mazorra, Visiting Assistant Professor. Suzanne McClelland, Visiting Associate Professor. Timothy McMahon, Visiting Instructor; B.F.A. Dennis McNett, Adjunct Assistant Professor; M.F.A. Jennifer Melby, Visiting Assistant Professor. Anne Messner, Adjunct Professor; B.F.A. Curtis Mitchell, Visiting Assistant Professor. Matthew Monteith, Visiting Assistant Professor. John Monti, Professor; M.F.A. Robert Morgan, Adjunct Professor; Ph.D. James Moroney, Associate Professor; M.F.A. Carrie Moyer, Visiting Associate Professor. Cyrilla Mozenter, Adjunct Professor; M.F.A. James Murphy, Visiting Assistant Professor. Dominique Nahas, Visiting Assistant Professor. Ross Neher, Adjunct Professor. Thirwell Nolen, Adjunct Assistant Professor. Coleman O'Connell, Visiting Assistant Professor. Lothar Osterburg, Adjunct Associate Professor. Philip Perkis, Visiting Professor. Tomaso Puliafito, Visiting Professor. Diana Puntar, Visiting Assistant Professor. Catherine Redmond, Adjunct Associate Professor; B.A. Judith Reiss, Visiting Professor. Jennifer Riley, Visiting Associate Professor. Corinne Robins, Visiting Associate Professor. Howard Rosenthal, Visiting Associate Professor; M.F.A. Mary Rozkewicz, Adjunct Associate Professor; B.F.A. Stuart Sachs, Visiting Assistant Professor. Miriam Schaer, Visiting Assistant Professor; B.F.A. Linda Schrank, Adjunct Professor; M.A. Carla Shapiro, Visiting Assistant Professor. Jean Shin, Adjunct Associate Professor. Gerald Siciliano, Visiting Assistant Professor; M.S. Elise Siegel, Visiting Assistant Professor. Lori Sikorski, Adjunct Assistant Professor; M.F.A. Robbin Silverberg, Adjunct Assistant Professor; B.A. Joseph Smith, Professor; M.F.A. Beecher Smith-Stackhouse, Visiting Instructor; B.F.A. Joseph Stauber, Adjunct Assistant Professor; M.F.A. Jeffrey Stone, Adjunct Associate Professor; M.F.A. Leila Tai Shenkin, Visiting Assistant Professor; M.A. Craig Taylor, Visiting Assistant Professor. Mickalene Thomas, Visiting Assistant Professor; M.FA. Seth Weiner, Visiting Instructor. Marjorie Welish, Adjunct Professor. Elizabeth Whalley, Visiting Assistant Professor; M.F.A. Kit White, Adjunct Assistant Professor. Jeanne Wilkinson, Visiting Associate Professor; M.A. Michael Womack, Visiting Instructor; M.F.A. Christopher Wright, Adjunct Assistant Professor; M.F.A. Bernard Yenelouis, Visiting Assistant Professor. Robert Zakarian, Professor.

History of Art and Design
Gayle Rodda Kurtz, Chair; Ph.D. Michelle Berenfeld, Visiting Assistant Professor; Ph.D. Diana Bramham, Visiting Instructor; M.A. Sam Bryan, Adjunct Associate Professor; Ph.D. Sandra Cheng, Visiting Assistant Professor; Ph.D. Edward DeCarbo, Adjunct Associate Professor; Ph.D. Andrew Deck, Visiting Assistant Professor. Mary Edwards, Adjunct Professor; Ph.D. Lisandra Estevez, Visiting Instructor. Amy Gansel, Visiting Assistant Professor. Diana Gisolfi, Professor; Ph.D. Paul Glassman, Visiting Instructor. Rachael Goldman, Visiting Instructor. Katherine Griffith, Visiting Assistant Professor; M.A. Dimitri Hazzikostas, Assistant Professor; Ph.D. Frima Fox Hofrichter; Ph.D. Anne Hrychuk, Visiting Instructor. Ellen Hurst, Visiting Instructor; Ph.D. Janet Kardon, Visiting Associate Professor. Jeehyun Kim, Visiting Instructor. Vivien Knussi, Adjunct Instructor; M.A. Marilyn Kushner, Visiting Professor; Ph.D. Dennis Longwell, Visiting Associate Professor. William Lorenzo, Visiting Instructor; B.F.A. Elizabeth Marcus, Visiting Assistant Professor. Leatrice Mendelsohn, Visiting Associate Professor; Ph.D. Marsha Morton, Professor; Ph.D. Jennifer Noonan, Visiting Instructor; Ph.D. Antoinette Owen, Visiting Associate Professor; M.A. Todor Petev, Visiting Instructor; M.A. Jason Petty, Visiting Assistant Professor. Joyce Polistena, Adjunct Associate Professor; Ph.D. Katarina V. Posch, Associate Professor; Ph.D. Edward Powers, Adjunct Assistant Professor; Ph.D. Kyunghee Pyun, Visiting Assistant Professor; Ph.D. Flavia Rando, Visiting Associate Professor. Vanessa Rocco, Visiting Assistant Professor; Ph.D. Elena Rossi-Snook, Visiting Assistant Professor. Ann Schoenfeld, Adjunct Assistant Professor; Ph.D. Dorothy Shepard, Adjunct Associate Professor; Ph.D. Sandra Sider, Visiting Assistant Professor. Denise Stone, Visiting Assistant Professor. Borhua Wang, Adjunct Associate Professor; Ph.D. Lisa West, Visiting Instructor. Constance Wiesman, Visiting Assistant Professor. Helena Winston, Visiting Instructor; M.S.

Industrial Design
Matthew Burger, Chair; B.I.D. Rick Goodwin, Assistant Chair; M.I.D. Leonard Bacich, Professor. Harvey Bernstein, Adjunct Professor; M.S. Fred Blumlein, Adjunct Professor. Gine Caspi, Visiting Professor. Linda Celentano, Adjunct Associate Professor; B.I.D. Gihyun Cho, Adjunct Professor. Allan Chochinov, Adjunct Associate Professor. Kevin Crowley, Visiting Assistant Professor. Lucia DeRespinis, Adjunct Professor; B.I.D. Patrick Fenton, Visiting Instructor. Kathryn Filla, Adjunct Professor. Colin Gentle, Visiting Instructor. Mark Goetz, Adjunct Professor. William Gordon, Visiting Instructor. Bruce Hannah, Professor; B.I.D. Kate Hixon, Adjunct Associate Professor. Benjamin Hopson, Visiting Instructor. Jeffrey Kapec, Visiting Associate Professor; B.I.D. Noah King, Visiting Instructor; B.I.D. Robert Langhorn, Visiting Assistant Professor. Jay Levy, Visiting Assistant Professor. Jong Lim, Adjunct Professor; M.F.A. Steven Mercurio, Visiting Associate Professor. Frank Millero III, Visiting Assistant Professor; M.I.D. Katrin Mueller-Russo, Adjunct Associate Professor. Samantha Murphy, Visiting Instructor. Shigeru Natsume, Visiting Associate Professor. Daniel November, Professor. Judith Nylen, Visiting Assistant Professor; M.L.S, M.F.A. Jeanne Pfordresher, Adjunct Instructor. Timothy Richartz, Adjunct Assistant Professor. Andrew Roberto, Visiting Instructor; M.F.A. Molly Roberts, Visiting Associate Professor; M.I.D. Willy Schwenzfeier, Visiting Instructor. Arthur Sempliner, Adjunct Assistant Professor. Martin Skalski, Professor. Jordan Steckel, Adjunct Associate Professor; B.F.A. Karen Stone, Adjunct Associate Professor; M.I.D. Irvin Tepper, Adjunct Professor; M.F.A. Jonathan Thayer, Assistant Professor; B.I.D. William Tolbert, Visiting Associate Professor; M.F.A. Brett Tom, Visiting Instructor. Scott Vandervoort, Adjunct Instructor. Kim Walter, Visiting Assistant Professor. Seth Weiner, Visiting Instructor. Joel Wennerstrom, Adjunct Assistant Professor; M.I.D. Julia Wheeler, Visiting Instructor. Hyukjae Yoo, Adjunct Associate Professor; M.I.D.

Interior Design
Anita Cooney, Chair; B.A. Jennifer Logun, Assistant Chair; M.Arch. Eric Ansel, Visiting Assistant Professor; M.F.A., M.Arch. Tarek Ashkar, Visiting Assistant Professor; M.Arch. Cynthia Atwood, Visiting Assistant Professor. Craig Bacheller II, Visiting Assistant Professor; M.Arch. Jonathan Baker, Visiting Assistant Professor; M.Arch. Emily Blitzer, Visiting Assistant Professor; B.A. Edward Brant, Visiting Assistant Professor. Alissa Bucher, Visiting Assistant Professor. Valeria Buchheit, Visiting Assistant Professor. Mary Burke, Visiting Assistant Professor. Amy Campos, Visiting Assistant Professor; M.Arch. Maneswar Cheemalapati, Visiting Assistant Professor. Ike Cheung, Visiting Assistant Professor; B.Arch. James Conti, Adjunct Associate Professor; M.F.A. Robin Drake, Visiting Assistant Professor; B.S. William Du Bose, Visiting Assistant Professor. Joann Eckstut, Visiting Assistant Professor; B.A. Jayme Elterman, Visiting Assistant Professor; B.A. Philip Farrell, Adjunct Professor; M.S. Alan Feltoon, Adjunct Assistant Professor. William Feuerman, Visiting Assistant Professor; M.S. Asdrubal Franco, Visiting Assistant Professor. Antonio Furgiuele, Visiting Assistant Professor. Jennifer Gieseking, Visiting Assistant Professor; M.A. Jacqueline Gross, Visiting Assistant Professor. Christopher Hall, Visiting Assistant Professor. Jennifer Hanlin, Visiting Assistant Professor; M.Arch. Kelly Hanson, Visiting Assistant Professor. Claudia Hernandez, Visiting Assistant Professor; M.S. Fred Kachelhofer, Visiting Assistant Professor. Mi-Young Kang, Visiting Assistant Professor; M.S. Mark Karlen, Professor; Ph.D. Sheryl Kasak, Visiting Assistant Professor; M.A. Poonam Khanna, Visiting Assistant Professor; M.A., M.S. Margaret Kirk, Visiting Instructor; M.Arch. Scott Larrabee, Visiting Assistant Professor. Barbara Lewandowska, Visiting Associate Professor. Jason Livingston, Visiting Assistant Professor; M.F.A. Cam Lorendo, Visiting Assistant Professor; B.A. Carmen Malvar, Adjunct Assistant Professor. William Mangold, Adjunct Assistant Professor; Ph.D. Gregory Marinic, Visiting Assistant Professor; M.Arch. Juan Matiz, Visiting Assistant Professor; B.Arch. Molly McKnight, Visiting Assistant Professor; B.Arch. Anthony Mekel, Adjunct Assistant Professor; B.Arch. Christopher Metz, Visiting Assistant Professor; B.Arch. Francine Monaco, Adjunct Associate Professor; B.Arch. Julie Moskovitz, Visiting Assistant Professor; M.Arch. Stephen Mullins, Visiting Assistant Professor; M.F.A. Tetsu Ohara, Visiting Assistant Professor; M.Arch. Jon Otis, Professor; M.S. Dae Park, Visiting Assistant Professor. Alexandra Summer, Adjunct Assistant Professor. James Supanick, Visiting Instructor; M.F.A. Anne Turyn, Adjunct Professor; M.F.A. Sarah van Ouwerkerk, Professor; M.F.A. Ellen Wallenstein, Adjunct Associate Professor; M.F.A. Gregory Webb, Adjunct Instructor.

sfai
san francisco. art. institute.
since 1871.

SAN FRANCISCO ART INSTITUTE

Program in Fine Arts and Liberal Arts

Programs of Study

San Francisco Art Institute (SFAI) consists of two schools: the School of Studio Practice and the School of Interdisciplinary Studies. The School of Studio Practice offers M.F.A. and low-residency summer M.F.A. degree programs and postbaccalaureate certificates in design and technology, film, new genres, painting, photography, printmaking, and sculpture. The School of Interdisciplinary Studies offers M.A. degree programs in the history and theory of contemporary art, urban studies, and exhibition and museum studies. All of SFAI's graduate programs are committed to creative research that investigates the relationship between inquiry and practice and how this dynamic manifests itself in contemporary and historical approaches to cultural production in times of accelerated paradigm shifts. In the graduate programs, students are trained to be inquisitive thinkers within an environment of rigorous studio practice and interdisciplinary study. Spheres of Interest, the graduate lecture series, engages students with the thoughts and productions of a wide array of international guest participants. The presentations, seminars, and one-on-one discussions are opportunities to grapple with productions, conditions, and perspectives that can stimulate other kinds of responses.

The Master of Fine Arts program develops the artist's vision through studio-based experiments and the understanding that the work of the artist is an essential part of society. In the two-year M.F.A. program, students explore studio production and theoretical work in a flexible structure that encourages individual development within an interdisciplinary context. Students are exposed to methodologies of inquiry that foster innovative, analytic, and speculative thinking skills necessary for artistic development and creative production. The low-residency summer M.F.A. program (three or four years) has the same rigor and faculty as the two-year M.F.A. program, except that it is designed for artists, teachers, and other art professionals who currently have an active studio practice and for whom a low-residency program accommodates their employment or academic schedule. The combination of intensive summer sessions and guided independent study gives students a strong sense of artistic community while allowing them to continue to develop work over a longer period of time. Participation in the M.F.A. Exhibition is the final requirement for the M.F.A. degree. In their final year, students prepare for this important event, which is the largest of its kind in the San Francisco Bay Area. A great deal of discussion ensues about the nature of work being produced as well as issues surrounding its presentation and exhibition. Noted for diverse, provocative, and innovative work, the M.F.A. Exhibition attracts significant critical attention from the public and draws curators, gallery directors, and collectors from the West Coast and beyond.

SFAI's Master of Arts in History and Theory of Contemporary Art provides an in-depth and critical understanding of the history of the ideas, conditions, institutions, and discourses surrounding contemporary art and culture and how these inform the study, interpretation, analysis, and exhibition of art today. The program's curriculum addresses complex issues such as the dismantling of the hierarchies of artistic mediums initiated by the historical avant-gardes, the globalization of culture, the intersection of Western and non-Western modernity, the role of technology in art making, and the question of authorship in the practice of contemporary art.

The Master of Arts in Urban Studies integrates courses and resources from the School of Studio Practice and School of Interdisciplinary Studies to create a unique platform for learning and social engagement. The program offers a studio- and research-based curriculum developed specifically to address the contributions of art, artists, and researchers to the understanding and shaping of the subjectivity of the city.

The Master of Arts in Exhibition and Museum Studies is founded on the understanding that museums and exhibitions are both historical objects and subjects. Through this program, students develop a thorough understanding of the history and roles of institutions of modernity (museums, historical societies, archives, libraries, architectural commissions) in contemporary culture, the economy of the art world, and the politics that affect it. The curriculum comprises curatorial models, exhibition systems, institutional mediation, and education and addresses such topics as historical preservation, heritage management, the ethics of trade in antiquities, and the complex issue of cross-cultural and cross-disciplinary curating involving works understood primarily as ethnographic, anthropologic, and archaeological.

SFAI's Postbaccalaureate Certificate program is ideal for students who want to prepare themselves and their portfolios for entrance into an M.F.A. program and for those who simply want to enhance their skills and knowledge without having specific plans to enter a graduate program. Students spend a year of intensive work in their studio workspace at SFAI's Graduate Center, either focusing on a specific area of inquiry or experimenting with a variety of media and ideas. The curriculum combines the tutorial aspects of the graduate program with the upper-division course work of the undergraduate program.

Research Facilities

Graduate Center facilities include a digital lab, film and sound studios, darkrooms, a wood shop, seminar classrooms, a gallery, and installation critique rooms where students can present finished works or works in progress.

Graduate students also use the resources at SFAI's main campus in San Francisco's Russian Hill neighborhood, which houses painting, drawing, and sculpture studios; photography studios and darkrooms; black-box studios for shooting film and video; and printmaking areas for lithography, intaglio, silkscreen, and digital printmaking. Postproduction facilities include darkrooms, mural printing, and large-scale digital photo output; Super-8 and 16 mm editing; digital video and Final Cut Pro editing; an HDCAM- and DVCAM-equipped video-finishing suite; black-and-white and color film processing for photography and film; and sound studios. Film and video production equipment includes sync and nonsync Super-8 and 16-mm cameras, standard NTSC and 24p digital video cameras, and a CineAlta HDCAM package. The lecture hall is equipped for 16-mm and digital projection and is available to students for screenings and performances. The Digital Media Studio is an interdisciplinary campus resource available to all students for both static and time-based digital work. Equipment includes G5 Dual Processor Power Macs, scanners, and digital video editing stations. In addition, the Digital Imaging Studio provides an array of large-format, archival, photo-quality Epson printers.

SFAI's Anne Bremer Memorial Library is a valuable resource for books and primary source material on artists. The library holds more than 29,000 volumes, including an outstanding collection of exhibition catalogues, artists' books, rare books, historic archives of original material documenting art in California since 1871, and subscriptions to more than 200 periodicals as well as collections of slides, audio- and videotapes, films, and DVDs.

Financial Aid

Graduate students are considered for Graduate Fellowships, loans, grants, and Federal Work-Study opportunities. The Graduate Fellowship program provides scholarship support for incoming graduate students who have demonstrated a particular suitability for SFAI through their art work and personal accomplishments. Application for all types of need-based financial aid administered by SFAI requires a completed application for admission and a valid FAFSA, which should include SFAI's federal school code of 003948. Students should visit the SFAI Web site for application deadlines to receive priority consideration for available financial aid funds.

Cost of Study

Tuition for full-time graduate study for the 2008–09 academic year was $32,174.

Living and Housing Costs

SFAI's Office of Student Affairs provides a range of services for students, including a residence hall, roommate-referral service, and housing bulletin boards. The Housing Coordinator advises students on housing options in the area. Although the cost of living in the Bay Area varies widely according to individual lifestyle, housing and food for a single student is estimated to average about $10,800 per academic year.

Student Group

The Legion of Graduate Students (LOGS) includes all graduate students and encourages participation of graduate alumni. LOGS oversees the Swell Gallery and the Alternative Lecture Series and serves as a forum for graduate students.

Location

SFAI's main campus was completed in 1926 in the residential neighborhood of Russian Hill. The architecture combines a historic Mediterranean-style building with a distinctive Modernist addition from 1970. The two buildings offer traditional studios, with natural light from windows and skylights; black-box performance, production, and editing studios; galleries and exhibition spaces for student work; and seminar, screening, and lecture spaces. The campus features spectacular views of San Francisco Bay, including the Golden Gate, Bay Bridge, and Richmond Bridge, as well as Alcatraz and Angel Island. Many of San Francisco's historic and diverse neighborhoods are also nearby, including North Beach, Chinatown, and the South of Market area, or SoMa, home to many of the city's major museums, including the San Francisco Museum of Modern Art and Yerba Buena Center for the Arts.

The Graduate Center occupies the second floor of a large converted industrial building along the San Francisco Bay, an area of artist lofts and art-related services. The 62,000-square-foot facility provides individual and group studios, many with natural light; 24-hour access; and convenience to public transportation. Potrero Hill, SoMa, and the Mission district are nearby.

The San Francisco Bay area is the country's sixth-largest metropolitan area and is home to an exciting art scene that includes museums, galleries, and alternative spaces. The area also offers a wealth of cultural and educational resources—opera, dance, traditional and experimental theater, a wide range of music, cinema, and libraries. Favored by a climate that is mild year-round, San Francisco is among the world's most livable cities.

The Institute

Founded in 1871 by artists, writers, and community leaders who possessed a cultural vision for the West, the San Francisco Art Association (SFAA) became a locus for artists and thinkers. The California School of Design (renamed California School of Fine Arts in 1916 and San Francisco Art Institute in 1961) was launched by SFAA two years later and has been central to the development of many of this country's most notable art movements.

Applying

All aspects of applications are reviewed by the faculty and the admissions staff. Admission decisions are made on an individual basis, taking into account artistic and/or scholastic achievement and personal maturity and dedication as well as academic background.

Deadlines vary according to semester and program—details and an online application form are available on the SFAI Web site at http://www.sfai.edu. Required are the artist's statement or statement of purpose; portfolio (M.F.A. only); transcripts of all undergraduate and graduate work, both completed and in progress; two letters of recommendation; and a personal interview. Additional requirements apply for international applicants.

Correspondence and Information

Office of Admissions
San Francisco Art Institute
800 Chestnut Street
San Francisco, California 94133

Phone: 415-749-4500
800-345-SFAI (7324)(toll-free)
E-mail: admissions@sfai.edu
Web site: http://www.sfai.edu

San Francisco Art Institute

THE FACULTY

With a faculty of more than 130, SFAI enjoys an extraordinary student-faculty ratio of 5:1. Students work closely with faculty members and develop important and lasting relationships that continue beyond graduation.

Faculty members include artists, curators, writers, historians, theorists, activists, critics, urbanists, designers, performers, philosophers, musicians, and scientists. Okwui Enwezor, Dean of Academic Affairs, is a curator and writer and was the artistic director of the 2006 Bienal Internacional de Arte Contemporaneo in Seville, Spain. Renée Green is Dean of Graduate Studies at SFAI, and her work has been seen throughout the world in museums, galleries, biennials, and festivals. Hou Hanru, Chair of SFAI's Exhibitions and Museum Studies program, is the curator of the Chinese pavilion at the 2007 Venice Biennale and director of the 2007 Istanbul Biennial. Trisha Donnelly's work was included in the 2004 and 2006 Whitney biennials. Martin Schmidt (of Matmos) has toured with Bjork and has a new CD, *The Rose Has Teeth in the Mouth of the Beast.* Caitlin Mitchell-Dayton's paintings were used in the film *Art School Confidential.* Henry Wessel's photographs were recently published as a five-volume boxed set by Steidl. Jon Phillips is an open-source programmer for Creative Commons. Mark Van Proyen is one of the editors of *AfterBurn: Reflections on Burning Man.* Amy Franceschini is the founder of Futurefarmers and has been involved in numerous projects aimed at raising public awareness of critical ecological issues. Thomas Humphrey is a nuclear physicist and director of exhibitions at the Exploratorium.

In addition to working with SFAI's esteemed full- and part-time faculty, students are introduced to a spectrum of visiting artists and scholars. SFAI provides students direct access to an exhibition program showcasing the work of regional and international artists as well as SFAI students; an extensive roster of lectures that brings more than 60 artists, designers, curators, and writers to campus every year; and film screenings, symposia, and panel discussions that engage in contemporary issues and ideas.

Key elements of SFAI's approach to the intersection of academic and public inquiries are the new fellowships sponsored by the Centers of Interdisciplinary Study. Internationally recognized artists work in residence for a minimum of five weeks. Fellowships provide artists with an environment to engage in the ongoing development of new ideas in their work, test those ideas, and teach and collaborate with SFAI students and faculty members. Recent Fellows include Raqs Media Collective, from New Delhi; Alfredo Jaar, an artist, architect, and filmmaker known for his public interventions; and Hilton Als, a staff writer for *The New Yorker* and recent coeditor of *White Noise: An Eminem Reader.*

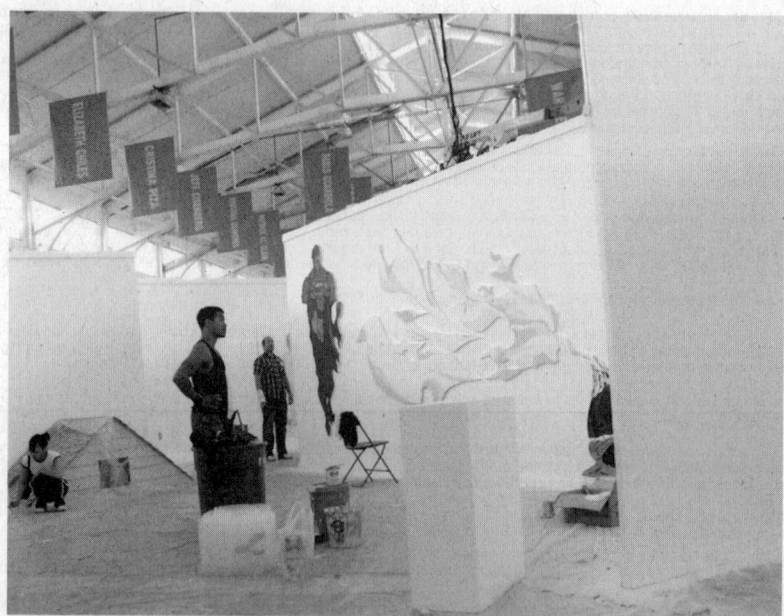

M.F.A. students installing work for the Graduate Exhibition.

SAVANNAH COLLEGE OF ART AND DESIGN

Graduate School

Savannah College of Art and Design

Programs of Study	Savannah College of Art and Design (SCAD) offers Master of Architecture (M.Arch.), Master of Arts (M.A.), Master of Arts in Teaching (M.A.T.), Master of Fine Arts (M.F.A.), and Master of Urban Design (M.U.D.) degrees as well as graduate certificates.
	The M.A. program is a one-year course of study requiring 45 credit hours. The M.F.A. and M.U.D. programs are two-year courses of study requiring 90 credit-hours. The M.A. and M.F.A. are offered in accessory design, advertising, animation, architectural history, design management, fashion, fibers, film and television, furniture design, graphic design, historic preservation, illustration, industrial design, interactive design and game development, interior design, luxury and fashion management, metals and jewelry, motion media design, painting, performing arts, photography, printmaking, production design, sculpture, sequential art, sound design, and visual effects. In addition, M.A. degrees are offered in art history, arts administration, cinema studies, commercial photography, design for sustainability, digital photography, documentary photography, illustration design, and international preservation. M.F.A. degrees in service design and writing are also available. The M.A.T. program requires 60 credit hours completed in one full year of intensive study and field experience.
	The professional Master of Architecture program requires 225 quarter hours: 180 undergraduate and 45 graduate. The postprofessional M.Arch. degree—for students with an accredited professional architecture degree who wish to pursue computer-aided design—requires 45 graduate quarter hours with an emphasis in either electronic design or urban design. The five-year professional M.Arch. degree is accredited by the National Architectural Accrediting Board.
	Online programs, including M.A. and M.F.A. degrees and graduate certificates, are offered via SCAD-eLearning.
Research Facilities	Architecture, interior design, and historic preservation facilities include an intranet of PCs configured with electronic-design software, including AutoCAD, Bentley Microstation V8, Adobe Photoshop, 3D Studio VIZ, SURFCAM, Autodesk Maya, and Revit. A video microscope, as well as architectural conservation, metals conservation, and paint-analysis labs also are available in the School of Building Arts.
	Animation, interactive design and game development, motion media design, and visual effects facilities offer ready access to high-end industry-standard equipment and software, including a Vicon motion capture studio, two green-screen stages, HD cameras, Cintiq monitors; Autodesk Maya, the Unreal game engine, Z Brush, Discreet 3ds Max, Photoshop, Illustrator, Premiere, After Effects, Flash, C++, and Actionscript.
	Fibers students work in a comprehensive facility with studios for screen printing, dyeing, weaving, sewing, felting, and papermaking, as well as CompuDobby looms, Jacquard looms, a Mimaki textile printer, Juki quilting machines, graduate studios, and classroom spaces. The facility also houses a dye lab and studios for hand weaving, silk screening, felting, and papermaking.
	Fashion studios are equipped with industry-standard dress forms, cutting tables, professional sewing machines, and specialty finishing equipment. Computer labs offer an Infinity Plus plotter for pattern making, Mimaki fabric printer, software including Kaledo, Vision Fashion Studio, Gerber Suite, Lectra U4ia, Virtual Fashion Pro, and online or print subscription services including WGSN, here & there, and Peclers.
	The Gulfstream Center for Furniture and Industrial Design in Savannah is a 44,000-square-foot state-of-the-art facility with studios, labs, and workshops; high-end computer labs; and the latest industry software, including AutoCAD, Autodesk Studio, Adobe Master Collection, Rhino 3-D, SolidWorks, and Autodesk Maya. The advanced technology lab includes computer numerical control (CNC) equipment for rapid prototyping and production, a laser cutter, and 3-D printers for producing ABS and polycarbonate 3-D models of computer-generated designs.
	Advertising, graphic design, illustration, and sequential art facilities include Macintosh computers with CD and DVD burners, scanners, black and white laser printers, light tables, and digital cameras. The Adobe Master Collection, Quark Xpress, and other graphics packages are available.
	Photography students use Macintosh digital imaging labs with extensive peripherals, wide-format inkjet printers, a Durst Theta printer, Imacon scanners, professional RA-4 color print processing machines for both negative and reversal papers, E-6 and C-41 color film processing machines, an alternative processes lab, studios, lighting equipment, view-camera systems, medium-format-camera systems, and digital SLR systems. Some labs are designated for graduate student use only.
	Metals and jewelry studios include an FDM Prodigy Plus rapid prototyping 3-D printer with capabilities for ABS or wax models of CAD prototypes and four-axis CNC milling machines.
	Film and television facilities include the Steadicam EFP and Super Panther Dolly, a chroma key/green screen studio, and a sound stage. The department houses Avid Adrenaline, Symphony, and Xpress DV workstations; MiniDV and DVC Pro cameras; Sony digital high-definition television cameras; 16mm, Super-16mm, and 35mm cameras; and an all-digital studio. Sound design equipment and software includes ten DH Pro Tools labs, two dedicated surround sound mix/mastering rooms, a MIDI lab, a recording studio for music production and Foley, two suites for dialog recording and editing, and a professionally equipped location sound cart for film production. Located adjacent to the High Museum of Art in midtown Atlanta, the sculpture facility is one of the finest in the Southeast. Designed by architect Renzo Piano, the facility houses a comprehensive wood and metal shop, a foundry for bronze and stainless steel, studios and support equipment, as well as exhibition space.
	Performing Arts facilities in Savannah include the 1,200-seat historic Lucas Theatre for the Arts, the 1,100-seat Trustees Theater, the ninety-seat Afifi Amphitheater at the Pei Ling Chan Garden for the Arts, and the 150-seat black-box Mondanaro Theater.
Financial Aid	Scholarships and fellowships are available to eligible incoming students based on academic and/or artistic achievement and financial need. For more information, students should visit http://www.scad.edu/scholarships.
Cost of Study	Graduate tuition for 2009–10 is $28,215.
Living and Housing Costs	Housing fees for the 2009–10 academic year range from $6700 for dormitory style to $8654 for an apartment-style unit with a separate bedroom. The basic meal plan rate per quarter is $1360.
Student Group	The total enrollment is more than 9,000 students, of whom 16 percent are graduate students. Approximately 20 percent of the graduate students are international.
Location	The College has locations in Savannah and Atlanta, Georgia, and Lacoste, France, with a Hong Kong location scheduled to open in fall 2010. Online programs are offered through SCAD-eLearning. SCAD–Savannah, the flagship campus, is the largest and offers a full university experience in the idyllic, creative environment of the beautiful coastal South. SCAD–Atlanta is located in Midtown Atlanta, the center of a growing metropolitan area of 5.1 million residents. SCAD–Lacoste, the study-abroad campus, offers immersion in the rich culture of the south of France. SCAD–Hong Kong (scheduled to open fall 2010) will be located in the historic North Kowloon Magistracy building in the Sham Sui Po community and will be the preeminent site for study of digital media in Asia. SCAD-eLearning is everywhere. Students anywhere in the world can earn graduate degrees through the online program. SCAD also offers certificate programs and individual graduate courses.
The College	The Savannah College of Art and Design exists to prepare talented students for professional creative careers, emphasizing learning through individual attention in a positively oriented university environment. The goal of the College is to nurture and cultivate the unique qualities of each student through an interesting curriculum, in an inspiring environment, under the leadership of involved professors.
	The Savannah College of Art and Design is a private, nonprofit institution accredited by the Commission on Colleges of the Southern Association of Colleges and Schools (1866 Southern Lane, Decatur, Georgia 30033-4097; telephone: 404-679-4501) to award bachelor's and master's degrees. The five-year professional M.Arch. degree program is accredited by the National Architectural Accrediting Board. The Master of Arts in Teaching degrees are approved by the Georgia Professional Standards Commission.
Applying	Admission requirements for graduate applicants include a completed application for admission; nonrefundable application fee ($25 for online; $50 for paper form); a bachelor's degree or its equivalent with an official transcript/mark sheet from each college/university attended; demonstration of English proficiency (for applicants whose first language is not English); three recommendations; a statement of purpose; a portfolio, writing submission, or audition; and résumé. An interview is recommended but not required. GRE scores are recommended. Applicants to the M.A.T. must have qualifying test scores on the Georgia Assessment for the Certification of Educators, the SAT, the ACT, or the GRE.
	Additionally, if applicable, applicants must provide any other documents or materials required to obtain a student visa. Portfolio requirements vary; applicants should consult the Web site (www.scad.edu/portfolio) for information. SCAD accepts applications on a rolling basis. Students may enter in the fall, winter, spring, or summer. Applications for the fall quarter should be completed by February 15 to ensure priority processing and scholarship consideration. After February 15, applications are still accepted, and scholarships are awarded until funds are no longer available. Graduate applicants who wish to enroll after fall quarter should submit completed application at least 60 days before the start of the intended quarter of enrollment. Those applying for financial aid should complete the online application and Free Application for Federal Student Aid (FAFSA). SCAD'S FAFSA code is 015022.
Correspondence and Information	SCAD–Savannah and SCAD-eLearning Admission Department Savannah College of Art and Design P.O. Box 2072 Savannah, Georgia 31402-2072 Phone: 912-525-5100 800-869-7223 (toll-free) E-mail: admission@scad.edu Web site: http://www.scad.edu SCAD–Atlanta Savannah College of Art and Design Admission Department P.O. Box 77300 Atlanta, Georgia 30357-1300 Phone: 404-253-2700 877-722-3285 (toll-free) E-mail: scadatl@scad.edu

Savannah College of Art and Design

THE FACULTY

A complete faculty listing is available online at http://www.scad.edu/academic/faculty/full1.cfm.

SCHOOL OF THE ART INSTITUTE OF CHICAGO

Graduate Division

Programs of Study

Graduate programs at the School of the Art Institute of Chicago (SAIC) leading to the M.F.A. in Studio degree are offered in the following studio areas: art and technology studies; ceramics; designed objects; design for emerging technologies; fiber and material studies; film, video, and new media; interior architecture; painting and drawing; performance; photography; printmedia; sculpture; sound; visual communication; and writing. Other advanced degree programs offered are an M.A. in Arts Administration and Policy; an M.A. in Art Education; an M.A. in Art Therapy; an M.A. in Modern Art History, Theory, and Criticism; an M.A. in Teaching; an M.A. in Visual and Critical Studies; an M.S. in Historic Preservation; a dual-degree M.A. in Modern Art History, Theory, and Criticism/M.A. in Arts Administration and Policy; and a Graduate Certificate in Art History, Theory, and Criticism. Since 2006 SAIC has offered the Master of Architecture; the Master of Architecture, with an emphasis in interior design; and the Master of Design in Designed Objects degrees.

Postbaccalaureate certificates in fashion, studio, and writing are also offered.

New programs offered by SAIC as of fall 2008 include a Master of Design in Fashion, Body, and Garment and a Master of Arts in New Arts Journalism.

Research Facilities

Among the facilities for research and study, in addition to the studio areas provided by individual departments, are the school library, with more than 85,000 books, periodicals, films, videos, records, CDs, and picture files; the 4,500-volume Joan Flasch Artists' Book Collection; and the Film Study Collections of 800 short and experimental films for class study. The Ryerson and Burnham libraries, the second-largest art and architecture reference libraries in the country, are housed in the Art Institute of Chicago museum and have approximately 220,000 volumes. Other resources include the Video Data Bank, with more than 600 artists' videotapes; the Gene Siskel Film Center; the Poetry Center; the Fashion Resource Center; and the Roger Brown Study Collection.

Financial Aid

Financial assistance for graduate students is available in the form of fellowships, merit and need-based scholarships, assistantships, grants, institutionally sponsored loans, Federal Perkins Loans, and Federal Work-Study Program awards. All students who wish to apply for financial assistance must file the Free Application for Federal Student Aid (FAFSA) form. All financial aid forms and instructions may be obtained through the School's Financial Aid office. Of the full-time graduate students, 83 percent are partially or completely funded.

Cost of Study

Tuition and fees for full-time M.F.A. graduate study (15 credit hours per term) for 2008–09 were $35,400 ($1180 per credit hour).

Living and Housing Costs

Estimated academic-year expenses for an independent, single student, exclusive of tuition, range from $8000 to $12,000, depending upon the housing choice a student makes. (This estimate includes room and board, transportation, supplies, and personal expenses.)

Student Group

Of a total enrollment of 2,463, there are 599 students registered in the Graduate Division. Approximately 65 percent are women, and about 18 percent are international students.

Location

The School of the Art Institute of Chicago offers the advantages of a central location in a large, culturally rich, metropolitan center. The Chicago area has a population of about 7 million and, as an urban center, offers a broad range of cultural activities, along with an efficient public transportation system and well-established, diversified neighborhoods.

The School

The Art Institute of Chicago, comprising the School and the museum, was founded under another name by a small group of artists in 1866. Their purpose was to provide an exceptional education in the studio arts in conjunction with exhibition opportunities. The small art school expanded from a rented facility to its present location in the heart of Chicago's downtown area. The School has become one of the largest independent schools of art and design in the country. Its modern facility adjoins the Art Institute of Chicago Museum, which was built for the World's Columbian Exhibition in 1893. The museum's extensive collection of masterpieces constitutes one of the finest in the world. The partnership between the museum and the School offers unlimited resources for research and study; students have extensive access to the permanent collection, the traveling exhibitions, the Prints and Drawings Room, and the Photography Study Center.

Applying

The School of the Art Institute of Chicago invites applications for admission from students of exceptional promise who have graduated from liberal arts colleges, fine arts schools, and state universities and colleges, as well as those who have completed partial M.F.A. degree programs at other schools. The Admissions Review Committee carefully reviews the portfolios and academic credentials of all applicants. Students are required to submit a portfolio of up to twenty examples of recent work, transcripts from each college previously attended, a statement of purpose, and two to three letters of recommendation. The M.F.A. (in studio areas) application deadline is January 10 for fall admission. Students interested in applying to other degree programs should visit http://www.saic.edu for application guidelines.

Correspondence and Information

Graduate Admissions
Admissions Office
School of the Art Institute of Chicago
36 South Wabash Avenue, Suite 1201
Chicago, Illinois 60603
Phone: 312-629-6100
         800-232-7242 (toll-free)
E-mail: admiss@saic.edu
Web site: http://www.saic.edu

School of the Art Institute of Chicago

THE FACULTY

ARCHITECTURE, INTERIOR ARCHITECTURE, AND DESIGNED OBJECTS
Hennie Reynders, Chair. Cynthia Coleman, Garret Eakin, Ellen Grimes, May Hawfield, Jaak Jurisson, Don Kalec, Linda Keane, Thomas Kong, Carl Ray Miller, Anders Nereim, Ben Nicholson, Helen Marie Nugent, Douglas Pancoast, Tristan Sterk.

ART AND TECHNOLOGY STUDIES
Benjamin Chang, Chair. Claudia Hart, Coordinator. Shawn Decker, Peter Gena, William Harper, Tiffany Holmes, Jason Hopkins, Eduardo Kac, John Manning, Dan Miller, Judd Morrissey, Greg Mowery.

ART EDUCATION
Karyn Sandlos, Chair and Director, Master of Arts in Teaching (MAT). Andres Hernandez, Director, Master of Arts in Art Education (MAAE). Jerome Hausman, Drea Howenstein, Rebecca Keller, Nicole Marroquinn, Angela Paterakis, Patricia Pelletier, Therese Quinn, David Rodriguez.

ART THERAPY
Catherine Moon, Chair. Danniel Anthon, Deborah Benke, Barbara Fish, William Miles, Joanne Ramseyer, Suellen Semekowski, Terri Sweig, Savneet Talwar, Randy Vick.

ARTS ADMINISTRATION AND POLICY
Nicholas Lowe, Chair. Bob Brodsky, John Corbett, Michael Dorf, Adelheid Mers, Amy Reichert, Michael Ryan, Rachel Weiss.

CERAMICS
Xavier Toubes, Chair. Thomas Laureman, William O'Brien, Patricia Rieger, Katherine Ross.

DESIGN FOR EMERGING TECHNOLOGIES
Anders Nereim, Coordinator. Benjamin Chang, Shawn Decker, Peter Gena, Linda Keane, John Manning, Carl Ray Miller, Dan Miller, Douglas Pancoast.

DESIGNED OBJECTS
Helen Maria Nugent, Coordinator. Linda Keane, Carl Ray Miller, Anders Nereim, Lisa Norton, Douglas Pancoast, Jim Termeer, Bruce Tharp.

FASHION
Andrea Reynders, Chair. Katrin Schnabl, Graduate Program Director. Sandra Michel Adams, Bambi Breakstone, Gillion Carrara, Nick Cave, Shane Gabier, Conrad Hamather, Anke Loh, Liat Smestad.

FIBER AND MATERIALS STUDIES
Anne Wilson, Chair. Amy Honchell, Graduate Coordinator. Marianne Fairbanks, Diana Guerrero-Macia, Kathryn Hixson, Joan Livingstone, Christy Matson, Ellen Rothenberg, Christine Tarkowski, Fraser Taylor.

FILM, VIDEO, AND NEW MEDIA
Gregg Bordowitz, Chair. Tatsuyuki Aoki, Jon Cates, Thomas Comerford, Sharon Couzin, Daniel Eisenberg, Shellie Fleming, Michele Mahoney, Mary Patten, John Petrakis, Anne Quirynen, Christopher Sullivan, Jim Trainor, Danielle Wilmouth.

HISTORIC PRESERVATION
Vincent L. Michael, Chair. Rolf Achilles, Craig Deller, Carol Dyson, Richard Friedman, Martha Frish, Yunxia Gao, Jean Guarino, Elaine Harrington, Donald Kalec, Charles Pipal, Anthony Rubano, Anne Sullivan, Terry Tatum, Neal Vogel, Tim Wittman, Carol Yetken.

LIBERAL ARTS
Raja Halwani, Chair. Paul Ashley, Romi Crawford, Calvin Forbes, Peter Gena, Barbara Guenther, James McManus, Karen Morris, Michael Nagelbach, Patrick Rivers, Kathryn Shaffer, Elizabeth Wright, Andrew Yang.

MODERN ART HISTORY, THEORY, AND CRITICISM
Kym Pinder, Chair. Nora Taylor, Director, Master of Arts in Modern Art History, Theory, and Criticism (MAAH). Rolf Achilles, Simon Anderson, Christine Atha, Shane Campbell, Gillion Carrara, Alan Cohen, Audrey Colby, Delinda Collier, Christopher Cutrone, Jim Elkins, Patricia Erens, David Getsy, Michael Golec, James Hugunin, Rebecca Keller, Kai Wood Mah, Deborah Mancoff, Stanley Murashige, Michael Newman, Daniel Quiles, Michael Rabe, David Raskin, Shawn Michelle Smith, Robin Stern, Charles Stuckey, Lisa Wainwright, Tim Wittman, James Yood.

NEW ARTS JOURNALISM
James Yood, Program Director. Cynthia Coleman, Margaret Hawkins, Tiffany Holmes, Michel Miner.

PAINTING AND DRAWING
Susanne Doremus, Chair. Candida Alvarez, Susanna Coffey, Dan Devening, Judith Geichman, Gaylen Gerber, Michelle Grabner, Sheridan Gustin, Philip Hanson, Richard Hull, Michiko Itatani, Susan Kraut, Marion Kryczka, José Lerma, Jim Lutes, Terry Myers, Jim Nutt, Elizabeth Ockwell, John Phillips, Frank Piatek, Scott Reeder, Tyson Reeder, Richard Rezec, Kay Rosen, Barbara Rossi, John Rozelle, Elizabeth Rupprecht, Jerry Saltz, Joanne Scott, Hazma Walker, Kevin Wolff.

PERFORMANCE
Faith Wilding, Chair. Werner Herterich, Lin Hixson, Mark Jeffery, Ginger Krebs, Trevor Martin, Roberto Sifuentes, Blair Thomas.

PHOTOGRAPHY
Barbara DeGenevieve, Chair. Daniel Bauer, Aimee Beaubien, Shannon Benine, Patty Carroll, Robert Clarke-Davis, Ken Fandell, Catherine Glass, Irena Knezevic, Alan Labb, Mayumi Lake, Jason Lazarus, Heidi Norton, Claire Pentecost, Karen Savage, Lewis Toby, Brian Ulrich.

PRINTMEDIA
Peter Power, Chair. Sally Alatalo, Jeanine Coupe-Ryding, Doug Huston, Myungah Hyon, Michael Miller, Mark Pascale, Karen Savage.

SCULPTURE
Laurie Palmer, Chair and Graduate Coordinator. José Ferreira, Preston Jackson, Mary Jane Jacob, Jin Soo Kim, Paul Martin, Adelheid Mers, Fred Nagelbach, Lisa Norton, Carolyn Ottmers, Stephen Reber, Richard Rezac, Frances Whitehead, James Zanzi.

SOUND
Shawn Decker, Chair. Nicholas Collins, John Corbett, Rob Drinkwater, Peter Gena, Eric Leonardson, Lou Mallozzi, Julia Miller, Robert Snyder, Lori Talley.

VISUAL AND CRITICAL STUDIES
Maud Lavin, Chair and Graduate Director. Gregg Bordowitz, Stanford Carpenter, James Elkins, Terri Kapsalis, Karen Morris, Patrick Rivers, Shawn Michelle Smith.

VISUAL COMMUNICATION
John Bowers, Chair. Frank DeBose, Alyson Beaton, Georgia Bockos, Gokhan Ersan, Stephen Farrell, Alysia Kaplan, B. J. Krivanek, Margaret MacNamara, Michael Miner, Jennifer Moody, Daniel Morgenthaler, Olivia Petrides, David Philmloe, Don Pollack, Catherine Ruggie-Saunders, Ann Tyler, Kimberly Viviano, Connie White.

WRITING
Sara Levine, Chair. Carol Anshaw, Rosellen Brown, Anne Calcagno, Elizabeth Cross, Mary Cross, Janet Desaulniers, Amy England, Calvin Forbes, Matthew Goulish, Joseph Grigley, James McManus, Michael Meyers, Beth Nugent, Beau O'Reilly, Elise Paschen, Bin Ramke, Jill Riddell, Ellen Rothenberg, Margaret Sloane, Leila Wilson.

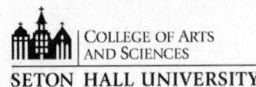

SETON HALL UNIVERSITY

Department of Art, Music, and Design
Master of Arts in Museum Professions

Program of Study	The Department of Art, Music and Design offers a Master of Arts (M.A.) in Museum Professions degree program to those interested in pursuing careers in museums and related cultural institutions. Balancing structure and flexibility, this cutting-edge program comprises a small number of core courses (including a mandatory internship), a choice of concentrations or tracks (in museum education, museum management, museum registration, or exhibition development), and four elective courses (for example, yearly seminars abroad in Amsterdam, Berlin, Paris, or Rome). Courses such as Exhibitions A–Z, Museums and Community, Museum Fundraising Fundamentals, Museum Technologies, and Object Care are offered on a rolling schedule.
	The program takes advantage of Seton Hall's own rich resources as well as the University's proximity to New York City, which boasts some of the finest museums in the world. Courses are taught by museum professionals from New York and New Jersey, and classes feature regular fieldtrips to museums as diverse as the Museum of Modern Art in midtown Manhattan, the Studio Museum in Harlem, the Newark Museum, and museums in Philadelphia, which are less than a two-hour drive away. Visiting lecturers from such institutions further enrich the curriculum. Museums have become complex, multipurpose organizations in the modern world; this program has been designed to meet the need for professionally trained employees.
	The 39-credit program (thirteen courses) may be followed on a full-time (three courses per semester) or part-time basis. The program can be completed in twenty months; however, many students take longer, depending on family and employment obligations. Courses are offered in the evenings and sometimes on weekends to accommodate those with full- or part-time jobs.
	Further details are available at http://www.shu.edu/academics/artsci/ma-museum-professions/index.cfm.
Research Facilities	The 155,000-square-foot Walsh Library has an excellent collection of the latest books and journals in museum studies, and it offers a variety of facilities, including carrels, group-study rooms, computer labs, and scholars' studies. Students have access to libraries and museums of the greater metropolitan area and their state-of-the-art resources. Library services include research support, bibliographic instruction, and interlibrary borrowing. Available technology includes CD-ROM databases, multimedia PC and Macintosh labs, electronic visual aids, and the Setoncat, an online catalog of the Walsh Library holdings that is accessible both on site and via the campus network.
	The Walsh Library Gallery offers a year-round program of art and history exhibitions. Students in the M.A. in Museum Professions program frequently are involved in the planning, implementation, and educational aspects of these exhibitions, especially when they enroll in the course entitled Producing an Exhibition.
Financial Aid	Graduate assistantships, which provide tuition benefits and a stipend, are offered on a competitive basis. Resident assistant positions, which offer housing only, are available as well. Students can apply for two types of federal student loans.
	To qualify for financial aid, students must take at least 6 credits per term. Additional information on financial aid and graduate assistantships is available at http://www.shu.edu/applying/graduate/grad-finaid.cfm.
Cost of Study	In 2009–10, tuition is $901 per credit. Full-time students pay $305 per semester in University and technology fees; part-time students pay $185.
Living and Housing Costs	Housing and living costs in South Orange and surrounding towns are comparable to most suburban cities, with studio and one-bedroom apartments renting for $750 to $1000 per month.
Student Group	Each year, about 20 students enter the program. The student body is diverse in age, ethnicity, and geographic origins, as students come from many states and countries. Some recently completed their undergraduate education; others are career changers who wish to prepare for new positions in museum environments. This diversity helps the program, as museums of today seek employees of diverse backgrounds. The students have strong collegial ties and are in close touch with faculty members. Indeed, the program fosters a sense of community.
Student Outcomes	Graduates and current students have held and are holding positions in such institutions as Children's Museum of Manhattan, New York City; Christie's Auction House, New York City; Citibank Art Advisory Service; Dallas Museum of Art, Texas; Edison National Historic Site, West Orange, New Jersey; El Museo del Barrio, New York City; Frick Collection, New York City; Guggenheim Museum, New York City; Hermitage Historic House, Ho-Ho-Kus, New Jersey; Historical Society of Princeton, New Jersey; International Center for Photography, New York City; JP Morgan Chase, Philanthropic Division, New York City; Jersey City Museum, New Jersey; Maritime Museum of San Diego, California; Metropolitan Museum of Art, New York City; Montclair Art Museum, New Jersey; Morris County Historical Society, Morristown, New Jersey; Museum of Arts and Design, New York City; Museum of Early Trades and Crafts, Madison, New Jersey; Museum of Jewish Heritage, New York City; Museum of Modern Art, New York City; Museum of the City of New York, New York City; National Air & Space Museum, Washington, D.C.; National Canal Museum, Easton, Pennsylvania; Newark Museum, Newark, New Jersey; Olana State Historic Site, Hudson, New York; Princeton Art Museum, Princeton, New Jersey; Ringling Museum of Art, Sarasota, Florida; Riverfront Center for the Arts, Millville, New Jersey; Ross Gallery of the University of Pennsylvania, Philadelphia, Pennsylvania; Rubin Museum of Art, New York City; Studio Museum in Harlem, New York City; Taft Museum, Cincinnati, Ohio; The Pew Charitable Trusts, Philadelphia, Pennsylvania; Vietnam Era Educational Center, Holmdel, New Jersey; Waterloo Village, New Jersey; and the Whitney Museum of American Art, New York City.
Location	Set in a suburban village, Seton Hall is a 5-minute drive from a 2,000-acre recreational reservation and a 30-minute bus or train ride to New York City with its wealth of museums and other cultural institutions. The campus buildings range from a nineteenth-century Victorian carriage house to a world-class fitness center. SOPAC, the South Orange Performing Arts Center, opened in November 2006 and features a five-screen Cineplex and a 415-seat theater center.
The University and The Program	Seton Hall University, founded in 1856, is the largest and oldest diocesan university in the country. It welcomes and educates men and women of all races, creeds, and ethnic origins. The Graduate Program in Museum Professions was founded in 1994 in order to prepare students for the challenges facing museums of the next century, which are to make museums relevant to a public of diverse backgrounds and traditions. At the graduate level, Seton Hall has more than sixty degree programs. The University is large enough to provide adequate facilities and resources, yet small enough to give individual attention to students.
Applying	Admission to the program is open to those with a baccalaureate degree in archaeology, anthropology, art history, or history or a degree in another field with a minimum of 12 undergraduate credits in one of those disciplines (these credits may be completed after conditional admission to the program). The program seeks students with a good academic record (preferable 3.0 or higher) and a strong desire to become a part of the museum world. An interview is necessary, as are two letters of recommendation, GRE scores (waived for applicants who have graduated more than five years ago), and a personal essay. Application forms are sent upon request or can be found online at http://www.shu.edu/academics/artsci/apply.cfm.
Correspondence and Information	Dr. Petra Chu, Director of Graduate Studies M.A. in Museum Professions Department of Art and Music Art Center Seton Hall University 400 South Orange Avenue South Orange, New Jersey 07079 Phone: 973-761-9430 or 9459 Fax: 973-275-2368 E-mail: museumgrad@shu.edu Web site: http://www.shu.edu/academics/artsci/ma-museum-professions/index.cfm

Seton Hall University

THE FACULTY

Director
Petra ten-Doesschate Chu, Ph.D., Columbia.

Full-Time Faculty
Petra ten-Doesschate Chu, Ph.D., Columbia.
Jürgen Heinrichs, Ph.D., Yale.
Susan Leshnoff, Ed.D., Columbia.
Janet Marstine, Ph.D., Pittsburgh.
Charlotte Nichols, Ph.D., NYU.

Adjunct Faculty
Jeanne Brasile, M.A., Seton Hall; Director, Walsh Library Gallery, Seton Hall.
Nicholas Holmes, LL.D., Michigan; In-House Legal Counsel, Whitney Museum of American Art
Lisa Mantone, M.A., William Patterson; Director of Development, The Museum of Modern Art.
Steven Miller, B.A., Bard; Director, The Morris Museum.
Antonia Moser, M.A., Seton Hall; Associate Registrar, Newark Museum.
Claudia Ocello, M.S., Bank Street College of Education; President and CEO of Museum Partners Consulting, LLC.
John Warren, M.S., Bank Street College of Education; Educational Specialist, National Parks of New York Harbor Education Center.
Katherine Witzig, M.A., Seton Hall; Collections Manager, Vietnam Era Educational Center.

Graduate faculty members of the Center for Public Service and the School of Education also participate in this program.

President's Hall.

The Arts Center.

TEMPLE UNIVERSITY
of the Commonwealth System of Higher Education

Tyler School of Art
Department of Art History

Programs of Study

The Department of Art History offers a course of study that leads to the M.A. and Ph.D. degrees. A special option combining art history courses with those given in the Graduate School of Business and Management is available to students studying for a master's degree who are interested in the administration of art collections and related cultural institutions. The graduate curriculum covers all areas of Western and Mediterranean art history, from ancient art to modern; it also introduces the student to a wide variety of critical methods and approaches. For Ph.D. students, the faculty concentrates on ancient/medieval, Renaissance/Baroque, and modern/contemporary art.

The objective of the master's degree program is to provide students with a thorough preparation for further graduate work or, for those for whom it is a terminal degree, specialized training as the foundation of a career. Requirements include 30 graduate credits; reading examinations in German and in French, Italian, or Spanish; a thesis; and a comprehensive examination. The fine arts administration option requires 36 graduate credits (15–18 in art history, 12–15 in business administration), a semester-long internship (6 credits, 20 hours per week), and the language and comprehensive examinations. It is expected that students will enter the program prepared to take language exams. The Ph.D. program is intended to prepare students for college teaching or for other research-oriented positions requiring advanced specialized study. The degree requires 60 graduate-level (5000-level or above) credits in art history beyond the B.A.; up to 9 of these credits may be taken in graduate-level courses, relevant to the student's field, outside the Department (but at Temple). Candidacy is granted upon acceptance of the dissertation proposal.

Research Facilities

Temple's library system contains nearly 2 million volumes and rich online resources; more than 60,000 books and periodicals are concerned with art and architecture. These holdings are supplemented by those of area libraries, including those at the University of Pennsylvania and Bryn Mawr College and at the Philadelphia Free Library. The research facilities of Washington, D.C.; Princeton University; and New York are only an hour or so away.

Financial Aid

The Department recommends full-time students for assistantships each term, with priority given to Ph.D. students. Funding is not normally available for M.A. candidates. Each assistantship carries a waiver of all tuition fees plus a stipend of $14,000 per academic year. Assistants are required to work 20 hours per week. Prestigious University-wide fellowships are awarded by the Graduate School upon recommendation by the Department; these provide full tuition and a stipend ($20,000). The Graduate School also awards Future Faculty Fellowships to students who intend to seek a terminal degree leading to a career in an area of academia underrepresented by their ethnic group. These fellowships are reserved for full-time students and provide funding of up to $14,000 per year plus full tuition remission. Loans, which are available only to American citizens, can be arranged through the Office of Financial Aid. The Department has a fellowship for predissertation study in Rome, which is awarded to a qualified student whose research will benefit by residence in Rome.

Cost of Study

In-state graduate tuition was $609 per credit in 2009–10; out-of-state graduate tuition was $897.

Living and Housing Costs

Minimum living expenses for the academic year are estimated at $15,000 for single students ($8600 for those commuting from home). Dormitory housing adjacent to the main campus of Temple is available.

Student Group

The Department accepts up to 15 students each year. While most are recent college graduates, others are returning students. The majority of students attend full-time; however, serious, qualified applicants are also admitted on a part-time basis. Graduate courses are held on weekdays, usually in the late afternoon.

Student Outcomes

Alumni from the master's program have pursued various options. Some attend Ph.D. programs at Temple and other institutions, while others teach at colleges and high schools. Several graduates are working in galleries or museums. The University's fine arts administration graduates tend to acquire positions in financial or developmental areas at art institutions, galleries, or museums.

Location

Philadelphia, the nation's fifth-largest city, is famous for its historic buildings and monuments and its outstanding museums—the Philadelphia Museum of Art, the University of Pennsylvania Museum, the Pennsylvania Academy of the Fine Arts, the Barnes Foundation, and the Rodin Museum. Among its cultural assets are the city's world-renowned orchestra, lively dance offerings, experimental and pre-Broadway theater, and film societies. The Jersey Shore and the Pocono Mountains are within an hour's drive.

The University and The Department

With more than 34,000 students and 1,700 faculty members, Temple University (a member institution of Pennsylvania's Commonwealth System of Higher Education) operates on two campuses in the Philadelphia area and on the Temple Abroad campuses in Rome and Tokyo; the Rome program is housed in the Villa Caproni, a nineteenth-century palazzo with classrooms and studios overlooking the Tiber. The Department of Art History is located on the main campus in the new Tyler School of Art building. This facility has faculty offices, a study lounge and computer facilities for graduate students, an auxiliary slide and digital image center, and a seminar room.

Applying

Although the Department makes admission decisions (on the basis of completed files) throughout the academic year, application deadlines for those applying for fellowships or assistantships are January 15 (for the following September) and October 15 (for the following January). Late applications are considered, but late applicants for assistantships or fellowships are at a disadvantage. In addition to an application form (available at http://www.temple.edu/grad) and a $50 fee (payable by credit card or bank account), two sets of the following credentials are required: a statement of goals (indicating the intended terminal degree), official transcripts of all undergraduate and graduate study, an original GRE score report form, a writing sample, and at least two letters of reference. International students must also send TOEFL scores. For the master's programs, applicants must hold a baccalaureate degree (any major). Students with an art history background are given preference. Because it is the objective of the program to give students training across the range of Western and Mediterranean art, students may be required to make up deficiencies in distribution at the discretion of the Director of Graduate Studies. Students seeking admission to the doctoral program must hold a master's degree in art history or in a related discipline, as determined at the discretion of the Director of Graduate Studies. Students admitted without a degree in art history are expected to take courses in areas where they are deficient. For both degrees, German is required, as is a second foreign language, usually French or Italian. When it is appropriate for a student's course of study, another relevant language may be substituted with the approval of the Director of Graduate Studies.

Correspondence and Information

For more information about the program:

Department of Art History
Temple University
2001 North 13th Street
Suite 210L
Philadelphia, Pennsylvania 19122
Phone: 215-777-9165
Fax: 215-777-9747
E-mail: arthisto@temple.edu

To request or return application forms:

Admissions Department
Tyler School of Art
Temple University
2001 North 13th Street
Philadelphia, Pennsylvania 19122
Phone: 215-777-8000

Temple University

THE FACULTY

Philip P. Betancourt, Laura H. Carnell Professor; Ph.D., Pennsylvania, 1970. Aegean Bronze Age and Greek art.
Elizabeth Bolman, Associate Professor; Ph.D., Bryn Mawr, 1997. Early medieval and Byzantine art.
Alan Braddock, Assistant Professor; Ph.D., Delaware, 2002. Nineteenth-century American art.
Tracy Cooper, Associate Professor; Ph.D., Princeton, 1990. Italian Renaissance and Baroque art and architecture.
Therese Dolan, Professor; Ph.D., Bryn Mawr, 1979. Nineteenth-century French art and criticism.
Jane DeRose Evans, Associate Professor; Ph.D., Pennsylvania, 1985. Roman art.
Susanna W. Gold, Lecturer; Ph.D., Pennsylvania, 2004. Nineteenth-century American art.
Marcia B. Hall, Professor; Ph.D., Harvard, 1967. Italian Renaissance art.
Gerald Silk, Professor and Chair; Ph.D., Virginia, 1976. Modern art.
Ashley West, Assistant Professor; Ph.D., Pennsylvania, 2006. Northern Baroque
Jonathan D. Kline, Ph.D., Temple, 2008. Italian Renaissance art.

A graduate assistant teaching at the Philadelphia Museum of Art.

Villa Caproni, Temple Abroad's headquarters in Rome.

Tyler School of Art on Temple's main campus in Philadelphia.

UNIVERSITY OF ROCHESTER

Department of Art and Art History
Visual and Cultural Studies Program

Program of Study

The Visual and Cultural Studies Program, housed in the Department of Art and Art History, offers students the chance to earn a master's or doctoral degree by doing intensive work simultaneously in several of Rochester's humanities departments. Primary faculty members for the Visual and Cultural Studies Program teach in the Departments of Art and Art History, Anthropology, English, and Modern Languages and Cultures, all in the College of Arts and Sciences. Students take courses in those departments and may also take courses in such departments as anthropology, history, music, and philosophy. About 20 faculty members participate in the program each year, including the Visual and Cultural Studies Steering Committee, which guides the program.

An innovative graduate program with a unique emphasis on visual and cultural representation, Rochester's Visual and Cultural Studies Program provides students with an opportunity to study critically and analyze culture from a social-historical perspective. The program stresses interpretation of art, film, and media within historical and ideological frameworks. Because the main contributing faculty members work in art and art history, film and media studies, and comparative literature, students are able to relate recent developments in literary and cultural theory to visual works and investigate the interrelationships between visual texts and critical theory.

All doctoral students take eight core courses: four in visual studies and four in critical theory. In addition, they take six electives, chosen from an extensive list of courses offered by the three primary departments; when appropriate, they may substitute courses from other disciplines. All students participate in the Visual and Cultural Studies Colloquium in the fall semester of their first year of study.

Most Ph.D. students spend 3½ years completing 60 credits of course work and 30 credits of research. After this, they take a qualifying exam, based on their reading and preliminary work on their dissertation. Students serve as teaching assistants for a number of introductory courses or as research assistants.

Research Facilities

The University's libraries contain holdings of 2.5 million volumes and 16,000 periodicals. Housed within the Rush Rhees Library, the Art and Music Library includes 40,000 books and bound journals, 300 journal subscriptions and standing orders for monograph series, and a growing collection of videotapes. The Visual Resource Collection at the University consists of more than 140,000 slides and mounted pictures. The University's Memorial Art Gallery also maintains its own library of 17,000 books and bound periodicals. The Film and Media Studies Center has several thousand films and videotapes available for viewing. Students can use the film and photograph collections at the world-renowned International Museum of Photography in the George Eastman House in Rochester.

Financial Aid

The Visual and Cultural Studies Steering Committee awards graduate teaching and research assistantships to students in the program. Tuition scholarships are also offered to qualified doctoral candidates. Assistantships currently carry an annual award of up to $15,000 beyond tuition. The University also awards Sproull Fellowships and Provost's Fellowships on a competitive basis, which carry a maximum stipend of $20,000 annually for up to two years. Students can receive extra funding by assisting in studio art courses or by teaching summer school.

Cost of Study

For the most up-to-date tuition costs, please see the University's Web site at http://www.rochester.edu/college/AAH/.

Living and Housing Costs

Accommodations for graduate students are available in four University-owned projects and in off-campus housing; for a brochure, a rate sheet, an application, and off-campus housing listings, applicants should write the Housing Coordinator at the Community Living Program, 020 Gates Wing, Susan B. Anthony Halls, P.O. Box 270468, Rochester, New York 14627-0468.

Student Group

The Department accepts 5 to 7 students each year, generally all of whom are full-time. Currently, there are 27 students in residence. The diverse graduate group is equally divided between men and women, and most students are receiving some form of financial aid.

Location

Located on the south shore of Lake Ontario, Rochester is the cultural and technological center of upstate New York. More than 800,000 residents of the metropolitan area can enjoy the Memorial Art Gallery, the George Eastman House (the world's leading museum and archive of photography and motion pictures), and the University's Eastman Theatre, where concerts are given by the Rochester Philharmonic Orchestra.

The University

The University, established in 1850, is private and coeducational. Four of the University's seven schools and colleges, including the College of Arts and Science, are located on the River Campus. The School of Medicine and Dentistry and the School of Nursing are within a 5-minute walk, and the Eastman School of Music is 2 miles away in the downtown area. Graduate work is carried on in each of the University's units. There are 1,000 full-time faculty members.

Applying

The deadline for applications is February 1 for the following September; offers of admission are sent to applicants on or about March 15. The application is available online only. Along with the online application, students should submit a personal statement, three letters of recommendation, official undergraduate and graduate transcripts, a writing sample, and GRE scores. International students must also supply TOEFL scores.

Correspondence and Information

Visual and Cultural Studies Program
Department of Art and Art History
424 Morey Hall, RC Box 270456
University of Rochester
Rochester, New York 14627

Phone: 585-275-9249
E-mail: art_arthist@cc.rochester.edu
Web site: http://www.rochester.edu/college/AAH/

University of Rochester

THE FACULTY AND THEIR RESEARCH

Visual and Cultural Studies Core Faculty and Associated Faculty

Janet Berlo, Professor of Art History/Visual and Cultural Studies; Ph.D., Yale. Native American art history and museum representation of Native peoples, Plains Indians drawings, Native American women and art, textiles and American visual culture.

Douglas Crimp, Fanny Knapp Allen Professor of Art History/Visual and Cultural Studies; Ph.D., CUNY. Contemporary art and criticism, race and representation, gay studies.

Thomas DiPiero, Professor of French/Visual and Cultural Studies; Ph.D., Cornell. French prose fiction of the seventeenth and eighteenth centuries.

Paul Duro, Professor of Art History/Visual and Cultural Studies and Chair, Department of Art and Art History; Ph.D., Essex (England). Theories of imitation in European painting, institutions of art.

Robert Foster, Professor of Anthropology; Ph.D., Chicago. Social theory, nationalism, globalization, mass consumption.

Susan Gustafson, Professor of German; Ph.D., Stanford. Eighteenth-century German literature, psychoanalysis, and feminism.

Rachel Haidu, Assistant Professor of Art History; Ph.D., Columbia. Postwar American and European art, history of photography.

Rosemary Kegl, Associate Professor of English; Ph.D., Cornell. Sixteenth- and seventeenth-century English literature, contemporary Marxist and feminist theory.

John Michael, Professor of English/Visual and Cultural Studies; Ph.D., Johns Hopkins. American literature, cultural studies, and critical theory.

Greta Niu, Assistant Professor of English; Ph.D., Duke. Film studies, Asian literature.

Joan Saab, Associate Professor of Art History/Visual and Cultural Studies and Director of the Program in Visual and Cultural Studies; Ph.D., NYU. Twentieth-century American history, media and culture, urban and community studies, popular culture, cultural studies.

Jeffrey Tucker, Associate Professor of English; Ph.D., Princeton. African American literature, twentieth-century American literature, science fiction.

Sharon Willis, Professor of French/Visual and Cultural Studies; Ph.D., Cornell. Modern French literature and literary theory, critical and feminist theory, film theory and visual analysis.

THE UNIVERSITY OF THE ARTS

Graduate Programs

Programs of Study
The University of the Arts (UArts), located on the Avenue of the Arts in Center City Philadelphia, offers graduate programs in art education; art education with a concentration in educational media; book arts/printmaking; ceramics, painting, and sculpture; industrial design; jazz studies; museum communication; museum education; museum exhibition, planning, and design; music education; teaching visual arts; postbaccalaureate certificate in crafts; postbaccalaureate teaching program (nondegree); and postbaccalaureate teaching program professional semester. The graduate programs offer an impressive combination of strengths: exceptionally accomplished faculty members, a remarkably individualized and interactive learning environment, access to outstanding facilities and resources, specialized studios, and programs of study that are both highly focused and highly flexible.

In the visual arts, programs include the Master of Arts in art education, which is designed to develop the studio, intellectual, and professional education background for educators; the Master of Arts in Teaching visual arts, which incorporates preparation for certification to teach art in grades K–12; the Master of Fine Arts in book arts/printmaking, which builds on the University's thirty-year tradition of involvement with the book and the printed image; and the Master of Fine Arts in ceramics, painting, or sculpture. These programs are designed to be completed in three years through part-time study. Also offered are the Master of Fine Arts in museum exhibition planning and design, which was developed with the support of the National Association of Museum Exhibition (NAME); the Master of Art in museum communication; the Master of Art in museum education; and the Master of Industrial Design.

In performance, the Master of Arts in Teaching in music education is a one-year-plus-summer program designed for students who have a bachelor's degree in music theory/composition, music history/literature, or other noneducation courses of study. The Master of Music in jazz studies is a one-year, 32-credit program. Designed as a finishing program in jazz performance, components of the program include advanced private instruction, hands-on internships and pedagogy study, and ensemble performances.

Research Facilities
Students use state-of-the-art digital-technology facilities, which include computer labs that support professional-level creative work, collaboration, and research. There is a dedicated Mac lab for graduate students and a wireless network throughout UArts buildings. In addition to multiple high-end graphics labs, the University hosts a New Media Center comprising two dual-platform digital laboratories that enable the integration of animation and 3-D modeling. Also available on campus are the Borowsky Center for Publication Arts; photography, film, and animation facilities with studios and darkrooms, video editing suites, and two Master Series Oxberry Animation stands; recording studios, state-of-the-art music technology MIDI studios and editing suites, and practice rooms; a bronze foundry and plaster workshop; and crafts studios and workshops for ceramics, metals, wood, glassblowing, papermaking, and fibers. Other important facilities include the digital forge 3-D printer, a bookbindery, and stone and metal welding shops.

Financial Aid
The Free Application for Federal Student Aid (FAFSA) must be filed by applicants for financial aid. Graduate teaching assistantships are available for qualified applicants. Some teaching and technical assistantships are awarded by the University of the Arts; the amounts of these awards vary.

Cost of Study
Tuition for 2009–10 is $30,700 plus applicable technology, book supplies, and activity fees.

Living and Housing Costs
There is limited University housing for graduate students.

Student Group
Students come from forty states and territories and thirty countries; about 5 percent of the total enrollment of 2,500 are international students. The graduate programs enrolled 218 students in 2008–09.

Location
The University of the Arts campus is located in the heart of Philadelphia's Avenue of the Arts, in the heart of the cultural community. The area has theaters, museums, galleries, music and dance facilities, restaurants, and shopping. Philadelphia offers a broad mix of strong cultural and educational experiences. In addition to being of historic importance, the city is also a supporter of the arts. Urban and sophisticated, it is also a series of small, close-knit neighborhoods. Fairmount Park, the largest city park in the world, provides facilities for boating, fishing, hiking, biking, picnicking, and relaxing.

The University
The University of the Arts is composed of the College of Art and Design, the College of Performing Arts, and the College of Media and Communication. The largest comprehensive educational institution of its kind in the United States, UArts prepares students for more than a hundred professional career paths in the visual, performing, and communication arts. The College of Art and Design is a professional community dedicated to the visual arts, where art is the primary and central concern. Founded in 1870 to train artists to translate the technological advances of the Industrial Revolution, it is today one of the nation's leading art colleges. The College of Performing Arts focuses on the areas of music, dance, acting, and musical theater. Founded in 1870 to educate musicians, it has expanded to offer demanding undergraduate programs of ballet, modern dance, and jazz dance as well as a program in theater arts. In 1996, the College of Media and Communication (CMAC) was founded and dedicated to the integration of art, technology, and communication. The College of Media and Communication offers undergraduate programs in writing, multimedia, and communication.

UArts sponsors a variety of activities that include social events, lectures, performances, and regular gallery and museum trips to New York City and Washington, D.C.

Applying
Required application materials include the University's Application for Graduate Study, a personal statement of intent, a nonrefundable fee of $60, official college transcripts, and at least three letters of recommendation. Portfolios must be submitted by applicants to the visual arts programs. An audition is required for applicants to the music program. International students must submit a Certification of Finance and TOEFL scores in the event the student's first language is other than English.

Applications for admission in September should be submitted by January 15 for priority consideration. Applications submitted after January 15 are considered on a space-available basis. Applications for January admission (art education, museum communications, museum education, and music only) should be submitted by the preceding November 15. Applications for the part-time M.F.A. (summer residence) should be submitted by January 1.

Correspondence and Information
Director of Admission
University of the Arts
320 South Broad Street
Philadelphia, Pennsylvania 19102
Phone: 215-717-6030
　　　800-616-ARTS (toll-free)
Fax: 215-717-6045
E-mail: admissions@uarts.edu
Web site: http://www.uarts.edu

University of the Arts

THE FACULTY

College of Art and Design
Paul Adorno, Adjunct Assistant Professor; M.S.Ed., Pennsylvania.
Jane Bedno, Professor Emeritus; J.D., William and Mary.
Rande Blank, Senior Lecturer; M.Ed., Beaver.
Gerard Brown, Senior Lecturer; M.F.A., Art Institute of Chicago.
Allegra Burnette, Senior Lecturer; M.F.A., University of the Arts.
Karen Clark-Schock, Adjunct Assistant Professor; Psy.D., Immaculata.
Raye Cohen, Adjunct Assistant Professor; M.F.A., M.A., University of the Arts.
David Comberg, Adjunct Associate Professor; M.F.A., Yale.
Richard Cress, Senior Lecturer; B.F.A., Virginia Commonwealth.
Tom Csaszar, Master Lecturer; B.F.A., Pennsylvania.
Alice Dommert, Senior Lecturer; M.F.A., University of the Arts.
Paul Flazone, Senior Lecturer; Ph.D. candidate, Pennsylvania.
Marita Fitzpatrick, Senior Lecturer; M.A.T., University of the Arts.
Virginia Fitzpatrick, Adjunct Associate Professor; Ph.D., Indiana.
Laura H. Foster, Adjunct Associate Professor; J.D., Baltimore.
Diane Foxman, Senior Lecturer; M.A., Goddard.
Nancy Gerber, Senior Lecturer; Psy.D., Immaculata.
Aaron Goldblatt, Adjunct Assistant Professor; M.F.A., Tyler.
Arlene Gostin, Associate Professor; M.A., Philadelphia College of Art.
Randy Granger, Adjunct Assistant Professor; B.F.A., Philadelphia College of Art.
James Green, Master Lecturer; M.L.S., Columbia, M.Ph., Yale.
Anthony Guido, Associate Professor; B.S.I.D., Ohio State.
Diane Hricko, Adjunct Assistant Professor; B.S., SUNY.
Jamer Hunt, Associate Professor; Ph.D., Rice.
Jeanne Jaffe, Professor; M.F.A., Alfred, College of Ceramics.
Lois M. Johnson, Professor; M.F.A., Wisconsin–Madison.
June Julian, Associate Professor; Ed.D., NYU.
Susan Kaye-Huntington, Adjunct Assistant Professor; Psy.D., Immaculata.
Nathan Knobler, Professor Emeritus; M.F.A., Florida State.
Peter Kruty, Master Lecturer; M.L.S., M.A., Alabama.
Hedi Kyle, Adjunct Professor; Dipl., Werk-Kunst Schule, Wiesbaden (Germany).
Sumi Maeshima, Senior Lecturer; M.F.A., University of the Arts.
Polly McKenna-Cress, Associate Professor; M.F.A., University of the Arts.
Jonas Milder, Associate Professor; M.I.D., Hochschule der Kuenste Berlin (Germany).
Slavko Milekic, Associate Professor; M.Sc., M.D., Belgrade (Yugoslavia); Ph.D., Connecticut.
Carol Moore, Associate Professor; M.F.A., Temple.
Eileen Neff, Adjunct Associate Professor; M.F.A., Temple.
Gerald Nichols, Professor; M.F.A., Pennsylvania.
Mary Phelan, Associate Professor; M.A., Wisconsin–Madison.
Amy Phillips-Iverson, Lecturer; M.A., University of the Arts.
Tom Porett, Professor; M.S., IIT.
Robin Rice, Adjunct Associate Professor; M.A., Missouri.
Susan Rodriguez, Adjunct Professor; M.Ed., Temple.
James Rosenthal, Senior Lecturer.
Barent Roth, Junior Lecturer; M.I.D., University of the Arts.
Pearl B. Schaeffer, Adjunct Associate Professor; M.F.A., University of the Arts.
Irene Sfakianos, Senior Lecturer; M.F.A., MIT.
Jennie Shanker, Adjunct Assistant Professor; M.F.A., Yale.
Patricia Smith, Associate Professor; M.A., Philadelphia College of Art.
Lori Spencer, Adjunct Associate Professor; M.F.A., University of the Arts.
Portia Hamilton Sperr, Adjunct Associate Professor; B.A., Barnard.
Patricia Stewart, Adjunct Associate Professor; B.A., Pennsylvania.
Barbara Suplee, Associate Professor; Ph.D., Penn State.
Jane Swanson, Lecturer; B.S., Iowa State.
Susan T. Viguers, Professor; Ph.D., Bryn Mawr.
Susan White, Senior Lecturer; M.F.A., University of the Arts.
Jo Ann Wright, Adjunct Assistant Professor; B.A., Rowan.
Mira Zergani, Senior Lecturer; B.A., Temple.

College of Performing Arts
Robert Brosh, Adjunct Associate Professor; D.A.., NYU.
Marc Dicciani, Professor; B.M., Philadelphia Musical Academy.
Annette DiMedio, Professor; Ph.D., Bryn Mawr.
William Garton, Senior Lecturer; M.A., Glassboro State.
Richard Genovese, Adjunct Assistant Professor; Certificate, Curtis.
Don Glanden, Professor; M.M., Rutgers.
Marjorie Goldberg, Senior Lecturer; B.M.E., Hartford (Hartt).
Patrick Jones, Head of M.A.T. Program; Ph.D., Penn State.
Michael Kennedy, Senior Lecturer; M.M., University of the Arts.
Ronald Kerber, Professor; B.M., Philadelphia College of the Performing Arts.
Jeffrey Kern, Associate Professor; M.M., Michigan.
Christopher Maute, Lecturer; B.M., University of the Arts.
Joseph Nero, Adjunct Associate Professor; Diploma, Curtis.
James Paxson, Adjunct Associate Professor.
Robert Quaile Jr., Senior Lecturer; B.M.E., Philadelphia Musical Academy.
Thomas Rudolph, Adjunct Assistant Professor; M.M., West Chester.
Gerald Veasley, Master Lecturer, B.A., Pennsylvania.
Gia Walton, Senior Lecturer; M.M., Temple.
Dennis Wasko, Adjunct Assistant Professor; B.M., Philadelphia College of the Performing Arts.

Section 4
Comparative and Interdisciplinary Arts

This section contains a directory of institutions offering graduate work in comparative and interdisciplinary arts. Additional information about programs listed in the directory may be obtained by writing directly to the dean of a graduate school or chair of a department at the address given in the directory.

For programs offering related work, see also in this book *Applied Arts and Design, Architecture, Art and Art History,* and *Performing Arts.* In another guide in this series:
Graduate Programs in Business, Education, Health, Information Studies, Law & Social Work
See *Subject Areas (Art Education)*

CONTENTS

Program Directory
Comparative and Interdisciplinary Arts   236

Comparative and Interdisciplinary Arts

Bradley University, Graduate School, Slane College of Communications and Fine Arts, Department of Art, Peoria, IL 61625-0002. Offers ceramics (MA, MFA); drawing/illustration (MA, MFA); interdisciplinary art (MA, MFA); painting (MA, MFA); photography (MA, MFA); printmaking (MA, MFA); sculpture (MA, MFA); visual communication and design (MA, MFA). *Accreditation:* NASAD. Part-time programs available. *Degree requirements:* For master's, comprehensive exam, thesis, final exhibit. *Entrance requirements:* For master's, portfolio, 2 letters of recommendation. Additional exam requirements/recommendations for international students: Required—TOEFL (minimum score 550 paper-based; 213 computer-based; 79 iBT).

Brigham Young University, Graduate Studies, College of Humanities, Department of Humanities, Classics, and Comparative Literature, Provo, UT 84602-1001. Offers comparative literature (MA); comparative studies (MA); humanities (MA). *Faculty:* 26 full-time (4 women). *Students:* 27 full-time (14 women). Average age 27. 15 applicants, 80% accepted, 6 enrolled. In 2008, 5 master's awarded. *Degree requirements:* For master's, 2 foreign languages, thesis. *Entrance requirements:* For master's, GRE, minimum GPA of 3.0 in last 60 hours. *Application deadline:* For fall admission, 3/1 for domestic and international students. Application fee: $50. Electronic applications accepted. *Expenses:* Tuition: Full-time $5160; part-time $287 per credit hour. Tuition and fees vary according to program and student's religious affiliation. *Financial support:* In 2008–09, 27 students received support, including 7 research assistantships (averaging $4,680 per year), 29 teaching assistantships; fellowships, career-related internships or fieldwork, institutionally sponsored loans, scholarships/grants, tuition waivers (full and partial), and student instructorships also available. Support available to part-time students. *Unit head:* Dr. Michael J. Call, Chair, 801-422-2550, Fax: 801-422-0305, E-mail: michael_call@byu.edu. *Application contact:* Carolyn Hone, Graduate Secretary for Humanities and Comparative Literature, 801-422-4430, Fax: 801-422-0305, E-mail: carolyn_hone@byu.edu.

Columbia College Chicago, Graduate School, Program in Interdisciplinary Arts, Chicago, IL 60605-1996. Offers interdisciplinary arts (MA); interdisciplinary book and paper arts (MFA). Part-time and evening/weekend programs available. *Students:* 53 full-time (43 women), 16 part-time (12 women); includes 6 minority (2 African Americans, 1 Asian American or Pacific Islander, 3 Hispanic Americans), 3 international. Average age 32. 35 applicants, 24 enrolled. In 2008, 22 master's awarded. *Degree requirements:* For master's, thesis. *Entrance requirements:* For master's, interview, minimum GPA of 3.0, portfolio, work sample. Additional exam requirements/recommendations for international students: Required—TOEFL (minimum score 550 paper-based; 213 computer-based). *Application deadline:* For fall admission, 2/2 for domestic and international students. Application fee: $55. Electronic applications accepted. *Expenses:* Tuition: Full-time $15,992; part-time $633 per credit hour. *Financial support:* Fellowships, career-related internships or fieldwork, Federal Work-Study, and scholarships/grants available. Support available to part-time students. Financial award application deadline: 8/13; financial award applicants required to submit FAFSA. *Unit head:* Michelle Citron, Department Chair, 312-369-7670, E-mail: mcitron@colum.edu. *Application contact:* Keith Cleveland, Office of Provost/Senior Vice President, 312-369-7261, Fax: 312-369-8022, E-mail: kcleveland@colum.edu.

Florida Atlantic University, Dorothy F. Schmidt College of Arts and Letters, Department of Comparative Studies, Boca Raton, FL 33431-0991. Offers PhD. Part-time programs available. *Students:* 36 full-time (27 women), 56 part-time (42 women); includes 17 minority (6 African Americans, 3 Asian Americans or Pacific Islanders, 8 Hispanic Americans), 9 international. Average age 44. 39 applicants, 49% accepted, 8 enrolled. In 2008, 8 doctorates awarded. *Degree requirements:* For doctorate, one foreign language, comprehensive exam, thesis/dissertation. *Entrance requirements:* For doctorate, GRE, minimum GPA of 3.5, 3 references. Additional exam requirements/recommendations for international students: Required—TOEFL. *Application deadline:* For fall admission, 2/1 priority date for domestic and international students. Applications are processed on a rolling basis. Application fee: $30. *Expenses:* Tuition, state resident: full-time $4867; part-time $270.40 per credit hour. Tuition, nonresident: full-time $16,486; part-time $915.87 per credit hour. *Financial support:* Teaching assistantships with tuition reimbursements available. *Faculty research:* Arts, humanities, social sciences. *Unit head:* Dr. Emily Stockard, Interim Director, 561-297-2817, Fax: 561-297-2058, E-mail: stockard@fau.edu. *Application contact:* Dr. Emily Stockard, Interim Director, 561-297-2817, Fax: 561-297-2058, E-mail: stockard@fau.edu.

Goddard College, Graduate Programs, Master of Fine Arts in Interdisciplinary Arts Program, Plainfield, VT 05667-9432. Offers MFA. Postbaccalaureate distance learning degree programs offered (minimal on-campus study). *Faculty:* 17 part-time/adjunct (13 women). *Students:* 98 full-time. Average age 42. 45 applicants, 73% accepted, 32 enrolled. *Degree requirements:* For master's, thesis. *Entrance requirements:* For master's, relevant undergraduate degree, transcripts, three letters of recommendation, study plan and resource list, interview, portfolio. *Application deadline:* Applications are processed on a rolling basis. Application fee: $40. Electronic applications accepted. *Expenses:* Tuition: Full-time $14,446. Full-time tuition and fees vary according to campus/location and program. Part-time tuition and fees vary according to course load and program. *Financial support:* In 2008–09, 90 students received support. Applicants required to submit FAFSA. *Unit head:* Prof. Bonnie Schock, Co-Director, 802-454-8311, Fax: 802-454-7835, E-mail: bonnie.schock@goddard.edu. *Application contact:* Phillip Robertson, Admissions Counselor, 800-906-8312 Ext. 221, Fax: 802-454-1029, E-mail: phillip.robertson@goddard.edu.

John F. Kennedy University, Graduate School of Holistic Studies, Department of Arts and Consciousness, Program in Transformative Arts, Pleasant Hill, CA 94523-4817. Offers MA. Part-time and evening/weekend programs available. *Degree requirements:* For master's, thesis or alternative. *Entrance requirements:* For master's, interview. Additional exam requirements/recommendations for international students: Required—TOEFL. *Expenses:* Contact institution.

Ohio University, Graduate College, College of Fine Arts, School of Interdisciplinary Arts, Athens, OH 45701-2979. Offers PhD. *Degree requirements:* For doctorate, 2 foreign languages, comprehensive exam, thesis/dissertation. *Entrance requirements:* For doctorate, GRE, MAT, master's degree. Additional exam requirements/recommendations for international students: Required—TOEFL. Electronic applications accepted. *Faculty research:* Comparative studies of theater, music, and the visual arts.

Simon Fraser University, Graduate Studies, Faculty of Arts and Social Sciences, School for the Contemporary Arts, Burnaby, BC V5A 1S6, Canada. Offers MFA. *Degree requirements:* For master's, thesis or alternative. *Entrance requirements:* For master's, minimum GPA of 3.0. Additional exam requirements/recommendations for international students: Required—TOEFL or IELTS. *Faculty research:* Dance theory, screenplays, drawing and painting, acting, electroacoustic music.

Section 5
Film, Television, and Video

This section contains a directory of institutions offering graduate work in film, television, and video, followed by in-depth entries submitted by institutions that chose to prepare detailed program descriptions. Additional information about programs listed in the directory but not augmented by an in-depth entry may be obtained by writing directly to the dean of a graduate school or chair of a department at the address given in the directory.

For programs offering related work, see also in this book *Art and Art History* and *Communication and Media*. In the other guides in this series:

Graduate Programs in Engineering & Applied Sciences
See *Telecommunications*
Graduate Programs in Business, Education, Health, Information Studies, Law & Social Work
See *Advertising and Public Relations*

CONTENTS

Program Directories

Film, Television, and Video Production 238
Film, Television, and Video Theory and Criticism 243

Close-Ups

See:
American University—Communication 681
Art Center College of Design—Design 115
Boston University—Communication 683
California College of the Arts—Art, Architecture, Design, and Writing 207
Columbia University—Film, Theater Arts, Visual Arts, and Writing 285
Miami International University of Art & Design—Art and Design 121
San Francisco Art Institute—Fine Arts 221
Savannah College of Art and Design—Art and Design 223
School of the Art Institute of Chicago—Graduate Studies in Art 225
University of Denver—Communication 707

Film, Television, and Video Production

Academy of Art University, Graduate Program, School of Animation and Visual Effects, San Francisco, CA 94105-3410. Offers 2D animation (MFA); 3D animation (MFA); 3D modeling (MFA); games (MFA); visual effects (MFA). Part-time programs available. Postbaccalaureate distance learning degree programs offered (no on-campus study). *Faculty:* 18 full-time (3 women), 45 part-time/adjunct (12 women). *Students:* 497 full-time (172 women), 200 part-time (73 women); includes 123 minority (31 African Americans, 3 American Indian/Alaska Native, 52 Asian Americans or Pacific Islanders, 37 Hispanic Americans), 362 international. Average age 28. 182 applicants. In 2008, 75 master's awarded. *Degree requirements:* For master's, final review. *Entrance requirements:* For master's, portfolio. *Application deadline:* For fall admission, 9/7 for domestic and international students; for spring admission, 2/2 for domestic and international students. Applications are processed on a rolling basis. Application fee: $100 ($500 for international students). Electronic applications accepted. *Expenses:* Tuition: Full-time $18,400; part-time $770 per term. Tuition and fees vary according to program. *Financial support:* Career-related internships or fieldwork and Federal Work-Study available. Support available to part-time students. Financial award application deadline: 8/10; financial award applicants required to submit FAFSA. *Unit head:* Tom Bertine, Director of Animation 3D, 800-544-ARTS, Fax: 415-263-4130, E-mail: info@academyart.edu. *Application contact:* Information Contact, 800-544-ARTS, Fax: 415-263-4130, E-mail: info@academyart.edu.

Academy of Art University, Graduate Program, School of Motion Pictures and Television, San Francisco, CA 94105-3410. Offers MFA. Part-time programs available. Postbaccalaureate distance learning degree programs offered (no on-campus study). *Faculty:* 6 full-time (2 women), 36 part-time/adjunct (12 women). *Students:* 185 full-time (71 women), 79 part-time (34 women); includes 62 minority (24 African Americans, 5 American Indian/Alaska Native, 15 Asian Americans or Pacific Islanders, 18 Hispanic Americans), 75 international. Average age 30. 73 applicants. In 2008, 12 master's awarded. *Degree requirements:* For master's, final review. *Entrance requirements:* For master's, portfolio. *Application deadline:* For fall admission, 9/7 for domestic and international students; for spring admission, 2/2 for domestic and international students. Applications are processed on a rolling basis. Application fee: $100 ($500 for international students). Electronic applications accepted. *Expenses:* Tuition: Full-time $18,400; part-time $770 per term. Tuition and fees vary according to program. *Financial support:* Career-related internships or fieldwork and Federal Work-Study available. Support available to part-time students. Financial award application deadline: 8/10; financial award applicants required to submit FAFSA. *Unit head:* Diane Baker, Director, 800-544-ARTS, E-mail: info@academyart.edu. *Application contact:* 800-544-ARTS, Fax: 415-263-4130, E-mail: info@academyart.edu.

American Film Institute Conservatory, Graduate Program, Los Angeles, CA 90027-1657. Offers cinematography (MFA); directing (MFA); editing (MFA); producing (MFA); production design (MFA); screenwriting (MFA). *Faculty:* 45 full-time (6 women), 64 part-time/adjunct (18 women). *Students:* 357 full-time (117 women); includes 65 minority (19 African Americans, 1 American Indian/Alaska Native, 21 Asian Americans or Pacific Islanders, 24 Hispanic Americans), 105 international. Average age 26. 651 applicants, 31% accepted, 140 enrolled. In 2008, 120 master's awarded. *Degree requirements:* For master's, thesis, production of film or screenplay, portfolio piece. *Entrance requirements:* For master's, portfolio, resumé, letters of recommendation, interview. Additional exam requirements/recommendations for international students: Required—TOEFL (minimum score 600 paper-based; 250 computer-based; 100 iBT). *Application deadline:* For fall admission, 12/1 for domestic and international students. Application fee: $75. *Expenses:* Tuition: Full-time $34,150. Required fees: $2300. *Financial support:* In 2008–09, 95 students received support, including 18 teaching assistantships with partial tuition reimbursements available (averaging $3,000 per year); career-related internships or fieldwork, scholarships/grants, and unspecified assistantships also available. Financial award application deadline: 4/15; financial award applicants required to submit FAFSA. *Faculty research:* Film production, TV production. *Unit head:* Robert Mandel, Dean, 323-856-7600, Fax: 323-467-4578. *Application contact:* Angela Wheaton, Admissions Counselor, 323-856-7842, Fax: 323-856-7720, E-mail: awheaton@afi.com.

American University, School of Communication, Film and Electronic Media Program, Washington, DC 20016-8001. Offers MFA. *Faculty:* 14 full-time (6 women). *Students:* 34 full-time (16 women), 39 part-time (19 women). 51 applicants, 73% accepted, 22 enrolled. In 2008, 141 master's awarded. *Degree requirements:* For master's, comprehensive exam, thesis or alternative. *Entrance requirements:* For master's, GRE General Test. Additional exam requirements/recommendations for international students: Required—TOEFL (minimum score 600 paper-based; 250 computer-based). *Application deadline:* For fall admission, 2/1 priority date for domestic and international students; for spring admission, 11/15 for domestic and international students. Applications are processed on a rolling basis. Application fee: $50. Electronic applications accepted. *Expenses:* Tuition: Full-time $21,204; part-time $1178 per credit hour. Required fees: $380. Part-time tuition and fees vary according to course load and program. *Financial support:* In 2008–09, 10 students received support, including 2 fellowships with partial tuition reimbursements available (averaging $13,000 per year), 2 research assistantships with partial tuition reimbursements available (averaging $11,000 per year), 4 teaching assistantships with partial tuition reimbursements available (averaging $11,000 per year); career-related internships or fieldwork, Federal Work-Study, institutionally sponsored loans, scholarships/grants, tuition waivers (partial), and unspecified assistantships also available. Financial award application deadline: 2/1. *Faculty research:* Documentary film production, social media, media and public policy, visual literacy, new technology. *Unit head:* Prof. John Douglass, Director, Film and Media Arts Division, 202-885-2045, Fax: 202-885-2019, E-mail: jdougla@american.edu. *Application contact:* Sharmeen Ahsan-Bracciale, Graduate Admissions Office, 202-885-2040, Fax: 202-885-2019, E-mail: sharmeen@american.edu.

American University, School of Communication, Film and Video Program, Washington, DC 20016-8001. Offers film and video (MA); producing film and video (MA). Part-time and evening/weekend programs available. *Faculty:* 14 full-time (6 women). *Students:* 14 full-time (4 women), 29 part-time (12 women). 95 applicants, 56% accepted, 32 enrolled. In 2008, 29 master's awarded. *Degree requirements:* For master's, comprehensive exam, thesis or alternative. *Entrance requirements:* For master's, GRE General Test. Additional exam requirements/recommendations for international students: Required—TOEFL (minimum score 660 paper-based; 250 computer-based). *Application deadline:* For fall admission, 2/1 priority date for domestic and international students; for spring admission, 11/15 for domestic and international students. Applications are processed on a rolling basis. Application fee: $50. Electronic applications accepted. *Expenses:* Tuition: Full-time $21,204; part-time $1178 per credit hour. Required fees: $380. Part-time tuition and fees vary according to course load and program. *Financial support:* In 2008–09, 2 research assistantships with partial tuition reimbursements (averaging $11,000 per year), 4 teaching assistantships with partial tuition reimbursements (averaging $11,000 per year) were awarded; career-related internships or fieldwork, Federal Work-Study, institutionally sponsored loans, scholarships/grants, tuition waivers (partial), and unspecified assistantships also available. Financial award application deadline: 2/1. *Faculty research:* Documentary film and video production, visual literacy, Eastern European cinema, media and public policy, social media. *Unit head:* Prof. John Douglass, Director, Film and Media Arts Division, 202-885-2045, Fax: 202-885-2019, E-mail: jdougla@american.edu. *Application contact:* Sharmeen Ahsan-Bracciale, Graduate Admissions Office, 202-885-2040, Fax: 202-885-2019, E-mail: sharmeen@american.edu.

See Close-Up on page 681.

American University, School of Communication, Weekend Programs in Communication, Washington, DC 20016-8001. Offers interactive journalism (MA); news media studies (MA); producing for film and video (MA); public communication (MA). *Accreditation:* ACEJMC. Part-time and evening/weekend programs available. *Faculty:* 5 part-time/adjunct (2 women). *Students:* 112 part-time (75 women). 137 applicants, 61% accepted, 61 enrolled. In 2008, 15 master's awarded. *Degree requirements:* For master's, comprehensive exam, thesis or alternative. *Entrance requirements:* Additional exam requirements/recommendations for international students: Required—TOEFL (minimum score 600 paper-based; 250 computer-based). *Application deadline:* For fall admission, 8/1 for domestic students. Applications are processed on a rolling basis. Application fee: $50. Electronic applications accepted. *Expenses:* Tuition: Full-time $21,204; part-time $1178 per credit hour. Required fees: $380. Part-time tuition and fees vary according to course load and program. *Financial support:* In 2008–09, 3 fellowships (averaging $3,500 per year) were awarded; institutionally sponsored loans also available. *Unit head:* Wendell Cochran, Journalism Weekend Program Director, 202-885-2075, E-mail: cochran@american.edu. *Application contact:* Sharmeen Ahsan-Bracciale, Graduate Admissions Office, 202-885-2040, Fax: 202-885-2019, E-mail: sharmeen@american.edu.

See Close-Up on page 681.

Antioch University McGregor, Graduate Programs, Individualized Liberal and Professional Studies Program, Yellow Springs, OH 45387-1609. Offers liberal and professional studies (MA), including counseling, creative writing, education, film studies, liberal studies, management, modern literature, psychology, theatre, visual arts. Part-time and evening/weekend programs available. Postbaccalaureate distance learning degree programs offered (minimal on-campus study). *Degree requirements:* For master's, thesis or alternative. *Entrance requirements:* For master's, resumé, 2 letters of reference. Electronic applications accepted. *Expenses:* Contact institution.

Arizona State University, Graduate College, College of Liberal Arts and Sciences, Division of Humanities, Program in Film and Media Studies, Tempe, AZ 85287. Offers American media and popular culture (MAS); film analysis (MLS); screenwriting (MAS).

Art Center College of Design, Graduate Division, Broadcast Cinema Department, Pasadena, CA 91103-1999. Offers MFA. *Accreditation:* NASAD. *Degree requirements:* For master's, thesis, studio project. *Entrance requirements:* For master's, portfolio. Additional exam requirements/recommendations for international students: Required—TOEFL (minimum score 100 iBT).

See Close-Up on page 115.

The Art Institute of California–San Francisco, Master of Fine Arts Program, San Francisco, CA 94102-4908. Offers computer animation (MFA).

Bob Jones University, Graduate Programs, Greenville, SC 29614. Offers accountancy (MS); Bible (MA); Bible translation (MA); Biblical studies (Certificate); broadcast management (MS); business administration (MBA); church history (MA, PhD); church ministries (MA); church music (MM); cinema and video production (MA); counseling (MS); curriculum and instruction (Ed D); divinity (M Div); dramatic production (MA); educational leadership (MS, Ed D, Ed S); elementary education (M Ed, MAT); English (M Ed, MA, MAT); fine arts (MA); graphic design (MA); history (M Ed, MA); illustration (MA); interpretative speech (MA); mathematics (M Ed, MAT); medical missions (Certificate); ministry (MM, D Min); multi-categorical special education (M Ed, MAT); music (M Ed); New Testament interpretation (PhD); Old Testament interpretation (PhD); orchestral instrument performance (MM); organ performance (MM); pastoral studies (MA); personnel services (MS, Ed S); piano pedagogy (MM); piano performance (MM); platform arts (MA); radio and television broadcasting (MS); rhetoric and public address (MA); secondary education (M Ed); studio art (MA); teaching Bible (MA); theology (MA, PhD); voice performance (MM); youth ministries (MA); M Div/MM.

Boston University, College of Communication, Department of Film and Television, Boston, MA 02215. Offers film production (MFA); film studies (MFA); screenwriting (MFA); television (MS); television management (MS); MBA/MS. *Degree requirements:* For master's, thesis. *Entrance requirements:* For master's, GMAT (MS in television management), GRE General Test, sample of written or creative work. Additional exam requirements/recommendations for international students: Required—TOEFL. Electronic applications accepted.

See Close-Up on page 683.

Bowling Green State University, Graduate College, College of Arts and Sciences, Department of Theatre and Film, Bowling Green, OH 43403. Offers MA, PhD. *Accreditation:* NAST. Part-time programs available. Terminal master's awarded for partial completion of doctoral program. *Degree requirements:* For master's, thesis or alternative; for doctorate, comprehensive exam, thesis/dissertation, 9 hour research tool. *Entrance requirements:* For master's and doctorate, GRE General Test. Additional exam requirements/recommendations for international students: Required—TOEFL. Electronic applications accepted. *Faculty research:* Theatre history, dramatic theory, cultural studies, performance studies, American theatre history.

Brigham Young University, Graduate Studies, College of Fine Arts and Communications, Department of Theatre and Media Arts, Provo, UT 84602-6404. Offers MA. MFA program accepts applications in odd-numbered years only. *Accreditation:* NAST. *Faculty:* 14 full-time (5 women). *Students:* 17 full-time (12 women), 1 part-time (0 women). Average age 34. In 2008, 6 master's awarded. *Degree requirements:* For master's, comprehensive exam, thesis, 32 hours, oral defense. *Entrance requirements:* For master's, GRE General Test, writing samples. Additional exam requirements/recommendations for international students: Required—TOEFL (minimum score 580 paper-based; 237 computer-based; 85 iBT). *Application deadline:* For fall admission, 2/1 priority date for domestic and international students. Application fee: $50. Electronic applications accepted. *Expenses:* Tuition: Full-time $5160; part-time $287 per credit hour. Tuition and fees vary according to program and student's religious affiliation. *Financial support:* In 2008–09, 18 students received support, including 3 research assistantships with partial tuition reimbursements available (averaging $3,500 per year), 12 teaching assistantships with partial tuition reimbursements available (averaging $3,500 per year); career-related internships or fieldwork, institutionally sponsored loans, scholarships/grants, health care benefits, tuition waivers (partial), unspecified assistantships, and administrative aides also available. Support available to part-time students. *Faculty research:* Media literacy, children's media, popular culture, theatre historiography, performance studies. *Unit head:* Dr. Rodger D. Sorensen, Department Chair, 801-422-8132, Fax: 801-422-0654, E-mail: rodger_sorensen@byu.edu. *Application contact:* Kim Poole, Secretary, 801-422-3750, Fax: 801-422-0654, E-mail: kim_poole@byu.edu.

Brooklyn College of the City University of New York, Division of Graduate Studies, Department of Television and Radio, Brooklyn, NY 11210-2889. Offers television and radio (MS); television production (MFA). MFA applicants admitted in fall of even-numbered years. Part-time and evening/weekend programs available. *Students:* 14 full-time (6 women), 38 part-time (19 women); includes 20 minority (16 African Americans, 2 Asian Americans or Pacific Islanders, 2 Hispanic Americans), 20 international. Average age 31. 33 applicants, 73% accepted, 14 enrolled. In 2008, 16 master's awarded. *Degree requirements:* For master's, comprehensive exam. *Entrance requirements:* For master's, GRE General Test or MAT, 12 credits in television/radio with a minimum B average, 2 letters of recommendation. *Application deadline:* For fall admission, 3/1 priority date for domestic students, 2/1 priority date for international students; for spring admission, 11/1 priority date for domestic students, 10/1 priority date for international students. Applications are processed on a rolling basis. Application fee: $125. Electronic applications accepted. *Expenses:* Tuition, state resident: full-time $7360; part-time $310 per credit hour. Tuition, nonresident: full-time $13,800; part-time $575 per credit hour. *Financial support:* Career-related internships or fieldwork, Federal Work-Study, and institutionally sponsored loans available. Support available to part-time students. Financial award application deadline: 5/1; financial award applicants required to submit FAFSA. *Faculty research:* Criticism, research methods, audience behavior, policy and regulation, program history, international television and radio. *Unit head:* Dr. George Rodman, Chairperson, 718-951-5555, E-mail: grodman@brooklyn.cuny.edu. *Application contact:* Hernan Sierra, Graduate Admissions Coordinator, 718-951-4536, Fax: 718-951-4506, E-mail: grads@brooklyn.cuny.edu.

California College of the Arts, Graduate Programs, Programs in Fine Art, San Francisco, CA 94107. Offers ceramics (MFA); film/video/performance (MFA); glass (MFA); jewelry/metal arts (MFA); painting/drawing (MFA); photography (MFA); printmaking (MFA); sculpture (MFA); textiles (MFA); wood/furniture (MFA). *Accreditation:* NASAD. *Degree requirements:* For master's, thesis, exhibit. *Entrance requirements:* For master's, appropriate bachelor's degree, portfolio. Additional exam requirements/recommendations for international students: Required—TOEFL (minimum score 600 paper-based; 250 computer-based). Electronic applications accepted.

California Institute of the Arts, School of Film/Video, Valencia, CA 91355-2340. Offers experimental animation (MFA); film directing (MFA, Adv C); film/video (Adv C). *Entrance requirements:* For master's, portfolio. Additional exam requirements/recommendations for international students: Required—TOEFL. Electronic applications accepted. *Faculty research:* Experimental and character animation, experimental film/video, video graphics.

California State University, Fullerton, Graduate Studies, College of the Arts, Department of Theatre and Dance, Fullerton, CA 92834-9480. Offers acting (MFA); acting and directing (MA); dance (MA); directing (MFA); dramatic literature/criticism (MA); oral interpretation (MA); playwriting (MA); technical theater (MA); technical theater and design (MFA); television (MA); theatre for children (MA); theatre history (MA). *Accreditation:* NASD; NAST (one or more programs are accredited). Part-time programs available. *Students:* 21 full-time (10 women), 3 part-time (2 women); includes 2 minority (both African Americans). Average age 29. 43 applicants, 26% accepted, 11 enrolled. In 2008, 3 master's awarded. *Degree requirements:* For master's, oral and written exam, project or thesis. *Entrance requirements:* For master's, major in theatre or related field, audition or interview, minimum GPA of 2.5 in last 60 units of course work. Application fee: $55. Tuition and fees vary according to degree level. *Financial support:* Teaching assistantships, career-related internships or fieldwork, Federal Work-Study, institutionally sponsored loans, and scholarships/grants available. Support available to part-time students. Financial award application deadline: 3/1. *Unit head:* Dr. Susan Hallman, Chair, 657-278-3628. *Application contact:* Gretchen Kanne, Adviser, 657-278-3628.

California State University, Los Angeles, Graduate Studies, College of Arts and Letters, Department of Communication Studies, Los Angeles, CA 90032-8530. Offers speech communication (MA); television, film and theatre (MFA). Part-time and evening/weekend programs available. *Faculty:* 12 full-time (3 women). *Students:* 64 full-time (37 women), 40 part-time (32 women); includes 47 minority (15 African Americans, 1 American Indian/Alaska Native, 13 Asian Americans or Pacific Islanders, 18 Hispanic Americans), 18 international. Average age 30. 88 applicants, 92% accepted, 47 enrolled. In 2008, 8 master's awarded. *Degree requirements:* For master's, comprehensive exam or thesis. *Entrance requirements:* For master's, minimum GPA of 2.75 in last 90 units of course work. Additional exam requirements/recommendations for international students: Required—TOEFL (minimum score 500 paper-based; 173 computer-based). *Application deadline:* For fall admission, 6/15 for domestic students, 5/1 for international students; for winter admission, 11/1 for domestic students, 9/1 for international students; for spring admission, 2/1 for domestic students, 10/1 for international students. Applications are processed on a rolling basis. Application fee: $55. Electronic applications accepted. *Expenses:* Tuition, nonresident: part-time $226 per credit. Required fees: $4019. *Financial support:* Career-related internships or fieldwork and Federal Work-Study available. Support available to part-time students. Financial award application deadline: 3/1. *Faculty research:* Organizational, interpersonal, intercultural, and instructional communication; rhetorical theories. *Unit head:* Dr. John Ramirez, Chair, 323-343-4200, Fax: 323-343-6467, E-mail: jramire4@calstatela.edu. *Application contact:* Dr. Jose L. Galvan, Dean of Graduate Studies, 323-343-3820, Fax: 323-343-5653, E-mail: jgalvan@cslanet.calstatela.edu.

California State University, Northridge, Graduate Studies, College of Arts, Media, and Communication, Department of Cinema and Television Arts, Northridge, CA 91330. Offers screenwriting (MA). *Faculty:* 2 part-time/adjunct. *Students:* 20 full-time (5 women), 21 part-time (8 women); includes 2 African Americans, 1 American Indian/Alaska Native, 3 Hispanic Americans, 2 international. Average age 35. 69 applicants, 36% accepted, 18 enrolled. In 2008, 11 master's awarded. *Entrance requirements:* For master's, GRE if cumulative undergraduate GPA below 3.0. *Unit head:* Robert Gustafson, Chair, 818-677-3192, E-mail: robert.gustafson@csun.edu. *Application contact:* Robert Gustafson, Chair, 818-677-3192, E-mail: robert.gustafson@csun.edu.

Carleton University, Faculty of Graduate Studies, Faculty of Arts and Social Sciences, School for Studies in Art and Culture, Program in Film Studies, Ottawa, ON K1S 5B6, Canada. Offers MA. *Degree requirements:* For master's, thesis. *Entrance requirements:* For master's, honors degree. Additional exam requirements/recommendations for international students: Required—TOEFL.

Carnegie Mellon University, School of Computer Science and College of Fine Arts, Program in Entertainment Technology, Pittsburgh, PA 15213-3891. Offers MET.

Central Michigan University, College of Graduate Studies, College of Communication and Fine Arts, School of Broadcasting and Cinematic Arts, Mount Pleasant, MI 48859. Offers electronic media management (MA); electronic media studies (MA); film theory and criticism (MA); media production (MA). Part-time programs available. *Faculty:* 12 full-time (2 women). *Students:* 23 (8 women); includes 1 African American, 1 Asian American or Pacific Islander, 1 Hispanic American. Average age 26. *Degree requirements:* For master's, thesis or alternative. *Entrance requirements:* For master's, undergraduate degree in broadcasting, film studies, or an associated discipline with minimum GPA of 2.7. *Application deadline:* Applications are processed on a rolling basis. Application fee: $35 ($45 for international students). Electronic applications accepted. *Expenses:* Tuition, state resident: full-time $3717; part-time $413 per credit. Tuition, nonresident: full-time $6894; part-time $766 per credit. *Financial support:* Fellowships with tuition reimbursements, teaching assistantships with tuition reimbursements, career-related internships or fieldwork, Federal Work-Study, unspecified assistantships, and out-of-state merit awards available. Financial award application deadline: 3/7. *Faculty research:* Multimedia production, film history and criticism, writing and promotions, international broadcasting and media systems, history of American broadcasting. *Unit head:* Dr. Peter B. Orlik, Chairperson, 989-774-3851, Fax: 989-774-2426, E-mail: peter.b.orlik@cmich.edu. *Application contact:* Dr. Patricia Williamson, Graduate Program Coordinator, 989-774-2561, Fax: 989-774-2426, E-mail: willi1pa@cmich.edu.

Chapman University, Graduate Studies, Dodge College of Film and Media Arts, Conservatory of Motion Pictures, Orange, CA 92866. Offers film and television producing (MFA); film production (MFA); film studies (MA); production design (MFA); screenwriting (MFA); JD/MFA; MBA/MFA. Part-time and evening/weekend programs available. *Faculty:* 34 full-time (7 women), 52 part-time/adjunct (16 women). *Students:* 230 full-time (86 women), 11 part-time (3 women); includes 31 minority (8 African Americans, 2 American Indian/Alaska Native, 7 Asian Americans or Pacific Islanders, 14 Hispanic Americans), 40 international. Average age 27. 342 applicants, 44% accepted, 85 enrolled. In 2008, 76 master's awarded. *Degree requirements:* For master's, thesis. *Entrance requirements:* For master's, GRE General Test, minimum undergraduate GPA of 2.5, portfolio. Additional exam requirements/recommendations for international students: Required—TOEFL (minimum score 550 paper-based). *Application deadline:* For fall admission, 3/1 priority date for domestic students. Application fee: $55. Electronic applications accepted. *Expenses:* Contact institution. *Financial support:* Fellowships, Federal Work-Study and scholarships/grants available. Financial award application deadline: 6/30; financial award applicants required to submit FAFSA. *Unit head:* Joseph Slowensky, Director, 714-744-7882, E-mail: jslowens@chapman.edu. *Application contact:* Jojo Delfin, Information Contact, 714-997-6786, E-mail: delfin@chapman.edu.

Chatham University, Program in Film and Digital Technology, Pittsburgh, PA 15232-2826. Offers emerging media (MFA). Part-time and evening/weekend programs available. *Students:* 9 full-time (6 women), 2 part-time (0 women). Average age 35. 16 applicants, 88% accepted, 10 enrolled. *Degree requirements:* For master's, thesis, capstone project. *Entrance requirements:* Additional exam requirements/recommendations for international students: Required—TOEFL (minimum score 600 paper-based; 250 computer-based; 100 iBT), IELTS (minimum score 6.5), TWE. *Application deadline:* For fall admission, 7/1 priority date for domestic students, 6/1 priority date for international students; for spring admission, 12/1 priority date for domestic students, 11/1 priority date for international students. Applications are processed on a rolling basis. Application fee: $45. Electronic applications accepted. *Expenses:* Tuition: Part-time $686 per credit. Tuition and fees vary according to program. *Financial support:* Applicants required to submit FAFSA. *Unit head:* Dr. Prajna Parasher, Director, 412-365-1182, E-mail: parasher@chatham.edu. *Application contact:* Dory Perry, Associate Director of Graduate Admissions, 412-365-2758, Fax: 412-365-1609, E-mail: gradadmissions@chatham.edu.

Columbia College Chicago, Graduate School, Department of Film and Video, Chicago, IL 60605-1996. Offers MFA. Part-time programs available. *Students:* 29 full-time (14 women), 30 part-time (19 women); includes 11 minority (8 African Americans, 1 Asian American or Pacific Islander, 2 Hispanic Americans), 3 international. Average age 32. 67 applicants, 10 enrolled. In 2008, 6 master's awarded. *Degree requirements:* For master's, thesis, film project. *Entrance requirements:* For master's, interview, minimum GPA of 3.0, portfolio or script. Additional exam requirements/recommendations for international students: Required—TOEFL (minimum score 550 paper-based; 213 computer-based). *Application deadline:* For fall admission, 1/5 for domestic and international students. Application fee: $55. Electronic applications accepted. *Expenses:* Tuition: Full-time $15,992; part-time $633 per credit hour. *Financial support:* Fellowships, career-related internships or fieldwork, Federal Work-Study, scholarships/grants, and unspecified assistantships available. Support available to part-time students. Financial award application deadline: 8/13; financial award applicants required to submit FAFSA. *Unit head:* Dr. Bruce Sheridan, Chairperson, 312-369-6710, Fax: 312-369-8044, E-mail: bsheridan@colum.edu. *Application contact:* Keith Cleveland, Office of Provost/Senior Vice President, 312-369-7261, Fax: 312-369-8022, E-mail: kcleveland@colum.edu.

Columbia University, School of the Arts, Film Division, New York, NY 10027. Offers directing (MFA); film studies (MA); producing (MFA); screen writing (MFA). *Degree requirements:* For master's, thesis. *Entrance requirements:* For master's, 3 letters of recommendation, writing sample, complete a scene, feature film treatment (optional visual submission). Additional exam requirements/recommendations for international students: Required—TOEFL (minimum score 600 paper-based; 250 computer-based; 100 iBT). Electronic applications accepted.

See Close-Up on page 285.

Concordia University, School of Graduate Studies, Faculty of Fine Arts, Department of Studio Arts, Montréal, QC H3G 1M8, Canada. Offers studio arts (MFA), including film production, open media, painting, photography, print media, sculpture, ceramics and fibers. *Degree requirements:* For master's, thesis or alternative. *Entrance requirements:* For master's, portfolio.

Concordia University, School of Graduate Studies, Faculty of Fine Arts, Mel Hoppenheim School of Cinema, Montréal, QC H3G 1M8, Canada. Offers film studies (MA).

Drexel University, College of Media Arts and Design, Philadelphia, PA 19104-2875. Offers design (MS), including digital media, fashion design, interior design, television management; media arts (MS); performing arts (MS), including arts administration; MS/MBA. *Accreditation:* NASAD. Part-time and evening/weekend programs available. *Entrance requirements:* For master's, interview. Additional exam requirements/recommendations for international students: Required—TOEFL. Electronic applications accepted. *Expenses:* Contact institution.

Drexel University, College of Media Arts and Design, Department of Design, Program in Television Management, Philadelphia, PA 19104-2875. Offers MS, MS/MBA.

Florida Atlantic University, Dorothy F. Schmidt College of Arts and Letters, School of Communication and Multimedia Studies, Boca Raton, FL 33431-0991. Offers communication studies (MA); film and video (Certificate); film studies (MA); multimedia journalism studies (MA). Part-time programs available. *Faculty:* 21 full-time (10 women), 14 part-time/adjunct (3 women). *Students:* 15 full-time (11 women), 10 part-time (5 women); includes 2 minority (1 Asian American or Pacific Islander, 1 Hispanic American), 3 international. Average age 29. 35 applicants, 37% accepted, 7 enrolled. In 2008, 8 master's awarded. *Degree requirements:* For master's, one foreign language, comprehensive exam (for some programs), thesis (for some programs). *Entrance requirements:* For master's, GRE General Test, minimum GPA of 3.0. *Application deadline:* For fall admission, 7/1 priority date for domestic students, 4/1 for international students; for spring admission, 11/1 for domestic students, 10/1 for international students. Applications are processed on a rolling basis. Application fee: $30. Electronic applications accepted. *Expenses:* Tuition, state resident: full-time $4867; part-time $270.40 per credit hour. Tuition, nonresident: full-time $16,486; part-time $915.87 per credit hour. *Financial support:* Teaching assistantships with partial tuition reimbursements, Federal Work-Study and institutionally sponsored loans available. Support available to part-time students. Financial award application deadline: 3/1. *Faculty research:* Cultural studies, gender studies, film, communication theory, journalism, new media. *Unit head:* Dr. Susan S. Reilly, Director, 561-297-1095, Fax: 561-297-2615, E-mail: sreilly@fau.edu. *Application contact:* Dr. Eric M. Freedman, Graduate Coordinator, 561-297-2534, Fax: 561-297-2615, E-mail: efreedma@fau.edu.

Florida State University, Graduate Studies, College of Motion Picture, Television, and Recording Arts, Tallahassee, FL 32306. Offers production (MFA); screen and play writing (MFA). *Degree requirements:* For master's, thesis, thesis project. *Entrance requirements:* For master's, GRE General Test, minimum GPA of 3.0, film/video experience. Additional exam requirements/recommendations for international students: Required—TOEFL (minimum score 550 paper-based; 253 computer-based; 80 iBT). *Faculty research:* Producing, screenwriting, directing, cinematography, editing.

George Mason University, College of Humanities and Social Sciences, Interdisciplinary Studies Program, Fairfax, VA 22030. Offers anthropology (MAIS); community college teaching (MAIS); folklore (MAIS); higher education (MAIS); individualized studies (MAIS); religion, cultures, and values (MAIS); video-based production (MAIS); women's studies (MAIS); zoo and aquarium leadership (MAIS). Part-time and evening/weekend programs available. *Degree requirements:* For master's, thesis optional. *Entrance requirements:* For master's, GRE, GMAT, or MAT, interview, minimum GPA of 3.0 in last 60 hours of course work. Electronic applications accepted.

Georgia State University, College of Arts and Sciences, Department of Communication, Atlanta, GA 30303-3083. Offers film/video/digital imaging (MA); human communication and social influence (MA); mass communication (MA); moving image studies (PhD); public communication (PhD). Part-time programs available. *Degree requirements:* For master's, one foreign language, thesis or alternative; for doctorate, comprehensive exam, thesis/dissertation. *Entrance requirements:* For master's and doctorate, GRE General Test. Additional exam requirements/recommendations for international students: Required—TOEFL (minimum score 80 computer-based). Electronic applications accepted. *Faculty research:* Critical/cultural studies, rhetoric studies, film/media studies, mass communications/journalism, audience studies.

Hofstra University, School of Communication, Department of Radio/Television/Film, Hempstead, NY 11549. Offers documentary studies and production (MFA), including documentary studies and production. Part-time and evening/weekend programs available. *Faculty:* 2 full-time (1 woman), 1 (woman) part-time/adjunct. *Students:* 6 full-time (2 women), 3 part-time (1 woman); includes 2 minority (1 Asian American or Pacific Islander, 1 Hispanic American). Average age 29. 18 applicants, 94% accepted, 6 enrolled. *Degree requirements:* For master's, thesis, thesis project. *Entrance requirements:* For master's, 2 letters of recommendation, essay, portfolio,

Film, Television, and Video Production

Hofstra University (continued)
interview. Additional exam requirements/recommendations for international students: Required—TOEFL (minimum score 550 paper-based; 213 computer-based; 80 iBT). *Application deadline:* Applications are processed on a rolling basis. Application fee: $60. Electronic applications accepted. *Expenses:* Tuition: Full-time $15,300; part-time $850 per credit. Required fees: $970; $165 per term. Tuition and fees vary according to program. *Financial support:* In 2008–09, 3 students received support, including 2 fellowships with full and partial tuition reimbursements available (averaging $3,400 per year); research assistantships with full and partial tuition reimbursements available, Federal Work-Study, institutionally sponsored loans, scholarships/grants, tuition waivers (full and partial), and unspecified assistantships also available. Support available to part-time students. Financial award applicants required to submit FAFSA. *Faculty research:* Community radio, indigenous movements, communication and development, animation, feminism and documentary, working class women, film aesthetics and theory, documentary television. *Unit head:* Dr. Christine Noschese, Director, 516-463-7141, E-mail: sphmjs@hofstra.edu. *Application contact:* Carol Drummer, Dean of Graduate Admissions, 516-463-4876, Fax: 516-463-4664, E-mail: gradstudent@hofstra.edu.

Hollins University, Graduate Programs, Program in Screenwriting and Film Studies, Roanoke, VA 24020-1603. Offers MA, MFA. Offered during summer only. Part-time programs available. *Faculty:* 1 full-time (0 women), 6 part-time/adjunct (2 women). *Students:* 37 full-time (21 women), 3 part-time (2 women); includes 8 minority (5 African Americans, 3 Hispanic Americans), 2 international. Average age 34. 30 applicants, 90% accepted, 15 enrolled. In 2008, 7 master's awarded. *Degree requirements:* For master's, one foreign language, comprehensive exam, thesis. *Entrance requirements:* For master's, letters of recommendation, portfolio. Additional exam requirements/recommendations for international students: Required—TOEFL (minimum score 550 paper-based; 213 computer-based; 79 iBT). *Application deadline:* For fall admission, 2/15 for domestic and international students. Application fee: $40. Electronic applications accepted. *Expenses:* Tuition: Full-time $26,720; part-time $590 per credit hour. Required fees: $280. *Financial support:* In 2008–09, 24 students received support, including 13 fellowships (averaging $700 per year); Federal Work-Study and scholarships/grants also available. Support available to part-time students. Financial award application deadline: 2/15; financial award applicants required to submit FAFSA. *Faculty research:* German film, women in film, censorship, minorities in film. *Unit head:* Dr. Klaus Phillips, Director, 540-362-6308, E-mail: kphillips@hollins.edu. *Application contact:* Cathy S. Koon, Manager of Graduate Services, 540-362-6326, Fax: 540-362-6288, E-mail: ckoon@hollins.edu.

Howard University, School of Communications, Department of Radio, Television and Film, Washington, DC 20059-0002. Offers film (MFA). Part-time programs available. *Degree requirements:* For master's, thesis optional. *Entrance requirements:* For master's, GRE General Test, minimum GPA of 3.0.

Humboldt State University, Graduate Studies, College of Arts, Humanities, and Social Sciences, Department of Theatre, Film and Dance, Arcata, CA 95521-8299. Offers theatre arts (MA, MFA), including film production (MA), production (MA), scenography (MFA). *Students:* 13 full-time (8 women), 2 part-time (1 woman); includes 2 minority (both Hispanic Americans). Average age 35. 23 applicants, 52% accepted, 9 enrolled. In 2008, 2 master's awarded. *Degree requirements:* For master's, thesis or alternative, qualifying exam. *Entrance requirements:* For master's, minimum GPA of 2.5. Additional exam requirements/recommendations for international students: Required—TOEFL (minimum score 500 paper-based; 173 computer-based). *Application deadline:* For fall admission, 4/15 for domestic students. Applications are processed on a rolling basis. Application fee: $55. *Expenses:* Tuition, state resident: full-time $5236. Tuition, nonresident: full-time $11,338. *Financial support:* Fellowships available. Financial award application deadline: 3/1; financial award applicants required to submit FAFSA. *Faculty research:* Physical theater, design, playwriting. *Unit head:* Bernadette Cheyne, Chair/Coordinator, 707-826-4606, Fax: 707-826-5494, E-mail: bmc3@humboldt.edu. *Application contact:* Ann Alter, Coordinator, 707-826-5495, Fax: 707-826-5494, E-mail: aea2@humboldt.edu.

Loyola Marymount University, School of Film and Television, Department of Production, Program in Production (Film and Television), Los Angeles, CA 90045-2659. Offers MFA. *Degree requirements:* For master's, thesis, film. *Entrance requirements:* For master's, GRE General Test. Electronic applications accepted.

Marywood University, Academic Affairs, Insalaco College of Creative Arts and Management, Department of Communication Arts, Program in Communication Arts, Scranton, PA 18509-1598. Offers corporate communication (Certificate); e-business (Certificate); health communication (Certificate); instructional technology (Certificate); interdisciplinary (MA); library science/information specialist (Certificate); media management (MA); production (MA).

Massachusetts College of Art and Design, Graduate Programs, Program in Fine Arts, Boston, MA 02115-5882. Offers ceramics (MFA); design (MFA); fibers (MFA); film (MFA); glass (MFA); media and performing arts (MFA); metals (MFA); painting (MFA); photography (MFA); printmaking (MFA); sculpture (MFA). *Accreditation:* NASAD. *Faculty:* 10 full-time (5 women), 8 part-time/adjunct (6 women). *Students:* 83 full-time (53 women), 17 part-time (10 women); includes 8 minority (1 American Indian/Alaska Native, 4 Asian Americans or Pacific Islanders, 3 Hispanic Americans), 15 international. Average age 34. 295 applicants, 24% accepted, 40 enrolled. In 2008, 37 master's awarded. *Degree requirements:* For master's, thesis, exhibit. *Entrance requirements:* For master's, 12 units of course work in art history, portfolio, resumé, college transcripts, statement of purpose, letters of reference, interview. Additional exam requirements/recommendations for international students: Required—TOEFL (minimum score 563 paper-based; 223 computer-based; 85 iBT); Recommended—IELTS (minimum score 6.5). *Application deadline:* For fall admission, 1/15 for domestic and international students; for spring admission, 11/1 for domestic students. Application fee: $75. *Expenses:* Tuition, area resident: Full-time $17,100; part-time $570 per credit. Tuition and fees vary according to program. *Financial support:* In 2008–09, 50 research assistantships (averaging $2,000 per year), 30 teaching assistantships (averaging $2,000 per year) were awarded; career-related internships or fieldwork, Federal Work-Study, and clerical/technical assistantships also available. Support available to part-time students. Financial award application deadline: 5/1; financial award applicants required to submit FAFSA. *Unit head:* George Creamer, Director, 617-879-7163, Fax: 617-879-7171, E-mail: creamer@massart.edu. *Application contact:* George Creamer, Director, 617-879-7163.

Miami International University of Art & Design, Program in Film, Miami, FL 33132-1418. Offers MFA. Postbaccalaureate distance learning degree programs offered.

See Close-Up on page 121.

Minneapolis College of Art and Design, Program in Visual Studies, Minneapolis, MN 55404-4347. Offers animation (MFA); comic art (MFA); drawing (MFA); filmmaking (MFA); fine arts (MFA); furniture design (MFA); graphic design (MFA); illustration (MFA); interactive media (MFA); painting (MFA); photography (MFA); printmaking (MFA); sculpture (MFA). *Accreditation:* NASAD. Part-time programs available. *Faculty:* 23 full-time (7 women), 9 part-time/adjunct (4 women). *Students:* 40 full-time (21 women), 1 (woman) part-time; includes 1 minority (American Indian/Alaska Native). Average age 27. 172 applicants, 24% accepted, 15 enrolled. In 2008, 7 master's awarded. *Degree requirements:* For master's, thesis, thesis exhibit. *Entrance requirements:* For master's, portfolio, resumé, 3 letters of recommendation, personal statement. Additional exam requirements/recommendations for international students: Required—TOEFL (minimum score 550 paper-based; 213 computer-based; 79 iBT). *Application deadline:* For fall admission, 1/15 for domestic and international students. Application fee: $50. Electronic applications accepted. *Expenses:* Tuition: Full-time $28,400; part-time $813 per credit. *Financial support:* In 2008–09, 23 students received support, including 15 teaching assistantships (averaging $6,000 per year); career-related internships or fieldwork, Federal Work-Study, scholarships/grants, and unspecified assistantships also available. Support available to part-time students. Financial award application deadline: 3/15; financial award applicants required to submit FAFSA. *Faculty research:* Visual arts. *Unit head:* Carole Fisher, Graduate Director, 612-874-3629, E-mail: carole_fisher@mcad.edu. *Application contact:* William Mullen, Vice President of Enrollment Management, 612-874-3762, Fax: 612-874-3701, E-mail: william_mullen@mcad.edu.

Montana State University, College of Graduate Studies, College of Arts and Architecture, Department of Media and Theatre Arts, Program in Science and Natural History Filmmaking, Bozeman, MT 59717. Offers MFA. *Degree requirements:* For master's, comprehensive exam. *Entrance requirements:* For master's, GRE General Test. Additional exam requirements/recommendations for international students: Required—TOEFL (minimum score 550 paper-based; 213 computer-based). *Faculty research:* Documentary, experimental video.

New York Film Academy, Program in Filmmaking–Hollywood, Los Angeles, CA 90068. Offers acting for film (MFA); filmmaking (MFA); producing (MFA); screenwriting (MFA).

New York Film Academy, Program in Filmmaking–New York, New York, NY 10003. Offers acting for film (MFA); filmmaking (MFA); producing (MFA); screenwriting (MFA).

New York Film Academy, Program in Filmmaking–United Arab Emirates, Abu Dhabi, CA 90068, United Arab Emirates. Offers acting for film (MFA); filmmaking (MFA); producing (MFA); screenwriting (MFA).

New York University, Tisch School of the Arts Asia, Singapore, NY 248923, Singapore. Offers animation and digital arts (MFA); dramatic writing (MFA); film production (MFA). *Entrance requirements:* Additional exam requirements/recommendations for international students: Required—TOEFL (minimum score 610 paper-based; 250 computer-based; 105 iBT). Electronic applications accepted.

New York University, Tisch School of the Arts and Graduate School of Arts and Science, Department of Cinema Studies, Program in Moving Image Archiving and Preservation, New York, NY 10012-1019. Offers MA. *Degree requirements:* For master's, internship. *Entrance requirements:* For master's, GRE. Additional exam requirements/recommendations for international students: Required—TOEFL or IELTS. Electronic applications accepted.

New York University, Tisch School of the Arts, Kanbar Institute of Film and Television, New York, NY 10012-1019. Offers MFA. *Degree requirements:* For master's, 4 films. *Entrance requirements:* For master's, portfolio. Additional exam requirements/recommendations for international students: Required—TOEFL or IELTS. Electronic applications accepted.

Northwestern University, The Graduate School, School of Communication, Department of Radio/Television/Film, Evanston, IL 60208. Offers MA, MFA, PhD. Admissions and degrees offered through The Graduate School. Part-time programs available. Terminal master's awarded for partial completion of doctoral program. *Degree requirements:* For master's, comprehensive exam or thesis; for doctorate, thesis/dissertation, qualifying exam. *Entrance requirements:* For master's and doctorate, GRE General Test. Additional exam requirements/recommendations for international students: Required—TOEFL. Electronic applications accepted. *Faculty research:* Art and new media, media theory and criticism, gender, media history, documentary.

Ohio University, Graduate College, College of Fine Arts, School of Film, Athens, OH 45701-2979. Offers film (MFA); film studies (MA). *Degree requirements:* For master's, one foreign language, thesis. *Entrance requirements:* Additional exam requirements/recommendations for international students: Required—TOEFL (minimum score 550 paper-based; 239 computer-based). Electronic applications accepted. *Faculty research:* Scriptwriting, sound, editing, cinematography, film theory, digital pest production.

Polytechnic Institute of NYU, Department of Electrical and Computer Engineering, Major in Image Processing, Brooklyn, NY 11201-2990. Offers Certificate. *Entrance requirements:* Additional exam requirements/recommendations for international students: Required—TOEFL (minimum score 550 paper-based; 213 computer-based); Recommended—IELTS (minimum score 6.5). Electronic applications accepted.

Regent University, Graduate School, School of Communication and the Arts, Virginia Beach, VA 23464-9800. Offers acting (MFA); acting and directing (MFA); cinema arts/television arts (MA); communication (MA, PhD); digital media (MA); directing for cinema/TV (MA); journalism (MA); producing for cinema/TV (MA); script and screenwriting (MFA); theatre (MA). Part-time programs available. Postbaccalaureate distance learning degree programs offered (minimal on-campus study). *Faculty:* 26 full-time (3 women), 15 part-time/adjunct (3 women). *Students:* 136 full-time (77 women), 163 part-time (90 women); includes 83 minority (59 African Americans, 3 American Indian/Alaska Native, 5 Asian Americans or Pacific Islanders, 16 Hispanic Americans), 15 international. Average age 32. 230 applicants, 63% accepted, 102 enrolled. In 2008, 53 master's, 16 doctorates awarded. *Degree requirements:* For master's, thesis or alternative; for doctorate, thesis/dissertation. *Entrance requirements:* For master's, GRE General Test or MAT, minimum undergraduate GPA of 3.0, writing sample, computer literacy survey, recommendation, resumé, interview, audition (MFA programs); for doctorate, GRE General Test, minimum graduate GPA of 3.0, writing sample, computer literacy survey, recommendation, interview, transcripts. Additional exam requirements/recommendations for international students: Required—TOEFL (minimum score 577 paper-based; 233 computer-based). *Application deadline:* For fall admission, 3/1 priority date for domestic students; for spring admission, 10/1 priority date for domestic students. Applications are processed on a rolling basis. Application fee: $50. Electronic applications accepted. *Expenses:* Contact institution. *Financial support:* Fellowships with full and partial tuition reimbursements, career-related internships or fieldwork, scholarships/grants, tuition waivers (full and partial), and unspecified assistantships available. Support available to part-time students. Financial award application deadline: 9/1; financial award applicants required to submit FAFSA. *Faculty research:* Southern gospel music, education and entertainment, celebrities and the media, journalism and ethics, C. S. Lewis. *Unit head:* Michael Patrick, Dean, 757-352-4970, Fax: 757-352-4279, E-mail: michpat@regent.edu. *Application contact:* Matthew Chadwick, Director of Admissions, 800-373-5504, Fax: 757-352-4381, E-mail: admissions@regent.edu.

Rochester Institute of Technology, Graduate Enrollment Services, College of Imaging Arts and Sciences, School of Photographic Arts and Sciences, Program in Imaging Arts, Rochester, NY 14623-5603. Offers MFA. *Accreditation:* NASAD. *Degree requirements:* For master's, thesis, exhibit. *Entrance requirements:* For master's, portfolio, minimum GPA of 3.0. Additional exam requirements/recommendations for international students: Required—TOEFL (minimum score 550 paper-based; 213 computer-based; 79 iBT).

St. Thomas University, School of Leadership Studies, Program in Electronic Media, Miami Gardens, FL 33054-6459. Offers MA.

San Diego State University, Graduate and Research Affairs, College of Professional Studies and Fine Arts, School of Theater, Television and Film, Program in Television, Film, and New Media Production, San Diego, CA 92182. Offers MA. *Entrance requirements:* For master's, GRE General Test, 3 letters of recommendation, resumé, sample reel, influential book list, influential films list, hobby list. Additional exam requirements/recommendations for international students: Required—TOEFL. Electronic applications accepted. *Faculty research:* Experimental film and television programs, documentary film, television research and production.

San Francisco Art Institute, Graduate Program, Department of Film, San Francisco, CA 94133. Offers MFA, Certificate. *Accreditation:* NASAD. Part-time programs available. *Degree requirements:* For master's and Certificate, oral reviews. *Entrance requirements:* For master's and Certificate, portfolio. Additional exam requirements/recommendations for international students: Required—TOEFL (minimum score 580 paper-based; 237 computer-based). Electronic applications accepted.

See Close-Up on page 221.

San Francisco Art Institute, Graduate Program, Department of New Genres, San Francisco, CA 94133. Offers new genres (Certificate); performance/video (MFA). *Accreditation:* NASAD.

Part-time programs available. *Degree requirements:* For master's and Certificate, oral reviews. *Entrance requirements:* For master's and Certificate, portfolio. Additional exam requirements/recommendations for international students: Required—TOEFL (minimum score 580 paper-based; 237 computer-based). Electronic applications accepted.

See Close-Up on page 221.

San Francisco State University, Division of Graduate Studies, College of Creative Arts, Department of Broadcast and Electronic Communication Arts, San Francisco, CA 94132-1722. Offers radio and television (MA).

San Francisco State University, Division of Graduate Studies, College of Creative Arts, Department of Cinema, San Francisco, CA 94132-1722. Offers cinema (MFA); cinema studies (MA).

San Jose State University, Graduate Studies and Research, College of Humanities and the Arts, Department of Television, Radio, Film and Theatre, San Jose, CA 95192-0001. Offers theatre arts (MA). *Accreditation:* NAST. *Degree requirements:* For master's, written exam. *Entrance requirements:* Additional exam requirements/recommendations for international students: Required—TOEFL (minimum score 570 paper-based). Electronic applications accepted.

Savannah College of Art and Design, Graduate School, Program in Animation, Savannah, GA 31402-3146. Offers MA, MFA. Part-time programs available. *Degree requirements:* For master's, thesis, internships. *Entrance requirements:* For master's, interview, portfolio. Additional exam requirements/recommendations for international students: Required—TOEFL (minimum score 450 paper-based; 133 computer-based). Electronic applications accepted. *Expenses:* Tuition: Full-time $28,215; part-time $3135 per course. One-time fee: $500.

Savannah College of Art and Design, Graduate School, Program in Film and Television, Savannah, GA 31402-3146. Offers MA, MFA. Part-time programs available. *Degree requirements:* For master's, thesis, internship. *Entrance requirements:* For master's, interview, videotape. Additional exam requirements/recommendations for international students: Required—TOEFL (minimum score 450 paper-based; 133 computer-based). Electronic applications accepted. *Expenses:* Tuition: Full-time $28,215; part-time $3135 per course. One-time fee: $500.

See Close-Up on page 223.

Savannah College of Art and Design, Graduate School, Program in Sound Design, Savannah, GA 31402-3146. Offers MA, MFA. Part-time programs available. *Degree requirements:* For master's, thesis, internships. *Entrance requirements:* For master's, interview, portfolio. Additional exam requirements/recommendations for international students: Required—TOEFL (minimum score 450 paper-based; 133 computer-based). *Expenses:* Tuition: Full-time $28,215; part-time $3135 per course. One-time fee: $500.

School of the Art Institute of Chicago, Graduate Division, Department of Film, Video, and New Media, Chicago, IL 60603-3103. Offers MFA. *Accreditation:* NASAD. *Degree requirements:* For master's, thesis exhibit. *Entrance requirements:* Additional exam requirements/recommendations for international students: Required—TOEFL, IELTS. Electronic applications accepted.

See Close-Up on page 225.

School of the Art Institute of Chicago, Graduate Division, Department of Sound, Chicago, IL 60603-3103. Offers MFA. *Entrance requirements:* Additional exam requirements/recommendations for international students: Required—TOEFL, IELTS.

See Close-Up on page 225.

School of Visual Arts, Graduate Programs, Program in Photography, Video and Related Media, New York, NY 10010-3994. Offers MFA. *Accreditation:* NASAD. *Degree requirements:* For master's, final review, project or thesis. *Entrance requirements:* For master's, portfolio. Additional exam requirements/recommendations for international students: Required—TOEFL (minimum score 550 paper-based; 213 computer-based; 79 iBT). Electronic applications accepted.

Southern Methodist University, Meadows School of the Arts, Division of Communication Arts, Dallas, TX 75275. Offers MA. Part-time and evening/weekend programs available. *Faculty:* 9 full-time (3 women), 6 part-time/adjunct (1 woman). *Students:* 12 full-time (7 women), 1 part-time (0 women); includes 2 minority (1 American Indian/Alaska Native, 1 Hispanic American), 5 international. Average age 30. 9 applicants, 78% accepted, 4 enrolled. In 2008, 6 master's awarded. *Degree requirements:* For master's, thesis or alternative. *Entrance requirements:* For master's, GRE General Test, minimum undergraduate GPA of 3.0 in major field during last 2 years. Additional exam requirements/recommendations for international students: Required—TOEFL (minimum score 550 paper-based; 213 computer-based; 80 iBT). *Application deadline:* For fall admission, 3/1 priority date for domestic and international students. Application fee: $75. *Financial support:* In 2008–09, 7 students received support, including 7 teaching assistantships (averaging $6,500 per year); research assistantships, scholarships/grants, tuition waivers (full), and unspecified assistantships also available. Financial award application deadline: 3/15. *Faculty research:* Digital sound, new technology, film and gender study, popular film and TV genres, Asian cinema. Total annual research expenditures: $10,000. *Unit head:* Rick Worland, Chair, 214-768-3708, Fax: 214-768-2784, E-mail: rworland@smu.edu. *Application contact:* Jean Cherry, Director of Graduate Admissions and Records, 214-768-3765, Fax: 214-768-3272, E-mail: jcherry@smu.edu.

Syracuse University, Graduate School, College of Visual and Performing Arts, Program in Film, Syracuse, NY 13244. Offers MFA.

Syracuse University, Graduate School, S. I. Newhouse School of Public Communications, Program in Documentary Film and History, Syracuse, NY 13244. Offers MA. *Entrance requirements:* For master's, GRE General Test.

Temple University, Graduate School, School of Communications and Theater, Department of Film and Media Arts, Philadelphia, PA 19122-6096. Offers MFA. Part-time programs available. *Degree requirements:* For master's, comprehensive exam, project. *Entrance requirements:* For master's, GRE General Test, minimum GPA of 3.0; exhibit. Additional exam requirements/recommendations for international students: Required—TOEFL (minimum score 550 paper-based; 213 computer-based; 79 iBT). Electronic applications accepted. *Faculty research:* Filmmaking and videography, documentary theory and practice, screenwriting, media culture studies, film studies.

The University of Alabama, Graduate School, College of Communication and Information Sciences, Department of Telecommunication and Film, Tuscaloosa, AL 35487-0152. Offers MA. *Faculty:* 8 full-time (2 women). *Students:* 8 full-time (6 women), 1 part-time (0 women); includes 1 minority (Hispanic American), 2 international. Average age 24. 7 applicants, 71% accepted, 3 enrolled. In 2008, 2 master's awarded. Terminal master's awarded for partial completion of doctoral program. *Degree requirements:* For master's, comprehensive exam, thesis or alternative. *Entrance requirements:* For master's, GRE, minimum GPA of 3.0. Additional exam requirements/recommendations for international students: Required—TOEFL (minimum score 600 paper-based; 79 iBT). *Application deadline:* For fall admission, 2/15 priority date for domestic students; for spring admission, 11/1 for domestic students. Applications are processed on a rolling basis. Application fee: $30. Electronic applications accepted. *Expenses:* Tuition, area resident: Full-time $6400. Tuition, state resident: full-time $6400. Tuition, nonresident: full-time $18,000. *Financial support:* In 2008–09, 6 students received support, including 2 research assistantships with tuition reimbursements available (averaging $9,825 per year), 2 teaching assistantships with tuition reimbursements available (averaging $9,825 per year); institutionally sponsored loans also available. Financial award application deadline: 2/15. *Faculty research:* Entertainment theory, news and public affairs, effects of telecommunications, management. Total annual research expenditures: $595,298. *Unit head:* Dr. Gary A. Copeland, Chair, 205-348-6350, Fax: 205-348-5162, E-mail: copeland@ua.edu. *Application contact:* Dr. Shuhua Zhou, Graduate Coordinator, 205-348-8653, Fax: 205-348-5162, E-mail: szhou@bama.ua.edu.

The University of British Columbia, Faculty of Arts, Creative Writing Program, Vancouver, BC V6T 1Z1, Canada. Offers creative writing (MFA); creative writing and film (MFA); creative writing and theatre (MFA). Part-time programs available. Postbaccalaureate distance learning degree programs offered (minimal on-campus study). *Degree requirements:* For master's, thesis. *Entrance requirements:* For master's, sample of written work. Additional exam requirements/recommendations for international students: Required—TOEFL (minimum score 550 paper-based; 213 computer-based). Electronic applications accepted. *Expenses:* Contact institution. *Faculty research:* Writing of fiction; poetry, creative nonfiction, plays for stage, screen, television, radio, writing for children and translation, song lyrics and libretto.

The University of British Columbia, Faculty of Arts and Faculty of Graduate Studies, Department of Theatre and Film, Film Program, Vancouver, BC V6T 1Z1, Canada. Offers creative writing and film production (MFA); film production (MFA, Diploma); film studies (MA). *Degree requirements:* For master's, thesis (MA), thesis or project (MFA). *Entrance requirements:* For master's, bachelor's degree in film production or equivalent, BA in film studies. Additional exam requirements/recommendations for international students: Required—TOEFL (minimum score 600 paper-based). Electronic applications accepted. *Faculty research:* Film history, theory, criticism; producing; experimental film.

University of California, Los Angeles, Graduate Division, Graduate School of Education and Information Studies, Department of Information Studies, Los Angeles, CA 90095. Offers archival studies (MLIS); informatics (MLIS); information studies (PhD); library and information science (Certificate); library studies (MLIS); moving image archive studies (MA); MBA/MLIS; MLIS/MA. *Accreditation:* ALA (one or more programs are accredited). *Faculty:* 13 full-time (7 women), 4 part-time/adjunct (3 women). *Students:* 164 full-time (114 women), 48 part-time (31 women); includes 76 minority (9 African Americans, 44 Asian Americans or Pacific Islanders, 23 Hispanic Americans), 7 international. Average age 29. 206 applicants, 68% accepted, 102 enrolled. In 2008, 85 master's, 2 doctorates awarded. Terminal master's awarded for partial completion of doctoral program. *Degree requirements:* For master's, thesis or alternative, professional portfolio; for doctorate, thesis/dissertation, oral and written qualifying exams. *Entrance requirements:* For master's, GRE General Test, previous course work in computer programming and statistics; for doctorate, GRE General Test, previous course work in statistics, 2 samples of research writing in English. Additional exam requirements/recommendations for international students: Required—TOEFL (paper-based 613, computer-based 220, iBT 87), IELTS (7) or TWE (5); Recommended—TWE (minimum score 5). *Application deadline:* For fall admission, 12/15 for domestic and international students. Applications are processed on a rolling basis. Application fee: $60 ($80 for international students). Electronic applications accepted. *Expenses:* Tuition, nonresident: full-time $14,694. Required fees: $9669.50. Full-time tuition and fees vary according to course load, degree level, program and student level. *Financial support:* In 2008–09, 57 students received support, including 35 fellowships (averaging $11,450 per year), 18 research assistantships with tuition reimbursements available (averaging $28,600 per year), 4 teaching assistantships with tuition reimbursements available (averaging $54,040 per year); career-related internships or fieldwork, Federal Work-Study, institutionally sponsored loans, scholarships/grants, and unspecified assistantships also available. Financial award application deadline: 3/1; financial award applicants required to submit FAFSA. *Faculty research:* Multimedia, digital libraries, archives and electronic records, interface design, information technology and preservation, preservation, access. *Unit head:* Anne J. Gilliland, Professor and Chair, 310-825-8799, E-mail: agilliland@ucla.edu. *Application contact:* Susan S. Abler, Student Affairs Officer, 310-825-5269, Fax: 310-206-4460, E-mail: abler@gseis.ucla.edu.

University of California, Los Angeles, Graduate Division, School of Theater, Film and Television, Department of Film, Television, and Digital Media, Los Angeles, CA 90034. Offers film and television (MA, MFA, PhD); MFA/MA. *Students:* 286 full-time (147 women); includes 77 minority (14 African Americans, 4 American Indian/Alaska Native, 25 Asian Americans or Pacific Islanders, 34 Hispanic Americans), 26 international. Average age 29. 968 applicants, 13% accepted, 81 enrolled. In 2008, 68 master's, 7 doctorates awarded. *Degree requirements:* For master's, comprehensive exam; for doctorate, one foreign language, thesis/dissertation, oral and written qualifying exams. *Entrance requirements:* For master's, film or TV project, animation, or script (MFA), 3.0 minimum GPA; for doctorate, GRE General Test, minimum undergraduate GPA of 3.0. Application fee: $60 ($80 for international students). Electronic applications accepted. *Expenses:* Tuition, nonresident: full-time $14,694. Required fees: $9669.50. Full-time tuition and fees vary according to course load, degree level, program and student level. *Financial support:* In 2008–09, 301 fellowships with full and partial tuition reimbursements, 20 research assistantships with full and partial tuition reimbursements, 133 teaching assistantships with full and partial tuition reimbursements were awarded; Federal Work-Study, institutionally sponsored loans, scholarships/grants, health care benefits, tuition waivers (full and partial), and unspecified assistantships also available. Financial award application deadline: 3/1; financial award applicants required to submit FAFSA. *Unit head:* Barbara Boyle, Chair, 310-825-8787. *Application contact:* Departmental Office, 310-825-8787, E-mail: info@tft.ucla.edu.

University of California, Santa Barbara, Graduate Division, College of Letters and Sciences, Division of Humanities and Fine Arts, Department of Film and Media Studies, Santa Barbara, CA 93106-4010. Offers PhD, MA/PhD. *Faculty:* 21 full-time (12 women). *Students:* 20 full-time (12 women). Average age 27. 112 applicants, 10% accepted, 5 enrolled. *Degree requirements:* For doctorate, one foreign language, comprehensive exam, thesis/dissertation. *Entrance requirements:* For doctorate, GRE, 3 letters of recommendation, statement of purpose, personal achievements/contributions statement, resumé/curriculum vitae, transcripts for post-secondary institutions attended. Additional exam requirements/recommendations for international students: Required—TOEFL (paper: 600, computer: 250, IBT: 100) or IELTS (7). *Application deadline:* For fall admission, 12/1 for domestic and international students. Application fee: $70 ($90 for international students). Electronic applications accepted. *Expenses:* Tuition, nonresident: full-time $25,149. Required fees: $10,143. Full-time tuition and fees vary according to campus/location, reciprocity agreements and student level. *Financial support:* In 2008–09, 20 students received support, including 10 fellowships with full and partial tuition reimbursements available (averaging $18,300 per year), 16 teaching assistantships with partial tuition reimbursements available (averaging $10,600 per year); career-related internships or fieldwork, Federal Work-Study, institutionally sponsored loans, scholarships/grants, health care benefits, tuition waivers (full and partial), and unspecified assistantships also available. Financial award application deadline: 12/1; financial award applicants required to submit FAFSA. *Faculty research:* Global media, broadcast history, cultural studies, film history and historiography, documentary film, film and ethnography, the Western and trauma and memory, classical and contemporary film theory, aesthetics, narrative, point of view, analysis, film history and theory, media studies, feminist theory, science and technology studies, contemporary art, post colonial media theory, Asian cinemas, cinema and media of the Americas. *Unit head:* Dr. Lisa Parks, Chair, 805-893-5547, Fax: 805-893-8630, E-mail: parks@filmandmedia.ucsb.edu. *Application contact:* Melany J. Miners, Graduate Program Assistant, 805-893-8535, Fax: 805-893-8630, E-mail: mminers@filmandmedia.ucsb.edu.

University of Central Arkansas, Graduate School, College of Fine Arts and Communication, Program in Digital Filmmaking, Conway, AR 72035-0001. Offers MFA. *Accreditation:* NASAD. *Degree requirements:* For master's, thesis. *Entrance requirements:* For master's, GRE General Test, minimum GPA of 2.7. Additional exam requirements/recommendations for international students: Required—TOEFL (minimum score 550 paper-based; 213 computer-based).

University of Central Florida, College of Arts and Humanities, Division of Film and Digital Media, Orlando, FL 32816. Offers entrepreneurial digital cinema (MFA); interactive entertainment (MS); visual language and interactive media (MA, MFA). *Faculty:* 28 full-time (10 women), 7

Film, Television, and Video Production

University of Central Florida (continued)
part-time/adjunct (3 women). *Students:* 72 full-time (13 women), 42 part-time (6 women); includes 28 minority (10 African Americans, 2 Asian Americans or Pacific Islanders, 16 Hispanic Americans), 6 international. In 2008, 59 master's awarded. *Expenses:* Tuition, area resident: Full-time $6816; part-time $284 per credit. Tuition, state resident: full-time $6816; part-time $1076 per credit. Tuition, nonresident: full-time $25,824. Required fees: $216; $9 per credit. *Financial support:* In 2008–09, 2 fellowships (averaging $10,000 per year), 2 research assistantships (averaging $5,480 per year), 13 teaching assistantships (averaging $7,100 per year) were awarded. *Unit head:* Dr. Jose Maunez-Cuadra, Interim Chair, 407-823-6100, E-mail: jmaunez@mail.ucf.edu. *Application contact:* Dr. Jose Maunez-Cuadra, Interim Chair, 407-823-6100, E-mail: jmaunez@mail.ucf.edu.

University of Denver, Division of Arts, Humanities and Social Sciences, School of Communication, Department of Mass Communications, Denver, CO 80208. Offers advertising management (MS); digital media studies (MA); mass communications (MA); public relations (MS); video production (MA). Part-time programs available. *Faculty:* 14 full-time (8 women), 4 part-time/adjunct (1 woman). *Students:* 3 full-time (1 woman), 42 part-time (30 women); includes 7 minority (1 African American, 6 Hispanic Americans), 3 international. Average age 27. In 2008, 17 master's awarded. *Degree requirements:* For master's, thesis (for some programs). *Entrance requirements:* For master's, GRE General Test. Additional exam requirements/recommendations for international students: Required—TOEFL, TWE. *Application deadline:* Applications are processed on a rolling basis. Application fee: $50. Electronic applications accepted. *Financial support:* In 2008–09, 4 research assistantships with full and partial tuition reimbursements (averaging $9,000 per year), 7 teaching assistantships with full and partial tuition reimbursements (averaging $10,000 per year) were awarded; career-related internships or fieldwork, Federal Work-Study, institutionally sponsored loans, and scholarships/grants also available. Support available to part-time students. Financial award application deadline: 3/1; financial award applicants required to submit FAFSA. *Faculty research:* Youth and civic engagement. Total annual research expenditures: $162,000. *Unit head:* Dr. Diane Waldman, Chair, 303-871-2008. *Application contact:* Information Contact, 303-871-2008, E-mail: mcom@du.edu.

See Close-Up on page 707.

The University of Iowa, Graduate College, College of Liberal Arts and Sciences, Department of Cinema and Comparative Literature, Program in Film and Video Production, Iowa City, IA 52242-1316. Offers MA, MFA. *Degree requirements:* For master's, thesis (for some programs), exam. *Entrance requirements:* For master's, GRE General Test, minimum GPA of 3.0. Additional exam requirements/recommendations for international students: Required—TOEFL (minimum score 550 paper-based; 213 computer-based; 81 iBT). Electronic applications accepted.

University of Memphis, Graduate School, College of Communication and Fine Arts, Department of Communication, Memphis, TN 38152. Offers communication (MA); communication arts (PhD); film and video production (MA). Part-time programs available. *Faculty:* 10 full-time (4 women). *Students:* 28 full-time (15 women), 17 part-time (9 women); includes 7 minority (all African Americans), 1 international. Average age 36. 24 applicants, 79% accepted, 12 enrolled. In 2008, 7 master's, 7 doctorates awarded. *Degree requirements:* For master's, comprehensive exam, thesis or alternative; for doctorate, comprehensive exam, thesis/dissertation. *Entrance requirements:* For master's and doctorate, GRE General Test. Additional exam requirements/recommendations for international students: Required—TOEFL (minimum score 550 paper-based; 210 computer-based). *Application deadline:* For fall admission, 8/1 for domestic students. Application fee: $35 ($60 for international students). *Expenses:* Tuition, area resident: Full-time $6242; part-time $330 per credit hour. Tuition, state resident: full-time $6242; part-time $330 per credit hour. Tuition, nonresident: full-time $17,828; part-time $815 per credit hour. Required fees: $1156. *Financial support:* Research assistantships with full tuition reimbursements, teaching assistantships with full tuition reimbursements, unspecified assistantships available. Financial award applicants required to submit FAFSA. *Faculty research:* Rhetoric, media studies, applied communication (health communication). *Unit head:* Dr. Mike Leff, Chair, 901-678-2565, Fax: 901-678-4331, E-mail: m_leff@bellsouth.net. *Application contact:* Dr. Sandra Sarkela, Coordinator of Graduate Studies, 901-678-3173, Fax: 901-678-4331, E-mail: ssarkela@memphis.edu.

University of Miami, Graduate School, School of Communication, Coral Gables, FL 33124. Offers communication (PhD); communication studies (MA); film studies (MA, PhD); motion pictures (MFA), including production, producing, and screenwriting; print journalism (MA); public relations (MA); Spanish language journalism (MA); television broadcast journalism (MA). *Accreditation:* ACEJMC. Part-time programs available. *Degree requirements:* For master's, comprehensive exam (for some programs), thesis (for some programs); for doctorate, comprehensive exam, thesis/dissertation. *Entrance requirements:* For master's, GRE General Test; for doctorate, GRE General Test, master's thesis or scholarly research. Additional exam requirements/recommendations for international students: Required—TOEFL (minimum score 600 paper-based; 250 computer-based; 100 iBT). Electronic applications accepted. *Faculty research:* Communication studies, mass communication, international/interpersonal communication, film studies, journalism.

University of Nevada, Las Vegas, Graduate College, College of Fine Arts, Department of Film, Las Vegas, NV 89154-5015. Offers screenwriting (MFA). Part-time programs available. *Faculty:* 6 full-time (0 women), 7 part-time/adjunct (0 women). *Students:* 5 full-time (2 women). Average age 40. 15 applicants, 20% accepted, 2 enrolled. In 2008, 3 master's awarded. *Degree requirements:* For master's, comprehensive exam, creative project. *Entrance requirements:* Additional exam requirements/recommendations for international students: Required—TOEFL (minimum score 550 paper-based; 213 computer-based), IELTS (minimum score 7). *Application deadline:* For fall admission, 1/15 priority date for domestic and international students. Applications are processed on a rolling basis. Application fee: $60 ($75 for international students). Electronic applications accepted. *Expenses:* Tuition, state resident: full-time $1414; part-time $198 per credit. Tuition, nonresident: full-time $12,509; part-time $415.75 per credit. International tuition: $14,249 full-time. Required fees: $4 per credit. $252 per semester. Tuition and fees vary according to course load. *Financial support:* In 2008–09, 5 students received support, including 5 teaching assistantships with partial tuition reimbursements available (averaging $10,000 per year); institutionally sponsored loans, scholarships/grants, health care benefits, and unspecified assistantships also available. Financial award application deadline: 3/1. *Faculty research:* Filmmaking: directing, producing, cinematography, editing; screenwriting; film archiving and restoration; film study publication; literary fiction. *Unit head:* Francisco Menendez, Chair/Professor, 702-895-4223, Fax: 702-895-4395, E-mail: francisco.menendez@unlv.edu. *Application contact:* Graduate College Admissions Evaluator, 702-895-3320, Fax: 702-895-4180, E-mail: gradcollege@unlv.edu.

University of New Orleans, Graduate School, College of Liberal Arts, Department of Film, Theatre and Communication Arts, New Orleans, LA 70148. Offers film production (MFA); theatre directing (MFA); theatre performance (MFA). *Accreditation:* NAST. *Degree requirements:* For master's, comprehensive exam, thesis. *Entrance requirements:* Additional exam requirements/recommendations for international students: Required—TOEFL (minimum score 550 paper-based; 213 computer-based; 79 iBT). Electronic applications accepted. *Faculty research:* Mass communication theory, nineteenth- and twentieth-century theater history, film criticism and history.

The University of North Carolina at Greensboro, Graduate School, College of Arts and Sciences, Department of Broadcasting and Cinema, Greensboro, NC 27412-5001. Offers film and video production (MFA).

University of North Carolina School of the Arts, School of Filmmaking, Winston-Salem, NC 27127-2188. Offers film music composition (MFA). *Faculty:* 3 full-time (0 women). *Students:* 7 full-time (0 women); includes 1 minority (Asian American or Pacific Islander). Average age 25. 6 applicants, 33% accepted, 2 enrolled. In 2008, 3 master's awarded. *Entrance requirements:* For master's, audition, performance, portfolio, interview. *Application deadline:* For fall admission, 4/1 priority date for domestic students. Applications are processed on a rolling basis. Application fee: $60 ($100 for international students). *Expenses:* Tuition, area resident: Full-time $3797. Tuition, state resident: full-time $3797. Tuition, nonresident: full-time $15,670. Required fees: $1791. *Financial support:* In 2008–09, fellowships (averaging $2,000 per year); career-related internships or fieldwork and Federal Work-Study also available. Support available to part-time students. Financial award application deadline: 3/15; financial award applicants required to submit FAFSA. *Unit head:* Jordan Kerner, Dean, 336-770-1330, Fax: 336-770-1339, E-mail: kernerj@uncsa.edu. *Application contact:* Sheeler Lawson, Director of Admissions, 336-770-3290, Fax: 336-770-3370, E-mail: admissions@uncsa.edu.

University of North Texas, Robert B. Toulouse School of Graduate Studies, College of Arts and Sciences, Department of Radio, Television and Film, Denton, TX 76203. Offers MA, MFA, MS. Part-time programs available. *Degree requirements:* For master's, thesis, thesis production (MFA). *Entrance requirements:* For master's, GRE General Test, 2 letters of recommendation, writing sample, goal statement (MA/MS), portfolio, 3 letters of recommendation, writing sample, goal statement (MFA). Additional exam requirements/recommendations for international students: Required—proof of English language proficiency required for non-native English speakers; Recommended—TOEFL (minimum score 550 paper-based; 213 computer-based). *Faculty research:* Media law and regulation, audio/video/film production, film and broadcasting history.

University of Oklahoma, Graduate College, College of Fine Arts, School of Art and Art History, Norman, OK 73019. Offers art (MA, MFA); art history (MA, MFA); ceramics (MFA); film and video (MFA); painting (MFA); photography (MFA); printmaking (MFA); visual communications (MFA). *Faculty:* 27 full-time (10 women), 2 part-time/adjunct (0 women). *Students:* 20 full-time (13 women), 12 part-time (10 women); includes 6 minority (2 African Americans, 4 American Indian/Alaska Native), 3 international. 28 applicants, 39% accepted, 9 enrolled. In 2008, 8 master's awarded. *Degree requirements:* For master's, thesis (MA), exhibit (MFA), departmental qualifying exam. *Entrance requirements:* For master's, GRE General Test (MA), bachelor's degree in art (MFA) or art history (MA), minimum GPA of 3.0 in last 60 undergraduate hours, 3 letters of recommendation, written research paper. Additional exam requirements/recommendations for international students: Required—TOEFL (minimum score 550 paper-based; 213 computer-based). *Application deadline:* For fall admission, 2/1 priority date for domestic students, 2/1 for international students; for spring admission, 10/1 for domestic and international students. Applications are processed on a rolling basis. Application fee: $40 ($90 for international students). Electronic applications accepted. *Expenses:* Tuition, state resident: full-time $3744; part-time $156 per credit hour. Tuition, nonresident: full-time $13,577; part-time $565.70 per credit hour. Required fees: $2415.40; $90.10 per credit hour. *Financial support:* In 2008–09, 16 students received support, including 14 research assistantships with partial tuition reimbursements available (averaging $10,014 per year), 4 teaching assistantships with partial tuition reimbursements available (averaging $9,586 per year); career-related internships or fieldwork, Federal Work-Study, institutionally sponsored loans, scholarships/grants, health care benefits, tuition waivers (partial), and unspecified assistantships also available. Support available to part-time students. Financial award application deadline: 4/7; financial award applicants required to submit FAFSA. *Faculty research:* Native American art history and art of the American West, contemporary and figurative sculpture, painting and print making, graphic design, media. Total annual research expenditures: $29,536. *Unit head:* Mary Jo Watson, Director, 405-325-2691, Fax: 405-325-1668, E-mail: mjwatson@ou.edu. *Application contact:* Jonathan Hils, Graduate Liaison, 405-325-2691, Fax: 405-325-1668, E-mail: hils@ou.edu.

University of Southern California, Graduate School, School of Cinematic Arts, Division of Animation and Digital Arts, Program in Film, Video, and Computer Animation, Los Angeles, CA 90089. Offers MFA. *Entrance requirements:* For master's, GRE General Test.

University of Southern California, Graduate School, School of Cinematic Arts, Division of Film and Television Production, Program in Film and Video Production, Los Angeles, CA 90089. Offers MFA.

University of Southern California, Graduate School, School of Cinematic Arts, Master's Program in Screen and Television Writing, Los Angeles, CA 90089. Offers MFA. *Entrance requirements:* For master's, GRE General Test. *Faculty research:* Filmmaking.

University of Southern California, Graduate School, School of Cinematic Arts, Program in Producing, Los Angeles, CA 90089. Offers MFA. *Degree requirements:* For master's, thesis, internship. *Entrance requirements:* For master's, GRE General Test. *Faculty research:* Motion pictures and television.

The University of Texas at Austin, Graduate School, College of Communication, Department of Radio-Television-Film, Austin, TX 78712-1111. Offers film and video production (MFA); radio-television-film (MA, PhD); screenwriting (MFA). *Degree requirements:* For master's, thesis (for some programs); for doctorate, thesis/dissertation. *Entrance requirements:* For master's and doctorate, GRE General Test. Electronic applications accepted. *Faculty research:* International communication, film studies, media and culture, telecommunication and new media, gender and sexuality.

University of the Sacred Heart, Graduate Programs, Department of Communication, San Juan, PR 00914-0383. Offers contemporary culture and media (MA); editing for media (MA); public relations (MA); publicity (MA); scriptwriting (MA). Part-time and evening/weekend programs available. *Degree requirements:* For master's, thesis.

University of Utah, The Graduate School, College of Fine Arts, Division of Film Studies, Salt Lake City, UT 84112-1107. Offers MFA. *Degree requirements:* For master's, comprehensive exam, film or video portfolio. *Entrance requirements:* For master's, minimum GPA of 3.0. Additional exam requirements/recommendations for international students: Required—TOEFL (minimum score 500 paper-based; 173 computer-based). *Faculty research:* Film history, criticism, cultural studies, production of narrative and documentary films.

University of Victoria, Faculty of Graduate Studies, Faculty of Fine Arts, Department of Visual Arts, Victoria, BC V8W 2Y2, Canada. Offers digital multimedia (MFA); drawing (MFA); painting (MFA); photography (MFA); sculpture (MFA); video (MFA). *Degree requirements:* For master's, exhibit, oral exam. *Entrance requirements:* For master's, portfolio, BFA. Additional exam requirements/recommendations for international students: Required—TOEFL (minimum score 575 paper-based; 233 computer-based), IELTS (minimum score 7). Electronic applications accepted.

University of Wisconsin–Milwaukee, Graduate School, Peck School of the Arts, Program in Performing Arts, Milwaukee, WI 53201-0413. Offers dance (MFA); film (MFA); theatre (MFA). Part-time programs available. *Faculty:* 35 full-time (21 women). *Students:* 18 full-time (12 women), 2 part-time (both women); includes 4 minority (2 African Americans, 1 Asian American or Pacific Islander, 1 Hispanic American), 1 international. Average age 33. 28 applicants, 21% accepted, 6 enrolled. In 2008, 17 master's awarded. *Degree requirements:* For master's, variable foreign language requirement, comprehensive exam, thesis or alternative. *Entrance*

Film, Television, and Video Theory and Criticism

requirements: For master's, audition, interview. Additional exam requirements/recommendations for international students: Required—TOEFL (minimum score 550 paper-based; 79 iBT), IELTS (minimum score 6.5). *Application deadline:* For fall admission, 1/1 priority date for domestic students; for spring admission, 9/1 for domestic students. Applications are processed on a rolling basis. Application fee: $45 ($75 for international students). *Expenses:* Tuition, area resident: Full-time $7320; part-time $165 per credit. Tuition, state resident: full-time $7320; part-time $165 per credit. Tuition, nonresident: full-time $17,840; part-time $714 per credit. Tuition and fees vary according to campus/location, program and reciprocity agreements. *Financial support:* In 2008–09, 13 teaching assistantships were awarded; career-related intern-

ships or fieldwork and unspecified assistantships also available. Support available to part-time students. Financial award application deadline: 4/15. *Unit head:* Simone Ferro, Representative, 414-229-4178, E-mail: sferro@uwm.edu. *Application contact:* General Information Contact, 414-229-4982, Fax: 414-229-6967, E-mail: gradschool@uwm.edu.

York University, Faculty of Graduate Studies, Faculty of Fine Arts, Program in Film, Toronto, ON M3J 1P3, Canada. Offers MA, MFA, PhD. *Degree requirements:* For master's, thesis. *Entrance requirements:* For master's, portfolio. Electronic applications accepted.

Film, Television, and Video Theory and Criticism

Boston University, College of Communication, Department of Film and Television, Boston, MA 02215. Offers film production (MFA); film studies (MFA); screenwriting (MFA); television (MS); television management (MS); MBA/MS. *Degree requirements:* For master's, thesis. *Entrance requirements:* For master's, GMAT (MS in television management), GRE General Test, sample of written or creative work. Additional exam requirements/recommendations for international students: Required—TOEFL. Electronic applications accepted.

See Close-Up on page 683.

California College of the Arts, Graduate Programs, Program in Visual and Critical Studies, San Francisco, CA 94107. Offers MA. *Degree requirements:* For master's, thesis, exhibit. *Entrance requirements:* For master's, appropriate bachelor's degree, portfolio. Additional exam requirements/recommendations for international students: Required—TOEFL (minimum score 600 paper-based; 250 computer-based). Electronic applications accepted.

See Close-Up on page 207.

Central Michigan University, College of Graduate Studies, College of Communication and Fine Arts, School of Broadcasting and Cinematic Arts, Mount Pleasant, MI 48859. Offers electronic media management (MA); electronic media studies (MA); film theory and criticism (MA); media production (MA). Part-time programs available. *Faculty:* 12 full-time (2 women). *Students:* 23 (8 women); includes 1 African American, 1 Asian American or Pacific Islander, 1 Hispanic American. Average age 26. *Degree requirements:* For master's, thesis or alternative. *Entrance requirements:* For master's, undergraduate degree in broadcasting, film studies, or an associated discipline with minimum GPA of 2.7. *Application deadline:* Applications are processed on a rolling basis. Application fee: $35 ($45 for international students). Electronic applications accepted. *Expenses:* Tuition, state resident: full-time $3717; part-time $413 per credit. Tuition, nonresident: full-time $6894; part-time $766 per credit. *Financial support:* Fellowships with tuition reimbursements, teaching assistantships with tuition reimbursements, career-related internships or fieldwork, Federal Work-Study, unspecified assistantships, and out-of-state merit awards available. Financial award application deadline: 3/7. *Faculty research:* Multimedia production, film history and criticism, writing and promotions, international broadcasting and media systems, history of American broadcasting. *Unit head:* Dr. Peter B. Orlik, Chairperson, 989-774-3851, Fax: 989-774-2426, E-mail: peter.b.orlik@cmich.edu. *Application contact:* Dr. Patricia Williamson, Graduate Program Coordinator, 989-774-2561, Fax: 989-774-2426, E-mail: willi1pa@cmich.edu.

Claremont Graduate University, Graduate Programs, School of Arts and Humanities, Department of English, Claremont, CA 91711-6160. Offers American studies (MA, PhD); critical theory (MA, PhD); early modern studies (MA, PhD); English (M Phil, MA, PhD); literary theory (PhD); literature (MA, PhD); literature and creative writing (MA); literature and film (MA); MBA/MA; MBA/PhD. Part-time programs available. *Faculty:* 2 full-time (1 woman), 2 part-time/adjunct (0 women). *Students:* 78 full-time (46 women), 12 part-time (9 women); includes 15 minority (1 African American, 2 American Indian/Alaska Native, 7 Asian Americans or Pacific Islanders, 5 Hispanic Americans), 2 international. Average age 35. In 2008, 9 master's, 11 doctorates awarded. *Entrance requirements:* For master's and doctorate, GRE General Test. Additional exam requirements/recommendations for international students: Required—TOEFL (minimum score 550 paper-based; 213 computer-based; 80 iBT). *Application deadline:* For fall admission, 2/1 priority date for domestic students. Applications are processed on a rolling basis. Application fee: $60. Electronic applications accepted. *Expenses:* Tuition: Full-time $33,698; part-time $1465 per unit. Required fees: $310; $155 per semester. Tuition and fees vary according to program. *Financial support:* Fellowships, Federal Work-Study, institutionally sponsored loans, and scholarships/grants available. Support available to part-time students. Financial award application deadline: 2/15; financial award applicants required to submit FAFSA. *Faculty research:* American, comparative, and English Renaissance literature; modernism; feminist literature and theory. *Unit head:* Wendy Martin, Chair, 909-621-8612, Fax: 909-607-1221, E-mail: wendy.martin@cgu.edu. *Application contact:* Justin Evans, Admissions Coordinator, 909-607-1278, Fax: 909-607-1221, E-mail: justin.evans@cgu.edu.

College of Staten Island of the City University of New York, Graduate Programs, Program in Cinema and Media Studies, Staten Island, NY 10314-6600. Offers MA. Part-time and evening/weekend programs available. *Faculty:* 5 full-time (2 women). *Students:* 15 part-time (7 women); includes 1 minority (Asian American or Pacific Islander), 5 international. Average age 31. 13 applicants, 54% accepted, 5 enrolled. In 2008, 4 master's awarded. *Degree requirements:* For master's, comprehensive exam, thesis optional, written thesis; original film, media or production thesis or written examination; 36 credits in cinema and media studies courses. *Entrance requirements:* For master's, bachelor's degree, 10-12 page critical writing sample on film or media topic, 3 letters of recommendation, 1-2 page statement of purpose. Additional exam requirements/recommendations for international students: Required—TOEFL (minimum score 550 paper-based; 213 computer-based; 79 iBT). *Application deadline:* For fall admission, 4/19 priority date for domestic and international students; for spring admission, 11/16 for domestic and international students. Applications are processed on a rolling basis. Application fee: $125. Electronic applications accepted. *Expenses:* Tuition, area resident: Full-time $6400; part-time $270 per credit. Tuition, nonresident: full-time $12,000; part-time $500 per credit. Required fees: $378; $113 per semester. *Financial support:* In 2008–09, 1 student received support, including 4 teaching assistantships (averaging $1,250 per year); career-related internships or fieldwork, Federal Work-Study, and scholarships/grants also available. Support available to part-time students. Financial award application deadline: 4/1; financial award applicants required to submit CSS PROFILE or FAFSA. *Unit head:* Dr. Matthew Solomon, Coordinator/Associate Professor, 718-982-2548, E-mail: cinemamasters@mail.csi.cuny.edu. *Application contact:* Sasha Spence, Assistant Director of Graduate Recruitment and Admissions, 718-982-2699, Fax: 718-982-2500, E-mail: spence@mail.csi.cuny.edu.

Concordia University, School of Graduate Studies, Faculty of Fine Arts, Mel Hoppenheim School of Cinema, Montréal, QC H3G 1M8, Canada. Offers film studies (MA).

Emory University, Graduate School of Arts and Sciences, Department of Film Studies, Atlanta, GA 30322-1100. Offers MA, PhD/Certificate. *Degree requirements:* For master's, comprehensive exam, thesis or alternative. *Entrance requirements:* For master's, GRE General Test, 3 letters of reference, 2 writing samples. Additional exam requirements/recommendations for international students: Required—TOEFL. Electronic applications accepted. *Faculty research:* International film history, film theory, film style, feminism and film, reception.

Emory University, Graduate School of Arts and Sciences, Department of Spanish and Portuguese, Atlanta, GA 30322-1100. Offers comparative literature (Certificate); film studies (Certificate); Spanish (PhD); women's studies (Certificate). *Degree requirements:* For doctorate, 2 foreign languages, comprehensive exam, thesis/dissertation. *Entrance requirements:* For doctorate, GRE General Test. Additional exam requirements/recommendations for international students: Required—TOEFL. Electronic applications accepted. *Faculty research:* Spanish literature, Spanish-American literature, literary theory, criticism, cultural studies.

Florida Atlantic University, Dorothy F. Schmidt College of Arts and Letters, School of Communication and Multimedia Studies, Boca Raton, FL 33431-0991. Offers communication studies (MA); film and video (Certificate); film studies (MA); multimedia journalism studies (MA). Part-time programs available. *Faculty:* 21 full-time (10 women), 14 part-time/adjunct (3 women). *Students:* 15 full-time (11 women), 10 part-time (5 women); includes 2 minority (1 Asian American or Pacific Islander, 1 Hispanic American), 3 international. Average age 29. 35 applicants, 37% accepted, 7 enrolled. In 2008, 8 master's awarded. *Degree requirements:* For master's, one foreign language, comprehensive exam (for some programs), thesis (for some programs). *Entrance requirements:* For master's, GRE General Test, minimum GPA of 3.0. *Application deadline:* For fall admission, 7/1 priority date for domestic students, 4/1 for international students; for spring admission, 11/1 for domestic students, 10/1 for international students. Applications are processed on a rolling basis. Application fee: $30. Electronic applications accepted. *Expenses:* Tuition, state resident: full-time $4867; part-time $270.40 per credit hour. Tuition, nonresident: full-time $16,486; part-time $915.87 per credit hour. *Financial support:* Teaching assistantships with partial tuition reimbursements, Federal Work-Study and institutionally sponsored loans available. Support available to part-time students. Financial award application deadline: 3/1. *Faculty research:* Cultural studies, gender studies, film, communication theory, journalism, new media. *Unit head:* Dr. Susan S. Reilly, Director, 561-297-1095, Fax: 561-297-2615, E-mail: sreilly@fau.edu. *Application contact:* Dr. Eric M. Freedman, Graduate Coordinator, 561-297-2534, Fax: 561-297-2615, E-mail: efreedma@fau.edu.

Hollins University, Graduate Programs, Program in Screenwriting and Film Studies, Roanoke, VA 24020-1603. Offers MA, MFA. Offered during summer only. Part-time programs available. *Faculty:* 1 full-time (0 women), 6 part-time/adjunct (2 women). *Students:* 37 full-time (21 women), 3 part-time (2 women); includes 8 minority (5 African Americans, 3 Hispanic Americans), 2 international. Average age 34. 30 applicants, 90% accepted, 15 enrolled. In 2008, 7 master's awarded. *Degree requirements:* For master's, one foreign language, comprehensive exam, thesis. *Entrance requirements:* For master's, letters of recommendation, portfolio. Additional exam requirements/recommendations for international students: Required—TOEFL (minimum score 550 paper-based; 213 computer-based; 79 iBT). *Application deadline:* For fall admission, 2/15 for domestic and international students. Application fee: $40. Electronic applications accepted. *Expenses:* Tuition: Full-time $26,720; part-time $590 per credit hour. Required fees: $280. *Financial support:* In 2008–09, 24 students received support, including 13 fellowships (averaging $700 per year); Federal Work-Study and scholarships/grants also available. Support available to part-time students. Financial award application deadline: 2/15; financial award applicants required to submit FAFSA. *Faculty research:* German film, women in film, censorship, minorities in film. *Unit head:* Dr. Klaus Phillips, Director, 540-362-6308, E-mail: kphillips@hollins.edu. *Application contact:* Cathy S. Koon, Manager of Graduate Services, 540-362-6326, Fax: 540-362-6288, E-mail: ckoon@hollins.edu.

Indiana University Bloomington, University Graduate School, College of Arts and Sciences, Department of Communication and Culture, Bloomington, IN 47405-7000. Offers film and media studies (PhD); performance and ethnography (PhD); rhetoric and public culture (PhD). *Faculty:* 24 full-time (12 women). *Students:* 81 full-time (45 women); includes 11 minority (2 African Americans, 1 American Indian/Alaska Native, 2 Asian Americans or Pacific Islanders, 6 Hispanic Americans), 10 international. Average age 32. 163 applicants, 20% accepted, 16 enrolled. In 2008, 5 master's, 11 doctorates awarded. *Degree requirements:* For master's, comprehensive exam; for doctorate, one foreign language, comprehensive exam, thesis/dissertation, student teaching. *Entrance requirements:* For master's and doctorate, GRE General Test (recommended), minimum GPA of 3.0, 3 letters of recommendation, writing sample. Additional exam requirements/recommendations for international students: Required—TOEFL (minimum score 550 paper-based; 213 computer-based). *Application deadline:* For winter admission, 1/1 for domestic students, 12/1 for international students. Application fee: $50 ($60 for international students). Electronic applications accepted. *Expenses:* Tuition, area resident: Part-time $291.97 per credit hour. Tuition, state resident: part-time $291.97 per credit hour. Tuition, nonresident: part-time $850.33 per credit hour. Required fees: $110 per semester. Tuition and fees vary according to course load and program. *Financial support:* In 2008–09, 65 students received support, including 4 fellowships with full tuition reimbursements available (averaging $18,000 per year), 61 teaching assistantships with full tuition reimbursements available (averaging $12,961 per year). Financial award application deadline: 4/15. *Faculty research:* Rhetoric and public culture, film and media studies, performance ethnography. *Unit head:* Prof. Gregory A. Waller, Chair, 812-855-2367, Fax: 812-855-6014, E-mail: cmcl@indiana.edu. *Application contact:* Kathy P. Teige, Graduate Secretary, 812-855-6389, Fax: 812-855-6014, E-mail: kteige@indiana.edu.

New York University, Tisch School of the Arts and Graduate School of Arts and Science, Department of Cinema Studies, New York, NY 10012-1019. Offers cinema studies (MA, PhD); moving image archiving and preservation (MA). *Degree requirements:* For master's, comprehensive exam; for doctorate, one foreign language, thesis/dissertation, 3 comprehensive

Film, Television, and Video Theory and Criticism

New York University *(continued)*
exams. *Entrance requirements:* For master's, GRE, sample of written work; for doctorate, GRE, master's degree, writing sample. Additional exam requirements/recommendations for international students: Required—TOEFL or IELTS. Electronic applications accepted. *Expenses:* Contact institution. *Faculty research:* History and aesthetics of American, European, and Third World cinemas; theory of film and the moving image; cultural studies; gay and lesbian media.

The Ohio State University, Graduate School, College of the Arts, Department of Photography and Cinema, Columbus, OH 43210. Offers MA. Electronic applications accepted.

Ohio University, Graduate College, College of Fine Arts, School of Film, Athens, OH 45701-2979. Offers film (MFA); film studies (MA). *Degree requirements:* For master's, one foreign language, thesis. *Entrance requirements:* Additional exam requirements/recommendations for international students: Required—TOEFL (minimum score 550 paper-based; 239 computer-based). Electronic applications accepted. *Faculty research:* Scriptwriting, sound, editing, cinematography, film theory, digital pest production.

San Francisco State University, Division of Graduate Studies, College of Creative Arts, Department of Cinema, San Francisco, CA 94132-1722. Offers cinema (MFA); cinema studies (MA).

Savannah College of Art and Design, Graduate School, Program in Cinema Studies, Savannah, GA 31402-3146. Offers MA. Part-time programs available. *Degree requirements:* For master's, thesis. *Entrance requirements:* For master's, interview. Additional exam requirements/recommendations for international students: Required—TOEFL (minimum score 450 paper-based; 133 computer-based). Electronic applications accepted. *Expenses:* Tuition: Full-time $28,215; part-time $3135 per course. One-time fee: $500.

Syracuse University, Graduate School, S. I. Newhouse School of Public Communications, Program in Documentary Film and History, Syracuse, NY 13244. Offers MA. *Entrance requirements:* For master's, GRE General Test.

Université de Montréal, Faculty of Arts and Sciences, Department of Art History and Film Studies, Montréal, QC H3C 3J7, Canada. Offers art history (MA, PhD); film studies (MA, PhD). *Faculty:* 27 full-time (13 women), 5 part-time/adjunct (1 woman). *Students:* 73 full-time (40 women), 74 part-time (47 women). 90 applicants, 57% accepted, 44 enrolled. In 2008, 23 master's, 3 doctorates awarded. *Degree requirements:* For master's, thesis. *Application deadline:* For fall admission, 2/1 priority date for domestic students; for winter admission, 11/1 priority date for domestic students; for spring admission, 2/1 priority date for domestic students. Application fee: $100. Electronic applications accepted. *Financial support:* Research assistantships, teaching assistantships available. *Faculty research:* Western art from the Middle Ages, classic and modern theory, modern and contemporary art, Canadian art. *Unit head:* Christine Bernier, Director, 514-343-6184, Fax: 514-343-2393, E-mail: christine_bernier@umontreal.ca. *Application contact:* Johanne Lamoureux, Information Contact: Art History, 514-343-5713, E-mail: johanne.lamoureux.2@umontreal.ca.

Université de Montréal, Faculty of Arts and Sciences, Department of Literatures and Modern Languages, Montréal, QC H3C 3J7, Canada. Offers German literature (PhD); German studies (MA); Hispanic literature (PhD); Hispanic studies (MA); literature and cinema (PhD). *Faculty:* 14 full-time (6 women), 1 (woman) part-time/adjunct. *Students:* 22 full-time (15 women), 23 part-time (16 women). 42 applicants, 45% accepted, 15 enrolled. In 2008, 13 master's awarded. Terminal master's awarded for partial completion of doctoral program. *Degree requirements:* For master's, 2 foreign languages, thesis; for doctorate, 2 foreign languages, thesis/dissertation, general exam. *Application deadline:* For fall admission, 2/1 priority date for domestic students; for winter admission, 11/1 priority date for domestic students; for spring admission, 2/1 priority date for domestic students. Application fee: $100. Electronic applications accepted. *Financial support:* Teaching assistantships available. *Unit head:* Georges Bastin, Director, 514-343-7050, Fax: 514-343-2255, E-mail: georges.bastin@umontreal.ca. *Application contact:* Nikola von Merveldt, Responsible for German Studies Program, 514-343-5905, Fax: 514-343-2255, E-mail: n.von.merveldt@umontreal.ca.

Université Laval, Faculty of Letters, Department of Literature, Programs in Literature and Arts of the Screen and Stage, Québec, QC G1K 7P4, Canada. Offers MA, PhD. Part-time programs available. Terminal master's awarded for partial completion of doctoral program. *Degree requirements:* For master's, thesis; for doctorate, comprehensive exam, thesis/dissertation. *Entrance requirements:* For master's and doctorate, linguistics exams, knowledge of French, knowledge of a second language. Electronic applications accepted.

The University of British Columbia, Faculty of Arts and Faculty of Graduate Studies, Department of Theatre and Film, Film Program, Vancouver, BC V6T 1Z1, Canada. Offers creative writing and film production (MFA); film production (MFA, Diploma); film studies (MA). *Degree requirements:* For master's, thesis (MA), thesis or project (MFA). *Entrance requirements:* For master's, bachelor's degree in film production or equivalent, BA in film studies. Additional exam requirements/recommendations for international students: Required—TOEFL (minimum score 600 paper-based). Electronic applications accepted. *Faculty research:* Film history, theory, criticism; producing; experimental film.

University of Chicago, Division of the Humanities, Committee on Cinema and Media Studies, Chicago, IL 60637-1513. Offers AM, PhD. *Degree requirements:* For master's, one foreign language, thesis; for doctorate, 2 foreign languages, thesis/dissertation.

The University of Iowa, Graduate College, College of Liberal Arts and Sciences, Department of Cinema and Comparative Literature, Program in Film Studies, Iowa City, IA 52242-1316. Offers MA, PhD. *Degree requirements:* For master's, thesis optional, exam; for doctorate, comprehensive exam, thesis/dissertation. *Entrance requirements:* For master's and doctorate, GRE General Test, minimum GPA of 3.0. Additional exam requirements/recommendations for international students: Required—TOEFL (minimum score 550 paper-based; 213 computer-based; 81 iBT). Electronic applications accepted.

The University of Kansas, Graduate Studies, College of Liberal Arts and Sciences, Department of Theatre and Film, Lawrence, KS 66045. Offers film and media studies (PhD); theatre (MA); theatre design (MFA), including scenography. *Faculty:* 24. *Students:* 36 full-time (13 women), 3 part-time (1 woman); includes 2 minority (both Asian Americans or Pacific Islanders), 8 international. Average age 34. 34 applicants, 59% accepted, 7 enrolled. In 2008, 4 master's, 2 doctorates awarded. *Degree requirements:* For master's, thesis; for doctorate, one foreign language, comprehensive exam, thesis/dissertation. *Entrance requirements:* For master's, GRE General Test, minimum GPA of 3.2; for doctorate, GRE General Test, minimum GPA of 3.5; MA or MFA in theatre, film, or related field. Additional exam requirements/recommendations for international students: Required—TOEFL. *Application deadline:* For fall admission, 1/1 priority date for domestic students, 1/1 for international students. Application fee: $45 ($55 for international students). Electronic applications accepted. *Expenses:* Tuition, area resident: Full-time $6122; part-time $255.10 per credit hour. Tuition, state resident: full-time $6122; part-time $255.10 per credit hour. Tuition, nonresident: full-time $14,629; part-time $609.55 per credit hour. Required fees: $847; $70.56 per credit hour. Tuition and fees vary according to course load and program. *Financial support:* Fellowships with tuition reimbursements, teaching assistantships with full and partial tuition reimbursements, Federal Work-Study, scholarships/grants, and unspecified assistantships available. Financial award application deadline: 1/1. *Faculty research:* Film history, theatre history, film theory, cultural studies, performance studies. *Unit head:* John Staniunas, Chair, 785-864-3511, Fax: 785-864-5251. *Application contact:* Henry Bial, Director of Graduate Studies, 785-864-3511, Fax: 785-331-5251, E-mail: tfdgs@ku.edu.

University of Miami, Graduate School, School of Communication, Coral Gables, FL 33124. Offers communication (PhD); communication studies (MA); film studies (MA, PhD); motion pictures (MFA), including production, producing, and screenwriting; print journalism (MA); public relations (MA); Spanish language journalism (MA); television broadcast journalism (MA). *Accreditation:* ACEJMC. Part-time programs available. *Degree requirements:* For master's, comprehensive exam (for some programs), thesis (for some programs); for doctorate, comprehensive exam, thesis/dissertation. *Entrance requirements:* For master's, GRE General Test; for doctorate, GRE General Test, master's thesis or scholarly research. Additional exam requirements/recommendations for international students: Required—TOEFL (minimum score 600 paper-based; 250 computer-based; 100 iBT). Electronic applications accepted. *Faculty research:* Communication studies, mass communication, international/interpersonal communication, film studies, journalism.

University of Michigan, Horace H. Rackham School of Graduate Studies, College of Literature, Science, and the Arts, Department of Screen Arts and Cultures, Ann Arbor, MI 48109. Offers PhD, Certificate. Part-time programs available. *Degree requirements:* For doctorate, one foreign language, comprehensive exam, thesis/dissertation; for Certificate, 15 credit hours (3 directed study). Electronic applications accepted. *Faculty research:* Transnational cinema, classical Hollywood cinema, silent cinema, film theory, television.

University of Southern California, Graduate School, School of Cinematic Arts, Programs in Critical Studies, Los Angeles, CA 90089. Offers MA, PhD. *Degree requirements:* For doctorate, thesis/dissertation. *Entrance requirements:* For master's and doctorate, GRE General Test. *Faculty research:* Transnational cinema, global media, television studies, American film history.

University of Wisconsin–Madison, Graduate School, College of Letters and Science, Department of Communication Arts, Madison, WI 53706-1380. Offers communication science (MA, PhD); film (MA, PhD); media and cultural studies (MA, PhD); rhetoric (MA, PhD). Terminal master's awarded for partial completion of doctoral program. *Degree requirements:* For master's, one foreign language, thesis (for some programs); for doctorate, one foreign language, thesis/dissertation. *Entrance requirements:* For master's and doctorate, GRE General Test, minimum GPA of 3.5. Electronic applications accepted.

Wilfrid Laurier University, Faculty of Graduate Studies, Faculty of Arts, Department of English and Film Studies, Waterloo, ON N2L 3C5, Canada. Offers MA, PhD. *Degree requirements:* For master's, thesis optional; for doctorate, thesis/dissertation. *Entrance requirements:* For master's, honours BA or the equivalent in English, minimum B+ in English courses above first year level; for doctorate, MA in English, minimum A- average in graduate work. Additional exam requirements/recommendations for international students: Recommended—TOEFL (minimum score 230 computer-based; 89 iBT). Electronic applications accepted. *Faculty research:* Gender and genre, Canadian studies, early modern studies, postcolonial studies, nineteenth century studies.

Yale University, Graduate School of Arts and Sciences, Department of East Asian Languages and Literatures, New Haven, CT 06520. Offers East Asian languages and literatures (PhD); East Asian languages and literatures and film studies (PhD). *Degree requirements:* For doctorate, 2 foreign languages, thesis/dissertation. *Entrance requirements:* For doctorate, GRE General Test.

Yale University, Graduate School of Arts and Sciences, Department of Slavic Languages and Literatures, New Haven, CT 06520. Offers medieval Slavic literature and philology (PhD); Polish literature (PhD); Russian literature (PhD); Slavic languages and literatures and film studies (PhD). *Degree requirements:* For doctorate, 3 foreign languages, thesis/dissertation. *Entrance requirements:* For doctorate, GRE General Test.

Yale University, Graduate School of Arts and Sciences, Interdisciplinary Program in Film Studies, New Haven, CT 06520. Offers PhD.

Section 6
Performing Arts

This section contains a directory of institutions offering graduate work in performing arts, followed by in-depth entries submitted by institutions that chose to prepare detailed program descriptions. Additional information about programs listed in the directory but not augmented by an in-depth entry may be obtained by writing directly to the dean of a graduate school or chair of a department at the address given in the directory.

For programs offering related work, see also in this book *Area and Cultural Studies, Art and Art History, Communication and Media,* and *Film, Television, and Video.* In another guide in this series: ***Graduate Programs in Business, Education, Health, Information Studies, Law & Social Work***

See *Leisure Studies and Recreation, Subject Areas (Music Education),* and *Physical Education and Kinesiology*

CONTENTS

Program Directories
Dance   246
Music   248
Theater   271
Therapies—Dance, Drama, and Music   283

Display
University of Hawaii at Manoa   279

Close-Ups
Columbia University   285
The New School: A University   287
Sarah Lawrence College   289
Southern Illinois University Carbondale   291
University of Southern California   293

See also:
California Institute of Integral Studies—Psychology   1105
Lesley University—Expressive Therapies   211
Naropa University—Graduate Studies   1121
Pratt Institute—Art and Design   219
Savannah College of Art and Design—Art and
    Design   223
School of the Art Institute of Chicago—Graduate
    Studies in Art   225
The University of the Arts—Graduate Studies   233

Dance

Arizona State University, Graduate College, Herberger College of the Arts, Department of Dance, Tempe, AZ 85287. Offers MFA. *Degree requirements:* For master's, thesis optional.

Bennington College, Graduate Programs, Program in Dance, Bennington, VT 05201. Offers MFA. Part-time programs available. *Faculty:* 3 full-time (2 women), 3 part-time/adjunct (2 women). *Students:* 1 (woman) full-time. Average age 44. 7 applicants, 14% accepted, 0 enrolled. *Degree requirements:* For master's, performances. *Application deadline:* For fall admission, 2/1 for domestic students. Application fee: $60. *Expenses:* Tuition: Full-time $20,640; part-time $2890 per course. One-time fee: $75. Tuition and fees vary according to program. *Financial support:* In 2008–09, 1 student received support, including 1 teaching assistantship; unspecified assistantships also available. Financial award application deadline: 4/1; financial award applicants required to submit FAFSA. *Faculty research:* Exploration of relationship between emergent improvisation and complex systems. *Unit head:* Terry Creach, Associate Dean for Academic Affairs/Dance, 802-440-4406, Fax: 802-440-4876, E-mail: tcreach@bennington.edu. *Application contact:* Mary Surdam, Admissions Coordinator, 802-440-4312, Fax: 802-440-4320, E-mail: admissions@bennington.edu.

California Institute of the Arts, School of Dance, Valencia, CA 91355-2340. Offers MFA, Adv C. *Accreditation:* NASD. *Degree requirements:* For master's, thesis presentation. *Entrance requirements:* For master's, audition, video of choreography. Additional exam requirements/recommendations for international students: Required—TOEFL.

California State University, Fullerton, Graduate Studies, College of the Arts, Department of Theatre and Dance, Fullerton, CA 92834-9480. Offers acting (MFA); acting and directing (MA); dance (MA); directing (MFA); dramatic literature/criticism (MA); oral interpretation (MA); playwriting (MA); technical theater (MA); technical theater and design (MFA); television (MA); theatre for children (MA); theatre history (MA). *Accreditation:* NASD; NAST (one or more programs are accredited). Part-time programs available. *Students:* 21 full-time (10 women), 3 part-time (2 women); includes 2 minority (both African Americans). Average age 29. 43 applicants, 26% accepted, 11 enrolled. In 2008, 3 master's awarded. *Degree requirements:* For master's, oral and written exam, project or thesis. *Entrance requirements:* For master's, major in theatre or related field, audition or interview, minimum GPA of 2.5 in last 60 units of course work. Application fee: $55. Tuition and fees vary according to degree level. *Financial support:* Teaching assistantships, career-related internships or fieldwork, Federal Work-Study, institutionally sponsored loans, and scholarships/grants available. Support available to part-time students. Financial award application deadline: 3/1. *Unit head:* Dr. Susan Hallman, Chair, 657-278-3628. *Application contact:* Gretchen Kanne, Adviser, 657-278-3628.

California State University, Long Beach, Graduate Studies, College of the Arts, Department of Dance, Long Beach, CA 90840. Offers MA, MFA. *Accreditation:* NASD. Part-time programs available. *Faculty:* 5 full-time (3 women). *Students:* 4 full-time (all women). Average age 36. 48 applicants, 48% accepted, 4 enrolled. *Degree requirements:* For master's, thesis. *Application deadline:* Applications are processed on a rolling basis. Application fee: $5. Electronic applications accepted. *Expenses:* Tuition, nonresident: full-time $11,160; part-time $372 per unit. Required fees: $4100; $1261 per semester. *Financial support:* Federal Work-Study, institutionally sponsored loans, scholarships/grants, and traineeships available. Financial award application deadline: 3/2. *Unit head:* Prof. Cyrus Parker-Jeanette, Chair, 562-985-4747, Fax: 562-985-7896, E-mail: cyparker@csulb.edu. *Application contact:* Prof. Coleen Dunagan, Graduate Advisor, 562-985-4747, Fax: 562-985-7896, E-mail: cdunagan@csulb.edu.

California State University, Sacramento, Graduate Studies, College of Arts and Letters, Department of Theatre and Dance, Sacramento, CA 95819-6048. Offers MA. *Accreditation:* NAST. Part-time programs available. *Degree requirements:* For master's, thesis or alternative, writing proficiency exam. *Entrance requirements:* For master's, GRE General Test, BA in drama or equivalent, minimum GPA of 2.5 during previous 2 years of course work. Additional exam requirements/recommendations for international students: Required—TOEFL. Electronic applications accepted.

Case Western Reserve University, School of Graduate Studies, Department of Theater and Dance, Cleveland, OH 44106. Offers acting (MFA); contemporary dance (MFA); dance (MA); theater (MFA). *Degree requirements:* For master's, thesis, oral presentation and defense, portfolio. *Entrance requirements:* For master's, audition, interview. Additional exam requirements/recommendations for international students: Required—TOEFL. Electronic applications accepted. *Faculty research:* Playwriting; history of theater; participation in professional area theaters in performing, design, acting, coaching.

The College at Brockport, State University of New York, School of Arts and Performance, Department of Dance, Brockport, NY 14420-2997. Offers MA, MFA. *Accreditation:* NASD. Part-time programs available. *Degree requirements:* For master's, thesis or alternative. *Entrance requirements:* For master's, local writing assessment assignment, audition/interview, minimum GPA of 3.0, letters of recommendation. Additional exam requirements/recommendations for international students: Required—TOEFL (minimum score 550 paper-based; 213 computer-based; 79 iBT). *Faculty research:* Choreography and performance, world dance and culture, dance process and theory, dance education, dance science and somatics.

Florida State University, Graduate Studies, College of Visual Arts, Theatre and Dance, Department of Dance, Tallahassee, FL 32306. Offers American dance studies (MA); dance (MFA); studio and related studies (MA). *Accreditation:* NASD. *Degree requirements:* For master's, comprehensive exam (for some programs), thesis (for some programs), technical proficiency (MFA), 1 foreign language (MA). *Entrance requirements:* For master's, GRE General Test (MA in American Dance Studies), audition, writing sample (MFA) Dance and MA Studio and related studies. Additional exam requirements/recommendations for international students: Required—TOEFL (minimum score 550 paper-based; 213 computer-based). Electronic applications accepted. *Faculty research:* Choreography, performance, dance and cultural significance, American dance history, dance technology.

George Mason University, College of Visual and Performing Arts, Program in Dance, Fairfax, VA 22030. Offers MFA. *Degree requirements:* For master's, choreographed performance. *Entrance requirements:* For master's, video of choreography or performance. Electronic applications accepted. *Faculty research:* Choreography, performance.

Hollins University, Graduate Programs, Program in Dance, Roanoke, VA 24020-1603. Offers MFA. *Faculty:* 2 full-time (1 woman), 2 part-time/adjunct (both women). *Students:* 17 full-time (14 women), 4 part-time (2 women); includes 6 minority (3 African Americans, 1 Asian American or Pacific Islander, 2 Hispanic Americans), 5 international. Average age 34. 72 applicants, 32% accepted, 15 enrolled. In 2008, 16 master's awarded. *Degree requirements:* For master's, thesis. *Entrance requirements:* For master's, videotape of selected works, 3 letters of recommendation, resumé. Additional exam requirements/recommendations for international students: Required—TOEFL (minimum score 550 paper-based; 213 computer-based; 79 iBT). *Application deadline:* For fall admission, 12/1 for domestic and international students. Application fee: $40. Electronic applications accepted. *Expenses:* Tuition: Full-time $26,720; part-time $590 per credit hour. Required fees: $280. *Financial support:* In 2008–09, 21 fellowships (averaging $3,362 per year) were awarded; teaching assistantships. Support available to part-time students. Financial award application deadline: 2/2. *Unit head:* Donna Faye Burchfield, Artistic Director, 540-362-6596, E-mail: dburchfield@hollins.edu. *Application contact:* Cathy S. Koon, Manager of Graduate Services, 540-362-6326, Fax: 540-362-6288, E-mail: ckoon@hollins.edu.

Mills College, Graduate Studies, Department of Dance, Oakland, CA 94613-1000. Offers dance (MA, MFA), including choreography and performance (MA). Part-time programs available. *Faculty:* 5 full-time (all women), 5 part-time/adjunct (3 women). *Students:* 19 full-time (all women); includes 3 minority (1 African American, 2 Asian Americans or Pacific Islanders). Average age 29. 41 applicants, 56% accepted, 10 enrolled. In 2008, 10 master's awarded. *Degree requirements:* For master's, comprehensive exam, thesis, performance. *Entrance requirements:* For master's, audition or tape. Additional exam requirements/recommendations for international students: Required—TOEFL. *Application deadline:* For fall admission, 2/1 priority date for domestic and international students. Applications are processed on a rolling basis. Application fee: $50. *Expenses:* Tuition: Full-time $25,072; part-time $6272 per course. Required fees: $880. *Financial support:* In 2008–09, 17 students received support, including 12 fellowships (averaging $5,708 per year), 10 teaching assistantships with partial tuition reimbursements available (averaging $5,014 per year); scholarships/grants and unspecified assistantships also available. Financial award application deadline: 2/1; financial award applicants required to submit FAFSA. *Faculty research:* Video and dance, modern dance technique, performance art, rhythmic analysis. *Unit head:* Sonya Delwaide, Head, 510-430-3258, E-mail: sdelwaid@mills.edu. *Application contact:* Marika Benko, Graduate Admission Specialist, 510-430-3309, Fax: 510-430-2159, E-mail: grad-studies@mills.edu.

New York University, Steinhardt School of Culture, Education and Human Development, Department of Music and Performing Arts Professions, Program in Dance Education, New York, NY 10012-1019. Offers MA, Ed D, PhD. Part-time and evening/weekend programs available. Terminal master's awarded for partial completion of doctoral program. *Degree requirements:* For master's, thesis (for some programs); for doctorate, thesis/dissertation. *Entrance requirements:* For master's, audition, interview; for doctorate, GRE General Test, audition, interview. Additional exam requirements/recommendations for international students: Required—TOEFL. *Faculty research:* Dance cognition and creativity, technology in dance, development of teacher expertise.

New York University, Tisch School of the Arts, Department of Dance, New York, NY 10012-1019. Offers MFA. *Entrance requirements:* For master's, audition. Additional exam requirements/recommendations for international students: Required—TOEFL or IELTS. Electronic applications accepted.

New York University, Tisch School of the Arts and Graduate School of Arts and Science, Department of Performance Studies, New York, NY 10012-1019. Offers MA, PhD. *Degree requirements:* For doctorate, one foreign language, comprehensive exam, thesis/dissertation, dissertation defense, qualifying exam. *Entrance requirements:* For master's, sample of written work; for doctorate, master's degree, writing sample. Additional exam requirements/recommendations for international students: Required—TOEFL or IELTS. Electronic applications accepted. *Expenses:* Contact institution. *Faculty research:* Performance theory, dance, folklore and festivals, postcolonial theory, anthropology and gender studies.

Northern Illinois University, Graduate School, College of Visual and Performing Arts, School of Theatre and Dance, De Kalb, IL 60115-2854. Offers MFA. *Accreditation:* NAST. Part-time programs available. *Degree requirements:* For master's, comprehensive exam, final project and defense. *Entrance requirements:* For master's, minimum GPA of 2.75, audition or portfolio. Additional exam requirements/recommendations for international students: Required—TOEFL (minimum score 550 paper-based; 213 computer-based). Electronic applications accepted. *Faculty research:* Theatre history, choreography, performance art spectacles, storytelling, computer visualization of the ethical space.

The Ohio State University, Graduate School, College of the Arts, Department of Dance, Program in Dance Studies, Columbus, OH 43210. Offers PhD. Electronic applications accepted.

Oklahoma City University, Margaret E. Petree College of Performing Arts, Ann Lacy School of American Dance and Arts Management, Oklahoma City, OK 73106-1402. Offers dance (MFA).

Purchase College, State University of New York, Conservatory of Dance, Purchase, NY 10577-1400. Offers MFA. *Students:* 13 full-time (11 women), 1 (woman) part-time; includes 3 minority (1 African American, 1 American Indian/Alaska Native, 1 Asian American or Pacific Islander), 5 international. Average age 29. 31 applicants, 35% accepted, 8 enrolled. In 2008, 1 master's awarded. *Degree requirements:* For master's, performance. *Entrance requirements:* For master's, audition. *Application deadline:* For fall admission, 3/15 priority date for domestic students. Applications are processed on a rolling basis. Application fee: $50. Electronic applications accepted. *Expenses:* Tuition, area resident: Full-time $6900; part-time $288 per credit. Tuition, state resident: full-time $6900; part-time $288 per credit. Tuition, nonresident: full-time $10,920; part-time $455 per credit. Required fees: $1461; $0.85 per credit. One-time fee: $75 full-time. *Financial support:* Fellowships, teaching assistantships, Federal Work-Study, scholarships/grants, and tuition waivers (partial) available. Support available to part-time students. Financial award application deadline: 3/15; financial award applicants required to submit FAFSA. *Unit head:* Stacey-Jo Marine, Interim Associate Dean, 914-251-6800, Fax: 914-251-6806. *Application contact:* Sabrina Johnston, Counselor, 914-251-6479, Fax: 914-251-6314, E-mail: admissn@purchase.edu.

Sam Houston State University, College of Arts and Sciences, Department of Theatre and Dance, Huntsville, TX 77341. Offers dance (MFA). *Faculty:* 2 full-time (both women), 1 part-time/adjunct (0 women). *Students:* 6 full-time (all women), 1 (woman) part-time; includes 2 minority (1 African American, 1 Hispanic American). Average age 24. 4 applicants, 100% accepted, 4 enrolled. In 2008, 5 master's awarded. *Degree requirements:* For master's, thesis, project. *Entrance requirements:* For master's, GRE General Test. Additional exam requirements/recommendations for international students: Required—TOEFL (minimum score 550 paper-based; 213 computer-based; 79 iBT). *Application deadline:* For fall admission, 8/1 for domestic and international students; for spring admission, 12/1 for domestic and international students. Applications are processed on a rolling basis. Application fee: $20. *Expenses:* Tuition, state resident: full-time $3564; part-time $198 per credit hour. Tuition, nonresident: full-time $8622; part-time $479 per credit hour. Required fees: $1290. Tuition and fees vary according to course load and campus/location. *Financial support:* Teaching assistantships, career-related internships or fieldwork, Federal Work-Study, and institutionally sponsored loans available. Financial award application deadline: 5/31; financial award applicants required to submit FAFSA. *Unit head:* Penelope Hasekoester, Chair, 936-294-1330, Fax: 936-294-3898, E-mail: drm_pah@shsu.edu. *Application contact:* Penelope Hasekoester, Chair, 936-294-1330, Fax: 936-294-3898, E-mail: drm_pah@shsu.edu.

Sarah Lawrence College, Graduate Studies, Program in Dance, Bronxville, NY 10708-5999. Offers MFA. *Faculty:* 25 part-time/adjunct (16 women). *Students:* 6 full-time (all women), 1 part-time (0 women); includes 1 minority (African American). 30 applicants, 40% accepted, 4 enrolled. In 2008, 6 master's awarded. *Degree requirements:* For master's, performance. *Entrance requirements:* For master's, audition, minimum B average in undergraduate course work. *Application deadline:* For fall admission, 1/15 for domestic and international students. Application fee: $60. *Expenses:* Tuition: Full-time $26,544; part-time $1106 per credit. Required fees: $450. Tuition and fees vary according to program. *Financial support:* Fellowships, career-related internships or fieldwork, scholarships/grants, and health care benefits available. Support available to part-time students. Financial award application deadline: 3/1; financial award applicants required to submit FAFSA. *Unit head:* Sara Rudner, Director, 914-395-2433. *Application contact:* Susan Guma, Dean of Graduate Studies, 914-395-2373, E-mail: sguma@mail.slc.edu.

See Close-Up on page 289.

Shenandoah University, Shenandoah Conservatory, Winchester, VA 22601-5195. Offers arts administration (MS); church music (MM, Certificate); composition (MM); conducting (MM); dance (MA, MFA, MS); dance accompanying (MM); music (MS); music education (MME, DMA); music therapy (MMT, Certificate); pedagogy (MM, DMA); performance (MM, DMA, Artist Diploma); piano accompanying (MM). *Accreditation:* NASM. Part-time and evening/weekend programs available. *Faculty:* 39 full-time (19 women), 21 part-time/adjunct (9 women).

Students: 71 full-time (42 women), 150 part-time (80 women); includes 14 minority (9 African Americans, 2 Asian Americans or Pacific Islanders, 3 Hispanic Americans), 32 international. Average age 40. 76 applicants, 96% accepted, 49 enrolled. In 2008, 24 master's, 10 doctorates, 7 other advanced degrees awarded. *Degree requirements:* For master's, comprehensive exam (for some programs), thesis (for some programs), internship (MS), recital (MM), research teaching project or thesis (MME), project (MA); for doctorate, comprehensive exam, thesis/dissertation (for some programs), dissertation or teaching project, recital; for other advanced degree, research project, recital. *Entrance requirements:* For master's, audition, minimum GPA of 2.5, writing sample, resumé; for doctorate, audition, minimum GPA of 3.25, 2 letters of recommendation, writing sample, resumé; for other advanced degree, bachelor or master's degree; minimum GPA of 2.5. Additional exam requirements/recommendations for international students: Required—TOEFL (minimum score 550 paper-based; 213 computer-based), IELTS (minimum score 6.5), Sakae Institute of Study Abroad (SISA): 550. *Application deadline:* Applications are processed on a rolling basis. Application fee: $30. Electronic applications accepted. *Expenses:* Tuition: Full-time $16,900; part-time $670 per credit. *Financial support:* In 2008–09, 154 students received support, including 26 teaching assistantships with partial tuition reimbursements available (averaging $5,870 per year); fellowships, career-related internships or fieldwork, institutionally sponsored loans, scholarships/grants, and unspecified assistantships also available. Support available to part-time students. Financial award application deadline: 3/15; financial award applicants required to submit FAFSA. *Faculty research:* Creative activity, performance practice, music therapy aging, composition, Motown music. Total annual research expenditures: $4,272. *Unit head:* Dr. Laurence A. Kaptain, Dean, 540-665-4600, Fax: 540-665-5402, E-mail: lkaptain@su.edu. *Application contact:* David Anthony, Dean of Admissions, 540-665-4581, Fax: 540-665-4627, E-mail: admit@su.edu.

Smith College, Graduate and Special Programs, Department of Dance, Northampton, MA 01063. Offers MFA. Part-time programs available. *Faculty:* 2 full-time (1 woman), 1 (woman) part-time/adjunct. *Students:* 7 part-time (all women); includes 1 minority (African American). Average age 28. 17 applicants, 24% accepted, 4 enrolled. In 2008, 4 master's awarded. *Degree requirements:* For master's, thesis performance. *Entrance requirements:* For master's, audition. Additional exam requirements/recommendations for international students: Required—TOEFL (minimum score 590 paper-based; 243 computer-based; 97 iBT). *Application deadline:* For fall admission, 1/15 for domestic and international students. Application fee: $60. *Financial support:* In 2008–09, 7 students received support, including 7 teaching assistantships with full tuition reimbursements available (averaging $5,955 per year); institutionally sponsored loans and scholarships/grants also available. Support available to part-time students. Financial award application deadline: 1/15; financial award applicants required to submit CSS PROFILE or FAFSA. *Unit head:* Rodger Blum, Chair, 413-585-3234, E-mail: rblum@smith.edu. *Application contact:* Susan Waltner, Graduate Student Adviser, 413-585-3236, E-mail: swaltner@smith.edu.

Southern Methodist University, Meadows School of the Arts, Division of Dance, Dallas, TX 75275. Offers MFA. *Accreditation:* NASD. *Faculty:* 9 full-time (6 women), 2 part-time/adjunct (both women). *Students:* 3 full-time (1 woman), 2 part-time (1 woman); includes 1 minority (African American), 1 international. Average age 35. *Degree requirements:* For master's, thesis or alternative, written qualifying exam. *Entrance requirements:* For master's, BA or BFA in dance, interview, professional-level experience. Additional exam requirements/recommendations for international students: Required—TOEFL (minimum score 550 paper-based; 213 computer-based; 80 iBT). *Application deadline:* For fall admission, 3/1 priority date for domestic and international students. Applications are processed on a rolling basis. Application fee: $75. *Financial support:* In 2008–09, 4 teaching assistantships (averaging $3,000 per year) were awarded; scholarships/grants and unspecified assistantships also available. Financial award application deadline: 3/1; financial award applicants required to submit FAFSA. *Faculty research:* Labanotation, dance preservation and documentation, dance history. *Unit head:* Myra Woodruff, Chair, 214-768-2718, Fax: 214-768-4540, E-mail: woodruff@smu.edu. *Application contact:* Jean Cherry, Director of Graduate Admissions and Records, 214-768-3765, Fax: 214-768-3272, E-mail: jcherry@smu.edu.

Temple University, Graduate School, Esther Boyer College of Music and Dance, Department of Dance, Philadelphia, PA 19122-6096. Offers Ed M, MFA, PhD. *Accreditation:* NASD. Part-time programs available. *Degree requirements:* For master's, thesis optional, professional project; for doctorate, thesis/dissertation. *Entrance requirements:* For master's and doctorate, minimum GPA of 3.0, audition/interview. Additional exam requirements/recommendations for international students: Required—TOEFL. Electronic applications accepted. *Faculty research:* Cultural studies, dance education, dance technology, aesthetics.

Texas Tech University, Graduate School, College of Visual and Performing Arts, Department of Theatre and Dance, Lubbock, TX 79409. Offers fine arts (PhD); theatre arts (MA, MFA), including arts administration (MFA), design (MFA), performance/pedagogy (MFA), playwriting (MFA), theatre management (MFA). *Accreditation:* NAST. Part-time programs available. *Faculty:* 10 full-time (5 women). *Students:* 37 full-time (18 women), 19 part-time (8 women); includes 6 minority (2 African Americans, 1 Asian American or Pacific Islander, 3 Hispanic Americans), 4 international. Average age 35. 42 applicants, 71% accepted, 16 enrolled. In 2008, 5 master's awarded. *Degree requirements:* For master's, variable foreign language requirement, thesis; for doctorate, thesis/dissertation. *Entrance requirements:* For master's and doctorate, GRE General Test. Additional exam requirements/recommendations for international students: Required—TOEFL (minimum score 550 paper-based; 213 computer-based). *Application deadline:* For fall admission, 3/1 priority date for international students; for spring admission, 11/1 priority date for international students. Applications are processed on a rolling basis. Application fee: $50 ($60 for international students). Electronic applications accepted. *Expenses:* Tuition, area resident: Part-time $194 per credit hour. Tuition, state resident: full-time $4648; part-time $194 per credit hour. Tuition, nonresident: full-time $11,392; part-time $475 per credit hour. Required fees: $2206; $69 per credit hour. $389 per semester. *Financial support:* In 2008–09, 41 students received support, including 27 teaching assistantships with partial tuition reimbursements available (averaging $10,419 per year); research assistantships with partial tuition reimbursements available, Federal Work-Study and institutionally sponsored loans also available. Support available to part-time students. Financial award application deadline: 4/15; financial award applicants required to submit FAFSA. *Faculty research:* New student plays program, theatre planning, dramaturgy; feminist theatre; arts administration; dance aesthetics. *Unit head:* Prof. Frederick B. Christoffel, Chair, 806-742-3601 Ext. 228, Fax: 806-742-1338, E-mail: fred.christoffel@ttu.edu. *Application contact:* Dr. James Bush, Graduate Adviser, 806-742-3601 Ext. 230, Fax: 806-742-1338, E-mail: james.bush@ttu.edu.

Texas Tech University, Graduate School, College of Visual and Performing Arts, Fine Arts Doctoral Program, Lubbock, TX 79409. Offers arts (PhD); music (PhD); theatre arts (PhD). *Accreditation:* NAST. *Students:* 50 full-time (22 women), 29 part-time (15 women); includes 9 minority (3 African Americans, 1 American Indian/Alaska Native, 1 Asian American or Pacific Islander, 4 Hispanic Americans), 10 international. Average age 36. 37 applicants, 70% accepted, 16 enrolled. In 2008, 4 doctorates awarded. *Degree requirements:* For doctorate, thesis/dissertation. *Entrance requirements:* For doctorate, GRE General Test. Additional exam requirements/recommendations for international students: Required—TOEFL (minimum score 550 paper-based; 213 computer-based). *Application deadline:* For fall admission, 3/1 priority date for international students; for spring admission, 11/1 priority date for international students. Applications are processed on a rolling basis. Application fee: $50 ($60 for international students). Electronic applications accepted. *Expenses:* Tuition, area resident: Part-time $194 per credit hour. Tuition, state resident: full-time $4648; part-time $194 per credit hour. Tuition, nonresident: full-time $11,392; part-time $475 per credit hour. Required fees: $2206; $69 per credit hour. $389 per semester. *Financial support:* Research assistantships with partial tuition reimbursements, teaching assistantships with partial tuition reimbursements available. Financial award application deadline: 4/15. *Faculty research:* Art criticism and theory, music, aesthetics, theatre arts. *Unit head:* Dr. Brian D. Steele, Director, 806-742-0700, Fax: 806-742-0695, E-mail: brian.steele@ttu.edu. *Application contact:* Dr. Brian D. Steele, Director, 806-742-0700, Fax: 806-742-0695, E-mail: brian.steele@ttu.edu.

Texas Woman's University, Graduate School, College of Arts and Sciences, School of the Arts, Department of Dance, Denton, TX 76201. Offers MA, MFA, PhD. *Accreditation:* NASD. *Faculty:* 5 full-time (4 women), 2 part-time/adjunct (1 woman). *Students:* 25 full-time (20 women), 11 part-time (10 women); includes 6 minority (2 African Americans, 2 Asian Americans or Pacific Islanders, 2 Hispanic Americans), 4 international. Average age 37. In 2008, 11 master's, 1 doctorate awarded. *Degree requirements:* For master's, thesis (for some programs), choreography portfolio, professional paper; for doctorate, comprehensive exam, thesis/dissertation. *Entrance requirements:* For master's, audition, 3 letters of recommendation, interview, writing sample, solo performance, resumé, personal essay, department program application information form; for doctorate, audition, portfolio, interview, 3 letters of reference, scholarly writing sample, resumé, personal essay, curriculum vitae, department program application information form, sample syllabus for university-level course. Additional exam requirements/recommendations for international students: Required—TOEFL (minimum score 550 paper-based; 213 computer-based; 79 iBT). *Application deadline:* For fall admission, 2/1 priority date for domestic and international students. Applications are processed on a rolling basis. Application fee: $30 ($50 for international students). Electronic applications accepted. *Expenses:* Tuition, state resident: full-time $3564; part-time $198 per semester hour. Tuition, nonresident: full-time $8622; part-time $479 per semester hour. Required fees: $1158; $64 per semester hour. Tuition and fees vary according to course load. *Financial support:* In 2008–09, 1 fellowship (averaging $10,000 per year), 9 research assistantships (averaging $11,862 per year), 9 teaching assistantships (averaging $11,862 per year) were awarded; career-related internships or fieldwork, Federal Work-Study, institutionally sponsored loans, scholarships/grants, traineeships, health care benefits, tuition waivers (partial), and unspecified assistantships also available. Support available to part-time students. Financial award application deadline: 3/1; financial award applicants required to submit FAFSA. *Faculty research:* Performance, choreography, pedagogy, somatic practices, theorizing artistic practice. *Unit head:* Dr. Penelope Hanstein, Chair, 940-898-2085, Fax: 940-898-2098, E-mail: dance@twu.edu. *Application contact:* Samuel Wheeler, Assistant Director of Admissions, 940-898-3188, Fax: 940-898-3081, E-mail: wheelersr@twu.edu.

Tufts University, Graduate School of Arts and Sciences, Department of Drama and Dance, Medford, MA 02155. Offers dance (MA, PhD); drama (MA); dramatic literature and criticism (PhD); theater history (PhD). Part-time programs available. Terminal master's awarded for partial completion of doctoral program. *Degree requirements:* For master's, one foreign language, thesis; for doctorate, 2 foreign languages, thesis/dissertation, oral exam, written general exam. *Entrance requirements:* For master's and doctorate, GRE General Test, writing sample. Additional exam requirements/recommendations for international students: Required—TOEFL (minimum score 600 paper-based; 250 computer-based; 80 iBT). Electronic applications accepted.

Tulane University, School of Liberal Arts, Department of Theatre and Dance, New Orleans, LA 70118-5669. Offers design and technical production (MFA). *Entrance requirements:* For master's, GRE General Test, minimum B average in undergraduate course work. Additional exam requirements/recommendations for international students: Required—TOEFL. Electronic applications accepted. *Faculty research:* Scene design, stage management, costume design, technical direction, lighting design.

Université du Québec à Montréal, Graduate Programs, Program in Dance, Montréal, QC H3C 3P8, Canada. Offers MA. Part-time programs available. *Degree requirements:* For master's, thesis optional. *Entrance requirements:* For master's, appropriate bachelor's degree or equivalent and proficiency in French.

University of California, Irvine, Office of Graduate Studies, Claire Trevor School of the Arts, Department of Dance, Irvine, CA 92697. Offers MFA. *Degree requirements:* For master's, thesis. *Entrance requirements:* For master's, minimum GPA of 3.0. Electronic applications accepted. *Faculty research:* Dance science, digital technology, history and theory, choreography.

University of California, Los Angeles, Graduate Division, School of the Arts and Architecture, Department of World Arts and Cultures, Los Angeles, CA 90095. Offers culture and performance (MA, PhD); dance (MFA). *Degree requirements:* For master's, comprehensive exam or thesis; for doctorate, one foreign language, thesis/dissertation, oral and written qualifying exams. *Entrance requirements:* For master's, minimum GPA of 3.0; for doctorate, GRE General Test, writing sample. Electronic applications accepted. *Expenses:* Tuition, nonresident: full-time $14,694. Required fees: $9669.50. Full-time tuition and fees vary according to course load, degree level, program and student level.

University of California, Riverside, Graduate Division, Department of Dance, Riverside, CA 92521. Offers critical dance studies (PhD); experimental choreography (MFA). *Faculty:* 9 full-time (8 women). *Students:* 33 full-time (30 women); includes 4 minority (2 African Americans, 1 Asian American or Pacific Islander, 1 Hispanic American), 9 international. Average age 31. 32 applicants, 41% accepted, 7 enrolled. In 2008, 5 doctorates awarded. *Degree requirements:* For doctorate, one foreign language, thesis/dissertation, qualifying exams. *Entrance requirements:* For master's, choreographed piece (MFA); for doctorate, GRE General Test, minimum GPA of 3.2, writing sample. Additional exam requirements/recommendations for international students: Required—TOEFL (minimum score 550 paper-based; 213 computer-based; 80 iBT). *Application deadline:* For fall admission, 1/5 priority date for domestic students, 2/1 for international students. Application fee: $70 ($85 for international students). Electronic applications accepted. *Expenses:* Tuition, nonresident: full-time $4898. Required fees: $10,362. *Financial support:* In 2008–09, fellowships with full tuition reimbursements (averaging $12,000 per year), teaching assistantships with full tuition reimbursements (averaging $15,600 per year) were awarded; research assistantships with tuition reimbursements, career-related internships or fieldwork, Federal Work-Study, institutionally sponsored loans, tuition waivers (full and partial), and unspecified assistantships also available. Financial award application deadline: 1/5; financial award applicants required to submit FAFSA. *Faculty research:* Movement analysis, cultural postcolonial gender studies of performance, theories of dance, anthropology of dance, history and reconstruction of dance. *Unit head:* Susan Rose, Chair, 951-827-6353, Fax: 951-827-4651, E-mail: susan.rose@ucr.edu. *Application contact:* Neil Greenberg, Graduate Adviser, 951-827-6481, Fax: 951-827-4651, E-mail: danceadvising@ucr.edu.

University of Colorado at Boulder, Graduate School, College of Arts and Sciences, Department of Theatre and Dance, Boulder, CO 80309. Offers dance (MFA); theatre (MA, PhD). Terminal master's awarded for partial completion of doctoral program. *Degree requirements:* For master's, comprehensive exam, thesis; for doctorate, one foreign language, thesis/dissertation. *Entrance requirements:* For master's, GRE General Test (MA), audition (MFA), minimum undergraduate GPA of 2.75. *Faculty research:* Performance choreography; pedagogy administration; body therapies; multi-media forms; film, video, and cultural studies; non-concert forms; music; poetry writing; literature; kinesiology (dance); theater history; theory and literature.

University of Hawaii at Manoa, Graduate Division, Colleges of Arts and Sciences, College of Arts and Humanities, Department of Theatre and Dance, Honolulu, HI 96822. Offers dance (MA, MFA); theatre (MA, MFA, PhD). *Entrance requirements:* Additional exam requirements/recommendations for international students: Required—TOEFL. *Faculty research:* Asian theatre, feminist theatre and dance, Russian theatre, Australian theatre.

University of Illinois at Urbana–Champaign, Graduate College, College of Fine and Applied Arts, Department of Dance, Champaign, IL 61820. Offers MFA. *Accreditation:* NASD. *Faculty:* 11 full-time (9 women). *Students:* 14 full-time (11 women); includes 1 minority (Hispanic American), 1 international. 29 applicants, 14% accepted, 4 enrolled. In 2008, 2 master's awarded. *Entrance requirements:* For master's, audition, minimum GPA of 3.0. Additional exam requirements/recommendations for international students: Required—TOEFL (minimum score 550 paper-based; 213 computer-based). *Application deadline:* Applications are processed on a rolling basis. Application fee: $60 ($75 for international students). Electronic applications accepted. *Financial support:* In 2008–09, 5 fellowships, 1 research assistantship, 12 teaching assistantships were awarded; tuition waivers (full and partial) also available. *Unit head:* Jan Erkert, Head, 217-333-1010, Fax: 217-333-3000, E-mail: erkert@illinois.edu. *Application contact:*

Dance

University of Illinois at Urbana–Champaign *(continued)*
Cynthia C. Howard, Program Coordinator, 217-333-1011, Fax: 217-333-3000, E-mail: choward1@illinois.edu.

The University of Iowa, Graduate College, College of Liberal Arts and Sciences, Department of Dance, Iowa City, IA 52242-1316. Offers MFA. *Degree requirements:* For master's, thesis, exam. *Entrance requirements:* For master's, minimum GPA of 3.0. Additional exam requirements/ recommendations for international students: Required—TOEFL (minimum score 550 paper-based; 213 computer-based; 81 iBT). Electronic applications accepted.

University of Maryland, College Park, Graduate Studies, College of Arts and Humanities, Department of Dance, College Park, MD 20742. Offers MFA. *Degree requirements:* For master's, final project. *Entrance requirements:* For master's, audition/interview, video tapes/ writing sample. Additional exam requirements/recommendations for international students: Required—TOEFL. Electronic applications accepted. *Faculty research:* Performance and choreography.

University of Michigan, Horace H. Rackham School of Graduate Studies, The School of Music, Theatre, and Dance, Department of Dance, Ann Arbor, MI 48109. Offers modern dance performance and choreography (MFA). Offered through the Horace H. Rackham School of Graduate Studies. *Accreditation:* NASD. *Degree requirements:* For master's, thesis. *Entrance requirements:* For master's, audition. Additional exam requirements/recommendations for international students: Required—TOEFL (minimum score 600 paper-based; 250 computer-based). Electronic applications accepted. *Faculty research:* Life forms software, Donald McKayles 'Rainbow Suite", Carlos Orta of Jose Limon, World Wide Rhythms concert.

University of Minnesota, Twin Cities Campus, Graduate School, College of Liberal Arts, Department of Theatre Arts and Dance, Minneapolis, MN 55455-0213. Offers design technology (MFA); theatre arts and dance (MA, PhD). *Accreditation:* NASD; NAST (one or more programs are accredited). Terminal master's awarded for partial completion of doctoral program. *Degree requirements:* For master's, thesis (for some programs), final creative project (MFA), foreign language (MA); for doctorate, one foreign language, thesis/dissertation, oral defense, written exams. *Entrance requirements:* For master's, GRE General Test, minimum GPA of 3.0, audition or portfolio; for doctorate, GRE General Test, minimum GPA of 3.0, writing sample, 1 foreign language. Additional exam requirements/recommendations for international students: Required—TOEFL (minimum score 550 paper-based; 213 computer-based; 79 iBT). Electronic applications accepted. *Faculty research:* Theatre history; Eastern European theatre; performance studies; medieval studies.

University of New Mexico, Graduate School, College of Fine Arts, Department of Theatre and Dance, Albuquerque, NM 87131-2039. Offers dramatic writing (MFA); theater and dance (MA). *Accreditation:* NASD; NAST. *Degree requirements:* For master's, comprehensive exam (for some programs), thesis (for some programs). *Entrance requirements:* For master's, minimum GPA of 3.0, undergraduate major in theatre, dance or closely related field, 3 letters of recommendation, letter of intent. Electronic applications accepted. *Faculty research:* Theater education and outreach, choreography, dramatic writing, dance history/criticism.

The University of North Carolina at Charlotte, Graduate School, College of Education, Program in Teacher Education, Charlotte, NC 28223-0001. Offers art education (K-12) (MAT); dance education (K-12) (MAT); elementary education (K-6) (MAT); English as a second language (K-12) (MAT); foreign language education (K-12) (MAT); general teacher education (MAT); middle grades education (6-9) (MAT); music education (K-12) (MAT); secondary education (9-12) (MAT); special education (K-12) (MAT); theatre education (K-12) (MAT). *Faculty:* 9 full-time (all women), 1 (woman) part-time/adjunct. *Students:* 23 full-time (15 women), 194 part-time (170 women); includes 33 minority (25 African Americans, 1 American Indian/Alaska Native, 5 Asian Americans or Pacific Islanders, 2 Hispanic Americans), 1 international. Average age 32. 116 applicants, 95% accepted, 91 enrolled. In 2008, 59 master's awarded. *Entrance requirements:* For master's, GRE or MAT. Additional exam requirements/recommendations for international students: Required—TOEFL (minimum score 557 paper-based; 220 computer-based). *Application deadline:* For fall admission, 7/1 for domestic students, 5/1 for international students; for spring admission, 11/1 for domestic students, 10/1 for international students. Applications are processed on a rolling basis. Application fee: $55. Electronic applications accepted. *Expenses:* Tuition, area resident: Full-time $2919; part-time $122 per credit hour. Tuition, state resident: full-time $2919; part-time $122 per credit hour. Tuition, nonresident: full-time $13,126; part-time $547 per credit hour. Required fees: $1779; $91 per credit hour. Tuition and fees vary according to program. *Financial support:* In 2008–09, 2 research assistantships (averaging $7,524 per year), 5 teaching assistantships (averaging $6,125 per year) were awarded; career-related internships or fieldwork, Federal Work-Study, institutionally sponsored loans, scholarships/grants, and unspecified assistantships also available. Support available to part-time students. Financial award application deadline: 4/1; financial award applicants required to submit FAFSA. *Unit head:* Dr. Kimberly J. Hartman, Coordinator, 704-687-8883, Fax: 704-687-6430, E-mail: khartman@email.uncc.edu. *Application contact:* Kathy B. Giddings, Director of Graduate Admissions, 704-687-3366, Fax: 704-687-3279, E-mail: agidding@uncc.edu.

The University of North Carolina at Greensboro, Graduate School, School of Health and Human Performance, Department of Dance, Greensboro, NC 27412-5001. Offers MA, MFA. *Accreditation:* NASD. *Degree requirements:* For master's, thesis. *Entrance requirements:* For master's, GRE General Test or MAT, audition or video (MFA). Additional exam requirements/ recommendations for international students: Required—TOEFL. Electronic applications accepted. *Faculty research:* Consciousness-raising images, perspectives on ballet.

University of Oklahoma, Graduate College, College of Fine Arts, School of Dance, Norman, OK 73019-0390. Offers MFA. *Faculty:* 5 full-time (2 women), 1 part-time/adjunct (0 women). *Students:* 6 full-time (all women); includes 1 minority (Hispanic American), 1 international. 7 applicants, 43% accepted, 3 enrolled. In 2008, 3 master's awarded. *Degree requirements:* For master's, comprehensive exam, departmental qualifying exams, solo performance or choreography of a work. *Entrance requirements:* For master's, minimum GPA of 3.0 or equivalent experience, resumé, audition, interview, 3 letters of reference, video, and personal choreography. Additional exam requirements/recommendations for international students: Required—TOEFL (minimum score 550 paper-based; 213 computer-based). *Application deadline:* For fall admission, 6/1 for domestic students, 4/1 for international students; for spring admission, 11/1 for domestic students, 9/1 for international students. Applications are processed on a rolling basis. Application fee: $40 ($90 for international students). Electronic applications accepted. *Expenses:* Tuition, state resident: full-time $3744; part-time $156 per credit hour. Tuition, nonresident: full-time $13,577; part-time $565.70 per credit hour. Required fees: $2415.40; $90.10 per credit hour. *Financial support:* In 2008–09, 2 students received support, including 4 fellowships with full tuition reimbursements available (averaging $6,000 per year), 5 teaching assistantships with partial tuition reimbursements available (averaging $14,937 per year); scholarships/grants, health care benefits, and unspecified assistantships also available. Financial award application deadline: 3/15; financial award applicants required to submit FAFSA. *Unit head:* Mary Margaret Holt, Director, 405-325-4051, Fax: 405-325-7024, E-mail: marymholt@ou.edu. *Application contact:* Jeremy Lindberg, Associate Professor/Graduate Liaison, 405-325-5312, Fax: 405-325-7024, E-mail: jlindberg@ou.edu.

University of Oregon, Graduate School, School of Music, Department of Dance, Eugene, OR 97403. Offers MA, MS. *Degree requirements:* For master's, thesis or alternative. *Entrance requirements:* For master's, minimum GPA of 3.0. Additional exam requirements/ recommendations for international students: Required—TOEFL. *Faculty research:* Choreography, dance history, dance pedagogy, scientific aspects of dance.

The University of Texas at Austin, Graduate School, College of Fine Arts, Department of Theatre and Dance, Austin, TX 78712-1111. Offers acting (MFA); dance (MFA); directing (MFA); drama and theatre for youth (MFA); performance as public practice (MA, MFA, PhD); playwriting (MFA); theatre technology (MFA); theatrical design (MFA). *Accreditation:* NASD. *Degree requirements:* For master's, thesis; for doctorate, variable foreign language requirement, thesis/dissertation. *Entrance requirements:* For master's and doctorate, GRE General Test.

University of Utah, The Graduate School, College of Fine Arts, Department of Ballet, Salt Lake City, UT 84112-1107. Offers MFA. *Degree requirements:* For master's, one foreign language, choreography projects, performance, teaching experience with written support. *Entrance requirements:* For master's, audition, videos/DVDs of teaching and choreography. Additional exam requirements/recommendations for international students: Required—TOEFL (minimum score 500 paper-based; 173 computer-based). *Faculty research:* Choreography, jazz, technique, fitness and dance injuries.

University of Utah, The Graduate School, College of Fine Arts, Department of Modern Dance, Salt Lake City, UT 84112-1107. Offers MA, MFA. *Degree requirements:* For master's, thesis, project, oral examination. *Entrance requirements:* For master's, audition, interview, minimum GPA of 3.0. Additional exam requirements/recommendations for international students: Required—TOEFL (minimum score 500 paper-based; 173 computer-based). Electronic applications accepted. *Faculty research:* Choreography, teaching methods, performance, cultural studies, dance technology.

University of Washington, Graduate School, College of Arts and Sciences, Program in Dance, Seattle, WA 98195. Offers MFA. *Degree requirements:* For master's, performance, project. *Entrance requirements:* For master's, 8 years of professional dance experience, resumé, performance DVD or VHS tape, 3 letters of reference. Electronic applications accepted. *Faculty research:* Choreography, history, anatomy.

University of Wisconsin–Milwaukee, Graduate School, Peck School of the Arts, Program in Performing Arts, Milwaukee, WI 53201-0413. Offers dance (MFA); film (MFA); theatre (MFA). Part-time programs available. *Faculty:* 35 full-time (21 women). *Students:* 18 full-time (12 women), 2 part-time (both women); includes 4 minority (2 African Americans, 1 Asian American or Pacific Islander, 1 Hispanic American), 1 international. Average age 33. 28 applicants, 21% accepted, 6 enrolled. In 2008, 17 master's awarded. *Degree requirements:* For master's, variable foreign language requirement, comprehensive exam, thesis or alternative. *Entrance requirements:* For master's, audition, interview. Additional exam requirements/recommendations for international students: Required—TOEFL (minimum score 550 paper-based; 79 iBT), IELTS (minimum score 6.5). *Application deadline:* For fall admission, 1/1 priority date for domestic students; for spring admission, 9/1 for domestic students. Applications are processed on a rolling basis. Application fee: $45 ($75 for international students). *Expenses:* Tuition, area resident: Full-time $7320; part-time $165 per credit. Tuition, state resident: full-time $7320; part-time $165 per credit. Tuition, nonresident: full-time $17,840; part-time $714 per credit. Tuition and fees vary according to campus/location, program and reciprocity agreements. *Financial support:* In 2008–09, 13 teaching assistantships were awarded; career-related internships or fieldwork and unspecified assistantships also available. Support available to part-time students. Financial award application deadline: 4/15. *Unit head:* Simone Ferro, Representative, 414-229-4178, E-mail: sferro@uwm.edu. *Application contact:* General Information Contact, 414-229-4982, Fax: 414-229-6967, E-mail: gradschool@uwm.edu.

York University, Faculty of Graduate Studies, Faculty of Fine Arts, Program in Dance, Toronto, ON M3J 1P3, Canada. Offers MA, MFA. *Degree requirements:* For master's, thesis or alternative. Electronic applications accepted.

Music

Alabama Agricultural and Mechanical University, School of Graduate Studies, School of Education, Area in Music Education, Huntsville, AL 35811. Offers music (MS); music education (M Ed). *Accreditation:* NCATE. Part-time and evening/weekend programs available. *Faculty:* 9 full-time (3 women), 7 part-time/adjunct (5 women). *Degree requirements:* For master's, comprehensive exam. *Entrance requirements:* For master's, GRE General Test. Additional exam requirements/recommendations for international students: Required—TOEFL (minimum score 500 paper-based; 173 computer-based; 61 iBT). *Application deadline:* For fall admission, 5/1 for domestic students. Applications are processed on a rolling basis. Application fee: $25. Electronic applications accepted. *Expenses:* Tuition, area resident: Full-time $3924; part-time $2616 per term. Tuition, nonresident: part-time $5234 per year. International tuition: $7848 full-time. Required fees: $198; $396 per credit hour. $2841 per term. One-time fee: $8498 full-time; $5682 part-time. Full-time tuition and fees vary according to program. *Financial support:* Career-related internships or fieldwork and traineeships available. Financial award application deadline: 4/1. *Faculty research:* Jazz and black music, Alabama folk music. *Unit head:* Dr. Horace Carney, Chairperson, 256-372-5512. *Application contact:* Dr. Horace Carney, Chairperson, 256-372-5512.

Alabama State University, School of Graduate Studies, Department of Music, Montgomery, AL 36101-0271. Offers instrumental music (M Ed); vocal/choral music (M Ed). *Accreditation:* NASM. Part-time programs available. *Degree requirements:* For master's, comprehensive exam. *Entrance requirements:* For master's, GRE General Test or MAT, graduate writing competency test. Additional exam requirements/recommendations for international students: Required—TOEFL (minimum score 500 paper-based; 173 computer-based). *Faculty research:* Computer applications.

Andrews University, School of Graduate Studies, College of Arts and Sciences, Department of Music, Berrien Springs, MI 49104. Offers M Mus, MA. *Accreditation:* NASM. *Faculty:* 8 full-time (5 women). *Students:* 21 full-time (10 women), 8 part-time (4 women); includes 8 minority (4 African Americans, 4 Hispanic Americans), 16 international. Average age 28. In 2008, 3 master's awarded. *Degree requirements:* For master's, variable foreign language requirement. *Entrance requirements:* For master's, GRE Subject Test, minimum undergraduate GPA of 2.6. Additional exam requirements/recommendations for international students: Required—TOEFL (minimum score 550 paper-based). *Application deadline:* Applications are processed on a rolling basis. Application fee: $40. *Expenses:* Tuition: Full-time $18,360; part-time $765 per credit hour. Required fees: $476; $765 per credit hour. $238 per semester. Tuition and fees vary according to degree level. *Unit head:* Dr. Carlos Flores, Chairman, 269-471-3555. *Application contact:* Carolyn Hurst, Supervisor of Graduate Admission, 800-253-2874, Fax: 269-471-6321, E-mail: graduate@andrews.edu.

Appalachian State University, Cratis D. Williams Graduate School, School of Music, Boone, NC 28608. Offers music education (MM); music performance (MM); music therapy (MMT). *Accreditation:* NASM. Part-time programs available. *Faculty:* 29 full-time (11 women), 2 part-time/adjunct (both women). *Students:* 25 full-time (13 women), 7 part-time (4 women); includes 2 minority (both African Americans), 1 international. 28 applicants, 86% accepted, 13 enrolled. In 2008, 9 master's awarded. *Degree requirements:* For master's, comprehensive exam, thesis or alternative. *Entrance requirements:* For master's, GRE General Test, 3 letters of reference, audition. Additional exam requirements/recommendations for international students: Required—TOEFL (minimum score 550 paper-based; 230 computer-based; 79 iBT), IELTS (minimum score 6.5). *Application deadline:* For fall admission, 7/1 for domestic students, 2/1 for international students; for spring admission, 11/1 for domestic students, 7/1 for international students. Applications are processed on a rolling basis. Application fee: $50. Electronic applications accepted. *Expenses:* Tuition, area resident: Full-time $2600; part-time $700 per course. Tuition, state resident: full-time $2600; part-time $700 per course. Tuition, nonresident: full-time $5000; part-time $3300 per course. Required fees: $2150; $330 per course. Tuition and fees vary according to campus/location. *Financial support:* In 2008–09, 16 research assistantships (averaging $7,000 per year) were awarded; fellowships, teaching assistantships, career-related internships or fieldwork, Federal Work-Study, scholarships/grants, tuition waivers (partial), and unspecified assistantships also available. Financial award application deadline: 4/1; financial award applicants required to submit FAFSA. *Faculty research:* Music of the holocaust, Celtic folk music, early 19th century performance practice, hypermeter and phase rhythm, world music, music and psychoneuroimmunology. Total annual research expenditures: $7,500. *Unit head:* Dr. William Harbinson, Dean, 828-262-6446, E-mail: harbinsonwg@appstate.edu. *Application contact:* Dr. Nancy Schneeloch-Bingham, Graduate Program Director, 828-262-6463, E-mail: schneelochna@appstate.edu.

Arizona State University, Graduate College, Herberger College of the Arts, School of Music, Tempe, AZ 85287. Offers composition (MM); music (MA, DMA); music education (MM); music therapy (MM); performance (MM). *Accreditation:* NASM. *Degree requirements:* For doctorate, thesis/dissertation. *Entrance requirements:* For master's, GRE or MAT; for doctorate, GRE.

Arkansas State University, Graduate School, College of Fine Arts, Department of Music, Jonesboro, State University, AR 72467. Offers music education (MME, SCCT); performance (MM). *Accreditation:* NASM (one or more programs are accredited). Part-time programs available. *Faculty:* 14 full-time (3 women), 2 part-time/adjunct (both women). *Students:* 3 full-time (2 women), 9 part-time (2 women); includes 1 minority (American Indian/Alaska Native), 1 international. Average age 30. 5 applicants, 100% accepted, 2 enrolled. In 2008, 8 master's, 1 other advanced degree awarded. *Degree requirements:* For master's, 2 foreign languages, comprehensive exam, thesis or alternative; for SCCT, comprehensive exam. *Entrance requirements:* For master's, GRE General Test or MAT (MME), university entrance exam, appropriate bachelor's degree, audition, official transcript; for SCCT, GRE General Test or MAT, interview, master's degree, official transcript. Additional exam requirements/recommendations for international students: Required—TOEFL (minimum score 550 paper-based; 213 computer-based; 79 iBT), IELTS (minimum score 6). *Application deadline:* For fall admission, 7/15 for domestic students, 7/1 for international students; for spring admission, 12/1 for domestic students, 11/13 for international students. Applications are processed on a rolling basis. Application fee: $30 ($40 for international students). Electronic applications accepted. *Expenses:* Tuition, state resident: full-time $3744; part-time $208 per credit hour. Tuition, nonresident: full-time $9540; part-time $530 per credit hour. International tuition: $7938 full-time. Required fees: $896; $47 per credit hour. $25 per term. One-time fee: $50. Tuition and fees vary according to course load and program. *Financial support:* In 2008–09, 7 students received support; teaching assistantships, career-related internships or fieldwork, scholarships/grants, and unspecified assistantships available. Financial award application deadline: 7/1; financial award applicants required to submit FAFSA. *Faculty research:* Classical period sacred choral music, film music, music theory, musical theatre, music business. *Unit head:* Dr. Tom O'Connor, Chair, 870-972-2094, Fax: 870-972-3932, E-mail: toconnor@astate.edu. *Application contact:* Dr. Andrew Sustich, Dean of the Graduate School, 870-972-3029, Fax: 870-972-3857, E-mail: sustich@astate.edu.

Austin Peay State University, College of Graduate Studies, College of Arts and Letters, Department of Music, Clarksville, TN 37044. Offers music education (M Mu); music performance (M Mu). *Accreditation:* NASM. Part-time programs available. *Faculty:* 11 full-time (6 women), 2 part-time/adjunct (1 woman). *Students:* 13 full-time (5 women), 5 part-time (1 woman); includes 2 minority (both African Americans), 1 international. Average age 30. 13 applicants, 100% accepted, 10 enrolled. In 2008, 12 master's awarded. *Degree requirements:* For master's, comprehensive exam, thesis optional. *Entrance requirements:* For master's, GRE General Test, diagnostic exams, audition, bachelor's degree, 3 letters of recommendation. Additional exam requirements/recommendations for international students: Required—TOEFL (minimum score 500 paper-based; 173 computer-based). *Application deadline:* For fall admission, 7/27 priority date for domestic students; for spring admission, 12/17 priority date for domestic students. Applications are processed on a rolling basis. Application fee: $25. Electronic applications accepted. *Expenses:* Tuition, area resident: Full-time $5772; part-time $305 per credit hour. Tuition, state resident: full-time $5772; part-time $305 per credit hour. Tuition, nonresident: full-time $16,664; part-time $778 per credit hour. Required fees: $1224. *Financial support:* In 2008–09, 10 research assistantships with full tuition reimbursements (averaging $6,996 per year) were awarded; career-related internships or fieldwork, Federal Work-Study, institutionally sponsored loans, scholarships/grants, and unspecified assistantships also available. Support available to part-time students. Financial award application deadline: 3/1; financial award applicants required to submit FAFSA. *Unit head:* Dr. Gail M. Robinson-Oturu, Chair, 931-221-7818, Fax: 931-221-7529, E-mail: oturug@apsu.edu. *Application contact:* Dr. Charles Pinder, Dean, College of Graduate Studies, 931-221-7414, Fax: 931-221-7641, E-mail: pinderc@apsu.edu.

Azusa Pacific University, School of Music, Azusa, CA 91702-7000. Offers education (M Mus); performance (M Mus). *Accreditation:* NASM. Part-time and evening/weekend programs available. *Degree requirements:* For master's, recital. *Entrance requirements:* For master's, interview, audition. Additional exam requirements/recommendations for international students: Required—TOEFL (minimum score 550 paper-based). *Faculty research:* Tribal music of northeast India, rare Motown recordings in England.

Baptist Theological Seminary at Richmond, Graduate and Professional Program, Richmond, VA 23227. Offers children and family ministry (M Div); Christian education (M Div); church music (M Div); theology (D Min); youth and student ministry (M Div); M Div/MS; M Div/MSW. *Accreditation:* ATS. Part-time programs available. Postbaccalaureate distance learning degree programs offered (minimal on-campus study). *Degree requirements:* For doctorate, one foreign language, comprehensive exam, thesis/dissertation, field study, independent study; for M Div, one foreign language, comprehensive exam (for some programs), thesis/dissertation optional, mission immersion experience, internship. *Entrance requirements:* For doctorate, MAT, M Div, 3 years of full-time ministry experience. Additional exam requirements/recommendations for international students: Required—TOEFL (minimum score 481 paper-based; 213 computer-based). *Faculty research:* New Testament studies, Old Testament studies, pastoral care, church history, theology.

Bard College, Conservatory of Music, The Conductors Institute, Annandale-on-Hudson, NY 12504. Offers MFA. *Entrance requirements:* For master's, resumé, 3 letters of recommendation.

Bard College, Conservatory of Music, Graduate Program in Vocal Arts, Annandale-on-Hudson, NY 12504. Offers MM. *Entrance requirements:* For master's, statement of interest, portfolio, 3 letters of recommendation, headshot, repertoire list.

Baylor University, Graduate School, School of Music, Waco, TX 76798. Offers church music (MM); collaborative piano (MM); composition (MM); conducting (MM); music history and literature (MM); music theory (MM); performance (MM); piano pedagogy and performance (MM); M Div/MM. *Accreditation:* NASM. *Students:* 13 full-time (7 women), 37 part-time (15 women); includes 3 minority (1 American Indian/Alaska Native, 2 Hispanic Americans), 4 international. In 2008, 26 master's awarded. *Degree requirements:* For master's, variable foreign language requirement, thesis (for some programs). *Entrance requirements:* For master's, GRE General Test. *Application deadline:* For fall admission, 8/1 for domestic students; for spring admission, 12/1 for domestic students. Applications are processed on a rolling basis. Application fee: $25. *Financial support:* In 2008–09, 43 teaching assistantships with full tuition reimbursements (averaging $5,990 per year) were awarded; Federal Work-Study and institutionally sponsored loans also available. *Unit head:* Dr. David Music, Graduate Program Director, 254-710-2360, Fax: 254-710-1191, E-mail: david_music@baylor.edu. *Application contact:* Melinda Coates, Administrative Assistant, 254-710-2360, Fax: 254-710-3870, E-mail: melinda_coats@baylor.edu.

Belmont University, College of Visual and Performing Arts, School of Music, Nashville, TN 37212-3757. Offers church music (MM); composition (MM); music education (MM); pedagogy (MM); performance (MM). *Accreditation:* NASM. Part-time programs available. *Faculty:* 26 full-time (8 women), 12 part-time/adjunct (3 women). *Students:* 13 full-time (10 women), 33 part-time (17 women); includes 5 minority (2 African Americans, 3 Hispanic Americans), 1 international. Average age 28. 19 applicants, 89% accepted, 13 enrolled. In 2008, 17 master's awarded. *Degree requirements:* For master's, comprehensive exam, thesis (for some programs). *Entrance requirements:* For master's, placement exam, GRE or MAT, audition, interview, minimum GPA of 2.75. Additional exam requirements/recommendations for international students: Required—TOEFL (minimum score 500 paper-based; 173 computer-based). *Application deadline:* For fall admission, 5/1 priority date for domestic students, 5/1 for international students; for spring admission, 11/1 priority date for domestic students, 11/1 for international students. Applications are processed on a rolling basis. Application fee: $50. Electronic applications accepted. *Expenses:* Tuition: Full-time $14,270; part-time $810 per credit hour. Required fees: $530; $280 per year. Tuition and fees vary according to degree level and program. *Financial support:* In 2008–09, 15 fellowships (averaging $2,000 per year), 5 teaching assistantships (averaging $2,000 per year) were awarded; career-related internships or fieldwork, scholarships/grants, and unspecified assistantships also available. Financial award application deadline: 3/1; financial award applicants required to submit FAFSA. *Unit head:* Dr. Robert Gregg, Director, 615-460-8111, Fax: 615-386-0239, E-mail: greggr@mail.belmont.edu. *Application contact:* Russ Cornwall, Graduate Secretary, 615-460-8117, Fax: 615-386-0239, E-mail: cornwallr@mail.belmont.edu.

Bennington College, Graduate Programs, Program in Music, Bennington, VT 05201. Offers MFA. Part-time programs available. *Faculty:* 5 full-time (1 woman), 14 part-time/adjunct (5 women). *Students:* 1 (woman) full-time, 1 part-time (0 women), 1 international. Average age 33. 7 applicants, 29% accepted, 0 enrolled. *Degree requirements:* For master's, thesis, concert performances. *Application deadline:* For fall admission, 2/1 for domestic students. Application fee: $60. *Expenses:* Tuition: Full-time $20,640; part-time $2890 per course. One-time fee: $75. Tuition and fees vary according to program. *Financial support:* In 2008–09, 2 students received support, including 2 teaching assistantships. Financial award application deadline: 4/1; financial award applicants required to submit FAFSA. *Unit head:* Allen Shawn, Director, 802-440-4525, E-mail: ashawn@bennington.edu. *Application contact:* Mary Surdam, Admissions Coordinator, 802-440-4312, Fax: 802-440-4320, E-mail: admissions@bennington.edu.

Bethesda Christian University, Graduate and Professional Programs, Anaheim, CA 92801. Offers biblical studies (MA); music (MA); theology (M Div). *Entrance requirements:* For M Div and master's, interview.

Birmingham-Southern College, Program in Music, Birmingham, AL 35254. Offers MM. *Accreditation:* NASM. *Entrance requirements:* For master's, 3 letters of recommendation, audition. Additional exam requirements/recommendations for international students: Required—TOEFL.

Bob Jones University, Graduate Programs, Greenville, SC 29614. Offers accountancy (MS); Bible (MA); Bible translation (MA); Biblical studies (Certificate); broadcast management (MS); business administration (MBA); church history (MA, PhD); church ministries (MA); church music (MM); cinema and video production (MA); counseling (MS); curriculum and instruction (Ed D); divinity (M Div); dramatic production (MA); educational leadership (MS, Ed D, Ed S); elementary education (M Ed, MAT); English (M Ed, MA, MAT); fine arts (MA); graphic design (MA); history (M Ed, MA); illustration (MA); interpretative speech (MA); mathematics (M Ed, MAT); medical missions (Certificate); ministry (MM, D Min); multi-categorical special education (M Ed, MAT); music (M Ed); New Testament interpretation (PhD); Old Testament interpretation (PhD); orchestral instrument performance (MM); organ performance (MM); pastoral studies (MA); personnel services (MS, Ed S); piano pedagogy (MM); piano performance (MM); platform arts (MA); radio and television broadcasting (MS); rhetoric and public address (MA); secondary education (M Ed); studio art (MA); teaching Bible (MA); theology (MA, PhD); voice performance (MM); youth ministries (MA); M Div/MM.

Boise State University, Graduate College, College of Arts and Sciences, Department of Music, Boise, ID 83725-0399. Offers music (MM); music education (MM); pedagogy (MM); performance (MM). *Accreditation:* NASM. Part-time programs available. *Degree requirements:* For master's, thesis optional. *Entrance requirements:* For master's, minimum GPA of 3.0, performance demonstration. Electronic applications accepted.

The Boston Conservatory, Graduate Division, Music Division, Boston, MA 02215. Offers music (MM, ADP, Certificate); music education (MM). Part-time programs available. *Degree requirements:* For master's, thesis (for some programs), recital; for other advanced degree, recital. *Entrance requirements:* For master's and other advanced degree, audition. Electronic applications accepted.

Boston University, College of Fine Arts, School of Music, Boston, MA 02215. Offers collaborative piano (MM, DMA); composition (MM, DMA); conducting (MM, Artist Diploma, Performance Diploma); historical performance (MM, DMA, Artist Diploma, Performance Diploma); music education (MM, DMA); music theory (MM); musicology (MM); opera performance (Certificate); performance (MM, DMA, Artist Diploma, Performance Diploma). *Accreditation:* NASM. Part-time programs available. *Degree requirements:* For master's, thesis; for doctorate, 2 foreign languages, thesis/dissertation. *Entrance requirements:* Additional exam requirements/recommendations for international students: Required—TOEFL. Electronic applications accepted.

Boston University, Graduate School of Arts and Sciences, Department of Music, Boston, MA 02215. Offers composition (MA); music education (MA); music history/theory (PhD); musicology (MA, PhD). *Accreditation:* NASM. *Degree requirements:* For master's, 2 foreign languages, comprehensive exam, thesis; for doctorate, 2 foreign languages, comprehensive exam, thesis/dissertation. *Entrance requirements:* For master's and doctorate, GRE General Test, musical composition or research paper, 3 letters of recommendation. Additional exam requirements/recommendations for international students: Required—TOEFL (minimum score 550 paper-based; 213 computer-based).

Bowling Green State University, Graduate College, College of Musical Arts, Bowling Green, OH 43403. Offers composition (MM); contemporary music (DMA), including composition, performance; ethnomusicology (MM); music education (MM), including choral, comprehensive, instrumental; music history (MM); music theory (MM); performance (MM). *Accreditation:* NASM. Part-time programs available. *Degree requirements:* For master's, thesis or alternative, recitals; for doctorate, comprehensive exam, thesis/dissertation. *Entrance requirements:* For master's, GRE General Test, diagnostic placement exams in music history and theory, audition, interview. Additional exam requirements/recommendations for international students: Required—TOEFL. Electronic applications accepted. *Faculty research:* Ethnomusicology.

Brandeis University, Graduate School of Arts and Sciences, Department of Music, Waltham, MA 02454-9110. Offers composition and theory (MA, MFA, PhD); music and women's studies (MA); musicology (MA, MFA, PhD). Part-time programs available. Terminal master's awarded for partial completion of doctoral program. *Degree requirements:* For master's, one foreign language, thesis or alternative; for doctorate, 2 foreign languages, comprehensive exam, thesis/dissertation. *Entrance requirements:* For master's, GRE General Test (musicology),

Music

Brandeis University (continued)

resumé, sample of work (music composition), letters of recommendation; for doctorate, GRE General Test (musicology), resumé, writing sample (musicology), letters of recommendation, sample of work—recording (composition). Additional exam requirements/recommendations for international students: Required—TOEFL (minimum score 600 paper-based; 250 computer-based; 100 iBT), IELTS (minimum score 7). Electronic applications accepted. *Faculty research:* History of theory; music of Monteverdi, Bach, Mozart, Lizst, and Wagner; compositional process; computer music.

Brandon University, School of Music, Brandon, MB R7A 6A9, Canada. Offers composition (M Mus); music education (M Mus); performance and literature (M Mus), including piano, strings. Part-time programs available. *Degree requirements:* For master's, comprehensive exam (for some programs), thesis (for some programs). *Entrance requirements:* For master's, B Mus. Additional exam requirements/recommendations for international students: Required—TOEFL (580 paper-based; 237 computer-based) or IELTS. Electronic applications accepted. *Faculty research:* Philosophy of music.

Brigham Young University, Graduate Studies, College of Fine Arts and Communications, School of Music, Provo, UT 84602-1001. Offers composition (MM); conducting (MM); music education (MA, MM); musicology (MA); performance (MM). *Accreditation:* NASM. *Faculty:* 46 full-time (8 women). *Students:* 54 full-time (28 women), 11 part-time (3 women); includes 5 minority (all Asian Americans or Pacific Islanders). Average age 29. 47 applicants, 57% accepted, 26 enrolled. In 2008, 25 master's awarded. *Degree requirements:* For master's, comprehensive exam (for some programs), thesis (for some programs), recital, project or composition (for some programs). *Entrance requirements:* For master's, graduate placement exam, minimum GPA of 3.0 in last 60 hours, bachelor of music degree. Additional exam requirements/recommendations for international students: Required—TOEFL (minimum score 580 paper-based; 237 computer-based; 85 iBT). *Application deadline:* For fall admission, 2/1 priority date for domestic students, 1/15 priority date for international students. Application fee: $50. Electronic applications accepted. *Expenses:* Tuition: Full-time $5160; part-time $287 per credit hour. Tuition and fees vary according to program and student's religious affiliation. *Financial support:* In 2008–09, 60 students received support, including 37 teaching assistantships (averaging $5,000 per year); research assistantships, career-related internships or fieldwork, institutionally sponsored loans, scholarships/grants, tuition waivers (partial), and unspecified assistantships also available. Support available to part-time students. Financial award application deadline: 2/1; financial award applicants required to submit FAFSA. *Faculty research:* Pergolesi, Louis Armstrong, rock and roll, Balinese gamelan. *Unit head:* Dr. Dale E. Monson, Director, 801-422-6304, Fax: 801-422-0533, E-mail: dale_monson@byu.edu. *Application contact:* Dr. Thomas L. Durham, Graduate Coordinator, 801-422-3226, Fax: 801-422-0533, E-mail: thomas_durham@byu.edu.

Brooklyn College of the City University of New York, Division of Graduate Studies, Conservatory of Music, Brooklyn, NY 11210-2889. Offers composition (MM); music (DMA, PhD); music education (MA); musicology (MA); performance (MM); performance practice (MA). The department offers courses at Brooklyn College that are creditable toward the CUNY doctoral degree (with permission of the executive officer of the doctoral program). Part-time programs available. *Students:* 64 full-time (36 women); includes 9 minority (4 African Americans, 1 Asian American or Pacific Islander, 4 Hispanic Americans), 19 international. Average age 29. 69 applicants, 74% accepted, 30 enrolled. In 2008, 22 master's awarded. *Degree requirements:* For master's, one foreign language, comprehensive exam, thesis. *Entrance requirements:* For master's, placement exam, 36 credits in music, audition, completed composition, writing sample. Additional exam requirements/recommendations for international students: Required—TOEFL (minimum score 550 paper-based; 213 computer-based; 79 iBT). *Application deadline:* For fall admission, 3/1 priority date for domestic students, 2/1 priority date for international students; for spring admission, 11/1 priority date for domestic students, 10/1 priority date for international students. Applications are processed on a rolling basis. Application fee: $125. Electronic applications accepted. *Expenses:* Tuition, state resident: full-time $7360; part-time $310 per credit hour. Tuition, nonresident: full-time $13,800; part-time $575 per credit hour. *Financial support:* Career-related internships or fieldwork, Federal Work-Study, institutionally sponsored loans, and scholarships/grants available. Support available to part-time students. Financial award application deadline: 5/1; financial award applicants required to submit FAFSA. *Faculty research:* American music, computer music. *Unit head:* Dr. Bruce MacIntyre, Chairperson, 718-951-5286, E-mail: brucem@brooklyn.cuny.edu. *Application contact:* Hernan Sierra, Graduate Admissions Coordinator, 718-951-4536, Fax: 718-951-4506, E-mail: grads@brooklyn.cuny.edu.

Brooklyn College of the City University of New York, Division of Graduate Studies, Program in Performance and Interactive Media Arts, Brooklyn, NY 11210-2889. Offers MFA, CAS. *Students:* 8 full-time (4 women), 10 part-time (6 women); includes 4 minority (2 African Americans, 2 Hispanic Americans), 2 international. Average age 33. 13 applicants, 62% accepted, 8 enrolled. In 2008, 5 master's, 1 other advanced degree awarded. *Entrance requirements:* For master's, 2 letters of recommendation, resumé, portfolio, interview; for CAS, 2 letters of recommendation. Additional exam requirements/recommendations for international students: Required—TOEFL (minimum score 500 paper-based; 173 computer-based; 61 iBT). *Application deadline:* For fall admission, 2/15 priority date for domestic students, 2/1 priority date for international students. Applications are processed on a rolling basis. Application fee: $125. Electronic applications accepted. *Expenses:* Tuition, state resident: full-time $7360; part-time $310 per credit hour. Tuition, nonresident: full-time $13,800; part-time $575 per credit hour. *Financial support:* Application deadline: 5/1. *Unit head:* Dr. John Jannone, Director, E-mail: jannone brooklyn.cuny.edu. *Application contact:* Hernan Sierra, Graduate Admissions Coordinator, 718-951-4536, Fax: 718-951-4506, E-mail: grads@brooklyn.cuny.edu.

Brown University, Graduate School, Department of Music, Providence, RI 02912. Offers electronic music and multimedia (PhD); ethnomusicology (PhD). *Degree requirements:* For doctorate, 2 foreign languages, comprehensive exam, thesis/dissertation, departmental qualifying exam. *Entrance requirements:* For doctorate, GRE General Test. *Faculty research:* Ethnomusicology.

Butler University, Jordan College of Fine Arts, Department of Music, Indianapolis, IN 46208-3485. Offers composition (MM); conducting (MM); music (MM); music education (MM); music history (MM); organ (MM); performance (MM). *Accreditation:* NASM. Part-time and evening/weekend programs available. *Faculty:* 14 full-time (3 women), 11 part-time/adjunct (5 women). *Students:* 23 full-time (10 women), 12 part-time (3 women); includes 1 minority (Hispanic American), 5 international. Average age 28. 38 applicants, 74% accepted, 9 enrolled. In 2008, 14 master's awarded. *Degree requirements:* For master's, thesis (for some programs). *Entrance requirements:* For master's, GRE General Test, GRE Subject Test, audition, interview. *Application deadline:* For fall admission, 8/15 priority date for domestic students. Applications are processed on a rolling basis. Application fee: $35. Electronic applications accepted. *Financial support:* In 2008–09, 15 teaching assistantships with full tuition reimbursements (averaging $2,500 per year) were awarded; fellowships, career-related internships or fieldwork, institutionally sponsored loans, and scholarships/grants also available. Support available to part-time students. Financial award application deadline: 7/15; financial award applicants required to submit FAFSA. *Unit head:* Dr. Daniel Bolin, Head, 317-940-9988, Fax: 317-940-9658, E-mail: dbolin@butler.edu. *Application contact:* Kathy Lang, Admission Representative, 317-940-9646, Fax: 317-940-9658, E-mail: klang@butler.edu.

California Baptist University, Program in Music, Riverside, CA 92504-3206. Offers conducting (MM); music education (MM); performance (MM). *Accreditation:* NASM. Part-time programs available. *Faculty:* 5 full-time (1 woman). *Students:* 16 full-time (9 women), 1 part-time (0 women); includes 5 minority (2 African Americans, 1 Asian American or Pacific Islander, 2 Hispanic Americans), 5 international. 15 applicants, 73% accepted, 9 enrolled. In 2008, 3 master's awarded. *Degree requirements:* For master's, thesis or alternative. *Entrance requirements:* For master's, minimum undergraduate GPA of 2.75. Additional exam requirements/recommendations for international students: Required—TOEFL (minimum score 575 paper-based; 230 computer-based; 89 iBT). *Application deadline:* For fall admission, 8/1 priority date for domestic students, 7/1 for international students; for spring admission, 12/1 priority date for domestic students, 10/15 for international students. Applications are processed on a rolling basis. Application fee: $45. Electronic applications accepted. *Expenses:* Tuition: Full-time $8172; part-time $454 per credit hour. Required fees: $510. *Financial support:* Federal Work-Study and scholarships/grants available. Support available to part-time students. Financial award applicants required to submit FAFSA. *Unit head:* Dr. Gary Bonner, Dean, School of Music, 951-343-4251, Fax: 951-343-4570, E-mail: gbonner@calbaptist.edu. *Application contact:* Gail Ronveaux, Dean of Graduate Enrollment, 951-343-5045, Fax: 951-343-5095, E-mail: graduateadmissions@calbaptist.edu.

California Institute of the Arts, School of Music, Valencia, CA 91355-2340. Offers African music (MFA, Adv C); composition (MFA, Adv C); composition/new media (MFA, Adv C); Indonesian music (MFA, Adv C); jazz (MFA, Adv C); North Indian music (MFA, Adv C); performance (MFA, Adv C); performer/composer (MFA, Adv C); voice (MFA, Adv C); world music performance (MFA). *Accreditation:* NASM. Part-time programs available. *Degree requirements:* For master's, composition or recital. *Entrance requirements:* For master's, audition or portfolio. Additional exam requirements/recommendations for international students: Required—TOEFL. Electronic applications accepted. *Faculty research:* Music composition and twentieth century performance practice, interactive multimedia and computer music, music cognition.

California State University, Chico, Graduate School, College of Humanities and Fine Arts, Department of Music, Chico, CA 95929-0805. Offers MA. *Accreditation:* NASM. *Degree requirements:* For master's, thesis or alternative, recital. *Entrance requirements:* For master's, GRE General Test, departmental exam, audition tape (off-campus applicants), music scores (for composers), 2 letters of recommendation, statement of purpose. Additional exam requirements/recommendations for international students: Required—TOEFL (minimum score 550 paper-based; 213 computer-based; 80 iBT), IELTS (minimum score 6.5). Electronic applications accepted.

California State University, East Bay, Academic Programs and Graduate Studies, College of Letters, Arts, and Social Sciences, Department of Music, Hayward, CA 94542-3000. Offers MA. *Accreditation:* NASM. Part-time programs available. *Degree requirements:* For master's, variable foreign language requirement, comprehensive exam, project, recital, or thesis. *Entrance requirements:* For master's, minimum GPA of 3.0 in field. Additional exam requirements/recommendations for international students: Required—TOEFL (minimum score 550 paper-based; 213 computer-based). Electronic applications accepted.

California State University, Fresno, Division of Graduate Studies, College of Arts and Humanities, Department of Music, Fresno, CA 93740-8027. Offers music (MA); music education (MA); performance (MA). *Accreditation:* NASM. Part-time programs available. *Degree requirements:* For master's, thesis or alternative. *Entrance requirements:* For master's, GRE General Test, BA in music, minimum GPA of 3.0. Additional exam requirements/recommendations for international students: Required—TOEFL. Electronic applications accepted. *Faculty research:* Technology transfer, folk art.

California State University, Fullerton, Graduate Studies, College of the Arts, Department of Music, Fullerton, CA 92834-9480. Offers music education (MA); music history and literature (MA); performance (MM); piano pedagogy (MA); theory-composition (MM). *Accreditation:* NASM. Part-time programs available. *Students:* 19 full-time (14 women), 59 part-time (32 women); includes 26 minority (2 African Americans, 18 Asian Americans or Pacific Islanders, 6 Hispanic Americans), 14 international. Average age 28. 63 applicants, 51% accepted, 25 enrolled. In 2008, 16 master's awarded. *Degree requirements:* For master's, comprehensive exam, project or thesis. *Entrance requirements:* For master's, audition, major in music or related field, minimum GPA of 2.5 in last 60 units of course work. Application fee: $55. Tuition and fees vary according to degree level. *Financial support:* Teaching assistantships, Federal Work-Study, institutionally sponsored loans, and scholarships/grants available. Support available to part-time students. Financial award application deadline: 3/1. *Unit head:* Dr. Marc Dickey, Chair, 657-278-3511. *Application contact:* Dr. Mitch Fennell, Adviser, 657-278-3511.

California State University, Long Beach, Graduate Studies, College of the Arts, Department of Music, Long Beach, CA 90840. Offers composition (MM); conducting-choral (MM); conducting-instrumental (MM); instrument/vocal performance (MM); jazz studies (MM); music (MA); opera performance (MM). *Accreditation:* NASM. Part-time programs available. *Faculty:* 21 full-time (5 women), 32 part-time/adjunct (10 women). *Students:* 38 full-time (19 women), 31 part-time (16 women); includes 14 minority (9 Asian Americans or Pacific Islanders, 5 Hispanic Americans), 9 international. Average age 36. 98 applicants, 48% accepted, 34 enrolled. *Degree requirements:* For master's, thesis or alternative, departmental qualifying exam. *Application deadline:* For fall admission, 5/1 for domestic students; for spring admission, 12/1 for domestic students. Applications are processed on a rolling basis. Application fee: $55. Electronic applications accepted. *Expenses:* Tuition, nonresident: full-time $11,160; part-time $372 per unit. Required fees: $4100; $1261 per semester. *Financial support:* Federal Work-Study, institutionally sponsored loans, and scholarships/grants available. Financial award application deadline: 3/2. *Unit head:* John A Carnahan, Chair, 562-985-4781, Fax: 562-985-2490, E-mail: jcarnaha@csulb.edu. *Application contact:* Dr. Leland Vail, Graduate Advisor, 562-985-4781, Fax: 562-985-2490, E-mail: lvail@csulb.edu.

California State University, Long Beach, Graduate Studies, College of the Arts, Department of Theatre Arts, Long Beach, CA 90840. Offers acting (MFA); dramatic writing (MFA); technical theatre/design (MFA); theatre management (MFA); MBA/MFA. *Accreditation:* NAST. Part-time programs available. *Faculty:* 6 full-time (3 women), 3 part-time/adjunct (0 women). *Students:* 27 full-time (17 women), 12 part-time (7 women); includes 3 minority (all Asian Americans or Pacific Islanders), 5 international. Average age 32. 24 applicants, 29% accepted, 5 enrolled. *Degree requirements:* For master's, thesis or alternative. *Application deadline:* For fall admission, 7/1 for domestic students; for spring admission, 12/1 for domestic students. Applications are processed on a rolling basis. Application fee: $55. Electronic applications accepted. *Expenses:* Tuition, nonresident: full-time $11,160; part-time $372 per unit. Required fees: $4100; $1261 per semester. *Financial support:* Research assistantships, teaching assistantships, Federal Work-Study, institutionally sponsored loans, scholarships/grants, and traineeships available. Financial award application deadline: 3/2. *Unit head:* Dr. Joanne L. Gordon, Chair, 562-985-7891, Fax: 562-985-2263, E-mail: jgordon@csulb.edu. *Application contact:* Barbara Matthews, Graduate Adviser, 562-985-4042, Fax: 562-985-2263, E-mail: jmatthew@csulb.edu.

California State University, Los Angeles, Graduate Studies, College of Arts and Letters, Department of Music, Los Angeles, CA 90032-8530. Offers music composition (MM); music education (MA); musicology (MA); performance (MM). *Accreditation:* NASM. Part-time and evening/weekend programs available. *Faculty:* 15 full-time (3 women), 8 part-time/adjunct (4 women). *Students:* 38 full-time (15 women), 43 part-time (20 women); includes 35 minority (5 African Americans, 11 Asian Americans or Pacific Islanders, 19 Hispanic Americans), 10 international. Average age 35. 26 applicants, 96% accepted, 15 enrolled. In 2008, 22 master's awarded. *Degree requirements:* For master's, comprehensive exam, project or thesis. *Entrance requirements:* For master's, audition. Additional exam requirements/recommendations for international students: Required—TOEFL (minimum score 500 paper-based; 173 computer-based). *Application deadline:* For fall admission, 6/15 for domestic students, 5/1 for international students; for winter admission, 11/1 for domestic students, 9/1 for international students; for spring admission, 2/1 for domestic students, 10/1 for international students. Applications are processed on a rolling basis. Application fee: $55. Electronic applications accepted. *Expenses:* Tuition, nonresident: part-time $226 per credit. Required fees: $4019. *Financial support:* Career-related internships or fieldwork and Federal Work-Study available. Support available to part-time students. Financial award application deadline: 3/1. *Faculty research:* Gregorian semiology, baroque opera. *Unit head:* Dr. George DeGraffenreid, Chair, 323-343-4060, Fax: 323-343-4063, E-mail: gdegraf@calstatela.edu. *Application contact:* Dr. Jose L. Galvan, Dean of Graduate Studies, 323-343-3820, Fax: 323-343-5653, E-mail: jgalvan@cslanet.calstatela.edu.

California State University, Northridge, Graduate Studies, College of Arts, Media, and Communication, Department of Music, Northridge, CA 91330. Offers composition (MM); conducting (MM); music education (MA); performance (MM). *Accreditation:* NASM. *Faculty:* 21 full-time (6 women), 46 part-time/adjunct (13 women). *Students:* 23 full-time (13 women), 32 part-time (21 women); includes 15 minority (3 African Americans, 6 Asian Americans or Pacific Islanders, 6 Hispanic Americans), 7 international. Average age 29. 93 applicants, 44% accepted, 29 enrolled. In 2008, 13 master's awarded. *Degree requirements:* For master's, thesis. *Entrance requirements:* For master's, audition, GRE General Test or minimum GPA of 3.0. Additional exam requirements/recommendations for international students: Required—TOEFL. *Application deadline:* For fall admission, 11/30 for domestic students. Application fee: $55. *Financial support:* Application deadline: 3/1. *Faculty research:* Touring program. *Unit head:* Dr. Ric Alviso, Chair, 816-677-2155, E-mail: ric.alviso@csun.edu. *Application contact:* John Roscigno, Graduate Advisor, 818-677-6834, E-mail: john.roscigno@csun.edu.

California State University, Sacramento, Graduate Studies, College of Arts and Letters, Department of Music, Sacramento, CA 95819-6048. Offers MM. *Accreditation:* NASM. Part-time programs available. *Degree requirements:* For master's, thesis or alternative, writing proficiency exam. *Entrance requirements:* For master's, BA in music or equivalent, minimum GPA of 2.5 during previous 2 years of course work. Additional exam requirements/recommendations for international students: Required—TOEFL. Electronic applications accepted.

Campbellsville University, School of Music, Campbellsville, KY 42718-2799. Offers church music (MM); music (MA); music education (MM). *Accreditation:* NASM. Part-time programs available. *Degree requirements:* For master's, thesis (for some programs), paper or recital. *Entrance requirements:* For master's, GRE General Test or PRAXIS, minimum GPA of 2.75. Additional exam requirements/recommendations for international students: Required—TOEFL (minimum score 550 paper-based). Electronic applications accepted. *Expenses:* Tuition: Full-time $6570; part-time $365 per credit hour. Required fees: $60 per term.

Capital University, Conservatory of Music, Columbus, OH 43209-2394. Offers music education (MM), including instrumental emphasis, Kodály emphasis. Program offered only in summer. *Accreditation:* NASM. Part-time programs available. *Degree requirements:* For master's, comprehensive exam, thesis or alternative, chamber performance exam. *Entrance requirements:* For master's, music theory exam, minimum undergraduate GPA of 3.0. Additional exam requirements/recommendations for international students: Required—TOEFL (minimum score 550 paper-based; 213 computer-based; 80 iBT). Electronic applications accepted. *Expenses:* Contact institution. *Faculty research:* Folk song research, Kodály method, performance, composition.

Cardinal Stritch University, College of Arts and Sciences, Music Department, Milwaukee, WI 53217-3985. Offers piano (MM). Part-time programs available. *Degree requirements:* For master's, comprehensive exam, recital permission audition. *Entrance requirements:* For master's, placement test in music theory and music history, 3 letters of recommendation, audition. Electronic applications accepted.

Carleton University, Faculty of Graduate Studies, Faculty of Arts and Social Sciences, School for Studies in Art and Culture, Program in Music and Culture, Ottawa, ON K1S 5B6, Canada. Offers MA.

Carnegie Mellon University, College of Fine Arts, School of Music, Pittsburgh, PA 15213-3891. Offers composition (MM); conducting (MM); instrumental performance (MM); music education (MM); vocal performance (MM). *Accreditation:* NASM. Part-time programs available. *Degree requirements:* For master's, comprehensive exam, recital. *Entrance requirements:* For master's, audition. *Faculty research:* Computer music, music history.

Case Western Reserve University, School of Graduate Studies, Department of Music, Cleveland, OH 44106. Offers early music (MA, D Mus A); music education (MA, PhD); music history (MA); musicology (PhD). *Accreditation:* NASM (one or more programs are accredited). *Degree requirements:* For doctorate, thesis/dissertation. *Entrance requirements:* For master's, audition. Additional exam requirements/recommendations for international students: Required—TOEFL. Electronic applications accepted. *Faculty research:* Early music performance practices; sixteenth-, seventeenth-, and twentieth-centuries; Mahler; wind ensemble direction; measurement/evaluation in music education.

The Catholic University of America, The Benjamin T. Rome School of Music, Washington, DC 20064. Offers MA, MM, MMSM, DMA, PhD, MSLS/MA. *Accreditation:* NASM. Part-time programs available. *Entrance requirements:* For master's, theory placement test, 2 letters of recommendation, list of publicly performed repertoire; for doctorate, school qualifying exam, 4 letters of recommendation list of publicly performed repertoire. Additional exam requirements/recommendations for international students: Required—TOEFL (minimum score 580 paper-based; 237 computer-based). Electronic applications accepted. *Faculty research:* Gregorian chant and related topics, Elizabeth Sprague Coolidge, performance-related topics.

Central Michigan University, College of Graduate Studies, College of Communication and Fine Arts, School of Music, Mount Pleasant, MI 48859. Offers conducting (MM); music composition (MM); music education (MM); music performance (MM); piano pedagogy (MM). *Accreditation:* NASM. Part-time programs available. *Faculty:* 28 full-time (11 women), 4 part-time/adjunct (1 woman). *Students:* 9 full-time (2 women), 23 part-time (9 women); includes 1 African American, 2 Asian Americans or Pacific Islanders, 1 Hispanic American, 1 international. Average age 29. *Degree requirements:* For master's, thesis or alternative. *Application deadline:* Applications are processed on a rolling basis. Application fee: $35 ($45 for international students). Electronic applications accepted. *Expenses:* Tuition, state resident: full-time $3717; part-time $413 per credit. Tuition, nonresident: full-time $6894; part-time $766 per credit. *Financial support:* Fellowships with tuition reimbursements, research assistantships with tuition reimbursements, teaching assistantships with tuition reimbursements, Federal Work-Study, unspecified assistantships, and out-of-state merit awards available. *Faculty research:* Music education, music composition, conducting, music performance, piano pedagogy. *Unit head:* Dr. Randi L'Hommedieu, Director, 989-774-3281, Fax: 989-774-3766, E-mail: randi.louis.l'hommedieu@cmich.edu. *Application contact:* Dr. Daniel L. Steele, Associate Dean and Graduate Coordinator, 989-774-1970, Fax: 989-774-3766, E-mail: steel1dl@cmich.edu.

Central Washington University, Graduate Studies, Research and Continuing Education, College of Arts and Humanities, Department of Music, Ellensburg, WA 98926. Offers MM. *Accreditation:* NASM. *Degree requirements:* For master's, thesis or alternative. *Entrance requirements:* For master's, minimum GPA of 3.0. Additional exam requirements/recommendations for international students: Required—TOEFL (minimum score 550 paper-based; 213 computer-based; 79 iBT). Electronic applications accepted.

City College of the City University of New York, Graduate School, College of Liberal Arts and Science, Division of the Humanities and Arts, Department of Music, New York, NY 10031-9198. Offers MA. Part-time programs available. *Degree requirements:* For master's, one foreign language, thesis. *Entrance requirements:* For master's, minimum GPA of 3.0, portfolio (composition), writing samples (history and theory), audition (performance). Additional exam requirements/recommendations for international students: Required—TOEFL (minimum score 575 paper-based; 233 computer-based). *Faculty research:* Tonal theory, American music, musicology, atonal theory, performance.

Claremont Graduate University, Graduate Programs, School of Arts and Humanities, Department of Music, Claremont, CA 91711-6160. Offers church music (MA, DCM); composition (MA, DMA); historical performance practices (MA, DMA); musicology (MA, PhD); performance (MA, DMA); MBA/PhD. Part-time programs available. *Faculty:* 3 full-time (1 woman). *Students:* 49 full-time (25 women), 6 part-time (3 women); includes 11 minority (5 Asian Americans or Pacific Islanders, 6 Hispanic Americans), 13 international. Average age 36. In 2008, 4 master's, 5 doctorates awarded. Terminal master's awarded for partial completion of doctoral program. *Degree requirements:* For master's, one foreign language, comprehensive exam, thesis (for

some programs), oral and written qualifying exams, recitals; for doctorate, 2 foreign languages, comprehensive exam, thesis/dissertation (for some programs), oral and written qualifying exams, oral defense of dissertation, recitals. *Entrance requirements:* For master's and doctorate, GRE General Test, auditions, compositions, or papers. Additional exam requirements/recommendations for international students: Required—TOEFL (minimum score 550 paper-based; 213 computer-based; 80 iBT). *Application deadline:* For fall admission, 2/1 priority date for domestic students. Applications are processed on a rolling basis. Application fee: $60. Electronic applications accepted. *Expenses:* Tuition: Full-time $33,698; part-time $1465 per unit. Required fees: $310; $155 per semester. Tuition and fees vary according to program. *Financial support:* Fellowships, research assistantships, teaching assistantships, Federal Work-Study, institutionally sponsored loans, and scholarships/grants available. Support available to part-time students. Financial award application deadline: 2/15; financial award applicants required to submit FAFSA. *Unit head:* Robert Zappulla, Chair, 909-607-9664, Fax: 909-607-3694, E-mail: robert.zappulla@cgu.edu. *Application contact:* Sylvia Quintana, Department Secretary, 909-607-3289, Fax: 909-607-1221, E-mail: sylvia.quintana@cgu.edu.

Cleveland Institute of Music, Graduate Programs, Cleveland, OH 44106-1776. Offers MM, DMA, AD, CPS. *Accreditation:* NASM (one or more programs are accredited). *Degree requirements:* For master's, comprehensive exam, recital; for doctorate, comprehensive exam, thesis/dissertation (for some programs), final projects; for other advanced degree, recital. *Entrance requirements:* For master's, theory placement tests, audition; for doctorate, diagnostic exams, theory placement test, audition; for other advanced degree, audition. Additional exam requirements/recommendations for international students: Required—TOEFL (minimum score 550 paper-based; 213 computer-based). Electronic applications accepted.

Cleveland State University, College of Graduate Studies, College of Liberal Arts and Social Sciences, Department of Music, Cleveland, OH 44115. Offers composition (MM); music education (MM); performance (MM). *Accreditation:* NASM. Part-time and evening/weekend programs available. *Faculty:* 14 full-time (6 women), 46 part-time/adjunct (14 women). *Students:* 15 full-time (4 women), 31 part-time (14 women); includes 8 minority (3 African Americans, 3 Asian Americans or Pacific Islanders, 2 Hispanic Americans). Average age 29. 37 applicants, 51% accepted, 15 enrolled. In 2008, 8 master's awarded. *Degree requirements:* For master's, comprehensive exam, thesis or recital. *Entrance requirements:* For master's, departmental assessment in music history, minimum undergraduate GPA of 2.75. Additional exam requirements/recommendations for international students: Required—TOEFL (minimum score 525 paper-based; 197 computer-based). *Application deadline:* For fall admission, 7/15 priority date for domestic students. Applications are processed on a rolling basis. Application fee: $30. *Financial support:* In 2008–09, 15 students received support, including 11 research assistantships with full tuition reimbursements available (averaging $3,612 per year); tuition waivers (partial) and unspecified assistantships also available. Financial award application deadline: 3/1. *Faculty research:* Ethnomusicology, classical-romantic music, new performance practices, electronic music, interdisciplinary studies. Total annual research expenditures: $121,000. *Unit head:* Dr. Eric E. Ziolek, Chairperson, 216-687-2301, Fax: 216-687-9279, E-mail: e.ziolek@csuohio.edu. *Application contact:* Dr. Birch Browning, Coordinator of Graduate Studies and Admission, 216-687-3768, Fax: 216-687-9279, E-mail: b.browning@csuohio.edu.

The College of Saint Rose, Graduate Studies, School of Arts and Humanities, Music Department, Program in Music, Albany, NY 12203-1419. Offers MA. *Accreditation:* NASM. *Degree requirements:* For master's, final project. *Entrance requirements:* For master's, audition, minimum undergraduate GPA of 3.0. Additional exam requirements/recommendations for international students: Required—TOEFL (minimum score 550 paper-based; 213 computer-based). Electronic applications accepted.

Colorado State University, Graduate School, College of Liberal Arts, Department of Music, Theater, and Dance, Fort Collins, CO 80523-1779. Offers music (MM). *Accreditation:* NASM. Part-time programs available. *Faculty:* 26 full-time (6 women). *Students:* 45 full-time (30 women), 37 part-time (27 women); includes 10 minority (3 African Americans, 5 Asian Americans or Pacific Islanders, 2 Hispanic Americans), 8 international. Average age 30. 63 applicants, 67% accepted, 28 enrolled. In 2008, 17 master's awarded. *Degree requirements:* For master's, variable foreign language requirement, comprehensive exam (for some programs), thesis (for some programs), 2 recitals, project. *Entrance requirements:* For master's, minimum GPA of 3.0, audition, bachelor's degree, letters of recommendation, statement of professional goals. Additional exam requirements/recommendations for international students: Required—TOEFL (minimum score 550 paper-based; 213 computer-based). *Application deadline:* For fall admission, 2/15 priority date for domestic students; for spring admission, 11/15 priority date for domestic students. Applications are processed on a rolling basis. Application fee: $50. Electronic applications accepted. *Expenses:* Tuition, area resident: Full-time $5620; part-time $312.25 per credit. Tuition, state resident: full-time $5620; part-time $312.25 per credit. Tuition, nonresident: full-time $17,253; part-time $958.50 per credit. Required fees: $1449.56; $82.35 per credit. *Financial support:* In 2008–09, 19 students received support, including 19 teaching assistantships with full and partial tuition reimbursements available (averaging $6,958 per year); fellowships, research assistantships with partial tuition reimbursements available, career-related internships or fieldwork, Federal Work-Study, scholarships/grants, traineeships, and unspecified assistantships also available. Financial award application deadline: 3/1; financial award applicants required to submit FAFSA. *Faculty research:* Neurobiology, musicology, music literacy, music learning, music therapy. *Unit head:* Dr. Michael H. Thaut, Chair, 970-491-5529, Fax: 970-491-7541, E-mail: michael.thaut@colostate.edu. *Application contact:* Dr. Eric Hollenbeck, Director of Graduate Studies, 970-491-4054, Fax: 970-491-7541, E-mail: eric.hollenbeck@colostate.edu.

Columbia University, Graduate School of Arts and Sciences, Division of Humanities, Department of Music, New York, NY 10027. Offers M Phil, MA, DMA, PhD. *Degree requirements:* For master's, 2 foreign languages, thesis or alternative; for doctorate, variable foreign language requirement, thesis/dissertation. *Entrance requirements:* For master's and doctorate, GRE General Test, GRE Subject Test, sample of written work. Additional exam requirements/recommendations for international students: Required—TOEFL. *Faculty research:* Historical musicology, ethnomusicology, composition and theory.

See Close-Up on page 285.

Concordia University, School of Graduate Studies, Faculty of Fine Arts, Department of Music, Montréal, QC H3G 1M8, Canada. Offers advanced music performance studies (Diploma). *Degree requirements:* For Diploma, performance, 2 recitals.

Concordia University Chicago, College of Graduate and Innovative Programs, Program in Church Music, River Forest, IL 60305-1499. Offers MCM. *Accreditation:* NASM. Part-time programs available. *Degree requirements:* For master's, composition, recital, or thesis. *Entrance requirements:* For master's, minimum GPA of 2.9, audition. Additional exam requirements/recommendations for international students: Required—TOEFL (minimum score 550 paper-based; 195 computer-based). Electronic applications accepted. *Faculty research:* Twentieth-century sacred choral music, liturgical context of sacred music after the Council of Trent, dance and music of J.S. Bach.

Concordia University Chicago, College of Graduate and Innovative Programs, Program in Music, River Forest, IL 60305-1499. Offers MA. Part-time programs available. *Degree requirements:* For master's, composition, recital, or thesis. *Entrance requirements:* For master's, minimum GPA of 2.9, audition. Additional exam requirements/recommendations for international students: Required—TOEFL (minimum score 550 paper-based; 195 computer-based). Electronic applications accepted.

Concordia University Wisconsin, Graduate Programs, School of Arts and Sciences, Program in Church Music, Mequon, WI 53097-2402. Offers MCM. *Degree requirements:* For master's, comprehensive exam, thesis or alternative. *Entrance requirements:* For master's, minimum

Music

Concordia University Wisconsin *(continued)*
GPA of 3.0. Additional exam requirements/recommendations for international students: Required—TOEFL.

Conservatorio de Musica, Program in Musical Performance, San Juan, PR 00918-2199. Offers instrumental performance (Diploma); vocal performance (Diploma). *Entrance requirements:* For degree, 3 letters of recommendation, audition, degree in music, minimum GPA of 2.5.

Converse College, Carroll McDaniel Petrie School of Music, Spartanburg, SC 29302-0006. Offers instrumental performance (M Mus); music education (M Mus); piano pedagogy (M Mus); vocal performance (M Mus). *Accreditation:* NASM. Part-time and evening/weekend programs available. *Degree requirements:* For master's, variable foreign language requirement, comprehensive exam, thesis (for some programs), recitals. *Entrance requirements:* For master's, NTE (music education), audition, 3 letters of recommendation. Additional exam requirements/recommendations for international students: Required—TOEFL. Electronic applications accepted. *Faculty research:* Chamber music, opera, performance, composition, recording.

Cornell University, Graduate School, Graduate Fields of Arts and Sciences, Field of Music, Ithaca, NY 14853-0001. Offers composition (DMA); musicology (PhD); performance practice (DMA); theory of music (MA). *Faculty:* 17 full-time (5 women). *Students:* 35 full-time (12 women); includes 3 minority (1 American Indian/Alaska Native, 1 Asian American or Pacific Islander, 1 Hispanic American), 18 international. Average age 29. 123 applicants, 11% accepted, 9 enrolled. In 2008, 5 master's, 8 doctorates awarded. *Degree requirements:* For doctorate, comprehensive exam, thesis/dissertation, 1 foreign language (DMA), 2 foreign languages (PhD). *Entrance requirements:* For doctorate, GRE General Test, 2 music papers; 2 recent scores (with recording) and 1 music paper (DMA composition); 1 music paper, recording and audition (DMA performance practice). Additional exam requirements/recommendations for international students: Required—TOEFL (minimum score 600 paper-based; 250 computer-based; 77 iBT). *Application deadline:* For fall admission, 1/15 for domestic students. Application fee: $70. Electronic applications accepted. *Expenses:* Tuition: Full-time $29,500. Required fees: $70. Full-time tuition and fees vary according to degree level, program and student level. *Financial support:* In 2008–09, 32 students received support, including 15 fellowships with full tuition reimbursements available, 17 teaching assistantships with full tuition reimbursements available; research assistantships with full tuition reimbursements available, institutionally sponsored loans, scholarships/grants, health care benefits, tuition waivers (full and partial), and unspecified assistantships also available. Financial award applicants required to submit FAFSA. *Faculty research:* Music history, music theory, performance practice, ethnomusicology, composition. *Unit head:* Director of Graduate Studies, 607-255-9078. *Application contact:* Graduate Field Assistant, 607-255-9078, E-mail: grad_music@cornell.edu.

The Curtis Institute of Music, Graduate Studies, Philadelphia, PA 19103-6107. Offers opera (MM). *Accreditation:* NASM. *Entrance requirements:* For master's, audition or performance in 2 or more principal roles or 6 major scenes.

Dalhousie University, Faculty of Arts and Social Science, Department of Musicology, Halifax, NS B3H 4R2, Canada. Offers MA. *Entrance requirements:* Additional exam requirements/recommendations for international students: Required—TOEFL, IELTS, CANTEST, CAEL, or Michigan English Language Assessment Battery. *Application deadline:* For fall admission, 6/1 for domestic students, 4/1 for international students; for winter admission, 11/15 for domestic students, 8/31 for international students; for spring admission, 2/29 for domestic students, 12/31 for international students. Application fee: $70. Electronic applications accepted. *Financial support:* Scholarships/grants and health care benefits available. *Unit head:* Dr. Jennifer Bain, Graduate Coordinator, 902-494-3867, Fax: 902-494-2801, E-mail: music@dal.ca. *Application contact:* April MacDonald, Secretary, 902-494-2418, Fax: 902-494-2801, E-mail: music@dal.ca.

Dartmouth College, Arts and Sciences Graduate Programs, Department of Music, Hanover, NH 03755. Offers electro-acoustic music (AM). *Degree requirements:* For master's, thesis or alternative. *Entrance requirements:* Additional exam requirements/recommendations for international students: Required—TOEFL. *Faculty research:* Composition and design of computer music software and related topics.

DePaul University, School of Music, Chicago, IL 60614. Offers applied music (performance) (MM, Certificate); jazz studies (MM), including composition, performance; music composition (MM); music education (MM). *Accreditation:* NASM (one or more programs are accredited). Part-time and evening/weekend programs available. *Faculty:* 11 full-time (2 women), 50 part-time/adjunct (14 women). *Students:* 61 full-time (23 women), 65 part-time (31 women); includes 13 minority (2 African Americans, 6 Asian Americans or Pacific Islanders, 5 Hispanic Americans), 26 international. Average age 24. 175 applicants, 46% accepted. In 2008, 40 master's, 5 Certificates awarded. *Degree requirements:* For master's, comprehensive exam, terminal project. *Entrance requirements:* For master's, bachelor's degree in music or related field, audition, minimum GPA of 3.0; for Certificate, master's degree in performance or related field. Additional exam requirements/recommendations for international students: Required—TOEFL (minimum score 550 paper-based; 213 computer-based; 80 iBT). *Application deadline:* For fall admission, 1/15 priority date for domestic and international students. Applications are processed on a rolling basis. Electronic applications accepted. *Expenses:* Contact institution. *Financial support:* In 2008–09, 4 fellowships with partial tuition reimbursements were awarded; teaching assistantships, career-related internships or fieldwork, Federal Work-Study, scholarships/grants, and tuition waivers also available. Support available to part-time students. Financial award application deadline: 1/15. *Unit head:* Dr. Donald E. Casey, Dean, 773-325-7256, E-mail: Dcasey@depaul.edu. *Application contact:* Ross Beacraft, Director of Admissions, 773-325-7444, Fax: 773-325-7429, E-mail: rbeacraf@depaul.edu.

Duke University, Graduate School, Department of Music, Durham, NC 27708. Offers music composition (AM, PhD); musicology (AM, PhD); performance practice (AM, PhD). Part-time programs available. Terminal master's awarded for partial completion of doctoral program. *Degree requirements:* For master's, 2 foreign languages; for doctorate, 3 foreign languages, thesis/dissertation. *Entrance requirements:* For master's and doctorate, GRE General Test. Additional exam requirements/recommendations for international students: Required—TOEFL (minimum score 550 paper-based; 213 computer-based; 83 iBT), IELTS (minimum score 7). Electronic applications accepted.

Duquesne University, Mary Pappert School of Music, Pittsburgh, PA 15282-0001. Offers music composition (MM); music education (MM); music performance (MM, AD); music technology (MM); music theory (MM); sacred music (MM). *Accreditation:* NASM. Part-time programs available. Postbaccalaureate distance learning degree programs offered (minimal on-campus study). *Faculty:* 26 full-time (8 women), 71 part-time/adjunct (18 women). *Students:* 71 full-time (35 women), 22 part-time (10 women); includes 8 minority (3 African Americans, 5 Asian Americans or Pacific Islanders, 26 international. Average age 23. 96 applicants, 81% accepted, 43 enrolled. In 2008, 41 master's, 11 ADs awarded. *Degree requirements:* For master's, comprehensive exam, thesis (for some programs), recital (music performance); for AD, recital. *Entrance requirements:* For master's, audition, minimum undergraduate QPA of 3.0 in music, portfolio of original compositions, theoretical papers, or music education experience; for AD, audition. Additional exam requirements/recommendations for international students: Required—TOEFL (minimum score 550 paper-based; 213 computer-based; 79 iBT). *Application deadline:* For fall admission, 9/1 priority date for domestic students; for spring admission, 12/1 for domestic students. Applications are processed on a rolling basis. Application fee: $50. *Expenses:* Contact institution. *Financial support:* In 2008–09, 45 fellowships with full and partial tuition reimbursements were awarded; career-related internships or fieldwork, Federal Work-Study, institutionally sponsored loans, and tuition waivers (full and partial) also available. Support available to part-time students. Financial award application deadline: 4/1. *Faculty research:* Performance; computer-assisted instruction in music at elementary and secondary levels; electronic music; contemporary music, theory, and analysis; development of on-line graduate

music courses. Total annual research expenditures: $7,500. *Unit head:* Dr. Edward W. Kocher, Dean, 412-396-6082, Fax: 412-396-1524, E-mail: kocher@duq.edu. *Application contact:* Peggy Eiseman, Administrative Assistant of Admissions, 412-396-5064, Fax: 412-396-5479, E-mail: eiseman@duq.edu.

East Carolina University, Graduate School, College of Fine Arts and Communication, School of Music, Greenville, NC 27858-4353. Offers music education (MM); music therapy (MM); performance (MM); theory and composition (MM). *Accreditation:* NASM. Part-time programs available. *Degree requirements:* For master's, comprehensive exam, thesis optional. *Entrance requirements:* For master's, GRE General Test or MAT. Additional exam requirements/recommendations for international students: Required—TOEFL.

Eastern Illinois University, Graduate School, College of Arts and Humanities, Department of Music, Charleston, IL 61920-3099. Offers MA. *Accreditation:* NASM. *Degree requirements:* For master's, thesis or alternative, recital.

Eastern Kentucky University, The Graduate School, College of Arts and Sciences, Department of Music, Richmond, KY 40475-3102. Offers choral conducting (MM); performance (MM); theory/composition (MM). *Accreditation:* NASM. Part-time programs available. *Degree requirements:* For master's, thesis optional. *Entrance requirements:* For master's, GRE General Test, minimum GPA of 2.5. *Faculty research:* Technology.

Eastern Michigan University, Graduate School, College of Arts and Sciences, Department of Communication and Theatre Arts, Program in Theatre, Ypsilanti, MI 48197. Offers interpretation/performance studies (MA); theatre arts (MA). Part-time and evening/weekend programs available. Postbaccalaureate distance learning degree programs offered (minimal on-campus study). *Degree requirements:* For master's, thesis or alternative. *Entrance requirements:* Additional exam requirements/recommendations for international students: Required—TOEFL.

Eastern Michigan University, Graduate School, College of Arts and Sciences, Department of Music and Dance, Ypsilanti, MI 48197. Offers music composition (MM); music education (MM); music pedagogy (MM); music performance (MM). *Accreditation:* NASM. Part-time and evening/weekend programs available. Postbaccalaureate distance learning degree programs offered (minimal on-campus study). *Entrance requirements:* Additional exam requirements/recommendations for international students: Required—TOEFL.

Eastern Washington University, Graduate Studies, College of Arts and Letters, Department of Music, Cheney, WA 99004-2431. Offers composition (MA); instrumental/vocal performance (MA); music education (MA); music history and literature (MA). *Accreditation:* NASM. Part-time programs available. *Degree requirements:* For master's, comprehensive exam, thesis or alternative. *Entrance requirements:* For master's, GRE General Test, minimum GPA of 3.0.

Emory University, Graduate School of Arts and Sciences, Department of Music, Atlanta, GA 30322-1100. Offers choral conducting (MM, MSM); organ performance (MM, MSM). *Accreditation:* NASM. *Degree requirements:* For master's, comprehensive exam, recital or worship service/recital. *Entrance requirements:* For master's, GRE General Test, audition, interview. Additional exam requirements/recommendations for international students: Required—TOEFL. Electronic applications accepted. *Faculty research:* 19th century criticism, Schenker, Bach Aria styles, contemporary passion music, Andriesson, cross-cultural research, organ performance.

Emporia State University, School of Graduate Studies, College of Liberal Arts and Sciences, Department of Music, Emporia, KS 66801-5087. Offers music education (MM), including instrumental, vocal; performance (MM). *Accreditation:* NASM. Part-time programs available. *Faculty:* 15 full-time (5 women), 3 part-time/adjunct (all women). *Students:* 3 full-time (2 women), 7 part-time (4 women), 3 international. 1 applicant, 100% accepted, 1 enrolled. In 2008, 5 master's awarded. *Degree requirements:* For master's, comprehensive exam or thesis. *Entrance requirements:* For master's, music qualifying exam, appropriate undergraduate degree. Additional exam requirements/recommendations for international students: Required—TOEFL (minimum score 450 paper-based; 133 computer-based). *Application deadline:* For fall admission, 8/15 priority date for domestic students. Applications are processed on a rolling basis. Application fee: $30 ($75 for international students). Electronic applications accepted. *Expenses:* Tuition, area resident: Full-time $3976; part-time $166 per credit hour. Tuition, state resident: full-time $3976; part-time $166 per credit hour. Tuition, nonresident: full-time $12,028; part-time $501 per credit hour. Required fees: $51 per credit hour. Tuition and fees vary according to campus/location. *Financial support:* In 2008–09, 2 research assistantships with full tuition reimbursements (averaging $7,059 per year), 2 teaching assistantships with full tuition reimbursements (averaging $6,841 per year) were awarded; Federal Work-Study, institutionally sponsored loans, health care benefits, and unspecified assistantships also available. Financial award application deadline: 3/15; financial award applicants required to submit FAFSA. *Unit head:* Dr. Allan D Comstock, Interim Chair, 620-341-5431, E-mail: acomstoc@emporia.edu. *Application contact:* Dr. Andrew Houchins, Graduate Coordinator, 620-341-6089, E-mail: ahouchin@emporia.edu.

Five Towns College, Department of Music, Dix Hills, NY 11746-6055. Offers jazz/commercial music (MM); music (DMA); music education (MM). Part-time programs available. *Degree requirements:* For master's, exams, major composition or capstone project, recital; for doctorate, comprehensive exam, thesis/dissertation, final oral exam. *Entrance requirements:* For master's, audition, bachelor's degree in music or music education, minimum GPA of 2.75, 36 hours of course work in performance; for doctorate, master's degree in music, minimum GPA of 3.0, 3 letters of recommendation. Additional exam requirements/recommendations for international students: Required—TOEFL (minimum score 550 paper-based; 213 computer-based; 80 iBT). *Faculty research:* Teaching methods, teaching strategies and techniques, analysis of modern music, jazz.

Florida Atlantic University, Barry Kaye College of Business, Program in Music Business Administration, Boca Raton, FL 33431-0991. Offers MS. Part-time programs available. *Students:* 3 full-time (2 women), 1 part-time (0 women); includes 2 minority (1 African American, 1 Asian American or Pacific Islander), 1 international. Average age 32. *Entrance requirements:* For master's, GMAT or GRE, minimum GPA of 3.0 for last two years of undergraduate work. *Application deadline:* For fall admission, 7/1 for domestic students, 2/15 for international students; for spring admission, 11/1 for domestic students, 7/15 for international students. *Expenses:* Tuition, state resident: full-time $4867; part-time $270.40 per credit hour. Tuition, nonresident: full-time $16,486; part-time $915.87 per credit hour. *Unit head:* Prof. Carl Riegel, Coordinator, 561-297-3684. *Application contact:* Fredrick G. Taylor, Graduate Adviser, 561-297-3196, Fax: 561-297-1315, E-mail: ftaylor@fau.edu.

Florida Atlantic University, Dorothy F. Schmidt College of Arts and Letters, Department of Music, Boca Raton, FL 33431-0991. Offers commercial music (MA); music history/literature (MA); performance (MA). *Accreditation:* NASM. Part-time programs available. *Faculty:* 17 full-time (8 women), 20 part-time/adjunct (4 women). *Students:* 14 full-time (9 women), 20 part-time (10 women); includes 10 minority (6 African Americans, 1 Asian American or Pacific Islander, 3 Hispanic Americans), 8 international. Average age 32. 23 applicants, 74% accepted, 4 enrolled. In 2008, 11 master's awarded. *Degree requirements:* For master's, lecture/recital or thesis. *Entrance requirements:* For master's, audition, minimum GPA of 3.0 in last 60 hours of course work, placement evaluations in music history and theory. *Application deadline:* For fall admission, 7/1 priority date for domestic students, 2/15 for international students; for spring admission, 11/1 for domestic students, 7/15 for international students. Applications are processed on a rolling basis. Application fee: $30. *Expenses:* Tuition, state resident: full-time $4867; part-time $270.40 per credit hour. Tuition, nonresident: full-time $16,486; part-time $915.87 per credit hour. *Financial support:* Fellowships with partial tuition reimbursements, teaching assistantships with partial tuition reimbursements, career-related internships or fieldwork, Federal Work-Study, and scholarships/grants available. Financial award application deadline: 5/1. *Faculty research:* Classical guitar history and literature, women composers, Mozart opera, composition, performance. *Unit head:* Dr. Heather J. Coltman, Chair, 561-297-3821, Fax:

561-297-2944, E-mail: coltman@fau.edu. *Application contact:* Dr. Heather J. Coltman, Chair, 561-297-3821, Fax: 561-297-2944, E-mail: coltman@fau.edu.

Florida International University, College of Architecture and the Arts, School of Music, Miami, FL 33199. Offers music (MM); music education (MS). Part-time and evening/weekend programs available. *Degree requirements:* For master's, thesis. *Entrance requirements:* For master's, minimum GPA of 3.0, audition or interview, depending area. Additional exam requirements/recommendations for international students: Required—TOEFL (minimum score 550 paper-based; 213 computer-based).

Florida State University, Graduate Studies, College of Arts and Sciences, Department of English, Tallahassee, FL 32306. Offers creative writing (MFA, PhD); literature (MA, PhD); rhetoric and composition (MA, PhD). Part-time programs available. *Degree requirements:* For master's, one foreign language, thesis or alternative; for doctorate, 2 foreign languages, thesis/dissertation. *Entrance requirements:* For master's, GRE General Test, GRE Subject Test (literature), sample of written work, 3 letters of recommendation; for doctorate, GRE General Test, sample of written work, 3 letters of recommendation. Electronic applications accepted. *Faculty research:* British literature, American literature, creative writing, rhetoric, multiethnic literature.

Florida State University, Graduate Studies, College of Music, Tallahassee, FL 32306. Offers accompanying (MM); arts administration (MA); choral conducting (MM); composition (MM, DM); ethnomusicology (MM); general music (MA); instrumental accompanying (MM); instrumental conducting (MM); jazz studies (MM); music education (MM Ed, PhD); music theory (MM, PhD); music therapy (MM); musicology (MM, PhD), including ethnomusicology (PhD), historical musicology; opera (MM); performance (MM, DM); piano pedagogy (MM); piano technology (MM); vocal accompanying (MM). *Accreditation:* NASM. *Degree requirements:* For master's, comprehensive exam (for some programs), thesis (for some programs), departmental qualifying exam; for doctorate, comprehensive exam (for some programs), thesis/dissertation, departmental qualifying exam. *Entrance requirements:* For master's and doctorate, audition, GRE General Test or minimum GPA of 3.0. Additional exam requirements/recommendations for international students: Required—TOEFL (minimum score 550 paper-based; 213 computer-based). Electronic applications accepted.

Fuller Theological Seminary, Graduate School of Theology, Pasadena, CA 91182. Offers Christian leadership (MACL); evangelism (MA); family life education (MA); ministry (M Div, D Min); pastoral ministry (MA); recovery ministry (MA); theology (MAT, Th M, PhD); worship music ministry (MA); worship, theology, and the arts (MA); youth, family, and culture (MA). M Div offered jointly with Denver Conservative Baptist Seminary. *Accreditation:* ACIPE; ATS (one or more programs are accredited). Part-time and evening/weekend programs available. *Degree requirements:* For doctorate, variable foreign language requirement, thesis/dissertation; for M Div, 2 foreign languages. *Entrance requirements:* For doctorate, GRE General Test. *Faculty research:* New Testament, Old Testament, systematic theology, history, practical theology.

Garrett-Evangelical Theological Seminary, Graduate and Professional Programs, Evanston, IL 60201-3298. Offers Bible and culture (PhD); Christian education (MA); Christian education and congregational studies (PhD); contemporary theology and culture (PhD); divinity (M Div); ethics, church, and society (MA); liturgical studies (PhD); ministry (D Min); music ministry (MA); pastoral care and counseling (MA); pastoral theology, personality, and culture (PhD); spiritual formation and evangelism (MA); theological studies (MTS); M Div/MSW. *Accreditation:* ACIPE; ATS (one or more programs are accredited). Part-time programs available. *Degree requirements:* For master's, thesis (for some programs); for doctorate, thesis/dissertation. *Entrance requirements:* For doctorate, GRE (PhD). Additional exam requirements/recommendations for international students: Required—TOEFL (minimum score 560 paper-based; 230 computer-based). Electronic applications accepted.

George Mason University, College of Visual and Performing Arts, Department of Music, Fairfax, VA 22030. Offers artist certificate (Certificate); composition (MA); conducting (MA); music (MM); music education (MA, Certificate); pedagogy and performance (MA); performance (MA). *Accreditation:* NASM. Part-time and evening/weekend programs available. *Degree requirements:* For master's, comprehensive exam, thesis (for some programs), recital for all but MM music education. *Entrance requirements:* For master's, BA or BM as appropriate for the desired master's program of study. Electronic applications accepted. *Expenses:* Contact institution.

Georgia Southern University, Jack N. Averitt College of Graduate Studies, College of Liberal Arts and Social Sciences, Department of Music, Statesboro, GA 30460. Offers MM. *Accreditation:* NASM. Part-time and evening/weekend programs available. *Students:* 9 full-time (1 woman), 10 part-time (1 woman); includes 5 minority (all African Americans), 1 international. Average age 27. 10 applicants, 80% accepted, 7 enrolled. In 2008, 4 master's awarded. *Degree requirements:* For master's, comprehensive exam. *Entrance requirements:* For master's, music theory and music history proficiency test, minimum GPA of 2.5, audition, letters of recommendation. Additional exam requirements/recommendations for international students: Required—TOEFL (minimum score 550 paper-based; 213 computer-based; 80 iBT). *Application deadline:* For fall admission, 3/1 priority date for domestic and international students; for spring admission, 10/1 priority date for domestic students, 10/1 for international students. Applications are processed on a rolling basis. Application fee: $50. Electronic applications accepted. *Expenses:* Tuition, area resident: Full-time $3840; part-time $160 per semester hour. Tuition, state resident: full-time $3840; part-time $160 per semester hour. Tuition, nonresident: full-time $15,336; part-time $639 per semester hour. Required fees: $1152. *Financial support:* In 2008–09, 17 students received support, including research assistantships with partial tuition reimbursements available (averaging $6,850 per year), teaching assistantships with partial tuition reimbursements available (averaging $6,850 per year); Federal Work-Study, scholarships/grants, tuition waivers (partial), and unspecified assistantships also available. Support available to part-time students. Financial award application deadline: 4/15; financial award applicants required to submit FAFSA. *Faculty research:* Music history and literature, technology in music, music composition, music performance, music/education. *Unit head:* Dr. Curtis Ricker, Acting Chair, 912-478-3396, Fax: 912-478-1295, E-mail: cricker@georgiasouthern.edu. *Application contact:* Office of Graduate Admissions, 912-478-5384, Fax: 912-478-0740, E-mail: gradadmissions@georgiasouthern.edu.

Georgia State University, College of Arts and Sciences, School of Music, Atlanta, GA 30303-3083. Offers M Mu. *Accreditation:* NASM. Part-time and evening/weekend programs available. *Degree requirements:* For master's, comprehensive exam, thesis (for some programs), recital, exam. *Entrance requirements:* For master's, GRE General Test or MAT (music education), GRE (composition), departmental supplemental form, audition. Additional exam requirements/recommendations for international students: Required—TOEFL. Electronic applications accepted. *Faculty research:* Teaching effectiveness assessment, computer music applications, arts/arts education policy, community music, psychology of music learning.

Graduate School and University Center of the City University of New York, Graduate Studies, Program in Music, New York, NY 10016-4039. Offers DMA, PhD. *Degree requirements:* For doctorate, 2 foreign languages, thesis/dissertation. *Entrance requirements:* For doctorate, GRE General Test. Additional exam requirements/recommendations for international students: Required—TOEFL. Electronic applications accepted.

Gratz College, Graduate Programs, Program in Jewish Music, Melrose Park, PA 19027. Offers MA, Certificate, MA/MA. Part-time programs available. *Degree requirements:* For master's, one foreign language, comprehensive exam, recital or thesis. *Entrance requirements:* For master's, audition, interview.

Hardin-Simmons University, Graduate School, School of Music, Abilene, TX 79698-0001. Offers church music (MM); music education (MM); music performance (MM); theory-composition (MM). *Accreditation:* NASM. Part-time programs available. *Faculty:* 14 full-time (4 women), 2 part-time/adjunct (1 woman). *Students:* 8 full-time (3 women), 4 part-time (3 women). Average age 28. 9 applicants, 89% accepted, 4 enrolled. In 2008, 2 master's awarded. *Degree requirements:* For master's, one foreign language, comprehensive exam, thesis (for some programs). *Entrance requirements:* For master's, minimum undergraduate GPA of 3.0 in major, 2.7 overall; performance; writing sample; demonstrated knowledge in chosen area. Additional exam requirements/recommendations for international students: Required—TOEFL (minimum score 550 paper-based; 213 computer-based; 75 iBT). *Application deadline:* For fall admission, 8/15 priority date for domestic students, 4/1 for international students; for spring admission, 1/5 priority date for domestic students, 9/1 for international students. Applications are processed on a rolling basis. Application fee: $50. *Expenses:* Tuition: Full-time $10,620; part-time $590 per credit hour. Required fees: $590; $110 per semester. Tuition and fees vary according to course load and degree level. *Financial support:* In 2008–09, 15 students received support, including 6 fellowships (averaging $1,467 per year); career-related internships or fieldwork and scholarships/grants also available. Support available to part-time students. Financial award application deadline: 6/30; financial award applicants required to submit FAFSA. *Unit head:* Dr. Leigh Anne Hunsaker, Director, 325-670-1391, Fax: 325-670-5873, E-mail: hunsaker@hsutx.edu. *Application contact:* Dr. Gary Stanlake, Dean of Graduate Studies, 325-670-1298, Fax: 325-670-1564, E-mail: gradoff@hsutx.edu.

Harvard University, Graduate School of Arts and Sciences, Department of Music, Cambridge, MA 02138. Offers composition (AM, PhD); musicology (AM); musicology and ethnomusicology (PhD); theory (AM, PhD). *Degree requirements:* For doctorate, 3 foreign languages, thesis/dissertation, composition, analytical paper. *Entrance requirements:* For master's and doctorate, GRE General Test. Additional exam requirements/recommendations for international students: Required—TOEFL. *Expenses:* Tuition: Full-time $32,556. Required fees: $1426. Full-time tuition and fees vary according to program and student level.

Hebrew College, Program in Jewish Studies, Newton Centre, MA 02459. Offers Jewish liturgical music (Certificate); Jewish music education (Certificate); Jewish studies (MA). Part-time and evening/weekend programs available. Postbaccalaureate distance learning degree programs offered (minimal on-campus study). *Degree requirements:* For master's, one foreign language. *Entrance requirements:* For master's, GRE, interview. Additional exam requirements/recommendations for international students: Required—TOEFL.

Hebrew Union College–Jewish Institute of Religion, School of Sacred Music, New York, NY 10012-1186. Offers MSM. *Degree requirements:* For master's, one foreign language, thesis, recital. *Entrance requirements:* For master's, GRE, minimum 2 years of college-level Hebrew, bachelor's degree in music or related area, trained singing voice. Additional exam requirements/recommendations for international students: Required—TOEFL. *Expenses:* Contact institution.

Hofstra University, School of Education, Health, and Human Services, Department of Curriculum and Teaching, Program in Music Education, Hempstead, NY 11549. Offers music education (MA, MS Ed); wind conducting (MA). Part-time programs available. *Students:* 8 full-time (2 women), 32 part-time (19 women); includes 5 minority (3 African Americans, 2 Hispanic Americans). Average age 27. 20 applicants, 90% accepted, 10 enrolled. In 2008, 22 master's awarded. *Degree requirements:* For master's, one foreign language, thesis (for some programs). *Entrance requirements:* For master's, 2 letters of recommendation, teacher certification (MA), essay. Additional exam requirements/recommendations for international students: Required—TOEFL (minimum score 550 paper-based; 213 computer-based; 80 iBT). *Application deadline:* Applications are processed on a rolling basis. Application fee: $60. Electronic applications accepted. *Expenses:* Tuition: Full-time $15,300; part-time $850 per credit. Required fees: $970; $165 per term. Tuition and fees vary according to program. *Financial support:* In 2008–09, 18 students received support, including 6 fellowships with full and partial tuition reimbursements available (averaging $3,333 per year); research assistantships with full and partial tuition reimbursements available, Federal Work-Study, institutionally sponsored loans, scholarships/grants, tuition waivers (full and partial), and unspecified assistantships also available. Support available to part-time students. Financial award applicants required to submit FAFSA. *Faculty research:* Creative thinking, musical thinking, curriculum design, teacher preparation. *Unit head:* Dr. Nathalie G. Robinson, Program Director, 516-463-4514, Fax: 516-463-6393, E-mail: musngr@hofstra.edu. *Application contact:* Carol Drummer, Dean of Graduate Admissions, 516-463-4876, Fax: 516-463-4664, E-mail: gradstudent@hofstra.edu.

Hollins University, Graduate Programs, Program in Liberal Studies, Roanoke, VA 24020-1603. Offers humanities (MALS); interdisciplinary studies (MALS); justice and legal studies (MALS); liberal studies (CAS); social science (MALS); visual and performing arts (MALS). Part-time and evening/weekend programs available. *Faculty:* 6 full-time (1 woman), 7 part-time/adjunct (4 women). *Students:* 20 full-time (17 women), 78 part-time (56 women); includes 14 minority (13 African Americans, 1 Hispanic American), 1 international. Average age 39. 33 applicants, 85% accepted, 23 enrolled. In 2008, 42 master's awarded. *Degree requirements:* For master's, thesis. *Entrance requirements:* For master's, letters of recommendation, interview. Additional exam requirements/recommendations for international students: Required—TOEFL (minimum score 550 paper-based; 213 computer-based; 79 iBT). *Application deadline:* For fall admission, 7/1 priority date for domestic and international students; for spring admission, 12/10 priority date for domestic and international students. Applications are processed on a rolling basis. Application fee: $40. Electronic applications accepted. *Expenses:* Tuition: Full-time $26,720; part-time $590 per credit hour. Required fees: $280. *Financial support:* In 2008–09, 53 students received support, including 2 fellowships (averaging $1,189 per year); Federal Work-Study and scholarships/grants also available. Support available to part-time students. Financial award application deadline: 7/15; financial award applicants required to submit FAFSA. *Faculty research:* Elderly blacks, film, feminist economics, US voting patterns, Wagner, diversity. *Unit head:* Dr. Edward A. Lynch, Director, 540-362-6475, Fax: 540-362-6288, E-mail: elynch@hollins.edu. *Application contact:* Cathy S. Koon, Manager of Graduate Services, 540-362-6326, Fax: 540-362-6288, E-mail: ckoon@hollins.edu.

Holy Names University, Graduate Division, Department of Music, Oakland, CA 94619-1699. Offers Kodaly specialist certificate (Certificate); Kodaly summer certificate (Certificate); music education with Kodaly emphasis (MM); piano pedagogy (MM); piano pedagogy with Suzuki emphasis (MM); vocal pedagogy (MM). *Faculty:* 2 full-time (1 woman), 7 part-time/adjunct (4 women). *Students:* 6 full-time (4 women), 10 part-time (9 women); includes 3 minority (all Asian Americans or Pacific Islanders), 2 international. Average age 35. 9 applicants, 100% accepted, 8 enrolled. In 2008, 3 master's awarded. *Degree requirements:* For master's, comprehensive exam, recital. *Entrance requirements:* For master's, audition, minimum undergraduate GPA of 2.6 overall, 3.0 in major. Additional exam requirements/recommendations for international students: Required—TOEFL (minimum score 550 paper-based; 213 computer-based; 80 iBT). *Application deadline:* For fall admission, 8/1 priority date for domestic and international students; for spring admission, 12/1 priority date for domestic and international students. Applications are processed on a rolling basis. Application fee: $65. *Expenses:* Tuition: Full-time $6255; part-time $695 per unit. Required fees: $340. Tuition and fees vary according to course load, program, reciprocity agreements and student's religious affiliation. *Financial support:* In 2008–09, 13 students received support. Scholarships/grants available. Support available to part-time students. Financial award application deadline: 3/2; financial award applicants required to submit FAFSA. *Faculty research:* Performance practice with special interest in baroque, Romantic, and twentieth-century instrumental and vocal music, choral pedagogy, Hungarian music education. *Unit head:* Dr. Steven Hofer, Chair of Music Department, 510-436-1244, E-mail: Hofer@hnu.edu. *Application contact:* 800-430-1321, Fax: 510-436-1325, E-mail: AdultEd@hnu.edu.

Hope International University, School of Graduate Studies, Programs in Ministry, Fullerton, CA 92831-3138. Offers Christian leadership (MCM); church music (MA); church music (Korean track) (MCM); church planting (MCM); intercultural studies (MCM); worship (MCM). Part-time and evening/weekend programs available. Postbaccalaureate distance learning degree programs offered (minimal on-campus study). *Degree requirements:* For master's, thesis (for some

Music

Hope International University (continued)

programs), project. *Entrance requirements:* For master's, minimum GPA of 3.0, MCM program requires an undergraduate degree in music, application, official transcripts, 2 references, statement of purpose. Additional exam requirements/recommendations for international students: Required—TOEFL (minimum score 550 paper-based; 213 computer-based; 86 iBT); Recommended—IELTS (minimum score 6.5). Electronic applications accepted. *Expenses:* Contact institution. *Faculty research:* Church dynamics, growth methodologies.

Houghton College, Greatbatch School of Music, Houghton, NY 14744. Offers collaborative studies (MMus); composition (MMus); conducting (MMus); music (MA); performance (MMus). *Accreditation:* NASM. *Degree requirements:* For master's, comprehensive exam (for some programs), thesis (for some programs), recitals (for some programs). *Entrance requirements:* For master's, bachelor of music or equivalent. Additional exam requirements/recommendations for international students: Required—TOEFL (minimum score 600 paper-based; 250 computer-based). Electronic applications accepted. *Faculty research:* Bach Studies; original compositions; professional performance; contemporary women composers; music in Christian worship.

Howard University, Graduate School, Division of Fine Arts, Department of Music, Washington, DC 20059-0002. Offers applied music (MM); instrument (MM Ed); jazz studies (MM); organ (MM Ed); piano (MM Ed); voice (MM Ed). *Accreditation:* NASM. Part-time programs available. *Degree requirements:* For master's, comprehensive exam, thesis or alternative, departmental qualifying exam, recital. *Entrance requirements:* For master's, minimum GPA of 3.0, bachelor's degree in music or music education. Additional exam requirements/recommendations for international students: Required—TOEFL.

Hunter College of the City University of New York, Graduate School, School of Arts and Sciences, Department of Music, New York, NY 10021-5085. Offers music (MA); music education (MA). Part-time and evening/weekend programs available. *Faculty:* 11 full-time (3 women), 6 part-time/adjunct (1 woman). *Students:* 40 part-time (21 women); includes 8 minority (1 African American, 6 Asian Americans or Pacific Islanders, 1 Hispanic American). Average age 33. 32 applicants, 47% accepted, 9 enrolled. In 2008, 17 master's awarded. *Degree requirements:* For master's, one foreign language, thesis, composition, essay, or recital; proficiency exam. *Entrance requirements:* For master's, undergraduate major in music (minimum 24 credits) or equivalent, sample of work, research paper. Additional exam requirements/recommendations for international students: Required—TOEFL. *Application deadline:* For fall admission, 4/1 for domestic students, 2/1 for international students; for spring admission, 11/1 for domestic students, 9/1 for international students. Applications are processed on a rolling basis. Application fee: $125. *Financial support:* In 2008–09, 4 fellowships (averaging $1,000 per year) were awarded; Federal Work-Study, tuition waivers (partial), and lesson stipends also available. Support available to part-time students. Financial award application deadline: 4/15. *Faculty research:* African and African-American music, Bach, Renaissance music, early romantic music, theory of tonal music. *Unit head:* Dr. Ruth DeFord, Department Chair, 212-772-5026, Fax: 212-772-5022, E-mail: ruth.deford@hunter.cuny.edu. *Application contact:* L.Pondie Burstein, Graduate Adviser, 212-772-5152, E-mail: HunterMusT@aol.com.

Illinois State University, Graduate School, College of Fine Arts, School of Music, Normal, IL 61790-2200. Offers MM, MM Ed. *Accreditation:* NASM. *Degree requirements:* For master's, thesis or alternative, performance. *Entrance requirements:* For master's, minimum GPA of 3.0 in music, 2.6 overall; auditions. *Faculty research:* Concerts on the Quad summer concert series.

Indiana State University, School of Graduate Studies, College of Arts and Sciences, Department of Music, Terre Haute, IN 47809-1401. Offers music performance (MM). *Accreditation:* NASM. *Degree requirements:* For master's, comprehensive exam, thesis (for some programs), departmental qualifying exam. Electronic applications accepted.

Indiana University Bloomington, Jacobs School of Music, Bloomington, IN 47405-7000. Offers MA, MM, MM/MLS, MME, MS, DM, DME, PhD, AD, Performance Diploma, Spec, MA/MLS. *Accreditation:* NASM (one or more programs are accredited). *Faculty:* 139 full-time (35 women), 11 part-time/adjunct (3 women). *Students:* 788 full-time (414 women), 97 part-time (49 women); includes 89 minority (21 African Americans, 2 American Indian/Alaska Native, 50 Asian Americans or Pacific Islanders, 16 Hispanic Americans), 245 international. Average age 29. 1,312 applicants, 34% accepted, 236 enrolled. In 2008, 170 master's, 46 doctorates, 68 other advanced degrees awarded. Terminal master's awarded for partial completion of doctoral program. *Degree requirements:* For master's, comprehensive exam (for some programs); for doctorate, comprehensive exam, thesis/dissertation. *Entrance requirements:* For master's and doctorate, GRE, audition, 3 letters of recommendation. Additional exam requirements/recommendations for international students: Required—TOEFL (minimum score 560 paper-based; 223 computer-based; 84 iBT). *Application deadline:* For fall admission, 12/1 for domestic and international students; for spring admission, 9/1 for domestic and international students. Applications are processed on a rolling basis. Application fee: $100 ($110 for international students). Electronic applications accepted. *Expenses:* Contact institution. *Financial support:* In 2008–09, 225 students received support, including 6 fellowships with full and partial tuition reimbursements available (averaging $17,000 per year), 85 teaching assistantships with full tuition reimbursements available (averaging $6,000 per year); research assistantships with tuition reimbursements available, Federal Work-Study, institutionally sponsored loans, scholarships/grants, tuition waivers (full and partial), and unspecified assistantships also available. Support available to part-time students. Financial award application deadline: 3/1; financial award applicants required to submit FAFSA. Total annual research expenditures: $8,300. *Unit head:* Gwyn Richards, Dean, 812-855-2435, E-mail: jln@indiana.edu. *Application contact:* Music Admissions, 812-855-7998, Fax: 812-856-6086, E-mail: musicadm@indiana.edu.

Indiana University Bloomington, University Graduate School, College of Arts and Sciences, Department of Communication and Culture, Bloomington, IN 47405-7000. Offers film and media studies (PhD); performance and ethnography (PhD); rhetoric and public culture (PhD). *Faculty:* 24 full-time (12 women). *Students:* 81 full-time (45 women); includes 11 minority (2 African Americans, 1 American Indian/Alaska Native, 2 Asian Americans or Pacific Islanders, 6 Hispanic Americans), 10 international. Average age 32. 163 applicants, 20% accepted, 16 enrolled. In 2008, 5 master's, 11 doctorates awarded. *Degree requirements:* For master's, comprehensive exam; for doctorate, one foreign language, comprehensive exam, thesis/dissertation, student teaching. *Entrance requirements:* For master's and doctorate, GRE General Test (recommended), minimum GPA of 3.0, 3 letters of recommendation, writing sample. Additional exam requirements/recommendations for international students: Required—TOEFL (minimum score 550 paper-based; 213 computer-based). *Application deadline:* For winter admission, 1/1 for domestic students, 12/1 for international students. Application fee: $50 ($60 for international students). Electronic applications accepted. *Expenses:* Tuition, area resident: Part-time $291.97 per credit hour. Tuition, state resident: part-time $291.97 per credit hour. Tuition, nonresident: part-time $850.33 per credit hour. Required fees: $110 per semester. Tuition and fees vary according to course load and program. *Financial support:* In 2008–09, 65 students received support, including 4 fellowships with full tuition reimbursements available (averaging $18,000 per year), 61 teaching assistantships with full tuition reimbursements available (averaging $12,961 per year). Financial award application deadline: 4/15. *Faculty research:* Rhetoric and public culture, film and media studies, performance ethnography. *Unit head:* Prof. Gregory A. Waller, Chair, 812-855-2367, Fax: 812-855-6014, E-mail: cmcl@indiana.edu. *Application contact:* Kathy P. Teige, Graduate Secretary, 812-855-6389, Fax: 812-855-6014, E-mail: kteige@indiana.edu.

Indiana University Bloomington, University Graduate School, College of Arts and Sciences, Department of Folklore and Ethnomusicology, Bloomington, IN 47408-3890. Offers folklore (MA, PhD), including ethnomusicology. Part-time programs available. *Faculty:* 12 full-time (5 women), 11 part-time/adjunct (6 women). *Students:* 88 full-time (51 women), 25 part-time (20 women); includes 24 minority (12 African Americans, 1 American Indian/Alaska Native, 5 Asian Americans or Pacific Islanders, 6 Hispanic Americans), 21 international. Average age 34. 89 applicants, 40% accepted, 10 enrolled. In 2008, 6 master's, 7 doctorates awarded. *Degree requirements:* For master's, one foreign language, comprehensive exam, thesis or alternative, project or thesis; for doctorate, 2 foreign languages, comprehensive exam, thesis/dissertation. *Entrance requirements:* For master's and doctorate, GRE General Test, minimum GPA of 3.0. Additional exam requirements/recommendations for international students: Required—TOEFL (minimum score 550 paper-based; 213 computer-based; 79 iBT). *Application deadline:* For fall admission, 1/15 for domestic students, 12/1 for international students. Application fee: $50 ($60 for international students). Electronic applications accepted. *Expenses:* Tuition, area resident: Part-time $291.97 per credit hour. Tuition, state resident: part-time $291.97 per credit hour. Tuition, nonresident: part-time $850.33 per credit hour. Required fees: $110 per semester. Tuition and fees vary according to course load and program. *Financial support:* In 2008–09, 38 students received support, including 5 fellowships with full tuition reimbursements available (averaging $15,000 per year), 21 research assistantships with full tuition reimbursements available (averaging $11,000 per year), 12 teaching assistantships with full tuition reimbursements available (averaging $11,000 per year); Federal Work-Study and unspecified assistantships also available. Financial award application deadline: 3/1; financial award applicants required to submit FAFSA. *Faculty research:* Narrative, performance studies, material culture, popular culture, music. *Unit head:* Dr. Portia Maultsby, Chair, 812-855-0395, Fax: 812-855-4008, E-mail: maultsby@indiana.edu. *Application contact:* Christopher Roush, Graduate Secretary, 812-855-0389, Fax: 812-855-4008, E-mail: croush@indiana.edu.

Indiana University of Pennsylvania, School of Graduate Studies and Research, College of Fine Arts, Department of Music and Music Education, Program in Music, Indiana, PA 15705-1087. Offers music education (MA); music history and literature (MA); music theory and composition (MA); performance (MA). *Accreditation:* NASM. Part-time programs available. *Faculty:* 11 full-time (4 women). *Students:* 10 full-time (4 women), 8 part-time (4 women), 1 international. Average age 29. 19 applicants, 47% accepted, 7 enrolled. In 2008, 4 master's awarded. *Degree requirements:* For master's, thesis optional. *Entrance requirements:* For master's, 2 letters of recommendation, audition. Additional exam requirements/recommendations for international students: Required—TOEFL. *Application deadline:* For fall admission, 7/1 priority date for domestic students; for spring admission, 11/1 for domestic students. Applications are processed on a rolling basis. Application fee: $30. *Expenses:* Tuition, area resident: Full-time $6430; part-time $357 per credit. Tuition, nonresident: full-time $10,288; part-time $572 per credit. Required fees: $1547.50; $107 per credit. $283 per year. *Financial support:* In 2008–09, 5 research assistantships with full and partial tuition reimbursements (averaging $4,896 per year) were awarded; fellowships, Federal Work-Study also available. Support available to part-time students. Financial award application deadline: 3/15; financial award applicants required to submit FAFSA. *Unit head:* Dr. Stephanie Caulder, Head, 724-357-4408, E-mail: Stephanie.Caulder@iup.edu. *Application contact:* Dr. Stephanie Caulder, Head, 724-357-4408, E-mail: Stephanie.Caulder@iup.edu.

Indiana University–Purdue University Indianapolis, School of Music, Indianapolis, IN 46202-2896. Offers music technology (MS). Part-time and evening/weekend programs available. Postbaccalaureate distance learning degree programs offered. *Degree requirements:* For master's, internship or final project. *Entrance requirements:* For master's, audition, minimum GPA of 3.0. Additional exam requirements/recommendations for international students: Required—TOEFL.

Indiana University South Bend, School of the Arts, South Bend, IN 46634-7111. Offers music (MM); studio teaching (MM). Part-time programs available. *Entrance requirements:* For master's, performance audition. *Faculty research:* Orchestral conducting.

Ithaca College, Division of Graduate and Professional Studies, School of Music, Program in Music and Music Education, Ithaca, NY 14850-7020. Offers composition (MM); conducting (MM); music education (MM, MS); performance (MM); Suzuki pedagogy (MM). *Accreditation:* NASM. Part-time programs available. *Faculty:* 58 full-time (22 women), 6 part-time/adjunct (4 women). *Students:* 35 full-time (21 women), 1 part-time (0 women); includes 1 minority (Hispanic American), 1 international. Average age 24. 109 applicants, 28% accepted, 21 enrolled. In 2008, 33 master's awarded. *Degree requirements:* For master's, comprehensive exam, thesis (for some programs). *Entrance requirements:* For master's, audition, minimum GPA of 3.0. Additional exam requirements/recommendations for international students: Required—TOEFL (minimum score 550 paper-based; 213 computer-based; 80 iBT). *Application deadline:* For fall admission, 3/1 for domestic and international students; for spring admission, 12/1 for domestic and international students. Applications are processed on a rolling basis. Application fee: $40. Electronic applications accepted. *Expenses:* Tuition: Full-time $18,090; part-time $603 per hour. *Financial support:* In 2008–09, 34 students received support, including 32 teaching assistantships (averaging $9,653 per year); career-related internships or fieldwork, Federal Work-Study, scholarships/grants, and unspecified assistantships also available. Support available to part-time students. Financial award application deadline: 4/1; financial award applicants required to submit FAFSA. *Faculty research:* Musical performance and performance studies, musical composition, music theory and analysis, music history and musicology, musical direction and conducting. *Unit head:* Dr. Timothy Johnson, Chairperson, Graduate Studies in Music, 607-274-3527, Fax: 607-274-1263, E-mail: gps@ithaca.edu. *Application contact:* Rob Gearhart, Interim Dean, Graduate and Professional Studies, 607-274-3527, Fax: 607-274-1263, E-mail: gps@ithaca.edu.

Jacksonville State University, College of Graduate Studies and Continuing Education, College of Arts and Sciences, Department of Music, Jacksonville, AL 36265-1602. Offers MA. *Accreditation:* NASM. Part-time and evening/weekend programs available. *Faculty:* 17 full-time (7 women), 1 part-time/adjunct (0 women). *Students:* 3 full-time (1 woman), 5 part-time (2 women); includes 2 minority (both African Americans). Average age 29. 6 applicants, 33% accepted, 2 enrolled. In 2008, 8 master's awarded. *Degree requirements:* For master's, comprehensive exam, thesis (for some programs). *Entrance requirements:* For master's, GRE General Test or MAT. *Application deadline:* Applications are processed on a rolling basis. Application fee: $30. Electronic applications accepted. *Expenses:* Tuition, area resident: Full-time $4560; part-time $225 per credit hour. Tuition, state resident: full-time $4560; part-time $450 per credit hour. Tuition, nonresident: full-time $9120; part-time $450 per credit hour. *Financial support:* Available to part-time students. Application deadline: 4/1; *Unit head:* Dr. Legare McIntosh, Head, 256-782-5560. *Application contact:* Dr. Jean Pugliese, Associate Dean, 256-782-8278, Fax: 256-782-5321, E-mail: pugliese@jsu.edu.

James Madison University, The Graduate School, College of Visual and Performing Arts, School of Music, Musical Arts Program, Harrisonburg, VA 22807. Offers DMA. Part-time programs available. *Students:* 15 full-time (6 women), 1 part-time (0 women); includes 2 minority (1 African American, 1 Hispanic American), 4 international. Average age 27. *Degree requirements:* For doctorate, comprehensive exam, written and oral exams. *Entrance requirements:* For doctorate, GRE General Test, written statement of future goals (professional and educational), 3 letters of recommendation, audition. Additional exam requirements/recommendations for international students: Required—TOEFL. *Application deadline:* For fall admission, 4/1 priority date for domestic students, 4/1 for international students; for spring admission, 4/1 priority date for domestic students, 4/1 for international students. Applications are processed on a rolling basis. Application fee: $55. Electronic applications accepted. *Expenses:* Tuition, area resident: Full-time $7008; part-time $292 per credit hour. Tuition, state resident: full-time $7008; part-time $292 per credit hour. Tuition, nonresident: full-time $20,352; part-time $848 per credit hour. *Financial support:* In 2008–09, 6 students received support. 14 doctoral assistantships ($14,500) available. Financial award application deadline: 3/1; financial award applicants required to submit FAFSA. *Unit head:* Dr. Jeffrey A. Showell, Academic Unit Head, 540-568-6197. *Application contact:* Dr. Mary Jane Speare, Graduate Coordinator, 540-568-6197.

The Jewish Theological Seminary, H. L. Miller Cantorial School and College of Jewish Music, New York, NY 10027-4649. Offers MSM. *Faculty:* 60 full-time (19 women), 73 part-time/adjunct (39 women). *Students:* 37 full-time (18 women), 1 (woman) part-time, 5 international.

Average age 31. 15 applicants, 53% accepted, 6 enrolled. In 2008, 10 master's awarded. *Degree requirements:* For master's, one foreign language, comprehensive exam, departmental qualifying exam, recitals. *Entrance requirements:* For master's, music aptitude test, audition, interview, 3 letters of recommendation. Additional exam requirements/recommendations for international students: Required—TOEFL. *Application deadline:* For fall admission, 1/1 priority date for domestic students. Applications are processed on a rolling basis. Application fee: $50. *Expenses:* Contact institution. *Financial support:* Fellowships, career-related internships or fieldwork available. Support available to part-time students. Financial award application deadline: 3/1; financial award applicants required to submit FAFSA. *Unit head:* Hazzan Henry Rosenblum, Dean, 212-678-8036, Fax: 212-678-8947, E-mail: herosenblum@jtsa.edu. *Application contact:* Rita Gordon, Admissions Coordinator, 212-678-8907, E-mail: rigordon@jtsa.edu.

The Johns Hopkins University, Peabody Conservatory of Music, Baltimore, MD 21218-2699. Offers MA, MM, DMA, AD, GPD. *Degree requirements:* For master's, thesis (for some programs), departmental qualifying exam, recital; for doctorate, 2 foreign languages, thesis/dissertation (for some programs), departmental qualifying exam, recitals; for other advanced degree, recitals. *Entrance requirements:* For master's and other advanced degree, audition; for doctorate, audition, interview. Additional exam requirements/recommendations for international students: Required—TOEFL (minimum score 550 paper-based; 213 computer-based; 79 iBT). *Expenses:* Contact institution.

The Juilliard School, Program in Music, New York, NY 10023-6588. Offers MM, DMA, Artist Diploma, Diploma. *Degree requirements:* For master's and other advanced degree, performance jury, recital; for doctorate, one foreign language, thesis/dissertation, performance jury, 3 recitals. *Entrance requirements:* For master's and other advanced degree, audition; for doctorate, audition, interview, dossier. Additional exam requirements/recommendations for international students: Required—TOEFL (minimum score 570 paper-based; 230 computer-based; 89 iBT). Electronic applications accepted.

Kansas State University, Graduate School, College of Arts and Sciences, Department of Music, Manhattan, KS 66506. Offers music education (MM); music education/band conducting (MM); music history and literature (MM); performance (MM); performance with pedagogy emphasis (MM); theory and composition (MM). *Accreditation:* NASM. Part-time programs available. *Faculty:* 18 full-time (5 women). *Students:* 15 full-time (7 women), 3 part-time (1 woman), 1 international. Average age 26. 11 applicants, 100% accepted, 9 enrolled. In 2008, 13 master's awarded. *Degree requirements:* For master's, thesis optional. *Entrance requirements:* For master's, GRE, audition (in person or recording), interview (music education). Additional exam requirements/recommendations for international students: Required—TOEFL (minimum score 600 paper-based). *Application deadline:* For fall admission, 2/1 priority date for domestic and international students; for spring admission, 10/1 priority date for domestic students, 8/1 priority date for international students. Applications are processed on a rolling basis. Application fee: $30 ($55 for international students). Electronic applications accepted. *Expenses:* Tuition, area resident: Full-time $6466; part-time $269.40 per credit hour. Tuition, state resident: full-time $6466; part-time $269.40 per credit hour. Tuition, nonresident: full-time $14,874; part-time $619.75 per credit hour. Required fees: $673; $23.40 per credit hour. Tuition and fees vary according to campus/location. *Financial support:* In 2008–09, 14 teaching assistantships with full tuition reimbursements (averaging $7,150 per year) were awarded; institutionally sponsored loans, scholarships/grants, and tuition waivers (full and partial) also available. Support available to part-time students. Financial award application deadline: 3/1; financial award applicants required to submit FAFSA. *Faculty research:* Music since 1945, music by women composers, American music, opera, current performance practices. Total annual research expenditures: $11,318. *Unit head:* Dr. Gary Mortenson, Head, 785-532-3828, Fax: 785-532-7732, E-mail: garym@ksu.edu. *Application contact:* Fred Burrack, Director, 785-532-5764, Fax: 785-532-7732, E-mail: fburrack@ksu.edu.

Kent State University, College of the Arts, Hugh A. Glauser School of Music, Kent, OH 44242-0001. Offers composition (MA); conducting (MM); ethnomusicology (MA); music education (MM, PhD); musicology (MA); musicology-ethnomusicology (PhD); performance (MM); theory (MA); theory and composition (PhD). *Accreditation:* NASM. *Degree requirements:* For master's, variable foreign language requirement, comprehensive exam, 2 recitals, essay and recital, or thesis; for doctorate, variable foreign language requirement, comprehensive exam, thesis/dissertation. *Entrance requirements:* For master's, diagnostic exams in music history and theory, audition, minimum GPA of 2.75; for doctorate, diagnostic exams in music history and theory, master's thesis or scholarly paper, minimum GPA of 3.0. Additional exam requirements/recommendations for international students: Required—TOEFL. Electronic applications accepted. *Faculty research:* Music composition, performance, teaching and history.

Lamar University, College of Graduate Studies, College of Fine Arts and Communication, Department of Music, Theatre, and Dance, Beaumont, TX 77710. Offers music education (MM Ed); music performance (MM); theatre (MS). *Accreditation:* NASM (one or more programs are accredited). *Faculty:* 7 full-time (3 women), 2 part-time/adjunct (both women). *Students:* 3 full-time (2 women), 3 part-time (2 women); includes 1 minority (African American). Average age 29. 2 applicants, 100% accepted, 1 enrolled. In 2008, 8 master's awarded. *Degree requirements:* For master's, comprehensive exam, thesis optional. *Entrance requirements:* For master's, GRE General Test, theory placement exams, audition. Additional exam requirements/recommendations for international students: Required—TOEFL. *Application deadline:* For fall admission, 8/1 for domestic students; for spring admission, 12/1 for domestic students. Applications are processed on a rolling basis. Application fee: $25 ($50 for international students). *Expenses:* Tuition, state resident: full-time $5000; part-time $195 per credit. Tuition, nonresident: full-time $12,376; part-time $476 per credit. Required fees: $1570. *Financial support:* In 2008–09, 4 fellowships with tuition reimbursements (averaging $2,000 per year), 2 teaching assistantships were awarded; institutionally sponsored loans and tuition waivers (partial) also available. Support available to part-time students. Financial award application deadline: 4/1. *Faculty research:* Performance: ensembles and personal. *Unit head:* Dr. L. Randolph Babin, Chair, 409-880-8144, Fax: 409-880-8143, E-mail: babinlr@hal.lamar.edu. *Application contact:* Dr. Robert M. Culbertson, Adviser, 409-880-8073, Fax: 409-880-8143, E-mail: culbertsrm@hal.lamar.edu.

Lee University, Program in Music, Cleveland, TN 37320-3450. Offers church music (MCM); music education (MME); performance (MMMP). *Accreditation:* NASM. Part-time programs available. *Faculty:* 31 full-time (6 women), 6 part-time/adjunct (3 women). *Students:* 12 full-time (6 women), 15 part-time (7 women); includes 3 minority (all African Americans), 2 international. Average age 29. 8 applicants, 100% accepted, 8 enrolled. In 2008, 7 master's awarded. *Degree requirements:* For master's, variable foreign language requirement, comprehensive exam, thesis, internship. *Entrance requirements:* For master's, audition, resumé, interview, minimum GPA of 2.75. *Application deadline:* For fall admission, 4/1 for domestic students; for spring admission, 10/1 for domestic students. Applications are processed on a rolling basis. Application fee: $25. *Expenses:* Tuition: Full-time $10,824; part-time $451 per credit. Required fees: $270; $200 per semester. Tuition and fees vary according to course load and program. *Financial support:* In 2008–09, teaching assistantships (averaging $2,275 per year); career-related internships or fieldwork, Federal Work-Study, institutionally sponsored loans, and scholarships/grants also available. Financial award application deadline: 3/1; financial award applicants required to submit FAFSA. *Unit head:* Dr. Jim W. Burns, Director, 423-614-8240, Fax: 423-614-8242, E-mail: gradmusic@leeuniversity.edu. *Application contact:* Vicki Glasscock, Graduate Admissions Director, 423-614-8059, E-mail: vglasscock@leeuniversity.edu.

Long Island University, C.W. Post Campus, School of Visual and Performing Arts, Department of Music, Brookville, NY 11548-1300. Offers music (MA); music education (MS). Part-time programs available. *Degree requirements:* For master's, thesis. *Entrance requirements:* For master's, GRE General Test (MA), GRE Subject Test in music, minimum undergraduate GPA of 3.0, 2 professional and/or academic letters of recommendation, current resumé. Electronic applications accepted. *Faculty research:* Performance, composing, musicology, conducting, computer-based music technology.

Longy School of Music, Conservatory at Longy, Cambridge, MA 02138. Offers chamber ensemble (Artist Diploma); collaborative piano (MM, Artist Diploma, GPD); composition (MM); Dalcroze eurhythmics (MM); early music (MM, Artist Diploma, GPD); instrumental performance (MM, Artist Diploma, GPD); modern American music (MM, GPD); opera performance (MM, GPD); organ performance (MM, Artist Diploma, GPD); piano performance (MM, Artist Diploma, GPD); vocal performance (MM, Artist Diploma, GPD). *Accreditation:* NASM. Part-time programs available. *Degree requirements:* For master's, thesis (for some programs), recital; for other advanced degree, recital. *Entrance requirements:* For master's and other advanced degree, audition. Additional exam requirements/recommendations for international students: Required—TOEFL (minimum score 500 paper-based; 173 computer-based; 61 iBT).

Louisiana State University and Agricultural and Mechanical College, Graduate School, College of Music and Dramatic Arts, School of Music, Baton Rouge, LA 70803. Offers music (MM, DMA, PhD); music education (PhD). *Accreditation:* NASM. Part-time programs available. Terminal master's awarded for partial completion of doctoral program. *Degree requirements:* For doctorate, thesis/dissertation (for some programs). *Entrance requirements:* For master's, minimum GPA of 3.0, audition/interview; for doctorate, GRE General Test, minimum GPA of 3.0, audition/interview. Additional exam requirements/recommendations for international students: Required—TOEFL (minimum score 550 paper-based; 213 computer-based; 79 iBT). Electronic applications accepted. *Faculty research:* Music education, music literature, formal and harmonic analysis, pedagogy, performance.

Loyola University New Orleans, College of Music and Fine Arts, New Orleans, LA 70118-6195. Offers music therapy (MMT); performance (MM). *Accreditation:* NASM. Part-time programs available. *Students:* 11 full-time (5 women), 4 part-time (all women); includes 4 minority (2 African Americans, 2 Hispanic Americans), 1 international. Average age 27. 10 applicants, 60% accepted, 5 enrolled. In 2008, 2 master's awarded. *Degree requirements:* For master's, comprehensive exam, thesis, comprehensive written and oral exams. *Entrance requirements:* For master's, performance audition, appropriate bachelor's degree, minimum GPA of 3.0, transcript, letters of recommendation, resumé, essay. Additional exam requirements/recommendations for international students: Required—TOEFL (minimum score 550 paper-based; 213 computer-based). *Application deadline:* For fall admission, 8/15 priority date for domestic and international students; for spring admission, 1/1 priority date for domestic and international students. Applications are processed on a rolling basis. Application fee: $20. Electronic applications accepted. *Expenses:* Contact institution. *Financial support:* Career-related internships or fieldwork, Federal Work-Study, institutionally sponsored loans, scholarships/grants, and unspecified assistantships available. Support available to part-time students. Financial award application deadline: 5/1; financial award applicants required to submit FAFSA. *Faculty research:* Music business, music therapy, musicology, music theory, music education. *Unit head:* Donald R. Boomgaarden, PhD, Dean, 504-865-3039, Fax: 504-865-2852, E-mail: deancmfa@loyno.edu. *Application contact:* Anthony A. Decuir, PhD, Associate Dean, 504-865-3037, Fax: 504-865-2852, E-mail: decuir@loyno.edu.

Lynchburg College, Graduate Studies, School of Communications and the Arts, Lynchburg, VA 24501-3199. Offers music (MA), including choral or instrumental conducting. Part-time and evening/weekend programs available. *Faculty:* 2 full-time (1 woman), 1 part-time/adjunct (0 women). *Students:* 3 part-time (all women); includes 1 minority (African American). Average age 38. 3 applicants, 67% accepted, 2 enrolled. *Degree requirements:* For master's, comprehensive exam. *Entrance requirements:* For master's, GRE, minimum undergraduate GPA of 3.0. Additional exam requirements/recommendations for international students: Required—TOEFL. *Application deadline:* For fall admission, 7/31 for domestic students, 6/1 for international students; for spring admission, 11/30 for domestic students, 10/1 for international students. Application fee: $30. *Expenses:* Tuition: Full-time $6750; part-time $375 per credit. *Financial support:* Career-related internships or fieldwork, scholarships/grants, and unspecified assistantships available. *Unit head:* Dr. Edward Polloway, Vice President for Graduate and Community Advancement, 434-544-8655, E-mail: polloway@lynchburg.edu. *Application contact:* Dr. Jong H. Kim, Program Coordinator, 434-544 Ext. 8443, E-mail: kim@lynchburg.edu.

Lynn University, Conservatory of Music, Boca Raton, FL 33431-5598. Offers music performance (MM); professional performance (Certificate). *Accreditation:* NASM. Part-time and evening/weekend programs available. *Degree requirements:* For Certificate, performance, recitals, orchestra, chamber music. *Entrance requirements:* For master's, resumé, 2 letters of recommendation, minimum undergraduate GPA of 3.0; for Certificate, bachelor's degree in music performance or equivalent, audition. Additional exam requirements/recommendations for international students: Required—TOEFL (minimum score 550 paper-based; 213 computer-based).

Manhattan School of Music, Graduate Programs, New York, NY 10027-4698. Offers composition (MM, DMA); jazz (MM, DMA); music performance (MM, DMA); orchestral performance (MM). *Faculty:* 50 full-time (0 women), 162 part-time/adjunct (74 women). *Students:* 505 full-time (286 women), 6 part-time (4 women); includes 77 minority (11 African Americans, 1 American Indian/Alaska Native, 46 Asian Americans or Pacific Islanders, 19 Hispanic Americans), 198 international. Average age 22. 1,439 applicants, 38% accepted, 265 enrolled. In 2008, 135 master's, 10 doctorates awarded. *Degree requirements:* For master's, recital; for doctorate, variable foreign language requirement, thesis/dissertation, departmental qualifying exam, recitals. *Entrance requirements:* For master's, audition, pre-screen CD, bachelor's degree; for doctorate, departmental exam, audition, interview, pre-screen CD, master's degree. Additional exam requirements/recommendations for international students: Required—TOEFL (minimum score 550 paper-based; 213 computer-based; 79 iBT). *Application deadline:* For fall admission, 12/1 for domestic and international students. Application fee: $100. Electronic applications accepted. *Expenses:* Tuition: Full-time $29,975; part-time $1300 per credit. Tuition and fees vary according to course load. *Financial support:* In 2008–09, 244 students received support, including 14 teaching assistantships with partial tuition reimbursements available (averaging $4,700 per year); Federal Work-Study, scholarships/grants, and tuition waivers (full and partial) also available. Support available to part-time students. Financial award application deadline: 3/1; financial award applicants required to submit FAFSA. *Unit head:* Dr. Marjorie Merryman, Dean of Academic Affairs, 212-749-2802 Ext. 4584, Fax: 212-749-5471, E-mail: mmerryman@msmnyc.edu. *Application contact:* Amy A. Anderson, Associate Dean for Enrollment Management, 917-493-4501, Fax: 212-749-3025, E-mail: aanderson@msmnyc.edu.

Manhattan School of Music, Professional Studies Certificate Program, New York, NY 10027-4698. Offers instrumental music (CPS), including accompanying, brass, composition, guitar, orchestral performance, organ, piano, strings, voice, woodwinds; vocal music (CPS), including accompanying, brass, composition, guitar, orchestral performance, organ, piano, strings, voice, woodwinds. *Faculty:* 50 full-time (0 women), 162 part-time/adjunct (74 women). *Students:* 35 full-time (24 women); includes 3 minority (1 African American, 2 Asian Americans or Pacific Islanders), 20 international. Average age 24. 139 applicants, 71% accepted, 33 enrolled. In 2008, 30 CPSs awarded. *Degree requirements:* For CPS, recital. *Entrance requirements:* For degree, audition, pre-screen CD. Additional exam requirements/recommendations for international students: Required—TOEFL (minimum score 550 paper-based; 213 computer-based). *Application deadline:* For fall admission, 12/1 for domestic and international students. Application fee: $100. Electronic applications accepted. *Expenses:* Tuition: Full-time $29,975; part-time $1300 per credit. Tuition and fees vary according to course load. *Financial support:* In 2008–09, 20 students received support. Federal Work-Study, scholarships/grants, and tuition waivers (full and partial) available. Support available to part-time students. Financial award application deadline: 3/1; financial award applicants required to submit FAFSA. *Unit head:* Dr. Marjorie Merryman, Dean of Academic Affairs, 212-749-2802 Ext. 4584, Fax: 212-749-5471, E-mail: mmerryman@msmnyc.edu. *Application contact:* Amy A. Anderson, Associate Dean for Enrollment Management, 917-493-4501, Fax: 212-749-3025, E-mail: aanderson@msmnyc.edu.

Mansfield University of Pennsylvania, Graduate Studies, Department of Music, Mansfield, PA 16933. Offers band conducting (MA); choral conducting (MA); performance (MA).

Music

Mansfield University of Pennsylvania (continued)
Accreditation: NASM. Part-time and evening/weekend programs available. *Faculty:* 7 full-time (4 women), 1 part-time/adjunct (0 women). *Students:* 6 full-time (3 women); includes 1 minority (African American), 1 international. Average age 27. 9 applicants, 67% accepted, 2 enrolled. In 2008, 2 degrees awarded. *Degree requirements:* For master's, comprehensive exam, thesis optional. *Entrance requirements:* For master's, minimum GPA of 3.0, audition. Additional exam requirements/recommendations for international students: Required—TOEFL (minimum score 550 paper-based; 220 computer-based). *Application deadline:* For fall admission, 8/1 priority date for domestic students, 6/1 for international students; for spring admission, 11/1 priority date for domestic students, 9/1 for international students. Applications are processed on a rolling basis. Application fee: $25. Electronic applications accepted. *Financial support:* Career-related internships or fieldwork and unspecified assistantships available. Financial award application deadline: 5/1; financial award applicants required to submit FAFSA. *Unit head:* Dr. Shellie Gregorich, Chairperson, 570-662-4714, E-mail: sgregori@mansfield.edu. *Application contact:* Christina Hale, Assistant Director of Enrollment Services/Graduate Admissions, 570-662-4812, Fax: 570-662-4121, E-mail: chale@mansfield.edu.

Marshall University, Academic Affairs Division, College of Fine Arts, Department of Music, Huntington, WV 25755. Offers MA. *Accreditation:* NASM. Evening/weekend programs available. *Degree requirements:* For master's, thesis optional.

McGill University, Faculty of Graduate and Postdoctoral Studies, Schulich School of Music, Montréal, QC H3A 2T5, Canada. Offers composition (M Mus, D Mus, PhD); music education (MA, PhD); music technology (MA, PhD); musicology (MA, PhD); performance (M Mus); performance studies (D Mus); sound recording (M Mus, PhD); theory (MA, PhD).

Memorial University of Newfoundland, School of Graduate Studies, Interdisciplinary Program in Ethnomusicology, St. John's, NL A1C 5S7, Canada. Offers MA, PhD. *Degree requirements:* For master's, thesis optional, research paper (non-thesis option); for doctorate, one foreign language, comprehensive exam, thesis/dissertation, oral defense of thesis. *Entrance requirements:* For master's, minimum B+ average with a B Mus or humanities/social sciences degree; for doctorate, MA in ethnomusicology or a related field.

Memorial University of Newfoundland, School of Graduate Studies, School of Music, St. John's, NL A1C 5S7, Canada. Offers conducting (MMus); performance pedagogy (MMus); performing (MMus). *Entrance requirements:* For master's, diagnostic exams measuring skills and knowledge in musical literacy, B Mus with first-class standing, audition (ca. 60 min. performance). Electronic applications accepted.

Mercer University, Graduate Studies, Macon Campus, School of Music, Macon, GA 31207-0003. Offers choral conducting (MM); church music (MM); performance (MM). *Degree requirements:* For master's, comprehensive exam, recitals. *Entrance requirements:* For master's, GRE, audition.

Meredith College, John E. Weems Graduate School, Department of Music, Raleigh, NC 27607-5298. Offers MM. *Accreditation:* NASM. Part-time and evening/weekend programs available. *Degree requirements:* For master's, thesis optional. *Entrance requirements:* For master's, audition, interview, letters of recommendation. Electronic applications accepted. *Expenses:* Contact institution.

Miami University, Graduate School, School of Fine Arts, Department of Music, Program in Music Performance, Oxford, OH 45056. Offers MM. *Entrance requirements:* For master's, audition, minimum undergraduate GPA of 3.0 during previous 2 years or 3.0 overall. Additional exam requirements/recommendations for international students: Required—TOEFL, TWE.

Michigan State University, The Graduate School, College of Music, East Lansing, MI 48824. Offers collaborative piano (M Mus); jazz studies (M Mus); music (PhD); music composition (M Mus, DMA); music conducting (M Mus, DMA); music education (M Mus); music performance (M Mus, DMA); music theory (M Mus); music therapy (M Mus); musicology (MA); piano pedagogy (M Mus). *Accreditation:* NASM. *Entrance requirements:* Additional exam requirements/recommendations for international students: Required—TOEFL. Electronic applications accepted.

Middle Tennessee State University, College of Graduate Studies, College of Liberal Arts, School of Music, Murfreesboro, TN 37132. Offers MA. *Accreditation:* NASM. Part-time and evening/weekend programs available. Postbaccalaureate distance learning degree programs offered. *Degree requirements:* For master's, one foreign language, comprehensive exam, thesis optional. *Entrance requirements:* For master's, GRE or MAT. Additional exam requirements/recommendations for international students: Required—TOEFL (paper-based 525; computer-based 195; IBT 71) or IELTS (6.0). Electronic applications accepted.

Middle Tennessee State University, College of Graduate Studies, College of Mass Communication, Department of Recording Industry, Murfreesboro, TN 37132. Offers recording arts and technologies (MFA). Part-time and evening/weekend programs available. Postbaccalaureate distance learning degree programs offered. *Degree requirements:* For master's, comprehensive exam, thesis optional. *Entrance requirements:* For master's, GRE. Additional exam requirements/recommendations for international students: Required—TOEFL (paper-based 525; computer-based 195; IBT 71) or IELTS (6.0). *Faculty research:* Digital audio, music production.

Midwestern Baptist Theological Seminary, Graduate and Professional Programs, Kansas City, MO 64118-4697. Offers Biblical archaeology (MA); Biblical languages (MA); Christian education (M Div, MACE); Christian foundations—lay ministry (Graduate Certificate); collegiate ministries (M Div); counseling (MA); educational ministry (D Ed Min); international church planting (M Div); ministry (M Div, D Min); North American church planting (M Div); sacred music (MCM); urban ministry (M Div); worship leadership (M Div); youth ministry (M Div). *Accreditation:* ATS. Part-time programs available. Postbaccalaureate distance learning degree programs offered (minimal on-campus study). *Degree requirements:* For doctorate, thesis/dissertation; for M Div, 2 foreign languages. *Entrance requirements:* For doctorate, MAT. Electronic applications accepted. *Faculty research:* Ministerial studies, Biblical and theological studies, missions, counseling.

Mills College, Graduate Studies, Department of Dance, Oakland, CA 94613-1000. Offers dance (MA, MFA), including choreography and performance (MA). Part-time programs available. *Faculty:* 5 full-time (all women), 5 part-time/adjunct (3 women). *Students:* 19 full-time (all women); includes 3 minority (1 African American, 2 Asian Americans or Pacific Islanders). Average age 29. 41 applicants, 56% accepted, 10 enrolled. In 2008, 10 master's awarded. *Degree requirements:* For master's, comprehensive exam, thesis, performance. *Entrance requirements:* For master's, audition or tape. Additional exam requirements/recommendations for international students: Required—TOEFL. *Application deadline:* For fall admission, 2/1 priority date for domestic and international students. Applications are processed on a rolling basis. Application fee: $50. *Expenses:* Tuition: Full-time $25,072; part-time $6272 per course. Required fees: $880. *Financial support:* In 2008–09, 17 students received support, including 12 fellowships (averaging $5,708 per year), 10 teaching assistantships with partial tuition reimbursements available (averaging $5,014 per year); scholarships/grants and unspecified assistantships also available. Financial award application deadline: 2/1; financial award applicants required to submit FAFSA. *Faculty research:* Video and dance, modern dance technique, performance art, rhythmic analysis. *Unit head:* Sonya Delwaide, Head, 510-430-3258, E-mail: sdelwaid@mills.edu. *Application contact:* Marika Benko, Graduate Admission Specialist, 510-430-3309, Fax: 510-430-2159, E-mail: grad-studies@mills.edu.

Mills College, Graduate Studies, Department of Music, Oakland, CA 94613-1000. Offers composition (MA); electronic music and recording media (MFA); music performance and literature (MFA). Part-time programs available. *Faculty:* 7 full-time (2 women), 3 part-time/adjunct (all women). *Students:* 41 full-time (13 women); includes 3 Hispanic Americans, 4 international. Average age 27. 53 applicants, 74% accepted, 19 enrolled. In 2008, 21 master's awarded. *Degree requirements:* For master's, variable foreign language requirement, thesis, performance or recital. *Entrance requirements:* For master's, tape. Additional exam requirements/recommendations for international students: Required—TOEFL. *Application deadline:* For fall admission, 2/1 priority date for domestic students; for spring admission, 11/1 for domestic students. Applications are processed on a rolling basis. Application fee: $50. Electronic applications accepted. *Expenses:* Tuition: Full-time $25,072; part-time $6272 per course. Required fees: $880. *Financial support:* In 2008–09, 35 students received support, including 17 fellowships (averaging $8,470 per year), 21 teaching assistantships with partial tuition reimbursements available (averaging $8,954 per year); scholarships/grants also available. Support available to part-time students. Financial award application deadline: 2/1; financial award applicants required to submit FAFSA. *Faculty research:* Electronic and computer music, twentieth century theory and performance practice, Mozart, music theory. *Unit head:* David Bernstein, Chairperson, 510-430-2171, Fax: 510-430-3314, E-mail: grad-studies@mills.edu. *Application contact:* Marika Benko, Graduate Admission Specialist, 510-430-3309, Fax: 510-430-2159, E-mail: grad-studies@mills.edu.

Minnesota State University Mankato, College of Graduate Studies, College of Arts and Humanities, Department of Music, Mankato, MN 56001. Offers MM, MT. *Accreditation:* NASM. *Students:* 3 full-time (2 women), 8 part-time (3 women). *Degree requirements:* For master's, comprehensive exam, thesis or alternative. *Entrance requirements:* For master's, minimum GPA of 3.0 during previous 2 years, audition or test. Additional exam requirements/recommendations for international students: Required—TOEFL. *Application deadline:* For fall admission, 7/1 priority date for domestic students; for spring admission, 11/1 for domestic students. Applications are processed on a rolling basis. Application fee: $40. Electronic applications accepted. *Financial support:* Research assistantships with full tuition reimbursements, teaching assistantships with full tuition reimbursements, career-related internships or fieldwork, Federal Work-Study, and institutionally sponsored loans available. Support available to part-time students. Financial award application deadline: 3/15. *Unit head:* Dr. John Lindberg, Chairperson, 507-389-2118. *Application contact:* 507-389-2321, E-mail: grad@mnsu.edu.

Mississippi College, Graduate School, College of Arts and Sciences, School of Christian Studies and the Arts, Department of Music, Clinton, MS 39058. Offers applied music performance (MM); conducting (MM); music education (MM); music performance: organ (MM); vocal pedagogy (MM). *Accreditation:* NASM. Part-time and evening/weekend programs available. *Degree requirements:* For master's, comprehensive exam, recital. *Entrance requirements:* For master's, GRE, minimum GPA of 2.5. Additional exam requirements/recommendations for international students: Recommended—IELTS. Electronic applications accepted.

Missouri State University, Graduate College, College of Arts and Letters, Department of Music, Springfield, MO 65804-0094. Offers music (MM), including conducting, music education, music pedagogy, music theory and composition, performance; secondary education (MS Ed), including music. *Accreditation:* NASM. Part-time programs available. *Faculty:* 23 full-time (8 women). *Students:* 18 full-time (7 women), 29 part-time (15 women), 2 international. Average age 28. 19 applicants, 95% accepted, 14 enrolled. In 2008, 15 master's awarded. *Degree requirements:* For master's, comprehensive exam, thesis or alternative. *Entrance requirements:* For master's, GRE, interview/audition (MM), 9-12 teaching certification (MS Ed). Additional exam requirements/recommendations for international students: Required—TOEFL (minimum score 550 paper-based; 213 computer-based; 79 iBT). *Application deadline:* For fall admission, 7/20 for domestic students, 5/1 for international students; for spring admission, 12/20 for domestic students, 9/1 for international students. Applications are processed on a rolling basis. Application fee: $35 ($50 for international students). Electronic applications accepted. *Expenses:* Tuition, state resident: full-time $3852; part-time $214 per credit hour. Tuition, nonresident: full-time $7524; part-time $418 per credit hour. Required fees: $230 per semester. Tuition and fees vary according to course level and course load. *Financial support:* In 2008–09, 2 research assistantships with full tuition reimbursements (averaging $7,340 per year), 7 teaching assistantships with full tuition reimbursements (averaging $7,340 per year) were awarded; Federal Work-Study, institutionally sponsored loans, scholarships/grants, tuition waivers (partial), and unspecified assistantships also available. Financial award application deadline: 3/31; financial award applicants required to submit FAFSA. *Faculty research:* Bulgarian violin literature, Ozarks fiddle music, carillon, nineteenth century piano. *Unit head:* Diane C Strickland, Head, 417-836-4122, Fax: 417-836-7665, E-mail: music@missouristate.edu. *Application contact:* Eric Eckert, Coordinator of Graduate Admissions and Recruitment, 417-836-5331, Fax: 417-836-6888.

Montclair State University, The Office of Graduate Admissions and Support Services, School of the Arts, Department of Music, Montclair, NJ 07043-1624. Offers music (AD); music education (MA); music therapy (MA); performance (MA, Certificate); theory/composition (MA). *Accreditation:* NASM. Part-time and evening/weekend programs available. *Faculty:* 11 full-time (7 women), 87 part-time/adjunct (38 women). *Students:* 14 full-time (11 women), 21 part-time (9 women); includes 3 minority (1 African American, 1 Asian American or Pacific Islander, 1 Hispanic American), 5 international. Average age 30. 20 applicants, 80% accepted, 14 enrolled. In 2008, 9 master's, 7 other advanced degrees awarded. *Degree requirements:* For master's, comprehensive exam, compositions, recitals, or thesis. *Entrance requirements:* For master's, GRE General Test, audition; undergraduate degree in music or at least 40 semester hours of work in theory, music history, performance; 2 letters of recommendation; teaching certificate (MA in music education). Additional exam requirements/recommendations for international students: Required—TOEFL (minimum score 83 computer-based). *Application deadline:* For fall admission, 6/1 for international students; for spring admission, 10/1 for international students. Applications are processed on a rolling basis. Application fee: $60. Electronic applications accepted. *Financial support:* In 2008–09, 2 research assistantships with full tuition reimbursements (averaging $7,000 per year) were awarded; Federal Work-Study, scholarships/grants, and unspecified assistantships also available. Support available to part-time students. Financial award application deadline: 3/1; financial award applicants required to submit FAFSA. *Unit head:* Prof. Robert Aldridge, Chairperson, 973-655-7212. *Application contact:* Amy Aiello, Associate Director of Admissions, 973-655-5147, Fax: 973-655-7869, E-mail: graduate.school@montclair.edu.

Morehead State University, Graduate Programs, Caudill College of Humanities, Department of Music, Morehead, KY 40351. Offers music education (MM); music performance (MM). *Accreditation:* NASM. Part-time and evening/weekend programs available. *Faculty:* 18 full-time (5 women), 1 (woman) part-time/adjunct. *Students:* 9 full-time (4 women), 12 part-time (7 women); includes 1 minority (African American). Average age 26. 13 applicants, 69% accepted, 5 enrolled. In 2008, 9 master's awarded. *Degree requirements:* For master's, oral and written exams. *Entrance requirements:* For master's, minimum GPA of 3.0 in music, 2.5 overall; audition. Additional exam requirements/recommendations for international students: Required—TOEFL (minimum score 550 paper-based; 173 computer-based). *Application deadline:* For fall admission, 8/1 priority date for domestic and international students; for spring admission, 12/1 priority date for domestic and international students. Applications are processed on a rolling basis. Application fee: $30 ($55 for international students). Electronic applications accepted. *Expenses:* Tuition, area resident: Full-time $6084; part-time $338 per credit hour. Tuition, state resident: full-time $6084; part-time $338 per credit hour. Tuition, nonresident: full-time $15,804; part-time $878 per credit hour. *Financial support:* In 2008–09, 1 teaching assistantship (averaging $6,000 per year) was awarded; career-related internships or fieldwork, Federal Work-Study, and unspecified assistantships also available. Financial award application deadline: 4/1; financial award applicants required to submit FAFSA. *Faculty research:* Musical instrument digital interface (MIDI) applications, tonal concepts of euphonium and baritone horn, digital synthesis, computer-assisted instruction in music, musical composition. *Unit head:* Dr. Curtis Hammond, Interim Department Chair, 606-783-2473, E-mail: s.mcbride@moreheadstate.edu. *Application contact:* Michelle Barber, Graduate Admissions Counselor, 606-783-2039, Fax: 606-783-5061, E-mail: m.barber@moreheadstate.edu.

Morgan State University, School of Graduate Studies, College of Liberal Arts, Department of Music, Baltimore, MD 21251. Offers MA. *Accreditation:* NASM. Part-time and evening/weekend programs available. *Degree requirements:* For master's, comprehensive exam, thesis.

Entrance requirements: Additional exam requirements/recommendations for international students: Required—TOEFL (minimum score 550 paper-based; 213 computer-based).

Murray State University, College of Humanities and Fine Arts, Program in Music, Murray, KY 42071. Offers music education (MME). *Accreditation:* NASM. Part-time programs available. *Entrance requirements:* For master's, GRE General Test or MAT. Additional exam requirements/recommendations for international students: Required—TOEFL.

New England Conservatory of Music, Graduate Program in Music, Boston, MA 02115-5000. Offers MM, DMA, Diploma. *Accreditation:* NASM (one or more programs are accredited). *Faculty:* 89 full-time (30 women), 127 part-time/adjunct (39 women). *Students:* 339 full-time (171 women), 19 part-time (14 women); includes 39 minority (9 African Americans, 2 American Indian/Alaska Native, 21 Asian Americans or Pacific Islanders, 7 Hispanic Americans), 138 international. Average age 25. 1,319 applicants, 30% accepted, 173 enrolled. In 2008, 148 master's, 167 doctorates, 35 other advanced degrees awarded. *Degree requirements:* For master's, thesis (for some programs), recital, 3 foreign languages (vocal majors); for doctorate, one foreign language, comprehensive exam, thesis/dissertation, qualifying exams, recital. *Entrance requirements:* For master's and Diploma, audition; for doctorate, music theory and musicology exam, audition. Additional exam requirements/recommendations for international students: Required—TOEFL (minimum score 550 paper-based; 213 computer-based; 79 iBT). *Application deadline:* For fall admission, 12/1 priority date for domestic and international students; for spring admission, 11/1 for domestic and international students. Applications are processed on a rolling basis. Application fee: $100. *Expenses:* Tuition: Full-time $32,900; part-time $2100 per credit. Required fees: $425. *Financial support:* In 2008–09, 342 students received support, including 330 fellowships with partial tuition reimbursements available (averaging $15,120 per year); teaching assistantships, Federal Work-Study, scholarships/grants, and tuition waivers (partial) also available. Support available to part-time students. Financial award application deadline: 12/1; financial award applicants required to submit FAFSA. *Unit head:* Tom Novak, Dean of the College, 617-585-1304, Fax: 617-585-1303, E-mail: tnovak@newenglandconservatory.edu. *Application contact:* Christina Daly, Director of Admissions, 617-585-1101, Fax: 617-585-1115, E-mail: christina.daly@newenglandconservatory.edu.

New Jersey City University, Graduate Studies and Continuing Education, College of Arts and Sciences, Department of Music, Dance and Theatre, Jersey City, NJ 07305-1597. Offers music education (MA); performance (MM). *Accreditation:* NASM. Evening/weekend programs available. *Degree requirements:* For master's, thesis optional, recital. *Entrance requirements:* For master's, GRE General Test or MAT. Additional exam requirements/recommendations for international students: Required—TOEFL.

New Mexico State University, Graduate School, College of Arts and Sciences, Department of Music, Las Cruces, NM 88003-8001. Offers conducting (MM); music education (MM); performance (MM). *Accreditation:* NASM. Part-time programs available. *Faculty:* 5 full-time (2 women), 1 part-time/adjunct (0 women). *Students:* 14 full-time (4 women), 5 part-time (2 women); includes 7 minority (1 African American, 1 Asian American or Pacific Islander, 5 Hispanic Americans), 5 international. Average age 30. 12 applicants, 100% accepted, 7 enrolled. In 2008, 5 master's awarded. *Degree requirements:* For master's, comprehensive exam (for some programs), thesis (for some programs), recital. *Entrance requirements:* For master's, diagnostic exam, audition, bachelor's degree or equivalent from an accredited institution. Additional exam requirements/recommendations for international students: Required—TOEFL. *Application deadline:* For fall admission, 7/1 priority date for domestic students; for spring admission, 11/1 for domestic students. Applications are processed on a rolling basis. Application fee: $30 ($50 for international students). Electronic applications accepted. *Expenses:* Contact institution. *Financial support:* In 2008–09, 11 students received support, including 6 teaching assistantships (averaging $14,483 per year); fellowships, Federal Work-Study and health care benefits also available. Support available to part-time students. Financial award application deadline: 3/1. *Faculty research:* Music education, contemporary wind band literature, performance. *Unit head:* Dr. Ken Van Winkle, Head, 575-646-2421, Fax: 575-646-8199, E-mail: kvanwink@nmsu.edu. *Application contact:* Dr. Lisa Van Winkle, Assistant Professor, 575-646-2523, Fax: 575-646-2472, E-mail: lvanwink@nmsu.edu.

New Orleans Baptist Theological Seminary, Graduate and Professional Programs, Division of Church Music Ministries, New Orleans, LA 70126-4858. Offers MMCM, DMA. *Accreditation:* NASM. *Degree requirements:* For doctorate, one foreign language, thesis/dissertation. *Entrance requirements:* For doctorate, GRE General Test.

The New School: A University, Mannes College The New School for Music, New York, NY 10024. Offers music performance (MM, PD). *Faculty:* 7 full-time (1 woman), 112 part-time/adjunct (44 women). *Students:* 188 full-time (120 women), 4 part-time (3 women); includes 20 minority (1 African American, 10 Asian Americans or Pacific Islanders, 9 Hispanic Americans), 108 international. Average age 25. 813 applicants, 30% accepted, 97 enrolled. In 2008, 59 master's, 16 other advanced degrees awarded. *Degree requirements:* For master's, recital, professional performance. *Entrance requirements:* For master's, audition. Additional exam requirements/recommendations for international students: Required—TOEFL (minimum score 550 paper-based; 213 computer-based). *Application deadline:* For fall admission, 11/15 for domestic students. Application fee: $100. *Expenses:* Tuition: Full-time $27,144; part-time $1508 per credit. Required fees: $355 per semester. *Financial support:* Fellowships with partial tuition reimbursements, research assistantships with partial tuition reimbursements, teaching assistantships with partial tuition reimbursements, career-related internships or fieldwork, Federal Work-Study, scholarships/grants, and tuition waivers (partial) available. Support available to part-time students. Financial award application deadline: 3/1; financial award applicants required to submit FAFSA. *Unit head:* Joel Lester, Dean, 212-580-0210 Ext. 4848. *Application contact:* Director of Admissions, 212-580-0210 Ext. 263.

New York University, Graduate School of Arts and Science, Department of Music, New York, NY 10012-1019. Offers composition and theory (MA, PhD); early music performance (Advanced Certificate); ethnomusicology (MA, PhD). Terminal master's awarded for partial completion of doctoral program. *Degree requirements:* For master's, one foreign language, thesis (for some programs), general exam; for doctorate, 2 foreign languages, thesis/dissertation, general and special exams. *Entrance requirements:* For master's, GRE General Test, bachelor's degree in liberal arts or music; for doctorate, GRE General Test, master's degree in music; for Advanced Certificate, bachelor's degree in music. Additional exam requirements/recommendations for international students: Required—TOEFL. *Faculty research:* Early music (nineteenth century), Wagner, Verdi, performance practice.

New York University, Steinhardt School of Culture, Education and Human Development, Department of Music and Performing Arts Professions, Program in Music Business, New York, NY 10012-1019. Offers MA. Part-time and evening/weekend programs available. *Degree requirements:* For master's, thesis (for some programs). *Entrance requirements:* For master's, interview, supplementary essay. Additional exam requirements/recommendations for international students: Required—TOEFL. *Faculty research:* Strategic marketing, new technologies, intellectual property, entrepreneurship.

New York University, Steinhardt School of Culture, Education and Human Development, Department of Music and Performing Arts Professions, Program in Music Performance and Composition, New York, NY 10012-1019. Offers MA, PhD. Part-time and evening/weekend programs available. Terminal master's awarded for partial completion of doctoral program. *Degree requirements:* For master's, thesis (for some programs); for doctorate, thesis/dissertation. *Entrance requirements:* For master's, audition; for doctorate, GRE General Test, audition, interview. Additional exam requirements/recommendations for international students: Required—TOEFL. *Faculty research:* Aesthetics, performance analysis, twentieth century music, music methodologies for arts criticism and analysis.

New York University, Steinhardt School of Culture, Education and Human Development, Department of Music and Performing Arts Professions, Program in Music Technology, New York, NY 10012-1019. Offers MM. Part-time and evening/weekend programs available. *Degree requirements:* For master's, thesis (for some programs). *Entrance requirements:* For master's, portfolio. Additional exam requirements/recommendations for international students: Required—TOEFL. *Faculty research:* Pattern processing in music, computer music, acoustics, music perception, interactive music systems.

New York University, Tisch School of the Arts, Graduate Musical Theatre Writing Program, New York, NY 10012-1019. Offers MFA. *Degree requirements:* For master's, full-length musical theatre work. *Entrance requirements:* For master's, interview, portfolio. Additional exam requirements/recommendations for international students: Required—TOEFL or IELTS. Electronic applications accepted.

The Nigerian Baptist Theological Seminary, Graduate Studies, Ogbomoso, Nigeria. Offers church music (M Div, M Th, Diploma); divinity (M Div); ministry (D Min); religious education (M Div, M Th, PhD); theological studies (MATS); theology (M Th, PhD). Part-time programs available. *Degree requirements:* For master's, thesis, 2 Nigerian languages; for M Div, thesis/dissertation (for some programs), 2 biblical languages; for Diploma, thesis or alternative.

Norfolk State University, School of Graduate Studies, School of Liberal Arts, Department of Music, Norfolk, VA 23504. Offers music (MM); music education (MM); performance (MM); theory and composition (MM). *Accreditation:* NASM. Part-time programs available. *Degree requirements:* For master's, thesis or alternative. *Entrance requirements:* For master's, minimum GPA of 2.7, letters of recommendation. Additional exam requirements/recommendations for international students: Required—TOEFL.

North Carolina Central University, Division of Academic Affairs, College of Liberal Arts, Department of Music, Durham, NC 27707-3129. Offers jazz studies (MM).

North Dakota State University, College of Graduate and Interdisciplinary Studies, College of Arts, Humanities and Social Sciences, Department of Music, Fargo, ND 58105. Offers M Ed, MM, DMA. *Accreditation:* NASM. *Students:* 13 full-time (5 women), 1 (woman) part-time; includes 1 Hispanic American, 2 international. In 2008, 2 master's, 5 doctorates awarded. *Degree requirements:* For master's, 2 foreign languages, comprehensive exam, thesis or alternative, recitals; for doctorate, 2 foreign languages, comprehensive exam, thesis/dissertation or alternative, recitals. *Entrance requirements:* For master's and doctorate, music history, music theory, performance audition. Additional exam requirements/recommendations for international students: Required—TOEFL (minimum score 525 paper-based; 197 computer-based; 71 iBT). *Application deadline:* Applications are processed on a rolling basis. Application fee: $45 ($60 for international students). Electronic applications accepted. *Financial support:* In 2008–09, 16 students received support; fellowships with full tuition reimbursements available, teaching assistantships with full tuition reimbursements available, tuition waivers (partial) and unspecified assistantships available. Support available to part-time students. Financial award applicants required to submit FAFSA. *Faculty research:* Performance, conducting. *Unit head:* Dr. John Miller, Director, Division of Fine Arts, 701-231-7932, E-mail: ej.miller@ndsu.edu. *Application contact:* Dr. Jo Ann Miller, Director, Graduate Studies, 701-231-7822, E-mail: jo.miller@ndsu.edu.

Northeastern Illinois University, Graduate College, College of Arts and Sciences, Department of Music, Program in Music, Chicago, IL 60625-4699. Offers MA. Part-time and evening/weekend programs available. *Degree requirements:* For master's, comprehensive exam, thesis optional, minimum GPA of 3.0. *Entrance requirements:* For master's, departmental exam, audition, minimum GPA of 2.75. Additional exam requirements/recommendations for international students: Required—TOEFL (minimum score 550 paper-based; 213 computer-based; 80 iBT). Electronic applications accepted. *Faculty research:* World music, computers as applied instruments, vocal pedagogy, vocal interpretation, jazz repertory.

Northern Arizona University, Graduate College, College of Arts and Letters, School of Music, Flagstaff, AZ 86011. Offers choral conducting (MM); instrumental conducting (MM); instrumental performance (MM); music education (MM); musicology (MM); theory and composition (MM); vocal performance (MM). *Accreditation:* NASM.

Northern Illinois University, Graduate School, College of Visual and Performing Arts, School of Music, De Kalb, IL 60115-2854. Offers MM, Performer's Certificate. *Accreditation:* NASM. Part-time programs available. *Degree requirements:* For master's, comprehensive exam, thesis optional, recital or project; for Performer's Certificate, recitals. *Entrance requirements:* For master's, minimum GPA of 2.75, appropriate bachelor's degree, audition, interview; for Performer's Certificate, minimum GPA of 2.75 (undergraduate), 3.2 (graduate); audition. Additional exam requirements/recommendations for international students: Required—TOEFL (minimum score 550 paper-based; 213 computer-based). Electronic applications accepted. *Faculty research:* Impact of music on urban children and acquisition of language skills, music in 17th century Madrid, Finnish music and culture, jazz studies.

Northwestern State University of Louisiana, Graduate Studies and Research, School of Creative and Performing Arts, Program in Music, Natchitoches, LA 71497. Offers MM. *Accreditation:* NASM. *Faculty:* 14 full-time (10 women), 1 (woman) part-time/adjunct. *Students:* 13 full-time (5 women), 1 part-time (0 women); includes 1 minority (African American), 3 international. Average age 27. 2 applicants, 100% accepted, 0 enrolled. In 2008, 4 master's awarded. *Degree requirements:* For master's, comprehensive exam, thesis or alternative. *Entrance requirements:* For master's, GRE General Test, minimum undergraduate GPA of 2.5. *Application deadline:* For fall admission, 8/1 priority date for domestic students; for spring admission, 1/10 for domestic students. Applications are processed on a rolling basis. Application fee: $20 ($30 for international students). *Financial support:* Application deadline: 7/15. *Application contact:* Dr. Steven G. Horton, Associate Provost/Dean, Graduate Studies, Research, and Information Systems, 318-357-5851, Fax: 318-357-5019, E-mail: grad_school@nsula.edu.

Northwestern University, The Graduate School, School of Communication, Department of Performance Studies, Evanston, IL 60208. Offers MA, PhD. Admissions and degrees offered through The Graduate School. Part-time programs available. Terminal master's awarded for partial completion of doctoral program. *Degree requirements:* For master's, recital; for doctorate, one foreign language, thesis/dissertation, recital. *Entrance requirements:* For master's and doctorate, GRE General Test. Additional exam requirements/recommendations for international students: Required—TOEFL. *Faculty research:* Adaptation/performance of literature, ethnography of performance, critical cultural studies, performance theory, intercultural performance, gender studies.

Northwestern University, Henry and Leigh Bienen School of Music, Department of Music Performance, Evanston, IL 60208. Offers collaborative arts (DM); conducting (MM, DM); jazz (MM); performance (MM), including string chamber music and orchestral literature; piano performance (MM, DM, CP); piano performance and collaborative arts (MM); piano performance and pedagogy (MM); string performance and pedagogy (MM); strings (MM, DM); strings, winds and percussion (CP); voice (MM, DM, CP); winds and percussion (MM, DM). *Accreditation:* NASM. *Degree requirements:* For master's, recital; for doctorate, comprehensive exam, thesis/dissertation, 3 recitals; for CP, 2 recitals. *Entrance requirements:* For master's, audition, preliminary tapes in voice, flute, percussion; for doctorate, written essay exam (theory and music history), audition, preliminary tapes; for CP, audition, preliminary tapes. Additional exam requirements/recommendations for international students: Required—TOEFL (minimum score 600 paper-based; 250 computer-based; 100 iBT).

Northwestern University, Henry and Leigh Bienen School of Music, Department of Music Studies, Evanston, IL 60208. Offers music composition (DM); music education (MM, PhD); music technology (MM); music technology/new media (DM); music theory (MM, PhD); musicology (MM, PhD). PhD admissions and degree offered through The Graduate School. *Accreditation:* NASM. *Degree requirements:* For doctorate, comprehensive exam, thesis/dissertation. *Entrance*

Music

Northwestern University (continued)

requirements: For master's, portfolio or research papers; for doctorate, GRE General Test (PhD), portfolio, research papers. Additional exam requirements/recommendations for international students: Required—TOEFL (minimum score 600 paper-based; 250 computer-based; 100 iBT), TOEFL (paper-based 560; computer-based 220) or IELTS (paper-based 6). *Faculty research:* Music cognition, cognitive learning, aesthetic education, computer music, technology in education.

Notre Dame de Namur University, Division of Academic Affairs, School of Arts and Humanities, Department of Music, Belmont, CA 94002-1908. Offers music (MFA, MM); pedagogy (MM); performance (MM). Part-time and evening/weekend programs available. *Faculty:* 3 full-time (2 women), 8 part-time/adjunct (4 women). *Students:* 8 full-time (6 women), 5 part-time (3 women); includes 2 minority (1 Asian American or Pacific Islander, 1 Hispanic American), 1 international. Average age 30. 6 applicants, 100% accepted, 5 enrolled. In 2008, 9 master's awarded. *Degree requirements:* For master's, exams. *Entrance requirements:* For master's, audition, appropriate bachelor's degree, minimum GPA of 2.5. Additional exam requirements/recommendations for international students: Required—TOEFL. *Application deadline:* For fall admission, 8/1 priority date for domestic students; for spring admission, 12/1 priority date for domestic students. Applications are processed on a rolling basis. Application fee: $50. Electronic applications accepted. *Expenses:* Tuition: Part-time $699 per unit. Required fees: $3 per unit. $35 per semester. *Financial support:* Available to part-time students. Applicants required to submit FAFSA. *Unit head:* Debra Lambert, Chair, 650-580-3694. *Application contact:* Candace Hallmark, Director of Graduate Admissions, 650-508-3592, Fax: 650-508-3426, E-mail: grad.admit@ndnu.edu.

Oakland University, Graduate Study and Lifelong Learning, College of Arts and Sciences, Department of Music, Rochester, MI 48309-4401. Offers music (MM); music education (PhD). *Accreditation:* NASM. *Entrance requirements:* For master's, minimum GPA of 3.0 for unconditional admission. Additional exam requirements/recommendations for international students: Required—TOEFL (minimum score 550 paper-based; 213 computer-based). Electronic applications accepted. *Expenses:* Contact institution.

Oberlin College, Conservatory of Music, Oberlin, OH 44074. Offers MM, MMT, AD. *Accreditation:* NASM. *Degree requirements:* For master's, 2 recitals. *Entrance requirements:* For master's, audition. Additional exam requirements/recommendations for international students: Required—TOEFL (minimum score 550 paper-based; 213 computer-based; 79 iBT). Electronic applications accepted.

The Ohio State University, Graduate School, College of the Arts, Department of Dance, Columbus, OH 43210. Offers choreography (MFA); dance (MA, MFA, PhD); dance and technology (MFA); dance studies (PhD); Labanotation (MFA); lighting (MFA); performance (MFA). *Accreditation:* NASD. *Degree requirements:* For master's, thesis optional. *Entrance requirements:* For master's, GRE General Test (MA); for doctorate, GRE General Test. Additional exam requirements/recommendations for international students: Recommended—TOEFL (minimum score 600 paper-based; 250 computer-based). Electronic applications accepted.

The Ohio State University, Graduate School, College of the Arts, School of Music, Columbus, OH 43210. Offers M Mus, MA, DMA, PhD. *Accreditation:* NASM. Part-time programs available. *Degree requirements:* For master's, thesis optional; for doctorate, 2 foreign languages, thesis/dissertation. *Entrance requirements:* For master's and doctorate, GRE General Test. Additional exam requirements/recommendations for international students: Recommended—TOEFL (minimum score 600 paper-based; 250 computer-based). Electronic applications accepted.

Ohio University, Graduate College, College of Fine Arts, School of Music, Athens, OH 45701-2979. Offers accompanying (MM); composition (MM); conducting (MM); history/literature (MM); music education (MM); music therapy (MM); performance (MM, Certificate); performance/pedagogy (MM); theory (MM). *Accreditation:* NASM. Postbaccalaureate distance learning degree programs offered (minimal on-campus study). *Degree requirements:* For master's, thesis (for some programs), oral exam. *Entrance requirements:* For master's, audition, interview, and/or portfolio. Additional exam requirements/recommendations for international students: Required—TOEFL.

Oklahoma City University, Margaret E. Petree College of Performing Arts, Wanda L. Bass School of Music, Oklahoma City, OK 73106-1402. Offers composition (MM); conducting (MM); musical theatre (MM); opera performance (MM); performance (MM). *Accreditation:* NASM. Part-time programs available. *Degree requirements:* For master's, thesis, departmental qualifying exam, recital. *Entrance requirements:* For master's, audition, bachelor's degree in music, minimum GPA of 3.0. Additional exam requirements/recommendations for international students: Required—TOEFL.

Oklahoma State University, College of Arts and Sciences, Department of Music, Stillwater, OK 74078. Offers pedagogy and performance (MM). *Accreditation:* NASM. *Faculty:* 27 full-time (12 women), 6 part-time/adjunct (3 women). *Students:* 7 full-time (3 women), 5 part-time (2 women); includes 1 minority (African American). Average age 30. 14 applicants, 43% accepted, 4 enrolled. In 2008, 4 master's awarded. *Degree requirements:* For master's, final project, oral exam. *Entrance requirements:* For master's, GRE, audition. Additional exam requirements/recommendations for international students: Required—TOEFL. *Application deadline:* For fall admission, 3/1 priority date for international students; for spring admission, 8/1 priority date for international students. Applications are processed on a rolling basis. Application fee: $40 ($75 for international students). Electronic applications accepted. *Expenses:* Tuition, state resident: full-time $3716.40; part-time $154.85 per credit hour. Tuition, nonresident: full-time $14,448; part-time $602 per credit hour. Required fees: $1772.40; $73.85 per credit hour. One-time fee: $50. Tuition and fees vary according to course load and campus/location. *Financial support:* In 2008–09, 8 teaching assistantships (averaging $9,828 per year) were awarded; career-related internships or fieldwork, Federal Work-Study, scholarships/grants, health care benefits, tuition waivers (partial), and unspecified assistantships also available. Support available to part-time students. Financial award application deadline: 3/1; financial award applicants required to submit FAFSA. *Faculty research:* Discovery and presentation of music literature of other countries, transportation of ancient music literature to modern notation. *Unit head:* Dr. Brant Adams, Head, 405-744-6133, Fax: 405-744-9324. *Application contact:* Dr. Gordon Emslie, Dean, 405-744-6368, Fax: 405-744-0355, E-mail: grad_i@okstate.edu.

Penn State University Park, Graduate School, College of Arts and Architecture, School of Music, State College, University Park, PA 16802-1503. Offers composition/theory (M Mus); conducting (M Mus); music education (MME, PhD); music theory (MA); music theory and history (MA); musicology (MA); performance (M Mus); piano, pedagogy and performance (M Mus); voice performance and pedagogy (M Mus). *Accreditation:* NASM.

Phillips Theological Seminary, Programs in Theology, Tulsa, OK 74116. Offers administration of church agencies (M Div); campus ministry (M Div); church-related social work (M Div); college and seminary teaching (M Div); global mission work (M Div); institutional chaplaincy (M Div); ministerial vocations in Christian education (M Div); ministry (D Min), including parish ministry, pastoral counseling, practices of ministry; ministry and culture (MAMC), including Christian education, congregational leadership, history and practice of Christian spirituality, theology, ethics, and culture; ministry of music (M Div); pastoral care and counseling (M Div); pastoral ministry (M Div); theological studies (MTS). *Accreditation:* ATS. Part-time programs available. Postbaccalaureate distance learning degree programs offered (minimal on-campus study). *Degree requirements:* For master's, thesis (for some programs); for doctorate, thesis/dissertation. *Entrance requirements:* For master's, minimum GPA of 2.5; for doctorate, M Div, minimum GPA of 3.0. *Faculty research:* Biblical studies, historical studies, theology and culture, practical theology, theology and film.

Pittsburg State University, Graduate School, College of Arts and Sciences, Department of Music, Pittsburg, KS 66762. Offers instrumental music education (MM); music history/music literature (MM); performance (MM), including orchestral performance, organ, piano, voice; theory and composition (MM); vocal music education (MM). *Accreditation:* NASM. *Degree requirements:* For master's, thesis or alternative.

Point Park University, Conservatory of Performing Arts, Pittsburgh, PA 15222-1984. Offers theatre arts-acting (MFA). *Faculty:* 4 full-time, 2 part-time/adjunct. *Students:* 6 full-time (3 women), 1 international. Average age 40. 17 applicants, 35% accepted, 6 enrolled. In 2008, 1 master's awarded. *Degree requirements:* For master's, comprehensive exam (for some programs), thesis or alternative. *Entrance requirements:* For master's, interview, undergraduate degree in related field, theatre experience. *Application deadline:* Applications are processed on a rolling basis. Application fee: $30. Electronic applications accepted. *Expenses:* Tuition: Full-time $11,880; part-time $660 per credit. Required fees: $486; $27 per credit. *Financial support:* In 2008–09, 5 students received support, including 5 teaching assistantships with full tuition reimbursements available (averaging $6,400 per year); Federal Work-Study and scholarships/grants also available. Support available to part-time students. Financial award application deadline: 5/1; financial award applicants required to submit FAFSA. *Unit head:* Ronald Allan-Lindblom, Dean/Artistic Producing Director, 412-392-3454, Fax: 412-392-2424, E-mail: rlindblom@pointpark.edu. *Application contact:* Lynn C. Ribar, Associate Director, Adult and Graduate Enrollment, 412-392-3908, Fax: 412-392-6164, E-mail: lribar@pointpark.edu.

Portland State University, Graduate Studies, School of Fine and Performing Arts, Department of Music, Portland, OR 97207-0751. Offers conducting (MMC); music education (MAT, MST); performance (MMP). *Accreditation:* NASM. Part-time programs available. *Faculty:* 25 full-time (10 women), 27 part-time/adjunct (8 women). *Students:* 15 full-time (8 women), 10 part-time (6 women); includes 2 minority (1 African American, 1 Hispanic American). Average age 30. 18 applicants, 50% accepted, 6 enrolled. In 2008, 11 master's awarded. *Degree requirements:* For master's, variable foreign language requirement, exit exam. *Entrance requirements:* For master's, departmental exam, GRE General Test, minimum GPA of 3.0 in upper-division course work or 2.75 overall. Additional exam requirements/recommendations for international students: Required—TOEFL (minimum score 550 paper-based; 213 computer-based). *Application deadline:* For fall admission, 8/1 priority date for domestic students, 8/1 for international students; for winter admission, 11/15 for domestic students, 10/1 for international students; for spring admission, 2/1 for domestic and international students. Applications are processed on a rolling basis. Application fee: $50. *Expenses:* Tuition, area resident: Full-time $8763; part-time $179 per credit hour. Tuition, state resident: full-time $8763; part-time $298 per credit hour. Tuition, nonresident: full-time $12,981; part-time $426 per credit hour. Required fees: $1242. One-time fee: $250. Tuition and fees vary according to course load and program. *Financial support:* Research assistantships with full tuition reimbursements, teaching assistantships with full tuition reimbursements, Federal Work-Study, scholarships/grants, and unspecified assistantships available. Support available to part-time students. Financial award application deadline: 3/1; financial award applicants required to submit FAFSA. *Faculty research:* Composition, music analysis, music history, jazz. Total annual research expenditures: $22,313. *Unit head:* Bryan Johanson, Chair, 503-725-3382, Fax: 503-725-8215. *Application contact:* Bryan Johanson, Chair, 503-725-3382, Fax: 503-725-8215.

Princeton University, Graduate School, Department of Music, Princeton, NJ 08544-1019. Offers composition (PhD); musicology (PhD). *Degree requirements:* For doctorate, variable foreign language requirement, thesis/dissertation. *Entrance requirements:* For doctorate, GRE General Test, sample of written work. Additional exam requirements/recommendations for international students: Required—TOEFL (minimum score 600 paper-based; 250 computer-based). Electronic applications accepted. *Faculty research:* Computer synthesis, history of Western music, comparative musicology, theory.

Purchase College, State University of New York, Conservatory of Music, Purchase, NY 10577-1400. Offers composition (MM); instrumental performance (MM); jazz studies (MM); studio composition (MM); voice and opera studies (MM). *Students:* 90 full-time (40 women), 5 part-time (all women); includes 6 minority (2 African Americans, 2 Asian Americans or Pacific Islanders, 2 Hispanic Americans), 27 international. Average age 30. 146 applicants, 37% accepted, 29 enrolled. In 2008, 33 master's awarded. *Degree requirements:* For master's, thesis or alternative, composition, performance. *Entrance requirements:* For master's, audition. *Application deadline:* For fall admission, 3/1 for domestic students. Application fee: $50. Electronic applications accepted. *Expenses:* Tuition, area resident: Full-time $6900; part-time $288 per credit. Tuition, state resident: full-time $6900; part-time $288 per credit. Tuition, nonresident: full-time $10,920; part-time $455 per credit. Required fees: $1461; $0.85 per credit. One-time fee: $75 full-time. *Financial support:* Fellowships, teaching assistantships, career-related internships or fieldwork, Federal Work-Study, scholarships/grants, and tuition waivers (partial) available. Support available to part-time students. Financial award application deadline: 3/15; financial award applicants required to submit FAFSA. *Unit head:* Robert Thompson, Interim Dean, 914-251-6700, Fax: 914-251-6739, E-mail: robert.thompson@purchase.edu. *Application contact:* Sabrina Johnston, Counselor, 914-251-6479, Fax: 914-251-6314, E-mail: admissn@purchase.edu.

Queens College of the City University of New York, Division of Graduate Studies, Arts and Humanities Division, Aaron Copland School of Music, Flushing, NY 11367-1597. Offers MA. Part-time programs available. *Degree requirements:* For master's, one foreign language, qualifying exams, recital. *Entrance requirements:* For master's, audition, bachelor's degree in music, minimum GPA of 3.0. Additional exam requirements/recommendations for international students: Required—TOEFL.

Radford University, College of Graduate and Professional Studies, College of Visual and Performing Arts, Department of Music, Radford, VA 24142. Offers music (MA); music education (MS); music therapy (MS). *Accreditation:* NASM. Part-time programs available. *Faculty:* 13 full-time (3 women), 2 part-time/adjunct (both women). *Students:* 16 full-time (12 women), 3 part-time (1 woman); includes 5 minority (4 African Americans, 1 Asian American or Pacific Islander), 1 international. Average age 28. 19 applicants, 79% accepted, 9 enrolled. In 2008, 7 master's awarded. *Degree requirements:* For master's, comprehensive exam, thesis or alternative. *Entrance requirements:* For master's, GRE, major field test in music or PRAXIS II (content knowledge), written diagnostics exams in music, minimum GPA of 2.75; 3 letters of reference. Additional exam requirements/recommendations for international students: Required—TOEFL (minimum score 550 paper-based; 213 computer-based; 79 iBT). *Application deadline:* For fall admission, 3/1 priority date for domestic students, 12/1 for international students; for spring admission, 10/1 for domestic students, 7/1 for international students. Applications are processed on a rolling basis. Application fee: $40. Electronic applications accepted. *Expenses:* Tuition, area resident: Full-time $4845; part-time $202 per credit. Tuition, state resident: full-time $4845; part-time $202 per credit. Tuition, nonresident: full-time $11,483; part-time $478 per credit. Required fees: $2349; $98 per credit. *Financial support:* In 2008–09, 13 students received support, including 7 research assistantships with partial tuition reimbursements available (averaging $8,000 per year), 4 teaching assistantships with partial tuition reimbursements available (averaging $8,700 per year); career-related internships or fieldwork, Federal Work-Study, institutionally sponsored loans, scholarships/grants, and unspecified assistantships also available. Financial award application deadline: 3/1; financial award applicants required to submit FAFSA. *Unit head:* Dr. Allen F. Wojtera, Chair, 540-831-5177, Fax: 540-831-6133, E-mail: awojtera@radford.edu. *Application contact:* Graduate Admissions, 540-831-5431, Fax: 540-831-6061, E-mail: gradcollege@radford.edu.

Regis University, College for Professional Studies, Program in Teacher Education, Denver, CO 80221-1099. Offers adult learning, training, and development (M Ed); curriculum, instruction, and assessment (M Ed); early childhood (M Ed); educational technology (Certificate); elementary (M Ed); ESL (M Ed); fine arts (M Ed), including arts, music; instructional technology (M Ed); professional leadership (M Ed); reading (M Ed); secondary (M Ed); self-designed (M Ed); space studies (M Ed); special education (M Ed); teacher licensure (M Ed). Program also offered in Henderson and Las Vegas (Summerlin), NV. Part-time and evening/weekend programs available. Postbaccalaureate distance learning degree programs offered (no on-campus study).

Degree requirements: For master's, thesis. *Entrance requirements:* For master's, essays, resumé, minimum GPA of 2.75, criminal background check. Additional exam requirements/recommendations for international students: Required—TOEFL (minimum score 213 computer-based), TWE (minimum score 5). Electronic applications accepted. *Faculty research:* Issues of equity in the middle school classroom, professional learning communities, school reform, socialinguistic and discursive obstacles to student integration, inclusive language arts curriculum.

Reinhardt College, Program in Music, Waleska, GA 30183-2981. Offers conducting (MM); music education (MM); piano pedagogy (MM).

Rice University, Graduate Programs, Shepherd School of Music, Houston, TX 77251-1892. Offers composition (MM, DMA); conducting (MM); history (MM); performance (MM, DMA); theory (MM). *Degree requirements:* For master's, thesis (for some programs), 2 recitals; for doctorate, one foreign language, comprehensive exam, thesis/dissertation, 4 recitals. *Entrance requirements:* For master's, minimum GPA of 3.0; for doctorate, GRE General Test, minimum GPA of 3.0. Additional exam requirements/recommendations for international students: Required—TOEFL (minimum score 600 paper-based; 250 computer-based; 90 iBT). Electronic applications accepted. *Faculty research:* Musicology, performance, theory, composition.

Roosevelt University, Graduate Division, Chicago College of Performing Arts, The Music Conservatory, Chicago, IL 60605-1394. Offers music (MM); piano pedagogy (Diploma). *Accreditation:* NASM. Part-time and evening/weekend programs available. *Expenses:* Tuition: Full-time $14,730; part-time $709 per credit. Required fees: $175 per semester. Tuition and fees vary according to course load and program.

Rowan University, Graduate School, College of Fine and Performing Arts, Program in Music, Glassboro, NJ 08028-1701. Offers performance (MM). *Accreditation:* NASM. Part-time and evening/weekend programs available. *Students:* 8 full-time (3 women), 3 part-time (0 women). Average age 29. 11 applicants, 45% accepted, 4 enrolled. In 2008, 2 master's awarded. *Degree requirements:* For master's, thesis (for some programs). *Entrance requirements:* Additional exam requirements/recommendations for international students: Required—TOEFL. *Application deadline:* Applications are processed on a rolling basis. Application fee: $50. Electronic applications accepted. *Expenses:* Tuition, area resident: Full-time $10,624; part-time $590 per credit. Tuition, state resident: full-time $10,624; part-time $590 per credit. Tuition, nonresident: full-time $10,624; part-time $590 per credit. Required fees: $2258; $124.90 per credit. *Financial support:* Career-related internships or fieldwork, scholarships/grants, health care benefits, and unspecified assistantships available. Support available to part-time students. *Unit head:* Dr. Mira Lalovic-Hand, Interim Associate Provost/Director of Graduate School, 856-256-5120, E-mail: Lalovic-hand@rowan.edu. *Application contact:* Karen Haynes, Graduate Coordinator, 856-256-4052, Fax: 856-256-4436, E-mail: Haynes@rowan.edu.

Rutgers, The State University of New Jersey, Newark, Graduate School, Program in Jazz History and Research, Newark, NJ 07102. Offers MA. *Entrance requirements:* For master's, GRE, minimum B average. Electronic applications accepted.

Rutgers, The State University of New Jersey, New Brunswick, Mason Gross School of the Arts, Program in Music, Piscataway, NJ 08854-8097. Offers collaborative piano (MM, DMA); conducting: choral (MM, DMA); conducting: instrumental (MM, DMA); conducting: orchestral (MM, DMA); jazz studies (MM); music (DMA, AD); music education (MM, DMA); music performance (MM). *Accreditation:* NASM. *Degree requirements:* For doctorate, one foreign language. *Entrance requirements:* For doctorate, audition. Additional exam requirements/recommendations for international students: Required—TOEFL (minimum score 550 paper-based; 213 computer-based). Electronic applications accepted. *Faculty research:* Performance, twentieth century music, jazz.

St. Cloud State University, School of Graduate Studies, College of Fine Arts and Humanities, Department of Music, St. Cloud, MN 56301-4498. Offers conducting and literature (MM); music education (MM); piano pedagogy (MM). *Accreditation:* NASM. *Degree requirements:* For master's, comprehensive exam (for some programs), thesis or alternative. *Entrance requirements:* For master's, GRE General Test, minimum GPA of 2.75. Additional exam requirements/recommendations for international students: Required—Michigan English Language Assessment Battery; Recommended—TOEFL (minimum score 550 paper-based; 213 computer-based), IELTS (minimum score 6.5). Electronic applications accepted.

Saint John's University, Saint John's School of Theology and Seminary, Collegeville, MN 56321. Offers divinity (M Div); liturgical music (MA); liturgical studies (MA); pastoral ministry (MA); theology (MA), including church history, liturgy, monastic studies, scripture, spirituality, systematics; M Div/MA. *Accreditation:* ATS. Part-time programs available. Postbaccalaureate distance learning degree programs offered (no on-campus study). *Degree requirements:* For master's, one foreign language, comprehensive exam (for some programs), thesis (for some programs). *Entrance requirements:* For master's, GRE General Test or MAT. Electronic applications accepted. *Faculty research:* Religious education, biblical literature.

Saint Joseph's College, Rensselaer Program of Church Music and Liturgy, Rensselaer, IN 47978. Offers church music and liturgy (MA); pastoral liturgy and music (Diploma). Offered during summer only. Part-time programs available. *Degree requirements:* For master's, thesis, research paper, service recital. *Entrance requirements:* For master's, entrance exams in music theory, conducting, keyboard, voice, and history.

St. Vladimir's Orthodox Theological Seminary, Graduate School of Theology, Crestwood, NY 10707-1699. Offers general theological studies (MA); liturgical music (MA); religious education (MA); theology (M Div, M Th, D Min); M Div/MA. MA in general theological studies, M Div offered jointly with St. Nersess Seminary. *Accreditation:* ATS. Part-time programs available. *Degree requirements:* For master's, one foreign language, thesis, fieldwork; for doctorate, thesis/dissertation, fieldwork; for M Div, one foreign language, thesis/dissertation, fieldwork. *Entrance requirements:* For doctorate, M Div, minimum GPA of 3.0. Additional exam requirements/recommendations for international students: Required—TOEFL (minimum score 250 computer-based).

Samford University, School of the Arts, Birmingham, AL 35229. Offers church music (MM); music (MME), including instrumental, vocal choral; piano pedagogy (MM). *Accreditation:* NASM. Part-time programs available. *Faculty:* 12 full-time (2 women), 9 part-time/adjunct (4 women). *Students:* 15 full-time (7 women), 5 part-time (3 women); includes 3 minority (1 African American, 1 American Indian/Alaska Native, 1 Asian American or Pacific Islander). Average age 26. 10 applicants, 80% accepted, 6 enrolled. In 2008, 3 master's awarded. *Degree requirements:* For master's, oral exams. *Entrance requirements:* For master's, GRE General Test or MAT, institutional graduate exam, minimum GPA of 3.0. Additional exam requirements/recommendations for international students: Required—TOEFL (minimum score 550 paper-based; 213 computer-based). *Application deadline:* For fall admission, 5/1 priority date for domestic students; for spring admission, 12/1 priority date for domestic students. Applications are processed on a rolling basis. Application fee: $35. *Expenses:* Tuition: Full-time $24,800; part-time $1007 per credit. Required fees: $110 per semester. *Financial support:* In 2008–09, 19 students received support, including research assistantships (averaging $4,000 per year); Federal Work-Study, scholarships/grants, and tuition waivers (partial) also available. Financial award application deadline: 9/1. *Faculty research:* Hymnology, choral techniques, assessment of music learning at elementary and secondary levels, piano pedagogy. *Unit head:* Dr. Joseph H. Hopkins, Dean, 205-726-2165, E-mail: jhhopkin@samford.edu. *Application contact:* Dr. Moya Nordlund, Director, Graduate Studies, 205-726-2651, Fax: 205-726-2165, E-mail: mlnordlu@samford.edu.

Sam Houston State University, College of Arts and Sciences, School of Music, Huntsville, TX 77341. Offers music (MM); music education (MM). *Accreditation:* NASM. Part-time programs available. *Faculty:* 9 full-time (0 women), 1 part-time/adjunct (0 women). *Students:* 13 full-time (4 women), 10 part-time (5 women); includes 5 minority (1 African American, 4 Hispanic Americans), 2 international. Average age 30. 15 applicants, 93% accepted, 11 enrolled. In 2008, 5 master's awarded. *Degree requirements:* For master's, thesis (for some programs), departmental qualifying exam. *Entrance requirements:* For master's, GRE General Test. Additional exam requirements/recommendations for international students: Required—TOEFL (minimum score 550 paper-based; 213 computer-based; 79 iBT). *Application deadline:* For fall admission, 8/1 for domestic and international students; for spring admission, 12/1 for domestic and international students. Applications are processed on a rolling basis. Application fee: $20. *Expenses:* Tuition, state resident: full-time $3564; part-time $198 per credit hour. Tuition, nonresident: full-time $8622; part-time $479 per credit hour. Required fees: $1290. Tuition and fees vary according to course load and campus/location. *Financial support:* Teaching assistantships, Federal Work-Study and scholarships/grants available. Financial award application deadline: 5/31; financial award applicants required to submit FAFSA. *Unit head:* Dr. James Bankhead, Chair, 936-294-3808, Fax: 936-294-3765, E-mail: bankhead@shsu.edu. *Application contact:* Scott Plugge, Advisor, 936-294-1393, E-mail: plugge@shsu.edu.

San Diego State University, Graduate and Research Affairs, College of Professional Studies and Fine Arts, School of Music and Dance, San Diego, CA 92182. Offers composition (acoustic and electronic) (MM); conducting (MM); ethnomusicology (MA); jazz studies (MM); musicology (MA); performance (MM); piano pedagogy (MA); theory (MA). *Degree requirements:* For master's, comprehensive exam (for some programs), thesis (for some programs). *Entrance requirements:* For master's, GRE General Test, bachelor's degree in related field, 2 letters of reference. Additional exam requirements/recommendations for international students: Required—TOEFL. Electronic applications accepted.

San Francisco Conservatory of Music, Graduate Division, San Francisco, CA 94102. Offers chamber music (MM); classical guitar (MM); composition (MM); conducting (MM); keyboards (MM); orchestral instruments (MM); voice (MM). *Accreditation:* NASM. Part-time programs available. *Degree requirements:* For master's, variable foreign language requirement, 2 recitals, departmental qualifying exam. *Entrance requirements:* For master's, audition, recommendations. Additional exam requirements/recommendations for international students: Required—TOEFL (minimum score 500 paper-based; 173 computer-based; 61 iBT). Electronic applications accepted.

San Francisco State University, Division of Graduate Studies, College of Creative Arts, School of Music and Dance, San Francisco, CA 94132-1722. Offers chamber music (MM); classical performance (MM); composition (MA); conducting (MM); music education (MA); music history (MA). *Accreditation:* NASM.

San Jose State University, Graduate Studies and Research, College of Humanities and the Arts, School of Music and Dance, San Jose, CA 95192-0001. Offers music (MA). *Accreditation:* NASM. *Degree requirements:* For master's, thesis or alternative. *Entrance requirements:* For master's, GRE. Additional exam requirements/recommendations for international students: Required—TOEFL (minimum score 590 paper-based). Electronic applications accepted.

Santa Clara University, School of Education, Counseling Psychology, and Pastoral Ministries, Program in Pastoral Ministries, Program in Liturgical Music, Santa Clara, CA 95053. Offers MA. Part-time and evening/weekend programs available. *Students:* 2 part-time (1 woman); includes 1 minority (Asian American or Pacific Islander). Average age 32. In 2008, 1 master's awarded. *Degree requirements:* For master's, comprehensive exam, thesis. *Entrance requirements:* Additional exam requirements/recommendations for international students: Required—TOEFL. *Application deadline:* Applications are processed on a rolling basis. *Expenses:* Contact institution. *Financial support:* Application deadline: 3/1; *Unit head:* Fr. Tom Powers, S.J., Director, 408-554-4322. *Application contact:* Fr. Tom Powers, S.J., Director, 408-554-4322.

Savannah College of Art and Design, Graduate School, Savannah, GA 31402-3146. Offers advertising design (MA, MFA); animation (MA, MFA); architectural history (MA, MFA); architecture (M Arch); art history (MA, MFA); arts administration (MA); broadcast design (MA, MFA); cinema studies (MA); commercial photography (MA); digital photography (MA); documentary photography (MA); fashion (MA, MFA); fibers (MA, MFA); film and television (MA, MFA); furniture design (MA, MFA); graphic design (MA, MFA); historic preservation (MA, MFA); illustration (MA, MFA); illustration design (MA); industrial design (MA, MFA); interactive design and game development (MA, MFA); interior design (MA, MFA); metals and jewelry (MA, MFA); painting (MA, MFA); performing arts (MA, MFA); photography (MA, MFA); printmaking (MA, MFA); production design (MA, MFA); professional education (MA); professional writing (MFA); sculpture (MA, MFA); sequential art (MA, MFA); sound design (MA, MFA); urban design and development (MA); visual effects (MA, MFA). Part-time programs available. Postbaccalaureate distance learning degree programs offered (no on-campus study). *Degree requirements:* For master's, thesis, internship. *Entrance requirements:* For master's, interview, 3 letters of recommendation. Additional exam requirements/recommendations for international students: Required—TOEFL (minimum score 500 paper-based; 133 computer-based). Electronic applications accepted. *Expenses:* Tuition: Full-time $28,215; part-time $3135 per course. One-time fee: $500. *Faculty research:* Urban planning for diverse communities, photovoltaics-powered environmental control, computer-aided design and virtual reality, multimedia design.

See Close-Up on page 223.

School of the Art Institute of Chicago, Graduate Division, Department of Performance, Chicago, IL 60603-3103. Offers MFA. *Entrance requirements:* Additional exam requirements/recommendations for international students: Required—TOEFL, IELTS.

See Close-Up on page 225.

Seabury-Western Theological Seminary, School of Theology, Evanston, IL 60201-2976. Offers advanced theological studies (Certificate); church music and liturgy (MTS); congregational development (D Min); preaching (D Min); theological studies (MA); theology (M Div, L Th). D Min in congregational development offered in summer only. *Accreditation:* ACIPE; ATS (one or more programs are accredited). Part-time programs available. *Degree requirements:* For master's, thesis; for doctorate, thesis/dissertation; for other advanced degree, thesis (for some programs). *Entrance requirements:* For M Div and master's, interview, sample of written work. *Faculty research:* Liturgical interpretations of baptism, trinitarian theology, congregational development, post modern biblical criticism-Matthew.

Shenandoah University, Shenandoah Conservatory, Winchester, VA 22601-5195. Offers arts administration (MS); church music (MM, Certificate); composition (MM); conducting (MM); dance (MA, MFA, MS); dance accompanying (MM); music (MS); music education (MME, DMA); music therapy (MMT, Certificate); pedagogy (MM, DMA); performance (MM, DMA, Artist Diploma); piano accompanying (MM). *Accreditation:* NASM. Part-time and evening/weekend programs available. *Faculty:* 39 full-time (19 women), 21 part-time/adjunct (9 women). *Students:* 71 full-time (42 women), 150 part-time (80 women); includes 14 minority (9 African Americans, 2 Asian Americans or Pacific Islanders, 3 Hispanic Americans), 32 international. Average age 40. 76 applicants, 96% accepted, 49 enrolled. In 2008, 24 master's, 10 doctorates, 7 other advanced degrees awarded. *Degree requirements:* For master's, comprehensive exam (for some programs), thesis (for some programs), internship (MS), recital (MM), research teaching project or thesis (MME), project (MA); for doctorate, comprehensive exam, thesis/dissertation (for some programs), dissertation or teaching project, recital; for other advanced degree, research project, recital. *Entrance requirements:* For master's, audition, minimum GPA of 2.5, writing sample, resumé; for doctorate, audition, minimum GPA of 3.25, 2 letters of recommendation, writing sample, resumé; for other advanced degree, bachelor or master's degree; minimum GPA of 2.5. Additional exam requirements/recommendations for international students: Required—TOEFL (minimum score 550 paper-based; 213 computer-based), IELTS (minimum score 6.5), Sakae Institute of Study Abroad (SISA): 550. *Application deadline:* Applications are processed on a rolling basis. Application fee: $30. Electronic applications accepted. *Expenses:* Tuition: Full-time $16,900; part-time $670 per credit. *Financial support:* In 2008–09, 154 students received support, including 26 teaching assistantships with partial tuition reimbursements available (averaging $5,870 per year); fellowships, career-

Music

Shenandoah University *(continued)*
related internships or fieldwork, institutionally sponsored loans, scholarships/grants, and unspecified assistantships also available. Support available to part-time students. Financial award application deadline: 3/15; financial award applicants required to submit FAFSA. *Faculty research:* Creative activity, performance practice, music therapy aging, composition, Motown music. Total annual research expenditures: $4,272. *Unit head:* Dr. Laurence A. Kaptain, Dean, 540-665-4600, Fax: 540-665-5402, E-mail: lkaptain@su.edu. *Application contact:* David Anthony, Dean of Admissions, 540-665-4581, Fax: 540-665-4627, E-mail: admit@su.edu.

Slippery Rock University of Pennsylvania, Graduate Studies (Recruitment), College of Humanities, Fine and Performing Arts, Department of English, Slippery Rock, PA 16057-1383. Offers literature and composition (MA); professional writing (MA). Part-time and evening/weekend programs available. *Degree requirements:* For master's, comprehensive exam (for some programs), thesis (for some programs). *Entrance requirements:* For master's, GRE General Test, MAT, minimum GPA of 2.75. *Application deadline:* For fall admission, 7/1 priority date for domestic and international students; for spring admission, 11/1 priority date for domestic and international students. Applications are processed on a rolling basis. Application fee: $25. Electronic applications accepted. *Expenses:* Tuition, area resident: Full-time $6430; part-time $357 per credit. Tuition, state resident: full-time $6430; part-time $357 per credit. Tuition, nonresident: full-time $10,288; part-time $572 per credit. Required fees: $2062; $158 per credit. *Financial support:* Career-related internships or fieldwork, Federal Work-Study, scholarships/grants, and unspecified assistantships available. Support available to part-time students. Financial award application deadline: 5/1; financial award applicants required to submit FAFSA. *Unit head:* Dr. Joseph McCarren, Graduate Coordinator, 724-738-2868, Fax: 724-738-4829, E-mail: joseph.mccarren@sru.edu. *Application contact:* Angela Piverotto, Interim Director of Graduate Studies, 724-738-2051, Fax: 724-738-2146, E-mail: graduate.admissions@sru.edu.

Southeastern Baptist Theological Seminary, Graduate and Professional Programs, Wake Forest, NC 27588-1889. Offers advanced biblical studies (M Div); Christian education (M Div, MACE); Christian ethics (PhD); Christian ministry (M Div); Christian planting (M Div); church music (MACM); counseling (MACO); evangelism (PhD); language (M Div); ministry (D Min); New Testament (PhD); Old Testament (PhD); philosophy (PhD); theology (Th M, PhD); women's studies (M Div). *Accreditation:* ACIPE; ATS (one or more programs are accredited). *Degree requirements:* For master's, thesis (for some programs), oral exam; for doctorate, thesis/dissertation, fieldwork; for M Div, supervised ministry. *Entrance requirements:* For master's, Cooperative English Test, minimum GPA of 2.0, M Div or equivalent (Th M); for doctorate, GRE General Test or MAT, Cooperative English Test, M Div or equivalent, 3 years of professional experience.

Southeastern Louisiana University, College of Arts, Humanities and Social Sciences, Department of Music and Dramatic Arts, Hammond, LA 70402. Offers music (M Mus). *Accreditation:* NASM. Part-time programs available. *Faculty:* 9 full-time (2 women). *Students:* 13 full-time (3 women), 2 part-time (0 women); includes 5 minority (all African Americans), 4 international. Average age 26. 5 applicants, 100% accepted, 5 enrolled. In 2008, 9 master's awarded. *Degree requirements:* For master's, comprehensive exam, thesis (for some programs), recital (for some programs). *Entrance requirements:* For master's, bachelor's degree in music, senior recital. Additional exam requirements/recommendations for international students: Required—TOEFL (minimum score 500 paper-based; 173 computer-based; 61 iBT). *Application deadline:* For fall admission, 7/15 priority date for domestic students, 6/1 priority date for international students; for spring admission, 12/1 priority date for domestic students, 10/1 priority date for international students. Applications are processed on a rolling basis. Application fee: $20 ($30 for international students). Electronic applications accepted. *Expenses:* Tuition, area resident: Full-time $2376. Tuition, state resident: full-time $2376. Tuition, nonresident: full-time $6876. Required fees: $1105. *Financial support:* In 2008–09, 13 students received support, including 13 research assistantships with full tuition reimbursements available (averaging $10,100 per year); career-related internships or fieldwork, Federal Work-Study, institutionally sponsored loans, scholarships/grants, unspecified assistantships, and administrative assistantships also available. Support available to part-time students. Financial award application deadline: 5/1; financial award applicants required to submit FAFSA. *Faculty research:* Music composition, pedagogical clinics, music and column editing, music theory, music performance. *Unit head:* Dr. David Evenson, Department Head, 985-549-2184, Fax: 985-549-2892, E-mail: devenson@selu.edu. *Application contact:* Sandra Meyers, Graduate Admissions Analyst, 985-549-2066, Fax: 985-549-5632, E-mail: admissions@selu.edu.

Southern Baptist Theological Seminary, School of Church Music and Worship, Louisville, KY 40280-0004. Offers church music (M Div, MCM, MM); church music and worship (DMA, DMM); worship (M Div, MAW). *Accreditation:* NASM. *Degree requirements:* For master's, comprehensive exam; for doctorate, one foreign language, thesis/dissertation. *Entrance requirements:* For doctorate, GRE General Test, MAT, auditions. Additional exam requirements/recommendations for international students: Required—TOEFL, TWE. *Faculty research:* Baptist hymnody, church music drama, keyboard literature, impact of contemporary pop culture on church music.

Southern Illinois University Carbondale, Graduate School, College of Liberal Arts, School of Music, Carbondale, IL 62901-4701. Offers composition and theory (MM); history and literature (MM); music education (MM); opera/music theater (MM); performance (MM); piano pedagogy (MM). *Accreditation:* NASM. Part-time programs available. *Degree requirements:* For master's, one foreign language, thesis or alternative. *Entrance requirements:* For master's, audition, minimum GPA of 2.7. Additional exam requirements/recommendations for international students: Required—TOEFL. *Faculty research:* Performance practices, historical research, operatic development.

Southern Illinois University Edwardsville, Graduate Studies and Research, College of Arts and Sciences, Department of Music, Program in Music, Edwardsville, IL 62026-0001. Offers music education (MM); music performance (MM). *Expenses:* Tuition, area resident: Full-time $5838. Tuition, nonresident: full-time $14,596. Required fees: $1525. *Application contact:* Dr. Darryl Coan, Director, 618-650-2012, E-mail: dcoan@siue.edu.

Southern Methodist University, Meadows School of the Arts, Division of Music, Dallas, TX 75275. Offers conducting (MM); music composition (MM); music education (MM); music history (MM); music theory (MM); performance (MM, Certificate); piano performance and pedagogy (MM); sacred music (MSM). *Accreditation:* NASM. Part-time programs available. *Faculty:* 32 full-time (11 women), 44 part-time/adjunct (16 women). *Students:* 22 full-time (10 women), 104 part-time (61 women); includes 22 minority (8 African Americans, 5 Asian Americans or Pacific Islanders, 9 Hispanic Americans), 34 international. Average age 27. 125 applicants, 70% accepted, 56 enrolled. In 2008, 26 master's, 13 Certificates awarded. *Degree requirements:* For master's, variable foreign language requirement, comprehensive exam, thesis (for some programs), project, recital, or thesis. *Entrance requirements:* For master's, placement exams in music history and theory, audition; bachelor's degree in music or equivalent; minimum GPA of 3.0; research paper in history, theory, education. Additional exam requirements/recommendations for international students: Required—TOEFL (minimum score 550 paper-based; 213 computer-based; 80 iBT). *Application deadline:* For fall admission, 3/1 priority date for domestic and international students; for spring admission, 11/1 for domestic and international students. Applications are processed on a rolling basis. Application fee: $75. *Financial support:* In 2008–09, 77 students received support, including 70 teaching assistantships with full and partial tuition reimbursements available (averaging $4,000 per year); career-related internships or fieldwork, Federal Work-Study, scholarships/grants, tuition waivers (full and partial), and unspecified assistantships also available. Financial award application deadline: 3/1; financial award applicants required to submit FAFSA. *Faculty research:* Music perception and cognition, computer-based instruction, music medicine and therapy, theoretical and historical analysis—medieval to contemporary. *Unit head:* Nancy Cochran, Director, 214-768-1951, Fax:

214-768-4669, E-mail: ncochran@smu.edu. *Application contact:* Jean Cherry, Director of Graduate Admissions and Records, 214-768-3765, Fax: 214-768-3272, E-mail: jcherry@smu.edu.

Southern Oregon University, Graduate Studies, School of Arts and Letters, Department of Music, Ashland, OR 97520. Offers MA, MS. Offered jointly with the American Band College. *Accreditation:* NASM. *Degree requirements:* For master's, comprehensive exam, thesis. *Entrance requirements:* For master's; GRE General Test, minimum GPA of 3.0.

Southwestern Baptist Theological Seminary, School of Church Music, Fort Worth, TX 76122-0000. Offers MACM, MAWSHP, MM, DMA, PhD, SPCM. *Accreditation:* NASM. Part-time programs available. Terminal master's awarded for partial completion of doctoral program. *Degree requirements:* For master's, comprehensive exam, thesis; for doctorate, comprehensive exam, thesis/dissertation. *Entrance requirements:* For master's, audition; for doctorate, MM or equivalent. Additional exam requirements/recommendations for international students: Required—TOEFL (minimum score 550 paper-based; 213 computer-based). Electronic applications accepted. *Faculty research:* Musicology, conducting, composition, pedagogy.

Southwestern Oklahoma State University, College of Arts and Sciences, Department of Music, Weatherford, OK 73096-3098. Offers music education (MM); performance (MM). *Accreditation:* NASM. Part-time programs available. *Degree requirements:* For master's, comprehensive exam, recital (music performance). *Entrance requirements:* For master's, minimum GPA of 2.5. Additional exam requirements/recommendations for international students: Required—TOEFL.

Stanford University, School of Humanities and Sciences, Department of Music, Stanford, CA 94305-9991. Offers computer-based music theory and acoustics (MA, PhD); music composition (MA, DMA); music history (MA); music, science, and technology (MA); musicology (PhD). Terminal master's awarded for partial completion of doctoral program. *Degree requirements:* For master's, variable foreign language requirement, thesis or alternative, project; for doctorate, variable foreign language requirement, thesis/dissertation (for some programs), qualifying, special area, and oral exams (PhD); composition project, lecture-demonstration exams (DMA). *Entrance requirements:* For master's and doctorate, GRE General Test, departmental theory/analysis test, samples of work. Additional exam requirements/recommendations for international students: Required—TOEFL. Electronic applications accepted.

State University of New York at Binghamton, Graduate School, School of Arts and Sciences, Department of Music, Binghamton, NY 13902-6000. Offers MA, MM. *Accreditation:* NASM. *Faculty:* 9 full-time (3 women), 27 part-time/adjunct (10 women). *Students:* 23 full-time (16 women), 5 part-time (4 women); includes 3 minority (1 African American, 2 Hispanic Americans), 3 international. Average age 25. 35 applicants, 60% accepted, 15 enrolled. In 2008, 7 master's awarded. *Degree requirements:* For master's, one foreign language, thesis. *Entrance requirements:* For master's, GRE General Test, GRE Subject Test. Additional exam requirements/recommendations for international students: Required—TOEFL. *Application deadline:* For fall admission, 4/15 priority date for domestic students, 1/15 priority date for international students; for spring admission, 11/1 for domestic students, 10/1 priority date for international students. Applications are processed on a rolling basis. Application fee: $60. Electronic applications accepted. *Expenses:* Tuition, area resident: Full-time $6900; part-time $288 per credit. Tuition, state resident: full-time $6900; part-time $288 per credit. Tuition, nonresident: full-time $10,920; part-time $455 per credit. Required fees: $1130. Part-time tuition and fees vary according to course load, program and student level. *Financial support:* In 2008–09, 11 students received support, including 2 fellowships with full tuition reimbursements available (averaging $9,500 per year), 9 teaching assistantships with full tuition reimbursements available (averaging $9,500 per year); career-related internships or fieldwork, Federal Work-Study, institutionally sponsored loans, scholarships/grants, health care benefits, and unspecified assistantships also available. Financial award application deadline: 2/15; financial award applicants required to submit FAFSA. *Unit head:* Dr. Timothy Perry, Chairperson, 607-777-2591, E-mail: tperry@binghamton.edu. *Application contact:* Victoria Williams, Recruiting and Admissions Coordinator, 607-777-2151, Fax: 607-777-2501, E-mail: vwilliam@binghamton.edu.

State University of New York at Fredonia, Graduate Studies, School of Music, Program in Music, Fredonia, NY 14063-1136. Offers MM. *Accreditation:* NASM. Part-time and evening/weekend programs available. *Degree requirements:* For master's, thesis optional.

State University of New York at New Paltz, Graduate School, School of Fine and Performing Arts, Department of Music, New Paltz, NY 12561. Offers music therapy (MS). Part-time programs available. *Students:* 17 full-time (13 women), 16 part-time (13 women); includes 6 minority (5 Asian Americans or Pacific Islanders, 1 Hispanic American), 2 international. Average age 28. 20 applicants, 65% accepted, 9 enrolled. *Degree requirements:* For master's, thesis. *Entrance requirements:* For master's, audition, minimum GPA of 3.0. Additional exam requirements/recommendations for international students: Required—TOEFL (minimum score 550 paper-based; 213 computer-based; 80 iBT). *Application deadline:* For fall admission, 5/15 for domestic and international students; for spring admission, 11/15 for domestic and international students. *Financial support:* In 2008–09, 2 students received support, including 2 teaching assistantships with partial tuition reimbursements available (averaging $5,000 per year). Financial award application deadline: 8/1. *Unit head:* Dr. Edward Lundergan, Chair, 845-257-3121, E-mail: lunderge@newpaltz.edu. *Application contact:* Prof. Mary Boyle, Coordinator, 845-257-2709, E-mail: boylem@newpaltz.edu.

State University of New York College at Potsdam, Crane School of Music, Potsdam, NY 13676. Offers composition (MM); history and literature (MM); music education (MM); music theory (MM); performance (MM). Part-time programs available. *Faculty:* 10 full-time (3 women). *Students:* 21 full-time (12 women), 4 part-time (1 woman); includes 2 minority (1 African American, 1 Asian American or Pacific Islander), 3 international. 32 applicants, 56% accepted, 18 enrolled. In 2008, 10 master's awarded. *Degree requirements:* For master's, variable foreign language requirement, thesis. *Entrance requirements:* For master's, audition, minimum GPA of 3.0. Additional exam requirements/recommendations for international students: Required—TOEFL (minimum score 550 paper-based; 213 computer-based; 80 iBT), IELTS (minimum score 6). *Application deadline:* For fall admission, 3/1 for domestic and international students. Applications are processed on a rolling basis. Application fee: $50. *Expenses:* Tuition, state resident: full-time $7390; part-time $328 per credit hour. Tuition, nonresident: full-time $12,085; part-time $552 per credit hour. Required fees: $952; $43.70 per credit hour. *Financial support:* In 2008–09, 1 student received support; teaching assistantships with full tuition reimbursements available, career-related internships or fieldwork, Federal Work-Study, scholarships/grants, and unspecified assistantships available. Support available to part-time students. Financial award application deadline: 3/1; financial award applicants required to submit FAFSA. *Unit head:* Dr. Alan Solomon, Dean, 315-267-2415, Fax: 315-267-2413, E-mail: solomon@potsdam.edu. *Application contact:* Peter Cutler, Graduate Admissions Counselor, 315-267-3154, Fax: 315-267-4802, E-mail: cutlerpj@potsdam.edu.

Stephen F. Austin State University, Graduate School, College of Fine Arts, School of Music, Nacogdoches, TX 75962. Offers MA, MM. *Accreditation:* NASM (one or more programs are accredited). Part-time programs available. *Degree requirements:* For master's, comprehensive exam, thesis optional. *Entrance requirements:* For master's, GRE General Test, audition. Additional exam requirements/recommendations for international students: Required—TOEFL. *Faculty research:* Music classroom methodology, serial music, seventeenth century sacred music, vocal pedagogy, organ duet literature.

Stony Brook University, State University of New York, Graduate School, College of Arts and Sciences, Department of Music, Program in Ethnomusicology, Stony Brook, NY 11794. Offers MA, PhD. *Entrance requirements:* For master's and doctorate, GRE, 3 letters of recommendation. Additional exam requirements/recommendations for international students: Required—TOEFL. *Application deadline:* For fall admission, 1/15 for domestic students.

Application fee: $60. *Expenses:* Tuition, area resident: Full-time $7880; part-time $328 per credit hour. Tuition, state resident: full-time $7880; part-time $328 per credit hour. Tuition, nonresident: full-time $13,250; part-time $552 per credit hour. Required fees: $848. *Financial support:* Teaching assistantships, scholarships/grants available. *Unit head:* Judith Lochhead, Graduate Director, 631-632-7330, Fax: 631-632-7404, E-mail: judith.lochhead@stonybrook.edu. *Application contact:* Judith Lochhead, Graduate Director, 631-632-7330, Fax: 631-632-7404, E-mail: judith.lochhead@stonybrook.edu.

Stony Brook University, State University of New York, Graduate School, College of Arts and Sciences, Department of Music, Program in Music History/Theory, Stony Brook, NY 11794. Offers MA, PhD. *Students:* 41 full-time (21 women), 2 part-time (both women); includes 4 minority (1 African American, 3 Hispanic Americans), 11 international. 106 applicants, 25% accepted. In 2008, 4 master's, 5 doctorates awarded. *Degree requirements:* For doctorate, thesis/dissertation. *Entrance requirements:* For master's and doctorate, GRE General Test. Additional exam requirements/recommendations for international students: Required—TOEFL. *Application deadline:* For fall admission, 1/15 for domestic students. Application fee: $60. Electronic applications accepted. *Expenses:* Tuition, area resident: Full-time $7880; part-time $328 per credit hour. Tuition, state resident: full-time $7880; part-time $328 per credit hour. Tuition, nonresident: full-time $13,250; part-time $552 per credit hour. Required fees: $848. *Unit head:* Dr. Daniel Weymouth, Chair, 631-632-7330. *Application contact:* Judith Lochhead, Director, 631-632-7330, Fax: 631-632-7404.

Stony Brook University, State University of New York, Graduate School, College of Arts and Sciences, Department of Music, Program in Music Performance, Stony Brook, NY 11794. Offers MM, DMA. *Students:* 187 full-time (110 women), 16 part-time (11 women); includes 29 minority (1 African American, 23 Asian Americans or Pacific Islanders, 5 Hispanic Americans), 77 international. 382 applicants, 22% accepted. In 2008, 10 master's, 35 doctorates awarded. *Degree requirements:* For doctorate, thesis/dissertation. *Entrance requirements:* For master's and doctorate, GRE General Test. Additional exam requirements/recommendations for international students: Required—TOEFL. *Application deadline:* For fall admission, 1/15 for domestic students. Application fee: $60. *Expenses:* Tuition, area resident: Full-time $7880; part-time $328 per credit hour. Tuition, state resident: full-time $7880; part-time $328 per credit hour. Tuition, nonresident: full-time $13,250; part-time $552 per credit hour. Required fees: $848. *Unit head:* Dr. Daniel Weymouth, Chair, 631-632-7330. *Application contact:* Judith Lochhead, Director, 631-632-7330, Fax: 631-632-7404.

Syracuse University, Graduate School, College of Visual and Performing Arts, Program in Composition, Syracuse, NY 13244. Offers M Mus.

Syracuse University, Graduate School, College of Visual and Performing Arts, Program in Conducting, Syracuse, NY 13244. Offers M Mu. *Accreditation:* NASM. Part-time programs available. *Entrance requirements:* For master's, audition, interview. Additional exam requirements/recommendations for international students: Required—TOEFL. Electronic applications accepted.

Syracuse University, Graduate School, College of Visual and Performing Arts, Program in Organ, Syracuse, NY 13244. Offers M Mus.

Syracuse University, Graduate School, College of Visual and Performing Arts, Program in Percussion, Syracuse, NY 13244. Offers M Mus.

Syracuse University, Graduate School, College of Visual and Performing Arts, Program in Piano, Syracuse, NY 13244. Offers M Mus.

Syracuse University, Graduate School, College of Visual and Performing Arts, Program in Strings, Syracuse, NY 13244. Offers M Mus.

Syracuse University, Graduate School, College of Visual and Performing Arts, Program in Voice, Syracuse, NY 13244. Offers M Mus.

Syracuse University, Graduate School, College of Visual and Performing Arts, Program in Wind Instruments, Syracuse, NY 13244. Offers M Mus.

Temple University, Graduate School, Esther Boyer College of Music and Dance, Department of Choral Activities, Philadelphia, PA 19122-6096. Offers MM. Part-time and evening/weekend programs available. *Entrance requirements:* Additional exam requirements/recommendations for international students: Required—TOEFL. Electronic applications accepted.

Temple University, Graduate School, Esther Boyer College of Music and Dance, Department of Instrumental Studies, Philadelphia, PA 19122-6096. Offers MM, DMA. Part-time programs available. *Entrance requirements:* Additional exam requirements/recommendations for international students: Required—TOEFL. Electronic applications accepted.

Temple University, Graduate School, Esther Boyer College of Music and Dance, Department of Music Studies, Philadelphia, PA 19122-6096. Offers composition (MM, DMA); music history (MM); music theory (MM). *Accreditation:* NASM. Part-time and evening/weekend programs available. *Degree requirements:* For master's, one foreign language, thesis (for some programs), compositions, recitals; for doctorate, one foreign language, thesis/dissertation, compositions, recitals. *Entrance requirements:* For doctorate, GRE or MAT. Additional exam requirements/recommendations for international students: Required—TOEFL. Electronic applications accepted. *Faculty research:* Computer composition, computer music synthesis, musical instrument digital interface (MIDI) applications.

Temple University, Graduate School, Esther Boyer College of Music and Dance, Department of Voice and Opera, Philadelphia, PA 19122-6096. Offers MM, DMA. *Accreditation:* NASM. Part-time and evening/weekend programs available. *Degree requirements:* For master's, compositions, recitals; for doctorate, compositions, 6 recitals. *Entrance requirements:* Additional exam requirements/recommendations for international students: Required—TOEFL. Electronic applications accepted.

Texas A&M University–Commerce, Graduate School, College of Arts and Sciences, Department of Music, Commerce, TX 75429-3011. Offers music (MA, MS); music composition (MA, MM); music education (MA, MM, MS); music literature (MA); music performance (MA, MM); music theory (MA, MM). *Accreditation:* NASM. Part-time programs available. *Degree requirements:* For master's, comprehensive exam, thesis (for some programs). *Entrance requirements:* For master's, GRE General Test. Electronic applications accepted.

Texas Christian University, College of Fine Arts, School of Music, Fort Worth, TX 76129-0002. Offers conducting (M Mus); music education (MM Ed); musicology (M Mus); organ performance (M Mus); piano (Artist Diploma); piano pedagogy (M Mus); piano performance (M Mus); string performance (M Mus); theory/composition (M Mus); vocal performance (M Mus); voice pedagogy (M Mus); wind and percussion performance (M Mus). *Accreditation:* NASM. Part-time and evening/weekend programs available. *Degree requirements:* For master's, one foreign language, thesis (for some programs). *Entrance requirements:* For master's, GRE General Test, audition or composition/theory, letters of recommendation. Additional exam requirements/recommendations for international students: Required—TOEFL. *Application deadline:* For fall admission, 3/1 for domestic students; for spring admission, 12/1 for domestic students. Applications are processed on a rolling basis. Application fee: $0. *Expenses:* Tuition: Full-time $17,640. *Financial support:* Unspecified assistantships available. Financial award application deadline: 3/1. *Unit head:* Dr. Richard Gipson, Director, 817-257-7602. *Application contact:* Dr. Joseph Butler, Associate Dean, College of Fine Arts, E-mail: j.butler@tcu.edu.

Texas Southern University, Graduate School, College of Liberal Arts and Behavioral Sciences, Department of Fine Arts, Houston, TX 77004-4584. Offers fine arts (MA); music (MA). Part-time programs available. *Faculty:* 2 full-time (1 woman). *Students:* 5 part-time (3 women); all minorities (all African Americans). Average age 33. 2 applicants, 100% accepted, 2 enrolled. *Degree requirements:* For master's, one foreign language, comprehensive exam, recital. *Entrance requirements:* For master's, GRE General Test, minimum GPA of 2.5. Additional exam requirements/recommendations for international students: Required—TOEFL. *Application deadline:* For fall admission, 7/15 priority date for domestic students. Application fee: $50 ($75 for international students). Electronic applications accepted. *Expenses:* Tuition, area resident: Full-time $1912; part-time $96 per credit hour. Tuition, state resident: full-time $1912; part-time $96 per credit hour. Tuition, nonresident: full-time $6302; part-time $343 per credit hour. Required fees: $3542. *Financial support:* Fellowships, teaching assistantships with partial tuition reimbursements, Federal Work-Study, institutionally sponsored loans, scholarships/grants, and unspecified assistantships available. Financial award application deadline: 5/1. *Faculty research:* Music theory, choral music, composition, percussion composition, ethnic musicology. *Unit head:* Dianne F. Jemison-Pollard, Chair, 713-313-7337, Fax: 713-313-1869, E-mail: jemison_dp@tsu.edu. *Application contact:* Dr. Gregory Maddox, Interim Dean of the Graduate School, 713-313-7011 Ext. 4410, Fax: 713-639-1876, E-mail: maddox_gh@tsu.edu.

Texas State University–San Marcos, Graduate School, College of Fine Arts and Communication, School of Music, Program in Music Performance, San Marcos, TX 78666. Offers MM. *Accreditation:* NASM. Part-time programs available. *Degree requirements:* For master's, comprehensive exam. *Entrance requirements:* For master's, minimum GPA of 2.75 in last 60 hours of course work. Additional exam requirements/recommendations for international students: Required—TOEFL (minimum score 550 paper-based; 213 computer-based). Electronic applications accepted.

Texas State University–San Marcos, Graduate School, College of Liberal Arts, Department of English, Program in Rhetoric and Composition, San Marcos, TX 78666. Offers MA. Part-time programs available. *Entrance requirements:* For master's, 3.25 in a minimum of 24 hours of undergrad English, 6 hours foreign language. Additional exam requirements/recommendations for international students: Required—TOEFL (minimum score 550 paper-based; 213 computer-based). Electronic applications accepted.

Texas Tech University, Graduate School, College of Visual and Performing Arts, Department of Theatre and Dance, Lubbock, TX 79409. Offers fine arts (PhD); theatre arts (MA, MFA), including arts administration (MFA), design (MFA), performance/pedagogy (MFA), playwriting (MFA), theatre management (MFA). *Accreditation:* NAST. Part-time programs available. *Faculty:* 10 full-time (5 women). *Students:* 37 full-time (18 women), 19 part-time (8 women); includes 6 minority (2 African Americans, 1 Asian American or Pacific Islander, 3 Hispanic Americans), 4 international. Average age 35. 42 applicants, 71% accepted, 16 enrolled. In 2008, 5 master's awarded. *Degree requirements:* For master's, variable foreign language requirement, thesis; for doctorate, thesis/dissertation. *Entrance requirements:* For master's and doctorate, GRE General Test. Additional exam requirements/recommendations for international students: Required—TOEFL (minimum score 550 paper-based; 213 computer-based). *Application deadline:* For fall admission, 3/1 priority date for international students; for spring admission, 11/1 priority date for international students. Applications are processed on a rolling basis. Application fee: $50 ($60 for international students). Electronic applications accepted. *Expenses:* Tuition, area resident: Part-time $194 per credit hour. Tuition, state resident: full-time $4648; part-time $194 per credit hour. Tuition, nonresident: full-time $11,392; part-time $475 per credit hour. Required fees: $2206; $69 per credit hour. $389 per semester. *Financial support:* In 2008–09, 41 students received support, including 27 teaching assistantships with partial tuition reimbursements available (averaging $10,419 per year); research assistantships with partial tuition reimbursements available, Federal Work-Study and institutionally sponsored loans also available. Support available to part-time students. Financial award application deadline: 4/15; financial award applicants required to submit FAFSA. *Faculty research:* New student plays program, theatre planning, dramaturgy; feminist theatre; arts administration; dance aesthetics. *Unit head:* Prof. Frederick B. Christoffel, Chair, 806-742-3601 Ext. 228, Fax: 806-742-1338, E-mail: fred.christoffel@ttu.edu. *Application contact:* Dr. James Bush, Graduate Adviser, 806-742-3601 Ext. 230, Fax: 806-742-1338, E-mail: james.bush@ttu.edu.

Texas Tech University, Graduate School, College of Visual and Performing Arts, Fine Arts Doctoral Program, Lubbock, TX 79409. Offers arts (PhD); music (PhD); theatre arts (PhD). *Accreditation:* NAST. *Students:* 50 full-time (22 women), 29 part-time (15 women); includes 9 minority (3 African Americans, 1 American Indian/Alaska Native, 1 Asian American or Pacific Islander, 4 Hispanic Americans), 10 international. Average age 36. 37 applicants, 70% accepted, 16 enrolled. In 2008, 4 doctorates awarded. *Degree requirements:* For doctorate, thesis/dissertation. *Entrance requirements:* For doctorate, GRE General Test. Additional exam requirements/recommendations for international students: Required—TOEFL (minimum score 550 paper-based; 213 computer-based). *Application deadline:* For fall admission, 3/1 priority date for international students; for spring admission, 11/1 priority date for international students. Applications are processed on a rolling basis. Application fee: $50 ($60 for international students). Electronic applications accepted. *Expenses:* Tuition, area resident: Part-time $194 per credit hour. Tuition, state resident: full-time $4648; part-time $194 per credit hour. Tuition, nonresident: full-time $11,392; part-time $475 per credit hour. Required fees: $2206; $69 per credit hour. $389 per semester. *Financial support:* Research assistantships with partial tuition reimbursements, teaching assistantships with partial tuition reimbursements available. Financial award application deadline: 4/15. *Faculty research:* Art criticism and theory, music, aesthetics, theatre arts. *Unit head:* Dr. Brian D. Steele, Director, 806-742-0700, Fax: 806-742-0695, E-mail: brian.steele@ttu.edu. *Application contact:* Dr. Brian D. Steele, Director, 806-742-0700, Fax: 806-742-0695, E-mail: brian.steele@ttu.edu.

Texas Tech University, Graduate School, College of Visual and Performing Arts, School of Music, Lubbock, TX 79409. Offers composition (MM, DMA); conducting (DMA); fine arts-music (PhD); music (MM Ed); music theory (MM); musicology (MM); pedagogy (MM); performance (MM, DMA); piano pedagogy (DMA). *Accreditation:* NASM. Part-time programs available. *Faculty:* 29 full-time (9 women), 1 part-time/adjunct (0 women). *Students:* 96 full-time (42 women), 29 part-time (14 women); includes 11 minority (3 African Americans, 1 American Indian/Alaska Native, 7 Hispanic Americans), 23 international. Average age 38. 108 applicants, 69% accepted, 34 enrolled. In 2008, 20 master's, 9 doctorates awarded. *Degree requirements:* For master's, thesis or alternative; for doctorate, thesis/dissertation. *Entrance requirements:* For master's and doctorate, GRE General Test. Additional exam requirements/recommendations for international students: Required—TOEFL (minimum score 550 paper-based; 213 computer-based). *Application deadline:* For fall admission, 3/1 priority date for international students; for spring admission, 11/1 priority date for international students. Applications are processed on a rolling basis. Application fee: $50 ($60 for international students). Electronic applications accepted. *Expenses:* Tuition, area resident: Part-time $194 per credit hour. Tuition, state resident: full-time $4648; part-time $194 per credit hour. Tuition, nonresident: full-time $11,392; part-time $475 per credit hour. Required fees: $2206; $69 per credit hour. $389 per semester. *Financial support:* In 2008–09, 96 students received support, including 71 teaching assistantships with partial tuition reimbursements available (averaging $7,591 per year); research assistantships with partial tuition reimbursements available, Federal Work-Study and institutionally sponsored loans also available. Support available to part-time students. Financial award application deadline: 4/15; financial award applicants required to submit FAFSA. *Faculty research:* Strategies for music pedagogy in grades K-12, performance practice of traditional music, role of the woman piano virtuoso, vernacular music center, voice health and culture. *Unit head:* Prof. William Ballenger, Director, 806-742-2270, Fax: 806-742-2294, E-mail: william.ballenger@ttu.edu. *Application contact:* Carin Wanner, Admissions and Scholarship Coordinator, 806-742-2270 Ext. 225, Fax: 806-742-2294, E-mail: melissacarin.wanner@ttu.edu.

Texas Woman's University, Graduate School, College of Arts and Sciences, School of the Arts, Department of Music and Drama, Denton, TX 76201. Offers drama (MA); music (MA). *Accreditation:* NASM. Part-time programs available. *Faculty:* 12 full-time (7 women), 5 part-time/adjunct (2 women). *Students:* 39 full-time (29 women), 23 part-time (17 women); includes 17 minority (4 African Americans, 1 American Indian/Alaska Native, 1 Asian American or Pacific Islander, 11 Hispanic Americans), 7 international. Average age 32. In 2008, 13 master's awarded. *Degree requirements:* For master's, thesis optional, project recital. *Entrance requirements:* For master's, music history/theory placement exam, audition, interview, sample of professional work, licensure as a music therapist, piano and aural skills. Additional exam

Music

Texas Woman's University (continued)
requirements/recommendations for international students: Required—TOEFL (minimum score 550 paper-based; 213 computer-based; 79 iBT). *Application deadline:* For fall admission, 4/1 for international students; for spring admission, 8/1 for international students. Applications are processed on a rolling basis. Application fee: $30 ($50 for international students). Electronic applications accepted. *Expenses:* Tuition, state resident: full-time $3564; part-time $198 per semester hour. Tuition, nonresident: full-time $8622; part-time $479 per semester hour. Required fees: $1158; $64 per semester hour. Tuition and fees vary according to course load. *Financial support:* In 2008–09, 7 research assistantships (averaging $9,684 per year), 1 teaching assistantship (averaging $9,684 per year) were awarded; career-related internships or fieldwork, Federal Work-Study, institutionally sponsored loans, scholarships/grants, traineeships, health care benefits, tuition waivers (partial), and unspecified assistantships also available. Support available to part-time students. Financial award application deadline: 3/1; financial award applicants required to submit FAFSA. *Faculty research:* Musical development in early childhood, little known or neglected compositions for flute (especially by women composers), relationship of visual art to piano music, pedagogical development of the singing voice, guided imagery and music. *Unit head:* Dr. James Chenevert, Chair, 940-898-2500, Fax: 940-898-2494, E-mail: jchenevert@twu.edu. *Application contact:* Samuel Wheeler, Assistant Director of Admissions, 940-898-3188, Fax: 940-898-3081, E-mail: wheelersr@twu.edu.

Towson University, College of Graduate Studies and Research, Program in Music Performance and Composition, Towson, MD 21252-0001. Offers MM. *Accreditation:* NASM. Part-time and evening/weekend programs available. *Degree requirements:* For master's, exam. *Entrance requirements:* For master's, audition, bachelor's degree in music or music education, minimum GPA of 3.0. Electronic applications accepted.

Trinity Lutheran Seminary, Graduate and Professional Programs, Columbus, OH 43209-2334. Offers church music (MA); divinity (M Div); lay ministry (MA); sacred theology (STM); theological studies (MTS); MSN/MTS; MTS/JD. *Accreditation:* ACIPE; ATS. Part-time programs available. *Degree requirements:* For master's, thesis (for some programs); for M Div, 2 foreign languages, internship. *Entrance requirements:* For master's, M Div or equivalent (STM). Additional exam requirements/recommendations for international students: Required—TOEFL (minimum score 500 paper-based).

Truman State University, Graduate School, College of Arts and Sciences, Program in Music, Kirksville, MO 63501-4221. Offers MA. *Accreditation:* NASM. *Degree requirements:* For master's, comprehensive exam, thesis or alternative. *Entrance requirements:* For master's, GRE General Test, minimum GPA of 3.0. Additional exam requirements/recommendations for international students: Required—TOEFL (minimum score 550 paper-based; 213 computer-based). Electronic applications accepted.

Tufts University, Graduate School of Arts and Sciences, Department of Music, Medford, MA 02155. Offers ethnomusicology (MA); music history and literature (MA); music theory and composition (MA). Part-time programs available. *Degree requirements:* For master's, one foreign language, thesis. *Entrance requirements:* For master's, writing sample or musical score. Additional exam requirements/recommendations for international students: Required—TOEFL (minimum score 550 paper-based; 213 computer-based; 80 iBT). Electronic applications accepted.

Tulane University, School of Liberal Arts, Department of Music, New Orleans, LA 70118-5669. Offers MA, MFA. *Degree requirements:* For master's, one foreign language, thesis (for some programs), recital or composition (MA). *Entrance requirements:* For master's, GRE General Test, minimum B average in undergraduate course work. Additional exam requirements/recommendations for international students: Required—TOEFL. Electronic applications accepted. *Faculty research:* New Orleans music, composition, piano, voice, music theatre, classical guitar.

Université de Montréal, Faculty of Music, Montréal, QC H3C 3J7, Canada. Offers composition (M Mus, D Mus); musicology and ethnomusicology (MA, PhD); orchestra conducting (M Mus, D Mus); orchestral repertoire (DESS); performance interpretation (DESS); voice and instruments interpretation (M Mus, D Mus). *Faculty:* 50 full-time (18 women), 45 part-time/adjunct (17 women). *Students:* 282 full-time (127 women), 4 part-time (3 women). 232 applicants, 43% accepted, 97 enrolled. In 2008, 54 master's, 21 doctorates, 11 other advanced degrees awarded. *Degree requirements:* For doctorate, thesis/dissertation, general exam. *Application deadline:* For fall admission, 2/1 priority date for domestic students; for winter admission, 11/1 priority date for domestic students; for spring admission, 2/1 priority date for domestic students. Application fee: $100. Electronic applications accepted. *Faculty research:* Semiology, music in Creole areas, computer-assisted composition, Argentinean tango. *Unit head:* Jacques Boucher, Dean, 514-343-6429, Fax: 514-343-5727, E-mail: jacques.boucher.2@umontreal.ca. *Application contact:* Sylvain Caron, Associate Dean Graduate Studies, 514-343-6428, Fax: 514-343-5727, E-mail: sylvain.caron@umontreal.ca.

Université Laval, Faculty of Music, Programs in Music, Québec, QC G1K 7P4, Canada. Offers composition (M Mus); instrumental didactics (M Mus); interpretation (M Mus); music education (M Mus, PhD); musicology (M Mus, PhD). Terminal master's awarded for partial completion of doctoral program. *Degree requirements:* For master's, thesis (for some programs); for doctorate, comprehensive exam, thesis/dissertation. *Entrance requirements:* For master's, English exam, audition, knowledge of French; for doctorate, English exam, knowledge of French, third language. Electronic applications accepted.

University at Buffalo, the State University of New York, Graduate School, College of Arts and Sciences, Department of Music, Buffalo, NY 14260. Offers historical musicology and music theory (PhD); music composition (MA, PhD); music history (MA); music performance (MM); music theory (MA). Terminal master's awarded for partial completion of doctoral program. *Degree requirements:* For master's, variable foreign language requirement, comprehensive exam (for some programs), thesis optional, recitals (MM); for doctorate, variable foreign language requirement, comprehensive exam, thesis/dissertation. *Entrance requirements:* For master's, GRE General Test, audition (MM), compositions, writing sample; for doctorate, GRE General Test, compositions, writing sample. Additional exam requirements/recommendations for international students: Required—TOEFL (minimum score 550 paper-based; 213 computer-based). Electronic applications accepted. *Faculty research:* Concert performance, analytical theory, musicology/history, computer composition.

The University of Akron, Graduate School, College of Fine and Applied Arts, School of Music, Program in Composition, Akron, OH 44325. Offers MM. *Degree requirements:* For master's, comprehensive exam, thesis or project. *Entrance requirements:* For master's, minimum GPA of 2.75, interview, audition. Additional exam requirements/recommendations for international students: Required—TOEFL (minimum score 550 paper-based; 213 computer-based; 79 iBT). Electronic applications accepted.

The University of Akron, Graduate School, College of Fine and Applied Arts, School of Music, Program in Music History and Literature, Akron, OH 44325. Offers MM. *Degree requirements:* For master's, comprehensive exam, thesis or project. *Entrance requirements:* For master's, minimum GPA of 2.75, interview, audition. Additional exam requirements/recommendations for international students: Required—TOEFL (minimum score 550 paper-based; 213 computer-based; 79 iBT). Electronic applications accepted.

The University of Akron, Graduate School, College of Fine and Applied Arts, School of Music, Program in Music Technology, Akron, OH 44325. Offers MM. *Degree requirements:* For master's, comprehensive exam, thesis or project. *Entrance requirements:* For master's, minimum GPA of 2.75, interview, audition. Additional exam requirements/recommendations for international students: Required—TOEFL (minimum score 550 paper-based; 213 computer-based; 79 iBT). Electronic applications accepted.

The University of Akron, Graduate School, College of Fine and Applied Arts, School of Music, Program in Performance, Akron, OH 44325. Offers MM. *Degree requirements:* For master's, comprehensive exam. *Entrance requirements:* For master's, minimum GPA of 2.75, interview, audition. Additional exam requirements/recommendations for international students: Required—TOEFL (minimum score 550 paper-based; 213 computer-based; 79 iBT). Electronic applications accepted.

The University of Akron, Graduate School, College of Fine and Applied Arts, School of Music, Program in Theory, Akron, OH 44325. Offers MM. *Degree requirements:* For master's, comprehensive exam, thesis optional, thesis or project. *Entrance requirements:* For master's, minimum GPA of 2.75, interview, audition. Additional exam requirements/recommendations for international students: Required—TOEFL (minimum score 550 paper-based; 213 computer-based; 79 iBT). Electronic applications accepted.

The University of Alabama, Graduate School, College of Arts and Sciences, Department of English, Tuscaloosa, AL 35487. Offers composition and rhetoric (PhD); creative writing (MFA), including fiction, poetry; literature (MA, PhD); rhetoric and composition (MA); teaching English as a second language (MATESOL). *Faculty:* 35 full-time (13 women). *Students:* 120 full-time (66 women), 16 part-time (12 women); includes 15 minority (8 African Americans, 2 American Indian/Alaska Native, 3 Asian Americans or Pacific Islanders, 2 Hispanic Americans), 5 international. Average age 28. 237 applicants, 20% accepted, 31 enrolled. In 2008, 21 master's, 2 doctorates awarded. *Degree requirements:* For master's, one foreign language, comprehensive exam, thesis (for some programs); for doctorate, 2 foreign languages, comprehensive exam, thesis/dissertation. *Entrance requirements:* For master's and doctorate, GRE, minimum GPA of 3.0, critical writing sample. Additional exam requirements/recommendations for international students: Required—TOEFL. *Application deadline:* For fall admission, 1/15 priority date for domestic students, 1/15 for international students. Application fee: $30. Electronic applications accepted. *Expenses:* Tuition, area resident: Full-time $6400. Tuition, state resident: full-time $6400. Tuition, nonresident: full-time $18,000. *Financial support:* In 2008–09, 7 fellowships with full tuition reimbursements (averaging $15,000 per year), 1 research assistantship (averaging $11,708 per year), 106 teaching assistantships with full tuition reimbursements (averaging $11,708 per year) were awarded; career-related internships or fieldwork, scholarships/grants, health care benefits, and unspecified assistantships also available. Financial award application deadline: 1/15. *Faculty research:* Critical theory; modern, Renaissance, and African-American literature. Total annual research expenditures: $8,282. *Unit head:* Dr. Catherine E. Davies, Director of Graduate Studies, 205-348-8499, E-mail: cdavies@bama.ua.edu. *Application contact:* Vernita W. James, Office Assistant II, 205-348-0766, Fax: 205-348-1388, E-mail: vwjames@bama.ua.edu.

The University of Alabama, Graduate School, College of Arts and Sciences, School of Music, Tuscaloosa, AL 35487. Offers arranging (MM); choral conducting (MM, DMA); composition (MM, DMA); music education (MA, PhD); music history (MM); performance (MM, DMA); theory (MM); wind conducting (MM, DMA). *Accreditation:* NASM. *Faculty:* 34 full-time (11 women), 1 (woman) part-time/adjunct. *Students:* 58 full-time (27 women), 21 part-time (12 women); includes 14 minority (6 African Americans, 4 Asian Americans or Pacific Islanders, 4 Hispanic Americans), 14 international. Average age 31. 58 applicants, 50% accepted, 21 enrolled. In 2008, 5 master's, 6 doctorates awarded. *Degree requirements:* For master's, comprehensive exam, thesis, oral and written exams, recital; for doctorate, comprehensive exam, thesis/dissertation, oral and written exams, recital. *Entrance requirements:* For master's and doctorate, audition. Additional exam requirements/recommendations for international students: Required—TOEFL, TOEFL or IELTS. *Application deadline:* For fall admission, 2/1 priority date for domestic and international students; for winter admission, 2/1 for domestic students, 2/1 priority date for international students; for spring admission, 2/1 priority date for domestic and international students. Applications are processed on a rolling basis. Application fee: $30. Electronic applications accepted. *Expenses:* Tuition, area resident: Full-time $6400. Tuition, state resident: full-time $6400. Tuition, nonresident: full-time $18,000. *Financial support:* In 2008–09, 22 students received support, including 1 fellowship with tuition reimbursement available (averaging $30,000 per year), 40 teaching assistantships with full and partial tuition reimbursements available (averaging $8,181 per year); Federal Work-Study, institutionally sponsored loans, and unspecified assistantships also available. Financial award application deadline: 7/14. *Faculty research:* Performance practice, musicology, theory, composition. Total annual research expenditures: $37,581. *Unit head:* Charles G. Snead, Director, 205-348-7110, Fax: 205-348-1473, E-mail: ssnead@music.ua.edu. *Application contact:* Dr. Marvin Johnson, Director of Graduate Studies, 205-348-6604, Fax: 205-348-1473, E-mail: mjohnson@music.ua.edu.

University of Alaska Fairbanks, College of Liberal Arts, Department of Music, Fairbanks, AK 99775-5660. Offers conducting (MA); music education (MA); music history (MA); music theory/composition (MA); performance (MA). *Accreditation:* NASM. Part-time programs available. *Faculty:* 11 full-time (3 women), 5 part-time/adjunct (2 women). *Students:* 4 full-time (1 woman), 4 part-time (2 women). Average age 40. 7 applicants, 29% accepted, 1 enrolled. In 2008, 1 master's awarded. *Degree requirements:* For master's, comprehensive exam, thesis or alternative, oral exam, oral defense. *Entrance requirements:* For master's, evaluative preliminary examination in music theory and history. Additional exam requirements/recommendations for international students: Required—TOEFL (minimum score 550 paper-based; 213 computer-based; 80 iBT). *Application deadline:* For fall admission, 6/1 for domestic students, 3/1 for international students; for spring admission, 10/15 for domestic students, 9/1 for international students. Applications are processed on a rolling basis. Application fee: $60. Electronic applications accepted. *Expenses:* Tuition, area resident: Full-time $5418; part-time $301 per credit. Tuition, state resident: full-time $5418; part-time $301 per credit. Tuition, nonresident: full-time $11,070; part-time $615 per credit. Required fees: $849; $25 per credit. $78 per semester. Tuition and fees vary according to course load and reciprocity agreements. *Financial support:* In 2008–09, 4 teaching assistantships (averaging $12,472 per year) were awarded; fellowships, Federal Work-Study, scholarships/grants, health care benefits, and unspecified assistantships also available. Support available to part-time students. Financial award application deadline: 7/1; financial award applicants required to submit FAFSA. *Faculty research:* Symphony, opera, jazz, chamber and solo performance. *Unit head:* Dr. John R. Hopkins, Department Chair, 907-474-7555, Fax: 907-474-6420, E-mail: fymusic@uaf.edu. *Application contact:* Dr. John R. Hopkins, Department Chair, 907-474-7555, Fax: 907-474-6420, E-mail: fymusic@uaf.edu.

University of Alberta, Faculty of Graduate Studies and Research, Department of Music, Edmonton, AB T6G 2E1, Canada. Offers applied music (M Mus); choral conducting (M Mus); composition (M Mus); music (PhD); organ and choral conductors (D Mus); piano (D Mus). *Degree requirements:* For master's, one foreign language, thesis; for doctorate, one foreign language, thesis/dissertation. *Entrance requirements:* Additional exam requirements/recommendations for international students: Required—TOEFL (minimum score 550 paper-based; 213 computer-based). Electronic applications accepted. *Faculty research:* Classical/Indian and West African music, popular music, choral conducting, theory and composition, musicology, applied music.

The University of Arizona, Graduate College, College of Fine Arts, School of Music, Tucson, AZ 85721. Offers composition (MM, A Mus D); conducting (MM, A Mus D); music education (MM, PhD); music theory (MM, PhD); musicology (MM); performance (MM, A Mus D). *Accreditation:* NASD (one or more programs are accredited); NASM (one or more programs are accredited). Part-time programs available. *Degree requirements:* For master's, thesis or alternative, orals; for doctorate, comprehensive exam, thesis/dissertation or alternative. *Entrance requirements:* For master's and doctorate, minimum GPA of 3.0, audition, 3 letters of recommendation, state of purpose. Additional exam requirements/recommendations for international students: Required—TOEFL (minimum score 550 paper-based). Electronic applications accepted. *Faculty research:* Music in general education, psychology of music learning, innovation in string music education, Zarzuela, Franz Liszt's work.

The University of Arizona, Graduate College, College of Humanities, Department of English, Rhetoric, Composition and the Teaching of English Program, Tucson, AZ 85721. Offers MA,

PhD. *Degree requirements:* For master's, one foreign language, comprehensive exam; for doctorate, one foreign language, comprehensive exam, thesis/dissertation. *Entrance requirements:* For master's, GRE, 3 letters of recommendation, minimum GPA of 3.0, statement of purpose, writing sample. Additional exam requirements/recommendations for international students: Required—TOEFL (minimum score 550 paper-based). Electronic applications accepted.

University of Arkansas, Graduate School, J. William Fulbright College of Arts and Sciences, Department of Music, Fayetteville, AR 72701-1201. Offers MM. *Accreditation:* NASM. *Entrance requirements:* For master's, GRE General Test.

The University of British Columbia, Faculty of Arts and Faculty of Graduate Studies, School of Music, Vancouver, BC V6T 1Z1, Canada. Offers M Mus, MA, DMA, PhD. Part-time programs available. *Degree requirements:* For master's, recital (M Mus), thesis (MA); for doctorate, one foreign language, comprehensive exam, thesis/dissertation (for some programs), public performance or composition (DMA), dissertation (PhD). *Entrance requirements:* For master's, audition/performance (M Mus); for doctorate, audition/performance (DMA). Additional exam requirements/recommendations for international students: Required—TOEFL (minimum score 580 paper-based; 237 computer-based; 93 iBT). Electronic applications accepted. *Faculty research:* Performance, composition, opera, musicology, ethnomusicology, theory.

University of Calgary, Faculty of Graduate Studies, Faculty of Fine Arts, Department of Music, Calgary, AB T2N 1N4, Canada. Offers M Mus, MA, PhD. *Degree requirements:* For master's, one foreign language, thesis; for doctorate, 2 foreign languages, thesis/dissertation. *Entrance requirements:* For master's, audition (performance), 3 compositions. Additional exam requirements/recommendations for international students: Required—TOEFL. Electronic applications accepted. *Faculty research:* Musicology, theory and composition, performance and performance practice, teaching methodology, folk music collection and analyses.

University of California, Berkeley, Graduate Division, College of Letters and Science, Department of Music, Berkeley, CA 94720-1500. Offers composition (PhD); ethnomusicology (PhD); musicology (PhD). *Degree requirements:* For doctorate, 2 foreign languages, thesis/dissertation, qualifying exam. *Entrance requirements:* For doctorate, GRE General Test, minimum GPA of 3.0, examples of work, 3 letters of recommendation. Additional exam requirements/recommendations for international students: Required—TOEFL (minimum score 570 paper-based; 230 computer-based). *Faculty research:* Historical musicology, music criticism, computer music.

University of California, Davis, Graduate Studies, Program in Music, Davis, CA 95616. Offers composition (MA, PhD); conducting (MA, PhD); musicology (MA, PhD). Terminal master's awarded for partial completion of doctoral program. *Degree requirements:* For master's, one foreign language, thesis; for doctorate, 2 foreign languages, thesis/dissertation. *Entrance requirements:* For master's, minimum GPA of 3.0; for doctorate, GRE, minimum GPA of 3.0. Additional exam requirements/recommendations for international students: Required—TOEFL (minimum score 550 paper-based; 213 computer-based). Electronic applications accepted.

University of California, Davis, Graduate Studies, Program in Performance Studies, Davis, CA 95616. Offers dramatic art (PhD). *Degree requirements:* For doctorate, 2 foreign languages, thesis/dissertation. *Entrance requirements:* For doctorate, GRE, minimum GPA of 3.25. Additional exam requirements/recommendations for international students: Required—TOEFL (minimum score 550 paper-based; 213 computer-based). Electronic applications accepted.

University of California, Irvine, Office of Graduate Studies, Claire Trevor School of the Arts, Department of Music, Irvine, CA 92697. Offers accompanying (MFA); choral conducting (MFA); composition and technology (MFA); guitar/lute performance (MFA); instrumental performance (MFA); jazz instrumental/composition (MFA); piano performance (MFA); vocal performance (MFA). *Degree requirements:* For master's, one foreign language, thesis. *Entrance requirements:* For master's, minimum GPA of 3.0. Electronic applications accepted. *Faculty research:* Composition, instrumental and choral performance, African-American music, Italian baroque music and performance practice.

University of California, Los Angeles, Graduate Division, College of Letters and Science, Department of Musicology, Los Angeles, CA 90095. Offers MA, PhD. *Students:* 29 full-time (19 women); includes 4 minority (1 American Indian/Alaska Native, 2 Asian Americans or Pacific Islanders, 1 Hispanic American), 4 international. Average age 27. 49 applicants, 10% accepted, 4 enrolled. In 2008, 6 master's, 6 doctorates awarded. Terminal master's awarded for partial completion of doctoral program. *Degree requirements:* For master's, one foreign language, thesis; for doctorate, 2 foreign languages, thesis/dissertation, oral and written qualifying exams. *Entrance requirements:* For master's, minimum GPA of 3.0, sample of written work, degree objective of Ph.D; for doctorate, minimum undergraduate GPA of 3.0, MA or equivalent in music, sample of written work. *Application deadline:* For fall admission, 12/1 for domestic and international students. Application fee: $60 ($80 for international students). Electronic applications accepted. *Expenses:* Tuition, nonresident: full-time $14,694. Required fees: $9669.50. Full-time tuition and fees vary according to course load, degree level, program and student level. *Financial support:* In 2008–09, 39 fellowships with full and partial tuition reimbursements, 14 research assistantships with full and partial tuition reimbursements, 21 teaching assistantships with full and partial tuition reimbursements were awarded; Federal Work-Study, health care benefits, tuition waivers (full and partial), and unspecified assistantships also available. Financial award application deadline: 3/1; financial award applicants required to submit FAFSA. *Unit head:* Dr. Raymond Knapp, Chair, 310-206-5187. *Application contact:* Departmental Office, 310-206-5187, E-mail: bvannost@humnet.ucla.edu.

University of California, Los Angeles, Graduate Division, School of the Arts and Architecture, Department of Ethnomusicology, Los Angeles, CA 90095. Offers MA, PhD. *Degree requirements:* For master's, one foreign language; for doctorate, 2 foreign languages, thesis/dissertation, oral and written qualifying exams. *Entrance requirements:* For master's, minimum GPA of 3.0, sample research paper, musical performance ability. Electronic applications accepted. *Expenses:* Tuition, nonresident: full-time $14,694. Required fees: $9669.50. Full-time tuition and fees vary according to course load, degree level, program and student level.

University of California, Los Angeles, Graduate Division, School of the Arts and Architecture, Department of Music, Los Angeles, CA 90095. Offers composition (MA, PhD); performance (MM, DMA). *Degree requirements:* For master's, one foreign language, thesis, final recital (MM), oral and written qualifying exams (MA); for doctorate, one foreign language, thesis/dissertation, oral/written qualifying exams; lecture recital (DMA); 2 foreign languages (PhD). *Entrance requirements:* For master's, departmental assessment exams, minimum GPA of 3.0, audition (MM); sample of work (MA); for doctorate, departmental assessment exams, minimum GPA of 3.0, audition (DMA); sample of work (PhD). Electronic applications accepted. *Expenses:* Tuition, nonresident: full-time $14,694. Required fees: $9669.50. Full-time tuition and fees vary according to course load, degree level, program and student level.

University of California, Riverside, Graduate Division, Department of Music, Riverside, CA 92521-0102. Offers composition (PhD); ethnomusicology (MA, PhD); musicology (PhD). *Faculty:* 10 full-time (3 women). *Students:* 30 full-time (10 women); includes 7 minority (3 Asian Americans or Pacific Islanders, 4 Hispanic Americans). Average age 31. 24 applicants, 63% accepted, 15 enrolled. In 2008, 5 master's awarded. Terminal master's awarded for partial completion of doctoral program. *Degree requirements:* For master's, one foreign language, comprehensive exam, thesis (for some programs), oral exams; for doctorate, one foreign language, comprehensive exam, thesis/dissertation, written and oral qualifying examination. *Entrance requirements:* For master's and doctorate, GRE General Test, minimum GPA of 3.2. Additional exam requirements/recommendations for international students: Required—TOEFL (minimum score 550 paper-based; 213 computer-based; 80 iBT). *Application deadline:* For fall admission, 5/1 for domestic students, 2/1 for international students; for winter admission, 9/1 for domestic students, 7/1 for international students; for spring admission, 12/1 for domestic students, 10/1 for international students. Applications are processed on a rolling basis. Application fee: $60 ($75 for international students). Electronic applications accepted. *Expenses:* Tuition,

nonresident: full-time $4898. Required fees: $10,362. *Financial support:* In 2008–09, 14 students received support, including fellowships with full and partial tuition reimbursements available (averaging $12,000 per year), teaching assistantships with partial tuition reimbursements available (averaging $16,500 per year); research assistantships, career-related internships or fieldwork, Federal Work-Study, institutionally sponsored loans, health care benefits, and tuition waivers (full and partial) also available. Financial award application deadline: 4/15; financial award applicants required to submit FAFSA. *Faculty research:* Composition, ethnomusicology (especially Southeast Asian and Asian-American music), cultural musicology, gender studies, performance practice. Total annual research expenditures: $60,695. *Unit head:* Dr. Walter Clark, Chair, 951-827-2114, Fax: 951-827-4651, E-mail: walter.clark@ucr.edu. *Application contact:* Dr. Tim Labor, Graduate Adviser, 951-827-5703, Fax: 951-827-4651, E-mail: timlabor@ucr.edu.

University of California, San Diego, Office of Graduate Studies, Department of Music, La Jolla, CA 92093. Offers MA, DMA, PhD. *Degree requirements:* For master's, thesis; for doctorate, thesis/dissertation. Electronic applications accepted. *Faculty research:* Computer music, extended instrumental techniques, comparison of brain wave resonances with musical resonances, composition, performance.

University of California, Santa Barbara, Graduate Division, College of Letters and Sciences, Division of Humanities and Fine Arts, Department of Music, Santa Barbara, CA 93106-6070. Offers brass (MM); composition (MA, PhD); conducting (MM, DMA); ethnomusicology (MA, PhD); feminist studies (PhD); keyboard (MM, DMA); musicology (MA, PhD); piano accompanying (MM); strings (MM, DMA); theory (MA, PhD); voice (MM, DMA); woodwinds (MM); MA/PhD; MM/DMA. *Faculty:* 28 full-time (6 women), 17 part-time/adjunct (6 women). *Students:* 71 full-time (34 women). Average age 30. 103 applicants, 31% accepted, 24 enrolled. In 2008, 13 master's, 11 doctorates awarded. Terminal master's awarded for partial completion of doctoral program. *Degree requirements:* For master's, variable foreign language requirement, comprehensive exam (for some programs), thesis (for some programs); for doctorate, variable foreign language requirement, comprehensive exam, thesis/dissertation. *Entrance requirements:* For master's, GRE, tape/audition, media (performance), portfolio (composition), writing sample, 3 letters of recommendation, statement of purpose, personal achievements/contributions statement, resumé/curriculum vitae, transcripts for post-secondary institutions attended; for doctorate, tape/audition (DMA), media (performance), portfolio (composition), writing sample, 3 letters of recommendation, statement of purpose, personal achievements/contributions statement, resumé/curriculum vitae, transcripts for post-secondary institutions attended. Additional exam requirements/recommendations for international students: Required—TOEFL (paper: 550, computer: 213, IBT: 80) or IELTS (7). Application fee: $70 ($90 for international students). Electronic applications accepted. *Expenses:* Tuition, nonresident: full-time $25,149. Required fees: $10,143. Full-time tuition and fees vary according to campus/location, reciprocity agreements and student level. *Financial support:* In 2008–09, 62 students received support, including 31 fellowships with full and partial tuition reimbursements available (averaging $7,700 per year), 2 research assistantships with full and partial tuition reimbursements available (averaging $6,200 per year), 42 teaching assistantships with partial tuition reimbursements available (averaging $8,500 per year); Federal Work-Study, institutionally sponsored loans, scholarships/grants, health care benefits, tuition waivers (full and partial), and unspecified assistantships also available. Financial award applicants required to submit FAFSA. *Faculty research:* Music theory, ethnomusicology, musicology, music performance, music composition. *Unit head:* Dr. Paul Berkowitz, Chair, Fax: 805-893-7194, E-mail: berkowit@music.ucsb.edu. *Application contact:* David L. Holmes, Student Affairs Officer, 805-893-4603, Fax: 805-893-7194, E-mail: dholmes@music.ucsb.edu.

University of California, Santa Cruz, Division of Graduate Studies, Division of the Arts, Department of Music, Santa Cruz, CA 95064. Offers music (MA, PhD); music composition (DMA). *Degree requirements:* For master's, one foreign language, thesis. *Entrance requirements:* For master's, GRE General Test. Electronic applications accepted. *Faculty research:* Western music history, new music, composition, ethnomusicology, musicology.

University of Central Arkansas, Graduate School, College of Fine Arts and Communication, Department of Music, Conway, AR 72035-0001. Offers choral conducting (MM); instrumental conducting (MM); music education (MM); music theory (MM); performance (MM). *Accreditation:* NASM. Part-time programs available. *Degree requirements:* For master's, comprehensive exam, thesis optional. *Entrance requirements:* For master's, GRE General Test, minimum GPA of 2.7. Additional exam requirements/recommendations for international students: Required—TOEFL (minimum score 550 paper-based; 213 computer-based).

University of Central Florida, College of Arts and Humanities, Department of Music, Orlando, FL 32816. Offers MA. *Accreditation:* NASM; NCATE. Part-time and evening/weekend programs available. *Students:* 10 full-time (4 women), 18 part-time (9 women); includes 5 minority (1 Asian American or Pacific Islander, 4 Hispanic Americans). *Entrance requirements:* For master's, GRE General Test. Additional exam requirements/recommendations for international students: Required—TOEFL. *Application deadline:* For fall admission, 7/15 for domestic students; for spring admission, 12/1 for domestic students. Application fee: $30. Electronic applications accepted. *Expenses:* Tuition, area resident: Full-time $6816; part-time $284 per credit. Tuition, state resident: Full-time $6816; part-time $1076 per credit. Tuition, nonresident: full-time $25,824. Required fees: $216; $9 per credit. *Financial support:* In 2008–09, 1 fellowship with partial tuition reimbursement (averaging $10,000 per year), 5 teaching assistantships with partial tuition reimbursements (averaging $8,600 per year) were awarded; career-related internships or fieldwork, Federal Work-Study, institutionally sponsored loans, tuition waivers (partial), and unspecified assistantships also available. Financial award application deadline: 3/1; financial award applicants required to submit FAFSA. *Unit head:* Dr. Johnny Pherigo, Chair, 407-823-2869, Fax: 407-823-3378, E-mail: jpherigo@mail.ucf.edu. *Application contact:* Dr. Johnny Pherigo, Chair, 407-823-2869, Fax: 407-823-3378, E-mail: jpherigo@mail.ucf.edu.

University of Central Missouri, The Graduate School, College of Arts, Humanities and Social Sciences, Department of Music, Warrensburg, MO 64093. Offers MA. *Accreditation:* NASM. Part-time programs available. *Degree requirements:* For master's, thesis (for some programs), comprehensive review, evaluation. *Entrance requirements:* For master's, minimum GPA of 2.5 in music, 30 hours of course work in music. Additional exam requirements/recommendations for international students: Required—TOEFL (minimum score 500 paper-based; 173 computer-based).

University of Central Oklahoma, College of Graduate Studies and Research, College of Arts, Media, and Design, Department of Music, Edmond, OK 73034-5209. Offers music education (MM); performance (MM). *Accreditation:* NASM. Part-time programs available. *Entrance requirements:* Additional exam requirements/recommendations for international students: Required—TOEFL (minimum score 550 paper-based; 213 computer-based). Electronic applications accepted. *Faculty research:* Opera/orchestral composition, western/world music, ethnomusicology, literature for librettos.

University of Chicago, Division of the Humanities, Department of Music, Chicago, IL 60637-1513. Offers AM, PhD. *Degree requirements:* For master's, 2 foreign languages, thesis; for doctorate, 3 foreign languages, thesis/dissertation. *Entrance requirements:* For master's and doctorate, GRE General Test. Additional exam requirements/recommendations for international students: Required—TOEFL.

University of Cincinnati, Graduate School, College-Conservatory of Music, Division of Composition, Musicology and Theory, Cincinnati, OH 45221. Offers composition (MM, DMA); music history (MM); music theory (MM, PhD); musicology (PhD). *Accreditation:* NASM. *Degree requirements:* For master's, variable foreign language requirement, comprehensive exam, thesis; for doctorate, variable foreign language requirement, comprehensive exam, thesis/dissertation. *Entrance requirements:* For master's and doctorate, GRE General Test, interview. Additional exam requirements/recommendations for international students: Required—TOEFL (minimum score 520 paper-based; 190 computer-based). Electronic applications accepted.

Music

University of Cincinnati, Graduate School, College-Conservatory of Music, Division of Ensembles and Conducting, Cincinnati, OH 45221. Offers choral conducting (MM, DMA); orchestral conducting (MM, DMA); wind conducting (MM, DMA). *Accreditation:* NASM. *Degree requirements:* For master's, comprehensive exam, conducting performances; for doctorate, one foreign language, comprehensive exam, thesis/dissertation, conducting performances, lecture recital. *Entrance requirements:* For master's and doctorate, GRE General Test, audition, interview. Additional exam requirements/recommendations for international students: Required—TOEFL (minimum score 520 paper-based; 190 computer-based). Electronic applications accepted.

University of Cincinnati, Graduate School, College-Conservatory of Music, Division of Keyboard Studies, Cincinnati, OH 45221. Offers MM, DMA, AD. *Degree requirements:* For master's, comprehensive exam; for doctorate, one foreign language, comprehensive exam, thesis/dissertation. *Entrance requirements:* For master's and doctorate, GRE General Test, audition; for AD, audition. Additional exam requirements/recommendations for international students: Required—TOEFL (minimum score 520 paper-based; 190 computer-based). Electronic applications accepted.

University of Cincinnati, Graduate School, College-Conservatory of Music, Division of Performance Studies, Cincinnati, OH 45221. Offers performance (MM, DMA, AD). MM, DMA, and AD are available for every instrument. *Accreditation:* NASM. *Degree requirements:* For master's, comprehensive exam, recitals; for doctorate, one foreign language, comprehensive exam, thesis/dissertation, recitals; for AD, recitals. *Entrance requirements:* For master's and doctorate, GRE General Test, audition. Additional exam requirements/recommendations for international students: Required—TOEFL (minimum score 520 paper-based; 190 computer-based). Electronic applications accepted. *Faculty research:* Performance, guest teaching.

University of Cincinnati, Graduate School, College-Conservatory of Music, Divisions of Opera, Musical Theater, Drama, and Arts Administration, Cincinnati, OH 45221. Offers arts administration (MA); directing (MFA); theater design and production (MFA); voice and opera (MM, DMA); MBA/MA. *Accreditation:* NAST (one or more programs are accredited). *Degree requirements:* For master's, final project. *Entrance requirements:* For master's, GMAT (MA), audition/interview. Additional exam requirements/recommendations for international students: Required—TOEFL (minimum score 520 paper-based; 190 computer-based). Electronic applications accepted.

University of Colorado at Boulder, Graduate School, College of Music, Boulder, CO 80309. Offers church music (M Mus); composition (M Mus, D Mus A); conducting (M Mus, D Mus A); music education (M Mus Ed, PhD); music literature (M Mus); musicology (PhD); pedagogy (M Mus, D Mus A); performance (M Mus, D Mus A). *Accreditation:* NASM. Terminal master's awarded for partial completion of doctoral program. *Degree requirements:* For master's, variable foreign language requirement, comprehensive exam, thesis or alternative, recital; for doctorate, variable foreign language requirement, thesis/dissertation. *Entrance requirements:* For master's, GRE General Test, GRE Subject Test (music literature), minimum undergraduate GPA of 2.75; for doctorate, GRE General Test, GRE Subject Test, audition, sample of research.

University of Colorado Denver, College of Arts and Media, Program in Recording Arts, Denver, CO 80217-3364. Offers MS. *Accreditation:* NASM. Part-time and evening/weekend programs available. *Degree requirements:* For master's, thesis or alternative. *Entrance requirements:* For master's, GRE General Test, minimum GPA of 2.75, portfolio, resumé, interview, 3 letters of recommendation. Additional exam requirements/recommendations for international students: Required—TOEFL (minimum score 500 paper-based; 173 computer-based). Electronic applications accepted.

University of Connecticut, Graduate School, School of Fine Arts, Department of Music, Field of Music, Storrs, CT 06269. Offers conducting (M Mus, DMA); historical musicology (MA); music (Performer's Certificate); music education (M Mus, PhD); music theory (MA); music theory and history (PhD); performance (M Mus, DMA). *Accreditation:* NASM. Terminal master's awarded for partial completion of doctoral program. *Degree requirements:* For master's, comprehensive exam; for doctorate, thesis/dissertation. *Entrance requirements:* For master's, GRE General Test, GRE Subject Test, audition; for doctorate, GRE Subject Test, MAT, audition. Additional exam requirements/recommendations for international students: Required—TOEFL (minimum score 550 paper-based; 213 computer-based). Electronic applications accepted.

University of Delaware, College of Arts and Sciences, Department of Music, Newark, DE 19716. Offers composition (MM); music education (MM); performance (MM). *Accreditation:* NASM. Part-time programs available. *Entrance requirements:* For master's, audition. Additional exam requirements/recommendations for international students: Required—TOEFL. Electronic applications accepted. *Faculty research:* Teaching of music.

University of Denver, Division of Arts, Humanities and Social Sciences, Lamont School of Music, Denver, CO 80208. Offers composition (MA); conducting (MA); jazz and commercial music (Certificate); music (MM); music education (MA); music history and literature (MA); Orff-Schulwerk (MA); performance (MA); piano pedagogy (MA); Suzuki pedagogy (MA); Suzuki teaching (Certificate); theory (MA). *Accreditation:* NASM. Part-time programs available. *Faculty:* 24 full-time (6 women), 42 part-time/adjunct (16 women). *Students:* 27 full-time (16 women), 38 part-time (21 women); includes 4 minority (2 African Americans, 1 Asian American or Pacific Islander, 1 Hispanic American), 9 international. Average age 27. In 2008, 14 master's, 1 other advanced degree awarded. *Degree requirements:* For master's, thesis (for some programs), recital or project, 2 years language (performance, music history and literature). *Entrance requirements:* For master's, GRE General Test, music history and theory qualifying exams. Additional exam requirements/recommendations for international students: Required—TOEFL. *Application deadline:* Applications are processed on a rolling basis. Application fee: $50. Electronic applications accepted. *Financial support:* In 2008–09, 37 teaching assistantships with full and partial tuition reimbursements (averaging $4,500 per year) were awarded; career-related internships or fieldwork, Federal Work-Study, institutionally sponsored loans, and scholarships/grants also available. Support available to part-time students. Financial award application deadline: 4/15; financial award applicants required to submit FAFSA. *Unit head:* Joseph Docksey, Director, 303-871-6986. *Application contact:* Information Contact, 303-871-6400.

University of Florida, Graduate School, College of Fine Arts, School of Music, Gainesville, FL 32611. Offers choral conducting (MM, PhD); composition/theory (MM, PhD); ethnomusicology (PhD); instrumental conducting (MM, PhD); music (MM, PhD); music education (MM, PhD); music history and literature (MM); musicology (PhD); performance (MM); sacred music (MM). *Accreditation:* NASM. *Degree requirements:* For master's, variable foreign language requirement, thesis; for doctorate, thesis/dissertation. *Entrance requirements:* For master's and doctorate, audition, GRE General Test or minimum GPA of 3.0. Additional exam requirements/recommendations for international students: Required—TOEFL (minimum score 550 paper-based; 213 computer-based). Electronic applications accepted.

University of Georgia, Graduate School, College of Arts and Sciences, School of Music, Athens, GA 30602. Offers MA, MM, DMA, PhD. *Accreditation:* NASM. *Degree requirements:* For master's, variable foreign language requirement, thesis (MA); for doctorate, variable foreign language requirement, thesis/dissertation. *Entrance requirements:* For master's and doctorate, GRE General Test. Electronic applications accepted.

University of Hartford, The Hartt School, West Hartford, CT 06117-1599. Offers choral conducting (MM Ed); composition (MM, DMA, Artist Diploma, Diploma); conducting (MM, DMA, Artist Diploma, Diploma), including choral (MM, Diploma), instrumental (MM, Diploma); early childhood education (MM Ed); instrumental conducting (MM Ed); Kodály (MM Ed); music (CAGS); music education (DMA, PhD); music history (MM); music theory (MM); pedagogy (MM Ed); performance (MM, MM Ed, DMA, Artist Diploma, Diploma); research (MM Ed); technology (MM Ed). Part-time programs available. *Degree requirements:* For master's, variable foreign language requirement, thesis (for some programs), recital; for doctorate, variable foreign language requirement, thesis/dissertation (for some programs), recital; for other advanced degree, recital. *Entrance requirements:* For master's, audition, letters of recommendation; for doctorate, proficiency exam, audition, interview, research paper; for other advanced degree, audition. Additional exam requirements/recommendations for international students: Required—TOEFL. Electronic applications accepted. *Expenses:* Contact institution.

University of Hawaii at Manoa, Graduate Division, Colleges of Arts and Sciences, College of Arts and Humanities, Department of Music, Honolulu, HI 96822. Offers M Mus, MA, PhD. *Accreditation:* NASM. Part-time programs available. *Degree requirements:* For master's, variable foreign language requirement, thesis optional; for doctorate, variable foreign language requirement, comprehensive exam, thesis/dissertation. *Entrance requirements:* For master's, diagnostic exams in acoustics theory, GRE General Test; for doctorate, diagnostic exams in music history and theory, GRE General Test. Additional exam requirements/recommendations for international students: Required—TOEFL (minimum score 540 paper-based; 207 computer-based; 76 iBT), IELTS (minimum score 5). *Faculty research:* Original compositions, nineteenth century German music, Korean and Indonesian music, piano/voice performance, Pacific music.

University of Houston, College of Liberal Arts and Social Sciences, Moores School of Music, Houston, TX 77204. Offers accompanying (MM); applied music (MM); composition (MM, DMA); conducting (DMA); music education (MM, DMA); music literature (MM); music performance and pedagogy (MM); music theory (MM); performance (DMA). *Accreditation:* NASM. Part-time programs available. *Faculty:* 28 full-time (6 women), 24 part-time/adjunct (11 women). *Students:* 105 full-time (55 women), 47 part-time (22 women); includes 20 minority (7 African Americans, 1 American Indian/Alaska Native, 5 Asian Americans or Pacific Islanders, 7 Hispanic Americans), 25 international. Average age 30. 113 applicants, 60% accepted, 49 enrolled. In 2008, 28 master's, 10 doctorates awarded. *Degree requirements:* For master's, variable foreign language requirement, thesis (for some programs), departmental comprehensive exam, recital; for doctorate, one foreign language, thesis/dissertation, departmental qualifying exam, recitals. *Entrance requirements:* For master's, GRE General Test, audition; for doctorate, GRE General Test, GRE Subject Test, audition. *Application deadline:* For fall admission, 7/1 priority date for domestic students. Applications are processed on a rolling basis. Application fee: $0 ($75 for international students). *Expenses:* Tuition, state resident: full-time $5164; part-time $287 per credit. Tuition, nonresident: full-time $10,222; part-time $568 per credit. *Financial support:* In 2008–09, 1 fellowship with full tuition reimbursement (averaging $10,000 per year), 51 teaching assistantships with full tuition reimbursements (averaging $10,000 per year) were awarded; career-related internships or fieldwork, Federal Work-Study, institutionally sponsored loans, scholarships/grants, health care benefits, and unspecified assistantships also available. Support available to part-time students. Financial award application deadline: 2/1. *Faculty research:* Twentieth century music, baroque music, history of music theory, music analysis. *Unit head:* David Ashley White, Chairperson, 713-743-3009, Fax: 713-743-3166, E-mail: daw@orpheus.music.uh.edu. *Application contact:* Howard Pollack, Director of Graduate Studies, 713-743-3314, Fax: 713-743-3166.

University of Idaho, College of Graduate Studies, College of Letters, Arts and Social Sciences, Lionel Hampton School of Music, Moscow, ID 83844-2282. Offers M Mus, MA. *Accreditation:* NASM. *Faculty:* 20 full-time, 3 part-time/adjunct. *Students:* 14 full-time, 6 part-time. Average age 28. In 2008, 8 master's awarded. *Degree requirements:* For master's, one foreign language, thesis or alternative. *Entrance requirements:* For master's, minimum GPA of 2.8. *Application deadline:* For fall admission, 8/1 for domestic students; for spring admission, 12/15 for domestic students. Application fee: $55 ($60 for international students). *Expenses:* Tuition, nonresident: full-time $10,080; part-time $336 per credit. Required fees: $5212; $267 per credit. Tuition and fees vary according to program. *Financial support:* Research assistantships, teaching assistantships available. Financial award application deadline: 2/15. *Unit head:* Dr. Kevin B. Woelfel, Director, 208-885-6231. *Application contact:* Dr. Kevin B. Woelfel, Director, 208-885-6231.

University of Illinois at Urbana–Champaign, Graduate College, College of Fine and Applied Arts, School of Music, Champaign, IL 61820. Offers music (M Mus, DMA, AD); music education (MME, MS, Ed D, PhD, CAS); musicology (PhD). *Accreditation:* NASM. *Faculty:* 73 full-time (14 women), 5 part-time/adjunct (3 women). *Students:* 292 full-time (146 women), 84 part-time (54 women); includes 27 minority (5 African Americans, 1 American Indian/Alaska Native, 16 Asian Americans or Pacific Islanders, 5 Hispanic Americans), 130 international. 554 applicants, 38% accepted, 84 enrolled. In 2008, 71 master's, 29 doctorates awarded. *Entrance requirements:* For master's and doctorate, minimum GPA of 3.0. Additional exam requirements/recommendations for international students: Required—TOEFL (minimum score 590 paper-based; 243 computer-based). *Application deadline:* Applications are processed on a rolling basis. Application fee: $60 ($75 for international students). Electronic applications accepted. *Financial support:* In 2008–09, 26 fellowships, 12 research assistantships, 135 teaching assistantships were awarded; tuition waivers (full and partial) also available. *Unit head:* Karl Kramer, Director, 217-244-2676, Fax: 217-244-4585, E-mail: kramerk@illinois.edu. *Application contact:* Jennifer Phillips, Office Manager, 217-333-1712, Fax: 217-244-4585, E-mail: jhorn@illinois.edu.

The University of Iowa, Graduate College, College of Liberal Arts and Sciences, School of Music, Iowa City, IA 52242-1316. Offers MA, MFA, DMA, PhD. *Accreditation:* NASM. *Degree requirements:* For master's, thesis (for some programs), exam; for doctorate, comprehensive exam, thesis/dissertation. *Entrance requirements:* For master's and doctorate, minimum GPA of 3.0. Additional exam requirements/recommendations for international students: Required—TOEFL (minimum score 550 paper-based; 213 computer-based; 81 iBT). Electronic applications accepted.

The University of Kansas, Graduate Studies, School of Music, Program in Music, Lawrence, KS 66045. Offers MM, DMA, PhD. *Faculty:* 56. *Students:* 117 full-time (53 women), 31 part-time (16 women); includes 20 minority (3 African Americans, 1 American Indian/Alaska Native, 6 Asian Americans or Pacific Islanders, 10 Hispanic Americans), 26 international. Average age 30. 143 applicants, 50% accepted, 39 enrolled. In 2008, 11 master's, 16 doctorates awarded. *Degree requirements:* For master's, comprehensive exam (for some programs), thesis (for some programs), recitals; for doctorate, comprehensive exam, thesis/dissertation, recitals (DMA). *Entrance requirements:* For master's, KU Musicology and Music Theory diagnostic exam, minimum GPA of 3.0, audition (performance); for doctorate, GRE (PhD); KU Musicology and Music Theory diagnostic exam, minimum GPA of 3.0, audition (DMA). Additional exam requirements/recommendations for international students: Required—TOEFL or IELTS (6.0). *Application deadline:* For fall admission, 12/15 priority date for domestic and international students; for spring admission, 5/15 priority date for domestic and international students. Applications are processed on a rolling basis. Application fee: $45 ($50 for international students). Electronic applications accepted. *Expenses:* Tuition, area resident: Full-time $6122; part-time $255.10 per credit hour. Tuition, state resident: full-time $6122; part-time $255.10 per credit hour. Tuition, nonresident: full-time $14,629; part-time $609.55 per credit hour. Required fees: $847; $70.56 per credit hour. Tuition and fees vary according to course load and program. *Financial support:* Fellowships with full tuition reimbursements, research assistantships with partial tuition reimbursements, teaching assistantships with full and partial tuition reimbursements, institutionally sponsored loans, scholarships/grants, and unspecified assistantships available. Financial award application deadline: 12/15; financial award applicants required to submit FAFSA. *Faculty research:* Musicology, music theory, church music, music composition, performance. *Unit head:* Lawrence Mallett, Chairperson, 785-864-3436, Fax: 785-864-5866, E-mail: music@ku.edu. *Application contact:* Director of Graduate Studies, 785-864-9699, Fax: 785-864-5866, E-mail: choir@ku.edu.

University of Kentucky, Graduate School, College of Fine Arts, Program in Music, Lexington, KY 40506-0032. Offers music (PhD); music composition (MM); music education (MM); music performance (MM); music theory (MA); musical arts (DMA); musicology (MA). *Accreditation:* NASM. Part-time and evening/weekend programs available. *Degree requirements:* For master's, variable foreign language requirement, comprehensive exam, thesis (for some programs); for doctorate, variable foreign language requirement, comprehensive exam, thesis/dissertation. *Entrance requirements:* For master's, GRE General Test, minimum undergraduate GPA of 2.75; for doctorate, GRE General Test, minimum undergraduate GPA of 2.75, graduate work GPA of 3.0. Additional exam requirements/recommendations for international students: Required—TOEFL (minimum score 550 paper-based; 213 computer-based). Electronic applications accepted. *Faculty research:* Musicology, music theory, jazz, music education, performance and conducting.

University of Lethbridge, School of Graduate Studies, Lethbridge, AB T1K 3M4, Canada. Offers accounting (MScM); addictions counseling (M Sc); agricultural biotechnology (M Sc); agricultural studies (M Sc, MA); anthropology (MA); archaeology (MA); art (MA); biochemistry (M Sc); biological sciences (M Sc); biomolecular science (PhD); biosystems and biodiversity (PhD); Canadian studies (MA); chemistry (M Sc); computer science (M Sc); computer science and geographical information science (M Sc); counseling psychology (M Ed); dramatic arts (MA); earth, space, and physical science (PhD); economics (MA); educational leadership (M Ed); English (MA); environmental science (M Sc); evolution and behavior (PhD); exercise science (M Sc); finance (MScM); French (MA); French/German (MA); French/Spanish (MA); general education (M Ed); general management (MScM); geography (M Sc, MA); German (MA); health sciences (M Sc, MA); history (MA); human resource management and labour relations (MScM); individualized multidisciplinary (M Sc, MA); information systems (MScM); international management (MScM); kinesiology (M Sc, MA); management (M Sc, MA); marketing (MScM); mathematics (M Sc); music (MA); Native American studies (MA); neuroscience (M Sc, PhD); new media (MA); nursing (M Sc); philosophy (MA); physics (M Sc); policy and strategy (MScM); political science (MA); psychology (M Sc, MA); religious studies (MA); sociology (MA); theoretical and computational science (PhD); urban and regional studies (MA). Part-time and evening/weekend programs available. *Degree requirements:* For doctorate, comprehensive exam, thesis/dissertation. *Entrance requirements:* For master's, GMAT (M Sc in management), bachelor's degree in related field, minimum GPA of 3.0 during previous 20 graded semester courses, 2 years teaching or related experience (M Ed); for doctorate, master's degree, minimum graduate GPA of 3.5. Additional exam requirements/recommendations for international students: Required—TOEFL. *Faculty research:* Movement and brain plasticity, gibberellin physiology, photosynthesis, carbon cycling, molecular properties of main-group ring components.

University of Louisiana at Lafayette, BI Moody III College of Business Administration MBA Program, College of the Arts, School of Music, Lafayette, LA 70504. Offers conducting (MM); pedagogy (MM); vocal and instrumental performance (MM). *Accreditation:* NASM. *Degree requirements:* For master's, thesis or alternative. *Entrance requirements:* For master's, GRE General Test, minimum GPA of 2.75. Additional exam requirements/recommendations for international students: Required—TOEFL (minimum score 550 paper-based; 213 computer-based). Electronic applications accepted. *Faculty research:* Nineteenth century American music, trumpet pedagogy, fifteenth century Renaissance polyphony, Charles Ives.

University of Louisiana at Monroe, Graduate School, College of Arts and Sciences, School of Visual and Performing Arts, Program in Music, Monroe, LA 71209-0001. Offers MM. *Accreditation:* NASM. Part-time programs available. *Faculty:* 6 full-time (2 women). *Students:* 8 full-time (2 women), 5 part-time (1 woman); includes 4 minority (3 African Americans, 1 Hispanic American). Average age 29. In 2008, 1 master's awarded. *Degree requirements:* For master's, thesis (for some programs). *Entrance requirements:* For master's, GRE, minimum GPA of 2.5. Additional exam requirements/recommendations for international students: Required—TOEFL (minimum score 500 paper-based; 173 computer-based; 61 iBT). *Application deadline:* For fall admission, 8/22 priority date for domestic students, 7/1 for international students; for winter admission, 12/12 priority date for domestic students; for spring admission, 1/17 for domestic students, 11/1 for international students. Applications are processed on a rolling basis. Application fee: $20 ($30 for international students). Electronic applications accepted. *Expenses:* Tuition, area resident: Full-time $2403; part-time $1202 per semester. Tuition, state resident: full-time $2403; part-time $1202 per semester. Tuition, nonresident: full-time $2403; part-time $1202 per semester. International tuition: $8352 full-time. Required fees: $1239.40; $141 per credit hour. *Financial support:* In 2008–09, 7 teaching assistantships with full tuition reimbursements (averaging $2,500 per year) were awarded; career-related internships or fieldwork, Federal Work-Study, and unspecified assistantships also available. Financial award application deadline: 4/1; financial award applicants required to submit FAFSA. *Unit head:* Dr. Mark R. Clark, Dean, 318-342-1569, Fax: 318-342-1599, E-mail: mclark@ulm.edu. *Application contact:* Dr. Mark R. Clark, Dean, 318-342-1569, Fax: 318-342-1599, E-mail: mclark@ulm.edu.

University of Louisville, Graduate School, School of Music, Program in Music History, Louisville, KY 40292-0001. Offers music history and literature (MM); musicology (PhD). *Accreditation:* NASM (one or more programs are accredited). Part-time programs available. *Degree requirements:* For master's, one foreign language, thesis; for doctorate, 2 foreign languages, thesis/dissertation. *Entrance requirements:* For master's, GRE General Test, music history and theory exam; for doctorate, GRE General Test. *Application deadline:* For fall admission, 3/15 priority date for domestic students; for winter admission, 10/1 priority date for domestic students. Applications are processed on a rolling basis. Application fee: $50. *Financial support:* Unspecified assistantships available. *Unit head:* Dr. Jean M. Christensen, Division Head, 502-852-0540, Fax: 502-852-0520, E-mail: jmchri01@gwise.louisville.edu. *Application contact:* Amanda Boyd, Admissions Counselor, 502-852-1623, Fax: 502-852-1874, E-mail: gomusic@louisville.edu.

University of Louisville, Graduate School, School of Music, Program in Music Performance, Louisville, KY 40292-0001. Offers performance (MM); theory and composition (MM). *Accreditation:* NASM. Part-time programs available. *Students:* 46 full-time (17 women), 8 part-time (4 women); includes 2 African Americans, 1 Asian American or Pacific Islander, 4 Hispanic Americans, 6 international. Average age 28. In 2008, 19 master's awarded. *Degree requirements:* For master's, 3 foreign languages, thesis (for some programs), recital. *Entrance requirements:* For master's, GRE General Test, music history and theory exam, jazz entrance exams (for jazz students), performance audition. *Application deadline:* For fall admission, 3/15 priority date for domestic students. Applications are processed on a rolling basis. Application fee: $50. *Financial support:* Teaching assistantships with tuition reimbursements, scholarships/grants and unspecified assistantships available. *Unit head:* John R. Jones, Division Head, 502-852-4342, Fax: 502-852-0520, E-mail: jrjone02@louisville.edu. *Application contact:* Amanda Boyd, Admissions Counselor, 502-852-1623, Fax: 502-852-1874, E-mail: gomusic@louisville.edu.

University of Maine, Graduate School, College of Liberal Arts and Sciences, School of Performing Arts, Department of Music, Orono, ME 04469. Offers MM. *Accreditation:* NASM. Part-time programs available. *Degree requirements:* For master's, rehearsal demonstration, recital. *Entrance requirements:* For master's, GRE General Test, audition. Additional exam requirements/recommendations for international students: Required—TOEFL. Electronic applications accepted. *Faculty research:* Curriculum development, rehearsal techniques, faculty development, pedagogical technology.

University of Manitoba, Faculty of Graduate Studies, Marcel A. Desautels Faculty of Music, Winnipeg, MB R3T 2N2, Canada. Offers M Mus.

University of Maryland, Baltimore County, Graduate School, College of Arts, Humanities and Social Sciences, Department of Music, Baltimore, MD 21250. Offers American contemporary music (Postbaccalaureate Certificate). Part-time programs available. *Faculty:* 9 full-time (4 women). *Students:* 3 full-time (2 women), 2 international. Average age 23. 4 applicants, 75% accepted, 3 enrolled. In 2008, 3 Postbaccalaureate Certificates awarded. *Entrance requirements:* For degree, minimum GPA of 3.0, resumé, reference letters, VHS tape of performance. *Application deadline:* For fall admission, 12/1 priority date for domestic and international students; for winter admission, 1/30 priority date for domestic and international students; for spring admission, 5/15 for domestic students, 3/1 for international students. Applications are processed on a rolling basis. Application fee: $50. *Faculty research:* Music, composition,

performance, music technology, contemporary music. *Unit head:* Dr. E. Michael Richards, Chair, 410-455-3064, E-mail: emrichards@umbc.edu. *Application contact:* Dr. Anna Rubin, Director, 410-455-3190, Fax: 410-455-1181, E-mail: airubin@umbc.edu.

University of Maryland, College Park, Graduate Studies, College of Arts and Humanities, School of Music, Program in Ethnomusicology, College Park, MD 20742. Offers MA. *Degree requirements:* For master's, comprehensive exam, thesis optional, oral defense. *Entrance requirements:* Additional exam requirements/recommendations for international students: Required—TOEFL.

University of Maryland, College Park, Graduate Studies, College of Arts and Humanities, School of Music, Program in Music, College Park, MD 20742. Offers M Ed, MA, MM, DMA, Ed D, PhD. *Entrance requirements:* Additional exam requirements/recommendations for international students: Required—TOEFL.

University of Massachusetts Amherst, Graduate School, College of Humanities and Fine Arts, Department of Music and Dance, Amherst, MA 01003. Offers music (MM, PhD). *Accreditation:* NASM. Part-time programs available. Terminal master's awarded for partial completion of doctoral program. *Degree requirements:* For master's, thesis or alternative; for doctorate, comprehensive exam, thesis/dissertation. *Entrance requirements:* For master's, GRE General Test, placement tests, original scores, research papers, audition or tape, and placement tests; for doctorate, GRE General Test, original scores, research papers, audition or tape, and placement tests. Additional exam requirements/recommendations for international students: Required—TOEFL (minimum score 550 paper-based; 213 computer-based; 79 iBT), IELTS (minimum score 6.5). Electronic applications accepted. *Expenses:* Tuition, area resident: Full-time $2640. Tuition, nonresident: full-time $9936. One-time fee: $332 full-time. Tuition and fees vary according to course load.

University of Massachusetts Lowell, College of Arts and Sciences, Department of Music, Lowell, MA 01854-2881. Offers music education (MM); sound recording technology (MM). *Accreditation:* NASM. Part-time programs available. *Degree requirements:* For master's, one foreign language, thesis. *Entrance requirements:* For master's, MAT, audition. Electronic applications accepted.

University of Memphis, Graduate School, College of Communication and Fine Arts, Rudi E. Scheidt School of Music, Memphis, TN 38152. Offers applied music (M Mu, DMA); composition (M Mu, DMA); conducting (M Mu, DMA); historical musicology (PhD); jazz and studio performance (M Mu); music education (M Mu, DMA); musicology (M Mu). *Accreditation:* NASM. Part-time programs available. *Faculty:* 34 full-time (9 women), 5 part-time/adjunct (3 women). *Students:* 69 full-time (29 women), 42 part-time (15 women); includes 18 minority (14 African Americans, 1 American Indian/Alaska Native, 1 Asian American or Pacific Islander, 2 Hispanic Americans), 27 international. Average age 32. 46 applicants, 80% accepted, 24 enrolled. In 2008, 25 master's, 13 doctorates awarded. Terminal master's awarded for partial completion of doctoral program. *Degree requirements:* For master's, comprehensive exam, thesis or alternative; for doctorate, one foreign language, comprehensive exam, thesis/dissertation, exam. *Entrance requirements:* For master's, GRE General Test or MAT, proficiency exam, audition; for doctorate, GRE General Test or MAT, proficiency exam, audition, master's degree. Additional exam requirements/recommendations for international students: Required—TOEFL. *Application deadline:* For fall admission, 8/1 for domestic students; for spring admission, 12/1 for domestic students. Applications are processed on a rolling basis. Application fee: $35 ($60 for international students). *Expenses:* Tuition, area resident: Full-time $6242; part-time $330 per credit hour. Tuition, state resident: full-time $6242; part-time $330 per credit hour. Tuition, nonresident: full-time $17,828; part-time $815 per credit hour. Required fees: $1156. *Financial support:* Research assistantships with full and partial tuition reimbursements, teaching assistantships with full and partial tuition reimbursements available. Financial award applicants required to submit FAFSA. *Faculty research:* Spanish Renaissance, twentieth century music, Project OPTIMUS, composition, musical performance, regional music, performance, performance practice, composition. *Unit head:* Dr. Patricia J. Hoy, Director, 901-678-2541, Fax: 901-678-3096, E-mail: phoy@memphis.edu. *Application contact:* Dr. John Baur, Assistant Director for Graduate Admissions, 901-678-3362, Fax: 901-678-3096, E-mail: jbaur@memphis.edu.

University of Miami, Graduate School, Frost School of Music, Department of Instrumental Performance, Coral Gables, FL 33124. Offers instrumental conducting (MM, DMA); instrumental performance (MM, DMA, AD); multiple woodwinds (MM, DMA). *Accreditation:* NASM. *Degree requirements:* For master's, thesis, recital paper, recital; for doctorate, thesis/dissertation, essay, 2 research tools, 3 recitals. *Entrance requirements:* For master's and doctorate, GRE General Test, audition. Additional exam requirements/recommendations for international students: Required—TOEFL (minimum score 550 paper-based; 213 computer-based; 59 iBT). Electronic applications accepted.

University of Miami, Graduate School, Frost School of Music, Department of Keyboard Performance, Coral Gables, FL 33124. Offers accompanying and chamber music (MM, DMA); keyboard performance and pedagogy (MM, DMA); piano performance (MM, DMA, AD). *Accreditation:* NASM. *Degree requirements:* For master's, thesis, recital paper, recital; for doctorate, thesis/dissertation, essay, 2 research tools, 3 recitals. *Entrance requirements:* For master's and doctorate, GRE General Test, audition. Additional exam requirements/recommendations for international students: Required—TOEFL (minimum score 555 paper-based; 213 computer-based; 59 iBT). Electronic applications accepted.

University of Miami, Graduate School, Frost School of Music, Department of Music Media and Industry, Coral Gables, FL 33124. Offers music business and entertainment industries (MM); music engineering (MS). *Accreditation:* NASM. *Degree requirements:* For master's, thesis, internship (MM, music business and entertainment industries), research project (MS). *Entrance requirements:* For master's, GRE General Test. Additional exam requirements/recommendations for international students: Required—TOEFL (minimum score 550 paper-based; 213 computer-based; 59 iBT). Electronic applications accepted.

University of Miami, Graduate School, Frost School of Music, Department of Musicology, Coral Gables, FL 33124. Offers MM. *Accreditation:* NASM. *Degree requirements:* For master's, thesis. *Entrance requirements:* For master's, GRE General Test. Additional exam requirements/recommendations for international students: Required—TOEFL (minimum score 550 paper-based; 213 computer-based; 59 iBT). Electronic applications accepted.

University of Miami, Graduate School, Frost School of Music, Department of Music Theory-Composition, Coral Gables, FL 33124. Offers composition (MM, DMA); electronic music (MM); media writing and production (MM); music theory (MM). *Accreditation:* NASM. *Degree requirements:* For master's, thesis; for doctorate, thesis/dissertation, essay. *Entrance requirements:* For master's and doctorate, GRE General Test, portfolio. Additional exam requirements/recommendations for international students: Required—TOEFL (minimum score 550 paper-based; 213 computer-based; 59 iBT). Electronic applications accepted.

University of Miami, Graduate School, Frost School of Music, Department of Studio Music and Jazz, Coral Gables, FL 33124. Offers jazz composition (DMA); jazz pedagogy (MM); jazz performance (MM, DMA); studio jazz writing (MM). *Accreditation:* NASM. *Degree requirements:* For master's, thesis. *Entrance requirements:* For master's and doctorate, GRE General Test, portfolio. Additional exam requirements/recommendations for international students: Required—TOEFL (minimum score 550 paper-based; 213 computer-based; 59 iBT). Electronic applications accepted.

University of Miami, Graduate School, Frost School of Music, Department of Vocal Performance, Coral Gables, FL 33124. Offers choral conducting (MM, DMA); vocal pedagogy (DMA); vocal performance (MM, DMA, AD). *Accreditation:* NASM. *Degree requirements:* For master's, 2 foreign languages, thesis, recital paper; for doctorate, thesis/dissertation, essay. *Entrance requirements:* For master's and doctorate, GRE General Test, audition. Additional

Music

University of Miami (continued)

exam requirements/recommendations for international students: Required—TOEFL (minimum score 550 paper-based; 213 computer-based; 59 iBT). Electronic applications accepted.

University of Michigan, Horace H. Rackham School of Graduate Studies, The School of Music, Theatre, and Dance, Ann Arbor, MI 48109. Offers MA, MFA, MM, A Mus D, PhD, Spec M, MBA/MM. *Accreditation:* NASM. *Entrance requirements:* For master's, audition, portfolio, interview. Additional exam requirements/recommendations for international students: Required—TOEFL (minimum score 560 paper-based; 237 computer-based). Electronic applications accepted.

University of Minnesota, Duluth, Graduate School, School of Fine Arts, Department of Music, Duluth, MN 55812-2496. Offers music education (MM); performance (MM). *Accreditation:* NASM. Part-time programs available. *Degree requirements:* For master's, comprehensive exam, thesis (for some programs), recital (MM in performance). *Entrance requirements:* For master's, audition, minimum GPA of 3.0, sample of written work, interview, bachelor's degree in music, video of teaching. Additional exam requirements/recommendations for international students: Required—TOEFL (minimum score 550 paper-based; 213 computer-based). *Faculty research:* Band composition, music aesthetics, learning theory, value theory, music advocacy.

University of Minnesota, Twin Cities Campus, Graduate School, College of Liberal Arts, School of Music, Minneapolis, MN 55455-0213. Offers MA, MM, DMA, PhD. *Accreditation:* NASM. *Degree requirements:* For master's, comprehensive exam, thesis (for some programs), foreign language (MA), recital (MM); for doctorate, comprehensive exam, thesis/dissertation (for some programs), 5 recitals (DMA); 2 foreign languages or computer languages, dissertation (PhD). *Entrance requirements:* For master's, GRE (MA); for doctorate, GRE (PhD). Additional exam requirements/recommendations for international students: Required—TOEFL (minimum score 550 paper-based; 213 computer-based; 79 iBT), IELTS (minimum score 6.5). Electronic applications accepted.

University of Mississippi, Graduate School, College of Liberal Arts, Department of Music, Oxford, University, MS 38677. Offers MM, DA. *Accreditation:* NASM. *Degree requirements:* For master's, thesis (for some programs); for doctorate, thesis/dissertation. *Entrance requirements:* For master's, GRE General Test, minimum GPA of 3.0; for doctorate, GRE General Test. Additional exam requirements/recommendations for international students: Required—TOEFL. Electronic applications accepted.

University of Missouri–Columbia, Graduate School, College of Arts and Sciences, School of Music, Columbia, MO 65211. Offers MA, MM. *Accreditation:* NASM. *Faculty:* 36 full-time (15 women), 5 part-time/adjunct (3 women). *Students:* 26 full-time (15 women), 2 part-time (1 woman), 5 international. Average age 25. 31 applicants, 58% accepted, 13 enrolled. In 2008, 16 master's awarded. *Degree requirements:* For master's, 3 foreign languages, thesis. *Entrance requirements:* For master's, GRE General Test, minimum GPA of 3.0. Additional exam requirements/recommendations for international students: Required—TOEFL (minimum score 500 paper-based; 173 computer-based; 61 iBT). *Application deadline:* For fall admission, 3/1 priority date for domestic students. Applications are processed on a rolling basis. Application fee: $45 ($60 for international students). *Financial support:* Fellowships, research assistantships, teaching assistantships, institutionally sponsored loans available. *Unit head:* Dr. Robert Shay, Department Chair, E-mail: shayr@missouri.edu. *Application contact:* Dr. Dan Willett, Director of Graduate Studies, 573-882-0933, E-mail: willettd@missouri.edu.

University of Missouri–Kansas City, Conservatory of Music, Kansas City, MO 64110-2499. Offers composition (MM, DMA); conducting (MM, DMA); music (MA); music education (MME, PhD); music history and literature (MM); music theory (MM); performance (MM, DMA). PhD is offered as an interdisciplinary degree through the School of Graduate Studies. *Accreditation:* NASM. Part-time programs available. *Faculty:* 52 full-time (20 women), 34 part-time/adjunct (19 women). *Students:* 151 full-time (73 women), 110 part-time (59 women); includes 17 minority (9 African Americans, 2 American Indian/Alaska Native, 3 Asian Americans or Pacific Islanders, 3 Hispanic Americans), 64 international. Average age 29. 146 applicants, 59% accepted, 80 enrolled. In 2008, 47 master's, 12 doctorates awarded. *Degree requirements:* For master's, variable foreign language requirement, comprehensive exam, thesis (for some programs); for doctorate, variable foreign language requirement, comprehensive exam, thesis/dissertation or alternative. *Entrance requirements:* For master's, minimum GPA of 3.0 in major, auditions (performance); for doctorate, minimum graduate GPA of 3.5, auditions (performance degrees), portfolio of compositions. Additional exam requirements/recommendations for international students: Required—TOEFL (minimum score 550 paper-based; 213 computer-based; 80 iBT). *Application deadline:* For fall admission, 1/15 priority date for domestic students, 1/15 for international students. Application fee: $45 ($50 for international students). *Expenses:* Tuition, state resident: full-time $5376; part-time $298.70 per credit hour. Tuition, nonresident: full-time $13,882; part-time $771.20 per credit hour. Required fees: $640.28; $34.65 per contact hour. $30 per semester. Tuition and fees vary according to course load and program. *Financial support:* In 2008–09, 51 teaching assistantships with partial tuition reimbursements (averaging $8,217 per year) were awarded; fellowships with partial tuition reimbursements, career-related internships or fieldwork, Federal Work-Study, institutionally sponsored loans, scholarships/grants, tuition waivers (partial), and unspecified assistantships also available. Support available to part-time students. Financial award application deadline: 3/1; financial award applicants required to submit FAFSA. *Faculty research:* Electro-acoustic composition, affective music responses, American music theatre, Russian choral music, music therapy and Alzheimer's. Total annual research expenditures: $8,559. *Unit head:* Peter Witte, Dean, 816-235-2731, Fax: 816-235-5265, E-mail: wittep@umkc.edu. *Application contact:* James Elswick, Associate Director, 816-235-2932, Fax: 816-235-5264, E-mail: cadmissions@umkc.edu.

The University of Montana, Graduate School, School of Fine Arts, Department of Music, Missoula, MT 59812-0002. Offers music (MM), including composition/technology, music education, musical theater, performance. *Accreditation:* NASM. *Entrance requirements:* For master's, GRE General Test, GRE Subject Test, portfolio.

University of Nebraska at Omaha, Graduate Studies and Research, College of Communication, Fine Arts and Media, Department of Music, Omaha, NE 68182. Offers MM. *Accreditation:* NASM. Part-time and evening/weekend programs available. *Degree requirements:* For master's, comprehensive exam, thesis (for some programs). *Entrance requirements:* For master's, departmental diagnostic exam, minimum GPA of 3.0. Additional exam requirements/recommendations for international students: Required—TOEFL (minimum score 500 paper-based; 173 computer-based; 61 iBT). Electronic applications accepted.

University of Nebraska–Lincoln, Graduate College, College of Arts and Sciences, Department of English, Lincoln, NE 68588-0333. Offers composition and rhetoric (MA, PhD); creative writing (MA, PhD); literature studies (MA, PhD). *Faculty:* 39 full-time (23 women). *Students:* 77 full-time (57 women), 54 part-time (36 women); includes 5 minority (3 African Americans, 2 Hispanic Americans), 6 international. In 2008, 11 master's, 15 doctorates awarded. *Degree requirements:* For master's, thesis optional; for doctorate, one foreign language, comprehensive exam, thesis/dissertation. *Entrance requirements:* For master's, writing sample; for doctorate, GRE General Test, writing sample. Additional exam requirements/recommendations for international students: Required—TOEFL (minimum score 600 paper-based; 250 computer-based). *Application deadline:* For fall admission, 1/15 for domestic and international students. Application fee: $40. Electronic applications accepted. *Expenses:* Tuition, state resident: full-time $4275; part-time $237.50 per credit hour. Tuition, nonresident: full-time $11,525; part-time $640.25 per credit hour. Required fees: $1068; $10.35 per credit hour. $440.70 per semester. Tuition and fees vary according to course load and program. *Financial support:* Fellowships, research assistantships, teaching assistantships, Federal Work-Study, health care benefits, and unspecified assistantships available. Support available to part-time students. Financial award application deadline: 1/15. *Faculty research:* Creative writing, composition and rhetoric, women's studies, North American literature, medieval/Renaissance studies. *Unit*

head: Dr. Linda Pratt, Chair, 402-472-3191, Fax: 402-472-1123. *Application contact:* Ginny Gross, Director of Graduate Admissions, 402-472-2878, Fax: 402-472-0589, E-mail: grad_admissions@unl.edu.

University of Nebraska–Lincoln, Graduate College, College of Fine and Performing Arts, School of Music, Lincoln, NE 68588. Offers composition (MM, DMA); conducting (MM, DMA); music education (MM, PhD); music history (MM); music theory (MM); performance (MM, DMA); piano pedagogy (MM); woodwind specialties (MM). *Accreditation:* NASM. *Faculty:* 37 full-time (11 women). *Students:* 73 full-time (30 women), 22 part-time (9 women); includes 2 African Americans, 1 Asian American or Pacific Islander, 1 Hispanic American, 16 international. Average age 31. In 2008, 30 master's, 12 doctorates awarded. *Degree requirements:* For master's, thesis optional; for doctorate, comprehensive exam, thesis/dissertation. *Entrance requirements:* For master's and doctorate, audition. Additional exam requirements/recommendations for international students: Required—TOEFL. *Application deadline:* For fall admission, 3/1 for domestic and international students; for spring admission, 12/1 for domestic students, 9/15 for international students. Application fee: $40. Electronic applications accepted. *Expenses:* Tuition, state resident: full-time $4275; part-time $237.50 per credit hour. Tuition, nonresident: full-time $11,525; part-time $640.25 per credit hour. Required fees: $1068; $10.35 per credit hour. $440.70 per semester. Tuition and fees vary according to course load and program. *Financial support:* Fellowships, research assistantships, teaching assistantships, Federal Work-Study and health care benefits available. Support available to part-time students. Financial award application deadline: 2/15. *Faculty research:* Mozart, Tchaikovsky, Josquin des Prez, practice of J. S. Bach's organ works, instructional strategies in music education. *Unit head:* Dr. Robert Fought, Interim Director, 402-472-2503. *Application contact:* Ginny Gross, Director of Graduate Admissions, 402-472-2878, Fax: 402-472-0589, E-mail: grad_admissions@unl.edu.

University of Nevada, Las Vegas, Graduate College, College of Fine Arts, Department of Music, Las Vegas, NV 89154-5025. Offers music (MM); musical arts (DMA). *Accreditation:* NASM. Part-time programs available. *Faculty:* 28 full-time (8 women), 19 part-time/adjunct (5 women). *Students:* 55 full-time (22 women), 37 part-time (17 women); includes 9 minority (2 African Americans, 1 American Indian/Alaska Native, 2 Asian Americans or Pacific Islanders, 4 Hispanic Americans), 13 international. Average age 31. 59 applicants, 90% accepted, 31 enrolled. In 2008, 26 master's, 2 doctorates awarded. *Degree requirements:* For master's, thesis optional, oral and/or written comprehensive exam; for doctorate, one foreign language, comprehensive exam, lecture-recital and document. *Entrance requirements:* Additional exam requirements/recommendations for international students: Required—TOEFL (minimum score 550 paper-based; 213 computer-based; 80 iBT), IELTS (minimum score 7). *Application deadline:* For fall admission, 5/1 priority date for domestic and international students; for spring admission, 11/15 priority date for domestic students, 10/1 for international students. Applications are processed on a rolling basis. Application fee: $60 ($75 for international students). Electronic applications accepted. *Expenses:* Tuition, state resident: full-time $1414; part-time $198 per credit. Tuition, nonresident: full-time $12,509; part-time $415.75 per credit. International tuition: $14,249 full-time. Required fees: $4 per credit. $252 per semester. Tuition and fees vary according to course load. *Financial support:* In 2008–09, 38 students received support, including 1 research assistantship with partial tuition reimbursement available (averaging $10,000 per year), 37 teaching assistantships with partial tuition reimbursements available (averaging $10,428 per year); institutionally sponsored loans, scholarships/grants, health care benefits, and unspecified assistantships also available. Financial award application deadline: 3/1. *Faculty research:* Richard Wagner, 17th-18th century repertoires, reception history; commissioned opera "Red Earth—Hunger"; music for winds and percussion; history of Las Vegas hotel bands 1940-1989; incorporation of technology into the music classroom. *Unit head:* Dr. Jonathan Good, Chair/Professor, 702-895-3332, Fax: 702-895-4239, E-mail: janathan.good@unlv.edu. *Application contact:* Graduate College Admissions Evaluator, 702-895-3320, Fax: 702-895-4180, E-mail: gradcollege@unlv.edu.

University of Nevada, Reno, Graduate School, College of Liberal Arts, Department of Music, Reno, NV 89557. Offers MA, MM. *Accreditation:* NASM. *Faculty:* 16 full-time (4 women). *Students:* 9 full-time (3 women), 11 part-time (6 women); includes 2 minority (1 African American, 1 Asian American or Pacific Islander), 1 international. Average age 33. 14 applicants, 86% accepted, 8 enrolled. In 2008, 9 master's awarded. *Degree requirements:* For master's, thesis optional. *Entrance requirements:* For master's, minimum GPA of 2.75. Additional exam requirements/recommendations for international students: Required—TOEFL (minimum score 500 paper-based; 173 computer-based; 61 iBT), IELTS (minimum score 6), TOFEL or IELTS. *Application deadline:* For fall admission, 3/1 priority date for domestic and international students; for spring admission, 11/1 priority date for domestic and international students. Applications are processed on a rolling basis. Application fee: $60 ($95 for international students). Electronic applications accepted. *Expenses:* Tuition, state resident: full-time $1710; part-time $1140 per semester. Tuition, nonresident: full-time $7115. Required fees: $158 per semester. *Financial support:* In 2008–09, 12 teaching assistantships with partial tuition reimbursements (averaging $14,000 per year) were awarded; Federal Work-Study, institutionally sponsored loans, health care benefits, and unspecified assistantships also available. Financial award application deadline: 3/1; financial award applicants required to submit FAFSA. *Faculty research:* Performance, conducting, music composition and arranging. Total annual research expenditures: $21,690. *Unit head:* Dr. Andrea Lenz, Graduate Program Director, 775-784-6145, E-mail: alenz@unr.edu. *Application contact:* Michele Sandberg, Application Contact, 775-784-7026, Fax: 775-784-6064, E-mail: gradschool@unr.edu.

University of New Hampshire, Graduate School, College of Liberal Arts, Department of Music, Durham, NH 03824. Offers music education (MA); music history (MA). *Accreditation:* NASM. *Faculty:* 17 full-time (3 women). *Students:* 6 full-time (4 women), 5 part-time (2 women). Average age 35. 6 applicants, 83% accepted, 3 enrolled. In 2008, 1 master's awarded. *Degree requirements:* For master's, one foreign language. *Entrance requirements:* For master's, audition. Additional exam requirements/recommendations for international students: Required—TOEFL (minimum score 550 paper-based; 213 computer-based; 80 iBT). *Application deadline:* For fall admission, 4/1 priority date for domestic students; for winter admission, 12/1 for domestic students. Applications are processed on a rolling basis. Application fee: $60. Electronic applications accepted. *Expenses:* Tuition, area resident: Full-time $9720; part-time $540 per credit hour. Tuition, nonresident: full-time $23,200; part-time $954 per credit hour. Required fees: $1446; $361.50 per term. *Financial support:* In 2008–09, 6 students received support, including 6 teaching assistantships; fellowships, research assistantships, career-related internships or fieldwork, Federal Work-Study, scholarships/grants, and tuition waivers (full and partial) also available. Support available to part-time students. Financial award application deadline: 2/15. *Unit head:* Dr. Rob Stibler, Chairperson, 603-862-2418. *Application contact:* Dr. Isabel Gray, Administrative Assistant, 603-862-2418, E-mail: grad.music@unh.edu.

University of New Mexico, Graduate School, College of Fine Arts, Department of Music, Albuquerque, NM 87131-2039. Offers M Mu. *Accreditation:* NASM. Part-time programs available. *Degree requirements:* For master's, thesis (for some programs), oral exam, recital in some programs. *Entrance requirements:* For master's, placement exams in music history and theory. Additional exam requirements/recommendations for international students: Required—TOEFL (minimum score 550 paper-based; 213 computer-based). Electronic applications accepted. *Faculty research:* Opera, twentieth century and contemporary music, performance, conducting.

University of New Orleans, Graduate School, College of Liberal Arts, Department of Music, New Orleans, LA 70148. Offers MM. *Accreditation:* NASM. Evening/weekend programs available. *Degree requirements:* For master's, recital. *Entrance requirements:* For master's, GRE General Test, audition. Additional exam requirements/recommendations for international students: Required—TOEFL (minimum score 550 paper-based; 213 computer-based; 79 iBT). Electronic applications accepted. *Faculty research:* American jazz, Czech music, Hispanic music.

The University of North Carolina at Chapel Hill, Graduate School, College of Arts and Sciences, Department of Music, Chapel Hill, NC 27599. Offers MA, PhD. Terminal master's awarded for partial completion of doctoral program. *Degree requirements:* For master's, one foreign language, thesis, theory and keyboard exams; for doctorate, 2 foreign languages, comprehensive exam, thesis/dissertation, theory and keyboard exams. *Entrance requirements:* For master's and doctorate, GRE General Test, department diagnostic exam, minimum GPA of 3.0. Additional exam requirements/recommendations for international students: Required—TOEFL. Electronic applications accepted. *Expenses:* Contact institution. *Faculty research:* Music theory, ethnomusicology, music history.

The University of North Carolina at Greensboro, Graduate School, School of Music, Greensboro, NC 27412-5001. Offers composition (MM); education (MM); music education (PhD); performance (MM, DMA). *Accreditation:* NASM. *Degree requirements:* For master's, variable foreign language requirement, thesis (for some programs), recital; for doctorate, comprehensive exam, thesis/dissertation, diagnostic exam, recital. *Entrance requirements:* For master's, GRE General Test, NTE, audition; for doctorate, GRE General Test, GRE Subject Test (music), audition. Additional exam requirements/recommendations for international students: Required—TOEFL. Electronic applications accepted.

University of North Carolina School of the Arts, School of Filmmaking, Winston-Salem, NC 27127-2188. Offers film music composition (MFA). *Faculty:* 3 full-time (0 women). *Students:* 7 full-time (0 women); includes 1 minority (Asian American or Pacific Islander). Average age 25. 6 applicants, 33% accepted, 2 enrolled. In 2008, 3 master's awarded. *Entrance requirements:* For master's, audition, performance, portfolio, interview. *Application deadline:* For fall admission, 4/1 priority date for domestic students. Applications are processed on a rolling basis. Application fee: $60 ($100 for international students). *Expenses:* Tuition, area resident: Full-time $3797. Tuition, state resident: full-time $3797. Tuition, nonresident: full-time $15,670. Required fees: $1791. *Financial support:* In 2008–09, fellowships (averaging $2,000 per year); career-related internships or fieldwork and Federal Work-Study also available. Support available to part-time students. Financial award application deadline: 3/15; financial award applicants required to submit FAFSA. *Unit head:* Jordan Kerner, Dean, 336-770-1330, Fax: 336-770-1339, E-mail: kernerj@uncsa.edu. *Application contact:* Sheeler Lawson, Director of Admissions, 336-770-3290, Fax: 336-770-3370, E-mail: admissions@uncsa.edu.

University of North Carolina School of the Arts, School of Music, Winston-Salem, NC 27127-2188. Offers music performance (MM), including chamber music performance, guitar performance, opera performance, organ performance, percussion performance, piano performance, strings performance, wind and brass performance; orchestral conducting (MM). *Faculty:* 30 full-time (9 women), 11 part-time/adjunct (3 women). *Students:* 60 full-time (19 women); includes 5 minority (3 African Americans, 1 American Indian/Alaska Native, 1 Hispanic American), 26 international. Average age 25. In 2008, 12 master's awarded. *Entrance requirements:* For master's, audition (music performance), interview, original score. *Application deadline:* For fall admission, 4/1 priority date for domestic students. Applications are processed on a rolling basis. Application fee: $60 ($100 for international students). *Expenses:* Tuition, area resident: Full-time $3797. Tuition, state resident: full-time $3797. Tuition, nonresident: full-time $15,670. Required fees: $1791. *Financial support:* In 2008–09, 8 fellowships with partial tuition reimbursements (averaging $2,000 per year), 10 teaching assistantships with partial tuition reimbursements (averaging $3,000 per year) were awarded; career-related internships or fieldwork and Federal Work-Study also available. Support available to part-time students. Financial award application deadline: 3/15; financial award applicants required to submit FAFSA. *Unit head:* Dr. Michael Rothkopf, Dean, 336-770-3251, Fax: 336-770-3248, E-mail: rothk@uncsa.edu. *Application contact:* Sheeler Lawson, Director of Admissions, 336-770-3290, Fax: 336-770-3370, E-mail: admissions@uncsa.edu.

University of North Dakota, Graduate School, College of Arts and Sciences, Department of Music, Grand Forks, ND 58202. Offers music (M Mus); music education (M Mus, DMEd). *Accreditation:* NASM. Part-time programs available. *Degree requirements:* For master's, comprehensive exam, thesis or alternative. *Entrance requirements:* For master's, minimum GPA of 3.0. Additional exam requirements/recommendations for international students: Required—TOEFL (minimum score 550 paper-based; 213 computer-based; 79 iBT), IELTS (minimum score 6.5). Electronic applications accepted.

University of Northern Colorado, Graduate School, College of Performing and Visual Arts, School of Music, Greeley, CO 80639. Offers collaborative keyboard (MM); conducting (MM); instrumental performance (MM); jazz studies (MM); music conducting (DA); music education (MM, DA); music history and literature (MM, DA); music performance (DA); music theory and composition (MM, DA); vocal performance (MM). *Accreditation:* NASM; NCATE (one or more programs are accredited). Part-time programs available. *Faculty:* 30 full-time (8 women). *Students:* 66 full-time (24 women), 23 part-time (10 women); includes 6 minority (2 African Americans, 2 Asian Americans or Pacific Islanders, 2 Hispanic Americans), 13 international. Average age 32. 78 applicants, 87% accepted, 39 enrolled. In 2008, 23 master's, 8 doctorates awarded. *Degree requirements:* For master's, comprehensive exam, thesis or alternative; for doctorate, comprehensive exam, thesis/dissertation. *Entrance requirements:* For master's, audition; for doctorate, GRE General Test, audition, 3 letters of recommendation. *Application deadline:* Applications are processed on a rolling basis. Application fee: $50 ($60 for international students). Electronic applications accepted. *Expenses:* Tuition, state resident: full-time $4370; part-time $242.75 per credit hour. Tuition, nonresident: full-time $12,366; part-time $687 per credit hour. Required fees: $664.20; $36.90 per credit hour. *Financial support:* In 2008–09, 30 research assistantships (averaging $4,101 per year), 17 teaching assistantships (averaging $5,787 per year) were awarded; fellowships, unspecified assistantships also available. Financial award application deadline: 3/1; financial award applicants required to submit FAFSA. *Unit head:* David Caffey, Director, 970-351-2679. *Application contact:* Linda Sisson, Graduate Student Admission Coordinator, 970-351-1807, Fax: 970-351-2371, E-mail: linda.sisson@unco.edu.

University of Northern Iowa, Graduate College, College of Humanities and Fine Arts, School of Music, Program in Music, Cedar Falls, IA 50614. Offers composition (MM); conducting (MM); music (MM); music history (MM); performance (MM). *Accreditation:* NASM. *Students:* 23 full-time (16 women), 8 part-time (6 women); includes 2 minority (1 African American, 1 Hispanic American), 8 international. 28 applicants, 54% accepted, 12 enrolled. In 2008, 10 master's awarded. *Degree requirements:* For master's, comprehensive exam, thesis or alternative. *Entrance requirements:* For master's, written diagnostic exam in theory, music history, expository writing skills and in the area of claimed competency, portfolio, tape recordings of compositions, in person auditions, minimum GPA of 3.0. Additional exam requirements/recommendations for international students: Required—TOEFL (minimum score 500 paper-based; 180 computer-based; 61 iBT). *Application deadline:* For fall admission, 8/1 priority date for domestic students. Applications are processed on a rolling basis. Application fee: $30 ($50 for international students). Electronic applications accepted. *Expenses:* Tuition, state resident: full-time $6446. Tuition, nonresident: full-time $14,874. Required fees: $852. *Financial support:* Career-related internships or fieldwork, Federal Work-Study, and tuition waivers (full and partial) available. Support available to part-time students. Financial award application deadline: 2/1. *Unit head:* Dr. Rebecca Burkhardt, Coordinator, 319-273-4723, Fax: 319-273-7320, E-mail: rebecca.burkhardt@uni.edu. *Application contact:* Laurie S. Russell, Record Analyst, 319-273-2623, Fax: 319-273-6792, E-mail: laurie.russell@uni.edu.

University of North Texas, Robert B. Toulouse School of Graduate Studies, College of Music, Denton, TX 76203. Offers composition (MM, DMA); jazz studies (MM); music (MA); music education (MM, MME, PhD); music theory (MM, PhD); musicology (MM, PhD); performance (MM, DMA). *Accreditation:* NASM. *Entrance requirements:* Additional exam requirements/recommendations for international students: Required—proof of English language proficiency; Recommended—TOEFL (minimum score 550 paper-based; 213 computer-based). *Faculty research:* Electro-acoustical music, intermedia, music and medicine, music performance.

University of Oklahoma, Graduate College, College of Fine Arts, School of Music, Norman, OK 73019-0390. Offers choral conducting (M Mus); conducting (M Mus Ed, DMA); general (M Mus Ed); instrumental (M Mus Ed); instrumental conducting (M Mus); music composition (M Mus, DMA); music education (M Mus Ed, PhD); music theory (M Mus); musicology (M Mus); organ (M Mus, DMA); piano (M Mus, DMA); voice (M Mus, DMA); wind/percussion/string (M Mus, DMA). *Accreditation:* NASM. *Faculty:* 54 full-time (16 women). *Students:* 101 full-time (57 women), 68 part-time (37 women); includes 17 minority (3 African Americans, 3 American Indian/Alaska Native, 6 Asian Americans or Pacific Islanders, 5 Hispanic Americans), 17 international. 84 applicants, 69% accepted, 30 enrolled. In 2008, 30 master's, 12 doctorates awarded. *Degree requirements:* For master's, variable foreign language requirement, thesis (for some programs), departmental qualifying exam, oral and preliminary exams; for doctorate, variable foreign language requirement, thesis/dissertation, departmental qualifying exam, general and oral exams. *Entrance requirements:* For master's, audition, BA in music, minimum GPA of 3.0; for doctorate, audition, minimum GPA of 3.0. Additional exam requirements/recommendations for international students: Required—TOEFL (minimum score 550 paper-based; 213 computer-based). *Application deadline:* For fall admission, 6/1 priority date for domestic students, 4/1 for international students; for spring admission, 11/1 for domestic students, 9/1 for international students. Applications are processed on a rolling basis. Application fee: $40 ($90 for international students). Electronic applications accepted. *Expenses:* Tuition, state resident: full-time $3744; part-time $156 per credit hour. Tuition, nonresident: full-time $13,577; part-time $565.70 per credit hour. Required fees: $2415.40; $90.10 per credit hour. *Financial support:* In 2008–09, 67 students received support, including 9 fellowships with full tuition reimbursements available (averaging $5,000 per year), 26 research assistantships with partial tuition reimbursements available (averaging $10,765 per year), 71 teaching assistantships with partial tuition reimbursements available (averaging $10,051 per year); unspecified assistantships also available. Financial award application deadline: 4/7; financial award applicants required to submit FAFSA. *Faculty research:* Piano pedagogy; vocal and instrumental performance; music education. Total annual research expenditures: $82,883. *Unit head:* Dr. Steven Curtis, Director, 405-325-2081, Fax: 405-325-7574, E-mail: scurtis@ou.edu. *Application contact:* Jan Russell, Office Assistant, 405-325-5393, Fax: 405-325-7574, E-mail: jrussell@ou.edu.

University of Oregon, Graduate School, School of Music, Program in Music, Eugene, OR 97403. Offers composition (M Mus, DMA, PhD); conducting (M Mus); jazz studies (M Mus); music (MA), including music history, music theory; music history (PhD); music theory (PhD); performance (M Mus, DMA); piano pedagogy (M Mus). *Entrance requirements:* For master's, minimum GPA of 3.0, audition (performance applicants), videotape or interview (conducting applicants); for doctorate, GRE General Test, minimum GPA of 3.0, audition (performance applicants), videotape or interview (conducting applicants). Additional exam requirements/recommendations for international students: Required—TOEFL.

University of Ottawa, Faculty of Graduate and Postdoctoral Studies, Faculty of Arts, Department of Music, Ottawa, ON K1N 6N5, Canada. Offers music (M Mus, MA); orchestral studies (Certificate); piano pedagogy research (Certificate). *Degree requirements:* For master's, thesis optional. *Entrance requirements:* For master's, honors degree or equivalent, minimum B+ average. Electronic applications accepted. *Faculty research:* Performance, theory, musicology.

University of Pennsylvania, School of Arts and Sciences, Graduate Group in Music, Philadelphia, PA 19104. Offers AM, PhD. Terminal master's awarded for partial completion of doctoral program. *Degree requirements:* For master's, variable foreign language requirement; for doctorate, variable foreign language requirement, thesis/dissertation. *Entrance requirements:* For master's and doctorate, GRE General Test, GRE Subject Test, samples of previous work. Additional exam requirements/recommendations for international students: Required—TOEFL. Electronic applications accepted.

University of Pittsburgh, School of Arts and Sciences, Department of Music, Pittsburgh, PA 15260. Offers composition and theory (MA, PhD); ethnomusicology (MA, PhD); musicology (MA, PhD). Part-time programs available. Terminal master's awarded for partial completion of doctoral program. *Degree requirements:* For master's, comprehensive exam, thesis, 1 foreign language (historical musicology); for doctorate, one foreign language, comprehensive exam, thesis/dissertation, 2 foreign languages (historical musicology). *Entrance requirements:* For master's and doctorate, GRE General Test, samples of work, references. Additional exam requirements/recommendations for international students: Required—TOEFL (minimum score 600 paper-based; 250 computer-based). Electronic applications accepted. *Faculty research:* Composition, ethnomusicology, historical musicology, intercultural musicology, jazz.

University of Pittsburgh, School of Arts and Sciences, Department of Theatre Arts, Pittsburgh, PA 15260. Offers performance pedagogy (MFA); theatre and performance studies (MA, PhD). *Accreditation:* NAST. Terminal master's awarded for partial completion of doctoral program. *Degree requirements:* For master's, comprehensive exam; for doctorate, one foreign language, comprehensive exam, thesis/dissertation. *Entrance requirements:* For master's and doctorate, GRE General Test, samples of written work. Additional exam requirements/recommendations for international students: Required—TOEFL. Electronic applications accepted. *Faculty research:* American theatre, Renaissance theatre, Asian theatre, dramatic structure, performance theory.

University of Portland, Graduate School, College of Arts and Sciences, Department of Performing and Fine Arts, Program in Music, Portland, OR 97203-5798. Offers MA. *Accreditation:* NASM. Part-time and evening/weekend programs available. *Faculty:* 4 full-time (0 women). *Students:* 1 (woman) full-time, 4 part-time (all women). Average age 34. In 2008, 1 master's awarded. *Degree requirements:* For master's, thesis optional. *Entrance requirements:* For master's, GRE General Test, minimum GPA of 3.0, resumé, 3 letters of recommendation, statement of goals, official transcripts. Additional exam requirements/recommendations for international students: Required—TOEFL (minimum score 600 paper-based; 100 iBT), IELTS (minimum score 7.5). *Application deadline:* For fall admission, 7/15 priority date for domestic and international students; for spring admission, 12/15 priority date for domestic and international students. Applications are processed on a rolling basis. Application fee: $50. *Expenses:* Tuition: Full-time $7380; part-time $8.20 per credit hour. *Financial support:* Federal Work-Study, scholarships/grants, and tuition waivers (partial) available. Financial award application deadline: 3/1; financial award applicants required to submit FAFSA. *Unit head:* Dr. Roger Doyle, Director, 502-943-7382, E-mail: doyle@up.edu. *Application contact:* Chris James Olinger, Administrative Assistant, 503-943-7107, Fax: 503-943-7315, E-mail: olingerc@up.edu.

University of Redlands, College of Arts and Sciences, School of Music, Redlands, CA 92373-0999. Offers MM. *Accreditation:* NASM. Part-time programs available. *Degree requirements:* For master's, comprehensive exam, thesis, 3 recitals, major conducted ensemble. *Entrance requirements:* For master's, GRE, bachelor's degree in music, minimum GPA of 2.75, audition, original scores. Additional exam requirements/recommendations for international students: Required—TOEFL (minimum score 550 paper-based). *Expenses:* Contact institution. *Faculty research:* Performance, composition.

University of Regina, Faculty of Graduate Studies and Research, Faculty of Fine Arts, Department of Music, Regina, SK S4S 0A2, Canada. Offers music (M Mus); music theory (MA); musicology (MA, PhD). *Faculty:* 10 full-time (6 women). *Students:* 4 full-time (2 women), 2 part-time (1 woman). 5 applicants, 60% accepted. *Degree requirements:* For master's, thesis (for some programs), recital, oral exam; for doctorate, thesis/dissertation. *Entrance requirements:* For master's, B Mus or equivalent. Additional exam requirements/recommendations for international students: Required—TOEFL (minimum score 580 paper-based; 237 computer-based; 88 iBT). *Application deadline:* For fall admission, 3/15 for domestic students. Application fee: $85 ($100 for international students). *Financial support:* In 2008–09, 1 fellowship (averaging $15,750 per year), research assistantships (averaging $13,875 per year), 1 teaching assistantship (averaging $13,060 per year) were awarded; scholarships/grants also available. Financial award application deadline: 6/15. *Faculty research:* Social status of 18th century musicians in the Habsburg Empire studies, electronic and computer music, piano performance. *Unit head:* Dr. Lynn Cavanagh, Head, 306-585-5507, Fax: 306-585-5780, E-mail: lynn.cavanagh@uregina.ca. *Application contact:* Randal Rogers, Graduate Program Coordinator, 306-585-4746, Fax: 306-585-5544, E-mail: randal.rogers@uregina.ca.

Music

University of Rhode Island, Graduate School, College of Arts and Sciences, Department of Music, Kingston, RI 02881. Offers MM. *Accreditation:* NASM. *Degree requirements:* For master's, thesis optional. *Expenses:* Tuition, state resident: full-time $8024; part-time $446 per credit. Tuition, nonresident: full-time $21,046; part-time $1169 per credit. Required fees: $1056; $26 per credit. $30 per semester. One-time fee: $95 part-time. *Unit head:* Dr. Ronald Lee, Chairman, 401-874-2431, E-mail: rlee@uri.edu. *Application contact:* Harold D. Bibb, Associate Dean of the Graduate School, 401-874-2262, Fax: 401-874-5491.

University of Rochester, Eastman School of Music, Rochester, NY 14627-0250. Offers composition (MA, MM, DMA, PhD); conducting (MM, DMA); education (MA, PhD); jazz studies/contemporary media (MM); music education (MM, DMA); musicology (MA, PhD); pedagogy of music theory (MA); performance and literature (MM, DMA); piano accompanying and chamber music (MM, DMA); theory (MA, PhD). *Accreditation:* NASM. Part-time programs available. *Degree requirements:* For master's, thesis (for some programs); for doctorate, comprehensive exam (for some programs), thesis/dissertation (for some programs). *Entrance requirements:* For master's and doctorate, GRE. *Expenses:* Contact institution.

University of Saskatchewan, College of Graduate Studies and Research, College of Arts and Sciences, Department of Music, Saskatoon, SK S7N 5A2, Canada. Offers MA. *Degree requirements:* For master's, thesis. *Entrance requirements:* Additional exam requirements/recommendations for international students: Required—TOEFL.

University of South Africa, College of Human Sciences, Pretoria, South Africa. Offers adult education (M Ed); African languages (MA, PhD); African politics (MA, PhD); Afrikaans (MA, PhD); ancient history (MA, PhD); ancient Near Eastern studies (MA, PhD); anthropology (MA, PhD); applied linguistics (MA); Arabic (MA, PhD); archaeology (MA); art history (MA); Biblical archaeology (MA); Biblical studies (M Th, D Th, PhD); Christian spirituality (M Th, D Th); church history (M Th, D Th); classical studies (MA, PhD); clinical psychology (MA); communication (MA, PhD); comparative education (M Ed, Ed D); consulting psychology (D Admin, D Com, PhD); curriculum studies (M Ed, Ed D); development studies (M Admin, MA, D Admin, PhD); didactics (M Ed, Ed D); education (M Tech); education management (M Ed, Ed D); educational psychology (M Ed); English (MA); environmental education (M Ed); French (MA, PhD); German (MA, PhD); Greek (MA); guidance and counseling (M Ed); health studies (MA, PhD), including health sciences education (MA), health services management (MA), medical and surgical nursing science (critical care general) (MA), midwifery and neonatal nursing science (MA), trauma and emergency care (MA); history (MA, PhD); history of education (Ed D); inclusive education (M Ed, Ed D); information and communications technology policy and regulation (MA); information science (MA, MIS, PhD); international politics (MA, PhD); Islamic studies (MA, PhD); Italian (MA, PhD); Judaica (MA, PhD); linguistics (MA, PhD); mathematical education (M Ed); mathematics education (MA); missiology (M Th, D Th); modern Hebrew (MA, PhD); musicology (MA, MMus, D Mus, PhD); natural science education (M Ed); New Testament (M Th, D Th); Old Testament (D Th); pastoral therapy (M Th, D Th); philosophy (MA); philosophy of education (M Ed, Ed D); politics (MA, PhD); Portuguese (MA, PhD); practical theology (M Th, D Th); psychology (MA, MS, PhD); psychology of education (M Ed, Ed D); public health (MA); religious studies (MA, D Th, PhD); Romance languages (MA); Russian (MA, PhD); Semitic languages (MA, PhD); social behavior studies in HIV/AIDS (MA); social science (mental health) (MA); social science in development studies (MA); social science in psychology (MA); social science in social work (MA); social science in sociology (MA); social work (MSW, DSW, PhD); socio-education (M Ed, Ed D); sociolinguistics (MA); sociology (MA, PhD); Spanish (MA, PhD); systematic theology (M Th, D Th); TESOL (teaching English to speakers of other languages) (MA); theological ethics (M Th, D Th); theory of literature (MA, PhD); urban ministries (D Th); urban ministry (M Th).

University of South Carolina, The Graduate School, School of Music, Columbia, SC 29208. Offers composition (MM, DMA); conducting (MM, DMA); jazz studies (MM); music education (MM Ed, PhD); music history (MM); music performance (Certificate); music theory (MM); opera theater (MM); performance (MM, DMA); piano pedagogy (MM, DMA). *Accreditation:* NASM (one or more programs are accredited). Part-time programs available. *Degree requirements:* For master's, 5 foreign languages, comprehensive exam, thesis (for some programs); for doctorate, one foreign language, comprehensive exam, thesis/dissertation; for Certificate, recitals. *Entrance requirements:* For master's and doctorate, GRE General Test or MAT, music diagnostic exam. Additional exam requirements/recommendations for international students: Required—TOEFL (minimum score 570 paper-based; 230 computer-based). Electronic applications accepted. *Expenses:* Contact institution. *Faculty research:* Music skills in pre-school children, evaluation of school performing ensembles.

The University of South Dakota, Graduate School, College of Fine Arts, Department of Music, Vermillion, SD 57069-2390. Offers MM. *Accreditation:* NASM. *Degree requirements:* For master's, thesis or alternative. *Entrance requirements:* For master's, minimum GPA of 2.7, audition or performance tape. Additional exam requirements/recommendations for international students: Required—TOEFL (minimum score 550 paper-based; 213 computer-based; 79 iBT). Electronic applications accepted.

University of Southern California, Graduate School, School of Music, Program in Early Music Performance, Los Angeles, CA 90089. Offers MA. *Accreditation:* NASM.

University of Southern California, Graduate School, School of Music, Program in Music History and Literature, Los Angeles, CA 90089. Offers MA. *Accreditation:* NASM. *Degree requirements:* For master's, 2 foreign languages. *Entrance requirements:* For master's, GRE General Test. *Faculty research:* Medieval, Renaissance, baroque, classical, Romantic, twentieth-century music.

University of Southern California, Graduate School, School of Music, Programs in Choral Music, Los Angeles, CA 90089. Offers MM, DMA. *Accreditation:* NASM. *Degree requirements:* For doctorate, thesis/dissertation. *Entrance requirements:* For doctorate, GRE.

University of Southern California, Graduate School, School of Music, Programs in Composition, Los Angeles, CA 90089. Offers MA, MM, DMA, PhD. *Accreditation:* NASM. *Degree requirements:* For doctorate, thesis/dissertation. *Entrance requirements:* For master's and doctorate, GRE General Test.

University of Southern California, Graduate School, School of Music, Programs in Jazz Studies, Los Angeles, CA 90089. Offers MM, DMA. *Accreditation:* NASM. Part-time programs available. *Degree requirements:* For master's, 2 recitals. *Faculty research:* Jazz improvisation, ear training, jazz history, music of black America.

University of Southern California, Graduate School, School of Music, Programs in Keyboard Collaborative Arts, Los Angeles, CA 90089. Offers MM, DMA, Graduate Certificate.

University of Southern California, Graduate School, School of Music, Programs in Organ Studies, Los Angeles, CA 90089. Offers MM, DMA, Graduate Certificate.

University of Southern California, Graduate School, School of Music, Programs in Strings, Los Angeles, CA 90089. Offers MM, DMA, Graduate Certificate.

University of Southern California, Graduate School, School of Music, Programs in Studio/Jazz Guitar, Los Angeles, CA 90089. Offers MM, DMA, Graduate Certificate.

University of Southern California, Graduate School, School of Music, Programs in Vocal Arts and Opera, Los Angeles, CA 90089. Offers MM, DMA, Graduate Certificate.

University of Southern California, Graduate School, School of Music, Programs in Winds and Percussion, Los Angeles, CA 90089. Offers MM, DMA, Graduate Certificate.

University of Southern Maine, College of Arts and Sciences, Program in Music, Portland, ME 04104-9300. Offers MM. *Accreditation:* NASM.

University of Southern Mississippi, Graduate School, College of Arts and Letters, School of Music, Hattiesburg, MS 39406-0001. Offers conducting (MM); history and literature (MM); music education (MME, PhD); performance (MM); performance and pedagogy (DMA); theory and composition (MM); woodwind performance (MM). *Accreditation:* NASM. *Faculty:* 34 full-time (12 women), 2 part-time/adjunct (1 woman). *Students:* 58 full-time (19 women), 30 part-time (10 women); includes 8 minority (4 African Americans, 4 Hispanic Americans), 17 international. Average age 32. 62 applicants, 56% accepted, 30 enrolled. In 2008, 28 master's, 13 doctorates awarded. Terminal master's awarded for partial completion of doctoral program. *Degree requirements:* For master's, comprehensive exam, thesis (for some programs); for doctorate, comprehensive exam, thesis/dissertation. *Entrance requirements:* For master's, GRE General Test, minimum GPA of 2.75 in last 60 hours; for doctorate, GRE General Test, minimum GPA of 3.5. Additional exam requirements/recommendations for international students: Required—TOEFL. *Application deadline:* For fall admission, 3/1 priority date for domestic students; for spring admission, 12/13 for domestic students. Applications are processed on a rolling basis. Application fee: $30. *Financial support:* In 2008–09, 1 fellowship with full tuition reimbursement (averaging $12,000 per year), 51 teaching assistantships with full tuition reimbursements (averaging $6,000 per year) were awarded; research assistantships, Federal Work-Study, scholarships/grants, tuition waivers (partial), and unspecified assistantships also available. Financial award application deadline: 3/15; financial award applicants required to submit FAFSA. *Faculty research:* Music theory, composition. *Unit head:* Dr. Charles Elliott, Director, 601-266-5543, Fax: 601-266-6427, E-mail: celliott@usm.edu. *Application contact:* Graduate Coordinator, 601-266-5369, Fax: 601-266-6427.

University of South Florida, Graduate School, College of The Arts, School of Music, Tampa, FL 33620-9951. Offers chamber music (MM); composition (MM); conducting (MM); electro-acoustic music (MM); jazz studies (MM), including composition, performance; music (MA); performance (MM), including percussion; piano pedagogy (MM); theory (MM). *Accreditation:* NASM. Part-time and evening/weekend programs available. *Faculty:* 24 full-time (6 women), 8 part-time/adjunct (5 women). *Students:* 61 full-time (31 women), 33 part-time (16 women); includes 11 minority (2 African Americans, 3 Asian Americans or Pacific Islanders, 6 Hispanic Americans), 13 international. 88 applicants, 61% accepted, 35 enrolled. In 2008, 38 master's, 1 doctorate awarded. *Degree requirements:* For master's, comprehensive exam, thesis. *Entrance requirements:* For master's, GRE General Test, diagnostic exam in theory and history, audition, portfolio, GPA 3.0. Additional exam requirements/recommendations for international students: Required—TOEFL (minimum score 550 paper-based; 213 computer-based). *Application deadline:* For fall admission, 2/15 priority date for domestic students, 3/15 for international students; for spring admission, 10/15 for domestic students, 6/1 for international students. Application fee: $30. *Expenses:* Tuition, state resident: full-time $2624.40; part-time $291.60 per credit hour. Tuition, nonresident: full-time $7822; part-time $869.13 per credit hour. *Financial support:* Fellowships with full tuition reimbursements, research assistantships with full tuition reimbursements, teaching assistantships with full tuition reimbursements, career-related internships or fieldwork, Federal Work-Study, scholarships/grants, health care benefits, and unspecified assistantships available. Financial award application deadline: 2/15. *Faculty research:* Medieval and Renaissance musicology, nonverbal conducting. Total annual research expenditures: $60,271. *Unit head:* Dr. Wade P. Weast, Director, 813-974-2311, Fax: 813-974-8721, E-mail: wweast@arts.usf.edu. *Application contact:* David Williams, Program Director, 813-974-2311, Fax: 813-974-8721, E-mail: dwilliams@arts.usf.edu.

The University of Tennessee, Graduate School, College of Arts and Sciences, Department of Theatre, Knoxville, TN 37996. Offers costume design (MFA); lighting design (MFA); performance (MFA); scene design (MFA); theatre technology (MFA). *Degree requirements:* For master's, thesis or alternative. *Entrance requirements:* For master's, audition, minimum GPA of 2.7. Additional exam requirements/recommendations for international students: Required—TOEFL. Electronic applications accepted. *Expenses:* Tuition, area resident: Part-time $348 per credit hour. Tuition, state resident: full-time $6262. Tuition, nonresident: full-time $18,920; part-time $1052 per credit hour. Required fees: $812; $36 per credit hour. Tuition and fees vary according to program.

The University of Tennessee, Graduate School, College of Arts and Sciences, School of Music, Knoxville, TN 37996. Offers accompanying (MM); choral conducting (MM); composition (MM); instrumental conducting (MM); jazz (MM); music education (MM); music theory (MM); musicology (MM); performance (MM); piano pedagogy and literature (MM). *Accreditation:* NASM. Part-time programs available. *Degree requirements:* For master's, thesis (for some programs). *Entrance requirements:* For master's, audition, minimum GPA of 2.7. Additional exam requirements/recommendations for international students: Required—TOEFL. Electronic applications accepted. *Expenses:* Tuition, area resident: Part-time $348 per credit hour. Tuition, state resident: full-time $6262. Tuition, nonresident: full-time $18,920; part-time $1052 per credit hour. Required fees: $812; $36 per credit hour. Tuition and fees vary according to program.

The University of Tennessee at Chattanooga, Graduate School, College of Arts and Sciences, Department of Music, Program in Music, Chattanooga, TN 37403. Offers MM. *Accreditation:* NASM. Part-time and evening/weekend programs available. *Faculty:* 10 full-time (1 woman), 3 part-time/adjunct (2 women). *Students:* 6 full-time (3 women), 12 part-time (7 women), 4 international. Average age 33. 7 applicants, 71% accepted, 4 enrolled. In 2008, 4 master's awarded. *Degree requirements:* For master's, comprehensive exam, thesis or alternative, senior recital. *Entrance requirements:* For master's, GRE General Test or MAT, bachelor's degree in music, audition for placement. Additional exam requirements/recommendations for international students: Required—TOEFL (minimum score 550 paper-based; 213 computer-based; 79 iBT); Recommended—IELTS (minimum score 6). *Application deadline:* For fall admission, 8/1 priority date for domestic students, 6/1 for international students; for spring admission, 12/1 priority date for domestic students, 10/1 for international students. Applications are processed on a rolling basis. Application fee: $30 ($35 for international students). *Expenses:* Tuition, area resident: Full-time $6150; part-time $281 per credit hour. Tuition, nonresident: full-time $16,710; part-time $867 per credit hour. Required fees: $1100; $128 per credit hour. $550 per semester. *Financial support:* In 2008–09, 4 fellowships with full and partial tuition reimbursements (averaging $2,750 per year) were awarded; career-related internships or fieldwork, Federal Work-Study, institutionally sponsored loans, scholarships/grants, tuition waivers (partial), and unspecified assistantships also available. Support available to part-time students. Financial award application deadline: 4/1; financial award applicants required to submit FAFSA. *Faculty research:* Music education, conducting, opera, vocal instruction, orchestras. *Unit head:* Dr. Monte C. Coulter, Coordinator, 423-425-4647, Fax: 423-425-4603, E-mail: monte-coulter@utc.edu. *Application contact:* Dr. Stephanie Bellar, Dean of Graduate Studies, 423-425-4666, Fax: 423-425-5223, E-mail: stephanie-bellar@utc.edu.

The University of Texas at Arlington, Graduate School, College of Liberal Arts, Department of Music, Arlington, TX 76019. Offers education (MM); performance (MM). *Accreditation:* NASM. Part-time and evening/weekend programs available. *Faculty:* 16 full-time (5 women), 2 part-time/adjunct (1 woman). *Students:* 13 full-time (6 women), 20 part-time (9 women); includes 6 minority (3 African Americans, 1 Asian American or Pacific Islander, 2 Hispanic Americans), 9 international. 25 applicants, 84% accepted, 17 enrolled. In 2008, 4 master's awarded. *Degree requirements:* For master's, comprehensive exam, thesis optional. *Entrance requirements:* For master's, GRE, 3 letters of recommendation, minimum GPA of 3.0 in last 60 hours of course work. Additional exam requirements/recommendations for international students: Required—TOEFL (minimum score 550 paper-based; 213 computer-based). *Application deadline:* For fall admission, 6/1 for domestic students. Application fee: $35 ($50 for international students). *Expenses:* Tuition, area resident: Full-time $6500. Tuition, state resident: full-time $6500. Tuition, nonresident: full-time $11,558. *Financial support:* In 2008–09, 2 research assistantships (averaging $6,500 per year), 5 teaching assistantships with partial tuition reimbursements (averaging $6,500 per year) were awarded; scholarships/grants also available. *Unit head:* Dr. John Burton, Chair, 817-272-3471, Fax: 817-272-3434. *Application contact:* Assistant Chair/Graduate Advisor.

The University of Texas at Austin, Graduate School, College of Fine Arts, Butler School of Music, Austin, TX 78712-1111. Offers M Music, DMA, PhD. *Accreditation:* NASM. Part-time programs available. *Degree requirements:* For master's, one foreign language, comprehensive exam, thesis (for some programs), recital for performance or composition majors; for doctorate, one foreign language, comprehensive exam, thesis/dissertation (for some programs), recital for performance or composition majors. *Entrance requirements:* For master's, GRE General Test (not required for performance or composition majors), audition (performance majors); for doctorate, GRE General Test (not required for performance or composition majors), audition (performance majors). Electronic applications accepted.

The University of Texas at El Paso, Graduate School, College of Liberal Arts, Department of Music, El Paso, TX 79968-0001. Offers music education (MM); music performance (MM). *Accreditation:* NASM. Part-time and evening/weekend programs available. *Degree requirements:* For master's, thesis. *Entrance requirements:* For master's, departmental exam. Additional exam requirements/recommendations for international students: Required—TOEFL. Electronic applications accepted.

The University of Texas at San Antonio, College of Liberal and Fine Arts, Department of Music, San Antonio, TX 78249-0617. Offers keyboard pedagogy (Graduate Certificate); keyboard performance (Graduate Certificate); music (MM). *Accreditation:* NASM. Part-time programs available. *Degree requirements:* For master's, one foreign language, comprehensive exam, thesis (for some programs), recital. *Entrance requirements:* For master's, GRE, audition, 3 letters of recommendation. Additional exam requirements/recommendations for international students: Required—TOEFL (minimum score 500 paper-based; 173 computer-based). Electronic applications accepted. *Faculty research:* Computer applications to music, psychology and music, music composition, music performance.

The University of Texas–Pan American, College of Arts and Humanities, Department of Music, Edinburg, TX 78541-2999. Offers ethnomusicology (M Mus); interdisciplinary studies (MAIS); music education (M Mus); performance (M Mus). Part-time programs available. *Degree requirements:* For master's, comprehensive exam, thesis optional, recital (performance). *Entrance requirements:* For master's, audition for performance area, bachelor's degree in music. *Faculty research:* Music history, instrumental pedagogy, vocal pedagogy, music education, ethnomusicology.

The University of the Arts, College of Performing Arts, School of Music, Program in Jazz Studies, Philadelphia, PA 19102-4944. Offers MM. Part-time programs available. *Degree requirements:* For master's, professional internship, recital. *Entrance requirements:* For master's, audition. Additional exam requirements/recommendations for international students: Required—TOEFL (minimum score 550 paper-based; 213 computer-based).

See Close-Up on page 233.

University of the Pacific, Conservatory of Music, Stockton, CA 95211-0197. Offers MA, MM. *Accreditation:* NASM. *Faculty:* 4 full-time (3 women), 3 part-time/adjunct (2 women). *Students:* 8 full-time (6 women), 10 part-time (8 women); includes 4 minority (2 Asian Americans or Pacific Islanders, 2 Hispanic Americans), 1 international. Average age 28. 16 applicants, 63% accepted, 6 enrolled. In 2008, 1 master's awarded. *Entrance requirements:* For master's, GRE General Test. Additional exam requirements/recommendations for international students: Required—TOEFL (minimum score 475 paper-based; 150 computer-based). *Application deadline:* For fall admission, 3/1 priority date for domestic students; for spring admission, 10/1 priority date for domestic students. Applications are processed on a rolling basis. Application fee: $75. *Expenses:* Tuition: Full-time $30,380; part-time $950 per unit. Required fees: $300. *Financial support:* Teaching assistantships, institutionally sponsored loans available. Support available to part-time students. Financial award application deadline: 3/1; financial award applicants required to submit FAFSA. *Unit head:* Dr. Steven Anderson, Dean, 209-946-2417. *Application contact:* Dr. Therese West, Chairperson, 209-946-3194.

The University of Toledo, College of Graduate Studies, College of Arts and Sciences, Department of Music, Toledo, OH 43606-3390. Offers performance (MMP). *Accreditation:* NASM. *Entrance requirements:* For master's, audition (performance), minimum A average in student teaching or teaching experience (music education). Electronic applications accepted.

University of Toronto, School of Graduate Studies, Humanities Division, Faculty of Music, Toronto, ON M5S 1A1, Canada. Offers composition (Mus M, Mus Doc); music education (Mus M, PhD); music performance (DMA); musicology/theory (MA, PhD). Part-time programs available. *Degree requirements:* For master's, comprehensive exam (for some programs), oral examination (Mus M in composition), 1 language (MA); for doctorate, thesis/dissertation (for some programs), recital of original works (Mus Doc), thesis (PhD). *Entrance requirements:* For master's, Bachelor of Music in area of specialization with minimum B average in final 2 years, original compositions (Mus M in composition); for doctorate, master's degree in area of specialization, minimum B+ average, at least 2 extended compositions (Mus Doc).

University of Trinity College, Faculty of Divinity, Toronto, ON M5S 1H8, Canada. Offers ministry (Diploma); ministry for church musicians (Diploma); theology (M Div, MTS, Th M, D Min, PhD, Th D, Diploma, L Th); M Div/MA. *Accreditation:* ATS. Part-time programs available. *Faculty:* 4 full-time (1 woman), 34 part-time/adjunct (7 women). *Students:* 51 full-time (19 women), 72 part-time (35 women). Average age 45. *Degree requirements:* For master's, 2 foreign languages, thesis (for some programs); for doctorate, 3 foreign languages, comprehensive exam, thesis/dissertation; for M Div, thesis/dissertation optional; for other advanced degree, thesis (for some programs). *Entrance requirements:* For M Div, interview; for master's, 1 language (modern or ancient), interview; for doctorate, 2 languages (modern and ancient). Additional exam requirements/recommendations for international students: Required—TOEFL, TWE. *Application deadline:* For fall admission, 3/31 priority date for domestic and international students; for winter admission, 12/31 for domestic and international students; for spring admission, 4/30 priority date for domestic and international students. Applications are processed on a rolling basis. Application fee: $0. Tuition and fees charges are reported in Canadian dollars. *Expenses:* Tuition: Full-time $5669 Canadian dollars; part-time $1889 Canadian dollars per course. Required fees: $400 Canadian dollars; $50 Canadian dollars per semester. Tuition and fees vary according to degree level. *Financial support:* Fellowships, teaching assistantships, career-related internships or fieldwork, institutionally sponsored loans, and bursaries available. Support available to part-time students. Financial award application deadline: 5/15. *Faculty research:* Interreligious dialogue, feminist theology, systematic theology, philosophy of religion, pastoral theology. *Unit head:* Dr. David Neelands, Dean, 416-978-7750, Fax: 416-978-4949, E-mail: divdean@trinity.utoronto.ca. *Application contact:* Rachel Richards, Administrative Assistant to the Dean, 416-978-2133, Fax: 416-978-4949, E-mail: divinity@trinity.utoronto.ca.

University of Utah, The Graduate School, College of Fine Arts, School of Music, Salt Lake City, UT 84112-1107. Offers M Mus, MA, DMA, PhD. *Accreditation:* NASM. *Degree requirements:* For master's, one foreign language, thesis (for some programs), 2 recitals, final oral exam; for doctorate, one foreign language, thesis/dissertation, final oral exam, 4 recitals (DMA). *Entrance requirements:* For master's and doctorate, placement exams, minimum GPA of 3.0, audition. Additional exam requirements/recommendations for international students: Required—TOEFL (minimum score 500 paper-based; 173 computer-based; 61 iBT). *Faculty research:* Music education, conducting, musicology, composition, performance.

University of Utah, The Graduate School, College of Humanities, Department of English, Salt Lake City, UT 84112-1107. Offers American studies (MA, PhD); British American literature (MA, PhD); creative writing (MFA, PhD); literature (PhD); rhetoric and composition (PhD). *Degree requirements:* For master's, one foreign language, thesis (for some programs), written exam; for doctorate, 2 foreign languages, comprehensive exam, thesis/dissertation. *Entrance requirements:* For master's and doctorate, GRE General Test, minimum GPA of 3.2. Additional exam requirements/recommendations for international students: Required—TOEFL (minimum score 500 paper-based; 173 computer-based; 120 iBT). Electronic applications accepted. *Faculty research:* Poetics and modern poetry, 19th and 20th century British and American literature, the American west, environmental studies, critical theory and race and gender studies.

University of Victoria, Faculty of Graduate Studies, Faculty of Fine Arts, School of Music, Victoria, BC V8W 2Y2, Canada. Offers composition (M Mus); musicology (MA, PhD); musicology with performance (MA); performance (M Mus). *Degree requirements:* For master's, 2 foreign languages, thesis; for doctorate, 2 foreign languages, thesis/dissertation, candidacy exam. *Entrance requirements:* For master's, theory placement test, audition or sample papers and compositions; for doctorate, audition or sample papers and compositions. Additional exam requirements/recommendations for international students: Required—TOEFL (minimum score 575 paper-based; 233 computer-based), IELTS (minimum score 7). Electronic applications accepted. *Faculty research:* Beethoven, Wagner, metrical structure in tonal music, French baroque, eighteenth century opera.

University of Virginia, College and Graduate School of Arts and Sciences, Department of Music, Charlottesville, VA 22903. Offers MA, PhD. *Faculty:* 17 full-time (5 women), 14 part-time/adjunct (4 women). *Students:* 30 full-time (12 women); includes 3 minority (1 American Indian/Alaska Native, 2 Asian Americans or Pacific Islanders), 4 international. Average age 30. 56 applicants, 9% accepted, 4 enrolled. In 2008, 1 master's, 2 doctorates awarded. *Degree requirements:* For master's, one foreign language, article-length paper; for doctorate, one foreign language, comprehensive exam, thesis/dissertation. *Entrance requirements:* For master's and doctorate, GRE General Test, 2 writing samples or portfolio. Additional exam requirements/recommendations for international students: Required—TOEFL (minimum score 600 paper-based; 250 computer-based; 90 iBT), IELTS (minimum score 7). *Application deadline:* For fall admission, 1/2 for domestic and international students. Applications are processed on a rolling basis. Application fee: $60. Electronic applications accepted. *Expenses:* Tuition, area resident: Full-time $10,452. Tuition, state resident: full-time $10,452. Tuition, nonresident: full-time $20,010. Required fees: $2176. Part-time tuition and fees vary according to course load and program. *Financial support:* Teaching assistantships available. Financial award applicants required to submit FAFSA. *Unit head:* Katherine E. Maus, Chair, 434-924-3052, Fax: 434-924-6033. *Application contact:* Katherine E. Maus, Chair, 434-924-3052, Fax: 434-924-6033.

University of Washington, Graduate School, College of Arts and Sciences, School of Music, Concentration in Choral Conducting, Seattle, WA 98195. Offers MM, DMA.

University of Washington, Graduate School, College of Arts and Sciences, School of Music, Concentration in Ethnomusicology, Seattle, WA 98195. Offers MA.

University of Washington, Graduate School, College of Arts and Sciences, School of Music, Concentration in Music History, Seattle, WA 98195. Offers MA, PhD.

University of Washington, Graduate School, College of Arts and Sciences, School of Music, Department of Choral Music, Seattle, WA 98195. Offers choral conducting (MM, DMA).

The University of Western Ontario, Faculty of Graduate Studies, Faculty of Arts and Humanities, Don Wright Faculty of Music, London, ON N6A 5B8, Canada. Offers music (M Mus, PhD); popular music and culture (MA). Part-time programs available. Terminal master's awarded for partial completion of doctoral program. *Degree requirements:* For master's, 2 foreign languages, thesis (for some programs), recital; for doctorate, 2 foreign languages, thesis/dissertation. *Entrance requirements:* For master's, honors degree in music; minimum A average in proposed area of concentration, B average overall; for doctorate, MA or equivalent. *Faculty research:* Systematic musicology, musicology, theory, music education.

University of West Georgia, Graduate School, College of Arts and Sciences, Department of Music, Program in Performance, Carrollton, GA 30118. Offers M Mus. *Accreditation:* NASM. Part-time programs available. *Students:* 1 (woman) full-time, 2 part-time (1 woman). 4 applicants, 100% accepted. *Degree requirements:* For master's, one foreign language, comprehensive exam, thesis optional, recitals. *Entrance requirements:* For master's, music qualifying exam, audition, minimum GPA of 2.5, performance evaluation. *Application deadline:* For fall admission, 7/18 priority date for domestic students; for spring admission, 11/27 for domestic students. Application fee: $30. Electronic applications accepted. *Expenses:* Contact institution. *Financial support:* In 2008–09, teaching assistantships with full tuition reimbursements (averaging $9,000 per year); career-related internships or fieldwork and unspecified assistantships also available. Financial award applicants required to submit FAFSA. *Faculty research:* Ethnomusicology, jazz performance, Latin American music, French music. *Unit head:* Dr. Kevin R. Hibbard, Chair, 678-8396516, E-mail: khibbard@westga.edu. *Application contact:* Dr. Charles W. Clark, Dean, 678-839-6508, E-mail: cclark@westga.edu.

University of Wisconsin–Madison, Graduate School, College of Letters and Science, School of Music, Program in Composition, Madison, WI 53706-1380. Offers MM, DMA. *Accreditation:* NASM. *Degree requirements:* For doctorate, thesis/dissertation.

University of Wisconsin–Madison, Graduate School, College of Letters and Science, School of Music, Program in Conducting, Madison, WI 53706-1380. Offers choral (MM, DMA); instrumental (MM, DMA); orchestral (MM, DMA). *Accreditation:* NASM. *Degree requirements:* For doctorate, thesis/dissertation.

University of Wisconsin–Madison, Graduate School, College of Letters and Science, School of Music, Program in Musicology and Ethnomusicology, Madison, WI 53706-1380. Offers ethnomusicology (MA, PhD); historical musicology (PhD); music history (MA). *Accreditation:* NASM. *Degree requirements:* For doctorate, 2 foreign languages, thesis/dissertation. *Entrance requirements:* For doctorate, GRE General Test.

University of Wisconsin–Madison, Graduate School, College of Letters and Science, School of Music, Program in Music Performance, Madison, WI 53706-1380. Offers MM, DMA. *Accreditation:* NASM. *Degree requirements:* For doctorate, one foreign language, thesis/dissertation.

University of Wisconsin–Madison, Graduate School, College of Letters and Science, School of Music, Program in Music Theory, Madison, WI 53706-1380. Offers MA, PhD. *Accreditation:* NASM. *Degree requirements:* For master's, thesis, 1 foreign language (MA); for doctorate, 2 foreign languages, thesis/dissertation. *Entrance requirements:* For master's, GRE General Test (MA); for doctorate, GRE General Test.

University of Wisconsin–Milwaukee, Graduate School, College of Letters and Sciences, Department of English, Milwaukee, WI 53201-0413. Offers creative writing (PhD); English (MA); linguistics (PhD); professional writing (PhD); professional writing and communication (Certificate); rhetoric and composition (PhD); MLIS/MA. *Faculty:* 40 full-time (19 women). *Students:* 107 full-time (64 women), 82 part-time (54 women); includes 13 minority (8 African Americans, 1 American Indian/Alaska Native, 2 Asian Americans or Pacific Islanders, 2 Hispanic Americans), 23 international. Average age 35. 187 applicants, 41% accepted, 34 enrolled. In 2008, 31 master's, 14 doctorates awarded. *Degree requirements:* For master's, thesis or alternative; for doctorate, one foreign language, thesis/dissertation. *Entrance requirements:* For master's, GRE General Test, GRE Subject Test; for doctorate, GRE. Additional exam requirements/recommendations for international students: Required—TOEFL (minimum score 550 paper-based; 79 iBT), IELTS (minimum score 6.5). *Application deadline:* For fall admission, 1/1 priority date for domestic students; for spring admission, 9/1 for domestic students. Applications are processed on a rolling basis. Application fee: $45 ($75 for international students). *Expenses:* Tuition, area resident: Full-time $7320; part-time $165 per credit. Tuition, state resident: full-time $7320; part-time $165 per credit. Tuition, nonresident: full-time $17,840; part-time $714 per credit. Tuition and fees vary according to campus/location, program and reciprocity agreements. *Financial support:* In 2008–09, 74 teaching assistantships were awarded; career-related internships or fieldwork and unspecified assistantships also available. Support available to part-time students. Financial award application deadline: 4/15. Total annual research expenditures: $53,677. *Unit head:* Tasha Oren, Representative, 414-229-2643, Fax: 414-229-

Music

University of Wisconsin–Milwaukee (continued)
2643, E-mail: tgoren@uwm.edu. *Application contact:* General Information Contact, 414-229-4982, Fax: 414-229-6967, E-mail: gradschool@uwm.edu.

University of Wisconsin–Milwaukee, Graduate School, Peck School of the Arts, Department of Music, Milwaukee, WI 53201-0413. Offers chamber music performance (Certificate); music composition (MM); music education (MM); music history and literature (MM); opera and vocal arts (Certificate); string pedagogy (MM); MLIS/MM. *Accreditation:* NASM. Part-time programs available. *Faculty:* 21 full-time (6 women). *Students:* 38 full-time (19 women), 28 part-time (14 women); includes 3 minority (2 Asian Americans or Pacific Islanders, 1 Hispanic American), 7 international. Average age 29. 63 applicants, 57% accepted, 27 enrolled. In 2008, 23 master's awarded. *Degree requirements:* For master's, variable foreign language requirement, comprehensive exam, thesis or alternative. *Entrance requirements:* For master's, GRE General Test, GRE Subject Test, audition, interview. Additional exam requirements/recommendations for international students: Required—TOEFL (minimum score 550 paper-based; 79 iBT), IELTS (minimum score 6.5). *Application deadline:* For fall admission, 1/1 priority date for domestic students; for spring admission, 9/1 for domestic students. Applications are processed on a rolling basis. Application fee: $45 ($75 for international students). *Expenses:* Tuition, area resident: Full-time $7320; part-time $165 per credit. Tuition, state resident: full-time $7320; part-time $165 per credit. Tuition, nonresident: full-time $17,840; part-time $714 per credit. Tuition and fees vary according to campus/location, program and reciprocity agreements. *Financial support:* In 2008–09, 14 teaching assistantships were awarded; career-related internships or fieldwork and unspecified assistantships also available. Support available to part-time students. Financial award application deadline: 4/15. *Unit head:* Timothy Noonan, Representative, 414-229-2286, Fax: 414-229-2776. *Application contact:* General Information Contact, 414-229-4982, Fax: 414-229-6967, E-mail: gradschool@uwm.edu.

University of Wyoming, Graduate School, College of Arts and Sciences, Department of Music, Laramie, WY 82070. Offers music education (MME); performance (MM). *Accreditation:* NASM. *Faculty:* 16 full-time (7 women), 4 part-time/adjunct (2 women). *Students:* 15 full-time (7 women), 3 part-time (1 woman), 7 international. Average age 27. 9 applicants, 56% accepted, 5 enrolled. In 2008, 2 master's awarded. *Degree requirements:* For master's, comprehensive exam, thesis or alternative. *Entrance requirements:* For master's, minimum GPA of 3.0. Additional exam requirements/recommendations for international students: Required—TOEFL (minimum score 540 paper-based; 207 computer-based). *Application deadline:* For fall admission, 3/1 priority date for domestic and international students. Application fee: $50. Electronic applications accepted. *Financial support:* In 2008–09, 8 students received support, including 7 teaching assistantships with full tuition reimbursements available (averaging $11,072 per year); unspecified assistantships also available. Financial award application deadline: 3/1. *Unit head:* Dr. David Brinkman, Head, 307-766-5242, Fax: 307-766-5326, E-mail: brinkman@uwyo.edu. *Application contact:* Dr. John Fadial, Assoc. Professor/Graduate Coordinator, 307-766*6337, Fax: 307-766-2697, E-mail: jfadial@uwyo.edu.

Virginia Commonwealth University, Graduate School, School of the Arts, Department of Music, Richmond, VA 23284-9005. Offers education (MM). *Accreditation:* NASM. *Degree requirements:* For master's, departmental qualifying exam, recital. *Entrance requirements:* For master's, department examination, audition or tapes, portfolio. *Faculty research:* Composition, conducting, education, performance.

Washington State University, Graduate School, College of Liberal Arts, School of Music and Theatre Arts, Pullman, WA 99164. Offers composition (MA); jazz (MA); music (MA); music education (MA); performance (MA). *Accreditation:* NASM. *Degree requirements:* For master's, comprehensive exam (for some programs), thesis (for some programs), oral exam. *Entrance requirements:* For master's, audition, minimum GPA of 3.0, 3 letters of recommendation, composition portfolio and recording (composition), writing sample and written philosophy (music education), writing sample (music history), in-depth audition (performance). Additional exam requirements/recommendations for international students: Required—TOEFL. Electronic applications accepted.

Washington University in St. Louis, Graduate School of Arts and Sciences, Department of Music, St. Louis, MO 63130-4899. Offers MM, PhD. *Students:* 24 full-time (16 women); includes 3 minority (1 African American, 1 Asian American or Pacific Islander, 1 Hispanic American). 31 applicants, 29% accepted, 4 enrolled. In 2008, 5 master's, 1 doctorate awarded. Terminal master's awarded for partial completion of doctoral program. *Degree requirements:* For master's, thesis or alternative; for doctorate, thesis/dissertation. *Entrance requirements:* For master's and doctorate, departmental exam, GRE General Test. *Application deadline:* For fall admission, 1/15 priority date for domestic students. Application fee: $45. Electronic applications accepted. *Financial support:* Fellowships, teaching assistantships, career-related internships or fieldwork, Federal Work-Study, institutionally sponsored loans, and tuition waivers (full and partial) available. Support available to part-time students. Financial award application deadline: 1/15. *Unit head:* Dr. Dolores Pesce, Chairman, 314-935-5566. *Application contact:* Assistant to the Dean, 314-935-6880, Fax: 314-935-4887.

Wayne State University, College of Fine, Performing and Communication Arts, Department of Music, Detroit, MI 48202. Offers choral conducting (MM); composition (MM); music (MA, MM); music education (MM); orchestral studies (Certificate); performance (MM); theory (MM). *Accreditation:* NASM. *Degree requirements:* For master's, variable foreign language requirement. *Entrance requirements:* For master's, audition, interview. Additional exam requirements/recommendations for international students: Required—TOEFL (minimum score 550 paper-based; 213 computer-based); Recommended—TWE (minimum score 6). Electronic applications accepted. *Faculty research:* Teacher training, pedagogy, musicology, composition/theory, conducting/performance practice.

Webster University, Leigh Gerdine College of Fine Arts, Department of Music, St. Louis, MO 63119-3194. Offers church music (MM); composition (MM); conducting (MM); jazz studies (MM); music (MA); music education (MM); performance (MM); piano (MM). *Accreditation:* NASM.

Wesleyan University, Graduate Programs, Department of Music, Middletown, CT 06459-0260. Offers ethnomusicology (PhD); music (MA). *Degree requirements:* For master's, one foreign language, thesis; for doctorate, one foreign language, thesis/dissertation. *Entrance requirements:* For master's, GRE General Test, GRE Subject Test; for doctorate, GRE Subject Test. Additional exam requirements/recommendations for international students: Required—TOEFL. Electronic applications accepted. *Faculty research:* African, African-American, Indonesian, European, and Euro-American music.

West Chester University of Pennsylvania, Office of Graduate Studies, College of Visual and Performing Arts, Department of Applied Music, West Chester, PA 19383. Offers accompanying (MM); performance (MM); piano pedagogy (MM, Certificate). Part-time and evening/weekend programs available. *Students:* 12 full-time (7 women), 11 part-time (7 women); includes 3 minority (1 African American, 1 Asian American or Pacific Islander, 1 Hispanic American), 1 international. Average age 29. 17 applicants, 94% accepted, 11 enrolled. In 2008, 6 master's awarded. *Degree requirements:* For master's, comprehensive exam, thesis optional, recital. *Entrance requirements:* For master's and Certificate, School of Music Graduate Admission Test (GAT), audition, interview. Additional exam requirements/recommendations for international students: Required—TOEFL (minimum score 550 paper-based; 213 computer-based; 80 iBT). *Application deadline:* For fall admission, 4/15 priority date for domestic students, 3/15 for international students; for spring admission, 10/15 for domestic students, 9/1 for international students. Applications are processed on a rolling basis. Application fee: $35. Electronic applications accepted. *Expenses:* Tuition, state resident: full-time $6430; part-time $357 per credit. Tuition, nonresident: full-time $10,288; part-time $572 per credit. Required fees: $652.50; $50 per credit. $67 per semester. *Financial support:* In 2008–09, 4 research assistantships with full and partial tuition reimbursements (averaging $5,000 per year) were awarded;

unspecified assistantships also available. Support available to part-time students. Financial award application deadline: 2/15; financial award applicants required to submit FAFSA. *Unit head:* Dr. Chris Hanning, Interim Chair, 610-436-4178, E-mail: channing@wcupa.edu. *Application contact:* Dr. J. Bryan Burton, Graduate Coordinator, 610-436-2222, E-mail: jburton@wcupa.edu.

West Chester University of Pennsylvania, Office of Graduate Studies, College of Visual and Performing Arts, Department of Music History and Literature, West Chester, PA 19383. Offers music history (MA). Part-time and evening/weekend programs available. *Students:* 4 part-time (2 women). Average age 29. 3 applicants, 67% accepted, 1 enrolled. In 2008, 1 master's awarded. *Degree requirements:* For master's, comprehensive exam, thesis optional, recital. *Entrance requirements:* For master's, School of Music Graduate Admission Test (GAT), audition, interview. Additional exam requirements/recommendations for international students: Required—TOEFL (minimum score 550 paper-based; 213 computer-based; 80 iBT). *Application deadline:* For fall admission, 4/15 priority date for domestic students, 3/15 for international students; for spring admission, 10/15 for domestic students, 9/1 for international students. Applications are processed on a rolling basis. Application fee: $35. Electronic applications accepted. *Expenses:* Tuition, state resident: full-time $6430; part-time $357 per credit. Tuition, nonresident: full-time $10,288; part-time $572 per credit. Required fees: $652.50; $50 per credit. $67 per semester. *Financial support:* In 2008–09, research assistantships with full and partial tuition reimbursements (averaging $5,000 per year); unspecified assistantships also available. Support available to part-time students. Financial award application deadline: 2/15; financial award applicants required to submit FAFSA. *Faculty research:* Musicology, 18th-century European music. *Unit head:* Dr. Scott Balthazar, Chair, 610-436-2284, E-mail: sbalthazar@wcupa.edu. *Application contact:* Dr. J. Bryan Burton, Graduate Coordinator, 610-436-2222, E-mail: jburton@wcupa.edu.

West Chester University of Pennsylvania, Office of Graduate Studies, College of Visual and Performing Arts, Department of Music Theory and Composition, West Chester, PA 19383. Offers music: theory and composition (MM). Part-time and evening/weekend programs available. *Students:* 1 (woman) full-time, 2 part-time (0 women); includes 1 minority (Asian American or Pacific Islander). Average age 38. 5 applicants, 100% accepted, 2 enrolled. *Degree requirements:* For master's, comprehensive exam, thesis optional, recital. *Entrance requirements:* For master's, School of Music Graduate Admission Test (GAT), audition, interview. Additional exam requirements/recommendations for international students: Required—TOEFL (minimum score 550 paper-based; 213 computer-based; 80 iBT). *Application deadline:* For fall admission, 4/15 priority date for domestic students, 3/15 for international students; for spring admission, 10/15 for domestic students, 9/1 for international students. Applications are processed on a rolling basis. Application fee: $35. Electronic applications accepted. *Expenses:* Tuition, state resident: full-time $6430; part-time $357 per credit. Tuition, nonresident: full-time $10,288; part-time $572 per credit. Required fees: $652.50; $50 per credit. $67 per semester. *Financial support:* In 2008–09, research assistantships with full and partial tuition reimbursements (averaging $5,000 per year); unspecified assistantships also available. Support available to part-time students. Financial award application deadline: 2/15; financial award applicants required to submit FAFSA. *Unit head:* Dr. Robert Maggio, Chair, 610-436-2646. *Application contact:* Dr. J. Bryan Burton, Graduate Coordinator, 610-436-2222, E-mail: jburton@wcupa.edu.

Western Carolina University, Graduate School, College of Fine and Performing Arts, School of Music, Cullowhee, NC 28723. Offers MM. Part-time programs available. *Degree requirements:* For master's, comprehensive exam, thesis. *Entrance requirements:* For master's, GRE, appropriate undergraduate, live audition and/or interview, passing music entrance exam. Additional exam requirements/recommendations for international students: Required—TOEFL (minimum score 550 paper-based; 270 computer-based; 79 iBT). *Faculty research:* Music experiences for K-12 students, marching band, sound mixing for television, music technology, choral methods, music history.

Western Illinois University, School of Graduate Studies, College of Fine Arts and Communication, School of Music, Macomb, IL 61455-1390. Offers MM. *Accreditation:* NASM. Part-time programs available. *Students:* 24 full-time (13 women), 9 part-time (5 women); includes 2 minority (1 African American, 1 Asian American or Pacific Islander), 7 international. Average age 29. 20 applicants, 65% accepted. In 2008, 12 master's awarded. *Degree requirements:* For master's, comprehensive exam, thesis or alternative. *Entrance requirements:* For master's, audition. Additional exam requirements/recommendations for international students: Required—TOEFL (minimum score 550 paper-based; 213 computer-based; 80 iBT). *Application deadline:* Applications are processed on a rolling basis. Application fee: $30. Electronic applications accepted. *Expenses:* Tuition, state resident: full-time $5696; part-time $237.34 per credit hour. Tuition, nonresident: full-time $11,392; part-time $474.68 per credit hour. Required fees: $1453; $60.55 per credit hour. *Financial support:* In 2008–09, 22 students received support, including 22 research assistantships with full tuition reimbursements available (averaging $7,040 per year). Financial award applicants required to submit FAFSA. *Unit head:* Dr. Bart Shanklin, Director, 309-298-1544. *Application contact:* Evelyn Hoing, Assistant Director of Graduate Studies, 309-298-1806, Fax: 309-298-2345, E-mail: grad-office@wiu.edu.

Western Michigan University, Graduate College, College of Fine Arts, School of Music, Kalamazoo, MI 49008-5202. Offers composition (MM); conducting (MM); music education (MM); music therapy (MM); performance (MM). *Accreditation:* NASM.

Western Oregon University, Graduate Programs, College of Liberal Arts and Sciences, Division of Creative Arts, Monmouth, OR 97361-1394. Offers contemporary music (MM). *Accreditation:* NASM. *Entrance requirements:* Additional exam requirements/recommendations for international students: Required—TOEFL (minimum score 550 paper-based; 213 computer-based; 79 iBT), IELTS (minimum score 6.5).

Western Washington University, Graduate School, College of Fine and Performing Arts, Department of Music, Bellingham, WA 98225-5996. Offers M Mus. *Accreditation:* NASM. Part-time programs available. *Degree requirements:* For master's, thesis. *Entrance requirements:* For master's, GRE General Test, department placement exams, audition, portfolio, minimum GPA of 3.0 in last 60 semester hours or last 90 quarter hours of course work. Additional exam requirements/recommendations for international students: Required—TOEFL (minimum score 567 paper-based; 227 computer-based). Electronic applications accepted. *Faculty research:* Baroque opera, historical music of the Silk Road, original composition, 20th century orchestral music, 13th century polyphony.

Westminster Choir College of Rider University, Graduate Programs in Music, Princeton, NJ 08540-3899. Offers choral conducting (MM); composition (MM); music education (MM, MME); organ performance (MM); piano accompanying and coaching (MM); piano pedagogy and performance (MM); piano performance (MM); sacred music (MM); vocal pedagogy and performance (MM); vocal training (MVP). Part-time programs available. *Degree requirements:* For master's, variable foreign language requirement, departmental qualifying exam. *Entrance requirements:* For master's, audition, interview, repertoire list, 2 letters of reference, resumé. Additional exam requirements/recommendations for international students: Required—TOEFL (minimum score 525 paper-based; 195 computer-based). Electronic applications accepted.

West Texas A&M University, College of Fine Arts and Humanities, Department of Music and Dance, Program in Music, Canyon, TX 79016-0001. Offers MA. *Accreditation:* NASM. Part-time programs available. *Degree requirements:* For master's, comprehensive exam, thesis optional. *Entrance requirements:* For master's, GRE General Test. Additional exam requirements/recommendations for international students: Required—TOEFL (minimum score 550 paper-based). Electronic applications accepted.

West Texas A&M University, College of Fine Arts and Humanities, Department of Music and Dance, Program in Performance, Canyon, TX 79016-0001. Offers MM. *Accreditation:* NASM. Part-time programs available. *Degree requirements:* For master's, comprehensive exam, thesis optional. *Entrance requirements:* For master's, GRE General Test. Additional exam requirements/recommendations for international students: Required—TOEFL (minimum score 550 paper-based). Electronic applications accepted.

West Virginia University, College of Creative Arts, Division of Music, Morgantown, WV 26506. Offers music composition (MM, DMA); music education (MM, PhD); music history (MM); music performance (MM, DMA); music theory (MM). *Accreditation:* NASM. *Degree requirements:* For master's, comprehensive exam, thesis (for some programs), recitals; for doctorate, variable foreign language requirement, comprehensive exam, thesis/dissertation, recitals (DMA). *Entrance requirements:* For master's, GRE General Test (music history), minimum GPA of 3.0, audition; for doctorate, GRE General Test (music education), minimum GPA of 3.0, audition. Additional exam requirements/recommendations for international students: Required—TOEFL. *Faculty research:* Jazz history, seventeenth century French court music, nineteenth century composition theory.

Wichita State University, Graduate School, College of Fine Arts, School of Music, Wichita, KS 67260. Offers music (MM); music education (MME). *Accreditation:* NASM. Part-time programs available. *Degree requirements:* For master's, one foreign language, thesis, recital, research project. *Entrance requirements:* For master's, GRE, audition, BM or BME. Additional exam requirements/recommendations for international students: Required—TOEFL. Electronic applications accepted.

William Paterson University of New Jersey, College of the Arts and Communication, Department of Music, Wayne, NJ 07470-8420. Offers MM. *Accreditation:* NASM. *Entrance requirements:* For master's, audition, minimum GPA of 2.75. Electronic applications accepted.

Winthrop University, College of Visual and Performing Arts, Department of Music, Rock Hill, SC 29733. Offers conducting (MM); music education (MME); performance (MM). *Accreditation:* NASM. Part-time programs available. *Degree requirements:* For master's, oral and written exams, recital (MM). *Entrance requirements:* For master's, GRE General Test, audition, minimum GPA of 3.0, 2 recitals. Electronic applications accepted.

Wright State University, School of Graduate Studies, College of Liberal Arts, Department of Music, Dayton, OH 45435. Offers music education (M Mus); performance (M Mus). *Accreditation:* NASM. Part-time programs available. *Degree requirements:* For master's, thesis or alternative, oral exam. *Entrance requirements:* For master's, theory placement test, BA in music. Additional exam requirements/recommendations for international students: Required—TOEFL. *Faculty research:* General music, current needs, role of teacher, expectations in music education.

Yale University, Graduate School of Arts and Sciences, Department of Music, New Haven, CT 06520. Offers music history (MA); music theory (MA). *Accreditation:* NASM. Terminal master's awarded for partial completion of doctoral program. *Degree requirements:* For master's, one foreign language; for doctorate, 3 foreign languages, thesis/dissertation. *Entrance requirements:* For doctorate, GRE General Test, GRE Subject Test.

Yale University, School of Music, New Haven, CT 06520. Offers MM, MMA, DMA, AD, Certificate. *Accreditation:* NASM. Terminal master's awarded for partial completion of doctoral program. *Degree requirements:* For master's, one foreign language, thesis (for some programs), recitals; for doctorate, one foreign language, thesis/dissertation, oral and written exam, recitals; for other advanced degree, one foreign language, recitals. *Entrance requirements:* For master's, departmental exams, audition; for doctorate, GRE, departmental exams in history and theory of music, audition; for other advanced degree, departmental exams in history and theory of music, audition. Additional exam requirements/recommendations for international students: Required—TOEFL (minimum score 550 paper-based; 213 computer-based; 79 iBT). Electronic applications accepted. *Expenses:* Contact institution. *Faculty research:* Performance, composition, conducting, music history and theory.

York University, Faculty of Graduate Studies, Faculty of Fine Arts, Program in Ethnomusicology and Musicology, Toronto, ON M3J 1P3, Canada. Offers composition (MA); musicology and ethnomusicology (MA, PhD). Part-time programs available. *Degree requirements:* For master's, one foreign language, thesis optional; for doctorate, 2 foreign languages, comprehensive exam, thesis/dissertation. *Entrance requirements:* For master's, portfolio. Electronic applications accepted.

Youngstown State University, Graduate School, College of Fine and Performing Arts, Dana School of Music, Youngstown, OH 44555-0001. Offers jazz studies (MM); music education (MM); music history and literature (MM); music theory and composition (MM); performance (MM). *Accreditation:* NASM. Part-time and evening/weekend programs available. *Degree requirements:* For master's, one foreign language, thesis optional, final qualifying exam. *Entrance requirements:* For master's, audition; GRE General Test or minimum GPA of 2.7. Additional exam requirements/recommendations for international students: Required—TOEFL. *Faculty research:* Teaching education, use of computers, conducting.

Theater

American Conservatory Theater, Program in Acting, San Francisco, CA 94108-5800. Offers MFA, Certificate. Certificate open only to applicants with undergraduate degree from a non-accredited institution. *Degree requirements:* For master's, thesis (for some programs), performance. *Entrance requirements:* For master's, audition, interview, appropriate bachelor's degree, 2 letters of recommendation.

Antioch University McGregor, Graduate Programs, Individualized Liberal and Professional Studies Program, Yellow Springs, OH 45387-1609. Offers liberal and professional studies (MA), including counseling, creative writing, education, film studies, liberal studies, management, modern literature, psychology, theatre, visual arts. Part-time and evening/weekend programs available. Postbaccalaureate distance learning degree programs offered (minimal on-campus study). *Degree requirements:* For master's, thesis or alternative. *Entrance requirements:* For master's, resumé, 2 letters of reference. Electronic applications accepted. *Expenses:* Contact institution.

Arcadia University, Graduate Studies, Department of Education, Glenside, PA 19038-3295. Offers art education (M Ed, MA Ed); biology education (MA Ed); chemistry education (MA Ed); child development (CAS); computer education (M Ed, CAS); computer education 7–12 (MA Ed); early childhood education (M Ed, CAS), including individualized (M Ed), master teacher (M Ed), research in child development (M Ed); educational leadership (M Ed, CAS); educational psychology (CAS); elementary education (M Ed, CAS); English education (MA Ed); environmental education (MA Ed, CAS); history education (MA Ed); language arts (M Ed, CAS); mathematics education (M Ed, MA Ed, CAS); music education (MA Ed); psychology (MA Ed); pupil personnel services (CAS); reading (M Ed, CAS); school library science (M Ed); science education (M Ed, CAS); secondary education (M Ed, CAS); special education (M Ed, Ed D, CAS); theater arts (MA Ed); written communication (MA Ed). *Accreditation:* NASAD. Part-time and evening/weekend programs available. Postbaccalaureate distance learning degree programs offered (minimal on-campus study). Electronic applications accepted.

Arizona State University, Graduate College, Herberger College of the Arts, School of Theatre and Film, Tempe, AZ 85287. Offers creative writing (playwriting) (MFA); theatre (MA, MFA, PhD). *Degree requirements:* For master's, thesis or alternative; for doctorate, thesis/dissertation. *Entrance requirements:* For master's, GRE or MAT.

Arkansas State University, Graduate School, College of Communications, Department of Communication Studies, Jonesboro, State University, AR 72467. Offers communication studies and theatre arts (MA); communication studies and theatre arts education (SCCT). Part-time programs available. *Faculty:* 5 full-time (2 women). *Students:* 4 full-time (2 women), 8 part-time (4 women); includes 2 minority (both African Americans), 2 international. Average age 29. 11 applicants, 91% accepted, 7 enrolled. In 2008, 7 master's awarded. *Degree requirements:* For master's, one foreign language, comprehensive exam, thesis or alternative. *Entrance requirements:* For master's, GRE General Test, appropriate bachelor's degree, writing sample, letter of recommendation, official transcript; for SCCT, GRE or MAT, appropriate master's degree, interview, official transcript. Additional exam requirements/recommendations for international students: Required—TOEFL (minimum score 550 paper-based; 213 computer-based; 79 iBT), IELTS (minimum score 6). *Application deadline:* For fall admission, 7/15 for domestic students, 7/1 for international students; for spring admission, 12/1 for domestic students, 11/13 for international students. Applications are processed on a rolling basis. Application fee: $30 ($40 for international students). Electronic applications accepted. *Expenses:* Tuition, state resident: full-time $3744; part-time $208 per credit hour. Tuition, nonresident: full-time $9540; part-time $530 per credit hour. International tuition: $7938 full-time. Required fees: $896; $47 per credit hour. $25 per term. One-time fee: $50. Tuition and fees vary according to course load and program. *Financial support:* In 2008–09, 4 students received support; teaching assistantships, career-related internships or fieldwork, scholarships/grants, and unspecified assistantships available. Financial award application deadline: 7/1; financial award applicants required to submit FAFSA. *Faculty research:* Business and professional speech development, communication consulting, speech communication, interpersonal communication, organizational training and development. *Unit head:* Dr. Thomas Bagland, Chair, 870-972-3091, Fax: 870-972-3856, E-mail: tbaglan@astate.edu. *Application contact:* Dr. Andrew Sustich, Dean of the Graduate School, 870-972-3029, Fax: 870-972-3857, E-mail: sustich@astate.edu.

Arkansas State University, Graduate School, College of Fine Arts, Department of Theatre, Jonesboro, State University, AR 72467. Offers communication studies and theatre arts (MA); communication studies and theatre arts education (SCCT). Part-time programs available. *Faculty:* 3 full-time (1 woman). *Students:* 1 (woman) full-time, 1 (woman) part-time; includes 1 minority (African American). Average age 38. 3 applicants, 100% accepted, 2 enrolled. In 2008, 1 other advanced degree awarded. *Degree requirements:* For master's, comprehensive exam, thesis or alternative; for SCCT, comprehensive exam. *Entrance requirements:* For master's, GRE General Test or MAT, appropriate bachelor's degree, official transcript, writing sample; for SCCT, GRE General Test or MAT, interview, master's degree, official transcript. Additional exam requirements/recommendations for international students: Required—TOEFL (minimum score 550 paper-based; 213 computer-based; 79 iBT), IELTS (minimum score 6). *Application deadline:* For fall admission, 7/15 for domestic students, 7/1 for international students; for spring admission, 12/1 for domestic students, 11/13 for international students. Applications are processed on a rolling basis. Application fee: $30 ($40 for international students). Electronic applications accepted. *Expenses:* Tuition, state resident: full-time $3744; part-time $208 per credit hour. Tuition, nonresident: full-time $9540; part-time $530 per credit hour. International tuition: $7938 full-time. Required fees: $896; $47 per credit hour. $25 per term. One-time fee: $50. Tuition and fees vary according to course load and program. *Financial support:* Teaching assistantships, career-related internships or fieldwork, scholarships/grants, and unspecified assistantships available. Financial award application deadline: 7/1; financial award applicants required to submit FAFSA. *Faculty research:* Acting, costume design and technology, directing and stage, makeup design and technology, voice and movement. *Unit head:* Bobby Simpson, Chair, 870-972-2037, Fax: 870-972-2830, E-mail: bsimpson@astate.edu. *Application contact:* Dr. Andrew Sustich, Dean of the Graduate School, 870-972-3029, Fax: 870-972-3857, E-mail: sustich@astate.edu.

Austin College, Program in Education, Sherman, TX 75909-4400. Offers art education (MA); elementary education (MA); middle school education (MA); music education (MA); physical education and coaching (MA); secondary education (MA); theatre education (MA). Part-time programs available. *Faculty:* 5 full-time (3 women), 1 (woman) part-time/adjunct. *Students:* 34 full-time (29 women), 1 (woman) part-time; includes 3 minority (1 Asian American or Pacific Islander, 2 Hispanic Americans). Average age 23. In 2008, 17 master's awarded. *Degree requirements:* For master's, one foreign language, thesis or alternative. *Entrance requirements:* For master's, Texas Academic Skills Program Test. *Application deadline:* For fall admission, 5/1 priority date for domestic students; for spring admission, 1/15 priority date for domestic students. Applications are processed on a rolling basis. Application fee: $35. Electronic applications accepted. *Financial support:* Career-related internships or fieldwork, Federal Work-Study, scholarships/grants, and unspecified assistantships available. Support available to part-time students. Financial award application deadline: 4/1; financial award applicants required to submit FAFSA. *Unit head:* Dr. Barbara Sylvester, Director of Teaching Program, 903-813-2327, Fax: 903-813-2326, E-mail: bsylvester@austincollege.edu. *Application contact:* Dr. Barbara Sylvester, Director of Teaching Program, 903-813-2327, Fax: 903-813-2326, E-mail: bsylvester@austincollege.edu.

Baylor University, Graduate School, College of Arts and Sciences, Department of Theatre Arts, Waco, TX 76798. Offers directing (MFA). *Accreditation:* NAST. *Students:* 7 full-time (5 women). In 2008, 2 master's awarded. *Degree requirements:* For master's, thesis. *Entrance requirements:* For master's, GRE General Test. *Application deadline:* Applications are processed on a rolling basis. Application fee: $25. *Financial support:* Fellowships, teaching assistantships, Federal Work-Study and institutionally sponsored loans available. *Unit head:* Dr. DeAnna Toten Beard, Graduate Program Director, 254-710-6486, Fax: 254-710-1765, E-mail: deanna_toten_beard@baylor.edu. *Application contact:* Renee Cluke, Administrative Assistant, 254-710-1861, Fax: 254-710-1765, E-mail: renee_cluke@baylor.edu.

Bob Jones University, Graduate Programs, Greenville, SC 29614. Offers accountancy (MS); Bible (MA); Bible translation (MA); Biblical studies (Certificate); broadcast management (MS); business administration (MBA); church history (MA, PhD); church ministries (MA); church music (MM); cinema and video production (MA); counseling (MS); curriculum and instruction (Ed D); divinity (M Div); dramatic production (MA); educational leadership (MS, Ed D, Ed S); elementary education (M Ed, MAT); English (M Ed, MA, MAT); fine arts (MA); graphic design (MA); history (M Ed, MA); illustration (MA); interpretative speech (MA); mathematics (M Ed, MAT); medical missions (Certificate); ministry (MM, D Min); multi-categorical special education (M Ed, MAT); music (M Ed); New Testament interpretation (PhD); Old Testament interpretation (PhD); orchestral instrument performance (MM); organ performance (MM); pastoral studies (MA); personnel services (MS, Ed S); piano pedagogy (MM); piano performance (MM); platform arts (MA); radio and television broadcasting (MS); rhetoric and public address (MA); secondary education (M Ed); studio art (MA); teaching Bible (MA); theology (MA, PhD); voice performance (MM); youth ministries (MA); M Div/MM.

The Boston Conservatory, Graduate Division, Theater Division, Boston, MA 02215. Offers MM. Part-time programs available. *Degree requirements:* For master's, performances. *Entrance requirements:* For master's, audition. Additional exam requirements/recommendations for international students: Required—TOEFL (minimum score 580 paper-based; 237 computer-based). Electronic applications accepted.

Boston University, College of Fine Arts, School of Theatre, Boston, MA 02215. Offers costume design (MFA); costume production (MFA); directing (MFA); lighting design (MFA);

Theater

Boston University (continued)
scene design (MFA); technical production (MFA, Certificate); theatre crafts (Certificate); theatre education (MFA). *Entrance requirements:* For master's, interview, portfolio. Additional exam requirements/recommendations for international students: Required—TOEFL.

Bowling Green State University, Graduate College, College of Arts and Sciences, Department of Theatre and Film, Bowling Green, OH 43403. Offers MA, PhD. *Accreditation:* NAST. Part-time programs available. Terminal master's awarded for partial completion of doctoral program. *Degree requirements:* For master's, thesis or alternative; for doctorate, comprehensive exam, thesis/dissertation, 9 hour research tool. *Entrance requirements:* For master's and doctorate, GRE General Test. Additional exam requirements/recommendations for international students: Required—TOEFL. Electronic applications accepted. *Faculty research:* Theatre history, dramatic theory, cultural studies, performance studies, American theatre history.

Brandeis University, Graduate School of Arts and Sciences, Department of Theater Arts, Waltham, MA 02454-9110. Offers acting (MFA); design (MFA). *Entrance requirements:* For master's, resumé, portfolio (design), letters of recommendation, audition (acting). Additional exam requirements/recommendations for international students: Required—TOEFL (minimum score 600 paper-based; 250 computer-based; 100 iBT), IELTS (minimum score 7). Electronic applications accepted. *Faculty research:* Acting, design, dramatic writing, dramaturgy.

Brigham Young University, Graduate Studies, College of Fine Arts and Communications, Department of Theatre and Media Arts, Provo, UT 84602-6404. Offers MA. MFA program accepts applications in odd-numbered years only. *Accreditation:* NAST. *Faculty:* 14 full-time (5 women). *Students:* 17 full-time (12 women), 1 part-time (0 women). Average age 34. In 2008, 6 master's awarded. *Degree requirements:* For master's, comprehensive exam, thesis, 32 hours, oral defense. *Entrance requirements:* For master's, GRE General Test, writing samples. Additional exam requirements/recommendations for international students: Required—TOEFL (minimum score 580 paper-based; 237 computer-based; 85 iBT). *Application deadline:* For fall admission, 2/1 priority date for domestic and international students. Application fee: $50. Electronic applications accepted. *Expenses:* Tuition: Full-time $5160; part-time $287 per credit hour. Tuition and fees vary according to program and student's religious affiliation. *Financial support:* In 2008–09, 18 students received support, including 3 research assistantships with partial tuition reimbursements available (averaging $3,500 per year), 12 teaching assistantships with partial tuition reimbursements available (averaging $3,500 per year); career-related internships or fieldwork, institutionally sponsored loans, scholarships/grants, health care benefits, tuition waivers (partial), unspecified assistantships, and administrative aides also available. Support available to part-time students. *Faculty research:* Media literacy, children's media, popular culture, theatre historiography, performance studies. *Unit head:* Dr. Rodger D. Sorensen, Department Chair, 801-422-8132, Fax: 801-422-0654, E-mail: rodger_sorensen@byu.edu. *Application contact:* Kim Poole, Secretary, 801-422-3750, Fax: 801-422-0654, E-mail: kim_poole@byu.edu.

Brooklyn College of the City University of New York, Division of Graduate Studies, Department of Theater, Brooklyn, NY 11210-2889. Offers acting (MFA); criticism and history (MA); design and technical production (MFA); directing (MFA); dramaturgy (MFA); performing arts management (MFA); theater (PhD). The department offers courses at Brooklyn College that are creditable toward the CUNY doctoral degree (with permission of the executive officer of the doctoral program). Part-time programs available. *Students:* 56 full-time (42 women), 14 part-time (5 women); includes 15 minority (3 African Americans, 2 Asian Americans or Pacific Islanders, 10 Hispanic Americans), 6 international. Average age 31. 145 applicants, 32% accepted, 33 enrolled. In 2008, 31 master's awarded. *Degree requirements:* For master's, thesis, professional residency. *Entrance requirements:* For master's, audition or interview, 18 credits in theater, 2 letters of recommendation, essay. Additional exam requirements/recommendations for international students: Required—TOEFL. *Application deadline:* For fall admission, 2/1 for domestic and international students. Application fee: $125. Electronic applications accepted. *Expenses:* Tuition, state resident: full-time $7360; part-time $310 per credit hour. Tuition, nonresident: full-time $13,800; part-time $575 per credit hour. *Financial support:* Career-related internships or fieldwork, Federal Work-Study, institutionally sponsored loans, and scholarships/grants available. Support available to part-time students. Financial award application deadline: 5/1; financial award applicants required to submit FAFSA. *Faculty research:* Multiculturalism and the arts, art education, arts collaboration. *Unit head:* Dr. Thomas Bullard, Chairperson, 718-951-5666, Fax: 718-951-4606, E-mail: tbullard@brooklyn.cuny.edu. *Application contact:* Hernan Sierra, Graduate Admissions Coordinator, 718-951-4536, Fax: 718-951-4506, E-mail: grads@brooklyn.cuny.edu.

Brown University, Graduate School, Department of Theatre, Speech, and Dance, Providence, RI 02912. Offers acting and directing (MFA); theatre and performance studies (PhD); theatre arts (AM). *Degree requirements:* For master's, thesis or alternative. *Entrance requirements:* For master's, GRE General Test.

California Institute of the Arts, School of Theatre, Valencia, CA 91355-2340. Offers acting (MFA, Adv C); design and technology (Adv C); directing (MFA); performing arts design and technology (MFA); theater management (MFA, Adv C); writing for performance (MFA). *Accreditation:* NAST. *Degree requirements:* For master's, thesis (for some programs), faculty review, performance or portfolio. *Entrance requirements:* For master's, audition or portfolio, interview. Additional exam requirements/recommendations for international students: Required—TOEFL. Electronic applications accepted.

California State University, Fullerton, Graduate Studies, College of the Arts, Department of Theatre and Dance, Fullerton, CA 92834-9480. Offers acting (MFA); acting and directing (MA); dance (MA); directing (MFA); dramatic literature/criticism (MA); oral interpretation (MA); playwriting (MA); technical theater (MA); technical theater and design (MFA); television (MA); theatre for children (MA); theatre history (MA). *Accreditation:* NASD; NAST (one or more programs are accredited). Part-time programs available. *Students:* 21 full-time (10 women), 3 part-time (2 women); includes 2 minority (both African Americans). Average age 29. 43 applicants, 26% accepted, 11 enrolled. In 2008, 3 master's awarded. *Degree requirements:* For master's, oral and written exam, project or thesis. *Entrance requirements:* For master's, major in theatre or related field, audition or interview, minimum GPA of 2.5 in last 60 units of course work. Application fee: $55. Tuition and fees vary according to degree level. *Financial support:* Teaching assistantships, career-related internships or fieldwork, Federal Work-Study, institutionally sponsored loans, and scholarships/grants available. Support available to part-time students. Financial award application deadline: 3/1. *Unit head:* Dr. Susan Hallman, Chair, 657-278-3628. *Application contact:* Gretchen Kanne, Adviser, 657-278-3628.

California State University, Long Beach, Graduate Studies, College of Business Administration, Long Beach, CA 90840. Offers accelerated (MBA); evening (MBA); fully employed (MBA); theatre management (MBA). *Accreditation:* AACSB. Part-time and evening/weekend programs available. *Faculty:* 20 full-time (3 women), 1 part-time/adjunct (0 women). *Students:* 93 full-time (34 women), 199 part-time (88 women); includes 92 minority (3 African Americans, 1 American Indian/Alaska Native, 54 Asian Americans or Pacific Islanders, 34 Hispanic Americans), 45 international. Average age 32. 464 applicants, 44% accepted, 66 enrolled. *Entrance requirements:* For master's, GMAT. *Application deadline:* For fall admission, 3/30 for domestic students. Applications are processed on a rolling basis. Application fee: $55. Electronic applications accepted. *Expenses:* Tuition, nonresident: full-time $11,160; part-time $372 per unit. Required fees: $4100; $1261 per semester. *Financial support:* Career-related internships or fieldwork and scholarships/grants available. Financial award application deadline: 3/2; financial award applicants required to submit FAFSA. *Faculty research:* Attitude formation theory, consumer motivation, gift giving, derivative and synthetic securities, financial applications of artificial intelligence. *Unit head:* Dr. Michael E. Solt, Dean, 562-985-5307, Fax: 562-985-5742, E-mail: msolt@csulb.edu. *Application contact:* Dr. H Michael Chung, Director, Graduate Programs and Executive Education, 562-985-5565, Fax: 562-985-5742, E-mail: hmchung@csulb.edu.

California State University, Long Beach, Graduate Studies, College of the Arts, Department of Theatre Arts, Long Beach, CA 90840. Offers MFA, dramatic writing (MFA); technical theatre/design (MFA); theatre management (MFA); MBA/MFA. *Accreditation:* NAST. Part-time programs available. *Faculty:* 6 full-time (3 women), 3 part-time/adjunct (0 women). *Students:* 27 full-time (17 women), 12 part-time (7 women); includes 3 minority (all Asian Americans or Pacific Islanders), 5 international. Average age 32. 24 applicants, 29% accepted, 5 enrolled. *Degree requirements:* For master's, thesis or alternative. *Application deadline:* For fall admission, 7/1 for domestic students; for spring admission, 12/1 for domestic students. Applications are processed on a rolling basis. Application fee: $55. Electronic applications accepted. *Expenses:* Tuition, nonresident: full-time $11,160; part-time $372 per unit. Required fees: $4100; $1261 per semester. *Financial support:* Research assistantships, teaching assistantships, Federal Work-Study, institutionally sponsored loans, scholarships/grants, and traineeships available. Financial award application deadline: 3/2. *Unit head:* Dr. Joanne L. Gordon, Chair, 562-985-7891, Fax: 562-985-2263, E-mail: jgordon@csulb.edu. *Application contact:* Barbara Matthews, Graduate Adviser, 562-985-4042, Fax: 562-985-2263, E-mail: jmatthew@csulb.edu.

California State University, Los Angeles, Graduate Studies, College of Arts and Letters, Department of Communication Studies, Los Angeles, CA 90032-8530. Offers speech communication (MA); television, film and theatre (MFA). Part-time and evening/weekend programs available. *Faculty:* 12 full-time (3 women). *Students:* 64 full-time (37 women), 40 part-time (32 women); includes 47 minority (15 African Americans, 1 American Indian/Alaska Native, 13 Asian Americans or Pacific Islanders, 18 Hispanic Americans), 18 international. Average age 30. 88 applicants, 92% accepted, 47 enrolled. In 2008, 8 master's awarded. *Degree requirements:* For master's, comprehensive exam or thesis. *Entrance requirements:* For master's, minimum GPA of 2.75 in last 90 units of course work. Additional exam requirements/recommendations for international students: Required—TOEFL (minimum score 500 paper-based; 173 computer-based). *Application deadline:* For fall admission, 6/15 for domestic students, 5/1 for international students; for winter admission, 11/1 for domestic students, 9/1 for international students; for spring admission, 2/1 for domestic students, 10/1 for international students. Applications are processed on a rolling basis. Application fee: $55. Electronic applications accepted. *Expenses:* Tuition, nonresident: part-time $226 per credit. Required fees: $4019. *Financial support:* Career-related internships or fieldwork and Federal Work-Study available. Support available to part-time students. Financial award application deadline: 3/1. *Faculty research:* Organizational, interpersonal, intercultural, and instructional communication; rhetorical theories. *Unit head:* Dr. John Ramirez, Chair, 323-343-4200, Fax: 323-343-6467, E-mail: jramire4@calstatela.edu. *Application contact:* Dr. Jose L. Galvan, Dean of Graduate Studies, 323-343-3820, Fax: 323-343-5653, E-mail: jgalvan@cslanet.calstatela.edu.

California State University, Los Angeles, Graduate Studies, College of Arts and Letters, Department of Theater Arts and Dance, Los Angeles, CA 90032-8530. Offers theater arts (MA). Part-time and evening/weekend programs available. *Faculty:* 4 full-time (3 women). *Students:* 7 full-time (5 women), 12 part-time (6 women); includes 8 minority (3 African Americans, 2 Asian Americans or Pacific Islanders, 3 Hispanic Americans), 2 international. Average age 34. 10 applicants, 100% accepted, 5 enrolled. In 2008, 2 master's awarded. *Degree requirements:* For master's, comprehensive exam, project or thesis. *Entrance requirements:* For master's, minimum GPA of 2.5, 30 units of course work in theater. Additional exam requirements/recommendations for international students: Required—TOEFL (minimum score 500 paper-based; 173 computer-based). *Application deadline:* For fall admission, 6/15 for domestic students, 5/1 for international students; for winter admission, 11/1 for domestic students, 9/1 for international students; for spring admission, 2/1 for domestic students, 10/1 for international students. Applications are processed on a rolling basis. Application fee: $55. Electronic applications accepted. *Expenses:* Tuition, nonresident: part-time $226 per credit. Required fees: $4019. *Financial support:* Federal Work-Study available. Support available to part-time students. Financial award application deadline: 3/1. *Faculty research:* Sondheim, Taiwanese theater, Australian theater, absurdism, dramaturgy. *Unit head:* Dr. Stephen Rothman, Acting Chair, 323-343-4110, Fax: 323-343-5567, E-mail: srothma@exchange.calstatela.edu. *Application contact:* Dr. Jose L. Galvan, Dean of Graduate Studies, 323-343-3820, Fax: 323-343-5653, E-mail: jgalvan@cslanet.calstatela.edu.

California State University, Northridge, Graduate Studies, College of Arts, Media, and Communication, Department of Theatre, Northridge, CA 91330. Offers MA. *Accreditation:* NAST. *Faculty:* 9 full-time (4 women), 19 part-time/adjunct (6 women). *Students:* 9 full-time (6 women), 10 part-time (7 women); includes 5 minority (2 African Americans, 3 Hispanic Americans). Average age 36. 20 applicants, 70% accepted, 5 enrolled. In 2008, 2 master's awarded. *Degree requirements:* For master's, thesis. *Entrance requirements:* For master's, GRE General Test or minimum GPA of 3.0. Additional exam requirements/recommendations for international students: Required—TOEFL. *Application deadline:* For fall admission, 11/30 for domestic students. Application fee: $55. *Financial support:* Application deadline: 3/1. *Unit head:* Prof. Peter Grego, Chair, 818-677-3086. *Application contact:* Prof. Peter Grego, Chair, 818-677-3086.

California State University, Sacramento, Graduate Studies, College of Arts and Letters, Department of Theatre and Dance, Sacramento, CA 95819-6048. Offers MA. *Accreditation:* NAST. Part-time programs available. *Degree requirements:* For master's, thesis or alternative, writing proficiency exam. *Entrance requirements:* For master's, GRE General Test, BA in drama or equivalent, minimum GPA of 2.5 during previous 2 years of course work. Additional exam requirements/recommendations for international students: Required—TOEFL. Electronic applications accepted.

California State University, Sacramento, Graduate Studies, College of Social Sciences and Interdisciplinary Studies, Liberal Arts Program, Sacramento, CA 95819-6048. Offers French (MA); German (MA); Spanish (MA); theater arts (MA). *Degree requirements:* For master's, writing proficiency exam. *Entrance requirements:* Additional exam requirements/recommendations for international students: Required—TOEFL. Electronic applications accepted.

California State University, San Bernardino, Graduate Studies, College of Arts and Letters, Department of Theatre Arts, San Bernardino, CA 92407-2397. Offers theatre arts (MA); theatre education (MA); theatre for youth (MA). *Accreditation:* NAST. *Faculty:* 5 full-time (3 women). *Students:* 12 full-time (9 women), 8 part-time (7 women); includes 10 minority (4 African Americans, 1 American Indian/Alaska Native, 1 Asian American or Pacific Islander, 4 Hispanic Americans). Average age 33. 15 applicants, 73% accepted, 9 enrolled. *Degree requirements:* For master's, thesis. *Entrance requirements:* For master's, Graduate Entrance Writing Exam. Application fee: $55. *Expenses:* Tuition, area resident: Full-time $1252; part-time $726 per quarter. Required fees: $334 per quarter. Tuition and fees vary according to degree level and student level. *Unit head:* Dr. Margaret Perry, Chair, 909-537-5876, E-mail: mperry@csusb.edu. *Application contact:* Olivia Rosas, Director of Admissions, 909-537-7577, Fax: 909-537-7034, E-mail: orosas@csusb.edu.

Carnegie Mellon University, College of Fine Arts, School of Drama, Pittsburgh, PA 15213-3890. Offers design (MFA); directing (MFA); dramatic writing (MFA); production technology and management (MFA). *Degree requirements:* For master's, thesis (for some programs). *Entrance requirements:* For master's, audition, portfolio review, interview. Additional exam requirements/recommendations for international students: Required—TOEFL. *Faculty research:* Developing voice and speech compact disc.

Case Western Reserve University, School of Graduate Studies, Department of Theater and Dance, Cleveland, OH 44106. Offers acting (MFA); contemporary dance (MFA); dance (MA); theater (MFA). *Degree requirements:* For master's, thesis, oral presentation and defense, portfolio. *Entrance requirements:* For master's, audition, interview. Additional exam requirements/recommendations for international students: Required—TOEFL. Electronic applications accepted. *Faculty research:* Playwriting; history of theater; participation in professional area theaters in performing, design, acting, coaching.

The Catholic University of America, School of Arts and Sciences, Department of Drama, Washington, DC 20064. Offers acting, directing, and playwriting (MFA); theatre history and criticism (MA). Part-time programs available. *Degree requirements:* For master's, variable foreign language requirement, comprehensive exam, thesis (for some programs). *Entrance requirements:* For master's, GRE General Test, 3 letters of recommendation, audition, resumé. Additional exam requirements/recommendations for international students: Required—TOEFL (minimum score 580 paper-based; 237 computer-based). Electronic applications accepted. *Faculty research:* Professional theater, Shakespearean stage history, feminist criticism, Strindberg theory, historiography.

Central Washington University, Graduate Studies, Research and Continuing Education, College of Arts and Humanities, Department of Theatre Arts, Ellensburg, WA 98926. Offers theatre production (MA). Part-time programs available. *Degree requirements:* For master's, thesis or alternative. *Entrance requirements:* For master's, minimum GPA of 3.0. Additional exam requirements/recommendations for international students: Required—TOEFL (minimum score 550 paper-based; 213 computer-based; 79 iBT). Electronic applications accepted.

Christopher Newport University, Graduate Studies, Department of Teacher Preparation, Newport News, VA 23606-2998. Offers art (PK-12) (MAT); biology (6-12) (MAT); computer science (6-12) (MAT); elementary (PK-6) (MAT); English (6-12) (MAT); French (PK-12) (MAT); history (6-12) (MAT); history and social science (MAT); mathematics (6-12) (MAT); music (PK-12) (MAT), including choral, instrumental; physics (6-12) (MAT); Spanish (PK-12) (MAT); theater (PK-12) (MAT). Part-time and evening/weekend programs available. *Degree requirements:* For master's, comprehensive exam, thesis or alternative. *Entrance requirements:* For master's, PRAXIS I, minimum GPA of 3.0. Electronic applications accepted. *Faculty research:* Early literacy development, instructional innovations, professional teaching standards, multicultural issues, aesthetic education.

Columbia University, Graduate School of Arts and Sciences, Program in Theatre, New York, NY 10027. Offers M Phil, MA, PhD. *Degree requirements:* For master's, one foreign language, thesis, written exam; for doctorate, 2 foreign languages, thesis/dissertation. *Entrance requirements:* For master's and doctorate, GRE General Test, writing sample. Additional exam requirements/recommendations for international students: Required—TOEFL.

Columbia University, School of the Arts, Theatre Arts Division, New York, NY 10027. Offers acting (MFA); directing (MFA); dramaturgy (MFA); playwriting (MFA); stage management (MFA); theater management (MFA); JD/MFA. *Degree requirements:* For master's, thesis, 2 internships. *Entrance requirements:* For master's, 3 letters of recommendation, resumé, other requirements vary by concentration. Additional exam requirements/recommendations for international students: Required—TOEFL (minimum score 600 paper-based; 250 computer-based; 100 iBT). Electronic applications accepted.

See Close-Up on page 285.

Cornell University, Graduate School, Graduate Fields of Arts and Sciences, Field of Theatre Arts, Ithaca, NY 14853-0001. Offers drama and the theatre (PhD); theatre history (PhD); theatre theory and aesthetics (PhD). *Faculty:* 17 full-time (7 women). *Students:* 12 full-time (7 women), 3 international. Average age 31. 26 applicants, 19% accepted, 2 enrolled. In 2008, 1 doctorate awarded. *Degree requirements:* For doctorate, 2 foreign languages, comprehensive exam, thesis/dissertation. *Entrance requirements:* For doctorate, GRE General Test, sample of written work, 3 letters of recommendation. Additional exam requirements/recommendations for international students: Required—TOEFL (minimum score 600 paper-based; 250 computer-based; 77 iBT). *Application deadline:* For fall admission, 1/15 for domestic students. Application fee: $70. Electronic applications accepted. *Expenses:* Tuition: Full-time $29,500. Required fees: $70. Full-time tuition and fees vary according to degree level, program and student level. *Financial support:* In 2008–09, 8 students received support, including 3 fellowships with full tuition reimbursements available, 5 teaching assistantships with full tuition reimbursements available; research assistantships with full tuition reimbursements available, institutionally sponsored loans, scholarships/grants, health care benefits, tuition waivers (full and partial), and unspecified assistantships also available. Financial award applicants required to submit FAFSA. *Faculty research:* Cultural studies and critical theory, seventeenth to twentieth-first century European and American theater, theory of the performing arts, film history and theory, feminism and theater. *Unit head:* Director of Graduate Studies, 607-254-2757, Fax: 607-254-2733. *Application contact:* Graduate Field Assistant, 607-254-2757, Fax: 607-254-2733, E-mail: theatre_grad@cornell.edu.

Dell'Arte School of Physical Theatre, MFA Program, Blue Lake, CA 95525. Offers ensemble based physical theatre (MFA). *Accreditation:* NAST. *Entrance requirements:* For master's, undergraduate degree, audition. Electronic applications accepted. *Faculty research:* Physical Theatre, International Theatre, Ensemble, Divised.

DePaul University, The Theatre School, Chicago, IL 60614. Offers acting (MFA); arts leadership (MFA); directing (MFA). *Faculty:* 18 full-time (9 women), 24 part-time/adjunct (13 women). *Students:* 39 full-time (20 women); includes 7 minority (6 African Americans, 1 Hispanic American). Average age 28. 233 applicants, 8% accepted, 14 enrolled. In 2008, 11 master's awarded. *Degree requirements:* For master's, comprehensive exam, thesis. *Entrance requirements:* For master's, audition or interview. Additional exam requirements/recommendations for international students: Required—TOEFL (minimum score 550 paper-based; 213 computer-based). *Application deadline:* For fall admission, 1/15 priority date for domestic and international students. Application fee: $65. Electronic applications accepted. *Expenses:* Contact institution. *Financial support:* In 2008–09, 38 students received support, including 38 fellowships (averaging $16,600 per year); career-related internships or fieldwork, Federal Work-Study, institutionally sponsored loans, and scholarships/grants also available. Financial award application deadline: 2/15; financial award applicants required to submit FAFSA. *Unit head:* John Culbert, Dean, 773-325-7954, Fax: 773-325-7920, E-mail: jculbert@depaul.edu. *Application contact:* Jason Beck, Director of Admissions, 773-325-7999, Fax: 773-325-7920, E-mail: jbeck1@depaul.edu.

Drake University, School of Education, Department of Teaching and Learning, Program in Secondary Education, Des Moines, IA 50311-4516. Offers art (MAT); biology (MAT); business (MAT); chemistry (MAT); English (MAT); general science (MAT); history-American (MAT); history-world (MAT); journalism (MAT); mathematics (MAT); physical science (MAT); physics (MAT); sociology (MAT); speech (MAT); speech communication (MAT); theatre (MAT). Part-time programs available. *Degree requirements:* For master's, comprehensive exam, thesis (for some programs), internships (for some programs). *Entrance requirements:* For master's, GRE General Test, MAT, or Drake Writing Assessment, resumé, 2 letters of recommendation. Additional exam requirements/recommendations for international students: Required—TOEFL (minimum score 550 paper-based; 213 computer-based). Electronic applications accepted. *Faculty research:* Counseling and rehabilitation, behavioral supports, inquiry-based science methods, teacher quality enhancement.

Eastern Michigan University, Graduate School, College of Arts and Sciences, Department of Communication and Theatre Arts, Program in Arts Administration, Ypsilanti, MI 48197. Offers theatre arts-arts administration (MA). Part-time and evening/weekend programs available. Postbaccalaureate distance learning degree programs offered (minimal on-campus study). *Entrance requirements:* Additional exam requirements/recommendations for international students: Required—TOEFL.

Eastern Michigan University, Graduate School, College of Arts and Sciences, Department of Communication and Theatre Arts, Program in Drama/Theatre for the Young, Ypsilanti, MI 48197. Offers MA, MFA. Part-time programs available. Postbaccalaureate distance learning degree programs offered (minimal on-campus study). *Degree requirements:* For master's, thesis optional. *Entrance requirements:* Additional exam requirements/recommendations for international students: Required—TOEFL.

Eastern Michigan University, Graduate School, College of Arts and Sciences, Department of Communication and Theatre Arts, Program in Theatre, Ypsilanti, MI 48197. Offers interpretation/performance studies (MA); theatre arts (MA). Part-time and evening/weekend programs available. Postbaccalaureate distance learning degree programs offered (minimal on-campus study). *Degree requirements:* For master's, thesis or alternative. *Entrance requirements:* Additional exam requirements/recommendations for international students: Required—TOEFL.

Emerson College, Graduate Studies, School of the Arts, Department of Performing Arts, Program in Theatre Education, Boston, MA 02116-4624. Offers MA. Part-time programs available. *Students:* 64 full-time (49 women), 15 part-time (11 women); includes 5 minority (4 African Americans, 1 Asian American or Pacific Islander), 1 international. Average age 27. 72 applicants, 82% accepted, 36 enrolled. In 2008, 30 master's awarded. *Degree requirements:* For master's, thesis optional. *Entrance requirements:* For master's, GRE General Test. Additional exam requirements/recommendations for international students: Required—TOEFL (minimum score 550 paper-based; 213 computer-based; 80 iBT), IELTS (minimum score 6.5). *Application deadline:* For fall admission, 6/1 priority date for domestic students, 5/1 for international students. Applications are processed on a rolling basis. Application fee: $60 ($75 for international students). Electronic applications accepted. *Expenses:* Tuition: Full-time $17,720; part-time $886 per credit. Required fees: $60 per year. One-time fee: $170. *Financial support:* In 2008–09, 13 students received support, including 2 fellowships with partial tuition reimbursements available (averaging $14,000 per year), 11 research assistantships with partial tuition reimbursements available (averaging $10,000 per year); teaching assistantships with partial tuition reimbursements available, career-related internships or fieldwork, Federal Work-Study, institutionally sponsored loans, scholarships/grants, and unspecified assistantships also available. Support available to part-time students. Financial award application deadline: 3/1; financial award applicants required to submit FAFSA. *Faculty research:* Theater. *Unit head:* Dr. Robert Colby, Graduate Program Director, 617-824-8780, E-mail: Robert_Colby@emerson.edu. *Application contact:* Office of Graduate Admission, 617-824-8610, Fax: 617-824-8614, E-mail: gradapp@emerson.edu.

Florida Atlantic University, Dorothy F. Schmidt College of Arts and Letters, Department of Theatre, Boca Raton, FL 33431-0991. Offers acting (MFA); design and technology (MFA). *Faculty:* 8 full-time (1 woman), 1 (woman) part-time/adjunct. *Students:* 22 full-time (13 women), 1 part-time (0 women); includes 1 minority (African American). Average age 29. 18 applicants, 72% accepted, 2 enrolled. In 2008, 5 master's awarded. *Degree requirements:* For master's, thesis, production. *Entrance requirements:* For master's, GRE General Test, minimum GPA of 3.0 during last 60 hours of undergraduate course work. *Application deadline:* For fall admission, 8/15 priority date for domestic students, 8/15 for international students. Applications are processed on a rolling basis. Application fee: $30. *Expenses:* Tuition, state resident: full-time $4867; part-time $270.40 per credit hour. Tuition, nonresident: full-time $16,486; part-time $915.87 per credit hour. *Financial support:* Fellowships, teaching assistantships with full tuition reimbursements, career-related internships or fieldwork, Federal Work-Study, and institutionally sponsored loans available. Support available to part-time students. Financial award application deadline: 3/31. *Faculty research:* Contemporary British theatre, Eastern European playwrights, Latin American drama. *Unit head:* Dr. Richard Gamble, Chair, 561-297-3815, Fax: 561-297-2180, E-mail: gamble@fau.edu. *Application contact:* Dr. Emily Stockard, Associate Dean, 561-297-2817, Fax: 561-297-2744, E-mail: stockard@fau.edu.

Florida State University, Graduate Studies, School of Theatre, Tallahassee, FL 32306. Offers acting (MFA); directing (MFA); lighting, costume, and scenic design (MFA); technical production (MFA); theater management (MFA); theatre (MA, MS, PhD). *Accreditation:* NAST. *Degree requirements:* For master's, one foreign language, comprehensive exam (for some programs), thesis (for some programs); for doctorate, one foreign language, comprehensive exam, thesis/dissertation. *Entrance requirements:* For master's, GRE General Test, writing sample (MA), interview (MFA), minimum undergraduate GPA of 3.0, audition (MFA in acting), portfolio (MFA). Additional exam requirements/recommendations for international students: Required—TOEFL. *Faculty research:* Gender theatre, performance theory, computers in theatre, dramaturgy, music theatre performance.

Fontbonne University, Graduate Programs, Department of Fine Arts, St. Louis, MO 63105-3098. Offers art (MA); fine arts (MFA); theater education (MA). Part-time and evening/weekend programs available. *Faculty:* 5 full-time (1 woman), 4 part-time/adjunct (all women). *Students:* 13 full-time (7 women), 5 part-time (2 women); includes 2 minority (1 African American, 1 Asian American or Pacific Islander), 2 international. Average age 35. In 2008, 15 master's awarded. *Degree requirements:* For master's, thesis exhibit (MFA). *Entrance requirements:* For master's, minimum GPA of 3.0, portfolio. *Application deadline:* For fall admission, 8/1 priority date for domestic students. Applications are processed on a rolling basis. Application fee: $25. *Expenses:* Tuition: Part-time $540 per credit hour. Required fees: $270 per year. *Financial support:* In 2008–09, teaching assistantships (averaging $2,500 per year). Support available to part-time students. Financial award application deadline: 4/1; financial award applicants required to submit FAFSA. *Unit head:* Catherine Connor-Talasek, Chairperson, 314-889-1431, Fax: 314-889-4545, E-mail: cconnor@fontbonne.edu. *Application contact:* Catherine Connor-Talasek, Chairperson, 314-889-1431, Fax: 314-889-4545, E-mail: cconnor@fontbonne.edu.

The George Washington University, Columbian College of Arts and Sciences, Department of Theatre and Dance, Washington, DC 20052. Offers classical acting (MFA); design (MFA). Part-time and evening/weekend programs available. *Faculty:* 11 full-time (6 women), 11 part-time/adjunct (8 women). *Students:* 18 full-time (8 women), 12 part-time (3 women), 2 international. Average age 36. In 2008, 14 master's awarded. *Degree requirements:* For master's, thesis. *Entrance requirements:* For master's, minimum GPA of 3.0, portfolio. Additional exam requirements/recommendations for international students: Required—TOEFL (minimum score 550 paper-based; 213 computer-based; 80 iBT). *Application deadline:* For fall admission, 8/1 priority date for domestic students; for spring admission, 10/1 priority date for domestic students. Applications are processed on a rolling basis. Application fee: $60. Electronic applications accepted. *Financial support:* In 2008–09, 2 students received support; fellowships with tuition reimbursements available, teaching assistantships with tuition reimbursements available, career-related internships or fieldwork, Federal Work-Study, and tuition waivers available. *Unit head:* Alan G. Wade, Interim Chair, 202-994-3664, E-mail: awade@gwu.edu. *Application contact:* Information Contact, 202-994-8072, E-mail: trdanews@gwu.edu.

Graduate School and University Center of the City University of New York, Graduate Studies, Program in Theatre, New York, NY 10016-4039. Offers PhD. *Degree requirements:* For doctorate, 2 foreign languages, thesis/dissertation. *Entrance requirements:* For doctorate, GRE General Test, writing sample. Additional exam requirements/recommendations for international students: Required—TOEFL. Electronic applications accepted.

Hollins University, Graduate Programs, Program in Playwriting, Roanoke, VA 24020-1603. Offers MFA. Part-time programs available. *Faculty:* 1 full-time (0 women), 2 part-time/adjunct (1 woman). *Students:* 11 full-time (7 women), 2 part-time (0 women); includes 1 minority (African American). Average age 39. 13 applicants, 100% accepted, 7 enrolled. *Degree requirements:* For master's, comprehensive exam, thesis. *Entrance requirements:* For master's, letters of recommendation, writing samples. Additional exam requirements/recommendations for international students: Required—TOEFL (minimum score 550 paper-based; 213 computer-based; 79 iBT). Application fee: $40. *Expenses:* Tuition: Full-time $26,720; part-time $590 per credit hour. Required fees: $280. *Financial support:* In 2008–09, 6 fellowships (averaging $1,027 per year) were awarded. *Unit head:* Todd Ristau, Director, 540-362-6386, E-mail: tristau@hollins.edu. *Application contact:* Cathy S. Koon, Manager of Graduate Services, 540-362-6326, Fax: 540-362-6288, E-mail: ckoon@hollins.edu.

Humboldt State University, Graduate Studies, College of Arts, Humanities, and Social Sciences, Department of Theatre, Film and Dance, Arcata, CA 95521-8299. Offers theatre arts (MA, MFA), including film production (MA), production (MA), scenography (MFA). *Students:* 13 full-time (8 women), 2 part-time (1 woman); includes 2 minority (both Hispanic Americans). Average age 35. 23 applicants, 52% accepted, 9 enrolled. In 2008, 2 master's awarded.

Theater

Humboldt State University (continued)

Degree requirements: For master's, thesis or alternative, qualifying exam. *Entrance requirements:* For master's, minimum GPA of 2.5. Additional exam requirements/recommendations for international students: Required—TOEFL (minimum score 500 paper-based; 173 computer-based). *Application deadline:* For fall admission, 4/15 for domestic students. Applications are processed on a rolling basis. Application fee: $55. *Expenses:* Tuition, state resident: full-time $5236. Tuition, nonresident: full-time $11,338. *Financial support:* Fellowships available. Financial award application deadline: 3/1; financial award applicants required to submit FAFSA. *Faculty research:* Physical theater, design, playwriting. *Unit head:* Bernadette Cheyne, Chair/Coordinator, 707-826-4606, Fax: 707-826-5494, E-mail: bmc3@humboldt.edu. *Application contact:* Ann Alter, Coordinator, 707-826-5495, Fax: 707-826-5494, E-mail: aea2@humboldt.edu.

Hunter College of the City University of New York, Graduate School, School of Arts and Sciences, Department of Theatre, New York, NY 10021-5085. Offers MA. Part-time and evening/weekend programs available. *Faculty:* 4 full-time (2 women). *Students:* 38 part-time (27 women); includes 4 minority (1 Asian American or Pacific Islander, 3 Hispanic Americans). Average age 36. 16 applicants, 69% accepted, 6 enrolled. In 2008, 11 master's awarded. *Degree requirements:* For master's, comprehensive exam, thesis. *Entrance requirements:* For master's, GRE General Test. Additional exam requirements/recommendations for international students: Required—TOEFL. *Application deadline:* For fall admission, 4/1 for domestic students, 2/1 for international students; for spring admission, 11/1 for domestic students, 9/1 for international students. Application fee: $125. *Financial support:* In 2008–09, 1 fellowship (averaging $3,000 per year), 4 teaching assistantships were awarded; research assistantships, career-related internships or fieldwork, Federal Work-Study, and tuition waivers (partial) also available. Support available to part-time students. Financial award application deadline: 4/15. *Faculty research:* Modern French mimes, acting techniques, directing, New York avant-garde theater and popular entertainment, playwriting. *Unit head:* Dr. Barbara Bosch, Chairperson, 212-772-5148/9, Fax: 212-650-3584, E-mail: bbosch@hunter.cuny.edu. *Application contact:* Mira Felner, Graduate Advisor, 212-772-4642, E-mail: theatre@hunter.cuny.edu.

Idaho State University, Office of Graduate Studies, College of Arts and Sciences, Program in Theatre and Dance, Pocatello, ID 83209. Offers theatre (MA). Part-time programs available. *Faculty:* 4 full-time (2 women). *Students:* 4 full-time (all women), 5 part-time (3 women). Average age 37. In 2008, 3 master's awarded. *Degree requirements:* For master's, comprehensive exam, thesis optional. *Entrance requirements:* For master's, GRE General Test (35th percentile or above on one of the 3 sections). Additional exam requirements/recommendations for international students: Required—TOEFL (minimum score 550 paper-based; 213 computer-based; 80 iBT). *Application deadline:* For fall admission, 7/1 for domestic students, 6/1 for international students; for spring admission, 12/1 for domestic students, 11/1 for international students. Applications are processed on a rolling basis. Application fee: $55. Electronic applications accepted. *Expenses:* Tuition, area resident: Full-time $3114; part-time $276 per credit hour. Tuition, state resident: full-time $3114; part-time $276 per credit hour. Tuition, nonresident: full-time $12,318; part-time $404 per credit hour. Required fees: $2360. Tuition and fees vary according to course load and reciprocity agreements. *Financial support:* In 2008–09, 3 teaching assistantships with full and partial tuition reimbursements (averaging $9,401 per year) were awarded; Federal Work-Study, institutionally sponsored loans, scholarships/grants, health care benefits, tuition waivers (full and partial), and unspecified assistantships also available. Support available to part-time students. Financial award application deadline: 1/1; financial award applicants required to submit FAFSA. *Faculty research:* Theatre history, technical theatre. *Unit head:* Chad Gross, Co-Chair, 208-282-3173, Fax: 208-282-6281, E-mail: groschad@isu.edu. *Application contact:* Ellen Combs, Graduate School Technical Records Specialist, 208-282-2150, Fax: 208-282-4847, E-mail: combelle@isu.edu.

Illinois State University, Graduate School, College of Fine Arts, School of Theatre, Normal, IL 61790-2200. Offers MA, MFA, MS. *Accreditation:* NAST. Part-time programs available. *Degree requirements:* For master's, variable foreign language requirement, thesis or alternative. *Entrance requirements:* For master's, sample of written work, minimum GPA of 3.0 in last 60 hours of course work. *Faculty research:* Illinois Shakespeare festival.

Indiana University Bloomington, University Graduate School, College of Arts and Sciences, Department of Theatre and Drama, Bloomington, IN 47405-7000. Offers acting (MFA); design and technology (MFA); directing (MFA); literature (MA, PhD); playwriting (MFA); theatre and drama (MAT); theatre history (MA, PhD); theory (MA, PhD). *Accreditation:* NAST. *Faculty:* 20 full-time (4 women). *Students:* 41 full-time (17 women), 3 part-time (2 women); includes 5 minority (2 African Americans, 1 American Indian/Alaska Native, 2 Hispanic Americans), 3 international. Average age 29. 65 applicants, 23% accepted, 15 enrolled. In 2008, 10 master's, 2 doctorates awarded. Terminal master's awarded for partial completion of doctoral program. *Degree requirements:* For master's, one foreign language, comprehensive exam, thesis, 30 credit hours (60 hours for MFA); for doctorate, 2 foreign languages, comprehensive exam, thesis/dissertation, 90 credit hours. *Entrance requirements:* For master's, audition, interview, portfolio or script analysis; for doctorate, GRE General Test. Additional exam requirements/recommendations for international students: Required—TOEFL (minimum score 550 paper-based; 213 computer-based; 80 iBT). *Application deadline:* For fall admission, 1/15 priority date for domestic students, 12/1 for international students. Application fee: $50 ($60 for international students). Electronic applications accepted. *Expenses:* Tuition, area resident: Part-time $291.97 per credit hour. Tuition, state resident: part-time $291.97 per credit hour. Tuition, nonresident: part-time $850.33 per credit hour. Required fees: $110 per semester. Tuition and fees vary according to course load and program. *Financial support:* In 2008–09, 38 students received support; fellowships with tuition reimbursements available, research assistantships with tuition reimbursements available, teaching assistantships with full tuition reimbursements available, career-related internships or fieldwork, Federal Work-Study, institutionally sponsored loans, scholarships/grants, health care benefits, and unspecified assistantships available. Financial award application deadline: 3/1. *Faculty research:* American, western European, world literature; history and theory; theatrical production, design and technology; acting; directing; playwriting. *Unit head:* Jonathan R. Michaelsen, Chairperson and Professor, 812-855-4535, Fax: 812-856-0698, E-mail: theatre@indiana.edu. *Application contact:* Barb Grinder, Administrative Secretary, 812-855-4535, Fax: 812-855-0698, E-mail: bgrinder@indiana.edu.

Kansas State University, Graduate School, College of Arts and Sciences, Department of Communication Studies, Theatre and Dance, Manhattan, KS 66505. Offers rhetoric/communication (MA); theatre (MA). *Faculty:* 16 full-time (8 women). *Students:* 30 full-time (24 women), 7 part-time (2 women); includes 4 minority (1 African American, 1 American Indian/Alaska Native, 1 Asian American or Pacific Islander, 1 Hispanic American), 1 international. Average age 27. 11 applicants, 100% accepted, 7 enrolled. In 2008, 12 master's awarded. *Degree requirements:* For master's, thesis or alternative. *Entrance requirements:* For master's, GRE General Test (recommended), minimum GPA of 3.0. Additional exam requirements/recommendations for international students: Required—TOEFL. *Application deadline:* For fall admission, 3/1 for domestic students, 2/1 priority date for international students; for spring admission, 10/1 for domestic students, 8/1 priority date for international students. Applications are processed on a rolling basis. Application fee: $30 ($55 for international students). *Expenses:* Tuition, area resident: Full-time $6466; part-time $269.40 per credit hour. Tuition, state resident: full-time $6466; part-time $269.40 per credit hour. Tuition, nonresident: full-time $14,874; part-time $619.75 per credit hour. Required fees: $673; $23.40 per credit hour. Tuition and fees vary according to campus/location. *Financial support:* In 2008–09, 27 teaching assistantships with full tuition reimbursements (averaging $10,111 per year) were awarded; career-related internships or fieldwork, institutionally sponsored loans, and scholarships/grants also available. Support available to part-time students. Financial award application deadline: 3/1; financial award applicants required to submit FAFSA. *Faculty research:* Drama therapy, directing, costume design, scenic design, and technical theatre mechanics and safety. *Unit head:* Charles Griffin, Head, 785-532-6860, Fax: 785-532-3714, E-mail: charlieg@ksu.edu. *Application contact:* William Schenck-Hamlin, Director, 785-532-6861, Fax: 785-532-3714, E-mail: billsh@ksu.edu.

Kent State University, College of the Arts, School of Theatre and Dance, Kent, OH 44242-0001. Offers acting (MFA); design and technology (MFA); theatre (MA, MFA). *Accreditation:* NAST. Part-time programs available. *Degree requirements:* For master's, thesis. *Entrance requirements:* For master's, GRE General Test, minimum GPA of 2.75. Additional exam requirements/recommendations for international students: Required—TOEFL. Electronic applications accepted. *Faculty research:* Scene design, costume design, lighting design, technical direction, musical theatre.

Lamar University, College of Graduate Studies, College of Fine Arts and Communication, Department of Music, Theatre, and Dance, Beaumont, TX 77710. Offers music education (MM Ed); music performance (MM); theatre (MS). *Accreditation:* NASM (one or more programs are accredited). *Faculty:* 7 full-time (3 women), 2 part-time/adjunct (both women). *Students:* 3 full-time (2 women), 3 part-time (2 women); includes 1 minority (African American). Average age 29. 2 applicants, 100% accepted, 1 enrolled. In 2008, 8 master's awarded. *Degree requirements:* For master's, comprehensive exam, thesis optional. *Entrance requirements:* For master's, GRE General Test, theory placement exams, audition. Additional exam requirements/recommendations for international students: Required—TOEFL. *Application deadline:* For fall admission, 8/1 for domestic students; for spring admission, 12/1 for domestic students. Applications are processed on a rolling basis. Application fee: $25 ($50 for international students). *Expenses:* Tuition, state resident: full-time $5000; part-time $195 per credit. Tuition, nonresident: full-time $12,376; part-time $476 per credit. Required fees: $1570. *Financial support:* In 2008–09, 4 fellowships with tuition reimbursements (averaging $2,000 per year), 2 teaching assistantships were awarded; institutionally sponsored loans and tuition waivers (partial) also available. Support available to part-time students. Financial award application deadline: 4/1. *Faculty research:* Performance: ensembles and personal. *Unit head:* Dr. L. Randolph Babin, Chair, 409-880-8144, Fax: 409-880-8143, E-mail: babinlr@hal.lamar.edu. *Application contact:* Dr. Robert M. Culbertson, Adviser, 409-880-8073, Fax: 409-880-8143, E-mail: culbertsrm@hal.lamar.edu.

Lindenwood University, Graduate Programs, School of Fine and Performing Arts, St. Charles, MO 63301-1695. Offers arts management (MA); communication arts (MA); studio art (MA, MFA); theatre (MA, MFA). Part-time programs available. *Faculty:* 21 full-time (10 women). *Students:* 28 full-time (18 women), 27 part-time (21 women); includes 8 minority (all African Americans), 7 international. Average age 35. In 2008, 16 master's awarded. *Degree requirements:* For master's, thesis (for some programs). *Entrance requirements:* For master's, audition or interview, minimum GPA of 3.0, official transcripts, submission of portfolio, essay, letter of recommendation. Additional exam requirements/recommendations for international students: Required—TOEFL (minimum score 550 paper-based; 213 computer-based; 80 iBT). *Application deadline:* For fall admission, 8/30 priority date for domestic and international students; for spring admission, 12/30 priority date for domestic and international students. Applications are processed on a rolling basis. Application fee: $30 ($100 for international students). Electronic applications accepted. *Expenses:* Tuition: Full-time $12,700; part-time $360 per credit hour. *Financial support:* Career-related internships or fieldwork, institutionally sponsored loans, tuition waivers (partial), and unspecified assistantships available. Financial award application deadline: 6/30; financial award applicants required to submit FAFSA. *Unit head:* Donnell Walsh, Dean of Fine Arts, 636-949-4853, Fax: 636-949-4910, E-mail: dwalsh@lindenwood.edu. *Application contact:* Brett Barger, Dean of Evening Admissions and Extension Campuses, 636-949-4934, Fax: 636-949-4109, E-mail: adultadmissions@lindenwood.edu.

Long Island University, C.W. Post Campus, School of Visual and Performing Arts, Department of Theatre, Film, Dance and Arts Management, Brookville, NY 11548-1300. Offers interactive multimedia (MA); theatre (MA). Part-time and evening/weekend programs available. *Degree requirements:* For master's, thesis. *Entrance requirements:* For master's, placement exam. Electronic applications accepted. *Faculty research:* Playwriting, intercultural dance and theatre, translation, Suzuki, set and costume design.

Louisiana State University and Agricultural and Mechanical College, Graduate School, College of Music and Dramatic Arts, Department of Theatre, Baton Rouge, LA 70803. Offers acting (MFA); directing (MFA); theatre (PhD); theatre design/technology (MFA). *Accreditation:* NAST. *Degree requirements:* For master's, thesis; for doctorate, one foreign language, thesis/dissertation. *Entrance requirements:* For master's, GRE General Test, audition, minimum GPA of 3.0; for doctorate, GRE General Test, minimum GPA of 3.0. Additional exam requirements/recommendations for international students: Required—TOEFL (minimum score 550 paper-based; 213 computer-based; 79 iBT). Electronic applications accepted. *Faculty research:* Acting, American drama, arts administration, theatre history, dramatic theory/literature, black drama.

Mary Baldwin College, Graduate Studies, Program in Shakespeare and Renaissance Literature in Performance, Staunton, VA 24401-3610. Offers acting (M Litt); directing (M Litt); Shakespeare and Renaissance literature in performance (MFA); teaching (M Litt). *Entrance requirements:* For master's, GRE (M Litt).

Massachusetts College of Art and Design, Graduate Programs, Program in Fine Arts, Boston, MA 02115-5882. Offers ceramics (MFA); design (MFA); fibers (MFA); film (MFA); glass (MFA); media and performing arts (MFA); metals (MFA); painting (MFA); photography (MFA); printmaking (MFA); sculpture (MFA). *Accreditation:* NASAD. *Faculty:* 10 full-time (5 women), 8 part-time/adjunct (6 women). *Students:* 83 full-time (53 women), 17 part-time (10 women); includes 8 minority (1 American Indian/Alaska Native, 4 Asian Americans or Pacific Islanders, 3 Hispanic Americans), 15 international. Average age 34. 295 applicants, 24% accepted, 40 enrolled. In 2008, 37 master's awarded. *Degree requirements:* For master's, thesis, exhibit. *Entrance requirements:* For master's, 12 units of course work in art history, portfolio, resumé, college transcripts, statement of purpose, letters of reference, interview. Additional exam requirements/recommendations for international students: Required—TOEFL (minimum score 563 paper-based; 223 computer-based; 85 iBT); Recommended—IELTS (minimum score 6.5). *Application deadline:* For fall admission, 1/15 for domestic and international students; for spring admission, 11/1 for domestic students. Application fee: $75. *Expenses:* Tuition, area resident: Full-time $17,100; part-time $570 per credit. Tuition and fees vary according to program. *Financial support:* In 2008–09, 50 research assistantships (averaging $2,000 per year), 30 teaching assistantships (averaging $2,000 per year) were awarded; career-related internships or fieldwork, Federal Work-Study, and clerical/technical assistantships also available. Support available to part-time students. Financial award application deadline: 5/1; financial award applicants required to submit FAFSA. *Unit head:* George Creamer, Director, 617-879-7163, Fax: 617-879-7171, E-mail: creamer@massart.edu. *Application contact:* George Creamer, Director, 617-879-7163.

Miami University, Graduate School, School of Fine Arts, Department of Theatre, Oxford, OH 45056. Offers MA. *Accreditation:* NAST. *Degree requirements:* For master's, thesis (for some programs), final exam. *Entrance requirements:* For master's, minimum undergraduate GPA of 3.0 during previous 2 years or 2.75 overall.

Michigan State University, The Graduate School, College of Arts and Letters, Department of Theatre, East Lansing, MI 48824. Offers MA, MFA. *Entrance requirements:* Additional exam requirements/recommendations for international students: Required—TOEFL. Electronic applications accepted.

Minnesota State University Mankato, College of Graduate Studies, College of Arts and Humanities, Department of Theatre and Dance, Mankato, MN 56001. Offers design/technology (MFA); performance (MFA); theatre arts (MA, MFA). *Students:* 12 full-time (6 women), 6 part-time (2 women). *Degree requirements:* For master's, one foreign language, comprehensive exam, thesis. *Entrance requirements:* For master's, minimum GPA of 3.0 during previous 2 years, 3 letters of recommendation, resumé of theatre work, audition. Additional exam requirements/recommendations for international students: Required—TOEFL. *Application deadline:* For fall admission, 7/1 priority date for domestic students, 5/1 for international students; for spring admission, 11/1 for domestic students, 10/1 for international students.

Applications are processed on a rolling basis. Application fee: $40. Electronic applications accepted. *Financial support:* Research assistantships with full tuition reimbursements, teaching assistantships with full tuition reimbursements, career-related internships or fieldwork, Federal Work-Study, institutionally sponsored loans, and unspecified assistantships available. Support available to part-time students. Financial award application deadline: 3/15; financial award applicants required to submit FAFSA. *Unit head:* Dr. Paul Hustoles, Chairperson, 507-389-2118. *Application contact:* 507-389-2321, E-mail: grad@mnsu.edu.

Missouri State University, Graduate College, College of Arts and Letters, Department of Theatre and Dance, Springfield, MO 65804-0094. Offers secondary education (MS Ed), including speech and theatre; theatre (MA). *Accreditation:* NAST. Part-time programs available. *Faculty:* 7 full-time (3 women). *Students:* 4 full-time (3 women), 2 part-time (both women). Average age 24. 5 applicants, 100% accepted, 4 enrolled. In 2008, 4 master's awarded. *Degree requirements:* For master's, comprehensive exam, thesis or alternative. *Entrance requirements:* For master's, minimum GPA of 3.0 (MA), 9-12 teaching certification (MS Ed). Additional exam requirements/recommendations for international students: Required—TOEFL (minimum score 550 paper-based; 213 computer-based; 79 iBT). *Application deadline:* For fall admission, 7/20 for domestic students, 5/1 for international students; for spring admission, 12/20 for domestic students, 9/1 for international students. Applications are processed on a rolling basis. Application fee: $35 ($50 for international students). Electronic applications accepted. *Expenses:* Tuition, state resident: full-time $3852; part-time $214 per credit hour. Tuition, nonresident: full-time $7524; part-time $418 per credit hour. Required fees: $230 per semester. Tuition and fees vary according to course level and course load. *Financial support:* Federal Work-Study, institutionally sponsored loans, scholarships/grants, and unspecified assistantships available. Financial award application deadline: 3/31; financial award applicants required to submit FAFSA. *Unit head:* Mark Biggs, Acting Head, 417-836-4400, Fax: 417-836-4234. *Application contact:* Eric Eckert, Coordinator of Admissions and Recruitment, 417-836-5331, Fax: 417-836-6888, E-mail: ericeckert@missouristate.edu.

Montclair State University, The Office of Graduate Admissions and Support Services, School of the Arts, Department of Theatre and Dance, Montclair, NJ 07043-1624. Offers theatre (MA), including arts management, production/stage management, theatre studies. *Accreditation:* NAST. Part-time and evening/weekend programs available. *Faculty:* 15 full-time (8 women), 42 part-time/adjunct (26 women). *Students:* 5 full-time (4 women), 20 part-time (14 women); includes 6 minority (5 African Americans, 1 Hispanic American). Average age 32. 16 applicants, 63% accepted, 7 enrolled. In 2008, 8 master's awarded. *Degree requirements:* For master's, comprehensive exam, thesis or alternative. *Entrance requirements:* For master's, GRE General Test, minimum GPA of 3.0, undergraduate degree or work in theatre, oral interpretation, broadcasting, speech communication or media; 2 letters of recommendation. Additional exam requirements/recommendations for international students: Required—TOEFL (minimum score 83 computer-based). *Application deadline:* For fall admission, 6/1 for international students; for spring admission, 10/1 for international students. Applications are processed on a rolling basis. Application fee: $60. Electronic applications accepted. *Financial support:* In 2008–09, 1 research assistantship with full tuition reimbursement (averaging $7,000 per year) was awarded; Federal Work-Study, scholarships/grants, and unspecified assistantships also available. Support available to part-time students. Financial award application deadline: 3/1; financial award applicants required to submit FAFSA. *Unit head:* Dr. Jane Peterson, Chairperson, 973-655-4217, E-mail: peterson@mail.montclair.edu. *Application contact:* Dr. Jane Peterson, Adviser, 973-655-4109, E-mail: petersonj@mail.montclair.edu.

Naropa University, Graduate Programs, Program in Theater: Contemporary Performance, Boulder, CO 80302-6697. Offers MFA. *Faculty:* 5 full-time (4 women), 7 part-time/adjunct (6 women). *Students:* 33 full-time (23 women); includes 9 minority (2 African Americans, 4 Asian Americans or Pacific Islanders, 3 Hispanic Americans), 2 international. Average age 32. 36 applicants, 56% accepted, 13 enrolled. In 2008, 14 master's awarded. *Degree requirements:* For master's, culminating projects and performances. *Entrance requirements:* For master's, interview, head shot, resumé, 3 letters of recommendation, letter of interest. Additional exam requirements/recommendations for international students: Required—TOEFL (minimum score 600 paper-based; 250 computer-based). *Application deadline:* For fall admission, 1/15 priority date for domestic and international students. Applications are processed on a rolling basis. Application fee: $60. Electronic applications accepted. *Expenses:* Tuition: Full-time $14,767; part-time $726 per credit hour. Required fees: $45 per term. *Financial support:* In 2008–09, 20 students received support, including 4 research assistantships (averaging $3,000 per year), 2 teaching assistantships with partial tuition reimbursements available (averaging $3,000 per year); Federal Work-Study, scholarships/grants, health care benefits, tuition waivers (partial), and unspecified assistantships also available. Support available to part-time students. Financial award application deadline: 3/1; financial award applicants required to submit FAFSA. *Unit head:* Wendell Beavers, Director, Performing Arts, 303-245-4640. *Application contact:* Kate Levene, Admissions Counselor, 303-245-4657, Fax: 303-546-3583, E-mail: klevene@naropa.edu.

See Close-Up on page 1121.

Naropa University, Graduate Programs, Program in Theater: Lecoq-Based Actor-Created Theater, Boulder, CO 80302-6697. Offers MFA. Part-time programs available. *Faculty:* 1 (woman) full-time. *Students:* 24 part-time (20 women); includes 3 minority (all Hispanic Americans), 3 international. Average age 27. 28 applicants, 82% accepted, 17 enrolled. In 2008, 14 master's awarded. *Degree requirements:* For master's, final student production. *Entrance requirements:* For master's, interview, head shot, 3 letters of recommendation, resumé, letter of interest. Additional exam requirements/recommendations for international students: Required—TOEFL (minimum score 600 paper-based; 250 computer-based). *Application deadline:* For fall admission, 1/15 priority date for domestic and international students. Applications are processed on a rolling basis. Application fee: $60. Electronic applications accepted. *Expenses:* Tuition: Full-time $14,767; part-time $726 per credit hour. Required fees: $45 per term. *Financial support:* In 2008–09, 8 students received support. Scholarships/grants and tuition waivers (partial) available. Support available to part-time students. Financial award application deadline: 3/1. *Unit head:* Amy Russell, Chair, 303-482-1032, E-mail: london@naropa.edu. *Application contact:* Kate Levene, Assistant Director of Admissions, 303-245-4657, Fax: 303-546-3583, E-mail: klevene@naropa.edu.

See Close-Up on page 1121.

National Theatre Conservatory, Department of Acting, Denver, CO 80204-2157. Offers MFA, Certificate. *Entrance requirements:* For master's, audition/interview.

The New School: A University, The New School for Drama, New York, NY 10014. Offers acting (MFA); directing (MFA); playwriting (MFA). *Faculty:* 5 full-time (2 women), 37 part-time/adjunct (20 women). *Students:* 124 full-time (73 women), 7 part-time (6 women); includes 19 minority (14 African Americans, 5 Hispanic Americans), 21 international. Average age 27. 358 applicants, 20% accepted, 50 enrolled. In 2008, 52 master's awarded. *Degree requirements:* For master's, thesis project. *Entrance requirements:* For master's, audition (acting), interview (directing and playwriting). Additional exam requirements/recommendations for international students: Required—TOEFL (minimum score 600 paper-based; 250 computer-based; 100 iBT). *Application deadline:* For fall admission, 1/10 priority date for domestic students. Application fee: $50. *Expenses:* Contact institution. *Financial support:* Federal Work-Study and scholarships/grants available. Financial award application deadline: 3/1; financial award applicants required to submit FAFSA. *Faculty research:* Translations of Vakhtangov, Metonymy and drama: essays on language and dramatic strategy; O'Neill, Sophocles. *Unit head:* Robert LuPone, Director, 212-229-5859 Ext. 2636, E-mail: luponer@newschool.edu. *Application contact:* Matthew Kelty, Director of Admissions, 212-229-5859, Fax: 212-229-5150, E-mail: keltym@newschool.edu.

See Close-Up on page 287.

New York University, Steinhardt School of Culture, Education and Human Development, Department of Music and Performing Arts Professions, Program in Educational Theatre, New York, NY 10012-1019. Offers educational theatre (Ed D, Advanced Certificate); educational theatre for colleges and communities (MA, PhD); educational theatre with English 7-12 (MA); teaching educational theatre, all grades (MA). Part-time and evening/weekend programs available. Terminal master's awarded for partial completion of doctoral program. *Degree requirements:* For master's, thesis (for some programs); for doctorate, thesis/dissertation. *Entrance requirements:* For master's, audition; for doctorate, GRE General Test, interview; for Advanced Certificate, master's degree. Additional exam requirements/recommendations for international students: Required—TOEFL. *Faculty research:* Theatre for young audiences, drama in education, applied theatre, arts education assessment, reflective praxis.

New York University, Tisch School of the Arts and Graduate School of Arts and Science, Department of Performance Studies, New York, NY 10012-1019. Offers MA, PhD. *Degree requirements:* For doctorate, one foreign language, comprehensive exam, thesis/dissertation, dissertation defense, qualifying exam. *Entrance requirements:* For master's, sample of written work; for doctorate, master's degree, writing sample. Additional exam requirements/recommendations for international students: Required—TOEFL or IELTS. Electronic applications accepted. *Expenses:* Contact institution. *Faculty research:* Performance theory, dance, folklore and festivals, postcolonial theory, anthropology and gender studies.

New York University, Tisch School of the Arts, Graduate Acting Program, New York, NY 10012-1019. Offers MFA. *Entrance requirements:* For master's, audition. Electronic applications accepted.

Northern Illinois University, Graduate School, College of Visual and Performing Arts, School of Theatre and Dance, De Kalb, IL 60115-2854. Offers MFA. *Accreditation:* NAST. Part-time programs available. *Degree requirements:* For master's, comprehensive exam, final project and defense. *Entrance requirements:* For master's, minimum GPA of 2.75, audition or portfolio. Additional exam requirements/recommendations for international students: Required—TOEFL (minimum score 550 paper-based; 213 computer-based). Electronic applications accepted. *Faculty research:* Theatre history, choreography, performance art spectacles, storytelling, computer visualization of the ethical space.

Northwestern University, The Graduate School, School of Communication, Department of Theatre, Evanston, IL 60208. Offers directing (MFA); stage design (MFA); theatre (MA). Admissions and degrees offered through The Graduate School. *Degree requirements:* For master's, thesis (MFA). *Entrance requirements:* For master's, GRE General Test. Additional exam requirements/recommendations for international students: Required—TOEFL. *Faculty research:* Critical analysis, theory and history of theatre and drama, philosophy of dance and movement, performance in multicultural contexts, storytelling, computer design process.

Northwestern University, The Graduate School, School of Communication, Interdisciplinary PhD Program in Theatre and Drama, Evanston, IL 60208. Offers PhD. Admissions and degree offered through The Graduate School. *Degree requirements:* For doctorate, thesis/dissertation, qualifying and final oral exams. *Entrance requirements:* For doctorate, GRE General Test, sample of written work. Additional exam requirements/recommendations for international students: Required—TOEFL. Electronic applications accepted. *Faculty research:* Theory and history of theatre and drama, performance theory, performance in multicultural contexts, critical analysis drama, theatre historiography.

The Ohio State University, Graduate School, College of the Arts, Department of Theatre, Columbus, OH 43210. Offers MA, MFA, PhD. *Accreditation:* NAST. *Degree requirements:* For master's, thesis (for some programs); for doctorate, one foreign language, thesis/dissertation. *Entrance requirements:* For master's, GRE General Test (MA); for doctorate, GRE General Test. Additional exam requirements/recommendations for international students: Recommended—TOEFL (minimum score 600 paper-based; 250 computer-based). Electronic applications accepted.

Ohio University, Graduate College, College of Fine Arts, School of Theater, Athens, OH 45701-2979. Offers MA, MFA. *Accreditation:* NAST. *Degree requirements:* For master's, thesis or alternative. *Entrance requirements:* For master's, minimum GPA of 3.0. Additional exam requirements/recommendations for international students: Required—TOEFL. Electronic applications accepted. *Faculty research:* Shakespearean performance, architecture, new plays, performance art, theory of comedy, playwriting.

Oklahoma City University, Margaret E. Petree College of Performing Arts, Department of Theatre, Oklahoma City, OK 73106-1402. Offers costume design (MA); technical theater (MA); theater (MA); theater for young audiences (MA). Part-time programs available. *Degree requirements:* For master's, thesis (for some programs). *Entrance requirements:* For master's, interview, audition, writing sample. Additional exam requirements/recommendations for international students: Required—TOEFL (minimum score 550 paper-based; 173 computer-based). *Faculty research:* Translation of plays, writing plays, dramaturgical research for plays and educational outreach materials.

Oklahoma State University, College of Arts and Sciences, Department of Theatre, Stillwater, OK 74078. Offers MA. *Accreditation:* NAST. *Faculty:* 9 full-time (4 women), 2 part-time/adjunct (1 woman). *Students:* 3 full-time (2 women); includes 1 minority (Hispanic American). Average age 24. 5 applicants, 60% accepted, 2 enrolled. In 2008, 4 master's awarded. *Degree requirements:* For master's, creative component or thesis. *Entrance requirements:* For master's, GRE. Additional exam requirements/recommendations for international students: Required—TOEFL. *Application deadline:* For fall admission, 3/1 priority date for international students; for spring admission, 8/1 priority date for international students. Applications are processed on a rolling basis. Application fee: $40 ($75 for international students). Electronic applications accepted. *Expenses:* Tuition, state resident: full-time $3716.40; part-time $154.85 per credit hour. Tuition, nonresident: full-time $14,448; part-time $602 per credit hour. Required fees: $1772.40; $73.85 per credit hour. One-time fee: $50. Tuition and fees vary according to course load and campus/location. *Financial support:* In 2008–09, 3 teaching assistantships (averaging $11,052 per year) were awarded; career-related internships or fieldwork, Federal Work-Study, scholarships/grants, health care benefits, tuition waivers (partial), and unspecified assistantships also available. Support available to part-time students. Financial award application deadline: 3/1; financial award applicants required to submit FAFSA. *Faculty research:* Historical scene painting and scenic art, Eastern European stage design, stage direction, voice and diction for the actor, stage choreography and dance. *Unit head:* Kevin Doolen, Head, 405-744-6094, Fax: 405-744-6509. *Application contact:* Dr. Gordon Emslie, Dean, 405-744-6368, Fax: 405-744-0355, E-mail: grad_i@okstate.edu.

Pace University, Dyson College of Arts and Sciences, The Actors Studio MFA, New York, NY 10038. Offers MFA.

Penn State University Park, Graduate School, College of Arts and Architecture, School of Theatre, State College, University Park, PA 16802-1503. Offers MFA. *Accreditation:* NAST.

Pittsburg State University, Graduate School, College of Arts and Sciences, Department of Communication, Pittsburg, KS 66762. Offers applied communication (MA); communication education (MA); theatre (MA). *Degree requirements:* For master's, thesis or alternative.

Point Park University, Conservatory of Performing Arts, Pittsburgh, PA 15222-1984. Offers theatre arts-acting (MFA). *Faculty:* 4 full-time, 2 part-time/adjunct. *Students:* 6 full-time (3 women), 1 international. Average age 40. 17 applicants, 35% accepted, 6 enrolled. In 2008, 1 master's awarded. *Degree requirements:* For master's, comprehensive exam (for some programs), thesis or alternative. *Entrance requirements:* For master's, interview, undergraduate degree in related field, theatre experience. *Application deadline:* Applications are processed on a rolling basis. Application fee: $30. Electronic applications accepted. *Expenses:* Tuition: Full-time $11,880; part-time $660 per credit. Required fees: $486; $27 per credit. *Financial support:* In 2008–09, 5 students received support, including 5 teaching assistantships with full tuition reimbursements available (averaging $6,400 per year); Federal Work-Study and

Theater

Point Park University (continued)
scholarships/grants also available. Support available to part-time students. Financial award application deadline: 5/1; financial award applicants required to submit FAFSA. *Unit head:* Ronald Allan-Lindblom, Dean/Artistic Producing Director, 412-392-3454, Fax: 412-392-2424, E-mail: rlindblom@pointpark.edu. *Application contact:* Lynn C. Ribar, Associate Director, Adult and Graduate Enrollment, 412-392-3908, Fax: 412-392-6164, E-mail: lribar@pointpark.edu.

Portland State University, Graduate Studies, School of Fine and Performing Arts, Department of Theater Arts, Portland, OR 97207-0751. Offers MA, MS, MA/MS. *Accreditation:* NAST. *Faculty:* 12 full-time (5 women), 10 part-time/adjunct (6 women). *Students:* 13 full-time (9 women), 5 part-time (all women); includes 2 minority (1 Asian American or Pacific Islander, 1 Hispanic American). Average age 33. 9 applicants, 100% accepted, 6 enrolled. In 2008, 2 master's awarded. *Degree requirements:* For master's, variable foreign language requirement, thesis or alternative. *Entrance requirements:* For master's, minimum GPA of 3.0 in upper-division course work or 2.75 overall, 24 credits in theater arts. Additional exam requirements/recommendations for international students: Required—TOEFL (minimum score 550 paper-based; 213 computer-based). *Application deadline:* For fall admission, 4/1 priority date for domestic students, 3/1 priority date for international students; for winter admission, 9/1 for domestic students; for spring admission, 11/1 for domestic students. Applications are processed on a rolling basis. Application fee: $50. *Expenses:* Tuition, area resident: Full-time $8763; part-time $179 per credit hour. Tuition, state resident: full-time $8763; part-time $298 per credit hour. Tuition, nonresident: full-time $12,981; part-time $426 per credit hour. Required fees: $1242. One-time fee: $250. Tuition and fees vary according to course load and program. *Financial support:* Research assistantships, teaching assistantships with full tuition reimbursements, career-related internships or fieldwork, Federal Work-Study, and unspecified assistantships available. Support available to part-time students. Financial award application deadline: 3/1; financial award applicants required to submit FAFSA. *Faculty research:* Design, acting/directing, scene/costume technology, dramatic literature, theater history. *Unit head:* Sarah Andrews-Collier, Chair, 503-725-4612, Fax: 503-725-4624, E-mail: andrews@pdx.edu. *Application contact:* Richard Wattenberg, Coordinator, 503-725-4602, Fax: 503-725-4624, E-mail: wattenbergr@pdx.edu.

Purchase College, State University of New York, Conservatory of Theatre Arts and Film, Purchase, NY 10577-1400. Offers theatre design (MFA); theatre technology (MFA). *Students:* 6 full-time (all women); 2 international. Average age 26. 9 applicants, 33% accepted, 3 enrolled. In 2008, 3 master's awarded. *Degree requirements:* For master's, thesis or alternative, performance. *Entrance requirements:* For master's, BFA, interview, portfolio. *Application deadline:* For fall admission, 3/1 for domestic students. Application fee: $50. Electronic applications accepted. *Expenses:* Tuition, area resident: Full-time $6900; part-time $288 per credit. Tuition, state resident: full-time $6900; part-time $288 per credit. Tuition, nonresident: full-time $10,920; part-time $455 per credit. Required fees: $1461; $0.85 per credit. One-time fee: $75 full-time. *Financial support:* Fellowships, teaching assistantships, career-related internships or fieldwork, Federal Work-Study, scholarships/grants, and tuition waivers (partial) available. Support available to part-time students. Financial award application deadline: 3/15; financial award applicants required to submit FAFSA. *Unit head:* Gregory Taylor, Interim Dean, 914-251-6831, E-mail: gregory.taylor@purchase.edu. *Application contact:* Sabrina Johnston, Counselor, 914-251-6479, Fax: 914-251-6314, E-mail: admissn@purchase.edu.

Purdue University, Graduate School, College of Liberal Arts, Department of Visual and Performing Arts, West Lafayette, IN 47907. Offers art and design (MA); theatre (MA, MFA). *Accreditation:* NASAD; NAST. Part-time programs available. *Degree requirements:* For master's, terminal exhibit, project, or thesis. *Entrance requirements:* Additional exam requirements/recommendations for international students: Required—TOEFL. Electronic applications accepted. *Faculty research:* Design, fine arts, photography, acting, directing, theatre technology.

Regent University, Graduate School, School of Communication and the Arts, Virginia Beach, VA 23464-9800. Offers acting (MFA); acting and directing (MFA); cinema arts/television arts (MA); communication (MA, PhD); digital media (MA); directing for cinema/TV (MA); journalism (MA); producing for cinema/TV (MA); script and screenwriting (MFA); theatre (MA). Part-time programs available. Postbaccalaureate distance learning degree programs offered (minimal on-campus study). *Faculty:* 26 full-time (3 women), 15 part-time/adjunct (3 women). *Students:* 136 full-time (77 women), 163 part-time (90 women); includes 83 minority (59 African Americans, 3 American Indian/Alaska Native, 5 Asian Americans or Pacific Islanders, 16 Hispanic Americans), 15 international. Average age 32. 230 applicants, 63% accepted, 102 enrolled. In 2008, 53 master's, 16 doctorates awarded. *Degree requirements:* For master's, thesis or alternative; for doctorate, thesis/dissertation. *Entrance requirements:* For master's, GRE General Test or MAT, minimum undergraduate GPA of 3.0, writing sample, computer literacy survey, recommendation, resumé, interview, audition (MFA programs); for doctorate, GRE General Test, minimum graduate GPA of 3.0, writing sample, computer literacy survey, recommendation, interview, transcripts. Additional exam requirements/recommendations for international students: Required—TOEFL (minimum score 577 paper-based; 233 computer-based). *Application deadline:* For fall admission, 3/1 priority date for domestic students; for spring admission, 10/1 priority date for domestic students. Applications are processed on a rolling basis. Application fee: $50. Electronic applications accepted. *Expenses:* Contact institution. *Financial support:* Fellowships with full and partial tuition reimbursements, career-related internships or fieldwork, scholarships/grants, tuition waivers (full and partial), and unspecified assistantships available. Support available to part-time students. Financial award application deadline: 9/1; financial award applicants required to submit FAFSA. *Faculty research:* Southern gospel music, education and entertainment, celebrities and the media, journalism and ethics, C. S. Lewis. *Unit head:* Michael Patrick, Dean, 757-352-4970, Fax: 757-352-4279, E-mail: michpat@regent.edu. *Application contact:* Matthew Chadwick, Director of Admissions, 800-373-5504, Fax: 757-352-4381, E-mail: admissions@regent.edu.

Rhode Island College, School of Graduate Studies, Faculty of Arts and Sciences, Department of Music, Theatre, and Dance, Providence, RI 02908-1991. Offers music education (MAT, MM Ed); theatre (MFA). Part-time and evening/weekend programs available. *Faculty:* 4 full-time (0 women), 7 part-time/adjunct (6 women). *Students:* 11 full-time (6 women), 8 part-time (6 women); includes 1 minority (African American). Average age 34. In 2008, 10 master's awarded. *Degree requirements:* For master's, comprehensive exam, thesis, final project (MFA). *Entrance requirements:* For master's, GRE General Test or MAT, exams in music education, theory, history and literature, audition, 3 letters of recommendation, evidence of musicianship, interview. Additional exam requirements/recommendations for international students: Recommended—TOEFL (minimum score 550 paper-based; 213 computer-based; 79 iBT). *Application deadline:* For fall admission, 4/1 for domestic students; for spring admission, 11/1 for domestic students. Applications are processed on a rolling basis. Application fee: $50. *Expenses:* Tuition, area resident: Full-time $6816; part-time $284 per credit hour. Tuition, state resident: full-time $6816; part-time $284 per credit hour. Tuition, nonresident: full-time $13,920; part-time $580 per credit hour. Required fees: $454; $16 per credit. $68 per term. *Financial support:* Teaching assistantships with full tuition reimbursements, Federal Work-Study, scholarships/grants, health care benefits, and unspecified assistantships available. Support available to part-time students. Financial award application deadline: 5/15; financial award applicants required to submit FAFSA. *Unit head:* Dr. James Taylor, Chair, 401-456-8639. *Application contact:* Graduate Studies, 401-456-8700.

Roosevelt University, Graduate Division, Chicago College of Performing Arts, Theatre Conservatory, Chicago, IL 60605-1394. Offers directing and dramaturgy (MFA); musical theatre (MFA); theatre (MA, MFA); theatre-directing (MA); theatre-performance (MFA). MA is a special 3-summer program for high school teachers only. *Degree requirements:* For master's, thesis production/performance. *Entrance requirements:* For master's, audition, interview, minimum GPA of 2.5. *Expenses:* Tuition: Full-time $14,730; part-time $709 per credit. Required fees: $175 per semester. Tuition and fees vary according to course load and program. *Faculty research:* Brecht, Shakespeare, contemporary and new work, fully mounted theatre.

Rowan University, Graduate School, College of Fine and Performing Arts, Program in Theatre, Glassboro, NJ 08028-1701. Offers theatre (MA); theatre education (MST). *Accreditation:* NAST. Part-time and evening/weekend programs available. *Students:* 1 (woman) full-time, 2 part-time (1 woman). Average age 47. 3 applicants, 0% accepted. In 2008, 2 master's awarded. *Degree requirements:* For master's, thesis. *Entrance requirements:* Additional exam requirements/recommendations for international students: Required—TOEFL. *Application deadline:* Applications are processed on a rolling basis. Application fee: $50. Electronic applications accepted. *Expenses:* Tuition, area resident: Full-time $10,624; part-time $590 per credit. Tuition, state resident: full-time $10,624; part-time $590 per credit. Tuition, nonresident: full-time $10,624; part-time $590 per credit. Required fees: $2258; $124.90 per credit. *Financial support:* Career-related internships or fieldwork, scholarships/grants, health care benefits, and unspecified assistantships available. Support available to part-time students. *Unit head:* Dr. Mira Lalovic-Hand, Interim Associate Provost/Director of Graduate School, 856-256-5120, E-mail: Lalovic-hand@rowan.edu. *Application contact:* Karen Haynes, Graduate Coordinator, 856-256-4052, Fax: 856-256-4436, E-mail: Haynes@rowan.edu.

Rutgers, The State University of New Jersey, New Brunswick, Mason Gross School of the Arts, Department of Theater Arts, Piscataway, NJ 08854-8097. Offers acting (MFA); design (MFA); directing (MFA); playwriting (MFA); stage management (MFA). *Degree requirements:* For master's, thesis (for some programs), performance project. *Entrance requirements:* For master's, audition, interview, portfolio. Electronic applications accepted. *Faculty research:* Faculty of working professional.

St. John's University, St. John's College of Liberal Arts and Sciences, Department of Speech, Communication Sciences and Theatre, Queens, NY 11439. Offers MA, Au D, Advanced Diploma. *Accreditation:* ASHA. Evening/weekend programs available. *Students:* 40 full-time (37 women), 118 part-time (111 women); includes 29 minority (10 African Americans, 8 Asian Americans or Pacific Islanders, 11 Hispanic Americans), 1 international. Average age 27. 405 applicants, 22% accepted, 38 enrolled. In 2008, 44 master's awarded. *Degree requirements:* For master's, comprehensive exam, thesis optional, internship. *Entrance requirements:* For master's, minimum GPA of 3.0. Additional exam requirements/recommendations for international students: Required—TOEFL (minimum score 500 paper-based; 173 computer-based; 61 iBT), IELTS (minimum score 5.5). *Application deadline:* For fall admission, 2/1 for domestic students, 5/1 priority date for international students; for spring admission, 10/1 for domestic students, 11/1 priority date for international students. Applications are processed on a rolling basis. Application fee: $70. Electronic applications accepted. *Expenses:* Contact institution. *Financial support:* Research assistantships, career-related internships or fieldwork and scholarships/grants available. Support available to part-time students. Financial award application deadline: 3/1; financial award applicants required to submit FAFSA. *Faculty research:* Bilingualism and adult and child language disorders, dysphagia speech motor control, electrophysiological measurement of hearing, central auditory processing disorders and auditory habilitation and rehabilitation. *Unit head:* Dr. Fredericka Bell-Berti, Chair, 718-990-6450, E-mail: bellf@stjohns.edu. *Application contact:* Kathleen Davis, Director of Graduate Admission, 718-990-2790, Fax: 718-990-5686, E-mail: gradhelp@stjohns.edu.

San Diego State University, Graduate and Research Affairs, College of Professional Studies and Fine Arts, School of Theater, Television and Film, San Diego, CA 92182. Offers television, film, and new media production (MA); theatre arts (MA, MFA). *Accreditation:* NAST. Part-time programs available. *Degree requirements:* For master's, thesis. *Entrance requirements:* For master's, GRE General Test, 3 letters of recommendation, interview. Additional exam requirements/recommendations for international students: Required—TOEFL. Electronic applications accepted.

San Francisco State University, Division of Graduate Studies, College of Creative Arts, Department of Theatre Arts, San Francisco, CA 94132-1722. Offers drama (MA); theatre arts (MFA), including design/technical production, performance. *Accreditation:* NAST.

San Jose State University, Graduate Studies and Research, College of Humanities and the Arts, Department of Television, Radio, Film and Theatre, San Jose, CA 95192-0001. Offers theatre arts (MA). *Accreditation:* NAST. *Degree requirements:* For master's, written exam. *Entrance requirements:* Additional exam requirements/recommendations for international students: Required—TOEFL (minimum score 570 paper-based). Electronic applications accepted.

Sarah Lawrence College, Graduate Studies, Program in Theater, Bronxville, NY 10708-5999. Offers MFA. *Faculty:* 25 part-time/adjunct (8 women). *Students:* 22 full-time (16 women), 1 (woman) part-time; includes 3 minority (all African Americans), 4 international. 67 applicants, 33% accepted, 12 enrolled. In 2008, 8 master's awarded. *Degree requirements:* For master's, portfolio. *Entrance requirements:* For master's, interview, minimum B average in undergraduate course work. Additional exam requirements/recommendations for international students: Required—TOEFL (minimum score 600 paper-based). *Application deadline:* For fall admission, 1/15 for domestic students. Application fee: $60. *Expenses:* Tuition: Full-time $26,544; part-time $1106 per credit. Required fees: $450. Tuition and fees vary according to program. *Financial support:* Fellowships, career-related internships or fieldwork, scholarships/grants, and unspecified assistantships available. Support available to part-time students. Financial award application deadline: 3/1. *Unit head:* John Dillon, Director, 914-395-2262. *Application contact:* Susan Guma, Dean of Graduate Studies, 914-395-2373, E-mail: sguma@mail.slc.edu.

See Close-Up on page 289.

Savannah College of Art and Design, Graduate School, Program in Production Design, Savannah, GA 31402-3146. Offers MA, MFA. Part-time programs available. *Degree requirements:* For master's, thesis. *Entrance requirements:* For master's, interview, portfolio. Additional exam requirements/recommendations for international students: Required—TOEFL (minimum score 450 paper-based; 133 computer-based). Electronic applications accepted. *Expenses:* Tuition: Full-time $28,215; part-time $3135 per course. One-time fee: $500.

Smith College, Graduate and Special Programs, Department of Theatre, Northampton, MA 01063. Offers playwriting (MFA). Part-time programs available. *Faculty:* 8 full-time (6 women). *Students:* 1 full-time (0 women). Average age 23. 8 applicants, 25% accepted. In 2008, 2 master's awarded. *Degree requirements:* For master's, one foreign language, thesis. *Entrance requirements:* Additional exam requirements/recommendations for international students: Required—TOEFL (minimum score 590 paper-based; 243 computer-based; 97 iBT). *Application deadline:* For fall admission, 4/1 for domestic students, 1/15 for international students. Application fee: $60. *Financial support:* In 2008–09, 1 student received support. Institutionally sponsored loans and scholarships/grants available. Support available to part-time students. Financial award application deadline: 1/15; financial award applicants required to submit CSS PROFILE or FAFSA. *Unit head:* Leonard Berkman, Graduate Adviser, 413-585-3206, E-mail: lberkman@smith.edu. *Application contact:* Leonard Berkman, Graduate Adviser, 413-585-3206, E-mail: lberkman@smith.edu.

Southern Illinois University Carbondale, Graduate School, College of Liberal Arts, Theater Department, Carbondale, IL 62901-4701. Offers speech/theater (PhD); theater (MFA). *Accreditation:* NAST (one or more programs are accredited). Part-time programs available. *Degree requirements:* For master's, thesis; for doctorate, thesis/dissertation. *Entrance requirements:* For master's, minimum GPA of 2.7; for doctorate, minimum GPA of 3.25. Additional exam requirements/recommendations for international students: Required—TOEFL. *Faculty research:* Scenography, theater performance, theater history, dramatic criticism, theater technology, playwriting.

See Close-Up on page 291.

Southern Methodist University, Meadows School of the Arts, Division of Theatre, Dallas, TX 75275. Offers acting (MFA); design (MFA). *Accreditation:* NAST. *Faculty:* 16 full-time (5 women), 3 part-time/adjunct (2 women). *Students:* 15 full-time (8 women); includes 2 minority (1 African

American, 1 Asian American or Pacific Islander). Average age 29. 10 applicants, 90% accepted, 9 enrolled. In 2008, 8 master's awarded. *Entrance requirements:* For master's, audition or interview. Additional exam requirements/recommendations for international students: Required—TOEFL (minimum score 550 paper-based; 213 computer-based; 80 iBT). *Application deadline:* For fall admission, 3/1 priority date for domestic and international students. Application fee: $75. *Financial support:* In 2008–09, 20 teaching assistantships (averaging $6,600 per year) were awarded; scholarships/grants and unspecified assistantships also available. Financial award application deadline: 3/1; financial award applicants required to submit FAFSA. *Faculty research:* European lighting techniques. *Unit head:* Cecil O'Neal, Chair, 214-768-2558, Fax: 214-768-1136, E-mail: coneal@smu.edu. *Application contact:* Jean Cherry, Director of Graduate Admissions and Records, 214-768-3765, Fax: 214-768-3272, E-mail: jcherry@smu.edu.

Stanford University, School of Humanities and Sciences, Department of Drama, Stanford, CA 94305-9991. Offers PhD. *Degree requirements:* For doctorate, one foreign language, thesis/dissertation, qualifying exams. *Entrance requirements:* For doctorate, GRE General Test, summary of production experience. Additional exam requirements/recommendations for international students: Required—TOEFL. Electronic applications accepted.

State University of New York at Binghamton, Graduate School, School of Arts and Sciences, Department of Theater, Binghamton, NY 13902-6000. Offers MA. *Faculty:* 12 full-time (4 women), 9 part-time/adjunct (2 women). *Students:* 7 full-time (6 women), 1 (woman) part-time, 2 international. Average age 35. 8 applicants, 63% accepted, 3 enrolled. In 2008, 2 master's awarded. *Degree requirements:* For master's, thesis. *Entrance requirements:* For master's, GRE General Test, GRE Subject Test. Additional exam requirements/recommendations for international students: Required—TOEFL. *Application deadline:* For fall admission, 4/15 priority date for domestic students, 1/15 priority date for international students; for spring admission, 11/1 for domestic students, 10/1 priority date for international students. Applications are processed on a rolling basis. Application fee: $60. Electronic applications accepted. *Expenses:* Tuition, area resident: Full-time $6900; part-time $288 per credit. Tuition, state resident: full-time $6900; part-time $288 per credit. Tuition, nonresident: full-time $10,920; part-time $455 per credit. Required fees: $1130. Part-time tuition and fees vary according to course load, program and student level. *Financial support:* In 2008–09, 3 students received support, including teaching assistantships with full and partial tuition reimbursements available (averaging $9,500 per year); fellowships, career-related internships or fieldwork, Federal Work-Study, institutionally sponsored loans, scholarships/grants, health care benefits, and unspecified assistantships also available. Financial award application deadline: 2/15; financial award applicants required to submit FAFSA. *Unit head:* Dr. John E. Vestal, Chairperson, 607-777-2360, E-mail: jvestal@binghamton.edu. *Application contact:* Victoria Williams, Recruiting and Admissions Coordinator, 607-777-2151, Fax: 607-777-2501, E-mail: vwilliam@binghamton.edu.

Stony Brook University, State University of New York, Graduate School, College of Arts and Sciences, Department of Theatre Arts, Program in Dramaturgy, Stony Brook, NY 11794. Offers MFA. *Students:* 15 full-time (12 women); includes 4 minority (1 Asian American or Pacific Islander, 3 Hispanic Americans), 2 international. Average age 29. 10 applicants, 90% accepted. *Degree requirements:* For master's, one foreign language, thesis. *Entrance requirements:* For master's, GRE General Test. Additional exam requirements/recommendations for international students: Required—TOEFL. *Application deadline:* For fall admission, 1/15 for domestic students. Application fee: $60. *Expenses:* Tuition, area resident: Full-time $7880; part-time $328 per credit hour. Tuition, state resident: full-time $7880; part-time $328 per credit hour. Tuition, nonresident: full-time $13,250; part-time $552 per credit hour. Required fees: $848. *Unit head:* Prof. Nick Mangano, Chair, 631-632-7300, Fax: 631-632-7258. *Application contact:* Michael Zelenak, Director of Graduate Studies, 631-632-7280.

Stony Brook University, State University of New York, Graduate School, College of Arts and Sciences, Department of Theatre Arts, Program in Theatre Arts, Stony Brook, NY 11794. Offers MA. Evening/weekend programs available. *Students:* 2 part-time (1 woman). Average age 35. 5 applicants, 100% accepted. *Degree requirements:* For master's, one foreign language, thesis. *Entrance requirements:* For master's, GRE General Test. Additional exam requirements/recommendations for international students: Required—TOEFL. *Application deadline:* For fall admission, 1/15 for domestic students. Application fee: $60. *Expenses:* Tuition, area resident: Full-time $7880; part-time $328 per credit hour. Tuition, state resident: full-time $7880; part-time $328 per credit hour. Tuition, nonresident: full-time $13,250; part-time $552 per credit hour. Required fees: $848. *Unit head:* Prof. Nick Mangano, Chair, 631-632-7300, Fax: 631-632-7258. *Application contact:* Michael Zelenak, Director of Graduate Studies, 631-632-7280.

Temple University, Graduate School, School of Communications and Theater, Department of Theater, Philadelphia, PA 19122-6096. Offers acting (MFA); design (MFA); directing (MFA). *Accreditation:* NAST. Part-time programs available. *Degree requirements:* For master's, thesis (for some programs). *Entrance requirements:* For master's, minimum GPA of 3.0; audition/interview, portfolio, or samples of written work. Additional exam requirements/recommendations for international students: Required—TOEFL (minimum score 550 paper-based; 213 computer-based; 79 iBT). Electronic applications accepted.

Texas A&M University–Commerce, Graduate School, College of Arts and Sciences, Department of Communication and Theatre, Commerce, TX 75429-3011. Offers theatre (MA, MS). Part-time programs available. *Degree requirements:* For master's, comprehensive exam, thesis (for some programs). *Entrance requirements:* For master's, GRE General Test. Electronic applications accepted. *Faculty research:* Theater history.

Texas State University–San Marcos, Graduate School, College of Fine Arts and Communication, Department of Theatre Arts and Dance, Program in Theatre Arts, San Marcos, TX 78666. Offers MA. Part-time and evening/weekend programs available. *Degree requirements:* For master's, comprehensive exam, thesis or alternative. *Entrance requirements:* For master's, GRE General Test, minimum GPA of 2.75 in last 60 hours of course work. Additional exam requirements/recommendations for international students: Required—TOEFL (minimum score 550 paper-based; 213 computer-based). Electronic applications accepted. *Faculty research:* Theatre history (especially nineteenth century American theatre), stage productions, playwriting.

Texas Tech University, Graduate School, College of Visual and Performing Arts, Department of Theatre and Dance, Lubbock, TX 79409. Offers fine arts (PhD); theatre arts (MA, MFA), including arts administration (MFA), design (MFA), performance/pedagogy (MFA), playwriting (MFA), theatre management (MFA). *Accreditation:* NAST. Part-time programs available. *Faculty:* 10 full-time (5 women). *Students:* 37 full-time (18 women), 19 part-time (8 women); includes 6 minority (2 African Americans, 1 Asian American or Pacific Islander, 3 Hispanic Americans), 4 international. Average age 35. 42 applicants, 71% accepted, 16 enrolled. In 2008, 5 master's awarded. *Degree requirements:* For master's, variable foreign language requirement, thesis; for doctorate, thesis/dissertation. *Entrance requirements:* For master's and doctorate, GRE General Test. Additional exam requirements/recommendations for international students: Required—TOEFL (minimum score 550 paper-based; 213 computer-based). *Application deadline:* For fall admission, 3/1 priority date for international students; for spring admission, 11/1 priority date for international students. Applications are processed on a rolling basis. Application fee: $50 ($60 for international students). Electronic applications accepted. *Expenses:* Tuition, area resident: Part-time $194 per credit hour. Tuition, state resident: full-time $4648; part-time $194 per credit hour. Tuition, nonresident: full-time $11,392; part-time $475 per credit hour. Required fees: $2206; $69 per credit hour. $389 per semester. *Financial support:* In 2008–09, 41 students received support, including 27 teaching assistantships with partial tuition reimbursements available (averaging $10,419 per year); research assistantships with partial tuition reimbursements available, Federal Work-Study and institutionally sponsored loans also available. Support available to part-time students. Financial award application deadline: 4/15; financial award applicants required to submit FAFSA. *Faculty research:* New student plays program, theatre planning, dramaturgy; feminist theatre; arts administration; dance aesthetics. *Unit head:* Prof. Frederick B. Christoffel, Chair, 806-742-3601 Ext. 228, Fax: 806-742-1338, E-mail: fred.christoffel@ttu.edu. *Application contact:* Dr. James Bush, Graduate Adviser, 806-742-3601 Ext. 230, Fax: 806-742-1338, E-mail: james.bush@ttu.edu.

Texas Tech University, Graduate School, College of Visual and Performing Arts, Fine Arts Doctoral Program, Lubbock, TX 79409. Offers arts (PhD); music (PhD); theatre arts (PhD). *Accreditation:* NAST. *Students:* 50 full-time (22 women), 29 part-time (15 women); includes 9 minority (3 African Americans, 1 American Indian/Alaska Native, 1 Asian American or Pacific Islander, 4 Hispanic Americans), 10 international. Average age 36. 37 applicants, 70% accepted, 16 enrolled. In 2008, 4 doctorates awarded. *Degree requirements:* For doctorate, thesis/dissertation. *Entrance requirements:* For doctorate, GRE General Test. Additional exam requirements/recommendations for international students: Required—TOEFL (minimum score 550 paper-based; 213 computer-based). *Application deadline:* For fall admission, 3/1 priority date for international students; for spring admission, 11/1 priority date for international students. Applications are processed on a rolling basis. Application fee: $50 ($60 for international students). Electronic applications accepted. *Expenses:* Tuition, area resident: Part-time $194 per credit hour. Tuition, state resident: full-time $4648; part-time $194 per credit hour. Tuition, nonresident: full-time $11,392; part-time $475 per credit hour. Required fees: $2206; $69 per credit hour. $389 per semester. *Financial support:* Research assistantships with partial tuition reimbursements, teaching assistantships with partial tuition reimbursements available. Financial award application deadline: 4/15. *Faculty research:* Art criticism and theory, music, aesthetics, theatre arts. *Unit head:* Dr. Brian D. Steele, Director, 806-742-0700, Fax: 806-742-0695, E-mail: brian.steele@ttu.edu. *Application contact:* Dr. Brian D. Steele, Director, 806-742-0700, Fax: 806-742-0695, E-mail: brian.steele@ttu.edu.

Texas Woman's University, Graduate School, College of Arts and Sciences, School of the Arts, Department of Music and Drama, Denton, TX 76201. Offers drama (MA); music (MA). *Accreditation:* NASM. Part-time programs available. *Faculty:* 12 full-time (7 women), 5 part-time/adjunct (2 women). *Students:* 39 full-time (29 women), 23 part-time (17 women); includes 17 minority (4 African Americans, 1 American Indian/Alaska Native, 1 Asian American or Pacific Islander, 11 Hispanic Americans), 7 international. Average age 32. In 2008, 13 master's awarded. *Degree requirements:* For master's, thesis optional, project recital. *Entrance requirements:* For master's, music history/theory placement exam, audition, interview, sample of professional work, licensure as a music therapist, piano and aural skills. Additional exam requirements/recommendations for international students: Required—TOEFL (minimum score 550 paper-based; 213 computer-based; 79 iBT). *Application deadline:* For fall admission, 4/1 for international students; for spring admission, 8/1 for international students. Applications are processed on a rolling basis. Application fee: $30 ($50 for international students). Electronic applications accepted. *Expenses:* Tuition, state resident: full-time $3564; part-time $198 per semester hour. Tuition, nonresident: full-time $8622; part-time $479 per semester hour. Required fees: $1158; $64 per semester hour. Tuition and fees vary according to course load. *Financial support:* In 2008–09, 7 research assistantships (averaging $9,684 per year), 1 teaching assistantship (averaging $9,684 per year) were awarded; career-related internships or fieldwork, Federal Work-Study, institutionally sponsored loans, scholarships/grants, traineeships, health care benefits, tuition waivers (partial), and unspecified assistantships also available. Support available to part-time students. Financial award application deadline: 3/1; financial award applicants required to submit FAFSA. *Faculty research:* Musical development in early childhood, little known or neglected compositions for flute (especially by women composers), relationship of visual art to piano music, pedagogical development of the singing voice, guided imagery and music. *Unit head:* Dr. James Chenevert, Chair, 940-898-2500, Fax: 940-898-2494, E-mail: jchenevert@twu.edu. *Application contact:* Samuel Wheeler, Assistant Director of Admissions, 940-898-3188, Fax: 940-898-3081, E-mail: wheelersr@twu.edu.

Towson University, College of Graduate Studies and Research, Program in Theatre, Towson, MD 21252-0001. Offers MFA. *Accreditation:* NAST. *Degree requirements:* For master's, thesis. *Entrance requirements:* For master's, audition or portfolio, interview, minimum GPA of 3.0. Electronic applications accepted. *Faculty research:* Playwriting, directing, entrepreneurship in the arts, movement theatre, design, drama.

Tufts University, Graduate School of Arts and Sciences, Department of Drama and Dance, Medford, MA 02155. Offers dance (MA, PhD); drama (MA); dramatic literature and criticism (PhD); theater history (PhD). Part-time programs available. Terminal master's awarded for partial completion of doctoral program. *Degree requirements:* For master's, one foreign language, thesis; for doctorate, 2 foreign languages, thesis/dissertation, oral exam, written general exam. *Entrance requirements:* For master's and doctorate, GRE General Test, writing sample. Additional exam requirements/recommendations for international students: Required—TOEFL (minimum score 600 paper-based; 250 computer-based; 80 iBT). Electronic applications accepted.

Tulane University, School of Liberal Arts, Department of Theatre and Dance, New Orleans, LA 70118-5669. Offers design and technical production (MFA). *Entrance requirements:* For master's, GRE General Test, minimum B average in undergraduate course work. Additional exam requirements/recommendations for international students: Required—TOEFL. Electronic applications accepted. *Faculty research:* Scene design, stage management, costume design, technical direction, lighting design.

Université de Sherbrooke, Faculty of Letters and Human Sciences, Department of Letters and Communications, Sherbrooke, QC J1K 2R1, Canada. Offers comparative Canadian literature (MA, PhD); French literature (MA, PhD); linguistics (MA); lit&erature de crèation (MA, PhD); theatre (MA). *Degree requirements:* For master's, thesis or alternative; for doctorate, thesis/dissertation. *Entrance requirements:* For master's, minimum GPA of 2.8; for doctorate, minimum GPA of 3.0.

Université Laval, Faculty of Letters, Department of Literature, Programs in Literature and Arts of the Screen and Stage, Québec, QC G1K 7P4, Canada. Offers MA, PhD. Part-time programs available. Terminal master's awarded for partial completion of doctoral program. *Degree requirements:* For master's, thesis; for doctorate, comprehensive exam, thesis/dissertation. *Entrance requirements:* For master's and doctorate, linguistics exams, knowledge of French, knowledge of a second language. Electronic applications accepted.

University at Albany, State University of New York, College of Arts and Sciences, Department of Theatre, Albany, NY 12222-0001. Offers MA. *Entrance requirements:* Additional exam requirements/recommendations for international students: Required—TOEFL (minimum score 550 paper-based; 213 computer-based). Electronic applications accepted.

The University of Akron, Graduate School, College of Fine and Applied Arts, School of Dance, Theatre, and Arts Administration, Program in Theatre Arts, Akron, OH 44325. Offers MA. *Degree requirements:* For master's, thesis optional. *Entrance requirements:* For master's, minimum GPA of 2.75, interview, personal statement. Additional exam requirements/recommendations for international students: Required—TOEFL (minimum score 550 paper-based; 213 computer-based; 79 iBT). Electronic applications accepted.

The University of Alabama, Graduate School, College of Arts and Sciences, Department of Theatre and Dance, Tuscaloosa, AL 35487. Offers acting (MFA); costume design (MFA); directing (MFA); scene design/technical production (MFA); stage management (MFA); theatre (MFA); theatre management/administration (MFA). *Accreditation:* NAST. *Faculty:* 11 full-time (2 women). *Students:* 31 full-time (15 women), 1 (woman) part-time; includes 1 minority (African American), 2 international. Average age 29. 29 applicants, 17% accepted, 4 enrolled. In 2008, 19 master's awarded. *Degree requirements:* For master's, thesis project. *Entrance requirements:* For master's, auditions/portfolio review. *Application deadline:* For fall admission, 7/6 for domestic students, 3/1 for international students. Applications are processed on a rolling basis. Application fee: $30. Electronic applications accepted. *Expenses:* Tuition, area resident: Full-time $6400. Tuition, state resident: full-time $6400. Tuition, nonresident: full-time $18,000. *Financial support:* In 2008–09, 18 research assistantships (averaging $11,508 per year), 21 teaching assistantships (averaging $11,508 per year) were awarded; Federal Work-Study and health care benefits also available. *Faculty research:* Arts management, theatre

Theater

The University of Alabama (continued)
history, practice and production. Total annual research expenditures: $1,941. *Unit head:* William Teague, Chairman and Professor, 205-348-5283, Fax: 205-348-9048, E-mail: wteague@as.ua.edu. *Application contact:* Pamela McCray, Recruiting Contact, 205-348-5283, Fax: 205-348-9048, E-mail: pmccray@bama.ua.edu.

University of Alberta, Faculty of Graduate Studies and Research, Department of Drama, Edmonton, AB T6G 2E1, Canada. Offers design (MFA); directing (MFA); drama (MA). *Degree requirements:* For master's, one foreign language, production thesis. *Faculty research:* Dramaturgy, history, theory and criticism, design.

The University of Arizona, Graduate College, College of Fine Arts, School of Theatre Arts, Tucson, AZ 85721. Offers MA, MFA. *Accreditation:* NAST. *Degree requirements:* For master's, comprehensive exam (for some programs), thesis (for some programs), production monograph. *Entrance requirements:* For master's, GRE, 3 letters of recommendation, statement of intent, portfolio. Additional exam requirements/recommendations for international students: Required—TOEFL (minimum score 550 paper-based; 213 computer-based). Electronic applications accepted. *Faculty research:* Modern and contemporary theater, cultural studies, musical theater, women and theater.

University of Arkansas, Graduate School, J. William Fulbright College of Arts and Sciences, Department of Drama, Fayetteville, AR 72701-1201. Offers MA, MFA. *Degree requirements:* For master's, thesis optional.

The University of British Columbia, Faculty of Arts, Creative Writing Program, Vancouver, BC V6T 1Z1, Canada. Offers creative writing (MFA); creative writing and film (MFA); creative writing and theatre (MFA). Part-time programs available. Postbaccalaureate distance learning degree programs offered (minimal on-campus study). *Degree requirements:* For master's, thesis. *Entrance requirements:* For master's, sample of written work. Additional exam requirements/recommendations for international students: Required—TOEFL (minimum score 550 paper-based; 213 computer-based). Electronic applications accepted. *Expenses:* Contact institution. *Faculty research:* Writing of fiction; poetry, creative nonfiction, plays for stage, screen, television, radio, writing for children and translation, song lyrics and libretto.

The University of British Columbia, Faculty of Arts and Faculty of Graduate Studies, Department of Theatre and Film, Theatre Program, Vancouver, BC V6T 1Z1, Canada. Offers theatre (MA, PhD); theatre design (MFA); theatre directing (MFA). *Degree requirements:* For master's, variable foreign language requirement, comprehensive exam, thesis; for doctorate, 2 foreign languages, comprehensive exam, thesis/dissertation. *Entrance requirements:* For master's, portfolio (MFA); for doctorate, MA or equivalent. Additional exam requirements/recommendations for international students: Required—TOEFL, TOEFL score of 550 paper-based, 213 computer-based required for MFA; score of 600 paper-based, 250 computer-based required for MA and PhD programs. *Faculty research:* Dramatic literature, theatrical history, criticism, playwriting, directing.

University of Calgary, Faculty of Graduate Studies, Faculty of Fine Arts, Department of Drama, Calgary, AB T2N 1N4, Canada. Offers design and technical theatre (MFA); directing (MFA); playwriting (MFA); theatre studies (MFA). *Degree requirements:* For master's, thesis. *Entrance requirements:* For master's, bachelor's degree in drama, minimum GPA of 3.0, portfolio (design and playwriting). Additional exam requirements/recommendations for international students: Required—TOEFL. *Faculty research:* Popular theatre, collective creation, technical design, dramaturgy, directing styles.

University of California, Berkeley, Graduate Division, Group in Performance Studies, Berkeley, CA 94720-1500. Offers PhD. *Degree requirements:* For doctorate, one foreign language, thesis/dissertation, qualifying exam. *Entrance requirements:* For doctorate, GRE General Test, sample of critical writing, 3 letters of recommendation. Additional exam requirements/recommendations for international students: Required—TOEFL. Electronic applications accepted. *Faculty research:* Postcolonial performance, gender, sexuality, and performance; political performance; dramatic literature and theory; race, ethnicity, performance.

University of California, Davis, Graduate Studies, Program in Dramatic Art, Davis, CA 95616. Offers acting (MFA); dramatic art (PhD). *Entrance requirements:* For master's, minimum GPA of 3.0, portfolio. Additional exam requirements/recommendations for international students: Required—TOEFL (minimum score 550 paper-based; 213 computer-based). Electronic applications accepted. *Faculty research:* Twentieth century performance and culture.

University of California, Davis, Graduate Studies, Program in Performance Studies, Davis, CA 95616. Offers dramatic art (PhD). *Degree requirements:* For doctorate, 2 foreign languages, thesis/dissertation. *Entrance requirements:* For doctorate, GRE, minimum GPA of 3.25. Additional exam requirements/recommendations for international students: Required—TOEFL (minimum score 550 paper-based; 213 computer-based). Electronic applications accepted.

University of California, Irvine, Office of Graduate Studies, Claire Trevor School of the Arts, Department of Drama, Irvine, CA 92697. Offers acting (MFA); design and stage management (MFA); directing (MFA); drama (MFA); drama and theatre (PhD). *Degree requirements:* For master's, comprehensive exam, thesis; for doctorate, one foreign language, thesis/dissertation. *Entrance requirements:* For master's, audition, interview, or portfolio; minimum GPA of 3.0; for doctorate, GRE, minimum GPA of 3.5, critical writing samples. Electronic applications accepted. *Faculty research:* Costume, scenery, and lighting design; production; theatre history, literature, and criticism.

University of California, Los Angeles, Graduate Division, School of Theater, Film and Television, Department of Theater, Los Angeles, CA 90095. Offers theater (MA, MFA); theater and performance studies (PhD). *Accreditation:* NAST. *Faculty:* 16. *Students:* 88 full-time (45 women); includes 23 minority (10 African Americans, 4 Asian Americans or Pacific Islanders, 9 Hispanic Americans), 6 international. Average age 27. 228 applicants, 17% accepted, 28 enrolled. In 2008, 22 master's, 5 doctorates awarded. *Degree requirements:* For master's, comprehensive exam or thesis; for doctorate, one foreign language, thesis/dissertation, oral and written exam. *Entrance requirements:* For master's, minimum GPA of 3.0, interview, portfolio, resumé, script, audition; for doctorate, GRE General Test, minimum undergraduate GPA of 3.0. Application fee: $60 ($80 for international students). Electronic applications accepted. *Expenses:* Tuition, nonresident: full-time $14,694. Required fees: $9669.50. Full-time tuition and fees vary according to course load, degree level, program and student level. *Financial support:* In 2008–09, 69 fellowships with full and partial tuition reimbursements, 6 research assistantships with full and partial tuition reimbursements, 53 teaching assistantships with full and partial tuition reimbursements were awarded; career-related internships or fieldwork, Federal Work-Study, institutionally sponsored loans, scholarships/grants, traineeships, health care benefits, tuition waivers (full and partial), and unspecified assistantships also available. Financial award application deadline: 3/1; financial award applicants required to submit FAFSA. *Unit head:* William D. Ward, Chair, 310-825-8787. *Application contact:* Departmental Office, 310-825-8787, E-mail: info@tft.ucla.edu.

University of California, San Diego, Office of Graduate Studies, Department of Theatre and Dance, La Jolla, CA 92093. Offers acting (MFA); design (MFA); directing (MFA); drama and theatre (PhD); playwriting (MFA); stage management (MFA); theatre (PhD). *Degree requirements:* For master's, thesis. *Entrance requirements:* For master's, GRE General Test (directing, playwriting). Electronic applications accepted.

University of California, Santa Barbara, Graduate Division, College of Letters and Sciences, Division of Humanities and Fine Arts, Department of Theatre and Dance, Santa Barbara, CA 93106-7060. Offers theater studies (MA, PhD), including European Medieval studies (PhD), feminist studies (PhD), theater studies (PhD); MA/PhD. *Faculty:* 7 full-time (3 women), 1 (woman) part-time/adjunct. *Students:* 22 full-time (15 women). Average age 33. 22 applicants, 36% accepted, 5 enrolled. In 2008, 3 master's, 5 doctorates awarded. Terminal master's awarded for partial completion of doctoral program. *Degree requirements:* For master's, variable foreign language requirement, comprehensive exam, thesis; for doctorate, one foreign language, comprehensive exam, thesis/dissertation. *Entrance requirements:* For master's and doctorate, GRE, sample of written work, 3 letters of recommendation, statement of purpose, personal achievements/contributions statement, resumé/curriculum vitae, transcripts for post-secondary institutions attended. Additional exam requirements/recommendations for international students: Required—TOEFL (paper: 550, computer: 213, IBT: 80) or IELTS (7). *Application deadline:* For fall admission, 1/5 for domestic and international students. Application fee: $70 ($90 for international students). Electronic applications accepted. *Expenses:* Tuition, nonresident: full-time $25,149. Required fees: $10,143. Full-time tuition and fees vary according to campus/location, reciprocity agreements and student level. *Financial support:* In 2008–09, 23 students received support, including 13 fellowships with full and partial tuition reimbursements available (averaging $11,600 per year), 29 teaching assistantships with partial tuition reimbursements available (averaging $11,500 per year); Federal Work-Study, scholarships/grants, traineeships, health care benefits, and unspecified assistantships also available. Support available to part-time students. Financial award application deadline: 1/5; financial award applicants required to submit FAFSA. *Faculty research:* Spanish/Latin American drama, performance studies and European theatre history, East Asian and Russian studies, playwriting, Medieval theatre. *Unit head:* Prof. Simon Williams, Chair, 805-893-5515, Fax: 805-893-7029, E-mail: williams@theaterdance.ucsb.edu. *Application contact:* Mary Tench, Graduate Program Assistant, 805-893-3147, Fax: 805-893-7029, E-mail: mtench@theaterdance.ucsb.edu.

University of California, Santa Cruz, Division of Graduate Studies, Division of the Arts, Department of Theater Arts, Santa Cruz, CA 95064. Offers Certificate.

University of Central Florida, College of Arts and Humanities, Department of Theatre, Orlando, FL 32816. Offers acting (MA); theatre for young audiences (MFA). *Faculty:* 25 full-time (10 women), 4 part-time/adjunct (2 women). *Students:* 53 full-time (34 women), 18 part-time (11 women); includes 5 minority (4 African Americans, 1 Hispanic American), 1 international. In 2008, 18 master's awarded. Application fee: $30. Electronic applications accepted. *Expenses:* Tuition, area resident: Full-time $6816; part-time $284 per credit. Tuition, state resident: full-time $6816; part-time $1076 per credit. Tuition, nonresident: full-time $25,824. Required fees: $216; $9 per credit. *Financial support:* In 2008–09, 39 research assistantships (averaging $6,700 per year), 18 teaching assistantships (averaging $4,000 per year) were awarded; fellowships also available. *Unit head:* Dr. Steven Chicurel, Interim Chair, 407-823-2862, Fax: 407-823-6446, E-mail: schicure@mail.ucf.edu. *Application contact:* Dr. Steven Chicurel, Interim Chair, 407-823-2862, Fax: 407-823-6446, E-mail: schicure@mail.ucf.edu.

University of Central Missouri, The Graduate School, College of Arts, Humanities and Social Sciences, Department of Theatre, Warrensburg, MO 64093. Offers MA. Part-time programs available. *Degree requirements:* For master's, comprehensive exam, research papers or thesis, oral exam. *Entrance requirements:* For master's, minimum GPA of 2.5 in major. Additional exam requirements/recommendations for international students: Required—TOEFL (minimum score 500 paper-based; 173 computer-based). Electronic applications accepted. *Faculty research:* Contemporary Theatre, Direct Theories, Performance Theories, Scenic Design, Design Technology.

University of Cincinnati, Graduate School, College-Conservatory of Music, Divisions of Opera, Musical Theater, Drama, and Arts Administration, Cincinnati, OH 45221. Offers arts administration (MA); directing (MFA); theater design and production (MFA); voice and opera (MM, DMA); MBA/MA. *Accreditation:* NAST (one or more programs are accredited). *Degree requirements:* For master's, final project. *Entrance requirements:* For master's, GMAT (MA), audition/interview. Additional exam requirements/recommendations for international students: Required—TOEFL (minimum score 520 paper-based; 190 computer-based). Electronic applications accepted.

University of Colorado at Boulder, Graduate School, College of Arts and Sciences, Department of Theatre and Dance, Boulder, CO 80309. Offers dance (MFA); theatre (MA, PhD). Terminal master's awarded for partial completion of doctoral program. *Degree requirements:* For master's, comprehensive exam, thesis; for doctorate, one foreign language, thesis/dissertation. *Entrance requirements:* For master's, GRE General Test (MA), audition (MFA), minimum undergraduate GPA of 2.75. *Faculty research:* Performance choreography; pedagogy administration; body therapies; multi-media forms; film, video, and cultural studies; non-concert forms; music; poetry writing; literature; kinesiology (dance); theater history; theory and literature.

University of Connecticut, Graduate School, School of Fine Arts, Department of Dramatic Arts, Field of Dramatic Arts, Storrs, CT 06269. Offers acting (MFA); costume design (MFA); lighting design (MFA); puppetry (MA, MFA); scenic design (MFA). *Degree requirements:* For master's, comprehensive exam. *Entrance requirements:* Additional exam requirements/recommendations for international students: Required—TOEFL (minimum score 550 paper-based; 213 computer-based). Electronic applications accepted.

University of Delaware, College of Arts and Sciences, Department of Theatre, Professional Theatre Training Program, Newark, DE 19716. Offers acting (MFA); stage management (MFA); technical production (MFA). Students are matriculated into program once every three years. *Entrance requirements:* For master's, audition, interview. Electronic applications accepted. *Faculty research:* Theatre training, acting, technical production, stage management.

University of Florida, Graduate School, College of Fine Arts, School of Theatre and Dance, Gainesville, FL 32611. Offers theatre (MFA). *Accreditation:* NAST. *Degree requirements:* For master's, thesis, creative project. *Entrance requirements:* For master's, audition/portfolio, bachelor's degree in theatre, interview, GRE General Test or minimum GPA of 3.0. Additional exam requirements/recommendations for international students: Required—TOEFL (minimum score 550 paper-based; 213 computer-based). Electronic applications accepted. *Faculty research:* Production, history of theatre, criticism.

University of Georgia, Graduate School, College of Arts and Sciences, Department of Theatre and Film Studies, Athens, GA 30602. Offers theatre (MFA, PhD). *Accreditation:* NAST. *Degree requirements:* For master's, comprehensive exam, written report; for doctorate, one foreign language, comprehensive exam, thesis/dissertation. *Entrance requirements:* For master's and doctorate, GRE General Test. Additional exam requirements/recommendations for international students: Required—TOEFL (minimum score 550 paper-based). Electronic applications accepted. *Faculty research:* Digital media, African-American theatre, Indian theatre, history of animation, vaudeville and popular culture history.

University of Guelph, Graduate Program Services, College of Arts, School of English and Theatre Studies, Program in Drama, Guelph, ON N1G 2W1, Canada. Offers MA. Part-time programs available. *Degree requirements:* For master's, thesis (for some programs). *Entrance requirements:* For master's, 2 letters of reference, 4-year honours undergraduate degree in English or drama. Additional exam requirements/recommendations for international students: Required—TOEFL. Electronic applications accepted. *Faculty research:* Canadian theatre, Renaissance, nineteenth and twentieth century drama and theatre, Shaw, theatre history, dramatic literature, performance theory.

University of Hawaii at Manoa, Graduate Division, Colleges of Arts and Sciences, College of Arts and Humanities, Department of Theatre and Dance, Honolulu, HI 96822. Offers dance (MA, MFA); theatre (MA, MFA, PhD). *Entrance requirements:* Additional exam requirements/recommendations for international students: Required—TOEFL. *Faculty research:* Asian theatre, feminist theatre and dance, Russian theatre, Australian theatre.

See Display on page 279.

University of Houston, College of Liberal Arts and Social Sciences, School of Theatre, Houston, TX 77204. Offers MA, MFA. Part-time programs available. *Faculty:* 6 full-time (1 woman), 3 part-time/adjunct (1 woman). *Students:* 39 full-time (19 women), 4 part-time (3 women); includes 11 minority (6 African Americans, 1 Asian American or Pacific Islander, 4 Hispanic Americans), 1 international. Average age 29. 31 applicants, 68% accepted, 18

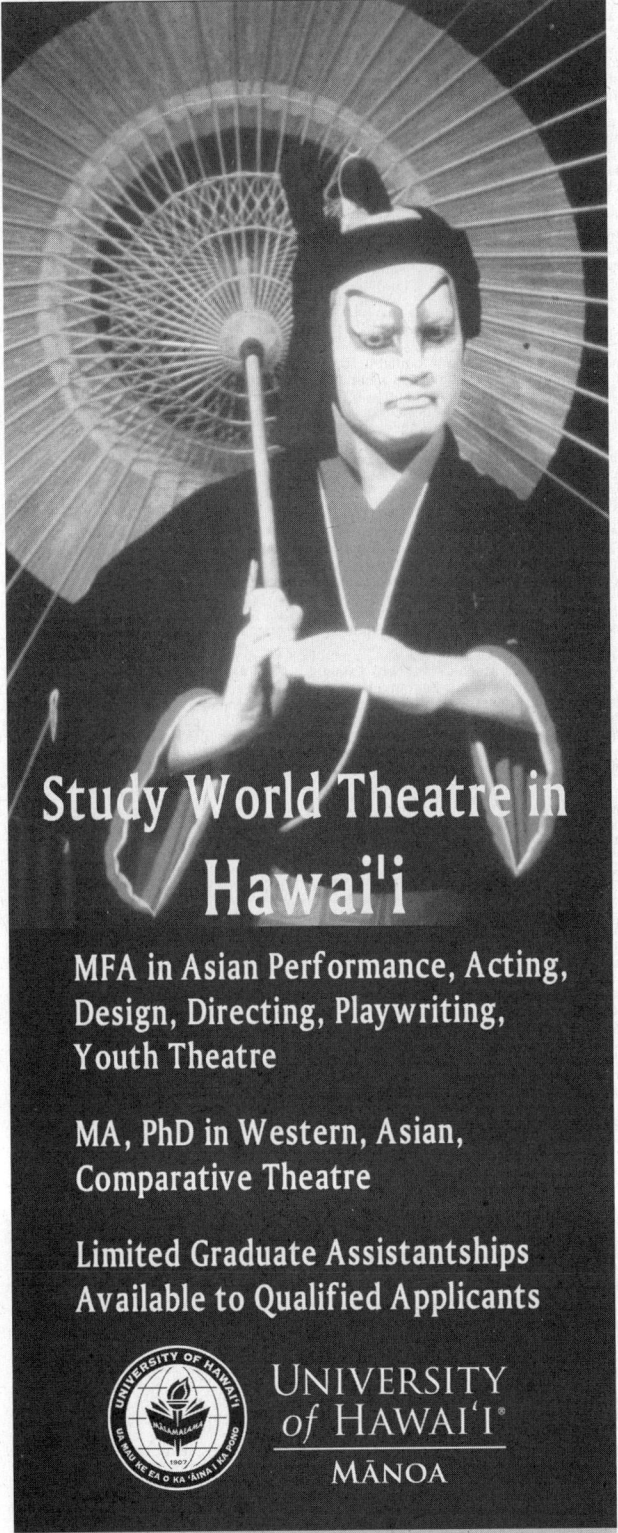
enrolled. In 2008, 4 master's awarded. *Degree requirements:* For master's, thesis optional. *Entrance requirements:* For master's, GRE General Test. Application fee: $25. *Expenses:* Tuition, state resident: full-time $5164; part-time $287 per credit. Tuition, nonresident: full-time $10,222; part-time $568 per credit. *Financial support:* In 2008–09, 35 teaching assistantships with full tuition reimbursements (averaging $9,300 per year) were awarded; career-related internships or fieldwork, Federal Work-Study, institutionally sponsored loans, scholarships/grants, health care benefits, and unspecified assistantships also available. Support available to part-time students. Financial award application deadline: 2/1. *Unit head:* Steven Wallace, Chairperson, 713-743-3003, Fax: 713-749-1420. *Application contact:* Steven Wallace, Chairperson, 713-743-3003, Fax: 713-749-1420.

University of Idaho, College of Graduate Studies, College of Letters, Arts and Social Sciences, Department of Theatre and Film, Moscow, ID 83844-2282. Offers theatre arts (MFA). *Faculty:* 7 full-time. *Students:* 23 full-time, 2 part-time. Average age 32. In 2008, 6 master's awarded. *Entrance requirements:* For master's, minimum GPA of 2.8. *Application deadline:* For fall admission, 8/1 for domestic students; for spring admission, 12/15 for domestic students. Application fee: $55 ($60 for international students). *Expenses:* Tuition, nonresident: full-time $10,080; part-time $336 per credit. Required fees: $5212; $267 per credit. Tuition and fees vary according to program. *Financial support:* Research assistantships, teaching assistantships available. Financial award application deadline: 2/15. *Unit head:* Dr. Dean Fields Panttaja, Chair, 208-885-6465. *Application contact:* Dr. Dean Fields Panttaja, Chair, 208-885-6465.

University of Illinois at Urbana–Champaign, Graduate College, College of Fine and Applied Arts, Department of Theatre, Champaign, IL 61820. Offers MA, MFA, PhD. *Accreditation:* NAST. *Faculty:* 15 full-time (6 women), 3 part-time/adjunct (2 women). *Students:* 58 full-time (34 women), 5 part-time (3 women); includes 6 minority (4 African Americans, 1 Asian American or Pacific Islander, 1 Hispanic American), 5 international. 71 applicants, 34% accepted, 21 enrolled. In 2008, 15 master's, 1 doctorate awarded. *Entrance requirements:* For master's, minimum GPA of 3.0; audition, portfolio or writing sample; for doctorate, writing sample; master's degree, minimum GPA of 3.0. Additional exam requirements/recommendations for international students: Required—TOEFL (minimum score 550 paper-based; 213 computer-based). *Application deadline:* Applications are processed on a rolling basis. Application fee: $60 ($75 for international students). Electronic applications accepted. *Financial support:* In 2008–09, 5 fellowships, 23 teaching assistantships were awarded; research assistantships, tuition waivers (full and partial) also available. *Unit head:* Brant Pope, Head, 217-333-2371, Fax: 217-244-1861, E-mail: brant@illinois.edu. *Application contact:* David Swinford, Admissions and Records Officer, 217-333-3538, Fax: 217-244-1861, E-mail: dswinfor@illinois.edu.

The University of Iowa, Graduate College, College of Liberal Arts and Sciences, Department of Theatre Arts, Iowa City, IA 52242-1316. Offers MFA. *Accreditation:* NAST. *Degree requirements:* For master's, thesis, exam. *Entrance requirements:* For master's, GRE, minimum GPA of 3.0. Additional exam requirements/recommendations for international students: Required—TOEFL (minimum score 550 paper-based; 213 computer-based; 81 iBT). Electronic applications accepted.

The University of Kansas, Graduate Studies, College of Liberal Arts and Sciences, Department of Theatre and Film, Lawrence, KS 66045. Offers film and media studies (PhD); theatre (MA); theatre design (MFA), including scenography. *Faculty:* 24. *Students:* 36 full-time (13 women), 3 part-time (1 woman); includes 2 minority (both Asian Americans or Pacific Islanders), 8 international. Average age 34. 34 applicants, 59% accepted, 7 enrolled. In 2008, 4 master's, 2 doctorates awarded. *Degree requirements:* For master's, thesis; for doctorate, one foreign language, comprehensive exam, thesis/dissertation. *Entrance requirements:* For master's, GRE General Test, minimum GPA of 3.2; for doctorate, GRE General Test, minimum GPA of 3.5; MA or MFA in theatre, film, or related field. Additional exam requirements/recommendations for international students: Required—TOEFL. *Application deadline:* For fall admission, 1/1 priority date for domestic students, 1/1 for international students. Application fee: $45 ($55 for international students). Electronic applications accepted. *Expenses:* Tuition, area resident: Full-time $6122; part-time $255.10 per credit hour. Tuition, state resident: full-time $6122; part-time $255.10 per credit hour. Tuition, nonresident: full-time $14,629; part-time $609.55 per credit hour. Required fees: $847; $70.56 per credit hour. Tuition and fees vary according to course load and program. *Financial support:* Fellowships with tuition reimbursements, teaching assistantships with full and partial tuition reimbursements, Federal Work-Study, scholarships/grants, and unspecified assistantships available. Financial award application deadline: 1/1. *Faculty research:* Film history, theatre history, film theory, cultural studies, performance studies. *Unit head:* John Staniunas, Chair, 785-864-3511, Fax: 785-864-5251. *Application contact:* Henry Bial, Director of Graduate Studies, 785-864-3511, Fax: 785-331-5251, E-mail: tfdgs@ku.edu.

University of Kentucky, Graduate School, College of Fine Arts, Program in Theatre, Lexington, KY 40506-0032. Offers MA. *Degree requirements:* For master's, comprehensive exam, thesis optional. *Entrance requirements:* For master's, GRE General Test, minimum undergraduate GPA of 2.75. Additional exam requirements/recommendations for international students: Required—TOEFL (minimum score 550 paper-based; 213 computer-based). Electronic applications accepted. *Faculty research:* Historical, critical, practical, theoretical, and experimental perspectives of acting, directing, design, performance, and dramaturgy.

University of Louisville, Graduate School, College of Arts and Sciences, Department of Theatre Arts, Louisville, KY 40292-0001. Offers performance (MFA). *Accreditation:* NAST. *Faculty:* 6 full-time (4 women), 1 (woman) part-time/adjunct. *Students:* 12 full-time (8 women); includes 7 African Americans. Average age 30. 10 applicants, 80% accepted, 4 enrolled. In 2008, 5 master's awarded. *Degree requirements:* For master's, thesis, performance project, monograph. *Entrance requirements:* For master's, GRE General Test, auditions and portfolio review. *Application deadline:* For spring admission, 4/15 priority date for domestic students. Applications are processed on a rolling basis. Application fee: $50. *Financial support:* In 2008–09, 12 students received support, including 11 teaching assistantships with full tuition reimbursements available (averaging $12,000 per year); scholarships/grants and health care benefits also available. Financial award application deadline: 3/15; financial award applicants required to submit FAFSA. *Faculty research:* Speech/dialects, especially for actors of color; African diaspora theatre; community acting and creation of new works; peace studies; African American theatre. Total annual research expenditures: $10,000. *Unit head:* Dr. Russell Vandenbroucke, Chair, 502-852-8444, Fax: 502-852-7235, E-mail: r.vandenbrouke@louisville.edu. *Application contact:* Libby Leggett, Director, Graduate Admissions, 502-852-3101, Fax: 502-852-6536, E-mail: gradadm@louisville.edu.

University of Maryland, College Park, Graduate Studies, College of Arts and Humanities, Department of Theatre, College Park, MD 20742. Offers MA, MFA, PhD. *Accreditation:* NAST. *Degree requirements:* For master's, comprehensive exam, thesis optional; for doctorate, thesis/dissertation. *Entrance requirements:* For master's, GRE General Test, minimum GPA of 3.0, writing sample, portfolio (MFA), 3 letters of recommendation; for doctorate, GRE General Test, writing sample. Additional exam requirements/recommendations for international students: Required—TOEFL. Electronic applications accepted. *Faculty research:* Theatre aesthetics, performance, history/theory, design and production.

University of Massachusetts Amherst, Graduate School, College of Humanities and Fine Arts, Department of Theater, Amherst, MA 01003. Offers MFA. Part-time programs available. *Degree requirements:* For master's, thesis. *Entrance requirements:* For master's, GRE General Test, resumé of production experience, two critical essays or design portfolio. Additional exam requirements/recommendations for international students: Required—TOEFL (minimum score 550 paper-based; 213 computer-based; 79 iBT), IELTS (minimum score 6.5). Electronic applications accepted. *Expenses:* Tuition, area resident: Full-time $2640. Tuition, nonresident: full-time $9936. One-time fee: $332 full-time. Tuition and fees vary according to course load.

University of Memphis, Graduate School, College of Communication and Fine Arts, Department of Theatre and Dance, Memphis, TN 38152. Offers theatre (MFA). *Accreditation:* NAST.

Theater

University of Memphis (continued)
Faculty: 10 full-time (4 women). *Students:* 15 full-time (9 women), 1 (woman) part-time, 1 international. Average age 29. 14 applicants, 36% accepted, 5 enrolled. In 2008, 4 master's awarded. *Degree requirements:* For master's, comprehensive exam, practicum. *Entrance requirements:* For master's, minimum GPA of 3.0 in major, 2.5 overall. *Application deadline:* For fall admission, 8/1 for domestic students; for spring admission, 12/1 for domestic students. Applications are processed on a rolling basis. Application fee: $35 ($60 for international students). *Expenses:* Tuition, area resident: Full-time $6242; part-time $330 per credit hour. Tuition, state resident: full-time $6242; part-time $330 per credit hour. Tuition, nonresident: full-time $17,828; part-time $815 per credit hour. Required fees: $1156. *Financial support:* Research assistantships with full tuition reimbursements, teaching assistantships with full tuition reimbursements, career-related internships or fieldwork, Federal Work-Study, and institutionally sponsored loans available. Financial award application deadline: 6/1; financial award applicants required to submit FAFSA. *Faculty research:* Theatre design, production management, Lessac vocal training, movement styles, directing. *Unit head:* Prof. Robert A. Hetherington, Chair, 901-678-2523, Fax: 901-678-4331, E-mail: rhether@memphis.edu. *Application contact:* Prof. Robert A. Hetherington, Chair, 901-678-2523, Fax: 901-678-4331, E-mail: rhether@memphis.edu.

University of Michigan, Horace H. Rackham School of Graduate Studies, The School of Music, Theatre, and Dance, Department of Theatre and Drama, Ann Arbor, MI 48109. Offers design (MFA); theatre (PhD). *Degree requirements:* For master's, thesis; for doctorate, one foreign language, thesis/dissertation, preliminary exam, qualifying exam. *Entrance requirements:* For master's, portfolio, interview, writing sample; for doctorate, GRE General Test, writing sample, interview. Additional exam requirements/recommendations for international students: Required—TOEFL (minimum score 600 paper-based; 250 computer-based). Electronic applications accepted. *Faculty research:* Silent film, avant-garde drama, popular entertainment.

University of Minnesota, Twin Cities Campus, Graduate School, College of Liberal Arts, Department of Theatre Arts and Dance, Minneapolis, MN 55455-0213. Offers design technology (MFA); theatre arts and dance (MA, PhD). *Accreditation:* NASD; NAST (one or more programs are accredited). Terminal master's awarded for partial completion of doctoral program. *Degree requirements:* For master's, thesis (for some programs), final creative project (MFA), foreign language (MA); for doctorate, one foreign language, thesis/dissertation, oral defense, written exams. *Entrance requirements:* For master's, GRE General Test, minimum GPA of 3.0, audition or portfolio; for doctorate, GRE General Test, minimum GPA of 3.0, writing sample, 1 foreign language. Additional exam requirements/recommendations for international students: Required—TOEFL (minimum score 550 paper-based; 213 computer-based; 79 iBT). Electronic applications accepted. *Faculty research:* Theatre history; Eastern European theatre; performance studies; medieval studies.

University of Missouri–Columbia, Graduate School, College of Arts and Sciences, Department of Theatre, Columbia, MO 65211. Offers MA, PhD. Part-time programs available. *Faculty:* 12 full-time (5 women). *Students:* 14 full-time (4 women), 11 part-time (6 women); includes 2 minority (1 African American, 1 Hispanic American). Average age 38. 22 applicants, 27% accepted, 5 enrolled. In 2008, 1 master's awarded. *Degree requirements:* For doctorate, thesis/dissertation. *Entrance requirements:* For master's and doctorate, GRE General Test, minimum GPA of 3.0. Additional exam requirements/recommendations for international students: Required—TOEFL (minimum score 650 paper-based; 280 computer-based; 114 iBT). *Application deadline:* For fall admission, 2/15 priority date for domestic students. Applications are processed on a rolling basis. Application fee: $45 ($60 for international students). *Financial support:* Fellowships, research assistantships, teaching assistantships, institutionally sponsored loans available. *Unit head:* Dr. Clyde Ruffin, Department Chair, E-mail: ruffinc@missouri.edu. *Application contact:* Marsha Miller, Office Support Staff II, 573-882-8281, E-mail: millermt@missouri.edu.

University of Missouri–Kansas City, College of Arts and Sciences, Theatre Department, Kansas City, MO 64110-2499. Offers acting (MFA); design technology (MFA); theatre (MA). *Accreditation:* NAST. *Faculty:* 17 full-time (6 women), 8 part-time/adjunct (3 women). *Students:* 66 full-time (34 women), 22 part-time (4 women); includes 14 minority (5 African Americans, 1 American Indian/Alaska Native, 1 Asian American or Pacific Islander, 7 Hispanic Americans), 1 international. Average age 27. 48 applicants, 67% accepted, 29 enrolled. In 2008, 23 master's awarded. *Degree requirements:* For master's, thesis. *Entrance requirements:* For master's, audition or portfolio, interview. Additional exam requirements/recommendations for international students: Required—TOEFL (minimum score 550 paper-based; 213 computer-based; 80 iBT). *Application deadline:* For fall admission, 3/1 priority date for domestic and international students; for spring admission, 11/1 priority date for domestic and international students. Applications are processed on a rolling basis. Application fee: $45 ($50 for international students). Electronic applications accepted. *Expenses:* Tuition, state resident: full-time $5376; part-time $298.70 per credit hour. Tuition, nonresident: full-time $13,882; part-time $771.20 per credit hour. Required fees: $640.28; $34.65 per contact hour. $30 per semester. Tuition and fees vary according to course load and program. *Financial support:* In 2008–09, 64 teaching assistantships with partial tuition reimbursements (averaging $11,379 per year) were awarded; fellowships with partial tuition reimbursements, career-related internships or fieldwork, Federal Work-Study, institutionally sponsored loans, and scholarships/grants also available. Financial award application deadline: 3/1; financial award applicants required to submit FAFSA. *Faculty research:* Contemporary Russian theatre, Shakespeare in performance, subtle energies in actor training, multi-channel sound, renovation of Zuni Pueblo historic Spanish mission. *Unit head:* Tom Mardikes, Chair, 816-235-2784, Fax: 816-235-6562, E-mail: mardikest@umkc.edu. *Application contact:* Cindy Stofiel, Student Affairs Representative, 816-235-2702, Fax: 816-235-6562, E-mail: stofielc@umkc.edu.

The University of Montana, Graduate School, School of Fine Arts, Department of Drama/Dance, Missoula, MT 59812-0002. Offers fine arts (MA, MFA), including acting (MFA), design/technology (MFA), directing (MFA), drama (MA), integrated arts and education (MA), media arts (MFA). *Accreditation:* NAST (one or more programs are accredited). *Degree requirements:* For master's, thesis or alternative. *Entrance requirements:* For master's, GRE General Test, audition, portfolio, production notebook.

The University of Montana, Graduate School, School of Fine Arts, Department of Music, Missoula, MT 59812-0002. Offers music (MM), including composition/technology, music education, musical theater, performance. *Accreditation:* NASM. *Entrance requirements:* For master's, GRE General Test, GRE Subject Test, portfolio.

University of Nebraska at Omaha, Graduate Studies and Research, College of Communication, Fine Arts and Media, Department of Theatre, Omaha, NE 68182. Offers MA. Part-time programs available. *Degree requirements:* For master's, comprehensive exam, thesis (for some programs). *Entrance requirements:* For master's, GRE General Test or MAT, minimum GPA of 3.0. Additional exam requirements/recommendations for international students: Required—TOEFL (minimum score 500 paper-based; 173 computer-based; 61 iBT). Electronic applications accepted.

University of Nebraska–Lincoln, Graduate College, College of Fine and Performing Arts, Johnny Carson School of Theatre and Film, Lincoln, NE 68588. Offers acting (MFA); costume (MFA); directing (MFA); stage design (MFA). *Accreditation:* NAST. *Faculty:* 10 full-time (4 women). *Students:* 16 full-time (7 women), 2 part-time (both women); includes 1 minority (African American). Average age 27. In 2008, 2 master's awarded. *Degree requirements:* For master's, thesis. *Entrance requirements:* For master's, audition, portfolio. Additional exam requirements/recommendations for international students: Required—TOEFL (minimum score 500 paper-based; 173 computer-based). *Application deadline:* For fall admission, 3/1 priority date for domestic students. Applications are processed on a rolling basis. Application fee: $40. Electronic applications accepted. *Expenses:* Tuition, state resident: full-time $4275; part-time $237.50 per credit hour. Tuition, nonresident: full-time $11,525; part-time $640.25 per credit hour. Required fees: $1068; $10.35 per credit hour. $440.70 per semester. Tuition and fees vary according to course load and program. *Financial support:* Fellowships, research assistantships, teaching assistantships, Federal Work-Study and health care benefits available. Support available to part-time students. Financial award application deadline: 2/15. *Faculty research:* American theatre history, British theatre history, modern American drama, contemporary performance, Elizabethan theatre history. *Unit head:* Prof. Jeffrey Elwell, Chair, 402-472-2072. *Application contact:* Prof. Jeffrey Elwell, Chair, 402-472-2072.

University of Nevada, Las Vegas, Graduate College, College of Fine Arts, Department of Theatre, Las Vegas, NV 89154-5036. Offers theatre arts (MA, MFA). *Accreditation:* NAST. Part-time programs available. *Faculty:* 13 full-time (2 women), 4 part-time/adjunct (2 women). *Students:* 38 full-time (20 women), 5 part-time (2 women); includes 2 minority (both Hispanic Americans), 2 international. Average age 31. 36 applicants, 42% accepted, 13 enrolled. In 2008, 12 master's awarded. *Degree requirements:* For master's, thesis (for some programs), creative project, oral exam. *Entrance requirements:* Additional exam requirements/recommendations for international students: Required—TOEFL (minimum score 550 paper-based; 213 computer-based; 80 iBT), IELTS (minimum score 7). *Application deadline:* For fall admission, 6/1 priority date for domestic students, 5/1 for international students. Applications are processed on a rolling basis. Application fee: $60 ($75 for international students). Electronic applications accepted. *Expenses:* Tuition, state resident: full-time $1414; part-time $198 per credit. Tuition, nonresident: full-time $12,509; part-time $415.75 per credit. International tuition: $14,249 full-time. Required fees: $4 per credit. $252 per semester. Tuition and fees vary according to course load. *Financial support:* In 2008–09, 31 students received support, including 16 research assistantships with partial tuition reimbursements available (averaging $10,000 per year), 15 teaching assistantships with partial tuition reimbursements available (averaging $10,000 per year); institutionally sponsored loans, scholarships/grants, health care benefits, and unspecified assistantships also available. Financial award application deadline: 3/1. *Faculty research:* Developing a professional/academic theatre model that is sustainable, curriculum development to seamlessly integrate stage and screen acting training, integrated voice and movement training (Lugering method), costume history. *Unit head:* Brackley Frayer, Chair/Associate Professor, 702-895-3666, Fax: 702-895-0833, E-mail: brackley.frayer@unlv.edu. *Application contact:* Graduate College Admissions Evaluator, 702-895-3320, Fax: 702-895-4180, E-mail: gradcollege@unlv.edu.

University of New Mexico, Graduate School, College of Fine Arts, Department of Theatre and Dance, Albuquerque, NM 87131-2039. Offers dramatic writing (MFA); theater and dance (MA). *Accreditation:* NASD; NAST. *Degree requirements:* For master's, comprehensive exam (for some programs), thesis (for some programs). *Entrance requirements:* For master's, minimum GPA of 3.0, undergraduate major in theatre, dance or closely related field, 3 letters of recommendation, letter of intent. Electronic applications accepted. *Faculty research:* Theater education and outreach, choreography, dramatic writing, dance history/criticism.

University of New Orleans, Graduate School, College of Liberal Arts, Department of Film, Theatre and Communication Arts, New Orleans, LA 70148. Offers film production (MFA); theatre directing (MFA); theatre performance (MFA). *Accreditation:* NAST. *Degree requirements:* For master's, comprehensive exam, thesis. *Entrance requirements:* Additional exam requirements/recommendations for international students: Required—TOEFL (minimum score 550 paper-based; 213 computer-based; 79 iBT). Electronic applications accepted. *Faculty research:* Mass communication theory, nineteenth- and twentieth-century theater history, film criticism and history.

The University of North Carolina at Chapel Hill, Graduate School, College of Arts and Sciences, Department of Dramatic Art, Chapel Hill, NC 27599. Offers acting (MFA); costume production (MFA); technical production (MFA). *Entrance requirements:* For master's, audition or portfolio.

The University of North Carolina at Charlotte, Graduate School, College of Education, Program in Teacher Education, Charlotte, NC 28223-0001. Offers art education (K-12) (MAT); dance education (K-12) (MAT); elementary education (K-6) (MAT); English as a second language (K-12) (MAT); foreign language education (K-12) (MAT); general teacher education (MAT); middle grades education (6-9) (MAT); music education (K-12) (MAT); secondary education (9-12) (MAT); special education (K-12) (MAT); theatre education (K-12) (MAT). *Faculty:* 9 full-time (all women), 1 (woman) part-time/adjunct. *Students:* 23 full-time (15 women), 194 part-time (170 women); includes 33 minority (25 African Americans, 1 American Indian/Alaska Native, 5 Asian Americans or Pacific Islanders, 2 Hispanic Americans), 1 international. Average age 32. 116 applicants, 95% accepted, 91 enrolled. In 2008, 59 master's awarded. *Entrance requirements:* For master's, GRE or MAT. Additional exam requirements/recommendations for international students: Required—TOEFL (minimum score 557 paper-based; 220 computer-based). *Application deadline:* For fall admission, 7/1 for domestic students, 5/1 for international students; for spring admission, 11/1 for domestic students, 10/1 for international students. Applications are processed on a rolling basis. Application fee: $55. Electronic applications accepted. *Expenses:* Tuition, area resident: Full-time $2919; part-time $122 per credit hour. Tuition, state resident: full-time $2919; part-time $122 per credit hour. Tuition, nonresident: full-time $13,126; part-time $547 per credit hour. Required fees: $1779; $91 per credit hour. Tuition and fees vary according to program. *Financial support:* In 2008–09, 2 research assistantships (averaging $7,524 per year), 5 teaching assistantships (averaging $6,125 per year) were awarded; career-related internships or fieldwork, Federal Work-Study, institutionally sponsored loans, scholarships/grants, and unspecified assistantships also available. Support available to part-time students. Financial award application deadline: 4/1; financial award applicants required to submit FAFSA. *Unit head:* Dr. Kimberly J. Hartman, Coordinator, 704-687-8883, Fax: 704-687-6430, E-mail: khartman@email.uncc.edu. *Application contact:* Kathy B. Giddings, Director of Graduate Admissions, 704-687-3366, Fax: 704-687-3279, E-mail: agidding@uncc.edu.

The University of North Carolina at Greensboro, Graduate School, College of Arts and Sciences, Department of Theater, Greensboro, NC 27412-5001. Offers acting (MFA); design (MFA); directing (MFA); theater education (M Ed); theater for youth (MFA). *Accreditation:* NAST. *Entrance requirements:* For master's, portfolio, interviews. Electronic applications accepted.

University of North Carolina School of the Arts, School of Design and Production, Winston-Salem, NC 27127-2188. Offers costume design (MFA); costume technology (MFA); scene design (MFA); scene painting/properties (MFA); sound design (MFA); stage automation (MFA); technical direction (MFA); wig and make-up design (MFA). *Faculty:* 19 full-time (4 women), 16 part-time/adjunct (6 women). *Students:* 66 full-time (39 women); includes 5 minority (1 African American, 4 Hispanic Americans), 2 international. Average age 25. 86 applicants, 77% accepted, 48 enrolled. In 2008, 11 master's awarded. *Degree requirements:* For master's, project. *Entrance requirements:* For master's, interview, portfolio. Additional exam requirements/recommendations for international students: Required—TOEFL. *Application deadline:* For fall admission, 4/1 priority date for domestic students. Applications are processed on a rolling basis. Application fee: $60 ($100 for international students). Electronic applications accepted. *Expenses:* Tuition, area resident: Full-time $3797. Tuition, state resident: full-time $3797. Tuition, nonresident: full-time $15,670. Required fees: $1791. *Financial support:* In 2008–09, 53 teaching assistantships with partial tuition reimbursements (averaging $1,500 per year) were awarded; career-related internships or fieldwork, Federal Work-Study, and unspecified assistantships also available. Support available to part-time students. Financial award application deadline: 3/15; financial award applicants required to submit FAFSA. *Unit head:* Joseph A. Tilford, Dean, 336-770-3214 Ext. 103, Fax: 336-770-3213. *Application contact:* Sheeler Lawson, Director of Admissions, 336-770-3290, Fax: 336-770-3370, E-mail: admissions@uncsa.edu.

University of North Dakota, Graduate School, College of Arts and Sciences, Department of Theatre Arts, Grand Forks, ND 58202. Offers MA. *Accreditation:* NAST. *Degree requirements:* For master's, comprehensive exam, thesis or alternative. *Entrance requirements:* For master's, minimum GPA of 3.0. Additional exam requirements/recommendations for international students:

Required—TOEFL (minimum score 550 paper-based; 213 computer-based; 79 iBT), IELTS (minimum score 6.5). Electronic applications accepted.

University of Oklahoma, Graduate College, College of Fine Arts, School of Drama, Norman, OK 73019. Offers acting (MFA); design (MFA); directing (MFA); drama (MA). *Accreditation:* NAST. *Faculty:* 8 full-time (4 women), 1 (woman) part-time/adjunct. *Students:* 12 full-time (7 women); includes 1 minority (Asian American or Pacific Islander), 3 international. 3 applicants, 100% accepted, 3 enrolled. In 2008, 6 master's awarded. *Degree requirements:* For master's, comprehensive exam, thesis (MA), departmental qualifying exam. *Entrance requirements:* For master's, BA with 36 hours in drama, auditions. Additional exam requirements/recommendations for international students: Required—TOEFL (minimum score 550 paper-based; 213 computer-based). *Application deadline:* For fall admission, 6/1 for domestic students, 4/1 for international students; for spring admission, 11/1 for domestic students, 9/1 for international students. Applications are processed on a rolling basis. Application fee: $40 ($90 for international students). Electronic applications accepted. *Expenses:* Tuition, state resident: full-time $3744; part-time $156 per credit hour. Tuition, nonresident: full-time $13,577; part-time $565.70 per credit hour. Required fees: $2415.40; $90.10 per credit hour. *Financial support:* In 2008–09, 5 students received support, including 5 research assistantships with partial tuition reimbursements available (averaging $9,586 per year), 7 teaching assistantships with partial tuition reimbursements available (averaging $9,586 per year); unspecified assistantships also available. Financial award application deadline: 4/7; financial award applicants required to submit FAFSA. *Faculty research:* Directing, costume design, lighting design, dramalurgy. *Unit head:* Dr. Tom Orr, Director, 405-325-4021, Fax: 405-325-0400, E-mail: thorr@ou.edu. *Application contact:* Dr. Judith Pender, Graduate Liaison, 405-325-5319, Fax: 405-325-0400, E-mail: jmpender@ou.edu.

University of Oregon, Graduate School, College of Arts and Sciences, Department of Theater Arts, Eugene, OR 97403. Offers MA, MFA, MS, PhD. *Degree requirements:* For master's, variable foreign language requirement, thesis or alternative; for doctorate, variable foreign language requirement, thesis/dissertation. *Entrance requirements:* For master's and doctorate, minimum GPA of 3.0. Additional exam requirements/recommendations for international students: Required—TOEFL.

University of Ottawa, Faculty of Graduate and Postdoctoral Studies, Faculty of Arts, Department of Theatre, Ottawa, ON K1N 6N5, Canada. Offers directing for theatre (MA). Electronic applications accepted. *Faculty research:* Lamise en scéne.

University of Pittsburgh, School of Arts and Sciences, Department of Theatre Arts, Pittsburgh, PA 15260. Offers performance pedagogy (MFA); theatre and performance studies (MA, PhD). *Accreditation:* NAST. Terminal master's awarded for partial completion of doctoral program. *Degree requirements:* For master's, comprehensive exam; for doctorate, one foreign language, comprehensive exam, thesis/dissertation. *Entrance requirements:* For master's and doctorate, GRE General Test, samples of written work. Additional exam requirements/recommendations for international students: Required—TOEFL. Electronic applications accepted. *Faculty research:* American theatre, Renaissance theatre, Asian theatre, dramatic structure, performance theory.

University of Portland, Graduate School, College of Arts and Sciences, Department of Performing and Fine Arts, Program in Drama, Portland, OR 97203-5798. Offers directing (MFA). *Accreditation:* NAST. Part-time and evening/weekend programs available. *Faculty:* 3 full-time (1 woman). *Students:* 5 full-time (1 woman). Average age 36. In 2008, 3 master's awarded. *Degree requirements:* For master's, thesis optional. *Entrance requirements:* For master's, GRE General Test, minimum GPA of 3.0, 3 letters of recommendation, resumé, statement of goals, official transcripts. Additional exam requirements/recommendations for international students: Required—TOEFL (minimum score 500 paper-based; 61 iBT), IELTS (minimum score 7). *Application deadline:* For fall admission, 7/15 priority date for domestic and international students; for spring admission, 12/15 priority date for domestic and international students. Applications are processed on a rolling basis. Application fee: $50. *Expenses:* Tuition: Full-time $7380; part-time $8.20 per credit hour. *Financial support:* Federal Work-Study and scholarships/grants available. Financial award application deadline: 3/1; financial award applicants required to submit FAFSA. *Unit head:* Lawrence Larsen, Director, 503-943-7396, E-mail: larsen@up.edu. *Application contact:* Chris James Olinger, Administrative Assistant, 503-943-7107, Fax: 503-943-7315, E-mail: olingerc@up.edu.

University of San Diego, College of Arts and Sciences, Program in Dramatic Arts, San Diego, CA 92110-2492. Offers MFA. *Faculty:* 3 full-time (2 women), 1 part-time/adjunct (0 women). *Students:* 14 full-time (6 women); includes 2 minority (1 Asian American or Pacific Islander, 1 Hispanic American). Average age 28. 354 applicants, 2% accepted, 7 enrolled. In 2008, 7 master's awarded. *Entrance requirements:* For master's, audition. Additional exam requirements/recommendations for international students: Required—TOEFL (minimum score 580 paper-based; 237 computer-based; 83 iBT), TWE. *Application deadline:* For fall admission, 1/3 for domestic and international students. Application fee: $45. *Expenses:* Tuition: Full-time $19,710; part-time $1129 per unit. Required fees: $154. Full-time tuition and fees vary according to course load and degree level. *Financial support:* In 2008–09, 14 students received support, including 14 fellowships with full tuition reimbursements available; career-related internships or fieldwork, Federal Work-Study, and institutionally sponsored loans also available. Financial award application deadline: 4/1; financial award applicants required to submit FAFSA. *Faculty research:* Drama, acting, instruction, voice and speech. *Unit head:* Richard Seer, Graduate Program Director, 619-260-8813, Fax: 619-231-5879. *Application contact:* Dr. John Mosby, Associate Director of Graduate Admissions, 619-260-4524, Fax: 619-260-4158, E-mail: grads@sandiego.edu.

University of Saskatchewan, College of Graduate Studies and Research, College of Arts and Sciences, Department of Drama, Saskatoon, SK S7N 5A2, Canada. Offers MA. *Degree requirements:* For master's, thesis. *Entrance requirements:* Additional exam requirements/recommendations for international students: Required—TOEFL.

University of South Carolina, The Graduate School, College of Arts and Sciences, Department of Theater and Dance, Columbia, SC 29208. Offers theater (MA, MAT, MFA). IMA and MAT offered in cooperation with the College of Education. *Accreditation:* NAST (one or more programs are accredited). *Degree requirements:* For master's, comprehensive exam, thesis. *Entrance requirements:* For master's, GRE General Test, GRE or MAT (for MAT degree), audition, interview (for MFA degree). Additional exam requirements/recommendations for international students: Required—TOEFL. Electronic applications accepted. *Faculty research:* Computer assisted design, rhetoric of science and technology, Alexander Technique, script analysis, Lessac Method.

University of South Carolina, The Graduate School, College of Education, Department of Instruction and Teacher Education, Program in Secondary Education, Columbia, SC 29208. Offers art education (IMA, MAT); business education (IMA, MAT); English (MAT); foreign language (MAT); health education (MAT); mathematics (MAT); science (IMA, MAT); secondary (Ed D); secondary education (MT, PhD); social studies (MAT); theatre and speech (MAT). IMA and MT offered jointly with the subject areas. *Accreditation:* NCATE. *Degree requirements:* For master's, comprehensive exam, thesis (for some programs), foreign language (MA); for doctorate, one foreign language, comprehensive exam, thesis/dissertation. *Entrance requirements:* For master's, GRE General Test or MAT, teaching certificate (IMA, M Ed), interview; for doctorate, GRE General Test or MAT, interview. *Faculty research:* Middle school programs, professional development, school collaboration.

The University of South Dakota, Graduate School, College of Fine Arts, Department of Theatre, Vermillion, SD 57069-2390. Offers MA, MFA. *Accreditation:* NAST. *Degree requirements:* For master's, thesis or alternative. *Entrance requirements:* For master's, GRE (MA), minimum GPA of 2.7, portfolio. Additional exam requirements/recommendations for international students: Required—TOEFL (minimum score 550 paper-based; 213 computer-based; 79 iBT). Electronic applications accepted.

University of Southern California, Graduate School, School of Theatre, Program in Acting, Los Angeles, CA 90089. Offers MFA. Postbaccalaureate distance learning degree programs offered (minimal on-campus study). *Entrance requirements:* For master's, 3 letters of recommendation, current headshot, audition.

See Close-Up on page 293.

University of Southern California, Graduate School, School of Theatre, Program in Dramatic Writing, Los Angeles, CA 90089. Offers MFA. *Entrance requirements:* For master's, GRE General Test, 3 letters of recommendation, play in standard Samuel French of Final Draft stage format, a synopsis of the play.

See Close-Up on page 293.

University of Southern Mississippi, Graduate School, College of Arts and Letters, Department of Theatre and Dance, Hattiesburg, MS 39406-0001. Offers theatre (MFA). *Accreditation:* NAST. Part-time programs available. *Faculty:* 8 full-time (2 women). *Students:* 20 full-time (10 women); includes 5 minority (1 African American, 1 American Indian/Alaska Native, 1 Asian American or Pacific Islander, 2 Hispanic Americans). Average age 28. 22 applicants, 45% accepted, 9 enrolled. In 2008, 8 master's awarded. *Degree requirements:* For master's, comprehensive exam, thesis or alternative, creative project. *Entrance requirements:* For master's, GRE General Test, minimum GPA of 3.0. Additional exam requirements/recommendations for international students: Required—TOEFL. *Application deadline:* For fall admission, 3/1 priority date for domestic students, 3/1 for international students. Applications are processed on a rolling basis. Application fee: $30. *Financial support:* In 2008–09, 20 teaching assistantships with full tuition reimbursements (averaging $7,065 per year) were awarded; research assistantships, career-related internships or fieldwork, Federal Work-Study, and unspecified assistantships also available. Support available to part-time students. Financial award application deadline: 3/15; financial award applicants required to submit FAFSA. *Faculty research:* Technical design, acting. *Unit head:* Louis Rackoff, Chair, 601-266-4994, Fax: 601-266-6423. *Application contact:* Shonna Breland, Manager of Graduate Admissions, 601-266-4369, Fax: 601-266-5138, E-mail: graduatestudies@usm.edu.

The University of Tennessee, Graduate School, College of Arts and Sciences, Department of Theatre, Knoxville, TN 37996. Offers costume design (MFA); lighting design (MFA); performance (MFA); scene design (MFA); theatre technology (MFA). *Degree requirements:* For master's, thesis or alternative. *Entrance requirements:* For master's, audition, minimum GPA of 2.7. Additional exam requirements/recommendations for international students: Required—TOEFL. Electronic applications accepted. *Expenses:* Tuition, area resident: Part-time $348 per credit hour. Tuition, state resident: full-time $6262. Tuition, nonresident: full-time $18,920; part-time $1052 per credit hour. Required fees: $812; $36 per credit hour. Tuition and fees vary according to program.

The University of Texas at Austin, Graduate School, College of Fine Arts, Department of Theatre and Dance, Austin, TX 78712-1111. Offers acting (MFA); dance (MFA); directing (MFA); drama and theatre for youth (MFA); performance as public practice (MA, MFA, PhD); playwriting (MFA); theatre technology (MFA); theatrical design (MFA). *Accreditation:* NASD. *Degree requirements:* For master's, thesis; for doctorate, variable foreign language requirement, thesis/dissertation. *Entrance requirements:* For master's and doctorate, GRE General Test.

The University of Texas–Pan American, College of Arts and Humanities, Department of Communications, Edinburg, TX 78541-2999. Offers communication (MA); theatre (MA). *Accreditation:* NAST. Part-time and evening/weekend programs available. *Degree requirements:* For master's, comprehensive exam, thesis or alternative. *Entrance requirements:* For master's, minimum GPA of 3.0. Additional exam requirements/recommendations for international students: Required—TOEFL. *Faculty research:* Rhetorical theory, intercultural and mass communication, American theatre, multicultural theatre and drama, television and film.

University of Toronto, School of Graduate Studies, Humanities Division, Centre for the Study of Drama, Toronto, ON M5S 1A1, Canada. Offers MA, PhD. Part-time programs available. *Degree requirements:* For doctorate, one foreign language, thesis/dissertation, language examination, qualifying examination, oral examination. *Entrance requirements:* For master's, minimum B+ average, significant coursework in drama and related disciplines, resumé, 2 letters of recommendation; for doctorate, minimum A- average, resumé, MA in drama; 2 letters of recommendation.

University of Victoria, Faculty of Graduate Studies, Faculty of Fine Arts, Department of Theatre, Victoria, BC V8W 2Y2, Canada. Offers design (MFA); directing (MFA); theatre history (MA). *Degree requirements:* For master's, thesis. *Entrance requirements:* Additional exam requirements/recommendations for international students: Required—TOEFL (minimum score 575 paper-based; 233 computer-based), IELTS (minimum score 7). Electronic applications accepted.

University of Virginia, College and Graduate School of Arts and Sciences, Department of Drama, Charlottesville, VA 22903. Offers MFA. *Faculty:* 18 full-time (8 women), 2 part-time/adjunct (both women). *Students:* 16 full-time (8 women); includes 2 minority (1 African American, 1 Asian American or Pacific Islander), 1 international. Average age 26. 42 applicants, 40% accepted, 16 enrolled. In 2008, 16 master's awarded. *Degree requirements:* For master's, thesis project. *Entrance requirements:* For master's, GRE General Test, resumé; 3 letters of recommendation. Additional exam requirements/recommendations for international students: Required—TOEFL (minimum score 600 paper-based; 250 computer-based; 90 iBT), IELTS (minimum score 7). *Application deadline:* For fall admission, 2/20 for domestic and international students. Applications are processed on a rolling basis. Application fee: $60. Electronic applications accepted. *Expenses:* Tuition, area resident: Full-time $10,452. Tuition, state resident: full-time $10,452. Tuition, nonresident: full-time $20,010. Required fees: $2176. Part-time tuition and fees vary according to course load and program. *Financial support:* Fellowships, teaching assistantships available. Financial award applicants required to submit FAFSA. *Faculty research:* Acting, scenic design, lighting design, technical direction, costume design/technology. *Unit head:* Tom Bloom, Chair, 434-924-3326, Fax: 434-924-1447, E-mail: drama@virginia.edu. *Application contact:* Tom Bloom, Chair, 434-924-3326, Fax: 434-924-1447, E-mail: drama@virginia.edu.

University of Washington, Graduate School, College of Arts and Sciences, School of Drama, Seattle, WA 98195. Offers acting (MFA); costume design (MFA); directing (MFA); dramatic theory (PhD); lighting design (MFA); scenic design (MFA); theatre and performance history (PhD). *Degree requirements:* For master's, thesis; for doctorate, one foreign language, comprehensive exam, thesis/dissertation. *Entrance requirements:* For master's, interview, minimum GPA of 3.0, portfolio; for doctorate, GRE General Test, minimum GPA of 3.0, writing sample. Additional exam requirements/recommendations for international students: Required—TOEFL. *Faculty research:* Semiotics, Suzuki actor training, modern American theatre, ethnic American theatre.

University of Wisconsin–Madison, Graduate School, College of Letters and Science, Department of Theatre and Drama, Madison, WI 53706-1380. Offers MA, MFA, PhD. *Accreditation:* NAST. Part-time programs available. *Degree requirements:* For master's, thesis; for doctorate, thesis/dissertation. *Entrance requirements:* For master's and doctorate, GRE. Electronic applications accepted. *Faculty research:* Theories and histories of dance, theatre and performance studies; Russian theatre and dance; postmodern performance; Holocaust drama; race and representation.

University of Wisconsin–Milwaukee, Graduate School, Peck School of the Arts, Program in Performing Arts, Milwaukee, WI 53201-0413. Offers dance (MFA); film (MFA); theatre (MFA). Part-time programs available. *Faculty:* 35 full-time (21 women). *Students:* 18 full-time (12 women), 2 part-time (both women); includes 4 minority (2 African Americans, 1 Asian American or Pacific Islander, 1 Hispanic American), 1 international. Average age 33. 28 applicants, 21% accepted, 6 enrolled. In 2008, 17 master's awarded. *Degree requirements:* For master's,

Theater

University of Wisconsin–Milwaukee (continued)
variable foreign language requirement, comprehensive exam, thesis or alternative. *Entrance requirements:* For master's, audition, interview. Additional exam requirements/recommendations for international students: Required—TOEFL (minimum score 550 paper-based; 79 iBT), IELTS (minimum score 6.5). *Application deadline:* For fall admission, 1/1 priority date for domestic students; for spring admission, 9/1 for domestic students. Applications are processed on a rolling basis. Application fee: $45 ($75 for international students). *Expenses:* Tuition, area resident: full-time $7320; part-time $165 per credit. Tuition, state resident: full-time $7320; part-time $165 per credit. Tuition, nonresident: full-time $17,840; part-time $714 per credit. Tuition and fees vary according to campus/location, program and reciprocity agreements. *Financial support:* In 2008–09, 13 teaching assistantships were awarded; career-related internships or fieldwork and unspecified assistantships also available. Support available to part-time students. Financial award application deadline: 4/15. *Unit head:* Simone Ferro, Representative, 414-229-4178, E-mail: sferro@uwm.edu. *Application contact:* General Information Contact, 414-229-4982, Fax: 414-229-6967, E-mail: gradschool@uwm.edu.

University of Wisconsin–Superior, Graduate Division, Department of Communicating Arts, Superior, WI 54880-4500. Offers mass communication (MA); speech communication (MA); theater (MA). Part-time programs available. *Degree requirements:* For master's, comprehensive exam, thesis or alternative, position paper or project. *Entrance requirements:* For master's, minimum GPA of 2.75. *Faculty research:* Multimedia technology, ethics in journalism, diversity, electronic portfolio assessment.

Utah State University, School of Graduate Studies, College of Humanities, Arts and Social Sciences, Department of Theatre Arts, Logan, UT 84322. Offers advanced technical practice (MFA); design (MFA); theatre arts (MA, MFA). *Degree requirements:* For master's, variable foreign language requirement, thesis (for some programs), summer internship (MFA). *Entrance requirements:* For master's, GRE General Test or MAT, portfolio (MFA), minimum GPA of 3.0, interview, BS or 20 semester credit. Additional exam requirements/recommendations for international students: Required—TOEFL. *Faculty research:* Seventeenth and eighteenth century Spanish theatre, Greek and Roman theatre, interpretation of literature for performance.

Villanova University, Graduate School of Liberal Arts and Sciences, Department of Theatre, Villanova, PA 19085-1699. Offers MA. Part-time and evening/weekend programs available. *Faculty:* 7 full-time (3 women), 1 (woman) part-time/adjunct. *Students:* 21 full-time (12 women), 11 part-time (9 women); includes 1 minority (Hispanic American). Average age 29. 18 applicants, 94% accepted, 10 enrolled. In 2008, 19 master's awarded. *Degree requirements:* For master's, comprehensive exam. *Entrance requirements:* For master's, GRE, minimum GPA of 3.0. *Application deadline:* For fall admission, 8/1 priority date for domestic students; for spring admission, 12/1 for domestic students. Applications are processed on a rolling basis. Application fee: $50. Electronic applications accepted. *Financial support:* Research assistantships, Federal Work-Study and scholarships/grants available. Financial award applicants required to submit FAFSA. *Unit head:* Fr. Richard Cannuli, Chairperson, 610-519-4760. *Application contact:* Dr. Gerald Long, Dean, Graduate School of Liberal Arts and Sciences, 610-519-7093, Fax: 610-519-7096.

Virginia Commonwealth University, Graduate School, School of the Arts, Department of Theatre, Richmond, VA 23284-9005. Offers acting (MFA); costume design (MFA); directing (MFA); pedagogy (MFA); scene design/technical theater (MFA). *Accreditation:* NAST. *Degree requirements:* For master's, thesis (for some programs). *Entrance requirements:* For master's, audition, portfolio. *Faculty research:* Dramatic literature, speech.

Virginia Polytechnic Institute and State University, Graduate School, College of Liberal Arts and Human Sciences, Department of Theatre Arts, Blacksburg, VA 24061. Offers arts administration (MFA); costume design (MFA); lighting design (MFA); property management (MFA); scenic design (MFA); stage management (MFA); technical theatre (MFA). *Accreditation:* NAST. *Entrance requirements:* Additional exam requirements/recommendations for international students: Required—TOEFL (minimum score 550 paper-based; 213 computer-based). Electronic applications accepted.

Wayne State University, College of Fine, Performing and Communication Arts, Department of Theatre, Detroit, MI 48202. Offers MA, MFA, PhD. *Accreditation:* NAST. *Degree requirements:* For master's, thesis (for some programs); for doctorate, one foreign language, thesis/dissertation. *Entrance requirements:* For master's, minimum GPA of 3.0, auditions, interviews; for doctorate, GRE, MA with minimum GPA of 3.3; directing experience; recommendations; scholarly paper; statement of goals. Additional exam requirements/recommendations for international students: Required—TOEFL (minimum score 550 paper-based; 213 computer-based); Recommended—TWE (minimum score 6). Electronic applications accepted. *Faculty research:* Dramatic criticism, lighting design, acting, directing, scenography.

Western Illinois University, School of Graduate Studies, College of Fine Arts and Communication, Department of Theatre and Dance, Macomb, IL 61455-1390. Offers acting (MFA); costume design (MFA); directing (MFA); lighting design/theatre technology (MFA); scenic design (MFA). Part-time programs available. *Students:* 32 full-time (12 women), 1 part-time (0 women); includes 1 minority (Asian American or Pacific Islander). Average age 29. 19 applicants, 58% accepted. In 2008, 7 master's awarded. *Degree requirements:* For master's, comprehensive exam, thesis or alternative, creative project, written exam. *Entrance requirements:* For master's, audition or interview. Additional exam requirements/recommendations for international students: Required—TOEFL (minimum score 550 paper-based; 213 computer-based; 80 iBT). *Application deadline:* Applications are processed on a rolling basis. Application fee: $30. Electronic applications accepted. *Expenses:* Tuition, state resident: full-time $5696; part-time $237.34 per credit hour. Tuition, nonresident: full-time $11,392; part-time $474.68 per credit hour. Required fees: $1453; $60.55 per credit hour. *Financial support:* In 2008–09, 29 students received support, including 26 research assistantships with full tuition reimbursements available (averaging $7,040 per year), 4 teaching assistantships with full tuition reimbursements available (averaging $8,120 per year). Financial award applicants required to submit FAFSA. *Unit head:* Dr. David Patrick, Chairperson, 309-298-1543. *Application contact:* Evelyn Hoing, Assistant Director of Graduate Studies, 309-298-1806, Fax: 309-298-2345, E-mail: grad-office@wiu.edu.

West Virginia University, College of Creative Arts, Division of Theatre and Dance, Morgantown, WV 26506. Offers acting (MFA); theatre design/technology (MFA). *Accreditation:* NAST. Part-time programs available. *Degree requirements:* For master's, thesis, oral defense. *Entrance requirements:* For master's, minimum GPA of 3.0, audition or portfolio. Additional exam requirements/recommendations for international students: Required—TOEFL. *Faculty research:* Professional directing, consulting, design.

Yale University, School of Drama, New Haven, CT 06520. Offers MFA, DFA, Certificate, MBA/MFA. *Degree requirements:* For master's, comprehensive exam (for some programs), thesis (for some programs); for doctorate, thesis/dissertation. *Entrance requirements:* For master's, in person audition (acting); portfolio, review (design); interview. Additional exam requirements/recommendations for international students: Required—TOEFL. Electronic applications accepted.

York University, Faculty of Graduate Studies, Faculty of Fine Arts, Program in Theatre, Toronto, ON M3J 1P3, Canada. Offers MFA. *Degree requirements:* For master's, thesis. Electronic applications accepted.

York University, Faculty of Graduate Studies, Faculty of Fine Arts, Program in Theatre Studies, Toronto, ON M3J 1P3, Canada. Offers MA, PhD.

Therapies—Dance, Drama, and Music

Antioch University New England, Graduate School, Department of Applied Psychology, Program in Dance/Movement Therapy and Counseling, Keene, NH 03431-3552. Offers M Ed, MA. *Degree requirements:* For master's, thesis, internship, practicum. *Entrance requirements:* For master's, previous course work and work experience in psychology, experience in dance or movement. Additional exam requirements/recommendations for international students: Required—TOEFL (minimum score 600 paper-based; 250 computer-based). Electronic applications accepted. *Expenses:* Contact institution. *Faculty research:* Research attitudes and needs of dance/movement therapists.

Appalachian State University, Cratis D. Williams Graduate School, School of Music, Boone, NC 28608. Offers music education (MM); music performance (MM); music therapy (MMT). *Accreditation:* NASM. Part-time programs available. *Faculty:* 29 full-time (11 women), 2 part-time/adjunct (both women). *Students:* 25 full-time (13 women), 7 part-time (4 women); includes 2 minority (both African Americans), 1 international. 28 applicants, 86% accepted, 13 enrolled. In 2008, 9 master's awarded. *Degree requirements:* For master's, comprehensive exam, thesis or alternative. *Entrance requirements:* For master's, GRE General Test, 3 letters of reference, audition. Additional exam requirements/recommendations for international students: Required—TOEFL (minimum score 550 paper-based; 230 computer-based; 79 iBT), IELTS (minimum score 6.5). *Application deadline:* For fall admission, 7/1 for domestic students, 2/1 for international students; for spring admission, 11/1 for domestic students, 7/1 for international students. Applications are processed on a rolling basis. Application fee: $50. Electronic applications accepted. *Expenses:* Tuition, area resident: Full-time $2600; part-time $700 per course. Tuition, state resident: full-time $2600; part-time $700 per course. Tuition, nonresident: full-time $5000; part-time $3300 per course. Required fees: $2150; $330 per course. Tuition and fees vary according to campus/location. *Financial support:* In 2008–09, 16 research assistantships (averaging $7,000 per year) were awarded; fellowships, teaching assistantships, career-related internships or fieldwork, Federal Work-Study, scholarships/grants, tuition waivers (partial), and unspecified assistantships also available. Financial award application deadline: 4/1; financial award applicants required to submit FAFSA. *Faculty research:* Music of the holocaust, Celtic folk music, early 19th century performance practice, hypermeter and phase rhythm, world music, music and psychoneuroimmunology. Total annual research expenditures: $7,500. *Unit head:* Dr. William Harbinson, Dean, 828-262-6446, E-mail: harbinsonwg@appstate.edu. *Application contact:* Dr. Nancy Schneeloch-Bingham, Graduate Program Director, 828-262-6463, E-mail: schneelochna@appstate.edu.

Arizona State University, Graduate College, Herberger College of the Arts, School of Music, Tempe, AZ 85287. Offers composition (MM); music (MA, DMA); music education (MM); music therapy (MM); performance (MM). *Accreditation:* NASM. *Degree requirements:* For doctorate, thesis/dissertation. *Entrance requirements:* For master's, GRE or MAT; for doctorate, GRE.

California Institute of Integral Studies, Graduate Programs, School of Professional Psychology, San Francisco, CA 94103. Offers clinical psychology (Psy D); community mental health (MA); drama therapy (MA); expressive arts therapy (MA); integral counseling psychology (MA); integral counseling, psychology-weekend (MA); somatic psychology (MA). *Accreditation:* APA. Part-time programs available. *Faculty:* 28 full-time, 59 part-time/adjunct. *Students:* 553 full-time (408 women), 88 part-time (69 women); includes 132 minority (25 African Americans, 3 American Indian/Alaska Native, 57 Asian Americans or Pacific Islanders, 47 Hispanic Americans). Average age 37. 506 applicants, 61% accepted, 181 enrolled. In 2008, 109 master's, 20 doctorates awarded. *Degree requirements:* For master's, comprehensive exam; for doctorate, comprehensive exam, thesis/dissertation. *Entrance requirements:* For master's, minimum GPA of 3.0, letters of recommendation, writing sample; for doctorate, GRE, MA in psychology or social work with appropriate practical experience for advanced standing, or BA with a minimum GPA of 3.1; letters of recommendation; writing sample. Additional exam requirements/recommendations for international students: Required—TOEFL. *Application deadline:* For fall admission, 2/1 priority date for domestic and international students; for spring admission, 10/15 priority date for domestic and international students. Applications are processed on a rolling basis. Application fee: $65. Electronic applications accepted. *Expenses:* Tuition: Part-time $815 per contact hour. Required fees: $270; $135 per semester. Tuition and fees vary according to degree level. *Financial support:* In 2008–09, 496 students received support; research assistantships with tuition reimbursements available, teaching assistantships with tuition reimbursements available, career-related internships or fieldwork, Federal Work-Study, institutionally sponsored loans, scholarships/grants, and tuition waivers (partial) available. Support available to part-time students. Financial award application deadline: 3/15; financial award applicants required to submit FAFSA. *Faculty research:* Somatic psychology, comparative psychology, art therapy, transpersonal psychology, eco-psychology. *Application contact:* David Townes, Senior Admissions Counselor, 415-575-6152, Fax: 415-575-1268, E-mail: dtownes@ciis.edu.

See Close-Up on page 1105.

Columbia College Chicago, Graduate School, Program in Dance/Movement Therapy, Chicago, IL 60605-1996. Offers MA, Certificate. Part-time programs available. *Students:* 29 full-time (28 women), 25 part-time (all women); includes 10 minority (4 African Americans, 1 American Indian/Alaska Native, 2 Asian Americans or Pacific Islanders, 3 Hispanic Americans), 1 international. Average age 28. In 2008, 15 master's awarded. *Degree requirements:* For master's, thesis, internship. *Entrance requirements:* For master's, movement assessment, interview, minimum GPA of 3.0. Additional exam requirements/recommendations for international students: Required—TOEFL (minimum score 550 paper-based; 213 computer-based). *Application deadline:* For fall admission, 1/5 for domestic and international students. Application fee: $55. *Expenses:* Tuition: Full-time $15,992; part-time $633 per credit hour. *Financial support:* Fellowships, career-related internships or fieldwork, Federal Work-Study, and scholarships/grants available. Support available to part-time students. Financial award application deadline: 8/13; financial award applicants required to submit FAFSA. *Unit head:* Susan Imus, Chairperson, 312-369-7097, Fax: 312-369-8054, E-mail: simus@colum.edu. *Application contact:* Keith Cleveland, Office of Provost/Senior Vice President, 312-369-7261, Fax: 312-369-8022, E-mail: kcleveland@colum.edu.

Drexel University, College of Nursing and Health Professions, Program in Creative Arts in Therapy, Specialization in Dance/Movement Therapy, Philadelphia, PA 19104-2875. Offers MA, PMC. Part-time programs available. *Degree requirements:* For master's, comprehensive exam, thesis. *Entrance requirements:* For master's, GRE General Test or MAT, audition, interview, minimum GPA of 2.75. Electronic applications accepted. *Faculty research:* Family nonverbal communication, early intervention, sexual abuse.

Drexel University, College of Nursing and Health Professions, Program in Creative Arts in Therapy, Specialization in Music Therapy, Philadelphia, PA 19104-2875. Offers MA, PMC. Part-time programs available. *Degree requirements:* For master's, comprehensive exam, thesis. *Entrance requirements:* For master's, GRE General Test or MAT, audition, interview, minimum GPA of 2.75. Electronic applications accepted. *Faculty research:* Early childhood intervention through creative art therapies, rhythm and dementia, music therapy and bulimia, assessment of adolescent suicide.

East Carolina University, Graduate School, College of Fine Arts and Communication, School of Music, Greenville, NC 27858-4353. Offers music education (MM); music therapy (MM); performance (MM); theory and composition (MM). *Accreditation:* NASM. Part-time programs available. *Degree requirements:* For master's, comprehensive exam, thesis optional. *Entrance requirements:* For master's, GRE General Test or MAT. Additional exam requirements/recommendations for international students: Required—TOEFL.

Florida State University, Graduate Studies, College of Music, Tallahassee, FL 32306. Offers accompanying (MM); arts administration (MA); choral conducting (MM); composition (MM, DM); ethnomusicology (MM); general music (MA); instrumental accompanying (MM); instrumental conducting (MM); jazz studies (MM); music education (MM Ed, PhD); music theory (MM, PhD); music therapy (MM); musicology (MM, PhD), including ethnomusicology (PhD), historical musicology; opera (MM); performance (MM, DM); piano pedagogy (MM); piano technology (MA); vocal accompanying (MM). *Accreditation:* NASM. *Degree requirements:* For master's, comprehensive exam (for some programs), thesis (for some programs), departmental qualifying exam; for doctorate, comprehensive exam (for some programs), thesis/dissertation, departmental qualifying exam. *Entrance requirements:* For master's and doctorate, audition, GRE General Test or minimum GPA of 3.0. Additional exam requirements/recommendations for international students: Required—TOEFL (minimum score 550 paper-based; 213 computer-based). Electronic applications accepted.

Georgia College & State University, Graduate School, School of Health Sciences, Program in Music Therapy, Milledgeville, GA 31061. Offers MMT. *Entrance requirements:* Additional exam requirements/recommendations for international students: Required—TOEFL. Electronic applications accepted.

Immaculata University, College of Graduate Studies, Program in Music Therapy, Immaculata, PA 19345. Offers MA. *Accreditation:* NASM. Part-time and evening/weekend programs available. *Degree requirements:* For master's, comprehensive exam, thesis optional. *Entrance requirements:* For master's, GRE General Test or MAT, minimum GPA of 3.0. Additional exam requirements/recommendations for international students: Required—TOEFL. Electronic applications accepted. *Faculty research:* Biofeedback music laboratory, experimental music therapy, virtual arts therapies, sound beam.

Lesley University, Graduate School of Arts and Social Sciences, Division of Expressive Therapies, Cambridge, MA 02138-2790. Offers art (MA); dance (MA); expressive therapies (MA, PhD, CAGS); music (MA). Terminal master's awarded for partial completion of doctoral program. *Degree requirements:* For master's, internship, practicum; for doctorate, thesis/dissertation. *Entrance requirements:* For master's, art portfolio, performance DVD; for doctorate, GRE or MAT. Additional exam requirements/recommendations for international students: Required—TOEFL (minimum score 550 paper-based; 213 computer-based; 80 iBT). *Expenses:* Tuition: Full-time $13,770; part-time $765 per credit hour. Required fees: $150. Tuition and fees vary according to course load, degree level, campus/location and program.

See Close-Up on page 211.

Loyola University New Orleans, College of Music and Fine Arts, New Orleans, LA 70118-6195. Offers music therapy (MMT); performance (MM). *Accreditation:* NASM. Part-time programs available. *Students:* 11 full-time (5 women), 4 part-time (all women); includes 4 minority (2 African Americans, 2 Hispanic Americans), 1 international. Average age 27. 10 applicants, 60% accepted, 5 enrolled. In 2008, 2 master's awarded. *Degree requirements:* For master's, comprehensive exam, thesis, comprehensive written and oral exams. *Entrance requirements:* For master's, performance audition, appropriate bachelor's degree, minimum GPA of 3.0, transcript, letters of recommendation, resumé, essay. Additional exam requirements/recommendations for international students: Required—TOEFL (minimum score 550 paper-based; 213 computer-based). *Application deadline:* For fall admission, 8/15 priority date for domestic and international students; for spring admission, 1/1 priority date for domestic and international students. Applications are processed on a rolling basis. Application fee: $20. Electronic applications accepted. *Expenses:* Contact institution. *Financial support:* Career-related internships or fieldwork, Federal Work-Study, institutionally sponsored loans, scholarships/grants, and unspecified assistantships available. Support available to part-time students. Financial award application deadline: 5/1; financial award applicants required to submit FAFSA. *Faculty research:* Music business, music therapy, musicology, music theory, music education. *Unit head:* Donald R. Boomgaarden, PhD, Dean, 504-865-3039, Fax: 504-865-2852, E-mail: deancmfa@loyno.edu. *Application contact:* Anthony A. Decuir, PhD, Associate Dean, 504-865-3037, Fax: 504-865-2852, E-mail: decuir@loyno.edu.

Maryville University of Saint Louis, School of Health Professions, Program in Music Therapy, St. Louis, MO 63141-7299. Offers MMT. *Accreditation:* NASM. Part-time programs available. *Students:* 3. In 2008, 1 master's awarded. *Entrance requirements:* For master's, music audition, interview, minimum undergraduate GPA of 3.0, 3 letters of recommendation. Additional exam requirements/recommendations for international students: Required—TOEFL (minimum score 550 paper-based). *Application deadline:* Applications are processed on a rolling basis. Application fee: $35. Electronic applications accepted. *Expenses:* Tuition: Full-time $19,650; part-time $605 per credit hour. Required fees: $100 per semester. Part-time tuition and fees vary according to degree level and program. *Financial support:* Applicants required to submit FAFSA. *Unit head:* Dr. Cynthia Briggs, Director, 314-529-9441, Fax: 314-529-9495, E-mail: cbriggs@maryville.edu. *Application contact:* Dr. Cynthia Briggs, Director, 314-529-9441, Fax: 314-529-9495, E-mail: cbriggs@maryville.edu.

Marywood University, Academic Affairs, Insalaco College of Creative Arts and Management, Music Department, Program in Music Therapy, Scranton, PA 18509-1598. Offers MMT, Certificate. *Accreditation:* NASM. Part-time and evening/weekend programs available. *Degree requirements:* For master's, comprehensive exam, thesis or alternative. *Entrance requirements:* For master's, GRE Subject Test, audition. Additional exam requirements/recommendations for international students: Required—TOEFL (minimum score 550 paper-based; 213 computer-based). Electronic applications accepted.

Michigan State University, The Graduate School, College of Music, East Lansing, MI 48824. Offers collaborative piano (M Mus); jazz studies (M Mus); music (PhD); music composition (M Mus, DMA); music conducting (M Mus, DMA); music education (M Mus); music performance (M Mus, DMA); music theory (M Mus); music therapy (M Mus); musicology (MA); piano pedagogy (M Mus). *Accreditation:* NASM. *Entrance requirements:* Additional exam requirements/recommendations for international students: Required—TOEFL. Electronic applications accepted.

Montclair State University, The Office of Graduate Admissions and Support Services, School of the Arts, Department of Music, Montclair, NJ 07043-1624. Offers music (AD); music education (MA); music therapy (MA); performance (MA, Certificate); theory/composition (MA). *Accreditation:* NASM. Part-time and evening/weekend programs available. *Faculty:* 11 full-time (7 women), 87 part-time/adjunct (38 women). *Students:* 14 full-time (11 women), 21 part-time (9 women); includes 3 minority (1 African American, 1 Asian American or Pacific Islander, 1 Hispanic American), 5 international. Average age 30. 20 applicants, 80% accepted, 14 enrolled. In 2008, 9 master's, 7 other advanced degrees awarded. *Degree requirements:* For master's, comprehensive exam, compositions, recitals, or thesis. *Entrance requirements:* For master's, GRE General Test, audition; undergraduate degree in music or at least 40 semester hours of work in theory, music history, performance; 2 letters of recommendation; teaching certificate (MA in music education). Additional exam requirements/recommendations for international students: Required—TOEFL (minimum score 83 computer-based). *Application deadline:* For fall admission, 6/1 for international students; for spring admission, 10/1 for international students. Applications are processed on a rolling basis. Application fee: $60. Electronic applications accepted. *Financial support:* In 2008–09, 2 research assistantships with full tuition reimbursements (averaging $7,000 per year) were awarded; Federal Work-Study, scholarships/grants, and unspecified assistantships also available. Support available to part-time students. Financial award application deadline: 3/1; financial award applicants required to submit FAFSA. *Unit head:* Prof. Robert Aldridge, Chairperson, 973-655-7212. *Application contact:* Amy Aiello, Associate Director of Admissions, 973-655-5147, Fax: 973-655-7869, E-mail: graduate.school@montclair.edu.

Naropa University, Graduate Programs, Program in Somatic Counseling Psychotherapy, Concentration in Dance/Movement Therapy, Boulder, CO 80302-6697. Offers MA. Part-time

Therapies—Dance, Drama, and Music

Naropa University (continued)

programs available. *Faculty:* 1 (woman) full-time, 11 part-time/adjunct (6 women). *Students:* 19 full-time (all women), 2 part-time (1 woman); includes 3 minority (all Hispanic Americans), 1 international. Average age 29. 26 applicants, 46% accepted, 8 enrolled. In 2008, 4 master's awarded. *Degree requirements:* For master's, comprehensive exam, thesis, internship, fieldwork, portfolio. *Entrance requirements:* For master's, in-person interview, course work in psychology and anatomy, experience in 3 forms of dance, resumé, letter of interest, 3 letters of recommendation. Additional exam requirements/recommendations for international students: Required—TOEFL (minimum score 600 paper-based; 250 computer-based). *Application deadline:* For fall admission, 1/15 priority date for domestic and international students. Applications are processed on a rolling basis. Application fee: $60. Electronic applications accepted. *Expenses:* Tuition: Full-time $14,767; part-time $726 per credit hour. Required fees: $45 per term. *Financial support:* In 2008–09, 11 students received support, including 4 research assistantships with partial tuition reimbursements available (averaging $3,000 per year), teaching assistantships with partial tuition reimbursements available (averaging $3,000 per year); career-related internships or fieldwork, Federal Work-Study, scholarships/grants, health care benefits, tuition waivers (partial), and unspecified assistantships also available. Support available to part-time students. Financial award application deadline: 3/1; financial award applicants required to submit FAFSA. *Unit head:* Zo?? Avstreih, Director, E-mail: movement@naropa.edu. *Application contact:* Donna McIntyre, Assistant Director of Admissions, 303-546-3555, Fax: 303-546-3583, E-mail: donna@naropa.edu.

See Close-Up on page 1121.

Nazareth College of Rochester, Graduate Studies, Department of Creative Arts Therapy, Program in Music Therapy, Rochester, NY 14618-3790. Offers MS. *Entrance requirements:* For master's, audition, minimum GPA of 3.0.

New York University, Steinhardt School of Culture, Education and Human Development, Department of Music and Performing Arts Professions, Program in Drama Therapy, New York, NY 10012-1019. Offers MA. *Degree requirements:* For master's, thesis (for some programs). *Entrance requirements:* For master's, audition, interview. Additional exam requirements/recommendations for international students: Required—TOEFL. *Faculty research:* Meaning of role in drama, therapy, and everyday life; clinical approaches to drama therapy; trauma effects on children.

New York University, Steinhardt School of Culture, Education and Human Development, Department of Music and Performing Arts Professions, Program in Music Therapy, New York, NY 10012-1019. Offers MA, DA. Part-time and evening/weekend programs available. *Degree requirements:* For master's, thesis (for some programs). *Entrance requirements:* For master's, audition, interview. Additional exam requirements/recommendations for international students: Required—TOEFL. *Faculty research:* Music therapy in special education, including autism and emotional disabilities.

Ohio University, Graduate College, College of Fine Arts, School of Music, Athens, OH 45701-2979. Offers accompanying (MM); composition (MM); conducting (MM); history/literature (MM); music education (MM); music therapy (MM); performance (MM, Certificate); performance/pedagogy (MM); theory (MM). *Accreditation:* NASM. Postbaccalaureate distance learning degree programs offered (minimal on-campus study). *Degree requirements:* For master's, thesis (for some programs), oral exam. *Entrance requirements:* For master's, audition, interview, and/or portfolio. Additional exam requirements/recommendations for international students: Required—TOEFL.

Pratt Institute, School of Art and Design, Programs in Creative Arts Therapy, Brooklyn, NY 11205-3899. Offers art therapy and creativity development (MPS); art therapy-special education (MPS); dance/movement therapy (MS). *Accreditation:* NASAD (one or more programs are accredited). Part-time programs available. *Faculty:* 3 full-time (all women), 19 part-time/adjunct (16 women). *Students:* 112 full-time (108 women), 1 (woman) part-time; includes 16 minority (5 African Americans, 3 Asian Americans or Pacific Islanders, 8 Hispanic Americans), 7 international. Average age 29. 196 applicants, 33% accepted, 35 enrolled. In 2008, 32 master's awarded. *Degree requirements:* For master's, thesis. *Entrance requirements:* For master's, bachelor's degree, transcripts, letters of recommendation, statement, portfolio. Additional exam requirements/recommendations for international students: Required—TOEFL (minimum score 600 paper-based; 250 computer-based). *Application deadline:* For fall admission, 2/1 for domestic and international students; for spring admission, 10/1 for domestic and international students. Applications are processed on a rolling basis. Application fee: $50 ($90 for international students). Electronic applications accepted. *Expenses:* Tuition: Full-time $20,412; part-time $1134 per credit. Required fees: $1190; $1190 per year. *Financial support:* Career-related internships or fieldwork, Federal Work-Study, institutionally sponsored loans, scholarships/grants, health care benefits, tuition waivers (full), and unspecified assistantships available. Support available to part-time students. Financial award application deadline: 2/1; financial award applicants required to submit FAFSA. *Faculty research:* Psychology and aesthetic interaction, art therapy and AIDS, art therapy and autism, art diagnosis. *Unit head:* Jean Davis, Chairperson, 718-636-3428, E-mail: jdavis@pratt.edu. *Application contact:* Young Hah, Director of Graduate Admissions, 718-636-3683, Fax: 718-399-4242, E-mail: yhah@pratt.edu.

See Close-Up on page 219.

Radford University, College of Graduate and Professional Studies, College of Visual and Performing Arts, Department of Music, Radford, VA 24142. Offers music (MA); music education (MS); music therapy (MS). *Accreditation:* NASM. Part-time programs available. *Faculty:* 13 full-time (3 women), 2 part-time/adjunct (both women). *Students:* 16 full-time (12 women), 3 part-time (1 woman); includes 5 minority (4 African Americans, 1 Asian American or Pacific Islander), 1 international. Average age 28. 19 applicants, 79% accepted, 9 enrolled. In 2008, 7 master's awarded. *Degree requirements:* For master's, comprehensive exam, thesis or alternative. *Entrance requirements:* For master's, GRE, major field test in music or PRAXIS II (content knowledge), written diagnostics exams in music, minimum GPA of 2.75; 3 letters of reference. Additional exam requirements/recommendations for international students: Required—TOEFL (minimum score 550 paper-based; 213 computer-based; 79 iBT). *Application deadline:* For fall admission, 3/1 priority date for domestic students, 12/1 for international students; for spring admission, 10/1 for domestic students, 7/1 for international students. Applications are processed on a rolling basis. Application fee: $40. Electronic applications accepted. *Expenses:* Tuition, area resident: Full-time $4845; part-time $202 per credit. Tuition, state resident: full-time $4845; part-time $202 per credit. Tuition, nonresident: full-time $11,483; part-time $478 per credit. Required fees: $2349; $98 per credit. *Financial support:* In 2008–09, 13 students received support, including 7 research assistantships with partial tuition reimbursements available (averaging $8,000 per year), 4 teaching assistantships with partial tuition reimbursements available (averaging $8,700 per year); career-related internships or fieldwork, Federal Work-Study, institutionally sponsored loans, scholarships/grants, and unspecified assistantships also available. Financial award application deadline: 3/1; financial award applicants required to submit FAFSA. *Unit head:* Dr. Allen F. Wojtera, Chair, 540-831-5177, Fax: 540-831-6133, E-mail: awojtera@radford.edu. *Application contact:* Graduate Admissions, 540-831-5431, Fax: 540-831-6061, E-mail: gradcollege@radford.edu.

Saint Mary-of-the-Woods College, Program in Music Therapy, Saint Mary-of-the-Woods, IN 47876. Offers MA. *Accreditation:* NASM. Part-time programs available. Postbaccalaureate distance learning degree programs offered (minimal on-campus study). *Degree requirements:* For master's, thesis or alternative, qualifying exam, portfolio completion. *Entrance requirements:* For master's, diagnostic music exam, audition. Electronic applications accepted.

Shenandoah University, Shenandoah Conservatory, Winchester, VA 22601-5195. Offers arts administration (MS); church music (MM, Certificate); composition (MM); conducting (MM); dance (MA, MFA, MS); dance accompanying (MM); music (MS); music education (MME, DMA); music therapy (MMT, Certificate); pedagogy (MM, DMA); performance (MM, DMA, Artist Diploma); piano accompanying (MM). *Accreditation:* NASM. Part-time and evening/weekend programs available. *Faculty:* 39 full-time (19 women), 21 part-time/adjunct (9 women). *Students:* 71 full-time (42 women), 150 part-time (80 women); includes 14 minority (9 African Americans, 2 Asian Americans or Pacific Islanders, 3 Hispanic Americans), 32 international. Average age 40. 76 applicants, 96% accepted, 49 enrolled. In 2008, 24 master's, 10 doctorates, 7 other advanced degrees awarded. *Degree requirements:* For master's, comprehensive exam (for some programs), thesis (for some programs), internship (MS), recital (MM), research teaching project or thesis (MME), project (MA); for doctorate, comprehensive exam, thesis/dissertation (for some programs), dissertation or teaching project, recital; for other advanced degree, research project, recital. *Entrance requirements:* For master's, audition, minimum GPA of 2.5, writing sample, resumé; for doctorate, audition, minimum GPA of 3.25, 2 letters of recommendation, writing sample, resumé; for other advanced degree, bachelor or master's degree; minimum GPA of 2.5. Additional exam requirements/recommendations for international students: Required—TOEFL (minimum score 550 paper-based; 213 computer-based), IELTS (minimum score 6.5), Sakae Institute of Study Abroad (SISA): 550. *Application deadline:* Applications are processed on a rolling basis. Application fee: $30. Electronic applications accepted. *Expenses:* Tuition: Full-time $16,900; part-time $670 per credit. *Financial support:* In 2008–09, 154 students received support, including 26 teaching assistantships with partial tuition reimbursements available (averaging $5,870 per year); fellowships, career-related internships or fieldwork, institutionally sponsored loans, scholarships/grants, and unspecified assistantships also available. Support available to part-time students. Financial award application deadline: 3/15; financial award applicants required to submit FAFSA. *Faculty research:* Creative activity, performance practice, music therapy aging, composition, Motown music. Total annual research expenditures: $4,272. *Unit head:* Dr. Laurence A. Kaptain, Dean, 540-665-4600, Fax: 540-665-5402, E-mail: lkaptain@su.edu. *Application contact:* David Anthony, Dean of Admissions, 540-665-4581, Fax: 540-665-4627, E-mail: admit@su.edu.

State University of New York at New Paltz, Graduate School, School of Fine and Performing Arts, Department of Music, New Paltz, NY 12561. Offers music therapy (MS). Part-time programs available. *Students:* 17 full-time (13 women), 16 part-time (13 women); includes 6 minority (5 Asian Americans or Pacific Islanders, 1 Hispanic American), 2 international. Average age 28. 20 applicants, 65% accepted, 9 enrolled. *Degree requirements:* For master's, thesis. *Entrance requirements:* For master's, audition, minimum GPA of 3.0. Additional exam requirements/recommendations for international students: Required—TOEFL (minimum score 550 paper-based; 213 computer-based; 80 iBT). *Application deadline:* For fall admission, 5/15 for domestic and international students; for spring admission, 11/15 for domestic and international students. *Financial support:* In 2008–09, 2 students received support, including 2 teaching assistantships with partial tuition reimbursements available (averaging $5,000 per year). Financial award application deadline: 8/1. *Unit head:* Dr. Edward Lundergan, Chair, 845-257-3121, E-mail: lunderge@newpaltz.edu. *Application contact:* Prof. Mary Boyle, Coordinator, 845-257-2709, E-mail: boylem@newpaltz.edu.

Temple University, Graduate School, Esther Boyer College of Music and Dance, Department of Music Education and Therapy, Philadelphia, PA 19122-6096. Offers music education (MM, PhD); music therapy (MMT, PhD). *Accreditation:* NASM. Part-time and evening/weekend programs available. *Degree requirements:* For master's, thesis; for doctorate, thesis/dissertation. *Entrance requirements:* Additional exam requirements/recommendations for international students: Required—TOEFL. Electronic applications accepted. *Faculty research:* Music learning theory, guided imagery in music, computer learning theory.

The University of Kansas, Graduate Studies, School of Music, Program in Music Therapy, Lawrence, KS 66045. Offers MME. *Faculty:* 8 full-time, 1 part-time/adjunct. *Students:* 20 full-time (19 women), 4 part-time (3 women); includes 1 minority (Asian American or Pacific Islander), 8 international. Average age 27. 12 applicants, 33% accepted, 3 enrolled. In 2008, 6 master's awarded. *Degree requirements:* For master's, comprehensive exam, thesis or alternative. *Entrance requirements:* For master's, GRE General Test, minimum undergraduate GPA of 3.0, video. Additional exam requirements/recommendations for international students: Required—TOEFL (minimum score 570 paper-based; 230 computer-based; 92 iBT), TOEFL or IELTS; Recommended—TWE. *Application deadline:* For fall admission, 3/15 priority date for domestic students, 3/15 for international students; for spring admission, 8/15 priority date for domestic students, 8/15 for international students. Application fee: $45 ($50 for international students). Electronic applications accepted. *Expenses:* Tuition, area resident: Full-time $6122; part-time $255.10 per credit hour. Tuition, state resident: full-time $6122; part-time $255.10 per credit hour. Tuition, nonresident: full-time $14,629; part-time $609.55 per credit hour. Required fees: $847; $70.56 per credit hour. Tuition and fees vary according to course load and program. *Financial support:* Fellowships, research assistantships with partial tuition reimbursements, teaching assistantships with full and partial tuition reimbursements, institutionally sponsored loans, scholarships/grants, and unspecified assistantships available. Financial award application deadline: 12/15; financial award applicants required to submit FAFSA. *Faculty research:* Music therapy in health, wellness, gerontology, pediatrics, early intervention, autism and hospice; Orff music therapy; influence of music on behavior. *Unit head:* Lawrence Mallett, Chairperson, 785-864-3436, Fax: 785-864-5866, E-mail: music@ku.edu. *Application contact:* Dr. James Daugherty, Director of Graduate Studies, 785-864-9637, Fax: 785-864-9640, E-mail: jdaugher@ku.edu.

University of Miami, Graduate School, Frost School of Music, Department of Music Education and Music Therapy, Coral Gables, FL 33124. Offers music education (MM, PhD, Spec M); music therapy (MM). *Accreditation:* NASM. *Degree requirements:* For master's, thesis; for doctorate, thesis/dissertation, 2 research tools; for Spec M, thesis, research project. *Entrance requirements:* For master's and doctorate, GRE General Test. Additional exam requirements/recommendations for international students: Required—TOEFL (minimum score 550 paper-based; 213 computer-based; 59 iBT). Electronic applications accepted.

University of the Pacific, Conservatory of Music, Program in Music Therapy, Stockton, CA 95211-0197. Offers MA. *Faculty:* 2 full-time (both women). *Students:* 6 full-time (4 women), 8 part-time (7 women); includes 3 minority (1 Asian American or Pacific Islander, 2 Hispanic Americans), 1 international. Average age 30. 11 applicants, 64% accepted, 5 enrolled. *Degree requirements:* For master's, thesis (for some programs). *Entrance requirements:* For master's, GRE General Test. Additional exam requirements/recommendations for international students: Required—TOEFL (minimum score 475 paper-based; 150 computer-based). Application fee: $75. *Expenses:* Tuition: Full-time $30,380; part-time $950 per unit. Required fees: $300. *Financial support:* Teaching assistantships, institutionally sponsored loans available. Support available to part-time students. Financial award application deadline: 3/1; financial award applicants required to submit FAFSA. *Unit head:* Dr. Therese West, Chairperson, 209-946-3194. *Application contact:* Dr. Therese West, Chairperson, 209-946-3194.

Western Michigan University, Graduate College, College of Fine Arts, School of Music, Kalamazoo, MI 49008-5202. Offers composition (MM); conducting (MM); music education (MM); music therapy (MM); performance (MM). *Accreditation:* NASM.

Wilfrid Laurier University, Faculty of Graduate Studies, Faculty of Music, Waterloo, ON N2L 3C5, Canada. Offers MMT. *Entrance requirements:* For master's, 1 year program: 4 year honours BA in music therapy with a minimum B average in final year, grade 6 RCM and grade 10 performance ability. 2 Year program: 4 year honours BA in an allied area (music or psychology) with a minimum B average in final year, grade 6 RCM, grade 10 performance ability. Additional exam requirements/recommendations for international students: Required—TOEFL (minimum score 230 computer-based; 89 iBT). Electronic applications accepted.

COLUMBIA UNIVERSITY

School of the Arts
Divisions of Film, Theatre Arts, Visual Arts, and Writing

Programs of Study

The School of the Arts offers M.F.A. degrees in film (directing, producing, and screenwriting), theater arts (acting, directing, dramaturgy, playwriting, stage management, and theater management), visual arts (digital media, drawing, new genres, painting, photography, printmaking, and sculpture), and writing (fiction, nonfiction, and poetry) and an M.A. degree in film studies. The School of the Arts accepts full-time students only. The Digital Media Center (DMC) offers a selection of courses in interactivity and advanced digital media applications. All DMC courses are interdisciplinary and open to School of the Arts students from all divisions. In addition, the Graduate School of Arts and Sciences offers the Ph.D. degree in drama and theater arts. The M.F.A. degree programs require 60 points of completed course work. All students take a core curriculum, which provides background in the history, theory, and literature of their field, and an understanding of the various disciplines taught within each division. During the first two years, students focus on workshops, lectures, and seminars in their particular disciplines. Students in film and theater arts partake in production crew work. Once the 60 points of course work are completed, each student concentrates on producing a thesis and/or completing internships under research arts status. The Division of Theatre Arts requires two professional internships; the Film and Writing Divisions recommend internships.

Research Facilities

The Film Division offers film and video production equipment, digital editing facilities, a sound stage, a screening room, and a film library. The Theatre Division offers two flexible-space theaters and two studios. In addition, there are various performing venues on campus that may be available for student productions. Each visual arts student is assigned a private studio (24-hour access) in Watson Hall on 115th Street and Prentis Hall on 125th Street. In addition, there are various spaces on campus where students have the opportunity to exhibit. The LeRoy Neiman Center for Print Studies provides the optimum environment to expose students to techniques in the production of intaglio, lithography, serigraphy, photography, and computer imaging. The University libraries house more than 6 million books, 4 million microfilms, and more than 26 million manuscripts. The library houses several special collections related to the arts, and it includes the Avery Architecture and Fine Arts Library. Students also have access to the Performing Arts Research Center of the New York Public Library at Lincoln Center as well as the vast holdings of the Central Research Library of the New York Public Library. There are dozens of special collections throughout New York City, such as the Film Study Center of the Museum of Modern Art, the Shubert Archives, and the Collections of the Players Club. New York City offers professional theaters, museums, galleries, movie theaters, concert halls, publishing companies, bookstores, and literary readings.

Financial Aid

The School seeks to work with students in arranging to cover costs through fellowships, scholarships, loans, and work-study. University scholarships, which are awarded by each division based upon merit, are limited. Departmental research assistantships, which carry tuition exemption plus a small stipend, are available, but generally only for second-year students. The Office of Student Affairs helps qualifying students arrange for federal financial aid.

Cost of Study

Tuition and fees for the 2007–08 school year were $39,800, based on full-time matriculation of 12 to 18 credits.

Living and Housing Costs

The University estimates that students need about $20,000 to cover living expenses and housing. University Apartment Housing is available to most graduate students, ranging from $565 to $1500 monthly, that offer furnished or unfurnished singles, suites, and studios to rent individually or to share. They also offer studio and one-bedroom apartments for married students.

Student Group

Columbia has an enrollment of approximately 22,000; 13,500 are graduate students. The School enrolled 778 full-time students in 2007–08: 318 students in film, 156 in theater arts, 256 in writing, and 48 in visual arts.

Location

Columbia University (including Barnard College and Teacher's College) occupies approximately eighteen square blocks in the Morningside Heights area of Manhattan. Its neighbors include Union Theological Seminary, Jewish Theological Seminary, the Manhattan School of Music, Riverside Church and the Interchurch Center, and the Cathedral of Saint John the Divine, the world's largest Gothic cathedral and home of a progressive arts program. Riverside Park and the Hudson River are a block away. The Upper West Side stretches south along Broadway for sixty blocks to Lincoln Center and beyond to the Theatre District and incorporates vital residential neighborhoods, some of the city's finest restaurants, and several theaters and museums, including the Apollo Theatre, the National Black Theatre, and City College.

The University and The School

Columbia, founded in 1754, is composed of fifteen undergraduate, graduate, and professional schools. In the late nineteenth century, Columbia became the first university to teach theater in the United States and, in 1914, the first to teach film courses. The School of Dramatic Arts and Painting and Sculpture was established in 1948, although the first drawing course was taught as early as 1881. These programs were joined by film, music composition, and writing in 1965 to form the School of the Arts. Columbia also offers undergraduate majors in dance, film studies, theater arts, visual arts, and writing.

Applying

Applications are accepted for the fall semester only. All deadlines are final. The application cost for fall 2008 is $100 for the online application and $120 for the paper application. The GRE is not required for application. International students are required to take the TOEFL prior to application; the minimum score required for admission is 600 on the written test, 250 on the computer-based test, and 100 on the Internet-based test.

Correspondence and Information

Admissions Office
School of the Arts
305 Dodge Hall, MC 1808
Columbia University
2960 Broadway
New York, New York 10027
Phone: 212-854-2134
E-mail: admissions-arts@columbia.edu
Web site: http://arts.columbia.edu

Columbia University

THE FACULTY

FILM
Jamal Joseph, Professor and Chair.
Bette Gordon, Associate Professor and Vice Chair.

Professors
Lewis Cole
Jane Gaines
Annette Insdorf
Nick Proferes
Janet Roach
Andrew Sarris

Associate Professors
Ira Deutchman
Bette Gordon
Jamal Joseph
Tom Kalin
Dan Kleinman
Richard Peña
James Schamus

Assistant Professors
Katherine Dieckmann
Trey Ellis
Eric Mendelsohn
Benjamin Ross

Adjunct Professors
Richard Brick
Lenore DeKoven
Leon Falk
Guy Gallo
Michael Hausman
Milena Jelinek
Peter Miner
Brendan Ward

Adjunct Associate Professors
David McKenna

Adjunct Assistant Professors
Chris Albers
Michael Barker
Henry Bean
Anthony Bregman
Adam Brooks
Joseph Cacaci
Patrick Downs
John Erman
John Fauer
David Ford
John Frankfurt
William Goldman
James V. Hart
Sabine Hoffman
Israel Horovitz
Malcolm Jamieson
David Jones
Jerome Kass
Chris Kelly
Jameel Khaja
Simon Kinberg
Alan Kingsberg
Sloane Klevin
Beth Kling
Darrell Larson
Christina Lazaridi
Andrew Lund
Mira Nair
Peter Parnell
Neil Pepe
Lee Percy
Frank Pugliese
Marie Reagan
Seth Rosenfeld
John Rubin
Maureen Ryan
Misael Sanchez
Malia Scotch-Marmo
Alex Sichel
Mary Jane Skalski
Edward Smith
Peter Sollett
Jeffrey Stanzler
Patrick Stettner
Fred Strype
Susanna Styron
Alan Taylor
Jim Taylor
Camilla Toniolo
Tzipi Trope
Adrien Weiss

Assistant Director of Instruction
Misael Sanchez

THEATER
Steven Chaikelson, Chair.

Professors
Arnold Aronson
Anne Bogart
Kristin Linklater
Andrei Serban

Associate Professors
Steven Chaikelson
Brian Kulick
Nikolaus Wolcz

Assistant Professor
Chuck Mee
Christian Parker

Adjunct Professors
Victoria Bailey
Bernard Gersten
Barry Grove
Paul Libin
Gerald Schoenfeld

Adjunct Associate Professors
Chris Boneau
James Leverett
Linda Winer

Adjunct Assistant Professors
Daniel Adamian
Barbara Allen
David Auster
Leslie Ayvazian
Robert Blacker
Gigi Bolt
Deborah Brevoort
Christopher Burney
Ben Cameron
Carolyn Casselman
Nancy Coyne
Beverly Emmons
Ragnar Freidank
James Freydberg
Robert Fried
David Grimm
Andy Hammerstein
Roy Harris
Hugh Hysell
Tom Kelly
Yurly Kordonskiy
Ruth Kreshka
Jeff Lee
Kelly Maurer
Maria Mileaf
Ira Mont
Gregory Mosher
Michael Naumann
Gene O'Donovan
Barney O'Hanlon
Frank Pugliese
William Russo
Micah Schraft
Larry Singer
David Stone
Livia Vanaver
Donna Walker-Kuhne
Dolphi Wertenbaker
J. Steven White
Robert Woodruff

Lecturers
Andrea Haring
Kelly Stuart
Ursula Wolcz

VISUAL ARTS
Gregory Amenoff, Chair.

Professors
Gregory Amenoff
Jon Kessler
Thomas Roma
Rirkrit Tiravanija
Kara Walker

Associate Professors
Tomas Vu Daniel

Assistant Professors
Dana Hoey
Gareth James
Blake Rayne
Paula Wilson

Adjunct Graduate Professors
Janine Antoni
Jackie Battenfield

Johanna Burton
Mark Dion
Liam Gillick
Rachel Harrison
Michael Joo
John Kelsey
John Miller
Matt Mullican
Jerry Saltz
Collier Schorr
Amy Sillman
Jeanne Silverthorne
Charline von Heyl

Visiting Graduate Critics
Vince Aletti
Gregg Bordowitz
Cecily Brown
Lynne Cooke
Liz Deschenes
Roe Ethridge
Jason Fox
Alfredo Jaar
John Kelsey
Jutta Koether
Christian Marclay
Allan McCollum
Sarah Morris
Dana Schutz
Gary Stephan
Cheyney Thompson
Steven Westfall
Terry Winters
Andrea Zittel

WRITING
Ben Marcus, Chair.

Professors
Lucie Brock-Broido
Nicholas Christopher
Richard Howard
Michael Janeway
Margo Jefferson
Binnie Kirshenbaum
Richard Locke
David Plante
Michael Scammell
Alan Ziegler

Associate Professors
Lis Harris
Jaime Manrique
Ben Marcus
Patricia O'Toole

Assistant Professors
Stacy D'Erasmo
Timothy Donnelly
Sam Lipsyte
Gary Shteyngart

Adjunct Professors
Eamon Grennan
Edith Grossman
Maureen Howard
Marie Howe
Phillip Lopate
Alice Quinn
Brenda Wineapple
James Wood

Adjunct Associate Professors
Steven O'Connor
Ben Taylor

Adjunct Assistant Professors
Esther Allen
Jonathan Dee
David Ebershoff
Darcy Frey
Samantha Gillison
Claire Harman
Bob Holman
Paul LaFarge
Victor LaValle
Ethan Nosowsky
Victoria Redel
Leslie Sharpe
Darcey Steinke
Rene Steinke
Bill Wadsworth
Mark Wunderlich

THE NEW SCHOOL: A UNIVERSITY

The New School for Drama

Program of Study

The New School for Drama offers a three-year intensive program dedicated to training artists in the fields of playwriting, directing, and acting. Students who successfully complete the program are awarded a Master of Fine Arts degree in playwriting, directing, or acting. The program is progressive—students begin with a course of self-discovery, explore technical craftsmanship in the second year, and finish by writing, directing, and acting in full productions, as well as developing a business plan for the transition from student to professional artist.

The actor is encouraged to stretch the fabric of his or her talent through a combination of disciplines—including the rigor of the Alexander Technique, an exacting voice and speech curriculum that universally coordinates several systems of training, as well as the acting techniques of Stanislavski. The playwright, through one-act festivals and main-stage productions, is trained within the context of real-world conditions that augment and enhance his or her individuality. The director is encouraged to learn what the word story means and how to express, conceive, and create visionary theater through main-stage and one-act productions.

The program at The New School for Drama relies on collaboration within each class. Playwrights work on their scripts in rehearsals and benefit from hearing and seeing their work performed. Directing and acting students work closely together as well. Playwrights, actors, and directors are all often represented (by both students and teachers) in rehearsals or in the classroom, giving them a glimpse of what it means to develop a new play. This crossover within a class lets students learn from their peers as well as from the instructors and allows students to develop important and long-lasting professional connections. A faculty of working professionals, through the discovery process, nurtures and guides each student's unique and original voice. Ultimately, students gain a rooted sense of who they are as individuals and how they may join, collaboratively, in finding their individual and collective artistic expression.

Research Facilities

The Herbert Robinson Drama Book and Script Collection contains more than 3,000 plays, screenplays, and books on film, theater history, and criticism.

A resource library of periodical, reference, and job-list materials is located in the Office of Career Development. In addition to such magazines as *Backstage, American Theatre,* and *ArtSearch,* the library contains information ranging from fellowship resources to directories of theaters, talent and casting agencies, and many other professional organizations. There is also a listing of internship opportunities, updated at the beginning of each week. The library also hosts an extensive lending library of plays, craft books, biographies, and industry guides—all for student use.

Financial Aid

Financial aid is available to matriculated degree candidates at The New School for Drama. Scholarships are merit-based, and assistance is granted on the basis of performance, starting with the audition or interview during the application phase and taking into account classroom performance and academic citizenship throughout the three years. All applicants for financial aid who are U.S. citizens or permanent residents must file the Free Application for Federal Student Assistance (FAFSA) each year in order to qualify for federally funded educational loans. International applicants may be considered for scholarships. Additional information is available from the Office of Financial Services at 212-229-8930.

Cost of Study

Tuition in 2009–10 is $16,925 per term, and fees are approximately $200 each term.

Living and Housing Costs

The University Housing Office maintains a comprehensive resource center with apartment listings. University-run apartments and residence halls are also available. The cost of housing, food, transportation, books, and living expenses averages $17,000 annually. For more information, students should go online to http://www.newschool.edu/studentservices.

Student Group

There are 170 students in the program; 169 attend on a full-time basis. Of these students, 108 are women, 32 are members of minority groups, and 27 are international students.

Location

With theater in the air and on its streets, as well as on its hundreds of stages, New York City provides an unrivaled curriculum in observation and a wealth of professional opportunities. Students are encouraged to take advantage of the museums, performance venues, and other cultural institutions that are only a walk or subway ride away. An extension of the classroom, the city also offers excellent professional and networking opportunities.

The University and The School

The New School pioneered the idea of lifelong university-level education for adults. It was created for teachers and students from different backgrounds who were willing to take risks for their intellectual and political beliefs. The New School for Drama has a legacy of vision. Artistic voices as distinctive as Tennessee Williams and Marlon Brando found their singularity at The New School, under the wing of Dramatic Workshop founder Erwin Piscator and a faculty that included Stella Adler and Lee Strasberg. Since 1994, the University has offered the M.F.A. in dramatic arts. Through its interrelated program of acting, directing, and playwriting, The New School for Drama is creative in its simplicity and original in its vision. The New School is forging the next generation of artists capable of meeting expectations of storytelling and of touching what is human about art.

A privately supported institution, The New School is accredited by the Commission on Higher Education of the Middle States Association of Colleges and Schools and chartered as a university by the Regents of the State of New York.

The eight schools that make up The New School are The New School for General Studies, The New School for Social Research, Milano The New School for Management and Urban Policy, Parsons The New School for Design, Eugene Lang College The New School for Liberal Arts, Mannes College The New School for Music, The New School for Drama, and The New School for Jazz and Contemporary Music.

Applying

An applicant to The New School for Drama must hold a bachelor's degree from an accredited college or university. A completed application, the $50 application fee, a statement of purpose, an artistic resume and a headshot, official transcripts of all undergraduate and graduate studies, and two letters of recommendation should be submitted to the University Admissions Office by January 10. Applicants are invited to audition based on application submissions.

Correspondence and Information

Office of Admissions
The New School for Drama
The New School
151 Bank Street
New York, New York 10014

Phone: 212-229-5859
E-mail: studentinfo@newschool.edu
Web site: http://www.newschool.edu/drama

The New School: A University

THE FACULTY

School Directors and Department Chairs

Robert LuPone, Director. A member of the Actors Studio, Mr. LuPone appeared on Broadway in *True West, A Thousand Clowns, A View from the Bridge, Late Nite Comic, Zoya's Apartment, Swing, St. Joan,* and *Nefertiti* and as Zach in *A Chorus Line.* Television credits include *Law & Order, Crossing Jordan, Swift Justice, Guiding Light, Mia—Child of Hollywood, American Tragedy, Palookaville, Sex and the City,* and Dr. Cusimano in *The Sopranos.* He received an Emmy nomination for his portrayal of Zach Grayson on *All My Children.* Film credits include *Nick of Time, Dead Presidents, The Doors, Jesus Christ Superstar, The Door in the Floor,* and the upcoming *Indocumentos.* LuPone is president of the board of ART/NY and artistic director of MCC Theater in New York City.

Paul Rudd, Associate Director. Mr. Rudd worked as a professional actor and director from 1967 to 1986 in New York City, both on- and off-Broadway, and in regional theaters around the country. His credits include the New York Shakespeare Festival/Public Theater, the Lincoln Center Theater, the Roundabout Theater, the Circle-in-the-Square, the Hudson Guild Theater, the Longwharf Theater, the Hartford Stage the Company, the Arena Stage, the American Repertory Theater, the Goodman Theater, the South Coast Repertory, and the San Diego Shakespeare Festival. Primarily a theater actor, Rudd has also worked in television and film productions of *End of Summer, A Family Reunion,* and *Beulah Land.* His roles include the central character of Brian Mallory in *Beacon Hill,* JFK in *Johnny We Hardly Knew Ye,* and guest appearances in episodes of *Moonlighting, Knot's Landing, Hart to Hart,* and *Murder, She Wrote.*

Ron Leibman, Chair of the Acting Department. A member of the Actors Studio, Mr. Leibman received the Tony Award and Drama Desk Award as Best Actor in Tony Kushner's Pulitzer Prize–winning *Angels in America.* Leibman won the Emmy Award as Best Actor for his work on *Kaz,* which he also created. Leibman has won Drama Desk Awards for *We Bombed in New Haven* (for which he also won a Theatre World Award), *Room Service, A Dybbuk,* and *Transfers,* and he won Obie Awards for his performance as Shylock in the New York Shakespeare Festival's *Merchant of Venice* and for his role in *Transfers.* Other Broadway appearances include *Rumors* and *I Ought To Be in Pictures* (both by Neil Simon), *Cop-Out* by John Guare, *The Deputy,* and *Dear Me, the Sky Is Falling.* His film work includes roles in *Norma Rae, Night Falls on Manhattan, Where's Poppa?, Slaughterhouse Five, Super Cops, The Hot Rock, Personal Velocity* (Sundance Grand Jury Prize winner), Paul Schrader's *Auto Focus,* and *Garden State.* Television credits include *Friends* (as Rachel's father), *Christmas Eve* (Golden Globe winner), *Central Park West, Law & Order,* a recurring role on *The Sopranos,* and numerous miniseries.

Pippin Parker, Chair of the Playwriting Department. Mr. Parker is a writer, director, and dramaturge. He is also a founding member and former artistic director of the Naked Angels theater company. His plays include *Anesthesia, Assisted Living,* and numerous one acts that have been produced in New York and Los Angeles. His radio play *A Gift* was broadcast on NPR's *The Next Big Thing.* Television credits include *The High Life* for HBO and the animated series *The Tick.* He was recently artistic director for the Naked Angels/Culture Project series, *The Democracy Project.*

Elinor Renfield, Chair of the Directing Department. Ms. Renfield began her training as a dancer with the Martha Graham Company in the 1950s. She attended the "old" High School of the Performing Arts and the Central School of Speech and Drama in London and earned an M.A. in theater at City University of New York. She has directed more than twenty-five new American plays since 1976 at the New York Shakespeare Festival, Playwrights Horizon, the American Place Theater, Ensemble Studio Theater, Theater for the New City, and Café La Mama. Her production of *Johnny Got His Gun* at the Circle Repertory won an Obie Award; her production of *The Diary of Anne Frank* won the Boston Theater Award; and her production of *Passion Play* by Peter Nichols at the Arena Stage in Washington, D.C., was nominated for a Helen Hayes Award. On Broadway, Renfield directed *Open Admissions* by Shirley Lauro at the Music Box.

Nova Thomas, Chair of the Voice and Speech Program. Ms. Thomas is an internationally acclaimed opera singer whose work has been characterized as "ravishing in sound and magical in stage appearance" (*OPERA*). Her roles have included Violetta in *La Traviata,* Leonora in *Il Trovatore,* Mimì in *La Bohème,* Desdemona in *Otello,* Lady Macbeth in *Macbeth,* all four heroines of *Les Contes d'Hoffman,* and the title roles of *Madama Butterfly, Norma, Anna Bolena, Tosca, Aida,* and *Turandot.* Her performances have taken her to the opera houses throughout the United States and the world. She has recorded the title role of *The Bohemian Girl* for DECCA records. A member of The New School for Drama faculty since its first year, she has coauthored and developed a three-year curriculum of voice and speech training uniquely designed to parallel and partner the Stanislavski-inspired system of training. Ms. Thomas serves on the national board of directors for the General H. Hugh Shelton Leadership Initiative, as well as several national scholarship committees. She is a recipient of The New School's Excellence in Teaching Award and the winner of a Lifetime Achievement Award from her home state of North Carolina for her contributions to the arts.

Tom Vasiliades, Chair of the Movement Program. Mr. Vasiliades trained and was certified at the American Center for the Alexander Technique in New York City. He is a member of the American Society for the Alexander Technique, Alexander Technique International, and the Society of Teachers for the Alexander Technique. After graduating from the American Center, he continued training in New York and London. He did postgraduate work with Barbara Kent, Glynn Macdonald, John Nicholls, Peggy Williams, and Walter Carrington, who carried on the training course after F.M. Alexander's death. Since the late 1970s, he has acted at regional theaters and in New York and in film and television. He has directed plays and produced two plays in New York, *The Sin Eaters* and *Triptych.* He has taught the Alexander Technique to many performers, including members of the Broadway cast of *Private Lives* with Alan Rickman and Lindsay Duncan.

ACTING

Ron Leibman, Chair.
Marcia Haufrecht
Gene Lasko
Karen Ludwig
Joseph Ragno
Paul Rudd
Arthur Storch
Mimi Turque
Robert Walden

Movement

Tom Vasiliades, Chair.
Teva Bjerken
Judith Grodowitz
Brendan McCall
Cynthia Reynolds
Rick Sordelet
Jean Taylor

Voice and Speech

Nova Thomas, Chair
Keith Buhl
Susan Cameron
Patricia Fletcher
Alba Quezada
Christopher Roselli

DIRECTING

Elinor Renfield, Chair.
Casey Biggs
Lou Jacob
Dorothy Lyman
Austin Pendleton
Jamie Richards

Design

Jack O'Connor
Jamie Richards

PLAYWRITING

Pippin Parker, Chair
Nicole Burdette
Laura Maria Censabella
Frank Pugliese
Christopher Shinn
Michael Weller

Script Analysis

Stephen Willems

Theater History

Jane Ann Crum
Beowulf Boritt
Donald Holder

SARAH LAWRENCE COLLEGE

Master of Fine Arts Programs

Programs of Study
Sarah Lawrence College offers advanced dance, theater, and writing students the opportunity to study with an outstanding faculty as they pursue the Master of Fine Arts degree at one of the nation's most selective liberal arts colleges. These programs follow the College's philosophy, which stresses a high degree of individual development that is essentially exploratory and noncompetitive in nature. Small seminar classes with individual student-faculty conferences allow close collaboration with faculty members in all three programs, and the opportunity for fieldwork is extensive and varied.

The dance and theater programs require two years of full-time study and completion of 36 course credits. The writing program offers both full-time and part-time study.

The program in dance is based on the premise that dance is a unique art form, calling for the integration of body, mind, and spirit. Daily modern and ballet technique classes are required of all graduate students. Basic physical skills, strength, and control are required for the central focus of the program—the creative use of the dance medium. The student is exposed to vital aspects of the art as a performer, creator, and observer, with music as an integral part. The curriculum centers on choreography, dance improvisation, music improvisation, composition, and the teaching of dance. Course work is offered with undergraduate dancers, and the dance program offers students an opportunity to grow under the guidance of an excellent faculty of dancers and dance scholars with professional experience in the New York area and abroad.

The theater program is based on the principle that learning comes through practical application, personal experience, and intensive workshops. Working with a faculty of New York City theater professionals, students explore playwriting, acting, directing, design, and technical work in small seminars, private tutorials, and collaborative projects.

The writing program offers an uncommon opportunity for students to develop as poets, creative nonfiction writers, or fiction writers under the close supervision of a nationally renowned faculty. At the center of the course of study are four successive seminars that students take during their two years in the program. In addition to the lively exchanges in these seminars, students participate in individual conferences with faculty members every two weeks. This distinctive aspect of the Sarah Lawrence program provides further intensive scrutiny of students' writing and helps them create the substantial body of work needed to fulfill the program's requirements.

Research Facilities
The College's facilities include classrooms, laboratories, a computer center, and a state-of-the-art sports center; a library with 202,265 books and 880 periodicals, which is linked by computer to more than 6,000 other libraries; the Performing Arts Center, which consists of four theaters, a dance studio, and a concert hall; a music building, including a music library; and the Center for Graduate Studies.

Financial Aid
Graduate students are welcome to apply for financial aid. There are two required forms for U.S. citizens (and other federally eligible students) and one form for international students. U.S. citizens should complete the Free Application for Federal Student Aid (FAFSA) and the Financial Aid PROFILE. International students may use the College's International Application for Financial Aid. There are links to all three forms at http://www.sarahlawrence.edu/finaid. March 1 is the College's preferential filing date. It is important that all applicants for financial aid complete either the PROFILE or the international application for aid at the same time as their application for admission. All financial aid is awarded on the basis of need. Students who complete the appropriate forms in a timely manner are automatically considered for all aid resources administered by Sarah Lawrence College. Grants (gift aid) and student loans comprise the two elements of a Sarah Lawrence financial aid package. Every federally eligible aid recipient is offered a student loan. Students are not required to accept the loan in order to receive Sarah Lawrence College gift aid. International students are advised to investigate financing opportunities offered by their government or private institutions. Detailed descriptions and a thorough explanation of financial aid procedures are available in *Financing Your Graduate Education at Sarah Lawrence College,* published and updated by the Office of Graduate Studies. A copy of the booklet is mailed to all students who apply to a graduate studies program.

Cost of Study
In 2009–10, tuition for the M.F.A. varies according to program. For more information, prospective students should visit http://www.slc.edu/student-accounts/Graduate_Tuition_and_Costs.php.

Living and Housing Costs
Estimated expenses for off-campus housing and food are $16,320 per year.

Student Group
Sarah Lawrence attracts students who seek a creative education and are eager to take responsibility for it. The College draws its graduate students from forty-nine states and thirty-one countries. Graduate programs are deliberately kept small. There are approximately 320 graduate students.

Location
The College is situated in the Bronxville/Yonkers suburban community in southern Westchester County, just 15 miles north of midtown Manhattan in New York City. Highways and a commuter railroad make it possible to reach the city in about 30 minutes, enabling students to take advantage of its social and cultural riches and its internship possibilities.

The College
Founded in 1926, Sarah Lawrence is a small, liberal arts college for men and women. It is a lively community of students, scholars, and artists, nationally renowned for its distinctive academic structure that combines small classes with individual student-faculty conferences.

Applying
Applicants for graduate studies must have received a Bachelor of Arts or an equivalent degree from an accredited college or university and have at least a 3.0 grade point average. Applicants should write to the College address to request information on a specific program.

Applicants are asked to complete the application form and to furnish transcripts of all undergraduate work and two letters of recommendation, preferably from former teachers. Personal interviews may be arranged with the program directors and with the director of graduate studies. The creative writing and the performing arts programs require demonstration of the candidate's ability. GRE scores are not required. Prospective students can apply online at https://data.slc.edu/graduate/index.php. Application deadlines vary according to the program. Students should visit the Web site at http://www.slc.edu/graduate/index.php.

Correspondence and Information
Susan Guma
Dean of Graduate Studies
Sarah Lawrence College
1 Mead Way
Bronxville, New York 10708
Phone: 914-395-2371
Fax: 914-395-2664
E-mail: grad@sarahlawrence.edu
Web site: http://www.sarahlawrence.edu

Sarah Lawrence College

THE FACULTY

Dance
Sara Rudner, Director; M.F.A., Bennington.
Emmy Devine, B.A., Connecticut.
Dan Hurlin, B.A., Sarah Lawrence.
Rose Anne Thom, B.A., McGill.
John Yannelli, M.F.A., Sarah Lawrence.

Theater
John Dillon, Director; M.F.A., Columbia (Danforth and Woodrow Wilson Fellow).
Ernest H. Abuba, Member, Ensemble Studio Theatre; Rockefeller Foundation Fellowship.
Edward Allen Baker, B.A., Rhode Island.
Lynn Book, M.F.A., Art Institute of Chicago.
Kevin Confoy, B.A., Rutgers.
Michael Early, M.F.A., Yale.
June Ekman, B.A., Goddard, Illinois; ACAT. Alexander Technique.
Christine Farrell, M.F.A., Columbia.
Nancy Franklin, Member, Actors Studio and Ensemble Studio Theatre.
Dan Hurlin, B.A., Sarah Lawrence.
Chris Jones, M.F.A., Carnegie Mellon.
Shirley Kaplan, A.A., Briarcliff, Academie de la Grande Chaumiere (Paris).
Doug MacHugh, M.F.A., Sarah Lawrence.
Greg MacPherson, B.A., Vermont.
John McCormack, B.A., Hamilton.
William D. McRee, M.F.A., Sarah Lawrence.
Cassandra Medley, Michigan.
Carol Ann Pelletier, B.A., Brandeis.
Paul Rudd, B.A., Fairfield.
Fanchon Miller Scheier, M.F.A., Sarah Lawrence.
Stuart Spencer, B.A., Lawrence Tech.
Sterling Swann, B.A., Vassar.
John Yannelli, M.F.A., Sarah Lawrence.

Writing/Creative Nonfiction
Vijay Seshadri, Director; M.F.A., Columbia.
Jo Ann Beard, M.A., Iowa.

Rachel Cohen, A.B., Harvard.
Stephen O'Connor, M.A., Berkeley.
Penny Wolfson, M.F.A., Sarah Lawrence.

Writing/Fiction
Brian Morton, Director; B.A., Sarah Lawrence.
Jo Ann Beard, M.A., Iowa.
Melvin Jules Bukiet, M.F.A., Columbia.
Carolyn Ferrell, M.A., CUNY, City College.
Myra Goldberg, M.A., CUNY Graduate Center.
Joshua Henkin, M.F.A., Michigan.
Kathleen Hill, Ph.D., Wisconsin.
William Melvin Kelley, Writer; Harvard.
Mary La Chapelle, M.F.A., Vermont.
Paul Lisicky, M.A., Rutgers.
Mary Morris, M.Phil., Columbia.
Dennia Nurkse, B.A., Harvard.
Victoria Redel, M.F.A., Iowa.
Lucy Rosenthal, M.F.A., Yale.
Joan Silber, M.A., NYU.

Writing/Poetry
Kate Knapp Johnson, Director; M.F.A., Sarah Lawrence.
Laure-Anne Bosselaar, M.F.A., National Institute for Performing Arts (Belgium).
Suzanne Gardinier, M.F.A., Columbia.
Marie Howe, M.F.A., Columbia.
Joan Larkin, M.A., Arizona.
Thomas Lux, B.A., Emerson; Iowa Writers Workshop.
Kevin Pilkington, M.A., Georgetown.
Victoria Redel, M.F.A., Iowa.
Vijay Seshadri, M.F.A., Columbia.

The Performing Arts Center houses a wide range of facilities, including the 117-seat Workshop Theatre and the 400-seat Reisinger Concert Hall.

SOUTHERN ILLINOIS UNIVERSITY CARBONDALE
Department of Theater

Programs of Study

The Department of Theater at Southern Illinois University Carbondale (SIUC) blends scholarship and practice in an academically based theater experience. The Department offers an M.F.A. in Theater with concentrations in directing, playwriting, costume, lighting, scenic design, and technical direction. The interdisciplinary Ph.D. program, with emphasis on theater history or playwriting, is administered through the Department of Speech Communication. The doctoral program allows students to explore a broad range of course work in the theater/speech communication arts, including American theater history, theory and criticism, dramaturgy, playwriting, intercultural communication, and pedagogy. Methodology classes are drawn from departments across the campus. Classes are small, providing many opportunities to work closely with faculty on a one-to-one basis. Courses of study are tailor made for each student.

The Department maintains two theaters. The McLeod Theater, a proscenium stage seating 520, was recently renovated with new rigging, sound and lighting control, and inventories. The Christian H. Moe Laboratory Theater, a flexible studio space seating up to 110, was also recently renovated with new lighting and sound systems, risers, and seating. The academic season in both theaters is designed to highlight contemporary theater and original works as well as the major historical periods of theater. Musicals and operas are fully produced and orchestrated in conjunction with the School of Music. The professional summer stock company (McLeod Summer Playhouse) offers a variety of plays and musicals. All of these productions provide opportunities for hands-on experience in all graduate programs.

Members of the Department of Theater faculty embrace both the academic and professional theater communities, regularly writing, performing, directing, designing for professional regional theaters, publishing articles and books, and presenting papers at national and international conferences. The faculty are members of their respective professional unions and associations. Faculty members actively prepare students for academic and professional careers through internships, conferences, and summer theater experiences.

Research Facilities

Southern Illinois University Carbondale offers outstanding research facilities. In addition to containing more than 2 million volumes, nearly 3 million microforms, and 12,000 current periodicals, Morris Library is also at the forefront of providing electronic access to information via its own network, the University's network, and the Internet. Multiple computer stations on each floor allow patrons to obtain information, often in full text, from local, state, national, and international sources. The library is a member of Illinet Online (IO), the statewide library automated catalog, circulation, and interlibrary loan system, and the national Online Computer Library Center (OCLC), the world's largest bibliographic network. Library holdings include a variety of special collections, including the papers of Erwin Piscator, Kathryn Dunham, the Abbey Theater, Marjorie Lawrence, Mordecai Gorelik, John Howard Lawson, and others.

Financial Aid

Financial aid is available in many forms. The Department offers assistantships, fellowships, scholarships, and a variety of work-study programs. Fellowships for promising minority students are available through the Proactive Recruitment of Multicultural Professionals for Tomorrow (PROMPT) Program, the Graduate Dean's Fellowship (GDF), the Illinois Minority Graduate Incentive Program (IMGIP), and the Illinois Consortium for Educational Opportunity Program (ICEOP). Assistantships and fellowships carry tuition scholarships. Student employment, loans, and other tuition scholarships are also available. About 70 percent of all graduate students receive some form of SIUC financial aid.

Cost of Study

In-state graduate tuition is $328 per credit hour in 2009–10. Out-of-state tuition is 2.5 times the in-state tuition rate ($820 per credit hour). Graduate students with at least a 25 percent appointment as a graduate assistant receive a tuition scholarship. Fees vary from $589.03 (1 credit hour) to $1557.50 (12 credit hours). Students with a graduate assistantship receive a 50 percent reduction in the primary care medical fee. New graduate students from Arkansas, Indiana, Kentucky, Missouri, and Tennessee qualify for the alternate tuition rate, which is equivalent to the in-state graduate tuition rate.

Living and Housing Costs

For married couples, students with families, and single graduate students, the University has 690 efficiency and one-, two-, three-, and four-bedroom apartments that rent for $499 to $720 per month in 2009–10. Residence halls for single graduate students are also available, as are accessible residence hall rooms and apartments for students with disabilities.

Student Group

The University's total enrollment exceeds 21,000, including more than 4,000 graduate students. Men and women come from all fifty states and more than 100 other countries. About 53 percent of the graduate students are women, 23 percent are international, and 13 percent are American minorities.

Location

SIUC is 350 miles south of Chicago and 100 miles southeast of St. Louis. Nestled in rolling hills bordered by the Ohio and Mississippi Rivers and enhanced by a mild climate, the area has state parks, national forests and wildlife refuges, and large lakes for outdoor recreation. Cultural offerings include theater, opera, concerts, art exhibits, and cinema. Educational facilities for the families of students are excellent.

The University and The Department

Southern Illinois University Carbondale is a comprehensive public university with a variety of general and professional education programs. The University offers associate, bachelor's, master's, and doctoral degrees and the J.D. and M.D. degrees. The University is fully accredited by the North Central Association of Colleges and Schools. The Graduate School has an essential role in the development and coordination of graduate instruction and research programs. The Graduate Council has academic responsibility for determining graduate standards, recommending new graduate programs and research centers, and establishing policies to facilitate the research effort. Southern Illinois University Carbondale is a state-funded university founded in 1869. The Theater Department is an accredited institutional member of the National Association of Schools of Theater (NAST).

Applying

Applications should be requested from the address given in the Correspondence and Information section. Each application must include a completed Departmental and Graduate School application form, three letters of recommendation, official transcripts from all colleges and universities previously attended, a personal statement of career goals, and GRE scores as well as a portfolio of theater work in the student's area of interest. The deadline for application is February 1 for the following fall. All materials should be sent directly to the Department of Theater.

Correspondence and Information

Dr. Ronald Naversen, Director of Graduate Studies
Department of Theater
Mail Code 6608
Southern Illinois University Carbondale
Carbondale, Illinois 62901

Phone: 618-453-5741
Fax: 618-453-7582
E-mail: rnav@siu.edu
Web site: http://www.siu.edu/~mcleod/

Southern Illinois University Carbondale

THE FACULTY AND THEIR RESEARCH

Susan Patrick Benson, Assistant Professor; M.F.A. (acting), Rutgers. Acting and voice.

Mary Bogumil, Associate Professor; Ph.D. (English), South Florida. Dramatic literature.

Joseph A. Brown, Director; Ph.D. (American studies), Yale. Black American studies.

Tim Fink, Associate Professor; M.F.A. (directing), Southern Illinois Carbondale; M.M. (voice), Arizona. Opera and musical theater.

Anne Fletcher, Associate Professor; Ph.D. (theater history), Tufts. History and dramaturgy.

Robert Holcombe, Associate Professor and Technical Director; M.F.A. (technical direction), Ohio. Theater health and safety.

Tom Kidd, Assistant Professor; M.F.A. (directing), Southern Illinois Carbondale. Acting and voice.

Lori Merrill-Fink, Associate Professor and Director of the University Honors Program; M.F.A. (acting), Arizona. Movement and acting.

Ronald Naversen, Professor; M.F.A. (scenic design), Carnegie-Mellon; Ph.D. (theater history), Southern Illinois Carbondale. Scene design painting and properties.

Olusegun Ojewuyi, Assistant Professor; M.F.A. (directing), Yale. Acting and directing.

David Rush, Professor; Ph.D., Illinois. Playwriting and analysis.

Mark K. Varns, Professor and Chair; M.F.A. (technical direction), Kansas. Lighting design and technical direction.

Wendi Zea, Assistant Professor; M.F.A. (costume design), Kent State. Costume design and technology.

UNIVERSITY OF SOUTHERN CALIFORNIA

USC School of Theatre
Programs in Acting and Dramatic Writing

Programs of Study	The University of Southern California (USC) School of Theatre currently offers M.F.A. degrees in acting and dramatic writing.
	The M.F.A. program in acting requires 72 units of course work, while the M.F.A. program in dramatic writing requires 64 units.
	USC School of Theatre offers conservatory-style training that combines rigorous academics with a rich artistic environment. The programs provide students with opportunities to develop and exercise their craft in a setting that parallels the professional theater world through practical and hands-on experience.
	The graduate programs in acting and dramatic writing are intensive, three-year programs taught by a faculty consisting first-rate master teachers and theater professionals working at the highest level in their respective fields. The School of Theatre faculty members have strong ties in the theater world and are sought out by leaders in the industry, the arts, and the media for their expertise.
	Students in the M.F.A. in Acting program perform in various workshops and productions in their first two years and a multiplay repertory in the third year. Every spring semester, the School presents Blueprints, the M.F.A. in Dramatic Writing Playwrights Workshop featuring the second-year writing students, and Under Construction, the Master of Fine Arts Play Project featuring the third-year writing students.
	The USC School of Theatre encourages students to fully explore their creative possibilities. The quality of programs and the lasting relationships students forge with faculty members and peers make USC a nurturing environment for developing theater skills and knowledge. An education at the University of Southern California is a unique and invaluable experience.
Research Facilities	The School of Theatre's active production program uses five theater facilities—the Bing Theatre is a traditional proscenium house with seating for 550 people; the Massman Theatre is a flexible performance space comparable to L.A. Equity Waiver and New York off-off-Broadway theaters with seating for 5 to 75 people; the Scene Dock Theatre is a flexible performance space with seating for 99 people; the new McClintock Theatre offers another space for performance opportunities seating 99 people; and the Village Gate Theatre is a cabaret-style performance space that comfortably seats 70 and is primarily reserved for student productions.
Financial Aid	Graduate students are eligible for various types of need-based assistance, and the School of Theatre offers a number of graduate scholarships ranging from 50 percent to 100 percent tuition remission. The average financial package consists of student work-study, educational loans, and a USC scholarship. Students interested in the M.F.A. in Dramatic Writing program are also eligible for teaching assistantships, which offer a tuition subsidy along with a monthly stipend.
Cost of Study	Based on the 2009–10 academic year, tuition and fees are approximately $33,430 for two semesters (12–18 units per semester).
Living and Housing Costs	The University estimates that students need approximately $17,000 per year if residing in on-campus housing or renting off-campus housing. The University Housing Office reserves numerous apartments for graduate students. All apartments are furnished and accommodate 1, 2, or 4 students.
Student Group	The School of Theatre consists of an estimated 500 students, of whom 40 are graduate students. Students are able to take advantage of a variety of student organizations within the School as well as around campus. Those students interested in pursuing a career in film or television are also encouraged to take advantage of the number of filming opportunities offered through the USC School of Cinematic Arts.
Location	The location of the University of Southern California—in the heart of the entertainment industry near major motion picture studios, performing arts centers, museums, and vibrant resident theatres—offers enrichment for the artist and the young professional that make the School of Theatre distinctive among colleges and universities in the United States.
The University and The School	The University of Southern California was founded in 1880. The School of Theatre is one of the premiere theater schools in the United States. Founded in 1945 by playwright and director William C. DeMille, the School is recognized internationally as a leader in theater education. The School blends artistic training in a conservatory environment with all the academic advantages of a major research university.
Applying	Applications are accepted for the fall semester only. The deadline for all M.F.A. programs is January 9, 2009. All applicants are required to submit a School of Theatre supplementary application, three letters of recommendation, an unofficial copy of transcripts, and a statement of purpose. Acting applicants must also submit a current headshot and a non-refundable $40 audition fee. Auditions are held in Los Angeles, New York, Chicago, and San Francisco. Dramatic writing applicants must also submit a play in standard Samuel French or Final Draft stage format, a synopsis of the play, and a GRE report. Applicants are encouraged to apply early because the number of students accepted is limited.
Correspondence and Information	Sergio Ramirez School of Theatre University of Southern California 1029 Childs Way, DRC 107 Los Angeles, California 90089-0791 Phone: 213-821-4163 E-mail: sotmfa@usc.edu Web site: http://theatre.usc.edu/mfa

University of Southern California

THE FACULTY AND THEIR AREAS OF FOCUS

Madeline Puzo, Dean.
Andrew J. Robinson, Senior Lecturer and Director of M.F.A. Acting.
Velina Hasu Houston, Associate Dean and Director of M.F.A. Dramatic Writing.
Luis Alfaro, Adjunct Faculty. Dramatic writing.
David Bridel, Senior Lecturer. Acting.
Paula Cizmar, Adjunct Faculty. Dramatic writing.
Charlotte Cornwell, Senior Lecturer. Acting.
Oliver Mayer, Assistant Professor. Dramatic writing.
Natsuko Ohama, Lecturer. Acting.
Jack Rowe, Senior Lecturer and Associate Dean. Acting.
Eric Trules, Lecturer. Acting.

ACADEMIC AND PROFESSIONAL PROGRAMS IN THE HUMANITIES

Section 7
History

This section contains a directory of institutions offering graduate work in history, followed by in-depth entries submitted by institutions that chose to prepare detailed program descriptions. Additional information about programs listed in the directory but not augmented by an in-depth entry may be obtained by writing directly to the dean of a graduate school or chair of a department at the address given in the directory.

For programs offering related work, see also in this book *Area and Cultural Studies, Architecture, Humanities, Political Science and International Affairs,* and *Sociology, Anthropology, and Archaeology.*

CONTENTS

Program Directories

History	298
History of Medicine	321
History of Science and Technology	321
Medieval and Renaissance Studies	323
Public History	325

Close-Ups

Seton Hall University	329
Southern Illinois University Carbondale	331
Villanova University	333

See also:

Central European University—Social Sciences and Humanities	349
The New School: A University—Political and Social Science	1251
Sarah Lawrence College—Women's History	621

History

Adams State College, The Graduate School, Department of History, Government and Philosophy, Alamosa, CO 81102. Offers history (MA).

American Public University System, AMU/APU Graduate Programs, Charles Town, WV 25414. Offers air warfare (MA Military Studies); American Revolution (MA Military Studies); business administration (MBA); Civil War (MA Military Studies); criminal justice (MA); defense management (MA Military Studies); emergency and disaster management (MA); environmental policy and management (MS); fire science management (MA); global engagement (MA); history (MA); homeland security (MA); humanities (MA); intelligence (MA Military Studies, MA Strategic Intelligence); international peace and conflict resolution (MA); international relations and conflict resolution (MA); joint warfare (MA Military Studies); land warfare international perspective (MA Military Studies); management (MA); military history (MA); military leadership (MA Military Studies); national security studies (MA); naval warfare international (MA Military Studies); naval warfare US (MA Military Studies); political science (MA); public administration (MA); public health (MA); security management (MA); space studies (MS); special ops/LIC (MA Military Studies); sports management (MA); transportation and logistics management (MA); transportation management (MA); unconventional warfare (MA Military Studies); World War II (MA Military Studies). Programs offered via distance learning only. Part-time and evening/weekend programs available. Postbaccalaureate distance learning degree programs offered (no on-campus study). *Degree requirements:* For master's, comprehensive exam. *Entrance requirements:* For master's, bachelor's degree or equivalent, minimum GPA of 2.7 in last 60 hours of course work. Electronic applications accepted. *Faculty research:* Military history, criminal justice, management performance, national security.

American University, College of Arts and Sciences, Department of History, Washington, DC 20016-8038. Offers MA, PhD. Part-time and evening/weekend programs available. *Faculty:* 20 full-time (9 women), 5 part-time/adjunct (4 women). *Students:* 51 full-time (29 women), 45 part-time (23 women); includes 8 minority (3 African Americans, 1 American Indian/Alaska Native, 2 Asian Americans or Pacific Islanders, 2 Hispanic Americans), 4 international. Average age 31. 131 applicants, 69% accepted, 31 enrolled. In 2008, 19 master's, 3 doctorates awarded. *Degree requirements:* For master's, comprehensive exam, thesis or alternative, tools of research in foreign language, methods, history or methodology; for doctorate, thesis/dissertation, tools of research, 2 seminars, 2 colloquia. *Entrance requirements:* For master's, GRE, two letters of recommendation; for doctorate, GRE, two letters of recommendation, sample of written work. Additional exam requirements/recommendations for international students: Required—TOEFL. *Application deadline:* For fall admission, 2/1 priority date for domestic students; for spring admission, 10/1 priority date for domestic students. Application fee: $80. *Expenses:* Tuition: Full-time $21,204; part-time $1178 per credit hour. Required fees: $380. Part-time tuition and fees vary according to course load and program. *Financial support:* In 2008–09, 20 students received support; fellowships, research assistantships with tuition reimbursements available, teaching assistantships with tuition reimbursements available, career-related internships or fieldwork, institutionally sponsored loans, tuition waivers (full and partial), and unspecified assistantships available. Financial award application deadline: 2/1. *Faculty research:* U.S. political and diplomatic history, modern European history, U.S. social and cultural history, recent U.S. history, early republic, modern Europe. *Unit head:* Dr. Robert Griffith, Chair, 202-885-2419, Fax: 202-885-6166, E-mail: bgriff@american.edu. *Application contact:* Kathleen Clowery, Director of Graduate Admissions, 202-885-3621, Fax: 202-885-1505, E-mail: clowery@american.edu.

American University of Beirut, Graduate Programs, Faculty of Arts and Sciences, Beirut, Lebanon. Offers anthropology (MA); Arabic language and literature (MA); archaeology (MA); biology (MS); chemistry (MS); computer science (MS); economics (MA); education (MA); English language (MA); English literature (MA); environmental policy planning (MSES); financial economics (MAFE); geology (MS); history (MA); mathematics (MA, MS); Middle Eastern studies (MA); philosophy (MA); physics (MS); political studies (MA); psychology (MA); public administration (MA); sociology (MA); statistics (MA, MS). Part-time programs available. *Degree requirements:* For master's, one foreign language, comprehensive exam, thesis (for some programs). *Entrance requirements:* For master's, GRE, letter of recommendation. Additional exam requirements/recommendations for international students: Required—TOEFL (minimum score 600 paper-based; 250 computer-based; 100 iBT), IELTS (minimum score 7.5). *Faculty research:* String theory and supergravity; computer graphics; algebra and number theory; popular Arabic literature; marine and freshwater biology; integrating science, math and technology.

Andrews University, School of Graduate Studies, College of Arts and Sciences, Department of History, Berrien Springs, MI 49104. Offers MA, MAT. Part-time programs available. *Faculty:* 5 full-time (3 women). In 2008, 1 master's awarded. *Degree requirements:* For master's, variable foreign language requirement, thesis optional. *Entrance requirements:* For master's, GRE Subject Test. *Application deadline:* Applications are processed on a rolling basis. Application fee: $43. *Expenses:* Tuition: Full-time $18,360; part-time $765 per credit hour. Required fees: $476; $765 per credit hour. $238 per semester. Tuition and fees vary according to degree level. *Financial support:* Fellowships, Federal Work-Study, institutionally sponsored loans, and unspecified assistantships available. Financial award application deadline: 6/1. *Faculty research:* American intellectual history, Civil War, American church history, modern German history. *Unit head:* Dr. Gary G. Land, Chairman, 269-471-3292. *Application contact:* Carolyn Hurst, Supervisor of Graduate Admission, 800-253-2874, Fax: 269-471-3228, E-mail: graduate@andrews.edu.

Angelo State University, College of Graduate Studies, College of Liberal and Fine Arts, Department of History, San Angelo, TX 76909. Offers MA. Part-time and evening/weekend programs available. *Faculty:* 3 full-time (0 women). *Students:* 2 full-time (both women), 6 part-time (2 women), 1 international. Average age 32. 5 applicants, 80% accepted, 4 enrolled. In 2008, 2 master's awarded. *Degree requirements:* For master's, comprehensive exam, thesis optional. *Entrance requirements:* For master's, GRE General Test. Additional exam requirements/recommendations for international students: Required—TOEFL or IELTS. *Application deadline:* For fall admission, 7/15 priority date for domestic students, 6/10 for international students; for spring admission, 12/1 priority date for domestic students, 11/1 for international students. Applications are processed on a rolling basis. Application fee: $40 ($50 for international students). Electronic applications accepted. *Financial support:* In 2008–09, 4 students received support. Federal Work-Study, scholarships/grants, and unspecified assistantships available. Support available to part-time students. Financial award application deadline: 3/1. *Unit head:* Dr. Virginia Noelke, Department Head, 325-942-2115. *Application contact:* Dr. Shirley Eoff, Graduate Advisor, 325-942-2118, E-mail: shirley.eoff@angelo.edu.

Appalachian State University, Cratis D. Williams Graduate School, Department of History, Boone, NC 28608. Offers history (MA); history education (MA); public history (MA). Part-time programs available. Postbaccalaureate distance learning degree programs offered (no on-campus study). *Faculty:* 26 full-time (8 women), 3 part-time/adjunct (1 woman). *Students:* 29 full-time (14 women), 18 part-time (5 women); includes 1 minority (American Indian/Alaska Native), 1 international. 27 applicants, 85% accepted, 23 enrolled. In 2008, 7 master's awarded. *Degree requirements:* For master's, one foreign language, comprehensive exam, thesis (for some programs). *Entrance requirements:* For master's, GRE General Test, 3 letters of recommendation. Additional exam requirements/recommendations for international students: Required—TOEFL (minimum score 570 paper-based; 230 computer-based; 79 iBT), IELTS (minimum score 6.5). *Application deadline:* For fall admission, 7/1 for domestic students, 2/1 for international students; for spring admission, 11/1 for domestic students, 7/1 for international students. Applications are processed on a rolling basis. Application fee: $50. Electronic applications accepted. *Expenses:* Tuition, area resident: Full-time $2600; part-time $700 per course. Tuition, state resident: full-time $2600; part-time $700 per course. Tuition, nonresident: full-time $5000; part-time $3300 per course. Required fees: $2150; $330 per course. Tuition and fees vary according to campus/location. *Financial support:* In 2008–09, 4 research assistantships (averaging $10,000 per year), 7 teaching assistantships (averaging $7,500 per year) were awarded; fellowships, career-related internships or fieldwork, Federal Work-Study, scholarships/grants, and unspecified assistantships also available. Financial award application deadline: 4/1; financial award applicants required to submit FAFSA. *Faculty research:* Women's history, social/cultural history, US history, Latin America, medieval studies. Total annual research expenditures: $155,791. *Unit head:* Dr. Michael Krenn, Chairperson, 828-262-2282, E-mail: krennml@appstate.edu. *Application contact:* Dr. James Goff, Graduate Program Director, 828-262-6019, E-mail: goffjr@appstate.edu.

Arizona State University, Graduate College, College of Liberal Arts and Sciences, Division of Humanities, Department of History, Tempe, AZ 85287. Offers East/Southeast Asian history (MA, PhD); European history (MA, PhD); Latin American studies (MA, PhD); North American history (MA, PhD); public history (MA). *Degree requirements:* For master's, thesis or alternative; for doctorate, 2 foreign languages, thesis/dissertation. *Entrance requirements:* For master's and doctorate, GRE.

Arkansas State University, Graduate School, College of Humanities and Social Sciences, Department of History, Jonesboro, State University, AR 72467. Offers history (MA); history education (SCCT); social science education (MSE). Part-time programs available. *Faculty:* 14 full-time (7 women), 2 part-time/adjunct (both women). *Students:* 8 full-time (3 women), 34 part-time (23 women); includes 5 minority (all African Americans). Average age 36. 29 applicants, 72% accepted, 12 enrolled. In 2008, 12 master's, 1 other advanced degree awarded. *Degree requirements:* For master's, comprehensive exam, thesis or alternative; for SCCT, comprehensive exam. *Entrance requirements:* For master's, GRE General Test or MAT, GMAT, appropriate bachelor's degree, letters of reference, official transcript, valid teaching certificate (for MSE); for SCCT, GRE General Test or MAT, interview, master's degree, letters of reference, official transcript. Additional exam requirements/recommendations for international students: Required—TOEFL (minimum score 550 paper-based; 213 computer-based; 79 iBT), IELTS (minimum score 6). *Application deadline:* For fall admission, 7/15 for domestic students, 7/1 for international students; for spring admission, 12/1 for domestic students, 11/13 for international students. Applications are processed on a rolling basis. Application fee: $30 ($40 for international students). Electronic applications accepted. *Expenses:* Tuition, state resident: full-time $3744; part-time $208 per credit hour. Tuition, nonresident: full-time $9540; part-time $530 per credit hour. International tuition: $7938 full-time. Required fees: $896; $47 per credit hour. $25 per term. One-time fee: $50. Tuition and fees vary according to course load and program. *Financial support:* In 2008–09, 10 students received support. Career-related internships or fieldwork, scholarships/grants, and unspecified assistantships available. Financial award application deadline: 7/1; financial award applicants required to submit FAFSA. *Faculty research:* US history, women's history, Islamic history, Eurasian perspectives, history of criminal justice. *Unit head:* Dr. Pamela Hronek, Chair, 870-972-3046, Fax: 870-972-2880, E-mail: phronek@astate.edu. *Application contact:* Dr. Andrew Sustich, Dean of the Graduate School, 870-972-3029, Fax: 870-972-3857, E-mail: sustich@astate.edu.

Arkansas Tech University, Graduate School, School of Liberal and Fine Arts, Russellville, AR 72801. Offers communication (MLA); English (M Ed, MA); fine arts (MLA); history (MA); multi-media journalism (MA); social science (MLA); social studies (M Ed); Spanish (MA, MLA); teaching English as a second language (MA, MLA). Part-time programs available. *Students:* 40 full-time (31 women), 81 part-time (60 women); includes 10 minority (3 African Americans, 2 American Indian/Alaska Native, 2 Asian Americans or Pacific Islanders, 3 Hispanic Americans), 19 international. Average age 33. In 2008, 70 master's awarded. *Degree requirements:* For master's, project. *Entrance requirements:* For master's, GRE General Test or MAT. Additional exam requirements/recommendations for international students: Required—TOEFL (minimum score 500 paper-based; 173 computer-based; 61 iBT). *Application deadline:* For fall admission, 3/1 priority date for domestic students, 5/1 priority date for international students; for winter admission, 10/1 priority date for international students; for spring admission, 10/1 priority date for domestic and international students. Applications are processed on a rolling basis. Application fee: $0 ($30 for international students). Electronic applications accepted. *Expenses:* Tuition, state resident: full-time $1575; part-time $175 per credit hour. Tuition, nonresident: full-time $3150; part-time $350 per credit hour. Tuition and fees vary according to course load. *Financial support:* In 2008–09, teaching assistantships with full tuition reimbursements (averaging $4,000 per year); career-related internships or fieldwork, Federal Work-Study, scholarships/grants, health care benefits, and unspecified assistantships also available. Support available to part-time students. Financial award application deadline: 4/15; financial award applicants required to submit FAFSA. *Unit head:* Dr. Georgena Duncan, Dean, 479-968-0266, Fax: 479-968-0275, E-mail: georgena.duncan@atu.edu. *Application contact:* Dr. Eldon G. Clary, Dean of Graduate School, 479-968-0398, Fax: 479-964-0542, E-mail: graduate.school@atu.edu.

Armstrong Atlantic State University, School of Graduate Studies, Program in History, Savannah, GA 31419-1997. Offers MA. Part-time and evening/weekend programs available. *Degree requirements:* For master's, one foreign language, comprehensive exam, thesis (for some programs). *Entrance requirements:* For master's, GRE General Test, minimum GPA of 3.0, letters of recommendation, BA in history or equivalent. Additional exam requirements/recommendations for international students: Required—TOEFL (minimum score 523 paper-based; 193 computer-based). Electronic applications accepted. *Faculty research:* Public history; European, Latin American, African, and United State history.

Ashland Theological Seminary, Graduate Programs, Ashland, OH 44805. Offers biblical and theological studies (MA, MAR), including New Testament (MA), Old Testament (MA); Christian ministry (MAPT); Christian studies (Diploma); clinical pastoral counseling (MACPC); historical studies (MA); ministry (D Min); pastoral counseling (MAPC); pastoral ministry (M Div); theological studies (MA). *Accreditation:* ATS. Part-time programs available. *Degree requirements:* For master's, comprehensive exam (for some programs), thesis (for some programs); for doctorate, thesis/dissertation; for M Div, 2 foreign languages. *Entrance requirements:* For M Div, minimum GPA of 2.75; for master's, minimum undergraduate GPA of 2.75; for doctorate, M Div, minimum undergraduate GPA of 3.0. Additional exam requirements/recommendations for international students: Required—TOEFL (minimum score 550 paper-based). Electronic applications accepted. *Faculty research:* Semitic languages and linguistics, rhetorical and social-scientific criticism, Anabaptist studies, inner spiritual healing, African-American clergy in film and literature.

Ashland University, College of Arts and Sciences, Program in American History and Government, Ashland, OH 44805-3702. Offers MAHG. Part-time programs available. *Faculty:* 5 full-time (0 women), 33 part-time/adjunct (2 women). *Students:* 41 full-time (19 women), 74 part-time (34 women); includes 9 minority (3 African Americans, 1 Asian American or Pacific Islander, 5 Hispanic Americans). Average age 38. 101 applicants, 69% accepted, 56 enrolled. In 2008, 1 master's awarded. *Degree requirements:* For master's, thesis optional. *Entrance requirements:* For master's, minimum GPA of 3.0. *Application deadline:* Applications are processed on a rolling basis. Application fee: $30. Electronic applications accepted. *Expenses:* Contact institution. *Financial support:* Application deadline: 4/15. *Faculty research:* American founding, United States Civil War, Progressive Era. *Unit head:* Dr. Peter W. Schramm, Executive Director, Ashbrook Center, 419-289-5414, Fax: 419-289-5425, E-mail: pschramm@ashland.edu. *Application contact:* Christina A Pascarella, Associate Director, 419-289-5411, Fax: 419-289-5425, E-mail: cpascare@ashland.edu.

Auburn University, Graduate School, College of Liberal Arts, Department of History, Auburn University, AL 36849. Offers MA, PhD. Part-time programs available. *Faculty:* 26 full-time (10 women). *Students:* 20 full-time (8 women), 49 part-time (17 women); includes 1 minority (Hispanic American), 1 international. Average age 38. 48 applicants, 52% accepted, 14 enrolled. In 2008, 9 master's, 4 doctorates awarded. *Degree requirements:* For master's, thesis, oral exam; for doctorate, 2 foreign languages, thesis/dissertation. *Entrance requirements:* For master's, GRE General Test; for doctorate, GRE General Test, master's degree with thesis. *Application deadline:* For fall admission, 7/7 for domestic students; for spring admission, 11/24 for domestic students. Applications are processed on a rolling basis. Application fee: $25 ($50 for international students). Electronic applications accepted. *Expenses:* Tuition, area resident: Full-time $5880; part-time $243 per credit hour. Tuition, state resident: full-time $5880; part-time $243 per credit hour. Tuition, nonresident: full-time $17,640; part-time $729 per credit hour. International tuition: $17,846 full-time. Required fees: $620. Tuition and fees vary according to program and reciprocity agreements. *Financial support:* Teaching assistantships, Federal Work-Study available. Support available to part-time students. Financial award application deadline: 3/15. *Unit head:* Dr. Tony Carey, Chair, 334-844-4360. *Application contact:* Dr. George Flowers, Dean of the Graduate School, 334-844-2125.

Ball State University, Graduate School, College of Sciences and Humanities, Department of History, Muncie, IN 47306-1099. Offers MA. *Faculty research:* European, British, and American history.

Baylor University, Graduate School, College of Arts and Sciences, Department of History, Waco, TX 76798. Offers MA. Part-time and evening/weekend programs available. *Students:* 17 full-time (7 women), 1 part-time (0 women); includes 1 minority (Hispanic American), 1 international. In 2008, 6 master's awarded. *Degree requirements:* For master's, comprehensive exam, thesis, foreign language translation exam. *Entrance requirements:* For master's, GRE General Test, 24 semester hours in history. *Application deadline:* For fall admission, 8/1 for domestic students. Applications are processed on a rolling basis. Application fee: $25. *Financial support:* Fellowships, research assistantships, Federal Work-Study and institutionally sponsored loans available. Financial award application deadline: 4/15. *Faculty research:* U.S. women's history, naval history, Chinese missions, late nineteenth century Germany, twentieth century urban U.S. *Unit head:* Dr. Barry Hankins, Graduate Program Director, 254-710-4667, Fax: 254-710-2551, E-mail: barry_hankins@baylor.edu. *Application contact:* Linda Conlon, Administrative Assistant, 254-710-6293, Fax: 254-710-3870.

Bob Jones University, Graduate Programs, Greenville, SC 29614. Offers accountancy (MS); Bible (MA); Bible translation (MA); Biblical studies (Certificate); broadcast management (MS); business administration (MBA); church history (MA, PhD); church ministries (MA); church music (MM); cinema and video production (MA); counseling (MS); curriculum and instruction (Ed D); divinity (M Div); dramatic production (MA); educational leadership (MS, Ed D, Ed S); elementary education (M Ed, MAT); English (M Ed, MA, MAT); fine arts (MA); graphic design (MA); history (M Ed, MA); illustration (MA); interpretative speech (MA); mathematics (M Ed, MAT); medical missions (Certificate); ministry (MM, D Min); multi-categorical special education (M Ed, MAT); music (M Ed); New Testament interpretation (PhD); Old Testament interpretation (PhD); orchestral instrument performance (MM); organ performance (MM); pastoral studies (MA); personnel services (MS, Ed S); piano pedagogy (MM); piano performance (MM); platform arts (MA); radio and television broadcasting (MS); rhetoric and public address (MA); secondary education (M Ed); studio art (MA); teaching Bible (MA); theology (MA, PhD); voice performance (MM); youth ministries (MA); M Div/MM.

Boise State University, Graduate College, College of Social Sciences and Public Affairs, Department of History, Boise, ID 83725-0399. Offers MA. Part-time programs available. *Degree requirements:* For master's, thesis. *Entrance requirements:* For master's, GRE General Test, minimum GPA of 3.0. Electronic applications accepted. *Faculty research:* Public history, American social and cultural history, European history, Third World history.

Boston College, Graduate School of Arts and Sciences, Department of History, Chestnut Hill, MA 02467-3800. Offers European national studies (MA); history (MA, PhD); medieval studies (MA). Terminal master's awarded for partial completion of doctoral program. *Degree requirements:* For master's, one foreign language, comprehensive exam, thesis optional; for doctorate, 2 foreign languages, comprehensive exam, thesis/dissertation. *Entrance requirements:* For master's and doctorate, GRE General Test, writing sample. Additional exam requirements/recommendations for international students: Required—TOEFL (minimum score 590 paper-based; 250 computer-based; 91 iBT). Electronic applications accepted. *Expenses:* Tuition: Part-time $1148 per credit. Required fees: $60. *Faculty research:* Modern and early modern European, U.S., Russian, and Soviet history; European and U.S. intellectual history.

Boston University, Graduate School of Arts and Sciences, Department of History, Boston, MA 02215. Offers MA, PhD. Terminal master's awarded for partial completion of doctoral program. *Degree requirements:* For master's, one foreign language; for doctorate, 2 foreign languages, comprehensive exam, thesis/dissertation. *Entrance requirements:* For master's and doctorate, GRE General Test, 2 letters of recommendation. Additional exam requirements/recommendations for international students: Required—TOEFL (minimum score 550 paper-based; 213 computer-based).

Bowling Green State University, Graduate College, College of Arts and Sciences, Department of History, Bowling Green, OH 43403. Offers history (MA, MAT, PhD); public history (MA); MA/MA. Part-time programs available. *Degree requirements:* For master's, thesis or alternative; for doctorate, one foreign language, comprehensive exam, thesis/dissertation. *Entrance requirements:* For master's and doctorate, GRE General Test. Additional exam requirements/recommendations for international students: Required—TOEFL. Electronic applications accepted. *Faculty research:* Policy history, modern Europe, recent United States history, East Asia, Latin America.

Brandeis University, Graduate School of Arts and Sciences, Department of History, Program in American History, Waltham, MA 02454-9110. Offers MA, PhD. Part-time programs available. Terminal master's awarded for partial completion of doctoral program. *Degree requirements:* For master's, one foreign language, thesis, colloquia, directed research, seminars; for doctorate, one foreign language, comprehensive exam, thesis/dissertation, colloquia, directed research, seminars. *Entrance requirements:* For master's and doctorate, GRE General Test, resumé, writing sample, letters of recommendation, statement of purpose. Additional exam requirements/recommendations for international students: Required—TOEFL (minimum score 600 paper-based; 250 computer-based; 100 iBT), IELTS (minimum score 7). Electronic applications accepted. *Faculty research:* American polity, social history, cultural, legal, colonial.

Brandeis University, Graduate School of Arts and Sciences, Department of History, Program in Comparative History, Waltham, MA 02454-9110. Offers MA, PhD. Part-time programs available. Terminal master's awarded for partial completion of doctoral program. *Degree requirements:* For master's, one foreign language, thesis, colloquia, seminar, research paper; for doctorate, 2 foreign languages, comprehensive exam, thesis/dissertation, colloquia, seminar, research paper. *Entrance requirements:* For master's and doctorate, GRE General Test, sample of written work, resumé, letters of recommendation, statement of purpose. Additional exam requirements/recommendations for international students: Required—TOEFL (minimum score 600 paper-based; 250 computer-based; 100 iBT), IELTS (minimum score 7). Electronic applications accepted. *Faculty research:* Early modern Europe, modern Europe, intellectual history, medieval.

Brock University, Faculty of Graduate Studies, Faculty of Humanities, Program in History, St. Catharines, ON L2S 3A1, Canada. Offers MA. Part-time programs available. *Degree requirements:* For master's, thesis optional. *Entrance requirements:* For master's, honors degree in history. Additional exam requirements/recommendations for international students: Required—TOEFL (minimum score 550 paper-based; 213 computer-based; 80 iBT), IELTS (minimum score 6.5), TWE (minimum score 4). Electronic applications accepted.

Brooklyn College of the City University of New York, Division of Graduate Studies, Department of History, Brooklyn, NY 11210-2889. Offers MA, PhD. The department offers courses at Brooklyn College that are creditable toward the CUNY doctoral degree (with permission of the executive officer of the doctoral program). Part-time and evening/weekend programs available. *Students:* 1 full-time (0 women), 47 part-time (15 women); includes 14 minority (8 African Americans, 1 Asian American or Pacific Islander, 5 Hispanic Americans). Average age 31. 42 applicants, 81% accepted, 20 enrolled. In 2008, 18 master's awarded.

Degree requirements: For master's, 30 credits. *Entrance requirements:* For master's, 12 credits in history, minimum GPA of 3.0 in major, 2 letters of recommendation. Additional exam requirements/recommendations for international students: Required—TOEFL. *Application deadline:* For fall admission, 3/1 priority date for domestic students, 2/1 priority date for international students; for spring admission, 11/1 priority date for domestic students, 10/1 priority date for international students. Applications are processed on a rolling basis. Application fee: $125. Electronic applications accepted. *Expenses:* Tuition, state resident: full-time $7360; part-time $310 per credit hour. Tuition, nonresident: full-time $13,800; part-time $575 per credit hour. *Financial support:* Federal Work-Study, institutionally sponsored loans, and scholarships/grants available. Support available to part-time students. Financial award application deadline: 5/1; financial award applicants required to submit FAFSA. *Faculty research:* Modern European, U.S., medieval, women's, Asian, and Caribbean history. *Unit head:* Dr. David Troyansky, Chairperson, 718-951-5303, E-mail: troyansky@brooklyn.cuny.edu. *Application contact:* Hernan Sierra, Graduate Admissions Coordinator, 718-951-4536, Fax: 718-951-4506, E-mail: grads@brooklyn.cuny.edu.

Brown University, Graduate School, Department of History, Providence, RI 02912. Offers MA, PhD. *Degree requirements:* For master's, thesis or alternative; for doctorate, variable foreign language requirement, thesis/dissertation, preliminary exam.

Buffalo State College, State University of New York, Graduate Studies and Research, Faculty of Natural and Social Sciences, Department of History and Social Studies, Buffalo, NY 14222-1095. Offers history (MA); secondary education (MS Ed), including social studies. Part-time and evening/weekend programs available. *Degree requirements:* For master's, one foreign language, thesis (for some programs), project (MS Ed). *Entrance requirements:* For master's, minimum GPA of 2.75, 30 hours in history (MA), 36 hours in history or social sciences (MS Ed). Additional exam requirements/recommendations for international students: Required—TOEFL (minimum score 550 paper-based; 213 computer-based).

Butler University, College of Liberal Arts and Sciences, Department of History, Indianapolis, IN 46208-3485. Offers MA. Part-time programs available. *Faculty:* 1 (woman) full-time. *Students:* 2 part-time (0 women). Average age 39. 4 applicants, 75% accepted, 0 enrolled. In 2008, 1 master's awarded. *Degree requirements:* For master's, thesis or alternative. *Entrance requirements:* For master's, GRE General Test, minimum GPA of 3.25 in undergraduate major. *Application deadline:* For fall admission, 8/15 priority date for domestic students. Applications are processed on a rolling basis. Application fee: $35. Electronic applications accepted. *Financial support:* Institutionally sponsored loans available. Support available to part-time students. Financial award applicants required to submit FAFSA. *Faculty research:* Gender issues in Africa, Indiana history, transnational migration, French Revolution. *Unit head:* Dr. Scott Swanson, Head, 317-940-9680, E-mail: sswanson@butler.edu. *Application contact:* Pamela Bender, Student Services Specialist, 317-940-8100, Fax: 317-940-8250, E-mail: pbender@butler.edu.

California Polytechnic State University, San Luis Obispo, College of Liberal Arts, Department of History, San Luis Obispo, CA 93407. Offers MA. Part-time programs available. *Faculty:* 2 full-time (0 women), 2 part-time/adjunct (1 woman). *Students:* 8 full-time (4 women), 24 part-time (5 women); includes 3 minority (all Hispanic Americans). Average age 30. 22 applicants, 77% accepted, 6 enrolled. In 2008, 7 master's awarded. *Degree requirements:* For master's, comprehensive exam (for some programs), thesis (for some programs). *Entrance requirements:* For master's, minimum GPA of 3.0 in last 90 quarter units of course work, writing sample. Additional exam requirements/recommendations for international students: Required—TOEFL (minimum score 550 paper-based; 213 computer-based), IELTS (minimum score 6), Either TOEFL or IELTS is acceptable. *Application deadline:* For fall admission, 5/1 for domestic students, 11/30 for international students; for winter admission, 10/1 for domestic students, 6/30 for international students; for spring admission, 1/15 for domestic students. Applications are processed on a rolling basis. Application fee: $55. Electronic applications accepted. *Expenses:* Tuition, nonresident: full-time $10,170; part-time $226 per unit. Required fees: $5751; $1265 per quarter. *Financial support:* Federal Work-Study and scholarships/grants available. Support available to part-time students. Financial award application deadline: 3/2; financial award applicants required to submit FAFSA. *Unit head:* Dr. Tom Trice, Graduate Coordinator, 805-756-2724, Fax: 805-756-5055, E-mail: ttrice@calpoly.edu. *Application contact:* Dr. Tom Trice, Graduate Coordinator, 805-756-2724, Fax: 805-756-5055, E-mail: ttrice@calpoly.edu.

California State Polytechnic University, Pomona, Academic Affairs, College of Letters, Arts, and Social Sciences, Program in History, Pomona, CA 91768-2557. Offers MA. Part-time programs available. *Students:* 2 full-time (0 women), 14 part-time (3 women); includes 6 minority (1 African American, 5 Hispanic Americans). Average age 36. 16 applicants, 56% accepted, 5 enrolled. In 2008, 5 master's awarded. *Degree requirements:* For master's, comprehensive exam (for some programs), thesis (for some programs). *Application deadline:* For fall admission, 5/1 priority date for domestic students; for winter admission, 10/15 priority date for domestic students; for spring admission, 1/20 priority date for domestic students. Applications are processed on a rolling basis. Application fee: $55. Electronic applications accepted. *Expenses:* Tuition, nonresident: full-time $7232; part-time $226 per credit. Required fees: $4272. One-time fee: $2694 part-time. Tuition and fees vary according to course load. *Unit head:* Dr. Daniel K. Lewis, Chair, 909-869-3869, E-mail: dklewis@csupomona.edu. *Application contact:* Dr. Daniel K. Lewis, Chair, 909-869-3869, E-mail: dklewis@csupomona.edu.

California State University, Bakersfield, Division of Graduate Studies, School of Humanities and Social Sciences, Program in History, Bakersfield, CA 93311-1022. Offers MA. *Degree requirements:* For master's, comprehensive exam or thesis. *Entrance requirements:* For master's, 2 letters of recommendation. *Faculty research:* American, European, Latin American, and modern Chinese history.

California State University, Chico, Graduate School, College of Humanities and Fine Arts, Department of History, Chico, CA 95929-0735. Offers MA. Part-time programs available. *Degree requirements:* For master's, thesis or alternative, oral exam. *Entrance requirements:* For master's, GRE General Test, 2 letters of recommendation, writing sample, statement of purpose. Additional exam requirements/recommendations for international students: Required—TOEFL (minimum score 550 paper-based; 213 computer-based; 80 iBT), IELTS (minimum score 6.5). Electronic applications accepted.

California State University, East Bay, Academic Programs and Graduate Studies, College of Letters, Arts, and Social Sciences, Department of History, Hayward, CA 94542-3000. Offers MA. Part-time and evening/weekend programs available. *Degree requirements:* For master's, one foreign language, comprehensive exam, thesis optional, project or thesis. *Entrance requirements:* For master's, minimum GPA of 3.0 in field. Additional exam requirements/recommendations for international students: Required—TOEFL (minimum score 550 paper-based; 213 computer-based). Electronic applications accepted.

California State University, Fresno, Division of Graduate Studies, College of Social Sciences, Department of History, Fresno, CA 93740-8027. Offers history-teaching option (MA); history-traditional track (MA). Part-time and evening/weekend programs available. *Degree requirements:* For master's, thesis or alternative. *Entrance requirements:* For master's, GRE General Test, minimum GPA of 3.0. Additional exam requirements/recommendations for international students: Required—TOEFL. Electronic applications accepted. *Faculty research:* International education, classical art history, improving teacher quality.

California State University, Fullerton, Graduate Studies, College of Humanities and Social Sciences, Department of History, Fullerton, CA 92834-9480. Offers MA. Part-time programs available. *Students:* 16 full-time (7 women), 58 part-time (21 women); includes 20 minority (3 African Americans, 3 Asian Americans or Pacific Islanders, 14 Hispanic Americans), 1 international. Average age 30. 49 applicants, 47% accepted, 11 enrolled. In 2008, 23 master's awarded. *Degree requirements:* For master's, comprehensive exam, project or thesis. *Entrance*

History

California State University, Fullerton *(continued)*
requirements: For master's, undergraduate major in history or related field, minimum GPA of 3.0. Application fee: $55. Tuition and fees vary according to degree level. *Financial support:* Teaching assistantships, career-related internships or fieldwork, Federal Work-Study, institutionally sponsored loans, and scholarships/grants available. Support available to part-time students. Financial award application deadline: 3/1. *Unit head:* Dr. William Haddad, Chair, 657-278-3474. *Application contact:* Dr. David Van Deventer, Adviser, 657-278-3474.

California State University, Long Beach, Graduate Studies, College of Liberal Arts, Department of History, Long Beach, CA 90840. Offers Africa and the Middle East (MA); ancient/Medieval Europe (MA); Asia (MA); Latin America (MA); modern Europe (MA); United States (MA); world (MA). Part-time and evening/weekend programs available. *Faculty:* 17 full-time (11 women), 2 part-time/adjunct (1 woman). *Students:* 9 full-time (4 women), 45 part-time (18 women); includes 15 minority (2 African Americans, 3 Asian Americans or Pacific Islanders, 10 Hispanic Americans), 1 international. Average age 35. 40 applicants, 50% accepted, 11 enrolled. *Degree requirements:* For master's, one foreign language, comprehensive exam or thesis. *Application deadline:* For fall admission, 3/1 for domestic students. Applications are processed on a rolling basis. Application fee: $55. Electronic applications accepted. *Expenses:* Tuition, nonresident: full-time $11,160; part-time $372 per unit. Required fees: $4100; $1261 per semester. *Financial support:* Research assistantships, Federal Work-Study, institutionally sponsored loans, and scholarships/grants available. Financial award application deadline: 3/2. *Faculty research:* All periods of European and American history, recent Asian and African history. *Unit head:* Dr. Nancy L Quam-Wickham, Graduate Advisor, 562-985-4431, Fax: 562-985-5431, E-mail: quamwick@csulb.edu. *Application contact:* Dr. Houri Berberian, Graduate Advisor, 562-985-4524, Fax: 562-985-4431, E-mail: hberber@csulb.edu.

California State University, Los Angeles, Graduate Studies, College of Natural and Social Sciences, Department of History, Los Angeles, CA 90032-8530. Offers MA. Part-time and evening/weekend programs available. *Faculty:* 5 full-time (2 women), 2 part-time/adjunct (1 woman). *Students:* 29 full-time (10 women), 64 part-time (24 women); includes 53 minority (4 African Americans, 1 American Indian/Alaska Native, 5 Asian Americans or Pacific Islanders, 43 Hispanic Americans), 5 international. Average age 32. 31 applicants, 100% accepted, 17 enrolled. In 2008, 12 master's awarded. *Degree requirements:* For master's, one foreign language, comprehensive exam or thesis. *Entrance requirements:* For master's, minimum GPA of 3.0, undergraduate major in history. Additional exam requirements/recommendations for international students: Required—TOEFL (minimum score 500 paper-based; 173 computer-based). *Application deadline:* For fall admission, 6/15 for domestic students, 5/1 for international students; for winter admission, 11/1 for domestic students, 9/1 for international students; for spring admission, 2/1 for domestic students, 10/1 for international students. Applications are processed on a rolling basis. Application fee: $55. Electronic applications accepted. *Expenses:* Tuition, nonresident: part-time $226 per credit. Required fees: $4019. *Financial support:* Federal Work-Study available. Support available to part-time students. Financial award application deadline: 3/1. *Faculty research:* Ancient and modern Europe, the Middle East, Latin America, U.S. history-Bill of Rights. *Unit head:* Dr. Cheryl A. Koos, Chair, 323-343-2020, Fax: 323-343-6431, E-mail: ckoos@calstatela.edu. *Application contact:* Dr. Jose L. Galvan, Dean of Graduate Studies, 323-343-3820, Fax: 323-343-5653, E-mail: jgalvan@cslanet.calstatela.edu.

California State University, Northridge, Graduate Studies, College of Social and Behavioral Sciences, Department of History, Northridge, CA 91330. Offers MA. *Faculty:* 17 full-time (5 women), 17 part-time/adjunct (6 women). *Students:* 37 full-time (16 women), 76 part-time (44 women); includes 28 minority (5 African Americans, 1 American Indian/Alaska Native, 5 Asian Americans or Pacific Islanders, 17 Hispanic Americans), 1 international. Average age 35. 71 applicants, 58% accepted, 29 enrolled. In 2008, 34 master's awarded. *Degree requirements:* For master's, one foreign language. *Entrance requirements:* For master's, GRE General Test or minimum GPA of 3.0, 2 letters of recommendation. Additional exam requirements/recommendations for international students: Required—TOEFL. *Application deadline:* For fall admission, 5/15 for domestic students; for spring admission, 11/1 for domestic students. Application fee: $55. *Financial support:* Fellowships, scholarships/grants available. Financial award application deadline: 3/1. *Unit head:* Dr. Thomas R. Maddux, Chair, 818-677-3566, E-mail: thomas.maddux@csun.edu. *Application contact:* Prof. Jeffrey Auerbach, Graduate Coordinator, 818-677-3566.

California State University, Stanislaus, College of Humanities and Social Sciences, Department of History, Turlock, CA 95382. Offers history (MA); international relations (MA); secondary school teachers (MA). Part-time programs available. *Degree requirements:* For master's, one foreign language, comprehensive exam, thesis or alternative. *Entrance requirements:* For master's, GRE General Test, minimum undergraduate GPA of 3.0, personal statement. Additional exam requirements/recommendations for international students: Required—TOEFL (minimum score 550 paper-based; 213 computer-based). Electronic applications accepted. *Faculty research:* History of Ancient Greece, history and ecology of the central valley, acculturation and gender.

Cardinal Stritch University, College of Arts and Sciences, Department of History, Milwaukee, WI 53217-3985. Offers MA. Part-time programs available. *Degree requirements:* For master's, comprehensive exam, research project. *Entrance requirements:* For master's, minimum GPA of 3.0, 2 letters of recommendation. Electronic applications accepted.

Carleton University, Faculty of Graduate Studies, Faculty of Arts and Social Sciences, Department of History, Ottawa, ON K1S 5B6, Canada. Offers MA, PhD. *Degree requirements:* For master's, one foreign language, thesis; for doctorate, one foreign language, thesis/dissertation. *Entrance requirements:* For master's, honors degree; for doctorate, master's degree. Additional exam requirements/recommendations for international students: Required—TOEFL. *Faculty research:* Canadian, American, British, modern French, and modern Russian history; international, medieval, and European intellectual history; women's history.

Carnegie Mellon University, College of Humanities and Social Sciences, Department of History, Pittsburgh, PA 15213-3891. Offers African and African-American diaspora (PhD); culture and power (PhD); gender and the family (PhD); history (MA, MS); history and policy (MA); labor and politics (PhD); science, technology, medicine and environment (PhD). Part-time programs available. *Degree requirements:* For doctorate, oral and written comprehensive exams, dissertation defense. *Entrance requirements:* For doctorate, GRE General Test. Additional exam requirements/recommendations for international students: Required—TOEFL. Electronic applications accepted. *Faculty research:* Anthropology and history, African American history, technology/environment, cultural history analysis.

Case Western Reserve University, School of Graduate Studies, Department of History, Cleveland, OH 44106. Offers MA, PhD. Part-time programs available. Terminal master's awarded for partial completion of doctoral program. *Degree requirements:* For master's, thesis; for doctorate, thesis/dissertation. *Entrance requirements:* For master's and doctorate, GRE General Test. Additional exam requirements/recommendations for international students: Required—TOEFL. Electronic applications accepted. *Faculty research:* American social history, social policy history, history of technology and science.

The Catholic University of America, School of Arts and Sciences, Department of History, Washington, DC 20064. Offers MA, PhD, JD/MA, MSLS/MA. Part-time programs available. *Degree requirements:* For master's, one foreign language, comprehensive exam, thesis or alternative; for doctorate, 2 foreign languages, comprehensive exam, thesis/dissertation, oral exams. *Entrance requirements:* For master's and doctorate, GRE General Test, 3 letters of recommendation. Additional exam requirements/recommendations for international students: Required—TOEFL (minimum score 580 paper-based; 237 computer-based). Electronic applications accepted. *Faculty research:* Medieval family law, U.S. liberalism, capitalism in Europe, Mexican rural society, urbanization in France.

Central Connecticut State University, School of Graduate Studies, School of Arts and Sciences, Department of History, New Britain, CT 06050-4010. Offers history (MA, Certificate); public history (MA); social studies (Certificate). Part-time and evening/weekend programs available. *Faculty:* 18 full-time (8 women), 20 part-time/adjunct (5 women). *Students:* 22 full-time (15 women), 45 part-time (31 women); includes 1 minority (American Indian/Alaska Native). Average age 30. 47 applicants, 57% accepted, 19 enrolled. In 2008, 7 master's, 2 other advanced degrees awarded. *Degree requirements:* For master's, comprehensive exam, thesis or alternative. *Entrance requirements:* For master's, minimum undergraduate GPA of 3.0, essay. Additional exam requirements/recommendations for international students: Required—TOEFL. *Application deadline:* For fall admission, 5/1 for domestic students; for spring admission, 12/1 for domestic students. Applications are processed on a rolling basis. Application fee: $50. Electronic applications accepted. *Expenses:* Tuition, area resident: Full-time $4377; part-time $420 per credit. Tuition, state resident: full-time $6566; part-time $420 per credit. Tuition, nonresident: full-time $12,195; part-time $420 per credit. Required fees: $3462. One-time fee: $62 part-time. *Financial support:* In 2008–09, 8 students received support, including 4 research assistantships; career-related internships or fieldwork, Federal Work-Study, scholarships/grants, and unspecified assistantships also available. Support available to part-time students. Financial award application deadline: 3/1; financial award applicants required to submit FAFSA. *Faculty research:* American West, African history, Eastern Europe, modern Middle East, East Asia. *Unit head:* Dr. Glenn Sunshine, Chair, 860-832-2800. *Application contact:* Dr. Glenn Sunshine, Chair, 860-832-2800.

Central European University, Graduate Studies, Department of History, Budapest, Hungary. Offers MA, PhD. Terminal master's awarded for partial completion of doctoral program. *Degree requirements:* For master's, one foreign language, thesis; for doctorate, one foreign language, comprehensive exam, thesis/dissertation. *Entrance requirements:* For master's and doctorate, interview. Additional exam requirements/recommendations for international students: Required—TOEFL (minimum score 570 paper-based; 230 computer-based). Electronic applications accepted. *Faculty research:* Early modern intellectual history; history of ideas; contemporary historiography comparative history of empires, symbolic geography, history of cultural and religious co-existence.

Central Michigan University, College of Graduate Studies, College of Humanities and Social and Behavioral Sciences, Department of History, Mount Pleasant, MI 48859. Offers European history (Graduate Certificate); history (MA, PhD); modern history (Graduate Certificate); United States history (Graduate Certificate). Offered jointly with the University of Stratclyde, Scotland. Part-time programs available. *Faculty:* 15 full-time (5 women). *Students:* 22 full-time (8 women), 15 part-time (2 women); includes 1 Hispanic American. Average age 30. *Degree requirements:* For master's, thesis or alternative; for doctorate, comprehensive exam, thesis/dissertation. Application fee: $35 ($45 for international students). Electronic applications accepted. *Expenses:* Tuition, state resident: full-time $3717; part-time $413 per credit. Tuition, nonresident: full-time $6894; part-time $766 per credit. *Financial support:* Fellowships with tuition reimbursements, research assistantships with tuition reimbursements, teaching assistantships with tuition reimbursements, Federal Work-Study, unspecified assistantships, and out-of-state merit awards available. *Faculty research:* Colonial and revolutionary United States history, modern European history, Latin American and transatlantic history, transnational and comparative history, United States social history. *Unit head:* Dr. Timothy D. Hall, Chairperson, 989-773-3374, Fax: 989-774-1156, E-mail: hall1td@cmich.edu. *Application contact:* Dr. Timothy D. Hall, Chairperson, 989-773-3374, Fax: 989-774-1156, E-mail: hall1td@cmich.edu.

Central Washington University, Graduate Studies, Research and Continuing Education, College of Arts and Humanities, Department of History, Ellensburg, WA 98926. Offers MA. *Degree requirements:* For master's, thesis or alternative. *Entrance requirements:* For master's, GRE General Test, minimum GPA of 3.0. Additional exam requirements/recommendations for international students: Required—TOEFL (minimum score 550 paper-based; 213 computer-based; 79 iBT). Electronic applications accepted.

Centro de Estudios Avanzados de Puerto Rico y el Caribe, Graduate Program in Puerto Rican and Caribbean Studies, Old San Juan, PR 00902-3970. Offers Puerto Rican and Caribbean history (MA, PhD); Puerto Rican and Caribbean literature (MA, PhD); Puerto Rican studies (MA). Part-time and evening/weekend programs available. *Degree requirements:* For master's, comprehensive exam, thesis; for doctorate, 2 foreign languages, comprehensive exam, thesis/dissertation. *Entrance requirements:* For master's and doctorate, interview. *Faculty research:* Literature, history, art, folklore, and culture of Puerto Rico and Caribbean countries.

Chicago State University, School of Graduate and Professional Studies, College of Arts and Sciences, Department of History, Philosophy, and Political Science, Chicago, IL 60628. Offers MA. Part-time and evening/weekend programs available. *Degree requirements:* For master's, thesis optional. *Entrance requirements:* For master's, minimum GPA of 2.75. Electronic applications accepted. *Faculty research:* Gregory the Great-use in later Middle Ages, Renaissance alchemy, Liberian wars, Waldo Frank, Sangalan oral traditions.

Christopher Newport University, Graduate Studies, Department of Teacher Preparation, Newport News, VA 23606-2998. Offers art (PK-12) (MAT); biology (6-12) (MAT); computer science (6-12) (MAT); elementary (PK-6) (MAT); English (6-12) (MAT); French (PK-12) (MAT); history (6-12) (MAT); history and social science (MAT); mathematics (6-12) (MAT); music (PK-12) (MAT), including choral, instrumental; physics (6-12) (MAT); Spanish (PK-12) (MAT); theater (PK-12) (MAT). Part-time and evening/weekend programs available. *Degree requirements:* For master's, comprehensive exam, thesis or alternative. *Entrance requirements:* For master's, PRAXIS I, minimum GPA of 3.0. Electronic applications accepted. *Faculty research:* Early literacy development, instructional innovations, professional teaching standards, multicultural issues, aesthetic education.

The Citadel, The Military College of South Carolina, Citadel Graduate College, Department of History, Charleston, SC 29409. Offers MA. Part-time and evening/weekend programs available. *Faculty:* 8 full-time (2 women). *Students:* 1 full-time (0 women), 12 part-time (2 women). Average age 33. *Degree requirements:* For master's, comprehensive exam, thesis optional. *Entrance requirements:* For master's, GRE (minimum 1000 and 4-6 on the writing assessment sections) or MAT (minimum 410), minimum undergraduate GPA of 2.5 (3.0 in major); 3 letters of recommendation; evidence of ability to conduct research and present findings. Additional exam requirements/recommendations for international students: Required—TOEFL (minimum score 550 paper-based; 213 computer-based). *Application deadline:* For fall admission, 3/1 for domestic students; for spring admission, 10/1 for domestic students. Application fee: $30. Electronic applications accepted. *Expenses:* Tuition, state resident: full-time $5850; part-time $325 per credit hour. Tuition, nonresident: full-time $9612; part-time $534 per credit hour. Required fees: $15 per semester. *Financial support:* Fellowships, health care benefits and unspecified assistantships available. Support available to part-time students. Financial award application deadline: 7/1; financial award applicants required to submit FAFSA. *Unit head:* Dr. Keith N. Knapp, Department Head, 843-953-5073, Fax: 843-953-7020, E-mail: keith.knapp@citadel.edu. *Application contact:* Dr. Katherine H. Grenier, Director of Graduate Studies, 843-953-6935, Fax: 843-953-7020, E-mail: grenierk@citadel.edu.

City College of the City University of New York, Graduate School, College of Liberal Arts and Science, Division of the Humanities and Arts, Department of History, New York, NY 10031-9198. Offers MA. Part-time programs available. *Degree requirements:* For master's, one foreign language, comprehensive exam, thesis. *Entrance requirements:* For master's, GRE. Additional exam requirements/recommendations for international students: Required—TOEFL (minimum score 500 paper-based; 173 computer-based). *Faculty research:* Latin American, European, Asian, urban, and architectural history.

Claremont Graduate University, Graduate Programs, School of Arts and Humanities, Department of History, Claremont, CA 91711-6160. Offers Africana history (Certificate); American studies and U.S. history (MA, PhD); archival studies (MA); early modern studies (MA, PhD); European studies (MA, PhD); oral history (MA, PhD); MBA/MA; MBA/PhD. *Faculty:* 3 full-time

(2 women). *Students:* 67 full-time (33 women), 8 part-time (3 women); includes 15 minority (1 African American, 3 Asian Americans or Pacific Islanders, 11 Hispanic Americans), 1 international. Average age 35. In 2008, 6 master's, 8 doctorates awarded. Terminal master's awarded for partial completion of doctoral program. *Entrance requirements:* For master's and doctorate, GRE General Test. Additional exam requirements/recommendations for international students: Required—TOEFL (minimum score 550 paper-based; 213 computer-based; 80 iBT). *Application deadline:* For fall admission, 2/1 priority date for domestic students. Applications are processed on a rolling basis. Application fee: $60. Electronic applications accepted. *Expenses:* Tuition: Full-time $33,698; part-time $1465 per unit. Required fees: $310; $155 per semester. Tuition and fees vary according to program. *Financial support:* Fellowships, research assistantships, Federal Work-Study, institutionally sponsored loans, and scholarships/grants available. Support available to part-time students. Financial award application deadline: 2/15; financial award applicants required to submit FAFSA. *Faculty research:* Intellectual and social history, cultural studies, gender studies, Western history, Chicano history. *Unit head:* Janet Farrell Brodie, Chair, 909-621-8880, Fax: 909-621-8609, E-mail: janet.brodie@cgu.edu. *Application contact:* Justin Evans, Admissions Coordinator, 909-607-1278, E-mail: justin.evans@cgu.edu.

Clark Atlanta University, School of Arts and Sciences, Department of History, Atlanta, GA 30314. Offers MA, DAH. Part-time programs available. *Faculty:* 3 full-time (0 women), 2 part-time/adjunct (both women). *Students:* 2 full-time (0 women), 8 part-time (6 women); includes all African Americans. Average age 39. 3 applicants, 67% accepted, 1 enrolled. In 2008, 1 master's awarded. *Degree requirements:* For master's, one foreign language, thesis. *Entrance requirements:* For master's, GRE General Test, minimum GPA of 2.5. Additional exam requirements/recommendations for international students: Required—TOEFL (minimum score 550 paper-based; 173 computer-based). *Application deadline:* For fall admission, 4/1 for domestic and international students; for spring admission, 11/1 for domestic and international students. Applications are processed on a rolling basis. Application fee: $40 ($55 for international students). Electronic applications accepted. *Expenses:* Tuition: Full-time $12,240; part-time $680 per credit hour. Required fees: $710; $355 per semester. *Financial support:* Career-related internships or fieldwork, Federal Work-Study, scholarships/grants, and unspecified assistantships available. Support available to part-time students. Financial award application deadline: 4/30; financial award applicants required to submit FAFSA. *Faculty research:* Education for public service. *Unit head:* Dr. Vicki Crawford, Chairperson, 404-880-6636, E-mail: vcrawfor@cau.edu. *Application contact:* Michelle Clark-Davis, Graduate Program Admissions, 404-880-6605, E-mail: cauadmissions@cau.edu.

Clark University, Graduate School, Department of History, Worcester, MA 01610-1477. Offers American history (PhD); history (MA, CAGS); holocaust history (PhD). *Faculty:* 12 full-time (5 women), 2 part-time/adjunct (0 women). *Students:* 18 full-time (9 women), 2 international. Average age 30. 42 applicants, 31% accepted, 9 enrolled. In 2008, 8 master's awarded. *Degree requirements:* For master's, thesis, oral exam; for doctorate, thesis/dissertation. *Entrance requirements:* Additional exam requirements/recommendations for international students: Required—TOEFL. *Application deadline:* For fall admission, 1/15 priority date for domestic students. Applications are processed on a rolling basis. Application fee: $50. *Expenses:* Tuition: Full-time $34,900; part-time $1091 per credit hour. Required fees: $30. *Financial support:* In 2008–09, fellowships with full and partial tuition reimbursements (averaging $11,850 per year), research assistantships with full and partial tuition reimbursements (averaging $11,850 per year), 3 teaching assistantships with full and partial tuition reimbursements (averaging $11,850 per year) were awarded; tuition waivers (full and partial) also available. *Faculty research:* American political history, comparative history, modern German and European history, Holocaust history, American family history. Total annual research expenditures: $90,000. *Unit head:* Dr. Drew McCoy, Chair, 508-793-7288. *Application contact:* Diane Fenner, Academic Secretary, 508-793-7288, Fax: 508-793-8816, E-mail: history@clarku.edu.

Clemson University, Graduate School, College of Architecture, Arts, and Humanities, Department of History, Clemson, SC 29634. Offers MA. Part-time programs available. *Faculty:* 23 full-time (8 women), 2 part-time/adjunct (0 women). *Students:* 18 full-time (6 women), 14 part-time (4 women); includes 1 minority (Asian American or Pacific Islander). Average age 31. 28 applicants, 54% accepted, 10 enrolled. In 2008, 11 master's awarded. *Degree requirements:* For master's, one foreign language, thesis. *Entrance requirements:* For master's, GRE General Test. Additional exam requirements/recommendations for international students: Required—TOEFL. *Application deadline:* For fall admission, 6/1 for domestic students, 4/15 for international students; for spring admission, 9/15 for international students. Application fee: $55. Full-time tuition and fees vary according to program. *Financial support:* In 2008–09, 1 research assistantship (averaging $10,000 per year), 15 teaching assistantships (averaging $10,100 per year) were awarded; career-related internships or fieldwork also available. Financial award application deadline: 2/15; financial award applicants required to submit FAFSA. *Faculty research:* American, European, British, and Third World history. Total annual research expenditures: $13,313. *Unit head:* Dr. Thomas Kuehn, Chair, 864-656-5361, Fax: 864-656-1015, E-mail: tjkuehn@clemson.edu. *Application contact:* Dr. Rod Andrew, Graduate Coordinator, 864-656-6706, Fax: 864-656-1015, E-mail: jrandre@clemson.edu.

Cleveland State University, College of Graduate Studies, College of Liberal Arts and Social Sciences, Department of History, Cleveland, OH 44115. Offers art history (MA); history (MA); museum studies (MA). Part-time and evening/weekend programs available. *Faculty:* 18 full-time (6 women), 10 part-time/adjunct (2 women). *Students:* 14 full-time (8 women), 17 part-time (8 women); includes 4 minority (all African Americans). Average age 34. 39 applicants, 51% accepted, 14 enrolled. In 2008, 20 master's awarded. *Degree requirements:* For master's, thesis optional. *Entrance requirements:* For master's, minimum GPA of 3.0, bachelor's degree in history. Additional exam requirements/recommendations for international students: Required—TOEFL (minimum score 525 paper-based; 197 computer-based). *Application deadline:* For fall admission, 7/15 priority date for domestic students. Applications are processed on a rolling basis. Application fee: $30. Electronic applications accepted. *Financial support:* In 2008–09, 7 students received support, including research assistantships with full tuition reimbursements available (averaging $8,600 per year); career-related internships or fieldwork and unspecified assistantships also available. *Faculty research:* African Diaspora, social history and the city, early modern Europe, local history. *Unit head:* Dr. Elizabeth A. Lehfeldt, Chairperson, 216-687-3920, Fax: 216-687-5592, E-mail: e.lehfeldt@csuohio.edu. *Application contact:* Dr. Robert S. Shelton, Graduate Director, 216-687-3927, E-mail: r.s.shelton@csuohio.edu.

The College at Brockport, State University of New York, School of Letters and Sciences, Department of History, Brockport, NY 14420-2997. Offers MA. Part-time and evening/weekend programs available. *Degree requirements:* For master's, thesis or alternative. *Entrance requirements:* For master's, GRE General Test (recommended), minimum GPA of 3.0, writing sample, letters of recommendation. Additional exam requirements/recommendations for international students: Required—TOEFL (minimum score 550 paper-based; 213 computer-based; 79 iBT). *Faculty research:* American history, women's history, European history, world history, cultural history.

College of Charleston, Graduate School, School of Humanities and Social Sciences, Program in History, Charleston, SC 29424-0001. Offers MA. Part-time and evening/weekend programs available. *Faculty:* 23 full-time (5 women), 2 part-time/adjunct (both women). *Students:* 22 full-time (13 women), 12 part-time (8 women); includes 3 minority (all African Americans). Average age 27. 29 applicants, 69% accepted, 15 enrolled. In 2008, 12 master's awarded. *Degree requirements:* For master's, comprehensive exam, thesis optional. *Entrance requirements:* For master's, GRE General Test or MAT, writing sample. Additional exam requirements/recommendations for international students: Required—TOEFL. *Application deadline:* For fall admission, 3/1 for domestic students; for spring admission, 10/15 for domestic students. Applications are processed on a rolling basis. Application fee: $45. Electronic applications accepted. *Expenses:* Tuition, area resident: Full-time $6624; part-time $368 per credit hour. Tuition, state resident: full-time $6624; part-time $368 per credit hour. Tuition, nonresident: full-time $16,074; part-time $893 per credit hour. Required fees: $30; $30 per course. One-time fee: $45. *Financial support:* In 2008–09, research assistantships (averaging $12,400 per year); career-related internships or fieldwork, Federal Work-Study, scholarships/grants, unspecified assistantships, and 2 graduate assistantships also available. Financial award application deadline: 6/1; financial award applicants required to submit FAFSA. *Faculty research:* Modern west Africa, labor history, Southern women's education, Native Americans, the Atlantic world. *Unit head:* Dr. William Scott Poole, Director, 843-953-4862, Fax: 843-953-6349, E-mail: poolews@cofc.edu. *Application contact:* Susan Hallatt, Director of Graduate Admissions, 843-953-5614, Fax: 843-953-1434, E-mail: hallatts@cofc.edu.

The College of Saint Rose, Graduate Studies, School of Arts and Humanities, Program in History/Political Science, Albany, NY 12203-1419. Offers MA. Part-time and evening/weekend programs available. *Degree requirements:* For master's, final paper/project, thesis or comprehensive exam. *Entrance requirements:* For master's, minimum undergraduate GPA of 3.0, 12 undergraduate credits in US history and/or political science. Additional exam requirements/recommendations for international students: Required—TOEFL (minimum score 550 paper-based; 213 computer-based). Electronic applications accepted.

College of Staten Island of the City University of New York, Graduate Programs, Program in History, Staten Island, NY 10314-6600. Offers MA. Part-time and evening/weekend programs available. *Faculty:* 4 full-time (1 woman). *Students:* 17 part-time (11 women); includes 2 minority (both Hispanic Americans), 1 international. Average age 33. 16 applicants, 88% accepted, 9 enrolled. In 2008, 2 master's awarded. *Degree requirements:* For master's, thesis. *Entrance requirements:* For master's, minimum GPA of 3.0 overall and in undergraduate history courses, 2 academic letters of recommendation, letter explaining interest. Additional exam requirements/recommendations for international students: Required—TOEFL (minimum score 550 paper-based; 213 computer-based; 79 iBT). *Application deadline:* Applications are processed on a rolling basis. Application fee: $125. Electronic applications accepted. *Expenses:* Tuition, area resident: Full-time $6400; part-time $270 per credit. Tuition, nonresident: full-time $12,000; part-time $500 per credit. Required fees: $378; $113 per semester. *Financial support:* Career-related internships or fieldwork, Federal Work-Study, and scholarships/grants available. Support available to part-time students. Financial award application deadline: 4/1; financial award applicants required to submit CSS PROFILE or FAFSA. *Unit head:* Dr. Catherine J. Lavender, PhD, Interim Coordinator, 718-982-2870 Ext. 2869, Fax: 718-982-2864, E-mail: historymakers@mail.csi.cuny.edu. *Application contact:* Sasha Spence, Assistant Director of Graduate Recruitment and Admissions, 718-982-2699, Fax: 718-982-2500, E-mail: spence@mail.csi.cuny.edu.

The College of William and Mary, Faculty of Arts and Sciences, Lyon Gardiner Tyler Department of History, Williamsburg, VA 23187-8795. Offers MA, PhD. Terminal master's awarded for partial completion of doctoral program. *Degree requirements:* For master's, one foreign language, comprehensive exam, thesis; for doctorate, one foreign language, comprehensive exam, thesis/dissertation. *Entrance requirements:* For master's and doctorate, GRE General Test, minimum GPA of 3.0. Additional exam requirements/recommendations for international students: Required—TOEFL. Electronic applications accepted. *Expenses:* Tuition, state resident: full-time $6400; part-time $300 per credit hour. Tuition, nonresident: full-time $19,720; part-time $800 per credit hour. International tuition: $19,720 full-time. Required fees: $3860. *Faculty research:* Early American, U.S., and comparative history.

Colorado State University, Graduate School, College of Liberal Arts, Department of History, Fort Collins, CO 80523-1776. Offers MA. Part-time programs available. *Faculty:* 20 full-time (9 women). *Students:* 36 full-time (21 women), 11 part-time (3 women); includes 6 minority (1 American Indian/Alaska Native, 5 Hispanic Americans), 1 international. Average age 29. 48 applicants, 46% accepted, 14 enrolled. In 2008, 12 master's awarded. *Degree requirements:* For master's, variable foreign language requirement, comprehensive exam (for some programs), thesis (for some programs), written and oral exams. *Entrance requirements:* For master's, GRE General Test, minimum GPA of 3.0, minimum 21 credits in history, personal statement, letters of recommendation. Additional exam requirements/recommendations for international students: Required—TOEFL. *Application deadline:* For fall admission, 2/1 priority date for domestic and international students; for spring admission, 11/1 for domestic and international students. Application fee: $50. Electronic applications accepted. *Expenses:* Tuition, area resident: Full-time $5620; part-time $312.25 per credit. Tuition, state resident: full-time $5620; part-time $312.25 per credit. Tuition, nonresident: full-time $17,253; part-time $958.50 per credit. Required fees: $1449.56; $82.35 per credit. *Financial support:* In 2008–09, 22 students received support, including 22 teaching assistantships with tuition reimbursements available (averaging $11,492 per year); fellowships, career-related internships or fieldwork, Federal Work-Study, institutionally sponsored loans, scholarships/grants, traineeships, and unspecified assistantships also available. Financial award application deadline: 3/1; financial award applicants required to submit FAFSA. *Faculty research:* U.S. history, world history, gender history, European history, environmental history. Total annual research expenditures: $44,036. *Unit head:* Dr. Douglas Yarrington, Professor and Chair, 970-491-6334, Fax: 970-491-2941, E-mail: doug.yarrington@colostate.edu. *Application contact:* Janet Ore, Graduate Studies Chair, 970-491-6334, Fax: 970-491-2941, E-mail: janet.ore@colostate.edu.

Columbia University, Graduate School of Arts and Sciences, Division of Social Sciences, Department of History, New York, NY 10027. Offers American history (M Phil, MA, PhD); history (M Phil, MA, PhD); JD/MA; JD/PhD. Part-time programs available. *Degree requirements:* For master's, one foreign language, thesis; for doctorate, variable foreign language requirement, thesis/dissertation. *Entrance requirements:* For master's and doctorate, GRE General Test, writing sample. Additional exam requirements/recommendations for international students: Required—TOEFL.

Concordia University, School of Graduate Studies, Faculty of Arts and Science, Department of History, Montréal, QC H3G 1M8, Canada. Offers MA, PhD. *Degree requirements:* For master's, one foreign language, thesis optional; for doctorate, one foreign language, comprehensive exam, thesis/dissertation. *Entrance requirements:* For master's, honors degree in history or equivalent. *Faculty research:* Canadian history, European social history, Canadian-American relations.

Converse College, School of Education and Graduate Studies, Program in Liberal Arts, Spartanburg, SC 29302-0006. Offers English (MLA); history (MLA); political science (MLA). *Degree requirements:* For master's, capstone paper. *Entrance requirements:* For master's, minimum GPA of 3.0, 2 recommendations.

Cornell University, Graduate School, Graduate Fields of Arts and Sciences, Field of History, Ithaca, NY 14853-0001. Offers African history (MA, PhD); American history (MA, PhD); ancient history (MA, PhD); early modern European history (MA, PhD); English history (MA, PhD); French history (MA, PhD); German history (MA, PhD); history of science (MA, PhD); Latin American history (MA, PhD); medieval Chinese history (MA, PhD); medieval history (MA, PhD); modern Chinese history (MA, PhD); modern European history (MA, PhD); modern Japanese history (MA, PhD); premodern Islamic history (MA, PhD); premodern Japanese history (MA, PhD); Renaissance history (MA, PhD); Russian history (MA, PhD); Southeast Asian history (MA, PhD). *Faculty:* 54 full-time (14 women). *Students:* 65 full-time (35 women); includes 12 minority (4 African Americans, 3 Asian Americans or Pacific Islanders, 5 Hispanic Americans), 19 international. Average age 31. 205 applicants, 8% accepted, 11 enrolled. In 2008, 12 master's, 6 doctorates awarded. Terminal master's awarded for partial completion of doctoral program. *Degree requirements:* For master's, thesis; for doctorate, 2 foreign languages, comprehensive exam, thesis/dissertation, 1 year of teaching experience. *Entrance requirements:* For master's and doctorate, GRE General Test, writing sample, 3 letters of recommendation. Additional exam requirements/recommendations for international students: Required—TOEFL (minimum score 550 paper-based; 213 computer-based; 77 iBT). *Application deadline:* For fall admission, 1/15 for domestic students. Application fee: $70. Electronic applications accepted. *Expenses:* Tuition: Full-time $29,500. Required fees: $70. Full-time tuition and fees vary according to degree level, program and student level. *Financial support:* In 2008–09, 54 students received support, including 27 fellowships with full tuition reimbursements available, 3 research assistantships with full tuition reimbursements available, 24 teaching assistantships

History

Cornell University (continued)

with full tuition reimbursements available; institutionally sponsored loans, scholarships/grants, health care benefits, tuition waivers (full and partial), and unspecified assistantships also available. Financial award applicants required to submit FAFSA. *Unit head:* Director of Graduate Studies, 607-255-6738, Fax: 607-255-0469. *Application contact:* Graduate Field Assistant, 607-255-6738, Fax: 607-255-0469, E-mail: history_grad_info@cornell.edu.

Dalhousie University, Faculty of Arts and Social Science, Department of History, Halifax, NS B3H 4R2, Canada. Offers MA, PhD. *Entrance requirements:* Additional exam requirements/recommendations for international students: Required—TOEFL, IELTS, 1 of 5 approved tests: TOEFL, IELTS, CANTEST, CAEL, Michigan English Language Assessment Battery. *Application deadline:* For fall admission, 6/1 for domestic students, 4/1 for international students; for winter admission, 10/31 for domestic students, 8/31 for international students; for spring admission, 2/28 for domestic students, 12/31 for international students. Application fee: $70. Electronic applications accepted. *Financial support:* Career-related internships or fieldwork, scholarships/grants, and health care benefits available. *Faculty research:* African, British, Russian, Canadian and Medieval history. *Unit head:* Dr. Chris Bell, Graduate Coordinator, 902-494-3586, Fax: 902-494-3349, E-mail: gradhist@dal.ca. *Application contact:* Valerie Peck, Graduate Administrator, 902-494-2011, Fax: 902-494-3349, E-mail: gradhist@dal.ca.

DePaul University, College of Liberal Arts and Sciences, Department of History, Chicago, IL 60614. Offers MA. Part-time and evening/weekend programs available. *Faculty:* 28 full-time (11 women), 7 part-time/adjunct (3 women). *Students:* 11 full-time (6 women), 15 part-time (5 women); includes 1 minority (Hispanic American). Average age 32. In 2008, 6 master's awarded. *Degree requirements:* For master's, thesis optional. *Entrance requirements:* For master's, GRE General Test, bachelor's degree in social science or history, or history minor. Additional exam requirements/recommendations for international students: Required—TOEFL. *Application deadline:* 4/1 priority date for domestic and international students. Applications are processed on a rolling basis. Application fee: $25. Electronic applications accepted. *Financial support:* In 2008–09, 3 students received support, including fellowships (averaging $7,000 per year); career-related internships or fieldwork, scholarships/grants, and tuition waivers (full) also available. Financial award application deadline: 5/1. *Faculty research:* U.S., Europe, Latin America, Asia, Africa. *Unit head:* Dr. Warren C. Schultz, Chairperson, 773-325-1561, Fax: 773-325-4764, E-mail: wschultz@depaul.edu. *Application contact:* Dr. Valentina K. Tikoff, Graduate Director, 773-325-1570, Fax: 773-325-4764, E-mail: vtikoff@depaul.edu.

Drake University, School of Education, Department of Teaching and Learning, Program in Secondary Education, Des Moines, IA 50311-4516. Offers art (MAT); biology (MAT); business (MAT); chemistry (MAT); English (MAT); general science (MAT); history-American (MAT); history-world (MAT); journalism (MAT); mathematics (MAT); physical science (MAT); physics (MAT); sociology (MAT); speech (MAT); speech communication (MAT); theatre (MAT). Part-time programs available. *Degree requirements:* For master's, comprehensive exam, thesis (for some programs), internships (for some programs). *Entrance requirements:* For master's, GRE General Test, MAT, or Drake Writing Assessment, resumé, 2 letters of recommendation. Additional exam requirements/recommendations for international students: Required—TOEFL (minimum score 550 paper-based; 213 computer-based). Electronic applications accepted. *Faculty research:* Counseling and rehabilitation, behavioral supports, inquiry-based science methods, teacher quality enhancement.

Drew University, Caspersen School of Graduate Studies, Program in Modern History and Literature, Madison, NJ 07940-1493. Offers MA, PhD. Part-time and evening/weekend programs available. Terminal master's awarded for partial completion of doctoral program. *Degree requirements:* For master's, one foreign language, thesis; for doctorate, 2 foreign languages, comprehensive exam, thesis/dissertation. *Entrance requirements:* For master's and doctorate, GRE General Test. *Faculty research:* History of the book, modern American history/European history, cultural and intellectual history, eighteenth- to twentieth-century history and literature, history of science.

Duke University, Graduate School, Department of History, Durham, NC 27708. Offers history (AM, PhD); Latin American studies (PhD); JD/AM; MD/PhD. *Degree requirements:* For doctorate, 2 foreign languages, thesis/dissertation. *Entrance requirements:* For doctorate, GRE General Test. Additional exam requirements/recommendations for international students: Required—TOEFL (minimum score 550 paper-based; 213 computer-based; 83 iBT), IELTS (minimum score 7). Electronic applications accepted.

Duquesne University, Graduate School of Liberal Arts, Department of History, Pittsburgh, PA 15282-0001. Offers archival, museum, and editing studies (MA); history (MA). Part-time and evening/weekend programs available. *Faculty:* 6 full-time (1 woman), 3 part-time/adjunct (1 woman). *Students:* 35 full-time (20 women), 8 part-time (5 women). Average age 26. 23 applicants, 96% accepted, 14 enrolled. In 2008, 15 master's awarded. *Degree requirements:* For master's, comprehensive exam (for some programs), thesis optional. *Entrance requirements:* For master's, GRE General Test, writing sample. Additional exam requirements/recommendations for international students: Required—TOEFL. *Application deadline:* For fall admission, 8/15 for domestic students, 5/1 for international students; for spring admission, 11/1 priority date for domestic students. Applications are processed on a rolling basis. Application fee: $50. Electronic applications accepted. *Expenses:* Tuition: Part-time $819 per credit. Required fees: $78 per credit. Tuition and fees vary according to course load. *Financial support:* In 2008–09, 4 research assistantships with full tuition reimbursements (averaging $4,800 per year) were awarded; career-related internships or fieldwork, Federal Work-Study, scholarships/grants, tuition waivers (full and partial), and unspecified assistantships also available. Support available to part-time students. Financial award application deadline: 5/1. *Faculty research:* American studies, immigration history, local social history, applied history, Eastern European history. *Unit head:* Dr. Holly Mayer, Chair, 412-396-6470. *Application contact:* Linda L. Rendulic, Assistant to the Dean, 412-396-6400, Fax: 412-396-5265, E-mail: rendulic@duq.edu.

East Carolina University, Graduate School, Thomas Harriot College of Arts and Sciences, Department of History, Greenville, NC 27858-4353. Offers American history (MA); European history (MA); maritime history (MA). Part-time and evening/weekend programs available. *Degree requirements:* For master's, one foreign language, comprehensive exam, thesis. *Entrance requirements:* For master's, GRE General Test, GRE Subject Test. Additional exam requirements/recommendations for international students: Required—TOEFL.

Eastern Illinois University, Graduate School, College of Arts and Humanities, Department of History, Charleston, IL 61920-3099. Offers historical administration (MA); history (MA).

Eastern Kentucky University, The Graduate School, College of Arts and Sciences, Department of History, Richmond, KY 40475-3102. Offers MA. Part-time programs available. *Degree requirements:* For master's, comprehensive exam, thesis optional. *Entrance requirements:* For master's, GRE General Test, GRE Subject Test, minimum GPA of 2.5. *Faculty research:* Twentieth-century U.S. history, Kentucky history, British history, world history, Eastern Europe.

Eastern Michigan University, Graduate School, College of Arts and Sciences, Department of History and Philosophy, Program in History, Ypsilanti, MI 48197. Offers history (MA); state and local history (Graduate Certificate). Part-time and evening/weekend programs available. Post-baccalaureate distance learning degree programs offered (minimal on-campus study). *Degree requirements:* For master's, thesis optional. *Entrance requirements:* Additional exam requirements/recommendations for international students: Required—TOEFL.

Eastern Washington University, Graduate Studies, College of Social and Behavioral Sciences, Department of History, Cheney, WA 99004-2431. Offers MA. *Degree requirements:* For master's, comprehensive exam, thesis optional. *Entrance requirements:* For master's, minimum GPA of 3.0.

East Stroudsburg University of Pennsylvania, Graduate School, College of Arts and Sciences, Department of History, East Stroudsburg, PA 18301-2999. Offers M Ed, MA. Part-time and evening/weekend programs available. *Faculty:* 5 full-time (0 women). *Students:* 15 full-time (6 women), 21 part-time (10 women); includes 3 minority (1 African American, 2 Hispanic Americans). Average age 33. In 2008, 6 master's awarded. *Degree requirements:* For master's, variable foreign language requirement, comprehensive exam, thesis (for some programs). *Entrance requirements:* For master's, Commonwealth of Pennsylvania Department of Education Certification Requirements (M Ed). Additional exam requirements/recommendations for international students: Required—TOEFL (minimum score 560 paper-based; 220 computer-based; 83 iBT). *Application deadline:* For fall admission, 7/31 priority date for domestic students, 5/1 priority date for international students; for spring admission, 11/30 for domestic students, 10/1 for international students. Applications are processed on a rolling basis. Application fee: $50. *Expenses:* Tuition, state resident: full-time $6430; part-time $357 per credit. Tuition, nonresident: full-time $10,288; part-time $572 per credit. *Financial support:* In 2008–09, 6 research assistantships with full and partial tuition reimbursements (averaging $1,877 per year) were awarded; Federal Work-Study and institutionally sponsored loans also available. Financial award application deadline: 3/1; financial award applicants required to submit FAFSA. *Unit head:* Dr. Lawrence Squeri, Graduate Coordinator, 570-422-3284, Fax: 570-422-3506, E-mail: lsqueri@po-box.esu.edu. *Application contact:* Kevin Quintero, Graduate Admissions Coordinator, 570-422-3890, Fax: 570-422-2711, E-mail: kquintero@po-box.esu.edu.

East Tennessee State University, School of Graduate Studies, College of Arts and Sciences, Department of History, Johnson City, TN 37614. Offers MA. Part-time and evening/weekend programs available. *Degree requirements:* For master's, comprehensive exam, thesis or alternative. *Entrance requirements:* For master's, GRE, bachelor's degree in history, minimum GPA of 3.0. Additional exam requirements/recommendations for international students: Required—TOEFL (minimum score 550 paper-based; 213 computer-based). *Faculty research:* Post-World War II German occupation, biographies of Eleanor Copenhaver Anderson and Harry M. Candill, the Miss America Pageant, encyclopedia of colonialism, the new Georgia campaign in the Pacific war.

Emory & Henry College, Graduate Programs, Emory, VA 24327-0947. Offers American history (MA Ed); professional studies (M Ed); reading specialist (MA Ed). Part-time and evening/weekend programs available. *Entrance requirements:* For master's, GRE or PRAXIS I, recommendations, writing sample, official transcripts.

Emory University, Graduate School of Arts and Sciences, Department of History, Atlanta, GA 30322-1100. Offers PhD. *Degree requirements:* For doctorate, 2 foreign languages, comprehensive exam, thesis/dissertation. *Entrance requirements:* For doctorate, GRE General Test, minimum GPA of 3.0. Electronic applications accepted. *Faculty research:* U.S., modern Europe, early modern Europe, medieval Europe, Latin America, Africa.

Emporia State University, School of Graduate Studies, College of Liberal Arts and Sciences, Department of Social Sciences, Program in History, Emporia, KS 66801-5087. Offers American history (MA); world history (MA). *Students:* 4 full-time (1 woman), 19 part-time (5 women). 5 applicants, 60% accepted, 3 enrolled. In 2008, 8 master's awarded. *Degree requirements:* For master's, comprehensive exam or thesis. *Entrance requirements:* For master's, 12 credit hours in history, minimum undergraduate GPA of 2.5, writing sample. Additional exam requirements/recommendations for international students: Required—TOEFL. *Application deadline:* For fall admission, 8/15 priority date for domestic students. Applications are processed on a rolling basis. Application fee: $30 ($75 for international students). Electronic applications accepted. *Expenses:* Tuition, area resident: Full-time $3976; part-time $166 per credit hour. Tuition, state resident: full-time $3976; part-time $166 per credit hour. Tuition, nonresident: full-time $12,028; part-time $501 per credit hour. Required fees: $51 per credit hour. Tuition and fees vary according to campus/location. *Financial support:* Federal Work-Study, institutionally sponsored loans, health care benefits, and unspecified assistantships available. Financial award application deadline: 3/15; financial award applicants required to submit FAFSA. *Faculty research:* Great Plains history. *Unit head:* Dr. Ellen Hansen, Chair, 620-341-5461, E-mail: ehansen@emporia.edu. *Application contact:* Dr. Deborah Gerish, Assistant Professor, 620-341-5579, E-mail: dgerish@emporia.edu.

Fairleigh Dickinson University, Metropolitan Campus, University College: Arts, Sciences, and Professional Studies, School of History, Political and International Studies, Program in History, Teaneck, NJ 07666-1914. Offers MA. *Students:* 2 part-time (both women). Average age 25. 3 applicants, 33% accepted, 0 enrolled. *Application deadline:* Applications are processed on a rolling basis. Application fee: $40. *Application contact:* Susan Brooman, University Director of Graduate Admissions, 201-692-2554, Fax: 201-692-2560, E-mail: globaleducation@fdu.edu.

Fayetteville State University, Graduate School, Department of Geography, History and Political Science, Fayetteville, NC 28301-4298. Offers history (MA); political science (MA). Part-time and evening/weekend programs available. *Degree requirements:* For master's, comprehensive exam, internship. *Entrance requirements:* For master's, GRE General Test. Electronic applications accepted.

Fitchburg State College, Division of Graduate and Continuing Education, Programs in History and Teaching History (Secondary Level), Fitchburg, MA 01420-2697. Offers MA, MAT, Certificate. *Accreditation:* NCATE. Part-time and evening/weekend programs available. *Students:* 1 full-time (0 women), 20 part-time (8 women); includes 1 minority (Hispanic American). Average age 36. 7 applicants, 100% accepted, 7 enrolled. In 2008, 4 master's awarded. *Entrance requirements:* For master's, GRE General Test or MAT, appropriate bachelor's degree, letters of recommendation, resumé. Additional exam requirements/recommendations for international students: Required—TOEFL (minimum score 550 paper-based; 213 computer-based; 79 iBT). *Application deadline:* Applications are processed on a rolling basis. Application fee: $25 ($50 for international students). *Expenses:* Tuition, state resident: full-time $3600; part-time $150 per credit. Tuition, nonresident: full-time $3600; part-time $150 per credit. Required fees: $109 per credit. *Financial support:* In 2008–09, research assistantships with partial tuition reimbursements (averaging $5,500 per year); Federal Work-Study, scholarships/grants, and unspecified assistantships also available. Support available to part-time students. Financial award application deadline: 3/1; financial award applicants required to submit FAFSA. *Unit head:* Dr. Laura Baker, Chair, 978-665-3379, Fax: 978-665-3658, E-mail: gce@fsc.edu. *Application contact:* Director of Admissions, 978-665-3144, Fax: 978-665-4540, E-mail: admissions@fsc.edu.

Florida Agricultural and Mechanical University, Division of Graduate Studies, Research, and Continuing Education, College of Arts and Sciences, Division of History and Political Sciences, Program in Applied Social Science, Tallahassee, FL 32307-3200. Offers African American history (MASS); criminal justice (MASS); economics (MASS); history (MASS); political science (MASS); public administration (MASS); public management (MASS); social work (MASS); sociology (MASS). Part-time programs available. *Degree requirements:* For master's, thesis optional. *Entrance requirements:* For master's, GRE General Test, minimum GPA of 3.0. *Faculty research:* Southern history, black history, election trends, presidential history.

Florida Atlantic University, Dorothy F. Schmidt College of Arts and Letters, Department of History, Boca Raton, FL 33431-0991. Offers environmental studies (Certificate); history (MA). Part-time programs available. *Faculty:* 19 full-time (8 women), 1 part-time/adjunct (0 women). *Students:* 13 full-time (6 women), 15 part-time (3 women); includes 4 minority (all Hispanic Americans). Average age 33. 28 applicants, 54% accepted, 8 enrolled. In 2008, 7 master's awarded. *Degree requirements:* For master's, one foreign language, thesis optional. *Entrance requirements:* For master's, GRE General Test, minimum GPA of 3.0. *Application deadline:* For fall admission, 6/1 priority date for domestic students, 2/15 for international students; for spring admission, 10/15 for domestic students, 8/15 for international students. Applications are processed on a rolling basis. Application fee: $30. Electronic applications accepted. *Expenses:* Tuition, state resident: full-time $4867; part-time $270.40 per credit hour. Tuition, nonresident: full-time $16,486; part-time $915.87 per credit hour. *Financial support:* Fellowships, research assistantships, teaching assistantships with tuition reimbursements, career-related internships or fieldwork, Federal Work-Study, and tuition waivers (partial) available. Support available to part-time students. Financial award application deadline: 3/1. *Faculty research:* Twentieth century America, U.S. urban history, Florida history, history of socialism, Latin America. *Unit head:* Dr. Patricia Kollander, Chair, 561-297-3841, Fax: 561-297-2704, E-mail: kollande@fau.edu. *Application contact:* Ben Lowe, Director of Graduate Programs, 561-297-3846, Fax: 561-297-2704, E-mail: bplowe@fau.edu.

Florida Gulf Coast University, College of Arts and Sciences, Program in History, Fort Myers, FL 33965-6565. Offers MA. Part-time and evening/weekend programs available. *Faculty:* 155 full-time (65 women), 123 part-time/adjunct (47 women). *Students:* 10 full-time (1 woman), 7 part-time (2 women); includes 2 minority (both Hispanic Americans). Average age 40. 15 applicants, 73% accepted, 9 enrolled. *Entrance requirements:* Additional exam requirements/recommendations for international students: Required—TOEFL (minimum score 550 paper-based; 213 computer-based). *Application deadline:* For fall admission, 2/15 priority date for domestic students; for spring admission, 10/1 for domestic students. Applications are processed on a rolling basis. Electronic applications accepted. *Unit head:* Eric Strahorn, Head, 239-590-7214, E-mail: estraho@fgcu.edu. *Application contact:* Patricia Rice, Executive Secretary, 239-590-7196, Fax: 239-590-7200, E-mail: price@fgcu.edu.

Florida International University, College of Arts and Sciences, Department of History, Miami, FL 33199. Offers MA, PhD. Part-time and evening/weekend programs available. *Degree requirements:* For master's, thesis optional; for doctorate, comprehensive exam, thesis/dissertation. *Entrance requirements:* For master's, GRE General Test, minimum 3.0 average, 2 letters of recommendation; for doctorate, GRE General Test, minimum GPA of 3.25, 2 letters of recommendation. Additional exam requirements/recommendations for international students: Required—TOEFL. *Faculty research:* European social history, American culture, Latin American culture and social history, Holocaust education.

Florida State University, Graduate Studies, College of Arts and Sciences, Department of History, Tallahassee, FL 32306. Offers historical administration (MA); history (MA, PhD). Part-time programs available. *Degree requirements:* For master's, one foreign language, comprehensive exam (for some programs), thesis (for some programs), internships; for doctorate, one foreign language, comprehensive exam, thesis/dissertation. *Entrance requirements:* For master's, GRE General Test, minimum GPA of 3.3, minimum 18 hours of course work in history; for doctorate, GRE General Test, minimum GPA of 3.3 (undergraduate), 3.65 (graduate). Additional exam requirements/recommendations for international students: Required—TOEFL (minimum score 550 paper-based; 213 computer-based; 80 iBT). Electronic applications accepted. *Faculty research:* Southern and Caribbean studies, Napoleon and the French Revolution, modern Europe, Latin America, U.S. intellectual and cultural history.

Fordham University, Graduate School of Arts and Sciences, Department of History, New York, NY 10458. Offers MA, PhD. Part-time and evening/weekend programs available. Terminal master's awarded for partial completion of doctoral program. *Degree requirements:* For master's, one foreign language, thesis optional; for doctorate, 2 foreign languages, comprehensive exam, thesis/dissertation. *Entrance requirements:* For master's and doctorate, GRE General Test. Additional exam requirements/recommendations for international students: Required—TOEFL (minimum score 650 paper-based; 280 computer-based). Electronic applications accepted.

Fort Hays State University, Graduate School, College of Arts and Sciences, Department of History, Hays, KS 67601-4099. Offers MA. *Degree requirements:* For master's, comprehensive exam, thesis or alternative. *Entrance requirements:* For master's, minimum undergraduate GPA of 3.0. Additional exam requirements/recommendations for international students: Required—TOEFL (minimum score 550 paper-based; 213 computer-based). Electronic applications accepted. *Faculty research:* Seventeenth century English legal history, Native American history, immigration history, Volga German settlement.

George Mason University, College of Humanities and Social Sciences, Department of History and Art History, Program in History, Fairfax, VA 22030. Offers MA, PhD. Evening/weekend programs available. *Degree requirements:* For master's, comprehensive exam; for doctorate, comprehensive exam, thesis/dissertation. *Entrance requirements:* For master's, GRE, 2 letters of recommendation, resumé; for doctorate, GRE, 3 letters of recommendation.

George Mason University, Graduate School of Education, Programs in Curriculum and Instruction, Fairfax, VA 22030. Offers early childhood education (M Ed); English as a second language (M Ed); gifted child education (M Ed); history (M Ed); instructional technology (M Ed); library media (M Ed); literacy and reading (M Ed); mathematics (M Ed); physical education (M Ed); science (M Ed); secondary education (M Ed); special education (M Ed, Graduate Certificate); teacher leadership (M Ed). Part-time and evening/weekend programs available. *Entrance requirements:* For master's, minimum GPA of 3.0 in last 60 hours. Electronic applications accepted.

Georgetown University, Graduate School of Arts and Sciences, Department of History, Washington, DC 20057-1035. Offers MA, PhD, MA/PhD, MS/MA. *Degree requirements:* For doctorate, 2 foreign languages, comprehensive exam, thesis/dissertation. *Entrance requirements:* For master's and doctorate, GRE General Test. Additional exam requirements/recommendations for international students: Required—TOEFL.

Georgetown University, Graduate School of Arts and Sciences, School of Continuing Studies, Washington, DC 20057. Offers American studies (MALS); Catholic studies (MALS); classical civilizations (MALS); ethics and the professions (MALS); human resources management (MPS); humanities (MALS); individualized study (MALS); international affairs (MALS); Islam and Muslim-Christian relations (MALS); journalism (MPS); liberal studies (DLS); literature and society (MALS); medieval and early modern European studies (MALS); public relations (MPS); real estate (MPS); religious studies (MALS); social and public policy (MALS); sports industry management (MPS); the theory and practice of American democracy (MALS); visual culture (MALS). *Entrance requirements:* Additional exam requirements/recommendations for international students: Required—TOEFL.

The George Washington University, Columbian College of Arts and Sciences, Department of History, Washington, DC 20052. Offers MA, PhD. Part-time and evening/weekend programs available. *Faculty:* 21 full-time (9 women), 18 part-time/adjunct (5 women). *Students:* 31 full-time (10 women), 42 part-time (20 women); includes 7 minority (1 African American, 2 American Indian/Alaska Native, 4 Asian Americans or Pacific Islanders), 2 international. Average age 33. 183 applicants, 34% accepted, 14 enrolled. In 2008, 17 master's, 7 doctorates awarded. Terminal master's awarded for partial completion of doctoral program. *Degree requirements:* For master's, one foreign language, comprehensive exam, thesis or alternative; for doctorate, 2 foreign languages, thesis/dissertation, general exam. *Entrance requirements:* For master's and doctorate, GRE General Test, minimum GPA of 3.0. Additional exam requirements/recommendations for international students: Required—TOEFL (minimum score 550 paper-based; 213 computer-based; 80 iBT). *Application deadline:* For fall admission, 1/15 priority date for domestic and international students; for spring admission, 10/1 priority date for domestic students, 9/1 priority date for international students. Applications are processed on a rolling basis. Application fee: $60. Electronic applications accepted. *Financial support:* In 2008–09, 28 students received support; fellowships with full tuition reimbursements available, teaching assistantships with tuition reimbursements available, career-related internships or fieldwork, Federal Work-Study, and tuition waivers available. Financial award application deadline: 1/15. *Unit head:* Tyler G. Anbinder, Chair, 202-994-6470, E-mail: anbinder@gwu.edu. *Application contact:* Information Contact, 202-994-6230, Fax: 202-994-6231, E-mail: history@www.gwu.edu.

Georgia College & State University, Graduate School, School of Liberal Arts and Sciences, Department of History and Geography, Program in History, Milledgeville, GA 31061. Offers MA.

Georgia Southern University, Jack N. Averitt College of Graduate Studies, College of Liberal Arts and Social Sciences, Department of History, Statesboro, GA 30460. Offers MA. Part-time programs available. *Students:* 17 full-time (8 women), 7 part-time (1 woman); includes 2 minority (both African Americans). Average age 31. 13 applicants, 92% accepted, 7 enrolled. In 2008, 5 master's awarded. *Degree requirements:* For master's, one foreign language, thesis optional, terminal exams. *Entrance requirements:* For master's, GRE General Test, minimum GPA of 3.0, undergraduate major in history or equivalent, letters of reference. Additional exam requirements/recommendations for international students: Required—TOEFL (minimum score 550 paper-based; 213 computer-based; 80 iBT). *Application deadline:* For fall admission, 3/1 priority date for domestic and international students; for spring admission, 10/1 priority date for domestic students, 10/1 for international students. Applications are processed on a rolling basis. Application fee: $50. Electronic applications accepted. *Expenses:* Tuition, area resident: Full-time $3840; part-time $160 per semester hour. Tuition, state resident: full-time $3840; part-time $160 per semester hour. Tuition, nonresident: full-time $15,336; part-time $639 per semester hour. Required fees: $1152. *Financial support:* In 2008–09, 17 students received support, including research assistantships with partial tuition reimbursements available (averaging $6,850 per year); teaching assistantships with partial tuition reimbursements available (averaging $6,850 per year); career-related internships or fieldwork, Federal Work-Study, scholarships/grants, tuition waivers (partial), and unspecified assistantships also available. Support available to part-time students. Financial award application deadline: 4/15; financial award applicants required to submit FAFSA. *Faculty research:* Women's/gender history, American South, Europe, history of religion. *Unit head:* Dr. Sandra Peacock, Chair, 912-478-5586, Fax: 912-478-0377, E-mail: speacock@georgiasouthern.edu. *Application contact:* 912-478-5384, Fax: 912-478-0740, E-mail: gradadmissions@georgiasouthern.edu.

Georgia State University, College of Arts and Sciences, Department of History, Program in History, Atlanta, GA 30303-3083. Offers MA, PhD. Part-time and evening/weekend programs available. *Degree requirements:* For master's, one foreign language, thesis, exam; for doctorate, 2 foreign languages, thesis/dissertation, exam. *Entrance requirements:* For master's, GRE General Test; for doctorate, GRE General Test, sample of written work. Additional exam requirements/recommendations for international students: Required—TOEFL. Electronic applications accepted. *Faculty research:* World, U.S. South, cultural history, public history, labor.

Graduate School and University Center of the City University of New York, Graduate Studies, Program in History, New York, NY 10016-4039. Offers PhD. *Degree requirements:* For doctorate, one foreign language, thesis/dissertation. *Entrance requirements:* For doctorate, GRE General Test, writing sample (15 pages). Additional exam requirements/recommendations for international students: Required—TOEFL. Electronic applications accepted.

Hardin-Simmons University, Graduate School, Cynthia Ann Parker College of Liberal Arts, Department of History, Abilene, TX 79698-0001. Offers MA. Part-time programs available. *Faculty:* 5 full-time (2 women). *Students:* 6 part-time (2 women). Average age 32. 4 applicants, 25% accepted, 0 enrolled. In 2008, 1 master's awarded. *Degree requirements:* For master's, one foreign language, comprehensive exam, thesis or alternative. *Entrance requirements:* For master's, GRE, minimum undergraduate GPA of 3.0 in history, 2.7 overall; 18 upper-level hours of course work in history; letters of recommendation; resumé; writing sample. Additional exam requirements/recommendations for international students: Required—TOEFL (minimum score 550 paper-based; 213 computer-based; 75 iBT). *Application deadline:* For fall admission, 8/15 priority date for domestic students, 4/1 for international students; for spring admission, 1/5 priority date for domestic students, 9/1 for international students. Applications are processed on a rolling basis. Application fee: $50. *Expenses:* Tuition: Full-time $10,620; part-time $590 per credit hour. Required fees: $590; $110 per semester. Tuition and fees vary according to course load and degree level. *Financial support:* In 2008–09, 4 students received support; fellowships, scholarships/grants available. Support available to part-time students. Financial award application deadline: 6/30; financial award applicants required to submit FAFSA. *Faculty research:* Vietnam, diplomatic history, Texas politics, Mexico and NAFTA, classical warfare. *Unit head:* Dr. Mark Beasley, Program Director, 325-670-1279, Fax: 325-670-1526, E-mail: mbeasley@hsutx.edu. *Application contact:* Dr. Gary Stanlake, Dean of Graduate Studies, 325-670-1298, Fax: 325-670-1564, E-mail: gradoff@hsutx.edu.

Harvard University, Graduate School of Arts and Sciences, Department of History, Cambridge, MA 02138. Offers African history (PhD); American history (PhD); ancient, medieval, early modern, and modern Europe (PhD), including Central Europe, Russia, Southeastern Europe, Western Europe; diplomatic history (PhD); East Asian history (PhD); economic and social history (PhD); intellectual history (PhD); Latin American history (PhD); Near Eastern history (PhD); oceanic history (PhD). *Degree requirements:* For doctorate, variable foreign language requirement, thesis/dissertation, oral general exam. *Entrance requirements:* For doctorate, GRE General Test, proficiency in 2 languages. Additional exam requirements/recommendations for international students: Required—TOEFL. *Expenses:* Tuition: Full-time $32,556. Required fees: $1426. Full-time tuition and fees vary according to program and student level.

High Point University, Norcross Graduate School, High Point, NC 27262-3598. Offers business administration (MBA); educational leadership (M Ed); elementary education (M Ed); history (MA); nonprofit management (MA); special education (M Ed); sport studies (MS). *Accreditation:* ACBSP; NCATE. Part-time and evening/weekend programs available. *Degree requirements:* For master's, comprehensive exam (for some programs), thesis (for some programs). *Entrance requirements:* For master's, GMAT (MBA), GRE, MAT, minimum GPA of 3.0. Additional exam requirements/recommendations for international students: Required—TOEFL (minimum score 550 paper-based). Electronic applications accepted.

Howard University, Graduate School, Department of History, Washington, DC 20059-0002. Offers African diaspora (MA, PhD); African history (MA, PhD); Latin America and the Caribbean (MA, PhD); public history (MA); United States history (MA, PhD). Part-time programs available. Terminal master's awarded for partial completion of doctoral program. *Degree requirements:* For master's, one foreign language, thesis optional; for doctorate, 2 foreign languages, comprehensive exam, thesis/dissertation. *Entrance requirements:* For master's, GRE General Test, minimum GPA of 3.0, 3 letters of recommendation; for doctorate, GRE General Test, minimum GPA of 3.5, 3 letters of recommendation. Additional exam requirements/recommendations for international students: Required—TOEFL. Electronic applications accepted. *Faculty research:* Africa diaspora, U.S. diplomatic relations, Caribbean economic history.

Hunter College of the City University of New York, Graduate School, School of Arts and Sciences, Department of History, New York, NY 10021-5085. Offers MA. *Faculty:* 7 full-time (2 women), 2 part-time/adjunct (1 woman). *Students:* 46 part-time (19 women); includes 4 minority (1 Asian American or Pacific Islander, 3 Hispanic Americans). Average age 36. 22 applicants, 55% accepted, 7 enrolled. In 2008, 4 master's awarded. *Degree requirements:* For master's, one foreign language, comprehensive exam, thesis, essay, language exam. *Entrance requirements:* For master's, GRE General Test, minimum of 18 credits in undergraduate history or related field. Additional exam requirements/recommendations for international students: Required—TOEFL. *Application deadline:* For fall admission, 4/1 for domestic students, 2/1 for international students; for spring admission, 11/1 for domestic students, 9/1 for international students. Application fee: $125. *Financial support:* Federal Work-Study, scholarships/grants, and tuition waivers (partial) available. Support available to part-time students. *Unit head:* Dr. Barbara Welter, Chair and Graduate Advisor, 212-772-5487, E-mail: bwelter@hunter.cuny.edu. *Application contact:* William Zlata, Director for Graduate Admissions, 212-772-4482, Fax: 212-650-3336, E-mail: admissions@hunter.cuny.edu.

Idaho State University, Office of Graduate Studies, College of Arts and Sciences, Department of History, Pocatello, ID 83209. Offers historical resources management (MA). Part-time programs available. *Faculty:* 7 full-time (2 women), 1 (woman) part-time/adjunct. *Students:* 4 full-time (0 women), 1 (woman) part-time, 1 international. Average age 31. *Degree requirements:* For master's, comprehensive exam, thesis optional, minimum of 30 credits, internship. *Entrance requirements:* For master's, GRE, 3 letters of recommendation, minimum of 18 upper division history credits, statement of interest in historical studies. Additional exam requirements/

History

Idaho State University (continued)

recommendations for international students: Required—TOEFL (minimum score 550 paper-based; 213 computer-based; 80 iBT). *Application deadline:* For fall admission, 7/1 for domestic students, 6/1 for international students; for spring admission, 12/1 for domestic students, 11/1 for international students. Applications are processed on a rolling basis. Application fee: $55. Electronic applications accepted. *Expenses:* Tuition, area resident: Full-time $3114; part-time $276 per credit hour. Tuition, state resident: full-time $3114; part-time $276 per credit hour. Tuition, nonresident: full-time $12,318; part-time $404 per credit hour. Required fees: $2360. Tuition and fees vary according to course load and reciprocity agreements. *Financial support:* In 2008–09, 1 research assistantship with full and partial tuition reimbursement (averaging $6,800 per year), 2 teaching assistantships with full and partial tuition reimbursements (averaging $9,401 per year) were awarded; career-related internships or fieldwork, Federal Work-Study, institutionally sponsored loans, scholarships/grants, health care benefits, tuition waivers (full and partial), and unspecified assistantships also available. Support available to part-time students. Financial award application deadline: 1/1; financial award applicants required to submit FAFSA. *Faculty research:* Historical GIS (geographic information systems), historical and urban geography, environmental history and environmental policy, United States political history, women's and gender history. *Unit head:* Dr. Laura Woodworth-Ney, Chairman, 208-282-2379, E-mail: woodlaur@isu.edu. *Application contact:* Ellen Combs, Graduate School Technical Records Specialist, 208-282-2150, Fax: 208-282-4847, E-mail: combelle@isu.edu.

Illinois State University, Graduate School, College of Arts and Sciences, Department of History, Normal, IL 61790-2200. Offers MA, MS. *Degree requirements:* For master's, thesis or alternative. *Entrance requirements:* For master's, GRE General Test, minimum GPA of 2.6 in last 60 hours of course work.

Indiana State University, School of Graduate Studies, College of Arts and Sciences, Department of History, Terre Haute, IN 47809-1401. Offers MA, MS. Part-time and evening/weekend programs available. *Degree requirements:* For master's, comprehensive exam (for some programs), thesis or alternative. *Entrance requirements:* For master's, equivalent of minor in geography or geology. Additional exam requirements/recommendations for international students: Required—TOEFL (minimum score 550 paper-based).

Indiana University Bloomington, University Graduate School, College of Arts and Sciences, Department of History, Bloomington, IN 47405-7000. Offers MA, MAT, PhD, MA/MLS. *Faculty:* 44 full-time (12 women), 34 part-time/adjunct (15 women). *Students:* 109 full-time (56 women), 21 part-time (12 women); includes 20 minority (8 African Americans, 3 Asian Americans or Pacific Islanders, 9 Hispanic Americans), 19 international. Average age 32. 232 applicants, 11% accepted, 20 enrolled. In 2008, 14 master's, 16 doctorates awarded. Terminal master's awarded for partial completion of doctoral program. *Degree requirements:* For master's, one foreign language, thesis optional; for doctorate, one foreign language, comprehensive exam, thesis/dissertation. *Entrance requirements:* For master's and doctorate, GRE General Test. Additional exam requirements/recommendations for international students: Required—TOEFL. *Application deadline:* For fall admission, 1/2 for domestic students, 12/1 for international students. Application fee: $50 ($60 for international students). Electronic applications accepted. *Expenses:* Tuition, area resident: Part-time $291.97 per credit hour. Tuition, state resident: part-time $291.97 per credit hour. Tuition, nonresident: part-time $850.33 per credit hour. Required fees: $110 per semester. Tuition and fees vary according to course load and program. *Financial support:* Fellowships with full tuition reimbursements, research assistantships with full tuition reimbursements, teaching assistantships with full tuition reimbursements, career-related internships or fieldwork, Federal Work-Study, institutionally sponsored loans, scholarships/grants, traineeships, health care benefits, and unspecified assistantships available. *Faculty research:* Medieval and early modern Europe, Russia, Latin America, Middle East, Great Britain, United States, Africa and African Diaspora, Europe, eastern Europe. *Unit head:* Dr. Claude Clegg, Chairman, 812-855-3236, Fax: 812-855-3378, E-mail: cclegg@indiana.edu. *Application contact:* Mary Medley-Byers, Admissions Secretary, 812-855-8233, Fax: 812-855-3378, E-mail: histadm@indiana.edu.

Indiana University of Pennsylvania, School of Graduate Studies and Research, College of Humanities and Social Sciences, Department of History, Program in History, Indiana, PA 15705-1087. Offers MA. Part-time programs available. *Faculty:* 9 full-time (3 women). *Students:* 9 full-time (6 women), 3 part-time (2 women). Average age 27. 13 applicants, 38% accepted, 4 enrolled. In 2008, 7 master's awarded. *Degree requirements:* For master's, thesis optional. *Entrance requirements:* For master's, GRE, 2 letters of recommendation. Additional exam requirements/recommendations for international students: Required—TOEFL. *Application deadline:* For spring admission, 11/1 for domestic students. Applications are processed on a rolling basis. Application fee: $30. *Expenses:* Tuition, area resident: Full-time $6430; part-time $357 per credit. Tuition, nonresident: full-time $10,288; part-time $572 per credit. Required fees: $1547.50; $107 per credit. $283 per year. *Financial support:* In 2008–09, 5 research assistantships with full and partial tuition reimbursements (averaging $3,390 per year) were awarded; fellowships, Federal Work-Study also available. Support available to part-time students. Financial award application deadline: 3/15; financial award applicants required to submit FAFSA. *Unit head:* Dr. Werner Lippert, Graduate Coordinator, 724-357-2573, E-mail: Werner.Lippert@iup.edu. *Application contact:* Dr. Tami Whited, Graduate Coordinator, 724-357-2573, E-mail: twhited@iup.edu.

Indiana University–Purdue University Indianapolis, Department of History, Indianapolis, IN 46202-2896. Offers history (MA); public history (MA); MA/MLS. Part-time and evening/weekend programs available. *Degree requirements:* For master's, one foreign language, thesis. *Entrance requirements:* For master's, GRE General Test, minimum GPA of 3.0.

Inter American University of Puerto Rico, Metropolitan Campus, Graduate Programs, Program in History, San Juan, PR 00919-1293. Offers MA.

Iona College, School of Arts and Science, Program in History, New Rochelle, NY 10801-1890. Offers MA. Part-time and evening/weekend programs available. *Faculty:* 7 full-time (1 woman). *Students:* 4 full-time (2 women), 15 part-time (10 women); includes 3 minority (1 African American, 2 Hispanic Americans). Average age 27. 10 applicants, 60% accepted, 1 enrolled. In 2008, 7 master's awarded. *Degree requirements:* For master's, one foreign language, thesis. *Entrance requirements:* For master's, undergraduate major in history or related field, minimum GPA of 3.0. Additional exam requirements/recommendations for international students: Required—TOEFL (minimum score 550 paper-based; 213 computer-based). *Application deadline:* Applications are processed on a rolling basis. Application fee: $50. Electronic applications accepted. *Expenses:* Tuition: Part-time $755 per credit. Required fees: $175 per term. *Financial support:* Unspecified assistantships available. Financial award application deadline: 4/15; financial award applicants required to submit FAFSA. *Faculty research:* Global studies, American diplomacy, Native Americans, foreign policy, Armenian history. *Unit head:* Dr. James Carroll, Chairman, 914-633-2694, E-mail: jcarroll@iona.edu. *Application contact:* Veronica Jarek-Prinz, Director of Graduate Admissions, 914-633-2420, Fax: 914-633-2277, E-mail: vjarekprinz@iona.edu.

Iowa State University of Science and Technology, Graduate College, College of Liberal Arts and Sciences, Department of History, Ames, IA 50011. Offers agricultural history and rural studies (PhD); history (MA); history of technology and science (MA, PhD). *Faculty:* 17 full-time (5 women). *Students:* 24 full-time (10 women), 10 part-time (2 women); includes 1 minority (Hispanic American), 4 international. 10 applicants, 70% accepted, 3 enrolled. In 2008, 9 master's, 3 doctorates awarded. *Degree requirements:* For master's, thesis or alternative; for doctorate, thesis/dissertation. *Entrance requirements:* For master's and doctorate, GRE General Test. Additional exam requirements/recommendations for international students: Required—TOEFL (minimum score 600 paper-based; 79 iBT), IELTS (7.0) or TOEFL. *Application deadline:* For fall admission, 1/15 priority date for domestic and international students. Applications are processed on a rolling basis. Application fee: $30 ($70 for international students). Electronic applications accepted. *Expenses:* Tuition, area resident: Full-time $6446; part-time $359 per credit. Tuition, state resident: full-time $6446; part-time $359 per credit. Tuition, nonresident: full-time $17,330; part-time $963 per credit. Required fees: $790; $249.25 per semester. Tuition and fees vary according to course load and program. *Financial support:* In 2008–09, 20 teaching assistantships with full and partial tuition reimbursements (averaging $12,150 per year) were awarded; research assistantships with full and partial tuition reimbursements, scholarships/grants, health care benefits, and unspecified assistantships also available. *Unit head:* Dr. Charles Dobbs, Chair, 515-294-7266, Fax: 515-294-6390, E-mail: cdobbs@iastate.edu. *Application contact:* Dr. Pamela Riney-Kehrberg, Information Contact, 515-294-1451, Fax: 515-294-6390.

Jackson State University, Graduate School, School of Liberal Arts, Department of History, Jackson, MS 39217. Offers MA. Part-time and evening/weekend programs available. *Degree requirements:* For master's, comprehensive exam, thesis or alternative. *Entrance requirements:* For master's, GRE General Test. Additional exam requirements/recommendations for international students: Required—TOEFL.

Jacksonville State University, College of Graduate Studies and Continuing Education, College of Arts and Sciences, Department of History, Jacksonville, AL 36265-1602. Offers MA. Part-time and evening/weekend programs available. *Faculty:* 10 full-time (2 women). *Students:* 14 full-time (5 women), 30 part-time (11 women); includes 3 minority (all African Americans). Average age 31. 15 applicants, 13% accepted, 2 enrolled. In 2008, 15 master's awarded. *Degree requirements:* For master's, comprehensive exam, thesis (for some programs). *Entrance requirements:* For master's, GRE General Test or MAT. *Application deadline:* Applications are processed on a rolling basis. Application fee: $30. Electronic applications accepted. *Expenses:* Tuition, area resident: Full-time $4560; part-time $225 per credit hour. Tuition, state resident: full-time $4560; part-time $450 per credit hour. Tuition, nonresident: full-time $9120; part-time $450 per credit hour. *Financial support:* In 2008–09, 28 students received support. Available to part-time students. Application deadline: 4/1; *Unit head:* Dr. Harvy Jackson, Head, 256-782-5622. *Application contact:* Dr. Jean Pugliese, Associate Dean, 256-782-8278, Fax: 256-782-5321, E-mail: pugliese@jsu.edu.

James Madison University, The Graduate School, College of Arts and Letters, Department of History, Harrisonburg, VA 22807. Offers MA. Part-time programs available. *Faculty:* 17 full-time (4 women), 3 part-time/adjunct (1 woman). *Students:* 25 full-time (10 women), 9 part-time (2 women); includes 1 minority (African American). Average age 27. In 2008, 7 master's awarded. *Degree requirements:* For master's, one foreign language, comprehensive exam, thesis, reading exam in a language. *Entrance requirements:* For master's, GRE General Test, GRE Subject Test, 2 letters of recommendation. Additional exam requirements/recommendations for international students: Required—TOEFL. *Application deadline:* For fall admission, 1/15 for domestic students. Applications are processed on a rolling basis. Application fee: $55. Electronic applications accepted. *Expenses:* Tuition, area resident: Full-time $7008; part-time $292 per credit hour. Tuition, state resident: full-time $7008; part-time $292 per credit hour. Tuition, nonresident: full-time $20,352; part-time $848 per credit hour. *Financial support:* In 2008–09, 12 students received support, including 3 teaching assistantships with full tuition reimbursements available (averaging $8,664 per year); Federal Work-Study and 9 graduate assistantships ($7,382) also available. Financial award application deadline: 3/1; financial award applicants required to submit FAFSA. *Unit head:* Dr. Michael J. Galgano, Academic Unit Head, 540-568-6132. *Application contact:* Lynette M. Bible, Director of Graduate Admissions, 540-568-6395, Fax: 540-568-7860, E-mail: biblelm@jmu.edu.

John Carroll University, Graduate School, Department of History, University Heights, OH 44118-4581. Offers MA. Part-time and evening/weekend programs available. *Degree requirements:* For master's, comprehensive exam, thesis (for some programs), research essay or thesis. *Entrance requirements:* For master's, GRE General Test, minimum 2.5 GPA average. Additional exam requirements/recommendations for international students: Required—TOEFL. Electronic applications accepted. *Faculty research:* Social history of Cleveland, early national Pennsylvania, modern Japanese journalism, Catholic Reformation.

The Johns Hopkins University, Zanvyl Krieger School of Arts and Sciences, Department of History, Baltimore, MD 21218-2699. Offers PhD. *Degree requirements:* For doctorate, variable foreign language requirement, comprehensive exam, thesis/dissertation. *Entrance requirements:* For doctorate, GRE General Test. Additional exam requirements/recommendations for international students: Required—TOEFL. Electronic applications accepted. *Faculty research:* American, European, Latin American, Chinese, and African history.

Kansas State University, Graduate School, College of Arts and Sciences, Department of History, Manhattan, KS 66506. Offers history (MA); security studies (MA, PhD). Part-time programs available. *Faculty:* 17 full-time (6 women), 2 part-time/adjunct (0 women). *Students:* 42 full-time (11 women), 72 part-time (17 women); includes 3 minority (all Asian Americans or Pacific Islanders), 7 international. Average age 29. 21 applicants, 67% accepted, 7 enrolled. In 2008, 4 master's, 2 doctorates awarded. *Degree requirements:* For master's, thesis (for some programs); for doctorate, one foreign language, thesis/dissertation, qualifying exam. *Entrance requirements:* For master's, GRE General Test or MAT, minimum undergraduate GPA of 3.0; for doctorate, GRE General Test or MAT. Additional exam requirements/recommendations for international students: Required—TOEFL (minimum score 600 paper-based). *Application deadline:* For fall admission, 5/1 for domestic students, 2/1 priority date for international students; for spring admission, 11/1 for domestic students, 8/1 priority date for international students. Applications are processed on a rolling basis. Application fee: $30 ($55 for international students). *Expenses:* Tuition, area resident: Full-time $6466; part-time $269.40 per credit hour. Tuition, state resident: full-time $6466; part-time $269.40 per credit hour. Tuition, nonresident: full-time $14,874; part-time $619.75 per credit hour. Required fees: $673; $23.40 per credit hour. Tuition and fees vary according to campus/location. *Financial support:* In 2008–09, 5 research assistantships (averaging $16,414 per year), 9 teaching assistantships with full tuition reimbursements (averaging $9,000 per year) were awarded; career-related internships or fieldwork, Federal Work-Study, institutionally sponsored loans, and scholarships/grants also available. Support available to part-time students. Financial award application deadline: 3/1; financial award applicants required to submit FAFSA. *Faculty research:* Environmental history, history of Christianity, American social history, history of war and society, history of international relations and diplomacy. Total annual research expenditures: $16,186. *Unit head:* Sue Zschoche, Head, 785-532-6730, Fax: 785-532-7004, E-mail: suez@ksu.edu. *Application contact:* Louise Breen, Recruiting Program Director, 785-532-0365, Fax: 785-532-7004, E-mail: breen@ksu.edu.

Kent State University, College of Arts and Sciences, Department of History, Kent, OH 44242-0001. Offers MA, PhD. Part-time programs available. *Degree requirements:* For master's, variable foreign language requirement, thesis optional; for doctorate, variable foreign language requirement, thesis/dissertation. *Entrance requirements:* For master's, GRE General Test, GRE Subject Test, minimum GPA of 2.75; for doctorate, GRE General Test, GRE Subject Test, minimum GPA of 3.0. Additional exam requirements/recommendations for international students: Required—TOEFL. Electronic applications accepted. *Faculty research:* African American, civil war, British empire, Latin America, public history.

Lakehead University, Graduate Studies, Department of History, Thunder Bay, ON P7B 5E1, Canada. Offers gerontology (MA); history (MA); women's studies (MA). Part-time programs available. *Degree requirements:* For master's, one foreign language, thesis. *Entrance requirements:* For master's, minimum B average. Additional exam requirements/recommendations for international students: Required—TOEFL. Tuition charges are reported in Canadian dollars. *Expenses:* Tuition, area resident: Full-time $6500 Canadian dollars. International tuition: $13,700 Canadian dollars full-time. *Faculty research:* Canadian history, British history, Russian/German history, women's studies.

Lamar University, College of Graduate Studies, College of Arts and Sciences, Department of History, Beaumont, TX 77710. Offers MA. Part-time programs available. *Faculty:* 6 full-time (0 women). *Students:* 2 full-time (1 woman), 7 part-time (3 women); includes 1 minority (African

American). Average age 43. 5 applicants, 40% accepted, 1 enrolled. In 2008, 4 master's awarded. *Degree requirements:* For master's, comprehensive exam (for some programs), thesis (for some programs). *Entrance requirements:* For master's, GRE General Test, minimum GPA of 2.5 in last 60 hours of undergraduate course work. Additional exam requirements/recommendations for international students: Required—TOEFL. *Application deadline:* For fall admission, 8/1 for domestic students; for spring admission, 12/1 for domestic students. Applications are processed on a rolling basis. Application fee: $25 ($50 for international students). *Expenses:* Tuition, state resident: full-time $5000; part-time $195 per credit. Tuition, nonresident: full-time $12,376; part-time $476 per credit. Required fees: $1570. *Financial support:* In 2008–09, fellowships (averaging $1,000 per year), teaching assistantships (averaging $2,000 per year) were awarded. Financial award application deadline: 4/1. *Faculty research:* Old South, nineteenth century reform, twentieth century US, religion in America's South, Renaissance/early modern Europe. *Unit head:* Dr. John Storey, Chair, 409-880-8511, Fax: 409-880-8710, E-mail: storeyjw@hal.lamar.edu. *Application contact:* Dr. Howell H. Gwin, Graduate Adviser, 409-880-8530, Fax: 409-880-8710, E-mail: gwinhh@hal.lamar.edu.

La Salle University, School of Arts and Sciences, Program in History, Philadelphia, PA 19141-1199. Offers MA. Part-time programs available.

Laurentian University, School of Graduate Studies and Research, Programme in History, Sudbury, ON P3E 2C6, Canada. Offers European history (MA); history of Northern Ontario (MA); North American history (MA). Part-time programs available. *Degree requirements:* For master's, thesis or alternative. *Entrance requirements:* For master's, honors degree with minimum second class. *Faculty research:* Franco-Ontarian history, northern Ontarian history, Canadian social history, European social history, Franco-Canadian history.

Lehigh University, College of Arts and Sciences, Department of History, Bethlehem, PA 18015. Offers MA, PhD. *Faculty:* 15 full-time (5 women), 1 (woman) part-time/adjunct. *Students:* 17 full-time (5 women), 20 part-time (5 women); includes 1 minority (Asian American or Pacific Islander), 4 international. Average age 33. 34 applicants, 53% accepted, 6 enrolled. In 2008, 14 master's awarded. *Degree requirements:* For master's, comprehensive exam or thesis; for doctorate, thesis/dissertation. *Entrance requirements:* For master's, GRE General Test, recommendations; for doctorate, GRE General Test, recommendations, writing samples. Additional exam requirements/recommendations for international students: Required—TOEFL. *Application deadline:* For winter admission, 1/15 priority date for domestic and international students. Applications are processed on a rolling basis. Application fee: $65. Electronic applications accepted. *Financial support:* In 2008–09, 7 students received support, including fellowships with full tuition reimbursements available (averaging $20,000 per year), research assistantships with full tuition reimbursements available (averaging $15,600 per year), teaching assistantships with full tuition reimbursements available (averaging $15,600 per year); career-related internships or fieldwork, Federal Work-Study, institutionally sponsored loans, scholarships/grants, tuition waivers (full and partial), and unspecified assistantships also available. Support available to part-time students. Financial award application deadline: 1/15. *Faculty research:* Colonial America, modern America, history of technology. *Unit head:* Dr. Stephen H. Cutcliffe, Chairman, 610-758-3360, Fax: 610-758-6554, E-mail: shc0@lehigh.edu. *Application contact:* Dr. Roger D. Simon, Graduate Coordinator, 610-758-3368, Fax: 610-758-6554, E-mail: rds2@lehigh.edu.

Lehman College of the City University of New York, Division of Arts and Humanities, Department of History, Bronx, NY 10468-1589. Offers MA. Part-time and evening/weekend programs available. *Degree requirements:* For master's, comprehensive exam, thesis. *Entrance requirements:* For master's, 18 undergraduate credits in history, minimum GPA of 2.7.

Lincoln University, School of Graduate Studies and Continuing Education, College of Liberal Arts, Education and Journalism, Department of Social and Behavioral Sciences, Jefferson City, MO 65102. Offers history (MA); social science (MA), including history, political science, sociology; sociology (MA); sociology/criminal justice (MA). Part-time and evening/weekend programs available. *Faculty:* 11 full-time (4 women), 4 part-time/adjunct (2 women). *Students:* 6 full-time (3 women), 21 part-time (11 women); includes 8 minority (all African Americans), 5 international. Average age 33. 13 applicants, 100% accepted, 9 enrolled. In 2008, 14 master's awarded. *Degree requirements:* For master's, comprehensive exam, thesis optional. *Entrance requirements:* For master's, GRE General Test or MAT, 15 undergraduate hours of course work in social science including 6 hours upper-division, with 9 hours in the area of concentration. Additional exam requirements/recommendations for international students: Required—TOEFL (minimum score 500 paper-based; 173 computer-based; 61 iBT). *Application deadline:* For fall admission, 7/1 priority date for domestic and international students; for spring admission, 12/1 priority date for domestic and international students. Applications are processed on a rolling basis. Application fee: $20. *Expenses:* Tuition, area resident: Full-time $4185; part-time $232.50 per credit hour. Tuition, nonresident: full-time $7767; part-time $431.50 per credit hour. Required fees: $270; $15 per credit hour. $252.50 per semester. One-time fee: $20. Tuition and fees vary according to course load. *Financial support:* Federal Work-Study and scholarships/grants available. Financial award application deadline: 4/1; financial award applicants required to submit FAFSA. *Faculty research:* Suicide prevention. *Unit head:* Dr. Debra F. Greene, Department Head, 573-681-5145, Fax: 573-681-5150, E-mail: greened@lincolnu.edu. *Application contact:* Irasema Steck, Administrative Assistant, 573-681-5247, Fax: 573-681-5106, E-mail: gradschool@lincolnu.edu.

Long Island University, Brooklyn Campus, Richard L. Conolly College of Liberal Arts and Sciences, Program in Social Science, Brooklyn, NY 11201-8423. Offers history (MS); United Nations studies (Certificate). Part-time and evening/weekend programs available. *Entrance requirements:* For master's, 2 letters of recommendation. Additional exam requirements/recommendations for international students: Required—TOEFL (minimum score 500 paper-based; 173 computer-based). Electronic applications accepted.

Long Island University, C.W. Post Campus, College of Liberal Arts and Sciences, Department of History, Brookville, NY 11548-1300. Offers MA. Part-time and evening/weekend programs available. *Degree requirements:* For master's, comprehensive exam or thesis. *Entrance requirements:* For master's, bachelor's degree in history, minimum GPA of 3.0. Electronic applications accepted. *Faculty research:* American slavery, women's studies, military history.

Louisiana State University and Agricultural and Mechanical College, Graduate School, College of Arts and Sciences, Department of History, Baton Rouge, LA 70803. Offers MA, PhD. Part-time programs available. Terminal master's awarded for partial completion of doctoral program. *Degree requirements:* For master's, thesis (for some programs), oral exam; for doctorate, one foreign language, thesis/dissertation, comprehensive written and oral exams. *Entrance requirements:* For master's and doctorate, GRE General Test, minimum GPA of 3.0. Additional exam requirements/recommendations for international students: Required—TOEFL (minimum score 550 paper-based; 213 computer-based; 79 iBT). Electronic applications accepted. *Faculty research:* U.S. South, Civil War; modern Europe, British; medieval history.

Louisiana Tech University, Graduate School, College of Liberal Arts, Department of History, Ruston, LA 71272. Offers MA. Part-time programs available. *Degree requirements:* For master's, thesis or alternative. *Entrance requirements:* For master's, GRE General Test.

Loyola University Chicago, Graduate School, Department of History, Chicago, IL 60611-2196. Offers history (MA, PhD); public history (MA). Part-time and evening/weekend programs available. *Faculty:* 20 full-time (8 women), 4 part-time/adjunct (1 woman). *Students:* 79 full-time (42 women), 36 part-time (19 women); includes 9 minority (4 African Americans, 1 American Indian/Alaska Native, 1 Asian American or Pacific Islander, 3 Hispanic Americans), 1 international. Average age 33. 134 applicants, 53% accepted, 31 enrolled. In 2008, 14 master's, 2 doctorates awarded. Terminal master's awarded for partial completion of doctoral program. *Degree requirements:* For master's, one foreign language, comprehensive exam, essay; for doctorate, 2 foreign languages, comprehensive exam, thesis/dissertation. *Entrance requirements:* For master's, GRE General Test, research paper; for doctorate, GRE General Test, seminar paper or master's thesis. Additional exam requirements/recommendations for international students: Required—TOEFL (minimum score 550 paper-based; 213 computer-based), IELTS. *Application deadline:* For fall admission, 5/1 for domestic students; for spring admission, 10/1 for domestic students. Applications are processed on a rolling basis. Application fee: $50. Electronic applications accepted. *Expenses:* Tuition: Full-time $13,500; part-time $750 per credit hour. Required fees: $60 per semester. Full-time tuition and fees vary according to program. *Financial support:* In 2008–09, 24 students received support, including 11 fellowships with full tuition reimbursements available (averaging $14,500 per year), 13 teaching assistantships with full tuition reimbursements available (averaging $15,000 per year); research assistantships with full tuition reimbursements available, Federal Work-Study also available. Financial award application deadline: 1/1; financial award applicants required to submit FAFSA. *Faculty research:* Medieval and early modern Europe, U.S. public history, U.S. urban history, gender history, Britain and Ireland. *Unit head:* Barbara Rosenwein, Chair, 773-508-2215, Fax: 773-508-2153, E-mail: brosen@luc.edu. *Application contact:* Dr. Suzanne Kaufman, Director, Graduate Programs, 773-508-2233, Fax: 773-508-2153, E-mail: skaufma@luc.edu.

Lynchburg College, Graduate Studies, School of Humanities and Social Sciences, Lynchburg, VA 24501-3199. Offers English (MA); history (MA). Part-time programs available. *Faculty:* 7 full-time (4 women), 1 part-time/adjunct (0 women). *Students:* 19 full-time (11 women), 18 part-time (11 women), 1 international. Average age 33. 30 applicants, 73% accepted, 13 enrolled. In 2008, 1 master's awarded. *Degree requirements:* For master's, comprehensive exam, thesis (for some programs). *Entrance requirements:* For master's, GRE, minimum undergraduate GPA of 3.0. Additional exam requirements/recommendations for international students: Required—TOEFL. *Application deadline:* For fall admission, 7/31 for domestic students, 6/1 for international students; for spring admission, 11/30 for domestic students, 10/1 for international students. Application fee: $30. *Expenses:* Tuition: Full-time $6750; part-time $375 per credit. *Financial support:* Career-related internships or fieldwork, Federal Work-Study, scholarships/grants, and unspecified assistantships available. *Unit head:* Dr. Edward Polloway, Vice President for Graduate and Community Advancement, 434-544-8655, E-mail: polloway@lynchburg.edu. *Application contact:* Dr. Kim McCabe, Dean, School of Humanities and Social Sciences, 434-544-8129, E-mail: McCabe@lynchburg.edu.

Marquette University, Graduate School, College of Arts and Sciences, Department of History, Milwaukee, WI 53201-1881. Offers European history (MA, PhD); medieval history (MA); Renaissance and Reformation (MA); United States history (MA, PhD). Part-time programs available. Terminal master's awarded for partial completion of doctoral program. *Degree requirements:* For master's, comprehensive exam, thesis or alternative; for doctorate, one foreign language, thesis/dissertation, qualifying exam. *Entrance requirements:* For master's, GRE General Test, GRE Subject Test; for doctorate, GRE General Test, writing sample. Additional exam requirements/recommendations for international students: Required—TOEFL. *Faculty research:* Social history, political history, diplomatic history, history of science, religious history.

Marshall University, Academic Affairs Division, College of Liberal Arts, Department of History, Huntington, WV 25755. Offers MA. *Degree requirements:* For master's, thesis optional.

McGill University, Faculty of Graduate and Postdoctoral Studies, Faculty of Arts, Department of History, Montréal, QC H3A 2T5, Canada. Offers history (MA, PhD); history of medicine (MA).

McMaster University, School of Graduate Studies, Faculty of Humanities, Department of History, Hamilton, ON L8S 4M2, Canada. Offers MA, PhD. Part-time programs available. *Degree requirements:* For master's, one foreign language, thesis or alternative; for doctorate, one foreign language, comprehensive exam, thesis/dissertation. *Entrance requirements:* For master's, honors BA in history, minimum B+ average. Additional exam requirements/recommendations for international students: Required—TOEFL (minimum score 580 paper-based; 237 computer-based). *Faculty research:* Canadian, European, British, U.S. history; ancient history.

Memorial University of Newfoundland, School of Graduate Studies, Department of History, St. John's, NL A1C 5S7, Canada. Offers MA, PhD. Part-time programs available. *Degree requirements:* For master's, thesis or comprehensive exam; for doctorate, one foreign language, comprehensive exam, thesis/dissertation, oral defense of thesis. *Entrance requirements:* For master's, honors degree or equivalent; for doctorate, master's degree. Electronic applications accepted. *Faculty research:* Canadian history, maritime history, Newfoundland history, social history, labor history.

Miami University, Graduate School, College of Arts and Sciences, Department of History, Oxford, OH 45056. Offers MA, PhD. Part-time programs available. *Degree requirements:* For master's, comprehensive exam, thesis, final exam; for doctorate, comprehensive exam, thesis/dissertation, final exam. *Entrance requirements:* For master's, minimum undergraduate GPA of 3.0 during previous 2 years or 2.75 overall. Additional exam requirements/recommendations for international students: Required—TOEFL (minimum score 550 paper-based; 213 computer-based), TWE (minimum score 4). Electronic applications accepted.

Michigan State University, The Graduate School, College of Arts and Letters, Department of History, East Lansing, MI 48824. Offers history (MA, PhD); history-secondary school teaching (MA). *Entrance requirements:* Additional exam requirements/recommendations for international students: Required—TOEFL. Electronic applications accepted.

Middle Tennessee State University, College of Graduate Studies, College of Liberal Arts, Department of History, Program in History, Murfreesboro, TN 37132. Offers MA. Part-time and evening/weekend programs available. Postbaccalaureate distance learning degree programs offered. *Degree requirements:* For master's, one foreign language, comprehensive exam, thesis. *Entrance requirements:* For master's, GRE. Additional exam requirements/recommendations for international students: Required—TOEFL (paper-based 525; computer-based 195; IBT 71) or IELTS (6.0).

Midwestern State University, Graduate Studies, College of Humanities and Social Sciences, Department of History, Wichita Falls, TX 76308. Offers MA. Part-time programs available. *Degree requirements:* For master's, one foreign language. *Entrance requirements:* For master's, GRE General Test. Additional exam requirements/recommendations for international students: Required—TOEFL (minimum score 550 paper-based; 213 computer-based). Electronic applications accepted. *Faculty research:* Conservation, Spanish borderlands, Jacksonian era, New Deal, Texas and the Southwest.

Millersville University of Pennsylvania, Graduate School, School of Humanities and Social Sciences, Department of History, Millersville, PA 17551-0302. Offers MA. Part-time and evening/weekend programs available. *Faculty:* 9 full-time (4 women), 7 part-time/adjunct (3 women). *Students:* 5 full-time (4 women), 12 part-time (3 women); includes 1 minority (Hispanic American). Average age 31. 3 applicants, 100% accepted, 2 enrolled. In 2008, 5 master's awarded. *Degree requirements:* For master's, thesis optional. *Entrance requirements:* Additional exam requirements/recommendations for international students: Required—TOEFL (minimum score 500 paper-based; 183 computer-based; 65 iBT), TOEFL may be replaced by IELTS with score of 6 or higher. *Application deadline:* For fall admission, 2/1 priority date for domestic and international students; for winter admission, 10/1 priority date for domestic and international students; for spring admission, 10/1 priority date for domestic and international students. Applications are processed on a rolling basis. Application fee: $40. Electronic applications accepted. *Expenses:* Tuition, state resident: full-time $6430; part-time $357 per credit. Tuition, nonresident: full-time $10,288; part-time $572 per credit. Required fees: $1937; $73.50 per credit. One-time fee: $88 part-time. Tuition and fees vary according to course load. *Financial support:* In 2008–09, 1 student received support, including 1 research assistantship with full tuition reimbursement available (averaging $5,000 per year); institutionally sponsored loans and unspecified assistantships also available. Support available to part-time students. Financial award application deadline: 3/15; financial award applicants required to submit FAFSA. *Faculty*

History

Millersville University of Pennsylvania (continued)
research: Social history of music, Vietnam War, women in Africa, Colonial Caribbean, Colonial New England. *Unit head:* Dr. Francis Bremer, Chair, 717-872-3548, Fax: 717-871-2485, E-mail: francis.bremer@millersville.edu. *Application contact:* Dr. Victor S. DeSantis, Dean of Graduate and Professional Studies, 717-872-3099, Fax: 717-872-3453, E-mail: victor.desantis@millersville.edu.

Minnesota State University Mankato, College of Graduate Studies, College of Social and Behavioral Sciences, Department of History, Mankato, MN 56001. Offers history (MA, MS); social studies (MS); teaching history (MS, MT). *Students:* 3 full-time (1 woman), 11 part-time (2 women). *Degree requirements:* For master's, one foreign language, comprehensive exam, thesis or alternative. *Entrance requirements:* For master's, minimum GPA of 3.0 during previous 2 years. Additional exam requirements/recommendations for international students: Required—TOEFL. *Application deadline:* For fall admission, 7/1 priority date for domestic students; for spring admission, 11/1 for domestic students. Applications are processed on a rolling basis. Application fee: $40. Electronic applications accepted. *Financial support:* Research assistantships, teaching assistantships with full tuition reimbursements, career-related internships or fieldwork, Federal Work-Study, institutionally sponsored loans, and unspecified assistantships available. Support available to part-time students. Financial award application deadline: 3/15. *Faculty research:* Charivaris, Lindbergh in the U.S., Dutch trade to South America in the seventeenth and eighteenth centuries. *Unit head:* Dr. Charles Piehl, Graduate Coordinator, 507-389-5316. *Application contact:* 507-389-2321, E-mail: grad@mnsu.edu.

Mississippi College, Graduate School, College of Arts and Sciences, School of Humanities and Social Sciences, Department of History and Political Science, Clinton, MS 39058. Offers administration of justice (MSS); history (M Ed, MA, MSS); paralegal studies (Certificate); political science (MSS); social sciences (M Ed, MSS). Part-time programs available. *Degree requirements:* For master's, one foreign language, comprehensive exam, thesis (for some programs). *Entrance requirements:* For master's, GRE or NTE, minimum GPA of 2.5. Additional exam requirements/recommendations for international students: Recommended—IELTS. Electronic applications accepted.

Mississippi State University, College of Arts and Sciences, Department of History, Mississippi State, MS 39762. Offers MA, PhD. Part-time programs available. *Degree requirements:* For master's, one foreign language, comprehensive exam, thesis optional; for doctorate, 2 foreign languages, thesis/dissertation, comprehensive oral and written exam. *Entrance requirements:* For master's, minimum GPA of 3.0; for doctorate, GRE General Test, writing sample, minimum graduate GPA of 3.0. Additional exam requirements/recommendations for international students: Required—TOEFL. *Faculty research:* U.S. political, diplomatic, military, social, and cultural history; modern Europe; Latin America; Asian history; African history.

Missouri State University, Graduate College, College of Humanities and Public Affairs, Department of History, Springfield, MO 65804-0094. Offers history (MA); secondary education (MS Ed), including history, social science. Part-time programs available. *Faculty:* 15 full-time (2 women). *Students:* 17 full-time (9 women), 42 part-time (18 women); includes 1 minority (Asian American or Pacific Islander). Average age 33. 18 applicants, 94% accepted, 10 enrolled. In 2008, 13 master's awarded. *Degree requirements:* For master's, comprehensive exam, thesis or alternative. *Entrance requirements:* For master's, minimum GPA of 2.75, 24 hours of undergraduate course work in history (MA), 9-12 teaching certification (MS Ed). Additional exam requirements/recommendations for international students: Required—TOEFL (minimum score 550 paper-based; 213 computer-based; 79 iBT). *Application deadline:* For fall admission, 7/20 priority date for domestic students, 5/1 for international students; for spring admission, 12/20 priority date for domestic students, 9/1 for international students. Applications are processed on a rolling basis. Application fee: $35 ($50 for international students). Electronic applications accepted. *Expenses:* Tuition, state resident: full-time $3852; part-time $214 per credit hour. Tuition, nonresident: full-time $7524; part-time $418 per credit hour. Required fees: $230 per semester. Tuition and fees vary according to course level and course load. *Financial support:* In 2008–09, 6 teaching assistantships with full tuition reimbursements (averaging $8,130 per year) were awarded; Federal Work-Study, scholarships/grants, and unspecified assistantships also available. Support available to part-time students. Financial award application deadline: 3/31; financial award applicants required to submit FAFSA. *Faculty research:* U.S. history, Native American history, Latin American history, women's history, ancient Near East. *Unit head:* Thomas S. Dicke, Head, 417-836-5511, Fax: 417-836-5523, E-mail: history@missouristate.edu. *Application contact:* Eric Eckert, Coordinator of Admissions and Recruitment, 417-836-5331, Fax: 417-836-6888, E-mail: ericeckert@missouristate.edu.

Monmouth University, Graduate School, Department of History, West Long Branch, NJ 07764-1898. Offers MA. Part-time and evening/weekend programs available. *Faculty:* 11 full-time (2 women). *Students:* 9 full-time (4 women), 49 part-time (21 women); includes 5 minority (all Hispanic Americans). Average age 37. 32 applicants, 100% accepted, 17 enrolled. In 2008, 11 master's awarded. *Degree requirements:* For master's, comprehensive exam, thesis or alternative. *Entrance requirements:* For master's, minimum GPA of 3.0 in major, 2.5 overall. Additional exam requirements/recommendations for international students: Required—TOEFL (minimum score 550 paper-based; 213 computer-based; 79 iBT), IELTS (minimum score 5), Michigan English Language Assessment Battery (minimum score: 77), Cambridge A, B, C. *Application deadline:* For fall admission, 7/15 priority date for domestic students, 6/1 for international students; for spring admission, 11/15 priority date for domestic students, 11/1 for international students. Applications are processed on a rolling basis. Application fee: $50. Electronic applications accepted. *Expenses:* Tuition: Full-time $13,914; part-time $773 per credit. Required fees: $628; $157 per semester. *Financial support:* In 2008–09, 31 students received support, including 30 fellowships (averaging $1,194 per year), 4 research assistantships (averaging $5,778 per year); career-related internships or fieldwork, scholarships/grants, tuition waivers (partial), and unspecified assistantships also available. Support available to part-time students. Financial award application deadline: 3/1; financial award applicants required to submit FAFSA. *Faculty research:* U.S. business; labor; British, German, and French Revolutions; Soviet Union; Africa. *Unit head:* Dr. Christopher DeRosa, Director, 732-571-4495, Fax: 732-263-5112, E-mail: cderosa@monmouth.edu. *Application contact:* Kevin Roane, Director, Office of Graduate Admission, 732-571-3452, Fax: 732-263-5123, E-mail: gradadm@monmouth.edu.

Montana State University, College of Graduate Studies, College of Letters and Science, Department of History, Bozeman, MT 59717. Offers MA, PhD. Part-time programs available. *Degree requirements:* For master's and doctorate, comprehensive exam. *Entrance requirements:* For master's and doctorate, GRE General Test. Additional exam requirements/recommendations for international students: Required—TOEFL (minimum score 550 paper-based; 213 computer-based). Electronic applications accepted. *Faculty research:* U.S. West, environmental history, science and technology history.

Montclair State University, The Office of Graduate Admissions and Support Services, College of Humanities and Social Sciences, Department of History, Montclair, NJ 07043-1624. Offers social sciences (MA), including history; social studies (Certificate). Part-time and evening/weekend programs available. *Faculty:* 16 full-time (7 women), 21 part-time/adjunct (5 women). *Students:* 2 full-time (0 women), 23 part-time (10 women); includes 1 minority (Hispanic American). Average age 35. 10 applicants, 80% accepted, 6 enrolled. *Degree requirements:* For master's, comprehensive exam. *Entrance requirements:* For master's, GRE General Test, 2 letters of recommendation. Additional exam requirements/recommendations for international students: Required—TOEFL (minimum score 550 paper-based; 213 computer-based). *Application deadline:* For fall admission, 6/1 for international students; for spring admission, 11/1 for international students. Applications are processed on a rolling basis. Application fee: $60. Electronic applications accepted. *Financial support:* Research assistantships with full tuition reimbursements, Federal Work-Study, scholarships/grants, and unspecified assistantships available. Support available to part-time students. Financial award application deadline: 3/1. *Unit head:* Dr. Michael Whelan, Chairperson, 973-655-7848. *Application contact:* Amy Aiello, Associate Director of Admissions, 973-655-5147, Fax: 973-655-7869, E-mail: graduate.school@montclair.edu.

Morgan State University, School of Graduate Studies, College of Liberal Arts, Department of History and Geography, Baltimore, MD 21251. Offers African-American studies (MA); history (MA, PhD). Part-time and evening/weekend programs available. *Degree requirements:* For master's, comprehensive exam, thesis; for doctorate, comprehensive exam, thesis/dissertation. *Entrance requirements:* For master's, minimum GPA of 2.5; for doctorate, GRE or MAT. Additional exam requirements/recommendations for international students: Required—TOEFL (minimum score 550 paper-based; 213 computer-based). *Faculty research:* Women's history, African diaspora history, urban history.

Murray State University, College of Humanities and Fine Arts, Program in History, Murray, KY 42071. Offers MA. Part-time programs available. *Degree requirements:* For master's, one foreign language, comprehensive exam, thesis (for some programs). *Entrance requirements:* For master's, GRE General Test. Additional exam requirements/recommendations for international students: Required—TOEFL.

National University, Academic Affairs, College of Letters and Sciences, Department of Art and Humanities, La Jolla, CA 92037-1011. Offers creative writing (MFA); English (MA); history (MA). Part-time and evening/weekend programs available. Postbaccalaureate distance learning degree programs offered (no on-campus study). *Faculty:* 19 full-time (6 women), 180 part-time/adjunct (92 women). *Students:* 208 full-time (153 women), 433 part-time (302 women); includes 137 minority (57 African Americans, 10 American Indian/Alaska Native, 19 Asian Americans or Pacific Islanders, 51 Hispanic Americans). Average age 38. 420 applicants, 100% accepted, 420 enrolled. In 2008, 152 master's awarded. *Degree requirements:* For master's, thesis (for some programs). *Entrance requirements:* For master's, interview, minimum GPA of 2.5. Additional exam requirements/recommendations for international students: Required—TOEFL (minimum score 550 paper-based; 213 computer-based; 79 iBT), IELTS (minimum score 6). *Application deadline:* Applications are processed on a rolling basis. Application fee: $60 ($65 for international students). Electronic applications accepted. *Expenses:* Tuition: Full-time $8694; part-time $322 per credit hour. Tuition and fees vary according to course load. *Financial support:* Career-related internships or fieldwork, institutionally sponsored loans, scholarships/grants, and tuition waivers (partial) available. Support available to part-time students. Financial award application deadline: 6/30; financial award applicants required to submit FAFSA. *Unit head:* Dr. Janet Baker, Chair, 858-642-8472, Fax: 858-642-8715, E-mail: jbaker@nu.edu. *Application contact:* Dominick Giovanniello, Associate Regional Dean—San Diego, 800-NAT-UNIV, Fax: 858-541-7792, E-mail: dgiovann@nu.edu.

Nebraska Wesleyan University, University College, Program in Historical Studies, Lincoln, NE 68504-2796. Offers MA. Part-time programs available. *Expenses:* Contact institution.

New Jersey Institute of Technology, Office of Graduate Studies, College of Science and Liberal Arts, Federated Department of History, Newark, NJ 07102. Offers MA, MAT. Part-time and evening/weekend programs available. *Faculty:* 6 full-time (2 women), 5 part-time/adjunct (2 women). *Entrance requirements:* For master's, GRE General Test, minimum B average in undergraduate course work. Additional exam requirements/recommendations for international students: Required—TOEFL (minimum score 550 paper-based; 213 computer-based; 79 iBT). *Application deadline:* For fall admission, 6/5 priority date for domestic students; for spring admission, 10/15 for domestic students. Applications are processed on a rolling basis. Application fee: $60. Electronic applications accepted. *Expenses:* Tuition, area resident: Full-time $13,780; part-time $750 per credit. Tuition, state resident: full-time $13,780; part-time $750 per credit. Tuition, nonresident: full-time $19,580; part-time $1033 per credit. Required fees: $1956; $197 per credit. *Financial support:* Fellowships with full and partial tuition reimbursements, research assistantships with full and partial tuition reimbursements, teaching assistantships with full and partial tuition reimbursements, career-related internships or fieldwork, Federal Work-Study, institutionally sponsored loans, and unspecified assistantships available. Financial award application deadline: 3/15. *Unit head:* Dr. Richard B. Sher, Chair, 973-596-3377, Fax: 973-762-3039, E-mail: richard.b.scherl@njit.edu. *Application contact:* Kathryn Kelly, Director of Admissions, 973-596-3300, Fax: 973-596-3461, E-mail: admissions@njit.edu.

New Mexico State University, Graduate School, College of Arts and Sciences, Department of History, Las Cruces, NM 88003-8001. Offers history (MA); public history (MA). Part-time programs available. *Faculty:* 11 full-time (4 women), 2 part-time/adjunct (0 women). *Students:* 36 full-time (16 women), 20 part-time (7 women); includes 15 minority (2 American Indian/Alaska Native, 13 Hispanic Americans), 1 international. Average age 32. 31 applicants, 90% accepted, 15 enrolled. In 2008, 7 master's awarded. *Degree requirements:* For master's, thesis (for some programs). *Entrance requirements:* For master's, 12 undergraduate history credits. Additional exam requirements/recommendations for international students: Required—TOEFL (minimum score 530 paper-based; 71 iBT). *Application deadline:* For fall admission, 7/1 priority date for domestic students; for spring admission, 11/1 for domestic students. Applications are processed on a rolling basis. Application fee: $30 ($50 for international students). Electronic applications accepted. *Expenses:* Tuition, area resident: Full-time $3890; part-time $212.85 per credit. Tuition, state resident: full-time $3890; part-time $212.85 per credit. Tuition, nonresident: full-time $13,916; part-time $630.55 per credit. Required fees: $1218; $609 per semester. *Financial support:* In 2008–09, 18 students received support, including 1 research assistantship with partial tuition reimbursement available (averaging $15,800 per year), 12 teaching assistantships with partial tuition reimbursements available (averaging $8,993 per year); fellowships, career-related internships or fieldwork, Federal Work-Study, and health care benefits also available. Support available to part-time students. Financial award application deadline: 3/1. *Faculty research:* U.S. Southwestern and border history, Latin American history, U.S. women's history, European history, history of science, U.S. diplomatic history, East Asian history. *Unit head:* Dr. Jeffrey P Brown, Head, 575-646-4601, Fax: 575-646-6096, E-mail: jbrown@nmsu.edu. *Application contact:* Dr. Jamie Bronstein, Director of Graduate Studies, 575-646-4200, Fax: 575-646-6096, E-mail: jbronste@nmsu.edu.

The New School: A University, The New School for Social Research, Committee on Historical Studies, New York, NY 10011. Offers MA, PhD. Part-time and evening/weekend programs available. *Faculty:* 8 full-time (4 women). *Students:* 13 full-time (5 women), 2 part-time (1 woman); includes 4 minority (1 African American, 1 Asian American or Pacific Islander, 2 Hispanic Americans), 2 international. Average age 28. In 2008, 4 master's awarded. Terminal master's awarded for partial completion of doctoral program. *Degree requirements:* For master's, thesis optional, exam or paper; for doctorate, variable foreign language requirement, thesis/dissertation, qualifying exam. *Entrance requirements:* For master's, GRE General Test; for doctorate, GRE General Test, MA. Additional exam requirements/recommendations for international students: Required—TOEFL (minimum score 600 paper-based; 250 computer-based; 100 iBT). *Application deadline:* For fall admission, 1/15 priority date for domestic students. Applications are processed on a rolling basis. Application fee: $50. *Expenses:* Tuition: Full-time $27,144; part-time $1508 per credit. Required fees: $355 per semester. *Financial support:* Fellowships, research assistantships, teaching assistantships, career-related internships or fieldwork, Federal Work-Study, scholarships/grants, and tuition waivers (full and partial) available. Support available to part-time students. Financial award application deadline: 3/1; financial award applicants required to submit FAFSA. *Faculty research:* Social movements, systemic change, culture and history. *Unit head:* Dr. David Plotke, Chair, 212-229-5747 Ext. 3087, Fax: 212-229-5315, E-mail: plotked@newschool.edu. *Application contact:* Robert MacDonald, Director of Admissions, 800-523-5710 Ext. 3007, Fax: 212-989-7102, E-mail: macdonar@newschool.edu.

See Close-Up on page 1251.

New York University, Graduate School of Arts and Science, Department of History, New York, NY 10012-1019. Offers African diaspora (PhD); African history (PhD); archival management and historical editing (Advanced Certificate); Atlantic history (PhD); French studies/history (PhD); Hebrew and Judaic studies/history (PhD); history (MA, PhD), including Europe (PhD),

Latin American and the Caribbean (PhD), United States (PhD), women's history (MA); Middle Eastern history (MA); Middle Eastern studies/history (PhD); public history (Advanced Certificate); world history (MA); JD/MA; MA/Advanced Certificate. Part-time programs available. Terminal master's awarded for partial completion of doctoral program. *Degree requirements:* For master's, seminar paper; for doctorate, one foreign language, thesis/dissertation, oral and written exams; for Advanced Certificate, internship. *Entrance requirements:* For master's, GRE General Test, minimum GPA of 3.0, writing sample; for doctorate, GRE. Additional exam requirements/recommendations for international students: Required—TOEFL. *Faculty research:* African, East Asian, Medieval, early modern, and modern European history; U.S. history; African and African diaspora; Latin American history; Atlantic World.

North Carolina Central University, Division of Academic Affairs, College of Liberal Arts, Department of History, Durham, NC 27707-3129. Offers MA. Part-time and evening/weekend programs available. *Degree requirements:* For master's, one foreign language, comprehensive exam, thesis. *Entrance requirements:* For master's, GRE, minimum GPA of 3.0 in major, 2.5 overall. Additional exam requirements/recommendations for international students: Required—TOEFL.

North Carolina State University, Graduate School, College of Humanities and Social Sciences, Department of History, Raleigh, NC 27695. Offers history (MA); public history (MA). Part-time and evening/weekend programs available. *Degree requirements:* For master's, thesis. *Entrance requirements:* For master's, GRE General Test. Electronic applications accepted. *Faculty research:* History of the United States, Europe, Asia Africa and the Middle East; history of science; intellectual, cultural, social, environmental and political history.

North Dakota State University, College of Graduate and Interdisciplinary Studies, College of Arts, Humanities and Social Sciences, Department of History, Fargo, ND 58105. Offers MA, MS, PhD. Part-time and evening/weekend programs available. *Faculty:* 9 full-time (1 woman), 2 part-time/adjunct (0 women). *Students:* 26 full-time (25 women), 22 part-time (19 women); includes 3 minority (1 African American, 1 American Indian/Alaska Native, 1 Hispanic American), 2 international. Average age 27. 11 applicants, 91% accepted, 10 enrolled. In 2008, 12 master's awarded. *Degree requirements:* For master's, one foreign language, comprehensive exam, thesis optional; for doctorate, 2 foreign languages, comprehensive exam, thesis/dissertation. *Entrance requirements:* For master's and doctorate, GRE General Test. Additional exam requirements/recommendations for international students: Required—TOEFL (minimum score 600 paper-based; 250 computer-based; 100 iBT). *Application deadline:* For fall admission, 2/10 priority date for domestic and international students. Applications are processed on a rolling basis. Application fee: $45 ($60 for international students). *Financial support:* In 2008–09, 9 students received support, including 1 fellowship with tuition reimbursement available (averaging $15,000 per year), 2 research assistantships with full tuition reimbursements available (averaging $9,400 per year), 4 teaching assistantships with full tuition reimbursements available (averaging $8,200 per year); career-related internships or fieldwork, Federal Work-Study, institutionally sponsored loans, and tuition waivers also available. Financial award application deadline: 3/15. *Faculty research:* Recent US, modern English, early modern European, North Dakota, Latin American, and Great Plains history. *Unit head:* Dr. John K. Cox, Head, 701-231-8654, Fax: 701-231-1047, E-mail: john.cox.l@ndsu.edu. *Application contact:* Dr. Jim Norris, Graduate Coordinator, 701-231-8827, Fax: 701-231-1047, E-mail: jim.norris@nodak.edu.

Northeastern Illinois University, Graduate College, College of Arts and Sciences, Department of History, Program in History, Chicago, IL 60625-4699. Offers MA. Part-time and evening/weekend programs available. *Degree requirements:* For master's, comprehensive exam, thesis optional, minimum GPA of 3.0. *Entrance requirements:* For master's, 24 undergraduate hours in history, minimum GPA of 2.75. Additional exam requirements/recommendations for international students: Required—TOEFL (minimum score 550 paper-based; 213 computer-based; 80 iBT). Electronic applications accepted. *Faculty research:* Africa; East Asia; European medieval, early-modern, and modern history; U.S. social, cultural, and intellectual history.

Northeastern University, College of Arts and Sciences, Department of History, Boston, MA 02115-5096. Offers history (MA); public history (MA); world history (PhD). Part-time and evening/weekend programs available. Terminal master's awarded for partial completion of doctoral program. *Degree requirements:* For master's, one foreign language, thesis or alternative, project; for doctorate, thesis/dissertation. *Entrance requirements:* For master's and doctorate, GRE General Test. Electronic applications accepted. *Faculty research:* World history, U.S. social history.

Northern Arizona University, Graduate College, College of Arts and Letters, Department of History, Flagstaff, AZ 86011. Offers MA, PhD. Part-time programs available. *Degree requirements:* For master's, thesis or departmental qualifying exam; for doctorate, thesis/dissertation. *Entrance requirements:* For master's and doctorate, GRE General Test. *Faculty research:* Twentieth-century U.S., U.S. trans-Mississippi West, Arizona and the Southwest, women's history, U.S. intellectual history.

Northern Illinois University, Graduate School, College of Liberal Arts and Sciences, Department of History, De Kalb, IL 60115-2854. Offers MA, PhD. Part-time programs available. Terminal master's awarded for partial completion of doctoral program. *Degree requirements:* For master's, variable foreign language requirement, comprehensive exam, thesis optional, research seminars; for doctorate, variable foreign language requirement, thesis/dissertation, candidacy exam, dissertation defense, research seminars. *Entrance requirements:* For master's, GRE General Test, minimum GPA of 2.75; for doctorate, GRE General Test, minimum undergraduate GPA of 2.75, graduate GPA of 3.2. Additional exam requirements/recommendations for international students: Required—TOEFL (minimum score 550 paper-based; 213 computer-based). Electronic applications accepted. *Faculty research:* History of the Carolingian empire, world history of early modern Europe, modern Irish history, history of the Ming dynasty.

Northwestern University, The Graduate School, Judd A. and Marjorie Weinberg College of Arts and Sciences, Department of History, Evanston, IL 60208. Offers PhD, JD/PhD. Admissions and degrees offered through The Graduate School. *Degree requirements:* For doctorate, variable foreign language requirement, thesis/dissertation, major and minor field exams. *Entrance requirements:* For doctorate, sample of written work. Additional exam requirements/recommendations for international students: Required—TOEFL. Electronic applications accepted. *Faculty research:* Medieval and early modern Europe, Africa, race and slavery, Atlantic history, gender.

Northwest Missouri State University, Graduate School, College of Arts and Sciences, Department of History, Humanities, and Political Science, Maryville, MO 64468-6001. Offers history (MA); teaching history (MS Ed). Part-time programs available. *Degree requirements:* For master's, comprehensive exam, thesis. *Entrance requirements:* For master's, GRE General Test, undergraduate major/minor in social studies/humanities, minimum undergraduate GPA of 2.5, writing sample. Additional exam requirements/recommendations for international students: Required—TOEFL (minimum score 550 paper-based; 213 computer-based).

Oakland University, Graduate Study and Lifelong Learning, College of Arts and Sciences, Department of History, Rochester, MI 48309-4401. Offers MA. Part-time and evening/weekend programs available. *Entrance requirements:* For master's, minimum GPA of 3.0 for unconditional admission. Additional exam requirements/recommendations for international students: Required—TOEFL (minimum score 550 paper-based; 213 computer-based). Electronic applications accepted.

The Ohio State University, Graduate School, College of Humanities, Department of History, Columbus, OH 43210. Offers MA, PhD. *Degree requirements:* For master's, thesis optional; for doctorate, variable foreign language requirement, thesis/dissertation. *Entrance requirements:* For master's and doctorate, GRE General Test. Additional exam requirements/recommendations for international students: Required—TOEFL (minimum score 600 paper-based; 250 computer-based). Electronic applications accepted.

Ohio University, Graduate College, College of Arts and Sciences, Department of History, Athens, OH 45701-2979. Offers MA, PhD. *Degree requirements:* For master's, one foreign language, thesis optional; for doctorate, 2 foreign languages, comprehensive exam, thesis/dissertation. *Entrance requirements:* For master's, GRE, minimum GPA of 3.0; for doctorate, GRE, minimum GPA of 3.0, completed M.A. Additional exam requirements/recommendations for international students: Required—TOEFL (minimum score 550 paper-based; 213 computer-based), IELTS (minimum score 6.5), TWE (minimum score 5). Electronic applications accepted. *Faculty research:* U.S. foreign relations, modern Europe, Latin America, southeast Asia, U.S. women.

Oklahoma State University, College of Arts and Sciences, Department of History, Stillwater, OK 74078. Offers applied history (MA); history (PhD). *Faculty:* 23 full-time (5 women), 3 part-time/adjunct (1 woman). *Students:* 18 full-time (7 women), 44 part-time (16 women); includes 7 minority (4 American Indian/Alaska Native, 2 Asian Americans or Pacific Islanders, 1 Hispanic American), 1 international. Average age 34. 48 applicants, 60% accepted, 18 enrolled. In 2008, 4 master's, 1 doctorate awarded. *Degree requirements:* For master's, thesis; for doctorate, comprehensive exam, thesis/dissertation. *Entrance requirements:* For master's and doctorate, GRE. Additional exam requirements/recommendations for international students: Required—TOEFL. *Application deadline:* For fall admission, 3/1 priority date for international students; for spring admission, 8/1 priority date for international students. Applications are processed on a rolling basis. Application fee: $40 ($75 for international students). Electronic applications accepted. *Expenses:* Tuition, state resident: full-time $3716.40; part-time $154.85 per credit hour. Tuition, nonresident: full-time $14,448; part-time $602 per credit hour. Required fees: $1772.40; $73.85 per credit hour. One-time fee: $50. Tuition and fees vary according to course load and campus/location. *Financial support:* In 2008–09, 1 research assistantship (averaging $10,038 per year), 23 teaching assistantships (averaging $15,267 per year) were awarded; career-related internships or fieldwork, Federal Work-Study, scholarships/grants, health care benefits, tuition waivers (partial), and unspecified assistantships also available. Support available to part-time students. Financial award application deadline: 3/1; financial award applicants required to submit FAFSA. *Faculty research:* U.S. history, The American West, Native American history, modern European history, women's history. *Unit head:* Dr. Michael F Logan, Head, 405-744-5678, Fax: 405-744-5400. *Application contact:* Dr. Gordon Emslie, Dean, 405-744-6368, Fax: 405-744-0355, E-mail: grad_i@okstate.edu.

Old Dominion University, College of Arts and Letters, Program in History, Norfolk, VA 23529. Offers MA. Part-time and evening/weekend programs available. *Faculty:* 16 full-time (7 women). *Students:* 14 full-time (5 women), 34 part-time (15 women); includes 4 minority (all African Americans). Average age 31. 41 applicants, 80% accepted, 20 enrolled. In 2008, 9 master's awarded. *Degree requirements:* For master's, comprehensive exam, thesis optional. *Entrance requirements:* For master's, GRE General Test, 24 credits in history with minimum GPA of 3.0. *Application deadline:* For fall admission, 6/1 for domestic students; for spring admission, 11/1 for domestic students. Applications are processed on a rolling basis. Application fee: $40. Electronic applications accepted. *Expenses:* Tuition, area resident: Full-time $7704; part-time $321 per credit. Tuition, state resident: full-time $7704; part-time $321 per credit. Tuition, nonresident: full-time $19,104; part-time $796 per credit. Required fees: $99 per semester. One-time fee: $40. *Financial support:* In 2008–09, 1 fellowship with full tuition reimbursement (averaging $8,000 per year), 6 teaching assistantships with partial tuition reimbursements (averaging $8,000 per year) were awarded; career-related internships or fieldwork and scholarships/grants also available. Support available to part-time students. Financial award application deadline: 2/15; financial award applicants required to submit FAFSA. *Faculty research:* History: maritime, American, European, modern Asia, and Africa. *Unit head:* Dr. Ingo K Heidbrink, Graduate Program Director, 757-683-3949, Fax: 757-683-5644, E-mail: histgpd@odu.edu. *Application contact:* Dr. Ingo K Heidbrink, Graduate Program Director, 757-683-3949, Fax: 757-683-5644, E-mail: histgpd@odu.edu.

Oregon State University, Graduate School, College of Liberal Arts, Department of History, Corvallis, OR 97331. Offers MA, MS, PhD.

Penn State University Park, Graduate School, College of the Liberal Arts, Department of History, State College, University Park, PA 16802-1503. Offers MA, PhD.

Pepperdine University, Seaver College, Humanities Division, Malibu, CA 90263. Offers American studies (MA); history (MA). *Degree requirements:* For master's, oral and written exams. *Entrance requirements:* For master's, GRE General Test, undergraduate major or 15 upper-division units in history. Additional exam requirements/recommendations for international students: Required—TOEFL.

Pittsburg State University, Graduate School, College of Arts and Sciences, Department of History, Pittsburg, KS 66762. Offers MA. *Degree requirements:* For master's, thesis or alternative.

Pontifical Catholic University of Puerto Rico, College of Arts and Humanities, Department of History, Ponce, PR 00717-0777. Offers MA. *Entrance requirements:* For master's, GRE General Test, minimum GPA of 2.75, 2 letters of recommendation.

Portland State University, Graduate Studies, College of Liberal Arts and Sciences, Department of History, Portland, OR 97207-0751. Offers MA. Part-time programs available. *Faculty:* 21 full-time (8 women), 6 part-time/adjunct (4 women). *Students:* 23 full-time (9 women), 26 part-time (15 women); includes 4 minority (2 American Indian/Alaska Native, 1 Asian American or Pacific Islander, 1 Hispanic American). Average age 34. 33 applicants, 52% accepted, 13 enrolled. In 2008, 11 master's awarded. *Degree requirements:* For master's, one foreign language, thesis, oral and written exams. *Entrance requirements:* For master's, GRE General Test, minimum GPA of 3.5 in upper-division history courses, 2 letters of recommendation, BA/BS in history. Additional exam requirements/recommendations for international students: Required—TOEFL (minimum score 550 paper-based; 213 computer-based). *Application deadline:* For fall admission, 2/15 for domestic and international students; for winter admission, 9/1 for domestic students, 6/1 for international students; for spring admission, 11/1 for domestic and international students. Application fee: $50. *Expenses:* Tuition, area resident: Full-time $8763; part-time $179 per credit hour. Tuition, state resident: full-time $8763; part-time $298 per credit hour. Tuition, nonresident: full-time $12,981; part-time $426 per credit hour. Required fees: $1242. One-time fee: $250. Tuition and fees vary according to course load and program. *Financial support:* In 2008–09, 2 research assistantships with full tuition reimbursements (averaging $11,238 per year) were awarded; teaching assistantships with full tuition reimbursements, career-related internships or fieldwork, Federal Work-Study, scholarships/grants, and unspecified assistantships also available. Support available to part-time students. Financial award application deadline: 3/1; financial award applicants required to submit FAFSA. *Faculty research:* Germany and Modern Europe, early modern France and England, Mexico in the 1920's, eighteenth century France, Reformation, U.S. cultural history. Total annual research expenditures: $6,689. *Unit head:* Dr. Thomas Luckett, Chair, 503-725-3917, Fax: 503-725-3953. *Application contact:* Dr. Richard Beyler, Graduate Coordinator, 503-725-3996, Fax: 503-725-3953, E-mail: beylerr@pdx.edu.

Princeton University, Graduate School, Department of Classics, Princeton, NJ 08544-1019. Offers classical and hellenic studies (PhD); classical philosophy (PhD); history (the ancient world) (PhD); literature and philology (PhD). *Degree requirements:* For doctorate, thesis/dissertation. *Entrance requirements:* For doctorate, GRE General Test, sample of written work. Additional exam requirements/recommendations for international students: Required—TOEFL (minimum score 600 paper-based; 250 computer-based). Electronic applications accepted.

Princeton University, Graduate School, Department of History, Princeton, NJ 08544-1019. Offers history (PhD); history of science (PhD). *Degree requirements:* For doctorate, variable foreign language requirement, comprehensive exam, thesis/dissertation. *Entrance requirements:* For doctorate, GRE General Test, sample of written work. Additional exam requirements/

History

Princeton University (continued)
recommendations for international students: Required—TOEFL (minimum score 600 paper-based; 250 computer-based). Electronic applications accepted. *Faculty research:* World comparative, Europe-early modern, modern, late antique, medieval.

Providence College, Graduate Studies, Department of History, Providence, RI 02918. Offers American history (MA); European history (MA). Part-time and evening/weekend programs available. *Faculty:* 11 full-time (3 women), 3 part-time/adjunct (0 women). *Students:* 17 full-time (9 women), 47 part-time (20 women), 1 international. Average age 31. 10 applicants, 100% accepted. In 2008, 26 master's awarded. *Degree requirements:* For master's, comprehensive exam, thesis optional. *Entrance requirements:* Additional exam requirements/recommendations for international students: Required—TOEFL (minimum score 550 paper-based; 213 computer-based; 80 iBT). *Application deadline:* For fall admission, 8/1 priority date for domestic and international students; for spring admission, 12/31 priority date for domestic students, 12/1 priority date for international students. Applications are processed on a rolling basis. Application fee: $55. *Expenses:* Tuition: Full-time $8991; part-time $333 per credit hour. One-time fee: $170. Tuition and fees vary according to program. *Financial support:* In 2008–09, 8 research assistantships with full tuition reimbursements (averaging $8,400 per year) were awarded; career-related internships or fieldwork, institutionally sponsored loans, and unspecified assistantships also available. Support available to part-time students. Financial award application deadline: 8/1; financial award applicants required to submit FAFSA. *Faculty research:* Modern Europe, American social and political history, Modern Ireland, Rhode Island, Eastern European history. *Unit head:* Dr. Paul O'Malley, Director of Graduate Program in History, 401-865-2193, Fax: 401-865-1193, E-mail: pomalley@providence.edu. *Application contact:* Phyllis S. Cardullo, Senior Administrative Coordinator, 401-865-2193, Fax: 401-865-1193, E-mail: pcardull@providence.edu.

Purdue University, Graduate School, College of Liberal Arts, Department of History, West Lafayette, IN 47907. Offers MA, PhD. Part-time programs available. *Degree requirements:* For master's, thesis optional; for doctorate, 2 foreign languages, thesis/dissertation. *Entrance requirements:* For master's and doctorate, GRE General Test, sample of written work. Additional exam requirements/recommendations for international students: Required—TOEFL. Electronic applications accepted. *Faculty research:* U.S. history, early modern and modern European history, global women's history, U.S. minority history, medieval history.

Purdue University Calumet, Graduate School, School of Liberal Arts and Social Sciences, Department of History and Political Science, Hammond, IN 46323-2094. Offers history (MA). Part-time and evening/weekend programs available. *Entrance requirements:* Additional exam requirements/recommendations for international students: Required—TOEFL. *Faculty research:* Mid-east, German history, US regional history, US social history, holocaust.

Queens College of the City University of New York, Division of Graduate Studies, Social Science Division, Department of History, Flushing, NY 11367-1597. Offers MA. Part-time and evening/weekend programs available. *Degree requirements:* For master's, one foreign language, comprehensive exam, thesis. *Entrance requirements:* For master's, minimum GPA of 3.0. Additional exam requirements/recommendations for international students: Required—TOEFL. *Faculty research:* Ancient, modern European, medieval, and American history.

Rhode Island College, School of Graduate Studies, Faculty of Arts and Sciences, Department of History, Providence, RI 02908-1991. Offers MA. Part-time and evening/weekend programs available. *Faculty:* 9 full-time (3 women), 1 (woman) part-time/adjunct. *Students:* 1 full-time (0 women), 6 part-time (2 women). Average age 31. In 2008, 2 master's awarded. *Degree requirements:* For master's, oral exam or thesis. *Entrance requirements:* For master's, GRE General Test and GRE Subject Test or MAT, 3 letters of recommendation, interview. Additional exam requirements/recommendations for international students: Recommended—TOEFL (minimum score 550 paper-based; 213 computer-based; 79 iBT). *Application deadline:* For fall admission, 4/1 for domestic students; for spring admission, 11/1 for domestic students. Applications are processed on a rolling basis. Application fee: $50. *Expenses:* Tuition, area resident: Full-time $6816; part-time $284 per credit hour. Tuition, state resident: full-time $6816; part-time $284 per credit hour. Tuition, nonresident: full-time $13,920; part-time $580 per credit hour. Required fees: $454; $16 per credit. $68 per term. *Financial support:* Teaching assistantships with full tuition reimbursements, Federal Work-Study, scholarships/grants, health care benefits, and unspecified assistantships available. Support available to part-time students. Financial award application deadline: 5/15; financial award applicants required to submit FAFSA. *Unit head:* Dr. Robert Cvornvek, Chair, 401-456-8039. *Application contact:* Graduate Studies, 401-456-8700.

Rice University, Graduate Programs, School of Humanities, Department of History, Houston, TX 77251-1892. Offers MA, PhD. Terminal master's awarded for partial completion of doctoral program. *Degree requirements:* For doctorate, one foreign language, comprehensive exam, thesis/dissertation. *Entrance requirements:* For master's and doctorate, GRE General Test, minimum GPA of 3.0. Additional exam requirements/recommendations for international students: Required—TOEFL (minimum score 600 paper-based; 250 computer-based; 90 iBT). *Faculty research:* Modern European and American military, modern British history, U.S. South, world history.

Roosevelt University, Graduate Division, College of Arts and Sciences, Department of History, Art, and Philosophy, Chicago, IL 60605-1394. Offers history (MA). Part-time and evening/weekend programs available. *Students:* 8 full-time (6 women), 22 part-time (12 women); includes 8 minority (4 African Americans, 4 Hispanic Americans). Average age 37. 62 applicants, 19% accepted, 5 enrolled. In 2008, 7 master's awarded. *Degree requirements:* For master's, thesis or alternative. *Application deadline:* For fall admission, 6/1 priority date for domestic students. Applications are processed on a rolling basis. Application fee: $25 ($35 for international students). *Expenses:* Tuition: Full-time $14,730; part-time $709 per credit. Required fees: $175 per semester. Tuition and fees vary according to course load and program. *Financial support:* Application deadline: 2/15. *Faculty research:* American social history, Holocaust, European history, African-American history, popular culture. *Unit head:* Susan Weininger, Head, 312-341-3711, E-mail: sweining@roosevelt.edu. *Application contact:* Joanne Canyon-Heller, Coordinator of Graduate Admission, 877-APPLY RU, Fax: 312-281-3356, E-mail: applyru@roosevelt.edu.

Rutgers, The State University of New Jersey, Camden, Graduate School of Arts and Sciences, Program in American and Public History, Camden, NJ 08102-1401. Offers MA. Part-time and evening/weekend programs available. *Degree requirements:* For master's, comprehensive exam. *Entrance requirements:* For master's, GRE General Test (full-time applicants), 3 letters of recommendation. Additional exam requirements/recommendations for international students: Required—TOEFL, IELTS. Electronic applications accepted. *Faculty research:* Women's history, military history, Afro-American history, urban history, history of technology.

Rutgers, The State University of New Jersey, Newark, Graduate School, Program in History, Newark, NJ 07102. Offers MA, MAT. Part-time and evening/weekend programs available. *Degree requirements:* For master's, one foreign language, comprehensive exam, thesis optional. *Entrance requirements:* For master's, GRE, minimum undergraduate B average. *Faculty research:* Global history, American history, American diplomatic and legal history, women's history, history of technology, environment and medicine.

Rutgers, The State University of New Jersey, New Brunswick, Graduate School, Program in History, Piscataway, NJ 08854-8097. Offers African-American history (PhD); early American history (PhD); early modern European history (PhD); east Asian history (PhD); global and comparative history (PhD); history (PhD); history of diplomacy and foreign relations (PhD); history of technology, environment and health (PhD); history of the Atlantic cultures and African diaspora (PhD); Latin American history (PhD); medieval history (PhD); modern European history (PhD); nineteenth and twentieth century American history (PhD); women's and gender history (PhD). *Degree requirements:* For doctorate, thesis/dissertation. *Entrance requirements:* For doctorate, GRE General Test, sample of written work. Electronic applications accepted. *Faculty research:* American history, European history, Afro-American history, women's history, Latin American history.

St. Cloud State University, School of Graduate Studies, College of Social Sciences, Department of History, St. Cloud, MN 56301-4498. Offers MA, MS. Part-time programs available. *Degree requirements:* For master's, thesis or alternative. *Entrance requirements:* For master's, GRE General Test, GRE Subject Test, minimum GPA of 2.75. Additional exam requirements/recommendations for international students: Required—Michigan English Language Assessment Battery; Recommended—TOEFL (minimum score 550 paper-based; 213 computer-based), IELTS (minimum score 6.5).

St. John's University, St. John's College of Liberal Arts and Sciences, Department of History, Queens, NY 11439. Offers history (MA); modern world history (DA). Part-time and evening/weekend programs available. *Students:* 7 full-time (5 women), 44 part-time (14 women); includes 10 minority (5 African Americans, 1 Asian American or Pacific Islander, 4 Hispanic Americans), 11 international. Average age 37. 25 applicants, 80% accepted, 11 enrolled. In 2008, 8 master's, 1 doctorate awarded. *Degree requirements:* For master's, one foreign language, comprehensive exam, thesis optional; for doctorate, one foreign language, comprehensive exam, thesis/dissertation, internship, practicum. *Entrance requirements:* For master's, minimum GPA of 3.0; for doctorate, interview; minimum GPA of 3.5 in history, 3.0 overall; writing sample. Additional exam requirements/recommendations for international students: Required—TOEFL (minimum score 500 paper-based; 173 computer-based; 61 iBT), IELTS (minimum score 5.5). *Application deadline:* For fall admission, 5/1 priority date for domestic and international students; for spring admission, 11/1 priority date for domestic and international students. Applications are processed on a rolling basis. Application fee: $70. Electronic applications accepted. *Expenses:* Tuition: Full-time $20,760; part-time $865 per credit. Required fees: $300; $150 per semester. Tuition and fees vary according to program. *Financial support:* Fellowships, research assistantships, scholarships/grants available. Support available to part-time students. Financial award application deadline: 3/1; financial award applicants required to submit FAFSA. *Faculty research:* European economic history, history of East Asian culture, Irish history. *Unit head:* Dr. Mauricio Borrero, Chair, 718-990-6228, E-mail: borrerom@stjohns.edu. *Application contact:* Kathleen Davis, Director of Graduate Admission, 718-990-2790, Fax: 718-990-5686, E-mail: gradhelp@stjohns.edu.

Saint Louis University, Graduate School, College of Arts and Sciences and Graduate School, Department of History, St. Louis, MO 63103-2097. Offers MA, MA-R, PhD. Part-time programs available. *Degree requirements:* For master's, one foreign language, comprehensive exam, thesis optional, comprehensive oral exam; for doctorate, 2 foreign languages, comprehensive exam, thesis/dissertation, preliminary oral and written exams. *Entrance requirements:* For master's and doctorate, GRE General Test, letters of recommendation, resumé, writing sample, goal statement, transcripts. Additional exam requirements/recommendations for international students: Required—TOEFL (minimum score 525 paper-based; 194 computer-based). Electronic applications accepted. *Faculty research:* Medieval Europe, Crusades, Byzantine Empire, US West and Borderlands, Early Modern Europe.

Saint Mary's University, Faculty of Arts, Department of History, Halifax, NS B3H 3C3, Canada. Offers MA. Part-time programs available. *Degree requirements:* For master's, one foreign language, comprehensive exam, thesis. *Entrance requirements:* For master's, honors degree. *Expenses:* Contact institution. *Faculty research:* Atlantic Canada, British Empire, history of science, South Africa.

Salem State College, School of Graduate Studies, Program in History, Salem, MA 01970-5353. Offers MA, MAT. Part-time and evening/weekend programs available. *Students:* 2 full-time (1 woman), 57 part-time (24 women). Average age 33. In 2008, 17 master's awarded. *Degree requirements:* For master's, one foreign language, thesis optional. *Entrance requirements:* For master's, GRE General Test, MAT. *Application deadline:* Applications are processed on a rolling basis. Application fee: $35. *Unit head:* Emerson Baker, Associate Professor, 978-542-6321, Fax: 978-542-7215, E-mail: ebaker@salemstate.edu. *Application contact:* Dr. Marc Glasser, Dean of the Graduate School, 978-542-6323, Fax: 978-542-7215.

Salisbury University, Graduate Division, Program in History, Salisbury, MD 21801-6837. Offers MA. Part-time programs available. *Faculty:* 10 full-time (3 women). *Students:* 6 full-time (0 women), 8 part-time (3 women). Average age 25. 8 applicants, 50% accepted, 1 enrolled. In 2008, 7 master's awarded. *Degree requirements:* For master's, comprehensive exam, thesis optional, 2 research and 3 reading seminars, final and oral exam. *Entrance requirements:* For master's, GRE General Test, minimum GPA of 3.0, 3 letters of recommendation. Additional exam requirements/recommendations for international students: Required—TOEFL (minimum score 550 paper-based; 213 computer-based). *Application deadline:* For fall admission, 5/15 for domestic students; for spring admission, 10/15 for domestic students. Application fee: $45. Electronic applications accepted. *Expenses:* Tuition, area resident: Part-time $270 per credit hour. Tuition, state resident: part-time $270 per credit hour. Tuition, nonresident: part-time $566 per credit hour. Required fees: $52 per credit hour. *Financial support:* In 2008–09, 3 students received support, including 3 research assistantships with partial tuition reimbursements available; career-related internships or fieldwork and scholarships/grants also available. Support available to part-time students. Financial award applicants required to submit FAFSA. *Faculty research:* History of science and technology, U. S. foreign relations, Maryland history, African-American history, medieval history. *Unit head:* Dr. Creston S. Long, Director, 410-548-5091, Fax: 410-677-5038, E-mail: cslong@salisbury.edu. *Application contact:* Mia C Vye, Administrative Assistant II, 410-548-4499, Fax: 410-677-5038, E-mail: mcvye@salisbury.edu.

Sam Houston State University, College of Humanities and Social Sciences, Department of History, Huntsville, TX 77341. Offers MA. Part-time and evening/weekend programs available. *Faculty:* 15 full-time (5 women). *Students:* 8 full-time (4 women), 54 part-time (13 women); includes 4 minority (1 Asian American or Pacific Islander, 3 Hispanic Americans). Average age 37. 35 applicants, 86% accepted, 24 enrolled. In 2008, 7 master's awarded. *Entrance requirements:* For master's, GRE General Test. Additional exam requirements/recommendations for international students: Required—TOEFL (minimum score 550 paper-based; 213 computer-based; 79 iBT). *Application deadline:* For fall admission, 8/1 for domestic students; for spring admission, 12/1 for domestic students. Application fee: $20. *Expenses:* Tuition, state resident: full-time $3564; part-time $198 per credit hour. Tuition, nonresident: full-time $8622; part-time $479 per credit hour. Required fees: $1290. Tuition and fees vary according to course load and campus/location. *Financial support:* Teaching assistantships, Federal Work-Study and institutionally sponsored loans available. Support available to part-time students. Financial award application deadline: 5/31; financial award applicants required to submit FAFSA. *Unit head:* Dr. Terry Bilhartz, Chair, 936-294-1483, Fax: 936-294-3938, E-mail: his_tdb@shsu.edu. *Application contact:* Dr. Mitchell Muehsam, Dean of Graduate Studies and Associate Vice President for Academic Affairs, 936-294-1971, Fax: 936-294-1271, E-mail: graduate@shsu.edu.

San Diego State University, Graduate and Research Affairs, College of Arts and Letters, Department of History, San Diego, CA 92182. Offers MA. *Degree requirements:* For master's, one foreign language. *Entrance requirements:* For master's, GRE General Test, bachelor's degree in related field. Additional exam requirements/recommendations for international students: Required—TOEFL. Electronic applications accepted. *Faculty research:* Latin American history, Filipino history.

San Francisco State University, Division of Graduate Studies, College of Behavioral and Social Sciences, Department of History, San Francisco, CA 94132-1722. Offers MA.

San Jose State University, Graduate Studies and Research, College of Social Sciences, Department of History, San Jose, CA 95192-0001. Offers history (MA); history education (MA). *Degree requirements:* For master's, comprehensive exam, thesis or alternative. *Entrance* requirements: For master's, bachelor's degree or 15 units of course work in history, minimum GPA of 3.0. Electronic applications accepted.

Sarah Lawrence College, Graduate Studies, Program in Women's History, Bronxville, NY 10708-5999. Offers MA. Part-time programs available. *Faculty:* 9 part-time/adjunct (8 women). *Students:* 26 full-time (25 women), 4 part-time (all women); includes 7 minority (2 African Americans, 2 Asian Americans or Pacific Islanders, 3 Hispanic Americans), 1 international. Average age 27. 48 applicants, 85% accepted, 18 enrolled. In 2008, 8 master's awarded. *Degree requirements:* For master's, thesis. *Entrance requirements:* For master's, previous course work in history, minimum B average in undergraduate course work. Additional exam requirements/recommendations for international students: Required—TOEFL (minimum score 600 paper-based). *Application deadline:* For fall admission, 2/1 priority date for domestic students. Applications are processed on a rolling basis. Application fee: $60. *Expenses:* Tuition: Full-time $26,544; part-time $1106 per credit. Required fees: $450. Tuition and fees vary according to program. *Financial support:* Fellowships, career-related internships or fieldwork available. Support available to part-time students. Financial award application deadline: 3/1; financial award applicants required to submit CSS PROFILE or FAFSA. *Unit head:* Priscilla Murolo, Director, 914-395-2405. *Application contact:* Susan Guma, Dean of Graduate Studies, 914-395-2373, E-mail: sguma@mail.slc.edu.

See Close-Up on page 621.

Seton Hall University, College of Arts and Sciences, Department of History, South Orange, NJ 07079-2697. Offers Catholic history (MA); European history (MA); global history (MA); US history (MA). Electronic applications accepted. *Faculty research:* Latin America Renaissance, Italy, Italian-American, urban African-American, law.

See Close-Up on page 329.

Shippensburg University of Pennsylvania, School of Graduate Studies, College of Arts and Sciences, Department of History and Philosophy, Shippensburg, PA 17257-2299. Offers applied history (MA, Certificate). Part-time and evening/weekend programs available. *Faculty:* 6 full-time (1 woman), 2 part-time/adjunct (0 women). *Students:* 23 full-time (11 women), 20 part-time (6 women). Average age 28. 36 applicants, 75% accepted, 18 enrolled. In 2008, 19 master's awarded. *Degree requirements:* For master's, thesis or internship. *Entrance requirements:* For master's, interview, 500-word statement of purpose (if undergraduate GPA is less than 2.75). Additional exam requirements/recommendations for international students: Required—TOEFL (minimum score 560 paper-based; 220 computer-based); Recommended—IELTS (minimum score 6). *Application deadline:* For fall admission, 3/1 for international students; for spring admission, 7/1 for international students. Applications are processed on a rolling basis. Application fee: $30. Electronic applications accepted. *Expenses:* Tuition, state resident: full-time $6430; part-time $357 per credit. Tuition, nonresident: full-time $10,288; part-time $572 per credit. Required fees: $1127; $38 per credit. One-time fee: $44 part-time. *Financial support:* In 2008–09, 10 research assistantships with full tuition reimbursements (averaging $5,000 per year) were awarded; career-related internships or fieldwork, scholarships/grants, unspecified assistantships, and resident hall directors, student payroll positions also available. Support available to part-time students. Financial award application deadline: 3/1; financial award applicants required to submit FAFSA. *Unit head:* Dr. Susan Rimby, Chairperson, 717-477-1621, Fax: 717-477-4062, E-mail: srrimb@ship.edu. *Application contact:* Renee Payne, Associate Dean of Graduate Admissions, 717-477-1231, Fax: 717-477-4016, E-mail: rmpayn@ship.edu.

Shippensburg University of Pennsylvania, School of Graduate Studies, College of Education and Human Services, Department of Teacher Education, Shippensburg, PA 17257-2299. Offers curriculum and instruction (M Ed), including biology, early childhood education, elementary education, English, foreign languages, geography/earth science, history, mathematics, middle school education; reading (M Ed). *Accreditation:* NCATE. Part-time and evening/weekend programs available. *Faculty:* 12 full-time (8 women), 7 part-time/adjunct (6 women). *Students:* 10 full-time (6 women), 171 part-time (154 women); includes 6 minority (2 African Americans, 2 Asian Americans or Pacific Islanders, 2 Hispanic Americans), 2 international. Average age 31. 56 applicants, 59% accepted, 24 enrolled. In 2008, 66 master's awarded. *Degree requirements:* For master's, comprehensive exam (for some programs), thesis optional, practicum or internship (for some programs). *Entrance requirements:* For master's, MAT (if GPA is below 2.75), interview, 3 letters of recommendation, writing sample of teaching background and future goals. Additional exam requirements/recommendations for international students: Required—TOEFL (minimum score 560 paper-based; 220 computer-based); Recommended—IELTS (minimum score 6). *Application deadline:* For fall admission, 6/1 priority date for domestic students, 3/1 for international students; for spring admission, 9/1 priority date for domestic students, 7/1 for international students. Applications are processed on a rolling basis. Application fee: $30. Electronic applications accepted. *Expenses:* Tuition, state resident: full-time $6430; part-time $357 per credit. Tuition, nonresident: full-time $10,288; part-time $572 per credit. Required fees: $1127; $38 per credit. One-time fee: $44 part-time. *Financial support:* In 2008–09, 5 research assistantships with full tuition reimbursements (averaging $5,000 per year) were awarded; career-related internships or fieldwork, scholarships/grants, unspecified assistantships, and resident hall directors, student payroll positions also available. Support available to part-time students. Financial award application deadline: 3/1; financial award applicants required to submit FAFSA. *Unit head:* Dr. Christine A. Royce, Chairperson, 717-477-1688, Fax: 717-477-4046, E-mail: caroyc@ship.edu. *Application contact:* Renee Payne, Associate Dean of Graduate Admissions, 717-477-1231, Fax: 717-477-4016, E-mail: rmpayn@ship.edu.

Simon Fraser University, Graduate Studies, Faculty of Arts and Social Sciences, Department of History, Burnaby, BC V5A 1S6, Canada. Offers MA, PhD. *Degree requirements:* For master's, one foreign language, thesis or alternative, project; for doctorate, one foreign language, comprehensive exam, thesis/dissertation. *Entrance requirements:* For master's, minimum GPA of 3.0; for doctorate, minimum GPA of 3.5. Additional exam requirements/recommendations for international students: Required—TOEFL or IELTS. *Faculty research:* Colonialism and imperialism, Canadian history, Middle East and Islam labor, Victorian intellect.

Slippery Rock University of Pennsylvania, Graduate Studies (Recruitment), College of Humanities, Fine and Performing Arts, Department of History, Slippery Rock, PA 16057-1383. Offers MA. Part-time and evening/weekend programs available. *Degree requirements:* For master's, comprehensive exam (for some programs), thesis (for some programs). *Entrance requirements:* For master's, GRE General Test, MAT, minimum GPA of 2.75. Additional exam requirements/recommendations for international students: Required—TOEFL (minimum score 550 paper-based; 213 computer-based). *Application deadline:* For fall admission, 7/1 priority date for domestic and international students; for spring admission, 11/1 priority date for domestic and international students. Applications are processed on a rolling basis. Application fee: $25. Electronic applications accepted. *Expenses:* Tuition, area resident: Full-time $6430; part-time $357 per credit. Tuition, state resident: full-time $6430; part-time $357 per credit. Tuition, nonresident: full-time $10,288; part-time $572 per credit. Required fees: $2062; $158 per credit. *Financial support:* Career-related internships or fieldwork, Federal Work-Study, scholarships/grants, and unspecified assistantships available. Support available to part-time students. Financial award application deadline: 5/1; financial award applicants required to submit FAFSA. *Unit head:* Dr. John Craig, Graduate Coordinator, 724-738-2406, Fax: 724-738-4762, E-mail: john.craig@sru.edu. *Application contact:* Angela Piverotto, Interim Director of Graduate Studies, 724-738-2051, Fax: 724-738-2146, E-mail: graduate.admissions@sru.edu.

Smith College, Graduate and Special Programs, Department of History, Northampton, MA 01063. Offers MAT. *Faculty:* 10 full-time (5 women), 1 (woman) part-time/adjunct. *Students:* 1 full-time (0 women). Average age 22. 2 applicants, 100% accepted, 1 enrolled. In 2008, 1 master's awarded. *Entrance requirements:* Additional exam requirements/recommendations for international students: Required—TOEFL (minimum score 590 paper-based; 243 computer-

based; 97 iBT). *Application deadline:* For fall admission, 4/15 for domestic students, 1/15 for international students; for spring admission, 12/1 for domestic students. Application fee: $60. *Financial support:* In 2008–09, 1 student received support. Career-related internships or fieldwork, institutionally sponsored loans, and scholarships/grants available. Support available to part-time students. Financial award application deadline: 1/15; financial award applicants required to submit CSS PROFILE or FAFSA. *Unit head:* Ernest Benz, Associate Professor, 413-585-3716, E-mail: ebenz@smith.edu. *Application contact:* Ruth Morgan, Administrative Assistant, 413-585-3050, Fax: 413-585-3054, E-mail: gradstdy@smith.edu.

Sonoma State University, School of Social Sciences, Department of History, Rohnert Park, CA 94928-3609. Offers MA. Part-time programs available. *Degree requirements:* For master's, thesis or alternative. *Entrance requirements:* For master's, GRE General Test or GRE Subject Test, minimum GPA of 3.0. *Faculty research:* Public historical studies.

Southeastern Louisiana University, College of Arts, Humanities and Social Sciences, Department of History and Political Science, Hammond, LA 70402. Offers history (MA). Part-time programs available. *Faculty:* 8 full-time (3 women). *Students:* 10 full-time (5 women), 38 part-time (21 women); includes 3 minority (all African Americans). Average age 31. 12 applicants, 100% accepted, 10 enrolled. In 2008, 4 master's awarded. *Degree requirements:* For master's, comprehensive exam, thesis optional. *Entrance requirements:* For master's, GRE General Test (900 or better), 30 undergraduate credits in history, minimum GPA of 2.5. Additional exam requirements/recommendations for international students: Required—TOEFL (minimum score 500 paper-based; 173 computer-based; 61 iBT). *Application deadline:* For fall admission, 7/15 priority date for domestic students, 6/1 priority date for international students; for spring admission, 12/1 priority date for domestic students, 10/1 priority date for international students. Applications are processed on a rolling basis. Application fee: $20 ($30 for international students). Electronic applications accepted. *Expenses:* Tuition, area resident: Full-time $2376. Tuition, state resident: full-time $2376. Tuition, nonresident: full-time $6876. Required fees: $1105. *Financial support:* In 2008–09, 10 students received support, including 10 teaching assistantships with full tuition reimbursements available (averaging $10,100 per year); career-related internships or fieldwork, Federal Work-Study, institutionally sponsored loans, unspecified assistantships, and administrative assistantships also available. Support available to part-time students. Financial award application deadline: 5/1; financial award applicants required to submit FAFSA. *Faculty research:* American history, British history, southern history, public history, European history. Total annual research expenditures: $38,146. *Unit head:* Dr. William B. Robison, Department Head, 985-549-2109, Fax: 985-549-2012, E-mail: wrobison@selu.edu. *Application contact:* Sandra Meyers, Graduate Admissions Analyst, 985-549-2066, Fax: 985-549-5632, E-mail: admissions@selu.edu.

Southeast Missouri State University, School of Graduate Studies, Department of History, Cape Girardeau, MO 63701. Offers MA. Part-time and evening/weekend programs available. *Faculty:* 9 full-time (1 woman). *Students:* 8 full-time (4 women), 26 part-time (20 women); includes 1 minority (African American). Average age 38. 7 applicants, 86% accepted. In 2008, 5 master's awarded. *Degree requirements:* For master's, comprehensive exam (for some programs), thesis or alternative. *Entrance requirements:* For master's, GRE, minimum undergraduate GPA of 2.75. Additional exam requirements/recommendations for international students: Required—TOEFL (minimum score 550 paper-based; 213 computer-based); Recommended—IELTS (minimum score 6). *Application deadline:* For fall admission, 8/1 for domestic students, 7/1 for international students; for spring admission, 11/21 for domestic students, 11/1 for international students. Applications are processed on a rolling basis. Application fee: $25 ($100 for international students). Electronic applications accepted. *Expenses:* Tuition, area resident: Part-time $213.30 per credit hour. Tuition, state resident: part-time $213.30 per credit hour. Tuition, nonresident: part-time $393.30 per credit hour. Required fees: $23.70 per credit hour. *Financial support:* In 2008–09, 5 students received support, including 3 research assistantships with full tuition reimbursements available (averaging $7,600 per year), 2 teaching assistantships with full tuition reimbursements available (averaging $7,600 per year); unspecified assistantships also available. Financial award applicants required to submit FAFSA. *Faculty research:* Modern America, historic preservation, world history. *Unit head:* Dr. Wayne H Bowen, Chairperson, 573-651-2179, E-mail: wbowen@semo.edu. *Application contact:* Marsha L. Arant, Senior Administrative Assistant, School of Graduate Studies, 573-651-2192, Fax: 573-651-2001, E-mail: marant@semo.edu.

Southern Connecticut State University, School of Graduate Studies, School of Arts and Sciences, Department of History, New Haven, CT 06515-1355. Offers MA, MS, MLS/MA. Part-time and evening/weekend programs available. *Degree requirements:* For master's, one foreign language, thesis. *Entrance requirements:* For master's, interview, undergraduate major or minor in history. Electronic applications accepted.

Southern Illinois University Carbondale, Graduate School, College of Liberal Arts, Department of History, Carbondale, IL 62901-4701. Offers MA, PhD. Part-time programs available. *Degree requirements:* For master's, one foreign language, research papers or thesis, written exams; for doctorate, 2 foreign languages, thesis/dissertation. *Entrance requirements:* For master's, GRE General Test, minimum GPA of 3.0; for doctorate, GRE General Test, minimum GPA of 3.25. Additional exam requirements/recommendations for international students: Required—TOEFL. *Faculty research:* American, Asian, European, and Latin American history, global history.

See Close-Up on page 331.

Southern Illinois University Edwardsville, Graduate Studies and Research, College of Arts and Sciences, Department of Historical Studies, Program in History, Edwardsville, IL 62026-0001. Offers MA. Part-time and evening/weekend programs available. *Students:* 4 full-time (all women), 30 part-time (12 women); includes 3 minority (all African Americans), 1 international. Average age 26. 20 applicants, 65% accepted. In 2008, 9 master's awarded. *Degree requirements:* For master's, one foreign language, thesis or alternative, final exam. *Entrance requirements:* For master's, GRE. Additional exam requirements/recommendations for international students: Required—TOEFL (minimum score 550 paper-based; 213 computer-based; 79 iBT), IELTS (minimum score 6.5). *Application deadline:* For fall admission, 2/28 for domestic students, 6/1 for international students; for spring admission, 10/1 for international students. Application fee: $30. Electronic applications accepted. *Expenses:* Tuition, area resident: Full-time $5838. Tuition, nonresident: full-time $14,596. Required fees: $1525. *Financial support:* In 2008–09, 2 research assistantships (averaging $8,064 per year), 13 teaching assistantships (averaging $8,064 per year) were awarded; fellowships also available. Financial award application deadline: 3/1; financial award applicants required to submit FAFSA. *Unit head:* Dr. Carole Frick, Director, 618-650-3237, E-mail: cfrick@siue.edu. *Application contact:* Dr. Carole Frick, Director, 618-650-3237, E-mail: cfrick@siue.edu.

Southern Methodist University, Dedman College, Clements Department of History, Dallas, TX 75275. Offers MA, PhD. Part-time programs available. *Faculty:* 22 full-time (6 women). *Students:* 20 full-time (7 women), 13 part-time (5 women); includes 8 minority (1 African American, 7 Hispanic Americans), 3 international. Average age 31. 21 applicants, 43% accepted, 7 enrolled. In 2008, 1 master's, 3 doctorates awarded. Terminal master's awarded for partial completion of doctoral program. *Degree requirements:* For master's, one foreign language, thesis, oral exam, thesis defense; for doctorate, one foreign language, thesis/dissertation, oral exam, dissertation defense. *Entrance requirements:* For master's and doctorate, GRE General Test, minimum GPA of 3.0, 12 undergraduate hours in advanced level history, writing sample. Additional exam requirements/recommendations for international students: Required—TOEFL. *Application deadline:* For fall admission, 2/1 priority date for domestic and international students. Applications are processed on a rolling basis. Application fee: $60. Electronic applications accepted. *Financial support:* In 2008–09, 20 students received support, including 12 fellowships with full tuition reimbursements available (averaging $16,000 per year), 1 research assistantship (averaging $30,000 per year); career-related internships or fieldwork, institutionally sponsored loans, scholarships/grants, health care benefits, and tuition waivers (full and partial) also available. Financial award application deadline: 2/1; financial award applicants required to

History

Southern Methodist University (continued)
submit FAFSA. *Faculty research:* US history, European history, Latin America, Africa/Middle East, China. *Unit head:* Dr. Kathleen A. Wellman, Chair, 214-768-2970, Fax: 214-768-2404, E-mail: hist@smu.edu. *Application contact:* Dr. Sherry L. Smith, Graduate Director, 214-768-1312, Fax: 214-768-2404, E-mail: hist@smu.edu.

Southern University and Agricultural and Mechanical College, Graduate School, College of Arts and Humanities, Department of History, Baton Rouge, LA 70813. Offers social sciences (MA). Part-time programs available. *Degree requirements:* For master's, thesis. *Entrance requirements:* For master's, GRE General Test. Additional exam requirements/recommendations for international students: Required—TOEFL (minimum score 525 paper-based; 193 computer-based).

Southwestern Assemblies of God University, Thomas F. Harrison School of Graduate Studies, Program in History, Waxahachie, TX 75165-5735. Offers MA.

Stanford University, School of Humanities and Sciences, Department of History, Stanford, CA 94305-9991. Offers MA, PhD. Terminal master's awarded for partial completion of doctoral program. *Degree requirements:* For doctorate, variable foreign language requirement, thesis/dissertation, oral exam. *Entrance requirements:* For master's and doctorate, GRE General Test. Additional exam requirements/recommendations for international students: Required—TOEFL. Electronic applications accepted.

State University of New York at Binghamton, Graduate School, School of Arts and Sciences, Department of History, Binghamton, NY 13902-6000. Offers MA, PhD. Part-time programs available. *Faculty:* 25 full-time (8 women), 2 part-time/adjunct (0 women). *Students:* 61 full-time (30 women), 46 part-time (29 women); includes 6 minority (1 African American, 1 Asian American or Pacific Islander, 4 Hispanic Americans), 14 international. Average age 32. 86 applicants, 38% accepted, 15 enrolled. In 2008, 14 master's, 8 doctorates awarded. Terminal master's awarded for partial completion of doctoral program. *Degree requirements:* For master's, one foreign language, thesis or alternative, written exam; for doctorate, variable foreign language requirement, comprehensive exam, thesis/dissertation. *Entrance requirements:* For master's and doctorate, GRE General Test, GRE Subject Test. Additional exam requirements/recommendations for international students: Required—TOEFL. *Application deadline:* For fall admission, 4/15 priority date for domestic students, 1/15 priority date for international students; for spring admission, 11/1 for domestic students, 10/1 priority date for international students. Applications are processed on a rolling basis. Application fee: $60. Electronic applications accepted. *Expenses:* Tuition, area resident: Full-time $6900; part-time $288 per credit. Tuition, state resident: full-time $6900; part-time $288 per credit. Tuition, nonresident: full-time $10,920; part-time $455 per credit. Required fees: $1130. Part-time tuition and fees vary according to course load, program and student level. *Financial support:* In 2008–09, 56 students received support, including 3 fellowships with full tuition reimbursements available (averaging $15,000 per year), 4 research assistantships with full tuition reimbursements available (averaging $15,000 per year), 44 teaching assistantships with full tuition reimbursements available (averaging $15,000 per year); career-related internships or fieldwork, Federal Work-Study, institutionally sponsored loans, scholarships/grants, health care benefits, tuition waivers (full), and unspecified assistantships also available. Financial award application deadline: 2/15; financial award applicants required to submit FAFSA. *Unit head:* Dr. Howard G. Brown, Chairperson, 607-777-6025, E-mail: hgbrown@binghamton.edu. *Application contact:* Victoria Williams, Recruiting and Admissions Coordinator, 607-777-2151, Fax: 607-777-2501, E-mail: vwilliam@binghamton.edu.

State University of New York at Oswego, Graduate Studies, College of Arts and Sciences, Department of History, Oswego, NY 13126. Offers MA. Part-time programs available. *Degree requirements:* For master's, thesis optional. *Entrance requirements:* For master's, writing sample. Additional exam requirements/recommendations for international students: Required—TOEFL (minimum score 560 paper-based; 220 computer-based).

State University of New York College at Cortland, Graduate Studies, School of Arts and Sciences, Department of History, Cortland, NY 13045. Offers MA, MS Ed. Part-time and evening/weekend programs available. *Degree requirements:* For master's, one foreign language, comprehensive exam (for some programs), thesis (for some programs). *Entrance requirements:* For master's, GRE General Test, GRE Subject Test. Additional exam requirements/recommendations for international students: Required—TOEFL.

Stephen F. Austin State University, Graduate School, College of Liberal Arts, Department of History, Nacogdoches, TX 75962. Offers MA. Part-time and evening/weekend programs available. *Degree requirements:* For master's, comprehensive exam. *Entrance requirements:* For master's, GRE General Test. Additional exam requirements/recommendations for international students: Required—TOEFL. *Faculty research:* U.S.-Third World foreign policy, racial attitudes of antebellum Southern whites, naval warfare in World War II, demography of East Texas, medieval sermons.

Stony Brook University, State University of New York, Graduate School, College of Arts and Sciences, Department of History, Stony Brook, NY 11794. Offers MA, PhD. Evening/weekend programs available. *Faculty:* 25 full-time (12 women), 3 part-time/adjunct (2 women). *Students:* 84 full-time (34 women), 6 part-time (4 women); includes 10 minority (6 African Americans, 1 Asian American or Pacific Islander, 3 Hispanic Americans), 24 international. Average age 33. 70 applicants, 33% accepted. In 2008, 9 master's, 6 doctorates awarded. *Degree requirements:* For doctorate, thesis/dissertation. *Entrance requirements:* For master's and doctorate, GRE General Test. Additional exam requirements/recommendations for international students: Required—TOEFL. *Application deadline:* For fall admission, 1/15 for domestic students. Application fee: $60. *Expenses:* Tuition, area resident: Full-time $7880; part-time $328 per credit hour. Tuition, state resident: full-time $7880; part-time $328 per credit hour. Tuition, nonresident: full-time $13,250; part-time $552 per credit hour. Required fees: $848. *Financial support:* In 2008–09, 33 teaching assistantships were awarded; fellowships, research assistantships also available. *Faculty research:* Social, cultural, and political history. Total annual research expenditures: $57,123. *Unit head:* Nancy Tomes, Chair, 631-632-7500, Fax: 631-632-7367. *Application contact:* Brooke Larson, Graduate Coordinator, 631-632-7500, Fax: 631-632-7367.

Sul Ross State University, School of Arts and Sciences, Department of Behavioral and Social Sciences, Program in History, Alpine, TX 79832. Offers MA. Part-time and evening/weekend programs available. *Degree requirements:* For master's, thesis optional. *Entrance requirements:* For master's, GRE General Test, minimum GPA of 2.5 in last 60 hours of undergraduate work. *Faculty research:* Borderland/Southwestern studies, British studies, women's history, Native American studies, local history.

Syracuse University, Graduate School, Maxwell School of Citizenship and Public Affairs, Program in History, Syracuse, NY 13244. Offers MA, PhD. Part-time programs available. Terminal master's awarded for partial completion of doctoral program. *Degree requirements:* For master's, comprehensive exam, thesis or alternative; for doctorate, 2 foreign languages, comprehensive exam, thesis/dissertation. *Entrance requirements:* For master's and doctorate, GRE General Test. Additional exam requirements/recommendations for international students: Required—TOEFL. Electronic applications accepted. *Faculty research:* American, Medieval, European, South East Asia, Russian.

Tarleton State University, College of Graduate Studies, College of Liberal and Fine Arts, Department of Social Sciences, Stephenville, TX 76402. Offers history (MA); political science (MA). Part-time and evening/weekend programs available. Postbaccalaureate distance learning degree programs offered (minimal on-campus study). *Faculty:* 7 full-time (2 women), 1 part-time/adjunct (0 women). *Students:* 8 full-time (3 women), 27 part-time (13 women); includes 7 minority (3 African Americans, 4 Hispanic Americans). Average age 36. 21 applicants, 67% accepted, 13 enrolled. In 2008, 11 master's awarded. *Degree requirements:* For master's, variable foreign language requirement, comprehensive exam, thesis optional. *Entrance requirements:* For master's, GRE General Test, minimum GPA of 3.0. Additional exam requirements/recommendations for international students: Required—TOEFL (minimum score 550 paper-based; 213 computer-based; 80 iBT). *Application deadline:* For fall admission, 8/5 priority date for domestic students; for spring admission, 12/1 for domestic students. Applications are processed on a rolling basis. Application fee: $30 ($130 for international students). Electronic applications accepted. *Expenses:* Tuition, area resident: Full-time $2853; part-time $158.50 per credit hour. Tuition, state resident: full-time $2853; part-time $158.50 per credit hour. Tuition, nonresident: full-time $7551; part-time $419.50 per credit hour. Required fees: $1040; $42 per credit hour. $124 per semester. Tuition and fees vary according to course load and campus/location. *Financial support:* In 2008–09, 2 research assistantships (averaging $13,200 per year) were awarded; teaching assistantships, career-related internships or fieldwork and Federal Work-Study also available. Support available to part-time students. Financial award application deadline: 5/1; financial award applicants required to submit FAFSA. *Unit head:* Dr. Malcom Cross, Department Head, 254-968-9627, Fax: 254-968-9798, E-mail: cross@tarleton.edu. *Application contact:* Information Contact, 254-968-9104, Fax: 254-968-9670, E-mail: gradoffice@tarleton.edu.

Teachers College, Columbia University, Graduate Faculty of Education, Department of Arts and Humanities, Program in History and Education, New York, NY 10027-6696. Offers Ed M, MA, Ed D, PhD. *Faculty:* 1 (woman) full-time. *Students:* 1 full-time (0 women), 13 part-time (9 women); includes 5 minority (4 African Americans, 1 Asian American or Pacific Islander). Average age 37. 16 applicants, 25% accepted, 0 enrolled. In 2008, 3 master's awarded. *Degree requirements:* For doctorate, thesis/dissertation. *Entrance requirements:* For master's, sample of historical writing (Ed M); for doctorate, sample of historical writing. *Application deadline:* For fall admission, 5/15 for domestic students; for spring admission, 12/1 for domestic students. Application fee: $75. *Expenses:* Tuition: Full-time $26,040; part-time $1085 per credit. Required fees: $720. *Financial support:* Career-related internships or fieldwork, Federal Work-Study, institutionally sponsored loans, and tuition waivers (full and partial) available. Support available to part-time students. Financial award application deadline: 2/1. *Faculty research:* History of American education. *Unit head:* Graeme Sullivan, Chair, 212-678-3799. *Application contact:* Mark E. Stearns, Associate Director of Admission, 212-678-3710, Fax: 212-678-4171.

Temple University, Graduate School, College of Liberal Arts, Department of History, Philadelphia, PA 19122-6096. Offers MA, PhD. Part-time and evening/weekend programs available. Terminal master's awarded for partial completion of doctoral program. *Degree requirements:* For doctorate, one foreign language, thesis/dissertation. *Entrance requirements:* For master's and doctorate, GRE General Test, minimum GPA of 3.0. Additional exam requirements/recommendations for international students: Required—TOEFL (minimum score 550 paper-based; 213 computer-based; 79 iBT). Electronic applications accepted. *Faculty research:* Third World; American military and diplomatic history; American social, cultural, and public history, European history.

Texas A&M International University, Office of Graduate Studies and Research, College of Arts and Sciences, Department of Social Sciences, Laredo, TX 78041-1900. Offers history (MA); political science (MA); public administration (MPA). *Degree requirements:* For master's, thesis (for some programs). *Entrance requirements:* For master's, GRE General Test. Additional exam requirements/recommendations for international students: Required—TOEFL (minimum score 550 paper-based; 213 computer-based).

Texas A&M University, College of Liberal Arts, Department of History, College Station, TX 77843. Offers MA, PhD. Part-time programs available. *Faculty:* 23. *Students:* 45 full-time (11 women), 25 part-time (6 women); includes 8 minority (2 African Americans, 6 Hispanic Americans), 3 international. Average age 32. In 2008, 9 master's, 4 doctorates awarded. Terminal master's awarded for partial completion of doctoral program. *Degree requirements:* For master's, one foreign language, thesis optional; for doctorate, 2 foreign languages, thesis/dissertation. *Entrance requirements:* For master's and doctorate, GRE General Test. Additional exam requirements/recommendations for international students: Required—TOEFL. *Application deadline:* For fall admission, 3/1 for domestic students. Application fee: $50 ($75 for international students). *Expenses:* Tuition, area resident: Full-time $3838.50. Tuition, state resident: full-time $3838.50. Tuition, nonresident: full-time $8897. Required fees: $2359.60. *Financial support:* In 2008–09, fellowships (averaging $4,000 per year); research assistantships, teaching assistantships with partial tuition reimbursements. Financial award application deadline: 2/1. *Faculty research:* Recent U.S. history, southwest, border studies, military history, Europe. *Unit head:* Dr. Walter L. Buenger, Head, 979-845-2571, E-mail: w-buenger@tamu.edu. *Application contact:* Albert S. Broussard, Coordinator, 979-845-7130, Fax: 979-862-4314.

Texas A&M University–Commerce, Graduate School, College of Arts and Sciences, Department of History, Commerce, TX 75429-3011. Offers history (MA, MS); social sciences (M Ed, MS). Part-time programs available. *Degree requirements:* For master's, comprehensive exam, thesis (for some programs). *Entrance requirements:* For master's, GRE General Test. Electronic applications accepted. *Faculty research:* American foreign policy, colonial America, Texas politics, Medieval England.

Texas A&M University–Corpus Christi, Graduate Studies and Research, College of Liberal Arts, Corpus Christi, TX 78412-5503. Offers English (MA); history (MA); psychology (MA); public administration (MPA); studio arts (MA, MFA). Part-time and evening/weekend programs available. *Degree requirements:* For master's, comprehensive exam, thesis (for some programs). *Entrance requirements:* For master's, GRE General Test. Additional exam requirements/recommendations for international students: Required—TOEFL. Electronic applications accepted.

Texas A&M University–Kingsville, College of Graduate Studies, College of Arts and Sciences, Program in History and Political Science, Kingsville, TX 78363. Offers MA, MS. Part-time and evening/weekend programs available. *Degree requirements:* For master's, comprehensive exam, thesis or alternative. *Entrance requirements:* For master's, GRE General Test. Additional exam requirements/recommendations for international students: Required—TOEFL.

Texas A&M University–Texarkana, Graduate Studies and Research, College of Arts and Sciences and Education, Texarkana, TX 75505-5518. Offers adult education (MS); curriculum and instruction (MS); education (MS); educational administration (M Ed); English (MA); history (MS); instructional technology (MS); interdisciplinary studies (MS); special education (M Ed, MS). Part-time and evening/weekend programs available. *Degree requirements:* For master's, comprehensive exam (for some programs), thesis optional. *Entrance requirements:* For master's, minimum GPA of 2.5 on last 60 hours of bachelor's degree. Additional exam requirements/recommendations for international students: Required—TOEFL. Electronic applications accepted.

Texas Christian University, AddRan College of Liberal Arts, Department of History, Fort Worth, TX 76129-0002. Offers MA, PhD. Part-time and evening/weekend programs available. *Degree requirements:* For master's, one foreign language, thesis; for doctorate, one foreign language, thesis/dissertation, qualifying exams. *Entrance requirements:* For master's and doctorate, GRE General Test. Additional exam requirements/recommendations for international students: Required—TOEFL. *Application deadline:* For fall admission, 3/1 for domestic students; for spring admission, 12/1 for domestic students. Applications are processed on a rolling basis. Application fee: $0. *Expenses:* Tuition: Full-time $17,640. *Financial support:* Fellowships, teaching assistantships, unspecified assistantships available. Financial award application deadline: 3/1. *Unit head:* Dr. Peter Worth, Chairperson, 817-257-7288, E-mail: p.worthing@tcu.edu. *Application contact:* Dr. Mike Butler, Associate Dean, AddRan College of Humanities and Social Sciences, E-mail: m.butler@tcu.edu.

Texas Southern University, Graduate School, College of Liberal Arts and Behavioral Sciences, Department of History and Geography, Houston, TX 77004-4584. Offers history (MA). Part-time and evening/weekend programs available. *Faculty:* 7 full-time (3 women). *Students:* 1 full-time (0 women), 5 part-time (3 women); includes 5 African Americans, 1 Asian American or Pacific Islander. Average age 36. 3 applicants, 100% accepted, 1 enrolled. *Degree requirements:* For master's, comprehensive exam, thesis optional. *Entrance requirements:* For master's, GRE General Test, minimum GPA of 2.5. Additional exam requirements/recommendations for international students: Required—TOEFL. *Application deadline:* For fall admission, 7/15 priority date for domestic students. Applications are processed on a rolling basis. Application fee: $50 ($75 for international students). *Expenses:* Tuition, area resident: Full-time $1912; part-time $96 per credit hour. Tuition, state resident: full-time $1912; part-time $96 per credit hour. Tuition, nonresident: full-time $6302; part-time $343 per credit hour. Required fees: $3542. *Financial support:* Research assistantships, teaching assistantships, Federal Work-Study and institutionally sponsored loans available. Financial award application deadline: 5/1. *Faculty research:* American, Colonial, African, Asian, and African-American history. *Unit head:* Dr. Ethopia Keleta, Chair, 713-313-7324, Fax: 713-313-4236, E-mail: keleta_ex@tsu.edu. *Application contact:* Dr. Gregory Maddox, Interim Dean of the Graduate School, 713-313-7011 Ext. 4410, Fax: 713-639-1876, E-mail: maddox_gh@tsu.edu.

Texas State University–San Marcos, Graduate School, College of Liberal Arts, Department of History, San Marcos, TX 78666. Offers M Ed, MA. Part-time programs available. *Degree requirements:* For master's, comprehensive exam, thesis (for some programs). *Entrance requirements:* For master's, GRE General Test, minimum GPA of 3.0 in history. Additional exam requirements/recommendations for international students: Required—TOEFL (minimum score 550 paper-based; 213 computer-based). Electronic applications accepted. *Faculty research:* American women, Texas and the Southwest, Hispanic Southwest, American-conservative movement, Mexico and Brazil.

Texas Tech University, Graduate School, College of Arts and Sciences, Department of History, Lubbock, TX 79409. Offers MA, PhD. Part-time programs available. *Faculty:* 19 full-time (4 women), 4 part-time/adjunct (1 woman). *Students:* 42 full-time (14 women), 35 part-time (11 women); includes 9 minority (1 African American, 3 Asian Americans or Pacific Islanders, 5 Hispanic Americans), 3 international. Average age 33. 38 applicants, 74% accepted, 11 enrolled. In 2008, 5 master's, 3 doctorates awarded. *Degree requirements:* For master's, one foreign language, thesis or alternative; for doctorate, 2 foreign languages, thesis/dissertation. *Entrance requirements:* For master's and doctorate, GRE General Test. Additional exam requirements/recommendations for international students: Required—TOEFL (minimum score 550 paper-based; 213 computer-based). *Application deadline:* For fall admission, 3/1 priority date for international students; for spring admission, 11/1 priority date for international students. Applications are processed on a rolling basis. Application fee: $50 ($60 for international students). Electronic applications accepted. *Expenses:* Tuition, area resident: Part-time $194 per credit hour. Tuition, state resident: full-time $4648; part-time $194 per credit hour. Tuition, nonresident: full-time $11,392; part-time $475 per credit hour. Required fees: $2206; $69 per credit hour. $389 per semester. *Financial support:* In 2008–09, 53 students received support, including 33 teaching assistantships with partial tuition reimbursements available (averaging $12,164 per year); research assistantships with partial tuition reimbursements available, Federal Work-Study and institutionally sponsored loans also available. Support available to part-time students. Financial award application deadline: 4/15; financial award applicants required to submit FAFSA. *Faculty research:* History of United States Southwest/West, the borderlands, history of Vietnam War and United States military history, history of Hispanics/Latinos and other U.S. minorities, history of Europe. Total annual research expenditures: $4,015. *Unit head:* Randy McBee, Chair, 806-742-1004, Fax: 806-742-1060, E-mail: randy.mcbee@ttu.edu. *Application contact:* Dr. Gretchen Adams, Graduate Adviser, 806-742-3744, Fax: 806-742-1060.

Texas Woman's University, Graduate School, College of Arts and Sciences, Department of History and Government, Denton, TX 76201. Offers government (MA); history (MA). Part-time and evening/weekend programs available. *Faculty:* 9 full-time (4 women), 5 part-time/adjunct (2 women). *Students:* 5 full-time (3 women), 29 part-time (26 women); includes 6 minority (2 African Americans, 1 Asian American or Pacific Islander, 3 Hispanic Americans), 2 international. Average age 36. In 2008, 12 master's awarded. *Degree requirements:* For master's, thesis. *Entrance requirements:* For master's, GRE (waived if completed a graduate degree), minimum GPA of 3.3, writing sample/portfolio. Additional exam requirements/recommendations for international students: Required—TOEFL (minimum score 550 paper-based; 213 computer-based; 79 iBT). *Application deadline:* For fall admission, 4/1 for international students; for spring admission, 8/1 for international students. Applications are processed on a rolling basis. Application fee: $30 ($50 for international students). Electronic applications accepted. *Expenses:* Tuition, state resident: full-time $3564; part-time $198 per semester hour. Tuition, nonresident: full-time $8622; part-time $479 per semester hour. Required fees: $1158; $64 per semester hour. Tuition and fees vary according to course load. *Financial support:* In 2008–09, 21 research assistantships (averaging $9,684 per year), 2 teaching assistantships (averaging $9,684 per year) were awarded; career-related internships or fieldwork, Federal Work-Study, institutionally sponsored loans, scholarships/grants, traineeships, health care benefits, and unspecified assistantships also available. Support available to part-time students. Financial award application deadline: 3/1; financial award applicants required to submit FAFSA. *Faculty research:* Recent American history, civil liberties, military history, legal studies, women and politics. *Unit head:* Dr. Mark Kessler, Chair, 940-898-2133, Fax: 940-898-2130, E-mail: HistoryGov@twu.edu. *Application contact:* Samuel Wheeler, Assistant Director of Admissions, 940-898-3188, Fax: 940-898-3081, E-mail: wheelersr@twu.edu.

Trinity Western University, Faculty of Graduate Studies, Program in Interdisciplinary Humanities, Langley, BC V2Y 1Y1, Canada. Offers general humanities (MAIH); specialized (MAIH), including English, history, philosophy. Part-time and evening/weekend programs available. Postbaccalaureate distance learning degree programs offered (minimal on-campus study). *Degree requirements:* For master's, 36 semester hours. *Entrance requirements:* For master's, strong undergraduate degree in Humanities or English, History or Philosophy. *Faculty research:* Literary theory, gender, medieval and early modern literature, philosophy of religion, Thomas Merton's poetics.

Tufts University, Graduate School of Arts and Sciences, Department of History, Medford, MA 02155. Offers MA, PhD. Terminal master's awarded for partial completion of doctoral program. *Degree requirements:* For master's, one foreign language; for doctorate, thesis/dissertation. *Entrance requirements:* For master's and doctorate, GRE General Test, writing sample. Additional exam requirements/recommendations for international students: Required—TOEFL (minimum score 550 paper-based; 213 computer-based; 80 iBT). Electronic applications accepted.

Tulane University, School of Liberal Arts, Department of History, New Orleans, LA 70118-5669. Offers MA, PhD. *Degree requirements:* For master's, one foreign language, thesis; for doctorate, variable foreign language requirement, thesis/dissertation. *Entrance requirements:* For master's, GRE General Test, minimum B average in undergraduate course work; for doctorate, GRE General Test. Additional exam requirements/recommendations for international students: Required—TOEFL. Electronic applications accepted.

Union Institute & University, Online MA Programs, Cincinnati, OH 45206-1925. Offers health and wellness (MA); history and culture (MA); leadership (MA); literature and writing (MA); psychology (MA). Part-time programs available. Postbaccalaureate distance learning degree programs offered (no on-campus study). *Degree requirements:* For master's, thesis. *Expenses:* Contact institution.

Universidad Adventista de las Antillas, EGECED Department, Mayagüez, PR 00681-0118. Offers curriculum and instruction (MA), including elementary, secondary biology, secondary history, secondary Spanish; education (MA), including ESL (elementary school level), ESL (high school level), school administration and supervision. *Degree requirements:* For master's, comprehensive exam (for some programs), thesis (for some programs). *Entrance requirements:* For master's, EXADEP or GRE, recommendations, transcripts (original). Electronic applications accepted.

Université de Moncton, Faculty of Arts and Social Sciences, Department of History and Geography, Moncton, NB E1A 3E9, Canada. Offers history (MA). *Degree requirements:* For master's, thesis, proficiency in English and French. *Entrance requirements:* For master's, honors degree in history, minimum GPA of 2.7. Electronic applications accepted. *Faculty research:* Economic and social history (Canada, France, Acadia), sociocultural history, women's history, labor history, history of the press.

Université de Montréal, Faculty of Arts and Sciences, Department of History, Montréal, QC H3C 3J7, Canada. Offers MA, PhD. *Faculty:* 24 full-time (5 women), 9 part-time/adjunct (2 women). *Students:* 54 full-time (26 women), 80 part-time (37 women). 58 applicants, 55% accepted, 30 enrolled. In 2008, 37 master's, 4 doctorates awarded. *Degree requirements:* For master's, thesis; for doctorate, thesis/dissertation, general exam. *Entrance requirements:* For doctorate, master's degree in related field. *Application deadline:* For fall admission, 2/1 priority date for domestic students; for winter admission, 11/1 priority date for domestic students; for spring admission, 2/1 priority date for domestic students. Applications are processed on a rolling basis. Application fee: $100. Electronic applications accepted. *Financial support:* In 2008–09, 15 fellowships (averaging $3,000 per year), 20 research assistantships (averaging $5,000 per year), 30 teaching assistantships (averaging $2,000 per year) were awarded; institutionally sponsored loans also available. Support available to part-time students. *Faculty research:* Preindustrial Quebec, Quebec working class, Quebec intellectual, diffusion of scientific thought, history of medicine. Total annual research expenditures: $550,000. *Unit head:* Michael J. Carley, Director, 514-343-6111 Ext. 41339, Fax: 514-343-2483, E-mail: michael.j.carley@umontreal.ca. *Application contact:* Christian Dessureault, Graduate Chairman, 514-343-6111 Ext. 41437, Fax: 514-343-2483, E-mail: christian.dessureault@umontreal.ca.

Université de Sherbrooke, Faculty of Letters and Human Sciences, Department of Human Sciences, Sherbrooke, QC J1K 2R1, Canada. Offers history (MA); philosophy (MA). *Degree requirements:* For master's, thesis. *Entrance requirements:* For master's, minimum GPA of 2.75. *Faculty research:* Political, social, and urban history; history of women.

Université du Québec à Montréal, Graduate Programs, Program in History, Montréal, QC H3C 3P8, Canada. Offers MA, PhD. Part-time programs available. *Degree requirements:* For master's, thesis; for doctorate, thesis/dissertation. *Entrance requirements:* For master's, appropriate bachelor's degree or equivalent, proficiency in French; for doctorate, appropriate master's degree or equivalent, proficiency in French.

Université Laval, Faculty of Letters, Department of History, Programs in History, Québec, QC G1K 7P4, Canada. Offers MA, PhD. Terminal master's awarded for partial completion of doctoral program. *Degree requirements:* For master's, thesis (for some programs); for doctorate, comprehensive exam, thesis/dissertation. *Entrance requirements:* For master's and doctorate, English exam (comprehension of written English), knowledge of French. Electronic applications accepted.

Université Laval, Faculty of Letters, Department of Literature, Programs in Ancient Civilization, Québec, QC G1K 7P4, Canada. Offers MA, PhD. Part-time programs available. Terminal master's awarded for partial completion of doctoral program. *Degree requirements:* For master's, thesis; for doctorate, comprehensive exam, thesis/dissertation. *Entrance requirements:* For master's and doctorate, English test (comprehension of written English), knowledge of French, knowledge of an ancient language. Electronic applications accepted.

University at Albany, State University of New York, College of Arts and Sciences, Department of History, Albany, NY 12222-0001. Offers history (MA, PhD); public history (Certificate). Part-time programs available. *Degree requirements:* For master's, variable foreign language requirement, exam, research paper or thesis; for doctorate, thesis/dissertation. *Entrance requirements:* For master's, minimum GPA of 3.0; for doctorate, GRE General Test, minimum GPA of 3.0. Additional exam requirements/recommendations for international students: Required—TOEFL (minimum score 550 paper-based; 213 computer-based). Electronic applications accepted. *Faculty research:* American history (all phases); public policy; European history (Medieval to modern); Asian, African, and Latin American history.

University at Buffalo, the State University of New York, Graduate School, College of Arts and Sciences, Department of History, Buffalo, NY 14260. Offers MA, PhD. Part-time programs available. Terminal master's awarded for partial completion of doctoral program. *Degree requirements:* For master's, project; for doctorate, variable foreign language requirement, thesis/dissertation, general exam. *Entrance requirements:* For master's and doctorate, GRE General Test. Additional exam requirements/recommendations for international students: Required—TOEFL. Electronic applications accepted. *Faculty research:* Early modern and modern European social, cultural and intellectual history; American social, cultural and political history; north and south Atlantic world history; Latin America; East Asian history; women's and gender history.

The University of Akron, Graduate School, Buchtel College of Arts and Sciences, Department of History, Akron, OH 44325. Offers MA, PhD. Part-time programs available. *Degree requirements:* For master's, one foreign language, thesis optional, written exams, seminars; for doctorate, 2 foreign languages, comprehensive exam, thesis/dissertation, written exams, oral exams. *Entrance requirements:* For master's, GRE, minimum GPA of 3.0, writing sample, letters of recommendation, letter of intent; for doctorate, GRE, minimum GPA of 3.5, writing sample, letters of recommendation. Additional exam requirements/recommendations for international students: Required—TOEFL (minimum score 580 paper-based; 237 computer-based; 92 iBT). Electronic applications accepted. *Faculty research:* European, American, and world history;.

The University of Alabama, Graduate School, College of Arts and Sciences, Department of History, Tuscaloosa, AL 35487. Offers MA, PhD. *Faculty:* 22 full-time (3 women). *Students:* 42 full-time (11 women), 16 part-time (5 women); includes 2 minority (both Hispanic Americans), 1 international. Average age 30. 52 applicants, 42% accepted, 10 enrolled. In 2008, 19 master's, 1 doctorate awarded. Terminal master's awarded for partial completion of doctoral program. *Degree requirements:* For master's, one foreign language, thesis optional, oral exam; for doctorate, 2 foreign languages, comprehensive exam, thesis/dissertation, oral exams, written exam. *Entrance requirements:* For master's and doctorate, GRE General Test. *Application deadline:* For fall admission, 5/1 for domestic students. Applications are processed on a rolling basis. Application fee: $30. *Expenses:* Tuition, area resident: full-time $6400. Tuition, state resident: full-time $6400. Tuition, nonresident: full-time $18,000. *Financial support:* In 2008–09, 29 students received support, including 6 fellowships with full tuition reimbursements available (averaging $10,000 per year), research assistantships (averaging $10,000 per year), 23 teaching assistantships with full tuition reimbursements available (averaging $10,200 per year); institutionally sponsored loans and unspecified assistantships also available. Financial award application deadline: 1/15. *Faculty research:* U.S., modern European, Latin American, military, and southern U.S. history. Total annual research expenditures: $100,080. *Unit head:* Dr. Michael Mendle, Chair, 205-348-7103. *Application contact:* Dr. Lisa Lindquist Dorr, Graduate Director, 205-348-1859, E-mail: ldorr@bama.ua.edu.

The University of Alabama at Birmingham, School of Social and Behavioral Sciences, Department of History, Birmingham, AL 35294. Offers MA. Part-time programs available. *Degree requirements:* For master's, variable foreign language requirement, thesis or alternative. *Entrance requirements:* For master's, GRE General Test or MAT. Electronic applications accepted. *Faculty research:* History of Europe, United States, Latin America, American South.

The University of Alabama in Huntsville, School of Graduate Studies, College of Liberal Arts, Department of History, Huntsville, AL 35899. Offers history (MA), including fifth year class A education certification. Part-time and evening/weekend programs available. *Faculty:* 6 full-time (2 women). *Students:* 2 full-time (1 woman), 10 part-time (4 women); includes 2 minority (both African Americans). Average age 30. 10 applicants, 70% accepted, 5 enrolled. In 2008, 4 master's awarded. *Degree requirements:* For master's, one foreign language, comprehensive exam, thesis or alternative, oral and written exams. *Entrance requirements:* For master's, GRE

History

The University of Alabama in Huntsville (continued)

General Test, minimum GPA of 3.0, bachelor's degree in history or related area. Additional exam requirements/recommendations for international students: Required—TOEFL (minimum score 500 paper-based; 173 computer-based; 62 iBT). *Application deadline:* For fall admission, 7/15 for domestic students, 4/1 for international students; for spring admission, 11/30 for domestic students, 9/1 for international students. Applications are processed on a rolling basis. Application fee: $40 ($50 for international students). Electronic applications accepted. *Expenses:* Tuition, area resident: Full-time $5214; part-time $323 per credit hour. Tuition, state resident: full-time $5214; part-time $323 per credit hour. Tuition, nonresident: full-time $11,444; part-time $705 per credit hour. Required fees: $540; $120 per semester. Tuition and fees vary according to course load. *Financial support:* In 2008–09, 5 students received support, including 1 research assistantship with full and partial tuition reimbursement available (averaging $8,460 per year); career-related internships or fieldwork, Federal Work-Study, institutionally sponsored loans, scholarships/grants, health care benefits, and unspecified assistantships also available. Support available to part-time students. Financial award application deadline: 4/1; financial award applicants required to submit FAFSA. *Faculty research:* American and European history, U.S. diplomatic history, Old South, ancient and medieval history, Latin American history. *Unit head:* Dr. Andrew Dunar, Chair, 256-824-6312, Fax: 256-824-6477, E-mail: dunara@uah.edu. *Application contact:* Kathy Biggs, Graduate Studies Admissions Manager, 256-824-6199, Fax: 256-824-6405, E-mail: deangrad@uah.edu.

University of Alaska Fairbanks, College of Liberal Arts, Department of Northern Studies, Fairbanks, AK 99775-6460. Offers environmental politics and policy (MA); Northern history (MA). Part-time programs available. *Faculty:* 7 full-time (3 women), 2 part-time/adjunct (both women). *Students:* 18 full-time (8 women), 18 part-time (12 women); includes 2 minority (1 African American, 1 American Indian/Alaska Native), 5 international. Average age 34. 24 applicants, 50% accepted, 11 enrolled. In 2008, 5 master's awarded. *Degree requirements:* For master's, comprehensive exam, thesis or alternative. *Entrance requirements:* Additional exam requirements/recommendations for international students: Required—TOEFL (minimum score 550 paper-based; 213 computer-based; 80 iBT). *Application deadline:* For fall admission, 6/1 for domestic students, 3/1 for international students; for spring admission, 10/15 for domestic students, 9/1 for international students. Applications are processed on a rolling basis. Application fee: $60. Electronic applications accepted. *Expenses:* Tuition, area resident: Full-time $5418; part-time $301 per credit. Tuition, state resident: full-time $5418; part-time $301 per credit. Tuition, nonresident: full-time $11,070; part-time $615 per credit. Required fees: $849; $25 per credit. $78 per semester. Tuition and fees vary according to course load and reciprocity agreements. *Financial support:* In 2008–09, 3 research assistantships (averaging $7,517 per year), 11 teaching assistantships (averaging $7,671 per year) were awarded; fellowships, career-related internships or fieldwork, Federal Work-Study, scholarships/grants, health care benefits, and unspecified assistantships also available. Support available to part-time students. Financial award application deadline: 1/1; financial award applicants required to submit FAFSA. *Faculty research:* Canadian history, environmental history, Native Alaskan history and art, fetal alcohol syndrome. *Unit head:* Dr. Judith S. Kleinfeld, Co-Director, 907-474-7126, Fax: 907-474-5817, E-mail: fynors@uaf.edu. *Application contact:* Dr. Judith S. Kleinfeld, Co-Director, 907-474-7126, Fax: 907-474-5817, E-mail: fynors@uaf.edu.

University of Alberta, Faculty of Graduate Studies and Research, Department of History and Classics, Edmonton, AB T6G 2E1, Canada. Offers ancient history (PhD); classical archaeology (MA, PhD); classical literature (PhD); classics (MA); history (MA, PhD). Part-time and evening/weekend programs available. *Degree requirements:* For master's, one foreign language, thesis (for some programs); for doctorate, one foreign language, thesis/dissertation. *Entrance requirements:* For master's, minimum B+ average; for doctorate, minimum A- average. Additional exam requirements/recommendations for international students: Required—TOEFL (minimum score 580 paper-based; 237 computer-based). Electronic applications accepted. *Faculty research:* Western Canada, classical archaeology, Britain, Eastern Europe, East Asia.

The University of Arizona, Graduate College, College of Social and Behavioral Sciences, Department of History, Tucson, AZ 85721. Offers MA, PhD. Part-time programs available. Terminal master's awarded for partial completion of doctoral program. *Degree requirements:* For master's, one foreign language, comprehensive exam, thesis optional; for doctorate, 2 foreign languages, comprehensive exam, thesis/dissertation. *Entrance requirements:* For master's, GRE, minimum GPA of 3.0, 3 letters of recommendation, writing sample; for doctorate, GRE General Test, minimum GPA of 3.0, 3 letters of recommendation, 2 writing samples. Additional exam requirements/recommendations for international students: Required—TOEFL (minimum score 550 paper-based). Electronic applications accepted. *Faculty research:* Latin American history, European history, U.S. history, women's history, global/environmental history.

University of Arkansas, Graduate School, J. William Fulbright College of Arts and Sciences, Department of History, Fayetteville, AR 72701-1201. Offers MA, PhD. Part-time programs available. *Degree requirements:* For master's, thesis optional; for doctorate, 2 foreign languages, thesis/dissertation. *Entrance requirements:* For master's, GRE General Test; for doctorate, GRE General Test, GRE Subject Test.

The University of British Columbia, Faculty of Arts and Faculty of Graduate Studies, Department of History, Vancouver, BC V6T 1Z1, Canada. Offers MA, PhD. Part-time programs available. *Degree requirements:* For master's, one foreign language, thesis, six 3-credit courses; for doctorate, one foreign language, comprehensive exam, thesis/dissertation, four 3-credit courses. *Entrance requirements:* Additional exam requirements/recommendations for international students: Required—TOEFL (minimum score 570 paper-based; 230 computer-based). Electronic applications accepted. *Faculty research:* Canadian, British, European, modern Chinese and Japanese history; international relations.

University of Calgary, Faculty of Graduate Studies, Faculty of Social Sciences, Department of History, Calgary, AB T2N 1N4, Canada. Offers MA, PhD. Part-time programs available. *Degree requirements:* For master's, one foreign language, thesis; for doctorate, one foreign language, thesis/dissertation, 3 written comprehensive exams, oral candidacy exam. *Entrance requirements:* For master's, minimum GPA of 3.4, writing sample; for doctorate, sample of written work, master's degree in history. Electronic applications accepted. *Faculty research:* Military history, Canadian history, Latin American history, gender/women's history, native history.

University of California, Berkeley, Graduate Division, College of Letters and Science, Department of History, Berkeley, CA 94720-1500. Offers PhD, MA/PhD. *Degree requirements:* For doctorate, variable foreign language requirement, comprehensive exam, thesis/dissertation. *Entrance requirements:* For doctorate, GRE General Test, minimum GPA of 3.0, 3 letters of recommendation, 2 copies of transcripts, statement of purpose, writing sample (not to exceed 10 pages). Additional exam requirements/recommendations for international students: Required—TOEFL (minimum score 570 paper-based; 230 computer-based; 68 iBT). Electronic applications accepted.

University of California, Berkeley, Graduate Division, Group in Ancient History and Mediterranean Archaeology, Berkeley, CA 94720-1500. Offers MA, PhD. *Degree requirements:* For master's, one foreign language, exam or thesis; for doctorate, 2 foreign languages, thesis/dissertation, qualifying exam. *Entrance requirements:* For master's and doctorate, GRE General Test, minimum GPA of 3.0, 3 letters of recommendation. Additional exam requirements/recommendations for international students: Required—TOEFL (minimum score 570 paper-based; 230 computer-based), TWE.

University of California, Davis, Graduate Studies, Program in History, Davis, CA 95616. Offers MA, PhD. Terminal master's awarded for partial completion of doctoral program. *Degree requirements:* For master's, one foreign language, comprehensive exam (for some programs), thesis (for some programs); for doctorate, 2 foreign languages, thesis/dissertation. *Entrance requirements:* For master's, GRE General Test, minimum GPA of 3.0, writing sample; for doctorate, GRE General Test, master's degree, writing sample. Additional exam requirements/recommendations for international students: Required—TOEFL (minimum score 550 paper-based; 213 computer-based). Electronic applications accepted. *Faculty research:* American social, cultural, and western history; modern and early history; modern European, East Asian, and Latin American history; history of science and medicine; cross-cultural history of women.

University of California, Irvine, Office of Graduate Studies, School of Humanities, Department of History, Irvine, CA 92697. Offers MA, PhD. *Degree requirements:* For doctorate, thesis/dissertation. *Entrance requirements:* For master's and doctorate, GRE General Test, minimum GPA of 3.0. Additional exam requirements/recommendations for international students: Required—TOEFL (minimum score 550 paper-based; 213 computer-based). Electronic applications accepted. *Faculty research:* European, U.S., Latin American, ancient, and East Asian history.

University of California, Los Angeles, Graduate Division, College of Letters and Science, Department of History, Los Angeles, CA 90095. Offers MA, PhD, MLIS/MA. *Students:* 195 full-time (100 women); includes 35 minority (8 African Americans, 3 American Indian/Alaska Native, 6 Asian Americans or Pacific Islanders, 18 Hispanic Americans), 20 international. Average age 30. 329 applicants, 29% accepted, 34 enrolled. In 2008, 42 master's, 31 doctorates awarded. Terminal master's awarded for partial completion of doctoral program. *Degree requirements:* For master's, one foreign language, comprehensive exam; for doctorate, variable foreign language requirement, thesis/dissertation, oral and written qualifying exams. *Entrance requirements:* For master's, GRE General Test, minimum GPA of 3.0, degree objective of Ph.D; for doctorate, GRE General Test, minimum undergraduate GPA of 3.0. *Application deadline:* For fall admission, 12/15 for domestic and international students. Application fee: $60 ($80 for international students). Electronic applications accepted. *Expenses:* Tuition, nonresident: full-time $14,694. Required fees: $9669.50. Full-time tuition and fees vary according to course load, degree level, program and student level. *Financial support:* In 2008–09, 160 fellowships with full and partial tuition reimbursements, 50 research assistantships with full and partial tuition reimbursements, 126 teaching assistantships with full and partial tuition reimbursements were awarded; Federal Work-Study, institutionally sponsored loans, scholarships/grants, health care benefits, tuition waivers (full and partial), and unspecified assistantships also available. Financial award application deadline: 3/1; financial award applicants required to submit FAFSA. *Unit head:* Dr. Edward Alpers, Chair, 310-206-9043. *Application contact:* Departmental Office, 310-206-2627, E-mail: gradoffice@history.ucla.edu.

University of California, Riverside, Graduate Division, Department of History, Riverside, CA 92521-0102. Offers archival management (MA); historic preservation (MA); history (MA, PhD); museum curatorship (MA). Part-time programs available. Terminal master's awarded for partial completion of doctoral program. *Degree requirements:* For master's, one foreign language, comprehensive exam, internship report and oral exams, or thesis; for doctorate, 2 foreign languages, thesis/dissertation, qualifying exams, teaching experience. *Entrance requirements:* For master's, GRE General Test, minimum GPA of 3.2; for doctorate, GRE General Test, MA in history, minimum GPA of 3.2. Additional exam requirements/recommendations for international students: Required—TOEFL (minimum score 550 paper-based; 213 computer-based; 80 iBT). Electronic applications accepted. *Expenses:* Tuition, nonresident: full-time $4898. Required fees: $10,362. *Faculty research:* Native American history, United States, public history, Russia, Europe.

University of California, San Diego, Office of Graduate Studies, Department of History, La Jolla, CA 92093. Offers history (MA, PhD); Judaic studies (MA); science studies (PhD). *Degree requirements:* For doctorate, thesis/dissertation. *Entrance requirements:* For master's and doctorate, GRE General Test. Electronic applications accepted.

University of California, Santa Barbara, Graduate Division, College of Letters and Sciences, Division of Humanities and Fine Arts, Department of History, Santa Barbara, CA 93106-9410. Offers feminist studies (PhD); global studies (PhD); public history (PhD); MA/PhD. *Faculty:* 40 full-time (17 women), 11 part-time/adjunct (6 women). *Students:* 120 full-time (62 women). Average age 34. 130 applicants, 38% accepted, 22 enrolled. In 2008, 9 doctorates awarded. Terminal master's awarded for partial completion of doctoral program. *Degree requirements:* For doctorate, comprehensive exam, thesis/dissertation, one or more languages depending on field of study. *Entrance requirements:* For doctorate, GRE, 3 letters of recommendation, statement of purpose, personal achievements/contributions statement, resumé/curriculum vitae, transcripts for post-secondary institutions attended. Additional exam requirements/recommendations for international students: Required—TOEFL (minimum score 550 paper-based; 213 computer-based; 80 iBT), IELTS (minimum score 7), TOEFL or IELTS. *Application deadline:* For fall admission, 12/5 for domestic and international students. Application fee: $70 ($90 for international students). Electronic applications accepted. *Expenses:* Tuition, nonresident: full-time $25,149. Required fees: $10,143. Full-time tuition and fees vary according to campus/location, reciprocity agreements and student level. *Financial support:* In 2008–09, 94 students received support, including 53 fellowships with full and partial tuition reimbursements available (averaging $8,600 per year), 2 research assistantships with full and partial tuition reimbursements available (averaging $7,400 per year), 70 teaching assistantships with partial tuition reimbursements available (averaging $9,400 per year); Federal Work-Study, institutionally sponsored loans, scholarships/grants, traineeships, health care benefits, tuition waivers (full and partial), and unspecified assistantships also available. Financial award application deadline: 12/5; financial award applicants required to submit FAFSA. *Faculty research:* Europe, U. S., Latin America, Africa, Middle East, East Asia. *Unit head:* Kenneth J. Moure, Chair, 805-893-2993, Fax: 805-893-8795, E-mail: moure@history.ucrb.edu. *Application contact:* Prof. Sharon Farmer, Director of Graduate Studies, 805-893-2543, Fax: 805-893-8795, E-mail: farmer@history.ucsb.edu.

University of California, Santa Cruz, Division of Graduate Studies, Division of Humanities, Department of History, Santa Cruz, CA 95064. Offers MA, PhD. *Degree requirements:* For doctorate, variable foreign language requirement, thesis/dissertation, qualifying exam. *Faculty research:* Comparative, interdisciplinary approach to history; the Americas, Asia, the Islamic world, and Europe since 1500; society history.

University of Central Arkansas, Graduate School, College of Liberal Arts, Department of History, Conway, AR 72035-0001. Offers MA. Part-time programs available. *Degree requirements:* For master's, one foreign language, comprehensive exam, thesis optional. *Entrance requirements:* For master's, GRE General Test, minimum GPA of 2.7. Additional exam requirements/recommendations for international students: Required—TOEFL (minimum score 550 paper-based; 213 computer-based). *Faculty research:* History Day, Russian culture.

University of Central Florida, College of Arts and Humanities, Department of History, Orlando, FL 32816. Offers history (MA); public history (MA). Part-time and evening/weekend programs available. *Faculty:* 27 full-time (13 women), 20 part-time/adjunct (6 women). *Students:* 13 full-time (2 women), 37 part-time (10 women); includes 9 minority (2 African Americans, 7 Hispanic Americans). Average age 34. In 2008, 10 master's awarded. *Degree requirements:* For master's, thesis, written exam. *Entrance requirements:* For master's, GRE General Test, minimum GPA of 3.0 in last 60 hours. Additional exam requirements/recommendations for international students: Required—TOEFL. *Application deadline:* For fall admission, 7/15 for domestic students; for spring admission, 12/1 for domestic students. Electronic applications accepted. *Expenses:* Tuition, area resident: Full-time $6816; part-time $284 per credit. Tuition, state resident: full-time $6816; part-time $1076 per credit. Tuition, nonresident: full-time $25,824. Required fees: $216; $9 per credit. *Financial support:* In 2008–09, 2 fellowships with partial tuition reimbursements (averaging $10,000 per year), 7 research assistantships with partial tuition reimbursements (averaging $4,000 per year), 8 teaching assistantships with partial tuition reimbursements (averaging $4,400 per year) were awarded; career-related internships or fieldwork, Federal Work-Study, institutionally sponsored loans, tuition waivers (partial), and unspecified assistantships also available. Financial award application deadline: 3/1; financial award applicants required to submit FAFSA. *Unit head:* Dr. Rosalind Beiler, Chair, 407-823-6467, E-mail: beiler@mail.ucf.edu. *Application contact:* Dr. Rosalind Beiler, Chair, 407-823-6467, E-mail: beiler@mail.ucf.edu.

University of Central Missouri, The Graduate School, College of Arts, Humanities and Social Sciences, Department of History and Anthropology, Warrensburg, MO 64093. Offers history (MA). Part-time programs available. *Degree requirements:* For master's, comprehensive exam. *Entrance requirements:* For master's, GRE Subject Test, 20 undergraduate hours of course work in history, minimum GPA of 2.75. Additional exam requirements/recommendations for international students: Required—TOEFL (minimum score 500 paper-based; 173 computer-based). *Faculty research:* American History, World History, Public History.

University of Central Oklahoma, College of Graduate Studies and Research, College of Liberal Arts, Department of History, Edmond, OK 73034-5209. Offers history (MA); museum studies (MA); social studies teaching (MA); Southwestern studies (MA). Part-time programs available. *Degree requirements:* For master's, thesis optional. *Entrance requirements:* Additional exam requirements/recommendations for international students: Required—TOEFL (minimum score 550 paper-based; 213 computer-based). Electronic applications accepted. *Faculty research:* China, Russia, civil war, American naval logistics.

University of Chicago, Division of Social Sciences, Department of History, Chicago, IL 60637-1513. Offers PhD. *Degree requirements:* For doctorate, variable foreign language requirement, thesis/dissertation, oral exams in 3 fields. *Entrance requirements:* For doctorate, GRE General Test. Additional exam requirements/recommendations for international students: Required—TOEFL, IELTS (minimum score 7). Electronic applications accepted.

University of Cincinnati, Graduate School, McMicken College of Arts and Sciences, Department of History, Cincinnati, OH 45221. Offers MA, PhD. Terminal master's awarded for partial completion of doctoral program. *Degree requirements:* For master's, comprehensive exam, thesis optional; for doctorate, comprehensive exam, thesis/dissertation. *Entrance requirements:* For master's, GRE General Test, BA in history; for doctorate, GRE General Test, MA in history. Additional exam requirements/recommendations for international students: Required—TOEFL (minimum score 600 paper-based). Electronic applications accepted. *Faculty research:* US cultural and social history, women's history, US and British intellectual history, modern Europe.

University of Colorado at Boulder, Graduate School, College of Arts and Sciences, Department of History, Boulder, CO 80309. Offers MA, PhD. Terminal master's awarded for partial completion of doctoral program. *Degree requirements:* For master's, comprehensive exam, thesis optional; for doctorate, one foreign language, thesis/dissertation. *Entrance requirements:* For master's, GRE General Test, minimum undergraduate GPA of 2.75; for doctorate, GRE General Test. *Faculty research:* History of the American West; early American history; history of women and gender; American political, social and intellectual history; early modern and modern European social history.

University of Colorado at Colorado Springs, Graduate School, College of Letters, Arts and Sciences, Department of History, Colorado Springs, CO 80933-7150. Offers MA. Part-time and evening/weekend programs available. *Faculty:* 5 full-time (1 woman). *Students:* 24 full-time (14 women), 16 part-time (9 women); includes 3 minority (1 African American, 1 American Indian/Alaska Native, 1 Hispanic American). Average age 36. 13 applicants, 92% accepted, 12 enrolled. In 2008, 11 master's awarded. *Degree requirements:* For master's, portfolio of 3-4 research projects, oral exam. *Entrance requirements:* For master's, minimum GPA of 2.75, writing sample. *Application deadline:* For fall admission, 3/1 for domestic students; for spring admission, 10/15 for domestic students. Applications are processed on a rolling basis. Application fee: $60 ($75 for international students). *Financial support:* Teaching assistantships available. *Faculty research:* U.S. to 1865, Latin America, India, medieval and modern Europe. Total annual research expenditures: $10,972. *Unit head:* Dr. Robert E. Sackett, Chair, 719-255-4079, Fax: 719-255-4068, E-mail: rsackett@uccs.edu. *Application contact:* Dr. Debbie Scott, Administrative Assistant, 719-255-4069, Fax: 719-255-4068, E-mail: dscott@uccs.edu.

University of Colorado Denver, College of Liberal Arts and Sciences, Department of History, Denver, CO 80217-3364. Offers MA. Part-time and evening/weekend programs available. *Degree requirements:* For master's, comprehensive exam, thesis. *Entrance requirements:* For master's, GRE General Test, interview, minimum GPA of 3.25. Additional exam requirements/recommendations for international students: Required—TOEFL (minimum score 525 paper-based; 197 computer-based). Electronic applications accepted.

University of Connecticut, Graduate School, College of Liberal Arts and Sciences, Department of History, Field of History, Storrs, CT 06269. Offers MA, PhD. Terminal master's awarded for partial completion of doctoral program. *Degree requirements:* For master's, comprehensive exam; for doctorate, thesis/dissertation. *Entrance requirements:* For master's and doctorate, GRE General Test. Additional exam requirements/recommendations for international students: Required—TOEFL (minimum score 550 paper-based; 213 computer-based). Electronic applications accepted.

University of Delaware, College of Arts and Sciences, Department of History, Hagley Program in the History of Technology and Industrialization, Newark, DE 19716. Offers MA, PhD. *Degree requirements:* For master's, thesis optional; for doctorate, comprehensive exam, thesis/dissertation. *Entrance requirements:* For master's and doctorate, interview. Electronic applications accepted.

University of Florida, Graduate School, College of Liberal Arts and Sciences, Department of History, Gainesville, FL 32611. Offers MA, PhD, JD/MA, JD/PhD. *Degree requirements:* For doctorate, thesis/dissertation. *Entrance requirements:* For master's and doctorate, GRE General Test, minimum GPA of 3.0. Additional exam requirements/recommendations for international students: Required—TOEFL (minimum score 550 paper-based; 213 computer-based). Electronic applications accepted. *Faculty research:* U.S. history, Florida studies, Latin American history, African history.

University of Georgia, Graduate School, College of Arts and Sciences, Department of History, Athens, GA 30602. Offers MA, PhD. *Degree requirements:* For master's, one foreign language, thesis; for doctorate, one foreign language, thesis/dissertation. *Entrance requirements:* For master's and doctorate, GRE General Test. Electronic applications accepted.

University of Guelph, Graduate Program Services, College of Arts, Department of History, Guelph, ON N1G 2W1, Canada. Offers MA, PhD. Part-time programs available. *Degree requirements:* For master's, one foreign language, thesis (for some programs); for doctorate, one foreign language, thesis/dissertation, 3 qualifying fields. *Entrance requirements:* For master's, minimum B+ average during previous 2 years of course work; for doctorate, minimum A-average in MA. Additional exam requirements/recommendations for international students: Required—TOEFL (minimum score 550 paper-based; 219 computer-based). Electronic applications accepted. *Faculty research:* Gender and family, Scottish history, rural and urban community studies, eighteenth century England, Canadian legal and social history, modern Europe.

University of Hawaii at Manoa, Graduate Division, Colleges of Arts and Sciences, College of Arts and Humanities, Department of History, Honolulu, HI 96822. Offers MA, PhD. Part-time programs available. *Degree requirements:* For master's, 2 foreign languages, thesis optional; for doctorate, 2 foreign languages, comprehensive exam, thesis/dissertation. *Entrance requirements:* For master's, GRE, minimum GPA of 3.0, writing sample; for doctorate, GRE, MA, sample of written work. Additional exam requirements/recommendations for international students: Required—TOEFL (minimum score 580 paper-based; 237 computer-based; 92 iBT), IELTS (minimum score 5). *Faculty research:* Asian, Pacific, world, American and European history.

University of Houston, College of Liberal Arts and Social Sciences, Department of History, Houston, TX 77204. Offers history (MA, PhD); public history (MA). Part-time programs available. *Faculty:* 24 full-time (9 women), 1 (woman) part-time/adjunct. *Students:* 52 full-time (27 women), 35 part-time (16 women); includes 15 minority (2 African Americans, 2 American Indian/Alaska Native, 1 Asian American or Pacific Islander, 10 Hispanic Americans), 1 international. Average age 38. 53 applicants, 43% accepted, 10 enrolled. In 2008, 6 master's, 6 doctorates awarded. Terminal master's awarded for partial completion of doctoral program. *Degree requirements:* For master's, one foreign language, thesis (for some programs); for doctorate, one foreign language, thesis/dissertation. *Entrance requirements:* For master's, GRE General Test, minimum GPA of 3.3; for doctorate, GRE General Test, minimum GPA of 3.67. Additional exam requirements/recommendations for international students: Required—TOEFL. *Application deadline:* For fall admission, 1/15 for domestic students; for spring admission, 11/1 for domestic students. Application fee: $25 ($100 for international students). *Expenses:* Tuition, state resident: full-time $5164; part-time $287 per credit. Tuition, nonresident: full-time $10,222; part-time $568 per credit. *Financial support:* In 2008–09, 3 research assistantships with full tuition reimbursements (averaging $10,000 per year), 33 teaching assistantships with full tuition reimbursements (averaging $10,000 per year) were awarded; career-related internships or fieldwork, Federal Work-Study, institutionally sponsored loans, scholarships/grants, health care benefits, and unspecified assistantships also available. Support available to part-time students. Financial award application deadline: 2/1. *Faculty research:* U.S., Latin American, European, social, and women's history. *Unit head:* Robert Buzzanco, Chairperson, 713-743-3008, Fax: 713-743-3216. *Application contact:* Robert Buzzanco, Chairperson, 713-743-3008, Fax: 713-743-3216.

University of Houston–Clear Lake, School of Human Sciences and Humanities, Programs in Humanities and Fine Arts, Houston, TX 77058-1098. Offers history (MA); humanities (MA); literature (MA). Part-time and evening/weekend programs available. Postbaccalaureate distance learning degree programs offered (minimal on-campus study). *Degree requirements:* For master's, thesis or alternative. *Entrance requirements:* For master's, GRE General Test. Additional exam requirements/recommendations for international students: Required—TOEFL (minimum score 550 paper-based; 213 computer-based). *Faculty research:* Digital media studies, Latin American history, labor history, Chaucer evolution versus creationism debate.

University of Idaho, College of Graduate Studies, College of Letters, Arts and Social Sciences, Department of History, Moscow, ID 83844-2282. Offers MA, MAT, PhD. *Faculty:* 8. *Students:* 15 full-time, 5 part-time. Average age 35. In 2008, 4 master's awarded. *Degree requirements:* For doctorate, thesis/dissertation. *Entrance requirements:* For master's, minimum GPA of 2.8; for doctorate, minimum undergraduate GPA of 2.8, 3.0 graduate. *Application deadline:* For fall admission, 8/1 for domestic students; for spring admission, 12/15 for domestic students. Application fee: $55 ($60 for international students). *Expenses:* Tuition, nonresident: full-time $10,080; part-time $336 per credit. Required fees: $5212; $267 per credit. Tuition and fees vary according to program. *Financial support:* Research assistantships, teaching assistantships available. Financial award application deadline: 2/15. *Unit head:* Dr. Richard Spence, Chair, 208-885-6228. *Application contact:* Dr. Richard Spence, Chair, 208-885-6228.

University of Illinois at Chicago, Graduate College, College of Liberal Arts and Sciences, Department of History, Chicago, IL 60607-7128. Offers MA, MAT, PhD. Part-time and evening/weekend programs available. *Degree requirements:* For master's, one foreign language, comprehensive exam; for doctorate, 2 foreign languages, comprehensive exam, thesis/dissertation. *Entrance requirements:* For master's and doctorate, GRE General Test, previous course work in a foreign language, minimum GPA of 3.0. Additional exam requirements/recommendations for international students: Required—TOEFL. Electronic applications accepted. *Faculty research:* American urban and immigration history, early modern European history, Eastern European history.

University of Illinois at Springfield, Graduate Programs, College of Liberal Arts and Sciences, Program in History, Springfield, IL 62703-5407. Offers MA. Part-time and evening/weekend programs available. *Faculty:* 9 full-time (4 women). *Students:* 17 full-time (10 women), 37 part-time (17 women); includes 9 minority (6 African Americans, 1 American Indian/Alaska Native, 2 Hispanic Americans). Average age 33. 33 applicants, 73% accepted, 17 enrolled. In 2008, 18 master's awarded. *Degree requirements:* For master's, thesis, internship, or historiography. *Entrance requirements:* For master's, BA in history or related field, minimum undergraduate GPA of 3.0, writing sample, statement of purpose. Additional exam requirements/recommendations for international students: Required—TOEFL (minimum score 500 paper-based; 176 computer-based; 61 iBT). *Application deadline:* Applications are processed on a rolling basis. Application fee: $50 ($60 for international students). Electronic applications accepted. *Expenses:* Tuition, state resident: full-time $6144; part-time $256 per credit hour. Tuition, nonresident: full-time $13,980; part-time $582.50 per credit hour. Required fees: $1800. *Financial support:* In 2008–09, research assistantships with full tuition reimbursements (averaging $8,109 per year), teaching assistantships with full tuition reimbursements (averaging $8,109 per year) were awarded; career-related internships or fieldwork, Federal Work-Study, scholarships/grants, health care benefits, and unspecified assistantships also available. Support available to part-time students. Financial award application deadline: 11/15; financial award applicants required to submit FAFSA. *Unit head:* Dr. Robert McGregor, Program Administrator, 217-206-7442, Fax: 217-206-6217, E-mail: mcgregor.robert@uis.edu. *Application contact:* Dr. Lynn Pardie, Office of Graduate Studies, 800-252-8533, Fax: 217-206-7623, E-mail: pardie.lynn@uis.edu.

University of Illinois at Urbana–Champaign, Graduate College, College of Liberal Arts and Sciences, Department of History, Champaign, IL 61820. Offers MA, PhD. *Faculty:* 42 full-time (16 women). *Students:* 96 full-time (41 women), 27 part-time (14 women); includes 23 minority (16 African Americans, 5 Asian Americans or Pacific Islanders, 2 Hispanic Americans), 19 international. 202 applicants, 9% accepted, 16 enrolled. In 2008, 10 master's, 4 doctorates awarded. *Entrance requirements:* For master's, GRE General Test, minimum GPA of 3.25; writing sample; for doctorate, GRE, minimum GPA of 3.5; writing sample. Additional exam requirements/recommendations for international students: Required—TOEFL (minimum score 600 paper-based; 250 computer-based). *Application deadline:* Applications are processed on a rolling basis. Application fee: $60 ($75 for international students). Electronic applications accepted. *Financial support:* In 2008–09, 59 fellowships, 20 research assistantships, 54 teaching assistantships were awarded; tuition waivers (full and partial) also available. *Unit head:* Antoinette Burton, Chairperson, 217-244-2075, Fax: 217-333-2297, E-mail: aburton@illinois.edu. *Application contact:* Elaine B. Sampson, Staff Secretary, 217-244-2591, Fax: 217-333-2297, E-mail: esampson@illinois.edu.

University of Indianapolis, Graduate Programs, College of Arts and Sciences, Department of History and Political Science, Indianapolis, IN 46227-3697. Offers history (MA); international relations (MA). Part-time and evening/weekend programs available. *Faculty:* 6 full-time (2 women). *Students:* 2 full-time (1 woman), 7 part-time (4 women). Average age 30. *Degree requirements:* For master's, thesis optional. *Entrance requirements:* For master's, GRE Subject Test, minimum GPA of 3.0, 3 letters of recommendation, statement of purpose. Additional exam requirements/recommendations for international students: Required—TOEFL (minimum score 550 paper-based; 213 computer-based). *Application deadline:* Applications are processed on a rolling basis. Application fee: $30. Electronic applications accepted. *Financial support:* Federal Work-Study available. Financial award application deadline: 5/1; financial award applicants required to submit FAFSA. *Unit head:* Dr. Lawrence Sondhaus, Chairperson, 317-788-2196, Fax: 317-788-3480, E-mail: sondhaus@uindy.edu. *Application contact:* Dr. Lawrence Sondhaus, Chairperson, 317-788-2196, Fax: 317-788-3480, E-mail: sondhaus@uindy.edu.

The University of Iowa, Graduate College, College of Liberal Arts and Sciences, Department of History, Iowa City, IA 52242-1316. Offers MA, PhD. *Degree requirements:* For master's, thesis optional, exam; for doctorate, comprehensive exam, thesis/dissertation. *Entrance requirements:* For master's and doctorate, GRE General Test, minimum GPA of 3.0. Additional exam requirements/recommendations for international students: Required—TOEFL (minimum score 550 paper-based; 213 computer-based; 81 iBT). Electronic applications accepted.

The University of Kansas, Graduate Studies, College of Liberal Arts and Sciences, Department of History, Lawrence, KS 66045. Offers MA, PhD. Part-time programs available. *Faculty:* 34. *Students:* 78 full-time (26 women), 8 part-time (4 women); includes 4 minority (3 American Indian/Alaska Native, 1 Hispanic American), 2 international. Average age 35. 80 applicants,

History

The University of Kansas *(continued)*
48% accepted, 21 enrolled. In 2008, 4 master's, 6 doctorates awarded. *Degree requirements:* For master's, variable foreign language requirement, 2 professional quality papers; for doctorate, variable foreign language requirement, comprehensive exam, thesis/dissertation. *Entrance requirements:* For master's and doctorate, GRE General Test, minimum GPA of 3.0. Additional exam requirements/recommendations for international students: Required—TOEFL. *Application deadline:* For fall admission, 12/1 for domestic students, 11/1 for international students. Application fee: $45 ($50 for international students). Electronic applications accepted. *Expenses:* Tuition, area resident: Full-time $6122; part-time $255.10 per credit hour. Tuition, state resident: full-time $6122; part-time $255.10 per credit hour. Tuition, nonresident: full-time $14,629; part-time $609.55 per credit hour. Required fees: $847; $70.56 per credit hour. Tuition and fees vary according to course load and program. *Financial support:* In 2008–09, 30 teaching assistantships with full and partial tuition reimbursements were awarded; fellowships with full and partial tuition reimbursements, research assistantships with full and partial tuition reimbursements, unspecified assistantships also available. Financial award application deadline: 12/1. *Faculty research:* Environment, military, early modern, East Asia, Russia/East Europe. *Unit head:* Paul Kelton, Graduate Director, 785-864-9441, Fax: 785-864-5046, E-mail: pkelton@ku.edu. *Application contact:* Ellen Garber, Graduate Program Administrator, 785-864-9438, Fax: 785-864-5046.

University of Kentucky, Graduate School, College of Arts and Sciences, Program in History, Lexington, KY 40506-0032. Offers MA, PhD. Part-time programs available. *Degree requirements:* For master's, one foreign language, comprehensive exam, thesis optional; for doctorate, variable foreign language requirement, comprehensive exam, thesis/dissertation. *Entrance requirements:* For master's, GRE General Test, minimum undergraduate GPA of 2.75; for doctorate, GRE General Test, minimum graduate GPA of 3.0. Additional exam requirements/recommendations for international students: Required—TOEFL (minimum score 550 paper-based; 213 computer-based). Electronic applications accepted. *Faculty research:* English, British, European history; U.S. social, political and diplomatic history; U.S. early national history; U.S. Southern history; Native American and African-American history.

University of Lethbridge, School of Graduate Studies, Lethbridge, AB T1K 3M4, Canada. Offers accounting (MScM); addictions counseling (M Sc); agricultural biotechnology (M Sc); agricultural studies (M Sc, MA); anthropology (MA); archaeology (MA); art (MA); biochemistry (M Sc); biological sciences (M Sc); biomolecular science (PhD); biosystems and biodiversity (PhD); Canadian studies (MA); chemistry (M Sc); computer science (M Sc); computer science and geographical information science (M Sc); counseling psychology (M Ed); dramatic arts (MA); earth, space, and physical science (PhD); economics (MA); educational leadership (M Ed); English (MA); environmental science (M Sc); evolution and behavior (PhD); exercise science (M Sc); finance (MScM); French (MA); French/German (MA); French/Spanish (MA); general education (M Ed); general management (MScM); geography (M Sc, MA); German (MA); health sciences (M Sc, MA); history (MA); human resource management and labour relations (MScM); individualized multidisciplinary (M Sc, MA); information systems (MScM); international management (MScM); kinesiology (M Sc, MA); management (M Sc, MA); marketing (MScM); mathematics (M Sc); music (MA); Native American studies (MA); neuroscience (M Sc, PhD); new media (MA); nursing (M Sc); philosophy (MA); physics (M Sc); policy and strategy (MScM); political science (MA); psychology (M Sc, MA); religious studies (MA); sociology (MA); theoretical and computational science (PhD); urban and regional studies (MA). Part-time and evening/weekend programs available. *Degree requirements:* For doctorate, comprehensive exam, thesis/dissertation. *Entrance requirements:* For master's, GMAT (M Sc in management), bachelor's degree in related field, minimum GPA of 3.0 during previous 20 graded semester courses, 2 years teaching or related experience (M Ed); for doctorate, master's degree, minimum graduate GPA of 3.5. Additional exam requirements/recommendations for international students: Required—TOEFL. *Faculty research:* Movement and brain plasticity, gibberellin physiology, photosynthesis, carbon cycling, molecular properties of main-group ring components.

University of Louisiana at Lafayette, BI Moody III College of Business Administration MBA Program, College of Liberal Arts, Department of History and Geography, Lafayette, LA 70504. Offers history (MA). Part-time programs available. *Degree requirements:* For master's, one foreign language, thesis or alternative. *Entrance requirements:* For master's, GRE General Test, minimum GPA of 2.75. Additional exam requirements/recommendations for international students: Required—TOEFL (minimum score 550 paper-based; 213 computer-based). Electronic applications accepted.

University of Louisiana at Monroe, Graduate School, College of Arts and Sciences, Department of History, Monroe, LA 71209-0001. Offers MA. Part-time and evening/weekend programs available. *Faculty:* 3 full-time (0 women). *Students:* 10 full-time (5 women), 5 part-time (1 woman); includes 3 African Americans. Average age 34. In 2008, 5 master's awarded. *Degree requirements:* For master's, thesis (for some programs). *Entrance requirements:* For master's, GRE General Test, minimum undergraduate GPA of 2.5. Additional exam requirements/recommendations for international students: Required—TOEFL (minimum score 500 paper-based; 173 computer-based; 61 iBT). *Application deadline:* For fall admission, 8/22 priority date for domestic students, 7/1 for international students; for winter admission, 12/12 priority date for domestic students; for spring admission, 1/17 for domestic students, 11/1 for international students. Applications are processed on a rolling basis. Application fee: $20 ($30 for international students). Electronic applications accepted. *Expenses:* Tuition, area resident: Full-time $2403; part-time $1202 per semester. Tuition, state resident: full-time $2403; part-time $1202 per semester. Tuition, nonresident: full-time $2403; part-time $1202 per semester. International tuition: $8352 full-time. Required fees: $1239.40; $141 per credit hour. *Financial support:* In 2008–09, 7 research assistantships with full tuition reimbursements (averaging $2,500 per year) were awarded; career-related internships or fieldwork, Federal Work-Study, and unspecified assistantships also available. Financial award application deadline: 4/1; financial award applicants required to submit FAFSA. *Faculty research:* Early Louisiana settlements, Soviet history, Louisiana "Tigers" in Civil War, Anglo-American relations, US/East European relations. *Unit head:* Dr. Ralph W Brown, Department Head, 318-342-1402, E-mail: rbrown@ulm.edu. *Application contact:* Dr. Ralph W Brown, Department Head, 318-342-1402, E-mail: rbrown@ulm.edu.

University of Louisville, Graduate School, College of Arts and Sciences, Department of History, Louisville, KY 40292-0001. Offers MA. Part-time programs available. *Faculty:* 17 full-time (4 women). *Students:* 11 full-time (6 women), 12 part-time (7 women); includes 1 American Indian/Alaska Native. Average age 32. 7 applicants, 100% accepted, 6 enrolled. In 2008, 6 master's awarded. *Degree requirements:* For master's, one foreign language, comprehensive exam (for some programs), thesis (for some programs). *Entrance requirements:* For master's, GRE General Test. Additional exam requirements/recommendations for international students: Required—TOEFL. *Application deadline:* For fall admission, 6/20 for domestic students, 5/1 for international students; for spring admission, 12/10 for domestic students, 11/1 for international students. Applications are processed on a rolling basis. Application fee: $50. Electronic applications accepted. *Financial support:* In 2008–09, 2 teaching assistantships with tuition reimbursements (averaging $12,000 per year) were awarded. Financial award applicants required to submit FAFSA. *Faculty research:* 19th century United States; British, British Empire; 20th century women's history; Turkey and the Middle East; world history. Total annual research expenditures: $1,200. *Unit head:* Dr. John McLeod, Chair, 502-852-6817, Fax: 502-852-0770, E-mail: john.mcleod@louisville.edu. *Application contact:* Libby Leggett, Director, Graduate Admissions, 502-852-3101, Fax: 502-852-6536, E-mail: gradadm@louisville.edu.

University of Maine, Graduate School, College of Liberal Arts and Sciences, Department of History, Orono, ME 04469. Offers MA, PhD. Terminal master's awarded for partial completion of doctoral program. *Degree requirements:* For master's, variable foreign language requirement, thesis optional; for doctorate, one foreign language, thesis/dissertation. *Entrance requirements:* For master's and doctorate, GRE General Test. Additional exam requirements/recommendations

for international students: Required—TOEFL. Electronic applications accepted. *Faculty research:* Canadian labor and working classes; American social, cultural, and urban history.

University of Manitoba, Faculty of Graduate Studies, Faculty of Arts, Department of History, Winnipeg, MB R3T 2N2, Canada. Offers archival studies (MA); history (MA, PhD). *Degree requirements:* For master's, thesis; for doctorate, one foreign language, thesis/dissertation.

University of Maryland, Baltimore County, Graduate School, College of Arts, Humanities and Social Sciences, Department of History, Baltimore, MD 21250. Offers historical studies (MA). Part-time and evening/weekend programs available. *Faculty:* 18 full-time (10 women), 10 part-time/adjunct (2 women). *Students:* 10 full-time (7 women), 67 part-time (41 women); includes 4 minority (2 African Americans, 2 Asian Americans or Pacific Islanders). Average age 30. 36 applicants, 69% accepted, 18 enrolled. In 2008, 16 master's awarded. *Degree requirements:* For master's, thesis or alternative. *Entrance requirements:* For master's, GRE General Test, minimum GPA of 3.0. Additional exam requirements/recommendations for international students: Required—TOEFL. *Application deadline:* For fall admission, 3/10 priority date for domestic students, 1/1 for international students; for spring admission, 11/1 priority date for domestic students, 5/1 for international students. Applications are processed on a rolling basis. Application fee: $50. Electronic applications accepted. *Financial support:* In 2008–09, 10 students received support, including 1 research assistantship with full tuition reimbursement available (averaging $11,324 per year), 9 teaching assistantships with full and partial tuition reimbursements available (averaging $11,324 per year); career-related internships or fieldwork, health care benefits, tuition waivers (partial), and unspecified assistantships also available. Financial award application deadline: 3/30; financial award applicants required to submit FAFSA. *Faculty research:* Archival administration, historical editing. Total annual research expenditures: $50,000. *Unit head:* Dr. Constantine Vaporis, Director, 410-455-2092, Fax: 410-455-1045, E-mail: vaporis@umbc.edu. *Application contact:* Carla Ison, Administrative Assistant, 410-455-2312, Fax: 410-455-1045, E-mail: ison@umbc.edu.

University of Maryland, College Park, Graduate Studies, College of Arts and Humanities, Department of History, College Park, MD 20742. Offers MA, PhD. *Degree requirements:* For master's, comprehensive exam, thesis optional; for doctorate, one foreign language, thesis/dissertation, oral and written exams. *Entrance requirements:* For master's, GRE General Test, minimum GPA of 3.25, writing sample, 3 letters of recommendation; for doctorate, GRE General Test, minimum GPA of 3.5. Additional exam requirements/recommendations for international students: Required—TOEFL. Electronic applications accepted. *Faculty research:* Ancient, British, East Asian, Latin American, and diplomatic history; papers of Samuel Gompers; Freedman and Southern Society; Caesarea excavations; Folger Institute.

University of Maryland, College Park, Graduate Studies, Interdepartmental Programs, Program in History, Library, and Information Services, College Park, MD 20742. Offers MA/MLS. *Entrance requirements:* Additional exam requirements/recommendations for international students: Required—TOEFL. Electronic applications accepted.

University of Massachusetts Amherst, Graduate School, College of Humanities and Fine Arts, Department of History, Amherst, MA 01003. Offers ancient history (MA); British Empire history (MA); European (medieval and modern) history (MA, PhD); Islamic history (MA); Latin American history (MA, PhD); modern global history (MA); public history (MA); science and technology history (MA); U.S. history (MA, PhD). Part-time programs available. Terminal master's awarded for partial completion of doctoral program. *Degree requirements:* For master's, one foreign language, thesis or alternative; for doctorate, one foreign language, comprehensive exam, thesis/dissertation. *Entrance requirements:* For master's and doctorate, GRE General Test, writing sample. Additional exam requirements/recommendations for international students: Required—TOEFL (minimum score 550 paper-based; 213 computer-based; 79 iBT), IELTS (minimum score 6.5). Electronic applications accepted. *Expenses:* Tuition, area resident: Full-time $2640. Tuition, nonresident: full-time $9936. One-time fee: $332 full-time. Tuition and fees vary according to course load. *Faculty research:* Ancient and medieval history; global and comparative history; public history; history of science, technology, medicine and the environment; history of women, gender, sexuality and family.

University of Massachusetts Boston, Office of Graduate Studies, College of Liberal Arts, Program in History, Boston, MA 02125-3393. Offers archival methods (MA); historical archaeology (MA); history (MA). Part-time and evening/weekend programs available. *Degree requirements:* For master's, thesis, oral exam. *Entrance requirements:* For master's, minimum GPA of 2.75. *Faculty research:* European intellectual history, American labor and social history in 19th century, colonial American Revolution, Afro-American Cold War.

University of Memphis, Graduate School, College of Arts and Sciences, Department of History, Memphis, TN 38152. Offers MA, PhD. Part-time programs available. *Faculty:* 21 full-time (5 women), 2 part-time/adjunct (0 women). *Students:* 61 full-time (30 women), 47 part-time (21 women); includes 18 minority (all African Americans), 1 international. Average age 38. 40 applicants, 85% accepted, 14 enrolled. In 2008, 10 master's, 7 doctorates awarded. Terminal master's awarded for partial completion of doctoral program. *Degree requirements:* For master's, comprehensive exam, thesis or alternative; for doctorate, one foreign language, comprehensive exam, thesis/dissertation. *Entrance requirements:* For master's, GRE General Test or MAT, minimum GPA of 3.0 in history, 18 undergraduate hours of course work in history; for doctorate, GRE General Test, GRE Subject Test, MA in history, minimum GPA of 3.25. *Application deadline:* For fall admission, 8/1 for domestic students; for spring admission, 12/1 for domestic students. Applications are processed on a rolling basis. Application fee: $35 ($60 for international students). Electronic applications accepted. *Expenses:* Tuition, area resident: Full-time $6242; part-time $330 per credit hour. Tuition, state resident: full-time $6242; part-time $330 per credit hour. Tuition, nonresident: full-time $17,828; part-time $815 per credit hour. Required fees: $1156. *Financial support:* Research assistantships with full tuition reimbursements, teaching assistantships with full tuition reimbursements, career-related internships or fieldwork and scholarships/grants available. Financial award applicants required to submit FAFSA. *Faculty research:* African/African-American history, mid-south regional studies, social cultural history, ancient Egyptian history. *Unit head:* Dr. Janann Sherman, Chairman, 901-678-2515, Fax: 907-678-2720, E-mail: sherman@memphis.edu. *Application contact:* Dr. James M. Blythe, Coordinator of Graduate Studies, 901-678-3381, Fax: 901-678-2720, E-mail: jmblythe@memphis.edu.

University of Miami, Graduate School, College of Arts and Sciences, Department of History, Coral Gables, FL 33124. Offers MA, PhD. Part-time programs available. Terminal master's awarded for partial completion of doctoral program. *Degree requirements:* For master's, one foreign language, comprehensive exam, thesis optional; for doctorate, one foreign language, comprehensive exam, thesis/dissertation. *Entrance requirements:* For master's and doctorate, GRE General Test, GRE Subject Test. Additional exam requirements/recommendations for international students: Required—TOEFL (minimum score 550 paper-based; 213 computer-based; 59 iBT). Electronic applications accepted. *Faculty research:* Latin American, European, U.S., and public history.

University of Michigan, Horace H. Rackham School of Graduate Studies, College of Literature, Science, and the Arts, Department of History, Ann Arbor, MI 48109. Offers PhD. *Degree requirements:* For doctorate, 2 foreign languages, thesis/dissertation, oral defense of dissertation, preliminary exam. *Entrance requirements:* For doctorate, GRE General Test, writing sample. Additional exam requirements/recommendations for international students: Required—TOEFL. Electronic applications accepted. *Faculty research:* Europe, Latin America, Africa, Asia, United States.

University of Michigan, Horace H. Rackham School of Graduate Studies, College of Literature, Science, and the Arts, Department of Women's Studies, Ann Arbor, MI 48109. Offers English and women's studies (PhD); history and women's studies (PhD); lesbian, gay, bisexual, transgender, queer (LGBTQ) studies (Certificate); psychology and women's studies (PhD); sociology and women's studies (PhD); women's studies (Certificate). *Degree requirements:*

For doctorate, variable foreign language requirement, thesis/dissertation. *Entrance requirements:* For doctorate, GRE General Test, previous undergraduate course work in women's studies. Electronic applications accepted. *Faculty research:* Gender issues; LGBTQ studies; sexuality; women and science; global feminism.

University of Michigan, Horace H. Rackham School of Graduate Studies, College of Literature, Science, and the Arts, Doctoral Program in Anthropology and History, Ann Arbor, MI 48109. Offers PhD. *Degree requirements:* For doctorate, 2 foreign languages, thesis/dissertation, oral defense of dissertation, preliminary exam. *Entrance requirements:* For doctorate, GRE General Test, writing sample. Additional exam requirements/recommendations for international students: Required—TOEFL. Electronic applications accepted. *Faculty research:* Historical anthropology.

University of Michigan, Horace H. Rackham School of Graduate Studies, College of Literature, Science, and the Arts, Interdepartmental Program in Greek and Roman History, Ann Arbor, MI 48109. Offers PhD, Certificate. *Degree requirements:* For doctorate, 4 foreign languages, comprehensive exam, thesis/dissertation, oral defense of dissertation, dissertation prospectus, preliminary exams. *Entrance requirements:* For doctorate, GRE, knowledge of classical Greek and Latin. Additional exam requirements/recommendations for international students: Required—TOEFL (minimum score 560 paper-based; 220 computer-based). Electronic applications accepted. *Faculty research:* Greek history, Roman history.

University of Minnesota, Twin Cities Campus, Graduate School, College of Liberal Arts, Department of Classical and Near Eastern Studies, Minneapolis, MN 55455-0213. Offers ancient and medieval art and archaeology (MA, PhD); classics (MA, PhD); Greek (MA, PhD); Latin (MA, PhD); religions in antiquity (MA). Part-time programs available. Terminal master's awarded for partial completion of doctoral program. *Degree requirements:* For master's, 2 foreign languages, comprehensive exam, thesis or alternative; for doctorate, variable foreign language requirement, comprehensive exam, thesis/dissertation. *Entrance requirements:* For master's and doctorate, GRE, 3 letters of recommendation, department application, writing sample, copies of transcripts, personal statement. Additional exam requirements/recommendations for international students: Required—TOEFL. Electronic applications accepted. *Faculty research:* Greek and Latin literature, archaeology, religions in antiquity, ancient Near East.

University of Minnesota, Twin Cities Campus, Graduate School, College of Liberal Arts, Department of History, Minneapolis, MN 55455-0213. Offers MA, PhD. *Degree requirements:* For master's, one foreign language, comprehensive exam, thesis or alternative; for doctorate, 2 foreign languages, comprehensive exam, thesis/dissertation. *Entrance requirements:* For doctorate, GRE General Test, writing sample, letters of recommendation. Additional exam requirements/recommendations for international students: Required—TOEFL (minimum score 550 paper-based; 213 computer-based). Electronic applications accepted. *Faculty research:* Early and modern United States; medieval, early modern and modern Europe; Africa; East and South Asia; Latin America.

University of Mississippi, Graduate School, College of Liberal Arts, Department of History, Oxford, University, MS 38677. Offers MA, PhD. *Degree requirements:* For doctorate, thesis/dissertation. *Entrance requirements:* For master's, GRE General Test, GRE Subject Test, minimum GPA of 3.0; for doctorate, GRE General Test, GRE Subject Test. Additional exam requirements/recommendations for international students: Required—TOEFL. Electronic applications accepted.

University of Missouri–Columbia, Graduate School, College of Arts and Sciences, Department of History, Columbia, MO 65211. Offers MA, PhD. *Faculty:* 26 full-time (8 women). *Students:* 24 full-time (10 women), 29 part-time (8 women); includes 4 minority (3 African Americans, 1 Asian American or Pacific Islander). Average age 34. 54 applicants, 48% accepted, 12 enrolled. In 2008, 7 master's, 6 doctorates awarded. *Degree requirements:* For master's, thesis; for doctorate, 2 foreign languages, thesis/dissertation. *Entrance requirements:* For master's and doctorate, GRE General Test, minimum GPA of 3.0. Additional exam requirements/recommendations for international students: Required—TOEFL (minimum score 500 paper-based; 173 computer-based; 61 iBT). *Application deadline:* For fall admission, 2/1 priority date for domestic students. Applications are processed on a rolling basis. Application fee: $45 ($60 for international students). *Financial support:* Fellowships, research assistantships, teaching assistantships, institutionally sponsored loans available. *Unit head:* Dr. John H. Wigger, Director of Graduate Studies, 573-882-6019, E-mail: wiggerj@missouri.edu. *Application contact:* Dr. John H. Wigger, Director of Graduate Studies, 573-882-6019, E-mail: wiggerj@missouri.edu.

University of Missouri–Kansas City, College of Arts and Sciences, Department of History, Kansas City, MO 64110-2499. Offers MA, PhD. PhD (interdisciplinary) offered through the School of Graduate Studies. Part-time programs available. *Faculty:* 17 full-time (8 women), 4 part-time/adjunct (2 women). *Students:* 3 full-time (1 woman), 25 part-time (15 women); includes 1 minority (Asian American or Pacific Islander). Average age 35. 18 applicants, 78% accepted, 12 enrolled. In 2008, 9 master's awarded. *Degree requirements:* For master's, thesis optional; for doctorate, one foreign language, thesis/dissertation. *Entrance requirements:* For master's, GRE General Test, minimum GPA of 3.0, 2 writing samples, 3 letters of recommendation; for doctorate, GRE General Test. Additional exam requirements/recommendations for international students: Required—TOEFL (minimum score 550 paper-based; 213 computer-based; 80 iBT). *Application deadline:* For fall admission, 3/15 for domestic and international students; for spring admission, 10/1 priority date for domestic students, 10/1 for international students. Applications are processed on a rolling basis. Application fee: $45 ($50 for international students). Electronic applications accepted. *Expenses:* Tuition, state resident: full-time $5376; part-time $298.70 per credit hour. Tuition, nonresident: full-time $13,882; part-time $771.20 per credit hour. Required fees: $640.28; $34.65 per contact hour. $30 per semester. Tuition and fees vary according to course load and program. *Financial support:* In 2008–09, 7 teaching assistantships with partial tuition reimbursements (averaging $14,878 per year) were awarded; fellowships with partial tuition reimbursements, research assistantships with partial tuition reimbursements, career-related internships or fieldwork, Federal Work-Study, institutionally sponsored loans, and tuition waivers (full and partial) also available. Support available to part-time students. Financial award application deadline: 3/1; financial award applicants required to submit FAFSA. *Faculty research:* U.S. history, Europe, women and gender, religious studies, history of science. Total annual research expenditures: $42,979. *Unit head:* Dr. Gary Ebersole, Chair, 816-235-1631, Fax: 816-235-5723, E-mail: ebersoleg@umkc.edu. *Application contact:* Dr. Andrew Bergerson, Principal Graduate Advisor, 816-235-1631, Fax: 816-235-5723, E-mail: BergersonA@umkc.edu.

The University of Montana, Graduate School, College of Arts and Sciences, Department of History, Missoula, MT 59812-0002. Offers MA, PhD. *Degree requirements:* For master's, thesis or additional course work/professional paper. *Entrance requirements:* For master's, GRE General Test. Additional exam requirements/recommendations for international students: Required—TOEFL.

University of Nebraska at Kearney, College of Graduate Study, College of Natural and Social Sciences, Department of History, Kearney, NE 68849-0001. Offers history (MA). Part-time and evening/weekend programs available. *Degree requirements:* For master's, thesis optional. *Entrance requirements:* For master's, GRE General Test, writing sample. Additional exam requirements/recommendations for international students: Required—TOEFL (minimum score 550 paper-based; 213 computer-based). Electronic applications accepted. *Faculty research:* Military history, labor history/labor and the law, state formation and nationalism, American intellectual history, Civil War and Reconstruction.

University of Nebraska at Omaha, Graduate Studies and Research, College of Arts and Sciences, Department of History, Omaha, NE 68182. Offers MA. Part-time and evening/weekend programs available. *Degree requirements:* For master's, comprehensive exam, thesis (for some programs). *Entrance requirements:* For master's, minimum GPA of 3.0, 21 hours of course work in history, statement of purpose, 2 letters of recommendation. Additional exam requirements/recommendations for international students: Required—TOEFL (minimum score 500 paper-based; 173 computer-based; 61 iBT). Electronic applications accepted.

University of Nebraska–Lincoln, Graduate College, College of Arts and Sciences, Department of History, Lincoln, NE 68588. Offers MA, PhD. *Faculty:* 27 full-time (11 women). *Students:* 24 full-time (9 women), 22 part-time (8 women); includes 1 minority (African American), 1 international. Average age 35. In 2008, 8 master's, 3 doctorates awarded. *Degree requirements:* For master's, thesis optional; for doctorate, one foreign language, comprehensive exam, thesis/dissertation. *Entrance requirements:* For master's and doctorate, GRE General Test, GRE Subject Test, writing sample. Additional exam requirements/recommendations for international students: Required—TOEFL (minimum score 575 paper-based; 233 computer-based). *Application deadline:* For fall admission, 1/15 priority date for domestic and international students. Applications are processed on a rolling basis. Application fee: $40. Electronic applications accepted. *Expenses:* Tuition, state resident: full-time $4275; part-time $237.50 per credit hour. Tuition, nonresident: full-time $11,525; part-time $640.25 per credit hour. Required fees: $1068; $10.35 per credit hour. $440.70 per semester. Tuition and fees vary according to course load and program. *Financial support:* Fellowships, research assistantships, teaching assistantships, Federal Work-Study, health care benefits, and unspecified assistantships available. Support available to part-time students. Financial award application deadline: 1/15. *Faculty research:* Military history, indigenous peoples, German history, American history (American West society and culture). *Unit head:* Dr. Ken Winkle, Chair, 402-472-2414, Fax: 402-472-8839. *Application contact:* Ginny Gross, Director of Graduate Admissions, 402-472-2878, Fax: 402-472-0589, E-mail: grad_admissions@unl.edu.

University of Nevada, Las Vegas, Graduate College, College of Liberal Arts, Department of History, Las Vegas, NV 89154-5020. Offers MA, PhD. Part-time programs available. *Faculty:* 25 full-time (8 women). *Students:* 26 full-time (13 women), 46 part-time (21 women); includes 4 minority (1 African American, 1 Asian American or Pacific Islander, 2 Hispanic Americans), 1 international. Average age 39. 37 applicants, 57% accepted, 12 enrolled. In 2008, 13 master's, 2 doctorates awarded. *Degree requirements:* For master's, one foreign language, comprehensive exam (for some programs), thesis (for some programs); for doctorate, 2 foreign languages, comprehensive exam, thesis/dissertation. *Entrance requirements:* For master's, minimum overall GPA of 3.0, 3.3 in history courses; for doctorate, GRE General Test, minimum overall GPA of 3.0, 3.3 in history courses. Additional exam requirements/recommendations for international students: Required—TOEFL (minimum score 550 paper-based; 213 computer-based; 80 iBT), IELTS (minimum score 7). *Application deadline:* For fall admission, 2/1 priority date for domestic and international students; for spring admission, 11/1 priority date for domestic students, 10/1 for international students. Applications are processed on a rolling basis. Application fee: $60 ($75 for international students). Electronic applications accepted. *Expenses:* Tuition, state resident: full-time $1414; part-time $198 per credit. Tuition, nonresident: full-time $12,509; part-time $415.75 per credit. International tuition: $14,249 full-time. Required fees: $4 per credit. $252 per semester. Tuition and fees vary according to course load. *Financial support:* In 2008–09, 26 students received support, including 1 fellowship (averaging $20,000 per year), 25 teaching assistantships with partial tuition reimbursements available (averaging $14,880 per year); institutionally sponsored loans, scholarships/grants, health care benefits, and unspecified assistantships also available. Financial award application deadline: 3/1. *Faculty research:* American West, public history, cultural history, urban history, gender and sexuality. *Unit head:* Dr. David Wrobel, Chair/Professor, 702-895-0810, Fax: 702-895-1782, E-mail: david.wrobel@unlv.edu. *Application contact:* Graduate College Admissions Evaluator, 702-895-3320, Fax: 702-895-4180, E-mail: gradcollege@unlv.edu.

University of Nevada, Reno, Graduate School, College of Liberal Arts, Department of History, Reno, NV 89557. Offers MA, PhD. *Faculty:* 17 full-time (7 women). *Students:* 9 full-time (3 women), 11 part-time (8 women); includes 4 minority (3 African Americans, 1 Hispanic American), 1 international. Average age 37. 11 applicants, 55% accepted, 3 enrolled. In 2008, 4 master's, 13 doctorates awarded. Terminal master's awarded for partial completion of doctoral program. *Degree requirements:* For master's, thesis optional; for doctorate, one foreign language, thesis/dissertation. *Entrance requirements:* For master's, GRE General Test, minimum GPA of 2.75; for doctorate, GRE General Test, minimum GPA of 3.0. Additional exam requirements/recommendations for international students: Required—TOEFL (minimum score 500 paper-based; 173 computer-based; 61 iBT), IELTS (minimum score 6), TOFEL or IELTS. *Application deadline:* For fall admission, 3/1 priority date for domestic and international students; for spring admission, 10/15 for domestic students, 10/15 priority date for international students. Applications are processed on a rolling basis. Application fee: $60 ($95 for international students). Electronic applications accepted. *Expenses:* Tuition, state resident: full-time $1710; part-time $1140 per semester. Tuition, nonresident: full-time $7115. Required fees: $158 per semester. *Financial support:* In 2008–09, research assistantships with partial tuition reimbursements (averaging $14,000 per year), 12 teaching assistantships with partial tuition reimbursements (averaging $14,000 per year) were awarded; Federal Work-Study, institutionally sponsored loans, scholarships/grants, health care benefits, and unspecified assistantships also available. Financial award application deadline: 3/1; financial award applicants required to submit FAFSA. *Faculty research:* History of medicine, science, environmental history, western America, social/cultural history. *Unit head:* Dr. Barbara Walker, Graduate Program Director, 775-784-6855, E-mail: bbwalker@unr.edu. *Application contact:* Michele Sandberg, Application Contact, 775-784-7026, Fax: 775-784-6064, E-mail: gradschool@unr.edu.

University of New Brunswick Fredericton, School of Graduate Studies, Faculty of Arts, Department of History, Fredericton, NB E3B 5A3, Canada. Offers MA, PhD. Part-time programs available. *Faculty:* 13 full-time (4 women), 6 part-time/adjunct (3 women). *Students:* 51 full-time (19 women), 10 part-time (5 women). In 2008, 16 master's, 3 doctorates awarded. *Degree requirements:* For master's, thesis; for doctorate, thesis/dissertation. *Entrance requirements:* For master's, minimum GPA of 3.0, resumé, writing sample and/or statement of research interests; for doctorate, minimum GPA of 3.0, statement of research interests, writing sample. Additional exam requirements/recommendations for international students: Required—TOEFL, TWE. *Application deadline:* For fall admission, 3/1 priority date for domestic students. Applications are processed on a rolling basis. Application fee: $50 Canadian dollars. Tuition and fees charges are reported in Canadian dollars. *Expenses:* Tuition, area resident: Full-time $5562 Canadian dollars. Tuition, nonresident: full-time $9450 Canadian dollars. Required fees: $333 Canadian dollars. *Financial support:* In 2008–09, 13 research assistantships, 2 teaching assistantships were awarded; fellowships, scholarships/grants also available. *Faculty research:* Canadian history, colonial North America, military/international, women's/gender history. *Unit head:* Dr. Steve Turner, Director of Graduate Studies (Acting), 506-458-7433, Fax: 506-453-5068, E-mail: turner@unb.ca. *Application contact:* Elizabeth Adshade, Graduate Secretary, 506-458-7471, Fax: 506-453-5068, E-mail: eliz@unb.ca.

University of New Hampshire, Graduate School, College of Liberal Arts, Department of History, Durham, NH 03824. Offers history (MA, PhD); museum studies (MA). Part-time programs available. *Faculty:* 24 full-time (13 women). *Students:* 27 full-time (20 women), 22 part-time (13 women); includes 3 minority (2 American Indian/Alaska Native, 1 Asian American or Pacific Islander), 2 international. Average age 35. 93 applicants, 39% accepted, 9 enrolled. In 2008, 8 master's, 1 doctorate awarded. *Degree requirements:* For master's, thesis or alternative; for doctorate, 2 foreign languages, thesis/dissertation. *Entrance requirements:* For master's and doctorate, GRE General Test. Additional exam requirements/recommendations for international students: Required—TOEFL (minimum score 550 paper-based; 213 computer-based; 80 iBT). *Application deadline:* For fall admission, 2/15 priority date for domestic students, 2/15 for international students. Applications are processed on a rolling basis. Application fee: $60. Electronic applications accepted. *Expenses:* Tuition, area resident: Full-time $9720; part-time $540 per credit hour. Tuition, nonresident: full-time $23,200; part-time $954 per credit hour. Required fees: $1446; $361.50 per term. *Financial support:* In 2008–09, 26 students received support, including 4 fellowships, 1 research assistantship, 16 teaching assistantships; career-related internships or fieldwork, Federal Work-Study, scholarships/grants, and tuition waivers (full and partial) also available. Support available to part-time students. Financial

History

University of New Hampshire *(continued)*
award application deadline: 2/15. *Unit head:* Dr. William Harris, Chairperson, 603-862-1764. *Application contact:* Susan Kilday, Administrative Assistant, 603-862-1764, E-mail: history.grad@unh.edu.

University of New Mexico, Graduate School, College of Arts and Sciences, Department of History, Albuquerque, NM 87131-2039. Offers MA, PhD. Part-time programs available. *Degree requirements:* For master's, one foreign language, comprehensive exam, thesis optional; for doctorate, one foreign language, comprehensive exam, thesis/dissertation. *Entrance requirements:* For master's, GRE, BA in history or equivalent; for doctorate, GRE, MA in history or equivalent. Additional exam requirements/recommendations for international students: Required—TOEFL. Electronic applications accepted. *Faculty research:* Western U.S. history, Latin American history, European and American history, Asian history, comparative gender and women's history.

University of New Orleans, Graduate School, College of Liberal Arts, Department of History, New Orleans, LA 70148. Offers history (MA); history teaching (MAHT). *Degree requirements:* For master's, one foreign language, thesis (for some programs). *Entrance requirements:* For master's, GRE General Test. Additional exam requirements/recommendations for international students: Required—TOEFL (minimum score 550 paper-based; 213 computer-based; 79 iBT). Electronic applications accepted. *Faculty research:* Recent U.S. political, military, urban, regional, and legal history.

University of North Alabama, College of Arts and Sciences, Department of History and Political Science, Florence, AL 35632-0001. Offers MA. *Faculty:* 7 part-time/adjunct (6 women). *Students:* 4 full-time (3 women), 18 part-time (6 women). In 2008, 2 master's awarded. *Expenses:* Tuition, area resident: Full-time $4704; part-time $196 per credit hour. Tuition, state resident: full-time $4704; part-time $196 per credit hour. Tuition, nonresident: full-time $9408; part-time $392 per credit hour. Required fees: $882. Tuition and fees vary according to course load and program. *Unit head:* Dr. Christopher Maynard, Chair, 256-765-4306, E-mail: camaynard@una.edu. *Application contact:* Kim Mauldin, Director of Admissions, 256-765-4608, Fax: 256-765-4960, E-mail: komauldin@una.edu.

The University of North Carolina at Chapel Hill, Graduate School, College of Arts and Sciences, Department of History, Chapel Hill, NC 27599. Offers MA, PhD. Terminal master's awarded for partial completion of doctoral program. *Degree requirements:* For master's, one foreign language, thesis, oral thesis defense; for doctorate, 2 foreign languages, comprehensive exam, thesis/dissertation, oral dissertation defense. *Entrance requirements:* For master's and doctorate, GRE General Test, minimum GPA of 3.0. Electronic applications accepted.

The University of North Carolina at Charlotte, Graduate School, College of Arts and Sciences, Department of History, Charlotte, NC 28223-0001. Offers MA. Part-time and evening/weekend programs available. *Faculty:* 26 full-time (9 women). *Students:* 12 full-time (6 women), 31 part-time (14 women); includes 3 minority (2 African Americans, 1 American Indian/Alaska Native), 1 international. Average age 29. 26 applicants, 81% accepted, 10 enrolled. In 2008, 3 master's awarded. *Degree requirements:* For master's, thesis or comprehensive exam. *Entrance requirements:* For master's, GRE General Test, minimum GPA of 3.0 in undergraduate major, 2.75 overall. Additional exam requirements/recommendations for international students: Required—TOEFL (minimum score 557 paper-based; 220 computer-based). *Application deadline:* For fall admission, 7/1 for domestic students, 5/1 for international students; for spring admission, 11/1 for domestic students, 10/1 for international students. Applications are processed on a rolling basis. Application fee: $55. Electronic applications accepted. *Expenses:* Tuition, area resident: Full-time $2919; part-time $122 per credit hour. Tuition, state resident: full-time $2919; part-time $122 per credit hour. Tuition, nonresident: full-time $13,126; part-time $547 per credit hour. Required fees: $1779; $91 per credit hour. Tuition and fees vary according to program. *Financial support:* In 2008–09, 1 research assistantship (averaging $7,000 per year), 19 teaching assistantships (averaging $8,961 per year) were awarded; career-related internships or fieldwork, Federal Work-Study, institutionally sponsored loans, scholarships/grants, unspecified assistantships, and 4 administrative assistantships ($9,813 average) also available. Support available to part-time students. Financial award application deadline: 4/1; financial award applicants required to submit FAFSA. *Faculty research:* Southern (United States) history, Latin American history, race and gender history, urban history, history of science, medicine, technology. Total annual research expenditures: $175,000. *Unit head:* Dr. John Smail, Chair, 704-687-4633, Fax: 704-687-3218, E-mail: jsmail@email.uncc.edu. *Application contact:* Kathy B. Giddings, Director of Graduate Admissions, 704-687-3366, Fax: 704-687-3279, E-mail: agidding@uncc.edu.

The University of North Carolina at Greensboro, Graduate School, College of Arts and Sciences, Department of History, Greensboro, NC 27412-5001. Offers historic preservation (Certificate); history (MA); museum studies (Certificate); U.S. history (PhD). Part-time programs available. *Entrance requirements:* For master's, GRE General Test. Additional exam requirements/recommendations for international students: Required—TOEFL. Electronic applications accepted. *Faculty research:* Simultaneous discovery in science, progressive social reform, Robert Mayer.

The University of North Carolina Wilmington, College of Arts and Sciences, Department of History, Wilmington, NC 28403-3297. Offers MA. Part-time programs available. *Students:* 16 full-time (12 women), 26 part-time (10 women); includes 1 minority (African American). Average age 28. 23 applicants, 65% accepted, 10 enrolled. In 2008, 8 master's awarded. *Degree requirements:* For master's, comprehensive exam, thesis. *Entrance requirements:* For master's, GRE General Test, minimum B average in undergraduate major. Additional exam requirements/recommendations for international students: Required—TOEFL (minimum score 550 paper-based; 217 computer-based; 79 iBT), IELTS (minimum score 6.5). *Application deadline:* For fall admission, 6/1 for domestic students. Applications are processed on a rolling basis. Application fee: $60. *Expenses:* Tuition, area resident: Full-time $4838. Tuition, state resident: full-time $4838. Tuition, nonresident: full-time $14,898. Required fees: $969.38 per semester. Tuition and fees vary according to course load, campus/location and program. *Financial support:* In 2008–09, 14 teaching assistantships with full and partial tuition reimbursements (averaging $9,500 per year) were awarded; career-related internships or fieldwork and Federal Work-Study also available. Support available to part-time students. Financial award application deadline: 3/15. *Unit head:* Dr. Susan P. McCaffray, Chair, 910-962-3308, Fax: 910-962-7011, E-mail: mccaffrays@uncw.edu. *Application contact:* Dr. David La Vere, Graduate Coordinator, 910-962-3315, E-mail: lavered@uncw.edu.

University of North Dakota, Graduate School, College of Arts and Sciences, Department of History, Grand Forks, ND 58202. Offers MA, DA, PhD. *Degree requirements:* For master's, thesis, final exam; for doctorate, comprehensive exam, thesis/dissertation, final exam. *Entrance requirements:* For master's, minimum GPA of 3.0; for doctorate, minimum GPA of 3.5. Additional exam requirements/recommendations for international students: Required—TOEFL (minimum score 550 paper-based; 213 computer-based; 79 iBT), IELTS (minimum score 6.5). Electronic applications accepted. *Faculty research:* U.S. history, Latin America, Russia, modern Europe, women studies.

University of Northern British Columbia, Office of Graduate Studies, Prince George, BC V2N 4Z9, Canada. Offers business administration (Diploma); community health science (M Sc); disability management (MA); education (M Ed); first nations studies (MA); gender studies (MA); history (MA); interdisciplinary studies (MA); international studies (MA); mathematical, computer and physical sciences (M Sc); natural resources and environmental studies (M Sc, MA, MNRES, PhD); political science (MA); psychology (M Sc, PhD); social work (MSW). Part-time and evening/weekend programs available. Postbaccalaureate distance learning degree programs offered (no on-campus study). *Degree requirements:* For master's, thesis; for doctorate,

thesis/dissertation. *Entrance requirements:* For master's, GRE, minimum B average in undergraduate course work; for doctorate, candidacy exam, minimum A average in graduate course work.

University of Northern Colorado, Graduate School, College of Humanities and Social Sciences, Program in History, Greeley, CO 80639. Offers MA. Part-time programs available. *Faculty:* 11 full-time (3 women). *Students:* 3 full-time (1 woman), 10 part-time (3 women); includes 1 minority (Hispanic American). Average age 39. 9 applicants, 78% accepted, 5 enrolled. In 2008, 2 master's awarded. *Degree requirements:* For master's, comprehensive exam, thesis or alternative. *Entrance requirements:* For master's, GRE, 3 letters of recommendation. *Application deadline:* Applications are processed on a rolling basis. Application fee: $50 ($60 for international students). Electronic applications accepted. *Expenses:* Tuition, state resident: full-time $4370; part-time $242.75 per credit hour. Tuition, nonresident: full-time $12,366; part-time $687 per credit hour. Required fees: $664.20; $36.90 per credit hour. *Financial support:* In 2008–09, 2 teaching assistantships (averaging $8,547 per year) were awarded. Financial award application deadline: 3/1; financial award applicants required to submit FAFSA. *Unit head:* Dr. Michael Welsh, Program Coordinator, 970-351-2905, Fax: 970-351-2199. *Application contact:* Linda Sisson, Graduate Student Admission Coordinator, 970-351-1807, Fax: 970-351-2371, E-mail: linda.sisson@unco.edu.

University of Northern Colorado, Graduate School, College of Humanities and Social Sciences, School of History, Philosophy and Political Science, Greeley, CO 80639. Offers history (MA). Part-time programs available. *Faculty:* 11 full-time (3 women). *Students:* 3 full-time (1 woman), 10 part-time (3 women); includes 1 minority (Hispanic American). Average age 39. 9 applicants, 78% accepted, 5 enrolled. In 2008, 2 master's awarded. *Degree requirements:* For master's, comprehensive exam, thesis or alternative. *Entrance requirements:* For master's, GRE, 3 letters of reference. *Application deadline:* Applications are processed on a rolling basis. Application fee: $50 ($60 for international students). Electronic applications accepted. *Expenses:* Tuition, state resident: full-time $4370; part-time $242.75 per credit hour. Tuition, nonresident: full-time $12,366; part-time $687 per credit hour. Required fees: $664.20; $36.90 per credit hour. *Financial support:* In 2008–09, 2 teaching assistantships (averaging $8,547 per year) were awarded; fellowships, research assistantships, unspecified assistantships also available. Financial award application deadline: 3/1; financial award applicants required to submit FAFSA. *Unit head:* Dr. Barry Rothaus, Director, 970-351-2905, Fax: 970-351-2199. *Application contact:* Linda Sisson, Graduate Student Admission Coordinator, 970-351-1807, Fax: 970-351-2371, E-mail: linda.sisson@unco.edu.

University of Northern Iowa, Graduate College, College of Social and Behavioral Sciences, Department of History, Cedar Falls, IA 50614. Offers MA. Part-time programs available. *Students:* 15 full-time (7 women), 7 part-time (4 women); includes 1 minority (Asian American or Pacific Islander). 21 applicants, 71% accepted, 10 enrolled. In 2008, 6 master's awarded. *Degree requirements:* For master's, comprehensive exam (for some programs), thesis or alternative. *Entrance requirements:* For master's, minimum GPA of 3.2. Additional exam requirements/recommendations for international students: Required—TOEFL (minimum score 500 paper-based; 180 computer-based; 61 iBT). *Application deadline:* For fall admission, 8/1 priority date for domestic students. Applications are processed on a rolling basis. Application fee: $30 ($50 for international students). Electronic applications accepted. *Expenses:* Tuition, state resident: full-time $6446. Tuition, nonresident: full-time $14,874. Required fees: $852. *Financial support:* Career-related internships or fieldwork, Federal Work-Study, scholarships/grants, and tuition waivers (full and partial) available. Support available to part-time students. Financial award application deadline: 2/1. *Unit head:* Dr. Robert Martin, Head, 319-273-2097, Fax: 319-273-5846, E-mail: robert.martin@uni.edu. *Application contact:* Laurie S. Russell, Record Analyst, 319-273-2623, Fax: 319-273-6792, E-mail: laurie.russell@uni.edu.

University of North Florida, College of Arts and Sciences, Department of History, Jacksonville, FL 32224-2645. Offers European history (MA); US history (MA). Part-time programs available. *Faculty:* 15 full-time (5 women). *Students:* 15 full-time (8 women), 23 part-time (14 women). Average age 31. 25 applicants, 68% accepted, 15 enrolled. In 2008, 9 master's awarded. *Degree requirements:* For master's, comprehensive exam (for some programs), thesis optional. *Entrance requirements:* For master's, GRE General Test, 3 letters of recommendation, minimum GPA of 3.0 in last 60 hours of course work. Additional exam requirements/recommendations for international students: Required—TOEFL (minimum score 500 paper-based; 173 computer-based). *Application deadline:* For fall admission, 7/1 priority date for domestic students, 5/1 for international students; for spring admission, 11/1 priority date for domestic students, 10/1 for international students. Applications are processed on a rolling basis. Application fee: $30. Electronic applications accepted. *Expenses:* Tuition, area resident: Full-time $5782.08; part-time $240.92 per credit hour. Tuition, state resident: full-time $5782.08; part-time $240.92 per credit hour. Tuition, nonresident: full-time $19,974; part-time $832.26 per credit hour. Required fees: $952.80; $39.70 per credit hour. *Financial support:* In 2008–09, 6 students received support, including 10 teaching assistantships (averaging $5,127 per year); career-related internships or fieldwork, Federal Work-Study, and tuition waivers (partial) also available. Support available to part-time students. Financial award application deadline: 4/1; financial award applicants required to submit FAFSA. *Unit head:* Dr. Dale Clifford, 904-620-2886, Fax: 904-620-1018, E-mail: clifford@unf.edu. *Application contact:* Dr. Phil Kaplan, Graduate Coordinator, 904-620-1863, Fax: 904-620-1018, E-mail: pkaplan@unf.edu.

University of North Texas, Robert B. Toulouse School of Graduate Studies, College of Arts and Sciences, Department of History, Denton, TX 76203. Offers MA, MS, PhD. Part-time programs available. Terminal master's awarded for partial completion of doctoral program. *Degree requirements:* For master's, one foreign language, comprehensive exam, thesis or alternative; for doctorate, 2 foreign languages, comprehensive exam, thesis/dissertation. *Entrance requirements:* For master's and doctorate, GRE General Test. Additional exam requirements/recommendations for international students: Required—proof of English language proficiency required for non-native English speakers; Recommended—TOEFL (minimum score 550 paper-based; 213 computer based). *Faculty research:* U.S. local, Texas, women and European history.

University of Notre Dame, Graduate School, College of Arts and Letters, Division of Humanities, Department of History, Notre Dame, IN 46556. Offers MA, PhD. *Faculty:* 31 full-time (9 women). *Students:* 70 full-time (29 women); includes 6 minority (1 African American, 3 Asian Americans or Pacific Islanders, 2 Hispanic Americans), 7 international. 189 applicants, 11% accepted, 14 enrolled. In 2008, 6 master's, 5 doctorates awarded. *Degree requirements:* For doctorate, one foreign language, thesis/dissertation, candidacy exam. *Entrance requirements:* For doctorate, GRE General Test. Additional exam requirements/recommendations for international students: Required—TOEFL (minimum score 600 paper-based; 250 computer-based; 80 iBT). *Application deadline:* For fall admission, 1/4 priority date for domestic students, 1/4 for international students. Application fee: $50. Electronic applications accepted. *Financial support:* Fellowships with full tuition reimbursements, research assistantships with full tuition reimbursements, teaching assistantships with full tuition reimbursements, tuition waivers (full) available. Financial award application deadline: 1/4. *Faculty research:* U.S., modern European and medieval history; history of European and U.S. religions; U.S. and European intellectual and cultural history; history of Central Europe. *Unit head:* Dr. Christopher Hamlin, Director of Graduate Studies, 574-631-4262, E-mail: history.1@nd.edu. *Application contact:* Dr. Barbara Turpin, Director of Graduate Admissions, 574-631-7706, Fax: 574-631-4183.

University of Oklahoma, Graduate College, College of Arts and Sciences, Department of History, Norman, OK 73019. Offers MA, PhD. Part-time and evening/weekend programs available. *Faculty:* 37 full-time (10 women). *Students:* 38 full-time (20 women), 22 part-time (10 women); includes 12 minority (6 American Indian/Alaska Native, 3 Asian Americans or Pacific Islanders, 3 Hispanic Americans). 17 applicants, 53% accepted, 8 enrolled. In 2008, 5 master's, 1 doctorate awarded. Terminal master's awarded for partial completion of doctoral program. *Degree requirements:* For master's, one foreign language, thesis or alternative, oral and written exams; for doctorate, 2 foreign languages, thesis/dissertation, oral and written exams.

Entrance requirements: For master's, GRE General Test, BA with 20 hours in history; for doctorate, GRE General Test. Additional exam requirements/recommendations for international students: Required—TOEFL (minimum score 550 paper-based; 213 computer-based). *Application deadline:* For fall admission, 4/1 for domestic and international students; for spring admission, 11/1 for domestic students, 9/1 for international students. Applications are processed on a rolling basis. Application fee: $40 ($90 for international students). Electronic applications accepted. *Expenses:* Tuition, state resident: full-time $3744; part-time $156 per credit hour. Tuition, nonresident: full-time $13,577; part-time $565.70 per credit hour. Required fees: $2415.40; $90.10 per credit hour. *Financial support:* In 2008–09, 27 students received support, including 9 fellowships with full tuition reimbursements available (averaging $4,421 per year), 4 research assistantships with partial tuition reimbursements available (averaging $16,978 per year), 28 teaching assistantships with partial tuition reimbursements available (averaging $14,023 per year); health care benefits and unspecified assistantships also available. Financial award application deadline: 1/31. *Faculty research:* Environmental, Western, Latin American and Native American history. Total annual research expenditures: $112,175. *Unit head:* Dr. Robert L. Griswold, Chair, 405-325-6002, Fax: 405-325-4503, E-mail: rgriswold@ou.edu. *Application contact:* Dr. Terry Rugeley, Professor, 405-625-6002, Fax: 405-325-4503, E-mail: trugeley@ou.edu.

University of Oregon, Graduate School, College of Arts and Sciences, Department of History, Eugene, OR 97403. Offers MA, PhD. *Degree requirements:* For master's, one foreign language, thesis or alternative, written exam; for doctorate, 2 foreign languages, thesis/dissertation, oral and written exams. *Entrance requirements:* For master's and doctorate, GRE General Test, minimum GPA of 3.0. Additional exam requirements/recommendations for international students: Required—TOEFL. *Faculty research:* U.S., European, East and Southeast Asian, Latin American, and ancient history.

University of Ottawa, Faculty of Graduate and Postdoctoral Studies, Faculty of Arts, Department of History, Ottawa, ON K1N 6N5, Canada. Offers MA, PhD. *Degree requirements:* For master's, 2 foreign languages, thesis or alternative; for doctorate, 2 foreign languages, thesis/dissertation, oral exam. *Entrance requirements:* For master's, honors degree or equivalent, minimum B average; for doctorate, master's degree, minimum B+ average. Electronic applications accepted. *Faculty research:* Canadian history.

University of Pennsylvania, School of Arts and Sciences, Graduate Group in Ancient History, Philadelphia, PA 19104. Offers AM, PhD. *Degree requirements:* For doctorate, 4 foreign languages, thesis/dissertation. Electronic applications accepted.

University of Pennsylvania, School of Arts and Sciences, Graduate Group in History, Philadelphia, PA 19104. Offers AM, PhD. Terminal master's awarded for partial completion of doctoral program. *Degree requirements:* For master's, thesis; for doctorate, one foreign language, thesis/dissertation. *Entrance requirements:* For master's and doctorate, GRE General Test. Additional exam requirements/recommendations for international students: Required—TOEFL. Electronic applications accepted.

University of Pittsburgh, School of Arts and Sciences, Department of History, Pittsburgh, PA 15260. Offers MA, PhD. Part-time programs available. Terminal master's awarded for partial completion of doctoral program. *Degree requirements:* For master's, one foreign language, oral exam, 1 seminar paper; for doctorate, 2 foreign languages, comprehensive exam, thesis/dissertation. *Entrance requirements:* For master's and doctorate, GRE General Test. Additional exam requirements/recommendations for international students: Required—TOEFL. Electronic applications accepted. *Faculty research:* Western Europe, Latin America, Russia, Eastern Europe, U.S., East Asia.

University of Puerto Rico, Río Piedras, College of Humanities, Department of History, San Juan, PR 00931-3300. Offers MA, PhD. Part-time programs available. *Degree requirements:* For master's, one foreign language, comprehensive exam, thesis; for doctorate, one foreign language, comprehensive exam, thesis/dissertation. *Entrance requirements:* For master's, PAEG or GRE, interview, minimum GPA of 3.0, 2 letters of recommendation; for doctorate, PAEG or GRE, interview, master's degree, minimum GPA of 3.0, 2 letters of recommendation.

University of Regina, Faculty of Graduate Studies and Research, Faculty of Arts, Department of History, Regina, SK S4S 0A2, Canada. Offers MA, PhD. *Faculty:* 13 full-time (2 women). *Students:* 9 full-time (3 women), 6 part-time (3 women). 5 applicants, 80% accepted, 1 enrolled. *Degree requirements:* For master's, thesis. *Entrance requirements:* Additional exam requirements/recommendations for international students: Required—TOEFL (minimum score 580 paper-based; 237 computer-based; 88 iBT). *Application deadline:* Applications are processed on a rolling basis. Application fee: $85 ($100 for international students). Electronic applications accepted. *Financial support:* In 2008–09, 1 fellowship (averaging $15,000 per year), 1 research assistantship (averaging $13,500 per year), 2 teaching assistantships (averaging $6,558 per year) were awarded; scholarships/grants also available. Financial award application deadline: 6/15. *Faculty research:* Canadian, English, United States, European, Asian, British, and Latin-American history. *Unit head:* Dr. Thomas Bredohl, Head, 306-585-4155, Fax: 306-585-4827, E-mail: thomas.bredohl@uregina.ca. *Application contact:* Dr. William Brennan, Graduate Program Coordinator, 306-585-4214, E-mail: william.brennan@uregina.ca.

University of Rhode Island, Graduate School, College of Arts and Sciences, Department of History, Kingston, RI 02881. Offers MA. *Degree requirements:* For master's, thesis optional. *Application deadline:* Applications are processed on a rolling basis. Application fee: $35. *Expenses:* Tuition, state resident: full-time $8024; part-time $446 per credit. Tuition, nonresident: full-time $21,046; part-time $1169 per credit. Required fees: $1056; $26 per credit. $30 per semester. One-time fee: $95 part-time. *Financial support:* Application deadline: 2/1. *Unit head:* Dr. Marie Jenkins Schwartz, Chair, 401-874-4900, E-mail: schwartz@uri.edu. *Application contact:* Harold D. Bibb, Associate Dean of the Graduate School, 401-874-2262, Fax: 401-874-5491.

University of Rochester, The College, Arts and Sciences, Department of History, Rochester, NY 14627-0250. Offers MA, PhD. Terminal master's awarded for partial completion of doctoral program. *Degree requirements:* For master's, one foreign language, thesis or alternative; for doctorate, 2 foreign languages, thesis/dissertation, comprehensive oral exam, qualifying exam. *Entrance requirements:* For master's and doctorate, GRE General Test, sample of written work. Additional exam requirements/recommendations for international students: Required—TOEFL.

University of San Diego, College of Arts and Sciences, Department of History, San Diego, CA 92110-2492. Offers MA. Part-time and evening/weekend programs available. *Faculty:* 3 full-time (2 women). *Students:* 7 full-time (2 women), 18 part-time (7 women); includes 6 minority (1 African American, 5 Hispanic Americans), 1 international. Average age 33. 28 applicants, 82% accepted, 10 enrolled. In 2008, 4 master's awarded. *Degree requirements:* For master's, thesis. *Entrance requirements:* For master's, GRE General Test, minimum GPA of 3.0. Additional exam requirements/recommendations for international students: Required—TOEFL (minimum score 580 paper-based; 237 computer-based; 83 iBT), TWE. *Application deadline:* For fall admission, 8/31 for domestic and international students; for spring admission, 11/15 for domestic and international students. Applications are processed on a rolling basis. Application fee: $45. Electronic applications accepted. *Expenses:* Tuition: Full-time $19,710; part-time $1129 per unit. Required fees: $154. Full-time tuition and fees vary according to course load and degree level. *Financial support:* In 2008–09, 15 students received support. Career-related internships or fieldwork, Federal Work-Study, institutionally sponsored loans, and unspecified assistantships available. Support available to part-time students. Financial award application deadline: 4/1; financial award applicants required to submit FAFSA. *Faculty research:* History of the American West, history of California, history of Mexico and Latin America, public history, environmental history. *Unit head:* Dr. Michael Gonzalez, Graduate Program Director, 619-260-4756, Fax: 619-260-2272, E-mail: michaelg@sandiego.edu. *Application contact:* Dr. John Mosby, Associate Director of Graduate Admissions, 619-260-4524, Fax: 619-260-4158, E-mail: grads@sandiego.edu.

University of Saskatchewan, College of Graduate Studies and Research, College of Arts and Sciences, Department of History, Saskatoon, SK S7N 5A2, Canada. Offers MA, PhD. Part-time programs available. *Degree requirements:* For master's, thesis; for doctorate, thesis/dissertation. *Entrance requirements:* Additional exam requirements/recommendations for international students: Required—TOEFL.

The University of Scranton, College of Graduate and Continuing Education, Department of History, Scranton, PA 18510. Offers MA. Part-time and evening/weekend programs available. *Faculty:* 11 full-time (2 women). *Students:* 4 full-time (2 women), 15 part-time (6 women). Average age 26. 14 applicants, 79% accepted. In 2008, 9 master's awarded. *Degree requirements:* For master's, comprehensive exam, thesis (for some programs), capstone experience. *Entrance requirements:* For master's, minimum GPA of 2.75. Additional exam requirements/recommendations for international students: Required—TOEFL (minimum score 500 paper-based; 173 computer-based), IELTS (minimum score 5.5). *Application deadline:* Applications are processed on a rolling basis. Application fee: $50. *Financial support:* In 2008–09, 2 students received support, including 2 teaching assistantships with full tuition reimbursements available (averaging $6,600 per year); fellowships, career-related internships or fieldwork, Federal Work-Study, and unspecified assistantships also available. Support available to part-time students. Financial award application deadline: 3/1. *Faculty research:* American, European, Latin American, Russian, and Chinese history. *Unit head:* Dr. Robert W. Shaffern, Director, 570-941-4360, Fax: 570-941-7625. *Application contact:* Joseph M. Roback, Director of Admissions, 570-941-4385, Fax: 570-941-5928, E-mail: roback j2@scranton.edu.

University of South Africa, College of Human Sciences, Pretoria, South Africa. Offers adult education (M Ed); African languages (MA, PhD); African politics (MA, PhD); Afrikaans (MA, PhD); ancient history (MA, PhD); ancient Near Eastern studies (MA, PhD); anthropology (MA, PhD); applied linguistics (MA); Arabic (MA, PhD); archaeology (MA); art history (MA); Biblical archaeology (MA); Biblical studies (M Th, D Th, PhD); Christian spirituality (M Th, D Th); church history (M Th, D Th); classical studies (MA, PhD); clinical psychology (MA); communication (MA, PhD); comparative education (M Ed, Ed D); consulting psychology (D Admin, D Com, PhD); curriculum studies (M Ed, Ed D); development studies (M Admin, MA, D Admin, PhD); didactics (M Ed, Ed D); education (M Tech); education management (M Ed, Ed D); educational psychology (M Ed); English (MA); environmental education (M Ed); French (MA, PhD); German (MA, PhD); Greek (MA); guidance and counseling (M Ed); health studies (MA, PhD), including health sciences education (MA), health services management (MA), medical and surgical nursing science (critical care general) (MA), midwifery and neonatal nursing science (MA), trauma and emergency care (MA); history (MA, PhD); history of education (Ed D); inclusive education (M Ed, Ed D); information and communications technology policy and regulation (MA); information science (MA, MIS, PhD); international politics (MA, PhD); Islamic studies (MA, PhD); Italian (MA, PhD); Judaica (MA, PhD); linguistics (MA, PhD); mathematical education (M Ed); mathematics education (MA); missiology (M Th, D Th); modern Hebrew (MA, PhD); musicology (MA, MMus, D Mus, PhD); natural science education (M Ed); New Testament (M Th, D Th); Old Testament (D Th); pastoral therapy (M Th, D Th); philosophy (MA); philosophy of education (M Ed, Ed D); politics (MA, PhD); Portuguese (MA, PhD); practical theology (M Th, D Th); psychology (MA, MS, PhD); psychology of education (M Ed, Ed D); public health (MA); religious studies (MA, D Th, PhD); Romance languages (MA); Russian (MA, PhD); Semitic languages (MA, PhD); social behavior studies in HIV/AIDS (MA); social science (mental health) (MA); social science in development studies (MA); social science in psychology (MA); social science in social work (MA); social science in sociology (MA); social work (MSW, DSW, PhD); socio-education (M Ed, Ed D); sociolinguistics (MA); sociology (MA, PhD); Spanish (MA, PhD); systematic theology (M Th, D Th); TESOL (teaching English to speakers of other languages) (MA); theological ethics (M Th, D Th); theory of literature (MA, PhD); urban ministries (D Th); urban ministry (M Th).

University of South Alabama, Graduate School, College of Arts and Sciences, Department of History, Mobile, AL 36688-0002. Offers MA. Part-time and evening/weekend programs available. *Faculty:* 13 full-time (5 women). *Students:* 12 full-time (2 women), 10 part-time (4 women); includes 1 minority (African American). 11 applicants, 91% accepted, 8 enrolled. In 2008, 2 master's awarded. *Degree requirements:* For master's, one foreign language, comprehensive exam, thesis optional. *Entrance requirements:* For master's, GRE General Test, GRE Subject Test, 21 hours of course work in history, minimum GPA of 3.0. *Application deadline:* For fall admission, 7/15 priority date for domestic students, 6/15 priority date for international students; for spring admission, 12/1 priority date for domestic students, 11/1 priority date for international students. Applications are processed on a rolling basis. Application fee: $35. *Expenses:* Tuition, area resident: Full-time $4656. Tuition, nonresident: full-time $9312. Required fees: $1102. *Financial support:* Fellowships, research assistantships available. Support available to part-time students. Financial award application deadline: 4/1. *Unit head:* Dr. Clarence Mohr, Chair, 251-460-6210. *Application contact:* Dr. Donald DeVore, PhD, Graduate Coordinator, 251-460-6210.

University of South Carolina, The Graduate School, College of Arts and Sciences, Department of History, Columbia, SC 29208. Offers history (MA, PhD); public history (MA, Certificate), including archives (MA), historic preservation (MA), museum (MA), museum management (Certificate); MLIS/MA. IMA and MAT offered in cooperation with the College of Education. Part-time programs available. Terminal master's awarded for partial completion of doctoral program. *Degree requirements:* For master's, one foreign language, thesis; for doctorate, one foreign language, thesis/dissertation. *Entrance requirements:* For master's and doctorate, GRE General Test. Additional exam requirements/recommendations for international students: Required—TOEFL. Electronic applications accepted. *Faculty research:* U.S. history; European history; Latin American history; history of science and technology.

The University of South Dakota, Graduate School, College of Arts and Sciences, Department of History, Vermillion, SD 57069-2390. Offers MA, JD/MA. Part-time programs available. *Degree requirements:* For master's, thesis (for some programs). *Entrance requirements:* For master's, GRE General Test, minimum GPA of 2.7. Additional exam requirements/recommendations for international students: Required—TOEFL (minimum score 550 paper-based; 213 computer-based; 79 iBT). Electronic applications accepted.

University of Southern California, Graduate School, College of Letters, Arts and Sciences, Department of History, Los Angeles, CA 90089. Offers PhD. Terminal master's awarded for partial completion of doctoral program. *Degree requirements:* For doctorate, 2 foreign languages, thesis/dissertation. *Entrance requirements:* For doctorate, GRE General Test. *Faculty research:* U.S., Latin America, Europe, Middle East, Central and East Asia.

University of Southern Mississippi, Graduate School, College of Arts and Letters, Department of History, Hattiesburg, MS 39406-0001. Offers MA, MS, PhD. Part-time programs available. *Faculty:* 16 full-time (6 women). *Students:* 28 full-time (4 women), 19 part-time (8 women); includes 2 minority (1 African American, 1 Hispanic American), 2 international. Average age 34. 33 applicants, 52% accepted, 10 enrolled. In 2008, 10 master's, 1 doctorate awarded. *Degree requirements:* For master's, one foreign language, comprehensive exam, thesis (for some programs); for doctorate, 2 foreign languages, comprehensive exam, thesis/dissertation. *Entrance requirements:* For master's, GRE General Test, minimum GPA of 3.0 in field of study, 2.75 in last 2 years; for doctorate, GRE General Test, minimum GPA of 3.5. Additional exam requirements/recommendations for international students: Required—TOEFL. *Application deadline:* For fall admission, 3/1 priority date for domestic students, 3/1 for international students. Applications are processed on a rolling basis. Application fee: $30. *Financial support:* In 2008–09, 1 fellowship with full tuition reimbursement (averaging $12,000 per year), 1 research assistantship with full tuition reimbursement (averaging $12,000 per year), 20 teaching assistantships with full tuition reimbursements (averaging $9,000 per year) were awarded; Federal Work-Study, scholarships/grants, and unspecified assistantships also available. Financial award application deadline: 3/15; financial award applicants required to submit FAFSA. *Faculty research:* Civil War, civil rights, modern European history, war history. *Unit head:* Dr. Phyllis

History

University of Southern Mississippi (continued)

Jestice, Chair, 601-266-4333, Fax: 601-266-4334. *Application contact:* Dr. Michael Niebarg, Graduate Coordinator, 601-266-4333, Fax: 601-266-4334.

University of South Florida, Graduate School, College of Arts and Sciences, Department of History, Tampa, FL 33620-9951. Offers MA, PhD. Part-time and evening/weekend programs available. *Faculty:* 17 full-time (8 women). *Students:* 17 full-time (9 women), 33 part-time (11 women); includes 5 minority (2 African Americans, 3 Hispanic Americans). 36 applicants, 36% accepted, 10 enrolled. In 2008, 21 master's awarded. *Degree requirements:* For master's, comprehensive exam, thesis optional; for doctorate, comprehensive exam, thesis/dissertation. *Entrance requirements:* For master's, GRE General Test, minimum GPA of 3.0 in last 60 hours, 2 letters of recommendation. Additional exam requirements/recommendations for international students: Required—TOEFL (minimum score 550 paper-based; 213 computer-based). *Application deadline:* For fall admission, 2/15 priority date for domestic students, 1/2 for international students; for spring admission, 10/15 priority date for domestic students, 6/1 for international students. Applications are processed on a rolling basis. Application fee: $30. Electronic applications accepted. *Expenses:* Tuition, state resident: full-time $2624.40; part-time $291.60 per credit hour. Tuition, nonresident: full-time $7822; part-time $869.13 per credit hour. *Financial support:* Application deadline: 4/1. *Faculty research:* U.S. history, European history, Latin American history, medieval history, ancient history. Total annual research expenditures: $147,649. *Unit head:* Dr. Fraser Ottanelli, Chairperson, 813-974-6209, Fax: 813-974-6228, E-mail: fraser@cas.usf.edu. *Application contact:* Barbara Berglund, Program Director, 813-974-6225, Fax: 813-974-6228, E-mail: berglund@cas.usf.edu.

The University of Tennessee, Graduate School, College of Arts and Sciences, Department of History, Knoxville, TN 37996. Offers American history (PhD); European history (PhD); history (MA). Part-time programs available. *Degree requirements:* For master's, thesis or alternative; for doctorate, one foreign language, thesis/dissertation. *Entrance requirements:* For master's and doctorate, GRE General Test, minimum GPA of 2.7. Additional exam requirements/recommendations for international students: Required—TOEFL. Electronic applications accepted. *Expenses:* Tuition, area resident: Part-time $348 per credit hour. Tuition, state resident: full-time $6262. Tuition, nonresident: full-time $18,920; part-time $1052 per credit hour. Required fees: $812; $36 per credit hour. Tuition and fees vary according to program.

The University of Texas at Arlington, Graduate School, College of Liberal Arts, Department of History, Arlington, TX 76019. Offers history (MA); transatlantic history (PhD). Part-time and evening/weekend programs available. *Faculty:* 16 full-time (4 women), 1 part-time/adjunct (0 women). *Students:* 32 full-time (16 women), 76 part-time (33 women); includes 14 minority (5 African Americans, 1 American Indian/Alaska Native, 2 Asian Americans or Pacific Islanders, 6 Hispanic Americans). 56 applicants, 89% accepted, 34 enrolled. In 2008, 18 master's, 7 doctorates awarded. *Degree requirements:* For master's, one foreign language, comprehensive exam (for some programs), thesis (for some programs); for doctorate, one foreign language; comprehensive exam, thesis/dissertation. *Entrance requirements:* For master's, GRE General Test, minimum GPA of 3.0 in last 60 hours, 3 letters of recommendation; for doctorate, GRE General Test, minimum graduate GPA of 3.5, 3 letters of recommendation, academic writing sample. Additional exam requirements/recommendations for international students: Required—TOEFL (minimum score 550 paper-based; 213 computer-based). *Application deadline:* For fall admission, 6/16 for domestic students. Applications are processed on a rolling basis. Application fee: $35 ($50 for international students). *Expenses:* Tuition, area resident: Full-time $6500. Tuition, state resident: full-time $6500. Tuition, nonresident: full-time $11,558. *Financial support:* In 2008–09, 4 fellowships with full tuition reimbursements (averaging $2,000 per year), 4 research assistantships (averaging $9,467 per year), 22 teaching assistantships (averaging $12,000 per year) were awarded; career-related internships or fieldwork also available. Financial award application deadline: 5/1; financial award applicants required to submit FAFSA. *Unit head:* Dr. Robert Fairbanks, Chair, 817-272-2861, Fax: 817-272-2852, E-mail: history@uta.edu. *Application contact:* Dr. Thomas Adam, Graduate Advisor, 817-272-2861, Fax: 817-272-2852, E-mail: adam@uta.edu.

The University of Texas at Austin, Graduate School, College of Liberal Arts, Department of History, Austin, TX 78712-1111. Offers MA, PhD. *Degree requirements:* For doctorate, thesis/dissertation. *Entrance requirements:* For master's and doctorate, GRE General Test. Electronic applications accepted. *Faculty research:* U.S., Latin American, European, African, Asian, and Middle Eastern history.

The University of Texas at Brownsville, Graduate Studies, College of Liberal Arts, Department of History, Brownsville, TX 78520-4991. Offers MAIS. Part-time and evening/weekend programs available. *Degree requirements:* For master's, comprehensive exam, thesis optional. *Entrance requirements:* For master's, GRE General Test. Additional exam requirements/recommendations for international students: Required—TOEFL.

The University of Texas at El Paso, Graduate School, College of Liberal Arts, Department of History, El Paso, TX 79968-0001. Offers border history (MA); history (MA, PhD). Part-time and evening/weekend programs available. *Degree requirements:* For master's, thesis optional; for doctorate, thesis/dissertation. *Entrance requirements:* For master's and doctorate, GRE General Test, minimum GPA of 3.0 in major. Additional exam requirements/recommendations for international students: Required—TOEFL. Electronic applications accepted.

The University of Texas at San Antonio, College of Liberal and Fine Arts, Department of History, San Antonio, TX 78249-0617. Offers MA. Part-time and evening/weekend programs available. *Degree requirements:* For master's, comprehensive exam, thesis optional. *Entrance requirements:* For master's, GRE, minimum GPA of 3.0 in last 60 hours. Additional exam requirements/recommendations for international students: Required—TOEFL (minimum score 500 paper-based; 173 computer-based). Electronic applications accepted.

The University of Texas at Tyler, College of Arts and Sciences, Department of History, Tyler, TX 75799-0001. Offers history (MA). Part-time and evening/weekend programs available. *Degree requirements:* For master's, one foreign language, comprehensive exam, thesis optional. *Entrance requirements:* For master's, GRE General Test, minimum GPA of 3.0. Additional exam requirements/recommendations for international students: Required—TOEFL (minimum score 79 computer-based). Electronic applications accepted. *Faculty research:* Early and modern U.S. history, early modern and modern European history.

The University of Texas of the Permian Basin, Office of Graduate Studies, College of Arts and Sciences, Department of History, Odessa, TX 79762-0001. Offers MA. Part-time and evening/weekend programs available. *Degree requirements:* For master's, comprehensive exam (for some programs), thesis (for some programs). *Entrance requirements:* For master's, GRE General Test. Additional exam requirements/recommendations for international students: Required—TOEFL (minimum score 550 paper-based; 213 computer-based).

The University of Texas–Pan American, College of Arts and Humanities, Department of History, Edinburg, TX 78541-2999. Offers MA, MAIS. Part-time and evening/weekend programs available. *Degree requirements:* For master's, comprehensive exam, thesis or alternative. *Entrance requirements:* For master's, GRE General Test, minimum GPA of 3.0. *Faculty research:* Texas-Mexican legacy, modern America, Southwest, labor, modern Europe.

The University of Toledo, College of Graduate Studies, College of Arts and Sciences, Department of History, Toledo, OH 43606-3390. Offers MA, PhD. Part-time programs available. *Degree requirements:* For doctorate, one foreign language, thesis/dissertation, oral and written exams. *Entrance requirements:* For master's, GRE General Test, minimum GPA of 2.7; for doctorate, GRE General Test, minimum GPA of 3.0. Electronic applications accepted. *Faculty research:* U.S. diplomatic history, U.S. history, urban history, public history, European history.

University of Toronto, School of Graduate Studies, Humanities Division, Department of History, Toronto, ON M5S 1A1, Canada. Offers MA, PhD. Part-time programs available. *Degree requirements:* For master's, one foreign language, thesis optional, thesis or research essay, French language exam; for doctorate, comprehensive exam, thesis/dissertation, oral examination/thesis defense. *Entrance requirements:* For master's, minimum B+ average or GPA of 3.3, 6 full academic year history courses; for doctorate, MA in history, minimum A– average or GPA of 3.7.

University of Tulsa, Graduate School, College of Arts and Sciences, Department of History, Tulsa, OK 74104-3189. Offers MA, MTA, JD/MA. Part-time programs available. *Faculty:* 9 full-time (2 women), 1 part-time/adjunct (0 women). *Students:* 7 full-time (3 women), 11 part-time (8 women); includes 1 minority (American Indian/Alaska Native). Average age 28. 5 applicants, 80% accepted, 3 enrolled. In 2008, 2 master's awarded. *Degree requirements:* For master's, one foreign language, comprehensive exam or oral defense of thesis. *Entrance requirements:* For master's, GRE General Test, writing sample. Additional exam requirements/recommendations for international students: Required—TOEFL (minimum score 575 paper-based; 231 computer-based; 91 iBT), IELTS (minimum score 6.5). *Application deadline:* Applications are processed on a rolling basis. Application fee: $40. Electronic applications accepted. *Expenses:* Tuition: Full-time $15,408; part-time $899 per credit hour. Required fees: $3.33 per credit hour. One-time fee: $200 full-time. Tuition and fees vary according to course load and program. *Financial support:* In 2008–09, 9 students received support, including 3 fellowships with full and partial tuition reimbursements available (averaging $9,332 per year), 1 research assistantship (averaging $11,594 per year), 5 teaching assistantships with full and partial tuition reimbursements available (averaging $10,435 per year); Federal Work-Study, scholarships/grants, tuition waivers (full and partial), and unspecified assistantships also available. Support available to part-time students. Financial award application deadline: 2/1; financial award applicants required to submit FAFSA. *Faculty research:* American history, ancient, medieval and modern European history, Latin American history, Russian history and Asian history. *Unit head:* Dr. Thomas Buoye, Chairperson, 918-631-2825, Fax: 918-631-2057, E-mail: thomas-buoye@utulsa.edu. *Application contact:* Dr. Christine Ruane, Adviser, 918-631-3814, Fax: 918-631-2057, E-mail: christine-ruane@utulsa.edu.

University of Utah, The Graduate School, College of Humanities, Department of History, Salt Lake City, UT 84112-1107. Offers MA, MS, PhD. Part-time and evening/weekend programs available. Terminal master's awarded for partial completion of doctoral program. *Degree requirements:* For master's, one foreign language, thesis (for some programs); for doctorate, 2 foreign languages, comprehensive exam, thesis/dissertation. *Entrance requirements:* For master's, GRE General Test, minimum GPA of 3.2; for doctorate, GRE General Test, minimum graduate GPA of 3.6. Additional exam requirements/recommendations for international students: Required—TOEFL (minimum score 500 paper-based; 173 computer-based). Electronic applications accepted. *Faculty research:* U.S. history, European history, U.S. African-American studies, Middle East, Latin America.

University of Utah, The Graduate School, College of Humanities, Program in Middle East Studies, Salt Lake City, UT 84112-1107. Offers anthropology (MA); Arabic (MA, PhD); Arabic and linguistics (MA, PhD); Hebrew (MA); history (MA, PhD); Persian (MA, PhD); political science (MA, PhD); Turkish (MA). Terminal master's awarded for partial completion of doctoral program. *Degree requirements:* For master's, 2 foreign languages, comprehensive exam, thesis optional; for doctorate, 3 foreign languages, comprehensive exam, thesis/dissertation. *Entrance requirements:* For master's, GRE General Test, minimum GPA of 3.2; for doctorate, GRE General Test, MA in Middle East studies or equivalent, minimum GPA of 3.2. Additional exam requirements/recommendations for international students: Required—TOEFL (minimum score 580 paper-based; 237 computer-based; 92 iBT). *Faculty research:* Arabic literature and linguistics, Islamic studies, Middle East history, political science, Judaic studies.

University of Vermont, Graduate College, College of Arts and Sciences, Department of History, Burlington, VT 05405. Offers MA. *Students:* 18 (9 women); includes 3 minority (1 African American, 1 Asian American or Pacific Islander, 1 Hispanic American). 25 applicants, 68% accepted, 7 enrolled. In 2008, 15 master's awarded. *Degree requirements:* For master's, thesis. *Entrance requirements:* For master's, GRE General Test, sample project. Additional exam requirements/recommendations for international students: Required—TOEFL (minimum score 550 paper-based; 213 computer-based; 80 iBT). *Application deadline:* For fall admission, 5/1 priority date for domestic students. Applications are processed on a rolling basis. Application fee: $40. Electronic applications accepted. *Expenses:* Tuition, state resident: part-time $488 per credit. Tuition, nonresident: part-time $1232 per credit. *Financial support:* Fellowships, research assistantships, teaching assistantships, career-related internships or fieldwork available. Financial award application deadline: 3/1. *Faculty research:* American, European, and Asian history. *Unit head:* Dr. Steven Zdatny, Chair, 802-656-3180. *Application contact:* Dr. Paul Deslandes, Coordinator, 802-656-3180.

University of Victoria, Faculty of Graduate Studies, Faculty of Humanities, Department of History, Victoria, BC V8W 2Y2, Canada. Offers MA, PhD. Part-time programs available. *Degree requirements:* For master's, one foreign language, thesis; for doctorate, one foreign language, comprehensive exam, thesis/dissertation. *Entrance requirements:* Additional exam requirements/recommendations for international students: Required—TOEFL (minimum score 600 paper-based; 250 computer-based), TWE. Electronic applications accepted. *Faculty research:* Canadian social history, Canadian gender history, Canadian native history, Canadian military history, British Columbian history, Western history, medieval history, world history.

University of Virginia, College and Graduate School of Arts and Sciences, Department of History, Charlottesville, VA 22903. Offers MA, PhD, JD/MA. *Faculty:* 36 full-time (9 women), 3 part-time/adjunct (0 women). *Students:* 111 full-time (39 women); includes 3 minority (2 African Americans, 1 Hispanic American), 13 international. Average age 30. 242 applicants, 23% accepted, 20 enrolled. In 2008, 21 master's, 20 doctorates awarded. *Degree requirements:* For master's, one foreign language, essay; for doctorate, variable foreign language requirement, comprehensive exam, thesis/dissertation. *Entrance requirements:* For master's and doctorate, GRE General Test, 2 or more letters of recommendation. Additional exam requirements/recommendations for international students: Required—TOEFL (minimum score 600 paper-based; 250 computer-based; 90 iBT), IELTS (minimum score 7). *Application deadline:* For fall admission, 12/1 for domestic and international students. Applications are processed on a rolling basis. Application fee: $60. Electronic applications accepted. *Expenses:* Tuition, area resident: Full-time $10,452. Tuition, state resident: full-time $10,452. Tuition, nonresident: full-time $20,010. Required fees: $2176. Part-time tuition and fees vary according to course load and program. *Financial support:* Fellowships, teaching assistantships available. Financial award application deadline: 12/1; financial award applicants required to submit FAFSA. *Unit head:* Duane J. Osheim, Chair, 434-924-7146, Fax: 434-924-7891, E-mail: history@virginia.edu. *Application contact:* Paul Kershaw, Director of Graduate Admissions, E-mail: pjk3p@virginia.edu.

University of Washington, Graduate School, College of Arts and Sciences, Department of History, Seattle, WA 98195. Offers MA, PhD. Part-time programs available. *Degree requirements:* For master's, one foreign language, comprehensive exam, thesis optional; for doctorate, one foreign language, comprehensive exam, thesis/dissertation. *Entrance requirements:* For master's and doctorate, GRE, minimum GPA of 3.0. Additional exam requirements/recommendations for international students: Required—TOEFL. Electronic applications accepted. *Faculty research:* U.S., Asia, Europe, comparative history.

University of Waterloo, Graduate Studies, Faculty of Arts, Department of Classical Studies, Waterloo, ON N2L 3G1, Canada. Offers ancient Mediterranean cultures (MA). *Degree requirements:* For master's, one foreign language. *Entrance requirements:* For master's, BA, B+. *Faculty research:* Ancient history, philosophy, anthropology, religion, culture.

University of Waterloo, Graduate Studies, Faculty of Arts, Department of History, Waterloo, ON N2L 3G1, Canada. Offers MA, PhD. Part-time and evening/weekend programs available. *Degree requirements:* For master's, one foreign language, thesis optional; for doctorate, one foreign language, thesis/dissertation. *Entrance requirements:* For master's, honors degree, minimum B+ average, resumé; for doctorate, master's degree, minimum A average, resumé, writing sample. Additional exam requirements/recommendations for international students: Required—TOEFL, TWE. Electronic applications accepted. *Faculty research:* Canadian, British, international, modern, European, and U.S. history; women's history; imperialism and slavery.

The University of Western Ontario, Faculty of Graduate Studies, Social Sciences Division, Department of History, London, ON N6A 5B8, Canada. Offers MA, PhD. Part-time programs available. *Degree requirements:* For master's, one foreign language, thesis (for some programs); for doctorate, one foreign language, thesis/dissertation. *Entrance requirements:* For master's, minimum B+ average on last 10 senior courses; for doctorate, minimum A- average on MA or last year honors degree. Additional exam requirements/recommendations for international students: Required—TOEFL. *Faculty research:* Canadian, U.S., Britain, Modern Europe, British Empire and Commonwealth Latin America.

University of West Florida, College of Arts and Sciences: Arts, Department of History, Pensacola, FL 32514-5750. Offers historic preservation (MA); history (MA); public history (MA). Part-time and evening/weekend programs available. *Faculty:* 6 full-time (1 woman), 1 part-time/adjunct (0 women). *Students:* 11 full-time (4 women), 28 part-time (12 women); includes 2 minority (1 African American, 1 Hispanic American). Average age 34. 29 applicants, 69% accepted, 13 enrolled. In 2008, 11 master's awarded. *Degree requirements:* For master's, thesis or alternative. *Entrance requirements:* For master's, GRE General Test, minimum GPA of 3.0, minimum 15 hours of upper-level history courses. Additional exam requirements/recommendations for international students: Required—TOEFL (minimum score 550 paper-based; 213 computer-based). *Application deadline:* For fall admission, 6/1 for domestic students, 5/15 for international students; for spring admission, 11/1 for domestic students, 10/1 for international students. Applications are processed on a rolling basis. Application fee: $30. *Expenses:* Tuition, state resident: full-time $6095; part-time $253.97 per credit hour. Tuition, nonresident: full-time $21,919; part-time $913.31 per credit hour. *Financial support:* In 2008–09, 3 research assistantships with partial tuition reimbursements (averaging $5,640 per year) were awarded; fellowships, teaching assistantships with partial tuition reimbursements, Federal Work-Study, institutionally sponsored loans, scholarships/grants, and unspecified assistantships also available. Financial award application deadline: 4/15; financial award applicants required to submit FAFSA. *Unit head:* Dr. John J. Clune, Chairperson, 850-474-2680. *Application contact:* Terry McCray, Assistant Director of Graduate Admissions, 850-473-7718, Fax: 850-473-7714, E-mail: gradadmissions@uwf.edu.

University of West Georgia, Graduate School, College of Arts and Sciences, Department of History, Program in History, Carrollton, GA 30118. Offers MA. *Students:* 21 full-time (13 women), 14 part-time (5 women); includes 2 minority (1 African American, 1 Hispanic American). Average age 33. In 2008, 6 master's awarded. Application fee: $30. *Expenses:* Tuition, state resident: full-time $2844; part-time $158 per semester hour. Tuition, nonresident: full-time $11,340; part-time $630 per semester hour. Required fees: $1120; $41.56 per semester hour. $186 per semester. Tuition and fees vary according to course load. *Unit head:* Dr. Howard Steve Goodson, Interim Chair, 678-839-6042, E-mail: hgoodson@westga.edu. *Application contact:* Dr. Charles W. Clark, Interim Dean, 678-839-6508, E-mail: cclark@westga.edu.

University of Windsor, Faculty of Graduate Studies, Faculty of Arts and Social Sciences, Department of History, Windsor, ON N9B 3P4, Canada. Offers MA. Part-time programs available. *Degree requirements:* For master's, thesis (for some programs). *Entrance requirements:* For master's, minimum B average. Additional exam requirements/recommendations for international students: Required—TOEFL (minimum score 600 paper-based; 250 computer-based). Electronic applications accepted. *Faculty research:* Gender history, social-history questions about class gender and national identity, divorce in France: 1792-1816, gender and sexuality in Western Europe during the high and later Middle Ages, U.S.-Canadian comparisons in women's history.

The University of Winnipeg, Graduate Studies, Department of History, Winnipeg, MB R3B 2E9, Canada. Offers MA. Part-time and evening/weekend programs available. *Degree requirements:* For master's, one foreign language, comprehensive exam or thesis. *Faculty research:* Canadian social history, European diplomacy, Indian history, colonial America, medieval history.

University of Wisconsin–Eau Claire, College of Arts and Sciences, Department of History, Eau Claire, WI 54702-4004. Offers MA. Part-time programs available. *Faculty:* 10 full-time (4 women). *Students:* 11 full-time (3 women), 21 part-time (10 women); includes 5 minority (4 American Indian/Alaska Native, 1 Hispanic American). Average age 31. 18 applicants, 78% accepted, 13 enrolled. In 2008, 5 master's awarded. *Degree requirements:* For master's, comprehensive exam, thesis optional, oral and written exams. *Entrance requirements:* For master's, minimum GPA of 3.15 during last 2 years, 3.3 in history, or 3.0 overall; research paper. Additional exam requirements/recommendations for international students: Required—TOEFL (minimum score 550 paper-based; 213 computer-based; 79 iBT). *Application deadline:* For fall admission, 3/1 priority date for domestic students, 6/1 priority date for international students; for spring admission, 11/1 priority date for international students. Applications are processed on a rolling basis. Application fee: $56. Electronic applications accepted. *Expenses:* Tuition, state resident: full-time $6426; part-time $400.60 per credit. Tuition, nonresident: full-time $17,560; part-time $975.32 per credit. One-time fee: $56 full-time. *Financial support:* In 2008–09, 19 students received support, including 2 fellowships (averaging $375 per year); Federal Work-Study and unspecified assistantships also available. Financial award application deadline: 3/1; financial award applicants required to submit FAFSA. *Unit head:* Dr. Kate Lang, Chair, 715-836-5501, Fax: 715-836-3540, E-mail: langkh@uwec.edu. *Application contact:* Kristina Anderson, Director of Admissions, 715-836-5415, Fax: 715-836-2409, E-mail: admissions@uwec.edu.

University of Wisconsin–Madison, Graduate School, College of Letters and Science, Department of History, Madison, WI 53706-1380. Offers African history (MA, PhD); Central Asian history (MA, PhD); comparative world history (MA, PhD); East Asian history (MA, PhD); European history (MA, PhD); gender and women's history (MA, PhD); Latin American and Caribbean history (MA, PhD); Middle Eastern history (MA, PhD); South Asian history (MA, PhD); Southeast Asian history (MA, PhD); United States history (MA, PhD). Terminal master's awarded for partial completion of doctoral program. *Degree requirements:* For master's, thesis (for some programs); for doctorate, variable foreign language requirement, thesis/dissertation. *Entrance requirements:* For master's and doctorate, GRE General Test. Additional exam requirements/recommendations for international students: Required—Michigan English Language Assessment Battery or TOEFL. Electronic applications accepted. *Faculty research:* American, African, European, Asian, Latin American, and Middle Eastern history.

University of Wisconsin–Milwaukee, Graduate School, College of Letters and Sciences, Department of History, Milwaukee, WI 53201-0413. Offers global history (PhD); history (MA); modern studies (PhD); urban history (PhD); MLIS/MA. Part-time programs available. *Faculty:* 32 full-time (15 women). *Students:* 44 full-time (22 women), 41 part-time (19 women); includes 9 minority (2 African Americans, 2 American Indian/Alaska Native, 1 Asian American or Pacific Islander, 4 Hispanic Americans), 1 international. Average age 34. 71 applicants, 58% accepted, 25 enrolled. In 2008, 12 master's awarded. *Degree requirements:* For master's, comprehensive exam, thesis or alternative; for doctorate, thesis/dissertation. *Entrance requirements:* For master's and doctorate, GRE General Test. Additional exam requirements/recommendations for international students: Required—TOEFL (minimum score 550 paper-based; 79 iBT), IELTS (minimum score 6.5). *Application deadline:* For fall admission, 1/1 priority date for domestic students; for spring admission, 9/1 for domestic students. Applications are processed on a rolling basis. Application fee: $45 ($75 for international students). *Expenses:* Tuition, area resident: Full-time $7320; part-time $165 per credit. Tuition, state resident: full-time $7320; part-time $165 per credit. Tuition, nonresident: full-time $17,840; part-time $714 per credit. Tuition and fees vary according to campus/location, program and reciprocity agreements. *Financial support:* In 2008–09, 21 teaching assistantships were awarded; career-related internships or fieldwork and unspecified assistantships also available. Support available to part-time students. Financial award application deadline: 4/15. Total annual research expenditures: $52,970. *Unit head:* Joe Austin, Representative, 414-229-4361, Fax: 414-229-2435, E-mail: jaustin@uwm.edu. *Application contact:* General Information Contact, 414-229-4982, Fax: 414-229-6967, E-mail: gradschool@uwm.edu.

University of Wisconsin–Stevens Point, College of Letters and Science, Department of History, Stevens Point, WI 54481-3897. Offers MST. *Students:* 1 full-time (0 women), 3 part-time (all women); includes 1 Hispanic American. *Degree requirements:* For master's, thesis or alternative. *Application deadline:* For fall admission, 5/1 priority date for domestic students. Applications are processed on a rolling basis. Application fee: $45. *Expenses:* Tuition, state resident: full-time $7410. Tuition, nonresident: full-time $17,756. Full-time tuition and fees vary according to reciprocity agreements. *Financial support:* Federal Work-Study and unspecified assistantships available. Financial award application deadline: 5/1; financial award applicants required to submit FAFSA. *Unit head:* Dr. Greg Summers, Chair, 715-346-2334, Fax: 715-346-4489. *Application contact:* Catherine Glennon, Director of Admissions, 715-346-2441, E-mail: admiss@uwsp.edu.

University of Wyoming, Graduate School, College of Arts and Sciences, Department of History, Laramie, WY 82070. Offers MA, MAT. Part-time programs available. *Faculty:* 9 full-time (2 women). *Students:* 14 full-time (5 women), 9 part-time (5 women); includes 2 minority (both Hispanic Americans), 1 international. Average age 30. 11 applicants, 100% accepted, 10 enrolled. In 2008, 9 master's awarded. *Degree requirements:* For master's, one foreign language, thesis (for some programs). *Entrance requirements:* For master's, GRE General Test, minimum GPA of 3.0, 12 semester hours of undergraduate course work in history. Additional exam requirements/recommendations for international students: Required—TOEFL. *Application deadline:* For fall admission, 2/1 priority date for domestic and international students. Applications are processed on a rolling basis. Application fee: $50. Electronic applications accepted. *Financial support:* In 2008–09, 9 students received support, including 7 teaching assistantships with tuition reimbursements available (averaging $10,062 per year); career-related internships or fieldwork, Federal Work-Study, institutionally sponsored loans, and health care benefits also available. Financial award application deadline: 3/1; financial award applicants required to submit FAFSA. *Faculty research:* American West, Native American history, nineteenth and twentieth century U.S. history, European history, Asian studies. Total annual research expenditures: $13,000. *Unit head:* Dr. Mark D. Potter, Head, 307-766-5101, Fax: 307-766-5192, E-mail: mpotter@uwyo.edu. *Application contact:* Douglas R. Johnson, Office Associate, 307-766-5101, E-mail: djohnson@uwyo.edu.

Utah State University, School of Graduate Studies, College of Humanities, Arts and Social Sciences, Department of History, Logan, UT 84322. Offers MA, MS. Part-time and evening/weekend programs available. *Degree requirements:* For master's, one foreign language, thesis. *Entrance requirements:* For master's, GRE General Test, minimum GPA of 3.0. Additional exam requirements/recommendations for international students: Required—TOEFL. Electronic applications accepted. *Faculty research:* U.S. race and ethnicity, early modern and modern Europe, environmental history, western regional history.

Valdosta State University, Graduate School, College of Arts and Sciences, Department of History, Valdosta, GA 31698. Offers MA. Part-time programs available. *Faculty:* 11 full-time (3 women). *Students:* 5 part-time (2 women). Average age 23. 4 applicants, 25% accepted, 1 enrolled. In 2008, 1 master's awarded. *Degree requirements:* For master's, one foreign language, thesis optional, comprehensive written and/or oral exams. *Entrance requirements:* For master's, GRE General Test, minimum GPA of 2.5. Additional exam requirements/recommendations for international students: Required—TOEFL (minimum score 523 paper-based; 193 computer-based). *Application deadline:* For fall admission, 5/15 for domestic and international students; for spring admission, 11/15 for domestic and international students. Applications are processed on a rolling basis. Application fee: $40. Electronic applications accepted. *Financial support:* In 2008–09, 1 research assistantship with full tuition reimbursement (averaging $2,452 per year), 1 teaching assistantship with full tuition reimbursement (averaging $2,800 per year) were awarded; scholarships/grants and unspecified assistantships also available. Support available to part-time students. Financial award application deadline: 7/1; financial award applicants required to submit FAFSA. *Faculty research:* Georgia history, U.S. history, Napoleonic France, American diplomatic history, English history. *Unit head:* Dr. Paul Riggs, Head, 229-333-5947, Fax: 229-249-4865. *Application contact:* Rebecca Waters, Coordinator of Graduate Admissions, 229-333-5694, Fax: 229-245-3853, E-mail: rlwaters@valdosta.edu.

Valparaiso University, Graduate Division, Program in Liberal Studies, Concentration in History, Valparaiso, IN 46383. Offers MALS, Post-Master's Certificate, JD/MALS. Part-time and evening/weekend programs available. *Students:* 5 full-time (2 women), 7 part-time (4 women); includes 1 minority (Asian American or Pacific Islander). Average age 32. In 2008, 4 master's awarded. *Entrance requirements:* For master's, minimum GPA of 3.0. Additional exam requirements/recommendations for international students: Required—TOEFL (minimum score 550 paper-based; 213 computer-based). *Application deadline:* Applications are processed on a rolling basis. Application fee: $30 ($50 for international students). Electronic applications accepted. *Financial support:* Available to part-time students. Applicants required to submit FAFSA. *Faculty research:* Regional Chinese history, British history, Martin Luther, Latin American history, African history. *Unit head:* Dr. David L. Rowland, Dean, Graduate Studies and Continuing Education, 219-464-5313, Fax: 219-464-5381, E-mail: David.Rowland@valpo.edu. *Application contact:* Jamie Haney, Coordinator of Recruitment Activities, 219-464-5313, Fax: 219-464-5381, E-mail: Jamie.Haney@valpo.edu.

Vanderbilt University, Graduate School, Department of History, Nashville, TN 37240-1001. Offers MA, MAT, PhD. *Faculty:* 38 full-time (10 women). *Students:* 48 full-time (26 women), 3 part-time (1 woman); includes 10 minority (5 African Americans, 1 American Indian/Alaska Native, 1 Asian American or Pacific Islander, 3 Hispanic Americans), 8 international. Average age 31. 131 applicants, 11% accepted, 10 enrolled. In 2008, 4 doctorates awarded. Terminal master's awarded for partial completion of doctoral program. *Degree requirements:* For doctorate, one foreign language, comprehensive exam, thesis/dissertation, final and qualifying exams. *Entrance requirements:* For doctorate, GRE General Test, sample of written work (recommended). Additional exam requirements/recommendations for international students: Required—TOEFL (minimum score 570 paper-based; 230 computer-based; 88 iBT). *Application deadline:* For fall admission, 1/15 for domestic and international students. Application fee: $0. Electronic applications accepted. *Financial support:* Fellowships with full tuition reimbursements, teaching assistantships with full tuition reimbursements, Federal Work-Study, institutionally sponsored loans, scholarships/grants, and health care benefits available. Financial award application deadline: 1/15; financial award applicants required to submit CSS PROFILE or FAFSA. *Faculty research:* Southern American history, recent U.S. history, intellectual and cultural history, European history, Latin American history. *Unit head:* Elizabeth Lunback, PhD, Chair, 615-322-2575, Fax: 615-343-6002, E-mail: elizabeth.lunbeck@vanderbilt.edu. *Application contact:* Katherine B. Crawford, PhD, Director of Graduate Studies, 615-322-3388, Fax: 615-343-6002, E-mail: kathering.b.crawford@vanderbilt.edu.

Villanova University, Graduate School of Liberal Arts and Sciences, Department of History, Villanova, PA 19085-1699. Offers MA. Part-time and evening/weekend programs available. *Faculty:* 12 full-time (6 women), 1 part-time/adjunct (0 women). *Students:* 17 full-time (12 women), 51 part-time (27 women); includes 8 minority (6 African Americans, 2 Hispanic Americans). Average age 28. 59 applicants, 80% accepted, 25 enrolled. In 2008, 29 master's awarded. *Degree requirements:* For master's, comprehensive exam, thesis optional. *Entrance requirements:* For master's, GRE General Test, minimum GPA of 3.0. Additional exam requirements/recommendations for international students: Required—TOEFL. *Application deadline:* For fall admission, 5/1 for domestic and international students; for spring admission, 11/15 for domestic and international students. Applications are processed on a rolling basis. Application fee: $50. Electronic applications accepted. *Financial support:* Research assistantships, Federal Work-Study and scholarships/grants available. Financial award applicants required to submit FAFSA. *Unit head:* Dr. Adele Lindenmeyr, Chairperson, 610-519-4660. *Application*

History

Villanova University (continued)

contact: Dr. Gerald Long, Dean, Graduate School of Liberal Arts and Sciences, 610-519-7093, Fax: 610-519-7096.

See Close-Up on page 333.

Virginia Commonwealth University, Graduate School, College of Humanities and Sciences, Department of History, Richmond, VA 23284-9005. Offers MA. Part-time programs available. *Degree requirements:* For master's, thesis optional. *Entrance requirements:* For master's, GRE General Test, 30 undergraduate credits in history.

Virginia Commonwealth University, Graduate School, School of the Arts, Department of Art History, Richmond, VA 23284-9005. Offers architectural history (MA); art history (MA, PhD); historical studies (MA); museum studies (MA). *Accreditation:* NASAD. *Degree requirements:* For master's, thesis; for doctorate, comprehensive exam, thesis/dissertation. *Entrance requirements:* For master's and doctorate, GRE General Test. *Faculty research:* Modern, nineteenth century, Renaissance, American, and Medieval art.

Virginia Polytechnic Institute and State University, Graduate School, College of Liberal Arts and Human Sciences, Department of History, Blacksburg, VA 24061. Offers MA. Part-time programs available. *Entrance requirements:* For master's, GRE General Test. Additional exam requirements/recommendations for international students: Required—TOEFL (minimum score 600 paper-based; 250 computer-based). Electronic applications accepted. *Faculty research:* History of the U.S.; race, class and gender; European (area studies); history of science and technology.

Virginia State University, School of Graduate Studies, Research, and Outreach, School of Liberal Arts and Education, Department of History, Petersburg, VA 23806-0001. Offers MA. *Degree requirements:* For master's, one foreign language, thesis (for some programs). *Entrance requirements:* For master's, GRE General Test, minimum GPA of 2.5.

Washington College, Graduate Programs, Department of History, Chestertown, MD 21620-1197. Offers MA. Part-time and evening/weekend programs available.

Washington State University, Graduate School, College of Liberal Arts, Department of History, Pullman, WA 99164. Offers early and modern European history (MA, PhD); environmental history (MA, PhD); Latin American history (MA, PhD); modern East Asia history (MA, PhD); public history (MA, PhD); US history (MA, PhD); women's history (MA, PhD); world history (MA, PhD). Part-time programs available. *Degree requirements:* For master's, comprehensive exam (for some programs), thesis, oral exam; for doctorate, one foreign language, comprehensive exam, thesis/dissertation, oral and written exam. *Entrance requirements:* For master's, GRE General Test, minimum GPA of 3.3, language background form, writing sample; for doctorate, GRE General Test, minimum GPA of 3.5, language background form, writing sample. Additional exam requirements/recommendations for international students: Required—TOEFL (minimum score 550 paper-based). Electronic applications accepted. *Faculty research:* Public, world, environmental, women and U.S. history.

Washington State University, Graduate School, College of Liberal Arts, Program in American Studies, Pullman, WA 99164. Offers ethnic studies (MA, PhD); feminist studies (MA, PhD); history (MA, PhD); literature (MA, PhD). *Degree requirements:* For master's, one foreign language, comprehensive exam (for some programs), thesis optional, oral exam; for doctorate, one foreign language, comprehensive exam (for some programs), thesis/dissertation, oral exam. *Entrance requirements:* For master's and doctorate, GRE General Test, minimum GPA of 3.0, writing sample, 3 letters of recommendation. Additional exam requirements/recommendations for international students: Required—TOEFL. *Faculty research:* The American West in multicultural perspective; nineteenth century historical, literary, and cultural studies; comparative American ethnic literatures and cultures; American cultures and the environment; American rhetoric.

Washington State University Vancouver, Graduate Programs, Program in History, Vancouver, WA 98686. Offers MA. Part-time programs available. *Degree requirements:* For master's, comprehensive exam (for some programs), thesis. *Entrance requirements:* For master's, GRE, minimum GPA of 3.0, writing sample, language background form, preferred field of study form, 3 letters of recommendation. Additional exam requirements/recommendations for international students: Required—TOEFL (minimum score 550 paper-based; 213 computer-based). *Faculty research:* Immigration, gender, slavery, labor, public history.

Washington University in St. Louis, Graduate School of Arts and Sciences, Department of History, St. Louis, MO 63130-4899. Offers American history (MA, PhD); Asian history (MA, PhD); British history (MA, PhD); European history (MA, PhD); Latin American history (MA, PhD); Middle Eastern history (MA, PhD). *Students:* 38 full-time (20 women); includes 6 minority (1 African American, 1 Asian American or Pacific Islander, 4 Hispanic Americans), 2 international. 71 applicants, 7% accepted, 2 enrolled. In 2008, 14 master's, 2 doctorates awarded. Terminal master's awarded for partial completion of doctoral program. *Degree requirements:* For master's, one foreign language, thesis (for some programs); for doctorate, 2 foreign languages, thesis/dissertation. *Entrance requirements:* For master's and doctorate, GRE General Test. *Application deadline:* For fall admission, 1/15 priority date for domestic students. Application fee: $45. Electronic applications accepted. *Financial support:* Fellowships, teaching assistantships, Federal Work-Study and institutionally sponsored loans available. Financial award application deadline: 1/15. *Unit head:* Dr. Jean Allman, Chairman, 314-935-5450. *Application contact:* Assistant to the Dean, 314-935-6880, Fax: 314-935-4887.

Wayne State University, College of Liberal Arts and Sciences, Department of History, Detroit, MI 48202. Offers MA, PhD, JD/MA. Evening/weekend programs available. *Degree requirements:* For doctorate, 2 foreign languages, thesis/dissertation, qualifying exam in 4 fields of history. *Entrance requirements:* For master's, GRE General Test, GRE Subject Test, minimum GPA of 3.0 in history, 2.75 overall; for doctorate, GRE General Test, GRE Subject Test, minimum GPA of 3.0. Additional exam requirements/recommendations for international students: Required—TOEFL (minimum score 550 paper-based; 213 computer-based); Recommended—TWE (minimum score 6). Electronic applications accepted. *Faculty research:* Labor and social history; citizenship and governance; modern U.S. history; early modern and modern European history; African-American history.

West Chester University of Pennsylvania, Office of Graduate Studies, College of Arts and Sciences, Department of History, West Chester, PA 19383. Offers history (M Ed, MA); holocaust and genocide studies (MA, Certificate); social studies/history (Teaching Certificate). Part-time and evening/weekend programs available. *Students:* 20 full-time (8 women), 34 part-time (16 women); includes 1 minority (African American). Average age 30. 38 applicants, 95% accepted, 21 enrolled. In 2008, 12 master's awarded. *Degree requirements:* For master's, thesis optional. *Entrance requirements:* For master's and other advanced degree, GMAT, GRE General Test, or MAT, statement of professional goals, writing sample, minimum GPA of 3.0 in history, three letters of recommendation. Additional exam requirements/recommendations for international students: Required—TOEFL (minimum score 550 paper-based; 213 computer-based; 80 iBT). *Application deadline:* For fall admission, 4/15 priority date for domestic students, 3/15 for international students; for spring admission, 10/15 for domestic students, 9/1 for international students. Applications are processed on a rolling basis. Application fee: $35. Electronic applications accepted. *Expenses:* Tuition, state resident: full-time $6430; part-time $357 per credit. Tuition, nonresident: full-time $10,288; part-time $572 per credit. Required fees: $652.50; $50 per credit. $67 per semester. *Financial support:* In 2008–09, 2 research assistantships with full and partial tuition reimbursements (averaging $5,000 per year) were awarded; unspecified assistantships also available. Support available to part-time students. Financial award application deadline: 2/15; financial award applicants required to submit FAFSA. *Faculty research:* Oral histories, siege of Leningrad. *Unit head:* Dr. Wayne Hanley, Chair, 610-436-2201, E-mail: whanley@wcupa.edu. *Application contact:* Dr. Jonathan Friedman, Director of the Holocaust/Genocide Education Center and Graduate Coordinator of Holocaust and Genocide Studies, 610-436-2972, E-mail: jfriedmans@wcupa.edu.

Western Carolina University, Graduate School, College of Arts and Sciences, Department of History, Cullowhee, NC 28723. Offers MA. Part-time and evening/weekend programs available. *Degree requirements:* For master's, one foreign language, comprehensive exam, thesis or alternative. *Entrance requirements:* For master's, GRE General Test, appropriate undergraduate, 3 letters of recommendation. Additional exam requirements/recommendations for international students: Required—TOEFL (minimum score 550 paper-based; 270 computer-based; 79 iBT). *Faculty research:* Social and economic history of the American South, Islamic world history, German history, social and political protest, medieval social history.

Western Connecticut State University, Division of Graduate Studies, School of Arts and Sciences, Department of History, Danbury, CT 06810-6885. Offers MA. Part-time programs available. *Faculty:* 3 full-time (1 woman), 1 part-time/adjunct (0 women). *Students:* 5 full-time (2 women), 26 part-time (13 women); includes 1 minority (African American). Average age 34. 54 applicants, 76% accepted, 9 enrolled. In 2008, 14 master's awarded. *Degree requirements:* For master's, thesis or alternative, thesis or research project, completion of program in 6 years with minimum cumulative GPA of 3.0. *Entrance requirements:* For master's, minimum GPA of 2.5. *Application deadline:* For fall admission, 8/5 priority date for domestic students; for spring admission, 1/5 priority date for domestic students. Applications are processed on a rolling basis. Application fee: $50. *Expenses:* Tuition, state resident: full-time $4377; part-time $363 per credit. Tuition, nonresident: full-time $12,195; part-time $363 per credit. Required fees: $3574; $60 per credit. Part-time tuition and fees vary according to degree level and program. *Financial support:* Available to part-time students. Application deadline: 5/1; *Unit head:* Dr. Michael Nolan, Assistant Professor, 203-837-8483, Fax: 203-837-8525, E-mail: nolanm@wcsu.edu. *Application contact:* Chris Shankle, Associate Director of Graduate Studies, 203-837-9005, Fax: 203-837-8326, E-mail: shanklec@wcsu.edu.

Western Illinois University, School of Graduate Studies, College of Arts and Sciences, Department of History, Macomb, IL 61455-1390. Offers MA. Part-time programs available. *Students:* 24 full-time (3 women), 11 part-time (4 women); includes 1 minority (African American). Average age 29. 16 applicants, 75% accepted. In 2008, 7 master's awarded. *Degree requirements:* For master's, thesis or alternative. *Entrance requirements:* Additional exam requirements/recommendations for international students: Required—TOEFL (minimum score 550 paper-based; 213 computer-based; 80 iBT). *Application deadline:* Applications are processed on a rolling basis. Application fee: $30. Electronic applications accepted. *Expenses:* Tuition, state resident: full-time $5696; part-time $237.34 per credit hour. Tuition, nonresident: full-time $11,392; part-time $474.68 per credit hour. Required fees: $1453; $60.55 per credit hour. *Financial support:* In 2008–09, 9 students received support, including 9 research assistantships with full tuition reimbursements available (averaging $7,040 per year); tuition waivers also available. Financial award applicants required to submit FAFSA. *Unit head:* Dr. Virginia Boynton, Chairperson, 309-298-1053. *Application contact:* Evelyn Hoing, Assistant Director of Graduate Studies, 309-298-1806, Fax: 309-298-2345, E-mail: grad-office@wiu.edu.

Western Kentucky University, Graduate Studies, Potter College of Arts and Letters, Department of History, Bowling Green, KY 42101. Offers MA, MA Ed. Part-time and evening/weekend programs available. Postbaccalaureate distance learning degree programs offered. *Degree requirements:* For master's, comprehensive exam, thesis optional, final exam. *Entrance requirements:* For master's, GRE General Test, minimum GPA of 2.75. Additional exam requirements/recommendations for international students: Required—TOEFL (minimum score 555 paper-based; 213 computer-based; 79 iBT). *Faculty research:* U.S.A, Europe, China, India, Latin America.

Western Michigan University, Graduate College, College of Arts and Sciences, Department of History, Kalamazoo, MI 49008-5202. Offers MA, PhD. *Degree requirements:* For master's, thesis optional, oral exams; for doctorate, thesis/dissertation, oral exam. *Entrance requirements:* For doctorate, GRE General Test.

Western Washington University, Graduate School, College of Humanities and Social Sciences, Department of History, Bellingham, WA 98225-5996. Offers MA. Part-time programs available. *Degree requirements:* For master's, one foreign language, comprehensive exam, thesis (for some programs). *Entrance requirements:* For master's, GRE General Test, minimum GPA of 3.0 in last 60 semester hours or last 90 quarter hours. Additional exam requirements/recommendations for international students: Required—TOEFL (minimum score 567 paper-based; 227 computer-based). Electronic applications accepted.

Westfield State College, Division of Graduate and Continuing Education, Department of History, Westfield, MA 01086. Offers M Ed. Part-time and evening/weekend programs available. *Faculty:* 2 full-time (0 women). *Students:* 6 part-time (4 women). Average age 38. In 2008, 3 master's awarded. *Degree requirements:* For master's, thesis. *Entrance requirements:* For master's, GRE General Test or MAT, minimum undergraduate GPA of 2.7. *Application deadline:* Applications are processed on a rolling basis. Application fee: $30. *Financial support:* Research assistantships, teaching assistantships, career-related internships or fieldwork, Federal Work-Study, and tuition waivers (full and partial) available. Support available to part-time students. Financial award application deadline: 4/1; financial award applicants required to submit CSS PROFILE. *Unit head:* Dr. John S. Ifkovic, Chair, 413-572-5692. *Application contact:* Michelle Janke, Admissions Coordinator, 413-572-8022, Fax: 413-572-5227, E-mail: mjanke@wsc.ma.edu.

West Texas A&M University, College of Education and Social Sciences, Department of History and Political Science, Program in History, Canyon, TX 79016-0001. Offers MA. Part-time and evening/weekend programs available. *Degree requirements:* For master's, comprehensive exam, thesis optional. *Entrance requirements:* For master's, GRE General Test. Additional exam requirements/recommendations for international students: Required—TOEFL (minimum score 550 paper-based). Electronic applications accepted. *Faculty research:* John B. Stetson Jr. (an American businessman in Warsaw), creation of kokugo in late Meiji Japan, canon law on cyberspace, Russian and American frontiers, Texas women of two cultures.

West Virginia University, Eberly College of Arts and Sciences, Department of History, Morgantown, WV 26506. Offers African history (MA, PhD); African-American history (MA, PhD); American history (MA, PhD); Appalachian/regional history (MA, PhD); East Asian history (MA, PhD); European history (MA, PhD); history of science and technology (MA, PhD); Latin American history (MA). Part-time programs available. *Degree requirements:* For master's, one foreign language, thesis (for some programs), oral exam, thesis defense; for doctorate, one foreign language, comprehensive exam, thesis/dissertation, dissertation defense. *Entrance requirements:* For master's, GRE General Test, minimum GPA of 3.0; for doctorate, GRE General Test. Additional exam requirements/recommendations for international students: Required—TOEFL (minimum score 550 paper-based), IELTS (minimum score 6.5). Electronic applications accepted. *Faculty research:* U.S., Appalachia, modern Europe, Africa, colonial and post-colonial societies.

Wichita State University, Graduate School, Fairmount College of Liberal Arts and Sciences, Department of History, Wichita, KS 67260. Offers MA. Part-time programs available. *Degree requirements:* For master's, one foreign language, comprehensive exam or thesis. *Entrance requirements:* For master's, GRE. Additional exam requirements/recommendations for international students: Required—TOEFL. Electronic applications accepted. *Faculty research:* U.S. history, European history, public history.

Wilfrid Laurier University, Faculty of Graduate Studies, Faculty of Arts, Department of History, Waterloo, ON N2L 3C5, Canada. Offers MA, PhD. *Degree requirements:* For master's, thesis optional; for doctorate, thesis/dissertation. *Entrance requirements:* For master's, honors BA degree or the equivalent in history, minimum B+ average in undergraduate course work, exclusive of first year level courses; for doctorate, MA in history, minimum A-average. Additional exam requirements/recommendations for international students: Required—TOEFL (minimum score 230 computer-based; 89 iBT). Electronic applications accepted. *Faculty research:* Canadian, early modern European, modern European, Scottish, race/class/imperialism/slavery, British, urban and rural, science/medicine/technology, gender/women's/family, international, United States.

William Paterson University of New Jersey, College of the Humanities and Social Sciences, Department of History, Wayne, NJ 07470-8420. Offers MA. *Entrance requirements:* For master's, GRE. Electronic applications accepted.

Winthrop University, College of Arts and Sciences, Department of History, Rock Hill, SC 29733. Offers MA. Part-time programs available. *Degree requirements:* For master's, one foreign language, thesis optional. *Entrance requirements:* For master's, GRE General Test or PRAXIS, 24 hours of history at the undergraduate level. Electronic applications accepted.

Worcester State College, Graduate Studies, Department of Education, Program in History, Worcester, MA 01602-2597. Offers M Ed. Part-time programs available. *Faculty:* 2 full-time (1 woman), 1 part-time/adjunct (0 women). *Students:* 1 full-time (0 women), 20 part-time (6 women); includes 2 minority (1 American Indian/Alaska Native, 1 Hispanic American). Average age 36. 11 applicants, 100% accepted, 7 enrolled. In 2008, 15 master's awarded. *Degree requirements:* For master's, comprehensive exam (for some programs), thesis optional. *Entrance requirements:* For master's, GRE General Test or MAT, 18 undergraduate credits in history, including US history and Western civilizations. Additional exam requirements/recommendations for international students: Required—TOEFL (minimum score 550 paper-based; 213 computer-based; 79 iBT). *Application deadline:* Applications are processed on a rolling basis. Application fee: $30. *Expenses:* Tuition, area resident: Full-time $2700; part-time $150 per credit. Tuition, state resident: full-time $2700; part-time $150 per credit. Tuition, nonresident: full-time $2700; part-time $150 per credit. Required fees: $1530; $85 per credit. *Financial support:* In 2008–09, 1 student received support, including 1 research assistantship with full tuition reimbursement available (averaging $4,800 per year); career-related internships or fieldwork, scholarships/grants, and unspecified assistantships also available. Financial award application deadline:

3/1; financial award applicants required to submit FAFSA. *Faculty research:* Labor history, Middle East politics, American-Russian relations, American–East Asian relations. *Unit head:* Dr. Charlotte Haller, Coordinator, 508-929-8046, Fax: 508-929-8155, E-mail: challer1@worcester.edu. *Application contact:* Nicole Brown, Assistant Dean of Graduate and Continuing Education, 508-929-8787, Fax: 508-929-8100, E-mail: nbrown@worcester.edu.

Wright State University, School of Graduate Studies, College of Liberal Arts, Department of History, Dayton, OH 45435. Offers MA. *Degree requirements:* For master's, thesis optional. *Entrance requirements:* For master's, GRE General Test, minimum GPA of 3.0 in history, 2.7 overall. Additional exam requirements/recommendations for international students: Required—TOEFL. *Faculty research:* U.S. religions; women's, Southern, European, and archival history.

Yale University, Graduate School of Arts and Sciences, Department of History, New Haven, CT 06520. Offers history (M Phil, MA, PhD); history of science and medicine (MA, PhD). Terminal master's awarded for partial completion of doctoral program. *Degree requirements:* For master's, one foreign language; for doctorate, 2 foreign languages, thesis/dissertation. *Entrance requirements:* For doctorate, GRE General Test.

York University, Faculty of Graduate Studies, Faculty of Arts, Program in History, Toronto, ON M3J 1P3, Canada. Offers MA, PhD. Part-time programs available. *Degree requirements:* For master's, thesis or alternative; for doctorate, one foreign language, comprehensive exam, thesis/dissertation, qualifying exam. Electronic applications accepted.

Youngstown State University, Graduate School, College of Liberal Arts and Social Sciences, Department of History, Youngstown, OH 44555-0001. Offers MA. Part-time programs available. *Degree requirements:* For master's, thesis optional, oral and written exams. *Entrance requirements:* For master's, minimum GPA of 2.75. Additional exam requirements/recommendations for international students: Required—TOEFL. *Faculty research:* Holocaust, Marxism, nineteenth- and twentieth-century United States, historic preservation, revolutionary France.

History of Medicine

Duke University, Graduate School, Department of History, Program in Medical Historian Training, Durham, NC 27708-0586. Offers MD/PhD.

McGill University, Faculty of Graduate and Postdoctoral Studies, Faculty of Arts, Department of History, Montréal, QC H3A 2T5, Canada. Offers history (MA, PhD); history of medicine (MA).

McGill University, Faculty of Graduate and Postdoctoral Studies, Faculty of Medicine, Department of Social Studies in Medicine, Montréal, QC H3A 2T5, Canada. Offers medical anthropology (MA, PhD); medical history (MA, PhD); medical sociology (MA, PhD).

Rutgers, The State University of New Jersey, New Brunswick, Graduate School, Program in History, Piscataway, NJ 08854-8097. Offers African-American history (PhD); early American history (PhD); early modern European history (PhD); east Asian history (PhD); global and comparative history (PhD); history (PhD); history of diplomacy and foreign relations (PhD); history of technology, environment and health (PhD); history of the Atlantic cultures and African diaspora (PhD); Latin American history (PhD); medieval history (PhD); modern European history (PhD); nineteenth and twentieth century American history (PhD); women's and gender history (PhD). *Degree requirements:* For doctorate, thesis/dissertation. *Entrance requirements:* For doctorate, GRE General Test, sample of written work. Electronic applications accepted.

Faculty research: American history, European history, Afro-American history, women's history, Latin American history.

Uniformed Services University of the Health Sciences, School of Medicine, Graduate Programs in the Biomedical Sciences and Public Health, Department of Medical History, Bethesda, MD 20814-4799. Offers MMH. Available to active duty military only. *Degree requirements:* For master's, comprehensive exam, thesis or alternative. *Entrance requirements:* For master's, GRE General Test, US citizenship, active military duty.

University of Minnesota, Twin Cities Campus, Graduate School, Program in the History of Science, Technology and Medicine, Minneapolis, MN 55455-0213. Offers MA, PhD. Part-time programs available. *Degree requirements:* For master's, one foreign language, thesis or alternative; for doctorate, 2 foreign languages, thesis/dissertation. *Entrance requirements:* For master's and doctorate, GRE General Test. *Faculty research:* History of infectious diseases, history of public health, history of evolutionary biology, history of infertility, women in science.

Yale University, Graduate School of Arts and Sciences, Department of History, Program in the History of Medicine and the Life Sciences, New Haven, CT 06520. Offers MS, PhD. *Degree requirements:* For doctorate, 2 foreign languages, thesis/dissertation. *Entrance requirements:* For doctorate, GRE General Test.

History of Science and Technology

Carnegie Mellon University, College of Humanities and Social Sciences, Department of History, Pittsburgh, PA 15213-3891. Offers African and African-American diaspora (PhD); culture and power (PhD); gender and the family (PhD); history (MA, MS); history and policy (MA); labor and politics (PhD); science, technology, medicine and environment (PhD). Part-time programs available. *Degree requirements:* For doctorate, oral and written comprehensive exams, dissertation defense. *Entrance requirements:* For doctorate, GRE General Test. Additional exam requirements/recommendations for international students: Required—TOEFL. Electronic applications accepted. *Faculty research:* Anthropology and history, African American history, technology/environment, cultural history analysis.

Cornell University, Graduate School, Graduate Fields of Arts and Sciences, Field of History, Ithaca, NY 14853-0001. Offers African history (MA, PhD); American history (MA, PhD); ancient history (MA, PhD); early modern European history (MA, PhD); English history (MA, PhD); French history (MA, PhD); German history (MA, PhD); history of science (MA, PhD); Latin American history (MA, PhD); medieval Chinese history (MA, PhD); medieval history (MA, PhD); modern Chinese history (MA, PhD); modern European history (MA, PhD); modern Japanese history (MA, PhD); premodern Islamic history (MA, PhD); premodern Japanese history (MA, PhD); Renaissance history (MA, PhD); Russian history (MA, PhD); Southeast Asian history (MA, PhD). *Faculty:* 54 full-time (14 women). *Students:* 65 full-time (35 women); includes 12 minority (4 African Americans, 3 Asian Americans or Pacific Islanders, 5 Hispanic Americans), 19 international. Average age 31. 205 applicants, 8% accepted, 11 enrolled. In 2008, 12 master's, 6 doctorates awarded. Terminal master's awarded for partial completion of doctoral program. *Degree requirements:* For master's, thesis; for doctorate, 2 foreign languages, comprehensive exam, thesis/dissertation, 1 year of teaching experience. *Entrance requirements:* For master's and doctorate, GRE General Test, writing sample, 3 letters of recommendation. Additional exam requirements/recommendations for international students: Required—TOEFL (minimum score 550 paper-based; 213 computer-based; 77 iBT). *Application deadline:* For fall admission, 1/15 for domestic students. Application fee: $70. Electronic applications accepted. *Expenses:* Tuition: Full-time $29,500. Required fees: $70. Full-time tuition and fees vary according to degree level, program and student level. *Financial support:* In 2008–09, 54 students received support, including 27 fellowships with full tuition reimbursements available, 3 research assistantships with full tuition reimbursements available, 24 teaching assistantships with full tuition reimbursements available; institutionally sponsored loans, scholarships/grants, health care benefits, tuition waivers (full and partial), and unspecified assistantships also available. Financial award applicants required to submit FAFSA. *Unit head:* Director of Graduate Studies, 607-255-6738, Fax: 607-255-0469. *Application contact:* Graduate Field Assistant, 607-255-6738, Fax: 607-255-0469, E-mail: history_grad_info@cornell.edu.

Cornell University, Graduate School, Graduate Fields of Arts and Sciences, Field of Science and Technology Studies, Ithaca, NY 14853-0001. Offers history and philosophy of science and technology (MA, PhD); social studies of science and technology (MA, PhD). *Faculty:* 20 full-time (10 women). *Students:* 22 full-time (14 women); includes 5 minority (1 African American,

4 Asian Americans or Pacific Islanders), 8 international. Average age 31. 38 applicants, 16% accepted, 3 enrolled. In 2008, 3 master's, 6 doctorates awarded. Terminal master's awarded for partial completion of doctoral program. *Degree requirements:* For master's, one foreign language, thesis; for doctorate, one foreign language, comprehensive exam, thesis/dissertation. *Entrance requirements:* For master's and doctorate, GRE General Test, writing sample, 3 letters of recommendation. Additional exam requirements/recommendations for international students: Required—TOEFL (minimum score 550 paper-based; 213 computer-based; 77 iBT). *Application deadline:* For fall admission, 1/10 for domestic students. Application fee: $70. Electronic applications accepted. *Expenses:* Tuition: Full-time $29,500. Required fees: $70. Full-time tuition and fees vary according to degree level, program and student level. *Financial support:* In 2008–09, 19 students received support, including 8 fellowships with full tuition reimbursements available, 1 research assistantship with full tuition reimbursement available, 10 teaching assistantships with full tuition reimbursements available; institutionally sponsored loans, scholarships/grants, health care benefits, tuition waivers (full and partial), and unspecified assistantships also available. Financial award applicants required to submit FAFSA. *Faculty research:* History, philosophy, sociology, politics, and policy of science and technology; gender, legal order, environment, and communication. *Unit head:* Director of Graduate Studies, 607-255-6234. *Application contact:* Graduate Field Assistant, 607-255-6234, E-mail: stsgradfield@cornell.edu.

Drexel University, College of Arts and Sciences, Department of History and Politics, Philadelphia, PA 19104-2875. Offers science, technology and society (MS). Part-time programs available. *Entrance requirements:* For master's, GRE. Additional exam requirements/recommendations for international students: Required—TOEFL. Electronic applications accepted.

Georgia Institute of Technology, Graduate Studies and Research, Ivan Allen College of Policy and International Affairs, School of History, Technology, and Society, Atlanta, GA 30332-0001. Offers history and sociology of technology and science (MS, PhD). Terminal master's awarded for partial completion of doctoral program. *Degree requirements:* For master's, research paper; for doctorate, one foreign language, comprehensive exam, thesis/dissertation. *Entrance requirements:* Additional exam requirements/recommendations for international students: Required—TOEFL. Electronic applications accepted. *Faculty research:* Industrialization, labor history, modern Europe, social history, sociology of science.

Harvard University, Graduate School of Arts and Sciences, Department of the History of Science, Cambridge, MA 02138. Offers AM, PhD. Terminal master's awarded for partial completion of doctoral program. *Degree requirements:* For master's, one foreign language; for doctorate, 2 foreign languages, thesis/dissertation. *Entrance requirements:* For master's and doctorate, GRE General Test. Additional exam requirements/recommendations for international students: Required—TOEFL. *Expenses:* Tuition: Full-time $32,556. Required fees: $1426. Full-time tuition and fees vary according to program and student level.

Indiana University Bloomington, University Graduate School, College of Arts and Sciences, Department of History and Philosophy of Science, Bloomington, IN 47405-7000. Offers MA,

History of Science and Technology

Indiana University Bloomington (continued)
PhD, MLS/MA. Part-time programs available. *Faculty:* 9 full-time (2 women). *Students:* 36 full-time (8 women), 4 part-time (0 women); includes 6 minority (3 Asian Americans or Pacific Islanders, 3 Hispanic Americans), 6 international. Average age 31. 41 applicants, 66% accepted, 9 enrolled. In 2008, 5 master's, 1 doctorate awarded. Terminal master's awarded for partial completion of doctoral program. *Degree requirements:* For master's, one foreign language, thesis optional; for doctorate, 2 foreign languages, thesis/dissertation. *Entrance requirements:* For master's and doctorate, GRE General Test. Additional exam requirements/recommendations for international students: Required—TOEFL. *Application deadline:* For fall admission, 1/15 priority date for domestic students, 12/15 for international students; for spring admission, 9/1 priority date for domestic students, 9/1 for international students. Applications are processed on a rolling basis. Application fee: $50 ($60 for international students). Electronic applications accepted. *Expenses:* Tuition, area resident: Part-time $291.97 per credit hour. Tuition, state resident: part-time $291.97 per credit hour. Tuition, nonresident: part-time $850.33 per credit hour. Required fees: $110 per semester. Tuition and fees vary according to course load and program. *Financial support:* In 2008–09, 14 students received support; fellowships with full tuition reimbursements available, research assistantships with full tuition reimbursements available, teaching assistantships with full tuition reimbursements available, Federal Work-Study, institutionally sponsored loans, scholarships/grants, health care benefits, and unspecified assistantships available. Support available to part-time students. Financial award application deadline: 3/1; financial award applicants required to submit FAFSA. *Faculty research:* History of scientific ideas, instruments, and institutions; foundations of physics; history of philosophy of science; history and philosophy of biology; early modern science and medicine. *Unit head:* Domenico Bertoloni Meli, Chair, 812-855-8746, E-mail: dbmeli@indiana.edu. *Application contact:* Peggy Roberts, Graduate Secretary, 812-855-3622, Fax: 812-855-3631, E-mail: hpscdept@indiana.edu.

Iowa State University of Science and Technology, Graduate College, College of Liberal Arts and Sciences, Department of History, Ames, IA 50011. Offers agricultural history and rural studies (PhD); history (MA); history of technology and science (MA, PhD). *Faculty:* 17 full-time (5 women). *Students:* 24 full-time (10 women), 10 part-time (2 women); includes 1 minority (Hispanic American), 4 international. 10 applicants, 70% accepted, 3 enrolled. In 2008, 9 master's, 3 doctorates awarded. *Degree requirements:* For master's, thesis or alternative; for doctorate, thesis/dissertation. *Entrance requirements:* For master's and doctorate, GRE General Test. Additional exam requirements/recommendations for international students: Required—TOEFL (minimum score 600 paper-based; 79 iBT), IELTS (7.0) or TOEFL. *Application deadline:* For fall admission, 1/15 priority date for domestic and international students. Applications are processed on a rolling basis. Application fee: $30 ($70 for international students). Electronic applications accepted. *Expenses:* Tuition, area resident: Full-time $6446; part-time $359 per credit. Tuition, state resident: full-time $6446; part-time $359 per credit. Tuition, nonresident: full-time $17,330; part-time $963 per credit. Required fees: $790; $249.25 per semester. Tuition and fees vary according to course load and program. *Financial support:* In 2008–09, 20 teaching assistantships with full and partial tuition reimbursements (averaging $12,150 per year) were awarded; research assistantships with full and partial tuition reimbursements, scholarships/grants, health care benefits, and unspecified assistantships also available. *Unit head:* Dr. Charles Dobbs, Chair, 515-294-7266, Fax: 515-294-6390, E-mail: cdobbs@iastate.edu. *Application contact:* Dr. Pamela Riney-Kehrberg, Information Contact, 515-294-1451, Fax: 515-294-6390.

The Johns Hopkins University, Zanvyl Krieger School of Arts and Sciences, Department of the History of Science and Technology, Baltimore, MD 21218-2699. Offers MA, PhD. Terminal master's awarded for partial completion of doctoral program. *Degree requirements:* For master's, one foreign language, thesis; for doctorate, 2 foreign languages, thesis/dissertation. *Entrance requirements:* For doctorate, GRE General Test. Additional exam requirements/recommendations for international students: Required—TOEFL (minimum score 600 paper-based; 250 computer-based). Electronic applications accepted. *Faculty research:* History of physical and biomedical sciences, history of technology, history of medicine (seventeenth–twentieth centuries).

Massachusetts Institute of Technology, School of Humanities, Arts, and Social Sciences, Program in Science, Technology, and Society, Cambridge, MA 02139-4307. Offers history, anthropology, and science, technology and society (PhD). *Degree requirements:* For doctorate, comprehensive exam, thesis/dissertation. *Entrance requirements:* For doctorate, GRE General Test. Additional exam requirements/recommendations for international students: Required—TOEFL (minimum score 577 paper-based; 233 computer-based). Electronic applications accepted. *Faculty research:* History of science; history of technology; sociology of science and technology; anthropology of science and technology; science, technology, and society.

Polytechnic Institute of NYU, Department of Humanities and Social Sciences, Major in History of Science, Brooklyn, NY 11201-2990. Offers MS. Part-time and evening/weekend programs available. *Degree requirements:* For master's, comprehensive exam (for some programs), thesis (for some programs). *Entrance requirements:* Additional exam requirements/recommendations for international students: Required—TOEFL (minimum score 550 paper-based; 213 computer-based); Recommended—IELTS (minimum score 6.5). Electronic applications accepted.

Princeton University, Graduate School, Department of History, Program in History of Science, Princeton, NJ 08544-1019. Offers PhD. *Degree requirements:* For doctorate, 2 foreign languages, thesis/dissertation. *Entrance requirements:* For doctorate, GRE General Test, sample of written work, 3 letters of recommendation. Additional exam requirements/recommendations for international students: Required—TOEFL (minimum score 600 paper-based; 250 computer-based). Electronic applications accepted. *Faculty research:* Early modern science, history of modern life sciences, history of physical sciences, history of modern technology, science and medicine in European expansion and colonialism.

Rensselaer Polytechnic Institute, Graduate School, School of Humanities and Social Sciences, Department of Science and Technology Studies, Troy, NY 12180-3590. Offers MS, PhD. Part-time programs available. Terminal master's awarded for partial completion of doctoral program. *Degree requirements:* For master's, thesis (for some programs); for doctorate, comprehensive exam, thesis/dissertation. *Entrance requirements:* For master's and doctorate, GRE General Test. Additional exam requirements/recommendations for international students: Required—TOEFL (minimum score 600 paper-based; 250 computer-based). Electronic applications accepted. *Faculty research:* Communities and technology, social dimensions of IT and biotechnology, ethics and policy, design.

Rutgers, The State University of New Jersey, New Brunswick, Graduate School, Program in History, Piscataway, NJ 08854-8097. Offers African-American history (PhD); early American history (PhD); early modern European history (PhD); east Asian history (PhD); global and comparative history (PhD); history (PhD); history of diplomacy and foreign relations (PhD); history of technology, environment and health (PhD); history of the Atlantic cultures and African diaspora (PhD); Latin American history (PhD); medieval history (PhD); modern European history (PhD); nineteenth and twentieth century American history (PhD); women's and gender history (PhD). *Degree requirements:* For doctorate, thesis/dissertation. *Entrance requirements:* For doctorate, GRE General Test, sample of written work. Electronic applications accepted. *Faculty research:* American history, European history, Afro-American history, women's history, Latin American history.

Uniformed Services University of the Health Sciences, School of Medicine, Graduate Programs in the Biomedical Sciences and Public Health, Bethesda, MD 20814-4799. Offers emerging infectious diseases (PhD); medical and clinical psychology (PhD), including clinical psychology, medical psychology; medical history (MMH); microbiology and immunology (PhD); molecular and cell biology (PhD); neuroscience (PhD); preventive medicine and biometrics (MPH, MSPH, MTMH, Dr PH, PhD), including environmental health science (PhD), medical zoology (PhD), public health (MPH, MSPH, Dr PH), tropical medicine and hygiene (MTMH).

Terminal master's awarded for partial completion of doctoral program. *Degree requirements:* For master's, comprehensive exam, thesis or alternative; for doctorate, comprehensive exam, thesis/dissertation, qualifying exam. *Entrance requirements:* For master's, GRE General Test; for doctorate, GRE General Test, minimum GPA of 3.0. Additional exam requirements/recommendations for international students: Required—TOEFL.

University of California, Berkeley, Graduate Division, College of Letters and Science, Group in Logic and the Methodology of Science, Berkeley, CA 94720-1500. Offers PhD. *Degree requirements:* For doctorate, qualifying exam, oral defense of dissertation. *Entrance requirements:* For doctorate, GRE General Test, minimum GPA of 3.5, 3 letters of recommendation. *Faculty research:* Set theory, recursion theory, theoretical computer science, philosophy of mathematics, philosophy of language.

University of California, San Diego, Office of Graduate Studies, Department of History, La Jolla, CA 92093. Offers history (MA, PhD); Judaic studies (MA); science studies (PhD). *Degree requirements:* For doctorate, thesis/dissertation. *Entrance requirements:* For master's and doctorate, GRE General Test. Electronic applications accepted.

University of California, San Francisco, Graduate Division, Department of History of Health Sciences, San Francisco, CA 94143. Offers MA, PhD, MD/PhD. Terminal master's awarded for partial completion of doctoral program. *Degree requirements:* For master's, 2 foreign languages, thesis; for doctorate, 2 foreign languages, thesis/dissertation. *Entrance requirements:* For master's and doctorate, GRE General Test.

University of Delaware, College of Arts and Sciences, Department of History, Hagley Program in the History of Technology and Industrialization, Newark, DE 19716. Offers MA, PhD. *Degree requirements:* For master's, thesis optional; for doctorate, comprehensive exam, thesis/dissertation. *Entrance requirements:* For master's and doctorate, interview. Electronic applications accepted.

University of Massachusetts Amherst, Graduate School, College of Humanities and Fine Arts, Department of History, Amherst, MA 01003. Offers ancient history (MA); British Empire history (MA); European (medieval and modern) history (MA, PhD); Islamic history (MA); Latin American history (MA, PhD); modern global history (MA); public history (MA); science and technology history (MA); U.S. history (MA, PhD). Part-time programs available. Terminal master's awarded for partial completion of doctoral program. *Degree requirements:* For master's, one foreign language, thesis or alternative; for doctorate, one foreign language, comprehensive exam, thesis/dissertation. *Entrance requirements:* For master's and doctorate, GRE General Test, writing sample. Additional exam requirements/recommendations for international students: Required—TOEFL (minimum score 550 paper-based; 213 computer-based; 79 iBT), IELTS (minimum score 6.5). Electronic applications accepted. *Expenses:* Tuition, area resident: Full-time $2640. Tuition, nonresident: full-time $9936. One-time fee: $332 full-time. Tuition and fees vary according to course load. *Faculty research:* Ancient and medieval history; global and comparative history; public history; history of science, technology, medicine and the environment; history of women, gender, sexuality and family.

University of Minnesota, Twin Cities Campus, Institute of Technology, Program in History of Science and Technology, Minneapolis, MN 55455-0213. Offers MA, PhD. Terminal master's awarded for partial completion of doctoral program. *Degree requirements:* For master's, one foreign language; for doctorate, 2 foreign languages, thesis/dissertation. *Entrance requirements:* For master's and doctorate, GRE General Test. *Faculty research:* History of physics, biology, and technology.

University of Notre Dame, Graduate School, College of Arts and Letters, Division of Humanities, Program in History and Philosophy of Science, Notre Dame, IN 46556. Offers MA, PhD. *Faculty:* 24 full-time (6 women). *Students:* 20 full-time (10 women); includes 1 minority (Hispanic American), 3 international. 34 applicants, 21% accepted, 5 enrolled. In 2008, 3 master's, 3 doctorates awarded. *Degree requirements:* For doctorate, 2 foreign languages, comprehensive exam, thesis/dissertation, candidacy exam. *Entrance requirements:* For doctorate, GRE General Test. Additional exam requirements/recommendations for international students: Required—TOEFL (minimum score 600 paper-based; 250 computer-based; 80 iBT). *Application deadline:* For fall admission, 1/15 priority date for domestic students, 1/15 for international students. Application fee: $50. Electronic applications accepted. *Financial support:* Fellowships with full tuition reimbursements, research assistantships with full tuition reimbursements, teaching assistantships with full tuition reimbursements, scholarships/grants and tuition waivers (full) available. Financial award application deadline: 2/1. *Faculty research:* Philosophy of physics, science and ethics, history and philosophy of biology, history of medicine and technology, history and philosophy of economics. *Unit head:* Dr. Don Howard, Director of Graduate Studies, 574-631-5015. *Application contact:* Dr. Barbara Turpin, Director of Graduate Admissions, 574-631-7706, Fax: 574-631-4183.

University of Oklahoma, Graduate College, College of Arts and Sciences, Department of History of Science, Norman, OK 73019. Offers MA, PhD. *Faculty:* 13 full-time (6 women). *Students:* 12 full-time (4 women), 5 part-time (3 women); includes 1 minority (American Indian/Alaska Native). 12 applicants, 67% accepted, 3 enrolled. In 2008, 4 master's, 1 doctorate awarded. Terminal master's awarded for partial completion of doctoral program. *Degree requirements:* For master's, one foreign language, thesis (for some programs); for doctorate, 2 foreign languages, thesis/dissertation. *Entrance requirements:* For master's, GRE, minimum GPA of 3.0 in last 60 hours, 3 letters of reference, writing sample; for doctorate, GRE. Additional exam requirements/recommendations for international students: Required—TOEFL (minimum score 550 paper-based; 213 computer-based). *Application deadline:* For fall admission, 1/15 priority date for domestic students, 4/1 for international students; for spring admission, 11/1 for domestic students, 9/1 for international students. Application fee: $40 ($90 for international students). Electronic applications accepted. *Expenses:* Tuition, state resident: full-time $3744; part-time $156 per credit hour. Tuition, nonresident: full-time $13,577; part-time $565.70 per credit hour. Required fees: $2415.40; $90.10 per credit hour. *Financial support:* In 2008–09, 3 students received support, including 3 fellowships with full tuition reimbursements available (averaging $5,000 per year), 2 research assistantships (averaging $13,904 per year), 7 teaching assistantships with partial tuition reimbursements available (averaging $16,014 per year); institutionally sponsored loans, scholarships/grants, health care benefits, and unspecified assistantships also available. Financial award applicants required to submit FAFSA. *Faculty research:* Science and religion, Medieval and early modern science, history of technology, history of science in America, natural and social sciences in the modern world. Total annual research expenditures: $141,839. *Unit head:* Steven Livesey, Professor and Department Chair, 405-325-2213, Fax: 405-325-2363, E-mail: slivesey@ou.edu. *Application contact:* Steven J Livesy, Department Chair, 405-325-6490, Fax: 405-325-2363, E-mail: slivesey@ou.edu.

University of Pennsylvania, School of Arts and Sciences, Graduate Group in the History and Sociology of Science, Philadelphia, PA 19104. Offers AM, PhD. *Degree requirements:* For master's, thesis or alternative; for doctorate, 2 foreign languages, thesis/dissertation. *Entrance requirements:* For master's and doctorate, GRE General Test. Additional exam requirements/recommendations for international students: Required—TOEFL. Electronic applications accepted.

University of Pittsburgh, School of Arts and Sciences, Department of History and Philosophy of Science, Pittsburgh, PA 15260. Offers MA, PhD. Terminal master's awarded for partial completion of doctoral program. *Degree requirements:* For master's, one foreign language, comprehensive exam; for doctorate, 2 foreign languages, comprehensive exam, thesis/dissertation. *Entrance requirements:* For master's and doctorate, GRE General Test. Additional exam requirements/recommendations for international students: Required—TOEFL (minimum score 550 paper-based; 213 computer-based). Electronic applications accepted. *Faculty research:* History and philosophy of biology, psychology, neuroscience; history and philosophy of physics; early modern science; rhetoric of science; philosophy of social science.

University of Toronto, School of Graduate Studies, Humanities Division, Institute for the History and Philosophy of Science and Technology, Toronto, ON M5S 1A1, Canada. Offers

MA, PhD. Part-time programs available. *Degree requirements:* For master's, one foreign language, thesis optional, reading ability in French or German; for doctorate, 2 foreign languages, thesis/dissertation, reading knowledge examinations, thesis defense. *Entrance requirements:* For master's, 2 letters of reference; for doctorate, 2 letters of reference, MA in history and philosophy of science and technology, minimum A– average. Additional exam requirements/recommendations for international students: Required—TOEFL (minimum score 580 paper-based; 237 computer-based), TWE (minimum score 5).

University of Wisconsin–Madison, Graduate School, College of Letters and Science, Department of History of Science, Madison, WI 53706-1380. Offers history of medicine (MA); history of science (MA, PhD). Terminal master's awarded for partial completion of doctoral program. *Degree requirements:* For master's, thesis; for doctorate, 2 foreign languages, thesis/dissertation. *Entrance requirements:* For master's and doctorate, GRE General Test. Electronic applications accepted. *Faculty research:* History of biology, physical sciences, technology, medicine.

Virginia Polytechnic Institute and State University, Graduate School, College of Liberal Arts and Human Sciences, Program in Science and Technology Studies, Blacksburg, VA 24061. Offers MS, PhD. *Entrance requirements:* Additional exam requirements/recommendations for international students: Required—TOEFL (minimum score 550 paper-based; 213 computer-based). Electronic applications accepted.

West Virginia University, Eberly College of Arts and Sciences, Department of History, Morgantown, WV 26506. Offers African history (MA, PhD); African-American history (MA, PhD); American history (MA, PhD); Appalachian/regional history (MA, PhD); East Asian history (MA, PhD); European history (MA, PhD); history of science and technology (MA, PhD); Latin American history (MA). Part-time programs available. *Degree requirements:* For master's, one foreign language, thesis (for some programs), oral exam, thesis defense; for doctorate, one foreign language, comprehensive exam, thesis/dissertation, dissertation defense. *Entrance requirements:* For master's, GRE General Test, minimum GPA of 3.0; for doctorate, GRE General Test. Additional exam requirements/recommendations for international students: Required—TOEFL (minimum score 550 paper-based), IELTS (minimum score 6.5). Electronic applications accepted. *Faculty research:* U.S., Appalachia, modern Europe, Africa, colonial and post-colonial societies.

Yale University, Graduate School of Arts and Sciences, Department of History, Program in the History of Medicine and the Life Sciences, New Haven, CT 06520. Offers MS, PhD. *Degree requirements:* For doctorate, 2 foreign languages, thesis/dissertation. *Entrance requirements:* For doctorate, GRE General Test.

Medieval and Renaissance Studies

California State University, Long Beach, Graduate Studies, College of Liberal Arts, Department of History, Long Beach, CA 90840. Offers Africa and the Middle East (MA); ancient/Medieval Europe (MA); Asia (MA); Latin America (MA); modern Europe (MA); United States (MA); world (MA). Part-time and evening/weekend programs available. *Faculty:* 17 full-time (11 women), 2 part-time/adjunct (1 woman). *Students:* 9 full-time (4 women), 45 part-time (18 women); includes 15 minority (2 African Americans, 3 Asian Americans or Pacific Islanders, 10 Hispanic Americans), 1 international. Average age 35. 40 applicants, 50% accepted, 11 enrolled. *Degree requirements:* For master's, one foreign language, comprehensive exam or thesis. *Application deadline:* For fall admission, 3/1 for domestic students. Applications are processed on a rolling basis. Application fee: $55. Electronic applications accepted. *Expenses:* Tuition, nonresident: full-time $11,160; part-time $372 per unit. Required fees: $4100; $1261 per semester. *Financial support:* Research assistantships, Federal Work-Study, institutionally sponsored loans, and scholarships/grants available. Financial award application deadline: 3/2. *Faculty research:* All periods of European and American history, recent Asian and African history. *Unit head:* Dr. Nancy L Quam-Wickham, Graduate Advisor, 562-985-4431, Fax: 562-985-5431, E-mail: quamwick@csulb.edu. *Application contact:* Dr. Houri Berberian, Graduate Advisor, 562-985-4524, Fax: 562-985-4431, E-mail: hberber@csulb.edu.

The Catholic University of America, School of Arts and Sciences, Department of History, Washington, DC 20064. Offers MA, PhD, JD/MA, MSLS/MA. Part-time programs available. *Degree requirements:* For master's, one foreign language, comprehensive exam, thesis or alternative; for doctorate, 2 foreign languages, comprehensive exam, thesis/dissertation, oral exams. *Entrance requirements:* For master's and doctorate, GRE General Test, 3 letters of recommendation. Additional exam requirements/recommendations for international students: Required—TOEFL (minimum score 580 paper-based; 237 computer-based). Electronic applications accepted. *Faculty research:* Medieval family law, U.S. liberalism, capitalism in Europe, Mexican rural society, urbanization in France.

The Catholic University of America, School of Arts and Sciences, Program in Medieval and Byzantine Studies, Washington, DC 20064. Offers Byzantine studies (MA, Certificate); medieval studies (MA, PhD, Certificate). Part-time programs available. Terminal master's awarded for partial completion of doctoral program. *Degree requirements:* For master's, 2 foreign languages, comprehensive exam, thesis or alternative; for doctorate, 3 foreign languages, comprehensive exam, thesis/dissertation. *Entrance requirements:* For master's and doctorate, GRE General Test, 3 letters of recommendation, writing sample. Additional exam requirements/recommendations for international students: Required—TOEFL (minimum score 580 paper-based; 237 computer-based). Electronic applications accepted.

Central European University, Graduate Studies, School of Social Sciences and Humanities, Budapest, Hungary. Offers economics (MA, PhD); gender studies (MA, PhD); international relations and European studies (MA, PhD); mathematics and its applications (MS, PhD); medieval studies (MA, PhD); nationalism studies (MA, PhD); philosophy (MA, PhD); political science (MA, PhD); public policy (MA, PhD); sociology and social anthropology (MA, PhD). Terminal master's awarded for partial completion of doctoral program. *Degree requirements:* For master's, one foreign language, thesis; for doctorate, one foreign language, comprehensive exam, thesis/dissertation. *Entrance requirements:* For master's, CEU subject tests, interview; for doctorate, GRE, CEU subject test, interview. Additional exam requirements/recommendations for international students: Required—TOEFL (minimum score 570 paper-based; 230 computer-based). Electronic applications accepted. *Faculty research:* Civil society, fiscal decentralization, party politics, political philosophy (especially Liberalism, theory of Democracy).

See Close-Up on page 349.

Columbia University, Graduate School of Arts and Sciences, Program in Liberal Studies, New York, NY 10027. Offers American studies (MA); East Asian studies (MA); human rights studies (MA); Islamic culture studies (MA); Jewish studies (MA); medieval studies (MA); modern European studies (MA); South Asian studies (MA). Part-time and evening/weekend programs available. *Degree requirements:* For master's, thesis.

Cornell University, Graduate School, Graduate Fields of Arts and Sciences, Field of Archaeology, Ithaca, NY 14853-0001. Offers environmental archaeology (MA); historical archaeology (MA); Latin American archaeology (MA); medieval archaeology (MA); Mediterranean and Near Eastern archaeology (MA); Stone Age archaeology (MA). *Faculty:* 12 full-time (3 women). *Students:* 4 full-time (3 women). Average age 27. 10 applicants, 40% accepted, 2 enrolled. *Degree requirements:* For master's, one foreign language, thesis. *Entrance requirements:* For master's, GRE General Test, 3 letters of recommendation, sample of written work. Additional exam requirements/recommendations for international students: Required—TOEFL (minimum score 550 paper-based; 213 computer-based; 77 iBT). *Application deadline:* For fall admission, 1/15 for domestic students. Application fee: $70. Electronic applications accepted. *Expenses:* Tuition: Full-time $29,500. Required fees: $70. Full-time tuition and fees vary according to degree level, program and student level. *Financial support:* In 2008–09, 4 students received support, including 1 fellowship with full tuition reimbursement available, 1 research assistantship with full tuition reimbursement available, 2 teaching assistantships with full tuition reimbursements available; institutionally sponsored loans, scholarships/grants, health care benefits, tuition waivers (full and partial), and unspecified assistantships also available. Financial award applicants required to submit FAFSA. *Faculty research:* Anatolia, Lydia, Sardis, classical and Hellenistic Greece; science in archaeology; North American Indians; Stone Age Africa; Maya trade. *Unit head:* Director of Graduate Studies, 607-255-6768, E-mail: blj7@cornell.edu. *Application contact:* Graduate Field Assistant, 607-255-6768, E-mail: dsd6@cornell.edu.

Cornell University, Graduate School, Graduate Fields of Arts and Sciences, Field of English Language and Literature, Ithaca, NY 14853-0001. Offers African-American literature (PhD); American literature after 1865 (PhD); American literature to 1865 (PhD); American studies (PhD); colonial and postcolonial literature (PhD); creative writing (MFA); cultural studies (PhD); dramatic literature (PhD); English poetry (PhD); English Renaissance to 1660 (PhD); lesbian, bisexual, and gay literature studies (PhD); literary criticism and theory (PhD); nineteenth century (PhD); Old and Middle English (PhD); prose fiction (PhD); Restoration and eighteenth century (PhD); twentieth century (PhD); women's literature (PhD); MFA/PhD. *Faculty:* 54 full-time (27 women). *Students:* 100 full-time (53 women); includes 24 minority (8 African Americans, 4 American Indian/Alaska Native, 6 Asian Americans or Pacific Islanders, 6 Hispanic Americans), 14 international. Average age 29. 821 applicants, 6% accepted, 23 enrolled. In 2008, 19 master's, 12 doctorates awarded. Terminal master's awarded for partial completion of doctoral program. *Degree requirements:* For master's, one foreign language, thesis; for doctorate, one foreign language, comprehensive exam, thesis/dissertation, teaching experience. *Entrance requirements:* For master's, GRE General Test, 3 letters of recommendation, creative writing sample; for doctorate, GRE General Test, GRE Subject Test (English), 3 letters of recommendation, writing sample. Additional exam requirements/recommendations for international students: Required—TOEFL (minimum score 600 paper-based; 250 computer-based; 77 iBT). *Application deadline:* For fall admission, 1/10 for domestic students. Application fee: $70. Electronic applications accepted. *Expenses:* Tuition: Full-time $29,500. Required fees: $70. Full-time tuition and fees vary according to degree level, program and student level. *Financial support:* In 2008–09, 96 students received support, including 41 fellowships with full tuition reimbursements available, 1 research assistantship with full tuition reimbursement available, 54 teaching assistantships with full tuition reimbursements available; institutionally sponsored loans, scholarships/grants, health care benefits, tuition waivers (full and partial), and unspecified assistantships also available. Financial award applicants required to submit FAFSA. *Faculty research:* English and American literature, women's writing, ethnic and post-colonial literature, critical theory, medievalism. *Unit head:* Director of Graduate Studies, 607-255-7989, Fax: 607-255-6661. *Application contact:* Graduate Field Assistant, 607-255-7989, Fax: 607-255-6661, E-mail: english_grad@cornell.edu.

Cornell University, Graduate School, Graduate Fields of Arts and Sciences, Field of History, Ithaca, NY 14853-0001. Offers African history (MA, PhD); American history (MA, PhD); ancient history (MA, PhD); early modern European history (MA, PhD); English history (MA, PhD); French history (MA, PhD); German history (MA, PhD); history of science (MA, PhD); Latin American history (MA, PhD); medieval Chinese history (MA, PhD); medieval history (MA, PhD); modern Chinese history (MA, PhD); modern European history (MA, PhD); modern Japanese history (MA, PhD); premodern Islamic history (MA, PhD); premodern Japanese history (MA, PhD); Renaissance history (MA, PhD); Russian history (MA, PhD); Southeast Asian history (MA, PhD). *Faculty:* 54 full-time (14 women). *Students:* 65 full-time (35 women); includes 12 minority (4 African Americans, 3 Asian Americans or Pacific Islanders, 5 Hispanic Americans), 19 international. Average age 31. 205 applicants, 8% accepted, 11 enrolled. In 2008, 12 master's, 6 doctorates awarded. Terminal master's awarded for partial completion of doctoral program. *Degree requirements:* For master's, thesis; for doctorate, 2 foreign languages, comprehensive exam, thesis/dissertation, 1 year of teaching experience. *Entrance requirements:* For master's and doctorate, GRE General Test, writing sample, 3 letters of recommendation. Additional exam requirements/recommendations for international students: Required—TOEFL (minimum score 550 paper-based; 213 computer-based; 77 iBT). *Application deadline:* For fall admission, 1/15 for domestic students. Application fee: $70. Electronic applications accepted. *Expenses:* Tuition: Full-time $29,500. Required fees: $70. Full-time tuition and fees vary according to degree level, program and student level. *Financial support:* In 2008–09, 54 students received support, including 27 fellowships with full tuition reimbursements available, 3 research assistantships with full tuition reimbursements available, 24 teaching assistantships with full tuition reimbursements available; institutionally sponsored loans, scholarships/grants, health care benefits, tuition waivers (full and partial), and unspecified assistantships also available. Financial award applicants required to submit FAFSA. *Unit head:* Director of Graduate Studies, 607-255-6738, Fax: 607-255-0469. *Application contact:* Graduate Field Assistant, 607-255-6738, Fax: 607-255-0469, E-mail: history_grad_info@cornell.edu.

Cornell University, Graduate School, Graduate Fields of Arts and Sciences, Field of History of Art and Archaeology, Ithaca, NY 14853. Offers American art (PhD); ancient art and archaeology (PhD); Asian art (PhD); baroque art (PhD); medieval art (PhD); modern art (PhD); Renaissance art (PhD); Southeast Asian art (PhD); theory and criticism (PhD). *Faculty:* 17 full-time (11 women). *Students:* 23 full-time (19 women); includes 4 minority (1 African American, 2 Asian Americans or Pacific Islanders, 1 Hispanic American), 7 international. Average age 33. 76 applicants, 8% accepted, 4 enrolled. In 2008, 1 doctorate awarded. *Degree requirements:* For doctorate, one foreign language, comprehensive exam, thesis/dissertation, general exams in 3 areas. *Entrance requirements:* For doctorate, GRE General Test, sample of written work, 3 letters of recommendation. Additional exam requirements/recommendations for international students: Required—TOEFL (minimum score 550 paper-based; 213 computer-based; 77 iBT). *Application deadline:* For fall admission, 1/15 for domestic students. Application fee: $70. Electronic applications accepted. *Expenses:* Tuition: Full-time $29,500. Required fees: $70. Full-time tuition and fees vary according to degree level, program and student level. *Financial support:* In 2008–09, 17 students received support, including 10 fellowships with full tuition reimbursements available, 1 research assistantship with full tuition reimbursement available, 6 teaching assistantships with full tuition reimbursements available; institutionally sponsored loans, scholarships/grants, health care benefits, tuition waivers (full and partial), and unspecified assistantships also available. Financial award applicants required to submit FAFSA. *Unit head:* Director of Graduate Studies, 607-255-4905, Fax: 607-255-0566, E-mail: art_history@cornell.edu. *Application contact:* Graduate Field Assistant, 607-255-4905, Fax: 607-255-0566, E-mail: art_history@cornell.edu.

Cornell University, Graduate School, Graduate Fields of Arts and Sciences, Field of Medieval Studies, Ithaca, NY 14853-0001. Offers medieval archaeology (PhD); medieval art (PhD);

Medieval and Renaissance Studies

Cornell University (continued)
medieval history (PhD); medieval literature (PhD); medieval music (PhD); medieval philology and linguistics (PhD); medieval philosophy (PhD). *Faculty:* 32 full-time (11 women). *Students:* 14 full-time (9 women), 1 international. Average age 30. 45 applicants, 11% accepted, 1 enrolled. In 2008, 3 doctorates awarded. *Degree requirements:* For doctorate, 3 foreign languages, comprehensive exam, thesis/dissertation, teaching experience. *Entrance requirements:* For doctorate, GRE General Test, 3 letters of recommendation, proficiency in Latin (recommended), 20 page writing sample on a Medieval topic. Additional exam requirements/recommendations for international students: Required—TOEFL (minimum score 600 paper-based; 250 computer-based; 77 iBT). *Application deadline:* For fall admission, 1/15 for domestic students. Application fee: $70. Electronic applications accepted. *Expenses:* Tuition: Full-time $29,500. Required fees: $70. Full-time tuition and fees vary according to degree level, program and student level. *Financial support:* In 2008–09, 14 students received support, including 5 fellowships with full tuition reimbursements available, 9 teaching assistantships with full tuition reimbursements available; research assistantships with full tuition reimbursements available, institutionally sponsored loans, scholarships/grants, health care benefits, tuition waivers (full and partial), and unspecified assistantships also available. Financial award applicants required to submit FAFSA. *Faculty research:* Interdisciplinary study of medieval culture, languages, literatures, history, archaeology. *Unit head:* Director of Graduate Studies, 607-255-8545. *Application contact:* Graduate Field Assistant, 607-255-8545, E-mail: medievalst@cornell.edu.

Duke University, Graduate School, Program in Medieval and Renaissance Studies, Durham, NC 27708. Offers Certificate.

Fordham University, Graduate School of Arts and Sciences, Center for Medieval Studies, New York, NY 10458. Offers MA, Certificate. Part-time and evening/weekend programs available. *Degree requirements:* For master's, thesis. *Entrance requirements:* For master's, GRE General Test. Additional exam requirements/recommendations for international students: Required—TOEFL (minimum score 650 paper-based; 280 computer-based). Electronic applications accepted. *Faculty research:* Medieval literature, Medieval history, Medieval philosophy, Medieval theology, Medieval fine arts, Anglo-Norman.

Georgetown University, Graduate School of Arts and Sciences, School of Continuing Studies, Washington, DC 20057. Offers American studies (MALS); Catholic studies (MALS); classical civilizations (MALS); ethics and the professions (MALS); human resources management (MPS); humanities (MALS); individualized study (MALS); international affairs (MALS); Islam and Muslim-Christian relations (MALS); journalism (MPS); liberal studies (DLS); literature and society (MALS); medieval and early modern European studies (MALS); public relations (MPS); real estate (MPS); religious studies (MALS); social and public policy (MALS); sports industry management (MPS); the theory and practice of American democracy (MALS); visual culture (MALS). *Entrance requirements:* Additional exam requirements/recommendations for international students: Required—TOEFL.

Graduate School and University Center of the City University of New York, Graduate Studies, Interdisciplinary Studies, New York, NY 10016-4039. Offers language in social context (PhD); medieval studies (PhD); public policy (MA, PhD); urban studies (MA, PhD); women's studies (MA, PhD). Terminal master's awarded for partial completion of doctoral program. *Degree requirements:* For master's, thesis; for doctorate, comprehensive exam, thesis/dissertation. *Entrance requirements:* For master's and doctorate, GRE General Test.

Harvard University, Graduate School of Arts and Sciences, Department of English and American Literature and Language, Cambridge, MA 02138. Offers critical theory (PhD); eighteenth-century literature (PhD); literature: nineteenth-century to the present (PhD); medieval literature and language (PhD); modern British and American literature (PhD); Renaissance literature (PhD). Terminal master's awarded for partial completion of doctoral program. *Degree requirements:* For doctorate, 2 foreign languages, thesis/dissertation, oral exam. *Entrance requirements:* For doctorate, GRE General Test, GRE Subject Test, writing sample. Additional exam requirements/recommendations for international students: Required—TOEFL. *Expenses:* Tuition: Full-time $32,556. Required fees: $1426. Full-time tuition and fees vary according to program and student level. *Faculty research:* Old and Middle English language and literature, drama, creative writing, transition to Romanticism, history and theory of criticism.

Indiana University Bloomington, University Graduate School, College of Arts and Sciences, Department of Germanic Studies, Bloomington, IN 47405-7000. Offers German philology and linguistics (PhD); German studies (MA, PhD), including German (MA), German literature and culture (MA), German literature and linguistics (MA); medieval German studies (PhD); teaching German (MAT). *Faculty:* 13 full-time (4 women), 6 part-time/adjunct (2 women). *Students:* 33 full-time (16 women), 4 part-time (2 women); includes 1 minority (Hispanic American), 9 international. Average age 30. 38 applicants, 29% accepted, 3 enrolled. In 2008, 6 master's, 3 doctorates awarded. Terminal master's awarded for partial completion of doctoral program. *Degree requirements:* For master's, one foreign language, project; for doctorate, one foreign language, comprehensive exam, thesis/dissertation. *Entrance requirements:* For master's, GRE General Test, BA in German or equivalent; for doctorate, GRE General Test, MA in German or equivalent. Additional exam requirements/recommendations for international students: Required—TOEFL. *Application deadline:* For fall admission, 1/15 priority date for domestic students, 12/15 for international students; for spring admission, 9/1 priority date for domestic students, 9/1 for international students. Applications are processed on a rolling basis. Application fee: $50 ($60 for international students). *Expenses:* Tuition, area resident: Part-time $291.97 per credit hour. Tuition, state resident: part-time $291.97 per credit hour. Tuition, nonresident: part-time $850.33 per credit hour. Required fees: $110 per semester. Tuition and fees vary according to course load and program. *Financial support:* In 2008–09, 7 fellowships with full and partial tuition reimbursements (averaging $20,000 per year), 1 research assistantship (averaging $13,025 per year), 22 teaching assistantships with full tuition reimbursements (averaging $13,025 per year) were awarded; Federal Work-Study, institutionally sponsored loans, scholarships/grants, and unspecified assistantships also available. Support available to part-time students. Financial award application deadline: 1/15; financial award applicants required to submit FAFSA. *Faculty research:* German (and European) literature: medieval to modern/postmodern, German and culture studies, Germanic philology, literary theory, literature and the other arts. *Unit head:* William Rasch, Department Chairman, 812-855-7947, Fax: 812-855-8292, E-mail: wrasch@indiana.edu. *Application contact:* Michelle Dunbar, Graduate Secretary, 812-855-7947, E-mail: midunbar@indiana.edu.

Marquette University, Graduate School, College of Arts and Sciences, Department of History, Milwaukee, WI 53201-1881. Offers European history (MA, PhD); medieval history (MA); Renaissance and Reformation (MA); United States history (MA, PhD). Part-time programs available. Terminal master's awarded for partial completion of doctoral program. *Degree requirements:* For master's, comprehensive exam, thesis or alternative; for doctorate, one foreign language, thesis/dissertation, qualifying exam. *Entrance requirements:* For master's, GRE General Test, GRE Subject Test; for doctorate, GRE General Test, writing sample. Additional exam requirements/recommendations for international students: Required—TOEFL. *Faculty research:* Social history, political history, diplomatic history, history of science, religious history.

Rutgers, The State University of New Jersey, New Brunswick, Graduate School, Program in History, Piscataway, NJ 08854-8097. Offers African-American history (PhD); early American history (PhD); early modern European history (PhD); east Asian history (PhD); global and comparative history (PhD); history (PhD); history of diplomacy and foreign relations (PhD); history of technology, environment and health (PhD); history of the Atlantic cultures and African diaspora (PhD); Latin American history (PhD); medieval history (PhD); modern European history (PhD); nineteenth and twentieth century American history (PhD); women's and gender history (PhD). *Degree requirements:* For doctorate, thesis/dissertation. *Entrance requirements:* For doctorate, GRE General Test, sample of written work. Electronic applications accepted. *Faculty research:* American history, European history, Afro-American history, women's history, Latin American history.

Southern Methodist University, Dedman College, Program in Medieval Studies, Dallas, TX 75275. Offers MA. Part-time programs available. *Students:* 2 part-time (1 woman). Average age 28. In 2008, 3 master's awarded. *Degree requirements:* For master's, 2 foreign languages, thesis. *Entrance requirements:* For master's, GRE General Test, minimum GPA of 3.0. *Application deadline:* Applications are processed on a rolling basis. Application fee: $60. Electronic applications accepted. *Financial support:* Federal Work-Study and institutionally sponsored loans available. *Faculty research:* Byzantine culture, medieval Europe, Arthurian literature, Chaucer, Romance. *Unit head:* Dr. Bonnie Wheeler, Director, 214-768-2949, Fax: 214-768-1234, E-mail: bwheeler@smu.edu. *Application contact:* Barbara Phillips, Assistant Dean, 214-768-4202, Fax: 214-768-4235, E-mail: bphillips@smu.edu.

University of California, Santa Barbara, Graduate Division, College of Letters and Sciences, Division of Humanities and Fine Arts, Department of French and Italian, Santa Barbara, CA 93106-4140. Offers French (MA, MABL, PhD), including applied linguistics (PhD), European Medieval studies (PhD), feminist studies (PhD), French (MABL, PhD); MA/PhD. French Language Institute available during summer sessions. *Faculty:* 21 full-time (12 women). *Students:* 11 full-time (7 women). Average age 31. 16 applicants, 63% accepted, 3 enrolled. In 2008, 1 master's, 5 doctorates awarded. Terminal master's awarded for partial completion of doctoral program. *Degree requirements:* For master's, 2 foreign languages, comprehensive exam; for doctorate, 2 foreign languages, comprehensive exam, thesis/dissertation. *Entrance requirements:* For master's, GRE, sample of written work, tape of spoken French, BA or the equivalent, 3 letters of recommendation, statement of purpose, personal achievements/contributions statement, resumé/curriculum vitae, transcripts for post-secondary institutions attended; for doctorate, GRE, sample of written work, tape of spoken French, MA or the equivalent, 3 letters of recommendation, statement of purpose, personal achievements/contributions statement, resumé/curriculum vitae, transcripts for post-secondary institutions attended. Additional exam requirements/recommendations for international students: Required—TOEFL (paper: 550, computer: 213, IBT: 80) or IELTS (7). *Application deadline:* For fall admission, 5/1 for domestic and international students; for winter admission, 10/1 for domestic and international students; for spring admission, 1/15 for domestic and international students. Application fee: $70 ($90 for international students). Electronic applications accepted. *Expenses:* Tuition, nonresident: full-time $25,149. Required fees: $10,143. Full-time tuition and fees vary according to campus/location, reciprocity agreements and student level. *Financial support:* In 2008–09, 11 students received support, including 5 fellowships with full and partial tuition reimbursements available (averaging $8,100 per year), 11 teaching assistantships with partial tuition reimbursements available (averaging $11,400 per year); career-related internships or fieldwork, Federal Work-Study, institutionally sponsored loans, scholarships/grants, traineeships, health care benefits, tuition waivers (full and partial), and unspecified assistantships also available. Financial award applicants required to submit FAFSA. *Faculty research:* French and Francophone studies, comparative literature, second language acquisition, applied linguistics, performance studies, feminist and gender studies. Total annual research expenditures: $2,500. *Unit head:* Prof. Jon Snyder, Chair, 805-893-2220, Fax: 805-893-8826, E-mail: snyder@frit.ucsb.edu. *Application contact:* Rosa Pinter, Graduate Staff Advisor, 805-893-3398, Fax: 805-893-8826, E-mail: pinter@frit.ucsb.edu.

University of California, Santa Barbara, Graduate Division, College of Letters and Sciences, Division of Humanities and Fine Arts, Department of Religious Studies, Santa Barbara, CA 93106-3130. Offers European Medieval studies (PhD); feminist studies (PhD); global studies (PhD); religious studies (MA, PhD); MA/PhD. *Faculty:* 18 full-time (8 women), 11 part-time/adjunct (5 women). *Students:* 86 full-time (33 women). Average age 31. 151 applicants, 31% accepted, 17 enrolled. In 2008, 7 master's, 6 doctorates awarded. Terminal master's awarded for partial completion of doctoral program. *Degree requirements:* For master's, one foreign language, comprehensive exam (for some programs), thesis (for some programs); for doctorate, one foreign language, thesis/dissertation. *Entrance requirements:* For master's, GRE General Test; for doctorate, GRE General Test, MA in related field, 3 letters of recommendation, statement of purpose, personal achievements/contributions statement, resumé/curriculum vitae, transcripts for post-secondary institutions attended. Additional exam requirements/recommendations for international students: Required—TOEFL (paper: 550, computer: 213, IBT: 80) or IELTS (7). *Application deadline:* For fall admission, 12/1 for domestic and international students. Application fee: $70 ($90 for international students). Electronic applications accepted. *Expenses:* Tuition, nonresident: full-time $25,149. Required fees: $10,143. Full-time tuition and fees vary according to campus/location, reciprocity agreements and student level. *Financial support:* In 2008–09, 67 students received support, including 29 fellowships with full and partial tuition reimbursements available (averaging $12,600 per year), 5 research assistantships with full and partial tuition reimbursements available (averaging $7,900 per year), 46 teaching assistantships with partial tuition reimbursements available (averaging $8,400 per year); career-related internships or fieldwork, Federal Work-Study, institutionally sponsored loans, scholarships/grants, traineeships, health care benefits, tuition waivers (full and partial), and unspecified assistantships also available. Financial award application deadline: 12/1; financial award applicants required to submit FAFSA. *Faculty research:* Religion and politics, religion and violence, contemporary spirituality, religious traditions, theoretical approaches to the study of religion, area studies. *Unit head:* Prof. Catherine L. Albanese, Chair, 805-893-3564, Fax: 805-893-2059, E-mail: albanese@religion.ucsb.edu. *Application contact:* Sally J. Lombrozo, Graduate Program Assistant, 805-893-2744, Fax: 805-893-2059, E-mail: lombrozo@religion.ucsb.edu.

University of California, Santa Barbara, Graduate Division, College of Letters and Sciences, Division of Humanities and Fine Arts, Department of Spanish and Portuguese, Santa Barbara, CA 93106-4150. Offers Hispanic languages and literature (PhD), including applied linguistics, European Medieval studies, feminist studies, Hispanic languages and literature; Portuguese (MA); Spanish (MA); Spanish and Portuguese (MA); MA/PhD. Spanish Language Institute available during summer session. *Faculty:* 16 full-time (6 women). *Students:* 29 full-time (16 women). Average age 30. 46 applicants, 39% accepted, 9 enrolled. In 2008, 4 master's, 2 doctorates awarded. *Degree requirements:* For master's, 2 foreign languages, comprehensive exam (for some programs), thesis optional; for doctorate, 2 foreign languages, comprehensive exam, thesis/dissertation. *Entrance requirements:* For master's, GRE, 2 writing samples, undergraduate major in Spanish or equivalent, 3 letters of recommendation, statement of purpose, personal achievements/contributions statement, resumé/curriculum vitae, transcripts for post-secondary institutions attended; for doctorate, GRE, 2 writing samples, master's degree, 3 letters of recommendation, statement of purpose, personal achievements/contributions statement, resumé/curriculum vitae, transcripts for post-secondary institutions attended. Additional exam requirements/recommendations for international students: Required—TOEFL (minimum score 550 paper-based; 213 computer-based; 80 iBT), IELTS (minimum score 7), TOEFL or IELTS. *Application deadline:* For fall admission, 3/1 for domestic and international students; for winter admission, 11/1 for domestic and international students; for spring admission, 2/1 for domestic and international students. Application fee: $70 ($90 for international students). Electronic applications accepted. *Expenses:* Tuition, nonresident: full-time $25,149. Required fees: $10,143. Full-time tuition and fees vary according to campus/location, reciprocity agreements and student level. *Financial support:* In 2008–09, 30 students received support, including 9 fellowships with full and partial tuition reimbursements available (averaging $7,000 per year), 29 teaching assistantships with partial tuition reimbursements available (averaging $11,500 per year); career-related internships or fieldwork, Federal Work-Study, institutionally sponsored loans, scholarships/grants, health care benefits, tuition waivers (full and partial), and unspecified assistantships also available. Financial award application deadline: 1/7; financial award applicants required to submit FAFSA. *Faculty research:* 19th century Spanish and Portuguese literature, Spanish and Spanish American literature, 19th and 20th century Portuguese and Brazilian literatures, Hispanic Linguistics, Catalan language and culture. *Unit head:* Prof. Francisco A. Lomeli, Chair, 805-893-5715, Fax: 805-893-8341, E-mail: lomeli@spanport.ucsb.edu. *Application contact:* Carol Conley, Graduate Program Assistant, 805-893-3162, Fax: 805-893-8341, E-mail: cconley@spanport.ucsb.edu.

University of California, Santa Barbara, Graduate Division, College of Letters and Sciences, Division of Humanities and Fine Arts, Department of Theatre and Dance, Santa Barbara, CA 93106-7060. Offers theater studies (MA, PhD), including European Medieval studies (PhD), feminist studies (PhD), theater studies (PhD); MA/PhD. *Faculty:* 7 full-time (3 women), 1 (woman) part-time/adjunct. *Students:* 22 full-time (15 women). Average age 33. 22 applicants, 36% accepted, 5 enrolled. In 2008, 3 master's, 5 doctorates awarded. Terminal master's awarded for partial completion of doctoral program. *Degree requirements:* For master's, variable foreign language requirement, comprehensive exam, thesis; for doctorate, one foreign language, comprehensive exam, thesis/dissertation. *Entrance requirements:* For master's and doctorate, GRE, sample of written work, 3 letters of recommendation, statement of purpose, personal achievements/contributions statement, resumé/curriculum vitae, transcripts for post-secondary institutions attended. Additional exam requirements/recommendations for international students: Required—TOEFL (paper: 550, computer: 213, IBT: 80) or IELTS (7). *Application deadline:* For fall admission, 1/5 for domestic and international students. Application fee: $70 ($90 for international students). Electronic applications accepted. *Expenses:* Tuition, nonresident: full-time $25,149. Required fees: $10,143. Full-time tuition and fees vary according to campus/location, reciprocity agreements and student level. *Financial support:* In 2008–09, 23 students received support, including 13 fellowships with full and partial tuition reimbursements available (averaging $11,600 per year), 29 teaching assistantships with partial tuition reimbursements available (averaging $11,500 per year); Federal Work-Study, scholarships/grants, traineeships, health care benefits, and unspecified assistantships also available. Support available to part-time students. Financial award application deadline: 1/5; financial award applicants required to submit FAFSA. *Faculty research:* Spanish/Latin American drama, performance studies and European theatre history, East Asian and Russian studies, playwriting, Medieval theatre. *Unit head:* Prof. Simon Williams, Chair, 805-893-5515, Fax: 805-893-7029, E-mail: williams@theaterdance.ucsb.edu. *Application contact:* Mary Tench, Graduate Program Assistant, 805-893-3147, Fax: 805-893-7029, E-mail: mtench@theaterdance.ucsb.edu.

University of Colorado at Boulder, Graduate School, College of Arts and Sciences, Department of Spanish and Portuguese, Boulder, CO 80309. Offers Hispanic linguistics (MA); medieval/early modern Hispanic literatures (PhD); Spanish literature (MA, PhD), including 18th and 19th century peninsular literature (MA), Golden Age (MA), medieval Iberian literature (MA). Part-time programs available. Terminal master's awarded for partial completion of doctoral program. *Degree requirements:* For master's, one foreign language, comprehensive exam, thesis or alternative; for doctorate, 2 foreign languages, thesis/dissertation. *Entrance requirements:* For master's, minimum undergraduate GPA of 2.75. *Faculty research:* Spanish peninsular and Spanish-American literatures; Hispanic linguistics; Medieval, Golden Age, eighteenth and nineteenth century literatures.

University of Connecticut, Graduate School, College of Liberal Arts and Sciences, Field of Medieval Studies, Storrs, CT 06269. Offers MA, PhD. Terminal master's awarded for partial completion of doctoral program. *Degree requirements:* For master's, comprehensive exam; for doctorate, 3 foreign languages, thesis/dissertation. *Entrance requirements:* For master's and doctorate, GRE General Test, GRE Subject Test. Additional exam requirements/recommendations for international students: Required—TOEFL (minimum score 550 paper-based; 213 computer-based). Electronic applications accepted.

University of Guelph, Graduate Program Services, College of Arts, School of English and Theatre Studies, Joint Program in Literary Studies/Theatre Studies in English, Guelph, ON N1G 2W1, Canada. Offers PhD. Part-time programs available. *Degree requirements:* For doctorate, one foreign language, comprehensive exam, thesis/dissertation. *Entrance requirements:* For doctorate, MA, 3 letters of reference, writing samples, resumé, minimum A- average in graduate course work. Additional exam requirements/recommendations for international students: Required—TOEFL. Electronic applications accepted. *Faculty research:* Canadian studies, Early Modern studies, Postcolonial studies, studies in gender and genre, 19th Century studies.

University of Michigan, Horace H. Rackham School of Graduate Studies, College of Literature, Science, and the Arts, Program in Medieval and Early Modern Studies, Ann Arbor, MI 48109. Offers Certificate. *Entrance requirements:* For degree, acceptance by Rackham Graduate School and A- average grade.

University of Minnesota, Twin Cities Campus, Graduate School, College of Liberal Arts, Department of German, Scandinavian, and Dutch, Minneapolis, MN 55455-0213. Offers Germanic studies: German and Scandinavian studies track (PhD); Germanic studies: German track (MA, PhD); Germanic studies: Germanic medieval studies track (MA, PhD); Germanic studies: Scandinavian studies track (MA); Germanic studies: teaching track (MA). Part-time programs available. Terminal master's awarded for partial completion of doctoral program. *Degree requirements:* For doctorate, 2 foreign languages, thesis/dissertation. *Entrance requirements:* For master's, GRE General Test, BA in German, Scandinavian, or equivalent; for doctorate, GRE General Test, MA in German, Scandinavian, or equivalent. Additional exam requirements/recommendations for international students: Required—TOEFL (minimum score 550 paper-based; 213 computer-based; 79 iBT). Electronic applications accepted. *Faculty research:* Cultural studies, literary theory, feminist criticism, film, Germanic philology.

University of Notre Dame, Graduate School, College of Arts and Letters, Division of Humanities, Medieval Institute, Notre Dame, IN 46556. Offers MMS, PhD. *Faculty:* 51 full-time (20 women). *Students:* 31 full-time (13 women); includes 1 minority (Hispanic American), 3 international. 75 applicants, 8% accepted, 4 enrolled. In 2008, 5 master's, 2 doctorates awarded. Terminal master's awarded for partial completion of doctoral program. *Degree requirements:* For master's, 3 foreign languages, comprehensive exam; for doctorate, 3 foreign languages, thesis/dissertation, candidacy exam. *Entrance requirements:* For master's and doctorate, GRE General Test. Additional exam requirements/recommendations for international students: Required—TOEFL (minimum score 600 paper-based; 250 computer-based; 80 iBT). *Application deadline:* For fall admission, 1/4 for international students. Application fee: $50. Electronic applications accepted. *Financial support:* Fellowships with full tuition reimbursements, research assistantships with full tuition reimbursements, teaching assistantships with full tuition reimbursements, tuition waivers (full) available. Financial award application deadline: 2/1. *Faculty research:* Medieval history, vernacular literatures, theology, philosophy, Ambrosiana manuscripts and drawings. *Unit head:* Dr. Olivia Remie Constable, Director, 574-631-6603, Fax: 574-631-8644. *Application contact:* Dr. Barbara Turpin, Director of Graduate Admissions, 574-631-7706, Fax: 574-631-4183.

University of Toronto, School of Graduate Studies, Humanities Division, Centre for Medieval Studies, Toronto, ON M5S 1A1, Canada. Offers MA, PhD. Part-time programs available. *Degree requirements:* For master's, one foreign language, thesis optional, 4 courses or 3 courses and a thesis; for doctorate, 3 foreign languages, thesis/dissertation, proficiency in Latin, German and French. *Entrance requirements:* For master's, letters of reference, minimum B+ average, course work in the medieval period; for doctorate, letters of reference, passing score on MA Latin examination. Additional exam requirements/recommendations for international students: Required—TOEFL (minimum score 580 paper-based; 237 computer-based), TWE (minimum score 5).

Western Michigan University, Graduate College, College of Arts and Sciences, Medieval Studies, Kalamazoo, MI 49008-5202. Offers MA. *Degree requirements:* For master's, one foreign language, thesis optional, oral exam.

Yale University, Graduate School of Arts and Sciences, Interdisciplinary Program in Medieval Studies, New Haven, CT 06520. Offers M Phil, PhD. *Entrance requirements:* For doctorate, GRE General Test.

Yale University, Graduate School of Arts and Sciences, Program in Renaissance Studies, New Haven, CT 06520. Offers PhD. *Degree requirements:* For doctorate, 3 foreign languages. *Entrance requirements:* For doctorate, GRE General Test.

Public History

Appalachian State University, Cratis D. Williams Graduate School, Department of History, Boone, NC 28608. Offers history (MA); history education (MA); public history (MA). Part-time programs available. Postbaccalaureate distance learning degree programs offered (no on-campus study). *Faculty:* 26 full-time (8 women), 3 part-time/adjunct (1 woman). *Students:* 29 full-time (14 women), 18 part-time (5 women); includes 1 minority (American Indian/Alaska Native), 1 international. 27 applicants, 85% accepted, 23 enrolled. In 2008, 7 master's awarded. *Degree requirements:* For master's, one foreign language, comprehensive exam, thesis (for some programs). *Entrance requirements:* For master's, GRE General Test, 3 letters of recommendation. Additional exam requirements/recommendations for international students: Required—TOEFL (minimum score 570 paper-based; 230 computer-based; 79 iBT), IELTS (minimum score 6.5). *Application deadline:* For fall admission, 7/1 for domestic students, 2/1 for international students; for spring admission, 11/1 for domestic students, 7/1 for international students. Applications are processed on a rolling basis. Application fee: $50. Electronic applications accepted. *Expenses:* Tuition, area resident: Full-time $2600; part-time $700 per course. Tuition, state resident: full-time $2600; part-time $700 per course. Tuition, nonresident: full-time $5000; part-time $3300 per course. Required fees: $2150; $330 per course. Tuition and fees vary according to campus/location. *Financial support:* In 2008–09, 4 research assistantships (averaging $10,000 per year), 7 teaching assistantships (averaging $7,500 per year) were awarded; fellowships, career-related internships or fieldwork, Federal Work-Study, scholarships/grants, and unspecified assistantships also available. Financial award application deadline: 4/1; financial award applicants required to submit FAFSA. *Faculty research:* Women's history, social/cultural history, US history, Latin America, medieval studies. Total annual research expenditures: $155,791. *Unit head:* Dr. Michael Krenn, Chairperson, 828-262-2282, E-mail: krennml@appstate.edu. *Application contact:* Dr. James Goff, Graduate Program Director, 828-262-6019, E-mail: goffjr@appstate.edu.

Arizona State University, Graduate College, College of Liberal Arts and Sciences, Division of Humanities, Department of History, Tempe, AZ 85287. Offers East/Southeast Asian history (MA, PhD); European history (MA, PhD); Latin American studies (MA, PhD); North American history (MA, PhD); public history (MA). *Degree requirements:* For master's, thesis or alternative; for doctorate, 2 foreign languages, thesis/dissertation. *Entrance requirements:* For master's and doctorate, GRE.

California State University, Sacramento, Graduate Studies, College of Arts and Letters, Department of History, Sacramento, CA 95819-6048. Offers public history (MA). Part-time programs available. *Degree requirements:* For master's, thesis or alternative, writing proficiency exam. *Entrance requirements:* For master's, GRE General Test, minimum GPA of 3.25 in history, 3.0 overall during previous 2 years; BA in history or equivalent. Additional exam requirements/recommendations for international students: Required—TOEFL. Electronic applications accepted.

Eastern Illinois University, Graduate School, College of Arts and Humanities, Department of History, Charleston, IL 61920-3099. Offers historical administration (MA); history (MA).

Florida State University, Graduate Studies, College of Arts and Sciences, Department of History, Tallahassee, FL 32306. Offers historical administration (MA); history (MA, PhD). Part-time programs available. *Degree requirements:* For master's, one foreign language, comprehensive exam (for some programs), thesis (for some programs), internships; for doctorate, one foreign language, comprehensive exam, thesis/dissertation. *Entrance requirements:* For master's, GRE General Test, minimum GPA of 3.3, minimum 18 hours of course work in history; for doctorate, GRE General Test, minimum GPA of 3.3 (undergraduate), 3.65 (graduate). Additional exam requirements/recommendations for international students: Required—TOEFL (minimum score 550 paper-based; 213 computer-based; 80 iBT). Electronic applications accepted. *Faculty research:* Southern and Caribbean studies, Napoleon and the French Revolution, modern Europe, Latin America, U.S. intellectual and cultural history.

Indiana University–Purdue University Indianapolis, Department of History, Indianapolis, IN 46202-2896. Offers history (MA); public history (MA); MA/MLS. Part-time and evening/weekend programs available. *Degree requirements:* For master's, one foreign language, thesis. *Entrance requirements:* For master's, GRE General Test, minimum GPA of 3.0.

Loyola University Chicago, Graduate School, Department of History, Chicago, IL 60611-2196. Offers history (MA, PhD); public history (MA). Part-time and evening/weekend programs available. *Faculty:* 20 full-time (8 women), 4 part-time/adjunct (1 woman). *Students:* 79 full-time (42 women), 36 part-time (19 women); includes 9 minority (4 African Americans, 1 American Indian/Alaska Native, 1 Asian American or Pacific Islander, 3 Hispanic Americans), 1 international. Average age 33. 134 applicants, 53% accepted, 31 enrolled. In 2008, 14 master's, 2 doctorates awarded. Terminal master's awarded for partial completion of doctoral program. *Degree requirements:* For master's, one foreign language, comprehensive exam, essay; for doctorate, 2 foreign languages, comprehensive exam, thesis/dissertation. *Entrance requirements:* For master's, GRE General Test, research paper; for doctorate, GRE General Test, seminar paper or master's thesis. Additional exam requirements/recommendations for international students: Required—TOEFL (minimum score 550 paper-based; 213 computer-based), IELTS. *Application deadline:* For fall admission, 5/1 for domestic students; for spring admission, 10/1 for domestic students. Applications are processed on a rolling basis. Application fee: $50. Electronic applications accepted. *Expenses:* Tuition: Full-time $13,500; part-time $750 per credit hour. Required fees: $60 per semester. Full-time tuition and fees vary according to program. *Financial support:* In 2008–09, 24 students received support, including 11 fellowships with full tuition reimbursements available (averaging $14,500 per year), 13 teaching assistantships with full tuition reimbursements available (averaging $15,000 per year); research assistantships with full tuition reimbursements available, Federal Work-Study also available. Financial award application deadline: 1/1; financial award applicants required to submit FAFSA. *Faculty research:* Medieval and early modern Europe, U.S. public history, U.S. urban history, gender history, Britain and Ireland. *Unit head:* Barbara Rosenwein, Chair, 773-508-2215, Fax: 773-508-2153, E-mail: brosen@luc.edu. *Application contact:* Dr. Suzanne Kaufman, Director, Graduate Programs, 773-508-2233, Fax: 773-508-2153, E-mail: skaufma@luc.edu.

Middle Tennessee State University, College of Graduate Studies, College of Liberal Arts, Department of History, Program in Public History, Murfreesboro, TN 37132. Offers PhD. Part-time and evening/weekend programs available. Postbaccalaureate distance learning degree programs offered. *Degree requirements:* For doctorate, one foreign language, comprehensive exam, thesis/dissertation. *Entrance requirements:* For doctorate, GRE. Additional exam

Public History

Middle Tennessee State University (continued)
requirements/recommendations for international students: Required—TOEFL (paper-based 525; computer-based 195; IBT 71) or IELTS (6.0).

New York University, Graduate School of Arts and Science, Department of History, New York, NY 10012-1019. Offers African diaspora (PhD); African history (PhD); archival management and historical editing (Advanced Certificate); Atlantic history (PhD); French studies/history (PhD); Hebrew and Judaic studies/history (PhD); history (MA, PhD), including Europe (PhD), Latin American and the Caribbean (PhD), United States (PhD), women's history (MA); Middle Eastern history (MA); Middle Eastern studies/history (PhD); public history (Advanced Certificate); world history (MA); JD/MA; MA/Advanced Certificate. Part-time programs available. Terminal master's awarded for partial completion of doctoral program. *Degree requirements:* For master's, seminar paper; for doctorate, one foreign language, thesis/dissertation, oral and written exams; for Advanced Certificate, internship. *Entrance requirements:* For master's, GRE General Test, minimum GPA of 3.0, writing sample; for doctorate, GRE. Additional exam requirements/recommendations for international students: Required—TOEFL. *Faculty research:* African, East Asian, Medieval, early modern, and modern European history; U.S. history; African and African diaspora; Latin American history; Atlantic World.

North Carolina State University, Graduate School, College of Humanities and Social Sciences, Department of History, Program in Public History, Raleigh, NC 27695. Offers MA. *Degree requirements:* For master's, thesis optional. *Entrance requirements:* For master's, GRE General Test. Electronic applications accepted.

Northeastern University, College of Arts and Sciences, Department of History, Boston, MA 02115-5096. Offers history (MA); public history (MA); world history (PhD). Part-time and evening/weekend programs available. Terminal master's awarded for partial completion of doctoral program. *Degree requirements:* For master's, one foreign language, thesis or alternative, project; for doctorate, thesis/dissertation. *Entrance requirements:* For master's and doctorate, GRE General Test. Electronic applications accepted. *Faculty research:* World history, U.S. social history.

Rutgers, The State University of New Jersey, Camden, Graduate School of Arts and Sciences, Program in American and Public History, Camden, NJ 08102-1401. Offers MA. Part-time and evening/weekend programs available. *Degree requirements:* For master's, comprehensive exam. *Entrance requirements:* For master's, GRE General Test (full-time applicants), 3 letters of recommendation. Additional exam requirements/recommendations for international students: Required—TOEFL, IELTS. Electronic applications accepted. *Faculty research:* Women's history, military history, Afro-American history, urban history, history of technology.

Shippensburg University of Pennsylvania, School of Graduate Studies, College of Arts and Sciences, Department of History and Philosophy, Shippensburg, PA 17257-2299. Offers applied history (MA, Certificate). Part-time and evening/weekend programs available. *Faculty:* 6 full-time (1 woman), 2 part-time/adjunct (0 women). *Students:* 23 full-time (11 women), 20 part-time (6 women). Average age 28. 36 applicants, 75% accepted, 18 enrolled. In 2008, 19 master's awarded. *Degree requirements:* For master's, thesis or internship. *Entrance requirements:* For master's, interview, 500-word statement of purpose (if undergraduate GPA is less than 2.75). Additional exam requirements/recommendations for international students: Required—TOEFL (minimum score 560 paper-based; 220 computer-based); Recommended—IELTS (minimum score 6). *Application deadline:* For fall admission, 3/1 for international students; for spring admission, 7/1 for international students. Applications are processed on a rolling basis. Application fee: $30. Electronic applications accepted. *Expenses:* Tuition, state resident: full-time $6430; part-time $357 per credit. Tuition, nonresident: full-time $10,288; part-time $572 per credit. Required fees: $1127; $38 per credit. One-time fee: $44 part-time. *Financial support:* In 2008–09, 10 research assistantships with full tuition reimbursements (averaging $5,000 per year) were awarded; career-related internships or fieldwork, scholarships/grants, unspecified assistantships, and resident hall directors, student payroll positions also available. Support available to part-time students. Financial award application deadline: 3/1; financial award applicants required to submit FAFSA. *Unit head:* Dr. Susan Rimby, Chairperson, 717-477-1621, Fax: 717-477-4062, E-mail: srrimb@ship.edu. *Application contact:* Renee Payne, Associate Dean of Graduate Admissions, 717-477-1231, Fax: 717-477-4016, E-mail: rmpayn@ship.edu.

Shippensburg University of Pennsylvania, School of Graduate Studies, College of Arts and Sciences, Department of Sociology and Anthropology, Shippensburg, PA 17257-2299. Offers organizational development and leadership (MS), including business, communications, education, environmental management, higher education, historical administration, individual and organizational development, public organizations, social structures and organizations. Part-time and evening/weekend programs available. *Faculty:* 4 full-time (3 women). *Students:* 12 full-time (2 women), 30 part-time (21 women); includes 5 minority (4 African Americans, 1 Asian American or Pacific Islander), 3 international. Average age 31. 39 applicants, 79% accepted, 17 enrolled. In 2008, 13 master's awarded. *Degree requirements:* For master's, capstone experience. *Entrance requirements:* For master's, interview (if GPA less than 2.75), resumé, goals statement. Additional exam requirements/recommendations for international students: Required—TOEFL (minimum score 560 paper-based; 220 computer-based); Recommended—IELTS (minimum score 6). *Application deadline:* For fall admission, 3/1 for international students; for spring admission, 7/1 for international students. Applications are processed on a rolling basis. Application fee: $30. Electronic applications accepted. *Expenses:* Tuition, state resident: full-time $6430; part-time $357 per credit. Tuition, nonresident: full-time $10,288; part-time $572 per credit. Required fees: $1127; $38 per credit. One-time fee: $44 part-time. *Financial support:* In 2008–09, 8 research assistantships with full tuition reimbursements (averaging $5,000 per year) were awarded; career-related internships or fieldwork, scholarships/grants, unspecified assistantships, and resident hall directors, student payroll positions also available. Support available to part-time students. Financial award applicants required to submit FAFSA. *Unit head:* Dr. Barbara Denison, Chairperson, 717-477-1735, Fax: 717-477-4011, E-mail: bjdeni@ship.edu. *Application contact:* Renee Payne, Associate Dean of Graduate Admissions, 717-477-1231, Fax: 717-477-4016, E-mail: rmpayn@ship.edu.

Simmons College, Graduate School of Library and Information Science and College of Arts and Sciences Graduate Studies, Program in History and Archives Management, Boston, MA 02115. Offers MS/MA. Part-time programs available. *Faculty:* 9 full-time (5 women), 11 part-time/adjunct (7 women). *Students:* 8 full-time (7 women), 149 part-time (122 women); includes 9 minority (1 African American, 1 American Indian/Alaska Native, 3 Asian Americans or Pacific Islanders, 4 Hispanic Americans). Average age 28. 45 applicants, 84% accepted, 22 enrolled. *Entrance requirements:* Additional exam requirements/recommendations for international students: Required—TOEFL (minimum score 550 paper-based; 213 computer-based; 79 iBT). *Application deadline:* For fall admission, 3/1 priority date for domestic students; for spring admission, 7/1 priority date for domestic students. Applications are processed on a rolling basis. Application fee: $50. Electronic applications accepted. *Expenses:* Contact institution. *Financial support:* In 2008–09, 29 students received support, including 2 fellowships (averaging $5,910 per year); scholarships/grants also available. Financial award application deadline: 3/1; financial award applicants required to submit FAFSA. *Faculty research:* History of women/gender, American history, cultural history, digital preservation, collective memory. *Application contact:* Sarah Petrakos, Assistant Dean, Admission & Recruitment, 617-521-2868, Fax: 617-521-3192, E-mail: gslisadm@simmons.edu.

Sonoma State University, School of Social Sciences, Program in Cultural Resources Management, Rohnert Park, CA 94928-3609. Offers MA. Part-time programs available. *Degree requirements:* For master's, thesis. *Entrance requirements:* For master's, minimum GPA of 3.0. *Faculty research:* Identification, evaluation, and preservation of cultural resources.

University at Albany, State University of New York, College of Arts and Sciences, Department of History, Albany, NY 12222-0001. Offers history (MA, PhD); public history (Certificate). Part-time programs available. *Degree requirements:* For master's, variable foreign language requirement, exam, research paper or thesis; for doctorate, thesis/dissertation. *Entrance requirements:* For master's, minimum GPA of 3.0; for doctorate, GRE General Test, minimum GPA of 3.0. Additional exam requirements/recommendations for international students: Required—TOEFL (minimum score 550 paper-based; 213 computer-based). Electronic applications accepted. *Faculty research:* American history (all phases); public policy; European history (Medieval to modern); Asian, African, and Latin American history.

University of Arkansas at Little Rock, Graduate School, College of Arts, Humanities, and Social Science, Department of History, Little Rock, AR 72204-1099. Offers public history (MA). Part-time programs available. *Degree requirements:* For master's, oral exam. *Entrance requirements:* For master's, GRE General Test, minimum GPA of 3.25 in history, 2.7 overall; 18 hours of art history. *Faculty research:* Historic preservation and restoration, museum studies, archives.

The University of British Columbia, Faculty of Arts, School of Library, Archival and Information Studies, Program in Archival Studies, Vancouver, BC V6T 1Z1, Canada. Offers MAS. *Degree requirements:* For master's, thesis optional. *Entrance requirements:* For master's, minimum GPA of 3.3 in undergraduate upper-division courses. Additional exam requirements/recommendations for international students: Required—TOEFL (minimum score 600 paper-based; 250 computer-based; 100 iBT). Electronic applications accepted. *Faculty research:* Diplomatics, electronic record, appraisal, descriptive standards, preservation.

The University of British Columbia, Faculty of Arts, School of Library, Archival and Information Studies, Program in Library, Archival and Information Studies, Vancouver, BC V6T 1Z1, Canada. Offers PhD. *Degree requirements:* For doctorate, thesis/dissertation. *Entrance requirements:* For doctorate, GRE, minimum GPA of 3.3 in MAS or MLIS. Other master's may be considered. Additional exam requirements/recommendations for international students: Required—TOEFL (minimum score 600 paper-based; 250 computer-based; 100 iBT). Electronic applications accepted. *Faculty research:* Computer systems/database design; library and archival management; archival description and organization; children's literature and youth services; interactive information retrieval.

University of Central Florida, College of Arts and Humanities, Department of History, Orlando, FL 32816. Offers history (MA); public history (MA). Part-time and evening/weekend programs available. *Faculty:* 27 full-time (13 women), 20 part-time/adjunct (6 women). *Students:* 13 full-time (2 women), 37 part-time (10 women); includes 9 minority (2 African Americans, 7 Hispanic Americans). Average age 34. In 2008, 10 master's awarded. *Degree requirements:* For master's, thesis, written exam. *Entrance requirements:* For master's, GRE General Test, minimum GPA of 3.0 in last 60 hours. Additional exam requirements/recommendations for international students: Required—TOEFL. *Application deadline:* For fall admission, 7/15 for domestic students; for spring admission, 12/1 for domestic students. Electronic applications accepted. *Expenses:* Tuition, area resident: Full-time $6816; part-time $284 per credit. Tuition, state resident: full-time $6816; part-time $1076 per credit. Tuition, nonresident: full-time $25,824. Required fees: $216; $9 per credit. *Financial support:* In 2008–09, 2 fellowships with partial tuition reimbursements (averaging $10,000 per year), 7 research assistantships with partial tuition reimbursements (averaging $4,000 per year), 8 teaching assistantships with partial tuition reimbursements (averaging $4,400 per year) were awarded; career-related internships or fieldwork, Federal Work-Study, institutionally sponsored loans, tuition waivers (partial), and unspecified assistantships also available. Financial award application deadline: 3/1; financial award applicants required to submit FAFSA. *Unit head:* Dr. Rosalind Beiler, Chair, 407-823-6467, E-mail: beiler@mail.ucf.edu. *Application contact:* Dr. Rosalind Beiler, Chair, 407-823-6467, E-mail: beiler@mail.ucf.edu.

University of Houston, College of Liberal Arts and Social Sciences, Department of History, Houston, TX 77204. Offers history (MA, PhD); public history (MA). Part-time programs available. *Faculty:* 24 full-time (9 women), 1 (woman) part-time/adjunct. *Students:* 52 full-time (27 women), 35 part-time (16 women); includes 15 minority (2 African Americans, 2 American Indian/Alaska Native, 1 Asian American or Pacific Islander, 10 Hispanic Americans), 1 international. Average age 38. 53 applicants, 43% accepted, 10 enrolled. In 2008, 6 master's, 6 doctorates awarded. Terminal master's awarded for partial completion of doctoral program. *Degree requirements:* For master's, one foreign language, thesis (for some programs); for doctorate, one foreign language, thesis/dissertation. *Entrance requirements:* For master's, GRE General Test, minimum GPA of 3.3; for doctorate, GRE General Test, minimum GPA of 3.67. Additional exam requirements/recommendations for international students: Required—TOEFL. *Application deadline:* For fall admission, 1/15 for domestic students; for spring admission, 11/1 for domestic students. Application fee: $25 ($100 for international students). *Expenses:* Tuition, state resident: full-time $5164; part-time $287 per credit. Tuition, nonresident: full-time $10,222; part-time $568 per credit. *Financial support:* In 2008–09, 3 research assistantships with full tuition reimbursements (averaging $10,000 per year), 33 teaching assistantships with full tuition reimbursements (averaging $10,000 per year) were awarded; career-related internships or fieldwork, Federal Work-Study, institutionally sponsored loans, scholarships/grants, health care benefits, and unspecified assistantships also available. Support available to part-time students. Financial award application deadline: 2/1. *Faculty research:* U.S., Latin American, European, social, and women's history. *Unit head:* Robert Buzzanco, Chairperson, 713-743-3008, Fax: 713-743-3216. *Application contact:* Robert Buzzanco, Chairperson, 713-743-3008, Fax: 713-743-3216.

University of Illinois at Springfield, Graduate Programs, College of Liberal Arts and Sciences, Program in History, Springfield, IL 62703-5407. Offers MA. Part-time and evening/weekend programs available. *Faculty:* 9 full-time (4 women). *Students:* 17 full-time (10 women), 37 part-time (17 women); includes 9 minority (6 African Americans, 1 American Indian/Alaska Native, 2 Hispanic Americans). Average age 33. 33 applicants, 73% accepted, 17 enrolled. In 2008, 18 master's awarded. *Degree requirements:* For master's, thesis, internship, or historiography. *Entrance requirements:* For master's, BA in history or related field, minimum undergraduate GPA of 3.0, writing sample, statement of purpose. Additional exam requirements/recommendations for international students: Required—TOEFL (minimum score 500 paper-based; 176 computer-based; 61 iBT). *Application deadline:* Applications are processed on a rolling basis. Application fee: $50 ($60 for international students). Electronic applications accepted. *Expenses:* Tuition, state resident: full-time $6144; part-time $256 per credit hour. Tuition, nonresident: full-time $13,980; part-time $582.50 per credit hour. Required fees: $1800. *Financial support:* In 2008–09, research assistantships with full tuition reimbursements (averaging $8,109 per year), teaching assistantships with full tuition reimbursements (averaging $8,109 per year) were awarded; career-related internships or fieldwork, Federal Work-Study, scholarships/grants, health care benefits, and unspecified assistantships also available. Support available to part-time students. Financial award application deadline: 11/15; financial award applicants required to submit FAFSA. *Unit head:* Dr. Robert McGregor, Program Administrator, 217-206-7442, Fax: 217-206-6217, E-mail: mcgregor.robert@uis.edu. *Application contact:* Dr. Lynn Pardie, Office of Graduate Studies, 800-252-8533, Fax: 217-206-7623, E-mail: pardie.lynn@uis.edu.

University of Massachusetts Amherst, Graduate School, College of Humanities and Fine Arts, Department of History, Amherst, MA 01003. Offers ancient history (MA); British Empire history (MA); European (medieval and modern) history (MA, PhD); Islamic history (MA); Latin American history (MA, PhD); modern global history (MA); public history (MA); science and technology history (MA); U.S. history (MA, PhD). Part-time programs available. Terminal master's awarded for partial completion of doctoral program. *Degree requirements:* For master's, one foreign language, thesis or alternative; for doctorate, one foreign language, comprehensive exam, thesis/dissertation. *Entrance requirements:* For master's and doctorate, GRE General Test, writing sample. Additional exam requirements/recommendations for international students: Required—TOEFL (minimum score 550 paper-based; 213 computer-based; 79 iBT), IELTS (minimum score 6.5), Electronic applications accepted. *Expenses:* Tuition, area resident: Full-time $2640. Tuition, nonresident: full-time $9936. One-time fee: $332 full-time. Tuition and fees vary according to course load. *Faculty research:* Ancient and medieval history; global and comparative history; public history; history of science, technology, medicine and the environment; history of women, gender, sexuality and family.

University of Massachusetts Boston, Office of Graduate Studies, College of Liberal Arts, Program in History, Boston, MA 02125-3393. Offers archival methods (MA); historical archaeology (MA); history (MA). Part-time and evening/weekend programs available. *Degree requirements:* For master's, thesis, oral exam. *Entrance requirements:* For master's, minimum GPA of 2.75. *Faculty research:* European intellectual history, American labor and social history in 19th century, colonial American Revolution, Afro-American Cold War.

University of South Carolina, The Graduate School, College of Arts and Sciences, Department of History, Program in Public History, Columbia, SC 29208. Offers archives (MA); historic preservation (MA); museum (MA); museum management (Certificate); MLIS/MA. *Degree requirements:* For master's, one foreign language, thesis, internship. *Entrance requirements:* For master's, GRE General Test, writing sample. Additional exam requirements/recommendations for international students: Required—TOEFL. Electronic applications accepted. *Faculty research:* Museum studies, historic preservation, archives administration.

The University of Texas at Austin, Graduate School, College of Liberal Arts, Department of Anthropology, Program in Folklore and Public Culture, Austin, TX 78712-1111. Offers MA, PhD. Part-time programs available. Terminal master's awarded for partial completion of doctoral program. *Degree requirements:* For master's, one foreign language, thesis, report; for doctorate, one foreign language, thesis/dissertation. *Entrance requirements:* For master's and doctorate, GRE General Test. Electronic applications accepted. *Faculty research:* Expressive culture, gender, genre, folklore and culture of British Isles, ethnography of speaking.

University of West Florida, College of Arts and Sciences: Arts, Department of History, Pensacola, FL 32514-5750. Offers historic preservation (MA); history (MA); public history (MA). Part-time and evening/weekend programs available. *Faculty:* 6 full-time (1 woman), 1 part-time/adjunct (0 women). *Students:* 11 full-time (4 women), 28 part-time (12 women); includes 2 minority (1 African American, 1 Hispanic American). Average age 34. 29 applicants, 69% accepted, 13 enrolled. In 2008, 11 master's awarded. *Degree requirements:* For master's, thesis or alternative. *Entrance requirements:* For master's, GRE General Test, minimum GPA of 3.0, minimum 15 hours of upper-level history courses. Additional exam requirements/recommendations for international students: Required—TOEFL (minimum score 550 paper-based; 213 computer-based). *Application deadline:* For fall admission, 6/1 for domestic students, 5/15 for international students; for spring admission, 11/1 for domestic students, 10/1 for international students. Applications are processed on a rolling basis. Application fee: $30. *Expenses:* Tuition, state resident: full-time $6095; part-time $253.97 per credit hour. Tuition, nonresident: full-time $21,919; part-time $913.31 per credit hour. *Financial support:* In 2008–09, 3 research assistantships with partial tuition reimbursements (averaging $5,640 per year) were awarded; fellowships, teaching assistantships with partial tuition reimbursements, Federal Work-Study, institutionally sponsored loans, scholarships/grants, and unspecified assistantships also available. Financial award application deadline: 4/15; financial award applicants required to submit FAFSA. *Unit head:* Dr. John J. Clune, Chairperson, 850-474-2680. *Application contact:* Terry McCray, Assistant Director of Graduate Admissions, 850-473-7718, Fax: 850-473-7714, E-mail: gradadmissions@uwf.edu.

Washington State University, Graduate School, College of Liberal Arts, Department of History, Pullman, WA 99164. Offers early and modern European history (MA, PhD); environmental history (MA, PhD); Latin American history (MA, PhD); modern East Asia history (MA, PhD); public history (MA, PhD); US history (MA, PhD); women's history (MA, PhD); world history (MA, PhD). Part-time programs available. *Degree requirements:* For master's, comprehensive exam (for some programs), thesis, oral exam; for doctorate, one foreign language, comprehensive exam, thesis/dissertation, oral and written exam. *Entrance requirements:* For master's, GRE General Test, minimum GPA of 3.3, language background form, writing sample; for doctorate, GRE General Test, minimum GPA of 3.5, language background form, writing sample. Additional exam requirements/recommendations for international students: Required—TOEFL (minimum score 550 paper-based). Electronic applications accepted. *Faculty research:* Public, world, environmental, women and U.S. history.

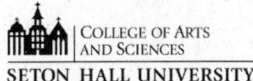

SETON HALL UNIVERSITY

Department of History

Programs of Study	The Department of History, located in the College of Arts and Sciences at Seton Hall University, offers a Master of Arts (M.A.) degree program with four concentrations: United States, European, global, and Catholic history. The program requires successful completion of ten courses (30 credits). All students must take an introductory course called The Historian's Craft, a minimum of one Program in Directed Readings (PDR) course, four courses in the chosen area of concentration, and electives in other areas. Advanced graduate students may choose either to conduct two semesters of thesis research and writing or to complete comprehensive written and oral examinations in the final semester of study.
	The master's program requires all students to pass a foreign language translation exam (proving reading knowledge) or demonstrate mastery of advanced statistical methods.
	This program is particularly attractive to K–12 teachers who are interested in an advanced degree in their field, as well as librarians and other professionals desiring a second advanced degree. It also provides a solid basis for those interested in continuing in a doctoral program.
	Seton Hall University undergraduates who have completed 75 credits toward their undergraduate degree in history, with at least 21 credits in history (at least seven courses) are eligible to apply to the combined B.A./M.A. program option and complete both degrees in five years.
	More information about graduate study in history at Seton Hall is available at http://www.shu.edu/academics/artsci/ma-history/.
Research Facilities	Students have access to Seton Hall's Walsh Library as well as libraries at area colleges and the many important research facilities in New York City. The Walsh Library is a pioneer in electronic research, making numerous online databases, journals, and resources available both on and off campus.
Financial Aid	Students may apply for graduate assistantships in the Department of History. Graduate assistants work for the Department or individual professors on special projects. The assistantships offer tuition remission and a stipend. Students should contact the Department of History for information about these graduate assistantships.
	Additional graduate assistantships are available through the Office of Graduate Programs. Graduate assistants work in a variety of campus positions and receive tuition benefits and a stipend. For more information, students should visit http://www.shu.edu/applying/graduate/grad-finaid.cfm.
Cost of Study	Tuition is $901 per credit; all courses are 3 credits. Fees are $305 per semester for full-time students and $185 per semester for part-time students. Students not on assistantships may, for a fee, lease an IBM laptop computer. All students have access to free computer training.
Living and Housing Costs	Housing and living costs in South Orange are comparable to most suburbs of major cities, with studio and one-bedroom apartments renting for $750 to $1200 per month.
Student Group	The M.A. program enrolls approximately 20 full-time and part-time students. Entering classes consist of 8 to 10 students per year.
Location	Seton Hall University, located in South Orange, New Jersey, is only 14 miles by train, bus, or car from New York City, offering students a unique cosmopolitan location complete with cultural, employment, and internship opportunities.
The University and The Department	Seton Hall is New Jersey's largest Catholic university. The University's diverse academic program is characterized by a strong teaching faculty and a wide range of academic choices. Students benefit from the personal attention generated by small classes and a low student-faculty ratio. At Seton Hall, students find people who are willing to listen, offer support, and help them get the most out of their education.
	The Department of History's faculty is distinguished by excellent scholarship and teaching. Faculty members regularly publish books and articles and participate in local, regional, and international conferences.
Applying	Applicants, other than dual-degree candidates, must have a baccalaureate degree, preferably in history or a history-related field, such as political science, geography, or economics. Students who have majored in other fields may be asked to take up to four undergraduate courses in history. Applicants must submit the Seton Hall University Graduate Application (available through a link on the Web site of the M.A. in History program at http://www.shu.edu/academics/artsci/ma-history/) as well as a personal statement, three letters of recommendation, and scores on the Graduate Record Examinations (GRE).
	Candidates applying for a graduate assistantship can find the online application at http://www.shu.edu/applying/graduate/grad-finaid.cfm. This application should be submitted with a statement of interest in the position and a writing sample. Students should contact the Department of History for more information on graduate assistantships.
Correspondence and Information	Dr. Dermot Quinn, Director of Graduate Studies Department of History College of Arts and Sciences Fahy Hall, Room 339 Seton Hall University 400 South Orange Avenue South Orange, New Jersey 07079 Phone: 973-275-2984 Fax: 973-761-7798 E-mail: quinnder@shu.edu Web site: http://www.shu.edu/academics/artsci/ma-history/

Seton Hall University

THE GRADUATE FACULTY AND THEIR RESEARCH

Tracey E. Billado, Ph.D., Emory. Medieval.
William J. Connell, Ph.D., Berkeley. Renaissance, Italy, Italian American.
Larry A. Greene, Ph.D., Columbia. United States, urban, African American.
Williamjames Hull Hoffer, J.D., Harvard; Ph.D., Johns Hopkins. United States, law, economy.
Nathaniel Knight, Ph.D., Columbia. Russia/Soviet Union, Eastern Europe.
Daniel J. Leab, Ph.D., Columbia. United States, labor, film.
Maxine N. Lurie, Ph.D., Wisconsin. United States, colonial and revolutionary, New Jersey.
Maxim Matusevich, Ph.D., Illinois at Urbana-Champaign. Global, Africa.
James P. McCartin, Ph.D., Notre Dame. United States, Catholic, religion and culture.
Mark C. Molesky, Ph.D., Harvard. Germany, France, intellectual.
Dermot A. Quinn, D.Phil., Oxford. England, Ireland, intellectual.
Thomas F. Rzeznik, Ph.D., Notre Dame. American religious.
Kirsten Schultz, Ph.D., NYU. Immigration, Latin America.

Southern™
Illinois University
Carbondale

SOUTHERN ILLINOIS UNIVERSITY CARBONDALE

Department of History
Ph.D. Program

Program of Study

The Department of History offers a Ph.D. degree in selected fields of United States, European, Middle Eastern/Asian, African, and Latin American history. It is possible to complete all requirements for the Ph.D. degree in three to four years of full-time study after the M.A. Most students spend two years completing classroom studies; thereafter, the time required for the completion of the dissertation varies considerably with the topic and the student. Ph.D. students are also encouraged to do internship work toward the development of career-related professional skills. Internships include teaching, training in innovative instructional technologies, editing at the Southern Illinois University Press, public history at the University museum, archive management at Morris Library, and similar approved activities at other venues.

The Department of History's graduate student body is small (between 55 and 65 students), allowing for close working relationships between faculty members and students. The faculty members are particularly strong in national and ethnic identity studies, local and regional studies, business and labor history, American studies, and gender and women's history. Students take regular courses and seminars in these and other areas, and they also arrange independent study courses and internships. Southern Illinois University Carbondale (SIUC) also has a cooperative Ph.D. program with SIU at Edwardsville (SIUE), which allows students to take courses on both campuses.

Students benefit from Departmental support for publishing and for travel to conferences. They may also participate in a very active History Graduate Student Association that provides a sense of community and a vehicle for organizing activities on campus.

Research Facilities

The Morris Library, with its collection of more than 2 million printed volumes and 4 million microfilm units, provides excellent support for research. More than one fourth of its holdings are in history or related areas, and it is particularly strong in U.S., European, and Latin American history. The library's special collections hold rare printed works and manuscripts to support historical research on many topics, including Irish studies, First Amendment freedoms, theater history, and Illinois history. The University is also home to the John Dewey Center, the Center for Irish Studies, and the Illinois Regional Archives Depository.

Financial Aid

Most qualified Ph.D. students receive support in the form of fellowships through programs such as the Illinois Minority Graduate Incentive Program (IMGIP) and the Illinois Consortium for Educational Opportunities Program (ICEOP) or through graduate fellowships, Morris Doctoral Fellowships, and dissertation research awards. Teaching assistantships or research assistantships are also available. All carry stipends (minimum of $11,000 for nine months) and remission of tuition. A maximum of forty-eight months of assistance is allowed. Application for these awards should be submitted by January 10.

Cost of Study

In-state graduate tuition is $328 per credit hour in 2009–10. Out-of-state tuition is 2.5 times the in-state tuition rate ($820 per credit hour). Graduate students with at least a 25 percent appointment as a graduate assistant receive a tuition scholarship. Fees vary from $589.03 (1 credit hour) to $1557.50 (12 credit hours). Students with a graduate assistantship receive a 50 percent reduction in the primary care medical fee. New graduate students from Arkansas, Indiana, Kentucky, Missouri, and Tennessee qualify for the alternate tuition rate, which is equivalent to the in-state graduate tuition rate.

Living and Housing Costs

For married couples, students with families, and single graduate students, the University has 690 efficiency and one-, two-, three-, and four-bedroom apartments that rent for $499 to $720 per month in 2009–10. Residence halls for single graduate students are also available, as are accessible residence hall rooms and apartments for students with disabilities.

Student Group

This program admits students seeking careers in academia and other areas of the workplace. There are between 30 and 35 students in the Ph.D. program (approximately 35 percent women), with at least half receiving financial assistance. Roughly one fourth of the students are part-time.

Student Outcomes

Graduates of the Ph.D. program in history have been very successful at obtaining tenure-track jobs with colleges and universities as well as jobs with museums and publications and editorial projects.

Location

SIUC is 350 miles south of Chicago and 100 miles southeast of St. Louis. Nestled in rolling hills bordered by the Ohio and Mississippi Rivers and enhanced by a mild climate, the area has state parks, national forests and wildlife refuges, and large lakes for outdoor recreation. Cultural offerings include theater, opera, concerts, art exhibits, and cinema. Educational facilities available for the families of students are excellent.

The University

Southern Illinois University Carbondale is a comprehensive public university with a variety of general and professional education programs. The University offers associate, bachelor's, master's, and doctoral degrees as well as the J.D. and M.D. degrees. The University is fully accredited by the North Central Association of Colleges and Schools. The Graduate School has an essential role in the development and coordination of graduate instruction and research programs. The Graduate Council has academic responsibility for determining graduate standards, recommending new graduate programs and research centers, and establishing policies to facilitate the research effort.

Applying

Applications should be requested from and sent to the Department. Each application must include the standard application forms, transcripts of all postsecondary school work, official GRE scores, three letters of recommendation, a statement of professional goals and interests, and the application fee. The deadline for application materials is January 10 for the following fall. Admission requires a grade point average in graduate work of at least 3.25 (A = 4.0).

Direct entry into the Ph.D. program from baccalaureate studies is possible for students of exceptional ability. This is demonstrated through extensive undergraduate course work of superior quality, excellent GRE scores, previous research experience, and letters of recommendation.

Correspondence and Information

Chasity Shea
Department of History
Southern Illinois University
Carbondale, Illinois 62901-4519

Phone: 618-453-4391
E-mail: cshea@siu.edu
Web site: http://www.siu.edu/~histsiu

Southern Illinois University Carbondale

THE FACULTY AND THEIR RESEARCH

(The number in parentheses in each entry represents the year in which the person joined the faculty.)

James Smith Allen, Professor; Ph.D., Tufts, 1979 (1991). European, modern France, social and cultural.
Jo Ann E. Argersinger, Professor; Ph.D., George Washington, 1980 (1998). U.S. labor.
Peter H. Argersinger, Professor; Ph.D., Wisconsin–Madison, 1970 (1998). U.S. political and rural, Gilded Age.
Jonathan J. Bean, Professor; Ph.D., Ohio State, 1994 (1995). U.S. economic and business.
Getahun Benti, Associate Professor; Ph.D., Michigan State, 2000 (2001). Modern Africa, urbanization-migration.
Michael Brown, Assistant Professor; Ph.D., Georgia, 2004 (2004). African American and Atlantic history.
Kay J. Carr, Associate Professor; Ph.D., Chicago, 1987 (1989). U.S. social, nineteenth century, Illinois, frontier, historical geography.
Mariola Espinosa, Assistant Professor; Ph.D., North Carolina, 2003 (2003). Latin American history.
Germaine Etienne, Assistant Professor; Ph.D., Massachusetts, 2004 (2004). African American history.
Holly S. Hurlburt, Associate Professor; Ph.D., Syracuse, 2000 (2001). Early modern Europe, Italy, women and gender.
Robbie Lieberman, Professor; Ph.D., Michigan, 1984 (1991). Contemporary U.S., war and peace, social movements.
Joseph Sramek, Assistant Professor; Ph.D., CUNY Graduate Center, 2007 (2007). South Asia and British Empire.
Rachel Stocking, Associate Professor; Ph.D., Stanford, 1994 (1994). Ancient and early medieval European, cultural and political, Spain.
Theodore R. Weeks, Professor; Ph.D., Berkeley, 1992 (1993). Russia/USSR East Central Europe, cultural and political, nationalism.
Jonathan S. Wiesen, Associate Professor; Ph.D., Brown, 1997 (1998). Modern Europe, Germany, Jewish.
David L. Wilson, Professor; Ph.D., Tennessee, 1974 (1974). United States foreign relations.
Hale Yilmaz, Assistant Professor; Ph.D., Utah, 2006 (2006). Middle East.
Gray Whaley, Assistant Professor; Ph.D., Oregon, 2002 (2002). Native America.
Natasha Zaretsky, Associate Professor; Ph.D., Brown, 2002 (2002). United States, cultural, family and gender.

Cross-Appointed Faculty

Jane H. Adams, Associate Professor (Anthropology); Ph.D., Illinois at Urbana-Champaign, 1987 (1987). U.S. rural, gender, social movements.
Pamela Smoot, Clinical Assistant Professor (Black American Studies); Ph.D., Michigan State, 1998 (1999), African-American history, archival administration.

Emeritus Faculty

Howard W. Allen, Professor Emeritus; Ph.D., Washington (Seattle), 1959 (1962).
Harry Ammon, Professor Emeritus; Ph.D., Virginia, 1948 (1950).
H. Arnold Barton, Professor Emeritus; Ph.D., Princeton, 1962 (1970).
Michael C. Batinski, Professor Emeritus; Ph.D., Northwestern, 1969 (1968). Early America.
Dale R. Bengtson, Assistant Professor Emeritus; Ph.D., Hartford Seminary, 1971 (1973). History of religions.
M. Browning Carrott, Professor Emeritus; Ph.D., Northwestern, 1966 (1967).
David E. Conrad, Professor Emeritus; Ph.D., Oklahoma, 1962 (1967).
Donald S. Detwiler, Professor Emeritus; D.Phil., Göttingen (Germany), 1961 (1967).
John E. Dotson, Professor Emeritus; Ph.D., Johns Hopkins, 1969 (1970). European medieval and renaissance, Italy, maritime.
Charles F. Fanning, Professor Emeritus; Ph.D., Pennsylvania, 1972 (1993). Ireland, Irish-American, immigration and ethic studies.
Robert L. Gold, Professor Emeritus; Ph.D., Iowa, 1964 (1965).
John S. Haller Jr., Emeritus Professor; Ph.D., Maryland, 1968 (1990). U.S. intellectual history, history of medicine and pharmacology.
James B. Murphy, Associate Professor Emeritus; Ph.D., LSU, 1968 (1968).
Edward J. O'Day, Associate Professor Emeritus; A.M., Indiana, 1956 (1962).
David P. Werlich, Professor Emeritus; Ph.D., Minnesota, 1968 (1968). Latin American Andean region.

SIUE Cooperative Ph.D. Faculty

Stefan Bradley, Assistant Professor; Ph.D., Missouri–Columbia, 2003. African Americans.
Anthony Cheeseboro, Assistant Professor; Ph.D., Michigan State, 1993. History of development, agriculture, and slavery.
Ching-chih Chen, Professor Emeritus; Ph.D., Harvard, 1973.
Leigh Anne Eubanks, Instructor; Ph.D. candidate, Cornell. Modern Europe.
Carole C. Frick, Associate Professor; Ph.D., UCLA, 1995. Renaissance/reformation and early modern history.
Stephen L. Hansen, Associate Professor; Ph.D., Illinois at Chicago, 1978. Civil War.
Alex Haskell, Assistant Professor; Ph.D., Johns Hopkins, 2004. Colonial U.S.
Christienne L. Hinz, Assistant Professor; Ph.D., Ohio State, 2001 (2001). Japanese history, business history, world history, women's history.
Thomas Jordan, Assistant Professor; Ph.D., Illinois at Urbana-Champaign, 1999. Latin America.
Rowena McClinton, Assistant Professor; Ph.D., Kentucky, 1996. Native American history, antebellum South and United States history since 1865.
Laura Milsk, Assistant Professor; Ph.D., Loyola Chicago, 2003. Museum studies.
Michael Moore, Assistant Professor, Ph.D., Michigan, 1996. Medieval Europe.
Norman E. Nordhauser, Professor Emeritus; Ph.D., Stanford, 1970. American economic history, history of American business.
Ellen Nore, Associate Professor; Ph.D., Stanford, 1980. Illinois history, women's history, progressive intellectuals, historiography.
Shirley J. Portwood, Professor; Ph.D., Washington (St. Louis), 1982. African American and women's history.
Eric Ruckh, Assistant Professor; Ph.D., California, Irvine, 1997. Critical theory.
Stephen E. Tamari, Assistant Professor; Ph.D., Georgetown, 1998 (2001). Middle East history, Ottoman Empire, Arab world, Arab-Israeli conflict.
John A. Taylor, Professor; Ph.D., Chicago. Britain and Colonial U.S.
Allison K. Thomason, Assistant Professor; Ph.D., Columbia, 1999. Ancient Near-Eastern and Greco-Roman history.
Anne Valk, Associate Professor; Ph.D., Duke, 1996. Public history, oral history, women's history, twentieth-century United States.
James J. Weingartner, Professor Emeritus; Ph.D., Wisconsin, 1967. Nazi Germany, the Holocaust, war crimes, World War II.

VILLANOVA UNIVERSITY

Graduate Studies in Liberal Arts and Sciences
Department of History

Program of Study

Villanova University is one of relatively few academic institutions in the country that offer only an M.A. degree in history, rather than the M.A. and Ph.D. The program seeks to encourage students' love of history and strengthen their analytical and interpretive skills to meet diverse career goals.

Over the course of an academic year (fall and spring semesters and a summer term), twenty-one different graduate seminars are typically offered that cover a broad range of historical periods, themes, and regions. The average class size is 11 to 12 students. During the fall and spring semesters, classes meet once a week for 2 hours in the late afternoon or early evening. During the summer, classes meet one evening each week for eight weeks. The program is especially strong in European and American history, but thematic and non-Western topics are an important part of the curriculum.

Program requirements include the successful completion of ten graduate courses and a passing score on the comprehensive examination. There is no formal language requirement. Students may begin taking courses in the fall, spring, or summer sessions and may take courses on a part-time (one course per session) or full-time basis. As many as two graduate courses in related disciplines, such as literature or political science, may be taken at Villanova. Students may also transfer a maximum of 6 credits for graduate courses taken at other institutions.

Research Facilities

The University Library contains more than 780,000 volumes and 5,600 current periodicals. The Philadelphia region, with its numerous other colleges and universities, museums, historical societies, and archival collections, offers a rich cultural and institutional environment for study and research in history.

Financial Aid

The Department has graduate assistantships and tuition scholarships for 15 full-time students. Graduate assistantships are awarded on a competitive basis. The assistantship in history included a waiver of all tuition and academic fees and a stipend of $6550 in 2008–09. A number of tuition scholarships are also available that provide a waiver of all tuition and academic fees.

In addition, the office of the director of financial aid administers the Federal Stafford Student Loan, the unsubsidized Federal Stafford Student Loan, and the Federal Supplemental Loans for Students.

Cost of Study

Graduate tuition was $610 per credit hour in 2008–09. In addition, there are a one-time application fee of $50 and a University fee of $30 each semester.

Living and Housing Costs

The area surrounding the University offers a wide selection of living quarters that are convenient to the campus, which is served by two suburban rail lines and buses. The University does not maintain accommodations for graduate students, but second-year students are eligible for positions as resident counselors in the dormitories.

Student Group

There is no typical graduate student in history at Villanova. The students comprise a large and diverse yet very congenial community. Many students enter the program directly from their undergraduate college. Others are completing graduate work in history while also engaged in careers in government service, law, business, or teaching. In any given semester, between 50 and 60 students take courses, approximately one third of whom are part-time students.

Student Outcomes

Many students continue to study toward a Ph.D. in history; recent graduates may be found in doctoral programs at Temple, Indiana Bloomington, the College of William and Mary, the University of Madrid, Brandeis, and other institutions. Other graduates pursue history-related careers in libraries, archives, or museums. Many have gone on to teaching or educational administration at the secondary or college level in places as diverse as Kuwait and West Point. Still other graduates work for government or nonprofit organizations, newspapers, or corporations.

Location

Located in the heart of the Delaware Valley's Main Line, the University occupies more than 200 handsomely landscaped acres in the town of Villanova, 12 miles west of Philadelphia. The location combines the advantages of a tranquil suburban setting with proximity to a large metropolitan city known for its outstanding historical, educational, and cultural resources.

The University

Villanova University is a private institution founded in 1842 by the Augustinian Fathers. Graduate programs were first administered separately in 1931. Currently, there are five academic units in addition to Graduate Studies: the Colleges of Arts and Sciences, Commerce and Finance, Engineering, and Nursing and the School of Law.

Applying

Applicants should have at least 18 undergraduate credits and a 3.0 average in history. The Graduate Record Examinations General Test is required for admission to the program. International applicants must take the TOEFL examination. Application deadlines are March 1 for fall admission, November 15 for spring admission, and May 1 for summer admission. The deadline is March 1 for those applying for a graduate assistantship.

Application forms and other information may be obtained from either the Department of History or the Office of Graduate Studies in the College of Liberal Arts and Sciences, Villanova University, 800 Lancaster Avenue, Villanova, Pennsylvania 19085 (phone: 610-519-7090, fax: 610-519-7096, e-mail: gradinformation@villanova.edu). Online submission of applications is also possible at http://www.villanova.edu/artsci/college/academics/graduate/.

Correspondence and Information

To discuss situation, qualifications, and goals:

Dr. R. Emmet McLaughlin, Director of the History Graduate Program
Department of History
Villanova University
Villanova, Pennsylvania 19085-1696

Phone: 610-519-4660
E-mail: emmet.mclaughlin@villanova.edu
Web site: http://www.villanova.edu/artsci/history/

Villanova University

THE FACULTY AND THEIR RESEARCH

Marc Gallicchio, Professor and Chair; Ph.D., Temple, 1986. U.S. foreign relations, American political and military history.

Hibba Abugideiri, Assistant Professor; Ph.D., Georgetown, 2001. Middle East history.

Craig Bailey, Assistant Professor; Ph.D., London, 2004. History of Ireland and Britain.

Judith Ann Giesberg, Associate Professor; Ph.D., Boston College, 1997. U.S. women's history.

Christopher Haas, Associate Professor; Ph.D., Michigan, 1988. Greece, Rome, late antiquity, early Christianity history.

Lynne Ann Hartnett, Assistant Professor; Ph.D., Boston College, 2000. Russian/Soviet history, European women's history.

Jeffrey A. Johnson, Professor; Ph.D., Princeton, 1980. History of science and technology.

Maghan Keita, Professor; Ph.D., Howard, 1988. African and world history.

Catherine Kerrison, Associate Professor; Ph.D., William and Mary, 1999. Colonial and revolutionary America, U.S. women's history.

Elizabeth Kolsky, Assistant Professor; Ph.D., Columbia, 2002. South Asian history.

Adele Lindenmeyr, Professor; Ph.D., Princeton, 1980. Russia and Soviet history, environmental history.

Lawrence Little, Associate Professor; Ph.D., Ohio State, 1993. African-American history.

Timothy McCall, Assistant Professor; Ph.D., Michigan, 2005. History of Renaissance art.

R. Emmet McLaughlin, Professor; Ph.D., Yale, 1980. Renaissance and Reformation history, early modern European history.

Charlene Mires, Associate Professor; Ph.D., Temple, 1997. American history, material culture, public history.

Paul Rosier, Associate Professor; Ph.D., Rochester, 1998. Modern and Native American history.

Rev. Joseph G. Ryan, O.S.A., Assistant Professor; Ph.D., American, 1997. American history, history of medicine.

Holly Sanders, Assistant Professor; Ph.D., Princeton, 2005. History of modern Asia.

Paul R. Steege, Associate Professor; Ph.D., Chicago, 1999. Post-1945 European history.

Rebecca L. Winer, Associate Professor; Ph.D., UCLA, 1996. Medieval Europe, European women's history, Jewish history.

Section 8
Humanities

This section contains a directory of institutions offering graduate work in humanities, followed by in-depth entries submitted by institutions that chose to prepare detailed program descriptions. Additional information about programs listed in the directory but not augmented by an in-depth entry may be obtained by writing directly to the dean of a graduate school or chair of a department at the address given in the directory.

For programs offering related work, see also in this book *Area and Cultural Studies, Geography, Interdisciplinary Studies, Philosophy, Political Science and International Affairs, Religious Studies,* and *Sociology, Anthropology, and Archaeology.* In another guide in this series:

Graduate Programs in Engineering & Applied Sciences
See *Management of Engineering and Technology*

CONTENTS

Program Directories

Humanities   336
Liberal Studies   339

Close-Ups
California Institute of Integral Studies   347
Central European University   349
Dartmouth College   351

See also:
The New School: A University—Political and Social
    Science   1251

Humanities

American Public University System, AMU/APU Graduate Programs, Charles Town, WV 25414. Offers air warfare (MA Military Studies); American Revolution (MA Military Studies); business administration (MBA); Civil War (MA Military Studies); criminal justice (MA); defense management (MA Military Studies); emergency and disaster management (MA); environmental policy and management (MS); fire science management (MA); global engagement (MA); history (MA); homeland security (MA); humanities (MA); intelligence (MA Military Studies, MA Strategic Intelligence); international peace and conflict resolution (MA); international relations and conflict resolution (MA); joint warfare (MA Military Studies); land warfare international perspective (MA Military Studies); management (MA); military history (MA); military leadership (MA Military Studies); national security studies (MA); naval warfare international (MA Military Studies); naval warfare US (MA Military Studies); political science (MA); public administration (MA); public health (MA); security management (MA); space studies (MS); special ops/LIC (MA Military Studies); sports management (MA); transportation and logistics management (MA); transportation management (MA); unconventional warfare (MA Military Studies); World War II (MA Military Studies). Programs offered via distance learning only. Part-time and evening/weekend programs available. Postbaccalaureate distance learning degree programs offered (no on-campus study). *Degree requirements:* For master's, comprehensive exam. *Entrance requirements:* For master's, bachelor's degree or equivalent, minimum GPA of 2.7 in last 60 hours of course work. Electronic applications accepted. *Faculty research:* Military history, criminal justice, management performance, national security.

Arcadia University, Graduate Studies, Program in Humanities, Glenside, PA 19038-3295. Offers fine arts, theater, and music (MAH); history, philosophy, and religion (MAH); literature and language (MAH). Part-time programs available. *Degree requirements:* For master's, thesis or alternative.

Brigham Young University, Graduate Studies, College of Humanities, Department of Humanities, Classics, and Comparative Literature, Provo, UT 84602-1001. Offers comparative literature (MA); comparative studies (MA); humanities (MA). *Faculty:* 26 full-time (4 women). *Students:* 27 full-time (14 women). Average age 27. 15 applicants, 80% accepted, 6 enrolled. In 2008, 5 master's awarded. *Degree requirements:* For master's, 2 foreign languages, thesis. *Entrance requirements:* For master's, GRE, minimum GPA of 3.0 in last 60 hours. *Application deadline:* For fall admission, 3/1 for domestic and international students. Application fee: $50. Electronic applications accepted. *Expenses:* Tuition: Full-time $5160; part-time $287 per credit hour. Tuition and fees vary according to program and student's religious affiliation. *Financial support:* In 2008–09, 27 students received support, including 7 research assistantships (averaging $4,680 per year), 29 teaching assistantships; fellowships, career-related internships or fieldwork, institutionally sponsored loans, scholarships/grants, tuition waivers (full and partial), and student instructorships also available. Support available to part-time students. *Unit head:* Dr. Michael J. Call, Chair, 801-422-2550, Fax: 801-422-0305, E-mail: michael_call@byu.edu. *Application contact:* Carolyn Hone, Graduate Secretary for Humanities and Comparative Literature, 801-422-4430, Fax: 801-422-0305, E-mail: carolyn_hone@byu.edu.

California Institute of Integral Studies, Graduate Programs, School of Consciousness and Transformation, San Francisco, CA 94103. Offers cultural anthropology and social transformation (MA); East-West psychology (MA, PhD); integrative health studies (MA); philosophy and religion (MA, PhD), including Asian and comparative studies, philosophy, cosmology, and consciousness, women's spirituality, women's spirituality flex format; social and cultural anthropology (PhD); transformative leadership (MA); transformative studies (PhD). Part-time and evening/weekend programs available. Postbaccalaureate distance learning degree programs offered (minimal on-campus study). *Faculty:* 29 full-time, 32 part-time/adjunct. *Students:* 334 full-time (218 women), 126 part-time (77 women); includes 102 minority (39 African Americans, 4 American Indian/Alaska Native, 35 Asian Americans or Pacific Islanders, 24 Hispanic Americans), 1 international. Average age 37. 223 applicants, 78% accepted, 110 enrolled. In 2008, 93 master's, 30 doctorates awarded. Terminal master's awarded for partial completion of doctoral program. *Degree requirements:* For master's; comprehensive exam (for some programs), thesis optional; for doctorate, comprehensive exam, thesis/dissertation. *Entrance requirements:* For master's, minimum GPA of 3.0, letters of recommendation, writing sample; for doctorate, master's degree, minimum GPA of 3.0, letters of recommendation, writing sample. Additional exam requirements/recommendations for international students: Required—TOEFL. *Application deadline:* For fall admission, 2/1 priority date for domestic and international students; for spring admission, 10/15 priority date for domestic and international students. Applications are processed on a rolling basis. Application fee: $65. Electronic applications accepted. *Expenses:* Tuition: Part-time $815 per contact hour. Required fees: $270; $135 per semester. Tuition and fees vary according to degree level. *Financial support:* In 2008–09, 271 students received support; research assistantships, teaching assistantships, career-related internships or fieldwork, Federal Work-Study, institutionally sponsored loans, scholarships/grants, and tuition waivers (partial) available. Support available to part-time students. Financial award application deadline: 3/15; financial award applicants required to submit FAFSA. *Faculty research:* Altered states of consciousness, dreams, cosmology, postcolonial studies, integrative health studies. *Application contact:* Allyson Werner, Senior Admissions Counselor, 415-575-6155, Fax: 415-575-1268.

See Close-Up on page 347.

California State University, Dominguez Hills, College of Arts and Humanities, Program in the Humanities, Carson, CA 90747-0001. Offers MA. Part-time and evening/weekend programs available. *Faculty:* 12 full-time (9 women), 4 part-time/adjunct (2 women). *Students:* 2 full-time (both women), 30 part-time (19 women); includes 12 minority (7 African Americans, 5 Hispanic Americans), 1 international. Average age 43. 12 applicants, 83% accepted, 3 enrolled. In 2008, 1 master's awarded. *Degree requirements:* For master's, thesis or alternative. *Entrance requirements:* For master's, minimum GPA of 3.0. *Application deadline:* For fall admission, 6/1 for domestic students. Applications are processed on a rolling basis. Application fee: $55. *Expenses:* Tuition, nonresident: part-time $339 per unit. Required fees: $1300 per semester. *Financial support:* Institutionally sponsored loans available. Support available to part-time students. Financial award application deadline: 8/1. *Faculty research:* African American music, postmodernism, cities of antiquity, Faust, African studies. *Unit head:* Dr. Lorna Fitzsimmons, Coordinator, 310-243-3036, E-mail: lfitzsimmons@csudh.edu. *Application contact:* Dr. Gayle Ball-Parker, Director of Admissions, 310-243-3645, E-mail: gball@csudh.edu.

California State University, Dominguez Hills, College of Extended and International Education, Humanities External Degree Program, Carson, CA 90747-0001. Offers MA. Part-time and evening/weekend programs available. Postbaccalaureate distance learning degree programs offered. *Faculty:* 8 full-time (4 women), 34 part-time/adjunct (13 women). *Students:* 6 full-time (3 women), 465 part-time (235 women); includes 53 minority (14 African Americans, 6 American Indian/Alaska Native, 10 Asian Americans or Pacific Islanders, 23 Hispanic Americans), 17 international. Average age 43. 88 applicants, 73% accepted, 50 enrolled. In 2008, 103 master's awarded. *Degree requirements:* For master's, thesis, advancement to candidacy essays. *Entrance requirements:* Additional exam requirements/recommendations for international students: Required—TOEFL. *Application deadline:* For fall admission, 6/1 for domestic and international students; for winter admission, 3/1 for domestic and international students; for spring admission, 11/1 for domestic and international students. Application fee: $55. *Expenses:* Contact institution. *Financial support:* Applicants required to submit FAFSA. *Faculty research:* 19th and 20th century literature, Arab history, Greek philosophy, ancient history, East Asian, Soviet cultural history, Native American history and culture, feminist studies. *Unit head:* Dr. Patricia Cherin, Coordinator, 310-243-3191, Fax: 310-516-4399, E-mail: huxonline@csudh.edu. *Application contact:* Lisa Ayers, Program Assistant, 310-243-3190, Fax: 310-516-4399, E-mail: layers@csudh.edu.

Carlow University, Humanities Division, Pittsburgh, PA 15213-3165. Offers creative writing (MFA), including fiction, nonfiction, poetry. Part-time and evening/weekend programs available. *Faculty:* 8 part-time/adjunct (4 women). *Students:* 30 part-time (27 women); includes 3 minority (all African Americans). Average age 41. In 2008, 8 master's awarded. *Degree requirements:* For master's, thesis or alternative. *Entrance requirements:* For master's, minimum GPA of 3.0, resumé, two essays, writing samples, two letters of recommendation. Additional exam requirements/recommendations for international students: Required—TOEFL (minimum score 550 paper-based; 213 computer-based). *Application deadline:* For fall admission, 6/15 priority date for domestic and international students; for spring admission, 11/15 priority date for domestic and international students. Applications are processed on a rolling basis. Application fee: $20. *Expenses:* Tuition: Part-time $700 per credit. *Financial support:* Career-related internships or fieldwork, Federal Work-Study, and scholarships/grants available. Support available to part-time students. Financial award application deadline: 4/1; financial award applicants required to submit FAFSA. *Unit head:* Ellie Wymard, PhD, Director of MFA Program, 412-578-6597, Fax: 412-578-8706, E-mail: wymardex@carlow.edu. *Application contact:* Jo Danhires, Administrative Assistant, Admissions, 412-578-6059, Fax: 412-578-6321, E-mail: gradstudies@carlow.edu.

Central European University, Graduate Studies, School of Social Sciences and Humanities, Budapest, Hungary. Offers economics (MA, PhD); gender studies (MA, PhD); international relations and European studies (MA, PhD); mathematics and its applications (MS, PhD); medieval studies (MA, PhD); nationalism studies (MA, PhD); philosophy (MA, PhD); political science (MA, PhD); public policy (MA, PhD); sociology and social anthropology (MA, PhD). Terminal master's awarded for partial completion of doctoral program. *Degree requirements:* For master's, one foreign language, thesis; for doctorate, one foreign language, comprehensive exam, thesis/dissertation. *Entrance requirements:* For master's, CEU subject tests, interview; for doctorate, GRE, CEU subject test, interview. Additional exam requirements/recommendations for international students: Required—TOEFL (minimum score 570 paper-based; 230 computer-based). Electronic applications accepted. *Faculty research:* Civil society, fiscal decentralization, party politics, political philosophy (especially Liberalism, theory of Democracy).

See Close-Up on page 349.

Central Michigan University, Central Michigan University Off-Campus Programs, Program in Humanities, Mount Pleasant, MI 48859. Offers MA. Part-time and evening/weekend programs available. *Entrance requirements:* For master's, minimum GPA of 2.7 in major. Additional exam requirements/recommendations for international students: Required—TOEFL. *Application deadline:* Applications are processed on a rolling basis. Application fee: $50. Electronic applications accepted. *Expenses:* Tuition, state resident: full-time $3717; part-time $413 per credit. Tuition, nonresident: full-time $6894; part-time $766 per credit. *Financial support:* Scholarships/grants available. Support available to part-time students. Financial award applicants required to submit FAFSA. *Unit head:* Dr. Ronald Primeau, Director, 989-774-3117, Fax: 989-774-7106, E-mail: ronald.r.primeau@cmich.edu. *Application contact:* 877-268-4636, E-mail: cmuoffcampus@cmich.edu.

Central Michigan University, College of Graduate Studies, College of Humanities and Social and Behavioral Sciences, Program in Humanities, Mount Pleasant, MI 48859. Offers humanities (MA), including contemporary issues in the humanities: race, class, and gender, images and ideas of self, Native American issues in modern culture, popular culture studies, the rise of industrial society. Part-time and evening/weekend programs available. *Students:* 3 full-time (1 woman), 7 part-time (4 women). Average age 37. *Degree requirements:* For master's, thesis or alternative. *Application deadline:* Applications are processed on a rolling basis. Application fee: $35 ($45 for international students). Electronic applications accepted. *Expenses:* Tuition, state resident: full-time $3717; part-time $413 per credit. Tuition, nonresident: full-time $6894; part-time $766 per credit. *Financial support:* Fellowships with tuition reimbursements, Federal Work-Study, unspecified assistantships, and out-of-state merit awards available. *Faculty research:* Rise of industrial society; images and ideas of self; contemporary issues of race, class, and gender; popular culture; Native American issues in modern culture. *Unit head:* Dr. Ronald Primeau, Director, 989-774-3117, Fax: 989-774-7106, E-mail: ronald.r.primeau@cmich.edu. *Application contact:* Judith L. Prince, Director of Graduate Student Services, 989-774-1059, Fax: 989-774-1857, E-mail: judith.l.prince@cmich.edu.

Claremont Graduate University, Graduate Programs, School of Arts and Humanities, Claremont, CA 91711-6160. Offers M Phil, MA, MFA, DCM, DMA, PhD, Certificate, MA/PhD, MBA/MA, MBA/PhD. Part-time programs available. *Faculty:* 12 full-time (2 women), 9 part-time/adjunct (1 woman). *Students:* 358 full-time (200 women), 47 part-time (25 women); includes 89 minority (19 African Americans, 3 American Indian/Alaska Native, 29 Asian Americans or Pacific Islanders, 38 Hispanic Americans), 26 international. Average age 35. In 2008, 64 master's, 27 doctorates awarded. *Degree requirements:* For doctorate, 2 foreign languages, comprehensive exam, thesis/dissertation, oral and written qualifying exams, oral defense of dissertation, recitals. *Entrance requirements:* For master's and doctorate, GRE General Test. Additional exam requirements/recommendations for international students: Required—TOEFL (minimum score 550 paper-based; 213 computer-based; 80 iBT). *Application deadline:* For fall admission, 2/1 priority date for domestic students. Applications are processed on a rolling basis. Application fee: $60. Electronic applications accepted. *Expenses:* Tuition: Full-time $33,698; part-time $1465 per unit. Required fees: $310; $155 per semester. Tuition and fees vary according to program. *Financial support:* Fellowships, research assistantships, teaching assistantships, Federal Work-Study, institutionally sponsored loans, and scholarships/grants available. Support available to part-time students. Financial award application deadline: 2/15; financial award applicants required to submit FAFSA. *Unit head:* Marc Redfield, Interim Dean, 909-607-3337, Fax: 909-607-1221, E-mail: marc.redfield@cgu.edu. *Application contact:* Justin Evans, Admissions Coordinator, 909-607-1278, Fax: 909-607-1221, E-mail: humanities@cgu.edu.

College of the Humanities and Sciences, Harrison Middleton University, Graduate Program, Tempe, AZ 85282. Offers education (MA, Ed D); humanities (MA); imaginative literature (MA); interdisciplinary studies (DA); jurisprudence (MA); natural science (MA); philosophy and religion (MA); social science (MA). Part-time and evening/weekend programs available. Postbaccalaureate distance learning degree programs offered (no on-campus study). Electronic applications accepted.

Concordia University, School of Graduate Studies, Faculty of Arts and Science, Program in Humanities, Montréal, QC H3G 1M8, Canada. Offers PhD. *Degree requirements:* For doctorate, one foreign language, comprehensive exam, thesis/dissertation.

Dominican University of California, Graduate Programs, School of Arts and Sciences, Program in Humanities, San Rafael, CA 94901-2298. Offers MA. Part-time programs available. *Faculty:* 7 full-time (3 women), 3 part-time/adjunct (1 woman). *Students:* 4 full-time (3 women), 38 part-time (28 women); includes 4 minority (1 African American, 1 American Indian/Alaska Native, 2 Hispanic Americans). Average age 46. 15 applicants, 53% accepted, 8 enrolled. In 2008, 9 master's awarded. *Degree requirements:* For master's, thesis or alternative. *Entrance requirements:* For master's, minimum GPA of 3.0, interview. Additional exam requirements/recommendations for international students: Required—TOEFL (minimum score 550 paper-based; 213 computer-based). *Application deadline:* Applications are processed on a rolling basis. Application fee: $40. Electronic applications accepted. *Expenses:* Tuition: Full-time $14,040; part-time $780 per unit. *Financial support:* In 2008–09, 18 students received support, including 7 fellowships (averaging $1,000 per year); scholarships/grants also available. Support available to part-time students. Financial award applicants required to submit FAFSA. *Unit head:* Dr. Craig Singleton, Director, 415-485-3275, Fax: 415-485-3205, E-mail: singleton@dominican.edu. *Application contact:* Shannon Lovelace, Assistant Director, 415-485-3246, Fax: 415-485-3214.

Drew University, Caspersen School of Graduate Studies, Program in Medical Humanities, Madison, NJ 07940-1493. Offers MMH, DMH, CMH. Part-time and evening/weekend programs available. *Degree requirements:* For master's, thesis; for doctorate, comprehensive exam. *Faculty research:* Biomedical ethics, medical narrative, history of medicine, medicine and the arts.

Duke University, Graduate School, Program in Humanities, Durham, NC 27708. Offers AM, JD/AM. Part-time programs available. *Entrance requirements:* For master's, GRE General Test. Additional exam requirements/recommendations for international students: Required—TOEFL (minimum score 550 paper-based; 213 computer-based; 83 iBT), IELTS (minimum score 7).

Florida State University, Graduate Studies, College of Arts and Sciences, Department of Interdisciplinary Humanities, Tallahassee, FL 32306. Offers American and Florida studies (MA, Certificate); interdisciplinary humanities (PhD). Part-time programs available. Terminal master's awarded for partial completion of doctoral program. *Degree requirements:* For master's, one foreign language; for doctorate, 2 foreign languages, thesis/dissertation. *Entrance requirements:* For master's, GRE General Test (minimum score: 1100), minimum GPA of 3.0; for doctorate, GRE General Test, minimum GPA of 3.0. Additional exam requirements/recommendations for international students: Required—TOEFL (minimum score 550 paper-based; 213 computer-based). Electronic applications accepted.

Georgetown University, Graduate School of Arts and Sciences, School of Continuing Studies, Washington, DC 20057. Offers American studies (MALS); Catholic studies (MALS); classical civilizations (MALS); ethics and the professions (MALS); human resources management (MPS); humanities (MALS); individualized study (MALS); international affairs (MALS); Islam and Muslim-Christian relations (MALS); journalism (MPS); liberal studies (DLS); literature and society (MALS); medieval and early modern European studies (MALS); public relations (MPS); real estate (MPS); religious studies (MALS); social and public policy (MALS); sports industry management (MPS); the theory and practice of American democracy (MALS); visual culture (MALS). *Entrance requirements:* Additional exam requirements/recommendations for international students: Required—TOEFL.

Hofstra University, College of Liberal Arts and Sciences, Department of Fine Arts, Art History, and Humanity, Hempstead, NY 11549. Offers comparative arts and culture (MA). Part-time programs available. *Faculty:* 4 full-time (0 women), 1 part-time/adjunct (0 women). *Students:* 2 full-time (both women), 7 part-time (4 women), 1 international. Average age 32. 2 applicants, 100% accepted, 0 enrolled. In 2008, 3 master's awarded. *Degree requirements:* For master's, thesis. *Entrance requirements:* For master's, letter of recommendation, interview, essay. Additional exam requirements/recommendations for international students: Required—TOEFL (minimum score 550 paper-based; 213 computer-based; 80 iBT). *Application deadline:* Applications are processed on a rolling basis. Application fee: $60. Electronic applications accepted. *Expenses:* Tuition: Full-time $15,300; part-time $850 per credit. Required fees: $970; $165 per term. Tuition and fees vary according to program. *Financial support:* In 2008–09, 3 students received support, including 2 fellowships with full and partial tuition reimbursements available (averaging $3,900 per year); research assistantships with full and partial tuition reimbursements available, Federal Work-Study, institutionally sponsored loans, scholarships/grants, and tuition waivers (full and partial) also available. Support available to part-time students. Financial award applicants required to submit FAFSA. *Unit head:* Prof. Alexander Mihailovic, Professor, 516-463-5435, Fax: 463-7082, E-mail: cllazm@hofstra.edu. *Application contact:* Carol Drummer, Dean of Graduate Admissions, 516-463-4876, Fax: 516-463-4664, E-mail: gradstudent@hofstra.edu.

Hollins University, Graduate Programs, Program in Liberal Studies, Roanoke, VA 24020-1603. Offers humanities (MALS); interdisciplinary studies (MALS); justice and legal studies (MALS); liberal studies (CAS); social science (MALS); visual and performing arts (MALS). Part-time and evening/weekend programs available. *Faculty:* 6 full-time (1 woman), 7 part-time/adjunct (4 women). *Students:* 20 full-time (17 women), 78 part-time (56 women); includes 14 minority (13 African Americans, 1 Hispanic American), 1 international. Average age 39. 33 applicants, 85% accepted, 23 enrolled. In 2008, 42 master's awarded. *Degree requirements:* For master's, thesis. *Entrance requirements:* For master's, letters of recommendation, interview. Additional exam requirements/recommendations for international students: Required—TOEFL (minimum score 550 paper-based; 213 computer-based; 79 iBT). *Application deadline:* For fall admission, 7/1 priority date for domestic and international students; for spring admission, 12/10 priority date for domestic and international students. Applications are processed on a rolling basis. Application fee: $40. Electronic applications accepted. *Expenses:* Tuition: Full-time $26,720; part-time $590 per credit hour. Required fees: $280. *Financial support:* In 2008–09, 53 students received support, including 2 fellowships (averaging $1,189 per year); Federal Work-Study and scholarships/grants also available. Support available to part-time students. Financial award application deadline: 7/15; financial award applicants required to submit FAFSA. *Faculty research:* Elderly blacks, film, feminist economics, US voting patterns, Wagner, diversity. *Unit head:* Dr. Edward A. Lynch, Director, 540-362-6475, Fax: 540-362-6288, E-mail: elynch@hollins.edu. *Application contact:* Cathy S. Koon, Manager of Graduate Services, 540-362-6326, Fax: 540-362-6288, E-mail: ckoon@hollins.edu.

Hood College, Graduate School, Program in Humanities, Frederick, MD 21701-8575. Offers MA. Part-time and evening/weekend programs available. *Faculty:* 6 full-time (4 women), 1 (woman) part-time/adjunct. *Students:* 1 (woman) full-time, 37 part-time (32 women), 2 international. Average age 35. 11 applicants, 91% accepted, 6 enrolled. In 2008, 6 master's awarded. *Degree requirements:* For master's, capstone/research project. *Entrance requirements:* For master's, minimum GPA of 2.75. Additional exam requirements/recommendations for international students: Required—TOEFL (minimum score 575 paper-based; 231 computer-based; 89 iBT). *Application deadline:* For fall admission, 7/15 for domestic and international students; for spring admission, 12/15 for domestic and international students. Applications are processed on a rolling basis. Application fee: $35. Electronic applications accepted. *Expenses:* Tuition: Full-time $6480. Required fees: $100; $50 per semester. *Financial support:* Applicants required to submit FAFSA. *Unit head:* Dr. Rusty Monhollon, Director, 301-696-3690, E-mail: monhollon@hood.edu. *Application contact:* Dr. Allen P. Flora, Dean of Graduate School, 301-696-3811, Fax: 301-696-3597, E-mail: gofurther@hood.edu.

Instituto Tecnológico y de Estudios Superiores de Monterrey, Campus Central de Veracruz, Graduate Programs, Córdoba, Mexico. Offers administration (MA); administration of information technologies (MTI); computer sciences (MCC); education (MEE); educational institution administration (MAD); educational technology (MTE); electronic commerce (MCE); finance (MAF); humanistic studies (MEH); international business for Latin America (MNL); marketing (MMT); science (MCP); technology management (MTT). Part-time and evening/weekend programs available. Postbaccalaureate distance learning degree programs offered (minimal on-campus study). *Degree requirements:* For master's, thesis (for some programs). *Entrance requirements:* For master's, PAEP College Board. Electronic applications accepted.

Instituto Tecnológico y de Estudios Superiores de Monterrey, Campus Ciudad de México, Virtual University Division, Ciudad de Mexico, Mexico. Offers administration of information technologies (MA); computer sciences (MA); education (MA, PhD); educational technology (MA); environmental engineering (MA); environmental systems (MA); humanistic studies (MA); industrial engineering (MA); international business for Latin America (MA); quality systems (MA); quality systems and productivity (MA). Part-time and evening/weekend programs available. Postbaccalaureate distance learning degree programs offered (minimal on-campus study). *Entrance requirements:* For master's and doctorate, Instituto entrance exam. Additional exam requirements/recommendations for international students: Required—TOEFL.

Instituto Tecnológico y de Estudios Superiores de Monterrey, Campus Ciudad Juárez, Program in Humanistic Studies, Ciudad Juárez, Mexico. Offers MEH.

Instituto Tecnológico y de Estudios Superiores de Monterrey, Campus Estado de México, Professional and Graduate Division, Estado de Mexico, Mexico. Offers administration of information technologies (MITA); architecture (M Arch); business administration (GMBA, MBA); computer sciences (MCS, PhD); education (M Ed); educational institution administration (MAD); educational technology and innovation (PhD); electronic commerce (MEC); environmental systems (MS); finance (MAF); humanistic studies (MHS); information sciences and knowledge management (MISKM); information systems (MS); manufacturing systems (MS); marketing (MEM); quality systems and productivity (MS); science and materials engineering (PhD); telecommunications management (MTM). Part-time programs available. Postbaccalaureate distance learning degree programs offered (minimal on-campus study). *Degree requirements:* For master's, one foreign language, thesis (for some programs); for doctorate, one foreign language, thesis/dissertation. *Entrance requirements:* For master's, E-PAEP 500, interview; for doctorate, E-PAEP 500, research proposal. Additional exam requirements/recommendations for international students: Required—TOEFL (minimum score 550 paper-based). *Faculty research:* Surface treatments by plasmas, mechanical properties, robotics, graphical computing, mechatronics security protocols.

Instituto Tecnológico y de Estudios Superiores de Monterrey, Campus Irapuato, Graduate Programs, Irapuato, Mexico. Offers administration (MBA); administration of information technology (MAIT); administration of telecommunications (MAT); architecture (M Arch); computer science (MCS); education (M Ed); educational administration (MEA); educational innovation and technology (DEIT); educational technology (MET); electronic commerce (MBA); environmental administration and planning (MEAP); environmental systems (MES); finances (MBA); humanistic studies (MHS); international management for Latin American executives (MIMLAE); library and information science (MLIS); manufacturing quality management (MMQM); marketing research (MBA).

John Carroll University, Graduate School, Program in Humanities, University Heights, OH 44118-4581. Offers MA. Part-time and evening/weekend programs available. *Degree requirements:* For master's, thesis optional, comprehensive research essay. *Entrance requirements:* For master's, minimum GPA of 2.75, interview. Electronic applications accepted. *Faculty research:* Modern French history, modern American Catholic history.

Laura and Alvin Siegal College of Judaic Studies, Graduate Programs, Beachwood, OH 44122-7116. Offers humanities (MA), including Holocaust studies; religious education (MAJS), including Jewish education, Judaic studies. Part-time and evening/weekend programs available. Postbaccalaureate distance learning degree programs offered (no on-campus study). *Degree requirements:* For master's, one foreign language, thesis. *Entrance requirements:* For master's, interview.

Laurentian University, School of Graduate Studies and Research, Programme in Humanities: Interpretation and Values, Sudbury, ON P3E 2C6, Canada. Offers MA. Part-time programs available. *Faculty research:* Modern Canadian literature; aboriginal languages and cultures; relation between ethics, religion, and the arts; narrative conventions; Renaissance drama and Reformation literature, Biblical and philosophical hermeneutics.

Marshall University, Academic Affairs Division, College of Liberal Arts, Program in Humanities, Huntington, WV 25755. Offers MA. Part-time and evening/weekend programs available. *Degree requirements:* For master's, thesis, comprehensive assessment. *Entrance requirements:* For master's, GRE General Test, MAT, bachelor's degree in humanities, minimum undergraduate GPA of 3.0.

Marymount University, School of Arts and Sciences, Program in Humanities, Arlington, VA 22207-4299. Offers MA. Part-time and evening/weekend programs available. *Students:* 1 (woman) full-time, 8 part-time (7 women); includes 3 minority (all African Americans). Average age 30. 4 applicants, 100% accepted, 2 enrolled. In 2008, 3 master's awarded. *Degree requirements:* For master's, thesis or alternative. *Entrance requirements:* For master's, minimum GPA of 3.0; undergraduate major in art history, English, history, or philosophy; 2 letters of recommendation; interview; writing sample; essay. Additional exam requirements/recommendations for international students: Required—TOEFL (minimum score 600 paper-based; 250 computer-based; 100 iBT). *Application deadline:* For fall admission, 7/1 for international students; for spring admission, 10/15 for international students. Applications are processed on a rolling basis. Application fee: $40. Electronic applications accepted. *Expenses:* Tuition: Full-time $12,420; part-time $690 per credit hour. Required fees: $126; $7 per credit hour. Tuition and fees vary according to degree level. *Financial support:* In 2008–09, 6 students received support. Career-related internships or fieldwork, Federal Work-Study, scholarships/grants, and unspecified assistantships available. Support available to part-time students. Financial award applicants required to submit FAFSA. *Unit head:* Dr. Mark Throwbridge, Director of Graduate Studies, 703-284-1564, Fax: 703-284-3859, E-mail: mark.throwbridge@marymount.edu. *Application contact:* Francesca Reed, Director, Graduate Admissions, 703-284-5901, Fax: 703-527-3815, E-mail: grad.admissions@marymount.edu.

Massachusetts Institute of Technology, School of Humanities, Arts, and Social Sciences, Program in Writing and Humanistic Studies, Cambridge, MA 02139-4307. Offers science writing (SM). *Degree requirements:* For master's, thesis, internship. *Entrance requirements:* For master's, GRE General Test. Electronic applications accepted.

Memorial University of Newfoundland, School of Graduate Studies, Interdisciplinary Programs in Humanities, St. John's, NL A1C 5S7, Canada. Offers M Phil. *Degree requirements:* For master's, comprehensive exam, journal. *Entrance requirements:* For master's, honors bachelor's degree. Electronic applications accepted. *Faculty research:* Western language, philosophy, literature, and history.

Michigan State University, College of Human Medicine and The Graduate School, Graduate Programs in Human Medicine, Program in Bioethics, Humanities, and Society, East Lansing, MI 48824. Offers MA. *Degree requirements:* For master's, thesis or alternative, oral defense of thesis. *Entrance requirements:* Additional exam requirements/recommendations for international students: Required—TOEFL (minimum score 550 paper-based; 213 computer-based), Michigan State University ELT (85), Michigan ELAB (83). Electronic applications accepted.

Mount St. Mary's College, Graduate Division, Program in Humanities, Los Angeles, CA 90049-1599. Offers MA. *Entrance requirements:* Additional exam requirements/recommendations for international students: Required—TOEFL.

National University, Academic Affairs, College of Letters and Sciences, Department of Art and Humanities, La Jolla, CA 92037-1011. Offers creative writing (MFA); English (MA); history (MA). Part-time and evening/weekend programs available. Postbaccalaureate distance learning degree programs offered (no on-campus study). *Faculty:* 19 full-time (6 women), 180 part-time/adjunct (92 women). *Students:* 208 full-time (153 women), 433 part-time (302 women); includes 137 minority (57 African Americans, 10 American Indian/Alaska Native, 19 Asian Americans or Pacific Islanders, 51 Hispanic Americans). Average age 38. 420 applicants, 100% accepted, 420 enrolled. In 2008, 152 master's awarded. *Degree requirements:* For master's, thesis (for some programs). *Entrance requirements:* For master's, interview, minimum GPA of 2.5. Additional exam requirements/recommendations for international students: Required—TOEFL (minimum score 550 paper-based; 213 computer-based; 79 iBT), IELTS (minimum score 6). *Application deadline:* Applications are processed on a rolling basis. Application fee: $60 ($65 for international students). Electronic applications accepted. *Expenses:* Tuition: Full-time $8694; part-time $322 per credit hour. Tuition and fees vary according to course load. *Financial support:* Career-related internships or fieldwork, institutionally sponsored loans, scholarships/grants, and tuition waivers (partial) available. Support available to part-time students. Financial award application deadline: 6/30; financial award applicants required to submit FAFSA. *Unit head:* Dr. Janet Baker, Chair, 858-642-8472, Fax: 858-642-8715, E-mail: jbaker@nu.edu. *Application contact:* Dominick Giovanniello, Associate Regional Dean—San Diego, 800-NAT-UNIV, Fax: 858-541-7792, E-mail: dgiovann@nu.edu.

Humanities

New York University, Graduate School of Arts and Science, Draper Interdisciplinary Program in Humanities and Social Thought, New York, NY 10012-1019. Offers humanities and social thought (MA); religion (Advanced Certificate); social theory (Advanced Certificate). Part-time programs available. *Degree requirements:* For master's, thesis, comprehensive exam or essay. *Entrance requirements:* For degree, master's degree. Additional exam requirements/recommendations for international students: Required—TOEFL. *Faculty research:* Art world, gender politics, global histories, literary cultures, the city.

Nova Southeastern University, Graduate School of Humanities and Social Sciences, Department of Multi-Disciplinary Studies, Fort Lauderdale, FL 33314-7796. Offers college student affairs (MS); college student personnel administration (Certificate); cross-disciplinary studies (MA); qualitative research (Certificate). Part-time programs available. Postbaccalaureate distance learning degree programs offered (no on-campus study). *Faculty:* 4 part-time/adjunct (2 women). *Students:* 24 full-time (15 women), 35 part-time (29 women); includes 24 minority (20 African Americans, 4 Hispanic Americans), 2 international. 45 applicants, 67% accepted, 30 enrolled. In 2008, 7 master's awarded. *Degree requirements:* For master's, comprehensive exam, thesis optional, portfolio. *Entrance requirements:* For master's, interview, minimum GPA of 3.0. Additional exam requirements/recommendations for international students: Required—TOEFL. *Application deadline:* For fall admission, 7/1 priority date for domestic and international students; for winter admission, 11/1 priority date for domestic and international students; for spring admission, 3/1 priority date for domestic and international students. Applications are processed on a rolling basis. Electronic applications accepted. *Financial support:* In 2008–09, 20 research assistantships with tuition reimbursements (averaging $15,600 per year) were awarded; career-related internships or fieldwork, Federal Work-Study, institutionally sponsored loans, and scholarships/grants also available. Financial award applicants required to submit CSS PROFILE. *Unit head:* Dr. Judith McKay, Senior Associate Dean, 954-262-3060, Fax: 954-262-3893, E-mail: mckayj@nsu.nova.edu. *Application contact:* Marcia Arango, Student Recruitment Coordinator, 954-262-3006, Fax: 954-262-3968, E-mail: marango@nsu.nova.edu.

Old Dominion University, College of Arts and Letters, Program in Humanities, Norfolk, VA 23529. Offers MA. Part-time and evening/weekend programs available. *Faculty:* 2 full-time (1 woman). *Students:* 16 full-time (15 women), 14 part-time (8 women); includes 3 minority (1 African American, 2 Hispanic Americans), 2 international. Average age 31. 27 applicants, 96% accepted. In 2008, 10 master's awarded. *Degree requirements:* For master's, thesis optional, project. *Entrance requirements:* For master's, GRE General Test, minimum GPA of 3.0. *Application deadline:* For fall admission, 7/1 for domestic students; for spring admission, 10/1 for domestic students. Applications are processed on a rolling basis. Application fee: $40. Electronic applications accepted. *Expenses:* Tuition, area resident: Full-time $7704; part-time $321 per credit. Tuition, state resident: full-time $7704; part-time $321 per credit. Tuition, nonresident: full-time $19,104; part-time $796 per credit. Required fees: $99 per semester. One-time fee: $40. *Financial support:* In 2008–09, 3 students received support, including 1 fellowship (averaging $4,000 per year), 2 research assistantships with tuition reimbursements available (averaging $8,000 per year); career-related internships or fieldwork, scholarships/grants, and unspecified assistantships also available. Financial award application deadline: 2/15; financial award applicants required to submit FAFSA. *Faculty research:* Media studies, communications, cultural studies, gender studies, American literature. *Unit head:* Dr. Dana Heller, Graduate Program Director, 757-683-3719, Fax: 757-683-6191, E-mail: humgpd@odu.edu. *Application contact:* Dr. Robert Wojtowicz, Associate Dean, 757-683-6077, Fax: 757-683-5746, E-mail: rwojtowi@odu.edu.

Penn State Harrisburg, Graduate School, School of Humanities, Middletown, PA 17057-4898. Offers American studies (MA); humanities (MA). Evening/weekend programs available.

Pepperdine University, Seaver College, Humanities Division, Malibu, CA 90263. Offers American studies (MA); history (MA). *Degree requirements:* For master's, oral and written exams. *Entrance requirements:* For master's, GRE General Test, undergraduate major or 15 upper-division units in history. Additional exam requirements/recommendations for international students: Required—TOEFL.

Polytechnic Institute of NYU, Department of Humanities and Social Sciences, Brooklyn, NY 11201-2990. Offers environment-behavior studies (MS); history of science (MS); integrated digital media (MS, Graduate Certificate); technical communication (Graduate Certificate); technical writing and specialized journalism (MS). Part-time and evening/weekend programs available. *Degree requirements:* For master's, comprehensive exam (for some programs), thesis (for some programs). *Entrance requirements:* Additional exam requirements/recommendations for international students: Required—TOEFL (minimum score 550 paper-based; 213 computer-based); Recommended—IELTS (minimum score 6.5). Electronic applications accepted. *Faculty research:* Trade magazine journalism, technical writing, financial reporting, medical and science reporting, industrial advertising and public relations.

Prescott College, Graduate Programs, Program in Humanities, Prescott, AZ 86301. Offers humanities (MA); student-directed independent study (MA). Part-time programs available. Postbaccalaureate distance learning degree programs offered (minimal on-campus study). *Faculty:* 1 (woman) full-time, 44 part-time/adjunct (26 women). *Students:* 19 full-time (13 women), 32 part-time (28 women); includes 11 minority (7 African Americans, 1 American Indian/Alaska Native, 1 Asian American or Pacific Islander, 2 Hispanic Americans). Average age 39. 28 applicants, 86% accepted, 15 enrolled. In 2008, 17 master's awarded. *Degree requirements:* For master's, thesis, fieldwork or internship, practicum. *Entrance requirements:* For master's, 2 letters of recommendation, resumé, official academic transcripts, personal statement, application form, proposed study plan. Additional exam requirements/recommendations for international students: Required—TOEFL (minimum score 500 paper-based; 173 computer-based). *Application deadline:* For fall admission, 3/15 priority date for domestic and international students; for spring admission, 9/15 priority date for domestic and international students. Applications are processed on a rolling basis. Application fee: $40. Electronic applications accepted. *Expenses:* Tuition: Full-time $13,608; part-time $567 per credit. Required fees: $50 per term. One-time fee: $182. Tuition and fees vary according to degree level. *Financial support:* Career-related internships or fieldwork, Federal Work-Study, and scholarships/grants available. Financial award applicants required to submit FAFSA. *Unit head:* Joan Clingan, Chair, 928-350-3208, Fax: 928-776-5151, E-mail: jclingan@prescott.edu. *Application contact:* Kerstin Alicki, Admissions Counselor, 877-350-2102, Fax: 928-776-5242, E-mail: admissions@prescott.edu.

St. Edward's University, New College, Program in Liberal Arts, Austin, TX 78704. Offers global issues (MLA); humanities (MLA); liberal arts (Certificate); social sciences (MLA). Part-time and evening/weekend programs available. *Students:* 9 full-time (4 women), 78 part-time (49 women); includes 22 minority (4 African Americans, 1 American Indian/Alaska Native, 2 Asian Americans or Pacific Islanders, 15 Hispanic Americans), 1 international. Average age 34. 33 applicants, 88% accepted, 25 enrolled. In 2008, 34 master's awarded. *Degree requirements:* For master's, minimum 24 resident hours. *Entrance requirements:* For master's, minimum GPA of 2.75 in last 60 hours of course work, interview. Additional exam requirements/recommendations for international students: Required—TOEFL (minimum score 550 paper-based; 213 computer-based; 79 iBT). *Application deadline:* For fall admission, 8/1 for domestic students, 7/1 for international students; for spring admission, 12/1 for domestic students, 11/1 for international students. Applications are processed on a rolling basis. Application fee: $45 ($50 for international students). Electronic applications accepted. *Expenses:* Tuition: Full-time $13,752; part-time $764 per credit hour. Required fees: $50 per semester. Full-time tuition and fees vary according to course load and program. *Financial support:* In 2008–09, 4 students received support. Scholarships/grants available. *Unit head:* Dr. Paula Marks, Director, 512-448-8702, Fax: 512-448-8492, E-mail: paulam@stewards.edu. *Application contact:* Kay L. Arnold, Graduate Admissions Coordinator, 512-233-1636, Fax: 512-428-1032, E-mail: kayla@stedwards.edu.

Salve Regina University, Graduate Studies, Program in Humanities, Newport, RI 02840-4192. Offers MA, PhD, CAGS. Part-time and evening/weekend programs available. Postbaccalaureate distance learning degree programs offered (no on-campus study). *Faculty:* 7 full-time (3 women), 6 part-time/adjunct (2 women). *Students:* 2 full-time (1 woman), 73 part-time (32 women); includes 3 minority (2 African Americans, 1 Asian American or Pacific Islander), 1 international. Average age 47. 30 applicants, 73% accepted, 20 enrolled. In 2008, 4 master's, 5 doctorates awarded. *Degree requirements:* For master's, thesis optional; for doctorate, one foreign language, comprehensive exam, thesis/dissertation. *Entrance requirements:* For master's, GMAT, GRE General Test, or MAT; for doctorate, GRE General Test. Additional exam requirements/recommendations for international students: Required—TOEFL (minimum score 600 paper-based; 250 computer-based; 100 iBT), TOEFL or IELTS. *Application deadline:* For fall admission, 3/15 priority date for domestic and international students; for spring admission, 9/15 priority date for domestic and international students. Applications are processed on a rolling basis. Application fee: $60. Electronic applications accepted. *Expenses:* Tuition: Part-time $395 per credit. Required fees: $40 per term. Tuition and fees vary according to degree level. *Financial support:* Career-related internships or fieldwork and Federal Work-Study available. Support available to part-time students. Financial award application deadline: 3/1; financial award applicants required to submit FAFSA. *Unit head:* Dr. Michael Budd, Director, 401-341-3284, E-mail: michael.budd@salve.edu. *Application contact:* Kelly Alverson, Graduate Admissions Counselor, 401-341-2153, Fax: 401-341-2973, E-mail: kelly.alverson@salve.edu.

Sam Houston State University, College of Humanities and Social Sciences, Huntsville, TX 77341. Offers MA, MPA, MS, PhD. *Faculty:* 53 full-time (19 women), 1 part-time/adjunct (0 women). *Students:* 124 full-time (96 women), 148 part-time (79 women); includes 40 minority (9 African Americans, 1 American Indian/Alaska Native, 13 Asian Americans or Pacific Islanders, 17 Hispanic Americans), 7 international. Average age 30. 239 applicants, 52% accepted, 103 enrolled. In 2008, 43 master's, 4 doctorates awarded. *Entrance requirements:* For master's, GRE General Test. Additional exam requirements/recommendations for international students: Required—TOEFL (minimum score 550 paper-based; 213 computer-based; 79 iBT). *Application deadline:* For fall admission, 8/1 for domestic students; for spring admission, 12/1 for domestic students. Application fee: $20. *Expenses:* Tuition, state resident: full-time $3564; part-time $198 per credit hour. Tuition, nonresident: full-time $8622; part-time $479 per credit hour. Required fees: $1290. Tuition and fees vary according to course load and campus/location. *Unit head:* Dr. John deCastro, Dean, 936-294-2200, Fax: 936-294-2207, E-mail: jmd018@shsu.edu. *Application contact:* Dr. Mitchell Muehsam, Dean of Graduate Studies and Associate Vice President for Academic Affairs, 936-294-1971, Fax: 936-294-1271, E-mail: graduate@shsu.edu.

San Francisco State University, Division of Graduate Studies, College of Humanities, Department of Humanities, San Francisco, CA 94132-1722. Offers MA. Part-time and evening/weekend programs available.

Stanford University, School of Humanities and Sciences, Department of Humanities, Stanford, CA 94305-9991. Offers MA. *Degree requirements:* For master's, one foreign language, thesis. *Entrance requirements:* For master's, GRE General Test. Additional exam requirements/recommendations for international students: Required—TOEFL. Electronic applications accepted.

Texas Tech University, Graduate School, College of Arts and Sciences, Department of Classical and Modern Languages and Literatures, Lubbock, TX 79409. Offers applied linguistics (MA); classics (MA); German (MA); Romance language (MA); Romance languages-French (MA); Romance languages-Spanish (MA, PhD). Part-time programs available. *Faculty:* 23 full-time (9 women), 1 (woman) part-time/adjunct. *Students:* 76 full-time (43 women), 21 part-time (14 women); includes 23 minority (1 African American, 1 Asian American or Pacific Islander, 21 Hispanic Americans), 26 international. Average age 32. 73 applicants, 75% accepted, 31 enrolled. In 2008, 20 master's, 2 doctorates awarded. *Degree requirements:* For master's, thesis or alternative; for doctorate, thesis/dissertation. *Entrance requirements:* For master's and doctorate, GRE General Test. Additional exam requirements/recommendations for international students: Required—TOEFL (minimum score 550 paper-based; 213 computer-based). *Application deadline:* For fall admission, 3/1 priority date for international students; for spring admission, 11/1 priority date for international students. Applications are processed on a rolling basis. Application fee: $50 ($60 for international students). Electronic applications accepted. *Expenses:* Tuition, area resident: Part-time $194 per credit hour. Tuition, state resident: full-time $4648; part-time $194 per credit hour. Tuition, nonresident: full-time $11,392; part-time $475 per credit hour. Required fees: $2206; $69 per credit hour. $389 per semester. *Financial support:* In 2008–09, 42 students received support, including 70 teaching assistantships with partial tuition reimbursements available (averaging $11,625 per year); research assistantships with partial tuition reimbursements available, Federal Work-Study and institutionally sponsored loans also available. Support available to part-time students. Financial award application deadline: 4/15; financial award applicants required to submit FAFSA. *Faculty research:* Literature, comparative literature, linguistics, culture, pedagogy. Total annual research expenditures: $65,397. *Unit head:* Dr. Julian Frederick Suppe, Chair and Professor, 806-742-4355, Fax: 806-742-3306, E-mail: frederick.suppe@ttu.edu. *Application contact:* Liz Hildebrand, Senior Advisor, 806-742-4055, Fax: 806-742-3306, E-mail: liz.hildebrand@ttu.edu.

Tiffin University, Program in Humanities, Tiffin, OH 44883-2161. Offers MH. *Entrance requirements:* For master's, work experience. Additional exam requirements/recommendations for international students: Required—TOEFL (minimum score 550 paper-based; 213 computer-based).

Towson University, College of Graduate Studies and Research, Program in Humanities, Towson, MD 21252-0001. Offers MA. Part-time and evening/weekend programs available. *Degree requirements:* For master's, thesis or alternative. *Entrance requirements:* For master's, 2 letters of recommendation, minimum GPA of 3.0, research paper, letter of intent. Additional exam requirements/recommendations for international students: Required—TOEFL. Electronic applications accepted.

Trinity Western University, Faculty of Graduate Studies, Program in Interdisciplinary Humanities, Langley, BC V2Y 1Y1, Canada. Offers general humanities (MAIH); specialized (MAIH), including English, history, philosophy. Part-time and evening/weekend programs available. Postbaccalaureate distance learning degree programs offered (minimal on-campus study). *Degree requirements:* For master's, 36 semester hours. *Entrance requirements:* For master's, strong undergraduate degree in Humanities or English, History or Philosophy. *Faculty research:* Literary theory, gender, medieval and early modern literature, philosophy of religion, Thomas Merton's poetics.

Universidad Nacional Pedro Henriquez Urena, Graduate School, Santo Domingo, Dominican Republic. Offers accounting and auditing (M Acct); animal production (M Agr); business administration (MBA, PhD); Caribbean tropical architecture (M Arch); conservation of monuments and cultural goods (M Arch); economics (M Econ); education (PhD); environmental engineering (MEE); horticulture (M Agr); hospital administration (PhD); humanities (PhD); international relations (MPS); management of natural resources (MNRM); project management (M Man, MPM); public administration (MPS); sanitary engineering (ME); social science (PhD); veterinary medicine (DVM).

University of California, Santa Cruz, Division of Graduate Studies, Division of Humanities, Program in the History of Consciousness, Santa Cruz, CA 95064. Offers PhD. *Degree requirements:* For doctorate, one foreign language, thesis/dissertation, qualifying exam. *Entrance requirements:* Additional exam requirements/recommendations for international students: Required—TOEFL (minimum score 550 paper-based; 220 computer-based). *Faculty research:* Interdisciplinary humanities and social sciences, political theory, cultural theory, feminist studies, literary theory.

University of Chicago, Division of the Humanities, Master of Arts Program in the Humanities, Chicago, IL 60637-1513. Offers MA. MAPH students take courses from faculty members of all departments at University of Chicago. Part-time programs available. *Degree requirements:* For master's, thesis. *Entrance requirements:* For master's, GRE General Test. Additional exam requirements/recommendations for international students: Required—TOEFL (minimum score 600 paper-based; 260 computer-based). Electronic applications accepted.

University of Colorado Denver, College of Liberal Arts and Sciences, Program in Humanities, Denver, CO 80217-3364. Offers MH. Part-time and evening/weekend programs available. *Degree requirements:* For master's, thesis or alternative. *Entrance requirements:* For master's, GRE or MAT, interview, minimum GPA of 2.75, writing sample. Additional exam requirements/recommendations for international students: Required—TOEFL (minimum score 525 paper-based; 197 computer-based). Electronic applications accepted.

University of Dallas, Braniff Graduate School of Liberal Arts, Program in Humanities, Irving, TX 75062-4736. Offers M Hum, MA. Part-time programs available. *Degree requirements:* For master's, one foreign language, comprehensive exam, thesis (for some programs). *Entrance requirements:* For master's, GRE General Test. Additional exam requirements/recommendations for international students: Required—TOEFL. *Faculty research:* Classical epic poetry, scholastic poetry, Renaissance drama, nineteenth and twentieth century Continental philosophy.

University of Houston–Clear Lake, School of Human Sciences and Humanities, Programs in Humanities and Fine Arts, Houston, TX 77058-1098. Offers history (MA); humanities (MA); literature (MA). Part-time and evening/weekend programs available. Postbaccalaureate distance learning degree programs offered (minimal on-campus study). *Degree requirements:* For master's, thesis or alternative. *Entrance requirements:* For master's, GRE General Test. Additional exam requirements/recommendations for international students: Required—TOEFL (minimum score 550 paper-based; 213 computer-based). *Faculty research:* Digital media studies, Latin American history, labor history, Chaucer evolution versus creationism debate.

University of Louisville, Graduate School, College of Arts and Sciences, Department of Humanities, Louisville, KY 40292-0001. Offers MA, PhD, MA/JD. *Students:* 27 full-time (19 women), 68 part-time (47 women); includes 7 African Americans, 3 Asian Americans or Pacific Islanders, 1 Hispanic American, 24 international. Average age 38. In 2008, 6 master's, 2 doctorates awarded. *Degree requirements:* For master's, one foreign language, comprehensive exam (for some programs), thesis (for some programs), internship, project; for doctorate, 2 foreign languages, thesis/dissertation, internship. *Entrance requirements:* For master's, GRE General Test; for doctorate, GRE General Test, letters of recommendation, writing sample. *Application deadline:* Applications are processed on a rolling basis. Application fee: $50. *Financial support:* In 2008–09, 10 teaching assistantships with tuition reimbursements (averaging $18,000 per year) were awarded; institutionally sponsored loans, scholarships/grants, and tuition waivers (partial) also available. *Unit head:* Elaine O. Wise, Chair, 502-852-7149, Fax: 502-852-0078, E-mail: elaine.wise@louisville.edu. *Application contact:* Libby Leggett, Director, Graduate Admissions, 502-852-3101, Fax: 502-852-6536, E-mail: gradadm@louisville.edu.

The University of Texas at Arlington, Graduate School, College of Liberal Arts, Graduate Humanities Program, Arlington, TX 76019. Offers MA. Part-time and evening/weekend programs available. *Faculty:* 6 full-time (1 woman). *Students:* 2 full-time (1 woman), 21 part-time (10 women); includes 5 minority (3 African Americans, 2 Hispanic Americans), 1 international. 18 applicants, 94% accepted, 9 enrolled. In 2008, 1 master's awarded. *Degree requirements:* For master's, one foreign language, thesis optional. *Entrance requirements:* For master's, GRE General Test. Additional exam requirements/recommendations for international students: Required—TOEFL (minimum score 550 paper-based; 213 computer-based). *Application deadline:* For fall admission, 6/16 for domestic students. Applications are processed on a rolling basis. Application fee: $35 ($50 for international students). *Expenses:* Tuition, area resident: Full-time $6500. Tuition, state resident: full-time $6500. Tuition, nonresident: full-time $11,558. *Financial support:* In 2008–09, 1 teaching assistantship (averaging $7,500 per year) was awarded. Financial award application deadline: 6/1; financial award applicants required to submit FAFSA. *Unit head:* Dr. Susan Hekman, Graduate Advisor, 817-272-2389, Fax: 817-272-5807, E-mail: hekman@uta.edu. *Application contact:* Dr. Susan Hekman, Graduate Advisor, 817-272-2389, Fax: 817-272-5807, E-mail: hekman@uta.edu.

The University of Texas at Dallas, School of Arts and Humanities, Richardson, TX 75083-0688. Offers arts and technology (MFA); emerging media and communications (MA); humanities (MA, MAT, PhD), including aesthetic studies, history of ideas, studies in literature. Part-time and evening/weekend programs available. *Faculty:* 52 full-time (15 women), 6 part-time/adjunct (2 women). *Students:* 201 full-time (107 women), 194 part-time (105 women); includes 82 minority (30 African Americans, 3 American Indian/Alaska Native, 23 Asian Americans or Pacific Islanders, 26 Hispanic Americans), 31 international. Average age 38. 173 applicants, 80% accepted, 83 enrolled. In 2008, 88 master's, 11 doctorates awarded. *Degree requirements:* For master's, one foreign language, portfolio; for doctorate, one foreign language, thesis/dissertation. *Entrance requirements:* For master's and doctorate, minimum GPA of 3.0 in undergraduate course work in field. Additional exam requirements/recommendations for international students: Required—TOEFL (minimum score 550 paper-based; 213 computer-based). *Application deadline:* For fall admission, 7/15 for domestic students, 5/1 priority date for international students; for spring admission, 11/15 for domestic students, 9/1 priority date for international students. Applications are processed on a rolling basis. Application fee: $50 ($100 for international students). Electronic applications accepted. *Expenses:* Tuition, area resident: Full-time $8320. Tuition, state resident: full-time $8320. Tuition, nonresident: full-time $15,054. Part-time tuition and fees vary according to course load. *Financial support:* In 2008–09, 10 research assistantships with tuition reimbursements (averaging $10,339 per year), 74 teaching assistantships with tuition reimbursements (averaging $10,152 per year) were awarded; fellowships, Federal Work-Study, institutionally sponsored loans, scholarships/grants, and unspecified assistantships also available. Support available to part-time students. Financial award application deadline: 4/30; financial award applicants required to submit FAFSA. *Faculty research:* Translation, science and the arts and humanities, intellectual and philosophical history, cultural studies. Total annual research expenditures: $165,892. *Unit head:* Dr. Dennis M. Kratz, Dean, 972-883-2984, Fax: 972-883-2989, E-mail: dkratz@utdallas.edu. *Application contact:* Dr. Michael Wilson, Associate Dean of Graduate Studies, 972-883-2756, Fax: 972-883-2989, E-mail: mwilson@utdallas.edu.

The University of Texas Medical Branch, Graduate School of Biomedical Sciences, Program in Medical Humanities, Galveston, TX 77555. Offers MA, PhD. *Students:* 15 full-time (9 women), 2 part-time (1 woman); includes 1 minority (Asian American or Pacific Islander), 1 international. Average age 39. 6 applicants, 83% accepted, 3 enrolled. In 2008, 1 master's, 2 doctorates awarded. *Degree requirements:* For master's, thesis; for doctorate, thesis/dissertation. *Entrance requirements:* For master's and doctorate, GRE General Test, writing sample. Additional exam requirements/recommendations for international students: Required—TOEFL (minimum score 550 paper-based; 213 computer-based). Application fee: $30 ($75 for international students). Electronic applications accepted. *Financial support:* In 2008–09, fellowships (averaging $25,000 per year), research assistantships with full tuition reimbursements (averaging $25,000 per year) were awarded; institutionally sponsored loans also available. Financial award applicants required to submit FAFSA. *Unit head:* Dr. Anne Hudson Jones, Director, 409-772-2376, Fax: 409-772-5640, E-mail: ahjones@utmb.edu. *Application contact:* Donna A. Vickers, Administrative Coordinator, 409-772-9396, Fax: 409-772-5640, E-mail: davicker@utmb.edu.

University of West Florida, College of Arts and Sciences: Arts, Program in Interdisciplinary Humanities, Pensacola, FL 32514-5750. Offers MA. Part-time and evening/weekend programs available. *Students:* 2 part-time (both women). Average age 46. In 2008, 1 master's awarded. *Degree requirements:* For master's, thesis. *Entrance requirements:* For master's, GRE General Test, minimum GPA of 3.0 in last 60 hours. Additional exam requirements/recommendations for international students: Required—TOEFL (minimum score 550 paper-based; 213 computer-based). *Application deadline:* For fall admission, 6/1 for domestic students, 5/15 for international students; for spring admission, 11/1 for domestic students, 10/1 for international students. Applications are processed on a rolling basis. Application fee: $30. *Expenses:* Tuition, state resident: full-time $6095; part-time $253.97 per credit hour. Tuition, nonresident: full-time $21,919; part-time $913.31 per credit hour. *Financial support:* Fellowships, research assistantships with partial tuition reimbursements, teaching assistantships, institutionally sponsored loans, scholarships/grants, and unspecified assistantships available. Financial award application deadline: 4/15; financial award applicants required to submit FAFSA. *Unit head:* Dr. Sally Ferguson, Chairperson, 850-474-2676. *Application contact:* Terry McCray, Assistant Director of Graduate Admissions, 850-473-7718, Fax: 850-473-7714, E-mail: gradadmissions@uwf.edu.

Villanova University, Graduate School of Liberal Arts and Sciences, Department of Humanities and Augustinian Tradition, Villanova, PA 19085-1699. Offers MA. Part-time and evening/weekend programs available. *Faculty:* 1 full-time (0 women), 1 part-time/adjunct (0 women). *Students:* 10 part-time (3 women); includes 1 minority (Asian American or Pacific Islander). Average age 32. 5 applicants, 80% accepted, 3 enrolled. *Degree requirements:* For master's, comprehensive exam. *Entrance requirements:* For master's, GRE, statement of objectives. Additional exam requirements/recommendations for international students: Required—TOEFL. *Application deadline:* For fall admission, 8/1 for domestic and international students; for spring admission, 12/1 for domestic and international students. Applications are processed on a rolling basis. Electronic applications accepted. *Financial support:* Research assistantships, Federal Work-Study available. Financial award applicants required to submit FAFSA. *Unit head:* Dr. Kevin Hughes. *Application contact:* Dr. Gerald Long, Dean, Graduate School of Liberal Arts and Sciences, 610-519-7093, Fax: 610-519-7096.

Virginia Commonwealth University, Graduate School, College of Humanities and Sciences, Richmond, VA 23284-9005. Offers MA, MFA, MPA, MS, MURP, PhD, CASR, CCJA, CPM, CURP, Certificate, Graduate Certificate, JD/MURP, MSW/Certificate. Part-time and evening/weekend programs available.

Wright State University, School of Graduate Studies, College of Liberal Arts, Interdisciplinary Program in Humanities, Dayton, OH 45435. Offers M Hum. *Degree requirements:* For master's, thesis or alternative. *Entrance requirements:* Additional exam requirements/recommendations for international students: Required—TOEFL.

York University, Faculty of Graduate Studies, Faculty of Arts, Program in Humanities, Toronto, ON M3J 1P3, Canada. Offers MA, PhD. Part-time programs available. *Degree requirements:* For master's, thesis or alternative; for doctorate, comprehensive exam, thesis/dissertation. *Entrance requirements:* Additional exam requirements/recommendations for international students: Required—TOEFL (minimum score 600 paper-based; 250 computer-based). Electronic applications accepted.

Liberal Studies

Abilene Christian University, Graduate School, Interdisciplinary Program in the Liberal Arts, Abilene, TX 79699-9100. Offers MLA. Part-time programs available. *Students:* 2 full-time (both women), 5 part-time (2 women). 4 applicants, 100% accepted, 3 enrolled. In 2008, 1 master's awarded. *Degree requirements:* For master's, comprehensive exam, thesis or alternative. *Entrance requirements:* For master's, GRE General Test, MAT. *Application deadline:* For fall admission, 4/1 priority date for domestic students; for spring admission, 11/1 for domestic students. Applications are processed on a rolling basis. Application fee: $40 ($45 for international students). Electronic applications accepted. *Expenses:* Tuition: Full-time $10,728; part-time $640 per hour. Required fees: $1090; $53.50 per hour. $10 per term. Tuition and fees vary according to campus/location. *Financial support:* In 2008–09, 5 students received support. Federal Work-Study available. Support available to part-time students. Financial award application deadline: 4/1; financial award applicants required to submit FAFSA. *Unit head:* Dr. David Merrell, Graduate Adviser, 325-674-2035, Fax: 325-674-6844, E-mail: merrelld@acu.edu. *Application contact:* William Horn, Graduate Admissions Counselor, 325-674-2656, Fax: 325-674-6717, E-mail: gradinfo@acu.edu.

Alaska Pacific University, Graduate Programs, Liberal Studies Department, Anchorage, AK 99508-4672. Offers self-designed study (MA).

Albertus Magnus College, Liberal Studies Program, New Haven, CT 06511-1189. Offers MALS. Part-time and evening/weekend programs available. *Degree requirements:* For master's, thesis. *Entrance requirements:* For master's, interview, writing sample.

Alvernia University, Graduate Studies, Program in Liberal Studies, Reading, PA 19607-1799. Offers MALS. Part-time and evening/weekend programs available. *Degree requirements:* For master's, thesis optional. *Entrance requirements:* For master's, MAT or GRE (alumni excluded). Electronic applications accepted.

Antioch University McGregor, Graduate Programs, Individualized Liberal and Professional Studies Program, Yellow Springs, OH 45387-1609. Offers liberal and professional studies (MA), including counseling, creative writing, education, film studies, liberal studies, management, modern literature, psychology, theatre, visual arts. Part-time and evening/weekend programs available. Postbaccalaureate distance learning degree programs offered (minimal on-campus study). *Degree requirements:* For master's, thesis or alternative. *Entrance requirements:* For master's, resumé, 2 letters of reference. Electronic applications accepted. *Expenses:* Contact institution.

Armstrong Atlantic State University, School of Graduate Studies, Program in Liberal and Professional Studies, Savannah, GA 31419-1997. Offers MALPS. Part-time programs available. *Degree requirements:* For master's, comprehensive exam, project. *Entrance requirements:* For master's, GRE, minimum GPA of 2.5, letters of recommendation. Additional exam requirements/recommendations for international students: Required—TOEFL (minimum score 523 paper-based; 193 computer-based).

Auburn University Montgomery, School of Liberal Arts, Montgomery, AL 36124-4023. Offers MLA. Part-time and evening/weekend programs available. *Faculty:* 30 full-time (10 women). *Students:* 4 full-time (2 women), 29 part-time (19 women); includes 8 minority (5 African Americans, 1 American Indian/Alaska Native, 2 Asian Americans or Pacific Islanders). Average age 38. In 2008, 6 master's awarded. *Degree requirements:* For master's, thesis. *Entrance requirements:* For master's, GRE or MAT. *Application deadline:* Applications are processed on a rolling basis. Application fee: $25. Electronic applications accepted. *Expenses:* Tuition, state resident: full-time $5088; part-time $212 per credit. Tuition, nonresident: full-time $15,264; part-time $636 per credit. Required fees: $234. *Financial support:* In 2008–09, 2 teaching assistantships were awarded; career-related internships or fieldwork and scholarships/grants also available. Support available to part-time students. Financial award application deadline: 3/1; financial award applicants required to submit FAFSA. *Unit head:* Dr. Steven Daniell, Interim Dean, 334-244-3382, Fax: 334-244-3740. *Application contact:* Dr. Eric Sterling, Professor, 334-244-3760, Fax: 334-244-3740, E-mail: esterlin@aum.edu.

Liberal Studies

Baker University, School of Professional and Graduate Studies, Program in Liberal Arts, Baldwin City, KS 66006-0065. Offers MLA. Program also offered in Overland Park, KS. Part-time and evening/weekend programs available. *Students:* 16 full-time (12 women), 95 part-time (64 women); includes 18 minority (10 African Americans, 6 American Indian/Alaska Native, 2 Hispanic Americans). Average age 38. In 2008, 12 master's awarded. *Degree requirements:* For master's, portfolio of learning. *Entrance requirements:* Additional exam requirements/recommendations for international students: Required—TOEFL (minimum score 600 paper-based; 250 computer-based). *Application deadline:* Applications are processed on a rolling basis. Application fee: $20. *Expenses:* Tuition: Full-time $9265; part-time $300 per credit hour. One-time fee: $2535 full-time. Tuition and fees vary according to course load, degree level and program. *Financial support:* Applicants required to submit FAFSA. *Unit head:* Dr. Marvin L. Hunt, Vice President and Dean, 913-491-4432, Fax: 913-491-0470, E-mail: marvin.hunt@bakeru.edu. *Application contact:* Dr. Marvin L. Hunt, Vice President and Dean, 913-491-4432, Fax: 913-491-0470, E-mail: marvin.hunt@bakeru.edu.

Barry University, School of Arts and Sciences, Interdisciplinary Program, Miami Shores, FL 33161-6695. Offers MA.

Boston University, Metropolitan College (Continuing Education), Department of Liberal Studies, Boston, MA 02215. Offers interdisciplinary studies (MLA). Part-time and evening/weekend programs available. *Degree requirements:* For master's, thesis. *Entrance requirements:* For master's, interview. Additional exam requirements/recommendations for international students: Required—TOEFL (minimum score 560 paper-based). Electronic applications accepted. *Faculty research:* Arts and gastronomy.

Bradley University, Graduate School, College of Liberal Arts and Sciences, Program in Liberal Studies, Peoria, IL 61625-0002. Offers MLS. Part-time and evening/weekend programs available. *Degree requirements:* For master's, comprehensive exam, colloquium. *Entrance requirements:* For master's, 2 letters of recommendation. Additional exam requirements/recommendations for international students: Required—TOEFL (minimum score 550 paper-based; 213 computer-based; 79 iBT). *Expenses:* Contact institution.

Brooklyn College of the City University of New York, Division of Graduate Studies, Liberal Studies Program, Brooklyn, NY 11210-2889. Offers MA. Part-time programs available. *Students:* 9 part-time (5 women); includes 5 minority (4 African Americans, 1 Hispanic American), 2 international. Average age 40. 4 applicants, 50% accepted, 0 enrolled. In 2008, 7 master's awarded. *Degree requirements:* For master's, thesis or alternative, final project. *Entrance requirements:* For master's, interview, 2 letters of recommendation, essay. Additional exam requirements/recommendations for international students: Required—TOEFL. *Application deadline:* For fall admission, 3/1 priority date for domestic students, 2/1 priority date for international students; for spring admission, 11/1 priority date for domestic students, 10/1 priority date for international students. Applications are processed on a rolling basis. Application fee: $125. Electronic applications accepted. *Expenses:* Tuition, state resident: full-time $7360; part-time $310 per credit hour. Tuition, nonresident: full-time $13,800; part-time $575 per credit hour. *Financial support:* Federal Work-Study, institutionally sponsored loans, and scholarships/grants available. Support available to part-time students. Financial award application deadline: 5/1; financial award applicants required to submit FAFSA. *Faculty research:* Language acquisition, Judaic biography, ecocriticism. *Unit head:* Dr. George Brinton, Director, 718-951-5281, E-mail: gabbc@brooklyn.cuny.edu. *Application contact:* Hernan Sierra, Graduate Admissions Coordinator, 718-951-4536, Fax: 718-951-4506, E-mail: grads@brooklyn.cuny.edu.

Brooklyn College of the City University of New York, Division of Graduate Studies, School of Education, Program in Childhood Education, Brooklyn, NY 11210-2889. Offers bilingual education (MS Ed); liberal arts (MS Ed); mathematics (MS Ed); science/environmental education (MS Ed). Part-time and evening/weekend programs available. *Students:* 11 full-time (8 women), 274 part-time (236 women); includes 154 minority (80 African Americans, 1 American Indian/Alaska Native, 14 Asian Americans or Pacific Islanders, 59 Hispanic Americans), 3 international. Average age 31. 157 applicants, 90% accepted, 104 enrolled. In 2008, 110 master's awarded. *Entrance requirements:* For master's, LAST, interview, previous course work in education, writing sample, resumé, 2 letters of recommendation. Additional exam requirements/recommendations for international students: Required—TOEFL (minimum score 500 paper-based; 173 computer-based; 61 iBT). *Application deadline:* For fall admission, 3/1 priority date for domestic students, 2/1 priority date for international students; for spring admission, 11/1 priority date for domestic students, 10/1 priority date for international students. Applications are processed on a rolling basis. Application fee: $125. Electronic applications accepted. *Expenses:* Tuition, state resident: full-time $7360; part-time $310 per credit hour. Tuition, nonresident: full-time $13,800; part-time $575 per credit hour. *Financial support:* Career-related internships or fieldwork, Federal Work-Study, institutionally sponsored loans, and scholarships/grants available. Support available to part-time students. Financial award application deadline: 5/1; financial award applicants required to submit FAFSA. *Faculty research:* Emotional intelligence, multiculturalism, arts immersion, the Holocaust. *Unit head:* Dr. Sharon O'Connor-Petruso, Program Head, 718-951-5214. *Application contact:* Hernan Sierra, Graduate Admissions Coordinator, 718-951-4536, Fax: 718-951-4506, E-mail: grads@brooklyn.cuny.edu.

California State University, Sacramento, Graduate Studies, College of Social Sciences and Interdisciplinary Studies, Liberal Arts Program, Sacramento, CA 95819-6048. Offers French (MA); German (MA); Spanish (MA); theater arts (MA). *Degree requirements:* For master's, writing proficiency exam. *Entrance requirements:* Additional exam requirements/recommendations for international students: Required—TOEFL. Electronic applications accepted.

Cardinal Stritch University, College of Arts and Sciences, Milwaukee, WI 53217-3985. Offers MA, MM, MS. Part-time and evening/weekend programs available. *Degree requirements:* For master's, thesis.

Clark University, Graduate School, College of Professional and Continuing Education, Program in Liberal Studies, Worcester, MA 01610-1477. Offers MALA. Part-time and evening/weekend programs available. *Students:* 1 (woman) part-time. Average age 54. In 2008, 3 master's awarded. *Degree requirements:* For master's, thesis optional. *Application deadline:* Applications are processed on a rolling basis. Application fee: $50. Electronic applications accepted. *Expenses:* Tuition: Full-time $34,900; part-time $1091 per credit hour. Required fees: $30. *Financial support:* Career-related internships or fieldwork available. Support available to part-time students. *Unit head:* Max E. Hess, Director of Graduate Studies, 508-793-7217, Fax: 508-793-7232. *Application contact:* Julia Parent, Director of Marketing, Communications, and Admissions, 508-793-7217, Fax: 508-793-7232, E-mail: jparent@clarku.edu.

Clayton State University, School of Graduate Studies, Program in Liberal Studies, Morrow, GA 30260-0285. Offers MALS. Part-time programs available. *Faculty:* 37 full-time (20 women). *Students:* 1 (woman) full-time, 17 part-time (13 women); includes 4 minority (all African Americans). Average age 42. 9 applicants, 44% accepted, 2 enrolled. In 2008, 1 master's awarded. *Degree requirements:* For master's, thesis optional. *Entrance requirements:* For master's, GRE. Additional exam requirements/recommendations for international students: Required—TOEFL (minimum score 550 paper-based; 213 computer-based; 80 iBT). *Application deadline:* For fall admission, 7/15 for domestic students, 5/1 for international students; for spring admission, 4/15 for domestic students, 2/1 for international students. Application fee: $50. Electronic applications accepted. *Expenses:* Contact institution. *Financial support:* Applicants required to submit FAFSA. *Unit head:* Dr. Wendy Burns-Ardolino, Director, Master of Arts in Liberal Studies, 678-466-4723, Fax: 678-466-4899, E-mail: mals@clayton.edu. *Application contact:* Melanie Nolan, Administrative Assistant, 678-466-4723, Fax: 678-466-4899, E-mail: mals@clayton.edu.

The College at Brockport, State University of New York, School of Letters and Sciences, Program in Liberal Studies, Brockport, NY 14420-2997. Offers MA. Part-time programs available. *Degree requirements:* For master's, portfolio. *Entrance requirements:* For master's, minimum GPA of 3.0, letters of recommendation, written statement of programmatic focus. Additional exam requirements/recommendations for international students: Required—TOEFL (minimum score 550 paper-based; 213 computer-based; 79 iBT).

College of Notre Dame of Maryland, Graduate Studies, Program in Liberal Studies, Baltimore, MD 21210-2476. Offers MA. Part-time and evening/weekend programs available. *Degree requirements:* For master's, thesis or alternative. *Entrance requirements:* For master's, minimum GPA of 3.0. Additional exam requirements/recommendations for international students: Required—TOEFL (minimum score 500 paper-based; 173 computer-based; 61 iBT). Electronic applications accepted.

College of Staten Island of the City University of New York, Graduate Programs, Program in Liberal Studies, Staten Island, NY 10314-6600. Offers MA. Evening/weekend programs available. *Faculty:* 3 full-time (0 women), 1 part-time/adjunct (0 women). *Students:* 26 part-time (14 women); includes 4 minority (1 Asian American or Pacific Islander, 3 Hispanic Americans), 2 international. Average age 36. 31 applicants, 77% accepted, 18 enrolled. In 2008, 11 master's awarded. *Degree requirements:* For master's, thesis, 30 credits. *Entrance requirements:* For master's, minimum undergraduate GPA of 3.0, interview. Additional exam requirements/recommendations for international students: Required—TOEFL (minimum score 550 paper-based; 213 computer-based; 79 iBT). *Application deadline:* Applications are processed on a rolling basis. Application fee: $125. Electronic applications accepted. *Expenses:* Tuition, area resident: Full-time $6400; part-time $270 per credit. Tuition, nonresident: full-time $12,000; part-time $500 per credit. Required fees: $378; $113 per semester. *Financial support:* Fellowships, research assistantships, teaching assistantships, career-related internships or fieldwork, Federal Work-Study, and scholarships/grants available. Support available to part-time students. Financial award application deadline: 4/1; financial award applicants required to submit CSS PROFILE or FAFSA. *Unit head:* Dr. David Traboulay, Coordinator, 718-982-2877, E-mail: mals@mail.csi.cuny.edu. *Application contact:* Sasha Spence, Assistant Director of Graduate Recruitment and Admissions, 718-982-2699, Fax: 718-982-2500, E-mail: spence@mail.csi.cuny.edu.

Columbia University, Graduate School of Arts and Sciences, Program in Liberal Studies, New York, NY 10027. Offers American studies (MA); East Asian studies (MA); human rights studies (MA); Islamic culture studies (MA); Jewish studies (MA); medieval studies (MA); modern European studies (MA); South Asian studies (MA). Part-time and evening/weekend programs available. *Degree requirements:* For master's, thesis.

Concordia University Chicago, College of Graduate and Innovative Programs, Program in Liberal Studies, River Forest, IL 60305-1499. Offers MA. *Entrance requirements:* Additional exam requirements/recommendations for international students: Required—TOEFL (minimum score 550 paper-based; 195 computer-based). Electronic applications accepted.

Converse College, School of Education and Graduate Studies, Program in Liberal Arts, Spartanburg, SC 29302-0006. Offers English (MLA); history (MLA); political science (MLA). *Degree requirements:* For master's, capstone paper. *Entrance requirements:* For master's, minimum GPA of 3.0, 2 recommendations.

Creighton University, Graduate School, College of Arts and Sciences, Program in Liberal Studies, Omaha, NE 68178-0001. Offers MLS. Part-time and evening/weekend programs available. *Degree requirements:* For master's, thesis (for some programs). *Entrance requirements:* For master's, 3 letters of recommendation. Additional exam requirements/recommendations for international students: Required—TOEFL (minimum score 550 paper-based; 213 computer-based; 80 iBT). Electronic applications accepted.

Dallas Baptist University, College of Adult Education, Liberal Arts Program, Dallas, TX 75211-9299. Offers arts (MLA); Christian ministry (MLA); English (MLA); English as a second language (MLA); fine arts (MLA); history (MLA); missions (MLA); political science (MLA). Part-time and evening/weekend programs available. *Faculty:* 68 full-time (30 women), 113 part-time/adjunct (47 women). *Students:* 1 full-time, 35 part-time. 16 applicants, 81% accepted, 10 enrolled. In 2008, 17 master's awarded. *Entrance requirements:* For master's, minimum GPA of 3.0. Additional exam requirements/recommendations for international students: Required—TOEFL. *Application deadline:* Applications are processed on a rolling basis. Application fee: $25. Electronic applications accepted. *Expenses:* Tuition: Part-time $558 per credit hour. *Financial support:* Federal Work-Study, institutionally sponsored loans, scholarships/grants, and tuition waivers (full and partial) available. Support available to part-time students. Financial award applicants required to submit FAFSA. *Faculty research:* Milton and seventeenth-century Puritans, inter-Biblical years, nineteenth-century literature, Latin American and Texas history. *Unit head:* Dr. John Tarwater, Director, 214-333-6830, Fax: 214-333-5558, E-mail: graduate@dbu.edu. *Application contact:* Kit P. Montgomery, Director of Graduate Programs, 214-333-5242, Fax: 214-333-5579, E-mail: graduate@dbu.edu.

Dartmouth College, Arts and Sciences Graduate Programs, Program in Liberal Studies, Hanover, NH 03755. Offers MALS. Part-time programs available. *Degree requirements:* For master's, thesis. *Entrance requirements:* Additional exam requirements/recommendations for international students: Required—TOEFL.

See Close-Up on page 351.

Dowling College, Programs in Arts and Sciences, Oakdale, NY 11769-1999. Offers integrated math and science (MS); liberal studies (MA). Part-time and evening/weekend programs available. *Degree requirements:* For master's, comprehensive exam, thesis. *Entrance requirements:* For master's, minimum undergraduate GPA of 3.0, 2 letters of recommendation. Additional exam requirements/recommendations for international students: Required—TOEFL (minimum score 550 paper-based). Electronic applications accepted.

Duke University, Graduate School, Program in Liberal Studies, Durham, NC 27708. Offers AM. Part-time and evening/weekend programs available. *Degree requirements:* For master's, thesis or alternative, final project. *Entrance requirements:* For master's, interview. Additional exam requirements/recommendations for international students: Required—IELTS (preferred) or TOEFL. Electronic applications accepted.

Duquesne University, School of Leadership and Professional Advancement, Pittsburgh, PA 15282-0001. Offers community leadership (MS); leadership and business ethics (MS); leadership and information technology (MS); leadership and liberal studies (MA); sports leadership (MS). Part-time and evening/weekend programs available. Postbaccalaureate distance learning degree programs offered (no on-campus study). *Faculty:* 1 full-time (0 women), 59 part-time/adjunct (30 women). *Students:* 535 (263 women); includes 51 minority (43 African Americans, 1 American Indian/Alaska Native, 3 Asian Americans or Pacific Islanders, 4 Hispanic Americans). 231 applicants, 84% accepted, 121 enrolled. In 2008, 134 master's awarded. *Degree requirements:* For master's, capstone course. *Entrance requirements:* For master's, professional work experience, 500-word essay. Additional exam requirements/recommendations for international students: Required—TOEFL. *Application deadline:* Applications are processed on a rolling basis. Application fee: $0. Electronic applications accepted. *Expenses:* Tuition: Part-time $819 per credit. Required fees: $78 per credit. Tuition and fees vary according to course load. *Financial support:* Applicants required to submit FAFSA. *Unit head:* Dr. Dorothy Bassett, PhD, Dean, 412-396-5839, Fax: 412-396-4711, E-mail: bassettd@duq.edu. *Application contact:* Marianne Leister, Director of Student Services, 412-396-4933, Fax: 412-396-5072, E-mail: leister@duq.edu.

East Tennessee State University, School of Graduate Studies, Division of Cross-Disciplinary Studies, Johnson City, TN 37614. Offers liberal studies (MALS). *Entrance requirements:* For master's, GRE. Additional exam requirements/recommendations for international students: Required—TOEFL (minimum score 550 paper-based; 213 computer-based).

Excelsior College, School of Liberal Arts, Albany, NY 12203-5159. Offers liberal studies (MA). Part-time and evening/weekend programs available. Postbaccalaureate distance learning degree programs offered (no on-campus study). *Degree requirements:* For master's, thesis or alternative. Electronic applications accepted.

Florida Atlantic University, Dorothy F. Schmidt College of Arts and Letters, Program in Liberal Studies, Boca Raton, FL 33431-0991. Offers MA. *Students:* 1 (woman) full-time, 6 part-time (3 women); includes 2 minority (1 African American, 1 Hispanic American). Average age 40. 11 applicants, 18% accepted, 0 enrolled. *Degree requirements:* For master's, thesis or alternative. *Entrance requirements:* For master's, GRE General Test. *Application deadline:* For fall admission, 2/1 priority date for domestic students, 2/1 for international students; for spring admission, 10/1 for domestic and international students. Applications are processed on a rolling basis. Application fee: $30. *Expenses:* Tuition, state resident: full-time $4867; part-time $270.40 per credit hour. Tuition, nonresident: full-time $16,486; part-time $915.87 per credit hour. *Unit head:* Dr. Clevis Headley, Director, 561-297-3920, E-mail: headley@fau.edu. *Application contact:* Dr. Emily Stockard, Associate Dean, 561-297-2817, Fax: 561-297-2744, E-mail: stockard@fau.edu.

Florida International University, College of Arts and Sciences, Program in Liberal Studies, Miami, FL 33199. Offers MA. *Entrance requirements:* For master's, minimum GPA of 3.0, letters of recommendation. Additional exam requirements/recommendations for international students: Required—TOEFL (minimum score 550 paper-based; 213 computer-based). Electronic applications accepted.

Fordham University, Graduate School of Arts and Sciences, Program in Humanities and Sciences, New York, NY 10458. Offers MA. Part-time and evening/weekend programs available. *Degree requirements:* For master's, final paper. *Entrance requirements:* Additional exam requirements/recommendations for international students: Required—TOEFL (minimum score 650 paper-based; 280 computer-based). Electronic applications accepted.

Fort Hays State University, Graduate School, College of Arts and Sciences, Center for Interdisciplinary Studies, Hays, KS 67601-4099. Offers liberal studies (MLS). Postbaccalaureate distance learning degree programs offered (minimal on-campus study). *Degree requirements:* For master's, comprehensive exam, thesis or alternative. *Entrance requirements:* Additional exam requirements/recommendations for international students: Required—TOEFL (minimum score 550 paper-based; 213 computer-based). Electronic applications accepted.

Georgetown University, Graduate School of Arts and Sciences, School of Continuing Studies, Washington, DC 20057. Offers American studies (MALS); Catholic studies (MALS); classical civilizations (MALS); ethics and the professions (MALS); human resources management (MPS); humanities (MALS); individualized study (MALS); international affairs (MALS); Islam and Muslim-Christian relations (MALS); journalism (MPS); liberal studies (DLS); literature and society (MALS); medieval and early modern European studies (MALS); public relations (MPS); real estate (MPS); religious studies (MALS); social and public policy (MALS); sports industry management (MPS); the theory and practice of American democracy (MALS); visual culture (MALS). *Entrance requirements:* Additional exam requirements/recommendations for international students: Required—TOEFL.

Graduate School and University Center of the City University of New York, Graduate Studies, Program in Liberal Studies, New York, NY 10016-4039. Offers MA. *Degree requirements:* For master's, thesis. *Entrance requirements:* For master's, GRE General Test. Additional exam requirements/recommendations for international students: Required—TOEFL. Electronic applications accepted.

Hamline University, Graduate School of Liberal Studies, St. Paul, MN 55104-1284. Offers MALS, MFA, CALS. Part-time and evening/weekend programs available. *Faculty:* 6 full-time (4 women), 13 part-time/adjunct (10 women). *Students:* 95 full-time (71 women), 127 part-time (97 women); includes 9 minority (7 African Americans, 1 American Indian/Alaska Native, 1 Hispanic American), 3 international. Average age 37. 66 applicants, 74% accepted, 37 enrolled. In 2008, 49 master's awarded. *Degree requirements:* For master's, thesis. *Entrance requirements:* For master's, 20 page writing sample (MFA), official transcripts, letters of recommendation. Additional exam requirements/recommendations for international students: Required—TOEFL (minimum score 550 paper-based), TWE (minimum score 5). *Application deadline:* For fall admission, 3/1 priority date for domestic students; for spring admission, 9/1 priority date for domestic students. Applications are processed on a rolling basis. Application fee: $0. Electronic applications accepted. *Expenses:* Contact institution. *Financial support:* Federal Work-Study available. Financial award applicants required to submit FAFSA. *Unit head:* Mary Francois Rockcastle, Dean, 651-523-2047, Fax: 651-523-2490, E-mail: mrockcastle@hamline.edu. *Application contact:* Rae A. Lenway, Director, Graduate Recruitment and Admission, 651-523-2900, Fax: 651-523-3058, E-mail: rlenway@hamline.edu.

Harvard University, Extension School, Cambridge, MA 02138-3722. Offers applied sciences (CAS); biotechnology (ALM); educational technologies (ALM); educational technology (CET); English for graduate and professional studies (DGP); environmental management (ALM, CEM); information technology (ALM); journalism (ALM); liberal arts (ALM); management (ALM, CM); mathematics for teaching (ALM); museum studies (ALM); premedical studies (Diploma); publication and communication (CPC). Part-time and evening/weekend programs available. *Degree requirements:* For master's, thesis. *Entrance requirements:* For master's, 3 completed graduate courses with grade of B or higher. Additional exam requirements/recommendations for international students: Required—TOEFL (minimum score 600 paper-based; 250 computer-based), TWE (minimum score 5). *Expenses:* Contact institution.

Henderson State University, Graduate Studies, Ellis College of Arts and Sciences, Arkadelphia, AR 71999-0001. Offers MLA. Part-time programs available. *Entrance requirements:* For master's, minimum GPA of 2.7, interview.

Hollins University, Graduate Programs, Program in Liberal Studies, Roanoke, VA 24020-1603. Offers humanities (MALS); interdisciplinary studies (MALS); justice and legal studies (MALS); liberal studies (CAS); social science (MALS); visual and performing arts (MALS). Part-time and evening/weekend programs available. *Faculty:* 6 full-time (1 woman), 7 part-time/adjunct (4 women). *Students:* 20 full-time (17 women), 78 part-time (56 women); includes 14 minority (13 African Americans, 1 Hispanic American), 1 international. Average age 39. 33 applicants, 85% accepted, 23 enrolled. In 2008, 42 master's awarded. *Degree requirements:* For master's, thesis. *Entrance requirements:* For master's, letters of recommendation, interview. Additional exam requirements/recommendations for international students: Required—TOEFL (minimum score 550 paper-based; 213 computer-based; 79 iBT). *Application deadline:* For fall admission, 7/1 priority date for domestic and international students; for spring admission, 12/10 priority date for domestic and international students. Applications are processed on a rolling basis. Application fee: $40. Electronic applications accepted. *Expenses:* Tuition: Full-time $26,720; part-time $590 per credit hour. Required fees: $280. *Financial support:* In 2008–09, 53 students received support, including 2 fellowships (averaging $1,189 per year); Federal Work-Study and scholarships/grants also available. Support available to part-time students. Financial award application deadline: 7/15; financial award applicants required to submit FAFSA. *Faculty research:* Elderly blacks, film, feminist economics, US voting patterns, Wagner, diversity. *Unit head:* Dr. Edward A. Lynch, Director, 540-362-6475, Fax: 540-362-6288, E-mail: elynch@hollins.edu. *Application contact:* Cathy S. Koon, Manager of Graduate Services, 540-362-6326, Fax: 540-362-6288, E-mail: ckoon@hollins.edu.

Houston Baptist University, College of Arts and Humanities, Program in Liberal Arts, Houston, TX 77074-3298. Offers MLA. Part-time and evening/weekend programs available. *Entrance requirements:* For master's, interview, minimum GPA of 2.5, writing sample. Additional exam requirements/recommendations for international students: Required—TOEFL (minimum score 550 paper-based; 213 computer-based).

Indiana University Kokomo, School of Arts and Sciences, Kokomo, IN 46904-9003. Offers liberal studies (MALS). *Degree requirements:* For master's, thesis. *Entrance requirements:* For master's, minimum GPA of 3.0. Additional exam requirements/recommendations for international students: Required—TOEFL. *Faculty research:* Bibliography and textual studies, comparative literature, current global issues/political science.

Indiana University–Purdue University Fort Wayne, College of Arts and Sciences, Program in Liberal Studies, Fort Wayne, IN 46805-1499. Offers MLS. Part-time programs available. *Students:* 4 full-time (all women), 22 part-time (13 women); includes 4 minority (2 African Americans, 1 Asian American or Pacific Islander, 1 Hispanic American), 1 international. Average age 41. 19 applicants, 100% accepted, 15 enrolled. In 2008, 2 master's awarded. *Entrance requirements:* For master's, minimum GPA of 3.0, major or minor in related area. Additional exam requirements/recommendations for international students: Required—TOEFL (minimum score 550 paper-based; 213 computer-based; 77 iBT). *Application deadline:* For fall admission, 8/1 for domestic students; for spring admission, 12/1 for domestic students. Applications are processed on a rolling basis. Application fee: $30. *Expenses:* Tuition, area resident: Full-time $4376; part-time $243 per credit. Tuition, state resident: full-time $4376; part-time $243 per credit. Tuition, nonresident: full-time $10,337; part-time $574 per credit. Required fees: $503; $27.95 per credit. Tuition and fees vary according to course load. *Financial support:* Scholarships/grants available. Support available to part-time students. Financial award application deadline: 3/1; financial award applicants required to submit FAFSA. *Unit head:* Dr. Michael E. Kaufmann, Director, 260-481-6760, Fax: 260-481-6985, E-mail: kaufmann@ipfw.edu. *Application contact:* Dr. Michael E. Kaufmann, Director, 260-481-6760, Fax: 260-481-6985, E-mail: kaufmann@ipfw.edu.

Indiana University–Purdue University Indianapolis, School of Liberal Arts, Indianapolis, IN 46202-2896. Offers MA, MS, XMA, PhD, Certificate, JD/MA, MA/MA, MD/MA, MPA/MA, MSN/MA.

Indiana University South Bend, College of Liberal Arts and Sciences, South Bend, IN 46634-7111. Offers applied mathematics and computer science (MS); applied psychology (MA); English (MA); liberal studies (MLS). Part-time and evening/weekend programs available. *Degree requirements:* For master's, thesis (for some programs). *Entrance requirements:* For master's, minimum GPA of 3.0. Additional exam requirements/recommendations for international students: Required—TOEFL. *Faculty research:* Artificial intelligence, bioinformatics, English language and literature, creative writing, computer networks.

Indiana University Southeast, Program in Liberal Studies, New Albany, IN 47150-6405. Offers MLS. *Degree requirements:* For master's, thesis or alternative. *Entrance requirements:* For master's, 3 letters of recommendation.

Jacksonville State University, College of Graduate Studies and Continuing Education, College of Arts and Sciences, Department of Liberal Studies, Jacksonville, AL 36265-1602. Offers MA. Part-time and evening/weekend programs available. *Students:* 4 full-time (2 women), 16 part-time (7 women); includes 9 minority (all African Americans), 1 international. Average age 32. 12 applicants, 42% accepted, 5 enrolled. In 2008, 6 master's awarded. *Degree requirements:* For master's, comprehensive exam, thesis (for some programs). *Application deadline:* Applications are processed on a rolling basis. Application fee: $30. Electronic applications accepted. *Expenses:* Tuition, area resident: Full-time $4560; part-time $225 per credit hour. Tuition, state resident: full-time $4560; part-time $450 per credit hour. Tuition, nonresident: full-time $9120; part-time $450 per credit hour. *Financial support:* In 2008–09, 14 students received support. Available to part-time students. Application deadline: 4/1; *Application contact:* Dr. Jean Pugliese, Associate Dean, 256-782-8278, Fax: 256-782-5321, E-mail: pugliese@jsu.edu.

The Johns Hopkins University, Zanvyl Krieger School of Arts and Sciences, Advanced Academic Programs, Program in Liberal Arts, Washington, DC 20036. Offers MA, Certificate. Part-time and evening/weekend programs available. *Degree requirements:* For master's, thesis. *Entrance requirements:* Additional exam requirements/recommendations for international students: Required—TOEFL (minimum score 250 computer-based; 100 iBT). Electronic applications accepted.

Kean University, School of Visual and Performing Arts, Program in Liberal Studies, Union, NJ 07083. Offers MA. Part-time and evening/weekend programs available. *Students:* 5 full-time (4 women), 15 part-time (8 women); includes 5 African Americans, 3 Hispanic Americans. Average age 38. 4 applicants, 75% accepted, 3 enrolled. In 2008, 8 master's awarded. *Degree requirements:* For master's, comprehensive exam, thesis, final project. *Entrance requirements:* For master's, minimum GPA of 3.0, 3 letters of recommendation, autobiographical essay, interview. *Application deadline:* For fall admission, 5/1 for domestic students; for spring admission, 11/1 for domestic students. Application fee: $60 ($150 for international students). Electronic applications accepted. *Expenses:* Tuition, state resident: full-time $10,128; part-time $422 per credit. Tuition, nonresident: full-time $13,728; part-time $572 per credit. Required fees: $2570; $107 per credit. Part-time tuition and fees vary according to course load, degree level and program. *Financial support:* In 2008–09, 4 research assistantships with full tuition reimbursements (averaging $3,217 per year) were awarded; unspecified assistantships also available. *Unit head:* Dr. John C. Gruesser, Program Coordinator, 908-737-4230, E-mail: jgruesse@kean.edu. *Application contact:* Steven Koch, Pre-Admissions Coordinator, 908-737-4723, Fax: 908-737-5965, E-mail: grad-adm@kean.edu.

Kent State University, College of Arts and Sciences, Program in Liberal Studies, Kent, OH 44242-0001. Offers MLS. Part-time programs available. *Degree requirements:* For master's, thesis. *Entrance requirements:* For master's, minimum GPA of 2.75. Electronic applications accepted.

Lake Forest College, Graduate Program in Liberal Studies, Lake Forest, IL 60045-2399. Offers MLS. Part-time and evening/weekend programs available. *Degree requirements:* For master's, thesis optional, 8 courses completed. *Entrance requirements:* For master's, interview, application, essay. *Faculty research:* Latin American film, the European Left, solid state chemistry, cast iron architecture, concepts of education in 19th century America.

Lock Haven University of Pennsylvania, Office of Graduate Studies, Department of Liberal Arts, Lock Haven, PA 17745-2390. Offers MLA. *Faculty:* 12 full-time (5 women), 1 (woman) part-time/adjunct. *Students:* 18 full-time (9 women), 7 part-time (4 women); includes 3 minority (all African Americans), 6 international. Average age 27. In 2008, 4 master's awarded. *Degree requirements:* For master's, thesis. *Entrance requirements:* For master's, minimum undergraduate GPA of 3.0. Additional exam requirements/recommendations for international students: Required—TOEFL. *Application deadline:* Applications are processed on a rolling basis. Application fee: $25. Electronic applications accepted. *Expenses:* Tuition, state resident: full-time $6430; part-time $357 per credit hour. Tuition, nonresident: full-time $10,288; part-time $572 per credit hour. Required fees: $1988; $144 per credit hour. One-time fee: $25. Tuition and fees vary according to course load. *Financial support:* Unspecified assistantships available. Financial award application deadline: 8/1. *Unit head:* Dr. Ellen P O'Hara-Mays, Graduate Coordinator, 570-893-2072, E-mail: poharama@lhup.edu. *Application contact:* Chris Rolley, Assistant Director of Admissions, 800-332-8900, Fax: 570-893-2734, E-mail: crolley@lhup.edu.

Louisiana State University and Agricultural and Mechanical College, Graduate School, College of Arts and Sciences, Interdepartmental Program in the Liberal Arts, Baton Rouge, LA 70803. Offers MALA. Part-time and evening/weekend programs available. *Degree requirements:* For master's, project or thesis. *Entrance requirements:* For master's, GRE General Test, minimum GPA of 3.0. Additional exam requirements/recommendations for international students: Required—TOEFL (minimum score 550 paper-based; 213 computer-based; 79 iBT). Electronic applications accepted.

Louisiana State University in Shreveport, College of Liberal Arts, Program in Liberal Arts, Shreveport, LA 71115-2399. Offers MA. Part-time and evening/weekend programs available. *Degree requirements:* For master's, comprehensive exam, thesis or alternative, 33 credit-hour curriculum. *Entrance requirements:* For master's, interview, minimum GPA of 3.0 during final 2

Liberal Studies

Louisiana State University in Shreveport (continued)
years of course work, statement of purpose. Additional exam requirements/recommendations for international students: Required—TOEFL (minimum score 500 paper-based; 173 computer-based; 61 iBT).

Loyola University Maryland, Graduate Programs, College of Arts and Sciences, Program in Liberal Studies, Baltimore, MD 21210-2699. Offers MMS. Part-time and evening/weekend programs available. *Faculty:* 4 full-time (0 women), 3 part-time/adjunct (0 women). *Students:* 2 full-time (1 woman), 50 part-time (33 women); includes 8 minority (7 African Americans, 1 Asian American or Pacific Islander). Average age 33. In 2008, 10 master's awarded. *Entrance requirements:* For master's, GRE General Test, GRE Subject Test (recommended). Additional exam requirements/recommendations for international students: Required—TOEFL (minimum score 550 paper-based; 213 computer-based). *Application deadline:* For fall admission, 9/1 priority date for domestic students; for spring admission, 1/1 priority date for domestic students. Applications are processed on a rolling basis. Application fee: $50. *Financial support:* Applicants required to submit FAFSA. *Unit head:* Dr. Randall Donaldson, Director, 410-617-2299, E-mail: liberalstudies@loyola.edu. *Application contact:* Maureen Faux, Interim Director, Graduate Admissions, 410-617-5020, Fax: 410-617-2002, E-mail: graduate@loyola.edu.

Madonna University, Program in Liberal Studies, Livonia, MI 48150-1173. Offers MALS.

Manhattanville College, Graduate Programs, Humanities and Social Sciences Programs, Program in Liberal Studies, Purchase, NY 10577-2132. Offers MA. Part-time and evening/weekend programs available. *Degree requirements:* For master's, thesis. *Entrance requirements:* For master's, interview, 2 letters of recommendation.

McDaniel College, Graduate and Professional Studies, Program in Liberal Studies, Westminster, MD 21157-4390. Offers MLA. Part-time and evening/weekend programs available. *Degree requirements:* For master's, final project. *Entrance requirements:* For master's, letters of reference (3). Additional exam requirements/recommendations for international students: Required—TOEFL (minimum score 213 computer-based).

Metropolitan State University, College of Arts and Sciences, St. Paul, MN 55106-5000. Offers computer science (MS); liberal studies (MA); technical communication (MS). Part-time and evening/weekend programs available. *Entrance requirements:* For master's, BA/BS; 2.75 GPA; resumée. Additional exam requirements/recommendations for international students: Required—TOEFL (minimum score 550 paper-based; 213 computer-based). *Faculty research:* Computer security, software engineering, distributed systems, document design, diffusing of innovations, social issues and communication technology.

Minnesota State University Moorhead, Graduate Studies, College of Arts and Humanities, Program in Liberal Studies, Moorhead, MN 56563-0002. Offers MLA. Part-time and evening/weekend programs available. *Degree requirements:* For master's, thesis, final oral exam. *Entrance requirements:* For master's, minimum GPA of 2.75. Additional exam requirements/recommendations for international students: Required—TOEFL (minimum score 570 paper-based; 230 computer-based). Electronic applications accepted.

Mississippi College, Graduate School, Program in Liberal Studies, Clinton, MS 39058. Offers MLS. Part-time programs available. *Degree requirements:* For master's, comprehensive exam, thesis optional. *Entrance requirements:* For master's, GRE, minimum GPA of 2.5. Additional exam requirements/recommendations for international students: Recommended—IELTS.

Monmouth University, Graduate School, Program in Liberal Arts, West Long Branch, NJ 07764-1898. Offers MA. Part-time and evening/weekend programs available. *Faculty:* 7 full-time (4 women), 1 (woman) part-time/adjunct. *Students:* 1 (woman) full-time, 9 part-time (4 women); includes 1 minority (African American). Average age 40. 7 applicants, 100% accepted, 4 enrolled. In 2008, 8 master's awarded. *Degree requirements:* For master's, thesis or alternative, project. *Entrance requirements:* For master's, minimum GPA of 3.0 in major, 2.5 overall. Additional exam requirements/recommendations for international students: Required—TOEFL (minimum score 550 paper-based; 213 computer-based; 79 iBT), IELTS (minimum score 5), Michigan English Language Assessment Battery (minimum score: 77), Cambridge A, B, C. *Application deadline:* For fall admission, 7/15 priority date for domestic students, 6/1 for international students; for spring admission, 11/15 priority date for domestic students, 11/1 for international students. Applications are processed on a rolling basis. Application fee: $50. Electronic applications accepted. *Expenses:* Tuition: Full-time $13,914; part-time $773 per credit. Required fees: $628; $157 per semester. *Financial support:* In 2008–09, 2 students received support, including 2 fellowships (averaging $1,550 per year); research assistantships, career-related internships or fieldwork, scholarships/grants, tuition waivers (partial), and unspecified assistantships also available. Support available to part-time students. Financial award application deadline: 3/1; financial award applicants required to submit FAFSA. *Faculty research:* Labor history, war and society, technology, historical archeology, art and society. *Unit head:* Dr. Richard Veit, Director, 732-571-4496, Fax: 732-263-5192. *Application contact:* Kevin Roane, Director, Office of Graduate Admission, 732-571-3452, Fax: 732-263-5123, E-mail: gradadm@monmouth.edu.

Nazareth College of Rochester, Graduate Studies, Department of Liberal Studies, Rochester, NY 14618-3790. Offers MA. *Entrance requirements:* For master's, minimum GPA of 3.0.

The New School: A University, The New School for Social Research, Committee on Liberal Studies, New York, NY 10011. Offers MA. Part-time and evening/weekend programs available. *Faculty:* 5 full-time (4 women), 5 part-time/adjunct (2 women). *Students:* 25 full-time (14 women), 21 part-time (16 women); includes 7 minority (4 African Americans, 3 Hispanic Americans), 8 international. Average age 29. In 2008, 13 master's awarded. *Degree requirements:* For master's, thesis. *Entrance requirements:* For master's, GRE General Test. Additional exam requirements/recommendations for international students: Required—TOEFL (minimum score 600 paper-based; 250 computer-based; 100 iBT). *Application deadline:* For fall admission, 1/15 priority date for domestic students. Applications are processed on a rolling basis. Application fee: $50. *Expenses:* Tuition: Full-time $27,144; part-time $1508 per credit. Required fees: $355 per semester. *Financial support:* Fellowships, research assistantships, teaching assistantships, career-related internships or fieldwork, Federal Work-Study, scholarships/grants, and tuition waivers (full and partial) available. Financial award application deadline: 3/1; financial award applicants required to submit FAFSA. *Faculty research:* Intellectual history, public intellectuals, popular culture. *Unit head:* Dr. Elzbieta Matynia, Director, 212-229-5580 Ext. 3138, E-mail: matynia@newschool.edu. *Application contact:* Robert MacDonald, Director of Admissions, 800-523-5710 Ext. 3007, Fax: 212-989-7102, E-mail: macdonar@newschool.edu.

See Close-Up on page 1251.

North Carolina State University, Graduate School, College of Humanities and Social Sciences, Program in Liberal Studies, Raleigh, NC 27695. Offers MA. Part-time and evening/weekend programs available. *Degree requirements:* For master's, thesis optional. Electronic applications accepted. *Faculty research:* Humanities, social sciences, sciences.

North Central College, Graduate Programs, Department of Liberal Studies, Naperville, IL 60566-7063. Offers MALS. Part-time and evening/weekend programs available. *Degree requirements:* For master's, project. *Entrance requirements:* For master's, interview. *Expenses:* Contact institution.

Northern Arizona University, Graduate College, College of Arts and Letters, Program in Sustainable Communities, Flagstaff, AZ 86011. Offers MA. Part-time programs available.

Northern Kentucky University, Office of Graduate Programs, College of Arts and Sciences, Program in Integrative Studies, Highland Heights, KY 41099. Offers civic engagement (Certificate); integrative studies (MA). Part-time and evening/weekend programs available. Postbaccalaureate distance learning degree programs offered (no on-campus study). *Students:* 5 full-time (3 women), 48 part-time (34 women); includes 6 minority (4 African Americans, 2 Asian Americans or Pacific Islanders). Average age 36. 34 applicants, 62% accepted, 21 enrolled. In 2008, 10 master's awarded. *Degree requirements:* For master's, thesis optional. *Entrance requirements:* For master's, minimum GPA of 3.0, resumé, 2 letters of recommendation, 1 letter of intent. Additional exam requirements/recommendations for international students: Required—TOEFL (minimum score 550 paper-based; 213 computer-based; 79 iBT), Michigan Test may be substituted only if taken at NKU (minimu score of 80); Recommended—IELTS (minimum score 6.5). *Application deadline:* For fall admission, 7/1 priority date for domestic students, 6/1 for international students; for spring admission, 12/1 priority date for domestic students, 10/1 for international students. Applications are processed on a rolling basis. Application fee: $40. Electronic applications accepted. *Expenses:* Tuition, area resident: Full-time $6642. Tuition, state resident: full-time $6642. Tuition, nonresident: full-time $11,682. *Financial support:* Unspecified assistantships available. Financial award applicants required to submit FAFSA. *Faculty research:* Religious studies, cyberculture, literature, history. *Unit head:* Dr. Debra Meyers, Director, 859-572-5831, Fax: 859-572-6185, E-mail: meyersde@nku.edu. *Application contact:* Dr. Peg Griffin, Director of Graduate Programs, 859-572-6934, Fax: 859-572-6670, E-mail: griffinp@nku.edu.

Northwestern University, The Graduate School, Interdepartmental Degree Programs, Interdisciplinary Program in Liberal Studies, Evanston, IL 60208. Offers MA. Admissions and degree offered through The Graduate School. Part-time and evening/weekend programs available. *Degree requirements:* For master's, thesis. *Entrance requirements:* For master's, writing sample. Additional exam requirements/recommendations for international students: Required—TOEFL. *Faculty research:* Urban and social history, literary criticism and comparative literature, women's studies, media and film criticism, philosophy.

Oakland University, Graduate Study and Lifelong Learning, College of Arts and Sciences, Program in Liberal Studies, Rochester, MI 48309-4401. Offers MA. *Entrance requirements:* For master's, minimum GPA of 3.0 for unconditional admission. Additional exam requirements/recommendations for international students: Required—TOEFL (minimum score 550 paper-based; 213 computer-based). Electronic applications accepted.

Occidental College, Graduate Studies, Department of Education, Program in Elementary Education, Los Angeles, CA 90041-3314. Offers liberal studies (MAT). Part-time programs available. *Degree requirements:* For master's, final exam, graduate synthesis paper. *Entrance requirements:* For master's, GRE General Test, minimum GPA of 3.0. Additional exam requirements/recommendations for international students: Required—TOEFL (minimum score 625 paper-based; 263 computer-based). *Expenses:* Contact institution.

Ohio Dominican University, Graduate Programs, Program in Liberal Studies, Columbus, OH 43219-2099. Offers MA. Part-time and evening/weekend programs available. *Degree requirements:* For master's, comprehensive exam or thesis. *Entrance requirements:* For master's, minimum undergraduate GPA of 3.0, 3 letters of recommendation. Additional exam requirements/recommendations for international students: Required—TOEFL (minimum score 550 paper-based; 213 computer-based).

Oklahoma City University, Petree College of Arts and Sciences, Program in Liberal Arts, Oklahoma City, OK 73106-1402. Offers art (MLA); general studies (MLA); leadership/management (MLA); literature (MLA); mass communications (MLA); philosophy (MLA); writing (MLA). Part-time and evening/weekend programs available. *Degree requirements:* For master's, comprehensive exam, thesis optional. *Entrance requirements:* Additional exam requirements/recommendations for international students: Required—TOEFL.

Queens College of the City University of New York, Division of Graduate Studies, Social Science Division, Program in Liberal Studies, Flushing, NY 11367-1597. Offers MALS. Part-time and evening/weekend programs available. *Degree requirements:* For master's, thesis. *Entrance requirements:* For master's, minimum GPA of 3.0. Additional exam requirements/recommendations for international students: Required—TOEFL.

Ramapo College of New Jersey, Program in Liberal Studies, Mahwah, NJ 07430. Offers MALS. Part-time and evening/weekend programs available. *Faculty:* 4 part-time/adjunct (3 women). *Students:* 36 part-time (26 women); includes 3 minority (1 African American, 2 Hispanic Americans), 2 international. 15 applicants, 100% accepted, 12 enrolled. In 2008, 4 degrees awarded. *Degree requirements:* For master's, thesis. *Entrance requirements:* For master's, minimum undergraduate GPA of 3.0, 2 letters of recommendation. Additional exam requirements/recommendations for international students: Required—TOEFL (minimum score 550 paper-based; 213 computer-based; 90 iBT). *Application deadline:* For fall admission, 9/1 priority date for domestic and international students; for spring admission, 1/30 priority date for domestic and international students. Applications are processed on a rolling basis. Application fee: $55. Electronic applications accepted. *Expenses:* Tuition, state resident: part-time $472.20 per credit. Tuition, nonresident: part-time $606.85 per credit. Required fees: $43.80 per credit. Part-time tuition and fees vary according to reciprocity agreements. *Financial support:* Tuition waivers (full) available. Financial award applicants required to submit FAFSA. *Faculty research:* History of science, women's studies, Native American studies, theology, genocide studies. *Unit head:* Dr. Anthony T. Padovano, Director, 201-684-7430, Fax: 201-684-7973, E-mail: apadovan@ramapo.edu. *Application contact:* Melissa C. Kupfer, MALS Secretary, 201-684-7709, Fax: 201-684-7973, E-mail: mkupfer@ramapo.edu.

Reed College, Graduate Program in Liberal Studies, Portland, OR 97202-8199. Offers MALS. Part-time and evening/weekend programs available. *Faculty:* 11 part-time/adjunct (5 women). *Students:* 37 part-time (20 women); includes 7 minority (2 African Americans, 3 Asian Americans or Pacific Islanders, 2 Hispanic Americans). Average age 39. 17 applicants, 41% accepted, 5 enrolled. In 2008, 5 master's awarded. *Degree requirements:* For master's, thesis, oral defense of thesis. *Entrance requirements:* For master's, interview, letters of recommendation. *Application deadline:* For fall admission, 7/1 priority date for domestic students; for spring admission, 12/1 priority date for domestic students. Applications are processed on a rolling basis. Application fee: $60. *Expenses:* Tuition: Part-time $3440 per unit. *Financial support:* In 2008–09, 5 students received support. Scholarships/grants and health care benefits available. Support available to part-time students. Financial award application deadline: 5/1; financial award applicants required to submit CSS PROFILE or FAFSA. *Unit head:* Barbara A. Amen, Director, Graduate Studies, 503-777-7259, Fax: 503-517-7345, E-mail: bamen@reed.edu. *Application contact:* Barbara A. Amen, Director, Graduate Studies, 503-777-7259, Fax: 503-517-7345, E-mail: bamen@reed.edu.

Rollins College, Hamilton Holt School, Program in Liberal Studies, Winter Park, FL 32789-4499. Offers MLS. Part-time and evening/weekend programs available. *Students:* 4 full-time (all women), 72 part-time (46 women); includes 8 minority (4 African Americans, 1 Asian American or Pacific Islander, 3 Hispanic Americans). Average age 41. In 2008, 9 master's awarded. *Degree requirements:* For master's, thesis. *Entrance requirements:* For master's, GRE or MAT, interview. Additional exam requirements/recommendations for international students: Required—TOEFL. *Application deadline:* For fall admission, 12/1 for domestic students; for spring admission, 4/1 for domestic students. Application fee: $50. Electronic applications accepted. *Expenses:* Contact institution. *Financial support:* Institutionally sponsored loans and scholarships/grants available. Support available to part-time students. *Unit head:* Dr. Patricia Lancaster, Director, 407-646-2237, Fax: 407-646-2363. *Application contact:* Christian Ricaurte, Coordinator of Records and Registration, 407-646-2653, Fax: 407-646-1551, E-mail: cricaurte@rollins.edu.

Rutgers, The State University of New Jersey, Camden, Graduate School of Arts and Sciences, Program in Liberal Studies, Camden, NJ 08102-1401. Offers MALS. Part-time and evening/weekend programs available. *Degree requirements:* For master's, thesis. *Entrance requirements:* For master's, 2 letters of recommendation, writing sample, statement of goals. Additional exam requirements/recommendations for international students: Required—TOEFL, IELTS. Electronic applications accepted. *Faculty research:* Psychology, English, history, philosphy, religion.

Rutgers, The State University of New Jersey, Newark, Graduate School, Program in Liberal Studies, Newark, NJ 07102. Offers MALS. Part-time and evening/weekend programs available. *Degree requirements:* For master's, thesis. *Entrance requirements:* For master's, minimum B average. Electronic applications accepted.

St. Edward's University, New College, Program in Liberal Arts, Austin, TX 78704. Offers global issues (MLA); humanities (MLA); liberal arts (Certificate); social sciences (MLA). Part-time and evening/weekend programs available. *Students:* 9 full-time (4 women), 78 part-time (49 women); includes 22 minority (4 African Americans, 1 American Indian/Alaska Native, 2 Asian Americans or Pacific Islanders, 15 Hispanic Americans), 1 international. Average age 34. 33 applicants, 88% accepted, 25 enrolled. In 2008, 34 master's awarded. *Degree requirements:* For master's, minimum 24 resident hours. *Entrance requirements:* For master's, minimum GPA of 2.75 in last 60 hours of course work, interview. Additional exam requirements/recommendations for international students: Required—TOEFL (minimum score 550 paper-based; 213 computer-based; 79 iBT). *Application deadline:* For fall admission, 8/1 for domestic students, 7/1 for international students; for spring admission, 12/1 for domestic students, 11/1 for international students. Applications are processed on a rolling basis. Application fee: $45 ($50 for international students). Electronic applications accepted. *Expenses:* Tuition: Full-time $13,752; part-time $764 per credit hour. Required fees: $50 per semester. Full-time tuition and fees vary according to course load and program. *Financial support:* In 2008–09, 4 students received support. Scholarships/grants available. *Unit head:* Dr. Paula Marks, Director, 512-448-8702, Fax: 512-448-8492, E-mail: paulam@stewards.edu. *Application contact:* Kay L. Arnold, Graduate Admissions Coordinator, 512-233-1636, Fax: 512-428-1032, E-mail: kayla@stedwards.edu.

St. Edward's University, School of Education, Program in Teaching, Austin, TX 78704. Offers curriculum leadership (Certificate); instructional technology (Certificate); mentoring and supervision (Certificate); sports management (Certificate); teaching (MA), including conflict resolution, initial teacher certification, liberal arts, organization development and training, sports management, teacher leadership. Part-time and evening/weekend programs available. *Students:* 7 full-time (4 women), 33 part-time (20 women); includes 9 minority (2 African Americans, 7 Hispanic Americans), 1 international. Average age 30. 21 applicants, 67% accepted, 10 enrolled. In 2008, 4 master's awarded. *Degree requirements:* For master's, minimum 24 resident hours. *Entrance requirements:* For master's, GRE General Test, minimum GPA of 3.0 in last 60 hours or 2.75 overall. Additional exam requirements/recommendations for international students: Required—TOEFL (minimum score 550 paper-based; 213 computer-based; 79 iBT). *Application deadline:* For fall admission, 8/1 for domestic students, 7/1 for international students; for spring admission, 12/1 for domestic students, 11/1 for international students. Applications are processed on a rolling basis. Application fee: $45 ($50 for international students). Electronic applications accepted. *Expenses:* Tuition: Full-time $13,752; part-time $764 per credit hour. Required fees: $50 per semester. Full-time tuition and fees vary according to course load and program. *Financial support:* In 2008–09, 4 students received support. Scholarships/grants available. *Unit head:* Dr. David Hollier, Director, 512-448-8666, Fax: 512-428-1372, E-mail: davidh@stedwards.edu. *Application contact:* Kay L. Arnold, Graduate Admissions Coordinator, 512-233-1636, Fax: 512-428-1032, E-mail: kayla@stedwards.edu.

St. John's College, Graduate Institute in Liberal Education, Annapolis, MD 21404. Offers liberal arts (MALA). Evening/weekend programs available. *Degree requirements:* For master's, thesis optional. *Entrance requirements:* Additional exam requirements/recommendations for international students: Required—TOEFL (minimum score 650 paper-based; 250 computer-based; 112 iBT), TWE (minimum score 5).

St. John's College, Graduate Institute in Liberal Education, Program in Liberal Arts, Santa Fe, NM 87505-4599. Offers MA. Evening/weekend programs available. *Entrance requirements:* For master's, 2 letters of recommendation. Additional exam requirements/recommendations for international students: Required—TOEFL, TWE.

St. John's University, St. John's College of Liberal Arts and Sciences, Program in Liberal Studies, Queens, NY 11439. Offers MA. Part-time and evening/weekend programs available. *Students:* 55 part-time (30 women); includes 11 minority (6 African Americans, 2 Asian Americans or Pacific Islanders, 3 Hispanic Americans), 8 international. Average age 38. 63 applicants, 52% accepted, 19 enrolled. In 2008, 5 master's awarded. *Entrance requirements:* Additional exam requirements/recommendations for international students: Required—TOEFL (minimum score 500 paper-based; 173 computer-based; 61 iBT), IELTS (minimum score 5.5). *Application deadline:* For fall admission, 5/1 priority date for domestic and international students; for spring admission, 11/1 priority date for domestic and international students. Application fee: $70. *Expenses:* Tuition: Full-time $20,760; part-time $865 per credit. Required fees: $300; $150 per semester. Tuition and fees vary according to program. *Financial support:* Career-related internships or fieldwork and scholarships/grants available. Support available to part-time students. *Unit head:* Fr. Jean-Pierre Ruiz, Director, 718-990-6467, E-mail: ruizj@stjohns.edu. *Application contact:* Kathleen Davis, Director of Graduate Admission, 718-990-2790, Fax: 718-990-5686, E-mail: gradhelp@stjohns.edu.

Saint Mary's College of California, School of Liberal Arts, Graduate Liberal Studies Program, Moraga, CA 94575. Offers MA. Not accepting new students at this time. Part-time and evening/weekend programs available. *Degree requirements:* For master's, thesis or final project. *Entrance requirements:* For master's, interview. *Expenses:* Contact institution. *Faculty research:* Philosophy, theology, classics, theatre, literature.

St. Norbert College, Program in Liberal Studies, De Pere, WI 54115-2099. Offers MA. *Expenses:* Tuition: Part-time $350 per credit hour. *Unit head:* Dr. Howard Ebert, Director, 920-403-3956, Fax: 920-403-4086, E-mail: howard.ebert@snc.edu. *Application contact:* Program Coordinator, Fax: 920-403-4086, E-mail: deette.radant@snc.edu.

San Diego State University, Graduate and Research Affairs, College of Arts and Letters, Program in Liberal Arts and Sciences, San Diego, CA 92182. Offers MA. Part-time and evening/weekend programs available. *Degree requirements:* For master's, thesis. *Entrance requirements:* For master's, GRE General Test. Additional exam requirements/recommendations for international students: Required—TOEFL. Electronic applications accepted.

Simon Fraser University, Graduate Studies, Faculty of Arts and Social Sciences, Program in Liberal Studies, Burnaby, BC V5A 1S6, Canada. Offers MALS. Part-time and evening/weekend programs available. *Degree requirements:* For master's, thesis or alternative. *Entrance requirements:* For master's, minimum GPA of 3.0. Additional exam requirements/recommendations for international students: Required—TOEFL or IELTS. *Faculty research:* Humanities, psychology, history, women's studies, English.

Skidmore College, Liberal Studies Program, Saratoga Springs, NY 12866-1632. Offers MA. Part-time programs available. Postbaccalaureate distance learning degree programs offered (minimal on-campus study). *Faculty:* 46 full-time (28 women), 27 part-time/adjunct (9 women). *Students:* 60 part-time (48 women); includes 5 minority (2 African Americans, 3 Hispanic Americans). Average age 42. 37 applicants, 73% accepted, 21 enrolled. In 2008, 14 master's awarded. *Degree requirements:* For master's, thesis. *Application deadline:* For fall admission, 6/1 priority date for domestic and international students; for spring admission, 10/1 priority date for domestic and international students. Applications are processed on a rolling basis. Application fee: $60. Electronic applications accepted. *Financial support:* In 2008–09, 6 students received support. Career-related internships or fieldwork and scholarships/grants available. Support available to part-time students. Financial award applicants required to submit FAFSA. *Unit head:* Dr. John Anzalone, Director, 518-580-5480, Fax: 518-580-5486, E-mail: mals@skidmore.edu. *Application contact:* Information Contact, 518-580-5480, Fax: 518-580-5486, E-mail: mals@skidmore.edu.

Spring Hill College, Graduate Programs, Program in Liberal Arts, Mobile, AL 36608-1791. Offers MLA. Part-time and evening/weekend programs available. *Faculty:* 9 full-time (3 women), 1 (woman) part-time/adjunct. *Students:* 1 full-time (0 women), 30 part-time (13 women); includes 6 minority (all African Americans). Average age 37. 20 applicants, 60% accepted, 4 enrolled. In 2008, 5 master's awarded. *Degree requirements:* For master's, capstone course. *Entrance requirements:* For master's, minimum undergraduate GPA of 3.0. Additional exam requirements/recommendations for international students: Required—TOEFL (minimum score 550 paper-based; 213 computer-based; 80 iBT), IELTS (minimum score 6.5). *Application deadline:* For fall admission, 8/1 priority date for domestic and international students; for spring admission, 12/1 priority date for domestic and international students. Applications are processed on a rolling basis. Application fee: $25 ($35 for international students). Electronic applications accepted. *Expenses:* Contact institution. *Financial support:* In 2008–09, 28 students received support. Career-related internships or fieldwork, scholarships/grants, and loans available. Support available to part-time students. Financial award applicants required to submit FAFSA. *Unit head:* Dr. Alexander R. Landi, Director, Master of Liberal Arts Program, 251-380-3056, Fax: 251-460-2115, E-mail: landi@shc.edu. *Application contact:* Donna B. Tarasavage, Director of Marketing and Recruiting, Graduate and Continuing Studies, 251-380-3094, Fax: 251-460-2190, E-mail: grad@shc.edu.

State University of New York at Plattsburgh, School of Business and Economics, Program in Liberal Studies, Plattsburgh, NY 12901-2681. Offers MA. Part-time and evening/weekend programs available. *Faculty:* 5 full-time (2 women), 2 part-time/adjunct (0 women). *Students:* 7 full-time (6 women), 23 part-time (12 women). Average age 37. 11 applicants, 100% accepted, 9 enrolled. In 2008, 27 master's awarded. *Degree requirements:* For master's, thesis. *Entrance requirements:* For master's, GRE, GMAT, or MAT. Additional exam requirements/recommendations for international students: Required—TOEFL (minimum score 550 paper-based; 213 computer-based; 79 iBT). *Application deadline:* For fall admission, 2/15 priority date for domestic students; for spring admission, 10/15 priority date for domestic students. Applications are processed on a rolling basis. Application fee: $75. *Expenses:* Tuition, area resident: Full-time $7880; part-time $328 per credit hour. Tuition, state resident: full-time $7880; part-time $328 per credit hour. Tuition, nonresident: full-time $13,250; part-time $552 per credit hour. Required fees: $1060. *Financial support:* Application deadline: 4/15; *Unit head:* Dr. Suzanne Catana, Coordinator, 518-792-5425, E-mail: catanasl@plattsburgh.edu. *Application contact:* Marguerite Adelman, Assistant Director, Graduate Admissions, 518-564-4723, Fax: 518-564-4722, E-mail: adelmaml@plattsburgh.edu.

State University of New York Empire State College, Graduate Studies, Program in Liberal Studies, Saratoga Springs, NY 12866-4391. Offers MA. Part-time and evening/weekend programs available. Postbaccalaureate distance learning degree programs offered (minimal on-campus study). *Degree requirements:* For master's, thesis. *Entrance requirements:* Additional exam requirements/recommendations for international students: Required—TOEFL (minimum score 600 paper-based; 250 computer-based). Electronic applications accepted.

Stony Brook University, State University of New York, School of Professional Development, Stony Brook, NY 11794. Offers biology -grade 7-12 (MAT); chemistry-grade 7-12 (MAT); coaching (Graduate Certificate); computer integrated engineering (Graduate Certificate); earth science-grade 7-12 (MAT); educational computing (Graduate Certificate); educational leadership (Advanced Certificate); English-grade 7-12 (MAT); environmental management (Graduate Certificate); environmental/occupational health and safety (Graduate Certificate); French-grade 7-12 (MAT); German-grade 7-12 (MAT); human resource management (Graduate Certificate); information systems management (Graduate Certificate); Italian-grade 7-12 (MAT); liberal studies (MA); liberal studies online (MA); mathematics-grade 7-12 (MAT); operation research (Graduate Certificate); physics-grade 7-12 (MAT); school administration and supervision (Graduate Certificate); school building leadership (Graduate Certificate); school district administration (Graduate Certificate); school district business leadership (Advanced Certificate); school district leadership (Graduate Certificate); social science and the professions (MPS), including environmental waste management, human resource management; social studies-grade 7-12 (MAT); Spanish-grade 7-12 (MAT); waste management (Graduate Certificate). Part-time and evening/weekend programs available. Postbaccalaureate distance learning degree programs offered. *Faculty:* 5 full-time (3 women), 131 part-time/adjunct (53 women). *Students:* 317 full-time (187 women), 1,200 part-time (773 women); includes 187 minority (77 African Americans, 2 American Indian/Alaska Native, 22 Asian Americans or Pacific Islanders, 86 Hispanic Americans), 11 international. Average age 28. In 2008, 597 master's, 234 other advanced degrees awarded. *Degree requirements:* For master's, one foreign language, thesis or alternative. *Application deadline:* Applications are processed on a rolling basis. Application fee: $62. *Expenses:* Tuition, area resident: Full-time $7880; part-time $328 per credit hour. Tuition, state resident: full-time $7880; part-time $328 per credit hour. Tuition, nonresident: full-time $13,250; part-time $552 per credit hour. Required fees: $848. *Financial support:* Fellowships, research assistantships, teaching assistantships, career-related internships or fieldwork available. Support available to part-time students. *Unit head:* Dr. Paul J. Edelson, Dean, 631-632-7052, Fax: 631-632-9046, E-mail: paul.edelson@stonybrook.edu. *Application contact:* Dr. Paul J. Edelson, Dean, 631-632-7052, Fax: 631-632-9046, E-mail: paul.edelson@stonybrook.edu.

Tarleton State University, College of Graduate Studies, Program in Liberal Studies, Stephenville, TX 76402. Offers MS. Part-time and evening/weekend programs available. *Students:* 3 full-time (2 women), 6 part-time (4 women); includes 3 minority (all African Americans). Average age 34. 11 applicants, 73% accepted, 7 enrolled. *Entrance requirements:* Additional exam requirements/recommendations for international students: Required—TOEFL (minimum score 550 paper-based; 213 computer-based; 80 iBT). *Application deadline:* For fall admission, 8/5 priority date for domestic students; for spring admission, 12/1 for domestic students. Applications are processed on a rolling basis. Application fee: $30 ($130 for international students). Electronic applications accepted. *Expenses:* Tuition, area resident: Full-time $2853; part-time $158.50 per credit hour. Tuition, state resident: full-time $2853; part-time $158.50 per credit hour. Tuition, nonresident: full-time $7551; part-time $419.50 per credit hour. Required fees: $1040; $42 per credit hour. $124 per semester. Tuition and fees vary according to course load and campus/location. *Financial support:* Application deadline: 5/1; *Unit head:* Dr. Linda M. Jones, Dean, 254-968-9104, Fax: 254-968-9670, E-mail: ljones@tarleton.edu. *Application contact:* Information Contact, 254-968-9104, Fax: 254-968-9670, E-mail: gradoffice@tarleton.edu.

Temple University, Graduate School, College of Liberal Arts, Program in Liberal Arts, Philadelphia, PA 19122-6096. Offers MLA. Part-time and evening/weekend programs available. *Degree requirements:* For master's, thesis, qualifying paper. *Entrance requirements:* Additional exam requirements/recommendations for international students: Required—TOEFL (minimum score 550 paper-based; 213 computer-based; 79 iBT). Electronic applications accepted.

Texas Christian University, Graduate Studies, Fort Worth, TX 76129-0002. Offers MLA. Part-time and evening/weekend programs available. *Entrance requirements:* Additional exam requirements/recommendations for international students: Required—TOEFL. *Application deadline:* For fall admission, 3/1 for domestic students; for spring admission, 12/1 for domestic students. Applications are processed on a rolling basis. Application fee: $0. *Expenses:* Tuition: Full-time $17,640. *Financial support:* Application deadline: 3/1. *Unit head:* Dr. Bonnie Melhart, Associate Provost for Academic Affairs, 817-257-7104, E-mail: b.melhart@tcu.edu. *Application contact:* Dr. Bonnie Melhart, Associate Provost for Academic Affairs, 817-257-7104, E-mail: b.melhart@tcu.edu.

Thomas Edison State College, Heavin School of Arts and Sciences, Program in Liberal Studies, Trenton, NJ 08608-1176. Offers homeland security (MALS). Part-time programs available. Postbaccalaureate distance learning degree programs offered (no on-campus study). *Students:* 85 part-time (56 women); includes 23 African Americans, 2 Asian Americans or Pacific Islanders, 6 Hispanic Americans. Average age 43. 39 applicants, 30 enrolled. In 2008, 20 master's awarded. *Degree requirements:* For master's, final project. *Entrance requirements:* For master's, bachelor's degree from a regionally-accredited college or university; minimum 2 letters of recommendation; 3-5 years of related working experience; current resumé. Additional exam requirements/recommendations for international students: Required—TOEFL (minimum

Liberal Studies

Thomas Edison State College (continued)

score 550 paper-based; 213 computer-based; 79 iBT). *Application deadline:* For fall admission, 8/15 priority date for domestic and international students; for winter admission, 11/15 priority date for domestic and international students; for spring admission, 2/15 priority date for domestic and international students. Applications are processed on a rolling basis. Application fee: $75. Electronic applications accepted. *Expenses:* Tuition, area resident: Part-time $465 per credit. Tuition, state resident: part-time $465 per credit. Tuition, nonresident: part-time $465 per credit. *Financial support:* Applicants required to submit FAFSA. *Unit head:* Dr. Susan Davenport, Dean, Heavin School of Arts and Sciences, 609-984-1130, Fax: 609-984-0740, E-mail: info@tesc.edu. *Application contact:* David Hoftiezer, Director of Admissions, 888-442-8372, Fax: 609-984-8447, E-mail: admissions@tesc.edu.

Towson University, College of Graduate Studies and Research, Program in Professional Studies, Towson, MD 21252-0001. Offers MA. Part-time and evening/weekend programs available. *Degree requirements:* For master's, thesis optional, exam. *Entrance requirements:* For master's, minimum GPA of 3.0, admission essay, official transcripts. Electronic applications accepted. *Faculty research:* History, World War II, counseling, marriage and family, human development.

Tulane University, Program in Liberal Arts, New Orleans, LA 70118-5669. Offers MLA. Part-time programs available. *Degree requirements:* For master's, thesis. *Entrance requirements:* For master's, GRE General Test, minimum B average in undergraduate course work. Additional exam requirements/recommendations for international students: Required—TOEFL.

University at Albany, State University of New York, College of Arts and Sciences, Liberal Studies Program, Albany, NY 12222-0001. Offers MA. *Entrance requirements:* Additional exam requirements/recommendations for international students: Required—TOEFL (minimum score 550 paper-based; 213 computer-based). Electronic applications accepted.

University of Arkansas at Little Rock, Graduate School, College of Arts, Humanities, and Social Science, Department of Philosophy and Liberal Studies, Little Rock, AR 72204-1099. Offers MALS. *Entrance requirements:* For master's, GRE.

University of Delaware, College of Arts and Sciences, Program in Liberal Studies, Newark, DE 19716. Offers MALS. Part-time and evening/weekend programs available. *Degree requirements:* For master's, thesis. Electronic applications accepted. *Faculty research:* British Raj, medical and scientific ethics, Jewish-American novelists, intellectual freedom.

University of Denver, University College, Denver, CO 80208. Offers applied communication (MAS, MPS, Certificate); computer information systems (MAS, Certificate); environmental policy and management (MAS, Certificate); geographic information systems (MAS, Certificate); human resource administration (MPS, Certificate); knowledge and information technologies (MAS); liberal studies (MLS, Certificate); modern languages (MLS, Certificate); organizational leadership (MPS, Certificate); security management (Certificate); technology management (MAS, Certificate), including 21st century strategic management (MAS), international markets (MAS), project management (MAS), research and development management (MAS); telecommunications (MAS, Certificate), including broadband (MAS), telecommunications management and policy (MAS), telecommunications technology (MAS), wireless networks (MAS). Part-time and evening/weekend programs available. Postbaccalaureate distance learning degree programs offered (no on-campus study). *Faculty:* 137 part-time/adjunct (55 women). *Students:* 28 full-time (15 women), 699 part-time (401 women); includes 129 minority (54 African Americans, 8 American Indian/Alaska Native, 22 Asian Americans or Pacific Islanders, 45 Hispanic Americans), 4 international. Average age 36. 845 applicants, 96% accepted, 326 enrolled. In 2008, 221 master's, 3 Certificates awarded. *Entrance requirements:* Additional exam requirements/recommendations for international students: Required—TOEFL (minimum score 550 paper-based; 213 computer-based). *Application deadline:* Applications are processed on a rolling basis. Application fee: $75. Electronic applications accepted. *Expenses:* Contact institution. *Financial support:* Applicants required to submit FAFSA. *Unit head:* Dr. James Davis, Dean, 303-871-2291, Fax: 303-871-4047, E-mail: jdavis@du.edu. *Application contact:* Information Contact, 303-871-3155.

University of Detroit Mercy, College of Liberal Arts and Education, Program in Liberal Studies, Detroit, MI 48221. Offers MALS. Part-time programs available.

The University of Findlay, Graduate and Professional Studies, College of Liberal Arts, Master of Arts Program in Liberal Studies, Findlay, OH 45840-3653. Offers MALS. Part-time and evening/weekend programs available. *Students:* 6 full-time (3 women), 19 part-time (15 women); includes 2 minority (1 American Indian/Alaska Native, 1 Hispanic American), 7 international. Average age 35. 9 applicants, 78% accepted, 6 enrolled. In 2008, 5 master's awarded. *Degree requirements:* For master's, thesis, cumulative project. *Entrance requirements:* For master's, minimum undergraduate GPA of 2.5 in last 64 hours of course work, 3 letters of recommendation, essay. Additional exam requirements/recommendations for international students: Required—TOEFL (minimum score 550 paper-based; 213 computer-based; 80 iBT). *Application deadline:* Applications are processed on a rolling basis. Application fee: $25. Electronic applications accepted. *Expenses:* Tuition: Full-time $10,350; part-time $7000 per credit hour. Required fees: $600; $30 per credit hour. $25 per semester. Tuition and fees vary according to course load and program. *Financial support:* Unspecified assistantships available. Financial award application deadline: 4/1; financial award applicants required to submit FAFSA. *Unit head:* Robert Cecire, PhD, Director, 419-434-5306, E-mail: rcecire@findlay.edu. *Application contact:* Heather Riffle, Assistant to the Dean, Graduate and Professional Studies, 419-434-4640, Fax: 419-434-5517, E-mail: riffle@findlay.edu.

University of Maine, Graduate School, Program in Liberal Studies, Orono, ME 04469. Offers MA. Part-time and evening/weekend programs available. *Degree requirements:* For master's, project. *Entrance requirements:* Additional exam requirements/recommendations for international students: Required—TOEFL. Electronic applications accepted.

University of Memphis, Graduate School, University College, Memphis, TN 38152. Offers liberal studies (MALS); merchandising and consumer science (MS), including consumer science and education; strategic leadership (MPS). Part-time and evening/weekend programs available. *Faculty:* 8 full-time (4 women). *Students:* 19 full-time (14 women), 83 part-time (59 women); includes 46 African Americans, 1 Asian American or Pacific Islander. Average age 41. 52 applicants, 85% accepted, 6 enrolled. In 2008, 43 master's awarded. *Degree requirements:* For master's, comprehensive exam, thesis (for some programs). *Entrance requirements:* For master's, MAT, GRE General Test (MS), interview (MALS). Additional exam requirements/recommendations for international students: Required—TOEFL (minimum score 550 paper-based; 210 computer-based). *Application deadline:* For fall admission, 7/1 for domestic students, 5/1 for international students; for spring admission, 11/1 for domestic students, 9/15 for international students. Applications are processed on a rolling basis. Application fee: $35 ($60 for international students). Electronic applications accepted. *Expenses:* Tuition, area resident: Full-time $6242; part-time $330 per credit hour. Tuition, state resident: full-time $6242; part-time $330 per credit hour. Tuition, nonresident: full-time $17,828; part-time $815 per credit hour. Required fees: $1156. *Financial support:* In 2008–09, 98 students received support; research assistantships with full tuition reimbursements available, teaching assistantships, unspecified assistantships available. Financial award application deadline: 6/1; financial award applicants required to submit FAFSA. *Faculty research:* Media ethics, history of psychiatry, public relations. Total annual research expenditures: $9,333. *Unit head:* Dr. Dan Lattimore, Dean, 901-678-2991. *Application contact:* Dr. Herbert McCree, Coordinator of Graduate Studies, 901-678-4171, Fax: 901-678-3363, E-mail: hmccree@memphis.edu.

University of Miami, Graduate School, College of Arts and Sciences, Program in Liberal Studies, Coral Gables, FL 33124. Offers MALS. Part-time and evening/weekend programs available. *Degree requirements:* For master's, thesis or alternative. *Entrance requirements:* For master's, minimum GPA of 3.0. Additional exam requirements/recommendations for international students: Required—TOEFL. Electronic applications accepted. *Expenses:* Contact institution.

University of Michigan–Dearborn, College of Arts, Sciences, and Letters, Master of Arts in Liberal Studies Program, Dearborn, MI 48128. Offers MA. Part-time and evening/weekend programs available. *Faculty:* 14 full-time (7 women). *Students:* 1 (woman) full-time, 30 part-time (16 women); includes 4 minority (2 African Americans, 1 Asian American or Pacific Islander, 1 Hispanic American). Average age 43. 12 applicants, 75% accepted, 9 enrolled. In 2008, 8 master's awarded. *Degree requirements:* For master's, thesis or alternative, capstone course. *Entrance requirements:* For master's, minimum GPA of 3.0, writing sample, interview, statement of purpose. Additional exam requirements/recommendations for international students: Required—TOEFL (minimum score 560 paper-based; 220 computer-based). *Application deadline:* For fall admission, 8/1 priority date for domestic students, 4/1 for international students; for winter admission, 12/1 priority date for domestic students, 11/1 for international students; for spring admission, 4/1 for domestic students, 3/1 for international students. Applications are processed on a rolling basis. Application fee: $60 ($75 for international students). *Financial support:* Scholarships/grants available. Support available to part-time students. Financial award application deadline: 4/1; financial award applicants required to submit FAFSA. *Faculty research:* History of science studies, consciousness, memory studies, early American history, environmental studies. *Unit head:* Dr. Jacqueline Vansant, Director, 313-593-5153, Fax: 313-583-6498, E-mail: jvansant@umd.umich.edu. *Application contact:* Carol Ligienza, Graduate Program Coordinator, CASL Graduate Programs, 313-593-1183, Fax: 313-583-6498, E-mail: caslgrad@umd.umich.edu.

University of Minnesota, Duluth, Graduate School, College of Liberal Arts, Department of Sociology/Anthropology, Liberal Studies Program, Duluth, MN 55812-2496. Offers MLS. Part-time and evening/weekend programs available. *Faculty research:* Nature of knowledge, cultural studies, language, literature, sociology.

University of New Hampshire, Graduate School, College of Liberal Arts, Program in Liberal Studies, Durham, NH 03824. Offers MALS. *Faculty:* 5 full-time (3 women). *Students:* 5 full-time (1 woman), 16 part-time (11 women); includes 1 minority (Asian American or Pacific Islander). Average age 39. 11 applicants, 91% accepted, 7 enrolled. In 2008, 3 master's awarded. *Entrance requirements:* Additional exam requirements/recommendations for international students: Required—TOEFL (minimum score 550 paper-based; 213 computer-based; 80 iBT). *Application deadline:* For fall admission, 4/1 for domestic and international students; for winter admission, 12/1 for domestic students. Applications are processed on a rolling basis. Application fee: $60. Electronic applications accepted. *Expenses:* Tuition, area resident: Full-time $9720; part-time $540 per credit hour. Tuition, nonresident: full-time $23,200; part-time $954 per credit hour. Required fees: $1446; $361.50 per term. *Financial support:* Fellowships, research assistantships, teaching assistantships available. Financial award application deadline: 2/15. *Unit head:* Dr. Warren Brown, Chairperson, 603-862-3225, E-mail: liberal.studies@unh.edu. *Application contact:* Dr. Warren Brown, Chairperson, 603-862-3225, E-mail: liberal.studies@unh.edu.

The University of North Carolina at Asheville, Graduate Studies, Asheville, NC 28804-3299. Offers MLA. Part-time and evening/weekend programs available. *Degree requirements:* For master's, thesis.

The University of North Carolina at Charlotte, Graduate School, College of Arts and Sciences, Program in Liberal Studies, Charlotte, NC 28223-0001. Offers MA. *Students:* 2 full-time (1 woman), 19 part-time (11 women); includes 3 minority (all African Americans). Average age 34. 5 applicants, 100% accepted, 5 enrolled. In 2008, 7 master's awarded. *Degree requirements:* For master's, comprehensive exam or project. *Entrance requirements:* For master's, GRE General Test or MAT, minimum GPA of 3.0 during previous 2 years, 2.75 overall. Additional exam requirements/recommendations for international students: Required—TOEFL (minimum score 557 paper-based; 220 computer-based). *Application deadline:* For fall admission, 7/1 for domestic students, 5/1 for international students; for spring admission, 11/1 for domestic students, 10/1 for international students. Applications are processed on a rolling basis. Application fee: $55. Electronic applications accepted. *Expenses:* Tuition, area resident: Full-time $2919; part-time $122 per credit hour. Tuition, state resident: full-time $2919; part-time $122 per credit hour. Tuition, nonresident: full-time $13,126; part-time $547 per credit hour. Required fees: $1779; $91 per credit hour. Tuition and fees vary according to program. *Financial support:* Career-related internships or fieldwork, Federal Work-Study, institutionally sponsored loans, scholarships/grants, and unspecified assistantships available. Support available to part-time students. Financial award application deadline: 4/1; financial award applicants required to submit FAFSA. *Unit head:* Dr. Alan Rauch, Director, 704-687-4312, Fax: 704-687-4347, E-mail: arauch@email.uncc.edu. *Application contact:* Kathy B. Giddings, Director of Graduate Admissions, 704-687-3366, Fax: 704-687-3279, E-mail: agidding@uncc.edu.

The University of North Carolina at Greensboro, Graduate School, Program in Liberal Studies, Greensboro, NC 27412-5001. Offers MALS. Electronic applications accepted.

The University of North Carolina Wilmington, College of Arts and Sciences, Interdisciplinary Program in Liberal Studies, Wilmington, NC 28403-3297. Offers MALS. Part-time programs available. *Students:* 16 full-time (10 women), 60 part-time (42 women); includes 14 minority (9 African Americans, 1 American Indian/Alaska Native, 1 Asian American or Pacific Islander, 3 Hispanic Americans), 1 international. Average age 38. 24 applicants, 75% accepted, 18 enrolled. In 2008, 22 master's awarded. *Degree requirements:* For master's, comprehensive exam, thesis or alternative, final project. *Entrance requirements:* For master's, minimum GPA of 3.0, writing sample. Additional exam requirements/recommendations for international students: Required—TOEFL (minimum score 550 paper-based; 217 computer-based; 79 iBT), IELTS (minimum score 6.5). *Application deadline:* For fall admission, 3/15 for domestic students. Application fee: $60. *Expenses:* Tuition, area resident: Full-time $4838. Tuition, state resident: full-time $4838. Tuition, nonresident: full-time $14,898. Required fees: $969.38 per semester. Tuition and fees vary according to course load, campus/location and program. *Financial support:* In 2008–09, 3 teaching assistantships (averaging $9,500 per year) were awarded. Financial award application deadline: 3/15. *Unit head:* Dr. Herb Berg, Director, 910-962-3299, E-mail: bergh@uncw.edu. *Application contact:* Dr. Herb Berg, Dean, Graduate School, 910-962-3299, E-mail: bergh@uncw.edu.

University of Oklahoma, Graduate College, College of Liberal Studies, Norman, OK 73019-0390. Offers administrative leadership (MLS); integrated studies (MLS); interprofessional human and health services (MLS); museum studies (MLS). Part-time programs available. Postbaccalaureate distance learning degree programs offered (no on-campus study). *Faculty:* 9 full-time (7 women), 24 part-time/adjunct (15 women). *Students:* 15 full-time (10 women), 328 part-time (178 women); includes 64 minority (39 African Americans, 15 American Indian/Alaska Native, 3 Asian Americans or Pacific Islanders, 7 Hispanic Americans). 96 applicants, 98% accepted, 81 enrolled. In 2008, 71 master's awarded. *Degree requirements:* For master's, thesis, research project, internship. *Entrance requirements:* For master's, minimum GPA of 3.0 in last 60 hours, writing sample. Additional exam requirements/recommendations for international students: Required—TOEFL (minimum score 550 paper-based; 213 computer-based). *Application deadline:* For fall admission, 7/15 priority date for domestic students, 4/1 for international students; for spring admission, 12/1 for domestic students, 9/1 for international students. Applications are processed on a rolling basis. Application fee: $40 ($90 for international students). Electronic applications accepted. *Expenses:* Tuition, state resident: full-time $3744; part-time $156 per credit hour. Tuition, nonresident: full-time $13,577; part-time $565.70 per credit hour. Required fees: $2415.40; $90.10 per credit hour. *Financial support:* In 2008–09, 144 students received support. Career-related internships or fieldwork, scholarships/grants, and tuition waivers (partial) available. Support available to part-time students. Financial award applicants required to submit FAFSA. *Faculty research:* Distance education, adult learning processes, student satisfaction, administrative leadership, organizations, museum studies. *Unit head:* Dr. James Pappas, Dean and Vice President for University Outreach, 405-325-

6361, Fax: 405-325-7196, E-mail: jpappas@ou.edu. *Application contact:* Dr. Julie Raadschelders, MA Program Coordinator, 405-325-1061, Fax: 405-325-9632, E-mail: jraadschelders@ou.edu.

University of Pennsylvania, School of Arts and Sciences, College of Liberal and Professional Studies, Program of Individualized Study, Philadelphia, PA 19104. Offers MLA.

University of St. Thomas, Program in Liberal Arts, Houston, TX 77006-4696. Offers MLA. Part-time and evening/weekend programs available. *Faculty:* 32 full-time (13 women), 8 part-time/adjunct (6 women). *Students:* 35 full-time (27 women), 99 part-time (72 women); includes 38 minority (16 African Americans, 2 Asian Americans or Pacific Islanders, 20 Hispanic Americans), 8 international. Average age 36. 51 applicants, 73% accepted, 31 enrolled. In 2008, 38 master's awarded. *Degree requirements:* For master's, thesis optional. *Entrance requirements:* For master's, minimum GPA of 2.5. Additional exam requirements/recommendations for international students: Required—TOEFL (minimum score 250 computer-based; 100 iBT). *Application deadline:* Applications are processed on a rolling basis. Application fee: $35. Electronic applications accepted. *Expenses:* Tuition: Full-time $13,554; part-time $753 per credit. Required fees: $224; $224 per year. *Financial support:* In 2008–09, 11 students received support. Federal Work-Study and scholarships/grants available. Support available to part-time students. Financial award application deadline: 3/1; financial award applicants required to submit FAFSA. *Unit head:* Dr. Ravi Srinivas, Dean, 713-525-6924, Fax: 713-525-6924, E-mail: srinivas@stthom.edu. *Application contact:* Kate Henderson, MLA Program Assistant, 713-525-3556, Fax: 713-525-6924, E-mail: henderlk@stthom.edu.

University of Southern Indiana, Graduate Studies, College of Liberal Arts, Program in Liberal Studies, Evansville, IN 47712-3590. Offers MA. Part-time and evening/weekend programs available. *Faculty:* 12 full-time (8 women). *Students:* 5 full-time (1 woman), 37 part-time (24 women); includes 3 minority (all African Americans), 1 international. Average age 36. 8 applicants, 100% accepted, 7 enrolled. In 2008, 11 master's awarded. *Entrance requirements:* For master's, minimum GPA of 2.5, resumé, interview. Additional exam requirements/recommendations for international students: Required—TOEFL (minimum score 550 paper-based; 213 computer-based; 79 iBT), IELTS (minimum score 6). *Application deadline:* For fall admission, 8/15 priority date for domestic students, 3/1 priority date for international students. Applications are processed on a rolling basis. Application fee: $25. *Expenses:* Tuition, area resident: Full-time $4374; part-time $243 per credit hour. Tuition, state resident: full-time $4374; part-time $243 per credit. Tuition, nonresident: full-time $8622; part-time $479 per credit hour. Required fees: $220; $22.75 per term. Tuition and fees vary according to course load and reciprocity agreements. *Financial support:* In 2008–09, 26 students received support. Federal Work-Study, scholarships/grants, tuition waivers (full and partial), and unspecified assistantships available. Financial award application deadline: 3/1; financial award applicants required to submit FAFSA. *Unit head:* Dr. Thomas M. Rivers, Director, 812-464-1753, E-mail: trivers@usi.edu. *Application contact:* Dr. Thomas M. Rivers, Director, 812-464-1753, E-mail: trivers@usi.edu.

University of South Florida, Graduate School, College of Arts and Sciences, Department of Humanities and American Studies, Program in Liberal Arts, Tampa, FL 33620-9951. Offers MLA. *Degree requirements:* For master's, comprehensive exam, thesis. *Entrance requirements:* For master's, GRE, minimum GPA of 3.0. Additional exam requirements/recommendations for international students: Required—TOEFL (minimum score 550 paper-based; 213 computer-based). *Application deadline:* For fall admission, 2/15 for domestic students, 1/2 for international students; for spring admission, 10/15 for domestic students, 6/1 for international students. Application fee: $30. *Expenses:* Tuition, state resident: full-time $2624.40; part-time $291.60 per credit hour. Tuition, nonresident: full-time $7822; part-time $869.13 per credit hour. *Unit head:* Daniel Belgrad, Program Director, 813-974-9384, Fax: 813-974-9409, E-mail: dbelgrad@cas.usf.edu. *Application contact:* Daniel Belgrad, Program Director, 813-974-9384, Fax: 813-974-9409, E-mail: dbelgrad@cas.usf.edu.

The University of Toledo, College of Graduate Studies, College of Arts and Sciences, Master of Liberal Studies Program, Toledo, OH 43606-3390. Offers MLS. Part-time and evening/weekend programs available. *Degree requirements:* For master's, thesis. *Entrance requirements:* For master's, interview, minimum GPA of 2.7. Electronic applications accepted.

University of Wisconsin–Milwaukee, Graduate School, College of Letters and Sciences, Interdepartmental Program in Liberal Studies, Milwaukee, WI 53201-0413. Offers MLS. *Faculty:* 10 full-time (3 women). *Students:* 7 full-time (4 women), 16 part-time (11 women); includes 4 minority (3 African Americans, 1 Hispanic American). Average age 37. 14 applicants, 79% accepted, 7 enrolled. In 2008, 6 master's awarded. *Entrance requirements:* For master's, interview, bachelor's degree. Additional exam requirements/recommendations for international students: Required—TOEFL (minimum score 600 paper-based; 79 iBT), IELTS (minimum score 7). Application fee: $45 ($75 for international students). *Expenses:* Tuition, area resident: Full-time $7320; part-time $165 per credit. Tuition, state resident: full-time $7320; part-time $165 per credit. Tuition, nonresident: full-time $17,840; part-time $714 per credit. Tuition and fees vary according to campus/location, program and reciprocity agreements. *Unit head:* Jeffrey R Hayes, Representative, 414-229-5963, E-mail: jhayes@uwm.edu. *Application contact:* General Information Contact, 414-229-4982, Fax: 414-229-6967, E-mail: gradschool@uwm.edu.

Ursuline College, School of Graduate Studies, Program in Liberal Studies, Pepper Pike, OH 44124-4398. Offers MALS. *Students:* 2 part-time (both women); includes 1 minority (African American). Average age 69. In 2008, 1 master's awarded. *Degree requirements:* For master's, thesis. *Entrance requirements:* For master's, minimum undergraduate GPA of 3.0. Additional exam requirements/recommendations for international students: Required—TOEFL (minimum score 500 paper-based; 173 computer-based). *Application deadline:* For fall admission, 8/1 priority date for domestic students. Applications are processed on a rolling basis. Application fee: $25. Electronic applications accepted. *Expenses:* Tuition: Full-time $13,590; part-time $775 per credit hour. Required fees: $220; $70 per semester. *Financial support:* In 2008–09, 5 students received support. Federal Work-Study available. Financial award application deadline: 3/1; financial award applicants required to submit FAFSA. *Unit head:* Dr. Tim Kinsella, Director, 440-646-8389, Fax: 440-684-6088, E-mail: tkinsell@ursuline.edu. *Application contact:* Lauren Anderson, Secretary, 440-646-8119, Fax: 440-684-6088, E-mail: gradsch@ursuline.edu.

Utica College, Liberal Studies Program, Utica, NY 13502-4892. Offers MS. Part-time and evening/weekend programs available. *Faculty:* 19 full-time (8 women). *Students:* 4 full-time (3 women), 33 part-time (26 women); includes 2 minority (1 African American, 1 Asian American or Pacific Islander), 1 international. Average age 33. In 2008, 3 master's awarded. *Degree requirements:* For master's, thesis or alternative, comprehensive exam or thesis. *Entrance requirements:* For master's, minimum GPA of 3.0. Additional exam requirements/recommendations for international students: Required—TOEFL (minimum score 525 paper-based; 195 computer-based). *Application deadline:* Applications are processed on a rolling basis. Application fee: $50. Electronic applications accepted. *Expenses:* Contact institution. *Financial support:* Career-related internships or fieldwork, scholarships/grants, tuition waivers (partial), and unspecified assistantships available. Support available to part-time students. Financial award application deadline: 3/15; financial award applicants required to submit FAFSA. *Unit head:* Dr. Lawrence Aaronson, Coordinator, Liberal Studies, 315-792-3092, E-mail: laaronson@utica.edu. *Application contact:* John D. Rowe, Director of Graduate Admissions, 315-792-3824, Fax: 315-792-3003, E-mail: jrowe@utica.edu.

Valparaiso University, Graduate Division, Program in Liberal Studies, Concentration in Human Behavior and Society, Valparaiso, IN 46383. Offers MALS, Post-Master's Certificate, JD/MALS. Part-time and evening/weekend programs available. *Students:* 7 full-time (5 women), 6 part-time (4 women); includes 1 minority (African American), 2 international. Average age 33. In 2008, 6 master's awarded. *Entrance requirements:* For master's, minimum GPA of 3.0. Additional exam requirements/recommendations for international students: Required—TOEFL (minimum score 550 paper-based; 213 computer-based). *Application deadline:* Applications are processed on a rolling basis. Application fee: $30 ($50 for international students). Electronic applications accepted. *Financial support:* Available to part-time students. Applicants required to submit FAFSA. *Unit head:* Dr. David L. Rowland, Dean, Graduate Studies and Continuing Education, 219-464-5313, Fax: 219-464-5381, E-mail: David.Rowland@valpo.edu. *Application contact:* Jamie Haney, Coordinator of Recruitment Activities, 219-464-5313, Fax: 219-464-5381, E-mail: Jamie.Haney@valpo.edu.

Valparaiso University, Graduate Division, Program in Liberal Studies, Individualized Program, Valparaiso, IN 46383. Offers MALS, JD/MALS. Part-time and evening/weekend programs available. *Students:* 2 full-time (both women), 6 part-time (5 women); includes 1 minority (African American), 1 international. Average age 33. In 2008, 2 master's awarded. *Entrance requirements:* For master's, minimum GPA of 3.0. Additional exam requirements/recommendations for international students: Required—TOEFL (minimum score 550 paper-based; 213 computer-based). *Application deadline:* Applications are processed on a rolling basis. Application fee: $30 ($50 for international students). Electronic applications accepted. *Financial support:* Available to part-time students. Applicants required to submit FAFSA. *Unit head:* Dr. David L. Rowland, Dean, Graduate Studies and Continuing Education, 219-464-5313, Fax: 219-464-5381, E-mail: David.Rowland@valpo.edu. *Application contact:* Jamie Haney, Coordinator of Recruitment Activities, 219-464-5313, Fax: 219-464-5381, E-mail: Jamie.Haney@valpo.edu.

Vanderbilt University, Graduate School, Program in Liberal Arts and Science, Nashville, TN 37240-1001. Offers MLAS. Part-time programs available. *Students:* 1 (woman) full-time, 70 part-time (45 women); includes 3 minority (all African Americans), 1 international. Average age 45. 30 applicants, 63% accepted, 12 enrolled. In 2008, 13 master's awarded. *Degree requirements:* For master's, thesis optional. *Entrance requirements:* For master's, GRE General Test. *Application deadline:* For fall admission, 1/15 priority date for domestic students, 1/15 for international students; for spring admission, 11/15 for domestic and international students. Applications are processed on a rolling basis. Application fee: $0. *Financial support:* Institutionally sponsored loans and tuition waivers (partial) available. *Unit head:* Martin Rapisarda, Associate Dean and Director, 615-343-3140, Fax: 615-343-8453, E-mail: martin.rapisarda@vanderbilt.edu. *Application contact:* Walter B. Bieschke, Program Coordinator for Graduate Admissions, 615-343-6321, Fax: 615-343-6687, E-mail: vandygrad@vanderbilt.edu.

Villanova University, Graduate School of Liberal Arts and Sciences, Program in Liberal Studies, Villanova, PA 19085-1699. Offers MA. Part-time and evening/weekend programs available. *Faculty:* 7 full-time (3 women). *Students:* 5 full-time (4 women), 19 part-time (16 women), 2 international. Average age 42. 14 applicants, 50% accepted, 5 enrolled. In 2008, 10 master's awarded. *Degree requirements:* For master's, comprehensive exam. *Entrance requirements:* For master's, minimum GPA of 3.0. *Application deadline:* For fall admission, 8/1 for domestic and international students; for spring admission, 12/1 for domestic and international students. Applications are processed on a rolling basis. Application fee: $50. Electronic applications accepted. *Financial support:* Research assistantships, Federal Work-Study available. Financial award applicants required to submit FAFSA. *Unit head:* Dr. Eugene McCarraher, Director, 610-519-4796, Fax: 610-519-4639, E-mail: eugene.mccarraher@villanova.edu. *Application contact:* Dr. Gerald Long, Dean, Graduate School of Liberal Arts and Sciences, 610-519-7093, Fax: 610-519-7096.

Wake Forest University, Graduate School of Arts and Sciences, Liberal Studies Program, Winston-Salem, NC 27109. Offers MALS. Part-time programs available. *Degree requirements:* For master's, thesis. *Entrance requirements:* Additional exam requirements/recommendations for international students: Required—TOEFL (minimum score 213 computer-based; 79 iBT).

Washburn University, College of Arts and Sciences, Program in Liberal Studies, Topeka, KS 66621. Offers MLS. Part-time and evening/weekend programs available. *Degree requirements:* For master's, thesis, 15 seminar hours. *Entrance requirements:* For master's, minimum GPA of 3.0. Electronic applications accepted. *Faculty research:* European architecture/history, British cultural studies movement, American military strategy/history.

Wesleyan University, Graduate Liberal Studies Program, Middletown, CT 06459-0260. Offers MALS, CAS. Part-time and evening/weekend programs available. *Degree requirements:* For master's, thesis optional; for CAS, thesis. *Entrance requirements:* For master's, application; for CAS, application, master's degree. Additional exam requirements/recommendations for international students: Required—TOEFL. *Expenses:* Contact institution. *Faculty research:* Interdisciplinary studies.

Western Illinois University, School of Graduate Studies, College of Arts and Sciences, Program in Liberal Arts and Sciences, Macomb, IL 61455-1390. Offers MLAS. *Students:* 2 part-time (1 woman). Average age 37. 4 applicants, 75% accepted. *Degree requirements:* For master's, thesis or alternative. *Entrance requirements:* Additional exam requirements/recommendations for international students: Required—TOEFL (minimum score 550 paper-based; 213 computer-based; 80 iBT). *Application deadline:* Applications are processed on a rolling basis. Application fee: $30. Electronic applications accepted. *Expenses:* Tuition, state resident: full-time $5696; part-time $237.34 per credit hour. Tuition, nonresident: full-time $11,392; part-time $474.68 per credit hour. Required fees: $1453; $60.55 per credit hour. *Financial support:* In 2008–09, research assistantships (averaging $7,020 per year). *Unit head:* Dr. Susan Martinelli, Associate Dean, 309-298-1828. *Application contact:* Evelyn Hoing, Assistant Director of Graduate Studies, 309-298-1806, Fax: 309-298-2345, E-mail: grad-office@wiu.edu.

West Virginia University, Eberly College of Arts and Sciences, Interdisciplinary Program in Liberal Studies, Morgantown, WV 26506. Offers MALS. Part-time programs available. *Degree requirements:* For master's, thesis or alternative. *Entrance requirements:* For master's, GRE General Test, minimum GPA of 3.0. Additional exam requirements/recommendations for international students: Required—TOEFL.

Wichita State University, Graduate School, Fairmount College of Liberal Arts and Sciences, Interdisciplinary Program in Liberal Studies, Wichita, KS 67260. Offers environmental science (MS). Participating faculty are from the Departments of Minority Studies, Philosophy, Religion, Social Work, and Women's Studies. Part-time programs available. *Degree requirements:* For master's, thesis optional, project. *Entrance requirements:* For master's, GRE, minimum GPA of 2.75. Additional exam requirements/recommendations for international students: Required—TOEFL. Electronic applications accepted.

Widener University, College of Arts and Sciences, Program in Liberal Studies, Chester, PA 19013-5792. Offers MA. Part-time and evening/weekend programs available. *Faculty:* 4 full-time (1 woman). *Students:* 12 part-time (9 women); includes 1 minority (African American). Average age 40. 3 applicants, 100% accepted. In 2008, 2 master's awarded. *Degree requirements:* For master's, thesis, project. *Entrance requirements:* For master's, interview, minimum undergraduate GPA of 3.0. *Application deadline:* Applications are processed on a rolling basis. Application fee: $25 ($300 for international students). *Expenses:* Contact institution. *Financial support:* Federal Work-Study and tuition waivers (full and partial) available. Financial award application deadline: 5/1. *Faculty research:* Contemporary analytical metaphysics, popular culture, British art, American literature, folklore. *Unit head:* Dr. Kenneth Skinner, Director, 610-499-4287, Fax: 610-499-4605, E-mail: kenneth.a.skinner@widener.edu. *Application contact:* Dr. Kenneth Skinner, Director, 610-499-4287, Fax: 610-499-4605, E-mail: kenneth.a.skinner@widener.edu.

Winthrop University, College of Arts and Sciences, Program in Liberal Arts, Rock Hill, SC 29733. Offers MLA. Part-time programs available. *Entrance requirements:* For master's, interview, minimum GPA of 3.0, 3-4 page essay. Electronic applications accepted.

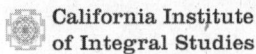
California Institute of Integral Studies

CALIFORNIA INSTITUTE OF INTEGRAL STUDIES
School of Consciousness and Transformation

Programs of Study

The mission of the School of Consciousness and Transformation at California Institute of Integral Studies (CIIS) is to conduct scholarly, interdisciplinary inquiry in the fields of anthropology, philosophy, East-West psychology, religion, transformative studies and leadership, integrative health studies, and women's spirituality. This mode of inquiry appreciates and challenges received traditions, enriching them with perspectives taken from feminist theory, ecological thought, consciousness studies, critical social theory, and new scientific paradigms. The School aims to support personal growth and development and to promote social action. The founding vision of an integral approach to education continues to inspire the School. Academic programs embody this integral vision by respecting the spiritual dimension of experience, incorporating different ways of knowing, and exposing students to the worldviews of diverse cultures.

Asian and Comparative Studies: M.A. and Ph.D. in philosophy and religion with a concentration in Asian and comparative studies. The Asian and comparative studies concentration offers a wide-ranging course of study in the world's spiritual and philosophical traditions. Students gain practical skills in research, teaching, language, translation, and cross-cultural communication. Areas of emphasis include Hinduism, Buddhism, and Chinese philosophy.

East-West Psychology: M.A. and Ph.D. in East-West psychology and a two-semester Advanced Certificate Program in Spiritual Counseling. Guided by an interest in pluralism, dialogue, and spiritual transformation, the East-West psychology program offers contemporary inquiry into Eastern and Western psychological and spiritual traditions while providing a larger context for productive explorations in transpersonal psychology, consciousness studies, depth psychology, spiritual counseling, and ecopsychology.

Integrative Health Studies: M.A. in integrative health studies. This nonclinical degree prepares its graduates to take leadership roles in the new field of integrative health, an exciting collaboration that combines the therapeutic treatment modalities of Western allopathic medicine with complementary and alternative healing systems, mind-body medicine, and spiritual healing traditions. The core curriculum includes the underlying methodology and philosophy foundational to complementary and alternative health-care systems and introduces new ideas in quantum physics that are bringing scientific and spiritual forms of healing together. Classes are offered in medical anthropology; global health issues; health policy and planning; grant writing; diversity training with program planning, evaluation, and assessment; and communication and health education.

Philosophy, Cosmology, and Consciousness: M.A. and Ph.D. in philosophy and religion with a concentration in philosophy, cosmology, and consciousness. The philosophy, cosmology, and consciousness concentration addresses the complex relations between philosophy, religion, science, and art as these practices converge to shape the view of self and the world. The program provides a solid foundation in the larger Western intellectual tradition, including ancient and esoteric thought and contemporary ecological, cosmological, evolutionary, religious, transpersonal, and feminist studies.

Social and Cultural Anthropology: M.A. in cultural anthropology and social transformation, emphasis in gender, ecology, and society; Ph.D. in social and cultural anthropology. CIIS's anthropology programs foster an interdisciplinary understanding of global systems through scholarship and action from perspectives that are sensitive to dynamics of power. They emphasize global ecology, social justice, postcolonial thought, critical social theory, and the integration of activism and scholarship. Students who have completed studies in the gender, ecology, and society program are eligible to apply to the social and cultural anthropology program, where they study the principles, theories, methods, actions, and interventions of anthropology-as-social-critique. Students in both programs benefit from close mentoring relationships with faculty members and have carried out research projects around the globe in such areas as sustainable development organizations, the homeless, land-use disputes, and social justice.

Transformative Studies: Ph.D. in transformative studies (online). Transformative studies provides students with the platform to pursue cutting-edge research in a field of their choosing. Under the mentorship of an adviser and in conjunction with a collaborative community of learners, students create a work of scholarship that is original, personally meaningful, and transdisciplinary. Students are exposed to a plurality of perspectives and disciplines and learn how to excavate the underlying assumptions and paradigms informing them. Students learn ways of inquiry that connect and contextualize in order to integrate different, even divergent, perspectives in a coherent way.

Transformative Leadership: M.A. in transformative leadership (online). In an era of complexity, challenges, and opportunities, there is a critical need for skilled leaders in a wide array of disciplines and settings—from education and the environment to businesses and local communities. The transformative leadership online M.A. program is for individuals who have the initiative, passion, and vision to facilitate positive social change and to make a significant contribution to the world. Transformative leadership students recognize that effective leadership requires specific skills in conflict resolution, group dynamics, and creative thinking. Also important is the ability to reflect on why change is needed, how it is conducted, and who is engaged in the process. The program invites students to engage in a profound questioning of these assumptions, along with their implications and applications to practice. Reflection and theory are united with practice by focusing on the development of capacities to envision, initiate, and engage in transformative change processes.

Women's Spirituality: M.A. and Ph.D. in philosophy and religion with a concentration in women's spirituality. One of the first accredited graduate programs in women's spirituality in the world, this program offers an experiential learning community that celebrates the contribution women have made in shaping and defining the spiritual throughout history and across cultures.

Research Facilities

The Laurance S. Rockefeller Library has collections of approximately 35,000 volumes (including numerous e-books), 290 periodicals (including electronic journals), 1,000 audiovisual materials (including audiocassettes, videotapes, and compact discs), and almost 1,000 CIIS dissertations and master's theses. The collections are especially strong in the areas of transpersonal and multicultural psychology, spirituality (particularly women's spirituality, Buddhism, Hinduism, Taoism, Confucianism, and wisdom traditions), integral studies, and studies of consciousness. Special collections include Alan Watts' and Haridas Chaudhuri's personal collections, the Langley-Porter collection of psychology and psychiatry, the Rogo collection of parapsychology, and a CIIS Institute Authors' collection.

Financial Aid

Financial assistance is awarded primarily on the basis of need. Financial aid consists of scholarships, loans, grants, and Federal Work-Study Program awards. There are a limited number of Institute scholarships. International students may obtain nonimmigrant visas and are eligible for part-time employment on the campus.

Cost of Study

In 2009–10, full-time annual tuition and fees are $15,300 for M.A. programs and $17,910 for doctoral programs.

Living and Housing Costs

There is no on-campus housing. Information about living and housing costs can be found on the CIIS Web site at http://www.ciis.edu/students/housing.

Student Group

Total enrollment in 2009–10 is 1,150. Twenty percent are students of color; 9 percent are international; and 70 percent are women.

The Institute

Founded in 1968 by the Indian philosopher, educator, and humanist Haridas Chaudhuri, California Institute of Integral Studies is a WASC-accredited institution of higher education and research dedicated to integrating mind, body, and spirit in service to individuals, communities, and the Earth. Certain programs offer online options or a combination of online and monthly weekend meetings. The Institute is defined by its value of cultural diversity as well as cultural coherence, multiple ways of knowing, spiritual development, a sense of community, emancipatory ideals, and ecological sustainability.

Applying

Decisions regarding admission are based on the potential for success in the chosen field of study by considering past academic achievement and motivation for educational and personal development and the congruence of the applicant's worldview with the Institute's mission and vision. Applicants to the M.A. programs must have earned a bachelor's degree from an accredited institution. A grade point average of 3.0 or higher is strongly recommended for all programs. Applicants to the Ph.D. and Psy.D. programs must have earned an M.A., preferably in a related discipline, with a minimum 3.1 GPA. Academic transcripts, the autobiographical and goal statements, a writing sample (if required), letters of recommendation (if required), resume (if required), and an interview are all considered in the admissions committee's decision. For specific program requirements, students should visit http://www.ciis.edu.

Correspondence and Information

Office of Admissions
California Institute of Integral Studies
1453 Mission Street
San Francisco, California 94103

Phone: 415-575-6154
Fax: 415-575-1268
E-mail: admissions@ciis.edu
Web site: http://www.ciis.edu

California Institute of Integral Studies

THE FACULTY AND THEIR RESEARCH

Asian Comparative Studies

Steven Goodman, Program Co-Director; Ph.D., Saskatchewan, 1984. Indo-Tibetan Buddhism, comparative philosophy, classical Tibetan language, Mahayana Buddhism, poetics.

Jim Ryan, Program Co-Director; Ph.D., Berkeley, 1985. Sanskrit, Hindi and Tamil, Hindu Tantrism, Jainism.

Rina Sircar, Haridas Chaudhuri Professor of South Asian and Comparative Philosophy; Ph.D., Gujarat (India), 1974; Ph.D., California Institute of Integral Studies, 1976. Buddhism, mindfulness, healing in the Theravada forest tradition, Pali language.

Yi Wu, Ph.D., University of Chinese Culture, 1970. Chinese philosophy, religion, and literature; Chinese language.

East-West Psychology

Brendan Collins, Ph.D., US International, 1977. Contemporary psychology, psychoanalysis, Western mystical and contemplative traditions.

Daniel Deslauriers, Ph.D., Montreal, 1989. Cross-cultural approaches to dreams, altered states, meditation, body-mind integrative practice.

Jorge Ferrer, Ph.D., California Institute of Integral Studies, 1999. Transpersonal psychology, epistemology, Buddhism and social engagement, sexuality and spirituality.

Janis Phelps, Ph.D., Connecticut, 1986. Child development, clinical studies in enhanced expectancies and treatment, mind-body wellness, Eastern disciplines, interaction of meditation and creativity.

Carol Whitfield, Ph.D., Graduate Theological Union, 1992; Ph.D., San Francisco School of Psychology, 1997. Synthesis of Western psychology and Eastern spirituality, Jungian psychotherapy.

Integrative Health Studies

Michael Denney, M.D., Ph.D., Pacifica Graduate. Fundamentals of integrative health studies, science, spirituality and healing, ethics of the healing relationship, psychosomatic counseling, holistic health and healing, alternative and complementary medicine and science.

Meg Jordan, Ph.D., CIIS, 1996, R.N. Medical anthropology, integrative medicine applications in clinical settings, methods of negotiating and resolving conflict among practitioners of differing licensure, philosophies, and healing modalities, welllness, fitness, and nutrition.

Mutombo Mpanya, Ph.D., Michigan, 1982. Global health, medical anthropology, health policy and planning, health costs, nutrition.

Ricki Pollycove, M.H.S., Berkeley, 1975; M.D., California, San Francisco, 1977. Integrative health approaches to women in midlife; integrative anatomy and physiology; psychosocial-spiritual healing; complementary, supportive, and therapeutic care as adjuncts in the treatment of breast cancer.

Arisika Razak, M.P.H., Berkeley, 1978; RN. Contemporary issues in women's health, women's embodiment of healing and sexuality, health issues of women of color, women's spirituality, diversity.

Philosophy, Cosmology, and Consciousness

Elizabeth Allison, Ph.D., Berkeley. Religious and spiritual discourse and practice in environmental action, environmental ethics, political ecology, religion and ecology, biodiversity conservation, climate change.

Sean Kelly, Ph.D., Ottawa, 1988. Transpersonal theory, Jungian thought, new paradigm studies.

Robert McDermott, Ph.D., Boston University, 1969. American philosophy, evolution of consciousness, modern spiritual masters, Rudolf Steiner.

Brian Swimme, Ph.D., Oregon, 1978. Evolutionary cosmology, science and spirituality, the role of humanity in the unfolding story of Earth.

Richard Tarnas, Ph.D., Saybrook Institute, 1976. History of Western thought and culture, depth psychology, archetypal studies, philosophy.

Social and Cultural Anthropology

Brian Keith Axel, Ph.D. Postcolonial thought; diaspora studies; historical anthropology; history of anthropology, globalization, nation, gender and sexuality; U.S., Europe, and South Asia.

Matthew Bronson, M.A., Berkeley, 1982. Accelerative teacher/trainer, intercultural communications, human learning potential, influence of indigenous languages on Spanish, linguistic analysis of discourses.

Angana Chatterji, Ph.D., California Institute of Integral Studies. Anthropology of development, participatory development, environmental management, gender, policy, research, postcolonial critique.

Mutombo Mpanya, Ph.D., Michigan, 1982. Twenty years with international development agencies in African countries, management of natural resources, economics, globalization, nonprofit sector.

Richard Shapiro, M.A., Ph.D. candidate, New School, 1981. Emancipatory education; cross-cultural study of subjectivity, gender, and European thought.

Transformative Studies/Transformative Leadership

Allan Combs, Ph.D. (neural psychology), Georgia, 1977. Integral psychology and philosophy; evolution of consciousness and spirituality; transformation of consciousness, dreaming, mind and brain, chaos, and complexity.

Riane Eisler, J.D., UCLA, 1965; President, Center for Partnership Studies. Developed study of relational dynamics, cultural transformation theory, and other new approaches to understanding systems maintenance and transformation; author of *The Power of Partnership*, among many other works introducing the new social categories of the partnership and domination systems as two underlying possibilities for structuring beliefs, institutions, and relations.

Ursula Fahim, Ph.D. (transformative learning and change), California Institute of Integral Studies, 2003. Women's leadership, inquiry and research methodologies, group process, collaborative creativity, intercultural communication.

Joanne Gozawa, Ph.D., California Institute of Integral Studies, 2000. Organic inquiry, learning community, transformative learning.

Constance Jones, Ph.D., Emory, 1977. History of Hindu movements in the United States, transformational learning, sociology of religion, new religious movements in the United States.

Bradford Keeney, Ph.D. (family therapy), Purdue, 1981. Ecstatic transformation, shaking medicine, wild conversation and absurd performance, n/om leadership, radical creativity, extreme improvisation.

Alfonso Montuori, Ph.D., Saybrook Institute, 1991. Systems and complexity theory, creativity, postmodernism, social change, cross-cultural theory.

Linda Jean Shepherd, Ph.D. (biochemistry), Penn State, 1976. Integral science, feminism, Jungian studies, ethnobotany, herbal studies, sustainability, building bridges between science and spirituality. Author of *Lifting the Veil: The Feminine Face of Science*.

Women's Spirituality

Lucia Chiavola Birnbaum, Ph.D., Berkeley, 1964. Feminist and cultural history and/or vernacular history of women and other subaltern classes.

Mara Lynn Keller, Ph.D., Yale, 1971. Ancient goddess cultures of Crete and Greece, holistic philosophy, ecofeminism, peace issues.

Arisika Razak, M.P.H., Berkeley, 1978. Reproductive health, ritual, embodiment of the sacred, perinatal care of African American women.

Charlene Spretnak, M.A., Berkeley, 1981. Women's spirituality, spirituality and art, ecological postmodernism, embodied/embedded philosophy and literature.

CENTRAL EUROPEAN UNIVERSITY

Graduate Programs in Social Sciences

Programs of Study

Central European University (CEU) offers graduate degrees in economics, environmental sciences and policy, gender studies, history, international relations and European studies, legal studies, mathematics and its applications, medieval studies, nationalism studies, philosophy, political science, public policy, and sociology and social anthropology. In addition, the CEU Business School offers an M.B.A., a Master of Science in information technology management, and executive programs. CEU typically has two types of master's degree programs: one-year master's programs, which take ten months to complete and normally require four years of undergraduate study, and Bologna-type two-year programs, which are specially designed for graduates of three-year undergraduate programs. CEU is a partner institution in several Erasmus Mundus consortia, offering the following two-year master's degree programs: environmental sciences, policy, and management (MESPOM); the Joint European Master in Women's and Gender Studies (GEMMA); and public policy (Mundus MAPP). Doctoral programs are offered on a full-time basis only and take three to six years to complete. A graduate research–intensive university, CEU promotes a combined emphasis on scholarship, research, and social engagement. Through both disciplinary depth and a strong comparative and transdisciplinary approach, studies at CEU focus on the diverse and changing social, economic, and political aspects and needs of societies in transition.

Research Facilities

The dissemination and pursuit of knowledge at CEU rests on the idea that nearly all of the major problems facing humanity today—e.g., poverty, climate change, democratization—require interdisciplinary cooperation from academics, experts, and policy makers. Much of this work is accomplished by programs conducted at the Research Centers of CEU. Thus, beyond the creation of knowledge in their respective academic disciplines, both CEU faculty members and accomplished visiting scholars engaged by these centers continually explore the sociocultural context of the contemporary state of learning.

The CEU library is the largest English-language academic library in the region. It collects materials in the fields of arts and literature, business studies, economics, environmental sciences, gender studies, history, international relations, legal studies, medieval studies, philosophy, political sciences, and social sciences. The library currently holds more than 250,000 documents in various formats, including 135,000 monographs, 1,600 periodical titles, and more than 10,000 papers, essays, and various research documents published by select academic and research institutions. The library offers access to a number of online sources, such as EBSCO Electronic Journals Service, Economist Intelligence Unit's Country Reports, International Financial Statistics (IFS), Westlaw International, and others.

The Open Society Archives (OSA) at CEU is another resource for the study and understanding of recent history—more specifically, the fascist and communist attempts to radically alter the course of human history. OSA is probably the richest international textual and audiovisual archive of the period of communism, a notable repository of documents from the era of the Cold War, and holds one of the largest collections of propaganda from the post–World War II period.

Financial Aid

CEU provides full and partial financial assistance to the majority of its students, regardless of their nationality. Detailed information about financial aid is available at http://www.ceu.hu/admissions/financialaid. The full CEU fellowship is an award that covers tuition and fees and medical insurance and provides a scholarship for living expenses. Candidates admitted into the CEU doctoral programs are eligible to receive the full CEU fellowship for three years, as well as research support grants and study-abroad funding. For students enrolled in the master's programs, CEU has established a diversified financial aid program, which offers full or partial financial assistance.

Financial aid is awarded primarily on the basis of merit.

Cost of Study

The tuition fee in 2009–10 is €10,000.

Living and Housing Costs

Students who do not receive financial aid need to budget approximately €6200 per academic year to cover their living costs in Budapest. These include housing in a shared apartment (or in the residence center), meals, local transportation, and incidentals. Travel, recreation, and other expenses vary with the individual and need to be budgeted separately. Information about the estimated cost of living is available at http://www.ceu.hu/studentlife/students/costofliving.

Student Group

One of the main characteristics of CEU's student body is the lack of a dominant national culture. Most of the students come from the countries in Central and Eastern Europe and the former Soviet Union. In addition, CEU has enrolled students from Western Europe, North America, Central and South America, Africa, and Asia. In 2008–09, CEU enrolled 1,541 students from ninety-six countries. Students are admitted on the basis of merit, without any specific country quotas. The University admits those with the highest academic achievement who share its mission and CEU's curriculum, which is tuned to that mission. In addition, CEU is looking to attract students with a sense of social responsibility who are transnationally inclined and have the potential to work for open and democratic societies.

Student Outcomes

CEU graduates—who now come from more than 100 countries around the world—represent a lively multicultural group of talented and motivated young scholars. They share a commitment to working for open and democratic societies and a desire to contribute to the public good. As of 2009, 27 percent of CEU's master's graduates are enrolled in doctoral and other graduate programs, and 73 percent have entered a professional career. Of those, 36 percent are employed in education and research institutions, 31 percent are in the business sector, 20 percent are in international organizations and public interest and advocacy groups, and 13 percent are in government.

Location

The University is located in Budapest, the political, cultural, intellectual, and economic center of Hungary. A city of outstanding architectural elegance, Budapest is brimming with restaurants, cafés, clubs, and shops. It offers something for everyone, including medieval and Roman areas, theaters and concert halls, sports facilities, and plenty of opportunities for recreation.

The University

Central European University is a U.S.-style graduate university with a focus on the social sciences and the humanities, accredited both in the United States and in Hungary, and located in Budapest, in the heart of Europe. The University is oriented to interdisciplinary research on, and the study of, social change and the policy implications of transition to open societies. In addition, emphasis is placed on European Union affairs, as well as on the special features of non-Western democracies.

Through their international experience at CEU, and exposure to a multitude of different—and sometimes opposing—points of view, students at the University develop a deep understanding of the intellectual and practical challenges arising along the shifting boundary between the local and the universal. They leave CEU with the knowledge and skills that enable them to pursue careers in academia, the government and the nongovernmental sectors, international organizations and research institutes, and missions of the United Nations, as well as business organizations at the national and international levels.

Applying

The application deadlines for 2010–11 are in January 2010. Details on the admission process are available at http://www.ceu.hu/admissions.

Application forms and documents are submitted online through the CEU Web site. A complete application package typically includes a statement of purpose or research outline, resume, academic records, two letters of recommendation, and proof of English language proficiency. Special requirements and subject tests may be requested by particular departments.

Correspondence and Information

Admissions Office
Central European University
Nador u.9
1051 Budapest
Hungary
Phone: 36-1-327-3009, 3272, 3210, or 3208
Fax: 36-1-327-3211
E-mail: admissions@ceu.hu
Web site: http://www.ceu.hu

Central European University

THE FACULTY AND THEIR RESEARCH

More than 300 professors from around the world teach at CEU. They come from countries including Albania, Australia, Austria, Belarus, Belgium, Bulgaria, Canada, Croatia, Cyprus, Denmark, Estonia, France, Germany, Hungary, Israel, Italy, Lebanon, Luxembourg, Malaysia, the Netherlands, Nigeria, New Zealand, Poland, Romania, Russia, Serbia, Slovakia, Slovenia, Switzerland, Turkey, Ukraine, the United Kingdom, and the United States. Among the faculty members are a large number of visiting professors who teach courses and give frequent lectures and seminars, thus giving students access to highly respected academics from other institutions.

Attracted by the University's academic excellence, by its social values and willingness to encourage intellectual risks, both renowned senior scholars and talented young faculty members have recognized CEU as an institution ready to organize resources and structures around promising new ideas. Even as CEU becomes increasingly global, the faculty's scholarship reflects its roots in this region. Their richly varied experiences have led naturally to a distinction found in both teaching and research at the University: an emphasis on the interplay between universal principles and local circumstances in shaping change.

SELECTED FACULTY

John Shattuck, CEU President and Rector; J.D., Yale. John Shattuck's career spans more than three decades in higher education, international diplomacy, foreign policy, and human rights. Previously CEO of the Kennedy Library Foundation, he is a former U.S. Ambassador to the Czech Republic and Assistant Secretary of State for Democracy, Human Rights and Labor under President Clinton, and also taught international relations at Tufts University. Prior to his government service, Shattuck was a vice president at Harvard University, taught at the Harvard Law School, and was a research associate at the Kennedy School of Government. He is the author of three books and has published more than fifty articles on human rights, civil liberties, international relations, public service, and higher education. In 2007 he was elected to the American Academy of Arts and Sciences and has received several honorary degrees.

Howard Robinson, CEU University Professor and Provost; Ph.D., Liverpool. Professor of philosophy at CEU and Honorary Research Fellow in the Department of Philosophy at the University of Liverpool; specializes in metaphysics, including the philosophy of religion and the philosophy of mind; has an interest in the history of philosophy.

Aziz Al-Azmeh, CEU University Professor; Ph.D., Oxford.

Peter Balazs, Professor; Ph.D., Hungarian Academy of Sciences.

Karoly Bard, Professor and Pro-Rector for Hungarian and European Union Affairs; Ph.D., Hungarian Academy of Sciences.

Gábor Betegh, Professor; Ph.D., Ecole des Hautes Etudes en Sciences Sociales, Paris and Eötvös Loránd, Budapest.

Andras Bozoki, Professor; Ph.D., Hungarian Academy of Sciences.

Rogers Brubaker, Recurrent Visiting Professor; Ph.D., Columbia.

Ayse Caglar, Professor; Ph.D., McGill.

Aleh Cherp, Associate Professor; Ph.D., Manchester.

László Csaba, Professor; Ph.D., Hungarian Academy of Sciences.

Francisca de Haan, Professor; Ph.D., Erasmus.

Nenad Dimitrijevic, Associate Professor; Ph.D., Novi Sad (Serbia).

John Earle, Professor; Ph.D., Stanford.

Béla Greskovits, Professor; Ph.D., Hungarian Academy of Sciences.

Julius Horvath, Professor; Ph.D., Southern Illinois at Carbondale.

Ferenc Huoranszki, Professor; Ph.D., Hungarian Academy of Sciences.

Erin Jenne, Associate Professor; Ph.D., Stanford.

János Kis, CEU University Professor; M.A., Eötvös Loránd (Budapest).

Gábor Klaniczay, CEU University Professor; Ph.D., Hungarian Academy of Sciences.

László Kontler, Professor; Ph.D., Hungarian Academy of Sciences.

János Kornai, CEU Distinguished Research Professor; Dr.Oec., Karl Marx (Budapest); Dr.Sc., Hungarian Academy of Sciences.

Andras Kovacs, Professor; Ph.D., Eötvös Loránd (Budapest).

Maria Kovacs, Professor; Ph.D., Hungarian Academy of Sciences.

Will Kymlicka, Recurrent Visiting Professor; D.Phil., Oxford.

Jozsef Laszlovszky, Professor; Ph.D., Hungarian Academy of Sciences.

Marvin Lazerson, Distinguished Research Professor (Professor Emeritus, University of Pennsylvania); Ph.D., Harvard.

László Mátyás, CEU University Professor; Ph.D., Hungarian Academy of Sciences.

Stefan Messmann, Professor; Ph.D., Fribourg (Switzerland).

Ruben Mnatsakanian, Professor; Ph.D., Moscow State.

Gheorghe Morosanu, Professor; Ph.D., Alexandru Ioan Cuza (Romania).

Wiktor Osiatynski, CEU University Professor; Ph.D., Polish Academy of Sciences.

Anton Pelinka, Professor; J.D., Vienna.

Istvan Perczel, Professor; Ph.D., Hungarian Academy of Sciences.

Prem Kumar Rajaram, Associate Professor; Ph.D., London School of Economics.

András Sajó, CEU University Professor; Ph.D., Hungarian Academy of Sciences.

Judit Sandor, Professor; Ph.D., Hungarian Academy of Sciences.

Diana Urge-Vorsatz, Professor; Ph.D., Berkeley.

Tibor Várady, CEU University Professor; S.J.D., Harvard.

Susan Zimmermann, Professor; Dr.habil., Linz (Austria); Dr.habil., Eötvös Loránd (Budapest).

SELECTED AREAS OF RESEARCH

Economics: Monetary economics; international macroeconomics; applied econometrics; labor economics; corporate governance; pension economics; stochastic analysis and mathematical finance; health economics; comparative economic institutions; macroeconomics; European integration.

Environmental Sciences and Policy: Management of ecological systems (special reference to freshwaters); state-of-the-environment assessments; environmental policy and law in countries in transition; environmental management and audit.

Gender Studies: Feminist theories and epistemology; interdisciplinary; intersections with race, class, and sexuality; local and transnational women's movement; comparative analysis; gender and post-state socialist societies; cultural studies; queer theory; globalization and postcolonialism; labor; literary studies; gender, nation, and state.

History: Interdisciplinary, transnational, comparative history of Europe, with a focus on Central Europe, Southeastern Europe, and Eastern Europe.

International Relations and European Studies: Ethnic conflicts; international refugee law; CIS member states foreign policy; international relations theory; international political theory; leading sectors and the variety of transnational capitalism in Eastern Europe; politics of economic policy making; political economy of international monetary relations; political economy of the European Union; European governance; European constitution; European cultural policy.

Legal Studies: Public law; free speech problems in a post-totalitarian context; constitutional transplant; institutional, constitutional, and human rights in the European Union law; data protection law; biotechnical and human rights; biomedical law and reproductive rights; international commercial arbitration; law and ethnicity; language and translation in international dispute settlement; Islamic banking and finance; southeastern European investment law; enforcement of contracts in Eastern Europe; transplant of war criminal law to the Balkans from Germany; comparative secured transactions law and the related reforms of the laws of emerging markets; comparative mortgage and housing programs; capital markets and securities regulation in emerging markets.

Mathematics and Its Applications: Algebra; algebraic geometry; approximation theory; combinatorics; computational geometry; computing; cryptology; evolutionary equations; dynamical systems; differential geometry; ergodic theory; fractals; functional analysis; graph theory; homological algebra; information theory; logic; number theory; numerical analysis; optimization; partial differential equations; probability theory; set theory; statistics; stochastic processes.

Medieval Studies: Social, cultural, and religious history of medieval east-central and southeastern Europe, such as nobility, law collections, rulership, urban evolution, Jewish minorities, cultural heritage, historical-environmental studies, monastic culture, hagiography, patristic traditions, interactions between medieval Latin and Greek Christianity and Slavia Orthodoxy, Christianity and Islam, and the broader world of Christian oikumene. Research projects are based on working with digitalized visual resources, manuscripts (Latin, Slavonic, Greek, and Siriac), and archaeological documentation.

Nationalism Studies: Empirical, theoretical, and normative issues connected to nationalism, self-determination and state-formation, ethnic conflict, minority protection, language and citizenship rights, constitutional design, and parliamentary mechanisms in ethnically divided societies.

Philosophy: History of philosophy ancient and modern; philosophy of language and logic, especially the nature of quantification, and semantics of externalism; philosophy of mind, especially dualism, the mind-body problem, and perception; metaphysics, especially agency, free will, causation, and idealism; political philosophy, especially liberalism, theory of democracy, and epistemology.

Political Science: Democratization and political economy (especially concerning eastern Europe and the EU); comparative and survey methods; analytical political theory; constitutional theory; normative and applied ethics; political obligation; democratic theory; discourse analysis; peacekeeping; media policy; bioethics; party politics; church-state relations; voting behavior.

Public Policy: Globalization; European integration and policy making; governance and policy reform; local government management; fiscal decentralization; comparative public budgeting; public finance; intergovernmental finance; public integrity; equal opportunity policies; rural development; economic culture; urban public transport management and policy; media and telecommunications policy; social policy; public-sector management; social network analysis; game theory.

Sociology and Social Anthropology: Empirical research using a wide variety of methodologies. Special research fields include comparative approaches to the theory and practice of development; modernity; globalization; state; politics of culture; migration; memory; civil society; inequalities; gender; the city and urban processes.

DARTMOUTH
1769

DARTMOUTH COLLEGE

Master of Arts in Liberal Studies

Program of Study	The Dartmouth Master of Arts in Liberal Studies (M.A.L.S.) Program was designed for individuals who want to engage in self-directed study in the liberal arts at the graduate level. A fundamental principle of liberal studies is the examination of accepted premises in traditional disciplines, and the M.A.L.S. Program affords students the opportunity to combine disparate disciplines in order to forge new areas of scholarly inquiry. Courses offered through the program have combined such disciplines as psychology and philosophy, history and sociology, art history and literature, geography and history, and many others. In addition, the program features courses that demonstrate breadth within a single discipline.

Candidates for the M.A.L.S. degree complete eight courses, three of which must be interdisciplinary; two summer symposia; and a thesis. At least one of the eight courses must be an independent study. A research methods course is offered in the summer as an alternative to the symposium. M.A.L.S. students pursue a self-designed liberal studies curriculum with the guidance of a faculty adviser and a faculty thesis committee. The program also offers concentrations in cultural studies, creative writing, and globalization studies. Each concentration consists of three courses in the area of concentration; three interdisciplinary M.A.L.S. courses; an independent study, also in the area of concentration; and one elective. Cultural studies courses encompass the subjects of race, class, gender, post-Colonial studies, and performance/media studies. Creative writing majors may pursue workshops in the genres of fiction, nonfiction, poetry, journalism, screenwriting, oral history, or playwriting. The globalization studies track combines history, politics, economics, sociology, and anthropology, and students may elect a regional focus. Candidates intending to concentrate in one of these areas should indicate their interest on their application but will be formally considered as concentrators after completing two M.A.L.S. courses.

Candidates for the M.A.L.S. Program may attend the program year-round on a full-time basis, part-time, summers only (for teachers and other professionals), or in a combination of these patterns. Students have six years from the time of entry to complete degree requirements. The program generally takes six to eight terms (1½ to 2 years) with full-time attendance, including thesis research and writing. After course work and the symposium requirements are fulfilled, students may remain on campus and formally enroll in thesis research, or they may work independently on their thesis off campus.

Research Facilities	Dartmouth's extensive facilities are available to all graduate students and visitors year-round. The College library's collection of more than a million volumes, the rich variety of computer network services, the Hopkins Center for the Performing Arts, the Hood Museum, Alumni Gym, and numerous other facilities and services offer many advantages to M.A.L.S. students. Resources that provide opportunities for students to engage in community activism, international and public affairs activities, and intellectual forums with guest speakers, debates, discussion groups, and student organizations include the Tucker Foundation, the John Sloan Dickey Center for International Affairs, the Nelson A. Rockefeller Center for Public Affairs, the Ethics Institute, the Humanities Center, and the Women's Resource Center, among many others.
Financial Aid	Financial assistance is available to M.A.L.S. students in the form of tuition scholarships and loans. M.A.L.S. Scholarships are awarded on the basis of financial need and academic merit. Teachers on the elementary and secondary school levels are considered a priority group for financial aid decisions; they are also encouraged to seek staff development funds from their home school. Many U.S. citizens are eligible for Federal Stafford Student Loans, Federal Perkins Loans, or veterans' benefits. Limited scholarship assistance is available for qualified international students. Both the Dartmouth Graduate Financial Aid Form and a link to the FAFSA form are available through the M.A.L.S. Web site. Inquiries about financial aid should be directed to the Executive Director of the program.
Cost of Study	Tuition for the M.A.L.S. Program is charged based upon enrollment per quarter, due to the flexible study options. Because Dartmouth College is on the quarter system, two courses per term are considered full-time study. During the 2008–09 academic year, the tuition per course was $4892. For two courses in one term, the tuition was $8561, and for three courses, $12,230. There is no charge for the summer symposium, research methods, or the writing workshop. Thesis research enrollment tuition is subsidized by the program for up to four terms.
Living and Housing Costs	Graduate student housing is available to M.A.L.S. students on a first-come, first-served basis with application deadlines in early spring of each year. The cost of this housing is from $800 to $1000. Local furnished apartments rent for an average of $700 to $800 per month. Married students have access to unfurnished apartments owned by Dartmouth that rent for $700 to $1200 per month.
Student Group	The M.A.L.S. Program offers enrollment on a full-time, part-time, or summers-only basis to accommodate both full-time graduate students and working professionals. Originally designed as a program for teachers to expand their cross-disciplinary knowledge, M.A.L.S. now satisfies a broad spectrum of academic and professional needs. M.A.L.S. has a typical enrollment of 75 to 90 students during the traditional academic year, with approximately 100 to 120 in the summer session.
Location	Dartmouth is located in Hanover, New Hampshire, a small New England town dating back to a few years before the College's founding in 1769. Situated in the Upper Valley of the Connecticut River between the White Mountains of New Hampshire and the Green Mountains of Vermont, Hanover combines the advantages of a rural setting with the resources of a university. The Dartmouth campus is about 2 hours by car from Boston and 3½ hours from Montreal. Local airports include Lebanon-Hanover, Manchester, and Burlington, and there is an Amtrak station approximately 15 minutes from campus in White River Junction, Vermont.
The Program and The College	The M.A.L.S. Program is in the Faculty of Arts and Sciences, which offers fifteen graduate programs in the natural sciences, social sciences, and humanities. Graduate programs are also offered by Dartmouth's professional schools, which include Dartmouth Medical School, Amos Tuck School of Business, and Thayer School of Engineering. All graduate programs maintain a favorable student-faculty ratio.
Applying	The M.A.L.S. applications committee requires the completion of an application form, three letters of professional/academic reference, a statement of purpose, and academic transcripts. Applications for admissions are available online through links on the M.A.L.S. Web site. Writing samples are optional but are recommended for candidates interested in the creative writing concentration. Submission of GRE scores is also optional. Applicants are strongly urged to schedule an admissions interview prior to the application deadline. Telephone interviews are also acceptable for people outside of the immediate area. Application deadlines are February 15 (for summer or fall enrollment) and July 15 (for winter or spring entry.)
Correspondence and Information	M.A.L.S. Program Dartmouth College 116 Wentworth, HB 6092 Hanover, New Hampshire 03755-3526 Phone: 603-646-3592 Fax: 603-646-3590 E-mail: mals.program@dartmouth.edu Web site: http://www.dartmouth.edu/~mals

Dartmouth College

THE FACULTY

Raúl Bueno, Ph.D., San Agustin (Peru); Professor of Spanish and Portuguese.
Ronald Edsforth, Ph.D., Michigan; Visiting Professor of History.
Carl B. Estabrook, Ph.D., Brown; Associate Professor of History.
Harvey Frommer, Ph.D., NYU; Visiting Professor of Liberal Studies.
Myrna Katz Frommer, Ph.D., NYU; Visiting Assistant Professor of Liberal Studies.
Cecilia Gaposchkin, Ph.D., Berkeley; Assistant Dean of Premajor Advising.
Jay Hull, Ph.D., Duke; Professor of Psychology.
Phyllis Katz, Ph.D., Columbia; Senior Lecturer in Classics and Women's Studies.
Barbara S. Kreiger, Ph.D., Brandeis; Senior Lecturer in English.
Sydney Lea, Ph.D., Yale; Visiting Professor of Poetry.
Alan Lelchuk, Ph.D., Stanford; Adjunct Professor of Liberal Studies.
Patricia McKee, Ph.D., Brandeis; Professor of English.
Klaus Milich; Ph.D., Humboldt (Berlin); Visiting Lecturer of American Literary and Cultural Studies.
Misagh Parsa, Ph.D., Michigan; Professor of Sociology.
Donald E. Pease Jr., Ph.D., Chicago; Professor of English.
William Phillips, M.F.A., USC; Visiting Associate Professor of Film.
Thomas Powers, Visiting Lecturer of Nonfiction Writing.
Regine Rosenthal, Ph.D., Munich; Visiting Professor of American and Jewish Studies.
Diederik Vandewalle, Ph.D., Columbia; Associate Professor of Government.
Keith Walker, Ph.D., Yale; Associate Professor of French and Italian and Liberal Studies.
Christopher Wren, M.A., Columbia; Visiting Professor of Journalism.

Administration

Lauren E. Clarke, Executive Director.
Carole Webber, Administrative Assistant.
Wole P. Ojurongbe, Administrator/Registrar.
Donald E. Pease Jr., Academic Chair.

Dartmouth Hall.

Section 9
Language and Literature

This section contains a directory of institutions offering graduate work in language and literature, followed by in-depth entries submitted by institutions that chose to prepare detailed program descriptions. Additional information about programs listed in the directory but not augmented by an in-depth entry may be obtained by writing directly to the dean of a graduate school or chair of a department at the address given in the directory.

For programs offering related work, see also in this book *Area and Cultural Studies, Communication and Media, Political Science and International Affairs,* and *Sociology, Anthropology, and Archaeology.* In another guide in this series:

Graduate Programs in Business, Education, Health, Information Studies, Law & Social Work

See *Special Focus* and *Subject Areas*

CONTENTS

Program Directories

Asian Languages	354
Celtic Languages	356
Chinese	356
Classics	357
Comparative Literature	361
English	366
French	394
German	403
Italian	409
Japanese	412
Near and Middle Eastern Languages	413
Portuguese	414
Romance Languages	416
Russian	418
Scandinavian Languages	419
Slavic Languages	420
Spanish	422

Announcements

Northwestern University	378
University of Pittsburgh	390

Close-Ups

Auburn University	435
Boston College	437
Bryn Mawr College	439
Saint Louis University–Madrid Campus	441
Seton Hall University	443
Southern Illinois University Carbondale	445
University of St. Thomas	447
Villanova University	449

See also:

Naropa University—Graduate Studies	1121
Seton Hall University—Asian Studies	623
Washington University in St. Louis—East Asian Studies	625

Asian Languages

Columbia University, Graduate School of Arts and Sciences, Division of Humanities, Department of East Asian Languages and Cultures, New York, NY 10027. Offers East Asian languages and cultures (M Phil, MA, PhD); Oriental studies (M Phil, MA, PhD). *Degree requirements:* For master's, one foreign language, comprehensive exam, thesis; for doctorate, 2 foreign languages, thesis/dissertation. *Entrance requirements:* For master's and doctorate, GRE General Test. Additional exam requirements/recommendations for international students: Required—TOEFL.

Columbia University, Graduate School of Arts and Sciences, Division of Humanities, Department of Middle East Languages and Cultures, New York, NY 10027. Offers Hebrew language and literature (M Phil, MA, PhD); Middle Eastern languages and cultures (M Phil, MA, PhD); South Asian languages and cultures (M Phil, MA, PhD). Part-time programs available. *Degree requirements:* For master's, thesis, oral and written exams; for doctorate, 3 foreign languages, thesis/dissertation. *Entrance requirements:* For master's and doctorate, GRE General Test. Additional exam requirements/recommendations for international students: Required—TOEFL. *Faculty research:* Indo-Iranian, Turkish, central Asian, and Armenian studies; Arabic and ancient Semitics.

Cornell University, Graduate School, Graduate Fields of Arts and Sciences, Field of East Asian Literature, Ithaca, NY 14853-0001. Offers Asian religions (MA, PhD); Chinese linguistics (MA, PhD); Chinese philology (MA, PhD); classical Chinese literature (MA, PhD); classical Japanese literature (MA, PhD); Japanese linguistics (MA, PhD); Korean literature (MA, PhD); modern Chinese literature (MA, PhD); modern Japanese literature (MA, PhD). *Faculty:* 14 full-time (6 women). *Students:* 18 full-time (9 women); includes 6 minority (all Asian Americans or Pacific Islanders), 9 international. Average age 34. 41 applicants, 7% accepted, 2 enrolled. In 2008, 2 master's, 3 doctorates awarded. *Degree requirements:* For master's, 2 foreign languages, thesis, teaching experience; for doctorate, 2 foreign languages, comprehensive exam, thesis/dissertation, teaching experience. *Entrance requirements:* For master's and doctorate, GRE General Test, 3 years of study in Chinese, Japanese, Korean, or Vietnamese, 3 letters of recommendation, academic writing sample. Additional exam requirements/recommendations for international students: Required—TOEFL (minimum score 600 paper-based; 250 computer-based; 77 iBT). *Application deadline:* For fall admission, 1/10 priority date for domestic students. Application fee: $70. Electronic applications accepted. *Expenses:* Tuition: Full-time $29,500. Required fees: $70. Full-time tuition and fees vary according to degree level, program and student level. *Financial support:* In 2008–09, 17 students received support, including 8 fellowships with full tuition reimbursements available, 2 research assistantships with full tuition reimbursements available, 7 teaching assistantships with full tuition reimbursements available; institutionally sponsored loans, scholarships/grants, health care benefits, tuition waivers (full and partial), and unspecified assistantships also available. Financial award applicants required to submit FAFSA. *Faculty research:* Vietnamese literature; Chinese literature, drama, and film; Japanese theater and literature; popular culture in East Asia; Korean literature; Asian linguistics. *Unit head:* Director of Graduate Studies, 607-255-9099. *Application contact:* Graduate Field Assistant, 607-255-9099, E-mail: east_asian_lit@cornell.edu.

Cornell University, Graduate School, Graduate Fields of Arts and Sciences, Field of Linguistics, Ithaca, NY 14853-0001. Offers applied linguistics (MA, PhD); East Asian linguistics (MA, PhD); English linguistics (MA, PhD); general linguistics (MA, PhD); Germanic linguistics (MA, PhD); Indo-European linguistics (MA, PhD); phonetics (MA, PhD); phonological theory (MA, PhD); Romance linguistics (MA, PhD); second language acquisition (MA, PhD); semantics (MA, PhD); Slavic linguistics (MA, PhD); sociolinguistics (MA, PhD); South Asian linguistics (MA, PhD); Southeast Asian linguistics (MA, PhD); syntactic theory (MA, PhD). *Faculty:* 15 full-time (6 women). *Students:* 32 full-time (15 women); includes 1 minority (Hispanic American), 16 international. Average age 30. 93 applicants, 16% accepted, 7 enrolled. In 2008, 5 master's, 7 doctorates awarded. Terminal master's awarded for partial completion of doctoral program. *Degree requirements:* For master's, one foreign language, thesis; for doctorate, one foreign language, comprehensive exam, thesis/dissertation. *Entrance requirements:* For master's and doctorate, GRE General Test, 2 letters of recommendation. Additional exam requirements/recommendations for international students: Required—TOEFL (minimum score 600 paper-based; 250 computer-based; 77 iBT). *Application deadline:* For fall admission, 1/15 for domestic students. Application fee: $70. Electronic applications accepted. *Expenses:* Tuition: Full-time $29,500. Required fees: $70. Full-time tuition and fees vary according to degree level, program and student level. *Financial support:* In 2008–09, 32 students received support, including 11 fellowships with full tuition reimbursements available, 4 research assistantships with full tuition reimbursements available, 17 teaching assistantships with full tuition reimbursements available; institutionally sponsored loans, scholarships/grants, health care benefits, tuition waivers (full and partial), and unspecified assistantships also available. Financial award applicants required to submit FAFSA. *Faculty research:* Phonology and phonetics; syntax and semantics; historical linguistics; philosophy of language; language acquisition. *Unit head:* Director of Graduate Studies, 607-255-1105. *Application contact:* Graduate Field Assistant, 607-255-1105, E-mail: lingfield@cornell.edu.

Harvard University, Graduate School of Arts and Sciences, Department of East Asian Languages and Civilizations, Cambridge, MA 02138. Offers Chinese (PhD); Japanese (PhD); Korean (PhD); Mongolian (PhD); Vietnamese (PhD). Terminal master's awarded for partial completion of doctoral program. *Degree requirements:* For doctorate, 3 foreign languages, thesis/dissertation, general exams. *Entrance requirements:* For doctorate, GRE General Test. Additional exam requirements/recommendations for international students: Required—TOEFL. *Expenses:* Tuition: Full-time $32,556. Required fees: $1426. Full-time tuition and fees vary according to program and student level. *Faculty research:* Central Asian literature, religion, and premodern history.

Harvard University, Graduate School of Arts and Sciences, Department of Sanskrit and Indian Studies, Cambridge, MA 02138. Offers Indian philosophy (AM, PhD); Pali (AM, PhD); Sanskrit (AM, PhD); Tibetan (AM, PhD); Urdu (AM, PhD). Terminal master's awarded for partial completion of doctoral program. *Degree requirements:* For master's, 3 foreign languages; for doctorate, 3 foreign languages, thesis/dissertation. *Entrance requirements:* For master's, GRE General Test; for doctorate, GRE General Test, proficiency in French and German. Additional exam requirements/recommendations for international students: Required—TOEFL. *Expenses:* Tuition: Full-time $32,556. Required fees: $1426. Full-time tuition and fees vary according to program and student level.

Indiana University Bloomington, University Graduate School, College of Arts and Sciences, Department of East Asian Languages and Cultures, Bloomington, IN 47405-7000. Offers Chinese (MA, PhD); East Asian languages and cultures (PhD); East Asian studies (MA); Japanese (MA, PhD); language pedagogy (MA). Part-time programs available. *Faculty:* 7 full-time (2 women). *Students:* 17 full-time (10 women), 11 part-time (7 women); includes 3 minority (1 African American, 1 Asian American or Pacific Islander, 1 Hispanic American), 7 international. Average age 33. 84 applicants, 30% accepted, 10 enrolled. In 2008, 6 master's, 1 doctorate awarded. *Degree requirements:* For master's, 2 foreign languages, thesis; for doctorate, 2 foreign languages, thesis/dissertation. *Entrance requirements:* Additional exam requirements/recommendations for international students: Required—TOEFL. *Application deadline:* For fall admission, 1/15 for domestic students, 12/15 for international students; for spring admission, 9/1 for domestic and international students. Applications are processed on a rolling basis. Application fee: $50 ($60 for international students). Electronic applications accepted. *Expenses:* Tuition, area resident: Part-time $291.97 per credit hour. Tuition, state resident: part-time $291.97 per credit hour. Tuition, nonresident: part-time $850.33 per credit hour. Required fees: $110 per semester. Tuition and fees vary according to course load and program. *Financial support:* Fellowships, teaching assistantships, Federal Work-Study, tuition waivers (full) available. Financial award application deadline: 3/1. *Faculty research:* Postwar/postmodern Japanese fiction, modern Chinese film and literature, classical Chinese

literature and philosophy, Chinese and Japanese linguistics and pedagogy, East Asian politics. *Unit head:* Robert Eno, Chair, 812-855-0856, E-mail: eno@indiana.edu. *Application contact:* Edith Sarra, Director of Graduate Studies, 812-855-4031, Fax: 812-855-6402, E-mail: eserra@indiana.edu.

Naropa University, Graduate Programs, Program in Indo-Tibetan Buddhism with Language, Boulder, CO 80302-6697. Offers MA. *Faculty:* 6 full-time (2 women), 10 part-time/adjunct (5 women). *Students:* 15 full-time (1 woman), 4 part-time (2 women); includes 3 minority (1 American Indian/Alaska Native, 1 Asian American or Pacific Islander, 1 Hispanic American), 1 international. Average age 32. 19 applicants, 84% accepted, 8 enrolled. In 2008, 5 master's awarded. *Degree requirements:* For master's, comprehensive exam, thesis. *Entrance requirements:* For master's, writing sample, interview (by phone or in-person), resumé, letter of interest, 3 letters of recommendation. Additional exam requirements/recommendations for international students: Required—TOEFL (minimum score 600 paper-based; 250 computer-based). *Application deadline:* For fall admission, 1/15 priority date for domestic and international students. Applications are processed on a rolling basis. Application fee: $60. Electronic applications accepted. *Expenses:* Tuition: Full-time $14,767; part-time $726 per credit hour. Required fees: $45 per term. *Financial support:* In 2008–09, 11 students received support, including 5 research assistantships with partial tuition reimbursements available (averaging $3,000 per year), 2 teaching assistantships with partial tuition reimbursements available (averaging $3,000 per year); career-related internships or fieldwork, Federal Work-Study, scholarships/grants, health care benefits, tuition waivers (partial), and unspecified assistantships also available. Support available to part-time students. Financial award application deadline: 3/1; financial award applicants required to submit FAFSA. *Unit head:* Roger Dorris, Co-Chair, 303-546-0937. *Application contact:* Donna McIntyre, Assistant Director of Admissions, 303-546-3555, Fax: 303-546-3583, E-mail: donna@naropa.edu.

See Close-Up on page 1121.

The Ohio State University, Graduate School, College of Humanities, Department of East Asian Languages and Literatures, Columbus, OH 43210. Offers Chinese (MA, PhD); Japanese (MA, PhD). *Degree requirements:* For master's, thesis optional; for doctorate, thesis/dissertation. *Entrance requirements:* For master's and doctorate, GRE (if applying for financial aid). Additional exam requirements/recommendations for international students: Required—TOEFL (minimum score 577 paper-based; 233 computer-based). Electronic applications accepted.

St. John's College, Graduate Institute in Liberal Education, Program in Eastern Classics, Santa Fe, NM 87505-4599. Offers MA. Part-time and evening/weekend programs available. *Entrance requirements:* For master's, 2 letters of recommendation. Additional exam requirements/recommendations for international students: Required—TOEFL, TWE. *Expenses:* Contact institution.

Seton Hall University, College of Arts and Sciences, Department of Asian Studies, South Orange, NJ 07079-2697. Offers MA. Part-time and evening/weekend programs available. *Degree requirements:* For master's, thesis optional. Electronic applications accepted. *Faculty research:* Modern Chinese history, contemporary Chinese politics, ancient Chinese history, Hinduism, Asian business, Japanese history.

See Close-Up on page 623.

University of California, Berkeley, Graduate Division, College of Letters and Science, Department of South and Southeast Asian Studies, Berkeley, CA 94720-1500. Offers Hindi (MA, PhD); Indonesian (MA, PhD); Sanskrit (MA, PhD); Tamil (MA, PhD). Terminal master's awarded for partial completion of doctoral program. *Degree requirements:* For master's, 2 foreign languages, thesis; for doctorate, 2 foreign languages, thesis/dissertation, oral qualifying exam. *Entrance requirements:* For master's and doctorate, GRE General Test, minimum GPA of 3.0, 3 letters of recommendation. Electronic applications accepted.

University of California, Irvine, Office of Graduate Studies, School of Humanities, Department of East Asian Languages and Literatures, Irvine, CA 92697. Offers Chinese (MA, PhD); East Asian languages and literatures (MA, PhD); Japanese (MA, PhD). *Degree requirements:* For doctorate, thesis/dissertation. *Entrance requirements:* For master's, GRE, minimum GPA of 3.0; for doctorate, GRE General Test, minimum GPA of 3.0. Additional exam requirements/recommendations for international students: Required—TOEFL (minimum score 550 paper-based; 213 computer-based). Electronic applications accepted. *Faculty research:* Chinese, Japanese, and Korean literature and culture; language and textual analysis; historical, social, and cultural dimensions of literary study.

University of California, Los Angeles, Graduate Division, College of Letters and Science, Department of Asian Languages and Cultures, Los Angeles, CA 90095. Offers MA, PhD. *Faculty:* 15. *Students:* 37 full-time (23 women); includes 11 minority (all Asian Americans or Pacific Islanders), 14 international. Average age 30. 54 applicants, 20% accepted, 8 enrolled. In 2008, 10 master's, 1 doctorate awarded. Terminal master's awarded for partial completion of doctoral program. *Degree requirements:* For master's, one foreign language, comprehensive exam or thesis; for doctorate, 2 foreign languages, thesis/dissertation, oral and written qualifying exams. *Entrance requirements:* For master's, GRE General Test, minimum GPA of 3.0, sample of written work; for doctorate, GRE General Test, minimum undergraduate GPA of 3.0, sample of research writing or thesis in English. Additional exam requirements/recommendations for international students: Required—TOEFL. *Application deadline:* For fall admission, 12/1 for domestic and international students. Application fee: $60 ($80 for international students). Electronic applications accepted. *Expenses:* Tuition, nonresident: full-time $14,694. Required fees: $9669.50. Full-time tuition and fees vary according to course load, degree level, program and student level. *Financial support:* In 2008–09, 49 fellowships with full and partial tuition reimbursements, 20 research assistantships with full and partial tuition reimbursements, 30 teaching assistantships with full and partial tuition reimbursements were awarded; Federal Work-Study, institutionally sponsored loans, scholarships/grants, health care benefits, tuition waivers (full and partial), and unspecified assistantships also available. Financial award application deadline: 3/1; financial award applicants required to submit FAFSA. *Unit head:* Dr. Lee Namhee, Chair, 310-794-2666. *Application contact:* Departmental Office, 310-206-8235, E-mail: alcgen@humnet.ucla.edu.

University of California, Santa Barbara, Graduate Division, College of Letters and Sciences, Division of Humanities and Fine Arts, Department of East Asian Languages and Cultural Studies, Santa Barbara, CA 93106-7075. Offers Asian Studies (MA), including Asian Studies, East Asian language and cultural studies; Asian studies (MA), including Asian Studies, East Asian language and cultural studies; East Asian language and cultural studies (PhD); MA/PhD. *Students:* 13 full-time (8 women). Average age 27. 76 applicants, 28% accepted, 6 enrolled. In 2008, 2 master's awarded. *Degree requirements:* For master's, one foreign language, thesis or alternative; for doctorate, 2 foreign languages, thesis/dissertation. *Entrance requirements:* For master's and doctorate, GRE, 3 letters of recommendation, statement of purpose, personal achievements/contributions statement, resumé/curriculum vitae, transcripts for post-secondary institutions attended. Additional exam requirements/recommendations for international students: Required—TOEFL (paper: 550, computer: 213, IBT: 80) or IELTS (7). *Application deadline:* For fall admission, 4/1 for domestic and international students. Application fee: $70 ($90 for international students). Electronic applications accepted. *Expenses:* Tuition, nonresident: full-time $25,149. Required fees: $10,143. Full-time tuition and fees vary according to campus/location, reciprocity agreements and student level. *Financial support:* In 2008–09, 10 students received support, including 5 fellowships with full and partial tuition reimbursements available (averaging $11,000 per year), 10 teaching assistantships with partial tuition reimbursements available (averaging $8,200 per year); Federal Work-Study, institutionally sponsored loans, scholarships/grants, health care benefits, and unspecified assistantships also available. Financial award application deadline: 12/15; financial award applicants required to submit FAFSA. *Faculty* *research:* Chinese literature, Chinese film, Japanese society, Japanese literature, East Asian cultural studies. *Unit head:* Dr. William Powell, Chair, 805-893-4455, Fax: 805-893-3011, E-mail: bpowell@religion.ucsb.edu. *Application contact:* Dr. Ronald Egan, Faculty Graduate Advisor, 805-893-3770, Fax: 805-893-3011, E-mail: ronegan@eastasian.ucsb.edu.

University of California, Santa Barbara, Graduate Division, College of Letters and Sciences, Division of Humanities and Fine Arts, Program in Comparative Literature, Santa Barbara, CA 93106-4130. Offers comparative literature (PhD); East Asian literatures (PhD); feminist studies (PhD); MA/PhD. *Faculty:* 56 full-time (24 women). *Students:* 24 full-time (18 women). Average age 29. 43 applicants, 40% accepted, 5 enrolled. In 2008, 5 doctorates awarded. Terminal master's awarded for partial completion of doctoral program. *Degree requirements:* For doctorate, 2 foreign languages, comprehensive exam, thesis/dissertation. *Entrance requirements:* For doctorate, GRE. Additional exam requirements/recommendations for international students: Required—TOEFL (paper: 550, computer: 213, IBT: 80) or IELTS (7). *Application deadline:* For fall admission, 12/15 for domestic and international students. Application fee: $70 ($90 for international students). Electronic applications accepted. *Expenses:* Tuition, nonresident: full-time $25,149. Required fees: $10,143. Full-time tuition and fees vary according to campus/location, reciprocity agreements and student level. *Financial support:* In 2008–09, 24 students received support, including 15 fellowships with full and partial tuition reimbursements available (averaging $6,900 per year), 1 research assistantship (averaging $10,600 per year), 18 teaching assistantships with partial tuition reimbursements available (averaging $10,400 per year); Federal Work-Study, institutionally sponsored loans, scholarships/grants, health care benefits, and tuition waivers (full and partial) also available. Financial award application deadline: 12/15; financial award applicants required to submit FAFSA. *Faculty research:* Media studies, literary theory, cultural studies, early-modern and modern literature, critical theory. *Unit head:* Prof. Elisabeth Weber, Chair, 805-893-3527, Fax: 805-893-2374, E-mail: weber@gss.ucsb.edu. *Application contact:* Sierra Gray, Graduate Program Assistant, 805-893-2131, Fax: 805-893-2374, E-mail: sierra@gss.ucsb.edu.

University of Chicago, Division of the Humanities, Department of East Asian Languages and Civilizations, Chicago, IL 60637-1513. Offers AM, PhD. Terminal master's awarded for partial completion of doctoral program. *Degree requirements:* For master's, one foreign language, thesis; for doctorate, 2 foreign languages, thesis/dissertation. *Entrance requirements:* For master's and doctorate, GRE General Test. Additional exam requirements/recommendations for international students: Required—TOEFL.

University of Chicago, Division of the Humanities, Department of South Asian Languages and Civilizations, Chicago, IL 60637-1513. Offers South Asian languages and civilizations (AM, PhD), including Bengali (PhD), Hindi (PhD), Sanskrit (PhD), Tamil (PhD), Urdu (PhD). Terminal master's awarded for partial completion of doctoral program. *Degree requirements:* For master's, one foreign language, thesis; for doctorate, 2 foreign languages, thesis/dissertation. *Entrance requirements:* For master's and doctorate, GRE General Test. Additional exam requirements/recommendations for international students: Required—TOEFL.

University of Hawaii at Manoa, Graduate Division, Colleges of Arts and Sciences, College of Language, Linguistics and Literature, Department of East Asian Languages and Literatures, Program in Korean, Honolulu, HI 96822. Offers MA, PhD. Part-time programs available. *Degree requirements:* For master's, 2 foreign languages, thesis optional; for doctorate, 2 foreign languages, comprehensive exam, thesis/dissertation. *Entrance requirements:* For master's and doctorate, GRE General Test. Additional exam requirements/recommendations for international students: Required—TOEFL (minimum score 560 paper-based; 220 computer-based; 83 iBT), IELTS (minimum score 5).

University of Illinois at Urbana–Champaign, Graduate College, College of Liberal Arts and Sciences, School of Literatures, Cultures and Linguistics, Department of East Asian Languages and Cultures, Champaign, IL 61820. Offers Asian studies (MA); East Asian languages and cultures (PhD). *Faculty:* 15 full-time (5 women), 1 (woman) part-time/adjunct. *Students:* 29 full-time (24 women), 8 part-time (all women); includes 2 minority (1 Asian American or Pacific Islander, 1 Hispanic American), 27 international. 76 applicants, 13% accepted, 9 enrolled. In 2008, 3 master's, 3 doctorates awarded. *Entrance requirements:* For master's, GRE General Test, minimum GPA of 3.0; writing sample; for doctorate, GRE, minimum GPA of 3.0; writing sample. Additional exam requirements/recommendations for international students: Required—TOEFL (minimum score 103 iBT). *Application deadline:* Applications are processed on a rolling basis. Application fee: $60 ($75 for international students). Electronic applications accepted. *Financial support:* In 2008–09, 10 fellowships, 1 research assistantship, 25 teaching assistantships were awarded; tuition waivers (full and partial) also available. *Unit head:* Karen Kelsky, Head, 217-244-9077, Fax: 217-244-2223, E-mail: kelsky@illinois.edu. *Application contact:* David Goodman, Director of Graduate Studies, 217-244-1432, Fax: 217-244-2223, E-mail: dgoodman@illinois.edu.

The University of Kansas, Graduate Studies, College of Liberal Arts and Sciences, Department of East Asian Languages and Cultures, Lawrence, KS 66045. Offers MA, MBA/MA. Part-time programs available. *Faculty:* 7. *Students:* 11 full-time (5 women), 3 part-time (2 women); includes 1 minority (Asian American or Pacific Islander), 3 international. Average age 31. 17 applicants, 29% accepted, 3 enrolled. In 2008, 1 master's awarded. *Degree requirements:* For master's, one foreign language, thesis. *Entrance requirements:* For master's, GRE, 3 letters of recommendation, statement of purpose, writing sample. Additional exam requirements/recommendations for international students: Required—TOEFL. *Application deadline:* For fall admission, 5/1 priority date for domestic students, 5/1 for international students; for spring admission, 12/1 priority date for domestic students, 12/1 for international students. Applications are processed on a rolling basis. Application fee: $45 ($55 for international students). Electronic applications accepted. *Expenses:* Tuition, area resident: Full-time $6122; part-time $255.10 per credit hour. Tuition, state resident: full-time $6122; part-time $255.10 per credit hour. Tuition, nonresident: full-time $14,629; part-time $609.55 per credit hour. Required fees: $847; $70.56 per credit hour. Tuition and fees vary according to course load and program. *Financial support:* Fellowships, teaching assistantships with full and partial tuition reimbursements, unspecified assistantships available. Financial award application deadline: 2/1. *Faculty research:* Gender relations in literature, ancient Chinese law, visual culture of modern Japan, Japanese language pedagogy, Chinese paleography, Korean shamanism, folklore, traditional Chinese and Japanese literature, Chinese linguistics and language pedagogy. *Unit head:* Margaret Childs, Chair and Graduate Director, 785-864-3100, E-mail: mgchilds@ku.edu. *Application contact:* Georgia Damis, Administrative Specialist, 785-864-3100, Fax: 785-864-4298, E-mail: ealc@ku.edu.

University of Michigan, Horace H. Rackham School of Graduate Studies, College of Literature, Science, and the Arts, Department of Asian Languages and Cultures, Ann Arbor, MI 48109. Offers MA, PhD. Terminal master's awarded for partial completion of doctoral program. *Degree requirements:* For master's, variable foreign language requirement, thesis; for doctorate, 2 foreign languages, thesis/dissertation, oral defense of dissertation, preliminary exam. *Entrance requirements:* For master's and doctorate, GRE General Test. Additional exam requirements/recommendations for international students: Required—TOEFL (minimum score 600 paper-based; 250 computer-based). Electronic applications accepted. *Faculty research:* Literature, linguistics, religion, philosophy, music, cinema.

University of Minnesota, Twin Cities Campus, Graduate School, College of Liberal Arts, Department of Asian Languages and Literatures, Minneapolis, MN 55455-0213. Offers Asian literatures, cultures, and media (PhD). *Degree requirements:* For doctorate, comprehensive exam, thesis/dissertation. *Entrance requirements:* For doctorate, GRE, 3 letters of recommendation. Additional exam requirements/recommendations for international students: Required—TOEFL (minimum score 550 paper-based; 213 computer-based), IELTS (minimum score 6.5). Electronic applications accepted. *Faculty research:* Gender studies, post-colonial theory, poetics and poetic theory, film studies, post modernist thought.

University of Oregon, Graduate School, College of Arts and Sciences, Department of East Asian Languages and Literature, Eugene, OR 97403. Offers Chinese (MA, PhD); Japanese (MA, PhD). *Entrance requirements:* Additional exam requirements/recommendations for international students: Required—TOEFL. *Faculty research:* Linguistics, pedagogy.

University of Southern California, Graduate School, College of Letters, Arts and Sciences, Department of East Asian Languages and Cultures, Los Angeles, CA 90089. Offers MA, PhD. *Degree requirements:* For master's, one foreign language, thesis; for doctorate, 2 foreign languages, thesis/dissertation. *Entrance requirements:* For master's and doctorate, GRE General Test. *Faculty research:* Premodern Chinese history, modern and classical Chinese literature, Japanese, Korea.

University of Southern California, Graduate School, College of Letters, Arts and Sciences, Department of Linguistics, Los Angeles, CA 90089. Offers East Asian linguistics (PhD); Hispanic linguistics (PhD); linguistics (PhD). *Degree requirements:* For doctorate, 2 foreign languages, thesis/dissertation. *Entrance requirements:* For doctorate, GRE General Test. *Faculty research:* Syntax, phonology, phonetics, semantics, sociolinguistics, psycholinguistics.

The University of Texas at Austin, Graduate School, College of Liberal Arts, Department of Asian Studies, Austin, TX 78712-1111. Offers Asian cultures and languages (MA, PhD); Asian studies (MA). Part-time programs available. *Degree requirements:* For master's, thesis; for doctorate, 3 foreign languages, thesis/dissertation. *Entrance requirements:* For master's and doctorate, GRE General Test. Electronic applications accepted. *Faculty research:* Modern Taiwanese fiction, modern Japanese literature, religious studies in South Asia during classical period.

University of Washington, Graduate School, College of Arts and Sciences, Department of Asian Languages and Literature, Seattle, WA 98195. Offers Buddhist studies (MA, PhD); Chinese language and literature (MA, PhD); Japanese language and literature (MA, PhD); Korean language and literature (MA, PhD); South Asian language and literature (MA, PhD). *Degree requirements:* For master's, 2 foreign languages, general exam, thesis or 2 research papers; for doctorate, 3 foreign languages, thesis/dissertation, general exam. *Entrance requirements:* For master's, GRE, minimum GPA of 3.0; for doctorate, GRE, master's degree in related field, minimum GPA of 3.0. Additional exam requirements/recommendations for international students: Required—TOEFL. Electronic applications accepted. *Faculty research:* Textual, linguistic, philological, and literary study of languages and literatures of Asia.

University of Wisconsin–Madison, Graduate School, College of Letters and Science, Department of Languages and Cultures of Asia, Madison, WI 53706-1380. Offers civilizations and cultures (PhD); languages and cultures of Asia (MA); languages and literatures (PhD); religions of Asia (PhD). Part-time programs available. Terminal master's awarded for partial completion of doctoral program. *Degree requirements:* For master's, one foreign language, thesis or alternative; for doctorate, 2 foreign languages, thesis/dissertation. *Entrance requirements:* For master's, minimum GPA of 3.0; for doctorate, minimum GPA of 3.25, master's degree. Electronic applications accepted. *Faculty research:* Literature, folklore, religion.

Washington University in St. Louis, Graduate School of Arts and Sciences, Department of Asian and Near Eastern Languages and Literatures, St. Louis, MO 63130-4899. Offers Chinese (MA); Chinese and comparative literature (PhD); Japanese (MA); Japanese and comparative literature (PhD). *Students:* 20 full-time (13 women); includes 1 minority (Hispanic American), 15 international. 9 applicants, 44% accepted, 2 enrolled. In 2008, 1 master's awarded. Terminal master's awarded for partial completion of doctoral program. *Degree requirements:* For master's, thesis optional; for doctorate, thesis/dissertation. *Entrance requirements:* For master's and doctorate, GRE General Test. *Application deadline:* For fall admission, 1/15 priority date for domestic students. Applications are processed on a rolling basis. Application fee: $45. Electronic applications accepted. *Financial support:* Teaching assistantships, Federal Work-Study, institutionally sponsored loans, and tuition waivers (full and partial) available. Support available to part-time students. Financial award application deadline: 1/15. *Unit head:* Dr. Fatemeh Keshavarz, Chairperson, 314-935-5156. *Application contact:* Assistant to the Dean, 314-935-6880, Fax: 314-935-4887.

Washington University in St. Louis, Graduate School of Arts and Sciences, Program in East Asian Studies, St. Louis, MO 63130-4899. Offers East Asian studies (MA); JD/MA. PhD offered through specific departments. *Students:* 16 full-time (8 women); includes 3 minority (1 American Indian/Alaska Native, 2 Asian Americans or Pacific Islanders), 6 international. 35 applicants, 26% accepted, 7 enrolled. In 2008, 6 master's awarded. *Entrance requirements:* For master's, GRE General Test. *Application deadline:* For fall admission, 1/15 priority date for domestic students. Application fee: $45. Electronic applications accepted. *Financial support:* Fellowships, research assistantships, teaching assistantships, tuition waivers available. Financial award application deadline: 1/15. *Unit head:* Dr. Letty Chen, Chairperson, 314-935-4448. *Application contact:* Assistant to the Dean, 314-935-6880, Fax: 314-935-4887.

See Close-Up on page 625.

Yale University, Graduate School of Arts and Sciences, Department of East Asian Languages and Literatures, New Haven, CT 06520. Offers East Asian languages and literatures (PhD); East Asian languages and literatures and film studies (PhD). *Degree requirements:* For doctorate, 2 foreign languages, thesis/dissertation. *Entrance requirements:* For doctorate, GRE General Test.

Celtic Languages

Harvard University, Graduate School of Arts and Sciences, Department of Celtic Languages and Literatures, Cambridge, MA 02138. Offers Irish (PhD); Welsh (PhD). *Degree requirements:* For doctorate, thesis/dissertation, proficiency in 2 Celtic languages; reading knowledge of French, German, and Latin. *Entrance requirements:* For doctorate, GRE General Test. Additional exam requirements/recommendations for international students: Required—TOEFL. *Expenses:* Tuition: Full-time $32,556. Required fees: $1426. Full-time tuition and fees vary according to program and student level.

Chinese

Arizona State University, Graduate College, College of Liberal Arts and Sciences, Division of Humanities, School of International Letters and Cultures, Program in Chinese, Tempe, AZ 85287. Offers MA.

Cornell University, Graduate School, Graduate Fields of Arts and Sciences, Field of East Asian Literature, Ithaca, NY 14853-0001. Offers Asian religions (MA, PhD); Chinese linguistics (MA, PhD); Chinese philology (MA, PhD); classical Chinese literature (MA, PhD); classical Japanese literature (MA, PhD); Japanese linguistics (MA, PhD); Korean literature (MA, PhD); modern Chinese literature (MA, PhD); modern Japanese literature (MA, PhD). *Faculty:* 14 full-time (6 women). *Students:* 18 full-time (9 women); includes 6 minority (all Asian Americans or Pacific Islanders), 9 international. Average age 34. 41 applicants, 7% accepted, 2 enrolled. In 2008, 2 master's, 3 doctorates awarded. *Degree requirements:* For master's, 2 foreign languages, thesis, teaching experience; for doctorate, 2 foreign languages, comprehensive exam, thesis/dissertation, teaching experience. *Entrance requirements:* For master's and doctorate, GRE General Test, 3 years of study in Chinese, Japanese, Korean, or Vietnamese, 3 letters of recommendation, academic writing sample. Additional exam requirements/recommendations for international students: Required—TOEFL (minimum score 600 paper-based; 250 computer-based; 77 iBT). *Application deadline:* For fall admission, 1/10 priority date for domestic students. Application fee: $70. Electronic applications accepted. *Expenses:* Tuition: Full-time $29,500. Required fees: $70. Full-time tuition and fees vary according to degree level, program and student level. *Financial support:* In 2008–09, 17 students received support, including 8 fellowships with full tuition reimbursements available, 2 research assistantships with full tuition reimbursements available, 7 teaching assistantships with full tuition reimbursements available; institutionally sponsored loans, scholarships/grants, health care benefits, tuition waivers (full and partial), and unspecified assistantships also available. Financial award applicants required to submit FAFSA. *Faculty research:* Vietnamese literature; Chinese literature, drama, and film; Japanese theater and literature; popular culture in East Asia; Korean literature; Asian linguistics. *Unit head:* Director of Graduate Studies, 607-255-9099. *Application contact:* Graduate Field Assistant, 607-255-9099, E-mail: east_asian_lit@cornell.edu.

Harvard University, Graduate School of Arts and Sciences, Department of East Asian Languages and Civilizations, Cambridge, MA 02138. Offers Chinese (PhD); Japanese (PhD); Korean (PhD); Mongolian (PhD); Vietnamese (PhD). Terminal master's awarded for partial completion of doctoral program. *Degree requirements:* For doctorate, 3 foreign languages, thesis/dissertation, general exams. *Entrance requirements:* For doctorate, GRE General Test. Additional exam requirements/recommendations for international students: Required—TOEFL. *Expenses:* Tuition: Full-time $32,556. Required fees: $1426. Full-time tuition and fees vary according to program and student level. *Faculty research:* Central Asian literature, religion, and premodern history.

Indiana University Bloomington, University Graduate School, College of Arts and Sciences, Department of East Asian Languages and Cultures, Bloomington, IN 47405-7000. Offers Chinese (MA, PhD); East Asian languages and cultures (PhD); East Asian studies (MA); Japanese (MA, PhD); language pedagogy (MA). Part-time programs available. *Faculty:* 7 full-time (2 women). *Students:* 17 full-time (10 women), 11 part-time (7 women); includes 3 minority (1 African American, 1 Asian American or Pacific Islander, 1 Hispanic American), 7 international. Average age 33. 84 applicants, 30% accepted, 10 enrolled. In 2008, 6 master's, 1 doctorate awarded. *Degree requirements:* For master's, 2 foreign languages, thesis; for doctorate, 2 foreign languages, thesis/dissertation. *Entrance requirements:* Additional exam requirements/recommendations for international students: Required—TOEFL. *Application deadline:* For fall admission, 1/15 for domestic students, 12/15 for international students; for spring admission, 9/1 for domestic and international students. Applications are processed on a rolling basis. Application fee: $50 ($60 for international students). Electronic applications accepted. *Expenses:* Tuition, area resident: Part-time $291.97 per credit hour. Tuition, state resident: part-time $291.97 per credit hour. Tuition, nonresident: part-time $850.33 per credit hour. Required fees: $110 per semester. Tuition and fees vary according to course load and program. *Financial support:* Fellowships, teaching assistantships, Federal Work-Study and tuition waivers (full) available. Financial award application deadline: 3/1. *Faculty research:* Postwar/postmodern Japanese fiction, modern Chinese film and literature, classical Chinese literature and philosophy, Chinese and Japanese linguistics and pedagogy, East Asian politics. *Unit head:* Robert Eno, Chair, 812-855-0856, E-mail: eno@indiana.edu. *Application contact:* Edith Sarra, Director of Graduate Studies, 812-855-4031, Fax: 812-855-6402, E-mail: eserra@indiana.edu.

Middlebury College, Language Schools, Chinese School, Middlebury, VT 05753. Offers MA. *Faculty:* 3 full-time (1 woman). *Students:* 21 full-time (17 women); includes 12 minority (all Asian Americans or Pacific Islanders). Average age 34. 37 applicants, 65% accepted, 22 enrolled. In 2008, 1 master's awarded. *Degree requirements:* For master's, one foreign language, teaching practicum. *Entrance requirements:* For master's, ACTFL OPI (for non-native speakers) or online adaptive test, 3 letters of recommendation, writing sample, curriculum vitae. Additional exam requirements/recommendations for international students: Required—TOEFL (only if student is applying to the Monterey option; paper-based minimum of 600, computer-based 250, iBT 100). *Application deadline:* Applications are processed on a rolling basis. Application fee: $55. Electronic applications accepted. *Financial support:* Fellowships, scholarships/grants available. Financial award applicants required to submit FAFSA. *Unit head:* Dr. Jianhua Bai, Director, 802-443-5520, Fax: 802-443-2075, E-mail: jbai@middlebury.edu. *Application contact:* Anna Sun, Coordinator, 802-443-5520, Fax: 802-443-2075, E-mail: sun@middlebury.edu.

The Ohio State University, Graduate School, College of Humanities, Department of East Asian Languages and Literatures, Columbus, OH 43210. Offers Chinese (MA, PhD); Japanese (MA, PhD). *Degree requirements:* For master's, thesis optional; for doctorate, thesis/dissertation. *Entrance requirements:* For master's and doctorate, GRE (if applying for financial aid). Additional exam requirements/recommendations for international students: Required—TOEFL (minimum score 577 paper-based; 233 computer-based). Electronic applications accepted.

San Francisco State University, Division of Graduate Studies, College of Humanities, Department of Foreign Languages and Literatures, Program in Chinese, San Francisco, CA 94132-1722. Offers MA.

Seton Hall University, College of Arts and Sciences, Department of Asian Studies, South Orange, NJ 07079-2697. Offers MA. Part-time and evening/weekend programs available. *Degree requirements:* For master's, thesis optional. Electronic applications accepted. *Faculty research:* Modern Chinese history, contemporary Chinese politics, ancient Chinese history, Hinduism, Asian business, Japanese history.

See Close-Up on page 623.

Stanford University, School of Humanities and Sciences, Department of Asian Languages, Stanford, CA 94305-9991. Offers Chinese (MA, PhD); Japanese (MA, PhD). Terminal master's awarded for partial completion of doctoral program. *Degree requirements:* For master's, one foreign language, thesis or an annotated translation of a literary or historical text; for doctorate, 2 foreign languages, thesis/dissertation, field exams. *Entrance requirements:* For master's and doctorate, GRE General Test. Additional exam requirements/recommendations for international students: Required—TOEFL. Electronic applications accepted.

University of Alberta, Faculty of Graduate Studies and Research, Department of East Asian Studies, Edmonton, AB T6G 2E1, Canada. Offers Chinese literature (MA); East Asian interdisciplinary studies (MA); Japanese literature (MA). Part-time programs available. *Degree requirements:* For master's, one foreign language, thesis. *Entrance requirements:* Additional exam requirements/recommendations for international students: Required—TOEFL. Electronic applications accepted. *Faculty research:* Classical Chinese poetry and poetics, Chinese philosophy, modern/contemporary Chinese literature, modern Japanese literature and culture, Japanese women's writing.

University of California, Berkeley, Graduate Division, College of Letters and Science, Department of East Asian Languages and Cultures, Berkeley, CA 94720-1500. Offers Chinese language (PhD); Japanese language (PhD). *Degree requirements:* For doctorate, one foreign language, thesis/dissertation, oral qualifying exam. *Entrance requirements:* For doctorate, GRE General Test, minimum GPA of 3.0, MA thesis, 3 letters of recommendation. Electronic applications accepted. *Faculty research:* Chinese and Japanese modern and classical texts, prose, and poetry; Chinese and Japanese linguistics.

University of California, Irvine, Office of Graduate Studies, School of Humanities, Department of East Asian Languages and Literatures, Irvine, CA 92697. Offers Chinese (MA, PhD); East Asian languages and literatures (MA, PhD); Japanese (MA, PhD). *Degree requirements:* For doctorate, thesis/dissertation. *Entrance requirements:* For master's, GRE, minimum GPA of 3.0; for doctorate, GRE General Test, minimum GPA of 3.0. Additional exam requirements/recommendations for international students: Required—TOEFL (minimum score 550 paper-based; 213 computer-based). Electronic applications accepted. *Faculty research:* Chinese, Japanese, and Korean literature and culture; language and textual analysis; historical, social, and cultural dimensions of literary study.

University of Colorado at Boulder, Graduate School, College of Arts and Sciences, Department of East Asian Languages and Civilizations, Boulder, CO 80309. Offers Chinese (MA, PhD); Japanese (MA, PhD). Part-time programs available. *Degree requirements:* For master's, comprehensive exam. *Entrance requirements:* For master's, BA in Chinese or Japanese, minimum undergraduate GPA of 3.0. Additional exam requirements/recommendations for international students: Required—TOEFL. *Faculty research:* Chinese and Japanese modern and classical literature, religions, linguistics, language pedagogy, pre-modern and contemporary fiction, sociolinguistics.

University of Hawaii at Manoa, Graduate Division, Colleges of Arts and Sciences, College of Language, Linguistics and Literature, Department of East Asian Languages and Literatures, Program in Chinese, Honolulu, HI 96822. Offers MA, PhD. Part-time programs available. *Degree requirements:* For master's, 2 foreign languages, thesis optional; for doctorate, 2 foreign languages, comprehensive exam, thesis/dissertation. *Entrance requirements:* For master's and doctorate, GRE General Test. Additional exam requirements/recommendations for international students: Required—TOEFL (minimum score 560 paper-based; 220 computer-based; 83 iBT), IELTS (minimum score 5).

University of Hawaii at Manoa, Graduate Division, School of Pacific and Asian Studies, Program in Asian Studies, Concentration in Chinese Studies, Honolulu, HI 96822. Offers Graduate Certificate. Part-time programs available. *Degree requirements:* For Graduate Certificate, one foreign language. *Entrance requirements:* For degree, GRE. Additional exam requirements/recommendations for international students: Required—TOEFL (minimum score 560 paper-based; 220 computer-based; 83 iBT), IELTS (minimum score 5).

University of Oregon, Graduate School, College of Arts and Sciences, Department of East Asian Languages and Literature, Eugene, OR 97403. Offers Chinese (MA, PhD); Japanese (MA, PhD). *Entrance requirements:* Additional exam requirements/recommendations for international students: Required—TOEFL. *Faculty research:* Linguistics, pedagogy.

University of Washington, Graduate School, College of Arts and Sciences, Department of Asian Languages and Literature, Seattle, WA 98195. Offers Buddhist studies (MA, PhD); Chinese language and literature (MA, PhD); Japanese language and literature (MA, PhD); Korean language and literature (MA, PhD); South Asian language and literature (MA, PhD). *Degree requirements:* For master's, 2 foreign languages, general exam, thesis or 2 research papers; for doctorate, 3 foreign languages, thesis/dissertation, general exam. *Entrance requirements:* For master's, GRE, minimum GPA of 3.0; for doctorate, GRE, master's degree in related field, minimum GPA of 3.0. Additional exam requirements/recommendations for international students: Required—TOEFL. Electronic applications accepted. *Faculty research:* Textual, linguistic, philological, and literary study of languages and literatures of Asia.

University of Wisconsin–Madison, Graduate School, College of Letters and Science, Department of East Asian Languages and Literature, Program in Chinese Literature, Madison, WI 53706-1380. Offers MA, PhD. Part-time programs available. Terminal master's awarded for partial completion of doctoral program. *Degree requirements:* For master's, one foreign language, seminars, written exam; for doctorate, 3 foreign languages, thesis/dissertation, seminars, preliminary exams, oral exam. *Entrance requirements:* For master's, bachelor's degree or equivalent in Chinese; for doctorate, master's degree or equivalent in Chinese. Electronic applications accepted. *Faculty research:* Chinese historical and modern linguistics, classical Chinese literary and cultural history, modern Chinese literary and cultural history, Chinese paleography.

Washington University in St. Louis, Graduate School of Arts and Sciences, Department of Asian and Near Eastern Languages and Literatures, St. Louis, MO 63130-4899. Offers Chinese (MA); Chinese and comparative literature (PhD); Japanese (MA); Japanese and comparative literature (PhD). *Students:* 20 full-time (13 women); includes 1 minority (Hispanic American), 15 international. 9 applicants, 44% accepted, 2 enrolled. In 2008, 1 master's awarded. Terminal master's awarded for partial completion of doctoral program. *Degree requirements:* For master's, thesis optional; for doctorate, thesis/dissertation. *Entrance requirements:* For master's and doctorate, GRE General Test. *Application deadline:* For fall admission, 1/15 priority date for domestic students. Applications are processed on a rolling basis. Application fee: $45. Electronic applications accepted. *Financial support:* Teaching assistantships, Federal Work-Study, institutionally sponsored loans, and tuition waivers (full and partial) available. Support available

to part-time students. Financial award application deadline: 1/15. *Unit head:* Dr. Fatemeh Keshavarz, Chairperson, 314-935-5156. *Application contact:* Assistant to the Dean, 314-935-6880, Fax: 314-935-4887.

Classics

Boston College, Graduate School of Arts and Sciences, Department of Classics, Chestnut Hill, MA 02467-3800. Offers classics (MA); Greek (MA); Latin (MA). Part-time programs available. *Degree requirements:* For master's, one foreign language, thesis optional. *Entrance requirements:* Additional exam requirements/recommendations for international students: Required—TOEFL (minimum score 590 paper-based; 250 computer-based; 91 iBT). *Expenses:* Tuition: Part-time $1148 per credit. Required fees: $60. *Faculty research:* Classical philology, ancient history, modern Greek.

Boston University, Graduate School of Arts and Sciences, Department of Classical Studies, Boston, MA 02215. Offers MA, PhD, MA/PhD. Terminal master's awarded for partial completion of doctoral program. *Degree requirements:* For master's, one foreign language, comprehensive exam; for doctorate, 2 foreign languages, comprehensive exam, thesis/dissertation. *Entrance requirements:* For master's and doctorate, GRE General Test, 3 letters of recommendation, scholarly writing sample, personal statement. Additional exam requirements/recommendations for international students: Required—TOEFL (minimum score 550 paper-based; 213 computer-based; 84 iBT). Electronic applications accepted. *Faculty research:* Homer and Hesiod, tragedy and comedy, classical tradition, fifth century Athenian history, empire literature and history.

Boston University, School of Education, Department of Curriculum and Teaching, Program in Latin and Classical Studies, Boston, MA 02215. Offers MAT. *Degree requirements:* For master's, comprehensive exam, thesis optional. *Entrance requirements:* For master's, GRE General Test or MAT. Additional exam requirements/recommendations for international students: Required—TOEFL. Electronic applications accepted.

Brandeis University, Graduate School of Arts and Sciences, Program in Classics, Waltham, MA 02454-9110. Offers Graduate Certificate. Part-time programs available. *Entrance requirements:* Additional exam requirements/recommendations for international students: Required—TOEFL (minimum score 600 paper-based; 250 computer-based; 100 iBT), IELTS (minimum score 7). Electronic applications accepted.

Brock University, Faculty of Graduate Studies, Faculty of Humanities, Program in Classics, St. Catharines, ON L2S 3A1, Canada. Offers MA. Part-time programs available. *Degree requirements:* For master's, thesis. *Entrance requirements:* For master's, honors degreee. Additional exam requirements/recommendations for international students: Required—TOEFL (minimum score 550 paper-based; 213 computer-based; 80 iBT), IELTS (minimum score 6.5), TWE (minimum score 4). Electronic applications accepted.

Brown University, Graduate School, Department of Classics, Providence, RI 02912. Offers MA, PhD. *Degree requirements:* For master's, one foreign language, thesis; for doctorate, 2 foreign languages, thesis/dissertation. *Entrance requirements:* For master's and doctorate, GRE General Test. *Faculty research:* Philology, archaeology, Sanskrit.

Bryn Mawr College, Graduate School of Arts and Sciences, Department of Greek, Latin, and Classical Studies, Bryn Mawr, PA 19010-2899. Offers MA, PhD. Part-time programs available. *Degree requirements:* For master's, 2 foreign languages, thesis; for doctorate, 3 foreign languages, comprehensive exam, thesis/dissertation. *Entrance requirements:* For master's and doctorate, GRE General Test. Additional exam requirements/recommendations for international students: Required—TOEFL (minimum score 600 paper-based; 250 computer-based).

See Close-Up on page 439.

The Catholic University of America, School of Arts and Sciences, Department of Greek and Latin, Washington, DC 20064. Offers classics (MA); Greek and Latin (PhD); Latin (MA); MSLS/MA. Part-time programs available. Terminal master's awarded for partial completion of doctoral program. *Degree requirements:* For master's, one foreign language, comprehensive exam; for doctorate, 2 foreign languages, comprehensive exam, thesis/dissertation. *Entrance requirements:* For master's and doctorate, GRE General Test, 3 letters of recommendation, writing sample. Additional exam requirements/recommendations for international students: Required—TOEFL (minimum score 580 paper-based; 237 computer-based). Electronic applications accepted. *Faculty research:* Greek and Latin patristics, medieval Latin, computers and classics, late antique history, late antique Byzantine art history.

Columbia University, Graduate School of Arts and Sciences, Division of Humanities, Department of Classics, New York, NY 10027. Offers M Phil, MA, PhD. *Degree requirements:* For master's, one foreign language, seminar paper; for doctorate, 3 foreign languages, thesis/dissertation. *Entrance requirements:* For master's, GRE General Test, reading knowledge of Greek or Latin; for doctorate, GRE General Test, reading knowledge of Greek and Latin. Additional exam requirements/recommendations for international students: Required—TOEFL. *Faculty research:* Greek and Latin literature, ancient philosophy.

Cornell University, Graduate School, Graduate Fields of Arts and Sciences, Field of Classics, Ithaca, NY 14853-0001. Offers ancient history (PhD); ancient philosophy (PhD); classical archaeology (PhD); classical myth (PhD); classical rhetoric (PhD); Greek and Latin language and linguistics (PhD); Greek language and literature (PhD); Indo-European linguistics (PhD); Latin language and literature (PhD); medieval and Renaissance Latin literature (PhD). *Faculty:* 25 full-time (6 women). *Students:* 16 full-time (3 women), 6 international. Average age 27. 61 applicants, 7% accepted, 1 enrolled. In 2008, 2 doctorates awarded. *Degree requirements:* For doctorate, 2 foreign languages, comprehensive exam, thesis/dissertation. *Entrance requirements:* For doctorate, GRE General Test, 3 letters of recommendation, sample of written work. Additional exam requirements/recommendations for international students: Required—TOEFL (minimum score 550 paper-based; 213 computer-based; 77 iBT). *Application deadline:* For fall admission, 1/15 for domestic students. Application fee: $70. Electronic applications accepted. *Expenses:* Tuition: Full-time $29,500. Required fees: $70. Full-time tuition and fees vary according to degree level, program and student level. *Financial support:* In 2008–09, 16 students received support, including 5 fellowships with full tuition reimbursements available, 11 teaching assistantships with full tuition reimbursements available; research assistantships with full tuition reimbursements available, institutionally sponsored loans, scholarships/grants, health care benefits, tuition waivers (full and partial), and unspecified assistantships also available. Financial award applicants required to submit FAFSA. *Faculty research:* Greek and Roman literature, ancient philosophy, Greek and Roman archaeology, ancient history, Indo-European linguistics. *Unit head:* Director of Graduate Studies, 607-255-3354. *Application contact:* Graduate Field Assistant, 607-255-3354, E-mail: classics@cornell.edu.

Dalhousie University, Faculty of Arts and Social Science, Department of Classics, Halifax, NS B3H 4R2, Canada. Offers MA, PhD. *Entrance requirements:* Additional exam requirements/ recommendations for international students: Required—TOEFL, IELTS, 1 of 5 approved tests: TOEFL, IELTS, CANTEST, CAEL, Michigan English Language Assessment Battery. *Application deadline:* For fall admission, 6/1 for domestic students, 4/1 for international students; for winter admission, 10/31 for domestic students, 8/31 for international students; for spring admission, 2/28 for domestic students, 12/31 for international students. Application fee: $70. Electronic

applications accepted. *Financial support:* In 2008–09, 10 students received support. Career-related internships or fieldwork, scholarships/grants, and health care benefits available. *Unit head:* Dr. Leona MacLeod, Chair, 902-494-2280, Fax: 902-494-2467, E-mail: claswww@ dal.ca. *Application contact:* Dr. Peter O'Brien, Graduate Coordinator, 902-494-3468, Fax: 902-494-2467, E-mail: claswww@dal.ca.

Duke University, Graduate School, Department of Classical Studies, Durham, NC 27708-0586. Offers PhD. *Degree requirements:* For doctorate, 2 foreign languages, thesis/dissertation. *Entrance requirements:* For doctorate, GRE General Test. Additional exam requirements/ recommendations for international students: Required—TOEFL (minimum score 550 paper-based; 213 computer-based; 83 iBT), IELTS (minimum score 7). Electronic applications accepted. *Faculty research:* Greek Bronze Age; classical and Roman archaeology; Pompeii and Hadrian; epigraphy, papyrology, and Latin paleography.

Florida State University, Graduate Studies, College of Arts and Sciences, Department of Classics, Tallahassee, FL 32306. Offers classical archaeology (MA); classical civilization (MA); classics (MA, PhD), including archaeology (PhD), literature and languages (PhD); Greek (MA); Greek and Latin (MA); Latin (MA). Part-time programs available. *Degree requirements:* For master's, one foreign language, comprehensive exam (for some programs), thesis (for some programs); for doctorate, 2 foreign languages, comprehensive exam, thesis/dissertation. *Entrance requirements:* For master's, GRE General Test, minimum GPA of 3.0; for doctorate, GRE General Test. Additional exam requirements/recommendations for international students: Required—TOEFL. Electronic applications accepted. *Faculty research:* Greek and Latin literature, mythology, classical archaeology, history, Roman religion.

Fordham University, Graduate School of Arts and Sciences, Department of Classical Languages and Literatures, New York, NY 10458. Offers classical Greek and Latin literature (MA); classics (PhD). Part-time and evening/weekend programs available. Terminal master's awarded for partial completion of doctoral program. *Degree requirements:* For master's, one foreign language, comprehensive exam; for doctorate, 2 foreign languages, comprehensive exam, thesis/dissertation. *Entrance requirements:* For master's and doctorate, GRE General Test. Additional exam requirements/recommendations for international students: Required—TOEFL (minimum score 650 paper-based; 280 computer-based). Electronic applications accepted.

Graduate School and University Center of the City University of New York, Graduate Studies, Program in Classics, New York, NY 10016-4039. Offers MA, PhD. *Degree requirements:* For master's, 2 foreign languages, thesis; for doctorate, 2 foreign languages, thesis/dissertation. *Entrance requirements:* For master's and doctorate, GRE General Test. Additional exam requirements/recommendations for international students: Required—TOEFL. Electronic applications accepted.

Graduate School and University Center of the City University of New York, Graduate Studies, Program in Comparative Literature, New York, NY 10016-4039. Offers comparative literature (MA, PhD), including classics (PhD), German (PhD), Italian (PhD). Terminal master's awarded for partial completion of doctoral program. *Degree requirements:* For master's, 2 foreign languages, comprehensive exam, thesis; for doctorate, 3 foreign languages, comprehensive exam, thesis/dissertation. *Entrance requirements:* For master's and doctorate, GRE General Test. Additional exam requirements/recommendations for international students: Required—TOEFL. Electronic applications accepted.

Harvard University, Graduate School of Arts and Sciences, Department of the Classics, Cambridge, MA 02138. Offers Byzantine Greek (PhD); classical archaeology (PhD); classical philology (PhD); classical philosophy (PhD); medieval Latin (PhD). *Degree requirements:* For doctorate, 4 foreign languages, thesis/dissertation, preliminary and special exams. *Entrance requirements:* For doctorate, GRE General Test. Additional exam requirements/recommendations for international students: Required—TOEFL. *Expenses:* Tuition: Full-time $32,556. Required fees: $1426. Full-time tuition and fees vary according to program and student level.

Heritage Christian University, Graduate Programs, Florence, AL 35630. Offers counseling (MM); Greek (MA); ministry (MM); New Testament (MA). *Degree requirements:* For master's, practicum (MM), major research paper (MA). *Entrance requirements:* For master's, MAT or GRE, bachelor's degree in Bible from an accredited college or university, minimum GPA of 2.75, 3 letters of recommendation.

Hunter College of the City University of New York, Graduate School, School of Arts and Sciences, Department of Classical and Oriental Studies, Program in Teaching Latin, New York, NY 10021-5085. Offers MA. Part-time and evening/weekend programs available. *Faculty:* 2 full-time (1 woman). *Students:* 2 full-time (0 women), 14 part-time (9 women). Average age 33. 3 applicants, 100% accepted, 2 enrolled. In 2008, 3 master's awarded. *Degree requirements:* For master's, one foreign language, comprehensive exam. *Entrance requirements:* For master's, undergraduate major in Latin or equivalent with a minimum GPA of 3.0, 2.8 overall; interview, 2 letters of recommendation. Additional exam requirements/recommendations for international students: Required—TOEFL. *Application deadline:* For fall admission, 4/28 for domestic students; for spring admission, 11/21 for domestic students. Application fee: $125. *Financial support:* Federal Work-Study, scholarships/grants, and tuition waivers (partial) available. Support available to part-time students. Financial award application deadline: 4/15. *Faculty research:* Late antique religion and social history, women in antiquity, Horace and lyric poetry, Roman comedy, Latin prose. *Unit head:* Dr. Ronnie Aucona, Director, 212-772-4960, E-mail: rancona@hunter. cuny.edu. *Application contact:* William Zlata, Director of Admissions, 212-772-4482, E-mail: admissions@hunter.cuny.edu.

Indiana University Bloomington, University Graduate School, College of Arts and Sciences, Department of Classical Studies, Bloomington, IN 47405. Offers MA, MAT, PhD. Part-time programs available. *Faculty:* 5 full-time (3 women). *Students:* 29 full-time (14 women), 3 part-time (2 women), 2 international. Average age 30. 16 applicants, 44% accepted, 3 enrolled. In 2008, 2 master's, 1 doctorate awarded. *Degree requirements:* For master's, 2 foreign languages, comprehensive exam; for doctorate, 3 foreign languages, thesis/dissertation. *Entrance requirements:* For master's and doctorate, GRE, minimum GPA of 3.0. Additional exam requirements/recommendations for international students: Required—TOEFL. *Application deadline:* For fall admission, 1/15 priority date for domestic students, 12/15 for international students; for spring admission, 9/1 priority date for domestic students, 9/1 for international students. Applications are processed on a rolling basis. Application fee: $50 ($60 for international students). *Expenses:* Tuition, area resident: Part-time $291.97 per credit hour. Tuition, state resident: part-time $291.97 per credit hour. Tuition, nonresident: part-time $850.33 per credit hour. Required fees: $110 per semester. Tuition and fees vary according to course load and program. *Financial support:* Fellowships with full tuition reimbursements, teaching assistantships with full tuition reimbursements, Federal Work-Study available. *Faculty research:* Roman literature (particularly Empire and late Latin), Greek drama, Homer, history of ideas, papyrology.

Classics

Indiana University Bloomington (continued)
Unit head: Prof. Matthew Christ, Chair, 812-855-6651. *Application contact:* Yvette Rollins, Graduate Secretary, 812-855-6651, E-mail: rollinsy@indiana.edu.

The Johns Hopkins University, Zanvyl Krieger School of Arts and Sciences, Department of Classics, Baltimore, MD 21218-2699. Offers PhD. Terminal master's awarded for partial completion of doctoral program. *Degree requirements:* For doctorate, 4 foreign languages, thesis/dissertation. *Entrance requirements:* For doctorate, GRE General Test. Additional exam requirements/recommendations for international students: Required—TOEFL (minimum score 600 paper-based; 250 computer-based), IELTS (minimum score 7). Electronic applications accepted. *Faculty research:* Greek culture and mythology, classical sculpture, Early Imperial Roman society.

Kent State University, College of Arts and Sciences, Department of Modern and Classical Language Studies, Kent, OH 44242-0001. Offers French literature (MA); French, Spanish, German and Latin pedagogy (MA); German literature (MA); Spanish literature (MA); translation (MA), including French, German, Japanese, Russian, Spanish; translation studies (PhD). Part-time and evening/weekend programs available. *Degree requirements:* For master's, one foreign language, comprehensive exam (for some programs), thesis (for some programs); for doctorate, comprehensive exam, thesis/dissertation (for some programs). *Entrance requirements:* For master's, minimum GPA of 3.0, writing sample, audio tape or CD; for doctorate, 3 recommendations. Additional exam requirements/recommendations for international students: Required—TOEFL (minimum score 197 computer-based). Electronic applications accepted. *Faculty research:* Literature, pedagogy, applied linguistics, translation studies.

Marshall University, Academic Affairs Division, College of Liberal Arts, Program in Latin, Huntington, WV 25755. Offers MA.

McMaster University, School of Graduate Studies, Faculty of Humanities, Department of Classics, Hamilton, ON L8S 4M2, Canada. Offers MA, PhD. *Degree requirements:* For master's, one foreign language, thesis or alternative; for doctorate, 2 foreign languages, comprehensive exam, thesis/dissertation. *Entrance requirements:* For master's, honors degree, minimum B+ average. Additional exam requirements/recommendations for international students: Required—TOEFL (minimum score 580 paper-based; 237 computer-based). *Faculty research:* Ancient history, art and archaeology, Latin language and literature, Greek language and literature.

Memorial University of Newfoundland, School of Graduate Studies, Department of Classics, St. John's, NL A1C 5S7, Canada. Offers MA. Part-time programs available. *Degree requirements:* For master's, one foreign language, thesis, language exam, translation exam, research essay. *Entrance requirements:* For master's, honors degree in related field, course work in Greek and Latin. Electronic applications accepted. *Faculty research:* Ancient history, historiography, literature, drama, philosophy, paleography, epigraphy, and textual criticism.

New York University, Graduate School of Arts and Science, Department of Classics, New York, NY 10012-1019. Offers classics (MA, PhD); poetics and theory (Advanced Certificate). Part-time programs available. *Degree requirements:* For master's, 4 foreign languages, exam or specialized project; for doctorate, 4 foreign languages, thesis/dissertation, exams. *Entrance requirements:* For master's, GRE General Test, knowledge of Greek and Latin history and literature, proficiency in Greek and Latin translation; for doctorate, GRE General Test. Additional exam requirements/recommendations for international students: Required—TOEFL. *Faculty research:* Greek and Latin literature, Greek and Roman history, epigraphy, Greek and Roman philosophy, classical archeology.

The Ohio State University, Graduate School, College of Humanities, Program in Classics, Columbus, OH 43210. Offers MA, PhD. Electronic applications accepted.

The Ohio State University, Graduate School, College of Humanities, Programs in Greek and Latin, Columbus, OH 43210. Offers ancient Greek (MA); Greek studies (MA, PhD); Latin studies (MA, PhD); modern Greek (MA, PhD). *Degree requirements:* For master's, 2 foreign languages; for doctorate, 2 foreign languages, thesis/dissertation. *Entrance requirements:* For master's and doctorate, GRE General Test. Additional exam requirements/recommendations for international students: Required—TOEFL (minimum score 600 paper-based; 250 computer-based). Electronic applications accepted.

Princeton University, Graduate School, Department of Classics, Princeton, NJ 08544-1019. Offers classical and hellenic studies (PhD); classical philosophy (PhD); history (the ancient world) (PhD); literature and philology (PhD). *Degree requirements:* For doctorate, thesis/dissertation. *Entrance requirements:* For doctorate, GRE General Test, sample of written work. Additional exam requirements/recommendations for international students: Required—TOEFL (minimum score 600 paper-based; 250 computer-based). Electronic applications accepted.

Queen's University at Kingston, School of Graduate Studies and Research, Faculty of Arts and Sciences, Department of Classics, Kingston, ON K7L 3N6, Canada. Offers classics, Greek, Latin (MA). Part-time programs available. *Degree requirements:* For master's, one foreign language, thesis (for some programs). *Entrance requirements:* For master's, 3 years of Latin, 2 years of Greek. Additional exam requirements/recommendations for international students: Required—TOEFL. Electronic applications accepted. *Faculty research:* Greek and Latin literature, Greek and Roman history, ancient philosophy, Greek archaeology.

Rutgers, The State University of New Jersey, New Brunswick, Graduate School, Department of Classics, Piscataway, NJ 08854-8097. Offers classics (MA, MAT, PhD); interdisciplinary classical studies and ancient history (MA, PhD). Part-time and evening/weekend programs available. Terminal master's awarded for partial completion of doctoral program. *Degree requirements:* For master's, 3 foreign languages, comprehensive exam, thesis or alternative; for doctorate, 3 foreign languages, comprehensive exam, thesis/dissertation. *Entrance requirements:* For master's and doctorate, GRE General Test. *Faculty research:* Greek and Latin literature, Greek and Roman social and political history, mythology, religion, ancient philosophy.

San Francisco State University, Division of Graduate Studies, College of Humanities, Department of Classics, San Francisco, CA 94132-1722. Offers MA. Part-time programs available.

Stanford University, School of Humanities and Sciences, Department of Classics, Stanford, CA 94305-9991. Offers MA, PhD. *Degree requirements:* For master's, 2 foreign languages, thesis or alternative; for doctorate, 4 foreign languages, thesis/dissertation, general exams. *Entrance requirements:* For master's and doctorate, GRE General Test. Additional exam requirements/recommendations for international students: Required—TOEFL. Electronic applications accepted.

Texas Tech University, Graduate School, College of Arts and Sciences, Department of Classical and Modern Languages and Literatures, Program in Classics, Lubbock, TX 79409. Offers MA. *Students:* 7 full-time (0 women), 1 part-time (0 women); includes 2 minority (1 Asian American or Pacific Islander, 1 Hispanic American). Average age 26. 9 applicants, 89% accepted, 5 enrolled. In 2008, 2 master's awarded. *Entrance requirements:* For master's, GRE General Test. Additional exam requirements/recommendations for international students: Required—TOEFL (minimum score 550 paper-based; 213 computer-based). *Application deadline:* For fall admission, 3/1 priority date for international students; for spring admission, 11/1 priority date for international students. Applications are processed on a rolling basis. Application fee: $50 ($60 for international students). Electronic applications accepted. *Expenses:* Tuition, area resident: Part-time $194 per credit hour. Tuition, state resident: full-time $4648; part-time $194 per credit hour. Tuition, nonresident: full-time $11,392; part-time $475 per credit hour. Required fees: $2206; $69 per credit hour. $389 per semester. *Financial support:* Research assistantships with partial tuition reimbursements, teaching assistantships with partial tuition reimbursements available. Financial award application deadline: 4/15. *Faculty*

research: Greek and Latin language; literature and criticism; art history; gender and sexuality. *Unit head:* Dr. David H.J. Larmour, Professor and Graduate Advisor, 806-742-3145 Ext. 260, Fax: 806-742-3306, E-mail: david.larmour@ttu.edu. *Application contact:* Liz Hildebrand, Senior Advisor, 806-742-4055, Fax: 806-742-3306, E-mail: liz.hildebrand@ttu.edu.

Tufts University, Graduate School of Arts and Sciences, Department of Classics, Medford, MA 02155. Offers classical archaeology (MA); classics (MA). Part-time programs available. *Degree requirements:* For master's, 2 foreign languages, comprehensive exam, thesis or alternative. *Entrance requirements:* For master's, GRE General Test, writing sample. Additional exam requirements/recommendations for international students: Required—TOEFL (minimum score 550 paper-based; 213 computer-based; 80 iBT). Electronic applications accepted.

Tulane University, School of Liberal Arts, Department of Classical Studies, New Orleans, LA 70118-5669. Offers MA. *Degree requirements:* For master's, 2 foreign languages, thesis or alternative. *Entrance requirements:* For master's, GRE General Test, minimum B average in undergraduate course work. Additional exam requirements/recommendations for international students: Required—TOEFL. Electronic applications accepted.

University at Buffalo, the State University of New York, Graduate School, College of Arts and Sciences, Department of Classics, Buffalo, NY 14260. Offers MA, PhD. Terminal master's awarded for partial completion of doctoral program. *Degree requirements:* For master's, 3 foreign languages, project; for doctorate, 4 foreign languages, thesis/dissertation, general and 2 special exams. *Entrance requirements:* For master's and doctorate, GRE General Test. Additional exam requirements/recommendations for international students: Required—TOEFL. Electronic applications accepted. *Expenses:* Contact institution. *Faculty research:* Greek and Latin literature, historiography, and epigraphy; Greek archaeology, mythology, and ancient philosophy; ancient and Roman religion and women's studies.

University of Alberta, Faculty of Graduate Studies and Research, Department of History and Classics, Edmonton, AB T6G 2E1, Canada. Offers ancient history (PhD); classical archaeology (MA, PhD); classical literature (PhD); classics (MA); history (MA, PhD). Part-time and evening/weekend programs available. *Degree requirements:* For master's, one foreign language, thesis (for some programs); for doctorate, one foreign language, thesis/dissertation. *Entrance requirements:* For master's, minimum B+ average; for doctorate, minimum A- average. Additional exam requirements/recommendations for international students: Required—TOEFL (minimum score 580 paper-based; 237 computer-based). Electronic applications accepted. *Faculty research:* Western Canada, classical archaeology, Britain, Eastern Europe, East Asia.

The University of Arizona, Graduate College, College of Humanities, Department of Classics, Tucson, AZ 85721. Offers MA. Part-time programs available. *Degree requirements:* For master's, one foreign language, comprehensive exam, thesis. *Entrance requirements:* For master's, GRE General Test, BA in classics, 2 letters of recommendation, letter of intent. Additional exam requirements/recommendations for international students: Required—TOEFL (minimum score 550 paper-based). Electronic applications accepted. *Faculty research:* Greek and Roman archaeology, ancient Greek, modern Greek, Latin, Greek and Roman religion, women in antiquity.

The University of British Columbia, Faculty of Arts and Faculty of Graduate Studies, Department of Classical, Near Eastern and Religious Studies, Programmes in Classics, Vancouver, BC V6T 1Z1, Canada. Offers ancient culture, religion, and ethnicity (MA); classical and near eastern archaeology (MA); classics (MA, PhD). Part-time programs available. *Degree requirements:* For master's, 2 foreign languages, thesis or comprehensive exam; for doctorate, 2 foreign languages, comprehensive exam, thesis/dissertation. *Entrance requirements:* For master's, upper second class standing; for doctorate, MA degree. Additional exam requirements/recommendations for international students: Required—TOEFL (minimum score 600 paper-based; 250 computer-based), IELTS (minimum score 7.5). Electronic applications accepted. *Faculty research:* Classical archaeology, ancient historians, late antiquity, ancient prose fiction, epigraphy.

University of Calgary, Faculty of Graduate Studies, Faculty of Humanities, Department of Greek and Roman Studies, Calgary, AB T2N 1N4, Canada. Offers MA, PhD. Part-time programs available. *Degree requirements:* For master's, one foreign language; for doctorate, 2 foreign languages, comprehensive exam, thesis/dissertation. *Entrance requirements:* For master's, BA in classics or related field, knowledge of Latin and/or Greek, minimum GPA of 3.7; for doctorate, MA in classics or related field, knowledge of Latin and Greek, GPA 3.7. Additional exam requirements/recommendations for international students: Required—TOEFL. Electronic applications accepted. *Faculty research:* Greek literature, Latin literature, Greek history, Roman history, classical archaeology.

University of California, Berkeley, Graduate Division, College of Letters and Science, Department of Classics, Berkeley, CA 94720-1500. Offers classical archaeology (MA, PhD); classics (MA, PhD); Greek (MA); Latin (MA). Terminal master's awarded for partial completion of doctoral program. *Degree requirements:* For master's, one foreign language, exams; for doctorate, 2 foreign languages, thesis/dissertation, qualifying exam. *Entrance requirements:* For master's and doctorate, GRE General Test, minimum GPA of 3.0, 3 letters of recommendation. Additional exam requirements/recommendations for international students: Required—TOEFL (minimum score 570 paper-based; 230 computer-based), TWE. *Faculty research:* Greek and Latin literature, textual criticism, history, archaeology and philosophy.

University of California, Irvine, Office of Graduate Studies, School of Humanities, Department of Classics, Irvine, CA 92697. Offers MA, PhD. Terminal master's awarded for partial completion of doctoral program. *Degree requirements:* For master's, one foreign language, thesis or alternative; for doctorate, 2 foreign languages, thesis/dissertation. *Entrance requirements:* For master's and doctorate, GRE General Test, minimum GPA of 3.0. Additional exam requirements/recommendations for international students: Required—TOEFL (minimum score 550 paper-based; 213 computer-based). Electronic applications accepted. *Faculty research:* Greek literature, computer application to Greek literature, Latin literature.

University of California, Los Angeles, Graduate Division, College of Letters and Science, Department of Classics, Los Angeles, CA 90095. Offers classics (MA, PhD); Greek (MA); Latin (MA). *Students:* 22 full-time (11 women). Average age 28. 61 applicants, 18% accepted, 5 enrolled. In 2008, 4 master's, 1 doctorate awarded. *Degree requirements:* For master's, 2 foreign languages, comprehensive exam; for doctorate, 2 foreign languages, thesis/dissertation, oral and written qualifying exams. *Entrance requirements:* For master's, GRE General Test, minimum GPA of 3.0, sample of written work; for doctorate, GRE General Test, minimum undergraduate GPA of 3.0, sample of written work, MA degree in classics. *Application deadline:* For fall admission, 12/15 for domestic and international students. Application fee: $60 ($80 for international students). Electronic applications accepted. *Expenses:* Tuition, nonresident: full-time $14,694. Required fees: $9669.50. Full-time tuition and fees vary according to course load, degree level, program and student level. *Financial support:* In 2008–09, 30 fellowships with full and partial tuition reimbursements, 2 research assistantships with full and partial tuition reimbursements, 2 teaching assistantships with full and partial tuition reimbursements were awarded; Federal Work-Study, institutionally sponsored loans, scholarships/grants, health care benefits, tuition waivers (full and partial), and unspecified assistantships also available. Financial award application deadline: 3/1; financial award applicants required to submit FAFSA. *Faculty research:* Homeric studies, archaeology, ancient comedy, ancient philosophy, Augustan poetry. *Unit head:* Dr. David Blank, Chair, 310-206-8652. *Application contact:* Departmental Office, 310-206-1590, E-mail: dabugheida@humnet.ucla.edu.

University of California, Riverside, Graduate Division, Tri-Campus Program in Classics, Riverside, CA 92521-0102. Offers PhD. *Degree requirements:* For doctorate, 3 foreign languages, comprehensive exam, thesis/dissertation. *Entrance requirements:* For doctorate, GRE, MA in classics. Additional exam requirements/recommendations for international students: Required—TOEFL (minimum score 550 paper-based; 213 computer-based; 80 iBT). Electronic applications accepted. *Expenses:* Tuition, nonresident: full-time $4898. Required fees: $10,362.

Faculty research: Rhetoric, Greek and Latin drama, Hellenistic poetry, Anglo-Latin literature, Greek and Latin prose.

University of California, Santa Barbara, Graduate Division, College of Letters and Sciences, Division of Humanities and Fine Arts, Department of Classics, Santa Barbara, CA 93106-3120. Offers ancient history (MA, PhD); classics (MA); literature and theory (PhD); MA/PhD. *Faculty:* 8 full-time (4 women). *Students:* 15 full-time (9 women). Average age 27. 30 applicants, 50% accepted, 4 enrolled. In 2008, 2 master's awarded. Terminal master's awarded for partial completion of doctoral program. *Degree requirements:* For master's, 3 foreign languages, comprehensive exam, thesis optional; for doctorate, 4 foreign languages, comprehensive exam, thesis/dissertation. *Entrance requirements:* For master's, GRE, BA in classics, minimum 2 years of college course work in Latin and Greek, writing sample, 3 letters of recommendation, statement of purpose, personal achievements/contributions statement, resumé/curriculum vitae, transcripts for post-secondary institutions attended; for doctorate, GRE, MA in classics, writing sample, 3 letters of recommendation, statement of purpose, personal achievements/contributions statement, resumé/curriculum vitae, transcripts for post-secondary institutions attended. Additional exam requirements/recommendations for international students: Required—TOEFL (minimum score 550 paper-based; 213 computer-based; 80 iBT), IELTS (minimum score 7), TOEFL or IELTS. *Application deadline:* For fall admission, 12/8 priority date for domestic and international students; for winter admission, 11/1 for domestic and international students; for spring admission, 2/1 for domestic and international students. Applications are processed on a rolling basis. Application fee: $70 ($90 for international students). Electronic applications accepted. *Expenses:* Tuition, nonresident: full-time $25,149. Required fees: $10,143. Full-time tuition and fees vary according to campus/location, reciprocity agreements and student level. *Financial support:* In 2008–09, 15 students received support, including 5 fellowships with full and partial tuition reimbursements available (averaging $4,600 per year), 1 research assistantship with partial tuition reimbursement available (averaging $1,600 per year), 14 teaching assistantships with partial tuition reimbursements available (averaging $10,500 per year); Federal Work-Study, institutionally sponsored loans, scholarships/grants, traineeships, health care benefits, tuition waivers (partial), unspecified assistantships, and readerships also available. Financial award application deadline: 12/8; financial award applicants required to submit FAFSA. *Faculty research:* Literary theory and cultural history, gender studies, Greek and Latin literature, Greek and Roman History, drama and performance. Total annual research expenditures: $35,000. *Unit head:* Prof. Robert Morstein-Marx, Chair, 805-893-3007, Fax: 805-893-4487, E-mail: morstein@classics.ucsb.edu. *Application contact:* Prof. Frances Hahn, Graduate Advisor, 805-893-3605, Fax: 805-893-4487, E-mail: fhahn@classics.ucsb.edu.

University of Chicago, Division of the Humanities, Department of Classics, Chicago, IL 60637-1513. Offers ancient philosophy (AM, PhD); classical archaeology (AM, PhD); classical languages and literatures (AM, PhD). Terminal master's awarded for partial completion of doctoral program. *Degree requirements:* For master's, one foreign language, thesis; for doctorate, 2 foreign languages, thesis/dissertation. *Entrance requirements:* For master's and doctorate, GRE General Test. Additional exam requirements/recommendations for international students: Required—TOEFL.

University of Cincinnati, Graduate School, McMicken College of Arts and Sciences, Department of Classics, Cincinnati, OH 45221. Offers MA, PhD. Part-time programs available. Terminal master's awarded for partial completion of doctoral program. *Degree requirements:* For master's, comprehensive exam (for some programs), thesis (for some programs); for doctorate, 2 foreign languages, comprehensive exam, thesis/dissertation. *Entrance requirements:* For master's and doctorate, GRE. Additional exam requirements/recommendations for international students: Required—TOEFL. Electronic applications accepted. *Faculty research:* Archaeology (bronze age and classical), philosophy (Greek and Latin), ancient history (Greek and Roman).

University of Colorado at Boulder, Graduate School, College of Arts and Sciences, Department of Classics, Boulder, CO 80309. Offers MA, PhD. Part-time programs available. Terminal master's awarded for partial completion of doctoral program. *Degree requirements:* For master's, one foreign language, comprehensive exam, thesis or alternative, oral exam; for doctorate, 4 foreign languages, comprehensive exam, thesis/dissertation. *Entrance requirements:* For master's, minimum undergraduate GPA of 2.75; for doctorate, master's degree in classics or related field. *Faculty research:* Roman and Greek history, Roman and Greek art and architecture, comparative literature, Greek philosophy, textual criticism, Greek and Latin poetry, Greek and Latin prose.

University of Florida, Graduate School, College of Liberal Arts and Sciences, Department of Classics, Gainesville, FL 32611. Offers classical studies (MA, PhD); Latin (MA, MAT, ML). Part-time programs available. Postbaccalaureate distance learning degree programs offered. *Degree requirements:* For master's, 2 foreign languages, thesis; for doctorate, 2 foreign languages, thesis/dissertation. *Entrance requirements:* For master's, GRE General Test, minimum GPA of 3.0; for doctorate, GRE General Test, minimum GPA of 3.0, MA in classical studies. Additional exam requirements/recommendations for international students: Required—TOEFL (minimum score 550 paper-based; 213 computer-based). Electronic applications accepted. *Faculty research:* Greek, literature, epigraphy.

University of Georgia, Graduate School, College of Arts and Sciences, Department of Classics, Athens, GA 30602. Offers classical languages (MA); Greek (MA); Latin (MA). *Degree requirements:* For master's, one foreign language, thesis. *Entrance requirements:* For master's, GRE General Test. Electronic applications accepted.

University of Illinois at Urbana–Champaign, Graduate College, College of Liberal Arts and Sciences, School of Literatures, Cultures and Linguistics, Department of the Classics, Champaign, IL 61820. Offers classical philology (PhD); classics (MA); teaching of Latin (MA). *Faculty:* 10 full-time (4 women). *Students:* 11 full-time (7 women), 1 part-time (0 women); includes 1 minority (Asian American or Pacific Islander), 2 international. 13 applicants, 54% accepted, 2 enrolled. In 2008, 9 master's awarded. *Entrance requirements:* For master's and doctorate, GRE, writing sample; minimum GPA of 3.0. Additional exam requirements/recommendations for international students: Required—TOEFL (minimum score 79 iBT). *Application deadline:* Applications are processed on a rolling basis. Application fee: $60 ($75 for international students). Electronic applications accepted. *Financial support:* In 2008–09, 4 fellowships, 11 teaching assistantships were awarded; research assistantships, tuition waivers (full and partial) also available. *Faculty research:* Greek and Latin language, papyrology, epigraphy, classical archaeology. *Unit head:* David Sansone, Head, 217-333-7573, Fax: 217-244-8430, E-mail: dsansone@illinois.edu. *Application contact:* Lynn Stanke, Administrative Secretary, 217-333-6269, Fax: 217-244-3050, E-mail: stanke@illinois.edu.

The University of Iowa, Graduate College, College of Liberal Arts and Sciences, Department of Classics, Iowa City, IA 52242-1316. Offers MA, PhD. *Degree requirements:* For master's, thesis optional, exam; for doctorate, comprehensive exam, thesis/dissertation. *Entrance requirements:* For master's and doctorate, GRE General Test, minimum GPA of 3.0. Additional exam requirements/recommendations for international students: Required—TOEFL (minimum score 550 paper-based; 213 computer-based; 81 iBT). Electronic applications accepted.

The University of Kansas, Graduate Studies, College of Liberal Arts and Sciences, Department of Classics, Lawrence, KS 66045. Offers MA. Part-time programs available. *Faculty:* 8 full-time (3 women), 3 part-time/adjunct (2 women). *Students:* 12 full-time (6 women), 1 part-time (0 women). Average age 26. 7 applicants, 71% accepted, 5 enrolled. In 2008, 6 master's awarded. *Degree requirements:* For master's, 3 foreign languages, comprehensive exam, thesis optional. *Entrance requirements:* For master's, GRE (recommended), 15 junior/senior hours of course work in Latin and/or Greek (recommended). Additional exam requirements/recommendations for international students: Required—TOEFL. *Application deadline:* For fall admission, 5/1 priority date for domestic students, 2/1 priority date for international students; for spring admission, 1/15 priority date for domestic students, 9/1 priority date for international students. Applications are processed on a rolling basis. Application fee: $45 ($50 for international students). Electronic applications accepted. *Expenses:* Tuition, area resident: Full-time $6122; part-time $255.10 per credit hour. Tuition, state resident: full-time $6122; part-time $255.10 per credit hour. Tuition, nonresident: full-time $14,629; part-time $609.55 per credit hour. Required fees: $847; $70.56 per credit hour. Tuition and fees vary according to course load and program. *Financial support:* Fellowships with full tuition reimbursements, teaching assistantships with full and partial tuition reimbursements, career-related internships or fieldwork, Federal Work-Study, scholarships/grants, traineeships, and unspecified assistantships available. Support available to part-time students. *Faculty research:* Greek and Roman literature, Greek cultural history, Roman cultural history, translation theory, sex and gender. *Unit head:* Pam Gordon, Chair, 785-864-3153, Fax: 785-864-5566, E-mail: pgordon@ku.edu. *Application contact:* Tara Welch, Graduate Director, 785-864-2395, Fax: 785-864-5566, E-mail: tswelch@ku.edu.

University of Kentucky, Graduate School, College of Arts and Sciences, Program in Modern and Classical Languages and Literatures, Lexington, KY 40506-0032. Offers classics (MA). Part-time programs available. *Degree requirements:* For master's, one foreign language, comprehensive exam, thesis optional. *Entrance requirements:* For master's, GRE General Test, minimum undergraduate GPA of 2.75. Additional exam requirements/recommendations for international students: Required—TOEFL (minimum score 550 paper-based; 213 computer-based). Electronic applications accepted. *Faculty research:* Erasmus, Renaissance Latin, Greek and Roman epic, Greek biography, early Christian literature, classical philosophy.

University of Manitoba, Faculty of Graduate Studies, Faculty of Arts, Department of Classics, Winnipeg, MB R3T 2N2, Canada. Offers MA. *Degree requirements:* For master's, thesis.

University of Maryland, College Park, Graduate Studies, College of Arts and Humanities, Department of Classics, College Park, MD 20742. Offers MA. *Degree requirements:* For master's, 2 foreign languages, thesis or alternative. *Entrance requirements:* For master's, writing sample, 3 letters of recommendation. Additional exam requirements/recommendations for international students: Required—TOEFL. Electronic applications accepted. *Faculty research:* Latin, Greek, and Roman culture.

University of Massachusetts Amherst, Graduate School, College of Humanities and Fine Arts, Department of Classics, Amherst, MA 01003. Offers Latin and classical humanities (MAT). Part-time programs available. *Degree requirements:* For master's, thesis or alternative. *Entrance requirements:* For master's, GRE General Test. Additional exam requirements/recommendations for international students: Required—TOEFL (minimum score 550 paper-based; 213 computer-based; 79 iBT), IELTS (minimum score 6.5). Electronic applications accepted. *Expenses:* Tuition, area resident: Full-time $2640. Tuition, nonresident: full-time $9936. One-time fee: $332 full-time. Tuition and fees vary according to course load.

University of Michigan, Horace H. Rackham School of Graduate Studies, College of Literature, Science, and the Arts, Department of Classical Studies, Ann Arbor, MI 48109. Offers classical studies (PhD); Greek (AM); Latin (AM); teaching Latin (MAT). Terminal master's awarded for partial completion of doctoral program. *Degree requirements:* For master's, one foreign language, comprehensive exam; for doctorate, 4 foreign languages, thesis/dissertation, oral defense of dissertation, preliminary exam. *Entrance requirements:* For master's, GRE General Test; for doctorate, GRE General Test, 3 years college-level Latin; 2 years college-level Greek. Additional exam requirements/recommendations for international students: Required—TOEFL (minimum score 560 paper-based; 220 computer-based). Electronic applications accepted. *Faculty research:* Greek and Latin literature, ancient history, papyrology, archaeology.

University of Michigan, Horace H. Rackham School of Graduate Studies, College of Literature, Science, and the Arts, Interdepartmental Program in Greek and Roman History, Ann Arbor, MI 48109. Offers PhD, Certificate. *Degree requirements:* For doctorate, 4 foreign languages, comprehensive exam, thesis/dissertation, oral defense of dissertation, dissertation prospectus, preliminary exams. *Entrance requirements:* For doctorate, GRE, knowledge of classical Greek and Latin. Additional exam requirements/recommendations for international students: Required—TOEFL (minimum score 560 paper-based; 220 computer-based). Electronic applications accepted. *Faculty research:* Greek history, Roman history.

University of Minnesota, Twin Cities Campus, Graduate School, College of Liberal Arts, Department of Classical and Near Eastern Studies, Minneapolis, MN 55455-0213. Offers ancient and medieval art and archaeology (MA, PhD); classics (MA, PhD); Greek (MA, PhD); Latin (MA, PhD); religions in antiquity (MA). Part-time programs available. Terminal master's awarded for partial completion of doctoral program. *Degree requirements:* For master's, 2 foreign languages, comprehensive exam, thesis or alternative; for doctorate, variable foreign language requirement, comprehensive exam, thesis/dissertation. *Entrance requirements:* For master's and doctorate, GRE, 3 letters of recommendation, department application, writing sample, copies of transcripts, personal statement. Additional exam requirements/recommendations for international students: Required—TOEFL. Electronic applications accepted. *Faculty research:* Greek and Latin literature, archaeology, religions in antiquity, ancient Near East.

University of Mississippi, Graduate School, College of Liberal Arts, Department of Classics, Oxford, University, MS 38677. Offers MA. *Degree requirements:* For master's, thesis. *Entrance requirements:* For master's, GRE General Test, minimum GPA of 3.0. Additional exam requirements/recommendations for international students: Required—TOEFL. Electronic applications accepted.

University of Missouri–Columbia, Graduate School, College of Arts and Sciences, Department of Classical Studies, Columbia, MO 65211. Offers MA, PhD. *Faculty:* 10 full-time (2 women). *Students:* 13 full-time (7 women), 8 part-time (0 women), 2 international. Average age 29. 29 applicants, 24% accepted, 4 enrolled. In 2008, 4 master's awarded. Terminal master's awarded for partial completion of doctoral program. *Degree requirements:* For master's, one foreign language; for doctorate, 2 foreign languages, thesis/dissertation. *Entrance requirements:* For master's and doctorate, GRE General Test, minimum GPA of 3.0. Additional exam requirements/recommendations for international students: Required—TOEFL (minimum score 500 paper-based; 173 computer-based; 61 iBT), IELTS (minimum score 5.5). *Application deadline:* For fall admission, 4/1 priority date for domestic students; for winter admission, 11/1 for domestic students. Applications are processed on a rolling basis. Application fee: $45 ($60 for international students). *Financial support:* Fellowships, research assistantships, teaching assistantships, institutionally sponsored loans available. *Unit head:* Dr. Dennis Trout, Department Chair, 573-884-8593, E-mail: troutd@missouri.edu. *Application contact:* Debbie Strodtman, Administrative Assistant, 573-882-0679, E-mail: strodtmand@missouri.edu.

University of Nebraska–Lincoln, Graduate College, College of Arts and Sciences, Department of Classics and Religious Studies, Lincoln, NE 68588. Offers MA. *Faculty:* 9 full-time (2 women). *Students:* 3 full-time (0 women). Average age 33. In 2008, 2 master's awarded. *Degree requirements:* For master's, thesis optional. *Entrance requirements:* For master's, GRE. Additional exam requirements/recommendations for international students: Required—TOEFL (minimum score 550 paper-based; 213 computer-based). *Application deadline:* For fall admission, 3/15 priority date for domestic students, 3/1 for international students. Applications are processed on a rolling basis. Application fee: $40. Electronic applications accepted. *Expenses:* Tuition, state resident: full-time $4275; part-time $237.50 per credit hour. Tuition, nonresident: full-time $11,525; part-time $640.25 per credit hour. Required fees: $1068; $10.35 per credit hour. $440.70 per semester. Tuition and fees vary according to course load and program. *Financial support:* Fellowships, research assistantships, teaching assistantships, Federal Work-Study, health care benefits, and unspecified assistantships available. Support available to part-time students. *Faculty research:* Greek and Latin poetry and prose, Greek and Latin linguistics, patristics, gnosticism, religion of late antiquity. *Unit head:* Dr. Sidnie W. Crawford, Chair, 402-472-2460. *Application contact:* Ginny Gross, Director of Graduate Admissions, 402-472-2878, Fax: 402-472-0589, E-mail: grad_admissions@unl.edu.

Classics

University of New Brunswick Fredericton, School of Graduate Studies, Faculty of Arts, Department of Classics and Ancient History, Fredericton, NB E3B 5A3, Canada. Offers classics (MA). Part-time programs available. *Faculty:* 5 full-time (2 women), 4 part-time/adjunct (1 woman). *Students:* 2 full-time (both women). *Degree requirements:* For master's, thesis. *Entrance requirements:* For master's, minimum GPA of 3.0, minimum of 18 credit hours or equivalent in either Greek or Latin. Additional exam requirements/recommendations for international students: Required—TOEFL, TWE. *Application deadline:* 1/31 for domestic and international students. Applications are processed on a rolling basis. Application fee: $50 Canadian dollars. Tuition and fees charges are reported in Canadian dollars. *Expenses:* Tuition, area resident: Full-time $5562 Canadian dollars. Tuition, nonresident: full-time $9450 Canadian dollars. Required fees: $333 Canadian dollars. *Financial support:* In 2008–09, 2 teaching assistantships were awarded. Financial award application deadline: 1/31. *Faculty research:* Roman history, silver-age Latin poetry, stamped roof tiles, Plato, early Christianity, Greek and Roman archaeology. *Unit head:* Prof. William Kerr, Director of Graduate Studies, 506-458-7507, Fax: 506-447-3072, E-mail: wkerr@unb.ca. *Application contact:* Susan Miller, Graduate Secretary, 506-453-4762, Fax: 506-447-3072, E-mail: smiller@unb.ca.

The University of North Carolina at Chapel Hill, Graduate School, College of Arts and Sciences, Department of Classics, Chapel Hill, NC 27599. Offers classical archaeology (MA, PhD); classics (MA, PhD). Terminal master's awarded for partial completion of doctoral program. *Degree requirements:* For master's, one foreign language, comprehensive exam, thesis; for doctorate, 2 foreign languages, comprehensive exam, thesis/dissertation. *Entrance requirements:* For master's and doctorate, GRE General Test, minimum GPA of 3.0. Electronic applications accepted.

The University of North Carolina at Greensboro, Graduate School, College of Arts and Sciences, Department of Classical Studies, Greensboro, NC 27412-5001. Offers Latin (M Ed). *Entrance requirements:* For master's, GRE General Test, MAT, or PRAXIS. Additional exam requirements/recommendations for international students: Required—TOEFL. Electronic applications accepted.

University of Oregon, Graduate School, College of Arts and Sciences, Department of Classics, Eugene, OR 97403. Offers classical civilization (MA); classics (MA), including Greek, Latin; Greek (MA); Latin (MA). Part-time programs available. *Degree requirements:* For master's, 2 foreign languages, thesis or alternative. *Entrance requirements:* For master's, GRE General Test, minimum GPA of 3.0. Additional exam requirements/recommendations for international students: Required—TOEFL. *Faculty research:* Roman religion, Greek philosophy, archaeology, Greek and Roman literature.

University of Ottawa, Faculty of Graduate and Postdoctoral Studies, Faculty of Arts, Department of Classics and Religious Studies, Ottawa, ON K1N 6N5, Canada. Offers classical studies (MA); religious studies (PhD). *Degree requirements:* For master's, comprehensive exam, thesis or alternative; for doctorate, comprehensive exam, thesis/dissertation. *Entrance requirements:* For master's, honors degree or equivalent, minimum B average; for doctorate, master's degree, minimum B+ average. Electronic applications accepted. *Faculty research:* Religions in Canada, including Amerindian and Inuit religions; religion and culture; late antiquity.

University of Pennsylvania, School of Arts and Sciences, Graduate Group in Classical Studies, Philadelphia, PA 19104. Offers AM, PhD. Terminal master's awarded for partial completion of doctoral program. *Degree requirements:* For master's, 3 foreign languages, thesis or alternative; for doctorate, 4 foreign languages, thesis/dissertation. *Entrance requirements:* For master's and doctorate, GRE General Test, undergraduate course work in classical language and history. Additional exam requirements/recommendations for international students: Required—TOEFL. Electronic applications accepted.

University of Pittsburgh, School of Arts and Sciences, Department of Classics, Pittsburgh, PA 15260. Offers MA, PhD. Part-time programs available. Terminal master's awarded for partial completion of doctoral program. *Degree requirements:* For master's, one foreign language, comprehensive exam, thesis optional; for doctorate, 2 foreign languages, comprehensive exam, thesis/dissertation. *Entrance requirements:* For master's, GRE General Test, background in Greek and Latin; for doctorate, GRE General Test, knowledge of Greek and Latin. Additional exam requirements/recommendations for international students: Required—TOEFL. Electronic applications accepted. *Faculty research:* Greek and Roman poetry, Greek drama, Greek and Roman historiography, Greek philosophy, societal organization.

University of South Africa, College of Human Sciences, Pretoria, South Africa. Offers adult education (M Ed); African languages (MA, PhD); African politics (MA, PhD); Afrikaans (MA, PhD); ancient history (MA, PhD); ancient Near Eastern studies (MA, PhD); anthropology (MA, PhD); applied linguistics (MA); Arabic (MA, PhD); archaeology (MA); art history (MA); Biblical archaeology (MA); Biblical studies (M Th, D Th, PhD); Christian spirituality (M Th, D Th); church history (M Th, D Th); classical studies (MA, PhD); clinical psychology (MA); communication (MA, PhD); comparative education (M Ed, Ed D); consulting psychology (D Admin, D Com, PhD); curriculum studies (M Ed, Ed D); development studies (M Admin, MA, D Admin, PhD); didactics (M Ed, Ed D); education (M Tech); education management (M Ed, Ed D); educational psychology (M Ed); English (MA); environmental education (M Ed); French (MA, PhD); German (MA, PhD); Greek (MA); guidance and counseling (M Ed); health studies (MA, PhD), including health sciences education (MA), health services management (MA), medical and surgical nursing science (critical care general) (MA), midwifery and neonatal nursing science (MA), trauma and emergency care (MA); history (MA, PhD); history of education (Ed D); inclusive education (M Ed, Ed D); information and communications technology policy and regulation (MA); information science (MA, MIS, PhD); international politics (MA, PhD); Islamic studies (MA, PhD); Italian (MA, PhD); Judaica (MA, PhD); linguistics (MA, PhD); mathematical education (M Ed); mathematics education (MA); missiology (M Th, D Th); modern Hebrew (MA, PhD); musicology (MA, MMus, D Mus, PhD); natural science education (M Ed); New Testament (M Th, D Th); Old Testament (D Th); pastoral therapy (M Th, D Th); philosophy (MA); philosophy of education (M Ed, Ed D); politics (MA, PhD); Portuguese (MA, PhD); practical theology (M Th, D Th); psychology (MA, MS, PhD); psychology of education (M Ed, Ed D); public health (MA); religious studies (MA, D Th, PhD); Romance languages (MA); Russian (MA, PhD); Semitic languages (MA, PhD); social behavior studies in HIV/AIDS (MA); social science (mental health) (MA); social science in development studies (MA); social science in psychology (MA); social science in social work (MA); social science in sociology (MA); social work (MSW, DSW, PhD); socio-education (M Ed, Ed D); sociolinguistics (MA); sociology (MA, PhD); Spanish (MA, PhD); systematic theology (M Th, D Th); TESOL (teaching English to speakers of other languages) (MA); theological ethics (M Th, D Th); theory of literature (MA, PhD); urban ministries (D Th); urban ministry (M Th).

University of Southern California, Graduate School, College of Letters, Arts and Sciences, Department of Classics, Los Angeles, CA 90089. Offers MA, PhD. *Degree requirements:* For doctorate, 4 foreign languages, thesis/dissertation. *Entrance requirements:* For master's and doctorate, GRE General Test.

University of South Florida, Graduate School, College of Arts and Sciences, Department of World Language Education, Tampa, FL 33620-9951. Offers classics: latin/greek (MA); French (MA); linguistics (MA); linguistics: ESL (MA); Spanish (MA). Part-time and evening/weekend programs available. *Faculty:* 17 full-time (10 women), 3 part-time/adjunct (2 women). *Students:* 36 full-time (26 women), 16 part-time (12 women); includes 21 minority (4 African Americans, 1 American Indian/Alaska Native, 1 Asian American or Pacific Islander, 15 Hispanic Americans), 9 international. 37 applicants, 73% accepted, 19 enrolled. In 2008, 19 master's awarded. *Degree requirements:* For master's, comprehensive exam, thesis. *Entrance requirements:* For master's, GRE General Test, minimum GPA of 3.0 in last 60 hours. Additional exam requirements/recommendations for international students: Required—TOEFL (minimum score 600 paper-based; 250 computer-based). *Application deadline:* For fall admission, 2/15 for domestic students, 1/2 for international students; for spring admission, 10/15 for domestic students. Application fee: $30. Electronic applications accepted. *Expenses:* Tuition, state resident: full-time $2624.40; part-time $291.60 per credit hour. Tuition, nonresident: full-time $7822; part-time $869.13 per credit hour. *Financial support:* Career-related internships or fieldwork, Federal Work-Study, institutionally sponsored loans, scholarships/grants, tuition waivers (partial), and unspecified assistantships available. Financial award application deadline: 6/30. *Faculty research:* Second language writing, academic literacy. Total annual research expenditures: $8,607. *Unit head:* Victor Peppard, Chairperson, 813-974-2012, Fax: 813-974-1718, E-mail: peppard@.cas.usf.edu. *Application contact:* Victor Peppard, Chairperson, 813-974-2012, Fax: 813-974-1718, E-mail: peppard@.cas.usf.edu.

The University of Texas at Austin, Graduate School, College of Liberal Arts, Department of Classics, Austin, TX 78712-1111. Offers MA, PhD. *Degree requirements:* For master's, 2 foreign languages, comprehensive exam, thesis; for doctorate, 4 foreign languages, comprehensive exam, thesis/dissertation. *Entrance requirements:* For master's, GRE General Test, proficiency in classics; for doctorate, GRE General Test, master's degree in classics. Electronic applications accepted.

University of Toronto, School of Graduate Studies, Humanities Division, Department of Classics, Toronto, ON M5S 1A1, Canada. Offers MA, PhD. Part-time programs available. *Degree requirements:* For master's, qualifying examinations, sight translation exams in Greek and Latin; for doctorate, thesis/dissertation, qualifying examinations, sight translation exams in Greek and Latin. *Entrance requirements:* For master's, minimum B+ average in final year of an undergraduate program in classics, 3–4 years of course work in Greek and Latin; for doctorate, minimum B+ average with at least one A–; MA in classics.

University of Vermont, Graduate College, College of Arts and Sciences, Department of Classics, Burlington, VT 05405. Offers Greek (MA); Greek and Latin (MAT); Latin (MA). *Students:* 9 (5 women). 11 applicants, 91% accepted, 3 enrolled. In 2008, 2 master's awarded. *Degree requirements:* For master's, one foreign language, thesis. *Entrance requirements:* For master's, GRE General Test. Additional exam requirements/recommendations for international students: Required—TOEFL (minimum score 550 paper-based; 213 computer-based; 80 iBT). *Application deadline:* For fall admission, 4/1 priority date for domestic students. Applications are processed on a rolling basis. Application fee: $40. Electronic applications accepted. *Expenses:* Tuition, state resident: part-time $488 per credit. Tuition, nonresident: part-time $1232 per credit. *Financial support:* Fellowships, teaching assistantships available. Financial award application deadline: 3/1. *Faculty research:* Early Greek literature. *Unit head:* Dr. Mark Usher, Chair, 802-656-3210. *Application contact:* Jacques Bailly, Coordinator, 802-656-3210.

University of Victoria, Faculty of Graduate Studies, Faculty of Humanities, Department of Greek and Roman Studies, Victoria, BC V8W 2Y2, Canada. Offers MA, PhD. PhD offered by special arrangement. Part-time programs available. *Degree requirements:* For master's, 3 foreign languages, thesis. *Entrance requirements:* For master's, knowledge of Greek and Latin. Additional exam requirements/recommendations for international students: Required—TOEFL (minimum score 575 paper-based; 233 computer-based), IELTS (minimum score 7). Electronic applications accepted. *Faculty research:* Roman social history, Roman archaeology and technology, Roman literature, Greek literature, Homer and tragedy, Greek historiography.

University of Virginia, College and Graduate School of Arts and Sciences, Department of Classics, Charlottesville, VA 22903. Offers MA, PhD. *Faculty:* 8 full-time (2 women). *Students:* 25 full-time (10 women); includes 3 minority (2 Asian Americans or Pacific Islanders, 1 Hispanic American), 2 international. Average age 29. 57 applicants, 28% accepted, 5 enrolled. In 2008, 4 master's, 3 doctorates awarded. *Degree requirements:* For master's, one foreign language, comprehensive exam, thesis, oral exam; for doctorate, 2 foreign languages, comprehensive exam, thesis/dissertation, oral exam. *Entrance requirements:* For master's and doctorate, GRE General Test, 2 letters of recommendation. Additional exam requirements/recommendations for international students: Required—TOEFL (minimum score 600 paper-based; 250 computer-based; 90 iBT), IELTS (minimum score 7). *Application deadline:* Applications are processed on a rolling basis. Application fee: $60. Electronic applications accepted. *Expenses:* Tuition, area resident: Full-time $10,452. Tuition, state resident: full-time $10,452. Tuition, nonresident: full-time $20,010. Required fees: $2176. Part-time tuition and fees vary according to course load and program. *Financial support:* Fellowships, teaching assistantships, unspecified assistantships available. Financial award application deadline: 1/3; financial award applicants required to submit FAFSA. *Unit head:* John Miller, Chair, 434-924-3008, Fax: 434-924-3062, E-mail: classics@virginia.edu. *Application contact:* Tony Woodman, Director of Graduate Admissions, E-mail: ajw6n@virginia.edu.

University of Washington, Graduate School, College of Arts and Sciences, Department of Classics, Seattle, WA 98195. Offers MA, PhD. Part-time programs available. Terminal master's awarded for partial completion of doctoral program. *Degree requirements:* For master's, one foreign language, thesis or alternative; for doctorate, 2 foreign languages, comprehensive exam, thesis/dissertation. *Entrance requirements:* For master's, GRE, bachelor's degree in classics, Greek, or Latin; minimum GPA of 3.0; for doctorate, GRE, minimum GPA of 3.0. Additional exam requirements/recommendations for international students: Required—TOEFL. Electronic applications accepted. *Faculty research:* Greek and Latin poetry, Greek and Roman cultural institutions, Greek and Latin historiography, ancient medicine, Greek tragedy.

University of Washington, Graduate School, College of Arts and Sciences, Department of Philosophy, Seattle, WA 98195. Offers classics and philosophy (PhD); philosophy (MA, PhD). Terminal master's awarded for partial completion of doctoral program. *Degree requirements:* For master's, 3 papers; for doctorate, thesis/dissertation, general exam. *Entrance requirements:* For master's and doctorate, GRE, minimum GPA of 3.0. Additional exam requirements/recommendations for international students: Required—TOEFL. *Faculty research:* History and philosophy of science, epistemology, Aristotle's metaphysics, ethics and politics, causation in modern philosophy.

The University of Western Ontario, Faculty of Graduate Studies, Faculty of Arts and Humanities, Department of Classical Studies, London, ON N6A 5B8, Canada. Offers MA. Part-time programs available. *Degree requirements:* For master's, one foreign language. *Entrance requirements:* For master's, honors degree, minimum B+ average, statement of interest. Additional exam requirements/recommendations for international students: Required—TOEFL. *Faculty research:* Greek literature, Roman history and law, ancient sport, Byzantine literature, Bronze Age archaeology.

University of Wisconsin–Madison, Graduate School, College of Letters and Science, Department of Classics, Madison, WI 53706-1380. Offers classics (MA, PhD); Greek (MA); Latin (MA). Part-time programs available. Terminal master's awarded for partial completion of doctoral program. *Degree requirements:* For master's, 3 foreign languages, oral and written exams; for doctorate, 4 foreign languages, thesis/dissertation, written exams. *Entrance requirements:* For master's, GRE; for doctorate, master's degree. Electronic applications accepted. *Faculty research:* Greek tragedy, Latin elegy, historiography, Homer, Greek lyric poetry.

University of Wisconsin–Milwaukee, Graduate School, College of Letters and Sciences, Interdepartmental Program in Foreign Language and Literature, Milwaukee, WI 53201-0413. Offers classics and Hebrew studies (MAFLL); comparative literature (MAFLL); French and Italian (MAFLL); German (MAFLL); Slavic studies (MAFLL); translation (Certificate). Part-time programs available. *Faculty:* 39 full-time (17 women). *Students:* 32 full-time (25 women), 28 part-time (19 women); includes 5 minority (1 Asian American or Pacific Islander, 4 Hispanic Americans), 22 international. Average age 32. 51 applicants, 65% accepted, 26 enrolled. In 2008, 19 master's awarded. *Degree requirements:* For master's, 2 foreign languages, thesis or alternative. *Entrance requirements:* Additional exam requirements/recommendations for international students: Required—TOEFL (minimum score 550 paper-based; 79 iBT), IELTS (minimum score 6.5). *Application deadline:* For fall admission, 1/1 priority date for domestic students; for spring admission, 9/1 for domestic students. Applications are processed on a rolling basis. Application fee: $45 ($75 for international students). *Expenses:* Tuition, area resident: Full-time $7320; part-time $165 per credit. Tuition, state resident: full-time $7320; part-time $165 per credit. Tuition, nonresident: full-time $17,840; part-time $714 per credit. Tuition and fees vary according to campus/location, program and reciprocity agreements. *Financial support:* In 2008–09, 2 research assistantships, 35 teaching assistantships were awarded; career-related internships or fieldwork and unspecified assistantships also available. Support available to part-time students. Financial award application deadline: 4/15. Total annual research expenditures: $43,420. *Unit head:* Gabrielle Verdier, Representative, 414-229-3346, Fax: 414-229-2741, E-mail: verdier@uwm.edu. *Application contact:* General Information Contact, 414-229-4982, Fax: 414-229-6967, E-mail: gradschool@uwm.edu.

Vanderbilt University, Graduate School, Department of Classical Studies, Nashville, TN 37240-1001. Offers classics (MA); Latin (MAT). *Faculty:* 15 full-time (8 women). *Students:* 7 full-time (4 women); includes 1 minority (Hispanic American). Average age 25. 37 applicants, 14% accepted, 4 enrolled. In 2008, 1 master's awarded. *Degree requirements:* For master's, 2 foreign languages, thesis. *Entrance requirements:* For master's, GRE General Test. Additional exam requirements/recommendations for international students: Required—TOEFL (minimum score 570 paper-based; 230 computer-based; 88 iBT). *Application deadline:* For fall admission, 1/15 for domestic and international students. Application fee: $0. Electronic applications accepted. *Financial support:* Fellowships with full and partial tuition reimbursements, teaching assistantships with full and partial tuition reimbursements, Federal Work-Study, institutionally sponsored loans, scholarships/grants, and health care benefits available. Financial award application deadline: 1/15; financial award applicants required to submit CSS PROFILE or FAFSA. *Faculty research:* Greek and Latin literature and language, Greek and Roman history, classical archaeology, philosophy, religion. *Unit head:* Barbara Tsakirgis, Chair, 615-322-2516, Fax: 615-343-7261, E-mail: barbara.tsakirgis@vanderbilt.edu. *Application contact:* Kathy L. Gaca, PhD, Director of Graduate Studies, 615-322-2516, Fax: 615-343-7261, E-mail: dgs.classics@vanderbilt.edu.

Washington University in St. Louis, Graduate School of Arts and Sciences, Department of Classics, St. Louis, MO 63130-4899. Offers MA. *Students:* 10 full-time (3 women); includes 2 minority (1 Asian American or Pacific Islander, 1 Hispanic American). 7 applicants, 57% accepted, 3 enrolled. In 2008, 5 master's awarded. *Degree requirements:* For master's, thesis or alternative. *Entrance requirements:* For master's, GRE General Test. *Application deadline:* For fall admission, 1/15 priority date for domestic students. Application fee: $45. Electronic applications accepted. *Financial support:* Teaching assistantships, Federal Work-Study, institutionally sponsored loans, and tuition waivers (full and partial) available. Support available to part-time students. Financial award application deadline: 1/15. *Unit head:* Dr. Judith Evans-Grubbs, Chairperson, 314-935-5123. *Application contact:* Assistant to the Dean, 314-935-6880, Fax: 314-935-4887.

Wayne State University, College of Liberal Arts and Sciences, Department of Classical and Modern Languages, Literatures, and Cultures, Program in Classics, Greek, and Latin, Detroit,

MI 48202. Offers classics (MA); Latin (MA). *Degree requirements:* For master's, thesis optional. *Entrance requirements:* For master's, GRE, bachelor's degree in Latin, Greek, or classics; letters of recommendation; personal statement; writing sample. Additional exam requirements/recommendations for international students: Required—TOEFL (minimum score 550 paper-based; 213 computer-based); Recommended—TWE (minimum score 6). Electronic applications accepted.

West Chester University of Pennsylvania, Office of Graduate Studies, College of Arts and Sciences, Department of Languages and Cultures, West Chester, PA 19383. Offers French (M Ed, MA, Teaching Certificate); German (Teaching Certificate); Latin (Teaching Certificate); Spanish (M Ed, MA, Teaching Certificate). Part-time and evening/weekend programs available. *Students:* 7 full-time (6 women), 14 part-time (all women); includes 2 minority (1 African American, 1 Hispanic American), 1 international. Average age 34. 16 applicants, 100% accepted, 8 enrolled. In 2008, 3 master's awarded. *Degree requirements:* For master's, one foreign language, comprehensive exam, thesis optional. *Entrance requirements:* For master's, GRE or MAT, placement test. Additional exam requirements/recommendations for international students: Required—TOEFL (minimum score 550 paper-based; 213 computer-based; 80 iBT). *Application deadline:* For fall admission, 4/15 priority date for domestic students, 3/15 for international students; for spring admission, 10/15 for domestic students, 9/1 for international students. Applications are processed on a rolling basis. Application fee: $35. Electronic applications accepted. *Expenses:* Tuition, state resident: full-time $6430; part-time $357 per credit. Tuition, nonresident: full-time $10,288; part-time $572 per credit. Required fees: $652.50; $50 per credit. $67 per semester. *Financial support:* In 2008–09, 1 research assistantship with full and partial tuition reimbursement (averaging $5,000 per year) was awarded; unspecified assistantships also available. Support available to part-time students. Financial award application deadline: 2/15; financial award applicants required to submit FAFSA. *Faculty research:* Implementation of world languages curriculum framework. *Unit head:* Dr. Jerry Williams, Chair, 610-436-2700, Fax: 610-436-3048, E-mail: jwilliams2@wcupa.edu. *Application contact:* Dr. Rebecca Pauly, Graduate Coordinator, 610-436-2382, E-mail: rpauly@wcupa.edu.

Wilfrid Laurier University, Faculty of Graduate Studies, Faculty of Arts, Department of Archaeology and Classical Studies, Waterloo, ON N2L 3C5, Canada. Offers MA. *Degree requirements:* For master's, thesis optional. *Entrance requirements:* For master's, minimum B+ average in last two undergraduate years (exclusive of first year level courses in those years). Additional exam requirements/recommendations for international students: Required—TOEFL.

Yale University, Graduate School of Arts and Sciences, Department of Classics, New Haven, CT 06520. Offers M Phil, MA, PhD. *Degree requirements:* For doctorate, 2 foreign languages, thesis/dissertation. *Entrance requirements:* For doctorate, GRE General Test.

Comparative Literature

American University, College of Arts and Sciences, Department of Literature, Program in Literature, Washington, DC 20016-8047. Offers MA. Part-time and evening/weekend programs available. *Students:* 22 full-time (18 women), 8 part-time (all women); includes 4 minority (1 African American, 1 American Indian/Alaska Native, 2 Asian Americans or Pacific Islanders), 2 international. Average age 26. 55 applicants, 89% accepted, 16 enrolled. In 2008, 11 master's awarded. *Degree requirements:* For master's, comprehensive exam, thesis or alternative. *Entrance requirements:* For master's, GRE, writing sample. Additional exam requirements/recommendations for international students: Required—TOEFL. *Application deadline:* For fall admission, 2/1 for domestic students. Application fee: $80. *Expenses:* Tuition: Full-time $21,204; part-time $1178 per credit hour. Required fees: $380. Part-time tuition and fees vary according to course load and program. *Financial support:* In 2008–09, 6 students received support; fellowships, research assistantships, teaching assistantships, career-related internships or fieldwork, Federal Work-Study, institutionally sponsored loans, and tuition waivers (full and partial) available. Support available to part-time students. Financial award application deadline: 2/1. *Faculty research:* British, American, African-American, and Third World literature; cinema studies; literary theory; feminist criticism. *Unit head:* Dr. Jonathon Loesberg, Chair, 202-885-2998, Fax: 202-885-2938, E-mail: jloesbe@american.edu. *Application contact:* Dr. Jonathon Loesberg, Chair, 202-885-2998, Fax: 202-885-2938, E-mail: jloesbe@american.edu.

The American University in Cairo, Graduate Studies and Research, School of Humanities and Social Sciences, Department of English and Comparative Literature, Cairo, Egypt. Offers MA. Part-time programs available. *Degree requirements:* For master's, one foreign language, thesis, proficiency in French or German. *Entrance requirements:* Additional exam requirements/recommendations for international students: Required—English entrance exam and/or TOEFL.

Antioch University McGregor, Graduate Programs, Individualized Liberal and Professional Studies Program, Yellow Springs, OH 45387-1609. Offers liberal and professional studies (MA), including counseling, creative writing, education, film studies, liberal studies, management, modern literature, psychology, theatre, visual arts. Part-time and evening/weekend programs available. Postbaccalaureate distance learning degree programs offered (minimal on-campus study). *Degree requirements:* For master's, thesis or alternative. *Entrance requirements:* For master's, resumé, 2 letters of reference. Electronic applications accepted. *Expenses:* Contact institution.

Arizona State University, Graduate College, College of Liberal Arts and Sciences, Division of Humanities, Department of English, Tempe, AZ 85287. Offers creative writing (MFA); English (MA, PhD), including comparative literature (MA), linguistics (MA), literature, rhetoric and composition (MA), rhetoric/composition and linguistics (PhD); teaching English to speakers of other languages (MTESOL). *Degree requirements:* For doctorate, thesis/dissertation. *Entrance requirements:* For master's and doctorate, GRE.

Brigham Young University, Graduate Studies, College of Humanities, Department of Humanities, Classics, and Comparative Literature, Provo, UT 84602-1001. Offers comparative literature (MA); comparative studies (MA); humanities (MA). *Faculty:* 26 full-time (4 women). *Students:* 27 full-time (14 women). Average age 27. 15 applicants, 80% accepted, 6 enrolled. In 2008, 5 master's awarded. *Degree requirements:* For master's, 2 foreign languages, thesis. *Entrance requirements:* For master's, GRE, minimum GPA of 3.0 in last 60 hours. *Application deadline:* For fall admission, 3/1 for domestic and international students. Application fee: $50. Electronic applications accepted. *Expenses:* Tuition: Full-time $5160; part-time $287 per credit hour. Tuition and fees vary according to program and student's religious affiliation. *Financial support:* In 2008–09, 27 students received support, including 7 research assistantships (averaging $4,680 per year), 29 teaching assistantships; fellowships, career-related internships or fieldwork, institutionally sponsored loans, scholarships/grants, tuition waivers (full and partial), and student instructorships also available. Support available to part-time students. *Unit head:* Dr. Michael J. Call, Chair, 801-422-2550, Fax: 801-422-0305, E-mail: michael_call@byu.edu. *Application contact:* Carolyn Hone, Graduate Secretary for Humanities and Comparative Literature, 801-422-4430, Fax: 801-422-0305, E-mail: carolyn_hone@byu.edu.

Brock University, Faculty of Graduate Studies, Faculty of Humanities, Program in Studies in Comparative Literatures and Arts, St. Catharines, ON L2S 3A1, Canada. Offers MA. *Degree requirements:* For master's, thesis optional. *Entrance requirements:* For master's, honors

degree. Additional exam requirements/recommendations for international students: Required—TOEFL (minimum score 550 paper-based; 213 computer-based; 80 iBT), IELTS (minimum score 6.5), TWE (minimum score 4). Electronic applications accepted.

Brown University, Graduate School, Department of Comparative Literature, Providence, RI 02912. Offers PhD. *Degree requirements:* For doctorate, 2 foreign languages, thesis/dissertation, preliminary exam. *Entrance requirements:* For doctorate, GRE General Test, GRE Subject Test.

California State University, Fullerton, Graduate Studies, College of Humanities and Social Sciences, Department of English and Comparative Literature, Fullerton, CA 92834-9480. Offers comparative literature (MA); English (MA). Part-time programs available. *Students:* 33 full-time (24 women), 81 part-time (66 women); includes 25 minority (1 African American, 8 Asian Americans or Pacific Islanders, 16 Hispanic Americans), 2 international. Average age 31. 73 applicants, 66% accepted, 34 enrolled. In 2008, 31 master's awarded. *Degree requirements:* For master's, comprehensive exam, thesis or alternative. *Entrance requirements:* For master's, minimum GPA of 3.0 in major, 2.5 in last 60 hours. Application fee: $55. Tuition and fees vary according to degree level. *Financial support:* Teaching assistantships, Federal Work-Study, institutionally sponsored loans, and scholarships/grants available. Support available to part-time students. Financial award application deadline: 3/1. *Unit head:* Dr. Joseph Sawicki, Chair, 657-278-3163. *Application contact:* Dr. Susan Jacobsen, Adviser, 657-278-3163.

California State University, Northridge, Graduate Studies, College of Humanities, Department of English, Northridge, CA 91330. Offers creative writing (MA); literature (MA); rhetoric and composition theory (MA). Part-time and evening/weekend programs available. *Faculty:* 33 full-time (16 women), 71 part-time/adjunct (60 women). *Students:* 42 full-time (27 women), 133 part-time (96 women); includes 38 minority (4 African Americans, 1 American Indian/Alaska Native, 14 Asian Americans or Pacific Islanders, 19 Hispanic Americans). Average age 34. 114 applicants, 74% accepted, 51 enrolled. In 2008, 40 master's awarded. *Degree requirements:* For master's, thesis or alternative. *Entrance requirements:* For master's, writing proficiency test, GRE General Test or minimum GPA of 3.0. Additional exam requirements/recommendations for international students: Required—TOEFL. *Application deadline:* For fall admission, 11/30 for domestic students. Application fee: $55. *Financial support:* Teaching assistantships available. Financial award application deadline: 3/1. *Faculty research:* Reading improvement, professional writing, Dickens, Shaw, English as a second language. *Unit head:* Dr. George Uba, Chair, 818-677-3434, E-mail: george.uba@csun.edu. *Application contact:* Dr. Marjie Seagoe, Graduate Studies Secretary, 818-677-3433.

Carleton University, Faculty of Graduate Studies, Faculty of Arts and Social Sciences, School for Languages, Literatures, and Comparative Literary Studies, Ottawa, ON K1S 5B6, Canada. Offers cultural mediations (PhD). *Entrance requirements:* Additional exam requirements/recommendations for international students: Required—TOEFL. *Faculty research:* Literary history, theory of literature, cross-cultural studies, modernism/postmodernism, comparative Canadian literature.

Carnegie Mellon University, College of Humanities and Social Sciences, Department of English, Pittsburgh, PA 15213-3891. Offers communication planning and design (M Des); literary and cultural studies (MA, PhD); professional writing (MAPW), including editing and publishing, policy and non-profit communication, public and media relations / corporate communications, science or healthcare communication, technical writing, writing for new media, writing for print media; rhetoric (MA, PhD). Part-time programs available. Terminal master's awarded for partial completion of doctoral program. *Degree requirements:* For doctorate, 2 foreign languages, comprehensive exam, thesis/dissertation. *Entrance requirements:* For master's and doctorate, GRE General Test. Additional exam requirements/recommendations for international students: Required—TOEFL, TWE. *Faculty research:* Cognitive processes in discourse with emphasis on writing, testing, and evaluation.

Case Western Reserve University, School of Graduate Studies, Department of English, Cleveland, OH 44106. Offers comparative literature (MA); English and American literature (MA, PhD). Part-time programs available. *Degree requirements:* For master's, written exam; for doctorate, one foreign language, thesis/dissertation, oral and written exams. *Entrance requirements:* For master's and doctorate, GRE General Test, sample of written work. Additional

Comparative Literature

Case Western Reserve University (continued)
exam requirements/recommendations for international students: Required—TOEFL. Electronic applications accepted. *Faculty research:* Sixteenth- to twentieth-century English literature, rhetorical and critical theory, women's studies, genre studies, Renaissance, America modernism, authorship.

Case Western Reserve University, School of Graduate Studies, Department of Modern Languages and Literatures and Department of English, Program in World Literature, Cleveland, OH 44106. Offers MA. *Degree requirements:* For master's, 2 foreign languages, written exam. *Entrance requirements:* For master's, GRE General Test, sample of written work. Additional exam requirements/recommendations for international students: Required—TOEFL. Electronic applications accepted. *Faculty research:* Literary theory, literary translation, Romanticism.

The Catholic University of America, School of Arts and Sciences, Program in Comparative Literature, Washington, DC 20064. Offers MA, PhD. Part-time programs available. *Degree requirements:* For master's, one foreign language, comprehensive exam, thesis or alternative; for doctorate, 2 foreign languages, comprehensive exam, thesis/dissertation, oral examination. *Entrance requirements:* For master's and doctorate, GRE General Test, 3 letters of recommendation, writing sample. Additional exam requirements/recommendations for international students: Required—TOEFL (minimum score 580 paper-based; 237 computer-based). Electronic applications accepted. *Faculty research:* Medieval literature, romanticism, religion and literature, modern literature, theory and criticism.

Claremont Graduate University, Graduate Programs, School of Arts and Humanities, Department of English, Claremont, CA 91711-6160. Offers American studies (MA, PhD); critical theory (MA, PhD); early modern studies (MA, PhD); English (M Phil, MA, PhD); literary theory (PhD); literature (MA, PhD); literature and creative writing (MA); literature and film (MA); MBA/MA; MBA/PhD. Part-time programs available. *Faculty:* 2 full-time (1 woman), 2 part-time/adjunct (0 women). *Students:* 78 full-time (46 women), 12 part-time (9 women); includes 15 minority (1 African American, 2 American Indian/Alaska Native, 7 Asian Americans or Pacific Islanders, 5 Hispanic Americans), 2 international. Average age 35. In 2008, 9 master's, 11 doctorates awarded. *Entrance requirements:* For master's and doctorate, GRE General Test. Additional exam requirements/recommendations for international students: Required—TOEFL (minimum score 550 paper-based; 213 computer-based; 80 iBT). *Application deadline:* For fall admission, 2/1 priority date for domestic students. Applications are processed on a rolling basis. Application fee: $60. Electronic applications accepted. *Expenses:* Tuition: Full-time $33,698; part-time $1465 per unit. Required fees: $310; $155 per semester. Tuition and fees vary according to program. *Financial support:* Fellowships, Federal Work-Study, institutionally sponsored loans, and scholarships/grants available. Support available to part-time students. Financial award application deadline: 2/15; financial award applicants required to submit FAFSA. *Faculty research:* American, comparative, and English Renaissance literature; modernism; feminist literature and theory. *Unit head:* Wendy Martin, Chair, 909-621-8612, Fax: 909-607-1221, E-mail: wendy.martin@cgu.edu. *Application contact:* Justin Evans, Admissions Coordinator, 909-607-1278, Fax: 909-607-1221, E-mail: justin.evans@cgu.edu.

College of the Humanities and Sciences, Harrison Middleton University, Graduate Program, Tempe, AZ 85282. Offers education (MA, Ed D); humanities (MA); imaginative literature (MA); interdisciplinary studies (DA); jurisprudence (MA); natural science (MA); philosophy and religion (MA); social science (MA). Part-time and evening/weekend programs available. Postbaccalaureate distance learning degree programs offered (no on-campus study). Electronic applications accepted.

Columbia University, Graduate School of Arts and Sciences, Division of Humanities, Department of English and Comparative Literature, New York, NY 10027. Offers comparative literature (M Phil, MA, PhD); English literature (M Phil, MA, PhD); literature-writing (M Phil, MA, PhD). Part-time programs available. *Degree requirements:* For master's, one foreign language, comprehensive exam, seminar papers; for doctorate, thesis/dissertation. *Entrance requirements:* For master's and doctorate, GRE General Test. Additional exam requirements/recommendations for international students: Required—TOEFL. *Faculty research:* Medieval through modern literature, drama, literary criticism.

Cornell University, Graduate School, Graduate Fields of Arts and Sciences, Field of Comparative Literature, Ithaca, NY 14853-0001. Offers PhD. *Faculty:* 36 full-time (16 women). *Students:* 29 full-time (21 women); includes 5 minority (3 Asian Americans or Pacific Islanders, 2 Hispanic Americans), 9 international. Average age 31. 89 applicants, 6% accepted, 3 enrolled. In 2008, 3 doctorates awarded. *Degree requirements:* For doctorate, 2 foreign languages, comprehensive exam, thesis/dissertation, teaching experience. *Entrance requirements:* For doctorate, GRE General Test, proficiency in 2 foreign literatures, writing sample, 3 letters of recommendation. Additional exam requirements/recommendations for international students: Required—TOEFL (minimum score 550 paper-based; 213 computer-based; 77 iBT). *Application deadline:* For fall admission, 1/10 for domestic students. Application fee: $70. Electronic applications accepted. *Expenses:* Tuition: Full-time $29,500. Required fees: $70. Full-time tuition and fees vary according to degree level, program and student level. *Financial support:* In 2008–09, 22 students received support, including 14 fellowships with full tuition reimbursements available, 8 teaching assistantships with full tuition reimbursements available; research assistantships with full tuition reimbursements available, institutionally sponsored loans, health care benefits, and tuition waivers (full and partial) also available. Financial award applicants required to submit FAFSA. *Faculty research:* Critical theory, European studies, Latin American studies, Asian studies. *Unit head:* Director of Graduate Studies, 607-255-4155. *Application contact:* Graduate Field Assistant, 607-255-4155, E-mail: complit@cornell.edu.

Dartmouth College, Arts and Sciences Graduate Programs, Comparative Literature Program, Hanover, NH 03755. Offers AM. *Degree requirements:* For master's, final paper, oral exams. *Entrance requirements:* For master's, proficiency in 2 languages. Additional exam requirements/recommendations for international students: Required—TOEFL. Electronic applications accepted.

Duke University, Graduate School, Program in Literature, Durham, NC 27708. Offers PhD. *Degree requirements:* For doctorate, 2 foreign languages, thesis/dissertation. *Entrance requirements:* For doctorate, GRE General Test. Additional exam requirements/recommendations for international students: Required—TOEFL (minimum score 550 paper-based; 213 computer-based; 83 iBT), IELTS (minimum score 7).

Emory University, Graduate School of Arts and Sciences, Department of Comparative Literature, Atlanta, GA 30322-1100. Offers comparative literature (PhD); English (Certificate); French (Certificate); Middle Eastern studies (PhD); philosophy (Certificate); psychoanalytic studies (PhD); religion (PhD); Spanish (Certificate); women studies (Certificate). *Degree requirements:* For doctorate, 2 foreign languages, comprehensive exam, thesis/dissertation. *Entrance requirements:* For doctorate, GRE General Test, minimum GPA of 3.0. Additional exam requirements/recommendations for international students: Required—TOEFL. Electronic applications accepted. *Faculty research:* Literary theory, psychoanalysis trauma and testimony, literature and religion, literature and technology, literature and philosophy, politics and global culture, literature and aesthetics.

Emory University, Graduate School of Arts and Sciences, Department of Spanish and Portuguese, Atlanta, GA 30322-1100. Offers comparative literature (Certificate); film studies (Certificate); Spanish (PhD); women's studies (Certificate). *Degree requirements:* For doctorate, 2 foreign languages, comprehensive exam, thesis/dissertation. *Entrance requirements:* For doctorate, GRE General Test. Additional exam requirements/recommendations for international students: Required—TOEFL. Electronic applications accepted. *Faculty research:* Spanish literature, Spanish-American literature, literary theory, criticism, cultural studies.

Fairleigh Dickinson University, Metropolitan Campus, University College: Arts, Sciences, and Professional Studies, Department of English, Philosophy, and Humanities, Program in English and Literature, Teaneck, NJ 07666-1914. Offers MA. *Students:* 3 full-time (2 women), 3 part-time (all women). Average age 25. 15 applicants, 93% accepted, 5 enrolled. In 2008, 3 master's awarded. Application fee: $40. *Application contact:* Susan Brooman, University Director of Graduate Admissions, 201-692-2554, Fax: 201-692-2560, E-mail: globaleducation@fdu.edu.

Florida Atlantic University, Dorothy F. Schmidt College of Arts and Letters, Department of Languages, Linguistics, and Comparative Literature, Boca Raton, FL 33431-0991. Offers comparative literature (MA); French (MA); linguistics (MA); Spanish (MA). Part-time programs available. *Faculty:* 23 full-time (20 women), 12 part-time/adjunct (10 women). *Students:* 18 full-time (15 women), 19 part-time (13 women); includes 17 minority (4 African Americans, 1 Asian American or Pacific Islander, 12 Hispanic Americans), 4 international. Average age 36. 24 applicants, 67% accepted, 6 enrolled. In 2008, 10 master's awarded. *Degree requirements:* For master's, one foreign language, comprehensive exam, thesis optional. *Entrance requirements:* For master's, GRE General Test, minimum GPA of 3.0. *Application deadline:* For fall admission, 7/1 priority date for domestic students, 2/15 for international students; for spring admission, 11/1 for domestic students, 7/15 for international students. Applications are processed on a rolling basis. Application fee: $30. *Expenses:* Tuition, state resident: full-time $4867; part-time $270.40 per credit hour. Tuition, nonresident: full-time $16,486; part-time $915.87 per credit hour. *Financial support:* Fellowships, research assistantships, teaching assistantships with partial tuition reimbursements, Federal Work-Study and tuition waivers (partial) available. Support available to part-time students. Financial award application deadline: 4/1. *Faculty research:* Modern European studies, modern Latin America, medieval Europe. *Unit head:* Dr. Michael Horswell, Chair, 561-297-3860, Fax: 561-297-2756, E-mail: horswell@fau.edu. *Application contact:* Dr. Emily Stockard, Associate Dean, 561-297-2817, Fax: 561-297-2744, E-mail: stockard@fau.edu.

Georgetown University, Graduate School of Arts and Sciences, School of Continuing Studies, Washington, DC 20057. Offers American studies (MALS); Catholic studies (MALS); classical civilizations (MALS); ethics and the professions (MALS); human resources management (MPS); humanities (MALS); individualized study (MALS); international affairs (MALS); Islam and Muslim-Christian relations (MALS); journalism (MPS); liberal studies (DLS); literature and society (MALS); medieval and early modern European studies (MALS); public relations (MPS); real estate (MPS); religious studies (MALS); social and public policy (MALS); sports industry management (MPS); the theory and practice of American democracy (MALS); visual culture (MALS). *Entrance requirements:* Additional exam requirements/recommendations for international students: Required—TOEFL.

Graduate School and University Center of the City University of New York, Graduate Studies, Program in Comparative Literature, New York, NY 10016-4039. Offers comparative literature (MA, PhD), including classics (PhD), German (PhD), Italian (PhD). Terminal master's awarded for partial completion of doctoral program. *Degree requirements:* For master's, 2 foreign languages, comprehensive exam, thesis; for doctorate, 3 foreign languages, comprehensive exam, thesis/dissertation. *Entrance requirements:* For master's and doctorate, GRE General Test. Additional exam requirements/recommendations for international students: Required—TOEFL. Electronic applications accepted.

Harvard University, Graduate School of Arts and Sciences, Department of Comparative Literature, Cambridge, MA 02138. Offers comparative literature (PhD); oral literature (PhD). *Degree requirements:* For doctorate, 4 foreign languages, thesis/dissertation, written and oral exams. *Entrance requirements:* For doctorate, GRE General Test, GRE Subject Test (recommended), sample of written work. Additional exam requirements/recommendations for international students: Required—TOEFL. *Expenses:* Tuition: Full-time $32,556. Required fees: $1426. Full-time tuition and fees vary according to program and student level.

Hofstra University, College of Liberal Arts and Sciences, Department of Comparative Literature and Languages, Hempstead, NY 11549. Offers applied linguistics (MA). Part-time programs available. *Faculty:* 2 full-time (0 women), 1 part-time/adjunct (0 women). *Students:* 2 part-time (both women). Average age 30. 3 applicants, 67% accepted, 1 enrolled. In 2008, 1 master's awarded. *Degree requirements:* For master's, thesis, 36 credits, capstone. *Entrance requirements:* For master's, bachelor's degree in related area, interview, 2 letters of recommendation. Additional exam requirements/recommendations for international students: Required—TOEFL (minimum score 550 paper-based; 213 computer-based; 80 iBT). *Application deadline:* Applications are processed on a rolling basis. Application fee: $60. Electronic applications accepted. *Expenses:* Tuition: Full-time $15,300; part-time $850 per credit. Required fees: $970; $165 per term. Tuition and fees vary according to program. *Financial support:* Fellowships with full and partial tuition reimbursements, research assistantships with full and partial tuition reimbursements, Federal Work-Study, institutionally sponsored loans, scholarships/grants, tuition waivers (full and partial), and unspecified assistantships available. Support available to part-time students. Financial award applicants required to submit FAFSA. *Faculty research:* Second language acquisition, second language writing. *Unit head:* Dr. George L. Greaney, Director, 516-463-5651, E-mail: cllglg@hofstra.edu. *Application contact:* Carol Drummer, Dean of Graduate Admissions, 516-463-4876, Fax: 516-463-4664, E-mail: gradstudent@hofstra.edu.

Indiana State University, School of Graduate Studies, College of Arts and Sciences, Department of English, Terre Haute, IN 47809-1401. Offers English teaching (MA); history (MA); literature (MA). Part-time and evening/weekend programs available. *Degree requirements:* For master's, one foreign language, thesis optional. *Entrance requirements:* For master's, minimum GPA of 2.75 in all English courses above freshman level. Additional exam requirements/recommendations for international students: Required—TOEFL (minimum score 550 paper-based). Electronic applications accepted.

Indiana University Bloomington, University Graduate School, College of Arts and Sciences, Department of Comparative Literature, Bloomington, IN 47405. Offers MA, MAT, PhD. Part-time programs available. *Faculty:* 6 full-time (3 women), 18 part-time/adjunct (11 women). *Students:* 37 full-time (30 women), 7 part-time (4 women); includes 5 minority (1 African American, 1 American Indian/Alaska Native, 2 Asian Americans or Pacific Islanders, 1 Hispanic American), 14 international. Average age 32. 58 applicants, 31% accepted, 6 enrolled. In 2008, 9 master's, 4 doctorates awarded. *Degree requirements:* For master's, 2 foreign languages, comprehensive exam (for some programs), thesis (for some programs); for doctorate, 3 foreign languages, comprehensive exam, thesis/dissertation. *Entrance requirements:* For master's, GRE, proficiency in 1 foreign language, writing sample; for doctorate, GRE, proficiency in 2 foreign languages, writing sample. Additional exam requirements/recommendations for international students: Required—TOEFL (minimum score 550 paper-based; 213 computer-based; 79 iBT). *Application deadline:* For fall admission, 1/15 priority date for domestic students, 12/15 priority date for international students. Application fee: $50 ($60 for international students). Electronic applications accepted. *Expenses:* Tuition, area resident: Part-time $291.97 per credit hour. Tuition, state resident: part-time $291.97 per credit hour. Tuition, nonresident: part-time $850.33 per credit hour. Required fees: $110 per semester. Tuition and fees vary according to course load and program. *Financial support:* In 2008–09, 9 students received support; fellowships with full tuition reimbursements available, research assistantships with partial tuition reimbursements available, teaching assistantships with full tuition reimbursements available, Federal Work-Study and unspecified assistantships available. Financial award application deadline: 1/15. *Faculty research:* East-West literary relations, film studies, translation, medieval studies, comparative arts. *Unit head:* Eileen Julien, Chairperson, 812-855-8422, Fax: 812-855-2688, E-mail: ejulien@indiana.edu. *Application contact:* Connie Sue May, Administrative Secretary, 812-855-9602, Fax: 812-855-2688, E-mail: csmay@indiana.edu.

The Johns Hopkins University, Zanvyl Krieger School of Arts and Sciences, Humanities Center, Baltimore, MD 21218-2699. Offers PhD. Part-time programs available. *Degree requirements:* For doctorate, 2 foreign languages, thesis/dissertation. *Entrance requirements:* For doctorate, GRE General Test, samples of written work. Additional exam requirements/recommendations for international students: Recommended—IELTS. Electronic applications accepted.

Kent State University, College of Arts and Sciences, Department of English, Kent, OH 44242-0001. Offers comparative literature (MA); creative writing (MFA); English (PhD); English for teachers (MA); literature and writing (MA); rhetoric and composition (PhD); teaching English as a second language (MA). Part-time programs available. Terminal master's awarded for partial completion of doctoral program. *Degree requirements:* For master's, one foreign language, thesis optional; for doctorate, one foreign language, thesis/dissertation, qualifying exams. *Entrance requirements:* For master's and doctorate, GRE General Test, writing sample, letters of recommendation. Additional exam requirements/recommendations for international students: Required—TOEFL (minimum score 600 paper-based). Electronic applications accepted. *Faculty research:* British and American literature, textual editing, rhetoric and composition, cultural studies, linguistic and critical theories.

Long Island University, Brooklyn Campus, Richard L. Conolly College of Liberal Arts and Sciences, Department of English, Brooklyn, NY 11201-8423. Offers English literature (MA); professional and creative writing (MA); teaching of writing (MA). Part-time and evening/weekend programs available. *Degree requirements:* For master's, thesis or alternative. *Entrance requirements:* For master's, 2 letters of recommendation. Additional exam requirements/recommendations for international students: Required—TOEFL (minimum score 550 paper-based; 173 computer-based). Electronic applications accepted.

Louisiana State University and Agricultural and Mechanical College, Graduate School, College of Arts and Sciences, Interdepartmental Program in Comparative Literature, Baton Rouge, LA 70803. Offers MA, PhD. Terminal master's awarded for partial completion of doctoral program. *Degree requirements:* For master's, 2 foreign languages, thesis optional; for doctorate, 2 foreign languages, thesis/dissertation. *Entrance requirements:* For master's and doctorate, GRE General Test, minimum GPA of 3.0. Additional exam requirements/recommendations for international students: Required—TOEFL (minimum score 550 paper-based; 213 computer-based; 79 iBT). Electronic applications accepted. *Faculty research:* World literature, Islamic studies, Dante, Foucault.

New York University, Graduate School of Arts and Science, Department of Comparative Literature, New York, NY 10012-1019. Offers MA, PhD. Part-time programs available. *Degree requirements:* For master's, 2 foreign languages, thesis; for doctorate, 3 foreign languages, thesis/dissertation. *Entrance requirements:* For master's and doctorate, GRE General Test. Additional exam requirements/recommendations for international students: Required—TOEFL. *Faculty research:* European and non-European literature and culture, comparative poetics, cultural studies, colonial and post-colonial literature and theory, philosophical issues and literary theory.

Northwestern University, The Graduate School, Interdepartmental Degree Programs, Program in Literature, Evanston, IL 60208. Offers MA. Part-time programs available. *Degree requirements:* For master's, thesis. *Entrance requirements:* For master's, writing sample. Additional exam requirements/recommendations for international students: Required—TOEFL. *Faculty research:* Sociology of literature, creative writing, women writers, modernism and post-modernism.

Northwestern University, The Graduate School, Judd A. and Marjorie Weinberg College of Arts and Sciences, Department of French and Italian, Evanston, IL 60208. Offers eighteenth-century studies (Certificate); French (PhD); French and comparative literature (PhD); Italian studies (Certificate). Admissions and degrees offered through The Graduate School. *Degree requirements:* For doctorate, one foreign language, thesis/dissertation, written and oral exams. *Entrance requirements:* For doctorate, GRE, writing sample, cassette recording. Additional exam requirements/recommendations for international students: Required—TOEFL. *Faculty research:* Francophone studies, 18th century contemporary theory.

Northwestern University, The Graduate School, Judd A. and Marjorie Weinberg College of Arts and Sciences, Program in Comparative Literary Studies, Evanston, IL 60208. Offers PhD. Admissions and degrees offered through The Graduate School. Part-time programs available. *Degree requirements:* For doctorate, 2 foreign languages, thesis/dissertation, preliminary exams. *Entrance requirements:* For doctorate, GRE General Test, sample of written work. Additional exam requirements/recommendations for international students: Required—TOEFL. *Faculty research:* The novel, modernism, post-colonial literature and theory, literature and the arts, Middle Ages and Renaissance, literature and philosophy.

Oklahoma City University, Petree College of Arts and Sciences, Program in Liberal Arts, Oklahoma City, OK 73106-1402. Offers art (MLA); general studies (MLA); leadership/management (MLA); literature (MLA); mass communications (MLA); philosophy (MLA); writing (MLA). Part-time and evening/weekend programs available. *Degree requirements:* For master's, comprehensive exam, thesis optional. *Entrance requirements:* Additional exam requirements/recommendations for international students: Required—TOEFL.

Penn State University Park, Graduate School, College of the Liberal Arts, Department of Languages and Literature, State College, University Park, PA 16802-1503. Offers comparative literature (MA, PhD); Russian and comparative literature (MA).

Princeton University, Graduate School, Department of Comparative Literature, Princeton, NJ 08544-1019. Offers PhD. *Degree requirements:* For doctorate, variable foreign language requirement, thesis/dissertation. *Entrance requirements:* For doctorate, GRE General Test, GRE Subject Test, sample of written work. Additional exam requirements/recommendations for international students: Required—TOEFL (minimum score 600 paper-based; 250 computer-based). Electronic applications accepted.

Purdue University, Graduate School, College of Liberal Arts, Program in Comparative Literature, West Lafayette, IN 47907. Offers MA, PhD. Part-time programs available. *Degree requirements:* For master's, one foreign language; for doctorate, 2 foreign languages, thesis/dissertation. *Entrance requirements:* For master's, GRE General Test, writing sample; for doctorate, GRE General Test. Additional exam requirements/recommendations for international students: Required—TOEFL. Electronic applications accepted. *Faculty research:* Theory and criticism, philosophy and aesthetics, East Asian literature, postcolonial literature, classics.

Rutgers, The State University of New Jersey, New Brunswick, Graduate School, Program in Comparative Literature, Piscataway, NJ 08854-8097. Offers MA, PhD. Part-time programs available. Terminal master's awarded for partial completion of doctoral program. *Degree requirements:* For master's, comprehensive exam; for doctorate, 3 foreign languages, thesis/dissertation, written and oral exams. *Entrance requirements:* For doctorate, GRE General Test, GRE Subject Test (recommended). Additional exam requirements/recommendations for international students: Required—TOEFL. Electronic applications accepted. *Faculty research:* Genres and periods, modern literary theory, psychoanalytic approaches to literature, literature and gender, cultural studies.

San Francisco State University, Division of Graduate Studies, College of Humanities, Department of Comparative and World Literature, San Francisco, CA 94132-1722. Offers comparative literature (MA). Part-time programs available. *Degree requirements:* For master's, one foreign language.

San Jose State University, Graduate Studies and Research, College of Humanities and the Arts, Department of English and Comparative Literature, San Jose, CA 95192-0001. Offers creative writing (MFA); literature (MA); secondary English education (Certificate). *Degree requirements:* For master's, one foreign language, thesis or alternative. *Entrance requirements:* For master's, GRE. Additional exam requirements/recommendations for international students: Required—TOEFL. Electronic applications accepted.

Stanford University, School of Humanities and Sciences, Department of Comparative Literature, Stanford, CA 94305-9991. Offers PhD. *Degree requirements:* For doctorate, 3 foreign languages, thesis/dissertation, qualification procedures. *Entrance requirements:* For doctorate, GRE General Test, GRE Subject Test. Additional exam requirements/recommendations for international students: Required—TOEFL. Electronic applications accepted.

Stanford University, School of Humanities and Sciences, Program in Modern Thought and Literature, Stanford, CA 94305-9991. Offers PhD. *Degree requirements:* For doctorate, 2 foreign languages, thesis/dissertation, qualifying paper, oral exam. *Entrance requirements:* For doctorate, GRE General Test. Additional exam requirements/recommendations for international students: Required—TOEFL. Electronic applications accepted.

State University of New York at Binghamton, Graduate School, School of Arts and Sciences, Department of Comparative Literature, Binghamton, NY 13902-6000. Offers MA, PhD. Part-time programs available. *Faculty:* 9 full-time (5 women), 2 part-time/adjunct (1 woman). *Students:* 27 full-time (17 women), 38 part-time (22 women); includes 10 minority (1 African American, 1 American Indian/Alaska Native, 5 Asian Americans or Pacific Islanders, 3 Hispanic Americans), 25 international. Average age 34. 46 applicants, 70% accepted, 12 enrolled. In 2008, 7 master's, 5 doctorates awarded. Terminal master's awarded for partial completion of doctoral program. *Degree requirements:* For master's, 2 foreign languages, thesis or alternative, written exam; for doctorate, 3 foreign languages, comprehensive exam, thesis/dissertation. *Entrance requirements:* For master's and doctorate, GRE General Test, GRE Subject Test. Additional exam requirements/recommendations for international students: Required—TOEFL. *Application deadline:* For fall admission, 4/15 priority date for domestic students, 1/15 priority date for international students; for spring admission, 11/1 for domestic students, 10/15 priority date for international students. Applications are processed on a rolling basis. Application fee: $60. Electronic applications accepted. *Expenses:* Tuition, area resident: Full-time $6900; part-time $288 per credit. Tuition, state resident: full-time $6900; part-time $288 per credit. Tuition, nonresident: full-time $10,920; part-time $455 per credit. Required fees: $1130. Part-time tuition and fees vary according to course load, program and student level. *Financial support:* In 2008–09, 20 students received support, including 1 fellowship with full tuition reimbursement available (averaging $14,500 per year), 18 teaching assistantships with full tuition reimbursements available (averaging $14,500 per year); research assistantships, career-related internships or fieldwork, Federal Work-Study, institutionally sponsored loans, scholarships/grants, health care benefits, and unspecified assistantships also available. Financial award application deadline: 2/15; financial award applicants required to submit FAFSA. *Unit head:* Dr. Luiza Moreira, Chairperson, 607-777-3673, E-mail: lmoreira@binghamton.edu. *Application contact:* Victoria Williams, Recruiting and Admissions Coordinator, 607-777-2151, Fax: 607-777-2501, E-mail: vwilliam@binghamton.edu.

Stony Brook University, State University of New York, Graduate School, College of Arts and Sciences, Department of Comparative Literary and Cultural Studies, Stony Brook, NY 11794. Offers comparative literature (MA, PhD); cultural studies (PhD). Evening/weekend programs available. *Faculty:* 7 full-time (1 woman). *Students:* 35 full-time (21 women), 4 part-time (3 women); includes 6 minority (5 Asian Americans or Pacific Islanders, 1 Hispanic American), 17 international. Average age 30. 101 applicants, 19% accepted. In 2008, 1 master's, 1 doctorate awarded. Terminal master's awarded for partial completion of doctoral program. *Degree requirements:* For master's, 2 foreign languages, exam; for doctorate, 3 foreign languages, comprehensive exam, thesis/dissertation. *Entrance requirements:* For master's and doctorate, GRE General Test, minimum GPA of 3.5 in major, 3.0 overall. Additional exam requirements/recommendations for international students: Required—TOEFL. *Application deadline:* For fall admission, 1/15 for domestic students. Application fee: $60. *Expenses:* Tuition, area resident: Full-time $7880; part-time $328 per credit hour. Tuition, state resident: full-time $7880; part-time $328 per credit hour. Tuition, nonresident: full-time $13,250; part-time $552 per credit hour. Required fees: $848. *Financial support:* In 2008–09, 24 teaching assistantships were awarded; fellowships, research assistantships also available. *Faculty research:* Literary theory, interdisciplinary studies, literary history. *Unit head:* Prof. Krin Gabbard, Chairman, 631-632-7456. *Application contact:* Dr. Kent Marks, Assistant Dean, Admissions and Records, 631-632-4723, Fax: 631-632-7243, E-mail: kmarks@notes.cc.sunysb.edu.

Université de Montréal, Faculty of Arts and Sciences, Department of Comparative Literature, Montréal, QC H3C 3J7, Canada. Offers comparative literature (MA); literature (PhD). *Faculty:* 11 full-time (4 women), 1 (woman) part-time/adjunct. *Students:* 41 full-time (26 women), 84 part-time (54 women). 39 applicants, 44% accepted, 14 enrolled. In 2008, 8 master's, 6 doctorates awarded. *Degree requirements:* For master's, 2 foreign languages, thesis; for doctorate, 3 foreign languages, thesis/dissertation, general exam. *Entrance requirements:* For doctorate, MA with minimum B+ average. *Application deadline:* For fall admission, 2/1 priority date for domestic students; for winter admission, 11/1 priority date for domestic students; for spring admission, 2/1 priority date for domestic students. Application fee: $100. Electronic applications accepted. *Financial support:* Fellowships, research assistantships, teaching assistantships available. *Unit head:* Terry Cochran, Graduate Chairman, 514-343-7130, Fax: 514-343-2211, E-mail: terry.cochran@umontreal.ca. *Application contact:* ??ric Savoy, Responsible for Graduate studies, 514-343-6340, Fax: 514-343-2211, E-mail: eric.savoy@umontreal.ca.

Université de Sherbrooke, Faculty of Letters and Human Sciences, Department of Letters and Communications, Sherbrooke, QC J1K 2R1, Canada. Offers comparative Canadian literature (MA, PhD); French literature (MA, PhD); linguistics (MA); lit&erature de crèation (MA, PhD); theatre (MA). *Degree requirements:* For master's, thesis or alternative; for doctorate, thesis/dissertation. *Entrance requirements:* For master's, minimum GPA of 2.8; for doctorate, minimum GPA of 3.0.

Université du Québec à Chicoutimi, Graduate Programs, Program in Literary Studies, Chicoutimi, QC G7H 2B1, Canada. Offers MA. Part-time programs available. *Degree requirements:* For master's, thesis optional. *Entrance requirements:* For master's, appropriate bachelor's degree, proficiency in French.

Université du Québec à Montréal, Graduate Programs, Program in Literary Studies, Montréal, QC H3C 3P8, Canada. Offers MA, PhD. Part-time programs available. *Degree requirements:* For master's, thesis; for doctorate, thesis/dissertation. *Entrance requirements:* For master's, appropriate bachelor's degree or equivalent, proficiency in French; for doctorate, appropriate master's degree or equivalent, proficiency in French.

Université du Québec à Montréal, Graduate Programs, Program in Semiology, Montréal, QC H3C 3P8, Canada. Offers PhD. Part-time programs available. *Degree requirements:* For doctorate, thesis/dissertation. *Entrance requirements:* For doctorate, appropriate master's degree or equivalent, proficiency in French.

Université du Québec à Rimouski, Graduate Programs, Program in Literary Studies, Rimouski, QC G5L 3A1, Canada. Offers MA, PhD. Part-time programs available. *Degree requirements:* For master's, thesis or alternative. *Entrance requirements:* For master's, appropriate bachelor's degree, proficiency in French.

Université du Québec à Trois-Rivières, Graduate Programs, Program in Literary Studies, Trois-Rivières, QC G9A 5H7, Canada. Offers MA. Part-time programs available. *Degree requirements:* For master's, thesis optional. *Entrance requirements:* For master's, appropriate bachelor's degree, proficiency in French.

Université Laval, Faculty of Letters, Department of Literature, Programs in Literary Studies, Québec, QC G1K 7P4, Canada. Offers MA, PhD. Part-time programs available. Terminal master's awarded for partial completion of doctoral program. *Degree requirements:* For master's, thesis; for doctorate, comprehensive exam, thesis/dissertation. *Entrance requirements:* For master's and doctorate, linguistics exams, knowledge of French, knowledge of a second language. Electronic applications accepted.

University at Buffalo, the State University of New York, Graduate School, College of Arts and Sciences, Department of Comparative Literature, Buffalo, NY 14260. Offers MA, PhD. Part-time programs available. Terminal master's awarded for partial completion of doctoral program. *Degree requirements:* For master's, one foreign language, exam or thesis; for doctorate, 2 foreign languages, comprehensive exam, thesis/dissertation. *Entrance requirements:* For master's and doctorate, GRE General Test, writing sample, 3 letters of recommendation. Additional exam requirements/recommendations for international students: Required—TOEFL

Comparative Literature

University at Buffalo, the State University of New York *(continued)*
(minimum score 550 paper-based; 213 computer-based). Electronic applications accepted. *Faculty research:* Theory; interaction between literature and philosophy; European, Francophone, African, American, and South American literature; postmodernism; postcolonialism.

University of Arkansas, Graduate School, Interdisciplinary Program in Comparative Literature and Cultural Studies, Fayetteville, AR 72701-1201. Offers classical studies (MA); comparative literature (PhD). *Degree requirements:* For master's, one foreign language, comprehensive exam, thesis optional; for doctorate, 2 foreign languages, comprehensive exam, thesis/dissertation. *Entrance requirements:* For master's and doctorate, GRE General Test. *Faculty research:* Literary and cultural theory, cultural studies, postcolonial theory, gender studies, world literature.

University of California, Berkeley, Graduate Division, College of Letters and Science, Department of Comparative Literature, Berkeley, CA 94720-1500. Offers PhD. *Degree requirements:* For doctorate, thesis/dissertation, 3 languages (department may require more for some programs), qualifying exam. *Entrance requirements:* For doctorate, GRE General Test, fluency in 1 foreign language (2 preferred), minimum GPA of 3.0, writing sample, 3 letters of recommendation.

University of California, Davis, Graduate Studies, Graduate Group in Comparative Literature, Davis, CA 95616. Offers PhD. *Degree requirements:* For doctorate, 3 foreign languages, thesis/dissertation. *Entrance requirements:* For doctorate, GRE General Test, minimum GPA of 3.0. Additional exam requirements/recommendations for international students: Required—TOEFL (minimum score 550 paper-based; 213 computer-based). Electronic applications accepted. *Faculty research:* Literary criticism, literary theory, gender history and literature, genre.

University of California, Irvine, Office of Graduate Studies, School of Humanities, Department of English and Comparative Literature, Program in Comparative Literature, Irvine, CA 92697. Offers MA, PhD. *Degree requirements:* For master's, one foreign language; for doctorate, 2 foreign languages, thesis/dissertation. *Entrance requirements:* For doctorate, GRE General Test, minimum GPA of 3.5, sample of written work, 3 letters of recommendation. Additional exam requirements/recommendations for international students: Required—TOEFL (minimum score 550 paper-based; 213 computer-based). Electronic applications accepted. *Faculty research:* Critical theory, feminist studies, Asian American studies.

University of California, Los Angeles, Graduate Division, College of Letters and Science, Department of Comparative Literature, Los Angeles, CA 90095. Offers MA, PhD. *Students:* 48 full-time (35 women); includes 11 minority (1 African American, 7 Asian Americans or Pacific Islanders, 3 Hispanic Americans), 4 international. Average age 28. 71 applicants, 11% accepted, 5 enrolled. In 2008, 3 master's, 8 doctorates awarded. Terminal master's awarded for partial completion of doctoral program. *Degree requirements:* For master's, 2 foreign languages, comprehensive exam; for doctorate, 2 foreign languages, thesis/dissertation, oral and written qualifying exams. *Entrance requirements:* For master's, GRE General Test, sample of written work, previous course work in literature, minimum GPA of 3.4 in upper-division course work, degree objective must be Ph.D. in FL literary proficiency; for doctorate, GRE General Test, sample of written work, MA in comparative literature. *Application deadline:* For fall admission, 12/1, for domestic and international students. Application fee: $60 ($80 for international students). Electronic applications accepted. *Expenses:* Tuition, nonresident: full-time $14,694. Required fees: $9669.50. Full-time tuition and fees vary according to course load, degree level, program and student level. *Financial support:* In 2008–09, 50 fellowships with full and partial tuition reimbursements, 15 research assistantships with full and partial tuition reimbursements, 36 teaching assistantships with full and partial tuition reimbursements were awarded; Federal Work-Study, institutionally sponsored loans, scholarships/grants, health care benefits, tuition waivers (full and partial), and unspecified assistantships also available. Financial award application deadline: 3/1; financial award applicants required to submit FAFSA. *Unit head:* Efrain Kristal, Chair, 310-206-0552. *Application contact:* Departmental Office, 310-825-7650, E-mail: klipp@humnet.ucla.edu.

University of California, Riverside, Graduate Division, Department of Comparative Literature and Foreign Languages, Riverside, CA 92521-0102. Offers comparative literature (MA, PhD). *Faculty:* 17 full-time (9 women), 16 part-time/adjunct (13 women). *Students:* 28 full-time (20 women); includes 3 minority (all Asian Americans or Pacific Islanders), 12 international. Average age 29. 41 applicants, 32% accepted, 10 enrolled. In 2008, 2 doctorates awarded. Terminal master's awarded for partial completion of doctoral program. *Degree requirements:* For master's, 3 foreign languages, comprehensive exam; for doctorate, 3 foreign languages, thesis/dissertation, qualifying exams. *Entrance requirements:* For master's and doctorate, GRE General Test, minimum GPA of 3.2. Additional exam requirements/recommendations for international students: Required—TOEFL (minimum score 550 paper-based; 213 computer-based; 80 iBT). *Application deadline:* For fall admission, 1/5 for domestic students, 2/1 for international students; for winter admission, 9/1 for domestic students, 7/1 for international students; for spring admission, 12/1 for domestic students, 10/1 for international students. Applications are processed on a rolling basis. Application fee: $70 ($85 for international students). Electronic applications accepted. *Expenses:* Tuition, nonresident: full-time $4898. Required fees: $10,362. *Financial support:* Fellowships with partial tuition reimbursements, research assistantships, teaching assistantships with partial tuition reimbursements, career-related internships or fieldwork, Federal Work-Study, institutionally sponsored loans, and tuition waivers (full and partial) available. Financial award application deadline: 1/5; financial award applicants required to submit FAFSA. *Faculty research:* French and German Enlightenment, modern drama and theatre, contemporary critical theory, East-West comparative studies, science fiction and fantasy. *Unit head:* Dr. Thomas F. Scanlon, Chair, 951-827-1462, Fax: 951-827-2160, E-mail: thomas.scanlon@ucr.edu. *Application contact:* Dr. Marguerite Waller, Graduate Advisor, 951-827-7859, Fax: 951-827-2160, E-mail: clhsgrad@ucr.edu.

University of California, San Diego, Office of Graduate Studies, Department of Literature, Program in Comparative Literature, La Jolla, CA 92093. Offers MA, PhD. *Degree requirements:* For master's, thesis; for doctorate, thesis/dissertation. *Entrance requirements:* For master's and doctorate, GRE General Test, GRE Subject Test. Electronic applications accepted. *Faculty research:* Problems of theory and method, relationship of the humanities to the social sciences.

University of California, Santa Barbara, Graduate Division, College of Letters and Sciences, Division of Humanities and Fine Arts, Program in Comparative Literature, Santa Barbara, CA 93106-4130. Offers comparative literature (PhD); East Asian literatures (PhD); feminist studies (PhD); MA/PhD. *Faculty:* 56 full-time (24 women). *Students:* 24 full-time (18 women). Average age 29. 43 applicants, 40% accepted, 5 enrolled. In 2008, 5 doctorates awarded. Terminal master's awarded for partial completion of doctoral program. *Degree requirements:* For doctorate, 2 foreign languages, comprehensive exam, thesis/dissertation. *Entrance requirements:* For doctorate, GRE. Additional exam requirements/recommendations for international students: Required—TOEFL (paper: 550, computer: 213, IBT: 80) or IELTS (7). *Application deadline:* For fall admission, 12/15 for domestic and international students. Application fee: $70 ($90 for international students). Electronic applications accepted. *Expenses:* Tuition, nonresident: full-time $25,149. Required fees: $10,143. Full-time tuition and fees vary according to campus/location, reciprocity agreements and student level. *Financial support:* In 2008–09, 24 students received support, including 15 fellowships with full and partial tuition reimbursements available (averaging $6,900 per year), 1 research assistantship (averaging $10,600 per year), 18 teaching assistantships with partial tuition reimbursements available (averaging $10,400 per year); Federal Work-Study, institutionally sponsored loans, scholarships/grants, health care benefits, and tuition waivers (full and partial) also available. Financial award application deadline: 12/15; financial award applicants required to submit FAFSA. *Faculty research:* Media studies, literary theory, cultural studies, early-modern and modern literature, critical theory. *Unit head:* Prof. Elisabeth Weber, Chair, 805-893-3527, Fax: 805-893-2374, E-mail: weber@gss.ucsb.edu.

Application contact: Sierra Gray, Graduate Program Assistant, 805-893-2131, Fax: 805-893-2374, E-mail: sierra@gss.ucsb.edu.

University of California, Santa Cruz, Division of Graduate Studies, Division of Humanities, Department of Literature, Santa Cruz, CA 95064. Offers MA, PhD. Terminal master's awarded for partial completion of doctoral program. *Degree requirements:* For master's, thesis; for doctorate, one foreign language, thesis/dissertation, qualifying exam. *Entrance requirements:* For master's, GRE General Test, writing sample, minimum GPA of 3.5; for doctorate, GRE General Test, minimum GPA of 3.5, writing sample. Electronic applications accepted. *Faculty research:* Comparative literature; German, Spanish, classical, American, and English literature.

University of Chicago, Division of the Humanities, Department of Comparative Literature, Chicago, IL 60637-1513. Offers AM, PhD. Terminal master's awarded for partial completion of doctoral program. *Degree requirements:* For master's, 2 foreign languages, thesis; for doctorate, 3 foreign languages, thesis/dissertation. *Entrance requirements:* For master's and doctorate, GRE General Test.

University of Colorado at Boulder, Graduate School, College of Arts and Sciences, Department of Comparative Literature, Boulder, CO 80309. Offers MA, PhD. Terminal master's awarded for partial completion of doctoral program. *Degree requirements:* For master's, 2 foreign languages, comprehensive exam, thesis or alternative; for doctorate, 3 foreign languages, comprehensive exam, thesis/dissertation. *Entrance requirements:* For master's, GRE General Test, minimum undergraduate GPA of 2.75; for doctorate, GRE General Test, MA in related field. *Faculty research:* Enlightenment to modern literature; literary theory and history; philosophy and literature; popular culture studies; reception, translation and interpretation; gender and sexual orientation; nationalism.

University of Connecticut, Graduate School, College of Liberal Arts and Sciences, Department of Modern and Classical Languages, Field of Comparative Literature and Cultural Studies, Storrs, CT 06269. Offers MA, PhD. Terminal master's awarded for partial completion of doctoral program. *Degree requirements:* For master's, comprehensive exam; for doctorate, thesis/dissertation. *Entrance requirements:* For master's and doctorate, GRE General Test, GRE Subject Test. Additional exam requirements/recommendations for international students: Required—TOEFL (minimum score 550 paper-based; 213 computer-based). Electronic applications accepted.

University of Dallas, Braniff Graduate School of Liberal Arts, Institute of Philosophic Studies, Program in Literature, Irving, TX 75062-4736. Offers PhD. *Degree requirements:* For doctorate, 2 foreign languages, comprehensive exam, thesis/dissertation, qualifying exams. *Entrance requirements:* For doctorate, GRE General Test. Additional exam requirements/recommendations for international students: Required—TOEFL. *Faculty research:* Medieval studies, modern literature, Renaissance, Shakespeare.

University of Georgia, Graduate School, College of Arts and Sciences, Department of Comparative Literature, Athens, GA 30602. Offers MA, PhD. *Degree requirements:* For master's, 2 foreign languages, thesis; for doctorate, one foreign language, thesis/dissertation. *Entrance requirements:* For master's and doctorate, GRE General Test. Electronic applications accepted.

University of Guelph, Graduate Program Services, College of Arts, School of English and Theatre Studies, Joint Program in Literary Studies/Theatre Studies in English, Guelph, ON N1G 2W1, Canada. Offers PhD. Part-time programs available. *Degree requirements:* For doctorate, one foreign language, comprehensive exam, thesis/dissertation. *Entrance requirements:* For doctorate, MA, 3 letters of reference, writing samples, resumé, minimum A- average in graduate course work. Additional exam requirements/recommendations for international students: Required—TOEFL. Electronic applications accepted. *Faculty research:* Canadian studies, Early Modern studies, Postcolonial studies, studies in gender and genre, 19th Century studies.

University of Illinois at Urbana–Champaign, Graduate College, College of Liberal Arts and Sciences, School of Literatures, Cultures and Linguistics, Program in Comparative and World Literature, Champaign, IL 61820. Offers comparative literature (MA, PhD). *Faculty:* 6 full-time (5 women), 1 (woman) part-time/adjunct. *Students:* 23 full-time (16 women), 5 part-time (4 women); includes 2 minority (1 Asian American or Pacific Islander, 1 Hispanic American), 13 international. 31 applicants, 26% accepted, 4 enrolled. In 2008, 6 master's, 2 doctorates awarded. *Entrance requirements:* For master's, minimum GPA of 3.0; writing sample. Additional exam requirements/recommendations for international students: Required—TOEFL (minimum score 105 iBT). *Application deadline:* Applications are processed on a rolling basis. Application fee: $60 ($75 for international students). Electronic applications accepted. *Financial support:* In 2008–09, 12 fellowships, 1 research assistantship, 20 teaching assistantships were awarded; tuition waivers (full and partial) also available. *Unit head:* Lawrence R. Schehr, Director, 217-244-2717, Fax: 217-244-4019, E-mail: schehr@illinois.edu. *Application contact:* Lynn Stanke, Secretary, 217-244-6269, Fax: 217-244-4019, E-mail: stanke@illinois.edu.

The University of Iowa, Graduate College, College of Liberal Arts and Sciences, Department of Cinema and Comparative Literature, Program in Comparative Literature, Iowa City, IA 52242-1316. Offers MA, PhD. *Degree requirements:* For master's, thesis optional, exam; for doctorate, comprehensive exam, thesis/dissertation. *Entrance requirements:* For master's and doctorate, GRE General Test, minimum GPA of 3.0. Additional exam requirements/recommendations for international students: Required—TOEFL (minimum score 520 paper-based; 213 computer-based; 81 iBT). Electronic applications accepted.

The University of Iowa, Graduate College, College of Liberal Arts and Sciences, Department of Cinema and Comparative Literature, Program in Comparative Literature Translation, Iowa City, IA 52242-1316. Offers MFA. *Degree requirements:* For master's, thesis, exam. *Entrance requirements:* For master's, GRE General Test, minimum GPA of 3.0. Additional exam requirements/recommendations for international students: Required—TOEFL (minimum score 550 paper-based; 213 computer-based; 81 iBT). Electronic applications accepted.

University of Maryland, College Park, Graduate Studies, College of Arts and Humanities, Department of English, Program in Comparative Literature, College Park, MD 20742. Offers MA, PhD. *Degree requirements:* For master's, thesis, oral defense; for doctorate, 3 foreign languages, thesis/dissertation, comprehensive exams in 4 areas. *Entrance requirements:* For master's, GRE General Test, minimum GPA of 3.0, foreign language, writing sample, 3 letters of recommendation; for doctorate, GRE General Test, minimum GPA of 3.0, foreign language, writing sample. Additional exam requirements/recommendations for international students: Required—TOEFL. Electronic applications accepted. *Faculty research:* Renaissance studies, drama, modern literature, postcolonial studies, feminist scholarship.

University of Massachusetts Amherst, Graduate School, College of Humanities and Fine Arts, Department of Languages, Literatures, and Cultures, Program in Comparative Literature, Amherst, MA 01003. Offers MA, PhD. Part-time programs available. Terminal master's awarded for partial completion of doctoral program. *Degree requirements:* For master's, 2 foreign languages, thesis or alternative; for doctorate, 2 foreign languages, comprehensive exam, thesis/dissertation. *Entrance requirements:* For master's and doctorate, GRE General Test, writing samples. Additional exam requirements/recommendations for international students: Required—TOEFL (minimum score 550 paper-based; 213 computer-based; 79 iBT), IELTS (minimum score 6.5). Electronic applications accepted. *Expenses:* Tuition, area resident: Full-time $2640. Tuition, nonresident: full-time $9936. One-time fee: $332 full-time. Tuition and fees vary according to course load.

University of Michigan, Horace H. Rackham School of Graduate Studies, College of Literature, Science, and the Arts, Department of Comparative Literature, Ann Arbor, MI 48109. Offers PhD. *Degree requirements:* For doctorate, 2 foreign languages, thesis/dissertation, oral defense of dissertation, preliminary exam. *Entrance requirements:* For doctorate, GRE General Test. Additional exam requirements/recommendations for international students: Required—TOEFL (paper 560; computer 220; iBT 84) or Michigan English Language Assessment Battery, IELTS

(6.5). Electronic applications accepted. *Faculty research:* Postcolonial theory, cultural studies, ideology of aesthetics, translation studies, medieval philosophy.

University of Minnesota, Twin Cities Campus, Graduate School, College of Liberal Arts, Department of Cultural Studies and Comparative Literature, Program in Comparative Literature, Minneapolis, MN 55455-0213. Offers PhD. *Degree requirements:* For doctorate, 3 foreign languages, thesis/dissertation. *Entrance requirements:* For doctorate, GRE General Test, sample of written work. Additional exam requirements/recommendations for international students: Required—TOEFL. *Faculty research:* Literary theory, emergent literatures, popular culture, postcolonial literature, gender and sexuality.

University of Missouri–Columbia, Graduate School, College of Arts and Sciences, Department of Romance Languages and Literature, Columbia, MO 65211. Offers French (MA, PhD); literature (MA); Spanish (MA, PhD); teaching (MA). *Faculty:* 24 full-time (11 women), 1 (woman) part-time/adjunct. *Students:* 8 full-time (6 women), 17 part-time (9 women); includes 10 minority (2 African Americans, 2 Asian Americans or Pacific Islanders, 6 Hispanic Americans), 4 international. Average age 36. 19 applicants, 37% accepted, 5 enrolled. In 2008, 6 master's, 2 doctorates awarded. Terminal master's awarded for partial completion of doctoral program. *Degree requirements:* For master's, one foreign language; for doctorate, 4 foreign languages, thesis/dissertation. *Entrance requirements:* For master's and doctorate, GRE General Test, minimum GPA of 3.0. Additional exam requirements/recommendations for international students: Required—TOEFL (minimum score 500 paper-based; 173 computer-based; 61 iBT). *Application deadline:* For fall admission, 1/15 priority date for domestic students. Applications are processed on a rolling basis. Application fee: $45 ($60 for international students). *Financial support:* Research assistantships, teaching assistantships, institutionally sponsored loans available. *Unit head:* Dr. Flore Zephir, Department Chair, E-mail: zephirf@missouri.edu. *Application contact:* Amy Rinck, Office Support Staff III, 573-882-5039, E-mail: rinckam@missouri.edu.

University of Nebraska–Lincoln, Graduate College, College of Arts and Sciences, Department of English, Lincoln, NE 68588-0333. Offers composition and rhetoric (MA, PhD); creative writing (MA, PhD); literature studies (MA, PhD). *Faculty:* 39 full-time (23 women). *Students:* 77 full-time (57 women), 54 part-time (36 women); includes 5 minority (3 African Americans, 2 Hispanic Americans), 6 international. In 2008, 11 master's, 15 doctorates awarded. *Degree requirements:* For master's, thesis optional; for doctorate, one foreign language, comprehensive exam, thesis/dissertation. *Entrance requirements:* For master's, writing sample; for doctorate, GRE General Test, writing sample. Additional exam requirements/recommendations for international students: Required—TOEFL (minimum score 600 paper-based; 250 computer-based). *Application deadline:* For fall admission, 1/15 for domestic and international students. Application fee: $40. Electronic applications accepted. *Expenses:* Tuition, state resident: full-time $4275; part-time $237.50 per credit hour. Tuition, nonresident: full-time $11,525; part-time $640.25 per credit hour. Required fees: $1068; $10.35 per credit hour. $440.70 per semester. Tuition and fees vary according to course load and program. *Financial support:* Fellowships, research assistantships, teaching assistantships, Federal Work-Study, health care benefits, and unspecified assistantships available. Support available to part-time students. Financial award application deadline: 1/15. *Faculty research:* Creative writing, composition and rhetoric, women's studies, North American literature, medieval/Renaissance studies. *Unit head:* Dr. Linda Pratt, Chair, 402-472-3191, Fax: 402-472-1123. *Application contact:* Ginny Gross, Director of Graduate Admissions, 402-472-2878, Fax: 402-472-0589, E-mail: grad_admissions@unl.edu.

University of New Hampshire, Graduate School, College of Liberal Arts, Department of English, Durham, NH 03824. Offers English (MFA, PhD); English education (MST); language and linguistics (MA); literature (MA); writing (MA). Part-time programs available. *Faculty:* 35 full-time (18 women). *Students:* 50 full-time (29 women), 66 part-time (44 women); includes 6 minority (1 African American, 3 Asian Americans or Pacific Islanders, 2 Hispanic Americans), 5 international. Average age 34. 267 applicants, 44% accepted, 37 enrolled. In 2008, 33 master's, 1 doctorate awarded. *Degree requirements:* For master's, one foreign language; for doctorate, 2 foreign languages, thesis/dissertation. *Entrance requirements:* For master's, GRE General Test, sample of written work; for doctorate, GRE General Test, GRE Subject Test, sample of written work. Additional exam requirements/recommendations for international students: Required—TOEFL (minimum score 550 paper-based; 213 computer-based; 80 iBT). *Application deadline:* For fall admission, 2/15 priority date for domestic students, 2/15 for international students. Applications are processed on a rolling basis. Application fee: $60. Electronic applications accepted. *Expenses:* Tuition, area resident: Full-time $9720; part-time $540 per credit hour. Tuition, nonresident: full-time $23,200; part-time $954 per credit hour. Required fees: $1446; $361.50 per term. *Financial support:* In 2008–09, 58 students received support, including 3 fellowships, 1 research assistantship, 47 teaching assistantships; career-related internships or fieldwork, Federal Work-Study, scholarships/grants, and tuition waivers (full and partial) also available. Support available to part-time students. Financial award application deadline: 2/15. *Unit head:* Dr. Andrew Merton, Chairperson, 603-862-3963. *Application contact:* Sue Smith, Administrative Assistant, 603-862-3963, E-mail: engl.grad@unh.edu.

University of New Mexico, Graduate School, College of Arts and Sciences, Department of Foreign Languages and Literature, Albuquerque, NM 87131-2039. Offers comparative literature and cultural studies (MA); French (MA); French studies (PhD); German studies (MA). Part-time programs available. *Degree requirements:* For master's, one foreign language, thesis optional; for doctorate, 2 foreign languages, thesis/dissertation. Electronic applications accepted. *Faculty research:* German, Russian, Italian, Japanese, French, Comparative Lit, culture studies, classics.

The University of North Carolina at Chapel Hill, Graduate School, College of Arts and Sciences, Curriculum in Comparative Literature, Chapel Hill, NC 27599. Offers MA, PhD. Terminal master's awarded for partial completion of doctoral program. *Degree requirements:* For master's, one foreign language, thesis, exams; for doctorate, 2 foreign languages, thesis/dissertation, exams. *Entrance requirements:* For master's and doctorate, GRE General Test, minimum GPA of 3.0. Additional exam requirements/recommendations for international students: Required—TOEFL (minimum score 600 paper-based; 250 computer-based). Electronic applications accepted. *Faculty research:* Realism, literature and medicine, Proust, literary theory, Arthurian romance.

University of Notre Dame, Graduate School, College of Arts and Letters, Division of Humanities, PhD Program in Literature, Notre Dame, IN 46556. Offers PhD. *Faculty:* 17 full-time (3 women). *Students:* 30 full-time (17 women); includes 6 minority (2 Asian Americans or Pacific Islanders, 4 Hispanic Americans), 7 international. 33 applicants, 27% accepted, 6 enrolled. *Degree requirements:* For doctorate, 3 foreign languages, thesis/dissertation, candidacy exam. *Entrance requirements:* For doctorate, GRE General Test. Additional exam requirements/recommendations for international students: Required—TOEFL (minimum score 600 paper-based; 250 computer-based; 80 iBT). *Application deadline:* For fall admission, 2/1 for domestic and international students. Application fee: $50. Electronic applications accepted. *Financial support:* Fellowships with full tuition reimbursements, research assistantships with full tuition reimbursements, teaching assistantships, tuition waivers (full) available. Financial award application deadline: 2/1. *Faculty research:* Interdisciplinary study of literature from a transitional and intercultural perspective; Classics, East Asian, French, German, Irish, Italian, Iberian and Latin American (Portuguese, Spanish). *Unit head:* Dr. Joseph Buttigieg, Director of Graduate Studies, 574-631-0481, E-mail: litprog@nd.edu. *Application contact:* Dr. Barbara Turpin, Director of Graduate Admissions, 574-631-7706, Fax: 574-631-4183.

University of Oregon, Graduate School, College of Arts and Sciences, Program in Comparative Literature, Eugene, OR 97403. Offers MA, PhD. Part-time programs available. Terminal master's awarded for partial completion of doctoral program. *Degree requirements:* For master's, 2 foreign languages, field exam; for doctorate, 2 foreign languages, thesis/dissertation, field exam. *Entrance requirements:* For master's, previous course work in English and literature, proficiency in 3 foreign languages, writing sample; for doctorate, previous course work in English and literature, proficiency in 2 foreign languages, writing sample. Additional exam requirements/recommendations for international students: Required—TOEFL. *Faculty research:* Critical theory, historical periods, interdisciplinary approach, Feminist studies.

University of Pennsylvania, School of Arts and Sciences, Graduate Group in Comparative Literature and Literary Theory, Philadelphia, PA 19104. Offers comparative literature (AM, PhD); literary theory (AM, PhD). *Degree requirements:* For master's, one foreign language, thesis; for doctorate, variable foreign language requirement, thesis/dissertation. *Entrance requirements:* For master's, GRE General Test, proficiency in 1 foreign language; for doctorate, GRE General Test, master's degree in a literature field, proficiency in 1 foreign language. Additional exam requirements/recommendations for international students: Required—TOEFL. Electronic applications accepted.

University of Puerto Rico, Río Piedras, College of Humanities, Department of Comparative Literature, San Juan, PR 00931-3300. Offers MA. Part-time programs available. *Degree requirements:* For master's, comprehensive exam, thesis. *Entrance requirements:* For master's, EXADEP, interview, minimum GPA of 3.0, letter of recommendation.

University of South Carolina, The Graduate School, College of Arts and Sciences, Department of Languages, Literatures, and Cultures, Columbia, SC 29208. Offers comparative literature (MA, PhD); foreign languages (MAT), including French, German, Spanish; French (MA); German (MA); Spanish (MA). MAT offered in cooperation with the College of Education. Part-time programs available. *Degree requirements:* For master's, one foreign language, comprehensive exam, thesis optional; for doctorate, 2 foreign languages, comprehensive exam, thesis/dissertation. *Entrance requirements:* For master's and doctorate, GRE General Test, writing sample. Additional exam requirements/recommendations for international students: Required—TOEFL (minimum score 230 computer-based; 75 iBT). Electronic applications accepted. *Faculty research:* Modern literature, linguistics, literature and culture, medieval literature, literary theory.

University of Southern California, Graduate School, College of Letters, Arts and Sciences, Department of Comparative Literature, Los Angeles, CA 90089. Offers MA, PhD. Terminal master's awarded for partial completion of doctoral program. *Degree requirements:* For master's, 2 foreign languages; for doctorate, 2 foreign languages, thesis/dissertation. *Entrance requirements:* For master's and doctorate, GRE General Test. *Faculty research:* Literary theory, film and literary, Asian-American literature, humanities and environment.

The University of Texas at Austin, Graduate School, College of Liberal Arts, Program in Comparative Literature, Austin, TX 78712-1111. Offers MA, PhD. *Degree requirements:* For master's, 2 foreign languages, report or thesis; for doctorate, 3 foreign languages, thesis/dissertation. *Entrance requirements:* For master's and doctorate, GRE General Test. Electronic applications accepted.

The University of Texas at Dallas, School of Arts and Humanities, Richardson, TX 75083-0688. Offers arts and technology (MFA); emerging media and communications (MA); humanities (MA, MAT, PhD), including aesthetic studies, history of ideas, studies in literature. Part-time and evening/weekend programs available. *Faculty:* 52 full-time (15 women), 6 part-time/adjunct (2 women). *Students:* 201 full-time (107 women), 194 part-time (105 women); includes 82 minority (30 African Americans, 3 American Indian/Alaska Native, 23 Asian Americans or Pacific Islanders, 26 Hispanic Americans), 31 international. Average age 38. 173 applicants, 80% accepted, 83 enrolled. In 2008, 88 master's, 11 doctorates awarded. *Degree requirements:* For master's, one foreign language, portfolio; for doctorate, one foreign language, thesis/dissertation. *Entrance requirements:* For master's and doctorate, minimum GPA of 3.0 in undergraduate course work in field. Additional exam requirements/recommendations for international students: Required—TOEFL (minimum score 550 paper-based; 213 computer-based). *Application deadline:* For fall admission, 7/15 for domestic students, 5/1 priority date for international students; for spring admission, 11/15 for domestic students, 9/1 priority date for international students. Applications are processed on a rolling basis. Application fee: $50 ($100 for international students). Electronic applications accepted. *Expenses:* Tuition, area resident: Full-time $8320. Tuition, state resident: full-time $8320. Tuition, nonresident: full-time $15,054. Part-time tuition and fees vary according to course load. *Financial support:* In 2008–09, 10 research assistantships with tuition reimbursements (averaging $10,339 per year), 74 teaching assistantships with tuition reimbursements (averaging $10,152 per year) were awarded; fellowships, Federal Work-Study, institutionally sponsored loans, scholarships/grants, and unspecified assistantships also available. Support available to part-time students. Financial award application deadline: 4/30; financial award applicants required to submit FAFSA. *Faculty research:* Translation, science and the arts and humanities, intellectual and philosophical history, cultural studies. Total annual research expenditures: $165,892. *Unit head:* Dr. Dennis M. Kratz, Dean, 972-883-2984, Fax: 972-883-2989, E-mail: dkratz@utdallas.edu. *Application contact:* Dr. Michael Wilson, Associate Dean of Graduate Studies, 972-883-2756, Fax: 972-883-2989, E-mail: mwilson@utdallas.edu.

University of Toronto, School of Graduate Studies, Humanities Division, Centre for Comparative Literature, Toronto, ON M5S 1A1, Canada. Offers MA, PhD. Part-time programs available. *Degree requirements:* For doctorate, thesis/dissertation. *Entrance requirements:* For master's and doctorate, 2 letters of recommendation, sample of work (short essay on a literary topic preferred), resumé.

University of Utah, The Graduate School, College of Humanities, Department of Languages and Literature, Salt Lake City, UT 84112-1107. Offers comparative literary and cultural studies (MA, PhD); French (MA, MALP); German (MA, MALP, PhD); language pedagogy (MALP); Spanish (MA, MALP, PhD); world languages with secondary teaching licensure (MA). Terminal master's awarded for partial completion of doctoral program. *Degree requirements:* For master's, standard proficiency in 2 languages other than English, comprehensive exam or thesis; for doctorate, comprehensive exam, standard proficiency in 2 languages other than English and language of study, advanced proficiency in 1 language other than English and language of study, dissertation. *Entrance requirements:* For master's, bachelor's degree or strong undergraduate record in target languages, GPA of 3.0, literature-survey courses; for doctorate, successful completion of MA and advanced proficiency in a target language. Additional exam requirements/recommendations for international students: Required—TOEFL (minimum score 500 paper-based; 173 computer-based). Electronic applications accepted. *Faculty research:* Literary theory, stylistics, Russian and Soviet literature, existentialism, theory of criticism.

University of Washington, Graduate School, College of Arts and Sciences, Department of Comparative Literature, Seattle, WA 98195. Offers MA, PhD. Part-time programs available. Terminal master's awarded for partial completion of doctoral program. *Degree requirements:* For master's, 2 foreign languages, thesis optional; for doctorate, 3 foreign languages, thesis/dissertation. *Entrance requirements:* For master's, GRE General Test, BA in comparative literature or equivalent, minimum GPA of 3.0, proficiency in 1 foreign language; for doctorate, GRE General Test, MA in comparative literature or equivalent, minimum GPA of 3.0, proficiency in 2 foreign languages. Additional exam requirements/recommendations for international students: Required—TOEFL. Electronic applications accepted. *Faculty research:* Literature and culture from classical antiquity to twentieth-century, literary theory and criticism.

The University of Western Ontario, Faculty of Graduate Studies, Faculty of Arts and Humanities, Department of Comparative Literature, London, ON N6A 5B8, Canada. Offers comparative literature (MA, PhD); Spanish (MA). Part-time programs available. *Degree requirements:* For master's, 2 foreign languages, thesis (for some programs). *Entrance requirements:* For master's, honors degree in Spanish or equivalent, minimum B average. Additional exam requirements/recommendations for international students: Required—TOEFL, TOEFL (comparative literature). *Faculty research:* Spanish golden age, Latin-American, romance, medieval, film.

University of Wisconsin–Madison, Graduate School, College of Letters and Science, Department of Comparative Literature, Madison, WI 53706-1380. Offers MA, PhD. Part-time programs available. Terminal master's awarded for partial completion of doctoral program.

Comparative Literature

University of Wisconsin–Madison (continued)
Degree requirements: For master's, one foreign language, second-year exam; for doctorate, 3 foreign languages, thesis/dissertation, 3 preliminary exams. *Entrance requirements:* For master's, GRE General Test, writing sample; for doctorate, GRE General Test. Electronic applications accepted. *Faculty research:* Literary theory, cultural criticism, classics through early modern literature, postmodernity, gender studies.

University of Wisconsin–Madison, Graduate School, College of Letters and Science, Department of East Asian Languages and Literature, Program in Chinese Literature, Madison, WI 53706-1380. Offers MA, PhD. Part-time programs available. Terminal master's awarded for partial completion of doctoral program. *Degree requirements:* For master's, one foreign language, seminars, written exam; for doctorate, 3 foreign languages, thesis/dissertation, seminars, preliminary exams, oral exam. *Entrance requirements:* For master's, bachelor's degree or equivalent in Chinese; for doctorate, master's degree or equivalent in Chinese. Electronic applications accepted. *Faculty research:* Chinese historical and modern linguistics, classical Chinese literary and cultural history, modern Chinese literary and cultural history, Chinese paleography.

University of Wisconsin–Madison, Graduate School, College of Letters and Science, Department of Scandinavian Studies, Madison, WI 53706-1380. Offers area studies (MA); folklore (PhD); literature (MA, PhD); philology (PhD). Part-time programs available. *Degree requirements:* For master's, 2 foreign languages, exam; for doctorate, thesis/dissertation, exam. *Entrance requirements:* For master's, minimum GPA of 3.25; for doctorate, minimum GPA of 3.5. Electronic applications accepted. *Faculty research:* Historical fiction, Icelandic poetry, nineteenth-century literature, theater, gender studies, folklore.

University of Wisconsin–Milwaukee, Graduate School, College of Letters and Sciences, Department of English, Milwaukee, WI 53201-0413. Offers creative writing (PhD); English (MA); linguistics (PhD); professional writing (PhD); professional writing and communication (Certificate); rhetoric and composition (PhD); MLIS/MA. *Faculty:* 40 full-time (19 women). *Students:* 107 full-time (64 women), 82 part-time (54 women); includes 13 minority (8 African Americans, 1 American Indian/Alaska Native, 2 Asian Americans or Pacific Islanders, 2 Hispanic Americans), 23 international. Average age 35. 187 applicants, 41% accepted, 34 enrolled. In 2008, 31 master's, 14 doctorates awarded. *Degree requirements:* For master's, thesis or alternative; for doctorate, one foreign language, thesis/dissertation. *Entrance requirements:* For master's, GRE General Test, GRE Subject Test; for doctorate, GRE. Additional exam requirements/recommendations for international students: Required—TOEFL (minimum score 550 paper-based; 79 iBT), IELTS (minimum score 6.5). *Application deadline:* For fall admission, 1/1 priority date for domestic students; for spring admission, 9/1 for domestic students. Applications are processed on a rolling basis. Application fee: $45 ($75 for international students). *Expenses:* Tuition, area resident: Full-time $7320; part-time $165 per credit. Tuition, state resident: full-time $7320; part-time $165 per credit. Tuition, nonresident: full-time $17,840; part-time $714 per credit. Tuition and fees vary according to campus/location, program and reciprocity agreements. *Financial support:* In 2008–09, 74 teaching assistantships were awarded; career-related internships or fieldwork and unspecified assistantships also available. Support available to part-time students. Financial award application deadline: 4/15. Total annual research expenditures: $35,677. *Unit head:* Tasha Oren, Representative, 414-229-2643, Fax: 414-229-2643, E-mail: tgoren@uwm.edu. *Application contact:* General Information Contact, 414-229-4982, Fax: 414-229-6967, E-mail: gradschool@uwm.edu.

University of Wisconsin–Milwaukee, Graduate School, College of Letters and Sciences, Interdepartmental Program in Foreign Language and Literature, Milwaukee, WI 53201-0413. Offers classics and Hebrew studies (MAFLL); comparative literature (MAFLL); French and Italian (MAFLL); German (MAFLL); Slavic studies (MAFLL); translation (Certificate). Part-time programs available. *Faculty:* 39 full-time (17 women). *Students:* 32 full-time (25 women), 28 part-time (19 women); includes 5 minority (1 Asian American or Pacific Islander, 4 Hispanic Americans), 22 international. Average age 32. 51 applicants, 65% accepted, 26 enrolled. In 2008, 19 master's awarded. *Degree requirements:* For master's, 2 foreign languages, thesis or alternative. *Entrance requirements:* Additional exam requirements/recommendations for international students: Required—TOEFL (minimum score 550 paper-based; 79 iBT), IELTS (minimum score 6.5). *Application deadline:* For fall admission, 1/1 priority date for domestic students; for spring admission, 9/1 for domestic students. Applications are processed on a rolling basis. Application fee: $45 ($75 for international students). *Expenses:* Tuition, area resident: Full-time $7320; part-time $165 per credit. Tuition, state resident: full-time $7320; part-time $165 per credit. Tuition, nonresident: full-time $17,840; part-time $714 per credit. Tuition and fees vary according to campus/location, program and reciprocity agreements. *Financial support:* In 2008–09, 2 research assistantships, 35 teaching assistantships were awarded; career-related internships or fieldwork and unspecified assistantships also available. Support available to part-time students. Financial award application deadline: 4/15. Total annual research expenditures: $43,420. *Unit head:* Gabrielle Verdier, Representative, 414-229-3346, Fax: 414-229-2741, E-mail: verdier@uwm.edu. *Application contact:* General Information Contact, 414-229-4982, Fax: 414-229-6967, E-mail: gradschool@uwm.edu.

Washington University in St. Louis, Graduate School of Arts and Sciences, Department of Asian and Near Eastern Languages and Literatures, St. Louis, MO 63130-4899. Offers Chinese (MA); Chinese and comparative literature (PhD); Japanese (MA); Japanese and comparative literature (PhD). *Students:* 20 full-time (13 women); includes 1 minority (Hispanic American), 15 international. 9 applicants, 44% accepted, 2 enrolled. In 2008, 1 master's awarded. Terminal master's awarded for partial completion of doctoral program. *Degree requirements:* For master's, thesis optional; for doctorate, thesis/dissertation. *Entrance requirements:* For master's and doctorate, GRE General Test. *Application deadline:* For fall admission, 1/15 priority date for domestic students. Applications are processed on a rolling basis. Application fee: $45. Electronic applications accepted. *Financial support:* Teaching assistantships, Federal Work-Study, institutionally sponsored loans, and tuition waivers (full and partial) available. Support available to part-time students. Financial award application deadline: 1/15. *Unit head:* Dr. Fatemeh Keshavarz, Chairperson, 314-935-5156. *Application contact:* Assistant to the Dean, 314-935-6880, Fax: 314-935-4887.

Washington University in St. Louis, Graduate School of Arts and Sciences, Program in Comparative Literature, St. Louis, MO 63130-4899. Offers MA, PhD. *Students:* 21 full-time (16 women); includes 1 minority (African American), 11 international. 23 applicants, 43% accepted, 8 enrolled. In 2008, 3 master's awarded. Terminal master's awarded for partial completion of doctoral program. *Degree requirements:* For master's, thesis or alternative; for doctorate, thesis/dissertation. *Entrance requirements:* For master's and doctorate, GRE General Test. *Application deadline:* For fall admission, 1/15 priority date for domestic students. Application fee: $45. Electronic applications accepted. *Financial support:* Fellowships, teaching assistantships, Federal Work-Study, institutionally sponsored loans, and tuition waivers (full and partial) available. Support available to part-time students. Financial award application deadline: 1/15. *Unit head:* Dr. Harriet Stone, Chairperson, 314-935-5170. *Application contact:* Assistant to the Dean, 314-935-6880, Fax: 314-935-4887.

Wayne State University, College of Liberal Arts and Sciences, Department of English, Program in Comparative Literature, Detroit, MI 48202. Offers MA. *Degree requirements:* For master's, one foreign language, essay or thesis. *Entrance requirements:* For master's, GRE General Test, minimum GPA of 3.25 in English, 3.0 overall. Additional exam requirements/recommendations for international students: Required—TOEFL (minimum score 550 paper-based; 213 computer-based); Recommended—TWE (minimum score 6). Electronic applications accepted.

Western Kentucky University, Graduate Studies, Potter College of Arts and Letters, Department of English, Bowling Green, KY 42101. Offers education (MA); English (MA Ed); literature (MA), including American literature, British literature, literary theory, women writers, world literature; teaching English as a second language (MA); writing (MA). Part-time and evening/weekend programs available. *Degree requirements:* For master's, comprehensive exam, thesis optional, final exam. *Entrance requirements:* For master's, GRE General Test, minimum GPA of 2.75. Additional exam requirements/recommendations for international students: Required—TOEFL (minimum score 555 paper-based; 213 computer-based; 79 iBT). *Faculty research:* Improving writing, linking teacher knowledge and performance, Victorian women writers, Kentucky women writers, Kentucky poets.

Yale University, Graduate School of Arts and Sciences, Department of Comparative Literature, New Haven, CT 06520. Offers PhD. *Degree requirements:* For doctorate, 2 foreign languages, thesis/dissertation. *Entrance requirements:* For doctorate, GRE General Test.

English

Abilene Christian University, Graduate School, College of Arts and Sciences, Department of English, Abilene, TX 79699-9100. Offers composition/rhetoric (MA); literature (MA); writing (MA). Part-time programs available. *Faculty:* 14 part-time/adjunct (5 women). *Students:* 11 full-time (7 women), 2 part-time (both women); includes 1 minority (Hispanic American), 1 international. 12 applicants, 50% accepted, 5 enrolled. In 2008, 6 master's awarded. *Degree requirements:* For master's, one foreign language, comprehensive exam, thesis optional. *Entrance requirements:* For master's, GRE General Test. *Application deadline:* For fall admission, 4/1 priority date for domestic students; for spring admission, 11/1 for domestic students. Applications are processed on a rolling basis. Application fee: $40 ($45 for international students). Electronic applications accepted. *Expenses:* Tuition: Full-time $10,728; part-time $640 per hour. Required fees: $1090; $53.50 per hour. $10 per term. Tuition and fees vary according to campus/location. *Financial support:* In 2008–09, 13 students received support; teaching assistantships, Federal Work-Study available. Support available to part-time students. Financial award application deadline: 4/1; financial award applicants required to submit FAFSA. *Faculty research:* Feminism, Shakespearean dimensions of new literature, poetic consciousness, deconstruction myths. *Unit head:* Dr. Dana McMichael, Graduate Adviser, 325-674-2253, Fax: 325-674-2408, E-mail: rankinw@acu.edu. *Application contact:* William Horn, Graduate Admissions Counselor, 325-674-2656, Fax: 325-674-6717, E-mail: gradinfo@acu.edu.

Acadia University, Faculty of Arts, Department of English, Wolfville, NS B4P 2R6, Canada. Offers MA. *Faculty:* 15 full-time (6 women). *Students:* 4 full-time (1 woman), 2 part-time (1 woman). Average age 25. 13 applicants, 46% accepted, 4 enrolled. In 2008, 3 master's awarded. *Degree requirements:* For master's, thesis. *Entrance requirements:* For master's, honors degree in English, minimum A- average. Additional exam requirements/recommendations for international students: Required—TOEFL (minimum score 630 paper-based; 267 computer-based; 93 iBT), IELTS (minimum score 6.5). *Application deadline:* For fall admission, 2/1 priority date for domestic students; for spring admission, 3/30 for domestic students. Applications are processed on a rolling basis. Application fee: $50. Tuition and fees charges are reported in Canadian dollars. *Expenses:* Tuition, area resident: Full-time $3873.50 Canadian dollars; part-time $844 Canadian dollars per course. Tuition, state resident: full-time $4634.50 Canadian dollars; part-time $844 Canadian dollars per course. Tuition, nonresident: full-time $9103 Canadian dollars; part-time $1687 Canadian dollars per course. Required fees: $503.22 Canadian dollars; $5 Canadian dollars per course. *Financial support:* In 2008–09, 4 students received support, including 4 teaching assistantships (averaging $9,000 per year); scholarships/grants and unspecified assistantships also available. Financial award application deadline: 2/1. *Faculty research:* Renaissance, Canadian, Medieval, Victorian, and Romantic literature. *Unit head:* Dr. Patricia Rigg, Chair, 902-585-1503, Fax: 902-585-1070, E-mail: patricia.rigg@acadiau.ca. *Application contact:* Christine Reed, Secretary, 902-585-1502, Fax: 902-585-1070, E-mail: christine.reed@acadiau.ca.

The American University in Cairo, Graduate Studies and Research, School of Humanities and Social Sciences, Department of English and Comparative Literature, Cairo, Egypt. Offers MA. Part-time programs available. *Degree requirements:* For master's, one foreign language, thesis, proficiency in French or German. *Entrance requirements:* Additional exam requirements/recommendations for international students: Required—English entrance exam and/or TOEFL.

American University of Beirut, Graduate Programs, Faculty of Arts and Sciences, Beirut, Lebanon. Offers anthropology (MA); Arabic language and literature (MA); archaeology (MA); biology (MS); chemistry (MS); computer science (MS); economics (MA); education (MA); English language (MA); English literature (MA); environmental policy planning (MSES); financial economics (MAFE); geology (MS); history (MA); mathematics (MA, MS); Middle Eastern studies (MA); philosophy (MA); physics (MS); political studies (MA); psychology (MA); public administration (MA); sociology (MA); statistics (MA, MS). Part-time programs available. *Degree requirements:* For master's, one foreign language, comprehensive exam, thesis (for some programs). *Entrance requirements:* For master's, GRE, letter of recommendation. Additional exam requirements/recommendations for international students: Required—TOEFL (minimum score 600 paper-based; 250 computer-based; 100 iBT), IELTS (minimum score 7.5). *Faculty research:* String theory and supergravity; computer graphics; algebra and number theory; popular Arabic literature; marine and freshwater biology; integrating science, math and technology.

Andrews University, School of Graduate Studies, College of Arts and Sciences, Department of English, Berrien Springs, MI 49104. Offers MA, MAT. Part-time programs available. *Faculty:* 10 full-time (4 women), 3 part-time/adjunct (2 women). *Students:* 12 full-time (7 women), 3 part-time (all women); includes 5 minority (1 African American, 3 Asian Americans or Pacific Islanders, 1 Hispanic American), 4 international. Average age 28. In 2008, 4 master's awarded. *Degree requirements:* For master's, one foreign language, thesis optional. *Entrance requirements:* For master's, GRE Subject Test. Additional exam requirements/recommendations for international students: Required—TOEFL (minimum score 550 paper-based). *Application deadline:* For fall admission, 8/15 for domestic students. Applications are processed on a rolling basis. Application fee: $40. *Expenses:* Tuition: Full-time $18,360; part-time $765 per credit hour. Required fees: $476; $765 per credit hour. $238 per semester. Tuition and fees vary according to degree level. *Financial support:* Fellowships, research assistantships, teaching assistantships, career-related internships or fieldwork and Federal Work-Study available. *Faculty research:* Christianity and literature, Victorian literature, social linguistics, rhetoric, American literature. *Unit head:* Dr. Douglas Jones, Chairperson, 269-471-3298. *Application contact:* Carolyn Hurst, Supervisor of Graduate Admission, 800-253-2874, Fax: 269-471-6321, E-mail: graduate@andrews.edu.

Angelo State University, College of Graduate Studies, College of Liberal and Fine Arts, Department of English, San Angelo, TX 76909. Offers MA. Part-time and evening/weekend programs available. *Faculty:* 5 full-time (2 women). *Students:* 2 full-time (1 woman), 13 part-time (8 women); includes 3 minority (all Hispanic Americans). Average age 27. 7 applicants, 100% accepted, 5 enrolled. In 2008, 7 master's awarded. *Degree requirements:* For master's, comprehensive exam, thesis optional. *Entrance requirements:* For master's, GRE General Test. Additional exam requirements/recommendations for international students: Required—TOEFL or IELTS. *Application deadline:* For fall admission, 7/15 priority date for domestic students, 6/10 for international students; for spring admission, 12/1 priority date for domestic students, 11/1 for international students. Applications are processed on a rolling basis. Application fee: $40 ($50 for international students). Electronic applications accepted. *Financial support:* In 2008–09, 9 students received support, including 4 teaching assistantships (averaging $10,251 per year); Federal Work-Study, scholarships/grants, and unspecified assistantships also available. Support available to part-time students. Financial award application deadline: 3/1; financial award applicants required to submit FAFSA. *Unit head:* Dr. John Wegner, Interim Department Head, 325-942-2273 Ext. 231, E-mail: john.wegner@angelo.edu. *Application contact:* Dr. Terry Dalrymple, Graduate Advisor, 325-942-2252 Ext. 225, E-mail: terry.dalrymple@angelo.edu.

Appalachian State University, Cratis D. Williams Graduate School, Department of English, Boone, NC 28608. Offers English (MA); English education (MA). Part-time programs available. Postbaccalaureate distance learning degree programs offered (no on-campus study). *Faculty:* 37 full-time (18 women). *Students:* 14 full-time (8 women), 25 part-time (13 women); includes 5 minority (2 African Americans, 3 Asian Americans or Pacific Islanders), 2 international. 28 applicants, 100% accepted, 7 enrolled. In 2008, 16 master's awarded. *Degree requirements:* For master's, one foreign language, comprehensive exam, thesis (for some programs). *Entrance requirements:* For master's, GRE General Test, 3 letters of recommendation. Additional exam requirements/recommendations for international students: Required—TOEFL (minimum score 570 paper-based; 230 computer-based; 79 iBT), IELTS (minimum score 6.5). *Application deadline:* For fall admission, 7/1 for domestic students, 2/1 for international students; for spring admission, 11/1 for domestic students, 7/1 for international students. Applications are processed on a rolling basis. Application fee: $50. Electronic applications accepted. *Expenses:* Tuition, area resident: Full-time $2600; part-time $700 per course. Tuition, state resident: full-time $2600; part-time $700 per course. Tuition, nonresident: full-time $5000; part-time $3300 per course. Required fees: $2150; $330 per course. Tuition and fees vary according to campus/location. *Financial support:* In 2008–09, 10 research assistantships (averaging $7,500 per year), 16 teaching assistantships (averaging $7,500 per year) were awarded; fellowships, career-related internships or fieldwork, Federal Work-Study, scholarships/grants, and unspecified assistantships also available. Financial award application deadline: 4/1; financial award applicants required to submit FAFSA. *Faculty research:* Contemporary Irish literature, Romantic psychology, cultural practices of everyday life, Gullah linguistics, Renaissance women's writing. Total annual research expenditures: $14,500. *Unit head:* Dr. James Ivory, Chair, 828-262-3098, E-mail: ivoryjm@appstate.edu. *Application contact:* Dr. Colin Ramsey, Graduate Program Director, 828-262-7390, E-mail: ramseyct@appstate.edu.

Arcadia University, Graduate Studies, Department of English, Glenside, PA 19038-3295. Offers MAE. Part-time and evening/weekend programs available. *Degree requirements:* For master's, thesis optional.

Arizona State University, Graduate College, College of Liberal Arts and Sciences, Division of Humanities, Department of English, Tempe, AZ 85287. Offers creative writing (MFA); English (MA, PhD), including comparative literature (MA), linguistics (MA), literature, rhetoric and composition (MA), rhetoric/composition and linguistics (PhD); teaching English to speakers of other languages (MTESOL). *Degree requirements:* For doctorate, thesis/dissertation. *Entrance requirements:* For master's and doctorate, GRE.

Arkansas State University, Graduate School, College of Humanities and Social Sciences, Department of English and Philosophy, Jonesboro, State University, AR 72467. Offers English (MA); English education (MSE, SCCT). Part-time programs available. *Faculty:* 14 full-time (4 women). *Students:* 9 full-time (2 women), 12 part-time (5 women); includes 1 minority (African American), 4 international. Average age 31. 17 applicants, 88% accepted, 9 enrolled. In 2008, 10 master's awarded. *Degree requirements:* For master's, one foreign language, comprehensive exam, thesis or alternative; for SCCT, comprehensive exam. *Entrance requirements:* For master's, GRE General Test or MAT, preliminary exam, appropriate bachelor's degree, official transcript, valid teaching certificate (for MSE); for SCCT, GRE General Test or MAT, interview, master's degree, official transcript. Additional exam requirements/recommendations for international students: Required—TOEFL (minimum score 550 paper-based; 213 computer-based; 79 iBT), IELTS (minimum score 6). *Application deadline:* For fall admission, 7/15 for domestic students, 7/1 for international students; for spring admission, 12/1 for domestic students, 11/13 for international students. Applications are processed on a rolling basis. Application fee: $30 ($40 for international students). Electronic applications accepted. *Expenses:* Tuition, state resident: full-time $3744; part-time $208 per credit hour. Tuition, nonresident: full-time $9540; part-time $530 per credit hour. International tuition: $7938 full-time. Required fees: $896; $47 per credit hour. $25 per term. One-time fee: $50. Tuition and fees vary according to course load and program. *Financial support:* In 2008–09, 10 students received support; teaching assistantships, career-related internships or fieldwork, scholarships/grants, and unspecified assistantships available. Financial award application deadline: 7/1; financial award applicants required to submit FAFSA. *Faculty research:* Cognitive science, critical race theory, history of English, linguistics, popular culture. *Unit head:* Dr. Charles Carr, Chair, 870-972-3043, Fax: 870-972-3045, E-mail: crcarr@astate.edu. *Application contact:* Dr. Andrew Sustich, Dean of the Graduate School, 870-972-3029, Fax: 870-972-3857, E-mail: sustich@astate.edu.

Arkansas Tech University, Graduate School, School of Liberal and Fine Arts, Russellville, AR 72801. Offers communication (MLA); English (M Ed, MA); fine arts (MLA); history (MA); multi-media journalism (MA); social science (MLA); social studies (M Ed); Spanish (MA, MLA); teaching English as a second language (MA, MLA). Part-time programs available. *Students:* 40 full-time (31 women), 81 part-time (60 women); includes 10 minority (3 African Americans, 2 American Indian/Alaska Native, 2 Asian Americans or Pacific Islanders, 3 Hispanic Americans), 19 international. Average age 33. In 2008, 70 master's awarded. *Degree requirements:* For master's, project. *Entrance requirements:* For master's, GRE General Test or MAT. Additional exam requirements/recommendations for international students: Required—TOEFL (minimum score 500 paper-based; 173 computer-based; 61 iBT). *Application deadline:* For fall admission, 3/1 priority date for domestic students, 5/1 priority date for international students; for winter admission, 10/1 priority date for international students; for spring admission, 10/1 priority date for domestic and international students. Applications are processed on a rolling basis. Application fee: $0 ($30 for international students). Electronic applications accepted. *Expenses:* Tuition, state resident: full-time $1575; part-time $175 per credit hour. Tuition, nonresident: full-time $3150; part-time $350 per credit hour. Tuition and fees vary according to course load. *Financial support:* In 2008–09, teaching assistantships with full tuition reimbursements (averaging $4,000 per year); career-related internships or fieldwork, Federal Work-Study, scholarships/grants, health care benefits, and unspecified assistantships also available. Support available to part-time students. Financial award application deadline: 4/15; financial award applicants required to submit FAFSA. *Unit head:* Dr. Georgena Duncan, Dean, 479-968-0266, Fax: 479-968-0275, E-mail: georgena.duncan@atu.edu. *Application contact:* Dr. Eldon G. Clary, Dean of Graduate School, 479-968-0398, Fax: 479-964-0542, E-mail: graduate.school@atu.edu.

Asbury College, Graduate Programs, Wilmore, KY 40390-1198. Offers biology: alternative certificate (MA Ed); chemistry: alternative certificate (MA Ed); English (Certificate); English as a second language (MA Ed); ESL (Certificate); French (Certificate); mathematics: alternative certificate (MA Ed); reading / writing (MA Ed); social studies (Certificate); Spanish (Certificate); special education (MA Ed); special education: alternative certificate (MA Ed). *Accreditation:* NCATE. Part-time programs available. *Degree requirements:* For master's, action research project, portfolio. *Entrance requirements:* For master's, PRAXIS/NTE, minimum GPA of 2.75, letters of recommendation. Additional exam requirements/recommendations for international students: Required—TOEFL (minimum score 550 paper-based).

Auburn University, Graduate School, College of Liberal Arts, Department of English, Auburn University, AL 36849. Offers MA, MTPC, PhD. Part-time programs available. *Faculty:* 67 full-time (38 women), 17 part-time/adjunct (8 women). *Students:* 25 full-time (19 women), 48 part-time (33 women); includes 3 minority (all African Americans), 2 international. Average age 30. 60 applicants, 53% accepted, 15 enrolled. In 2008, 21 master's, 4 doctorates awarded. *Degree requirements:* For master's, one foreign language, thesis optional, written exam; for doctorate, 2 foreign languages, thesis/dissertation, oral and written exams. *Entrance requirements:* For master's, GRE General Test, sample of written work; for doctorate, GRE General Test, GRE Subject Test, sample of written work. *Application deadline:* For fall admission, 7/7 for domestic students; for spring admission, 11/24 for domestic students. Applications are processed on a rolling basis. Application fee: $25 ($50 for international students). Electronic applications accepted. *Expenses:* Tuition, area resident: Full-time $5880; part-time $243 per credit hour. Tuition, state resident: full-time $5880; part-time $243 per credit hour. Tuition, nonresident: full-time $17,640; part-time $729 per credit hour. International tuition: $17,846 full-time. Required fees: $620. Tuition and fees vary according to program and reciprocity agreements. *Financial support:* Fellowships, teaching assistantships, Federal Work-Study available. Support available to part-time students. Financial award application deadline: 3/15. *Faculty research:* English literature, American literature, linguistics, rhetoric and composition, literary theory. *Unit head:* Dr. George W. Crandell, Head, 334-844-4620. *Application contact:* Dr. George Flowers, Dean of the Graduate School, 334-844-2125.

See Close-Up on page 435.

Austin Peay State University, College of Graduate Studies, College of Arts and Letters, Department of Languages and Literature, Clarksville, TN 37044. Offers English (MA). Part-time programs available. Postbaccalaureate distance learning degree programs offered (minimal on-campus study). *Faculty:* 8 full-time (4 women). *Students:* 13 full-time (12 women), 14 part-time (11 women); includes 3 minority (all African Americans). Average age 35. 20 applicants, 100% accepted, 15 enrolled. In 2008, 7 master's awarded. *Degree requirements:* For master's, comprehensive exam, thesis optional. *Entrance requirements:* For master's, GRE General Test, 3 letters of recommendation, bachelor's degree. Additional exam requirements/recommendations for international students: Required—TOEFL (minimum score 500 paper-based; 173 computer-based). *Application deadline:* For fall admission, 7/27 priority date for domestic students; for spring admission, 12/17 priority date for domestic students. Applications are processed on a rolling basis. Application fee: $25. Electronic applications accepted. *Expenses:* Tuition, area resident: Full-time $5772; part-time $305 per credit hour. Tuition, state resident: full-time $5772; part-time $305 per credit hour. Tuition, nonresident: full-time $16,664; part-time $778 per credit hour. Required fees: $1224. *Financial support:* In 2008–09, 11 research assistantships with full tuition reimbursements (averaging $6,996 per year) were awarded; career-related internships or fieldwork, Federal Work-Study, institutionally sponsored loans, scholarships/grants, and unspecified assistantships also available. Support available to part-time students. Financial award application deadline: 3/1; financial award applicants required to submit FAFSA. *Faculty research:* English literature, creative writing, American literature, linguistics. *Unit head:* Dr. David Guest, Professor/Chair, 931-221-7891, Fax: 931-221-7219, E-mail: mcnabbw@apsu.edu. *Application contact:* Dr. Charles Pinder, Dean, College of Graduate Studies, 931-221-7414, Fax: 931-221-7641, E-mail: pinderc@apsu.edu.

Ball State University, Graduate School, College of Sciences and Humanities, Department of English, Muncie, IN 47306-1099. Offers English (MA, PhD), including composition, creative writing (MA), general (MA), literature; linguistics (MA, PhD), including applied linguistics (PhD); linguistics and teaching English to speakers of other languages (MA); teaching English to speakers of other languages (MA). *Degree requirements:* For doctorate, variable foreign language requirement, thesis/dissertation. *Entrance requirements:* For master's, GRE General Test, writing sample; for doctorate, GRE General Test, GRE Subject Test, minimum graduate GPA of 3.2, writing sample. *Faculty research:* American literature; literary editing; Medieval, Renaissance, and eighteenth century British literature; rhetoric.

Baylor University, Graduate School, College of Arts and Sciences, Department of English, Waco, TX 76798. Offers MA, PhD. Part-time programs available. *Faculty:* 19 full-time (6 women). *Students:* 31 full-time (28 women), 37 part-time (25 women); includes 3 minority (1 American Indian/Alaska Native, 2 Hispanic Americans), 3 international. 25 applicants, 88% accepted. In 2008, 9 master's, 4 doctorates awarded. *Degree requirements:* For master's, one foreign language, thesis; for doctorate, 2 foreign languages, thesis/dissertation. *Entrance requirements:* For master's, GRE General Test, 18 hours of upper-level course work in English; for doctorate, GRE General Test. *Application deadline:* For fall admission, 3/15 priority date for domestic students. Applications are processed on a rolling basis. Application fee: $25. Electronic applications accepted. *Financial support:* In 2008–09, 10 research assistantships, 28 teaching assistantships were awarded; fellowships, Federal Work-Study, institutionally sponsored loans, unspecified assistantships, and laboratory assistantships also available. *Faculty research:* Nineteenth century British literature, Renaissance studies, American studies, Medieval studies, rhetoric and composition. Total annual research expenditures: $48,400. *Unit head:* Dr. Jay Losey, Graduate Program Director, 254-710-1768, Fax: 254-710-3894, E-mail: jay_losey@baylor.edu. *Application contact:* Lois Avey, Administrative Assistant, 254-710-1768, Fax: 254-710-3870, E-mail: lois_avey@baylor.edu.

Belmont University, College of Arts and Sciences, Department of English, Nashville, TN 37212-3757. Offers literature (MA); writing (MA). Part-time and evening/weekend programs available. *Faculty:* 16 full-time (12 women). *Students:* 2 full-time (both women), 37 part-time (31 women); includes 3 minority (2 African Americans, 1 Hispanic American). Average age 28. 15 applicants, 80% accepted, 11 enrolled. In 2008, 10 master's awarded. *Degree requirements:* For master's, one foreign language, comprehensive exam (for some programs), thesis optional. *Entrance requirements:* For master's, GRE, letters of recommendation, writing sample. Additional exam requirements/recommendations for international students: Required—TOEFL. *Application deadline:* For fall admission, 8/1 for domestic students; for spring admission, 12/1 for domestic students. Applications are processed on a rolling basis. Application fee: $50. Electronic applications accepted. *Expenses:* Contact institution. *Financial support:* In 2008–09, 20 students received support. Federal Work-Study and scholarships/grants available. Financial award applicants required to submit FAFSA. *Faculty research:* Gender, autobiography, folklore, Shakespeare, editing. *Unit head:* Dr. James Wells, Director, 615-460-6239, Fax: 615-460-5720, E-mail: james.wells@mail.belmont.edu. *Application contact:* Dr. James Wells, Director, 615-460-6239, Fax: 615-460-5720, E-mail: james.wells@mail.belmont.edu.

Bemidji State University, School of Graduate Studies, College of Arts and Letters, Department of English, Bemidji, MN 56601-2699. Offers MA, MS. Part-time programs available. *Degree requirements:* For master's, one foreign language, thesis. *Entrance requirements:* For master's, letters of Rec. Additional exam requirements/recommendations for international students: Required—TOEFL. Electronic applications accepted. *Faculty research:* Creative writing; modern languages; film; electronic writing; rhetoric and composition; literary criticism.

Bennington College, Graduate Programs, The Bennington Writing Seminars, Bennington, VT 05201. Offers creative writing (MFA). Postbaccalaureate distance learning degree programs offered (minimal on-campus study). *Faculty:* 15 full-time (5 women), 6 part-time/adjunct (3 women). *Students:* 103 full-time (76 women); includes 6 minority (3 African Americans, 3 Hispanic Americans), 2 international. Average age 38. 165 applicants, 35% accepted, 28 enrolled. In 2008, 50 master's awarded. *Degree requirements:* For master's, thesis, collection of essays or poems, or collection of short stories and/or a novel. *Entrance requirements:* For master's, manuscript. *Application deadline:* For fall admission, 3/1 for domestic students; for spring admission, 9/1 for domestic students. Application fee: $60. *Expenses:* Contact institution. *Financial support:* In 2008–09, 6 students received support. Scholarships/grants available. Financial award application deadline: 4/1; financial award applicants required to submit FAFSA. *Unit head:* Sven Birkerts, Director, Writing Seminars, 802-440-4452, Fax: 802-440-4453, E-mail: writing@bennington.edu. *Application contact:* Victoria Clausi, Associate Director of Writing Seminars, 802-440-4454, Fax: 802-440-4453, E-mail: writing@bennington.edu.

English

Bob Jones University, Graduate Programs, Greenville, SC 29614. Offers accountancy (MS); Bible (MA); Bible translation (MA); Biblical studies (Certificate); broadcast management (MS); business administration (MBA); church history (MA, PhD); church ministries (MA); church music (MM); cinema and video production (MA); counseling (MS); curriculum and instruction (Ed D); divinity (M Div); dramatic production (MA); educational leadership (MS, Ed D, Ed S); elementary education (M Ed, MAT); English (M Ed, MA, MAT); fine arts (MA); graphic design (MA); history (M Ed, MA); illustration (MA); interpretative speech (MA); mathematics (M Ed, MAT); medical missions (Certificate); ministry (MM, D Min); multi-categorical special education (M Ed, MAT); music (M Ed); New Testament interpretation (PhD); Old Testament interpretation (PhD); orchestral instrument performance (MM); organ performance (MM); pastoral studies (MA); personnel services (MS, Ed S); piano pedagogy (MM); piano performance (MM); platform arts (MA); radio and television broadcasting (MS); rhetoric and public address (MA); secondary education (M Ed); studio art (MA); teaching Bible (MA); theology (MA, PhD); voice performance (MM); youth ministries (MA); M Div/MM.

Boise State University, Graduate College, College of Arts and Sciences, Department of English, Program in English, Boise, ID 83725-0399. Offers MA. Part-time programs available. *Degree requirements:* For master's, thesis. *Entrance requirements:* For master's, GRE General Test, minimum GPA of 3.0. Electronic applications accepted.

Boston College, Graduate School of Arts and Sciences, Department of English, Chestnut Hill, MA 02467-3800. Offers MA, PhD. *Degree requirements:* For master's, one foreign language, thesis optional; for doctorate, 2 foreign languages, thesis/dissertation. *Entrance requirements:* For master's and doctorate, GRE General Test, GRE Subject Test. Additional exam requirements/recommendations for international students: Required—TOEFL (minimum score 590 paper-based; 250 computer-based; 91 iBT). Electronic applications accepted. *Expenses:* Tuition: Part-time $1148 per credit. Required fees: $60. *Faculty research:* English and American literature, critical theory.

Boston University, Graduate School of Arts and Sciences, Department of English, Boston, MA 02215. Offers creative writing (MA); English (MA, PhD). Terminal master's awarded for partial completion of doctoral program. *Degree requirements:* For master's, one foreign language, thesis; for doctorate, 2 foreign languages, comprehensive exam, thesis/dissertation, qualifying/oral exam. *Entrance requirements:* For master's and doctorate, GRE General Test, GRE Subject Test, sample of written work, 2 letters of recommendation. Additional exam requirements/recommendations for international students: Required—TOEFL (minimum score 550 paper-based; 213 computer-based).

Bowie State University, Graduate Programs, Program in English, Bowie, MD 20715-9465. Offers MA. Part-time and evening/weekend programs available. *Entrance requirements:* For master's, minimum 2.5 GPA, English Degree. Electronic applications accepted.

Bowling Green State University, Graduate College, College of Arts and Sciences, Department of English, Program in English, Bowling Green, OH 43403. Offers English (MA, PhD); literature (MA); rhetoric and writing (PhD); scientific and technical communication (MA). Part-time programs available. *Degree requirements:* For master's, thesis or alternative; for doctorate, comprehensive exam, thesis/dissertation, foreign language or proficiency in Old English. *Entrance requirements:* For master's and doctorate, GRE General Test. Additional exam requirements/recommendations for international students: Required—TOEFL. Electronic applications accepted. *Faculty research:* Postmodern literary theory, rhetorical theory, ethnic American literature, literature and culture, composition pedagogy.

Bradley University, Graduate School, College of Liberal Arts and Sciences, Department of English, Peoria, IL 61625-0002. Offers MA. Part-time programs available. *Degree requirements:* For master's, comprehensive exam. *Entrance requirements:* For master's, writing sample, 2 letters of recommendation. Additional exam requirements/recommendations for international students: Required—TOEFL (minimum score 550 paper-based; 213 computer-based; 79 iBT).

Brandeis University, Graduate School of Arts and Sciences, Department of English and American Literature, Waltham, MA 02454-9110. Offers English and American literature (MA, PhD); English and women's studies (MA). Part-time programs available. *Degree requirements:* For master's, one foreign language, thesis, symposium; for doctorate, 2 foreign languages, thesis/dissertation, field exam, symposium presentation, prospectus defense. *Entrance requirements:* For master's, GRE General Test, resumé, sample of work, letters of recommendation; for doctorate, GRE General Test, GRE Subject Test, resumé, sample of work, letters of recommendation. Additional exam requirements/recommendations for international students: Required—TOEFL (minimum score 600 paper-based; 250 computer-based; 100 iBT), IELTS (minimum score 7). Electronic applications accepted. *Faculty research:* Feminist and gender theory, American literature, Anglophone literature, early modern literature, modernism.

Bridgewater State College, School of Graduate Studies, School of Arts and Sciences, Department of English, Bridgewater, MA 02325-0001. Offers MA, MAT. Part-time and evening/weekend programs available. *Degree requirements:* For master's, one foreign language, comprehensive exam, thesis optional. *Entrance requirements:* For master's, GRE General Test.

Brigham Young University, Graduate Studies, College of Humanities, Department of English, Provo, UT 84602-1001. Offers MA. *Faculty:* 54 full-time (18 women). *Students:* 79 full-time (52 women), 2 part-time (0 women). Average age 25. 69 applicants, 51% accepted, 25 enrolled. In 2008, 36 master's awarded. *Degree requirements:* For master's, thesis. *Entrance requirements:* For master's, GRE General Test. Additional exam requirements/recommendations for international students: Required—TOEFL. *Application deadline:* For fall admission, 1/15 for domestic students. Application fee: $50. Electronic applications accepted. *Expenses:* Tuition: Full-time $5160; part-time $287 per credit hour. Tuition and fees vary according to program and student's religious affiliation. *Financial support:* In 2008–09, 72 students received support, including 10 research assistantships (averaging $3,000 per year), 62 teaching assistantships (averaging $6,000 per year); career-related internships or fieldwork, institutionally sponsored loans, scholarships/grants, and tuition waivers (partial) also available. Support available to part-time students. Financial award application deadline: 3/15. *Faculty research:* English literature, American literature, rhetoric, creative writing. *Unit head:* Prof. Ed Cutler, Head, 801-422-3581, Fax: 801-422-0221, E-mail: ed_cutler@byu.edu. *Application contact:* Lou Ann C. Crisler, Graduate Secretary, 801-422-8673, Fax: 801-422-0221, E-mail: louann_crisler@byu.edu.

Brock University, Faculty of Graduate Studies, Faculty of Humanities, Program in English, St. Catharines, ON L2S 3A1, Canada. Offers MA. Part-time programs available. *Degree requirements:* For master's, thesis optional. *Entrance requirements:* For master's, honours in English. Additional exam requirements/recommendations for international students: Required—TOEFL (minimum score 550 paper-based; 213 computer-based; 80 iBT), IELTS (minimum score 6.5), TWE (minimum score 4). Electronic applications accepted. *Faculty research:* Literary theory, Canadian literature, Milton and 17th century American literature, 19th century American literature, British Romantic literature and culture.

Brooklyn College of the City University of New York, Division of Graduate Studies, Department of English, Brooklyn, NY 11210-2889. Offers creative writing (MFA), including fiction, playwriting, poetry; English (MA, PhD). The department offers courses at Brooklyn College that are creditable toward the CUNY doctoral degree (with permission of the executive officer of the doctoral program). Part-time and evening/weekend programs available. *Students:* 20 full-time (15 women), 164 part-time (100 women); includes 37 minority (21 African Americans, 8 Asian Americans or Pacific Islanders, 8 Hispanic Americans), 7 international. Average age 30. 457 applicants, 29% accepted, 68 enrolled. In 2008, 70 master's awarded. *Degree requirements:* For master's, one foreign language, comprehensive exam (for some programs), thesis (for some programs). *Entrance requirements:* For master's, advanced undergraduate courses in English, 2 letters of recommendation, writing sample, statement of purpose. Additional

exam requirements/recommendations for international students: Required—TOEFL. *Application deadline:* For fall admission, 3/1 priority date for domestic students, 2/1 for international students; for spring admission, 11/1 for domestic students, 10/1 for international students. Applications are processed on a rolling basis. Application fee: $125. Electronic applications accepted. *Expenses:* Tuition, state resident: full-time $7360; part-time $310 per credit hour. Tuition, nonresident: full-time $13,800; part-time $575 per credit hour. *Financial support:* Federal Work-Study, institutionally sponsored loans, and scholarships/grants available. Support available to part-time students. Financial award application deadline: 5/1; financial award applicants required to submit FAFSA. *Faculty research:* Cultural studies, medieval literature, Virginia Woolf. *Unit head:* Dr. Ellen Tremper, Chairperson, 718-951-5195, E-mail: etremper@brooklyn.cuny.edu. *Application contact:* Hernan Sierra, Graduate Admissions Coordinator, 718-951-4536, Fax: 718-951-4506, E-mail: grads@brooklyn.cuny.edu.

Brown University, Graduate School, Department of English, Program in Literatures and Cultures in English, Providence, RI 02912. Offers MA, PhD. *Degree requirements:* For doctorate, variable foreign language requirement, thesis/dissertation. *Entrance requirements:* For master's and doctorate, GRE General Test, GRE Subject Test.

Bucknell University, Graduate Studies, College of Arts and Sciences, Department of English, Lewisburg, PA 17837. Offers MA. Part-time programs available. *Degree requirements:* For master's, one foreign language, thesis. *Entrance requirements:* For master's, GRE General Test, GRE Subject Test, minimum GPA of 2.8. Additional exam requirements/recommendations for international students: Required—TOEFL.

Buffalo State College, State University of New York, Graduate Studies and Research, Faculty of Arts and Humanities, Department of English, Buffalo, NY 14222-1095. Offers English (MA); secondary education (MS Ed), including English. Part-time and evening/weekend programs available. *Degree requirements:* For master's, thesis or project, 1 foreign language (MS Ed). *Entrance requirements:* For master's, minimum GPA of 2.75, 36 hours in English, New York teaching certificate (MS Ed). Additional exam requirements/recommendations for international students: Required—TOEFL (minimum score 550 paper-based; 213 computer-based).

Butler University, College of Liberal Arts and Sciences, Department of English, Indianapolis, IN 46208-3485. Offers MA. Part-time and evening/weekend programs available. *Faculty:* 2 full-time (1 woman). *Students:* 4 full-time (3 women), 20 part-time (14 women), 3 international. Average age 37. 32 applicants, 56% accepted, 15 enrolled. In 2008, 7 master's awarded. *Entrance requirements:* For master's, GRE General Test, GRE Subject Test. *Application deadline:* For fall admission, 8/15 priority date for domestic students. Applications are processed on a rolling basis. Application fee: $35. Electronic applications accepted. *Financial support:* Applicants required to submit FAFSA. *Faculty research:* Modern poetry, ethnic literature, liberal education, Chaucer, ethics. *Unit head:* Dr. Hilene Flanzbaum, Head, 317-940-9860, E-mail: hflanzba@butler.edu. *Application contact:* Pamela Bender, Student Services Specialist, 317-940-8100, Fax: 317-940-8250, E-mail: pbender@butler.edu.

California Baptist University, Program in English, Riverside, CA 92504-3206. Offers English pedagogy (MA); literature (MA); teaching English as a second language (TESOL) (MA). Part-time programs available. *Faculty:* 5 full-time (4 women), 2 part-time/adjunct (1 woman). *Students:* 4 full-time (all women), 27 part-time (20 women); includes 5 minority (1 African American, 1 Asian American or Pacific Islander, 3 Hispanic Americans), 5 international. 17 applicants, 59% accepted, 10 enrolled. In 2008, 10 master's awarded. *Degree requirements:* For master's, thesis (for some programs). *Entrance requirements:* For master's, minimum undergraduate GPA of 2.75, 18 semester hours of course work in English beyond freshman level. Additional exam requirements/recommendations for international students: Required—TOEFL (minimum score 575 paper-based; 230 computer-based; 89 iBT). *Application deadline:* For fall admission, 8/1 priority date for domestic students, 7/1 priority date for international students; for spring admission, 12/1 priority date for domestic students, 10/15 priority date for international students. Applications are processed on a rolling basis. Application fee: $45. Electronic applications accepted. *Expenses:* Tuition: Full-time $8172; part-time $454 per credit hour. Required fees: $510. *Financial support:* Federal Work-Study available. Support available to part-time students. Financial award applicants required to submit FAFSA. *Unit head:* Dr. Jennifer Newton, Director, 951-343-4276, Fax: 951-343-4661, E-mail: jnewton@calbaptist.edu. *Application contact:* Gail Ronveaux, Dean of Graduate Enrollment, 951-343-5045, Fax: 951-343-5095, E-mail: graduateadmissions@calbaptist.edu.

California Polytechnic State University, San Luis Obispo, College of Liberal Arts, Department of English, San Luis Obispo, CA 93407. Offers MA. Part-time programs available. *Faculty:* 4 full-time (3 women). *Students:* 9 full-time (all women), 18 part-time (10 women); includes 4 minority (1 Asian American or Pacific Islander, 3 Hispanic Americans). Average age 27. 28 applicants, 71% accepted, 11 enrolled. In 2008, 15 master's awarded. *Degree requirements:* For master's, one foreign language, comprehensive exam. *Entrance requirements:* For master's, minimum GPA of 3.0 in last 90 quarter units of course work, writing sample. Additional exam requirements/recommendations for international students: Required—TOEFL (minimum score 550 paper-based; 213 computer-based), IELTS (minimum score 6), Either TOEFL or IELTS is acceptable. *Application deadline:* For fall admission, 7/1 for domestic students, 11/30 for international students; for winter admission, 11/1 for domestic students, 6/30 for international students; for spring admission, 2/1 for domestic students. Applications are processed on a rolling basis. Application fee: $55. *Expenses:* Tuition, nonresident: full-time $10,170; part-time $226 per unit. Required fees: $5751; $1265 per quarter. *Financial support:* Teaching assistantships, career-related internships or fieldwork, Federal Work-Study, institutionally sponsored loans, and tutorships, writing laboratory assistantships available. Support available to part-time students. Financial award application deadline: 3/2; financial award applicants required to submit FAFSA. *Faculty research:* Feminist literary criticism, modern British novel, literary theory, Shakespeare, Victorian literature. *Unit head:* Dr. Debora Schwartz, Graduate Coordinator, 805-756-2636, Fax: 805-756-6374, E-mail: dschwart@calpoly.edu. *Application contact:* Dr. Debora Schwartz, Graduate Coordinator, 805-756-2636, Fax: 805-756-6374, E-mail: dschwart@calpoly.edu.

California State Polytechnic University, Pomona, Academic Affairs, College of Letters, Arts, and Social Sciences, Program in English, Pomona, CA 91768-2557. Offers MA. Part-time programs available. *Students:* 19 full-time (13 women), 58 part-time (40 women); includes 32 minority (3 African Americans, 10 Asian Americans or Pacific Islanders, 19 Hispanic Americans), 2 international. Average age 31. 34 applicants, 62% accepted, 14 enrolled. In 2008, 29 master's awarded. *Degree requirements:* For master's, one foreign language, thesis or alternative. *Application deadline:* For fall admission, 5/1 priority date for domestic students; for winter admission, 10/15 priority date for domestic students; for spring admission, 1/20 priority date for domestic students. Applications are processed on a rolling basis. Application fee: $55. Electronic applications accepted. *Expenses:* Tuition, nonresident: full-time $7232; part-time $226 per credit. Required fees: $4272. One-time fee: $2694 part-time. Tuition and fees vary according to course load. *Financial support:* In 2008–09, 2 fellowships were awarded; Federal Work-Study and institutionally sponsored loans also available. Support available to part-time students. Financial award application deadline: 3/2; financial award applicants required to submit FAFSA. *Unit head:* Dr. Karen A. Russikoff, Coordinator, 909-869-3836, E-mail: krussikoff@csupomona.edu. *Application contact:* Scott J. Duncan, Director, Admissions, 909-869-3258, Fax: 909-869-4529, E-mail: sjduncan@csupomona.edu.

California State University, Bakersfield, Division of Graduate Studies, School of Humanities and Social Sciences, Program in English, Bakersfield, CA 93311-1022. Offers MA. *Degree requirements:* For master's, comprehensive exam or thesis. *Entrance requirements:* For master's, GRE General Test, GRE Subject Test (literature), minimum GPA of 2.5 for last 90 quarter units. Additional exam requirements/recommendations for international students: Required—TOEFL (minimum score 550 paper-based; 213 computer-based).

California State University, Chico, Graduate School, College of Humanities and Fine Arts, Department of English, Program in English, Chico, CA 95929-0830. Offers MA. *Degree requirements:* For master's, thesis. *Entrance requirements:* For master's, GRE General Test, Two letters of recommendation, Statement of Purpose, writing sample. Additional exam requirements/recommendations for international students: Required—TOEFL (minimum score 550 paper-based; 213 computer-based; 80 iBT), IELTS (minimum score 6.5).

California State University, Dominguez Hills, College of Arts and Humanities, Department of English, Carson, CA 90747-0001. Offers English (MA); rhetoric and composition (Certificate); teaching English as a second language (Certificate). Part-time and evening/weekend programs available. *Faculty:* 15 full-time (5 women). *Students:* 27 full-time (15 women), 52 part-time (32 women); includes 38 minority (11 African Americans, 6 Asian Americans or Pacific Islanders, 21 Hispanic Americans), 3 international. Average age 36. 46 applicants, 87% accepted, 25 enrolled. In 2008, 28 master's awarded. *Degree requirements:* For master's, comprehensive exam (for some programs), thesis or alternative. *Entrance requirements:* For master's, minimum GPA of 3.0 in last 60 units. Additional exam requirements/recommendations for international students: Required—TOEFL (minimum score 550 paper-based; 213 computer-based). *Application deadline:* Applications are processed on a rolling basis. Application fee: $55. Electronic applications accepted. *Expenses:* Tuition, nonresident: part-time $339 per unit. Required fees: $1300 per semester. *Faculty research:* Gender studies, transnationalism, discourse analysis, visual culture, Shakespeare. *Unit head:* Dr. Helen Oesterheld, Chair, 310-243-3322, E-mail: hoesterheld@csudh.edu. *Application contact:* 310-243-3600.

California State University, East Bay, Academic Programs and Graduate Studies, College of Letters, Arts, and Social Sciences, Department of English, Hayward, CA 94542-3000. Offers MA. Part-time and evening/weekend programs available. *Degree requirements:* For master's, one foreign language, comprehensive exam, thesis optional. *Entrance requirements:* For master's, minimum GPA of 3.0 in field. Additional exam requirements/recommendations for international students: Required—TOEFL (minimum score 550 paper-based; 213 computer-based). Electronic applications accepted.

California State University, Fresno, Division of Graduate Studies, College of Arts and Humanities, Department of English, Fresno, CA 93740-8027. Offers composition theory (MA); creative writing (MFA); literature (MA). Part-time and evening/weekend programs available. *Degree requirements:* For master's, one foreign language, thesis. *Entrance requirements:* For master's, GRE General Test, minimum GPA of 3.0, writing sample. Additional exam requirements/recommendations for international students: Required—TOEFL. Electronic applications accepted. *Faculty research:* American literature, Renaissance literature, foreign literature.

California State University, Fullerton, Graduate Studies, College of Humanities and Social Sciences, Department of English and Comparative Literature, Fullerton, CA 92834-9480. Offers comparative literature (MA); English (MA). Part-time programs available. *Students:* 33 full-time (24 women), 81 part-time (66 women); includes 25 minority (1 African American, 8 Asian Americans or Pacific Islanders, 16 Hispanic Americans), 2 international. Average age 31. 73 applicants, 66% accepted, 34 enrolled. In 2008, 31 master's awarded. *Degree requirements:* For master's, comprehensive exam, thesis or alternative. *Entrance requirements:* For master's, minimum GPA of 3.0 in major, 2.5 in last 60 hours. Application fee: $55. Tuition and fees vary according to degree level. *Financial support:* Teaching assistantships, Federal Work-Study, institutionally sponsored loans, and scholarships/grants available. Support available to part-time students. Financial award application deadline: 3/1. *Unit head:* Dr. Joseph Sawicki, Chair, 657-278-3163. *Application contact:* Dr. Susan Jacobsen, Adviser, 657-278-3163.

California State University, Long Beach, Graduate Studies, College of Liberal Arts, Department of English, Long Beach, CA 90840. Offers creative writing (MFA); English (MA). Part-time programs available. *Faculty:* 50 full-time (24 women), 78 part-time/adjunct (45 women). *Students:* 60 full-time (42 women), 114 part-time (78 women); includes 43 minority (5 African Americans, 1 American Indian/Alaska Native, 17 Asian Americans or Pacific Islanders, 20 Hispanic Americans). Average age 34. *Degree requirements:* For master's, one foreign language, comprehensive exam or thesis. *Entrance requirements:* For master's, GRE Subject Test, minimum GPA of 3.0 in English. *Application deadline:* For fall admission, 5/1 for domestic students. Applications are processed on a rolling basis. Application fee: $55. Electronic applications accepted. *Expenses:* Tuition, nonresident: full-time $11,160; part-time $372 per unit. Required fees: $4100; $1261 per semester. *Financial support:* Federal Work-Study, institutionally sponsored loans, and scholarships/grants available. Financial award application deadline: 3/2. *Faculty research:* English and American literature, literary theory, linguistics, rhetoric and composition. *Unit head:* Dr. Eileen S. Klink, Chair, 562-985-4223, Fax: 562-985-2369, E-mail: eklink@csulb.edu. *Application contact:* Dr. Beth Lau, Graduate Adviser, 562-985-42852, Fax: 562-985-4223, E-mail: blau@csulb.edu.

California State University, Los Angeles, Graduate Studies, College of Arts and Letters, Department of English, Los Angeles, CA 90032-8530. Offers MA. Part-time and evening/weekend programs available. *Faculty:* 5 full-time (2 women), 3 part-time/adjunct (2 women). *Students:* 15 full-time (9 women), 76 part-time (49 women); includes 31 minority (5 African Americans, 1 American Indian/Alaska Native, 6 Asian Americans or Pacific Islanders, 19 Hispanic Americans), 5 international. Average age 35. 36 applicants, 100% accepted, 12 enrolled. In 2008, 26 master's awarded. *Degree requirements:* For master's, comprehensive exam or thesis. *Entrance requirements:* Additional exam requirements/recommendations for international students: Required—TOEFL (minimum score 500 paper-based; 173 computer-based). *Application deadline:* For fall admission, 6/15 for domestic students, 5/1 for international students; for winter admission, 11/1 for domestic students, 9/1 for international students; for spring admission, 2/1 for domestic students, 10/1 for international students. Applications are processed on a rolling basis. Application fee: $55. Electronic applications accepted. *Expenses:* Tuition, nonresident: part-time $226 per credit. Required fees: $4019. *Financial support:* Federal Work-Study available. Support available to part-time students. Financial award application deadline: 3/1. *Faculty research:* English and American literature, linguistics, composition. *Unit head:* Dr. Hema Chari, Acting Chair, 323-343-4140, Fax: 323-343-6470, E-mail: hchari@calstatela.edu. *Application contact:* Dr. Jose L. Galvan, Dean of Graduate Studies, 323-343-3820, Fax: 323-343-5653, E-mail: jgalvan@cslanet.calstatela.edu.

California State University, Northridge, Graduate Studies, College of Humanities, Department of English, Northridge, CA 91330. Offers creative writing (MA); literature (MA); rhetoric and composition theory (MA). Part-time and evening/weekend programs available. *Faculty:* 33 full-time (16 women), 71 part-time/adjunct (60 women). *Students:* 42 full-time (27 women), 133 part-time (96 women); includes 38 minority (4 African Americans, 1 American Indian/Alaska Native, 14 Asian Americans or Pacific Islanders, 19 Hispanic Americans). Average age 34. 114 applicants, 74% accepted, 51 enrolled. In 2008, 40 master's awarded. *Degree requirements:* For master's, thesis or alternative. *Entrance requirements:* For master's, writing proficiency test, GRE General Test or minimum GPA of 3.0. Additional exam requirements/recommendations for international students: Required—TOEFL. *Application deadline:* For fall admission, 11/30 for domestic students. Application fee: $55. *Financial support:* Teaching assistantships available. Financial award application deadline: 3/1. *Faculty research:* Reading improvement, professional writing, Dickens, Shaw, English as a second language. *Unit head:* Dr. George Uba, Chair, 818-677-3434, E-mail: george.uba@csun.edu. *Application contact:* Dr. Marjie Seagoe, Graduate Studies Secretary, 818-677-3433.

California State University, Sacramento, Graduate Studies, College of Arts and Letters, Department of English, Sacramento, CA 95819-6048. Offers creative writing (MA); teaching English to speakers of other languages (MA). Part-time programs available. *Degree requirements:* For master's, thesis, project, or comprehensive exam; writing proficiency exam. *Entrance requirements:* For master's, portfolio (creative writing); minimum GPA of 3.0 in English, 2.75 overall during previous 2 years. Additional exam requirements/recommendations for international students: Required—TOEFL. Electronic applications accepted. *Faculty research:* Teaching composition, remedial writing.

California State University, San Bernardino, Graduate Studies, College of Arts and Letters, Department of English, San Bernardino, CA 92407-2397. Offers creative writing (MFA); English composition (MA). Part-time and evening/weekend programs available. *Faculty:* 18 full-time (12 women), 1 (woman) part-time/adjunct. *Students:* 68 full-time (45 women), 48 part-time (35 women); includes 41 minority (14 African Americans, 1 American Indian/Alaska Native, 7 Asian Americans or Pacific Islanders, 19 Hispanic Americans), 1 international. Average age 36. 46 applicants, 63% accepted, 23 enrolled. In 2008, 28 master's awarded. *Degree requirements:* For master's, one foreign language, thesis. *Entrance requirements:* For master's, BA in English or linguistics, minimum GPA of 3.0. Additional exam requirements/recommendations for international students: Required—TOEFL. *Application deadline:* For fall admission, 8/31 priority date for domestic students. Application fee: $55. *Expenses:* Tuition, area resident: Full-time $1252; part-time $726 per quarter. Required fees: $334 per quarter. Tuition and fees vary according to degree level and student level. *Financial support:* Research assistantships, teaching assistantships, career-related internships or fieldwork, Federal Work-Study, institutionally sponsored loans, and writing center tutorships available. Support available to part-time students. Financial award application deadline: 3/1. *Faculty research:* Composition and literary theory, theatrical theory, creative writing, relationship between evaluating writing and teaching composition. *Unit head:* Dr. Juan Delgado, Chair, 909-537-5834, Fax: 909-537-7086, E-mail: jdelgado@csusb.edu. *Application contact:* Olivia Rosas, Director of Admissions, 909-537-7577, Fax: 909-537-7034, E-mail: orosas@csusb.edu.

California State University, San Marcos, College of Arts and Sciences, Program in Literature and Writing Studies, San Marcos, CA 92096-0001. Offers MA. Part-time and evening/weekend programs available. *Degree requirements:* For master's, one foreign language, thesis. *Entrance requirements:* For master's, GRE General Test, minimum GPA of 3.0, writing sample. *Faculty research:* Postcolonialism, feminism rhetoric, cultural studies, creative writing, critical theory.

California State University, Stanislaus, College of Humanities and Social Sciences, Department of English, Turlock, CA 95382. Offers English (MA); literature (MA); rhetoric and teaching of writing (MA); TESOL (MA, Certificate). Part-time programs available. *Degree requirements:* For master's, one foreign language, comprehensive exam, thesis. *Entrance requirements:* For master's, GRE General Test, minimum GPA of 3.0, 2 letters of reference, personal statement; for Certificate, minimum GPA of 3.0, 2 letters of reference. Additional exam requirements/recommendations for international students: Required—TOEFL (minimum score 550 paper-based; 213 computer-based), TWE (minimum score 4). Electronic applications accepted. *Faculty research:* Transnational literacies, Renaissance and Medieval literature, abolition writings and slave narratives, qualitative writing.

Carleton University, Faculty of Graduate Studies, Faculty of Arts and Social Sciences, Department of English Language and Literature, Ottawa, ON K1S 5B6, Canada. Offers MA, PhD. *Degree requirements:* For master's, thesis optional. *Entrance requirements:* For master's, honors degree. Additional exam requirements/recommendations for international students: Required—TOEFL. *Faculty research:* British, Canadian, American, and Commonwealth literatures; English language and writing; literary criticism; social and historical context of literature.

Carnegie Mellon University, College of Humanities and Social Sciences, Department of English, Pittsburgh, PA 15213-3891. Offers communication planning and design (M Des); literary and cultural studies (MA, PhD); professional writing (MAPW), including editing and publishing, policy and non-profit communication, public and media relations / corporate communications, science or healthcare communication, technical writing, writing for new media, writing for print media; rhetoric (MA, PhD). Part-time programs available. Terminal master's awarded for partial completion of doctoral program. *Degree requirements:* For doctorate, 2 foreign languages, comprehensive exam, thesis/dissertation. *Entrance requirements:* For master's and doctorate, GRE General Test. Additional exam requirements/recommendations for international students: Required—TOEFL, TWE. *Faculty research:* Cognitive processes in discourse with emphasis on writing, testing, and evaluation.

Case Western Reserve University, School of Graduate Studies, Department of English, Cleveland, OH 44106. Offers comparative literature (MA); English and American literature (MA, PhD). Part-time programs available. *Degree requirements:* For master's, written exam; for doctorate, one foreign language, thesis/dissertation, oral and written exams. *Entrance requirements:* For master's and doctorate, GRE General Test, sample of written work. Additional exam requirements/recommendations for international students: Required—TOEFL. Electronic applications accepted. *Faculty research:* Sixteenth- to twentieth-century English literature, rhetorical and critical theory, women's studies, genre studies, Renaissance, America modernism, authorship.

The Catholic University of America, School of Arts and Sciences, Department of English Language and Literature, Washington, DC 20064. Offers English language and literature (MA, PhD); rhetoric (MA, PhD); MSLS/MA. Part-time and evening/weekend programs available. Terminal master's awarded for partial completion of doctoral program. *Degree requirements:* For master's, one foreign language, comprehensive exam, thesis or alternative; for doctorate, 2 foreign languages, comprehensive exam, thesis/dissertation. *Entrance requirements:* For master's and doctorate, GRE General Test, 3 letters of recommendation, writing sample. Additional exam requirements/recommendations for international students: Required—TOEFL (minimum score 580 paper-based; 237 computer-based). Electronic applications accepted. *Faculty research:* Medieval literature, theory and history of rhetoric, modern Irish literature, religion and literature, English and American drama.

Central Connecticut State University, School of Graduate Studies, School of Arts and Sciences, Department of English, Program in English, New Britain, CT 06050-4010. Offers MA, Certificate. Part-time and evening/weekend programs available. *Students:* 22 full-time (10 women), 29 part-time (20 women); includes 3 minority (1 African American, 2 Hispanic Americans). Average age 31. 27 applicants, 59% accepted, 9 enrolled. In 2008, 8 master's, 5 other advanced degrees awarded. *Degree requirements:* For master's, comprehensive exam, thesis or alternative. *Entrance requirements:* For master's, minimum undergraduate GPA of 3.0. Additional exam requirements/recommendations for international students: Required—TOEFL. *Application deadline:* For fall admission, 7/1 for domestic students; for spring admission, 12/1 for domestic students. Applications are processed on a rolling basis. Application fee: $50. Electronic applications accepted. *Expenses:* Tuition, area resident: Full-time $4377; part-time $420 per credit. Tuition, state resident: full-time $6566; part-time $420 per credit. Tuition, nonresident: full-time $12,195; part-time $420 per credit. Required fees: $3462. One-time fee: $62 part-time.

Central Michigan University, College of Graduate Studies, College of Humanities and Social and Behavioral Sciences, Department of English Language and Literature, Mount Pleasant, MI 48859. Offers English composition and communication (MA); English language and literature (MA), including children's and young adult literature, creative writing, general concentration; teaching English to speakers of other languages (TESOL) (MA). Part-time and evening/weekend programs available. *Faculty:* 17 full-time (8 women), 11 part-time/adjunct (7 women). *Students:* 16 full-time (5 women), 53 part-time (32 women); includes 1 African American, 1 American Indian/Alaska Native, 2 Hispanic Americans, 8 international. Average age 32. *Degree requirements:* For master's, thesis or alternative. *Application deadline:* Applications are processed on a rolling basis. Application fee: $35 ($45 for international students). Electronic applications accepted. *Expenses:* Tuition, state resident: full-time $3717; part-time $413 per credit. Tuition, nonresident: full-time $6894; part-time $766 per credit. *Financial support:* Fellowships with tuition reimbursements, research assistantships with tuition reimbursements, teaching assistantships with tuition reimbursements, career-related internships or fieldwork, Federal Work-Study, unspecified assistantships, and out-of-state merit awards available. *Faculty research:* Composition theory, science fiction history and bibliography, children's and young adult literature, nineteenth century American literature, applied linguistics. *Unit head:* Dr. Marcia Taylor, Chairperson, 989-774-3171, Fax: 989-774-1271, E-mail: taylo1mm@cmich.edu. *Application*

English

Central Michigan University *(continued)*
contact: Dr. Jeffrey A. Weinstock, Coordinator, Graduate Studies in English, 989-774-3101, Fax: 989-774-1271, E-mail: weins1ja@cmich.edu.

Central Washington University, Graduate Studies, Research and Continuing Education, College of Arts and Humanities, Department of English, Ellensburg, WA 98926. Offers English (MA); teaching English as a second language (MA). Part-time programs available. *Degree requirements:* For master's, thesis or alternative. *Entrance requirements:* For master's, GRE General Test, minimum GPA of 3.0, writing sample. Additional exam requirements/recommendations for international students: Required—TOEFL (minimum score 550 paper-based; 213 computer-based; 79 iBT). Electronic applications accepted.

Chapman University, Graduate Studies, Wilkinson College of Humanities and Social Sciences, Department of English, Orange, CA 92866. Offers creative writing (MFA); English (MA). Part-time and evening/weekend programs available. *Faculty:* 18 full-time (8 women), 22 part-time/adjunct (10 women). *Students:* 40 full-time (21 women), 37 part-time (28 women); includes 7 minority (1 African American, 1 American Indian/Alaska Native, 3 Asian Americans or Pacific Islanders, 2 Hispanic Americans). Average age 30. 57 applicants, 67% accepted, 25 enrolled. In 2008, 28 master's awarded. *Degree requirements:* For master's, comprehensive exam (for some programs), thesis (for some programs). *Entrance requirements:* For master's, GRE or MAT, minimum undergraduate GPA of 2.5. Additional exam requirements/recommendations for international students: Required—TOEFL (minimum score 550 paper-based; 213 computer-based; 80 iBT). *Application deadline:* For fall admission, 5/1 priority date for domestic students. Applications are processed on a rolling basis. Application fee: $50. Electronic applications accepted. *Expenses:* Contact institution. *Financial support:* Fellowships, Federal Work-Study and scholarships/grants available. Financial award application deadline: 3/2; financial award applicants required to submit FAFSA. *Unit head:* Dr. Paul Gulino, Department Chair, 714-997-6750, E-mail: gulino@chapman.edu. *Application contact:* Priscilla Garcia Powers, Graduate Admission Counselor, 714-997-6711, E-mail: pgarcia@chapman.edu.

Chicago State University, School of Graduate and Professional Studies, College of Arts and Sciences, Department of English, Chicago, IL 60628. Offers creative writing (MFA); English (MA). *Degree requirements:* For master's, comprehensive exam. *Entrance requirements:* For master's, minimum GPA of 2.75.

The Citadel, The Military College of South Carolina, Citadel Graduate College, Department of English, Charleston, SC 29409. Offers MA. Part-time and evening/weekend programs available. *Faculty:* 3 full-time (1 woman). *Students:* 5 part-time (all women); includes 1 minority (African American). Average age 27. In 2008, 4 master's awarded. *Degree requirements:* For master's, one foreign language, comprehensive exam, thesis optional. *Entrance requirements:* For master's, GRE (minimum 1000 with at least a 4 on the Writing Assessment section) or MAT (minimum 403), minimum undergraduate GPA of 2.5 (3.0 in major); 2 letters of recommendation from former professors or recent supervisors; 2-page statement about educational goals and interest in a graduate program in English; writing sample showing ability to perform literary analysis and to conduct research. Additional exam requirements/recommendations for international students: Required—TOEFL (minimum score 550 paper-based; 213 computer-based). *Application deadline:* Applications are processed on a rolling basis. Application fee: $30. Electronic applications accepted. *Expenses:* Tuition, state resident: full-time $5850; part-time $325 per credit hour. Tuition, nonresident: full-time $9612; part-time $534 per credit hour. Required fees: $15 per semester. *Financial support:* Research assistantships, career-related internships or fieldwork, health care benefits, and unspecified assistantships available. Support available to part-time students. Financial award application deadline: 7/1; financial award applicants required to submit FAFSA. *Faculty research:* Renaissance literature; eighteenth and nineteenth century British literature; eighteenth, nineteenth, and twentieth century American literature. *Unit head:* Dr. David G. Allen, Department Head, 843-953-5134, Fax: 843-953-1881, E-mail: allend@citadel.edu. *Application contact:* Dr. James M. Hutchisson, Graduate Coordinator, 843-953-5139, Fax: 843-953-1881, E-mail: hutchissonj@citadel.edu.

City College of the City University of New York, Graduate School, College of Liberal Arts and Science, Division of the Humanities and Arts, Department of English, Program in English and American Literature, New York, NY 10031-9198. Offers MA. *Degree requirements:* For master's, one foreign language, comprehensive exam, thesis. *Entrance requirements:* For master's, GRE, minimum GPA of 3.0. Additional exam requirements/recommendations for international students: Required—TOEFL (minimum score 600 paper-based; 250 computer-based).

Claremont Graduate University, Graduate Programs, School of Arts and Humanities, Department of English, Claremont, CA 91711-6160. Offers American studies (MA, PhD); critical theory (MA, PhD); early modern studies (MA, PhD); English (M Phil, MA, PhD); literary theory (PhD); literature (MA, PhD); literature and creative writing (MA); literature and film (MA); MBA/MA; MBA/PhD. Part-time programs available. *Faculty:* 2 full-time (1 woman), 2 part-time/adjunct (0 women). *Students:* 78 full-time (46 women), 12 part-time (9 women); includes 15 minority (1 African American, 2 American Indian/Alaska Native, 7 Asian Americans or Pacific Islanders, 5 Hispanic Americans), 2 international. Average age 35. In 2008, 9 master's, 11 doctorates awarded. *Entrance requirements:* For master's and doctorate, GRE General Test. Additional exam requirements/recommendations for international students: Required—TOEFL (minimum score 550 paper-based; 213 computer-based; 80 iBT). *Application deadline:* For fall admission, 2/1 priority date for domestic students. Applications are processed on a rolling basis. Application fee: $60. Electronic applications accepted. *Expenses:* Tuition: Full-time $33,698; part-time $1465 per unit. Required fees: $310; $155 per semester. Tuition and fees vary according to program. *Financial support:* Fellowships, Federal Work-Study, institutionally sponsored loans, and scholarships/grants available. Support available to part-time students. Financial award application deadline: 2/15; financial award applicants required to submit FAFSA. *Faculty research:* American, comparative, and English Renaissance literature; modernism; feminist literature and theory. *Unit head:* Wendy Martin, Chair, 909-621-8612, Fax: 909-607-1221, E-mail: wendy.martin@cgu.edu. *Application contact:* Justin Evans, Admissions Coordinator, 909-607-1278, Fax: 909-607-1221, E-mail: justin.evans@cgu.edu.

Clarion University of Pennsylvania, Office of Research and Graduate Studies, College of Arts and Sciences, Department of English, Clarion, PA 16214. Offers MA. *Degree requirements:* For master's, thesis optional. *Entrance requirements:* For master's, GRE General Test, minimum QPA of 2.75. Additional exam requirements/recommendations for international students: Required—TOEFL (minimum score 550 paper-based; 213 computer-based; 80 iBT). Electronic applications accepted.

Clark Atlanta University, School of Arts and Sciences, Department of English, Atlanta, GA 30314. Offers MA, DAH. Part-time programs available. *Faculty:* 5 full-time (3 women). *Students:* 8 full-time (6 women), 26 part-time (24 women); includes 24 minority (all African Americans). Average age 32. 6 applicants, 83% accepted, 5 enrolled. In 2008, 1 doctorate awarded. *Degree requirements:* For master's, one foreign language, thesis. *Entrance requirements:* For master's, GRE General Test, minimum GPA of 2.5. Additional exam requirements/recommendations for international students: Required—TOEFL (minimum score 500 paper-based; 173 computer-based). *Application deadline:* For fall admission, 4/1 for domestic and international students; for spring admission, 11/1 for domestic and international students. Applications are processed on a rolling basis. Application fee: $40 ($55 for international students). *Expenses:* Tuition: Full-time $12,240; part-time $680 per credit hour. Required fees: $710; $355 per semester. *Financial support:* Career-related internships or fieldwork, Federal Work-Study, scholarships/grants, and unspecified assistantships available. Support available to part-time students. Financial award application deadline: 4/30; financial award applicants required to submit FAFSA. *Unit head:* Dr. Alma Vineyard, Chairperson, 404-880-6067, E-mail: avineyard@cau.edu. *Application contact:* Michelle Clark-Davis, Graduate Program Admissions, 404-880-6605, E-mail: cauadmissions@cau.edu.

Clark University, Graduate School, Department of English, Worcester, MA 01610-1477. Offers MA. Part-time programs available. *Faculty:* 9 full-time (6 women), 12 part-time/adjunct (6 women). *Students:* 13 full-time (9 women), 5 part-time (4 women); includes 1 minority (African American), 5 international. Average age 27. 16 applicants, 100% accepted, 13 enrolled. In 2008, 8 master's awarded. *Degree requirements:* For master's, thesis, oral exam. *Entrance requirements:* For master's, GRE Subject Test. Additional exam requirements/recommendations for international students: Required—TOEFL. *Application deadline:* For fall admission, 2/1 priority date for domestic students. Applications are processed on a rolling basis. Application fee: $50. *Expenses:* Tuition: Full-time $34,900; part-time $1091 per credit hour. Required fees: $30. *Financial support:* In 2008–09, fellowships with tuition reimbursements (averaging $10,300 per year), research assistantships with full and partial tuition reimbursements (averaging $10,300 per year), 4 teaching assistantships with full and partial tuition reimbursements (averaging $10,300 per year) were awarded; career-related internships or fieldwork and tuition waivers (partial) also available. Support available to part-time students. Financial award application deadline: 2/15. *Faculty research:* Writings of James Fenimore Cooper, Renaissance literature, American literature, medieval literature, Victorian literature. *Unit head:* Dr. Virginia Vaughan, Chair, 508-793-7142. *Application contact:* Terri Rutkiewicz, Academic Secretary, 508-793-7142, Fax: 508-793-8892, E-mail: engma@clarku.edu.

Clemson University, Graduate School, College of Architecture, Arts, and Humanities, Department of English, Clemson, SC 29634. Offers English (MA); professional communication (MA); rhetorics, communication and information design (PhD). Part-time programs available. *Faculty:* 29 full-time (13 women), 4 part-time/adjunct (0 women). *Students:* 93 full-time (57 women), 19 part-time (15 women); includes 12 minority (7 African Americans, 2 Asian Americans or Pacific Islanders, 3 Hispanic Americans), 7 international. Average age 30. 87 applicants, 64% accepted, 40 enrolled. In 2008, 27 master's, 1 doctorate awarded. *Degree requirements:* For master's, one foreign language, thesis optional, oral exam. *Entrance requirements:* For master's, GRE General Test, minimum GPA of 3.0. *Application deadline:* For fall admission, 6/1 priority date for domestic students, 4/15 for international students; for spring admission, 12/1 for domestic students, 9/15 for international students. Applications are processed on a rolling basis. Application fee: $50. Full-time tuition and fees vary according to program. *Financial support:* In 2008–09, 1 fellowship (averaging $10,000 per year), 16 research assistantships (averaging $11,535 per year), 73 teaching assistantships (averaging $14,589 per year) were awarded. Financial award application deadline: 4/1; financial award applicants required to submit FAFSA. *Faculty research:* American and British literature, rhetoric and composition, literary theory, Southern American literature. Total annual research expenditures: $36,553. *Unit head:* Dr. Lee Morrissey, Department Chair, 864-656-3151, E-mail: lmorris@clemson.edu. *Application contact:* Dr. Michelle Martin, Associate Department Chair, 864-656-5413, Fax: 864-656-5344, E-mail: mmichel@clemson.edu.

Cleveland State University, College of Graduate Studies, College of Liberal Arts and Social Sciences, Department of English, Cleveland, OH 44115. Offers creative writing (MFA); English (MA). Part-time and evening/weekend programs available. *Faculty:* 19 full-time (8 women), 29 part-time/adjunct (13 women). *Students:* 22 full-time (14 women), 63 part-time (45 women); includes 10 minority (9 African Americans, 1 Asian American or Pacific Islander), 3 international. Average age 34, 43 applicants, 53% accepted, 14 enrolled. In 2008, 17 master's awarded. *Degree requirements:* For master's, comprehensive exam, thesis. *Entrance requirements:* For master's, minimum GPA of 2.75, undergraduate concentration in English, writing sample, portfolio. Additional exam requirements/recommendations for international students: Required—TOEFL (525 paper-based; 197 computer-based) or IELTS (6 paper-based). *Application deadline:* For fall admission, 7/18 priority date for domestic students, 5/15 for international students; for spring admission, 12/15 for domestic students, 11/1 for international students. Applications are processed on a rolling basis. Application fee: $30. Electronic applications accepted. *Financial support:* In 2008–09, 20 students received support, including 1 fellowship (averaging $1,000 per year), 5 research assistantships with full and partial tuition reimbursements available (averaging $3,480 per year), 7 teaching assistantships with full and partial tuition reimbursements available (averaging $3,480 per year); Federal Work-Study, institutionally sponsored loans, tuition waivers (full and partial), and unspecified assistantships also available. Support available to part-time students. Financial award application deadline: 2/15. *Faculty research:* Literary history and criticism, linguistics, literature. Total annual research expenditures: $5,000. *Unit head:* Dr. David M. Larson, Chairperson, 216-687-3951, Fax: 216-687-6943, E-mail: d.larson@csuohio.edu. *Application contact:* Dr. Jennifer M. Jeffers, Graduate Director, 216-687-3975, Fax: 216-687-6943, E-mail: j.m.jeffers53@csuohio.edu.

The College at Brockport, State University of New York, School of Letters and Sciences, Department of English, Brockport, NY 14420-2997. Offers MA. Part-time programs available. *Degree requirements:* For master's, thesis. *Entrance requirements:* For master's, minimum GPA of 3.0, letters of recommendation, writing sample. Additional exam requirements/recommendations for international students: Required—TOEFL (minimum score 550 paper-based; 213 computer-based; 79 iBT). *Faculty research:* British and American literature, creative writing, film studies, children's literature, Ancient and Modern World Literature.

College of Charleston, Graduate School, School of Humanities and Social Sciences, Program in English, Charleston, SC 29424-0001. Offers MA. Part-time and evening/weekend programs available. *Faculty:* 29 full-time (16 women), 1 part-time/adjunct (0 women). *Students:* 21 full-time (17 women), 13 part-time (9 women); includes 2 minority (both Hispanic Americans), 1 international. Average age 27. 24 applicants, 75% accepted, 14 enrolled. In 2008, 11 master's awarded. *Degree requirements:* For master's, one foreign language, comprehensive exam, thesis optional. *Entrance requirements:* For master's, GRE General Test or MAT, minimum GPA of 2.5 overall, 3.0 in major; 2 letters of recommendation; writing sample. Additional exam requirements/recommendations for international students: Required—TOEFL. *Application deadline:* For fall admission, 6/1 for domestic students; for spring admission, 11/1 for domestic students. Application fee: $45. Electronic applications accepted. *Expenses:* Tuition, area resident: Full-time $6624; part-time $368 per credit hour. Tuition, state resident: full-time $6624; part-time $368 per credit hour. Tuition, nonresident: full-time $16,074; part-time $893 per credit hour. Required fees: $30; $30 per course. One-time fee: $45. *Financial support:* In 2008–09, 5 research assistantships (averaging $12,400 per year) were awarded; fellowships, scholarships/grants and unspecified assistantships also available. Financial award application deadline: 6/1; financial award applicants required to submit FAFSA. *Unit head:* Dr. Susan Farrell, Director, 843-953-5664, Fax: 843-953-3180, E-mail: farrells@cofc.edu. *Application contact:* Susan Hallatt, Director of Graduate Admissions, 843-953-5614, Fax: 843-953-1434, E-mail: hallatts@cofc.edu.

The College of New Jersey, Graduate Division, School of Culture and Society, Department of English, Program in English, Ewing, NJ 08628. Offers MA. Part-time and evening/weekend programs available. *Entrance requirements:* For master's, GRE, minimum GPA of 3.0 in field or 2.75 overall. Additional exam requirements/recommendations for international students: Required—TOEFL. Electronic applications accepted.

The College of Saint Rose, Graduate Studies, School of Arts and Humanities, Department of English, Albany, NY 12203-1419. Offers MA. Part-time and evening/weekend programs available. *Degree requirements:* For master's, thesis optional, advanced project. *Entrance requirements:* For master's, 24 credits in English, minimum undergraduate GPA of 3.2, writing sample. Additional exam requirements/recommendations for international students: Required—TOEFL (minimum score 550 paper-based; 213 computer-based). Electronic applications accepted.

College of Staten Island of the City University of New York, Graduate Programs, Program in English, Staten Island, NY 10314-6600. Offers MA. Part-time and evening/weekend programs available. *Faculty:* 5 full-time (4 women). *Students:* 3 full-time (1 woman), 34 part-time (23 women); includes 3 minority (all African Americans), 2 international. Average age 32. 42 applicants, 95% accepted, 24 enrolled. In 2008, 7 master's awarded. *Degree requirements:* For master's, comprehensive exam, 3-hour written exam, 2 papers. *Entrance requirements:* For master's, 32 undergraduate credits in English, minimum GPA of 3.0. Additional exam requirements/recommendations for international students: Required—TOEFL (minimum score 550 paper-based; 213 computer-based; 79 iBT). *Application deadline:* Applications are processed on a rolling basis. Application fee: $125. Electronic applications accepted. *Expenses:* Tuition, area resident: Full-time $6400; part-time $270 per credit. Tuition, nonresident: full-time $12,000; part-time $500 per credit. Required fees: $378; $113 per semester. *Financial support:* Career-related internships or fieldwork, Federal Work-Study, institutionally sponsored loans, scholarships/grants, and institutional work-study available. Support available to part-time students. Financial award application deadline: 4/1; financial award applicants required to submit CSS PROFILE or FAFSA. *Unit head:* Dr. Maryann Feola, Coordinator, 718-982-3666, Fax: 718-982-3643, E-mail: englishmasters@mail.csi.cuny.edu. *Application contact:* Sasha Spence, Assistant Director of Graduate Recruitment Admissions, 718-982-2699, Fax: 718-982-2500, E-mail: spence@mail.csi.cuny.edu.

Columbia University, Graduate School of Arts and Sciences, Division of Humanities, Department of English and Comparative Literature, New York, NY 10027. Offers comparative literature (M Phil, MA, PhD); English literature (M Phil, MA, PhD); literature-writing (M Phil, MA, PhD). Part-time programs available. *Degree requirements:* For master's, one foreign language, comprehensive exam, seminar papers; for doctorate, thesis/dissertation. *Entrance requirements:* For master's and doctorate, GRE General Test. Additional exam requirements/recommendations for international students: Required—TOEFL. *Faculty research:* Medieval through modern literature, drama, literary criticism.

Concordia University, School of Graduate Studies, Faculty of Arts and Science, Department of English, Program in English, Montréal, QC H3G 1M8, Canada. Offers MA. *Degree requirements:* For master's, one foreign language, thesis optional. *Entrance requirements:* For master's, honors degree in English, minimum GPA of 3.3 in English literature.

Converse College, School of Education and Graduate Studies, Program in Liberal Arts, Spartanburg, SC 29302-0006. Offers English (MLA); history (MLA); political science (MLA). *Degree requirements:* For master's, capstone paper. *Entrance requirements:* For master's, minimum GPA of 3.0, 2 recommendations.

Cornell University, Graduate School, Graduate Fields of Arts and Sciences, Field of English Language and Literature, Ithaca, NY 14853-0001. Offers African-American literature (PhD); American literature after 1865 (PhD); American literature to 1865 (PhD); American studies (PhD); colonial and postcolonial literature (PhD); creative writing (MFA); cultural studies (PhD); dramatic literature (PhD); English poetry (PhD); English Renaissance to 1660 (PhD); lesbian, bisexual, and gay literature studies (PhD); literary criticism and theory (PhD); nineteenth century (PhD); Old and Middle English (PhD); prose fiction (PhD); Restoration and eighteenth century (PhD); twentieth century (PhD); women's literature (PhD); MFA/PhD. *Faculty:* 54 full-time (27 women). *Students:* 100 full-time (53 women); includes 24 minority (8 African Americans, 4 American Indian/Alaska Native, 6 Asian Americans or Pacific Islanders, 6 Hispanic Americans), 14 international. Average age 29. 821 applicants, 6% accepted, 23 enrolled. In 2008, 19 master's, 12 doctorates awarded. Terminal master's awarded for partial completion of doctoral program. *Degree requirements:* For master's, one foreign language, thesis; for doctorate, one foreign language, comprehensive exam, thesis/dissertation, teaching experience. *Entrance requirements:* For master's, GRE General Test, 3 letters of recommendation, creative writing sample; for doctorate, GRE General Test, GRE Subject Test (English), 3 letters of recommendation, writing sample. Additional exam requirements/recommendations for international students: Required—TOEFL (minimum score 600 paper-based; 250 computer-based; 77 iBT). *Application deadline:* For fall admission, 1/10 for domestic students. Application fee: $70. Electronic applications accepted. *Expenses:* Tuition: Full-time $29,500. Required fees: $70. Full-time tuition and fees vary according to degree level, program and student level. *Financial support:* In 2008–09, 96 students received support, including 41 fellowships with full tuition reimbursements available, 1 research assistantship with full tuition reimbursement available, 54 teaching assistantships with full tuition reimbursements available; institutionally sponsored loans, scholarships/grants, health care benefits, tuition waivers (full and partial), and unspecified assistantships also available. Financial award applicants required to submit FAFSA. *Faculty research:* English and American literature, women's writing, ethnic and post-colonial literature, critical theory, medievalism. *Unit head:* Director of Graduate Studies, 607-255-7989, Fax: 607-255-6661. *Application contact:* Graduate Field Assistant, 607-255-7989, Fax: 607-255-6661, E-mail: english_grad@cornell.edu.

Cornell University, Graduate School, Graduate Fields of Arts and Sciences, Field of Linguistics, Ithaca, NY 14853-0001. Offers applied linguistics (MA, PhD); East Asian linguistics (MA, PhD); English linguistics (MA, PhD); general linguistics (MA, PhD); Germanic linguistics (MA, PhD); Indo-European linguistics (MA, PhD); phonetics (MA, PhD); phonological theory (MA, PhD); Romance linguistics (MA, PhD); second language acquisition (MA, PhD); semantics (MA, PhD); Slavic linguistics (MA, PhD); sociolinguistics (MA, PhD); South Asian linguistics (MA, PhD); Southeast Asian linguistics (MA, PhD); syntactic theory (MA, PhD). *Faculty:* 15 full-time (6 women). *Students:* 32 full-time (15 women); includes 1 minority (Hispanic American), 16 international. Average age 30. 93 applicants, 16% accepted, 7 enrolled. In 2008, 5 master's, 7 doctorates awarded. Terminal master's awarded for partial completion of doctoral program. *Degree requirements:* For master's, one foreign language, thesis; for doctorate, one foreign language, comprehensive exam, thesis/dissertation. *Entrance requirements:* For master's and doctorate, GRE General Test, 2 letters of recommendation. Additional exam requirements/recommendations for international students: Required—TOEFL (minimum score 600 paper-based; 250 computer-based; 77 iBT). *Application deadline:* For fall admission, 1/15 for domestic students. Application fee: $70. Electronic applications accepted. *Expenses:* Tuition: Full-time $29,500. Required fees: $70. Full-time tuition and fees vary according to degree level, program and student level. *Financial support:* In 2008–09, 32 students received support, including 11 fellowships with full tuition reimbursements available, 4 research assistantships with full tuition reimbursements available, 17 teaching assistantships with full tuition reimbursements available; institutionally sponsored loans, scholarships/grants, health care benefits, tuition waivers (full and partial), and unspecified assistantships also available. Financial award applicants required to submit FAFSA. *Faculty research:* Phonology and phonetics; syntax and semantics; historical linguistics; philosophy of language; language acquisition. *Unit head:* Director of Graduate Studies, 607-255-1105. *Application contact:* Graduate Field Assistant, 607-255-1105, E-mail: lingfield@cornell.edu.

Creighton University, Graduate School, College of Arts and Sciences, Department of English, Omaha, NE 68178-0001. Offers MA. Part-time programs available. *Degree requirements:* For master's, thesis optional. *Entrance requirements:* For master's, GRE Subject Test in English, 10-15 page writing sample, 3 letters of recommendation. Additional exam requirements/recommendations for international students: Required—TOEFL (minimum score 550 paper-based; 213 computer-based; 80 iBT). Electronic applications accepted.

Dalhousie University, Faculty of Arts and Social Science, Department of English, Halifax, NS B3H 4R2, Canada. Offers MA, PhD. *Students:* 37 full-time (22 women), 1 (woman) part-time. 65 applicants, 20% accepted. *Entrance requirements:* Additional exam requirements/recommendations for international students: Required—TOEFL, IELTS, 1 of 5 approved tests: TOEFL, IELTS, CANTEST, CAEL, Michigan English Language Assessment Battery. *Application deadline:* For fall admission, 6/1 for domestic students, 4/1 for international students; for winter admission, 10/31 for domestic students, 8/31 for international students; for spring admission, 2/28 for domestic students, 12/31 for international students. Application fee: $70. Electronic applications accepted. *Financial support:* Career-related internships or fieldwork, scholarships/grants, and health care benefits available. *Faculty research:* Victorian, Canadian, Renaissance, eighteenth-century, and modern literature. *Unit head:* Dr. Christina Luckyj, Chair, 902-494-6924, Fax: 902-494-2176, E-mail: gradengl@dal.ca. *Application contact:* Dr. Rohan Maitzen, Graduate Coordinator, 902-494-6924, Fax: 902-494-2176, E-mail: gradengl@dal.ca.

DePaul University, College of Liberal Arts and Sciences, Department of English, Program in English, Chicago, IL 60604-2287. Offers MA. *Unit head:* Dr. William Fahrenbach, Chairperson, 773-325-1776, E-mail: bfahrenb@depaul.edu. *Application contact:* Dr. Lesley Kordecki, Director, 773-325-1786, Fax: 773-325-8607, E-mail: lkordeck@depaul.edu.

Drew University, Caspersen School of Graduate Studies, Program in English Literature, Madison, NJ 07940-1493. Offers MA, PhD. Part-time programs available. Terminal master's awarded for partial completion of doctoral program. *Degree requirements:* For master's, one foreign language, thesis; for doctorate, 2 foreign languages, comprehensive exam, thesis/dissertation. *Entrance requirements:* For master's and doctorate, GRE General Test. *Faculty research:* British literature/American literature, Victorian literature, Shakespeare, Cather studies, postmodernity.

Drew University, Caspersen School of Graduate Studies, Program in Modern History and Literature, Madison, NJ 07940-1493. Offers MA, PhD. Part-time and evening/weekend programs available. Terminal master's awarded for partial completion of doctoral program. *Degree requirements:* For master's, one foreign language, thesis; for doctorate, 2 foreign languages, comprehensive exam, thesis/dissertation. *Entrance requirements:* For master's and doctorate, GRE General Test. *Faculty research:* History of the book, modern American history/European history, cultural and intellectual history, eighteenth- to twentieth-century history and literature, history of science.

Duke University, Graduate School, Department of English, Durham, NC 27708. Offers PhD, JD/AM. *Degree requirements:* For doctorate, 2 foreign languages, thesis/dissertation. *Entrance requirements:* For doctorate, GRE General Test. Additional exam requirements/recommendations for international students: Required—TOEFL (minimum score 550 paper-based; 213 computer-based; 83 iBT), IELTS (minimum score 7). Electronic applications accepted.

Duquesne University, Graduate School of Liberal Arts, Program in English, Pittsburgh, PA 15282-0001. Offers MA, PhD. Part-time and evening/weekend programs available. *Faculty:* 17 full-time (10 women), 29 part-time/adjunct (17 women). *Students:* 64 full-time (47 women), 16 part-time (12 women), 2 international. Average age 25. 71 applicants, 52% accepted, 20 enrolled. In 2008, 14 master's, 2 doctorates awarded. *Degree requirements:* For master's, one foreign language, comprehensive exam, thesis or alternative; for doctorate, 2 foreign languages, comprehensive exam, thesis/dissertation. *Entrance requirements:* For master's and doctorate, GRE General Test, bachelor's degree in English, writing sample. Additional exam requirements/recommendations for international students: Required—TOEFL. *Application deadline:* For fall admission, 2/1 priority date for domestic and international students. Applications are processed on a rolling basis. Application fee: $50. Electronic applications accepted. *Expenses:* Tuition: Part-time $819 per credit. Required fees: $78 per credit. Tuition and fees vary according to course load. *Financial support:* In 2008–09, 1 research assistantship with full tuition reimbursement (averaging $13,000 per year), 21 teaching assistantships with full tuition reimbursements (averaging $13,000 per year) were awarded; Federal Work-Study, scholarships/grants, tuition waivers (partial), and unspecified assistantships also available. Support available to part-time students. Financial award application deadline: 5/1. *Unit head:* Dr. Magali Michael, Chair, 412-396-6440. *Application contact:* Dr. Daniel Howard, Director of Graduate Studies in English, 412-396-6420.

East Carolina University, Graduate School, Thomas Harriot College of Arts and Sciences, Department of English, Greenville, NC 27858-4353. Offers MA. Part-time and evening/weekend programs available. *Degree requirements:* For master's, one foreign language, comprehensive exam, thesis optional. *Entrance requirements:* For master's, GRE General Test, MAT (MA Ed). Additional exam requirements/recommendations for international students: Required—TOEFL.

Eastern Illinois University, Graduate School, College of Arts and Humanities, Department of English, Charleston, IL 61920-3099. Offers MA. Part-time programs available. *Entrance requirements:* For master's, GRE General Test.

Eastern Kentucky University, The Graduate School, College of Arts and Sciences, Department of English and Theatre, Richmond, KY 40475-3102. Offers creative writing (MFA); English (MA). Part-time and evening/weekend programs available. *Degree requirements:* For master's, thesis optional. *Entrance requirements:* For master's, GRE General Test, minimum GPA of 2.5, minor in English with 3.0 GPA. *Faculty research:* Old English, Victorian studies, women's studies, rhetoric, popular culture, novel studies.

Eastern Michigan University, Graduate School, College of Arts and Sciences, Department of English Language and Literature, Program in Children's Literature, Ypsilanti, MI 48197. Offers MA. Part-time and evening/weekend programs available. Postbaccalaureate distance learning degree programs offered (minimal on-campus study). *Entrance requirements:* Additional exam requirements/recommendations for international students: Required—TOEFL.

Eastern Michigan University, Graduate School, College of Arts and Sciences, Department of English Language and Literature, Program in English Linguistics, Ypsilanti, MI 48197. Offers MA. Part-time and evening/weekend programs available. Postbaccalaureate distance learning degree programs offered (minimal on-campus study). *Degree requirements:* For master's, thesis (for some programs). *Entrance requirements:* Additional exam requirements/recommendations for international students: Required—TOEFL.

Eastern Michigan University, Graduate School, College of Arts and Sciences, Department of English Language and Literature, Program in Literature, Ypsilanti, MI 48197. Offers MA, Graduate Certificate. Part-time and evening/weekend programs available. Postbaccalaureate distance learning degree programs offered (minimal on-campus study). *Entrance requirements:* Additional exam requirements/recommendations for international students: Required—TOEFL.

Eastern New Mexico University, Graduate School, College of Liberal Arts and Sciences, Department of Languages and Literature, Portales, NM 88130. Offers English (MA). Part-time programs available. *Degree requirements:* For master's, one foreign language, thesis optional. *Entrance requirements:* For master's, minimum GPA of 2.5. Electronic applications accepted.

Eastern Washington University, Graduate Studies, College of Arts and Letters, Department of English, Cheney, WA 99004-2431. Offers literature (MA); rhetoric, composition, and technical communication (MA); teaching English as a second language (MA). *Degree requirements:* For master's, comprehensive exam, thesis or alternative. *Entrance requirements:* For master's, GRE General Test, minimum GPA of 3.0.

East Tennessee State University, School of Graduate Studies, College of Arts and Sciences, Department of English, Johnson City, TN 37614. Offers MA. Part-time and evening/weekend programs available. *Degree requirements:* For master's, oral defense of thesis. *Entrance requirements:* For master's, GRE General Test or GRE Subject Test, minimum undergraduate GPA of 3.0 in English. Additional exam requirements/recommendations for international students: Required—TOEFL (minimum score 550 paper-based; 213 computer-based). *Faculty research:* Appalachian studies, women's studies, sports images in religion, British and American literature.

Elmhurst College, Graduate Programs, Program in English Studies, Elmhurst, IL 60126-3296. Offers MA. Part-time and evening/weekend programs available. *Faculty:* 2 full-time (1 woman). *Students:* 17 part-time (13 women); includes 1 minority (Asian American or Pacific Islander). Average age 28. 10 applicants, 70% accepted, 5 enrolled. In 2008, 12 master's awarded. *Degree requirements:* For master's, thesis optional. *Entrance requirements:* For master's, 3 recommendations. Additional exam requirements/recommendations for international students: Required—TOEFL (minimum score 550 paper-based; 213 computer-based). *Application deadline:* Applications are processed on a rolling basis. Application fee: $25. Electronic applications accepted. *Expenses:* Tuition: Part-time $675 per semester hour. Tuition and fees vary according to program. *Financial support:* In 2008–09, 5 students received support. Federal Work-Study and scholarships/grants available. Support available to part-time students. Financial award application deadline: 6/1; financial award applicants required to submit FAFSA. *Unit head:* Dr. John E. Bohnert, Dean of Graduate Studies, 630-617-3069,

English

Elmhurst College (continued)
Fax: 630-617-5501, E-mail: gradadm@elmhurst.edu. *Application contact:* Elizabeth D. Kuebler, Director of Adult and Graduate Admission, 630-617-3069, Fax: 630-617-5501, E-mail: betsyk@elmhurst.edu.

Emory University, Graduate School of Arts and Sciences, Department of Comparative Literature, Atlanta, GA 30322-1100. Offers comparative literature (PhD); English (Certificate); French (Certificate); Middle Eastern studies (PhD); philosophy (Certificate); psychoanalytic studies (PhD); religion (PhD); Spanish (Certificate); women studies (Certificate). *Degree requirements:* For doctorate, 2 foreign languages, comprehensive exam, thesis/dissertation. *Entrance requirements:* For doctorate, GRE General Test, minimum GPA of 3.0. Additional exam requirements/recommendations for international students: Required—TOEFL. Electronic applications accepted. *Faculty research:* Literary theory, psychoanalysis trauma and testimony, literature and religion, literature and technology, literature and philosophy, politics and global culture, literature and aesthetics.

Emory University, Graduate School of Arts and Sciences, Department of English, Atlanta, GA 30322-1100. Offers PhD. *Degree requirements:* For doctorate, one foreign language, comprehensive exam, thesis/dissertation. *Entrance requirements:* For doctorate, GRE General Test, minimum GPA of 3.0. Additional exam requirements/recommendations for international students: Required—TOEFL. Electronic applications accepted. *Faculty research:* American literature, renaissance literature, twentieth century poetry, Irish literature, cultural studies.

Emporia State University, School of Graduate Studies, College of Liberal Arts and Sciences, Department of English, Emporia, KS 66801-5087. Offers MA. Part-time programs available. *Faculty:* 14 full-time (6 women), 1 (woman) part-time/adjunct. *Students:* 9 full-time (7 women), 11 part-time (6 women); includes 2 minority (both Hispanic Americans), 2 international. 5 applicants, 100% accepted, 5 enrolled. In 2008, 6 master's awarded. *Degree requirements:* For master's, comprehensive exam or thesis. *Entrance requirements:* For master's, appropriate undergraduate degree, writing sample. Additional exam requirements/recommendations for international students: Required—TOEFL (minimum score 575 paper-based). *Application deadline:* For fall admission, 8/15 priority date for domestic students. Applications are processed on a rolling basis. Application fee: $30 ($75 for international students). Electronic applications accepted. *Expenses:* Tuition, area resident: Full-time $3976; part-time $166 per credit hour. Tuition, state resident: full-time $3976; part-time $166 per credit hour. Tuition, nonresident: full-time $12,028; part-time $501 per credit hour. Required fees: $51 per credit hour. Tuition and fees vary according to campus/location. *Financial support:* In 2008–09, 14 teaching assistantships with full tuition reimbursements (averaging $7,610 per year) were awarded; Federal Work-Study, institutionally sponsored loans, health care benefits, and unspecified assistantships also available. Financial award application deadline: 3/15; financial award applicants required to submit FAFSA. *Unit head:* Dr. Jim Hoy, Interim Chair, 620-341-5216, E-mail: jhoy@emporia.edu. *Application contact:* Dr. Mel Storm, Graduate Coordinator, 620-341-5563, E-mail: mstorm@emporia.edu.

Fairleigh Dickinson University, Metropolitan Campus, University College: Arts, Sciences, and Professional Studies, Department of English, Philosophy, and Humanities, Program in English and Literature, Teaneck, NJ 07666-1914. Offers MA. *Students:* 3 full-time (2 women), 3 part-time (all women). Average age 25. 15 applicants, 93% accepted, 5 enrolled. In 2008, 3 master's awarded. Application fee: $40. *Application contact:* Susan Brooman, University Director of Graduate Admissions, 201-692-2554, Fax: 201-692-2560, E-mail: globaleducation@fdu.edu.

Fayetteville State University, Graduate School, Program in English, Fayetteville, NC 28301-4298. Offers MA. Part-time and evening/weekend programs available. *Degree requirements:* For master's, comprehensive exam, thesis, internship. *Entrance requirements:* For master's, GRE General Test. Electronic applications accepted. *Faculty research:* Online film culture; literature and pre-Raphaelite, Symbolist, and Surrealist painting; aesthetics of African-American gospel music; power of sheltered instruction.

Fitchburg State College, Division of Graduate and Continuing Education, Programs in English and Teaching English (Secondary Level), Fitchburg, MA 01420-2697. Offers MA, MAT, Certificate. *Accreditation:* NCATE. Part-time and evening/weekend programs available. *Students:* 1 full-time (0 women), 28 part-time (23 women); includes 1 minority (African American). Average age 35. 9 applicants, 78% accepted, 5 enrolled. In 2008, 7 master's awarded. *Entrance requirements:* For master's, GRE General Test or MAT, letters of recommendation, resumé. Additional exam requirements/recommendations for international students: Required—TOEFL (minimum score 550 paper-based; 213 computer-based; 79 iBT). *Application deadline:* Applications are processed on a rolling basis. Application fee: $25 ($50 for international students). *Expenses:* Tuition, state resident: full-time $3600; part-time $150 per credit. Tuition, nonresident: full-time $3600; part-time $150 per credit. Required fees: $109 per credit. *Financial support:* In 2008–09, research assistantships with partial tuition reimbursements (averaging $5,500 per year); Federal Work-Study, scholarships/grants, and unspecified assistantships also available. Support available to part-time students. Financial award application deadline: 3/1; financial award applicants required to submit FAFSA. *Unit head:* Dr. Chola Chisunka, Chair, 978-665-3445, Fax: 978-665-3658, E-mail: gce@fsc.edu. *Application contact:* Director of Admissions, 978-665-3144, Fax: 978-665-4540, E-mail: admissions@fsc.edu.

Florida Atlantic University, Dorothy F. Schmidt College of Arts and Letters, Department of English, Boca Raton, FL 33431-0991. Offers British and American literature (MA); creative nonfiction (MFA); creative writing (MA); fiction (MFA); multicultural literatures and literacies (MA); poetry (MFA); science fiction and fantasy (MA); teaching English (MAT). Part-time programs available. *Faculty:* 49 full-time (24 women), 17 part-time/adjunct (7 women). *Students:* 51 full-time (28 women), 29 part-time (26 women); includes 16 minority (4 African Americans, 1 American Indian/Alaska Native, 2 Asian Americans or Pacific Islanders, 9 Hispanic Americans), 1 international. Average age 31. 53 applicants, 57% accepted, 16 enrolled. In 2008, 27 master's awarded. *Degree requirements:* For master's, one foreign language, thesis. *Entrance requirements:* For master's, GRE General Test, minimum GPA of 3.0, writing samples, 2 letters of recommendation. *Application deadline:* For fall admission, 3/1 for domestic students, 2/15 for international students; for spring admission, 11/1 for domestic students, 7/15 for international students. Applications are processed on a rolling basis. Application fee: $30. Electronic applications accepted. *Expenses:* Tuition, state resident: full-time $4867; part-time $270.40 per credit hour. Tuition, nonresident: full-time $16,486; part-time $915.87 per credit hour. *Financial support:* Fellowships, teaching assistantships with partial tuition reimbursements, Federal Work-Study and tuition waivers available. Support available to part-time students. Financial award application deadline: 3/1. *Faculty research:* African-American writers, critical theory, British American, Asian American. *Unit head:* Dr. Wenying Xu, Chair, 561-297-2065, Fax: 561-297-3807, E-mail: wxu@fau.edu. *Application contact:* Dr. Andrew Furman, Director of Graduate Studies, 561-297-3835, Fax: 561-297-3807, E-mail: afurman@fau.edu.

Florida Gulf Coast University, College of Arts and Sciences, Program in English, Fort Myers, FL 33965-6565. Offers MA. *Faculty:* 155 full-time (65 women), 123 part-time/adjunct (47 women). *Students:* 16 full-time (12 women), 8 part-time (4 women); includes 2 minority (1 Asian American or Pacific Islander, 1 Hispanic American). Average age 31. 31 applicants, 42% accepted, 8 enrolled. In 2008, 11 master's awarded. *Entrance requirements:* For master's, GRE General Test, minimum GPA of 3.0. Additional exam requirements/recommendations for international students: Required—TOEFL (minimum score 550 paper-based; 213 computer-based). *Application deadline:* For fall admission, 2/15 for domestic students. Application fee: $30. *Unit head:* Joe Wisdom, Chair, 239-590-7157, E-mail: jwisdom@fgcu.edu. *Application contact:* Patricia Rice, Executive Secretary, 239-590-7196, Fax: 239-590-7200, E-mail: price@fgcu.edu.

Florida International University, College of Arts and Sciences, Department of English, Program in English, Miami, FL 33199. Offers MA. Part-time and evening/weekend programs available. *Degree requirements:* For master's, thesis. *Entrance requirements:* For master's, GRE General Test, writing examples, minimum GPA of 3.0, letters of recommendation. Additional exam requirements/recommendations for international students: Required—TOEFL (minimum score 550 paper-based; 213 computer-based). Electronic applications accepted.

Florida State University, Graduate Studies, College of Arts and Sciences, Department of English, Tallahassee, FL 32306. Offers creative writing (MFA, PhD); literature (MA, PhD); rhetoric and composition (MA, PhD). Part-time programs available. *Degree requirements:* For master's, one foreign language, thesis or alternative; for doctorate, 2 foreign languages, thesis/dissertation. *Entrance requirements:* For master's, GRE General Test, GRE Subject Test (literature), sample of written work, 3 letters of recommendation; for doctorate, GRE General Test, sample of written work, 3 letters of recommendation. Electronic applications accepted. *Faculty research:* British literature, American literature, creative writing, rhetoric, multiethnic literature.

Fordham University, Graduate School of Arts and Sciences, Department of English Language and Literature, New York, NY 10458. Offers MA, PhD. Part-time and evening/weekend programs available. Terminal master's awarded for partial completion of doctoral program. *Degree requirements:* For master's, one foreign language, comprehensive exam, thesis optional; for doctorate, 2 foreign languages, comprehensive exam, thesis/dissertation. *Entrance requirements:* For master's, GRE General Test; for doctorate, GRE General Test, GRE Subject Test. Additional exam requirements/recommendations for international students: Required—TOEFL (minimum score 650 paper-based; 280 computer-based). Electronic applications accepted. *Faculty research:* 19th century British and American literature, Shakespeare and early modern drama, Aesthetic theory, Old Norse, poetics of race and gender, Anglo-Norman.

Fort Hays State University, Graduate School, College of Arts and Sciences, Department of English, Hays, KS 67601-4099. Offers MA. *Degree requirements:* For master's, comprehensive exam, thesis or alternative. *Entrance requirements:* Additional exam requirements/recommendations for international students: Required—TOEFL (minimum score 550 paper-based; 213 computer-based). Electronic applications accepted. *Faculty research:* Eisenhower and Hansen papers, Celtic literature and culture, poetry of Robert Frost.

Gannon University, School of Graduate Studies, College of Humanities, Education, and Social Sciences, School of Humanities, Program in English, Erie, PA 16541-0001. Offers MA. Part-time and evening/weekend programs available. *Students:* 5 full-time (2 women), 17 part-time (12 women). Average age 30. 19 applicants, 84% accepted, 11 enrolled. In 2008, 2 master's awarded. *Degree requirements:* For master's, thesis. *Entrance requirements:* For master's, interview. Additional exam requirements/recommendations for international students: Required—TOEFL (minimum score 500 paper-based; 173 computer-based). *Application deadline:* Applications are processed on a rolling basis. Application fee: $25. Electronic applications accepted. *Expenses:* Tuition: Full-time $13,050; part-time $725 per credit. Required fees: $502; $16 per credit. Tuition and fees vary according to course load, degree level, campus/location and program. *Financial support:* In 2008–09, 5 teaching assistantships (averaging $6,300 per year) were awarded; career-related internships or fieldwork and scholarships/grants also available. Financial award application deadline: 7/1; financial award applicants required to submit FAFSA. *Unit head:* Dr. Penelope Smith, Chair, 814-871-7748, E-mail: smith006@gannon.edu. *Application contact:* Kara Morgan, Assistant Director of Graduate Admissions, 814-871-5831, Fax: 814-871-5827, E-mail: graduate@gannon.edu.

Gardner-Webb University, Graduate School, Department of English, Boiling Springs, NC 28017. Offers English (MA); English education (MA). Part-time and evening/weekend programs available. *Degree requirements:* For master's, comprehensive exam. *Entrance requirements:* For master's, GRE General Test, MAT, or NTE; PRAXIS, minimum GPA of 2.5. Electronic applications accepted.

George Mason University, College of Humanities and Social Sciences, Department of English, Fairfax, VA 22030. Offers creative writing (MFA); English (MA); English literature (MA); linguistics (MA); professional writing and editing (MA, Certificate); teaching English as a second language (Certificate); teaching writing and literature (MA). *Degree requirements:* For master's, thesis (for some programs). *Entrance requirements:* For master's, minimum GPA of 3.0 in last 60 hours of course work. Electronic applications accepted. *Faculty research:* Literature, professional writing and editing, writing of fiction or poetry.

Georgetown University, Graduate School of Arts and Sciences, Department of English, Washington, DC 20057. Offers British and American literature (MA). *Degree requirements:* For master's, thesis or alternative, independent study, oral exam. *Entrance requirements:* For master's, GRE General Test. Additional exam requirements/recommendations for international students: Required—TOEFL.

The George Washington University, Columbian College of Arts and Sciences, Department of English, Washington, DC 20052. Offers MA, PhD. Part-time and evening/weekend programs available. *Faculty:* 33 full-time (17 women), 27 part-time/adjunct (18 women). *Students:* 20 full-time (15 women), 17 part-time (14 women); includes 5 minority (1 African American, 4 Asian Americans or Pacific Islanders), 3 international. Average age 30. 98 applicants, 43% accepted, 11 enrolled. In 2008, 16 master's, 10 doctorates awarded. Terminal master's awarded for partial completion of doctoral program. *Degree requirements:* For master's, one foreign language, comprehensive exam, thesis or alternative; for doctorate, 2 foreign languages, thesis/dissertation, general exam. *Entrance requirements:* For master's and doctorate, GRE General Test, GRE Subject Test, minimum GPA of 3.0, writing sample. Additional exam requirements/recommendations for international students: Required—TOEFL (minimum score 550 paper-based; 213 computer-based; 80 iBT). *Application deadline:* For fall admission, 1/15 priority date for domestic and international students; for spring admission, 10/1 priority date for domestic students, 9/1 priority date for international students. Applications are processed on a rolling basis. Application fee: $60. Electronic applications accepted. *Financial support:* In 2008–09, 18 students received support; fellowships with tuition reimbursements available, teaching assistantships with tuition reimbursements available, Federal Work-Study available. Financial award application deadline: 1/15. *Unit head:* Jeffrey Jerome Cohen, Chair, 202-994-6180, E-mail: jjcohen@gwu.edu. *Application contact:* Jeffrey Jerome Cohen, Chair, 202-994-6180, E-mail: jjcohen@gwu.edu.

Georgia College & State University, Graduate School, School of Liberal Arts and Sciences, Department of English, Speech, and Journalism, Program in English, Milledgeville, GA 31061. Offers MA. *Degree requirements:* For master's, one foreign language, comprehensive exam, thesis. *Entrance requirements:* For master's, GRE (minimum score: 550 verbal, 4.5 analytical), undergraduate major in English, minimum GPA of 3.0, letters of recommendation.

Georgia Southern University, Jack N. Averitt College of Graduate Studies, College of Liberal Arts and Social Sciences, Department of Literature and Philosophy, Statesboro, GA 30460. Offers English (MA). Part-time programs available. *Students:* 18 full-time (14 women), 7 part-time (3 women); includes 3 minority (all African Americans). Average age 27. 14 applicants, 86% accepted, 10 enrolled. In 2008, 3 master's awarded. *Degree requirements:* For master's, one foreign language, thesis optional, terminal exams. *Entrance requirements:* For master's, GRE General Test, minimum GPA of 3.0, letters of reference. Additional exam requirements/recommendations for international students: Required—TOEFL (minimum score 550 paper-based; 213 computer-based; 80 iBT). *Application deadline:* For fall admission, 3/1 priority date for domestic and international students; for spring admission, 10/1 priority date for domestic students, 10/1 for international students. Applications are processed on a rolling basis. Application fee: $50. Electronic applications accepted. *Expenses:* Tuition, area resident: Full-time $3840; part-time $160 per semester hour. Tuition, state resident: full-time $3840; part-time $160 per semester hour. Tuition, nonresident: full-time $15,336; part-time $639 per semester hour. Required fees: $1152. *Financial support:* In 2008–09, 21 students received support, including research assistantships with partial tuition reimbursements available (averaging $6,850 per year), teaching assistantships with partial tuition reimbursements available (averaging $6,850 per year); career-related internships or fieldwork, Federal Work-Study, scholarships/grants, tuition waivers (partial), and unspecified assistantships also available. Support available to part-time students. Financial award application deadline: 4/15; financial award applicants required to submit FAFSA. *Faculty research:* The fiction of Nuguib Mahfouz and Shusako Enato, a book-length collection of essays on playwright Paula Vogel, a critical edition of math, Gregory Lewis' Tales of Wonder (1800), ongoing studies in the dramatic works of English poet John Dryden, post modern childhoods, post modern poetries. *Unit head:* David Dudley, Chair, 912-478-5471, E-mail: dldudley@georgiasouthern.edu. *Application contact:* 912-478-5384, Fax: 912-478-0740, E-mail: gradadmissions@georgiasouthern.edu.

Georgia State University, College of Arts and Sciences, Department of English, Atlanta, GA 30303-3083. Offers creative writing (MA, MFA, PhD); English (MA, PhD); fiction (MFA); literary studies and composition (MA, PhD); poetry (MFA); rhetoric (MA, PhD). Part-time and evening/weekend programs available. *Degree requirements:* For master's, one foreign language, thesis; for doctorate, 2 foreign languages, comprehensive exam, thesis/dissertation, exam. *Entrance requirements:* For master's and doctorate, GRE General Test. Additional exam requirements/recommendations for international students: Required—TOEFL. Electronic applications accepted. *Faculty research:* Literary biography, folklore, Southern literature, medieval literature.

Governors State University, College of Arts and Sciences, Program in English, University Park, IL 60466-0975. Offers MA. Part-time and evening/weekend programs available. *Degree requirements:* For master's, thesis or alternative. *Entrance requirements:* For master's, bachelor's degree in related field.

Graduate School and University Center of the City University of New York, Graduate Studies, Program in English, New York, NY 10016-4039. Offers PhD. *Degree requirements:* For doctorate, 2 foreign languages, thesis/dissertation. *Entrance requirements:* For doctorate, GRE General Test, GRE Subject Test, writing sample, curriculum vitae. Additional exam requirements/recommendations for international students: Required—TOEFL. Electronic applications accepted.

Grambling State University, School of Graduate Studies and Research, College of Education, Department of Educational Leadership, Grambling, LA 71245. Offers curriculum and instruction (Ed D); developmental education (MS, Ed D), including curriculum and instruction: reading (Ed D), English (MS), guidance and counseling (MS), higher education administration (Ed D), instructional systems and technology (Ed D), mathematics (MS), reading (MS), science (MS), student development and personnel services (Ed D); educational leadership (MS, Ed D). Part-time and evening/weekend programs available. *Faculty:* 12 full-time (5 women), 1 part-time/adjunct (0 women). *Students:* 25 full-time (23 women), 88 part-time (62 women); includes 83 minority (81 African Americans, 1 American Indian/Alaska Native, 1 Asian American or Pacific Islander), 5 international. Average age 41. In 2008, 3 doctorates awarded. *Degree requirements:* For master's, comprehensive exam, thesis (for some programs); for doctorate, comprehensive exam, thesis/dissertation. *Entrance requirements:* For master's, GRE, minimum GPA of 2.5 on last degree; for doctorate, GRE (minimum 1000, 500 on Verbal), master's degree, minimum GPA of 3.0 on last degree. Additional exam requirements/recommendations for international students: Required—TOEFL (minimum score 500 paper-based; 173 computer-based; 61 iBT). *Application deadline:* For fall admission, 7/1 for domestic and international students; for spring admission, 12/1 for domestic and international students. Applications are processed on a rolling basis. Application fee: $20 ($30 for international students). Electronic applications accepted. *Expenses:* Tuition, area resident: Full-time $3637; part-time $134 per credit hour. Tuition, nonresident: full-time $7651; part-time $134 per credit hour. Required fees: $1225; $134 per credit hour. $430 per semester. *Financial support:* In 2008–09, 8 research assistantships (averaging $7,594 per year) were awarded; health care benefits, tuition waivers (full), and unspecified assistantships also available. Financial award application deadline: 5/31; financial award applicants required to submit FAFSA. *Unit head:* Dr. Olatunde Ogunyemi, Director, 318-274-6105, Fax: 318-274-2799, E-mail: ogunyemio@gram.edu. *Application contact:* Laketha Richards, Administrative Assistant III, 318-274-6105, Fax: 318-274-6249, E-mail: richardsl@gram.edu.

Grand Valley State University, College of Liberal Arts and Sciences, English Department, Allendale, MI 49401-9403. Offers MA. *Faculty:* 11 full-time (7 women). *Students:* 8 full-time (5 women), 30 part-time (22 women); includes 1 minority (Hispanic American). Average age 34. 11 applicants, 82% accepted, 8 enrolled. In 2008, 8 master's awarded. *Entrance requirements:* Additional exam requirements/recommendations for international students: Required—TOEFL. Application fee: $30. *Financial support:* In 2008–09, 1 research assistantship with full and partial tuition reimbursement (averaging $8,000 per year) was awarded. *Faculty research:* Literary history, philosophy and literature, feminist issues in literature. *Unit head:* Dr. Jill VanAntwerp, Chair, 616-331-3405, E-mail: vanantwj@gvsu.edu. *Application contact:* Dr. Ben Lockerd, Information Contact, 616-331-3575, E-mail: lockerdb@gvsu.edu.

Hardin-Simmons University, Graduate School, Cynthia Ann Parker College of Liberal Arts, Department of English, Abilene, TX 79698-0001. Offers MA. Part-time programs available. *Faculty:* 4 full-time (2 women). *Students:* 1 (woman) full-time, 6 part-time (all women); includes 2 minority (both Hispanic Americans). Average age 30. 5 applicants, 40% accepted, 2 enrolled. In 2008, 4 master's awarded. *Degree requirements:* For master's, one foreign language, comprehensive exam, thesis or alternative. *Entrance requirements:* For master's, minimum undergraduate GPA of 3.0 in English, 2.7 overall; writing sample; letters of recommendation; interview. Additional exam requirements/recommendations for international students: Required—TOEFL (minimum score 550 paper-based; 213 computer-based; 75 iBT). *Application deadline:* For fall admission, 8/15 priority date for domestic students, 4/1 for international students; for spring admission, 1/5 priority date for domestic students, 9/1 for international students. Applications are processed on a rolling basis. Application fee: $50. *Expenses:* Tuition: Full-time $10,620; part-time $590 per credit hour. Required fees: $590; $110 per semester. Tuition and fees vary according to course load and degree level. *Financial support:* In 2008–09, 9 students received support, including 2 fellowships (averaging $1,200 per year); scholarships/grants also available. Support available to part-time students. Financial award application deadline: 6/30; financial award applicants required to submit FAFSA. *Faculty research:* Milton, Tennyson, American Romantic period, Derek Walcott, woman's literature. *Unit head:* Dr. Laura Pogue, Program Director, 325-670-1366, Fax: 325-670-5859, E-mail: lpogue@hsutx.edu. *Application contact:* Dr. Gary Stanlake, Dean of Graduate Studies, 325-670-1298, Fax: 325-670-1564, E-mail: gradoff@hsutx.edu.

Harvard University, Extension School, Cambridge, MA 02138-3722. Offers applied sciences (CAS); biotechnology (ALM); educational technologies (ALM); educational technology (CET); English for graduate and professional studies (DGP); environmental management (ALM, CEM); information technology (ALM); journalism (ALM); liberal arts (ALM); management (ALM, CM); mathematics for teaching (ALM); museum studies (ALM); premedical studies (Diploma); publication and communication (CPC). Part-time and evening/weekend programs available. *Degree requirements:* For master's, thesis. *Entrance requirements:* For master's, 3 completed graduate courses with grade of B or higher. Additional exam requirements/recommendations for international students: Required—TOEFL (minimum score 600 paper-based; 250 computer-based), TWE (minimum score 5). *Expenses:* Contact institution.

Harvard University, Graduate School of Arts and Sciences, Department of English and American Literature and Language, Cambridge, MA 02138. Offers critical theory (PhD); eighteenth-century literature (PhD); literature: nineteenth-century to the present (PhD); medieval literature and language (PhD); modern British and American literature (PhD); Renaissance literature (PhD). Terminal master's awarded for partial completion of doctoral program. *Degree requirements:* For doctorate, 2 foreign languages, thesis/dissertation, oral exam. *Entrance requirements:* For doctorate, GRE General Test, GRE Subject Test, writing sample. Additional exam requirements/recommendations for international students: Required—TOEFL. *Expenses:* Tuition: Full-time $32,556. Required fees: $1426. Full-time tuition and fees vary according to program and student level. *Faculty research:* Old and Middle English language and literature, drama, creative writing, transition to Romanticism, history and theory of criticism.

Heritage University, Graduate Programs in Education, Program in Professional Studies, Toppenish, WA 98948-9599. Offers bilingual education/ESL (M Ed); biology (M Ed); English and literature (M Ed); reading/literacy (M Ed); special education (M Ed). Part-time and evening/weekend programs available. *Degree requirements:* For master's, comprehensive exam (for some programs), thesis (for some programs).

Hofstra University, College of Liberal Arts and Sciences, Department of English, Hempstead, NY 11549. Offers English and creative writing (MA); English literature (MA). Part-time programs available. *Faculty:* 12 full-time (7 women). *Students:* 16 full-time (9 women), 18 part-time (15 women); includes 1 minority (Hispanic American). Average age 31. 41 applicants, 73% accepted, 14 enrolled. In 2008, 15 master's awarded. *Degree requirements:* For master's, thesis optional. *Entrance requirements:* For master's, writing sample, essay, minimum GPA of 3.0 in literature courses. Additional exam requirements/recommendations for international students: Required—TOEFL (minimum score 550 paper-based; 213 computer-based; 80 iBT). *Application deadline:* Applications are processed on a rolling basis. Application fee: $60. Electronic applications accepted. *Expenses:* Tuition: Full-time $15,300; part-time $850 per credit. Required fees: $970; $165 per term. Tuition and fees vary according to program. *Financial support:* In 2008–09, 13 students received support, including 5 fellowships with full and partial tuition reimbursements available (averaging $2,605 per year), 1 research assistantship with full and partial tuition reimbursement available (averaging $14,220 per year); Federal Work-Study, institutionally sponsored loans, scholarships/grants, and tuition waivers (full and partial) also available. Support available to part-time students. Financial award applicants required to submit FAFSA. *Faculty research:* Herman Melville, disability studies, Early American literature, Queer Theory, twentieth century popular culture. *Unit head:* Dr. Joseph A. Fichtelberg, Chairperson, 516-463-5455, Fax: 516-463-6395, E-mail: engjaf@hofstra.edu. *Application contact:* Carol Drummer, Dean of Graduate Admissions, 516-463-4876, Fax: 516-463-4664, E-mail: gradstudent@hofstra.edu.

Hollins University, Graduate Programs, Program in Children's Literature, Roanoke, VA 24020-1603. Offers MA, MFA. Offered during summer only. Part-time programs available. *Faculty:* 12 part-time/adjunct (9 women). *Students:* 74 full-time (70 women), 6 part-time (all women); includes 6 minority (2 African Americans, 1 Asian American or Pacific Islander, 3 Hispanic Americans), 2 international. Average age 34. 44 applicants, 98% accepted, 28 enrolled. In 2008, 14 master's awarded. *Degree requirements:* For master's, one foreign language, comprehensive exam, thesis. *Entrance requirements:* For master's, letters of recommendation, portfolio. Additional exam requirements/recommendations for international students: Required—TOEFL (minimum score 550 paper-based; 213 computer-based; 79 iBT). *Application deadline:* For fall admission, 2/15 for domestic and international students. Application fee: $40. Electronic applications accepted. *Expenses:* Tuition: Full-time $26,720; part-time $590 per credit hour. Required fees: $280. *Financial support:* In 2008–09, 48 students received support, including 30 fellowships (averaging $921 per year); Federal Work-Study, scholarships/grants, and unspecified assistantships also available. Support available to part-time students. Financial award application deadline: 2/15; financial award applicants required to submit FAFSA. *Faculty research:* Fantasy, children's film, gender studies, mythology and folk tales, children's poetry, young adult fiction. *Unit head:* Amanda Cockrell, Director, 540-362-6024, Fax: 540-362-6642, E-mail: acockrell@hollins.edu. *Application contact:* Cathy S. Koon, Manager of Graduate Services, 540-362-6326, Fax: 540-362-6288, E-mail: ckoon@hollins.edu.

Howard University, Graduate School, Department of English, Washington, DC 20059-0002. Offers MA, PhD. Part-time programs available. *Degree requirements:* For master's, one foreign language, comprehensive exam, thesis; for doctorate, 2 foreign languages, comprehensive exam, thesis/dissertation, qualifying exam. *Entrance requirements:* For master's, GRE General Test, minimum GPA of 3.0; for doctorate, GRE General Test.

Humboldt State University, Graduate Studies, College of Arts, Humanities, and Social Sciences, Department of English, Arcata, CA 95521-8299. Offers English (MA), including international program, literature, teaching of writing. *Students:* 29 full-time (19 women), 7 part-time (3 women); includes 2 minority (1 African American, 1 Hispanic American). Average age 31. 24 applicants, 63% accepted, 4 enrolled. In 2008, 5 master's awarded. *Degree requirements:* For master's, one foreign language, thesis or alternative, qualifying exam. *Entrance requirements:* For master's, GRE, minimum GPA of 3.0, 3 letters of recommendation, sample of writing. Additional exam requirements/recommendations for international students: Required—TOEFL (minimum score 500 paper-based; 173 computer-based). *Application deadline:* For fall admission, 3/1 for domestic students; for spring admission, 11/1 for domestic students. Applications are processed on a rolling basis. Application fee: $55. *Expenses:* Tuition, state resident: full-time $5236. Tuition, nonresident: full-time $11,338. *Financial support:* Teaching assistantships, career-related internships or fieldwork, Federal Work-Study, and institutionally sponsored loans available. Financial award application deadline: 3/1; financial award applicants required to submit FAFSA. *Faculty research:* Teaching of writing, literature. *Unit head:* Dr. Susan Bennett, Chair, 707-826-3758, Fax: 707-826-5939, E-mail: sgb1@humboldt.edu. *Application contact:* Dr. Michael S. Eldridge, Graduate Coordinator, 707-826-5906, Fax: 707-826-5939, E-mail: me2@humboldt.edu.

Hunter College of the City University of New York, Graduate School, School of Arts and Sciences, Department of English, Program in British and American Literature, New York, NY 10021-5085. Offers MA. Part-time and evening/weekend programs available. *Faculty:* 32 full-time (17 women). *Students:* 62 part-time (34 women); includes 8 minority (4 African Americans, 2 Asian Americans or Pacific Islanders, 2 Hispanic Americans). Average age 33. 40 applicants, 58% accepted, 0 enrolled. In 2008, 25 master's awarded. *Degree requirements:* For master's, one foreign language, comprehensive exam, thesis, essay. *Entrance requirements:* For master's, GRE General Test, minimum 18 credits of course work in English, excluding journalism and writing. Additional exam requirements/recommendations for international students: Required—TOEFL. *Application deadline:* For fall admission, 4/1 for domestic students, 2/1 for international students; for spring admission, 11/1 for domestic students, 9/1 for international students. Application fee: $125. *Financial support:* Federal Work-Study and tuition waivers (partial) available. Support available to part-time students. Financial award application deadline: 4/15. *Unit head:* Dr. Christina Alfar, Associate Professor, 212-772-5187, E-mail: calfar@hunter.cuny.edu. *Application contact:* David Carlson, Education Adviser, 212-772-5074, E-mail: dcarlson@hunter.cuny.edu.

Idaho State University, Office of Graduate Studies, College of Arts and Sciences, Department of English, Pocatello, ID 83209. Offers MA, DA, PhD, Post-Master's Certificate. Part-time programs available. *Faculty:* 20 full-time (7 women). *Students:* 27 full-time (15 women), 28 part-time (16 women); includes 3 minority (1 Asian American or Pacific Islander, 2 Hispanic Americans), 4 international. Average age 38. In 2008, 3 master's, 4 doctorates awarded. *Degree requirements:* For master's, one foreign language, comprehensive exam, thesis optional; for doctorate, one foreign language, comprehensive exam, thesis/dissertation, 2 papers, 2 teaching internships; for Post-Master's Certificate, 6 credits of elective linguistics, practicum. *Entrance requirements:* For master's, GRE General Test, general literature exam, minimum GPA of 3.0, 3 letters of recommendation; for doctorate, GRE General Test, GRE Subject Test, minimum GPA of 3.5, writing examples, 3 letters of recommendation, master's degree in English; for Post-Master's Certificate, GRE, bachelor's degree, minimum undergraduate GPA of 3.0 in last 2 years, 3 letters of recommendation, knowledge of second language. Additional exam requirements/recommendations for international students: Required—TOEFL (minimum score 550 paper-based; 213 computer-based; 80 iBT). *Application deadline:* For fall admission, 7/1 for domestic students, 6/1 for international students; for spring admission, 12/1 for domestic students, 11/1 for international students. Applications are processed on a rolling basis. Application fee: $55. Electronic applications accepted. *Expenses:* Tuition, area resident: Full-time $3114; part-time $276 per credit hour. Tuition, state resident: full-time $3114; part-time $276 per credit hour. Tuition, nonresident: full-time $12,318; part-time $404 per credit hour. Required fees:

English

Idaho State University (continued)

$2360. Tuition and fees vary according to course load and reciprocity agreements. *Financial support:* In 2008–09, 1 research assistantship (averaging $6,800 per year), 21 teaching assistantships with full and partial tuition reimbursements (averaging $9,401 per year) were awarded; fellowships with full and partial tuition reimbursements, career-related internships or fieldwork, Federal Work-Study, institutionally sponsored loans, scholarships/grants, health care benefits, tuition waivers (full and partial), and unspecified assistantships also available. Support available to part-time students. Financial award application deadline: 1/1; financial award applicants required to submit FAFSA. *Faculty research:* American literature, Renaissance literature, composition and rhetoric, Intermountain West studies, ethics. *Unit head:* Dr. Terry O. Engebretsen, Chairman, 208-282-2478, Fax: 208-282-4472, E-mail: engeterr@isu.edu. *Application contact:* Ellen Combs, Graduate School Technical Records Specialist, 208-282-2150, Fax: 208-282-4847, E-mail: combelle@isu.edu.

Illinois State University, Graduate School, College of Arts and Sciences, Department of English, Program in English, Normal, IL 61790-2200. Offers English (MA, MS); English studies (PhD). *Degree requirements:* For doctorate, thesis/dissertation, 2 terms of residency. *Entrance requirements:* For master's, GRE General Test, minimum GPA of 3.0 in last 60 hours; for doctorate, GRE General Test.

Indiana State University, School of Graduate Studies, College of Arts and Sciences, Department of English, Terre Haute, IN 47809-1401. Offers English teaching (MA); history (MA); literature (MA). Part-time and evening/weekend programs available. *Degree requirements:* For master's, one foreign language, thesis optional. *Entrance requirements:* For master's, minimum GPA of 2.75 in all English courses above freshman level. Additional exam requirements/recommendations for international students: Required—TOEFL (minimum score 550 paper-based). Electronic applications accepted.

Indiana University Bloomington, University Graduate School, College of Arts and Sciences, Department of English, Bloomington, IN 47405-7000. Offers composition, literacy, and culture (PhD); creative writing (MA, MFA), including fiction, poetry; language (MA); literature (MA, PhD); writing (MA). Part-time programs available. *Faculty:* 51 full-time (23 women). *Students:* 180 full-time (115 women), 22 part-time (12 women); includes 25 minority (6 African Americans, 10 Asian Americans or Pacific Islanders, 9 Hispanic Americans), 10 international. Average age 30. 627 applicants, 11% accepted, 32 enrolled. In 2008, 27 master's, 11 doctorates awarded. Terminal master's awarded for partial completion of doctoral program. *Degree requirements:* For master's, one foreign language, thesis (for some programs); for doctorate, 2 foreign languages, thesis/dissertation, qualifying exam. *Entrance requirements:* For master's, GRE General Test, GRE Subject Test (for all but MFA and MA in creative writing), minimum GPA of 3.5; for doctorate, GRE General Test, GRE Subject Test, minimum GPA of 3.7. Additional exam requirements/recommendations for international students: Required—TOEFL. *Application deadline:* For fall admission, 1/15 priority date for domestic students, 12/15 for international students. Application fee: $50 ($60 for international students). Electronic applications accepted. *Expenses:* Tuition, area resident: Part-time $291.97 per credit hour. Tuition, state resident: part-time $291.97 per credit hour. Tuition, nonresident: part-time $850.33 per credit hour. Required fees: $110 per semester. Tuition and fees vary according to course load and program. *Financial support:* In 2008–09, 22 fellowships (averaging $14,337 per year), 1 research assistantship (averaging $7,500 per year), 136 teaching assistantships (averaging $13,000 per year) were awarded; career-related internships or fieldwork and health care benefits also available. Financial award application deadline: 2/1. *Unit head:* George Hutchinson, Chair, 812-855-8225, E-mail: gbhutchi@indiana.edu. *Application contact:* Patricia Ingham, Director of Admissions, 812-855-0521, Fax: 812-855-9535, E-mail: pingham@indiana.edu.

Indiana University of Pennsylvania, School of Graduate Studies and Research, College of Humanities and Social Sciences, Department of English, Program in Composition and Teaching English to Speakers of Other Languages, Indiana, PA 15705-1087. Offers composition and teaching English to speakers of other languages (PhD); teaching English (MAT); teaching English to speakers of other languages (MA). *Faculty:* 31 full-time (17 women). *Students:* 57 full-time (29 women), 145 part-time (98 women); includes 10 minority (4 African Americans, 1 American Indian/Alaska Native, 3 Asian Americans or Pacific Islanders, 2 Hispanic Americans), 72 international. Average age 37. 187 applicants, 34% accepted, 29 enrolled. In 2008, 20 master's, 12 doctorates awarded. *Degree requirements:* For master's, thesis optional; for doctorate, one foreign language, comprehensive exam, thesis/dissertation. *Entrance requirements:* For master's and doctorate, 2 letters of recommendation. Additional exam requirements/recommendations for international students: Required—TOEFL. *Application deadline:* For fall admission, 7/1 priority date for domestic students; for spring admission, 11/1 for domestic students. Applications are processed on a rolling basis. Application fee: $30. *Expenses:* Tuition, area resident: Full-time $6430; part-time $357 per credit. Tuition, nonresident: full-time $10,288; part-time $572 per credit. Required fees: $1547.50; $107 per credit. $283 per year. *Financial support:* In 2008–09, 2 fellowships (averaging $2,666 per year), 19 research assistantships with full and partial tuition reimbursements (averaging $5,841 per year), 11 teaching assistantships with partial tuition reimbursements (averaging $12,355 per year) were awarded. Financial award application deadline: 3/15; financial award applicants required to submit FAFSA. *Unit head:* Dr. Ben Rafoth, Graduate Coordinator, 724-357-2272. *Application contact:* Dr. Ben Rafoth, Graduate Coordinator, 724-357-2272.

Indiana University of Pennsylvania, School of Graduate Studies and Research, College of Humanities and Social Sciences, Department of English, Program in Literature and Criticism, Indiana, PA 15705-1087. Offers generalist (MA); literature (MA); literature and criticism (PhD). *Faculty:* 31 full-time (17 women). *Students:* 75 full-time (40 women), 96 part-time (57 women); includes 10 minority (8 African Americans, 1 Asian American or Pacific Islander, 1 Hispanic American), 33 international. Average age 39. 133 applicants, 47% accepted, 44 enrolled. In 2008, 20 master's, 16 doctorates awarded. *Degree requirements:* For master's, thesis optional; for doctorate, one foreign language, comprehensive exam, thesis/dissertation. *Entrance requirements:* For master's and doctorate, 2 letters of recommendation. Additional exam requirements/recommendations for international students: Required—TOEFL. *Application deadline:* For fall admission, 7/1 priority date for domestic students; for spring admission, 11/1 for domestic students. Applications are processed on a rolling basis. Application fee: $30. *Expenses:* Tuition, area resident: Full-time $6430; part-time $357 per credit. Tuition, nonresident: full-time $10,288; part-time $572 per credit. Required fees: $1547.50; $107 per credit. $283 per year. *Financial support:* In 2008–09, 5 fellowships (averaging $1,600 per year), 22 research assistantships with full and partial tuition reimbursements (averaging $5,753 per year), 11 teaching assistantships with partial tuition reimbursements (averaging $12,355 per year) were awarded. Financial award application deadline: 3/15; financial award applicants required to submit FAFSA. *Unit head:* Dr. David Downing, Graduate Coordinator, 724-357-3963, E-mail: David.Downing@iup.edu. *Application contact:* Dr. David Downing, Graduate Coordinator, 724-357-3963, E-mail: David.Downing@iup.edu.

Indiana University–Purdue University Fort Wayne, College of Arts and Sciences, Department of English and Linguistics, Fort Wayne, IN 46805-1499. Offers English (MA, MAT); TENL (teaching English as a new language) (Certificate). Part-time programs available. *Faculty:* 28 full-time (14 women). *Students:* 8 full-time (5 women), 30 part-time (21 women); includes 2 minority (1 African American, 1 Hispanic American). Average age 36. 13 applicants, 100% accepted, 10 enrolled. In 2008, 11 master's, 1 other advanced degree awarded. *Degree requirements:* For master's, one foreign language, thesis (for some programs), teaching certificate (MAT). *Entrance requirements:* For master's, GRE General Test, minimum GPA of 3.0, major or minor in English, 3 letters of recommendation; for Certificate, bachelor's degree with minimum GPA of 2.5. Additional exam requirements/recommendations for international students: Required—TOEFL (minimum score 600 paper-based; 260 computer-based). *Application deadline:* For fall admission, 8/1 for domestic students; for spring admission, 10/15 for domestic students. Applications are processed on a rolling basis. Application fee: $30. *Expenses:* Tuition, area resident: Full-time $4376; part-time $243 per credit. Tuition, state resident: full-time $4376; part-time $243 per credit. Tuition, nonresident: full-time $10,337; part-time $574 per credit. Required fees: $503; $27.95 per credit. Tuition and fees vary according to course load. *Financial support:* In 2008–09, 10 teaching assistantships with partial tuition reimbursements (averaging $12,740 per year) were awarded; career-related internships or fieldwork, scholarships/grants, and unspecified assistantships also available. Support available to part-time students. Financial award application deadline: 3/1; financial award applicants required to submit FAFSA. *Faculty research:* Romanticism, Appalachian students' lives, studying Spenser's erotic poetry. Total annual research expenditures: $55,201. *Unit head:* Dr. Hardin Aasand, Chairperson, 260-481-6750, Fax: 260-481-6985, E-mail: aasandh@ipfw.edu. *Application contact:* Dr. Michael Stapleton, Graduate Program Director, 260-481-6772, Fax: 260-481-6985.

Indiana University–Purdue University Indianapolis, Department of English, Indianapolis, IN 46202-2896. Offers English (MA); teaching English (MA). *Entrance requirements:* For master's, GRE.

Indiana University South Bend, College of Liberal Arts and Sciences, South Bend, IN 46634-7111. Offers applied mathematics and computer science (MS); applied psychology (MA); English (MA); liberal studies (MLS). Part-time and evening/weekend programs available. *Degree requirements:* For master's, thesis (for some programs). *Entrance requirements:* For master's, minimum GPA of 3.0. Additional exam requirements/recommendations for international students: Required—TOEFL. *Faculty research:* Artificial intelligence, bioinformatics, English language and literature, creative writing, computer networks.

Inter American University of Puerto Rico, Metropolitan Campus, Graduate Programs, Program in English, San Juan, PR 00919-1293. Offers MA.

Iona College, School of Arts and Science, Department of English, New Rochelle, NY 10801-1890. Offers MA. Part-time and evening/weekend programs available. *Faculty:* 13 full-time (6 women). *Students:* 3 full-time (2 women), 18 part-time (12 women); includes 1 minority (African American). Average age 33. 10 applicants, 80% accepted, 8 enrolled. In 2008, 5 master's awarded. *Degree requirements:* For master's, one foreign language, thesis or alternative. *Entrance requirements:* For master's, minimum GPA of 3.0. Additional exam requirements/recommendations for international students: Required—TOEFL (minimum score 550 paper-based; 213 computer-based). *Application deadline:* Applications are processed on a rolling basis. Application fee: $50. Electronic applications accepted. *Expenses:* Tuition: Part-time $755 per credit. Required fees: $175 per term. *Financial support:* Tuition waivers (partial) and unspecified assistantships available. Support available to part-time students. Financial award application deadline: 4/15; financial award applicants required to submit FAFSA. *Faculty research:* Victorian fiction, women's studies, nineteenth century American literature, Irish literature, Shakespeare. *Unit head:* Dr. Hugh Short, Chair, 914-637-7725, E-mail: hshort@iona.edu. *Application contact:* Veronica Jarek-Prinz, Director of Graduate Admissions, 914-633-2420, Fax: 914-633-2277, E-mail: vjarekprinz@iona.edu.

Iowa State University of Science and Technology, Graduate College, College of Liberal Arts and Sciences, Department of English, Ames, IA 50011. Offers English (MA); rhetoric and professional communication (PhD). *Faculty:* 51 full-time (25 women), 10 part-time/adjunct (7 women). *Students:* 89 full-time (57 women), 34 part-time (22 women); includes 4 minority (1 African American, 3 Hispanic Americans), 28 international. 106 applicants, 58% accepted, 37 enrolled. In 2008, 31 master's awarded. *Degree requirements:* For master's, thesis or alternative; for doctorate, thesis/dissertation. *Entrance requirements:* For master's, GRE General Test, sample of written work, resumé, portfolio in creative writing; for doctorate, GRE General Test, sample of written work, resumé. Additional exam requirements/recommendations for international students: Required—TOEFL (minimum score 600 paper-based; 100 iBT), IELTS (7.0) or TOEFL. *Application deadline:* For fall admission, 1/5 priority date for domestic and international students. Application fee: $30 ($70 for international students). Electronic applications accepted. *Expenses:* Tuition, area resident: Full-time $6446; part-time $359 per credit. Tuition, state resident: full-time $6446; part-time $359 per credit. Tuition, nonresident: full-time $17,330; part-time $963 per credit. Required fees: $790; $249.25 per semester. Tuition and fees vary according to course load and program. *Financial support:* In 2008–09, 14 research assistantships with full and partial tuition reimbursements (averaging $16,308 per year), 79 teaching assistantships with full and partial tuition reimbursements (averaging $16,308 per year) were awarded; fellowships, scholarships/grants, health care benefits, and unspecified assistantships also available. *Faculty research:* Creative writing, literature, rhetoric, composition and professional communication, teaching English as a second language, applied linguistics. *Unit head:* Dr. Charles Kostelnick, Chair, 515-294-2477, Fax: 515-294-2125, E-mail: englgrad@iastate.edu. *Application contact:* Dr. Constance Post, Director of Graduate Education, 515-294-3175, E-mail: englgrad@iastate.edu.

Jackson State University, Graduate School, School of Liberal Arts, Department of English and Modern Foreign Languages, Jackson, MS 39217. Offers English (MA); teaching English (MAT). Part-time and evening/weekend programs available. *Degree requirements:* For master's, comprehensive exam, thesis or alternative. *Entrance requirements:* For master's, GRE General Test. Additional exam requirements/recommendations for international students: Required—TOEFL.

Jacksonville State University, College of Graduate Studies and Continuing Education, College of Arts and Sciences, Department of English, Jacksonville, AL 36265-1602. Offers MA. Part-time and evening/weekend programs available. *Faculty:* 5 full-time (2 women). *Students:* 4 full-time (3 women), 18 part-time (12 women); includes 2 minority (1 African American, 1 Hispanic American), 1 international. Average age 27. 10 applicants, 50% accepted, 3 enrolled. In 2008, 7 master's awarded. *Degree requirements:* For master's, comprehensive exam, thesis (for some programs). *Entrance requirements:* For master's, GRE General Test or MAT. *Application deadline:* Applications are processed on a rolling basis. Application fee: $30. Electronic applications accepted. *Expenses:* Tuition, area resident: Full-time $4560; part-time $225 per credit hour. Tuition, state resident: full-time $4560; part-time $450 per credit hour. Tuition, nonresident: full-time $9120; part-time $450 per credit hour. *Financial support:* In 2008–09, 18 students received support. Available to part-time students. Application deadline: 4/1; *Unit head:* Dr. Robert Felgar, Head, 256-782-5413. *Application contact:* Dr. Jean Pugliese, Associate Dean, 256-782-8278, Fax: 256-782-5321, E-mail: pugliese@jsu.edu.

James Madison University, The Graduate School, College of Arts and Letters, Department of English, Harrisonburg, VA 22807. Offers MA. Part-time programs available. *Faculty:* 10 full-time (7 women). *Students:* 10 full-time (7 women), 7 part-time (5 women); includes 1 minority (African American). Average age 27. In 2008, 15 master's awarded. *Degree requirements:* For master's, one foreign language, thesis, reading exam in languages, formal exam based on required reading list. *Entrance requirements:* For master's, GRE General Test, GRE Subject Test, 2 letters of recommendation, writing sample. Additional exam requirements/recommendations for international students: Required—TOEFL. *Application deadline:* For fall admission, 2/10 priority date for domestic students. Applications are processed on a rolling basis. Application fee: $55. Electronic applications accepted. *Expenses:* Tuition, area resident: Full-time $7008; part-time $292 per credit hour. Tuition, state resident: full-time $7008; part-time $292 per credit hour. Tuition, nonresident: full-time $20,352; part-time $848 per credit hour. *Financial support:* In 2008–09, 8 students received support, including 6 teaching assistantships with full tuition reimbursements available (averaging $8,664 per year); Federal Work-Study and 2 graduate assistantships ($7,382) also available. Financial award application deadline: 3/1; financial award applicants required to submit FAFSA. *Unit head:* Dr. Mark L. Parker, Academic Unit Head, 540-568-6797. *Application contact:* Lynette M. Bible, Director of Graduate Admissions, 540-568-6395, Fax: 540-568-7860, E-mail: biblelm@jmu.edu.

John Carroll University, Graduate School, Department of English, University Heights, OH 44118-4581. Offers MA. Part-time and evening/weekend programs available. *Degree requirements:* For master's, comprehensive exam, thesis (for some programs), research essay or thesis. *Entrance requirements:* For master's, GRE General Test, GRE Subject Test, minimum 3.0 GPA, writing sample. Additional exam requirements/recommendations for international students: Required—TOEFL. Electronic applications accepted. *Faculty research:* Postcolonial literature, African-American literature, Renaissance poetry, Anglo-Saxon literature, American literature.

The Johns Hopkins University, Zanvyl Krieger School of Arts and Sciences, Department of English, Baltimore, MD 21218-2699. Offers English and American literature (PhD). *Degree requirements:* For doctorate, 2 foreign languages, comprehensive exam, thesis/dissertation, 10 seminars, 2 oral exams. Electronic applications accepted. *Faculty research:* 19th century British, 18th century, Renaissance, American, cultural studies.

Kansas State University, Graduate School, College of Arts and Sciences, Department of English, Manhattan, KS 66506. Offers MA. Part-time programs available. *Faculty:* 26 full-time (15 women), 2 part-time/adjunct (0 women). *Students:* 62 full-time (40 women), 9 part-time (6 women); includes 3 minority (all Hispanic Americans), 5 international. Average age 27. 63 applicants, 75% accepted, 30 enrolled. In 2008, 27 master's awarded. *Degree requirements:* For master's, one foreign language, thesis optional. *Entrance requirements:* For master's, GRE, minimum B average in English. Additional exam requirements/recommendations for international students: Required—TOEFL. *Application deadline:* For fall admission, 2/1 priority date for domestic and international students; for spring admission, 9/1 priority date for domestic students, 8/1 priority date for international students. Applications are processed on a rolling basis. Application fee: $30 ($55 for international students). Electronic applications accepted. *Expenses:* Tuition, area resident: Full-time $6466; part-time $269.40 per credit hour. Tuition, state resident: full-time $6466; part-time $269.40 per credit hour. Tuition, nonresident: full-time $14,874; part-time $619.75 per credit hour. Required fees: $673; $23.40 per credit hour. Tuition and fees vary according to campus/location. *Financial support:* In 2008–09, 43 teaching assistantships with full tuition reimbursements (averaging $10,063 per year) were awarded; career-related internships or fieldwork, Federal Work-Study, institutionally sponsored loans, scholarships/grants, and tuition waivers (full) also available. Support available to part-time students. Financial award application deadline: 3/1; financial award applicants required to submit FAFSA. *Faculty research:* Cultural studies, children's literature, American literature, rhetorical and composition theory, British literature. Total annual research expenditures: $2,650. *Unit head:* Karin Westman, Head, 785-532-2190, Fax: 785-532-2192, E-mail: westmank@ksu.edu. *Application contact:* Greg Eiselein, Director, 785-532-0386, Fax: 785-532-2192, E-mail: eiselei@ksu.edu.

Kent State University, College of Arts and Sciences, Department of English, Kent, OH 44242-0001. Offers comparative literature (MA); creative writing (MFA); English (PhD); English for teachers (MA); literature and writing (MA); rhetoric and composition (PhD); teaching English as a second language (MA). Part-time programs available. Terminal master's awarded for partial completion of doctoral program. *Degree requirements:* For master's, one foreign language, thesis optional; for doctorate, one foreign language, thesis/dissertation, qualifying exams. *Entrance requirements:* For master's and doctorate, GRE General Test, writing sample, letters of recommendation. Additional exam requirements/recommendations for international students: Required—TOEFL (minimum score 600 paper-based). Electronic applications accepted. *Faculty research:* British and American literature, textual editing, rhetoric and composition, cultural studies, linguistic and critical theories.

Kutztown University of Pennsylvania, College of Graduate Studies and Extended Learning, College of Liberal Arts and Sciences, Program in English, Kutztown, PA 19530-0730. Offers MA. Part-time and evening/weekend programs available. *Faculty:* 7 full-time (3 women). *Students:* 5 full-time (3 women), 16 part-time (12 women); includes 1 minority (Hispanic American). Average age 30. 20 applicants, 65% accepted, 4 enrolled. In 2008, 9 master's awarded. *Degree requirements:* For master's, one foreign language, comprehensive exam, thesis optional. *Entrance requirements:* For master's, GRE General Test. Additional exam requirements/recommendations for international students: Required—TOEFL. *Application deadline:* For fall admission, 8/15 priority date for domestic and international students; for spring admission, 12/15 priority date for domestic and international students. Applications are processed on a rolling basis. Application fee: $35. Electronic applications accepted. *Expenses:* Tuition, area resident: Full-time $6430; part-time $357 per credit. Tuition, state resident: full-time $6430; part-time $357 per credit. Tuition, nonresident: full-time $10,288; part-time $572 per credit. Required fees: $1360; $72 per credit. $67 per semester. *Financial support:* Career-related internships or fieldwork, Federal Work-Study, scholarships/grants, and unspecified assistantships available. Financial award application deadline: 3/1; financial award applicants required to submit FAFSA. *Faculty research:* Women science fiction writers, Joyce Cary, myth and symbol, folklore, Victorian revision modes. *Unit head:* Dr. Janice Chernekoff, Chairperson, 610-683-4353, Fax: 610-683-4355, E-mail: cherneko@kutztown.edu. *Application contact:* Dr. Linda Matthews, Interim Dean of Graduate Studies, 610-683-4201, Fax: 610-683-1393, E-mail: graduate@kutztown.edu.

Lakehead University, Graduate Studies, Faculty of Social Sciences and Humanities, Department of English, Thunder Bay, ON P7B 5E1, Canada. Offers English (MA); women's studies (MA). Part-time and evening/weekend programs available. *Degree requirements:* For master's, one foreign language, thesis optional. *Entrance requirements:* For master's, minimum B average. Additional exam requirements/recommendations for international students: Required—TOEFL. Tuition charges are reported in Canadian dollars. *Expenses:* Tuition, area resident: Full-time $6500 Canadian dollars. International tuition: $13,700 Canadian dollars full-time. *Faculty research:* Rhetoric and literary studies, children's literature, nineteenth- and twentieth-century American literature, modern literature, women's studies.

Lamar University, College of Graduate Studies, College of Arts and Sciences, Department of English and Foreign Languages, Beaumont, TX 77710. Offers English (MA). Part-time and evening/weekend programs available. *Faculty:* 10 full-time (2 women). *Students:* 2 full-time (1 woman), 18 part-time (15 women); includes 2 minority (1 African American, 1 Hispanic American). Average age 35. 9 applicants, 56% accepted, 4 enrolled. In 2008, 1 master's awarded. *Degree requirements:* For master's, one foreign language, thesis optional, practicum. *Entrance requirements:* For master's, GRE General Test, minimum GPA of 2.5 in last 60 hours of undergraduate course work. Additional exam requirements/recommendations for international students: Required—TOEFL. *Application deadline:* For fall admission, 8/1 for domestic students; for spring admission, 12/1 for domestic students. Applications are processed on a rolling basis. Application fee: $25 ($50 for international students). *Expenses:* Tuition, state resident: full-time $5000; part-time $195 per credit. Tuition, nonresident: full-time $12,376; part-time $476 per credit. Required fees: $1570. *Financial support:* In 2008–09, 6 students received support, including 4 teaching assistantships (averaging $8,000 per year); career-related internships or fieldwork, Federal Work-Study, and institutionally sponsored loans also available. Support available to part-time students. Financial award application deadline: 4/1. *Faculty research:* British, Renaissance, nineteenth century, and American literature; creative writing; modern literature; African-American literature. *Unit head:* Dr. Joe E. Nordgren, Chair, 409-880-8558, Fax: 409-880-8591, E-mail: nordgrenje@hal.lamar.edu. *Application contact:* Dr. James W. Westgate, Assistant Dean, 409-880-7978, E-mail: westgate@hal.lamar.edu.

La Sierra University, College of Arts and Sciences, Department of English and Communication, Riverside, CA 92515. Offers communication (MA), including public relations/advertising, theory emphasis; English (MA), including literary emphasis, writing emphasis. Part-time programs available. *Degree requirements:* For master's, one foreign language. *Entrance requirements:* For master's, GRE General Test.

Lehigh University, College of Arts and Sciences, Department of English, Bethlehem, PA 18015. Offers MA, PhD. *Faculty:* 18 full-time (9 women). *Students:* 39 full-time (22 women), 11 part-time (8 women); includes 1 minority (Asian American or Pacific Islander), 1 international. Average age 32. 51 applicants, 12% accepted, 3 enrolled. In 2008, 5 master's, 4 doctorates awarded. Terminal master's awarded for partial completion of doctoral program. *Degree requirements:* For master's, thesis; for doctorate, one foreign language, comprehensive exam, thesis/dissertation. *Entrance requirements:* For master's, GRE Subject Test (literature), GRE General Test, minimum GPA of 3.0 in undergraduate English courses; for doctorate, GRE Subject Test (literature), GRE General Test, minimum GPA of 3.5 in MA coursework. Additional exam requirements/recommendations for international students: Required—TOEFL (minimum score 620 paper-based; 260 computer-based; 96 iBT). *Application deadline:* For fall admission, 1/2 priority date for domestic and international students. Application fee: $65. Electronic applications accepted. *Financial support:* In 2008–09, 3 fellowships with full tuition reimbursements (averaging $22,000 per year), 31 teaching assistantships with full tuition reimbursements (averaging $16,400 per year) were awarded; career-related internships or fieldwork, Federal Work-Study, institutionally sponsored loans, scholarships/grants, tuition waivers (full and partial), and unspecified assistantships also available. Support available to part-time students. Financial award application deadline: 1/2. *Faculty research:* Literature and social justice, narrative theory, modernism, transatlantic study, literature and medicine. *Unit head:* Dr. Barry M. Kroll, Chairperson, 610-758-3311, Fax: 610-758-6616, E-mail: bmk3@lehigh.edu. *Application contact:* Dr. Dawn Keetley, Director of Graduate Studies, 610-758-5926, Fax: 610-758-6616, E-mail: dek7@lehigh.edu.

Lehman College of the City University of New York, Division of Arts and Humanities, Department of English, Bronx, NY 10468-1589. Offers MA. *Degree requirements:* For master's, thesis. *Entrance requirements:* For master's, GRE, 18 upper-level credits in U.S. or English literature.

Long Island University, Brooklyn Campus, Richard L. Conolly College of Liberal Arts and Sciences, Department of English, Brooklyn, NY 11201-8423. Offers English literature (MA); professional and creative writing (MA); teaching of writing (MA). Part-time and evening/weekend programs available. *Degree requirements:* For master's, thesis or alternative. *Entrance requirements:* For master's, 2 letters of recommendation. Additional exam requirements/recommendations for international students: Required—TOEFL (minimum score 550 paper-based; 173 computer-based). Electronic applications accepted.

Long Island University, C.W. Post Campus, College of Liberal Arts and Sciences, Department of English, Brookville, NY 11548-1300. Offers English (MA); English for adolescence education (MS). Part-time and evening/weekend programs available. *Degree requirements:* For master's, comprehensive exam (for some programs), thesis (for some programs). *Entrance requirements:* For master's, minimum GPA of 3.5 in major, 3.0 overall; 21 credits of English. Electronic applications accepted. *Faculty research:* English Renaissance, Sinclair Lewis: The Early Years, puppetry archives, Irish-American Experiences: literature of memory, Henry James's anxiety of Poe's influence.

Longwood University, Office of Graduate Studies, Department of English and Modern Languages, Farmville, VA 23909. Offers 6-12 initial teaching/licensure (MA); creative writing (MA); English education and writing (MA); literature (MA). Part-time programs available. *Degree requirements:* For master's, comprehensive exam (for some programs), thesis (for some programs). *Entrance requirements:* For master's, minimum GPA of 2.75. Additional exam requirements/recommendations for international students: Required—TOEFL (minimum score 550 paper-based; 213 computer-based).

Louisiana State University and Agricultural and Mechanical College, Graduate School, College of Arts and Sciences, Department of English, Baton Rouge, LA 70803. Offers creative writing (MFA); English (MA, PhD). Part-time programs available. Terminal master's awarded for partial completion of doctoral program. *Degree requirements:* For master's, comprehensive exam; for doctorate, one foreign language, comprehensive exam, thesis/dissertation. *Entrance requirements:* For master's, GRE General Test, minimum GPA of 3.0; for doctorate, GRE General Test, GRE Subject Test, minimum GPA of 3.0. Additional exam requirements/recommendations for international students: Required—TOEFL (minimum score 550 paper-based; 213 computer-based; 79 iBT). Electronic applications accepted. *Faculty research:* American literature, British literature, cultural studies, rhetoric and composition, folklore.

Louisiana Tech University, Graduate School, College of Liberal Arts, Department of English, Ruston, LA 71272. Offers MA. Part-time programs available. *Degree requirements:* For master's, thesis or alternative. *Entrance requirements:* For master's, GRE General Test.

Loyola Marymount University, College of Liberal Arts, Department of English, Los Angeles, CA 90045-2659. Offers creative writing (MA); literature (MA), including). Part-time and evening/weekend programs available. *Degree requirements:* For master's, comprehensive exam. *Entrance requirements:* For master's, GRE General Test, minimum GPA of 3.0. Additional exam requirements/recommendations for international students: Required—TOEFL (minimum score 600 paper-based; 250 computer-based). Electronic applications accepted.

Loyola University Chicago, Graduate School, Department of English, Chicago, IL 60611-2196. Offers MA, PhD. Part-time and evening/weekend programs available. *Faculty:* 21 full-time (8 women). *Students:* 55 full-time (32 women), 4 part-time (2 women); includes 6 minority (2 African Americans, 2 Asian Americans or Pacific Islanders, 2 Hispanic Americans), 2 international. Average age 29. 152 applicants, 26% accepted, 17 enrolled. In 2008, 12 master's, 6 doctorates awarded. Terminal master's awarded for partial completion of doctoral program. *Degree requirements:* For master's, comprehensive exam, thesis or alternative; for doctorate, one foreign language, comprehensive exam, thesis/dissertation. *Entrance requirements:* For master's and doctorate, GRE General Test, GRE Subject Test. Additional exam requirements/recommendations for international students: Required—TOEFL, IELTS. *Application deadline:* For fall admission, 6/1 for domestic students. Applications are processed on a rolling basis. Application fee: $50. Electronic applications accepted. *Expenses:* Tuition: Full-time $13,500; part-time $750 per credit hour. Required fees: $60 per semester. Full-time tuition and fees vary according to program. *Financial support:* In 2008–09, 26 students received support, including 5 fellowships with full tuition reimbursements available (averaging $13,500 per year), research assistantships with full tuition reimbursements available (averaging $10,000 per year), 21 teaching assistantships with full tuition reimbursements available (averaging $10,000 per year); Federal Work-Study, institutionally sponsored loans, tuition waivers (partial), and unspecified assistantships also available. Support available to part-time students. Financial award application deadline: 1/15; financial award applicants required to submit FAFSA. *Faculty research:* Medieval and Renaissance studies, Romantic period, literary history and theory, American studies, modernism and postmodernism. *Unit head:* Dr. Pamela Caughie, Chair, 773-508-2240, Fax: 773-508-8696, E-mail: pcaughi@luc.edu. *Application contact:* Maureen Taylor, Graduate Program Secretary, 773-508-2255, Fax: 773-508-8696, E-mail: mtaylo3@luc.edu.

Lynchburg College, Graduate Studies, School of Humanities and Social Sciences, Lynchburg, VA 24501-3199. Offers English (MA); history (MA). Part-time programs available. *Faculty:* 7 full-time (4 women), 1 part-time/adjunct (0 women). *Students:* 19 full-time (11 women), 18 part-time (11 women), 1 international. Average age 33. 30 applicants, 73% accepted, 13 enrolled. In 2008, 1 master's awarded. *Degree requirements:* For master's, comprehensive exam, thesis (for some programs). *Entrance requirements:* For master's, GRE, minimum undergraduate GPA of 3.0. Additional exam requirements/recommendations for international students: Required—TOEFL. *Application deadline:* For fall admission, 7/31 for domestic students, 6/1 for international students; for spring admission, 11/30 for domestic students, 10/1 for international students. Application fee: $30. *Expenses:* Tuition: Full-time $6750; part-time $375 per credit. *Financial support:* Career-related internships or fieldwork, Federal Work-Study, scholarships/grants, and unspecified assistantships available. *Unit head:* Dr. Edward Polloway, Vice President for Graduate and Community Advancement, 434-544-8655, E-mail: polloway@lynchburg.edu. *Application contact:* Dr. Kim McCabe, Dean, School of Humanities and Social Sciences, 434-544-8129, E-mail: McCabe@lynchburg.edu.

Marquette University, Graduate School, College of Arts and Sciences, Department of English, Milwaukee, WI 53201-1881. Offers American literature (PhD); British and American literature (MA); British literature (PhD). Part-time programs available. Terminal master's awarded for partial completion of doctoral program. *Degree requirements:* For master's, comprehensive

English

Marquette University (continued)
exam, thesis or alternative; for doctorate, one foreign language, thesis/dissertation, qualifying exam. *Entrance requirements:* For master's and doctorate, GRE General Test, GRE Subject Test. Additional exam requirements/recommendations for international students: Required—TOEFL. *Faculty research:* Discourse analysis, cultural studies, textual criticism, literary history, literary theory.

Marshall University, Academic Affairs Division, College of Liberal Arts, Department of English, Huntington, WV 25755. Offers MA. *Degree requirements:* For master's, one foreign language, thesis optional. *Entrance requirements:* For master's, GRE General Test.

Mary Baldwin College, Graduate Studies, Program in Shakespeare and Renaissance Literature in Performance, Staunton, VA 24401-3610. Offers acting (M Litt); directing (M Litt); Shakespeare and Renaissance literature in performance (MFA); teaching (M Litt). *Entrance requirements:* For master's, GRE (M Litt).

Marygrove College, Graduate Division, Program in English, Detroit, MI 48221-2599. Offers MA.

Marymount University, School of Arts and Sciences, Program in Literature and Languages, Arlington, VA 22207-4299. Offers MA. Part-time and evening/weekend programs available. *Faculty:* 4 full-time (all women), 1 (woman) part-time/adjunct. *Students:* 2 full-time (both women), 12 part-time (9 women); includes 2 minority (both African Americans), 1 international. Average age 37. 8 applicants, 100% accepted, 3 enrolled. In 2008, 5 master's awarded. *Degree requirements:* For master's, thesis or alternative. *Entrance requirements:* For master's, 2 letters of recommendation, interview, minimum undergraduate GPA of 3.0 with major in English or other humanities discipline, writing sample, essay. Additional exam requirements/recommendations for international students: Required—TOEFL (minimum score 600 paper-based; 250 computer-based; 100 iBT). *Application deadline:* For fall admission, 7/1 for international students; for spring admission, 10/15 for international students. Applications are processed on a rolling basis. Application fee: $40. Electronic applications accepted. *Expenses:* Tuition: Full-time $12,420; part-time $690 per credit hour. Required fees: $126; $7 per credit hour. Tuition and fees vary according to degree level. *Financial support:* In 2008–09, 9 students received support; research assistantships with full tuition reimbursements available, career-related internships or fieldwork, Federal Work-Study, scholarships/grants, and unspecified assistantships available. Support available to part-time students. Financial award applicants required to submit FAFSA. *Unit head:* Dr. Susan Fay, Chair, Literature and Languages, 703-284-3858, Fax: 703-284-3859, E-mail: susan.fay@marymount.edu. *Application contact:* Francesca Reed, Director, Graduate Admissions, 703-284-5901, Fax: 703-527-3815, E-mail: grad.admissions@marymount:edu.

McGill University, Faculty of Graduate and Postdoctoral Studies, Faculty of Arts, Department of English, Montréal, QC H3A 2T5, Canada. Offers MA, PhD. Electronic applications accepted.

McMaster University, School of Graduate Studies, Faculty of Humanities, Department of English and Cultural Studies, Hamilton, ON L8S 4M2, Canada. Offers cultural studies and critical theory (MA); English (MA, PhD). Part-time programs available. *Degree requirements:* For master's, one foreign language, thesis; for doctorate, one foreign language, comprehensive exam, thesis/dissertation. *Entrance requirements:* For master's, honors degree, minimum B+ average in at least 6 full courses of English beyond year 1; for doctorate, MA; minimum A-average in two of three courses. Additional exam requirements/recommendations for international students: Required—TOEFL (minimum score 580 paper-based; 237 computer-based). *Faculty research:* Literary theory, feminist theory, literature of migration, Bakhting globalization.

McNeese State University, Doré School of Graduate Studies, College of Liberal Arts, Department of English and Foreign Languages, Program in English, Lake Charles, LA 70609. Offers MA. Evening/weekend programs available. *Faculty:* 15 full-time (9 women). *Students:* 6 full-time (3 women), 6 part-time (all women); includes 3 minority (1 African American, 1 Asian American or Pacific Islander, 1 Hispanic American). In 2008, 8 master's awarded. *Degree requirements:* For master's, one foreign language, thesis or alternative. *Entrance requirements:* For master's, GRE. *Application deadline:* For fall admission, 5/15 priority date for domestic and international students; for spring admission, 10/15 priority date for domestic and international students. Applications are processed on a rolling basis. Application fee: $20 ($30 for international students). *Expenses:* Tuition, area resident: Full-time $2386. Tuition, state resident: full-time $2386. Required fees: $885. Tuition and fees vary according to course load. *Financial support:* Teaching assistantships available. Financial award application deadline: 5/1. *Faculty research:* Textual criticism, seventeenth century literature, American women writers, Romanticism and the origins of diplomacy. *Unit head:* Dr. Joe L. Cash, Head, 337-475-5326, Fax: 337-475-5327, E-mail: jcash@mcneese.edu. *Application contact:* Dr. George F. Mead, Interim Dean of Dore' School of Graduate Studies, 337-475-5396, Fax: 337-475-5397, E-mail: admissions@mcneese.edu.

Memorial University of Newfoundland, School of Graduate Studies, Department of English Language and Literature, St. John's, NL A1C 5S7, Canada. Offers MA, PhD. *Degree requirements:* For master's, thesis optional; for doctorate, one foreign language, comprehensive exam, thesis/dissertation, oral thesis defense, minimum 3 semesters of full-time study. *Entrance requirements:* For master's, honors degree. Electronic applications accepted. *Faculty research:* American, British, Canadian, and Anglo-Irish literature; Newfoundland literature.

Mercy College, School of Liberal Arts, Program in English Literature, Dobbs Ferry, NY 10522-1189. Offers MA. Part-time and evening/weekend programs available. Postbaccalaureate distance learning degree programs offered (no on-campus study). *Students:* 4 full-time (3 women), 46 part-time (36 women); includes 3 African Americans, 1 Asian American or Pacific Islander, 3 Hispanic Americans, 1 international. Average age 36. 34 applicants, 68% accepted, 18 enrolled. In 2008, 7 master's awarded. *Degree requirements:* For master's, comprehensive exam, thesis. *Entrance requirements:* For master's, two letters of reference; BA/BS in English with minimum GPA of 3.0 or BA/BS in related subject area with a minor in English literature or BA/BS in another discipline demonstrating the potential to succeed in a graduate program; statement of purpose; essay. Additional exam requirements/recommendations for international students: Required—TOEFL (minimum score 600 paper-based; 250 computer-based; 100 iBT). *Application deadline:* For fall admission, 8/1 for international students. Applications are processed on a rolling basis. Application fee: $40. Electronic applications accepted. *Expenses:* Tuition: Full-time $12,330; part-time $685 per credit. Required fees: $240; $120 per semester. Tuition and fees vary according to program. *Financial support:* In 2008–09, 19 students received support. Career-related internships or fieldwork, Federal Work-Study, scholarships/grants, and unspecified assistantships available. Support available to part-time students. Financial award applicants required to submit FAFSA. *Unit head:* Dr. Joel N. Feimer, Program Director, 914-245-6100 Ext. 2235, E-mail: jfeimer@mercy.edu. *Application contact:* Dr. Joel N. Feimer, Program Director, 914-245-6100 Ext. 2235, E-mail: jfeimer@mercy.edu.

Miami University, Graduate School, College of Arts and Sciences, Department of English, Oxford, OH 45056. Offers composition and rhetoric (MA, PhD); creative writing (MA); criticism (PhD); English and American literature and language (PhD); English education (MAT); library theory (PhD); literature (MA, MAT, PhD); technical and scientific communication (MTSC). Part-time programs available. *Degree requirements:* For master's, final exam; for doctorate, 2 foreign languages, comprehensive exam, thesis/dissertation, final exams. *Entrance requirements:* For master's, minimum undergraduate GPA of 3.0 during previous 2 years or 2.75 overall; for doctorate, GRE General Test, GRE Subject Test, minimum GPA of 2.75 (undergraduate), 3.0 (graduate). Additional exam requirements/recommendations for international students: Required—TOEFL (minimum score 550 paper-based; 213 computer-based), TWE (minimum score 4). Electronic applications accepted.

Michigan State University, The Graduate School, College of Arts and Letters, Department of English, East Lansing, MI 48824. Offers English (PhD); literature in English (MA). *Entrance requirements:* For master's, GRE General Test, minimum GPA of 3.25, 2 years of foreign language or American Sign Language study, 3 letters of recommendation; for doctorate, GRE General Test, master's degree in English, 2 years of foreign language study, 3 letters of recommendation. Additional exam requirements/recommendations for international students: Required—TOEFL. Electronic applications accepted.

Middlebury College, Bread Loaf School of English, Middlebury, VT 05753. Offers M Litt, MA. Offered during summer only. *Faculty:* 54 full-time. *Students:* 496 full-time; includes 19 minority (12 African Americans, 1 American Indian/Alaska Native, 4 Asian Americans or Pacific Islanders, 2 Hispanic Americans). Average age 30. In 2008, 72 master's awarded. *Application deadline:* Applications are processed on a rolling basis. Application fee: $55. Electronic applications accepted. *Financial support:* In 2008–09, 242 students received support, including 36 fellowships; scholarships/grants also available. Support available to part-time students. *Unit head:* Dr. James Maddox, Director, 802-443-5418, Fax: 802-443-2060, E-mail: blse@breadnet.middlebury.edu. *Application contact:* Language Schools Office, 802-443-5510, Fax: 802-443-2075.

Middle Tennessee State University, College of Graduate Studies, College of Liberal Arts, Department of English, Murfreesboro, TN 37132. Offers MA, PhD. Part-time and evening/weekend programs available. Postbaccalaureate distance learning degree programs offered. *Degree requirements:* For master's, one foreign language, comprehensive exam, thesis optional; for doctorate, one foreign language, comprehensive exam, thesis/dissertation. *Entrance requirements:* For master's and doctorate, GRE. Additional exam requirements/recommendations for international students: Required—TOEFL (paper-based 525; computer-based 195; IBT 71) or IELTS (6.0). Electronic applications accepted.

Midwestern State University, Graduate Studies, College of Humanities and Social Sciences, Department of English, Wichita Falls, TX 76308. Offers MA. Part-time and evening/weekend programs available. *Degree requirements:* For master's, one foreign language, thesis optional. *Entrance requirements:* For master's, GRE General Test, MAT or GMAT. Additional exam requirements/recommendations for international students: Required—TOEFL (minimum score 550 paper-based; 213 computer-based). Electronic applications accepted. *Faculty research:* Jung and literature, Shakespeare, Oscar Hahn, origins of language, modern American literature.

Millersville University of Pennsylvania, Graduate School, School of Humanities and Social Sciences, Department of English, Millersville, PA 17551-0302. Offers English (MA); English education (M Ed). Part-time programs available. *Faculty:* 24 full-time (13 women), 12 part-time/adjunct (9 women). *Students:* 10 full-time (5 women), 22 part-time (15 women); includes 4 minority (2 African Americans, 1 Asian American or Pacific Islander, 1 Hispanic American). Average age 30. 7 applicants, 100% accepted, 6 enrolled. In 2008, 12 master's awarded. *Degree requirements:* For master's, one foreign language, thesis optional. *Entrance requirements:* For master's, GRE or MAT. Additional exam requirements/recommendations for international students: Required—TOEFL (minimum score 500 paper-based; 183 computer-based; 65 iBT), TOEFL may be replaced by IELTS with score of 6 or higher. *Application deadline:* For fall admission, 2/1 priority date for domestic and international students; for winter admission, 10/1 priority date for domestic and international students; for spring admission, 10/1 priority date for domestic and international students. Applications are processed on a rolling basis. Application fee: $40. Electronic applications accepted. *Expenses:* Tuition, state resident: full-time $6430; part-time $357 per credit. Tuition, nonresident: full-time $10,288; part-time $572 per credit. Required fees: $1937; $73.50 per credit. One-time fee: $88 part-time. Tuition and fees vary according to course load. *Financial support:* In 2008–09, 11 students received support, including 11 research assistantships with full and partial tuition reimbursements available (averaging $4,611 per year); institutionally sponsored loans and unspecified assistantships also available. Support available to part-time students. Financial award application deadline: 3/15; financial award applicants required to submit FAFSA. *Faculty research:* Literary criticism, rhetoric and composition studies, distance teaching, creative writing, journalism history. Total annual research expenditures: $7,500. *Unit head:* Dr. Beverly Schneller, Chair, 717-871-2342, Fax: 717-871-2446, E-mail: beverly.schneller@millersville.edu. *Application contact:* Dr. Victor S. DeSantis, Dean of Graduate and Professional Studies, 717-872-3099, Fax: 717-872-3453, E-mail: victor.desantis@millersville.edu.

Mills College, Graduate Studies, Department of English, Oakland, CA 94613-1000. Offers book art and creative writing (MFA); creative writing, poetry (MFA); creative writing, prose (MFA); English and American literature (MA). Part-time programs available. *Faculty:* 9 full-time (7 women), 24 part-time/adjunct (20 women). *Students:* 94 full-time (67 women), 7 part-time (6 women); includes 29 minority (13 African Americans, 8 Asian Americans or Pacific Islanders, 8 Hispanic Americans). Average age 30. 154 applicants, 86% accepted, 50 enrolled. In 2008, 37 master's awarded. *Degree requirements:* For master's, comprehensive exam, thesis. *Entrance requirements:* For master's, manuscript, writing sample. Additional exam requirements/recommendations for international students: Required—TOEFL. *Application deadline:* For fall admission, 2/1 priority date for domestic students; for spring admission, 11/1 for domestic students. Applications are processed on a rolling basis. Application fee: $50. Electronic applications accepted. *Expenses:* Tuition: Full-time $25,072; part-time $6272 per course. Required fees: $880. *Financial support:* In 2008–09, 86 students received support, including 83 fellowships (averaging $6,994 per year), 28 teaching assistantships with partial tuition reimbursements available (averaging $2,430 per year); scholarships/grants also available. Support available to part-time students. Financial award application deadline: 2/1; financial award applicants required to submit FAFSA. *Faculty research:* Creative writing, African-American literature, Victorian women writers, theories of sexuality, Shakespeare. *Unit head:* Dr. Cynthia Scheinberg, Chair, 510-430-2213, E-mail: cyns@mills.edu. *Application contact:* Marika Benko, Graduate Admission Specialist, 510-430-3309, Fax: 510-430-2159, E-mail: grad-studies@mills.edu.

Minnesota State University Mankato, College of Graduate Studies, College of Arts and Humanities, Department of English, Mankato, MN 56001. Offers creative writing (MFA); English (MA, MS); English literature (MA); teaching English (MS, MT); teaching English as a second language (MA, Certificate); technical communication (Certificate). Part-time programs available. *Students:* 36 full-time (20 women), 107 part-time (82 women). *Degree requirements:* For master's, one foreign language, comprehensive exam, thesis or alternative. *Entrance requirements:* For master's, minimum GPA of 3.0 during previous 2 years, writing sample (MFA). Additional exam requirements/recommendations for international students: Required—TOEFL. *Application deadline:* Applications are processed on a rolling basis. Application fee: $40. Electronic applications accepted. *Financial support:* Research assistantships with full tuition reimbursements, teaching assistantships with full tuition reimbursements, career-related internships or fieldwork, Federal Work-Study, and unspecified assistantships available. Financial award application deadline: 3/15; financial award applicants required to submit FAFSA. *Faculty research:* Keats and Christianity. *Unit head:* Dr. John Banschbach, Chairperson, 507-389-2117. *Application contact:* 507-389-2321, E-mail: grad@mnsu.edu.

Mississippi College, Graduate School, College of Arts and Sciences, School of Humanities and Social Sciences, Department of English, Clinton, MS 39058. Offers M Ed, MA. Part-time and evening/weekend programs available. *Degree requirements:* For master's, one foreign language, comprehensive exam, thesis or alternative. *Entrance requirements:* For master's, GRE or NTE, minimum GPA of 2.5. Additional exam requirements/recommendations for international students: Recommended—IELTS. Electronic applications accepted.

Mississippi State University, College of Arts and Sciences, Department of English, Mississippi State, MS 39762. Offers MA. Part-time programs available. *Degree requirements:* For master's, thesis optional, comprehensive oral or written exam. *Entrance requirements:* For master's, GRE General Test, minimum GPA of 2.75. Additional exam requirements/recommendations for international students: Required—TOEFL. *Faculty research:* Literary criticism, linguistics, textual editing, editing *Mississippi Quarterly*, Southern literature.

Missouri State University, Graduate College, College of Arts and Letters, Department of English, Springfield, MO 65804-0094. Offers English and writing (MA); secondary education (MS Ed), including English. Part-time and evening/weekend programs available. *Faculty:* 26 full-time (15 women). *Students:* 33 full-time (20 women), 56 part-time (35 women), 8 international. Average age 29. 31 applicants, 100% accepted, 22 enrolled. In 2008, 39 master's awarded. *Degree requirements:* For master's, one foreign language, comprehensive exam, thesis or alternative. *Entrance requirements:* For master's, GRE (MA), minimum GPA of 3.0 (MA), 9-12 teacher certification (MS Ed). Additional exam requirements/recommendations for international students: Required—TOEFL (minimum score 550 paper-based; 213 computer-based; 79 iBT). *Application deadline:* For fall admission, 7/20 for domestic students, 5/1 for international students; for spring admission, 12/20 for domestic students, 9/1 for international students. Applications are processed on a rolling basis. Application fee: $35 ($50 for international students). Electronic applications accepted. *Expenses:* Tuition, state resident: full-time $3852; part-time $214 per credit hour. Tuition, nonresident: full-time $7524; part-time $418 per credit hour. Required fees: $230 per semester. Tuition and fees vary according to course level and course load. *Financial support:* In 2008–09, 37 teaching assistantships with full tuition reimbursements (averaging $7,340 per year) were awarded; Federal Work-Study, institutionally sponsored loans, scholarships/grants, and unspecified assistantships also available. Support available to part-time students. Financial award application deadline: 3/31; financial award applicants required to submit FAFSA. *Faculty research:* Renaissance literature, William Blake, autobiography, Georgian theatre, TESOL. *Unit head:* Dr. W. D. Blackmon, Head, 417-836-5107, Fax: 417-836-6940, E-mail: wdblackon@missouristate.edu. *Application contact:* Eric Eckert, Coordinator of Graduate Admissions and Recruitment, 417-836-5331, Fax: 417-836-6888, E-mail: ericeckert@missouristate.edu.

Monmouth University, Graduate School, Department of English, West Long Branch, NJ 07764-1898. Offers MA. Part-time and evening/weekend programs available. *Faculty:* 11 full-time (7 women). *Students:* 8 full-time (5 women), 20 part-time (16 women); includes 1 minority (African American). Average age 31. 18 applicants, 100% accepted, 10 enrolled. In 2008, 3 master's awarded. *Degree requirements:* For master's, comprehensive exam (for some programs), thesis (for some programs), 30 credits. *Entrance requirements:* For master's, minimum overall GPA of 2.75, at least 15 credits in literary studies. Additional exam requirements/recommendations for international students: Required—TOEFL (minimum score 550 paper-based; 213 computer-based; 79 iBT), IELTS (minimum score 5), Michigan English Language Assessment Battery (minimum score: 77), Cambridge A, B, C. *Application deadline:* For fall admission, 7/15 for domestic students, 6/1 for international students; for spring admission, 11/15 for domestic students, 11/1 for international students. Application fee: $50. *Expenses:* Tuition: Full-time $13,914; part-time $773 per credit. Required fees: $628; $157 per semester. *Financial support:* In 2008–09, 19 students received support, including 18 fellowships (averaging $1,830 per year), 4 research assistantships (averaging $5,778 per year); scholarships/grants, tuition waivers (partial), and unspecified assistantships also available. Support available to part-time students. *Faculty research:* Renaissance and medieval literature, 19th century America literature, 18th century British literature and women's studies, Old English and Middle English, African diasposa and African post colonial literature. *Unit head:* Dr. Hiede Estes, Program Director, 732-571-7547, E-mail: hestes@monmouth.edu. *Application contact:* Kevin Roane, Director, Office of Graduate Admission, 732-571-3452, Fax: 732-263-5123, E-mail: gradadm@monmouth.edu.

Montana State University, College of Graduate Studies, College of Letters and Science, Department of English, Bozeman, MT 59717. Offers MA. Part-time programs available. *Degree requirements:* For master's, comprehensive exam. *Entrance requirements:* For master's, GRE General Test. Additional exam requirements/recommendations for international students: Required—TOEFL (minimum score 550 paper-based; 213 computer-based). Electronic applications accepted. *Faculty research:* British literature, American literature, global literacy, English pedagogy, Western literature.

Montclair State University, The Office of Graduate Admissions and Support Services, College of Humanities and Social Sciences, Department of English, Montclair, NJ 07043-1624. Offers MA, Certificate. Part-time and evening/weekend programs available. *Faculty:* 39 full-time (21 women), 64 part-time/adjunct (48 women). *Students:* 14 full-time (12 women), 40 part-time (31 women); includes 1 minority (Asian American or Pacific Islander). Average age 32. 27 applicants, 52% accepted, 9 enrolled. In 2008, 15 master's awarded. *Degree requirements:* For master's, thesis. *Entrance requirements:* For master's, GRE General Test, minimum GPA of 3.0, 2 letters of recommendation. Additional exam requirements/recommendations for international students: Required—TOEFL (minimum score 83 computer-based). *Application deadline:* For fall admission, 4/1 for domestic and international students; for spring admission, 11/1 for domestic and international students. Applications are processed on a rolling basis. Application fee: $60. Electronic applications accepted. *Financial support:* In 2008–09, 6 research assistantships with full tuition reimbursements (averaging $7,000 per year) were awarded; Federal Work-Study, scholarships/grants, and unspecified assistantships also available. Support available to part-time students. Financial award application deadline: 3/1; financial award applicants required to submit FAFSA. *Unit head:* Dr. Dan Bronson, Chairperson, 973-655-4274. *Application contact:* Amy Aiello, Associate Director of Admissions, 973-655-5147, Fax: 973-655-7869, E-mail: graduate.school@montclair.edu.

Morehead State University, Graduate Programs, Caudill College of Humanities, Department of English, Foreign Languages, and Philosophy, Morehead, KY 40351. Offers English (MA). Part-time and evening/weekend programs available. *Faculty:* 10 full-time (2 women), 1 part-time/adjunct (0 women). *Students:* 9 full-time (7 women), 37 part-time (29 women); includes 3 minority (2 African Americans, 1 Asian American or Pacific Islander). Average age 31. 34 applicants, 79% accepted, 25 enrolled. In 2008, 7 master's awarded. *Degree requirements:* For master's, comprehensive exam, thesis optional. *Entrance requirements:* For master's, GRE General Test, minimum GPA of 3.0 in English, 2.5 overall; undergraduate major or minor in English. Additional exam requirements/recommendations for international students: Required—TOEFL (minimum score 500 paper-based; 173 computer-based). *Application deadline:* For fall admission, 8/1 priority date for domestic and international students; for spring admission, 12/1 priority date for domestic and international students. Applications are processed on a rolling basis. Application fee: $30 ($55 for international students). *Expenses:* Tuition, area resident: Full-time $6084; part-time $338 per credit hour. Tuition, state resident: full-time $6084; part-time $338 per credit hour. Tuition, nonresident: full-time $15,804; part-time $878 per credit hour. *Financial support:* In 2008–09, 4 teaching assistantships (averaging $6,000 per year) were awarded; career-related internships or fieldwork, Federal Work-Study, and unspecified assistantships also available. Financial award application deadline: 4/1; financial award applicants required to submit FAFSA. *Faculty research:* Nineteenth and twentieth century American literature, linguistics, Victorian literature, modern British literature, creative writing. *Unit head:* Dr. Philip Krummrich, Chair, 606-783-2185, Fax: 606-783-5346, E-mail: p.krummrich@moreheadstate.edu. *Application contact:* Michelle Barber, Graduate Admissions Counselor, 606-783-2039, Fax: 606-783-5061, E-mail: m.barber@moreheadstate.edu.

Morgan State University, School of Graduate Studies, College of Liberal Arts, Department of English, Baltimore, MD 21251. Offers MA, PhD. Part-time programs available. *Degree requirements:* For master's, comprehensive exam, thesis; for doctorate, comprehensive exam, thesis/dissertation. *Entrance requirements:* For master's, GRE, minimum GPA of 2.5; for doctorate, GRE. Additional exam requirements/recommendations for international students: Required—TOEFL (minimum score 550 paper-based; 213 computer-based). *Faculty research:* African and African-American studies, nineteenth century American literature, rhetoric, women's studies, children's literature.

Mount Mary College, Graduate Programs, Program in English, Milwaukee, WI 53222-4597. Offers MA. Evening/weekend programs available. *Faculty:* 1 (woman) full-time, 10 part-time/adjunct (7 women). *Students:* 32 full-time (29 women), 26 part-time (all women); includes 14 minority (7 African Americans, 1 American Indian/Alaska Native, 6 Hispanic Americans). Average age 39. 20 applicants, 80% accepted, 15 enrolled. *Degree requirements:* For master's, comprehensive exam, thesis or alternative. *Entrance requirements:* For master's, minimum GPA of 2.75. Additional exam requirements/recommendations for international students: Required—TOEFL (minimum score 500 paper-based; 173 computer-based). *Application deadline:* For fall admission, 8/1 priority date for domestic and international students; for spring admission, 12/1 priority date for domestic and international students. Applications are processed on a rolling basis. Application fee: $35 ($75 for international students). Electronic applications accepted. *Expenses:* Tuition: Part-time $545 per credit. *Financial support:* Career-related internships or fieldwork available. Financial award application deadline: 5/1; financial award applicants required to submit FAFSA. *Unit head:* Dr. Kristi Siegel, Director, 414-258-4810 Ext. 287, E-mail: siegelkr@mtmary.edu. *Application contact:* Dr. Kristi Siegel, Director, 414-258-4810 Ext. 287, E-mail: siegelkr@mtmary.edu.

Murray State University, College of Humanities and Fine Arts, Department of English and Philosophy, Program in English, Murray, KY 42071. Offers MA. Part-time programs available. *Degree requirements:* For master's, comprehensive exam, thesis (for some programs).

National University, Academic Affairs, College of Letters and Sciences, Department of Art and Humanities, La Jolla, CA 92037-1011. Offers creative writing (MFA); English (MA); history (MA). Part-time and evening/weekend programs available. Postbaccalaureate distance learning degree programs offered (no on-campus study). *Faculty:* 19 full-time (6 women), 180 part-time/adjunct (92 women). *Students:* 208 full-time (153 women), 433 part-time (302 women); includes 137 minority (57 African Americans, 10 American Indian/Alaska Native, 19 Asian Americans or Pacific Islanders, 51 Hispanic Americans). Average age 38. 420 applicants, 100% accepted, 420 enrolled. In 2008, 152 master's awarded. *Degree requirements:* For master's, thesis (for some programs). *Entrance requirements:* For master's, interview, minimum GPA of 2.5. Additional exam requirements/recommendations for international students: Required—TOEFL (minimum score 550 paper-based; 213 computer-based; 79 iBT), IELTS (minimum score 6). *Application deadline:* Applications are processed on a rolling basis. Application fee: $60 ($65 for international students). Electronic applications accepted. *Expenses:* Tuition: Full-time $8694; part-time $322 per credit hour. Tuition and fees vary according to course load. *Financial support:* Career-related internships or fieldwork, institutionally sponsored loans, scholarships/grants, and tuition waivers (partial) available. Support available to part-time students. Financial award application deadline: 6/30; financial award applicants required to submit FAFSA. *Unit head:* Dr. Janet Baker, Chair, 858-642-8472, Fax: 858-642-8715, E-mail: jbaker@nu.edu. *Application contact:* Dominick Giovanniello, Associate Regional Dean—San Diego, 800-NAT-UNIV, Fax: 858-541-7792, E-mail: dgiovann@nu.edu.

New Mexico Highlands University, Graduate Studies, College of Arts and Sciences, Department of Humanities, Las Vegas, NM 87701. Offers English (MA), including creative writing, language, rhetoric and composition, literature. *Faculty:* 12 full-time (6 women). *Students:* 12 full-time (6 women), 4 part-time (3 women); includes 3 minority (all Hispanic Americans), 1 international. Average age 30. 10 applicants, 70% accepted, 5 enrolled. In 2008, 5 master's awarded. *Degree requirements:* For master's, comprehensive exam, thesis. *Entrance requirements:* For master's, minimum undergraduate GPA of 3.0. Additional exam requirements/recommendations for international students: Required—TOEFL (minimum score 540 paper-based; 207 computer-based). *Application deadline:* For fall admission, 8/1 priority date for domestic students. Applications are processed on a rolling basis. Application fee: $15. *Expenses:* Tuition, state resident: full-time $2880; part-time $120 per credit hour. Tuition, nonresident: full-time $4234; part-time $176 per credit hour. International tuition: $5645 full-time. One-time fee: $20. *Financial support:* In 2008–09, 8 students received support, including teaching assistantships with full and partial tuition reimbursements available (averaging $6,500 per year); career-related internships or fieldwork, Federal Work-Study, institutionally sponsored loans, scholarships/grants, tuition waivers (full and partial), and unspecified assistantships also available. Support available to part-time students. Financial award application deadline: 3/1; financial award applicants required to submit FAFSA. *Faculty research:* 20th century literature, life path writing in homeless shelters, native American philosophy, medieval intellectual and cultural history, creating pedagogical tools for teaching law. *Unit head:* Dr. Brandon Kempner, Department Head, 505-454-3286, E-mail: bkempner@nmhu.edu. *Application contact:* Diane Trujillo, Administrative Assistant, Graduate Studies, 505-454-3266, Fax: 505-426-2117, E-mail: dtrujillo@nmhu.edu.

New Mexico State University, Graduate School, College of Arts and Sciences, Department of English, Las Cruces, NM 88003-8001. Offers creative writing (MFA); English (MA); rhetoric and professional communication (PhD). Part-time programs available. *Faculty:* 20 full-time (12 women), 2 part-time/adjunct (0 women). *Students:* 73 full-time (39 women), 36 part-time (24 women); includes 15 minority (3 American Indian/Alaska Native, 12 Hispanic Americans), 9 international. Average age 32. 135 applicants, 41% accepted, 40 enrolled. In 2008, 25 master's, 2 doctorates awarded. *Degree requirements:* For master's, one foreign language, thesis (for some programs); for doctorate, comprehensive exam, thesis/dissertation, internship. *Entrance requirements:* For master's and doctorate, sample of written work. *Application deadline:* For fall admission, 2/1 for domestic and international students. Application fee: $30 ($50 for international students). Electronic applications accepted. *Expenses:* Tuition, area resident: Full-time $3890; part-time $212.85 per credit. Tuition, state resident: full-time $3890; part-time $212.85 per credit. Tuition, nonresident: full-time $13,916; part-time $630.55 per credit. Required fees: $1218; $609 per semester. *Financial support:* In 2008–09, 81 students received support, including 3 research assistantships (averaging $9,217 per year), 53 teaching assistantships (averaging $15,623 per year); fellowships, career-related internships or fieldwork, Federal Work-Study, institutionally sponsored loans, scholarships/grants, health care benefits, and unspecified assistantships also available. Financial award application deadline: 2/1; financial award applicants required to submit FAFSA. *Faculty research:* Composition research, history and theory of rhetoric, technical/professional communication, creative writing, English and American literature. *Unit head:* Dr. Elizabeth Schirmer, Head, 575-646-1733, Fax: 575-646-7725, E-mail: eschirme@nmsu.edu. *Application contact:* Dr. Elizabeth Schirmer, Director of Graduate Studies, 575-646-1733, E-mail: eschirme@nmsu.edu.

New York University, Graduate School of Arts and Science, Department of English, Program in English and American Literature, New York, NY 10012-1019. Offers MA, PhD. *Degree requirements:* For master's, one foreign language, thesis or alternative, qualifying exams, special project; for doctorate, one foreign language, thesis/dissertation. *Entrance requirements:* For master's, GRE General Test. Additional exam requirements/recommendations for international students: Required—TOEFL.

North Carolina Agricultural and Technical State University, Graduate School, College of Arts and Sciences, Department of English, Greensboro, NC 27411. Offers English (MA); English and Afro-American literature (MA); Engligh education (MS). Part-time and evening/weekend programs available. *Degree requirements:* For master's, comprehensive exam, qualifying exam. *Entrance requirements:* For master's, GRE General Test, minimum GPA of 3.0.

North Carolina Central University, Division of Academic Affairs, College of Liberal Arts, Department of English and Mass Communication, Durham, NC 27707-3129. Offers English (MA). Part-time and evening/weekend programs available. *Degree requirements:* For master's, one foreign language, comprehensive exam, thesis. *Entrance requirements:* For master's, GRE, minimum GPA of 3.0 in major, 2.5 overall. Additional exam requirements/recommendations for international students: Required—TOEFL. *Faculty research:* Victorian literature, African-American literature, women's studies, literature and film, twentieth-century literature.

North Carolina State University, Graduate School, College of Humanities and Social Sciences, Department of English, Program in English, Raleigh, NC 27695. Offers MA. *Degree requirements:* For master's, thesis. *Entrance requirements:* For master's, GRE General Test. Electronic applications accepted. *Faculty research:* Creative writing, linguistics, rhetoric and composition, rhetoric and technical communication, film studies.

English

North Dakota State University, College of Graduate and Interdisciplinary Studies, College of Arts, Humanities and Social Sciences, Department of English, Fargo, ND 58105. Offers MA, MS. Part-time programs available. *Faculty:* 12 full-time (6 women), 1 part-time/adjunct (0 women). *Students:* 21 full-time (15 women), 13 part-time (11 women), 2 international. Average age 31. 33 applicants, 61% accepted, 14 enrolled. In 2008, 11 master's awarded. *Degree requirements:* For master's, one foreign language, thesis. *Entrance requirements:* Additional exam requirements/recommendations for international students: Required—TOEFL (minimum score 600 paper-based; 250 computer-based; 100 iBT), IELTS (minimum score 7). *Application deadline:* For fall admission, 4/1 priority date for domestic students; for spring admission, 12/15 priority date for domestic students. Applications are processed on a rolling basis. Application fee: $45 ($60 for international students). Electronic applications accepted. *Financial support:* In 2008–09, 3 fellowships with full tuition reimbursements (averaging $12,150 per year), 1 research assistantship (averaging $3,000 per year), 18 teaching assistantships with full tuition reimbursements (averaging $8,100 per year) were awarded; Federal Work-Study, institutionally sponsored loans, and scholarships/grants also available. Support available to part-time students. Financial award application deadline: 5/1. *Faculty research:* American and English literature, women's studies, language attitudes, composition practices, computers and composition. *Unit head:* Dr. Dale Sullivan, Head, 701-231-7143, Fax: 701-231-1047, E-mail: dale.sullivan@ndsu.edu. *Application contact:* Dr. Dale Sullivan, Head, 701-231-7143, Fax: 701-231-1047, E-mail: dale.sullivan@ndsu.edu.

Northeastern Illinois University, Graduate College, College of Arts and Sciences, Department of English, Programs in English, Chicago, IL 60625-4699. Offers composition/writing (MA); literature (MA). Part-time and evening/weekend programs available. *Degree requirements:* For master's, comprehensive exam, thesis optional, minimum GPA of 3.0. *Entrance requirements:* For master's, 30 hours of undergraduate course work in literature and composition (literature), BA in English or approval (composition/writing), minimum GPA of 2.75. Additional exam requirements/recommendations for international students: Required—TOEFL (minimum score 550 paper-based; 213 computer-based; 80 iBT). Electronic applications accepted. *Faculty research:* Arthurian literature, Southern American literature, rhetoric and theories of authorship.

Northeastern State University, Graduate College, College of Liberal Arts, Department of Languages and Literature, Tahlequah, OK 74464-2399. Offers English (MA), including literature, rhetoric/composition. *Students:* 13 full-time (8 women), 42 part-time (29 women); includes 12 minority (1 African American, 10 American Indian/Alaska Native, 1 Hispanic American). In 2008, 14 master's awarded. *Degree requirements:* For master's, thesis. *Entrance requirements:* For master's, GRE or MAT, minimum GPA of 2.5. Additional exam requirements/recommendations for international students: Required—TOEFL (minimum score 213 computer-based). *Application deadline:* For fall admission, 6/1 priority date for domestic students. Applications are processed on a rolling basis. Application fee: $0 ($25 for international students). Electronic applications accepted. *Financial support:* Application deadline: 3/1. *Unit head:* Dr. Jacqueline Wilcox, Chair, 918-456-5511 Ext. 3609, E-mail: wilcoxj@nsuok.edu. *Application contact:* Margie Railey, Administrative Assistant, 918-456-5511 Ext. 2093, Fax: 918-458-2061, E-mail: railey@nsouk.edu.

Northeastern University, College of Arts and Sciences, Department of English, Boston, MA 02115-5096. Offers cinema studies (Certificate); English (MA, PhD); women's studies (Certificate). Part-time and evening/weekend programs available. *Degree requirements:* For master's, one foreign language, comprehensive exam; for doctorate, 2 foreign languages, comprehensive exam, thesis/dissertation, qualifying exams. *Entrance requirements:* For master's and doctorate, GRE General Test, GRE Subject Test, sample of written work. Additional exam requirements/recommendations for international students: Required—TOEFL. *Faculty research:* Literature, creative writing, composition studies, linguistics.

Northern Arizona University, Graduate College, College of Arts and Letters, Department of English, Program in English, Flagstaff, AZ 86011. Offers creative writing (MA); general English (MA); literacy, technology and professional writing (MA); literature (MA); secondary English education (MA). *Degree requirements:* For master's, departmental qualifying exam. *Entrance requirements:* For master's, GRE General Test, GRE Subject Test.

Northern Illinois University, Graduate School, College of Liberal Arts and Sciences, Department of English, De Kalb, IL 60115-2854. Offers MA, PhD. Part-time programs available. Terminal master's awarded for partial completion of doctoral program. *Degree requirements:* For master's, variable foreign language requirement, comprehensive exam, thesis optional; for doctorate, variable foreign language requirement, thesis/dissertation, candidacy exam, dissertation defense. *Entrance requirements:* For master's, GRE General Test, minimum GPA of 2.75; for doctorate, GRE General Test, minimum GPA of 2.75 (undergraduate), 3.2 (graduate). Additional exam requirements/recommendations for international students: Required—TOEFL (minimum score 550 paper-based; 213 computer-based). Electronic applications accepted. *Faculty research:* 19th century English literature, linguistic programs, portfolio assembly, Mideast literature, old English folklore.

Northern Kentucky University, Office of Graduate Programs, College of Arts and Sciences, Program in English, Highland Heights, KY 41099. Offers English (MA). Part-time and evening/weekend programs available. *Students:* 4 full-time (3 women), 26 part-time (21 women); includes 4 minority (2 African Americans, 2 Hispanic Americans). Average age 36. 37 applicants, 84% accepted, 29 enrolled. *Degree requirements:* For master's, comprehensive exam (for some programs), thesis optional, capstone project via comprehensive exam or thesis. *Entrance requirements:* For master's, minimum GPA of 3.0, two letters of reference. Additional exam requirements/recommendations for international students: Required—TOEFL (minimum score 550 paper-based; 213 computer-based; 79 iBT), Michigan Test may be substituted only if taken at NKU (minimu score of 80); Recommended—IELTS (minimum score 6.5). *Application deadline:* For fall admission, 7/1 priority date for domestic students, 6/1 priority date for international students. Applications are processed on a rolling basis. Application fee: $40. Electronic applications accepted. *Expenses:* Tuition, area resident: Full-time $6642. Tuition, state resident: full-time $6642. Tuition, nonresident: full-time $11,682. *Financial support:* Unspecified assistantships available. Financial award applicants required to submit FAFSA. *Faculty research:* Professional writing and new media studies, composition and rhetoric, literary studies, creative writing, cinema studies. *Unit head:* Dr. Roxanne Kent-Drury, Coordinator, 859-572-6636, E-mail: rkdrury@nku.edu. *Application contact:* Dr. Peg Griffin, Director of Graduate Programs, 859-572-6934, Fax: 859-572-6670, E-mail: griffinp@nku.edu.

Northern Michigan University, College of Graduate Studies, College of Arts and Sciences, Department of English, Marquette, MI 49855-5301. Offers creative writing (MFA); literature (MA); pedagogy (MA); writing (MA). Part-time programs available. *Degree requirements:* For master's, thesis or alternative. *Entrance requirements:* For master's, minimum GPA of 2.75.

Northwestern State University of Louisiana, Graduate Studies and Research, Department of Language and Communication, Natchitoches, LA 71497. Offers English (MA). *Faculty:* 7 full-time (2 women), 2 part-time/adjunct (1 woman). *Students:* 18 full-time (11 women), 11 part-time (8 women); includes 5 minority (4 African Americans, 1 American Indian/Alaska Native). Average age 31. 8 applicants, 88% accepted, 5 enrolled. In 2008, 6 master's awarded. *Degree requirements:* For master's, one foreign language, comprehensive exam, thesis or alternative. *Entrance requirements:* For master's, GRE General Test, minimum undergraduate GPA of 2.5. *Application deadline:* For fall admission, 8/1 priority date for domestic students; for spring admission, 1/10 for domestic students. Applications are processed on a rolling basis. Application fee: $20 ($30 for international students). *Financial support:* Application deadline: 7/15. *Unit head:* Dr. Lisa Abney, Chairman, 318-357-6166, Fax: 318-357-5942, E-mail: abney@nsula.edu. *Application contact:* Dr. Steven G. Horton, Associate Provost/Dean, Graduate Studies, Research, and Information Systems, 318-357-5851, Fax: 318-357-5019, E-mail: grad_school@nsula.edu.

Northwestern University, The Graduate School, Judd A. and Marjorie Weinberg College of Arts and Sciences, Department of English, Evanston, IL 60208. Offers MA, PhD. Admissions and degrees offered through The Graduate School. Terminal master's awarded for partial completion of doctoral program. *Degree requirements:* For master's, thesis; for doctorate, one foreign language, thesis/dissertation, oral and written qualifying exam. *Entrance requirements:* For master's and doctorate, GRE General Test, sample of written work. Additional exam requirements/recommendations for international students: Required—TOEFL. Electronic applications accepted. *Faculty research:* Renaissance literature, theatre and drama, American literature, modern European contemporary literature, poetry, cultural history.

Announcement: Small, highly selective doctoral program oriented toward research. Departmental strengths include medieval, early modern, American, Victorian, cultural history, and critical theory. Close contact with senior faculty members; closely supervised teaching. Doctoral students are supported by fellowships and teaching assistantships for five academic years and four summers. Web site: www.english.northwestern.edu.

Northwest Missouri State University, Graduate School, College of Arts and Sciences, Department of English, Maryville, MO 64468-6001. Offers English (MA); English with speech emphasis (MA); teaching English (option 1) (MS Ed); teaching English with speech emphasis (MS Ed). Part-time programs available. *Degree requirements:* For master's, comprehensive exam, thesis optional. *Entrance requirements:* For master's, GRE General Test, minimum undergraduate GPA of 2.5, writing sample. Additional exam requirements/recommendations for international students: Required—TOEFL (minimum score 550 paper-based; 213 computer-based).

Notre Dame de Namur University, Division of Academic Affairs, School of Arts and Humanities, Department of English, Belmont, CA 94002-1908. Offers English (MA); teaching English to speakers of other languages (Certificate). Part-time and evening/weekend programs available. *Faculty:* 5 full-time (2 women), 5 part-time/adjunct (3 women). *Students:* 3 full-time (all women), 15 part-time (12 women); includes 4 minority (1 Asian American or Pacific Islander, 3 Hispanic Americans), 1 international. Average age 28. 6 applicants, 100% accepted, 4 enrolled. In 2008, 10 master's awarded. *Degree requirements:* For master's, thesis optional, exam. *Entrance requirements:* For master's, minimum GPA of 2.5, writing sample. Additional exam requirements/recommendations for international students: Required—TOEFL. *Application deadline:* For fall admission, 8/1 priority date for domestic students; for spring admission, 12/1 priority date for domestic students. Applications are processed on a rolling basis. Application fee: $50 ($500 for international students). Electronic applications accepted. *Expenses:* Tuition: Part-time $699 per unit. Required fees: $3 per unit. $35 per semester. *Financial support:* Career-related internships or fieldwork available. Support available to part-time students. Financial award applicants required to submit FAFSA. *Unit head:* Jacqueline Berger, Director, 650-508-3730. *Application contact:* Candace Hallmark, Assistant Director of Graduate Admissions, 650-508-3592, Fax: 650-508-3426, E-mail: grad.admit@ndnu.edu.

Oakland University, Graduate Study and Lifelong Learning, College of Arts and Sciences, Department of English, Rochester, MI 48309-4401. Offers MA. Part-time and evening/weekend programs available. *Entrance requirements:* For master's, minimum GPA of 3.0 for unconditional admission. Additional exam requirements/recommendations for international students: Required—TOEFL (minimum score 550 paper-based; 213 computer-based). Electronic applications accepted.

The Ohio State University, Graduate School, College of Humanities, Department of English, Columbus, OH 43210. Offers MA, MFA, PhD. *Degree requirements:* For master's, one foreign language, thesis or written exam; for doctorate, one foreign language, thesis/dissertation. *Entrance requirements:* For master's and doctorate, GRE General Test. Additional exam requirements/recommendations for international students: Required—TOEFL (minimum score 600 paper-based; 250 computer-based). Electronic applications accepted.

Ohio University, Graduate College, College of Arts and Sciences, Department of English Language and Literature, Athens, OH 45701-2979. Offers MA, PhD. Part-time programs available. *Degree requirements:* For master's, one foreign language, thesis or alternative; for doctorate, one foreign language, comprehensive exam, thesis/dissertation, oral exam, public lecture. *Entrance requirements:* For master's, GRE General Test, minimum GPA of 3.0; for doctorate, GRE General Test, minimum GPA of 3.0, master's degree in English. Additional exam requirements/recommendations for international students: Required—TOEFL (minimum score 600 paper-based; 260 computer-based). Electronic applications accepted. *Faculty research:* Environmental literature, post-colonial studies, print culture, film in popular culture, computers in pedagogy.

Oklahoma State University, College of Arts and Sciences, Department of English, Stillwater, OK 74078. Offers creative writing (MA); English (MFA); literature (PhD). *Faculty:* 52 full-time (30 women), 2 part-time/adjunct (both women). *Students:* 3 full-time (2 women), 131 part-time (77 women); includes 14 minority (4 African Americans, 6 American Indian/Alaska Native, 2 Asian Americans or Pacific Islanders, 2 Hispanic Americans), 19 international. Average age 32. 134 applicants, 40% accepted, 24 enrolled. In 2008, 16 master's, 6 doctorates awarded. *Degree requirements:* For master's, comprehensive exam, thesis; for doctorate, comprehensive exam, thesis/dissertation. *Entrance requirements:* For master's, GRE General Test, minimum GPA of 3.0, writing sample; for doctorate, GRE General Test, minimum GPA of 3.5, writing sample. Additional exam requirements/recommendations for international students: Required—TOEFL. *Application deadline:* For fall admission, 3/1 priority date for international students; for spring admission, 8/1 priority date for international students. Applications are processed on a rolling basis. Application fee: $40 ($75 for international students). Electronic applications accepted. *Expenses:* Tuition, state resident: full-time $3716.40; part-time $154.85 per credit hour. Tuition, nonresident: full-time $14,448; part-time $602 per credit hour. Required fees: $1772.40; $73.85 per credit hour. One-time fee: $50. Tuition and fees vary according to course load and campus/location. *Financial support:* In 2008–09, 5 research assistantships (averaging $10,399 per year), 79 teaching assistantships (averaging $14,715 per year) were awarded; career-related internships or fieldwork, Federal Work-Study, scholarships/grants, health care benefits, tuition waivers (partial), and unspecified assistantships also available. Support available to part-time students. Financial award application deadline: 3/1; financial award applicants required to submit FAFSA. *Faculty research:* American and British novel, poetry, and autobiography; Native American languages and literature; institutional history of American film, history, and adaptations; rhetoric and theories of human communication; learning strategies of second language learners. *Unit head:* Dr. Carol Moder, Head, 405-744-9474, Fax: 405-744-6326. *Application contact:* Dr. Gordon Emslie, Dean, 405-744-6368, Fax: 405-744-0355, E-mail: grad_i@okstate.edu.

Old Dominion University, College of Arts and Letters, Doctoral Program in English, Norfolk, VA 23529. Offers PhD. Part-time and evening/weekend programs available. Postbaccalaureate distance learning degree programs offered (minimal on-campus study). *Faculty:* 16 full-time (9 women). *Students:* 9 full-time (6 women), 22 part-time (20 women); includes 7 minority (6 African Americans, 1 Hispanic American), 1 international. Average age 36. 32 applicants, 38% accepted, 6 enrolled. *Degree requirements:* For doctorate, one foreign language, comprehensive exam, thesis/dissertation. *Entrance requirements:* For doctorate, GRE General Test, MA in English or related field with minimum GPA of 3.5, writing sample, resumé. Additional exam requirements/recommendations for international students: Required—TOEFL. *Application deadline:* For fall admission, 2/15 for domestic students. Application fee: $40. Electronic applications accepted. *Expenses:* Tuition, area resident: Full-time $7704; part-time $321 per credit. Tuition, state resident: full-time $7704; part-time $321 per credit. Tuition, nonresident: full-time $19,104; part-time $796 per credit. Required fees: $99 per semester. One-time fee: $40. *Financial support:* In 2008–09, 13 students received support, including 3 fellowships with full tuition reimbursements available (averaging $15,000 per year), 1 research assistantship with full tuition reimbursement available (averaging $15,000 per year), 9 teaching assistantships with full tuition reimbursements available (averaging $15,000 per year); career-related internships or fieldwork, scholarships/grants, and unspecified assistantships also available. Support available to part-time students. Financial award application deadline: 2/15; financial award applicants required to submit FAFSA. *Faculty research:* New media studies, rhetorical history and theory, digital studies, writing studies, professional writing and document design, linguistics, textual studies, literary studies. *Unit head:* Dr. Joyce Neff, Graduate Program Director, 757-683-6875, Fax: 757-683-3241, E-mail: jneff@odu.edu. *Application contact:* Dr. Robert Wojtowicz, Associate Dean, 757-683-6077, Fax: 757-683-5746, E-mail: rwojtowi@odu.edu.

Old Dominion University, College of Arts and Letters, Master's in English Program, Norfolk, VA 23529. Offers MA. Part-time and evening/weekend programs available. Postbaccalaureate distance learning degree programs offered (minimal on-campus study). *Faculty:* 17 full-time (8 women). *Students:* 22 full-time (17 women), 42 part-time (32 women); includes 11 minority (8 African Americans, 2 Asian Americans or Pacific Islanders, 1 Hispanic American), 1 international. Average age 31. 56 applicants, 66% accepted, 30 enrolled. In 2008, 27 master's awarded. *Degree requirements:* For master's, comprehensive exam, thesis optional. *Entrance requirements:* For master's, GRE General Test, 24 hours in English, minimum B average, sample of written work. Additional exam requirements/recommendations for international students: Required—TOEFL. *Application deadline:* For fall admission, 6/1 priority date for domestic students; for winter admission, 11/1 priority date for domestic students; for spring admission, 3/1 priority date for domestic students. Applications are processed on a rolling basis. Application fee: $40. Electronic applications accepted. *Expenses:* Tuition, area resident: Full-time $7704; part-time $321 per credit. Tuition, state resident: full-time $7704; part-time $321 per credit. Tuition, nonresident: full-time $19,104; part-time $796 per credit. Required fees: $99 per semester. One-time fee: $40. *Financial support:* In 2008–09, 3 fellowships with tuition reimbursements (averaging $15,000 per year), 3 research assistantships with partial tuition reimbursements (averaging $8,119 per year), 14 teaching assistantships with partial tuition reimbursements (averaging $12,000 per year) were awarded; career-related internships or fieldwork, scholarships/grants, and unspecified assistantships also available. Support available to part-time students. Financial award application deadline: 2/15; financial award applicants required to submit FAFSA. *Faculty research:* Literary theory, composition theory, professional writing, rhetoric, British and American literature. Total annual research expenditures: $3,451. *Unit head:* Dr. Jeffrey H. Richards, Graduate Program Director, 757-683-4032, Fax: 757-683-3241, E-mail: jhrichar@odu.edu. *Application contact:* Dr. Jeffrey H. Richards, Graduate Program Director, 757-683-4032, Fax: 757-683-3241, E-mail: jhrichar@odu.edu.

Old Dominion University, Darden College of Education, Programs in Secondary Education, Norfolk, VA 23529. Offers biology (MS Ed); chemistry (MS Ed); English (MS Ed); instructional technology (MS Ed); library science (MS Ed); secondary education (MS Ed). *Accreditation:* NCATE. Part-time and evening/weekend programs available. Postbaccalaureate distance learning degree programs offered (minimal on-campus study). *Faculty:* 28 full-time (11 women). *Students:* 61 full-time (45 women), 165 part-time (118 women); includes 56 minority (31 African Americans, 13 Asian Americans or Pacific Islanders, 12 Hispanic Americans). Average age 34. 54 applicants, 91% accepted. In 2008, 114 master's awarded. *Degree requirements:* For master's, comprehensive exam, thesis, writing exam. *Entrance requirements:* For master's, GRE General Test or MAT, PRAXIS I (for licensure), minimum GPA of 2.8, teaching certificate. Additional exam requirements/recommendations for international students: Required—TOEFL. *Application deadline:* Applications are processed on a rolling basis. Application fee: $40. Electronic applications accepted. *Expenses:* Tuition, area resident: Full-time $7704; part-time $321 per credit. Tuition, state resident: full-time $7704; part-time $321 per credit. Tuition, nonresident: full-time $19,104; part-time $796 per credit. Required fees: $99 per semester. One-time fee: $40. *Financial support:* In 2008–09, 58 students received support, including fellowships (averaging $15,000 per year), 2 research assistantships with tuition reimbursements available (averaging $9,000 per year), 3 teaching assistantships with tuition reimbursements available (averaging $12,500 per year); career-related internships or fieldwork, Federal Work-Study, institutionally sponsored loans, scholarships/grants, and tuition waivers (partial) also available. Support available to part-time students. Financial award application deadline: 2/15; financial award applicants required to submit FAFSA. *Faculty research:* Mathematics retraining, writing project for teachers, geography teaching, reading. *Unit head:* Dr. Robert Lucking, Graduate Program Director, 757-683-5545, Fax: 757-683-5862, E-mail: rlucking@odu.edu. *Application contact:* Dr. Robert Lucking, Graduate Program Director, 757-683-5545, Fax: 757-683-5862, E-mail: rlucking@odu.edu.

Oregon State University, Graduate School, College of Liberal Arts, Department of English, Corvallis, OR 97331. Offers MA, MAIS, MFA. *Degree requirements:* For master's, one foreign language, thesis. *Entrance requirements:* For master's, minimum GPA of 3.0 in last 90 hours of course work. Additional exam requirements/recommendations for international students: Required—TOEFL. *Faculty research:* Composition and rhetoric, American literature theory, American renaissance, gender studies, English drama.

Our Lady of the Lake University of San Antonio, College of Arts and Sciences, Program in English, San Antonio, TX 78207-4689. Offers English and communication arts (MA); English and literature (MA); English education (MA); writing (MA). Part-time and evening/weekend programs available. *Students:* 12 full-time (11 women), 7 part-time (all women); includes 14 minority (1 African American, 13 Hispanic Americans). Average age 31. In 2008, 15 master's awarded. *Degree requirements:* For master's, comprehensive exam, thesis optional. *Entrance requirements:* For master's, GRE General Test or MAT, minimum GPA of 3.0 in last 60 hours, 2.5 overall. Additional exam requirements/recommendations for international students: Required—TOEFL. *Application deadline:* Applications are processed on a rolling basis. Application fee: $25 ($50 for international students). Electronic applications accepted. *Expenses:* Tuition: Full-time $11,970; part-time $665 per credit hour. Required fees: $500; $250 per term. *Financial support:* Research assistantships, teaching assistantships, career-related internships or fieldwork, Federal Work-Study, institutionally sponsored loans, and tuition waivers (partial) available. Financial award application deadline: 4/15. *Faculty research:* Writing theory and research, contemporary Southern literature, popular culture, poetry, literature of the Southwest. *Unit head:* Dr. Leah Larson, Chair, 210-434-2387 Ext. 2260, E-mail: larsl@lake.ollusa.edu. *Application contact:* 210-434-6711, Fax: 210-431-4036, E-mail: gradadm@lake.ollusa.edu.

Penn State University Park, Graduate School, College of the Liberal Arts, Department of English, State College, University Park, PA 16802-1503. Offers MA, MFA, PhD.

Pittsburg State University, Graduate School, College of Arts and Sciences, Department of English, Pittsburg, KS 66762. Offers MA. *Degree requirements:* For master's, thesis or alternative. *Faculty research:* American fiction, American poetry, British fiction, British poetry, composition theory.

Portland State University, Graduate Studies, College of Liberal Arts and Sciences, Department of English, Portland, OR 97207-0751. Offers MA, MA/MS. Part-time and evening/weekend programs available. *Faculty:* 39 full-time (20 women), 36 part-time/adjunct (17 women). *Students:* 103 full-time (72 women), 93 part-time (67 women); includes 11 minority (1 African American, 2 American Indian/Alaska Native, 6 Asian Americans or Pacific Islanders, 2 Hispanic Americans), 5 international. Average age 34. 181 applicants, 54% accepted, 59 enrolled. In 2008, 74 master's awarded. *Degree requirements:* For master's, one foreign language, comprehensive exam (for some programs), thesis (for some programs), oral and written exams. *Entrance requirements:* For master's, minimum GPA of 3.25 in upper-division course work and English courses or 2.75 overall, 3 letters of recommendation. Additional exam requirements/recommendations for international students: Required—TOEFL (minimum score 600 paper-based). *Application deadline:* For fall admission, 1/18 for domestic and international students; for winter admission, 9/1 for domestic and international students; for spring admission, 11/1 for domestic and international students. Application fee: $50. *Expenses:* Tuition, area resident: Full-time $8763; part-time $179 per credit hour. Tuition, state resident: full-time $8763; part-time $298 per credit hour. Tuition, nonresident: full-time $12,981; part-time $426 per credit hour. Required fees: $1242. One-time fee: $250. Tuition and fees vary according to course load and program. *Financial support:* In 2008–09, 17 teaching assistantships with full tuition reimbursements (averaging $6,661 per year) were awarded; research assistantships, career-related internships or fieldwork, Federal Work-Study, scholarships/grants, and unspecified assistantships also available. Support available to part-time students. Financial award application deadline: 3/1; financial award applicants required to submit FAFSA. *Faculty research:* American literature and cultural studies, Medieval and British literature, writing prose fiction and poetry, rhetoric and composition, women's literature. *Unit head:* Dr. Jennifer Ruth, Interim Chair, 503-725-3521, Fax: 503-725-3561. *Application contact:* Nixie Stark, Program Administrator, 503-725-3521, Fax: 503-725-3561, E-mail: starkn@pdx.edu.

Prairie View A&M University, College of Arts and Sciences, Department of Languages and Communication, Prairie View, TX 77446-0519. Offers English (MA). Part-time programs available. *Degree requirements:* For master's, comprehensive exam, thesis, exit exam. *Entrance requirements:* For master's, GRE General Test, bachelor's degree in English or equivalent. Additional exam requirements/recommendations for international students: Required—TOEFL. *Faculty research:* Composition, rhetoric, technical writing, literature, communication, pedagogy in general and literature, online teaching.

Princeton University, Graduate School, Department of English, Princeton, NJ 08544-1019. Offers PhD. *Degree requirements:* For doctorate, 2 foreign languages, thesis/dissertation. *Entrance requirements:* For doctorate, GRE General Test, GRE Subject Test, sample of written work. Additional exam requirements/recommendations for international students: Required—TOEFL (minimum score 600 paper-based; 250 computer-based). Electronic applications accepted.

Purdue University, Graduate School, College of Liberal Arts, Department of English, West Lafayette, IN 47907. Offers creative writing (MFA); literature (MA, PhD), including linguistics, literature and philosophy (PhD), rhetoric and composition, theory and cultural studies (PhD). Part-time programs available. *Degree requirements:* For master's, one foreign language; for doctorate, one foreign language, thesis/dissertation. *Entrance requirements:* For master's and doctorate, GRE General Test, sample of written work. Additional exam requirements/recommendations for international students: Required—TOEFL. Electronic applications accepted. *Faculty research:* Cultural studies, postmodern narrative, contemporary women writers, composition theory, slave narratives.

Purdue University Calumet, Graduate School, School of Liberal Arts and Social Sciences, Department of English and Philosophy, Hammond, IN 46323-2094. Offers English (MA). Part-time and evening/weekend programs available. Postbaccalaureate distance learning degree programs offered (minimal on-campus study). *Degree requirements:* For master's, comprehensive exam, thesis optional. *Entrance requirements:* Additional exam requirements/recommendations for international students: Required—TOEFL. Electronic applications accepted. *Faculty research:* English literature, American literature, critical theory, women's studies, historical philosophy.

Queens College of the City University of New York, Division of Graduate Studies, Arts and Humanities Division, Department of English, Flushing, NY 11367-1597. Offers creative writing (MA); English language and literature (MA). Part-time and evening/weekend programs available. *Degree requirements:* For master's, one foreign language, thesis (for some programs), oral exam (English language and literature). *Entrance requirements:* For master's, manuscript (creative writing), minimum GPA of 3.0. Additional exam requirements/recommendations for international students: Required—TOEFL.

Queen's University at Kingston, School of Graduate Studies and Research, Faculty of Arts and Sciences, Department of English Language and Literature, Kingston, ON K7L 3N6, Canada. Offers MA, PhD. *Degree requirements:* For master's, one foreign language, thesis optional; for doctorate, 2 foreign languages, comprehensive exam, thesis/dissertation. *Entrance requirements:* For master's, B.A.H. upper 2nd class standing, 10 full courses in English; for doctorate, M.A. upper 2nd class standing. Additional exam requirements/recommendations for international students: Required—TOEFL, TWE. *Faculty research:* Renaissance, 18th century, post colonial, Canadian, 19th century.

Radford University, College of Graduate and Professional Studies, College of Humanities and Behavioral Sciences, Department of English, Radford, VA 24142. Offers MA, MS. Part-time programs available. *Faculty:* 21 full-time (10 women), 1 (woman) part-time/adjunct. *Students:* 24 full-time (15 women), 7 part-time (6 women); includes 2 minority (1 American Indian/Alaska Native, 1 Asian American or Pacific Islander). Average age 29. 18 applicants, 94% accepted, 10 enrolled. In 2008, 12 master's awarded. *Degree requirements:* For master's, comprehensive exam, thesis (for some programs). *Entrance requirements:* For master's, GRE, minimum GPA of 2.75; 2 letters of reference; sample of expository writing. Additional exam requirements/recommendations for international students: Required—TOEFL (minimum score 550 paper-based; 213 computer-based; 79 iBT). *Application deadline:* For fall admission, 3/1 priority date for domestic students, 12/1 for international students; for spring admission, 10/1 for domestic students, 7/1 for international students. Applications are processed on a rolling basis. Application fee: $40. Electronic applications accepted. *Expenses:* Tuition, area resident: Full-time $4845; part-time $202 per credit. Tuition, state resident: full-time $4845; part-time $202 per credit. Tuition, nonresident: full-time $11,483; part-time $478 per credit. Required fees: $2349; $98 per credit. *Financial support:* In 2008–09, 23 students received support, including 5 research assistantships with partial tuition reimbursements available (averaging $8,000 per year), 12 teaching assistantships with partial tuition reimbursements available (averaging $8,700 per year); career-related internships or fieldwork, Federal Work-Study, institutionally sponsored loans, scholarships/grants, and unspecified assistantships also available. Financial award application deadline: 3/1; financial award applicants required to submit FAFSA. *Unit head:* Dr. Rosemary F. Guruswamy, Chair, 540-831-5285, Fax: 540-831-6800, E-mail: rguruswa@radford.edu. *Application contact:* Graduate Admissions, 540-831-5431, Fax: 540-831-6061, E-mail: gradcollege@radford.edu.

Rhode Island College, School of Graduate Studies, Faculty of Arts and Sciences, Department of English, Providence, RI 02908-1991. Offers creative writing (MA); English (MA). Part-time and evening/weekend programs available. *Faculty:* 15 full-time (8 women). *Students:* 4 full-time (all women), 15 part-time (9 women); includes 1 minority (Asian American or Pacific Islander). Average age 36. In 2008, 7 master's awarded. *Degree requirements:* For master's, thesis (for some programs). *Entrance requirements:* For master's, GRE General Test, 3 letters of recommendation, interview. Additional exam requirements/recommendations for international students: Recommended—TOEFL (minimum score 550 paper-based; 213 computer-based; 79 iBT). *Application deadline:* For fall admission, 4/1 for domestic students; for spring admission, 11/1 for domestic students. Applications are processed on a rolling basis. Application fee: $50. *Expenses:* Tuition, area resident: Full-time $6816; part-time $284 per credit hour. Tuition, state resident: full-time $6816; part-time $284 per credit hour. Tuition, nonresident: full-time $13,920; part-time $580 per credit hour. Required fees: $454; $16 per credit. $68 per term. *Financial support:* Teaching assistantships with full tuition reimbursements, career-related internships or fieldwork, Federal Work-Study, scholarships/grants, health care benefits, and unspecified assistantships available. Support available to part-time students. Financial award application deadline: 5/15; financial award applicants required to submit FAFSA. *Unit head:* Dr. Maureen Reddy, Chair, 401-456-8028. *Application contact:* Graduate Studies, 401-456-8700.

Rice University, Graduate Programs, School of Humanities, Department of English, Houston, TX 77251-1892. Offers MA, PhD. Terminal master's awarded for partial completion of doctoral program. *Degree requirements:* For master's, comprehensive exam, thesis (for some programs); for doctorate, comprehensive exam, thesis/dissertation. *Entrance requirements:* For master's and doctorate, GRE General Test, minimum GPA of 3.0. Additional exam requirements/recommendations for international students: Required—TOEFL (minimum score 600 paper-based; 250 computer-based; 90 iBT). Electronic applications accepted. *Faculty research:* Traditional periods and genres (excluding Old English), literary criticism and theory, Victorian literature, feminist literature, Renaissance literature, American literature, African-American literature.

English

Rivier College, School of Graduate Studies, Department of English, Nashua, NH 03060. Offers English (MA, MAT); writing and literature (MA); MA/MAT. Part-time and evening/weekend programs available. *Degree requirements:* For master's, comprehensive exam (for some programs). *Entrance requirements:* For master's, GRE Subject Test.

Roosevelt University, Graduate Division, College of Arts and Sciences, Department of Literature and Languages, Program in English, Chicago, IL 60605-1394. Offers MA. Part-time and evening/weekend programs available. *Students:* 3 full-time (all women), 6 part-time (4 women); includes 2 minority (both Hispanic Americans). Average age 31. 56 applicants, 36% accepted, 3 enrolled. In 2008, 2 master's awarded. *Degree requirements:* For master's, one foreign language, thesis or alternative. *Application deadline:* For fall admission, 6/1 priority date for domestic students. Applications are processed on a rolling basis. Application fee: $25 ($35 for international students). *Expenses:* Tuition: Full-time $14,730; part-time $709 per credit. Required fees: $175 per semester. Tuition and fees vary according to course load and program. *Financial support:* Research assistantships available. Financial award application deadline: 2/15. *Faculty research:* Eighteenth-century Victorian literature and culture, creative writing, eighteenth through twentieth century literature, American literature and culture. *Unit head:* Bonnie Gunzenhauser, Chair. *Application contact:* Joanne Canyon-Heller, Coordinator of Graduate Admission, 877-APPLY RU, Fax: 312-281-3356, E-mail: applyru@roosevelt.edu.

Rosemont College, Graduate School, Program in English and Publishing and English Literature, Rosemont, PA 19010-1699. Offers English and publishing (MA); English literature (MA). Part-time programs available. *Degree requirements:* For master's, comprehensive exam (for some programs), thesis. *Entrance requirements:* For master's, Baccalaureat Degree 3.0 college GPA, statement of purpose, 3 letters of recommendation. Additional exam requirements/recommendations for international students: Required—TOEFL. Electronic applications accepted.

Rutgers, The State University of New Jersey, Camden, Graduate School of Arts and Sciences, Program in English, Camden, NJ 08102-1401. Offers MA. Part-time and evening/weekend programs available. *Degree requirements:* For master's, comprehensive exam, thesis optional. *Entrance requirements:* For master's, GRE General Test, 3 letters of recommendation, writing sample, statement of goals. Additional exam requirements/recommendations for international students: Required—TOEFL, IELTS. *Faculty research:* British literature; American literature; women's studies; literary, poetic, and rhetorical theory; creative writing.

Rutgers, The State University of New Jersey, Newark, Graduate School, Program in English, Newark, NJ 07102. Offers MA. Part-time and evening/weekend programs available. *Degree requirements:* For master's, one foreign language, comprehensive exam, thesis optional. *Entrance requirements:* For master's, GRE, minimum undergraduate B average. Electronic applications accepted. *Faculty research:* British and American literature, cultural studies, literary theory, minority literatures.

Rutgers, The State University of New Jersey, New Brunswick, Graduate School, Program of Literatures in English, Piscataway, NJ 08854-8097. Offers PhD. *Degree requirements:* For doctorate, one foreign language, thesis/dissertation, qualifying exam. *Entrance requirements:* For doctorate, GRE General Test, GRE Subject Test, writing sample, 3 letters of recommendation. Additional exam requirements/recommendations for international students: Required—TOEFL. Electronic applications accepted. *Faculty research:* Medieval literature; Renaissance; African American literature; 18th century British literature; feminism, gender, and sexuality; postcolonial studies.

St. Bonaventure University, School of Graduate Studies, School of Arts and Sciences, Department of English, St. Bonaventure, NY 14778-2284. Offers MA. Part-time programs available. *Degree requirements:* For master's, one foreign language, comprehensive exam, thesis optional. *Entrance requirements:* For master's, GRE Subject Test. Additional exam requirements/recommendations for international students: Required—TOEFL. *Faculty research:* Victorian, Renaissance, American, modern British, and Romantic literature.

St. Cloud State University, School of Graduate Studies, College of Fine Arts and Humanities, Department of English, St. Cloud, MN 56301-4498. Offers English (MA, MS); teaching English as a second language (MA). Part-time programs available. *Degree requirements:* For master's, thesis or alternative. *Entrance requirements:* For master's, GRE General Test, minimum GPA of 2.75. Additional exam requirements/recommendations for international students: Required—Michigan English Language Assessment Battery; Recommended—TOEFL (minimum score 550 paper-based; 213 computer-based), IELTS (minimum score 6.5). Electronic applications accepted.

St. John's University, St. John's College of Liberal Arts and Sciences, Department of English, Queens, NY 11439. Offers MA, DA. Part-time and evening/weekend programs available. *Students:* 7 full-time (5 women), 66 part-time (45 women); includes 15 minority (3 African Americans, 3 Asian Americans or Pacific Islanders, 9 Hispanic Americans), 1 international. Average age 33. 58 applicants, 64% accepted, 26 enrolled. In 2008, 25 master's awarded. *Degree requirements:* For master's, thesis optional; for doctorate, one foreign language, comprehensive exam, thesis/dissertation, residency. *Entrance requirements:* For master's, GRE General Test, GRE Subject Test, minimum GPA of 3.0; for doctorate, GRE General Test, GRE Subject Test, interview; minimum GPA of 3.5 in literature, 3.0 overall; writing sample. Additional exam requirements/recommendations for international students: Required—TOEFL (minimum score 500 paper-based; 173 computer-based; 61 iBT), IELTS (minimum score 5.5). *Application deadline:* For fall admission, 5/1 priority date for domestic and international students; for spring admission, 11/1 priority date for domestic and international students. Applications are processed on a rolling basis. Application fee: $70. Electronic applications accepted. *Expenses:* Tuition: Full-time $20,760; part-time $865 per credit. Required fees: $300; $150 per semester. Tuition and fees vary according to program. *Financial support:* Fellowships, research assistantships, scholarships/grants available. Support available to part-time students. Financial award application deadline: 3/1; financial award applicants required to submit FAFSA. *Faculty research:* Modern comparative drama, literary theories and criticism, nineteenth and early twentieth century American literature, Chaucer, Elizabethan drama. *Unit head:* Dr. Stephen Sicari, Chair, 718-990-6390, E-mail: sicaris@stjohns.edu. *Application contact:* Kathleen Davis, Director of Graduate Admission, 718-990-2790, Fax: 718-990-5686, E-mail: gradhelp@stjohns.edu.

Saint Louis University, Graduate School, College of Arts and Sciences and Graduate School, Department of English, St. Louis, MO 63103-2097. Offers MA, MA-R, PhD. Part-time programs available. *Degree requirements:* For master's, one foreign language, comprehensive exam, thesis optional, comprehensive oral exam; for doctorate, 2 foreign languages, comprehensive exam, thesis/dissertation, preliminary oral and written exams. *Entrance requirements:* For master's, GRE General Test, GRE Subject Test, letters of recommendation, resumé, writing sample, interview, goal statement, transcripts; for doctorate, GRE General Test, GRE Subject Test, letters of recommendation, resumé, writing sample, interview, goal statement, writing sample. Additional exam requirements/recommendations for international students: Required—TOEFL (minimum score 550 paper-based; 213 computer-based). *Faculty research:* English literature, American literature, post-colonial literature, composition, literary theory.

Saint Louis University–Madrid Campus, Graduate Programs, Program in English, Madrid, Spain. Offers MA. Part-time programs available. *Faculty:* 67 full-time (40 women), 1 part-time/adjunct (0 women). *Students:* 4 full-time (2 women), 7 part-time (3 women). Average age 28. 9 applicants, 100% accepted, 5 enrolled. In 2008, 2 master's awarded. *Degree requirements:* For master's, one foreign language, comprehensive exam, thesis optional. *Entrance requirements:* For master's, GRE General Test, GRE Subject Test, 3 letters of recommendation, writing sample, curriculum vitae. *Application deadline:* For fall admission, 3/31 for domestic and international students; for winter admission, 12/1 for domestic and international students; for spring admission, 2/1 for domestic and international students. Applications are processed on a rolling basis. Application fee: $40. Tuition and fees charges are reported in euros. *Expenses:* Tuition: Full-time 4920 euros; part-time 410 euros per credit. One-time fee: 200 euros. Tuition and fees vary according to course load. *Financial support:* In 2008–09, 11 students received support; teaching assistantships with full tuition reimbursements available, career-related internships or fieldwork, Federal Work-Study, scholarships/grants, health care benefits, tuition waivers (full and partial), and unspecified assistantships available. Financial award application deadline: 5/30; financial award applicants required to submit FAFSA. *Faculty research:* English, Irish and American literature, literary theory, translation, linguistics. *Unit head:* Dr. Paul Anthony Vita, Chair, 34-91-554-58-58, Fax: 34-91-554-62-02, E-mail: vitap@madrid.slu.edu. *Application contact:* Stephanie Reina, Admissions Counselor and Graduate Programs Coordinator, 34-91-554-58-58, Fax: 34-91-554-62-02, E-mail: graduate_admissions@madrid.slu.edu.

St. Mary's University, Graduate School, Department of English and Communication Studies, Program in English Literature and Language, San Antonio, TX 78228-8507. Offers MA. Part-time programs available. *Faculty:* 2 full-time (both women). *Students:* 5 full-time (3 women), 13 part-time (8 women); includes 9 minority (all Hispanic Americans). Average age 29. 6 applicants, 67% accepted, 3 enrolled. In 2008, 2 master's awarded. *Degree requirements:* For master's, comprehensive exam. *Entrance requirements:* For master's, GRE. Additional exam requirements/recommendations for international students: Required—TOEFL (minimum score 550 paper-based; 213 computer-based; 80 iBT). *Application deadline:* Applications are processed on a rolling basis. Application fee: $0. Electronic applications accepted. *Expenses:* Tuition: Full-time $12,006; part-time $667 per credit hour. Required fees: $440; $220 per semester. *Financial support:* In 2008–09, 4 students received support, including 3 fellowships (averaging $2,133 per year), 1 research assistantship (averaging $4,500 per year). Financial award application deadline: 3/31. *Unit head:* Dr. Gwendolyn Diaz, Director, 210-436-3107, E-mail: gdiaz@stmarytx.edu. *Application contact:* Dr. Henry Flores, Dean of the Graduate School, 210-436-3101, Fax: 210-431-2220, E-mail: hflores@stmarytx.edu.

Saint Xavier University, Graduate Studies, School of Arts and Sciences, Department of English, Chicago, IL 60655-3105. Offers English (CAS); literary studies (MA); teaching of writing (MA); writing pedagogy (CAS). Part-time and evening/weekend programs available. *Entrance requirements:* For master's, MAT or GRE, minimum GPA of 3.0.

Salem State College, School of Graduate Studies, Program in English, Salem, MA 01970-5353. Offers English (MA, MAT, MA/MAT); English as a second language (MAT); MA/MAT. Part-time and evening/weekend programs available. *Students:* 18 full-time (14 women), 60 part-time (41 women); includes 3 minority (1 African American, 1 Asian American or Pacific Islander, 1 Hispanic American), 2 international. Average age 33. In 2008, 22 master's awarded. *Degree requirements:* For master's, one foreign language. *Entrance requirements:* For master's, GRE General Test, MAT. *Application deadline:* Applications are processed on a rolling basis. Application fee: $35. *Unit head:* Lisa Mulman, Coordinator, 978-542-6321, E-mail: lmulman@salemstate.edu. *Application contact:* Dr. Marc Glasser, Dean of the Graduate School, 978-542-6323, Fax: 978-542-7215.

Salisbury University, Graduate Division, Program in English, Salisbury, MD 21801-6837. Offers composition, language and rhetoric (MA); literature (MA); teaching English to speakers of other languages (MA). Part-time and evening/weekend programs available. *Faculty:* 19 full-time (7 women), 1 part-time/adjunct (0 women). *Students:* 11 full-time (8 women), 23 part-time (15 women); includes 3 minority (2 African Americans, 1 Hispanic American), 1 international. Average age 29. 21 applicants, 67% accepted, 10 enrolled. In 2008, 22 master's awarded. *Degree requirements:* For master's, comprehensive exam (for some programs), thesis optional. *Entrance requirements:* For master's, GRE General Test, MAT or PRAXIS, minimum GPA of 3.0, 2 letters of recommendation. Additional exam requirements/recommendations for international students: Required—TOEFL (minimum score 550 paper-based; 213 computer-based). *Application deadline:* For fall admission, 8/1 for domestic students; for spring admission, 1/1 for domestic students. Applications are processed on a rolling basis. Application fee: $45. Electronic applications accepted. *Expenses:* Tuition, area resident: Part-time $270 per credit hour. Tuition, state resident: part-time $270 per credit hour. Tuition, nonresident: part-time $566 per credit hour. Required fees: $52 per credit hour. *Financial support:* In 2008–09, 13 students received support, including 13 teaching assistantships with full tuition reimbursements available; career-related internships or fieldwork and scholarships/grants also available. Support available to part-time students. Financial award applicants required to submit FAFSA. *Faculty research:* Shakespeare, Keats, J. D. Salinger, Samuel Johnson, post colonial theory. *Unit head:* Dr. John D. Kalb, Graduate Program Director, 410-543-6049, Fax: 410-548-2142, E-mail: jdkalb@salisbury.edu. *Application contact:* Dr. John D. Kalb, Graduate Program Director, 410-543-6049, Fax: 410-548-2142, E-mail: jdkalb@salisbury.edu.

Sam Houston State University, College of Humanities and Social Sciences, Department of English and Foreign Languages, Huntsville, TX 77341. Offers English (MA). Part-time and evening/weekend programs available. *Faculty:* 7 full-time (2 women). *Students:* 10 full-time (7 women), 35 part-time (24 women); includes 1 minority (Asian American or Pacific Islander). Average age 32. 23 applicants, 100% accepted, 18 enrolled. In 2008, 8 master's awarded. *Degree requirements:* For master's, comprehensive exam, thesis optional. *Entrance requirements:* For master's, GRE General Test. Additional exam requirements/recommendations for international students: Required—TOEFL (minimum score 550 paper-based; 213 computer-based; 79 iBT). *Application deadline:* For fall admission, 8/1 for domestic students; for spring admission, 12/31 for domestic students. Applications are processed on a rolling basis. Application fee: $20. *Expenses:* Tuition, state resident: full-time $3564; part-time $198 per credit hour. Tuition, nonresident: full-time $8622; part-time $479 per credit hour. Required fees: $1290. Tuition and fees vary according to course load and campus/location. *Financial support:* Teaching assistantships, Federal Work-Study and institutionally sponsored loans available. Support available to part-time students. Financial award application deadline: 5/31; financial award applicants required to submit FAFSA. *Unit head:* Dr. Bill Bridges, Chair, 936-294-1402, Fax: 936-294-1408, E-mail: eng_cwb@shsu.edu. *Application contact:* Dr. Paul Child, Advisor, 936-294-1412, E-mail: eng_pwc@shsu.edu.

San Diego State University, Graduate and Research Affairs, College of Arts and Letters, Department of English and Comparative Literature, San Diego, CA 92182. Offers creative writing (MFA); English (MA). *Degree requirements:* For master's, one foreign language, comprehensive exam (for some programs), thesis (for some programs). *Entrance requirements:* For master's, GRE General Test, minimum GPA of 2.85, writing sample, 3 letters of recommendation. Additional exam requirements/recommendations for international students: Required—TOEFL. Electronic applications accepted.

San Francisco State University, Division of Graduate Studies, College of Humanities, Department of English Language and Literature, Program in Composition, San Francisco, CA 94132-1722. Offers MA, Certificate. Part-time programs available. *Degree requirements:* For master's, comprehensive exam. *Entrance requirements:* Additional exam requirements/recommendations for international students: Required—TOEFL, TWE.

San Francisco State University, Division of Graduate Studies, College of Humanities, Department of English Language and Literature, Program in Literature, San Francisco, CA 94132-1722. Offers MA. Part-time programs available.

San Jose State University, Graduate Studies and Research, College of Humanities and the Arts, Department of English and Comparative Literature, San Jose, CA 95192-0001. Offers creative writing (MFA); literature (MA); secondary English education (Certificate). *Degree requirements:* For master's, one foreign language, thesis or alternative. *Entrance requirements:* For master's, GRE. Additional exam requirements/recommendations for international students: Required—TOEFL. Electronic applications accepted.

Seton Hall University, College of Arts and Sciences, Department of English, South Orange, NJ 07079-2697. Offers MA. Part-time and evening/weekend programs available. *Degree requirements:* For master's, one foreign language, comprehensive exam, thesis optional, research seminars. Electronic applications accepted. *Faculty research:* The essay, modern poetry, the novel, medieval poetry, Renaissance drama.

See Close-Up on page 443.

Sewanee: The University of the South, Sewanee School of Letters, Sewanee, TN 37383-1000. Offers American literature and English literature (MA); creative writing (MFA). Programs offered only during the summer. Part-time programs available. *Faculty:* 8 full-time (3 women). *Students:* 36 full-time (20 women), 6 part-time (2 women); includes 3 minority (2 African Americans, 1 Asian American or Pacific Islander). Average age 31. 20 applicants, 95% accepted, 12 enrolled. *Degree requirements:* For master's, thesis (for some programs). *Entrance requirements:* For master's, writing sample, 2 letters of recommendation. *Application deadline:* For spring admission, 2/1 priority date for domestic and international students. Applications are processed on a rolling basis. Application fee: $40. Electronic applications accepted. *Expenses:* Contact institution. *Financial support:* Application deadline: 4/1; *Unit head:* Dr. John M Grammer, Director, 931-598-1483, Fax: 931-598-3303, E-mail: jgrammer@sewanee.edu. *Application contact:* Margaret D Binnicker, Coordinator, 931-598-1636, Fax: 931-598-3303, E-mail: mbinnick@sewanee.edu.

Simmons College, College of Arts and Sciences Graduate Studies, Program in Children's Literature, Boston, MA 02115. Offers children's literature (MA); writing for children (MFA); MA/MFA; MAT/MA. Part-time programs available. *Faculty:* 3 full-time (all women), 5 part-time/adjunct (3 women). *Students:* 3 full-time (all women), 18 part-time (17 women); includes 1 minority (Asian American or Pacific Islander). Average age 31. 71 applicants, 68% accepted, 37 enrolled. In 2008, 11 master's awarded. *Degree requirements:* For master's, thesis optional. *Entrance requirements:* For master's, writing portfolio (for MFA). Additional exam requirements/recommendations for international students: Required—TOEFL (minimum score 600 paper-based; 250 computer-based; 100 iBT). *Application deadline:* For fall admission, 8/1 priority date for domestic and international students; for winter admission, 12/15 priority date for domestic and international students; for spring admission, 5/1 priority date for domestic and international students. Applications are processed on a rolling basis. Application fee: $35. Electronic applications accepted. *Expenses:* Contact institution. *Financial support:* In 2008–09, 5 students received support, including 2 fellowships, 1 research assistantship (averaging $2,000 per year), 8 teaching assistantships (averaging $2,000 per year); scholarships/grants and unspecified assistantships also available. Financial award application deadline: 3/1; financial award applicants required to submit FAFSA. *Faculty research:* Construction of childhood and adolescence, gender and reading, narratology and young adult relation, queer theory and children's literature, bio criticism. *Unit head:* Dr. Cathryn Mercier, Associate Dean, Director—Center for the Study of Children's Literature, 617-521-2541. *Application contact:* Kristen Haack, Director, Graduate Studies Admission, 617-521-2917, Fax: 617-521-3058, E-mail: gsa@simmons.edu.

Simmons College, College of Arts and Sciences Graduate Studies, Program in English, Boston, MA 02115. Offers MA, MAT/MA. Part-time programs available. *Faculty:* 10 full-time (4 women). *Students:* 5 full-time (all women), 20 part-time (19 women); includes 1 minority (Asian American or Pacific Islander). Average age 26. 31 applicants, 58% accepted, 8 enrolled. In 2008, 12 master's awarded. *Degree requirements:* For master's, one foreign language, thesis optional. *Entrance requirements:* For master's, analytical writing sample. Additional exam requirements/recommendations for international students: Required—TOEFL (minimum score 600 paper-based; 250 computer-based; 100 iBT). *Application deadline:* For fall admission, 8/1 priority date for domestic and international students; for winter admission, 12/15 priority date for domestic and international students; for spring admission, 5/1 priority date for domestic and international students. Applications are processed on a rolling basis. Application fee: $35. Electronic applications accepted. *Expenses:* Contact institution. *Financial support:* In 2008–09, 9 students received support, including research assistantships (averaging $2,000 per year), 12 teaching assistantships (averaging $2,000 per year); scholarships/grants and unspecified assistantships also available. Financial award application deadline: 3/1; financial award applicants required to submit FAFSA. *Faculty research:* Postcolonial literature and theory, film studies, 19th century American women writers, creative writing, psychoanalysis and race. *Unit head:* Dr. Pamela Bromberg, Professor of English, 617-521-2214 Ext. 2176. *Application contact:* Kristen Haack, Director, Graduate Studies Admission, 617-521-2917, Fax: 617-521-3058, E-mail: gsa@simmons.edu.

Simon Fraser University, Graduate Studies, Faculty of Arts and Social Sciences, Department of English, Burnaby, BC V5A 1S6, Canada. Offers MA, PhD. Part-time programs available. *Degree requirements:* For master's, one foreign language, thesis or alternative; for doctorate, one foreign language, thesis/dissertation, field exams. *Entrance requirements:* For master's, minimum GPA of 3.0; for doctorate, minimum GPA of 3.5. Additional exam requirements/recommendations for international students: Required—TOEFL or IELTS. *Faculty research:* Literary criticism, literature and psychoanalysis, Renaissance drama and poetry, Shakespeare, Canadian and American literature.

Slippery Rock University of Pennsylvania, Graduate Studies (Recruitment), College of Humanities, Fine and Performing Arts, Department of English, Slippery Rock, PA 16057-1383. Offers literature and composition (MA); professional writing (MA). Part-time and evening/weekend programs available. *Degree requirements:* For master's, comprehensive exam (for some programs), thesis (for some programs). *Entrance requirements:* For master's, GRE General Test, MAT, minimum GPA of 2.75. *Application deadline:* For fall admission, 7/1 priority date for domestic and international students; for spring admission, 11/1 priority date for domestic and international students. Applications are processed on a rolling basis. Application fee: $25. Electronic applications accepted. *Expenses:* Tuition, area resident: Full-time $6430; part-time $357 per credit. Tuition, state resident: full-time $6430; part-time $357 per credit. Tuition, nonresident: full-time $10,288; part-time $572 per credit. Required fees: $2062; $158 per credit. *Financial support:* Career-related internships or fieldwork, Federal Work-Study, scholarships/grants, and unspecified assistantships available. Support available to part-time students. Financial award application deadline: 5/1; financial award applicants required to submit FAFSA. *Unit head:* Dr. Joseph McCarren, Graduate Coordinator, 724-738-2868, Fax: 724-738-4829, E-mail: joseph.mccarren@sru.edu. *Application contact:* Angela Piverotto, Interim Director of Graduate Studies, 724-738-2051, Fax: 724-738-2146, E-mail: graduate.admissions@sru.edu.

Sonoma State University, School of Arts and Humanities, Department of English, Rohnert Park, CA 94928-3609. Offers American literature (MA); creative writing (MA); English literature (MA); world literature (MA). Part-time and evening/weekend programs available. *Degree requirements:* For master's, one foreign language, thesis or alternative. *Entrance requirements:* For master's, minimum GPA of 2.5. *Faculty research:* Women writers, international literature in English, literature of fantasy.

South Dakota State University, Graduate School, College of Arts and Science, Department of English, Brookings, SD 57007. Offers MA. Part-time programs available. *Faculty:* 9 full-time (3 women). *Students:* 1 (woman) full-time, 27 part-time (16 women); includes 3 minority (2 Asian Americans or Pacific Islanders, 1 Hispanic American). 10 applicants, 90% accepted, 9 enrolled. In 2008, 5 master's awarded. *Degree requirements:* For master's, comprehensive exam (for some programs), thesis (for some programs), oral and written exams. *Entrance requirements:* For master's, minimum GPA of 2.75. Additional exam requirements/recommendations for international students: Required—TOEFL (minimum score 600 paper-based; 250 computer-based; 100 iBT). *Application deadline:* For fall admission, 4/15 priority date for international students; for spring admission, 8/15 priority date for international students. Applications are processed on a rolling basis. Application fee: $35. *Financial support:* In 2008–09, 14 teaching assistantships with partial tuition reimbursements (averaging $15,750 per year) were awarded; unspecified assistantships also available. *Faculty research:* English and American literature topics, regional literature (Midwestern), women's literature, Lakota literature and culture, rhetoric and writing. *Unit head:* Dr. Kathleen Donovan, Head, 605-688-5191, Fax: 605-688-5192, E-mail: kathleen.donovan@sdstate.edu. *Application contact:* Dr. Jason McEntee, Graduate Coordinator, 605-688-5191, Fax: 605-688-5192, E-mail: jason.mcentee@sdstate.edu.

Southeastern Louisiana University, College of Arts, Humanities and Social Sciences, Department of English, Hammond, LA 70402. Offers MA. Part-time and evening/weekend programs available. *Faculty:* 14 full-time (8 women). *Students:* 18 full-time (9 women), 31 part-time (19 women); includes 9 minority (all African Americans). Average age 29. 16 applicants, 94% accepted, 11 enrolled. In 2008, 12 master's awarded. *Degree requirements:* For master's, one foreign language, comprehensive exam, thesis optional. *Entrance requirements:* For master's, GRE General Test (850 or better), 24 undergraduate credit hours in English, minimum GPA of 2.5. Additional exam requirements/recommendations for international students: Required—TOEFL (minimum score 500 paper-based; 173 computer-based; 61 iBT). *Application deadline:* For fall admission, 7/15 priority date for domestic students, 6/1 priority date for international students; for spring admission, 12/1 priority date for domestic students, 10/1 priority date for international students. Applications are processed on a rolling basis. Application fee: $20 ($30 for international students). Electronic applications accepted. *Expenses:* Tuition, area resident: Full-time $2376. Tuition, state resident: full-time $2376. Tuition, nonresident: full-time $6876. Required fees: $1105. *Financial support:* In 2008–09, 2 students received support, including 1 fellowship with full tuition reimbursement available (averaging $11,400 per year), 1 teaching assistantship with full tuition reimbursement available (averaging $10,100 per year); career-related internships or fieldwork, Federal Work-Study, institutionally sponsored loans, scholarships/grants, unspecified assistantships, and administrative assistantships also available. Support available to part-time students. Financial award application deadline: 5/1; financial award applicants required to submit FAFSA. *Faculty research:* Native American, composition/rhetoric, postcolonial, Chaucer, professional writing. *Unit head:* Dr. David Hanson, Department Head, 985-549-2100, Fax: 985-549-5021, E-mail: dhanson@selu.edu. *Application contact:* Sandra Meyers, Graduate Admissions Analyst, 985-549-2066, Fax: 985-549-5632, E-mail: admissions@selu.edu.

Southeast Missouri State University, School of Graduate Studies, Department of English, Cape Girardeau, MO 63701-4799. Offers English (MA); teaching English to speakers of other languages (MA). Part-time and evening/weekend programs available. Postbaccalaureate distance learning degree programs offered (no on-campus study). *Faculty:* 16 full-time (9 women). *Students:* 24 full-time (15 women), 66 part-time (58 women); includes 2 minority (1 African American, 1 Hispanic American), 4 international. Average age 35. 39 applicants, 92% accepted. In 2008, 35 master's awarded. *Degree requirements:* For master's, comprehensive exam (for some programs), thesis or alternative. *Entrance requirements:* For master's, minimum undergraduate GPA of 2.5. Additional exam requirements/recommendations for international students: Required—TOEFL (minimum score 550 paper-based; 213 computer-based); Recommended—IELTS (minimum score 6). *Application deadline:* For fall admission, 8/1 for domestic students, 7/1 for international students; for spring admission, 11/21 for domestic students, 11/1 for international students. Applications are processed on a rolling basis. Application fee: $25 ($100 for international students). Electronic applications accepted. *Expenses:* Tuition, area resident: Part-time $213.30 per credit hour. Tuition, state resident: part-time $213.30 per credit hour. Tuition, nonresident: part-time $393.30 per credit hour. Required fees: $23.70 per credit hour. *Financial support:* In 2008–09, 16 students received support, including 16 teaching assistantships with full tuition reimbursements available (averaging $7,600 per year); unspecified assistantships also available. Financial award applicants required to submit FAFSA. *Faculty research:* Literature, writing, linguistics, education, TESOL. *Unit head:* Dr. Carol Scates, Chairperson and Graduate Program Coordinator, 573-651-2156, E-mail: cscates@semo.edu. *Application contact:* Marsha L. Arant, Senior Administrative Assistant, School of Graduate Studies, 573-651-2192, Fax: 573-651-2001, E-mail: marant@semo.edu.

Southern Connecticut State University, School of Graduate Studies, School of Arts and Sciences, Department of English, New Haven, CT 06515-1355. Offers MA, MS, MLS/MS. Part-time and evening/weekend programs available. *Degree requirements:* For master's, one foreign language, thesis or alternative. *Entrance requirements:* For master's, interview. Electronic applications accepted.

Southern Illinois University Carbondale, Graduate School, College of Liberal Arts, Department of English, Carbondale, IL 62901-4701. Offers composition (MA, PhD), including composition, literature, rhetoric; creative writing (MFA). *Degree requirements:* For master's, one foreign language, thesis; for doctorate, 2 foreign languages, thesis/dissertation. *Entrance requirements:* For master's, GRE General Test, GRE Subject Test, minimum GPA of 2.7; for doctorate, GRE General Test, GRE Subject Test, minimum GPA of 3.25. Additional exam requirements/recommendations for international students: Required—TOEFL. *Faculty research:* British literature, English literature, modern Continental literature, literary criticism and theory, film studies, Irish studies.

See Close-Up on page 445.

Southern Illinois University Edwardsville, Graduate Studies and Research, College of Arts and Sciences, Department of English Language and Literature, Program in American and English Literature, Edwardsville, IL 62026-0001. Offers MA, Postbaccalaureate Certificate. Part-time programs available. *Students:* 6 full-time (3 women), 16 part-time (11 women); includes 3 minority (1 African American, 1 Asian American or Pacific Islander, 1 Hispanic American). Average age 26. 22 applicants, 45% accepted. In 2008, 4 master's awarded. *Degree requirements:* For master's, one foreign language, thesis or alternative, written papers, oral examination. *Entrance requirements:* Additional exam requirements/recommendations for international students: Required—TOEFL (minimum score 550 paper-based; 213 computer-based; 79 iBT), IELTS (minimum score 6.5). *Application deadline:* For fall admission, 7/20 for domestic students, 6/1 for international students; for spring admission, 12/14 for domestic students, 10/1 for international students. Applications are processed on a rolling basis. Application fee: $30. Electronic applications accepted. *Expenses:* Tuition, area resident: Full-time $5838. Tuition, nonresident: full-time $14,596. Required fees: $1525. *Financial support:* Fellowships with full tuition reimbursements, research assistantships with full tuition reimbursements, teaching assistantships with full tuition reimbursements, Federal Work-Study, institutionally sponsored loans, and unspecified assistantships available. Support available to part-time students. Financial award application deadline: 3/1; financial award applicants required to submit FAFSA. *Unit head:* Dr. Eileen Joy, Director, 618-650-3971, E-mail: ejoy@siue.edu. *Application contact:* Dr. Eileen Joy, Director, 618-650-3971, E-mail: ejoy@siue.edu.

Southern Methodist University, Dedman College, Department of English, Dallas, TX 75275. Offers MA, PhD. *Faculty:* 18 full-time (6 women). *Students:* 13 full-time (6 women), 1 (woman) part-time; includes 1 minority (African American). Average age 27. 63 applicants, 16% accepted, 6 enrolled. In 2008, 5 master's awarded. Terminal master's awarded for partial completion of doctoral program. *Degree requirements:* For master's, one foreign language, comprehensive exam, thesis optional, oral exam; for doctorate, one foreign language, comprehensive exam, thesis/dissertation. *Entrance requirements:* For master's, GRE General Test, minimum GPA of 3.0; for doctorate, GRE General Test, minimum GPA of 3.5, BA in English or other appropriate field. Additional exam requirements/recommendations for international students: Required—TOEFL (minimum score 550 paper-based). *Application deadline:* For fall admission, 1/15 priority date for domestic and international students. Application fee: $75. Electronic applications accepted. *Financial support:* In 2008–09, 12 students received support, including 12 fellowships with full tuition reimbursements available (averaging $24,800 per year); health care benefits and tuition waivers (full) also available. Financial award application deadline: 1/15. *Faculty research:* British/American literature, critical theory, medieval studies, gender studies, book history. *Unit head:* Prof. Nina Schwartz, Chair, 214-768-2946, Fax: 214-768-1234, E-mail: nschwart@smu.edu. *Application contact:* Prof. Darryl Dickson-Carr, Director of Graduate Studies, 214-768-4689, Fax: 214-768-1234, E-mail: dcarr@smu.edu.

Stanford University, School of Humanities and Sciences, Department of English, Stanford, CA 94305-9991. Offers MA, PhD. Terminal master's awarded for partial completion of doctoral program. *Degree requirements:* For master's, one foreign language, thesis (for some programs);

English

Stanford University (continued)
for doctorate, 2 foreign languages, thesis/dissertation, oral exam. *Entrance requirements:* For master's and doctorate, GRE General Test, GRE Subject Test. Additional exam requirements/recommendations for international students: Required—TOEFL. Electronic applications accepted.

State University of New York at Binghamton, Graduate School, School of Arts and Sciences, Department of English, Binghamton, NY 13902-6000. Offers MA, PhD. Part-time programs available. *Faculty:* 32 full-time (16 women), 26 part-time/adjunct (14 women). *Students:* 65 full-time (30 women), 52 part-time (35 women); includes 12 minority (2 African Americans, 1 American Indian/Alaska Native, 3 Asian Americans or Pacific Islanders, 6 Hispanic Americans), 9 international. Average age 32. 121 applicants, 53% accepted, 19 enrolled. In 2008, 14 master's, 13 doctorates awarded. Terminal master's awarded for partial completion of doctoral program. *Degree requirements:* For master's, thesis (for some programs), written exam; for doctorate, one foreign language, comprehensive exam, thesis/dissertation. *Entrance requirements:* For master's and doctorate, GRE General Test, GRE Subject Test, critical writing sample. Additional exam requirements/recommendations for international students: Required—TOEFL. *Application deadline:* For fall admission, 4/15 priority date for domestic students, 1/15 priority date for international students; for spring admission, 11/1 for domestic students, 10/1 priority date for international students. Applications are processed on a rolling basis. Application fee: $60. Electronic applications accepted. *Expenses:* Tuition, area resident: Full-time $6900; part-time $288 per credit. Tuition, state resident: full-time $6900; part-time $288 per credit. Tuition, nonresident: full-time $10,920; part-time $455 per credit. Required fees: $1130. Part-time tuition and fees vary according to course load, program and student level. *Financial support:* In 2008–09, 58 students received support, including 4 fellowships with full tuition reimbursements available (averaging $15,000 per year), 45 teaching assistantships with full tuition reimbursements available (averaging $15,000 per year); research assistantships, career-related internships or fieldwork, Federal Work-Study, institutionally sponsored loans, scholarships/grants, health care benefits, and unspecified assistantships also available. Financial award application deadline: 2/15; financial award applicants required to submit FAFSA. *Unit head:* Dr. David Bartine, Chairperson, 607-777-2169, E-mail: dbartine@binghamton.edu. *Application contact:* Victoria Williams, Recruiting and Admissions Coordinator, 607-777-2151, Fax: 607-777-2501, E-mail: vwilliam@binghamton.edu.

State University of New York at Fredonia, Graduate Studies, Department of English, Fredonia, NY 14063-1136. Offers MA, MS Ed. Part-time and evening/weekend programs available. *Degree requirements:* For master's, thesis optional.

State University of New York at New Paltz, Graduate School, School of Liberal Arts and Sciences, Department of English, New Paltz, NY 12561. Offers MA. Part-time and evening/weekend programs available. *Faculty:* 12 full-time (4 women). *Students:* 16 full-time (11 women), 39 part-time (23 women); includes 4 minority (1 African American, 1 Asian American or Pacific Islander, 2 Hispanic Americans), 1 international. Average age 28. 25 applicants, 80% accepted, 19 enrolled. In 2008, 21 master's awarded. *Degree requirements:* For master's, comprehensive exam, thesis (for some programs), foreign language proficiency exam. *Entrance requirements:* For master's, minimum GPA of 3.0, 10-15 page writing sample. Additional exam requirements/recommendations for international students: Required—TOEFL (minimum score 550 paper-based; 213 computer-based; 80 iBT). *Application deadline:* For fall admission, 5/15 priority date for domestic students, 5/15 for international students; for spring admission, 11/15 for domestic and international students. Application fee: $50. Electronic applications accepted. *Financial support:* In 2008–09, 20 students received support, including 2 research assistantships with partial tuition reimbursements available (averaging $5,000 per year), 17 teaching assistantships with partial tuition reimbursements available (averaging $5,000 per year); career-related internships or fieldwork, Federal Work-Study, institutionally sponsored loans, and tuition waivers (full) also available. Financial award application deadline: 8/1; financial award applicants required to submit FAFSA. *Faculty research:* Twentieth-century British literature, Hemingway and Modernism, British Modernist fiction, Faulkner and the Southern Renaissance, revisionary approaches to early twentieth-century literature. *Unit head:* Dr. Thomas Olsen, Chair, 845-257-2723, E-mail: olsent@newpaltz.edu. *Application contact:* Dr. Daniel Kempton, Graduate Coordinator, 845-257-2728, E-mail: kemptond@newpaltz.edu.

State University of New York at Oswego, Graduate Studies, College of Arts and Sciences, Department of English, Oswego, NY 13126. Offers MA. Part-time programs available. *Degree requirements:* For master's, thesis optional. *Entrance requirements:* Additional exam requirements/recommendations for international students: Required—TOEFL (minimum score 560 paper-based; 220 computer-based).

State University of New York College at Cortland, Graduate Studies, School of Arts and Sciences, Department of English, Cortland, NY 13045. Offers MA, MAT, MS Ed. Part-time and evening/weekend programs available. *Degree requirements:* For master's, one foreign language, comprehensive exam, thesis (for some programs). *Entrance requirements:* For master's, GRE General Test.

State University of New York College at Potsdam, School of Arts and Sciences, Department of English and Communication, Potsdam, NY 13676. Offers English and communication (MA). Part-time and evening/weekend programs available. *Faculty:* 6 full-time (3 women), 1 (woman) part-time/adjunct. *Students:* 14 full-time (7 women), 9 part-time (7 women), 1 international. 13 applicants, 77% accepted, 8 enrolled. In 2008, 6 master's awarded. *Degree requirements:* For master's, one foreign language, thesis or alternative. *Entrance requirements:* For master's, minimum GPA of 3.0 in last 60 hours of undergraduate course work. Additional exam requirements/recommendations for international students: Required—TOEFL (minimum score 550 paper-based; 213 computer-based; 80 iBT), IELTS (minimum score 6). *Application deadline:* For fall admission, 4/1 priority date for domestic and international students; for spring admission, 10/15 priority date for domestic and international students. Applications are processed on a rolling basis. Application fee: $50. *Expenses:* Tuition, state resident: full-time $7390; part-time $328 per credit hour. Tuition, nonresident: full-time $12,085; part-time $552 per credit hour. Required fees: $952; $43.70 per credit hour. *Financial support:* In 2008–09, 1 student received support; teaching assistantships with full tuition reimbursements available, Federal Work-Study and unspecified assistantships available. Support available to part-time students. Financial award application deadline: 3/1; financial award applicants required to submit FAFSA. *Unit head:* Dr. Lisa Wilson, Director of Graduate Studies, English and Communication, 315-267-2004, Fax: 315-267-3256, E-mail: wilsonlm@potsdam.edu. *Application contact:* Peter Cutler, Graduate Admissions Counselor, 315-267-3154, Fax: 315-267-4802, E-mail: cutlerpj@potsdam.edu.

State University of New York College at Potsdam, School of Education and Professional Studies, Program in Secondary Education, Potsdam, NY 13676. Offers English (MST); mathematics (with grades 5-6 extension) (MST); science (MST), including biology, chemistry, earth science, physics; social studies (MS Ed); Social Studies (with grades 5-6 extension) (MST). *Accreditation:* NCATE. *Faculty:* 10 full-time (4 women), 3 part-time/adjunct (all women). *Students:* 63 full-time (36 women), 7 part-time (3 women); includes 2 minority (1 African American, 1 Hispanic American), 11 international. 19 applicants, 63% accepted, 9 enrolled. In 2008, 48 master's awarded. *Degree requirements:* For master's, thesis optional, culminating experience. *Entrance requirements:* For master's, minimum GPA of 2.75 in last 60 hours of course work (3.0 for English program). Additional exam requirements/recommendations for international students: Required—TOEFL (minimum score 550 paper-based; 213 computer-based; 80 iBT), IELTS (minimum score 6). *Application deadline:* For fall admission, 4/1 priority date for domestic and international students; for spring admission, 10/15 priority date for domestic and international students. Applications are processed on a rolling basis. Application fee: $50. *Expenses:* Tuition, state resident: full-time $7390; part-time $328 per credit hour. Tuition, nonresident: full-time $12,085; part-time $552 per credit hour. Required fees: $952; $43.70 per credit hour. *Financial support:* Fellowships, teaching assistantships, career-related internships or fieldwork, Federal Work-Study, scholarships/grants, and unspecified assistantships available. Support available to part-time students. Financial award application deadline: 3/1; financial award applicants required to submit FAFSA. *Unit head:* Dr. Peter Brouwer, Chairperson, 315-267-3018, Fax: 315-267-4802, E-mail: brouweps@potsdam.edu. *Application contact:* Peter Cutler, Graduate Admissions Counselor, 315-267-3154, Fax: 315-267-4802, E-mail: cutlerpj@potsdam.edu.

Stephen F. Austin State University, Graduate School, College of Liberal Arts, Department of English and Philosophy, Nacogdoches, TX 75962. Offers English (MA). *Degree requirements:* For master's, comprehensive exam. *Entrance requirements:* For master's, GRE General Test. Additional exam requirements/recommendations for international students: Required—TOEFL. *Faculty research:* Creative writing, Latin American literature, modern American literature, modern British literature, literature for children.

Stetson University, College of Arts and Sciences, Division of Humanities, Department of English, DeLand, FL 32723. Offers MA. *Students:* 4 part-time (all women). Average age 27. In 2008, 2 master's awarded. *Degree requirements:* For master's, thesis. *Entrance requirements:* For master's, GRE General Test. *Application deadline:* For fall admission, 3/1 priority date for domestic students; for spring admission, 11/1 for domestic students. Applications are processed on a rolling basis. Application fee: $25. *Unit head:* Dr. Joseph Witek, Director, 386-822-7720. *Application contact:* Diana Belian, Office of Graduate Studies, 386-822-7075, Fax: 386-822-7388, E-mail: dbelian@stetson.edu.

Stony Brook University, State University of New York, Graduate School, College of Arts and Sciences, Department of Comparative Literary and Cultural Studies, Stony Brook, NY 11794. Offers comparative literature (MA, PhD); cultural studies (PhD). Evening/weekend programs available. *Faculty:* 7 full-time (1 woman). *Students:* 35 full-time (21 women), 4 part-time (3 women); includes 6 minority (5 Asian Americans or Pacific Islanders, 1 Hispanic American), 17 international. Average age 30. 101 applicants, 19% accepted. In 2008, 1 master's, 1 doctorate awarded. Terminal master's awarded for partial completion of doctoral program. *Degree requirements:* For master's, 2 foreign languages, exam; for doctorate, 3 foreign languages, comprehensive exam, thesis/dissertation. *Entrance requirements:* For master's and doctorate, GRE General Test, minimum GPA of 3.5 in major, 3.0 overall. Additional exam requirements/recommendations for international students: Required—TOEFL. *Application deadline:* For fall admission, 1/15 for domestic students. Application fee: $60. *Expenses:* Tuition, area resident: Full-time $7880; part-time $328 per credit hour. Tuition, state resident: full-time $7880; part-time $328 per credit hour. Tuition, nonresident: full-time $13,250; part-time $552 per credit hour. Required fees: $848. *Financial support:* In 2008–09, 24 teaching assistantships were awarded; fellowships, research assistantships also available. *Faculty research:* Literary theory, interdisciplinary studies, literary history. *Unit head:* Prof. Krin Gabbard, Chairman, 631-632-7456. *Application contact:* Dr. Kent Marks, Assistant Dean, Admissions and Records, 631-632-4723, Fax: 631-632-7243, E-mail: kmarks@notes.cc.sunysb.edu.

Stony Brook University, State University of New York, Graduate School, College of Arts and Sciences, Department of English, Stony Brook, NY 11794. Offers composition studies (Certificate); English (MA, PhD); English education (MAT). MAT offered through the School of Professional Development. Evening/weekend programs available. *Faculty:* 25 full-time (10 women), 1 part-time/adjunct. *Students:* 77 full-time (46 women), 23 part-time (18 women); includes 12 minority (5 African Americans, 3 Asian Americans or Pacific Islanders, 4 Hispanic Americans), 5 international. Average age 32. 154 applicants, 23% accepted. In 2008, 16 master's, 7 doctorates awarded. Terminal master's awarded for partial completion of doctoral program. *Degree requirements:* For doctorate, thesis/dissertation. *Entrance requirements:* For master's and doctorate, GRE General Test. Additional exam requirements/recommendations for international students: Required—TOEFL. *Application deadline:* For fall admission, 1/15 for domestic students. Application fee: $60. *Expenses:* Tuition, area resident: Full-time $7880; part-time $328 per credit hour. Tuition, state resident: full-time $7880; part-time $328 per credit hour. Tuition, nonresident: full-time $13,250; part-time $552 per credit hour. Required fees: $848. *Financial support:* In 2008–09, 42 teaching assistantships were awarded; fellowships, research assistantships also available. *Faculty research:* American literature, British literature, literary critical theory, rhetoric and composition theory, women's studies. *Unit head:* Dr. Stephen Spector, Chair, 631-632-7420, Fax: 631-632-7568. *Application contact:* Dr. Helen M. Cooper, Director, 631-632-7784, Fax: 631-632-7568, E-mail: hcooper@notes.cc.sunysb.edu.

Sul Ross State University, School of Arts and Sciences, Department of Languages and Literature, Alpine, TX 79832. Offers English (MA). Part-time and evening/weekend programs available. *Degree requirements:* For master's, thesis optional. *Entrance requirements:* For master's, GRE General Test, minimum GPA of 2.5 in last 60 hours of undergraduate work. *Faculty research:* Narrative theory, feminist literary criticism, autobiography studies, multiculturalism, biblical narrative.

Syracuse University, Graduate School, College of Arts and Sciences, Programs in English, Syracuse, NY 13244. Offers MA, PhD. *Entrance requirements:* For master's and doctorate, GRE General Test. Additional exam requirements/recommendations for international students: Required—TOEFL.

Tarleton State University, College of Graduate Studies, College of Liberal and Fine Arts, Department of English and Languages, Stephenville, TX 76402. Offers English (MA). Part-time and evening/weekend programs available. *Faculty:* 6 full-time (4 women). *Students:* 5 full-time (1 woman), 6 part-time (5 women). Average age 33. 4 applicants, 75% accepted, 2 enrolled. In 2008, 1 master's awarded. *Degree requirements:* For master's, comprehensive exam, thesis (for some programs). *Entrance requirements:* For master's, GRE General Test, minimum GPA of 3.0. Additional exam requirements/recommendations for international students: Required—TOEFL (minimum score 550 paper-based; 213 computer-based; 80 iBT). *Application deadline:* For fall admission, 8/5 priority date for domestic students; for spring admission, 12/1 for domestic students. Applications are processed on a rolling basis. Application fee: $30 ($130 for international students). Electronic applications accepted. *Expenses:* Tuition, area resident: Full-time $2853; part-time $158.50 per credit hour. Tuition, state resident: full-time $2853; part-time $158.50 per credit hour. Tuition, nonresident: full-time $7551; part-time $419.50 per credit hour. Required fees: $1040; $42 per credit hour. $124 per semester. Tuition and fees vary according to course load and campus/location. *Financial support:* In 2008–09, 5 research assistantships (averaging $14,133 per year) were awarded; teaching assistantships, career-related internships or fieldwork and Federal Work-Study also available. Support available to part-time students. Financial award application deadline: 5/1; financial award applicants required to submit FAFSA. *Unit head:* Dr. Jeanelle Barrett, Head, 254-968-9039, Fax: 254-968-1931, E-mail: jbarrett@tarleton.edu. *Application contact:* Information Contact, 254-968-9104, Fax: 254-968-9670, E-mail: gradoffice@tarleton.edu.

Temple University, Graduate School, College of Liberal Arts, Department of English, Philadelphia, PA 19122-6096. Offers creative writing (MA); English (MA, PhD). Part-time programs available. *Degree requirements:* For doctorate, 2 foreign languages, thesis/dissertation. *Entrance requirements:* For master's and doctorate, GRE General Test, minimum GPA of 3.0. Additional exam requirements/recommendations for international students: Required—TOEFL (minimum score 550 paper-based; 213 computer-based; 79 iBT). Electronic applications accepted. *Faculty research:* Renaissance, Victorian, Modern British, and American literature; critical theory; composition.

Tennessee State University, The School of Graduate Studies and Research, College of Arts and Sciences, Department of Languages, Literature, and Philosophy, Nashville, TN 37209-1561. Offers English (MA). *Faculty:* 16 full-time (9 women), 3 part-time/adjunct (2 women). *Students:* 11 full-time (8 women), 12 part-time (8 women); includes 15 minority (all African Americans). Average age 27. 22 applicants, 45% accepted, 6 enrolled. In 2008, 3 master's awarded. *Degree requirements:* For master's, thesis optional. *Entrance requirements:* For master's, GRE General Test or MAT. *Application deadline:* For fall admission, 3/1 priority date for domestic students, 4/1 priority date for international students. Applications are processed on a rolling basis. Application fee: $25. Electronic applications accepted. *Faculty research:* American literature, British literature, Anglo/Saxon literature, cultural/women's studies. *Unit* *head:* Dr. Warren Wescott, Head, 615-963-5715, E-mail: wwescott@tnstate.edu. *Application contact:* Dr. Jo Helen Railsback, Graduate Coordinator, 615-963-5724.

Tennessee Technological University, Graduate School, College of Arts and Sciences, Department of English, Cookeville, TN 38505. Offers MA. Part-time programs available. *Degree requirements:* For master's, thesis. *Entrance requirements:* For master's, GRE General Test. Additional exam requirements/recommendations for international students: Required—TOEFL.

Texas A&M International University, Office of Graduate Studies and Research, College of Arts and Sciences, Department of Language and Literature, Laredo, TX 78041-1900. Offers English (MA); Hispanic studies (PhD); Spanish (MA). *Entrance requirements:* For master's, GRE General Test. Additional exam requirements/recommendations for international students: Required—TOEFL (minimum score 550 paper-based; 213 computer-based).

Texas A&M University, College of Liberal Arts, Department of English, College Station, TX 77843. Offers MA, PhD. *Faculty:* 35. *Students:* 106 full-time (72 women), 15 part-time (12 women); includes 14 minority (5 African Americans, 1 American Indian/Alaska Native, 2 Asian Americans or Pacific Islanders, 6 Hispanic Americans), 26 international. Average age 24. In 2008, 16 master's, 7 doctorates awarded. Terminal master's awarded for partial completion of doctoral program. *Degree requirements:* For master's, one foreign language, thesis optional; for doctorate, 2 foreign languages, thesis/dissertation. *Entrance requirements:* For master's and doctorate, GRE General Test, sample of written work. Additional exam requirements/recommendations for international students: Required—TOEFL. *Application deadline:* For fall admission, 2/1 priority date for domestic and international students; for spring admission, 10/1 priority date for domestic and international students. Applications are processed on a rolling basis. Application fee: $50 ($75 for international students). Electronic applications accepted. *Expenses:* Tuition, area resident: Full-time $3838.50. Tuition, state resident: full-time $3838.50. Tuition, nonresident: full-time $8897. Required fees: $2359.60. *Financial support:* In 2008–09, fellowships with partial tuition reimbursements (averaging $10,000 per year), research assistantships with partial tuition reimbursements (averaging $12,000 per year), teaching assistantships with partial tuition reimbursements (averaging $12,000 per year) were awarded; career-related internships or fieldwork, Federal Work-Study, institutionally sponsored loans, scholarships/grants, and unspecified assistantships also available. Financial award application deadline: 4/1. *Faculty research:* American, Renaissance, Medieval, textual studies, discourse studies. *Unit head:* Dr. Jimmie Killingworth, Head, 979-845-3890, E-mail: killingworth@tamu.edu. *Application contact:* Howard Marchitello, Director of Graduate Programs, 979-845-9836, Fax: 979-862-2292, E-mail: info-grad@english.tamu.edu.

Texas A&M University–Commerce, Graduate School, College of Arts and Sciences, Department of Literature and Languages, Commerce, TX 75429-3011. Offers college teaching of English (PhD); English (MA, MS); Spanish (MA). Part-time programs available. Terminal master's awarded for partial completion of doctoral program. *Degree requirements:* For master's, comprehensive exam, thesis (for some programs); for doctorate, one foreign language, thesis/dissertation, departmental qualifying exam. *Entrance requirements:* For master's and doctorate, GRE General Test. Electronic applications accepted. *Faculty research:* Latino literature, American film studies, ethnographic research, Willa Carter.

Texas A&M University–Corpus Christi, Graduate Studies and Research, College of Liberal Arts, Program in English, Corpus Christi, TX 78412-5503. Offers MA. Part-time and evening/weekend programs available. *Degree requirements:* For master's, comprehensive exam, thesis (for some programs). *Entrance requirements:* For master's, GRE General Test. Additional exam requirements/recommendations for international students: Required—TOEFL. Electronic applications accepted.

Texas A&M University–Kingsville, College of Graduate Studies, College of Arts and Sciences, Department of Language and Literature, Kingsville, TX 78363. Offers English (MA, MS); Spanish (MA). Part-time and evening/weekend programs available. *Degree requirements:* For master's, comprehensive exam, thesis or alternative. *Entrance requirements:* For master's, GRE General Test, minimum GPA of 3.0. Additional exam requirements/recommendations for international students: Required—TOEFL. *Faculty research:* Linguistics, culture, Spanish American literature, Spanish peninsular literature, American literature.

Texas A&M University–Texarkana, Graduate Studies and Research, College of Arts and Sciences and Education, Texarkana, TX 75505-5518. Offers adult education (MS); curriculum and instruction (MS); education (MS); educational administration (M Ed); English (MA); history (MS); instructional technology (MS); interdisciplinary studies (MS); special education (M Ed, MS). Part-time and evening/weekend programs available. *Degree requirements:* For master's, comprehensive exam (for some programs), thesis optional. *Entrance requirements:* For master's, minimum GPA of 2.5 on last 60 hours of bachelor's degree. Additional exam requirements/recommendations for international students: Required—TOEFL. Electronic applications accepted.

Texas Christian University, AddRan College of Liberal Arts, Department of English, Fort Worth, TX 76129-0002. Offers MA, PhD. Part-time and evening/weekend programs available. *Degree requirements:* For master's, one foreign language, thesis, candidacy exam; for doctorate, one foreign language, thesis/dissertation, diagnostic exam, qualifying exam. *Entrance requirements:* For master's and doctorate, GRE General Test. Additional exam requirements/recommendations for international students: Required—TOEFL. *Application deadline:* For fall admission, 3/1 for domestic students; for spring admission, 12/1 for domestic students. Applications are processed on a rolling basis. Application fee: $0. *Expenses:* Tuition: Full-time $17,640. *Financial support:* Fellowships, teaching assistantships, unspecified assistantships available. Financial award application deadline: 3/1. *Unit head:* Dr. Brad Lucas, Chairperson, 817-257-7240. *Application contact:* Dr. Mike Butler, Associate Dean, AddRan College of Liberal Arts, E-mail: m.butler@tcu.edu.

Texas Southern University, Graduate School, College of Liberal Arts and Behavioral Sciences, Department of English, Houston, TX 77004-4584. Offers MA. Part-time programs available. *Faculty:* 5 full-time (1 woman). *Students:* 6 full-time (all women), 3 part-time (2 women); includes all African Americans. Average age 33. 7 applicants, 100% accepted, 5 enrolled. In 2008, 4 master's awarded. *Degree requirements:* For master's, one foreign language, comprehensive exam, thesis. *Entrance requirements:* For master's, GRE General Test, minimum GPA of 2.5. Additional exam requirements/recommendations for international students: Required—TOEFL. *Application deadline:* For fall admission, 7/15 priority date for domestic students. Applications are processed on a rolling basis. Application fee: $50 ($75 for international students). *Expenses:* Tuition, area resident: Full-time $1912; part-time $96 per credit hour. Tuition, state resident: full-time $1912; part-time $96 per credit hour. Tuition, nonresident: full-time $6302; part-time $343 per credit hour. Required fees: $3542. *Financial support:* Fellowships, teaching assistantships, Federal Work-Study and institutionally sponsored loans available. Financial award application deadline: 5/1. *Faculty research:* Linguistics, teaching of English, African-American literature, African literature, developmental English. *Unit head:* Dr. Rhonda Saldivar, Interim Chair, 713-313-7536, Fax: 713-313-7538, E-mail: saldivar_rx@tsu.edu. *Application contact:* Dr. Gregory Maddox, Interim Dean of the Graduate School, 713-313-7011 Ext. 4410, Fax: 713-639-1876, E-mail: maddox_gh@tsu.edu.

Texas State University–San Marcos, Graduate School, College of Liberal Arts, Department of English, Program in Literature, San Marcos, TX 78666. Offers MA. Part-time and evening/weekend programs available. *Degree requirements:* For master's, comprehensive exam. *Entrance requirements:* For master's, minimum GPA of 2.75 in last 60 hours, 24 undergraduate hours of course work in English (12 advanced) with minimum GPA of 3.25, 6 hours of course work in foreign language. Additional exam requirements/recommendations for international students: Required—TOEFL (minimum score 550 paper-based; 213 computer-based). Electronic applications accepted.

Texas Tech University, Graduate School, College of Arts and Sciences, Department of English, Lubbock, TX 79409. Offers English (MA, PhD); technical communication (MA); technical communication and rhetoric (PhD). Part-time programs available. *Faculty:* 37 full-time (14 women), 3 part-time/adjunct (all women). *Students:* 100 full-time (37 women), 82 part-time (52 women); includes 19 minority (4 African Americans, 3 American Indian/Alaska Native, 6 Asian Americans or Pacific Islanders, 6 Hispanic Americans), 11 international. Average age 35. 188 applicants, 38% accepted, 33 enrolled. In 2008, 24 master's, 12 doctorates awarded. *Degree requirements:* For master's, one foreign language, thesis (for some programs); for doctorate, thesis/dissertation. *Entrance requirements:* For master's and doctorate, GRE General Test. Additional exam requirements/recommendations for international students: Required—TOEFL (minimum score 550 paper-based; 213 computer-based). *Application deadline:* For fall admission, 3/1 priority date for international students; for spring admission, 11/1 priority date for international students. Applications are processed on a rolling basis. Application fee: $50 ($60 for international students). Electronic applications accepted. *Expenses:* Tuition, area resident: Part-time $194 per credit hour. Tuition, state resident: full-time $4648; part-time $194 per credit hour. Tuition, nonresident: full-time $11,392; part-time $475 per credit hour. Required fees: $2206; $69 per credit hour. $389 per semester. *Financial support:* In 2008–09, 109 students received support, including 1 research assistantship with partial tuition reimbursement available (averaging $16,357 per year), 82 teaching assistantships with partial tuition reimbursements available (averaging $14,350 per year); Federal Work-Study and institutionally sponsored loans also available. Support available to part-time students. Financial award application deadline: 4/15; financial award applicants required to submit FAFSA. *Faculty research:* Computers and writing; technical communication and rhetoric; creative writing; nineteenth century studies; literature of social justice and the environment. Total annual research expenditures: $54,723. *Unit head:* Dr. Sam Dragga, Chair, 806-742-2501, Fax: 806-742-0989, E-mail: sam.dragga@ttu.edu. *Application contact:* Dr. Sean Grass, Director of Graduate Studies, 806-742-2501, Fax: 806-742-0989, E-mail: english.gradadvisor@ttu.edu.

Texas Woman's University, Graduate School, College of Arts and Sciences, Department of English, Speech, and Foreign Languages, Denton, TX 76201. Offers English (MA); rhetoric (PhD). Part-time programs available. *Faculty:* 11 full-time (6 women), 4 part-time/adjunct (2 women). *Students:* 10 full-time (all women), 49 part-time (43 women); includes 10 minority (4 African Americans, 1 American Indian/Alaska Native, 2 Asian Americans or Pacific Islanders, 3 Hispanic Americans), 1 international. Average age 37. In 2008, 8 master's, 4 doctorates awarded. *Degree requirements:* For master's, one foreign language, comprehensive exam, thesis; for doctorate, 2 foreign languages, comprehensive exam, thesis/dissertation. *Entrance requirements:* For master's, GRE General Test (minimum score: Verbal 500, Quantitative 350), 3 letters of reference, interview, minimum GPA of 3.0; for doctorate, GRE General Test, writing sample, 3 letters of reference, interview, minimum GPA of 3.0 on previous upper-division and graduate work. Additional exam requirements/recommendations for international students: Recommended—TOEFL (minimum score 600 paper-based; 213 computer-based; 79 iBT). *Application deadline:* For fall admission, 4/1 for international students; for spring admission, 8/1 for international students. Applications are processed on a rolling basis. Application fee: $30 ($50 for international students). Electronic applications accepted. *Expenses:* Tuition, state resident: full-time $3564; part-time $198 per semester hour. Tuition, nonresident: full-time $8622; part-time $479 per semester hour. Required fees: $1158; $64 per semester hour. Tuition and fees vary according to course load. *Financial support:* In 2008–09, 19 research assistantships (averaging $10,530 per year), 14 teaching assistantships (averaging $10,530 per year) were awarded; career-related internships or fieldwork, Federal Work-Study, institutionally sponsored loans, scholarships/grants, traineeships, health care benefits, and unspecified assistantships also available. Support available to part-time students. Financial award application deadline: 3/1; financial award applicants required to submit FAFSA. *Faculty research:* British and American literature, rhetoric: historical and applied, composition studies and technology, literary theory and criticism, women's literature and feminist rhetoric. *Unit head:* Dr. Bruce Krajewski, Chair, 940-898-2324, Fax: 940-898-2297, E-mail: gwest@twu.edu. *Application contact:* Samuel Wheeler, Assistant Director of Admissions, 940-898-3188, Fax: 940-898-3081, E-mail: wheelersr@twu.edu.

Trinity College, Graduate Programs, Department of English, Hartford, CT 06106-3100. Offers MA. Part-time and evening/weekend programs available. *Degree requirements:* For master's, thesis. *Entrance requirements:* For master's, minimum GPA of 3.0.

Trinity Western University, Faculty of Graduate Studies, Program in Interdisciplinary Humanities, Langley, BC V2Y 1Y1, Canada. Offers general humanities (MAIH); specialized (MAIH), including English, history, philosophy. Part-time and evening/weekend programs available. Postbaccalaureate distance learning degree programs offered (minimal on-campus study). *Degree requirements:* For master's, 36 semester hours. *Entrance requirements:* For master's, strong undergraduate degree in Humanities or English, History or Philosophy. *Faculty research:* Literary theory, gender, medieval and early modern literature, philosophy of religion, Thomas Merton's poetics.

Truman State University, Graduate School, College of Arts and Sciences, Program in English, Kirksville, MO 63501-4221. Offers MA. *Degree requirements:* For master's, thesis. *Entrance requirements:* For master's, GRE General Test, minimum GPA of 3.0. Additional exam requirements/recommendations for international students: Required—TOEFL (minimum score 550 paper-based; 213 computer-based). Electronic applications accepted.

Tufts University, Graduate School of Arts and Sciences, Department of English, Medford, MA 02155. Offers MA, PhD. Terminal master's awarded for partial completion of doctoral program. *Degree requirements:* For master's, one foreign language, thesis; for doctorate, 2 foreign languages, thesis/dissertation. *Entrance requirements:* For master's and doctorate, GRE General Test, GRE Subject Test, writing sample. Additional exam requirements/recommendations for international students: Required—TOEFL (minimum score 550 paper-based; 213 computer-based; 80 iBT). Electronic applications accepted.

Tulane University, School of Liberal Arts, Department of English, New Orleans, LA 70118-5669. Offers MA, PhD. *Degree requirements:* For master's, one foreign language, thesis or alternative; for doctorate, 2 foreign languages, thesis/dissertation. *Entrance requirements:* For master's, GRE General Test, minimum B average in undergraduate course work; for doctorate, GRE General Test. Additional exam requirements/recommendations for international students: Required—TOEFL. Electronic applications accepted.

Universidad de las Américas–Puebla, Division of Graduate Studies, School of Humanities, Program in Literature, Puebla, Mexico. Offers MA. Part-time and evening/weekend programs available. *Degree requirements:* For master's, one foreign language, thesis. *Entrance requirements:* Additional exam requirements/recommendations for international students: Required—TOEFL. *Faculty research:* Women in literature, Mexican and Hispanic literature.

Université de Montréal, Faculty of Arts and Sciences, Department of English Studies, Montréal, QC H3C 3J7, Canada. Offers MA, PhD. *Faculty:* 10 full-time (4 women). *Students:* 42 full-time (21 women), 44 part-time (28 women). 39 applicants, 26% accepted, 9 enrolled. In 2008, 8 master's awarded. *Degree requirements:* For doctorate, thesis/dissertation, general exam. *Entrance requirements:* For master's, BA in English with minimum B+ average; for doctorate, MA in English with minimum B+ average. *Application deadline:* For fall admission, 2/1 priority date for domestic students; for winter admission, 11/1 priority date for domestic students; for spring admission, 2/1 priority date for domestic students. Application fee: $100. Electronic applications accepted. *Financial support:* Teaching assistantships available. *Faculty research:* British, Canadian, and American literature. *Unit head:* Robert Schwartzwald, Director, 514-343-7926, Fax: 514-343-6443, E-mail: robert.schwartzwald@umontreal.ca. *Application contact:* Lianne Moyes, Information Contact, 514-343-2218, Fax: 514-343-6443, E-mail: lianne.moyes@umontreal.ca.

Université Laval, Faculty of Letters, Department of Literature, Programs in Ancient Civilization, Québec, QC G1K 7P4, Canada. Offers MA, PhD. Part-time programs available. Terminal master's awarded for partial completion of doctoral program. *Degree requirements:* For master's, thesis; for doctorate, comprehensive exam, thesis/dissertation. *Entrance requirements:* For

English

Université Laval (continued)

master's and doctorate, English test (comprehension of written English), knowledge of French, knowledge of an ancient language. Electronic applications accepted.

Université Laval, Faculty of Letters, Department of Literature, Programs in English Literatures, Québec, QC G1K 7P4, Canada. Offers MA, PhD. Part-time programs available. Terminal master's awarded for partial completion of doctoral program. *Degree requirements:* For master's, thesis (for some programs); for doctorate, comprehensive exam, thesis/dissertation. *Entrance requirements:* For master's, French exam, knowledge of English; for doctorate, French exam, knowledge of English, knowledge of a third language. Electronic applications accepted.

University at Albany, State University of New York, College of Arts and Sciences, Department of English, Albany, NY 12222-0001. Offers MA, PhD. *Degree requirements:* For master's, one foreign language; for doctorate, one foreign language, comprehensive exam, thesis/dissertation, residency. *Entrance requirements:* For master's and doctorate, GRE General Test, GRE Subject Test. Additional exam requirements/recommendations for international students: Required—TOEFL (minimum score 550 paper-based; 213 computer-based). Electronic applications accepted. *Faculty research:* Women playwrights; critical literary theory; poetry and poetics; media history, writing and reporting; creative non-fiction.

University at Buffalo, the State University of New York, Graduate School, College of Arts and Sciences, Department of English, Buffalo, NY 14260. Offers MA, PhD. Part-time programs available. Terminal master's awarded for partial completion of doctoral program. *Degree requirements:* For master's, thesis or alternative; for doctorate, thesis/dissertation, departmental qualifying exam. *Entrance requirements:* For master's and doctorate, GRE General Test, sample of written work. Additional exam requirements/recommendations for international students: Required—TOEFL. Electronic applications accepted. *Faculty research:* Psychoanalysis, early modern British literature, poetics, 19th century American literature.

The University of Akron, Graduate School, Buchtel College of Arts and Sciences, Department of English, Akron, OH 44325. Offers composition (MA); creative writing (MFA); literature (MA). Part-time programs available. *Degree requirements:* For master's, thesis optional. *Entrance requirements:* For master's, BA in English, minimum GPA of 2.75, writing portfolio, letters of recommendation. Additional exam requirements/recommendations for international students: Required—TOEFL (minimum score 580 paper-based; 237 computer-based; 92 iBT). Electronic applications accepted. *Faculty research:* British and American literary studies, literary theory, creative writing, applied linguistics.

The University of Alabama, Graduate School, College of Arts and Sciences, Department of English, Tuscaloosa, AL 35487. Offers composition and rhetoric (PhD); creative writing (MFA), including fiction, poetry; literature (MA, PhD); rhetoric and composition (MA); teaching English as a second language (MATESOL). *Faculty:* 35 full-time (13 women). *Students:* 120 full-time (66 women), 16 part-time (12 women); includes 15 minority (8 African Americans, 2 American Indian/Alaska Native, 3 Asian Americans or Pacific Islanders, 2 Hispanic Americans), 5 international. Average age 28. 237 applicants, 20% accepted, 31 enrolled. In 2008, 21 master's, 2 doctorates awarded. *Degree requirements:* For master's, one foreign language, comprehensive exam, thesis (for some programs); for doctorate, 2 foreign languages, comprehensive exam, thesis/dissertation. *Entrance requirements:* For master's and doctorate, GRE, minimum GPA of 3.0, critical writing sample. Additional exam requirements/recommendations for international students: Required—TOEFL. *Application deadline:* For fall admission, 1/15 priority date for domestic students, 1/15 for international students. Application fee: $30. Electronic applications accepted. *Expenses:* Tuition, area resident: Full-time $6400. Tuition, state resident: full-time $6400. Tuition, nonresident: full-time $18,000. *Financial support:* In 2008–09, 7 fellowships with full tuition reimbursements (averaging $15,000 per year), 1 research assistantship (averaging $11,708 per year), 106 teaching assistantships with full tuition reimbursements (averaging $11,708 per year) were awarded; career-related internships or fieldwork, scholarships/grants, health care benefits, and unspecified assistantships also available. Financial award application deadline: 1/15. *Faculty research:* Critical theory; modern, Renaissance, and African-American literature. Total annual research expenditures: $8,282. *Unit head:* Dr. Catherine E. Davies, Director of Graduate Studies, 205-348-8499, E-mail: cdavies@bama.ua.edu. *Application contact:* Vernita W. James, Office Assistant II, 205-348-0766, Fax: 205-348-1388, E-mail: vwjames@bama.ua.edu.

The University of Alabama at Birmingham, School of Arts and Humanities, Department of English, Birmingham, AL 35294. Offers MA. *Degree requirements:* For master's, one foreign language, comprehensive exam, thesis optional. *Entrance requirements:* For master's, GRE General Test or MAT, minimum GPA of 2.75. Electronic applications accepted.

The University of Alabama in Huntsville, School of Graduate Studies, College of Liberal Arts, Department of English, Huntsville, AL 35899. Offers English (MA); teaching of English to speakers of other languages (Certificate); technical communications (Certificate). Part-time and evening/weekend programs available. *Faculty:* 19 full-time (10 women). *Students:* 22 full-time (16 women), 43 part-time (34 women); includes 11 minority (8 African Americans, 1 American Indian/Alaska Native, 2 Hispanic Americans). Average age 32. 32 applicants, 75% accepted, 20 enrolled. In 2008, 20 master's, 7 other advanced degrees awarded. *Degree requirements:* For master's, one foreign language, comprehensive exam, thesis or alternative, oral and written exams. *Entrance requirements:* For master's and Certificate, GRE General Test, minimum GPA of 3.0. Additional exam requirements/recommendations for international students: Required—TOEFL (minimum score 500 paper-based; 173 computer-based; 62 iBT). *Application deadline:* For fall admission, 7/15 for domestic students, 4/1 for international students; for spring admission, 11/30 for domestic students, 9/1 for international students. Applications are processed on a rolling basis. Application fee: $40 ($50 for international students). Electronic applications accepted. *Expenses:* Tuition, area resident: Full-time $5214; part-time $323 per credit hour. Tuition, state resident: full-time $5214; part-time $323 per credit hour. Tuition, nonresident: full-time $11,444; part-time $705 per credit hour. Required fees: $540; $120 per semester. Tuition and fees vary according to course load. *Financial support:* In 2008–09, 7 students received support, including 4 teaching assistantships with full and partial tuition reimbursements available (averaging $8,460 per year); career-related internships or fieldwork, Federal Work-Study, institutionally sponsored loans, scholarships/grants, health care benefits, and unspecified assistantships also available. Support available to part-time students. Financial award application deadline: 4/1; financial award applicants required to submit FAFSA. *Faculty research:* American and British literature, linguistics, technical writing, women's studies, rhetoric. *Unit head:* Dr. Rose Norman, Chair, 256-824-6320, Fax: 256-824-6949, E-mail: normanr@uah.edu. *Application contact:* Kathy Biggs, Graduate Studies Admissions Manager, 256-824-6199, Fax: 256-824-6405, E-mail: deangrad@uah.edu.

University of Alaska Anchorage, College of Arts and Sciences, Department of English, Anchorage, AK 99508-8060. Offers MA. Part-time programs available. *Degree requirements:* For master's, comprehensive exam, thesis or alternative. *Entrance requirements:* For master's, GRE General Test, GRE Subject Test, portfolio, minimum GPA of 3.5, writing sample. Additional exam requirements/recommendations for international students: Required—TOEFL (minimum score 550 paper-based; 213 computer-based). *Faculty research:* The rhetoric of essays, American and American Indian literature, linguistics, Shakespeare, literature of war.

University of Alaska Fairbanks, College of Liberal Arts, Department of English, Fairbanks, AK 99775-5720. Offers creative writing (MFA); literature (MA); MA/MFA. Part-time programs available. *Faculty:* 16 full-time (7 women), 2 part-time/adjunct (1 woman). *Students:* 33 full-time (14 women), 13 part-time (12 women); includes 5 minority (2 American Indian/Alaska Native, 2 Asian Americans or Pacific Islanders, 1 Hispanic American). Average age 32. 55 applicants, 51% accepted, 16 enrolled. In 2008, 3 master's awarded. *Degree requirements:* For master's, comprehensive exam, thesis or alternative, oral exams, oral defense. *Entrance requirements:* For master's, GRE General Test, academic writing sample. Additional exam requirements/recommendations for international students: Required—TOEFL (minimum score 550 paper-

based; 213 computer-based; 80 iBT). *Application deadline:* For fall admission, 6/1 for domestic students, 3/1 for international students; for spring admission, 10/15 for domestic students, 9/1 for international students. Applications are processed on a rolling basis. Application fee: $60. Electronic applications accepted. *Expenses:* Tuition, area resident: Full-time $5418; part-time $301 per credit. Tuition, state resident: full-time $5418; part-time $301 per credit. Tuition, nonresident: full-time $11,070; part-time $615 per credit. Required fees: $849; $25 per credit. $78 per semester. Tuition and fees vary according to course load and reciprocity agreements. *Financial support:* In 2008–09, 1 research assistantship (averaging $13,330 per year), 26 teaching assistantships (averaging $11,844 per year) were awarded; fellowships, Federal Work-Study, scholarships/grants, health care benefits, and unspecified assistantships also available. Support available to part-time students. Financial award application deadline: 7/1; financial award applicants required to submit FAFSA. *Faculty research:* Traditional Alaskan native literature, British literature, pedagogy, American literature, rhetoric/composition history. *Unit head:* Dr. Cooper Burns, Department Chair, 907-474-7193, Fax: 907-474-5247, E-mail: faengl@uaf.edu. *Application contact:* Dr. Cooper Burns, Department Chair, 907-474-7193, Fax: 907-474-5247, E-mail: faengl@uaf.edu.

University of Alberta, Faculty of Graduate Studies and Research, Department of English and Film Studies, Edmonton, AB T6G 2E1, Canada. Offers English (MA, PhD). Part-time and evening/weekend programs available. *Degree requirements:* For master's, one foreign language, thesis optional; for doctorate, 2 foreign languages, thesis/dissertation. *Entrance requirements:* For master's, honors BA or equivalent; for doctorate, honors BA and MA. Additional exam requirements/recommendations for international students: Required—TOEFL (minimum score 600 paper-based). Electronic applications accepted. *Faculty research:* Women's writing, postcolonial theory, Victorian literature, Renaissance literature, Canadian literature.

The University of Arizona, Graduate College, College of Humanities, Department of English, Tucson, AZ 85721. Offers creative writing (MFA); English (MA, PhD); rhetoric, composition and the teaching of English (MA, PhD). Part-time programs available. Terminal master's awarded for partial completion of doctoral program. *Degree requirements:* For master's, one foreign language, comprehensive exam; for doctorate, one foreign language, comprehensive exam, thesis/dissertation, preliminary and qualifying exams. *Entrance requirements:* For master's, GRE General Test, GRE Subject Test, sample of written work, 3 letters of recommendation, minimum GPA of 3.0, statement of purpose; for doctorate, GRE General Test, GRE Subject Test (literature), sample of written work, 3 letters of recommendation, minimum GPA of 3.0, statement of purpose. Additional exam requirements/recommendations for international students: Required—TOEFL (minimum score 550 paper-based). Electronic applications accepted. *Faculty research:* Literature, women's studies, Southwestern literature, feminist theory.

University of Arkansas, Graduate School, J. William Fulbright College of Arts and Sciences, Department of English, Program in English, Fayetteville, AR 72701-1201. Offers MA, PhD. *Degree requirements:* For master's, thesis; for doctorate, thesis/dissertation. *Entrance requirements:* For master's, GRE General Test; for doctorate, GRE General Test, GRE Subject Test. *Faculty research:* Creative writing, seventeenth century literature, twentieth century literature, American literature.

The University of British Columbia, Faculty of Arts and Faculty of Graduate Studies, Department of English, Vancouver, BC V6T 1Z1, Canada. Offers MA, PhD. *Degree requirements:* For master's, thesis or alternative, non-thesis 30 credits, with thesis 21 credits; for doctorate, one foreign language, comprehensive exam, thesis/dissertation. *Entrance requirements:* For master's, 4 year BA; for doctorate, MA. Additional exam requirements/recommendations for international students: Required—TOEFL (minimum score 615 paper-based; 258 computer-based; 104 iBT), IELTS (minimum score 8). Electronic applications accepted. *Faculty research:* English, American, Canadian, and Commonwealth post-colonial literature; English language; rhetoric.

The University of British Columbia, Faculty of Arts, School of Library, Archival and Information Studies, Children's Literature Program, Vancouver, BC V6T 1Z1, Canada. Offers MA. Part-time programs available. *Degree requirements:* For master's, thesis. *Entrance requirements:* For master's, minimum GPA of 3.3 in undergraduate upper-division courses. Additional exam requirements/recommendations for international students: Required—TOEFL (minimum score 600 paper-based; 250 computer-based; 100 iBT). Electronic applications accepted. *Faculty research:* Language and literacy education; writing children's literature; teaching children's literature.

University of Calgary, Faculty of Graduate Studies, Faculty of Humanities, Department of English, Calgary, AB T2N 1N4, Canada. Offers MA, PhD. Part-time programs available. *Degree requirements:* For master's, one foreign language, comprehensive exam (for some programs), thesis; for doctorate, one foreign language, thesis/dissertation, candidacy exam. *Entrance requirements:* Additional exam requirements/recommendations for international students: Required—TOEFL (minimum score 600 paper-based; 250 computer-based). Electronic applications accepted. *Faculty research:* Various national and period literatures, creative writing, literary theory, gender and women's studies, postcolonial literatures.

University of California, Berkeley, Graduate Division, College of Letters and Science, Department of English, Berkeley, CA 94720-1500. Offers PhD. *Degree requirements:* For doctorate, 2 foreign languages, thesis/dissertation, qualifying exam. *Entrance requirements:* For doctorate, GRE General Test, GRE Subject Test, minimum GPA of 3.0, writing sample, 3 letters of recommendation.

University of California, Davis, Graduate Studies, Program in English, Davis, CA 95616. Offers creative writing (MA); English (MA, PhD). Terminal master's awarded for partial completion of doctoral program. *Degree requirements:* For master's, one foreign language, thesis optional; for doctorate, 2 foreign languages, thesis/dissertation. *Entrance requirements:* For master's and doctorate, GRE General Test, GRE Subject Test, minimum GPA of 3.0, writing sample. Additional exam requirements/recommendations for international students: Required—TOEFL (minimum score 550 paper-based; 213 computer-based). Electronic applications accepted. *Faculty research:* Feminist theory, ethnic literature, literary theory, history of literature, literature of nature.

University of California, Irvine, Office of Graduate Studies, School of Humanities, Department of English and Comparative Literature, English Summer Program, Irvine, CA 92697. Offers MA. Offered during summer only. *Degree requirements:* For master's, thesis. *Entrance requirements:* For master's, GRE General Test, GRE Subject Test, writing sample, 3 letters of recommendation. Electronic applications accepted. *Expenses:* Contact institution. *Faculty research:* Shakespeare, American multiculturalism, literary theory.

University of California, Irvine, Office of Graduate Studies, School of Humanities, Department of English and Comparative Literature, Program in English, Irvine, CA 92697. Offers English (MA); English and American literature (PhD). Terminal master's awarded for partial completion of doctoral program. *Degree requirements:* For master's, one foreign language, comprehensive exam; for doctorate, 2 foreign languages, comprehensive exam, thesis/dissertation. *Entrance requirements:* For doctorate, GRE General Test, GRE Subject Test, minimum GPA of 3.5, sample of written work, 3 letters of recommendation. Additional exam requirements/recommendations for international students: Required—TOEFL (minimum score 550 paper-based; 213 computer-based). Electronic applications accepted. *Faculty research:* Critical theory, literary history, cultural studies.

University of California, Los Angeles, Graduate Division, College of Letters and Science, Department of English, Los Angeles, CA 90095. Offers MA, PhD. *Students:* 101 full-time (58 women); includes 24 minority (6 African Americans, 8 Asian Americans or Pacific Islanders, 10 Hispanic Americans), 2 international. Average age 28. 286 applicants, 14% accepted, 20 enrolled. In 2008, 10 master's, 15 doctorates awarded. Terminal master's awarded for partial completion of doctoral program. *Degree requirements:* For master's, comprehensive exam or thesis; for doctorate, 2 foreign languages, thesis/dissertation, oral and written qualifying exams.

Entrance requirements: For master's, GRE General Test, GRE Subject Test (literature), minimum GPA of 3.0, sample of written work, degree objective of Ph.D; for doctorate, GRE General Test, GRE Subject Test (literature), minimum GPA of 3.5 (undergraduate), 3.7 (graduate), sample of written work. *Application deadline:* For fall admission, 12/15 for domestic and international students. Application fee: $60 ($80 for international students). Electronic applications accepted. *Expenses:* Tuition, nonresident: full-time $14,694. Required fees: $9669.50. Full-time tuition and fees vary according to course load, degree level, program and student level. *Financial support:* In 2008–09, 96 fellowships with full and partial tuition reimbursements, 30 research assistantships with full and partial tuition reimbursements, 75 teaching assistantships with full and partial tuition reimbursements were awarded; Federal Work-Study, institutionally sponsored loans, scholarships/grants, health care benefits, tuition waivers (full and partial), and unspecified assistantships also available. Financial award application deadline: 3/1; financial award applicants required to submit FAFSA. *Unit head:* Dr. Rafael Perez-Torrez, Chair, 310-825-3927. *Application contact:* Departmental Office, 310-825-3927, E-mail: graduate@english.ucla.edu.

University of California, Riverside, Graduate Division, Department of English, Riverside, CA 92521-0102. Offers MA, PhD. *Faculty:* 27 full-time (15 women). *Students:* 86 full-time (57 women); includes 20 minority (3 African Americans, 1 American Indian/Alaska Native, 10 Asian Americans or Pacific Islanders, 6 Hispanic Americans), 3 international. Average age 31. In 2008, 5 master's, 11 doctorates awarded. *Degree requirements:* For master's, one foreign language, comprehensive exam; for doctorate, 2 foreign languages, thesis/dissertation, qualifying exams. *Entrance requirements:* For master's and doctorate, GRE General Test, minimum GPA of 3.5. Additional exam requirements/recommendations for international students: Required—TOEFL (minimum score 550 paper-based; 213 computer-based; 80 iBT). *Application deadline:* For fall admission, 3/31 for domestic students, 2/1 priority date for international students. Applications are processed on a rolling basis. Application fee: $60 ($75 for international students). Electronic applications accepted. *Expenses:* Tuition, nonresident: full-time $4898. Required fees: $10,362. *Financial support:* In 2008–09, fellowships with full and partial tuition reimbursements (averaging $12,000 per year), teaching assistantships with full and partial tuition reimbursements (averaging $16,500 per year) were awarded; research assistantships with tuition reimbursements, career-related internships or fieldwork, Federal Work-Study, institutionally sponsored loans, and tuition waivers (full and partial) also available. Financial award application deadline: 12/10; financial award applicants required to submit FAFSA. *Faculty research:* Critical theory, cultural and film studies, lesbian and gay studies, minority and feminist discourses, rhetoric and composition. *Unit head:* Prof. Deborah Willis, Chair, 951-827-1458, Fax: 951-827-3967, E-mail: deborah.willis@ucr.edu. *Application contact:* Tina M. Feldmann, Graduate Program Assistant, 951-827-1454, Fax: 951-827-3967, E-mail: english@ucr.edu.

University of California, San Diego, Office of Graduate Studies, Department of Literature, Program in Literatures in English, La Jolla, CA 92093. Offers MA. *Degree requirements:* For master's, thesis. *Entrance requirements:* For master's, GRE General Test, GRE Subject Test. Electronic applications accepted.

University of California, Santa Barbara, Graduate Division, College of Letters and Sciences, Division of Humanities and Fine Arts, Department of English, Santa Barbara, CA 93106-3170. Offers English (PhD); feminist studies (PhD); global studies (PhD); MA/PhD. *Faculty:* 26 full-time (13 women), 17 part-time/adjunct (12 women). *Students:* 81 full-time (43 women). Average age 30. 151 applicants, 19% accepted, 13 enrolled. In 2008, 12 doctorates awarded. Terminal master's awarded for partial completion of doctoral program. *Degree requirements:* For doctorate, one foreign language, comprehensive exam, thesis/dissertation. *Entrance requirements:* For doctorate, GRE General Test, GRE Subject Test (literature), sample of written work, 3 letters of recommendation, statement of purpose, personal achievements/contributions statement, resumé/curriculum vitae, transcripts for post-secondary institutions attended. Additional exam requirements/recommendations for international students: Required—TOEFL (paper: 550, computer: 213, IBT: 80) or IELTS (7). *Application deadline:* For fall admission, 12/15 for domestic and international students. Application fee: $70 ($90 for international students). Electronic applications accepted. *Expenses:* Tuition, nonresident: full-time $25,149. Required fees: $10,143. Full-time tuition and fees vary according to campus/location, reciprocity agreements and student level. *Financial support:* In 2008–09, 70 students received support, including 32 fellowships with full and partial tuition reimbursements available (averaging $10,800 per year), 6 research assistantships with full and partial tuition reimbursements available (averaging $4,200 per year), 54 teaching assistantships with partial tuition reimbursements available (averaging $10,800 per year); Federal Work-Study, institutionally sponsored loans, scholarships/grants, health care benefits, tuition waivers (full and partial), and unspecified assistantships also available. Financial award application deadline: 12/15; financial award applicants required to submit FAFSA. *Faculty research:* Renaissance literature, 18th century literature, American literature, race and ethnic studies, literature and theory of technology/media/information. *Unit head:* Prof. Alan Liu, Chair, 805-893-3478, Fax: 805-893-4622, E-mail: ayliu@english.ucsb.edu. *Application contact:* Chelsea Houdyshell, Staff Graduate Advisor, 805-893-2639, Fax: 805-893-4622, E-mail: chelsea@english.ucsb.edu.

University of California, Santa Cruz, Division of Graduate Studies, Division of Humanities, Department of Literature, Santa Cruz, CA 95064. Offers MA, PhD. Terminal master's awarded for partial completion of doctoral program. *Degree requirements:* For master's, thesis; for doctorate, one foreign language, thesis/dissertation, qualifying exam. *Entrance requirements:* For master's, GRE General Test, writing sample, minimum GPA of 3.5; for doctorate, GRE General Test, minimum GPA of 3.5, writing sample. Electronic applications accepted. *Faculty research:* Comparative literature; German, Spanish, classical, American, and English literature.

University of Central Arkansas, Graduate School, College of Liberal Arts, Department of English, Conway, AR 72035-0001. Offers MA. Part-time programs available. *Degree requirements:* For master's, comprehensive exam, thesis optional. *Entrance requirements:* For master's, GRE General Test, minimum GPA of 2.7. Additional exam requirements/recommendations for international students: Required—TOEFL (minimum score 550 paper-based; 213 computer-based). *Faculty research:* Writing project.

University of Central Florida, College of Arts and Humanities, Department of English, Program in English, Orlando, FL 32816. Offers creative writing (MFA); English (MA). *Students:* 31 full-time (21 women), 47 part-time (33 women); includes 15 minority (5 African Americans, 1 Asian American or Pacific Islander, 9 Hispanic Americans). In 2008, 38 master's awarded. *Expenses:* Tuition, area resident: Full-time $6816; part-time $284 per credit. Tuition, state resident: full-time $6816; part-time $1076 per credit. Tuition, nonresident: full-time $25,824. Required fees: $216; $9 per credit. *Financial support:* In 2008–09, 3 fellowships (averaging $8,500 per year), 13 research assistantships (averaging $5,000 per year), 11 teaching assistantships (averaging $5,600 per year) were awarded.

University of Central Missouri, The Graduate School, College of Arts, Humanities and Social Sciences, Department of English and Philosophy, Warrensburg, MO 64093. Offers English (MA); teaching English as a second language (MA). Part-time programs available. *Degree requirements:* For master's, comprehensive exam. *Entrance requirements:* For master's, minimum GPA of 2.75 overall and in major, 18 hours of course work in English. Additional exam requirements/recommendations for international students: Required—TOEFL (minimum score 500 paper-based; 173 computer-based).

University of Central Oklahoma, College of Graduate Studies and Research, College of Liberal Arts, Department of English, Edmond, OK 73034-5209. Offers composition skills (MA); contemporary literature (MA); creative writing (MA); teaching English as a second language (MA); traditional studies (MA). Part-time programs available. *Degree requirements:* For master's, one foreign language. *Entrance requirements:* For master's, 24 hours of course work in English language and literature. Additional exam requirements/recommendations for international students: Required—TOEFL (minimum score 550 paper-based; 213 computer-based). Electronic applications accepted. *Faculty research:* John Milton, Harriet Beecher Stowe.

University of Chicago, Division of the Humanities, Department of English Language and Literature, Chicago, IL 60637-1513. Offers AM, PhD. *Degree requirements:* For master's, one foreign language, thesis; for doctorate, 2 foreign languages, thesis/dissertation. *Entrance requirements:* For master's and doctorate, GRE General Test, GRE Subject Test (English). Additional exam requirements/recommendations for international students: Required—TOEFL.

University of Cincinnati, Graduate School, McMicken College of Arts and Sciences, Department of English, Cincinnati, OH 45221. Offers MA, MAT, PhD. Part-time programs available. Terminal master's awarded for partial completion of doctoral program. *Degree requirements:* For master's, one foreign language, thesis (for some programs); for doctorate, 2 foreign languages, thesis/dissertation. *Entrance requirements:* For master's, GRE General Test, letters of recommendation (3), writing samples; for doctorate, GRE General Test, GRE Subject Test, letters of recommendation (3), writing samples. Additional exam requirements/recommendations for international students: Required—TOEFL. Electronic applications accepted. *Faculty research:* Literature/theory, creative writing, composition, professional writing/editing, linguistics.

University of Colorado at Boulder, Graduate School, College of Arts and Sciences, Department of English, Boulder, CO 80309. Offers literature (MA, PhD), including creative writing (MA). Part-time programs available. *Degree requirements:* For master's, one foreign language, comprehensive exam, thesis or alternative; for doctorate, 2 foreign languages, comprehensive exam, thesis/dissertation. *Entrance requirements:* For master's, GRE General Test, GRE Subject Test, minimum undergraduate GPA of 3.0; for doctorate, GRE General Test, GRE Subject Test. *Faculty research:* Creative writing (MA), language, critical theory, literature.

University of Colorado at Boulder, Graduate School, College of Arts and Sciences, Department of Spanish and Portuguese, Boulder, CO 80309. Offers Hispanic linguistics (MA); medieval/early modern Hispanic literatures (PhD); Spanish literature (MA, PhD), including 18th and 19th century peninsular literature (MA), Golden Age (MA), medieval Iberian literature (MA). Part-time programs available. Terminal master's awarded for partial completion of doctoral program. *Degree requirements:* For master's, one foreign language, comprehensive exam, thesis or alternative; for doctorate, 2 foreign languages, thesis/dissertation. *Entrance requirements:* For master's, minimum undergraduate GPA of 2.75. *Faculty research:* Spanish peninsular and Spanish-American literatures; Hispanic linguistics; Medieval, Golden Age, eighteenth and nineteenth century literatures.

University of Colorado Denver, College of Liberal Arts and Sciences, Department of English, Denver, CO 80217-3364. Offers applied linguistics (MA); English studies (MA); literature (MA); teaching English to speakers of other languages (Certificate); teaching of writing (MA). Part-time and evening/weekend programs available. *Degree requirements:* For master's, thesis optional. *Entrance requirements:* For master's, GRE General Test, minimum GPA of 3.0. Additional exam requirements/recommendations for international students: Required—TOEFL (minimum score 550 paper-based). Electronic applications accepted.

University of Connecticut, Graduate School, College of Liberal Arts and Sciences, Department of English, Field of English, Storrs, CT 06269. Offers MA, PhD. Terminal master's awarded for partial completion of doctoral program. *Degree requirements:* For master's, comprehensive exam; for doctorate, thesis/dissertation. *Entrance requirements:* For master's and doctorate, GRE General Test, GRE Subject Test. Additional exam requirements/recommendations for international students: Required—TOEFL (minimum score 550 paper-based; 213 computer-based). Electronic applications accepted.

University of Dallas, Braniff Graduate School of Liberal Arts, Department of English, Irving, TX 75062-4736. Offers English literature (MA, MEL). Part-time programs available. *Degree requirements:* For master's, one foreign language. *Entrance requirements:* For master's, GRE General Test. *Faculty research:* Modern literature, Renaissance, Shakespeare, medieval studies.

University of Dayton, Graduate School, College of Arts and Sciences, Department of English, Dayton, OH 45469-1300. Offers MA. Part-time and evening/weekend programs available. *Faculty:* 18 full-time (7 women). *Students:* 25 full-time (22 women), 11 part-time (9 women); includes 6 minority (4 African Americans, 1 Asian American or Pacific Islander, 1 Hispanic American). Average age 29. 41 applicants, 73% accepted, 9 enrolled. In 2008, 8 master's awarded. *Degree requirements:* For master's, thesis optional. *Entrance requirements:* For master's, minimum GPA of 3.0, 24 upper level credit hours of course work in English. Additional exam requirements/recommendations for international students: Required—TOEFL (minimum score 550 paper-based; 213 computer-based; 80 iBT). *Application deadline:* For fall admission, 4/4 priority date for domestic students, 3/1 priority date for international students; for winter admission, 7/1 priority date for international students; for spring admission, 1/1 priority date for international students. Applications are processed on a rolling basis. Application fee: $0 ($50 for international students). Electronic applications accepted. *Expenses:* Tuition: Full-time $6950; part-time $1737.50 per semester. Required fees: $25 per semester. Tuition and fees vary according to course level, course load, degree level and program. *Financial support:* In 2008–09, 13 teaching assistantships with full tuition reimbursements (averaging $9,891 per year) were awarded; institutionally sponsored loans, health care benefits, and unspecified assistantships also available. Financial award applicants required to submit FAFSA. *Faculty research:* Religion and literature, rhetoric and composition, teaching literature and writing and creative writing. Total annual research expenditures: $6,000. *Unit head:* Dr. Sheila Hughes, Chair, 937-229-3434, Fax: 937-229-3563, E-mail: sheila.hughes@notes.udayton.edu. *Application contact:* Angela Jones-Glukhov, Associate Director of Graduate Admissions, 937-229-4305, Fax: 937-229-4729, E-mail: jonesgas@notes.udayton.edu.

University of Delaware, College of Arts and Sciences, Department of English, Newark, DE 19716. Offers English and American literature (MA, PhD); MA/PhD. Terminal master's awarded for partial completion of doctoral program. *Degree requirements:* For master's, one foreign language, thesis optional; for doctorate, 2 foreign languages, comprehensive exam, thesis/dissertation, specialty exam. *Entrance requirements:* For master's and doctorate, GRE General Test, GRE Subject Test. Additional exam requirements/recommendations for international students: Required—TOEFL (minimum score 550 paper-based; 213 computer-based). Electronic applications accepted. *Faculty research:* Significant strengths in American literature and culture, material cultural studies, Renaissance studies, archival studies.

University of Denver, Division of Arts, Humanities and Social Sciences, Department of English, Denver, CO 80208. Offers MA, PhD. Part-time programs available. *Faculty:* 18 full-time (8 women), 5 part-time/adjunct (2 women). *Students:* 29 full-time (19 women), 8 part-time (6 women); includes 2 minority (1 African American, 1 Asian American or Pacific Islander), 1 international. Average age 34. In 2008, 2 master's, 4 doctorates awarded. *Degree requirements:* For master's, one foreign language, thesis; for doctorate, 2 foreign languages, thesis/dissertation. *Entrance requirements:* For master's and doctorate, GRE General Test, GRE Subject Test. Additional exam requirements/recommendations for international students: Required—TOEFL. *Application deadline:* Applications are processed on a rolling basis. Application fee: $50. Electronic applications accepted. *Financial support:* In 2008–09, 31 teaching assistantships with full and partial tuition reimbursements (averaging $12,000 per year) were awarded; Federal Work-Study, institutionally sponsored loans, and scholarships/grants also available. Support available to part-time students. Financial award application deadline: 2/1; financial award applicants required to submit FAFSA. *Faculty research:* Cultural studies, creative nonfiction, eighteenth century colonial literature, multicultural literature, Cervantes. *Unit head:* Dr. Ann Dobyns, Chair, 303-871-2266. *Application contact:* Information Contact, 303-871-2266, E-mail: kheeps@du.edu.

University of Florida, Graduate School, College of Liberal Arts and Sciences, Department of English, Gainesville, FL 32611. Offers creative writing (MFA); English (MA, PhD). *Degree requirements:* For master's, variable foreign language requirement, thesis or alternative; for doctorate, thesis/dissertation. *Entrance requirements:* For master's and doctorate, GRE General Test, minimum GPA of 3.0. Additional exam requirements/recommendations for international

English

University of Florida (continued)

students: Required—TOEFL (minimum score 550 paper-based; 213 computer-based). Electronic applications accepted.

University of Georgia, Graduate School, College of Arts and Sciences, Department of English, Athens, GA 30602. Offers creative writing (MFA, PhD); English (MA, MAT, PhD). *Degree requirements:* For master's, one foreign language, thesis (MA); for doctorate, 2 foreign languages, thesis/dissertation. *Entrance requirements:* For master's and doctorate, GRE General Test. Additional exam requirements/recommendations for international students: Required—TWE. Electronic applications accepted.

University of Guam, Office of Graduate Studies, College of Liberal Arts and Social Sciences, Department of English, Mangilao, GU 96923. Offers MA. *Entrance requirements:* For master's, GRE. Additional exam requirements/recommendations for international students: Required—TOEFL.

University of Guelph, Graduate Program Services, College of Arts, School of English and Theatre Studies, Program in English, Guelph, ON N1G 2W1, Canada. Offers MA. Part-time programs available. *Degree requirements:* For master's, thesis (for some programs). *Entrance requirements:* For master's, letters of reference, 4-year honours undergraduate degree in English or drama. Additional exam requirements/recommendations for international students: Required—TOEFL. Electronic applications accepted. *Faculty research:* Post-colonial literature, Canadian literature, children's literature, Scottish literature, American literature, cultural studies.

University of Hawaii at Manoa, Graduate Division, Colleges of Arts and Sciences, College of Language, Linguistics and Literature, Department of English, Honolulu, HI 96822. Offers MA, PhD. Part-time programs available. *Degree requirements:* For master's, 2 foreign languages, thesis optional; for doctorate, 2 foreign languages, comprehensive exam, thesis/dissertation. *Entrance requirements:* For master's, GRE General Test; for doctorate, GRE General Test, GRE Subject Test. Additional exam requirements/recommendations for international students: Required—TOEFL (minimum score 600 paper-based; 250 computer-based; 100 iBT), IELTS (minimum score 7). *Faculty research:* British and American literature, creative writing, cultural studies, rhetoric and composition.

University of Houston, College of Liberal Arts and Social Sciences, Department of English, Houston, TX 77204. Offers applied English linguistics (MA); English and American literature (MA, PhD); literature and creative writing (MA, MFA, PhD). Postbaccalaureate distance learning degree programs offered. *Faculty:* 21 full-time (10 women), 7 part-time/adjunct (3 women). *Students:* 78 full-time (35 women), 49 part-time (39 women); includes 21 minority (4 African Americans, 1 American Indian/Alaska Native, 10 Asian Americans or Pacific Islanders, 6 Hispanic Americans), 4 international. Average age 33. 197 applicants, 24% accepted, 22 enrolled. In 2008, 28 master's, 13 doctorates awarded. *Degree requirements:* For master's, one foreign language, thesis (for some programs); for doctorate, 2 foreign languages, comprehensive exam, thesis/dissertation. *Entrance requirements:* For master's, GRE General Test, GRE Subject Test, minimum GPA of 3.0 in last 60 hours of course work; for doctorate, GRE General Test, GRE Subject Test, writing sample. Additional exam requirements/recommendations for international students: Required—TOEFL. *Application deadline:* For fall admission, 1/1 priority date for domestic students. Applications are processed on a rolling basis. Application fee: $50. *Expenses:* Tuition, state resident: full-time $5164; part-time $287 per credit. Tuition, nonresident: full-time $10,222; part-time $568 per credit. *Financial support:* In 2008–09, 2 fellowships with full tuition reimbursements (averaging $7,100 per year), 68 teaching assistantships with full tuition reimbursements (averaging $12,250 per year) were awarded; career-related internships or fieldwork, Federal Work-Study, institutionally sponsored loans, scholarships/grants, health care benefits, and unspecified assistantships also available. Support available to part-time students. Financial award application deadline: 2/1. *Unit head:* Wyman Henderson, Chairperson, 713-743-3004, Fax: 713-743-3215, E-mail: whh@uh.edu. *Application contact:* Ruby Jones, Advising Assistant, 713-743-2941, Fax: 713-743-3215, E-mail: rjones@uh.edu.

University of Houston–Clear Lake, School of Human Sciences and Humanities, Programs in Humanities and Fine Arts, Houston, TX 77058-1098. Offers history (MA); humanities (MA); literature (MA). Part-time and evening/weekend programs available. Postbaccalaureate distance learning degree programs offered (minimal on-campus study). *Degree requirements:* For master's, thesis or alternative. *Entrance requirements:* For master's, GRE General Test. Additional exam requirements/recommendations for international students: Required—TOEFL (minimum score 550 paper-based; 213 computer-based). *Faculty research:* Digital media studies, Latin American history, labor history, Chaucer evolution versus creationism debate.

University of Houston–Downtown, College of Humanities and Social Sciences, Department of English, Houston, TX 77002-1001. Offers professional writing and technical communication (MS). Part-time and evening/weekend programs available. *Faculty:* 11 full-time (7 women). *Students:* 3 full-time (2 women), 19 part-time (17 women); includes 10 minority (8 African Americans, 1 Asian American or Pacific Islander, 1 Hispanic American). Average age 37. 6 applicants, 83% accepted, 5 enrolled. In 2008, 4 master's awarded. *Degree requirements:* For master's, thesis optional, graduation portfolio with oral defense. *Entrance requirements:* For master's, GRE (including Analytical Writing section), personal application statement, resumé, writing sample, 3 letters of recommendation. Additional exam requirements/recommendations for international students: Required—TOEFL (minimum score 600 paper-based; 250 computer-based; 86 iBT). *Application deadline:* For fall admission, 3/15 for domestic and international students; for spring admission, 11/15 for domestic and international students. Application fee: $35 ($60 for international students). Electronic applications accepted. *Expenses:* Tuition, area resident: Full-time $3060; part-time $170 per credit hour. Tuition, state resident: full-time $3060; part-time $170 per credit hour. Tuition, nonresident: full-time $7488; part-time $416 per credit hour. International tuition: $7570 full-time. Required fees: $854; $307 per term. Tuition and fees vary according to course load. *Financial support:* Applicants required to submit FAFSA. *Faculty research:* Environmental rhetoric, instructional design, usability, assessment, presentation slides. *Unit head:* Dr. Robert Jarrett, Chair, 713-221-8013, Fax: 713-226-5205, E-mail: JarrettR@uhd.edu. *Application contact:* Dr. Ann Jennings, Coordinator of MS in Professional Writing and Technical Communication and Professor, Department of English, 713-221-8013, Fax: 713-226-5205, E-mail: mspwtc@uhd.edu.

University of Idaho, College of Graduate Studies, College of Letters, Arts and Social Sciences, Department of English, Program in English, Moscow, ID 83844-2282. Offers MA, MAT. *Students:* 13 full-time, 4 part-time. Average age 30. In 2008, 2 master's awarded. *Entrance requirements:* For master's, minimum GPA of 2.8. *Application deadline:* For fall admission, 8/1 for domestic students; for spring admission, 12/15 for domestic students. Application fee: $55 ($60 for international students). *Expenses:* Tuition, nonresident: full-time $10,080; part-time $336 per credit. Required fees: $5212; $267 per credit. Tuition and fees vary according to program. *Financial support:* Research assistantships, teaching assistantships available. Financial award application deadline: 2/15. *Unit head:* Dr. Kurt Olsson, Chair, 208-883-6156. *Application contact:* Dr. Kurt Olsson, Chair, 208-883-6156.

University of Illinois at Chicago, Graduate College, College of Liberal Arts and Sciences, Department of English, Chicago, IL 60607-7128. Offers English (MA, PhD), including creative writing (PhD), English education (MA), English studies, writing (MA); linguistics (MA), including teaching English to speakers of other languages/applied linguistics. Part-time and evening/weekend programs available. *Degree requirements:* For doctorate, variable foreign language requirement, thesis/dissertation, written and oral exams. *Entrance requirements:* For master's, GRE General Test, GRE Subject Test; for doctorate, GRE General Test, GRE Subject Test, minimum GPA of 2.0. Additional exam requirements/recommendations for international students: Required—TOEFL. Electronic applications accepted. *Faculty research:* Literary history and theory.

University of Illinois at Springfield, Graduate Programs, College of Liberal Arts and Sciences, Program in English, Springfield, IL 62703-5407. Offers MA. Part-time and evening/weekend programs available. *Faculty:* 13 full-time (8 women). *Students:* 5 full-time (all women), 22 part-time (14 women); includes 1 minority (Asian American or Pacific Islander). Average age 32. 13 applicants, 62% accepted, 5 enrolled. In 2008, 9 master's awarded. *Degree requirements:* For master's, comprehensive exam, thesis, or project. *Entrance requirements:* For master's, GRE General Test, analytical writing sample, two letters of recommendation. Additional exam requirements/recommendations for international students: Required—TOEFL (minimum score 500 paper-based; 176 computer-based; 61 iBT). *Application deadline:* Applications are processed on a rolling basis. Application fee: $50 ($60 for international students). Electronic applications accepted. *Expenses:* Tuition, state resident: full-time $6144; part-time $256 per credit hour. Tuition, nonresident: full-time $13,980; part-time $582.50 per credit hour. Required fees: $1800. *Financial support:* In 2008–09, research assistantships (averaging $8,109 per year), teaching assistantships (averaging $8,109 per year) were awarded; career-related internships or fieldwork, Federal Work-Study, scholarships/grants, health care benefits, and unspecified assistantships also available. Support available to part-time students. Financial award application deadline: 11/15; financial award applicants required to submit FAFSA. *Unit head:* Dr. James Ottery, Program Administrator, 217-206-7443, Fax: 217-206-6217, E-mail: ottery.james@uis.edu. *Application contact:* Dr. Lynn Pardie, Office of Graduate Studies, 800-252-8533, Fax: 217-206-7623, E-mail: pardie.lynn@uis.edu.

University of Illinois at Urbana–Champaign, Graduate College, College of Liberal Arts and Sciences, Department of English, Champaign, IL 61820. Offers creative writing (MFA); English (MA, PhD). *Faculty:* 59 full-time (25 women), 2 part-time/adjunct (1 woman). *Students:* 88 full-time (63 women), 67 part-time (36 women); includes 12 minority (4 African Americans, 1 American Indian/Alaska Native, 5 Asian Americans or Pacific Islanders, 2 Hispanic Americans), 12 international. 361 applicants, 16% accepted, 26 enrolled. In 2008, 20 master's, 15 doctorates awarded. *Entrance requirements:* For master's, GRE General Test, GRE Subject Test, minimum GPA of 3.0; writing sample. Additional exam requirements/recommendations for international students: Required—TOEFL (minimum score 550 paper-based; 213 computer-based). *Application deadline:* Applications are processed on a rolling basis. Application fee: $60 ($75 for international students). Electronic applications accepted. *Financial support:* In 2008–09, 76 fellowships, 11 research assistantships, 124 teaching assistantships were awarded; tuition waivers (full and partial) also available. *Faculty research:* English and American literature, cultural studies and critical theory. *Unit head:* Perry Perry, Head, 217-333-2391, Fax: 217-333-4321, E-mail: cperry@illinois.edu. *Application contact:* Stephanie Shockey, Secretary, 217-244-3646, Fax: 217-333-4321, E-mail: shockey@illinois.edu.

University of Indianapolis, Graduate Programs, College of Arts and Sciences, Department of English Language and Literature, Indianapolis, IN 46227-3697. Offers English (MA). Part-time and evening/weekend programs available. *Faculty:* 5 full-time (3 women), 2 part-time/adjunct (both women). *Students:* 4 full-time (all women), 7 part-time (all women); includes 1 minority (Hispanic American), 2 international. Average age 33. *Entrance requirements:* For master's, GRE Subject Test, minimum GPA of 2.5. Additional exam requirements/recommendations for international students: Required—TOEFL (minimum score 550 paper-based; 213 computer-based). *Application deadline:* Applications are processed on a rolling basis. Application fee: $30. Electronic applications accepted. *Financial support:* Federal Work-Study available. Financial award application deadline: 5/1; financial award applicants required to submit FAFSA. *Unit head:* Dr. William R. Dynes, Chair, 317-788-2072, Fax: 317-788-3480. *Application contact:* Dr. William R. Dynes, Chair, 317-788-2072, Fax: 317-788-3480.

The University of Iowa, Graduate College, College of Liberal Arts and Sciences, Department of English, Iowa City, IA 52242-1316. Offers English (PhD); literary criticism (PhD); literary history (PhD); literary studies (MA); nonfiction writing (MFA); rhetorical theory and stylistics (PhD); writer's workshop (MFA); JD/PhD. *Degree requirements:* For master's, thesis (for some programs), exam; for doctorate, comprehensive exam, thesis/dissertation. *Entrance requirements:* For master's and doctorate, GRE General Test, minimum GPA of 3.0. Additional exam requirements/recommendations for international students: Required—TOEFL (minimum score 640 paper-based; 273 computer-based; 112 iBT). Electronic applications accepted.

The University of Kansas, Graduate Studies, College of Liberal Arts and Sciences, Department of English, Lawrence, KS 66045. Offers creative writing (MFA); English (MA, PhD). Part-time programs available. *Faculty:* 37. *Students:* 92 full-time (61 women), 12 part-time (5 women); includes 9 minority (5 African Americans, 4 Hispanic Americans), 3 international. Average age 33. 166 applicants, 24% accepted, 21 enrolled. In 2008, 19 master's, 13 doctorates awarded. *Degree requirements:* For master's, one foreign language, comprehensive exam (for some programs), thesis or alternative; for doctorate, 2 foreign languages, comprehensive exam, thesis/dissertation. *Entrance requirements:* For master's and doctorate, GRE General Test, minimum GPA of 3.3. Additional exam requirements/recommendations for international students: Required—TOEFL. *Application deadline:* For fall admission, 1/1 priority date for domestic and international students. Applications are processed on a rolling basis. Application fee: $45 ($55 for international students). Electronic applications accepted. *Expenses:* Tuition, area resident: Full-time $6122; part-time $255.10 per credit hour. Tuition, state resident: full-time $6122; part-time $255.10 per credit hour. Tuition, nonresident: full-time $14,629; part-time $609.55 per credit hour. Required fees: $847; $70.56 per credit hour. Tuition and fees vary according to course load and program. *Financial support:* Fellowships, research assistantships, teaching assistantships with full and partial tuition reimbursements, unspecified assistantships available. Financial award application deadline: 1/1. *Faculty research:* African-American literature, 20th century American literature, Renaissance literature, creative writing. *Unit head:* Dorice Elliott, Chair, 785-864-4520, E-mail: delliott@ku.edu. *Application contact:* Joseph Harrington, Director of Graduate Studies, 785-864-4520, E-mail: j-harrington@ku.edu.

University of Kentucky, Graduate School, College of Arts and Sciences, Program in English, Lexington, KY 40506-0032. Offers MA, PhD. *Degree requirements:* For master's, one foreign language, comprehensive exam, thesis optional; for doctorate, one foreign language, comprehensive exam, thesis/dissertation. *Entrance requirements:* For master's, GRE General Test, minimum undergraduate GPA of 2.75; for doctorate, GRE General Test, minimum graduate GPA of 3.0. Additional exam requirements/recommendations for international students: Required—TOEFL (minimum score 550 paper-based; 213 computer-based). Electronic applications accepted.

University of Lethbridge, School of Graduate Studies, Lethbridge, AB T1K 3M4, Canada. Offers accounting (MScM); addictions counseling (M Sc); agricultural biotechnology (M Sc); agricultural studies (M Sc, MA); anthropology (MA); archaeology (MA); art (MA); biochemistry (M Sc); biological sciences (M Sc); biomolecular science (PhD); biosystems and biodiversity (PhD); Canadian studies (MA); chemistry (M Sc); computer science (M Sc); computer science and geographical information science (M Sc); counseling psychology (M Ed); dramatic arts (MA); earth, space, and physical science (PhD); economics (MA); educational leadership (M Ed); English (MA); environmental science (M Sc); evolution and behavior (PhD); exercise science (M Sc); finance (MScM); French (MA); French/German (MA); French/Spanish (MA); general education (M Ed); general management (MScM); geography (M Sc, MA); German (MA); health sciences (M Sc, MA); history (MA); human resource management and labour relations (MScM); individualized multidisciplinary (M Sc, MA); information systems (MScM); international management (MScM); kinesiology (M Sc, MA); management (M Sc, MA); marketing (MScM); mathematics (M Sc); music (MA); Native American studies (MA); neuroscience (M Sc, PhD); new media (MA); nursing (M Sc); philosophy (MA); physics (M Sc); policy and strategy (MScM); political science (MA); psychology (M Sc, MA); religious studies (MA); sociology (MA); theoretical and computational science (PhD); urban and regional studies (MA). Part-time and evening/weekend programs available. *Degree requirements:* For doctorate, comprehensive exam, thesis/dissertation. *Entrance requirements:* For master's, GMAT (M Sc in management), bachelor's degree in related field, minimum GPA of 3.0 during previous 20 graded semester courses, 2 years teaching or related experience (M Ed); for doctorate, master's degree, minimum graduate GPA of 3.5. Additional exam requirements/recommendations for international students: Required—TOEFL. *Faculty research:* Movement and brain plasticity, gibberellin physiology, photosynthesis, carbon cycling, molecular properties of main-group ring components.

University of Louisiana at Lafayette, BI Moody III College of Business Administration MBA Program, College of Liberal Arts, Department of English, Lafayette, LA 70504. Offers British and American literature (MA), including creative writing, folklore, rhetoric; creative writing (PhD); literature (PhD); rhetoric (PhD). Part-time programs available. Terminal master's awarded for partial completion of doctoral program. *Degree requirements:* For master's, one foreign language, thesis or alternative; for doctorate, 2 foreign languages, comprehensive exam, thesis/dissertation. *Entrance requirements:* For master's, GRE General Test, minimum GPA of 2.75; for doctorate, GRE General Test, minimum GPA of 3.0. Additional exam requirements/recommendations for international students: Required—TOEFL (minimum score 550 paper-based; 213 computer-based). Electronic applications accepted. *Faculty research:* Composition theory, Southern literature, medieval literature.

University of Louisiana at Monroe, Graduate School, College of Arts and Sciences, Department of English, Monroe, LA 71209-0001. Offers MA. Part-time and evening/weekend programs available. *Faculty:* 7 full-time (4 women). *Students:* 8 full-time (6 women), 2 part-time (both women); includes 1 minority (Hispanic American). Average age 29. In 2008, 5 master's awarded. *Degree requirements:* For master's, one foreign language, thesis (for some programs). *Entrance requirements:* For master's, GRE General Test (minimum verbal and quantitative score: 900), minimum GPA of 3.0. Additional exam requirements/recommendations for international students: Required—TOEFL (minimum score 500 paper-based; 173 computer-based; 61 iBT), TOEFL or Michigan English Language Assessment Battery. *Application deadline:* For fall admission, 8/22 priority date for domestic students, 7/1 for international students; for winter admission, 12/12 priority date for domestic students; for spring admission, 1/17 for domestic students, 11/1 for international students. Applications are processed on a rolling basis. Application fee: $20 ($30 for international students). Electronic applications accepted. *Expenses:* Tuition, area resident: Full-time $2403; part-time $1202 per semester. Tuition, state resident: full-time $2403; part-time $1202 per semester. Tuition, nonresident: full-time $2403; part-time $1202 per semester. International tuition: $8352 full-time. Required fees: $1239.40; $141 per credit hour. *Financial support:* In 2008–09, 7 teaching assistantships with full tuition reimbursements (averaging $2,600 per year) were awarded; career-related internships or fieldwork, Federal Work-Study, institutionally sponsored loans, and unspecified assistantships also available. Financial award application deadline: 4/1; financial award applicants required to submit FAFSA. *Faculty research:* Creative writing, American literature, British literature, multicultural literature, literary theory. *Unit head:* Dr. Fleming J. McClelland, Interim Head, 318-342-1485, Fax: 318-342-1491, E-mail: mcclelland@ulm.edu. *Application contact:* Dr. Julia Guernsey-Shaw, Information Contact, 318-342-1496, E-mail: shaw@ulm.edu.

University of Louisville, Graduate School, College of Arts and Sciences, Department of English, Program in English, Louisville, KY 40292. Offers creative writing (MA); literature (MA); rhetoric and composition (MA). Part-time and evening/weekend programs available. *Faculty:* 40 full-time (24 women). *Students:* 33 full-time (19 women), 29 part-time (18 women); includes 4 African Americans, 2 Asian Americans or Pacific Islanders, 1 international. Average age 28. 58 applicants, 95% accepted, 33 enrolled. In 2008, 16 master's awarded. *Degree requirements:* For master's, one foreign language, thesis or culminating project. *Entrance requirements:* For master's, GRE General Test, 10-15 page critical writing sample, 2 academic letters of recommendation, transcripts of all college work;. Additional exam requirements/recommendations for international students: Required—TOEFL (minimum score 600 paper-based; 210 computer-based; 100 iBT). *Application deadline:* For fall admission, 1/5 priority date for domestic and international students; for spring admission, 12/1 for domestic students. Applications are processed on a rolling basis. Application fee: $50. Electronic applications accepted. *Financial support:* In 2008–09, 19 students received support, including 18 teaching assistantships with full tuition reimbursements available (averaging $15,500 per year); health care benefits and unspecified assistantships also available. Financial award application deadline: 1/5. *Faculty research:* English literatures and cultures; American literatures and cultures; critical theory and cultural studies; rhetoric and composition; creative writing. Total annual research expenditures: $278,898. *Unit head:* Dr. Susan Griffin, Chair, 502-852-6801, Fax: 502-852-4182, E-mail: smgriff01@louisville.edu. *Application contact:* Libby Leggett, Director, Graduate Admissions, 502-852-3101, Fax: 502-852-6536, E-mail: gradadm@louisville.edu.

University of Louisville, Graduate School, College of Arts and Sciences, Department of English, Program in English Rhetoric and Composition, Louisville, KY 40292. Offers rhetoric and composition (PhD). Part-time programs available. *Faculty:* 40 full-time (24 women). *Students:* 39 full-time (21 women), 3 part-time (2 women); includes 5 African Americans, 3 international. Average age 34. 33 applicants, 33% accepted, 8 enrolled. In 2008, 4 doctorates awarded. *Degree requirements:* For doctorate, 2 foreign languages, comprehensive exam, thesis/dissertation. *Entrance requirements:* For doctorate, GRE General Test, 15-20 page critical writing sample, 1000-word statement of professional goals, 3 academic letters of recommendation, application for graduate teaching assistantship (resumé + statement of teaching philosophy), transcripts of all college work. Additional exam requirements/recommendations for international students: Required—TOEFL (minimum score 600 paper-based; 210 computer-based; 100 iBT). *Application deadline:* For fall admission, 1/5 priority date for domestic and international students. Application fee: $50. Electronic applications accepted. *Financial support:* In 2008–09, 28 students received support, including 4 fellowships with full tuition reimbursements available (averaging $19,992 per year), 4 teaching assistantships with full tuition reimbursements available (averaging $19,992 per year); health care benefits and fellowships, teaching assistantships also available. Financial award application deadline: 1/5. *Faculty research:* Literacy studies, including global literacies; cultural studies; historical rhetoric; composition studies; rhetorical theory. *Unit head:* Dr. Susan Griffin, Chair, 502-852-6801, Fax: 502-852-4182, E-mail: smgriff01@louisville.edu. *Application contact:* Libby Leggett, Director, Graduate Admissions, 502-852-3108, Fax: 502-852-3111, E-mail: gradadm@louisville.edu.

University of Maine, Graduate School, College of Liberal Arts and Sciences, Department of English, Orono, ME 04469. Offers MA. Part-time and evening/weekend programs available. *Degree requirements:* For master's, one foreign language, thesis optional. *Entrance requirements:* For master's, GRE General Test, minimum GPA of 3.0. Additional exam requirements/recommendations for international students: Required—TOEFL. Electronic applications accepted. *Faculty research:* Contemporary poetics, contemporary criticism, composition theory and pedagogy, feminist approaches to literature.

University of Manitoba, Faculty of Graduate Studies, Faculty of Arts, Department of English, Film, and Theatre, Winnipeg, MB R3T 2N2, Canada. Offers English (MA, PhD). *Degree requirements:* For master's, one foreign language, thesis; for doctorate, one foreign language, thesis/dissertation.

University of Maryland, College Park, Graduate Studies, College of Arts and Humanities, Department of English, Program in English Language and Literature, College Park, MD 20742. Offers MA, PhD. *Degree requirements:* For master's, thesis optional; for doctorate, one foreign language, thesis/dissertation, oral and written exams. *Entrance requirements:* For master's, GRE General Test, minimum GPA of 3.5, writing sample, 3 letters of recommendation; for doctorate, GRE General Test, minimum GPA of 3.7, writing sample. Additional exam requirements/recommendations for international students: Required—TOEFL. Electronic applications accepted.

University of Massachusetts Amherst, Graduate School, College of Humanities and Fine Arts, Department of English, Amherst, MA 01003. Offers creative writing (MFA); English and American literature (MA, PhD). Part-time programs available. Terminal master's awarded for partial completion of doctoral program. *Degree requirements:* For master's, one foreign language, thesis optional; for doctorate, one foreign language, comprehensive exam, thesis/dissertation. *Entrance requirements:* For master's, GRE General Test, GRE Subject Test (MA), writing sample (MFA); for doctorate, GRE General Test, GRE Subject Test. Additional exam requirements/recommendations for international students: Required—TOEFL (minimum score 550 paper-based; 213 computer-based; 79 iBT), IELTS (minimum score 6.5). Electronic applications accepted. *Expenses:* Tuition, area resident: Full-time $2640. Tuition, nonresident: full-time $9936. One-time fee: $332 full-time. Tuition and fees vary according to course load.

University of Massachusetts Boston, Office of Graduate Studies, College of Liberal Arts, Program in English, Boston, MA 02125-3393. Offers MA. Part-time and evening/weekend programs available. *Degree requirements:* For master's, one foreign language, final project. *Entrance requirements:* For master's, minimum GPA of 2.75. *Faculty research:* Working class literature, women writers, British fiction, composition theory, modern American literature.

University of Memphis, Graduate School, College of Arts and Sciences, Department of English, Memphis, TN 38152. Offers creative writing (MFA); English (MA, Graduate Certificate); writing and language studies (PhD). Part-time programs available. *Faculty:* 36 full-time (17 women), 2 part-time/adjunct (both women). *Students:* 83 full-time (48 women), 112 part-time (90 women); includes 36 minority (33 African Americans, 2 Asian Americans or Pacific Islanders, 1 Hispanic American), 11 international. Average age 35. 100 applicants, 84% accepted, 27 enrolled. In 2008, 44 master's, 2 doctorates, 13 other advanced degrees awarded. Terminal master's awarded for partial completion of doctoral program. *Degree requirements:* For master's, one foreign language, comprehensive exam, thesis or alternative; for doctorate, 2 foreign languages, comprehensive exam, thesis/dissertation. *Entrance requirements:* For master's, GRE General Test or MAT, minimum GPA of 2.5; for doctorate, GRE General Test, minimum GPA of 3.0. *Application deadline:* For fall admission, 8/1 for domestic students; for spring admission, 12/1 for domestic students. Applications are processed on a rolling basis. Application fee: $35 ($60 for international students). *Expenses:* Tuition, area resident: Full-time $6242; part-time $330 per credit hour. Tuition, state resident: full-time $6242; part-time $330 per credit hour. Tuition, nonresident: full-time $17,828; part-time $815 per credit hour. Required fees: $1156. *Financial support:* Research assistantships with full tuition reimbursements, teaching assistantships with full tuition reimbursements available. Financial award applicants required to submit FAFSA. *Faculty research:* American literature, cultural studies, ESL/linguistics, composition studies/professional writing. *Unit head:* Dr. Eric C. Link, Chair, 901-678-2651, Fax: 901-678-2226, E-mail: eclink@memphis.edu. *Application contact:* Dr. Verner D. Mitchell, Director, Graduate Studies, 901-678-3099, Fax: 901-678-2226, E-mail: vdmtchll@memphis.edu.

University of Miami, Graduate School, College of Arts and Sciences, Department of English, Coral Gables, FL 33124. Offers creative writing (MFA); English (MA, PhD). Part-time programs available. Terminal master's awarded for partial completion of doctoral program. *Degree requirements:* For master's, one foreign language, thesis optional; for doctorate, one foreign language, thesis/dissertation. *Entrance requirements:* For master's and doctorate, GRE General Test. Electronic applications accepted. *Faculty research:* Anglo-Irish literature, feminist criticism and theory, Caribbean literature, early modern literature and culture, postcolonial and ethnic studies.

University of Michigan, Horace H. Rackham School of Graduate Studies, College of Literature, Science, and the Arts, Department of English Language and Literature, Ann Arbor, MI 48109. Offers creative writing (MFA); English and education (PhD); English and women's studies (PhD); English language and literature (PhD). *Degree requirements:* For doctorate, 2 foreign languages, comprehensive exam, thesis/dissertation, oral defense of dissertation, preliminary exam. *Entrance requirements:* For doctorate, GRE General Test, GRE Subject Test, writing sample. Additional exam requirements/recommendations for international students: Required—TOEFL (minimum score 620 paper-based; 260 computer-based; 106 iBT). Electronic applications accepted. *Faculty research:* Post colonialism, modernism, early modern, American, British.

University of Michigan, Horace H. Rackham School of Graduate Studies, College of Literature, Science, and the Arts, Department of Women's Studies, Ann Arbor, MI 48109. Offers English and women's studies (PhD); history and women's studies (PhD); lesbian, gay, bisexual, transgender, queer (LGBTQ) studies (Certificate); psychology and women's studies (PhD); sociology and women's studies (PhD); women's studies (Certificate). *Degree requirements:* For doctorate, variable foreign language requirement, thesis/dissertation. *Entrance requirements:* For doctorate, GRE General Test, previous undergraduate course work in women's studies. Electronic applications accepted. *Faculty research:* Gender issues; LGBTQ studies; sexuality; women and science; global feminism.

University of Michigan–Flint, College of Arts and Sciences, Program in English, Flint, MI 48502-1950. Offers MA. Part-time programs available. *Faculty:* 9 full-time (4 women), 1 (woman) part-time/adjunct. *Students:* 8 full-time (5 women), 46 part-time (32 women); includes 8 minority (6 African Americans, 1 Asian American or Pacific Islander, 1 Hispanic American). Average age 36. 31 applicants, 77% accepted, 18 enrolled. *Entrance requirements:* Additional exam requirements/recommendations for international students: Required—TOEFL (minimum score 550 paper-based; 220 computer-based), IELTS (minimum score 6.5). *Application deadline:* For fall admission, 8/1 priority date for domestic students, 5/1 priority date for international students; for winter admission, 11/15 priority date for domestic students, 9/15 priority date for international students; for spring admission, 3/15 priority date for domestic students, 1/15 priority date for international students. Application fee: $55. *Expenses:* Contact institution. *Financial support:* Federal Work-Study, scholarships/grants, and unspecified assistantships available. Support available to part-time students. Financial award application deadline: 6/1; financial award applicants required to submit FAFSA. *Unit head:* Dr. Tom Foster, Program Director, 810-762-3285, E-mail: tfos@umflint.edu. *Application contact:* Bradley T. Maki, Director of Graduate Admissions, 810-762-3171, Fax: 810-766-6789, E-mail: bmaki@umflint.edu.

University of Minnesota, Duluth, Graduate School, College of Liberal Arts, Department of English, Duluth, MN 55812-2496. Offers MA. Part-time programs available. *Degree requirements:* For master's, one foreign language, comprehensive exam, 2 extended papers or projects. *Entrance requirements:* For master's, GRE General Test, minimum GPA of 3.0. Additional exam requirements/recommendations for international students: Required—TOEFL (minimum score 213 computer-based). *Faculty research:* British cultural studies, Irish literature, American studies, linguistics, information design.

University of Minnesota, Twin Cities Campus, Graduate School, College of Liberal Arts, Department of English, Minneapolis, MN 55455-0213. Offers MA, MFA, PhD. Part-time programs available. Terminal master's awarded for partial completion of doctoral program. *Degree requirements:* For master's, one foreign language, thesis or alternative; for doctorate, 2 foreign languages, thesis/dissertation. *Entrance requirements:* For master's and doctorate, GRE General Test. Additional exam requirements/recommendations for international students: Required—TOEFL. Electronic applications accepted. *Faculty research:* British and American literature, postcolonial literature, feminist studies in literature, composition and creative writing, cultural studies.

University of Mississippi, Graduate School, College of Liberal Arts, Department of English, Oxford, University, MS 38677. Offers MA, MFA, PhD. *Degree requirements:* For master's, one foreign language, thesis; for doctorate, 2 foreign languages, thesis/dissertation. *Entrance requirements:* For master's, GRE General Test, minimum GPA of 3.0; for doctorate, GRE General Test. Additional exam requirements/recommendations for international students: Required—TOEFL.

University of Missouri–Columbia, Graduate School, College of Arts and Sciences, Department of English, Columbia, MO 65211. Offers MA, PhD. *Faculty:* 59 full-time (37 women), 5 part-time/adjunct (1 woman). *Students:* 65 full-time (35 women), 45 part-time (29 women); includes 8 minority (4 African Americans, 1 American Indian/Alaska Native, 1 Asian American or Pacific Islander, 2 Hispanic Americans), 6 international. Average age 32. 149 applicants, 12% accepted, 18 enrolled. In 2008, 16 master's, 13 doctorates awarded. Terminal master's awarded for partial completion of doctoral program. *Degree requirements:* For doctorate, 2 foreign languages, thesis/dissertation. *Entrance requirements:* For master's and doctorate, GRE General Test, minimum GPA of 3.0. Additional exam requirements/recommendations for international students:

English

University of Missouri–Columbia (continued)

Required—TOEFL (minimum score 500 paper-based; 173 computer-based; 61 iBT). *Application deadline:* For fall admission, 1/15 priority date for domestic students. Applications are processed on a rolling basis. Application fee: $45 ($60 for international students). *Financial support:* Fellowships, research assistantships, teaching assistantships, institutionally sponsored loans available. *Unit head:* Dr. Pat Okker, Department Chair, 573-882-6066, E-mail: okkerp@missouri.edu. *Application contact:* Vickie Thorp, Secretary Sr, 573-882-4676, E-mail: thorpv@missouri.edu.

University of Missouri–Kansas City, College of Arts and Sciences, Department of English, Kansas City, MO 64110-2499. Offers MA, PhD. PhD (interdisciplinary) offered through the School of Graduate Studies. Part-time and evening/weekend programs available. *Faculty:* 20 full-time (14 women), 16 part-time/adjunct (12 women). *Students:* 5 full-time (2 women), 46 part-time (28 women); includes 5 minority (all African Americans). Average age 32. 34 applicants, 59% accepted, 19 enrolled. In 2008, 17 master's awarded. *Degree requirements:* For master's, one foreign language; for doctorate, 2 foreign languages, comprehensive exam, thesis/dissertation. *Entrance requirements:* For master's, GRE General Test, writing sample, statement of purpose, 3 letters of recommendation. Additional exam requirements/recommendations for international students: Required—TOEFL (minimum score 550 paper-based; 213 computer-based; 80 iBT). *Application deadline:* For fall admission, 1/15 for domestic students, 1/15 priority date for international students. Applications are processed on a rolling basis. Application fee: $45 ($50 for international students). Electronic applications accepted. *Expenses:* Tuition, state resident: full-time $5376; part-time $298.70 per credit hour. Tuition, nonresident: full-time $13,882; part-time $771.20 per credit hour. Required fees: $640.28; $34.65 per contact hour. $30 per semester. Tuition and fees vary according to course load and program. *Financial support:* In 2008–09, 2 research assistantships (averaging $11,328 per year), 13 teaching assistantships (averaging $13,731 per year) were awarded; career-related internships or fieldwork, Federal Work-Study, and institutionally sponsored loans also available. Support available to part-time students. Financial award application deadline: 3/1; financial award applicants required to submit FAFSA. *Faculty research:* Creative writing: poetry and prose, computational linguistics, rhetoric and composition, African American and British literature, print culture. Total annual research expenditures: $234,094. *Unit head:* Dr. Jeff Rydberg-Cox, Co-Chair, 816-235-2560, Fax: 816-235-1308, E-mail: rydbergcoxj@umkc.edu. *Application contact:* Dr. Joan Dean, Director of Graduate Studies, 816-235-2555, E-mail: deanj@umkc.edu.

University of Missouri–St. Louis, College of Arts and Sciences, Department of English, St. Louis, MO 63121. Offers American literature (MA); creative writing (MFA); English (MA); English literature (MA); linguistics (MA); teaching of writing (Graduate Certificate). Part-time and evening/weekend programs available. *Faculty:* 19 full-time (12 women), 1 part-time/adjunct (0 women). *Students:* 14 full-time (8 women), 98 part-time (71 women); includes 10 minority (8 African Americans, 1 Asian American or Pacific Islander, 1 Hispanic American). Average age 32. In 2008, 21 master's awarded. *Degree requirements:* For master's, thesis optional. *Entrance requirements:* For master's, writing sample. Additional exam requirements/recommendations for international students: Required—TOEFL (minimum score 550 paper-based; 213 computer-based). *Application deadline:* For fall admission, 7/1 priority date for domestic and international students; for spring admission, 12/1 priority date for domestic and international students. Applications are processed on a rolling basis. Application fee: $35 ($40 for international students). Electronic applications accepted. *Expenses:* Tuition, area resident: Full-time $5377; part-time $298.70 per credit hour. Tuition, nonresident: full-time $13,381; part-time $472.50 per credit hour. Required fees: $4078; $52 per credit hour. *Financial support:* In 2008–09, 2 research assistantships (averaging $9,000 per year), 4 teaching assistantships with full and partial tuition reimbursements (averaging $9,000 per year) were awarded. Financial award applicants required to submit FAFSA. *Faculty research:* Victorian literature, Shakespeare and Renaissance literature, eighteenth century literature, composition theory. *Unit head:* Dr. Frank Grady, Director of Graduate Studies, 314-516-5541, Fax: 314-516-5781, E-mail: fgrady@umsl.edu. *Application contact:* 314-516-5458, Fax: 314-516-5310, E-mail: gradadm@umsl.edu.

The University of Montana, Graduate School, College of Arts and Sciences, Department of English, Program in Literature, Missoula, MT 59812-0002. Offers MA. *Degree requirements:* For master's, thesis optional. *Entrance requirements:* For master's, GRE General Test, sample of written work. Additional exam requirements/recommendations for international students: Required—TOEFL. *Faculty research:* Literary history, cultural studies, criticism and theory, Western studies.

University of Montevallo, College of Arts and Sciences, Department of English, Montevallo, AL 35115. Offers English literature (MA). Part-time programs available. *Students:* 1 (woman) full-time, 6 part-time (all women); includes 1 minority (Asian American or Pacific Islander). In 2008, 5 master's awarded. *Degree requirements:* For master's, comprehensive exam, thesis optional. *Entrance requirements:* For master's, GRE General Test, MAT, minimum undergraduate GPA of 2.75 in last 60 hours or 2.5 overall, bachelor's degree in English or equivalent. Additional exam requirements/recommendations for international students: Required—TOEFL (minimum score 550 paper-based; 213 computer-based). *Application deadline:* For fall admission, 7/15 for domestic students; for spring admission, 11/15 for domestic students. Application fee: $25. *Expenses:* Tuition, state resident: full-time $5280; part-time $220 per credit hour. Tuition, nonresident: full-time $10,560; part-time $440 per credit hour. Required fees: $482; $113 per semester. One-time fee: $25 part-time. *Financial support:* Federal Work-Study, scholarships/grants, and unspecified assistantships available. *Unit head:* Dr. Jim Murphy, Chair, 205-665-6420, E-mail: murphyj@montevallo.edu. *Application contact:* Dr. Jim Murphy, Chair, 205-665-6420, E-mail: murphyj@montevallo.edu.

University of Nebraska at Kearney, College of Graduate Study, College of Fine Arts and Humanities, Department of English, Kearney, NE 68849-0001. Offers creative writing (MA); literature (MA). Part-time and evening/weekend programs available. *Degree requirements:* For master's, thesis optional. *Entrance requirements:* For master's, GRE General Test, writing samples. Additional exam requirements/recommendations for international students: Required—TOEFL (minimum score 550 paper-based; 213 computer-based). Electronic applications accepted. *Faculty research:* Narrative theory, popular culture, western and plains literature, women's studies, media studies.

University of Nebraska at Omaha, Graduate Studies and Research, College of Arts and Sciences, Department of English, Omaha, NE 68182. Offers advanced writing (Certificate); English (MA); teaching English to speakers of other languages (Certificate); technical communication (Certificate). Part-time and evening/weekend programs available. *Degree requirements:* For master's, comprehensive exam, thesis (for some programs). *Entrance requirements:* For master's, minimum GPA of 3.0, statement of purpose, 3 letters of recommendation, writing sample. Additional exam requirements/recommendations for international students: Required—TOEFL (minimum score 600 paper-based; 250 computer-based; 100 iBT). Electronic applications accepted.

University of Nebraska–Lincoln, Graduate College, College of Arts and Sciences, Department of English, Lincoln, NE 68588-0333. Offers composition and rhetoric (MA, PhD); creative writing (MA, PhD); literature studies (MA, PhD). *Faculty:* 39 full-time (23 women). *Students:* 77 full-time (57 women), 54 part-time (36 women); includes 5 minority (3 African Americans, 2 Hispanic Americans), 6 international. In 2008, 11 master's, 15 doctorates awarded. *Degree requirements:* For master's, thesis optional; for doctorate, one foreign language, comprehensive exam, thesis/dissertation. *Entrance requirements:* For master's, writing sample; for doctorate, GRE General Test, writing sample. Additional exam requirements/recommendations for international students: Required—TOEFL (minimum score 600 paper-based; 250 computer-based). *Application deadline:* For fall admission, 1/15 for domestic and international students. Application fee: $40. Electronic applications accepted. *Expenses:* Tuition, state resident: full-time $4275; part-time $237.50 per credit hour. Tuition, nonresident: full-time $11,525; part-time $640.25 per credit hour. Required fees: $1068; $10.35 per credit hour. $440.70 per semester. Tuition and fees vary according to course load and program. *Financial support:* Fellowships, research assistantships, teaching assistantships, Federal Work-Study, health care benefits, and unspecified assistantships available. Support available to part-time students. Financial award application deadline: 1/15. *Faculty research:* Creative writing, composition and rhetoric, women's studies, North American literature, medieval/Renaissance studies. *Unit head:* Dr. Linda Pratt, Chair, 402-472-3191, Fax: 402-472-1123. *Application contact:* Ginny Gross, Director of Graduate Admissions, 402-472-2878, Fax: 402-472-0589, E-mail: grad_admissions@unl.edu.

University of Nevada, Las Vegas, Graduate College, College of Liberal Arts, Department of English, Las Vegas, NV 89154-5011. Offers creative writing (MFA); English (MA, PhD). Part-time programs available. *Faculty:* 32 full-time (12 women), 5 part-time/adjunct (0 women). *Students:* 66 full-time (31 women), 21 part-time (14 women); includes 4 minority (1 Asian American or Pacific Islander, 3 Hispanic Americans), 4 international. Average age 35. 172 applicants, 23% accepted, 25 enrolled. In 2008, 16 master's, 3 doctorates awarded. *Degree requirements:* For master's, one foreign language, comprehensive exam, thesis (for some programs); for doctorate, 2 foreign languages, comprehensive exam, thesis/dissertation. *Entrance requirements:* For master's, GRE General Test (Verbal); for doctorate, GRE General Test (Verbal and Subject). Additional exam requirements/recommendations for international students: Required—TOEFL (minimum score 550 paper-based; 213 computer-based; 80 iBT), IELTS (minimum score 7). *Application deadline:* For fall admission, 2/15 priority date for domestic and international students. Applications are processed on a rolling basis. Application fee: $60 ($75 for international students). Electronic applications accepted. *Expenses:* Tuition, state resident: full-time $1414; part-time $198 per credit. Tuition, nonresident: full-time $12,509; part-time $415.75 per credit. International tuition: $14,249 full-time. Required fees: $4 per credit. $252 per semester. Tuition and fees vary according to course load. *Financial support:* In 2008–09, 69 students received support, including 5 research assistantships with partial tuition reimbursements available (averaging $19,400 per year), 64 teaching assistantships with partial tuition reimbursements available (averaging $11,803 per year); institutionally sponsored loans, scholarships/grants, health care benefits, and unspecified assistantships also available. Financial award application deadline: 3/1. *Faculty research:* Contemporary poetry and fiction, Renaissance literature and Renaissance studies, Post-Structuralist literary theory and criticism, business and professional writing, 19th and 20th century British and American literature. *Unit head:* Dr. Richard Harp, Chair/Professor, 702-895-0919, Fax: 702-895-4801, E-mail: richard.harp@unlv.edu. *Application contact:* Graduate College Admissions Evaluator, 702-895-3320, Fax: 702-895-4180, E-mail: gradcollege@unlv.edu.

University of Nevada, Reno, Graduate School, College of Liberal Arts, Department of English, Reno, NV 89557. Offers MA, MATE, PhD. *Faculty:* 21 full-time (10 women). *Students:* 26 full-time (16 women), 49 part-time (28 women); includes 3 minority (1 Asian American or Pacific Islander, 2 Hispanic Americans), 3 international. Average age 34. 62 applicants, 40% accepted, 21 enrolled. In 2008, 10 master's, 2 doctorates awarded. Terminal master's awarded for partial completion of doctoral program. *Degree requirements:* For master's, variable foreign language requirement, thesis optional; for doctorate, variable foreign language requirement, thesis/dissertation. *Entrance requirements:* For master's, GRE General Test, minimum GPA of 2.75; for doctorate, GRE General Test, minimum GPA of 3.0. Additional exam requirements/recommendations for international students: Required—TOEFL (minimum score 500 paper-based; 173 computer-based; 61 iBT), IELTS (minimum score 6). *Application deadline:* For fall admission, 2/1 for domestic students, 2/1 priority date for international students. Application fee: $60 ($95 for international students). Electronic applications accepted. *Expenses:* Tuition, state resident: full-time $1710; part-time $1140 per semester. Tuition, nonresident: full-time $7115. Required fees: $158 per semester. *Financial support:* In 2008–09, 1 research assistantship with partial tuition reimbursement (averaging $14,000 per year), 40 teaching assistantships with partial tuition reimbursements (averaging $14,000 per year) were awarded; Federal Work-Study, institutionally sponsored loans, scholarships/grants, health care benefits, and unspecified assistantships also available. Financial award application deadline: 3/1; financial award applicants required to submit FAFSA. *Faculty research:* Translating Persian/Iraqi literature, Shakespearean literature, modern American literature, composition and rhetoric. Total annual research expenditures: $22,489. *Unit head:* Dr. Don Hardy, Graduate Program Director, 775-784-8689. *Application contact:* Michele Sandberg, Application Contact, 775-784-7026, Fax: 775-784-6064, E-mail: gradschool@unr.edu.

University of New Brunswick Fredericton, School of Graduate Studies, Faculty of Arts, Department of English, Fredericton, NB E3B 5A3, Canada. Offers MA, PhD. Part-time programs available. *Faculty:* 15 full-time (7 women), 1 (woman) part-time/adjunct. *Students:* 45 full-time (19 women), 5 part-time (2 women). Average age 25. 62 applicants, 53% accepted, 15 enrolled. In 2008, 10 master's, 1 doctorate awarded. *Degree requirements:* For master's, thesis; for doctorate, comprehensive exam, thesis/dissertation. *Entrance requirements:* For master's and doctorate, minimum GPA of 3.7. Additional exam requirements/recommendations for international students: Required—TOEFL (minimum score 550 paper-based), TWE (minimum score 4). *Application deadline:* 1/31 priority date for domestic and international students. Applications are processed on a rolling basis. Application fee: $50 Canadian dollars. Tuition and fees charges are reported in Canadian dollars. *Expenses:* Tuition, area resident: Full-time $5562 Canadian dollars. Tuition, nonresident: full-time $9450 Canadian dollars. Required fees: $333 Canadian dollars. *Financial support:* In 2008–09, 14 research assistantships were awarded; fellowships, teaching assistantships, health care benefits also available. Financial award application deadline: 1/31. *Faculty research:* Creative writing, Canadian literature, Post Colonial literature, Early Modern literature, scholarly editing and textual studies. *Unit head:* Dr. Randall Martin, Director of Graduate Studies, 506-458-7407, Fax: 506-453-5069, E-mail: martin@unb.ca. *Application contact:* Theresa Keenan, Graduate Secretary, 506-451-6809, Fax: 506-453-5069, E-mail: tkeenan@unb.ca.

University of New Hampshire, Graduate School, College of Liberal Arts, Department of English, Durham, NH 03824. Offers English (MFA, PhD); English education (MST); language and linguistics (MA); literature (MA); writing (MA). Part-time programs available. *Faculty:* 35 full-time (18 women). *Students:* 50 full-time (29 women), 66 part-time (44 women); includes 6 minority (1 African American, 3 Asian Americans or Pacific Islanders, 2 Hispanic Americans), 5 international. Average age 34. 267 applicants, 44% accepted, 37 enrolled. In 2008, 33 master's, 1 doctorate awarded. *Degree requirements:* For master's, one foreign language; for doctorate, 2 foreign languages, thesis/dissertation. *Entrance requirements:* For master's, GRE General Test, sample of written work; for doctorate, GRE General Test, GRE Subject Test, sample of written work. Additional exam requirements/recommendations for international students: Required—TOEFL (minimum score 550 paper-based; 213 computer-based; 80 iBT). *Application deadline:* For fall admission, 2/15 priority date for domestic students, 2/15 for international students. Applications are processed on a rolling basis. Application fee: $60. Electronic applications accepted. *Expenses:* Tuition, area resident: Full-time $9720; part-time $540 per credit hour. Tuition, nonresident: full-time $23,200; part-time $954 per credit hour. Required fees: $1446; $361.50 per term. *Financial support:* In 2008–09, 58 students received support, including 3 fellowships, 1 research assistantship, 47 teaching assistantships; career-related internships or fieldwork, Federal Work-Study, scholarships/grants, and tuition waivers (full and partial) also available. Support available to part-time students. Financial award application deadline: 2/15. *Unit head:* Dr. Andrew Merton, Chairperson, 603-862-3963. *Application contact:* Sue Smith, Administrative Assistant, 603-862-3963, E-mail: engl.grad@unh.edu.

University of New Mexico, Graduate School, College of Arts and Sciences, Department of English, Program in English, Albuquerque, NM 87131-2039. Offers MA, PhD. *Degree requirements:* For master's, one foreign language, comprehensive exam (for some programs), thesis (for some programs), portfolio; for doctorate, 2 foreign languages, comprehensive exam, thesis/dissertation. *Entrance requirements:* For master's, GRE General Test, GRE Subject Test (literature MA); for doctorate, GRE General Test, GRE Subject Test. *Faculty research:* American literature, Native American literature, Chicano literature, British and Irish literature, rhetoric and writing.

English

University of New Orleans, Graduate School, College of Liberal Arts, Department of English, Program in English, New Orleans, LA 70148. Offers MA. Part-time and evening/weekend programs available. *Degree requirements:* For master's, one foreign language, thesis (for some programs). *Entrance requirements:* For master's, GRE General Test. Additional exam requirements/recommendations for international students: Required—TOEFL (minimum score 550 paper-based; 213 computer-based; 79 iBT). Electronic applications accepted.

University of North Alabama, College of Arts and Sciences, Department of English, Florence, AL 35632-0001. Offers MAEN. Part-time and evening/weekend programs available. *Faculty:* 7 part-time/adjunct (3 women). *Students:* 8 full-time (6 women), 15 part-time (12 women). Average age 32. In 2008, 12 master's awarded. *Application deadline:* For fall admission, 7/1 priority date for domestic students; for spring admission, 12/1 for domestic students. Applications are processed on a rolling basis. Application fee: $25. Electronic applications accepted. *Expenses:* Tuition, area resident: Full-time $4704; part-time $196 per credit hour. Tuition, state resident: full-time $4704; part-time $196 per credit hour. Tuition, nonresident: full-time $9408; part-time $392 per credit hour. Required fees: $882. Tuition and fees vary according to course load and program. *Unit head:* Dr. Ronald Smith, Chair, 256-765-4238, Fax: 256-765-4239, E-mail: resmith@una.edu. *Application contact:* Kim Mauldin, Director of Admissions, 256-765-4608, Fax: 256-765-4960, E-mail: komauldin@una.edu.

The University of North Carolina at Chapel Hill, Graduate School, College of Arts and Sciences, Department of English, Chapel Hill, NC 27599. Offers MA, PhD. *Degree requirements:* For master's, one foreign language, comprehensive exam, thesis; for doctorate, 2 foreign languages, comprehensive exam, thesis/dissertation. *Entrance requirements:* For master's and doctorate, GRE General Test, GRE Subject Test, minimum GPA of 3.0 for last 2 undergraduate years, writing sample. Additional exam requirements/recommendations for international students: Required—TOEFL. Electronic applications accepted. *Faculty research:* African American, Southern, period studies, genre studies, critical theory/culture studies.

The University of North Carolina at Charlotte, Graduate School, College of Arts and Sciences, Department of English, Charlotte, NC 28223-0001. Offers English (MA); English education (MA). Part-time and evening/weekend programs available. *Faculty:* 34 full-time (17 women). *Students:* 30 full-time (21 women), 44 part-time (36 women); includes 8 minority (6 African Americans, 1 Asian American or Pacific Islander, 1 Hispanic American), 1 international. Average age 30. 41 applicants, 83% accepted, 24 enrolled. In 2008, 21 master's awarded. *Degree requirements:* For master's, comprehensive exam. *Entrance requirements:* For master's, GRE General Test, minimum undergraduate GPA of 3.0 in major, 2.75 overall. Additional exam requirements/recommendations for international students: Required—TOEFL (minimum score 557 paper-based; 220 computer-based). *Application deadline:* For fall admission, 7/15 for domestic students, 5/1 for international students; for spring admission, 11/15 for domestic students, 10/1 for international students. Applications are processed on a rolling basis. Application fee: $55. Electronic applications accepted. *Expenses:* Tuition, area resident: Full-time $2919; part-time $122 per credit hour. Tuition, state resident: full-time $2919; part-time $122 per credit hour. Tuition, nonresident: full-time $13,126; part-time $547 per credit hour. Required fees: $1779; $91 per credit hour. Tuition and fees vary according to program. *Financial support:* In 2008–09, 2 research assistantships (averaging $5,000 per year), 25 teaching assistantships (averaging $7,404 per year) were awarded; career-related internships or fieldwork, Federal Work-Study, institutionally sponsored loans, scholarships/grants, unspecified assistantships, and 1 administrative assistantship ($9,500) also available. Support available to part-time students. Financial award application deadline: 4/1; financial award applicants required to submit FAFSA. *Faculty research:* English as a second language (ESL), composition theory and pedagogy, children's literature, technical and professional writing, English for specific purposes (ESP). Total annual research expenditures: $700,000. *Unit head:* Dr. Cyril H. Knoblauch, Chair, 704-687-2296, Fax: 704-687-3961, E-mail: chknobla@email.uncc.edu. *Application contact:* Kathy B. Giddings, Director of Graduate Admissions, 704-687-3366, Fax: 704-687-3279, E-mail: agidding@uncc.edu.

The University of North Carolina at Greensboro, Graduate School, College of Arts and Sciences, Department of English, Program in English, Greensboro, NC 27412-5001. Offers American literature (PhD); English (M Ed, MA); English literature (PhD); rhetoric and composition (PhD). *Degree requirements:* For master's, comprehensive exam, thesis or alternative; for doctorate, variable foreign language requirement, thesis/dissertation, preliminary exam. *Entrance requirements:* For master's, GRE General Test, GRE Subject Test, minimum GPA of 3.0; for doctorate, GRE General Test, GRE Subject Test, critical writing sample, minimum GPA of 3.0. Additional exam requirements/recommendations for international students: Required—TOEFL. Electronic applications accepted.

The University of North Carolina Wilmington, College of Arts and Sciences, Department of English, Wilmington, NC 28403-3297. Offers MA. *Faculty:* 26 full-time (13 women). *Students:* 13 full-time (11 women), 24 part-time (12 women); includes 1 minority (African American). Average age 27. 25 applicants, 68% accepted, 14 enrolled. In 2008, 17 master's awarded. *Degree requirements:* For master's, comprehensive exam, thesis. *Entrance requirements:* For master's, GRE General Test, minimum B average in undergraduate major. Additional exam requirements/recommendations for international students: Required—TOEFL (minimum score 550 paper-based; 217 computer-based; 79 iBT), IELTS (minimum score 6.5). *Application deadline:* For fall admission, 3/1 for domestic students. Applications are processed on a rolling basis. Application fee: $60. *Expenses:* Tuition, area resident: Full-time $4838. Tuition, state resident: full-time $4838. Tuition, nonresident: full-time $14,898. Required fees: $969.38 per semester. Tuition and fees vary according to course load, campus/location and program. *Financial support:* In 2008–09, 9 teaching assistantships with full and partial tuition reimbursements (averaging $9,500 per year) were awarded; career-related internships or fieldwork and Federal Work-Study also available. Support available to part-time students. Financial award application deadline: 3/15. *Unit head:* Dr. Keith Newlin, Chair, 910-962-3615, Fax: 910-962-7186, E-mail: nowlink@uncw.edu. *Application contact:* Dr. Colleen Reilly, Graduate Coordinator, 910-962-7548, E-mail: reillyc@uncw.edu.

University of North Dakota, Graduate School, College of Arts and Sciences, Department of English, Grand Forks, ND 58202. Offers MA, PhD. *Degree requirements:* For master's, one foreign language, comprehensive exam, thesis or alternative; for doctorate, one foreign language, comprehensive exam, thesis/dissertation. *Entrance requirements:* For master's and doctorate, GRE General Test, minimum GPA of 3.0. Additional exam requirements/recommendations for international students: Required—TOEFL (minimum score 550 paper-based; 213 computer-based; 79 iBT), IELTS (minimum score 6.5). Electronic applications accepted. *Faculty research:* Creative writing, rhetorical theory, cinema, American literature, European literature.

University of Northern Colorado, Graduate School, College of Humanities and Social Sciences, School of English Language and Literature, Program in English, Greeley, CO 80639. Offers MA. Part-time programs available. *Faculty:* 9 full-time (4 women). *Students:* 18 full-time (10 women), 3 part-time (0 women); includes 2 minority (1 Asian American or Pacific Islander, 1 Hispanic American). Average age 31. 16 applicants, 94% accepted, 7 enrolled. In 2008, 5 master's awarded. *Degree requirements:* For master's, comprehensive exam. *Entrance requirements:* For master's, GRE General Test, 2 letters of recommendation. *Application deadline:* Applications are processed on a rolling basis. Application fee: $50 ($60 for international students). Electronic applications accepted. *Expenses:* Tuition, state resident: full-time $4370; part-time $242.75 per credit hour. Tuition, nonresident: full-time $12,366; part-time $687 per credit hour. Required fees: $664.20; $36.90 per credit hour. *Financial support:* In 2008–09, 6 research assistantships (averaging $5,009 per year), 16 teaching assistantships (averaging $9,169 per year) were awarded; unspecified assistantships also available. Financial award application deadline: 3/1; financial award applicants required to submit FAFSA. *Unit head:* Dr. Marcus Embry, Program Coordinator, 970-351-2971, Fax: 970-351-3378. *Application contact:* Linda Sisson, Graduate Student Admission Coordinator, 970-351-1807, Fax: 970-351-2371, E-mail: linda.sisson@unco.edu.

University of Northern Iowa, Graduate College, College of Humanities and Fine Arts, Department of English Language and Literature, Cedar Falls, IA 50614. Offers English (MA); teaching English to speakers of other languages (MA). Part-time and evening/weekend programs available. *Students:* 38 full-time (25 women), 17 part-time (15 women); includes 3 minority (1 African American, 2 Asian Americans or Pacific Islanders), 10 international. 56 applicants, 52% accepted, 20 enrolled. In 2008, 20 master's awarded. *Degree requirements:* For master's, one foreign language, comprehensive exam, thesis or alternative, portfolio. *Entrance requirements:* For master's, minimum GPA of 3.0. Additional exam requirements/recommendations for international students: Required—TOEFL (minimum score 600 paper-based; 250 computer-based; 100 iBT). *Application deadline:* For fall admission, 8/1 priority date for domestic students. Applications are processed on a rolling basis. Application fee: $30 ($50 for international students). Electronic applications accepted. *Expenses:* Tuition, state resident: full-time $6446. Tuition, nonresident: full-time $14,874. Required fees: $852. *Financial support:* Career-related internships or fieldwork, Federal Work-Study, scholarships/grants, and tuition waivers (full and partial) available. Support available to part-time students. Financial award application deadline: 2/1. *Unit head:* Dr. Jeffrey S. Copeland, Head, 319-273-3855, Fax: 319-273-5807, E-mail: jeffrey.copeland@uni.edu. *Application contact:* Laurie S. Russell, Record Analyst, 319-273-2623, Fax: 319-273-6792, E-mail: laurie.russell@uni.edu.

University of North Florida, College of Arts and Sciences, Department of English, Jacksonville, FL 32224-2645. Offers MA. Part-time and evening/weekend programs available. *Faculty:* 14 full-time (6 women). *Students:* 14 full-time (12 women), 48 part-time (40 women); includes 6 minority (3 African Americans, 3 Hispanic Americans), 1 international. Average age 32. 37 applicants, 57% accepted, 9 enrolled. In 2008, 23 master's awarded. *Degree requirements:* For master's, comprehensive exam, thesis optional. *Entrance requirements:* For master's, GRE General Test, minimum GPA of 3.0 in last 60 hours, writing sample. Additional exam requirements/recommendations for international students: Required—TOEFL (minimum score 500 paper-based; 173 computer-based). *Application deadline:* For fall admission, 7/6 priority date for domestic students, 5/1 for international students; for spring admission, 11/1 priority date for domestic students, 10/1 for international students. Applications are processed on a rolling basis. Application fee: $30. Electronic applications accepted. *Expenses:* Tuition, area resident: Full-time $5782.08; part-time $240.92 per credit hour. Tuition, state resident: full-time $5782.08; part-time $240.92 per credit hour. Tuition, nonresident: full-time $19,974; part-time $832.26 per credit hour. Required fees: $952.80; $39.70 per credit hour. *Financial support:* In 2008–09, 29 students received support; research assistantships, teaching assistantships, Federal Work-Study and tuition waivers (partial) available. Support available to part-time students. Financial award application deadline: 4/1; financial award applicants required to submit FAFSA. *Faculty research:* Genre, period, and individual author studies in British, American, and world literature; literary criticism and theory—psychological, new historical and cultural, deconstructive, feminist, narrative, mythic; film and popular culture; online poetry publishing. *Unit head:* Dr. Samuel A. Kimball, Chair, 904-620-2273, Fax: 904-620-3940, E-mail: skimball@unf.edu. *Application contact:* Dr. Jason Mauro, Graduate Coordinator, 904-620-2273, Fax: 904-620-3940, E-mail: jmauro@unf.edu.

University of North Texas, Robert B. Toulouse School of Graduate Studies, College of Arts and Sciences, Department of English, Denton, TX 76203. Offers creative writing (MA); English (MA, PhD); English as a second language (MA); linguistics (MA); Technical writing (MA). Terminal master's awarded for partial completion of doctoral program. *Degree requirements:* For master's, one foreign language, comprehensive exam, thesis optional; for doctorate, one foreign language, comprehensive exam, thesis/dissertation. *Entrance requirements:* For master's, GRE General Test, 3.0 GPA, personal statement, current vita/resumé, writing sample for creative writing program; for doctorate, GRE General Test, 3.5 GPA, 3 letters of recommendation, personal statement, writing sample. Additional exam requirements/recommendations for international students: Required—proof of English language proficiency required for non-native English speakers; Recommended—TOEFL (minimum score 550 paper-based; 213 computer-based). *Faculty research:* Creative writing, British and American literature, composition and rhetoric.

University of Notre Dame, Graduate School, College of Arts and Letters, Division of Humanities, Department of English, Notre Dame, IN 46556. Offers creative writing (MFA); English (MA, PhD). *Faculty:* 46 full-time (21 women). *Students:* 62 full-time (36 women); includes 11 minority (2 African Americans, 1 Asian American or Pacific Islander, 8 Hispanic Americans), 6 international. 224 applicants, 8% accepted, 10 enrolled. In 2008, 5 master's, 6 doctorates awarded. *Degree requirements:* For doctorate, one foreign language, thesis/dissertation, candidacy exam. *Entrance requirements:* For master's, GRE General Test, minimum GPA of 3.0; for doctorate, GRE General Test, GRE Subject Test, minimum GPA of 3.0. Additional exam requirements/recommendations for international students: Required—TOEFL (minimum score 600 paper-based; 250 computer-based; 80 iBT). *Application deadline:* For fall admission, 1/1 priority date for domestic students, 1/1 for international students. Applications are processed on a rolling basis. Application fee: $50. Electronic applications accepted. *Financial support:* Fellowships with full tuition reimbursements, research assistantships with full tuition reimbursements, teaching assistantships with full tuition reimbursements, tuition waivers (full) available. Financial award application deadline: 1/1. *Faculty research:* Early modern studies (medieval/Renaissance), modern British studies (18th-20th centuries), American Studies, literature and philosophy, Irish studies. *Unit head:* Dr. Jesse Lander, Director of Graduate Studies, 574-631-6618, E-mail: english.13@nd.edu. *Application contact:* Dr. Barbara Turpin, Director of Graduate Admissions, 574-631-7706, Fax: 574-631-4183.

University of Oklahoma, Graduate College, College of Arts and Sciences, Department of English, Norman, OK 73019-0390. Offers MA, PhD. *Faculty:* 31 full-time (13 women). *Students:* 48 full-time (30 women), 6 part-time (5 women); includes 12 minority (2 African Americans, 8 American Indian/Alaska Native, 2 Hispanic Americans), 3 international. 41 applicants, 61% accepted, 12 enrolled. In 2008, 13 master's, 5 doctorates awarded. *Degree requirements:* For master's, one foreign language, thesis or alternative, qualifying exam; for doctorate, 2 foreign languages, thesis/dissertation, qualifying exam. *Entrance requirements:* For master's, GRE General Test, minimum GPA of 3.0, BA with 27 hours of course work in English or 15 hours of upper-level courses; for doctorate, GRE General Test, GRE Subject Test (English literature), minimum graduate GPA of 3.5. Additional exam requirements/recommendations for international students: Required—TOEFL (minimum score 550 paper-based; 213 computer-based). *Application deadline:* For fall admission, 4/1 priority date for domestic students, 4/1 for international students; for spring admission, 11/1 for domestic students, 9/1 for international students. Applications are processed on a rolling basis. Application fee: $40 ($90 for international students). Electronic applications accepted. *Expenses:* Tuition, state resident: full-time $3744; part-time $156 per credit hour. Tuition, nonresident: full-time $13,577; part-time $565.70 per credit hour. Required fees: $2415.40; $90.10 per credit hour. *Financial support:* In 2008–09, 33 students received support, including 1 fellowship with full tuition reimbursement available (averaging $2,500 per year), 4 research assistantships with partial tuition reimbursements available (averaging $12,990 per year), 48 teaching assistantships with partial tuition reimbursements available (averaging $12,168 per year); scholarships/grants, health care benefits, tuition waivers (full and partial), and unspecified assistantships also available. Financial award application deadline: 3/1; financial award applicants required to submit FAFSA. *Faculty research:* Native American studies, medieval/early modern studies, modern contemporary literature, literary theory. Total annual research expenditures: $29,875. *Unit head:* David Mair, Chair, 405-325-4661, Fax: 405-325-0831, E-mail: dmair@ou.edu. *Application contact:* Dr. Timothy S Murphy, Graduate Liaison, 405-325-4661, Fax: 405-325-0831, E-mail: tmurphy@ou.edu.

University of Oregon, Graduate School, College of Arts and Sciences, Department of English, Eugene, OR 97403. Offers MA, PhD. Terminal master's awarded for partial completion of doctoral program. *Degree requirements:* For master's, one foreign language; for doctorate, 2 foreign languages, thesis/dissertation. *Entrance requirements:* For master's, GRE General Test; for doctorate, GRE Subject Test (English literature), minimum GPA of 3.5. Additional exam requirements/recommendations for international students: Required—TOEFL. *Faculty*

English

University of Oregon (continued)
research: Old and Middle English, women writers, critical theory, literature and the environment, rhetoric and composition.

University of Ottawa, Faculty of Graduate and Postdoctoral Studies, Faculty of Arts, Department of English, Ottawa, ON K1N 6N5, Canada. Offers MA, PhD. Part-time and evening/weekend programs available. *Degree requirements:* For master's, one foreign language, thesis optional; for doctorate, 2 foreign languages, comprehensive exam, thesis/dissertation. *Entrance requirements:* For master's, honors degree or equivalent, minimum B average; for doctorate, master's degree, minimum B+ average. Electronic applications accepted. *Faculty research:* Anglo-Saxon and medieval literature.

University of Pennsylvania, School of Arts and Sciences, Graduate Group in English, Philadelphia, PA 19104. Offers AM, PhD. Terminal master's awarded for partial completion of doctoral program. *Degree requirements:* For master's, one foreign language; for doctorate, 2 foreign languages, thesis/dissertation, oral and written qualifying exams. *Entrance requirements:* For master's, GRE General Test, GRE Subject Test, sample of written work; for doctorate, GRE General Test, GRE Subject Test. Additional exam requirements/recommendations for international students: Required—TOEFL. Electronic applications accepted. *Faculty research:* Renaissance literature and intellectual theory, feminist studies, literary theory.

University of Pittsburgh, School of Arts and Sciences, Department of English, Pittsburgh, PA 15260. Offers cultural and critical studies (PhD); English (MA); writing (MFA). Part-time programs available. *Degree requirements:* For master's, one foreign language; for doctorate, 2 foreign languages, comprehensive exam, thesis/dissertation. *Entrance requirements:* For master's and doctorate, GRE General Test, writing sample. Additional exam requirements/recommendations for international students: Required—TOEFL. *Faculty research:* Cultural studies, literary history and theory, film, composition.

Announcement: Graduate programs stimulate work across literary history, critical and cultural theory, composition, film, and creative writing. MA and PhD courses articulate theoretical issues through historical investigations of discursive practices ranging from canonical British and American literature to film and student writing. Special attention to social conditions of literary and critical writing, pedagogical practices, and the interrelationships of reading and writing, film and literature, and critical theory, composition, and literary study. MFA offers specializations in poetry, fiction, and creative nonfiction; includes training in criticism and theory; final manuscript of professional quality.

University of Puerto Rico, Mayagüez Campus, Graduate Studies, College of Arts and Sciences, Department of English, Mayagüez, PR 00681-9000. Offers English education (MA). Part-time programs available. *Degree requirements:* For master's, comprehensive exam, thesis optional. *Entrance requirements:* For master's, course work in linguistics or language, American literature, British literature, and structure/grammar or syntax. *Faculty research:* Teaching English as a second language, linguistics, American literature, British literature.

University of Puerto Rico, Río Piedras, College of Humanities, Department of English, San Juan, PR 00931-3300. Offers MA, PhD. Part-time programs available. *Degree requirements:* For master's, one foreign language, comprehensive exam, thesis; for doctorate, residency. *Entrance requirements:* For master's, PAEG or GRE, interview, minimum GPA of 3.0, 2 letters of recommendation; for doctorate, PAEG or GRE, minimum GPA of 3.0, 3 letters of recommendation, interview.

University of Regina, Faculty of Graduate Studies and Research, Faculty of Arts, Department of English, Regina, SK S4S 0A2, Canada. Offers MA, PhD. Part-time programs available. *Faculty:* 23 full-time (10 women). *Students:* 12 full-time (7 women), 16 part-time (9 women). 17 applicants, 88% accepted. In 2008, 6 master's awarded. *Degree requirements:* For master's, thesis optional; for doctorate, thesis/dissertation. *Entrance requirements:* For master's, writing sample. Additional exam requirements/recommendations for international students: Required—TOEFL (minimum score 580 paper-based; 237 computer-based; 88 iBT). *Application deadline:* For fall admission, 3/15 for international students. Application fee: $85 ($100 for international students). Electronic applications accepted. *Financial support:* In 2008–09, 7 fellowships (averaging $15,930 per year), 2 research assistantships (averaging $13,720 per year), 2 teaching assistantships (averaging $6,650 per year) were awarded; scholarships/grants also available. Financial award application deadline: 6/15. *Faculty research:* British, American, Canadian and post-colonial literature. *Unit head:* Dr. Dorothy Lane, Head, 306-585-4465, Fax: 306-585-5429, E-mail: dorothy.lane@uregina.ca. *Application contact:* Dr. Ken Probert, Graduate Program Coordinator, 306-585-4432, Fax: 306-585-5429, E-mail: ken.probert@uregina.ca.

University of Rhode Island, Graduate School, College of Arts and Sciences, Department of English, Kingston, RI 02881. Offers MA, PhD. *Application deadline:* Applications are processed on a rolling basis. Application fee: $35. *Expenses:* Tuition, state resident: full-time $8024; part-time $446 per credit. Tuition, nonresident: full-time $21,046; part-time $1169 per credit. Required fees: $1056; $26 per credit. $30 per semester. One-time fee: $95 part-time. *Unit head:* Dr. Stephen Barber, Chair, 401-874-9088, E-mail: engchair@gmail.com. *Application contact:* Harold D. Bibb, Associate Dean of the Graduate School, 401-874-2262, Fax: 401-874-5491.

University of Rochester, The College, Arts and Sciences, Department of English, Rochester, NY 14627-0250. Offers MA, PhD. Terminal master's awarded for partial completion of doctoral program. *Degree requirements:* For doctorate, one foreign language, thesis/dissertation, qualifying exam. *Entrance requirements:* For master's and doctorate, GRE General Test. Additional exam requirements/recommendations for international students: Required—TOEFL.

University of St. Thomas, Graduate Studies, College of Arts and Sciences, Graduate Program in English, St. Paul, MN 55105-1096. Offers MA. Part-time and evening/weekend programs available. *Degree requirements:* For master's, essay. *Entrance requirements:* For master's, minimum GPA of 3.0, previous course work in literature, sample of written work. Additional exam requirements/recommendations for international students: Required—TOEFL. *Expenses:* Contact institution. *Faculty research:* Multicultural literature, literature and theory, regional writers.

See Close-Up on page 447.

University of Saskatchewan, College of Graduate Studies and Research, College of Arts and Sciences, Department of English, Saskatoon, SK S7N 5A2, Canada. Offers MA, PhD. *Degree requirements:* For master's, one foreign language, thesis; for doctorate, one foreign language, thesis/dissertation. *Entrance requirements:* Additional exam requirements/recommendations for international students: Required—TOEFL.

University of South Africa, College of Human Sciences, Pretoria, South Africa. Offers adult education (M Ed); African languages (MA, PhD); African politics (MA, PhD); Afrikaans (MA, PhD); ancient history (MA, PhD); ancient Near Eastern studies (MA, PhD); anthropology (MA, PhD); applied linguistics (MA); Arabic (MA, PhD); archaeology (MA); art history (MA); Biblical archaeology (MA); Biblical studies (M Th, D Th, PhD); Christian spirituality (M Th, D Th); church history (M Th, D Th); classical studies (MA, PhD); clinical psychology (MA); communication (MA, PhD); comparative education (M Ed, Ed D); consulting psychology (D Admin, D Com, PhD); curriculum studies (M Ed, Ed D); development studies (M Admin, MA, D Admin, PhD); didactics (M Ed, Ed D); education (M Tech); education management (M Ed, Ed D); educational psychology (M Ed); English (MA); environmental education (M Ed); French (MA, PhD); German (MA, PhD); Greek (MA); guidance and counseling (M Ed); health studies (MA, PhD), including health sciences education (MA), health services management (MA), medical and surgical nursing science (critical care general) (MA), midwifery and neonatal nursing science (MA), trauma and emergency care (MA); history (MA, PhD); history of education (Ed D); inclusive education (M Ed, Ed D); information and communications technology policy and regulation (MA); information science (MA, MIS, PhD); international politics (MA, PhD); Islamic studies (MA, PhD); Italian (MA, PhD); Judaica (MA, PhD); linguistics (MA, PhD); mathematical education (M Ed); mathematics education (MA); missiology (M Th, D Th); modern Hebrew (MA, PhD); musicology (MA, MMus, D Mus, PhD); natural science education (M Ed); New Testament (M Th, D Th); Old Testament (D Th); pastoral therapy (M Th, D Th); philosophy (MA); philosophy of education (M Ed, Ed D); politics (MA, PhD); Portuguese (MA, PhD); practical theology (M Th, D Th); psychology (MA, MS, PhD); psychology of education (M Ed, Ed D); public health (MA); religious studies (MA, D Th, PhD); Romance languages (MA); Russian (MA, PhD); Semitic languages (MA, PhD); social behavior studies in HIV/AIDS (MA); social science (mental health) (MA); social science in development studies (MA); social science in psychology (MA); social science in social work (MA); social science in sociology (MA); social work (MSW, DSW, PhD); socio-education (M Ed, Ed D); sociolinguistics (MA); sociology (MA, PhD); Spanish (MA, PhD); systematic theology (M Th, D Th); TESOL (teaching English to speakers of other languages) (MA); theological ethics (M Th, D Th); theory of literature (MA, PhD); urban ministries (D Th); urban ministry (M Th).

University of South Alabama, Graduate School, College of Arts and Sciences, Department of English, Mobile, AL 36688-0002. Offers MA. Part-time and evening/weekend programs available. *Faculty:* 16 full-time (7 women), 1 part-time/adjunct (0 women). *Students:* 24 full-time (15 women), 18 part-time (13 women); includes 35 minority (32 African Americans, 2 American Indian/Alaska Native, 1 Asian American or Pacific Islander). 23 applicants, 70% accepted, 10 enrolled. In 2008, 4 master's awarded. *Degree requirements:* For master's, one foreign language, comprehensive exam, thesis optional. *Entrance requirements:* For master's, GRE General Test, BA in English or 40 hours of course work in English, minimum GPA of 3.0. *Application deadline:* For fall admission, 7/15 priority date for domestic students, 5/15 priority date for international students; for spring admission, 12/1 priority date for domestic students, 11/1 priority date for international students. Applications are processed on a rolling basis. Application fee: $35. *Expenses:* Tuition, area resident: Full-time $4656. Tuition, nonresident: full-time $9312. Required fees: $1102. *Financial support:* Research assistantships available. Support available to part-time students. Financial award application deadline: 4/1. *Unit head:* Dr. Sue Walker, Chair, 251-460-6146. *Application contact:* Dr. Sue Walker, Chair, 251-460-6146.

University of South Carolina, The Graduate School, College of Arts and Sciences, Department of English Language and Literature, Columbia, SC 29208. Offers creative writing (MFA); English (MA, PhD); English education (MAT); MLIS/MA. MAT offered in cooperation with the College of Education. Part-time programs available. *Degree requirements:* For master's, one foreign language, comprehensive exam, thesis; for doctorate, 2 foreign languages, comprehensive exam, thesis/dissertation. *Entrance requirements:* For master's, GRE General Test (MFA), GRE Subject Test (MA, MAT), sample of written work; for doctorate, GRE General Test, GRE Subject Test, sample of written work. Additional exam requirements/recommendations for international students: Required—TOEFL. Electronic applications accepted. *Faculty research:* American literature, British literature, composition and rhetoric, linguistics, speech communication.

The University of South Dakota, Graduate School, College of Arts and Sciences, Department of English, Vermillion, SD 57069-2390. Offers MA, PhD. *Degree requirements:* For master's, comprehensive exam (for some programs), thesis (for some programs); for doctorate, comprehensive exam, thesis/dissertation. *Entrance requirements:* For master's, minimum GPA of 3.0, writing sample; for doctorate, GRE, minimum GPA of 3.0, writing sample. Additional exam requirements/recommendations for international students: Required—TOEFL (minimum score 620 paper-based; 260 computer-based; 105 iBT). Electronic applications accepted.

University of Southern California, Graduate School, College of Letters, Arts and Sciences, Department of English, Los Angeles, CA 90089. Offers English and American literature (MA, PhD); English literature and creative writing (PhD). Terminal master's awarded for partial completion of doctoral program. *Degree requirements:* For doctorate, one foreign language, thesis/dissertation. *Entrance requirements:* For doctorate, GRE General Test, GRE Subject Test. *Faculty research:* Creative writing and literature, early modern studies, gender and sexuality, narrative studies, poetry and poetics, media, film and popular culture.

University of Southern Mississippi, Graduate School, College of Arts and Letters, Department of English, Hattiesburg, MS 39406-0001. Offers MA, PhD. *Faculty:* 20 full-time (11 women), 2 part-time/adjunct (0 women). *Students:* 55 full-time (31 women), 24 part-time (17 women); includes 5 minority (2 African Americans, 1 American Indian/Alaska Native, 2 Hispanic Americans), 3 international. Average age 32. 67 applicants, 67% accepted, 21 enrolled. In 2008, 12 master's, 9 doctorates awarded. *Degree requirements:* For master's, one foreign language, comprehensive exam, thesis; for doctorate, 2 foreign languages, comprehensive exam, thesis/dissertation. *Entrance requirements:* For master's, GRE General Test, minimum GPA of 3.0 in field of study, 2.75 in last 2 years; for doctorate, GRE General Test, minimum GPA of 3.5. Additional exam requirements/recommendations for international students: Required—TOEFL. *Application deadline:* For fall admission, 3/15 priority date for domestic students, 3/15 for international students. Application fee: $30. Electronic applications accepted. *Financial support:* In 2008–09, 1 fellowship (averaging $14,000 per year), 2 research assistantships with full tuition reimbursements (averaging $10,000 per year), 44 teaching assistantships with full tuition reimbursements (averaging $10,000 per year) were awarded; Federal Work-Study, institutionally sponsored loans, scholarships/grants, and unspecified assistantships also available. Financial award application deadline: 3/15; financial award applicants required to submit FAFSA. *Faculty research:* English and American literature, critical theory and cultural studies, creative writing. *Unit head:* Dr. W. Michael Mays, Chair, 601-266-4319, Fax: 601-266-5757, E-mail: michael.mays@usm.edu. *Application contact:* Dr. Jameela Lares, Graduate Coordinator, 601-266-4320, Fax: 601-266-5757.

University of South Florida, Graduate School, College of Arts and Sciences, Department of English, Tampa, FL 33620-9951. Offers MA, MFA, PhD. Part-time and evening/weekend programs available. *Faculty:* 21 full-time (13 women), 1 part-time/adjunct (0 women). *Students:* 76 full-time (45 women), 52 part-time (35 women); includes 7 minority (2 African Americans, 1 American Indian/Alaska Native, 4 Hispanic Americans), 5 international. 112 applicants, 51% accepted, 43 enrolled. In 2008, 15 master's, 6 doctorates awarded. *Degree requirements:* For master's, comprehensive exam, thesis (for some programs); for doctorate, comprehensive exam, thesis/dissertation. *Entrance requirements:* For master's, GRE General Test, minimum GPA of 3.5; for doctorate, GRE General Test, minimum GPA of 3.7. Additional exam requirements/recommendations for international students: Required—TOEFL (minimum score 550 paper-based; 213 computer-based). *Application deadline:* For fall admission, 2/1 for domestic students, 1/2 for international students. Applications are processed on a rolling basis. Application fee: $30. Electronic applications accepted. *Expenses:* Tuition, state resident: full-time $2624.40; part-time $291.60 per credit hour. Tuition, nonresident: full-time $7822; part-time $869.13 per credit hour. *Financial support:* Scholarships/grants and unspecified assistantships available. Financial award application deadline: 6/30; financial award applicants required to submit FAFSA. *Faculty research:* British and American literature, rhetoric and composition. Total annual research expenditures: $70,499. *Unit head:* Hunt Hawkins, Chairperson, 813-974-9420, Fax: 813-974-2270, E-mail: hhawkins@cas.usf.edu. *Application contact:* Dr. Laura Runge, Program Director, 813-974-9469, Fax: 813-974-2270, E-mail: runge@chuma.cas.usf.edu.

The University of Tennessee, Graduate School, College of Arts and Sciences, Department of English, Knoxville, TN 37996. Offers MA, PhD. Part-time programs available. *Degree requirements:* For master's, one foreign language, thesis or alternative; for doctorate, one foreign language, thesis/dissertation. *Entrance requirements:* For master's, GRE General Test, minimum GPA of 2.7; for doctorate, GRE General Test, GRE Subject Test, minimum GPA of 2.7. Additional exam requirements/recommendations for international students: Required—TOEFL. Electronic applications accepted. *Expenses:* Tuition, area resident: Part-time $348 per credit hour. Tuition, state resident: full-time $6262. Tuition, nonresident: full-time $18,920;

part-time $1052 per credit hour. Required fees: $812; $36 per credit hour. Tuition and fees vary according to program.

The University of Tennessee at Chattanooga, Graduate School, College of Arts and Sciences, Department of English, Program in English, Chattanooga, TN 37403. Offers MA. Part-time and evening/weekend programs available. *Faculty:* 13 full-time (7 women). *Students:* 20 full-time (8 women), 33 part-time (25 women); includes 2 minority (both African Americans). Average age 30. 25 applicants, 80% accepted, 16 enrolled. In 2008, 18 master's awarded. *Degree requirements:* For master's, comprehensive exam, thesis. *Entrance requirements:* For master's, GRE General Test or GRE Subject Test in literature, minimum GPA of 3.0 in English. Additional exam requirements/recommendations for international students: Required—TOEFL (minimum score 550 paper-based; 213 computer-based; 79 iBT); Recommended—IELTS (minimum score 6). *Application deadline:* For fall admission, 8/1 priority date for domestic students, 6/1 for international students; for spring admission, 12/1 priority date for domestic students, 10/1 for international students. Applications are processed on a rolling basis. Application fee: $30 ($35 for international students). *Expenses:* Tuition, area resident: Full-time $6150; part-time $281 per credit hour. Tuition, nonresident: full-time $16,710; part-time $867 per credit hour. Required fees: $1100; $128 per credit hour. $550 per semester. *Financial support:* In 2008–09, 5 fellowships with full and partial tuition reimbursements (averaging $3,300 per year) were awarded; career-related internships or fieldwork, Federal Work-Study, institutionally sponsored loans, scholarships/grants, tuition waivers (partial), and unspecified assistantships also available. Support available to part-time students. Financial award application deadline: 4/1. *Faculty research:* Technical writing, African-American literature, Milton, creative writing and poetry, American modernism and gender theory. Total annual research expenditures: $68,600. *Unit head:* Dr. Joyce Smith, Director of Graduate Programs, 423-425-4623, Fax: 423-425-2282, E-mail: joyce-smith@utc.edu. *Application contact:* Dr. Stephanie Bellar, Dean of Graduate Studies, 423-425-4666, Fax: 423-425-5223, E-mail: stephanie-bellar@utc.edu.

The University of Texas at Arlington, Graduate School, College of Liberal Arts, Department of English, Arlington, TX 76019. Offers English (MA); literature (PhD). Part-time and evening/weekend programs available. *Faculty:* 16 full-time (9 women). *Students:* 14 full-time (10 women), 86 part-time (58 women); includes 14 minority (6 African Americans, 2 Asian Americans or Pacific Islanders, 6 Hispanic Americans), 3 international. 54 applicants, 83% accepted, 27 enrolled. In 2008, 7 master's, 7 doctorates awarded. *Degree requirements:* For master's, thesis optional, thesis or comprehensive exam; for doctorate, one foreign language, comprehensive exam, thesis/dissertation. *Entrance requirements:* For master's, GRE General Test, minimum 5-page writing sample, minimum GPA of 3.0, 3 letters of recommendation; for doctorate, GRE General Test, minimum graduate GPA of 3.5, writing sample, 3 letters of recommendation. Additional exam requirements/recommendations for international students: Required—TOEFL (minimum score 550 paper-based; 213 computer-based). *Application deadline:* For fall admission, 6/16 for domestic students. Applications are processed on a rolling basis. Application fee: $35 ($50 for international students). *Expenses:* Tuition, area resident: Full-time $6500. Tuition, state resident: full-time $6500. Tuition, nonresident: full-time $11,558. *Financial support:* In 2008–09, 4 fellowships (averaging $2,000 per year) were awarded; scholarships/grants also available. Financial award application deadline: 5/1; financial award applicants required to submit FAFSA. *Faculty research:* Rhetoric composition, American literature, British literature, cultural studies, women's studies. *Unit head:* Dr. Wendy Faris, Chair, 817-272-2692, Fax: 817-272-2718, E-mail: wbfaris@uta.edu. *Application contact:* Dr. Tim Morris, Associate Chair for Graduate Studies, 817-272-2739, E-mail: morris@uta.edu.

The University of Texas at Austin, Graduate School, College of Liberal Arts, Department of English, Austin, TX 78712-1111. Offers creative writing (MA); English (MA, PhD). Part-time programs available. Terminal master's awarded for partial completion of doctoral program. *Degree requirements:* For master's, 2 foreign languages; for doctorate, variable foreign language requirement. *Entrance requirements:* For master's and doctorate, GRE General Test. Electronic applications accepted.

The University of Texas at Brownsville, Graduate Studies, College of Liberal Arts, Department of English, Brownsville, TX 78520-4991. Offers English (MA); interdisciplinary studies (MAIS). Part-time and evening/weekend programs available. *Degree requirements:* For master's, comprehensive exam or thesis. *Entrance requirements:* For master's, GRE General Test. Additional exam requirements/recommendations for international students: Required—TOEFL. *Faculty research:* Sandra Cisneros, Nathaniel Hawthorne, Rodolfo Araya, Isabel Allende, linguistics.

The University of Texas at El Paso, Graduate School, College of Liberal Arts, Department of English, El Paso, TX 79968-0001. Offers English and American literature (MA); rhetoric and composition (PhD); rhetoric and writing studies (MA); teaching English (MAT). Part-time and evening/weekend programs available. *Degree requirements:* For master's, thesis optional. *Entrance requirements:* For master's, GRE General Test, minimum GPA of 3.0. Additional exam requirements/recommendations for international students: Required—TOEFL. Electronic applications accepted. *Faculty research:* Literature, creative writing, literary theory.

The University of Texas at San Antonio, College of Liberal and Fine Arts, Department of English, Classics and Philosophy, San Antonio, TX 78249-0617. Offers creative writing (Graduate Certificate); English (MA, PhD). Part-time and evening/weekend programs available. *Degree requirements:* For master's, comprehensive exam, thesis optional; for doctorate, comprehensive exam, thesis/dissertation. *Entrance requirements:* For master's, GRE General Test, minimum GPA of 3.3 on all upper division English courses; for doctorate, GRE General Test. Additional exam requirements/recommendations for international students: Required—TOEFL (minimum score 500 paper-based; 173 computer-based). Electronic applications accepted. *Faculty research:* English and American literature, linguistics.

The University of Texas at Tyler, College of Arts and Sciences, Department of Literature and Languages, Tyler, TX 75799-0001. Offers English (MA); interdisciplinary studies (MAIS). Part-time and evening/weekend programs available. *Degree requirements:* For master's, one foreign language, comprehensive exam, thesis optional. *Entrance requirements:* For master's, GRE General Test, minimum GPA of 3.0, four semesters—or the equivalent—of one foreign language. Additional exam requirements/recommendations for international students: Required—TOEFL (minimum score 79 computer-based). Electronic applications accepted. *Faculty research:* Medieval and Tudor drama, Shakespeare, British Romanticism, British and Irish modernism, American realism, Greek drama, Nineteenth Century American literature.

The University of Texas of the Permian Basin, Office of Graduate Studies, College of Arts and Sciences, Department of Literature and Languages, Program in English, Odessa, TX 79762-0001. Offers MA. Part-time and evening/weekend programs available. *Degree requirements:* For master's, comprehensive exam (for some programs), thesis (for some programs). *Entrance requirements:* For master's, GRE General Test. Additional exam requirements/recommendations for international students: Required—TOEFL (minimum score 550 paper-based; 213 computer-based).

The University of Texas–Pan American, College of Arts and Humanities, Department of English, Edinburg, TX 78541-2999. Offers English (MA, MAIS); English as a second language (MA). Part-time and evening/weekend programs available. *Degree requirements:* For master's, comprehensive exam, thesis optional. *Entrance requirements:* For master's, GRE General Test, minimum GPA of 3.0. *Faculty research:* Oral vs. literary culture, Borderland literature, Mexican-American literature, topics in British and American literature, discourse analysis.

University of the District of Columbia, College of Arts and Sciences, Department of English, Program in English Composition and Rhetoric, Washington, DC 20008-1175. Offers MA. *Degree requirements:* For master's, comprehensive exam. *Entrance requirements:* For master's, writing proficiency exam.

The University of Toledo, College of Graduate Studies, College of Arts and Sciences, Department of English Language and Literature, Toledo, OH 43606-3390. Offers English as a second language (MA); literature (MA); teaching of writing (Certificate). Part-time programs available. *Degree requirements:* For master's, one foreign language. *Entrance requirements:* For master's, minimum GPA of 2.7. Electronic applications accepted. *Faculty research:* Literary criticism, linguistics, creative writing, folklore and cultural studies.

University of Toronto, School of Graduate Studies, Humanities Division, Department of English, Toronto, ON M5S 1A1, Canada. Offers MA, PhD. Part-time programs available. *Degree requirements:* For master's, thesis optional; for doctorate, 2 foreign languages, thesis/dissertation. *Entrance requirements:* For master's, minimum B+ average, 2 letters of reference, portfolio (creative writing program); for doctorate, minimum A– average, 2 letters of reference, writing sample.

University of Tulsa, Graduate School, College of Arts and Sciences, Department of English Language and Literature, Tulsa, OK 74104-3189. Offers MA, MTA, PhD, JD/MA. Part-time and evening/weekend programs available. *Faculty:* 13 full-time (5 women), 1 (woman) part-time/adjunct. *Students:* 41 full-time (24 women), 11 part-time (5 women), 5 international. Average age 29. 45 applicants, 64% accepted, 15 enrolled. In 2008, 5 master's, 5 doctorates awarded. *Degree requirements:* For master's, independent research project; for doctorate, one foreign language, comprehensive exam, thesis/dissertation. *Entrance requirements:* For master's and doctorate, GRE General Test. Additional exam requirements/recommendations for international students: Required—TOEFL (minimum score 575 paper-based; 231 computer-based; 91 iBT), IELTS (minimum score 6.5). *Application deadline:* For fall admission, 2/1 priority date for domestic students. Applications are processed on a rolling basis. Application fee: $40. Electronic applications accepted. *Expenses:* Tuition: Full-time $15,408; part-time $899 per credit hour. Required fees: $3.33 per credit hour. One-time fee: $200 full-time. Tuition and fees vary according to course load and program. *Financial support:* In 2008–09, 36 students received support, including 8 fellowships with full and partial tuition reimbursements available (averaging $7,938 per year), 1 research assistantship with full and partial tuition reimbursement available (averaging $14,337 per year), 22 teaching assistantships with full and partial tuition reimbursements available (averaging $11,949 per year); Federal Work-Study, scholarships/grants, tuition waivers (full and partial), and unspecified assistantships also available. Support available to part-time students. Financial award application deadline: 2/1; financial award applicants required to submit FAFSA. *Faculty research:* Women's literature, modern British, Irish, and American literature, 19th century poetry and prose, literary theory, Renaissance literature. Total annual research expenditures: $164,883. *Unit head:* Dr. Lars Engle, Chairperson, 918-631-2807, Fax: 918-631-3033, E-mail: lars-engle@utulsa.edu. *Application contact:* Dr. Laura Stevens, Advisor, 918-631-2859, Fax: 918-631-3033, E-mail: laura-stevens@utulsa.edu.

University of Utah, The Graduate School, College of Humanities, Department of English, Salt Lake City, UT 84112-1107. Offers American studies (MA, PhD); British American literature (MA, PhD); creative writing (MFA, PhD); literature (PhD); rhetoric and composition (PhD). *Degree requirements:* For master's, one foreign language, thesis (for some programs), written exam; for doctorate, 2 foreign languages, comprehensive exam, thesis/dissertation. *Entrance requirements:* For master's and doctorate, GRE General Test, minimum GPA of 3.2. Additional exam requirements/recommendations for international students: Required—TOEFL (minimum score 500 paper-based; 173 computer-based; 120 iBT). Electronic applications accepted. *Faculty research:* Poetics and modern poetry, 19th and 20th century British and American literature, the American west, environmental studies, critical theory and race and gender studies.

University of Vermont, Graduate College, College of Arts and Sciences, Department of English, Burlington, VT 05405. Offers MA. *Students:* 29 (17 women); includes 3 minority (1 African American, 2 Asian Americans or Pacific Islanders). 54 applicants, 94% accepted, 12 enrolled. In 2008, 8 master's awarded. *Degree requirements:* For master's, one foreign language, thesis. *Entrance requirements:* For master's, GRE General Test, Writing sample. Additional exam requirements/recommendations for international students: Required—TOEFL (minimum score 550 paper-based; 213 computer-based; 80 iBT). *Application deadline:* For fall admission, 2/15 priority date for domestic students. Applications are processed on a rolling basis. Application fee: $40. Electronic applications accepted. *Expenses:* Tuition, state resident: part-time $488 per credit. Tuition, nonresident: part-time $1232 per credit. *Financial support:* Fellowships, teaching assistantships available. Financial award application deadline: 3/1. *Unit head:* Dr. LoKangaka Losambe, Chair, 802-656-3056. *Application contact:* Dr. A. Barnaby, Coordinator, 802-656-3056.

University of Victoria, Faculty of Graduate Studies, Faculty of Humanities, Department of English, Victoria, BC V8W 2Y2, Canada. Offers MA, PhD. Part-time programs available. *Degree requirements:* For master's, one foreign language, thesis (for some programs); for doctorate, 2 foreign languages, comprehensive exam, thesis/dissertation, candidacy exam. *Entrance requirements:* For master's, minimum A- average in last 2 years of undergraduate course work, writing sample, resumé; for doctorate, minimum A- average in graduate course work, writing sample, resumé. Additional exam requirements/recommendations for international students: Required—TOEFL (minimum score 630 paper-based; 267 computer-based). Electronic applications accepted. *Faculty research:* Critical theory, nineteenth century literature, postcolonialism/multiculturalism, medieval and Renaissance literature, cultural theory.

University of Virginia, College and Graduate School of Arts and Sciences, Department of English Language and Literature, Program in English, Charlottesville, VA 22903. Offers MA, PhD. *Students:* 160 full-time (96 women); includes 11 minority (6 African Americans, 3 Asian Americans or Pacific Islanders, 2 Hispanic Americans), 6 international. Average age 29. 441 applicants, 18% accepted, 33 enrolled. In 2008, 30 master's, 15 doctorates awarded. *Degree requirements:* For master's, one foreign language, oral exam or thesis; for doctorate, 2 foreign languages, comprehensive exam, thesis/dissertation. *Entrance requirements:* For master's and doctorate, GRE General Test, GRE Subject Test, 3 letters of recommendation; 2 writing samples. Additional exam requirements/recommendations for international students: Required—TOEFL (minimum score 600 paper-based; 250 computer-based; 90 iBT), IELTS (minimum score 7). *Application deadline:* For fall admission, 1/2 for domestic and international students. Applications are processed on a rolling basis. Application fee: $60. Electronic applications accepted. *Expenses:* Tuition, area resident: Full-time $10,452. Tuition, state resident: full-time $10,452. Tuition, nonresident: full-time $20,010. Required fees: $2176. Part-time tuition and fees vary according to course load and program. *Financial support:* Fellowships, teaching assistantships available. Financial award applicants required to submit FAFSA. *Unit head:* Jahan Ramazani, Chair, 434-924-7105, Fax: 434-924-1478, E-mail: rr5m@virginia.edu. *Application contact:* Peter Baker, Director of Graduate Admissions, E-mail: psb6m@virginia.edu.

University of Virginia, Curry School of Education, Department of Curriculum, Instruction, and Special Education, Program in Curriculum and Instruction, Charlottesville, VA 22903. Offers curriculum and instruction (M Ed, Ed S); elementary (M Ed, Ed D); English (M Ed, Ed D); foreign language (M Ed); mathematics (M Ed, Ed D); reading (M Ed, Ed D, Ed S); science (Ed D); social studies (M Ed). *Students:* 22 full-time (19 women), 31 part-time (25 women); includes 3 minority (1 African American, 2 Hispanic Americans), 2 international. Average age 33. 182 applicants, 93% accepted, 16 enrolled. In 2008, 178 master's, 1 doctorate, 15 other advanced degrees awarded. *Degree requirements:* For master's, comprehensive exam (for some programs); for doctorate, comprehensive exam, thesis/dissertation; for Ed S, comprehensive exam. *Entrance requirements:* For master's, doctorate, and Ed S, GRE General Test, 2 letters of recommendation. Additional exam requirements/recommendations for international students: Required—TOEFL (minimum score 600 paper-based; 250 computer-based; 90 iBT), IELTS (minimum score 7). *Application deadline:* Applications are processed on a rolling basis. Application fee: $60. Electronic applications accepted. *Expenses:* Tuition, area resident: Full-time $10,452. Tuition, state resident: full-time $10,452. Tuition, nonresident: full-time $20,010. Required fees: $2176. Part-time tuition and fees vary according to course load and program. *Financial support:* Fellowships with tuition reimbursements, research assistantships with tuition reimbursements, teaching assistantships with tuition reimbursements available. Financial award application deadline: 1/5; financial award applicants required to submit FAFSA.

English

University of Washington, Graduate School, College of Arts and Sciences, Department of English, Seattle, WA 98195. Offers creative writing (MFA); English as a second language (MAT); English literature and language (MA, MAT, PhD). Part-time programs available. Terminal master's awarded for partial completion of doctoral program. *Degree requirements:* For master's, one foreign language, thesis (for some programs); for doctorate, one foreign language, thesis/dissertation. *Entrance requirements:* For master's, GRE General Test, GRE Subject Test (for English (MA, MAT) only), minimum GPA of 3.0; for doctorate, GRE General Test, GRE Subject Test. Additional exam requirements/recommendations for international students: Required— TOEFL. Electronic applications accepted. *Faculty research:* English and American literature, critical theory, creative writing, language theory.

University of Waterloo, Graduate Studies, Faculty of Arts, Department of English, Language and Literature, Waterloo, ON N2L 3G1, Canada. Offers English language and literature (PhD); literary studies (MA); rhetoric and communication design (MA). Part-time programs available. *Degree requirements:* For master's, one foreign language, thesis optional; for doctorate, 2 foreign languages, thesis/dissertation. *Entrance requirements:* For master's, honors degree, minimum B+ average; for doctorate, master's degree, minimum A- average. Additional exam requirements/recommendations for international students: Required—TOEFL, TWE. Electronic applications accepted. *Faculty research:* Shakespeare, American literature, rhetoric, Romantics, moderns.

The University of Western Ontario, Faculty of Graduate Studies, Faculty of Arts and Humanities, Department of English, London, ON N6A 5B8, Canada. Offers Canadian literature (MA); English (PhD); English literature (MA). *Degree requirements:* For master's, one foreign language, thesis or alternative; for doctorate, 2 foreign languages, thesis/dissertation, qualifying exam. *Entrance requirements:* For master's, minimum A average in appropriate field; for doctorate, MA or equivalent, minimum A average. Additional exam requirements/recommendations for international students: Required—TOEFL (minimum score 630 paper-based; 267 computer-based). *Faculty research:* Renaissance, nineteenth-century, modern, and postcolonial literature.

University of West Florida, College of Arts and Sciences: Arts, Department of English and Foreign Languages, Pensacola, FL 32514-5750. Offers creative writing (MA); literature (MA). Part-time and evening/weekend programs available. *Faculty:* 7 full-time (2 women). *Students:* 7 full-time (4 women), 29 part-time (22 women); includes 4 minority (1 African American, 1 American Indian/Alaska Native, 2 Asian Americans or Pacific Islanders). Average age 31. 20 applicants, 80% accepted, 12 enrolled. In 2008, 2 master's awarded. *Degree requirements:* For master's, thesis. *Entrance requirements:* For master's, GRE General Test, minimum GPA of 3.0. Additional exam requirements/recommendations for international students: Required— TOEFL (minimum score 550 paper-based; 213 computer-based). *Application deadline:* For fall admission, 6/1 for domestic students, 5/15 for international students; for spring admission, 11/1 for domestic students, 10/1 for international students. Applications are processed on a rolling basis. Application fee: $30. *Expenses:* Tuition, state resident: full-time $6095; part-time $253.97 per credit hour. Tuition, nonresident: full-time $21,919; part-time $913.31 per credit hour. *Financial support:* In 2008–09, 6 research assistantships with partial tuition reimbursements (averaging $2,187 per year), 9 teaching assistantships with partial tuition reimbursements (averaging $4,556 per year) were awarded; scholarships/grants, tuition waivers (partial), and unspecified assistantships also available. Support available to part-time students. Financial award application deadline: 4/15; financial award applicants required to submit FAFSA. *Faculty research:* Faulkner, Shakespeare, American humor, women's studies, poetry. *Unit head:* Dr. Bob Yeager, Chairperson, 850-474-2923. *Application contact:* Terry McCray, Assistant Director of Graduate Admissions, 850-473-7718, Fax: 850-473-7714, E-mail: gradadmissions@uwf.edu.

University of West Georgia, Graduate School, College of Arts and Sciences, Department of English and Philosophy, Carrollton, GA 30118. Offers English (MA). Part-time and evening/weekend programs available. *Faculty:* 20 full-time (11 women). *Students:* 1 (woman) full-time, 22 part-time (16 women); includes 2 minority (both African Americans). Average age 38. 13 applicants, 92% accepted, 1 enrolled. In 2008, 6 master's awarded. *Degree requirements:* For master's, one foreign language, comprehensive exam, thesis optional. *Entrance requirements:* For master's, GRE General Test, NTE, undergraduate degree in English, minimum GPA of 3.2. *Application deadline:* For fall admission, 7/18 priority date for domestic students; for spring admission, 11/27 for domestic students. Application fee: $30. Electronic applications accepted. *Expenses:* Tuition, state resident: full-time $2844; part-time $158 per semester hour. Tuition, nonresident: full-time $11,340; part-time $630 per semester hour. Required fees: $1120; $41.56 per semester hour. $186 per semester. Tuition and fees vary according to course load. *Financial support:* In 2008–09, 10 students received support, including 10 research assistantships with full tuition reimbursements available (averaging $4,000 per year); career-related internships or fieldwork and unspecified assistantships also available. Support available to part-time students. Financial award application deadline: 7/18; financial award applicants required to submit FAFSA. *Unit head:* Dr. Randy J. Hendricks, Chair, 678-839-6512, Fax: 678-839-4849, E-mail: rhendric@westga.edu. *Application contact:* Dr. Charles W. Clark, Dean, 678-839-6508, E-mail: cclark@westga.edu.

University of Windsor, Faculty of Graduate Studies, Faculty of Arts and Social Sciences, Department of English Language, Literature and Creative Writing, Windsor, ON N9B 3P4, Canada. Offers English: creative writing and language and literature (MA); English: language and literature (MA). Part-time programs available. *Degree requirements:* For master's, thesis. *Entrance requirements:* For master's, minimum B average, portfolio. Additional exam requirements/recommendations for international students: Required—TOEFL (minimum score 600 paper-based; 250 computer-based). Electronic applications accepted. *Faculty research:* Use of gender-related terms in popular culture; international and Aboriginal literatures; expression of cultural identity; critical analysis of authors: Pope, Munroe, Lady Morgan, Orwell, Thomas; the 'feminine' voice in literature and contemporary culture.

University of Wisconsin–Eau Claire, College of Arts and Sciences, Program in English, Eau Claire, WI 54702-4004. Offers MA. Part-time programs available. *Faculty:* 25 full-time (15 women), 2 part-time/adjunct (1 woman). *Students:* 7 full-time (3 women), 14 part-time (8 women); includes 1 minority (Asian American or Pacific Islander). Average age 31. 10 applicants, 70% accepted, 7 enrolled. In 2008, 6 master's awarded. *Degree requirements:* For master's, thesis, written exam, written project (oral defense). *Entrance requirements:* For master's, minimum GPA of 3.25 in English, 2.75 overall. Additional exam requirements/recommendations for international students: Required—TOEFL (minimum score 550 paper-based; 213 computer-based; 79 iBT). *Application deadline:* For fall admission, 7/1 priority date for domestic students, 6/1 priority date for international students; for spring admission, 12/1 priority date for domestic students, 11/1 priority date for international students. Applications are processed on a rolling basis. Application fee: $56. Electronic applications accepted. *Expenses:* Tuition, state resident: full-time $6426; part-time $400.60 per credit. Tuition, nonresident: full-time $17,560; part-time $975.32 per credit. One-time fee: $56 full-time. *Financial support:* In 2008–09, 15 students received support, including 1 fellowship (averaging $500 per year); Federal Work-Study and unspecified assistantships also available. Financial award application deadline: 3/1; financial award applicants required to submit FAFSA. *Unit head:* Dr. Jack Bushnell, Chair, 715-836-2639, Fax: 715-836-5996, E-mail: bushnejp@uwec.edu. *Application contact:* Kristina Anderson, Director of Admissions, 715-836-5415, Fax: 715-836-2409, E-mail: admissions@uwec.edu.

University of Wisconsin–Madison, Graduate School, College of Letters and Science, Department of English, Madison, WI 53706-1380. Offers applied English linguistics (MA); composition and rhetoric (PhD); creative writing (MFA); English language and linguistics (PhD); literary studies (MA, PhD). *Degree requirements:* For doctorate, thesis/dissertation.

University of Wisconsin–Milwaukee, Graduate School, College of Letters and Sciences, Department of English, Milwaukee, WI 53201-0413. Offers creative writing (PhD); English (MA); linguistics (PhD); professional writing (PhD); professional writing and communication (Certificate); rhetoric and composition (PhD); MLIS/MA. *Faculty:* 40 full-time (19 women).

Students: 107 full-time (64 women), 82 part-time (54 women); includes 13 minority (8 African Americans, 1 American Indian/Alaska Native, 2 Asian Americans or Pacific Islanders, 2 Hispanic Americans), 23 international. Average age 35. 187 applicants, 41% accepted, 34 enrolled. In 2008, 31 master's, 14 doctorates awarded. *Degree requirements:* For master's, thesis or alternative; for doctorate, one foreign language, thesis/dissertation. *Entrance requirements:* For master's, GRE General Test, GRE Subject Test; for doctorate, GRE. Additional exam requirements/recommendations for international students: Required—TOEFL (minimum score 550 paper-based; 79 iBT), IELTS (minimum score 6.5). *Application deadline:* For fall admission, 1/1 priority date for domestic students; for spring admission, 9/1 for domestic students. Applications are processed on a rolling basis. Application fee: $45 ($75 for international students). *Expenses:* Tuition, area resident: Full-time $7320; part-time $165 per credit. Tuition, state resident: full-time $7320; part-time $165 per credit. Tuition, nonresident: full-time $17,840; part-time $714 per credit. Tuition and fees vary according to campus/location, program and reciprocity agreements. *Financial support:* In 2008–09, 74 teaching assistantships were awarded; career-related internships or fieldwork and unspecified assistantships also available. Support available to part-time students. Financial award application deadline: 4/15. Total annual research expenditures: $53,677. *Unit head:* Tasha Oren, Representative, 414-229-2643, Fax: 414-229-2643, E-mail: tgoren@uwm.edu. *Application contact:* General Information Contact, 414-229-4982, Fax: 414-229-6967, E-mail: gradschool@uwm.edu.

University of Wisconsin–Oshkosh, The Office of Graduate Studies, College of Letters and Science, Department of English, Oshkosh, WI 54901. Offers MA. Part-time programs available. *Degree requirements:* For master's, thesis or alternative. *Entrance requirements:* For master's, GRE. Additional exam requirements/recommendations for international students: Required—TOEFL (minimum score 550 paper-based; 213 computer-based; 79 iBT). Electronic applications accepted.

University of Wisconsin–Stevens Point, College of Letters and Science, Department of English, Stevens Point, WI 54481-3897. Offers MST. *Students:* 5 full-time (4 women), 9 part-time (7 women). *Degree requirements:* For master's, thesis or alternative. *Application deadline:* For fall admission, 5/1 priority date for domestic students. Applications are processed on a rolling basis. Application fee: $45. *Expenses:* Tuition, state resident: full-time $7410. Tuition, nonresident: full-time $17,756. Full-time tuition and fees vary according to reciprocity agreements. *Financial support:* Federal Work-Study and unspecified assistantships available. Financial award application deadline: 5/1; financial award applicants required to submit FAFSA. *Unit head:* Dr. Michael Williams, Chair, 715-346-4757, Fax: 715-346-4215. *Application contact:* Catherine Glennon, Director of Admissions, 715-346-2441, E-mail: admiss@uwsp.edu.

University of Wyoming, Graduate School, College of Arts and Sciences, Department of English, Laramie, WY 82070. Offers creative writing (MFA); English (MA). Part-time programs available. *Faculty:* 28 full-time (14 women), 5 part-time/adjunct (3 women). *Students:* 35 full-time (17 women), 10 part-time (6 women); includes 1 minority (Hispanic American), 1 international. Average age 28. 72 applicants, 26% accepted, 13 enrolled. In 2008, 9 master's awarded. *Degree requirements:* For master's, thesis or alternative, internship. *Entrance requirements:* For master's, GRE General Test, minimum GPA of 3.0. *Application deadline:* For fall admission, 3/1 priority date for domestic students; for spring admission, 12/1 for domestic students. Applications are processed on a rolling basis. Application fee: $50. Electronic applications accepted. *Financial support:* In 2008–09, 14 teaching assistantships were awarded; institutionally sponsored loans also available. Financial award application deadline: 3/1. *Faculty research:* Literature and theory, creative writing, English as a second language, ethnic and women's studies, composition. *Unit head:* Dr. Peter Parolin, Department Chair, Professor, 307-766-6452, Fax: 307-766-3189, E-mail: parolin@uwyo.edu. *Application contact:* Rachel Michelle Ferrell, MFA in Creative Writing Program Coordinator, 307-766-2867, Fax: 307-766-2697, E-mail: cw@uwyo.edu.

Utah State University, School of Graduate Studies, College of Humanities, Arts and Social Sciences, Department of English, Logan, UT 84322. Offers American studies (MA, MS), including folklore, western American literature and culture; English (MA, MS), including literature and writing, technical writing. Part-time and evening/weekend programs available. *Degree requirements:* For master's, thesis or alternative. *Entrance requirements:* For master's, GRE General Test or MAT, minimum GPA of 3.0, recommendation letters, writing samples. Additional exam requirements/recommendations for international students: Required—TOEFL. *Faculty research:* Scottish enlightenment, material culture, composition theory, creative nonfiction, literary criticism.

Valdosta State University, Graduate School, College of Arts and Sciences, Department of English, Valdosta, GA 31698. Offers MA. Part-time programs available. *Faculty:* 22 full-time (13 women). *Students:* 4 full-time (3 women), 12 part-time (7 women); includes 1 minority (Asian American or Pacific Islander). Average age 25. 14 applicants, 50% accepted, 3 enrolled. In 2008, 4 master's awarded. *Degree requirements:* For master's, one foreign language, thesis, comprehensive written and/or oral exams. *Entrance requirements:* For master's, GRE General Test, minimum GPA of 3.0. Additional exam requirements/recommendations for international students: Required—TOEFL (minimum score 523 paper-based; 193 computer-based). *Application deadline:* For fall admission, 7/1 for domestic and international students; for spring admission, 11/1 for domestic and international students. Applications are processed on a rolling basis. Application fee: $40. Electronic applications accepted. *Financial support:* In 2008–09, 4 students received support, including 2 research assistantships with full tuition reimbursements available (averaging $2,452 per year), 2 teaching assistantships with full tuition reimbursements available (averaging $2,800 per year); institutionally sponsored loans, scholarships/grants, and unspecified assistantships also available. Support available to part-time students. Financial award application deadline: 7/1; financial award applicants required to submit FAFSA. *Faculty research:* American literature. *Unit head:* Dr. Mark Smith, Head, 229-333-5946, E-mail: marksmit@valdosta.edu. *Application contact:* Rebecca Waters, Coordinator of Graduate Admissions, 229-333-5694, Fax: 229-245-3853, E-mail: rlwaters@valdosta.edu.

Valparaiso University, Graduate Division, Program in Liberal Studies, Concentration in English, Valparaiso, IN 46383. Offers MALS, Post-Master's Certificate, JD/MALS. Part-time and evening/weekend programs available. *Students:* 2 full-time (1 woman), 7 part-time (all women); includes 2 minority (both African Americans), 1 international. Average age 32. In 2008, 8 master's awarded. *Entrance requirements:* For master's, minimum GPA of 3.0. Additional exam requirements/recommendations for international students: Required—TOEFL (minimum score 550 paper-based; 213 computer-based). *Application deadline:* Applications are processed on a rolling basis. Application fee: $30 ($50 for international students). Electronic applications accepted. *Financial support:* Available to part-time students. Applicants required to submit FAFSA. *Unit head:* Dr. David L. Rowland, Dean, Graduate Studies and Continuing Education, 219-464-5313, Fax: 219-464-5381, E-mail: David.Rowland@valpo.edu. *Application contact:* Jamie Haney, Coordinator of Recruitment Activities, 219-464-5313, Fax: 219-464-5381, E-mail: Jamie.Haney@valpo.edu.

Vanderbilt University, Graduate School, Department of English, Nashville, TN 37240-1001. Offers MA, MAT, PhD. *Faculty:* 51 full-time (25 women). *Students:* 37 full-time (25 women), 2 part-time (both women); includes 10 minority (4 African Americans, 2 American Indian/Alaska Native, 3 Asian Americans or Pacific Islanders, 1 Hispanic American), 1 international. Average age 29. 402 applicants, 4% accepted, 7 enrolled. In 2008, 6 master's, 8 doctorates awarded. *Degree requirements:* For master's, thesis; for doctorate, one foreign language, comprehensive exam, thesis/dissertation, final and qualifying exams. *Entrance requirements:* For master's and doctorate, GRE General Test, sample of written work. Additional exam requirements/recommendations for international students: Required—TOEFL (minimum score 570 paper-based; 230 computer-based; 88 iBT). *Application deadline:* For fall admission, 1/15 for domestic and international students. Application fee: $0. Electronic applications accepted. *Financial support:* Fellowships with full and partial tuition reimbursements, research assistantships with full and partial tuition reimbursements, teaching assistantships with full tuition reimbursements,

Federal Work-Study, institutionally sponsored loans, scholarships/grants, and health care benefits available. Financial award application deadline: 1/15; financial award applicants required to submit CSS PROFILE or FAFSA. *Faculty research:* British, American, and Anglophone literature, film, cultural studies, and literary theory. *Unit head:* Jay Clayton, PhD, Chair, 615-322-2542, Fax: 615-343-8028, E-mail: jay.clayton@vanderbilt.edu. *Application contact:* Kathryn Schwarz, PhD, Director of Graduate Studies, 615-322-2541, Fax: 615-343-8028, E-mail: kathryn.schwarz@vanderbilt.edu.

Villanova University, Graduate School of Liberal Arts and Sciences, Department of English, Villanova, PA 19085-1699. Offers MA. Part-time and evening/weekend programs available. *Faculty:* 9 full-time (6 women). *Students:* 28 full-time (16 women), 27 part-time (16 women); includes 3 minority (1 African American, 2 Asian Americans or Pacific Islanders). Average age 28. 41 applicants, 71% accepted, 16 enrolled. In 2008, 10 master's awarded. *Degree requirements:* For master's, comprehensive exam, thesis optional. *Entrance requirements:* For master's, GRE General Test, GRE Subject Test, minimum GPA of 3.0, writing sample. *Application deadline:* For fall admission, 7/1 for domestic and international students; for spring admission, 11/15 for domestic and international students. Applications are processed on a rolling basis. Application fee: $50. Electronic applications accepted. *Financial support:* Research assistantships, Federal Work-Study and scholarships/grants available. Financial award applicants required to submit FAFSA. *Unit head:* Dr. Evan Radcliffe, Chairperson, 610-519-4630. *Application contact:* Dr. Gerald Long, Dean, Graduate School of Liberal Arts and Sciences, 610-519-7093, Fax: 610-519-7096.

See Close-Up on page 449.

Virginia Commonwealth University, Graduate School, College of Humanities and Sciences, Department of English, Program in English, Richmond, VA 23284-9005. Offers literature (MA); writing and rhetoric (MA).

Virginia Polytechnic Institute and State University, Graduate School, College of Liberal Arts and Human Sciences, Department of English, Blacksburg, VA 24061. Offers creative writing (MFA); English (MA); rhetoric and writing (PhD). *Entrance requirements:* For master's, GRE General Test, GRE Subject Test. Additional exam requirements/recommendations for international students: Required—TOEFL (minimum score 600 paper-based; 250 computer-based). Electronic applications accepted. *Faculty research:* Critical theory, feminist criticism, textual editing, literary history.

Virginia State University, School of Graduate Studies, Research, and Outreach, School of Liberal Arts and Education, Department of Languages and Literature, Petersburg, VA 23806-0001. Offers English (MA). Part-time and evening/weekend programs available. *Degree requirements:* For master's, one foreign language, thesis (for some programs). *Entrance requirements:* For master's, GRE General Test. *Faculty research:* Writing and learning instruction, high-risk students, twentieth-century literature.

Wake Forest University, Graduate School of Arts and Sciences, Department of English, Winston-Salem, NC 27109. Offers MA. Part-time programs available. *Degree requirements:* For master's, one foreign language, thesis. *Entrance requirements:* For master's, GRE General Test, GRE Subject Test, writing sample. Additional exam requirements/recommendations for international students: Required—TOEFL (minimum score 213 computer-based; 79 iBT). Electronic applications accepted. *Faculty research:* Modern and contemporary poetry, feminist criticism and theory, Irish literature, British Commonwealth literature, medieval poetry.

Washington College, Graduate Programs, Department of English, Chestertown, MD 21620-1197. Offers MA. Part-time and evening/weekend programs available.

Washington State University, Graduate School, College of Liberal Arts, Department of English, Pullman, WA 99164. Offers composition (MA); English (MA, PhD); teaching of English (MA). *Degree requirements:* For master's, one foreign language, comprehensive exam (for some programs), thesis (for some programs), oral exam; for doctorate, 2 foreign languages, comprehensive exam, thesis/dissertation, oral exam, written exam. *Entrance requirements:* For master's and doctorate, GRE General Test, GRE Subject Test, minimum GPA of 3.0, 10 page writing sample, 3 letters of recommendation. Additional exam requirements/recommendations for international students: Required—TOEFL. *Faculty research:* Nationalism and gender in the American West, slavery and exploitation in 19th century Britain, photography and the color line, D.H. Lawrence and Mexico, social movement cultures and the arts.

Washington State University, Graduate School, College of Liberal Arts, Program in American Studies, Pullman, WA 99164. Offers ethnic studies (MA, PhD); feminist studies (MA, PhD); history (MA, PhD); literature (MA, PhD). *Degree requirements:* For master's, one foreign language, comprehensive exam (for some programs), thesis optional, oral exam; for doctorate, one foreign language, comprehensive exam (for some programs), thesis/dissertation, oral exam. *Entrance requirements:* For master's and doctorate, GRE General Test, minimum GPA of 3.0, writing sample, 3 letters of recommendation. Additional exam requirements/recommendations for international students: Required—TOEFL. *Faculty research:* The American West in multicultural perspective; nineteenth century historical, literary, and cultural studies; comparative American ethnic literatures and cultures; American cultures and the environment; American rhetoric.

Washington University in St. Louis, Graduate School of Arts and Sciences, Department of English and American Literature, St. Louis, MO 63130-4899. Offers English and American literature (MA, PhD); writing (MFAW). *Students:* 78 full-time (58 women); includes 1 minority (Asian American or Pacific Islander), 3 international. 122 applicants, 16% accepted, 9 enrolled. In 2008, 4 master's, 11 doctorates awarded. Terminal master's awarded for partial completion of doctoral program. *Degree requirements:* For master's, thesis or written exam; for doctorate, 2 foreign languages, thesis/dissertation. *Entrance requirements:* For master's and doctorate, GRE General Test, sample of written work. *Application deadline:* For fall admission, 1/3 for domestic students. Application fee: $45. Electronic applications accepted. *Financial support:* Fellowships, research assistantships, teaching assistantships, career-related internships or fieldwork, Federal Work-Study, institutionally sponsored loans, and tuition waivers (full and partial) available. Support available to part-time students. Financial award application deadline: 1/15. *Unit head:* Dr. Vincent Sherry, Chairman, 314-935-5120. *Application contact:* Kathy Schneider, Academic Coordinator, 314-935-5120.

Wayne State University, College of Liberal Arts and Sciences, Department of English, Detroit, MI 48202. Offers comparative literature (MA); English (MA, PhD). *Degree requirements:* For master's, one foreign language, essay or thesis; for doctorate, one foreign language, thesis/dissertation. *Entrance requirements:* For master's, GRE General Test, minimum GPA of 3.25 in English, 3.0 overall, statement of purpose; references; sample essay; for doctorate, GRE General Test, GRE Subject Test, statement of purpose, references, sample essay. Additional exam requirements/recommendations for international students: Required—TOEFL (minimum score 550 paper-based; 213 computer-based); Recommended—TWE (minimum score 6). Electronic applications accepted. *Faculty research:* English and American literature, cultural studies, composition, linguistics, film.

Weber State University, College of Arts and Humanities, Program in English, Ogden, UT 84408-1001. Offers MENG. Part-time and evening/weekend programs available. *Degree requirements:* For master's, one foreign language, additional course hours, thesis or research project. *Entrance requirements:* For master's, MAT or GRE, 3 letter of recommendation, transcript, writing sample, bachelor's degree. *Faculty research:* Victoria literature, Middle East women writers, Irish literature (Seamus Heanes).

West Chester University of Pennsylvania, Office of Graduate Studies, College of Arts and Sciences, Department of English, West Chester, PA 19383. Offers English (MA, Teaching Certificate); English—non-thesis option (MA); TESL (MA, Certificate). Part-time and evening/weekend programs available. *Students:* 23 full-time (11 women), 70 part-time (56 women); includes 6 minority (4 African Americans, 1 Asian American or Pacific Islander, 1 Hispanic American), 2 international. Average age 36. 52 applicants, 100% accepted, 23 enrolled. In 2008, 45 master's, 1 other advanced degree awarded. *Degree requirements:* For master's, thesis optional. *Entrance requirements:* For master's, writing sample, three letters of recommendation, interview, minimum GPA of 2.8, one foreign language (for TESL); for other advanced degree, goals statement. Additional exam requirements/recommendations for international students: Required—TOEFL (minimum score 550 paper-based; 213 computer-based; 80 iBT). *Application deadline:* For fall admission, 4/15 priority date for domestic students, 3/15 for international students; for spring admission, 10/15 for domestic students, 9/1 for international students. Applications are processed on a rolling basis. Application fee: $35. Electronic applications accepted. *Expenses:* Tuition, state resident: full-time $6430; part-time $357 per credit. Tuition, nonresident: full-time $10,288; part-time $572 per credit. Required fees: $652.50; $50 per credit. $67 per semester. *Financial support:* In 2008–09, 15 research assistantships with full and partial tuition reimbursements (averaging $5,000 per year) were awarded; unspecified assistantships also available. Support available to part-time students. Financial award application deadline: 2/15; financial award applicants required to submit FAFSA. *Faculty research:* William Smith, Sara Winnemucca Hopkins, literacy practices for students at risk. *Unit head:* Dr. Anne Herzog, Chair, 610-436-2822, E-mail: aherzog@wcupa.edu. *Application contact:* Dr. Carolyn Sorisio, Graduate Coordinator for English, 610-436-2745, E-mail: kfitts@wcupa.edu.

Western Carolina University, Graduate School, College of Arts and Sciences, Department of English, Cullowhee, NC 28723. Offers English (MA); teaching English as a second language or foreign language (MA). Part-time and evening/weekend programs available. *Degree requirements:* For master's, one foreign language, comprehensive exam, thesis (for some programs). *Entrance requirements:* For master's, GRE General Test, appropriate undergraduate, writing sample, 3 letters of recommendation. Additional exam requirements/recommendations for international students: Required—TOEFL (minimum score 550 paper-based; 270 computer-based; 79 iBT). *Faculty research:* TESOL, language assessment, applied linguistics, poetry, folk and fairy tales, post World War II British literature, Appalachian and southern literature.

Western Connecticut State University, Division of Graduate Studies, School of Arts and Sciences, Department of English, Danbury, CT 06810-6885. Offers English (MA); literature option (MA); TESOL option (MA); writing option (MA). Part-time programs available. *Faculty:* 5 full-time (2 women). *Students:* 8 full-time (5 women), 35 part-time (26 women); includes 6 minority (2 African Americans, 1 Asian American or Pacific Islander, 3 Hispanic Americans), 2 international. Average age 40. 23 applicants, 48% accepted, 11 enrolled. In 2008, 10 master's awarded. *Degree requirements:* For master's, thesis (for writing option), completion of program in 6 years with minimum cumulative GPA of 3.0. *Entrance requirements:* For master's, minimum GPA of 2.5, writing sample. *Application deadline:* For fall admission, 8/5 priority date for domestic students; for spring admission, 1/5 priority date for domestic students. Applications are processed on a rolling basis. Application fee: $50. *Expenses:* Tuition, state resident: full-time $4377; part-time $363 per credit. Tuition, nonresident: full-time $12,195; part-time $363 per credit. Required fees: $3574; $60 per credit. Part-time tuition and fees vary according to degree level and program. *Financial support:* Teaching assistantships, career-related internships or fieldwork available. Support available to part-time students. Financial award application deadline: 5/1; financial award applicants required to submit FAFSA. *Unit head:* Dr. Shouhua Qi, Co-Coordinator, 203-837-9048, Fax: 203-837-8525, E-mail: qis@wcsu.edu. *Application contact:* Chris Shankle, Associate Director of Graduate Studies, 203-837-9005, Fax: 203-837-8326, E-mail: shanklec@wcsu.edu.

Western Illinois University, School of Graduate Studies, College of Arts and Sciences, Department of English and Journalism, Macomb, IL 61455-1390. Offers English (MA, Certificate). Part-time programs available. *Students:* 18 full-time (9 women), 23 part-time (19 women); includes 1 minority (Hispanic American), 1 international. Average age 30. 18 applicants, 72% accepted. In 2008, 22 master's awarded. *Degree requirements:* For master's, thesis or alternative. *Entrance requirements:* Additional exam requirements/recommendations for international students: Required—TOEFL (minimum score 575 paper-based; 230 computer-based; 88 iBT). *Application deadline:* Applications are processed on a rolling basis. Application fee: $30. Electronic applications accepted. *Expenses:* Tuition, state resident: full-time $5696; part-time $237.34 per credit hour. Tuition, nonresident: full-time $11,392; part-time $474.68 per credit hour. Required fees: $1453; $60.55 per credit hour. *Financial support:* In 2008–09, 15 students received support, including 7 research assistantships with full tuition reimbursements available (averaging $7,040 per year), 8 teaching assistantships with full tuition reimbursements available (averaging $8,120 per year). Financial award applicants required to submit FAFSA. *Unit head:* Dr. Joan Livingston-Webber, Chairperson, 309-298-1103. *Application contact:* Evelyn Hoing, Assistant Director of Graduate Studies, 309-298-1806, Fax: 309-298-2345, E-mail: grad-office@wiu.edu.

Western Kentucky University, Graduate Studies, Potter College of Arts and Letters, Department of English, Bowling Green, KY 42101. Offers education (MA); English (MA Ed); literature (MA), including American literature, British literature, literary theory, women writers, world literature; teaching English as a second language (MA); writing (MA). Part-time and evening/weekend programs available. *Degree requirements:* For master's, comprehensive exam, thesis optional, final exam. *Entrance requirements:* For master's, GRE General Test, minimum GPA of 2.75. Additional exam requirements/recommendations for international students: Required—TOEFL (minimum score 555 paper-based; 213 computer-based; 79 iBT). *Faculty research:* Improving writing, linking teacher knowledge and performance, Victorian women writers, Kentucky women writers, Kentucky poets.

Western Michigan University, Graduate College, College of Arts and Sciences, Department of English, Kalamazoo, MI 49008-5202. Offers creative writing (MFA); English (MA, PhD); English education (MA, PhD); professional writing (MA). *Degree requirements:* For master's, oral exams; for doctorate, one foreign language, thesis/dissertation, oral exam, written exams. *Entrance requirements:* For master's and doctorate, GRE General Test, GRE Subject Test.

Western Washington University, Graduate School, College of Humanities and Social Sciences, Department of English, Bellingham, WA 98225-5996. Offers MA. Part-time programs available. *Degree requirements:* For master's, one foreign language, comprehensive exam, thesis (for some programs). *Entrance requirements:* For master's, GRE General Test, writing sample, minimum GPA of 3.0 in last 60 semester hours or last 90 quarter hours of course work. Additional exam requirements/recommendations for international students: Required—TOEFL (minimum score 567 paper-based; 227 computer-based). Electronic applications accepted. *Faculty research:* Literature and technology, film, composition and rhetoric, technical writing, critical and cultural theory.

Westfield State College, Division of Graduate and Continuing Education, Department of English, Westfield, MA 01086. Offers MA. Part-time and evening/weekend programs available. *Faculty:* 3 full-time (2 women). *Students:* 2 full-time (both women), 15 part-time (9 women). Average age 39. In 2008, 2 master's awarded. *Degree requirements:* For master's, one foreign language, thesis. *Entrance requirements:* For master's, GRE General Test, MAT, minimum undergraduate GPA of 2.7, undergraduate course work in English. *Application deadline:* Applications are processed on a rolling basis. Application fee: $30. *Financial support:* In 2008–09, 1 research assistantship with tuition reimbursement (averaging $1,600 per year) was awarded; teaching assistantships, career-related internships or fieldwork, Federal Work-Study, and tuition waivers (full and partial) also available. Financial award application deadline: 4/1; financial award applicants required to submit CSS PROFILE. *Unit head:* Dr. Marilyn Sandidge, Director, 413-572-5330. *Application contact:* Michelle Janke, Admissions Coordinator, 413-572-8022, Fax: 413-572-5227, E-mail: mjanke@wsc.ma.edu.

West Texas A&M University, College of Fine Arts and Humanities, Department of English and Modern Languages, Canyon, TX 79016-0001. Offers English (MA). Part-time and evening/weekend programs available. *Degree requirements:* For master's, comprehensive exam, thesis optional. *Entrance requirements:* For master's, GRE General Test. Additional exam requirements/recommendations for international students: Required—TOEFL (minimum score 550 paper-

English

West Texas A&M University (continued)
based). Electronic applications accepted. *Faculty research:* Medieval studies, composition theory, literary criticism, Evelyn Scott, transformation of literacy in computer mediated communication.

West Virginia University, Eberly College of Arts and Sciences, Department of English, Morgantown, WV 26506. Offers creative writing (MFA); English (MA, PhD); literary/cultural studies (MA, PhD); writing (MA). Part-time and evening/weekend programs available. *Degree requirements:* For master's, one foreign language, thesis optional; for doctorate, one foreign language, thesis/dissertation, preliminary exam. *Entrance requirements:* For master's, GRE General Test, minimum GPA of 3.0; for doctorate, GRE General Test, GRE Subject Test, minimum GPA of 3.0. Additional exam requirements/recommendations for international students: Required—TOEFL. Electronic applications accepted. *Faculty research:* American studies, gender studies, media studies, cultural studies.

Wichita State University, Graduate School, Fairmount College of Liberal Arts and Sciences, Department of English, Wichita, KS 67260. Offers creative writing (MA, MFA); English (MA, MFA). Part-time and evening/weekend programs available. *Degree requirements:* For master's, comprehensive exam. *Entrance requirements:* For master's, GRE, writing sample (MFA). Additional exam requirements/recommendations for international students: Required—TOEFL. Electronic applications accepted.

Wilfrid Laurier University, Faculty of Graduate Studies, Faculty of Arts, Department of English and Film Studies, Waterloo, ON N2L 3C5, Canada. Offers MA, PhD. *Degree requirements:* For master's, thesis optional; for doctorate, thesis/dissertation. *Entrance requirements:* For master's, honours BA or the equivalent in English, minimum B+ in English courses above first year level; for doctorate, MA in English, minimum A- average in graduate work. Additional exam requirements/recommendations for international students: Recommended—TOEFL (minimum score 230 computer-based; 89 iBT). Electronic applications accepted. *Faculty research:* Gender and genre, Canadian studies, early modern studies, postcolonial studies, nineteenth century studies.

William Paterson University of New Jersey, College of the Humanities and Social Sciences, Department of English, Wayne, NJ 07470-8420. Offers MA. Part-time and evening/weekend programs available. *Degree requirements:* For master's, thesis, essay, manuscript, portfolio. *Entrance requirements:* For master's, GRE General Test, MAT, minimum GPA of 2.75. Electronic applications accepted. *Faculty research:* Thornton Wilder notebooks and diaries, minimal grammar text, Senhora text, Frank O'Hara biography, Caresse Crosby biography.

Winona State University, College of Liberal Arts, Department of English, Winona, MN 55987-5838. Offers MA, MS. Part-time programs available. *Degree requirements:* For master's, thesis or alternative.

Winthrop University, College of Arts and Sciences, Department of English, Rock Hill, SC 29733. Offers MA. Part-time and evening/weekend programs available. *Degree requirements:*

For master's, one foreign language, thesis optional. *Entrance requirements:* For master's, GRE General Test, MAT or PRAXIS, 24 undergraduate English hours. Electronic applications accepted.

Wright State University, School of Graduate Studies, College of Liberal Arts, Department of English Language and Literatures, Dayton, OH 45435. Offers composition and rhetoric (MA); English (MA); literature (MA); teaching English to speakers of other languages (MA). *Degree requirements:* For master's, thesis optional, portfolio. *Entrance requirements:* For master's, 20 hours in upper-level English. Additional exam requirements/recommendations for international students: Required—TOEFL. *Faculty research:* American literature, world literature in English, applied linguistics, writing theory and pedagogy.

Xavier University, College of Arts and Sciences, Department of English, Cincinnati, OH 45207. Offers MA. Part-time and evening/weekend programs available. *Faculty:* 12 full-time (4 women). *Students:* 7 full-time (5 women), 12 part-time (8 women). Average age 30. 18 applicants, 61% accepted, 7 enrolled. In 2008, 5 master's awarded. *Degree requirements:* For master's, one foreign language, comprehensive exam, thesis optional. *Entrance requirements:* For master's, GRE, 2 letters of recommendation, writing sample, official undergraduate transcripts with minimum GPA of 3.2. Additional exam requirements/recommendations for international students: Required—TOEFL (minimum score 550 paper-based; 213 computer-based; 79 iBT). *Application deadline:* Applications are processed on a rolling basis. Application fee: $35. Electronic applications accepted. Tuition and fees vary according to course load, degree level and program. *Financial support:* In 2008–09, 14 students received support. Tuition waivers (partial) and unspecified assistantships available. Financial award applicants required to submit FAFSA. *Faculty research:* British literature, American literature, linguistics, literary theory, composition studies. *Unit head:* Dr. Alison Russell, Chair, 513-745-3275, Fax: 513-745-3065, E-mail: russell@xavier.edu. *Application contact:* Dr. Alison Russell, Chair, 513-745-3275, Fax: 513-745-3065, E-mail: russell@xavier.edu.

Yale University, Graduate School of Arts and Sciences, Department of English Language and Literature, New Haven, CT 06520. Offers MA, PhD. Terminal master's awarded for partial completion of doctoral program. *Degree requirements:* For master's, 2 foreign languages; for doctorate, 3 foreign languages, thesis/dissertation. *Entrance requirements:* For master's and doctorate, GRE General Test, GRE Subject Test.

York University, Faculty of Graduate Studies, Faculty of Arts, Program in English, Toronto, ON M3J 1P3, Canada. Offers MA, PhD. Part-time programs available. *Degree requirements:* For master's, thesis or alternative; for doctorate, one foreign language, comprehensive exam, thesis/dissertation. Electronic applications accepted.

Youngstown State University, Graduate School, College of Liberal Arts and Social Sciences, Department of English, Youngstown, OH 44555-0001. Offers MA. Part-time programs available. *Degree requirements:* For master's, portfolio. *Entrance requirements:* For master's, bachelor's degree in English, minimum GPA of 2.7. Additional exam requirements/recommendations for international students: Required—TOEFL. *Faculty research:* Technical communications, multi-cultural literacy, children's literature, women's literature, film study, linguistics.

French

American University, College of Arts and Sciences, Department of Language and Foreign Studies, Program in French, Washington, DC 20016-8045. Offers translation (Certificate). Part-time and evening/weekend programs available. *Students:* 1 (woman) full-time, 4 part-time (all women), 1 international. Average age 29. *Degree requirements:* For Certificate, minimum 15 credit hours related course work. *Entrance requirements:* For degree, bachelor's degree in French or evidence of French proficiency plus BA in any field. Additional exam requirements/recommendations for international students: Required—TOEFL. *Application deadline:* For fall admission, 2/1 for domestic students; for spring admission, 10/1 for domestic students. Application fee: $50. *Expenses:* Tuition: Full-time $21,204; part-time $1178 per credit hour. Required fees: $380. Part-time tuition and fees vary according to course load and program. *Financial support:* Fellowships, career-related internships or fieldwork, Federal Work-Study, and institutionally sponsored loans available. Financial award application deadline: 2/1. *Faculty research:* Literature, language, modern French politics, contemporary French society, the civilization of Quebec, business French and translation studies.

Arizona State University, Graduate College, College of Liberal Arts and Sciences, Division of Humanities, School of International Letters and Cultures, Program in French, Tempe, AZ 85287. Offers MA. *Degree requirements:* For master's, thesis or alternative. *Entrance requirements:* For master's, GRE.

Asbury College, Graduate Programs, Wilmore, KY 40390-1198. Offers biology: alternative certificate (MA Ed); chemistry: alternative certificate (MA Ed); English (Certificate); English as a second language (MA Ed); ESL (Certificate); French (Certificate); mathematics: alternative certificate (MA Ed); reading / writing (MA Ed); social studies (Certificate); Spanish (Certificate); special education (MA Ed); special education: alternative certificate (MA Ed). *Accreditation:* NCATE. Part-time programs available. *Degree requirements:* For master's, action research project, portfolio. *Entrance requirements:* For master's, PRAXIS/NTE, minimum GPA of 2.75, letters of recommendation. Additional exam requirements/recommendations for international students: Required—TOEFL (minimum score 550 paper-based).

Bennington College, Graduate Programs, Program in Teaching a Second Language, Bennington, VT 05201. Offers education (MATSL); foreign language education (MATSL); French (MATSL); Spanish (MATSL). Part-time programs available. *Faculty:* 2 full-time (1 woman), 4 part-time/adjunct (all women). *Students:* 21 part-time (20 women); includes 4 minority (1 African American, 3 Hispanic Americans), 1 international. Average age 41. 14 applicants, 71% accepted, 9 enrolled. In 2008, 4 master's awarded. *Degree requirements:* For master's, one foreign language, 2 major projects and presentations. *Entrance requirements:* For master's, Oral Proficiency Interview (OPI). Additional exam requirements/recommendations for international students: Required—TOEFL (minimum score 577 paper-based; 233 computer-based; 91 iBT). *Application deadline:* For spring admission, 4/1 priority date for domestic and international students. Applications are processed on a rolling basis. Application fee: $60. *Expenses:* Contact institution. *Financial support:* In 2008–09, 2 students received support. Scholarships/grants available. Financial award application deadline: 4/1; financial award applicants required to submit FAFSA. *Faculty research:* Acquisition, evaluation, assessment, conceptual teaching and learning content-driven communication, applied linguistics. *Unit head:* Carol Meyer, Director, 802-440-4375, E-mail: cmeyer@bennington.edu. *Application contact:* Nancy Pearlman, Assistant Director, MATSL, 802-440-4710, E-mail: matsl@bennington.edu.

Boston College, Graduate School of Arts and Sciences, Department of Romance Languages and Literatures, Chestnut Hill, MA 02467-3800. Offers French (MA, PhD); Italian (MA); medieval language (PhD); Spanish (MA, PhD). Part-time programs available. Terminal master's awarded for partial completion of doctoral program. *Degree requirements:* For master's, one foreign language; for doctorate, 2 foreign languages, thesis/dissertation. *Entrance requirements:* Additional exam requirements/recommendations for international students: Required—TOEFL (minimum score 590 paper-based; 250 computer-based; 91 iBT). Electronic applications accepted. *Expenses:* Tuition: Part-time $1148 per credit. Required fees: $60. *Faculty research:*

Spanish-American literature, philology, medieval French romance and troubadour/trouvere lyrics, Golden Age Peninsular literature, secondary language acquisition and pedagogy.
See Close-Up on page 437.

Boston University, Graduate School of Arts and Sciences, Department of Romance Studies, Boston, MA 02215. Offers French language and literature (MA, PhD); Hispanic language and literatures (MA, PhD). Terminal master's awarded for partial completion of doctoral program. *Degree requirements:* For master's, one foreign language, comprehensive exam; for doctorate, 2 foreign languages, comprehensive exam, thesis/dissertation. *Entrance requirements:* For master's and doctorate, GRE General Test, sample of written work, 3 letters of recommendation. Additional exam requirements/recommendations for international students: Required—TOEFL (minimum score 550 paper-based; 213 computer-based).

Bowling Green State University, Graduate College, College of Arts and Sciences, Department of Romance and Classical Studies, Program in French, Bowling Green, OH 43403. Offers French (MA); French education (MAT). Part-time programs available. *Degree requirements:* For master's, one foreign language, thesis or alternative. *Entrance requirements:* For master's, GRE General Test. Additional exam requirements/recommendations for international students: Required—TOEFL. Electronic applications accepted. *Faculty research:* Francophone literature, French cinema, business French, nineteenth and twentieth century literature.

Brigham Young University, Graduate Studies, College of Humanities, Department of French and Italian, Provo, UT 84602. Offers French studies (MA). *Faculty:* 12 full-time (1 woman). *Students:* 4 full-time (2 women), 7 part-time (4 women); includes 2 minority (both Hispanic Americans). Average age 28. 4 applicants, 100% accepted, 4 enrolled. In 2008, 4 master's awarded. *Degree requirements:* For master's, one foreign language, thesis. *Entrance requirements:* For master's, GRE General Test, BA in French. Additional exam requirements/recommendations for international students: Required—TOEFL. *Application deadline:* For fall admission, 2/28 for domestic and international students; for winter admission, 9/1 for domestic students, 6/30 for international students. Application fee: $50. Electronic applications accepted. *Expenses:* Tuition: Full-time $5160; part-time $287 per credit hour. Tuition and fees vary according to program and student's religious affiliation. *Financial support:* In 2008–09, 9 students received support, including 1 research assistantship (averaging $3,500 per year), 5 teaching assistantships (averaging $8,480 per year); career-related internships or fieldwork, institutionally sponsored loans, scholarships/grants, and tuition waivers (full and partial) also available. Support available to part-time students. *Faculty research:* Francophone studies, Medieval literature, Provençal literature, existentialism, second language acquisition. *Unit head:* Dr. Yvon R. Lebras, Department Chair, 801-422-2288, Fax: 901-422-0260, E-mail: yvon_lebras@byu.edu. *Application contact:* Dr. Corry L. Cropper, Graduate Coordinator, 801-422-4484, Fax: 801-422-0260, E-mail: corry_cropper@byu.edu.

Brooklyn College of the City University of New York, Division of Graduate Studies, Department of Modern Languages and Literature, Brooklyn, NY 11210-2889. Offers French (MA); modern languages and literature (PhD); Spanish (MA). The department offers courses at Brooklyn College that are creditable toward the CUNY doctoral degree (with permission of the executive officer of the doctoral program). *Students:* 1 full-time (0 women), 24 part-time (15 women); includes 18 minority (8 African Americans, 10 Hispanic Americans), 5 international. Average age 37. 12 applicants, 100% accepted, 7 enrolled. In 2008, 8 master's awarded. *Degree requirements:* For master's, comprehensive exam or research paper. *Entrance requirements:* For master's, 18 credits in advanced courses in Spanish, 2 letters of recommendation. Additional exam requirements/recommendations for international students: Required—TOEFL. *Application deadline:* For fall admission, 3/1 priority date for domestic students, 2/1 priority date for international students; for spring admission, 11/1 priority date for domestic students, 10/1 priority date for international students. Applications are processed on a rolling basis. Application fee: $125. Electronic applications accepted. *Expenses:* Tuition, state resident: full-time $7360; part-time $310 per credit hour. Tuition, nonresident: full-time $13,800; part-time $575 per credit hour. *Financial support:* Federal Work-Study, institutionally sponsored loans, and scholarships/grants available. Support available to part-time students. Financial award application deadline: 5/1; financial award applicants required to submit FAFSA. *Faculty research:* Latin American contemporary novel; Caribbean female contemporary literature; 19th and 20th century Spanish novel; 20th century Mexican poetry. *Unit head:* Dr. William Childers, Chairperson, 718-951-5451, E-mail: wchilders@brooklyn.cuny.edu. *Application contact:* Hernan Sierra, Graduate Admissions Coordinator, 718-951-4536, Fax: 718-951-4506, E-mail: grads@brooklyn.cuny.edu.

Brown University, Graduate School, Department of French Studies, Providence, RI 02912. Offers PhD, MA/PhD. *Degree requirements:* For doctorate, variable foreign language requirement, thesis/dissertation, preliminary exam.

Bryn Mawr College, Graduate School of Arts and Sciences, Department of French, Bryn Mawr, PA 19010-2899. Offers MA, PhD. Part-time programs available. *Degree requirements:* For master's, one foreign language, thesis. *Entrance requirements:* For master's, GRE General Test. Additional exam requirements/recommendations for international students: Required— TOEFL (minimum score 600 paper-based; 250 computer-based).

California State University, Fullerton, Graduate Studies, College of Humanities and Social Sciences, Department of Modern Languages and Literatures, Fullerton, CA 92834-9480. Offers French (MA); German (MA); Spanish (MA); teaching English to speakers of other languages (MS). Part-time programs available. *Students:* 63 full-time (49 women), 79 part-time (65 women); includes 70 minority (21 Asian Americans or Pacific Islanders, 49 Hispanic Americans), 23 international. Average age 32. 118 applicants, 56% accepted, 43 enrolled. In 2008, 28 master's awarded. *Degree requirements:* For master's, comprehensive exam, thesis or alternative. *Entrance requirements:* For master's, minimum GPA of 2.5 in last 60 hours of course work, undergraduate major in a language. Application fee: $55. Tuition and fees vary according to degree level. *Financial support:* Federal Work-Study, institutionally sponsored loans, and scholarships/grants available. Support available to part-time students. Financial award application deadline: 3/1. *Unit head:* Dr. Janet Eyring, Chair, 657-278-3534. *Application contact:* Admissions/Applications, 657-278-2300.

California State University, Long Beach, Graduate Studies, College of Liberal Arts, Department of Romance, German, and Russian Languages and Literature, Program in French, Long Beach, CA 90840. Offers MA. Part-time programs available. *Students:* 8 full-time (4 women), 7 part-time (5 women); includes 4 minority (1 African American, 2 Asian Americans or Pacific Islanders, 1 Hispanic American), 1 international. Average age 35. 9 applicants, 67% accepted, 4 enrolled. *Degree requirements:* For master's, one foreign language, comprehensive exam, thesis optional. *Entrance requirements:* For master's, BA in French. *Application deadline:* For fall admission, 7/1 for domestic students. Applications are processed on a rolling basis. Application fee: $55. Electronic applications accepted. *Expenses:* Tuition, nonresident: full-time $11,160; part-time $372 per unit. Required fees: $4100; $1261 per semester. *Financial support:* Federal Work-Study, institutionally sponsored loans, and scholarships/grants available. Financial award application deadline: 3/2. *Faculty research:* Eighteenth century encyclopedism, development of the novel, Chanson de Roland. *Unit head:* Dr. Clorinda Donato, Co-Director, 562-985-4318, Fax: 562-985-4259, E-mail: cdonato@csulb.edu. *Application contact:* Dr. Stephen Flect, Co-Director, 562-985-4318, Fax: 562-985-4259, E-mail: sfleck@csulb.edu.

California State University, Los Angeles, Graduate Studies, College of Arts and Letters, Department of Modern Languages and Literatures, Los Angeles, CA 90032-8530. Offers French (MA); Spanish (MA). Part-time and evening/weekend programs available. *Faculty:* 5 full-time (2 women), 1 (woman) part-time/adjunct. *Students:* 26 full-time (18 women), 31 part-time (26 women); includes 41 minority (1 African American, 2 Asian Americans or Pacific Islanders, 38 Hispanic Americans), 5 international. Average age 36. 15 applicants, 100% accepted, 7 enrolled. In 2008, 6 master's awarded. *Degree requirements:* For master's, comprehensive exam. *Entrance requirements:* Additional exam requirements/recommendations for international students: Required—TOEFL (minimum score 500 paper-based; 173 computer-based). *Application deadline:* For fall admission, 6/15 for domestic students, 5/1 for international students; for winter admission, 11/1 for domestic students, 9/1 for international students; for spring admission, 2/1 for domestic students, 10/1 for international students. Applications are processed on a rolling basis. Application fee: $55. Electronic applications accepted. *Expenses:* Tuition, nonresident: part-time $226 per credit. Required fees: $4019. *Financial support:* Federal Work-Study available. Support available to part-time students. Financial award application deadline: 3/1. *Faculty research:* French literature, language teaching and methodology, Spanish poetry, Spanish-American fiction and poetry. *Unit head:* Dr. Sachiko Matsunaga, Chair, 323-343-4230, Fax: 323-343-4234, E-mail: smatsun@calstatela.edu. *Application contact:* Dr. Jose L. Galvan, Dean of Graduate Studies, 323-343-3820, Fax: 323-343-5653, E-mail: jgalvan@cslanet.calstatela.edu.

California State University, Sacramento, Graduate Studies, College of Social Sciences and Interdisciplinary Studies, Liberal Arts Program, Sacramento, CA 95819-6048. Offers French (MA); German (MA); Spanish (MA); theater arts (MA). *Degree requirements:* For master's, writing proficiency exam. *Entrance requirements:* Additional exam requirements/ recommendations for international students: Required—TOEFL. Electronic applications accepted.

Carleton University, Faculty of Graduate Studies, Faculty of Arts and Social Sciences, Department of French, Ottawa, ON K1S 5B6, Canada. Offers MA. *Degree requirements:* For master's, thesis optional. *Entrance requirements:* For master's, honors degree. *Faculty research:* French, French Canadian and Acadian literatures and linguistics, Francophone studies, rhetorical studies.

Case Western Reserve University, School of Graduate Studies, Department of Modern Languages and Literatures, Program in French, Cleveland, OH 44106. Offers MA. Part-time programs available. Terminal master's awarded for partial completion of doctoral program. *Degree requirements:* For master's, one foreign language, thesis or alternative. *Entrance requirements:* For master's, GRE General Test. Additional exam requirements/recommendations for international students: Required—TOEFL. Electronic applications accepted. *Faculty research:* Eighteenth- and nineteenth-century literature (novel, poetry, drama), literary theory, women's studies, cultural criticism.

Central Connecticut State University, School of Graduate Studies, School of Arts and Sciences, Department of Modern Languages, Program in Modern Language, New Britain, CT 06050-4010. Offers French (MA); Italian (Certificate); modern language (MA). Part-time and evening/weekend programs available. *Students:* 5 full-time (3 women), 30 part-time (25 women); includes 17 minority (all Hispanic Americans). Average age 36. 13 applicants, 100% accepted, 5 enrolled. In 2008, 5 master's awarded. *Degree requirements:* For master's, one foreign language, comprehensive exam, thesis or alternative. *Entrance requirements:* For master's, minimum undergraduate GPA of 2.7, 24 credits of undergraduate courses in either Italian or Spanish. Additional exam requirements/recommendations for international students: Required— TOEFL. *Application deadline:* For fall admission, 7/1 for domestic students; for spring admission, 12/1 for domestic students. Applications are processed on a rolling basis. Application fee: $50. Electronic applications accepted. *Expenses:* Tuition, area resident: full-time $4377; part-time $420 per credit. Tuition, state resident: full-time $6566; part-time $420 per credit. Tuition, nonresident: full-time $12,195; part-time $420 per credit. Required fees: $3462. One-time fee: $62 part-time. *Faculty research:* Twentieth century French theater, seventeenth century French literature, French Middle Ages.

Cleveland State University, College of Graduate Studies, College of Liberal Arts and Social Sciences, Department of Modern Languages, Cleveland, OH 44115. Offers French (M Ed); Spanish (M Ed, MA), including language and linguistics (MA), Latin American studies (MA), peninsular studies (MA), Spanish (MA). Part-time and evening/weekend programs available. *Faculty:* 12 full-time (9 women). *Students:* 7 full-time (6 women), 11 part-time (8 women); includes 7 minority (1 African American, 6 Hispanic Americans), 1 international. Average age 37. 11 applicants, 100% accepted, 8 enrolled. In 2008, 9 master's awarded. *Degree*

requirements: For master's, one foreign language, comprehensive exam, thesis optional, study abroad. *Entrance requirements:* For master's, undergraduate major in Spanish or equivalent, essay in Spanish, writing sample. Additional exam requirements/recommendations for international students: Required—TOEFL (minimum score 525 paper-based; 197 computer-based). *Application deadline:* For fall admission, 7/25 priority date for domestic students; for spring admission, 12/15 priority date for domestic students. Applications are processed on a rolling basis. Application fee: $30. Electronic applications accepted. *Financial support:* In 2008–09, 6 students received support, including 6 teaching assistantships with full tuition reimbursements available (averaging $7,030 per year); Federal Work-Study also available. *Faculty research:* Second language acquisition, sociolinguistics, contemporary Spanish novel, Arabic diaspora in Latin America, border literature. *Unit head:* Dr. Tama L. Engelking, Chairperson, 216-523-7175, Fax: 216-687-4650, E-mail: t.engelking@csuohio.edu. *Application contact:* Dr. Antonio Medina-Rivera, Graduate Director, 216-523-7168, Fax: 216-687-4650, E-mail: a.medinarivera@csuohio.edu.

Columbia University, Graduate School of Arts and Sciences, Division of Humanities, Department of French and Romance Philology, New York, NY 10027. Offers French and Romance philology (M Phil, PhD); Romance languages (MA). Part-time programs available. *Degree requirements:* For master's, one foreign language, thesis, written exam; for doctorate, 2 foreign languages, thesis/dissertation. *Entrance requirements:* For master's and doctorate, GRE General Test, knowledge of Latin, writing sample. Additional exam requirements/ recommendations for international students: Required—TOEFL. *Faculty research:* Theory of literature, literary semiotics, poetics.

Columbia University, Graduate School of Arts and Sciences, Program in French Cultural Studies, New York, NY 10027. Offers MA. Program offered in Paris, France. *Expenses:* Contact institution.

Concordia University, School of Graduate Studies, Faculty of Arts and Science, Department of Études Françaises, Montréal, QC H3G 1M8, Canada. Offers écriture (Certificate); anglais-français en langue et techniques de localisation (Certificate); littératures francophones et résonances médiatiques (MA); traductologie (MA); translation (Diploma). *Degree requirements:* For other advanced degree, one foreign language.

Cornell University, Graduate School, Graduate Fields of Arts and Sciences, Field of Romance Studies, Ithaca, NY 14853-0001. Offers French linguistics (PhD); French literature (PhD); Hispanic literature (PhD); Italian linguistics (PhD); Italian literature (PhD); Romance linguistics (PhD); Spanish linguistics (PhD). *Faculty:* 30 full-time (14 women). *Students:* 50 full-time (24 women); includes 10 minority (all Hispanic Americans), 18 international. Average age 30. 99 applicants, 15% accepted, 8 enrolled. In 2008, 5 doctorates awarded. *Degree requirements:* For doctorate, 2 foreign languages, comprehensive exam, thesis/dissertation. *Entrance requirements:* For doctorate, GRE General Test, sample of written work, 3 letters of recommendation. Additional exam requirements/recommendations for international students: Required—TOEFL (minimum score 550 paper-based; 213 computer-based; 77 iBT). *Application deadline:* For fall admission, 1/15 for domestic students. Application fee: $70. Electronic applications accepted. *Expenses:* Tuition: Full-time $29,500. Required fees: $70. Full-time tuition and fees vary according to degree level, program and student level. *Financial support:* In 2008–09, 46 students received support, including 16 fellowships with full tuition reimbursements available, 30 teaching assistantships with full tuition reimbursements available; research assistantships with full tuition reimbursements available, institutionally sponsored loans, scholarships/grants, health care benefits, tuition waivers (full and partial), and unspecified assistantships also available. Financial award applicants required to submit FAFSA. *Faculty research:* Literary theory, Hispanic studies, French studies, gender studies. *Unit head:* Director of Graduate Studies, 607-255-8222. *Application contact:* Graduate Field Assistant, 607-255-4246, E-mail: romance_studies@cornell.edu.

Dalhousie University, Faculty of Arts and Social Science, Department of French, Halifax, NS B3H 4R2, Canada. Offers MA, PhD. *Entrance requirements:* Additional exam requirements/ recommendations for international students: Required—TOEFL, IELTS, 1 of 5 approved tests: TOEFL, IELTS, CANTEST, CAEL, Michigan English Language Assessment Battery. *Application deadline:* For fall admission, 6/1 for domestic students, 4/1 for international students; for winter admission, 10/31 for domestic students, 8/31 for international students; for spring admission, 2/28 for domestic students, 12/31 for international students. Application fee: $70. Electronic applications accepted. *Financial support:* Career-related internships or fieldwork, scholarships/ grants, and health care benefits available. *Faculty research:* Literature, linguistics, French civilization, French and Francophone literature of all periods, translation and cultural studies. *Unit head:* Dr. Irene Oore, Chair, 902-494-6813, Fax: 902-494-1626, E-mail: french@dal.ca. *Application contact:* Elizabeth Price, Graduate Coordinator, 902-494-2430, Fax: 902-494-1626, E-mail: french@dal.ca.

Duke University, Graduate School, Department of Romance Studies, Durham, NC 27708. Offers French (PhD); Spanish (PhD); JD/AM. *Degree requirements:* For doctorate, 2 foreign languages, thesis/dissertation. *Entrance requirements:* For doctorate, GRE General Test. Additional exam requirements/recommendations for international students: Required—TOEFL (minimum score 550 paper-based; 213 computer-based; 83 iBT), IELTS (minimum score 7). Electronic applications accepted.

Eastern Michigan University, Graduate School, College of Arts and Sciences, Department of Foreign Languages and Bilingual Studies, Program in Foreign Languages, Ypsilanti, MI 48197. Offers French (MA); German (MA); German for business (Graduate Certificate); Hispanic language and cultures (Graduate Certificate); Japanese business practices (Graduate Certificate); Spanish (MA). Part-time and evening/weekend programs available. Post-baccalaureate distance learning degree programs offered (minimal on-campus study). *Degree requirements:* For master's, one foreign language, thesis optional. *Entrance requirements:* Additional exam requirements/recommendations for international students: Required—TOEFL.

Emory University, Graduate School of Arts and Sciences, Department of Comparative Literature, Atlanta, GA 30322-1100. Offers comparative literature (PhD); English (Certificate); French (Certificate); Middle Eastern studies (PhD); philosophy (Certificate); psychoanalytic studies (PhD); religion (PhD); Spanish (Certificate); women studies (Certificate). *Degree requirements:* For doctorate, 2 foreign languages, comprehensive exam, thesis/dissertation. *Entrance requirements:* For doctorate, GRE General Test, minimum GPA of 3.0. Additional exam requirements/recommendations for international students: Required—TOEFL. Electronic applications accepted. *Faculty research:* Literary theory, psychoanalysis trauma and testimony, literature and religion, literature and technology, literature and philosophy, politics and global culture, literature and aesthetics.

Emory University, Graduate School of Arts and Sciences, Department of French and Italian, Atlanta, GA 30322-1100. Offers French (PhD); French and educational studies (PhD). *Degree requirements:* For doctorate, one foreign language, comprehensive exam, thesis/dissertation. *Entrance requirements:* For doctorate, GRE General Test. Electronic applications accepted. *Faculty research:* French literature through multidisciplinary critical approaches, second language acquisition theory.

Florida Atlantic University, Dorothy F. Schmidt College of Arts and Letters, Department of Languages, Linguistics, and Comparative Literature, Boca Raton, FL 33431-0991. Offers comparative literature (MA); French (MA); linguistics (MA); Spanish (MA). Part-time programs available. *Faculty:* 23 full-time (20 women), 12 part-time/adjunct (10 women). *Students:* 18 full-time (15 women), 19 part-time (13 women); includes 17 minority (4 African Americans, 1 Asian American or Pacific Islander, 12 Hispanic Americans), 4 international. Average age 36. 24 applicants, 67% accepted, 6 enrolled. In 2008, 10 master's awarded. *Degree requirements:* For master's, one foreign language, comprehensive exam, thesis optional. *Entrance requirements:* For master's, GRE General Test, minimum GPA of 3.0. *Application deadline:* For fall admission, 7/1 priority date for domestic students, 2/15 for international students; for spring

French

Florida Atlantic University (continued)
admission, 11/1 for domestic students, 7/15 for international students. Applications are processed on a rolling basis. Application fee: $30. *Expenses:* Tuition, state resident: full-time $4867; part-time $270.40 per credit hour. Tuition, nonresident: full-time $16,486; part-time $915.87 per credit hour. *Financial support:* Fellowships, research assistantships, teaching assistantships with partial tuition reimbursements, Federal Work-Study and tuition waivers (partial) available. Support available to part-time students. Financial award application deadline: 4/1. *Faculty research:* Modern European studies, modern Latin America, medieval Europe. *Unit head:* Dr. Michael Horswell, Chair, 561-297-3860, Fax: 561-297-2756, E-mail: horswell@fau.edu. *Application contact:* Dr. Emily Stockard, Associate Dean, 561-297-2817, Fax: 561-297-2744, E-mail: stockard@fau.edu.

Florida State University, Graduate Studies, College of Arts and Sciences, Department of Modern Languages, Program in French, Tallahassee, FL 32306. Offers MA, PhD. Part-time programs available. Terminal master's awarded for partial completion of doctoral program. *Degree requirements:* For master's, thesis optional; for doctorate, thesis/dissertation, reading knowledge of French and 2 other languages. *Entrance requirements:* For master's and doctorate, GRE General Test or minimum GPA of 3.0. Additional exam requirements/recommendations for international students: Required—TOEFL (minimum score 550 paper-based; 213 computer-based). Electronic applications accepted. *Faculty research:* Twentieth century European novel, Renaissance and Middle Ages literature, second language acquisition.

Georgia State University, College of Arts and Sciences, Department of Modern and Classical Languages, Program in French, Atlanta, GA 30303-3083. Offers MA. Part-time and evening/weekend programs available. *Degree requirements:* For master's, one foreign language, thesis or alternative, general exam. *Entrance requirements:* For master's, GRE General Test. Additional exam requirements/recommendations for international students: Required—TOEFL. Electronic applications accepted. *Faculty research:* French literature of the sixteenth-, eighteenth-, nineteenth-, and twentieth-centuries.

Georgia State University, College of Arts and Sciences, Department of Modern and Classical Languages, Program in Translation and Interpretation, Atlanta, GA 30303-3083. Offers French (Certificate); German (Certificate); Spanish (Certificate). Electronic applications accepted.

Graduate School and University Center of the City University of New York, Graduate Studies, Program in French, New York, NY 10016-4039. Offers PhD. *Degree requirements:* For doctorate, 2 foreign languages, thesis/dissertation. *Entrance requirements:* For doctorate, GRE General Test, writing samples (1 for applicants with BA, 2 for applicants with master's). Additional exam requirements/recommendations for international students: Required—TOEFL. Electronic applications accepted.

Harvard University, Graduate School of Arts and Sciences, Department of Romance Languages and Literatures, Cambridge, MA 02138. Offers French (AM, PhD); Italian (AM, PhD); Portuguese (AM, PhD); Spanish (AM, PhD). Terminal master's awarded for partial completion of doctoral program. *Degree requirements:* For master's, 2 foreign languages; for doctorate, 2 foreign languages, thesis/dissertation. *Entrance requirements:* For master's and doctorate, GRE General Test, sample of written work. Additional exam requirements/recommendations for international students: Required—TOEFL. *Expenses:* Tuition: Full-time $32,556. Required fees: $1426. Full-time tuition and fees vary according to program and student level.

Hofstra University, School of Education, Health, and Human Services, Department of Curriculum and Teaching, Program in Foreign Language Education, Hempstead, NY 11549. Offers foreign language education (MA, MS Ed), including French, German, Russian, Spanish. Part-time and evening/weekend programs available. *Students:* 2 full-time (both women), 4 part-time (3 women); includes 3 minority (all Hispanic Americans). Average age 32. 7 applicants, 71% accepted, 0 enrolled. In 2008, 2 master's awarded. *Degree requirements:* For master's, one foreign language, thesis. *Entrance requirements:* For master's, 2 letters of recommendation, teacher certification (MA), essay. Additional exam requirements/recommendations for international students: Required—TOEFL (minimum score 550 paper-based; 213 computer-based; 80 iBT). *Application deadline:* Applications are processed on a rolling basis. Application fee: $60. Electronic applications accepted. *Expenses:* Tuition: Full-time $15,300; part-time $850 per credit. Required fees: $970; $165 per term. Tuition and fees vary according to program. *Financial support:* In 2008–09, 1 student received support; fellowships with full and partial tuition reimbursements available, research assistantships with full and partial tuition reimbursements available, Federal Work-Study, institutionally sponsored loans, scholarships/grants, and tuition waivers (full and partial) available. Support available to part-time students. Financial award applicants required to submit FAFSA. *Faculty research:* Contemporary Spanish cultural studies, twentieth century Spanish theater, identity and post-coloniality, Romance philology, politics of language, decolonization, Spanish imperial Africa and Latin America, twentieth century Latin American poetry. Total annual research expenditures: $5,000. *Unit head:* Dr. David Powell, Chairperson, 516-463-5485, Fax: 516-463-2310, E-mail: rlldap@hofstra.edu. *Application contact:* Carol Drummer, Dean of Graduate Admissions, 516-463-4876, Fax: 516-463-4664, E-mail: gradstudent@hofstra.edu.

Howard University, Graduate School, Department of Modern Languages and Literatures, Washington, DC 20059-0002. Offers French (MA); Spanish (MA). Part-time programs available. *Degree requirements:* For master's, one foreign language, comprehensive exam, thesis. *Entrance requirements:* For master's, GRE General Test, writing samples in English and French or Spanish. *Faculty research:* African literature in French, Spanish linguistics, Spanish Peninsular literature, Spanish sociolinguistics.

Hunter College of the City University of New York, Graduate School, School of Arts and Sciences, Department of Romance Languages, Program in French, New York, NY 10021-5085. Offers French (MA); French education (MA). Part-time and evening/weekend programs available. *Faculty:* 3 full-time (1 woman). *Students:* 1 (woman) full-time, 4 part-time (2 women). Average age 30. 4 applicants, 50% accepted, 2 enrolled. In 2008, 3 master's awarded. *Degree requirements:* For master's, 2 foreign languages, comprehensive exam, thesis optional. *Entrance requirements:* For master's, GRE General Test, GRE Subject Test, ability to read, speak, and write French; interview. Additional exam requirements/recommendations for international students: Required—TOEFL. *Application deadline:* For fall admission, 4/1 for domestic students, 2/1 for international students; for spring admission, 11/1 for domestic students, 9/1 for international students. Application fee: $125. *Financial support:* Fellowships, Federal Work-Study, scholarships/grants, and tuition waivers (partial) available. Support available to part-time students. Financial award application deadline: 4/15. *Faculty research:* Contemporary French theater, Villiers-dell Isle-Adam, Voltaire, medieval folklore, fin-de-siécle. *Unit head:* Prof. Marlene Barloum, Graduate Advisor, 212-650-3511, E-mail: mbarloum@hunter.cuny.edu. *Application contact:* William Zlata, Director for Graduate Admissions, 212-772-4482, Fax: 212-650-3336, E-mail: admissions@hunter.cuny.edu.

Illinois State University, Graduate School, College of Arts and Sciences, Department of Foreign Languages, Literatures and Cultures, Normal, IL 61790-2200. Offers French (MA); French and German (MA); French and Spanish (MA); German (MA); German and Spanish (MA); Spanish (MA). *Degree requirements:* For master's, variable foreign language requirement, comprehensive exam, 1 term of residency. *Entrance requirements:* For master's, GRE General Test, minimum GPA of 2.8 in last 60 hours of course work.

Indiana University Bloomington, University Graduate School, College of Arts and Sciences, Department of French and Italian, Bloomington, IN 47405-7000. Offers French (MA, PhD), including French instruction (MA), French linguistics, French literature; Italian (MA, PhD). Part-time programs available. *Faculty:* 19 full-time (7 women). *Students:* 79 full-time (50 women); includes 5 minority (1 African American, 1 American Indian/Alaska Native, 1 Asian American or Pacific Islander, 2 Hispanic Americans), 34 international. Average age 30. 46 applicants, 70% accepted, 15 enrolled. In 2008, 18 master's, 6 doctorates awarded. Terminal master's awarded for partial completion of doctoral program. *Degree requirements:* For master's,

one foreign language, comprehensive exam, thesis optional; for doctorate, 2 foreign languages, comprehensive exam, thesis/dissertation. *Entrance requirements:* For master's and doctorate, GRE General Test. Additional exam requirements/recommendations for international students: Required—TOEFL (minimum score 550 paper-based; 213 computer-based; 79 iBT). *Application deadline:* For fall admission, 1/15 priority date for domestic students, 12/1 priority date for international students; for spring admission, 9/1 priority date for domestic and international students. Application fee: $50 ($60 for international students). Electronic applications accepted. *Expenses:* Tuition, area resident: Part-time $291.97 per credit hour. Tuition, state resident: part-time $291.97 per credit hour. Tuition, nonresident: part-time $850.33 per credit hour. Required fees: $110 per semester. Tuition and fees vary according to course load and program. *Financial support:* In 2008–09, 46 students received support, including 2 fellowships with partial tuition reimbursements available (averaging $15,000 per year), 7 research assistantships with partial tuition reimbursements available (averaging $13,025 per year), 37 teaching assistantships with partial tuition reimbursements available (averaging $13,025 per year). Financial award application deadline: 1/15. *Faculty research:* All periods of French and Italian literature and various areas of French linguistics, including the novel and political theory, literature and fine arts, literary theory, postcolonialism, French-Creole studies, French literature of Africa and its Diaspora, humanism, medieval folklore and mythology, humor in medieval and renaissance literature, cinema Old Occitan and Old French, emigration, second lang. acquisition, syntax, sociolinguistics, phonology, and lexicography. *Unit head:* Prof. Emanuel Mickel, Interim Chairman, 812-855-5458, Fax: 812-855-8877, E-mail: fritchr@indiana.edu. *Application contact:* Jocelyn Karlan, Secretary, 812-855-1088, Fax: 812-855-8877, E-mail: fritgs@indiana.edu.

The Johns Hopkins University, Zanvyl Krieger School of Arts and Sciences, Department of German and Romance Languages, Baltimore, MD 21218-2699. Offers French (PhD); German (PhD); Italian (PhD); romance languages (PhD); Spanish (PhD). *Degree requirements:* For doctorate, 2 foreign languages, thesis/dissertation. *Entrance requirements:* For doctorate, GRE General Test. Additional exam requirements/recommendations for international students: Required—TOEFL (minimum score 600 paper-based; 250 computer-based). Electronic applications accepted.

Kansas State University, Graduate School, College of Arts and Sciences, Department of Modern Languages, Manhattan, KS 66506. Offers French (MA); German (MA); Spanish (MA). Part-time and evening/weekend programs available. Postbaccalaureate distance learning degree programs offered (minimal on-campus study). *Faculty:* 15 full-time (7 women). *Students:* 18 full-time (11 women), 10 part-time (8 women); includes 4 minority (all Hispanic Americans), 11 international. Average age 32. 6 applicants, 100% accepted, 6 enrolled. In 2008, 4 master's awarded. *Degree requirements:* For master's, thesis optional. *Entrance requirements:* For master's, teaching certificate. Additional exam requirements/recommendations for international students: Required—TOEFL (minimum score 560 paper-based). *Application deadline:* For fall admission, 2/1 priority date for domestic and international students; for spring admission, 10/1 for domestic students, 8/1 priority date for international students. Applications are processed on a rolling basis. Application fee: $30 ($55 for international students). *Expenses:* Tuition, area resident: full-time $6466; part-time $269.40 per credit hour. Tuition, state resident: full-time $6466; part-time $269.40 per credit hour. Tuition, nonresident: full-time $14,874; part-time $619.75 per credit hour. Required fees: $673; $23.40 per credit hour. Tuition and fees vary according to campus/location. *Financial support:* In 2008–09, 13 teaching assistantships with full tuition reimbursements (averaging $10,546 per year) were awarded; fellowships, Federal Work-Study, institutionally sponsored loans, and scholarships/grants also available. Support available to part-time students. Financial award application deadline: 3/1; financial award applicants required to submit FAFSA. *Faculty research:* Second language acquisitions; Chicano literature; Francophone literature; cultural studies; German, French, Spanish, and Spanish-American literature from the Middle Ages to the modern era. *Unit head:* Robert Corum, Head, 785-532-1987, Fax: 785-532-7004, E-mail: corum@ksu.edu. *Application contact:* Claire Dehon, Director, 785-532-1929, Fax: 785-532-7004, E-mail: dehoncl@ksu.edu.

Kent State University, College of Arts and Sciences, Department of Modern and Classical Language Studies, Kent, OH 44242-0001. Offers French literature (MA); French, Spanish, German and Latin pedagogy (MA); German literature (MA); Spanish literature (MA); translation (MA), including French, German, Japanese, Russian, Spanish; translation studies (PhD). Part-time and evening/weekend programs available. *Degree requirements:* For master's, one foreign language, comprehensive exam (for some programs), thesis (for some programs); for doctorate, comprehensive exam, thesis/dissertation (for some programs). *Entrance requirements:* For master's, minimum GPA of 3.0, writing sample, audio tape or CD; for doctorate, 3 recommendations. Additional exam requirements/recommendations for international students: Required—TOEFL (minimum score 197 computer-based). Electronic applications accepted. *Faculty research:* Literature, pedagogy, applied linguistics, translation studies.

Louisiana State University and Agricultural and Mechanical College, Graduate School, College of Arts and Sciences, Department of French Studies, Baton Rouge, LA 70803. Offers French literature and linguistics (MA, PhD). Terminal master's awarded for partial completion of doctoral program. *Degree requirements:* For master's, thesis optional; for doctorate, 2 foreign languages, thesis/dissertation. *Entrance requirements:* For master's and doctorate, GRE General Test, minimum GPA of 3.0. Additional exam requirements/recommendations for international students: Required—TOEFL (minimum score 550 paper-based; 213 computer-based; 79 iBT). Electronic applications accepted. *Faculty research:* French literature of all periods, modern critical theory, linguistics, cinema, Francophonia.

McGill University, Faculty of Graduate and Postdoctoral Studies, Faculty of Arts, Department of French Language and Literature, Montréal, QC H3A 2T5, Canada. Offers MA, PhD.

McMaster University, School of Graduate Studies, Faculty of Humanities, Department of French, Hamilton, ON L8S 4M2, Canada. Offers MA. Part-time and evening/weekend programs available. *Degree requirements:* For master's, thesis or alternative. *Entrance requirements:* For master's, honors degree in French, minimum B+ average. Additional exam requirements/recommendations for international students: Required—TOEFL (minimum score 580 paper-based; 237 computer-based). *Faculty research:* Medieval literature, eighteenth- and nineteenth-century literature, twentieth-century French and Francophone literature, linguistics.

Memorial University of Newfoundland, School of Graduate Studies, Department of French and Spanish, St. John's, NL A1C 5S7, Canada. Offers French studies (MA). Part-time programs available. *Degree requirements:* For master's, one foreign language, thesis. *Entrance requirements:* For master's, honors degree (minimum 2nd class standing). Electronic applications accepted. *Faculty research:* French and French-Canadian literature, literary theory, linguistics, philosophy, translation, Francophone culture.

Miami University, Graduate School, College of Arts and Sciences, Department of French and Italian, Oxford, OH 45056. Offers French (MA). Part-time programs available. *Degree requirements:* For master's, thesis, final exam. *Entrance requirements:* For master's, GRE General Test, minimum undergraduate GPA of 3.0 during previous 2 years or 2.75 overall. Additional exam requirements/recommendations for international students: Required—TOEFL (minimum score 550 paper-based; 213 computer-based), TWE (minimum score 4). Electronic applications accepted.

Michigan State University, The Graduate School, College of Arts and Letters, Department of French, Classics, and Italian, East Lansing, MI 48824. Offers French (MA); French language and literature (PhD). *Entrance requirements:* Additional exam requirements/recommendations for international students: Required—TOEFL. Electronic applications accepted.

Middlebury College, Language Schools, French School, Middlebury, VT 05753. Offers MA, DML. *Faculty:* 32 full-time (12 women). *Students:* 82 full-time (68 women); includes 12 minority (3 African Americans, 4 Asian Americans or Pacific Islanders, 5 Hispanic Americans). Average age 30. 186 applicants, 63% accepted, 90 enrolled. In 2008, 29 master's, 2 doctorates awarded. *Degree requirements:* For master's, one foreign language; for doctorate, 2 foreign languages, comprehensive exam, thesis/dissertation, residence abroad, teaching experience. *Entrance requirements:* For master's, placement exam, 3 letters of recommendation, writing sample; for doctorate, 1st and 2nd language placement exam, 3 letters of recommendation, writing sample. *Application deadline:* Applications are processed on a rolling basis. Application fee: $55. Electronic applications accepted. *Financial support:* Fellowships, scholarships/grants available. Financial award applicants required to submit FAFSA. *Unit head:* Dr. Aline Germain-Rutherford, Director, 802-443-5526, Fax: 802-443-2075. *Application contact:* Sheila Schwaneflugel, Coordinator, 802-443-5526, Fax: 802-443-2075, E-mail: keim@middlebury.edu.

Millersville University of Pennsylvania, Graduate School, School of Humanities and Social Sciences, Department of Foreign Languages, Program in French, Millersville, PA 17551-0302. Offers M Ed, MA. Part-time programs available. *Faculty:* 9 full-time (5 women), 4 part-time/adjunct (3 women). In 2008, 1 master's awarded. *Degree requirements:* For master's, comprehensive exam, thesis optional. *Entrance requirements:* For master's, GRE or MAT. Additional exam requirements/recommendations for international students: Required—TOEFL (minimum score 500 paper-based; 183 computer-based; 65 iBT), TOEFL may be replaced by IELTS with score of 6 or higher. *Application deadline:* For fall admission, 2/1 priority date for domestic and international students; for winter admission, 10/1 priority date for domestic and international students; for spring admission, 10/1 priority date for domestic and international students. Applications are processed on a rolling basis. Application fee: $40. Electronic applications accepted. *Expenses:* Tuition, state resident: full-time $6430; part-time $357 per credit. Tuition, nonresident: full-time $10,288; part-time $572 per credit. Required fees: $1937; $73.50 per credit. One-time fee: $88 part-time. Tuition and fees vary according to course load. *Financial support:* Research assistantships, institutionally sponsored loans and unspecified assistantships available. Support available to part-time students. Financial award application deadline: 3/15; financial award applicants required to submit FAFSA. *Unit head:* Dr. Christine M. Gaudry-Hudson, Coordinator of Foreign Language Graduate Program, 717-872-3663, E-mail: christine.gaudry-hudson@millersville.edu. *Application contact:* Dr. Victor S. DeSantis, Dean of Graduate Studies, 717-872-3099, Fax: 717-872-3453, E-mail: victor.desantis@millersville.edu.

Minnesota State University Mankato, College of Graduate Studies, College of Arts and Humanities, Department of Modern Languages, Program in French, Mankato, MN 56001. Offers MAT, MS. *Students:* 1 (woman) full-time. *Degree requirements:* For master's, one foreign language, comprehensive exam, thesis or alternative. *Entrance requirements:* For master's, minimum GPA of 3.0 during previous 2 years. Additional exam requirements/recommendations for international students: Required—TOEFL. *Application deadline:* For fall admission, 7/1 priority date for domestic students; for spring admission, 11/1 for domestic students. Applications are processed on a rolling basis. Application fee: $40. Electronic applications accepted. *Financial support:* Research assistantships, teaching assistantships with full tuition reimbursements, unspecified assistantships available. Financial award application deadline: 3/15; financial award applicants required to submit FAFSA. *Unit head:* Dr. John Janc, Graduate Coordinator, 507-389-1817. *Application contact:* 507-389-2321, E-mail: grad@mnsu.edu.

Mississippi State University, College of Arts and Sciences, Department of Foreign Languages, Mississippi State, MS 39762. Offers French (MA); French/German (MA); German (MA); Spanish (MA); Spanish/French (MA); Spanish/German (MA). Part-time programs available. *Degree requirements:* For master's, one foreign language, thesis optional, comprehensive oral or written exam. *Entrance requirements:* For master's, minimum GPA of 2.75. Additional exam requirements/recommendations for international students: Required—TOEFL (minimum score 525 paper-based). *Faculty research:* French, German, Spanish literature from medieval to present; gender and cultural studies in French; Spanish American literature; foreign language methodology; linguistics.

Missouri State University, Graduate College, College of Arts and Letters, Department of Modern and Classical Languages, Springfield, MO 65804-0094. Offers secondary education (MS Ed), including French, German, Spanish. Part-time programs available. *Faculty:* 5 full-time (2 women). *Students:* 2 full-time (1 woman), 2 part-time (both women). Average age 30. 1 applicant, 100% accepted, 0 enrolled. In 2008, 4 master's awarded. *Entrance requirements:* For master's, grades 9-12 teaching certification. Additional exam requirements/recommendations for international students: Required—TOEFL (minimum score 550 paper-based; 213 computer-based; 79 iBT), IELTS (minimum score 6). *Application deadline:* For fall admission, 7/20 priority date for domestic students, 5/1 for international students; for spring admission, 12/20 priority date for domestic students, 9/1 for international students. Applications are processed on a rolling basis. Application fee: $35 ($50 for international students). Electronic applications accepted. *Expenses:* Tuition, state resident: full-time $3852; part-time $214 per credit hour. Tuition, nonresident: full-time $7524; part-time $418 per credit hour. Required fees: $230 per semester. Tuition and fees vary according to course level and course load. *Financial support:* Federal Work-Study, institutionally sponsored loans, scholarships/grants, and unspecified assistantships available. Financial award applicants required to submit FAFSA. *Unit head:* Dr. Madeleine Kernen, Head, 417-836-7626, E-mail: mcl@missouristate.edu. *Application contact:* Eric Eckert, Coordinator of Admissions and Recruitment, 417-836-5331, Fax: 417-836-6888, E-mail: ericeckert@missouristate.edu.

Montclair State University, The Office of Graduate Admissions and Support Services, College of Education and Human Services, Department of Curriculum and Teaching, Montclair, NJ 07043-1624. Offers education (M Ed); educational technology (M Ed); learning disabled teacher consultant (Certificate); school library media specialist (Certificate); teaching (MAT, Certificate), including art (MAT), biological science (MAT), early childhood education (P-3) (MAT), earth science (MAT), elementary education (K-8) (MAT), English (MAT), French (MAT), health and physical education (MAT), health education (MAT), home economics (MAT), mathematics (MAT), music (MAT), physical education (MAT), physical science (MAT), social studies (MAT), Spanish (MAT), teacher of ESL (MAT), teacher of students with disabilities (MAT). Part-time and evening/weekend programs available. *Faculty:* 14 full-time (10 women), 23 part-time/adjunct (17 women). *Students:* 103 full-time (61 women), 98 part-time (73 women); includes 15 minority (8 African Americans, 3 Asian Americans or Pacific Islanders, 4 Hispanic Americans), 3 international. Average age 31. 56 applicants, 63% accepted, 33 enrolled. In 2008, 196 master's, 2 other advanced degrees awarded. *Degree requirements:* For master's, comprehensive exam, field experience. *Entrance requirements:* For master's, PRAXIS II, minimum GPA of 2.67, 2 letters of recommendation. Additional exam requirements/recommendations for international students: Required—TOEFL (minimum score 83 computer-based). *Application deadline:* For fall admission, 2/15 for domestic and international students; for spring admission, 9/15 for domestic and international students. Applications are processed on a rolling basis. Application fee: $60. Electronic applications accepted. *Financial support:* In 2008–09, 7 research assistantships with full tuition reimbursements (averaging $7,000 per year) were awarded; Federal Work-Study, scholarships/grants, and unspecified assistantships also available. Support available to part-time students. Financial award application deadline: 3/1; financial award applicants required to submit FAFSA. *Unit head:* Dr. David Keiser, Chairperson, 973-655-7199. *Application contact:* Amy Aiello, Associate Director of Admissions, 973-655-5147, Fax: 973-655-7869, E-mail: graduate.school@montclair.edu.

Montclair State University, The Office of Graduate Admissions and Support Services, College of Humanities and Social Sciences, Department of French, German and Russian, Montclair, NJ 07043-1624. Offers French (MA, Certificate), including French literature (MA), French studies (MA). Part-time and evening/weekend programs available. *Faculty:* 8 full-time (5 women), 20 part-time/adjunct (17 women). *Students:* 3 full-time (1 woman), 14 part-time (8 women); includes 3 minority (all African Americans), 2 international. Average age 37. 4 applicants, 75% accepted, 3 enrolled. In 2008, 5 master's awarded. *Degree requirements:* For master's, comprehensive exam, thesis optional. *Entrance requirements:* For master's, GRE General Test, 24 credits of undergraduate course work in French, 2 letters of recommendation. Additional exam requirements/recommendations for international students: Required—TOEFL (minimum score 83 computer-based). *Application deadline:* For fall admission, 6/1 for international students; for spring admission, 11/1 for international students. Applications are processed on a rolling basis. Application fee: $60. Electronic applications accepted. *Financial support:* In 2008–09, 1 research assistantship with full tuition reimbursement (averaging $7,000 per year) was awarded; Federal Work-Study, scholarships/grants, and unspecified assistantships also available. Support available to part-time students. Financial award application deadline: 3/1; financial award applicants required to submit FAFSA. *Unit head:* Dr. Lois Oppenheim, Chairperson, 973-655-4283. *Application contact:* Amy Aiello, Associate Director of Admissions, 973-655-5147, Fax: 973-655-7869, E-mail: graduate.school@montclair.edu.

New York University, Graduate School of Arts and Science, Center for French Civilization and Culture, Department of French, New York, NY 10012-1019. Offers French (PhD); French language and civilization (MA); French literature (MA); Romance languages and literatures (MA). Part-time programs available. Terminal master's awarded for partial completion of doctoral program. *Degree requirements:* For master's, one foreign language, thesis (for some programs); for doctorate, one foreign language, thesis/dissertation. *Entrance requirements:* For master's and doctorate, GRE General Test, proficiency in French. Additional exam requirements/recommendations for international students: Required—TOEFL. *Faculty research:* French and Francophone literature, literary theory, and history; rhetoric and poetics; cultural history; theater and cinema.

New York University, Graduate School of Arts and Science, Center for French Civilization and Culture, Institute of French Studies, New York, NY 10012-1019. Offers French civilization (PhD); French studies (MA, PhD, Advanced Certificate); French studies and anthropology (PhD); French studies and history (PhD); French studies and journalism (MA); French studies and sociology (PhD); JD/MA; MBA/MA. Part-time programs available. Terminal master's awarded for partial completion of doctoral program. *Degree requirements:* For master's, one foreign language, comprehensive exam; for doctorate, one foreign language, thesis/dissertation, qualifying exam. *Entrance requirements:* For master's and doctorate, GRE General Test, knowledge of French. Additional exam requirements/recommendations for international students: Required—TOEFL. *Faculty research:* Contemporary French society, politics, economy, and culture; French history since 1789; French cultural studies, French colonialism and the post-colonial world; France and the European community.

North Carolina State University, Graduate School, College of Humanities and Social Sciences, Department of Foreign Languages and Literatures, Program in French Language and Literature, Raleigh, NC 27695. Offers MA. *Degree requirements:* For master's, thesis optional. *Entrance requirements:* For master's, fluency in French. Electronic applications accepted. *Faculty research:* 19th-century visual culture, translation, cinema, modern theater, linguistics.

Northern Illinois University, Graduate School, College of Liberal Arts and Sciences, Department of Foreign Languages and Literatures, De Kalb, IL 60115-2854. Offers French (MA); Spanish (MA). Part-time programs available. *Degree requirements:* For master's, one foreign language, comprehensive exam, thesis or alternative, language proficiency exam. *Entrance requirements:* For master's, GRE General Test, interview, minimum GPA of 2.75, undergraduate major in French or Spanish. Additional exam requirements/recommendations for international students: Required—TOEFL (minimum score 550 paper-based; 213 computer-based). Electronic applications accepted. *Faculty research:* Francophone women writers, prosodies of French and Italian, early Spanish drama, business German, history of Burmese literature.

Northwestern University, The Graduate School, Judd A. and Marjorie Weinberg College of Arts and Sciences, Department of French and Italian, Evanston, IL 60208. Offers eighteenth-century studies (Certificate); French (PhD); French and comparative literature (PhD); Italian studies (Certificate). Admissions and degrees offered through The Graduate School. *Degree requirements:* For doctorate, one foreign language, thesis/dissertation, written and oral exams. *Entrance requirements:* For doctorate, GRE, writing sample, cassette recording. Additional exam requirements/recommendations for international students: Required—TOEFL. *Faculty research:* Francophone studies, 18th century contemporary theory.

The Ohio State University, Graduate School, College of Humanities, Department of French and Italian, Columbus, OH 43210. Offers French (MA, PhD); Italian (MA). *Degree requirements:* For master's, variable foreign language requirement, thesis optional; for doctorate, variable foreign language requirement, thesis/dissertation. *Entrance requirements:* For master's and doctorate, GRE General Test. Additional exam requirements/recommendations for international students: Required—TOEFL. Electronic applications accepted. *Faculty research:* Italian and Romance linguistics.

Ohio University, Graduate College, College of Arts and Sciences, Department of Modern Languages, Athens, OH 45701-2979. Offers French (MA); Spanish (MA). Part-time programs available. *Degree requirements:* For master's, 2 foreign languages, comprehensive exam, thesis optional. *Entrance requirements:* For master's, oral and written samples. Additional exam requirements/recommendations for international students: Required—TOEFL (minimum score 500 paper-based). Electronic applications accepted. *Faculty research:* French and Spanish language and literature.

Penn State University Park, Graduate School, College of the Liberal Arts, Department of French, State College, University Park, PA 16802-1503. Offers MA, PhD.

Portland State University, Graduate Studies, College of Liberal Arts and Sciences, Department of Foreign Languages and Literatures, Portland, OR 97207-0751. Offers foreign literature and language (MA); French (MA); German (MA); Japanese (MA); Spanish (MA). Part-time programs available. *Faculty:* 43 full-time (27 women), 28 part-time/adjunct (19 women). *Students:* 29 full-time (24 women), 17 part-time (11 women); includes 6 minority (1 African American, 1 Asian American or Pacific Islander, 4 Hispanic Americans), 11 international. Average age 32. 23 applicants, 91% accepted, 20 enrolled. In 2008, 14 master's awarded. *Degree requirements:* For master's, one foreign language, thesis (for some programs). *Entrance requirements:* Additional exam requirements/recommendations for international students: Required—TOEFL (minimum score 550 paper-based; 213 computer-based). *Application deadline:* For fall admission, 4/1 for domestic students, 3/1 for international students; for winter admission, 9/1 for domestic students, 7/1 for international students; for spring admission, 11/1 for domestic and international students. Applications are processed on a rolling basis. Application fee: $50. *Expenses:* Tuition, area resident: Full-time $8763; part-time $179 per credit hour. Tuition, state resident: full-time $8763; part-time $298 per credit hour. Tuition, nonresident: full-time $12,981; part-time $426 per credit hour. Required fees: $1242. One-time fee: $250. Tuition and fees vary according to course load and program. *Financial support:* In 2008–09, 6 teaching assistantships with full tuition reimbursements (averaging $9,359 per year) were awarded; research assistantships with full tuition reimbursements, Federal Work-Study, scholarships/grants, and unspecified assistantships also available. Support available to part-time students. Financial award application deadline: 3/1; financial award applicants required to submit FAFSA. *Faculty research:* Foreign language pedagogy, applied and social linguistics, literary history and criticism. Total annual research expenditures: $6,847. *Unit head:* Dr. Sandra F. Freels, Chair, 503-725-3522, Fax: 503-725-5276. *Application contact:* Karen Popp, Office Coordinator, 503-725-3522, E-mail: poppk@pdx.edu.

Princeton University, Graduate School, Department of French and Italian, Princeton, NJ 08544-1019. Offers French language and literature (PhD). *Degree requirements:* For doctorate, variable foreign language requirement, thesis/dissertation. *Entrance requirements:* For doctorate, GRE General Test, sample of written work. Additional exam requirements/recommendations for international students: Required—TOEFL (minimum score 600 paper-based; 250 computer-based). Electronic applications accepted.

Purdue University, Graduate School, College of Liberal Arts, Department of Foreign Languages and Literatures, West Lafayette, IN 47907. Offers French (MA, MAT, PhD), including French (MA, PhD), French education (MAT); German (MA, MAT, PhD), including German (MA, PhD), German education (MAT); Spanish (MA, MAT, PhD), including Spanish (MA, PhD), Spanish

French

Purdue University (continued)
education (MAT). Terminal master's awarded for partial completion of doctoral program. *Degree requirements:* For master's, one foreign language; for doctorate, 2 foreign languages, thesis/dissertation. *Entrance requirements:* For master's and doctorate, GRE, writing sample, sample recording of English and language of study. Additional exam requirements/recommendations for international students: Required—TOEFL. Electronic applications accepted. *Faculty research:* Linguistics, semiotics, literary criticism, pedagogy.

Queens College of the City University of New York, Division of Graduate Studies, Arts and Humanities Division, Department of European Languages and Literatures, Program in French, Flushing, NY 11367-1597. Offers MA. Part-time and evening/weekend programs available. *Degree requirements:* For master's, 2 foreign languages, comprehensive exam, thesis or alternative. *Entrance requirements:* For master's, minimum GPA of 3.0. Additional exam requirements/recommendations for international students: Required—TOEFL.

Queen's University at Kingston, School of Graduate Studies and Research, Faculty of Arts and Sciences, Department of French Studies, Kingston, ON K7L 3N6, Canada. Offers MA, PhD. Part-time programs available. *Degree requirements:* For master's, thesis or 4 credits and oral exam; for doctorate, one foreign language, comprehensive exam, thesis/dissertation. *Entrance requirements:* For master's, minimum B+ average; for doctorate, minimum 80% average. Additional exam requirements/recommendations for international students: Required—TOEFL (minimum score 550 paper-based; 213 computer-based). Electronic applications accepted. *Faculty research:* Reception of Quebec literature in English Canada, autobiography and postcolonialism, irony in women's writing, critical editions of renaissance authors, aspectual systems and grammatical categories.

Rice University, Graduate Programs, School of Humanities, Department of French Studies, Houston, TX 77251-1892. Offers MA, PhD. Terminal master's awarded for partial completion of doctoral program. *Degree requirements:* For master's, one foreign language, thesis, 2 advanced research papers; for doctorate, one foreign language, thesis/dissertation. *Entrance requirements:* For master's, GRE General Test, sample of written work, minimum GPA of 3.0, BA in French studies or related field; for doctorate, GRE, BA or MA in French studies or related field, sample of written work. Additional exam requirements/recommendations for international students: Required—TOEFL (minimum score 600 paper-based; 250 computer-based; 90 iBT). Electronic applications accepted. *Faculty research:* Linguistics, modern philosophy, modern history, gender and traditional studies.

Rider University, Department of Graduate Education, Leadership and Counseling, Teacher Certification Program, Lawrenceville, NJ 08648-3001. Offers business education (Certificate); elementary education (Certificate); English as a second language (Certificate); English education (Certificate); mathematics education (Certificate); preschool to grade 3 (Certificate); science education (Certificate); social studies education (Certificate); world languages (Certificate), including French, German, Spanish. Part-time programs available. *Degree requirements:* For Certificate, internship, professional portfolio. *Entrance requirements:* For degree, PRAXIS, resumé. Additional exam requirements/recommendations for international students: Required—TOEFL (minimum score 550 paper-based; 213 computer-based). Electronic applications accepted. *Faculty research:* Conceptual foundations for optimal development of creativity; creative theory, cognitive processes in mathematics learning, teacher collaboration.

Rutgers, The State University of New Jersey, New Brunswick, Graduate School, Program in French, Piscataway, NJ 08854-8097. Offers French (MA, PhD); French studies (MAT). Part-time and evening/weekend programs available. Terminal master's awarded for partial completion of doctoral program. *Degree requirements:* For master's, one foreign language, written and oral exams (MA); for doctorate, 3 foreign languages, thesis/dissertation, qualifying exam. *Entrance requirements:* For master's and doctorate, GRE General Test. *Faculty research:* Literatures in French, literary history and theory, rhetoric and poetics.

Saint Louis University, Graduate School, College of Arts and Sciences and Graduate School, Department of Modern and Classical Languages, St. Louis, MO 63103-2097. Offers French (MA); Spanish (MA). Part-time programs available. *Degree requirements:* For master's, one foreign language, comprehensive exam, thesis/dissertation (for Spanish). *Entrance requirements:* For master's, GRE General Test or MAT, letters of recommendation, resumé, interview, transcripts, goal statement. Additional exam requirements/recommendations for international students: Required—TOEFL (minimum score 525 paper-based; 194 computer-based). Electronic applications accepted. *Faculty research:* Culture studies, literature studies, foreign language acquisition.

San Francisco State University, Division of Graduate Studies, College of Humanities, Department of Foreign Languages and Literatures, Program in French, San Francisco, CA 94132-1722. Offers MA.

San Jose State University, Graduate Studies and Research, College of Humanities and the Arts, Department of Foreign Languages, Program in French, San Jose, CA 95192-0001. Offers MA. *Degree requirements:* For master's, 2 foreign languages, thesis or alternative, departmental qualifying exam. *Entrance requirements:* Additional exam requirements/recommendations for international students: Required—TOEFL (minimum score 580 paper-based). Electronic applications accepted.

Simon Fraser University, Graduate Studies, Faculty of Arts and Social Sciences, Department of French, Burnaby, BC V5A 1S6, Canada. Offers MA. *Degree requirements:* For master's, one foreign language, thesis or alternative. *Entrance requirements:* For master's, minimum GPA of 3.0. Additional exam requirements/recommendations for international students: Required—TOEFL or IELTS. *Faculty research:* French linguistics, Creole linguistics, French literature of the Middle Ages and Ancient Régime, modern and contemporary French literature, French Canadian language and literature.

Smith College, Graduate and Special Programs, Department of French Language and Literature, Northampton, MA 01063. Offers MAT. Part-time programs available. *Faculty:* 9 full-time (7 women). *Degree requirements:* For master's, one foreign language. *Entrance requirements:* Additional exam requirements/recommendations for international students: Required—TOEFL (minimum score 590 paper-based; 243 computer-based; 97 iBT). *Application deadline:* For fall admission, 4/1 for domestic students, 1/15 for international students; for spring admission, 12/1 for domestic students. Application fee: $60. *Financial support:* Career-related internships or fieldwork, institutionally sponsored loans, and scholarships/grants available. Support available to part-time students. Financial award application deadline: 1/15; financial award applicants required to submit CSS PROFILE or FAFSA. *Unit head:* Mary Ellen Birkett, Chair, 413-585-3351, E-mail: mbirkett@smith.edu. *Application contact:* Ruth Morgan, Administrative Assistant, 413-585-3050, Fax: 413-585-3054, E-mail: gradstdy@smith.edu.

Stanford University, School of Humanities and Sciences, Department of French and Italian, Stanford, CA 94305-9991. Offers French (MA, PhD); Italian (MA, PhD). Terminal master's awarded for partial completion of doctoral program. *Degree requirements:* For master's, one foreign language, written exam; for doctorate, 2 foreign languages, thesis/dissertation, oral exam. *Entrance requirements:* For master's and doctorate, GRE General Test. Additional exam requirements/recommendations for international students: Required—TOEFL. Electronic applications accepted.

State University of New York at Binghamton, Graduate School, School of Arts and Sciences, Department of Romance Languages and Literatures, Program in French, Binghamton, NY 13902-6000. Offers MA. *Students:* 1 (woman) part-time. Average age 35. 2 applicants, 100% accepted, 1 enrolled. *Degree requirements:* For master's, one foreign language, comprehensive exam, thesis or alternative. *Entrance requirements:* For master's, GRE General Test, GRE Subject Test. Additional exam requirements/recommendations for international students: Required—TOEFL. *Application deadline:* For fall admission, 4/15 priority date for

domestic students, 1/15 priority date for international students; for spring admission, 11/1 for domestic students, 10/1 priority date for international students. Applications are processed on a rolling basis. Application fee: $60. Electronic applications accepted. *Expenses:* Tuition, area resident: Full-time $6900; part-time $288 per credit. Tuition, state resident: full-time $6900; part-time $288 per credit. Tuition, nonresident: full-time $10,920; part-time $455 per credit. Required fees: $1130. Part-time tuition and fees vary according to course load, program and student level. *Financial support:* Fellowships, research assistantships, teaching assistantships; career-related internships or fieldwork, Federal Work-Study, institutionally sponsored loans, and unspecified assistantships available. Support available to part-time students. Financial award application deadline: 2/15. *Unit head:* Dr. Antonio Sobejano-Moran, Chairperson, 607-777-4635, E-mail: antobianco@msn.com. *Application contact:* Victoria Williams, Recruiting and Admissions Coordinator, 607-777-2151, Fax: 607-777-2501, E-mail: vwilliam@binghamton.edu.

Stony Brook University, State University of New York, Graduate School, College of Arts and Sciences, Department of European Languages, Literatures, and Cultures, Program in French, Stony Brook, NY 11794. Offers Romance languages (MA). Evening/weekend programs available. *Degree requirements:* For master's, one foreign language. *Entrance requirements:* For master's, GRE General Test. Additional exam requirements/recommendations for international students: Required—TOEFL. *Application deadline:* For fall admission, 1/15 for domestic students. Application fee: $60. *Expenses:* Tuition, area resident: Full-time $7880; part-time $328 per credit hour. Tuition, state resident: full-time $7880; part-time $328 per credit hour. Tuition, nonresident: full-time $13,250; part-time $552 per credit hour. Required fees: $848. *Unit head:* Prosper Sanou, Coordinator, 631-632-7440, E-mail: prosper.sanou@stonybrook.edu. *Application contact:* Dr. Andrea Fedi, Director of Graduate Studies, 631-632-7438, Fax: 631-632-9612.

Syracuse University, Graduate School, College of Arts and Sciences, Program in French and Francophone Studies, Syracuse, NY 13244. Offers MA. Part-time programs available. *Entrance requirements:* For master's, GRE General Test, GRE Subject Test. Additional exam requirements/recommendations for international students: Required—TOEFL. Electronic applications accepted.

Texas Tech University, Graduate School, College of Arts and Sciences, Department of Classical and Modern Languages and Literatures, Program in Romance Languages-French, Lubbock, TX 79409. Offers MA. *Students:* 20 full-time (13 women), 3 part-time (all women); includes 10 minority (1 African American, 9 Hispanic Americans), 4 international. Average age 29. 16 applicants, 81% accepted, 5 enrolled. In 2008, 5 master's awarded. *Entrance requirements:* For master's, GRE General Test. Additional exam requirements/recommendations for international students: Required—TOEFL (minimum score 550 paper-based; 213 computer-based). *Application deadline:* For fall admission, 3/1 priority date for international students; for spring admission, 11/1 priority date for international students. Applications are processed on a rolling basis. Application fee: $50 ($60 for international students). Electronic applications accepted. *Expenses:* Tuition, area resident: Part-time $194 per credit hour. Tuition, state resident: full-time $4648; part-time $194 per credit hour. Tuition, nonresident: full-time $11,392; part-time $475 per credit hour. Required fees: $2206; $69 per credit hour. $389 per semester. *Financial support:* Application deadline: 4/15. *Faculty research:* French and Francophone literature, French cinema, French and Francophone culture, business French. *Unit head:* Dr. Diane Wood, Professor and Graduate Advisor of French, 806-742-3145 Ext. 258, Fax: 806-742-3306, E-mail: diane.wood@ttu.edu. *Application contact:* Liz Hildebrand, Senior Advisor, 806-742-4055, Fax: 806-742-3306, E-mail: liz.hildebrand@ttu.edu.

Tufts University, Graduate School of Arts and Sciences, Program in French, Medford, MA 02155. Offers MA. Part-time programs available. *Degree requirements:* For master's, one foreign language. *Entrance requirements:* For master's, GRE General Test, writing sample. Additional exam requirements/recommendations for international students: Required—TOEFL (minimum score 550 paper-based; 213 computer-based; 80 iBT). Electronic applications accepted.

Tulane University, School of Liberal Arts, Department of French and Italian, New Orleans, LA 70118-5669. Offers French (MA, PhD). *Degree requirements:* For master's, one foreign language, thesis or alternative; for doctorate, 2 foreign languages, thesis/dissertation. *Entrance requirements:* For master's, GRE General Test, minimum B average in undergraduate course work; for doctorate, GRE General Test. Additional exam requirements/recommendations for international students: Required—TOEFL. Electronic applications accepted.

Université de Moncton, Faculty of Arts and Social Sciences, Department of French Studies, Moncton, NB E1A 3E9, Canada. Offers MA, PhD. Part-time programs available. Terminal master's awarded for partial completion of doctoral program. *Degree requirements:* For master's, thesis, proficiency in French; for doctorate, thesis/dissertation, proficiency in French. *Entrance requirements:* For master's, honors degree in French; for doctorate, MA in French. Electronic applications accepted. *Faculty research:* Language, linguistics, literature, ethnology, Acadian studies.

Université de Montréal, Faculty of Arts and Sciences, Department of French Literature, Montréal, QC H3C 3J7, Canada. Offers MA, PhD. *Faculty:* 31 full-time (10 women). *Students:* 57 full-time (36 women), 126 part-time (91 women). 95 applicants, 41% accepted, 37 enrolled. In 2008, 33 master's, 5 doctorates awarded. *Degree requirements:* For master's, one foreign language, thesis; for doctorate, one foreign language, thesis/dissertation, general exam. *Application deadline:* For fall admission, 2/1 priority date for domestic students; for winter admission, 11/1 priority date for domestic students; for spring admission, 2/1 priority date for domestic students. Application fee: $100. Electronic applications accepted. *Financial support:* Fellowships, research assistantships, teaching assistantships available. *Faculty research:* Literary history, literary genres, critical edition, creative writing, Quebecois literature. *Unit head:* Benoit Melan??on, Director, 514-343-6213, Fax: 514-343-2256, E-mail: benoit.melancon@umontreal.ca. *Application contact:* Jean-Philippe Beaulieu, Graduate Chairman, 514-343-6559, Fax: 514-343-2256, E-mail: jean-philippe.beaulieu@umontreal.ca.

Université de Sherbrooke, Faculty of Letters and Human Sciences, Department of Letters and Communications, Sherbrooke, QC J1K 2R1, Canada. Offers comparative Canadian literature (MA, PhD); French literature (MA, PhD); linguistics (MA); lit&erature de crèation (MA, PhD); theatre (MA). *Degree requirements:* For master's, thesis or alternative; for doctorate, thesis/dissertation. *Entrance requirements:* For master's, minimum GPA of 2.8; for doctorate, minimum GPA of 3.0.

Université du Québec à Chicoutimi, Graduate Programs, Program in Didactics of French-Mother Tongue, Chicoutimi, QC G7H 2B1, Canada. Offers Diploma. Part-time programs available. *Entrance requirements:* For degree, appropriate bachelor's degree, proficiency in French.

University at Albany, State University of New York, College of Arts and Sciences, Department of Languages, Literatures, and Cultures, Program in French, Albany, NY 12222-0001. Offers MA, PhD. *Degree requirements:* For master's, one foreign language; for doctorate, thesis/dissertation.

University at Buffalo, the State University of New York, Graduate School, College of Arts and Sciences, Department of Romance Languages and Literatures, Buffalo, NY 14260. Offers French (MA, PhD); Spanish (MA, PhD). Part-time programs available. Terminal master's awarded for partial completion of doctoral program. *Degree requirements:* For master's, one foreign language, project; for doctorate, 2 foreign languages, thesis/dissertation. *Entrance requirements:* For master's and doctorate, GRE. Additional exam requirements/recommendations for international students: Required—TOEFL (minimum score 550 paper-based; 213 computer-based; 79 iBT). Electronic applications accepted. *Faculty research:* Romance linguistics, cultural studies, literary studies, literature and philosophy.

The University of Alabama, Graduate School, College of Arts and Sciences, Department of Modern Languages and Classics, Tuscaloosa, AL 35487. Offers French (MA, PhD); French and Spanish (PhD); German (MA); Romance languages (MA, PhD); Spanish (MA, PhD). Part-time programs available. *Faculty:* 21 full-time (11 women). *Students:* 45 full-time (35 women), 12 part-time (7 women); includes 13 minority (6 African Americans, 7 Hispanic Americans), 11 international. Average age 32. 25 applicants, 68% accepted, 11 enrolled. In 2008, 17 master's, 4 doctorates awarded. *Degree requirements:* For master's, comprehensive exam, thesis optional; for doctorate, one foreign language, thesis/dissertation, preliminary exam. *Entrance requirements:* For master's and doctorate, minimum GPA of 3.0, writing sample. Additional exam requirements/recommendations for international students: Required—TOEFL or IELTS. *Application deadline:* For fall admission, 7/6 priority date for domestic students, 1/15 priority date for international students; for spring admission, 12/6 priority date for domestic students, 6/1 priority date for international students. Applications are processed on a rolling basis. Application fee: $31. Electronic applications accepted. *Expenses:* Tuition, area resident: Full-time $6400. Tuition, state resident: full-time $6400. Tuition, nonresident: full-time $18,000. *Financial support:* In 2008–09, 7 students received support, including 1 fellowship, research assistantships with full tuition reimbursements available (averaging $10,291 per year), 6 teaching assistantships with full tuition reimbursements available (averaging $10,291 per year); career-related internships or fieldwork, Federal Work-Study, institutionally sponsored loans, and scholarships/grants also available. Financial award application deadline: 7/14. *Faculty research:* Non-English literature, linguistics, culture, film. Total annual research expenditures: $9,630. *Unit head:* Dr. Michael Picone, Chair and Professor, 205-348-5054, Fax: 205-348-2042, E-mail: mpicone@bama.ua.edu. *Application contact:* Dr. K. Barbara Fischer, Graduate Director and Associate Professor, 205-348-8465, Fax: 205-348-2042, E-mail: bfischer@bama.ua.edu.

University of Alberta, Faculty of Graduate Studies and Research, Department of Modern Languages and Cultural Studies, Edmonton, AB T6G 2E1, Canada. Offers applied linguistics (Germanic, Romance, Slavic) (MA); French language, literatures and linguistics (PhD); French language, literatures, and linguistics (MA); Germanic languages, literatures and linguistics (PhD); Germanic languages, literatures, and linguistics (MA); Italian studies (MA); Slavic languages and literatures (Russian, Ukrainian) (MA, PhD); Slavic linguistics (Russian, Ukrainian) (MA, PhD); Spanish and Latin American studies (MA, PhD); Ukrainian folklore (MA, PhD). Part-time programs available. *Degree requirements:* For master's, one foreign language, thesis; for doctorate, 2 foreign languages, comprehensive exam, thesis/dissertation. *Entrance requirements:* For master's and doctorate, 1 language other than English. Additional exam requirements/recommendations for international students: Required—Michigan English Language Assessment Battery or TOEFL (paper score 550; computer score 213). Electronic applications accepted. *Faculty research:* Russian/Ukrainian studies; German studies; contemporary Latin American, French and Francophone studies; Italian studies.

The University of Arizona, Graduate College, College of Humanities, Department of French and Italian, Tucson, AZ 85721. Offers French (MA, PhD). Part-time programs available. *Degree requirements:* For doctorate, one foreign language, comprehensive exam, thesis/dissertation. *Entrance requirements:* For master's and doctorate, minimum GPA of 3.5, 3 letters of reference, statement of purpose, writing sample in French, audio sample. Additional exam requirements/recommendations for international students: Required—TOEFL (minimum score 550 paper-based; 213 computer-based; 80 iBT). Electronic applications accepted. *Faculty research:* French literature (history, criticism, and theory), Francophone literature and culture, second language acquisition and teaching.

University of Arkansas, Graduate School, J. William Fulbright College of Arts and Sciences, Department of Foreign Languages, Program in French, Fayetteville, AR 72701-1201. Offers MA. *Degree requirements:* For master's, variable foreign language requirement.

The University of British Columbia, Faculty of Arts and Faculty of Graduate Studies, Department of French, Hispanic and Italian Studies, Vancouver, BC V6T 1Z1, Canada. Offers French (MA, PhD); Hispanic studies (MA, PhD). Part-time programs available. *Degree requirements:* For master's, thesis optional; for doctorate, 2 foreign languages, comprehensive exam, thesis/dissertation. *Entrance requirements:* For master's, BA degree; for doctorate, MA degree. Additional exam requirements/recommendations for international students: Required—TOEFL (minimum score 550 paper-based; 213 computer-based; 80 iBT). Electronic applications accepted. *Faculty research:* Medieval and Renaissance literature, modern literature, romance philology and linguistics, cultural studies, women's literature.

University of California, Berkeley, Graduate Division, College of Letters and Science, Department of French, Berkeley, CA 94720-1500. Offers PhD. *Degree requirements:* For doctorate, one foreign language, thesis/dissertation, qualifying exam. *Entrance requirements:* For doctorate, minimum GPA of 3.0, 3 letters of recommendation.

University of California, Berkeley, Graduate Division, Group in Romance Languages and Literature, Program in French, Berkeley, CA 94720-1500. Offers PhD. *Entrance requirements:* For doctorate, GRE General Test, 3 letters of recommendation.

University of California, Davis, Graduate Studies, Program in French, Davis, CA 95616. Offers PhD. Part-time programs available. *Degree requirements:* For doctorate, thesis/dissertation. *Entrance requirements:* For doctorate, GRE General Test, minimum GPA of 3.0. Additional exam requirements/recommendations for international students: Required—TOEFL (minimum score 550 paper-based; 213 computer-based). Electronic applications accepted. *Faculty research:* Art and art criticism, Francophone literature, travel narrative, colonial and postcolonial studies and romance linguistics.

University of California, Irvine, Office of Graduate Studies, School of Humanities, Department of French and Italian, Irvine, CA 92697. Offers French (MA, PhD). *Degree requirements:* For doctorate, thesis/dissertation. *Entrance requirements:* For master's and doctorate, GRE General Test, minimum GPA of 3.0. Additional exam requirements/recommendations for international students: Required—TOEFL (minimum score 550 paper-based; 213 computer-based). Electronic applications accepted. *Faculty research:* Montaigne, psychoanalysis, feminism and the problem of repression, aesthetics of nationalism and the limits of culture.

University of California, Los Angeles, Graduate Division, College of Letters and Science, Department of French and Francophone Studies, Los Angeles, CA 90034. Offers MA, PhD. *Students:* 22 full-time (18 women); includes 3 minority (1 African American, 2 Hispanic Americans), 2 international. Average age 29. 21 applicants, 62% accepted, 8 enrolled. In 2008, 1 master's, 5 doctorates awarded. Terminal master's awarded for partial completion of doctoral program. *Degree requirements:* For master's, one foreign language, comprehensive exam; for doctorate, 2 foreign languages, thesis/dissertation, oral and written qualifying exams. *Entrance requirements:* For master's, GRE General Test, minimum GPA of 3.0, sample of written work in French, degree objective of Ph.D; for doctorate, GRE General Test, MA in French or equivalent; minimum undergraduate GPA of 3.0; sample of written work in French. *Application deadline:* For fall admission, 12/15 for domestic and international students. Application fee: $60 ($80 for international students). Electronic applications accepted. *Expenses:* Tuition, nonresident: full-time $14,694. Required fees: $9669.50. Full-time tuition and fees vary according to course load, degree level, program and student level. *Financial support:* In 2008–09, 24 fellowships with full and partial tuition reimbursements, 3 research assistantships with full and partial tuition reimbursements, 13 teaching assistantships with full and partial tuition reimbursements were awarded; Federal Work-Study, institutionally sponsored loans, health care benefits, tuition waivers (full and partial), and unspecified assistantships also available. Financial award applicants required to submit FAFSA. *Unit head:* Dr. Dominic Thomas, Chair, 310-825-1145. *Application contact:* Departmental Office, 310-825-1145, E-mail: allen@humnet.ucla.edu.

University of California, San Diego, Office of Graduate Studies, Department of Literature, Program in French Literature, La Jolla, CA 92093. Offers MA. *Degree requirements:* For master's, thesis. *Entrance requirements:* For master's, GRE General Test, GRE Subject Test. Electronic applications accepted.

University of California, Santa Barbara, Graduate Division, College of Letters and Sciences, Division of Humanities and Fine Arts, Department of French and Italian, Santa Barbara, CA 93106-4140. Offers French (MA, MABL, PhD), including applied linguistics (PhD), European Medieval studies (PhD), feminist studies (PhD), French (MABL, PhD); MA/PhD. French Language Institute available during summer sessions. *Faculty:* 21 full-time (12 women). *Students:* 11 full-time (7 women). Average age 31. 16 applicants, 63% accepted, 3 enrolled. In 2008, 1 master's, 5 doctorates awarded. Terminal master's awarded for partial completion of doctoral program. *Degree requirements:* For master's, 2 foreign languages, comprehensive exam; for doctorate, 2 foreign languages, comprehensive exam, thesis/dissertation. *Entrance requirements:* For master's, GRE, sample of written work, tape of spoken French, BA or the equivalent, 3 letters of recommendation, statement of purpose, personal achievements/contributions statement, resumé/curriculum vitae, transcripts for post-secondary institutions attended; for doctorate, GRE, sample of written work, tape of spoken French, MA or the equivalent, 3 letters of recommendation, statement of purpose, personal achievements/contributions statement, resumé/curriculum vitae, transcripts for post-secondary institutions attended. Additional exam requirements/recommendations for international students: Required—TOEFL (paper: 550, computer: 213, IBT: 80) or IELTS (7). *Application deadline:* For fall admission, 5/1 for domestic and international students; for winter admission, 10/1 for domestic and international students; for spring admission, 1/15 for domestic and international students. Application fee: $70 ($90 for international students). Electronic applications accepted. *Expenses:* Tuition, nonresident: full-time $25,149. Required fees: $10,143. Full-time tuition and fees vary according to campus/location, reciprocity agreements and student level. *Financial support:* In 2008–09, 11 students received support, including 5 fellowships with full and partial tuition reimbursements available (averaging $8,100 per year), 11 teaching assistantships with partial tuition reimbursements available (averaging $11,400 per year); career-related internships or fieldwork, Federal Work-Study, institutionally sponsored loans, scholarships/grants, traineeships, health care benefits, tuition waivers (full and partial), and unspecified assistantships also available. Financial award applicants required to submit FAFSA. *Faculty research:* French and Francophone studies, comparative literature, second language acquisition, applied linguistics, performance studies, feminist and gender studies. Total annual research expenditures: $2,500. *Unit head:* Prof. Jon Snyder, Chair, 805-893-2220, Fax: 805-893-8826, E-mail: snyder@frit.ucsb.edu. *Application contact:* Rosa Pinter, Graduate Staff Advisor, 805-893-3398, Fax: 805-893-8826, E-mail: pinter@frit.ucsb.edu.

University of California, Santa Barbara, Summer Sessions, Santa Barbara, CA 93106-2010. Offers French (MA); Spanish (MA). In 2008, 17 master's awarded. *Degree requirements:* For master's, comprehensive exam (for some programs). *Entrance requirements:* For master's, GRE, 3 letters of recommendation, statement of purpose, personal achievements/contributions statement, resumé/curriculum vitae, transcripts for post-secondary institutions attended. Additional exam requirements/recommendations for international students: Required—TOEFL (paper: 550, computer: 213, IBT: 80) or IELTS (7). Application fee: $70 ($90 for international students). Electronic applications accepted. *Expenses:* Contact institution. *Financial support:* Scholarships/grants available. Financial award applicants required to submit FAFSA. *Unit head:* Dr. Loy Lytle, Dean of Summer Sessions, 805-893-2706, Fax: 805-893-7306, E-mail: low.lytle@els.ucsb.edu. *Application contact:* Program Manager, 805-893-7053, Fax: 805-893-7306, E-mail: language.institutes@summersessions.ucsb.edu.

University of Chicago, Division of the Humanities, Department of Romance Languages and Literatures, Chicago, IL 60637-1513. Offers French (AM, PhD); Italian (AM, PhD); Spanish (AM, PhD). Terminal master's awarded for partial completion of doctoral program. *Degree requirements:* For master's, 2 foreign languages, thesis; for doctorate, 3 foreign languages, thesis/dissertation. *Entrance requirements:* For master's and doctorate, GRE General Test, GRE Subject Test. Additional exam requirements/recommendations for international students: Required—TOEFL.

University of Cincinnati, Graduate School, McMicken College of Arts and Sciences, Department of Romance Languages and Literature, Program in French, Cincinnati, OH 45221. Offers MA, PhD. Terminal master's awarded for partial completion of doctoral program. *Degree requirements:* For master's, thesis optional; for doctorate, 2 foreign languages, thesis/dissertation. *Entrance requirements:* For master's, minimum GPA of 3.0. Electronic applications accepted.

University of Colorado at Boulder, Graduate School, College of Arts and Sciences, Department of French and Italian, Boulder, CO 80309. Offers French (MA, PhD). Terminal master's awarded for partial completion of doctoral program. *Degree requirements:* For master's, 2 foreign languages, comprehensive exam, thesis or alternative; for doctorate, 3 foreign languages, thesis/dissertation. *Entrance requirements:* For master's, GRE General Test, minimum undergraduate GPA of 3.0; for doctorate, GRE General Test. *Faculty research:* All periods of French literature from the Middle Ages to the present (including Francophone literature, cultural studies and literary theory).

University of Connecticut, Graduate School, College of Liberal Arts and Sciences, Department of Modern and Classical Languages, Field of French, Storrs, CT 06269. Offers MA, PhD. Terminal master's awarded for partial completion of doctoral program. *Degree requirements:* For master's, comprehensive exam; for doctorate, thesis/dissertation. *Entrance requirements:* For master's and doctorate, GRE General Test, GRE Subject Test. Additional exam requirements/recommendations for international students: Required—TOEFL (minimum score 550 paper-based; 213 computer-based). Electronic applications accepted.

University of Delaware, College of Arts and Sciences, Department of Foreign Languages and Literatures, Newark, DE 19716. Offers foreign languages and literatures (MA), including French, German, Spanish; foreign languages pedagogy (MA), including French, German, Spanish. *Degree requirements:* For master's, one foreign language, comprehensive exam, thesis optional. *Entrance requirements:* For master's, GRE General Test, letters of recommendation, writing sample. Additional exam requirements/recommendations for international students: Required—TOEFL. Electronic applications accepted. *Faculty research:* Medieval to Modern French and Spanish literature, Twentieth Century German, French, Spanish literature by women, computer-assisted instruction.

University of Florida, Graduate School, College of Liberal Arts and Sciences, Department of Romance Languages and Literatures, Program in French, Gainesville, FL 32611. Offers MA, PhD. *Degree requirements:* For master's, thesis optional; for doctorate, one foreign language, thesis/dissertation. *Entrance requirements:* For master's and doctorate, GRE General Test, minimum GPA of 3.0. Additional exam requirements/recommendations for international students: Required—TOEFL (minimum score 550 paper-based; 213 computer-based). Electronic applications accepted. *Faculty research:* Medieval, sixteenth, seventeenth, nineteenth, and twentieth century French literature.

University of Georgia, Graduate School, College of Arts and Sciences, Department of Romance Languages, Program in French, Athens, GA 30602. Offers MA, MAT. *Degree requirements:* For master's, one foreign language, thesis (MA). *Entrance requirements:* For master's, GRE General Test. Electronic applications accepted.

University of Guelph, Graduate Program Services, College of Arts, School of Languages and Literatures, Guelph, ON N1G 2W1, Canada. Offers European studies (MA); French studies (MA). *Entrance requirements:* For master's, BA Honours or equivalent. Electronic applications accepted. *Faculty research:* Sociolinguistics, poetics and politics of literature, language acquisition.

University of Hawaii at Manoa, Graduate Division, Colleges of Arts and Sciences, College of Language, Linguistics and Literature, Department of Languages and Literatures of Europe and the Americas, Program in French, Honolulu, HI 96822. Offers MA. Part-time programs available. *Degree requirements:* For master's, one foreign language, thesis optional. *Entrance*

French

University of Hawaii at Manoa (continued)

requirements: Additional exam requirements/recommendations for international students: Required—TOEFL (minimum score 580 paper-based; 237 computer-based; 92 iBT), IELTS (minimum score 5).

University of Houston, College of Liberal Arts and Social Sciences, Department of Modern and Classical Languages, Houston, TX 77204. Offers French (MA); Spanish (MA, PhD); MBA/MA. Part-time and evening/weekend programs available. Postbaccalaureate distance learning degree programs offered. *Faculty:* 8 full-time (5 women), 1 (woman) part-time/adjunct. *Students:* 27 full-time (21 women), 46 part-time (34 women); includes 48 minority (1 African American, 2 Asian Americans or Pacific Islanders, 45 Hispanic Americans), 7 international. Average age 38. 23 applicants, 83% accepted, 12 enrolled. In 2008, 11 master's, 4 doctorates awarded. Terminal master's awarded for partial completion of doctoral program. *Degree requirements:* For master's, one foreign language, thesis optional; for doctorate, 3 foreign languages, thesis/dissertation. *Entrance requirements:* For master's and doctorate, GRE General Test. Additional exam requirements/recommendations for international students: Required—TOEFL. *Application deadline:* For fall admission, 2/28 priority date for domestic students; for spring admission, 10/30 priority date for domestic students. Application fee: $25 ($75 for international students). *Expenses:* Tuition, state resident: full-time $5164; part-time $287 per credit. Tuition, nonresident: full-time $10,222; part-time $568 per credit. *Financial support:* In 2008–09, 5 research assistantships with full tuition reimbursements (averaging $10,600 per year), 18 teaching assistantships with full tuition reimbursements (averaging $10,600 per year) were awarded; career-related internships or fieldwork, Federal Work-Study, institutionally sponsored loans, scholarships/grants, health care benefits, and unspecified assistantships also available. Support available to part-time students. Financial award application deadline: 2/1; financial award applicants required to submit FAFSA. *Faculty research:* Hispanic literature and language in the U.S., Golden Age, women. *Unit head:* Dr. Marc Zimmerman, Chairperson, 713-743-3007, Fax: 713-743-0935, E-mail: mzimmerm@mail.uh.edu. *Application contact:* Debra Frazier, Graduate Analyst, 713-743-2991, Fax: 713-743-2990.

University of Illinois at Chicago, Graduate College, College of Liberal Arts and Sciences, Department of Spanish, French, Italian and Portuguese, Program in French, Chicago, IL 60607-7128. Offers MA. Part-time programs available. *Degree requirements:* For master's, one foreign language, thesis optional, exam. *Entrance requirements:* For master's, minimum GPA of 2.75. Additional exam requirements/recommendations for international students: Required—TOEFL. Electronic applications accepted. *Faculty research:* French civilization, feminist theory, French theater, sociology of literature, narrative theory.

University of Illinois at Urbana–Champaign, Graduate College, College of Liberal Arts and Sciences, School of Literatures, Cultures and Linguistics, Department of French, Champaign, IL 61820. Offers MA, PhD. *Faculty:* 14 full-time (7 women). *Students:* 14 full-time (10 women), 16 part-time (10 women); includes 1 minority (Asian American or Pacific Islander), 7 international. 37 applicants, 32% accepted, 7 enrolled. In 2008, 2 master's, 2 doctorates awarded. *Entrance requirements:* For master's, GRE, minimum GPA of 3.0, 2 writing samples in French; for doctorate, GRE, minimum GPA of 3.5, 2 writing samples in French. Additional exam requirements/recommendations for international students: Required—TOEFL (minimum score 550 paper-based; 213 computer-based; 79 iBT), IELTS (minimum score 6.5), TOEFL or IELTS. *Application deadline:* Applications are processed on a rolling basis. Application fee: $60 ($75 for international students). Electronic applications accepted. *Financial support:* In 2008–09, 6 fellowships, 1 research assistantship, 31 teaching assistantships were awarded; tuition waivers (full and partial) also available. *Unit head:* Armine Mortimer, Head, 217-333-2000, Fax: 217-244-2223, E-mail: armine@illinois.edu. *Application contact:* Lynn Stanke, Office Support Specialist, 217-333-6269, Fax: 217-244-3050, E-mail: slclgradservices@illinois.edu.

The University of Iowa, Graduate College, College of Liberal Arts and Sciences, Department of French and Italian, Iowa City, IA 52242-1316. Offers French (MA, PhD). *Degree requirements:* For master's, thesis optional, exam; for doctorate, comprehensive exam, thesis/dissertation. *Entrance requirements:* For master's and doctorate, GRE General Test, minimum GPA of 3.0. Additional exam requirements/recommendations for international students: Required—TOEFL (minimum score 550 paper-based; 213 computer-based; 81 iBT). Electronic applications accepted.

The University of Kansas, Graduate Studies, College of Liberal Arts and Sciences, Department of French and Italian, Lawrence, KS 66045-7590. Offers French (MA, PhD). Part-time programs available. *Faculty:* 11 full-time (6 women), 2 part-time/adjunct (both women). *Students:* 27 full-time (19 women), 1 (woman) part-time, 7 international. Average age 33. 14 applicants, 71% accepted, 9 enrolled. In 2008, 5 master's, 1 doctorate awarded. *Degree requirements:* For master's, one foreign language, comprehensive exam, thesis optional; for doctorate, 2 foreign languages, comprehensive exam, thesis/dissertation. *Entrance requirements:* For master's and doctorate, GRE. Additional exam requirements/recommendations for international students: Required—TOEFL, IELTS. *Application deadline:* For fall admission, 1/15 priority date for domestic and international students. Applications are processed on a rolling basis. Application fee: $45 ($50 for international students). Electronic applications accepted. *Expenses:* Tuition, area resident: Full-time $6122; part-time $255.10 per credit hour. Tuition, state resident: full-time $6122; part-time $255.10 per credit hour. Tuition, nonresident: full-time $14,629; part-time $609.55 per credit hour. Required fees: $847; $70.56 per credit hour. Tuition and fees vary according to course load and program. *Financial support:* Fellowships, teaching assistantships with full tuition reimbursements, unspecified assistantships available. Financial award applicants required to submit FAFSA. *Faculty research:* French literature and cultural studies; Francophone literature, film. *Unit head:* Van Kelly, Chair, 785-864-4056, Fax: 785-864-5179, E-mail: vkelly@ku.edu. *Application contact:* Bruce Hayes, Associate Professor, 785-864-9028, E-mail: bhayes@ku.edu.

University of Kentucky, Graduate School, College of Arts and Sciences, Program in French, Lexington, KY 40506-0032. Offers MA. *Degree requirements:* For master's, one foreign language, comprehensive exam. *Entrance requirements:* For master's, GRE General Test, minimum undergraduate GPA of 2.75. Additional exam requirements/recommendations for international students: Required—TOEFL (minimum score 550 paper-based; 213 computer-based). Electronic applications accepted. *Faculty research:* The fables of Marie DeFrance, Rabelais and reading; the family romance in eighteenth century narrative; women of Dada and surrealism; postcolonialism; postmodernism.

University of Lethbridge, School of Graduate Studies, Lethbridge, AB T1K 3M4, Canada. Offers accounting (MScM); addictions counseling (M Sc); agricultural biotechnology (M Sc); agricultural studies (M Sc, MA); anthropology (MA); archaeology (MA); art (MA); biochemistry (M Sc); biological sciences (M Sc); biomolecular science (PhD); biosystems and biodiversity (PhD); Canadian studies (MA); chemistry (M Sc); computer science (M Sc); computer science and geographical information science (M Sc); counseling psychology (M Ed); dramatic arts (MA); earth, space, and physical science (PhD); economics (MA); educational leadership (M Ed); English (MA); environmental science (M Sc); evolution and behavior (PhD); exercise science (M Sc); finance (MScM); French (MA); French/German (MA); French/Spanish (MA); general education (M Ed); general management (MScM); geography (M Sc, MA); German (MA); health sciences (M Sc, MA); history (MA); human resource management and labour relations (MScM); individualized multidisciplinary (M Sc, MA); information systems (MScM); international management (MScM); kinesiology (M Sc, MA); management (M Sc, MA); marketing (MScM); mathematics (M Sc); music (MA); Native American studies (MA); neuroscience (M Sc, PhD); new media (MA); nursing (M Sc); philosophy (MA); physics (M Sc); policy and strategy (MScM); political science (MA); psychology (M Sc, MA); religious studies (MA); sociology (MA); theoretical and computational science (PhD); urban and regional studies (MA). Part-time and evening/weekend programs available. *Degree requirements:* For doctorate, comprehensive exam, thesis/dissertation. *Entrance requirements:* For master's, GMAT (M Sc in management), bachelor's degree in related field, minimum GPA of 3.0 during previous 20 graded semester courses, 2 years teaching or related experience (M Ed); for doctorate, master's degree, minimum graduate GPA of 3.5. Additional exam requirements/recommendations for international students: Required—TOEFL. *Faculty research:* Movement and brain plasticity, gibberellin physiology, photosynthesis, carbon cycling, molecular properties of main-group ring components.

University of Louisiana at Lafayette, BI Moody III College of Business Administration MBA Program, College of Liberal Arts, Department of Modern Languages, Program in Francophone Studies, Lafayette, LA 70504. Offers PhD. *Degree requirements:* For doctorate, 2 foreign languages, comprehensive exam, thesis/dissertation. *Entrance requirements:* For doctorate, GRE General Test, minimum GPA of 2.75. Additional exam requirements/recommendations for international students: Required—TOEFL (minimum score 550 paper-based; 213 computer-based). Electronic applications accepted. *Faculty research:* Louisiana folklore, eighteenth century French literature, contemporary criticism.

University of Louisiana at Lafayette, BI Moody III College of Business Administration MBA Program, College of Liberal Arts, Department of Modern Languages, Program in French, Lafayette, LA 70504. Offers MA. Part-time programs available. *Degree requirements:* For master's, 2 foreign languages, thesis or alternative. *Entrance requirements:* For master's, GRE General Test, minimum GPA of 2.75. Additional exam requirements/recommendations for international students: Required—TOEFL (minimum score 550 paper-based; 213 computer-based). Electronic applications accepted. *Faculty research:* Louisiana studies, nineteenth century French literature, Francophone studies.

University of Louisville, Graduate School, College of Arts and Sciences, Department of Classical and Modern Languages, Program in French, Louisville, KY 40292-0001. Offers MA. Part-time programs available. *Faculty:* 5 full-time (3 women). *Students:* 7 full-time (5 women), 11 part-time (4 women); includes 2 minority (both African Americans), 1 international. Average age 39. 5 applicants, 100% accepted, 4 enrolled. In 2008, 6 master's awarded. *Degree requirements:* For master's, one foreign language, thesis optional. *Application deadline:* Applications are processed on a rolling basis. Application fee: $50. Electronic applications accepted. *Financial support:* In 2008–09, 3 students received support, including 3 teaching assistantships with full tuition reimbursements available (averaging $12,000 per year); institutionally sponsored loans and scholarships/grants also available. Financial award applicants required to submit FAFSA. *Faculty research:* Medieval Occitan, 18th and 19th century French literature, contemporary French media, applied French linguistics, cultural studies. *Unit head:* Dr. Augustus Mastri, Chair, 502-852-6686, Fax: 502-852-8885, E-mail: aamast01@louisville.edu. *Application contact:* Libby Leggett, Director, Graduate Admissions, 502-852-3101, Fax: 502-852-6536, E-mail: gradadm@louisville.edu.

University of Maine, Graduate School, College of Liberal Arts and Sciences, Department of Modern Languages and Classics, Orono, ME 04469. Offers French (MA, MAT). Part-time programs available. *Degree requirements:* For master's, one foreign language, thesis (for some programs). *Entrance requirements:* For master's, GRE General Test. Additional exam requirements/recommendations for international students: Required—TOEFL. Electronic applications accepted. *Faculty research:* Narratology, poetics, Quebec literature, theater, women's studies.

University of Manitoba, Faculty of Graduate Studies, Faculty of Arts, Department of French, Spanish and Italian, Winnipeg, MB R3T 2N2, Canada. Offers French (MA, PhD). *Degree requirements:* For master's, one foreign language, thesis; for doctorate, 2 foreign languages, thesis/dissertation.

University of Maryland, College Park, Graduate Studies, College of Arts and Humanities, School of Languages, Literature, and Cultures, Modern French Studies Program, College Park, MD 20742. Offers PhD. *Entrance requirements:* Additional exam requirements/recommendations for international students: Required—TOEFL.

University of Maryland, College Park, Graduate Studies, College of Arts and Humanities, School of Languages, Literature, and Cultures, Program in French Language and Literature, College Park, MD 20742. Offers MA. *Degree requirements:* For master's, one foreign language, comprehensive exam, thesis or alternative. *Entrance requirements:* For master's, GRE General Test, GRE Subject Test, minimum GPA of 3.0, 3 letters of recommendation. Additional exam requirements/recommendations for international students: Required—TOEFL. Electronic applications accepted.

University of Maryland, College Park, Graduate Studies, College of Arts and Humanities, School of Languages, Literature, and Cultures, Program in Second Language Acquisition and Application, College Park, MD 20742. Offers French (MA); German (MA); Japanese (MA); Russian (MA); second language instruction (PhD); second language learning (PhD); second language measurement and assessment (PhD); second language use (PhD); Spanish (MA). *Entrance requirements:* For master's, BA or BS in related field, demonstrated language competency, 3 letters of reference. Electronic applications accepted. *Faculty research:* Second language acquisition, pedagogical perspectives, technological applications, language use in professional contexts.

University of Massachusetts Amherst, Graduate School, College of Humanities and Fine Arts, Department of Languages, Literatures, and Cultures, Program in French and Francophone Studies, Amherst, MA 01003. Offers French and Francophone studies (MA, MAT, PhD). Part-time programs available. *Degree requirements:* For master's, thesis or alternative. *Entrance requirements:* For master's, GRE General Test. Additional exam requirements/recommendations for international students: Required—TOEFL (minimum score 550 paper-based; 213 computer-based; 79 iBT), IELTS (minimum score 6.5). Electronic applications accepted. *Expenses:* Tuition, area resident: Full-time $2640. Tuition, nonresident: full-time $9936. One-time fee: $332 full-time. Tuition and fees vary according to course load.

University of Memphis, Graduate School, College of Arts and Sciences, Department of Foreign Languages and Literatures, Memphis, TN 38152. Offers French (MA); Spanish (MA). Part-time programs available. *Faculty:* 12 full-time (7 women), 1 part-time/adjunct (0 women). *Students:* 11 full-time (3 women), 10 part-time (all women); includes 7 minority (3 African Americans, 1 American Indian/Alaska Native, 3 Hispanic Americans), 2 international. Average age 34. 11 applicants, 100% accepted, 3 enrolled. In 2008, 9 master's awarded. *Degree requirements:* For master's, one foreign language, comprehensive exam, thesis optional. *Entrance requirements:* For master's, GRE General Test. *Application deadline:* For fall admission, 8/1 for domestic students; for spring admission, 12/1 for domestic students. Applications are processed on a rolling basis. Application fee: $35 ($60 for international students). *Expenses:* Tuition, area resident: Full-time $6242; part-time $330 per credit hour. Tuition, state resident: full-time $6242; part-time $330 per credit hour. Tuition, nonresident: full-time $17,828; part-time $815 per credit hour. Required fees: $1156. *Financial support:* Research assistantships with full tuition reimbursements, teaching assistantships with full tuition reimbursements available. Financial award applicants required to submit FAFSA. *Faculty research:* Spanish-American short story, Latin American women writers, French women of letters, Avevedo and Cervantes, 19th and 20th century peninsular literature, Brazilian culture and literature. *Unit head:* Dr. Ralph Albanese, Chairman, 901-678-2506, Fax: 901-678-5338, E-mail: ralbanes@memphis.edu. *Application contact:* Dr. Fernando Burgos, Coordinator of Graduate Studies, 901-678-3158, Fax: 901-678-5338, E-mail: fburgos@memphis.edu.

University of Miami, Graduate School, College of Arts and Sciences, Department of Modern Languages and Literatures, Coral Gables, FL 33124. Offers romance studies (PhD), including French, Spanish. *Degree requirements:* For doctorate, 2 foreign languages, thesis/dissertation, area exam, qualifying exam. *Entrance requirements:* For doctorate, 1 writing sample in English and 1 writing sample in French or Spanish, minimum GPA of 3.0; oral interview; letters of recommendation. Additional exam requirements/recommendations for international students: Required—TOEFL (minimum score 550 paper-based; 213 computer-based; 59 iBT), GRE General Test (recommended). Electronic applications accepted. *Faculty research:* Transatlantic studies, Caribbean studies, comparative literature, gender theory, cultural studies.

University of Michigan, Horace H. Rackham School of Graduate Studies, College of Literature, Science, and the Arts, Department of Romance Languages and Literatures, Program in French, Ann Arbor, MI 48109. Offers PhD. *Degree requirements:* For doctorate, 2 foreign languages, thesis/dissertation, oral defense of dissertation, preliminary exams. *Entrance requirements:* For doctorate, GRE General Test. Additional exam requirements/recommendations for international students: Required—TOEFL or Michigan English Language Assessment Battery. Electronic applications accepted. *Faculty research:* Comparative Romance studies, medieval and early modern studies, postcolonial and minority literatures, culture and materiality, reflection on the nature and function of scholarship.

University of Minnesota, Twin Cities Campus, Graduate School, College of Liberal Arts, Department of French and Italian, Minneapolis, MN 55455-0213. Offers French (MA, PhD). Part-time programs available. *Degree requirements:* For master's, one foreign language, comprehensive exam, thesis optional; for doctorate, one foreign language, thesis/dissertation, individualized exam on topic areas. *Entrance requirements:* For master's and doctorate, GRE, minimum GPA of 3.25 (recommended). Additional exam requirements/recommendations for international students: Required—TOEFL (minimum score 550 paper-based; 213 computer-based). Electronic applications accepted. *Faculty research:* Francophone literature, cultural studies, feminism, critical theory, medieval studies.

University of Mississippi, Graduate School, College of Liberal Arts, Department of Modern Languages, Oxford, University, MS 38677. Offers French (MA); German (MA); Spanish (MA). *Degree requirements:* For master's, thesis (for some programs). *Entrance requirements:* For master's, GRE General Test, minimum GPA of 3.0. Additional exam requirements/recommendations for international students: Required—TOEFL. Electronic applications accepted.

University of Missouri–Columbia, Graduate School, College of Arts and Sciences, Department of Romance Languages and Literature, Program in French, Columbia, MO 65211. Offers MA, PhD. *Students:* 2 full-time (1 woman). Average age 25. 3 applicants, 33% accepted, 1 enrolled. In 2008, 2 master's awarded. *Degree requirements:* For master's, one foreign language; for doctorate, 4 foreign languages, thesis/dissertation. *Entrance requirements:* For master's and doctorate, GRE General Test, minimum GPA of 3.0. Additional exam requirements/recommendations for international students: Required—TOEFL (minimum score 500 paper-based; 173 computer-based; 61 iBT). *Application deadline:* For fall admission, 1/15 priority date for domestic students. Applications are processed on a rolling basis. Application fee: $45 ($60 for international students). *Financial support:* Research assistantships, teaching assistantships, institutionally sponsored loans available.

The University of Montana, Graduate School, College of Arts and Sciences, Department of Modern and Classical Languages and Literatures, Missoula, MT 59812-0002. Offers French (MA); German (MA); Spanish (MA). *Degree requirements:* For master's, one foreign language. *Entrance requirements:* For master's, GRE General Test. Additional exam requirements/recommendations for international students: Required—TOEFL.

University of Nebraska–Lincoln, Graduate College, College of Arts and Sciences, Department of Modern Languages and Literatures, Lincoln, NE 68588. Offers French (MA, PhD); German (MA, PhD); Spanish (MA, PhD). *Faculty:* 20 full-time (9 women). *Students:* 28 full-time (16 women), 12 part-time (9 women); includes 9 minority (1 African American, 1 Asian American or Pacific Islander, 7 Hispanic Americans), 17 international. Average age 34. In 2008, 6 master's, 1 doctorate awarded. *Degree requirements:* For master's, thesis optional; for doctorate, comprehensive exam, thesis/dissertation. *Entrance requirements:* For master's and doctorate, writing sample in target language. Additional exam requirements/recommendations for international students: Required—TOEFL (minimum score 550 paper-based; 213 computer-based). *Application deadline:* For fall admission, 2/1 for domestic and international students. Applications are processed on a rolling basis. Application fee: $40. Electronic applications accepted. *Expenses:* Tuition, state resident: full-time $4275; part-time $237.50 per credit hour. Tuition, nonresident: full-time $11,525; part-time $640.25 per credit hour. Required fees: $1068; $10.35 per credit hour. $440.70 per semester. Tuition and fees vary according to course load and program. *Financial support:* Fellowships, research assistantships, teaching assistantships, Federal Work-Study, health care benefits, and unspecified assistantships available. Support available to part-time students. Financial award application deadline: 2/15. *Faculty research:* French, German, and Spanish language, literature, and culture. *Unit head:* Dr. Russell Ganim, Chair, 402-472-3745, Fax: 402-472-0327. *Application contact:* Dr. Dieter Karch, Graduate Chair, 402-472-3745, E-mail: modlang2@unl.edu.

University of Nevada, Reno, Graduate School, College of Liberal Arts, Department of Foreign Languages and Literatures, Reno, NV 89557. Offers French (MA); German (MA); Spanish (MA). *Faculty:* 18 full-time (8 women). *Students:* 11 full-time (6 women), 9 part-time (5 women); includes 4 minority (1 Asian American or Pacific Islander, 3 Hispanic Americans), 1 international. Average age 32. 10 applicants, 90% accepted, 6 enrolled. In 2008, 7 master's awarded. *Degree requirements:* For master's, one foreign language, thesis optional. *Entrance requirements:* For master's, GRE General Test, minimum GPA of 2.75. Additional exam requirements/recommendations for international students: Required—TOEFL (minimum score 500 paper-based; 173 computer-based; 61 iBT), IELTS (minimum score 6), TOFEL or IELTS. *Application deadline:* For fall admission, 3/1 priority date for domestic and international students; for spring admission, 11/1 priority date for domestic and international students. Applications are processed on a rolling basis. Application fee: $60 ($95 for international students). *Expenses:* Tuition, state resident: full-time $1710; part-time $1140 per semester. Tuition, nonresident: full-time $7115. Required fees: $158 per semester. *Financial support:* In 2008–09, 1 research assistantship with partial tuition reimbursement (averaging $14,000 per year), 10 teaching assistantships with partial tuition reimbursements (averaging $14,000 per year) were awarded; Federal Work-Study, institutionally sponsored loans, scholarships/grants, health care benefits, and unspecified assistantships also available. Financial award application deadline: 3/1; financial award applicants required to submit FAFSA. *Faculty research:* Thirteenth century mysticism, contemporary Spanish and Latin American poetry and theater, French interrelation between narration and photography, exile literature and Holocaust. Total annual research expenditures: $4,341. *Unit head:* Dr. Darrell Lockhart, Graduate Program Director, 775-784-6055, E-mail: lockhart@unr.edu. *Application contact:* Michele Sandberg, Application Contact, 775-784-7026, Fax: 775-784-6064, E-mail: gradschool@unr.edu.

University of New Mexico, Graduate School, College of Arts and Sciences, Department of Foreign Languages and Literature, Albuquerque, NM 87131-2039. Offers comparative literature and cultural studies (MA); French (MA); French studies (PhD); German studies (MA). Part-time programs available. *Degree requirements:* For master's, one foreign language, thesis optional; for doctorate, 2 foreign languages, thesis/dissertation. Electronic applications accepted. *Faculty research:* German, Russian, Italian, Japanese, French, Comparative Lit, culture studies, classics.

The University of North Carolina at Chapel Hill, Graduate School, College of Arts and Sciences, Department of Romance Languages, Chapel Hill, NC 27599. Offers French (MA, PhD); Italian (MA, PhD); Portuguese (MA, PhD); Romance languages (MA, PhD); Romance philology (MA, PhD); Spanish (MA, PhD). *Degree requirements:* For master's, one foreign language, comprehensive exam, thesis; for doctorate, 2 foreign languages, comprehensive exam, thesis/dissertation. *Entrance requirements:* For master's and doctorate, GRE General Test, minimum GPA of 3.0. Additional exam requirements/recommendations for international students: Required—TOEFL (minimum score 550 paper-based; 213 computer-based). Electronic applications accepted.

The University of North Carolina at Greensboro, Graduate School, College of Arts and Sciences, Department of Romance Languages, Program in French, Greensboro, NC 27412-5001. Offers MA. *Degree requirements:* For master's, one foreign language, comprehensive exam, thesis or alternative. *Entrance requirements:* For master's, GRE General Test, 3-5 minute tape demonstrating foreign language proficiency, composition in French, sample paper in English. Additional exam requirements/recommendations for international students: Required—TOEFL. Electronic applications accepted.

University of Northern Iowa, Graduate College, College of Humanities and Fine Arts, Department of Modern Languages, Program in French, Cedar Falls, IA 50614. Offers French (MA); teaching English to speakers of other languages/French (MA). Part-time and evening/weekend programs available. *Students:* 4 full-time (3 women), 5 part-time (4 women), 2 international. 2 applicants, 50% accepted, 1 enrolled. In 2008, 5 master's awarded. *Degree requirements:* For master's, one foreign language, comprehensive exam, thesis or alternative. *Entrance requirements:* For master's, minimum GPA of 3.0, valid teaching license, documentation of successful teaching experience. Additional exam requirements/recommendations for international students: Required—TOEFL (minimum score 600 paper-based; 250 computer-based; 100 iBT). *Application deadline:* For fall admission, 8/1 priority date for domestic students. Applications are processed on a rolling basis. Application fee: $30 ($50 for international students). Electronic applications accepted. *Expenses:* Tuition, state resident: full-time $6446. Tuition, nonresident: full-time $14,874. Required fees: $852. *Financial support:* Career-related internships or fieldwork, Federal Work-Study, and tuition waivers (full and partial) available. Support available to part-time students. Financial award application deadline: 2/1. *Unit head:* Dr. Anne Lair, Coordinator, 319-273-2183, Fax: 319-273-2848, E-mail: anne.lair@uni.edu. *Application contact:* Laurie S. Russell, Record Analyst, 319-273-2623, Fax: 319-273-6792, E-mail: laurie.russell@uni.edu.

University of North Texas, Robert B. Toulouse School of Graduate Studies, College of Arts and Sciences, Department of Foreign Languages and Literatures, Denton, TX 76203. Offers French (MA); Spanish (MA). Part-time programs available. *Degree requirements:* For master's, 2 foreign languages, comprehensive exam, thesis optional, proficiency in a second foreign language. *Entrance requirements:* For master's, GRE General Test, minimum undergraduate GPA of 3.0, curriculum vita, 250 word essay in French or Spanish, 12 advanced credita in French or Spanish. Additional exam requirements/recommendations for international students: Recommended—TOEFL (minimum score 550 paper-based; 213 computer-based). *Faculty research:* Literature of Austria, France, Germany, Latin America, Spain; culture/civilization; applied linguistics.

University of Notre Dame, Graduate School, College of Arts and Letters, Division of Humanities, Department of Romance Languages and Literatures, Notre Dame, IN 46556. Offers French and Francophone studies (MA); Iberian and Latin American studies (MA); Italian studies (MA); Romance literatures (MA). *Faculty:* 25 full-time (10 women), 4 part-time/adjunct (all women). *Students:* 17 full-time (12 women); includes 4 minority (all Hispanic Americans), 2 international. 30 applicants, 47% accepted, 11 enrolled. In 2008, 11 master's awarded. *Degree requirements:* For master's, 2 foreign languages, comprehensive exam, thesis optional. *Entrance requirements:* For master's, GRE General Test, BA in target language. Additional exam requirements/recommendations for international students: Required—TOEFL (minimum score 600 paper-based; 250 computer-based; 80 iBT). *Application deadline:* For fall admission, 2/1 priority date for domestic students, 2/1 for international students. Application fee: $50. Electronic applications accepted. *Financial support:* Teaching assistantships with full tuition reimbursements, tuition waivers (full) available. Financial award application deadline: 2/1. *Faculty research:* Literature of discovery and exploration, modern literature, literary criticism, medieval literature, feminist critical theory. *Unit head:* Dr. John Welle, Director of Graduate Studies, 574-631-6887, E-mail: al.romland.1@nd.edu. *Application contact:* Dr. Barbara Turpin, Director of Graduate Admissions, 574-631-7706, Fax: 574-631-4183.

University of Oklahoma, Graduate College, College of Arts and Sciences, Department of Modern Languages, Program in French, Norman, OK 73019. Offers MA, PhD, MBA/MA. Part-time programs available. *Students:* 10 full-time (8 women); includes 2 minority (1 African American, 1 Hispanic American), 4 international. 3 applicants, 100% accepted, 2 enrolled. *Degree requirements:* For master's, 2 foreign languages, comprehensive exam, thesis optional, departmental qualifying exam; for doctorate, 3 foreign languages, comprehensive exam, thesis/dissertation, departmental qualifying exam. *Entrance requirements:* For master's, BA in French or equivalent, minimum GPA of 3.0 in last 60 hours, 3 letters of recommendation. Additional exam requirements/recommendations for international students: Required—TOEFL (minimum score 550 paper-based; 213 computer-based). *Application deadline:* For fall admission, 6/1 priority date for domestic students, 4/1 for international students; for spring admission, 11/1 for domestic students, 9/1 for international students. Applications are processed on a rolling basis. Application fee: $40 ($90 for international students). Electronic applications accepted. *Expenses:* Tuition, state resident: full-time $3744; part-time $156 per credit hour. Tuition, nonresident: full-time $13,577; part-time $565.70 per credit hour. Required fees: $2415.40; $90.10 per credit hour. *Financial support:* In 2008–09, 2 students received support. Scholarships/grants, health care benefits, and unspecified assistantships available. Financial award applicants required to submit FAFSA. *Faculty research:* French and Francophone literature and cultural studies; history of medicine; critical theory; food and culture; European culture and identity. *Unit head:* Dr. Pamela Genova, Chair, 405-325-6181, Fax: 405-325-0103, E-mail: genova@ou.edu. *Application contact:* Dr. Logan E. Whalen, Graduate Liaison, 405-325-5088, Fax: 405-325-0103, E-mail: mlllgradinfo@ou.edu.

University of Oregon, Graduate School, College of Arts and Sciences, Department of Romance Languages, Program in French, Eugene, OR 97403. Offers MA. Part-time programs available. *Degree requirements:* For master's, one foreign language. *Entrance requirements:* For master's, GRE General Test, minimum GPA of 3.0. Additional exam requirements/recommendations for international students: Required—TOEFL.

University of Ottawa, Faculty of Graduate and Postdoctoral Studies, Faculty of Arts, Department of Lettres Françaises, Ottawa, ON K1N 6N5, Canada. Offers MA, PhD. *Degree requirements:* For master's, thesis or alternative; for doctorate, thesis/dissertation, oral exam. *Entrance requirements:* For master's, honors degree or equivalent, minimum B average; for doctorate, master's degree, minimum B+ average. Electronic applications accepted. *Faculty research:* Littérature française, du Moyen-Âge á nos jours; littérature québécoise, des origines au XXe siećle; création littéraire.

University of Pennsylvania, School of Arts and Sciences, Graduate Group in Romance Languages, Philadelphia, PA 19104. Offers French (AM, PhD); Italian (AM, PhD); Spanish (AM, PhD). Terminal master's awarded for partial completion of doctoral program. *Degree requirements:* For master's, one foreign language, thesis or alternative; for doctorate, 2 foreign languages, thesis/dissertation. *Entrance requirements:* For master's and doctorate, GRE General Test. Additional exam requirements/recommendations for international students: Required—TOEFL. Electronic applications accepted. *Faculty research:* Literary theory and criticism, cultural studies, history of Romance literatures, gender studies.

University of Pittsburgh, School of Arts and Sciences, Department of French and Italian, Program in French, Pittsburgh, PA 15260. Offers MA, PhD. Part-time programs available. Terminal master's awarded for partial completion of doctoral program. *Degree requirements:* For master's, 2 foreign languages, comprehensive exam, seminar paper; for doctorate, 3 foreign languages, comprehensive exam, thesis/dissertation, dissertation defense. *Entrance requirements:* For master's and doctorate, GRE General Test, interview, 2 writing samples, essay. Additional exam requirements/recommendations for international students: Required—TOEFL (minimum score 554 paper-based; 213 computer-based; 80 iBT). Electronic applications accepted. *Faculty research:* Literature and politics, literature and the arts, intellectual history of European modernity, French cinema, Francophone studies.

University of Regina, Faculty of Graduate Studies and Research, Faculty of Arts, Department of French, Regina, SK S4S 0A2, Canada. Offers MA. *Faculty:* 5 full-time (1 woman), 1 part-time/adjunct (0 women). *Students:* 1 (woman) full-time, 1 part-time (0 women). 2 applicants, 100% accepted. *Degree requirements:* For master's, thesis, 2 seminar presentations. *Entrance requirements:* Additional exam requirements/recommendations for international students: Required—TOEFL (minimum score 580 paper-based; 237 computer-based; 88 iBT). *Application deadline:* Applications are processed on a rolling basis. Application fee: $85 ($100 for international students). Electronic applications accepted. *Financial support:* Fellowships, research assistantships, teaching assistantships, scholarships/grants available. Financial award application

French

University of Regina (continued)
deadline: 6/15. *Faculty research:* Literature of the sixteenth through twentieth centuries in France, French Canadian literature, literary criticism, translation, history of ideas. *Unit head:* Dr. Emmanuel Aito, Graduate Program Coordinator, 306-585-4323, Fax: 306-585-4827, E-mail: emmanuel.aito@uregina.ca. *Application contact:* Dr. Emmanuel Aito, Graduate Program Coordinator, 306-585-4323, Fax: 306-585-4827, E-mail: emmanuel.aito@uregina.ca.

University of Saskatchewan, College of Graduate Studies and Research, College of Arts and Sciences, Department of Languages and Linguistics, Saskatoon, SK S7N 5A2, Canada. Offers MA. *Degree requirements:* For master's, 2 foreign languages, thesis. *Entrance requirements:* Additional exam requirements/recommendations for international students: Required—TOEFL.

University of South Africa, College of Human Sciences, Pretoria, South Africa. Offers adult education (M Ed); African languages (MA, PhD); African politics (MA, PhD); Afrikaans (MA, PhD); ancient history (MA, PhD); ancient Near Eastern studies (MA, PhD); anthropology (MA, PhD); applied linguistics (MA); Arabic (MA, PhD); archaeology (MA); art history (MA); Biblical archaeology (MA); Biblical studies (M Th, D Th, PhD); Christian spirituality (M Th, D Th); church history (M Th, D Th); classical studies (MA, PhD); clinical psychology (MA); communication (MA, PhD); comparative education (M Ed, Ed D); consulting psychology (D Admin, D Com, PhD); curriculum studies (M Ed, Ed D); development studies (M Admin, MA, D Admin, PhD); didactics (M Ed, Ed D); education (M Tech); education management (M Ed, Ed D); educational psychology (M Ed); English (MA); environmental education (M Ed); French (MA, PhD); German (MA, PhD); Greek (MA); guidance and counseling (M Ed); health studies (MA, PhD), including health sciences education (MA), health services management (MA), medical and surgical nursing science (critical care general) (MA), midwifery and neonatal nursing science (MA), trauma and emergency care (MA); history (MA, PhD); history of education (Ed D); inclusive education (M Ed, Ed D); information and communications technology policy and regulation (MA); information science (MA, MIS, PhD); international politics (MA, PhD); Islamic studies (MA, PhD); Italian (MA, PhD); Judaica (MA, PhD); linguistics (MA, PhD); mathematical education (M Ed); mathematics education (MA); missiology (M Th, D Th); modern Hebrew (MA, PhD); musicology (MA, MMus, D Mus, PhD); natural science education (M Ed); New Testament (M Th, D Th); Old Testament (D Th); pastoral therapy (M Th, D Th); philosophy (MA); philosophy of education (M Ed, Ed D); politics (MA, PhD); Portuguese (MA, PhD); practical theology (M Th, D Th); psychology (MA, MS, PhD); psychology of education (M Ed, Ed D); public health (MA); religious studies (MA, D Th, PhD); Romance languages (MA); Russian (MA, PhD); Semitic languages (MA, PhD); social behavior studies in HIV/AIDS (MA); social science (mental health) (MA); social science in development studies (MA); social science in psychology (MA); social science in social work (MA); social science in sociology (MA); social work (MSW, DSW, PhD); socio-education (M Ed, Ed D); sociolinguistics (MA); sociology (MA, PhD); Spanish (MA, PhD); systematic theology (M Th, D Th); TESOL (teaching English to speakers of other languages) (MA); theological ethics (M Th, D Th); theory of literature (MA, PhD); urban ministries (D Th); urban ministry (M Th).

University of South Carolina, The Graduate School, College of Arts and Sciences, Department of Languages, Literatures, and Cultures, Columbia, SC 29208. Offers comparative literature (MA, PhD); foreign languages (MAT), including French, German, Spanish; French (MA); German (MA); Spanish (MA). MAT offered in cooperation with the College of Education. Part-time programs available. *Degree requirements:* For master's, one foreign language, comprehensive exam, thesis optional; for doctorate, 2 foreign languages, comprehensive exam, thesis/dissertation. *Entrance requirements:* For master's and doctorate, GRE General Test, writing sample. Additional exam requirements/recommendations for international students: Required—TOEFL (minimum score 230 computer-based; 75 iBT). Electronic applications accepted. *Faculty research:* Modern literature, linguistics, literature and culture, medieval literature, literary theory.

University of Southern California, Graduate School, College of Letters, Arts and Sciences, Department of French and Italian, Los Angeles, CA 90089. Offers French (MA, PhD). *Degree requirements:* For doctorate, one foreign language, thesis/dissertation. *Entrance requirements:* For doctorate, GRE General Test. *Faculty research:* French renaissance, French women writers autobiographical writing.

University of South Florida, Graduate School, College of Arts and Sciences, Department of World Language Education, Program in French, Tampa, FL 33620-9951. Offers MA. *Students:* 10 full-time (7 women), 3 part-time (all women); includes 6 minority (3 African Americans, 1 American Indian/Alaska Native, 2 Hispanic Americans), 4 international. 14 applicants, 79% accepted, 8 enrolled. In 2008, 2 master's awarded. *Degree requirements:* For master's, comprehensive exam, thesis. *Entrance requirements:* For master's, 36 hours of graduate course work in French, minimum GPA of 3.0. Additional exam requirements/recommendations for international students: Required—TOEFL (minimum score 550 paper-based; 213 computer-based). *Application deadline:* For fall admission, 2/15 for domestic students, 1/2 for international students; for spring admission, 10/15 for domestic students, 6/1 for international students. Application fee: $30. *Expenses:* Tuition, state resident: full-time $2624.40; part-time $291.60 per credit hour. Tuition, nonresident: full-time $7822; part-time $869.13 per credit hour. *Unit head:* Roberta Tucker, Program Director, 813-974-2762, Fax: 813-974-1718, E-mail: tucker@cas.usf.edu. *Application contact:* Roberta Tucker, Program Director, 813-974-2762, Fax: 813-974-1718, E-mail: tucker@cas.usf.edu.

The University of Tennessee, Graduate School, College of Arts and Sciences, Department of Modern Foreign Languages and Literatures, Program in French, Knoxville, TN 37996. Offers MA. *Degree requirements:* For master's, one foreign language, thesis or alternative. *Entrance requirements:* For master's, minimum GPA of 2.7. Additional exam requirements/recommendations for international students: Required—TOEFL. Electronic applications accepted. *Expenses:* Tuition, area resident: Part-time $348 per credit hour. Tuition, state resident: full-time $6262. Tuition, nonresident: full-time $18,920; part-time $1052 per credit hour. Required fees: $812; $36 per credit hour. Tuition and fees vary according to program.

The University of Tennessee, Graduate School, College of Arts and Sciences, Department of Modern Foreign Languages and Literatures, Program in Modern Foreign Languages, Knoxville, TN 37996. Offers applied linguistics (PhD); French (PhD); German (PhD); Italian (PhD); Portuguese (PhD); Russian (PhD); Spanish (PhD). *Degree requirements:* For doctorate, 2 foreign languages, thesis/dissertation. *Entrance requirements:* For doctorate, minimum GPA of 2.7. Additional exam requirements/recommendations for international students: Required—TOEFL. Electronic applications accepted. *Expenses:* Tuition, area resident: Part-time $348 per credit hour. Tuition, state resident: full-time $6262. Tuition, nonresident: full-time $18,920; part-time $1052 per credit hour. Required fees: $812; $36 per credit hour. Tuition and fees vary according to program.

The University of Texas at Arlington, Graduate School, College of Liberal Arts, Department of Modern Languages, Arlington, TX 76019. Offers French (MA); Spanish (MA). Part-time and evening/weekend programs available. *Faculty:* 7 full-time (5 women), 1 (woman) part-time/adjunct. *Students:* 9 full-time (6 women), 26 part-time (19 women); includes 16 minority (6 African Americans, 10 Hispanic Americans), 2 international. 24 applicants, 79% accepted, 10 enrolled. In 2008, 3 master's awarded. *Degree requirements:* For master's, 2 foreign languages, comprehensive exam, thesis optional. *Entrance requirements:* For master's, GRE General Test, minimum GPA of 3.0, 3 letters of recommendation. Additional exam requirements/recommendations for international students: Required—TOEFL (minimum score 550 paper-based; 213 computer-based). *Application deadline:* For fall admission, 6/16 for domestic students. Applications are processed on a rolling basis. Application fee: $35 ($50 for international students). *Expenses:* Tuition, area resident: Full-time $6500. Tuition, state resident: full-time $6500. Tuition, nonresident: full-time $11,558. *Financial support:* In 2008–09, teaching assistantships (averaging $6,600 per year); research assistantships. Financial award application deadline: 6/1; financial award applicants required to submit FAFSA. *Unit head:* Dr. A. Raymond Elliott, Chair, 817-272-3161, Fax: 817-272-5408, E-mail: elliott@uta.edu. *Application contact:* Dr. Antoinette Sol, Graduate Advisor, 817-272-3161, Fax: 817-272-5408, E-mail: amsol@uta.edu.

The University of Texas at Austin, Graduate School, College of Liberal Arts, Department of French and Italian, Austin, TX 78712-1111. Offers French (MA, PhD); French linguistics (MA, PhD); Italian studies (MA, PhD); Romance linguistics (MA, PhD). Part-time programs available. *Degree requirements:* For master's, one foreign language, thesis; for doctorate, 2 foreign languages, thesis/dissertation. *Entrance requirements:* For master's, GRE General Test, minimum GPA of 3.0, bachelor's degree in French or equivalent; for doctorate, GRE General Test, minimum GPA of 3.0, master's degree in French. Additional exam requirements/recommendations for international students: Required—TOEFL. Electronic applications accepted. *Faculty research:* Nineteenth-century Italian literature, Italian Renaissance, twentieth-century French literature, Francophone literature, fifteenth-century literature and culture.

The University of Toledo, College of Graduate Studies, College of Arts and Sciences, Department of Foreign Languages, Toledo, OH 43606-3390. Offers French (MA); German (MA); Spanish (MA). Part-time programs available. *Degree requirements:* For master's, one foreign language, comprehensive reading exam in 1 additional foreign language. Electronic applications accepted.

University of Toronto, School of Graduate Studies, Humanities Division, Department of French, Toronto, ON M5S 1A1, Canada. Offers French language and literature (MA, PhD). Part-time programs available. *Degree requirements:* For master's, research essay; for doctorate, one foreign language, thesis/dissertation, field exam. *Entrance requirements:* For master's, 2 letters of reference, writing sample, minimum B+ average overall and in French, undergraduate major in French; for doctorate, 7 courses in French language and literature, minimum A- average, writing sample.

University of Utah, The Graduate School, College of Humanities, Department of Languages and Literature, Salt Lake City, UT 84112-1107. Offers comparative literary and cultural studies (MA, PhD); French (MA, MALP); German (MA, MALP, PhD); language pedagogy (MALP); Spanish (MA, MALP, PhD); world languages with secondary teaching licensure (MA). Terminal master's awarded for partial completion of doctoral program. *Degree requirements:* For master's, standard proficiency in 2 languages other than English, comprehensive exam or thesis; for doctorate, comprehensive exam, standard proficiency in 2 languages other than English and language of study, advanced proficiency in 1 language other than English and language of study, dissertation. *Entrance requirements:* For master's, bachelor's degree or strong undergraduate record in target languages, GPA of 3.0, literature-survey courses; for doctorate, successful completion of MA and advanced proficiency in a target language. Additional exam requirements/recommendations for international students: Required—TOEFL (minimum score 500 paper-based; 173 computer-based). Electronic applications accepted. *Faculty research:* Literary theory, stylistics, Russian and Soviet literature, existentialism, theory of criticism.

University of Vermont, Graduate College, College of Arts and Sciences, Department of Romance Languages, Burlington, VT 05405. Offers French (MA). *Students:* 5 (3 women); includes 1 minority (American Indian/Alaska Native). 4 applicants, 75% accepted, 1 enrolled. *Degree requirements:* For master's, one foreign language. *Entrance requirements:* For master's, GRE General Test. Additional exam requirements/recommendations for international students: Required—TOEFL (minimum score 550 paper-based; 213 computer-based; 80 iBT). *Application deadline:* For fall admission, 8/1 priority date for domestic students. Applications are processed on a rolling basis. Application fee: $40. Electronic applications accepted. *Expenses:* Tuition, state resident: part-time $488 per credit. Tuition, nonresident: part-time $1232 per credit. *Financial support:* Fellowships, teaching assistantships available. Financial award application deadline: 3/1. *Faculty research:* French, French-Canadian, and French-African literature. *Unit head:* Dr. G. Nunley, Chairperson, 802-656-3196. *Application contact:* Dr. J. Whatley, Coordinator, 802-656-3196.

University of Victoria, Faculty of Graduate Studies, Faculty of Humanities, Department of French, Victoria, BC V8W 2Y2, Canada. Offers literature (MA); teaching emphasis (MA). Part-time and evening/weekend programs available. *Degree requirements:* For master's, 2 foreign languages, thesis optional. *Entrance requirements:* For master's, BA in French. Additional exam requirements/recommendations for international students: Required—TOEFL (minimum score 575 paper-based; 233 computer-based), IELTS (minimum score 7). Electronic applications accepted. *Faculty research:* French-Canadian literature, stylistics, comparative literature, Francophone literature.

University of Virginia, College and Graduate School of Arts and Sciences, Department of French, Charlottesville, VA 22903. Offers MA, PhD. *Faculty:* 13 full-time (10 women), 2 part-time/adjunct (both women). *Students:* 34 full-time (23 women); includes 1 minority (African American), 4 international. Average age 28. 29 applicants, 62% accepted, 7 enrolled. In 2008, 7 master's, 4 doctorates awarded. *Degree requirements:* For master's, one foreign language, comprehensive exam; for doctorate, one foreign language, comprehensive exam, thesis/dissertation. *Entrance requirements:* For master's and doctorate, GRE General Test, minimum GPA of 3.0 in major & overall; 2 letters of recommendation; writing sample. Additional exam requirements/recommendations for international students: Required—TOEFL (minimum score 600 paper-based; 250 computer-based; 90 iBT), IELTS (minimum score 7). *Application deadline:* For fall admission, 12/1 for domestic and international students. Applications are processed on a rolling basis. Application fee: $60. Electronic applications accepted. *Expenses:* Tuition, area resident: Full-time $10,452. Tuition, state resident: full-time $10,452. Tuition, nonresident: full-time $20,010. Required fees: $2176. Part-time tuition and fees vary according to course load and program. *Financial support:* Fellowships, teaching assistantships available. Financial award applicants required to submit FAFSA. *Unit head:* John Lyons, 434-924-7158, Fax: 434-924-7157. *Application contact:* Amy Ogden, Director of Graduate Studies, 434-924-1393, Fax: 434-924-7157, E-mail: avo2n@virginia.edu.

University of Washington, Graduate School, College of Arts and Sciences, Department of Romance Languages and Literature, Division of French and Italian Studies, Seattle, WA 98195. Offers French (MA, PhD); Italian (MA). Terminal master's awarded for partial completion of doctoral program. *Degree requirements:* For master's, 2 foreign languages, exam; for doctorate, 3 foreign languages, thesis/dissertation, exam. *Entrance requirements:* For master's and doctorate, GRE General Test, minimum GPA of 3.0. Additional exam requirements/recommendations for international students: Required—TOEFL. Electronic applications accepted. *Faculty research:* Interdisciplinary studies, literary theory and criticism, film, major periods of French and Italian literature, Francophonie.

University of Waterloo, Graduate Studies, Faculty of Arts, Department of French Studies, Waterloo, ON N2L 3G1, Canada. Offers French (MA, PhD). Part-time programs available. *Entrance requirements:* For master's, honors degree, minimum B average, course work and assignments in French, resumé. Additional exam requirements/recommendations for international students: Required—TOEFL, TWE. Electronic applications accepted. *Faculty research:* French and Quebec literature: Middle Ages through twentieth century, phonology of Acadian dialect, computerized scholarly editions of medieval and Renaissance texts.

The University of Western Ontario, Faculty of Graduate Studies, Faculty of Arts and Humanities, Department of French, London, ON N6A 5B8, Canada. Offers Canadian literature (MA); French (MA, PhD). MA (Canadian literature) offered in cooperation with Department of English. *Degree requirements:* For master's, thesis or alternative; for doctorate, one foreign language, thesis/dissertation. *Entrance requirements:* For master's, minimum B average, honors degree, 2 years of teaching experience (MAT); for doctorate, MA or equivalent, minimum B average in French. Additional exam requirements/recommendations for international students: Required—TOEFL. Electronic applications accepted.

University of Wisconsin–Madison, Graduate School, College of Letters and Science, Department of French and Italian, Program in French, Madison, WI 53706-1380. Offers MA,

PhD. Part-time programs available. *Degree requirements:* For master's, one foreign language; for doctorate, one foreign language, thesis/dissertation. *Entrance requirements:* For master's and doctorate, GRE. Electronic applications accepted. *Faculty research:* Francophone literature; French literature, culture, linguistics, and language pedagogy.

University of Wisconsin–Madison, Graduate School, College of Letters and Science, Department of French and Italian, Program in French Studies, Madison, WI 53706-1380. Offers MFS, Certificate. Part-time programs available. *Degree requirements:* For master's, one foreign language, thesis, internship; for Certificate, one foreign language, internship. *Entrance requirements:* For master's, GRE. Electronic applications accepted. *Faculty research:* International development, European citizenship, French and business, foreign language education, agricultural economics.

University of Wisconsin–Milwaukee, Graduate School, College of Letters and Sciences, Interdepartmental Program in Foreign Language and Literature, Milwaukee, WI 53201-0413. Offers classics and Hebrew studies (MAFLL); comparative literature (MAFLL); French and Italian (MAFLL); German (MAFLL); Slavic studies (MAFLL); translation (Certificate). Part-time programs available. *Faculty:* 39 full-time (17 women). *Students:* 32 full-time (25 women), 28 part-time (19 women); includes 5 minority (1 Asian American or Pacific Islander, 4 Hispanic Americans), 22 international. Average age 32. 51 applicants, 65% accepted, 26 enrolled. In 2008, 19 master's awarded. *Degree requirements:* For master's, 2 foreign languages, thesis or alternative. *Entrance requirements:* Additional exam requirements/recommendations for international students: Required—TOEFL (minimum score 550 paper-based; 79 iBT), IELTS (minimum score 6.5). *Application deadline:* For fall admission, 1/1 priority date for domestic students; for spring admission, 9/1 for domestic students. Applications are processed on a rolling basis. Application fee: $45 ($75 for international students). *Expenses:* Tuition, area resident: Full-time $7320; part-time $165 per credit. Tuition, state resident: full-time $7320; part-time $165 per credit. Tuition, nonresident: full-time $17,840; part-time $714 per credit. Tuition and fees vary according to campus/location, program and reciprocity agreements. *Financial support:* In 2008–09, 2 research assistantships, 35 teaching assistantships were awarded; career-related internships or fieldwork and unspecified assistantships also available. Support available to part-time students. Financial award application deadline: 4/15. Total annual research expenditures: $43,420. *Unit head:* Gabrielle Verdier, Representative, 414-229-3346, Fax: 414-229-2741, E-mail: verdier@uwm.edu. *Application contact:* General Information Contact, 414-229-4982, Fax: 414-229-6967, E-mail: gradschool@uwm.edu.

University of Wyoming, Graduate School, College of Arts and Sciences, Department of Modern and Classical Languages, Program in French, Laramie, WY 82070. Offers MA. Part-time programs available. *Faculty:* 2 full-time (0 women). *Students:* 2 part-time (both women). Average age 23. 2 applicants, 100% accepted, 2 enrolled. In 2008, 1 master's awarded. *Degree requirements:* For master's, one foreign language, thesis or alternative. *Entrance requirements:* For master's, GRE General Test, minimum GPA of 3.0. *Application deadline:* For fall admission, 4/1 priority date for domestic students. Applications are processed on a rolling basis. Application fee: $50. *Financial support:* In 2008–09, 2 teaching assistantships with full tuition reimbursements (averaging $10,696 per year) were awarded; institutionally sponsored loans also available. Financial award application deadline: 3/1. *Faculty research:* Poetry, Asian literature, medieval literature, nineteenth- and twentieth century literature. *Unit head:* Dr. Philip Holt, Head, 307-766-4177, Fax: 307-766-2727, E-mail: pholt@uwyo.edu. *Application contact:* Dr. Kevin S. Larsen, Graduate Adviser, 307-766-2294, Fax: 307-766-2727, E-mail: klarsen@uwyo.edu.

Vanderbilt University, Graduate School, Department of French and Italian, Nashville, TN 37240-1001. Offers French (MA, MAT, PhD). *Faculty:* 19 full-time (14 women). *Students:* 10 full-time (6 women); includes 1 minority (Hispanic American). Average age 30. 33 applicants, 18% accepted, 3 enrolled. In 2008, 1 master's awarded. Terminal master's awarded for partial completion of doctoral program. *Degree requirements:* For master's, one foreign language, comprehensive exam; for doctorate, 2 foreign languages, comprehensive exam, thesis/dissertation, final and qualifying exams. *Entrance requirements:* For master's and doctorate, GRE General Test. Additional exam requirements/recommendations for international students: Required—TOEFL (minimum score 570 paper-based; 230 computer-based; 88 iBT). *Application deadline:* For fall admission, 1/15 for domestic and international students. Application fee: $0. Electronic applications accepted. *Financial support:* Fellowships with full and partial tuition reimbursements, teaching assistantships with full and partial tuition reimbursements, career-related internships or fieldwork, Federal Work-Study, institutionally sponsored loans, scholarships/grants, and health care benefits available. Financial award application deadline: 1/15; financial award applicants required to submit CSS PROFILE or FAFSA. *Faculty research:* Baudelaire, Rabelais, voyage literature, postcolonial literature, medieval epic. *Unit head:* Lynn Ramey, PhD, Chair, 615-322-6900, Fax: 615-343-6909, E-mail: lynn.ramey@vanderbilt.edu. *Application contact:* Robert Barsky, Director of Graduate Studies, 615-322-6900, Fax: 615-343-6909, E-mail: robert.barsky@vanderbilt.edu.

Washington University in St. Louis, Graduate School of Arts and Sciences, Department of Romance Languages and Literatures, Program in French, St. Louis, MO 63130-4899. Offers MA, PhD. *Students:* 22 full-time (17 women); includes 3 minority (all African Americans), 8 international. 12 applicants, 67% accepted, 5 enrolled. In 2008, 1 master's, 2 doctorates awarded. Terminal master's awarded for partial completion of doctoral program. *Degree requirements:* For master's, thesis or alternative; for doctorate, thesis/dissertation. *Entrance requirements:* For master's and doctorate, GRE General Test. *Application deadline:* For fall admission, 1/15 priority date for domestic students. Application fee: $45. Electronic applications accepted. *Financial support:* Fellowships, teaching assistantships available. Financial award application deadline: 1/15. *Unit head:* Dr. Elzbieta Sklodowska, Chairperson, 314-935-5175. *Application contact:* Assistant to the Dean, 314-935-6880, Fax: 314-935-4887.

Wayne State University, College of Liberal Arts and Sciences, Department of Classical and Modern Languages, Literatures, and Cultures, Program in French, Detroit, MI 48202. Offers MA. *Degree requirements:* For master's, one foreign language, thesis optional. *Entrance requirements:* For master's, GRE General Test, minimum GPA of 3.0. Additional exam requirements/recommendations for international students: Required—TOEFL (minimum score 550 paper-based; 213 computer-based); Recommended—TWE (minimum score 6). Electronic applications accepted. *Faculty research:* Renaissance lyric, eighteenth century theatre and poetry, Quebecois literature, nineteenth century prose, twentieth century novel and criticism.

West Chester University of Pennsylvania, Office of Graduate Studies, College of Arts and Sciences, Department of Languages and Cultures, West Chester, PA 19383. Offers French (M Ed, MA, Teaching Certificate); German (Teaching Certificate); Latin (Teaching Certificate); Spanish (M Ed, MA, Teaching Certificate). Part-time and evening/weekend programs available. *Students:* 7 full-time (6 women), 14 part-time (all women); includes 2 minority (1 African American, 1 Hispanic American), 1 international. Average age 34. 16 applicants, 100% accepted, 8 enrolled. In 2008, 3 master's awarded. *Degree requirements:* For master's, one foreign language, comprehensive exam, thesis optional. *Entrance requirements:* For master's, GRE or MAT, placement test. Additional exam requirements/recommendations for international students: Required—TOEFL (minimum score 550 paper-based; 213 computer-based; 80 iBT). *Application deadline:* For fall admission, 4/15 priority date for domestic students, 3/15 for international students; for spring admission, 10/15 for domestic students, 9/1 for international students. Applications are processed on a rolling basis. Application fee: $35. Electronic applications accepted. *Expenses:* Tuition, state resident: full-time $6430; part-time $357 per credit. Tuition, nonresident: full-time $10,288; part-time $572 per credit. Required fees: $652.50; $50 per credit. $67 per semester. *Financial support:* In 2008–09, 1 research assistantship with full and partial tuition reimbursement (averaging $5,000 per year) was awarded; unspecified assistantships also available. Support available to part-time students. Financial award application deadline: 2/15; financial award applicants required to submit FAFSA. *Faculty research:* Implementation of world languages curriculum framework. *Unit head:* Dr. Jerry Williams, Chair, 610-436-2700, Fax: 610-436-3048, E-mail: jwilliams2@wcupa.edu. *Application contact:* Dr. Rebecca Pauly, Graduate Coordinator, 610-436-2382, E-mail: rpauly@wcupa.edu.

West Virginia University, Eberly College of Arts and Sciences, Department of Foreign Languages, Morgantown, WV 26506. Offers French (MA); linguistics (MA); Spanish (MA); teaching English to speakers of other languages (MA). Part-time programs available. *Degree requirements:* For master's, one foreign language, comprehensive exam (for some programs), thesis optional. *Entrance requirements:* For master's, minimum GPA of 3.0. Electronic applications accepted. *Faculty research:* French, German, and Spanish literature; foreign language pedagogy; English as a second language; cultural studies; linguistics.

Yale University, Graduate School of Arts and Sciences, Department of French, New Haven, CT 06520. Offers M Phil, MA, PhD. *Degree requirements:* For doctorate, 3 foreign languages, thesis/dissertation. *Entrance requirements:* For doctorate, GRE General Test.

York University, Faculty of Graduate Studies, Glendon College, Program in French Studies, Toronto, ON M3J 1P3, Canada. Offers MA. *Degree requirements:* For master's, thesis or alternative. Electronic applications accepted.

German

Arizona State University, Graduate College, College of Liberal Arts and Sciences, Division of Humanities, School of International Letters and Cultures, Program in German, Tempe, AZ 85287. Offers MA. *Degree requirements:* For master's, thesis or alternative. *Entrance requirements:* For master's, GRE.

Bowling Green State University, Graduate College, College of Arts and Sciences, Department of German, Russian, and East Asian Languages, Bowling Green, OH 43403. Offers German (MA, MAT); MA/MA. Part-time programs available. *Degree requirements:* For master's, one foreign language, thesis or alternative. *Entrance requirements:* For master's, GRE General Test. Additional exam requirements/recommendations for international students: Required—TOEFL. Electronic applications accepted.

Brigham Young University, Graduate Studies, College of Humanities, Department of Germanic and Slavic Languages, Provo, UT 84602. Offers German studies (MA). *Faculty:* 16 full-time (4 women), 2 part-time/adjunct (both women). *Students:* 5 full-time (all women), 1 (woman) part-time; includes 1 minority (Hispanic American). Average age 24. 3 applicants, 67% accepted, 2 enrolled. In 2008, 2 master's awarded. *Degree requirements:* For master's, 2 foreign languages, comprehensive exam, thesis. *Entrance requirements:* For master's, GRE General Test, bachelor's degree in German or related field. Additional exam requirements/recommendations for international students: Required—TOEFL (minimum score 213 computer-based). *Application deadline:* For fall admission, 2/1 priority date for domestic and international students. Application fee: $50. Electronic applications accepted. *Expenses:* Tuition: Full-time $5160; part-time $287 per credit hour. Tuition and fees vary according to program and student's religious affiliation. *Financial support:* In 2008–09, 5 students received support, including 4 teaching assistantships with full and partial tuition reimbursements available (averaging $7,580 per year); career-related internships or fieldwork, institutionally sponsored loans, scholarships/grants, tuition waivers (full and partial), and unspecified assistantships also available. Support available to part-time students. Financial award application deadline: 6/15. *Faculty research:* Second language acquisition, modern German literature, critical theory, German women authors, German dialects, German cinema, German drama. Total annual research expenditures: $4,450. *Unit head:* Dr. David K. Hart, Chair, 801-422-4923, Fax: 801-422-0268, E-mail: david_hart@byu.edu. *Application contact:* AnnMarie Hamar, Secretary to the Chair, 801-422-4923, Fax: 801-422-0268, E-mail: annmarie_hamar@byu.edu.

Brown University, Graduate School, Department of German Studies, Providence, RI 02912. Offers PhD, MA/PhD. *Degree requirements:* For doctorate, 2 foreign languages, thesis/dissertation, preliminary exam. *Entrance requirements:* For doctorate, GRE General Test.

California State University, Fullerton, Graduate Studies, College of Humanities and Social Sciences, Department of Modern Languages and Literatures, Fullerton, CA 92834-9480. Offers French (MA); German (MA); Spanish (MA); teaching English to speakers of other languages (MS). Part-time programs available. *Students:* 63 full-time (49 women), 79 part-time (65 women); includes 70 minority (21 Asian Americans or Pacific Islanders, 49 Hispanic Americans), 23 international. Average age 32. 118 applicants, 56% accepted, 43 enrolled. In 2008, 28 master's awarded. *Degree requirements:* For master's, comprehensive exam, thesis or alternative. *Entrance requirements:* For master's, minimum GPA of 2.5 in last 60 hours of course work, undergraduate major in a language. Application fee: $55. Tuition and fees vary according to degree level. *Financial support:* Federal Work-Study, institutionally sponsored loans, and scholarships/grants available. Support available to part-time students. Financial award application deadline: 3/1. *Unit head:* Dr. Janet Eyring, Chair, 657-278-3534. *Application contact:* Admissions/Applications, 657-278-2300.

California State University, Long Beach, Graduate Studies, College of Liberal Arts, Department of Romance, German, and Russian Languages and Literature, Program in German, Long Beach, CA 90840. Offers MA. Part-time programs available. *Students:* 5 full-time (3 women), 7 part-time (4 women); includes 3 minority (1 American Indian/Alaska Native, 2 Hispanic Americans). Average age 39. 5 applicants, 80% accepted, 4 enrolled. *Degree requirements:* For master's, one foreign language, comprehensive exam or thesis. *Application deadline:* For fall admission, 7/1 for domestic students. Applications are processed on a rolling basis. Application fee: $55. Electronic applications accepted. *Expenses:* Tuition, nonresident: full-time $11,160; part-time $372 per unit. Required fees: $4100; $1261 per semester. *Financial support:* Federal Work-Study, institutionally sponsored loans, and scholarships/grants available. Financial award application deadline: 3/2. *Faculty research:* Contemporary German society, baroque, Goethe, Wagner. *Unit head:* Dr. Lisa Vollendorf, Chair, 562-985-4318, Fax: 562-985-4259, E-mail: lvollend@csulb.edu. *Application contact:* Dr. Jeffrey High, Program Director, 562-985-5381, Fax: 562-985-2463, E-mail: jhigh@csulb.edu.

California State University, Sacramento, Graduate Studies, College of Social Sciences and Interdisciplinary Studies, Liberal Arts Program, Sacramento, CA 95819-6048. Offers French (MA); German (MA); Spanish (MA); theater arts (MA). *Degree requirements:* For master's, writing proficiency exam. *Entrance requirements:* Additional exam requirements/recommendations for international students: Required—TOEFL. Electronic applications accepted.

Columbia University, Graduate School of Arts and Sciences, Division of Humanities, Department of Germanic Languages, New York, NY 10027. Offers M Phil, MA, PhD. Part-time

German

Columbia University *(continued)*
programs available. *Degree requirements:* For master's, one foreign language, written exam; for doctorate, 2 foreign languages, thesis/dissertation. *Entrance requirements:* For master's and doctorate, GRE General Test, GRE Subject Test, sample of written work. Additional exam requirements/recommendations for international students: Required—TOEFL. *Faculty research:* German language and literature, comparative literature.

Cornell University, Graduate School, Graduate Fields of Arts and Sciences, Field of Germanic Studies, Ithaca, NY 14853-0001. Offers German area studies (MA, PhD); German intellectual history (MA, PhD); Germanic linguistics (MA, PhD); Germanic literature (MA, PhD); old Norse (MA, PhD). *Faculty:* 17 full-time (8 women). *Students:* 17 full-time (9 women); includes 3 minority (1 American Indian/Alaska Native, 1 Asian American or Pacific Islander, 1 Hispanic American), 6 international. Average age 29. 35 applicants, 20% accepted, 4 enrolled. In 2008, 2 doctorates awarded. Terminal master's awarded for partial completion of doctoral program. *Degree requirements:* For master's, one foreign language, thesis; for doctorate, 2 foreign languages, comprehensive exam, thesis/dissertation. *Entrance requirements:* For master's and doctorate, GRE General Test, fluency in German, writing sample, 2 letters of recommendation. Additional exam requirements/recommendations for international students: Required—TOEFL (minimum score 550 paper-based; 213 computer-based; 77 iBT). *Application deadline:* For fall admission, 1/15 for domestic students. Application fee: $70. Electronic applications accepted. *Expenses:* Tuition: Full-time $29,500. Required fees: $70. Full-time tuition and fees vary according to degree level, program and student level. *Financial support:* In 2008–09, 15 students received support, including 6 fellowships with full tuition reimbursements available, 9 teaching assistantships with full tuition reimbursements available; research assistantships with full tuition reimbursements available, institutionally sponsored loans, scholarships/grants, health care benefits, tuition waivers (full and partial), and unspecified assistantships also available. Financial award applicants required to submit FAFSA. *Faculty research:* Women's studies, minority literature, literature and intellectual history, theater and film studies, continental philosophy. *Unit head:* Director of Graduate Studies, 607-255-4047. *Application contact:* Graduate Field Assistant, 607-255-4047, E-mail: germanic_studies@cornell.edu.

Cornell University, Graduate School, Graduate Fields of Arts and Sciences, Field of Linguistics, Ithaca, NY 14853-0001. Offers applied linguistics (MA, PhD); East Asian linguistics (MA, PhD); English linguistics (MA, PhD); general linguistics (MA, PhD); Germanic linguistics (MA, PhD); Indo-European linguistics (MA, PhD); phonetics (MA, PhD); phonological theory (MA, PhD); Romance linguistics (MA, PhD); second language acquisition (MA, PhD); semantics (MA, PhD); Slavic linguistics (MA, PhD); sociolinguistics (MA, PhD); South Asian linguistics (MA, PhD); Southeast Asian linguistics (MA, PhD); syntactic theory (MA, PhD). *Faculty:* 15 full-time (6 women). *Students:* 32 full-time (15 women); includes 1 minority (Hispanic American), 16 international. Average age 30. 93 applicants, 16% accepted, 7 enrolled. In 2008, 5 master's, 7 doctorates awarded. Terminal master's awarded for partial completion of doctoral program. *Degree requirements:* For master's, one foreign language, thesis; for doctorate, one foreign language, comprehensive exam, thesis/dissertation. *Entrance requirements:* For master's and doctorate, GRE General Test, 2 letters of recommendation. Additional exam requirements/recommendations for international students: Required—TOEFL (minimum score 600 paper-based; 250 computer-based; 77 iBT). *Application deadline:* For fall admission, 1/15 for domestic students. Application fee: $70. Electronic applications accepted. *Expenses:* Tuition: Full-time $29,500. Required fees: $70. Full-time tuition and fees vary according to degree level, program and student level. *Financial support:* In 2008–09, 32 students received support, including 11 fellowships with full tuition reimbursements available, 4 research assistantships with full tuition reimbursements available, 17 teaching assistantships with full tuition reimbursements available; institutionally sponsored loans, scholarships/grants, health care benefits, tuition waivers (full and partial), and unspecified assistantships also available. Financial award applicants required to submit FAFSA. *Faculty research:* Phonology and phonetics; syntax and semantics; historical linguistics; philosophy of language; language acquisition. *Unit head:* Director of Graduate Studies, 607-255-1105. *Application contact:* Graduate Field Assistant, 607-255-1105, E-mail: lingfield@cornell.edu.

Dalhousie University, Faculty of Arts and Social Science, Department of German, Halifax, NS B3H 4R2, Canada. Offers MA. *Entrance requirements:* Additional exam requirements/recommendations for international students: Required—TOEFL, IELTS, 1 of 5 approved tests: TOEFL, IELTS, CANTEST, CAEL, Michigan English Language Assessment Battery. *Application deadline:* For fall admission, 6/1 for domestic students, 4/1 for international students; for winter admission, 10/31 for domestic students, 8/31 for international students; for spring admission, 2/28 for domestic students, 12/31 for international students. Application fee: $70. Electronic applications accepted. *Financial support:* Career-related internships or fieldwork, scholarships/grants, and health care benefits available. *Faculty research:* Baroque age in Germany, literature and philosophy of German idealism, twentieth-century German culture, aesthetics, reception of the Islamic Orient, reception of Greek and Roman antiquity; realism and ornament. *Unit head:* Dr. Jane Curran, Chair, 902-494-1091, Fax: 902-494-2719, E-mail: german@dal.ca. *Application contact:* Annett Gaudig, Administrative Secretary, 902-494-2161, Fax: 902-494-2719, E-mail: german@dal.ca.

Duke University, Graduate School, Interdisciplinary Program in German Studies, Durham, NC 27708-0256. Offers PhD. Part-time programs available. *Degree requirements:* For doctorate, thesis/dissertation. *Entrance requirements:* For doctorate, GRE General Test. Additional exam requirements/recommendations for international students: Required—TOEFL (minimum score 550 paper-based; 213 computer-based; 83 iBT), IELTS (minimum score 7). Electronic applications accepted.

Eastern Michigan University, Graduate School, College of Arts and Sciences, Department of Foreign Languages and Bilingual Studies, Program in Foreign Languages, Ypsilanti, MI 48197. Offers French (MA); German (MA); German for business (Graduate Certificate); Hispanic language and cultures (Graduate Certificate); Japanese business practices (Graduate Certificate); Spanish (MA). Part-time and evening/weekend programs available. Post-baccalaureate distance learning degree programs offered (minimal on-campus study). *Degree requirements:* For master's, one foreign language, thesis optional. *Entrance requirements:* Additional exam requirements/recommendations for international students: Required—TOEFL.

Florida State University, Graduate Studies, College of Arts and Sciences, Department of Modern Languages, Program in German, Tallahassee, FL 32306. Offers MA. *Degree requirements:* For master's, thesis optional. *Entrance requirements:* For master's, GRE General Test or minimum GPA of 3.0. Additional exam requirements/recommendations for international students: Required—TOEFL (minimum score 550 paper-based; 213 computer-based). Electronic applications accepted.

Georgetown University, Graduate School of Arts and Sciences, BMW Center for German and European Studies, Washington, DC 20057. Offers MA, MA/JD, MA/PhD. *Degree requirements:* For master's, 2 foreign languages, comprehensive exam. *Entrance requirements:* For master's, GRE General Test. Additional exam requirements/recommendations for international students: Required—TOEFL. *Faculty research:* Trans-Atlantic relations, European Union, German and European Studies.

Georgetown University, Graduate School of Arts and Sciences, Department of German, Washington, DC 20057. Offers MA, MS, PhD, MA/PhD. *Degree requirements:* For master's, 2 foreign languages, research project; for doctorate, 3 foreign languages, thesis/dissertation. *Entrance requirements:* For master's, GRE General Test. Additional exam requirements/recommendations for international students: Required—TOEFL.

Georgia State University, College of Arts and Sciences, Department of Modern and Classical Languages, Program in German, Atlanta, GA 30303-3083. Offers MA. Evening/weekend programs available. *Degree requirements:* For master's, one foreign language, thesis or alternative, general exam. *Entrance requirements:* For master's, GRE General Test. Additional

exam requirements/recommendations for international students: Required—TOEFL. Electronic applications accepted. *Faculty research:* Medieval and twentieth-century German literature.

Georgia State University, College of Arts and Sciences, Department of Modern and Classical Languages, Program in Translation and Interpretation, Atlanta, GA 30303-3083. Offers French (Certificate); German (Certificate); Spanish (Certificate). Electronic applications accepted.

Graduate School and University Center of the City University of New York, Graduate Studies, Program in Comparative Literature, New York, NY 10016-4039. Offers comparative literature (MA, PhD), including classics (PhD), German (PhD), Italian (PhD). Terminal master's awarded for partial completion of doctoral program. *Degree requirements:* For master's, 2 foreign languages, comprehensive exam, thesis; for doctorate, 3 foreign languages, comprehensive exam, thesis/dissertation. *Entrance requirements:* For master's and doctorate, GRE General Test. Additional exam requirements/recommendations for international students: Required—TOEFL. Electronic applications accepted.

Graduate School and University Center of the City University of New York, Graduate Studies, Program in Germanic Languages and Literatures, New York, NY 10016-4039. Offers MA, PhD. *Degree requirements:* For master's, one foreign language, thesis; for doctorate, 2 foreign languages, thesis/dissertation. *Entrance requirements:* For master's and doctorate, GRE General Test.

Harvard University, Graduate School of Arts and Sciences, Department of Germanic Languages and Literatures, Cambridge, MA 02138. Offers German (PhD); Scandinavian (PhD). Terminal master's awarded for partial completion of doctoral program. *Degree requirements:* For doctorate, 2 foreign languages, thesis/dissertation, exams. *Entrance requirements:* For doctorate, GRE General Test, German writing sample. Additional exam requirements/recommendations for international students: Required—TOEFL. *Expenses:* Tuition: Full-time $32,556. Required fees: $1426. Full-time tuition and fees vary according to program and student level.

Hofstra University, School of Education, Health, and Human Services, Department of Curriculum and Teaching, Program in Foreign Language Education, Hempstead, NY 11549. Offers foreign language education (MA, MS Ed), including French, German, Russian, Spanish. Part-time and evening/weekend programs available. *Students:* 2 full-time (both women), 4 part-time (3 women); includes 3 minority (all Hispanic Americans). Average age 32. 7 applicants, 71% accepted, 0 enrolled. In 2008, 2 master's awarded. *Degree requirements:* For master's, one foreign language, thesis. *Entrance requirements:* For master's, 2 letters of recommendation, teacher certification (MA), essay. Additional exam requirements/recommendations for international students: Required—TOEFL (minimum score 550 paper-based; 213 computer-based; 80 iBT). *Application deadline:* Applications are processed on a rolling basis. Application fee: $60. Electronic applications accepted. *Expenses:* Tuition: Full-time $15,300; part-time $850 per credit. Required fees: $970; $165 per term. Tuition and fees vary according to program. *Financial support:* In 2008–09, 1 student received support; fellowships with full and partial tuition reimbursements available, research assistantships with full and partial tuition reimbursements available, Federal Work-Study, institutionally sponsored loans, scholarships/grants, and tuition waivers (full and partial) available. Support available to part-time students. Financial award applicants required to submit FAFSA. *Faculty research:* Contemporary Spanish cultural studies, twentieth century Spanish theater, identity and post-coloniality, Romance philology, politics of language, decolonization, Spanish imperial Africa and Latin America, twentieth century Latin American poetry. Total annual research expenditures: $5,000. *Unit head:* Dr. David Powell, Chairperson, 516-463-5485, Fax: 516-463-2310, E-mail: rlldap@hofstra.edu. *Application contact:* Carol Drummer, Dean of Graduate Admissions, 516-463-4876, Fax: 516-463-4664, E-mail: gradstudent@hofstra.edu.

Illinois State University, Graduate School, College of Arts and Sciences, Department of Foreign Languages, Literatures and Cultures, Normal, IL 61790-2200. Offers French (MA); French and German (MA); French and Spanish (MA); German (MA); German and Spanish (MA); Spanish (MA). *Degree requirements:* For master's, variable foreign language requirement, comprehensive exam, 1 term of residency. *Entrance requirements:* For master's, GRE General Test, minimum GPA of 2.8 in last 60 hours of course work.

Indiana University Bloomington, University Graduate School, College of Arts and Sciences, Department of Germanic Studies, Bloomington, IN 47405-7000. Offers German philology and linguistics (PhD); German studies (MA, PhD), including German (MA), German literature and culture (MA), German literature and linguistics (MA); medieval German studies (PhD); teaching German (MAT). *Faculty:* 13 full-time (4 women), 6 part-time/adjunct (2 women). *Students:* 33 full-time (16 women), 4 part-time (2 women); includes 1 minority (Hispanic American), 9 international. Average age 30. 38 applicants, 29% accepted, 3 enrolled. In 2008, 6 master's, 3 doctorates awarded. Terminal master's awarded for partial completion of doctoral program. *Degree requirements:* For master's, one foreign language, project; for doctorate, one foreign language, comprehensive exam, thesis/dissertation. *Entrance requirements:* For master's, GRE General Test, BA in German or equivalent; for doctorate, GRE General Test, MA in German or equivalent. Additional exam requirements/recommendations for international students: Required—TOEFL. *Application deadline:* For fall admission, 1/15 priority date for domestic students, 12/15 for international students; for spring admission, 9/1 priority date for domestic students, 9/1 for international students. Applications are processed on a rolling basis. Application fee: $50 ($60 for international students). *Expenses:* Tuition, area resident: Part-time $291.97 per credit hour. Tuition, state resident: part-time $291.97 per credit hour. Tuition, nonresident: part-time $850.33 per credit hour. Required fees: $110 per semester. Tuition and fees vary according to course load and program. *Financial support:* In 2008–09, 7 fellowships with full and partial tuition reimbursements (averaging $20,000 per year), 1 research assistantship (averaging $13,025 per year), 22 teaching assistantships with full tuition reimbursements (averaging $13,025 per year) were awarded; Federal Work-Study, institutionally sponsored loans, scholarships/grants, and unspecified assistantships also available. Support available to part-time students. Financial award application deadline: 1/15; financial award applicants required to submit FAFSA. *Faculty research:* German (and European) literature: medieval to modern/postmodern, German and culture studies, Germanic philology, literary theory, literature and the other arts. *Unit head:* William Rasch, Department Chairman, 812-855-7947, Fax: 812-855-8292, E-mail: wrasch@indiana.edu. *Application contact:* Michelle Dunbar, Graduate Secretary, 812-855-7947, E-mail: midunbar@indiana.edu.

The Johns Hopkins University, Zanvyl Krieger School of Arts and Sciences, Department of German and Romance Languages, Baltimore, MD 21218-2699. Offers French (PhD); German (PhD); Italian (PhD); romance languages (PhD); Spanish (PhD). *Degree requirements:* For doctorate, 2 foreign languages, thesis/dissertation. *Entrance requirements:* For doctorate, GRE General Test. Additional exam requirements/recommendations for international students: Required—TOEFL (minimum score 600 paper-based; 250 computer-based). Electronic applications accepted.

Kansas State University, Graduate School, College of Arts and Sciences, Department of Modern Languages, Manhattan, KS 66506. Offers French (MA); German (MA); Spanish (MA). Part-time and evening/weekend programs available. Postbaccalaureate distance learning degree programs offered (minimal on-campus study). *Faculty:* 15 full-time (7 women). *Students:* 18 full-time (11 women), 10 part-time (8 women); includes 4 minority (all Hispanic Americans), 11 international. Average age 32. 6 applicants, 100% accepted, 6 enrolled. In 2008, 4 master's awarded. *Degree requirements:* For master's, thesis optional. *Entrance requirements:* For master's, teaching certificate. Additional exam requirements/recommendations for international students: Required—TOEFL (minimum score 560 paper-based). *Application deadline:* For fall admission, 2/1 priority date for domestic and international students; for spring admission, 10/1 for domestic students, 8/1 priority date for international students. Applications are processed on a rolling basis. Application fee: $30 ($55 for international students). *Expenses:* Tuition, area resident: Full-time $6466; part-time $269.40 per credit hour. Tuition, state resident: full-time $6466; part-time $269.40 per credit hour. Tuition, nonresident: full-time $14,874; part-time $619.75 per credit hour. Required fees: $673; $23.40 per credit hour. Tuition and fees vary according to campus/location. *Financial support:* In 2008–09, 13 teaching assistantships with full tuition reimbursements (averaging $10,546 per year) were awarded; fellowships, Federal Work-Study, institutionally sponsored loans, and scholarships/grants also available. Support available to part-time students. Financial award application deadline: 3/1; financial award applicants required to submit FAFSA. *Faculty research:* Second language acquisitions; Chicano literature; Francophone literature; cultural studies; German, French, Spanish, and Spanish-American literature from the Middle Ages to the modern era. *Unit head:* Robert Corum, Head, 785-532-1987, Fax: 785-532-7004, E-mail: corum@ksu.edu. *Application contact:* Claire Dehon, Director, 785-532-1929, Fax: 785-532-7004, E-mail: dehoncl@ksu.edu.

Kent State University, College of Arts and Sciences, Department of Modern and Classical Language Studies, Kent, OH 44242-0001. Offers French literature (MA); French, Spanish, German and Latin pedagogy (MA); German literature (MA); Spanish literature (MA); translation (MA), including French, German, Japanese, Russian, Spanish; translation studies (PhD). Part-time and evening/weekend programs available. *Degree requirements:* For master's, one foreign language, comprehensive exam (for some programs), thesis (for some programs); for doctorate, comprehensive exam, thesis/dissertation (for some programs). *Entrance requirements:* For master's, minimum GPA of 3.0, writing sample, audio tape or CD; for doctorate, 3 recommendations. Additional exam requirements/recommendations for international students: Required—TOEFL (minimum score 197 computer-based). Electronic applications accepted. *Faculty research:* Literature, pedagogy, applied linguistics, translation studies.

McGill University, Faculty of Graduate and Postdoctoral Studies, Faculty of Arts, Department of German Studies, Montréal, QC H3A 2T5, Canada. Offers MA, PhD.

Memorial University of Newfoundland, School of Graduate Studies, Department of German and Russian, St. John's, NL A1C 5S7, Canada. Offers German language and literature (M Phil, MA). Part-time programs available. *Degree requirements:* For master's, one foreign language, thesis (for some programs), comprehensive exam (M Phil). *Entrance requirements:* For master's, honors degree (minimum 2nd class standing). Electronic applications accepted. *Faculty research:* German literature from the Middle Ages to the twentieth century, German studies.

Michigan State University, The Graduate School, College of Arts and Letters, Department of Linguistics and Germanic, Slavic, Asian, and African Languages, East Lansing, MI 48824. Offers German studies (MA, PhD); linguistics (MA, PhD); teaching English to speakers of other languages (MA). Part-time and evening/weekend programs available. *Entrance requirements:* For master's, GRE General Test, minimum GPA of 3.2 in last 2 undergraduate years, 2 years of college-level foreign language, 3 letters of recommendation, portfolio (German studies); for doctorate, GRE General Test, minimum graduate GPA of 3.5, 3 letters of recommendation, master's degree or sufficient graduate course work in linguistics or language of study, master's thesis or major research paper. Additional exam requirements/recommendations for international students: Required—TOEFL. Electronic applications accepted.

Middlebury College, Language Schools, German School, Middlebury, VT 05753. Offers MA, DML. *Faculty:* 5 full-time (2 women). *Students:* 26 full-time (12 women); includes 1 minority (Hispanic American). Average age 30. 47 applicants, 70% accepted, 30 enrolled. In 2008, 15 master's awarded. *Degree requirements:* For master's, one foreign language; for doctorate, 2 foreign languages, comprehensive exam, thesis/dissertation, residence abroad, teaching experience. *Entrance requirements:* For master's, placement exam, 3 letters of recommendation. *Application deadline:* Applications are processed on a rolling basis. Application fee: $55. Electronic applications accepted. *Financial support:* Scholarships/grants available. Financial award applicants required to submit FAFSA. *Unit head:* Dr. Doris Kirchner, Director, 802-443-5203, Fax: 802-443-2075, E-mail: dkirchner@middlebury.edu. *Application contact:* Christina Ellison, Coordinator, 802-443-5203, Fax: 802-443-2075, E-mail: ccartwri@middlebury.edu.

Millersville University of Pennsylvania, Graduate School, School of Humanities and Social Sciences, Department of Foreign Languages, Program in German, Millersville, PA 17551-0302. Offers M Ed, MA. Part-time programs available. *Faculty:* 9 full-time (5 women), 4 part-time/adjunct (3 women). *Students:* 2 part-time (both women). Average age 27. In 2008, 3 master's awarded. *Degree requirements:* For master's, comprehensive exam, thesis optional. *Entrance requirements:* For master's, GRE or MAT. Additional exam requirements/recommendations for international students: Required—TOEFL (minimum score 500 paper-based; 183 computer-based; 65 iBT), TOEFL may be replaced by IELTS with score of 6 or higher. *Application deadline:* For fall admission, 2/1 priority date for domestic and international students; for winter admission, 10/1 priority date for domestic and international students; for spring admission, 10/1 priority date for domestic and international students. Applications are processed on a rolling basis. Application fee: $40. Electronic applications accepted. *Expenses:* Tuition, state resident: full-time $6430; part-time $357 per credit. Tuition, nonresident: full-time $10,288; part-time $572 per credit. Required fees: $1937; $73.50 per credit. One-time fee: $88 part-time. Tuition and fees vary according to course load. *Financial support:* Research assistantships, institutionally sponsored loans and unspecified assistantships available. Support available to part-time students. Financial award application deadline: 3/15; financial award applicants required to submit FAFSA. *Unit head:* Dr. Christine M. Gaudry-Hudson, Coordinator of Foreign Language Graduate Program, 717-872-3663, E-mail: christine.gaudry-hudson@millersville.edu. *Application contact:* Dr. Victor S. DeSantis, Dean of Graduate and Professional Studies, 717-872-3099, Fax: 717-872-3453, E-mail: victor.desantis@millersville.edu.

Mississippi State University, College of Arts and Sciences, Department of Foreign Languages, Mississippi State, MS 39762. Offers French (MA); French/German (MA); German (MA); Spanish (MA); Spanish/French (MA); Spanish/German (MA). Part-time programs available. *Degree requirements:* For master's, one foreign language, thesis optional, comprehensive oral or written exam. *Entrance requirements:* For master's, minimum GPA of 2.75. Additional exam requirements/recommendations for international students: Required—TOEFL (minimum score 525 paper-based). *Faculty research:* French, German, Spanish literature from medieval to present; gender and cultural studies in French; Spanish American literature; foreign language methodology; linguistics.

Missouri State University, Graduate College, College of Arts and Letters, Department of Modern and Classical Languages, Springfield, MO 65804-0094. Offers secondary education (MS Ed), including French, German, Spanish. Part-time programs available. *Faculty:* 5 full-time (2 women). *Students:* 2 full-time (1 woman), 2 part-time (both women). Average age 30. 1 applicant, 100% accepted, 0 enrolled. In 2008, 4 master's awarded. *Entrance requirements:* For master's, grades 9-12 teaching certification. Additional exam requirements/recommendations for international students: Required—TOEFL (minimum score 550 paper-based; 213 computer-based; 79 iBT), IELTS (minimum score 6). *Application deadline:* For fall admission, 7/20 priority date for domestic students, 5/1 for international students; for spring admission, 12/20 priority date for domestic students, 9/1 for international students. Applications are processed on a rolling basis. Application fee: $35 ($50 for international students). Electronic applications accepted. *Expenses:* Tuition, state resident: full-time $3852; part-time $214 per credit hour. Tuition, nonresident: full-time $7524; part-time $418 per credit hour. Required fees: $230 per semester. Tuition and fees vary according to course level and course load. *Financial support:* Federal Work-Study, institutionally sponsored loans, scholarships/grants, and unspecified assistantships available. Financial award applicants required to submit FAFSA. *Unit head:* Dr. Madeleine Kernen, Head, 417-836-7626, E-mail: mcl@missouristate.edu. *Application contact:* Eric Eckert, Coordinator of Admissions and Recruitment, 417-836-5331, Fax: 417-836-6888, E-mail: ericeckert@missouristate.edu.

New York University, Graduate School of Arts and Science, Department of German, New York, NY 10012-1019. Offers German studies and critical thought (MA, PhD). Part-time programs available. Terminal master's awarded for partial completion of doctoral program. *Degree requirements:* For master's, one foreign language, thesis; for doctorate, 2 foreign languages, thesis/dissertation. *Entrance requirements:* For master's, GRE Subject Test; for doctorate, GRE Subject Test, sample of written work. Additional exam requirements/recommendations for international students: Required—TOEFL. *Faculty research:* Eighteenth to twentieth century literature, culture and critical thought, film and visual culture, philosophy, critical theory.

Northwestern University, The Graduate School, Judd A. and Marjorie Weinberg College of Arts and Sciences, Program in German Literature and Critical Thought, Evanston, IL 60208. Offers PhD. Admissions and degrees offered through The Graduate School. *Degree requirements:* For doctorate, one foreign language, thesis/dissertation. *Entrance requirements:* For doctorate, GRE General Test. Additional exam requirements/recommendations for international students: Required—TOEFL. Electronic applications accepted. *Faculty research:* Eighteenth through twentieth century German literature, comparative literature, theory, philosophy, language pedagogy.

The Ohio State University, Graduate School, College of Humanities, Department of Germanic Languages and Literatures, Columbus, OH 43210. Offers MA, PhD. *Degree requirements:* For master's, one foreign language, thesis optional; for doctorate, 2 foreign languages, thesis/dissertation. *Entrance requirements:* For master's and doctorate, GRE General Test. Additional exam requirements/recommendations for international students: Required—TOEFL (minimum score 600 paper-based; 250 computer-based). Electronic applications accepted. *Faculty research:* German literature, Germanic philology, linguistics.

Penn State University Park, Graduate School, College of the Liberal Arts, Department of Germanic and Slavic Languages and Literatures, State College, University Park, PA 16802-1503. Offers German (MA, PhD). *Faculty research:* Literature, literary theory, culture, language pedagogy.

Portland State University, Graduate Studies, College of Liberal Arts and Sciences, Department of Foreign Languages and Literatures, Portland, OR 97207-0751. Offers foreign literature and language (MA); French (MA); German (MA); Japanese (MA); Spanish (MA). Part-time programs available. *Faculty:* 43 full-time (27 women), 28 part-time/adjunct (19 women). *Students:* 29 full-time (24 women), 17 part-time (11 women); includes 6 minority (1 African American, 1 Asian American or Pacific Islander, 4 Hispanic Americans), 11 international. Average age 32. 23 applicants, 91% accepted, 20 enrolled. In 2008, 14 master's awarded. *Degree requirements:* For master's, one foreign language, thesis (for some programs). *Entrance requirements:* Additional exam requirements/recommendations for international students: Required—TOEFL (minimum score 550 paper-based; 213 computer-based). *Application deadline:* For fall admission, 4/1 for domestic students, 3/1 for international students; for winter admission, 9/1 for domestic students, 7/1 for international students; for spring admission, 11/1 for domestic and international students. Applications are processed on a rolling basis. Application fee: $50. *Expenses:* Tuition, area resident: Full-time $8763; part-time $179 per credit hour. Tuition, state resident: full-time $8763; part-time $298 per credit hour. Tuition, nonresident: full-time $12,981; part-time $426 per credit hour. Required fees: $1242. One-time fee: $250. Tuition and fees vary according to course load and program. *Financial support:* In 2008–09, 6 teaching assistantships with full tuition reimbursements (averaging $9,359 per year) were awarded; research assistantships with full tuition reimbursements, Federal Work-Study, scholarships/grants, and unspecified assistantships also available. Support available to part-time students. Financial award application deadline: 3/1; financial award applicants required to submit FAFSA. *Faculty research:* Foreign language pedagogy, applied and social linguistics, literary history and criticism. Total annual research expenditures: $6,847. *Unit head:* Dr. Sandra F. Freels, Chair, 503-725-3522, Fax: 503-725-5276. *Application contact:* Karen Popp, Office Coordinator, 503-725-3522, E-mail: poppk@pdx.edu.

Princeton University, Graduate School, Department of German, Princeton, NJ 08544-1019. Offers PhD. *Degree requirements:* For doctorate, 2 foreign languages, thesis/dissertation. *Entrance requirements:* For doctorate, GRE General Test. Additional exam requirements/recommendations for international students: Required—TOEFL (minimum score 600 paper-based; 250 computer-based). Electronic applications accepted.

Purdue University, Graduate School, College of Liberal Arts, Department of Foreign Languages and Literatures, West Lafayette, IN 47907. Offers French (MA, MAT, PhD), including French (MA, PhD), French education (MAT); German (MA, MAT, PhD), including German (MA, PhD), German education (MAT); Spanish (MA, MAT, PhD), including Spanish (MA, PhD), Spanish education (MAT). Terminal master's awarded for partial completion of doctoral program. *Degree requirements:* For master's, one foreign language; for doctorate, 2 foreign languages, thesis/dissertation. *Entrance requirements:* For master's and doctorate, GRE, writing sample, sample recording of English and language of study. Additional exam requirements/recommendations for international students: Required—TOEFL. Electronic applications accepted. *Faculty research:* Linguistics, semiotics, literary criticism, pedagogy.

Queen's University at Kingston, School of Graduate Studies and Research, Faculty of Arts and Sciences, Department of German Language and Literature, Kingston, ON K7L 3N6, Canada. Offers MA, PhD. Part-time programs available. *Degree requirements:* For master's, thesis optional; for doctorate, one foreign language, comprehensive exam, thesis/dissertation. *Entrance requirements:* For master's, 7 German courses, honors bachelors degree in German; for doctorate, MA or equivalent in German. Additional exam requirements/recommendations for international students: Required—TOEFL. Electronic applications accepted. *Faculty research:* Goethe and Weimar classicism, Romanticism, nineteenth- and twentieth-century German literature.

Rider University, Department of Graduate Education, Leadership and Counseling, Teacher Certification Program, Lawrenceville, NJ 08648-3001. Offers business education (Certificate); elementary education (Certificate); English as a second language (Certificate); English education (Certificate); mathematics education (Certificate); preschool to grade 3 (Certificate); science education (Certificate); social studies education (Certificate); world languages (Certificate), including French, German, Spanish. Part-time programs available. *Degree requirements:* For Certificate, internship, professional portfolio. *Entrance requirements:* For degree, PRAXIS, resumé. Additional exam requirements/recommendations for international students: Required—TOEFL (minimum score 550 paper-based; 213 computer-based). Electronic applications accepted. *Faculty research:* Conceptual foundations for optimal development of creativity; creative theory, cognitive processes in mathematics learning, teacher collaboration.

Rutgers, The State University of New Jersey, New Brunswick, Graduate School, Program in German, Piscataway, NJ 08854-8097. Offers German (MAT, PhD); German literature (MA, PhD). Part-time and evening/weekend programs available. Terminal master's awarded for partial completion of doctoral program. *Degree requirements:* For master's, one foreign language, comprehensive exam, thesis or alternative; for doctorate, 2 foreign languages, comprehensive exam, thesis/dissertation. *Entrance requirements:* For master's and doctorate, GRE General Test. Additional exam requirements/recommendations for international students: Required—TOEFL. Electronic applications accepted. *Faculty research:* Literature and ideology; early German novella; narrative structures, mythology, psychology, and realist literature; German-American cultural history; literary theory and aesthetics; German film.

San Francisco State University, Division of Graduate Studies, College of Humanities, Department of Foreign Languages and Literatures, Program in German, San Francisco, CA 94132-1722. Offers MA.

Stanford University, School of Humanities and Sciences, Department of German Studies, Stanford, CA 94305-9991. Offers MA, PhD. *Degree requirements:* For master's, one foreign language, oral exam; for doctorate, 2 foreign languages, thesis/dissertation, oral exam, qualifying paper and exam. *Entrance requirements:* For master's and doctorate, GRE General Test. Additional exam requirements/recommendations for international students: Required—TOEFL. Electronic applications accepted.

Texas Tech University, Graduate School, College of Arts and Sciences, Department of Classical and Modern Languages and Literatures, Program in German, Lubbock, TX 79409. Offers MA. *Students:* 6 full-time (2 women), 4 part-time (3 women), 3 international. Average

German

Texas Tech University (continued)

age 34. 6 applicants, 100% accepted, 4 enrolled. In 2008, 2 master's awarded. *Entrance requirements:* For master's, GRE General Test. Additional exam requirements/recommendations for international students: Required—TOEFL (minimum score 550 paper-based; 213 computer-based). *Application deadline:* For fall admission, 3/1 priority date for international students; for spring admission, 11/1 priority date for international students. Applications are processed on a rolling basis. Application fee: $50 ($60 for international students). Electronic applications accepted. *Expenses:* Tuition, area resident: Part-time $194 per credit hour. Tuition, state resident: full-time $4648; part-time $194 per credit hour. Tuition, nonresident: full-time $11,392; part-time $475 per credit hour. Required fees: $2206; $69 per credit hour. $389 per semester. *Financial support:* Research assistantships with partial tuition reimbursements, teaching assistantships with partial tuition reimbursements available. Financial award application deadline: 4/15. *Faculty research:* German literature, Goethe, business German, German culture, German in the southwest. *Unit head:* Dr. Charles A. Grair, Graduate Advisor and Associate Professor of German, 806-742-3145 Ext. 275, Fax: 806-742-3306, E-mail: charles.grair@ttu.edu. *Application contact:* Liz Hildebrand, Senior Advisor, 806-742-4055, Fax: 806-742-3306, E-mail: liz.hildebrand@ttu.edu.

Tufts University, Graduate School of Arts and Sciences, Department of Russian and German, Medford, MA 02155. Offers German (MA). Part-time programs available. *Degree requirements:* For master's, one foreign language, oral and written exam. *Entrance requirements:* Additional exam requirements/recommendations for international students: Required—TOEFL (minimum score 550 paper-based; 213 computer-based; 80 iBT). Electronic applications accepted.

Université de Montréal, Faculty of Arts and Sciences, Department of Literatures and Modern Languages, Program in German Studies, Montréal, QC H3C 3J7, Canada. Offers MA. *Students:* 6 full-time (2 women), 7 part-time (5 women). 7 applicants, 43% accepted, 2 enrolled. In 2008, 4 master's awarded. *Degree requirements:* For master's, 2 foreign languages, thesis. *Application deadline:* For fall admission, 2/1 priority date for domestic students; for winter admission, 11/1 priority date for domestic students; for spring admission, 2/1 priority date for domestic students. Application fee: $100. Electronic applications accepted. *Financial support:* Teaching assistantships available. *Unit head:* Nikola von Merveldt, Responsible for German Studies Program, 514-343-5905, Fax: 514-343-2255, E-mail: n.von.merveldt@umontreal.ca. *Application contact:* Nikola von Merveldt, Responsible for German Studies Program, 514-343-5905, Fax: 514-343-2255, E-mail: n.von.merveldt@umontreal.ca.

The University of Alabama, Graduate School, College of Arts and Sciences, Department of Modern Languages and Classics, Tuscaloosa, AL 35487. Offers French (MA, PhD); French and Spanish (PhD); German (MA); Romance languages (MA, PhD); Spanish (MA, PhD). Part-time programs available. *Faculty:* 21 full-time (11 women). *Students:* 45 full-time (35 women), 12 part-time (7 women); includes 13 minority (6 African Americans, 7 Hispanic Americans), 11 international. Average age 32. 25 applicants, 68% accepted, 11 enrolled. In 2008, 17 master's, 4 doctorates awarded. *Degree requirements:* For master's, comprehensive exam, thesis optional; for doctorate, one foreign language, thesis/dissertation, preliminary exam. *Entrance requirements:* For master's and doctorate, minimum GPA of 3.0, writing sample. Additional exam requirements/recommendations for international students: Required—TOEFL or IELTS. *Application deadline:* For fall admission, 7/6 priority date for domestic students, 1/15 priority date for international students; for spring admission, 12/6 priority date for domestic students, 6/1 priority date for international students. Applications are processed on a rolling basis. Application fee: $31. Electronic applications accepted. *Expenses:* Tuition, area resident: Full-time $6400. Tuition, state resident: full-time $6400. Tuition, nonresident: full-time $18,000. *Financial support:* In 2008–09, 7 students received support, including 1 fellowship, research assistantships with full tuition reimbursements available (averaging $10,291 per year), 6 teaching assistantships with full tuition reimbursements available (averaging $10,291 per year); career-related internships or fieldwork, Federal Work-Study, institutionally sponsored loans, and scholarships/grants also available. Financial award application deadline: 7/14. *Faculty research:* Non-English literature, linguistics, culture, film. Total annual research expenditures: $9,630. *Unit head:* Dr. Michael Picone, Chair and Professor, 205-348-5054, Fax: 205-348-2042, E-mail: mpicone@bama.ua.edu. *Application contact:* Dr. K. Barbara Fischer, Graduate Director and Associate Professor, 205-348-8465, Fax: 205-348-2042, E-mail: bfischer@bama.ua.edu.

University of Alberta, Faculty of Graduate Studies and Research, Department of Modern Languages and Cultural Studies, Edmonton, AB T6G 2E1, Canada. Offers applied linguistics (Germanic, Romance, Slavic) (MA); French language, literatures and linguistics (PhD); French language, literatures, and linguistics (MA); Germanic languages, literatures and linguistics (PhD); Germanic languages, literatures, and linguistics (MA); Italian studies (MA); Slavic languages and literatures (Russian, Ukrainian) (MA, PhD); Slavic linguistics (Russian, Ukrainian) (MA, PhD); Spanish and Latin American studies (MA, PhD); Ukrainian folklore (MA, PhD). Part-time programs available. *Degree requirements:* For master's, one foreign language, thesis; for doctorate, 2 foreign languages, comprehensive exam, thesis/dissertation. *Entrance requirements:* For master's and doctorate, 1 language other than English. Additional exam requirements/recommendations for international students: Required—Michigan English Language Assessment Battery or TOEFL (paper score 550; computer score 213). Electronic applications accepted. *Faculty research:* Russian/Ukrainian studies; German studies; contemporary Latin American, French and Francophone studies; Italian studies.

The University of Arizona, Graduate College, College of Humanities, Department of German Studies, Tucson, AZ 85721. Offers German (MA, PhD). *Degree requirements:* For master's, one foreign language, comprehensive exam, oral exam; for doctorate, 2 foreign languages, comprehensive exam, thesis/dissertation, oral exam, oral defense. *Entrance requirements:* For master's, GRE, minimum GPA of 3.0, 3 letters of recommendation, statement of purpose, audio sample. Additional exam requirements/recommendations for international students: Required—TOEFL (minimum score 550 paper-based). Electronic applications accepted. *Faculty research:* Literature, language, and foreign language pedagogy; computer-assisted text analysis.

University of Arkansas, Graduate School, J. William Fulbright College of Arts and Sciences, Department of Foreign Languages, Program in German, Fayetteville, AR 72701-1201. Offers MA. *Degree requirements:* For master's, variable foreign language requirement.

The University of British Columbia, Faculty of Arts and Faculty of Graduate Studies, Department of Central, Eastern and Northern European Studies, Vancouver, BC V6T 1Z1, Canada. Offers Germanic studies (MA, PhD). Part-time programs available. *Degree requirements:* For master's, one foreign language, thesis optional, exam; for doctorate, comprehensive exam, thesis/dissertation. *Entrance requirements:* For master's, BA in German; for doctorate, MA in German. Additional exam requirements/recommendations for international students: Required—TOEFL (minimum score 550 paper-based; 213 computer-based). Electronic applications accepted. *Faculty research:* Second language acquisition, media theory, performance theory, gender studies, cultural studies.

University of Calgary, Faculty of Graduate Studies, Faculty of Humanities, Department of Germanic, Slavic and East Asian Studies, Calgary, AB T2N 1N4, Canada. Offers German (MA). Part-time programs available. *Degree requirements:* For master's, one foreign language, thesis. *Entrance requirements:* Additional exam requirements/recommendations for international students: Required—TOEFL. Electronic applications accepted. *Faculty research:* German language and linguistics, second language acquisition, medieval and early modern literature and culture, twentieth century German literature.

University of California, Berkeley, Graduate Division, College of Letters and Science, Department of German, Berkeley, CA 94720-1500. Offers PhD. *Degree requirements:* For doctorate, 2 foreign languages, thesis/dissertation, qualifying exam. *Entrance requirements:* For doctorate, GRE General Test, minimum GPA of 3.0, writing sample, 3 letters of recommendation. Electronic applications accepted. *Faculty research:* German literature/culture, film, Germanic linguistics, second-language acquisition.

University of California, Davis, Graduate Studies, Program in German, Davis, CA 95616. Offers MA, PhD. Terminal master's awarded for partial completion of doctoral program. *Degree requirements:* For master's, comprehensive exam (for some programs), thesis (for some programs); for doctorate, thesis/dissertation. *Entrance requirements:* For master's, GRE; for doctorate, GRE, master's degree or equivalent. Additional exam requirements/recommendations for international students: Required—TOEFL (minimum score 550 paper-based; 213 computer-based). Electronic applications accepted. *Faculty research:* Sixteenth to twentieth century medieval literature, critical theory, women's studies.

University of California, Irvine, Office of Graduate Studies, School of Humanities, Department of German, Irvine, CA 92697. Offers MA, PhD. *Degree requirements:* For doctorate, thesis/dissertation. *Entrance requirements:* For master's and doctorate, GRE General Test, minimum GPA of 3.0. Additional exam requirements/recommendations for international students: Required—TOEFL (minimum score 550 paper-based; 213 computer-based). Electronic applications accepted. *Faculty research:* Goethe yearbook, fin de siècle theory, Thomas Mann.

University of California, Los Angeles, Graduate Division, College of Letters and Science, Department of Germanic Languages, Program in Germanic Languages, Los Angeles, CA 90095. Offers MA, PhD. *Students:* 14 full-time (7 women); includes 3 minority (2 Asian Americans or Pacific Islanders, 1 Hispanic American), 2 international. Average age 32. 13 applicants, 69% accepted, 3 enrolled. In 2008, 3 doctorates awarded. Terminal master's awarded for partial completion of doctoral program. *Degree requirements:* For master's, one foreign language, comprehensive exam or thesis; for doctorate, 2 foreign languages, oral and written qualifying exams. *Entrance requirements:* For master's, GRE General Test, BA in German with minimum GPA of 3.0, sample of written work; for doctorate, GRE General Test, minimum undergraduate GPA of 3.0, MA in German or equivalent, sample of written work. *Application deadline:* For fall admission, 12/15 for domestic and international students. Application fee: $60 ($80 for international students). Electronic applications accepted. *Expenses:* Tuition, nonresident: full-time $14,694. Required fees: $9669.50. Full-time tuition and fees vary according to course load, degree level, program and student level. *Financial support:* In 2008–09, 10 fellowships with full and partial tuition reimbursements, 5 research assistantships with full and partial tuition reimbursements, 10 teaching assistantships with full and partial tuition reimbursements were awarded; Federal Work-Study, health care benefits, tuition waivers (full and partial), and unspecified assistantships also available. Financial award applicants required to submit FAFSA. *Unit head:* Dr. James Schultz, Chair, 310-825-5195. *Application contact:* Departmental Office, 310-825-3955, E-mail: allen@humnet.ucla.edu.

University of California, San Diego, Office of Graduate Studies, Department of Literature, Program in German Literature, La Jolla, CA 92093. Offers MA. *Degree requirements:* For master's, thesis. *Entrance requirements:* For master's, GRE General Test, GRE Subject Test. Electronic applications accepted.

University of California, Santa Barbara, Graduate Division, College of Letters and Sciences, Division of Humanities and Fine Arts, Department of Germanic, Slavic, and Semitic Studies, Santa Barbara, CA 93106-4130. Offers Germanic languages and literature (MA, PhD), including applied linguistics (PhD), feminist studies (PhD); MA/PhD. *Faculty:* 7 full-time (4 women). *Students:* 2 full-time (0 women). Average age 31. 6 applicants, 50% accepted, 1 enrolled. In 2008, 1 master's awarded. Terminal master's awarded for partial completion of doctoral program. *Degree requirements:* For master's, 2 foreign languages, comprehensive exam, thesis; for doctorate, 3 foreign languages, comprehensive exam, thesis/dissertation. *Entrance requirements:* For master's and doctorate, GRE. Additional exam requirements/recommendations for international students: Required—TOEFL (minimum score 550 paper-based; 213 computer-based; 80 iBT), IELTS (minimum score 7), TOEFL or IELTS. *Application deadline:* For fall admission, 12/31 priority date for domestic students, 5/1 priority date for international students; for winter admission, 11/1 priority date for domestic and international students; for spring admission, 2/1 priority date for domestic and international students. Applications are processed on a rolling basis. Application fee: $70 ($90 for international students). Electronic applications accepted. *Expenses:* Tuition, nonresident: full-time $25,149. Required fees: $10,143. Full-time tuition and fees vary according to campus/location, reciprocity agreements and student level. *Financial support:* In 2008–09, 2 students received support, including 2 fellowships with full and partial tuition reimbursements available (averaging $10,100 per year), 1 teaching assistantship with partial tuition reimbursement available (averaging $11,600 per year); Federal Work-Study, institutionally sponsored loans, scholarships/grants, health care benefits, and tuition waivers (full and partial) also available. Financial award application deadline: 12/31; financial award applicants required to submit FAFSA. *Faculty research:* Critical theory, media technology, psychoanalysis, German romanticism, Goethe. *Unit head:* Prof. Elisabeth Weber, Chair, 805-893-3527, Fax: 805-893-2374, E-mail: weber@gss.ucsb.edu. *Application contact:* Sierra Gray, Graduate Program Assistant, 805-893-2131, Fax: 805-893-2374, E-mail: sierra@gss.ucsb.edu.

University of Chicago, Division of the Humanities, Department of Germanic Languages and Literatures, Chicago, IL 60637-1513. Offers AM, PhD. Terminal master's awarded for partial completion of doctoral program. *Degree requirements:* For master's, one foreign language, thesis; for doctorate, 2 foreign languages, thesis/dissertation. *Entrance requirements:* For master's and doctorate, GRE General Test. Additional exam requirements/recommendations for international students: Required—TOEFL.

University of Cincinnati, Graduate School, McMicken College of Arts and Sciences, Department of German Studies, Cincinnati, OH 45221. Offers MA, PhD. Part-time programs available. Terminal master's awarded for partial completion of doctoral program. *Degree requirements:* For master's, one foreign language, thesis or alternative; for doctorate, 3 foreign languages, thesis/dissertation. *Entrance requirements:* For master's, GRE General Test; for doctorate, GRE General Test, MA in German or equivalent. Additional exam requirements/recommendations for international students: Required—TOEFL (minimum score 560 paper-based). Electronic applications accepted. *Faculty research:* German literary culture, language and linguistics, medieval and early modern, German-Jewish literature, 20th and 21st century German literature and film.

University of Colorado at Boulder, Graduate School, College of Arts and Sciences, Department of Germanic and Slavic Languages, Boulder, CO 80309. Offers German (MA). Part-time programs available. *Degree requirements:* For master's, 2 foreign languages, comprehensive exam, thesis or alternative. *Entrance requirements:* For master's, minimum undergraduate GPA of 2.75. *Faculty research:* Eighteenth-, nineteenth-, and twentieth-century literature, culture and thought; intellectual history; film; philosophy; social and political theory; German, Scandanavian, and comparative literature.

University of Connecticut, Graduate School, College of Liberal Arts and Sciences, Department of Modern and Classical Languages, Field of German, Storrs, CT 06269. Offers MA, PhD. Terminal master's awarded for partial completion of doctoral program. *Degree requirements:* For master's, comprehensive exam; for doctorate, thesis/dissertation. *Entrance requirements:* For master's and doctorate, GRE General Test. Additional exam requirements/recommendations for international students: Required—TOEFL (minimum score 550 paper-based; 213 computer-based). Electronic applications accepted.

University of Delaware, College of Arts and Sciences, Department of Foreign Languages and Literatures, Newark, DE 19716. Offers foreign languages and literatures (MA), including French, German, Spanish; foreign languages pedagogy (MA), including French, German, Spanish. *Degree requirements:* For master's, one foreign language, comprehensive exam, thesis optional. *Entrance requirements:* For master's, GRE General Test, letters of recommendation, writing sample. Additional exam requirements/recommendations for international students: Required—TOEFL. Electronic applications accepted. *Faculty research:* Medieval to

Modern French and Spanish literature, Twentieth Century German, French, Spanish literature by women, computer-assisted instruction.

University of Florida, Graduate School, College of Liberal Arts and Sciences, Department of Germanic and Slavic Studies, Gainesville, FL 32611. Offers German (MA, PhD). *Degree requirements:* For master's, thesis or alternative; for doctorate, thesis/dissertation. *Entrance requirements:* For master's and doctorate, GRE General Test, minimum GPA of 3.0. Additional exam requirements/recommendations for international students: Required—TOEFL (minimum score 550 paper-based; 213 computer-based). Electronic applications accepted. *Faculty research:* Literature and language, film and media.

University of Georgia, Graduate School, College of Arts and Sciences, Department of Germanic and Slavic Studies, Athens, GA 30602. Offers German (MA, MAT). *Degree requirements:* For master's, one foreign language, thesis. *Entrance requirements:* For master's, GRE General Test. Electronic applications accepted.

University of Illinois at Chicago, Graduate College, College of Liberal Arts and Sciences, Department of Germanic Studies, Chicago, IL 60607-7128. Offers MA, PhD. Part-time programs available. Terminal master's awarded for partial completion of doctoral program. *Degree requirements:* For master's, thesis optional, exam; for doctorate, 2 foreign languages, thesis/dissertation. *Entrance requirements:* For master's and doctorate, GRE General Test, minimum GPA of 2.75. Additional exam requirements/recommendations for international students: Required—TOEFL. Electronic applications accepted. *Faculty research:* German literature.

University of Illinois at Urbana–Champaign, Graduate College, College of Liberal Arts and Sciences, School of Literatures, Cultures and Linguistics, Department of Germanic Languages and Literatures, Champaign, IL 61820. Offers German (MA, PhD). *Faculty:* 9 full-time (7 women). *Students:* 16 full-time (11 women), 3 part-time (2 women), 3 international. 21 applicants, 57% accepted, 6 enrolled. In 2008, 6 master's, 2 doctorates awarded. *Entrance requirements:* For master's and doctorate, minimum GPA of 3.0; writing sample. Additional exam requirements/recommendations for international students: Required—TOEFL (minimum score 79 iBT). *Application deadline:* Applications are processed on a rolling basis. Application fee: $60 ($75 for international students). Electronic applications accepted. *Financial support:* In 2008–09, 5 fellowships, 3 research assistantships, 22 teaching assistantships were awarded; tuition waivers (full and partial) also available. *Unit head:* Mara Wade, Head, 217-333-9353, Fax: 217-244-2223, E-mail: mwade@illinois.edu. *Application contact:* Lynn Stanke, Secretary, 217-333-6269, Fax: 217-244-3050, E-mail: stanke@illinois.edu.

The University of Iowa, Graduate College, College of Liberal Arts and Sciences, Department of German, Iowa City, IA 52242-1316. Offers MA, PhD. *Degree requirements:* For master's, thesis optional, exam; for doctorate, comprehensive exam, thesis/dissertation. *Entrance requirements:* For master's and doctorate, GRE General Test, minimum GPA of 3.0. Additional exam requirements/recommendations for international students: Required—TOEFL (minimum score 550 paper-based; 213 computer-based; 81 iBT). Electronic applications accepted.

The University of Kansas, Graduate Studies, College of Liberal Arts and Sciences, Department of Germanic Languages and Literatures, Lawrence, KS 66045. Offers German (MA, PhD). Part-time programs available. *Faculty:* 7. *Students:* 20 full-time (13 women); includes 1 minority (Asian American or Pacific Islander), 8 international. Average age 31. 7 applicants, 86% accepted, 4 enrolled. In 2008, 1 master's, 1 doctorate awarded. *Degree requirements:* For master's, one foreign language, comprehensive exam, thesis optional, final oral exam; for doctorate, 2 foreign languages, comprehensive exam, thesis/dissertation, final oral exam. *Entrance requirements:* For master's, GRE, undergraduate major in German or equivalent; for doctorate, GRE, MA in German. Additional exam requirements/recommendations for international students: Required—TOEFL. *Application deadline:* For fall admission, 1/15 priority date for domestic and international students. Applications are processed on a rolling basis. Application fee: $45 ($50 for international students). Electronic applications accepted. *Expenses:* Tuition, area resident: Full-time $6122; part-time $255.10 per credit hour. Tuition, state resident: full-time $6122; part-time $255.10 per credit hour. Tuition, nonresident: full-time $14,629; part-time $609.55 per credit hour. Required fees: $847; $70.56 per credit hour. Tuition and fees vary according to course load and program. *Financial support:* Fellowships, research assistantships with full tuition reimbursements, teaching assistantships with full tuition reimbursements, Federal Work-Study, institutionally sponsored loans, and unspecified assistantships available. Support available to part-time students. Financial award application deadline: 1/30; financial award applicants required to submit FAFSA. *Faculty research:* Humanism, eighteenth to twentieth century literature, Germanic linguistics, German-American studies, German applied linguistics, German philology. *Unit head:* William Keel, Chair, 785-864-4803, Fax: 785-864-4298, E-mail: wkeel@ku.edu. *Application contact:* Leonie Marx, Graduate Director, 785-864-4803, Fax: 785-864-4298, E-mail: marx@ku.edu.

University of Kentucky, Graduate School, College of Arts and Sciences, Program in German, Lexington, KY 40506-0032. Offers MA. *Degree requirements:* For master's, one foreign language, comprehensive exam, thesis optional. *Entrance requirements:* For master's, GRE General Test, minimum undergraduate GPA of 2.75. Additional exam requirements/recommendations for international students: Required—TOEFL (minimum score 550 paper-based; 213 computer-based). Electronic applications accepted. *Faculty research:* Medieval studies, literature from Enlightenment to present, literary theory, intellectual history, gender studies.

University of Lethbridge, School of Graduate Studies, Lethbridge, AB T1K 3M4, Canada. Offers accounting (MScM); addictions counseling (M Sc); agricultural biotechnology (M Sc); agricultural studies (M Sc, MA); anthropology (MA); archaeology (MA); art (MA); biochemistry (M Sc); biological sciences (M Sc); biomolecular science (PhD); biosystems and biodiversity (PhD); Canadian studies (MA); chemistry (M Sc); computer science (M Sc); computer science and geographical information science (M Sc); counseling psychology (M Ed); dramatic arts (MA); earth, space, and physical science (PhD); economics (MA); educational leadership (M Ed); English (MA); environmental science (M Sc); evolution and behavior (PhD); exercise science (M Sc); finance (MScM); French (MA); French/German (MA); French/Spanish (MA); general education (M Ed); general management (MScM); geography (M Sc, MA); German (MA); health sciences (M Sc, MA); history (MA); human resource management and labour relations (MScM); individualized multidisciplinary (M Sc, MA); information systems (MScM); international management (MScM); kinesiology (M Sc, MA); management (M Sc, MA); marketing (MScM); mathematics (M Sc); music (MA); Native American studies (MA); neuroscience (M Sc, PhD); new media (MA); nursing (M Sc); philosophy (MA); physics (M Sc); policy and strategy (MScM); political science (MA); psychology (M Sc, MA); religious studies (MA); sociology (MA); theoretical and computational science (PhD); urban and regional studies (MA). Part-time and evening/weekend programs available. *Degree requirements:* For doctorate, comprehensive exam, thesis/dissertation. *Entrance requirements:* For master's, GMAT (M Sc in management), bachelor's degree in related field, minimum GPA of 3.0 during previous 20 graded semester courses, 2 years teaching or related experience (M Ed); for doctorate, master's degree, minimum graduate GPA of 3.5. Additional exam requirements/recommendations for international students: Required—TOEFL. *Faculty research:* Movement and brain plasticity, gibberellin physiology, photosynthesis, carbon cycling, molecular properties of main-group ring components.

University of Manitoba, Faculty of Graduate Studies, Faculty of Arts, Department of German and Slavic Studies, Winnipeg, MB R3T 2N2, Canada. Offers German language and literature (MA); Slavic languages and literatures (MA). *Degree requirements:* For master's, one foreign language, thesis or alternative.

University of Maryland, College Park, Graduate Studies, College of Arts and Humanities, School of Languages, Literature, and Cultures, Department of Germanic Studies, College Park, MD 20742. Offers Germanic language and literature (MA, PhD). *Degree requirements:* For master's, one foreign language, comprehensive exam, thesis optional, exams; for doctorate, 2 foreign languages, comprehensive exam, thesis/dissertation, reading exam, oral defense. *Entrance requirements:* For master's, GRE General Test, writing sample, 3 letters of recommendation; for doctorate, GRE General Test, MA in German or related discipline. Additional exam requirements/recommendations for international students: Required—TOEFL. Electronic applications accepted. *Faculty research:* Language pedagogy, Germanic philology, medieval culture.

University of Maryland, College Park, Graduate Studies, College of Arts and Humanities, School of Languages, Literature, and Cultures, Program in Second Language Acquisition and Application, College Park, MD 20742. Offers French (MA); German (MA); Japanese (MA); Russian (MA); second language instruction (PhD); second language learning (PhD); second language measurement and assessment (PhD); second language use (PhD); Spanish (MA). *Entrance requirements:* For master's, BA or BS in related field, demonstrated language competency, 3 letters of reference. Electronic applications accepted. *Faculty research:* Second language acquisition, pedagogical perspectives, technological applications, language use in professional contexts.

University of Massachusetts Amherst, Graduate School, College of Humanities and Fine Arts, Department of Languages, Literatures, and Cultures, Programs in German and Scandinavian Studies, Amherst, MA 01003. Offers MA, PhD. Part-time programs available. Terminal master's awarded for partial completion of doctoral program. *Degree requirements:* For master's, thesis or alternative; for doctorate, 2 foreign languages, comprehensive exam, thesis/dissertation. *Entrance requirements:* For master's and doctorate, writing sample in English and German. Additional exam requirements/recommendations for international students: Required—TOEFL (minimum score 550 paper-based; 213 computer-based; 79 iBT), IELTS (minimum score 6.5). Electronic applications accepted. *Expenses:* Tuition, area resident: Full-time $2640. Tuition, nonresident: full-time $9936. One-time fee: $332 full-time. Tuition and fees vary according to course load.

University of Michigan, Horace H. Rackham School of Graduate Studies, College of Literature, Science, and the Arts, Department of Germanic Languages and Literatures, Ann Arbor, MI 48109. Offers German (AM, PhD). *Degree requirements:* For doctorate, one foreign language, thesis/dissertation, oral defense of dissertation, preliminary exam. *Entrance requirements:* For master's and doctorate, GRE General Test. Additional exam requirements/recommendations for international students: Required—TOEFL (minimum score 560 paper-based; 220 computer-based). Electronic applications accepted. *Faculty research:* German history, German literature, literary theory, film, political and social theory.

University of Minnesota, Twin Cities Campus, Graduate School, College of Liberal Arts, Department of German, Scandinavian, and Dutch, Minneapolis, MN 55455-0213. Offers Germanic studies: German and Scandinavian studies track (PhD); Germanic studies: German track (MA, PhD); Germanic studies: Germanic medieval studies track (MA, PhD); Germanic studies: Scandinavian studies track (MA); Germanic studies: teaching track (MA). Part-time programs available. Terminal master's awarded for partial completion of doctoral program. *Degree requirements:* For doctorate, 2 foreign languages, thesis/dissertation. *Entrance requirements:* For master's, GRE General Test, BA in German, Scandinavian, or equivalent; for doctorate, GRE General Test, MA in German, Scandinavian, or equivalent. Additional exam requirements/recommendations for international students: Required—TOEFL (minimum score 550 paper-based; 213 computer-based; 79 iBT). Electronic applications accepted. *Faculty research:* Cultural studies, literary theory, feminist criticism, film, Germanic philology.

University of Mississippi, Graduate School, College of Liberal Arts, Department of Modern Languages, Oxford, University, MS 38677. Offers French (MA); German (MA); Spanish (MA). *Degree requirements:* For master's, thesis (for some programs). *Entrance requirements:* For master's, GRE General Test, minimum GPA of 3.0. Additional exam requirements/recommendations for international students: Required—TOEFL. Electronic applications accepted.

University of Missouri–Columbia, Graduate School, College of Arts and Sciences, Department of German and Russian Studies, Columbia, MO 65211. Offers German (MA). *Faculty:* 13 full-time (6 women). *Students:* 16 full-time (11 women), 1 (woman) part-time, 9 international. Average age 28. 7 applicants, 86% accepted, 6 enrolled. In 2008, 3 master's awarded. *Entrance requirements:* For master's, GRE General Test, minimum GPA of 3.0. Additional exam requirements/recommendations for international students: Required—TOEFL (minimum score 500 paper-based; 173 computer-based; 61 iBT). *Application deadline:* For fall admission, 3/1 priority date for domestic students. Applications are processed on a rolling basis. Application fee: $45 ($60 for international students). *Financial support:* Research assistantships, teaching assistantships, institutionally sponsored loans available. *Unit head:* Dr. Carsten Strathausen, Department Chair, E-mail: strathaussenc@missouri.edu. *Application contact:* Jennifer Arnold, 573-882-4328, E-mail: arnoldj@missouri.edu.

The University of Montana, Graduate School, College of Arts and Sciences, Department of Modern and Classical Languages and Literatures, Missoula, MT 59812-0002. Offers French (MA); German (MA); Spanish (MA). *Degree requirements:* For master's, one foreign language. *Entrance requirements:* For master's, GRE General Test. Additional exam requirements/recommendations for international students: Required—TOEFL.

University of Nebraska–Lincoln, Graduate College, College of Arts and Sciences, Department of Modern Languages and Literatures, Lincoln, NE 68588. Offers French (MA, PhD); German (MA, PhD); Spanish (MA, PhD). *Faculty:* 20 full-time (9 women). *Students:* 28 full-time (16 women), 12 part-time (9 women); includes 9 minority (1 African American, 1 Asian American or Pacific Islander, 7 Hispanic Americans), 17 international. Average age 34. In 2008, 6 master's, 1 doctorate awarded. *Degree requirements:* For master's, thesis optional; for doctorate, comprehensive exam, thesis/dissertation. *Entrance requirements:* For master's and doctorate, writing sample in target language. Additional exam requirements/recommendations for international students: Required—TOEFL (minimum score 550 paper-based; 213 computer-based). *Application deadline:* For fall admission, 2/1 for domestic and international students. Applications are processed on a rolling basis. Application fee: $40. Electronic applications accepted. *Expenses:* Tuition, state resident: full-time $4275; part-time $237.50 per credit hour. Tuition, nonresident: full-time $11,525; part-time $640.25 per credit hour. Required fees: $1068; $10.35 per credit hour. $440.70 per semester. Tuition and fees vary according to course load and program. *Financial support:* Fellowships, research assistantships, teaching assistantships, Federal Work-Study, health care benefits, and unspecified assistantships available. Support available to part-time students. Financial award application deadline: 2/15. *Faculty research:* French, German, and Spanish language, literature, and culture. *Unit head:* Dr. Russell Ganim, Chair, 402-472-3745, Fax: 402-472-0327. *Application contact:* Dr. Dieter Karch, Graduate Chair, 402-472-3745, E-mail: modlang2@unl.edu.

University of Nevada, Reno, Graduate School, College of Liberal Arts, Department of Foreign Languages and Literatures, Reno, NV 89557. Offers French (MA); German (MA); Spanish (MA). *Faculty:* 18 full-time (8 women). *Students:* 11 full-time (6 women), 9 part-time (5 women); includes 4 minority (1 Asian American or Pacific Islander, 3 Hispanic Americans), 1 international. Average age 32. 10 applicants, 90% accepted, 6 enrolled. In 2008, 7 master's awarded. *Degree requirements:* For master's, one foreign language, thesis optional. *Entrance requirements:* For master's, GRE General Test, minimum GPA of 2.75. Additional exam requirements/recommendations for international students: Required—TOEFL (minimum score 500 paper-based; 173 computer-based; 61 iBT), IELTS (minimum score 6), TOFEL or IELTS. *Application deadline:* For fall admission, 3/1 priority date for domestic and international students; for spring admission, 11/1 priority date for domestic and international students. Applications are processed on a rolling basis. Application fee: $60 ($95 for international students). *Expenses:* Tuition, state resident: full-time $1710; part-time $1140 per semester. Tuition, nonresident: full-time $7115. Required fees: $158 per semester. *Financial support:* In 2008–09, 1 research assistantship with partial tuition reimbursement (averaging $14,000 per year), 10 teaching assistantships with partial tuition reimbursements (averaging $14,000 per year) were awarded; Federal Work-Study, institutionally sponsored loans, scholarships/grants, health care benefits, and unspecified assistantships also available. Financial award application deadline: 3/1; financial award applicants required to submit FAFSA. *Faculty research:* Thirteenth century mysticism,

German

University of Nevada, Reno (continued)
contemporary Spanish and Latin American poetry and theater, French interrelation between narration and photography, exile literature and Holocaust. Total annual research expenditures: $4,341. *Unit head:* Dr. Darrell Lockhart, Graduate Program Director, 775-784-6055, E-mail: lockhart@unr.edu. *Application contact:* Michele Sandberg, Application Contact, 775-784-7026, Fax: 775-784-6064, E-mail: gradschool@unr.edu.

University of New Mexico, Graduate School, College of Arts and Sciences, Department of Foreign Languages and Literature, Albuquerque, NM 87131-2039. Offers comparative literature and cultural studies (MA); French (MA); French studies (PhD); German studies (MA). Part-time programs available. *Degree requirements:* For master's, one foreign language, thesis optional; for doctorate, 2 foreign languages, thesis/dissertation. Electronic applications accepted. *Faculty research:* German, Russian, Italian, Japanese, French, Comparative Lit, culture studies, classics.

The University of North Carolina at Chapel Hill, Graduate School, College of Arts and Sciences, Department of Germanic Languages, Chapel Hill, NC 27599. Offers literature and linguistics (MA, PhD). Part-time programs available. Terminal master's awarded for partial completion of doctoral program. *Degree requirements:* For master's, comprehensive exam, thesis; for doctorate, one foreign language, comprehensive exam, thesis/dissertation. *Entrance requirements:* For master's and doctorate, GRE General Test, minimum GPA of 3.0. *Faculty research:* Gender and sexuality, literature and politics, German and Jewish culture, medieval through modern literature, Germanic linguistics.

University of Northern Iowa, Graduate College, College of Humanities and Fine Arts, Department of Modern Languages, Program in German, Cedar Falls, IA 50614. Offers German (MA); teaching English to speakers of other languages/German (MA). Part-time and evening/weekend programs available. *Students:* 5 full-time (all women), 1 part-time (0 women), 5 international. 4 applicants, 75% accepted, 1 enrolled. In 2008, 2 master's awarded. *Degree requirements:* For master's, one foreign language, comprehensive exam, thesis or alternative. *Entrance requirements:* For master's, minimum GPA of 3.0, valid teaching license, documentation of successful teaching experience. Additional exam requirements/recommendations for international students: Required—TOEFL (minimum score 600 paper-based; 250 computer-based; 100 iBT). *Application deadline:* For fall admission, 8/1 priority date for domestic students. Applications are processed on a rolling basis. Application fee: $30 ($50 for international students). *Expenses:* Tuition, state resident: full-time $6446. Tuition, nonresident: full-time $14,874. Required fees: $852. *Financial support:* Career-related internships or fieldwork, Federal Work-Study, and tuition waivers (full and partial) available. Support available to part-time students. Financial award application deadline: 2/1. *Unit head:* Dr. Cheryl Roberts, Graduate Coordinator, 319-273-2200, Fax: 319-273-2848, E-mail: cheryl.roberts@uni.edu. *Application contact:* Laurie S. Russell, Record Analyst, 319-273-2623, Fax: 319-273-6792, E-mail: laurie.russell@uni.edu.

University of Oklahoma, Graduate College, College of Arts and Sciences, Department of Modern Languages, Program in German, Norman, OK 73019. Offers MA, MBA/MA. Part-time programs available. *Students:* 5 full-time (3 women), 1 international. In 2008, 1 master's awarded. *Degree requirements:* For master's, 2 foreign languages, comprehensive exam, thesis optional, departmental qualifying exam. *Entrance requirements:* For master's, BA with 25 hours in German or equivalent, minimum GPA of 3.0 in last 60 hours, 3 letters of recommendation. Additional exam requirements/recommendations for international students: Required—TOEFL (minimum score 550 paper-based; 213 computer-based). *Application deadline:* For fall admission, 6/1 priority date for domestic students, 4/1 for international students; for spring admission, 11/1 for domestic students, 9/1 for international students. Applications are processed on a rolling basis. Application fee: $40 ($90 for international students). Electronic applications accepted. *Expenses:* Tuition, state resident: full-time $3744; part-time $156 per credit hour. Tuition, nonresident: full-time $13,577; part-time $565.70 per credit hour. Required fees: $2415.40; $90.10 per credit hour. *Financial support:* In 2008–09, 5 students received support. Scholarships/grants, health care benefits, and unspecified assistantships available. Financial award applicants required to submit FAFSA. *Faculty research:* Film studies; German literature and culture studies; fin-de-siecle Austria; Arthurian romance; the Goethe era. *Unit head:* Dr. Pamela Genova, Chair, 405-325-6181, Fax: 405-325-0103, E-mail: genova@ou.edu. *Application contact:* Dr. Logan E. Whalen, Graduate Liaison, 405-325-5088, Fax: 405-325-0103, E-mail: mlllgradinfo@ou.edu.

University of Oregon, Graduate School, College of Arts and Sciences, Department of Germanic Languages and Literatures, Eugene, OR 97403. Offers MA, PhD. *Degree requirements:* For master's, 2 foreign languages, thesis or alternative; for doctorate, 3 foreign languages, thesis/dissertation. *Entrance requirements:* For master's and doctorate, minimum GPA of 3.0. Additional exam requirements/recommendations for international students: Required—TOEFL. *Faculty research:* Medieval language and literature, eighteenth to twentieth century literature and philosophy, literary theory, feminist literature and theory, psychoanalysis and literature.

University of Pennsylvania, School of Arts and Sciences, Graduate Group in Germanic Languages, Philadelphia, PA 19104. Offers AM, PhD. Terminal master's awarded for partial completion of doctoral program. *Degree requirements:* For master's, one foreign language, thesis or alternative; for doctorate, one foreign language, comprehensive exam, thesis/dissertation. *Entrance requirements:* For master's and doctorate, GRE General Test.

University of Pittsburgh, School of Arts and Sciences, Department of Germanic Languages and Literatures, Pittsburgh, PA 15260. Offers MA, PhD. Part-time programs available. Terminal master's awarded for partial completion of doctoral program. *Degree requirements:* For master's, one foreign language, comprehensive exam (for some programs), thesis (for some programs); for doctorate, one foreign language, comprehensive exam, thesis/dissertation. *Entrance requirements:* For master's, bachelor's degree in German, minimum GPA of 3.0 or equivalent. Additional exam requirements/recommendations for international students: Required—TOEFL. Electronic applications accepted. *Faculty research:* Age of Goethe, German film, postwar culture, German-Jewish culture.

University of Saskatchewan, College of Graduate Studies and Research, College of Arts and Sciences, Department of Languages and Linguistics, Saskatoon, SK S7N 5A2, Canada. Offers MA. *Degree requirements:* For master's, 2 foreign languages, thesis. *Entrance requirements:* Additional exam requirements/recommendations for international students: Required—TOEFL.

University of South Africa, College of Human Sciences, Pretoria, South Africa. Offers adult education (M Ed); African languages (MA, PhD); African politics (MA, PhD); Afrikaans (MA, PhD); ancient history (MA, PhD); ancient Near Eastern studies (MA, PhD); anthropology (MA, PhD); applied linguistics (MA); Arabic (MA, PhD); archaeology (MA); art history (MA); Biblical archaeology (MA); Biblical studies (M Th, D Th, PhD); Christian spirituality (M Th, D Th); church history (M Th, D Th); classical studies (MA, PhD); clinical psychology (MA); communication (MA, PhD); comparative education (M Ed, Ed D); consulting psychology (D Admin, D Com, PhD); curriculum studies (M Ed, Ed D); development studies (M Admin, MA, D Admin, PhD); didactics (M Ed, Ed D); education (M Tech); education management (M Ed, Ed D); educational psychology (M Ed); English (MA); environmental education (M Ed); French (MA, PhD); German (MA, PhD); Greek (MA); guidance and counseling (M Ed); health studies (MA, PhD), including health sciences education (MA), health services management (MA), medical and surgical nursing science (critical care general) (MA), midwifery and neonatal nursing science (MA), trauma and emergency care (MA); history (MA, PhD); history of education (Ed D); inclusive education (M Ed, Ed D); information and communications technology policy and regulation (MA); information science (MA, MIS, PhD); international politics (MA, PhD); Islamic studies (MA, PhD); Italian (MA, PhD); Judaica (MA, PhD); linguistics (MA, PhD); mathematical education (M Ed); mathematics education (MA); missiology (M Th, D Th); modern Hebrew (MA, PhD); musicology (MA, MMus, D Mus, PhD); natural science education (M Ed); New Testament (M Th, D Th); Old Testament (D Th); pastoral therapy (M Th, D Th); philosophy (MA); philosophy of education (M Ed, Ed D); politics (MA, PhD); Portuguese (MA, PhD); practical theology (M Th, D Th); psychology (MA, MS, PhD); psychology of education (M Ed, Ed D); public health (MA); religious studies (MA, D Th, PhD); Romance languages (MA); Russian (MA, PhD); Semitic languages (MA, PhD); social behavior studies in HIV/AIDS (MA); social science (mental health) (MA); social science in development studies (MA); social science in psychology (MA); social science in social work (MA); social science in sociology (MA); social work (MSW, DSW, PhD); socio-education (M Ed, Ed D); sociolinguistics (MA); sociology (MA, PhD); Spanish (MA, PhD); systematic theology (M Th, D Th); TESOL (teaching English to speakers of other languages) (MA); theological ethics (M Th, D Th); theory of literature (MA, PhD); urban ministries (D Th); urban ministry (M Th).

University of South Carolina, The Graduate School, College of Arts and Sciences, Department of Languages, Literatures, and Cultures, Columbia, SC 29208. Offers comparative literature (MA, PhD); foreign languages (MAT), including French, German, Spanish; French (MA); German (MA); Spanish (MA). MAT offered in cooperation with the College of Education. Part-time programs available. *Degree requirements:* For master's, one foreign language, comprehensive exam, thesis optional; for doctorate, 2 foreign languages, comprehensive exam, thesis/dissertation. *Entrance requirements:* For master's and doctorate, GRE General Test, writing sample. Additional exam requirements/recommendations for international students: Required—TOEFL (minimum score 230 computer-based; 75 iBT). Electronic applications accepted. *Faculty research:* Modern literature, linguistics, literature and culture, medieval literature, literary theory.

The University of Tennessee, Graduate School, College of Arts and Sciences, Department of Modern Foreign Languages and Literatures, Program in German, Knoxville, TN 37996. Offers MA. Part-time programs available. *Degree requirements:* For master's, one foreign language, thesis or alternative. *Entrance requirements:* For master's, minimum GPA of 2.7. Additional exam requirements/recommendations for international students: Required—TOEFL. Electronic applications accepted. *Expenses:* Tuition, area resident: Part-time $348 per credit hour. Tuition, state resident: full-time $6262. Tuition, nonresident: full-time $18,920; part-time $1052 per credit hour. Required fees: $812; $36 per credit hour. Tuition and fees vary according to program.

The University of Tennessee, Graduate School, College of Arts and Sciences, Department of Modern Foreign Languages and Literatures, Program in Modern Foreign Languages, Knoxville, TN 37996. Offers applied linguistics (PhD); French (PhD); German (PhD); Italian (PhD); Portuguese (PhD); Russian (PhD); Spanish (PhD). *Degree requirements:* For doctorate, 2 foreign languages, thesis/dissertation. *Entrance requirements:* For doctorate, minimum GPA of 2.7. Additional exam requirements/recommendations for international students: Required—TOEFL. Electronic applications accepted. *Expenses:* Tuition, area resident: Part-time $348 per credit hour. Tuition, state resident: full-time $6262. Tuition, nonresident: full-time $18,920; part-time $1052 per credit hour. Required fees: $812; $36 per credit hour. Tuition and fees vary according to program.

The University of Texas at Austin, Graduate School, College of Liberal Arts, Department of Germanic Studies, Austin, TX 78712-1111. Offers MA, PhD. *Degree requirements:* For master's, one foreign language, thesis or alternative; for doctorate, 2 foreign languages, thesis/dissertation. *Entrance requirements:* For master's and doctorate, GRE General Test. *Faculty research:* Germanic languages and culture (German, Austrian, Swiss, Dutch, Danish, Norwegian, Swedish, Yiddish), language pedagogy and linguistics.

The University of Toledo, College of Graduate Studies, College of Arts and Sciences, Department of Foreign Languages, Toledo, OH 43606-3390. Offers French (MA); German (MA); Spanish (MA). Part-time programs available. *Degree requirements:* For master's, one foreign language, comprehensive reading exam in 1 additional foreign language. Electronic applications accepted.

University of Toronto, School of Graduate Studies, Humanities Division, Department of Germanic Languages and Literatures, Toronto, ON M5S 1A1, Canada. Offers MA, PhD. Part-time programs available. *Degree requirements:* For master's, thesis optional, German language competence exam; for doctorate, thesis/dissertation, qualifying exam, thesis defense. *Entrance requirements:* For master's, 7 two-semester courses in German language and literature, minimum B+ average, 3 letters of recommendation; for doctorate, MA in German, minimum A– average, 3 letters of recommendation, writing sample, resumé.

University of Utah, The Graduate School, College of Humanities, Department of Languages and Literature, Salt Lake City, UT 84112-1107. Offers comparative literary and cultural studies (MA, PhD); French (MA, MALP); German (MA, MALP, PhD); language pedagogy (MALP); Spanish (MA, MALP, PhD); world languages with secondary teaching licensure (MA). Terminal master's awarded for partial completion of doctoral program. *Degree requirements:* For master's, standard proficiency in 2 languages other than English, comprehensive exam or thesis; for doctorate, comprehensive exam, standard proficiency in 2 languages other than English and language of study, advanced proficiency in 1 language other than English and language of study, dissertation. *Entrance requirements:* For master's, bachelor's degree or strong undergraduate record in target languages, GPA of 3.0, literature-survey courses; for doctorate, successful completion of MA and advanced proficiency in a target language. Additional exam requirements/recommendations for international students: Required—TOEFL (minimum score 500 paper-based; 173 computer-based). Electronic applications accepted. *Faculty research:* Literary theory, stylistics, Russian and Soviet literature, existentialism, theory of criticism.

University of Vermont, Graduate College, College of Arts and Sciences, Department of German and Russian, Burlington, VT 05405. Offers German (MA). In 2008, 1 master's awarded. *Degree requirements:* For master's, one foreign language, thesis. *Entrance requirements:* For master's, GRE General Test. Additional exam requirements/recommendations for international students: Required—TOEFL (minimum score 550 paper-based; 213 computer-based; 80 iBT). *Application deadline:* For fall admission, 4/1 priority date for domestic students. Applications are processed on a rolling basis. Application fee: $40. Electronic applications accepted. *Expenses:* Tuition, state resident: part-time $488 per credit. Tuition, nonresident: part-time $1232 per credit. *Financial support:* Fellowships, teaching assistantships available. Financial award application deadline: 3/1. *Faculty research:* Medieval and eighteenth and nineteenth century literature, folklore. *Unit head:* Dr. W. Mieder, Chairperson, 802-656-3430. *Application contact:* Dr. D. Scrase, Coordinator, 802-656-3430.

University of Victoria, Faculty of Graduate Studies, Faculty of Humanities, Department of Germanic and Slavic Studies, Victoria, BC V8W 2Y2, Canada. Offers German studies (MA). Part-time programs available. *Degree requirements:* For master's, 2 foreign languages, oral defense of thesis. *Entrance requirements:* For master's, BA in German, minimum B+ average in undergraduate course work. Additional exam requirements/recommendations for international students: Required—TOEFL (minimum score 575 paper-based; 233 computer-based), IELTS (minimum score 7). Electronic applications accepted. *Faculty research:* Nineteenth and twentieth century German literature, literature and music, language acquisition, eighteenth and twentieth century drama and theater, military history.

University of Virginia, College and Graduate School of Arts and Sciences, Department of Germanic Languages and Literatures, Charlottesville, VA 22903. Offers German (MA, PhD). *Faculty:* 13 full-time (7 women). *Students:* 14 full-time (5 women), 6 international. Average age 28. 7 applicants, 71% accepted, 2 enrolled. In 2008, 4 master's, 1 doctorate awarded. *Degree requirements:* For master's, one foreign language, comprehensive exam, thesis; for doctorate, one foreign language, comprehensive exam, thesis/dissertation. *Entrance requirements:* For master's and doctorate, GRE General Test, 3 letters of recommendation; critical writing sample. Additional exam requirements/recommendations for international students: Required—TOEFL (minimum score 600 paper-based; 250 computer-based; 90 iBT), IELTS (minimum score 7). *Application deadline:* For fall admission, 1/15 for domestic and international students. Applications are processed on a rolling basis. Application fee: $60. Electronic applications accepted.

Expenses: Tuition, area resident: Full-time $10,452. Tuition, state resident: full-time $10,452. Tuition, nonresident: full-time $20,010. Required fees: $2176. Part-time tuition and fees vary according to course load and program. *Financial support:* Applicants required to submit FAFSA. *Unit head:* Grossman Jeffrey, Chair, 434-924-3530, Fax: 434-924-6700, E-mail: germandepartment@virginia.edu. *Application contact:* Benjamin Bennett, 434-924-6695, E-mail: bkb@virginia.edu.

University of Washington, Graduate School, College of Arts and Sciences, Department of Germanics, Seattle, WA 98195. Offers MA, PhD. Part-time programs available. Terminal master's awarded for partial completion of doctoral program. *Degree requirements:* For master's, one foreign language, 2 research papers; for doctorate, 2 foreign languages, thesis/dissertation, 3 research papers. *Entrance requirements:* For master's and doctorate, GRE, minimum GPA of 3.0. Additional exam requirements/recommendations for international students: Required—TOEFL. Electronic applications accepted. *Faculty research:* Modern German literature, Germanic linguistics and philology, language pedagogy, literary theory, cinema studies.

University of Waterloo, Graduate Studies, Faculty of Arts, Department of Germanic and Slavic Studies, Waterloo, ON N2L 3G1, Canada. Offers German (MA, PhD); Russian (MA). Part-time and evening/weekend programs available. *Degree requirements:* For master's, one foreign language, thesis optional; for doctorate, 2 foreign languages, comprehensive exam, thesis/dissertation. *Entrance requirements:* For master's, honors degree, minimum B average; for doctorate, master's degree, minimum B average. Additional exam requirements/recommendations for international students: Required—TOEFL, TWE. Electronic applications accepted. *Faculty research:* Medieval theatre; history and literature; German and Russian literary relations; seventeenth, eighteenth, nineteenth, and twentieth century German literature.

University of Wisconsin–Madison, Graduate School, College of Letters and Science, Department of German, Madison, WI 53706-1380. Offers MA, PhD. Part-time programs available. Terminal master's awarded for partial completion of doctoral program. *Degree requirements:* For master's, one foreign language, comprehensive exam, thesis optional; for doctorate, 2 foreign languages, comprehensive exam, thesis/dissertation. *Entrance requirements:* For master's and doctorate, GRE. Electronic applications accepted. *Faculty research:* Literature, culture/linguistics, film, Dutch.

University of Wisconsin–Milwaukee, Graduate School, College of Letters and Sciences, Interdepartmental Program in Foreign Language and Literature, Milwaukee, WI 53201-0413. Offers classics and Hebrew studies (MAFLL); comparative literature (MAFLL); French and Italian (MAFLL); German (MAFLL); Slavic studies (MAFLL); translation (Certificate). Part-time programs available. *Faculty:* 39 full-time (17 women). *Students:* 32 full-time (25 women), 28 part-time (19 women); includes 5 minority (1 Asian American or Pacific Islander, 4 Hispanic Americans), 22 international. Average age 32. 51 applicants, 65% accepted, 26 enrolled. In 2008, 19 master's awarded. *Degree requirements:* For master's, 2 foreign languages, thesis or alternative. *Entrance requirements:* Additional exam requirements/recommendations for international students: Required—TOEFL (minimum score 550 paper-based; 79 iBT), IELTS (minimum score 6.5). *Application deadline:* For fall admission, 1/1 priority date for domestic students; for spring admission, 9/1 for domestic students. Applications are processed on a rolling basis. Application fee: $45 ($75 for international students). *Expenses:* Tuition, area resident: Full-time $7320; part-time $165 per credit. Tuition, state resident: full-time $7320; part-time $165 per credit. Tuition, nonresident: full-time $17,840; part-time $714 per credit. Tuition and fees vary according to campus/location, program and reciprocity agreements. *Financial support:* In 2008–09, 2 research assistantships, 35 teaching assistantships were awarded; career-related internships or fieldwork and unspecified assistantships also available. Support available to part-time students. Financial award application deadline: 4/15. Total annual research expenditures: $43,420. *Unit head:* Gabrielle Verdier, Representative, 414-229-3346, Fax: 414-229-2741, E-mail: verdier@uwm.edu. *Application contact:* General Information Contact, 414-229-4982, Fax: 414-229-6967, E-mail: gradschool@uwm.edu.

University of Wyoming, Graduate School, College of Arts and Sciences, Department of Modern and Classical Languages, Program in German, Laramie, WY 82070. Offers MA. Part-time programs available. *Faculty:* 3 full-time (1 woman). *Students:* 3 full-time (2 women), 2 international. Average age 26. 1 applicant, 100% accepted. *Degree requirements:* For master's, one foreign language, thesis or alternative. *Entrance requirements:* For master's, GRE General Test, minimum GPA of 3.0. *Application deadline:* For fall admission, 4/1 priority date for domestic students. Applications are processed on a rolling basis. Application fee: $50. *Financial support:* In 2008–09, 2 teaching assistantships with full tuition reimbursements (averaging $10,696 per year) were awarded; institutionally sponsored loans also available. Financial award application deadline: 3/1. *Faculty research:* East German literature, German literature, theatre, poetry. *Unit head:* Dr. Philip Holt, Head, 307-766-4177, Fax: 307-766-2727, E-mail: pholt@uwyo.edu. *Application contact:* Dr. Kevin S. Larsen, Graduate Adviser, 307-766-2294, Fax: 307-766-2727, E-mail: klarsen@uwyo.edu.

Vanderbilt University, Graduate School, Department of Germanic and Slavic Languages, Nashville, TN 37240-1001. Offers German (MA, MAT, PhD). *Faculty:* 8 full-time (5 women). *Students:* 16 full-time (10 women); includes 1 minority (Asian American or Pacific Islander), 5 international. Average age 31. 14 applicants, 43% accepted, 2 enrolled. In 2008, 4 master's awarded. Terminal master's awarded for partial completion of doctoral program. *Degree requirements:* For master's, one foreign language, comprehensive exam; for doctorate, 2 foreign languages, comprehensive exam, thesis/dissertation, qualifying and final exams. *Entrance requirements:* For master's and doctorate, GRE General Test, sample of written work. Additional exam requirements/recommendations for international students: Required—TOEFL (minimum score 570 paper-based; 230 computer-based; 88 iBT). *Application deadline:* For fall admission, 1/15 for domestic and international students. Application fee: $0. Electronic applications accepted. *Financial support:* Fellowships with full and partial tuition reimbursements, teaching assistantships with full and partial tuition reimbursements, career-related internships or fieldwork, Federal Work-Study, institutionally sponsored loans, scholarships/grants, and health care benefits available. Financial award application deadline: 1/15; financial award applicants required to submit CSS PROFILE or FAFSA. *Faculty research:* 1750 to present, Middle Ages, baroque, language pedagogy, linguistics. *Unit head:* Dieter H. O. Sevin, PhD, Chair, 615-322-2611, Fax: 615-343-7258, E-mail: dieter.h.sevin@vanderbilt.edu. *Application contact:* Christoph Zeller, PhD, Director of Graduate Studies, 615-322-2611, Fax: 615-343-7258, E-mail: christoph.zeller@vanderbilt.edu.

Washington University in St. Louis, Graduate School of Arts and Sciences, Department of Germanic Languages and Literature, St. Louis, MO 63130-4899. Offers MA, PhD. *Students:* 42 full-time (29 women); includes 3 minority (1 African American, 1 American Indian/Alaska Native, 1 Asian American or Pacific Islander), 3 international. 21 applicants, 57% accepted, 7 enrolled. In 2008, 6 master's, 2 doctorates awarded. Terminal master's awarded for partial completion of doctoral program. *Degree requirements:* For master's, thesis optional; for doctorate, thesis/dissertation. *Entrance requirements:* For master's and doctorate, GRE General Test, sample of written work. *Application deadline:* For fall admission, 1/15 priority date for domestic students. Application fee: $45. Electronic applications accepted. *Financial support:* Fellowships, research assistantships, teaching assistantships, career-related internships or fieldwork, Federal Work-Study, institutionally sponsored loans, and tuition waivers (full and partial) available. Support available to part-time students. Financial award application deadline: 1/15. *Unit head:* Dr. Stephan K. Schindler, Chairperson, 314-935-5160. *Application contact:* Assistant to the Dean, 314-935-6880, Fax: 314-935-4887.

Wayne State University, College of Liberal Arts and Sciences, Department of Classical and Modern Languages, Literatures, and Cultures, Program in German and Slavic Studies, Detroit, MI 48202. Offers German (MA); language learning (MA); modern languages (PhD); Russian (MA). *Degree requirements:* For master's, one foreign language, thesis or alternative; for doctorate, 2 foreign languages, thesis/dissertation. *Entrance requirements:* For master's and doctorate, minimum GPA of 3.0. Additional exam requirements/recommendations for international students: Required—TOEFL (minimum score 550 paper-based; 213 computer-based); Recommended—TWE (minimum score 6). Electronic applications accepted. *Faculty research:* Exile and Holocaust, minority literature, gender studies, fairytale studies, sociolinguistics.

West Chester University of Pennsylvania, Office of Graduate Studies, College of Arts and Sciences, Department of Languages and Cultures, West Chester, PA 19383. Offers French (M Ed, MA, Teaching Certificate); German (Teaching Certificate); Latin (Teaching Certificate); Spanish (M Ed, MA, Teaching Certificate). Part-time and evening/weekend programs available. *Students:* 7 full-time (6 women), 14 part-time (all women); includes 2 minority (1 African American, 1 Hispanic American), 1 international. Average age 34. 16 applicants, 100% accepted, 8 enrolled. In 2008, 3 master's awarded. *Degree requirements:* For master's, one foreign language, comprehensive exam, thesis optional. *Entrance requirements:* For master's, GRE or MAT, placement test. Additional exam requirements/recommendations for international students: Required—TOEFL (minimum score 550 paper-based; 213 computer-based; 80 iBT). *Application deadline:* For fall admission, 4/15 priority date for domestic students, 3/15 for international students; for spring admission, 10/15 for domestic students, 9/1 for international students. Applications are processed on a rolling basis. Application fee: $35. Electronic applications accepted. *Expenses:* Tuition, state resident: full-time $6430; part-time $357 per credit. Tuition, nonresident: full-time $10,288; part-time $572 per credit. Required fees: $652.50; $50 per credit. $67 per semester. *Financial support:* In 2008–09, 1 research assistantship with full and partial tuition reimbursement (averaging $5,000 per year) was awarded; unspecified assistantships also available. Support available to part-time students. Financial award application deadline: 2/15; financial award applicants required to submit FAFSA. *Faculty research:* Implementation of world languages curriculum framework. *Unit head:* Dr. Jerry Williams, Chair, 610-436-2700, Fax: 610-436-3048, E-mail: jwilliams2@wcupa.edu. *Application contact:* Dr. Rebecca Pauly, Graduate Coordinator, 610-436-2382, E-mail: rpauly@wcupa.edu.

Yale University, Graduate School of Arts and Sciences, Department of German, New Haven, CT 06520. Offers PhD. Terminal master's awarded for partial completion of doctoral program. *Degree requirements:* For doctorate, 3 foreign languages, thesis/dissertation. *Entrance requirements:* For doctorate, GRE General Test.

Italian

Boston College, Graduate School of Arts and Sciences, Department of Romance Languages and Literatures, Chestnut Hill, MA 02467-3800. Offers French (MA, PhD); Italian (MA); medieval language (PhD); Spanish (MA, PhD). Part-time programs available. Terminal master's awarded for partial completion of doctoral program. *Degree requirements:* For master's, one foreign language; for doctorate, 2 foreign languages, thesis/dissertation. *Entrance requirements:* Additional exam requirements/recommendations for international students: Required—TOEFL (minimum score 590 paper-based; 250 computer-based; 91 iBT). Electronic applications accepted. *Expenses:* Tuition: Part-time $1148 per credit. Required fees: $60. *Faculty research:* Spanish-American literature, philology, medieval French romance and troubadour/trouvere lyrics, Golden Age Peninsular literature, secondary language acquisition and pedagogy.

See Close-Up on page 437.

Brown University, Graduate School, Department of Italian Studies, Providence, RI 02912. Offers PhD, MA/PhD. Terminal master's awarded for partial completion of doctoral program. *Degree requirements:* For doctorate, 2 foreign languages, thesis/dissertation, preliminary exam.

Central Connecticut State University, School of Graduate Studies, School of Arts and Sciences, Department of Modern Languages, Program in Modern Language, New Britain, CT 06050-4010. Offers French (MA); Italian (Certificate); modern language (MA). Part-time and evening/weekend programs available. *Students:* 5 full-time (3 women), 30 part-time (25 women); includes 17 minority (all Hispanic Americans). Average age 36. 13 applicants, 100% accepted, 5 enrolled. In 2008, 5 master's awarded. *Degree requirements:* For master's, one foreign language, comprehensive exam, thesis or alternative. *Entrance requirements:* For master's, minimum undergraduate GPA of 2.7, 24 credits of undergraduate courses in either Italian or Spanish. Additional exam requirements/recommendations for international students: Required—TOEFL. *Application deadline:* For fall admission, 7/1 for domestic students; for spring admission, 12/1 for domestic students. Applications are processed on a rolling basis. Application fee: $50. Electronic applications accepted. *Expenses:* Tuition, area resident: Full-time $4377; part-time $420 per credit. Tuition, state resident: full-time $6566; part-time $420 per credit. Tuition, nonresident: full-time $12,195; part-time $420 per credit. Required fees: $3462. One-time fee: $62 part-time. *Faculty research:* Twentieth century French theater, seventeenth century French literature, French Middle Ages.

Columbia University, Graduate School of Arts and Sciences, Division of Humanities, Department of Italian, New York, NY 10027. Offers M Phil, MA, PhD. Part-time programs available. *Degree requirements:* For master's, one foreign language, oral and written exams; for doctorate, 2 foreign languages, thesis/dissertation. *Entrance requirements:* For master's and doctorate, GRE General Test, writing sample. Additional exam requirements/recommendations for international students: Required—TOEFL. *Faculty research:* Medieval and Renaissance Italian literature; Italian poetry, prose, and theater; modern and contemporary Italian literature.

Cornell University, Graduate School, Graduate Fields of Arts and Sciences, Field of Romance Studies, Ithaca, NY 14853-0001. Offers French linguistics (PhD); French literature (PhD); Hispanic literature (PhD); Italian linguistics (PhD); Italian literature (PhD); Romance linguistics (PhD); Spanish linguistics (PhD). *Faculty:* 30 full-time (14 women). *Students:* 50 full-time (24 women); includes 10 minority (all Hispanic Americans), 18 international. Average age 30. 99 applicants, 15% accepted, 8 enrolled. In 2008, 5 doctorates awarded. *Degree requirements:* For doctorate, 2 foreign languages, comprehensive exam, thesis/dissertation. *Entrance requirements:* For doctorate, GRE General Test, sample of written work, 3 letters of recommendation. Additional exam requirements/recommendations for international students: Required—TOEFL (minimum score 550 paper-based; 213 computer-based; 77 iBT). *Application deadline:* For fall admission, 1/15 for domestic students. Application fee: $70. Electronic applications accepted. *Expenses:* Tuition: Full-time $29,500. Required fees: $70. Full-time tuition and fees vary according to degree level, program and student level. *Financial support:* In 2008–09, 46 students received support, including 16 fellowships with full tuition reimbursements available, 30 teaching assistantships with full tuition reimbursements available; research assistantships with full tuition reimbursements available, institutionally sponsored loans, scholarships/grants, health care benefits, tuition waivers (full and partial), and unspecified

Italian

Cornell University (continued)

assistantships also available. Financial award applicants required to submit FAFSA. *Faculty research:* Literary theory, Hispanic studies, French studies, gender studies. *Unit head:* Director of Graduate Studies, 607-255-8222. *Application contact:* Graduate Field Assistant, 607-255-4246, E-mail: romance_studies@cornell.edu.

Florida State University, Graduate Studies, College of Arts and Sciences, Department of Modern Languages, Program in Italian Studies, Tallahassee, FL 32306. Offers MA. *Entrance requirements:* For master's, GRE General Test or minimum GPA of 3.0. Additional exam requirements/recommendations for international students: Required—TOEFL (minimum score 550 paper-based; 213 computer-based). Electronic applications accepted.

Graduate School and University Center of the City University of New York, Graduate Studies, Program in Comparative Literature, New York, NY 10016-4039. Offers comparative literature (MA, PhD), including classics (PhD), German (PhD), Italian (PhD). Terminal master's awarded for partial completion of doctoral program. *Degree requirements:* For master's, 2 foreign languages, comprehensive exam, thesis; for doctorate, 3 foreign languages, comprehensive exam, thesis/dissertation. *Entrance requirements:* For master's and doctorate, GRE General Test. Additional exam requirements/recommendations for international students: Required—TOEFL. Electronic applications accepted.

Harvard University, Graduate School of Arts and Sciences, Department of Romance Languages and Literatures, Cambridge, MA 02138. Offers French (AM, PhD); Italian (AM, PhD); Portuguese (AM, PhD); Spanish (AM, PhD). Terminal master's awarded for partial completion of doctoral program. *Degree requirements:* For master's, 2 foreign languages; for doctorate, 2 foreign languages, thesis/dissertation. *Entrance requirements:* For master's and doctorate, GRE General Test, sample of written work. Additional exam requirements/recommendations for international students: Required—TOEFL. *Expenses:* Tuition: Full-time $32,556. Required fees: $1426. Full-time tuition and fees vary according to program and student level.

Hunter College of the City University of New York, Graduate School, School of Arts and Sciences, Department of Romance Languages, Program in Italian, New York, NY 10021-5085. Offers Italian (MA); Italian education (MA). *Faculty:* 2 full-time (both women). *Students:* 9 part-time (6 women). Average age 43. 3 applicants, 33% accepted, 1 enrolled. *Degree requirements:* For master's, 2 foreign languages, comprehensive exam, thesis optional. *Entrance requirements:* For master's, GRE General Test, GRE Subject Test, ability to read, speak, and write Italian; interview. Additional exam requirements/recommendations for international students: Required—TOEFL. *Application deadline:* For fall admission, 4/1 for domestic students, 2/1 for international students; for spring admission, 11/1 for domestic students, 9/1 for international students. Application fee: $125. *Financial support:* Federal Work-Study, scholarships/grants, and tuition waivers (partial) available. Support available to part-time students. Financial award application deadline: 4/15. *Faculty research:* Dante, Middle Ages, Renaissance, contemporary Italian novel and poetry, late Renaissance and baroque. *Unit head:* Dr. Paolo Fasoli, Graduate Co-Adviser, 212-772-5129, Fax: 212-772-5094, E-mail: pfasoli@hunter.cuny.edu. *Application contact:* William Zlata, Director for Graduate Admissions, 212-772-4482, Fax: 212-650-3336, E-mail: admissions@hunter.cuny.edu.

Indiana University Bloomington, University Graduate School, College of Arts and Sciences, Department of French and Italian, Bloomington, IN 47405-7000. Offers French (MA, PhD), including French instruction (MA), French linguistics, French literature; Italian (MA, PhD). Part-time programs available. *Faculty:* 19 full-time (7 women). *Students:* 79 full-time (50 women); includes 5 minority (1 African American, 1 American Indian/Alaska Native, 1 Asian American or Pacific Islander, 2 Hispanic Americans), 34 international. Average age 30. 46 applicants, 70% accepted, 15 enrolled. In 2008, 18 master's, 6 doctorates awarded. Terminal master's awarded for partial completion of doctoral program. *Degree requirements:* For master's, one foreign language, comprehensive exam, thesis optional; for doctorate, 2 foreign languages, comprehensive exam, thesis/dissertation. *Entrance requirements:* For master's and doctorate, GRE General Test. Additional exam requirements/recommendations for international students: Required—TOEFL (minimum score 550 paper-based; 213 computer-based; 79 iBT). *Application deadline:* For fall admission, 1/15 priority date for domestic students, 12/1 priority date for international students; for spring admission, 9/1 priority date for domestic and international students. Application fee: $50 ($60 for international students). Electronic applications accepted. *Expenses:* Tuition, area resident: Part-time $291.97 per credit hour. Tuition, state resident: part-time $291.97 per credit hour. Tuition, nonresident: part-time $850.33 per credit hour. Required fees: $110 per semester. Tuition and fees vary according to course load and program. *Financial support:* In 2008–09, 46 students received support, including 2 fellowships with partial tuition reimbursements available (averaging $15,000 per year), 7 research assistantships with partial tuition reimbursements available (averaging $13,025 per year), 37 teaching assistantships with partial tuition reimbursements available (averaging $13,025 per year). Financial award application deadline: 1/15. *Faculty research:* All periods of French and Italian literature and various areas of French linguistics, including the novel and political theory, literature and fine arts, literary theory, postcolonialism, French-Creole studies, French literature of Africa and its Diaspora, humanism, medieval folklore and mythology, humor in medieval and renaissance literature, cinema Old Occitan and Old French, emigration, second lang. acquisition, syntax, sociolinguistics, phonology, and lexicography. *Unit head:* Prof. Emanuel Mickel, Interim Chairman, 812-855-5458, Fax: 812-855-8877, E-mail: fritchr@indiana.edu. *Application contact:* Jocelyn Karlan, Secretary, 812-855-1088, Fax: 812-855-8877, E-mail: fritgs@indiana.edu.

Iona College, School of Arts and Science, Program in Foreign Languages, New Rochelle, NY 10801-1890. Offers Italian (MA); Spanish (MA). Part-time and evening/weekend programs available. *Faculty:* 5 full-time (2 women), 3 part-time/adjunct (1 woman). *Students:* 18 part-time (14 women); includes 3 minority (1 African American, 2 Hispanic Americans). Average age 32. 3 applicants, 67% accepted, 1 enrolled. *Degree requirements:* For master's, thesis or alternative. *Entrance requirements:* For master's, minimum GPA of 3.0. Additional exam requirements/recommendations for international students: Required—TOEFL (minimum score 550 paper-based; 213 computer-based). *Application deadline:* Applications are processed on a rolling basis. Application fee: $50. Electronic applications accepted. *Expenses:* Tuition: Part-time $755 per credit. Required fees: $175 per term. *Financial support:* Unspecified assistantships available. Support available to part-time students. Financial award application deadline: 4/15; financial award applicants required to submit FAFSA. *Faculty research:* Contemporary Spanish literature, linguistics, language acquisition, female Hispanic literature, Latina authors. *Unit head:* Dr. Thomas E. Mussio, Chair, 914-637-2737, E-mail: TMussio@iona.edu. *Application contact:* Veronica Jarek-Prinz, Director of Graduate Admissions, 914-633-2420, Fax: 914-633-2277, E-mail: vjarekprinz@iona.edu.

The Johns Hopkins University, Zanvyl Krieger School of Arts and Sciences, Department of German and Romance Languages, Baltimore, MD 21218-2699. Offers French (PhD); German (PhD); Italian (PhD); romance languages (PhD); Spanish (PhD). *Degree requirements:* For doctorate, 2 foreign languages, thesis/dissertation. *Entrance requirements:* For doctorate, GRE General Test. Additional exam requirements/recommendations for international students: Required—TOEFL (minimum score 600 paper-based; 250 computer-based). Electronic applications accepted.

McGill University, Faculty of Graduate and Postdoctoral Studies, Faculty of Arts, Department of Italian Studies, Montréal, QC H3A 2T5, Canada. Offers MA, PhD.

Middlebury College, Language Schools, Italian School, Middlebury, VT 05753. Offers MA, DML. *Faculty:* 15 full-time (3 women). *Students:* 65 full-time (47 women); includes 6 minority (all Hispanic Americans). Average age 33. 106 applicants, 82% accepted, 67 enrolled. In 2008, 34 master's awarded. *Degree requirements:* For master's, one foreign language; for doctorate, 2 foreign languages, comprehensive exam, thesis/dissertation, residence abroad, teaching experience. *Entrance requirements:* For master's, placement exam, 3 letters of recommendation, writing sample. *Application deadline:* Applications are processed on a rolling basis. Application fee: $55. Electronic applications accepted. *Financial support:* Scholarships/grants available. *Unit head:* Dr. Antonio Vitti, Director, 802-443-5727, Fax: 802-443-2075, E-mail: acvitti@middlebury.edu. *Application contact:* Kara Gennarelli, Coordinator, 802-443-5727, Fax: 802-443-2075, E-mail: kgennar@middlebury.edu.

Montclair State University, The Office of Graduate Admissions and Support Services, College of Humanities and Social Sciences, Department of Spanish and Italian, Montclair, NJ 07043-1624. Offers Italian (Certificate); Spanish (MA, Certificate); translating and interpreting Spanish (Certificate). Part-time and evening/weekend programs available. *Faculty:* 18 full-time (10 women), 25 part-time/adjunct (19 women). *Students:* 2 full-time (both women), 18 part-time (16 women); includes 6 minority (2 African Americans, 2 American Indian/Alaska Native, 2 Hispanic Americans), 1 international. Average age 35. 6 applicants, 100% accepted, 2 enrolled. In 2008, 6 master's awarded. *Degree requirements:* For master's, comprehensive exam, thesis or alternative. *Entrance requirements:* For master's, GRE General Test, BA in Spanish or at least 24 undergraduate credits of Spanish, 2 letters of recommendation. Additional exam requirements/recommendations for international students: Required—TOEFL (minimum score 83 computer-based). *Application deadline:* For fall admission, 6/1 for international students; for spring admission, 11/1 for international students. Applications are processed on a rolling basis. Application fee: $60. Electronic applications accepted. *Financial support:* In 2008–09, 1 research assistantship with full tuition reimbursement (averaging $7,000 per year) was awarded; Federal Work-Study, scholarships/grants, and unspecified assistantships also available. Support available to part-time students. Financial award application deadline: 3/1; financial award applicants required to submit FAFSA. *Unit head:* Dr. Diana Guemaraz Cruz, Chairperson, 973-655-7506. *Application contact:* Amy Aiello, Associate Director of Admissions, 973-655-5147, Fax: 973-655-7869, E-mail: graduate.school@montclair.edu.

New York University, Graduate School of Arts and Science, Department of Italian Studies, New York, NY 10012-1019. Offers Italian (MA, PhD); Italian studies (MA). Part-time programs available. Terminal master's awarded for partial completion of doctoral program. *Degree requirements:* For master's, one foreign language, thesis; for doctorate, 3 foreign languages, thesis/dissertation. *Entrance requirements:* For master's, GRE General Test, sample of written work; for doctorate, GRE General Test. Additional exam requirements/recommendations for international students: Required—TOEFL. *Faculty research:* Dante, early modern literature, fascism and culture, contemporary literature, feminist theory.

Northwestern University, The Graduate School, Judd A. and Marjorie Weinberg College of Arts and Sciences, Department of French and Italian, Evanston, IL 60208. Offers eighteenth-century studies (Certificate); French (PhD); French and comparative literature (PhD); Italian studies (Certificate). Admissions and degrees offered through The Graduate School. *Degree requirements:* For doctorate, one foreign language, thesis/dissertation, written and oral exams. *Entrance requirements:* For doctorate, GRE, writing sample, cassette recording. Additional exam requirements/recommendations for international students: Required—TOEFL. *Faculty research:* Francophone studies, 18th century contemporary theory.

The Ohio State University, Graduate School, College of Humanities, Department of French and Italian, Columbus, OH 43210. Offers French (MA, PhD); Italian (MA). *Degree requirements:* For master's, variable foreign language requirement, thesis optional; for doctorate, variable foreign language requirement, thesis/dissertation. *Entrance requirements:* For master's and doctorate, GRE General Test. Additional exam requirements/recommendations for international students: Required—TOEFL. Electronic applications accepted. *Faculty research:* Italian and Romance linguistics.

Queens College of the City University of New York, Division of Graduate Studies, Arts and Humanities Division, Department of European Languages and Literatures, Program in Italian, Flushing, NY 11367-1597. Offers MA. Part-time and evening/weekend programs available. *Degree requirements:* For master's, 2 foreign languages, comprehensive exam, thesis or alternative. *Entrance requirements:* For master's, minimum GPA of 3.0. Additional exam requirements/recommendations for international students: Required—TOEFL.

Rutgers, The State University of New Jersey, New Brunswick, Graduate School, Program in Italian, Piscataway, NJ 08854-8097. Offers Italian (MA, PhD); Italian literature and literary criticism (MA); language, literature and culture (MAT). Part-time and evening/weekend programs available. Terminal master's awarded for partial completion of doctoral program. *Degree requirements:* For master's, one foreign language, comprehensive exam (for some programs), thesis optional; for doctorate, 2 foreign languages, thesis/dissertation, qualifying exam. *Entrance requirements:* For master's and doctorate, GRE General Test. Additional exam requirements/recommendations for international students: Required—TOEFL. *Faculty research:* Literature.

San Francisco State University, Division of Graduate Studies, College of Humanities, Department of Foreign Languages and Literatures, Program in Italian, San Francisco, CA 94132-1722. Offers MA.

Stanford University, School of Humanities and Sciences, Department of French and Italian, Stanford, CA 94305-9991. Offers French (MA, PhD); Italian (MA, PhD). Terminal master's awarded for partial completion of doctoral program. *Degree requirements:* For master's, one foreign language, written exam; for doctorate, 2 foreign languages, thesis/dissertation, oral exam. *Entrance requirements:* For master's and doctorate, GRE General Test. Additional exam requirements/recommendations for international students: Required—TOEFL. Electronic applications accepted.

State University of New York at Binghamton, Graduate School, School of Arts and Sciences, Department of Romance Languages and Literatures, Program in Italian, Binghamton, NY 13902-6000. Offers MA. *Students:* 3 part-time (all women), 1 international. Average age 23. 1 applicant, 0% accepted. In 2008, 1 master's awarded. *Degree requirements:* For master's, one foreign language, comprehensive exam, thesis or alternative. *Entrance requirements:* For master's, GRE General Test, GRE Subject Test. Additional exam requirements/recommendations for international students: Required—TOEFL. *Application deadline:* For fall admission, 4/15 priority date for domestic students, 1/15 priority date for international students; for spring admission, 11/1 for domestic students, 10/1 priority date for international students. Applications are processed on a rolling basis. Application fee: $60. Electronic applications accepted. *Expenses:* Tuition, area resident: Full-time $6900; part-time $288 per credit. Tuition, state resident: full-time $6900; part-time $288 per credit. Tuition, nonresident: full-time $10,920; part-time $455 per credit. Required fees: $1130. Part-time tuition and fees vary according to course load, program and student level. *Financial support:* Fellowships, research assistantships, teaching assistantships, career-related internships or fieldwork, Federal Work-Study, institutionally sponsored loans, scholarships/grants, health care benefits, and unspecified assistantships available. Financial award application deadline: 2/15; financial award applicants required to submit FAFSA. *Unit head:* Dr. Antonio Sobejano-Moran, Chairperson, 607-777-4635, E-mail: antobianco@msn.com. *Application contact:* Victoria Williams, Recruiting and Admissions Coordinator, 607-777-2151, Fax: 607-777-2501, E-mail: vwilliam@binghamton.edu.

Stony Brook University, State University of New York, Graduate School, College of Arts and Sciences, Department of European Languages, Literatures, and Cultures, Program in Italian, Stony Brook, NY 11794. Offers MA. Evening/weekend programs available. *Degree requirements:* For master's, one foreign language. *Entrance requirements:* For master's, GRE General Test. Additional exam requirements/recommendations for international students: Required—TOEFL. *Application deadline:* For fall admission, 1/15 for domestic students. Application fee: $60. *Expenses:* Tuition, area resident: Full-time $7880; part-time $328 per credit hour. Tuition, state resident: full-time $7880; part-time $328 per credit hour. Tuition, nonresident: full-time $13,250; part-time $552 per credit hour. Required fees: $848. *Unit head:* Charles Franco, Coordinator, 631-632-1494, E-mail: charles.franco@stonybrook.edu. *Application contact:* Dr. Andrea Fedi, Director of Graduate Studies, 631-632-7438, Fax: 631-632-9612.

Italian

University at Albany, State University of New York, College of Arts and Sciences, Department of Languages, Literatures, and Cultures, Program in Italian, Albany, NY 12222-0001. Offers MA.

University of Alberta, Faculty of Graduate Studies and Research, Department of Modern Languages and Cultural Studies, Edmonton, AB T6G 2E1, Canada. Offers applied linguistics (Germanic, Romance, Slavic) (MA); French language, literatures and linguistics (PhD); French language, literatures, and linguistics (MA); Germanic languages, literatures and linguistics (PhD); Germanic languages, literatures, and linguistics (MA); Italian studies (MA); Slavic languages and literatures (Russian, Ukrainian) (MA, PhD); Slavic linguistics (Russian, Ukrainian) (MA, PhD); Spanish and Latin American studies (MA, PhD); Ukrainian folklore (MA, PhD). Part-time programs available. *Degree requirements:* For master's, one foreign language, thesis; for doctorate, 2 foreign languages, comprehensive exam, thesis/dissertation. *Entrance requirements:* For master's and doctorate, 1 language other than English. Additional exam requirements/recommendations for international students: Required—Michigan English Language Assessment Battery or TOEFL (paper score 550; computer score 213). Electronic applications accepted. *Faculty research:* Russian/Ukrainian studies; German studies; contemporary Latin American, French and Francophone studies; Italian studies.

University of California, Berkeley, Graduate Division, College of Letters and Science, Department of Italian Studies, Berkeley, CA 94720-1500. Offers PhD. *Degree requirements:* For doctorate, one foreign language, thesis/dissertation, oral and written qualifying exams. *Entrance requirements:* For doctorate, GRE General Test, minimum GPA of 3.0, 3 letters of recommendation. Additional exam requirements/recommendations for international students: Required—TOEFL (minimum score 570 paper-based; 230 computer-based). *Faculty research:* Literature and culture of Italy in Middle Ages and the Renaissance, literature and culture of Italy in nineteenth- and twentieth-centuries, Italian film studies, interdisciplinary cultural studies.

University of California, Berkeley, Graduate Division, Group in Romance Languages and Literature, Program in Italian, Berkeley, CA 94720-1500. Offers PhD. *Entrance requirements:* For doctorate, GRE General Test, 3 letters of recommendation.

University of California, Los Angeles, Graduate Division, College of Letters and Science, Department of Italian, Los Angeles, CA 90095. Offers MA, PhD. *Students:* 23 full-time (17 women); includes 2 minority (both Hispanic Americans), 1 international. Average age 30. 14 applicants, 43% accepted, 4 enrolled. In 2008, 4 master's, 1 doctorate awarded. Terminal master's awarded for partial completion of doctoral program. *Degree requirements:* For master's, one foreign language, comprehensive exam or thesis; for doctorate, 2 foreign languages, thesis/dissertation, oral and written qualifying exams. *Entrance requirements:* For master's, GRE General Test, minimum GPA of 3.0, sample of written work; statement of purpose; for doctorate, GRE General Test, minimum undergraduate GPA of 3.0, sample of written work; statement of purpose. *Application deadline:* For fall admission, 12/15 for domestic and international students. Application fee: $60 ($80 for international students). Electronic applications accepted. *Expenses:* Tuition, nonresident: full-time $14,694. Required fees: $9669.50. Full-time tuition and fees vary according to course load, degree level, program and student level. *Financial support:* In 2008–09, 23 fellowships with full and partial tuition reimbursements, 5 research assistantships with full and partial tuition reimbursements, 17 teaching assistantships with full and partial tuition reimbursements were awarded; Federal Work-Study, institutionally sponsored loans, health care benefits, tuition waivers (full and partial), and unspecified assistantships also available. Financial award application deadline: 3/1. *Unit head:* Chair. *Application contact:* Departmental Office, 310-825-1940, E-mail: allen@humnet.ucla.edu.

University of Chicago, Division of the Humanities, Department of Romance Languages and Literatures, Chicago, IL 60637-1513. Offers French (AM, PhD); Italian (AM, PhD); Spanish (AM, PhD). Terminal master's awarded for partial completion of doctoral program. *Degree requirements:* For master's, 2 foreign languages, thesis; for doctorate, 3 foreign languages, thesis/dissertation. *Entrance requirements:* For master's and doctorate, GRE General Test, GRE Subject Test. Additional exam requirements/recommendations for international students: Required—TOEFL.

University of Connecticut, Graduate School, College of Liberal Arts and Sciences, Department of Modern and Classical Languages, Field of Italian, Storrs, CT 06269. Offers MA, PhD. Terminal master's awarded for partial completion of doctoral program. *Degree requirements:* For master's, comprehensive exam; for doctorate, thesis/dissertation. *Entrance requirements:* For master's, GRE General Test. Additional exam requirements/recommendations for international students: Required—TOEFL (minimum score 550 paper-based; 213 computer-based). Electronic applications accepted.

University of Illinois at Urbana–Champaign, Graduate College, College of Liberal Arts and Sciences, School of Literatures, Cultures and Linguistics, Department of Spanish, Italian and Portuguese, Champaign, IL 61820. Offers Italian (MA, PhD); Portuguese (MA, PhD); Spanish (MA, PhD). *Faculty:* 17 full-time (10 women), 1 part-time/adjunct (0 women). *Students:* 50 full-time (38 women), 7 part-time (6 women); includes 4 minority (all Hispanic Americans), 31 international. 55 applicants, 44% accepted, 14 enrolled. In 2008, 10 master's, 4 doctorates awarded. *Entrance requirements:* For master's, GRE General Test, minimum GPA of 3.0; writing sample; for doctorate, GRE, minimum GPA of 3.0; writing sample. Additional exam requirements/recommendations for international students: Required—TOEFL (minimum score 88 iBT). *Application deadline:* Applications are processed on a rolling basis. Application fee: $60 ($75 for international students). Electronic applications accepted. *Financial support:* In 2008–09, 15 fellowships, 1 research assistantship, 48 teaching assistantships were awarded; tuition waivers (full and partial) also available. *Unit head:* Diane Musumeci, Head, 217-244-3250, Fax: 217-244-8430, E-mail: musumeci@illinois.edu. *Application contact:* Lynn Stanke, Secretary, 217-333-6269, Fax: 217-244-3050, E-mail: stanke@illinois.edu.

The University of North Carolina at Chapel Hill, Graduate School, College of Arts and Sciences, Department of Romance Languages, Chapel Hill, NC 27599. Offers French (MA, PhD); Italian (MA, PhD); Portuguese (MA, PhD); Romance languages (MA, PhD); Romance philology (MA, PhD); Spanish (MA, PhD). *Degree requirements:* For master's, one foreign language, comprehensive exam, thesis; for doctorate, 2 foreign languages, comprehensive exam, thesis/dissertation. *Entrance requirements:* For master's and doctorate, GRE General Test, minimum GPA of 3.0. Additional exam requirements/recommendations for international students: Required—TOEFL (minimum score 550 paper-based; 213 computer-based). Electronic applications accepted.

University of Notre Dame, Graduate School, College of Arts and Letters, Division of Humanities, Department of Romance Languages and Literatures, Notre Dame, IN 46556. Offers French and Francophone studies (MA); Iberian and Latin American studies (MA); Italian studies (MA); Romance literatures (MA). *Faculty:* 25 full-time (10 women), 4 part-time/adjunct (all women). *Students:* 17 full-time (12 women); includes 4 minority (all Hispanic Americans), 2 international. 30 applicants, 47% accepted, 11 enrolled. In 2008, 11 master's awarded. *Degree requirements:* For master's, 2 foreign languages, comprehensive exam, thesis optional. *Entrance requirements:* For master's, GRE General Test, BA in target language. Additional exam requirements/recommendations for international students: Required—TOEFL (minimum score 600 paper-based; 250 computer-based; 80 iBT). *Application deadline:* For fall admission, 2/1 priority date for domestic students, 2/1 for international students. Application fee: $50. Electronic applications accepted. *Financial support:* Teaching assistantships with full tuition reimbursements, tuition waivers (full) available. Financial award application deadline: 2/1. *Faculty research:* Literature of discovery and exploration, modern literature, literary criticism, medieval literature, feminist critical theory. *Unit head:* Dr. John Welle, Director of Graduate Studies, 574-631-6887, E-mail: al.romland.1@nd.edu. *Application contact:* Dr. Barbara Turpin, Director of Graduate Admissions, 574-631-7706, Fax: 574-631-4183.

University of Oregon, Graduate School, College of Arts and Sciences, Department of Romance Languages, Program in Italian, Eugene, OR 97403. Offers MA. Part-time programs available. *Degree requirements:* For master's, variable foreign language requirement. *Entrance requirements:* For master's, GRE General Test, minimum GPA of 3.0. Additional exam requirements/recommendations for international students: Required—TOEFL.

University of Pennsylvania, School of Arts and Sciences, Graduate Group in Romance Languages, Philadelphia, PA 19104. Offers French (AM, PhD); Italian (AM, PhD); Spanish (AM, PhD). Terminal master's awarded for partial completion of doctoral program. *Degree requirements:* For master's, one foreign language, thesis or alternative; for doctorate, 2 foreign languages, thesis/dissertation. *Entrance requirements:* For master's and doctorate, GRE General Test. Additional exam requirements/recommendations for international students: Required—TOEFL. Electronic applications accepted. *Faculty research:* Literary theory and criticism, cultural studies, history of Romance literatures, gender studies.

University of Pittsburgh, School of Arts and Sciences, Department of French and Italian, Program in Italian, Pittsburgh, PA 15260. Offers MA. Part-time programs available. *Degree requirements:* For master's, 2 foreign languages, comprehensive exam, seminar paper. *Entrance requirements:* For master's, minimum GPA of 3.0, writing sample. Additional exam requirements/recommendations for international students: Required—TOEFL (minimum score 554 paper-based; 213 computer-based; 80 iBT). *Faculty research:* Seventeenth and eighteenth century literature, twentieth century holocaust literature, theater, opera, Dante and his reception, humanism.

University of South Africa, College of Human Sciences, Pretoria, South Africa. Offers adult education (M Ed); African languages (MA, PhD); African politics (MA, PhD); Afrikaans (MA, PhD); ancient history (MA, PhD); ancient Near Eastern studies (MA, PhD); anthropology (MA, PhD); applied linguistics (MA); Arabic (MA, PhD); archaeology (MA); art history (MA); Biblical archaeology (MA); Biblical studies (M Th, D Th, PhD); Christian spirituality (M Th, D Th); church history (M Th, D Th); classical studies (MA, PhD); clinical psychology (MA); communication (MA, PhD); comparative education (M Ed, Ed D); consulting psychology (D Admin, D Com, PhD); curriculum studies (M Ed, Ed D); development studies (M Admin, MA, D Admin, PhD); didactics (M Ed, Ed D); education (M Tech); education management (M Ed, Ed D); educational psychology (M Ed); English (MA); environmental education (M Ed); French (MA, PhD); German (MA, PhD); Greek (MA); guidance and counseling (M Ed); health studies (MA, PhD), including health sciences education (MA), health services management (MA), medical and surgical nursing science (critical care general) (MA), midwifery and neonatal nursing science (MA), trauma and emergency care (MA); history (MA, PhD); history of education (Ed D); inclusive education (M Ed, Ed D); information and communications technology policy and regulation (MA); information science (MA, MIS, PhD); international politics (MA, PhD); Islamic studies (MA, PhD); Italian (MA, PhD); Judaica (MA, PhD); linguistics (MA, PhD); mathematical education (M Ed); mathematics education (MA); missiology (M Th, D Th); modern Hebrew (MA, PhD); musicology (MA, MMus, D Mus, PhD); natural science education (M Ed); New Testament (M Th, D Th); Old Testament (D Th); pastoral therapy (M Th, D Th); philosophy (MA); philosophy of education (M Ed, Ed D); politics (MA, PhD); Portuguese (MA, PhD); practical theology (M Th, D Th); psychology (MA, MS, PhD); psychology of education (M Ed, Ed D); public health (MA); religious studies (MA, D Th, PhD); Romance languages (MA); Russian (MA, PhD); Semitic languages (MA, PhD); social behavior studies in HIV/AIDS (MA); social science (mental health) (MA); social science in development studies (MA); social science in psychology (MA); social science in social work (MA); social science in sociology (MA); social work (MSW, DSW, PhD); socio-education (M Ed, Ed D); sociolinguistics (MA); sociology (MA, PhD); Spanish (MA, PhD); systematic theology (M Th, D Th); TESOL (teaching English to speakers of other languages) (MA); theological ethics (M Th, D Th); theory of literature (MA, PhD); urban ministries (D Th); urban ministry (M Th).

The University of Tennessee, Graduate School, College of Arts and Sciences, Department of Modern Foreign Languages and Literatures, Program in Modern Foreign Languages, Knoxville, TN 37996. Offers applied linguistics (PhD); French (PhD); German (PhD); Italian (PhD); Portuguese (PhD); Russian (PhD); Spanish (PhD). *Degree requirements:* For doctorate, 2 foreign languages, thesis/dissertation. *Entrance requirements:* For doctorate, minimum GPA of 2.7. Additional exam requirements/recommendations for international students: Required—TOEFL. Electronic applications accepted. *Expenses:* Tuition, area resident: Part-time $348 per credit hour. Tuition, state resident: full-time $6262. Tuition, nonresident: full-time $18,920; part-time $1052 per credit hour. Required fees: $812; $36 per credit hour. Tuition and fees vary according to program.

The University of Texas at Austin, Graduate School, College of Liberal Arts, Department of French and Italian, Austin, TX 78712-1111. Offers French (MA, PhD); French linguistics (MA, PhD); Italian studies (MA, PhD); Romance linguistics (MA, PhD). Part-time programs available. *Degree requirements:* For master's, one foreign language, thesis; for doctorate, 2 foreign languages, thesis/dissertation. *Entrance requirements:* For master's, GRE General Test, minimum GPA of 3.0, bachelor's degree in French or equivalent; for doctorate, GRE General Test, minimum GPA of 3.0, master's degree in French. Additional exam requirements/recommendations for international students: Required—TOEFL. Electronic applications accepted. *Faculty research:* Nineteenth-century Italian literature, Italian Renaissance, twentieth-century French literature, Francophone literature, fifteenth-century literature and culture.

University of Toronto, School of Graduate Studies, Humanities Division, Department of Italian Studies, Toronto, ON M5S 1A1, Canada. Offers MA, PhD. Part-time programs available. *Degree requirements:* For doctorate, 2 foreign languages, comprehensive exam, thesis/dissertation, oral defense, language exam(s). *Entrance requirements:* For master's, minimum B average in last 2 years in Italian; minimum B average in final year, overall; 2 letters of recommendation; for doctorate, MA in Italian, minimum A– average.

University of Victoria, Faculty of Graduate Studies, Faculty of Humanities, Department of Hispanic and Italian Studies, Victoria, BC V8W 2Y2, Canada. Offers Hispanic and Italian studies (MA); Hispanic studies (MA). *Degree requirements:* For master's, one foreign language, comprehensive exam, thesis (for some programs). *Entrance requirements:* For master's, undergraduate major in Hispanic studies, minimum B+ average. Additional exam requirements/recommendations for international students: Required—TOEFL (minimum score 575 paper-based; 233 computer-based), IELTS (minimum score 7). Electronic applications accepted. *Faculty research:* Medieval/Renaissance Spanish and Italian literature, Golden Age literature, Latin American literature.

University of Virginia, College and Graduate School of Arts and Sciences, Department of Spanish, Italian and Portuguese, Program in Italian, Charlottesville, VA 22903. Offers MA. *Students:* 7 full-time (5 women), 1 (woman) part-time; includes 2 minority (both Hispanic Americans), 6 international. Average age 30. 6 applicants, 83% accepted, 4 enrolled. In 2008, 3 master's awarded. *Degree requirements:* For master's, one foreign language, comprehensive exam, thesis. *Entrance requirements:* For master's, GRE General Test, BA in Italian; 2 letters of recommendation. Additional exam requirements/recommendations for international students: Required—TOEFL (minimum score 600 paper-based; 250 computer-based; 90 iBT), IELTS (minimum score 7). *Application deadline:* For fall admission, 12/1 for domestic and international students. Applications are processed on a rolling basis. Application fee: $60. Electronic applications accepted. *Expenses:* Tuition, area resident: Full-time $10,452. Tuition, state resident: full-time $10,452. Tuition, nonresident: full-time $20,010. Required fees: $2176. Part-time tuition and fees vary according to course load and program. *Financial support:* Teaching assistantships available. Financial award applicants required to submit FAFSA. *Application contact:* Enrico Cesaretti, Director of Graduate Admissions, 434-924-7159.

University of Washington, Graduate School, College of Arts and Sciences, Department of Romance Languages and Literature, Division of French and Italian Studies, Seattle, WA 98195. Offers French (MA, PhD); Italian (MA). Terminal master's awarded for partial completion of doctoral program. *Degree requirements:* For master's, 2 foreign languages, exam; for doctorate, 3 foreign languages, thesis/dissertation, exam. *Entrance requirements:* For master's and doctorate, GRE General Test, minimum GPA of 3.0. Additional exam requirements/

Italian

University of Washington (continued)
recommendations for international students: Required—TOEFL. Electronic applications accepted. *Faculty research:* Interdisciplinary studies, literary theory and criticism, film, major periods of French and Italian literature, Francophonie.

University of Wisconsin–Madison, Graduate School, College of Letters and Science, Department of French and Italian, Program in Italian, Madison, WI 53706-1380. Offers MA, PhD. Part-time programs available. *Degree requirements:* For master's, one foreign language; for doctorate, 2 foreign languages, thesis/dissertation. *Entrance requirements:* For master's and doctorate, GRE. Electronic applications accepted. *Faculty research:* Italian literature, culture, linguistics, cinema, and language.

University of Wisconsin–Milwaukee, Graduate School, College of Letters and Sciences, Interdepartmental Program in Foreign Language and Literature, Milwaukee, WI 53201-0413. Offers classics and Hebrew studies (MAFLL); comparative literature (MAFLL); French and Italian (MAFLL); German (MAFLL); Slavic studies (MAFLL); translation (Certificate). Part-time programs available. *Faculty:* 39 full-time (17 women). *Students:* 32 full-time (25 women), 28 part-time (19 women); includes 5 minority (1 Asian American or Pacific Islander, 4 Hispanic Americans), 22 international. Average age 32. 51 applicants, 65% accepted, 26 enrolled. In 2008, 19 master's awarded. *Degree requirements:* For master's, 2 foreign languages, thesis or alternative. *Entrance requirements:* Additional exam requirements/recommendations for international students: Required—TOEFL (minimum score 550 paper-based; 79 iBT), IELTS (minimum score 6.5). *Application deadline:* For fall admission, 1/1 priority date for domestic

students; for spring admission, 9/1 for domestic students. Applications are processed on a rolling basis. Application fee: $45 ($75 for international students). *Expenses:* Tuition, area resident: Full-time $7320; part-time $165 per credit. Tuition, state resident: full-time $7320; part-time $165 per credit. Tuition, nonresident: full-time $17,840; part-time $714 per credit. Tuition and fees vary according to campus/location, program and reciprocity agreements. *Financial support:* In 2008–09, 2 research assistantships, 35 teaching assistantships were awarded; career-related internships or fieldwork and unspecified assistantships also available. Support available to part-time students. Financial award application deadline: 4/15. Total annual research expenditures: $43,420. *Unit head:* Gabrielle Verdier, Representative, 414-229-3346, Fax: 414-229-2741, E-mail: verdier@uwm.edu. *Application contact:* General Information Contact, 414-229-4982, Fax: 414-229-6967, E-mail: gradschool@uwm.edu.

Wayne State University, College of Liberal Arts and Sciences, Department of Classical and Modern Languages, Literatures, and Cultures, Program in Italian, Detroit, MI 48202. Offers MA. *Degree requirements:* For master's, one foreign language, thesis optional. *Entrance requirements:* For master's, GRE General Test, minimum GPA of 3.0. Additional exam requirements/recommendations for international students: Required—TOEFL (minimum score 550 paper-based; 213 computer-based); Recommended—TWE (minimum score 6). Electronic applications accepted. *Faculty research:* Renaissance lyric, modern theatre, Dante and Bocaccio, modern novel.

Yale University, Graduate School of Arts and Sciences, Department of Italian Language and Literature, New Haven, CT 06520. Offers PhD. *Degree requirements:* For doctorate, 3 foreign languages, thesis/dissertation. *Entrance requirements:* For doctorate, GRE General Test.

Japanese

Arizona State University, Graduate College, College of Liberal Arts and Sciences, Division of Humanities, School of International Letters and Cultures, Program in Japanese, Tempe, AZ 85287. Offers MA.

Cornell University, Graduate School, Graduate Fields of Arts and Sciences, Field of East Asian Literature, Ithaca, NY 14853-0001. Offers Asian religions (MA, PhD); Chinese linguistics (MA, PhD); Chinese philology (MA, PhD); classical Chinese literature (MA, PhD); classical Japanese literature (MA, PhD); Japanese linguistics (MA, PhD); Korean literature (MA, PhD); modern Chinese literature (MA, PhD); modern Japanese literature (MA, PhD). *Faculty:* 14 full-time (6 women). *Students:* 18 full-time (9 women); includes 6 minority (all Asian Americans or Pacific Islanders), 9 international. Average age 34. 41 applicants, 7% accepted, 2 enrolled. In 2008, 2 master's, 3 doctorates awarded. *Degree requirements:* For master's, 2 foreign languages, thesis, teaching experience; for doctorate, 2 foreign languages, comprehensive exam, thesis/dissertation, teaching experience. *Entrance requirements:* For master's and doctorate, GRE General Test, 3 years of study in Chinese, Japanese, Korean, or Vietnamese, 3 letters of recommendation, academic writing sample. Additional exam requirements/recommendations for international students: Required—TOEFL (minimum score 600 paper-based; 250 computer-based; 77 iBT). *Application deadline:* For fall admission, 1/10 priority date for domestic students. Application fee: $70. Electronic applications accepted. *Expenses:* Tuition: Full-time $29,500. Required fees: $70. Full-time tuition and fees vary according to degree level, program and student level. *Financial support:* In 2008–09, 17 students received support, including 8 fellowships with full tuition reimbursements available, 2 research assistantships with full tuition reimbursements available, 7 teaching assistantships with full tuition reimbursements available; institutionally sponsored loans, scholarships/grants, health care benefits, tuition waivers (full and partial), and unspecified assistantships also available. Financial award applicants required to submit FAFSA. *Faculty research:* Vietnamese literature; Chinese literature, drama, and film; Japanese theater and literature; popular culture in East Asia; Korean literature; Asian linguistics. *Unit head:* Director of Graduate Studies, 607-255-9099. *Application contact:* Graduate Field Assistant, 607-255-9099, E-mail: east_asian_lit@cornell.edu.

Eastern Michigan University, Graduate School, College of Arts and Sciences, Department of Foreign Languages and Bilingual Studies, Program in Foreign Languages, Ypsilanti, MI 48197. Offers French (MA); German (MA); German for business (Graduate Certificate); Hispanic language and cultures (Graduate Certificate); Japanese business practices (Graduate Certificate); Spanish (MA). Part-time and evening/weekend programs available. Post-baccalaureate distance learning degree programs offered (minimal on-campus study). *Degree requirements:* For master's, one foreign language, thesis optional. *Entrance requirements:* Additional exam requirements/recommendations for international students: Required—TOEFL.

Harvard University, Graduate School of Arts and Sciences, Department of East Asian Languages and Civilizations, Cambridge, MA 02138. Offers Chinese (PhD); Japanese (PhD); Korean (PhD); Mongolian (PhD); Vietnamese (PhD). Terminal master's awarded for partial completion of doctoral program. *Degree requirements:* For doctorate, 3 foreign languages, thesis/dissertation, general exams. *Entrance requirements:* For doctorate, GRE General Test. Additional exam requirements/recommendations for international students: Required—TOEFL. *Expenses:* Tuition: Full-time $32,556. Required fees: $1426. Full-time tuition and fees vary according to program and student level. *Faculty research:* Central Asian literature, religion, and premodern history.

Indiana University Bloomington, University Graduate School, College of Arts and Sciences, Department of East Asian Languages and Cultures, Bloomington, IN 47405-7000. Offers Chinese (MA, PhD); East Asian languages and cultures (PhD); East Asian studies (MA); Japanese (MA, PhD); language pedagogy (MA). Part-time programs available. *Faculty:* 7 full-time (2 women). *Students:* 17 full-time (10 women), 11 part-time (7 women); includes 3 minority (1 African American, 1 Asian American or Pacific Islander, 1 Hispanic American), 7 international. Average age 33. 84 applicants, 30% accepted, 10 enrolled. In 2008, 6 master's, 1 doctorate awarded. *Degree requirements:* For master's, 2 foreign languages, thesis; for doctorate, 2 foreign languages, thesis/dissertation. *Entrance requirements:* Additional exam requirements/recommendations for international students: Required—TOEFL. *Application deadline:* For fall admission, 1/15 for domestic students, 12/15 for international students; for spring admission, 9/1 for domestic and international students. Applications are processed on a rolling basis. Application fee: $50 ($60 for international students). Electronic applications accepted. *Expenses:* Tuition, area resident: Part-time $291.97 per credit hour. Tuition, state resident: part-time $291.97 per credit hour. Tuition, nonresident: part-time $850.33 per credit hour. Required fees: $110 per semester. Tuition and fees vary according to course load and program. *Financial support:* Fellowships, teaching assistantships, Federal Work-Study and tuition waivers (full) available. Financial award application deadline: 3/1. *Faculty research:* Postwar/postmodern Japanese fiction, modern Chinese film and literature, classical Chinese literature and philosophy, Chinese and Japanese linguistics and pedagogy, East Asian politics. *Unit head:* Robert Eno, Chair, 812-855-0856, E-mail: eno@indiana.edu. *Application contact:* Edith Sarra, Director of Graduate Studies, 812-855-4031, Fax: 812-855-6402, E-mail: eserra@indiana.edu.

Kent State University, College of Arts and Sciences, Department of Modern and Classical Language Studies, Kent, OH 44242-0001. Offers French literature (MA); French, Spanish, German and Latin pedagogy (MA); German literature (MA); Spanish literature (MA); translation (MA), including French, German, Japanese, Russian, Spanish; translation studies (PhD). Part-time and evening/weekend programs available. *Degree requirements:* For master's, one

foreign language, comprehensive exam (for some programs), thesis (for some programs); for doctorate, comprehensive exam, thesis/dissertation (for some programs). *Entrance requirements:* For master's, minimum GPA of 3.0, writing sample, audio tape or CD; for doctorate, 3 recommendations. Additional exam requirements/recommendations for international students: Required—TOEFL (minimum score 197 computer-based). Electronic applications accepted. *Faculty research:* Literature, pedagogy, applied linguistics, translation studies.

The Ohio State University, Graduate School, College of Humanities, Department of East Asian Languages and Literatures, Program in Japanese, Columbus, OH 43210. Offers MA, PhD. Electronic applications accepted.

Portland State University, Graduate Studies, College of Liberal Arts and Sciences, Department of Foreign Languages and Literatures, Portland, OR 97207-0751. Offers foreign literature and language (MA); French (MA); German (MA); Japanese (MA); Spanish (MA). Part-time programs available. *Faculty:* 43 full-time (27 women), 28 part-time/adjunct (19 women). *Students:* 29 full-time (24 women), 17 part-time (11 women); includes 6 minority (1 African American, 1 Asian American or Pacific Islander, 4 Hispanic Americans), 11 international. Average age 32. 23 applicants, 91% accepted, 20 enrolled. In 2008, 14 master's awarded. *Degree requirements:* For master's, one foreign language, thesis (for some programs). *Entrance requirements:* Additional exam requirements/recommendations for international students: Required—TOEFL (minimum score 550 paper-based; 213 computer-based). *Application deadline:* For fall admission, 4/1 for domestic students, 3/1 for international students; for winter admission, 9/1 for domestic students, 7/1 for international students; for spring admission, 11/1 for domestic and international students. Applications are processed on a rolling basis. Application fee: $50. *Expenses:* Tuition, area resident: Full-time $8763; part-time $179 per credit hour. Tuition, state resident: full-time $8763; part-time $298 per credit hour. Tuition, nonresident: full-time $12,981; part-time $426 per credit hour. Required fees: $1242. One-time fee: $250. Tuition and fees vary according to course load and program. *Financial support:* In 2008–09, 6 teaching assistantships with full tuition reimbursements (averaging $9,359 per year) were awarded; research assistantships with full tuition reimbursements, Federal Work-Study, scholarships/grants, and unspecified assistantships also available. Support available to part-time students. Financial award application deadline: 3/1; financial award applicants required to submit FAFSA. *Faculty research:* Foreign language pedagogy, applied and social linguistics, literary history and criticism. Total annual research expenditures: $6,847. *Unit head:* Dr. Sandra F. Freels, Chair, 503-725-3522, Fax: 503-725-5276. *Application contact:* Karen Popp, Office Coordinator, 503-725-3522, E-mail: poppk@pdx.edu.

San Francisco State University, Division of Graduate Studies, College of Humanities, Department of Foreign Languages and Literatures, Program in Japanese, San Francisco, CA 94132-1722. Offers MA.

Stanford University, School of Humanities and Sciences, Department of Asian Languages, Stanford, CA 94305-9991. Offers Chinese (MA, PhD); Japanese (MA, PhD). Terminal master's awarded for partial completion of doctoral program. *Degree requirements:* For master's, one foreign language, thesis or an annotated translation of a literary or historical text; for doctorate, 2 foreign languages, thesis/dissertation, field exams. *Entrance requirements:* For master's and doctorate, GRE General Test. Additional exam requirements/recommendations for international students: Required—TOEFL. Electronic applications accepted.

University at Buffalo, the State University of New York, Graduate School, Graduate School of Education, Department of Learning and Instruction, Buffalo, NY 14260. Offers adolescence education (Certificate); biology (Ed M); chemistry (Ed M); childhood education (Ed M); early childhood and childhood education with bilingual extension (Ed M); early childhood education (Ed M); earth science (Ed M); elementary education (Ed D, PhD); English (Ed M); English education (PhD); English for speakers of other languages (Ed M); foreign and second language education (PhD); French (Ed M); general education (Ed M); German (Ed M); Italian (Ed M); Japanese (Ed M); Latin (Ed M); literary specialist (Ed M); mathematics (Ed M); mathematics education (PhD); mentoring teachers (Certificate); music education (Ed M, Certificate); physics (Ed M); reading education (PhD); Russian (Ed M); school administrator and supervisor (Certificate); science education (PhD); social studies (Ed M); Spanish (Ed M); special education (PhD); teaching and leading for diversity (Certificate); teaching English to speakers of other languages (Ed M). Part-time and evening/weekend programs available. Postbaccalaureate distance learning degree programs offered (no on-campus study). Terminal master's awarded for partial completion of doctoral program. *Degree requirements:* For master's, comprehensive exam; for doctorate, thesis/dissertation, research analysis exam, research experience component. *Entrance requirements:* For doctorate, GRE General Test or MAT, interview, writing sample, letters of recommendation. Additional exam requirements/recommendations for international students: Required—TOEFL (minimum score 600 paper-based; 250 computer-based). Electronic applications accepted. *Faculty research:* Science assessment, state-level testing, early learning, literacy, second language acquisition.

University of Alberta, Faculty of Graduate Studies and Research, Department of East Asian Studies, Edmonton, AB T6G 2E1, Canada. Offers Chinese literature (MA); East Asian interdisciplinary studies (MA); Japanese literature (MA). Part-time programs available. *Degree requirements:* For master's, one foreign language, thesis. *Entrance requirements:* Additional exam requirements/recommendations for international students: Required—TOEFL. Electronic applications accepted. *Faculty research:* Classical Chinese poetry and poetics, Chinese philosophy, modern/contemporary Chinese literature, modern Japanese literature and culture, Japanese women's writing.

University of California, Berkeley, Graduate Division, College of Letters and Science, Department of East Asian Languages and Cultures, Berkeley, CA 94720-1500. Offers Chinese language (PhD); Japanese language (PhD). *Degree requirements:* For doctorate, one foreign language, thesis/dissertation, oral qualifying exam. *Entrance requirements:* For doctorate, GRE General Test, minimum GPA of 3.0, MA thesis, 3 letters of recommendation. Electronic applications accepted. *Faculty research:* Chinese and Japanese modern and classical texts, prose, and poetry; Chinese and Japanese linguistics.

University of California, Irvine, Office of Graduate Studies, School of Humanities, Department of East Asian Languages and Literatures, Irvine, CA 92697. Offers Chinese (MA, PhD); East Asian languages and literatures (MA, PhD); Japanese (MA, PhD). *Degree requirements:* For doctorate, thesis/dissertation. *Entrance requirements:* For master's, GRE, minimum GPA of 3.0; for doctorate, GRE General Test, minimum GPA of 3.0. Additional exam requirements/recommendations for international students: Required—TOEFL (minimum score 550 paper-based; 213 computer-based). Electronic applications accepted. *Faculty research:* Chinese, Japanese, and Korean literature and culture; language and textual analysis; historical, social, and cultural dimensions of literary study.

University of Colorado at Boulder, Graduate School, College of Arts and Sciences, Department of East Asian Languages and Civilizations, Boulder, CO 80309. Offers Chinese (MA, PhD); Japanese (MA, PhD). Part-time programs available. *Degree requirements:* For master's, comprehensive exam. *Entrance requirements:* For master's, BA in Chinese or Japanese, minimum undergraduate GPA of 3.0. Additional exam requirements/recommendations for international students: Required—TOEFL. *Faculty research:* Chinese and Japanese modern and classical literature, religions, linguistics, language pedagogy, pre-modern and contemporary fiction, sociolinguistics.

University of Hawaii at Manoa, Graduate Division, Colleges of Arts and Sciences, College of Language, Linguistics and Literature, Department of East Asian Languages and Literatures, Program in Japanese, Honolulu, HI 96822. Offers MA, PhD. Part-time programs available. *Degree requirements:* For master's, 2 foreign languages, thesis optional; for doctorate, 2 foreign languages, comprehensive exam, thesis/dissertation. *Entrance requirements:* For master's and doctorate, GRE General Test. Additional exam requirements/recommendations for international students: Required—TOEFL (minimum score 560 paper-based; 220 computer-based; 83 iBT), IELTS (minimum score 5).

University of Hawaii at Manoa, Graduate Division, School of Pacific and Asian Studies, Program in Asian Studies, Concentration in Japanese Studies, Honolulu, HI 96822. Offers Graduate Certificate. Part-time programs available. *Degree requirements:* For Graduate Certificate, one foreign language. *Entrance requirements:* For degree, GRE. Additional exam requirements/recommendations for international students: Required—TOEFL (minimum score 560 paper-based; 220 computer-based; 83 iBT), IELTS (minimum score 5).

University of Maryland, College Park, Graduate Studies, College of Arts and Humanities, School of Languages, Literature, and Cultures, Program in Second Language Acquisition and Application, College Park, MD 20742. Offers French (MA); German (MA); Japanese (MA); Russian (MA); second language instruction (PhD); second language learning (PhD); second language measurement and assessment (PhD); second language use (PhD); Spanish (MA). *Entrance requirements:* For master's, BA or BS in related field, demonstrated language competency, 3 letters of reference. Electronic applications accepted. *Faculty research:* Second language acquisition, pedagogical perspectives, technological applications, language use in professional contexts.

University of Oregon, Graduate School, College of Arts and Sciences, Department of East Asian Languages and Literature, Eugene, OR 97403. Offers Chinese (MA, PhD); Japanese (MA, PhD). *Entrance requirements:* Additional exam requirements/recommendations for international students: Required—TOEFL. *Faculty research:* Linguistics, pedagogy.

University of Washington, Graduate School, College of Arts and Sciences, Department of Asian Languages and Literature, Seattle, WA 98195. Offers Buddhist studies (MA, PhD); Chinese language and literature (MA, PhD); Japanese language and literature (MA, PhD); Korean language and literature (MA, PhD); South Asian language and literature (MA, PhD). *Degree requirements:* For master's, 2 foreign languages, general exam, thesis or 2 research papers; for doctorate, 3 foreign languages, thesis/dissertation, general exam. *Entrance requirements:* For master's, GRE, minimum GPA of 3.0; for doctorate, GRE, master's degree in related field, minimum GPA of 3.0. Additional exam requirements/recommendations for international students: Required—TOEFL. Electronic applications accepted. *Faculty research:* Textual, linguistic, philological, and literary study of languages and literatures of Asia.

University of Wisconsin–Madison, Graduate School, College of Letters and Science, Department of East Asian Languages and Literature, Program in Japanese Linguistics, Madison, WI 53706-1380. Offers MA, PhD. Part-time programs available. Terminal master's awarded for partial completion of doctoral program. *Degree requirements:* For master's, one foreign language, seminars, written exam; for doctorate, 3 foreign languages, thesis/dissertation, seminars, preliminary exams, oral exam. *Entrance requirements:* For master's, GRE General Test, bachelor's degree or equivalent in Japanese; for doctorate, GRE General Test, master's degree or equivalent in Japanese. Electronic applications accepted. *Faculty research:* Modern and historical Japanese linguistics, modern Japanese fiction and poetry, classical Japanese literature, language pedagogy.

Washington University in St. Louis, Graduate School of Arts and Sciences, Department of Asian and Near Eastern Languages and Literatures, St. Louis, MO 63130-4899. Offers Chinese (MA); Chinese and comparative literature (PhD); Japanese (MA); Japanese and comparative literature (PhD). *Students:* 20 full-time (13 women); includes 1 minority (Hispanic American), 15 international. 9 applicants, 44% accepted, 2 enrolled. In 2008, 1 master's awarded. Terminal master's awarded for partial completion of doctoral program. *Degree requirements:* For master's, thesis optional; for doctorate, thesis/dissertation. *Entrance requirements:* For master's and doctorate, GRE General Test. *Application deadline:* For fall admission, 1/15 priority date for domestic students. Applications are processed on a rolling basis. Application fee: $45. Electronic applications accepted. *Financial support:* Teaching assistantships, Federal Work-Study, institutionally sponsored loans, and tuition waivers (full and partial) available. Support available to part-time students. Financial award application deadline: 1/15. *Unit head:* Dr. Fatemeh Keshavarz, Chairperson, 314-935-5156. *Application contact:* Assistant to the Dean, 314-935-6880, Fax: 314-935-4887.

Near and Middle Eastern Languages

The American University in Cairo, Graduate Studies and Research, School of Humanities and Social Sciences, Department of Arabic Studies, Cairo, Egypt. Offers Arab language and literature (MA); Islamic art and architecture (MA); Islamic studies (Diploma); Middle East studies (MA, Diploma); Middle Eastern history (MA). Part-time programs available. *Degree requirements:* For master's, thesis optional, proficiency in French or German. *Entrance requirements:* Additional exam requirements/recommendations for international students: Required—English entrance exam and/or TOEFL. Electronic applications accepted. *Faculty research:* History of early Islam, Ayubbid, and Mamluk periods; nineteenth- and twentieth-century Middle East Islamic jurisprudence; contemporary Arabic literary criticism.

American University of Beirut, Graduate Programs, Faculty of Arts and Sciences, Beirut, Lebanon. Offers anthropology (MA); Arabic language and literature (MA); archaeology (MA); biology (MS); chemistry (MS); computer science (MS); economics (MA); education (MA); English language (MA); English literature (MA); environmental policy planning (MSES); financial economics (MAFE); geology (MS); history (MA); mathematics (MA, MS); Middle Eastern studies (MA); philosophy (MA); physics (MS); political studies (MA); psychology (MA); public administration (MA); sociology (MA); statistics (MA, MS). Part-time programs available. *Degree requirements:* For master's, one foreign language, comprehensive exam, thesis (for some programs). *Entrance requirements:* For master's, GRE, letter of recommendation. Additional exam requirements/recommendations for international students: Required—TOEFL (minimum score 600 paper-based; 250 computer-based; 100 iBT), IELTS (minimum score 7.5). *Faculty research:* String theory and supergravity; computer graphics; algebra and number theory; popular Arabic literature; marine and freshwater biology; integrating science, math and technology.

Brandeis University, Graduate School of Arts and Sciences, Department of Near Eastern and Judaic Studies, Waltham, MA 02454-9110. Offers Near Eastern and Judaic studies (MA, PhD); Near Eastern and Judaic studies and sociology (PhD); Near Eastern and Judaic studies and women's studies (MA); teaching of Hebrew (MAT). Part-time programs available. Terminal master's awarded for partial completion of doctoral program. *Degree requirements:* For master's, one foreign language, comprehensive exam, thesis or alternative; for doctorate, 3 foreign languages, comprehensive exam, thesis/dissertation. *Entrance requirements:* For master's and doctorate, GRE General Test (recommended), letters of recommendation, transcripts, statement of purpose. Additional exam requirements/recommendations for international students: Required—TOEFL (minimum score 600 paper-based; 250 computer-based; 100 iBT), IELTS (minimum score 7). Electronic applications accepted. *Faculty research:* Ancient Near East and Bible, philosophy, history, modern Middle East, Islamic studies.

The Catholic University of America, School of Arts and Sciences, Department of Semitic and Egyptian Languages and Literature, Washington, DC 20064. Offers MA, PhD. *Degree requirements:* For master's, 2 foreign languages, comprehensive exam, thesis or alternative; for doctorate, 2 foreign languages, comprehensive exam, thesis/dissertation. *Entrance requirements:* For master's and doctorate, GRE General Test, 3 letters of recommendation. Additional exam requirements/recommendations for international students: Required—TOEFL (minimum score 580 paper-based; 237 computer-based). Electronic applications accepted. *Faculty research:* Christian history and literature of the Near East, Hebrew Bible.

Columbia University, Graduate School of Arts and Sciences, Division of Humanities, Department of Middle East Languages and Cultures, New York, NY 10027. Offers Hebrew language and literature (M Phil, MA, PhD); Middle Eastern languages and cultures (M Phil, MA, PhD); South Asian languages and cultures (M Phil, MA, PhD). Part-time programs available. *Degree requirements:* For master's, thesis, oral and written exams; for doctorate, 3 foreign languages, thesis/dissertation. *Entrance requirements:* For master's and doctorate, GRE General Test. Additional exam requirements/recommendations for international students: Required—TOEFL. *Faculty research:* Indo-Iranian, Turkish, central Asian, and Armenian studies; Arabic and ancient Semitics.

Georgetown University, Graduate School of Arts and Sciences, Department of Arabic and Islamic Studies, Washington, DC 20057. Offers Arabic area studies (PhD); Islamic studies (MA, PhD); linguistics (MA, PhD). *Degree requirements:* For master's, comprehensive exam, research project; for doctorate, one foreign language, comprehensive exam, thesis/dissertation. *Entrance requirements:* Additional exam requirements/recommendations for international students: Required—TOEFL.

Harvard University, Graduate School of Arts and Sciences, Department of Near Eastern Languages and Civilizations, Cambridge, MA 02138. Offers Akkadian and Sumerian (AM, PhD); Arabic (AM, PhD); Armenian (AM, PhD); biblical history (AM, PhD); Hebrew (AM, PhD); Indo-Muslim culture (AM, PhD); Iranian (AM, PhD); Jewish history and literature (AM, PhD); Persian (AM, PhD); Semitic philology (AM, PhD); Syro-Palestinian archaeology (AM, PhD); Turkish (AM, PhD). *Degree requirements:* For doctorate, variable foreign language requirement, thesis/dissertation, general exams. *Entrance requirements:* For master's, GRE General Test; for doctorate, GRE General Test, proficiency in a Near Eastern language. Additional exam requirements/recommendations for international students: Required—TOEFL. *Expenses:* Tuition: Full-time $32,556. Required fees: $1426. Full-time tuition and fees vary according to program and student level.

Hebrew Union College–Jewish Institute of Religion, School of Graduate Studies, Program in Hebrew Letters, New York, NY 10012-1186. Offers DHL. *Degree requirements:* For doctorate, one foreign language, thesis/dissertation. *Entrance requirements:* For doctorate, GRE. Additional exam requirements/recommendations for international students: Required—TOEFL. *Expenses:* Contact institution. *Faculty research:* Philosophy and theology, Bible, Hebrew, pastoral care, history and Rabbinics.

Indiana University Bloomington, University Graduate School, College of Arts and Sciences, Department of Near Eastern Languages and Cultures, Bloomington, IN 47405-7000. Offers MA, PhD. Part-time programs available. *Faculty:* 5 full-time (2 women). *Students:* 41 full-time (17 women), 6 part-time (1 woman); includes 3 minority (2 Asian Americans or Pacific Islanders, 1 Hispanic American), 26 international. Average age 31. 40 applicants, 58% accepted, 8 enrolled. In 2008, 10 master's, 2 doctorates awarded. Terminal master's awarded for partial completion of doctoral program. *Degree requirements:* For master's, 2 foreign languages, thesis or alternative; for doctorate, 3 foreign languages, thesis/dissertation. *Entrance requirements:* For master's and doctorate, GRE General Test. Additional exam requirements/recommendations for international students: Required—TOEFL. *Application deadline:* For fall admission, 1/15 priority date for domestic students, 12/15 for international students; for spring admission, 9/1 priority date for domestic students, 9/1 for international students. Applications are processed on a rolling basis. Application fee: $50 ($60 for international students). *Expenses:* Tuition, area resident: Part-time $291.97 per credit hour. Tuition, state resident: part-time $291.97 per credit hour. Tuition, nonresident: part-time $850.33 per credit hour. Required fees: $110 per semester. Tuition and fees vary according to course load and program. *Financial support:* Fellowships with full and partial tuition reimbursements, research assistantships with full and partial tuition reimbursements, teaching assistantships with full and partial tuition reimbursements, Federal Work-Study, institutionally sponsored loans, tuition waivers (full and partial), and unspecified assistantships available. Financial award application deadline: 3/1; financial award applicants required to submit FAFSA. *Faculty research:* Classical and modern Arabic literature and linguistics, biblical and modern Hebrew studies, Persian language and literature, Islamic civilization, Iranian history and language. *Unit head:* Dr. Nazif Shahrani, Chair, 812-855-4858. *Application contact:* Elaine Wright, Administrative Secretary, 812-855-5993.

The Ohio State University, Graduate School, College of Humanities, Department of Near Eastern Languages and Cultures, Columbus, OH 43210. Offers MA, PhD. *Degree requirements:* For master's, thesis optional. *Entrance requirements:* For master's and doctorate, GRE General

Near and Middle Eastern Languages

The Ohio State University (continued)

Test. Additional exam requirements/recommendations for international students: Required—TOEFL (minimum score 600 paper-based; 250 computer-based). Electronic applications accepted.

Oral Roberts University, School of Theology and Missions, Tulsa, OK 74171-0001. Offers biblical literature (MA), including advanced languages, Judaic-Christian studies; Christian counseling (MA), including marriage and family therapy; Christian education (MA); divinity (M Div); missions (MA); practical theology (MA); theological/historical studies (MA); theology (D Min). *Accreditation:* ATS; NASM. Part-time programs available. Postbaccalaureate distance learning degree programs offered (minimal on-campus study). *Degree requirements:* For master's, thesis (for some programs), practicum/internship; for doctorate, thesis/dissertation, applied research project; for M Div, one foreign language, field experience. *Entrance requirements:* For M Div and master's, GRE General Test or MAT, minimum GPA of 2.5; for doctorate, M Div, minimum GPA of 3.0, 3 years of full-time ministry experience. Additional exam requirements/recommendations for international students: Required—TOEFL (minimum score 500 paper-based; 213 computer-based; 79 iBT). Electronic applications accepted.

University of California, Los Angeles, Graduate Division, College of Letters and Science, Department of Near Eastern Languages and Cultures, Los Angeles, CA 90034. Offers MA, PhD. *Students:* 46 full-time (21 women); includes 3 minority (1 Asian American or Pacific Islander, 2 Hispanic Americans), 1 international. Average age 28. 60 applicants, 35% accepted, 7 enrolled. In 2008, 4 master's, 2 doctorates awarded. *Degree requirements:* For master's, one foreign language, comprehensive exam; for doctorate, 2 foreign languages, thesis/dissertation, oral and written qualifying exams. *Entrance requirements:* For master's and doctorate, GRE General Test, minimum GPA of 3.25, sample of written work recommended. Additional exam requirements/recommendations for international students: Required—TOEFL. *Application deadline:* For fall admission, 12/1 for domestic and international students. Application fee: $60 ($80 for international students). Electronic applications accepted. *Expenses:* Tuition, nonresident: full-time $14,694. Required fees: $9669.50. Full-time tuition and fees vary according to course load, degree level, program and student level. *Financial support:* In 2008–09, 29 fellowships with full and partial tuition reimbursements, 24 research assistantships with full and partial tuition reimbursements, 21 teaching assistantships with full and partial tuition reimbursements were awarded; Federal Work-Study, institutionally sponsored loans, scholarships/grants, health care benefits, tuition waivers (full and partial), and unspecified assistantships also available. Financial award application deadline: 3/1; financial award applicants required to submit FAFSA. *Unit head:* Dr. Elizabeth Carter, Chair, 310-206-5474. *Application contact:* Departmental Office, 310-825-4165, E-mail: nreast@humnet.ucla.edu.

University of Chicago, Division of the Humanities, Department of Near Eastern Languages and Civilizations, Chicago, IL 60637-1513. Offers AM, PhD. Terminal master's awarded for partial completion of doctoral program. *Degree requirements:* For master's, one foreign language, comprehensive exam, thesis; for doctorate, 2 foreign languages, comprehensive exam, thesis/dissertation. *Entrance requirements:* For master's and doctorate, GRE General Test. Additional exam requirements/recommendations for international students: Required—TOEFL.

University of Maryland, College Park, Graduate Studies, College of Arts and Humanities, The Arabic Flagship Program, College Park, MD 20742. Offers Graduate Certificate.

University of Maryland, College Park, Graduate Studies, College of Arts and Humanities, The Persian Flagship Program, College Park, MD 20742. Offers MPS, Graduate Certificate.

University of Michigan, Horace H. Rackham School of Graduate Studies, College of Literature, Science, and the Arts, Department of Near Eastern Studies, Ann Arbor, MI 48109. Offers ancient Israel/Hebrew Bible (AM, PhD); Arabic (AM, PhD); Armenian (AM, PhD); early Christian studies (AM, PhD); Egyptology (AM, PhD); Hebrew (AM, PhD); Islamic studies (AM, PhD); Mesopotamian and ancient Near Eastern studies (AM, PhD); Persian (AM, PhD); teaching of Arabic as a foreign Language (AM); Turkish (AM, PhD). Part-time programs available. Terminal master's awarded for partial completion of doctoral program. *Degree requirements:* For master's, 2 foreign languages; for doctorate, 4 foreign languages, oral defense of dissertation, preliminary exam. *Entrance requirements:* For master's, GRE General Test; for doctorate, GRE General Test, master's degree. Additional exam requirements/recommendations for international students: Required—TOEFL (minimum score 560 paper-based; 220 computer-based; 84 iBT). *Faculty research:* Middle and Near Eastern literatures, languages, cultures from ancient times to the present.

University of South Africa, College of Human Sciences, Pretoria, South Africa. Offers adult education (M Ed); African languages (MA, PhD); African politics (MA, PhD); Afrikaans (MA, PhD); ancient history (MA, PhD); ancient Near Eastern studies (MA, PhD); anthropology (MA, PhD); applied linguistics (MA); Arabic (MA, PhD); archaeology (MA); art history (MA); Biblical archaeology (MA); Biblical studies (M Th, D Th, PhD); Christian spirituality (M Th, D Th); church history (M Th, D Th); classical studies (MA, PhD); clinical psychology (MA); communication (MA, PhD); comparative education (M Ed, Ed D); consulting psychology (D Admin, D Com, PhD); curriculum studies (M Ed, Ed D); development studies (M Admin, MA, D Admin, PhD); didactics (M Ed, Ed D); education (M Tech); education management (M Ed, Ed D); educational psychology (M Ed); English (MA); environmental education (M Ed); French (MA, PhD); German (MA, PhD); Greek (MA); guidance and counseling (M Ed); health studies (MA, PhD), including health sciences education (MA), health services management (MA), medical and surgical nursing science (critical care general) (MA), midwifery and neonatal nursing science (MA), trauma and emergency care (MA); history (MA, PhD); history of education (Ed D); inclusive education (M Ed, Ed D); information and communications technology policy and regulation (MA); information science (MA, MIS, PhD); international politics (MA, PhD); Islamic studies (MA, PhD); Italian (MA, PhD); Judaica (MA, PhD); linguistics (MA, PhD); mathematical education (M Ed); mathematics education (MA); missiology (M Th, D Th); modern Hebrew (MA, PhD); musicology (MA, MMus, D Mus, PhD); natural science education (M Ed); New Testament (M Th, D Th); Old Testament (D Th); pastoral therapy (M Th, D Th); philosophy (MA); philosophy of education (M Ed, Ed D); politics (MA, PhD); Portuguese (MA, PhD); practical theology (M Th, D Th); psychology (MA, MS, PhD); psychology of education (M Ed, Ed D); public health (MA); religious studies (MA, D Th, PhD); Romance languages (MA); Russian (MA, PhD); Semitic languages (MA, PhD); social behavior studies in HIV/AIDS (MA); social science (mental health) (MA); social science in development studies (MA); social science in psychology (MA); social science in social work (MA); social science in sociology (MA); social work (MSW, DSW, PhD); socio-education (M Ed, Ed D); sociolinguistics (MA); sociology (MA, PhD); Spanish (MA, PhD); systematic theology (M Th, D Th); TESOL (teaching English to speakers of other languages) (MA); theological ethics (M Th, D Th); theory of literature (MA, PhD); urban ministries (D Th); urban ministry (M Th).

The University of Texas at Austin, Graduate School, College of Liberal Arts, Department of Middle Eastern Studies, Austin, TX 78712-1111. Offers Arabic (MA, PhD); Hebrew (MA). *Degree requirements:* For master's, one foreign language, comprehensive exam, thesis; for doctorate, 2 foreign languages, comprehensive exam, thesis/dissertation. *Entrance requirements:* For master's and doctorate, GRE General Test. Additional exam requirements/recommendations for international students: Required—TOEFL. Electronic applications accepted. *Faculty research:* Islamic studies, Persian language and literature, Hebrew language, Jewish studies, Arabic literature and language.

University of Utah, The Graduate School, College of Humanities, Program in Middle East Studies, Salt Lake City, UT 84112-1107. Offers anthropology (MA); Arabic (MA, PhD); Arabic and linguistics (MA, PhD); Hebrew (MA); history (MA, PhD); Persian (MA, PhD); political science (MA, PhD); Turkish (MA). Terminal master's awarded for partial completion of doctoral program. *Degree requirements:* For master's, 2 foreign languages, comprehensive exam, thesis optional; for doctorate, 3 foreign languages, comprehensive exam, thesis/dissertation. *Entrance requirements:* For master's, GRE General Test, minimum GPA of 3.2; for doctorate, GRE General Test, MA in Middle East studies or equivalent, minimum GPA of 3.2. Additional exam requirements/recommendations for international students: Required—TOEFL (minimum score 580 paper-based; 237 computer-based; 92 iBT). *Faculty research:* Arabic literature and linguistics, Islamic studies, Middle East history, political science, Judaic studies.

University of Wisconsin–Madison, Graduate School, College of Letters and Science, Department of Hebrew and Semitic Studies, Madison, WI 53706-1380. Offers MA, PhD. Terminal master's awarded for partial completion of doctoral program. *Degree requirements:* For master's, 2 foreign languages; for doctorate, thesis/dissertation. *Entrance requirements:* For master's and doctorate, GRE. Electronic applications accepted. *Faculty research:* Biblical language and literature, Northwest Semitic languages.

Yale University, Graduate School of Arts and Sciences, Department of Near Eastern Languages and Civilizations, New Haven, CT 06520. Offers Arabic and Islamic studies (MA, PhD); archaeology of the ancient Near East (MA, PhD); Assyriology (MA, PhD); Egyptology (MA, PhD); Graeco-Arabic studies (MA, PhD); Northwest Semitic, Bible, comparative Semitics (MA, PhD). *Degree requirements:* For doctorate, 2 foreign languages, thesis/dissertation. *Entrance requirements:* For doctorate, GRE General Test.

Portuguese

Brigham Young University, Graduate Studies, College of Humanities, Department of Spanish and Portuguese, Provo, UT 84602. Offers Portuguese linguistics (MA); Portuguese literature (MA); Spanish linguistics (MA); Spanish teaching (MA); Spanish/Latin American Literature (MA); Spanish/Peninsular literature (MA). Part-time programs available. *Faculty:* 32 full-time (5 women). *Students:* 15 full-time (7 women), 24 part-time (13 women); includes 6 minority (all Hispanic Americans), 8 international. Average age 29. 19 applicants, 74% accepted, 14 enrolled. In 2008, 12 master's awarded. *Degree requirements:* For master's, one foreign language, comprehensive exam, thesis, 1 semester of teaching. *Entrance requirements:* For master's, minimum GPA of 3.5 in Spanish or Portuguese, 3.3 overall. Additional exam requirements/recommendations for international students: Required—TOEFL (minimum score 580 paper-based; 237 computer-based). *Application deadline:* For fall admission, 2/1 for domestic and international students. Application fee: $50. Electronic applications accepted. *Expenses:* Tuition: Full-time $5160; part-time $287 per credit hour. Tuition and fees vary according to program and student's religious affiliation. *Financial support:* In 2008–09, 39 students received support, including 39 teaching assistantships with partial tuition reimbursements available (averaging $6,574 per year); institutionally sponsored loans, scholarships/grants, tuition waivers (partial), and unspecified assistantships also available. Support available to part-time students. Financial award application deadline: 7/21. *Faculty research:* Mexican prose; Latin American theater, literature, phonetics, and phonology; pedagogy; classical Portuguese literature; Peninsular prose and theater. *Unit head:* Dr. Alvin F. Sherman, Chair, 801-422-3107, Fax: 801-422-0628, E-mail: alvin_sherman@byu.edu. *Application contact:* Arwen T. Wyatt, Graduate Secretary, 801-422-2196, Fax: 801-422-0628, E-mail: arwen_wyatt@byu.edu.

Emory University, Graduate School of Arts and Sciences, Department of Spanish and Portuguese, Atlanta, GA 30322-1100. Offers comparative literature (Certificate); film studies (Certificate); Spanish (PhD); women's studies (Certificate). *Degree requirements:* For doctorate, 2 foreign languages, comprehensive exam, thesis/dissertation. *Entrance requirements:* For doctorate, GRE General Test. Additional exam requirements/recommendations for international students: Required—TOEFL. Electronic applications accepted. *Faculty research:* Spanish literature, Spanish-American literature, literary theory, criticism, cultural studies.

Harvard University, Graduate School of Arts and Sciences, Department of Romance Languages and Literatures, Cambridge, MA 02138. Offers French (AM, PhD); Italian (AM, PhD); Portuguese (AM, PhD); Spanish (AM, PhD). Terminal master's awarded for partial completion of doctoral program. *Degree requirements:* For master's, 2 foreign languages; for doctorate, 2 foreign languages, thesis/dissertation. *Entrance requirements:* For master's and doctorate, GRE General Test, sample of written work. Additional exam requirements/recommendations for international students: Required—TOEFL. *Expenses:* Tuition: Full-time $32,556. Required fees: $1426. Full-time tuition and fees vary according to program and student level.

Indiana University Bloomington, University Graduate School, College of Arts and Sciences, Department of Spanish and Portuguese, Bloomington, IN 47405-7000. Offers Hispanic linguistics (MA, PhD); Hispanic literature (MA); Luso-Brazilian literature (MA); Luso-Brazilian studies (PhD); Spanish literatures (PhD); teaching Spanish (MAT). *Faculty:* 18 full-time (10 women). *Students:* 75 full-time (39 women), 6 part-time (4 women); includes 17 minority (all Hispanic Americans), 17 international. Average age 30. 53 applicants, 36% accepted, 16 enrolled. In 2008, 7 master's, 7 doctorates awarded. *Degree requirements:* For master's, one foreign language; for doctorate, 3 foreign languages, thesis/dissertation. *Entrance requirements:* For master's, GRE General Test, GRE Subject Test, bachelor's degree in Portuguese or Spanish, minimum GPA of 3.25; for doctorate, GRE General Test, GRE Subject Test, master's degree in Portuguese or Spanish, minimum GPA of 3.25. Additional exam requirements/recommendations for international students: Required—TOEFL. *Application deadline:* For fall admission, 1/15 priority date for domestic students, 12/15 for international students; for spring admission, 9/1 for domestic and international students. Application fee: $50 ($60 for international students). *Expenses:* Tuition, area resident: Part-time $291.97 per credit hour. Tuition, state resident: part-time $291.97 per credit hour. Tuition, nonresident: part-time $850.33 per credit hour. Required fees: $110 per semester. Tuition and fees vary according to course load and program. *Financial support:* Fellowships with full tuition reimbursements, research assistantships, teaching assistantships with full tuition reimbursements, Federal Work-Study available. Financial award application deadline: 1/15. *Faculty research:* Spanish American literature, Spanish peninsular literature, Luso-Brazilian studies, Catalan studies. *Unit head:* Josep Miguel Sobrer, Chair, 812-855-8498. *Application contact:* Steven Wagschal, Student Contact, 812-855-9194, E-mail: swagscha@indiana.edu.

Michigan State University, The Graduate School, College of Arts and Letters, Department of Spanish and Portuguese, East Lansing, MI 48824. Offers applied Spanish linguistics (MA); Hispanic cultural studies (PhD); Hispanic literatures (MA). *Entrance requirements:* Additional exam requirements/recommendations for international students: Required—TOEFL. Electronic applications accepted.

New York University, Graduate School of Arts and Science, Department of Spanish and Portuguese Languages and Literatures, New York, NY 10012-1019. Offers Portuguese (MA, PhD); Spanish (PhD); Spanish and Latin American literatures and cultures (MA); Spanish language and translation (MA). Part-time programs available. *Degree requirements:* For master's, 2 foreign languages, thesis; for doctorate, 2 foreign languages, thesis/dissertation. *Entrance requirements:* For master's, GRE General Test; for doctorate, GRE General Test, master's degree. Additional exam requirements/recommendations for international students: Required—TOEFL. *Faculty research:* Gender and sexuality, transatlantic studies, literacy and cultural theories, colonial and post colonial studies, autobiography and modern subjectivities.

The Ohio State University, Graduate School, College of Humanities, Department of Spanish and Portuguese, Columbus, OH 43210. Offers MA, PhD. *Degree requirements:* For master's, thesis optional; for doctorate, thesis/dissertation. *Entrance requirements:* For master's and doctorate, GRE General Test. Additional exam requirements/recommendations for international students: Required—TOEFL (minimum score 600 paper-based; 250 computer-based). Electronic applications accepted.

Princeton University, Graduate School, Department of Spanish and Portuguese Languages and Cultures, Princeton, NJ 08544-1019. Offers PhD. *Degree requirements:* For doctorate, variable foreign language requirement, thesis/dissertation. *Entrance requirements:* For doctorate, GRE General Test, sample of written work. Additional exam requirements/recommendations for international students: Required—TOEFL (minimum score 600 paper-based; 250 computer-based). Electronic applications accepted.

Tulane University, School of Liberal Arts, Department of Spanish and Portuguese, New Orleans, LA 70118-5669. Offers Portuguese (MA); Spanish (MA); Spanish and Portuguese (PhD). *Degree requirements:* For master's, 2 foreign languages; for doctorate, 2 foreign languages, thesis/dissertation. *Entrance requirements:* For master's, GRE General Test, minimum B average in undergraduate course work; for doctorate, GRE General Test. Additional exam requirements/recommendations for international students: Required—TOEFL. Electronic applications accepted.

University of California, Los Angeles, Graduate Division, College of Letters and Science, Department of Spanish and Portuguese, Program in Portuguese, Los Angeles, CA 90095. Offers MA. *Students:* 1 full-time. In 2008, 1 master's awarded. *Degree requirements:* For master's, one foreign language, comprehensive exam or thesis. *Entrance requirements:* For master's, GRE General Test, minimum GPA of 3.0, sample of written work (recommended). *Application deadline:* For fall admission, 12/31 for domestic and international students. Application fee: $60 ($80 for international students). Electronic applications accepted. *Expenses:* Tuition, nonresident: full-time $14,694. Required fees: $9669.50. Full-time tuition and fees vary according to course load, degree level, program and student level. *Financial support:* In 2008–09, 2 fellowships with full and partial tuition reimbursements were awarded; teaching assistantships with full and partial tuition reimbursements, Federal Work-Study, institutionally sponsored loans, health care benefits, tuition waivers, and unspecified assistantships also available. Financial award applicants required to submit FAFSA. *Unit head:* Dr. Ruiz Teofilo, Chair, 310-825-1036. *Application contact:* Departmental Office, 310-825-1036, E-mail: peinado@humnet.ucla.edu.

University of California, Santa Barbara, Graduate Division, College of Letters and Sciences, Division of Humanities and Fine Arts, Department of Spanish and Portuguese, Santa Barbara, CA 93106-4150. Offers Hispanic languages and literature (PhD), including applied linguistics, European Medieval studies, feminist studies, Hispanic languages and literature; Portuguese (MA); Spanish (MA); Spanish and Portuguese (MA); MA/PhD. Spanish Language Institute available during summer session. *Faculty:* 16 full-time (6 women). *Students:* 29 full-time (16 women). Average age 30. 46 applicants, 39% accepted, 9 enrolled. In 2008, 4 master's, 2 doctorates awarded. *Degree requirements:* For master's, 2 foreign languages, comprehensive exam (for some programs), thesis optional; for doctorate, 2 foreign languages, comprehensive exam, thesis/dissertation. *Entrance requirements:* For master's, GRE, 2 writing samples, undergraduate major in Spanish or equivalent, 3 letters of recommendation, statement of purpose, personal achievements/contributions statement, resumé/curriculum vitae, transcripts for post-secondary institutions attended; for doctorate, GRE, 2 writing samples, master's degree, 3 letters of recommendation, statement of purpose, personal achievements/contributions statement, resumé/curriculum vitae, transcripts for post-secondary institutions attended. Additional exam requirements/recommendations for international students: Required—TOEFL (minimum score 550 paper-based; 213 computer-based; 80 iBT), IELTS (minimum score 7), TOEFL or IELTS. *Application deadline:* For fall admission, 3/1 for domestic and international students; for winter admission, 11/1 for domestic and international students; for spring admission, 2/1 for domestic and international students. Application fee: $70 ($90 for international students). Electronic applications accepted. *Expenses:* Tuition, nonresident: full-time $25,149. Required fees: $10,143. Full-time tuition and fees vary according to campus/location, reciprocity agreements and student level. *Financial support:* In 2008–09, 30 students received support, including 9 fellowships with full and partial tuition reimbursements available (averaging $7,000 per year), 29 teaching assistantships with partial tuition reimbursements available (averaging $11,500 per year); career-related internships or fieldwork, Federal Work-Study, institutionally sponsored loans, scholarships/grants, health care benefits, tuition waivers (full and partial), and unspecified assistantships also available. Financial award application deadline: 1/7; financial award applicants required to submit FAFSA. *Faculty research:* 19th century Spanish and Portuguese literature, Spanish and Spanish American literature, 19th and 20th century Portuguese and Brazilian literatures, Hispanic Linguistics, Catalan language and culture. *Unit head:* Prof. Francisco A. Lomeli, Chair, 805-893-5715, Fax: 805-893-8341, E-mail: lomeli@spanport.ucsb.edu. *Application contact:* Carol Conley, Graduate Program Assistant, 805-893-3162, Fax: 805-893-8341, E-mail: cconley@spanport.ucsb.edu.

University of Illinois at Urbana–Champaign, Graduate College, College of Liberal Arts and Sciences, School of Literatures, Cultures and Linguistics, Department of Spanish, Italian and Portuguese, Champaign, IL 61820. Offers Italian (MA, PhD); Portuguese (MA, PhD); Spanish (MA, PhD). *Faculty:* 17 full-time (10 women), 1 part-time/adjunct (0 women). *Students:* 50 full-time (38 women), 7 part-time (6 women); includes 4 minority (all Hispanic Americans), 31 international. 55 applicants, 44% accepted, 14 enrolled. In 2008, 10 master's, 4 doctorates awarded. *Entrance requirements:* For master's, GRE General Test, minimum GPA of 3.0; writing sample; for doctorate, GRE, minimum GPA of 3.0; writing sample. Additional exam requirements/recommendations for international students: Required—TOEFL (minimum score 88 iBT). *Application deadline:* Applications are processed on a rolling basis. Application fee: $60 ($75 for international students). Electronic applications accepted. *Financial support:* In 2008–09, 15 fellowships, 1 research assistantship, 48 teaching assistantships were awarded; tuition waivers (full and partial) also available. *Unit head:* Diane Musumeci, Head, 217-244-3250, Fax: 217-244-8430, E-mail: musumeci@illinois.edu. *Application contact:* Lynn Stanke, Secretary, 217-333-6269, Fax: 217-244-3050, E-mail: stanke@illinois.edu.

University of Maryland, College Park, Graduate Studies, College of Arts and Humanities, School of Languages, Literature, and Cultures, Department of Spanish and Portuguese, College Park, MD 20742. Offers MA, PhD. *Degree requirements:* For master's, comprehensive exam, thesis optional, scholarly paper; for doctorate, 2 foreign languages, thesis/dissertation. *Entrance requirements:* For master's, minimum GPA of 3.0, interview, sample research paper, minimum of 12 credits in upper-level literature, 3 letters of recommendation; for doctorate, minimum GPA of 3.0, interview, sample research paper, minimum of 12 credits in upper-level literature. Additional exam requirements/recommendations for international students: Required—TOEFL. Electronic applications accepted.

University of Massachusetts Amherst, Graduate School, College of Humanities and Fine Arts, Department of Languages, Literatures, and Cultures, Programs in Hispanic Literatures, Cultures and Linguistics, Amherst, MA 01003. Offers Hispanic literatures, cultures and linguistics (MA, PhD), including Hispanic literatures, cultures and linguistics (MA), teaching Spanish (MA); teaching Spanish (MAT). Part-time programs available. Terminal master's awarded for partial completion of doctoral program. *Degree requirements:* For master's, one foreign language, thesis or alternative; for doctorate, 2 foreign languages, comprehensive exam, thesis/dissertation. *Entrance requirements:* For master's and doctorate, GRE General Test, sample academic term paper. Additional exam requirements/recommendations for international students: Required—TOEFL (minimum score 550 paper-based; 213 computer-based; 79 iBT), IELTS (minimum score 6.5). Electronic applications accepted. *Expenses:* Tuition, area resident: Full-time $2640. Tuition, nonresident: full-time $9936. One-time fee: $332 full-time. Tuition and fees vary according to course load.

University of Massachusetts Dartmouth, Graduate School, College of Arts and Sciences, Department of Portuguese, North Dartmouth, MA 02747-2300. Offers Luso-Afro-Brazilian studies (PhD); Portuguese (MA). Part-time programs available. *Faculty:* 6 full-time (2 women), 1 part-time/adjunct (0 women). *Students:* 10 full-time (6 women), 11 part-time (6 women); includes 6 minority (1 African American, 1 Asian American or Pacific Islander, 4 Hispanic Americans), 2 international. Average age 34. 5 applicants, 100% accepted, 2 enrolled. In 2008, 1 master's awarded. *Degree requirements:* For master's, comprehensive exam (for some programs). *Entrance requirements:* For master's, GRE (recommended), 10-page writing sample; for doctorate, GRE. Additional exam requirements/recommendations for international students: Required—TOEFL (minimum score 500 paper-based). *Application deadline:* For fall admission, 4/20 priority date for domestic students, 2/20 priority date for international students; for spring admission, 11/15 priority date for domestic students, 9/15 priority date for international students. Applications are processed on a rolling basis. Application fee: $40 ($60 for international students). Electronic applications accepted. *Expenses:* Tuition, state resident: full-time $2071; part-time $86.29 per credit. Tuition, nonresident: full-time $8099; part-time $337.46 per credit. Required fees: $7946. Tuition and fees vary according to class time, course load and reciprocity agreements. *Financial support:* In 2008–09, 2 research assistantships with full tuition reimbursements (averaging $17,025 per year), 8 teaching assistantships with full tuition reimbursements (averaging $16,000 per year) were awarded. Financial award application deadline: 3/1; financial award applicants required to submit FAFSA. *Unit head:* Victor J Mendes, Director, Graduate Studies, 508-999-8338, Fax: 508-999-9272, E-mail: vmendes@umassd.edu. *Application contact:* Elan Turcotte-Shamski, Graduate Admissions Officer, 508-999-8604, Fax: 508-999-8183, E-mail: graduate@umassd.edu.

University of Minnesota, Twin Cities Campus, Graduate School, College of Liberal Arts, Department of Spanish and Portuguese Studies, Minneapolis, MN 55455-0213. Offers Hispanic and Luso-Brazilian literatures and linguistics (PhD); Hispanic linguistics (MA); Hispanic literature (MA); Lusophone literature (MA). *Degree requirements:* For master's, 2 foreign languages, comprehensive exam, thesis or alternative; for doctorate, 2 foreign languages, comprehensive exam, thesis/dissertation. *Entrance requirements:* For master's and doctorate, GRE General Test, samples of written work, 3 letters of recommendation, voice sample, statement of purpose. Additional exam requirements/recommendations for international students: Required—TOEFL (minimum score 550 paper-based; 213 computer-based; 79 iBT). Electronic applications accepted. *Faculty research:* Sociohistorical approaches to literature and culture, feminist studies, literary theory, ideologies and literature, pragmatics and sociolinguistics.

University of New Mexico, Graduate School, College of Arts and Sciences, Department of Spanish and Portuguese, Albuquerque, NM 87131-2039. Offers Portuguese (MA); Spanish (MA); Spanish and Portuguese (PhD). Part-time programs available. *Degree requirements:* For master's, one foreign language, comprehensive exam, thesis optional; for doctorate, one foreign language, comprehensive exam, thesis/dissertation. *Entrance requirements:* For master's, GRE, BA in Spanish or Portuguese, letters of recommendation, letter of intent; for doctorate, GRE, 3 letters of recommendation, letter of intent, sample research paper. Additional exam requirements/recommendations for international students: Required—TOEFL (minimum score 550 paper-based; 213 computer-based), Michigan English Language Assessment Battery. Electronic applications accepted. *Faculty research:* Spanish literature in Spain, Latin America, and the U.S. Spanish Southwest from its inception to present day; gender and genre studies including film, linguistic variation and change, and psycholinguistics in Spanish.

The University of North Carolina at Chapel Hill, Graduate School, College of Arts and Sciences, Department of Romance Languages, Chapel Hill, NC 27599. Offers French (MA, PhD); Italian (MA, PhD); Portuguese (MA, PhD); Romance languages (MA, PhD); Romance philology (MA, PhD); Spanish (MA, PhD). *Degree requirements:* For master's, one foreign language, comprehensive exam, thesis; for doctorate, 2 foreign languages, comprehensive exam, thesis/dissertation. *Entrance requirements:* For master's and doctorate, GRE General Test, minimum GPA of 3.0. Additional exam requirements/recommendations for international students: Required—TOEFL (minimum score 550 paper-based; 213 computer-based). Electronic applications accepted.

University of South Africa, College of Human Sciences, Pretoria, South Africa. Offers adult education (M Ed); African languages (MA, PhD); African politics (MA, PhD); Afrikaans (MA, PhD); ancient history (MA, PhD); ancient Near Eastern studies (MA, PhD); anthropology (MA, PhD); applied linguistics (MA); Arabic (MA, PhD); archaeology (MA); art history (MA); Biblical archaeology (MA); Biblical studies (M Th, D Th, PhD); Christian spirituality (M Th, D Th); church history (M Th, D Th); classical studies (MA, PhD); clinical psychology (MA); communication (MA, PhD); comparative education (M Ed, Ed D); consulting psychology (D Admin, D Com, PhD); curriculum studies (M Ed, Ed D); development studies (M Admin, MA, D Admin, PhD); didactics (M Ed, Ed D); education (M Tech); education management (M Ed, Ed D); educational psychology (M Ed); English (MA); environmental education (M Ed); French (MA, PhD); German (MA, PhD); Greek (MA); guidance and counseling (M Ed); health studies (MA, PhD), including health sciences education (MA), health services management (MA), medical and surgical nursing science (critical care general) (MA), midwifery and neonatal nursing science (MA), trauma and emergency care (MA); history (MA, PhD); history of education (Ed D); inclusive education (M Ed, Ed D); information and communications technology policy and regulation (MA); information science (MA, MIS, PhD); international politics (MA, PhD); Islamic studies (MA, PhD); Italian (MA, PhD); Judaica (MA, PhD); linguistics (MA, PhD); mathematical education (M Ed); mathematics education (MA); missiology (M Th, D Th); modern Hebrew (MA, PhD); musicology (MA, MMus, D Mus, PhD); natural science education (M Ed); New Testament (M Th, D Th); Old Testament (D Th); pastoral therapy (M Th, D Th); philosophy (MA); philosophy of education (M Ed, Ed D); politics (MA, PhD); Portuguese (MA, PhD); practical theology (M Th, D Th); psychology (MA, MS, PhD); psychology of education (M Ed, Ed D); public health (MA); religious studies (MA, D Th, PhD); Romance languages (MA); Russian (MA, PhD); Semitic languages (MA, PhD); social behavior studies in HIV/AIDS (MA); social science (mental health) (MA); social science in development studies (MA); social science in psychology (MA); social science in social work (MA); social science in sociology (MA); social work (MSW, DSW, PhD); socio-education (M Ed, Ed D); sociolinguistics (MA); sociology (MA, PhD); Spanish (MA, PhD); systematic theology (M Th, D Th); TESOL (teaching English to speakers of other languages) (MA); theological ethics (M Th, D Th); theory of literature (MA, PhD); urban ministries (D Th); urban ministry (M Th).

The University of Tennessee, Graduate School, College of Arts and Sciences, Department of Modern Foreign Languages and Literatures, Program in Modern Foreign Languages, Knoxville, TN 37996. Offers applied linguistics (PhD); French (PhD); German (PhD); Italian (PhD); Portuguese (PhD); Russian (PhD); Spanish (PhD). *Degree requirements:* For doctorate, 2 foreign languages, thesis/dissertation. *Entrance requirements:* For doctorate, minimum GPA of 2.7. Additional exam requirements/recommendations for international students: Required—TOEFL. Electronic applications accepted. *Expenses:* Tuition, area resident: Part-time $348 per credit hour. Tuition, state resident: full-time $6262. Tuition, nonresident: full-time $18,920; part-time $1052 per credit hour. Required fees: $812; $36 per credit hour. Tuition and fees vary according to program.

The University of Texas at Austin, Graduate School, College of Liberal Arts, Department of Spanish and Portuguese, Austin, TX 78712-1111. Offers Hispanic linguistics (MA, PhD); Hispanic literature (MA, PhD); Luso-Brazilian literature (MA, PhD). *Degree requirements:* For master's, 2 foreign languages, thesis or alternative; for doctorate, 3 foreign languages, thesis/dissertation. *Entrance requirements:* For master's and doctorate, GRE General Test. Electronic applications accepted.

Portuguese

University of Toronto, School of Graduate Studies, Humanities Division, Department of Spanish and Portuguese, Toronto, ON M5S 1A1, Canada. Offers MA, PhD. Part-time programs available. *Degree requirements:* For doctorate, thesis/dissertation. *Entrance requirements:* For master's, minimum B average in final year, 2 letters of reference; for doctorate, minimum A– average, 2 letters of reference, writing sample. Additional exam requirements/recommendations for international students: Required—TOEFL, Michigan English Language Assessment Battery, IELTS or COPE.

University of Washington, Graduate School, College of Arts and Sciences, Department of Romance Languages and Literature, Division of Spanish and Portuguese Studies, Seattle, WA 98195. Offers Hispanic literary and cultural studies (MA). *Degree requirements:* For master's, 2 foreign languages, thesis optional, exam. *Entrance requirements:* For master's, GRE General Test, minimum GPA of 3.0. Additional exam requirements/recommendations for international students: Required—TOEFL. Electronic applications accepted. *Faculty research:* Medieval through modern Spanish literature and film, Latin American literature, poetry and essay, pan-Hispanic ballad, Hispanic cultural studies, second language acquisition and applied linguistics.

University of Wisconsin–Madison, Graduate School, College of Letters and Science, Department of Spanish and Portuguese, Program in Portuguese, Madison, WI 53706-1380. Offers MA, PhD. *Degree requirements:* For master's, one foreign language; for doctorate, 2 foreign languages, thesis/dissertation. *Entrance requirements:* For master's, GRE (recommended), minimum GPA of 3.25 in Spanish or Portuguese; for doctorate, GRE (recommended), minimum graduate GPA of 3.4. Additional exam requirements/recommendations for international students: Required—TOEFL. Electronic applications accepted. *Faculty research:* Portuguese and Brazilian literature.

Vanderbilt University, Graduate School, Department of Spanish and Portuguese, Nashville, TN 37240-1001. Offers Portuguese (MA); Spanish (MA, MAT, PhD); Spanish and Portuguese (PhD). *Faculty:* 22 full-time (7 women). *Students:* 25 full-time (12 women), 1 part-time (0 women); includes 2 minority (1 African American, 1 American Indian/Alaska Native), 12 international. Average age 30. 47 applicants, 17% accepted, 4 enrolled. In 2008, 6 master's, 6 doctorates awarded. *Degree requirements:* For master's, one foreign language, thesis; for doctorate, 2 foreign languages, thesis/dissertation, final and qualifying exams. *Entrance requirements:* For master's, GRE General Test; for doctorate, GRE General Test, writing sample in Spanish. Additional exam requirements/recommendations for international students: Required—TOEFL (minimum score 570 paper-based; 230 computer-based; 88 iBT). *Application deadline:* For fall admission, 1/15 for domestic and international students. Application fee: $0. Electronic applications accepted. *Financial support:* Fellowships with full and partial tuition reimbursements, teaching assistantships with full tuition reimbursements, Federal Work-Study, institutionally sponsored loans, and health care benefits available. Financial award application deadline: 1/15; financial award applicants required to submit CSS PROFILE or FAFSA. *Faculty research:* Spanish, Portuguese, and Latin American literatures; foreign language pedagogy; Renaissance and baroque poetry; nineteenth century Spanish novel. *Unit head:* Cathy L. Jrade, PhD, Chair, 615-322-6930, Fax: 615-343-7260, E-mail: cathy.l.jrade@vanderbilt.edu. *Application contact:* Christina Karageorgou-Bastea, PhD, Director of Graduate Studies, 615-322-6930, Fax: 615-343-7260, E-mail: christina.karageorgou@vanderbilt.edu.

Yale University, Graduate School of Arts and Sciences, Department of Spanish and Portuguese, New Haven, CT 06520. Offers Latin American literature (PhD); Luso-Brazilian and Spanish/Spanish American literatures (PhD); Spanish peninsular literature (PhD). Terminal master's awarded for partial completion of doctoral program. *Degree requirements:* For doctorate, 3 foreign languages, thesis/dissertation. *Entrance requirements:* For doctorate, GRE General Test.

Romance Languages

Appalachian State University, Cratis D. Williams Graduate School, Department of Foreign Languages and Literatures, Boone, NC 28608. Offers romance languages (MA), including Spanish or French teaching. Part-time programs available. Postbaccalaureate distance learning degree programs offered (no on-campus study). *Faculty:* 15 full-time (8 women). *Students:* 6 full-time (4 women), 10 part-time (8 women); includes 4 minority (all Hispanic Americans). 9 applicants, 89% accepted, 8 enrolled. In 2008, 5 master's awarded. *Degree requirements:* For master's, one foreign language, comprehensive exam, thesis optional. *Entrance requirements:* For master's, GRE General Test, 3 letters of recommendation. Additional exam requirements/recommendations for international students: Required—TOEFL (minimum score 570 paper-based; 230 computer-based; 79 iBT), IELTS (minimum score 6.5), TOEFL or IELTS. *Application deadline:* For fall admission, 7/1 for domestic students, 2/1 for international students; for spring admission, 11/1 for domestic students, 7/1 for international students. Applications are processed on a rolling basis. Application fee: $50. Electronic applications accepted. *Expenses:* Tuition, area resident: Full-time $2600; part-time $700 per course. Tuition, state resident: full-time $2600; part-time $700 per course. Tuition, nonresident: full-time $5000; part-time $3300 per course. Required fees: $2150; $330 per course. Tuition and fees vary according to campus/location. *Financial support:* In 2008–09, 2 research assistantships (averaging $7,000 per year) were awarded; fellowships, teaching assistantships, career-related internships or fieldwork and unspecified assistantships also available. Financial award application deadline: 4/1; financial award applicants required to submit FAFSA. *Faculty research:* French and Spanish literature, Latin American culture, teaching foreign languages. Total annual research expenditures: $166,000. *Unit head:* Dr. Richard Carp, Chairperson, 828-262-3096, Fax: 828-262-3095, E-mail: carprm@appstate.edu. *Application contact:* Dr. Beverly Moser, Graduate Coordinator, 828-262-2929, E-mail: moserba@appstate.edu.

Boston University, Graduate School of Arts and Sciences, Department of Romance Studies, Boston, MA 02215. Offers French language and literature (MA, PhD); Hispanic language and literatures (MA, PhD). Terminal master's awarded for partial completion of doctoral program. *Degree requirements:* For master's, one foreign language, comprehensive exam; for doctorate, 2 foreign languages, comprehensive exam, thesis/dissertation. *Entrance requirements:* For master's and doctorate, GRE General Test, sample of written work, 3 letters of recommendation. Additional exam requirements/recommendations for international students: Required—TOEFL (minimum score 550 paper-based; 213 computer-based).

Clark Atlanta University, School of Arts and Sciences, Department of Foreign Languages, Atlanta, GA 30314. Offers Romance languages (MA, DAH). Part-time programs available. *Faculty:* 3 full-time (1 woman). *Students:* 1 (woman) full-time, 1 part-time (0 women); both minorities (both African Americans). Average age 37. 1 applicant, 100% accepted, 1 enrolled. *Degree requirements:* For master's, one foreign language, thesis. *Entrance requirements:* For master's, GRE General Test, minimum GPA of 2.5. Additional exam requirements/recommendations for international students: Required—TOEFL (minimum score 500 paper-based; 173 computer-based). *Application deadline:* For fall admission, 4/1 for domestic and international students; for spring admission, 11/1 for domestic and international students. Applications are processed on a rolling basis. Application fee: $40 ($55 for international students). *Expenses:* Tuition: Full-time $12,240; part-time $680 per credit hour. Required fees: $710; $355 per semester. *Financial support:* Career-related internships or fieldwork, Federal Work-Study, scholarships/grants, and unspecified assistantships available. Support available to part-time students. Financial award application deadline: 4/30; financial award applicants required to submit FAFSA. *Unit head:* Dr. Laurent Monye, Chairperson, 404-880-8547, E-mail: lmonye@cau.edu. *Application contact:* Michelle Clark-Davis, Graduate Program Admissions, 404-880-6605, E-mail: cauadmissions@cau.edu.

Columbia University, Graduate School of Arts and Sciences, Division of Humanities, Department of French and Romance Philology, New York, NY 10027. Offers French and Romance philology (M Phil, PhD); Romance languages (MA). Part-time programs available. *Degree requirements:* For master's, one foreign language, thesis, written exam; for doctorate, 2 foreign languages, thesis/dissertation. *Entrance requirements:* For master's and doctorate, GRE General Test, knowledge of Latin, writing sample. Additional exam requirements/recommendations for international students: Required—TOEFL. *Faculty research:* Theory of literature, literary semiotics, poetics.

Cornell University, Graduate School, Graduate Fields of Arts and Sciences, Field of Linguistics, Ithaca, NY 14853-0001. Offers applied linguistics (MA, PhD); East Asian linguistics (MA, PhD); English linguistics (MA, PhD); general linguistics (MA, PhD); Germanic linguistics (MA, PhD); Indo-European linguistics (MA, PhD); phonetics (MA, PhD); phonological theory (MA, PhD); Romance linguistics (MA, PhD); second language acquisition (MA, PhD); semantics (MA, PhD); Slavic linguistics (MA, PhD); sociolinguistics (MA, PhD); South Asian linguistics (MA, PhD); Southeast Asian linguistics (MA, PhD); syntactic theory (MA, PhD). *Faculty:* 15 full-time (6 women). *Students:* 32 full-time (15 women); includes 1 minority (Hispanic American), 16 international. Average age 30. 93 applicants, 16% accepted, 7 enrolled. In 2008, 5 master's, 7 doctorates awarded. Terminal master's awarded for partial completion of doctoral program. *Degree requirements:* For master's, one foreign language, thesis; for doctorate, one foreign language, comprehensive exam, thesis/dissertation. *Entrance requirements:* For master's and doctorate, GRE General Test, 2 letters of recommendation. Additional exam requirements/recommendations for international students: Required—TOEFL (minimum score 600 paper-based; 250 computer-based; 77 iBT). *Application deadline:* For fall admission, 1/15 for domestic students. Application fee: $70. Electronic applications accepted. *Expenses:* Tuition: Full-time $29,500. Required fees: $70. Full-time tuition and fees vary according to degree level, program and student level. *Financial support:* In 2008–09, 32 students received support, including 11 fellowships with full tuition reimbursements available, 4 research assistantships with full tuition reimbursements available, 17 teaching assistantships with full tuition reimbursements available; institutionally sponsored loans, scholarships/grants, health care benefits, tuition waivers (full and partial), and unspecified assistantships also available. Financial award applicants required to submit FAFSA. *Faculty research:* Phonology and phonetics; syntax and semantics; historical linguistics; philosophy of language; language acquisition. *Unit head:* Director of Graduate Studies, 607-255-1105. *Application contact:* Graduate Field Assistant, 607-255-1105, E-mail: lingfield@cornell.edu.

Cornell University, Graduate School, Graduate Fields of Arts and Sciences, Field of Romance Studies, Ithaca, NY 14853-0001. Offers French linguistics (PhD); French literature (PhD); Hispanic literature (PhD); Italian linguistics (PhD); Italian literature (PhD); Romance linguistics (PhD); Spanish linguistics (PhD). *Faculty:* 30 full-time (14 women). *Students:* 50 full-time (24 women); includes 10 minority (all Hispanic Americans), 18 international. Average age 30. 99 applicants, 15% accepted, 8 enrolled. In 2008, 5 doctorates awarded. *Degree requirements:* For doctorate, 2 foreign languages, comprehensive exam, thesis/dissertation. *Entrance requirements:* For doctorate, GRE General Test, sample of written work, 3 letters of recommendation. Additional exam requirements/recommendations for international students: Required—TOEFL (minimum score 550 paper-based; 213 computer-based; 77 iBT). *Application deadline:* For fall admission, 1/15 for domestic students. Application fee: $70. Electronic applications accepted. *Expenses:* Tuition: Full-time $29,500. Required fees: $70. Full-time tuition and fees vary according to degree level, program and student level. *Financial support:* In 2008–09, 46 students received support, including 16 fellowships with full tuition reimbursements available, 30 teaching assistantships with full tuition reimbursements available; research assistantships with full tuition reimbursements available, institutionally sponsored loans, scholarships/grants, health care benefits, tuition waivers (full and partial), and unspecified assistantships also available. Financial award applicants required to submit FAFSA. *Faculty research:* Literary theory, Hispanic studies, French studies, gender studies. *Unit head:* Director of Graduate Studies, 607-255-8222. *Application contact:* Graduate Field Assistant, 607-255-4246, E-mail: romance_studies@cornell.edu.

Hunter College of the City University of New York, Graduate School, School of Arts and Sciences, Department of Romance Languages, New York, NY 10021-5085. Offers French (MA), including French, French education; Italian (MA), including Italian, Italian education; Spanish (MA), including Spanish, Spanish education. Part-time and evening/weekend programs available. *Faculty:* 8 full-time (5 women). *Students:* 1 (woman) full-time, 23 part-time (16 women); includes 6 minority (all Hispanic Americans). Average age 38. 14 applicants, 50% accepted, 4 enrolled. In 2008, 11 master's awarded. *Degree requirements:* For master's, 2 foreign languages, comprehensive exam, thesis optional. *Entrance requirements:* For master's, GRE General Test, GRE Subject Test, interview, proficiency in chosen language. Additional exam requirements/recommendations for international students: Required—TOEFL. *Application deadline:* For fall admission, 4/1 for domestic students, 2/1 for international students; for spring admission, 11/1 for domestic students, 9/1 for international students. Application fee: $125. *Financial support:* Fellowships, Federal Work-Study, scholarships/grants, and tuition waivers (partial) available. Support available to part-time students. Financial award application deadline: 4/15. *Unit head:* Dr. Giuseppe Carlo DiScipio, Chair, 212-772-5108, Fax: 212-772-5094, E-mail: gdiscipi@hunter.cuny.edu. *Application contact:* William Zlata, Director for Graduate Admissions, 212-772-4482, Fax: 212-650-3336, E-mail: admissions@hunter.cuny.edu.

The Johns Hopkins University, Zanvyl Krieger School of Arts and Sciences, Department of German and Romance Languages, Baltimore, MD 21218-2699. Offers French (PhD); German (PhD); Italian (PhD); romance languages (PhD); Spanish (PhD). *Degree requirements:* For doctorate, 2 foreign languages, thesis/dissertation. *Entrance requirements:* For doctorate, GRE General Test. Additional exam requirements/recommendations for international students: Required—TOEFL (minimum score 600 paper-based; 250 computer-based). Electronic applications accepted.

Michigan State University, The Graduate School, College of Arts and Letters, Department of French, Classics, and Italian, East Lansing, MI 48824. Offers French (MA); French language and literature (PhD). *Entrance requirements:* Additional exam requirements/recommendations for international students: Required—TOEFL. Electronic applications accepted.

New York University, Graduate School of Arts and Science, Center for French Civilization and Culture, Department of French, New York, NY 10012-1019. Offers French (PhD); French language and civilization (MA); French literature (MA); Romance languages and literatures (MA). Part-time programs available. Terminal master's awarded for partial completion of doctoral program. *Degree requirements:* For master's, one foreign language, thesis (for some programs); for doctorate, one foreign language, thesis/dissertation. *Entrance requirements:* For master's and doctorate, GRE General Test, proficiency in French. Additional exam requirements/recommendations for international students: Required—TOEFL. *Faculty research:*

French and Francophone literature, literary theory, and history; rhetoric and poetics; cultural history; theater and cinema.

New York University, Graduate School of Arts and Science, Department of Spanish and Portuguese Languages and Literatures, New York, NY 10012-1019. Offers Portuguese (MA, PhD); Spanish (PhD); Spanish and Latin American literatures and cultures (MA); Spanish language and translation (MA). Part-time programs available. *Degree requirements:* For master's, 2 foreign languages, thesis; for doctorate, 2 foreign languages, thesis/dissertation. *Entrance requirements:* For master's, GRE General Test; for doctorate, GRE General Test, master's degree. Additional exam requirements/recommendations for international students: Required—TOEFL. *Faculty research:* Gender and sexuality, transatlantic studies, literacy and cultural theories, colonial and post colonial studies, autobiography and modern subjectivities.

Northern Illinois University, Graduate School, College of Liberal Arts and Sciences, Department of Foreign Languages and Literatures, De Kalb, IL 60115-2854. Offers French (MA); Spanish (MA). Part-time programs available. *Degree requirements:* For master's, one foreign language, comprehensive exam, thesis or alternative, language proficiency exam. *Entrance requirements:* For master's, GRE General Test, interview, minimum GPA of 2.75, undergraduate major in French or Spanish. Additional exam requirements/recommendations for international students: Required—TOEFL (minimum score 550 paper-based; 213 computer-based). Electronic applications accepted. *Faculty research:* Francophone women writers, prosodies of French and Italian, early Spanish drama, business German, history of Burmese literature.

Queens College of the City University of New York, Division of Graduate Studies, Arts and Humanities Division, Department of European Languages and Literatures, Flushing, NY 11367-1597. Offers French (MA); Italian (MA). Part-time and evening/weekend programs available. *Degree requirements:* For master's, 2 foreign languages, comprehensive exam, thesis or alternative. *Entrance requirements:* For master's, minimum GPA of 3.0. Additional exam requirements/recommendations for international students: Required—TOEFL.

San Diego State University, Graduate and Research Affairs, College of Arts and Letters, Department of European Studies, San Diego, CA 92182. Offers MA. *Degree requirements:* For master's, one foreign language. *Entrance requirements:* For master's, GRE General Test. Additional exam requirements/recommendations for international students: Required—TOEFL. Electronic applications accepted.

Stony Brook University, State University of New York, Graduate School, College of Arts and Sciences, Department of European Languages, Literatures, and Cultures, Program in French, Stony Brook, NY 11794. Offers Romance languages (MA). Evening/weekend programs available. *Degree requirements:* For master's, one foreign language. *Entrance requirements:* For master's, GRE General Test. Additional exam requirements/recommendations for international students: Required—TOEFL. *Application deadline:* For fall admission, 1/15 for domestic students. Application fee: $60. *Expenses:* Tuition, area resident: Full-time $7880; part-time $328 per credit hour. Tuition, state resident: full-time $7880; part-time $328 per credit hour. Tuition, nonresident: full-time $13,250; part-time $552 per credit hour. Required fees: $848. *Unit head:* Prosper Sanou, Coordinator, 631-632-7440, E-mail: prosper.sanou@stonybrook.edu. *Application contact:* Dr. Andrea Fedi, Director of Graduate Studies, 631-632-7438, Fax: 631-632-9612.

Texas Tech University, Graduate School, College of Arts and Sciences, Department of Classical and Modern Languages and Literatures, Lubbock, TX 79409. Offers applied linguistics (MA); classics (MA); German (MA); Romance language (MA); Romance languages-French (MA); Romance languages-Spanish (MA, PhD). Part-time programs available. *Faculty:* 23 full-time (9 women), 1 (woman) part-time/adjunct. *Students:* 76 full-time (43 women), 21 part-time (14 women); includes 23 minority (1 African American, 1 Asian American or Pacific Islander, 21 Hispanic Americans), 26 international. Average age 32. 73 applicants, 75% accepted, 31 enrolled. In 2008, 20 master's, 2 doctorates awarded. *Degree requirements:* For master's, thesis or alternative; for doctorate, thesis/dissertation. *Entrance requirements:* For master's and doctorate, GRE General Test. Additional exam requirements/recommendations for international students: Required—TOEFL (minimum score 550 paper-based; 213 computer-based). *Application deadline:* For fall admission, 3/1 priority date for international students; for spring admission, 11/1 priority date for international students. Applications are processed on a rolling basis. Application fee: $50 ($60 for international students). Electronic applications accepted. *Expenses:* Tuition, area resident: Part-time $194 per credit hour. Tuition, state resident: full-time $4648; part-time $194 per credit hour. Tuition, nonresident: full-time $11,392; part-time $475 per credit hour. Required fees: $2206; $69 per credit hour. $389 per semester. *Financial support:* In 2008–09, 42 students received support, including 70 teaching assistantships with partial tuition reimbursements available (averaging $11,625 per year); research assistantships with partial tuition reimbursements available, Federal Work-Study and institutionally sponsored loans also available. Support available to part-time students. Financial award application deadline: 4/15; financial award applicants required to submit FAFSA. *Faculty research:* Literature, comparative literature, linguistics, culture, pedagogy. Total annual research expenditures: $65,397. *Unit head:* Dr. Julian Frederick Suppe, Chair and Professor, 806-742-4355, Fax: 806-742-3306, E-mail: frederick.suppe@ttu.edu. *Application contact:* Liz Hildebrand, Senior Advisor, 806-742-4055, Fax: 806-742-3306, E-mail: liz.hildebrand@ttu.edu.

University at Buffalo, the State University of New York, Graduate School, College of Arts and Sciences, Department of Romance Languages and Literatures, Buffalo, NY 14260. Offers French (MA, PhD); Spanish (MA, PhD). Part-time programs available. Terminal master's awarded for partial completion of doctoral program. *Degree requirements:* For master's, one foreign language, project; for doctorate, 2 foreign languages, thesis/dissertation. *Entrance requirements:* For master's and doctorate, GRE. Additional exam requirements/recommendations for international students: Required—TOEFL (minimum score 550 paper-based; 213 computer-based; 79 iBT). Electronic applications accepted. *Faculty research:* Romance linguistics, cultural studies, literary studies, literature and philosophy.

The University of Alabama, Graduate School, College of Arts and Sciences, Department of Modern Languages and Classics, Tuscaloosa, AL 35487. Offers French (MA, PhD); French and Spanish (PhD); German (MA); Romance languages (MA, PhD); Spanish (MA, PhD). Part-time programs available. *Faculty:* 21 full-time (11 women). *Students:* 45 full-time (35 women), 12 part-time (7 women); includes 13 minority (6 African Americans, 7 Hispanic Americans), 11 international. Average age 32. 25 applicants, 68% accepted, 11 enrolled. In 2008, 17 master's, 4 doctorates awarded. *Degree requirements:* For master's, comprehensive exam, thesis optional; for doctorate, one foreign language, thesis/dissertation, preliminary exam. *Entrance requirements:* For master's and doctorate, minimum GPA of 3.0, writing sample. Additional exam requirements/recommendations for international students: Required—TOEFL or IELTS. *Application deadline:* For fall admission, 7/6 priority date for domestic students, 1/15 priority date for international students; for spring admission, 12/6 priority date for domestic students, 6/1 priority date for international students. Applications are processed on a rolling basis. Application fee: $31. Electronic applications accepted. *Expenses:* Tuition, area resident: Full-time $6400. Tuition, state resident: full-time $6400. Tuition, nonresident: full-time $18,000. *Financial support:* In 2008–09, 7 students received support, including 1 fellowship, research assistantships with full tuition reimbursements available (averaging $10,291 per year), 6 teaching assistantships with full tuition reimbursements available (averaging $10,291 per year); career-related internships or fieldwork, Federal Work-Study, institutionally sponsored loans, and scholarships/grants also available. Financial award application deadline: 7/14. *Faculty research:* Non-English literature, linguistics, culture, film. Total annual research expenditures: $9,630. *Unit head:* Dr. Michael Picone, Chair and Professor, 205-348-5054, Fax: 205-348-2042, E-mail: mpicone@bama.ua.edu. *Application contact:* Dr. K. Barbara Fischer, Graduate Director and Associate Professor, 205-348-8465, Fax: 205-348-2042, E-mail: bfischer@bama.ua.edu.

University of California, Berkeley, Graduate Division, Group in Romance Languages and Literature, Berkeley, CA 94720-1500. Offers French (PhD); Italian (PhD); Spanish (PhD). *Degree requirements:* For doctorate, thesis/dissertation, qualifying exam. *Entrance requirements:* For doctorate, GRE General Test, minimum GPA of 3.0, 3 letters of recommendation. Additional exam requirements/recommendations for international students: Required—TOEFL (minimum score 570 paper-based; 230 computer-based).

University of Chicago, Division of the Humanities, Department of Romance Languages and Literatures, Chicago, IL 60637-1513. Offers French (AM, PhD); Italian (AM, PhD); Spanish (AM, PhD). Terminal master's awarded for partial completion of doctoral program. *Degree requirements:* For master's, 2 foreign languages, thesis; for doctorate, 3 foreign languages, thesis/dissertation. *Entrance requirements:* For master's and doctorate, GRE General Test, GRE Subject Test. Additional exam requirements/recommendations for international students: Required—TOEFL.

University of Cincinnati, Graduate School, McMicken College of Arts and Sciences, Department of Romance Languages and Literature, Cincinnati, OH 45221. Offers French (MA, PhD); Romance languages and literatures (PhD); Spanish (MA, PhD). Terminal master's awarded for partial completion of doctoral program. *Degree requirements:* For master's, 2 foreign languages, comprehensive exam, thesis optional; for doctorate, 3 foreign languages, comprehensive exam, thesis/dissertation. *Entrance requirements:* For master's, minimum GPA of 3.0; for doctorate, MA or equivalent in French or Spanish language and literature. Additional exam requirements/recommendations for international students: Required—TOEFL (minimum score 520 paper-based; 190 computer-based). Electronic applications accepted. *Faculty research:* Teaching methods in Spanish, Spanish theater, Old French, Francophone studies, poetry.

University of Georgia, Graduate School, College of Arts and Sciences, Department of Romance Languages, Program in Romance Languages, Athens, GA 30602. Offers MA, MAT, PhD. *Degree requirements:* For master's, one foreign language, thesis (MA); for doctorate, one foreign language, thesis/dissertation. *Entrance requirements:* For master's and doctorate, GRE General Test. Electronic applications accepted.

University of Miami, Graduate School, College of Arts and Sciences, Department of Modern Languages and Literatures, Coral Gables, FL 33124. Offers romance studies (PhD), including French, Spanish. *Degree requirements:* For doctorate, 2 foreign languages, thesis/dissertation, area exam, qualifying exam. *Entrance requirements:* For doctorate, 1 writing sample in English and 1 writing sample in French or Spanish, minimum GPA of 3.0; oral interview; letters of recommendation. Additional exam requirements/recommendations for international students: Required—TOEFL (minimum score 550 paper-based; 213 computer-based; 59 iBT), GRE General Test (recommended). Electronic applications accepted. *Faculty research:* Transatlantic studies, Caribbean studies, comparative literature, gender theory, cultural studies.

University of Michigan, Horace H. Rackham School of Graduate Studies, College of Literature, Science, and the Arts, Department of Romance Languages and Literatures, Ann Arbor, MI 48109. Offers French (PhD); Romance linguistics (PhD); Spanish (PhD). *Degree requirements:* For doctorate, 2 foreign languages, thesis/dissertation, oral defense of dissertation, preliminary exams. *Entrance requirements:* For doctorate, GRE General Test. Additional exam requirements/recommendations for international students: Required—TOEFL or Michigan English Language Assessment Battery. Electronic applications accepted. *Faculty research:* Comparative Romance studies, medieval and early modern studies, postcolonial and minority literatures, culture and materiality, reflection on the nature and function of scholarship.

University of Missouri–Columbia, Graduate School, College of Arts and Sciences, Department of Romance Languages and Literature, Columbia, MO 65211. Offers French (MA, PhD); literature (MA); Spanish (MA, PhD); teaching (MA). *Faculty:* 24 full-time (11 women), 1 (woman) part-time/adjunct. *Students:* 8 full-time (6 women), 17 part-time (9 women); includes 10 minority (2 African Americans, 2 Asian Americans or Pacific Islanders, 6 Hispanic Americans), 4 international. Average age 36. 19 applicants, 37% accepted, 5 enrolled. In 2008, 6 master's, 2 doctorates awarded. Terminal master's awarded for partial completion of doctoral program. *Degree requirements:* For master's, one foreign language; for doctorate, 4 foreign languages, thesis/dissertation. *Entrance requirements:* For master's and doctorate, GRE General Test, minimum GPA of 3.0. Additional exam requirements/recommendations for international students: Required—TOEFL (minimum score 500 paper-based; 173 computer-based; 61 iBT). *Application deadline:* For fall admission, 1/15 priority date for domestic students. Applications are processed on a rolling basis. Application fee: $45 ($60 for international students). *Financial support:* Research assistantships, teaching assistantships, institutionally sponsored loans available. *Unit head:* Dr. Flore Zephir, Department Chair, E-mail: zephirf@missouri.edu. *Application contact:* Amy Rinck, Office Support Staff III, 573-882-5039, E-mail: rinckam@missouri.edu.

University of Missouri–Kansas City, College of Arts and Sciences, Department of Foreign Languages and Literatures, Kansas City, MO 64110-2499. Offers Romance languages and literatures (MA). Part-time programs available. *Faculty:* 11 full-time (4 women), 19 part-time/adjunct (12 women). *Students:* 3 full-time (1 woman), 21 part-time (16 women); includes 11 minority (2 African Americans, 9 Hispanic Americans). Average age 34. 11 applicants, 100% accepted, 9 enrolled. In 2008, 11 master's awarded. *Degree requirements:* For master's, 2 foreign languages. *Entrance requirements:* For master's, GRE General Test, minimum GPA of 2.75, 2 letters of recommendation. Additional exam requirements/recommendations for international students: Required—TOEFL (minimum score 550 paper-based; 213 computer-based; 80 iBT). *Application deadline:* For fall admission, 4/1 priority date for domestic and international students; for spring admission, 11/1 priority date for domestic and international students. Applications are processed on a rolling basis. Application fee: $45 ($50 for international students). Electronic applications accepted. *Expenses:* Tuition, state resident: full-time $5376; part-time $298.70 per credit hour. Tuition, nonresident: full-time $13,882; part-time $771.20 per credit hour. Required fees: $640.28; $34.65 per contact hour. $30 per semester. Tuition and fees vary according to course load and program. *Financial support:* In 2008–09, 5 students received support, including 1 teaching assistantship with full tuition reimbursement available (averaging $10,500 per year); Federal Work-Study, institutionally sponsored loans, and tuition waivers (full and partial) also available. Support available to part-time students. Financial award application deadline: 3/1; financial award applicants required to submit FAFSA. *Faculty research:* Literary analyses; psychology and literature; narrative techniques, poetic structure, and style; literature, politics, and society (especially Latin America). *Unit head:* Dr. Kathy Krause, Chair, 816-235-1340, Fax: 816-235-1312, E-mail: krausek@umkc.edu. *Application contact:* Jennifer DeHaemers, Director of Admissions, 816-235-1111, Fax: 816-235-5544, E-mail: admit@umkc.edu.

University of New Orleans, Graduate School, College of Liberal Arts, Department of Foreign Languages, New Orleans, LA 70148. Offers MA. Part-time and evening/weekend programs available. *Degree requirements:* For master's, one foreign language, thesis optional. *Entrance requirements:* For master's, GRE General Test, minimum B average. Additional exam requirements/recommendations for international students: Required—TOEFL (minimum score 550 paper-based; 213 computer-based; 79 iBT). Electronic applications accepted. *Faculty research:* Translation studies, Michelet, Scève, Spanish canzoniero, theories of representation.

The University of North Carolina at Chapel Hill, Graduate School, College of Arts and Sciences, Department of Romance Languages, Chapel Hill, NC 27599. Offers French (MA, PhD); Italian (MA, PhD); Portuguese (MA, PhD); Romance languages (MA, PhD); Romance philology (MA, PhD); Spanish (MA, PhD). *Degree requirements:* For master's, one foreign language, comprehensive exam, thesis; for doctorate, 2 foreign languages, comprehensive exam, thesis/dissertation. *Entrance requirements:* For master's and doctorate, GRE General Test, minimum GPA of 3.0. Additional exam requirements/recommendations for international students: Required—TOEFL (minimum score 550 paper-based; 213 computer-based). Electronic applications accepted.

Romance Languages

University of Notre Dame, Graduate School, College of Arts and Letters, Division of Humanities, Department of Romance Languages and Literatures, Notre Dame, IN 46556. Offers French and Francophone studies (MA); Iberian and Latin American studies (MA); Italian studies (MA); Romance literatures (MA). *Faculty:* 25 full-time (10 women), 4 part-time/adjunct (all women). *Students:* 17 full-time (12 women); includes 4 minority (all Hispanic Americans), 2 international. 30 applicants, 47% accepted, 11 enrolled. In 2008, 11 master's awarded. *Degree requirements:* For master's, 2 foreign languages, comprehensive exam, thesis optional. *Entrance requirements:* For master's, GRE General Test, BA in target language. Additional exam requirements/recommendations for international students: Required—TOEFL (minimum score 600 paper-based; 250 computer-based; 80 iBT). *Application deadline:* For fall admission, 2/1 priority date for domestic students, 2/1 for international students. Application fee: $50. Electronic applications accepted. *Financial support:* Teaching assistantships with full tuition reimbursements, tuition waivers (full) available. Financial award application deadline: 2/1. *Faculty research:* Literature of discovery and exploration, modern literature, literary criticism, medieval literature, feminist critical theory. *Unit head:* Dr. John Welle, Director of Graduate Studies, 574-631-6887, E-mail: al.romland.1@nd.edu. *Application contact:* Dr. Barbara Turpin, Director of Graduate Admissions, 574-631-7706, Fax: 574-631-4183.

University of Oregon, Graduate School, College of Arts and Sciences, Department of Romance Languages, Program in Romance Languages, Eugene, OR 97403. Offers MA, PhD. Part-time programs available. *Degree requirements:* For master's, 2 foreign languages; for doctorate, 2 foreign languages, thesis/dissertation. *Entrance requirements:* For master's and doctorate, GRE General Test, minimum GPA of 3.0. Additional exam requirements/recommendations for international students: Required—TOEFL.

University of Pennsylvania, School of Arts and Sciences, Graduate Group in Romance Languages, Philadelphia, PA 19104. Offers French (AM, PhD); Italian (AM, PhD); Spanish (AM, PhD). Terminal master's awarded for partial completion of doctoral program. *Degree requirements:* For master's, one foreign language, thesis or alternative; for doctorate, 2 foreign languages, thesis/dissertation. *Entrance requirements:* For master's and doctorate, GRE General Test. Additional exam requirements/recommendations for international students: Required—TOEFL. Electronic applications accepted. *Faculty research:* Literary theory and criticism, cultural studies, history of Romance literatures, gender studies.

University of South Africa, College of Human Sciences, Pretoria, South Africa. Offers adult education (M Ed); African languages (MA, PhD); African politics (MA, PhD); Afrikaans (MA, PhD); ancient history (MA, PhD); ancient Near Eastern studies (MA, PhD); anthropology (MA, PhD); applied linguistics (MA); Arabic (MA, PhD); archaeology (MA); art history (MA); Biblical archaeology (MA); Biblical studies (M Th, D Th, PhD); Christian spirituality (M Th, D Th); church history (M Th, D Th); classical studies (MA, PhD); clinical psychology (MA); communication (MA, PhD); comparative education (M Ed, Ed D); consulting psychology (D Admin, D Com, PhD); curriculum studies (M Ed, Ed D); development studies (M Admin, MA, D Admin, PhD); didactics (M Ed, Ed D); education (M Tech); education management (M Ed, Ed D); educational psychology (M Ed); English (MA); environmental education (M Ed); French (MA, PhD); German (MA, PhD); Greek (MA); guidance and counseling (M Ed); health studies (MA, PhD), including health sciences education (MA), health services management (MA), medical and surgical nursing science (critical care general) (MA), midwifery and neonatal nursing science (MA), trauma and emergency care (MA); history (MA, PhD); history of education (Ed D); inclusive education (M Ed, Ed D); information and communications technology policy and regulation (MA); information science (MA, MIS, PhD); international politics (MA, PhD); Islamic studies (MA, PhD); Italian (MA, PhD); Judaica (MA, PhD); linguistics (MA, PhD); mathematical education (M Ed); mathematics education (MA); missiology (M Th, D Th); modern Hebrew (MA, PhD); musicology (MA, MMus, D Mus, PhD); natural science education (M Ed); New Testament (M Th, D Th); Old Testament (D Th); pastoral therapy (M Th, D Th); philosophy (MA); philosophy of education (M Ed, Ed D); politics (MA, PhD); Portuguese (MA, PhD); practical theology (M Th, D Th); psychology (MA, MS, PhD); psychology of education (M Ed, Ed D); public health (MA); religious studies (MA, D Th, PhD); Romance languages (MA); Russian (MA, PhD); Semitic languages (MA, PhD); social behavior studies in HIV/AIDS (MA); social science (mental health) (MA); social science in development studies (MA); social science in psychology (MA); social science in social work (MA); social science in sociology (MA); social work (MSW, DSW, PhD); socio-education (M Ed, Ed D); sociolinguistics (MA); sociology (MA, PhD); Spanish (MA, PhD); systematic theology (M Th, D Th); TESOL (teaching English to speakers of other languages) (MA); theological ethics (M Th, D Th); theory of literature (MA, PhD); urban ministries (D Th); urban ministry (M Th).

The University of Texas at Austin, Graduate School, College of Liberal Arts, Department of French and Italian, Austin, TX 78712-1111. Offers French (MA, PhD); French linguistics (MA, PhD); Italian studies (MA, PhD); Romance linguistics (MA, PhD). Part-time programs available. *Degree requirements:* For master's, one foreign language, thesis; for doctorate, 2 foreign languages, thesis/dissertation. *Entrance requirements:* For master's, GRE General Test, minimum GPA of 3.0, bachelor's degree in French or equivalent; for doctorate, GRE General Test, minimum GPA of 3.0, master's degree in French. Additional exam requirements/recommendations for international students: Required—TOEFL. Electronic applications accepted. *Faculty research:* Nineteenth-century Italian literature, Italian Renaissance, twentieth-century French literature, Francophone literature, fifteenth-century literature and culture.

University of Virginia, College and Graduate School of Arts and Sciences, Department of Spanish, Italian and Portuguese, Charlottesville, VA 22903. Offers Italian (MA); Spanish (MA, PhD). *Faculty:* 19 full-time (9 women), 2 part-time/adjunct (both women). *Students:* 57 full-time (42 women), 1 (woman) part-time; includes 5 minority (all Hispanic Americans), 12 international. Average age 27. 57 applicants, 72% accepted, 26 enrolled. In 2008, 13 master's, 6 doctorates awarded. *Degree requirements:* For master's, comprehensive exam, thesis; for doctorate, one foreign language, comprehensive exam, thesis/dissertation. *Entrance requirements:* For master's and doctorate, GRE General Test, GRE Subject Test, 2 letters of recommendation. Additional exam requirements/recommendations for international students: Required—TOEFL (minimum score 600 paper-based; 250 computer-based; 90 iBT), IELTS (minimum score 7). *Application deadline:* For fall admission, 12/1 for domestic and international students. Applications are processed on a rolling basis. Application fee: $60. Electronic applications accepted. *Expenses:* Tuition, area resident: Full-time $10,452. Tuition, state resident: full-time $10,452. Tuition, nonresident: full-time $20,010. Required fees: $2176. Part-time tuition and fees vary according to course load and program. *Financial support:* Fellowships, teaching assistantships available. Financial award applicants required to submit FAFSA. *Unit head:* Mar??a-In??s Lagos, Chair, 434-924-7159, Fax: 434-924-7160, E-mail: sipinfo@virginia.edu. *Application contact:* Mar??a-In??s Lagos, Chair, 434-924-7159, Fax: 434-924-7160, E-mail: sipinfo@virginia.edu.

University of Washington, Graduate School, College of Arts and Sciences, Department of Romance Languages and Literature, Seattle, WA 98195. Offers French and Italian studies (MA, PhD), including French, Italian (MA); Spanish and Portuguese (MA), including Hispanic literary and cultural studies. Terminal master's awarded for partial completion of doctoral program. *Degree requirements:* For master's, 2 foreign languages, thesis optional, exam; for doctorate, 3 foreign languages, thesis/dissertation, exams. *Entrance requirements:* For master's and doctorate, GRE General Test, minimum GPA of 3.0. Additional exam requirements/recommendations for international students: Required—TOEFL. Electronic applications accepted.

Washington University in St. Louis, Graduate School of Arts and Sciences, Department of Romance Languages and Literatures, St. Louis, MO 63130-4899. Offers French (MA, PhD); Spanish (MA, PhD). *Students:* 63 full-time (49 women); includes 9 minority (3 African Americans, 6 Hispanic Americans), 30 international. 41 applicants, 39% accepted, 8 enrolled. In 2008, 2 master's, 2 doctorates awarded. Terminal master's awarded for partial completion of doctoral program. *Degree requirements:* For master's, thesis or alternative; for doctorate, thesis/dissertation. *Entrance requirements:* For master's and doctorate, GRE General Test. *Application deadline:* For fall admission, 1/15 priority date for domestic students. Application fee: $45. Electronic applications accepted. *Financial support:* Fellowships, teaching assistantships, Federal Work-Study, institutionally sponsored loans, and tuition waivers (full and partial) available. Support available to part-time students. Financial award application deadline: 1/15. *Unit head:* Dr. Elzbieta Sklodowska, Chairperson, 314-935-5175. *Application contact:* Assistant to the Dean, 314-935-6880, Fax: 314-935-4887.

Russian

American University, College of Arts and Sciences, Department of Language and Foreign Studies, Program in Russian, Washington, DC 20016-8045. Offers translation (Certificate). Part-time and evening/weekend programs available. *Students:* 2 part-time (1 woman). Average age 26. In 2008, 1 Certificate awarded. *Degree requirements:* For Certificate, 15 credit hour minimum in related course work. *Entrance requirements:* For degree, bachelor's degree in Russian or evidence of Russian proficiency plus a BA. Additional exam requirements/recommendations for international students: Required—TOEFL. *Application deadline:* For fall admission, 2/1 for domestic students; for spring admission, 10/1 for domestic students. Application fee: $50. *Expenses:* Tuition: Full-time $21,204; part-time $1178 per credit hour. Required fees: $380. Part-time tuition and fees vary according to course load and program. *Financial support:* Fellowships, career-related internships or fieldwork, Federal Work-Study, and institutionally sponsored loans available. Financial award application deadline: 2/1. *Faculty research:* Culture, literature, and area studies; technology-assisted language instruction; linguistics.

Boston College, Graduate School of Arts and Sciences, Department of Slavic and Eastern Languages, Program in Russian and Slavic Languages and Literature, Chestnut Hill, MA 02467-3800. Offers MA, MA/JD, MBA/MA. Part-time programs available. *Degree requirements:* For master's, 3 foreign languages, comprehensive exam, thesis or alternative. *Entrance requirements:* Additional exam requirements/recommendations for international students: Required—TOEFL (minimum score 550 paper-based; 213 computer-based). Electronic applications accepted. *Expenses:* Tuition: Part-time $1148 per credit. Required fees: $60. *Faculty research:* Structural analysis of language, poetry and semiotic systems.

Brown University, Graduate School, Department of Slavic Languages, Providence, RI 02912. Offers Russian language and literature (AM); Slavic languages (AM); Slavic studies (PhD). *Degree requirements:* For master's, one foreign language; for doctorate, 2 foreign languages, thesis/dissertation, preliminary exam.

Bryn Mawr College, Graduate School of Arts and Sciences, Department of Russian, Bryn Mawr, PA 19010-2899. Offers MA, PhD. Part-time programs available. *Degree requirements:* For master's, one foreign language, thesis; for doctorate, 2 foreign languages, comprehensive exam, thesis/dissertation. *Entrance requirements:* For master's and doctorate, GRE General Test. Additional exam requirements/recommendations for international students: Required—TOEFL (minimum score 600 paper-based; 250 computer-based).

Columbia University, Graduate School of Arts and Sciences, Division of Humanities, Department of Slavic Languages, New York, NY 10027. Offers Russian literature (M Phil, MA, PhD); Slavic languages (M Phil, MA, PhD). *Degree requirements:* For master's, one foreign language, thesis; for doctorate, 2 foreign languages, thesis/dissertation. *Entrance requirements:* For master's and doctorate, GRE General Test. Additional exam requirements/recommendations for international students: Required—TOEFL. *Faculty research:* Polish, Serbo-Croatian, Czechoslovakian, medieval and modern Russian literature.

Harvard University, Graduate School of Arts and Sciences, Department of Slavic Languages and Literatures, Cambridge, MA 02138. Offers Polish (PhD); Russian (PhD); Serbo-Croatian (PhD); Slavic philology (PhD); Ukrainian (PhD). *Degree requirements:* For doctorate, 4 foreign languages, thesis/dissertation. *Entrance requirements:* For doctorate, GRE General Test, writing sample. Additional exam requirements/recommendations for international students: Required—TOEFL. *Expenses:* Tuition: Full-time $32,556. Required fees: $1426. Full-time tuition and fees vary according to program and student level.

Hofstra University, School of Education, Health, and Human Services, Department of Curriculum and Teaching, Program in Foreign Language Education, Hempstead, NY 11549. Offers foreign language education (MA, MS Ed), including French, German, Russian, Spanish. Part-time and evening/weekend programs available. *Students:* 2 full-time (both women), 4 part-time (3 women); includes 3 minority (all Hispanic Americans). Average age 32. 7 applicants, 71% accepted, 0 enrolled. In 2008, 2 master's awarded. *Degree requirements:* For master's, one foreign language, thesis. *Entrance requirements:* For master's, 2 letters of recommendation, teacher certification (MA), essay. Additional exam requirements/recommendations for international students: Required—TOEFL (minimum score 550 paper-based; 213 computer-based; 80 iBT). *Application deadline:* Applications are processed on a rolling basis. Application fee: $60. Electronic applications accepted. *Expenses:* Tuition: Full-time $15,300; part-time $850 per credit. Required fees: $970; $165 per term. Tuition and fees vary according to program. *Financial support:* In 2008–09, 1 student received support; fellowships with full and partial tuition reimbursements available, research assistantships with full and partial tuition reimbursements available, Federal Work-Study, institutionally sponsored loans, scholarships/grants, and tuition waivers (full and partial) available. Support available to part-time students. Financial award applicants required to submit FAFSA. *Faculty research:* Contemporary Spanish cultural studies, twentieth century Spanish theater, identity and post-coloniality, Romance philology, politics of language, decolonization, Spanish imperial Africa and Latin America, twentieth century Latin American poetry. Total annual research expenditures: $5,000. *Unit head:* Dr. David Powell, Chairperson, 516-463-5485, Fax: 516-463-2310, E-mail: rlldap@hofstra.edu. *Application contact:* Carol Drummer, Dean of Graduate Admissions, 516-463-4876, Fax: 516-463-4664, E-mail: gradstudent@hofstra.edu.

Kent State University, College of Arts and Sciences, Department of Modern and Classical Language Studies, Kent, OH 44242-0001. Offers French literature (MA); French, Spanish, German and Latin pedagogy (MA); German literature (MA); Spanish literature (MA); translation (MA), including French, German, Japanese, Russian, Spanish; translation studies (PhD). Part-time and evening/weekend programs available. *Degree requirements:* For master's, one foreign language, comprehensive exam (for some programs), thesis (for some programs); for doctorate, comprehensive exam, thesis/dissertation (for some programs). *Entrance requirements:* For master's, minimum GPA of 3.0, writing sample, audio tape or CD; for doctorate, 3 recommendations. Additional exam requirements/recommendations for international students: Required—TOEFL (minimum score 197 computer-based). Electronic applications accepted. *Faculty research:* Literature, pedagogy, applied linguistics, translation studies.

McGill University, Faculty of Graduate and Postdoctoral Studies, Faculty of Arts, Department of Russian and Slavic Studies, Montréal, QC H3A 2T5, Canada. Offers Russian literature (MA, PhD).

Middlebury College, Language Schools, Russian School, Middlebury, VT 05753. Offers MA, DML. *Faculty:* 6 full-time (3 women). *Students:* 23 full-time (18 women); includes 1 minority (Asian American or Pacific Islander). Average age 33. 57 applicants, 58% accepted, 27 enrolled. In 2008, 6 master's awarded. *Degree requirements:* For master's, one foreign language; for doctorate, 2 foreign languages, comprehensive exam, thesis/dissertation. *Entrance requirements:* For master's, placement exam, 3 letters of recommendation, writing sample. *Application deadline:* Applications are processed on a rolling basis. Application fee: $55. Electronic applications accepted. *Financial support:* Scholarships/grants available. *Unit head:* Dr. Benjamin Rifkin, Director, 802-443-5230, Fax: 802-443-2075, E-mail: brifkin@middlebury.edu. *Application contact:* John Stokes, Coordinator, 802-443-5230, Fax: 802-443-2075, E-mail: jstokes@middlebury.edu.

New York University, Graduate School of Arts and Science, Department of Russian and Slavic Studies, New York, NY 10012-1019. Offers Russian literature (MA); Slavic literature (MA). Part-time programs available. *Degree requirements:* For master's, one foreign language, comprehensive exam, thesis. *Entrance requirements:* For master's, GRE General Test, minimum 3 years of undergraduate Russian or equivalent. Additional exam requirements/recommendations for international students: Required—TOEFL. *Faculty research:* Modern Russian literature and art, contemporary Russian and East European literature, literary theory, Slavic linguistics, Russian journalism.

Penn State University Park, Graduate School, College of the Liberal Arts, Department of Languages and Literature, State College, University Park, PA 16802-1503. Offers comparative literature (MA, PhD); Russian and comparative literature (MA).

Princeton University, Graduate School, Department of Slavic Languages and Literatures, Princeton, NJ 08544-1019. Offers Russian and Slavic linguistics (PhD); Russian literature (PhD). *Degree requirements:* For doctorate, variable foreign language requirement, thesis/dissertation. *Entrance requirements:* For doctorate, GRE General Test. Additional exam requirements/recommendations for international students: Required—TOEFL (minimum score 600 paper-based; 250 computer-based). Electronic applications accepted.

Stanford University, School of Humanities and Sciences, Department of Slavic Languages and Literatures, Stanford, CA 94305-9991. Offers Russian (MA); Slavic languages and literatures (PhD). Terminal master's awarded for partial completion of doctoral program. *Degree requirements:* For master's, one foreign language, thesis or alternative; for doctorate, 3 foreign languages, thesis/dissertation. *Entrance requirements:* For master's and doctorate, GRE General Test. Additional exam requirements/recommendations for international students: Required—TOEFL. Electronic applications accepted.

University at Albany, State University of New York, College of Arts and Sciences, Department of Languages, Literatures, and Cultures, Program in Russian, Albany, NY 12222-0001. Offers Russian (MA); Russian translation (Certificate). *Faculty research:* Translation, phonology and morphology of modern Russian.

The University of Arizona, Graduate College, College of Humanities, Department of Russian and Slavic Studies, Tucson, AZ 85721. Offers Russian (M Ed, MA). Part-time programs available. *Degree requirements:* For master's, one foreign language, comprehensive exam (for some programs), thesis (for some programs). *Entrance requirements:* For master's, department language proficiency exam, minimum GPA of 3.0, statement of purpose, 3 letters of recommendation, audio sample. Additional exam requirements/recommendations for international students: Required—TOEFL (minimum score 550 paper-based). Electronic applications accepted. *Faculty research:* Russian literature, language/pedagogy, linguistics, Russian culture.

University of California, Berkeley, Graduate Division, College of Letters and Science, Department of Slavic Languages and Literatures, Berkeley, CA 94720-1500. Offers Czech (PhD), including Czech linguistics, Czech literature; Polish (PhD), including Polish linguistics, Polish literature; Russian (PhD), including Russian linguistics, Russian literature; Serbo-Croatian (PhD), including Serbo-Croatian linguistics, Serbo-Croatian literature. Terminal master's awarded for partial completion of doctoral program. *Degree requirements:* For doctorate, thesis/dissertation, oral and written exams. *Entrance requirements:* For doctorate, GRE General Test, minimum GPA of 3.0, 3 letters of recommendation. Additional exam requirements/recommendations for international students: Required—TOEFL (minimum score 570 paper-based; 230 computer-based). Electronic applications accepted.

University of Michigan, Horace H. Rackham School of Graduate Studies, College of Literature, Science, and the Arts, Department of Slavic Languages and Literatures, Ann Arbor, MI 48109. Offers Russian (AM); Slavic languages and literatures (PhD). *Degree requirements:* For master's, 2 foreign languages, comprehensive exam; for doctorate, 3 foreign languages, comprehensive exam, thesis/dissertation, oral defense of dissertation, preliminary exam. *Entrance requirements:* For master's, GRE General Test, 3rd year foreign language proficiency; for doctorate, GRE General Test, master's degree. Additional exam requirements/recommendations for international students: Required—TOEFL (minimum score 560 paper-based; 220 computer-based). Electronic applications accepted. *Faculty research:* Russian literature (all periods), Polish literature, Slavic linguistics, Czech literature, Ukrainian literature.

The University of North Carolina at Chapel Hill, Graduate School, College of Arts and Sciences, Department of Slavic Languages and Literatures, Chapel Hill, NC 27599. Offers Polish literature (PhD); Russian literature (MA, PhD); Serbo-Croatian literature (PhD); Slavic linguistics (MA, PhD). Part-time programs available. Terminal master's awarded for partial completion of doctoral program. *Degree requirements:* For master's, 2 foreign languages, comprehensive exam, thesis; for doctorate, 4 foreign languages, comprehensive exam, thesis/dissertation. *Entrance requirements:* For master's and doctorate, GRE General Test, minimum GPA of 3.0. Electronic applications accepted. *Faculty research:* Russian cultural studies, literary translation, sociolinguistics, cognitive linguistics, émigré literature.

University of Oregon, Graduate School, College of Arts and Sciences, Program in Russian and East European Studies, Eugene, OR 97403. Offers MA. Part-time programs available. *Degree requirements:* For master's, 2 foreign languages, thesis. *Entrance requirements:* For master's, GRE General Test (recommended), minimum GPA of 3.0. Additional exam requirements/recommendations for international students: Required—TOEFL. *Faculty research:* L. N. Tolstoy's middle years, Russian folklore in eighteenth century contexts, Bulgarian syntax, medieval Bulgarian texts, contemporary Russian culture film.

University of South Africa, College of Human Sciences, Pretoria, South Africa. Offers adult education (M Ed); African languages (MA, PhD); African politics (MA, PhD); Afrikaans (MA, PhD); ancient history (MA, PhD); ancient Near Eastern studies (MA, PhD); anthropology (MA, PhD); applied linguistics (MA); Arabic (MA, PhD); archaeology (MA); art history (MA); Biblical archaeology (MA); Biblical studies (M Th, D Th, PhD); Christian spirituality (M Th, D Th); church history (M Th, D Th); classical studies (MA, PhD); clinical psychology (MA); communication (MA, PhD); comparative education (M Ed, Ed D); consulting psychology (D Admin, D Com, PhD); curriculum studies (M Ed, Ed D); development studies (M Admin, MA, D Admin, PhD); didactics (M Ed, Ed D); education (M Tech); education management (M Ed, Ed D); educational psychology (M Ed); English (MA); environmental education (M Ed); French (MA, PhD); German (MA, PhD); Greek (MA); guidance and counseling (M Ed); health studies (MA, PhD), including health sciences education (MA), health services management (MA), medical and surgical nursing science (critical care general) (MA), midwifery and neonatal nursing science (MA), trauma and emergency care (MA); history (MA, PhD); history of education (Ed D); inclusive education (M Ed, Ed D); information and communications technology policy and regulation (MA); information science (MA, MIS, PhD); international politics (MA, PhD); Islamic studies (MA, PhD); Italian (MA, PhD); Judaica (MA, PhD); linguistics (MA, PhD); mathematical education (M Ed); mathematics education (MA); missiology (M Th, D Th); modern Hebrew (MA, PhD); musicology (MA, MMus, D Mus, PhD); natural science education (M Ed); New Testament (M Th, D Th); Old Testament (D Th); pastoral therapy (M Th, D Th); philosophy (MA); philosophy of education (M Ed, Ed D); politics (MA, PhD); Portuguese (MA, PhD); practical theology (M Th, D Th); psychology (MA, MS, PhD); psychology of education (M Ed, Ed D); public health (MA); religious studies (MA, D Th, PhD); Romance languages (MA); Russian (MA, PhD); Semitic languages (MA, PhD); social behavior studies in HIV/AIDS (MA); social science (mental health) (MA); social science in development studies (MA); social science in psychology (MA); social science in social work (MA); social science in sociology (MA); social work (MSW, DSW, PhD); socio-education (M Ed, Ed D); sociolinguistics (MA); sociology (MA, PhD); Spanish (MA, PhD); systematic theology (M Th, D Th); TESOL (teaching English to speakers of other languages) (MA); theological ethics (M Th, D Th); theory of literature (MA, PhD); urban ministries (D Th); urban ministry (M Th).

The University of Tennessee, Graduate School, College of Arts and Sciences, Department of Modern Foreign Languages and Literatures, Program in Modern Foreign Languages, Knoxville, TN 37996. Offers applied linguistics (PhD); French (PhD); German (PhD); Italian (PhD); Portuguese (PhD); Russian (PhD); Spanish (PhD). *Degree requirements:* For doctorate, 2 foreign languages, thesis/dissertation. *Entrance requirements:* For doctorate, minimum GPA of 2.7. Additional exam requirements/recommendations for international students: Required—TOEFL. Electronic applications accepted. *Expenses:* Tuition, area resident: Part-time $348 per credit hour. Tuition, state resident: full-time $6262. Tuition, nonresident: full-time $18,920; part-time $1052 per credit hour. Required fees: $812; $36 per credit hour. Tuition and fees vary according to program.

University of Washington, Graduate School, College of Arts and Sciences, Department of Slavic Languages and Literatures, Seattle, WA 98195. Offers Russian literature (MA, PhD); Slavic linguistics (MA, PhD). *Degree requirements:* For master's, 2 foreign languages, thesis optional; for doctorate, 3 foreign languages, thesis/dissertation. *Entrance requirements:* For master's and doctorate, GRE General Test, minimum GPA of 3.0. Additional exam requirements/recommendations for international students: Required—TOEFL. Electronic applications accepted. *Faculty research:* Modern and medieval East European languages and literatures, comparative literature, Russian folk literature, Slavic literary theory and criticism, computerized morphology of Russian.

University of Waterloo, Graduate Studies, Faculty of Arts, Department of Germanic and Slavic Studies, Waterloo, ON N2L 3G1, Canada. Offers German (MA, PhD); Russian (MA). Part-time and evening/weekend programs available. *Degree requirements:* For master's, one foreign language, thesis optional; for doctorate, 2 foreign languages, comprehensive exam, thesis/dissertation. *Entrance requirements:* For master's, honors degree, minimum B average; for doctorate, master's degree, minimum B average. Additional exam requirements/recommendations for international students: Required—TOEFL, TWE. Electronic applications accepted. *Faculty research:* Medieval theatre; history and literature; German and Russian literary relations; seventeenth, eighteenth, nineteenth, and twentieth century German literature.

Wayne State University, College of Liberal Arts and Sciences, Department of Classical and Modern Languages, Literatures, and Cultures, Program in German and Slavic Studies, Detroit, MI 48202. Offers German (MA); language learning (MA); modern languages (PhD); Russian (MA). *Degree requirements:* For master's, one foreign language, thesis or alternative; for doctorate, 2 foreign languages, thesis/dissertation. *Entrance requirements:* For master's and doctorate, minimum GPA of 3.0. Additional exam requirements/recommendations for international students: Required—TOEFL (minimum score 550 paper-based; 213 computer-based); Recommended—TWE (minimum score 6). Electronic applications accepted. *Faculty research:* Exile and Holocaust, minority literature, gender studies, fairytale studies, sociolinguistics.

Yale University, Graduate School of Arts and Sciences, Department of Slavic Languages and Literatures, New Haven, CT 06520. Offers medieval Slavic literature and philology (PhD); Polish literature (PhD); Russian literature (PhD); Slavic languages and literatures and film studies (PhD). *Degree requirements:* For doctorate, 3 foreign languages, thesis/dissertation. *Entrance requirements:* For doctorate, GRE General Test.

Scandinavian Languages

Cornell University, Graduate School, Graduate Fields of Arts and Sciences, Field of Germanic Studies, Ithaca, NY 14853-0001. Offers German area studies (MA, PhD); German intellectual history (MA, PhD); Germanic linguistics (MA, PhD); Germanic literature (MA, PhD); old Norse (MA, PhD). *Faculty:* 17 full-time (8 women). *Students:* 17 full-time (9 women); includes 3 minority (1 American Indian/Alaska Native, 1 Asian American or Pacific Islander, 1 Hispanic American), 6 international. Average age 29. 35 applicants, 20% accepted, 4 enrolled. In 2008, 2 doctorates awarded. Terminal master's awarded for partial completion of doctoral program. *Degree requirements:* For master's, one foreign language, thesis; for doctorate, 2 foreign languages, comprehensive exam, thesis/dissertation. *Entrance requirements:* For master's and doctorate, GRE General Test, fluency in German, writing sample, 2 letters of recommendation. Additional exam requirements/recommendations for international students: Required—TOEFL (minimum score 550 paper-based; 213 computer-based; 77 iBT). *Application deadline:* For fall admission, 1/15 for domestic students. Application fee: $70. Electronic applications accepted. *Expenses:* Tuition: Full-time $29,500. Required fees: $70. Full-time tuition and fees vary according to degree level, program and student level. *Financial support:* In 2008–09, 15 students received support, including 6 fellowships with full tuition reimbursements available, 9 teaching assistantships with full tuition reimbursements available; research assistantships with full tuition reimbursements available, institutionally sponsored loans, scholarships/grants, health care benefits, tuition waivers (full and partial), and unspecified assistantships also available. Financial award applicants required to submit FAFSA. *Faculty research:* Women's studies, minority literature, literature and intellectual history, theater and film studies, continental philosophy. *Unit head:* Director of Graduate Studies, 607-255-4047. *Application contact:* Graduate Field Assistant, 607-255-4047, E-mail: germanic_studies@cornell.edu.

Harvard University, Graduate School of Arts and Sciences, Department of Germanic Languages and Literatures, Cambridge, MA 02138. Offers German (PhD); Scandinavian (PhD). Terminal master's awarded for partial completion of doctoral program. *Degree requirements:* For doctorate, 2 foreign languages, thesis/dissertation, exams. *Entrance requirements:* For doctorate, GRE General Test, German writing sample. Additional exam requirements/recommendations for international students: Required—TOEFL. *Expenses:* Tuition: Full-time $32,556. Required fees: $1426. Full-time tuition and fees vary according to program and student level.

Scandinavian Languages

University of California, Berkeley, Graduate Division, College of Letters and Science, Department of Scandinavian Languages and Literatures, Berkeley, CA 94720-1500. Offers PhD. *Degree requirements:* For doctorate, 2 foreign languages, thesis/dissertation, 3 field papers, qualifying exam. *Entrance requirements:* For doctorate, GRE General Test, minimum GPA of 3.0, MA in Scandinavian language or equivalent, 3 letters of recommendation. Additional exam requirements/recommendations for international students: Required—TOEFL (minimum score 570 paper-based; 230 computer-based). *Faculty research:* Modern literatures, old Norse language and literatures, folklore, film, interdisciplinary.

University of California, Los Angeles, Graduate Division, College of Letters and Science, Department of Germanic Languages, Program in Scandinavian, Los Angeles, CA 90095. Offers MA. *Students:* 1 full-time. 2 applicants, 50% accepted, 1 enrolled. *Degree requirements:* For master's, one foreign language, comprehensive exam. *Entrance requirements:* For master's, GRE General Test, sample of written work. *Application deadline:* For fall admission, 12/15 for domestic and international students. Application fee: $60 ($80 for international students). Electronic applications accepted. *Expenses:* Tuition, nonresident: full-time $14,694. Required fees: $9669.50. Full-time tuition and fees vary according to course load, degree level, program and student level. *Financial support:* Fellowships with full and partial tuition reimbursements, research assistantships with full and partial tuition reimbursements, teaching assistantships with full and partial tuition reimbursements, Federal Work-Study, institutionally sponsored loans, and health care benefits available. Financial award application deadline: 3/1; financial award applicants required to submit FAFSA. *Unit head:* Timothy Tangherlini, Vice Chair, 310-825-9754. *Application contact:* Departmental Office, 310-825-6828, E-mail: allen@humnet.ucla.edu.

University of Massachusetts Amherst, Graduate School, College of Humanities and Fine Arts, Department of Languages, Literatures, and Cultures, Programs in German and Scandinavian Studies, Amherst, MA 01003. Offers MA, PhD. Part-time programs available. Terminal master's awarded for partial completion of doctoral program. *Degree requirements:* For master's, thesis or alternative; for doctorate, 2 foreign languages, comprehensive exam, thesis/dissertation. *Entrance requirements:* For master's and doctorate, writing sample in English and German. Additional exam requirements/recommendations for international students: Required—TOEFL (minimum score 550 paper-based; 213 computer-based; 79 iBT), IELTS

(minimum score 6.5). Electronic applications accepted. *Expenses:* Tuition, area resident: Full-time $2640. Tuition, nonresident: full-time $9936. One-time fee: $332 full-time. Tuition and fees vary according to course load.

University of Minnesota, Twin Cities Campus, Graduate School, College of Liberal Arts, Department of German, Scandinavian, and Dutch, Minneapolis, MN 55455-0213. Offers Germanic studies: German and Scandinavian studies track (PhD); Germanic studies: German track (MA, PhD); Germanic studies: Germanic medieval studies track (MA, PhD); Germanic studies: Scandinavian studies track (MA); Germanic studies: teaching track (MA). Part-time programs available. Terminal master's awarded for partial completion of doctoral program. *Degree requirements:* For doctorate, 2 foreign languages, thesis/dissertation. *Entrance requirements:* For master's, GRE General Test, BA in German, Scandinavian, or equivalent; for doctorate, GRE General Test, MA in German, Scandinavian, or equivalent. Additional exam requirements/recommendations for international students: Required—TOEFL (minimum score 550 paper-based; 213 computer-based; 79 iBT). Electronic applications accepted. *Faculty research:* Cultural studies, literary theory, feminist criticism, film, Germanic philology.

University of Washington, Graduate School, College of Arts and Sciences, Department of Scandinavian Studies, Seattle, WA 98195. Offers MA, PhD. *Degree requirements:* For master's, one foreign language, comprehensive exam, thesis optional; for doctorate, 2 foreign languages, comprehensive exam, thesis/dissertation. *Entrance requirements:* For master's, GRE, BA in Scandinavian or equivalent, minimum GPA of 3.0; for doctorate, GRE, master's degree, minimum GPA of 3.0. Additional exam requirements/recommendations for international students: Required—TOEFL. *Faculty research:* Scandinavian folklore, history, and politics; medieval to modern Scandinavian literature; Scandinavian fiction, poetry, drama, literary history, and theory.

University of Wisconsin–Madison, Graduate School, College of Letters and Science, Department of Scandinavian Studies, Madison, WI 53706-1380. Offers area studies (MA); folklore (PhD); literature (MA, PhD); philology (PhD). Part-time programs available. *Degree requirements:* For master's, 2 foreign languages, exam; for doctorate, thesis/dissertation, exam. *Entrance requirements:* For master's, minimum GPA of 3.25; for doctorate, minimum GPA of 3.5. Electronic applications accepted. *Faculty research:* Historical fiction, Icelandic poetry, nineteenth-century literature, theater, gender studies, folklore.

Slavic Languages

Boston College, Graduate School of Arts and Sciences, Department of Slavic and Eastern Languages, Program in Russian and Slavic Languages and Literature, Chestnut Hill, MA 02467-3800. Offers MA, MA/JD, MBA/MA. Part-time programs available. *Degree requirements:* For master's, 3 foreign languages, comprehensive exam, thesis or alternative. *Entrance requirements:* Additional exam requirements/recommendations for international students: Required—TOEFL (minimum score 550 paper-based; 213 computer-based). Electronic applications accepted. *Expenses:* Tuition: Part-time $1148 per credit. Required fees: $60. *Faculty research:* Structural analysis of language, poetry and semiotic systems.

Brown University, Graduate School, Department of Slavic Languages, Providence, RI 02912. Offers Russian language and literature (AM); Slavic languages (AM); Slavic studies (PhD). *Degree requirements:* For master's, one foreign language; for doctorate, 2 foreign languages, thesis/dissertation, preliminary exam.

Columbia University, Graduate School of Arts and Sciences, Division of Humanities, Department of Slavic Languages, New York, NY 10027. Offers Russian literature (M Phil, MA, PhD); Slavic languages (M Phil, MA, PhD). *Degree requirements:* For master's, one foreign language, thesis; for doctorate, 2 foreign languages, thesis/dissertation. *Entrance requirements:* For master's and doctorate, GRE General Test. Additional exam requirements/recommendations for international students: Required—TOEFL. *Faculty research:* Polish, Serbo-Croatian, Czechoslovakian, medieval and modern Russian literature.

Cornell University, Graduate School, Graduate Fields of Arts and Sciences, Field of Linguistics, Ithaca, NY 14853-0001. Offers applied linguistics (MA, PhD); East Asian linguistics (MA, PhD); English linguistics (MA, PhD); general linguistics (MA, PhD); Germanic linguistics (MA, PhD); Indo-European linguistics (MA, PhD); phonetics (MA, PhD); phonological theory (MA, PhD); Romance linguistics (MA, PhD); second language acquisition (MA, PhD); semantics (MA, PhD); Slavic linguistics (MA, PhD); sociolinguistics (MA, PhD); South Asian linguistics (MA, PhD); Southeast Asian linguistics (MA, PhD); syntactic theory (MA, PhD). *Faculty:* 15 full-time (6 women). *Students:* 32 full-time (15 women); includes 1 minority (Hispanic American), 16 international. Average age 30. 93 applicants, 16% accepted, 7 enrolled. In 2008, 5 master's, 7 doctorates awarded. Terminal master's awarded for partial completion of doctoral program. *Degree requirements:* For master's, one foreign language, thesis; for doctorate, one foreign language, comprehensive exam, thesis/dissertation. *Entrance requirements:* For master's and doctorate, GRE General Test, 2 letters of recommendation. Additional exam requirements/recommendations for international students: Required—TOEFL (minimum score 600 paper-based; 250 computer-based; 77 iBT). *Application deadline:* For fall admission, 1/15 for domestic students. Application fee: $70. Electronic applications accepted. *Expenses:* Tuition: Full-time $29,500. Required fees: $70. Full-time tuition and fees vary according to degree level, program and student level. *Financial support:* In 2008–09, 32 students received support, including 11 fellowships with full tuition reimbursements available, 4 research assistantships with full tuition reimbursements available, 17 teaching assistantships with full tuition reimbursements available; institutionally sponsored loans, scholarships/grants, health care benefits, tuition waivers (full and partial), and unspecified assistantships also available. Financial award applicants required to submit FAFSA. *Faculty research:* Phonology and phonetics; syntax and semantics; historical linguistics; philosophy of language; language acquisition. *Unit head:* Director of Graduate Studies, 607-255-1105. *Application contact:* Graduate Field Assistant, 607-255-1105, E-mail: lingfield@cornell.edu.

Duke University, Graduate School, Department of Slavic Languages and Literatures, Durham, NC 27708. Offers AM. Part-time programs available. *Entrance requirements:* For master's, GRE General Test. Additional exam requirements/recommendations for international students: Required—TOEFL (minimum score 550 paper-based; 213 computer-based; 83 iBT), IELTS (minimum score 7). Electronic applications accepted.

Florida State University, Graduate Studies, College of Arts and Sciences, Department of Modern Languages, Program in Slavic Languages/Russian, Tallahassee, FL 32306. Offers Slavic languages and literatures (MA). *Degree requirements:* For master's, thesis optional. *Entrance requirements:* For master's, GRE General Test or minimum GPA of 3.0. Additional exam requirements/recommendations for international students: Required—TOEFL (minimum score 550 paper-based; 213 computer-based). Electronic applications accepted. *Faculty research:* Contemporary literature, emigré literature, Old Russian word formation, political rhetoric, structure of modern Russian.

Harvard University, Graduate School of Arts and Sciences, Department of Slavic Languages and Literatures, Cambridge, MA 02138. Offers Polish (PhD); Russian (PhD); Serbo-Croatian (PhD); Slavic philology (PhD); Ukrainian (PhD). *Degree requirements:* For doctorate, 4 foreign languages, thesis/dissertation. *Entrance requirements:* For doctorate, GRE General Test, writing sample. Additional exam requirements/recommendations for international students:

Required—TOEFL. *Expenses:* Tuition: Full-time $32,556. Required fees: $1426. Full-time tuition and fees vary according to program and student level.

Indiana University Bloomington, University Graduate School, College of Arts and Sciences, Department of Slavic Languages and Literatures, Bloomington, IN 47405. Offers MA, MAT, PhD. Part-time programs available. *Faculty:* 8 full-time (3 women). *Students:* 12 full-time (11 women), 4 international. Average age 29. 8 applicants, 88% accepted, 2 enrolled. In 2008, 1 master's awarded. Terminal master's awarded for partial completion of doctoral program. *Degree requirements:* For master's, variable foreign language requirement; for doctorate, variable foreign language requirement, comprehensive exam, thesis/dissertation. *Entrance requirements:* For master's, GRE General Test. Additional exam requirements/recommendations for international students: Required—TOEFL. *Application deadline:* Applications are processed on a rolling basis. Application fee: $50 ($60 for international students). *Expenses:* Tuition, area resident: Part-time $291.97 per credit hour. Tuition, state resident: part-time $291.97 per credit hour. Tuition, nonresident: part-time $850.33 per credit hour. Required fees: $110 per semester. Tuition and fees vary according to course load and program. *Financial support:* In 2008–09, 1 fellowship with full tuition reimbursement, 5 teaching assistantships with full tuition reimbursements were awarded; research assistantships with full tuition reimbursements. Financial award application deadline: 2/1. *Faculty research:* Russian stress, Slavic accentology and morphophonemics, Eastern European literature, Bible translation. *Unit head:* Dr. Steven Franks, Chair, 812-855-9906, E-mail: feldstei@indiana.edu. *Application contact:* Tricia Wall, Summer Program and Student Services Assistant, 812-855-2608, Fax: 812-855-2107.

New York University, Graduate School of Arts and Science, Department of Russian and Slavic Studies, New York, NY 10012-1019. Offers Russian literature (MA); Slavic literature (MA). Part-time programs available. *Degree requirements:* For master's, one foreign language, comprehensive exam, thesis. *Entrance requirements:* For master's, GRE General Test, minimum 3 years of undergraduate Russian or equivalent. Additional exam requirements/recommendations for international students: Required—TOEFL. *Faculty research:* Modern Russian literature and art, contemporary Russian and East European literature, literary theory, Slavic linguistics, Russian journalism.

Northwestern University, The Graduate School, Judd A. and Marjorie Weinberg College of Arts and Sciences, Department of Slavic Languages and Literature, Evanston, IL 60208. Offers PhD. Admissions and degrees offered through The Graduate School. Part-time programs available. *Degree requirements:* For doctorate, 3 foreign languages, thesis/dissertation. *Entrance requirements:* For doctorate, GRE General Test. Additional exam requirements/recommendations for international students: Required—TOEFL. *Faculty research:* Russian poetry and prose, nineteenth- through twentieth-centuries, translation and Russian culture, Russian intellectual history, Slavic literature and nationalism, Polish poetry.

The Ohio State University, Graduate School, College of Humanities, Department of Slavic and East European Languages and Literatures, Columbus, OH 43210. Offers Slavic and East European studies (MA); Slavic languages and literatures (MA, PhD). *Degree requirements:* For master's, variable foreign language requirement, thesis optional; for doctorate, variable foreign language requirement, thesis/dissertation. *Entrance requirements:* For master's and doctorate, GRE General Test. Additional exam requirements/recommendations for international students: Required—TOEFL (minimum score 600 paper-based; 250 computer-based). Electronic applications accepted. *Faculty research:* Polish literature.

Princeton University, Graduate School, Department of Slavic Languages and Literatures, Princeton, NJ 08544-1019. Offers Russian and Slavic linguistics (PhD); Russian literature (PhD). *Degree requirements:* For doctorate, variable foreign language requirement, thesis/dissertation. *Entrance requirements:* For doctorate, GRE General Test. Additional exam requirements/recommendations for international students: Required—TOEFL (minimum score 600 paper-based; 250 computer-based). Electronic applications accepted.

Stanford University, School of Humanities and Sciences, Department of Slavic Languages and Literatures, Stanford, CA 94305-9991. Offers Russian (MA); Slavic languages and literatures (PhD). Terminal master's awarded for partial completion of doctoral program. *Degree requirements:* For master's, one foreign language, thesis or alternative; for doctorate, 3 foreign languages, thesis/dissertation. *Entrance requirements:* For master's and doctorate, GRE General Test. Additional exam requirements/recommendations for international students: Required—TOEFL. Electronic applications accepted.

University of Alberta, Faculty of Graduate Studies and Research, Department of Modern Languages and Cultural Studies, Edmonton, AB T6G 2E1, Canada. Offers applied linguistics (Germanic, Romance, Slavic) (MA); French language, literatures and linguistics (PhD); French language, literatures, and linguistics (MA); Germanic languages, literatures and linguistics (PhD); Germanic languages, literatures, and linguistics (MA); Italian studies (MA); Slavic languages and literatures (Russian, Ukrainian) (MA, PhD); Slavic linguistics (Russian, Ukrainian) (MA, PhD); Spanish and Latin American studies (MA, PhD); Ukrainian folklore (MA, PhD). Part-time programs available. *Degree requirements:* For master's, one foreign language, thesis; for doctorate, 2 foreign languages, comprehensive exam, thesis/dissertation. *Entrance requirements:* For master's and doctorate, 1 language other than English. Additional exam requirements/recommendations for international students: Required—Michigan English Language Assessment Battery or TOEFL (paper score 550; computer score 213). Electronic applications accepted. *Faculty research:* Russian/Ukrainian studies; German studies; contemporary Latin American, French and Francophone studies; Italian studies.

University of California, Berkeley, Graduate Division, College of Letters and Science, Department of Slavic Languages and Literatures, Berkeley, CA 94720-1500. Offers Czech (PhD), including Czech linguistics, Czech literature; Polish (PhD), including Polish linguistics, Polish literature; Russian (PhD), including Russian linguistics, Russian literature; Serbo-Croatian (PhD), including Serbo-Croatian linguistics, Serbo-Croatian literature. Terminal master's awarded for partial completion of doctoral program. *Degree requirements:* For doctorate, thesis/dissertation, oral and written exams. *Entrance requirements:* For doctorate, GRE General Test, minimum GPA of 3.0, 3 letters of recommendation. Additional exam requirements/recommendations for international students: Required—TOEFL (minimum score 570 paper-based; 230 computer-based). Electronic applications accepted.

University of California, Los Angeles, Graduate Division, College of Letters and Science, Department of Slavic Languages and Literatures, Los Angeles, CA 90095. Offers MA, PhD. *Students:* 13 full-time (8 women); includes 2 minority (1 American Indian/Alaska Native, 1 Hispanic American). Average age 28. 12 applicants, 50% accepted, 2 enrolled. In 2008, 1 master's, 2 doctorates awarded. Terminal master's awarded for partial completion of doctoral program. *Degree requirements:* For master's, 2 foreign languages, comprehensive exam; for doctorate, 2 foreign languages, thesis/dissertation, oral and written qualifying exams. *Entrance requirements:* For master's, GRE General Test, minimum GPA of 3.0, sample of written work; for doctorate, GRE General Test, minimum undergraduate GPA of 3.0, proficiency in French and German, sample of written work. *Application deadline:* For fall admission, 1/15 for domestic and international students. Application fee: $60 ($80 for international students). Electronic applications accepted. *Expenses:* Tuition, nonresident: full-time $14,694. Required fees: $9669.50. Full-time tuition and fees vary according to course load, degree level, program and student level. *Financial support:* In 2008–09, 15 fellowships with full and partial tuition reimbursements, 6 research assistantships with full and partial tuition reimbursements, 5 teaching assistantships with full and partial tuition reimbursements were awarded; Federal Work-Study, institutionally sponsored loans, scholarships/grants, health care benefits, tuition waivers (full and partial), and unspecified assistantships also available. Financial award application deadline: 3/1; financial award applicants required to submit FAFSA. *Unit head:* Dr. David MacFadyen, Chair, 310-825-8724. *Application contact:* Departmental Office, 310-825-3856, E-mail: slavic@humnet.ucla.edu.

University of Chicago, Division of the Humanities, Department of Slavic Languages and Literatures, Chicago, IL 60637-1513. Offers AM, PhD. Terminal master's awarded for partial completion of doctoral program. *Degree requirements:* For master's, one foreign language; for doctorate, 2 foreign languages, thesis/dissertation. *Entrance requirements:* For master's and doctorate, GRE General Test. Additional exam requirements/recommendations for international students: Required—TOEFL.

University of Illinois at Urbana–Champaign, Graduate College, College of Liberal Arts and Sciences, School of Literatures, Cultures and Linguistics, Department of Slavic Languages and Literatures, Champaign, IL 61820. Offers MA, PhD. *Faculty:* 6 full-time (1 woman), 1 part-time/adjunct (0 women). *Students:* 7 full-time (6 women), 1 part-time (0 women), 3 international. 8 applicants, 75% accepted, 3 enrolled. In 2008, 1 master's awarded. *Entrance requirements:* For master's and doctorate, GRE, minimum GPA of 3.0; writing sample. Additional exam requirements/recommendations for international students: Required—TOEFL (minimum score 79 iBT). *Application deadline:* Applications are processed on a rolling basis. Application fee: $60 ($75 for international students). Electronic applications accepted. *Financial support:* In 2008–09, 5 fellowships, 1 research assistantship, 5 teaching assistantships were awarded; tuition waivers (full and partial) also available. *Unit head:* Harriet Murav, Head, 217-344-3066, Fax: 217-333-7310, E-mail: hlmurav@illinois.edu. *Application contact:* Lynn Stanke, Secretary, 217-333-6269, Fax: 217-244-3050, E-mail: stanke@illinois.edu.

The University of Kansas, Graduate Studies, College of Liberal Arts and Sciences, Department of Slavic Languages and Literatures, Lawrence, KS 66045. Offers MA, PhD. Part-time programs available. *Faculty:* 9. *Students:* 13 full-time (10 women), 1 international. Average age 30. 9 applicants, 78% accepted, 4 enrolled. In 2008, 5 master's, 1 doctorate awarded. Terminal master's awarded for partial completion of doctoral program. *Degree requirements:* For master's, one foreign language, comprehensive exam, thesis or alternative; for doctorate, 3 foreign languages, comprehensive exam, thesis/dissertation, 2nd Slavic language. *Entrance requirements:* For master's, GRE, BA in Slavic languages and literatures or the equivalent; for doctorate, GRE, MA in Slavic languages and literatures. Additional exam requirements/recommendations for international students: Required—TOEFL. *Application deadline:* For winter admission, 1/31 priority date for domestic and international students. Applications are processed on a rolling basis. Application fee: $45 ($55 for international students). Electronic applications accepted. *Expenses:* Tuition, area resident: Full-time $6122; part-time $255.10 per credit hour. Tuition, state resident: full-time $6122; part-time $255.10 per credit hour. Tuition, nonresident: full-time $14,629; part-time $609.55 per credit hour. Required fees: $847; $70.56 per credit hour. Tuition and fees vary according to course load and program. *Financial support:* Fellowships with tuition reimbursements, teaching assistantships with full and partial tuition reimbursements, Federal Work-Study, institutionally sponsored loans, scholarships/grants, and unspecified assistantships available. Financial award application deadline: 1/31. *Faculty research:* Russian and south Slavic linguistics, Polish and Russian literature, folklore, Russian intellectual history. *Unit head:* Prof. Marc L. Greenberg, Chair, 785-864-3313, Fax: 785-864-4298, E-mail: mlg@ku.edu. *Application contact:* Prof. Maria Carlson, Graduate Director, 785-864-3313, Fax: 785-864-4298, E-mail: mcarlson@ku.edu.

University of Manitoba, Faculty of Graduate Studies, Faculty of Arts, Department of German and Slavic Studies, Winnipeg, MB R3T 2N2, Canada. Offers German language and literature (MA); Slavic languages and literatures (MA). *Degree requirements:* For master's, one foreign language, thesis or alternative.

University of Michigan, Horace H. Rackham School of Graduate Studies, College of Literature, Science, and the Arts, Department of Slavic Languages and Literatures, Ann Arbor, MI 48109. Offers Russian (AM); Slavic languages and literatures (PhD). *Degree requirements:* For master's, 2 foreign languages, comprehensive exam; for doctorate, 3 foreign languages, comprehensive exam, thesis/dissertation, oral defense of dissertation, preliminary exam. *Entrance requirements:* For master's, GRE General Test, 3rd year foreign language proficiency; for doctorate, GRE General Test, master's degree. Additional exam requirements/recommendations for international students: Required—TOEFL (minimum score 560 paper-based; 220 computer-based). Electronic applications accepted. *Faculty research:* Russian literature (all periods), Polish literature, Slavic linguistics, Czech literature, Ukrainian literature.

The University of North Carolina at Chapel Hill, Graduate School, College of Arts and Sciences, Department of Slavic Languages and Literatures, Chapel Hill, NC 27599. Offers Polish literature (PhD); Russian literature (MA, PhD); Serbo-Croatian literature (PhD); Slavic linguistics (MA, PhD). Part-time programs available. Terminal master's awarded for partial completion of doctoral program. *Degree requirements:* For master's, 2 foreign languages, comprehensive exam, thesis; for doctorate, 4 foreign languages, comprehensive exam, thesis/dissertation. *Entrance requirements:* For master's and doctorate, GRE General Test, minimum GPA of 3.0. Electronic applications accepted. *Faculty research:* Russian cultural studies, literary translation, sociolinguistics, cognitive linguistics, émigré literature.

University of Pittsburgh, School of Arts and Sciences, Department of Slavic Languages and Literatures, Pittsburgh, PA 15260. Offers MA, PhD. Part-time programs available. Terminal master's awarded for partial completion of doctoral program. *Degree requirements:* For master's, one foreign language, comprehensive exam; for doctorate, 2 foreign languages, comprehensive exam, thesis/dissertation. *Entrance requirements:* For master's and doctorate, GRE General Test. Additional exam requirements/recommendations for international students: Required—TOEFL. *Faculty research:* Contemporary Russian literature and culture, Russian cinema.

University of Southern California, Graduate School, College of Letters, Arts and Sciences, Department of Slavic Languages and Literatures, Los Angeles, CA 90089. Offers MA, PhD. *Degree requirements:* For master's, one foreign language; for doctorate, 3 foreign languages, thesis/dissertation. *Entrance requirements:* For doctorate, GRE General Test. *Faculty research:* Russian avant-garde art, Russian poetry, literacy criticism, Slavic linguistics, symbolism.

The University of Texas at Austin, Graduate School, College of Liberal Arts, Department of Slavic and Eurasian Studies, Austin, TX 78712-1111. Offers Slavic languages (MA, PhD). *Degree requirements:* For master's, 2 foreign languages, thesis; for doctorate, 3 foreign languages, thesis/dissertation. *Entrance requirements:* For master's and doctorate, GRE General Test. Electronic applications accepted. *Faculty research:* Slavic linguistics; applied linguistics; Russian, Czech, and Slavic literature and culture.

University of Toronto, School of Graduate Studies, Humanities Division, Department of Slavic Languages and Literatures, Toronto, ON M5S 1A1, Canada. Offers MA, PhD. Part-time programs available. *Degree requirements:* For doctorate, comprehensive exam, thesis/dissertation. *Entrance requirements:* For master's, BA in related area; minimum A– average in Slavic courses taken in final year, writing sample, 2 letters of recommendation; for doctorate, MA in Slavic languages and literatures, minimum A– average, writing sample, 2 letters of recommendation.

University of Virginia, College and Graduate School of Arts and Sciences, Department of Slavic Languages and Literatures, Charlottesville, VA 22903. Offers MA, PhD. *Faculty:* 5 full-time (2 women). *Students:* 14 full-time (10 women); includes 9 Hispanic Americans, 2 international. Average age 27. 11 applicants, 73% accepted, 2 enrolled. In 2008, 2 master's awarded. *Degree requirements:* For master's, one foreign language, comprehensive exam, thesis (for some programs); for doctorate, one foreign language, comprehensive exam, thesis/dissertation. *Entrance requirements:* For master's and doctorate, GRE General Test, 2 letters of recommendation; writing sample in English. Additional exam requirements/recommendations for international students: Required—TOEFL (minimum score 600 paper-based; 250 computer-based; 90 iBT), IELTS (minimum score 7). *Application deadline:* Applications are processed on a rolling basis. Application fee: $60. Electronic applications accepted. *Expenses:* Tuition, area resident: Full-time $10,452. Tuition, state resident: full-time $10,452. Tuition, nonresident: full-time $20,010. Required fees: $2176. Part-time tuition and fees vary according to course load and program. *Financial support:* Teaching assistantships available. Financial award application deadline: 1/15; financial award applicants required to submit FAFSA. *Unit head:* Julian W. Connolly, Chair, 434-924-3548, Fax: 434-982-2744, E-mail: slavic@virginia.edu. *Application contact:* Julian W. Connolly, Chair, 434-924-3548, Fax: 434-982-2744, E-mail: slavic@virginia.edu.

University of Washington, Graduate School, College of Arts and Sciences, Department of Slavic Languages and Literatures, Seattle, WA 98195. Offers Russian literature (MA, PhD); Slavic linguistics (MA, PhD). *Degree requirements:* For master's, 2 foreign languages, thesis optional; for doctorate, 3 foreign languages, thesis/dissertation. *Entrance requirements:* For master's and doctorate, GRE General Test, minimum GPA of 3.0. Additional exam requirements/recommendations for international students: Required—TOEFL. Electronic applications accepted. *Faculty research:* Modern and medieval East European languages and literatures, comparative literature, Russian folk literature, Slavic literary theory and criticism, computerized morphology of Russian.

University of Wisconsin–Madison, Graduate School, College of Letters and Science, Department of Slavic Languages and Literature, Madison, WI 53706-1380. Offers MA, PhD. Part-time programs available. Terminal master's awarded for partial completion of doctoral program. *Degree requirements:* For doctorate, thesis/dissertation. *Entrance requirements:* For master's and doctorate, GRE General Test. Additional exam requirements/recommendations for international students: Required—TOEFL. Electronic applications accepted. *Faculty research:* Polish literature, linguistics, South Slavic literature, second language acquisition, nineteenth and twentieth-century Russian literature.

University of Wisconsin–Milwaukee, Graduate School, College of Letters and Sciences, Interdepartmental Program in Foreign Language and Literature, Milwaukee, WI 53201-0413. Offers classics and Hebrew studies (MAFLL); comparative literature (MAFLL); French and Italian (MAFLL); German (MAFLL); Slavic studies (MAFLL); translation (Certificate). Part-time programs available. *Faculty:* 39 full-time (17 women). *Students:* 32 full-time (25 women), 28 part-time (19 women); includes 5 minority (1 Asian American or Pacific Islander, 4 Hispanic Americans), 22 international. Average age 32. 51 applicants, 65% accepted, 26 enrolled. In 2008, 19 master's awarded. *Degree requirements:* For master's, 2 foreign languages, thesis or alternative. *Entrance requirements:* Additional exam requirements/recommendations for international students: Required—TOEFL (minimum score 550 paper-based; 79 iBT), IELTS (minimum score 6.5). *Application deadline:* For fall admission, 1/1 priority date for domestic students; for spring admission, 9/1 for domestic students. Applications are processed on a rolling basis. Application fee: $45 ($75 for international students). *Expenses:* Tuition, area resident: Full-time $7320; part-time $165 per credit. Tuition, state resident: full-time $7320; part-time $165 per credit. Tuition, nonresident: full-time $17,840; part-time $714 per credit. Tuition and fees vary according to campus/location, program and reciprocity agreements. *Financial support:* In 2008–09, 2 research assistantships, 35 teaching assistantships were awarded; career-related internships or fieldwork and unspecified assistantships also available. Support available to part-time students. Financial award application deadline: 4/15. Total annual research expenditures: $43,420. *Unit head:* Gabrielle Verdier, Representative, 414-229-3346, Fax: 414-229-2741, E-mail: verdier@uwm.edu. *Application contact:* General Information Contact, 414-229-4982, Fax: 414-229-6967, E-mail: gradschool@uwm.edu.

Yale University, Graduate School of Arts and Sciences, Department of Slavic Languages and Literatures, New Haven, CT 06520. Offers medieval Slavic literature and philology (PhD); Polish literature (PhD); Russian literature (PhD); Slavic languages and literatures and film studies (PhD). *Degree requirements:* For doctorate, 3 foreign languages, thesis/dissertation. *Entrance requirements:* For doctorate, GRE General Test.

Spanish

American University, College of Arts and Sciences, Department of Language and Foreign Studies, Program in Spanish: Latin American Studies, Washington, DC 20016-8045. Offers Spanish: Latin American studies (MA); translation (Certificate). Part-time and evening/weekend programs available. *Students:* 17 full-time (13 women), 10 part-time (8 women); includes 9 minority (5 African Americans, 4 Hispanic Americans), 2 international. Average age 26. 23 applicants, 96% accepted, 7 enrolled. In 2008, 11 master's, 5 other advanced degrees awarded. *Degree requirements:* For master's, one foreign language, comprehensive exam, thesis or alternative, research requirement. *Entrance requirements:* For master's, GRE, bachelor's degree in language or equivalent, essay in Spanish, minimum GPA of 3.2, statement of purpose; for Certificate, bachelor's degree in Spanish or BA in any field plus Spanish proficiency. Additional exam requirements/recommendations for international students: Required—TOEFL. *Application deadline:* For fall admission, 2/1 for domestic students; for spring admission, 10/1 for domestic students. Application fee: $80. *Expenses:* Tuition: Full-time $21,204; part-time $1178 per credit hour. Required fees: $380. Part-time tuition and fees vary according to course load and program. *Financial support:* Fellowships, career-related internships or fieldwork, Federal Work-Study, and institutionally sponsored loans available. Financial award application deadline: 2/1. *Faculty research:* Latin American culture, literature, and history; computer-aided instruction.

Arizona State University, Graduate College, College of Liberal Arts and Sciences, Division of Humanities, School of International Letters and Cultures, Program in Spanish, Tempe, AZ 85287. Offers MA, PhD. *Degree requirements:* For master's, thesis or alternative; for doctorate, thesis/dissertation. *Entrance requirements:* For master's and doctorate, GRE.

Arkansas Tech University, Graduate School, School of Liberal and Fine Arts, Russellville, AR 72801. Offers communication (MLA); English (M Ed, MA); fine arts (MLA); history (MA); multi-media journalism (MA); social science (MLA); social studies (M Ed); Spanish (MA, MLA); teaching English as a second language (MA, MLA). Part-time programs available. *Students:* 40 full-time (31 women), 81 part-time (60 women); includes 10 minority (3 African Americans, 2 American Indian/Alaska Native, 2 Asian Americans or Pacific Islanders, 3 Hispanic Americans), 19 international. Average age 33. In 2008, 70 master's awarded. *Degree requirements:* For master's, project. *Entrance requirements:* For master's, GRE General Test or MAT. Additional exam requirements/recommendations for international students: Required—TOEFL (minimum score 500 paper-based; 173 computer-based; 61 iBT). *Application deadline:* For fall admission, 3/1 priority date for domestic students, 5/1 priority date for international students; for winter admission, 10/1 priority date for international students; for spring admission, 10/1 priority date for domestic and international students. Applications are processed on a rolling basis. Application fee: $0 ($30 for international students). Electronic applications accepted. *Expenses:* Tuition, state resident: full-time $1575; part-time $175 per credit hour. Tuition, nonresident: full-time $3150; part-time $350 per credit hour. Tuition and fees vary according to course load. *Financial support:* In 2008–09, teaching assistantships with full tuition reimbursements (averaging $4,000 per year); career-related internships or fieldwork, Federal Work-Study, scholarships/grants, health care benefits, and unspecified assistantships also available. Support available to part-time students. Financial award application deadline: 4/15; financial award applicants required to submit FAFSA. *Unit head:* Dr. Georgena Duncan, Dean, 479-968-0266, Fax: 479-968-0275, E-mail: georgena.duncan@atu.edu. *Application contact:* Dr. Eldon G. Clary, Dean of Graduate School, 479-968-0398, Fax: 479-964-0542, E-mail: graduate.school@atu.edu.

Asbury College, Graduate Programs, Wilmore, KY 40390-1198. Offers biology: alternative certificate (MA Ed); chemistry: alternative certificate (MA Ed); English (Certificate); English as a second language (MA Ed); ESL (Certificate); French (Certificate); mathematics: alternative certificate (MA Ed); reading / writing (MA Ed); social studies (Certificate); Spanish (Certificate); special education (MA Ed); special education: alternative certificate (MA Ed). *Accreditation:* NCATE. Part-time programs available. *Degree requirements:* For master's, action research project, portfolio. *Entrance requirements:* For master's, PRAXIS/NTE, minimum GPA of 2.75, letters of recommendation. Additional exam requirements/recommendations for international students: Required—TOEFL (minimum score 550 paper-based).

Auburn University, Graduate School, College of Liberal Arts, Department of Foreign Languages and Literatures, Auburn University, AL 36849. Offers Spanish (MA, MHS). Part-time programs available. *Faculty:* 33 full-time (18 women), 9 part-time/adjunct (7 women). *Students:* 18 full-time (14 women), 16 part-time (13 women); includes 10 minority (6 African Americans, 4 Hispanic Americans). Average age 30. 16 applicants, 75% accepted, 11 enrolled. In 2008, 8 master's awarded. *Degree requirements:* For master's, one foreign language, comprehensive exam, thesis (for some programs). *Entrance requirements:* For master's, GRE General Test. *Application deadline:* For fall admission, 7/7 for domestic students; for spring admission, 11/24 for domestic students. Applications are processed on a rolling basis. Application fee: $25 ($50 for international students). Electronic applications accepted. *Expenses:* Tuition, area resident: Full-time $5880; part-time $243 per credit hour. Tuition, state resident: full-time $5880; part-time $243 per credit hour. Tuition, nonresident: full-time $17,640; part-time $729 per credit hour. International tuition: $17,846 full-time. Required fees: $620. Tuition and fees vary according to program and reciprocity agreements. *Financial support:* Fellowships, teaching assistantships, Federal Work-Study available. Support available to part-time students. Financial award application deadline: 3/15. *Unit head:* Dr. Robert G. Weigel, Chair, 334-844-4345, Fax: 334-844-6378. *Application contact:* Dr. George Flowers, Dean of the Graduate School, 334-844-2125.

Baylor University, Graduate School, College of Arts and Sciences, Department of Modern Foreign Languages, Waco, TX 76798. Offers Spanish (MA). *Students:* 3 full-time (all women); includes 2 minority (both Hispanic Americans). In 2008, 5 master's awarded. *Entrance requirements:* For master's, GRE General Test. *Application deadline:* Applications are processed on a rolling basis. Application fee: $25. *Unit head:* Dr. Baudelio Garza, Graduate Program Director, 254-710-3711, Fax: 254-710-3799, E-mail: baudelio_garza@baylor.edu. *Application contact:* Ann Westbrook, Administrative Assistant, 254-710-6027, Fax: 254-710-3870, E-mail: ann_westbrook@baylor.edu.

Bennington College, Graduate Programs, Program in Teaching a Second Language, Bennington, VT 05201. Offers education (MATSL); foreign language education (MATSL); French (MATSL); Spanish (MATSL). Part-time programs available. *Faculty:* 2 full-time (1 woman), 4 part-time/adjunct (all women). *Students:* 21 part-time (20 women); includes 4 minority (1 African American, 3 Hispanic Americans), 1 international. Average age 41. 14 applicants, 71% accepted, 9 enrolled. In 2008, 4 master's awarded. *Degree requirements:* For master's, one foreign language, 2 major projects and presentations. *Entrance requirements:* For master's, Oral Proficiency Interview (OPI). Additional exam requirements/recommendations for international students: Required—TOEFL (minimum score 577 paper-based; 233 computer-based; 91 iBT). *Application deadline:* For spring admission, 4/1 priority date for domestic and international students. Applications are processed on a rolling basis. Application fee: $60. *Expenses:* Contact institution. *Financial support:* In 2008–09, 2 students received support. Scholarships/grants available. Financial award application deadline: 4/1; financial award applicants required to submit FAFSA. *Faculty research:* Acquisition, evaluation, assessment, conceptual teaching and learning content-driven communication, applied linguistics. *Unit head:* Carol Meyer, Director, 802-440-4375, E-mail: cmeyer@bennington.edu. *Application contact:* Nancy Pearlman, Assistant Director, MATSL, 802-440-4710, E-mail: matsl@bennington.edu.

Boston College, Graduate School of Arts and Sciences, Department of Romance Languages and Literatures, Chestnut Hill, MA 02467-3800. Offers French (MA, PhD); Italian (MA); medieval language (PhD); Spanish (MA, PhD). Part-time programs available. Terminal master's awarded for partial completion of doctoral program. *Degree requirements:* For master's, one foreign language; for doctorate, 2 foreign languages, thesis/dissertation. *Entrance requirements:* Additional exam requirements/recommendations for international students: Required—TOEFL (minimum score 590 paper-based; 250 computer-based; 91 iBT). Electronic applications accepted. *Expenses:* Tuition: Part-time $1148 per credit. Required fees: $60. *Faculty research:* Spanish-American literature, philology, medieval French romance and troubadour/trouvere lyrics, Golden Age Peninsular literature, secondary language acquisition and pedagogy.

See Close-Up on page 437.

Boston University, Graduate School of Arts and Sciences, Department of Romance Studies, Boston, MA 02215. Offers French language and literature (MA, PhD); Hispanic language and literatures (MA, PhD). Terminal master's awarded for partial completion of doctoral program. *Degree requirements:* For master's, one foreign language, comprehensive exam; for doctorate, 2 foreign languages, comprehensive exam, thesis/dissertation. *Entrance requirements:* For master's and doctorate, GRE General Test, sample of written work, 3 letters of recommendation. Additional exam requirements/recommendations for international students: Required—TOEFL (minimum score 550 paper-based; 213 computer-based).

Bowling Green State University, Graduate College, College of Arts and Sciences, Department of Romance and Classical Studies, Program in Spanish, Bowling Green, OH 43403. Offers Spanish (MA); Spanish education (MAT). Part-time programs available. *Degree requirements:* For master's, one foreign language, thesis or alternative. *Entrance requirements:* For master's, GRE General Test. Additional exam requirements/recommendations for international students: Required—TOEFL. Electronic applications accepted. *Faculty research:* U.S. Latino literature and culture, Latin American film and popular culture, applied linguistics, Spanish popular culture.

Brigham Young University, Graduate Studies, College of Humanities, Department of Spanish and Portuguese, Provo, UT 84602. Offers Portuguese linguistics (MA); Portuguese literature (MA); Spanish linguistics (MA); Spanish teaching (MA); Spanish/Latin American literature (MA); Spanish/Peninsular literature (MA). Part-time programs available. *Faculty:* 32 full-time (5 women). *Students:* 15 full-time (7 women), 24 part-time (13 women); includes 6 minority (all Hispanic Americans), 8 international. Average age 29. 19 applicants, 74% accepted, 14 enrolled. In 2008, 12 master's awarded. *Degree requirements:* For master's, one foreign language, comprehensive exam, thesis, 1 semester of teaching. *Entrance requirements:* For master's, minimum GPA of 3.5 in Spanish or Portuguese, 3.3 overall. Additional exam requirements/recommendations for international students: Required—TOEFL (minimum score 580 paper-based; 237 computer-based). *Application deadline:* For fall admission, 2/1 for domestic and international students. Application fee: $50. Electronic applications accepted. *Expenses:* Tuition: Full-time $5160; part-time $287 per credit hour. Tuition and fees vary according to program and student's religious affiliation. *Financial support:* In 2008–09, 39 students received support, including 39 teaching assistantships with partial tuition reimbursements available (averaging $6,574 per year); institutionally sponsored loans, scholarships/grants, tuition waivers (partial), and unspecified assistantships also available. Support available to part-time students. Financial award application deadline: 7/21. *Faculty research:* Mexican prose; Latin American theater, literature, phonetics, and phonology; pedagogy; classical Portuguese literature; Peninsular prose and theater. *Unit head:* Dr. Alvin F. Sherman, Chair, 801-422-3107, Fax: 801-422-0628, E-mail: alvin_sherman@byu.edu. *Application contact:* Arwen T. Wyatt, Graduate Secretary, 801-422-2196, Fax: 801-422-0628, E-mail: arwen_wyatt@byu.edu.

Brooklyn College of the City University of New York, Division of Graduate Studies, Department of Modern Languages and Literature, Brooklyn, NY 11210-2889. Offers French (MA); modern languages and literature (PhD); Spanish (MA). The department offers courses at Brooklyn College that are creditable toward the CUNY doctoral degree (with permission of the executive officer of the doctoral program). *Students:* 1 full-time (0 women), 24 part-time (15 women); includes 18 minority (8 African Americans, 10 Hispanic Americans), 5 international. Average age 37. 12 applicants, 100% accepted, 7 enrolled. In 2008, 8 master's awarded. *Degree requirements:* For master's, comprehensive exam or research paper. *Entrance requirements:* For master's, 18 credits in advanced courses in Spanish, 2 letters of recommendation. Additional exam requirements/recommendations for international students: Required—TOEFL. *Application deadline:* For fall admission, 3/1 priority date for domestic students, 2/1 priority date for international students; for spring admission, 11/1 priority date for domestic students, 10/1 priority date for international students. Applications are processed on a rolling basis. Application fee: $125. Electronic applications accepted. *Expenses:* Tuition, state resident: full-time $7360; part-time $310 per credit hour. Tuition, nonresident: full-time $13,800; part-time $575 per credit hour. *Financial support:* Federal Work-Study, institutionally sponsored loans, and scholarships/grants available. Support available to part-time students. Financial award application deadline: 5/1; financial award applicants required to submit FAFSA. *Faculty research:* Latin American contemporary novel; Caribbean female contemporary literature; 19th and 20th century Spanish novel; 20th century Mexican poetry. *Unit head:* Dr. William Childers, Chairperson, 718-951-5451, E-mail: wchilders@brooklyn.cuny.edu. *Application contact:* Hernan Sierra, Graduate Admissions Coordinator, 718-951-4536, Fax: 718-951-4506, E-mail: grads@brooklyn.cuny.edu.

California State University, Bakersfield, Division of Graduate Studies, School of Humanities and Social Sciences, Program in Spanish, Bakersfield, CA 93311-1022. Offers MA. *Degree requirements:* For master's, capstone course.

California State University, Fresno, Division of Graduate Studies, College of Arts and Humanities, Department of Modern and Classical Languages and Literatures, Fresno, CA 93740-8027. Offers Spanish (MA). Part-time programs available. *Degree requirements:* For master's, one foreign language, thesis or alternative. *Entrance requirements:* For master's, GRE General Test, BA in Spanish, minimum GPA of 3.0. Additional exam requirements/recommendations for international students: Required—TOEFL. Electronic applications accepted.

California State University, Fullerton, Graduate Studies, College of Humanities and Social Sciences, Department of Modern Languages and Literatures, Fullerton, CA 92834-9480. Offers French (MA); German (MA); Spanish (MA); teaching English to speakers of other languages (MS). Part-time programs available. *Students:* 63 full-time (49 women), 79 part-time (65 women); includes 70 minority (21 Asian Americans or Pacific Islanders, 49 Hispanic Americans), 23 international. Average age 32. 118 applicants, 56% accepted, 43 enrolled. In 2008, 28 master's awarded. *Degree requirements:* For master's, comprehensive exam, thesis or alternative. *Entrance requirements:* For master's, minimum GPA of 2.5 in last 60 hours of course work, undergraduate major in a language. Application fee: $55. Tuition and fees vary according to degree level. *Financial support:* Federal Work-Study, institutionally sponsored loans, and scholarships/grants available. Support available to part-time students. Financial award application deadline: 3/1. *Unit head:* Dr. Janet Eyring, Chair, 657-278-3534. *Application contact:* Admissions/Applications, 657-278-2300.

California State University, Long Beach, Graduate Studies, College of Liberal Arts, Department of Romance, German, and Russian Languages and Literature, Program in Spanish, Long Beach, CA 90840. Offers MA. Part-time programs available. *Students:* 16 full-time (15 women), 26 part-time (22 women); includes 31 minority (1 Asian American or Pacific Islander, 30 Hispanic Americans), 3 international. Average age 32. 24 applicants, 54% accepted, 10 enrolled. *Degree requirements:* For master's, one foreign language, thesis or alternative, research paper. *Entrance requirements:* For master's, BA in Spanish. *Application deadline:* For fall admission, 7/1 for domestic students. Applications are processed on a rolling basis. Application fee: $55. Electronic applications accepted. *Expenses:* Tuition, nonresident: full-time $11,160; part-time $372 per unit. Required fees: $4100; $1261 per semester. *Financial support:* Federal Work-Study, institutionally sponsored loans, and scholarships/grants available. Financial award application deadline: 3/2. *Faculty research:* Literary translation, literature and politics, women writers, Latin American poetry, Latin American theatre. *Unit head:* Dr. Lisa Vollendorf,

Chair, 562-985-4318, Fax: 562-985-4259, E-mail: lvollend@csulb.edu. *Application contact:* Dr. Bonnie Gasior, Program Director, 562-985-4318, Fax: 562-985-4259, E-mail: bgasior@csulb.edu.

California State University, Los Angeles, Graduate Studies, College of Arts and Letters, Department of Modern Languages and Literatures, Los Angeles, CA 90032-8530. Offers French (MA); Spanish (MA). Part-time and evening/weekend programs available. *Faculty:* 5 full-time (2 women), 1 (woman) part-time/adjunct. *Students:* 26 full-time (18 women), 31 part-time (26 women); includes 41 minority (1 African American, 2 Asian Americans or Pacific Islanders, 38 Hispanic Americans), 5 international. Average age 36. 15 applicants, 100% accepted, 7 enrolled. In 2008, 6 master's awarded. *Degree requirements:* For master's, comprehensive exam. *Entrance requirements:* Additional exam requirements/recommendations for international students: Required—TOEFL (minimum score 500 paper-based; 173 computer-based). *Application deadline:* For fall admission, 6/15 for domestic students, 5/1 for international students; for winter admission, 11/1 for domestic students, 9/1 for international students; for spring admission, 2/1 for domestic students, 10/1 for international students. Applications are processed on a rolling basis. Application fee: $55. Electronic applications accepted. *Expenses:* Tuition, nonresident: part-time $226 per credit. Required fees: $4019. *Financial support:* Federal Work-Study available. Support available to part-time students. Financial award application deadline: 3/1. *Faculty research:* French literature, language teaching and methodology, Spanish poetry, Spanish-American fiction and poetry. *Unit head:* Dr. Sachiko Matsunaga, Chair, 323-343-4230, Fax: 323-343-4234, E-mail: smatsun@calstatela.edu. *Application contact:* Dr. Jose L. Galvan, Dean of Graduate Studies, 323-343-3820, Fax: 323-343-5653, E-mail: jgalvan@cslanet.calstatela.edu.

California State University, Northridge, Graduate Studies, College of Humanities, Department of Modern and Classical Languages and Literatures, Northridge, CA 91330. Offers Spanish (MA). Part-time and evening/weekend programs available. *Faculty:* 12 full-time (4 women), 22 part-time/adjunct (15 women). *Students:* 12 full-time (9 women), 11 part-time (6 women); includes 20 Hispanic Americans. Average age 36. 24 applicants, 46% accepted, 4 enrolled. In 2008, 9 master's awarded. *Degree requirements:* For master's, one foreign language. *Entrance requirements:* For master's, GRE General Test or minimum GPA of 3.0. Additional exam requirements/recommendations for international students: Required—TOEFL. *Application deadline:* For fall admission, 11/30 for domestic students. Application fee: $55. *Financial support:* Application deadline: 3/1. *Unit head:* Dr. Brian Castronovo, Chair, 818-677-3467, E-mail: brian.castronovo@csun.edu. *Application contact:* Dr. Brian Castronovo, Chair, 818-677-3467, E-mail: brian.castronovo@csun.edu.

California State University, Sacramento, Graduate Studies, College of Social Sciences and Interdisciplinary Studies, Liberal Arts Program, Sacramento, CA 95819-6048. Offers French (MA); German (MA); Spanish (MA); theater arts (MA). *Degree requirements:* For master's, writing proficiency exam. *Entrance requirements:* Additional exam requirements/recommendations for international students: Required—TOEFL. Electronic applications accepted.

California State University, San Bernardino, Graduate Studies, College of Arts and Letters, Department of World Languages and Literatures, San Bernardino, CA 92407-2397. Offers Spanish (MA). Part-time and evening/weekend programs available. *Students:* 7 full-time (5 women), 18 part-time (14 women); includes 19 minority (all Hispanic Americans), 2 international. Average age 35. 13 applicants, 54% accepted, 5 enrolled. In 2008, 5 master's awarded. *Degree requirements:* For master's, comprehensive exam, advancement to candidacy. *Application deadline:* Applications are processed on a rolling basis. Application fee: $55. *Expenses:* Tuition, area resident: Full-time $1252; part-time $726 per quarter. Required fees: $334 per quarter. Tuition and fees vary according to degree level and student level. *Financial support:* Career-related internships or fieldwork, Federal Work-Study, and institutionally sponsored loans available. Support available to part-time students. *Unit head:* Dan Whitaker, Chair, 909-537-5855, Fax: 909-537-7091, E-mail: dwhitake@csusb.edu. *Application contact:* Olivia Rosas, Director of Admissions, 909-537-7577, Fax: 909-537-7034, E-mail: orosas@csusb.edu.

California State University, San Marcos, College of Arts and Sciences, Program in World Languages, San Marcos, CA 92096-0001. Offers Spanish (MA). Part-time and evening/weekend programs available. *Degree requirements:* For master's, 2 foreign languages, exam. *Entrance requirements:* For master's, GRE General Test, minimum GPA of 2.5, minimum GPA of 3.0 in upper division Spanish courses. Electronic applications accepted. *Faculty research:* Applied linguistics, golden age Spanish literature, Latin American literature, poetry, Chicano studies.

The Catholic University of America, School of Arts and Sciences, Department of Modern Languages and Literatures, Washington, DC 20064. Offers French (MA, PhD); Italian (MA); Romance languages and literatures (MA, PhD); Spanish (MA, PhD). Part-time programs available. *Degree requirements:* For master's, one foreign language, comprehensive exam, thesis or alternative; for doctorate, 2 foreign languages, comprehensive exam, thesis/dissertation. *Entrance requirements:* For master's and doctorate, GRE General Test, 3 letters of recommendation. Additional exam requirements/recommendations for international students: Required—TOEFL (minimum score 580 paper-based; 237 computer-based). Electronic applications accepted.

Central Connecticut State University, School of Graduate Studies, School of Arts and Sciences, Department of Modern Languages, Program in Spanish, New Britain, CT 06050-4010. Offers Spanish (MS, Certificate); Spanish language and Hispanic culture (MA). Specialization in Spanish language and Hispanic cultures offered jointly with the University of Salamanca, Spain. Part-time and evening/weekend programs available. *Students:* 1 (woman) full-time, 6 part-time (all women); includes 1 minority (Hispanic American). Average age 34. 6 applicants, 50% accepted, 3 enrolled. In 2008, 1 master's, 1 other advanced degree awarded. *Degree requirements:* For master's, one foreign language, comprehensive exam, thesis or alternative. *Entrance requirements:* For master's, minimum undergraduate GPA of 2.7, 24 credits of undergraduate courses in either Italian or Spanish. Additional exam requirements/recommendations for international students: Required—TOEFL. *Application deadline:* For fall admission, 7/1 for domestic students; for spring admission, 12/1 for domestic students. Applications are processed on a rolling basis. Application fee: $50. Electronic applications accepted. *Expenses:* Tuition, area resident: Full-time $4377; part-time $420 per credit. Tuition, state resident: full-time $6566; part-time $420 per credit. Tuition, nonresident: full-time $12,195; part-time $420 per credit. Required fees: $3462. One-time fee: $62 part-time. *Faculty research:* Linguistics, nineteenth to twentieth century Spanish literature, Spanish Golden Age prose/drama.

Central Michigan University, College of Graduate Studies, College of Humanities and Social and Behavioral Sciences, Department of Foreign Languages, Literatures, and Cultures, Mount Pleasant, MI 48859. Offers Spanish (MA). Part-time programs available. *Faculty:* 5 full-time (4 women). *Students:* 12 part-time (9 women). Average age 28. *Degree requirements:* For master's, thesis or alternative. *Application deadline:* Applications are processed on a rolling basis. Application fee: $35 ($45 for international students). Electronic applications accepted. *Expenses:* Tuition, state resident: full-time $3717; part-time $413 per credit. Tuition, nonresident: full-time $6894; part-time $766 per credit. *Financial support:* Fellowships with tuition reimbursements, unspecified assistantships and out-of-state merit awards available. *Unit head:* Dr. Susan Knight, Chairperson, 989-774-3786, Fax: 989-774-2323, E-mail: knigh1sm@umich.edu. *Application contact:* Dr. Alejandra Rengifo, Graduate Program Coordinator, 989-774-6513, Fax: 989-774-2323, E-mail: rengi1a@cmich.edu.

City College of the City University of New York, Graduate School, College of Liberal Arts and Science, Division of the Humanities and Arts, Department of Foreign Languages, New York, NY 10031-9198. Offers Spanish (MA). *Degree requirements:* For master's, one foreign language, comprehensive exam, thesis or alternative. *Entrance requirements:* For master's,

minimum GPA of 3.0. Additional exam requirements/recommendations for international students: Required—TOEFL (minimum score 500 paper-based; 173 computer-based).

Cleveland State University, College of Graduate Studies, College of Liberal Arts and Social Sciences, Department of Modern Languages, Cleveland, OH 44115. Offers French (M Ed); Spanish (M Ed, MA), including language and linguistics (MA), Latin American studies (MA), peninsular studies (MA), Spanish (MA). Part-time and evening/weekend programs available. *Faculty:* 12 full-time (9 women). *Students:* 7 full-time (6 women), 11 part-time (8 women); includes 7 minority (1 African American, 6 Hispanic Americans), 1 international. Average age 37. 11 applicants, 100% accepted, 8 enrolled. In 2008, 9 master's awarded. *Degree requirements:* For master's, one foreign language, comprehensive exam, thesis optional, study abroad. *Entrance requirements:* For master's, undergraduate major in Spanish or equivalent, essay in Spanish, writing sample. Additional exam requirements/recommendations for international students: Required—TOEFL (minimum score 525 paper-based; 197 computer-based). *Application deadline:* For fall admission, 7/25 priority date for domestic students; for spring admission, 12/15 priority date for domestic students. Applications are processed on a rolling basis. Application fee: $30. Electronic applications accepted. *Financial support:* In 2008–09, 6 students received support, including 6 teaching assistantships with full tuition reimbursements available (averaging $7,030 per year); Federal Work-Study also available. *Faculty research:* Second language acquisition, sociolinguistics, contemporary Spanish novel, Arabic diaspora in Latin America, border literature. *Unit head:* Dr. Tama L. Engelking, Chairperson, 216-523-7175, Fax: 216-687-4650, E-mail: t.engelking@csuohio.edu. *Application contact:* Dr. Antonio Medina-Rivera, Graduate Director, 216-523-7168, Fax: 216-687-4650, E-mail: a.medinarivera@csuohio.edu.

The College of New Jersey, Graduate Division, School of Culture and Society, Department of Modern Language, Ewing, NJ 08628. Offers applied Spanish studies (MA). *Entrance requirements:* For master's, GRE, minimum GPA of 3.0 in field or 2.75 overall. Additional exam requirements/recommendations for international students: Required—TOEFL. Electronic applications accepted.

Columbia University, Graduate School of Arts and Sciences, Division of Humanities, Department of Spanish and Portuguese, New York, NY 10027. Offers M Phil, MA, PhD. Part-time programs available. *Degree requirements:* For master's, one foreign language, written exam; for doctorate, 3 foreign languages, thesis/dissertation. *Entrance requirements:* For master's and doctorate, GRE General Test, GRE Subject Test, sample of written work. Additional exam requirements/recommendations for international students: Required—TOEFL. *Faculty research:* Literary theory and criticism, Spain's Golden Age: sixteenth- and seventeenth-centuries, contemporary Spanish American literature.

Cornell University, Graduate School, Graduate Fields of Arts and Sciences, Field of Romance Studies, Ithaca, NY 14853-0001. Offers French linguistics (PhD); French literature (PhD); Hispanic literature (PhD); Italian linguistics (PhD); Italian literature (PhD); Romance linguistics (PhD); Spanish linguistics (PhD). *Faculty:* 30 full-time (14 women). *Students:* 50 full-time (24 women); includes 10 minority (all Hispanic Americans), 18 international. Average age 30. 99 applicants, 15% accepted, 8 enrolled. In 2008, 5 doctorates awarded. *Degree requirements:* For doctorate, 2 foreign languages, comprehensive exam, thesis/dissertation. *Entrance requirements:* For doctorate, GRE General Test, sample of written work, 3 letters of recommendation. Additional exam requirements/recommendations for international students: Required—TOEFL (minimum score 550 paper-based; 213 computer-based; 77 iBT). *Application deadline:* For fall admission, 1/15 for domestic students. Application fee: $70. Electronic applications accepted. *Expenses:* Tuition: Full-time $29,500. Required fees: $70. Full-time tuition and fees vary according to degree level, program and student level. *Financial support:* In 2008–09, 46 students received support, including 16 fellowships with full tuition reimbursements available, 30 teaching assistantships with full tuition reimbursements available; research assistantships with full tuition reimbursements available, institutionally sponsored loans, scholarships/grants, health care benefits, tuition waivers (full and partial), and unspecified assistantships also available. Financial award applicants required to submit FAFSA. *Faculty research:* Literary theory, Hispanic studies, French studies, gender studies. *Unit head:* Director of Graduate Studies, 607-255-8222. *Application contact:* Graduate Field Assistant, 607-255-4246, E-mail: romance_studies@cornell.edu.

Duke University, Graduate School, Department of Romance Studies, Durham, NC 27708. Offers French (PhD); Spanish (PhD); JD/AM. *Degree requirements:* For doctorate, 2 foreign languages, thesis/dissertation. *Entrance requirements:* For doctorate, GRE General Test. Additional exam requirements/recommendations for international students: Required—TOEFL (minimum score 550 paper-based; 213 computer-based; 83 iBT), IELTS (minimum score 7). Electronic applications accepted.

Eastern Michigan University, Graduate School, College of Arts and Sciences, Department of Foreign Languages and Bilingual Studies, Program in Foreign Languages, Ypsilanti, MI 48197. Offers French (MA); German (MA); German for business (Graduate Certificate); Hispanic language and cultures (Graduate Certificate); Japanese business practices (Graduate Certificate); Spanish (MA). Part-time and evening/weekend programs available. Post-baccalaureate distance learning degree programs offered (minimal on-campus study). *Degree requirements:* For master's, one foreign language, thesis optional. *Entrance requirements:* Additional exam requirements/recommendations for international students: Required—TOEFL.

Emory University, Graduate School of Arts and Sciences, Department of Comparative Literature, Atlanta, GA 30322-1100. Offers comparative literature (PhD); English (Certificate); French (Certificate); Middle Eastern studies (PhD); philosophy (Certificate); psychoanalytic studies (PhD); religion (PhD); Spanish (Certificate); women studies (Certificate). *Degree requirements:* For doctorate, 2 foreign languages, comprehensive exam, thesis/dissertation. *Entrance requirements:* For doctorate, GRE General Test, minimum GPA of 3.0. Additional exam requirements/recommendations for international students: Required—TOEFL. Electronic applications accepted. *Faculty research:* Literary theory, psychoanalysis trauma and testimony, literature and religion, literature and technology, literature and philosophy, politics and global culture, literature and aesthetics.

Emory University, Graduate School of Arts and Sciences, Department of Spanish and Portuguese, Atlanta, GA 30322-1100. Offers comparative literature (Certificate); film studies (Certificate); Spanish (PhD); women's studies (Certificate). *Degree requirements:* For doctorate, 2 foreign languages, comprehensive exam, thesis/dissertation. *Entrance requirements:* For doctorate, GRE General Test. Additional exam requirements/recommendations for international students: Required—TOEFL. Electronic applications accepted. *Faculty research:* Spanish literature, Spanish-American literature, literary theory, criticism, cultural studies.

Florida Atlantic University, Dorothy F. Schmidt College of Arts and Letters, Department of Languages, Linguistics, and Comparative Literature, Boca Raton, FL 33431-0991. Offers comparative literature (MA); French (MA); linguistics (MA); Spanish (MA). Part-time programs available. *Faculty:* 23 full-time (20 women), 12 part-time/adjunct (10 women). *Students:* 18 full-time (15 women), 19 part-time (13 women); includes 17 minority (4 African Americans, 1 Asian American or Pacific Islander, 12 Hispanic Americans), 4 international. Average age 36. 24 applicants, 67% accepted, 6 enrolled. In 2008, 10 master's awarded. *Degree requirements:* For master's, one foreign language, comprehensive exam, thesis optional. *Entrance requirements:* For master's, GRE General Test, minimum GPA of 3.0. *Application deadline:* For fall admission, 7/1 priority date for domestic students, 2/15 for international students; for spring admission, 11/1 for domestic students, 7/15 for international students. Applications are processed on a rolling basis. Application fee: $30. *Expenses:* Tuition, state resident: full-time $4867; part-time $270.40 per credit hour. Tuition, nonresident: full-time $16,486; part-time $915.87 per credit hour. *Financial support:* Fellowships, research assistantships, teaching assistantships with partial tuition reimbursements, Federal Work-Study and tuition waivers (partial) available. Support available to part-time students. Financial award application deadline: 4/1. *Faculty research:* Modern European studies, modern Latin America, medieval Europe. *Unit*

Spanish

Florida Atlantic University (continued)
head: Dr. Michael Horswell, Chair, 561-297-3860, Fax: 561-297-2756, E-mail: horswell@fau.edu. *Application contact:* Dr. Emily Stockard, Associate Dean, 561-297-2817, Fax: 561-297-2744, E-mail: stockard@fau.edu.

Florida International University, College of Arts and Sciences, Department of Modern Languages, Miami, FL 33199. Offers Spanish (MA, PhD). Part-time and evening/weekend programs available. *Degree requirements:* For master's, 2 foreign languages, thesis or alternative; for doctorate, 3 foreign languages, comprehensive exam, thesis/dissertation. *Entrance requirements:* For master's, 2 letters of recommendation, minimum GPA of 3.0; for doctorate, GRE General Test or EXADEP, minimum GPA of 3.0, writing example. Additional exam requirements/recommendations for international students: Required—TOEFL (minimum score 550 paper-based; 213 computer-based). Electronic applications accepted. *Faculty research:* Contemporary Spanish/Spanish-American literature, Spanish/Spanish-American linguistics, traductology.

Florida State University, Graduate Studies, College of Arts and Sciences, Department of Modern Languages, Program in Spanish, Tallahassee, FL 32306. Offers MA, PhD. Terminal master's awarded for partial completion of doctoral program. *Degree requirements:* For master's, thesis optional; for doctorate, 2 foreign languages, thesis/dissertation. *Entrance requirements:* For master's and doctorate, GRE General Test or minimum GPA of 3.0. Additional exam requirements/recommendations for international students: Required—TOEFL (minimum score 550 paper-based; 213 computer-based). Electronic applications accepted. *Faculty research:* Latin American theater, Hispanic literature of the United States, twentieth century Latin American poetry, Spanish American colonial.

Framingham State College, Division of Graduate and Continuing Education, Program in Spanish, Framingham, MA 01701-9101. Offers M Ed.

Georgetown University, Graduate School of Arts and Sciences, Department of Spanish and Portuguese, Washington, DC 20057. Offers Spanish (MS, PhD), including Hispanic literature, Spanish linguistics, Spanish literature; MS/PhD. *Degree requirements:* For master's, one foreign language, research project; for doctorate, 3 foreign languages, thesis/dissertation. *Entrance requirements:* Additional exam requirements/recommendations for international students: Required—TOEFL.

Georgia Southern University, Jack N. Averitt College of Graduate Studies, College of Liberal Arts and Social Sciences, Department of Foreign Languages, Statesboro, GA 30460. Offers Spanish (MA). Part-time and evening/weekend programs available. *Students:* 3 full-time (all women), 9 part-time (8 women); includes 4 minority (all Hispanic Americans). Average age 33. 2 applicants, 100% accepted, 1 enrolled. In 2008, 1 master's awarded. *Degree requirements:* For master's, one foreign language, thesis optional. *Entrance requirements:* For master's, GRE, minimum GPA of 3.0. Additional exam requirements/recommendations for international students: Required—TOEFL (minimum score 550 paper-based; 213 computer-based; 80 iBT). *Application deadline:* For fall admission, 3/1 priority date for domestic and international students; for spring admission, 10/1 priority date for domestic students, 10/1 for international students. Applications are processed on a rolling basis. Application fee: $50. Electronic applications accepted. *Expenses:* Tuition, area resident: Full-time $3840; part-time $160 per semester hour. Tuition, state resident: full-time $3840; part-time $160 per semester hour. Tuition, nonresident: full-time $15,336; part-time $639 per semester hour. Required fees: $1152. *Financial support:* In 2008–09, 8 students received support, including research assistantships with partial tuition reimbursements available (averaging $6,850 per year), teaching assistantships with partial tuition reimbursements available (averaging $6,850 per year); career-related internships or fieldwork, Federal Work-Study, scholarships/grants, tuition waivers (partial), and unspecified assistantships also available. Support available to part-time students. Financial award application deadline: 4/15. *Unit head:* Dr. Donnie Richards, Chair, 912-478-5282, Fax: 912-478-0652, E-mail: forlangs@georgiasouthern.edu. *Application contact:* 912-478-5384, Fax: 912-478-0740, E-mail: gradadmissions@georgiasouthern.edu.

Georgia State University, College of Arts and Sciences, Department of Modern and Classical Languages, Program in Spanish, Atlanta, GA 30303-3083. Offers MA. Evening/weekend programs available. *Degree requirements:* For master's, one foreign language, thesis or alternative, general exam. *Entrance requirements:* For master's, GRE General Test. Additional exam requirements/recommendations for international students: Required—TOEFL. Electronic applications accepted. *Faculty research:* Spanish and Latin-American literature.

Georgia State University, College of Arts and Sciences, Department of Modern and Classical Languages, Program in Translation and Interpretation, Atlanta, GA 30303-3083. Offers French (Certificate); German (Certificate); Spanish (Certificate). Electronic applications accepted.

Graduate School and University Center of the City University of New York, Graduate Studies, Program in Hispanic and Luso-Brazilian Literatures and Languages, New York, NY 10016-4039. Offers PhD. *Degree requirements:* For doctorate, 2 foreign languages, thesis/dissertation. *Entrance requirements:* For doctorate, GRE General Test. Additional exam requirements/recommendations for international students: Required—TOEFL. Electronic applications accepted.

Harvard University, Graduate School of Arts and Sciences, Department of Romance Languages and Literatures, Cambridge, MA 02138. Offers French (AM, PhD); Italian (AM, PhD); Portuguese (AM, PhD); Spanish (AM, PhD). Terminal master's awarded for partial completion of doctoral program. *Degree requirements:* For master's, 2 foreign languages; for doctorate, 2 foreign languages, thesis/dissertation. *Entrance requirements:* For master's and doctorate, GRE General Test, sample of written work. Additional exam requirements/recommendations for international students: Required—TOEFL. *Expenses:* Tuition: Full-time $32,556. Required fees: $1426. Full-time tuition and fees vary according to program and student level.

Hofstra University, College of Liberal Arts and Sciences, Department of Romance Languages and Literatures, Hempstead, NY 11549. Offers Spanish (MA). *Accreditation:* NCATE. Part-time and evening/weekend programs available. *Faculty:* 4 full-time (1 woman), 2 part-time/adjunct (1 woman). *Students:* 2 full-time (both women), 4 part-time (3 women); includes 4 minority (1 Asian American or Pacific Islander, 3 Hispanic Americans). Average age 32. 2 applicants, 100% accepted, 1 enrolled. In 2008, 7 master's awarded. *Degree requirements:* For master's, one foreign language, thesis. *Entrance requirements:* For master's, essay. Additional exam requirements/recommendations for international students: Required—TOEFL (minimum score 550 paper-based; 213 computer-based; 80 iBT). *Application deadline:* Applications are processed on a rolling basis. Application fee: $60. Electronic applications accepted. *Expenses:* Tuition: Full-time $15,300; part-time $850 per credit. Required fees: $970; $165 per term. Tuition and fees vary according to program. *Financial support:* In 2008–09, 6 students received support, including 1 fellowship with full and partial tuition reimbursement available (averaging $3,500 per year); research assistantships with full and partial tuition reimbursements available, Federal Work-Study, institutionally sponsored loans, scholarships/grants, and tuition waivers (full and partial) also available. Support available to part-time students. Financial award applicants required to submit FAFSA. *Faculty research:* Contemporary Spanish cultural studies, twentieth century Spanish theater, identity and post-coloniality, Romance philology, politics of language, decolonization, Spanish imperial Africa and Latin America, twentieth century Latin American poetry. Total annual research expenditures: $5,000. *Unit head:* Dr. Benita Sampedro, Chairperson, 516-463-4521, Fax: 516-463-2310, E-mail: benita.sampedro@hofstra.edu. *Application contact:* Carol Drummer, Dean of Graduate Admissions, 516-463-4876, Fax: 516-463-4664, E-mail: gradstudent@hofstra.edu.

Hofstra University, School of Education, Health, and Human Services, Department of Curriculum and Teaching, Program in Foreign Language Education, Hempstead, NY 11549. Offers foreign language education (MA, MS Ed), including French, German, Russian, Spanish. Part-time and evening/weekend programs available. *Students:* 2 full-time (both women), 4

part-time (3 women); includes 3 minority (all Hispanic Americans). Average age 32. 7 applicants, 71% accepted, 0 enrolled. In 2008, 2 master's awarded. *Degree requirements:* For master's, one foreign language, thesis. *Entrance requirements:* For master's, 2 letters of recommendation, teacher certification (MA), essay. Additional exam requirements/recommendations for international students: Required—TOEFL (minimum score 550 paper-based; 213 computer-based; 80 iBT). *Application deadline:* Applications are processed on a rolling basis. Application fee: $60. Electronic applications accepted. *Expenses:* Tuition: Full-time $15,300; part-time $850 per credit. Required fees: $970; $165 per term. Tuition and fees vary according to program. *Financial support:* In 2008–09, 1 student received support; fellowships with full and partial tuition reimbursements available, research assistantships with full and partial tuition reimbursements available, Federal Work-Study, institutionally sponsored loans, scholarships/grants, and tuition waivers (full and partial) available. Support available to part-time students. Financial award applicants required to submit FAFSA. *Faculty research:* Contemporary Spanish cultural studies, twentieth century Spanish theater, identity and post-coloniality, Romance philology, politics of language, decolonization, Spanish imperial Africa and Latin America, twentieth century Latin American poetry. Total annual research expenditures: $5,000. *Unit head:* Dr. David Powell, Chairperson, 516-463-5485, Fax: 516-463-2310, E-mail: rlldap@hofstra.edu. *Application contact:* Carol Drummer, Dean of Graduate Admissions, 516-463-4876, Fax: 516-463-4664, E-mail: gradstudent@hofstra.edu.

Howard University, Graduate School, Department of Modern Languages and Literatures, Washington, DC 20059-0002. Offers French (MA); Spanish (MA). Part-time programs available. *Degree requirements:* For master's, one foreign language, comprehensive exam, thesis. *Entrance requirements:* For master's, GRE General Test, writing samples in English and French or Spanish. *Faculty research:* African literature in French, Spanish linguistics, Spanish Peninsular literature, Spanish sociolinguistics.

Hunter College of the City University of New York, Graduate School, School of Arts and Sciences, Department of Romance Languages, Program in Spanish, New York, NY 10021-5085. Offers Spanish (MA); Spanish education (MA). Part-time and evening/weekend programs available. *Faculty:* 4 full-time (3 women). *Students:* 10 part-time (8 women); includes 6 minority (all Hispanic Americans). Average age 40. 7 applicants, 57% accepted, 1 enrolled. In 2008, 8 master's awarded. *Degree requirements:* For master's, 2 foreign languages, comprehensive exam, thesis optional. *Entrance requirements:* For master's, GRE General Test, GRE Subject Test, ability to read, speak, and write Spanish; interview. Additional exam requirements/recommendations for international students: Required—TOEFL. *Application deadline:* For fall admission, 4/1 for domestic students, 2/1 for international students; for spring admission, 11/1 for domestic students, 9/1 for international students. Application fee: $125. *Financial support:* Federal Work-Study and tuition waivers (partial) available. Support available to part-time students. Financial award application deadline: 4/15. *Faculty research:* Galician studies, contemporary Spanish poetry, Lope de Vega, comparative Hispanic literatures, contemporary Hispanic poetry. *Unit head:* Dr. James O. Pellier, Graduate Advisor, 212-772-5625, E-mail: jpellice@hunter.cuny.edu. *Application contact:* William Zlata, Director for Graduate Admissions, 212-772-4482, Fax: 212-650-3336, E-mail: admissions@hunter.cuny.edu.

Illinois State University, Graduate School, College of Arts and Sciences, Department of Foreign Languages, Literatures and Cultures, Normal, IL 61790-2200. Offers French (MA); French and German (MA); French and Spanish (MA); German (MA); German and Spanish (MA); Spanish (MA). *Degree requirements:* For master's, variable foreign language requirement, comprehensive exam, 1 term of residency. *Entrance requirements:* For master's, GRE General Test, minimum GPA of 2.8 in last 60 hours of course work.

Indiana University Bloomington, University Graduate School, College of Arts and Sciences, Department of Spanish and Portuguese, Bloomington, IN 47405-7000. Offers Hispanic linguistics (MA, PhD); Hispanic literature (MA); Luso-Brazilian literature (MA); Luso-Brazilian studies (PhD); Spanish literatures (PhD); teaching Spanish (MAT). *Faculty:* 18 full-time (10 women). *Students:* 75 full-time (39 women), 6 part-time (4 women); includes 17 minority (all Hispanic Americans), 17 international. Average age 30. 53 applicants, 36% accepted, 16 enrolled. In 2008, 7 master's, 7 doctorates awarded. *Degree requirements:* For master's, one foreign language; for doctorate, 3 foreign languages, thesis/dissertation. *Entrance requirements:* For master's, GRE General Test, GRE Subject Test, bachelor's degree in Portuguese or Spanish, minimum GPA of 3.25; for doctorate, GRE General Test, GRE Subject Test, master's degree in Portuguese or Spanish, minimum GPA of 3.25. Additional exam requirements/recommendations for international students: Required—TOEFL. *Application deadline:* For fall admission, 1/15 priority date for domestic students, 12/15 for international students; for spring admission, 9/1 for domestic and international students. Application fee: $50 ($60 for international students). *Expenses:* Tuition, area resident: Part-time $291.97 per credit hour. Tuition, state resident: part-time $291.97 per credit hour. Tuition, nonresident: part-time $850.33 per credit hour. Required fees: $110 per semester. Tuition and fees vary according to course load and program. *Financial support:* Fellowships with full tuition reimbursements, research assistantships, teaching assistantships with full tuition reimbursements, Federal Work-Study available. Financial award application deadline: 1/15. *Faculty research:* Spanish American literature, Spanish peninsular literature, Luso-Brazilian studies, Catalan studies. *Unit head:* Josep Miguel Sobrer, Chair, 812-855-8498. *Application contact:* Steven Wagschal, Student Contact, 812-855-9194, E-mail: swagscha@indiana.edu.

Inter American University of Puerto Rico, Metropolitan Campus, Graduate Programs, Program in Spanish, San Juan, PR 00919-1293. Offers MA. Part-time and evening/weekend programs available. *Degree requirements:* For master's, one foreign language, comprehensive exam. *Entrance requirements:* For master's, GRE or EXADEP, interview, minimum GPA of 2.5, 6 credits each of Spanish literature and Hispanic-American literature. Electronic applications accepted.

Inter American University of Puerto Rico, Ponce Campus, Graduate School, Mercedita, PR 00715-1602. Offers accounting (MBA); biology (M Ed); chemistry (M Ed); criminal justice (MA); elementary education (M Ed); English as a Second Language (M Ed); finance (MBA); history (M Ed); human resources (MBA); marketing (MBA); mathematics (M Ed); Spanish (M Ed). *Entrance requirements:* For master's, minimum GPA of 2.5.

Iona College, School of Arts and Science, Program in Foreign Languages, New Rochelle, NY 10801-1890. Offers Italian (MA); Spanish (MA). Part-time and evening/weekend programs available. *Faculty:* 5 full-time (2 women), 3 part-time/adjunct (1 woman). *Students:* 18 part-time (14 women); includes 3 minority (1 African American, 2 Hispanic Americans). Average age 32. 3 applicants, 67% accepted, 1 enrolled. *Degree requirements:* For master's, thesis or alternative. *Entrance requirements:* For master's, minimum GPA of 3.0. Additional exam requirements/recommendations for international students: Required—TOEFL (minimum score 550 paper-based; 213 computer-based). *Application deadline:* Applications are processed on a rolling basis. Application fee: $50. Electronic applications accepted. *Expenses:* Tuition: Part-time $755 per credit. Required fees: $175 per term. *Financial support:* Unspecified assistantships available. Support available to part-time students. Financial award application deadline: 4/15; financial award applicants required to submit FAFSA. *Faculty research:* Contemporary Spanish literature, linguistics, language acquisition, female Hispanic literature, Latina authors. *Unit head:* Dr. Thomas E. Mussio, Chair, 914-637-2737, E-mail: TMussio@iona.edu. *Application contact:* Veronica Jarek-Prinz, Director of Graduate Admissions, 914-633-2420, Fax: 914-633-2277, E-mail: vjarekprinz@iona.edu.

The Johns Hopkins University, Zanvyl Krieger School of Arts and Sciences, Department of German and Romance Languages, Baltimore, MD 21218-2699. Offers French (PhD); German (PhD); Italian (PhD); romance languages (PhD); Spanish (PhD). *Degree requirements:* For doctorate, 2 foreign languages, thesis/dissertation. *Entrance requirements:* For doctorate, GRE General Test. Additional exam requirements/recommendations for international students: Required—TOEFL (minimum score 600 paper-based; 250 computer-based). Electronic applications accepted.

Kansas State University, Graduate School, College of Arts and Sciences, Department of Modern Languages, Manhattan, KS 66506. Offers French (MA); German (MA); Spanish (MA). Part-time and evening/weekend programs available. Postbaccalaureate distance learning degree programs offered (minimal on-campus study). *Faculty:* 15 full-time (7 women). *Students:* 18 full-time (11 women), 10 part-time (8 women); includes 4 minority (all Hispanic Americans), 11 international. Average age 32. 6 applicants, 100% accepted, 6 enrolled. In 2008, 4 master's awarded. *Degree requirements:* For master's, thesis optional. *Entrance requirements:* For master's, teaching certificate. Additional exam requirements/recommendations for international students: Required—TOEFL (minimum score 560 paper-based). *Application deadline:* For fall admission, 2/1 priority date for domestic and international students; for spring admission, 10/1 for domestic students, 8/1 priority date for international students. Applications are processed on a rolling basis. Application fee: $30 ($55 for international students). *Expenses:* Tuition, area resident: Full-time $6466; part-time $269.40 per credit hour. Tuition, state resident: full-time $6466; part-time $269.40 per credit hour. Tuition, nonresident: full-time $14,874; part-time $619.75 per credit hour. Required fees: $673; $23.40 per credit hour. Tuition and fees vary according to campus/location. *Financial support:* In 2008–09, 13 teaching assistantships with full tuition reimbursements (averaging $10,546 per year) were awarded; fellowships, Federal Work-Study, institutionally sponsored loans, and scholarships/grants also available. Support available to part-time students. Financial award application deadline: 3/1; financial award applicants required to submit FAFSA. *Faculty research:* Second language acquisitions; Chicano literature; Francophone literature; cultural studies; German, French, Spanish, and Spanish-American literature from the Middle Ages to the modern era. *Unit head:* Robert Corum, Head, 785-532-1987, Fax: 785-532-7004, E-mail: corum@ksu.edu. *Application contact:* Claire Dehon, Director, 785-532-1929, Fax: 785-532-7004, E-mail: dehoncl@ksu.edu.

Kean University, College of Education, Program in Instruction and Curriculum, Union, NJ 07083. Offers bilingual/bicultural education (MA); classroom instruction (MA); earth science (MA); mathematics/science/computer education (MA); teaching (MA); teaching English as a second language (MA); world languages (Spanish) (MA). *Accreditation:* NCATE. Part-time and evening/weekend programs available. *Faculty:* 17 full-time (7 women). *Students:* 34 full-time (28 women), 163 part-time (128 women); includes 12 African Americans, 4 Asian Americans or Pacific Islanders, 55 Hispanic Americans, 5 international. Average age 33. 59 applicants, 93% accepted, 40 enrolled. In 2008, 70 master's awarded. *Degree requirements:* For master's, 2 foreign languages, comprehensive exam, thesis. *Entrance requirements:* For master's, GRE General Test or MAT, PRAXIS, minimum GPA of 3.0, 2 letters of recommendation, interview, teacher certification (for some programs). *Application deadline:* For fall admission, 5/1 for domestic students; for spring admission, 11/1 for domestic students. Application fee: $60 ($150 for international students). Electronic applications accepted. *Expenses:* Tuition, state resident: full-time $10,128; part-time $422 per credit. Tuition, nonresident: full-time $13,728; part-time $572 per credit. Required fees: $2570; $107 per credit. Part-time tuition and fees vary according to course load, degree level and program. *Financial support:* In 2008–09, 2 research assistantships with full tuition reimbursements (averaging $3,217 per year) were awarded; unspecified assistantships also available. *Unit head:* Dr. Thomas Walsh, Program Coordinator, 908-737-4296, E-mail: twalsh@kean.edu. *Application contact:* Steven Koch, Pre-Admissions Coordinator, 908-737-4723, Fax: 908-737-5965, E-mail: grad-adm@kean.edu.

Kent State University, College of Arts and Sciences, Department of Modern and Classical Language Studies, Kent, OH 44242-0001. Offers French literature (MA); French, Spanish, German and Latin pedagogy (MA); German literature (MA); Spanish literature (MA); translation (MA), including French, German, Japanese, Russian, Spanish; translation studies (PhD). Part-time and evening/weekend programs available. *Degree requirements:* For master's, one foreign language, comprehensive exam (for some programs), thesis (for some programs); for doctorate, comprehensive exam, thesis/dissertation (for some programs). *Entrance requirements:* For master's, minimum GPA of 3.0, writing sample, audio tape or CD; for doctorate, 3 recommendations. Additional exam requirements/recommendations for international students: Required—TOEFL (minimum score 197 computer-based). Electronic applications accepted. *Faculty research:* Literature, pedagogy, applied linguistics, translation studies.

Lehman College of the City University of New York, Division of Arts and Humanities, Department of Languages and Literatures, Bronx, NY 10468-1589. Offers Spanish (MA). Part-time and evening/weekend programs available. *Degree requirements:* For master's, one foreign language.

Long Island University, C.W. Post Campus, College of Liberal Arts and Sciences, Department of Foreign Languages, Brookville, NY 11548-1300. Offers Spanish (MA); Spanish education (MS). Part-time programs available. *Degree requirements:* For master's, 2 foreign languages, comprehensive exam, thesis or alternative. *Entrance requirements:* For master's, 24 credits of undergraduate Spanish. Electronic applications accepted. *Faculty research:* Making of superhero, dialogue in the 19th century novel, nicknames, Menendez Pidal and Spanish School of Philology, women writers of Latin America.

Loyola University Chicago, Graduate School, Department of Modern Languages and Literatures, Chicago, IL 60611-2196. Offers Spanish (MA). Part-time and evening/weekend programs available. *Faculty:* 6 full-time (4 women), 1 part-time/adjunct (0 women). *Students:* 16 full-time (9 women), 8 part-time (5 women); includes 8 minority (1 African American, 7 Hispanic Americans). Average age 32. 15 applicants, 87% accepted, 4 enrolled. In 2008, 9 master's awarded. *Degree requirements:* For master's, 2 foreign languages, comprehensive exam, thesis or alternative. *Entrance requirements:* Additional exam requirements/recommendations for international students: Required—TOEFL. Application fee: $50. *Expenses:* Tuition: Full-time $13,500; part-time $750 per credit hour. Required fees: $60 per semester. Full-time tuition and fees vary according to program. *Financial support:* In 2008–09, 6 students received support, including 3 teaching assistantships with full tuition reimbursements available (averaging $10,000 per year); scholarships/grants also available. Financial award applicants required to submit FAFSA. *Faculty research:* Linguistics, Latin American contemporary narrative, Latin American culture and civilization, Hispanic women's studies, twentieth century peninsular writing, Golden Age, Don Quixote. *Unit head:* Dr. Olympia Gonzalez, Chair, 773-508-2872, Fax: 773-508-3514, E-mail: ogonzal@luc.edu. *Application contact:* Dr. Olympia Gonzalez, Chair, 773-508-2872, Fax: 773-508-3514, E-mail: ogonzal@luc.edu.

Marquette University, Graduate School, College of Arts and Sciences, Department of Foreign Languages and Literatures, Milwaukee, WI 53201-1881. Offers Spanish (MA, MAT). Part-time programs available. *Degree requirements:* For master's, one foreign language, comprehensive exam or thesis. *Entrance requirements:* Additional exam requirements/recommendations for international students: Required—TOEFL. *Faculty research:* Magic realism, African-Hispanic literature, women studies, Hispanic linguistics.

Marshall University, Academic Affairs Division, College of Liberal Arts, Program in Spanish, Huntington, WV 25755. Offers MA.

Miami University, Graduate School, College of Arts and Sciences, Department of Spanish and Portuguese, Oxford, OH 45056. Offers Spanish (MA). Part-time programs available. *Degree requirements:* For master's, thesis (for some programs), final exam. *Entrance requirements:* For master's, minimum undergraduate GPA of 3.0 during previous 2 years or 2.75 overall. Additional exam requirements/recommendations for international students: Required—TOEFL (minimum score 550 paper-based; 213 computer-based), TWE (minimum score 4). Electronic applications accepted.

Michigan State University, The Graduate School, College of Arts and Letters, Department of Spanish and Portuguese, East Lansing, MI 48824. Offers applied Spanish linguistics (MA); Hispanic cultural studies (PhD); Hispanic literatures (MA). *Entrance requirements:* Additional exam requirements/recommendations for international students: Required—TOEFL. Electronic applications accepted.

Middlebury College, Language Schools, Spanish School, Middlebury, VT 05753. Offers MA, DML. *Faculty:* 30 full-time (14 women). *Students:* 173 full-time (119 women); includes 35 minority (3 African Americans, 1 American Indian/Alaska Native, 2 Asian Americans or Pacific Islanders, 29 Hispanic Americans). Average age 30. 339 applicants, 70% accepted, 182 enrolled. In 2008, 66 master's, 4 doctorates awarded. *Degree requirements:* For master's, one foreign language; for doctorate, 2 foreign languages, comprehensive exam, thesis/dissertation, residence abroad, teaching experience. *Entrance requirements:* For master's, placement exam, 3 letters of recommendation, writing sample. Application fee: $55. Electronic applications accepted. *Financial support:* Scholarships/grants available. *Unit head:* Dr. Jacobo Sefami, Director, 802-443-5539, Fax: 802-443-2075, E-mail: jsefami@middlebury.edu. *Application contact:* Audrey LaRock, Coordinator, 802-443-5539, Fax: 802-443-2075, E-mail: larock@middlebury.edu.

Millersville University of Pennsylvania, Graduate School, School of Humanities and Social Sciences, Department of Foreign Languages, Program in Spanish, Millersville, PA 17551-0302. Offers M Ed, MA. Part-time programs available. *Faculty:* 9 full-time (5 women), 4 part-time/adjunct (3 women). *Students:* 1 (woman) full-time, 6 part-time (all women); includes 1 minority (Hispanic American). Average age 33. 2 applicants, 100% accepted, 0 enrolled. In 2008, 4 master's awarded. *Degree requirements:* For master's, comprehensive exam, thesis optional. *Entrance requirements:* For master's, GRE or MAT. Additional exam requirements/recommendations for international students: Required—TOEFL (minimum score 500 paper-based; 183 computer-based; 65 iBT), TOEFL may be replaced by IELTS with score of 6 or higher. *Application deadline:* For fall admission, 2/1 priority date for domestic and international students; for winter admission, 10/1 priority date for domestic and international students; for spring admission, 10/1 priority date for domestic and international students. Applications are processed on a rolling basis. Application fee: $40. Electronic applications accepted. *Expenses:* Tuition, state resident: full-time $6430; part-time $357 per credit. Tuition, nonresident: full-time $10,288; part-time $572 per credit. Required fees: $1937; $73.50 per credit. One-time fee: $88 part-time. Tuition and fees vary according to course load. *Financial support:* Research assistantships, institutionally sponsored loans and unspecified assistantships available. Support available to part-time students. Financial award application deadline: 3/15; financial award applicants required to submit FAFSA. *Unit head:* Dr. Christine M. Gaudry-Hudson, Coordinator of Foreign Language Graduate Program, 717-872-3663, E-mail: christine.gaudry-hudson@millersville.edu. *Application contact:* Dr. Victor S. DeSantis, Dean of Graduate and Professional Studies, 717-872-3099, Fax: 717-872-3453, E-mail: victor.desantis@millersville.edu.

Minnesota State University Mankato, College of Graduate Studies, College of Arts and Humanities, Department of Modern Languages, Program in Spanish, Mankato, MN 56001. Offers MAT, MS. *Students:* 3 full-time (all women), 10 part-time (4 women). *Degree requirements:* For master's, one foreign language, comprehensive exam, thesis. *Entrance requirements:* For master's, minimum GPA of 3.0 during previous 2 years. *Application deadline:* For fall admission, 7/1 priority date for domestic students; for spring admission, 11/1 for domestic students. Applications are processed on a rolling basis. Application fee: $40. Electronic applications accepted. *Financial support:* Research assistantships with full tuition reimbursements, teaching assistantships with full tuition reimbursements, career-related internships or fieldwork, Federal Work-Study, institutionally sponsored loans, and unspecified assistantships available. Support available to part-time students. Financial award application deadline: 3/15. *Unit head:* Dr. Kimberly Contag, Graduate Coordinator, 507-389-5358. *Application contact:* 507-389-2321, E-mail: grad@mnsu.edu.

Mississippi State University, College of Arts and Sciences, Department of Foreign Languages, Mississippi State, MS 39762. Offers French (MA); French/German (MA); German (MA); Spanish (MA); Spanish/French (MA); Spanish/German (MA). Part-time programs available. *Degree requirements:* For master's, one foreign language, thesis optional, comprehensive oral or written exam. *Entrance requirements:* For master's, minimum GPA of 2.75. Additional exam requirements/recommendations for international students: Required—TOEFL (minimum score 525 paper-based). *Faculty research:* French, German, Spanish literature from medieval to present; gender and cultural studies in French; Spanish American literature; foreign language methodology; linguistics.

Missouri State University, Graduate College, College of Arts and Letters, Department of Modern and Classical Languages, Springfield, MO 65804-0094. Offers secondary education (MS Ed), including French, German, Spanish. Part-time programs available. *Faculty:* 5 full-time (2 women). *Students:* 2 full-time (1 woman), 2 part-time (both women). Average age 30. 1 applicant, 100% accepted, 0 enrolled. In 2008, 4 master's awarded. *Entrance requirements:* For master's, grades 9-12 teaching certification. Additional exam requirements/recommendations for international students: Required—TOEFL (minimum score 550 paper-based; 213 computer-based; 79 iBT), IELTS (minimum score 6). *Application deadline:* For fall admission, 7/20 priority date for domestic students, 5/1 for international students; for spring admission, 12/20 priority date for domestic students, 9/1 for international students. Applications are processed on a rolling basis. Application fee: $35 ($50 for international students). Electronic applications accepted. *Expenses:* Tuition, state resident: full-time $3852; part-time $214 per credit hour. Tuition, nonresident: full-time $7524; part-time $418 per credit hour. Required fees: $230 per semester. Tuition and fees vary according to course level and course load. *Financial support:* Federal Work-Study, institutionally sponsored loans, scholarships/grants, and unspecified assistantships available. Financial award applicants required to submit FAFSA. *Unit head:* Dr. Madeleine Kernen, Head, 417-836-7626, E-mail: mcl@missouristate.edu. *Application contact:* Eric Eckert, Coordinator of Admissions and Recruitment, 417-836-5331, Fax: 417-836-6888, E-mail: ericeckert@missouristate.edu.

Montclair State University, The Office of Graduate Admissions and Support Services, College of Education and Human Services, Department of Curriculum and Teaching, Montclair, NJ 07043-1624. Offers education (M Ed); educational technology (M Ed); learning disabled teacher consultant (Certificate); school library media specialist (Certificate); teaching (MAT, Certificate), including art (MAT), biological science (MAT), early childhood education (P-3) (MAT), earth science (MAT), elementary education (K-8) (MAT), English (MAT), French (MAT), health and physical education (MAT), health education (MAT), home economics (MAT), mathematics (MAT), music (MAT), physical education (MAT), physical science (MAT), social studies (MAT), Spanish (MAT), teacher of ESL (MAT), teacher of students with disabilities (MAT). Part-time and evening/weekend programs available. *Faculty:* 14 full-time (10 women), 23 part-time/adjunct (17 women). *Students:* 103 full-time (61 women), 98 part-time (73 women); includes 15 minority (8 African Americans, 3 Asian Americans or Pacific Islanders, 4 Hispanic Americans), 3 international. Average age 31. 56 applicants, 63% accepted, 33 enrolled. In 2008, 196 master's, 2 other advanced degrees awarded. *Degree requirements:* For master's, comprehensive exam, field experience. *Entrance requirements:* For master's, PRAXIS II, minimum GPA of 2.67, 2 letters of recommendation. Additional exam requirements/recommendations for international students: Required—TOEFL (minimum score 83 computer-based). *Application deadline:* For fall admission, 2/15 for domestic and international students; for spring admission, 9/15 for domestic and international students. Applications are processed on a rolling basis. Application fee: $60. Electronic applications accepted. *Financial support:* In 2008–09, 7 research assistantships with full tuition reimbursements (averaging $7,000 per year) were awarded; Federal Work-Study, scholarships/grants, and unspecified assistantships also available. Support available to part-time students. Financial award application deadline: 3/1; financial award applicants required to submit FAFSA. *Unit head:* Dr. David Keiser, Chairperson, 973-655-7199. *Application contact:* Amy Aiello, Associate Director of Admissions, 973-655-5147, Fax: 973-655-7869, E-mail: graduate.school@montclair.edu.

Montclair State University, The Office of Graduate Admissions and Support Services, College of Humanities and Social Sciences, Department of Spanish and Italian, Montclair, NJ 07043-1624. Offers Italian (Certificate); Spanish (MA, Certificate); translating and interpreting Spanish (Certificate). Part-time and evening/weekend programs available. *Faculty:* 18 full-time (10 women), 25 part-time/adjunct (19 women). *Students:* 2 full-time (both women), 18 part-time (16 women); includes 6 minority (2 African Americans, 2 American Indian/Alaska Native, 2

Spanish

Montclair State University (continued)

Hispanic Americans), 1 international. Average age 35. 6 applicants, 100% accepted, 2 enrolled. In 2008, 6 master's awarded. *Degree requirements:* For master's, comprehensive exam, thesis or alternative. *Entrance requirements:* For master's, GRE General Test, BA in Spanish or at least 24 undergraduate credits of Spanish, 2 letters of recommendation. Additional exam requirements/recommendations for international students: Required—TOEFL (minimum score 83 computer-based). *Application deadline:* For fall admission, 6/1 for international students; for spring admission, 11/1 for international students. Applications are processed on a rolling basis. Application fee: $60. Electronic applications accepted. *Financial support:* In 2008–09, 1 research assistantship with full tuition reimbursement (averaging $7,000 per year) was awarded; Federal Work-Study, scholarships/grants, and unspecified assistantships also available. Support available to part-time students. Financial award application deadline: 3/1; financial award applicants required to submit FAFSA. *Unit head:* Dr. Diana Guemaraz Cruz, Chairperson, 973-655-7506. *Application contact:* Amy Aiello, Associate Director of Admissions, 973-655-5147, Fax: 973-655-7869, E-mail: graduate.school@montclair.edu.

New Mexico State University, Graduate School, College of Arts and Sciences, Department of Languages and Linguistics, Las Cruces, NM 88003-8001. Offers Spanish (MA). Part-time programs available. *Faculty:* 9 full-time (3 women). *Students:* 27 full-time (18 women), 7 part-time (5 women); includes 14 minority (all Hispanic Americans), 14 international. Average age 33. 21 applicants, 95% accepted, 10 enrolled. In 2008, 8 master's awarded. *Degree requirements:* For master's, one foreign language, comprehensive exam, thesis optional, oral and written exams. *Entrance requirements:* For master's, sample of written work in Spanish, cassette tape in Spanish, 3 letters of reference. *Application deadline:* For fall admission, 2/15 for domestic students; for spring admission, 10/12 for domestic students. Applications are processed on a rolling basis. Application fee: $30 ($50 for international students). Electronic applications accepted. *Expenses:* Tuition, area resident: Full-time $3890; part-time $212.85 per credit. Tuition, state resident: full-time $3890; part-time $212.85 per credit. Tuition, nonresident: full-time $13,916; part-time $630.55 per credit. Required fees: $1218; $609 per semester. *Financial support:* In 2008–09, 19 students received support, including 1 research assistantship (averaging $25,500 per year), 18 teaching assistantships (averaging $14,483 per year); Federal Work-Study, institutionally sponsored loans, scholarships/grants, health care benefits, and unspecified assistantships also available. Support available to part-time students. Financial award application deadline: 3/1. *Faculty research:* Spanish-American literature, U.S. Hispanic and Chicano literature and border culture, Hispanic linguistics, French and German literature and linguistics. *Unit head:* Dr. Richard Rundell, Head, 575-646-3408, Fax: 575-646-7876, E-mail: rrundell@nmsu.edu. *Application contact:* Elena Luna, Coordinator, 575-646-3498, Fax: 575-646-7721, E-mail: rosluna@nmsu.edu.

New York University, Graduate School of Arts and Science, Department of Spanish and Portuguese Languages and Literatures, New York, NY 10012-1019. Offers Portuguese (MA, PhD); Spanish (PhD); Spanish and Latin American literatures and cultures (MA); Spanish language and translation (MA). Part-time programs available. *Degree requirements:* For master's, 2 foreign languages, thesis; for doctorate, 2 foreign languages, thesis/dissertation. *Entrance requirements:* For master's, GRE General Test; for doctorate, GRE General Test, master's degree. Additional exam requirements/recommendations for international students: Required—TOEFL. *Faculty research:* Gender and sexuality, transatlantic studies, literacy and cultural theories, colonial and post colonial studies, autobiography and modern subjectivities.

North Carolina State University, Graduate School, College of Humanities and Social Sciences, Department of Foreign Languages and Literatures, Program in Spanish Language and Literature, Raleigh, NC 27695. Offers MA. *Degree requirements:* For master's, thesis optional. *Entrance requirements:* For master's, fluency in Spanish. Electronic applications accepted. *Faculty research:* Applied linguistics, technology-assisted language instruction, Latin-American literature and culture, 20th and 21st Century Spanish narrative and film, children's literature.

Northern Illinois University, Graduate School, College of Liberal Arts and Sciences, Department of Foreign Languages and Literatures, De Kalb, IL 60115-2854. Offers French (MA); Spanish (MA). Part-time programs available. *Degree requirements:* For master's, one foreign language, comprehensive exam, thesis or alternative, language proficiency exam. *Entrance requirements:* For master's, GRE General Test, interview, minimum GPA of 2.75, undergraduate major in French or Spanish. Additional exam requirements/recommendations for international students: Required—TOEFL (minimum score 550 paper-based; 213 computer-based). Electronic applications accepted. *Faculty research:* Francophone women writers, prosodies of French and Italian, early Spanish drama, business German, history of Burmese literature.

Nova Southeastern University, Fischler School of Education and Human Services, Graduate Teacher Education Program, Fort Lauderdale, FL 33314-7796. Offers athletic administration (MS); brain research (MS, Ed S); charter school education/leadership (MS); cognitive and behavioral disabilities (MS); computer science education (Ed S); computer science education (K-12) (MS); curriculum and teaching (Ed S); curriculum, instruction and technology (MS); curriculum, instruction, management and administration (Ed S); early childhood education (MS); early literacy and reading (Ed S); early literacy education (MS); education technology (MS); educational leadership (administration K–12) (MS, Ed S); educational media (Ed S); educational media (K-12) (MS); elementary education (MS, Ed S), including ESOL endorsement (MS); English education (MS, Ed S); environmental education (MS); exceptional student education (MS), including ESOL endorsement; gifted education (MS, Ed S); interdisciplinary arts education (MS); management and administration of educational programs (MS); mathematics (MS); mathematics education (Ed S); multicultural early intervention (MS); pre-kindergarten/primary (MS); preschool education (MS); reading (MS); reading and TESOL (MS); reading education (Ed S); science (MS); science education (Ed S); secondary education (MS); social studies (MS, Ed S); Spanish language (MS); special education and reading (MS); teaching and learning (MA, MS), including curriculum and instruction (MA), elementary mathematics (MA), elementary reading (MA), K-12 technology integration (MA); teaching English to speakers of other languages (MS, Ed S); technology management and administration (Ed S); urban studies education (MS). Part-time and evening/weekend programs available. Postbaccalaureate distance learning degree programs offered (minimal on-campus study). *Faculty:* 72 full-time (43 women), 385 part-time/adjunct (252 women). *Students:* 489 full-time (407 women), 876 part-time (771 women); includes 787 minority (652 African Americans, 3 American Indian/Alaska Native, 7 Asian Americans or Pacific Islanders, 125 Hispanic Americans), 3 international. Average age 37. 2,610 applicants, 72% accepted, 1352 enrolled. In 2008, 682 other advanced degrees awarded. *Degree requirements:* For master's and Ed S, thesis, practicum, internship. *Entrance requirements:* For master's, MAT, GRE, CLAST, CBEST, PRAXIS I, GKT, minimum GPA of 2.5; for Ed S, MAT or GRE, master's degree, teaching certificate, minimum GPA of 3.0. Additional exam requirements/recommendations for international students: Required—TSE recommended 50; Recommended—TOEFL (minimum score 550 paper-based; 213 computer-based; 80 iBT), IELTS (minimum score 6). *Application deadline:* For fall admission, 9/25 priority date for domestic and international students; for winter admission, 2/23 priority date for domestic and international students; for spring admission, 4/25 priority date for domestic and international students. Applications are processed on a rolling basis. Application fee: $50. Electronic applications accepted. *Financial support:* Federal Work-Study available. Support available to part-time students. Financial award application deadline: 4/15; financial award applicants required to submit FAFSA. *Faculty research:* School effectiveness, critical thinking, leadership skills acquisition, child education, multicultural education. *Unit head:* Dr. Ronald Kern, Dean of Academic Affairs, 800-986-3223 Ext. 7809, Fax: 954-262-3606, E-mail: rk429@nsu.nova.edu. *Application contact:* Dr. Jennifer Quinones Nottingham, Dean of Student Affairs, 800-986-3223 Ext. 1559.

The Ohio State University, Graduate School, College of Humanities, Department of Spanish and Portuguese, Columbus, OH 43210. Offers MA, PhD. *Degree requirements:* For master's, thesis optional; for doctorate, thesis/dissertation. *Entrance requirements:* For master's and doctorate, GRE General Test. Additional exam requirements/recommendations for international students: Required—TOEFL (minimum score 600 paper-based; 250 computer-based). Electronic applications accepted.

Ohio University, Graduate College, College of Arts and Sciences, Department of Modern Languages, Athens, OH 45701-2979. Offers French (MA); Spanish (MA). Part-time programs available. *Degree requirements:* For master's, 2 foreign languages, comprehensive exam, thesis optional. *Entrance requirements:* For master's, oral and written samples. Additional exam requirements/recommendations for international students: Required—TOEFL (minimum score 500 paper-based). Electronic applications accepted. *Faculty research:* French and Spanish language and literature.

Penn State University Park, Graduate School, College of the Liberal Arts, Department of Spanish, Italian, and Portuguese, State College, University Park, PA 16802-1503. Offers Spanish (MA, PhD).

Pontifical Catholic University of Puerto Rico, College of Arts and Humanities, Department of Hispanic Studies, Ponce, PR 00717-0777. Offers grammar and writing (Professional Certificate); Hispanic studies (MA). Part-time and evening/weekend programs available. *Degree requirements:* For master's, variable foreign language requirement, comprehensive exam, thesis or alternative. *Entrance requirements:* For master's, GRE General Test, 2 letters of recommendation, interview, minimum GPA of 2.75. Electronic applications accepted.

Portland State University, Graduate Studies, College of Liberal Arts and Sciences, Department of Foreign Languages and Literatures, Portland, OR 97207-0751. Offers foreign literature and language (MA); French (MA); German (MA); Japanese (MA); Spanish (MA). Part-time programs available. *Faculty:* 43 full-time (27 women), 28 part-time/adjunct (19 women). *Students:* 29 full-time (24 women), 17 part-time (11 women); includes 6 minority (1 African American, 1 Asian American or Pacific Islander, 4 Hispanic Americans), 11 international. Average age 32. 23 applicants, 91% accepted, 20 enrolled. In 2008, 14 master's awarded. *Degree requirements:* For master's, one foreign language, thesis (for some programs). *Entrance requirements:* Additional exam requirements/recommendations for international students: Required—TOEFL (minimum score 550 paper-based; 213 computer-based). *Application deadline:* For fall admission, 4/1 for domestic students, 3/1 for international students; for winter admission, 9/1 for domestic students, 7/1 for international students; for spring admission, 11/1 for domestic and international students. Applications are processed on a rolling basis. Application fee: $50. *Expenses:* Tuition, area resident: Full-time $8763; part-time $179 per credit hour. Tuition, state resident: full-time $8763; part-time $298 per credit hour. Tuition, nonresident: full-time $12,981; part-time $426 per credit hour. Required fees: $1242. One-time fee: $250. Tuition and fees vary according to course load and program. *Financial support:* In 2008–09, 6 teaching assistantships with full tuition reimbursements (averaging $9,359 per year) were awarded; research assistantships with full tuition reimbursements, Federal Work-Study, scholarships/grants, and unspecified assistantships also available. Support available to part-time students. Financial award application deadline: 3/1; financial award applicants required to submit FAFSA. *Faculty research:* Foreign language pedagogy, applied and social linguistics, literary history and criticism. Total annual research expenditures: $6,847. *Unit head:* Dr. Sandra F. Freels, Chair, 503-725-3522, Fax: 503-725-5276. *Application contact:* Karen Popp, Office Coordinator, 503-725-3522, E-mail: poppk@pdx.edu.

Princeton University, Graduate School, Department of Spanish and Portuguese Languages and Cultures, Princeton, NJ 08544-1019. Offers PhD. *Degree requirements:* For doctorate, variable foreign language requirement, thesis/dissertation. *Entrance requirements:* For doctorate, GRE General Test, sample of written work. Additional exam requirements/recommendations for international students: Required—TOEFL (minimum score 600 paper-based; 250 computer-based). Electronic applications accepted.

Purdue University, Graduate School, College of Liberal Arts, Department of Foreign Languages and Literatures, West Lafayette, IN 47907. Offers French (MA, MAT, PhD), including French (MA, PhD), French education (MAT); German (MA, MAT, PhD), including German (MA, PhD), German education (MAT); Spanish (MA, MAT, PhD), including Spanish (MA, PhD), Spanish education (MAT). Terminal master's awarded for partial completion of doctoral program. *Degree requirements:* For master's, one foreign language; for doctorate, 2 foreign languages, thesis/dissertation. *Entrance requirements:* For master's and doctorate, GRE, writing sample, sample recording of English and language of study. Additional exam requirements/recommendations for international students: Required—TOEFL. Electronic applications accepted. *Faculty research:* Linguistics, semiotics, literary criticism, pedagogy.

Queens College of the City University of New York, Division of Graduate Studies, Arts and Humanities Division, Department of Hispanic Languages and Literatures, Program in Spanish, Flushing, NY 11367-1597. Offers MA. Part-time and evening/weekend programs available. *Degree requirements:* For master's, 2 foreign languages, comprehensive exam, thesis or alternative. *Entrance requirements:* For master's, minimum GPA of 3.0. Additional exam requirements/recommendations for international students: Required—TOEFL.

Queen's University at Kingston, School of Graduate Studies and Research, Faculty of Arts and Sciences, Department of Spanish and Italian, Kingston, ON K7L 3N6, Canada. Offers Spanish language and literature (MA). Part-time programs available. *Degree requirements:* For master's, one foreign language, thesis. *Entrance requirements:* Additional exam requirements/recommendations for international students: Required—TOEFL. Electronic applications accepted. *Faculty research:* Golden Age, nineteenth- and twentieth-century Peninsular novel, literary theory, colonial Latin America, nineteenth-and-twentieth century Latin America.

Rice University, Graduate Programs, School of Humanities, Department of Hispanic Studies, Houston, TX 77251-1892. Offers Spanish (MA). Part-time programs available. *Degree requirements:* For master's, one foreign language, thesis. *Entrance requirements:* For master's, GRE General Test, minimum GPA of 3.0. Additional exam requirements/recommendations for international students: Required—TOEFL (minimum score 600 paper-based; 250 computer-based; 90 iBT). Electronic applications accepted. *Faculty research:* Golden Age Spanish literature, Modern Spanish literature, modern Latin American literature, linguistics and Hispanic cultural studies.

Rider University, Department of Graduate Education, Leadership and Counseling, Teacher Certification Program, Lawrenceville, NJ 08648-3001. Offers business education (Certificate); elementary education (Certificate); English as a second language (Certificate); English education (Certificate); mathematics education (Certificate); preschool to grade 3 (Certificate); science education (Certificate); social studies education (Certificate); world languages (Certificate), including French, German, Spanish. Part-time programs available. *Degree requirements:* For Certificate, internship, professional portfolio. *Entrance requirements:* For degree, PRAXIS, resumé. Additional exam requirements/recommendations for international students: Required—TOEFL (minimum score 550 paper-based; 213 computer-based). Electronic applications accepted. *Faculty research:* Conceptual foundations for optimal development of creativity; creative theory, cognitive processes in mathematics learning, teacher collaboration.

Roosevelt University, Graduate Division, College of Arts and Sciences, Department of Literature and Languages, Program in Spanish, Chicago, IL 60605-1394. Offers MA. Part-time and evening/weekend programs available. *Students:* 13 part-time (9 women); includes 4 minority (1 African American, 3 Hispanic Americans). Average age 36. 14 applicants, 57% accepted, 5 enrolled. In 2008, 5 master's awarded. *Degree requirements:* For master's, variable foreign language requirement, thesis or alternative. *Entrance requirements:* For master's, BA in Spanish or the equivalent. *Application deadline:* For fall admission, 6/1 priority date for domestic students. Applications are processed on a rolling basis. Application fee: $25 ($35 for international students). *Expenses:* Tuition: Full-time $14,730; part-time $709 per credit. Required fees: $175 per semester. Tuition and fees vary according to course load and program. *Financial support:* Scholarships/grants available. Financial award application deadline: 2/15. *Faculty research:* Latin American narrative, feminism, Hispanic cultures, twentieth century

Hispanic literature, Latino studies. *Unit head:* Priscilla Archibald, Chair, 312-341-3670. *Application contact:* Joanne Canyon-Heller, Coordinator of Graduate Admission, 877-APPLY RU, Fax: 312-281-3356, E-mail: applyru@roosevelt.edu.

Rutgers, The State University of New Jersey, New Brunswick, Graduate School, Program in Spanish, Piscataway, NJ 08854-8097. Offers bilingualism and second language acquisition (MA, PhD); Spanish (MA, MAT, PhD); Spanish literature (MA, PhD); translation (MA). Part-time programs available. *Degree requirements:* For master's, comprehensive exam (for some programs), thesis (for some programs); for doctorate, 2 foreign languages, comprehensive exam, thesis/dissertation. *Entrance requirements:* For master's and doctorate, GRE General Test. Additional exam requirements/recommendations for international students: Required—TOEFL. Electronic applications accepted. *Faculty research:* Hispanic literature, Luso-Brazilian literature, Spanish linguistics, Spanish translation.

St. John's University, St. John's College of Liberal Arts and Sciences, Department of Languages and Literatures, Queens, NY 11439. Offers languages and literatures (Adv C); Spanish (MA). Part-time and evening/weekend programs available. *Students:* 3 full-time (1 woman), 9 part-time (8 women); includes 9 minority (1 African American, 8 Hispanic Americans), 1 international. Average age 29. 9 applicants, 89% accepted, 4 enrolled. In 2008, 10 master's awarded. *Degree requirements:* For master's, thesis optional. *Entrance requirements:* For master's, 24 credits of undergraduate course work in languages with 18 credits in Spanish, minimum GPA of 3.0. Additional exam requirements/recommendations for international students: Required—TOEFL (minimum score 500 paper-based; 173 computer-based; 61 iBT), IELTS (minimum score 5.5). *Application deadline:* For fall admission, 5/1 priority date for domestic and international students; for spring admission, 11/1 priority date for domestic and international students. Applications are processed on a rolling basis. Application fee: $70. Electronic applications accepted. *Expenses:* Tuition: Full-time $20,760; part-time $865 per credit. Required fees: $300; $150 per semester. Tuition and fees vary according to program. *Financial support:* Research assistantships, scholarships/grants available. Support available to part-time students. Financial award application deadline: 3/1; financial award applicants required to submit FAFSA. *Unit head:* Dr. Nicholas J. Toscano, Chair, 718-990-5250, E-mail: toscanon@stjohns.edu. *Application contact:* Kathleen Davis, Director of Graduate Admission, 718-990-2790, Fax: 718-990-5686, E-mail: gradhelp@stjohns.edu.

Saint Louis University, Graduate School, College of Arts and Sciences and Graduate School, Department of Modern and Classical Languages, St. Louis, MO 63103-2097. Offers French (MA); Spanish (MA). Part-time programs available. *Degree requirements:* For master's, one foreign language, comprehensive exam, thesis/dissertation (for Spanish). *Entrance requirements:* For master's, GRE General Test or MAT, letters of recommendation, resumé, interview, transcripts, goal statement. Additional exam requirements/recommendations for international students: Required—TOEFL (minimum score 525 paper-based; 194 computer-based). Electronic applications accepted. *Faculty research:* Culture studies, literature studies, foreign language acquisition.

Saint Louis University–Madrid Campus, Graduate Programs, Program in Spanish Language and Literature, Madrid, Spain. Offers MA. Part-time programs available. *Faculty:* 6 full-time (4 women), 4 part-time/adjunct (3 women). *Students:* 12 full-time (11 women), 8 part-time (6 women). 14 applicants, 71% accepted, 6 enrolled. In 2008, 6 master's awarded. *Degree requirements:* For master's, one foreign language, comprehensive exam, thesis optional. *Entrance requirements:* For master's, GRE General Test or MAT, 3 letters of recommendation, curriculum vitae, writing sample. *Application deadline:* For fall admission, 5/30 for domestic and international students; for spring admission, 10/30 for domestic and international students. Applications are processed on a rolling basis. Application fee: $40. Tuition and fees charges are reported in euros. *Expenses:* Tuition: Full-time 4920 euros; part-time 410 euros per credit. One-time fee: 200 euros. Tuition and fees vary according to course load. *Financial support:* In 2008–09, 1 student received support, including 2 research assistantships with partial tuition reimbursements available (averaging $2,000 per year); teaching assistantships, career-related internships or fieldwork, Federal Work-Study, scholarships/grants, health care benefits, and unspecified assistantships also available. Financial award application deadline: 5/30; financial award applicants required to submit FAFSA. *Faculty research:* Spanish and Latin American literature, linguistics, cultural studies, gender studies. *Unit head:* Dr. Angeles Encinar, Chair, 34-91-554-58-58 Ext. 219, Fax: 34-91-554-62-02, E-mail: encinara@madrid.sluiberica.slu.edu. *Application contact:* Stephanie Reina, Graduate Programs Coordinator and Admissions Counselor, 34-91-554-58-58, Fax: 34-91-554-62-02, E-mail: graduate_admissions@madrid.slu.edu.

See Close-Up on page 441.

Salem State College, School of Graduate Studies, Program in Spanish, Salem, MA 01970-5353. Offers MAT. Part-time and evening/weekend programs available. *Students:* 3 full-time (2 women), 26 part-time (24 women); includes 1 minority (Hispanic American). Average age 33. In 2008, 4 master's awarded. Application fee: $35. *Unit head:* Dr. Nicole Sherf, Coordinator, 978-542-6468, E-mail: nsherf@salemstate.edu. *Application contact:* Dr. Marc Glasser, Dean of the Graduate School, 978-542-6323, Fax: 978-542-7215.

San Diego State University, Graduate and Research Affairs, College of Arts and Letters, Department of Spanish and Portuguese Languages and Literatures, San Diego, CA 92182. Offers Spanish (MA). *Degree requirements:* For master's, one foreign language. *Entrance requirements:* For master's, GRE General Test, 3 letters of reference. Additional exam requirements/recommendations for international students: Required—TOEFL. Electronic applications accepted. *Faculty research:* New strategies for teaching foreign languages.

San Francisco State University, Division of Graduate Studies, College of Humanities, Department of Foreign Languages and Literatures, Program in Spanish, San Francisco, CA 94132-1722. Offers MA. Part-time programs available. Electronic applications accepted.

San Jose State University, Graduate Studies and Research, College of Humanities and the Arts, Department of Foreign Languages, Program in Spanish, San Jose, CA 95192-0001. Offers MA. *Degree requirements:* For master's, 2 foreign languages, thesis or alternative. Electronic applications accepted.

Simmons College, College of Arts and Sciences Graduate Studies, Program in Spanish, Boston, MA 02115. Offers MA, MAT/MA. Part-time programs available. *Faculty:* 4 full-time (all women). *Students:* 3 full-time (all women), 2 part-time (both women); includes 2 minority (1 Asian American or Pacific Islander, 1 Hispanic American). Average age 25. 7 applicants, 0% accepted, 0 enrolled. In 2008, 4 master's awarded. *Degree requirements:* For master's, one foreign language. *Entrance requirements:* For master's, analytical writing samples in Spanish. Additional exam requirements/recommendations for international students: Required—TOEFL (minimum score 600 paper-based; 250 computer-based; 100 iBT). *Application deadline:* For fall admission, 8/1 priority date for domestic and international students; for winter admission, 12/15 priority date for domestic and international students; for spring admission, 5/1 priority date for domestic and international students. Applications are processed on a rolling basis. Application fee: $35. Electronic applications accepted. *Financial support:* In 2008–09, 1 student received support. Scholarships/grants and unspecified assistantships available. Financial award application deadline: 3/1; financial award applicants required to submit FAFSA. *Faculty research:* Latin American contemporary fiction, women writers, medieval Spanish literature, Golden Age Spanish literature, contemporary Spanish literature. *Unit head:* Dr. Raquel Maria Halty, Professor of Spanish & Director, Graduate Program in Spanish, 617-521-2182, Fax: 617-521-3090, E-mail: raquel.halty@simmons.edu. *Application contact:* Kristen Haack, Director, Graduate Studies Admission, 617-521-2917, Fax: 617-521-3058, E-mail: gsa@simmons.edu.

Stanford University, School of Humanities and Sciences, Department of Spanish and Portuguese, Stanford, CA 94305-9991. Offers Spanish (MA, PhD). Terminal master's awarded for partial completion of doctoral program. *Degree requirements:* For master's, 2 foreign languages; for doctorate, 3 foreign languages, thesis/dissertation, oral exam. *Entrance*

requirements: For master's and doctorate, GRE General Test. Additional exam requirements/recommendations for international students: Required—TOEFL. Electronic applications accepted.

State University of New York at Binghamton, Graduate School, School of Arts and Sciences, Department of Romance Languages and Literatures, Program in Spanish, Binghamton, NY 13902-6000. Offers Spanish (MA); translation (Certificate). *Students:* 5 full-time (4 women), 1 (woman) part-time; includes 1 minority (Hispanic American), 1 international. Average age 24. 5 applicants, 80% accepted, 4 enrolled. In 2008, 4 master's awarded. *Degree requirements:* For master's, one foreign language, comprehensive exam, thesis or alternative. *Entrance requirements:* For master's, GRE General Test, GRE Subject Test. Additional exam requirements/recommendations for international students: Required—TOEFL. *Application deadline:* For fall admission, 4/15 priority date for domestic students, 1/15 priority date for international students; for spring admission, 11/1 for domestic students, 10/1 priority date for international students. Applications are processed on a rolling basis. Application fee: $60. Electronic applications accepted. *Expenses:* Tuition, area resident: Full-time $6900; part-time $288 per credit. Tuition, state resident: full-time $6900; part-time $288 per credit. Tuition, nonresident: full-time $10,920; part-time $455 per credit. Required fees: $1130. Part-time tuition and fees vary according to course load, program and student level. *Financial support:* Fellowships, research assistantships, teaching assistantships, career-related internships or fieldwork, Federal Work-Study, institutionally sponsored loans, scholarships/grants, health care benefits, and unspecified assistantships available. Financial award application deadline: 2/15; financial award applicants required to submit FAFSA. *Unit head:* Dr. Antonio Sobejano-Moran, Chairperson, 607-777-4635, E-mail: antobianco@msn.com. *Application contact:* Victoria Williams, Recruiting and Admissions Coordinator, 607-777-2151, Fax: 607-777-2501, E-mail: vwilliam@binghamton.edu.

Syracuse University, Graduate School, College of Arts and Sciences, Program in Spanish Language, Literature and Culture, Syracuse, NY 13244. Offers MA. Part-time programs available. *Entrance requirements:* For master's, GRE General Test. Additional exam requirements/recommendations for international students: Required—TOEFL. Electronic applications accepted.

Temple University, Graduate School, College of Liberal Arts, Department of Spanish and Portuguese, Philadelphia, PA 19122-6096. Offers Spanish (MA, PhD). Part-time and evening/weekend programs available. Terminal master's awarded for partial completion of doctoral program. *Degree requirements:* For master's, one foreign language; for doctorate, 2 foreign languages, thesis/dissertation. *Entrance requirements:* For master's and doctorate, GRE General Test, minimum GPA of 3.0. Additional exam requirements/recommendations for international students: Required—TOEFL (minimum score 550 paper-based; 213 computer-based; 79 iBT). Electronic applications accepted. *Faculty research:* Spanish American literature, Spanish Peninsular literature, Hispanic linguistics.

Texas A&M International University, Office of Graduate Studies and Research, College of Arts and Sciences, Department of Language and Literature, Laredo, TX 78041-1900. Offers English (MA); Hispanic studies (PhD); Spanish (MA). *Entrance requirements:* For master's, GRE General Test. Additional exam requirements/recommendations for international students: Required—TOEFL (minimum score 550 paper-based; 213 computer-based).

Texas A&M University, College of Liberal Arts, Department of Hispanic Studies, College Station, TX 77843. Offers MA, PhD. *Faculty:* 11. *Students:* 27 full-time (13 women), 16 part-time (15 women); includes 21 minority (1 Asian American or Pacific Islander, 20 Hispanic Americans), 5 international. In 2008, 2 master's, 1 doctorate awarded. *Expenses:* Tuition, area resident: full-time $3838.50. Tuition, state resident: full-time $3838.50. Tuition, nonresident: full-time $8897. Required fees: $2359.60. *Unit head:* Larry Mitchell, Head, 979-845-2164, E-mail: j-mitchell@tamu.edu. *Application contact:* Dr., Associate Dean.

Texas A&M University–Commerce, Graduate School, College of Arts and Sciences, Department of Literature and Languages, Commerce, TX 75429-3011. Offers college teaching of English (PhD); English (MA, MS); Spanish (MA). Part-time programs available. Terminal master's awarded for partial completion of doctoral program. *Degree requirements:* For master's, comprehensive exam, thesis (for some programs); for doctorate, one foreign language, thesis/dissertation, departmental qualifying exam. *Entrance requirements:* For master's and doctorate, GRE General Test. Electronic applications accepted. *Faculty research:* Latino literature, American film studies, ethnographic research, Willa Carter.

Texas A&M University–Kingsville, College of Graduate Studies, College of Arts and Sciences, Department of Language and Literature, Kingsville, TX 78363. Offers English (MA, MS); Spanish (MA). Part-time and evening/weekend programs available. *Degree requirements:* For master's, comprehensive exam, thesis or alternative. *Entrance requirements:* For master's, GRE General Test, minimum GPA of 3.0. Additional exam requirements/recommendations for international students: Required—TOEFL. *Faculty research:* Linguistics, culture, Spanish American literature, Spanish peninsular literature, American literature.

Texas State University–San Marcos, Graduate School, College of Liberal Arts, Department of Modern Languages, Program in Spanish, San Marcos, TX 78666. Offers MA. Part-time and evening/weekend programs available. *Degree requirements:* For master's, one foreign language, comprehensive exam, internship (MAT), thesis (MA). *Entrance requirements:* For master's, minimum GPA of 3.0 in last 12 undergraduate hours of advanced Spanish with 6 hours in literature. Additional exam requirements/recommendations for international students: Required—TOEFL (minimum score 550 paper-based; 213 computer-based). Electronic applications accepted. *Faculty research:* Hispanic literature, linguistics, literary theory, computer-assisted language instruction, Hispanic philology.

Texas Tech University, Graduate School, College of Arts and Sciences, Department of Classical and Modern Languages and Literatures, Program in Romance Languages-Spanish, Lubbock, TX 79409. Offers MA, PhD. Part-time programs available. *Students:* 21 full-time (12 women), 11 part-time (7 women); includes 11 minority (all Hispanic Americans), 7 international. Average age 39. 14 applicants, 50% accepted, 3 enrolled. In 2008, 2 doctorates awarded. *Degree requirements:* For master's, one foreign language, thesis optional; for doctorate, one foreign language, comprehensive exam, thesis/dissertation. *Entrance requirements:* For master's and doctorate, GRE General Test. Additional exam requirements/recommendations for international students: Required—TOEFL (minimum score 550 paper-based; 213 computer-based). *Application deadline:* For fall admission, 3/1 priority date for international students; for spring admission, 11/1 priority date for international students. Applications are processed on a rolling basis. Application fee: $50 ($60 for international students). Electronic applications accepted. *Expenses:* Tuition, area resident: Part-time $194 per credit hour. Tuition, state resident: full-time $4648; part-time $194 per credit hour. Tuition, nonresident: full-time $11,392; part-time $475 per credit hour. Required fees: $2206; $69 per credit hour. $389 per semester. *Financial support:* Research assistantships with partial tuition reimbursements, teaching assistantships with partial tuition reimbursements available. Financial award application deadline: 4/15. *Faculty research:* Peninsular literature, Latin-American literature, Portuguese language and literature, Spanish linguistics. *Unit head:* Dr. Genaro Perez, Professor and Graduate Advisor of Spanish, 806-742-3145 Ext. 281, Fax: 806-742-3306, E-mail: genaro.perez@ttu.edu. *Application contact:* Dr. Genaro Perez, Professor and Graduate Advisor of Spanish, 806-742-3145 Ext. 281, Fax: 806-742-3306, E-mail: genaro.perez@ttu.edu.

Tulane University, School of Liberal Arts, Department of Spanish and Portuguese, New Orleans, LA 70118-5669. Offers Portuguese (MA); Spanish (MA); Spanish and Portuguese (PhD). *Degree requirements:* For master's, 2 foreign languages; for doctorate, 2 foreign languages, thesis/dissertation. *Entrance requirements:* For master's, GRE General Test, minimum B average in undergraduate course work; for doctorate, GRE General Test. Additional exam requirements/recommendations for international students: Required—TOEFL. Electronic applications accepted.

Universidad Adventista de las Antillas, EGECED Department, Mayagüez, PR 00681-0118. Offers curriculum and instruction (MA), including elementary, secondary biology, secondary

Spanish

Universidad Adventista de las Antillas (continued)
history, secondary Spanish; education (MA), including ESL (elementary school level), ESL (high school level), school administration and supervision. *Degree requirements:* For master's, comprehensive exam (for some programs), thesis (for some programs). *Entrance requirements:* For master's, EXADEP or GRE, recommendations, transcripts (original). Electronic applications accepted.

Universidad Autonoma de Guadalajara, Graduate Programs, Guadalajara, Mexico. Offers advertising and corporate communications (MA); architecture (M Arch); business (MBA); computational science (MCC); education (Ed M, Ed D); English-Spanish translation (MA); fiscal law (MA); international business (MIB); international corporate law (LL M); internet technologies (MS); labor health (MS); manufacturing systems (MMS); market research (MBA); philosophy (MA, PhD); quality systems (MQS); renewable energy (MS); teaching mathematics (MA).

Université de Montréal, Faculty of Arts and Sciences, Department of Literatures and Modern Languages, Program in Hispanic Studies, Montréal, QC H3C 3J7, Canada. Offers MA. *Students:* 16 full-time (13 women), 16 part-time (11 women). 10 applicants, 40% accepted, 4 enrolled. In 2008, 9 master's awarded. *Degree requirements:* For master's, 2 foreign languages, thesis. *Application deadline:* For fall admission, 2/1 priority date for domestic students; for winter admission, 11/1 priority date for domestic students; for spring admission, 2/1 priority date for domestic students. Application fee: $100. Electronic applications accepted. *Financial support:* Research assistantships, teaching assistantships, scholarships/grants available. *Faculty research:* Spanish literature and culture, Latin American literature and culture. *Unit head:* Javier Rubiera, Responsible, 514-343-5892, Fax: 514-343-2255, E-mail: javier.rubiera@umontreal.ca. *Application contact:* Javier Rubiera, Responsible, 514-343-5892, Fax: 514-343-2255, E-mail: javier.rubiera@umontreal.ca.

Université Laval, Faculty of Letters, Department of Literature, Programs in Spanish Literatures, Québec, QC G1K 7P4, Canada. Offers MA, PhD. Part-time programs available. Terminal master's awarded for partial completion of doctoral program. *Degree requirements:* For master's, thesis; for doctorate, comprehensive exam, thesis/dissertation. *Entrance requirements:* For master's and doctorate, linguistics exams, knowledge of French and Spanish. Electronic applications accepted.

University at Albany, State University of New York, College of Arts and Sciences, Department of Languages, Literatures, and Cultures, Program in Spanish, Albany, NY 12222-0001. Offers MA, PhD. *Degree requirements:* For doctorate, thesis/dissertation. *Entrance requirements:* For doctorate, GRE General Test.

University at Buffalo, the State University of New York, Graduate School, College of Arts and Sciences, Department of Romance Languages and Literatures, Buffalo, NY 14260. Offers French (MA, PhD); Spanish (MA, PhD). Part-time programs available. Terminal master's awarded for partial completion of doctoral program. *Degree requirements:* For master's, one foreign language, project; for doctorate, 2 foreign languages, thesis/dissertation. *Entrance requirements:* For master's and doctorate, GRE. Additional exam requirements/recommendations for international students: Required—TOEFL (minimum score 550 paper-based; 213 computer-based; 79 iBT). Electronic applications accepted. *Faculty research:* Romance linguistics, cultural studies, literary studies, literature and philosophy.

The University of Akron, Graduate School, Buchtel College of Arts and Sciences, Department of Modern Languages, Program in Spanish, Akron, OH 44325. Offers MA. Part-time and evening/weekend programs available. *Degree requirements:* For master's, one foreign language, comprehensive exam, thesis optional, oral exam, essay, research paper. *Entrance requirements:* For master's, interview, minimum GPA of 3.0, proficiency in Spanish, letters of recommendation. Additional exam requirements/recommendations for international students: Required—TOEFL (minimum score 550 paper-based; 213 computer-based; 79 iBT). Electronic applications accepted.

The University of Alabama, Graduate School, College of Arts and Sciences, Department of Modern Languages and Classics, Tuscaloosa, AL 35487. Offers French (MA, PhD); French and Spanish (PhD); German (MA); Romance languages (MA, PhD); Spanish (MA, PhD). Part-time programs available. *Faculty:* 21 full-time (11 women). *Students:* 45 full-time (35 women), 12 part-time (7 women); includes 13 minority (6 African Americans, 7 Hispanic Americans), 11 international. Average age 32. 25 applicants, 68% accepted, 11 enrolled. In 2008, 17 master's, 4 doctorates awarded. *Degree requirements:* For master's, comprehensive exam, thesis optional; for doctorate, one foreign language, thesis/dissertation, preliminary exam. *Entrance requirements:* For master's and doctorate, minimum GPA of 3.0, writing sample. Additional exam requirements/recommendations for international students: Required—TOEFL or IELTS. *Application deadline:* For fall admission, 7/6 priority date for domestic students, 1/15 priority date for international students; for spring admission, 12/6 priority date for domestic students, 6/1 priority date for international students. Applications are processed on a rolling basis. Application fee: $31. Electronic applications accepted. *Expenses:* Tuition, area resident: Full-time $6400. Tuition, state resident: Full-time $6400. Tuition, nonresident: full-time $18,000. *Financial support:* In 2008–09, 7 students received support, including 1 fellowship, research assistantships with full tuition reimbursements available (averaging $10,291 per year), 6 teaching assistantships with full tuition reimbursements available (averaging $10,291 per year); career-related internships or fieldwork, Federal Work-Study, institutionally sponsored loans, and scholarships/grants also available. Financial award application deadline: 7/14. *Faculty research:* Non-English literature, linguistics, culture, film. Total annual research expenditures: $9,630. *Unit head:* Dr. Michael Picone, Chair and Professor, 205-348-5054, Fax: 205-348-2042, E-mail: mpicone@bama.ua.edu. *Application contact:* Dr. K. Barbara Fischer, Graduate Director and Associate Professor, 205-348-8465, Fax: 205-348-2042, E-mail: bfischer@bama.ua.edu.

The University of Arizona, Graduate College, College of Humanities, Department of Spanish and Portuguese, Tucson, AZ 85721. Offers Spanish (M Ed, MA, PhD). Terminal master's awarded for partial completion of doctoral program. *Degree requirements:* For master's, one foreign language, comprehensive exam, thesis optional; for doctorate, 3 foreign languages, comprehensive exam, thesis/dissertation. *Entrance requirements:* For master's, GRE General Test, BA in Spanish, minimum GPA of 3.3, writing sample, 3 letters of recommendation, statement of purpose; for doctorate, GRE General Test, BA in Spanish, writing sample, minimum GPA of 3.4, 3 letters of recommendation, statement of purpose. Additional exam requirements/recommendations for international students: Required—TOEFL (minimum score 550 paper-based; 213 computer-based). *Faculty research:* Spanish and Latin American literature and linguistics, literary theory.

University of Arkansas, Graduate School, J. William Fulbright College of Arts and Sciences, Department of Foreign Languages, Program in Spanish, Fayetteville, AR 72701-1201. Offers MA. *Degree requirements:* For master's, one foreign language, comprehensive exam, thesis optional. *Entrance requirements:* Additional exam requirements/recommendations for international students: Required—TOEFL (minimum score 550 paper-based; 213 computer-based), IELTS (minimum score 6.5). Electronic applications accepted. *Faculty research:* Medieval and Golden Age poetry, colonial Latin America, contemporary Latin America.

University of California, Berkeley, Graduate Division, College of Letters and Science, Department of Hispanic Languages and Literature, Berkeley, CA 94720-1500. Offers PhD. *Degree requirements:* For doctorate, thesis/dissertation, qualifying exam. *Entrance requirements:* For doctorate, GRE General Test, minimum GPA of 3.0, 3 letters of recommendation. Additional exam requirements/recommendations for international students: Required—TOEFL (minimum score 570 paper-based; 230 computer-based).

University of California, Berkeley, Graduate Division, Group in Romance Languages and Literature, Program in Spanish, Berkeley, CA 94720-1500. Offers PhD. *Entrance requirements:* For doctorate, GRE General Test, 3 letters of recommendation.

University of California, Davis, Graduate Studies, Program in Spanish, Davis, CA 95616. Offers MA, PhD. Terminal master's awarded for partial completion of doctoral program. *Degree requirements:* For master's, comprehensive exam (for some programs), thesis (for some programs); for doctorate, 2 foreign languages, thesis/dissertation. *Entrance requirements:* For master's, GRE General Test, minimum GPA of 3.0; for doctorate, GRE General Test, master's degree, minimum GPA of 3.0. Additional exam requirements/recommendations for international students: Required—TOEFL (minimum score 550 paper-based; 213 computer-based). *Faculty research:* Medieval Spanish language and literature, Spanish linguistics, Latin American literature, nineteenth century Peninsular literature.

University of California, Irvine, Office of Graduate Studies, School of Humanities, Department of Spanish and Portuguese, Irvine, CA 92697. Offers Spanish (MA, MAT, PhD). *Degree requirements:* For doctorate, thesis/dissertation. *Entrance requirements:* For master's and doctorate, GRE General Test, minimum GPA of 3.0. Additional exam requirements/recommendations for international students: Required—TOEFL (minimum score 550 paper-based; 213 computer-based). Electronic applications accepted. *Faculty research:* Latin American literature, Spanish literature, Spanish linguistics in Creole studies, Hispanic literature in the U.S., Luso-Brazilian literature.

University of California, Los Angeles, Graduate Division, College of Letters and Science, Department of Spanish and Portuguese, Program in Spanish, Los Angeles, CA 90095. Offers MA. *Students:* 5 full-time. 32 applicants, 16% accepted, 3 enrolled. In 2008, 6 master's awarded. Terminal master's awarded for partial completion of doctoral program. *Degree requirements:* For master's, one foreign language, comprehensive exam or thesis. *Entrance requirements:* For master's, GRE General Test, minimum GPA of 3.0, sample of written work (recommended). *Application deadline:* For fall admission, 12/31 for domestic and international students. Application fee: $60. Electronic applications accepted. *Expenses:* Tuition, nonresident: full-time $14,694. Required fees: $9669.50. Full-time tuition and fees vary according to course load, degree level, program and student level. *Financial support:* In 2008–09, 2 fellowships with full and partial tuition reimbursements, 3 teaching assistantships with full and partial tuition reimbursements were awarded; research assistantships with full and partial tuition reimbursements, Federal Work-Study, institutionally sponsored loans, scholarships/grants, health care benefits, tuition waivers (full and partial), and unspecified assistantships also available. Financial award applicants required to submit FAFSA. *Unit head:* Dr. Ruiz Teofilo, Chair, 310-825-1036. *Application contact:* Departmental Office, 310-825-1036, E-mail: peinado@humnet.ucla.edu.

University of California, Riverside, Graduate Division, Department of Hispanic Studies, Riverside, CA 92521-0102. Offers Spanish (MA, PhD). *Faculty:* 8 full-time (3 women). *Students:* 23 full-time (14 women); includes 18 minority (all Hispanic Americans), 2 international. Average age 34. 14 applicants, 21% accepted, 3 enrolled. In 2008, 6 master's, 1 doctorate awarded. Terminal master's awarded for partial completion of doctoral program. *Degree requirements:* For master's, one foreign language, comprehensive exam; for doctorate, one foreign language, thesis/dissertation, qualifying exams, 1 quarter of teaching experience. *Entrance requirements:* For master's and doctorate, GRE General Test, minimum GPA of 3.2. Additional exam requirements/recommendations for international students: Required—TOEFL (minimum score 550 paper-based; 213 computer-based; 80 iBT). *Application deadline:* For fall admission, 1/5 for domestic students, 2/1 for international students; for winter admission, 9/1 for domestic students, 7/1 for international students; for spring admission, 12/1 for domestic students, 10/1 for international students. Applications are processed on a rolling basis. Application fee: $60 ($75 for international students). Electronic applications accepted. *Expenses:* Tuition, nonresident: full-time $4898. Required fees: $10,362. *Financial support:* In 2008–09, fellowships with tuition reimbursements (averaging $12,000 per year), teaching assistantships with tuition reimbursements (averaging $16,500 per year) were awarded; career-related internships or fieldwork, Federal Work-Study, institutionally sponsored loans, scholarships/grants, health care benefits, and tuition waivers (full and partial) also available. Financial award application deadline: 1/5; financial award applicants required to submit FAFSA. *Faculty research:* Spanish literature of sixteenth, seventeenth and twentieth century; pre-Columbian and colonial Latin American literature; nineteenth and twentieth century Latin American literature. *Unit head:* Dr. David E. Hevzberger, Chair, 951-827-5007 Ext. 11462, Fax: 951-827-2160, E-mail: david.herzberger@ucr.edu. *Application contact:* Dr. Benjamin Liu, Graduate Advisor, 951-827-1569, Fax: 951-827-2294, E-mail: clhsgrad@ucr.edu.

University of California, San Diego, Office of Graduate Studies, Department of Literature, Program in Spanish Literature, La Jolla, CA 92093. Offers MA. *Degree requirements:* For master's, thesis. *Entrance requirements:* For master's, GRE General Test, GRE Subject Test. Electronic applications accepted.

University of California, Santa Barbara, Graduate Division, College of Letters and Sciences, Division of Humanities and Fine Arts, Department of Spanish and Portuguese, Santa Barbara, CA 93106-4150. Offers Hispanic languages and literature (PhD), including applied linguistics, European Medieval studies, feminist studies, Hispanic languages and literature; Portuguese (MA); Spanish (MA); Spanish and Portuguese (MA); MA/PhD. Spanish Language Institute available during summer session. *Faculty:* 16 full-time (6 women). *Students:* 29 full-time (16 women). Average age 30. 46 applicants, 39% accepted, 9 enrolled. In 2008, 4 master's, 2 doctorates awarded. *Degree requirements:* For master's, 2 foreign languages, comprehensive exam (for some programs), thesis optional; for doctorate, 2 foreign languages, comprehensive exam, thesis/dissertation. *Entrance requirements:* For master's, GRE, 2 writing samples, undergraduate major in Spanish or equivalent, 3 letters of recommendation, statement of purpose, personal achievements/contributions statement, resumé/curriculum vitae, transcripts for post-secondary institutions attended; for doctorate, GRE, 2 writing samples, master's degree, 3 letters of recommendation, statement of purpose, personal achievements/contributions statement, resumé/curriculum vitae, transcripts for post-secondary institutions attended. Additional exam requirements/recommendations for international students: Required—TOEFL (minimum score 550 paper-based; 213 computer-based; 80 iBT), IELTS (minimum score 7), TOEFL or IELTS. *Application deadline:* For fall admission, 3/1 for domestic and international students; for winter admission, 11/1 for domestic and international students; for spring admission, 2/1 for domestic and international students. Application fee: $70 ($90 for international students). Electronic applications accepted. *Expenses:* Tuition, nonresident: full-time $25,149. Required fees: $10,143. Full-time tuition and fees vary according to campus/location, reciprocity agreements and student level. *Financial support:* In 2008–09, 30 students received support, including 9 fellowships with full and partial tuition reimbursements available (averaging $7,000 per year), 29 teaching assistantships with partial tuition reimbursements available (averaging $11,500 per year); career-related internships or fieldwork, Federal Work-Study, institutionally sponsored loans, scholarships/grants, health care benefits, tuition waivers (full and partial), and unspecified assistantships also available. Financial award application deadline: 1/7; financial award applicants required to submit FAFSA. *Faculty research:* 19th century Spanish and Portuguese literature, Spanish and Spanish American literature, 19th and 20th century Portuguese and Brazilian literatures, Hispanic Linguistics, Catalan language and culture. *Unit head:* Prof. Francisco A. Lomeli, Chair, 805-893-5715, Fax: 805-893-8341, E-mail: lomeli@spanport.ucsb.edu. *Application contact:* Carol Conley, Graduate Program Assistant, 805-893-3162, Fax: 805-893-8341, E-mail: cconley@spanport.ucsb.edu.

University of California, Santa Barbara, Summer Sessions, Santa Barbara, CA 93106-2010. Offers French (MA); Spanish (MA). In 2008, 17 master's awarded. *Degree requirements:* For master's, comprehensive exam (for some programs). *Entrance requirements:* For master's, GRE, 3 letters of recommendation, statement of purpose, personal achievements/contributions statement, resumé/curriculum vitae, transcripts for post-secondary institutions attended. Additional exam requirements/recommendations for international students: Required—TOEFL (paper: 550, computer: 213, IBT: 80) or IELTS (7). Application fee: $70 ($90 for international students). Electronic applications accepted. *Expenses:* Contact institution. *Financial support:* Scholarships/grants available. Financial award applicants required to submit FAFSA. *Unit head:* Dr. Loy Lytle, Dean of Summer Sessions, 805-893-2706, Fax: 805-893-7306, E-mail: low.lytle@els.ucsb.edu. *Application contact:* Program Manager, 805-893-7053, Fax: 805-893-7306, E-mail: language.institutes@summersessions.ucsb.edu.

University of Central Florida, College of Arts and Humanities, Department of Modern Languages and Literatures, Program in Spanish, Orlando, FL 32816. Offers MA. Part-time and evening/weekend programs available. *Students:* 4 full-time (3 women), 17 part-time (13 women); includes 17 minority (all Hispanic Americans). In 2008, 7 master's awarded. *Degree requirements:* For master's, one foreign language, comprehensive exam, thesis or alternative. *Entrance requirements:* For master's, GRE General Test, minimum GPA of 3.0 in last 60 hours. Additional exam requirements/recommendations for international students: Required—TOEFL. *Application deadline:* For fall admission, 6/1 for domestic students; for spring admission, 12/1 for domestic students. Application fee: $30. Electronic applications accepted. *Expenses:* Tuition, area resident: Full-time $6816; part-time $284 per credit. Tuition, state resident: full-time $6816; part-time $1076 per credit. Tuition, nonresident: full-time $25,824. Required fees: $216; $9 per credit. *Financial support:* In 2008–09, 2 research assistantships with partial tuition reimbursements (averaging $6,800 per year), 2 teaching assistantships with partial tuition reimbursements (averaging $7,800 per year) were awarded; career-related internships or fieldwork, Federal Work-Study, institutionally sponsored loans, tuition waivers (partial), and unspecified assistantships also available. Financial award application deadline: 3/1; financial award applicants required to submit FAFSA.

University of Chicago, Division of the Humanities, Department of Romance Languages and Literatures, Chicago, IL 60637-1513. Offers French (AM, PhD); Italian (AM, PhD); Spanish (AM, PhD). Terminal master's awarded for partial completion of doctoral program. *Degree requirements:* For master's, 2 foreign languages, thesis; for doctorate, 3 foreign languages, thesis/dissertation. *Entrance requirements:* For master's and doctorate, GRE General Test, GRE Subject Test. Additional exam requirements/recommendations for international students: Required—TOEFL.

University of Cincinnati, Graduate School, McMicken College of Arts and Sciences, Department of Romance Languages and Literature, Program in Spanish, Cincinnati, OH 45221. Offers MA, PhD. Terminal master's awarded for partial completion of doctoral program. *Degree requirements:* For master's, thesis optional; for doctorate, 2 foreign languages, thesis/dissertation. *Entrance requirements:* For master's, minimum GPA of 3.0. Electronic applications accepted. *Faculty research:* Applied linguistics, Spanish essay, Latin American culture, women's studies, poetry.

University of Colorado at Boulder, Graduate School, College of Arts and Sciences, Department of Spanish and Portuguese, Boulder, CO 80309. Offers Hispanic linguistics (MA); medieval/early modern Hispanic literatures (PhD); Spanish literature (MA, PhD), including 18th and 19th century peninsular literature (MA), Golden Age (MA), medieval Iberian literature (MA). Part-time programs available. Terminal master's awarded for partial completion of doctoral program. *Degree requirements:* For master's, one foreign language, comprehensive exam, thesis or alternative; for doctorate, 2 foreign languages, thesis/dissertation. *Entrance requirements:* For master's, minimum undergraduate GPA of 2.75. *Faculty research:* Spanish peninsular and Spanish-American literatures; Hispanic linguistics; Medieval, Golden Age, eighteenth and nineteenth century literatures.

University of Colorado Denver, College of Liberal Arts and Sciences, Department of Modern Languages, Denver, CO 80217-3364. Offers Spanish (MA). *Entrance requirements:* For master's, GRE, minimum undergraduate GPA of 2.5, 3.0 in all Spanish courses. Additional exam requirements/recommendations for international students: Required—TOEFL.

University of Connecticut, Graduate School, College of Liberal Arts and Sciences, Department of Modern and Classical Languages, Field of Spanish, Storrs, CT 06269. Offers MA, PhD. Terminal master's awarded for partial completion of doctoral program. *Degree requirements:* For master's, one foreign language, comprehensive exam; for doctorate, 2 foreign languages, thesis/dissertation. *Entrance requirements:* For master's and doctorate, GRE General Test, GRE Subject Test. Additional exam requirements/recommendations for international students: Required—TOEFL (minimum score 550 paper-based; 213 computer-based). Electronic applications accepted.

University of Delaware, College of Arts and Sciences, Department of Foreign Languages and Literatures, Newark, DE 19716. Offers foreign languages and literatures (MA), including French, German, Spanish; foreign languages pedagogy (MA), including French, German, Spanish. *Degree requirements:* For master's, one foreign language, comprehensive exam, thesis optional. *Entrance requirements:* For master's, GRE General Test, letters of recommendation, writing sample. Additional exam requirements/recommendations for international students: Required—TOEFL. Electronic applications accepted. *Faculty research:* Medieval to Modern French and Spanish literature, Twentieth Century German, French, Spanish literature by women, computer-assisted instruction.

University of Florida, Graduate School, College of Liberal Arts and Sciences, Department of Romance Languages and Literatures, Program in Spanish, Gainesville, FL 32611. Offers MA, PhD. *Degree requirements:* For master's, one foreign language, thesis optional; for doctorate, one foreign language, thesis/dissertation. *Entrance requirements:* For master's and doctorate, GRE General Test, minimum GPA of 3.0. Additional exam requirements/recommendations for international students: Required—TOEFL (minimum score 550 paper-based; 213 computer-based). Electronic applications accepted. *Faculty research:* Peninsular literature, Latin American literature, Hispanic linguistics.

University of Georgia, Graduate School, College of Arts and Sciences, Department of Romance Languages, Program in Spanish, Athens, GA 30602. Offers MA, MAT. *Degree requirements:* For master's, one foreign language, thesis (MA). *Entrance requirements:* For master's, GRE General Test. Electronic applications accepted.

University of Hawaii at Manoa, Graduate Division, Colleges of Arts and Sciences, College of Language, Linguistics and Literature, Department of Languages and Literatures of Europe and the Americas, Program in Spanish, Honolulu, HI 96822. Offers MA. Part-time programs available. *Degree requirements:* For master's, one foreign language, thesis optional. *Entrance requirements:* For master's, GRE General Test. Additional exam requirements/recommendations for international students: Required—TOEFL (minimum score 580 paper-based; 237 computer-based; 92 iBT), IELTS (minimum score 5).

University of Houston, College of Liberal Arts and Social Sciences, Department of Modern and Classical Languages, Houston, TX 77204. Offers French (MA); Spanish (MA, PhD); MBA/MA. Part-time and evening/weekend programs available. Postbaccalaureate distance learning degree programs offered. *Faculty:* 8 full-time (5 women), 1 (woman) part-time/adjunct. *Students:* 27 full-time (21 women), 46 part-time (34 women); includes 48 minority (1 African American, 2 Asian Americans or Pacific Islanders, 45 Hispanic Americans), 7 international. Average age 38. 23 applicants, 83% accepted, 12 enrolled. In 2008, 11 master's, 4 doctorates awarded. Terminal master's awarded for partial completion of doctoral program. *Degree requirements:* For master's, one foreign language, thesis optional; for doctorate, 3 foreign languages, thesis/dissertation. *Entrance requirements:* For master's and doctorate, GRE General Test. Additional exam requirements/recommendations for international students: Required—TOEFL. *Application deadline:* For fall admission, 2/28 priority date for domestic students; for spring admission, 10/30 priority date for domestic students. Application fee: $25 ($75 for international students). *Expenses:* Tuition, state resident: full-time $5164; part-time $287 per credit. Tuition, nonresident: full-time $10,222; part-time $568 per credit. *Financial support:* In 2008–09, 5 research assistantships with full tuition reimbursements (averaging $10,600 per year), 18 teaching assistantships with full tuition reimbursements (averaging $10,600 per year) were awarded; career-related internships or fieldwork, Federal Work-Study, institutionally sponsored loans, scholarships/grants, health care benefits, and unspecified assistantships also available. Support available to part-time students. Financial award application deadline: 2/1; financial award applicants required to submit FAFSA. *Faculty research:* Hispanic literature and language in the U.S., Golden Age, women. *Unit head:* Dr. Marc Zimmerman, Chairperson, 713-743-3007, Fax: 713-743-0935, E-mail: mzimmerm@mail.uh.edu. *Application contact:* Debra Frazier, Graduate Analyst, 713-743-2991, Fax: 713-743-2990.

University of Illinois at Chicago, Graduate College, College of Liberal Arts and Sciences, Department of Spanish, French, Italian and Portuguese, Program in Hispanic Studies, Chicago, IL 60607-7128. Offers Hispanic linguistics (MA, PhD); Hispanic literary and cultural studies (MA, PhD). Part-time programs available. Terminal master's awarded for partial completion of doctoral program. *Degree requirements:* For master's, one foreign language, departmental qualifying exam. *Entrance requirements:* For master's, GRE General Test, minimum GPA of 2.75, undergraduate major in Spanish. Additional exam requirements/recommendations for international students: Required—TOEFL. Electronic applications accepted.

University of Illinois at Urbana–Champaign, Graduate College, College of Liberal Arts and Sciences, School of Literatures, Cultures and Linguistics, Department of Spanish, Italian and Portuguese, Champaign, IL 61820. Offers Italian (MA, PhD); Portuguese (MA, PhD); Spanish (MA, PhD). *Faculty:* 17 full-time (10 women), 1 part-time/adjunct (0 women). *Students:* 50 full-time (38 women), 7 part-time (6 women); includes 4 minority (all Hispanic Americans), 31 international. 55 applicants, 44% accepted, 14 enrolled. In 2008, 10 master's, 4 doctorates awarded. *Entrance requirements:* For master's, GRE General Test, minimum GPA of 3.0; writing sample; for doctorate, GRE, minimum GPA of 3.0; writing sample. Additional exam requirements/recommendations for international students: Required—TOEFL (minimum score 88 iBT). *Application deadline:* Applications are processed on a rolling basis. Application fee: $60 ($75 for international students). Electronic applications accepted. *Financial support:* In 2008–09, 15 fellowships, 1 research assistantship, 48 teaching assistantships were awarded; tuition waivers (full and partial) also available. *Unit head:* Diane Musumeci, Head, 217-244-3250, Fax: 217-244-8430, E-mail: musumeci@illinois.edu. *Application contact:* Lynn Stanke, Secretary, 217-333-6269, Fax: 217-244-3050, E-mail: stanke@illinois.edu.

The University of Iowa, Graduate College, College of Liberal Arts and Sciences, Department of Spanish and Portuguese, Iowa City, IA 52242-1316. Offers Spanish (MA, PhD). *Degree requirements:* For master's, thesis optional, exam; for doctorate, comprehensive exam, thesis/dissertation. *Entrance requirements:* For master's and doctorate, minimum GPA of 3.0. Additional exam requirements/recommendations for international students: Required—TOEFL (minimum score 600 paper-based; 250 computer-based; 100 iBT). Electronic applications accepted.

The University of Kansas, Graduate Studies, College of Liberal Arts and Sciences, Department of Spanish and Portuguese, Lawrence, KS 66045. Offers Spanish (MA, PhD). *Faculty:* 16. *Students:* 35 full-time (19 women), 1 (woman) part-time; includes 4 minority (all Hispanic Americans), 7 international. Average age 30. 25 applicants, 60% accepted, 7 enrolled. In 2008, 11 master's, 3 doctorates awarded. *Degree requirements:* For master's, 2 foreign languages; for doctorate, 3 foreign languages, thesis/dissertation. *Entrance requirements:* Additional exam requirements/recommendations for international students: Required—TOEFL. *Application deadline:* For fall admission, 5/15 priority date for domestic students, 12/15 priority date for international students; for spring admission, 10/15 priority date for domestic students, 5/15 priority date for international students. Applications are processed on a rolling basis. Application fee: $45 ($55 for international students). Electronic applications accepted. *Expenses:* Tuition, area resident: Full-time $6122; part-time $255.10 per credit hour. Tuition, state resident: full-time $6122; part-time $255.10 per credit hour. Tuition, nonresident: full-time $14,629; part-time $609.55 per credit hour. Required fees: $847; $70.56 per credit hour. Tuition and fees vary according to course load and program. *Financial support:* Fellowships with tuition reimbursements, research assistantships, teaching assistantships with full and partial tuition reimbursements, unspecified assistantships available. Financial award application deadline: 1/15. *Faculty research:* Latin American literary and cultural studies; medieval, early modern and contemporary Spanish literary and cultural studies. *Unit head:* Dr. Jill Kuhnheim, Chair, 785-864-3851, Fax: 785-864-4298, E-mail: spanport@ku.edu. *Application contact:* Rhonda Cook, Graduate Coordinator, 785-864-3851, Fax: 785-864-4298, E-mail: rcook@ku.edu.

University of Lethbridge, School of Graduate Studies, Lethbridge, AB T1K 3M4, Canada. Offers accounting (MScM); addictions counseling (M Sc); agricultural biotechnology (M Sc); agricultural studies (M Sc, MA); anthropology (MA); archaeology (MA); art (MA); biochemistry (M Sc); biological sciences (M Sc); biomolecular science (PhD); biosystems and biodiversity (PhD); Canadian studies (MA); chemistry (M Sc); computer science (M Sc); computer science and geographical information science (M Sc); counseling psychology (M Ed); dramatic arts (MA); earth, space, and physical science (PhD); economics (MA); educational leadership (M Ed); English (MA); environmental science (M Sc); evolution and behavior (PhD); exercise science (M Sc); finance (MScM); French (MA); French/German (MA); French/Spanish (MA); general education (M Ed); general management (MScM); geography (M Sc, MA); German (MA); health sciences (M Sc, MA); history (MA); human resource management and labour relations (MScM); individualized multidisciplinary (M Sc, MA); information systems (MScM); international management (MScM); kinesiology (M Sc, MA); management (M Sc, MA); marketing (MScM); mathematics (M Sc); music (MA); Native American studies (MA); neuroscience (M Sc, PhD); new media (MA); nursing (M Sc); philosophy (MA); physics (M Sc); policy and strategy (MScM); political science (MA); psychology (M Sc, MA); religious studies (MA); sociology (MA); theoretical and computational science (PhD); urban and regional studies (MA). Part-time and evening/weekend programs available. *Degree requirements:* For doctorate, comprehensive exam, thesis/dissertation. *Entrance requirements:* For master's, GMAT (M Sc in management), bachelor's degree in related field, minimum GPA of 3.0 during previous 20 graded semester courses, 2 years teaching or related experience (M Ed); for doctorate, master's degree, minimum graduate GPA of 3.5. Additional exam requirements/recommendations for international students: Required—TOEFL. *Faculty research:* Movement and brain plasticity, gibberellin physiology, photosynthesis, carbon cycling, molecular properties of main-group ring components.

University of Louisville, Graduate School, College of Arts and Sciences, Department of Classical and Modern Languages, Program in Spanish, Louisville, KY 40292-0001. Offers MA. *Students:* 12 full-time (9 women), 12 part-time (7 women); includes 4 Hispanic Americans, 3 international. Average age 27. In 2008, 14 master's awarded. *Degree requirements:* For master's, one foreign language, thesis optional. *Entrance requirements:* For master's, GRE General Test. *Application deadline:* Applications are processed on a rolling basis. Application fee: $50. *Unit head:* Dr. Mary Makris, Acting Chair, 502-852-0491, Fax: 502-852-8885, E-mail: mmakris@louisville.edu. *Application contact:* Libby Leggett, Director, Graduate Admissions, 502-852-3101, Fax: 502-852-6536, E-mail: gradadm@louisville.edu.

University of Maryland, College Park, Graduate Studies, College of Arts and Humanities, School of Languages, Literature, and Cultures, Department of Spanish and Portuguese, College Park, MD 20742. Offers MA, PhD. *Degree requirements:* For master's, comprehensive exam, thesis optional, scholarly paper; for doctorate, 2 foreign languages, thesis/dissertation. *Entrance requirements:* For master's, minimum GPA of 3.0, interview, sample research paper, minimum of 12 credits in upper-level literature, 3 letters of recommendation; for doctorate, minimum GPA of 3.0, interview, sample research paper, minimum of 12 credits in upper-level literature. Additional exam requirements/recommendations for international students: Required—TOEFL. Electronic applications accepted.

University of Maryland, College Park, Graduate Studies, College of Arts and Humanities, School of Languages, Literature, and Cultures, Program in Second Language Acquisition and Application, College Park, MD 20742. Offers French (MA); German (MA); Japanese (MA); Russian (MA); second language instruction (PhD); second language learning (PhD); second language measurement and assessment (PhD); second language use (PhD); Spanish (MA). *Entrance requirements:* For master's, BA or BS in related field, demonstrated language competency, 3 letters of reference. Electronic applications accepted. *Faculty research:* Second

Spanish

University of Maryland, College Park (continued)
language acquisition, pedagogical perspectives, technological applications, language use in professional contexts.

University of Massachusetts Amherst, Graduate School, College of Humanities and Fine Arts, Department of Languages, Literatures, and Cultures, Programs in Hispanic Literatures, Cultures and Linguistics, Amherst, MA 01003. Offers Hispanic literatures, cultures and linguistics (MA, PhD), including Hispanic literatures, cultures and linguistics (MA), teaching Spanish (MA); teaching Spanish (MAT). Part-time programs available. Terminal master's awarded for partial completion of doctoral program. *Degree requirements:* For master's, one foreign language, thesis or alternative; for doctorate, 2 foreign languages, comprehensive exam, thesis/dissertation. *Entrance requirements:* For master's and doctorate, GRE General Test, sample academic term paper. Additional exam requirements/recommendations for international students: Required—TOEFL (minimum score 550 paper-based; 213 computer-based; 79 iBT), IELTS (minimum score 6.5). Electronic applications accepted. *Expenses:* Tuition, area resident: Full-time $2640. Tuition, nonresident: full-time $9936. One-time fee: $332 full-time. Tuition and fees vary according to course load.

University of Memphis, Graduate School, College of Arts and Sciences, Department of Foreign Languages and Literatures, Memphis, TN 38152. Offers French (MA); Spanish (MA). Part-time programs available. *Faculty:* 12 full-time (7 women), 1 part-time/adjunct (0 women). *Students:* 11 full-time (3 women), 10 part-time (all women); includes 7 minority (3 African Americans, 1 American Indian/Alaska Native, 3 Hispanic Americans), 2 international. Average age 34. 11 applicants, 100% accepted, 3 enrolled. In 2008, 9 master's awarded. *Degree requirements:* For master's, one foreign language, comprehensive exam, thesis optional. *Entrance requirements:* For master's, GRE General Test. *Application deadline:* For fall admission, 8/1 for domestic students; for spring admission, 12/1 for domestic students. Applications are processed on a rolling basis. Application fee: $35 ($60 for international students). *Expenses:* Tuition, area resident: Full-time $6242; part-time $330 per credit hour. Tuition, state resident: full-time $6242; part-time $330 per credit hour. Tuition, nonresident: full-time $17,828; part-time $815 per credit hour. Required fees: $1156. *Financial support:* Research assistantships with full tuition reimbursements, teaching assistantships with full tuition reimbursements available. Financial award applicants required to submit FAFSA. *Faculty research:* Spanish-American short story, Latin American women writers, French women of letters, Avevedo and Cervantes, 19th and 20th century peninsular literature, Brazilian culture and literature. *Unit head:* Dr. Ralph Albanese, Chairman, 901-678-2506, Fax: 901-678-5338, E-mail: ralbanes@memphis.edu. *Application contact:* Dr. Fernando Burgos, Coordinator of Graduate Studies, 901-678-3158, Fax: 901-678-5338, E-mail: fburgos@memphis.edu.

University of Miami, Graduate School, College of Arts and Sciences, Department of Modern Languages and Literatures, Coral Gables, FL 33124. Offers romance studies (PhD), including French, Spanish. *Degree requirements:* For doctorate, 2 foreign languages, thesis/dissertation, area exam, qualifying exam. *Entrance requirements:* For doctorate, 1 writing sample in English and 1 writing sample in French or Spanish, minimum GPA of 3.0; oral interview; letters of recommendation. Additional exam requirements/recommendations for international students: Required—TOEFL (minimum score 550 paper-based; 213 computer-based; 59 iBT), GRE General Test (recommended). Electronic applications accepted. *Faculty research:* Transatlantic studies, Caribbean studies, comparative literature, gender theory, cultural studies.

University of Miami, Graduate School, School of Communication, Coral Gables, FL 33124. Offers communication (PhD); communication studies (MA); film studies (MA, PhD); motion pictures (MFA), including production, producing, and screenwriting; print journalism (MA); public relations (MA); Spanish language journalism (MA); television broadcast journalism (MA). *Accreditation:* ACEJMC. Part-time programs available. *Degree requirements:* For master's, comprehensive exam (for some programs), thesis (for some programs); for doctorate, comprehensive exam, thesis/dissertation. *Entrance requirements:* For master's, GRE General Test; for doctorate, GRE General Test, master's thesis or scholarly research. Additional exam requirements/recommendations for international students: Required—TOEFL (minimum score 600 paper-based; 250 computer-based; 100 iBT). Electronic applications accepted. *Faculty research:* Communication studies, mass communication, international/interpersonal communication, film studies, journalism.

University of Michigan, Horace H. Rackham School of Graduate Studies, College of Literature, Science, and the Arts, Department of Romance Languages and Literatures, Program in Spanish, Ann Arbor, MI 48109. Offers PhD. *Degree requirements:* For doctorate, 2 foreign languages, thesis/dissertation, oral defense of dissertation, preliminary exams. *Entrance requirements:* For doctorate, GRE General Test. Additional exam requirements/recommendations for international students: Required—TOEFL or Michigan English Language Assessment Battery. Electronic applications accepted. *Faculty research:* Comparative Romance studies, medieval and early modern studies, postcolonial and minority literatures, culture and materiality, reflection in the nature and function of scholarship.

University of Minnesota, Twin Cities Campus, Graduate School, College of Liberal Arts, Department of Spanish and Portuguese Studies, Minneapolis, MN 55455-0213. Offers Hispanic and Luso-Brazilian literatures and linguistics (PhD); Hispanic linguistics (MA); Hispanic literature (MA); Lusophone literature (MA). *Degree requirements:* For master's, 2 foreign languages, comprehensive exam, thesis or alternative; for doctorate, 2 foreign languages, comprehensive exam, thesis/dissertation. *Entrance requirements:* For master's and doctorate, GRE General Test, samples of written work, 3 letters of recommendation, voice sample, statement of purpose. Additional exam requirements/recommendations for international students: Required—TOEFL (minimum score 550 paper-based; 213 computer-based; 79 iBT). Electronic applications accepted. *Faculty research:* Sociohistorical approaches to literature and culture, feminist studies, literary theory, ideologies and literature, pragmatics and sociolinguistics.

University of Mississippi, Graduate School, College of Liberal Arts, Department of Modern Languages, Oxford, University, MS 38677. Offers French (MA); German (MA); Spanish (MA). *Degree requirements:* For master's, thesis (for some programs). *Entrance requirements:* For master's, GRE General Test, minimum GPA of 3.0. Additional exam requirements/recommendations for international students: Required—TOEFL. Electronic applications accepted.

University of Missouri–Columbia, Graduate School, College of Arts and Sciences, Department of Romance Languages and Literature, Program in Spanish, Columbia, MO 65211. Offers MA, PhD. *Students:* 5 full-time (4 women), 4 part-time (1 woman); includes 4 minority (1 Asian American or Pacific Islander, 3 Hispanic Americans), 2 international. Average age 34. 9 applicants, 44% accepted, 2 enrolled. In 2008, 4 master's awarded. *Degree requirements:* For master's, one foreign language; for doctorate, 4 foreign languages, thesis/dissertation. *Entrance requirements:* For master's and doctorate, GRE General Test, minimum GPA of 3.0. Additional exam requirements/recommendations for international students: Required—TOEFL (minimum score 500 paper-based; 173 computer-based). *Application deadline:* For fall admission, 1/15 priority date for domestic students. Applications are processed on a rolling basis. Application fee: $45 ($60 for international students). *Financial support:* Research assistantships, teaching assistantships, institutionally sponsored loans available. *Unit head:* Director of Graduate Studies. *Application contact:* Director of Graduate Studies.

The University of Montana, Graduate School, College of Arts and Sciences, Department of Modern and Classical Languages and Literatures, Missoula, MT 59812-0002. Offers French (MA); German (MA); Spanish (MA). *Degree requirements:* For master's, one foreign language. *Entrance requirements:* For master's, GRE General Test. Additional exam requirements/recommendations for international students: Required—TOEFL.

University of Nebraska–Lincoln, Graduate College, College of Arts and Sciences, Department of Modern Languages and Literatures, Lincoln, NE 68588. Offers French (MA, PhD); German (MA, PhD); Spanish (MA, PhD). *Faculty:* 20 full-time (9 women). *Students:* 28 full-time (16 women), 12 part-time (9 women); includes 9 minority (1 African American, 1 Asian American or Pacific Islander, 7 Hispanic Americans), 17 international. Average age 34. In 2008, 6 master's, 1 doctorate awarded. *Degree requirements:* For master's, thesis optional; for doctorate, comprehensive exam, thesis/dissertation. *Entrance requirements:* For master's and doctorate, writing sample in target language. Additional exam requirements/recommendations for international students: Required—TOEFL (minimum score 550 paper-based; 213 computer-based). *Application deadline:* For fall admission, 2/1 for domestic and international students. Applications are processed on a rolling basis. Application fee: $40. Electronic applications accepted. *Expenses:* Tuition, state resident: full-time $4275; part-time $237.50 per credit hour. Tuition, nonresident: full-time $11,525; part-time $640.25 per credit hour. Required fees: $1068; $10.35 per credit hour. $440.70 per semester. Tuition and fees vary according to course load and program. *Financial support:* Fellowships, research assistantships, teaching assistantships, Federal Work-Study, health care benefits, and unspecified assistantships available. Support available to part-time students. Financial award application deadline: 2/15. *Faculty research:* French, German, and Spanish language, literature, and culture. *Unit head:* Dr. Russell Ganim, Chair, 402-472-3745, Fax: 402-472-0327. *Application contact:* Dr. Dieter Karch, Graduate Chair, 402-472-3745, E-mail: modlang2@unl.edu.

University of Nevada, Las Vegas, Graduate College, College of Liberal Arts, Department of Foreign Languages, Las Vegas, NV 89154-5047. Offers Hispanic studies (MA); Spanish translation (Certificate). Part-time programs available. *Faculty:* 5 full-time (4 women). *Students:* 2 full-time (both women), 10 part-time (6 women); includes 7 minority (1 Asian American or Pacific Islander, 6 Hispanic Americans). Average age 40. 12 applicants, 50% accepted, 4 enrolled. In 2008, 3 master's, 1 other advanced degree awarded. *Degree requirements:* For master's and Certificate, one foreign language, comprehensive exam. *Entrance requirements:* Additional exam requirements/recommendations for international students: Required—TOEFL (minimum score 550 paper-based; 213 computer-based; 80 iBT), IELTS (minimum score 7). *Application deadline:* For fall admission, 8/1 priority date for domestic students, 5/1 for international students; for spring admission, 12/1 priority date for domestic students, 10/1 for international students. Applications are processed on a rolling basis. Application fee: $60 ($75 for international students). Electronic applications accepted. *Expenses:* Tuition, state resident: full-time $1414; part-time $198 per credit. Tuition, nonresident: full-time $12,509; part-time $415.75 per credit. International tuition: $14,249 full-time. Required fees: $4 per credit. $252 per semester. Tuition and fees vary according to course load. *Financial support:* In 2008–09, 2 students received support, including 2 teaching assistantships with partial tuition reimbursements available (averaging $10,000 per year); institutionally sponsored loans, scholarships/grants, health care benefits, and unspecified assistantships also available. Financial award application deadline: 3/1. *Faculty research:* Second language acquisition/Romance languages, Old French, sociolinguistics/Romance languages, Spanish poetry of the 20's and 30's, post-Spanish Civil War women's fiction. *Unit head:* Dr. Ralph Buechler, Chair/Associate Professor, 702-895-3546, Fax: 702-895-3431, E-mail: ralph.buechler@unlv.edu. *Application contact:* Graduate College Admissions Evaluator, 702-895-3320, Fax: 702-895-4180, E-mail: gradcollege@unlv.edu.

University of Nevada, Reno, Graduate School, College of Liberal Arts, Department of Foreign Languages and Literatures, Reno, NV 89557. Offers French (MA); German (MA); Spanish (MA). *Faculty:* 18 full-time (8 women). *Students:* 11 full-time (6 women), 9 part-time (5 women); includes 4 minority (1 Asian American or Pacific Islander, 3 Hispanic Americans), 1 international. Average age 32. 10 applicants, 90% accepted, 6 enrolled. In 2008, 7 master's awarded. *Degree requirements:* For master's, one foreign language, thesis optional. *Entrance requirements:* For master's, GRE General Test, minimum GPA of 2.75. Additional exam requirements/recommendations for international students: Required—TOEFL (minimum score 500 paper-based; 173 computer-based; 61 iBT), IELTS (minimum score 6), TOFEL or IELTS. *Application deadline:* For fall admission, 3/1 priority date for domestic and international students; for spring admission, 11/1 priority date for domestic and international students. Applications are processed on a rolling basis. Application fee: $60 ($95 for international students). *Expenses:* Tuition, state resident: full-time $1710; part-time $1140 per semester. Tuition, nonresident: full-time $7115. Required fees: $158 per semester. *Financial support:* In 2008–09, 1 research assistantship with partial tuition reimbursement (averaging $14,000 per year), 10 teaching assistantships with partial tuition reimbursements (averaging $14,000 per year) were awarded; Federal Work-Study, institutionally sponsored loans, scholarships/grants, health care benefits, and unspecified assistantships also available. Financial award application deadline: 3/1; financial award applicants required to submit FAFSA. *Faculty research:* Thirteenth century mysticism, contemporary Spanish and Latin American poetry and theater, French interrelation between narration and photography, exile literature and Holocaust. Total annual research expenditures: $4,341. *Unit head:* Dr. Darrell Lockhart, Graduate Program Director, 775-784-6055, E-mail: lockhart@unr.edu. *Application contact:* Michele Sandberg, Application Contact, 775-784-7026, Fax: 775-784-6064, E-mail: gradschool@unr.edu.

University of New Hampshire, Graduate School, College of Liberal Arts, Program in Spanish, Durham, NH 03824. Offers MA. *Faculty:* 9 full-time (6 women). *Students:* 8 full-time (7 women), 11 part-time (7 women); includes 5 minority (all Hispanic Americans), 2 international. Average age 36. 11 applicants, 82% accepted, 7 enrolled. In 2008, 4 master's awarded. *Degree requirements:* For master's, one foreign language, thesis or alternative. *Entrance requirements:* Additional exam requirements/recommendations for international students: Required—TOEFL (minimum score 550 paper-based; 213 computer-based; 80 iBT). *Application deadline:* For fall admission, 4/1 priority date for domestic students, 4/1 for international students; for winter admission, 12/1 for domestic students; for spring admission, 12/1 priority date for domestic students. Applications are processed on a rolling basis. Application fee: $60. Electronic applications accepted. *Expenses:* Tuition, area resident: Full-time $9720; part-time $540 per credit hour. Tuition, nonresident: full-time $23,200; part-time $954 per credit hour. Required fees: $1446; $361.50 per term. *Financial support:* In 2008–09, 4 students received support, including 4 teaching assistantships; fellowships, research assistantships, career-related internships or fieldwork, Federal Work-Study, scholarships/grants, and tuition waivers (full and partial) also available. Support available to part-time students. Financial award application deadline: 2/15. *Unit head:* Dr. Piero Garofalo, Chairperson, 603-862-4005. *Application contact:* Holly Harris, Administrative Assistant, 603-862-3121, E-mail: spanish.master@unh.edu.

University of New Mexico, Graduate School, College of Arts and Sciences, Department of Spanish and Portuguese, Albuquerque, NM 87131-2039. Offers Portuguese (MA); Spanish (MA); Spanish and Portuguese (PhD). Part-time programs available. *Degree requirements:* For master's, one foreign language, comprehensive exam, thesis optional; for doctorate, one foreign language, comprehensive exam, thesis/dissertation. *Entrance requirements:* For master's, GRE, BA in Spanish or Portuguese, letters of recommendation, letter of intent; for doctorate, GRE, 3 letters of recommendation, letter of intent, sample research paper. Additional exam requirements/recommendations for international students: Required—TOEFL (minimum score 550 paper-based; 213 computer-based), Michigan English Language Assessment Battery. Electronic applications accepted. *Faculty research:* Spanish literature in Spain, Latin America, and the U.S. Spanish Southwest from its inception to present day; gender and genre studies including film, linguistic variation and change, and psycholinguistics in Spanish.

The University of North Carolina at Chapel Hill, Graduate School, College of Arts and Sciences, Department of Romance Languages, Chapel Hill, NC 27599. Offers French (MA, PhD); Italian (MA, PhD); Portuguese (MA, PhD); Romance languages (MA, PhD); Romance philology (MA, PhD); Spanish (MA, PhD). *Degree requirements:* For master's, one foreign language, comprehensive exam, thesis; for doctorate, 2 foreign languages, comprehensive exam, thesis/dissertation. *Entrance requirements:* For master's and doctorate, GRE General Test, minimum GPA of 3.0. Additional exam requirements/recommendations for international students: Required—TOEFL (minimum score 550 paper-based; 213 computer-based). Electronic applications accepted.

The University of North Carolina at Charlotte, Graduate School, College of Arts and Sciences, Department of Languages and Culture Studies, Charlotte, NC 28223-0001. Offers

Latin American studies (MA); Spanish (MA). Part-time and evening/weekend programs available. *Faculty:* 22 full-time (12 women), 1 part-time/adjunct (0 women). *Students:* 13 full-time (11 women), 19 part-time (12 women); includes 13 minority (4 African Americans, 9 Hispanic Americans). Average age 28. 26 applicants, 92% accepted, 18 enrolled. In 2008, 13 master's awarded. *Degree requirements:* For master's, thesis optional. *Entrance requirements:* For master's, GRE, 3 letters of reference, minimum GPA of 2.75. Additional exam requirements/recommendations for international students: Required—TOEFL (minimum score 557 paper-based; 220 computer-based). *Application deadline:* For fall admission, 7/15 for domestic students, 5/1 for international students; for spring admission, 11/15 for domestic students, 10/1 for international students. Applications are processed on a rolling basis. Application fee: $55. Electronic applications accepted. *Expenses:* Tuition, area resident: Full-time $2919; part-time $122 per credit hour. Tuition, state resident: full-time $2919; part-time $122 per credit hour. Tuition, nonresident: full-time $13,126; part-time $547 per credit hour. Required fees: $1779; $91 per credit hour. Tuition and fees vary according to program. *Financial support:* In 2008–09, 4 teaching assistantships (averaging $6,250 per year) were awarded; career-related internships or fieldwork, Federal Work-Study, institutionally sponsored loans, scholarships/grants, unspecified assistantships, and 3 administrative assistantships ($9,667 average) also available. Support available to part-time students. Financial award application deadline: 4/1; financial award applicants required to submit FAFSA. *Faculty research:* Twentieth and twenty-first century Spanish literature, Central American literature, Caribbean literature, Mexican literature, literature of the Southern Cone. *Unit head:* Robert L. Reimer, Chair, 704-687-8767, Fax: 704-687-3496. *Application contact:* Kathy B. Giddings, Director of Graduate Admissions, 704-687-3366, Fax: 704-687-3279, E-mail: agidding@uncc.edu.

The University of North Carolina at Greensboro, Graduate School, College of Arts and Sciences, Department of Romance Languages, Program in Spanish, Greensboro, NC 27412-5001. Offers advanced Spanish language and Hispanic cultural studies (Certificate); Spanish (MA). *Degree requirements:* For master's, one foreign language, comprehensive exam, thesis or alternative. *Entrance requirements:* For master's, GRE General Test, 3-5 minute tape demonstrating foreign language proficiency, composition in Spanish, sample paper in English. Additional exam requirements/recommendations for international students: Required—TOEFL. Electronic applications accepted.

University of Northern Colorado, Graduate School, College of Humanities and Social Sciences, School of Modern Languages and Cultural Studies, Program in Foreign Languages, Greeley, CO 80639. Offers Spanish/teaching (MA). Part-time programs available. *Faculty:* 12 full-time (6 women). *Students:* 2 part-time (1 woman); includes 1 minority (Hispanic American). Average age 38. In 2008, 11 master's awarded. *Degree requirements:* For master's, comprehensive exam, thesis or alternative. *Entrance requirements:* For master's, minimum undergraduate GPA of 3.0, BA in Spanish, 1 year of secondary teaching. *Application deadline:* Applications are processed on a rolling basis. Application fee: $50 ($60 for international students). Electronic applications accepted. *Expenses:* Tuition, state resident: full-time $4370; part-time $242.75 per credit hour. Tuition, nonresident: full-time $12,366; part-time $687 per credit hour. Required fees: $664.20; $36.90 per credit hour. *Financial support:* In 2008–09, 1 teaching assistantship (averaging $11,969 per year) was awarded; fellowships, research assistantships, unspecified assistantships also available. Financial award application deadline: 3/1; financial award applicants required to submit FAFSA. *Unit head:* Dr. Joy Landeira, Program Coordinator, 970-351-2221, Fax: 970-351-1571. *Application contact:* Linda Sisson, Graduate Student Admission Coordinator, 970-351-1807, Fax: 970-351-2371, E-mail: linda.sisson@unco.edu.

University of Northern Iowa, Graduate College, College of Humanities and Fine Arts, Department of Modern Languages, Program in Spanish, Cedar Falls, IA 50614. Offers Spanish (MA); teaching English to speakers of other languages/Spanish (MA). Part-time and evening/weekend programs available. *Students:* 8 full-time (6 women), 2 part-time (both women); includes 2 minority (both Hispanic Americans), 2 international. 11 applicants, 100% accepted, 5 enrolled. In 2008, 13 master's awarded. *Degree requirements:* For master's, one foreign language, comprehensive exam, thesis or alternative. *Entrance requirements:* For master's, minimum GPA of 3.0, valid teaching license, documentation of successful teaching experience. Additional exam requirements/recommendations for international students: Required—TOEFL (minimum score 600 paper-based; 250 computer-based; 100 iBT). *Application deadline:* For fall admission, 8/1 priority date for domestic students. Applications are processed on a rolling basis. Application fee: $30 ($50 for international students). Electronic applications accepted. *Expenses:* Tuition, state resident: full-time $6446. Tuition, nonresident: full-time $14,874. Required fees: $852. *Financial support:* Career-related internships or fieldwork, Federal Work-Study, and tuition waivers (full and partial) available. Support available to part-time students. Financial award application deadline: 2/1. *Unit head:* Dr. Juan Carlos, Coordinator, 319-273-2200, Fax: 319-273-2848. *Application contact:* Laurie S. Russell, Record Analyst, 319-273-2623, Fax: 319-273-6792, E-mail: laurie.russell@uni.edu.

University of North Texas, Robert B. Toulouse School of Graduate Studies, College of Arts and Sciences, Department of Foreign Languages and Literatures, Denton, TX 76203. Offers French (MA); Spanish (MA). Part-time programs available. *Degree requirements:* For master's, 2 foreign languages, comprehensive exam, thesis optional, proficiency in a second foreign language. *Entrance requirements:* For master's, GRE General Test, minimum undergraduate GPA of 3.0, curriculum vita, 250 word essay in French or Spanish, 12 advanced credita in French or Spanish. Additional exam requirements/recommendations for international students: Recommended—TOEFL (minimum score 550 paper-based; 213 computer-based). *Faculty research:* Literature of Austria, France, Germany, Latin America, Spain; culture/civilization; applied linguistics.

University of Notre Dame, Graduate School, College of Arts and Letters, Division of Humanities, Department of Romance Languages and Literatures, Notre Dame, IN 46556. Offers French and Francophone studies (MA); Iberian and Latin American studies (MA); Italian studies (MA); Romance literatures (MA). *Faculty:* 25 full-time (10 women), 4 part-time/adjunct (all women). *Students:* 17 full-time (12 women); includes 4 minority (all Hispanic Americans), 2 international. 30 applicants, 47% accepted, 11 enrolled. In 2008, 11 master's awarded. *Degree requirements:* For master's, 2 foreign languages, comprehensive exam, thesis optional. *Entrance requirements:* For master's, GRE General Test, BA in target language. Additional exam requirements/recommendations for international students: Required—TOEFL (minimum score 600 paper-based; 250 computer-based; 80 iBT). *Application deadline:* For fall admission, 2/1 priority date for domestic students, 2/1 for international students. Application fee: $50. Electronic applications accepted. *Financial support:* Teaching assistantships with full tuition reimbursements, tuition waivers (full) available. Financial award application deadline: 2/1. *Faculty research:* Literature of discovery and exploration, modern literature, literary criticism, medieval literature, feminist critical theory. *Unit head:* Dr. John Welle, Director of Graduate Studies, 574-631-6887, E-mail: al.romland.1@nd.edu. *Application contact:* Dr. Barbara Turpin, Director of Graduate Admissions, 574-631-7706, Fax: 574-631-4183.

University of Oklahoma, Graduate College, College of Arts and Sciences, Department of Modern Languages, Program in Spanish, Norman, OK 73019. Offers MA, PhD, MBA/MA. Part-time programs available. *Students:* 17 full-time (12 women), 3 part-time (all women); includes 7 minority (all Hispanic Americans), 3 international. 6 applicants, 67% accepted, 3 enrolled. In 2008, 4 master's, 1 doctorate awarded. *Degree requirements:* For master's, one foreign language, comprehensive exam, thesis optional, departmental qualifying exam; for doctorate, 2 foreign languages, comprehensive exam, thesis/dissertation, departmental qualifying exam. *Entrance requirements:* For master's, BA in Spanish literature, minimum GPA of 3.0 in last 60 hours, 3 letters of recommendation; for doctorate, MA in Spanish, 3 letters of recommendation, minimum graduate GPA of 3.5. Additional exam requirements/recommendations for international students: Required—TOEFL (minimum score 550 paper-based; 213 computer-based). *Application deadline:* For fall admission, 4/1 for domestic and international students; for spring admission, 10/1 for domestic students, 9/1 for international students. Application fee: $40 ($90 for international students). Electronic applications accepted. *Expenses:* Tuition, state resident: full-time $3744; part-time $156 per credit hour. Tuition, nonresident: full-time $13,577; part-time $565.70 per credit hour. Required fees: $2415.40; $90.10 per credit hour. *Financial support:* In 2008–09, 4 students received support. Scholarships/grants, health care benefits, and unspecified assistantships available. Financial award applicants required to submit FAFSA. *Faculty research:* Spanish and Latin American literatures, 20th century literature of Latin American social issues; women writers; medieval and early modern Intellectual history; Golden Age Drama. *Unit head:* Dr. Pamela Genova, Chairperson, 405-325-6181, Fax: 405-325-0103, E-mail: pgenova@ou.edu. *Application contact:* Dr. Logan E. Whalen, Graduate Liaison, 405-325-5088, Fax: 405-325-0103, E-mail: mllgradinfo@ou.edu.

University of Oregon, Graduate School, College of Arts and Sciences, Department of Romance Languages, Program in Spanish, Eugene, OR 97403. Offers MA. Part-time programs available. *Degree requirements:* For master's, one foreign language. *Entrance requirements:* For master's, GRE General Test, minimum GPA of 3.0. Additional exam requirements/recommendations for international students: Required—TOEFL.

University of Ottawa, Faculty of Graduate and Postdoctoral Studies, Faculty of Arts, Department of Modern Languages and Literatures, Ottawa, ON K1N 6N5, Canada. Offers Spanish (MA, PhD). Part-time and evening/weekend programs available. *Degree requirements:* For master's, one foreign language, thesis or alternative; for doctorate, one foreign language, comprehensive exam, thesis/dissertation. *Entrance requirements:* For master's, BA with honors in Spanish, minimum B average; for doctorate, MA in Spanish or equivalent, minimum B average. Electronic applications accepted. *Faculty research:* Spanish American literature, Mexican literature and film studies, Spanish golden age literature, twentieth century Spanish literature, Hispanic linguistics with special emphasis on linguistic theory.

University of Pennsylvania, School of Arts and Sciences, Graduate Group in Romance Languages, Philadelphia, PA 19104. Offers French (AM, PhD); Italian (AM, PhD); Spanish (AM, PhD). Terminal master's awarded for partial completion of doctoral program. *Degree requirements:* For master's, one foreign language, thesis or alternative; for doctorate, 2 foreign languages, thesis/dissertation. *Entrance requirements:* For master's and doctorate, GRE General Test. Additional exam requirements/recommendations for international students: Required—TOEFL. Electronic applications accepted. *Faculty research:* Literary theory and criticism, cultural studies, history of Romance literatures, gender studies.

University of Pittsburgh, School of Arts and Sciences, Department of Hispanic Languages and Literatures, Pittsburgh, PA 15260. Offers MA, PhD. Part-time programs available. Terminal master's awarded for partial completion of doctoral program. *Degree requirements:* For master's, one foreign language, comprehensive exam (for some programs), thesis or alternative, research paper; for doctorate, 2 foreign languages, comprehensive exam, thesis/dissertation. *Entrance requirements:* Additional exam requirements/recommendations for international students: Required—TOEFL (minimum score 550 paper-based; 213 computer-based; 80 iBT). Electronic applications accepted. *Faculty research:* Latin American, Luso-Brazilian, and peninsular literature; cultural theory; cultural studies; race, ethnicity, and post-colonial studies.

University of Pittsburgh, School of Arts and Sciences, Department of Linguistics, Program in Hispanic Linguistics, Pittsburgh, PA 15260. Offers MA, PhD. *Degree requirements:* For master's, one foreign language, thesis; for doctorate, 2 foreign languages, comprehensive exam, thesis/dissertation. *Entrance requirements:* For master's, GRE General Test; for doctorate, GRE General Test, MA in Linguistics. Additional exam requirements/recommendations for international students: Required—TOEFL (minimum score 600 paper-based; 250 computer-based). Electronic applications accepted. *Faculty research:* Hispanic Linguistics.

University of Rhode Island, Graduate School, College of Arts and Sciences, Department of Modern and Classical Languages and Literatures, Kingston, RI 02881. Offers Spanish (MA). *Degree requirements:* For master's, one foreign language. Application fee: $35. *Expenses:* Tuition, state resident: full-time $8024; part-time $446 per credit. Tuition, nonresident: full-time $21,046; part-time $1169 per credit. Required fees: $1056; $26 per credit. $30 per semester. One-time fee: $95 part-time. *Unit head:* Dr. Joseph Morello, Head, 401-874-4699, E-mail: morello@uri.edu. *Application contact:* Harold D. Bibb, Associate Dean of the Graduate School, 401-874-2262, Fax: 401-874-5491.

University of South Africa, College of Human Sciences, Pretoria, South Africa. Offers adult education (M Ed); African languages (MA, PhD); African politics (MA, PhD); Afrikaans (MA, PhD); ancient history (MA, PhD); ancient Near Eastern studies (MA, PhD); anthropology (MA, PhD); applied linguistics (MA); Arabic (MA, PhD); archaeology (MA); art history (MA); Biblical archaeology (MA); Biblical studies (M Th, D Th, PhD); Christian spirituality (M Th, D Th); church history (M Th, D Th); classical studies (MA, PhD); clinical psychology (MA); communication (MA, PhD); comparative education (M Ed, Ed D); consulting psychology (D Admin, D Com, PhD); curriculum studies (M Ed, Ed D); development studies (M Admin, MA, D Admin, PhD); didactics (M Ed, Ed D); education (M Tech); education management (M Ed, Ed D); educational psychology (M Ed); English (MA); environmental education (M Ed); French (MA, PhD); German (MA, PhD); Greek (MA); guidance and counseling (M Ed); health studies (MA, PhD), including health sciences education (MA), health services management (MA), medical and surgical nursing science (critical care general) (MA), midwifery and neonatal nursing science (MA), trauma and emergency care (MA); history (MA, PhD); history of education (Ed D); inclusive education (M Ed, Ed D); information and communications technology policy and regulation (MA); information science (MA, MIS, PhD); international politics (MA, PhD); Islamic studies (MA, PhD); Italian (MA, PhD); Judaica (MA, PhD); linguistics (MA, PhD); mathematical education (M Ed); mathematics education (MA); missiology (M Th, D Th); modern Hebrew (MA, PhD); musicology (MA, MMus, D Mus, PhD); natural science education (M Ed); New Testament (M Th, D Th); Old Testament (D Th); pastoral therapy (M Th, D Th); philosophy (MA); philosophy of education (M Ed, Ed D); politics (MA, PhD); Portuguese (MA, PhD); practical theology (M Th, D Th); psychology (MA, MS, PhD); psychology of education (M Ed, Ed D); public health (MA); religious studies (MA, D Th, PhD); Romance languages (MA); Russian (MA, PhD); Semitic languages (MA, PhD); social behavior studies in HIV/AIDS (MA); social science (mental health) (MA); social science in development studies (MA); social science in psychology (MA); social science in social work (MA); social science in sociology (MA); social work (MSW, DSW, PhD); socio-education (M Ed, Ed D); sociolinguistics (MA); sociology (MA, PhD); Spanish (MA, PhD); systematic theology (M Th, D Th); TESOL (teaching English to speakers of other languages) (MA); theological ethics (M Th, D Th); theory of literature (MA, PhD); urban ministries (D Th); urban ministry (M Th).

University of South Carolina, The Graduate School, College of Arts and Sciences, Department of Languages, Literatures, and Cultures, Columbia, SC 29208. Offers comparative literature (MA, PhD); foreign languages (MAT), including French, German, Spanish; French (MA); German (MA); Spanish (MA). MAT offered in cooperation with the College of Education. Part-time programs available. *Degree requirements:* For master's, one foreign language, comprehensive exam, thesis optional; for doctorate, 2 foreign languages, comprehensive exam, thesis/dissertation. *Entrance requirements:* For master's and doctorate, GRE General Test, writing sample. Additional exam requirements/recommendations for international students: Required—TOEFL (minimum score 230 computer-based; 75 iBT). Electronic applications accepted. *Faculty research:* Modern literature, linguistics, literature and culture, medieval literature, literary theory.

University of South Florida, Graduate School, College of Arts and Sciences, Department of World Language Education, Program in Spanish, Tampa, FL 33620-9951. Offers MA. *Students:* 11 full-time (9 women), 5 part-time (3 women); includes 10 minority (all Hispanic Americans), 3 international. 9 applicants, 89% accepted, 7 enrolled. In 2008, 7 master's awarded. *Degree requirements:* For master's, comprehensive exam, thesis. *Entrance requirements:* For master's, minimum GPA of 3.0, 36 hours of graduate course work in French. Additional exam requirements/recommendations for international students: Required—TOEFL (minimum score 550 paper-based; 213 computer-based). *Application deadline:* For fall admission, 2/15 for domestic students, 1/2 for international students; for spring admission, 10/15 for domestic students, 6/1

Spanish

University of South Florida (continued)
for international students. Application fee: $30. *Expenses:* Tuition, state resident: full-time $2624.40; part-time $291.60 per credit hour. Tuition, nonresident: full-time $7822; part-time $869.13 per credit hour. *Unit head:* Madeline Camara, Program Director, 813-974-3924, Fax: 813-974-1718, E-mail: mcamara@cas.usf.edu. *Application contact:* Tom Rogers, Contact Person, 813-974-2548, Fax: 813-974-1718, E-mail: tmroger3@chuma1.cas.usf.edu.

The University of Tennessee, Graduate School, College of Arts and Sciences, Department of Modern Foreign Languages and Literatures, Program in Modern Foreign Languages, Knoxville, TN 37996. Offers applied linguistics (PhD); French (PhD); German (PhD); Italian (PhD); Portuguese (PhD); Russian (PhD); Spanish (PhD). *Degree requirements:* For doctorate, 2 foreign languages, thesis/dissertation. *Entrance requirements:* For doctorate, minimum GPA of 2.7. Additional exam requirements/recommendations for international students: Required—TOEFL. Electronic applications accepted. *Expenses:* Tuition, area resident: Part-time $348 per credit hour. Tuition, state resident: full-time $6262. Tuition, nonresident: full-time $18,920; part-time $1052 per credit hour. Required fees: $812; $36 per credit hour. Tuition and fees vary according to program.

The University of Tennessee, Graduate School, College of Arts and Sciences, Department of Modern Foreign Languages and Literatures, Program in Spanish, Knoxville, TN 37996. Offers MA. *Degree requirements:* For master's, one foreign language, thesis or alternative. *Entrance requirements:* For master's, minimum GPA of 2.7. Additional exam requirements/recommendations for international students: Required—TOEFL. Electronic applications accepted. *Expenses:* Tuition, area resident: Part-time $348 per credit hour. Tuition, state resident: full-time $6262. Tuition, nonresident: full-time $18,920; part-time $1052 per credit hour. Required fees: $812; $36 per credit hour. Tuition and fees vary according to program.

The University of Texas at Arlington, Graduate School, College of Liberal Arts, Department of Modern Languages, Arlington, TX 76019. Offers French (MA); Spanish (MA). Part-time and evening/weekend programs available. *Faculty:* 7 full-time (5 women), 1 (woman) part-time/adjunct. *Students:* 9 full-time (6 women), 26 part-time (19 women); includes 16 minority (6 African Americans, 10 Hispanic Americans), 2 international. 24 applicants, 79% accepted, 10 enrolled. In 2008, 3 master's awarded. *Degree requirements:* For master's, 2 foreign languages, comprehensive exam, thesis optional. *Entrance requirements:* For master's, GRE General Test, minimum GPA of 3.0, 3 letters of recommendation. Additional exam requirements/recommendations for international students: Required—TOEFL (minimum score 550 paper-based; 213 computer-based). *Application deadline:* For fall admission, 6/16 for domestic students. Applications are processed on a rolling basis. Application fee: $35 ($50 for international students). *Expenses:* Tuition, area resident: Full-time $6500. Tuition, state resident: full-time $6500. Tuition, nonresident: full-time $11,558. *Financial support:* In 2008–09, teaching assistantships (averaging $6,600 per year); research assistantships. Financial award application deadline: 6/1; financial award applicants required to submit FAFSA. *Unit head:* Dr. A. Raymond Elliott, Chair, 817-272-3161, Fax: 817-272-5408, E-mail: elliott@uta.edu. *Application contact:* Dr. Antoinette Sol, Graduate Advisor, 817-272-3161, Fax: 817-272-5408, E-mail: amsol@uta.edu.

The University of Texas at Austin, Graduate School, College of Liberal Arts, Department of Spanish and Portuguese, Austin, TX 78712-1111. Offers Hispanic linguistics (MA, PhD); Hispanic literature (MA, PhD); Luso-Brazilian literature (MA, PhD). *Degree requirements:* For master's, 2 foreign languages, thesis or alternative; for doctorate, 3 foreign languages, thesis/dissertation. *Entrance requirements:* For master's and doctorate, GRE General Test. Electronic applications accepted.

The University of Texas at Brownsville, Graduate Studies, College of Liberal Arts, Department of Modern Languages, Brownsville, TX 78520-4991. Offers interdisciplinary studies (MAIS); Spanish (MA). Part-time and evening/weekend programs available. *Degree requirements:* For master's, comprehensive exam, thesis optional. *Entrance requirements:* For master's, GRE General Test, letters of recommendation, interview. Additional exam requirements/recommendations for international students: Required—TOEFL. *Faculty research:* Children's literature, Hispanic folklore, translation.

The University of Texas at El Paso, Graduate School, College of Liberal Arts, Department of Creative Writing, El Paso, TX 79968-0001. Offers creative writing in English (MFA); creative writing in Spanish (MFA). Part-time and evening/weekend programs available. *Degree requirements:* For master's, thesis. *Entrance requirements:* For master's, departmental exam (creative writing in Spanish), minimum GPA of 3.0. Additional exam requirements/recommendations for international students: Required—TOEFL. Electronic applications accepted.

The University of Texas at San Antonio, College of Liberal and Fine Arts, Department of Modern Languages and Literatures, San Antonio, TX 78249-0617. Offers Spanish (MA); Spanish translation studies (Graduate Certificate). Part-time and evening/weekend programs available. *Degree requirements:* For master's, one foreign language, comprehensive exam, thesis optional. *Entrance requirements:* For master's, GRE, minimum GPA of 3.0, sample of written and spoken work. Additional exam requirements/recommendations for international students: Required—TOEFL (minimum score 500 paper-based; 173 computer-based). Electronic applications accepted.

The University of Texas of the Permian Basin, Office of Graduate Studies, College of Arts and Sciences, Department of Literature and Languages, Odessa, TX 79762-0001. Offers English (MA); Spanish (MA). *Degree requirements:* For master's, comprehensive exam (for some programs), thesis (for some programs). *Entrance requirements:* For master's, GRE General Test. Additional exam requirements/recommendations for international students: Required—TOEFL (minimum score 550 paper-based; 213 computer-based).

The University of Texas–Pan American, College of Arts and Humanities, Department of Modern Languages and Literatures, Edinburg, TX 78541-2999. Offers Spanish (MA). Part-time programs available. *Degree requirements:* For master's, comprehensive exam, thesis or alternative. *Entrance requirements:* For master's, GRE General Test, minimum GPA of 3.0. *Faculty research:* Latin American literature, women's literature, Caribbean literature, Latina/o studies, sociolinguistics, applied linguistics, creative writing.

The University of Toledo, College of Graduate Studies, College of Arts and Sciences, Department of Foreign Languages, Toledo, OH 43606-3390. Offers French (MA); German (MA); Spanish (MA). Part-time programs available. *Degree requirements:* For master's, one foreign language, comprehensive reading exam in 1 additional foreign language. Electronic applications accepted.

University of Toronto, School of Graduate Studies, Humanities Division, Department of Spanish and Portuguese, Toronto, ON M5S 1A1, Canada. Offers MA, PhD. Part-time programs available. *Degree requirements:* For doctorate, thesis/dissertation. *Entrance requirements:* For master's, minimum B average in final year, 2 letters of reference; for doctorate, minimum A– average, 2 letters of reference, writing sample. Additional exam requirements/recommendations for international students: Required—TOEFL, Michigan English Language Assessment Battery, IELTS or COPE.

University of Utah, The Graduate School, College of Humanities, Department of Languages and Literature, Salt Lake City, UT 84112-1107. Offers comparative literary and cultural studies (MA, PhD); French (MA, MALP); German (MA, MALP, PhD); language pedagogy (MALP); Spanish (MA, MALP, PhD); world languages with secondary teaching licensure (MA). Terminal master's awarded for partial completion of doctoral program. *Degree requirements:* For master's, standard proficiency in 2 languages other than English, comprehensive exam or thesis; for doctorate, comprehensive exam, standard proficiency in 2 languages other than English and language of study, advanced proficiency in 1 language other than English and language of study, dissertation. *Entrance requirements:* For master's, bachelor's degree or strong undergraduate record in target languages, GPA of 3.0, literature-survey courses; for doctorate, successful completion of MA and advanced proficiency in a target language. Additional exam requirements/recommendations for international students: Required—TOEFL (minimum score 500 paper-based; 173 computer-based). Electronic applications accepted. *Faculty research:* Literary theory, stylistics, Russian and Soviet literature, existentialism, theory of criticism.

University of Virginia, College and Graduate School of Arts and Sciences, Department of Spanish, Italian and Portuguese, Program in Spanish, Charlottesville, VA 22903. Offers MA, PhD. *Students:* 50 full-time (37 women); includes 5 minority (all Hispanic Americans), 6 international. Average age 27. 51 applicants, 71% accepted, 22 enrolled. In 2008, 10 master's, 6 doctorates awarded. *Degree requirements:* For master's, one foreign language, comprehensive exam, thesis; for doctorate, 2 foreign languages, comprehensive exam, thesis/dissertation. *Entrance requirements:* For master's, GRE General Test, GRE Subject Test, 2 letters of recommendation; for doctorate, GRE General Test, GRE Subject Test, 2 letters of recommendation; a writing sample. Additional exam requirements/recommendations for international students: Required—TOEFL (minimum score 600 paper-based; 250 computer-based; 90 iBT), IELTS (minimum score 7). *Application deadline:* For fall admission, 12/1 for domestic and international students. Applications are processed on a rolling basis. Application fee: $60. Electronic applications accepted. *Expenses:* Tuition, area resident: Full-time $10,452. Tuition, state resident: full-time $10,452. Tuition, nonresident: full-time $20,010. Required fees: $2176. Part-time tuition and fees vary according to course load and program. *Financial support:* Fellowships, teaching assistantships available. Financial award applicants required to submit FAFSA. *Unit head:* E. Michael Gerli, Director of Graduate Studies (Spanish), 434-924-7159, E-mail: sipinfo@virginia.edu. *Application contact:* Enrico Cesaretti, Director of Graduate Admissions, 434-924-7159, E-mail: sipinfo@virginia.edu.

University of Washington, Graduate School, College of Arts and Sciences, Department of Romance Languages and Literature, Division of Spanish and Portuguese Studies, Seattle, WA 98195. Offers Hispanic literary and cultural studies (MA). *Degree requirements:* For master's, 2 foreign languages, thesis optional, exam. *Entrance requirements:* For master's, GRE General Test, minimum GPA of 3.0. Additional exam requirements/recommendations for international students: Required—TOEFL. Electronic applications accepted. *Faculty research:* Medieval through modern Spanish literature and film, Latin American literature, poetry and essay, pan-Hispanic ballad, Hispanic cultural studies, second language acquisition and applied linguistics.

The University of Western Ontario, Faculty of Graduate Studies, Faculty of Arts and Humanities, Department of Comparative Literature, London, ON N6A 5B8, Canada. Offers comparative literature (MA, PhD); Spanish (MA). Part-time programs available. *Degree requirements:* For master's, 2 foreign languages, thesis (for some programs). *Entrance requirements:* For master's, honors degree in Spanish or equivalent, minimum B average. Additional exam requirements/recommendations for international students: Required—TOEFL, TOEFL (comparative literature). *Faculty research:* Spanish golden age, Latin-American, romance, medieval, film.

University of Wisconsin–Madison, Graduate School, College of Letters and Science, Department of Spanish and Portuguese, Program in Spanish, Madison, WI 53706-1380. Offers MA, PhD. *Degree requirements:* For master's, one foreign language; for doctorate, 2 foreign languages, thesis/dissertation. *Entrance requirements:* For master's, GRE (recommended), minimum GPA of 3.25 in Spanish or Portuguese; for doctorate, GRE (recommended), minimum graduate GPA of 3.4, writing sample. Additional exam requirements/recommendations for international students: Required—TOEFL. Electronic applications accepted. *Faculty research:* Hispanic linguistics, Spanish and Spanish-American literature.

University of Wisconsin–Milwaukee, Graduate School, College of Letters and Sciences, Department of Spanish, Milwaukee, WI 53201-0413. Offers Spanish (MA); translation (Certificate). *Faculty:* 7 full-time (3 women). *Entrance requirements:* For master's, bachelor's degree. *Expenses:* Tuition, area resident: Full-time $7320; part-time $165 per credit. Tuition, state resident: full-time $7320; part-time $165 per credit. Tuition, nonresident: full-time $17,840; part-time $714 per credit. Tuition and fees vary according to campus/location, program and reciprocity agreements. *Financial support:* In 2008–09, 15 teaching assistantships were awarded. Total annual research expenditures: $2,567. *Unit head:* Jeffrey Oxford, Chair, 414-229-4257, E-mail: oxford@uwm.edu. *Application contact:* General Information Contact, 414-229-4982, Fax: 414-229-6967, E-mail: gradschool@uwm.edu.

University of Wyoming, Graduate School, College of Arts and Sciences, Department of Modern and Classical Languages, Program in Spanish, Laramie, WY 82070. Offers MA. Part-time programs available. *Faculty:* 5 full-time (1 woman). *Students:* 6 full-time (4 women), 5 part-time (3 women). Average age 33. 4 applicants, 75% accepted, 3 enrolled. In 2008, 6 master's awarded. *Degree requirements:* For master's, one foreign language, thesis or alternative. *Entrance requirements:* For master's, GRE General Test, minimum GPA of 3.0. *Application deadline:* For fall admission, 4/1 priority date for domestic students. Applications are processed on a rolling basis. Application fee: $50. *Financial support:* In 2008–09, 4 students received support, including teaching assistantships with full tuition reimbursements available (averaging $10,696 per year); institutionally sponsored loans also available. Financial award application deadline: 3/1. *Faculty research:* Peninsular literature, Latin American literature, theatre, science and literature, linguistics. *Unit head:* Dr. Philip Holt, Head, 307-766-4177, Fax: 307-766-2727, E-mail: pholt@uwyo.edu. *Application contact:* Dr. Kevin S. Larsen, Graduate Adviser, 307-766-2294, Fax: 307-766-2727, E-mail: klarsen@uwyo.edu.

Vanderbilt University, Graduate School, Department of Spanish and Portuguese, Nashville, TN 37240-1001. Offers Portuguese (MA); Spanish (MA, MAT, PhD); Spanish and Portuguese (PhD). *Faculty:* 22 full-time (7 women). *Students:* 25 full-time (12 women), 1 part-time (0 women); includes 2 minority (1 African American, 1 American Indian/Alaska Native), 12 international. Average age 30. 47 applicants, 17% accepted, 4 enrolled. In 2008, 6 master's, 6 doctorates awarded. *Degree requirements:* For master's, one foreign language, thesis; for doctorate, 2 foreign languages, thesis/dissertation, final and qualifying exams. *Entrance requirements:* For master's, GRE General Test; for doctorate, GRE General Test, writing sample in Spanish. Additional exam requirements/recommendations for international students: Required—TOEFL (minimum score 570 paper-based; 230 computer-based; 88 iBT). *Application deadline:* For fall admission, 1/15 for domestic and international students. Application fee: $0. Electronic applications accepted. *Financial support:* Fellowships with full and partial tuition reimbursements, teaching assistantships with full tuition reimbursements, Federal Work-Study, institutionally sponsored loans, and health care benefits available. Financial award application deadline: 1/15; financial award applicants required to submit CSS PROFILE or FAFSA. *Faculty research:* Spanish, Portuguese, and Latin American literatures; foreign language pedagogy; Renaissance and baroque poetry; nineteenth century Spanish novel. *Unit head:* Cathy L. Jrade, PhD, Chair, 615-322-6930, Fax: 615-343-7260, E-mail: cathy.l.jrade@vanderbilt.edu. *Application contact:* Christina Karageorgou-Bastea, PhD, Director of Graduate Studies, 615-322-6930, Fax: 615-343-7260, E-mail: christina.karageorgou@vanderbilt.edu.

Washington State University, Graduate School, College of Liberal Arts, Department of Foreign Languages and Cultures, Pullman, WA 99164. Offers foreign languages with emphasis in Spanish (MA). *Degree requirements:* For master's, comprehensive exam (for some programs), thesis (for some programs), 4 written exams, oral exam, master's paper. *Entrance requirements:* For master's, minimum GPA of 3.0, speech tapes, writing sample, 3 letters of recommendation. Additional exam requirements/recommendations for international students: Required—TOEFL (minimum score 550 paper-based). Electronic applications accepted. *Faculty research:* Spanish and Latin American literature, film, and culture; pedagogy; computer-aided instruction.

Washington University in St. Louis, Graduate School of Arts and Sciences, Department of Romance Languages and Literatures, Program in Spanish, St. Louis, MO 63130-4899. Offers MA, PhD. *Students:* 41 full-time (32 women); includes 6 minority (all Hispanic Americans), 22 international. 29 applicants, 28% accepted, 3 enrolled. In 2008, 1 master's awarded. Terminal master's awarded for partial completion of doctoral program. *Degree requirements:* For master's, thesis or alternative; for doctorate, thesis/dissertation. *Entrance requirements:* For master's and doctorate, GRE General Test. *Application deadline:* For fall admission, 1/15 priority date for domestic students. Application fee: $45. Electronic applications accepted. *Financial support:* Fellowships, teaching assistantships, tuition waivers (full and partial) available. Financial award application deadline: 1/15. *Unit head:* Dr. Elzbieta Sklodowska, Chairperson, 314-935-5175. *Application contact:* Assistant to the Dean, 314-935-6880, Fax: 314-935-4887.

Wayne State University, College of Liberal Arts and Sciences, Department of Classical and Modern Languages, Literatures, and Cultures, Program in Spanish, Detroit, MI 48202. Offers MA. *Degree requirements:* For master's, one foreign language, thesis optional. *Entrance requirements:* For master's, GRE General Test, minimum GPA of 3.0. Additional exam requirements/recommendations for international students: Required—TOEFL (minimum score 550 paper-based; 213 computer-based); Recommended—TWE (minimum score 6). Electronic applications accepted. *Faculty research:* Drama of the Golden Age, eighteenth century humanism, Romanticism, twentieth century essay.

West Chester University of Pennsylvania, Office of Graduate Studies, College of Arts and Sciences, Department of Languages and Cultures, West Chester, PA 19383. Offers French (M Ed, MA, Teaching Certificate); German (Teaching Certificate); Latin (Teaching Certificate); Spanish (M Ed, MA, Teaching Certificate). Part-time and evening/weekend programs available. *Students:* 7 full-time (6 women), 14 part-time (all women); includes 2 minority (1 African American, 1 Hispanic American), 1 international. Average age 34. 16 applicants, 100% accepted, 8 enrolled. In 2008, 3 master's awarded. *Degree requirements:* For master's, one foreign language, comprehensive exam, thesis optional. *Entrance requirements:* For master's, GRE or MAT, placement test. Additional exam requirements/recommendations for international students: Required—TOEFL (minimum score 550 paper-based; 213 computer-based; 80 iBT). *Application deadline:* For fall admission, 4/15 priority date for domestic students, 3/15 for international students; for spring admission, 10/15 for domestic students, 9/1 for international students. Applications are processed on a rolling basis. Application fee: $35. Electronic applications accepted. *Expenses:* Tuition, state resident: full-time $6430; part-time $357 per credit. Tuition, nonresident: full-time $10,288; part-time $572 per credit. Required fees: $652.50; $50 per credit. $67 per semester. *Financial support:* In 2008–09, 1 research assistantship with full and partial tuition reimbursement (averaging $5,000 per year) was awarded; unspecified assistantships also available. Support available to part-time students. Financial award application deadline: 2/15; financial award applicants required to submit FAFSA. *Faculty research:* Implementation of world languages curriculum framework. *Unit head:* Dr. Jerry Williams, Chair, 610-436-2700, Fax: 610-436-3048, E-mail: jwilliams2@wcupa.edu. *Application contact:* Dr. Rebecca Pauly, Graduate Coordinator, 610-436-2382, E-mail: rpauly@wcupa.edu.

Western Michigan University, Graduate College, College of Arts and Sciences, Department of Foreign Languages and Literatures, Kalamazoo, MI 49008-5202. Offers Spanish (MA, PhD). *Degree requirements:* For master's, oral exam.

West Virginia University, Eberly College of Arts and Sciences, Department of Foreign Languages, Morgantown, WV 26506. Offers French (MA); linguistics (MA); Spanish (MA); teaching English to speakers of other languages (MA). Part-time programs available. *Degree requirements:* For master's, one foreign language, comprehensive exam (for some programs), thesis optional. *Entrance requirements:* For master's, minimum GPA of 3.0. Electronic applications accepted. *Faculty research:* French, German, and Spanish literature; foreign language pedagogy; English as a second language; cultural studies; linguistics.

Wichita State University, Graduate School, Fairmount College of Liberal Arts and Sciences, Department of Modern and Classical Languages and Literatures, Wichita, KS 67260. Offers Spanish (MA). Part-time programs available. *Degree requirements:* For master's, one foreign language, comprehensive exam. *Entrance requirements:* For master's, GRE. Additional exam requirements/recommendations for international students: Required—TOEFL. Electronic applications accepted.

Winthrop University, College of Arts and Sciences, Program in Spanish, Rock Hill, SC 29733. Offers MA. Part-time programs available. *Entrance requirements:* For master's, GRE General Test and PRAXIS, minimum GPA of 3.0, 24 hours of undergraduate Spanish, or interview. Electronic applications accepted.

Worcester State College, Graduate Studies, Department of Education, Program in Spanish, Worcester, MA 01602-2597. Offers M Ed. Part-time programs available. *Faculty:* 2 full-time (both women). *Students:* 11 part-time (8 women); includes 3 minority (all Hispanic Americans). Average age 32. 8 applicants, 63% accepted, 2 enrolled. In 2008, 3 master's awarded. *Degree requirements:* For master's, comprehensive exam (for some programs), thesis optional. *Entrance requirements:* Additional exam requirements/recommendations for international students: Required—TOEFL (minimum score 550 paper-based; 213 computer-based; 79 iBT). *Application deadline:* Applications are processed on a rolling basis. *Expenses:* Tuition, area resident: Full-time $2700; part-time $150 per credit. Tuition, state resident: full-time $2700; part-time $150 per credit. Tuition, nonresident: full-time $2700; part-time $150 per credit. Required fees: $1530; $85 per credit. *Financial support:* Career-related internships or fieldwork, scholarships/grants, and unspecified assistantships available. Financial award application deadline: 3/1; financial award applicants required to submit FAFSA. *Unit head:* Dr. Juan Orbe, Head, 508-929-8704, Fax: 508-929-8174, E-mail: jorbe@worcester.edu. *Application contact:* Nicole Brown, Assistant Dean of Graduate and Continuing Education, 508-929-8787, Fax: 508-929-8100, E-mail: nbrown@worcester.edu.

Yale University, Graduate School of Arts and Sciences, Department of Spanish and Portuguese, New Haven, CT 06520. Offers Latin American literature (PhD); Luso-Brazilian and Spanish/Spanish American literatures (PhD); Spanish peninsular literature (PhD). Terminal master's awarded for partial completion of doctoral program. *Degree requirements:* For doctorate, 3 foreign languages, thesis/dissertation. *Entrance requirements:* For doctorate, GRE General Test.

AUBURN UNIVERSITY

College of Liberal Arts
Department of English

Programs of Study
Programs of study in the Department of English at Auburn University lead to the Master of Arts (M.A.), the Master of Technical and Professional Communication (M.T.P.C.), and the Doctorate (Ph.D.) degrees. There is also a non-degree option. The Department offers a wide range of courses in American, British, and comparative literatures; literary theory; creative writing; linguistics; rhetoric and composition; and technical and professional communication. The Department seeks to enroll 6–8 new Ph.D. students and 12–15 new master's level students each year. More than 70 students are currently enrolled in our graduate programs, about half of whom are Ph.D. students. There are slightly more women than men enrolled in our program.

Functioning as a terminal degree and as preparation for doctoral study, Auburn University's M.A. enhances students' previous training. Minimum requirements are eight courses and a thesis (thesis option) or ten courses (nonthesis option). Students must also demonstrate reading ability in a foreign language. Students can focus course work in any of the above listed areas or combine courses from several areas to create an individualized program of study. Two courses from another department may be approved as a minor within this degree program. In addition to course work, students must pass a written examination.

The M.T.P.C. prepares students for careers as professional writers, technical editors and communicators, and teachers of technical and professional communication, as well as for doctoral work-study. Students take four required courses, three electives in English, and three courses in a coordinated minor field. Students must also pass a comprehensive exam and submit a portfolio of work.

Auburn's Ph.D. program ranks ninth nationally among low-cost schools with low student-faculty ratios and high graduate placement rates in the online Guide to Graduate Programs (sponsored by the Alfred P. Sloan Foundation and the Burroughs Wellcome Fund). The program prepares students to become scholars and to teach in higher education. It requires a minimum of sixteen courses beyond the B.A. or seven courses beyond the M.A. Working in consultation with their advisory committees, doctoral students balance broad preparation with the development of three specialized areas for their written and oral examinations. These areas include topics in literature (e.g., major authors, literary genres and periods, critical theory) and language (e.g., composition, linguistics, stylistics, rhetoric). Doctoral students must demonstrate a reading knowledge of two 'or extensive knowledge of one foreign language. The Ph.D. program requires candidates to write and defend a dissertation.

Research Facilities
The University and the English Department offer graduate students ready access to current technologies. Draughon Library, a member of the Association of Research Libraries, is a leader in computer-assisted research tools and facilities. It houses nearly 3 million volumes and has nearly 3 million items on microform, including full and current collections in English studies. Additionally, the library receives over 35,000 current periodicals, many of which are available online, and provides access to more than 200 databases.

Financial Aid
All students admitted to graduate degree programs in English are offered financial aid in the form of a renewable graduate teaching assistantship. The current stipend is $13,528 for M.A. and M.T.P.C. students and $14,212 for Ph.D. students. The teaching assistantship additionally covers tuition except for a small matriculation fee each semester. Each year, 5 highly ranked entering students receive an additional fellowship. Minority doctoral students are eligible for a renewable financial aid package of approximately $20,000 per year.

Entering master's-level graduate assistants co-teach two sections with experienced instructors. Returning graduate assistants typically teach three sections of introductory composition yearly. Doctoral-level graduate assistants may request to teach world literature. The Department also offers support for professional travel.

Living and Housing Costs
Room and board for an individual cost approximately $7500 annually. There is a variety of affordable housing from which to choose, including rental apartments, duplexes, and town houses.

Student Group
The Department seeks to enroll 6–8 new Ph.D. students and 12–15 new master's-level students each year. More than 70 graduate students are currently enrolled in graduate programs; about half of them are Ph.D. students. There are slightly more women than men enrolled in the Ph.D. program.

Student Outcomes
Recent graduates of the master's programs have advanced to doctoral or other professional programs at Auburn and other colleges and universities, including Cornell, Emory, Florida, Georgia, North Carolina, Pittsburgh, South Carolina, Texas, Tufts, and Wisconsin; others have entered law or divinity school or have begun careers in teaching, editing, professional and technical writing, and program administration in the U.S. and abroad. Ninety percent of M.T.P.C. graduates obtain suitable positions within three months of graduation. Recent graduates of the Ph.D. program have found tenure-track positions at Alabama State, Gainesville State College, Huntington College, Middle Tennessee State, Saint Louis University, Seton Hall, Oregon State University, the Savannah College of Art and Design, Stephen F. Austin State University, and Wisconsin–Eau Claire. Some Ph.D. graduates have also established successful careers in software development, editing, and humanities administration.

Location
The University is located in Auburn, Alabama, 60 miles from Montgomery, home of the Alabama Shakespeare Festival and the Civil Rights Memorial, and 120 miles from both Birmingham and Atlanta. All three cities are easily accessible by interstate highways. Gulf Coast beaches are about 4 hours away by car. Although the area has a population of more than 100,000, Auburn affords the security, seclusion, and clean air of a small town in rural surroundings. There are many recreational opportunities.

The University and The Department
Chartered in 1856 as a private college, Auburn University is now Alabama's public land-grant institution and the largest university in the state, enrolling almost 24,000 students, including more than 3,000 graduate students. Auburn operates on the semester system. English is the largest single department in the University. Among its graduate faculty are 5 named chairs. The Department plays a vital role in the University's core curriculum, teaching writing and world literature courses to every Auburn student. The Department sponsors conferences and colloquia, lectures, readings, and discussion groups and is home to three professional journals: *Southern Humanities Review, IEEE,* and *Literary Imagination: Review of the Association of Literary Scholars and Critics,* which is published by Oxford University Press. Each spring, the English Graduate Association sponsors a research colloquium.

Applying
Graduate students matriculate in the fall semester, when graduate assistantship appointments begin. Review of applications begins in January; initial offers of admission are made in late winter or early spring. Successful applicants present strong undergraduate preparation, competitive GRE scores, and cogent writing samples and statements of purpose. Applications and information requests can be processed online through the Department's Web site from links on http://media.cla.auburn.eud/english/gs/index.cfm.

Correspondence and Information
Coordinator of Graduate Studies
Department of English
9030 Haley Center
Auburn University
Auburn, Alabama 36849-5203

Phone: 334-844-4620
Fax: 334-844-9027
E-mail: gradenglish@auburn.edu
Web site: http://www.auburn.edu/english/gs/

Auburn University

THE FACULTY AND THEIR RESEARCH

Chantel Acevedo, Assistant Professor; M.F.A., Miami (Florida), 1999. Fiction.

Paula R. Backscheider, Professor and West Point Stevens–H. M. Philpott Eminent Scholar in English; Ph.D., Purdue, 1972. Restoration and eighteenth-century literature, the novel and novel theory, feminist criticism and theory.

Craig Bertolet, Associate Professor; Ph.D., Penn State, 1995. Medieval literature.

Jon Bolton, Associate Professor; Ph.D., Maryland, 1996. Twentieth-century British literature.

Peter Campion, Assistant Professor; M.A., Boston College, 2000. Poetry.

Alicia Carroll, Associate Professor; Ph.D., CUNY Graduate Center, 1995. Nineteenth-century British fiction.

Miriam Marty Clark, Associate Professor; Ph.D., North Carolina at Chapel Hill, 1986. Twentieth-century literature, the short story, poetry.

George W. Crandell, Professor; Ph.D., Texas, 1985. Twentieth-century American literature, bibliography, textual criticism, Tennessee Williams.

Jeremy M. Downes, Associate Professor; Ph.D., Wisconsin, 1991. Poetry, poetics, poetry writing, the epic.

R. James Goldstein, Professor; Ph.D., Virginia, 1987. Medieval literature, critical theory.

Christopher Keirstead, Assistant Professor; Ph.D., Delaware, 1999. Nineteenth-century British poetry, travel literature.

Virginia M. Kouidis, Associate Professor; Ph.D., Iowa, 1972. American literature, twentieth-century English and American literature, modern poetry, women's literature, feminist criticism.

Dan Latimer, Professor; Ph.D., Michigan, 1972. Criticism, comparative literature, modernism, symbolism.

Jo Mackiewicz, Assistant Professor; Ph.D., Georgetown, 2001. Technical and professional communication, applied linguistics.

Trimiko Melancon, Assistant Professor; Ph.D., Massachusetts Amherst, 2006. African American literature.

Susanna Morris, Assistant Professor; Ph.D., Emory, 2007. African American literature.

Thomas E. Nunnally, Associate Professor; Ph.D., Georgia, 1985. Historical English linguistics, Old English language and literature, grammatical theories, usage study.

Constance C. Relihan, Ph.D., Minnesota, 1989. Renaissance literature, prose fiction before 1700, Shakespeare, early women writers.

Anya Riehl, Assistant Professor; Ph.D., Illinois at Chicago, 2007. Early modern British literature.

Kevin Roozen, Assistant Professor; Ph.D., Illinois at Urbana-Champaign, 2005. Composition and rhetoric.

Joyce Rothschild, Assistant Professor; Ph.D., Maryland, 1983. Technical communication, professional editing.

James Emmett Ryan, Associate Professor; Ph.D., North Carolina at Chapel Hill, 1999. Nineteenth-century American literature, religion and literature.

Robin Sabino, Associate Professor; Ph.D., Pennsylvania, 1990. Sociolinguistics, ESL, phonetics/phonology, grammatical theory.

Michelle A. Sidler, Assistant Professor; Ph.D., Purdue, 1998. Composition and rhetoric, literary theory.

Marc Silverstein, Hollifield Associate Professor of English Literature; Ph.D., Brown, 1989. Contemporary drama, critical theory, drama as a genre, postmodernism.

Sunny Stalter, Assistant Professor; Ph.D., Rutgers, 2007. Twentieth-century American literature, modernism, American studies.

Isabelle Thompson, Professor; Ed.D., Duke, 1982. Composition and rhetoric, technical communication.

Joanne Tong, Assistant Professor; Ph.D., UCLA, 2005. British Romanticism.

Judy Troy, Professor and Alumni Writer in Residence; M.A., Indiana, 1981. Fiction writing, the short story, twentieth-century American fiction.

Donald R. Wehrs, Associate Professor; Ph.D., Virginia, 1986. The novel, eighteenth-century British literature, critical theory.

Stewart Whittemore, Assistant Professor; Ph.D., Michigan State, 2008. Rhetoric, technical and professional communication.

Hilary E. Wyss, Associate Professor; Ph.D., North Carolina at Chapel Hill, 1998. Early American literature, Native American literature, American studies.

Susan Youngblood, Assistant Professor; Ph.D., Texas Tech, 2008. Technical communication and rhetoric, risk communication.

Matt Zarnowiecki, Assistant Professor; Ph.D., Columbia, 2007. Early modern British literature.

BOSTON COLLEGE

Graduate School of Arts and Sciences
Department of Romance Languages and Literatures

Programs of Study

The Department of Romance Languages and Literatures at Boston College offers an extensive program of language, literature, and culture in French, Italian, and Hispanic studies on the Chestnut Hill, Massachusetts, campus and in many countries overseas through a variety of international partnerships. The Department offers Master of Arts (M.A.) degrees in French, Hispanic, and Italian literature and culture and Master of Arts in Teaching (M.A.T.) degrees in French and Hispanic studies. Ph.D. degrees are available in French and Hispanic literature or studies. The master's program in French, Hispanic, or Italian literature and culture requires 30 credits (10 courses) in Romance languages and literatures. M.A. candidates may receive a maximum of 9 credits for courses taken in languages/literatures other than the primary language/literature of study, including courses on literary theory, pedagogy, and linguistics. Included in this limit, and with the approval of the Graduate Studies Committee, up to 6 credits may be earned from courses in related areas of study.

The Master of Arts in Teaching program is administered through the Lynch Graduate School of Education in cooperation with the Department of Romance Languages and Literatures. Applicants to the M.A.T. program should apply directly to the Lynch Graduate School of Education. The program provides certification and continued professional development for primary and secondary school teachers of French and Hispanic studies. Students must complete a minimum of 30 credits, with an average of B or better. A minimum of 15 credits must be completed in the School of Education.

The department also offers a three-year M.A./M.B.A. in French or Hispanic Studies, and International Management degree in coordination with the Carroll School of Management.

The program of doctoral study in French, Hispanic, or Italian studies is designed to build on each candidate's strengths and develop individual interests that culminate in fields of specialization—the springboards for a professional academic career. Students enroll in Plan I or Plan II of the Ph.D. program. Plan I involves in-depth work in one literature and culture. In Plan II, students work concurrently in two languages and literatures. One of the most frequently pursued fields in the Plan II doctoral program is the exceptional Medieval Studies program. Students choose two of the following literatures: medieval Catalan, French, Italian, Spanish, or Provençal. Boston College offers a rich array of courses in medieval studies in such departments as Theology, History, Philosophy, Fine Arts, and Political Science. Students entering with an M.A. who are accepted for the doctoral program are granted transfer credit for the M.A. degree or its equivalent of 30 credits. The M.A. equivalency of foreign degrees is determined, whenever appropriate, through communication with the Bureau of Comparative Education of the Division of the International Education in Washington, D.C. Students with a bachelor's degree entering the Ph.D. program must take a course of study equivalent to that required for the M.A. in French or Hispanic literatures. After earning 30 credits, students are evaluated as potential Ph.D. candidates.

The Graduate School of Arts and Sciences stipulates that a student must complete all requirements for the M.A. degree within five consecutive years from the date of acceptance into the program. Despite the University's five-year time limit for finishing the M.A. degree, the Department fully expects students to complete all requirements within two years of entering the program.

Research Facilities

Boston College provides its students with state-of-the-art facilities for learning, including a full range of computer services, online access to databases, and a library system with more than 1.9 million books, periodicals, and government documents and 3.4 million microform units. The library's membership in the Boston Library Consortium provides access to ten major research libraries in the Boston area, and an interlibrary loan system provides further resources.

The Language Laboratory serves the language learning and teaching needs of Boston College's language departments, students of English as a foreign language, and the community at large from its center in Lyons Hall. The facility provides access to installed and portable equipment for use with audio, video, cable television, Internet, and multimedia language-learning tools. The lab has an extensive catalog of resources in seventeen languages to facilitate language learning and teaching and to promote cultural awareness.

Financial Aid

The following forms of financial assistance are available to students in the Department: teaching fellowships, graduate assistantships, and two Fellow-in-Residence positions. Appointments and awards are competitive and are based on the candidate's academic background and experience. For those seeking teaching fellowships, an interview in French, Italian, or Spanish is required. For more information about Boston College's financial assistance or government grants, students should contact the Office of Student Services.

Cost of Study

The tuition rate for the Graduate School of Arts and Sciences is $1182 per credit for the 2009–10 year. The student activities fee ranges from $25 to $50 per semester, depending on the number of credits taken. The cost of books varies by semester. Additional fees may apply.

Living and Housing Costs

Rental housing is plentiful in the surrounding cities and towns. Many different types of housing are available, ranging from one-room rentals in large Victorian homes to triple-decker brownstones and apartment high-rises. Allston-Brighton and Jamaica Plain are among the nearby Boston neighborhoods that attract students from many colleges and universities because of their diverse communities and relative affordability. Graduate students also have found Newton, Brookline, Waltham, Watertown, and Boston's West Roxbury neighborhood attractive places to live. Boston College's Off-Campus Housing Office is available to assist in the housing search. The Off-Campus Housing Office maintains an extensive database of available rental listings, roommates, and helpful local realtors.

Student Group

There are more than 50 students enrolled in the Department's various degree programs in 2009–10.

Location

The Graduate School of Arts and Sciences is located on the Chestnut Hill campus of Boston College, approximately 6 miles west of the city of Boston, Massachusetts. Boston offers students the opportunity to experience one of the oldest cities in the U.S., with museums, a symphony orchestra, and world championship professional basketball, baseball, ice hockey, and football teams. The city of Boston also offers a wide variety of shopping, dining, and cultural experiences—all located on the beautiful Boston Harbor and Charles River.

The College and The School

Founded in 1863, Boston College is one of the oldest Jesuit-sponsored universities in the United States. It has professional and graduate schools, doctoral programs, research institutes, community service programs, an excellent faculty, and rich resources of libraries, research equipment, computers, and other facilities. A coeducational university, it has an enrollment of approximately 9,000 undergraduate and 4,700 graduate and professional students representing every state and nearly 100 countries. Boston College confers degrees in more than fifty fields of study through its eleven schools and colleges. It has more than 600 full-time faculty members committed to both teaching and research.

The Graduate School of Arts and Sciences is the oldest of the seven graduate and professional schools at Boston College. The Graduate School offers programs of study in the humanities, social sciences, and natural sciences, leading to the degrees of Doctor of Philosophy (Ph.D.), Master of Arts (M.A.), and Master of Science (M.S.). In addition, the Graduate School offers numerous dual-degree options in cooperation with the Graduate School of Social Work, the Lynch School of Education, the Carroll School of Management, and the Boston College Law School. Non-degree-seeking students may be admitted into the Graduate School as Special Students. The Graduate School of Arts and Sciences operates on a semester calendar, with the fall semester running from late August until mid-December and the spring semester running from late January until late May.

Applying

Students are generally admitted only in the fall semester. The deadline for applying for the fall semester is January 2. Candidates for all Master of Arts programs should have an undergraduate major or its equivalent in the appropriate field, including advanced composition and surveys of the pertinent literatures. Because all courses in the Department are conducted in French, Italian, or Spanish, students are expected to enter the program with sufficiently advanced oral and written proficiency to perform with ease in the linguistic environment. Applicants must submit a completed application directly to the Graduate School of Arts and Sciences. Along with the application, students must submit official transcripts of all undergraduate study, three letters of recommendation for those applying to the Ph.D. program and two for those applying to the M.A. program, a statement of purpose, a writing sample in the selected Romance language, a $70 nonrefundable application fee, and GRE scores for those applying to the Ph.D. program.

Correspondence and Information

Department of Romance Languages and Literatures
Lyons Hall, Room 304
Boston College
140 Commonwealth Avenue
Chestnut Hill, Massachusetts 02467-3804

Phone: 617-552-3820
Fax: 617-552-2064
E-mail: rll@bc.edu
Web site: http://www.bc.edu/schools/cas/romlang

Boston College

THE FACULTY AND THEIR RESEARCH

Norman Araujo, Associate Professor of French; Ph.D., Harvard. Nineteenth-century French literature, with emphasis on the novel.

Sarah H. Beckjord, Assistant Professor of Spanish; Ph.D., Columbia. Colonial Spanish-American literature, with an emphasis on historiography; nineteenth-century Spanish-American literature.

Stephen C. Bold, Associate Professor of French; Ph.D., NYU. Seventeenth-century French literature, especially philosophical literature, theater, and literature and the arts; linguistics.

Matilda Tomaryn Bruckner, Professor of French; Ph.D., Yale. Medieval French literature, especially twelfth- and thirteenth-century Romance, verse and prose narrative, troubadour and trouvère lyric.

Dwayne E. Carpenter, Professor of Spanish; Ph.D., Berkeley; Ph.D., Graduate Theological Union. Medieval Spanish literature and history, textual criticism, Jewish-Muslim-Christian relations.

Rena A. Lamparska, Associate Professor of Italian; Ph.D., Harvard. Modern Italian literature, with emphasis on the late seventeenth- and eighteenth-century literary theories; Gregorio Caloprese, Giacomo Leopardi, Luigi Pirandello, Italo Calvino.

Kathy Lee, Adjunct Assistant Professor of Spanish; Ph.D., Yale. Nineteenth- and twentieth-century Peninsular literature.

Ernesto Livón-Grosman, Assistant Professor of Hispanic Studies; Ph.D., NYU. Latin-American poetry, autobiography, literary theory.

Irene Mizrahi, Associate Professor of Spanish; Ph.D., Connecticut. Nineteenth- and twentieth-century Spanish literature, Spanish Romanticism (Gustavo Adolfo Bécquer), generation of 1914 (José Ortega y Gasset), contemporary theater (Buero Vallejo), current critical theory.

Franco Mormando, Associate Professor of Italian; Ph.D., Harvard. Popular and Ecclesiastical literature and preaching, fifteenth to seventeenth centuries, social context of Renaissance and Baroque art.

Ourida Mostefai, Associate Professor of French; Ph.D., NYU. Eighteenth-century French literature, Rousseau, polemical literature.

Kevin Newmark, Associate Professor of French; Ph.D., Yale. Nineteenth- and twentieth-century French literature, literary theory.

Elizabeth Rhodes, Associate Professor of Spanish; Ph.D., Bryn Mawr. Early modern Spanish literature, theology and religious culture, women's studies and feminist theory, needle arts.

Harry L. Rosser, Associate Professor of Spanish; Ph.D., North Carolina at Chapel Hill. Latin-American novel, short prose fiction, essay, Latin-American studies, applied linguistics.

Laurie Shepard, Associate Professor of Italian; Ph.D., Boston College. Status of opinion in medieval and Renaissance public discourse, Boccaccio's readers in the fourteenth and fifteenth centuries, coblas esparsa and the decline of the troubadour tradition.

BRYN MAWR COLLEGE

Graduate School of Arts and Sciences
Department of Greek, Latin, and Classical Studies

Programs of Study

The Department of Greek, Latin, and Classical Studies at Bryn Mawr College offers M.A. and Ph.D. degrees in Greek, Latin, and classical languages. In cooperation with the Department of Classical and Near Eastern Archaeology, it also offers the M.A. and Ph.D. in classical studies. It is one of three independent departments that comprise the Graduate Group in Archaeology, Classics, and History of Art.

The focus of the Department has always been on the precise study of ancient texts. Rigorous training in philology and literary analysis is its hallmark. Seminars in Greek tragedy, poetry, history, religion, and magic; Latin poetry, rhetoric, and history; and late antique and early Christian writers are offered regularly. Students are also encouraged to explore the reception of classical texts and the relationship between texts and material culture through interdisciplinary seminars and internships in Philadelphia-area museums and libraries, under the auspices of the Graduate Group. Course work and the M.A. thesis can normally be completed within three years. Ph.D. preliminary examinations should be taken in the fourth or fifth year, followed by the dissertation. For the Ph.D., the median time-to-degree of recent graduates is 8.5 years.

Students are encouraged to develop their own research projects in consultation with a faculty adviser. Recent dissertation projects include Vergilian imitation in Silius Italicus' Punica, Sedulius and Vergil, Female Friendship in Antiquity, Ovid's Remedia Amoris and the Heroides, and Rome's Appropriation of Egypt.

Seventy percent of Ph.D. graduates of the past ten years hold college or university positions teaching classics. M.A. graduates typically teach in public and private secondary schools.

Research Facilities

The reference collection for classics is housed in the award-winning Rhys Carpenter Library, inaugurated in 1997, which is also a specialized library for archaeology and the history of art. Fully wired carrels are available to all students in the Graduate Group in Archaeology, Classics, and History of Art. In addition to the more than 135,000 volumes in Carpenter Library, the tri-college library consortium of Bryn Mawr, Haverford, and Swarthmore Colleges contains over 2 million volumes. Bryn Mawr currently subscribes to more than 300 periodicals and serials in classics and in archaeology. Online reference sources include the TLG, Dyabola, Library of Latin Texts, and *l'Année philologique*. The special collections in the Mariam Coffin Canaday Library include significant resources for classics, including one of the largest collections of incunables in the United States.

Financial Aid

Bryn Mawr offers a number of fellowships for full-time study, as well as grants, tuition awards, and summer stipends. Fellowship stipends begin at $17,500, including a summer stipend, and can be guaranteed for multiple years. Special awards include Areté (Excellence) Fellowships with a package of $20,000 including a health insurance subsidy. Each year, the Department offers two part-time teaching assistantships with stipends of $7000 plus a health insurance subsidy; assistantship stipends can be supplemented by grants to a maximum of $15,000. For students in the Graduate Group in Archaeology, Classics, and History of Art, additional competitive fellowships and curatorial internships for multidisciplinary study are available with twelve-month stipends of $20,000 plus a health insurance subsidy. Currently, 70 percent of the students enrolled in the program in Greek, Latin, and Classical Studies receive some form of financial aid.

Cost of Study

Full-time tuition, consisting of six courses per year, is $31,340; part-time tuition is $5290 per course. Units of supervised work cost $845, and the fee for maintaining matriculation (continuing enrollment) is $430 per semester.

Living and Housing Costs

Students live locally or in Philadelphia. Shared apartments can be rented for $600 to $900 per month, studio apartments begin at $800 per month, and food costs are about $200 per month. Other expenses include transportation (about $165 per month if commuting from Philadelphia) and health insurance (approximately $2500 per year for domestic students and approximately $1500 for international students).

Student Group

In 2009–10, there are 19 students enrolled in classics: 14 women and 5 men. Four students have progressed to Ph.D. candidacy, 3 are candidates for the M.A., and the remaining are in course work.

Student Outcomes

Ph.D. graduates of the past ten years are currently teaching at Carleton University; Christopher Newport University; Fresno Pacific University; Kent State University; Lewis and Clark College; Rutgers University, Newark; and Yale University.

Location

Bryn Mawr is a suburb of Philadelphia, the fifth-largest city in the U.S. It is well served by rail lines and by bus. Philadelphia is renowned for music, museums, and sports, and it is also a culinary mecca, with restaurants serving many cuisines. The metropolitan area has more than 100 museums and fifty colleges and universities, with a total population of 220,000 students.

The College and The Department

Bryn Mawr is a liberal arts college for women, founded in 1885. It was the first college to offer graduate education through the Ph.D. and the first U.S. institution to offer fellowships to women for graduate study. Throughout its history, the College has been committed first and foremost to providing the most rigorous and challenging education to women and, in the Graduate School of Arts and Sciences, also to men. The current enrollment is 1,300 undergraduate students, 150 graduate students in the Graduate School of Arts and Sciences, and about 250 students in the Graduate School of Social Work and Social Research.

Classics has always been a preeminent field of instruction at Bryn Mawr; even the College hymn is in Greek. The Department's tradition of outstanding scholarship and teaching was established by such faculty members as Lily Ross Taylor (1927–1952), Agnes Kirsopp Michaels (1934–1975), Richmond Lattimore (1935–1971), and Mabel Lang (1945–1988). The Department is known worldwide as the home of *The Bryn Mawr Classical Review*, edited by Professor Richard Hamilton, and the *Bryn Mawr Commentaries*.

Applying

Application for admission and financial aid should be made on the form available from the Graduate School of Arts and Sciences. Applicants can also download this form from the Graduate School's Web site at http://www.brynmawr.edu/gsas/. The deadline for admission with financial aid is January 4, 2010. Applications for admission without financial aid are accepted until June 30, 2010.

Students admitted to graduate work in classics typically have demonstrated exceptional aptitude in at least one classical language, excellent command of written English, and a predilection for independent thinking and research. Applicants must submit GRE scores; TOEFL scores, if not native speakers of English; a statement of interest; and a recent research paper or critical essay. Prerequisites include at least three years at the undergraduate level of Greek or Latin. For a degree in classical languages, three years of Greek and Latin are prerequisites.

Students are encouraged to contact the Department and to visit. The Department Web site is http://www.brynmawr.edu/gradgroup/classics/.

Correspondence and Information

Lea Miller, Program Assistant
Graduate School of Arts and Sciences
Bryn Mawr College
101 North Merion Avenue
Bryn Mawr, Pennsylvania 19010
Phone: 610-526-5072
Fax: 610-526-5076
E-mail: lrmiller@brynmawr.edu
Web site: http://www.brynmawr.edu/gsas/

Bryn Mawr College

THE FACULTY AND THEIR RESEARCH

Annette Baertschi, Assistant Professor; Ph.D., Humboldt, 2006. Post-Augustan poetry, ancient magic, Latin meter, reception.

Catherine Conybeare, Associate Professor; Ph.D., Toronto, 1997. Late antique and early medieval Latin prose, cultural history, critical theory.

Radcliffe G. Edmonds III, Associate Professor; Ph.D., Chicago, 1999. Greek myth, Greco-Roman religion and magic, Greek philosophy.

Richard Hamilton, Paul Shorey Professor of Greek; Ph.D., Michigan, 1971. Greek lyric poetry, Greek drama, Greek religion.

Russell T. Scott, Doreen C. Spitzer Professor of Latin and Classical Studies; Ph.D., Yale, 1964. Roman history and historiography, Latin literature, Roman archaeology.

Affiliated Faculty

Mehmet-Ali Ataç, Assistant Professor, Department of Classical and Near Eastern Archaeology; Ph.D., Harvard, 2003. Visual and intellectual traditions of the ancient Near East; Neo-Assyrian art and architecture, ancient Near Eastern and Egyptian kingship.

A. A. Donohue, Professor, Department of Classical and Near Eastern Archaeology; Ph.D., NYU, 1984. History and historiography of classical art.

Robert Germany, Assistant Professor, Haverford College; Ph.D., Chicago, 2008. Roman comedy, the ancient novel, the Homeric hymns, magic in Latin literature, seventeenth- and eighteenth-century German reception of classics.

Peter Magee, Associate Professor, Department of Classical and Near Eastern Archaeology; Ph.D., Sydney, 1996. Archaeology of South Asia, Iran, and Arabia; ancient imperialism; field methods; materials analysis.

Bret Mulligan, Assistant Professor, Haverford College; Ph.D., Brown. Greek and Latin epic and epistolography, late antique Greek and Latin literature, the classical tradition.

Deborah H. Roberts, Professor, Haverford College; Ph.D., Yale. Greek tragedy, Latin poetry, reception and translation of classical literature, literary theory.

James C. Wright, Professor, Department of Classical and Near Eastern Archaeology; Ph.D., Bryn Mawr, 1978. Prehistory of the Aegean basin, settlement forms and architecture of classical Greece, theory and method in archaeology.

SAINT LOUIS UNIVERSITY–MADRID CAMPUS

Master's in Spanish Language and Literature and Master's in English

Programs of Study

Two programs of study are offered: Master of Arts degree in Spanish and the dual-degree Master's in English. Both programs are accredited by the North Central Association of Schools and Colleges (NCA). The M.A. in English, offered jointly with the Universidad Autónoma de Madrid (UAM), is also recognized as *Formación Permanente del Profesorado* (8 Apartado de la Resolución de 27 de April de 1997, B.O.E. de 25 de Mayo) for English teachers in Spain.

The Master of Arts degree program in Spanish is specifically designed for students interested in pursuing concentrated studies in a combination of Spanish language and Hispanic cultures and literature. The curriculum is suited to those individuals planning, or already engaged in, professional careers such as teaching or international affairs. The program also prepares students who wish to continue study in a Ph.D. degree program in Spanish or a related field.

Students who choose to enroll in the program at the Madrid Campus have the opportunity to immerse themselves in Spanish culture, taking with them not only a graduate degree and a stronger knowledge of Spanish language and literature, but also the experience of studying a language in its native country. Participants perfect their oral and written Spanish communication skills and broaden their knowledge of the rich Spanish literature and culture as they study with Ph.D. faculty members, all of whom are native Spanish speakers.

The program may be completed during a series of five-week summer sessions (usually three, four, or five summers). It may also be completed through attending classes during the traditional academic year, complemented by a summer or two. If students choose to spend three summers in Madrid, each summer they take two M.A. courses, each worth 3 credits, and two *Cursos de Perfeccionamiento* or optional M.A. courses, each worth 2 credits. Throughout their program, a full-time faculty member serves as their adviser. During their last session, students take the final written and oral exams.

Cursos de Perfeccionamiento, designed for secondary school teachers of Spanish, are in-service language and literature classes that allow students to earn from 2 to 8 credits by taking from one to four enrichment courses.

Saint Louis University's master's degree in English can be earned at both its Madrid and St. Louis campuses. Those students pursuing the degree in Spain meet the same admissions requirements and follow the same program as those pursuing the degree in the U.S. This dual-degree program seeks primarily to engage students in a disciplined study of texts drawn from the full experience of English and American literature. Giving due recognition to the history of the English literary tradition as it has unfolded from the Middle Ages to the present, the M.A. in English also alerts students to the exciting developments in the realm of literary theory and offers them opportunities for exploring the interpretation of English literature with the writings of other cultures and with issues raised in other fields.

Classes are taught by American and European Ph.D. faculty members from both Saint Louis University and the Universidad Autónoma de Madrid, providing a unique, international perspective on British, North American, and Anglophone literature. The individualized course of study allows students to select ten graduate seminars from such areas as the traditional periods and genres of literature in English, literary theory, linguistics, the teaching of writing, and translation.

Students completing the one- to two-year program (30 credits in the U.S. system, 70 in the European [ECTS]) earn a Master of Arts in English from Saint Louis University and a *Máster en Estudios Culturales y Anglo-norteamericanos* from the Universidad Autónoma de Madrid.

Courses in Madrid are offered on a trimester basis (October-December, January-March, April-June), to accommodate the European academic calendar. Students also take two seminars during a six-week summer session in St. Louis, Missouri. At the conclusion of their course work, students take a 1-hour oral examination on a reading list, which they have a hand in shaping.

Research Facilities

The resources of the Madrid Campus Library are bilingual in nature and designed primarily to meet the needs of the students studying at this campus. The 9,000 books and 60 journals that compose its collection respond to specific bibliographies that supplement courses offered. Furthermore, the Madrid Campus Library offers students and faculty members access to all electronic resources available at the University's main campus in St. Louis, Missouri, via the SLU proxy server and to other electronic research aids via the Pius XII library in St. Louis, Missouri.

In addition, M.A. students may request reading privileges at all libraries in Madrid and Europe, including Spain's National Library *(Biblioteca Nacional)*, the country's foremost research library; the Center of North American Studies Library; the British Studies Information Center; and the British Council Library. Interlibrary loan facilities are also available, with exceptionally fast access to current periodicals via the British Library (UK) Document Supply Service as well as several Spanish research libraries.

The UAM libraries support both a B.A. and a Ph.D. program in English language and literature. The libraries of the Universidad Autónoma de Madrid contain more than 500,000 books and 4,500 periodical subscriptions. The UAM's online services provide direct links to databases, information resources, electronic journals, and catalogs of other university libraries in Madrid and around the world.

Financial Aid

U.S. citizens may apply U.S. federal financial aid to their studies at Saint Louis University–Madrid Campus. All students are eligible to apply for work-study grants. Awards are made only after a student gains full admission to the program.

Cost of Study

Costs for the 2008–09 academic year were €410 per credit hour. Students may enroll on a full-time or part-time basis. Costs for *Cursos de Perfeccionamiento* were €360 per credit.

Living and Housing Costs

During the traditional academic year, most graduate students choose to rent apartments near the campus. While prices vary according to apartment size and neighborhood, two-bedroom apartments usually start at €1000 per month in Madrid. Students may also take part in the Madrid campus residential housing program, which allows them to live in a Spanish household. Costs range from €550 to €740 per month, depending on board plan and kitchen privileges, and other factors.

During the summer, housing is available for individuals in University-run shared apartments. For couples and families, arrangements can be made to live in private apartments.

Student Group

Students enrolled in the graduate programs at the Madrid Campus come from across the United States and Europe. During the academic year, the campus hosts up to 20 graduate students; during the summer session, up to 60 students.

Location

Madrid, Spain's capital, with a population of more than 4 million, is politically, culturally, and geographically the heart of Spain. The campus is located in the university quarter of Madrid, overlooking the Sierra de Guatarrama Mountains, only 20 minutes by metro from Puerta del Sol. Surrounded by other private Spanish universities, the campus' location facilitates interaction between the University's Spanish, international, and American students.

M.A. in English students also pursue courses during the summer in the St. Louis campus of Saint Louis University, an architecturally rich urban campus located in the center of the city. The Universidad Autónoma de Madrid's spacious campus, located in Cantoblanco, is a few kilometers north of Madrid and is easily accessible via public transport.

The University

Saint Louis University is a Catholic, Jesuit university and leading research institution. Founded in 1818, the University strives to foster the intellectual and spiritual growth of its students through a broad array of undergraduate, graduate, and professional degree programs on campuses in St. Louis, Missouri, and Madrid, Spain. The Madrid Campus was the first American university program in Spain and the first free-standing campus in Europe operated by a U.S.-based university.

Applying

Spanish Language and Literature: Applications are evaluated for evidence of preparation for advanced study of language and literature and the likelihood of academic success. Applicants need to submit a classified (degree-seeking) application (included in the application packet and available online), an application fee of US$40, Graduate Record Examinations (GRE) General Test or Miller Analogies Test scores, official transcripts of all academic work completed in undergraduate, graduate, and/or professional schools, three letters of recommendation (forms are included in the application packet and are available online), a biographical goal statement of 500 words that addresses the applicant's intellectual and professional goals, a writing sample, and a curriculum vitae.

To be considered for October admission, candidates must submit materials by March 1; for January, by December 1; and for April, by February 1.

Students should make arrangements to take the Graduate Record Examinations (GRE) or Miller Analogies Test as soon as possible and have the score reports sent directly to Saint Louis University. All other materials should be sent directly to the Madrid Campus.

Cursos candidates must submit an online application as a visiting U.S. student for the second summer session, an application fee of $45 (payable online), and official transcripts of all academic work completed. Though not required, it is highly recommended that students submit at least one letter of recommendation from their department chair, principal, or other professional contact. To be considered for summer admission, all documents must be received by Saint Louis University–Madrid Campus by April 30.

English: Applications are reviewed by faculty members from both Saint Louis University and the Universidad Autónoma de Madrid. Candidates are evaluated for evidence of preparation for advanced study of literature and the likelihood of academic success.

Applicants should hold a B.A. or *Licenciatura* in English or the equivalent, with an excellent academic record. Saint Louis University's Graduate School of Arts and Sciences also requires evidence of competence or successful study of a classical or modern foreign language. Native speakers of a language other than English fulfill this requirement automatically. Candidates must submit an application, undergraduate academic transcripts, three letters of recommendation, Graduate Record Examinations (GRE) scores (both general and subject tests), a current CV, a 500-word statement of purpose, a writing sample, and a $40 application fee.

To be considered for October admission, candidates must submit materials by March 1; for January, by December 1; and for April, by February 1.

Correspondence and Information

Graduate Admissions
Saint Louis University–Madrid Campus
Avenida del Valle, 34
28003 Madrid, España

Phone: 34-91-554-5858
Fax: 34-91-554-6202
E-mail: graduate_admissions@madrid.slu.edu
Web site: http://spain.slu.edu

Saint Louis University, Madrid

THE FACULTY AND THEIR RESEARCH

Master's in Spanish Language and Literature

Aitor Bikandi, Ph.D., Cincinnati. Nineteenth- and twentieth-century peninsular narrative, cultural studies, peninsular film.

Xelo Candel, Ph.D., Universidad de Valencia. Twentieth-century Latin American and peninsular poetry, golden age poetry, cultural studies.

Angeles Encinar, Ph.D., Washington (St. Louis). Nineteenth- and twentieth-century peninsular narrative, twentieth-century Latin American narrative, women's narrative.

Cristina Matute, Ph.D., Universidad Autónoma de Madrid. History of Spanish grammar, Spanish phonetics and phonology, linguistics.

Alicia Ramos, Ph.D., Northwestern. Twentieth-century peninsular narrative, twentieth-century peninsular thought, medieval literature, survey of Hispanic narrative and film.

Rafael Reig, Ph.D., SUNY at Stony Brook. Nineteenth- and twentieth-century peninsular narrative, creative writing.

Maria Teresa Rodriguez, Ph.D., Universidad Autónoma de Madrid. History of Spanish grammar, Spanish phonetics and phonology, linguistics.

Master's Program in English

Sara van den Berg, Chair, Department of English; Ph.D., Yale. Ben Jonson, Milton, seventeenth-century literature, psychoanalytic theory, medicine and the humanities.

Stephen Casmier, Ph.D., Université de Nice-Sophia Antipolis (France). African American literature, theory and expressive culture, African literature, twentieth-century American literature.

Anne Day Dewey, Ph.D., Stanford. American poetry, twentieth-century American literature, women's poetry.

Anthony Hasler, Ph.D., Cambridge. Chaucer, medieval literature, late medieval/early modern British literature, drama.

Georgia Johnston, Ph.D., Rutgers. Twentieth-century British literature, autobiography, creative writing (poetry).

Matthew Kineen, Ph.D., Wisconsin. Theory of genres, comparative literature.

María Lozano, Program Director; Ph.D., Universidad de Zaragoza (Spain). Twentieth-century American literature.

Anne McCabe, Ph.D., Aston (England). Systemic functional linguistics, contrastive rhetoric, text linguistics/analysis, teaching writing, English for academic purposes, teacher development.

Janice McIntire-Strasburg, Ph.D., Nevada. Computers and writing, Mark Twain, American literature, Native American literature.

Eulalia Piñero, Ph.D., Universidad Complutense de Madrid (Spain). Ethnic American literaturas.

Esteban Pujals, Ph.D., Universidad Complutense de Madrid (Spain). Twentieth-century American poetry.

Julia Salmerón, Ph.D., Hull (England). Gender studies, twentieth-century British literature.

Pilar Somacarrera, Ph.D., Universidad de Salamanca (Spain). Canadian literature, postcolonial literaturas.

Maura Tarnoff, Ph.D., Virginia. Renaissance literature.

Paul Vita, Chair, Department of English (Madrid Campus); Ph.D., Columbia. Nineteenth-century British literature and narrative theory.

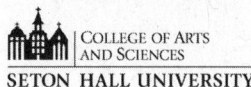

SETON HALL UNIVERSITY

Department of English
English Literature and Writing

Programs of Study	The Department of English at Seton Hall University offers a Master of Arts degree program with three options: literature, writing, and creative writing. The program requires 30 credits, with at least 6 credits at the 7000 level. All students are required to take the 12 credit "hub," which includes ENGL 6010: Introduction to Literary Research; two literature electives (one American, one British); and ENGL 7011: Studies in Criticism. Students then follow a "spoke" of 18 credits (in literature, writing, or creative writing); students in the literature spoke generally write a thesis.
	Recent courses include the African-American Literary Experience, Studies in Medieval Literature, the English Novel, American Literature 1900–1945, Shakespeare, Studies in Victorian Literature, Modern Rhetoric and Writing, Art and Craft of Writing, Modern British Drama, the American Renaissance, Renaissance Literature, and Composition Workshop.
	The master's program requires all students to pass a foreign language translation exam (demonstrating reading knowledge) and a comprehensive exam, generally taken in the student's last semester.
	The literature spoke provides a good basis for students interested in continuing in a doctoral program. Students have recently gone on to Ph.D. programs at the University of Tulsa; the University of California, Riverside; Temple; Michigan State; Fordham; Drew; Lehigh; and the University of Edinburgh. The literature spoke is also well suited to secondary-school English teachers.
	The writing spoke is particularly attractive to secondary school teachers and students who are interested in teaching at two-year colleges; many students who seek careers in editing and publishing also select this option. Students pursuing this spoke have gone on to careers in medical editing, public relations, educational publishing, and teaching.
	The creative writing spoke is designed for students interested in becoming writers, teaching creative writing, or hoping to pursue an M.F.A or Ph.D. in creative writing. Students have recently gone on to programs at The New School and CUNY.
	Further information is available online at http://www.shu.edu/academics/artsci/ma-english/index.cfm.
Research Facilities	Students have access to the Seton Hall Library as well as libraries at area colleges and the many important research facilities in New York City. Seton Hall's Walsh Library is a pioneer in electronic research facilities, making numerous online databases and resources available both on and off campus.
	The Language Resource Center (LRC) in the College of Arts and Sciences houses the theater-style Screening Room and a state-of-the-art computer workstation area. All computers have keyboards installed in a number of languages, including Arabic, Chinese, and Japanese, and have Internet access, video recording and editing software, and connections to a VCR/DVD combo for viewing. The LRC provides DVDs, videos, and other media in Arabic, Chinese, English, French, German, Italian, Japanese, Spanish, Russian, and other languages and offers self-paced language learning materials for Seton Hall community members who wish to study a language on their own.
Financial Aid	The teaching assistantship program allows Master of Arts students to teach freshman English courses. Teaching assistants receive extensive training during the summer. They then teach two sections of First-Year Writing each semester. The teaching assistantships cover tuition (but not fees) and provide an additional stipend of $8500 for the academic year. Teaching assistants are also given an IBM laptop computer and participate in Seton Hall's Mobile Computing program, which brings information technology into the classroom. Students should contact the Department of English for information about applying for one of these positions.
	Graduate assistantships are also available through the Office of Graduate Programs (http://www.shu.edu/applying/graduate/grad-finaid.cfm). Graduate assistants work in a variety of campus positions and receive tuition remission and a stipend.
Cost of Study	In 2009–10, tuition is $901 per credit. Full-time students pay $305 per semester in University and technology fees; part-time students pay $185.
Living and Housing Costs	Housing and living costs in South Orange and surrounding towns are comparable to most suburban cities, with studio and one-bedroom apartments renting for $750 to $1000 per month.
Student Group	The master's program enrolls approximately 30 students. Eight students receive teaching assistantships, which cover tuition and provide a stipend of $8500 per year. About half of the program's students are enrolled part-time. Entering classes consist of 12 to 18 students.
Location	Seton Hall University is located in the Village of South Orange, New Jersey, only 14 miles (or a 30-minute direct train ride) from New York City. The University's proximity to New York City allows students to take advantage of all the city has to offer while living in a charming suburban area.
The University and The Department	Seton Hall is New Jersey's only Catholic university. The University's diverse academic program is characterized by a strong teaching faculty and a wide range of academic choices. Students benefit from the personal attention generated by small classes and a low student-faculty ratio. At Seton Hall, students find people who are willing to listen, offer support, and help them get the most out of their education.
	The Department of English's faculty members are distinguished by their scholarship and their love of teaching. Senior faculty members contribute their years of commitment to excellent teaching, while the junior faculty members—a growing number from eminent graduate programs across the country—bring energy, enthusiasm, and new areas of expertise to their classes. Faculty members regularly publish articles and books and take part in local, regional, and international conferences. Students are encouraged to join faculty members at conferences and to participate in them, as well. The Department is active in its graduate students' professional development, sponsoring seminars for students who are interested in continuing their study in doctoral programs; publishing their work, both creative and scholarly; or exploring the academic job market.
Applying	Students who have completed 18 credits or more of undergraduate study in English (at least six semester-long courses) are eligible to apply to this program, which seeks to provide them with a comprehensive background in English and literature. For applications, students should visit http://www.shu.edu/academics/artsci/apply-graduate.cfm.
	Students must submit the general Seton Hall University Graduate Application, which includes three letters of recommendation, a resume, and a personal statement. All applicants must take the GRE General Test before an admissions decision can be made. Candidates applying for a teaching assistantship should also submit the TA application, a statement of interest in the position, and a writing sample by March 15 of their application year. The Graduate Application should be returned to the Office of Graduate Programs or submitted online; however, the TA application should be sent directly to the Director of Graduate Studies, Department of English, Seton Hall University, South Orange, New Jersey 07079.
Correspondence and Information	Dr. Angela Weisl, Director of Graduate Studies Department of English College of Arts and Sciences Fahy Hall, Room 362 Seton Hall University 400 South Orange Avenue South Orange, New Jersey 07042 Phone: 973-275-5889 Fax: 973-761-9453 E-mail: angela.weisl@shu.edu Web site: http://www.shu.edu/academics/artsci/ma-english/index.cfm

Seton Hall University

THE GRADUATE FACULTY AND THEIR RESEARCH

Mary McAleer Balkun, Ph.D., NYU. Early American literature, African American literature, women's studies.
Martha C. Carpentier, Ph.D., Fordham. Modern British literature, feminist theory.
Jonathan Farina, Ph.D., NYU. Nineteenth-century literature, the novel.
Karen Bloom Gevirtz, Ph.D., Emory. Eighteenth-century literature, women's studies, the rise of the novel.
Jeffrey Gray, Ph.D., California, Riverside. Modern and contemporary poetry, post-colonial literature, literary theory.
Chrysanthy M. Grieco, Ph.D., Drew. Shakespeare, drama, nineteenth-century literature.
Edmund Jones, Ph.D., NYU. Composition theory.
James R. Lindroth, Ph.D., NYU. American literature, 1900–present; film studies.
Nathan Oates, PhD., Missouri–Columbia. Fiction, American literature.
Kelly Shea, Ph.D., Penn State. Creative nonfiction, composition theory.
Mark Svenvold, M.F.A., Iowa. Poetry, creative non-fiction.
John Wargacki, Ph.D., NYU. Hart Crane, American poetry and literature in spirituality.
Angela Jane Weisl, Ph.D., Columbia. Chaucer, medieval literature, women's studies.
Leigh Winser, Ph.D., Columbia. Milton, Renaissance nondramatic literature, Shakespeare.

SOUTHERN ILLINOIS UNIVERSITY CARBONDALE

Department of English
Ph.D. in English

Programs of Study	The Doctor of Philosophy degree (Ph.D.) in English at Southern Illinois University Carbondale (SIUC) prepares graduates for careers in the field of higher education as scholars and educators, with course work, qualifying examinations, and dissertations in the full range of literary areas, including critical theory, cultural studies, and rhetoric and composition.
	Students benefit from a wide range of specializations, including medieval and Renaissance literature, British literature (eighteenth, nineteenth, and twentieth centuries), American literature (nineteenth century and modern), literary theory, cultural studies, gender studies, writing studies, and popular culture.
	The Department of English also maintains a highly regarded Irish and Irish immigration studies program that is complemented by Morris Library's special collections of internationally recognized manuscript and archival holdings and that affords graduate students the opportunity for study abroad at the University College, Galway.
	The Ph.D. program is designed as a four- to five-year program for full-time students. Its residency requirement is satisfied by completion of 24 semester hours of graduate credit before the qualifying examinations followed by 24 semester hours of dissertation credit. The doctoral program maintains a research-tool requirement consisting of two foreign languages or one foreign language and course work in a field of study directly related to the dissertation. The doctoral student's course work is developed in consultation with an advisory committee to suit his or her particular needs. Qualifying examinations cover one major and two minor areas of study as chosen by the student in consultation with the committee. Upon successful completion of the examinations, the student is advanced to candidacy and proceeds directly to the dissertation prospectus and writing the dissertation. Once the dissertation is completed, the student presents an oral defense of the dissertation before the committee, including any designated outside readers. A successful defense means that the student has completed all requirements for the Ph.D. degree.
Research Facilities	SIUC's Morris Library contains more than 2.5 million volumes, 3 million microfilms, and more than 12,000 current serial subscriptions. Library users have electronic access to a statewide automated catalog system and nearly 600 electronic data files and CD-ROM products via workstations located throughout the building. The library's special collections are extensive in areas pertinent to graduate students and research and include papers, manuscripts, letters, and research materials in American and British expatriate literature; twentieth-century philosophy, especially John Dewey and the Open Court press; the Irish literary renaissance; literary modernism, with an especially strong collection of James Joyce materials; and proletariat theater. The Humanities Library is particularly rich in both traditional and contemporary monographs and periodicals.
Financial Aid	SIUC offers a number of competitive fellowships to full-time graduate students. Awards are made by the Graduate School on the recommendation of the Graduate Studies Committee. For further information, students should contact the Graduate School. The deadline for applicants for fellowships is usually one month earlier than the deadline for graduate assistantships. Almost all M.F.A. students hold graduate assistantships that provide stipends for the academic year and full remission of tuition. The application deadline for admission with assistantship support is early February, with student notification before April 1.
Cost of Study	In-state graduate tuition is $328 per credit hour in 2009–10. Out-of-state tuition is 2.5 times the in-state tuition rate ($820 per credit hour). Graduate students with at least a 25 percent appointment as a graduate assistant receive a tuition scholarship. Fees vary from $589.03 (1 credit hour) to $1557.50 (12 credit hours). Students with a graduate assistantship receive a 50 percent reduction in the Primary Care Medical Fee. New graduate students from Arkansas, Indiana, Kentucky, Missouri, and Tennessee qualify for the alternate tuition rate, which is equivalent to the in-state graduate tuition rate.
Living and Housing Costs	For married couples, students with families, and single graduate students, the University has 690 efficiency and one-, two-, three-, and four-bedroom apartments that rent for $499 to $720 per month in 2009–10. Residence halls for single graduate students are also available, as are accessible residence hall rooms and apartments for students with disabilities.
Student Group	The University's total enrollment exceeds 21,000, including more than 4,000 graduate students. Men and women come from all 50 states and more than 100 other countries. About 53 percent of the graduate students are women, 23 percent are international, and 13 percent are members of American minority groups.
Location	SIUC is 350 miles south of Chicago and 100 miles southeast of St. Louis. Nestled in rolling hills bordered by the Ohio and Mississippi Rivers and enhanced by a mild climate, the area has state parks, national forests and wildlife refuges, and large lakes for outdoor recreation. Cultural offerings include theater, opera, concerts, art exhibits, and cinema. Educational facilities for the families of students are excellent.
The University	Southern Illinois University Carbondale is a comprehensive public university with a variety of general and professional education programs. The University offers bachelor's, associate, master's, and doctoral degrees; the J.D. degree; and the M.D. degree. The University is fully accredited by the North Central Association of Colleges and Schools. The Graduate School has an essential role in the development and coordination of graduate instruction and research programs. The Graduate Council has academic responsibility for determining graduate standards, recommending new graduate programs and research centers, and establishing policies to facilitate the research effort. Southern Illinois University Carbondale is a state-funded university founded in 1869.
Applying	Applicants to the Ph.D. program must complete all forms in the application package, including a separate application for admission to the Graduate School, a nonrefundable processing fee of $40, three letters of recommendation, a statement of purpose, and a writing sample. International students must submit TOEFL scores and a statement showing sufficient financial support at the time of application. The minimum GPA required for admission to SIUC's Graduate School is 2.7, out of 4.0.
	Application materials for admission, including graduate assistantship support, are available from the Department of English. Application material is also available online at the Departmental Web site. Separate application forms for fellowships are available from the Graduate School.
Correspondence and Information	Michael R. Molino, Director of Graduate Studies Graduate Studies in English Department of English Southern Illinois University Carbondale Carbondale, Illinois 62901-4503 Phone: 618-453-6894 E-mail: gradengl@siu.edu Web site: http://www.siu.edu/departments/english

Southern Illinois University Carbondale

THE FACULTY AND THEIR RESEARCH

Michael L. Humphries, Associate Professor and Chair; Ph.D., Claremont, 1990. Classical literature, mythology and folklore, biblical literature.

Mark Addison Amos, Associate Professor; Ph.D., Duke, 1994. Middle English literature and culture, continental medieval literature, issues of representation, gender studies.

David J. Anthony, Associate Professor; Ph.D., Michigan, 1998. Nineteenth-century American literature; studies of emotion, race, and mass culture.

Mary L. Bogumil, Assistant Professor; Ph.D., South Florida, 1988. Modern and contemporary British and American drama and fiction, multiculturalism.

George Boulukos, Assistant Professor; Ph.D., Texas at Austin, 1998. Eighteenth-century British literature.

Edward J. Brunner, Professor; Ph.D., Iowa, 1974. Modern American literature, twentieth-century poetry.

Anne Chandler, Associate Professor; Ph.D., Duke, 1995. Eighteenth-century English literature, the novel.

Jane N. Cogie, Associate Professor and Director, Writing Center; Ph.D., Iowa, 1984. Rhetoric and composition.

K. K. Collins, Associate Professor; Ph.D., Vanderbilt, 1976. Nineteenth-century English literature.

Kevin J. H. Dettmar, Professor; Ph.D., UCLA, 1990. Twentieth-century English literature.

Ronda L. Dively, Associate Professor and Director, Undergraduate Studies; D.A., Illinois State, 1994. Rhetoric and composition, English education.

Jane Dougherty, Assistant Professor; Ph.D., Tufts, 2001. Irish studies.

Charles F. Fanning, Professor and Director, Irish and Irish Immigration Studies; Ph.D., Pennsylvania, 1972. Twentieth-century poetry, Irish literature, immigration and ethnicity studies.

Robert Elliott Fox, Professor; Ph.D., SUNY at Buffalo, 1976. American literature, African and African American literature, science fiction.

Rodney Jones, Professor; M.F.A., North Carolina at Greensboro, 1973. Poetry writing.

Judy Jordan, Assistant Professor; M.F.A., Utah, 2000; M.F.A., Virginia, 1995. Creative writing, poetry.

Allison E. Joseph, Associate Professor; M.F.A., Indiana, 1992. Poetry writing.

Elizabeth Klaver, Professor; Ph.D., California, Riverside, 1990. Modern American literature, postmodernism, drama, literary theory.

Mary E. Lamb, Professor; Ph.D., Columbia, 1975. Renaissance literature, feminist and gender studies.

E. Beth Lordan, Professor and Assistant to the Chair; M.F.A., Cornell, 1987. Fiction writing.

Michael Magnuson, Associate Professor and Director, Creative Writing; M.F.A., Florida, 1997. Fiction writing.

Lisa J. McClure, Associate Professor; D.A., Michigan, 1988. Rhetoric and composition.

Scott J. McEathron, Associate Professor; Ph.D., Duke, 1993. Nineteenth-century English literature.

Michael R. Molino, Associate Professor and Director, Graduate Studies; Ph.D., 1986. Twentieth-century British and Irish literature.

R. Gerald Nelms, Associate Professor; Ph.D., Ohio State, 1990. Rhetoric and composition, linguistics, oral history.

Ryan Netzley, Assistant Professor; Ph.D., Penn State, 2002. Milton, seventeenth-century British literature.

Anita R. Riedlinger, Associate Professor; Ph.D., NYU, 1985. Old and middle English literature.

Jeremy Wells, Assistant Professor; Ph.D., Michigan, 2000. Nineteenth-century American literature, Southern literature.

Clarisse Zimra, Associate Professor; Ph.D., Washington (Seattle), 1974. Literary theory, continental and Caribbean literature.

UNIVERSITY OF ST. THOMAS

Department of English
Master of Arts Program

Program of Study	The Department offers a general Master of Arts program that allows for great flexibility. Students may take courses in English and American literature, multicultural literature, critical theory, women's literature, rhetoric, and writing pedagogy. The program requires 30 semester credits: 12 credits of required courses, 15 credits of electives, and 3 credits for a master's essay.
Research Facilities	The University has four libraries that contain more than 815,000 volumes and provide access to 88,000 electronic book titles. The libraries also have over 2,500 current subscriptions to periodicals and allow access to 32,000 electronic titles. In addition to reference and general collections, the O'Shaughnessy-Frey Library Center houses a robust media collection, the Luxembourg Collection, the Celtic Collection (one of the most outstanding of its kind in the country), and a notable Chesterton-Belloc Collection. The Archbishop Ireland Memorial Library, the theology library, is strong in areas ancillary to the study of language and literature. Through Cooperating Libraries in Consortium (CLIC), the University has access to seven other local academic libraries giving access to over 2,000,000 volumes. The CLIC libraries jointly maintain an electronic catalog that can be accessed off campus. CLIC can also access the libraries in four Midwestern states through Minitex. The University also participates in international interlibrary loan systems.
Financial Aid	Three full-time and eight part-time fellowships are available for students of exceptional academic promise. The three full-time fellowships, renewable until completion of the degree, provide a tuition waiver and a stipend of $5000 per semester. Students holding full-time fellowships must ordinarily take three courses each semester and maintain a minimum 3.5 GPA. The eight part-time scholarships offer a tuition waiver for one course per semester until completion of the degree. The University of St. Thomas also administers two federal loan programs (Stafford subsidized and unsubsidized loans) and one Minnesota program (SELF). SELF is non-need based. These loan programs are open to full- and part-time students.
Cost of Study	Tuition for 2008–09 was $647 per credit for both in-state and out-of-state students. A health-care center provides services for minor illnesses free of charge. Students may purchase medical insurance through the University. Students with a valid ID may use all athletic and other facilities.
Living and Housing Costs	Off-campus housing is available within convenient walking distance of the campus.
Student Group	The Department enrolls 65 to 70 master's degree students (full-time and part-time) each semester; the student body profile includes a wide range of ages, careers, and goals. Class enrollments are kept low to allow for close faculty-student interaction. Students are invited to participate fully in the intellectual and social life of the Department, which includes a colloquium series, academic conference presentations, and off-campus graduate events. Master's students also have representation on the Graduate Committee.
Location	The metropolitan area of St. Paul and Minneapolis regularly ranks at or near the top of the lists of the most desirable cities in the country. The Twin Cities are the home of the renowned Guthrie Theater, two world-class orchestras, The Loft (one of the largest literary centers in the country), several museums, galleries, and more than 100 small, live theaters. Numerous lakes, parks, and recreational areas are within minutes of both downtowns.
The University and The Department	Founded in 1885, the University of St. Thomas is a comprehensive, coeducational, Catholic university. Inspired by Catholic intellectual tradition, the University of St. Thomas educates students to be morally responsible leaders who think critically, act wisely, and work skillfully for the common good. More than 10,500 students attend St. Thomas, with slightly more than half at the graduate level. Graduate programs emphasize the integration of theory with practice, enhance the professional competence and ethical judgments of their students, and foster both personal growth and an appreciation of lifelong learning.
	The Department of English has 26 full-time faculty members. Two academic journals are edited by the English faculty members and published by the University of St. Thomas: *LOGOS: A Journal of Catholic Thought and Culture* and *New Hibernia Review*.
Applying	Requirements for admission are a bachelor's degree, a minimum undergraduate GPA of 3.0, at least five courses beyond the first year or introductory level in language or literature (earning a grade of B or better), three letters of recommendation (at least one must be from a former professor), and a writing sample that demonstrates critical or analytical skills. The application fee is $50. Application deadlines are March 1 for the summer and fall and October 1 for the spring.
Correspondence and Information	Dr. Catherine Craft-Fairchild Director of Graduate Studies in English Department of English University of St. Thomas Mail #JRC 333 2115 Summit Avenue St. Paul, Minnesota 55105 Phone: 651-962-5628 800-328-6819 Ext. 2-5628 (toll-free) Fax: 651-962-5623 E-mail: gradenglish@stthomas.edu Web site: http://www.stthomas.edu/gradenglish

University of St. Thomas

THE FACULTY

Young-Ok An, Ph.D., USC. Romanticism, eighteenth- and nineteenth-century British literature, literary theory, postcolonialism and cultural critique.

Matthew Batt, Ph.D., Utah. Creative nonfiction, prose writing.

Heather Bouwman, Ph.D., Illinois at Urbana–Champaign. Colonial and early American literature, Native American literature, poetry as genre, American poetry.

Susan Callaway, Ph.D., Wisconsin–Milwaukee; Director, The Center for Writing. Composition theory and pedagogy, writing center theory and administration, writing across the curriculum.

Kanishka Chowdhury, Ph.D., Purdue. Postcolonial literature and theory, world literature, cultural theory.

Catherine Craft-Fairchild, Ph.D., Rochester. Restoration and eighteenth-century British literature, feminist theory, psychoanalysis and film theory, history of the novel.

Alexis Easley, Ph.D., Oregon. Victorian studies, British literature, the novel, literary geography, new historicism, gender studies, media history, multicultural literatures, creative writing, composition theory/pedagogy.

Carmela Garritano, Ph.D., Michigan State. Feminist and postcolonial theory, African and Third World literature and film.

(John) Chris Hallman, M.F.A., Iowa; M.A., Johns Hopkins. Creative nonfiction, prose writing.

Michael C. Jordan, Ph.D., North Carolina at Chapel Hill. Comparative literature, literary theory, Classical Greek literature, philosophical anthropology, history and theory of liberal education.

Paul Lai, M.A., North Carolina at Chapel Hill. Asian American literature, transnational feminist studies, cultural studies.

Kelli Larson, Ph.D., Michigan State. Eighteenth- and nineteenth-century and modern American literature.

(David) Todd Lawrence, Ph.D., Missouri–Columbia. African-American literature and culture, African diasporic studies, folklore and folkloristics, the Black Arts Movement.

Juan Li, Ph.D., Washington (Seattle). Discourse theory and analysis, linguistics and English language study, language and ideology, rhetoric and stylistics.

Raymond MacKenzie, Ph.D., Kansas State. Milton, Nineteenth- and twentieth-century British literature, literary criticism.

Michael Mikolajczak, Ph.D., Wisconsin–Milwaukee. Sixteenth- and seventeenth-century British literature, Shakespeare, Milton, religion and literature, rhetoric.

Leslie Adrienne Miller, Ph.D., Texas at Houston. Contemporary American poetry, rhetorical theory and criticism, British romanticism, medieval literature.

Amy Muse, Ph.D., Auburn. Drama, theater and revolutionary movements, Romanticism, eighteenth- and nineteenth-century literature and theater culture, writing and civic education.

Lon Otto, Ph.D., Indiana. Creative writing, novel since World War II, modern poetry, short story, travel writing, Faulkner.

Joan Piorkowski, Ph.D., Temple. Eighteenth-century British and Gothic literature, basic writing.

Brenda J. Powell, Ph.D., North Carolina at Chapel Hill. Literature by women, mythology, classical literature, multicultural literature.

Thomas Dillon Redshaw, Ph.D., NYU; Senior Fellow, Institute of Irish Studies, Queen's University (Belfast). Modern and contemporary Irish literature, British literature between the wars, seventeenth-century British literature.

Andrew Scheiber, Ph.D., Michigan State; Department Chair. Nineteenth- and twentieth-century American literature, literary criticism, literature and linguistics, women's studies, history of the novel, African-American literature.

Erika Scheurer, Ph.D., Massachusetts Amherst. Composition theory and pedagogy, Dickinson.

Martin Warren, Ph.D., Minnesota. Medieval literature, religion and literature, linguistics, hypertext and literacy.

VILLANOVA UNIVERSITY

Graduate Program in
English Language and Literature

Program of Study	Villanova has been granting its master's degree in English language and literature for more than half a century. Villanova weds this sense of history with a keen awareness of the contemporary, interdisciplinary spirit of literary study. The curriculum balances a traditional, historical understanding of literary periods with newer, theoretically based considerations of writing and reading. This range of approaches provides students with expertise in much of the literature written in English, highly refined interpretive skills, and familiarity with the major intellectual currents shaping the discipline of literary study today.
	All courses are conducted as small seminars, with a maximum enrollment of 15 students. Course work provides a broad range of study in a variety of areas, and the thesis or field exam provides focus within a particular field. The thesis offers an opportunity for sustained critical examination of a work, author, or topic, while the field examination is taken on a list of works compiled in consultation with the student's adviser within a field of the student's choosing.
	To satisfy the requirements for the master's degree, students must complete a minimum of 30 credits, including successful completion of a thesis or an oral/written field examination. Students are expected to take at least one course in British literature before 1800 and another in American literature before 1900. An average grade of at least a B must be maintained to remain in the program. Students usually complete the curriculum in two years, taking two or three courses each semester, but may pursue their studies on a part-time basis, in which case they are allowed a period of six years to earn the degree.
	At all stages, the program is deeply committed to the individual student's development and maturation as a literary scholar. Upon matriculation, each student is assigned an adviser, who assists in planning the individual course of study. After successful completion of 9 credits, the student may request an adviser with particular expertise in the student's area of interest.
Research Facilities	The Falvey Memorial Library at Villanova University houses more than 600,000 volumes and 3,000 periodicals. An interlibrary loan system operates with the efficiency of e-mail. Special holdings include the McGarrity and Worthington collections, major resources of literature and periodicals about Irish history, Irish-American relations, and writings by and about James Joyce. The library is located in the middle of the campus and includes numerous public-use computer stations that are equipped with sophisticated search engines and data-retrieval mechanisms.
Financial Aid	Applicants may compete for full financial awards, including tuition remission and a yearly stipend of approximately $13,000, which are renewable for a second year. Tuition scholarships (tuition remission without a stipend) are also offered and are renewable for the second year. The work these awards require ranges from helping individual faculty members with research materials to assisting in the University Writing and Learning Center.
	Since classes in the master's program meet in the evenings, students without financial aid are often able to support their graduate study through daytime employment outside the University.
Cost of Study	Fees and expenses for graduate students in 2009–10 were $50 for the application fee, $585 per credit for tuition, and $30 per semester for general University fees.
Living and Housing Costs	A variety of affordable housing possibilities are available near the Villanova University campus. Housing costs vary in accordance with the option chosen. Villanova University does not provide on-campus housing for graduate students.
Student Group	There are usually about 50 students matriculated in the program, and the ratio of men to women is approximately 2:3. While some graduate students are dedicated to becoming professors of English, others are seeking the master's because they want to learn more about the discipline in order to decide whether a Ph.D. is right for them, they wish to advance their careers as teachers of secondary school, or they simply love literature and want to immerse themselves in it. Some students come directly from undergraduate programs, while others have pursued other careers and are returning to school to pursue a lifelong ambition.
Student Outcomes	In recent years, recipients of the master's degree in English from Villanova have been admitted to highly competitive Ph.D. programs, including Harvard, Johns Hopkins, Ohio State, Penn State, Princeton, Rutgers, UCLA, and the Universities of Kansas, Maryland, North Carolina, Pennsylvania, and Wisconsin. Others have elected to use the degree to pursue teaching positions at the excellent secondary schools adjacent to the University. Still others have chosen to pursue careers in publishing and other fields, including business and law, which demand the verbal acumen and analytical rigor Villanova's program cultivates.
Location	Villanova is situated on the historic Main Line, in a beautiful western suburb of Philadelphia. Philadelphia offers a wide variety of museums, libraries, concerts, and other cultural opportunities. Home to the greatest variety of eighteenth-century buildings in America, the city is also enjoying a renaissance in modern architecture, restaurants, and the performing arts. By car or train, the campus is only 30 minutes from downtown. It is 2 minutes from the Blue Route (Route 476) and 5 minutes from the Pennsylvania Turnpike, the Schuylkill Expressway, and Route 202. With ample parking and mass transit stops right on campus grounds, students can travel easily to and from the campus by car, bus, or train.
The University and The Department	Founded in 1842 by the friars of the Order of St. Augustine, Villanova is a comprehensive Roman Catholic institution that welcomes students of all faiths. Roughly 10,000 students attend the University, including 6,000 undergraduates and 4,000 graduate students. The Department of English at Villanova includes a number of distinguished critics, whose scholarship has earned them national and international recognition. They are well acquainted with the methods and values of current scholarship in English literature, and they seek equally to deepen the student's acquaintance with these critical discourses and develop each student's individual critical sensibility.
Applying	Villanova typically requires that applicants have at least 18 undergraduate credits and a 3.0 average in English. However, the University occasionally accepts applications from candidates who majored in related fields.
	Applicants should send the three letters of recommendation (at least two of which should be from former professors), a writing sample of approximately ten pages, and a one-page personal statement to the Graduate English Program, Department of English, Villanova University, 800 Lancaster Avenue, Villanova, Pennsylvania 19085-1699; they should send the application for admission, the nonrefundable application fee, all official postsecondary transcripts, and the GRE scores from both the General Test and the English Subject Test to the Graduate Studies Office, College of Liberal Arts and Sciences, Villanova University, 800 Lancaster Avenue, Villanova, Pennsylvania 19085-1699. Application forms are available online at Villanova's Graduate School Web site. The deadline for receipt of applications for the fall semester is March 1 and for the spring semester, November 15.
Correspondence and Information	Director of Graduate Studies Department of English Villanova University Villanova, Pennsylvania 19085
	Phone: 610-519-7826 Fax: 610-519-6913 E-mail: gradinfo@email.villanova.edu Web site: www.gradenglish.villanova.edu

Villanova University

THE FACULTY AND THEIR RESEARCH

Chiji Akoma, Associate Professor; Ph.D., SUNY at Binghamton. Postcolonial literature.

Michael Berthold, Associate Professor; Ph.D., Harvard. Nineteenth-century American literature, slave narrative, American Gothic.

Cristina Maria Cervone, Assistant Professor; Ph.D., Virginia. Medieval studies, poetics, history of the English language.

Charles L. Cherry, Professor; Ph.D., North Carolina. British Romanticism, madness and imagination, history of ideas.

Alice A. Dailey, Assistant Professor; Ph.D., UCLA. Renaissance literature.

Heather Hicks, Associate Professor; Ph.D., Duke. Post–World War II American fiction, postmodern theory, contemporary cultural studies.

Karyn L. Hollis, Associate Professor; Ph.D., USC. Composition studies.

Crystal J. Lucky, Associate Professor; Ph.D., Pennsylvania. African American literature, nineteenth-century African American church history, literary pedagogy.

Jean Lutes, Associate Professor; Ph.D., Wisconsin–Madison. Modern American fiction.

Hugh Ormsby-Lennon, Associate Professor; Ph.D., Pennsylvania. Augustan literature, eighteenth-century cultural studies, eighteenth-century Anglo-Irish literature, literary theory.

Megan Quigley, Assistant Professor; Ph.D., Yale. British and Irish Modernism.

Evan Radcliffe, Associate Professor; Ph.D., Cornell. British Romanticism, the French Revolution controversy, historicism.

Jill Rappaport, Assistant Professor; Ph.D., Virginia. Victorian literature and cultural history.

Lisa Sewell, Associate Professor; Ph.D., Tufts. Contemporary American poetry, poetics.

Lauren E. Shohet, Associate Professor; Ph.D., Brown. Renaissance and seventeenth-century literature, cultural studies, literary theory, gender studies.

Deborah A. Thomas, Professor; Ph.D., Rochester. Victorian literature and culture, Dickens, Thackeray, nineteenth-century British women's writing.

Section 10
Linguistic Studies

This section contains a directory of institutions offering graduate work in linguistic studies, followed by an in-depth entry submitted by an institution that chose to prepare a detailed program description. Additional information about programs listed in the directory but not augmented by an in-depth entry may be obtained by writing directly to the dean of a graduate school or chair of a department at the address given in the directory.

For programs offering related work, see also in this book *Area and Cultural Studies, Language and Literature,* and *Sociology, Anthropology, and Archaeology.*

CONTENTS

Program Directories

Linguistics   452
Translation and Interpretation   460

Close-Up

Monterey Institute of International Studies   463

Linguistics

Arizona State University, Graduate College, College of Liberal Arts and Sciences, Division of Humanities, Department of English, Tempe, AZ 85287. Offers creative writing (MFA); English (MA, PhD), including comparative literature (MA), linguistics (MA), literature, rhetoric and composition (MA), rhetoric/composition and linguistics (PhD); teaching English to speakers of other languages (MTESOL). *Degree requirements:* For doctorate, thesis/dissertation. *Entrance requirements:* For master's and doctorate, GRE.

Ball State University, Graduate School, College of Sciences and Humanities, Department of English, Program in Linguistics, Muncie, IN 47306-1099. Offers applied linguistics (PhD). *Faculty research:* Descriptive and theoretical linguistics.

Biola University, School of Intercultural Studies, La Mirada, CA 90639-0001. Offers applied linguistics (MA); intercultural education (PhD); intercultural studies (MAICS); missiology (D Miss); missions (MA); teaching English to speakers of other languages (MA, Certificate). Part-time and evening/weekend programs available. Terminal master's awarded for partial completion of doctoral program. *Degree requirements:* For master's, one foreign language, comprehensive exam; for doctorate, one foreign language, comprehensive exam, thesis/dissertation. *Entrance requirements:* For master's, minimum undergraduate GPA of 3.0; for doctorate, MA, 3 years of ministry experience, minimum graduate GPA of 3.3. Additional exam requirements/recommendations for international students: Required—TOEFL (minimum score 550 paper-based; 213 computer-based). Electronic applications accepted.

Boston College, Graduate School of Arts and Sciences, Department of Slavic and Eastern Languages, Program in Linguistics, Chestnut Hill, MA 02467-3800. Offers MA, MA/JD, MBA/MA. Part-time programs available. *Degree requirements:* For master's, 3 foreign languages, comprehensive exam, thesis or alternative. Electronic applications accepted. *Expenses:* Tuition: Part-time $1148 per credit. Required fees: $60.

Boston University, Graduate School of Arts and Sciences, Program in Applied Linguistics, Boston, MA 02215. Offers MA, PhD. Part-time programs available. Terminal master's awarded for partial completion of doctoral program. *Degree requirements:* For master's, one foreign language, project; for doctorate, 2 foreign languages, thesis/dissertation, 1 book review, 2 research papers, oral exam. *Entrance requirements:* For master's and doctorate, GRE General Test. Additional exam requirements/recommendations for international students: Required—TOEFL. Electronic applications accepted. *Faculty research:* Psycholinguistics, sociolinguistics, neurolinguistics, language acquisition, American Sign Language.

Brandeis University, Graduate School of Arts and Sciences, Program in Computational Linguistics, Waltham, MA 02454-9110. Offers MA.

Brigham Young University, Graduate Studies, College of Humanities, Department of Linguistics and English Language, Provo, UT 84602. Offers general linguistics (MA); teaching English as a second language (MA, Certificate). Part-time programs available. *Faculty:* 20 full-time (4 women). *Students:* 85 full-time (65 women); includes 18 minority (1 African American, 15 Asian Americans or Pacific Islanders, 2 Hispanic Americans), 6 international. Average age 30. 57 applicants, 82% accepted, 45 enrolled. In 2008, 9 master's, 24 other advanced degrees awarded. *Degree requirements:* For master's, 2 foreign languages, thesis. *Entrance requirements:* For master's, GRE General Test, minimum GPA of 3.6 in last 60 hours of course work. Additional exam requirements/recommendations for international students: Required—TOEFL (minimum score 580 paper-based; 237 computer-based; 90 iBT), TWE. *Application deadline:* 1/15 for domestic and international students. Application fee: $50. Electronic applications accepted. *Expenses:* Tuition: Full-time $5160; part-time $287 per credit hour. Tuition and fees vary according to program and student's religious affiliation. *Financial support:* In 2008–09, 51 students received support, including 6 fellowships with partial tuition reimbursements available (averaging $4,333 per year), 15 research assistantships with partial tuition reimbursements available (averaging $2,545 per year), 15 teaching assistantships with partial tuition reimbursements available (averaging $1,921 per year); career-related internships or fieldwork, institutionally sponsored loans, scholarships/grants, tuition waivers (partial), unspecified assistantships, and student instructorships also available. Support available to part-time students. Financial award application deadline: 3/28. *Faculty research:* TESOL, second language acquisition, computational linguistics, semiotics and semantics, computer-assisted language instruction. Total annual research expenditures: $9,435. *Unit head:* Dr. William G. Eggington, Chair, 801-422-2937, Fax: 801-422-0906, E-mail: bill_eggington@byu.edu. *Application contact:* Phyllis Ann Daniel, Secretary, 801-422-2937, Fax: 801-422-0906, E-mail: phyllis_daniel@byu.edu.

Brown University, Graduate School, Department of Cognitive and Linguistic Sciences, Providence, RI 02912. Offers cognitive science (Sc M, PhD); linguistics (AM, PhD). *Degree requirements:* For master's, one foreign language, thesis or alternative; for doctorate, 2 foreign languages, thesis/dissertation.

California State University, Fresno, Division of Graduate Studies, College of Arts and Humanities, Department of Linguistics, Fresno, CA 93740-8027. Offers linguistics (MA), including Teaching English as a second language. Part-time and evening/weekend programs available. *Degree requirements:* For master's, comprehensive exam. *Entrance requirements:* For master's, GRE General Test, minimum GPA of 3.0. Additional exam requirements/recommendations for international students: Required—TOEFL. Electronic applications accepted. *Faculty research:* Communication systems, bilingual education, animal communication, conflict resolution, literacy programs.

California State University, Fullerton, Graduate Studies, College of Humanities and Social Sciences, Program in Linguistics, Fullerton, CA 92834-9480. Offers analysis of specific language structures (MA); anthropological linguistics (MA); applied linguistics (MA); communication and semantics (MA); disorders of communication (MA); experimental phonetics (MA). Part-time programs available. *Students:* 14 full-time (8 women), 6 part-time (5 women); includes 2 minority (both Hispanic Americans), 10 international. Average age 32. 19 applicants, 68% accepted, 6 enrolled. In 2008, 9 master's awarded. *Degree requirements:* For master's, one foreign language, thesis or alternative, project. *Entrance requirements:* For master's, minimum GPA of 3.0, undergraduate major in linguistics or related field. Application fee: $55. Tuition and fees vary according to degree level. *Financial support:* Career-related internships or fieldwork, Federal Work-Study, institutionally sponsored loans, and scholarships/grants available. Support available to part-time students. Financial award application deadline: 3/1. *Unit head:* Dr. Franz Muller-Gotama, Adviser, 657-278-2441. *Application contact:* Dr. Franz Muller-Gotama, Adviser, 657-278-2441.

California State University, Long Beach, Graduate Studies, College of Liberal Arts, Department of Linguistics, Long Beach, CA 90840. Offers general linguistics (MA); language and culture (MA); special concentration (MA); teaching English as a second language (MA). Part-time and evening/weekend programs available. *Faculty:* 8 full-time (6 women), 1 part-time/adjunct (0 women). *Students:* 41 full-time (32 women), 36 part-time (28 women); includes 17 minority (1 African American, 9 Asian Americans or Pacific Islanders, 7 Hispanic Americans), 33 international. Average age 34. 47 applicants, 62% accepted, 15 enrolled. *Degree requirements:* For master's, one foreign language, comprehensive exam, thesis optional. *Application deadline:* For fall admission, 5/1 for domestic students. Applications are processed on a rolling basis. Application fee: $55. Electronic applications accepted. *Expenses:* Tuition, nonresident: full-time $11,160; part-time $372 per unit. Required fees: $4100; $1261 per semester. *Financial support:* Teaching assistantships, career-related internships or fieldwork, Federal Work-Study, institutionally sponsored loans, and scholarships/grants available. Financial award application deadline: 3/2. *Faculty research:* Pedagogy of language instruction, role of language in society, Khmer language instruction. *Unit head:* Dr. Malcolm A Finney, Chair, 562-985-5792, Fax: 562-985-2593, E-mail: mfinney@csulb.edu. *Application contact:* Dr. Xiaoping Liang, Graduate Advisor, 562-985-8509, Fax: 562-985-5792, E-mail: xliang@csulb.edu.

California State University, Northridge, Graduate Studies, College of Humanities, Linguistics Program, Northridge, CA 91330. Offers MA. Part-time and evening/weekend programs available. *Faculty:* 3 part-time/adjunct (all women). *Students:* 13 full-time (9 women), 27 part-time (26 women); includes 11 minority (6 Asian Americans or Pacific Islanders, 5 Hispanic Americans), 8 international. Average age 34. 24 applicants, 58% accepted, 9 enrolled. In 2008, 8 master's awarded. *Degree requirements:* For master's, one foreign language, comprehensive exam, thesis, or project. *Entrance requirements:* For master's, GRE General Test or minimum GPA of 3.0. Additional exam requirements/recommendations for international students: Required—TOEFL (minimum score 563 paper-based; 223 computer-based; 85 iBT). *Application deadline:* For fall admission, 11/30 for domestic students. Application fee: $55. *Financial support:* Application deadline: 3/1. *Faculty research:* Ethnography of communication, stylistics, natural language processing, linguistics and humor, Otomanguean phonology and reconstruction. *Unit head:* Dr. Sabrina Peck, Coordinator, 818-677-3453, E-mail: sabrina.peck@csun.edu. *Application contact:* Dr. Sabrina Peck, Coordinator, 818-677-3453, E-mail: sabrina.peck@csun.edu.

Carleton University, Faculty of Graduate Studies, Faculty of Arts and Social Sciences, School of Linguistics and Applied Language Studies, Ottawa, ON K1S 5B6, Canada. Offers applied language studies (MA). *Degree requirements:* For master's, thesis optional. *Entrance requirements:* For master's, honors degree. Additional exam requirements/recommendations for international students: Required—TOEFL or CAEL. *Faculty research:* Language learning, acquisition and use of first and/or second languages in a variety of professional and academic contexts.

Carnegie Mellon University, College of Humanities and Social Sciences, Department of Modern Languages, Pittsburgh, PA 15213-3891. Offers second language acquisition (PhD). *Degree requirements:* For doctorate, one foreign language, comprehensive exam, thesis/dissertation. *Entrance requirements:* For doctorate, GRE General Test. Additional exam requirements/recommendations for international students: Required—TOEFL.

Case Western Reserve University, School of Graduate Studies, Department of Cognitive Science, Cleveland, OH 44106. Offers cognitive linguistics (MA). Part-time programs available. *Degree requirements:* For master's, thesis. *Entrance requirements:* For master's, GRE, writing sample, recommendations. Additional exam requirements/recommendations for international students: Required—TOEFL. Electronic applications accepted. *Faculty research:* Application of metaphor and conceptual integration theories to a wide range of non-linguistic phenomena.

Cleveland State University, College of Graduate Studies, College of Liberal Arts and Social Sciences, Department of Modern Languages, Cleveland, OH 44115. Offers French (M Ed); Spanish (M Ed, MA), including language and linguistics (MA), Latin American studies (MA), peninsular studies (MA), Spanish (MA). Part-time and evening/weekend programs available. *Faculty:* 12 full-time (9 women). *Students:* 7 full-time (6 women), 11 part-time (8 women); includes 7 minority (1 African American, 6 Hispanic Americans), 1 international. Average age 37. 11 applicants, 100% accepted, 8 enrolled. In 2008, 9 master's awarded. *Degree requirements:* For master's, one foreign language, comprehensive exam, thesis optional, study abroad. *Entrance requirements:* For master's, undergraduate major in Spanish or equivalent, essay in Spanish, writing sample. Additional exam requirements/recommendations for international students: Required—TOEFL (minimum score 525 paper-based; 197 computer-based). *Application deadline:* For fall admission, 7/25 priority date for domestic students; for spring admission, 12/15 priority date for domestic students. Applications are processed on a rolling basis. Application fee: $30. Electronic applications accepted. *Financial support:* In 2008–09, 6 students received support, including 6 teaching assistantships with full tuition reimbursements available (averaging $7,030 per year); Federal Work-Study also available. *Faculty research:* Second language acquisition, sociolinguistics, contemporary Spanish novel, Arabic diaspora in Latin America, border literature. *Unit head:* Dr. Tama I. Engelking, Chairperson, 216-523-7175, Fax: 216-687-4650, E-mail: t.engelking@csuohio.edu. *Application contact:* Dr. Antonio Medina-Rivera, Graduate Director, 216-523-7168, Fax: 216-687-4650, E-mail: a.medinarivera@csuohio.edu.

Concordia University, School of Graduate Studies, Faculty of Arts and Science, Department of Education, Program in Applied Linguistics, Montréal, QC H3G 1M8, Canada. Offers applied linguistics (MA); teaching English as a second language (Certificate).

Cornell University, Graduate School, Graduate Fields of Arts and Sciences, Field of Asian Studies, Ithaca, NY 14853-0001. Offers East Asian linguistics (MA); East Asian studies (MA); South Asian linguistics (MA); South Asian studies (MA); Southeast Asian linguistics (MA); Southeast Asian studies (MA). *Faculty:* 50 full-time (20 women). *Students:* 8 full-time (2 women); includes 4 minority (1 African American, 2 Asian Americans or Pacific Islanders, 1 Hispanic American), 3 international. Average age 31. 55 applicants, 29% accepted, 5 enrolled. In 2008, 3 master's awarded. *Degree requirements:* For master's, one foreign language, thesis. *Entrance requirements:* For master's, GRE General Test, 3 letters of recommendation. Additional exam requirements/recommendations for international students: Required—TOEFL (minimum score 550 paper-based; 213 computer-based; 77 iBT). *Application deadline:* Applications are processed on a rolling basis. Application fee: $70. Electronic applications accepted. *Expenses:* Tuition: Full-time $29,500. Required fees: $70. Full-time tuition and fees vary according to degree level, program and student level. *Financial support:* In 2008–09, 5 students received support, including 1 fellowship with full tuition reimbursement available, 4 research assistantships with full tuition reimbursements available; teaching assistantships with full tuition reimbursements available, institutionally sponsored loans, scholarships/grants, health care benefits, tuition waivers (full and partial), and unspecified assistantships also available. Financial award applicants required to submit FAFSA. *Faculty research:* East Asian studies, South Asian studies, Southeast Asian studies. *Unit head:* Director of Graduate Studies, 607-255-9099, Fax: 607-255-1345. *Application contact:* Graduate Field Assistant, 607-255-9099, Fax: 607-255-1345, E-mail: asian@cornell.edu.

Cornell University, Graduate School, Graduate Fields of Arts and Sciences, Field of Linguistics, Ithaca, NY 14853-0001. Offers applied linguistics (MA, PhD); East Asian linguistics (MA, PhD); English linguistics (MA, PhD); general linguistics (MA, PhD); Germanic linguistics (MA, PhD); Indo-European linguistics (MA, PhD); phonetics (MA, PhD); phonological theory (MA, PhD); Romance linguistics (MA, PhD); second language acquisition (MA, PhD); semantics (MA, PhD); Slavic linguistics (MA, PhD); sociolinguistics (MA, PhD); South Asian linguistics (MA, PhD); Southeast Asian linguistics (MA, PhD); syntactic theory (MA, PhD). *Faculty:* 15 full-time (6 women). *Students:* 32 full-time (15 women); includes 1 minority (Hispanic American), 16 international. Average age 30. 93 applicants, 16% accepted, 7 enrolled. In 2008, 5 master's, 7 doctorates awarded. Terminal master's awarded for partial completion of doctoral program. *Degree requirements:* For master's, one foreign language, thesis; for doctorate, one foreign language, comprehensive exam, thesis/dissertation. *Entrance requirements:* For master's and doctorate, GRE General Test, 2 letters of recommendation. Additional exam requirements/recommendations for international students: Required—TOEFL (minimum score 600 paper-based; 250 computer-based; 77 iBT). *Application deadline:* For fall admission, 1/15 for domestic students. Application fee: $70. Electronic applications accepted. *Expenses:* Tuition: Full-time $29,500. Required fees: $70. Full-time tuition and fees vary according to degree level, program and student level. *Financial support:* In 2008–09, 32 students received support, including 11 fellowships with full tuition reimbursements available, 4 research assistantships with full tuition reimbursements available, 17 teaching assistantships with full tuition reimbursements available; institutionally sponsored loans, scholarships/grants, health care benefits, tuition waivers (full and partial), and unspecified assistantships also available. Financial award applicants required to submit FAFSA. *Faculty research:* Phonology and phonetics; syntax and semantics; historical linguistics; philosophy of language; language acquisition. *Unit head:* Director of Graduate

Studies, 607-255-1105. *Application contact:* Graduate Field Assistant, 607-255-1105, E-mail: lingfield@cornell.edu.

Eastern Michigan University, Graduate School, College of Arts and Sciences, Department of English Language and Literature, Program in English Linguistics, Ypsilanti, MI 48197. Offers MA. Part-time and evening/weekend programs available. Postbaccalaureate distance learning degree programs offered (minimal on-campus study). *Degree requirements:* For master's, thesis (for some programs). *Entrance requirements:* Additional exam requirements/recommendations for international students: Required—TOEFL.

Florida Atlantic University, Dorothy F. Schmidt College of Arts and Letters, Department of Languages, Linguistics, and Comparative Literature, Boca Raton, FL 33431-0991. Offers comparative literature (MA); French (MA); linguistics (MA); Spanish (MA). Part-time programs available. *Faculty:* 23 full-time (20 women), 12 part-time/adjunct (10 women). *Students:* 18 full-time (15 women), 19 part-time (13 women); includes 17 minority (4 African Americans, 1 Asian American or Pacific Islander, 12 Hispanic Americans), 4 international. Average age 36. 24 applicants, 67% accepted, 6 enrolled. In 2008, 10 master's awarded. *Degree requirements:* For master's, one foreign language, comprehensive exam, thesis optional. *Entrance requirements:* For master's, GRE General Test, minimum GPA of 3.0. *Application deadline:* For fall admission, 7/1 priority date for domestic students, 2/15 for international students; for spring admission, 11/1 for domestic students, 7/15 for international students. Applications are processed on a rolling basis. Application fee: $30. *Expenses:* Tuition, state resident: full-time $4867; part-time $270.40 per credit hour. Tuition, nonresident: full-time $16,486; part-time $915.87 per credit hour. *Financial support:* Fellowships, research assistantships, teaching assistantships with partial tuition reimbursements, Federal Work-Study and tuition waivers (partial) available. Support available to part-time students. Financial award application deadline: 4/1. *Faculty research:* Modern European studies, modern Latin America, medieval Europe. *Unit head:* Dr. Michael Horswell, Chair, 561-297-3860, Fax: 561-297-2756, E-mail: horswell@fau.edu. *Application contact:* Dr. Emily Stockard, Associate Dean, 561-297-2817, Fax: 561-297-2744, E-mail: stockard@fau.edu.

Florida International University, College of Arts and Sciences, Department of English, Program in Linguistics, Miami, FL 33199. Offers MA. Part-time and evening/weekend programs available. *Degree requirements:* For master's, thesis or alternative. *Entrance requirements:* For master's, GRE General Test (for students receiving an assistantship), minimum GPA of 3.0. Additional exam requirements/recommendations for international students: Required—TOEFL (minimum score 550 paper-based; 213 computer-based). Electronic applications accepted.

Gallaudet University, The Graduate School, Department of Linguistics, Washington, DC 20002-3625. Offers MA, PhD. Part-time programs available. *Degree requirements:* For master's, thesis optional. *Entrance requirements:* For master's, GRE General Test or MAT. Electronic applications accepted.

George Mason University, College of Humanities and Social Sciences, Department of English, Fairfax, VA 22030. Offers creative writing (MFA); English (MA); English literature (MA); linguistics (MA); professional writing and editing (MA, Certificate); teaching English as a second language (Certificate); teaching writing and literature (MA). *Degree requirements:* For master's, thesis (for some programs). *Entrance requirements:* For master's, minimum GPA of 3.0 in last 60 hours of course work. Electronic applications accepted. *Faculty research:* Literature, professional writing and editing, writing of fiction or poetry.

Georgetown University, Graduate School of Arts and Sciences, Department of Linguistics, Washington, DC 20057. Offers bilingual education (Certificate); language and communication (MA); linguistics (MS, PhD), including applied linguistics, computational linguistics, sociolinguistics, theoretical linguistics; teaching English as a second language (MAT, Certificate); teaching English as a second language and bilingual education (MAT). Terminal master's awarded for partial completion of doctoral program. *Degree requirements:* For master's, one foreign language, comprehensive exam, optional research project; for doctorate, 2 foreign languages, comprehensive exam, thesis/dissertation. *Entrance requirements:* For master's and doctorate, 18 undergraduate credits in a foreign language. Additional exam requirements/recommendations for international students: Required—TOEFL.

Georgia State University, College of Arts and Sciences, Department of Applied Linguistics and English as a Second Language, Atlanta, GA 30303-3083. Offers applied linguistics (MA, PhD). Part-time programs available. *Degree requirements:* For master's, one foreign language, portfolio; for doctorate, one foreign language, comprehensive exam, thesis/dissertation, qualifying paper. *Entrance requirements:* For master's, GRE General Test; for doctorate, GRE. Additional exam requirements/recommendations for international students: Required—TOEFL (minimum score 600 paper-based; 250 computer-based; 97 iBT), TWE (minimum score 5). Electronic applications accepted. *Faculty research:* Native language and second language, second language literacy, intercultural communication, classroom-centered research, learning styles/strategies.

Graduate Institute of Applied Linguistics, Graduate Programs, Dallas, TX 75236. Offers applied linguistics (MA, Certificate); language development (MA). Part-time programs available. *Degree requirements:* For master's, one foreign language, comprehensive exam (for some programs), thesis (for some programs). *Entrance requirements:* For master's, GRE. Additional exam requirements/recommendations for international students: Required—TOEFL (minimum score 577 paper-based; 233 computer-based; 90 iBT). Electronic applications accepted. *Faculty research:* Minority languages, endangered languages, language documentation.

Graduate School and University Center of the City University of New York, Graduate Studies, Program in Anthropology, New York, NY 10016-4039. Offers anthropological linguistics (PhD); archaeology (PhD); cultural anthropology (PhD); physical anthropology (PhD). *Degree requirements:* For doctorate, one foreign language, thesis/dissertation. *Entrance requirements:* For doctorate, GRE General Test. Additional exam requirements/recommendations for international students: Required—TOEFL. Electronic applications accepted.

Graduate School and University Center of the City University of New York, Graduate Studies, Program in Linguistics, New York, NY 10016-4039. Offers MA, PhD. Terminal master's awarded for partial completion of doctoral program. *Degree requirements:* For master's, one foreign language, thesis; for doctorate, 2 foreign languages, thesis/dissertation. *Entrance requirements:* For master's and doctorate, GRE General Test. Additional exam requirements/recommendations for international students: Required—TOEFL. Electronic applications accepted.

Harvard University, Graduate School of Arts and Sciences, Department of Linguistics, Cambridge, MA 02138. Offers descriptive linguistics (PhD); historical linguistics (PhD); theoretical linguistics (PhD). *Degree requirements:* For doctorate, 4 foreign languages, thesis/dissertation, field exam, Indo-European language exam, research paper. *Entrance requirements:* For doctorate, GRE General Test. Additional exam requirements/recommendations for international students: Required—TOEFL. *Expenses:* Tuition: Full-time $32,556. Required fees: $1426. Full-time tuition and fees vary according to program and student level.

Hofstra University, College of Liberal Arts and Sciences, Department of Comparative Literature and Languages, Hempstead, NY 11549. Offers applied linguistics (MA). Part-time programs available. *Faculty:* 2 full-time (0 women), 1 part-time/adjunct (0 women). *Students:* 2 part-time (both women). Average age 30. 3 applicants, 67% accepted, 1 enrolled. In 2008, 1 master's awarded. *Degree requirements:* For master's, thesis, 36 credits, capstone. *Entrance requirements:* For master's, bachelor's degree in related area, interview, 2 letters of recommendation. Additional exam requirements/recommendations for international students: Required—TOEFL (minimum score 550 paper-based; 213 computer-based; 80 iBT). *Application deadline:* Applications are processed on a rolling basis. Application fee: $60. Electronic applications accepted. *Expenses:* Tuition: Full-time $15,300; part-time $850 per credit. Required fees: $970; $165 per term. Tuition and fees vary according to program. *Financial support:* Fellowships with full and partial tuition reimbursements, research assistantships with full and partial tuition reimbursements, Federal Work-Study, institutionally sponsored loans, scholarships/grants, tuition waivers (full and partial), and unspecified assistantships available. Support available to part-time students. Financial award applicants required to submit FAFSA. *Faculty research:* Second language acquisition, second language writing. *Unit head:* Dr. George L. Greaney, Director, 516-463-5651, E-mail: cllglg@hofstra.edu. *Application contact:* Carol Drummer, Dean of Graduate Admissions, 516-463-4876, Fax: 516-463-4664, E-mail: gradstudent@hofstra.edu.

Hofstra University, School of Education, Health, and Human Services, Department of Curriculum and Teaching, Hempstead, NY 11549. Offers business education (MS Ed); early childhood education (MA, MS Ed), including early childhood and childhood education (MS Ed), early childhood education (MA, MS Ed, Ed D); educational technology (CAS); elementary education (MA, MS Ed); elementary education-math/science/technology (MA); English education (MA, MS Ed); fine arts education (MA, MS Ed); foreign language education (MA, MS Ed), including foreign language education; learning and teaching (Ed D), including applied linguistics, art education, arts and humanities, early childhood education (MA, MS Ed, Ed D), English education, human development, learning and teaching, math education, math, science, and technology, multicultural education, physical education, science education (MA, MS Ed, Ed D), social studies education, special education; mathematics education (MA, MS Ed); middle level education (Advanced Certificate), including middle school extension (grades 5-6), middle school extension (grades 7-9); music education (MA, MS Ed), including music education, wind conducting (MA); science education (MA, MS Ed), including science education (MA, MS Ed, Ed D); secondary education (Advanced Certificate); social studies education (MA, MS Ed); TESL/bilingual education (MA, MS Ed, CAS), including bilingual education (MA), bilingual extension education (CAS), TESOL (MS Ed, CAS). *Accreditation:* NCATE. Part-time and evening/weekend programs available. Postbaccalaureate distance learning degree programs offered. *Faculty:* 26 full-time (18 women), 28 part-time/adjunct (16 women). *Students:* 250 full-time (187 women), 258 part-time (208 women); includes 80 minority (26 African Americans, 12 Asian Americans or Pacific Islanders, 42 Hispanic Americans). Average age 28. 376 applicants, 83% accepted, 171 enrolled. In 2008, 273 master's, 17 other advanced degrees awarded. Terminal master's awarded for partial completion of doctoral program. *Degree requirements:* For master's, one foreign language, comprehensive exam (for some programs), thesis (for some programs), electronic portfolio, student teaching, fieldwork, curriculum project, exit project; for doctorate, comprehensive exam, thesis/dissertation; for other advanced degree, one foreign language, comprehensive exam, electronic portfolio. *Entrance requirements:* For master's, letters of recommendation, interview, teaching certificate (MA), essay, portfolio; for doctorate, GRE, 3 letters of recommendation, essay, interview, 2 years full-time teaching; for other advanced degree, letters of recommendation, interview, teaching certificate, essay, portfolio. Additional exam requirements/recommendations for international students: Required—TOEFL (minimum score 550 paper-based; 213 computer-based; 80 iBT). *Application deadline:* Applications are processed on a rolling basis. Application fee: $60. Electronic applications accepted. *Expenses:* Tuition: Full-time $15,300; part-time $850 per credit. Required fees: $970; $165 per term. Tuition and fees vary according to program. *Financial support:* In 2008–09, 298 students received support, including 55 fellowships with full and partial tuition reimbursements available (averaging $3,410 per year), 7 research assistantships with full and partial tuition reimbursements available (averaging $13,199 per year); career-related internships or fieldwork, Federal Work-Study, institutionally sponsored loans, scholarships/grants, health care benefits, tuition waivers (full and partial), unspecified assistantships, and tuition vouchers for cooperating teachers also available. Support available to part-time students. Financial award applicants required to submit FAFSA. *Faculty research:* Problem-based learning. Total annual research expenditures: $6,000. *Unit head:* Dr. Judith Kaufman, Chairperson, 516-463-6566, Fax: 516-463-6196, E-mail: catjsk@hofstra.edu. *Application contact:* Carol Drummer, Dean of Graduate Admissions, 516-463-4876, Fax: 516-463-4664, E-mail: gradstudent@hofstra.edu.

Indiana State University, School of Graduate Studies, College of Arts and Sciences, Department of Languages, Literatures, and Linguistics, Terre Haute, IN 47809-1401. Offers linguistics/teaching English as a second language (MA); TESL/TEFL (CAS). *Degree requirements:* For master's, comprehensive exam. Electronic applications accepted.

Indiana University Bloomington, University Graduate School, College of Arts and Sciences, Department of French and Italian, Bloomington, IN 47405-7000. Offers French (MA, PhD), including French instruction (MA), French linguistics, French literature; Italian (MA, PhD). Part-time programs available. *Faculty:* 19 full-time (7 women). *Students:* 79 full-time (50 women); includes 5 minority (1 African American, 1 American Indian/Alaska Native, 1 Asian American or Pacific Islander, 2 Hispanic Americans), 34 international. Average age 30. 46 applicants, 70% accepted, 15 enrolled. In 2008, 18 master's, 6 doctorates awarded. Terminal master's awarded for partial completion of doctoral program. *Degree requirements:* For master's, one foreign language, comprehensive exam, thesis optional; for doctorate, 2 foreign languages, comprehensive exam, thesis/dissertation. *Entrance requirements:* For master's and doctorate, GRE General Test. Additional exam requirements/recommendations for international students: Required—TOEFL (minimum score 550 paper-based; 213 computer-based; 79 iBT). *Application deadline:* For fall admission, 1/15 priority date for domestic students, 12/1 priority date for international students; for spring admission, 9/1 priority date for domestic and international students. Application fee: $50 ($60 for international students). Electronic applications accepted. *Expenses:* Tuition, area resident: Part-time $291.97 per credit hour. Tuition, state resident: part-time $291.97 per credit hour. Tuition, nonresident: part-time $850.33 per credit hour. Required fees: $110 per semester. Tuition and fees vary according to course load and program. *Financial support:* In 2008–09, 46 students received support, including 2 fellowships with partial tuition reimbursements available (averaging $15,000 per year), 7 research assistantships with partial tuition reimbursements available (averaging $13,025 per year), 37 teaching assistantships with partial tuition reimbursements available (averaging $13,025 per year). Financial award application deadline: 1/15. *Faculty research:* All periods of French and Italian literature and various areas of French linguistics, including the novel and political theory, literature and fine arts, literary theory, postcolonialism, French-Creole studies, French literature of Africa and its Diaspora, humanism, medieval folklore and mythology, humor in medieval and renaissance literature, cinema Old Occitan and Old French, emigration, second lang. acquisition, syntax, sociolinguistics, phonology, and lexicography. *Unit head:* Prof. Emanuel Mickel, Interim Chairman, 812-855-5458, Fax: 812-855-8877, E-mail: fritchr@indiana.edu. *Application contact:* Jocelyn Karlan, Secretary, 812-855-1088, Fax: 812-855-8877, E-mail: fritgs@indiana.edu.

Indiana University Bloomington, University Graduate School, College of Arts and Sciences, Department of Germanic Studies, Bloomington, IN 47405-7000. Offers German philology and linguistics (PhD); German studies (MA, PhD), including German (MA), German literature and culture (MA), German literature and linguistics (MA); medieval German studies (PhD); teaching German (MAT). *Faculty:* 13 full-time (4 women), 6 part-time/adjunct (2 women). *Students:* 33 full-time (16 women), 4 part-time (2 women); includes 1 minority (Hispanic American), 9 international. Average age 30. 38 applicants, 29% accepted, 3 enrolled. In 2008, 6 master's, 3 doctorates awarded. Terminal master's awarded for partial completion of doctoral program. *Degree requirements:* For master's, one foreign language, project; for doctorate, one foreign language, comprehensive exam, thesis/dissertation. *Entrance requirements:* For master's, GRE General Test, BA in German or equivalent; for doctorate, GRE General Test, MA in German or equivalent. Additional exam requirements/recommendations for international students: Required—TOEFL. *Application deadline:* For fall admission, 1/15 priority date for domestic students, 12/15 for international students; for spring admission, 9/1 priority date for domestic students, 9/1 for international students. Applications are processed on a rolling basis. Application fee: $50 ($60 for international students). *Expenses:* Tuition, area resident: Part-time $291.97 per credit hour. Tuition, state resident: part-time $291.97 per credit hour. Tuition, nonresident: part-time $850.33 per credit hour. Required fees: $110 per semester. Tuition and fees vary according to course load and program. *Financial support:* In 2008–09, 7 fellowships with full and partial tuition reimbursements (averaging $20,000 per year), 1 research assistantship

Linguistics

Indiana University Bloomington (continued)
(averaging $13,025 per year), 22 teaching assistantships with full tuition reimbursements (averaging $13,025 per year) were awarded; Federal Work-Study, institutionally sponsored loans, scholarships/grants, and unspecified assistantships also available. Support available to part-time students. Financial award application deadline: 1/15; financial award applicants required to submit FAFSA. *Faculty research:* German (and European) literature: medieval to modern/postmodern, German and culture studies, Germanic philology, literary theory, literature and the other arts. *Unit head:* William Rasch, Department Chairman, 812-855-7947, Fax: 812-855-8292, E-mail: wrasch@indiana.edu. *Application contact:* Michelle Dunbar, Graduate Secretary, 812-855-7947, E-mail: midunbar@indiana.edu.

Indiana University Bloomington, University Graduate School, College of Arts and Sciences, Department of Linguistics, Bloomington, IN 47405-7000. Offers African languages and linguistics (PhD); computational linguistics (MA, PhD); linguistics (MA, PhD). *Faculty:* 10 full-time (1 woman), 18 part-time/adjunct (7 women). *Students:* 73 full-time (37 women), 9 part-time (6 women); includes 5 minority (3 African Americans, 2 Hispanic Americans), 33 international. Average age 32. 74 applicants, 46% accepted, 10 enrolled. In 2008, 4 master's, 8 doctorates awarded. Terminal master's awarded for partial completion of doctoral program. *Degree requirements:* For master's, one foreign language, thesis optional; for doctorate, one foreign language, comprehensive exam, thesis/dissertation, proficiency in research tool appropriate to research area. *Entrance requirements:* For master's and doctorate, GRE General Test. Additional exam requirements/recommendations for international students: Required—TOEFL (minimum score 580 paper-based; 237 computer-based). *Application deadline:* For fall admission, 1/15 priority date for domestic students, 12/1 priority date for international students. Application fee: $50 ($60 for international students). Electronic applications accepted. *Expenses:* Tuition, area resident: Part-time $291.97 per credit hour. Tuition, state resident: part-time $291.97 per credit hour. Tuition, nonresident: part-time $850.33 per credit hour. Required fees: $110 per semester. Tuition and fees vary according to course load and program. *Financial support:* In 2008–09, 29 students received support, including 2 fellowships with full tuition reimbursements available (averaging $15,000 per year), 2 research assistantships with full tuition reimbursements available (averaging $13,500 per year), 9 teaching assistantships with full tuition reimbursements available (averaging $12,240 per year); unspecified assistantships also available. *Faculty research:* African linguistics and language, semantics, phonology, syntactic theory, historical linguistics, phonetics-phonology, syntax, sociolinguistics, computational linguistics. Total annual research expenditures: $100,000. *Unit head:* Dr. Stuart Davis, Chair, 812-855-6456, Fax: 812-855-5363, E-mail: davis@indiana.edu. *Application contact:* Marilyn Estep, Secretary, 812-855-6456, Fax: 812-855-5363, E-mail: estepm@indiana.edu.

Indiana University of Pennsylvania, School of Graduate Studies and Research, College of Humanities and Social Sciences, Department of English, Indiana, PA 15705-1087. Offers composition and teaching English to speakers of other languages (MA, MAT, PhD), including composition and teaching English to speakers of other languages (PhD), teaching English (MAT), teaching English to speakers of other languages (MA); literature and criticism (MA, PhD), including generalist (MA), literature (MA), literature and criticism (PhD); rhetoric and linguistics (PhD). Part-time programs available. *Faculty:* 31 full-time (17 women). *Students:* 132 full-time (69 women), 241 part-time (155 women); includes 20 minority (12 African Americans, 1 American Indian/Alaska Native, 4 Asian Americans or Pacific Islanders, 3 Hispanic Americans), 105 international. Average age 36. 320 applicants, 39% accepted, 73 enrolled. In 2008, 40 master's, 28 doctorates awarded. *Degree requirements:* For master's, thesis optional; for doctorate, one foreign language, comprehensive exam, thesis/dissertation. *Entrance requirements:* For master's and doctorate, 2 letters of recommendation. Additional exam requirements/recommendations for international students: Required—TOEFL. *Application deadline:* For fall admission, 7/1 priority date for domestic students; for spring admission, 11/1 for domestic students. Applications are processed on a rolling basis. Application fee: $30. *Expenses:* Tuition, area resident: Full-time $6430; part-time $357 per credit. Tuition, nonresident: full-time $10,288; part-time $572 per credit. Required fees: $1547.50; $107 per credit. $283 per year. *Financial support:* In 2008–09, 7 fellowships (averaging $2,000 per year), 41 research assistantships with full and partial tuition reimbursements (averaging $5,808 per year), 22 teaching assistantships with partial tuition reimbursements (averaging $12,355 per year) were awarded. Financial award application deadline: 3/15; financial award applicants required to submit FAFSA. *Unit head:* Dr. Gail I. Berlin, Chairperson, 724-357-2261, E-mail: ivy@iup.edu. *Application contact:* Dr. Gail I. Berlin, Chairperson, 724-357-2261, E-mail: ivy@iup.edu.

Instituto Tecnologico de Santo Domingo, Graduate School, Santo Domingo, Dominican Republic. Offers applied linguistics (MA); corporate finance (M Mgmt); education (M Ed); engineering (M Eng), including data telecommunications, industrial engineering, sanitary and environmental engineering, structural engineering; environmental science (M En S), including environmental education, environmental management, marine and coastal ecosystems, natural resources management; human resources administration (M Mgmt); management (M Mgmt); psychology (MA); social science (M Ed). *Entrance requirements:* For master's, birth certificate, minimum GPA of 2.0.

Louisiana State University and Agricultural and Mechanical College, Graduate School, College of Arts and Sciences, Interdepartmental Program in Linguistics, Baton Rouge, LA 70803. Offers MA, PhD. Terminal master's awarded for partial completion of doctoral program. *Degree requirements:* For master's, one foreign language, thesis or alternative; for doctorate, one foreign language, thesis/dissertation. *Entrance requirements:* For master's, GRE General Test, minimum GPA of 3.0; for doctorate, GRE General Test. Additional exam requirements/recommendations for international students: Required—TOEFL (minimum score 550 paper-based; 213 computer-based; 79 iBT). Electronic applications accepted. *Faculty research:* Neurolinguistics, speech science, ESL, Hispanic linguistics, anthropological linguistics.

Massachusetts Institute of Technology, School of Humanities, Arts, and Social Sciences, Department of Linguistics and Philosophy, Linguistics Section, Cambridge, MA 02139-4307. Offers PhD. *Degree requirements:* For doctorate, one foreign language, comprehensive exam, thesis/dissertation. *Entrance requirements:* Additional exam requirements/recommendations for international students: Required—TOEFL (minimum score 577 paper-based; 233 computer-based). Electronic applications accepted.

McGill University, Faculty of Graduate and Postdoctoral Studies, Faculty of Arts, Department of Linguistics, Montréal, QC H3A 2T5, Canada. Offers language acquisition (PhD); linguistics (MA, PhD).

Memorial University of Newfoundland, School of Graduate Studies, Department of Linguistics, St. John's, NL A1C 5S7, Canada. Offers MA, PhD. *Degree requirements:* For master's, one foreign language, thesis optional, comprehensive exam or thesis; for doctorate, 2 foreign languages, comprehensive exam, thesis/dissertation, oral defense of thesis. *Entrance requirements:* For master's, BA in linguistics; for doctorate, master's degree in linguistics. Electronic applications accepted. *Faculty research:* Aboriginal languages of eastern North America, historical/comparative linguistics, languages and dialects of Newfoundland and Labrador.

Michigan State University, The Graduate School, College of Arts and Letters, Department of Linguistics and Germanic, Slavic, Asian, and African Languages, East Lansing, MI 48824. Offers German studies (MA, PhD); linguistics (MA, PhD); teaching English to speakers of other languages (MA). Part-time and evening/weekend programs available. *Entrance requirements:* For master's, GRE General Test, minimum GPA of 3.2 in last 2 undergraduate years, 2 years of college-level foreign language, 3 letters of recommendation, portfolio (German studies); for doctorate, GRE General Test, minimum graduate GPA of 3.5, 3 letters of recommendation, master's degree or sufficient graduate course work in linguistics or language of study, master's thesis or major research paper. Additional exam requirements/recommendations for international students: Required—TOEFL. Electronic applications accepted.

Michigan State University, The Graduate School, College of Arts and Letters, Department of Spanish and Portuguese, East Lansing, MI 48824. Offers applied Spanish linguistics (MA); Hispanic cultural studies (PhD); Hispanic literatures (MA). *Entrance requirements:* Additional exam requirements/recommendations for international students: Required—TOEFL. Electronic applications accepted.

Midwestern Baptist Theological Seminary, Graduate and Professional Programs, Kansas City, MO 64118-4697. Offers Biblical archaeology (MA); Biblical languages (MA); Christian education (M Div, MACE); Christian foundations—lay ministry (Graduate Certificate); collegiate ministries (M Div); counseling (MA); educational ministry (D Ed Min); international church planting (M Div); ministry (M Div, D Min); North American church planting (M Div); sacred music (MCM); urban ministry (M Div); worship leadership (M Div); youth ministry (M Div). *Accreditation:* ATS. Part-time programs available. Postbaccalaureate distance learning degree programs offered (minimal on-campus study). *Degree requirements:* For doctorate, thesis/dissertation; for M Div, 2 foreign languages. *Entrance requirements:* For doctorate, MAT. Electronic applications accepted. *Faculty research:* Ministerial studies, Biblical and theological studies, missions, counseling.

Montclair State University, The Office of Graduate Admissions and Support Services, College of Humanities and Social Sciences, Department of Linguistics, Montclair, NJ 07043-1624. Offers applied linguistics (MA); teacher of English as a second language (Certificate). Part-time and evening/weekend programs available. *Faculty:* 6 full-time (5 women), 18 part-time/adjunct (16 women). *Students:* 4 full-time (all women), 22 part-time (19 women); includes 6 minority (3 African Americans, 2 Asian Americans or Pacific Islanders, 1 Hispanic American), 3 international. Average age 33. 11 applicants, 55% accepted, 5 enrolled. In 2008, 6 master's awarded. *Degree requirements:* For master's, comprehensive exam. *Entrance requirements:* For master's, GRE General Test, 2 letters of recommendation. Additional exam requirements/recommendations for international students: Required—TOEFL (minimum score 83 computer-based). *Application deadline:* For fall admission, 6/1 for international students; for spring admission, 10/1 for international students. Applications are processed on a rolling basis. Application fee: $60. Electronic applications accepted. *Financial support:* In 2008–09, 1 research assistantship with full tuition reimbursement (averaging $7,000 per year) was awarded; Federal Work-Study, scholarships/grants, and unspecified assistantships also available. Support available to part-time students. Financial award application deadline: 3/1; financial award applicants required to submit FAFSA. *Unit head:* Dr. Eileen Fitzpatrick, Chairperson, 973-655-4480. *Application contact:* Dr. Steve Seegmiller, Adviser, 973-655-7500, E-mail: seegmillerm@mail.montclair.edu.

New York University, Graduate School of Arts and Science, Department of Linguistics, New York, NY 10012-1019. Offers MA, PhD. Part-time programs available. Terminal master's awarded for partial completion of doctoral program. *Degree requirements:* For master's, one foreign language, comprehensive exam, thesis optional; for doctorate, one foreign language, thesis/dissertation, 2 publishable papers. *Entrance requirements:* For master's and doctorate, GRE General Test. Additional exam requirements/recommendations for international students: Required—TOEFL. *Faculty research:* Phonology, syntax, sociolinguistics, cognitive science.

Northeastern Illinois University, Graduate College, College of Arts and Sciences, Department of Linguistics, Program in Linguistics, Chicago, IL 60625-4699. Offers MA. Part-time and evening/weekend programs available. *Degree requirements:* For master's, one foreign language, comprehensive exam, thesis optional, minimum GPA of 3.0. *Entrance requirements:* For master's, 9 undergraduate hours in a foreign language or equivalent, minimum GPA of 2.75. Additional exam requirements/recommendations for international students: Required—TOEFL (minimum score 550 paper-based; 213 computer-based; 80 iBT). Electronic applications accepted. *Faculty research:* Acquisition of literacy, Mayan language, Rotuman language, English as a second language methodology, Farsi language.

Northern Arizona University, Graduate College, College of Arts and Letters, Department of English, Programs in Teaching English as a Second Language/Applied Linguistics, Flagstaff, AZ 86011. Offers applied linguistics (PhD); teaching English as a second language (MA); teaching English as a second language/English as a second language (Certificate). *Degree requirements:* For master's, departmental qualifying exam; for doctorate, thesis/dissertation. *Entrance requirements:* For master's and doctorate, GRE General Test.

Northwestern University, The Graduate School, Judd A. and Marjorie Weinberg College of Arts and Sciences, Department of Linguistics, Evanston, IL 60208. Offers MA, PhD, JD/PhD. Admissions and degrees offered through The Graduate School. Part-time programs available. Terminal master's awarded for partial completion of doctoral program. *Degree requirements:* For master's, one foreign language, thesis; for doctorate, 2 foreign languages, thesis/dissertation, 2 qualifying papers. *Entrance requirements:* For master's and doctorate, GRE General Test. Additional exam requirements/recommendations for international students: Required—TOEFL. Electronic applications accepted. *Faculty research:* Theoretical linguistics, empirical approaches to the study of language, language and cognition.

Oakland University, Graduate Study and Lifelong Learning, College of Arts and Sciences, Department of Linguistics, Rochester, MI 48309-4401. Offers linguistics (MA); teaching English as a second language (Certificate). Part-time and evening/weekend programs available. *Entrance requirements:* For master's, minimum GPA of 3.0 for unconditional admission. Additional exam requirements/recommendations for international students: Required—TOEFL (minimum score 550 paper-based; 213 computer-based).

The Ohio State University, Graduate School, College of Humanities, Department of Linguistics, Columbus, OH 43210. Offers MA, PhD. *Degree requirements:* For master's, one foreign language, exam or thesis; for doctorate, 2 foreign languages, thesis/dissertation, exam. *Entrance requirements:* For master's and doctorate, GRE General Test. Additional exam requirements/recommendations for international students: Required—TOEFL (minimum score 600 paper-based; 250 computer-based). Electronic applications accepted. *Faculty research:* Experimental phonetics, nonlinear phonology, process morphology (synchronically and diachronically), syntactic theory (GB, GPSG, HPSG, Categorical Grammar, Relational Grammar), Montague semantics.

Ohio University, Graduate College, College of Arts and Sciences, Department of Linguistics, Athens, OH 45701-2979. Offers applied linguistics/TESOL (MA). Part-time programs available. *Degree requirements:* For master's, one foreign language, thesis or alternative. *Entrance requirements:* For master's, minimum GPA of 3.0. Additional exam requirements/recommendations for international students: Required—TOEFL (minimum score 600 paper-based; 250 computer-based); Recommended—TWE (minimum score 5). Electronic applications accepted. *Faculty research:* Syntax, language learning, language teaching, computers for teaching, sociolinguistics.

Old Dominion University, College of Arts and Letters, Program in Applied Linguistics, Norfolk, VA 23529. Offers MA. Part-time and evening/weekend programs available. *Faculty:* 4 full-time (3 women). *Students:* 13 full-time (10 women), 10 part-time (8 women); includes 2 minority (both Asian Americans or Pacific Islanders), 2 international. Average age 29. 17 applicants, 88% accepted, 11 enrolled. In 2008, 12 master's awarded. *Degree requirements:* For master's, one foreign language, comprehensive exam, thesis optional. *Entrance requirements:* For master's, GRE General Test, sample of written work, 12 hours in English, minimum B average. Additional exam requirements/recommendations for international students: Required—TOEFL (minimum score 570 paper-based; 213 computer-based; 80 iBT). *Application deadline:* For fall admission, 6/1 priority date for domestic and international students; for spring admission, 11/1 priority date for domestic and international students. Applications are processed on a rolling basis. Application fee: $40. Electronic applications accepted. *Expenses:* Tuition, area resident: Full-time $7704; part-time $321 per credit. Tuition, state resident: full-time $7704; part-time $321 per credit. Tuition, nonresident: full-time $19,104; part-time $796 per credit. Required fees: $99 per semester. One-time fee: $40. *Financial support:* In 2008–09, 6 students received support, including 1 research assistantship with partial tuition reimbursement available (averaging

$8,000 per year), 3 teaching assistantships with partial tuition reimbursements available (averaging $8,000 per year); career-related internships or fieldwork, institutionally sponsored loans, and unspecified assistantships also available. Financial award application deadline: 2/15. *Faculty research:* Discourse analysis, phonology, syntax, first and second language acquisition, gender, sociolinguistics. *Unit head:* Dr. Joanne Scheibman, Graduate Program Director, 757-683-3879, Fax: 757-683-3241, E-mail: lingpd@odu.edu. *Application contact:* Dr. Robert Wojtowicz, Associate Dean, 757-683-6077, Fax: 757-683-5746, E-mail: rwojtowi@odu.edu.

Purdue University, Graduate School, College of Liberal Arts, Department of English, West Lafayette, IN 47907. Offers creative writing (MFA); literature (MA, PhD), including linguistics, literature and philosophy (PhD), rhetoric and composition, theory and cultural studies (PhD). Part-time programs available. *Degree requirements:* For master's, one foreign language; for doctorate, one foreign language, thesis/dissertation. *Entrance requirements:* For master's and doctorate, GRE General Test, sample of written work. Additional exam requirements/recommendations for international students: Required—TOEFL. Electronic applications accepted. *Faculty research:* Cultural studies, postmodern narrative, contemporary women writers, composition theory, slave narratives.

Purdue University, Graduate School, College of Liberal Arts, Department of Speech, Language, and Hearing Sciences, West Lafayette, IN 47907. Offers audiology (MS, Au D, PhD); linguistics (MS, PhD); speech and hearing science (MS, PhD); speech-language pathology (MS, PhD). *Accreditation:* ASHA. *Degree requirements:* For master's, thesis optional; for doctorate, thesis/dissertation. *Entrance requirements:* For master's and doctorate, GRE. Additional exam requirements/recommendations for international students: Required—TOEFL. Electronic applications accepted. *Faculty research:* Psychoacoustics, speech perception, speech physiology, stuttering, child language.

Purdue University, Graduate School, College of Liberal Arts, Program in Linguistics, West Lafayette, IN 47907. Offers MS, PhD. *Entrance requirements:* For master's and doctorate, GRE, minimum GPA of 3.4. Additional exam requirements/recommendations for international students: Required—TOEFL. Electronic applications accepted. *Faculty research:* Sign languages, sociolinguistics and African American English, computational linguistics, indigenous languages, theoretical linguistics.

Queens College of the City University of New York, Division of Graduate Studies, Arts and Humanities Division, Department of Linguistics and Communication Disorders, Program in Applied Linguistics, Flushing, NY 11367-1597. Offers MA. Part-time and evening/weekend programs available. *Degree requirements:* For master's, thesis optional. *Entrance requirements:* For master's, minimum GPA of 3.0. Additional exam requirements/recommendations for international students: Required—TOEFL.

Rice University, Graduate Programs, School of Humanities, Department of Linguistics, Houston, TX 77251-1892. Offers MA, PhD. Terminal master's awarded for partial completion of doctoral program. *Degree requirements:* For master's, one foreign language, thesis; for doctorate, 2 foreign languages, thesis/dissertation, 3 research papers. *Entrance requirements:* For master's and doctorate, GRE General Test, minimum GPA of 3.0. Additional exam requirements/recommendations for international students: Required—TOEFL (minimum score 600 paper-based; 250 computer-based; 90 iBT). Electronic applications accepted. *Faculty research:* Typology, fieldwork and language description, cognitive grammar, historical linguistics, corpus linguistics.

Rutgers, The State University of New Jersey, New Brunswick, Graduate School, Department of Linguistics, Piscataway, NJ 08854-8097. Offers PhD. *Degree requirements:* For doctorate, thesis/dissertation, 2 qualifying papers. *Entrance requirements:* For doctorate, GRE General Test, 3 letters of recommendation, statement of purpose, writing sample, transcripts. Electronic applications accepted. *Faculty research:* Theoretical linguistics, syntax, semantics, phonology, computational linguistics, phoenetics.

San Diego State University, Graduate and Research Affairs, College of Arts and Letters, Department of Linguistics and Oriental Languages, San Diego, CA 92182. Offers applied linguistics and English as a second language (CAL); computational linguistics (MA); English as a second language/applied linguistics (MA); general linguistics (MA). *Degree requirements:* For master's, one foreign language, comprehensive exam, thesis optional. *Entrance requirements:* For master's, GRE General Test, 2 letters of recommendation. Additional exam requirements/recommendations for international students: Required—TOEFL (minimum score 570 paper-based). Electronic applications accepted. *Faculty research:* Cross-cultural linguistic studies of semantics.

San Francisco State University, Division of Graduate Studies, College of Humanities, Department of English Language and Literature, Program in Linguistics, San Francisco, CA 94132-1722. Offers MA. Part-time programs available. *Degree requirements:* For master's, 2 foreign languages, thesis (for some programs). *Faculty research:* Mental lexicon, endangered languages, language and gender, linguistics, discourse analysis.

San Jose State University, Graduate Studies and Research, College of Humanities and the Arts, Department of Linguistics and Language Development, San Jose, CA 95192-0001. Offers computational linguistics (Certificate); linguistics (MA, Certificate); teaching English to speakers of other languages (MA, Certificate). *Entrance requirements:* Additional exam requirements/recommendations for international students: Required—TOEFL (minimum score 570 paper-based; 230 computer-based). Electronic applications accepted.

Simon Fraser University, Graduate Studies, Faculty of Arts and Social Sciences, Department of Linguistics, Burnaby, BC V5A 1S6, Canada. Offers MA, PhD. *Degree requirements:* For master's, one foreign language, thesis; for doctorate, 2 foreign languages, thesis/dissertation. *Entrance requirements:* For master's, minimum GPA of 3.0; for doctorate, minimum GPA of 3.5. Additional exam requirements/recommendations for international students: Required—TOEFL or IELTS. *Faculty research:* History of linguistics, syntactic theory, relational grammar, experimental phonetics, pragmatics.

Southern Illinois University Carbondale, Graduate School, College of Liberal Arts, Department of Applied Linguistics, Carbondale, IL 62901-4701. Offers applied linguistics (MA); teaching English to speakers of other languages (MA). *Degree requirements:* For master's, one foreign language, thesis. *Entrance requirements:* For master's, minimum GPA of 3.0. Additional exam requirements/recommendations for international students: Required—TOEFL. *Faculty research:* Theory and methods, second language acquisition, pidgin and Creole languages, cognitive grammar.

Stanford University, School of Humanities and Sciences, Department of Linguistics, Stanford, CA 94305-9991. Offers MA, PhD. *Degree requirements:* For master's, one foreign language, thesis; for doctorate, 2 foreign languages, thesis/dissertation, oral exam, qualifying papers. *Entrance requirements:* For master's and doctorate, GRE General Test. Additional exam requirements/recommendations for international students: Required—TOEFL. Electronic applications accepted.

Stony Brook University, State University of New York, Graduate School, College of Arts and Sciences, Department of Linguistics, Program in Linguistics, Stony Brook, NY 11794. Offers MA, PhD. *Faculty:* 10 full-time (5 women). *Students:* 25 full-time (19 women), 2 part-time (both women); includes 1 Asian American or Pacific Islander, 16 international. Average age 31. 43 applicants, 23% accepted. In 2008, 2 master's, 4 doctorates awarded. *Application deadline:* For fall admission, 1/15 for domestic students. Application fee: $60. *Expenses:* Tuition, area resident: Full-time $7880; part-time $328 per credit hour. Tuition, state resident: full-time $7880; part-time $328 per credit hour. Tuition, nonresident: full-time $13,250; part-time $552 per credit hour. Required fees: $848. *Financial support:* Fellowships, research assistantships, teaching assistantships available. *Unit head:* Dr. Robert Hoberman, Chair, 631-632-7774, Fax: 631-632-9789. *Application contact:* Michelle Carbone, 631-632-7774, Fax: 631-632-9789.

Syracuse University, Graduate School, College of Arts and Sciences, Program in Linguistic Studies, Syracuse, NY 13244. Offers MA. Part-time programs available. *Entrance requirements:* For master's, GRE General Test. Additional exam requirements/recommendations for international students: Required—TOEFL. Electronic applications accepted.

Teachers College, Columbia University, Graduate Faculty of Education, Department of Arts and Humanities, Program in Applied Linguistics, New York, NY 10027-6696. Offers Ed M, MA, Ed D. Part-time and evening/weekend programs available. *Faculty:* 4 full-time (3 women), 5 part-time/adjunct. *Students:* 6 full-time (all women), 65 part-time (55 women); includes 26 minority (8 African Americans, 18 Asian Americans or Pacific Islanders), 11 international. Average age 34. 66 applicants, 38% accepted, 11 enrolled. In 2008, 22 master's, 4 doctorates awarded. Terminal master's awarded for partial completion of doctoral program. *Degree requirements:* For doctorate, variable foreign language requirement, thesis/dissertation. *Application deadline:* For fall admission, 5/15 for domestic students; for spring admission, 12/1 for domestic students. Application fee: $75. *Expenses:* Tuition: Full-time $26,040; part-time $1085 per credit. Required fees: $720. *Financial support:* Fellowships, research assistantships, teaching assistantships, career-related internships or fieldwork, Federal Work-Study, institutionally sponsored loans, and tuition waivers (full and partial) available. Support available to part-time students. Financial award application deadline: 2/1. *Faculty research:* Linguistics applied to education and other professions, sociolinguistics and second language acquisition, rude speech and social rules of speaking. *Unit head:* Graeme Sullivan, Chair, 212-678-3799. *Application contact:* Mark E. Stearns, Associate Director of Admission, 212-678-3710, Fax: 212-678-4171.

Temple University, Health Sciences Center and Graduate School, College of Health Professions, Department of Communication Sciences, Program in Linguistics, Philadelphia, PA 19122-6096. Offers MA. Part-time and evening/weekend programs available. *Degree requirements:* For master's, comprehensive exam. *Entrance requirements:* For master's, GRE General Test, minimum GPA of 3.0. Additional exam requirements/recommendations for international students: Required—TOEFL (minimum score 550 paper-based; 213 computer-based; 79 iBT). Electronic applications accepted. *Faculty research:* Generative syntax, generative phonology, formal semantics, sociolinguistics.

Texas Tech University, Graduate School, College of Arts and Sciences, Department of Classical and Modern Languages and Literatures, Masters in Applied Linguistics Program, Lubbock, TX 79409. Offers MA. *Students:* 22 full-time (16 women), 2 part-time (1 woman), 12 international. Average age 28. 28 applicants, 75% accepted, 14 enrolled. In 2008, 11 master's awarded. *Entrance requirements:* Additional exam requirements/recommendations for international students: Required—TOEFL (minimum score 550 paper-based; 213 computer-based). *Application deadline:* For fall admission, 3/1 priority date for international students; for spring admission, 11/1 priority date for international students. Application fee: $50 ($60 for international students). *Expenses:* Tuition, area resident: Part-time $194 per credit hour. Tuition, state resident: full-time $4648; part-time $194 per credit hour. Tuition, nonresident: full-time $11,392; part-time $475 per credit hour. Required fees: $2206; $69 per credit hour. $389 per semester. *Financial support:* Research assistantships available. *Faculty research:* Second language acquisition; second language instruction; language processing; assessment; general linguistics. *Unit head:* Dr. Bill VanPatten, Director and Professor, 860-742-3145 Ext. 232, Fax: 860-742-3306, E-mail: bill.vanpatten@ttu.edu. *Application contact:* Liz Hildebrand, Senior Advisor, 806-742-4055, Fax: 806-742-3306, E-mail: liz.hildebrand@ttu.edu.

Trinity Western University, Faculty of Graduate Studies, Program in Linguistics, Langley, BC V2Y 1Y1, Canada. Offers MA. *Degree requirements:* For master's, 39 seminar hours; essay (for non-thesis students). *Entrance requirements:* For master's, BA; minimum GPA of 2.7, 3.0 in last two years; 12 seminar hours; linguistic prerequisites; 1 foreign language. Additional exam requirements/recommendations for international students: Required—TOEFL (minimum score 600 paper-based; 250 computer-based). Electronic applications accepted. *Expenses:* Contact institution. *Faculty research:* Syntax, phonology, tone, historical and comparative, discourse analysis.

Universidad de las Américas–Puebla, Division of Graduate Studies, School of Humanities, Program in Applied Linguistics, Puebla, Mexico. Offers linguistics (MA). Part-time and evening/weekend programs available. *Degree requirements:* For master's, one foreign language, thesis. *Entrance requirements:* Additional exam requirements/recommendations for international students: Required—TOEFL. *Faculty research:* English linguistics, teaching English to speakers of other languages.

Université de Montréal, Faculty of Arts and Sciences, Department of Linguistics and Translation, Montréal, QC H3C 3J7, Canada. Offers linguistics and translation (MA, PhD, DESS). *Faculty:* 33 full-time (14 women), 1 (woman) part-time/adjunct. *Students:* 65 full-time (49 women), 123 part-time (90 women). 193 applicants, 37% accepted, 58 enrolled. In 2008, 28 master's, 2 doctorates, 18 other advanced degrees awarded. *Degree requirements:* For master's, thesis, general exam; for doctorate, thesis/dissertation, general exam. *Application deadline:* For fall admission, 2/1 priority date for domestic students; for winter admission, 11/1 priority date for domestic students; for spring admission, 2/1 priority date for domestic students. Application fee: $100. Electronic applications accepted. *Unit head:* Mireille Tremblay, Chairman, 514-343-6675, Fax: 514-343-2284, E-mail: mireille.tremblay.4@umontreal.ca. *Application contact:* Gilles Belanger, Conseillor (Traduction), 514-343-6024, Fax: 514-343-2284, E-mail: gilles.belanger@umontreal.ca.

Université de Sherbrooke, Faculty of Letters and Human Sciences, Department of Letters and Communications, Sherbrooke, QC J1K 2R1, Canada. Offers comparative Canadian literature (MA, PhD); French literature (MA, PhD); linguistics (MA); lit&erature de crèation (MA, PhD); theatre (MA). *Degree requirements:* For master's, thesis or alternative; for doctorate, thesis/dissertation. *Entrance requirements:* For master's, minimum GPA of 2.8; for doctorate, minimum GPA of 3.0.

Université du Québec à Chicoutimi, Graduate Programs, Program in Linguistics, Chicoutimi, QC G7H 2B1, Canada. Offers MA. Part-time programs available. *Degree requirements:* For master's, thesis. *Entrance requirements:* For master's, appropriate bachelor's degree, proficiency in French.

Université du Québec à Montréal, Graduate Programs, Program in Linguistics, Montréal, QC H3C 3P8, Canada. Offers MA, PhD. Part-time programs available. *Degree requirements:* For master's, thesis optional; for doctorate, thesis/dissertation. *Entrance requirements:* For master's, appropriate bachelor's degree or equivalent, proficiency in French; for doctorate, appropriate master's degree or equivalent, proficiency in French.

Université Laval, Faculty of Letters, Department of Languages, Linguistics and Translations, Programs in Linguistics, Québec, QC G1K 7P4, Canada. Offers MA, PhD. Terminal master's awarded for partial completion of doctoral program. *Degree requirements:* For master's, thesis (for some programs); for doctorate, comprehensive exam, thesis/dissertation. *Entrance requirements:* For master's, English test (comprehension of written English), knowledge of French; for doctorate, English exam (comprehension of written English), knowledge of French. Electronic applications accepted.

University at Buffalo, the State University of New York, Graduate School, College of Arts and Sciences, Department of Linguistics, Buffalo, NY 14260. Offers MA, PhD. Terminal master's awarded for partial completion of doctoral program. *Degree requirements:* For master's, exam, project, or thesis; for doctorate, one foreign language, thesis/dissertation, qualifying paper. *Entrance requirements:* For master's and doctorate, GRE General Test. Additional exam requirements/recommendations for international students: Required—TOEFL (minimum score

Linguistics

University at Buffalo, the State University of New York (continued)
600 paper-based; 250 computer-based). Electronic applications accepted. *Faculty research:* Cognitive linguistics, cross-linguistic studies, psycholinguistics, syntax, semantics.

University of Alaska Fairbanks, College of Liberal Arts, Program in Linguistics, Fairbanks, AK 99775-6280. Offers applied linguistics (MA), including language documentation, second language acquisition teacher education. Part-time programs available. *Faculty:* 2 full-time (both women), 2 part-time/adjunct (1 woman). *Students:* 3 full-time (2 women), 24 part-time (22 women); includes 18 minority (17 American Indian/Alaska Native, 1 Asian American or Pacific Islander), 1 international. Average age 42. 8 applicants, 38% accepted, 3 enrolled. *Degree requirements:* For master's, comprehensive exam, thesis or alternative. *Entrance requirements:* Additional exam requirements/recommendations for international students: Required—TOEFL (minimum score 550 paper-based; 213 computer-based; 80 iBT). *Application deadline:* For fall admission, 6/1 for domestic students, 3/1 for international students; for spring admission, 10/15 for domestic students, 9/1 for international students. Application fee: $60. *Expenses:* Tuition, area resident: Full-time $5418; part-time $301 per credit. Tuition, state resident: full-time $5418; part-time $301 per credit. Tuition, nonresident: full-time $11,070; part-time $615 per credit. Required fees: $849; $25 per credit. $78 per semester. Tuition and fees vary according to course load and reciprocity agreements. *Financial support:* In 2008–09, 2 research assistantships (averaging $25,033 per year), 1 teaching assistantship (averaging $9,354 per year) were awarded; fellowships, career-related internships or fieldwork, Federal Work-Study, scholarships/grants, health care benefits, and unspecified assistantships also available. Support available to part-time students. Financial award application deadline: 7/1; financial award applicants required to submit FAFSA. *Faculty research:* Second language acquisition/teaching, INUPIAQ, Athabaskan languages, language maintenance and shift, phonology, morphology. *Unit head:* Dr. Anna Berge, Program Head, 907-474-7876, Fax: 907-474-6586, E-mail: ffamb@uaf.edu. *Application contact:* Dr. Anna Berge, Program Head, 907-474-7876, Fax: 907-474-6586, E-mail: ffamb@uaf.edu.

University of Alberta, Faculty of Graduate Studies and Research, Department of Linguistics, Edmonton, AB T6G 2E1, Canada. Offers experimental linguistics (M Sc, PhD). *Degree requirements:* For master's, thesis (for some programs); for doctorate, thesis/dissertation. *Entrance requirements:* For master's, BA in linguistics; for doctorate, M Sc or MA in linguistics. Additional exam requirements/recommendations for international students: Required—TOEFL. *Faculty research:* Experimental phonetics, psycholinguistics, phonology, endangered languages, language acquisition.

University of Alberta, Faculty of Graduate Studies and Research, Department of Modern Languages and Cultural Studies, Edmonton, AB T6G 2E1, Canada. Offers applied linguistics (Germanic, Romance, Slavic) (MA); French language, literatures and linguistics (PhD); French language, literatures, and linguistics (MA); Germanic languages, literatures and linguistics (PhD); Germanic languages, literatures, and linguistics (MA); Italian studies (MA); Slavic languages and literatures (Russian, Ukrainian) (MA, PhD); Slavic linguistics (Russian, Ukrainian) (MA, PhD); Spanish and Latin American studies (MA, PhD); Ukrainian folklore (MA, PhD). Part-time programs available. *Degree requirements:* For master's, one foreign language, thesis; for doctorate, 2 foreign languages, comprehensive exam, thesis/dissertation. *Entrance requirements:* For master's and doctorate, 1 language other than English. Additional exam requirements/recommendations for international students: Required—Michigan English Language Assessment Battery or TOEFL (paper score 550; computer score 213). Electronic applications accepted. *Faculty research:* Russian/Ukrainian studies; German studies; contemporary Latin American, French and Francophone studies; Italian studies.

The University of Arizona, Graduate College, College of Social and Behavioral Sciences, Department of Linguistics, Tucson, AZ 85721. Offers human language technology (MS); linguistics and anthropology (PhD); Native American linguistics (MA); theoretical linguistics (PhD). PhD in linguistics and anthropology offered jointly with Department of Anthropology. Terminal master's awarded for partial completion of doctoral program. *Degree requirements:* For master's, one foreign language, thesis; for doctorate, one foreign language, comprehensive exam, thesis/dissertation. *Entrance requirements:* For master's, GRE General Test (MS), writing sample, statement of purpose, 3 letters of recommendation, departmental application, minimum GPA of 3.0; for doctorate, GRE General Test, writing sample, statement of purpose, 3 letters of recommendation, departmental application, minimum GPA of 3.0. Additional exam requirements/recommendations for international students: Required—TOEFL (minimum score 550 paper-based; 213 computer-based). Electronic applications accepted. *Faculty research:* Semantic, syntactic, morphological, and phonological theories of natural languages; native languages of the American Southwest, psycholinguistics and computational linguistics.

The University of British Columbia, Faculty of Arts and Faculty of Graduate Studies, Department of Linguistics, Vancouver, BC V6T 1Z1, Canada. Offers MA, PhD. Part-time programs available. *Degree requirements:* For master's, one foreign language, thesis optional; for doctorate, 2 foreign languages, thesis/dissertation, 2 qualifying papers. *Entrance requirements:* Additional exam requirements/recommendations for international students: Required—TOEFL (minimum score 550 paper-based; 213 computer-based). Electronic applications accepted. *Faculty research:* Linguistic theory (phonology, syntax, semantics), Native American languages, African languages, first language acquisition, experimental phonetics.

University of Calgary, Faculty of Graduate Studies, Faculty of Social Sciences, Department of Linguistics, Calgary, AB T2N 1N4, Canada. Offers MA, PhD. *Degree requirements:* For master's, one foreign language, thesis; for doctorate, one foreign language, comprehensive exam, thesis/dissertation. *Entrance requirements:* For doctorate, MA. Additional exam requirements/recommendations for international students: Required—TOEFL (minimum score 560 paper-based; 220 computer-based). Electronic applications accepted. *Faculty research:* Theoretical linguistics, historical linguistics, language acquisition, Amerindian.

University of California, Berkeley, Graduate Division, College of Letters and Science, Department of Linguistics, Berkeley, CA 94720-1500. Offers PhD. *Degree requirements:* For doctorate, thesis/dissertation, qualifying exam. *Entrance requirements:* For doctorate, GRE General Test, minimum GPA of 3.0, 3 letters of recommendation.

University of California, Davis, Graduate Studies, Graduate Group in Linguistics, Davis, CA 95616. Offers applied linguistics (MA, PhD); linguistics (MA). *Degree requirements:* For master's, one foreign language, comprehensive exam (for some programs), thesis (for some programs); for doctorate, thesis/dissertation. *Entrance requirements:* For master's and doctorate, GRE General Test, minimum GPA of 3.0. Additional exam requirements/recommendations for international students: Required—TOEFL (minimum score 550 paper-based; 213 computer-based). Electronic applications accepted. *Faculty research:* Grammatical analysis and theory, sociolinguistics, historical linguistics, Romance linguistics, neurolinguistics.

University of California, Los Angeles, Graduate Division, College of Letters and Science, Department of Applied Linguistics and Teaching English as a Second Language, Program in Applied Linguistics, Los Angeles, CA 90095. Offers PhD. *Students:* 40 full-time (30 women); includes 5 minority (3 Asian Americans or Pacific Islanders, 2 Hispanic Americans), 20 international. Average age 33. 37 applicants, 24% accepted, 4 enrolled. In 2008, 9 doctorates awarded. *Degree requirements:* For doctorate, one foreign language, thesis/dissertation, oral and written qualifying exams. *Entrance requirements:* For doctorate, GRE General Test, MA in relevant field, thesis or related research paper. *Application deadline:* For fall admission, 12/15 for domestic students. Application fee: $60. Electronic applications accepted. *Expenses:* Tuition, nonresident: full-time $14,694. Required fees: $9669.50. Full-time tuition and fees vary according to course load, degree level, program and student level. *Financial support:* In 2008–09, 33 fellowships with full and partial tuition reimbursements, 13 research assistantships with full and partial tuition reimbursements, 20 teaching assistantships with full and partial tuition reimbursements were awarded; Federal Work-Study, institutionally sponsored loans, scholarships/grants, and tuition waivers (full and partial) also available. Financial award application deadline: 3/1; financial award applicants required to submit FAFSA. *Unit head:* Dr. Lyle F. Bachman, Chair, 310-825-4631. *Application contact:* Departmental Office, 310-825-4631, Fax: 310-206-4118, E-mail: lyn@humnet.ucla.edu.

University of California, Los Angeles, Graduate Division, College of Letters and Science, Department of Linguistics, Los Angeles, CA 90095. Offers MA, PhD. *Students:* 28 full-time (15 women); includes 2 minority (1 Asian American or Pacific Islander, 1 Hispanic American), 11 international. Average age 25. 130 applicants, 15% accepted, 7 enrolled. In 2008, 7 doctorates awarded. Terminal master's awarded for partial completion of doctoral program. *Degree requirements:* For master's, one foreign language, comprehensive exam or thesis; for doctorate, thesis/dissertation, oral and written qualifying exams. *Entrance requirements:* For master's, GRE General Test, minimum GPA of 3.0, sample of written work; statement of purpose; degree objective of Ph.D; for doctorate, GRE General Test, minimum undergraduate GPA of 3.0, sample of written work; statement of purpose. *Application deadline:* For fall admission, 12/15 for domestic and international students. Application fee: $60 ($80 for international students). Electronic applications accepted. *Expenses:* Tuition, nonresident: full-time $14,694. Required fees: $9669.50. Full-time tuition and fees vary according to course load, degree level, program and student level. *Financial support:* In 2008–09, 40 fellowships with full and partial tuition reimbursements, 24 research assistantships with full and partial tuition reimbursements, 34 teaching assistantships with full and partial tuition reimbursements were awarded; Federal Work-Study, institutionally sponsored loans, scholarships/grants, health care benefits, tuition waivers (full and partial), and unspecified assistantships also available. Financial award application deadline: 3/1; financial award applicants required to submit FAFSA. *Faculty research:* Phonetics, nonlinear phonology, formal syntax, formal semantics, natural language processing. *Unit head:* Dr. Anoop Mahajan, Chair, 310-825-5060. *Application contact:* Departmental Office, 310-825-0634, E-mail: linguist@humnet.ucla.edu.

University of California, San Diego, Office of Graduate Studies, Department of Linguistics, La Jolla, CA 92093. Offers PhD. *Degree requirements:* For doctorate, thesis/dissertation. *Entrance requirements:* For doctorate, GRE General Test. Electronic applications accepted.

University of California, San Diego, Office of Graduate Studies, Interdisciplinary Program in Cognitive Science, La Jolla, CA 92093. Offers cognitive science/anthropology (PhD); cognitive science/communication (PhD); cognitive science/computer science and engineering (PhD); cognitive science/linguistics (PhD); cognitive science/neuroscience (PhD); cognitive science/philosophy (PhD); cognitive science/psychology (PhD); cognitive science/sociology (PhD). Admissions offered through affiliated departments. *Degree requirements:* For doctorate, thesis/dissertation. *Entrance requirements:* For doctorate, GRE General Test, acceptance into one of the 8 participating departments. *Faculty research:* Language and cognition, philosophy of mind, visual perception, biological anthropology, sociolinguistics.

University of California, Santa Barbara, Graduate Division, College of Letters and Sciences, Division of Humanities and Fine Arts, Department of French and Italian, Santa Barbara, CA 93106-4140. Offers French (MA, MABL, PhD), including applied linguistics (PhD), European Medieval studies (PhD), feminist studies (PhD), French (MABL, PhD); MA/PhD. French Language Institute available during summer sessions. *Faculty:* 21 full-time (12 women). *Students:* 11 full-time (7 women). Average age 31. 16 applicants, 63% accepted, 3 enrolled. In 2008, 1 master's, 5 doctorates awarded. Terminal master's awarded for partial completion of doctoral program. *Degree requirements:* For master's, 2 foreign languages, comprehensive exam; for doctorate, 2 foreign languages, comprehensive exam, thesis/dissertation. *Entrance requirements:* For master's, GRE, sample of written work, tape of spoken French, BA or the equivalent, 3 letters of recommendation, statement of purpose, personal achievements/contributions statement, resumé/curriculum vitae, transcripts for post-secondary institutions attended; for doctorate, GRE, sample of written work, tape of spoken French, MA or the equivalent, 3 letters of recommendation, statement of purpose, personal achievements/contributions statement, resumé/curriculum vitae, transcripts for post-secondary institutions attended. Additional exam requirements/recommendations for international students: Required—TOEFL (paper: 550, computer: 213, IBT: 80) or IELTS (7). *Application deadline:* For fall admission, 5/1 for domestic and international students; for winter admission, 10/1 for domestic and international students; for spring admission, 1/15 for domestic and international students. Application fee: $70 ($90 for international students). Electronic applications accepted. *Expenses:* Tuition, nonresident: full-time $25,149. Required fees: $10,143. Full-time tuition and fees vary according to campus/location, reciprocity agreements and student level. *Financial support:* In 2008–09, 11 students received support, including 5 fellowships with full and partial tuition reimbursements available (averaging $8,100 per year), 11 teaching assistantships with partial tuition reimbursements available (averaging $11,400 per year); career-related internships or fieldwork, Federal Work-Study, institutionally sponsored loans, scholarships/grants, traineeships, health care benefits, tuition waivers (full and partial), and unspecified assistantships also available. Financial award applicants required to submit FAFSA. *Faculty research:* French and Francophone studies, comparative literature, second language acquisition, applied linguistics, performance studies, feminist and gender studies. Total annual research expenditures: $2,500. *Unit head:* Prof. Jon Snyder, Chair, 805-893-2220, Fax: 805-893-8826, E-mail: snyder@frit.ucsb.edu. *Application contact:* Rosa Pinter, Graduate Staff Advisor, 805-893-3398, Fax: 805-893-8826, E-mail: pinter@frit.ucsb.edu.

University of California, Santa Barbara, Graduate Division, College of Letters and Sciences, Division of Humanities and Fine Arts, Department of Germanic, Slavic, and Semitic Studies, Santa Barbara, CA 93106-4130. Offers Germanic languages and literature (MA, PhD), including applied linguistics (PhD), feminist studies (PhD); MA/PhD. *Faculty:* 7 full-time (4 women). *Students:* 2 full-time (0 women). Average age 31. 6 applicants, 50% accepted, 1 enrolled. In 2008, 1 master's awarded. Terminal master's awarded for partial completion of doctoral program. *Degree requirements:* For master's, 2 foreign languages, comprehensive exam, thesis; for doctorate, 3 foreign languages, comprehensive exam, thesis/dissertation. *Entrance requirements:* For master's and doctorate, GRE. Additional exam requirements/recommendations for international students: Required—TOEFL (minimum score 550 paper-based; 213 computer-based; 80 iBT), IELTS (minimum score 7), TOEFL or IELTS. *Application deadline:* For fall admission, 12/31 priority date for domestic students, 5/1 priority date for international students; for winter admission, 11/1 priority date for domestic and international students; for spring admission, 2/1 priority date for domestic and international students. Applications are processed on a rolling basis. Application fee: $70 ($90 for international students). Electronic applications accepted. *Expenses:* Tuition, nonresident: full-time $25,149. Required fees: $10,143. Full-time tuition and fees vary according to campus/location, reciprocity agreements and student level. *Financial support:* In 2008–09, 2 students received support, including 2 fellowships with full and partial tuition reimbursements available (averaging $10,100 per year), 1 teaching assistantship with partial tuition reimbursement available (averaging $11,600 per year); Federal Work-Study, institutionally sponsored loans, scholarships/grants, health care benefits, and tuition waivers (full and partial) also available. Financial award application deadline: 12/31; financial award applicants required to submit FAFSA. *Faculty research:* Critical theory, media technology, psychoanalysis, German romanticism, Goethe. *Unit head:* Prof. Elisabeth Weber, Chair, 805-893-3527, Fax: 805-893-2374, E-mail: weber@gss.ucsb.edu. *Application contact:* Sierra Gray, Graduate Program Assistant, 805-893-2131, Fax: 805-893-2374, E-mail: sierra@gss.ucsb.edu.

University of California, Santa Barbara, Graduate Division, College of Letters and Sciences, Division of Humanities and Fine Arts, Department of Linguistics, Santa Barbara, CA 93106-3100. Offers applied linguistics (PhD); cognitive science (PhD); human development (PhD); language, interaction, and social organizations (PhD); MA/PhD. *Faculty:* 23 full-time (12 women). *Students:* 25 full-time (14 women). Average age 32. 63 applicants, 17% accepted, 5 enrolled. In 2008, 5 doctorates awarded. *Degree requirements:* For doctorate, one foreign language, comprehensive exam, thesis/dissertation, 48 units of coursework, minimum GPA of 3.7. *Entrance requirements:* For doctorate, GRE, 3 letters of recommendation, statement of purpose, personal achievements/contributions statement, resumé/curriculum vitae, transcripts for post-secondary institutions attended. Additional exam requirements/recommendations for international students: Required—TOEFL (minimum score 550 paper-based; 213 computer-based; 80 iBT), IELTS (minimum score 7), TOEFL or IELTS. *Application deadline:* For fall admission, 12/1 priority date for domestic and international students. Application fee: $70 ($90 for international students). Electronic applications accepted. *Expenses:* Tuition, nonresident: full-time $25,149. Required fees: $10,143. Full-time tuition and fees vary according to campus/location, reciprocity agreements and student level. *Financial support:* In 2008–09, 24 students received support, including 19 fellowships with full and partial tuition reimbursements available (averaging $12,400 per year), 1 research assistantship with full and partial tuition reimbursement available (averaging $3,000 per year), 13 teaching assistantships with partial tuition reimbursements available (averaging $5,600 per year); Federal Work-Study, institutionally sponsored loans, scholarships/grants, health care benefits, and unspecified assistantships also available. Financial award application deadline: 12/1; financial award applicants required to submit FAFSA. *Faculty research:* Language, race and subcultural identities among California teenagers; language acquisition, psycholinguisticss; language documentation, fieldwork; syntax of nominalization in 5 Tibeto-Burman languages; perceptual correlates of syllable weight. *Unit head:* Prof. Patricia M. Clancy, Chair, 805-893-8658, Fax: 805-893-7769, E-mail: pclancy@linguistics.ucsb.edu. *Application contact:* Mary Rae Staton, Graduate Program Assistant, 805-893-3776, Fax: 805-893-7769, E-mail: staton@linguistics.ucsb.edu.

University of California, Santa Barbara, Graduate Division, College of Letters and Sciences, Division of Humanities and Fine Arts, Department of Spanish and Portuguese, Santa Barbara, CA 93106-4150. Offers Hispanic languages and literature (PhD), including applied linguistics, European Medieval studies, feminist studies, Hispanic languages and literature; Portuguese (MA); Spanish (MA); Spanish and Portuguese (MA); MA/PhD. Spanish Language Institute available during summer session. *Faculty:* 16 full-time (6 women). *Students:* 29 full-time (16 women). Average age 30. 46 applicants, 39% accepted, 9 enrolled. In 2008, 4 master's, 2 doctorates awarded. *Degree requirements:* For master's, 2 foreign languages, comprehensive exam (for some programs), thesis optional; for doctorate, 2 foreign languages, comprehensive exam, thesis/dissertation. *Entrance requirements:* For master's, GRE, 2 writing samples, undergraduate major in Spanish or equivalent, 3 letters of recommendation, statement of purpose, personal achievements/contributions statement, resumé/curriculum vitae, transcripts for post-secondary institutions attended; for doctorate, GRE, 2 writing samples, master's degree, 3 letters of recommendation, statement of purpose, personal achievements/contributions statement, resumé/curriculum vitae, transcripts for post-secondary institutions attended. Additional exam requirements/recommendations for international students: Required—TOEFL (minimum score 550 paper-based; 213 computer-based; 80 iBT), IELTS (minimum score 7), TOEFL or IELTS. *Application deadline:* For fall admission, 3/1 for domestic and international students; for winter admission, 11/1 for domestic and international students; for spring admission, 2/1 for domestic and international students. Application fee: $70 ($90 for international students). Electronic applications accepted. *Expenses:* Tuition, nonresident: full-time $25,149. Required fees: $10,143. Full-time tuition and fees vary according to campus/location, reciprocity agreements and student level. *Financial support:* In 2008–09, 30 students received support, including 9 fellowships with full and partial tuition reimbursements available (averaging $7,000 per year), 29 teaching assistantships with partial tuition reimbursements available (averaging $11,500 per year); career-related internships or fieldwork, Federal Work-Study, institutionally sponsored loans, scholarships/grants, health care benefits, tuition waivers (full and partial), and unspecified assistantships also available. Financial award application deadline: 1/7; financial award applicants required to submit FAFSA. *Faculty research:* 19th century Spanish and Portuguese literature, Spanish and Spanish American literature, 19th and 20th century Portuguese and Brazilian literatures, Hispanic Linguistics, Catalan language and culture. *Unit head:* Prof. Francisco A. Lomeli, Chair, 805-893-5715, Fax: 805-893-8341, E-mail: lomeli@spanport.ucsb.edu. *Application contact:* Carol Conley, Graduate Program Assistant, 805-893-3162, Fax: 805-893-8341, E-mail: cconley@spanport.ucsb.edu.

University of California, Santa Cruz, Division of Graduate Studies, Division of Humanities, Linguistics Research Center, Santa Cruz, CA 95064. Offers MA, PhD. Terminal master's awarded for partial completion of doctoral program. *Degree requirements:* For master's, one foreign language, research paper; for doctorate, one foreign language, thesis/dissertation, qualifying exam. *Entrance requirements:* For master's and doctorate, GRE General Test. *Faculty research:* Phonological, morphological, syntactic, and semantic theory; computational linguistics.

University of Chicago, Division of the Humanities, Department of Linguistics, Chicago, IL 60637-1513. Offers anthropology and linguistics (PhD); linguistics (AM, PhD). Terminal master's awarded for partial completion of doctoral program. *Degree requirements:* For master's, one foreign language, thesis; for doctorate, 2 foreign languages, thesis/dissertation. *Entrance requirements:* For master's and doctorate, GRE General Test. Additional exam requirements/recommendations for international students: Required—TOEFL.

University of Colorado at Boulder, Graduate School, College of Arts and Sciences, Department of Linguistics, Boulder, CO 80309. Offers MA, PhD. Part-time programs available. Terminal master's awarded for partial completion of doctoral program. *Degree requirements:* For master's, comprehensive exam, thesis optional; for doctorate, one foreign language, thesis/dissertation. *Entrance requirements:* For master's, GRE General Test, minimum undergraduate GPA of 2.75; for doctorate, GRE General Test. *Faculty research:* Synchronic linguistics, discourse analysis, language acquisition, diachronic linguistics, lexicography, American Indian linguistics, psycholinguistics, African linguistics.

University of Colorado Denver, College of Liberal Arts and Sciences, Department of English, Denver, CO 80217-3364. Offers applied linguistics (MA); English studies (MA); literature (MA); teaching English to speakers of other languages (Certificate); teaching of writing (MA). Part-time and evening/weekend programs available. *Degree requirements:* For master's, thesis optional. *Entrance requirements:* For master's, GRE General Test, minimum GPA of 3.0. Additional exam requirements/recommendations for international students: Required—TOEFL (minimum score 550 paper-based). Electronic applications accepted.

University of Connecticut, Graduate School, College of Liberal Arts and Sciences, Department of Linguistics, Field of Linguistics, Storrs, CT 06269. Offers MA, PhD. *Degree requirements:* For doctorate, thesis/dissertation. *Entrance requirements:* For doctorate, GRE General Test. Additional exam requirements/recommendations for international students: Required—TOEFL (minimum score 550 paper-based; 213 computer-based). Electronic applications accepted.

University of Delaware, College of Arts and Sciences, Department of Linguistics, Newark, DE 19716. Offers MA, PhD. *Degree requirements:* For doctorate, one foreign language, comprehensive exam, thesis/dissertation, publishable research papers. *Entrance requirements:* For master's, GRE General Test; for doctorate, GRE General Test, writing sample. Additional exam requirements/recommendations for international students: Required—TOEFL (minimum score 600 paper-based; 250 computer-based). Electronic applications accepted. *Faculty research:* East Asian, Austronesian and Romance languages, phonology, phonetics, syntax, cognitive science, semantics, psycholinguistics, language acquisition, endangered languages.

University of Florida, Graduate School, College of Liberal Arts and Sciences, Program in Linguistics, Gainesville, FL 32611. Offers linguistics (MA, PhD); teaching English as a second language (Certificate). *Degree requirements:* For master's, one foreign language, comprehensive exam, thesis optional; for doctorate, 2 foreign languages, thesis/dissertation, qualifying exam. *Entrance requirements:* For master's and doctorate, GRE General Test, minimum GPA of 3.0. Additional exam requirements/recommendations for international students: Required—TOEFL (minimum score 550 paper-based; 213 computer-based). Electronic applications accepted. *Faculty research:* Theoretical, applied, and descriptive linguistics.

University of Georgia, Graduate School, College of Arts and Sciences, Program in Linguistics, Athens, GA 30602. Offers MA, PhD. *Degree requirements:* For master's, one foreign language, thesis; for doctorate, 2 foreign languages, comprehensive exam, thesis/dissertation. *Entrance requirements:* For master's and doctorate, GRE General Test. Electronic applications accepted. *Expenses:* Contact institution. *Faculty research:* Applied linguistics, English linguistics, dialectology, lexicography, discourse analysis.

University of Hawaii at Manoa, Graduate Division, Colleges of Arts and Sciences, College of Language, Linguistics and Literature, Department of Linguistics, Honolulu, HI 96822. Offers MA, PhD. Part-time programs available. Terminal master's awarded for partial completion of doctoral program. *Degree requirements:* For master's, 2 foreign languages, thesis optional; for doctorate, 2 foreign languages, comprehensive exam, thesis/dissertation. *Entrance requirements:* For master's and doctorate, GRE General Test. Additional exam requirements/recommendations for international students: Required—TOEFL (minimum score 600 paper-based; 250 computer-based; 100 iBT), IELTS (minimum score 7). *Faculty research:* Languages of the Pacific and Asia.

University of Houston, College of Liberal Arts and Social Sciences, Department of English, Houston, TX 77204. Offers applied English linguistics (MA); English and American literature (MA, PhD); literature and creative writing (MA, MFA, PhD). Postbaccalaureate distance learning degree programs offered. *Faculty:* 21 full-time (10 women), 7 part-time/adjunct (3 women). *Students:* 78 full-time (35 women), 49 part-time (39 women); includes 21 minority (4 African Americans, 1 American Indian/Alaska Native, 10 Asian Americans or Pacific Islanders, 6 Hispanic Americans), 4 international. Average age 33. 197 applicants, 24% accepted, 22 enrolled. In 2008, 28 master's, 13 doctorates awarded. *Degree requirements:* For master's, one foreign language, thesis (for some programs); for doctorate, 2 foreign languages, comprehensive exam, thesis/dissertation. *Entrance requirements:* For master's, GRE General Test, GRE Subject Test, minimum GPA of 3.0 in last 60 hours of course work; for doctorate, GRE General Test, GRE Subject Test, writing sample. Additional exam requirements/recommendations for international students: Required—TOEFL. *Application deadline:* For fall admission, 1/1 priority date for domestic students. Applications are processed on a rolling basis. Application fee: $50. *Expenses:* Tuition, state resident: full-time $5164; part-time $287 per credit. Tuition, nonresident: full-time $10,222; part-time $568 per credit. *Financial support:* In 2008–09, 2 fellowships with full tuition reimbursements (averaging $7,100 per year), 68 teaching assistantships with full tuition reimbursements (averaging $12,250 per year) were awarded; career-related internships or fieldwork, Federal Work-Study, institutionally sponsored loans, scholarships/grants, health care benefits, and unspecified assistantships also available. Support available to part-time students. Financial award application deadline: 2/1. *Unit head:* Wyman Henderson, Chairperson, 713-743-3004, Fax: 713-743-3215, E-mail: whh@uh.edu. *Application contact:* Ruby Jones, Advising Assistant, 713-743-2941, Fax: 713-743-3215, E-mail: rjones@uh.edu.

University of Illinois at Chicago, Graduate College, College of Liberal Arts and Sciences, Department of English, Program in Linguistics, Chicago, IL 60607-7128. Offers teaching English to speakers of other languages/applied linguistics (MA). Part-time programs available. *Degree requirements:* For master's, one foreign language, comprehensive exam, thesis (for some programs). *Entrance requirements:* For master's, minimum GPA of 3.0. Additional exam requirements/recommendations for international students: Required—TOEFL. Electronic applications accepted. *Faculty research:* Second language acquisition, methodology of second language teaching, lexicography, language, sex and gender.

University of Illinois at Urbana–Champaign, Graduate College, College of Liberal Arts and Sciences, School of Literatures, Cultures and Linguistics, Department of Linguistics, Champaign, IL 61820. Offers linguistics (MA, PhD); teaching of English as a second language (MA). *Faculty:* 17 full-time (5 women), 2 part-time/adjunct (0 women). *Students:* 72 full-time (47 women), 36 part-time (26 women); includes 6 minority (1 African American, 4 Asian Americans or Pacific Islanders, 1 Hispanic American), 56 international. 195 applicants, 22% accepted, 23 enrolled. In 2008, 24 master's, 12 doctorates awarded. *Entrance requirements:* For master's, GRE, minimum GPA of 3.0; writing sample; for doctorate, GRE, minimum GPA of 3.5; writing sample. Additional exam requirements/recommendations for international students: Required—TOEFL (minimum score 88 iBT). *Application deadline:* Applications are processed on a rolling basis. Application fee: $60 ($75 for international students). Electronic applications accepted. *Financial support:* In 2008–09, 19 fellowships, 21 research assistantships, 66 teaching assistantships were awarded; tuition waivers (full and partial) also available. *Unit head:* Elabbas Benmamoun, Head, 217-333-7129, E-mail: benmamou@illinois.edu. *Application contact:* Lynn Stanke, Office Support Specialist, 217-333-6269, Fax: 217-244-3050, E-mail: stanke@illinois.edu.

The University of Iowa, Graduate College, College of Liberal Arts and Sciences, Department of Linguistics, Iowa City, IA 52242-1316. Offers linguistics (MA, PhD); linguistics with TESL (MA). Linguistics with TESL option offered as part of dual degree that begins at undergraduate level. *Degree requirements:* For master's, thesis optional, exam; for doctorate, comprehensive exam, thesis/dissertation. *Entrance requirements:* For master's and doctorate, GRE General Test, minimum GPA of 3.0. Additional exam requirements/recommendations for international students: Required—TOEFL (minimum score 600 paper-based; 250 computer-based; 100 iBT). Electronic applications accepted.

The University of Kansas, Graduate Studies, College of Liberal Arts and Sciences, Department of Linguistics, Lawrence, KS 66045. Offers MA, PhD. Part-time programs available. *Faculty:* 8. *Students:* 34 full-time (13 women), 2 part-time (1 woman), 23 international. Average age 33. 34 applicants, 65% accepted, 10 enrolled. In 2008, 7 master's, 2 doctorates awarded. Terminal master's awarded for partial completion of doctoral program. *Degree requirements:* For master's, one foreign language, thesis or alternative; for doctorate, one foreign language, thesis/dissertation. *Entrance requirements:* For master's and doctorate, GRE General Test, resumé, 3 letters of recommendation. Additional exam requirements/recommendations for international students: Required—TOEFL. *Application deadline:* For fall admission, 1/5 priority date for domestic students, 1/5 for international students. Application fee: $45 ($55 for international students). Electronic applications accepted. *Expenses:* Tuition, area resident: Full-time $6122; part-time $255.10 per credit hour. Tuition, state resident: full-time $6122; part-time $255.10 per credit hour. Tuition, nonresident: full-time $14,629; part-time $609.55 per credit hour. Required fees: $847; $70.56 per credit hour. Tuition and fees vary according to course load and program. *Financial support:* Fellowships with full and partial tuition reimbursements, research assistantships with full and partial tuition reimbursements, teaching assistantships with full and partial tuition reimbursements, unspecified assistantships available. Financial award application deadline: 1/1. *Faculty research:* Phonetics and phonology, syntax, psycholinguistics, neurolinguistics, language acquisition. *Unit head:* Dr. Allard Jongman, Chair, 785-864-3450, Fax: 785-864-5724, E-mail: liguistics@ku.edu. *Application contact:* Corinna Johnson, Department Secretary, 785-864-3450, Fax: 785-864-5724, E-mail: linguistics@ku.edu.

University of Manitoba, Faculty of Graduate Studies, Faculty of Arts, Department of Linguistics, Winnipeg, MB R3T 2N2, Canada. Offers MA, PhD.

University of Maryland, Baltimore County, Graduate School, College of Arts, Humanities and Social Sciences, Department of Modern Languages and Linguistics, Program in Intercultural Communication, Baltimore, MD 21250. Offers MA. Part-time and evening/weekend programs available. *Faculty:* 18 full-time (6 women), 3 part-time/adjunct (2 women). *Students:* 19 full-time (17 women), 17 part-time (12 women); includes 5 minority (1 African American, 2 Asian Americans or Pacific Islanders, 2 Hispanic Americans), 10 international. 25 applicants, 64% accepted, 12 enrolled. In 2008, 18 master's awarded. *Degree requirements:* For master's, one foreign language, comprehensive exam (for some programs), thesis (for some programs). *Entrance requirements:* For master's, GRE General Test, minimum GPA of 3.0, 3 letters of recommendation, self-evaluation and statement of support, resumé. Additional exam requirements/recommendations for international students: Required—TOEFL (minimum score 213 computer-based). *Application deadline:* For fall admission, 1/31 for domestic and international students. Applications are processed on a rolling basis. Application fee: $45. Electronic applications accepted. *Financial support:* In 2008–09, 8 students received support, including 4 teaching assistantships with full tuition reimbursements available (averaging $11,324 per year); tuition waivers also available. Financial award applicants required to submit FAFSA.

Linguistics

University of Maryland, Baltimore County (continued)
Faculty research: Comparative television research-cross-cultural; cultural studies; social developments in Latin America; intercultural communication; French civilization and cultural studies; language, gender and sexuality; sociolinguistics; African linguistics; immigrants in U. S. and Latin American societies. *Unit head:* Dr. Edward Larkey, Director, 410-455-2104, Fax: 410-455-1025, E-mail: larkey@umbc.edu. *Application contact:* Dr. Edward Larkey, Director, 410-455-2104, Fax: 410-455-1025, E-mail: larkey@umbc.edu.

University of Maryland, College Park, Graduate Studies, College of Arts and Humanities, Department of Linguistics, College Park, MD 20742. Offers MA, PhD. *Degree requirements:* For master's, thesis or alternative; for doctorate, thesis/dissertation. *Entrance requirements:* For master's, GRE General Test, minimum GPA of 3.0, sample of work, 3 letters of recommendation; for doctorate, GRE General Test, minimum GPA of 3.0, sample of work. Additional exam requirements/recommendations for international students: Required—TOEFL. Electronic applications accepted. *Faculty research:* Psycholinguistics, computational linguistics.

University of Massachusetts Amherst, Graduate School, College of Humanities and Fine Arts, Department of Linguistics, Amherst, MA 01003. Offers MA, PhD. Part-time programs available. Terminal master's awarded for partial completion of doctoral program. *Degree requirements:* For master's, thesis or alternative; for doctorate, comprehensive exam, thesis/dissertation. *Entrance requirements:* For master's and doctorate, GRE General Test. Additional exam requirements/recommendations for international students: Required—TOEFL (minimum score 550 paper-based; 213 computer-based; 79 iBT), IELTS (minimum score 6.5). Electronic applications accepted. *Expenses:* Tuition, area resident: Full-time $2640. Tuition, nonresident: full-time $9936. One-time fee: $332 full-time. Tuition and fees vary according to course load.

University of Massachusetts Boston, Office of Graduate Studies, College of Liberal Arts, Program in Applied Linguistics, Boston, MA 02125-3393. Offers bilingual education (MA); English as a second language (MA); foreign language pedagogy (MA). Part-time and evening/weekend programs available. *Degree requirements:* For master's, one foreign language, comprehensive exam. *Entrance requirements:* For master's, minimum GPA of 2.75. *Faculty research:* Multicultural theory and curriculum development, foreign language pedagogy, language and culture, applied psycholinguistics, bilingual education.

University of Michigan, Horace H. Rackham School of Graduate Studies, College of Literature, Science, and the Arts, Department of Linguistics, Ann Arbor, MI 48109. Offers general linguistics (PhD); linguistics and Germanic languages and literatures (PhD). *Degree requirements:* For doctorate, 2 foreign languages, thesis/dissertation, oral defense of dissertation. *Entrance requirements:* For doctorate, GRE General Test. Additional exam requirements/recommendations for international students: Required—TOEFL (minimum score 620 paper-based; 260 computer-based), TOEFL or Michigan English Language Assessment Battery. Electronic applications accepted. *Faculty research:* Broad-based approach to linguistics as a cognitive and social science including theoretical, experimental and computational approaches.

University of Michigan, Horace H. Rackham School of Graduate Studies, College of Literature, Science, and the Arts, Department of Romance Languages and Literatures, Ann Arbor, MI 48109. Offers French (PhD); Romance linguistics (PhD); Spanish (PhD). *Degree requirements:* For doctorate, 2 foreign languages, thesis/dissertation, oral defense of dissertation, preliminary exams. *Entrance requirements:* For doctorate, GRE General Test. Additional exam requirements/recommendations for international students: Required—TOEFL or Michigan English Language Assessment Battery. Electronic applications accepted. *Faculty research:* Comparative Romance studies, medieval and early modern studies, postcolonial and minority literatures, culture and materiality, reflection on the nature and function of scholarship.

University of Minnesota, Twin Cities Campus, Graduate School, College of Liberal Arts, Institute of Linguistics, English as a Second Language, and Slavic Languages and Literatures (ILES), Program in Linguistics, Minneapolis, MN 55455-0213. Offers MA, PhD. Terminal master's awarded for partial completion of doctoral program. *Degree requirements:* For master's, one foreign language, comprehensive exam, thesis; for doctorate, 2 foreign languages, comprehensive exam, thesis/dissertation. *Entrance requirements:* For master's and doctorate, GRE General Test, 3 letters of recommendation, unit questionnaire. Additional exam requirements/recommendations for international students: Required—TOEFL (minimum score 550 paper-based; 213 computer-based). Electronic applications accepted. *Faculty research:* Pragmatics and language processing, syntactic theory, language policy and planning, contact linguistics, language and cognition.

University of Missouri–St. Louis, College of Arts and Sciences, Department of English, St. Louis, MO 63121. Offers American literature (MA); creative writing (MFA); English (MA); English literature (MA); linguistics (MA); teaching of writing (Graduate Certificate). Part-time and evening/weekend programs available. *Faculty:* 19 full-time (12 women), 1 part-time/adjunct (0 women). *Students:* 14 full-time (8 women), 98 part-time (71 women); includes 10 minority (8 African Americans, 1 Asian American or Pacific Islander, 1 Hispanic American). Average age 32. In 2008, 21 master's awarded. *Degree requirements:* For master's, thesis optional. *Entrance requirements:* For master's, writing sample. Additional exam requirements/recommendations for international students: Required—TOEFL (minimum score 550 paper-based; 213 computer-based). *Application deadline:* For fall admission, 7/1 priority date for domestic and international students; for spring admission, 12/1 priority date for domestic and international students. Applications are processed on a rolling basis. Application fee: $35 ($40 for international students). Electronic applications accepted. *Expenses:* Tuition, area resident: Full-time $5377; part-time $298.70 per credit hour. Tuition, nonresident: full-time $13,381; part-time $472.50 per credit hour. Required fees: $4078; $52 per credit hour. *Financial support:* In 2008–09, 2 research assistantships (averaging $9,000 per year), 4 teaching assistantships with full and partial tuition reimbursements (averaging $9,000 per year) were awarded. Financial award applicants required to submit FAFSA. *Faculty research:* Victorian literature, Shakespeare and Renaissance literature, eighteenth century literature, composition theory. *Unit head:* Dr. Frank Grady, Director of Graduate Studies, 314-516-5541, Fax: 314-516-5781, E-mail: fgrady@umsl.edu. *Application contact:* 314-516-5458, Fax: 314-516-5310, E-mail: gradadm@umsl.edu.

The University of Montana, Graduate School, College of Arts and Sciences, Department of Anthropology, Missoula, MT 59812-0002. Offers anthropology (MA); cultural heritage (MA); cultural heritage studies (PhD); forensic anthropology (MA); historical anthropology (PhD); linguistics (MA). *Degree requirements:* For master's, thesis (for some programs). *Entrance requirements:* For master's, GRE General Test. Additional exam requirements/recommendations for international students: Required—TOEFL. *Faculty research:* Historical preservation, plateau-plains archaeology and ethnohistory.

The University of Montana, Graduate School, College of Arts and Sciences, Program in Linguistics, Missoula, MT 59812-0002. Offers MA. *Entrance requirements:* For master's, GRE General Test. Additional exam requirements/recommendations for international students: Required—TOEFL.

University of New Hampshire, Graduate School, College of Liberal Arts, Department of English, Durham, NH 03824. Offers English (MFA, PhD); English education (MST); language and linguistics (MA); literature (MA); writing (MA). Part-time programs available. *Faculty:* 35 full-time (18 women). *Students:* 50 full-time (29 women), 66 part-time (44 women); includes 6 minority (1 African American, 3 Asian Americans or Pacific Islanders, 2 Hispanic Americans), 5 international. Average age 34. 267 applicants, 44% accepted, 37 enrolled. In 2008, 33 master's, 1 doctorate awarded. *Degree requirements:* For master's, one foreign language; for doctorate, 2 foreign languages, thesis/dissertation. *Entrance requirements:* For master's, GRE General Test, sample of written work; for doctorate, GRE General Test, GRE Subject Test, sample of written work. Additional exam requirements/recommendations for international students: Required—TOEFL (minimum score 550 paper-based; 213 computer-based; 80 iBT). *Application deadline:* For fall admission, 2/15 priority date for domestic students, 2/15 for international students. Applications are processed on a rolling basis. Application fee: $60. Electronic applications accepted. *Expenses:* Tuition, area resident: Full-time $9720; part-time $540 per credit hour. Tuition, nonresident: full-time $23,200; part-time $954 per credit hour. Required fees: $1446; $361.50 per term. *Financial support:* In 2008–09, 58 students received support, including 3 fellowships, 1 research assistantship, 47 teaching assistantships; career-related internships or fieldwork, Federal Work-Study, scholarships/grants, and tuition waivers (full and partial) also available. Support available to part-time students. Financial award application deadline: 2/15. *Unit head:* Dr. Andrew Merton, Chairperson, 603-862-3963. *Application contact:* Sue Smith, Administrative Assistant, 603-862-3963, E-mail: engl.grad@unh.edu.

University of New Mexico, Graduate School, College of Arts and Sciences, Department of Linguistics, Albuquerque, NM 87131-2039. Offers MA, PhD. Part-time programs available. Terminal master's awarded for partial completion of doctoral program. *Degree requirements:* For master's, comprehensive exam, thesis optional; for doctorate, 2 foreign languages, comprehensive exam, thesis/dissertation. *Entrance requirements:* For master's, minimum GPA of 3.0, letters of recommendation, letter of intent; for doctorate, MA in linguistics or equivalent, paper of publishable quality, 3 letters of recommendation, letter of intent. Electronic applications accepted. *Faculty research:* Functional/cognitive linguistics, sociolinguistics, Spanish linguistics, Native American linguistics, signed language linguistics.

University of New Mexico, Graduate School, College of Education, Department of Language, Literacy and Sociocultural Studies, Program in Educational Linguistics, Albuquerque, NM 87131-2039. Offers Ed D, PhD. Part-time programs available. *Degree requirements:* For doctorate, comprehensive exam, thesis/dissertation. *Entrance requirements:* For doctorate, masters in linguistics, or complementary field, recommended. Additional exam requirements/recommendations for international students: Required—TOEFL. Electronic applications accepted. *Faculty research:* Bilingualism, language maintenance and loss, bilingual deaf education, Spanish dialectical studies, English as a second language writing/composition, Native American language issues, language and thought, creativity and collaboration.

The University of North Carolina at Chapel Hill, Graduate School, College of Arts and Sciences, Department of Germanic Languages, Chapel Hill, NC 27599. Offers literature and linguistics (MA, PhD). Part-time programs available. Terminal master's awarded for partial completion of doctoral program. *Degree requirements:* For master's, comprehensive exam, thesis; for doctorate, one foreign language, comprehensive exam, thesis/dissertation. *Entrance requirements:* For master's and doctorate, GRE General Test, minimum GPA of 3.0. *Faculty research:* Gender and sexuality, literature and politics, German and Jewish culture, medieval through modern literature, Germanic linguistics.

The University of North Carolina at Chapel Hill, Graduate School, College of Arts and Sciences, Department of Linguistics, Chapel Hill, NC 27599. Offers MA, PhD. Terminal master's awarded for partial completion of doctoral program. *Degree requirements:* For master's, one foreign language, comprehensive exam, thesis; for doctorate, 2 foreign languages, comprehensive exam, thesis/dissertation. *Entrance requirements:* For master's and doctorate, GRE General Test, minimum GPA of 3.0. Additional exam requirements/recommendations for international students: Required—TOEFL (minimum score 550 paper-based; 213 computer-based). Electronic applications accepted. *Faculty research:* Phonetics, phonology, syntax, historical linguistics, Indo-European.

University of North Dakota, Graduate School, College of Arts and Sciences, Program in Linguistics, Grand Forks, ND 58202. Offers MA. *Degree requirements:* For master's, one foreign language, thesis, final examination. *Entrance requirements:* For master's, minimum GPA of 3.0. Additional exam requirements/recommendations for international students: Required—TOEFL (minimum score 550 paper-based; 213 computer-based; 79 iBT), IELTS (minimum score 6.5). Electronic applications accepted. *Faculty research:* Practice-based field studies.

University of North Texas, Robert B. Toulouse School of Graduate Studies, College of Arts and Sciences, Department of English, Denton, TX 76203. Offers creative writing (MA); English (MA, PhD); English as a second language (MA); linguistics (MA); Technical writing (MA). Terminal master's awarded for partial completion of doctoral program. *Degree requirements:* For master's, one foreign language, comprehensive exam, thesis optional; for doctorate, one foreign language, comprehensive exam, thesis/dissertation. *Entrance requirements:* For master's, GRE General Test, 3.0 GPA, personal statement, current vita/resumé, writing sample for creative writing program; for doctorate, GRE General Test, 3.5 GPA, 3 letters of recommendation, personal statement, writing sample. Additional exam requirements/recommendations for international students: Required—proof of English language proficiency required for non-native English speakers; Recommended—TOEFL (minimum score 550 paper-based; 213 computer-based). *Faculty research:* Creative writing, British and American literature, composition and rhetoric.

University of Oregon, Graduate School, College of Arts and Sciences, Department of Linguistics, Eugene, OR 97403. Offers MA, PhD. Terminal master's awarded for partial completion of doctoral program. *Degree requirements:* For master's, 2 foreign languages; for doctorate, thesis/dissertation. *Entrance requirements:* For master's and doctorate, GRE General Test, minimum GPA of 3.0. Additional exam requirements/recommendations for international students: Required—TOEFL. *Faculty research:* Functional syntax, discourse, empirical methods.

University of Ottawa, Faculty of Graduate and Postdoctoral Studies, Faculty of Arts, Department of Linguistics, Ottawa, ON K1N 6N5, Canada. Offers MA, PhD. *Degree requirements:* For master's, one foreign language, thesis or alternative; for doctorate, 2 foreign languages, comprehensive exam, thesis/dissertation. *Entrance requirements:* For master's, honors degree or equivalent, minimum B average; for doctorate, master's degree, minimum B+ average. Electronic applications accepted. *Faculty research:* Empirical linguistics, formal linguistics.

University of Pennsylvania, Graduate School of Education, Division of Language in Education, Programs in Teaching English to Speakers of Other Languages and Intercultural Communication, Philadelphia, PA 19104. Offers educational linguistics (PhD); intercultural communication (MS Ed); teaching English to speakers of other languages (MS Ed). Part-time programs available. Postbaccalaureate distance learning degree programs offered (minimal on-campus study). Terminal master's awarded for partial completion of doctoral program. *Degree requirements:* For master's, comprehensive exam, thesis (for some programs); for doctorate, one foreign language, thesis/dissertation, preliminary exam. *Entrance requirements:* For master's and doctorate, GRE General Test or MAT. Additional exam requirements/recommendations for international students: Required—TOEFL. Electronic applications accepted. *Expenses:* Contact institution. *Faculty research:* Second language acquisition, social linguistics, English as a second language.

University of Pennsylvania, School of Arts and Sciences, Graduate Group in Linguistics, Philadelphia, PA 19104. Offers AM, PhD. Terminal master's awarded for partial completion of doctoral program. *Degree requirements:* For master's, thesis; for doctorate, 2 foreign languages, thesis/dissertation. *Entrance requirements:* For master's and doctorate, GRE General Test. Additional exam requirements/recommendations for international students: Required—TOEFL. Electronic applications accepted.

University of Pittsburgh, School of Arts and Sciences, Department of Linguistics, Pittsburgh, PA 15260. Offers applied linguistics (PhD); Hispanic linguistics (MA, PhD); linguistics (MA); sociolinguistics (PhD). Part-time programs available. Terminal master's awarded for partial completion of doctoral program. *Degree requirements:* For master's, one foreign language, thesis; for doctorate, 2 foreign languages, comprehensive exam, thesis/dissertation. *Entrance requirements:* For master's, GRE General Test; for doctorate, GRE General Test, MA in linguistics. Additional exam requirements/recommendations for international students: Required—TOEFL (minimum score 600 paper-based; 250 computer-based). Electronic applications accepted. *Faculty research:* Second language acquisition, applied linguistics, sociolinguistics, language contact.

University of Puerto Rico, Río Piedras, College of Humanities, Department of Linguistics, San Juan, PR 00931-3300. Offers MA. Part-time programs available. *Degree requirements:* For master's, one foreign language, comprehensive exam, thesis. *Entrance requirements:* For master's, PAEG or GRE, interview, minimum GPA of 3.0, letter of recommendation (2).

University of Regina, Faculty of Graduate Studies and Research, Faculty of Arts, Program in Linguistics, Regina, SK S4S 0A2, Canada. Offers MA. Offered as special case program. Part-time programs available. *Faculty:* 4 full-time (0 women). *Students:* 1 applicant, 0% accepted. *Degree requirements:* For master's, thesis. *Entrance requirements:* Additional exam requirements/recommendations for international students: Required—TOEFL (minimum score 580 paper-based; 237 computer-based). *Application deadline:* Applications are processed on a rolling basis. Application fee: $85 ($100 for international students). Electronic applications accepted. *Financial support:* Fellowships, research assistantships, teaching assistantships, scholarships/grants available. Financial award application deadline: 6/15. *Faculty research:* Phonology, morphology, syntax, semantics, Amerindian linguistics. *Unit head:* Dr. Arok Wolvengrey, Program Coordinator, 790-790-5950 Ext. 3310, E-mail: awolvengrey@firstnations.university.ca. *Application contact:* Dr. Arok Wolvengrey, Program Coordinator, 790-790-5950 Ext. 3310, E-mail: awolvengrey@firstnations.university.ca.

University of South Africa, College of Human Sciences, Pretoria, South Africa. Offers adult education (M Ed); African languages (MA, PhD); African politics (MA, PhD); Afrikaans (MA, PhD); ancient history (MA, PhD); ancient Near Eastern studies (MA, PhD); anthropology (MA, PhD); applied linguistics (MA); Arabic (MA, PhD); archaeology (MA); art history (MA); Biblical archaeology (MA); Biblical studies (M Th, D Th, PhD); Christian spirituality (M Th, D Th); church history (M Th, D Th); classical studies (MA, PhD); clinical psychology (MA); communication (MA, PhD); comparative education (M Ed, Ed D); consulting psychology (D Admin, D Com, PhD); curriculum studies (M Ed, Ed D); development studies (M Admin, MA, D Admin, PhD); didactics (M Ed, Ed D); education (M Tech); education management (M Ed, Ed D); educational psychology (M Ed); English (MA); environmental education (M Ed); French (MA, PhD); German (MA, PhD); Greek (MA); guidance and counseling (M Ed); health studies (MA, PhD), including health sciences education (MA), health services management (MA), medical and surgical nursing science (critical care general) (MA), midwifery and neonatal nursing science (MA), trauma and emergency care (MA); history (MA, PhD); history of education (Ed D); inclusive education (M Ed, Ed D); information and communications technology policy and regulation (MA); information science (MA, MIS, PhD); international politics (MA, PhD); Islamic studies (MA, PhD); Italian (MA, PhD); Judaica (MA, PhD); linguistics (MA, PhD); mathematical education (M Ed); mathematics education (MA); missiology (M Th, D Th); modern Hebrew (MA, PhD); musicology (MA, MMus, D Mus, PhD); natural science education (M Ed); New Testament (M Th, D Th); Old Testament (D Th); pastoral therapy (M Th, D Th); philosophy (MA); philosophy of education (M Ed, Ed D); politics (MA, PhD); Portuguese (MA, PhD); practical theology (M Th, D Th); psychology (MA, MS, PhD); psychology of education (M Ed, Ed D); public health (MA); religious studies (MA, D Th, PhD); Romance languages (MA); Russian (MA, PhD); Semitic languages (MA, PhD); social behavior studies in HIV/AIDS (MA); social science (mental health) (MA); social science in development studies (MA); social science in psychology (MA); social science in social work (MA); social science in sociology (MA); social work (MSW, DSW, PhD); socio-education (M Ed, Ed D); sociolinguistics (MA); sociology (MA, PhD); Spanish (MA, PhD); systematic theology (M Th, D Th); TESOL (teaching English to speakers of other languages) (MA); theological ethics (M Th, D Th); theory of literature (MA, PhD); urban ministries (D Th); urban ministry (M Th).

University of South Carolina, The Graduate School, College of Arts and Sciences, Linguistics Program, Columbia, SC 29208. Offers linguistics (MA, PhD); teaching English to speakers of other languages (Certificate). Part-time programs available. Terminal master's awarded for partial completion of doctoral program. *Degree requirements:* For master's, one foreign language, comprehensive exam, thesis optional; for doctorate, 3 foreign languages, comprehensive exam, thesis/dissertation. *Entrance requirements:* For master's and Certificate, GRE General Test, minimum GPA of 3.0; for doctorate, GRE General Test, minimum GPA of 3.5. Additional exam requirements/recommendations for international students: Required—TOEFL. Electronic applications accepted. *Faculty research:* Second language acquisition, sociolinguistics, syntax, historical linguistics and phonology.

University of Southern California, Graduate School, College of Letters, Arts and Sciences, Department of Linguistics, Los Angeles, CA 90089. Offers East Asian linguistics (PhD); Hispanic linguistics (PhD); linguistics (PhD). *Degree requirements:* For doctorate, 2 foreign languages, thesis/dissertation. *Entrance requirements:* For doctorate, GRE General Test. *Faculty research:* Syntax, phonology, phonetics, semantics, sociolinguistics, psycholinguistics.

University of South Florida, Graduate School, College of Arts and Sciences, Department of World Language Education, Program in Linguistics, Tampa, FL 33620-9951. Offers MA. *Students:* 12 full-time (9 women), 6 part-time (4 women); includes 4 minority (1 African American, 1 Asian American or Pacific Islander, 2 Hispanic Americans), 2 international. 14 applicants, 57% accepted, 4 enrolled. In 2008, 8 master's awarded. *Degree requirements:* For master's, one foreign language, comprehensive exam, thesis optional. *Entrance requirements:* For master's, GRE (minimum score: 430 verbal reasoning, 4.5 analytical writing), GPA of 3.0 or higher in upper level of undergraduate studies. Additional exam requirements/recommendations for international students: Required—TOEFL (minimum score 250 computer-based; 100 iBT). *Application deadline:* For fall admission, 2/15 for domestic students, 1/2 for international students; for spring admission, 10/15 for domestic students. Application fee: $30. Electronic applications accepted. *Expenses:* Tuition, state resident: full-time $2624.40; part-time $291.60 per credit hour. Tuition, nonresident: full-time $7822; part-time $869.13 per credit hour. *Unit head:* Camilla Va'squez, Program Director, 813-974-7378, Fax: 813-974-1718, E-mail: cvasquez@cas.usf.edu. *Application contact:* Camilla Va'squez, Program Director, 813-974-7378, Fax: 813-974-1718, E-mail: cvasquez@cas.usf.edu.

The University of Tennessee, Graduate School, College of Arts and Sciences, Department of Modern Foreign Languages and Literatures, Program in Modern Foreign Languages, Knoxville, TN 37996. Offers applied linguistics (PhD); French (PhD); German (PhD); Italian (PhD); Portuguese (PhD); Russian (PhD); Spanish (PhD). *Degree requirements:* For doctorate, 2 foreign languages, thesis/dissertation. *Entrance requirements:* For doctorate, minimum GPA of 2.7. Additional exam requirements/recommendations for international students: Required—TOEFL. Electronic applications accepted. *Expenses:* Tuition, area resident: Part-time $348 per credit hour. Tuition, state resident: full-time $6262. Tuition, nonresident: full-time $18,920; part-time $1052 per credit hour. Required fees: $812; $36 per credit hour. Tuition and fees vary according to program.

The University of Texas at Arlington, Graduate School, College of Liberal Arts, Department of Linguistics and TESOL, Program in Linguistics, Arlington, TX 76019. Offers MA, PhD. Part-time and evening/weekend programs available. *Faculty:* 7 full-time (2 women). *Students:* 23 full-time (12 women), 39 part-time (21 women); includes 5 minority (4 Asian Americans or Pacific Islanders, 1 Hispanic American), 16 international. 29 applicants, 86% accepted, 18 enrolled. In 2008, 6 master's, 6 doctorates awarded. Terminal master's awarded for partial completion of doctoral program. *Degree requirements:* For master's, one foreign language, comprehensive exam (for some programs), thesis optional; for doctorate, 2 foreign languages, comprehensive exam, thesis/dissertation, qualifying exam, dissertation proposal defense, professional development. *Entrance requirements:* For master's, GRE General Test, minimum undergraduate GPA of 3.0, 9 credits of undergraduate foundation courses; for doctorate, GRE General Test, 30 hours of graduate work in linguistics or a related discipline, minimum GPA of 3.5. Additional exam requirements/recommendations for international students: Required—TOEFL (minimum score 550 paper-based; 213 computer-based). *Application deadline:* For fall admission, 6/16 for domestic students. Applications are processed on a rolling basis. Application fee: $35 ($50 for international students). *Expenses:* Tuition, area resident: Full-time $6500. Tuition, state resident: full-time $6500. Tuition, nonresident: full-time $11,558. *Financial support:* In 2008–09, 52 students received support, including 10 fellowships (averaging $1,000 per year), 1 research assistantship, 4 teaching assistantships; career-related internships or fieldwork and institutionally sponsored loans also available. Financial award application deadline: 3/1; financial award applicants required to submit FAFSA. *Faculty research:* Field linguistics, discourse analysis, text linguistics, phonology, teaching English as a second language. *Unit head:* Dr. Jerrold Edmonson, Chair, 817-272-3133, Fax: 817-272-2731, E-mail: jerry@uta.edu. *Application contact:* Dr. Laurel Stvan, Graduate Advisor, 817-272-3133, Fax: 817-272-2731.

The University of Texas at Austin, Graduate School, College of Liberal Arts, Department of French and Italian, Austin, TX 78712-1111. Offers French (MA, PhD); French linguistics (MA, PhD); Italian studies (MA, PhD); Romance linguistics (MA, PhD). Part-time programs available. *Degree requirements:* For master's, one foreign language, thesis; for doctorate, 2 foreign languages, thesis/dissertation. *Entrance requirements:* For master's, GRE General Test, minimum GPA of 3.0, bachelor's degree in French or equivalent; for doctorate, GRE General Test, minimum GPA of 3.0, master's degree in French. Additional exam requirements/recommendations for international students: Required—TOEFL. Electronic applications accepted. *Faculty research:* Nineteenth-century Italian literature, Italian Renaissance, twentieth-century French literature, Francophone literature, fifteenth-century literature and culture.

The University of Texas at Austin, Graduate School, College of Liberal Arts, Department of Linguistics, Austin, TX 78712-1111. Offers MA, PhD. *Degree requirements:* For master's, one foreign language, thesis; for doctorate, 2 foreign languages, thesis/dissertation. *Entrance requirements:* For master's and doctorate, GRE General Test. Electronic applications accepted. *Faculty research:* Theoretical linguistics, sociolinguistics, documentary and descriptive linguistics, computational linguistics.

The University of Texas at El Paso, Graduate School, College of Liberal Arts, Department of Languages and Linguistics, El Paso, TX 79968-0001. Offers linguistics (MA). Part-time and evening/weekend programs available. *Degree requirements:* For master's, thesis optional. *Entrance requirements:* For master's, departmental exam, GRE General Test, sample of written work, minimum GPA of 3.0. Additional exam requirements/recommendations for international students: Required—TOEFL. Electronic applications accepted.

University of Toronto, School of Graduate Studies, Humanities Division, Department of Linguistics, Toronto, ON M5S 1A1, Canada. Offers MA, PhD. Part-time programs available. *Degree requirements:* For master's, 2 foreign languages; for doctorate, thesis/dissertation, oral thesis proposal. *Entrance requirements:* For master's, BA in linguistics; for doctorate, MA in linguistics.

University of Utah, The Graduate School, College of Humanities, Department of Linguistics, Salt Lake City, UT 84112-1107. Offers applied linguistics (MA, PhD); linguistics (MA, PhD). Part-time programs available. Postbaccalaureate distance learning degree programs offered (minimal on-campus study). *Degree requirements:* For master's and doctorate, 2 foreign languages, comprehensive exam. *Entrance requirements:* For master's and doctorate, GRE General Test, minimum undergraduate GPA of 3.0. Additional exam requirements/recommendations for international students: Required—TOEFL (minimum score 600 paper-based; 250 computer-based). Electronic applications accepted. *Faculty research:* American Indian languages, applied linguistics phonology, sociolinguistics, syntax.

University of Utah, The Graduate School, College of Humanities, Program in Middle East Studies, Salt Lake City, UT 84112-1107. Offers anthropology (MA); Arabic (MA, PhD); Arabic and linguistics (MA, PhD); Hebrew (MA); history (MA, PhD); Persian (MA, PhD); political science (MA, PhD); Turkish (MA). Terminal master's awarded for partial completion of doctoral program. *Degree requirements:* For master's, 2 foreign languages, comprehensive exam, thesis optional; for doctorate, 3 foreign languages, comprehensive exam, thesis/dissertation. *Entrance requirements:* For master's, GRE General Test, minimum GPA of 3.2; for doctorate, GRE General Test, MA in Middle East studies or equivalent, minimum GPA of 3.2. Additional exam requirements/recommendations for international students: Required—TOEFL (minimum score 580 paper-based; 237 computer-based; 92 iBT). *Faculty research:* Arabic literature and linguistics, Islamic studies, Middle East history, political science, Judaic studies.

University of Victoria, Faculty of Graduate Studies, Faculty of Humanities, Department of Linguistics, Victoria, BC V8W 2Y2, Canada. Offers applied linguistics (MA); linguistics (MA, PhD). Part-time programs available. *Degree requirements:* For master's, one foreign language, thesis, colloquium; for doctorate, 2 foreign languages, comprehensive exam, thesis/dissertation, candidacy exam. *Entrance requirements:* For master's, GRE; for doctorate, GRE, sample of written work. Additional exam requirements/recommendations for international students: Required—TOEFL. Electronic applications accepted. *Faculty research:* Grammatical theory, syntactic analysis, morphology, Western Amerindian languages, Salishan, applied linguistics.

University of Virginia, College and Graduate School of Arts and Sciences, Program in Linguistics, Charlottesville, VA 22903. Offers MA. *Students:* 12 full-time (8 women); includes 1 minority (Hispanic American), 1 international. Average age 27. 13 applicants, 69% accepted, 3 enrolled. In 2008, 3 master's awarded. *Degree requirements:* For master's, one foreign language, comprehensive exam, thesis optional, reading knowledge of French or German. *Entrance requirements:* For master's, GRE General Test. Additional exam requirements/recommendations for international students: Required—TOEFL (minimum score 600 paper-based; 250 computer-based; 90 iBT), IELTS (minimum score 7). *Application deadline:* For fall admission, 2/15 for domestic and international students. Applications are processed on a rolling basis. Application fee: $60. Electronic applications accepted. *Expenses:* Tuition, area resident: Full-time $10,452. Tuition, state resident: full-time $10,452. Tuition, nonresident: full-time $20,010. Required fees: $2176. Part-time tuition and fees vary according to course load and program. *Financial support:* Teaching assistantships available. Financial award applicants required to submit FAFSA. *Unit head:* Eve Danziger, E-mail: ed8c@virginia.edu. *Application contact:* Eve Danziger, E-mail: ed8c@virginia.edu.

University of Washington, Graduate School, College of Arts and Sciences, Department of Linguistics, Seattle, WA 98195. Offers computational linguistics (MA); linguistics (MA, PhD); Romance linguistics (MA, PhD). Part-time programs available. Terminal master's awarded for partial completion of doctoral program. *Degree requirements:* For master's, one foreign language, thesis; for doctorate, 2 foreign languages, thesis/dissertation. *Entrance requirements:* For master's, GRE General Test, minimum GPA of 3.0; for doctorate, GRE, minimum GPA of 3.0. Additional exam requirements/recommendations for international students: Required—TOEFL. Electronic applications accepted. *Faculty research:* Syntax, phonology, semantics, phonetics, sociolinguistics.

University of Washington, Graduate School, College of Arts and Sciences, Department of Slavic Languages and Literatures, Seattle, WA 98195. Offers Russian literature (MA, PhD); Slavic linguistics (MA, PhD). *Degree requirements:* For master's, 2 foreign languages, thesis optional; for doctorate, 3 foreign languages, thesis/dissertation. *Entrance requirements:* For master's and doctorate, GRE General Test, minimum GPA of 3.0. Additional exam requirements/recommendations for international students: Required—TOEFL. Electronic applications accepted. *Faculty research:* Modern and medieval East European languages and literatures, comparative literature, Russian folk literature, Slavic literary theory and criticism, computerized morphology of Russian.

University of Wisconsin–Madison, Graduate School, College of Letters and Science, Department of East Asian Languages and Literature, Program in Japanese Linguistics, Madison, WI 53706-1380. Offers MA, PhD. Part-time programs available. Terminal master's awarded for partial completion of doctoral program. *Degree requirements:* For master's, one foreign language, seminars, written exam; for doctorate, 3 foreign languages, thesis/dissertation, seminars, preliminary exams, oral exam. *Entrance requirements:* For master's, GRE General Test, bachelor's degree or equivalent in Japanese; for doctorate, GRE General Test, master's degree or equivalent in Japanese. Electronic applications accepted. *Faculty research:* Modern and historical Japanese linguistics, modern Japanese fiction and poetry, classical Japanese literature, language pedagogy.

Linguistics

University of Wisconsin–Madison, Graduate School, College of Letters and Science, Department of English, Madison, WI 53706-1380. Offers applied English linguistics (MA); composition and rhetoric (PhD); creative writing (MFA); English language and linguistics (PhD); literary studies (MA, PhD). *Degree requirements:* For doctorate, thesis/dissertation.

University of Wisconsin–Madison, Graduate School, College of Letters and Science, Department of Linguistics, Madison, WI 53706-1380. Offers MA, PhD. Part-time programs available. Terminal master's awarded for partial completion of doctoral program. *Degree requirements:* For master's, 2 foreign languages; for doctorate, 3 foreign languages, thesis/dissertation. Electronic applications accepted. *Faculty research:* Formal linguistics, acoustic phonetics, American studies, Indo-European linguistics.

University of Wisconsin–Milwaukee, Graduate School, College of Letters and Sciences, Department of English, Milwaukee, WI 53201-0413. Offers creative writing (PhD); English (MA); linguistics (PhD); professional writing (PhD); professional writing and communication (Certificate); rhetoric and composition (PhD); MLIS/MA. *Faculty:* 40 full-time (19 women). *Students:* 107 full-time (64 women), 82 part-time (54 women); includes 13 minority (8 African Americans, 1 American Indian/Alaska Native, 2 Asian Americans or Pacific Islanders, 2 Hispanic Americans), 23 international. Average age 35. 187 applicants, 41% accepted, 34 enrolled. In 2008, 31 master's, 14 doctorates awarded. *Degree requirements:* For master's, thesis or alternative; for doctorate, one foreign language, thesis/dissertation. *Entrance requirements:* For master's, GRE General Test, GRE Subject Test; for doctorate, GRE. Additional exam requirements/recommendations for international students: Required—TOEFL (minimum score 550 paper-based; 79 iBT), IELTS (minimum score 6.5). *Application deadline:* For fall admission, 1/1 priority date for domestic students; for spring admission, 9/1 for domestic students. Applications are processed on a rolling basis. Application fee: $45 ($75 for international students). *Expenses:* Tuition, area resident: Full-time $7320; part-time $165 per credit. Tuition, state resident: full-time $7320; part-time $165 per credit. Tuition, nonresident: full-time $17,840; part-time $714 per credit. Tuition and fees vary according to campus/location, program and reciprocity agreements. *Financial support:* In 2008–09, 74 teaching assistantships were awarded; career-related internships or fieldwork and unspecified assistantships also available. Support available to part-time students. Financial award application deadline: 4/15. Total annual research expenditures: $53,677. *Unit head:* Tasha Oren, Representative, 414-229-2643, Fax: 414-229-2643, E-mail: tgoren@uwm.edu. *Application contact:* General Information Contact, 414-229-4982, Fax: 414-229-6967, E-mail: gradschool@uwm.edu.

Wayne State University, College of Liberal Arts and Sciences, Interdisciplinary Program in Linguistics, Detroit, MI 48202. Offers MA. *Degree requirements:* For master's, one foreign language, thesis. *Entrance requirements:* Additional exam requirements/recommendations for international students: Required—TOEFL (minimum score 550 paper-based; 213 computer-based); Recommended—TWE (minimum score 6). Electronic applications accepted. *Faculty research:* Formal linguistics, psycholinguistics, sociolinguistics, historical linguistics, language acquisition.

West Virginia University, Eberly College of Arts and Sciences, Department of Foreign Languages, Morgantown, WV 26506. Offers French (MA); linguistics (MA); Spanish (MA); teaching English to speakers of other languages (MA). Part-time programs available. *Degree requirements:* For master's, one foreign language, comprehensive exam (for some programs), thesis optional. *Entrance requirements:* For master's, minimum GPA of 3.0. Electronic applications accepted. *Faculty research:* French, German, and Spanish literature; foreign language pedagogy; English as a second language; cultural studies; linguistics.

Yale University, Graduate School of Arts and Sciences, Department of Linguistics, New Haven, CT 06520. Offers PhD. *Degree requirements:* For doctorate, 2 foreign languages, thesis/dissertation. *Entrance requirements:* For doctorate, GRE General Test.

York University, Faculty of Graduate Studies, Faculty of Arts, Program in Theoretical and Applied Linguistics, Toronto, ON M3J 1P3, Canada. Offers MA, PhD. *Degree requirements:* For master's, thesis.

Translation and Interpretation

American University, College of Arts and Sciences, Department of Language and Foreign Studies, Program in French, Washington, DC 20016-8045. Offers translation (Certificate). Part-time and evening/weekend programs available. *Students:* 1 (woman) full-time, 4 part-time (all women), 1 international. Average age 29. *Degree requirements:* For Certificate, minimum 15 credit hours related course work. *Entrance requirements:* For degree, bachelor's degree in French or evidence of French proficiency plus BA in any field. Additional exam requirements/recommendations for international students: Required—TOEFL. *Application deadline:* For fall admission, 2/1 for domestic students; for spring admission, 10/1 for domestic students. Application fee: $50. *Expenses:* Tuition: Full-time $21,204; part-time $1178 per credit hour. Required fees: $380. Part-time tuition and fees vary according to course load and program. *Financial support:* Fellowships, career-related internships or fieldwork, Federal Work-Study, and institutionally sponsored loans available. Financial award application deadline: 2/1. *Faculty research:* Literature, language, modern French politics, contemporary French society, the civilization of Quebec, business French and translation studies.

American University, College of Arts and Sciences, Department of Language and Foreign Studies, Program in Russian, Washington, DC 20016-8045. Offers translation (Certificate). Part-time and evening/weekend programs available. *Students:* 2 part-time (1 woman). Average age 26. In 2000, 1 Certificate awarded. *Degree requirements:* For Certificate, 15 credit hour minimum in related course work. *Entrance requirements:* For degree, bachelor's degree in Russian or evidence of Russian proficiency plus a BA. Additional exam requirements/recommendations for international students: Required—TOEFL. *Application deadline:* For fall admission, 2/1 for domestic students; for spring admission, 10/1 for domestic students. Application fee: $50. *Expenses:* Tuition: Full-time $21,204; part-time $1178 per credit hour. Required fees: $380. Part-time tuition and fees vary according to course load and program. *Financial support:* Fellowships, career-related internships or fieldwork, Federal Work-Study, and institutionally sponsored loans available. Financial award application deadline: 2/1. *Faculty research:* Culture, literature, and area studies; technology-assisted language instruction; linguistics.

American University, College of Arts and Sciences, Department of Language and Foreign Studies, Program in Spanish: Latin American Studies, Washington, DC 20016-8045. Offers Spanish: Latin American studies (MA); translation (Certificate). Part-time and evening/weekend programs available. *Students:* 17 full-time (13 women), 10 part-time (8 women); includes 9 minority (5 African Americans, 4 Hispanic Americans), 2 international. Average age 26. 23 applicants, 96% accepted, 7 enrolled. In 2008, 11 master's, 5 other advanced degrees awarded. *Degree requirements:* For master's, one foreign language, comprehensive exam, thesis or alternative, research requirement. *Entrance requirements:* For master's, GRE, bachelor's degree in language or equivalent, essay in Spanish, minimum GPA of 3.2, statement of purpose; for Certificate, bachelor's degree in Spanish or BA in any field plus Spanish proficiency. Additional exam requirements/recommendations for international students: Required—TOEFL. *Application deadline:* For fall admission, 2/1 for domestic students; for spring admission, 10/1 for domestic students. Application fee: $80. *Expenses:* Tuition: Full-time $21,204; part-time $1178 per credit hour. Required fees: $380. Part-time tuition and fees vary according to course load and program. *Financial support:* Fellowships, career-related internships or fieldwork, Federal Work-Study, and institutionally sponsored loans available. Financial award application deadline: 2/1. *Faculty research:* Latin American culture, literature, and history; computer-aided instruction.

American University of Sharjah, Graduate Programs, Sharjah, United Arab Emirates. Offers business (EMBA, MBA); chemical engineering (MS Ch E); civil engineering (MSCE); computer engineering (MS); electrical engineering (MSEE); mechanical engineering (MSME); mechatronics engineering (MS); public administration (MPA); teaching English to speakers of other languages (MA); translation and interpreting (MA); urban planning (MUP). Part-time and evening/weekend programs available. *Faculty:* 35 full-time (7 women). *Students:* 66 full-time (36 women), 188 part-time (83 women). Average age 28. 302 applicants, 65% accepted, 131 enrolled. In 2008, 74 master's awarded. *Entrance requirements:* For master's, GMAT (MBA). Additional exam requirements/recommendations for international students: Required—TOEFL (minimum score 550 paper-based; 213 computer-based; 80 iBT), TWE (minimum score 5). *Application deadline:* For fall admission, 7/30 priority date for domestic students, 7/15 priority date for international students; for spring admission, 12/31 priority date for domestic students, 12/16 for international students. Applications are processed on a rolling basis. Application fee: $300. Electronic applications accepted. Tuition and fees charges are reported in United Arab Emirates dirhams. *Expenses:* Tuition: Full-time 58,500 United Arab Emirates dirhams; part-time 3250 United Arab Emirates dirhams per credit hour. One-time fee: 300 United Arab Emirates dirhams. *Faculty research:* Chemical engineering, civil engineering, computer engineering, electrical engineering, linguistics, translation. *Unit head:* Ghada S Sami, Admissions Manager, 971-65151006 Ext. 1006, Fax: 971-65151020, E-mail: graduateadmission@aus.edu. *Application contact:* Ghada S Sami, Admissions Manager, 971-65151006 Ext. 1006, Fax: 971-65151020, E-mail: graduateadmission@aus.edu.

Babel University School of Translation, Program in Translation, Honolulu, HI 96815-1302. Offers MS. Part-time and evening/weekend programs available. Postbaccalaureate distance learning degree programs offered (no on-campus study). *Degree requirements:* For master's, comprehensive exam, thesis. *Entrance requirements:* For master's, translation exam. Additional exam requirements/recommendations for international students: Recommended—TOEFL (minimum score 550 paper-based).

College of Charleston, Graduate School, School of Languages, Cultures, and World Affairs, Program in Healthcare and Medical Interpreting, Charleston, SC 29424-0001. Offers Certificate. *Faculty:* 4 full-time (2 women). *Students:* 3 part-time (all women); includes 2 African Americans. Average age 25. 6 applicants, 83% accepted. In 2008, 2 Certificates awarded. *Entrance requirements:* For degree, language exam, minimum GPA of 3.0. Additional exam requirements/recommendations for international students: Required—TOEFL. *Application deadline:* For fall admission, 6/15 for domestic students; for spring admission, 11/1 for domestic students. Application fee: $50. *Expenses:* Contact institution. *Unit head:* Dr. Gladys Matthews, Director, 843-953-5718, E-mail: matthewsg@cofc.edu. *Application contact:* Susan Hallatt, Director of Graduate Admissions, 843-953-5614, Fax: 843-953-1434, E-mail: hallatts@cofc.edu.

Concordia University, School of Graduate Studies, Faculty of Arts and Science, Department of Études Françaises, Montréal, QC H3G 1M8, Canada. Offers écriture (Certificate); anglais-français en langue et techniques de localisation (Certificate); littératures francophones et résonances médiatiques (MA); traductologie (MA); translation (Diploma). *Degree requirements:* For other advanced degree, one foreign language.

Georgia State University, College of Arts and Sciences, Department of Modern and Classical Languages, Program in Translation and Interpretation, Atlanta, GA 30303-3083. Offers French (Certificate); German (Certificate); Spanish (Certificate). Electronic applications accepted.

Kent State University, College of Arts and Sciences, Department of Modern and Classical Language Studies, Kent, OH 44242-0001. Offers French literature (MA); French, Spanish, German and Latin pedagogy (MA); German literature (MA); Spanish literature (MA); translation (MA), including French, German, Japanese, Russian, Spanish; translation studies (PhD). Part-time and evening/weekend programs available. *Degree requirements:* For master's, one foreign language, comprehensive exam (for some programs), thesis (for some programs); for doctorate, comprehensive exam, thesis/dissertation (for some programs). *Entrance requirements:* For master's, minimum GPA of 3.0, writing sample, audio tape or CD; for doctorate, 3 recommendations. Additional exam requirements/recommendations for international students: Required—TOEFL (minimum score 197 computer-based). Electronic applications accepted. *Faculty research:* Literature, pedagogy, applied linguistics, translation studies.

Marygrove College, Graduate Division, Program in Modern Language Translation, Detroit, MI 48221-2599. Offers Certificate.

Montclair State University, The Office of Graduate Admissions and Support Services, College of Humanities and Social Sciences, Department of Spanish and Italian, Montclair, NJ 07043-1624. Offers Italian (Certificate); Spanish (MA, Certificate); translating and interpreting Spanish (Certificate). Part-time and evening/weekend programs available. *Faculty:* 18 full-time (10 women), 25 part-time/adjunct (19 women). *Students:* 2 full-time (both women), 18 part-time (16 women); includes 6 minority (2 African Americans, 2 American Indian/Alaska Native, 2 Hispanic Americans), 1 international. Average age 35. 6 applicants, 100% accepted, 2 enrolled. In 2008, 6 master's awarded. *Degree requirements:* For master's, comprehensive exam, thesis or alternative. *Entrance requirements:* For master's, GRE General Test, BA in Spanish or at least 24 undergraduate credits of Spanish, 2 letters of recommendation. Additional exam requirements/recommendations for international students: Required—TOEFL (minimum score 83 computer-based). *Application deadline:* For fall admission, 6/1 for international students; for spring admission, 11/1 for international students. Applications are processed on a rolling basis. Application fee: $60. Electronic applications accepted. *Financial support:* In 2008–09, 1 research assistantship with full tuition reimbursement (averaging $7,000 per year) was awarded; Federal Work-Study, scholarships/grants, and unspecified assistantships also available. Support available to part-time students. Financial award application deadline: 3/1; financial award applicants required to submit FAFSA. *Unit head:* Dr. Diana Guemaraz Cruz, Chairperson, 973-655-7506. *Application contact:* Amy Aiello, Associate Director of Admissions, 973-655-5147, Fax: 973-655-7869, E-mail: graduate.school@montclair.edu.

Monterey Institute of International Studies, Graduate School of Translation and Interpretation, Monterey, CA 93940-2691. Offers conference interpretation (MA); translation (MA); translation and interpretation (MA); translation and localization management (MA). *Students:* 184 full-time (140 women), 5 part-time (2 women); includes 32 minority (3 African Americans, 13 Asian Americans or Pacific Islanders, 16 Hispanic Americans), 108 international. Average age 27. 236 applicants, 72% accepted, 122 enrolled. In 2008, 86 master's awarded. *Degree requirements:* For master's, one foreign language, thesis or alternative, exams. *Entrance requirements:* For master's, minimum GPA of 3.0, proficiency in a foreign language. Additional exam requirements/recommendations for international students: Required—TOEFL (minimum score 600 paper-based; 250 computer-based; 100 iBT). *Application deadline:* For fall admission, 3/15 priority date for domestic and international students; for spring admission, 10/1 priority date for domestic and international students. Applications are processed on a rolling basis.

Application fee: $50. Electronic applications accepted. *Expenses:* Tuition: Full-time $29,300; part-time $1400 per credit. Required fees: $56. *Financial support:* In 2008–09, 177 students received support. Career-related internships or fieldwork, Federal Work-Study, institutionally sponsored loans, scholarships/grants, tuition waivers (partial), and unspecified assistantships available. Support available to part-time students. Financial award application deadline: 3/15; financial award applicants required to submit FAFSA. *Faculty research:* Assessment and testing in translation and interpretation, translation and interpretation pedagogy and curricula, integration of translation technology, language policy and planning. *Unit head:* Dr. Chuanyun Bao, Dean, 831-647-4170, Fax: 831-647-3560, E-mail: gsti@miis.edu. *Application contact:* 831-647-4123, Fax: 831-647-6405, E-mail: admit@miis.edu.

See Close-Up on page 463.

Rutgers, The State University of New Jersey, New Brunswick, Graduate School, Program in Spanish, Piscataway, NJ 08854-8097. Offers bilingualism and second language acquisition (MA, PhD); Spanish (MA, MAT, PhD); Spanish literature (MA, PhD); translation (MA). Part-time programs available. *Degree requirements:* For master's, comprehensive exam (for some programs), thesis (for some programs); for doctorate, 2 foreign languages, comprehensive exam, thesis/dissertation. *Entrance requirements:* For master's and doctorate, GRE General Test. Additional exam requirements/recommendations for international students: Required— TOEFL. Electronic applications accepted. *Faculty research:* Hispanic literature, Luso-Brazilian literature, Spanish linguistics, Spanish translation.

State University of New York at Binghamton, Graduate School, School of Arts and Sciences, Department of Romance Languages and Literatures, Program in Spanish, Binghamton, NY 13902-6000. Offers Spanish (MA); translation (Certificate). *Students:* 5 full-time (4 women), 1 (woman) part-time; includes 1 minority (Hispanic American), 1 international. Average age 24. 5 applicants, 80% accepted, 4 enrolled. In 2008, 4 master's awarded. *Degree requirements:* For master's, one foreign language, comprehensive exam, thesis or alternative. *Entrance requirements:* For master's, GRE General Test, GRE Subject Test. Additional exam requirements/recommendations for international students: Required—TOEFL. *Application deadline:* For fall admission, 4/15 priority date for domestic students, 1/15 priority date for international students; for spring admission, 11/1 for domestic students, 10/1 priority date for international students. Applications are processed on a rolling basis. Application fee: $60. Electronic applications accepted. *Expenses:* Tuition, area resident: Full-time $6900; part-time $288 per credit. Tuition, state resident: full-time $6900; part-time $288 per credit. Tuition, nonresident: full-time $10,920; part-time $455 per credit. Required fees: $1130. Part-time tuition and fees vary according to course load, program and student level. *Financial support:* Fellowships, research assistantships, teaching assistantships, career-related internships or fieldwork, Federal Work-Study, institutionally sponsored loans, scholarships/grants, health care benefits, and unspecified assistantships available. Financial award application deadline: 2/15; financial award applicants required to submit FAFSA. *Unit head:* Dr. Antonio Sobejano-Moran, Chairperson, 607-777-4635, E-mail: antobianco@msn.com. *Application contact:* Victoria Williams, Recruiting and Admissions Coordinator, 607-777-2151, Fax: 607-777-2501, E-mail: vwilliam@binghamton.edu.

State University of New York at Binghamton, Graduate School, School of Arts and Sciences, Translation Research and Instruction Program, Binghamton, NY 13902-6000. Offers Certificate. Part-time programs available. *Faculty:* 1 (woman) part-time/adjunct. *Students:* 11 full-time (10 women), 10 part-time (5 women); includes 3 minority (1 African American, 2 Hispanic Americans), 8 international. Average age 32. 14 applicants, 71% accepted, 5 enrolled. In 2008, 4 Certificates awarded. *Entrance requirements:* For degree, GRE General Test. *Application deadline:* For fall admission, 4/15 priority date for domestic students, 1/15 priority date for international students; for spring admission, 11/1 for domestic students, 10/1 priority date for international students. Applications are processed on a rolling basis. Application fee: $60. Electronic applications accepted. *Expenses:* Tuition, area resident: Full-time $6900; part-time $288 per credit. Tuition, state resident: full-time $6900; part-time $288 per credit. Tuition, nonresident: full-time $10,920; part-time $455 per credit. Required fees: $1130. Part-time tuition and fees vary according to course load, program and student level. *Financial support:* In 2008–09, 1 student received support, including 1 research assistantship (averaging $7,055 per year); teaching assistantships with full tuition reimbursements available. Financial award application deadline: 2/15. *Unit head:* Rosemary Arrojo, Director, 607-777-6555, E-mail: rarrojo@binghamton.edu. *Application contact:* Victoria Williams, Recruiting and Admissions Coordinator, 607-777-2151, Fax: 607-777-2501, E-mail: vwilliam@binghamton.edu.

Universidad Autonoma de Guadalajara, Graduate Programs, Guadalajara, Mexico. Offers advertising and corporate communications (MA); architecture (M Arch); business (MBA); computational science (MCC); education (Ed M, Ed D); English-Spanish translation (MA); fiscal law (MA); international business (MIB); international corporate law (LL M); internet technologies (MS); labor health (MS); manufacturing systems (MMS); market research (MBA); philosophy (MA, PhD); quality systems (MQS); renewable energy (MS); teaching mathematics (MA).

Université de Montréal, Faculty of Arts and Sciences, Department of Linguistics and Translation, Montréal, QC H3C 3J7, Canada. Offers linguistics and translation (MA, PhD, DESS). *Faculty:* 33 full-time (14 women), 1 (woman) part-time/adjunct. *Students:* 65 full-time (49 women), 123 part-time (90 women). 193 applicants, 37% accepted, 58 enrolled. In 2008, 28 master's, 2 doctorates, 18 other advanced degrees awarded. *Degree requirements:* For master's, thesis, general exam; for doctorate, thesis/dissertation, general exam. *Application deadline:* For fall admission, 2/1 priority date for domestic students; for winter admission, 11/1 priority date for domestic students; for spring admission, 2/1 priority date for domestic students. Application fee: $100. Electronic applications accepted. *Unit head:* Mireille Tremblay, Chairman, 514-343-6675, Fax: 514-343-2284, E-mail: mireille.tremblay.4@umontreal.ca. *Application contact:* Gilles Belanger, Conseillor (Traduction), 514-343-6024, Fax: 514-343-2284, E-mail: gilles.belanger@umontreal.ca.

Université Laval, Faculty of Letters, Department of Languages, Linguistics and Translations, Programs in Terminology and Translation, Québec, QC G1K 7P4, Canada. Offers MA, Diploma. Part-time programs available. *Degree requirements:* For master's, thesis (for some programs). *Entrance requirements:* For master's and Diploma, knowledge of French and English. Electronic applications accepted.

University at Albany, State University of New York, College of Arts and Sciences, Department of Languages, Literatures, and Cultures, Program in Russian, Albany, NY 12222-0001. Offers Russian (MA); Russian translation (Certificate). *Faculty research:* Translation, phonology and morphology of modern Russian.

University of Arkansas, Graduate School, J. William Fulbright College of Arts and Sciences, Department of English, Program in Translation, Fayetteville, AR 72701-1201. Offers MFA. *Degree requirements:* For master's, thesis.

University of Denver, University College, Denver, CO 80208. Offers applied communication (MAS, MPS, Certificate); computer information systems (MAS, Certificate); environmental policy and management (MAS, Certificate); geographic information systems (MAS, Certificate); human resource administration (MPS, Certificate); knowledge and information technologies (MAS); liberal studies (MLS, Certificate); modern languages (MLS, Certificate); organizational leadership (MPS, Certificate); security management (Certificate); technology management (MAS, Certificate), including 21st century strategic management (MAS); international markets (MAS); project management (MAS); research and development management (MAS); telecommunications (MAS, Certificate), including broadband (MAS), telecommunications management and policy (MAS), telecommunications technology (MAS); wireless networks (MAS). Part-time and evening/weekend programs available. Postbaccalaureate distance learning degree programs offered (no on-campus study). *Faculty:* 137 part-time/adjunct (55 women). *Students:* 28 full-time

(15 women), 699 part-time (401 women); includes 129 minority (54 African Americans, 8 American Indian/Alaska Native, 22 Asian Americans or Pacific Islanders, 45 Hispanic Americans), 4 international. Average age 36. 845 applicants, 96% accepted, 326 enrolled. In 2008, 221 master's, 3 Certificates awarded. *Entrance requirements:* Additional exam requirements/recommendations for international students: Required—TOEFL (minimum score 550 paper-based; 213 computer-based). *Application deadline:* Applications are processed on a rolling basis. Application fee: $75. Electronic applications accepted. *Expenses:* Contact institution. *Financial support:* Applicants required to submit FAFSA. *Unit head:* Dr. James Davis, Dean, 303-871-2291, Fax: 303-871-4047, E-mail: jdavis@du.edu. *Application contact:* Information Contact, 303-871-3155.

The University of Iowa, Graduate College, College of Liberal Arts and Sciences, Department of Cinema and Comparative Literature, Program in Comparative Literature Translation, Iowa City, IA 52242-1316. Offers MFA. *Degree requirements:* For master's, thesis, exam. *Entrance requirements:* For master's, GRE General Test, minimum GPA of 3.0. Additional exam requirements/recommendations for international students: Required—TOEFL (minimum score 550 paper-based; 213 computer-based; 81 iBT). Electronic applications accepted.

University of Nevada, Las Vegas, Graduate College, College of Liberal Arts, Department of Foreign Languages, Las Vegas, NV 89154-5047. Offers Hispanic studies (MA); Spanish translation (Certificate). Part-time programs available. *Faculty:* 5 full-time (4 women). *Students:* 2 full-time (both women), 10 part-time (6 women); includes 7 minority (1 Asian American or Pacific Islander, 6 Hispanic Americans). Average age 40. 12 applicants, 50% accepted, 4 enrolled. In 2008, 3 master's, 1 other advanced degree awarded. *Degree requirements:* For master's and Certificate, one foreign language, comprehensive exam. *Entrance requirements:* Additional exam requirements/recommendations for international students: Required—TOEFL (minimum score 550 paper-based; 213 computer-based; 80 iBT), IELTS (minimum score 7). *Application deadline:* For fall admission, 8/1 priority date for domestic students, 5/1 for international students; for spring admission, 12/1 priority date for domestic students, 10/1 for international students. Applications are processed on a rolling basis. Application fee: $60 ($75 for international students). Electronic applications accepted. *Expenses:* Tuition, state resident: full-time $1414; part-time $198 per credit. Tuition, nonresident: full-time $12,509; part-time $415.75 per credit. International tuition: $14,249 full-time. Required fees: $4 per credit. $252 per semester. Tuition and fees vary according to course load. *Financial support:* In 2008–09, 2 students received support, including 2 teaching assistantships with partial tuition reimbursements available (averaging $10,000 per year); institutionally sponsored loans, scholarships/grants, health care benefits, and unspecified assistantships also available. Financial award application deadline: 3/1. *Faculty research:* Second language acquisition/Romance languages, Old French, sociolinguistics/Romance languages, Spanish poetry of the 20's and 30's, post-Spanish Civil War women's fiction. *Unit head:* Dr. Ralph Buechler, Chair/Associate Professor, 702-895-3546, Fax: 702-895-3431, E-mail: ralph.buechler@unlv.edu. *Application contact:* Graduate College Admissions Evaluator, 702-895-3320, Fax: 702-895-4180, E-mail: gradcollege@unlv.edu.

University of Ottawa, Faculty of Graduate and Postdoctoral Studies, Faculty of Arts, Institute of Canadian Studies, Ottawa, ON K1N 6N5, Canada. Offers economics (PhD); English (PhD); geography (PhD); history (PhD); lettres Françaises (PhD); linguistics (PhD); philosophy (PhD); political science (PhD); psychology (PhD); religious studies (PhD); translation studies (PhD). *Degree requirements:* For doctorate, comprehensive exam, thesis/dissertation.

University of Ottawa, Faculty of Graduate and Postdoctoral Studies, Faculty of Arts, School of Translation and Interpretation, Ottawa, ON K1N 6N5, Canada. Offers interpreting (MA); Spanish translation (MA); translation (MA); translation studies (PhD). *Degree requirements:* For master's, one foreign language, thesis or alternative, research paper; for doctorate, thesis/dissertation, doctoral exam. *Entrance requirements:* For master's, school-administered exam, honors degree or equivalent, minimum B average; for doctorate, master's degree, minimum B+ average. Electronic applications accepted. *Faculty research:* Theory of translation, Spanish translation, conference interpreting, legal translation, translation-oriented lexicology and terminology.

University of Puerto Rico, Río Piedras, College of Humanities, Program in Translation, San Juan, PR 00931-3300. Offers MA, Certificate. Part-time and evening/weekend programs available. *Degree requirements:* For master's, 2 foreign languages, comprehensive exam, thesis. *Entrance requirements:* For master's, PAEG, minimum GPA of 3.0, graduate-level knowledge of 2 languages (English, French, or Spanish), letter of recommendation.

The University of Texas at San Antonio, College of Liberal and Fine Arts, Department of Modern Languages and Literatures, San Antonio, TX 78249-0617. Offers Spanish (MA); Spanish translation studies (Graduate Certificate). Part-time and evening/weekend programs available. *Degree requirements:* For master's, one foreign language, comprehensive exam, thesis optional. *Entrance requirements:* For master's, GRE, minimum GPA of 3.0, sample of written and spoken work. Additional exam requirements/recommendations for international students: Required—TOEFL (minimum score 500 paper-based; 173 computer-based). Electronic applications accepted.

University of Wisconsin–Milwaukee, Graduate School, College of Letters and Sciences, Department of Spanish, Milwaukee, WI 53201-0413. Offers Spanish (MA); translation (Certificate). *Faculty:* 7 full-time (3 women). *Entrance requirements:* For master's, bachelor's degree. *Expenses:* Tuition, area resident: Full-time $7320; part-time $165 per credit. Tuition, state resident: full-time $7320; part-time $165 per credit. Tuition, nonresident: full-time $17,840; part-time $714 per credit. Tuition and fees vary according to campus/location, program and reciprocity agreements. *Financial support:* In 2008–09, 15 teaching assistantships were awarded. Total annual research expenditures: $2,567. *Unit head:* Jeffrey Oxford, Chair, 414-229-4257, E-mail: oxford@uwm.edu. *Application contact:* General Information Contact, 414-229-4982, Fax: 414-229-6967, E-mail: gradschool@uwm.edu.

University of Wisconsin–Milwaukee, Graduate School, College of Letters and Sciences, Interdepartmental Program in Foreign Language and Literature, Milwaukee, WI 53201-0413. Offers classics and Hebrew studies (MAFLL); comparative literature (MAFLL); French and Italian (MAFLL); German (MAFLL); Slavic studies (MAFLL); translation (Certificate). Part-time programs available. *Faculty:* 39 full-time (17 women). *Students:* 32 full-time (25 women), 28 part-time (19 women); includes 5 minority (1 Asian American or Pacific Islander, 4 Hispanic Americans), 22 international. Average age 32. 51 applicants, 65% accepted, 26 enrolled. In 2008, 19 master's awarded. *Degree requirements:* For master's, 2 foreign languages, thesis or alternative. *Entrance requirements:* Additional exam requirements/recommendations for international students: Required—TOEFL (minimum score 550 paper-based; 79 iBT), IELTS (minimum score 6.5). *Application deadline:* For fall admission, 1/1 priority date for domestic students; for spring admission, 9/1 for domestic students. Applications are processed on a rolling basis. Application fee: $45 ($75 for international students). *Expenses:* Tuition, area resident: Full-time $7320; part-time $165 per credit. Tuition, state resident: full-time $7320; part-time $165 per credit. Tuition, nonresident: full-time $17,840; part-time $714 per credit. Tuition and fees vary according to campus/location, program and reciprocity agreements. *Financial support:* In 2008–09, 2 research assistantships, 35 teaching assistantships were awarded; career-related internships or fieldwork and unspecified assistantships also available. Support available to part-time students. Financial award application deadline: 4/15. Total annual research expenditures: $43,420. *Unit head:* Gabrielle Verdier, Representative, 414-229-3346, Fax: 414-229-2741, E-mail: verdier@uwm.edu. *Application contact:* General Information Contact, 414-229-4982, Fax: 414-229-6967, E-mail: gradschool@uwm.edu.

York University, Faculty of Graduate Studies, Glendon College, Program in Translation, Toronto, ON M3J 1P3, Canada. Offers MA. *Degree requirements:* For master's, thesis or alternative. *Entrance requirements:* For master's, professional translating experience. Electronic applications accepted.

Monterey Institute
of International Studies
An affiliate of Middlebury College

MONTEREY INSTITUTE OF INTERNATIONAL STUDIES

Translation and Interpretation

Programs of Study	The Graduate School of Translation, Interpretation, and Language Education (GSTILE) offers Master of Arts degrees in four areas of translation and interpretation: translation and interpretation (M.A.T.I.), conference interpretation (M.A.C.I.), translation (M.A.T.), and translation and localization management (M.A.T.L.M.). Each is designed to be a four-semester, 60-credit program. Students must demonstrate fluency in English and one or more of the following languages: Chinese, French, German, Japanese, Korean, Russian, or Spanish. Requirements for the advanced-entry, one-year Master of Arts degree programs are either two or more years of professional experience or a graduate degree in translation and interpretation. Nondegree certificates are offered in court or medical interpreting (Spanish only) and in the teaching of translation and interpretation.

In the first semester, all students take the same required courses: Basic Translation and Introduction to Interpretation. All students then specialize, based on their degree program and career interests. M.A.T.L.M. students may take interpretation as an elective, and accounting and computer-assisted translation courses are part of the curriculum during the first semester.

The M.A.T.I. program is a balanced mix of translation and interpretation courses, while the M.A.T. program concentrates on written, sight, and computer-assisted translation. The M.A.C.I. program focuses on simultaneous and consecutive interpretation, while the M.A.T.L.M. program incorporates business courses offered through the Institute's M.B.A. program in addition to translation technology courses. The Monterey Institute offers a variety of practicum and other courses that provide unique opportunities for interpreters-in-training to hone their skills. Translation students gain valuable training in project management, software localization, and specialized terminology in other courses.

The Translation and Interpretation program is a member of the Conférence Internationale Permanente d'Instituts Universitaires de Traducteurs et Interprètes (CIUTI) and participates in exchanges with CIUTI schools worldwide. Students may opt for a year of overseas study to consolidate their languages. The School's faculty members—experienced translators, interpreters, and educators—are dedicated to excellence and outstanding performance as both professors and working professionals. They are committed to helping students develop the analytical skills, cultural literacy, conduct, competence, and professional integrity needed to become superior professionals. |
| **Research Facilities** | Innovative and challenging curricula at the Institute require appropriate facilities and cutting-edge technology. Classrooms vary in size from large halls where plenary sessions with simultaneous interpretation can be held to smaller classrooms and labs befitting seminar-style classes for 5 to 15 students.

State-of-the-art multimedia and interpreting labs simulate professional environments. Interpretation students have access to three facilities that are equipped for simultaneous interpretation: a conference room with eight booths that conform to ISO specifications and two labs with twelve booths each. The Irvine Auditorium, site of international conferences, multilingual courses, and guest presentations, has four simultaneous interpreting booths and a seating capacity of 275.

Brahler and Gentner portable interpreting equipment transforms any classroom into a multilingual seminar, giving students further opportunities to provide and practice interpretation for Institute classes and events. To keep pace with the dynamic localization industry, GSTILE teaches computer-assisted translation and develops partnerships with high-technology firms. GSTILE students also work in a multimedia, computer-assisted translation and interpretation laboratory where video is distributed from cable, satellite broadcasts, or the Internet, and localized versions of software and translation tools are available. A unique speech bank makes speeches in all GSTILE languages available for student practice via the Internet.

The William Tell Coleman Library includes 95,000 volumes, more than 500 print periodicals, over 50 online databases, more than 400 academic journals, about thirty-five newspapers, and approximately 15,000 electronic books. One third of the collection is in languages other than English.

The Max Kade Language and Technology Center is a fully equipped language-learning center. It provides multimedia classrooms and conference rooms with state-of-the-art technology, including a multimedia resource center and the campus Teaching and Learning Collaborative.

In addition to numerous computer labs, the campus is fully networked utilizing the latest wireless standards. Every student is encouraged, for flexibility, to have a personal laptop computer adapted for wireless connectivity. |
| **Financial Aid** | Candidates with a minimum grade point average of 3.0 on a 4.0 scale (or equivalent) are invited to compete for merit scholarships; amounts range from $4000 to $15,000 per year. Scholarships are renewable for a second year depending upon the recipient's program and academic performance. Veterans of military service or orphans/dependants of veterans may be eligible for veteran's benefits. The Monterey Institute Grant is awarded to students demonstrating exceptional financial need who do not qualify for merit scholarships. Other scholarships may be awarded by outside foundations.

Under the Federal Stafford Loan program, students may borrow up to $8500 in subsidized loans, or $20,500 in unsubsidized loans less any subsidized amount. Graduate PLUS Loans cover the cost of attendance minus other financial aid resources. The Federal Work-Study Program allows students to work up to $4000 per academic year, working a maximum of 20 hours per week. |
Cost of Study	Tuition and fees for 2009–10 are $31,056.
Living and Housing Costs	The estimated variable expenses for books, supplies, housing, food, local transportation, personal expenses, and health insurance is $17,530.
Student Group	Institute enrollment is approximately 800. About one third of the students are from outside the United States, representing more than sixty countries. More than 90 percent of students from the U.S. have worked or studied abroad. More than fifty languages are spoken by students on campus. Language classes are regularly offered in English, Spanish, Arabic, French, Russian, Japanese, Chinese (Mandarin), and German. Other languages are offered by request.
Student Outcomes	GSTILE is one of the few translation and interpretation schools in the world to have a resident director of career management. Each year, thirty to forty employers participate in the Translation and Interpretation Job and Internship Fair, and ten to twelve more recruit on campus outside the fair. About 100 employers post jobs with the GSTILE career manager each year on a continuous basis. International and U.S. employers are in business, educational, government, nonprofit, and translation and interpretation agency sectors. About one third of all 1,400 translation and interpretation alumni are freelancers seeking contracts from all work sectors.

Of those seeking employment in the class of 2008, 80 percent found translation, interpretation, project management, and translation and interpretation teaching jobs with employers or launched independent contracting businesses within three months of graduation. More than 75 percent of the last three graduating classes had translation- and/or interpretation-related internships or summer jobs while students; most were paid. Selected employers in the last three years include Apple Computer; Bank for International Settlements (Switzerland); Bank of Korea; Bureau of International Recycling (Belgium); Chinese Times (San Francisco); Citigroup Asset Management (Japan); Daiwa Institute of Research (Japan); Eriksen, Inc. (Brooklyn, New York); Foreign Broadcast Information Service (Washington, D.C.); Honda Kaihatsu Kogyo (U.S.); Inter-American Investment Corporation (Washington, D.C.); Korean Ministry of Forestry and Agriculture; Lionbridge Technologies (U.S.); Lucile Packard Children's Hospital (Stanford, California); Microsoft Asia (Japan); Monterey County Office of Education; Nikon Research (U.S.); Samsung Electronics; SAP (Germany); Sun Microsystems (San Jose, California); Toyota Techno Service Corporation (Japan); and the Yuda Institute of Business Technology (China).

Many of the School's alumni provide freelance and staff translation and interpretation for international organizations, including the United Nations Secretariat, UN Criminal Tribunals, Free Trade Area of the Americas, International Civil Aviation Organization, and the World Intellectual Property Organization, in addition to governments worldwide. More information can be found at http://faculty.miis.edu/gsticareers. |
| **Location** | The Monterey Institute is situated in one of the most spectacular natural environments in the world. The Monterey Peninsula is 130 miles south of San Francisco on California's central coast, surrounded by ocean and mountains. Silicon Valley is only a short drive away. With a population of 100,000, the area combines a variety of rich cultural resources and agricultural activities. |
| **The Institute** | Opened in 1955 with summer classes in language and culture, the Monterey Institute of Foreign Studies was the first institute dedicated to the then-revolutionary concept that a living language should be taught as such: French in French, German in German, etc. Full-year degree programs began in 1961. By 1979, the Institute had grown to international distinction and was renamed the Monterey Institute of International Studies.

In December 2005, the Institute became an affiliate of Middlebury College, one of the world's premier colleges, located in Middlebury, Vermont. Middlebury College is renowned for its international programs, its summer language schools, and schools abroad (currently in China, France, Germany, Italy, Russia, Spain, Argentina, Brazil, Chile, Mexico, and Uruguay). The affiliation between Middlebury College and the Monterey Institute gives these two prestigious institutions further enriched curriculum and a bicoastal presence as well as a unique opportunity, through their extensive international programs and networks, to build greater global connections. Students at the Monterey Institute are pioneering partners, with members of the administration and faculty on both campuses, in building this international venture. |
| **Applying** | Applicants to the master's programs in translation and interpretation must have a U.S. bachelor's degree or the equivalent. Application may be made at any time, provided it is received at least two months prior to the applicant's proposed semester of enrollment or three months in advance for international students residing in their home countries.

Students should visit the Monterey Institute's Web site for complete information on admission requirements and the deadlines for scholarship and financial aid. |
| **Correspondence and Information** | Admissions Office
Monterey Institute of International Studies
460 Pierce Street
Monterey, California 93940
Phone: 831-647-4123
        800-824-7235 (toll-free within the U.S.)
Fax: 831-647-6405
E-mail: admit@miis.edu
Web site: http://www.miis.edu |

Monterey Institute of International Studies

THE FACULTY AND THEIR RESEARCH

Program Heads

John Balcom, Associate Professor and Chinese Program Head; Ph.D., Washington (St. Louis). Translation of Chinese and English.

Marcos Celesia, Associate Professor and Spanish Program Head; Licenliate, Universidad del Salvador (Argentina). Simultaneous and consecutive interpretation and translation of English and Spanish.

Jacolyn Harmer, Professor and German Program Head; M.A., Monterey Institute; Commission of the European Union Stage (Brussels); DEA (Diplome d'Etudes Approfondies) Candidate, Geneva (ETI). Simultaneous and consecutive interpretation and translation of German, French, Spanish, and English.

Julie Johnson, Associate Professor and French Program Head; M.A., Monterey Institute. Simultaneous and consecutive interpretation and translation of French and English.

Rosa Kavenoki, Associate Professor and Russian Program Head; Ph.D., Saint Petersburg State Pedagogical University. Simultaneous and consecutive interpretation and translation of Russian and English.

Miryoung Sohn, Assistant Professor and Korean Program Head, Interpreting and Translations; M.A., Hankuk University of Foreign Studies (Korea). Simultaneous and consecutive interpretation and translation of Korean and English.

Yun-Hyang Lee, Associate Professor; M.A., Hankuk University of Foreign Studies (Korea); Ph.D. candidate. Simultaneous and consecutive interpretation and translation of Korean and English.

Kayoko Takeda, Assistant Professor and Japanese Program Head; Ph.D., Simultaneous and consecutive interpretation and translation of Japanese and English.

Professors

Renee Jourdenais, Dean; Ph.D., Georgetown, Second language acquisition, sociolinguistics, applied linguistics research, language assessment, pedagogy, psycholinguistics.

Lydia Longstreth Hunt, Professor Emerita; Ph.D., NYU. Simultaneous and consecutive interpretation and translation of Spanish and English.

Diane de Terra, Ph.D., London. Simultaneous and consecutive interpretation of English, French, and Spanish; cross-cultural communication; international development; applied anthropology.

Ryoko Yamazaki Winter, Professor Emerita; Ed.D., San Francisco. Simultaneous and consecutive interpretation of Japanese and English.

Associate Professors

Laura Burian, M.A., Monterey Institute. Simultaneous and consecutive interpretation and translation of Chinese and English.

Carl Fehlandt, M.A., Translation Certificate, Monterey Institute. International studies, Spanish language and literature.

Mike Gillen, M.B.A., Monterey Institute. Translation of Russian and English.

Holly Mikkelson, M.A., Monterey Institute. Court interpreting, medical interpreting, translation and interpretation of Spanish and English.

Andrea Hoffman Miller, M.A., Translation and Interpretation, Monterey Institute. Simultaneous and consecutive interpretation and translation of German and English.

Lynette Xiaojing Shi, M.A., Hawaii; Diploma, Beijing Foreign Studies University. Simultaneous and consecutive interpretation and translation of Chinese and English.

Zinan Ye, M.A., University of the Pacific. Translation of Chinese and English.

Assistant Professors

Yoonji Choi, M.A., Translation and Interpretation, Monterey Institute. Translation, software localization, simultaneous and consecutive interpretation of Korean and English.

Antonio Canizales Gonzales, M.A., Ottawa. Translation and interpretation of Spanish and English.

Masaru Kawase, M.A., Keio (Tokyo). Simultaneous and consecutive interpretation of Japanese and English.

Barry Olsen, M.A., Conference Interpretation, Monterey Institute. Simultaneous and consecutive interpretation, translation of English and Spanish.

Tanya Pound, M.A., Toronto. Translation of Japanese and English.

Section 11
Philosophy and Ethics

This section contains a directory of institutions offering graduate work in philosophy and ethics, followed by an in-depth entry submitted by an institution that chose to prepare a detailed program description. Additional information about programs listed in the directory but not augmented by an in-depth entry may be obtained by writing directly to the dean of a graduate school or chair of a department at the address given in the directory.

For programs offering related work, see also in this book *Area and Cultural Studies, History, Humanities, Religious Studies,* and *Social Sciences.*

CONTENTS

Program Directories

Ethics   466
Philosophy   468

Close-Up
Southern Illinois University Carbondale   479

See also:
American University—International Service   861
California Institute of Integral Studies—Humanities   347
Central European University—Social Sciences and
    Humanities   349
The New School: A University—Political and Social
    Science   1251

Ethics

American University, College of Arts and Sciences, Department of Philosophy and Religion, Washington, DC 22016-8056. Offers ethics, peace, and global affairs (MA); philosophy (MA), including history of philosophy, philosophy and social policy. Part-time and evening/weekend programs available. *Faculty:* 9 full-time (5 women), 6 part-time/adjunct (3 women). *Students:* 8 full-time (4 women), 6 part-time (1 woman); includes 4 minority (1 African American, 2 Asian Americans or Pacific Islanders, 1 Hispanic American). Average age 25. 38 applicants, 55% accepted, 5 enrolled. In 2008, 10 master's awarded. *Degree requirements:* For master's, one foreign language, comprehensive exam, thesis (for some programs). *Entrance requirements:* For master's, GRE, writing sample. Additional exam requirements/recommendations for international students: Required—TOEFL. *Application deadline:* For fall admission, 2/1 for domestic students; for spring admission, 10/1 for domestic students. Application fee: $80. *Expenses:* Tuition: Full-time $21,204; part-time $1178 per credit hour. Required fees: $380. Part-time tuition and fees vary according to course load and program. *Financial support:* Fellowships, teaching assistantships, Federal Work-Study and institutionally sponsored loans available. Support available to part-time students. Financial award application deadline: 2/1. *Faculty research:* Oriental religion, classical and medieval philosophy, philosophy of law and ethics, comparative religion, philosophy of science. *Unit head:* Dr. Amy Oliver, Chair, 202-885-2140. *Application contact:* Kathleen Clowery, Director, Graduate Admissions, 202-885-3621, Fax: 202-885-1505.

American University, School of International Service, Washington, DC 20016-8071. Offers comparative and regional studies (Certificate); cross-cultural communication (Certificate); development management (MS); ethics, peace, and global affairs (MA); European studies (Certificate); global environmental policy (MA, Certificate); international affairs (MA), including comparative and regional studies, environmental policy, international economic policy, international politics, natural resources and sustainable development, U.S. foreign policy; international communication (MA, Certificate); international development (MA, Certificate); international development management (Certificate); international economic policy (Certificate); international economic relations (Certificate); international media (MA); international peace and conflict resolution (MA, Certificate); international relations (PhD); international service (MIS); peace building (Certificate); the Americas (Certificate); United States foreign policy (Certificate); JD/MA. Part-time and evening/weekend programs available. *Faculty:* 70 full-time (28 women), 51 part-time/adjunct (20 women). *Students:* 519 full-time (317 women), 335 part-time (205 women); includes 157 minority (54 African Americans, 2 American Indian/Alaska Native, 45 Asian Americans or Pacific Islanders, 56 Hispanic Americans), 116 international. Average age 27. 1,901 applicants, 58% accepted, 277 enrolled. In 2008, 358 master's, 5 doctorates, 9 other advanced degrees awarded. Terminal master's awarded for partial completion of doctoral program. *Degree requirements:* For master's, one foreign language, comprehensive exam, thesis or alternative; for doctorate, one foreign language, comprehensive exam, thesis/dissertation, research practicum; for Certificate, minimum 15 credit hours related course work. *Entrance requirements:* For master's, GRE, 24 credits of course work in related social sciences, minimum GPA of 3.5, 2 letters of recommendation, bachelor's degree, resumé, statement of purpose; for doctorate, GRE, 2 letters of recommendation, 24 credits in related social sciences; for Certificate, bachelor's degree. Additional exam requirements/recommendations for international students: Required—TOEFL (minimum score 600 paper-based; 250 computer-based; 100 iBT). *Application deadline:* For fall admission, 1/15 priority date for domestic students; for spring admission, 10/1 priority date for domestic students. Applications are processed on a rolling basis. Application fee: $50. *Expenses:* Tuition: Full-time $21,204; part-time $1178 per credit hour. Required fees: $380. Part-time tuition and fees vary according to course load and program. *Financial support:* Career-related internships or fieldwork, Federal Work-Study, and institutionally sponsored loans available. Financial award application deadline: 1/15. *Faculty research:* International intellectual property, international environmental issues, international law and legal order, international telecommunications/technology, international sustainable development. *Unit head:* Dr. Louis W. Goodman, Dean, 202-885-1600, Fax: 202-885-2494. *Application contact:* Yasmin Quianzon, Director of Graduate Admissions and Financial Aid, 202-885-2496, Fax: 202-885-1109.

See Close-Up on page 861.

Azusa Pacific University, Haggard School of Theology, Program in Religion: Theology and Ethics, Azusa, CA 91702-7000. Offers MAR.

Biola University, Talbot School of Theology, La Mirada, CA 90639-0001. Offers Bible exposition (MA); biblical and theological studies (MA); Christian education (MACE); Christian ministry and leadership (MA); divinity (M Div); education (PhD); ministry (MA Min); New Testament (MA); Old Testament (MA); philosophy of religion and ethics (MA); spiritual formation (MA); spiritual formation and soul care (MA); theology (MA, Th M, D Min). *Accreditation:* ATS. Part-time and evening/weekend programs available. *Degree requirements:* For master's, variable foreign language requirement, thesis or alternative; for doctorate, variable foreign language requirement, thesis/dissertation; for M Div, thesis/dissertation or alternative. *Entrance requirements:* For M Div, minimum GPA of 2.6; for master's, minimum undergraduate GPA of 3.0; for doctorate, minimum GPA of 3.25. Additional exam requirements/recommendations for international students: Required—TOEFL (minimum score 550 paper-based; 213 computer-based). *Faculty research:* Moral development; biological, medical, and social ethics; ancient Near Eastern historical philosophy.

Chicago Theological Seminary, Graduate and Professional Programs, Chicago, IL 60637-1507. Offers preaching (D Min); religion and health (D Min); religious studies (MA); spirituality and spiritual direction (D Min); theology (M Div); theology, ethics and the human sciences (PhD); M Div/MSW. *Accreditation:* ACIPE; ATS. Part-time programs available. *Faculty:* 13 full-time (5 women). *Students:* 71 full-time (32 women), 139 part-time (76 women); includes 54 minority (45 African Americans, 6 Asian Americans or Pacific Islanders, 3 Hispanic Americans), 33 international. *Degree requirements:* For master's, thesis; for doctorate, 2 foreign languages, comprehensive exam, thesis/dissertation; for M Div, thesis/dissertation. *Entrance requirements:* For doctorate, GRE General Test. Additional exam requirements/recommendations for international students: Required—TOEFL (minimum score 217 computer-based). *Application deadline:* For fall admission, 2/15 priority date for domestic and international students; for spring admission, 11/1 for domestic and international students. Application fee: $50. *Financial support:* Fellowships, institutionally sponsored loans, scholarships/grants, and tuition waivers (partial) available. Support available to part-time students. Financial award application deadline: 3/1; financial award applicants required to submit FAFSA. *Faculty research:* Bible, culture and hermeneutics, theology, gender and sexuality, black faith and life, spirituality and psychology, practical theology. Total annual research expenditures: $150,000. *Unit head:* Dr. Theodore W. Jennings, Acting Dean, 773-752-5757, Fax: 773-752-1903, E-mail: tjennings@ctschicago.edu. *Application contact:* Rev. Lin Sanford Keppert, Director of Admissions, Recruitment and Financial Aid, E-mail: lkeppert@ctschicago.edu.

Claremont Graduate University, Graduate Programs, School of Religion, Claremont, CA 91711-6160. Offers Hebrew Bible (MA, PhD); history of Christianity and religions of North America (MA, PhD); New Testament (MA, PhD); philosophy of religion and theology (MA, PhD); theology, ethics and culture (MA, PhD); women's studies in religion (MA, PhD); MA/PhD; MBA/PhD. Part-time programs available. *Faculty:* 7 full-time (2 women), 2 part-time/adjunct (0 women). *Students:* 231 full-time (96 women), 4 part-time (2 women); includes 32 minority (13 African Americans, 11 Asian Americans or Pacific Islanders, 8 Hispanic Americans), 29 international. Average age 37. In 2008, 13 master's, 16 doctorates awarded. Terminal master's awarded for partial completion of doctoral program. *Entrance requirements:* For master's and doctorate, GRE General Test. Additional exam requirements/recommendations for international students: Required—TOEFL (minimum score 550 paper-based; 213 computer-based; 80 iBT). *Application deadline:* For fall admission, 2/1 priority date for domestic students. Applications are processed on a rolling basis. Application fee: $60. Electronic applications accepted. *Expenses:* Tuition: Full-time $33,698; part-time $1465 per unit. Required fees: $310; $155 per semester. Tuition and fees vary according to program. *Financial support:* Fellowships, research assistantships, teaching assistantships, Federal Work-Study, institutionally sponsored loans, and scholarships/grants available. Support available to part-time students. Financial award application deadline: 2/15; financial award applicants required to submit FAFSA. *Unit head:* Karen Torjesen, Dean, 909-607-3214, Fax: 909-621-9587, E-mail: karen.torjesen@cgu.edu. *Application contact:* Brent Smith, Recruiter, 909-607-2653, Fax: 909-607-9587, E-mail: brent.smith@cgu.edu.

Drew University, Caspersen School of Graduate Studies, Program in Religion and Society, Madison, NJ 07940-1493. Offers anthropology of religion (MA, PhD); Christian social ethics (MA, PhD); psychology and religion (MA, PhD); sociology of religion (MA, PhD). Part-time programs available. Terminal master's awarded for partial completion of doctoral program. *Degree requirements:* For master's, one foreign language, thesis; for doctorate, 2 foreign languages, comprehensive exam, thesis/dissertation. *Entrance requirements:* For master's and doctorate, GRE General Test. *Faculty research:* Liberation theory, feminist critique, social science critique of religion.

Drew University, Caspersen School of Graduate Studies, Program in Theological and Religious Studies, Madison, NJ 07940-1493. Offers historical studies (MA, PhD); Methodist studies (PhD); philosophy of religion (MA, PhD); systematic theology (MA, PhD); theological ethics (MA, PhD). *Accreditation:* ATS. Part-time programs available. Terminal master's awarded for partial completion of doctoral program. *Degree requirements:* For master's, one foreign language, thesis; for doctorate, 2 foreign languages, comprehensive exam, thesis/dissertation. *Entrance requirements:* For master's and doctorate, GRE General Test. *Faculty research:* History and theology of religion, postmodern theologies, patristics.

Duquesne University, School of Leadership and Professional Advancement, Pittsburgh, PA 15282-0001. Offers community leadership (MS); leadership and business ethics (MS); leadership and information technology (MS); leadership and liberal studies (MA); sports leadership (MS). Part-time and evening/weekend programs available. Postbaccalaureate distance learning degree programs offered (no on-campus study). *Faculty:* 1 full-time (0 women), 59 part-time/adjunct (30 women). *Students:* 535 (263 women); includes 51 minority (43 African Americans, 1 American Indian/Alaska Native, 3 Asian Americans or Pacific Islanders, 4 Hispanic Americans). 231 applicants, 84% accepted, 121 enrolled. In 2008, 134 master's awarded. *Degree requirements:* For master's, capstone course. *Entrance requirements:* For master's, professional work experience, 500-word essay. Additional exam requirements/recommendations for international students: Required—TOEFL. *Application deadline:* Applications are processed on a rolling basis. Application fee: $0. Electronic applications accepted. *Expenses:* Tuition: Part-time $819 per credit. Required fees: $78 per credit. Tuition and fees vary according to course load. *Financial support:* Applicants required to submit FAFSA. *Unit head:* Dr. Dorothy Bassett, PhD, Dean, 412-396-5839, Fax: 412-396-4711, E-mail: bassettd@duq.edu. *Application contact:* Marianne Leister, Director of Student Services, 412-396-4933, Fax: 412-396-5072, E-mail: leister@duq.edu.

Fordham University, Graduate School of Arts and Sciences, Center for Ethics Education Program, New York, NY 10458. Offers health care ethics (Certificate). Part-time programs available. *Entrance requirements:* Additional exam requirements/recommendations for international students: Required—TOEFL. Electronic applications accepted.

Freed-Hardeman University, Program in Business Administration, Henderson, TN 38340-2399. Offers accounting (MBA); corporate responsibility (MBA); leadership (MBA). *Accreditation:* ACBSP. Part-time and evening/weekend programs available. Postbaccalaureate distance learning degree programs offered (no on-campus study). *Faculty:* 4 full-time (2 women), 1 part-time/adjunct (0 women). *Students:* 6 full-time (3 women), 34 part-time (14 women); includes 4 minority (all African Americans). Average age 30. 26 applicants, 85% accepted, 20 enrolled. In 2008, 11 master's awarded. *Entrance requirements:* For master's, GMAT. Additional exam requirements/recommendations for international students: Required—TOEFL (minimum score 500 paper-based; 173 computer-based). *Application deadline:* For fall admission, 8/17 for domestic students. Application fee: $35. *Expenses:* Tuition: Full-time $4284; part-time $357 per credit hour. Required fees: $16 per credit hour. *Financial support:* Career-related internships or fieldwork, Federal Work-Study, institutionally sponsored loans, scholarships/grants, and unspecified assistantships available. Support available to part-time students. Financial award applicants required to submit FAFSA. *Unit head:* Dr. Tom Deberry, Director of Graduate Studies, School of Business, 731-989-6659, E-mail: tdeberry@fhu.edu. *Application contact:* Dr. Samuel T. Jones, Vice President for Academics, 731-989-6004, Fax: 731-989-6945, E-mail: sjones@fhu.edu.

Georgetown University, Graduate School of Arts and Sciences, School of Continuing Studies, Washington, DC 20057. Offers American studies (MALS); Catholic studies (MALS); classical civilizations (MALS); ethics and the professions (MALS); human resources management (MPS); humanities (MALS); individualized study (MALS); international affairs (MALS); Islam and Muslim-Christian relations (MALS); journalism (MPS); liberal studies (DLS); literature and society (MALS); medieval and early modern European studies (MALS); public relations (MPS); real estate (MPS); religious studies (MALS); social and public policy (MALS); sports industry management (MPS); the theory and practice of American democracy (MALS); visual culture (MALS). *Entrance requirements:* Additional exam requirements/recommendations for international students: Required—TOEFL.

Graduate Theological Union, Graduate Programs, Berkeley, CA 94709-1212. Offers art and religion (MA, PhD); biblical languages (MA); biblical studies (Old and New Testament) (MA, PhD, Th D); Buddhist studies (MA); Christian spirituality (MA, PhD); cultural and historical studies of religions (MA, PhD); ethics and social theory (PhD); history (MA, PhD, Th D); homiletics (MA, PhD, Th D); interdisciplinary studies (PhD, Th D); Jewish studies (MA, PhD, Certificate); liturgical studies (MA, PhD, Th D); Near Eastern religions (PhD); Orthodox Christian studies (MA); Orthodox studies (Certificate); religion and psychology (MA, PhD); religion and society/ethics and social theory (MA); systematic and philosophical theology (MA, PhD, Th D); women's studies in religion (Certificate); MA/M Div. *Accreditation:* ATS. Terminal master's awarded for partial completion of doctoral program. *Degree requirements:* For master's, one foreign language, thesis; for doctorate, one foreign language, comprehensive exam, thesis/dissertation. *Entrance requirements:* For master's, GRE General Test; for doctorate, GRE General Test, MA or M Div. Additional exam requirements/recommendations for international students: Required—TOEFL. Electronic applications accepted.

Lutheran Theological Seminary, Graduate and Professional Programs, Saskatoon, SK S7N 0X3, Canada. Offers Biblical studies (MTS); church history (MTS); ethics/church and society (MTS); history of Christianity (STM); New Testament (STM); Old Testament (STM); pastoral studies (STM); pastoral theology (MTS); systematic theology (MTS); systematic theology and philosophy of religion (STM); theology (M Div, D Div). *Accreditation:* ATS. Part-time programs available. *Degree requirements:* For master's, thesis; for M Div, Greek, Hebrew.

Marquette University, Graduate School, College of Arts and Sciences, Department of Philosophy, Milwaukee, WI 53201-1881. Offers ancient philosophy (MA, PhD); British empiricism and analytic philosophy (MA, PhD); Christian philosophy (MA, PhD); early modern European philosophy (MA, PhD); ethics (MA, PhD); German philosophy (MA, PhD); medieval philosophy (MA, PhD); phenomenology and existentialism (MA, PhD); philosophy of religion (MA, PhD); social and applied philosophy (MA). Part-time programs available. Terminal master's awarded for partial completion of doctoral program. *Degree requirements:* For master's, one foreign language, comprehensive exam, thesis; for doctorate, 2 foreign languages, thesis/dissertation, qualifying exams. *Entrance requirements:* For master's and doctorate, GRE General Test.

Additional exam requirements/recommendations for international students: Required—TOEFL. *Faculty research:* Aristotle, Augustine, Descartes, Hegel, Heidegger.

Marquette University, Graduate School, College of Arts and Sciences, Department of Theology, Milwaukee, WI 53201-1881. Offers ethics (PhD); historical theology (MA, PhD); religious studies (PhD), including scriptural theology (MA, PhD); systematic theology (MA, PhD); theology (MA), including scriptural theology (MA, PhD); theology and society (PhD). Part-time programs available. Terminal master's awarded for partial completion of doctoral program. *Degree requirements:* For master's, one foreign language, comprehensive exam, thesis or alternative; for doctorate, 2 foreign languages, thesis/dissertation, qualifying exam. *Entrance requirements:* For master's and doctorate, GRE General Test. Additional exam requirements/recommendations for international students: Required—TOEFL. *Faculty research:* Old Testament theology, New Testament theology, church history, Christian ethics.

Phillips Theological Seminary, Programs in Theology, Tulsa, OK 74116. Offers administration of church agencies (M Div); campus ministry (M Div); church-related social work (M Div); college and seminary teaching (M Div); global mission work (M Div); institutional chaplaincy (M Div); ministerial vocations in Christian education (M Div); ministry (D Min), including parish ministry, pastoral counseling, practices of ministry; ministry and culture (MAMC), including Christian education, congregational leadership, history and practice of Christian spirituality, theology, ethics, and culture; ministry of music (M Div); pastoral care and counseling (M Div); pastoral ministry (M Div); theological studies (MTS). *Accreditation:* ATS. Part-time programs available. Postbaccalaureate distance learning degree programs offered (minimal on-campus study). *Degree requirements:* For master's, thesis (for some programs); for doctorate, thesis/dissertation. *Entrance requirements:* For master's, minimum GPA of 2.5; for doctorate, M Div, minimum GPA of 3.0. *Faculty research:* Biblical studies, historical studies, theology and culture, practical theology, theology and film.

St. Edward's University, School of Management and Business, Program in Organizational Leadership and Ethics, Austin, TX 78704. Offers MS. Part-time and evening/weekend programs available. *Students:* 1 (woman) full-time, 45 part-time (29 women); includes 14 minority (7 African Americans, 7 Hispanic Americans). Average age 39. 19 applicants, 84% accepted, 14 enrolled. In 2008, 23 master's awarded. *Degree requirements:* For master's, minimum 24 hours in residence. *Entrance requirements:* For master's, GMAT or GRE General Test, minimum GPA of 2.75 in last 60 hours of course work. Additional exam requirements/recommendations for international students: Required—TOEFL (minimum score 550 paper-based; 213 computer-based; 79 iBT). *Application deadline:* For fall admission, 8/1 for domestic students, 7/1 for international students; for spring admission, 12/1 for domestic students, 11/1 for international students. Applications are processed on a rolling basis. Application fee: $45 ($50 for international students). Electronic applications accepted. *Expenses:* Tuition: Full-time $13,752; part-time $764 per credit hour. Required fees: $50 per semester. Full-time tuition and fees vary according to course load and program. *Financial support:* In 2008–09, 1 student received support. Scholarships/grants available. *Faculty research:* Business ethics. *Unit head:* Dr. Tom Sechrest, Director, 512-637-1954, Fax: 512-448-8492, E-mail: thomasl@stedwards.edu. *Application contact:* Benjamin Jimenez, Recruiting Coordinator, 512-233-1694, Fax: 512-428-1032, E-mail: benjij@stedwards.edu.

Southeastern Baptist Theological Seminary, Graduate and Professional Programs, Wake Forest, NC 27588-1889. Offers advanced biblical studies (M Div); Christian education (M Div, MACE); Christian ethics (PhD); Christian ministry (M Div); Christian planting (M Div); church music (MACM); counseling (MACO); evangelism (PhD); language (M Div); ministry (D Min); New Testament (PhD); Old Testament (PhD); philosophy (PhD); theology (Th M, PhD); women's studies (M Div). *Accreditation:* ACIPE; ATS (one or more programs are accredited). *Degree requirements:* For master's, thesis (for some programs), oral exam; for doctorate, thesis/dissertation, fieldwork; for M Div, supervised ministry. *Entrance requirements:* For master's, Cooperative English Test, minimum GPA of 2.0, M Div or equivalent (Th M); for doctorate, GRE General Test or MAT, Cooperative English Test, M Div or equivalent, 3 years of professional experience.

Suffolk University, College of Arts and Sciences, Program in Ethics and Public Policy, Boston, MA 02108-2770. Offers MS. Part-time and evening/weekend programs available. *Degree requirements:* For master's, internship or thesis. *Entrance requirements:* For master's, GRE General Test, MAT, GMAT, statement of professional goals, official transcripts, 2 letters of recommendation, resumé. Additional exam requirements/recommendations for international students: Required—TOEFL (minimum score 550 paper-based; 213 computer-based; 80 iBT). Electronic applications accepted. *Expenses:* Contact institution. *Faculty research:* History of philosophy, ethics, political philosophy, continental philosophy and phenomenology, applied ethics.

Université de Sherbrooke, Faculty of Theology, Ethics and Philosophy, Sherbrooke, QC J1K 2R1, Canada. Offers applied ethics (Diploma); human science of religions (MA); intercultural training (Diploma); philosophy (MA, PhD); spiritual anthropology (Diploma); theology (MA, PhD, Diploma). Part-time and evening/weekend programs available. Postbaccalaureate distance learning degree programs offered. Terminal master's awarded for partial completion of doctoral program. *Entrance requirements:* For master's, bachelor's degree in related discipline; for doctorate, master's degree in related discipline. *Faculty research:* Faith and culture interrelation.

Université du Québec à Chicoutimi, Graduate Programs, Program in Ethics, Chicoutimi, QC G7H 2B1, Canada. Offers Diploma. *Entrance requirements:* For degree, appropriate bachelor's degree, proficiency in French.

Université du Québec à Rimouski, Graduate Programs, Program in Ethics, Rimouski, QC G5L 3A1, Canada. Offers MA, Diploma. Part-time programs available. *Degree requirements:* For master's, thesis. *Entrance requirements:* For master's, appropriate bachelor's degree, proficiency in French.

Université Laval, Faculty of Theology and Religious Sciences, Program in Applied Ethics, Québec, QC G1K 7P4, Canada. Offers DESS. Part-time programs available. *Entrance requirements:* For degree, knowledge of French. Electronic applications accepted.

University of Baltimore, Graduate School, The Yale Gordon College of Liberal Arts, Program in Legal and Ethical Studies, Baltimore, MD 21201-5779. Offers MA. Part-time and evening/weekend programs available. *Faculty:* 14 full-time (7 women), 12 part-time/adjunct (4 women). *Students:* 19 full-time (7 women), 78 part-time (49 women); includes 63 minority (41 African Americans, 1 American Indian/Alaska Native, 21 Hispanic Americans), 1 international. Average age 34. 51 applicants, 57% accepted, 25 enrolled. In 2008, 22 master's awarded. *Degree requirements:* For master's, thesis optional. *Entrance requirements:* For master's, minimum GPA of 3.0. Additional exam requirements/recommendations for international students: Required—TOEFL (minimum score 550 paper-based; 213 computer-based). *Application deadline:* For fall admission, 8/1 for domestic students, 6/1 for international students; for spring admission, 12/1 for domestic students, 11/1 for international students. Applications are processed on a rolling basis. Application fee: $45. Electronic applications accepted. *Expenses:* Tuition, state resident: part-time $568 per credit. Tuition, nonresident: part-time $824 per credit. Required fees: $250 per semester. *Financial support:* In 2008–09, 3 research assistantships were awarded; fellowships, career-related internships or fieldwork and Federal Work-Study also available. Support available to part-time students. Financial award application deadline: 4/1; financial award applicants required to submit FAFSA. *Faculty research:* Morality in law and economics, religion in lawmaking, comparative legal history, law and social change, critical issues in constitutional law, theories of justice. Total annual research expenditures: $24,077. *Unit head:* Dr. Jeffrey Sawyer, Director, 410-837-5320, E-mail: jsawyer@ubalt.edu. *Application contact:* Kevin Nies, Assistant Director, Office of Graduate Admission, 410-837-6565, E-mail: Knies@ubalt.edu.

University of Nevada, Las Vegas, Graduate College, College of Liberal Arts, Department of Political Science, Program in Ethics and Policy Studies, Las Vegas, NV 89154-5029. Offers MA. Part-time programs available. *Faculty:* 2 full-time (0 women), 2 part-time/adjunct (both women). *Students:* 9 part-time (2 women); includes 5 minority (1 African American, 1 American Indian/Alaska Native, 1 Asian American or Pacific Islander, 2 Hispanic Americans). Average age 35. 2 applicants, 100% accepted, 1 enrolled. In 2008, 1 master's awarded. *Degree requirements:* For master's, thesis. *Entrance requirements:* For master's, GRE General Test. Additional exam requirements/recommendations for international students: Required—TOEFL (minimum score 550 paper-based; 213 computer-based; 80 iBT), IELTS (minimum score 7). *Application deadline:* For fall admission, 2/1 priority date for domestic and international students; for spring admission, 10/1 priority date for domestic and international students. Applications are processed on a rolling basis. Application fee: $60 ($75 for international students). Electronic applications accepted. *Expenses:* Tuition, state resident: full-time $1414; part-time $198 per credit. Tuition, nonresident: full-time $12,509; part-time $415.75 per credit. International tuition: $14,249 full-time. Required fees: $4 per credit. $252 per semester. Tuition and fees vary according to course load. *Financial support:* Institutionally sponsored loans, scholarships/grants, health care benefits, and unspecified assistantships available. Financial award application deadline: 3/1. *Faculty research:* Immigration and crime policy, ancient and contemporary political theory. *Unit head:* Dr. Mehran Tamadonfar, Chair/Associate Professor, 702-895-5258, Fax: 702-895-1065, E-mail: mehram.tamadonfar@unlv.edu. *Application contact:* Graduate College Admissions Evaluator, 702-895-3320, Fax: 702-895-4180, E-mail: gradcollege@unlv.edu.

University of North Florida, College of Arts and Sciences, Department of Philosophy, Jacksonville, FL 32224-2645. Offers applied ethics (Graduate Certificate); practical philosophy and applied ethics (MA). Part-time and evening/weekend programs available. *Faculty:* 11 full-time (5 women). *Students:* 11 full-time (5 women), 5 part-time (3 women); includes 3 minority (1 African American, 1 Asian American or Pacific Islander, 1 Hispanic American). Average age 33. 13 applicants, 85% accepted, 7 enrolled. In 2008, 3 master's awarded. *Entrance requirements:* For master's, GRE General Test, minimum GPA of 3.0 in last 60 hours, 3 letters of recommendation, writing sample. Additional exam requirements/recommendations for international students: Required—TOEFL (minimum score 500 paper-based). *Application deadline:* For fall admission, 3/1 priority date for domestic students, 3/1 for international students. Applications are processed on a rolling basis. Application fee: $30. Electronic applications accepted. *Expenses:* Tuition, area resident: Full-time $5782.08; part-time $240.92 per credit hour. Tuition, state resident: full-time $5782.08; part-time $240.92 per credit hour. Tuition, nonresident: full-time $19,974; part-time $832.26 per credit hour. Required fees: $952.80; $39.70 per credit hour. *Financial support:* In 2008–09, 2 students received support, including 4 teaching assistantships (averaging $6,450 per year). Financial award application deadline: 4/1; financial award applicants required to submit FAFSA. *Faculty research:* Late modern philosophy, pragmatism, religion and American culture, hermeneutics, philosophy of mind. Total annual research expenditures: $24,367. *Unit head:* Dr. Hans Herbert Koegler, 904-620-1330, Fax: 904-620-1840, E-mail: hkoegler@unf.edu. *Application contact:* Dr. Andrew Buchwalter, Graduate Coordinator, 904-620-1155, Fax: 904-620-1840, E-mail: abuchwal@unf.edu.

University of Pennsylvania, Wharton School, Legal Studies and Business Ethics Department, Philadelphia, PA 19104. Offers MBA, PhD.

University of South Africa, College of Human Sciences, Pretoria, South Africa. Offers adult education (M Ed); African languages (MA, PhD); African politics (MA, PhD); Afrikaans (MA, PhD); ancient history (MA, PhD); ancient Near Eastern studies (MA, PhD); anthropology (MA, PhD); applied linguistics (MA); Arabic (MA, PhD); archaeology (MA); art history (MA); Biblical archaeology (MA); Biblical studies (M Th, D Th, PhD); Christian spirituality (M Th, D Th); church history (M Th, D Th); classical studies (MA, PhD); clinical psychology (MA); communication (MA, PhD); comparative education (M Ed, Ed D); consulting psychology (D Admin, D Com, PhD); curriculum studies (M Ed, Ed D); development studies (M Admin, MA, D Admin, PhD); didactics (M Ed, Ed D); education (M Tech); education management (M Ed, Ed D); educational psychology (M Ed); English (MA); environmental education (M Ed); French (MA, PhD); German (MA, PhD); Greek (MA); guidance and counseling (M Ed); health studies (MA, PhD), including health sciences education (MA), health services management (MA), medical and surgical nursing science (critical care general) (MA), midwifery and neonatal nursing science (MA), trauma and emergency care (MA); history (MA, PhD); history of education (Ed D); inclusive education (M Ed, Ed D); information and communications technology policy and regulation (MA); information science (MA, MIS, PhD); international politics (MA, PhD); Islamic studies (MA, PhD); Italian (MA, PhD); Judaica (MA, PhD); linguistics (MA, PhD); mathematical education (M Ed); mathematics education (MA); missiology (M Th, D Th); modern Hebrew (MA, PhD); musicology (MA, MMus, D Mus, PhD); natural science education (M Ed); New Testament (M Th, D Th); Old Testament (D Th); pastoral therapy (M Th, D Th); philosophy (MA); philosophy of education (M Ed, Ed D); politics (MA, PhD); Portuguese (MA, PhD); practical theology (M Th, D Th); psychology (MA, MS, PhD); psychology of education (M Ed, Ed D); public health (MA); religious studies (MA, D Th, PhD); Romance languages (MA); Russian (MA, PhD); Semitic languages (MA, PhD); social behavior studies in HIV/AIDS (MA); social science (mental health) (MA); social science in development studies (MA); social science in psychology (MA); social science in social work (MA); social science in sociology (MA); social work (MSW, DSW, PhD); socio-education (M Ed, Ed D); sociolinguistics (MA); sociology (MA, PhD); Spanish (MA, PhD); systematic theology (M Th, D Th); TESOL (teaching English to speakers of other languages) (MA); theological ethics (M Th, D Th); theory of literature (MA, PhD); urban ministries (D Th); urban ministry (M Th).

Valparaiso University, Graduate Division, Program in Liberal Studies, Concentration in Ethics and Values, Valparaiso, IN 46383. Offers MALS, Post-Master's Certificate, JD/MALS. Part-time and evening/weekend programs available. *Students:* 1 full-time (0 women), 2 part-time (both women); includes 1 minority (Hispanic American). Average age 40. In 2008, 2 master's awarded. *Entrance requirements:* For master's, minimum GPA of 3.0. Additional exam requirements/recommendations for international students: Required—TOEFL (minimum score 550 paper-based; 213 computer-based). *Application deadline:* Applications are processed on a rolling basis. Application fee: $30 ($50 for international students). Electronic applications accepted. *Financial support:* Available to part-time students. Applicants required to submit FAFSA. *Unit head:* Dr. David L. Rowland, Dean, Graduate Studies and Continuing Education, 219-464-5313, Fax: 219-464-5381, E-mail: David.Rowland@valpo.edu. *Application contact:* Jamie Haney, Coordinator of Recruitment Activities, 219-464-5313, Fax: 219-464-5381, E-mail: Jamie.Haney@valpo.edu.

Warner Pacific College, Graduate Programs, Portland, OR 97215-4099. Offers biblical and theological studies (MA); biblical studies (M Rel); education (M Ed); management/organizational leadership (MS); pastoral ministries (M Rel); religion and ethics (M Rel); teaching (MA); theology (M Rel). Part-time programs available. *Degree requirements:* For master's, thesis or alternative, Presentation of Defense. *Entrance requirements:* For master's, interview, minimum GPA of 2.5, letters of recommendations. *Faculty research:* New Testament studies, nineteenth-century Wesleyan theology, preaching and church growth, Christian ethics.

West Chester University of Pennsylvania, Office of Graduate Studies, College of Arts and Sciences, Department of Philosophy, West Chester, PA 19383. Offers business ethics (Certificate); healthcare ethics (Certificate); philosophy (MA). Part-time and evening/weekend programs available. *Students:* 16 full-time (6 women), 12 part-time (5 women); includes 1 minority (African American), 1 international. Average age 31. 21 applicants, 90% accepted, 11 enrolled. In 2008, 3 master's awarded. *Degree requirements:* For master's, thesis optional, thesis or comprehensive exam. *Entrance requirements:* For master's, GRE or writing sample, three letters of reference. Additional exam requirements/recommendations for international students: Required—TOEFL (minimum score 550 paper-based; 213 computer-based; 80 iBT). *Application deadline:* For fall admission, 4/15 priority date for domestic students, 3/15 for international students; for spring admission, 10/15 for domestic students, 9/1 for international students. Applications are processed on a rolling basis. Application fee: $35. Electronic applications accepted. *Expenses:* Tuition, state resident: full-time $6430; part-time $357 per credit.

Ethics

West Chester University of Pennsylvania *(continued)*
Tuition, nonresident: full-time $10,288; part-time $572 per credit. Required fees: $652.50; $50 per credit. $67 per semester. *Financial support:* In 2008–09, 5 research assistantships with full and partial tuition reimbursements (averaging $5,000 per year) were awarded; unspecified assistantships also available. Support available to part-time students. Financial award application deadline: 2/15; financial award applicants required to submit FAFSA. *Faculty research:* International studies. *Unit head:* Dr. Joan Woolfrey, Chair, 610-436-1004, E-mail: jwoolfrey@wcupa.edu. *Application contact:* Dr. Helen Daley Schroepfer, Graduate Coordinator, 610-436-2429, E-mail: hschroepfer@wcupa.edu.

Wilfrid Laurier University, Waterloo Lutheran Seminary, Waterloo, ON N2L 3C5, Canada. Offers Christian ethics (M Th); divinity (M Div); homiletics (M Th); ministry (D Min); pastoral counseling (M Th); spirituality in a health care setting (Diploma); theological studies (MTS); theology (Diploma); M Div/MTS/MSW. *Accreditation:* ATS. Part-time programs available. *Degree requirements:* For master's, one foreign language, thesis (for some programs); for doctorate, thesis/dissertation; for M Div, one foreign language, thesis/dissertation. *Entrance requirements:* For M Div, denominational endorsement; for master's, M Div, 2 units of clinical pastoral education (M Th); for doctorate, M Div, 3 years of ministry experience, proficiency in a foreign language, basic training in clinical pastoral education. Additional exam requirements/recommendations for international students: Required—TOEFL (minimum score 573 paper-based; 230 computer-based; 89 iBT), IELTS (minimum score 7). Electronic applications accepted. *Expenses:* Contact institution. *Faculty research:* Biblical study, church history, systematic theology.

Philosophy

American University, College of Arts and Sciences, Department of Philosophy and Religion, Washington, DC 22016-8056. Offers ethics, peace, and global affairs (MA); philosophy (MA), including history of philosophy, philosophy and social policy. Part-time and evening/weekend programs available. *Faculty:* 9 full-time (5 women), 6 part-time/adjunct (3 women). *Students:* 8 full-time (4 women), 6 part-time (1 woman); includes 4 minority (1 African American, 2 Asian Americans or Pacific Islanders, 1 Hispanic American). Average age 25. 38 applicants, 55% accepted, 5 enrolled. In 2008, 10 master's awarded. *Degree requirements:* For master's, one foreign language, comprehensive exam, thesis (for some programs). *Entrance requirements:* For master's, GRE, writing sample. Additional exam requirements/recommendations for international students: Required—TOEFL. *Application deadline:* For fall admission, 2/1 for domestic students; for spring admission, 10/1 for domestic students. Application fee: $80. *Expenses:* Tuition: Full-time $21,204; part-time $1178 per credit hour. Required fees: $380. Part-time tuition and fees vary according to course load and program. *Financial support:* Fellowships, teaching assistantships, Federal Work-Study and institutionally sponsored loans available. Support available to part-time students. Financial award application deadline: 2/1. *Faculty research:* Oriental religion, classical and medieval philosophy, philosophy of law and ethics, comparative religion, philosophy of science. *Unit head:* Dr. Amy Oliver, Chair, 202-885-2140. *Application contact:* Kathleen Clowery, Director, Graduate Admissions, 202-885-3621, Fax: 202-885-1505.

American University of Beirut, Graduate Programs, Faculty of Arts and Sciences, Beirut, Lebanon. Offers anthropology (MA); Arabic language and literature (MA); archaeology (MA); biology (MS); chemistry (MS); computer science (MS); economics (MA); education (MA); English language (MA); English literature (MA); environmental policy planning (MSES); financial economics (MAFE); geology (MS); history (MA); mathematics (MA, MS); Middle Eastern studies (MA); philosophy (MA); physics (MS); political studies (MA); psychology (MA); public administration (MA); sociology (MA); statistics (MA, MS). Part-time programs available. *Degree requirements:* For master's, one foreign language, comprehensive exam, thesis (for some programs). *Entrance requirements:* For master's, GRE, letter of recommendation. Additional exam requirements/recommendations for international students: Required—TOEFL (minimum score 600 paper-based; 250 computer-based; 100 iBT), IELTS (minimum score 7.5). *Faculty research:* String theory and supergravity; computer graphics; algebra and number theory; popular Arabic literature; marine and freshwater biology; integrating science, math and technology.

Arizona State University, Graduate College, College of Liberal Arts and Sciences, Division of Humanities, Department of Philosophy, Tempe, AZ 85287. Offers MA, PhD. *Degree requirements:* For master's, thesis. *Entrance requirements:* For master's, GRE.

Baylor University, Graduate School, College of Arts and Sciences, Department of Philosophy, Waco, TX 76798. Offers MA, PhD. *Students:* 27 full-time (4 women), 2 part-time (both women); includes 1 minority (Asian American or Pacific Islander), 2 international. In 2008, 3 master's, 5 doctorates awarded. *Degree requirements:* For master's, one foreign language, thesis or alternative. *Entrance requirements:* For master's, GRE General Test. Additional exam requirements/recommendations for international students: Required—TOEFL. *Application deadline:* Applications are processed on a rolling basis. Application fee: $25. *Financial support:* Teaching assistantships, Federal Work-Study, institutionally sponsored loans, and unspecified assistantships available. *Unit head:* Dr. Bob Roberts, Graduate Program Director, 254-710-6363, Fax: 254-710-3838, E-mail: robert_roberts@baylor.edu. *Application contact:* Marilyn McKinney, Administrative Assistant, 254-710-4237, Fax: 254-710-3870, E-mail: marilyn_mckinney@baylor.edu.

Boston College, Graduate School of Arts and Sciences, Department of Philosophy, Chestnut Hill, MA 02467-3800. Offers MA, PhD. Terminal master's awarded for partial completion of doctoral program. *Degree requirements:* For master's, one foreign language, thesis optional; for doctorate, 2 foreign languages, thesis/dissertation. *Entrance requirements:* For master's and doctorate, GRE General Test. Additional exam requirements/recommendations for international students: Required—TOEFL (minimum score 590 paper-based; 250 computer-based; 91 iBT). *Expenses:* Tuition: Part-time $1148 per credit. Required fees: $60. *Faculty research:* History of philosophy, metaphysics, ethics.

Boston University, Graduate School of Arts and Sciences, Department of Philosophy, Boston, MA 02215. Offers MA, PhD, JD/MA. Terminal master's awarded for partial completion of doctoral program. *Degree requirements:* For master's, one foreign language, thesis; for doctorate, one foreign language, comprehensive exam, thesis/dissertation. *Entrance requirements:* For master's and doctorate, GRE General Test, sample of written work, 3 letters of recommendation. Additional exam requirements/recommendations for international students: Required—TOEFL (minimum score 600 paper-based; 250 computer-based).

Bowling Green State University, Graduate College, College of Arts and Sciences, Department of Philosophy, Bowling Green, OH 43403. Offers applied philosophy (PhD); institutional theory and history (PhD); philosophy (MA). Part-time programs available. Terminal master's awarded for partial completion of doctoral program. *Degree requirements:* For master's, thesis or alternative; for doctorate, comprehensive exam, thesis/dissertation, foreign language or research tool. *Entrance requirements:* For master's and doctorate, GRE General Test. Additional exam requirements/recommendations for international students: Required—TOEFL. Electronic applications accepted. *Faculty research:* Moral philosophy and ethics, political and social philosophy, decision theory, applied ethics, public policy.

Brock University, Faculty of Graduate Studies, Faculty of Humanities, Program in Philosophy, St. Catharines, ON L2S 3A1, Canada. Offers MA. Part-time programs available. *Degree requirements:* For master's, thesis optional. *Entrance requirements:* For master's, honors BA in philosophy. Additional exam requirements/recommendations for international students: Required—TOEFL (minimum score 550 paper-based; 213 computer-based; 80 iBT), IELTS (minimum score 6.5), TWE (minimum score 4). Electronic applications accepted. *Faculty research:* Contemporary continental philosophy, Chinese and comparative philosophy, Indian philosophy, ethics.

Brown University, Graduate School, Department of Philosophy, Providence, RI 02912. Offers MA, PhD. *Degree requirements:* For master's, thesis or alternative; for doctorate, variable foreign language requirement, thesis/dissertation. *Entrance requirements:* For master's and doctorate, GRE General Test.

California Institute of Integral Studies, Graduate Programs, School of Consciousness and Transformation, San Francisco, CA 94103. Offers cultural anthropology and social transformation (MA); East-West psychology (MA, PhD); integrative health studies (MA); philosophy and religion (MA, PhD), including Asian and comparative studies, philosophy, cosmology, and consciousness, women's spirituality, women's spirituality flex format; social and cultural anthropology (PhD); transformative leadership (MA); transformative studies (PhD). Part-time and evening/weekend programs available. Postbaccalaureate distance learning degree programs offered (minimal on-campus study). *Faculty:* 29 full-time, 32 part-time/adjunct. *Students:* 334 full-time (218 women), 126 part-time (77 women); includes 102 minority (39 African Americans, 4 American Indian/Alaska Native, 35 Asian Americans or Pacific Islanders, 24 Hispanic Americans), 1 international. Average age 37. 223 applicants, 78% accepted, 110 enrolled. In 2008, 93 master's, 30 doctorates awarded. Terminal master's awarded for partial completion of doctoral program. *Degree requirements:* For master's, comprehensive exam (for some programs), thesis optional; for doctorate, comprehensive exam, thesis/dissertation. *Entrance requirements:* For master's, minimum GPA of 3.0, letters of recommendation, writing sample; for doctorate, master's degree, minimum GPA of 3.0, letters of recommendation, writing sample. Additional exam requirements/recommendations for international students: Required—TOEFL. *Application deadline:* For fall admission, 2/1 priority date for domestic and international students; for spring admission, 10/15 priority date for domestic and international students. Applications are processed on a rolling basis. Application fee: $65. Electronic applications accepted. *Expenses:* Tuition: Part-time $815 per contact hour. Required fees: $270; $135 per semester. Tuition and fees vary according to degree level. *Financial support:* In 2008–09, 271 students received support; research assistantships, teaching assistantships, career-related internships or fieldwork, Federal Work-Study, institutionally sponsored loans, scholarships/grants, and tuition waivers (partial) available. Support available to part-time students. Financial award application deadline: 3/15; financial award applicants required to submit FAFSA. *Faculty research:* Altered states of consciousness, dreams, cosmology, postcolonial studies, integrative health studies. *Application contact:* Allyson Werner, Senior Admissions Counselor, 415-575-6155, Fax: 415-575-1268.

See Close-Up on page 347.

California State University, Long Beach, Graduate Studies, College of Liberal Arts, Department of Philosophy, Long Beach, CA 90840. Offers MA. Part-time programs available. *Faculty:* 8 full-time (2 women), 1 part-time/adjunct (0 women). *Students:* 5 full-time (1 woman), 17 part-time (4 women); includes 6 minority (1 African American, 2 Asian Americans or Pacific Islanders, 3 Hispanic Americans), 2 international. Average age 38. 31 applicants, 32% accepted, 2 enrolled. *Degree requirements:* For master's, comprehensive exam or thesis. *Application deadline:* For fall admission, 7/1 for domestic students. Applications are processed on a rolling basis. Application fee: $55. Electronic applications accepted. *Expenses:* Tuition, nonresident: full-time $11,160; part-time $372 per unit. Required fees: $4100; $1261 per semester. *Financial support:* Federal Work-Study, institutionally sponsored loans, and scholarships/grants available. Financial award application deadline: 3/2. *Faculty research:* Philosophy of science, ethics. *Unit head:* Dr. Martin Herman, Chair, 562-985-4331, Fax: 562-985-7135, E-mail: mherman@csulb.edu. *Application contact:* Dr. Charles Wallis, Graduate Advisor, 562-985-4245, Fax: 562-985-4331, E-mail: cwallis@csulb.edu.

California State University, Los Angeles, Graduate Studies, College of Arts and Letters, Department of Philosophy, Los Angeles, CA 90032-8530. Offers MA. Part-time and evening/weekend programs available. *Faculty:* 5 full-time (3 women). *Students:* 19 full-time (2 women), 29 part-time (11 women); includes 20 minority (2 African Americans, 1 American Indian/Alaska Native, 6 Asian Americans or Pacific Islanders, 11 Hispanic Americans), 2 international. Average age 33. 31 applicants, 100% accepted, 14 enrolled. In 2008, 10 master's awarded. *Degree requirements:* For master's, comprehensive exam. *Entrance requirements:* Additional exam requirements/recommendations for international students: Required—TOEFL (minimum score 500 paper-based; 173 computer-based). *Application deadline:* For fall admission, 6/15 for domestic students, 5/1 for international students; for winter admission, 11/1 for domestic students, 9/1 for international students; for spring admission, 2/1 for domestic students, 10/1 for international students. Applications are processed on a rolling basis. Application fee: $55. Electronic applications accepted. *Expenses:* Tuition, nonresident: part-time $226 per credit. Required fees: $4019. *Financial support:* Career-related internships or fieldwork and Federal Work-Study available. Support available to part-time students. Financial award application deadline: 3/1. *Faculty research:* Aesthetics, philosophy of language, ethics, philosophy of science, history of philosophy. *Unit head:* Dr. Mark Balaguer, Chair, 323-343-4180, Fax: 323-343-4193, E-mail: mbalago@calstatela.edu. *Application contact:* Dr. Jose L. Galvan, Dean of Graduate Studies, 323-343-3820, Fax: 323-343-5653, E-mail: jgalvan@cslanet.calstatela.edu.

Carleton University, Faculty of Graduate Studies, Faculty of Arts and Social Sciences, Department of Philosophy, Ottawa, ON K1S 5B6, Canada. Offers MA. *Degree requirements:* For master's, thesis optional. *Entrance requirements:* For master's, honors degree. Additional exam requirements/recommendations for international students: Required—TOEFL. *Faculty research:* Application of philosophical theory to issues of current concern, history of philosophy, contemporary philosophy in North America and Europe.

Carnegie Mellon University, College of Humanities and Social Sciences, Department of Philosophy, Pittsburgh, PA 15213-3891. Offers logic and computation (MS); logic, computation and methodology (PhD); philosophy (MA). Part-time programs available. *Degree requirements:* For master's, thesis; for doctorate, comprehensive exam, thesis/dissertation. *Entrance requirements:* For master's and doctorate, GRE General Test. Additional exam requirements/recommendations for international students: Required—TOEFL. Electronic applications accepted. *Faculty research:* Philosophy of science, artificial intelligence.

The Catholic University of America, School of Philosophy, Washington, DC 20064. Offers MA, PhD, Ph L, JD/MA. Part-time programs available. *Degree requirements:* For master's, one foreign language, thesis, oral exam; for doctorate, 2 foreign languages, comprehensive exam, thesis/dissertation, oral exam. *Entrance requirements:* For master's and doctorate, GRE General Test, previous course work in symbolic logic, 3 letters of recommendation, minimum GPA of

3.0, interview. Additional exam requirements/recommendations for international students: Required—TOEFL (minimum score 580 paper-based; 237 computer-based). Electronic applications accepted. *Faculty research:* Metaphysics; history of ancient, medieval, and modern philosophy; twentieth century Continental philosophy, especially Husserl and Heidegger.

Central European University, Graduate Studies, School of Social Sciences and Humanities, Budapest, Hungary. Offers economics (MA, PhD); gender studies (MA, PhD); international relations and European studies (MA, PhD); mathematics and its applications (MS, PhD); medieval studies (MA, PhD); nationalism studies (MA, PhD); philosophy (MA, PhD); political science (MA, PhD); public policy (MA, PhD); sociology and social anthropology (MA, PhD). Terminal master's awarded for partial completion of doctoral program. *Degree requirements:* For master's, one foreign language, thesis; for doctorate, one foreign language, comprehensive exam, thesis/dissertation. *Entrance requirements:* For master's, CEU subject tests, interview; for doctorate, GRE, CEU subject test, interview. Additional exam requirements/recommendations for international students: Required—TOEFL (minimum score 570 paper-based; 230 computer-based). Electronic applications accepted. *Faculty research:* Civil society, fiscal decentralization, party politics, political philosophy (especially Liberalism, theory of Democracy).

See Close-Up on page 349.

Claremont Graduate University, Graduate Programs, School of Arts and Humanities, Department of Philosophy, Claremont, CA 91711-6160. Offers MA, PhD, MA/PhD, MBA/MA, MBA/PhD. Part-time programs available. *Faculty:* 3 full-time (1 woman). *Students:* 33 full-time (9 women), 7 part-time (1 woman); includes 11 minority (1 African American, 1 American Indian/Alaska Native, 4 Asian Americans or Pacific Islanders, 5 Hispanic Americans). Average age 38. In 2008, 3 master's, 1 doctorate awarded. *Degree requirements:* For doctorate, research folio. *Entrance requirements:* For master's and doctorate, GRE General Test. Additional exam requirements/recommendations for international students: Required—TOEFL (minimum score 550 paper-based; 213 computer-based; 80 iBT). *Application deadline:* For fall admission, 2/1 priority date for domestic students. Applications are processed on a rolling basis. Application fee: $60. Electronic applications accepted. *Expenses:* Tuition: Full-time $33,698; part-time $1465 per unit. Required fees: $310; $155 per semester. Tuition and fees vary according to program. *Financial support:* Fellowships, research assistantships, Federal Work-Study, institutionally sponsored loans, and scholarships/grants available. Support available to part-time students. Financial award application deadline: 2/15; financial award applicants required to submit FAFSA. *Faculty research:* Ancient philosophy, philosophy of science, probability theory, philosophical logic, philosophy of logic. *Unit head:* Patricia Easton, Chair, 909-607-9440, Fax: 909-607-1221, E-mail: patricia.easton@cgu.edu. *Application contact:* Justin Evans, Admissions Coordinator, 909-607-1278, Fax: 909-607-1221, E-mail: justin.evans@cgu.edu.

Cleveland State University, College of Graduate Studies, College of Liberal Arts and Social Sciences, Department of Philosophy, Cleveland, OH 44115. Offers bioethics (MA, Certificate), including bioethics (MA); philosophy (MA), including philosophy. Part-time and evening/weekend programs available. *Faculty:* 8 full-time (4 women), 1 part-time/adjunct (0 women). *Students:* 6 full-time (2 women), 8 part-time (5 women); includes 4 minority (3 African Americans, 1 Hispanic American), 1 international. Average age 30. 13 applicants, 46% accepted, 2 enrolled. In 2008, 4 master's awarded. *Degree requirements:* For master's, comprehensive exam, thesis optional. *Entrance requirements:* For master's, minimum GPA of 2.75. Additional exam requirements/recommendations for international students: Required—TOEFL (minimum score 525 paper-based; 197 computer-based). *Application deadline:* For fall admission, 5/1 priority date for domestic and international students. Applications are processed on a rolling basis. Application fee: $30. *Financial support:* In 2008–09, research assistantships with full tuition reimbursements (averaging $3,480 per year), 6 teaching assistantships with full tuition reimbursements (averaging $3,480 per year) were awarded; tuition waivers (full) and unspecified assistantships also available. *Faculty research:* Ethics, history of philosophy, bioethics, social and political philosophy. *Unit head:* Dr. Diane Steinberg, Chairperson, 216-687-3900, Fax: 216-523-7482, E-mail: d.steinberg@csuohio.edu. *Application contact:* Dr. Giannina Pianalto, Director of Graduate Admissions, 216-687-5599, Fax: 216-687-5400, E-mail: g.pianalto@csuohio.edu.

Collège Dominicain de Philosophie et de Théologie, Graduate Programs, Program in Philosophy, Ottawa, ON K1R 7G3, Canada. Offers MA Ph, PhD. Part-time and evening/weekend programs available. *Degree requirements:* For master's, thesis; for doctorate, 3 foreign languages, thesis/dissertation, candidacy exam. *Entrance requirements:* For master's, honors degree in philosophy, minimum B average in undergraduate course work; for doctorate, master's degree in philosophy, minimum A average in graduate course work.

College of the Humanities and Sciences, Harrison Middleton University, Graduate Program, Tempe, AZ 85282. Offers education (MA, Ed D); humanities (MA); imaginative literature (MA); interdisciplinary studies (DA); jurisprudence (MA); natural science (MA); philosophy and religion (MA); social science (MA). Part-time and evening/weekend programs available. Post-baccalaureate distance learning degree programs offered (no on-campus study). Electronic applications accepted.

Colorado State University, Graduate School, College of Liberal Arts, Department of Philosophy, Fort Collins, CO 80523-1781. Offers MA. Part-time programs available. *Faculty:* 14 full-time (3 women), 1 part-time/adjunct (0 women). *Students:* 17 full-time (2 women), 13 part-time (2 women); includes 1 minority (Hispanic American), 1 international. Average age 30. 16 applicants, 69% accepted, 8 enrolled. In 2008, 7 master's awarded. *Degree requirements:* For master's, variable foreign language requirement, comprehensive exam (for some programs), thesis (for some programs). *Entrance requirements:* For master's, GRE General Test, minimum GPA of 3.25, 3 letters of recommendation, writing sample, statement of purpose. Additional exam requirements/recommendations for international students: Required—TOEFL. *Application deadline:* For fall admission, 2/15 priority date for domestic and international students; for spring admission, 8/1 priority date for domestic and international students. Applications are processed on a rolling basis. Application fee: $50. Electronic applications accepted. *Expenses:* Tuition, area resident: Full-time $5620; part-time $312.25 per credit. Tuition, state resident: full-time $5620; part-time $312.25 per credit. Tuition, nonresident: full-time $17,253; part-time $958.50 per credit. Required fees: $1449.56; $82.35 per credit. *Financial support:* In 2008–09, 13 students received support, including 13 teaching assistantships with full tuition reimbursements available (averaging $12,225 per year); fellowships, research assistantships, career-related internships or fieldwork, Federal Work-Study, institutionally sponsored loans, scholarships/grants, traineeships, and unspecified assistantships also available. Support available to part-time students. Financial award application deadline: 3/1; financial award applicants required to submit FAFSA. *Faculty research:* Animal ethics, environmental ethics, history of philosophy, comparative philosophy, epistemology. *Unit head:* Dr. Jane E. Kneller, Chair, 970-491-7614, Fax: 970-491-4900, E-mail: jane.kneller@colostate.edu. *Application contact:* Dr. Michael Losonsky, Graduate Studies Coordinator, 970-491-6734, Fax: 970-491-4900, E-mail: losonsky@lamar.colostate.edu.

Columbia University, Graduate School of Arts and Sciences, Division of Humanities, Department of Philosophy, New York, NY 10027. Offers M Phil, MA, PhD, JD/MA, JD/PhD. Part-time programs available. *Degree requirements:* For master's, one foreign language; for doctorate, 2 foreign languages, thesis/dissertation. *Entrance requirements:* For master's and doctorate, GRE General Test, writing sample. Additional exam requirements/recommendations for international students: Required—TOEFL.

Columbia University, Graduate School of Arts and Sciences, Division of Natural Sciences, Department of Physics, Program in Philosophical Foundations of Physics, New York, NY 10027. Offers MA.

Concordia University, School of Graduate Studies, Faculty of Arts and Science, Department of Philosophy, Montréal, QC H3G 1M8, Canada. Offers MA. *Degree requirements:* For master's, comprehensive exam, thesis or alternative. *Entrance requirements:* For master's, honors degree in philosophy or equivalent. *Faculty research:* Anglo-American analytic thought, Continental thought, pragmatic thought.

Cornell University, Graduate School, Graduate Fields of Arts and Sciences, Field of Philosophy, Ithaca, NY 14853-0001. Offers PhD. *Faculty:* 18 full-time (5 women). *Students:* 43 full-time (10 women); includes 4 minority (2 African Americans, 2 Hispanic Americans), 20 international. Average age 31. 271 applicants, 7% accepted, 7 enrolled. In 2008, 4 doctorates awarded. *Degree requirements:* For doctorate, comprehensive exam, thesis/dissertation, teaching experience. *Entrance requirements:* For doctorate, sample of written work in philosophy, 2 letters of recommendation. Additional exam requirements/recommendations for international students: Required—TOEFL (minimum score 550 paper-based; 213 computer-based; 77 iBT). *Application deadline:* For fall admission, 1/15 for domestic students. Application fee: $70. Electronic applications accepted. *Expenses:* Tuition: Full-time $29,500. Required fees: $70. Full-time tuition and fees vary according to degree level, program and student level. *Financial support:* In 2008–09, 34 students received support, including 13 fellowships with full tuition reimbursements available, 21 teaching assistantships with full tuition reimbursements available; research assistantships with full tuition reimbursements available, institutionally sponsored loans, scholarships/grants, health care benefits, tuition waivers (full and partial), and unspecified assistantships also available. Financial award applicants required to submit FAFSA. *Unit head:* Director of Graduate Studies, 607-255-3687, Fax: 607-255-8177. *Application contact:* Graduate Field Assistant, 607-255-3687, Fax: 607-255-8177, E-mail: philosophy@cornell.edu.

Dalhousie University, Faculty of Arts and Social Science, Department of Philosophy, Halifax, NS B3H 4R2, Canada. Offers MA, PhD. *Entrance requirements:* For doctorate, MA in philosophy. Additional exam requirements/recommendations for international students: Required—TOEFL, IELTS, 1 of 5 approved tests: TOEFL, IELTS, CANTEST, CAEL, Michigan English Language Assessment Battery. *Application deadline:* For fall admission, 6/1 for domestic students, 4/1 for international students; for winter admission, 10/31 for domestic students, 8/31 for international students; for spring admission, 2/28 for domestic students, 12/31 for international students. Application fee: $70. Electronic applications accepted. *Financial support:* Career-related internships or fieldwork, scholarships/grants, and health care benefits available. *Faculty research:* Ethical and political philosophy; epistemology; philosophy of language, history, and logic; bioethics; feminist theory. *Unit head:* Dr. Micheal Hymers, Graduate Coordinator, 902-494-3810, Fax: 902-494-3518, E-mail: dalphil@dal.ca. *Application contact:* Laurie Finlay, Graduate Administrator, 902-494-3548, Fax: 902-494-3518, E-mail: laurie.finlay@dal.ca.

DePaul University, College of Liberal Arts and Sciences, Department of Philosophy, Chicago, IL 60604-2287. Offers MA, PhD. Part-time and evening/weekend programs available. *Faculty:* 21 full-time (8 women). *Students:* 19 full-time (10 women), 30 part-time (15 women); includes 3 minority (2 African Americans, 1 Hispanic American), 9 international. Average age 29. 157 applicants, 4% accepted, 6 enrolled. In 2008, 6 master's, 2 doctorates awarded. Terminal master's awarded for partial completion of doctoral program. *Degree requirements:* For master's, one foreign language, thesis optional, 11 courses in philosophy; for doctorate, 2 foreign languages, thesis/dissertation, oral exam, 28 courses in philosophy. *Entrance requirements:* For master's, GRE General Test, sample of written work, BA, two letters of recommendation; for doctorate, GRE General Test, MA in philosophy, sample of written work, two letters of recommendation. Additional exam requirements/recommendations for international students: Required—TOEFL. *Application deadline:* For fall admission, 12/15 for domestic students; for winter admission, 12/15 for domestic students. Applications are processed on a rolling basis. Application fee: $40. Electronic applications accepted. *Financial support:* In 2008–09, 12 fellowships with full tuition reimbursements (averaging $18,000 per year), 24 teaching assistantships with full tuition reimbursements (averaging $15,500 per year) were awarded; tuition waivers (partial) also available. Financial award application deadline: 12/15. *Faculty research:* German idealism, contemporary Continental philosophy, social and political philosophy, critical race theory, Renaissance and early modern philosophy. *Unit head:* Richard A. Lee, Chair, 773-325-4502, Fax: 773-325-7268, E-mail: rlee17@depaul.edu. *Application contact:* Avery M Goldman, Director of Recruitment, 773-325-4811, Fax: 773-325-7268, E-mail: agoldman@depaul.edu.

Dominican School of Philosophy and Theology, Graduate Programs, Department of Philosophy, Berkeley, CA 94708. Offers MA, MA/MA. Part-time programs available. *Degree requirements:* For master's, one foreign language, thesis. *Entrance requirements:* For master's, GRE General Test, minimum GPA of 3.0. Additional exam requirements/recommendations for international students: Required—TOEFL (minimum score 550 paper-based; 68 computer-based). *Faculty research:* Pre-modernism philosophy, philosophy and science, human suffering, philosophy of language, classical philosophy.

Duke University, Graduate School, Department of Philosophy, Durham, NC 27708. Offers AM, PhD, JD/AM. *Degree requirements:* For doctorate, one foreign language, thesis/dissertation. *Entrance requirements:* For doctorate, GRE General Test. Additional exam requirements/recommendations for international students: Required—TOEFL (minimum score 550 paper-based; 213 computer-based; 83 iBT), IELTS (minimum score 7). Electronic applications accepted.

Duquesne University, Graduate School of Liberal Arts, Department of Philosophy, Pittsburgh, PA 15282-0001. Offers MA, PhD. Part-time and evening/weekend programs available. *Faculty:* 10 full-time (3 women), 4 part-time/adjunct (2 women). *Students:* 94 full-time (17 women), 4 part-time (2 women); includes 1 minority (Hispanic American), 10 international. Average age 32. 83 applicants, 49% accepted, 19 enrolled. In 2008, 8 master's, 3 doctorates awarded. Terminal master's awarded for partial completion of doctoral program. *Degree requirements:* For master's, one foreign language; for doctorate, 2 foreign languages, comprehensive exam, thesis/dissertation. *Entrance requirements:* For master's, GRE General Test, bachelor's degree in philosophy, minimum GPA of 3.5; for doctorate, GRE General Test, master's degree in philosophy, minimum GPA of 3.75. Additional exam requirements/recommendations for international students: Required—TOEFL. *Application deadline:* For fall admission, 2/15 for domestic and international students. Application fee: $50. Electronic applications accepted. *Expenses:* Tuition: Part-time $819 per credit. Required fees: $78 per credit. Tuition and fees vary according to course load. *Financial support:* In 2008–09, 3 research assistantships with full tuition reimbursements (averaging $5,000 per year), 12 teaching assistantships with full tuition reimbursements (averaging $10,000 per year) were awarded; Federal Work-Study, scholarships/grants, tuition waivers (partial), and unspecified assistantships also available. Financial award application deadline: 5/1. *Faculty research:* Phenomenology, twentieth century Continental philosophy, history of philosophy. *Unit head:* Dr. James Swindal, Chair, 412-396-6572. *Application contact:* Linda L. Rendulic, Assistant to the Dean, 412-396-6400, Fax: 412-396-5265, E-mail: rendulic@duq.edu.

Emory University, Graduate School of Arts and Sciences, Department of Comparative Literature, Atlanta, GA 30322-1100. Offers comparative literature (PhD); English (Certificate); French (Certificate); Middle Eastern studies (PhD); philosophy (Certificate); psychoanalytic studies (PhD); religion (PhD); Spanish (Certificate); women studies (Certificate). *Degree requirements:* For doctorate, 2 foreign languages, comprehensive exam, thesis/dissertation. *Entrance requirements:* For doctorate, GRE General Test, minimum GPA of 3.0. Additional exam requirements/recommendations for international students: Required—TOEFL. Electronic applications accepted. *Faculty research:* Literary theory, psychoanalysis trauma and testimony, literature and religion, literature and technology, literature and philosophy, politics and global culture, literature and aesthetics.

Emory University, Graduate School of Arts and Sciences, Department of Philosophy, Atlanta, GA 30322-1100. Offers PhD. *Degree requirements:* For doctorate, 2 foreign languages, comprehensive exam, thesis/dissertation. *Entrance requirements:* For doctorate, GRE General Test, minimum GPA of 3.0. Additional exam requirements/recommendations for international students: Required—TOEFL. Electronic applications accepted. *Faculty research:* History of philosophy, German idealism, twentieth century Continental philosophy, ethics, social theory.

Philosophy

Florida State University, Graduate Studies, College of Arts and Sciences, Department of Philosophy, Tallahassee, FL 32306. Offers history and philosophy of science (MA); philosophy (MA, PhD). Terminal master's awarded for partial completion of doctoral program. *Degree requirements:* For master's, one foreign language, comprehensive exam (for some programs), thesis (for some programs); for doctorate, one foreign language, thesis/dissertation. *Entrance requirements:* For master's and doctorate, GRE General Test. Additional exam requirements/recommendations for international students: Required—TOEFL (minimum score 550 paper-based; 213 computer-based; 80 iBT). Electronic applications accepted. *Faculty research:* Philosophy of biology, Greek philosophy, ethics, action theory, philosophy of mind.

Fordham University, Graduate School of Arts and Sciences, Department of Philosophy, New York, NY 10458. Offers philosophical resources (MA); philosophy (MA, PhD). Part-time and evening/weekend programs available. Terminal master's awarded for partial completion of doctoral program. *Degree requirements:* For master's, one foreign language, comprehensive exam; for doctorate, 2 foreign languages, comprehensive exam, thesis/dissertation. *Entrance requirements:* For master's and doctorate, GRE General Test. Additional exam requirements/recommendations for international students: Required—TOEFL (minimum score 650 paper-based; 280 computer-based). Electronic applications accepted. *Faculty research:* Contemporary continental philosophy (including German idealism), philosophy of religion, medieval philosophy, ethics, epistemology.

Franciscan University of Steubenville, Graduate Programs, Department of Philosophy, Steubenville, OH 43952-1763. Offers MA. Part-time programs available. *Degree requirements:* For master's, one foreign language, thesis. *Entrance requirements:* For master's, minimum undergraduate GPA of 3.0.

George Mason University, College of Humanities and Social Sciences, Department of Philosophy, Fairfax, VA 22030.

Georgetown University, Graduate School of Arts and Sciences, Department of Philosophy, Washington, DC 20057. Offers bioethics (MA); philosophy (PhD); JD/MA; JD/PhD; MD/PhD. *Degree requirements:* For master's, thesis or alternative; for doctorate, 2 foreign languages, comprehensive exam, thesis/dissertation. *Entrance requirements:* For master's and doctorate, GRE General Test. Additional exam requirements/recommendations for international students: Required—TOEFL.

The George Washington University, Columbian College of Arts and Sciences, Trachtenberg School of Public Policy and Public Administration, Washington, DC 20052. Offers public administration (MPA), including budget and public finance, federal policy, politics, and management, international development management, managing public organizations, managing state and local governments, nonprofit management, policy analysis and evaluation, public administration, public-private policy and management; public policy (MA, MPP), including environmental and resource policy (MA), philosophy and social policy (MA), women's studies (MA); public policy and administration (PhD); JD/MPP; MPA/JD; PhD/MPP. Part-time and evening/weekend programs available. *Faculty:* 19 full-time (8 women), 12 part-time/adjunct (3 women). *Students:* 82 full-time (57 women), 130 part-time (80 women); includes 28 minority (9 African Americans, 1 American Indian/Alaska Native, 10 Asian Americans or Pacific Islanders, 8 Hispanic Americans), 28 international. Average age 31. 225 applicants, 38% accepted, 31 enrolled. In 2008, 64 master's, 7 doctorates awarded. *Degree requirements:* For doctorate, thesis/dissertation, general exam. *Entrance requirements:* For master's, GRE General Test, minimum GPA of 3.0; for doctorate, GRE General Test, interview, minimum GPA of 3.0. Additional exam requirements/recommendations for international students: Required—TOEFL (minimum score 600 paper-based; 250 computer-based; 100 iBT). *Application deadline:* For fall admission, 1/15 priority date for domestic and international students; for spring admission, 10/1 priority date for domestic students, 9/1 priority date for international students. Applications are processed on a rolling basis. Application fee: $60. Electronic applications accepted. *Financial support:* In 2008–09, 87 students received support; fellowships, teaching assistantships, institutionally sponsored loans and tuition waivers available. Financial award application deadline: 1/15. *Unit head:* Dr. Joseph J. Cordes, Director, 202-994-5826, Fax: 202-994-8913, E-mail: cordes@gwu.edu. *Application contact:* Information Contact, 202-994-8500, Fax: 202-994-8913, E-mail: pubpol@gwu.edu.

The George Washington University, Columbian College of Arts and Sciences, Trachtenberg School of Public Policy and Public Administration, Interdisciplinary Programs in Public Policy, Program in Philosophy and Social Policy, Washington, DC 20052. Offers MA. *Students:* 13 full-time (7 women), 10 part-time (5 women); includes 3 minority (all African Americans), 2 international. Average age 26. 15 applicants, 87% accepted, 8 enrolled. In 2008, 5 master's awarded. *Degree requirements:* For master's, comprehensive exam, thesis or alternative. *Entrance requirements:* For master's, GRE General Test, interview, minimum GPA of 3.0. Additional exam requirements/recommendations for international students: Required—TOEFL (minimum score 600 paper-based; 250 computer-based; 100 iBT). *Application deadline:* For fall admission, 4/1 priority date for domestic and international students; for spring admission, 10/1 priority date for domestic students, 9/1 priority date for international students. Applications are processed on a rolling basis. Application fee: $60. Electronic applications accepted. *Financial support:* In 2008–09, 2 students received support; fellowships with tuition reimbursements available, Federal Work-Study and institutionally sponsored loans available. Financial award application deadline: 1/15. *Unit head:* Dr. William B. Griffith, Chair and Academic Director, 202-994-8684, E-mail: wbg@gwu.edu. *Application contact:* Information Contact, 202-994-6265, Fax: 202-994-8683, E-mail: philosop@gwu.edu.

Georgia State University, College of Arts and Sciences, Department of Philosophy, Atlanta, GA 30302-4089. Offers MA, MA/JD. Part-time programs available. *Degree requirements:* For master's, thesis. *Entrance requirements:* For master's, GRE General Test, sample of written work. Additional exam requirements/recommendations for international students: Required—TOEFL. Electronic applications accepted. *Faculty research:* Ethics, ancient philosophy, Kant, philosophy of mind, epistemology.

Gonzaga University, College of Arts and Sciences, Program in Philosophy, Spokane, WA 99258. Offers MA. Part-time programs available. *Degree requirements:* For master's, comprehensive exam. *Entrance requirements:* For master's, GRE General Test or MAT, minimum GPA of 3.0. Additional exam requirements/recommendations for international students: Required—TOEFL.

Graduate School and University Center of the City University of New York, Graduate Studies, Program in Philosophy, New York, NY 10016-4039. Offers MA, PhD. Terminal master's awarded for partial completion of doctoral program. *Degree requirements:* For master's, thesis; for doctorate, one foreign language, comprehensive exam, thesis/dissertation. *Entrance requirements:* For master's, GRE General Test; for doctorate, GRE General Test, 3 letters of recommendation, writing sample. Additional exam requirements/recommendations for international students: Required—TOEFL. Electronic applications accepted.

Harvard University, Graduate School of Arts and Sciences, Department of Philosophy, Cambridge, MA 02138. Offers classical philosophy (PhD); philosophy (PhD). *Degree requirements:* For doctorate, 2 foreign languages, thesis/dissertation, final exams. *Entrance requirements:* For doctorate, GRE General Test. Additional exam requirements/recommendations for international students: Required—TOEFL. *Expenses:* Tuition: Full-time $32,556. Required fees: $1426. Full-time tuition and fees vary according to program and student level.

Harvard University, Graduate School of Arts and Sciences, Department of Sanskrit and Indian Studies, Cambridge, MA 02138. Offers Indian philosophy (AM, PhD); Pali (AM, PhD); Sanskrit (AM, PhD); Tibetan (AM, PhD); Urdu (AM, PhD). Terminal master's awarded for partial completion of doctoral program. *Degree requirements:* For master's, 3 foreign languages; for doctorate, 3 foreign languages, thesis/dissertation. *Entrance requirements:* For master's, GRE General Test; for doctorate, GRE General Test, proficiency in French and German. Additional exam requirements/recommendations for international students: Required—TOEFL. *Expenses:* Tuition: Full-time $32,556. Required fees: $1426. Full-time tuition and fees vary according to program and student level.

Harvard University, Graduate School of Arts and Sciences, Department of the Classics, Cambridge, MA 02138. Offers Byzantine Greek (PhD); classical archaeology (PhD); classical philology (PhD); classical philosophy (PhD); medieval Latin (PhD). *Degree requirements:* For doctorate, 4 foreign languages, thesis/dissertation, preliminary and special exams. *Entrance requirements:* For doctorate, GRE General Test. Additional exam requirements/recommendations for international students: Required—TOEFL. *Expenses:* Tuition: Full-time $32,556. Required fees: $1426. Full-time tuition and fees vary according to program and student level.

Howard University, Graduate School, Department of Philosophy, Washington, DC 20059-0002. Offers MA. Part-time programs available. *Degree requirements:* For master's, one foreign language, comprehensive exam, thesis. *Entrance requirements:* For master's, GRE General Test. Additional exam requirements/recommendations for international students: Required—TOEFL. *Faculty research:* African and African-American philosophy, social and political philosophy, ethics, philosophy of culture, applied philosophy.

Indiana University Bloomington, University Graduate School, College of Arts and Sciences, Department of Philosophy, Bloomington, IN 47405-7000. Offers MA, PhD. *Faculty:* 17 full-time (5 women). *Students:* 37 full-time (8 women), 1 part-time (0 women); includes 3 minority (1 Asian American or Pacific Islander, 2 Hispanic Americans), 5 international. Average age 30. 118 applicants, 10% accepted, 2 enrolled. In 2008, 3 master's, 6 doctorates awarded. Terminal master's awarded for partial completion of doctoral program. *Degree requirements:* For master's, thesis; for doctorate, comprehensive exam, thesis/dissertation, qualifying paper. *Entrance requirements:* For master's and doctorate, GRE General Test, writing sample. Additional exam requirements/recommendations for international students: Required—TOEFL. *Application deadline:* For fall admission, 1/15 priority date for domestic students, 12/15 for international students; for spring admission, 9/1 priority date for domestic students, 9/1 for international students. Applications are processed on a rolling basis. Application fee: $50 ($60 for international students). Electronic applications accepted. *Expenses:* Tuition, area resident: Part-time $291.97 per credit hour. Tuition, state resident: part-time $291.97 per credit hour. Tuition, nonresident: part-time $850.33 per credit hour. Required fees: $110 per semester. Tuition and fees vary according to course load and program. *Financial support:* In 2008–09, 32 students received support, including 2 fellowships with partial tuition reimbursements available (averaging $16,000 per year), 2 teaching assistantships with partial tuition reimbursements available (averaging $15,000 per year); research assistantships. Financial award application deadline: 4/15. *Faculty research:* Algebraic logic, cognitive science, history of modern philosophy, ancient and Jewish philosophy, Medieval logic and semantics, epistomology, ethics, history, philosophy of mind, philosophy of language. *Unit head:* Timothy W. O'Connor, Chair and Professor, 812-855-1093, Fax: 812-855-3777, E-mail: toconnor@indiana.edu. *Application contact:* Linda J. Harl, Department Secretary, 812-855-9503, Fax: 812-855-3777, E-mail: lharl@indiana.edu.

Indiana University–Purdue University Indianapolis, School of Liberal Arts, Department of Philosophy, Indianapolis, IN 46202-2896. Offers American philosophy (Certificate); bioethics (Certificate); philosophy (MA); JD/MA; MD/MA. Part-time programs available. *Degree requirements:* For master's, thesis optional. *Entrance requirements:* For master's, GRE. Additional exam requirements/recommendations for international students: Required—TOEFL. Electronic applications accepted. *Faculty research:* American philosophy, Peirce bioethics, metaphysics, ethical theory.

Institute for Christian Studies, Graduate Programs, Toronto, ON M5T 1R4, Canada. Offers education (M Phil F, PhD); history of philosophy (M Phil F, PhD); philosophical aesthetics (M Phil F, PhD); philosophy of religion (M Phil F, PhD); political theory (M Phil F, PhD); systematic philosophy (M Phil F, PhD); theology (M Phil F, PhD); worldview studies (MWS). Part-time programs available. Postbaccalaureate distance learning degree programs offered (minimal on-campus study). *Degree requirements:* For master's, one foreign language, thesis; for doctorate, 2 foreign languages, thesis/dissertation. *Entrance requirements:* For master's and doctorate, philosophy background. Additional exam requirements/recommendations for international students: Required—TOEFL (minimum score 600 paper-based; 250 computer-based). *Faculty research:* Human rights, anthropology of self, medieval discourse, gender and body, post-modern thought; biblical hermeneutics, creational aesthetics, ecumenism, epistemology, political theory and public policy, relational psychotherapy.

The Johns Hopkins University, Zanvyl Krieger School of Arts and Sciences, Department of Philosophy, Baltimore, MD 21218-2699. Offers MA, PhD. *Degree requirements:* For doctorate, thesis/dissertation. *Entrance requirements:* For master's and doctorate, GRE General Test. Additional exam requirements/recommendations for international students: Required—TOEFL. Electronic applications accepted. *Faculty research:* Historical and analytical research on range of philosophical topics.

Kent State University, College of Arts and Sciences, Department of Philosophy, Kent, OH 44242-0001. Offers MA. Part-time programs available. *Degree requirements:* For master's, thesis optional. *Entrance requirements:* For master's, GRE, minimum GPA of 3.0. Electronic applications accepted.

Louisiana State University and Agricultural and Mechanical College, Graduate School, College of Arts and Sciences, Department of Philosophy and Religious Studies, Baton Rouge, LA 70803. Offers philosophy (MA). Part-time programs available. *Degree requirements:* For master's, one foreign language, thesis (for some programs). *Entrance requirements:* For master's, GRE General Test, minimum GPA of 3.0. Additional exam requirements/recommendations for international students: Required—TOEFL (minimum score 550 paper-based; 213 computer-based; 79 iBT). Electronic applications accepted. *Faculty research:* Analytic philosophy, continental philosophy, history of philosophy, philosophy and religion, existential value theory.

Loyola Marymount University, College of Liberal Arts, Department of Philosophy, Program in Philosophy, Los Angeles, CA 90045-2659. Offers MA. *Entrance requirements:* For master's, GRE General Test. Additional exam requirements/recommendations for international students: Required—TOEFL (minimum score 600 paper-based).

Loyola University Chicago, Graduate School, Department of Philosophy, Chicago, IL 60611-2196. Offers health care ethics (MA); philosophy (MA, PhD); social philosophy (MA). Part-time and evening/weekend programs available. *Faculty:* 28 full-time (7 women), 4 part-time/adjunct (2 women). *Students:* 102 full-time (22 women), 15 part-time (3 women); includes 13 minority (4 African Americans, 7 Asian Americans or Pacific Islanders, 2 Hispanic Americans), 12 international. Average age 33. 224 applicants, 21% accepted, 26 enrolled. In 2008, 24 master's, 4 doctorates awarded. Terminal master's awarded for partial completion of doctoral program. *Degree requirements:* For master's, oral exam; for doctorate, one foreign language, thesis/dissertation, oral exam. *Entrance requirements:* For master's and doctorate, GRE General Test. Additional exam requirements/recommendations for international students: Required—TOEFL. *Application deadline:* For fall admission, 1/15 priority date for domestic students. Application fee: $50. Electronic applications accepted. *Expenses:* Tuition: Full-time $13,500; part-time $750 per credit hour. Required fees: $60 per semester. Full-time tuition and fees vary according to program. *Financial support:* In 2008–09, 6 fellowships with full tuition reimbursements (averaging $20,000 per year), 4 research assistantships with full tuition reimbursements (averaging $18,000 per year), 15 teaching assistantships with full tuition reimbursements (averaging $18,000 per year) were awarded; institutionally sponsored loans also available. Financial award application deadline: 1/15; financial award applicants required to submit FAFSA. *Faculty research:* Social philosophy, ethics, medical ethics, analytic philosophy, contemporary Continental philosophy. *Unit head:* Dr. Paul Moser, Chair, 773-508-8481, Fax: 773-508-3292, E-mail: acutrof@luc.edu. *Application contact:* Dr. Andrew Cutrofello, Graduate Program Director, 773-508-8481, Fax: 773-508-2292, E-mail: acutrof@luc.edu.

Marquette University, Graduate School, College of Arts and Sciences, Department of Philosophy, Milwaukee, WI 53201-1881. Offers ancient philosophy (MA, PhD); British empiricism and analytic philosophy (MA, PhD); Christian philosophy (MA, PhD); early modern European philosophy (MA, PhD); ethics (MA, PhD); German philosophy (MA, PhD); medieval philosophy (MA, PhD); phenomenology and existentialism (MA, PhD); philosophy of religion (MA, PhD); social and applied philosophy (MA). Part-time programs available. Terminal master's awarded for partial completion of doctoral program. *Degree requirements:* For master's, one foreign language, comprehensive exam, thesis; for doctorate, 2 foreign languages, thesis/dissertation, qualifying exams. *Entrance requirements:* For master's and doctorate, GRE General Test. Additional exam requirements/recommendations for international students: Required—TOEFL. *Faculty research:* Aristotle, Augustine, Descartes, Hegel, Heidegger.

Massachusetts Institute of Technology, School of Humanities, Arts, and Social Sciences, Department of Linguistics and Philosophy, Philosophy Section, Cambridge, MA 02139-4307. Offers PhD. *Degree requirements:* For doctorate, comprehensive exam, thesis/dissertation. *Entrance requirements:* Additional exam requirements/recommendations for international students: Required—TOEFL (minimum score 577 paper-based; 233 computer-based). Electronic applications accepted. *Faculty research:* Metaphysics; philosophy of mind; philosophy of language; ethics; political philosophy.

McGill University, Faculty of Graduate and Postdoctoral Studies, Faculty of Arts, Department of Philosophy, Montréal, QC H3A 2T5, Canada. Offers bioethics (MA); philosophy (PhD).

McMaster University, School of Graduate Studies, Faculty of Humanities, Department of Philosophy, Hamilton, ON L8S 4M2, Canada. Offers MA, PhD. Part-time programs available. *Degree requirements:* For master's, thesis; for doctorate, one foreign language, thesis/dissertation. *Entrance requirements:* For master's, honors degree in philosophy; minimum average B+; for doctorate, master's degree in philosophy. Additional exam requirements/recommendations for international students: Required—TOEFL (minimum score 580 paper-based; 237 computer-based). *Faculty research:* Twentieth-century European philosophy, twentieth-century Anglo-American philosophy, political philosophy, ethics, argumentation.

Memorial University of Newfoundland, School of Graduate Studies, Department of Philosophy, St. John's, NL A1C 5S7, Canada. Offers MA. Part-time programs available. *Degree requirements:* For master's, thesis. *Entrance requirements:* For master's, first-class undergraduate degree in philosophy. Electronic applications accepted. *Faculty research:* History of philosophy, philosophy of science, phenomenology and existentialism, contemporary metaphysics.

Miami University, Graduate School, College of Arts and Sciences, Department of Philosophy, Oxford, OH 45056. Offers MA. *Degree requirements:* For master's, thesis, final exam. *Entrance requirements:* For master's, minimum undergraduate GPA of 3.0 during previous 2 years or 2.75 overall. Additional exam requirements/recommendations for international students: Required—TOEFL (minimum score 550 paper-based; 213 computer-based), TWE (minimum score 4). Electronic applications accepted.

Michigan State University, The Graduate School, College of Arts and Letters, Department of Philosophy, East Lansing, MI 48824. Offers MA, PhD. *Entrance requirements:* Additional exam requirements/recommendations for international students: Required—TOEFL. Electronic applications accepted.

Montclair State University, The Office of Graduate Admissions and Support Services, College of Education and Human Services, Center of Pedagogy, Montclair, NJ 07043-1624. Offers mathematics education (Ed D); philosophy for children (Ed D). Part-time programs available. *Students:* 6 full-time (3 women), 15 part-time (9 women); includes 2 African Americans, 1 Asian American or Pacific Islander, 4 international. Average age 40. 8 applicants, 38% accepted, 1 enrolled. In 2008, 1 doctorate awarded. *Degree requirements:* For doctorate, thesis/dissertation. *Entrance requirements:* For doctorate, GRE, 3 letters of recommendation. Additional exam requirements/recommendations for international students: Required—TOEFL (minimum score 117 computer-based). *Application deadline:* For fall admission, 2/1 for domestic students, 11/15 for international students. Application fee: $60. Electronic applications accepted. *Financial support:* In 2008–09, 1 research assistantship with full tuition reimbursement (averaging $7,000 per year) was awarded; institutionally sponsored loans and scholarships/grants also available. Financial award application deadline: 3/1; financial award applicants required to submit FAFSA. *Unit head:* Jennifer Robinson, Director, 973-655-4262. *Application contact:* Amy Aiello, Associate Director of Admissions, 973-655-5147, Fax: 973-655-7869, E-mail: graduate.school@montclair.edu.

Montclair State University, The Office of Graduate Admissions and Support Services, College of Education and Human Services, Department of Educational Foundations, Montclair, NJ 07043-1624. Offers critical thinking (M Ed); philosophy for children (M Ed, Ed D, Certificate). Part-time and evening/weekend programs available. *Faculty:* 9 full-time (3 women), 13 part-time/adjunct (6 women). *Students:* 7 part-time (all women); includes 1 minority (Hispanic American). Average age 38. In 2008, 28 master's awarded. *Degree requirements:* For master's, comprehensive exam, field experience; for doctorate, comprehensive exam, thesis/dissertation. *Entrance requirements:* For master's, GRE or MAT, minimum GPA of 2.67, 2 letters of recommendation, teaching certificate; for doctorate, GRE General Test, 3 years of classroom teaching experience, interview, writing sample. Additional exam requirements/recommendations for international students: Required—TOEFL (minimum score 117 computer-based). *Application deadline:* For fall admission, 2/1 for domestic students, 2/15 for international students; for spring admission, 10/15 for domestic and international students. Applications are processed on a rolling basis. Application fee: $60. Electronic applications accepted. *Financial support:* In 2008–09, 2 research assistantships with full tuition reimbursements (averaging $7,000 per year) were awarded; Federal Work-Study and scholarships/grants also available. Support available to part-time students. Financial award application deadline: 3/1; financial award applicants required to submit FAFSA. *Unit head:* Dr. Jeremy Price, Chairperson, 973-655-7039. *Application contact:* Amy Aiello, Associate Director of Admissions, 973-655-5147, Fax: 973-655-7869, E-mail: graduate.school@montclair.edu.

The New School: A University, The New School for Social Research, Department of Philosophy, New York, NY 10011. Offers MA, DS Sc, PhD. Part-time and evening/weekend programs available. *Faculty:* 11 full-time (3 women), 3 part-time/adjunct (0 women). *Students:* 143 full-time (45 women), 51 part-time (12 women); includes 19 minority (6 African Americans, 4 Asian Americans or Pacific Islanders, 9 Hispanic Americans), 45 international. Average age 31. In 2008, 21 master's, 7 doctorates awarded. Terminal master's awarded for partial completion of doctoral program. *Degree requirements:* For master's, one foreign language, exam or thesis; for doctorate, 2 foreign languages, thesis/dissertation, qualifying exam. *Entrance requirements:* For master's, GRE General Test; for doctorate, GRE General Test, MA. Additional exam requirements/recommendations for international students: Required—TOEFL (minimum score 600 paper-based; 250 computer-based). *Application deadline:* For fall admission, 1/15 priority date for domestic students. Applications are processed on a rolling basis. Application fee: $50. *Expenses:* Tuition: Full-time $27,144; part-time $1508 per credit. Required fees: $355 per semester. *Financial support:* Fellowships, research assistantships, teaching assistantships, career-related internships or fieldwork, Federal Work-Study, scholarships/grants, and tuition waivers (full and partial) available. Financial award application deadline: 3/1; financial award applicants required to submit FAFSA. *Faculty research:* Continental philosophy, history of philosophy, political philosophy, aesthetics, pragmatism. *Unit head:* Dr. Simon Critchley, Chair, 212-229-5707, E-mail: critchls@newschool.edu. *Application contact:* Robert MacDonald, Director of Admissions, 800-523-5710 Ext. 3007, Fax: 212-989-7102, E-mail: macdonar@newschool.edu.

See Close-Up on page 1251.

New York University, Graduate School of Arts and Science, Department of Philosophy, New York, NY 10012-1019. Offers MA, PhD, JD/MA, JD/PhD, MD/MA. Part-time programs available. *Degree requirements:* For master's, thesis or alternative; for doctorate, one foreign language,

thesis/dissertation. *Entrance requirements:* For master's and doctorate, GRE General Test, sample of written work. Additional exam requirements/recommendations for international students: Required—TOEFL. *Faculty research:* Philosophy of mind and language, metaphysics, ethics and political philosophy.

Northern Illinois University, Graduate School, College of Liberal Arts and Sciences, Department of Philosophy, De Kalb, IL 60115-2854. Offers MA. Part-time programs available. *Degree requirements:* For master's, comprehensive exam, thesis optional. *Entrance requirements:* For master's, GRE General Test, minimum GPA of 2.75, writing sample, major or minor in philosophy. Additional exam requirements/recommendations for international students: Required—TOEFL (minimum score 550 paper-based; 213 computer-based). Electronic applications accepted. *Faculty research:* Epistemology, philosophy of biology, animal rights, philosophy of war, international ethics.

Northwestern University, The Graduate School, Judd A. and Marjorie Weinberg College of Arts and Sciences, Department of Philosophy, Evanston, IL 60208. Offers PhD. Admissions and degrees offered through The Graduate School. *Degree requirements:* For doctorate, 2 foreign languages, thesis/dissertation. *Entrance requirements:* For doctorate, GRE General Test, sample of written work. Additional exam requirements/recommendations for international students: Required—TOEFL. Electronic applications accepted. *Faculty research:* Phenomenology, philosophy of science, history of philosophy, ethics, social and political philosophy, epistemology.

The Ohio State University, Graduate School, College of Humanities, Department of Philosophy, Columbus, OH 43210. Offers MA, PhD. *Degree requirements:* For master's, thesis optional; for doctorate, thesis/dissertation. *Entrance requirements:* For master's and doctorate, GRE General Test. Additional exam requirements/recommendations for international students: Required—TOEFL (minimum score 600 paper-based; 250 computer-based). Electronic applications accepted.

Ohio University, Graduate College, College of Arts and Sciences, Department of Philosophy, Athens, OH 45701-2979. Offers MA. Part-time programs available. *Degree requirements:* For master's, thesis. *Entrance requirements:* For master's, GRE, 28 hours. in philosophy including logic, ancient and modern; minimum GPA of 3.0. Additional exam requirements/recommendations for international students: Required—TOEFL. *Faculty research:* Ethics, phenomenology, applied ethics, Aristotle, Kant, epistemology.

Oklahoma City University, Petree College of Arts and Sciences, Program in Liberal Arts, Oklahoma City, OK 73106-1402. Offers art (MLA); general studies (MLA); leadership/management (MLA); literature (MLA); mass communications (MLA); philosophy (MLA); writing (MLA). Part-time and evening/weekend programs available. *Degree requirements:* For master's, comprehensive exam, thesis optional. *Entrance requirements:* Additional exam requirements/recommendations for international students: Required—TOEFL.

Oklahoma State University, College of Arts and Sciences, Department of Philosophy, Stillwater, OK 74078. Offers MA. *Faculty:* 15 full-time (7 women), 3 part-time/adjunct (0 women). *Students:* 6 full-time (2 women), 10 part-time (2 women); includes 3 minority (2 African Americans, 1 American Indian/Alaska Native), 1 international. Average age 29. 15 applicants, 67% accepted, 7 enrolled. In 2008, 6 master's awarded. *Degree requirements:* For master's, comprehensive exam, thesis. *Entrance requirements:* For master's, GRE, 2 letters of recommendation. Additional exam requirements/recommendations for international students: Required—TOEFL. *Application deadline:* For fall admission, 3/1 priority date for international students; for spring admission, 8/1 priority date for international students. Applications are processed on a rolling basis. Application fee: $40 ($75 for international students). Electronic applications accepted. *Expenses:* Tuition, state resident: full-time $3716.40; part-time $154.85 per credit hour. Tuition, nonresident: full-time $14,448; part-time $602 per credit hour. Required fees: $1772.40; $73.85 per credit hour. One-time fee: $50. Tuition and fees vary according to course load and campus/location. *Financial support:* In 2008–09, 9 teaching assistantships (averaging $12,706 per year) were awarded; career-related internships or fieldwork, Federal Work-Study, scholarships/grants, health care benefits, tuition waivers (partial), and unspecified assistantships also available. Support available to part-time students. Financial award application deadline: 3/1; financial award applicants required to submit FAFSA. *Faculty research:* Theoretical and applied ethics, history and philosophy of science, east/west comparative philosophy, social/political/legal philosophy, truth and theory of knowledge. *Unit head:* Dr. Doren Recker, Head, 405-744-0487, Fax: 405-744-4635. *Application contact:* Dr. Gordon Emslie, Dean, 405-744-6368, Fax: 405-744-0355, E-mail: grad_i@okstate.edu.

Oregon State University, Graduate School, College of Liberal Arts, Department of Philosophy, Corvallis, OR 97331.

Penn State University Park, Graduate School, College of the Liberal Arts, Department of Philosophy, State College, University Park, PA 16802-1503. Offers classical American philosophy (MA, PhD); contemporary European philosophy (MA, PhD); history of philosophy (MA, PhD).

Princeton University, Graduate School, Department of Classics, Princeton, NJ 08544-1019. Offers classical and hellenic studies (PhD); classical philosophy (PhD); history (the ancient world) (PhD); literature and philology (PhD). *Degree requirements:* For doctorate, thesis/dissertation. *Entrance requirements:* For doctorate, GRE General Test, sample of written work. Additional exam requirements/recommendations for international students: Required—TOEFL (minimum score 600 paper-based; 250 computer-based). Electronic applications accepted.

Princeton University, Graduate School, Department of Philosophy, Princeton, NJ 08544-1019. Offers classical philosophy (PhD); philosophy (PhD); philosophy of science (PhD). *Degree requirements:* For doctorate, variable foreign language requirement, thesis/dissertation. *Entrance requirements:* For doctorate, GRE General Test, sample of written work. Additional exam requirements/recommendations for international students: Required—TOEFL (minimum score 600 paper-based; 250 computer-based). Electronic applications accepted.

Princeton University, Graduate School, Department of Politics, Princeton, NJ 08544-1019. Offers political philosophy (PhD); politics (PhD). *Degree requirements:* For doctorate, comprehensive exam, thesis/dissertation, teaching experience. *Entrance requirements:* For doctorate, GRE General Test, sample of written work, letters of recommendation. Additional exam requirements/recommendations for international students: Required—TOEFL (minimum score 600 paper-based; 250 computer-based). Electronic applications accepted. *Faculty research:* American politics, comparative politics, formal and quantitative methods, international relations, public law, political theory.

Purdue University, Graduate School, College of Liberal Arts, Department of Philosophy, West Lafayette, IN 47907. Offers MA, PhD. Part-time programs available. Terminal master's awarded for partial completion of doctoral program. *Degree requirements:* For master's, thesis optional; for doctorate, one foreign language, thesis/dissertation. *Entrance requirements:* For master's and doctorate, GRE General Test. Additional exam requirements/recommendations for international students: Required—TOEFL. Electronic applications accepted. *Faculty research:* Continental philosophy, ethics and social philosophy, analytic philosophy, history of philosophy, logic.

Queen's University at Kingston, School of Graduate Studies and Research, Faculty of Arts and Sciences, Department of Philosophy, Kingston, ON K7L 3N6, Canada. Offers MA, PhD. Part-time programs available. *Degree requirements:* For master's, thesis; for doctorate, comprehensive exam, thesis/dissertation. *Entrance requirements:* Additional exam requirements/recommendations for international students: Required—TOEFL. Electronic applications accepted. *Faculty research:* Ethics, social and political philosophy, philosophy of language, epistemology, metaphysics.

Rice University, Graduate Programs, School of Humanities, Department of Philosophy, Houston, TX 77251-1892. Offers MA, PhD. *Degree requirements:* For master's, one foreign language,

Philosophy

Rice University (continued)
thesis; for doctorate, one foreign language, thesis/dissertation. *Entrance requirements:* For master's and doctorate, GRE General Test, minimum GPA of 3.0. Additional exam requirements/recommendations for international students: Required—TOEFL (minimum score 600 paper-based; 250 computer-based; 90 iBT). Electronic applications accepted. *Faculty research:* Metaphysics, philosophy of law, philosophy of science, medical ethics, philosophy of language.

Rutgers, The State University of New Jersey, New Brunswick, Graduate School, Program in Philosophy, Piscataway, NJ 08854-8097. Offers PhD. *Degree requirements:* For doctorate, comprehensive exam, thesis/dissertation. *Entrance requirements:* For doctorate, GRE General Test, writing sample. Electronic applications accepted. *Faculty research:* Philosophy of mind, epistemology, philosophy of language, philosophy of science, metaphysics.

St. John's University, St. John's College of Liberal Arts and Sciences, Department of Philosophy, Queens, NY 11439. Offers MA. Part-time and evening/weekend programs available. *Entrance requirements:* Additional exam requirements/recommendations for international students: Required—TOEFL (minimum score 500 paper-based; 173 computer-based; 61 iBT), IELTS (minimum score 5.5). *Application deadline:* For fall admission, 5/1 priority date for domestic and international students; for spring admission, 11/1 priority date for domestic and international students. *Expenses:* Tuition: Full-time $20,760; part-time $865 per credit. Required fees: $300; $150 per semester. Tuition and fees vary according to program. *Financial support:* Career-related internships or fieldwork and scholarships/grants available. Support available to part-time students. *Unit head:* Dr. Paul Gaffney, Chair, 718-990-5256. *Application contact:* Kathleen Davis, Director of Graduate Admission, 718-990-2790, Fax: 718-990-5686, E-mail: gradhelp@stjohns.edu.

Saint Louis University, Graduate School, College of Arts and Sciences and Graduate School, Department of Philosophy, St. Louis, MO 63103-2097. Offers MA, MA-R, PhD. Part-time programs available. *Degree requirements:* For master's, one foreign language, thesis, comprehensive oral and written exams; for doctorate, 2 foreign languages, thesis/dissertation, preliminary exams, comprehensive oral and written exams. *Entrance requirements:* For master's and doctorate, GRE General Test, letters of recommendation, resumé, writing sample, interview, goal statement, transcripts. Additional exam requirements/recommendations for international students: Required—TOEFL (minimum score 550 paper-based; 213 computer-based). Electronic applications accepted. *Faculty research:* Medieval philosophy, philosophy of religion, political philosophy, ethics, epistemology.

Saint Mary's University, Faculty of Arts, Department of Philosophy, Halifax, NS B3H 3C3, Canada. Offers MA. *Degree requirements:* For master's, thesis. *Entrance requirements:* For master's, GRE, honors degree, minimum B+ average. Additional exam requirements/recommendations for international students: Required—TOEFL. *Faculty research:* History of philosophy, analytic philosophy, ethics, social philosophy, logic.

San Diego State University, Graduate and Research Affairs, College of Arts and Letters, Department of Philosophy, San Diego, CA 92182. Offers MA. Part-time programs available. *Entrance requirements:* For master's, GRE General Test. Additional exam requirements/recommendations for international students: Required—TOEFL. Electronic applications accepted. *Faculty research:* Ancient philosophy, modern philosophy, philosophy of technology, logic, philosophy of mind.

San Francisco State University, Division of Graduate Studies, College of Humanities, Department of Philosophy, San Francisco, CA 94132-1722. Offers philosophy (MA); teaching critical thinking (Certificate). Part-time programs available.

San Jose State University, Graduate Studies and Research, College of Humanities and the Arts, Department of Philosophy, San Jose, CA 95192-0001. Offers MA, Certificate. *Degree requirements:* For master's, one foreign language, thesis or alternative. Electronic applications accepted.

Simon Fraser University, Graduate Studies, Faculty of Arts and Social Sciences, Department of Philosophy, Burnaby, BC V5A 1S6, Canada. Offers MA, PhD. Terminal master's awarded for partial completion of doctoral program. *Degree requirements:* For master's, thesis or alternative; for doctorate, thesis/dissertation. *Entrance requirements:* For master's, minimum GPA of 3.33; for doctorate, minimum GPA of 3.67. Additional exam requirements/recommendations for international students: Required—TOEFL or IELTS. Electronic applications accepted. *Faculty research:* Epistemology, philosophy of mind, philosophy of science, value theory, logic.

Southeastern Baptist Theological Seminary, Graduate and Professional Programs, Wake Forest, NC 27588-1889. Offers advanced biblical studies (M Div); Christian education (M Div, MACE); Christian ethics (PhD); Christian ministry (M Div); Christian planting (M Div); church music (MACM); counseling (MACO); evangelism (PhD); language (M Div); ministry (D Min); New Testament (PhD); Old Testament (PhD); philosophy (PhD); theology (Th M, PhD); women's studies (M Div). *Accreditation:* ACIPE; ATS (one or more programs are accredited). *Degree requirements:* For master's, thesis (for some programs), oral exam; for doctorate, thesis/dissertation, fieldwork; for M Div, supervised ministry. *Entrance requirements:* For master's, Cooperative English Test, minimum GPA of 2.0, M Div or equivalent (Th M); for doctorate, GRE General Test or MAT, Cooperative English Test, M Div or equivalent, 3 years of professional experience.

Southern Baptist Theological Seminary, School of Theology, Louisville, KY 40280-0004. Offers biblical and theological studies (M Div); biblical counseling (M Div, MA, D Min); biblical spirituality (D Min); Christian ministry (M Div); expository preaching (D Min); pastoral studies (M Div); theological studies (MA); theology (Th M, PhD); theology and arts (MA); theology and law (MA); worldview and apologetics (M Div). *Accreditation:* ATS. Part-time and evening/weekend programs available. Postbaccalaureate distance learning degree programs offered (minimal on-campus study). *Degree requirements:* For master's, 2 foreign languages, thesis; for doctorate, 4 foreign languages, thesis/dissertation; for M Div, 2 foreign languages. *Entrance requirements:* For master's, GRE General Test, MAT, M Div; for doctorate, GRE General Test, MAT, interview, M Div, field essay. Additional exam requirements/recommendations for international students: Required—TOEFL, TWE. *Faculty research:* Biblical studies, contemporary theology, church history, pastoral care, ministry/missions studies.

Southern Evangelical Seminary, Veritas Graduate School of Apologetics and Counter-Cult Ministry, Matthews, NC 28105. Offers apologetics (MA, D Min, PhD, Certificate); Islamic studies (MA); Jewish studies (MA); philosophy (MA); religion (MA). *Accreditation:* ATS. Part-time and evening/weekend programs available. Postbaccalaureate distance learning degree programs offered (minimal on-campus study). *Degree requirements:* For master's, thesis optional; for doctorate, comprehensive exam (for some programs), thesis/dissertation. *Entrance requirements:* Additional exam requirements/recommendations for international students: Required—TOEFL (minimum score 600 paper-based; 250 computer-based).

Southern Illinois University Carbondale, Graduate School, College of Liberal Arts, Department of Philosophy, Carbondale, IL 62901-4701. Offers MA, PhD. *Degree requirements:* For master's, one foreign language, thesis; for doctorate, 2 foreign languages, thesis/dissertation. *Entrance requirements:* For master's, GRE General Test, minimum GPA of 2.7; for doctorate, GRE General Test, minimum GPA of 3.25. Additional exam requirements/recommendations for international students: Required—TOEFL. *Faculty research:* Continental philosophy, American philosophy, philosophy of mind, Asian philosophy.

See Close-Up on page 479.

Stanford University, School of Humanities and Sciences, Department of Philosophy, Stanford, CA 94305-9991. Offers MA, PhD. Terminal master's awarded for partial completion of doctoral program. *Degree requirements:* For master's, oral exam; for doctorate, thesis/dissertation, oral exam. *Entrance requirements:* For master's and doctorate, GRE General Test. Additional exam requirements/recommendations for international students: Required—TOEFL. Electronic applications accepted.

State University of New York at Binghamton, Graduate School, School of Arts and Sciences, Department of Philosophy, Binghamton, NY 13902-6000. Offers MA, PhD. *Faculty:* 14 full-time (4 women), 4 part-time/adjunct (0 women). *Students:* 2 full-time (0 women); includes 1 minority (African American). Average age 28. 9 applicants, 22% accepted, 2 enrolled. In 2008, 5 master's awarded. *Degree requirements:* For master's, 2 foreign languages, thesis or alternative; for doctorate, thesis/dissertation. *Entrance requirements:* For master's and doctorate, GRE General Test, GRE Subject Test. Additional exam requirements/recommendations for international students: Required—TOEFL. *Application deadline:* For fall admission, 4/15 priority date for domestic students, 1/15 priority date for international students; for spring admission, 11/1 for domestic students, 10/1 priority date for international students. Applications are processed on a rolling basis. Application fee: $60. Electronic applications accepted. *Expenses:* Tuition, area resident: Full-time $6900; part-time $288 per credit. Tuition, state resident: full-time $6900; part-time $288 per credit. Tuition, nonresident: full-time $10,920; part-time $455 per credit. Required fees: $1130. Part-time tuition and fees vary according to course load, program and student level. *Financial support:* In 2008–09, 36 students received support, including 10 fellowships with full tuition reimbursements available (averaging $14,500 per year), 22 teaching assistantships with full tuition reimbursements available (averaging $14,500 per year); research assistantships, career-related internships or fieldwork, Federal Work-Study, institutionally sponsored loans, scholarships/grants, health care benefits, and unspecified assistantships also available. Financial award application deadline: 2/15; financial award applicants required to submit FAFSA. *Unit head:* Dr. Bat-Ami Bar-On, Chairperson, 607-777-6198, E-mail: ami@binghamton.edu. *Application contact:* Victoria Williams, Recruiting and Admissions Coordinator, 607-777-2151, Fax: 607-777-2501, E-mail: vwilliam@binghamton.edu.

State University of New York at Binghamton, Graduate School, School of Arts and Sciences, Philosophy, Interpretation and Culture Program, Binghamton, NY 13902-6000. Offers MA, PhD. *Students:* 21 full-time (11 women), 32 part-time (13 women); includes 15 minority (7 African Americans, 2 Asian Americans or Pacific Islanders, 6 Hispanic Americans), 18 international. Average age 35. 40 applicants, 53% accepted, 10 enrolled. In 2008, 3 master's, 6 doctorates awarded. Application fee: $60. *Expenses:* Tuition, area resident: Full-time $6900; part-time $288 per credit. Tuition, state resident: full-time $6900; part-time $288 per credit. Tuition, nonresident: full-time $10,920; part-time $455 per credit. Required fees: $1130. Part-time tuition and fees vary according to course load, program and student level. *Financial support:* In 2008–09, 10 students received support, including 8 teaching assistantships with full tuition reimbursements available (averaging $14,500 per year); career-related internships or fieldwork, Federal Work-Study, institutionally sponsored loans, scholarships/grants, health care benefits, and unspecified assistantships also available. Financial award application deadline: 2/15; financial award applicants required to submit FAFSA. *Unit head:* Dr. William Haver, Director, 607-777-3827. *Application contact:* Victoria Williams, Recruiting and Admissions Coordinator, 607-777-2151, Fax: 607-777-2501, E-mail: vwilliam@binghamton.edu.

State University of New York at Binghamton, Graduate School, School of Arts and Sciences, Program in Social, Political, Ethical and Legal Philosophy, Binghamton, NY 13902-6000. Offers MA, PhD. *Students:* 19 full-time (8 women), 12 part-time (4 women); includes 5 minority (2 African Americans, 2 Asian Americans or Pacific Islanders, 1 Hispanic American), 6 international. Average age 29. 53 applicants, 34% accepted, 5 enrolled. In 2008, 2 master's, 1 doctorate awarded. Application fee: $60. *Expenses:* Tuition, area resident: Full-time $6900; part-time $288 per credit. Tuition, state resident: full-time $6900; part-time $288 per credit. Tuition, nonresident: full-time $10,920; part-time $455 per credit. Required fees: $1130. Part-time tuition and fees vary according to course load, program and student level. *Unit head:* Dr. Bat-Ami Bar-On, Chairperson, 607-777-6198, E-mail: ami@binghamton.edu. *Application contact:* Victoria Williams, Recruiting and Admissions Coordinator, 607-777-2151, Fax: 607-777-2501, E-mail: vwilliam@binghamton.edu.

Stony Brook University, State University of New York, Graduate School, College of Arts and Sciences, Department of Philosophy, Stony Brook, NY 11794. Offers MA, PhD. Evening/weekend programs available. *Faculty:* 23 full-time (6 women). *Students:* 94 full-time (35 women), 14 part-time (5 women); includes 15 minority (2 African Americans, 1 American Indian/Alaska Native, 2 Asian Americans or Pacific Islanders, 10 Hispanic Americans), 17 international. Average age 29. 254 applicants, 19% accepted. In 2008, 23 master's, 9 doctorates awarded. *Degree requirements:* For doctorate, one foreign language, thesis/dissertation. *Entrance requirements:* For master's and doctorate, GRE General Test. Additional exam requirements/recommendations for international students: Required—TOEFL. *Application deadline:* For fall admission, 1/15 for domestic students. Application fee: $60. *Expenses:* Tuition, area resident: Full-time $7880; part-time $328 per credit hour. Tuition, state resident: full-time $7880; part-time $328 per credit hour. Tuition, nonresident: full-time $13,250; part-time $552 per credit hour. Required fees: $848. *Financial support:* In 2008–09, 42 teaching assistantships were awarded; fellowships, research assistantships also available. *Faculty research:* Philosophy of science, philosophy of language, analytical philosophy, phenomenology, structuralism. *Unit head:* Dr. Robert Crease, Chair, 631-632-7590, Fax: 631-632-7522. *Application contact:* Dr. Harvey Cormier, Director of Graduate Studies, 631-632-7312, Fax: 631-632-7522, E-mail: harvey.cormier@notes.cc.sunysb.edu.

Syracuse University, Graduate School, College of Arts and Sciences, Program in Philosophy, Syracuse, NY 13244. Offers MA, PhD. Part-time and evening/weekend programs available. Terminal master's awarded for partial completion of doctoral program. *Degree requirements:* For master's, thesis or alternative; for doctorate, thesis/dissertation. *Entrance requirements:* For master's and doctorate, GRE Writing Test, writing sample. Additional exam requirements/recommendations for international students: Required—TOEFL. Electronic applications accepted. *Faculty research:* Ethics, metaphysics, epistemology, philosophy of language.

Temple University, Graduate School, College of Liberal Arts, Department of Philosophy, Philadelphia, PA 19122-6096. Offers MA, PhD. Part-time programs available. Terminal master's awarded for partial completion of doctoral program. *Degree requirements:* For master's, thesis or alternative; for doctorate, one foreign language, thesis/dissertation. *Entrance requirements:* For master's and doctorate, GRE General Test. Additional exam requirements/recommendations for international students: Required—TOEFL (minimum score 550 paper-based; 213 computer-based; 79 iBT). Electronic applications accepted. *Faculty research:* Philosophy of mind, aesthetics, philosophy of science, nineteenth century German philosophy, phenomenology.

Texas A&M University, College of Liberal Arts, Department of Philosophy and Humanities, College Station, TX 77843. Offers philosophy (MA, PhD). Part-time programs available. *Faculty:* 9. *Students:* 24 full-time (5 women), 4 part-time (1 woman); includes 4 minority (1 American Indian/Alaska Native, 3 Hispanic Americans). Average age 27. In 2008, 11 master's, 2 doctorates awarded. Terminal master's awarded for partial completion of doctoral program. *Degree requirements:* For master's, thesis optional; for doctorate, comprehensive exam, thesis/dissertation. *Entrance requirements:* For master's, GRE General Test, letter of recommendation, resumé, writing sample; for doctorate, GRE General Test, letters of recommendation, resumé, writing sample. *Application deadline:* For fall admission, 1/15 for domestic students, 3/1 for international students; for winter admission, 8/1 for international students; for spring admission, 10/15 priority date for domestic students. Application fee: $50 ($75 for international students). Electronic applications accepted. *Expenses:* Tuition, area resident: Full-time $3838.50. Tuition, state resident: full-time $3838.50. Tuition, nonresident: full-time $8897. Required fees: $2359.60. *Financial support:* In 2008–09, fellowships with partial tuition reimbursements (averaging $16,000 per year), research assistantships with partial tuition reimbursements (averaging $15,000 per year), teaching assistantships with partial tuition reimbursements (averaging $9,000 per year) were awarded; career-related internships or fieldwork, institutionally sponsored loans, scholarships/grants, and unspecified assistantships also available. Financial award application deadline: 1/15; financial award applicants required to submit FAFSA. *Faculty research:* American philosophy, applied ethics, philosophy of mind, philosophy of religion, history and philosophy of logic. *Unit head:* Dr. Daniel Conway, Head, 979-845-5696, E-mail: conway@tamu.edu. *Application contact:* Dr., Graduate Advisor, 979-845-7133, E-mail: philstaff@www-phil.tamu.edu.

Texas Tech University, Graduate School, College of Arts and Sciences, Department of Philosophy, Lubbock, TX 79409. Offers MA. Part-time programs available. *Faculty:* 9 full-time (2 women). *Students:* 15 full-time (2 women), 3 part-time (2 women); includes 2 minority (1 African American, 1 Hispanic American), 3 international. Average age 28. 27 applicants, 63% accepted, 7 enrolled. In 2008, 7 master's awarded. *Degree requirements:* For master's, thesis or alternative. *Entrance requirements:* For master's, GRE General Test. Additional exam requirements/recommendations for international students: Required—TOEFL (minimum score 550 paper-based; 213 computer-based). *Application deadline:* For fall admission, 3/1 priority date for international students; for spring admission, 11/1 priority date for international students. Applications are processed on a rolling basis. Application fee: $50 ($60 for international students). Electronic applications accepted. *Expenses:* Tuition, area resident: Part-time $194 per credit hour. Tuition, state resident: full-time $4648; part-time $194 per credit hour. Tuition, nonresident: full-time $11,392; part-time $475 per credit hour. Required fees: $2206; $69 per credit hour. $389 per semester. *Financial support:* In 2008–09, 15 students received support, including 14 teaching assistantships with partial tuition reimbursements available (averaging $11,150 per year); research assistantships with partial tuition reimbursements available, Federal Work-Study and institutionally sponsored loans also available. Support available to part-time students. Financial award application deadline: 4/15; financial award applicants required to submit FAFSA. *Faculty research:* Aesthetics, ethics, history of philosophy, philosophy of mind, philosophy of science. Total annual research expenditures: $50,734. *Unit head:* Dr. Peder G. Christiansen, Chair, 806-742-3275 Ext. 323, Fax: 806-742-0730, E-mail: peder.christiansen@ttu.edu. *Application contact:* Dr. Daniel O. Nathan, Director of Graduate Studies, 806-742-0373 Ext. 340, Fax: 806-742-0730, E-mail: daniel.nathan@ttu.edu.

Trinity Western University, Faculty of Graduate Studies, Program in Interdisciplinary Humanities, Langley, BC V2Y 1Y1, Canada. Offers general humanities (MAIH); specialized (MAIH), including English, history, philosophy. Part-time and evening/weekend programs available. Postbaccalaureate distance learning degree programs offered (minimal on-campus study). *Degree requirements:* For master's, 36 semester hours. *Entrance requirements:* For master's, strong undergraduate degree in Humanities or English, History or Philosophy. *Faculty research:* Literary theory, gender, medieval and early modern literature, philosophy of religion, Thomas Merton's poetics.

Tufts University, Graduate School of Arts and Sciences, Department of Philosophy, Medford, MA 02155. Offers MA. *Degree requirements:* For master's, one foreign language, comprehensive exam, departmental qualifying exam. *Entrance requirements:* For master's, GRE General Test, writing sample. Additional exam requirements/recommendations for international students: Required—TOEFL (minimum score 550 paper-based; 213 computer-based; 80 iBT). Electronic applications accepted.

Tulane University, School of Liberal Arts, Department of Philosophy, New Orleans, LA 70118-5669. Offers MA, PhD. *Degree requirements:* For master's, thesis or alternative; for doctorate, one foreign language, thesis/dissertation. *Entrance requirements:* For master's, GRE General Test, minimum B average in undergraduate course work; for doctorate, GRE General Test. Additional exam requirements/recommendations for international students: Required—TOEFL. Electronic applications accepted.

Universidad Autonoma de Guadalajara, Graduate Programs, Guadalajara, Mexico. Offers advertising and corporate communications (MA); architecture (M Arch); business (MBA); computational science (MCC); education (Ed M, Ed D); English-Spanish translation (MA); fiscal law (MA); international business (MIB); international corporate law (LL M); internet technologies (MS); labor health (MS); manufacturing systems (MMS); market research (MBA); philosophy (MA, PhD); quality systems (MQS); renewable energy (MS); teaching mathematics (MA).

Université de Montréal, Faculty of Arts and Sciences, Department of Philosophy, Montréal, QC H3C 3J7, Canada. Offers MA, PhD. *Faculty:* 29 full-time (4 women), 5 part-time/adjunct (1 woman). *Students:* 52 full-time (16 women), 134 part-time (37 women). 70 applicants, 60% accepted, 37 enrolled. In 2008, 33 master's, 1 doctorate awarded. *Degree requirements:* For master's, 2 foreign languages, thesis; for doctorate, thesis/dissertation, general exam. *Application deadline:* For fall admission, 2/1 priority date for domestic students; for winter admission, 11/1 priority date for domestic students; for spring admission, 2/1 priority date for domestic students. Application fee: $100. Electronic applications accepted. *Financial support:* Fellowships, teaching assistantships available. Support available to part-time students. *Faculty research:* Ancient and modern philosophy; logic and philosophy of language, ethics, and politics; contemporary Continental philosophy. *Unit head:* Daniel Dumouchel, Director, 514-343-7693, Fax: 514-343-7899, E-mail: daniel.dumouchel@umontreal.ca. *Application contact:* Frederic Bouchard, Responsible for Graduate Studies, 514-343-6848, Fax: 514-343-7899, E-mail: f.bouchard@umontreal.ca.

Université de Sherbrooke, Faculty of Letters and Human Sciences, Department of Human Sciences, Sherbrooke, QC J1K 2R1, Canada. Offers history (MA); philosophy (MA). *Degree requirements:* For master's, thesis. *Entrance requirements:* For master's, minimum GPA of 2.75. *Faculty research:* Political, social, and urban history; history of women.

Université de Sherbrooke, Faculty of Theology, Ethics and Philosophy, Sherbrooke, QC J1K 2R1, Canada. Offers applied ethics (Diploma); human science of religions (MA); intercultural training (Diploma); philosophy (MA, PhD); spiritual anthropology (Diploma); theology (MA, PhD, Diploma). Part-time and evening/weekend programs available. Postbaccalaureate distance learning degree programs offered. Terminal master's awarded for partial completion of doctoral program. *Entrance requirements:* For master's, bachelor's degree in related discipline; for doctorate, master's degree in related discipline. *Faculty research:* Faith and culture interrelation.

Université du Québec à Montréal, Graduate Programs, Program in Philosophy, Montréal, QC H3C 3P8, Canada. Offers MA, PhD. Part-time programs available. *Degree requirements:* For master's, thesis; for doctorate, thesis/dissertation. *Entrance requirements:* For master's, appropriate bachelor's degree or equivalent, proficiency in French; for doctorate, appropriate master's degree or equivalent, proficiency in French.

Université du Québec à Trois-Rivières, Graduate Programs, Program in Philosophy, Trois-Rivières, QC G9A 5H7, Canada. Offers MA, PhD. Part-time programs available. *Degree requirements:* For master's, thesis; for doctorate, thesis/dissertation. *Entrance requirements:* For master's, appropriate bachelor's degree, proficiency in French; for doctorate, appropriate master's degree, proficiency in French.

Université Laval, Faculty of Philosophy, Programs in Philosophy, Québec, QC G1K 7P4, Canada. Offers MA, PhD. Terminal master's awarded for partial completion of doctoral program. *Degree requirements:* For master's, thesis; for doctorate, comprehensive exam, thesis/dissertation. *Entrance requirements:* For master's and doctorate, French exam. Electronic applications accepted.

University at Albany, State University of New York, College of Arts and Sciences, Department of Philosophy, Albany, NY 12222-0001. Offers MA, PhD. *Degree requirements:* For master's, one foreign language, thesis; for doctorate, thesis/dissertation. *Entrance requirements:* For master's and doctorate, GRE General Test. Additional exam requirements/recommendations for international students: Required—TOEFL (minimum score 550 paper-based; 213 computer-based). Electronic applications accepted. *Faculty research:* Philosophical logic, ethics, ancient philosophy/metaphysics, aesthetics, biomedical ethics.

University at Buffalo, the State University of New York, Graduate School, College of Arts and Sciences, Department of Philosophy, Buffalo, NY 14260. Offers MA, PhD. Terminal master's awarded for partial completion of doctoral program. *Degree requirements:* For master's, variable foreign language requirement, thesis or alternative; for doctorate, variable foreign language requirement, comprehensive exam, thesis/dissertation. *Entrance requirements:* For master's, GRE General Test, minimum GPA of 2.67; for doctorate, GRE General Test, minimum GPA of 3.0. Additional exam requirements/recommendations for international students: Required—TOEFL (minimum score 550 paper-based; 213 computer-based). Electronic applications accepted. *Faculty research:* Logic, metaphysics (historical and contemporary), aesthetics, epistemology, ethics (historical and contemporary), ontology.

University of Alberta, Faculty of Graduate Studies and Research, Department of Philosophy, Edmonton, AB T6G 2E1, Canada. Offers MA, PhD. Part-time programs available. *Degree requirements:* For master's, thesis; for doctorate, thesis/dissertation. *Entrance requirements:* Additional exam requirements/recommendations for international students: Required—TOEFL (minimum score 550 paper-based; 213 computer-based). Electronic applications accepted. *Faculty research:* Philosophy of science, cognitive science, social and political philosophy, philosophy of language and logic, environmental aesthetics.

The University of Arizona, Graduate College, College of Social and Behavioral Sciences, Department of Philosophy, Tucson, AZ 85721. Offers MA, PhD, JD/PhD. Part-time programs available. Terminal master's awarded for partial completion of doctoral program. *Degree requirements:* For master's, exams, qualifying paper; for doctorate, thesis/dissertation, preliminary exams. *Entrance requirements:* For master's and doctorate, GRE General Test, 3 letters of recommendation, statement of purpose, writing sample. Additional exam requirements/recommendations for international students: Required—TOEFL (minimum score 550 paper-based). Electronic applications accepted. *Faculty research:* Law, social, and political philosophy; epistemology; philosophy of mind; cognitive science.

University of Arkansas, Graduate School, J. William Fulbright College of Arts and Sciences, Department of Philosophy, Fayetteville, AR 72701-1201. Offers MA, PhD. Part-time programs available. *Degree requirements:* For master's, thesis; for doctorate, 2 foreign languages, thesis/dissertation.

The University of British Columbia, Faculty of Arts and Faculty of Graduate Studies, Department of Philosophy, Vancouver, BC V6T 1Z1, Canada. Offers MA, PhD. *Accreditation:* NCATE. Part-time programs available. *Degree requirements:* For master's, thesis (for some programs); for doctorate, comprehensive exam, thesis/dissertation. *Entrance requirements:* For master's, honors BA or BA/BS with upper second class standing, minimum GPA of 3.3; for doctorate, MA or honors BA with first class standing, MA or BA with first class standing in philosophy. Additional exam requirements/recommendations for international students: Required—TOEFL (minimum score 550 paper-based; 213 computer-based; 80 iBT). Electronic applications accepted. *Faculty research:* Ethics and applied ethics, metaphysics and epistemology, history of philosophy, philosophy of science, philosophy of biology.

University of Calgary, Faculty of Graduate Studies, Faculty of Humanities, Department of Philosophy, Calgary, AB T2N 1N4, Canada. Offers MA, PhD. Part-time programs available. *Degree requirements:* For master's, comprehensive exam (for some programs), thesis (for some programs); for doctorate, thesis/dissertation, candidacy exam. *Entrance requirements:* Additional exam requirements/recommendations for international students: Required—TOEFL (minimum score 550 paper-based; 213 computer-based). Electronic applications accepted. *Faculty research:* Ethics and political philosophy, metaphysics, philosophy of mind, philosophy of language.

University of California, Berkeley, Graduate Division, College of Letters and Science, Department of Philosophy, Berkeley, CA 94720-1500. Offers PhD. *Degree requirements:* For doctorate, thesis/dissertation, qualifying exam. *Entrance requirements:* For doctorate, GRE General Test, minimum GPA of 3.0, writing sample, 3 letters of recommendation.

University of California, Davis, Graduate Studies, Program in Philosophy, Davis, CA 95616. Offers MA, PhD. Terminal master's awarded for partial completion of doctoral program. *Degree requirements:* For doctorate, thesis/dissertation. *Entrance requirements:* For master's and doctorate, GRE General Test, minimum GPA of 3.0. Additional exam requirements/recommendations for international students: Required—TOEFL (minimum score 550 paper-based; 213 computer-based). Electronic applications accepted. *Faculty research:* Moral and political philosophy, philosophy of language, metaphysics, philosophy of science, history of philosophy.

University of California, Irvine, Office of Graduate Studies, School of Humanities, Department of Philosophy, Irvine, CA 92697. Offers MA, PhD. *Degree requirements:* For master's, thesis; for doctorate, thesis/dissertation. *Entrance requirements:* For master's and doctorate, GRE General Test, minimum GPA of 3.0. Additional exam requirements/recommendations for international students: Required—TOEFL (minimum score 550 paper-based; 213 computer-based). Electronic applications accepted. *Faculty research:* Philosophy of action and decision theory, philosophy of language, philosophy of mathematics, virtue ethics, modern and contemporary Continental philosophy.

University of California, Irvine, Office of Graduate Studies, School of Social Sciences, Department of Logic and Philosophy of Science, Irvine, CA 92697. Offers philosophy (PhD). *Entrance requirements:* For doctorate, GRE, minimum GPA of 3.0. Additional exam requirements/recommendations for international students: Required—TOEFL (minimum score 550 paper-based; 213 computer-based).

University of California, Los Angeles, Graduate Division, College of Letters and Science, Department of Philosophy, Los Angeles, CA 90095. Offers MA, PhD. *Students:* 52 full-time (19 women); includes 5 minority (2 Asian Americans or Pacific Islanders, 3 Hispanic Americans), 3 international. Average age 28. 185 applicants, 6% accepted, 5 enrolled. In 2008, 9 master's, 5 doctorates awarded. Terminal master's awarded for partial completion of doctoral program. *Degree requirements:* For master's, one foreign language, comprehensive exam; for doctorate, one foreign language, thesis/dissertation, oral and written qualifying exams, teaching experience. *Entrance requirements:* For master's, GRE General Test, minimum GPA of 3.0, sample of written work, degree objective of Ph.D; for doctorate, GRE General Test, minimum undergraduate GPA of 3.0, sample of written work. Additional exam requirements/recommendations for international students: Required—TOEFL. *Application deadline:* For fall admission, 1/10 for domestic and international students. Application fee: $60 ($80 for international students). Electronic applications accepted. *Expenses:* Tuition, nonresident: full-time $14,694. Required fees: $9669.50. Full-time tuition and fees vary according to course load, degree level, program and student level. *Financial support:* In 2008–09, 55 fellowships with full and partial tuition reimbursements, 9 research assistantships with full and partial tuition reimbursements, 40 teaching assistantships with full and partial tuition reimbursements were awarded; Federal Work-Study, institutionally sponsored loans, scholarships/grants, health care benefits, tuition waivers (full and partial), and unspecified assistantships also available. Financial award application deadline: 3/1. *Unit head:* Dr. John Carriero, Chair, 310-206-3475. *Application contact:* Departmental Office, 310-206-1356, E-mail: alaven@humnet.ucla.edu.

University of California, Riverside, Graduate Division, Department of Philosophy, Riverside, CA 92521-0102. Offers MA, PhD. Terminal master's awarded for partial completion of doctoral program. *Degree requirements:* For master's, logic exam, professional paper; for doctorate, one foreign language, thesis/dissertation, logic exam, proposition papers, qualifying exams. *Entrance requirements:* For master's, GRE General Test, minimum GPA of 3.2; for doctorate, GRE General Test, master's degree in philosophy, minimum GPA of 3.2. Additional exam requirements/recommendations for international students: Required—TOEFL (minimum score 550 paper-based; 213 computer-based; 80 iBT). Electronic applications accepted. *Expenses:* Tuition, nonresident: full-time $4898. Required fees: $10,362. *Faculty research:* Moral philosophy, philosophy of science, history of philosophy, philosophy of language, Continental philosophy.

Philosophy

University of California, San Diego, Office of Graduate Studies, Department of Philosophy, La Jolla, CA 92093. Offers philosophy (PhD); science studies (PhD). *Degree requirements:* For doctorate, thesis/dissertation. *Entrance requirements:* For doctorate, GRE General Test, GRE Subject Test. Electronic applications accepted.

University of California, San Diego, Office of Graduate Studies, Interdisciplinary Program in Cognitive Science, La Jolla, CA 92093. Offers cognitive science/anthropology (PhD); cognitive science/communication (PhD); cognitive science/computer science and engineering (PhD); cognitive science/linguistics (PhD); cognitive science/neuroscience (PhD); cognitive science/philosophy (PhD); cognitive science/psychology (PhD); cognitive science/sociology (PhD). Admissions offered through affiliated departments. *Degree requirements:* For doctorate, thesis/dissertation. *Entrance requirements:* For doctorate, GRE General Test, acceptance into one of the 8 participating departments. *Faculty research:* Language and cognition, philosophy of mind, visual perception, biological anthropology, sociolinguistics.

University of California, Santa Barbara, Graduate Division, College of Letters and Sciences, Division of Humanities and Fine Arts, Department of Philosophy, Santa Barbara, CA 93106-6070. Offers PhD, MA/PhD. *Faculty:* 11 full-time (1 woman). *Students:* 33 full-time (3 women). Average age 29. 83 applicants, 23% accepted, 5 enrolled. In 2008, 3 doctorates awarded. Terminal master's awarded for partial completion of doctoral program. *Degree requirements:* For doctorate, comprehensive exam (for some programs), thesis/dissertation. *Entrance requirements:* For doctorate, GRE, writing sample, 3 letters of recommendation, statement of purpose, personal achievements/contributions statement, resumé/curriculum vitae, transcripts for post-secondary institutions attended. Additional exam requirements/recommendations for international students: Required—TOEFL (paper: 550, computer: 213, IBT: 80) or IELTS (7). *Application deadline:* For fall admission, 5/1 for domestic and international students; for winter admission, 11/1 for domestic and international students; for spring admission, 2/1 for domestic and international students. Application fee: $70 ($90 for international students). Electronic applications accepted. *Expenses:* Tuition, nonresident: full-time $25,149. Required fees: $10,143. Full-time tuition and fees vary according to campus/location, reciprocity agreements and student level. *Financial support:* In 2008–09, 34 students received support, including 8 fellowships with full and partial tuition reimbursements available (averaging $13,200 per year), 30 teaching assistantships with partial tuition reimbursements available (averaging $10,700 per year); Federal Work-Study, institutionally sponsored loans, scholarships/grants, health care benefits, tuition waivers (full and partial), and unspecified assistantships also available. Financial award application deadline: 1/15; financial award applicants required to submit FAFSA. *Faculty research:* Epistemology, philosophy of language, philosophy of mind, philosophy of logic, metaphysics. *Unit head:* Prof. Voula Tsouna, Chair, 805-893-3122, Fax: 805-893-8221, E-mail: vtsouna@philosophy.ucsb.edu. *Application contact:* Marsha Bonney, Graduate Program Assistant, 805-893-3122, Fax: 805-893-8221, E-mail: mbonney@philosophy.ucsb.edu.

University of California, Santa Cruz, Division of Graduate Studies, Division of Humanities, Department of Philosophy, Santa Cruz, CA 95064. Offers MA, PhD. *Degree requirements:* For doctorate, thesis/dissertation, qualifying exam. *Entrance requirements:* For master's and doctorate, GRE, official transcripts, 3 letters of recommendation. Additional exam requirements/recommendations for international students: Required—TOEFL.

University of Chicago, Division of the Humanities, Department of Philosophy, Chicago, IL 60637-1513. Offers ancient philosophy (AM, PhD); philosophy (AM, PhD). Terminal master's awarded for partial completion of doctoral program. *Degree requirements:* For master's, thesis; for doctorate, one foreign language, thesis/dissertation. *Entrance requirements:* For master's and doctorate, GRE General Test. Additional exam requirements/recommendations for international students: Required—TOEFL.

University of Cincinnati, Graduate School, McMicken College of Arts and Sciences, Department of Philosophy, Cincinnati, OH 45221. Offers MA, PhD. Terminal master's awarded for partial completion of doctoral program. *Degree requirements:* For master's, thesis; for doctorate, one foreign language, comprehensive exam, thesis/dissertation. *Entrance requirements:* For master's and doctorate, GRE General Test, BA in philosophy or equivalent experience. Additional exam requirements/recommendations for international students: Required—TOEFL (minimum score 240 computer-based). Electronic applications accepted.

University of Colorado at Boulder, Graduate School, College of Arts and Sciences, Department of Philosophy, Boulder, CO 80309. Offers MA, PhD. Terminal master's awarded for partial completion of doctoral program. *Degree requirements:* For master's, comprehensive exam, thesis; for doctorate, one foreign language, thesis/dissertation, logic and qualifying papers, oral exam. *Entrance requirements:* For master's, GRE General Test, writing sample, minimum undergraduate GPA of 2.75; for doctorate, GRE General Test, writing sample. *Faculty research:* Metaphysics and epistemology, classical philosophy, moral and political philosophy, philosophy of science.

University of Connecticut, Graduate School, College of Liberal Arts and Sciences, Department of Philosophy, Field of Philosophy, Storrs, CT 06269. Offers MA, PhD. Terminal master's awarded for partial completion of doctoral program. *Degree requirements:* For master's, comprehensive exam; for doctorate, 2 foreign languages, thesis/dissertation. *Entrance requirements:* For master's and doctorate, GRE General Test. Additional exam requirements/recommendations for international students: Required—TOEFL (minimum score 550 paper-based; 213 computer-based). Electronic applications accepted.

University of Dallas, Braniff Graduate School of Liberal Arts, Institute of Philosophic Studies, Doctoral Program in Philosophy, Irving, TX 75062-4736. Offers PhD. *Degree requirements:* For doctorate, 2 foreign languages, comprehensive exam, thesis/dissertation, qualifying exams. *Entrance requirements:* For doctorate, GRE General Test. *Faculty research:* Aesthetics, postmodernism, Hegel, ethics, Aristotle.

University of Dallas, Braniff Graduate School of Liberal Arts, Master's Program in Philosophy, Irving, TX 75062-4736. Offers MA. *Degree requirements:* For master's, one foreign language, comprehensive exam, thesis. *Entrance requirements:* For master's, GRE General Test. Additional exam requirements/recommendations for international students: Required—TOEFL. *Faculty research:* Aesthetics, postmodernism, Hegel, ethics, Aristotle.

University of Florida, Graduate School, College of Liberal Arts and Sciences, Department of Philosophy, Gainesville, FL 32611. Offers MA, PhD. *Degree requirements:* For master's, thesis or alternative; for doctorate, thesis/dissertation. *Entrance requirements:* For master's and doctorate, GRE General Test, minimum GPA of 3.0. Additional exam requirements/recommendations for international students: Required—TOEFL (minimum score 550 paper-based; 213 computer-based). Electronic applications accepted. *Faculty research:* History of philosophy, ethics, philosophy of the mind, philosophy of science, philosophy of language.

University of Georgia, Graduate School, College of Arts and Sciences, Department of Philosophy, Athens, GA 30602. Offers MA, PhD. Part-time programs available. *Degree requirements:* For master's, one foreign language, thesis; for doctorate, one foreign language, thesis/dissertation. *Entrance requirements:* For master's and doctorate, GRE General Test. Additional exam requirements/recommendations for international students: Required—TOEFL. Electronic applications accepted.

University of Guelph, Graduate Program Services, College of Arts, Department of Philosophy, Guelph, ON N1G 2W1, Canada. Offers MA, PhD. Part-time programs available. *Degree requirements:* For master's, thesis (for some programs); for doctorate, one foreign language, thesis/dissertation. *Entrance requirements:* For master's, minimum B- average during previous 2 years of course work; for doctorate, minimum B average. Additional exam requirements/recommendations for international students: Required—TOEFL (minimum score 550 paper-based; 213 computer-based). Electronic applications accepted. *Faculty research:* Philosophy of science, ethics, modern philosophy, social philosophy, Continental philosophy.

University of Hawaii at Manoa, Graduate Division, Colleges of Arts and Sciences, College of Arts and Humanities, Department of Philosophy, Honolulu, HI 96822. Offers MA, PhD. Part-time programs available. *Degree requirements:* For master's, variable foreign language requirement, thesis optional, culminating exam; for doctorate, variable foreign language requirement, comprehensive exam, thesis/dissertation, final oral presentation. *Entrance requirements:* For master's and doctorate, GRE General Test. Additional exam requirements/recommendations for international students: Required—TOEFL (minimum score 600 paper-based; 250 computer-based; 100 iBT), IELTS (minimum score 7). *Faculty research:* Renaissance philosophy, Indian philosophy, logic, ethics, philosophy of science, philosophy of mathematics, Chinese philosophy.

University of Houston, College of Liberal Arts and Social Sciences, Department of Philosophy, Houston, TX 77204. Offers MA. Part-time programs available. *Faculty:* 8 full-time (3 women), 2 part-time/adjunct (0 women). *Students:* 16 full-time (2 women), 13 part-time (4 women); includes 8 minority (2 Asian Americans or Pacific Islanders, 6 Hispanic Americans), 3 international. Average age 31. 31 applicants, 97% accepted, 8 enrolled. In 2008, 10 master's awarded. *Degree requirements:* For master's, one foreign language, thesis optional. *Entrance requirements:* For master's, GRE General Test, minimum of 18 hours of course work in philosophy. *Application deadline:* For fall admission, 7/15 for domestic students. Applications are processed on a rolling basis. Application fee: $15. *Expenses:* Tuition, state resident: full-time $5164; part-time $287 per credit. Tuition, nonresident: full-time $10,222; part-time $568 per credit. *Financial support:* In 2008–09, 9 teaching assistantships with full tuition reimbursements (averaging $10,600 per year) were awarded; career-related internships or fieldwork, Federal Work-Study, institutionally sponsored loans, scholarships/grants, health care benefits, and unspecified assistantships also available. Support available to part-time students. Financial award application deadline: 3/10. *Faculty research:* Skepticism, nominalism, liberalism, history of philosophy, cognitive science. *Unit head:* Dr. Cynthia Freeland, Chairperson, 713-743-3010, Fax: 713-743-5162, E-mail: cfreeland@uh.edu. *Application contact:* Gregory Brown, Director of Graduate Studies, 713-743-3202, Fax: 713-743-2990, E-mail: gbrown@jetson.uh.edu.

University of Illinois at Chicago, Graduate College, College of Liberal Arts and Sciences, Department of Philosophy, Chicago, IL 60607-7128. Offers MA, PhD. Terminal master's awarded for partial completion of doctoral program. *Degree requirements:* For doctorate, thesis/dissertation, preliminary exams. *Entrance requirements:* For master's and doctorate, minimum GPA of 2.75. Additional exam requirements/recommendations for international students: Required—TOEFL. Electronic applications accepted. *Faculty research:* Philosophy of science, philosophy of language, epistemology and metaphysics, ethics, aesthetics.

University of Illinois at Urbana–Champaign, Graduate College, College of Liberal Arts and Sciences, Department of Philosophy, Champaign, IL 61820. Offers MA, PhD, PhD/JD. *Faculty:* 11 full-time (1 woman), 3 part-time/adjunct (1 woman). *Students:* 32 full-time (6 women), 4 part-time (1 woman); includes 1 minority (Hispanic American), 3 international. 79 applicants, 10% accepted, 6 enrolled. In 2008, 4 master's, 3 doctorates awarded. *Entrance requirements:* For doctorate, GRE, minimum GPA of 3.0; writing sample. Additional exam requirements/recommendations for international students: Required—TOEFL (minimum score 600 paper-based; 100 iBT). *Application deadline:* Applications are processed on a rolling basis. Application fee: $60 ($75 for international students). Electronic applications accepted. *Financial support:* In 2008–09, 10 fellowships, 2 research assistantships, 35 teaching assistantships were awarded; tuition waivers (full and partial) also available. *Unit head:* Robert C. Cummins, Chair, 217-333-2889, Fax: 217-244-8355, E-mail: rcummins@illinois.edu. *Application contact:* Peggy Wells, Office Support Specialist, 217-333-2889, Fax: 217-244-8355, E-mail: pwells@illinois.edu.

The University of Iowa, Graduate College, College of Liberal Arts and Sciences, Department of Philosophy, Iowa City, IA 52242-1316. Offers MA, PhD, JD/MA. *Degree requirements:* For master's, thesis optional, exam; for doctorate, comprehensive exam, thesis/dissertation. *Entrance requirements:* For master's, GRE General Test or LSAT, minimum GPA of 3.0; for doctorate, GRE General Test, minimum GPA of 3.0. Additional exam requirements/recommendations for international students: Required—TOEFL (minimum score 550 paper-based; 213 computer-based; 81 iBT). Electronic applications accepted.

The University of Kansas, Graduate Studies, College of Liberal Arts and Sciences, Department of Philosophy, Lawrence, KS 66045. Offers MA, PhD, JD/MA. *Faculty:* 13 full-time (2 women). *Students:* 40 full-time (10 women), 3 part-time (1 woman); includes 3 minority (2 Asian Americans or Pacific Islanders, 1 Hispanic American), 1 international. Average age 32. 21 applicants, 62% accepted, 10 enrolled. In 2008, 6 master's, 5 doctorates awarded. Terminal master's awarded for partial completion of doctoral program. *Degree requirements:* For master's, comprehensive exam, thesis or alternative; for doctorate, one foreign language, comprehensive exam, thesis/dissertation. *Entrance requirements:* For master's and doctorate, GRE. Additional exam requirements/recommendations for international students: Required—TOEFL. *Application deadline:* For fall admission, 2/1 priority date for domestic students, 6/15 for international students. Applications are processed on a rolling basis. Application fee: $45 ($50 for international students). Electronic applications accepted. *Expenses:* Tuition, area resident: Full-time $6122; part-time $255.10 per credit hour. Tuition, state resident: full-time $6122; part-time $255.10 per credit hour. Tuition, nonresident: full-time $14,629; part-time $609.55 per credit hour. Required fees: $847; $70.56 per credit hour. Tuition and fees vary according to course load and program. *Financial support:* Fellowships with full and partial tuition reimbursements, research assistantships with full and partial tuition reimbursements, teaching assistantships with full and partial tuition reimbursements available. Financial award application deadline: 1/5. *Faculty research:* Theoretical and applied ethics, social and political philosophy, history of philosophy, analytic philosophy, philosophy of mind and language. *Unit head:* Ben Eggleston, Chair, 785-864-2332, E-mail: eggleston@ku.edu. *Application contact:* Ben Eggleston, Chair, 785-864-2332, E-mail: eggleston@ku.edu.

University of Kentucky, Graduate School, College of Arts and Sciences, Program in Philosophy, Lexington, KY 40506-0032. Offers MA, PhD. *Degree requirements:* For master's, one foreign language, comprehensive exam, thesis; for doctorate, one foreign language, comprehensive exam, thesis/dissertation. *Entrance requirements:* For master's, GRE General Test, minimum undergraduate GPA of 2.75; for doctorate, GRE General Test, minimum graduate GPA of 3.0. Additional exam requirements/recommendations for international students: Required—TOEFL (minimum score 550 paper-based; 213 computer-based). Electronic applications accepted. *Faculty research:* History of philosophy, history and philosophy of science, ethics, social and political philosophy.

University of Lethbridge, School of Graduate Studies, Lethbridge, AB T1K 3M4, Canada. Offers accounting (MScM); addictions counseling (M Sc); agricultural biotechnology (M Sc); agricultural studies (M Sc, MA); anthropology (MA); archaeology (MA); art (MA); biochemistry (M Sc); biological sciences (M Sc); biomolecular science (PhD); biosystems and biodiversity (PhD); Canadian studies (MA); chemistry (M Sc); computer science (M Sc); computer science and geographical information science (M Sc); counseling psychology (M Ed); dramatic arts (MA); earth, space, and physical science (PhD); economics (MA); educational leadership (M Ed); English (MA); environmental science (M Sc); evolution and behavior (PhD); exercise science (M Sc); finance (MScM); French (MA); French/German (MA); French/Spanish (MA); general education (M Ed); general management (MScM); geography (M Sc, MA); German (MA); health sciences (M Sc, MA); history (MA); human resource management and labour relations (MScM); individualized multidisciplinary (M Sc, MA); information systems (MScM); international management (MScM); kinesiology (M Sc, MA); management (M Sc, MA); marketing (MScM); mathematics (M Sc); music (MA); Native American studies (MA); neuroscience (M Sc, PhD); new media (MA); nursing (M Sc); philosophy (MA); physics (M Sc); policy and strategy (MScM); political science (MA); psychology (M Sc, MA); religious studies (MA); sociology (MA); theoretical and computational science (PhD); urban and regional studies (MA). Part-time and evening/weekend programs available. *Degree requirements:* For doctorate, comprehensive exam, thesis/dissertation. *Entrance requirements:* For master's, GMAT (M Sc in management), bachelor's degree in related field, minimum GPA of 3.0 during previous 20 graded semester courses, 2 years teaching or related experience (M Ed); for doctorate, master's degree, minimum graduate GPA of 3.5. Additional exam requirements/recommendations for international students: Required—TOEFL. *Faculty research:* Movement and brain plasticity, gibberellin physiology, photosynthesis, carbon cycling, molecular properties of main-group ring components.

University of Louisville, Graduate School, College of Arts and Sciences, Department of Philosophy, Louisville, KY 40292-0001. Offers MA. *Students:* 1 part-time. Average age 56. *Degree requirements:* For master's, one foreign language, thesis or alternative. *Entrance requirements:* For master's, GRE General Test. *Application deadline:* Applications are processed on a rolling basis. Application fee: $50. *Unit head:* Dr. Robert Kimball, Chair, 502-852-0488, Fax: 502-852-0459, E-mail: robert.kimball@louisville.edu. *Application contact:* Libby Leggett, Director, Graduate Admissions, 502-852-3101, Fax: 502-852-6536, E-mail: gradadm@louisville.edu.

University of Manitoba, Faculty of Graduate Studies, Faculty of Arts, Department of Philosophy, Winnipeg, MB R3T 2N2, Canada. Offers MA. *Degree requirements:* For master's, variable foreign language requirement, thesis or alternative.

University of Maryland, College Park, Graduate Studies, College of Arts and Humanities, Department of Philosophy, College Park, MD 20742. Offers MA, PhD. *Degree requirements:* For master's, thesis optional; for doctorate, thesis/dissertation, 2 semesters of undergraduate teaching, qualification in symbolic logic. *Entrance requirements:* For master's, GRE General Test, minimum GPA of 3.0, philosophy paper, writing sample, 3 letters of recommendation; for doctorate, GRE General Test, minimum GPA of 3.0, philosophy paper, writing sample. Electronic applications accepted. *Faculty research:* Contemporary British and American philosophy, the relationship between philosophy and other disciplines, ethical and conceptual issues in public policy.

University of Massachusetts Amherst, Graduate School, College of Humanities and Fine Arts, Department of Philosophy, Amherst, MA 01003. Offers MA, PhD. Part-time programs available. Terminal master's awarded for partial completion of doctoral program. *Degree requirements:* For master's, thesis optional; for doctorate, comprehensive exam, thesis/dissertation. *Entrance requirements:* For master's and doctorate, GRE General Test, writing sample, 3 letters of recommendation. Additional exam requirements/recommendations for international students: Required—TOEFL (minimum score 550 paper-based; 213 computer-based; 79 iBT), IELTS (minimum score 6.5). Electronic applications accepted. *Expenses:* Tuition, area resident: Full-time $2640. Tuition, nonresident: full-time $9936. One-time fee: $332 full-time. Tuition and fees vary according to course load.

University of Memphis, Graduate School, College of Arts and Sciences, Department of Philosophy, Memphis, TN 38152. Offers MA, PhD. Part-time programs available. *Faculty:* 10 full-time (3 women). *Students:* 29 full-time (15 women), 6 part-time (3 women); includes 12 minority (9 African Americans, 3 Asian Americans or Pacific Islanders), 5 international. Average age 30. 101 applicants, 18% accepted, 14 enrolled. In 2008, 11 master's, 2 doctorates awarded. Terminal master's awarded for partial completion of doctoral program. *Degree requirements:* For master's, thesis optional, 2 written comprehensive exams; for doctorate, 2 foreign languages, thesis/dissertation, area and qualifying exams. *Entrance requirements:* For master's, GRE General Test, minimum GPA of 2.5, 18 hours of undergraduate course work in philosophy; for doctorate, GRE General Test, minimum GPA of 3.0, bachelor's degree in philosophy. *Application deadline:* For fall admission, 2/1 for domestic students. Application fee: $35 ($60 for international students). Electronic applications accepted. *Expenses:* Tuition, area resident: Full-time $6242; part-time $330 per credit hour. Tuition, state resident: full-time $6242; part-time $330 per credit hour. Tuition, nonresident: full-time $17,828; part-time $815 per credit hour. Required fees: $1156. *Financial support:* Fellowships with full tuition reimbursements, research assistantships with full tuition reimbursements, teaching assistantships with full tuition reimbursements, tuition waivers (full) available. Financial award applicants required to submit FAFSA. *Faculty research:* Continental philosophy, ethics, analytic philosophy, feminist theory, Africana philosophy. *Unit head:* Dr. Deborah Tollefsen, Chair, 901-678-2535, Fax: 901-678-4365, E-mail: dtollfsn@memphis.edu. *Application contact:* Dr. Mary Beth Mader, Coordinator of Admission, 901-678-4526.

University of Miami, Graduate School, College of Arts and Sciences, Department of Philosophy, Coral Gables, FL 33124. Offers MA, PhD. Part-time programs available. Terminal master's awarded for partial completion of doctoral program. *Degree requirements:* For master's, thesis or alternative; for doctorate, comprehensive exam, thesis/dissertation. *Entrance requirements:* For master's, GRE General Test; for doctorate, GRE General Test, minimum GPA of 3.0, 3 letters of recommendation, writing sample. Additional exam requirements/recommendations for international students: Required—TOEFL. Electronic applications accepted. *Faculty research:* Ethics, epistemology, pragmatism, philosophy of science, metaphysics.

University of Michigan, Horace H. Rackham School of Graduate Studies, College of Literature, Science, and the Arts, Department of Philosophy, Ann Arbor, MI 48109. Offers AM, PhD. Terminal master's awarded for partial completion of doctoral program. *Degree requirements:* For doctorate, one foreign language, thesis/dissertation, oral defense of dissertation. *Entrance requirements:* For master's and doctorate, GRE General Test, 3 letters of recommendation, writing sample. Additional exam requirements/recommendations for international students: Required—TOEFL. Electronic applications accepted. *Faculty research:* Ethics, metaphysics, philosophy of language and mind, political and social philosophy, philosophy of science.

University of Minnesota, Twin Cities Campus, Graduate School, College of Liberal Arts, Department of Philosophy, Minneapolis, MN 55455-0213. Offers MA, PhD. Part-time programs available. Terminal master's awarded for partial completion of doctoral program. *Degree requirements:* For master's, thesis (for some programs); for doctorate, thesis/dissertation. *Entrance requirements:* For master's and doctorate, GRE, references, writing sample. Additional exam requirements/recommendations for international students: Required—TOEFL (paper-based 550; computer-based 213), IELTS (score 6.5), or Michigan English Language Assessment Battery (score 80). Electronic applications accepted. *Faculty research:* Philosophy of science; ethics and social/political philosophy; logic, language, and mind.

University of Mississippi, Graduate School, College of Liberal Arts, Department of Philosophy and Religions, Oxford, University, MS 38677. Offers philosophy (MA). *Degree requirements:* For master's, thesis. *Entrance requirements:* For master's, GRE General Test, minimum GPA of 3.0. Additional exam requirements/recommendations for international students: Required—TOEFL. Electronic applications accepted.

University of Missouri–Columbia, Graduate School, College of Arts and Sciences, Department of Philosophy, Columbia, MO 65211. Offers MA, PhD. *Faculty:* 17 full-time (3 women), 1 part-time/adjunct (0 women). *Students:* 17 full-time (4 women), 10 part-time (0 women); includes 2 minority (1 American Indian/Alaska Native, 1 Asian American or Pacific Islander), 4 international. Average age 29. 43 applicants, 30% accepted, 7 enrolled. In 2008, 6 master's, 7 doctorates awarded. Terminal master's awarded for partial completion of doctoral program. *Degree requirements:* For doctorate, one foreign language, thesis/dissertation. *Entrance requirements:* For master's and doctorate, GRE General Test, minimum GPA of 3.0. Additional exam requirements/recommendations for international students: Required—TOEFL (minimum score 500 paper-based; 173 computer-based; 61 iBT). *Application deadline:* For fall admission, 2/1 priority date for domestic students. Applications are processed on a rolling basis. Application fee: $45 ($60 for international students). *Financial support:* Fellowships, research assistantships, teaching assistantships, institutionally sponsored loans available. Financial award application deadline: 2/1. *Unit head:* Dr. Andrew Melnyk, Department Chair, E-mail: melnyka@missouri.edu. *Application contact:* Jonni Paxton, Administrative Assistant, 573-882-2871, E-mail: paxtonj@missouri.edu.

University of Missouri–St. Louis, College of Arts and Sciences, Department of Philosophy, St. Louis, MO 63121. Offers MA. *Faculty:* 10 full-time (3 women). *Students:* 15 full-time (3 women), 15 part-time (2 women); includes 3 minority (1 African American, 1 American Indian/Alaska Native, 1 Asian American or Pacific Islander), 2 international. Average age 28. 5 applicants. In 2008, 8 master's awarded. *Entrance requirements:* For master's, writing sample, 3 letters of recommendation. Additional exam requirements/recommendations for international students: Required—TOEFL (minimum score 550 paper-based; 213 computer-based). *Application deadline:* For fall admission, 7/1 priority date for domestic and international students; for spring admission, 12/1 priority date for domestic and international students. Applications are processed on a rolling basis. Application fee: $35 ($40 for international students). Electronic applications accepted. *Expenses:* Tuition, area resident: Full-time $5377; part-time $298.70 per credit hour. Tuition, nonresident: full-time $13,381; part-time $472.50 per credit hour. Required fees: $4078; $52 per credit hour. *Financial support:* In 2008–09, 1 research assistantship with full and partial tuition reimbursement (averaging $5,000 per year), 13 teaching assistantships with full and partial tuition reimbursements (averaging $5,000 per year) were awarded. Financial award applicants required to submit FAFSA. *Faculty research:* Ethics, philosophy and history of science, philosophical social science, aesthetics. *Unit head:* Dr. Eric Wiland, Graduate Program Director, 314-516-5631, Fax: 314-516-5816, E-mail: wiland@umsl.edu. *Application contact:* 314-516-5458, Fax: 314-516-6996, E-mail: gradadm@umsl.edu.

The University of Montana, Graduate School, College of Arts and Sciences, Department of Philosophy, Missoula, MT 59812-0002. Offers MA. *Degree requirements:* For master's, thesis or additional course work/professional paper. *Entrance requirements:* For master's, GRE General Test. Additional exam requirements/recommendations for international students: Required—TOEFL (minimum score 525 paper-based; 197 computer-based). *Faculty research:* Philosophy of law, natural science, feminism, and technology; environmental, business, and medical ethics.

University of Nebraska–Lincoln, Graduate College, College of Arts and Sciences, Department of Philosophy, Lincoln, NE 68588. Offers MA, PhD. *Faculty:* 12 full-time (3 women). *Students:* 23 full-time (2 women), 9 part-time (4 women); includes 3 Asian Americans or Pacific Islanders, 2 Hispanic Americans, 1 international. Average age 33. In 2008, 2 master's, 1 doctorate awarded. *Degree requirements:* For master's, thesis optional; for doctorate, comprehensive exam, thesis/dissertation. *Entrance requirements:* For master's and doctorate, GRE General Test, writing sample. Additional exam requirements/recommendations for international students: Required—TOEFL (minimum score 600 paper-based; 250 computer-based). *Application deadline:* For fall admission, 1/31 priority date for domestic students, 3/1 for international students. Applications are processed on a rolling basis. Application fee: $40. Electronic applications accepted. *Expenses:* Tuition, state resident: full-time $4275; part-time $237.50 per credit hour. Tuition, nonresident: full-time $11,525; part-time $640.25 per credit hour. Required fees: $1068; $10.35 per credit hour. $440.70 per semester. Tuition and fees vary according to course load and program. *Financial support:* Fellowships, research assistantships, teaching assistantships, Federal Work-Study, health care benefits, and unspecified assistantships available. Support available to part-time students. Financial award application deadline: 1/15. *Faculty research:* Ethics, epistemology, metaphysics, cognitive science, history of philosophy. *Unit head:* Dr. Joseph Mendola, Chair, 402-472-0528, Fax: 402-472-0626. *Application contact:* Ginny Gross, Director of Graduate Admissions, 402-472-2878, Fax: 402-472-0589, E-mail: grad_admissions@unl.edu.

University of Nevada, Reno, Graduate School, College of Liberal Arts, Department of Philosophy, Reno, NV 89557. Offers MA. *Faculty:* 9 full-time (2 women). *Students:* 3 full-time (1 woman), 7 part-time (0 women). Average age 37. 11 applicants, 64% accepted, 5 enrolled. In 2008, 13 master's awarded. *Degree requirements:* For master's, thesis optional. *Entrance requirements:* For master's, GRE General Test, minimum GPA of 2.75. Additional exam requirements/recommendations for international students: Required—TOEFL (minimum score 500 paper-based; 173 computer-based; 61 iBT), IELTS (minimum score 6), TOFEL or IELTS. *Application deadline:* For fall admission, 3/1 priority date for domestic and international students; for spring admission, 11/1 priority date for domestic and international students. Applications are processed on a rolling basis. Application fee: $60 ($95 for international students). Electronic applications accepted. *Expenses:* Tuition, state resident: full-time $1710; part-time $1140 per semester. Tuition, nonresident: full-time $7115. Required fees: $158 per semester. *Financial support:* Teaching assistantships with partial tuition reimbursements, Federal Work-Study, institutionally sponsored loans, scholarships/grants, health care benefits, and unspecified assistantships available. Financial award application deadline: 3/1; financial award applicants required to submit FAFSA. *Faculty research:* Ancient philosophy (Aristotle), ethics, political theory, violence, Continental philosophy. *Unit head:* Dr. Christopher Williams, Graduate Program Director, 775-784-4287, E-mail: ctw@unr.edu. *Application contact:* Michele Sandberg, Application Contact, 775-784-7026, Fax: 775-784-6064, E-mail: gradschool@unr.edu.

University of New Brunswick Fredericton, School of Graduate Studies, Policy Studies Program, Fredericton, NB E3B 5A3, Canada. Offers people, property and alternative dispute resolution (M Phil); philosophy politics and economics (M Phil); sustainable development (M Phil). *Faculty:* 6 full-time (2 women), 13 part-time/adjunct (2 women). *Students:* 16 full-time (9 women), 4 part-time (3 women). In 2008, 3 master's awarded. *Entrance requirements:* For master's, minimum GPA of 3.5, BA. Additional exam requirements/recommendations for international students: Required—TOEFL (minimum score 600 paper-based), TWE (minimum score 5). Application fee: $50 Canadian dollars. Tuition and fees charges are reported in Canadian dollars. *Expenses:* Tuition, area resident: Full-time $5562 Canadian dollars. Tuition, nonresident: full-time $9450 Canadian dollars. Required fees: $333 Canadian dollars. *Financial support:* In 2008–09, 4 research assistantships, 1 teaching assistantship were awarded. *Unit head:* Dr. Linda Eyre, Dean of Graduate Studies, 506-447-3044, Fax: 506-453-4817, E-mail: gradidst@unb.ca. *Application contact:* Janet Amurault, Graduate Secretary, 506-458-7558, Fax: 506-453-4817, E-mail: jamiraul@unb.ca.

University of New Mexico, Graduate School, College of Arts and Sciences, Department of Philosophy, Albuquerque, NM 87131-2039. Offers MA, PhD. Part-time programs available. Terminal master's awarded for partial completion of doctoral program. *Degree requirements:* For master's, thesis (for some programs); for doctorate, one foreign language, comprehensive exam, thesis/dissertation. *Entrance requirements:* For master's and doctorate, GRE. Additional exam requirements/recommendations for international students: Required—TOEFL. Electronic applications accepted. *Faculty research:* History of philosophy, ethics, philosophy of art and literature, Asian philosophy, continental philosophy, philosophy of language.

The University of North Carolina at Chapel Hill, Graduate School, College of Arts and Sciences, Department of Philosophy, Chapel Hill, NC 27599. Offers MA, PhD. *Degree requirements:* For master's, comprehensive exam, thesis; for doctorate, comprehensive exam, thesis/dissertation. *Entrance requirements:* For master's and doctorate, GRE General Test, minimum GPA of 3.0.

University of North Florida, College of Arts and Sciences, Department of Philosophy, Jacksonville, FL 32224-2645. Offers applied ethics (Graduate Certificate); practical philosophy and applied ethics (MA). Part-time and evening/weekend programs available. *Faculty:* 11 full-time (5 women). *Students:* 11 full-time (5 women), 5 part-time (3 women); includes 3 minority (1 African American, 1 Asian American or Pacific Islander, 1 Hispanic American). Average age 33. 13 applicants, 85% accepted, 7 enrolled. In 2008, 3 master's awarded. *Entrance requirements:* For master's, GRE General Test, minimum GPA of 3.0 in last 60 hours, 3 letters of recommendation, writing sample. Additional exam requirements/recommendations for international students: Required—TOEFL (minimum score 500 paper-based). *Application deadline:* For fall admission, 3/1 priority date for domestic students, 3/1 for international students. Applications are processed on a rolling basis. Application fee: $30. Electronic applications accepted. *Expenses:* Tuition, area resident: Full-time $5782.08; part-time $240.92 per credit hour. Tuition, state resident: full-time $5782.08; part-time $240.92 per credit hour. Tuition, nonresident: full-time $19,974; part-time $832.26 per credit hour. Required fees: $952.80; $39.70 per credit hour. *Financial support:* In 2008–09, 2 students received support, including 4 teaching assistantships (averaging $6,450 per year). Financial award application deadline: 4/1; financial award applicants required to submit FAFSA. *Faculty research:* Late

Philosophy

University of North Florida (continued)
modern philosophy, pragmatism, religion and American culture, hermeneutics, philosophy of mind. Total annual research expenditures: $24,367. *Unit head:* Dr. Hans Herbert Koegler, 904-620-1330, Fax: 904-620-1840, E-mail: hkoegler@unf.edu. *Application contact:* Dr. Andrew Buchwalter, Graduate Coordinator, 904-620-1155, Fax: 904-620-1840, E-mail: abuchwal@unf.edu.

University of North Texas, Robert B. Toulouse School of Graduate Studies, College of Arts and Sciences, Department of Philosophy and Religion Studies, Denton, TX 76203. Offers philosophy (MA, PhD). *Degree requirements:* For master's, one foreign language, thesis or alternative. *Entrance requirements:* For master's, GRE General Test. Additional exam requirements/recommendations for international students: Required—proof of English language proficiency required for non-native English speakers; Recommended—TOEFL (minimum score 550 paper-based; 213 computer-based).

University of Notre Dame, Graduate School, College of Arts and Letters, Division of Humanities, Department of Philosophy, Notre Dame, IN 46556. Offers PhD. *Faculty:* 43 full-time (4 women), 4 part-time/adjunct (0 women). *Students:* 72 full-time (19 women); includes 1 American Indian/Alaska Native, 3 Asian Americans or Pacific Islanders, 2 Hispanic Americans, 8 international. 275 applicants, 9% accepted, 8 enrolled. In 2008, 3 doctorates awarded. *Degree requirements:* For doctorate, 2 foreign languages, thesis/dissertation, candidacy exam. *Entrance requirements:* For doctorate, GRE General Test. Additional exam requirements/recommendations for international students: Required—TOEFL (minimum score 600 paper-based; 250 computer-based; 80 iBT). *Application deadline:* For fall admission, 1/15 for domestic and international students. Application fee: $50. Electronic applications accepted. *Financial support:* Fellowships with full tuition reimbursements, research assistantships with full tuition reimbursements, teaching assistantships with full tuition reimbursements, tuition waivers (full) available. Financial award application deadline: 1/15. *Faculty research:* History of philosophy, ethics, philosophy of science and logic, philosophy of religion, Continental philosophy, metaphysics. *Unit head:* Dr. Patricia Blanchette, Director of Graduate Studies, 574-631-6471, E-mail: ndphilo.1@nd.edu. *Application contact:* Dr. Barbara Turpin, Director of Graduate Admissions, 574-631-7706, Fax: 574-631-4183.

University of Oklahoma, Graduate College, College of Arts and Sciences, Department of Philosophy, Norman, OK 73019. Offers MA, PhD. Part-time and evening/weekend programs available. *Faculty:* 15 full-time (4 women). *Students:* 24 full-time (4 women), 9 part-time (1 woman); includes 3 minority (2 American Indian/Alaska Native, 1 Asian American or Pacific Islander). 24 applicants, 75% accepted, 6 enrolled. In 2008, 1 master's, 2 doctorates awarded. Terminal master's awarded for partial completion of doctoral program. *Degree requirements:* For master's, thesis optional; for doctorate, thesis/dissertation, oral and written exams. *Entrance requirements:* For master's and doctorate, GRE General Test, 3 letters of recommendation, writing sample. Additional exam requirements/recommendations for international students: Required—TOEFL (minimum score 550 paper-based; 213 computer-based). *Application deadline:* For fall admission, 2/1 priority date for domestic and international students; for spring admission, 11/1 for domestic students, 9/1 for international students. Applications are processed on a rolling basis. Application fee: $40 ($90 for international students). Electronic applications accepted. *Expenses:* Tuition, state resident: full-time $3744; part-time $156 per credit hour. Tuition, nonresident: full-time $13,577; part-time $565.70 per credit hour. Required fees: $2415.40; $90.10 per credit hour. *Financial support:* In 2008–09, 16 students received support, including 3 fellowships (averaging $3,333 per year), 1 research assistantship with partial tuition reimbursement available (averaging $16,538 per year), 20 teaching assistantships with partial tuition reimbursements available (averaging $12,582 per year); health care benefits and unspecified assistantships also available. Financial award application deadline: 2/28; financial award applicants required to submit FAFSA. *Faculty research:* Analytic philosophy. Total annual research expenditures: $30,385. *Unit head:* Dr. Hugh Benson, Chair, 405-325-6324, Fax: 405-325-2660, E-mail: hbenson@ou.edu. *Application contact:* Wayne Riggs, Graduate Director, 405-325-5950, Fax: 405-325-2660, E-mail: wriggs@ou.edu.

University of Oregon, Graduate School, College of Arts and Sciences, Department of Philosophy, Eugene, OR 97403. Offers MA, PhD. Terminal master's awarded for partial completion of doctoral program. *Degree requirements:* For master's, one foreign language, thesis or alternative; for doctorate, one foreign language, thesis/dissertation. *Entrance requirements:* For master's and doctorate, GRE General Test. Additional exam requirements/recommendations for international students: Required—TOEFL. *Faculty research:* Social and political philosophy, feminist philosophy, American philosophy, aesthetics, philosophy of mind.

University of Ottawa, Faculty of Graduate and Postdoctoral Studies, Faculty of Arts, Department of Philosophy, Ottawa, ON K1N 6N5, Canada. Offers MA, PhD. *Degree requirements:* For master's, thesis or alternative; for doctorate, comprehensive exam, thesis/dissertation. *Entrance requirements:* For master's, honors degree or equivalent, minimum B average; for doctorate, master's degree, minimum B+ average. Electronic applications accepted. *Faculty research:* History of philosophy (ancient, medieval, modern and contemporary); metaphysics/epistemology; value theory: political philosophy, ethics.

University of Pennsylvania, School of Arts and Sciences, Graduate Group in Philosophy, Philadelphia, PA 19104. Offers AM, PhD, JD/PhD. Terminal master's awarded for partial completion of doctoral program. *Degree requirements:* For master's, thesis; for doctorate, thesis/dissertation, 1 year of teaching experience. Electronic applications accepted.

University of Pittsburgh, School of Arts and Sciences, Department of History and Philosophy of Science, Pittsburgh, PA 15260. Offers MA, PhD. Terminal master's awarded for partial completion of doctoral program. *Degree requirements:* For master's, one foreign language, comprehensive exam; for doctorate, 2 foreign languages, comprehensive exam, thesis/dissertation. *Entrance requirements:* For master's and doctorate, GRE General Test. Additional exam requirements/recommendations for international students: Required—TOEFL (minimum score 550 paper-based; 213 computer-based). Electronic applications accepted. *Faculty research:* History and philosophy of biology, psychology, neuroscience; history and philosophy of physics; early modern science; rhetoric of science; philosophy of social science.

University of Pittsburgh, School of Arts and Sciences, Department of Philosophy, Pittsburgh, PA 15260. Offers MA, PhD. Terminal master's awarded for partial completion of doctoral program. *Degree requirements:* For master's, one foreign language; for doctorate, one foreign language, thesis/dissertation. *Entrance requirements:* For master's and doctorate, GRE General Test. Additional exam requirements/recommendations for international students: Required—TOEFL (minimum score 550 paper-based; 213 computer-based; 79 iBT), IELTS (minimum score 6.5). Electronic applications accepted. *Faculty research:* Metaphysics and epistemology, ethics, philosophy of science, history of philosophy.

University of Puerto Rico, Río Piedras, College of Humanities, Department of Philosophy, San Juan, PR 00931-3300. Offers MA. Part-time programs available. *Degree requirements:* For master's, one foreign language, comprehensive exam, thesis. *Entrance requirements:* For master's, PAEG or GRE, interview, minimum GPA of 3.0, letter of recommendation (2).

University of Regina, Faculty of Graduate Studies and Research, Faculty of Arts, Department of Philosophy, Regina, SK S4S 0A2, Canada. Offers philosophy (MA); social and political thought (MA). *Faculty:* 9 full-time (3 women). *Students:* 3 full-time (2 women). 2 applicants, 100% accepted. *Degree requirements:* For master's, thesis. *Entrance requirements:* Additional exam requirements/recommendations for international students: Required—TOEFL (minimum score 580 paper-based; 237 computer-based; 88 iBT). *Application deadline:* Applications are processed on a rolling basis. Application fee: $85 ($100 for international students). Electronic applications accepted. *Financial support:* Fellowships, research assistantships, teaching assistantships, scholarships/grants available. Financial award application deadline: 6/15. *Faculty research:* History of philosophy, ethics, aesthetics, metaphysics, epistemology. *Unit head:* Dr. Eldon Soifer, Head, 306-585-4301, Fax: 306-585-4827, E-mail: eldon.soifer@uregina.ca. *Application contact:* Dr. Eldon Soifer, Head, 306-585-4301, Fax: 306-585-4827, E-mail: eldon.soifer@uregina.ca.

University of Regina, Faculty of Graduate Studies and Research, Faculty of Arts, Program in Social and Political Thought, Regina, SK S4S 0A2, Canada. Offers MA. *Faculty:* 9 full-time (3 women). *Students:* 5 full-time (1 woman), 4 part-time (0 women). 3 applicants, 100% accepted. In 2008, 1 master's awarded. *Degree requirements:* For master's, thesis. *Entrance requirements:* Additional exam requirements/recommendations for international students: Required—TOEFL (minimum score 580 paper-based; 237 computer-based; 88 iBT). *Application deadline:* For fall admission, 3/15 for domestic students. Application fee: $85 ($100 for international students). Electronic applications accepted. *Financial support:* In 2008–09, 1 fellowship (averaging $15,000 per year), 1 research assistantship (averaging $13,500 per year), 1 teaching assistantship (averaging $6,558 per year) were awarded. *Unit head:* Dr. Shadia Drury, Program Coordinator, 306-585-4073, E-mail: shadia.drury@uregina.ca. *Application contact:* Dr. Shadia Drury, Program Coordinator, 306-585-4073, E-mail: shadia.drury@uregina.ca.

University of Rochester, The College, Arts and Sciences, Department of Philosophy, Rochester, NY 14627-0250. Offers MA, PhD. Terminal master's awarded for partial completion of doctoral program. *Degree requirements:* For doctorate, thesis/dissertation, qualifying exam. *Entrance requirements:* For master's, GRE General Test; for doctorate, GRE General Test, sample of written work. Additional exam requirements/recommendations for international students: Required—TOEFL.

University of St. Thomas, Center for Thomistic Studies, Houston, TX 77006-4696. Offers philosophy (MA, PhD). Part-time programs available. *Faculty:* 6 full-time (1 woman). *Students:* 14 full-time (2 women), 12 part-time (1 woman); includes 5 minority (2 African Americans, 3 Asian Americans or Pacific Islanders), 3 international. Average age 32. 21 applicants, 43% accepted, 7 enrolled. In 2008, 1 master's, 2 doctorates awarded. Terminal master's awarded for partial completion of doctoral program. *Degree requirements:* For master's, one foreign language, comprehensive exam, thesis (for some programs); for doctorate, 2 foreign languages, comprehensive exam, thesis/dissertation, MA level Latin exam (completed prior to 3rd semester of study). *Entrance requirements:* For master's, minimum GPA of 3.0, minimum 18 hours of undergraduate course work in philosophy, 3 letters of recommendation from professional educators qualified to evaluate the applicant's academic background, writing sample; for doctorate, MA in philosophy. *Application deadline:* For fall admission, 2/1 priority date for domestic students. Applications are processed on a rolling basis. Application fee: $35. Electronic applications accepted. *Expenses:* Tuition: Full-time $13,554; part-time $753 per credit. Required fees: $224; $224 per year. *Financial support:* In 2008–09, 13 students received support. Federal Work-Study, scholarships/grants, and unspecified assistantships available. Support available to part-time students. Financial award application deadline: 3/1; financial award applicants required to submit FAFSA. *Unit head:* Dr. Mary Catherine Sommers, Director, 713-525-3591, Fax: 713-942-3464, E-mail: sommers@stthom.edu. *Application contact:* Pamela Butler, Administrative Assistant II, 713-525-3591, Fax: 713-942-3464, E-mail: butlerp@stthom.edu.

University of Saskatchewan, College of Graduate Studies and Research, College of Arts and Sciences, Department of Philosophy, Saskatoon, SK S7N 5A2, Canada. Offers MA. *Degree requirements:* For master's, thesis. *Entrance requirements:* Additional exam requirements/recommendations for international students: Required—TOEFL.

University of South Africa, College of Human Sciences, Pretoria, South Africa. Offers adult education (M Ed); African languages (MA, PhD); African politics (MA, PhD); Afrikaans (MA, PhD); ancient history (MA, PhD); ancient Near Eastern studies (MA, PhD); anthropology (MA, PhD); applied linguistics (MA); Arabic (MA, PhD); archaeology (MA); art history (MA); Biblical archaeology (MA); Biblical studies (M Th, D Th, PhD); Christian spirituality (M Th, D Th); church history (M Th, D Th); classical studies (MA, PhD); clinical psychology (MA); communication (MA, PhD); comparative education (M Ed, Ed D); consulting psychology (D Admin, D Com, PhD); curriculum studies (M Ed, Ed D); development studies (M Admin, MA, D Admin, PhD); didactics (M Ed, Ed D); education (M Tech); education management (M Ed, Ed D); educational psychology (M Ed); English (MA); environmental education (M Ed); French (MA, PhD); German (MA, PhD); Greek (MA); guidance and counseling (M Ed); health studies (MA, PhD), including health sciences education (MA), health services management (MA), medical and surgical nursing science (critical care general) (MA), midwifery and neonatal nursing science (MA), trauma and emergency care (MA); history (MA, PhD); history of education (Ed D); inclusive education (M Ed, Ed D); information and communications technology policy and regulation (MA); information science (MA, MIS, PhD); international politics (MA, PhD); Islamic studies (MA, PhD); Italian (MA, PhD); Judaica (MA, PhD); linguistics (MA, PhD); mathematical education (M Ed); mathematics education (MA); missiology (M Th, D Th); modern Hebrew (MA, PhD); musicology (MA, MMus, D Mus, PhD); natural science education (M Ed); New Testament (M Th, D Th); Old Testament (D Th); pastoral therapy (M Th, D Th); philosophy (MA); philosophy of education (M Ed, Ed D); politics (MA, PhD); Portuguese (MA, PhD); practical theology (M Th, D Th); psychology (MA, MS, PhD); psychology of education (M Ed, Ed D); public health (MA); religious studies (MA, D Th, PhD); Romance languages (MA); Russian (MA, PhD); Semitic languages (MA, PhD); social behavior studies in HIV/AIDS (MA); social science (mental health) (MA); social science in development studies (MA); social science in psychology (MA); social science in social work (MA); social science in sociology (MA); social work (MSW, DSW, PhD); socio-education (M Ed, Ed D); sociolinguistics (MA); sociology (MA, PhD); Spanish (MA, PhD); systematic theology (M Th, D Th); TESOL (teaching English to speakers of other languages) (MA); theological ethics (M Th, D Th); theory of literature (MA, PhD); urban ministries (D Th); urban ministry (M Th).

University of South Carolina, The Graduate School, College of Arts and Sciences, Department of Philosophy, Columbia, SC 29208. Offers MA, PhD. Part-time programs available. *Degree requirements:* For master's, one foreign language, comprehensive exam, thesis optional; for doctorate, one foreign language, comprehensive exam, thesis/dissertation, candidacy exam. *Entrance requirements:* For master's and doctorate, GRE General Test, 18 hours in philosophy, 3 letters of recommendation, writing sample. Additional exam requirements/recommendations for international students: Required—TOEFL (minimum score 590 paper-based; 243 computer-based). Electronic applications accepted. *Faculty research:* History of philosophy, ethics, philosophy of science, social philosophy.

University of Southern California, Graduate School, College of Letters, Arts and Sciences, School of Philosophy, Los Angeles, CA 90089. Offers MA, PhD. Terminal master's awarded for partial completion of doctoral program. *Degree requirements:* For master's, one foreign language, thesis or alternative; for doctorate, one foreign language, thesis/dissertation. *Entrance requirements:* For master's, GRE; for doctorate, GRE General Test. *Faculty research:* History of modern philosophy, philosophy of mind and language, moral and political philosophy, epistomology, meta physics.

University of Southern Mississippi, Graduate School, College of Arts and Letters, Department of Philosophy and Religion, Hattiesburg, MS 39406-0001. Offers philosophy (MA). Part-time programs available. *Faculty:* 6 full-time (1 woman). *Students:* 5 full-time (0 women), 5 part-time (1 woman); includes 2 minority (1 African American, 1 Hispanic American). Average age 30. 4 applicants, 50% accepted, 2 enrolled. In 2008, 1 master's awarded. *Degree requirements:* For master's, one foreign language, comprehensive exam, thesis. *Entrance requirements:* For master's, GRE General Test, minimum GPA of 3.0 in philosophy, 2.75 last 60 hours. Additional exam requirements/recommendations for international students: Required—TOEFL. *Application deadline:* For fall admission, 3/1 for domestic and international students. Applications are processed on a rolling basis. Application fee: $30. *Financial support:* In 2008–09, 6 teaching assistantships with full tuition reimbursements (averaging $6,000 per year) were awarded; research assistantships, Federal Work-Study, scholarships/grants, and unspecified assistantships also available. Financial award application deadline: 3/15; financial award applicants required to submit FAFSA. *Faculty research:* Philosophy of religion, American philosophy, Oriental philosophy, philosophy of medicine. *Unit head:* Dr. David Holley, Chair, 601-266-4518,

Fax: 601-266-5800. *Application contact:* Dr. Paula Smithka, Graduate Coordinator, 601-266-4518, Fax: 601-266-5800.

University of South Florida, Graduate School, College of Arts and Sciences, Department of Philosophy, Tampa, FL 33620-9951. Offers MA, PhD. Part-time and evening/weekend programs available. *Faculty:* 13 full-time (4 women), 1 part-time/adjunct (0 women). *Students:* 44 full-time (11 women), 30 part-time (4 women); includes 10 minority (2 African Americans, 8 Hispanic Americans), 2 international. 47 applicants, 64% accepted, 12 enrolled. In 2008, 7 master's, 1 doctorate awarded. Terminal master's awarded for partial completion of doctoral program. *Degree requirements:* For master's, one foreign language, comprehensive exam, thesis or alternative; for doctorate, 2 foreign languages, comprehensive exam, thesis/dissertation. *Entrance requirements:* For master's, GRE General Test, minimum GPA of 3.0 in last 60 hours, writing sample, statement of purpose, references; for doctorate, GRE General Test, writing sample, statement of purpose, references. Additional exam requirements/recommendations for international students: Required—TOEFL (minimum score 550 paper-based; 213 computer-based). *Application deadline:* For fall admission, 2/15 for domestic students, 1/2 for international students; for spring admission, 10/15 for domestic students, 6/1 for international students. Application fee: $30. Electronic applications accepted. *Expenses:* Tuition, state resident: full-time $2624.40; part-time $291.60 per credit hour. Tuition, nonresident: full-time $7822; part-time $869.13 per credit hour. *Financial support:* In 2008–09, 34 students received support; fellowships with partial tuition reimbursements available, teaching assistantships with partial tuition reimbursements available, health care benefits and unspecified assistantships available. Financial award application deadline: 1/2. *Faculty research:* Ancient philosophy, social philosophy, ethics, continental philosophy, philosophy of science. Total annual research expenditures: $104,989. *Unit head:* Dr. Roger Ariew, Chairperson, 813-974-8207, Fax: 813-974-5914, E-mail: rariew@cas.usf.edu. *Application contact:* Darlene Corcoran, Academic Program Specialist, 813-974-5955, Fax: 813-974-5914, E-mail: dcorcoran@chuma1.cas.usf.edu.

The University of Tennessee, Graduate School, College of Arts and Sciences, Department of Philosophy, Knoxville, TN 37996. Offers medical ethics (MA, PhD); philosophy (MA, PhD); religious studies (MA). Part-time programs available. *Degree requirements:* For master's, thesis or alternative; for doctorate, one foreign language, thesis/dissertation. *Entrance requirements:* For master's and doctorate, GRE General Test, minimum GPA of 2.7. Additional exam requirements/recommendations for international students: Required—TOEFL. Electronic applications accepted. *Expenses:* Tuition, area resident: Part-time $348 per credit hour. Tuition, state resident: full-time $6262. Tuition, nonresident: full-time $18,920; part-time $1052 per credit hour. Required fees: $812; $36 per credit hour. Tuition and fees vary according to program.

The University of Texas at Austin, Graduate School, College of Liberal Arts, Department of Philosophy, Austin, TX 78712-1111. Offers PhD. Part-time programs available. Terminal master's awarded for partial completion of doctoral program. *Degree requirements:* For doctorate, one foreign language, thesis/dissertation. *Entrance requirements:* For doctorate, GRE General Test. Electronic applications accepted. *Faculty research:* Ancient philosophy, cognitive science, continental philosophy, history and philosophy of science.

The University of Toledo, College of Graduate Studies, College of Arts and Sciences, Department of Philosophy, Toledo, OH 43606-3390. Offers MA. Part-time programs available. *Degree requirements:* For master's, exam. Electronic applications accepted. *Faculty research:* History of philosophy, ethics, social/political philosophy, philosophy of science, European philosophy.

University of Toronto, School of Graduate Studies, Humanities Division, Department of Philosophy, Toronto, ON M5S 1A1, Canada. Offers MA, PhD. Part-time programs available. *Degree requirements:* For doctorate, one foreign language, thesis/dissertation. *Entrance requirements:* For master's, GRE, 6 courses in philosophy; minimum A– average in philosophy courses; B overall, 2 letters of reference, writing sample; for doctorate, GRE, MA in philosophy, minimum A– average, 2 letters of reference, writing sample. Additional exam requirements/recommendations for international students: Required—TOEFL (minimum score 600 paper-based), TWE (minimum score 5).

University of Utah, The Graduate School, College of Humanities, Department of Philosophy, Salt Lake City, UT 84112-1107. Offers MA, MS, PhD. Part-time programs available. *Degree requirements:* For master's, comprehensive exam, thesis or alternative; for doctorate, thesis/dissertation, qualifying oral exam. *Entrance requirements:* For master's, GRE General Test, minimum undergraduate GPA of 3.0; for doctorate, GRE General Test. Additional exam requirements/recommendations for international students: Required—TOEFL (minimum score 500 paper-based; 173 computer-based). *Faculty research:* Social philosophy, ethics, metaphysics, political philosophy, logic.

University of Victoria, Faculty of Graduate Studies, Faculty of Humanities, Department of Philosophy, Victoria, BC V8W 2Y2, Canada. Offers MA. Part-time and evening/weekend programs available. *Degree requirements:* For master's, thesis. *Entrance requirements:* For master's, writing sample. Additional exam requirements/recommendations for international students: Required—TOEFL (minimum score 575 paper-based; 233 computer-based), IELTS (minimum score 7). *Faculty research:* Ethics, metaphysics, philosophy of mind, history of philosophy, political philosophy.

University of Virginia, College and Graduate School of Arts and Sciences, Department of Philosophy, Charlottesville, VA 22903. Offers MA, PhD, JD/MA. *Faculty:* 13 full-time (3 women), 1 part-time/adjunct (0 women). *Students:* 31 full-time (8 women), 4 international. Average age 30. 127 applicants, 9% accepted, 6 enrolled. In 2008, 5 master's, 2 doctorates awarded. *Degree requirements:* For master's, 2 papers; for doctorate, thesis/dissertation, 2 papers. *Entrance requirements:* For master's and doctorate, GRE General Test, GRE Subject Test, 3 letters of recommendation; writing sample. Additional exam requirements/recommendations for international students: Required—TOEFL (minimum score 600 paper-based; 250 computer-based; 90 iBT), IELTS. *Application deadline:* For fall admission, 1/5 for domestic and international students. Applications are processed on a rolling basis. Application fee: $60. Electronic applications accepted. *Expenses:* Tuition, area resident: Full-time $10,452. Tuition, state resident: full-time $10,452. Tuition, nonresident: full-time $20,010. Required fees: $2176. Part-time tuition and fees vary according to course load and program. *Financial support:* Fellowships, teaching assistantships available. Financial award applicants required to submit FAFSA. *Unit head:* Jorge Secada, Chair, 434-924-7701, Fax: 434-924-6927. *Application contact:* Mitch Green, Director of Graduate Admissions, E-mail: msg6m@virginia.edu.

University of Washington, Graduate School, College of Arts and Sciences, Department of Philosophy, Seattle, WA 98195. Offers classics and philosophy (PhD); philosophy (MA, PhD). Terminal master's awarded for partial completion of doctoral program. *Degree requirements:* For master's, 3 papers; for doctorate, thesis/dissertation, general exam. *Entrance requirements:* For master's and doctorate, GRE, minimum GPA of 3.0. Additional exam requirements/recommendations for international students: Required—TOEFL. *Faculty research:* History and philosophy of science, epistemology, Aristotle's metaphysics, ethics and politics, causation in modern philosophy.

University of Waterloo, Graduate Studies, Faculty of Arts, Department of Philosophy, Waterloo, ON N2L 3G1, Canada. Offers MA, PhD. *Degree requirements:* For master's, thesis or alternative; for doctorate, one foreign language, thesis/dissertation. *Entrance requirements:* For master's, honors degree, minimum B+ average, writing sample, resumé; for doctorate, master's degree, minimum A- average, resumé. Additional exam requirements/recommendations for international students: Required—TOEFL, TWE. Electronic applications accepted. *Faculty research:* Logic, ethics, social/political, cognitive science, philosophy of science.

The University of Western Ontario, Faculty of Graduate Studies, Faculty of Arts and Humanities, Department of Philosophy, London, ON N6A 5B8, Canada. Offers MA, PhD. *Degree requirements:* For master's, 1 competency exam; for doctorate, comprehensive exam, thesis/dissertation, 2 competency exams. *Entrance requirements:* For master's, honors degree, statement of philosophical interests. Additional exam requirements/recommendations for international students: Required—TOEFL (minimum score 600 paper-based; 250 computer-based). Electronic applications accepted. *Faculty research:* Philosophy of science, history of philosophy, philosophy of law, ethics, epistemology.

University of Windsor, Faculty of Graduate Studies, Faculty of Arts and Social Sciences, Department of Philosophy, Windsor, ON N9B 3P4, Canada. Offers MA. Part-time programs available. *Degree requirements:* For master's, thesis. *Entrance requirements:* For master's, minimum B average. Additional exam requirements/recommendations for international students: Required—TOEFL (minimum score 600 paper-based; 250 computer-based). Electronic applications accepted. *Faculty research:* Informal logic, contemporary Continental philosophy, epistemology.

University of Wisconsin–Madison, Graduate School, College of Letters and Science, Department of Philosophy, Madison, WI 53706-1380. Offers MA, PhD. Part-time programs available. Terminal master's awarded for partial completion of doctoral program. *Degree requirements:* For master's, thesis, preliminary exams; for doctorate, thesis/dissertation, preliminary exams. *Entrance requirements:* For doctorate, GRE, BA in philosophy or related area. Additional exam requirements/recommendations for international students: Required—TOEFL. Electronic applications accepted. *Faculty research:* History of philosophy, logic, philosophy of science, philosophy of mind, metaphysics.

University of Wisconsin–Milwaukee, Graduate School, College of Letters and Sciences, Department of Philosophy, Milwaukee, WI 53201-0413. Offers MA. Part-time programs available. *Faculty:* 15 full-time (4 women). *Students:* 21 full-time (4 women), 2 part-time (1 woman); includes 3 minority (1 American Indian/Alaska Native, 2 Asian Americans or Pacific Islanders), 2 international. Average age 28. 97 applicants, 22% accepted, 11 enrolled. In 2008, 10 master's awarded. *Degree requirements:* For master's, thesis or alternative. *Entrance requirements:* For master's, GRE General Test. Additional exam requirements/recommendations for international students: Required—TOEFL (minimum score 550 paper-based; 79 iBT), IELTS (minimum score 6.5). *Application deadline:* For fall admission, 1/1 priority date for domestic students; for spring admission, 9/1 for domestic students. Applications are processed on a rolling basis. Application fee: $45 ($75 for international students). *Expenses:* Tuition, area resident: Full-time $7320; part-time $165 per credit. Tuition, state resident: full-time $7320; part-time $165 per credit. Tuition, nonresident: full-time $17,840; part-time $714 per credit. Tuition and fees vary according to campus/location, program and reciprocity agreements. *Financial support:* In 2008–09, 18 teaching assistantships were awarded; career-related internships or fieldwork and unspecified assistantships also available. Support available to part-time students. Financial award application deadline: 4/15. Total annual research expenditures: $107,264. *Unit head:* Robert Schwartz, Representative, 414-229-5216, Fax: 414-229-5022, E-mail: schwartz@uwm.edu. *Application contact:* Carla Bagnoli, General Information Contact, 414-229-5215, Fax: 414-229-6967, E-mail: cbagnoli@uwm.edu.

University of Wyoming, Graduate School, College of Arts and Sciences, Department of Philosophy, Laramie, WY 82070. Offers MA. Part-time programs available. *Faculty:* 6 full-time (1 woman). *Students:* 5 full-time (0 women), 2 part-time (1 woman). Average age 30. 7 applicants, 86% accepted, 4 enrolled. In 2008, 4 master's awarded. *Degree requirements:* For master's, thesis, logic proficiency, first-year paper. *Entrance requirements:* For master's, GRE General Test, minimum GPA of 3.0. Additional exam requirements/recommendations for international students: Required—TOEFL (minimum score 525 paper-based; 197 computer-based). *Application deadline:* For spring admission, 2/1 priority date for domestic students, 2/1 for international students. Applications are processed on a rolling basis. Application fee: $50. Electronic applications accepted. *Financial support:* In 2008–09, 25 teaching assistantships with full tuition reimbursements (averaging $11,072 per year) were awarded; health care benefits also available. Financial award application deadline: 2/1. *Faculty research:* Philosophy of science, political and ethical theory, philosophy of language, epistemology, philosophy of mind, early modern philosophy. *Unit head:* Dr. Ed Sherline, Head, 307-766-3204, E-mail: sherline@uwyo.edu. *Application contact:* Dr. Franz-Peter Griesmaier, Graduate Advisor, 307-766-3231, E-mail: fpg@uwyo.edu.

Vanderbilt University, Graduate School, Department of Philosophy, Nashville, TN 37240-1001. Offers MA, PhD. *Faculty:* 21 full-time (5 women). *Students:* 45 full-time (21 women), 1 part-time (0 women); includes 3 minority (1 African American, 1 American Indian/Alaska Native, 1 Hispanic American), 3 international. Average age 32. 179 applicants, 6% accepted, 7 enrolled. In 2008, 3 master's, 5 doctorates awarded. Terminal master's awarded for partial completion of doctoral program. *Degree requirements:* For doctorate, one foreign language, comprehensive exam, thesis/dissertation, final and qualifying exams. *Entrance requirements:* For doctorate, GRE General Test, writing sample. Additional exam requirements/recommendations for international students: Required—TOEFL (minimum score 570 paper-based; 230 computer-based; 88 iBT). *Application deadline:* For fall admission, 1/15 for domestic and international students. Application fee: $0. Electronic applications accepted. *Financial support:* Fellowships with full tuition reimbursements, teaching assistantships with full tuition reimbursements, Federal Work-Study, institutionally sponsored loans, scholarships/grants, and health care benefits available. Financial award application deadline: 1/15; financial award applicants required to submit CSS PROFILE or FAFSA. *Faculty research:* Ancient, medieval, and modern philosophy; philosophy of science; ethics; philosophy of language; philosophy of religion. *Unit head:* Jeffrey Tlumak, Chair, 615-322-2637, Fax: 615-343-7259, E-mail: jeffrey.tlumak@vanderbilt.edu. *Application contact:* Robert Talisse, Director of Graduate Studies, 615-322-2637, Fax: 615-343-7259, E-mail: robert.talisse@vanderbilt.edu.

Villanova University, Graduate School of Liberal Arts and Sciences, Department of Philosophy, Villanova, PA 19085-1699. Offers PhD. Part-time and evening/weekend programs available. *Faculty:* 8 full-time (3 women). *Students:* 52 full-time (17 women); includes 2 minority (1 Asian American or Pacific Islander, 1 Hispanic American), 5 international. Average age 29. 111 applicants, 9% accepted, 10 enrolled. In 2008, 3 doctorates awarded. *Degree requirements:* For doctorate, 2 foreign languages, comprehensive exam, thesis/dissertation. *Entrance requirements:* For doctorate, GRE General Test, GRE Subject Test, minimum GPA of 3.5. *Application deadline:* For fall admission, 2/1 for domestic and international students. Applications are processed on a rolling basis. Application fee: $50. Electronic applications accepted. *Financial support:* Research assistantships, teaching assistantships, Federal Work-Study available. Financial award applicants required to submit FAFSA. *Unit head:* Dr. Walter Brogan, Chairman, 610-519-4690. *Application contact:* Dr. Gerald Long, Dean, Graduate School of Liberal Arts and Sciences, 610-519-7093, Fax: 610-519-7096.

Virginia Polytechnic Institute and State University, Graduate School, College of Liberal Arts and Human Sciences, Department of Philosophy, Blacksburg, VA 24061. Offers MA. *Entrance requirements:* For master's, GRE General Test. Additional exam requirements/recommendations for international students: Required—TOEFL (minimum score 550 paper-based; 213 computer-based). Electronic applications accepted. *Faculty research:* History of philosophy, ethics, history and philosophy of science and philosophy.

Washington State University, Graduate School, College of Liberal Arts, Department of Philosophy, Pullman, WA 99164. Offers MA. *Degree requirements:* For master's, comprehensive exam (for some programs), thesis (for some programs). *Entrance requirements:* For master's, GRE, minimum GPA of 3.0, 3 letters of recommendation, writing sample. Additional exam requirements/recommendations for international students: Required—TOEFL. *Faculty research:* Philosophy of language and mind, philosophy of race and ethnicity, social and political philosophy.

Washington University in St. Louis, Graduate School of Arts and Sciences, Department of Philosophy, St. Louis, MO 63130-4899. Offers philosophy (MA, PhD); philosophy/neuroscience/psychology (PhD). *Students:* 22 full-time (7 women), 1 international. 104 applicants, 6% accepted, 3 enrolled. In 2008, 6 master's, 4 doctorates awarded. Terminal master's awarded

Philosophy

Washington University in St. Louis (continued)
for partial completion of doctoral program. *Degree requirements:* For master's, thesis optional; for doctorate, thesis/dissertation. *Entrance requirements:* For master's and doctorate, GRE General Test, sample of written work. *Application deadline:* For fall admission, 1/15 priority date for domestic students. Application fee: $45. Electronic applications accepted. *Financial support:* Fellowships, teaching assistantships, career-related internships or fieldwork, Federal Work-Study, institutionally sponsored loans, and tuition waivers (full and partial) available. Support available to part-time students. Financial award application deadline: 1/15. *Unit head:* Dr. Mark Rollins, Chairperson, 314-935-5119. *Application contact:* Assistant to the Dean, 314-935-6880, Fax: 314-935-4887.

Wayne State University, College of Liberal Arts and Sciences, Department of Philosophy, Detroit, MI 48202. Offers MA, PhD. Terminal master's awarded for partial completion of doctoral program. *Degree requirements:* For master's, thesis; for doctorate, one foreign language, thesis/dissertation. *Entrance requirements:* For master's, GRE General Test or minimum GPA of 3.0; for doctorate, undergraduate GPA of at least 3.0. Additional exam requirements/recommendations for international students: Required—TOEFL (minimum score 550 paper-based; 213 computer-based); Recommended—TWE (minimum score 6). Electronic applications accepted. *Faculty research:* Metaphysics; ancient philosophy; philosophy of art; ethics; philosophy of science.

West Chester University of Pennsylvania, Office of Graduate Studies, College of Arts and Sciences, Department of Philosophy, West Chester, PA 19383. Offers business ethics (Certificate); healthcare ethics (Certificate); philosophy (MA). Part-time and evening/weekend programs available. *Students:* 16 full-time (6 women), 12 part-time (5 women); includes 1 minority (African American), 1 international. Average age 31. 21 applicants, 90% accepted, 11 enrolled. In 2008, 3 master's awarded. *Degree requirements:* For master's, thesis optional, thesis or comprehensive exam. *Entrance requirements:* For master's, GRE or writing sample, three letters of reference. Additional exam requirements/recommendations for international students: Required—TOEFL (minimum score 550 paper-based; 213 computer-based; 80 iBT).

Application deadline: For fall admission, 4/15 priority date for domestic students, 3/15 for international students; for spring admission, 10/15 for domestic students, 9/1 for international students. Applications are processed on a rolling basis. Application fee: $35. Electronic applications accepted. *Expenses:* Tuition, state resident: full-time $6430; part-time $357 per credit. Tuition, nonresident: full-time $10,288; part-time $572 per credit. Required fees: $652.50; $50 per credit. $67 per semester. *Financial support:* In 2008–09, 5 research assistantships with full and partial tuition reimbursements (averaging $5,000 per year) were awarded; unspecified assistantships also available. Support available to part-time students. Financial award application deadline: 2/15; financial award applicants required to submit FAFSA. *Faculty research:* International studies. *Unit head:* Dr. Joan Woolfrey, Chair, 610-436-1004, E-mail: jwoolfrey@wcupa.edu. *Application contact:* Dr. Helen Daley Schroepfer, Graduate Coordinator, 610-436-2429, E-mail: hschroepfer@wcupa.edu.

Western Michigan University, Graduate College, College of Arts and Sciences, Department of Philosophy, Kalamazoo, MI 49008-5202. Offers MA. *Degree requirements:* For master's, thesis optional.

Wilfrid Laurier University, Faculty of Graduate Studies, Faculty of Arts, Department of Philosophy, Waterloo, ON N2L 3C5, Canada. Offers MA. *Entrance requirements:* For master's, Honours BA in philosophy or equivalent with a minimum B+ in philosophy and in final year. Additional exam requirements/recommendations for international students: Required—TOEFL (minimum score 230 computer-based; 89 iBT). Electronic applications accepted. *Faculty research:* Self, agency, community.

Yale University, Graduate School of Arts and Sciences, Department of Philosophy, New Haven, CT 06520. Offers PhD. *Degree requirements:* For doctorate, 2 foreign languages, thesis/dissertation. *Entrance requirements:* For doctorate, GRE General Test.

York University, Faculty of Graduate Studies, Faculty of Arts, Program in Philosophy, Toronto, ON M3J 1P3, Canada. Offers MA, PhD. Part-time programs available. *Degree requirements:* For master's, thesis or alternative; for doctorate, one foreign language, thesis/dissertation. Electronic applications accepted.

SOUTHERN ILLINOIS UNIVERSITY CARBONDALE

Department of Philosophy
Ph.D. Program

Programs of Study

The Department of Philosophy at Southern Illinois University Carbondale (SIUC) offers the Ph.D. degree, centered on a diverse, pluralistic curriculum in several contemporary philosophical traditions and in the history of philosophy. It is internationally recognized for its strength, especially in American philosophy, including pragmatism, idealism, and process philosophy. It also offers strengths in nineteenth- and twentieth-century Continental philosophy, value studies (ethics, social and political philosophy, aesthetics), and philosophy of religion. In addition, the Department regularly offers courses in the history of ancient, medieval, and modern philosophy; Asian philosophy (Indian philosophy, Chinese philosophy, Buddhism, Islamic philosophy); metaphysics; philosophy of mind; epistemology; feminist philosophy; and philosophy of science and technology. The 15 faculty members of the Department are all committed teachers and active scholars, both nationally and internationally.

The program is designed for students looking to teach philosophy at the college level. Students pursuing the Ph.D. must complete a rigorous schedule of 30 semester hours of course work beyond the M.A. All students must demonstrate competence in formal logic during the first year of residence, as required for the M.A. degree, and also demonstrate a background in the history of philosophy by passing the Department's M.A. comprehensive examination on the history of philosophy. Incoming doctoral students are expected to take this examination within the first year after entering the Ph.D. program. Students must fulfill a research tool requirement by showing an extensive knowledge and usage of one foreign language and completing a seminar in the history of the analytic movement. All candidates must pass a written preliminary examination on the following three areas: metaphysics, epistemology, and value fields (ethics, social philosophy, and aesthetics). These examinations are normally taken only after the student has accumulated at least 24 hours of credit beyond the M.A. degree. Upon completion of 30 hours course work, students must complete a dissertation to satisfy all degree requirements.

Opportunities to enhance studies are offered through lecture series and opportunities to study abroad in countries such as Greece, Egypt, Germany, France, Japan, and Iran.

Research Facilities

The Center for Dewey Studies is widely recognized internationally as one of the leading research centers for the study of American philosophy. SIUC's Morris Library also provides excellent research facilities, with more than 2 million volumes, an extensive collection of philosophical journals, and important archives in American philosophy, including the Open Court papers of Paul Carus as well as the papers of John Dewey, J. H. Tufts, Stephen Pepper, Edward Scribner Ames, and Henry Weiman.

Financial Aid

In addition to various scholarships awarded through the Graduate School, the Department of Philosophy offers approximately thirty graduate assistantship appointments of 25 to 50 percent, which currently pay $5301 to $11,898 plus a tuition waiver.

Cost of Study

In-state graduate tuition is $328 per credit hour in 2009–10. Out-of-state tuition is 2.5 times the in-state tuition rate ($820 per credit hour). Graduate students with at least a 25 percent appointment as a graduate assistant receive a tuition scholarship. Fees vary from $589.03 (1 credit hour) to $1557.50 (12 credit hours). Students with a graduate assistantship receive a 50 percent reduction in the primary care medical fee. New graduate students from Arkansas, Indiana, Kentucky, Missouri, and Tennessee qualify for the alternate tuition rate, which is equivalent to the in-state graduate tuition rate.

Living and Housing Costs

For married couples, students with families, and single graduate students, the University has 690 efficiency and one-, two-, three-, and four-bedroom apartments that rent for $499 to $720 per month in 2009–10. Residence halls for single graduate students are also available, as are accessible residence hall rooms and apartments for students with disabilities.

Student Group

The more than 60 graduate students are encouraged to take an active role in the Department. They have their own Graduate Philosophy Union; host their own weekly colloquium, Agora; publish *Kinesis,* one of the oldest and most respected graduate journals; and annually host their own conference, Building Bridges, which aims to promote dialogue across disciplines and philosophical traditions.

Location

SIUC is 350 miles south of Chicago and 100 miles southeast of St. Louis. Nestled in rolling hills bordered by the Ohio and Mississippi Rivers and enhanced by a mild climate, the area has state parks, national forests and wildlife refuges, and large lakes for outdoor recreation, including the 240,000 acres of the Shawnee National Forest. Cultural offerings include theater, opera, concerts, art exhibits, and cinema. Educational facilities for the families of students are excellent.

The University and The Department

Southern Illinois University Carbondale is a comprehensive public university with a variety of general and professional education programs. The University offers bachelor's and associate degrees, master's and doctoral degrees, the J.D. degree, and the M.D. degree. The University is fully accredited by the North Central Association of Colleges and Schools. The Graduate School has an essential role in the development and coordination of graduate instruction and research programs. The Graduate Council has academic responsibility for determining graduate standards, recommending new graduate programs and research centers, and establishing policies to facilitate the research effort. Southern Illinois University Carbondale is a state-funded university founded in 1869. The Department of Philosophy is part of the College of Liberal Arts.

Applying

Interested students should apply online at https://www.gradapp.siu.edu/. A completed application includes a completed application form with a $45 nonrefundable application fee, an official transcript from each college attended, a sample of the applicant's written work, three letters of recommendation from individuals who are familiar with the applicant's academic work (to be sent directly to the Academic Secretary), a personal statement, and Graduate Record Examination scores (required for fellowship applications and assistantships but not for admission to the program). International students are also required to submit TOEFL scores of at least 550 (paper-based test) or 220 (computer-based test) and a copy of their passport.

For students to be properly considered for financial assistance, applications should be completed by the end of December.

Correspondence and Information

Rich Black
Academic Secretary
Department of Philosophy
980 Faner Drive, Mailcode 4505
Southern Illinois University
Carbondale, Illinois 62901
Phone: 618-453-7429
Fax: 618-453-7428
E-mail: phildept@siu.edu
Web site: http://www.siu.edu/~philos/

Southern Illinois University Carbondale

THE FACULTY AND THEIR RESEARCH

Thomas Alexander, Professor; Ph.D., Emory, 1984. American philosophy, aesthetics, classical philosophy, Dewey.

Douglas Anderson, Professor; Ph.D., Penn State, 1984. History of philosophy and American philosophy, philosophy's relationship to other dimensions of culture, Charles Peirce and the history of pragmatism.

Randall E. Auxier, Professor; Ph.D., Emory, 1992. American philosophy, post-Kantian Continental philosophy, process and systematic philosophy/theology, history of philosophy, metaphysics, moral philosophy and theology, political theory, philosophy of education.

Sara Beardsworth, Associate Professor; Ph.D., Warwick (England), 1994. Nineteenth- and twentieth-century European philosophy.

Douglas L. Berger, Assistant Professor; Ph.D., Temple, 2000. Classical and contemporary Brahminical and Indian Buddhist philosophies, classical Chinese philosophy, cross-cultural philosophical hermeneutics.

David S. Clarke Jr., Professor Emeritus; Ph.D., Emory, 1964.

Gerard Delahoussaye, Assistant Professor; Ph.D., Ottawa, 2004. Medieval philosophy, John Duns Scotus.

Elizabeth R. Eames, Professor Emerita; Ph.D., Bryn Mawr, 1951.

Eugenia Gatens-Robinson, Associate Professor Emerita; Ph.D., Southern Illinois at Carbondale, 1983.

Garth J. Gillan, Professor Emeritus; Ph.D., Duquesne, 1966.

Robert Hahn, Professor; Ph.D., Yale, 1976. Greek philosophy, Aristotle, Kant, history of philosophy.

Larry Hickman, Professor; Ph.D., Texas at Austin, 1971. Classical American philosophy (Peirce, Mead, James, Dewey), philosophy of technology, philosophy of culture.

John Howie, Professor Emeritus; Ph.D., Boston University, 1965.

Matthew J. Kelly, Associate Professor Emeritus; Ph.D., Notre Dame, 1963.

Pat Manfredi, Associate Professor; Ph.D., Notre Dame. Metaphysics, philosophy of mind, epistemology, recent analytic philosophy.

George Kimball Plochmann, Professor Emeritus; Ph.D., Chicago, 1950.

George Schedler, Professor and Chair; Ph.D., California, San Diego, 1973; J.D., Southern Illinois, 1987. Philosophy of law, social philosophy, ethics.

Anthony Steinbock, Professor; Ph.D., SUNY at Stony Brook, 1993. Contemporary French and German philosophy, phenomenology, social ontology, aesthetics.

Kenneth W. Stikkers, Professor; Ph.D., DePaul, 1982. American philosophy, Continental philosophy, ethics, Scheler, James.

Stephen Tyman, Associate Professor; Ph.D., Toronto, 1980. Eighteenth- and nineteenth-century European philosophy, phenomenology, and existentialism.

Andrew Youpa, Assistant Professor; Ph.D., California, Irvine, 2002. Modern philosophy, modern moral philosophy, contemporary moral philosophy.

Section 12
Religious Studies

This section contains a directory of institutions offering graduate work in religious studies, followed by in-depth entries submitted by institutions that chose to prepare detailed program descriptions. Additional information about programs listed in the directory but not augmented by an in-depth entry may be obtained by writing directly to the dean of a graduate school or chair of a department at the address given in the directory.

For programs offering related work, see also in this book *Area and Cultural Studies, History, Humanities,* and *Philosophy.* In another guide in this series:

Graduate Programs in Business, Education, Health, Information Studies, Law & Social Work

See *Subject Areas (Religious Education)*

CONTENTS

Program Directories

Missions and Missiology 482
Pastoral Ministry and Counseling 485
Religion 497
Theology 508

Announcement

St. Mary's Seminary and University 522

Close-Ups

The Jewish Theological Seminary
   Graduate Studies 529
   Rabbinical Studies 531
Seton Hall University 533

See also:

Argosy University, Sarasota—Psychology and
   Behavioral Sciences 1091
California Institute of Integral Studies—Humanities 347
Naropa University—Graduate Studies 1121

Missions and Missiology

Abilene Christian University, Graduate School, College of Biblical Studies, Graduate School of Theology, Program in Missions, Abilene, TX 79699-9100. Offers MA. Part-time programs available. *Students:* 4 full-time (all women), 1 (woman) part-time; includes 1 minority (African American). 3 applicants, 33% accepted, 0 enrolled. *Entrance requirements:* For master's, GRE, MAT. *Application deadline:* For fall admission, 4/1 priority date for domestic students; for spring admission, 11/1 for domestic students. Applications are processed on a rolling basis. Application fee: $40 ($45 for international students). Electronic applications accepted. *Expenses:* Tuition: Full-time $10,728; part-time $640 per hour. Required fees: $1090; $53.50 per hour. $10 per term. Tuition and fees vary according to campus/location. *Financial support:* Teaching assistantships, career-related internships or fieldwork available. Financial award application deadline: 4/1; financial award applicants required to submit FAFSA. *Faculty research:* Animism, contextualization, missions education. *Unit head:* Dr. Chris Flanders, Graduate Adviser, 325-674-3742, Fax: 325-674-6180, E-mail: clf03c@acu.edu. *Application contact:* William Horn, Graduate Admissions Counselor, 325-674-2656, Fax: 325-674-6717, E-mail: gradinfo@acu.edu.

Alliance Theological Seminary, Graduate and Professional Programs, Nyack, NY 10960. Offers Christian ministry (MPS); counseling (MA); intercultural studies (MA); missions (MPS); New Testament (MA); Old Testament (MA); theology (M Div); urban ministry (MPS). *Accreditation:* ATS. Part-time programs available. *Degree requirements:* For master's, comprehensive exam (for some programs), thesis optional, internships; for M Div, 2 foreign languages, internship. *Entrance requirements:* Proficiency in New Testament Greek, minimum GPA of 2.5 (undergraduate). Additional exam requirements/recommendations for international students: Required—TOEFL (minimum score 550 paper-based; 213 computer-based).

Ambrose University College, Ambrose Seminary, Calgary, AB T2P 3T5, Canada. Offers biblical/theological studies (MA); Chinese ministries (Certificate); Christian studies (Diploma); church education (M Div); intercultural ministries (M Div, MA, Certificate, Diploma); leadership and ministry (MA, Certificate, Diploma); pastoral ministries (M Div). *Accreditation:* ATS (one or more programs are accredited). Part-time programs available. *Degree requirements:* For master's, 2 foreign languages, internship; for M Div, one foreign language, internship. *Entrance requirements:* For master's, bachelor degree. Additional exam requirements/recommendations for international students: Required—TOEFL or IELTS. Electronic applications accepted. *Faculty research:* Evangelicalism and sociology, missiological trends, chaplaincy, intertestamental studies, postmodernism.

Anderson University, School of Theology, Anderson, IN 46012-3495. Offers missions (MA); theology (M Div, MTS, D Min). *Accreditation:* ACIPE; ATS. Part-time programs available. *Degree requirements:* For master's, one foreign language, thesis, integrative senior seminar; for doctorate, thesis/dissertation; for M Div, thesis/dissertation (for some programs). *Faculty research:* Small-church/bivocational ministry, women in ministry.

Asbury Theological Seminary, Graduate and Professional Programs, Wilmore, KY 40390-1199. Offers MA, MAC, MACE, MACL, MAPC, MAXM, MAYM, Th M, D Miss, PhD, Certificate. *Accreditation:* ATS. Part-time programs available. Postbaccalaureate distance learning degree programs offered (minimal on-campus study). *Faculty:* 67 full-time (15 women), 74 part-time/adjunct (14 women). *Students:* 708 full-time (219 women), 852 part-time (263 women); includes 110 minority (59 African Americans, 10 American Indian/Alaska Native, 12 Asian Americans or Pacific Islanders, 29 Hispanic Americans), 156 international. Average age 25. 765 applicants, 75% accepted, 364 enrolled. In 2008, 95 master's, 15 doctorates, 38 other advanced degrees awarded. Terminal master's awarded for partial completion of doctoral program. *Degree requirements:* For master's, thesis (for some programs); for doctorate, thesis/dissertation, qualifying exam. *Entrance requirements:* For master's, minimum GPA of 2.75; for doctorate, minimum GPA of 3.0. Additional exam requirements/recommendations for international students: Required—TOEFL, IELTS. *Application deadline:* Applications are processed on a rolling basis. Application fee: $50. Electronic applications accepted. *Expenses:* Tuition: Full-time $12,474; part-time $462 per credit hour. Required fees: $50; $30 per year. Tuition and fees vary according to course load, degree level, campus/location and program. *Financial support:* In 2008–09, 1,317 students received support. Career-related internships or fieldwork, Federal Work-Study, institutionally sponsored loans, and scholarships/grants available. Support available to part-time students. Financial award applicants required to submit FAFSA. *Unit head:* Dr. Leslie A. Andrews, Provost, 859-858-2206, Fax: 859-858-2025, E-mail: leslie.andrews@asburyseminary.edu. *Application contact:* Janelle Vernon, Admissions Director, 859-858-2211, Fax: 859-858-2287, E-mail: admissions.office@asburyseminary.edu.

Assemblies of God Theological Seminary, Graduate and Professional Programs, Springfield, MO 65802. Offers biblical preaching (D Min); Christian ministries (MA); divinity (M Div); intercultural studies (D Miss, PhD); missional leadership (D Min); relief and development (D Miss); self-design study (D Min); women in leadership (D Min). *Accreditation:* ATS. Part-time and evening/weekend programs available. Postbaccalaureate distance learning degree programs offered (minimal on-campus study). *Faculty:* 16 full-time (3 women), 21 part-time/adjunct (4 women). *Students:* 220 full-time (69 women), 226 part-time (49 women); includes 49 minority (11 African Americans, 5 American Indian/Alaska Native, 11 Asian Americans or Pacific Islanders, 22 Hispanic Americans), 7 international. Average age 36. *Degree requirements:* For master's, analytical reflection paper or comprehensive exam; for doctorate, thesis/dissertation; for M Div, one foreign language, analytical reflection paper. *Entrance requirements:* For M Div, minimum GPA of 2.0; for master's, minimum GPA of 2.5; for doctorate, minimum GPA of 3.0. Additional exam requirements/recommendations for international students: Required—TOEFL (minimum score 550 paper-based; 213 computer-based; 80 iBT). *Application deadline:* For fall admission, 7/1 priority date for domestic students, 6/1 priority date for international students; for spring admission, 12/1 priority date for domestic students, 11/1 priority date for international students. Applications are processed on a rolling basis. Application fee: $35. Electronic applications accepted. *Financial support:* Career-related internships or fieldwork, Federal Work-Study, and scholarships/grants available. Support available to part-time students. Financial award application deadline: 7/15; financial award applicants required to submit FAFSA. *Unit head:* Stephen Lim, Academic Dean, 417-268-1000, Fax: 417-268-1001, E-mail: slim@agts.edu. *Application contact:* Stephen Lim, Academic Dean, 417-268-1000, Fax: 417-268-1001, E-mail: slim@agts.edu.

Associated Mennonite Biblical Seminary, Graduate and Professional Programs, Elkhart, IN 46517-1999. Offers Christian formation (MA); divinity (M Div); mission and evangelism (MA); peace studies (MA); theological studies (MA, Certificate). *Accreditation:* ACIPE; ATS. Part-time programs available. *Degree requirements:* For master's, comprehensive exam, thesis optional; for M Div, integration paper. *Entrance requirements:* For M Div, master's, and Certificate, 3 letters of reference. Additional exam requirements/recommendations for international students: Required—TOEFL (minimum score 550 paper-based; 213 computer-based). Electronic applications accepted. *Faculty research:* Biblical studies, theology, church history, church leadership.

Baptist Bible College of Pennsylvania, Baptist Bible Seminary, Clarks Summit, PA 18411-1297. Offers biblical studies (PhD); church planting (M Div); global missions (M Div); military chaplaincy (M Div); ministry (M Min, D Min); pastor of church education (M Div); pastor of outreach (M Div); pastoral counseling (M Div); pastoral leadership (M Div); theology (M Div, Th M); youth pastor (M Div). Part-time and evening/weekend programs available. Postbaccalaureate distance learning degree programs offered (minimal on-campus study). Terminal master's awarded for partial completion of doctoral program. *Degree requirements:* For master's, 2 foreign languages, thesis; for doctorate, 2 foreign languages, comprehensive exam (for some programs), thesis/dissertation, oral exam; for M Div, 2 foreign languages, thesis/dissertation, oral exam. *Entrance requirements:* For doctorate, Greek and Hebrew entrance exams (PhD). Electronic applications accepted.

Bethel Seminary, Graduate and Professional Programs, St. Paul, MN 55112-6998. Offers applied ministry (MA); biblical studies (MATS, Certificate); children's and family ministry (MACFM); Christian education (MACE); Christian thought (M Div, MACT); church leadership (D Min); community ministry leadership (MA, Certificate); congregation and family care (D Min); global and contextual studies (MA, MATS); historical studies (MATS); lay ministry (Certificate); marriage and family studies (M Div); marriage and family therapy (MAMFT, Certificate); pastoral ministries (M Div); spiritual formation (Certificate); theological studies (MATS, Certificate); transformational leadership (MATL); youth ministries (MACE). *Accreditation:* ACIPE; ATS (one or more programs are accredited). Part-time and evening/weekend programs available. Postbaccalaureate distance learning degree programs offered (minimal on-campus study). *Faculty:* 26 full-time (2 women), 93 part-time/adjunct (29 women). *Students:* 397 full-time (124 women), 707 part-time (299 women); includes 218 minority (123 African Americans, 1 American Indian/Alaska Native, 67 Asian Americans or Pacific Islanders, 27 Hispanic Americans), 14 international. Average age 36. 470 applicants, 90% accepted, 270 enrolled. In 2008, 63 first professional degrees, 101 master's, 10 doctorates awarded. *Degree requirements:* For master's, variable foreign language requirement, thesis (for some programs); for doctorate, thesis/dissertation; for M Div, one foreign language. *Entrance requirements:* For M Div, letters of reference; for master's, letters of reference, transcripts, personal statement; for doctorate, M Div, letters of reference, essays, organizational support. Additional exam requirements/recommendations for international students: Required—TOEFL (minimum score 550 paper-based; 213 computer-based). *Application deadline:* For fall admission, 8/1 priority date for domestic students, 3/1 for international students; for winter admission, 12/1 priority date for domestic students; for spring admission, 3/1 priority date for domestic students. Applications are processed on a rolling basis. Application fee: $20. Electronic applications accepted. *Financial support:* In 2008–09, 688 students received support, including 20 teaching assistantships; career-related internships or fieldwork, Federal Work-Study, scholarships/grants, and tuition waivers (full) also available. Financial award application deadline: 7/15; financial award applicants required to submit FAFSA. *Faculty research:* Nature of theology, ethics, biblical commentaries, nature of God, science and theology. *Unit head:* Dr. Leland Eliason, Executive Vice President and Provost, 651-638-6182. *Application contact:* Joseph V. Dworak, Director of Admissions, 651-638-6288, Fax: 651-638-6002, E-mail: j-dworak@bethel.edu.

Biblical Theological Seminary, Graduate and Professional Programs, Hatfield, PA 19440-2499. Offers advanced missional leadership (D Min); advanced pastoral studies (Certificate); biblical counseling (Certificate); biblical studies (MA, Certificate); counseling (MA); ministry (MA); missional theology (MA); theology (M Div); youth ministry (Certificate). *Accreditation:* ATS. Part-time programs available. Postbaccalaureate distance learning degree programs offered. *Degree requirements:* For M Div, thesis/dissertation. *Entrance requirements:* Additional exam requirements/recommendations for international students: Required—TOEFL (minimum score 550 paper-based; 213 computer-based). *Faculty research:* Old Testament narrative, Old Testament historiography, Hebrew syntax, parables, addictions.

Biola University, School of Intercultural Studies, La Mirada, CA 90639-0001. Offers applied linguistics (MA); intercultural education (PhD); intercultural studies (MAICS); missiology (D Miss); missions (MA); teaching English to speakers of other languages (MA, Certificate). Part-time and evening/weekend programs available. Terminal master's awarded for partial completion of doctoral program. *Degree requirements:* For master's, one foreign language, comprehensive exam; for doctorate, one foreign language, comprehensive exam, thesis/dissertation. *Entrance requirements:* For master's, minimum undergraduate GPA of 3.0; for doctorate, MA, 3 years of ministry experience, minimum graduate GPA of 3.3. Additional exam requirements/recommendations for international students: Required—TOEFL (minimum score 550 paper-based; 213 computer-based). Electronic applications accepted.

Briercrest Seminary, Graduate Programs, Program in Christian Ministries, Caronport, SK S0H 0S0, Canada. Offers leadership (MA); marriage and family counseling (MA); missions (MA); pastoral counseling (MA); worship (MA); youth and family ministry (MA). Part-time programs available. *Degree requirements:* For master's, comprehensive exam, thesis optional. *Entrance requirements:* Additional exam requirements/recommendations for international students: Required—TOEFL (minimum score 550 paper-based; 213 computer-based).

Calvin Theological Seminary, Graduate and Professional Programs, Grand Rapids, MI 49546-4387. Offers divinity (M Div); educational ministry (MA); historical theology (PhD); missions: church growth (MA); philosophical and moral theology (PhD); systematic theology (PhD); theological studies (MTS); theology (Th M). *Accreditation:* ACIPE; ATS. Part-time programs available. *Degree requirements:* For master's, thesis (for some programs); for doctorate, 4 foreign languages, comprehensive exam, thesis/dissertation; for M Div, 2 foreign languages. *Entrance requirements:* For doctorate, GRE General Test, Hebrew, Greek, and a modern foreign language. Additional exam requirements/recommendations for international students: Required—TOEFL (minimum score 550 paper-based; 213 computer-based), TWE (minimum score 4). Electronic applications accepted. *Faculty research:* Recent Trinity theory, Christian anthropology, Proverbs, reformed confessions, Paul's view of law.

Catholic Theological Union at Chicago, Graduate and Professional Programs, Chicago, IL 60615-5698. Offers biblical spirituality (Certificate); cross-cultural ministries (D Min); cross-cultural missions (Certificate); divinity (M Div); liturgical studies (Certificate); liturgy (D Min); pastoral studies (MAPS, Certificate); spiritual formation (Certificate); spirituality (D Min); theology (MA); M Div/MA; M Div/MSW; M Div/PhD. *Accreditation:* ACIPE; ATS (one or more programs are accredited). Part-time and evening/weekend programs available. *Degree requirements:* For master's, one foreign language, comprehensive exam (for some programs), thesis (for some programs); for doctorate, thesis/dissertation. *Entrance requirements:* For doctorate, master's degree, 5 years of active ministry. *Faculty research:* Doctrine, sacraments, ethics, Bible.

Central Baptist Theological Seminary, Graduate and Professional Programs, Shawnee, KS 66226. Offers missional church studies (MA); theological studies (MA); theology (M Div, Diploma). *Accreditation:* ACIPE; ATS (one or more programs are accredited). Part-time programs available. *Degree requirements:* For master's, thesis optional, MMPI, Myers-Briggs, Enneagram; for M Div, thesis/dissertation optional. *Entrance requirements:* For master's, accredited bachelor's degree with minimum GPA of 2.3. Additional exam requirements/recommendations for international students: Required—TOEFL (minimum score 547 paper-based; 210 computer-based; 77 iBT). Electronic applications accepted.

Columbia International University, Columbia Biblical Seminary and School of Missions, Columbia, SC 29230-3122. Offers academic ministries (M Div); bible exposition (M Div, MABE); biblical studies (Certificate); counseling ministries (Certificate); divinity (M Div); educational ministries (M Div, MAEM, Certificate); intercultural studies (M Div, MAIS, Certificate); leadership (D Min); leadership for evangelism/mobilization (MALM); member care (D Min); ministry (Certificate); missions (D Min); pastoral counseling and spiritual formation (M Div, MAPS); preaching (D Min); theology (MA). *Accreditation:* ATS (one or more programs are accredited). Part-time and evening/weekend programs available. *Degree requirements:* For master's, integrative seminar; for doctorate, comprehensive exam, thesis/dissertation; for M Div, internship. *Entrance requirements:* For master's, minimum GPA of 2.7; for doctorate, 3 years of ministerial experience, M Div. Additional exam requirements/recommendations for international students: Required—TOEFL. Electronic applications accepted.

Dallas Baptist University, College of Adult Education, Liberal Arts Program, Dallas, TX 75211-9299. Offers arts (MLA); Christian ministry (MLA); English (MLA); English as a second language (MLA); fine arts (MLA); history (MLA); missions (MLA); political science (MLA). Part-time and evening/weekend programs available. *Faculty:* 68 full-time (30 women), 113 part-time/adjunct (47 women). *Students:* 1 full-time, 35 part-time. 16 applicants, 81% accepted, 10 enrolled. In 2008, 17 master's awarded. *Entrance requirements:* For master's, minimum GPA of 3.0. Additional exam requirements/recommendations for international students: Required—TOEFL. *Application deadline:* Applications are processed on a rolling basis.

Application fee: $25. Electronic applications accepted. *Expenses:* Tuition: Part-time $558 per credit hour. *Financial support:* Federal Work-Study, institutionally sponsored loans, scholarships/grants, and tuition waivers (full and partial) available. Support available to part-time students. Financial award applicants required to submit FAFSA. *Faculty research:* Milton and seventeenth-century Puritans, inter-Biblical years, nineteenth-century literature, Latin American and Texas history. *Unit head:* Dr. John Tarwater, Director, 214-333-6830, Fax: 214-333-5558, E-mail: graduate@dbu.edu. *Application contact:* Kit P. Montgomery, Director of Graduate Programs, 214-333-5242, Fax: 214-333-5579, E-mail: graduate@dbu.edu.

Dallas Baptist University, College of Adult Education, Professional Development Program, Dallas, TX 75211-9299. Offers accounting (MA); church leadership (MA); counseling (MA); criminal justice (MA); English as a second language (MA); finance (MA); higher education (MA); leadership studies (MA); management (MA); management information systems (MA); marketing (MA); missions (MA). Part-time and evening/weekend programs available. *Faculty:* 68 full-time (30 women), 113 part-time/adjunct (47 women). *Students:* 10 full-time, 83 part-time. 30 applicants, 47% accepted. In 2008, 39 master's awarded. *Entrance requirements:* For master's, minimum GPA of 3.0. Additional exam requirements/recommendations for international students: Required—TOEFL, IELTS. Application fee: $25. *Expenses:* Tuition: Part-time $558 per credit hour. *Financial support:* Federal Work-Study, institutionally sponsored loans, scholarships/grants, and tuition waivers (full and partial) available. Support available to part-time students. Financial award applicants required to submit FAFSA. *Unit head:* Dr. John Tarwater, Acting Director, 214-333-6830, Fax: 214-333-5558, E-mail: graduate@dbu.edu. *Application contact:* Kit P. Montgomery, Director of Graduate Programs, 214-333-5242, Fax: 214-333-5579, E-mail: graduate@dbu.edu.

Dallas Baptist University, Gary Cook School of Leadership, Program in Christian Education, Dallas, TX 75211-9299. Offers adult ministry (MA); business ministry (MA); childhood ministry (MA); collegiate ministry (MA); communication ministry (MA); counseling ministry (MA); education ministry (MA); general ministry (MA); missions ministry (MA); student ministry (MA); worship ministry (MA). Part-time and evening/weekend programs available. *Faculty:* 68 full-time (30 women), 113 part-time/adjunct (47 women). *Students:* 13 full-time, 55 part-time. 45 applicants. In 2008, 22 master's awarded. *Entrance requirements:* For master's, minimum GPA of 3.0. Additional exam requirements/recommendations for international students: Required—TOEFL. *Application deadline:* Applications are processed on a rolling basis. Application fee: $25. Electronic applications accepted. *Expenses:* Tuition: Part-time $558 per credit hour. *Financial support:* Federal Work-Study, institutionally sponsored loans, scholarships/grants, and tuition waivers (full and partial) available. Support available to part-time students. Financial award applicants required to submit FAFSA. *Unit head:* Dr. Judy Morris, Director, 214-333-5246, Fax: 214-333-5115, E-mail: graduate@dbu.edu. *Application contact:* Kit P. Montgomery, Director of Graduate Programs, 214-333-5242, Fax: 214-333-5579, E-mail: graduate@dbu.edu.

Dallas Baptist University, Gary Cook School of Leadership, Program in Global Leadership, Dallas, TX 75211-9299. Offers business communication (MA); Christian education/missions (MA); ESL (MA); general studies (MA); global studies (MA); international business (MA); missions (MA); worship/missions (MA). Part-time and evening/weekend programs available. *Faculty:* 68 full-time (30 women), 113 part-time/adjunct (47 women). *Students:* 11 full-time, 26 part-time. 15 applicants, 40% accepted. *Entrance requirements:* For master's, minimum GPA of 3.0. Additional exam requirements/recommendations for international students: Required—TOEFL, IELTS. Application fee: $25. *Expenses:* Tuition: Part-time $558 per credit hour. *Financial support:* Federal Work-Study, institutionally sponsored loans, scholarships/grants, and tuition waivers (full and partial) available. Support available to part-time students. Financial award applicants required to submit FAFSA. *Unit head:* Dr. Bob Garrett, Director, 214-333-5292, Fax: 214-333-6955, E-mail: graduate@dbu.edu. *Application contact:* Kit P. Montgomery, Director of Graduate Programs, 214-333-5242, Fax: 214-333-5579, E-mail: graduate@dbu.edu.

Dallas Theological Seminary, Graduate Programs, Dallas, TX 75204-6499. Offers academic ministries (Th M); Bible translation (Th M); biblical and theological studies (CGS); biblical counseling (MA, Th M); biblical exegesis and linguistics (MA); biblical exposition (PhD); biblical studies (MA); Christian education (MA, D Min); cross-cultural ministries (MA, Th M); educational leadership (Th M); evangelism and discipleship (Th M); interdisciplinary studies (Th M); media and communication (MA); media arts in ministry (Th M); ministry (D Min); New Testament studies (Th M, PhD); Old Testament studies (PhD); parachurch ministries (Th M); pastoral ministries (Th M); sacred theology (STM); theological studies (PhD); women's ministry (Th M). *Accreditation:* ATS (one or more programs are accredited). Part-time and evening/weekend programs available. *Degree requirements:* For master's, variable foreign language requirement, thesis (for some programs); for doctorate, 2 foreign languages, thesis/dissertation. *Entrance requirements:* Additional exam requirements/recommendations for international students: Required—TOEFL, TWE. *Application deadline:* For fall admission, 7/1 priority date for domestic students, 1/15 for international students; for winter admission, 11/1 priority date for domestic students; for spring admission, 11/1 priority date for domestic students. Applications are processed on a rolling basis. Application fee: $30. Electronic applications accepted. *Financial support:* Career-related internships or fieldwork, institutionally sponsored loans, scholarships/grants, and tuition waivers (full and partial) available. Financial award application deadline: 2/28. *Unit head:* Dr. Mark L. Bailey, President, 214-841-3676, Fax: 214-841-3565. *Application contact:* Josh Bleeker, Director of Admissions, 214-841-3661, Fax: 214-841-3664, E-mail: admissions@dts.edu.

Eastern University, Palmer Theological Seminary, Program in Renewal of the Church for Mission, St. Davids, PA 19087-3696. Offers D Min. *Degree requirements:* For doctorate, thesis/dissertation.

Emmanuel School of Religion, Graduate and Professional Programs, Johnson City, TN 37601-9438. Offers Christian care and counseling (M Div); Christian doctrine (M Div); Christian education (M Div); Christian ministries (M Div); church history (M Div, MAR); ministry (D Min); New Testament (M Div, MAR); Old Testament (M Div, MAR); urban ministry (M Div); world mission (M Div). *Accreditation:* ACIPE; ATS. Part-time programs available. *Faculty:* 12 full-time (2 women), 2 part-time/adjunct (0 women). *Students:* 86 full-time (26 women), 42 part-time (10 women); includes 5 minority (4 African Americans, 1 Hispanic American), 14 international. Average age 32. 47 applicants, 98% accepted, 34 enrolled. In 2008, 16 first professional degrees, 6 master's, 2 doctorates awarded. *Degree requirements:* For master's, 2 foreign languages, thesis; for M Div, 2 foreign languages, thesis/dissertation or alternative. *Entrance requirements:* For doctorate, GRE General Test, Minnesota Multiphasic Personality Inventory, M Div or equivalent. *Application deadline:* For fall admission, 8/1 priority date for domestic students. Applications are processed on a rolling basis. Application fee: $25. *Expenses:* Tuition: Full-time $7800; part-time $325 per credit. Required fees: $122.50 per semester. Tuition and fees vary according to degree level and program. *Financial support:* In 2008–09, 90 students received support, including 10 teaching assistantships with partial tuition reimbursements available; career-related internships or fieldwork, institutionally sponsored loans, scholarships/grants, and tuition waivers (partial) also available. Support available to part-time students. Financial award application deadline: 4/1; financial award applicants required to submit FAFSA. *Faculty research:* Theology of Old Testament prophets, spiritual formation for Christian leaders, history of African churches and religions, social world of early Christianity, lay pastoral counseling. Total annual research expenditures: $12,000. *Unit head:* Dr. Rollin A Ramsaran, Dean and Professor of New Testament, 423-461-1524, Fax: 423-926-6198, E-mail: RamsaranR@esr.edu. *Application contact:* Shelley Gasser, Administrative Assistant for Admissions, 423-461-1535, Fax: 423-926-6198, E-mail: GasserS@esr.edu.

Fuller Theological Seminary, Graduate School of Theology, Pasadena, CA 91182. Offers Christian leadership (MACL); evangelism (MA); family life education (MA); ministry (M Div, D Min); pastoral ministry (MA); recovery ministry (MA); theology (MAT, Th M, PhD); worship music ministry (MA); worship, theology, and the arts (MA); youth, family, and culture (MA). M Div offered jointly with Denver Conservative Baptist Seminary. *Accreditation:* ACIPE; ATS (one or more programs are accredited). Part-time and evening/weekend programs available. *Degree requirements:* For doctorate, variable foreign language requirement, thesis/dissertation; for M Div, 2 foreign languages. *Entrance requirements:* For doctorate, GRE General Test. *Faculty research:* New Testament, Old Testament, systematic theology, history, practical theology.

Fuller Theological Seminary, School of Intercultural Studies, Program in Global Ministries, Pasadena, CA 91182. Offers global leadership (MA); global ministries (D Min); global ministry (Korean language) (D Min). *Degree requirements:* For doctorate, one foreign language, thesis/dissertation. *Entrance requirements:* For doctorate, qualifying exam.

Fuller Theological Seminary, School of Intercultural Studies, Program in Intercultural Studies, Pasadena, CA 91182. Offers cross-cultural studies (MA); intercultural studies (MA, Th M, PhD); intercultural studies (Korean language) (MA). *Degree requirements:* For master's, one foreign language, thesis optional; for doctorate, one foreign language, thesis/dissertation. *Entrance requirements:* For doctorate, qualifying exam, minimum GPA of 3.7, Th M and MA degrees from Graduate School of World Mission. Additional exam requirements/recommendations for international students: Required—TOEFL.

Fuller Theological Seminary, School of Intercultural Studies, Program in Missiology, Pasadena, CA 91182. Offers missiology (D Miss); missiology (Korean language) (Th M). *Degree requirements:* For doctorate, one foreign language, thesis/dissertation. *Entrance requirements:* For doctorate, qualifying exam, minimum GPA of 3.4 (D Miss), 3.7 (PhD), Th M and MA degrees from Graduate School of World Mission. Additional exam requirements/recommendations for international students: Required—TOEFL.

Gardner-Webb University, M. Christopher White School of Divinity, Boiling Springs, NC 28017. Offers Christian education (M Div); ministry (D Min); missiology (M Div); pastoral care and counseling (M Div); pastoral ministry (M Div); M Div/MA. *Accreditation:* ACIPE; ATS. Part-time programs available. *Degree requirements:* For M Div, 2 foreign languages. *Entrance requirements:* For M Div, minimum GPA of 2.0; for doctorate, minimum GPA of 2.75. *Expenses:* Contact institution. *Faculty research:* Jewish Christian dialogue, Islam.

George Fox University, George Fox Evangelical Seminary, Newberg, OR 97132-2697. Offers divinity (M Div); ministry (D Min), including global missional leadership, leadership and spiritual formation, leadership in the emerging culture; ministry leadership (MA); spiritual formation (MA); spiritual formation and discipleship (Certificate); theological studies (MA). *Accreditation:* ACIPE; ATS. Part-time and evening/weekend programs available. Postbaccalaureate distance learning degree programs offered (minimal on-campus study). *Faculty:* 7 full-time (2 women), 17 part-time/adjunct (7 women). *Students:* 51 full-time (6 women), 289 part-time (94 women); includes 27 minority (6 African Americans, 2 American Indian/Alaska Native, 15 Asian Americans or Pacific Islanders, 4 Hispanic Americans), 6 international. Average age 41. 134 applicants, 94% accepted, 97 enrolled. In 2008, 9 first professional degrees, 18 master's, 20 doctorates, 5 other advanced degrees awarded. *Degree requirements:* For master's, variable foreign language requirement, thesis optional, internship; for doctorate, thesis/dissertation. *Entrance requirements:* Additional exam requirements/recommendations for international students: Required—TOEFL (minimum score 550 paper-based; 213 computer-based; 80 iBT). *Application deadline:* For fall admission, 7/1 for domestic and international students; for spring admission, 11/1 for domestic and international students. Applications are processed on a rolling basis. Application fee: $40. Electronic applications accepted. *Expenses:* Contact institution. *Financial support:* In 2008–09, 33 students received support. Career-related internships or fieldwork and scholarships/grants available. Financial award application deadline: 5/1; financial award applicants required to submit FAFSA. *Unit head:* Dr. Chuck Conniry, Vice President and Dean, George Fox Evangelical Seminary, 503-554-6152, E-mail: cconniry@georgefox.edu. *Application contact:* Sheila Bartlett, Admissions Counselor, 800-631-0921, Fax: 503-554-6122, E-mail: sbartlett@georgefox.edu.

Global University, Graduate School of Theology, Springfield, MO 65804. Offers biblical studies (MA); divinity (M Div); ministerial studies (MA), including education, leadership, missions, New Testament, Old Testament. Part-time and evening/weekend programs available. Postbaccalaureate distance learning degree programs offered (no on-campus study). *Faculty:* 10 full-time (1 woman), 83 part-time/adjunct (10 women). *Students:* 200 full-time (27 women), 175 part-time (48 women); includes 250 minority (150 African Americans, 25 American Indian/Alaska Native, 50 Asian Americans or Pacific Islanders, 25 Hispanic Americans). Average age 49. 148 applicants, 94% accepted, 139 enrolled. In 2008, 1 first professional degree, 27 master's awarded. *Degree requirements:* For master's, thesis (for some programs). *Entrance requirements:* For M Div, minimum undergraduate GPA of 3.0; for master's, minimum undergraduate GPA of 3.0, 15 undergraduate credit hours of course work in Bible or theology. *Application deadline:* Applications are processed on a rolling basis. Application fee: $50. Electronic applications accepted. *Expenses:* Tuition: Full-time $3690; part-time $205 per credit hour. Required fees: $205 per credit hour. One-time fee: $50 full-time. *Faculty research:* Higher education, cross-cultural missions. *Unit head:* Dr. Carl Chrisner, Dean, 417-862-9533 Ext. 2237, Fax: 417-869-5623, E-mail: cchrisner@globaluniversity.edu. *Application contact:* Jody Patterson, Graduate Student Enrollment Representative, 417-862-9533 Ext. 2347, Fax: 417-862-0863, E-mail: gradenroll@globaluniversity.edu.

Gordon-Conwell Theological Seminary, Graduate and Professional Programs, South Hamilton, MA 01982. Offers Biblical languages (MABL); church history (MACH); counseling (MACO); ministry (D Min); missions/evangelism (MAME); New Testament (MANT); Old Testament (MAOT); religion (MAR); theology (M Div, MATH, Th M, Th D). *Accreditation:* ACIPE; ATS (one or more programs are accredited). Part-time and evening/weekend programs available. *Degree requirements:* For master's, one foreign language, thesis optional; for doctorate, 2 foreign languages, thesis/dissertation; for M Div, 2 foreign languages. *Entrance requirements:* For M Div and master's, minimum GPA of 2.5; for doctorate, minimum GPA of 3.0.

Grace Theological Seminary, Graduate and Professional Programs, Winona Lake, IN 46590-9907. Offers biblical studies (Certificate); camp administration (MA); counseling (M Div); exegetical studies (MA); intercultural studies (M Div, MA); local church studies (MA); pastoral studies (M Div); theological studies (MA); theology (D Min, Diploma). *Accreditation:* ATS. Part-time programs available. Postbaccalaureate distance learning degree programs offered (no on-campus study). *Degree requirements:* For master's, thesis optional; for doctorate, 2 foreign languages, thesis/dissertation; for M Div, 2 foreign languages, thesis/dissertation optional. *Entrance requirements:* For M Div and master's, MAT, minimum GPA of 2.5. Electronic applications accepted. *Faculty research:* Biblical theology, language, and church ministries.

Grand Rapids Theological Seminary of Cornerstone University, Graduate Programs, Grand Rapids, MI 49525-5897. Offers biblical counseling (MA); Biblical counseling (M Div); chaplaincy (M Div); Christian education (M Div, MA); intercultural studies (M Div, MA); New Testament (MA, Th M); Old Testament (MA, Th M); pastoral studies (M Div); systematic theology (MA); theology (Th M). *Accreditation:* ATS. Part-time programs available. Postbaccalaureate distance learning degree programs offered (minimal on-campus study). *Entrance requirements:* Additional exam requirements/recommendations for international students: Required—TOEFL (minimum score 577 paper-based; 233 computer-based; 90 iBT). Electronic applications accepted.

Hope International University, School of Graduate Studies, Programs in Ministry, Fullerton, CA 92831-3138. Offers Christian leadership (MCM); church music (MA); church music (Korean track) (MCM); church planting (MCM); intercultural studies (MCM); worship (MCM). Part-time and evening/weekend programs available. Postbaccalaureate distance learning degree programs offered (minimal on-campus study). *Degree requirements:* For master's, thesis (for some programs), project. *Entrance requirements:* For master's, minimum GPA of 3.0, MCM program requires an undergraduate degree in music, application, official transcripts, 2 references, statement of purpose. Additional exam requirements/recommendations for international students: Required—TOEFL (minimum score 550 paper-based; 213 computer-based; 86 iBT); Recommended—IELTS (minimum score 6.5). Electronic applications accepted. *Expenses:* Contact institution. *Faculty research:* Church dynamics, growth methodologies.

Missions and Missiology

Knox Theological Seminary, Graduate Programs, Program in Evangelism, Fort Lauderdale, FL 33308. Offers ME. Part-time and evening/weekend programs available. *Entrance requirements:* Additional exam requirements/recommendations for international students: Required—TOEFL, TWE (minimum score 5).

Luther Rice University, Graduate Programs, Lithonia, GA 30038-2454. Offers Bible/theology (M Div); Christian education (M Div); Christian studies (MA); church ministry (D Min); counseling (M Div); discipleship counseling (MA); ministry (M Div, MA); missions/evangelism (M Div). Part-time programs available. Postbaccalaureate distance learning degree programs offered (no on-campus study). *Degree requirements:* For doctorate, thesis/dissertation. *Entrance requirements:* Additional exam requirements/recommendations for international students: Required—TOEFL (minimum score 500 paper-based; 173 computer-based).

Mennonite Brethren Biblical Seminary, School of Theology, Program in Intercultural Mission, Fresno, CA 93727-5097. Offers MA.

Midwestern Baptist Theological Seminary, Graduate and Professional Programs, Kansas City, MO 64118-4697. Offers Biblical archaeology (MA); Biblical languages (MA); Christian education (M Div, MACE); Christian foundations—lay ministry (Graduate Certificate); collegiate ministries (M Div); counseling (MA); educational ministry (D Ed Min); international church planting (M Div); ministry (M Div, D Min); North American church planting (M Div); sacred music (MCM); urban ministry (M Div); worship leadership (M Div); youth ministry (M Div). *Accreditation:* ATS. Part-time programs available. Postbaccalaureate distance learning degree programs offered (minimal on-campus study). *Degree requirements:* For doctorate, thesis/dissertation; for M Div, 2 foreign languages. *Entrance requirements:* For doctorate, MAT. Electronic applications accepted. *Faculty research:* Ministerial studies, Biblical and theological studies, missions, counseling.

Nazarene Theological Seminary, Graduate and Professional Programs, Kansas City, MO 64131-1263. Offers Christian education (MA); intercultural studies (MA); theological studies (MA); theology (M Div, D Min). *Accreditation:* ACIPE; ATS. Part-time programs available. *Degree requirements:* For master's, comprehensive exam (for some programs), thesis (for some programs); for doctorate, thesis/dissertation. *Entrance requirements:* Additional exam requirements/recommendations for international students: Required—TOEFL. Electronic applications accepted.

Northern Baptist Theological Seminary, Graduate and Professional Programs, Lombard, IL 60148-5698. Offers Biblical studies (MA); Christian ministries (MACM); divinity (M Div); ministry (D Min); missional church (MA); theology (MA). *Accreditation:* ATS. Part-time programs available. *Faculty:* 6 full-time (1 woman), 30 part-time/adjunct (5 women). *Students:* 127 full-time (38 women), 20 part-time (13 women); includes 67 minority (51 African Americans, 12 Asian Americans or Pacific Islanders, 4 Hispanic Americans), 3 international. Average age 40. *Degree requirements:* For doctorate, thesis/dissertation; for M Div, field experience. *Entrance requirements:* For doctorate, 3 years in the ministry post-M Div. Additional exam requirements/recommendations for international students: Required—TOEFL. *Application deadline:* For fall admission, 9/1 priority date for domestic students, 2/1 priority date for international students; for winter admission, 12/1 priority date for domestic students; for spring admission, 3/1 priority date for domestic students. Applications are processed on a rolling basis. Application fee: $35. Electronic applications accepted. *Expenses:* Tuition: Full-time $15,800; part-time $440 per credit. Required fees: $100 per quarter. Tuition and fees vary according to degree level. *Financial support:* Career-related internships or fieldwork and scholarships/grants available. Support available to part-time students. Financial award application deadline: 9/1. *Faculty research:* Theology, worship studies, church history, evangelism, Bible. *Unit head:* Alistair Brown, Dean, 630-620-2103, Fax: 630-620-2190. *Application contact:* Greg Henson, Executive Director of External Relations, 630-620-2180, Fax: 630-620-2190, E-mail: admissions@seminary.edu.

Northwest Nazarene University, Graduate Studies, Program in Religion, Nampa, ID 83686-5897. Offers Christian education (MA); missional leadership (MA); pastoral ministry (MA); religion (M Div); spiritual formation (MA). Part-time and evening/weekend programs available. Postbaccalaureate distance learning degree programs offered (no on-campus study). *Faculty:* 10 full-time (2 women), 24 part-time/adjunct (5 women). *Students:* 135 full-time (36 women), 11 part-time (5 women); includes 17 minority (8 African Americans, 1 American Indian/Alaska Native, 5 Asian Americans or Pacific Islanders, 3 Hispanic Americans). In 2008, 42 master's awarded. *Application deadline:* Applications are processed on a rolling basis. Application fee: $50. Electronic applications accepted. *Unit head:* Dr. Jay Akkerman, Director, Graduate Studies, 208-467-8437, Fax: 208-467-8252. *Application contact:* Jill Jones, Program Assistant, 208-467-8368, Fax: 208-467-8252, E-mail: jdjones@nnu.edu.

Oral Roberts University, School of Theology and Missions, Tulsa, OK 74171-0001. Offers biblical literature (MA), including advanced languages, Judaic-Christian studies; Christian counseling (MA), including marriage and family therapy; Christian education (MA); divinity (M Div); missions (MA); practical theology (MA); theological/historical studies (MA); theology (D Min). *Accreditation:* ATS; NASM. Part-time programs available. Postbaccalaureate distance learning degree programs offered (minimal on-campus study). *Degree requirements:* For master's, thesis (for some programs), practicum/internship; for doctorate, thesis/dissertation, applied research project; for M Div, one foreign language, field experience. *Entrance requirements:* For M Div and master's, GRE General Test or MAT, minimum GPA of 2.5; for doctorate, M Div, minimum GPA of 3.0, 3 years of full-time ministry experience. Additional exam requirements/recommendations for international students: Required—TOEFL (minimum score 500 paper-based; 213 computer-based; 79 iBT). Electronic applications accepted.

Phillips Theological Seminary, Programs in Theology, Tulsa, OK 74116. Offers administration of church agencies (M Div); campus ministry (M Div); church-related social work (M Div); college and seminary teaching (M Div); global mission work (M Div); institutional chaplaincy (M Div); ministerial vocations in Christian education (M Div); ministry (D Min), including parish ministry, pastoral counseling, practices of ministry; ministry and culture (MAMC), including Christian education, congregational leadership, history and practice of Christian spirituality, theology, ethics, and culture; ministry of music (M Div); pastoral care and counseling (M Div); pastoral ministry (M Div); theological studies (MTS). *Accreditation:* ATS. Part-time programs available. Postbaccalaureate distance learning degree programs offered (minimal on-campus study). *Degree requirements:* For master's, thesis (for some programs); for doctorate, thesis/dissertation. *Entrance requirements:* For master's, minimum GPA of 2.5; for doctorate, M Div, minimum GPA of 3.0. *Faculty research:* Biblical studies, historical studies, theology and culture, practical theology, theology and film.

Providence College and Theological Seminary, Theological Seminary, Otterburne, MB R0A 1G0, Canada. Offers children's ministry (Certificate); Christian studies (MA, Certificate); counseling (MA); cross-cultural discipleship (Certificate); divinity (M Div); educational studies (MA), including counseling psychology, educational ministries, student development, teaching English to speakers of other languages, training teachers of English to speakers of other languages; global studies (MA); lay counseling (Diploma); ministry (D Min); teaching English to speakers of other languages (Certificate); theological studies (MA); training teacher of English to speakers of other languages (Certificate); youth ministry (Certificate). *Accreditation:* ATS. Part-time programs available. *Degree requirements:* For master's, variable foreign language requirement, thesis (for some programs); for doctorate, thesis/dissertation; for M Div, 2 foreign languages, comprehensive exam, thesis/dissertation (for some programs). *Entrance requirements:* Additional exam requirements/recommendations for international students: Recommended—TOEFL (minimum score 550 paper-based; 213 computer-based). *Faculty research:* Studies in Isaiah, theology of sin.

Reformed Theological Seminary–Jackson Campus, Graduate and Professional Programs, Jackson, MS 39209-3099. Offers Bible, theology, and missions (Certificate); biblical studies (MA); Christian education (M Div, MA); counseling (M Div); divinity (M Div, Diploma); marriage and family therapy (MA); ministry (D Min); missions (M Div, MA, D Min); New Testament (Th M); Old Testament (Th M); theological studies (MA); theology (Th M); M Div/MA. *Accreditation:* AAMFT/COAMFTE (one or more programs are accredited); ATS (one or more programs are accredited). *Degree requirements:* For master's, thesis (for some programs), fieldwork; for doctorate, 2 foreign languages, thesis/dissertation; for M Div, 2 foreign languages, thesis/dissertation (for some programs). *Entrance requirements:* For M Div and master's, minimum GPA of 2.6; for doctorate, minimum GPA of 3.0. Additional exam requirements/recommendations for international students: Required—TOEFL.

Regent University, Graduate School, School of Divinity, Virginia Beach, VA 23464-9800. Offers Biblical studies (MA); leadership and renewal (D Min); missiology (M Div, MA); practical theology (M Div, MA); renewal studies (PhD); M Div/M Ed; M Div/MA; M Div/MBA; M Ed/MA; MBA/MA. *Accreditation:* ACIPE; ATS. Part-time programs available. Postbaccalaureate distance learning degree programs offered (minimal on-campus study). *Faculty:* 21 full-time (4 women), 24 part-time/adjunct (5 women). *Students:* 194 full-time (90 women), 391 part-time (164 women); includes 249 minority (217 African Americans, 3 American Indian/Alaska Native, 11 Asian Americans or Pacific Islanders, 18 Hispanic Americans), 19 international. Average age 38. 320 applicants, 65% accepted, 137 enrolled. In 2008, 39 first professional degrees, 36 master's, 29 doctorates awarded. *Degree requirements:* For master's, comprehensive exam, thesis or alternative, internship; for doctorate, thesis/dissertation or alternative; for M Div, internship. *Entrance requirements:* For M Div, GRE General Test or MAT, minimum undergraduate GPA of 3.0, minimum 3 years of ministry experience, transcripts, recommendations; for master's, GRE General Test or MAT, minimum undergraduate GPA of 2.75, writing sample, clergy recommendation, transcripts; for doctorate, M Div or theological master's degree; minimum graduate GPA of 3.5 (PhD), 3.0 (D Min); recommendations; writing sample; transcripts. Additional exam requirements/recommendations for international students: Required—TOEFL (minimum score 577 paper-based; 233 computer-based). *Application deadline:* For fall admission, 5/1 priority date for domestic students. Applications are processed on a rolling basis. Application fee: $50. Electronic applications accepted. *Expenses:* Contact institution. *Financial support:* Fellowships with full and partial tuition reimbursements, career-related internships or fieldwork, scholarships/grants, tuition waivers (full and partial), and unspecified assistantships available. Support available to part-time students. Financial award application deadline: 9/1; financial award applicants required to submit FAFSA. *Faculty research:* Greek and Hebrew, theology, spiritual formation, global missions and world Christianity, women's studies. *Unit head:* Dr. Michael Palmer, Dean, 757-352-4406, Fax: 757-352-4597, E-mail: mpalmer@regent.edu. *Application contact:* Matthew Chadwick, Director of Admissions, 800-373-5504, Fax: 757-352-4381, E-mail: admissions@regent.edu.

Saint Paul University, Faculty of Human Sciences, Program in Mission and Interreligious Studies, Ottawa, ON K1S 1C4, Canada. Offers MA. *Degree requirements:* For master's, one foreign language, thesis. *Entrance requirements:* For master's, honors BA in mission, minimum B average. *Faculty research:* Theology of mission; mission and sociology; history of mission; faith, religion, and culture; world religions; practice of mission; religious anthropology; sociocultural anthropology.

Simpson University, A.W. Tozer Theological Seminary, Redding, CA 96003-8606. Offers Christian leadership (MA); Christian studies (MA); intercultural studies (MA); ministry (M Div). Part-time and evening/weekend programs available. Postbaccalaureate distance learning degree programs offered (minimal on-campus study). *Degree requirements:* For master's, student portfolio. *Entrance requirements:* For master's, GRE General Test (if undergraduate GPA is below 2.5), 2 letters of reference, Christian Experience statement. Additional exam requirements/recommendations for international students: Required—TOEFL. Electronic applications accepted. *Expenses:* Contact institution.

Southeastern Baptist Theological Seminary, Graduate and Professional Programs, Wake Forest, NC 27588-1889. Offers advanced biblical studies (M Div); Christian education (M Div, MACE); Christian ethics (PhD); Christian ministry (M Div); Christian planting (M Div); church music (MACM); counseling (MACO); evangelism (PhD); language (M Div); ministry (D Min); New Testament (PhD); Old Testament (PhD); philosophy (PhD); theology (Th M, PhD); women's studies (M Div). *Accreditation:* ACIPE; ATS (one or more programs are accredited). *Degree requirements:* For master's, thesis (for some programs), oral exam; for doctorate, thesis/dissertation, fieldwork; for M Div, supervised ministry. *Entrance requirements:* For master's, Cooperative English Test, minimum GPA of 2.0, M Div or equivalent (Th M); for doctorate, GRE General Test or MAT, Cooperative English Test, M Div or equivalent, 3 years of professional experience.

Southern Adventist University, School of Religion, Collegedale, TN 37315-0370. Offers Biblical and theological studies (MA); church leadership and management (MA); church ministry and homiletics (MA); evangelism and world mission (MA); religious studies (MA). Summer program only. Part-time programs available. *Degree requirements:* For master's, comprehensive exam, thesis (for some programs). *Entrance requirements:* For master's, GRE. Additional exam requirements/recommendations for international students: Required—TOEFL (minimum score 550 paper-based). *Faculty research:* Biblical archaeology.

Southern Baptist Theological Seminary, Billy Graham School of Missions, Evangelism and Church Growth, Louisville, KY 40280-0004. Offers Christian mission/world religion (PhD); evangelism/church growth (PhD); ministry (D Min); missiology (MA, D Miss); missions, evangelism and church growth (M Div); religion (Th M); theological studies (MA). *Accreditation:* ATS. Part-time and evening/weekend programs available. Postbaccalaureate distance learning degree programs offered (minimal on-campus study). *Degree requirements:* For master's and M Div, 2 foreign languages; for doctorate, 4 foreign languages, thesis/dissertation. *Entrance requirements:* For doctorate, GRE General Test, MAT, field essay, M Div. Additional exam requirements/recommendations for international students: Required—TOEFL, TWE. *Faculty research:* Assimilation of church congregants, effective methodologies of evangelism, expectations of church members, spiritual warfare literature, formative church discipline.

Southern Evangelical Seminary, Graduate School of Ministry and Missions, Matthews, NC 28105. Offers apologetics (Certificate); Christian education (MA); church ministry (MA, Certificate); divinity (Certificate), including apologetics (M Div, Certificate); Islamic studies (Certificate); theology (M Div), including apologetics (M Div, Certificate), Biblical studies; youth ministry (MA). Part-time and evening/weekend programs available. Postbaccalaureate distance learning degree programs offered. *Degree requirements:* For master's, thesis (for some programs); for M Div, one foreign language. *Entrance requirements:* Additional exam requirements/recommendations for international students: Required—TOEFL (minimum score 600 paper-based; 250 computer-based).

Southwestern Assemblies of God University, Thomas F. Harrison School of Graduate Studies, Program in Theological Studies, Waxahachie, TX 75165-5735. Offers Bible and theology (MS); Biblical studies (M Div); counseling (M Div); cross cultural missions (M Div); practical theology (M Div); theological studies (M Div). Postbaccalaureate distance learning degree programs offered. *Degree requirements:* For master's, comprehensive written and oral exams. *Entrance requirements:* For master's, GRE General Test, minimum GPA of 2.5. Electronic applications accepted.

Southwestern Christian University, Program in Ministry, Bethany, OK 73008-0340. Offers church planting (M Min); church revitalization and renewal (M Min); intercultural studies (M Min); leadership (M Min); life coaching (M Min); pastoral ministries (M Min); work place ministries (M Min). Part-time programs available. *Degree requirements:* For master's, thesis. *Entrance requirements:* For master's, minimum GPA of 2.5. Additional exam requirements/recommendations for international students: Required—TOEFL (minimum score 500 paper-based). Electronic applications accepted.

Taylor College and Seminary, Graduate and Professional Programs, Edmonton, AB T6J 4T3, Canada. Offers Christian studies (Diploma); intercultural studies (MA, Diploma); theology

(M Div, MTS). *Accreditation:* ATS. Part-time programs available. *Degree requirements:* For master's, comprehensive exam, thesis optional. *Entrance requirements:* Additional exam requirements/recommendations for international students: Required—TOEFL (minimum score 550 paper-based; 213 computer-based), IELTS (minimum score 6.5). *Faculty research:* Biblical studies, administration and organization, world religions.

Trinity Episcopal School for Ministry, Graduate Programs, Ambridge, PA 15003-2397. Offers Anglican studies (Diploma); basic Christian studies (Diploma); divinity (M Div); ministry (D Min); mission and evangelism (MAME, Diploma); religion (MAR); youth ministry (Diploma). *Accreditation:* ATS (one or more programs are accredited). Part-time programs available. *Degree requirements:* For master's, thesis optional; for doctorate, thesis/dissertation; for M Div, thesis/dissertation optional, Greek and Hebrew. *Entrance requirements:* Additional exam requirements/recommendations for international students: Required—TOEFL. *Faculty research:* Pauline Epistles, contemporary theology, history of Anglican liturgy, book of Ruth, biblical theology.

Trinity International University, Trinity Evangelical Divinity School, Deerfield, IL 60015-1284. Offers Biblical and Near Eastern archaeology and languages (MA); Christian studies (MA, Certificate); Christian thought (MA); church history (MA, Th M); congregational ministry: pastor-teacher (M Div); congregational ministry: team ministry (M Div); counseling ministries (MA); counseling psychology (MA); cross-cultural ministry (M Div); educational studies (PhD); evangelism (MA); history of Christianity in America (MA); intercultural studies (MA, PhD); leadership and ministry management (D Min); military chaplaincy (D Min); ministry (MA); mission and evangelism (Th M); missions and evangelism (D Min); New Testament (MA, Th M); Old Testament (Th M); Old Testament and Semitic languages (MA); pastoral care (M Div); pastoral care and counseling (D Min); pastoral counseling and psychology (Th M); pastoral theology (Th M); philosophy of religion (MA); preaching (D Min); religion (MA); research ministry (M Div); systematic theology (Th M); theological studies (PhD); urban ministry (MA). *Accreditation:* ATS (one or more programs are accredited). Part-time programs available. Postbaccalaureate distance learning degree programs offered (minimal on-campus study). *Degree requirements:* For master's, comprehensive exam, thesis, fieldwork; for doctorate, comprehensive exam (for some programs), thesis/dissertation; for M Div, 2 foreign languages, fieldwork; for Certificate, comprehensive exam, integrative papers. *Entrance requirements:* For M Div, GRE, MAT; for master's, GRE, MAT, minimum cumulative undergraduate GPA of 3.0; for doctorate, GRE, minimum cumulative graduate GPA of 3.2; for Certificate, GRE, MAT, minimum undergraduate GPA of 2.5. Additional exam requirements/recommendations for international students: Required—TOEFL (minimum score 580 paper-based; 237 computer-based), TWE (minimum score 4). Electronic applications accepted.

Tyndale University College & Seminary, Graduate Programs, Toronto, ON M2M 4B3, Canada. Offers Biblical studies (M Div); Christian foundations (MTS); Christian studies (Diploma); counseling (M Div); educational ministry (M Div); missions (M Div, Diploma); pastoral and Chinese ministry (M Div); pastoral ministry (M Div); Pentecostal studies (MTS); spiritual formation (M Div, Diploma); theological studies (M Div); theology (Th M); worship and liturgy (M Div, MTS); youth and family ministry (M Div). *Accreditation:* ATS. Part-time programs available. Postbaccalaureate distance learning degree programs offered (no on-campus study). *Degree requirements:* For M Div, one foreign language, thesis/dissertation optional. *Entrance requirements:* For M Div, master's, and Diploma, minimum C+ average in undergraduate course work. Additional exam requirements/recommendations for international students: Required—TOEFL (minimum score 570 paper-based; 230 computer-based), TWE (minimum score 5). Electronic applications accepted. *Faculty research:* Canadian church history, Chinese church history, Old Testament, counseling ministries (narrative therapy), world religions.

University of South Africa, College of Human Sciences, Pretoria, South Africa. Offers adult education (M Ed); African languages (MA, PhD); African politics (MA, PhD); Afrikaans (MA, PhD); ancient history (MA, PhD); ancient Near Eastern studies (MA, PhD); anthropology (MA, PhD); applied linguistics (MA); Arabic (MA, PhD); archaeology (MA); art history (MA); Biblical archaeology (MA); Biblical studies (M Th, D Th, PhD); Christian spirituality (M Th, D Th); church history (M Th, D Th); classical studies (MA, PhD); clinical psychology (MA); communication (MA, PhD); comparative education (M Ed, Ed D); consulting psychology (D Admin, D Com, PhD); curriculum studies (M Ed, Ed D); development studies (M Admin, MA, D Admin, PhD); didactics (M Ed, Ed D); education (M Tech); education management (M Ed, Ed D); educational psychology (M Ed); English (MA); environmental education (M Ed); French (MA, PhD); German (MA, PhD); Greek (MA); guidance and counseling (M Ed); health studies (MA, PhD), including health sciences education (MA), health services management (MA), medical and surgical nursing science (critical care general) (MA), midwifery and neonatal nursing science (MA), trauma and emergency care (MA); history (MA, PhD); history of education (Ed D); inclusive education (M Ed, Ed D); information and communications technology policy and regulation (MA); information science (MA, MIS, PhD); international politics (MA, PhD); Islamic studies (MA, PhD); Italian (MA, PhD); Judaica (MA, PhD); linguistics (MA, PhD); mathematical education (M Ed); mathematics education (MA); missiology (M Th, D Th); modern Hebrew (MA, PhD); musicology (MA, MMus, D Mus, PhD); natural science education (M Ed); New Testament (M Th, D Th); Old Testament (D Th); pastoral therapy (M Th, D Th); philosophy (MA); philosophy of education (M Ed, Ed D); politics (MA, PhD); Portuguese (MA, PhD); practical theology (M Th, D Th); psychology (MA, MS, PhD); psychology of education (M Ed, Ed D); public health (MA); religious studies (MA, D Th, PhD); Romance languages (MA); Russian (MA, PhD); Semitic languages (MA, PhD); social behavior studies in HIV/AIDS (MA); social science (mental health) (MA); social science in development studies (MA); social science in psychology (MA); social science in social work (MA); social science in sociology (MA); social work (MSW, DSW, PhD); socio-education (M Ed, Ed D); sociolinguistics (MA); sociology (MA, PhD); Spanish (MA, PhD); systematic theology (M Th, D Th); TESOL (teaching English to speakers of other languages) (MA); theological ethics (M Th, D Th); theory of literature (MA, PhD); urban ministries (D Th); urban ministry (M Th).

Wesley Biblical Seminary, Graduate Programs, Jackson, MS 39206. Offers Biblical literature (MA); Christian studies (MA); evangelism (M Div); family life ministry (M Div); honors research (M Div); missions (M Div); pastoral ministry (M Div); teaching (M Div); theology (MA). *Accreditation:* ATS. Part-time programs available. *Degree requirements:* For master's, thesis. *Entrance requirements:* Additional exam requirements/recommendations for international students: Required—TOEFL. Electronic applications accepted. *Faculty research:* Patristics, missiology, culture, hermeneutics.

Western Seminary, Graduate Programs, Program in Specialized Ministry, Portland, OR 97215-3367. Offers children / youth at risk (MA); coaching (MA); evangelism and equipping (MA); pastoral care to women (MA); youth and family ministry (MA); youth ministry (MA). *Degree requirements:* For master's, practicum.

Westminster Theological Seminary, Graduate and Professional Programs, Philadelphia, PA 19118. Offers apologetics (Th M); Biblical and urban studies (Certificate); Biblical counseling (MA); biblical studies (MAR); Christian studies (Certificate); church history (Th M); counseling (M Div); general studies (M Div, MAR); hermeneutics and Bible interpretations (PhD); historical and theological studies (PhD); historical theology (Th M); New Testament (Th M); Old Testament (Th M); pastoral counseling (D Min); pastoral ministry (M Div, D Min); systematic theology (Th M); theological studies (MAR); urban missions (M Div, MA, MAR, D Min). *Accreditation:* ATS. Part-time programs available. Terminal master's awarded for partial completion of doctoral program. *Degree requirements:* For master's, thesis (for some programs); for doctorate, 4 foreign languages, comprehensive exam (for some programs), thesis/dissertation; for M Div, 2 foreign languages. *Entrance requirements:* For doctorate, GRE General Test. Additional exam requirements/recommendations for international students: Required—TOEFL, TWE.

Wheaton College, Graduate School, Department of Intercultural Studies, Wheaton, IL 60187-5593. Offers evangelism (MA); intercultural studies (MA); intercultural studies/teaching English as a second language (MA); missions (MA); teaching English as a second language (Certificate). Part-time programs available. *Degree requirements:* For master's, thesis or alternative. *Entrance requirements:* For master's, GRE General Test, MAT. Electronic applications accepted.

Pastoral Ministry and Counseling

Abilene Christian University, Graduate School, College of Biblical Studies, Graduate School of Theology, Program in Ministry, Abilene, TX 79699-9100. Offers D Min. Part-time programs available. *Students:* 21 part-time (0 women), 2 international. 8 applicants, 75% accepted, 6 enrolled. In 2008, 6 doctorates awarded. *Degree requirements:* For doctorate, one foreign language, thesis/dissertation. *Entrance requirements:* For doctorate, GRE, MAT. *Application deadline:* For fall admission, 4/1 priority date for domestic students; for spring admission, 11/1 for domestic students. Applications are processed on a rolling basis. Application fee: $40 ($45 for international students). *Expenses:* Tuition: Full-time $10,728; part-time $640 per hour. Required fees: $1090; $53.50 per hour. $10 per term. Tuition and fees vary according to campus/location. *Financial support:* In 2008–09, 6 students received support. Application deadline: 4/1; *Faculty research:* Church growth, ministry evaluation, leadership. *Unit head:* Dr. Charles Siburt, Graduate Adviser, 325-674-3732, Fax: 325-674-6180, E-mail: siburt@bible.acu.edu. *Application contact:* William Horn, Graduate Admissions Counselor, 325-674-2656, Fax: 325-674-6717, E-mail: gradinfo@acu.edu.

Abilene Christian University, Graduate School, College of Biblical Studies, Graduate School of Theology, Programs in Christian Ministry, Abilene, TX 79699-9100. Offers MACM. Part-time programs available. *Students:* 16 full-time (5 women), 29 part-time (10 women); includes 3 minority (1 American Indian/Alaska Native, 2 Hispanic Americans), 4 international. 13 applicants, 77% accepted, 7 enrolled. In 2008, 9 master's awarded. *Degree requirements:* For master's, comprehensive exam. *Entrance requirements:* For master's, GRE General Test or MAT. *Application deadline:* For fall admission, 4/1 priority date for domestic students; for spring admission, 11/1 for domestic students. Applications are processed on a rolling basis. Application fee: $40 ($45 for international students). Electronic applications accepted. *Expenses:* Tuition: Full-time $10,728; part-time $640 per hour. Required fees: $1090; $53.50 per hour. $10 per term. Tuition and fees vary according to campus/location. *Financial support:* In 2008–09, 22 students received support. Application deadline: 4/1; *Faculty research:* Program innovation, instruments for educational evaluation. *Unit head:* Dr. Tim Sensing, Graduate Advisor, 325-674-3792, Fax: 325-674-6180, E-mail: sensingt@acu.edu. *Application contact:* William Horn, Graduate Admissions Counselor, 325-674-2656, Fax: 325-674-6717, E-mail: gradinfo@acu.edu.

Alliance Theological Seminary, Graduate and Professional Programs, Nyack, NY 10960. Offers Christian ministry (MPS); counseling (MA); intercultural studies (MA); missions (MPS); New Testament (MA); Old Testament (MA); theology (M Div); urban ministry (MPS). *Accreditation:* ATS. Part-time programs available. *Degree requirements:* For master's, comprehensive exam (for some programs), thesis optional, internships; for M Div, 2 foreign languages, internship. *Entrance requirements:* Proficiency in New Testament Greek, minimum GPA of 2.5 (undergraduate). Additional exam requirements/recommendations for international students: Required—TOEFL (minimum score 550 paper-based; 213 computer-based).

Ambrose University College, Ambrose Seminary, Calgary, AB T2P 3T5, Canada. Offers biblical/theological studies (MA); Chinese ministries (Certificate); Christian studies (Diploma); church education (M Div); intercultural ministries (M Div, MA, Certificate, Diploma); leadership and ministry (MA, Certificate, Diploma); pastoral ministries (M Div). *Accreditation:* ATS (one or more programs are accredited). Part-time programs available. *Degree requirements:* For master's, 2 foreign languages, internship; for M Div, one foreign language, internship. *Entrance requirements:* For master's, bachelor degree. Additional exam requirements/recommendations for international students: Required—TOEFL or IELTS. Electronic applications accepted. *Faculty research:* Evangelicalism and sociology, missiological trends, chaplaincy, intertestamental studies, postmodernism.

American Baptist Seminary of the West, Graduate and Professional Programs, Berkeley, CA 94704-3029. Offers community leadership (MA); theology (M Div, MA). *Accreditation:* ACIPE; ATS (one or more programs are accredited). Part-time and evening/weekend programs available. *Faculty:* 4 full-time (all women), 5 part-time/adjunct (0 women). *Students:* 50 full-time (29 women), 21 part-time (11 women); includes 50 minority (44 African Americans, 6 Asian Americans or Pacific Islanders), 13 international. *Entrance requirements:* For M Div, minimum GPA of 2.5; for master's, minimum GPA of 3.0. Additional exam requirements/recommendations for international students: Required—TOEFL (minimum score 550 paper-based; 250 computer-based). *Application deadline:* For fall admission, 4/15 priority date for domestic students, 4/15 for international students. Applications are processed on a rolling basis. Application fee: $25. Electronic applications accepted. *Expenses:* Tuition: Full-time $12,750; part-time $500 per credit. Required fees: $240 per semester. One-time fee: $250. Tuition and fees vary according to degree level. *Financial support:* Career-related internships or fieldwork, institutionally sponsored loans, scholarships/grants, tuition waivers (partial), and tuition discount available. Support available to part-time students. Financial award application deadline: 4/15; financial award applicants required to submit FAFSA. *Unit head:* Dr. Paul M. Martin, President for the Interim, 510-841-1905 Ext. 224, Fax: 510-841-2446, E-mail: pmartin@absw.edu. *Application contact:* Rev. Michelle M. Holmes, Vice President, 510-841-1905 Ext. 225, Fax: 510-841-2446, E-mail: mmholmes@absw.edu.

Amridge University, Graduate and Professional Programs, Montgomery, AL 36117. Offers behavioral leadership and management (MA); biblical studies (MA, PhD); family therapy (D Min); leadership and management (MS); marriage and family therapy (M Div, MA, PhD), including marriage and family therapy (PhD), professional counseling (PhD); ministerial leadership (M Div, MS); pastoral counseling (M Div, MS); practical theology (MA); professional counseling (M Div, MA); theology (M Div, D Min). *Accreditation:* ATS. Part-time and evening/weekend programs available. Postbaccalaureate distance learning degree programs offered (no on-campus study). *Faculty:* 44 full-time (9 women), 18 part-time/adjunct (7 women). *Students:* 131 full-time (61 women), 218 part-time (119 women); includes 174 minority (164 African Americans, 1 American Indian/Alaska Native, 1 Asian American or Pacific Islander, 8 Hispanic Americans). Average age 35. *Degree requirements:* For master's, one foreign language, comprehensive exam (for some programs), thesis (for some programs); for doctorate, comprehensive exam (for some programs), thesis/dissertation; for M Div, comprehensive exam (for some programs). *Entrance requirements:* For M Div, master's, and doctorate, GRE General Test or MAT. Additional exam requirements/recommendations for international students: Required—TOEFL. *Application deadline:* For fall admission, 9/1 priority date for domestic students; for spring admission, 1/1 priority date for domestic students. Applications are processed on a rolling basis. Application fee: $75. Electronic applications accepted. *Expenses:* Tuition:

Pastoral Ministry and Counseling

Amridge University (continued)
Full-time $9630; part-time $535 per semester hour. Required fees: $600 per term. Tuition and fees vary according to course load and degree level. *Financial support:* Federal Work-Study and scholarships/grants available. Support available to part-time students. Financial award applicants required to submit FAFSA. *Faculty research:* Homiletics, hermeneutics, ancient Near Eastern history. *Unit head:* Rick Johnson, Director of Enrollment Management, 800-351-4040 Ext. 7513, Fax: 334-387-3878, E-mail: rickjohnson@amridgeuniversity.edu. *Application contact:* Ora Davis, Admissions Officer, 334-387-3877 Ext. 7524, Fax: 334-387-3878, E-mail: oradavis@amridgeuniversity.edu.

Anderson University, School of Christian Ministry, Anderson, SC 29621-4035. Offers M Min. Postbaccalaureate distance learning degree programs offered. *Degree requirements:* For master's, capstone course, ministry project. *Entrance requirements:* For master's, copy of official transcripts, 3 references.

Andrews University, School of Graduate Studies, Seventh-day Adventist Theological Seminary, Berrien Springs, MI 49104. Offers ministry (M Div, D Min); pastoral ministry (MA); religious education (MA, Ed D, PhD, Ed S); theology (M Th, Th D); youth ministry (MA). *Accreditation:* ATS. *Faculty:* 35 full-time (3 women), 1 (woman) part-time/adjunct. *Students:* 377 full-time (63 women), 494 part-time (46 women); includes 336 minority (173 African Americans, 3 American Indian/Alaska Native, 43 Asian Americans or Pacific Islanders, 117 Hispanic Americans), 239 international. Average age 41. In 2008, 103 first professional degrees, 26 master's, 23 doctorates, 3 other advanced degrees awarded. *Degree requirements:* For master's, thesis optional; for doctorate, variable foreign language requirement, thesis/dissertation; for M Div, one foreign language, thesis/dissertation optional. *Entrance requirements:* For master's, GRE Subject Test, minimum GPA of 2.0. Additional exam requirements/recommendations for international students: Required—TOEFL (minimum score 550 paper-based). *Application deadline:* Applications are processed on a rolling basis. Application fee: $40. *Expenses:* Tuition: Full-time $18,360; part-time $765 per credit hour. Required fees: $476; $765 per credit hour. $238 per semester. Tuition and fees vary according to degree level. *Financial support:* Fellowships, research assistantships, teaching assistantships, career-related internships or fieldwork, Federal Work-Study, and institutionally sponsored loans available. *Unit head:* Dr. Denis Fortin, Dean, 269-471-3537. *Application contact:* Carolyn Hurst, Director, 800-253-2874, Fax: 269-471-6321.

Anna Maria College, Graduate Division, Program in Pastoral Ministry, Paxton, MA 01612. Offers MA. Part-time and evening/weekend programs available. *Faculty:* 1 full-time (0 women), 2 part-time/adjunct (0 women). *Students:* 18 part-time (12 women); includes 1 minority (American Indian/Alaska Native). Average age 46. In 2008, 4 master's awarded. *Degree requirements:* For master's, pastoral project. *Entrance requirements:* For master's, interview. Additional exam requirements/recommendations for international students: Required—TOEFL (minimum score 500 paper-based). *Application deadline:* For fall admission, 3/1 priority date for domestic and international students; for spring admission, 11/1 priority date for domestic and international students. Applications are processed on a rolling basis. Application fee: $40. Electronic applications accepted. *Expenses:* Tuition: Part-time $1400 per course. *Financial support:* Applicants required to submit FAFSA. *Unit head:* Dr. Michael Boover, Director, 508-849-3431, Fax: 508-849-3343, E-mail: mboover@annamaria.edu. *Application contact:* Dennis Braun, Director, Graduate Studies and Continuing Education, 508-849-3293, Fax: 508-819-3362, E-mail: dbraun@annamaria.edu.

Aquinas Institute of Theology, Graduate and Professional Programs, St. Louis, MO 63108. Offers biblical studies (Certificate); health care mission (MAHCM); ministry (M Div); pastoral care (Certificate); pastoral ministry (MAPM); pastoral studies (MAPS); preaching (D Min); spiritual direction (Certificate); theology (M Div, MA); Thomistic studies (Certificate); M Div/MA; MAPS/MSW. *Accreditation:* ATS (one or more programs are accredited). Part-time and evening/weekend programs available. Postbaccalaureate distance learning degree programs offered (minimal on-campus study). *Faculty:* 17 full-time (10 women), 4 part-time/adjunct (2 women). *Students:* 74 full-time (25 women), 193 part-time (127 women); includes 37 minority (16 African Americans, 1 American Indian/Alaska Native, 10 Asian Americans or Pacific Islanders, 10 Hispanic Americans), 12 international. Average age 41. 76 applicants, 87% accepted, 56 enrolled. In 2008, 42 master's, 8 doctorates awarded. *Degree requirements:* For master's, one foreign language, comprehensive exam, thesis or major paper; for doctorate, thesis/dissertation. *Entrance requirements:* For M Div and master's, MAT; for doctorate, 3 years of ministerial experience, 6 hours of graduate course work in homiletics, M Div or the equivalent, minimum GPA of 3.0. Additional exam requirements/recommendations for international students: Required—TOEFL. *Application deadline:* For fall admission, 3/15 priority date for domestic and international students; for spring admission, 11/15 priority date for domestic and international students. Applications are processed on a rolling basis. Application fee: $50. *Expenses:* Tuition: Full-time $14,784; part-time $616 per credit hour. Required fees: $195 per semester. Tuition and fees vary according to course load. *Financial support:* Career-related internships or fieldwork, scholarships/grants, health care benefits, and tuition waivers (partial) available. Support available to part-time students. Financial award application deadline: 3/15; financial award applicants required to submit CSS PROFILE or FAFSA. *Faculty research:* Theology of preaching, hermeneutics, lay ecclesiastical ministry, pastoral and practical theology. *Unit head:* Fr. Gregory Heille, Academic Dean, 314-256-8800, Fax: 314-256-8888, E-mail: heille@ai.edu. *Application contact:* David Werthmann, Director of Admissions, 314-256-8806, Fax: 314-256-8888, E-mail: admissions@ai.edu.

Argosy University, Sarasota, College of Psychology and Behavioral Sciences, Sarasota, FL 34235. Offers community counseling (MA); counseling psychology (Ed D); counselor education and supervision (Ed D); forensic psychology (MA); marriage and family therapy (MA); mental health counseling (MA); organizational leadership (Ed D); pastoral community counseling (Ed D); school counseling (MA, Ed S); school psychology (MA).

See Close-Up on page 1091.

Asbury Theological Seminary, Graduate and Professional Programs, Wilmore, KY 40390-1199. Offers MA, MAC, MACE, MACL, MAPC, MAXM, MAYM, Th M, D Miss, PhD, Certificate. *Accreditation:* ATS. Part-time programs available. Postbaccalaureate distance learning degree programs offered (minimal on-campus study). *Faculty:* 67 full-time (15 women), 74 part-time/adjunct (14 women). *Students:* 708 full-time (219 women), 852 part-time (263 women); includes 110 minority (59 African Americans, 10 American Indian/Alaska Native, 12 Asian Americans or Pacific Islanders, 29 Hispanic Americans), 156 international. Average age 25. 765 applicants, 75% accepted, 364 enrolled. In 2008, 95 master's, 15 doctorates, 38 other advanced degrees awarded. Terminal master's awarded for partial completion of doctoral program. *Degree requirements:* For master's, thesis (for some programs); for doctorate, thesis/dissertation, qualifying exam. *Entrance requirements:* For master's, minimum GPA of 2.75; for doctorate, minimum GPA of 3.0. Additional exam requirements/recommendations for international students: Required—TOEFL, IELTS. *Application deadline:* Applications are processed on a rolling basis. Application fee: $50. Electronic applications accepted. *Expenses:* Tuition: Full-time $12,474; part-time $462 per credit hour. Required fees: $50; $30 per year. Tuition and fees vary according to course level, course load, degree level, campus/location and program. *Financial support:* In 2008–09, 1,317 students received support. Career-related internships or fieldwork, Federal Work-Study, institutionally sponsored loans, and scholarships/grants available. Support available to part-time students. Financial award applicants required to submit FAFSA. *Unit head:* Dr. Leslie A. Andrews, Provost, 859-858-2206, Fax: 859-858-2025, E-mail: leslie.andrews@asburyseminary.edu. *Application contact:* Janelle Vernon, Admissions Director, 859-858-2211, Fax: 859-858-2287, E-mail: admissions.office@asburyseminary.edu.

Ashland Theological Seminary, Graduate Programs, Ashland, OH 44805. Offers biblical and theological studies (MA, MAR), including New Testament (MA), Old Testament (MA); Christian ministry (MAPT); Christian studies (Diploma); clinical pastoral counseling (MACPC); historical studies (MA); ministry (D Min); pastoral counseling (MAPC); pastoral ministry (M Div); theological studies (MA). *Accreditation:* ATS. Part-time programs available. *Degree requirements:* For master's, comprehensive exam (for some programs), thesis (for some programs); for doctorate, thesis/dissertation; for M Div, 2 foreign languages. *Entrance requirements:* For M Div, minimum GPA of 2.75; for master's, minimum undergraduate GPA of 2.75; for doctorate, M Div, minimum undergraduate GPA of 3.0. Additional exam requirements/recommendations for international students: Required—TOEFL (minimum score 550 paper-based). Electronic applications accepted. *Faculty research:* Semitic languages and linguistics, rhetorical and social-scientific criticism, Anabaptist studies, inner spiritual healing, African-American clergy in film and literature.

Assemblies of God Theological Seminary, Graduate and Professional Programs, Springfield, MO 65802. Offers biblical preaching (D Min); Christian ministries (MA); divinity (M Div); intercultural studies (D Miss, PhD); missional leadership (D Min); relief and development (D Miss); self-design study (D Min); women in leadership (D Min). *Accreditation:* ATS. Part-time and evening/weekend programs available. Postbaccalaureate distance learning degree programs offered (minimal on-campus study). *Faculty:* 16 full-time (3 women), 21 part-time/adjunct (4 women). *Students:* 220 full-time (69 women), 226 part-time (49 women); includes 49 minority (11 African Americans, 5 American Indian/Alaska Native, 11 Asian Americans or Pacific Islanders, 22 Hispanic Americans), 7 international. Average age 36. *Degree requirements:* For master's, analytical reflection paper or comprehensive exam; for doctorate, thesis/dissertation; for M Div, one foreign language, analytical reflection paper. *Entrance requirements:* For M Div, minimum GPA of 2.0; for master's, minimum GPA of 2.5; for doctorate, minimum GPA of 3.0. Additional exam requirements/recommendations for international students: Required—TOEFL (minimum score 550 paper-based; 213 computer-based; 80 iBT). *Application deadline:* For fall admission, 7/1 priority date for domestic students, 6/1 priority date for international students; for spring admission, 12/1 priority date for domestic students, 11/1 priority date for international students. Applications are processed on a rolling basis. Application fee: $35. Electronic applications accepted. *Financial support:* Career-related internships or fieldwork, Federal Work-Study, and scholarships/grants available. Support available to part-time students. Financial award application deadline: 7/15; financial award applicants required to submit FAFSA. *Unit head:* Stephen Lim, Academic Dean, 417-268-1000, Fax: 417-268-1001, E-mail: slim@agts.edu. *Application contact:* Stephen Lim, Academic Dean, 417-268-1000, Fax: 417-268-1001, E-mail: slim@agts.edu.

The Athenaeum of Ohio, Graduate Programs, Cincinnati, OH 45230-5900. Offers biblical studies (MABS); divinity (M Div); lay ministry (Certificate); pastoral counseling (MAPC); pastoral ministry (MA); theology (MA Th); M Div/MA Th; M Div/MABS; M Div/MAPC. *Accreditation:* ATS (one or more programs are accredited). Part-time and evening/weekend programs available. *Degree requirements:* For master's, one foreign language, comprehensive exam (for some programs), thesis optional; for M Div, comprehensive exam.

Austin Presbyterian Theological Seminary, Graduate and Professional Programs, Austin, TX 78705-5797. Offers divinity (M Div); ministry (D Min); theological studies (MA); M Div/MATS; M Div/MSSW. *Accreditation:* ACIPE; ATS. Part-time programs available. *Degree requirements:* For doctorate, thesis/dissertation; for M Div, Greek, Hebrew. *Entrance requirements:* References. Additional exam requirements/recommendations for international students: Required—TOEFL (minimum score 550 paper-based; 213 computer-based; 79 iBT). *Faculty research:* Mystical theology, religious pluralism, narrative preaching, social ethics, pastoral care and healing.

Ave Maria University, Graduate Programs, Ave Maria, FL 34142. Offers pastoral theology (MTS); theology (MA, PhD). Terminal master's awarded for partial completion of doctoral program. *Degree requirements:* For master's, one foreign language, thesis; for doctorate, 3 foreign languages, comprehensive exam, thesis/dissertation. *Entrance requirements:* For master's, GRE; for doctorate, GRE, M Div or equivalent; MA or MTS in religion, theology, or philosophy; bachelor's degree with strong background in religion, theology, and/or philosophy.

Ave Maria University, Institute for Pastoral Theology, Ave Maria, FL 34142. Offers MTS. Part-time and evening/weekend programs available.

Azusa Pacific University, Haggard School of Theology, Program in Divinity, Azusa, CA 91702-7000. Offers M Div.

Azusa Pacific University, Haggard School of Theology, Program in Ministry Management, Azusa, CA 91702-7000. Offers MAMM.

Azusa Pacific University, Haggard School of Theology, Program in Pastoral Studies, Azusa, CA 91702-7000. Offers MAPS.

Azusa Pacific University, Haggard School of Theology, Program in Worship Leadership, Azusa, CA 91702-7000. Offers MAWL.

Bakke Graduate University, Programs in Pastoral Ministry and Business, Seattle, WA 98104. Offers business (MBA); global urban ministry (MA); social and civic entrepreneurship (MA); transformational leadership for the global city (D Min). Part-time programs available. Postbaccalaureate distance learning degree programs offered (minimal on-campus study). *Faculty:* 6 full-time (2 women), 29 part-time/adjunct (2 women). *Students:* 56 full-time (12 women), 149 part-time (31 women); includes 87 minority (50 African Americans, 1 American Indian/Alaska Native, 28 Asian Americans or Pacific Islanders, 8 Hispanic Americans). Average age 36. In 2008, 8 master's, 19 doctorates awarded. *Degree requirements:* For master's, thesis; for doctorate, thesis/dissertation. *Entrance requirements:* For master's, 2 years of ministry experience, BA in biblical studies or theology; for doctorate, 3 years of ministry experience, M Div. Additional exam requirements/recommendations for international students: Required—TOEFL (minimum score 60 computer-based). *Application deadline:* For fall admission, 7/1 priority date for domestic students; for winter admission, 12/1 for domestic students; for spring admission, 3/15 for domestic students. Applications are processed on a rolling basis. Application fee: $75 ($25 for international students). Electronic applications accepted. *Expenses:* Tuition: Full-time $3800; part-time $1700 per course. Tuition and fees vary according to course level. *Financial support:* In 2008–09, 46 students received support. Scholarships/grants and tuition waivers (partial) available. Financial award applicants required to submit CSS PROFILE. *Faculty research:* Theological systems, church management, worship. *Unit head:* Dr. Grace Barnes, Academic Dean, 206-264-9100 Ext. 119, Fax: 206-264-8828, E-mail: graceb@bgu.edu. *Application contact:* Lauren Geiser, Assistant Registrar, 206-246-9100 Ext. 122, Fax: 206-264-8828, E-mail: laureng@bgu.edu.

Baptist Bible College, Graduate School of Theology, Springfield, MO 65803-3498. Offers biblical counseling (MA); biblical studies (MA); church ministry (MA); intercultural studies (MA); theology (M Div). Part-time programs available. *Degree requirements:* For master's, 2 foreign languages, thesis (for some programs); for M Div, 2 foreign languages, thesis/dissertation (for some programs). *Entrance requirements:* For master's, outcomes test. Electronic applications accepted.

Baptist Bible College of Pennsylvania, Baptist Bible Seminary, Clarks Summit, PA 18411-1297. Offers biblical studies (PhD); church planting (M Div); global missions (M Div); military chaplaincy (M Div); ministry (M Min, D Min); pastor of church education (M Div); pastor of outreach (M Div); pastoral counseling (M Div); pastoral leadership (M Div); theology (M Div, Th M); youth pastor (M Div). Part-time and evening/weekend programs available. Postbaccalaureate distance learning degree programs offered (minimal on-campus study). Terminal master's awarded for partial completion of doctoral program. *Degree requirements:* For master's, 2 foreign languages, thesis; for doctorate, 2 foreign languages, comprehensive exam (for some programs), thesis/dissertation, oral exam; for M Div, 2 foreign languages, thesis/dissertation, oral exam. *Entrance requirements:* For doctorate, Greek and Hebrew entrance exams (PhD). Electronic applications accepted.

Baptist Bible College of Pennsylvania, Graduate School, Clarks Summit, PA 18411-1297. Offers biblical ministries (MS); Christian school education (MS); counseling (MS). Part-time and evening/weekend programs available. Postbaccalaureate distance learning degree programs offered (no on-campus study). *Entrance requirements:* Additional exam requirements/recommendations for international students: Required—TOEFL.

Baptist Theological Seminary at Richmond, Graduate and Professional Program, Richmond, VA 23227. Offers children and family ministry (M Div); Christian education (M Div); church music (M Div); theology (D Min); youth and student ministry (M Div); M Div/MS; M Div/MSW. *Accreditation:* ATS. Part-time programs available. Postbaccalaureate distance learning degree programs offered (minimal on-campus study). *Degree requirements:* For doctorate, one foreign language, comprehensive exam, thesis/dissertation, field study, independent study; for M Div, one foreign language, comprehensive exam (for some programs), thesis/dissertation optional, mission immersion experience, internship. *Entrance requirements:* For doctorate, MAT, M Div, 3 years of full-time ministry experience. Additional exam requirements/recommendations for international students: Required—TOEFL (minimum score 481 paper-based; 213 computer-based). *Faculty research:* New Testament studies, Old Testament studies, pastoral care, church history, theology.

Barry University, School of Arts and Sciences, Department of Theology and Philosophy, Miami Shores, FL 33161-6695. Offers ministry (D Min); pastoral ministry for Hispanics (MA); pastoral theology (MA); practical theology (MA). *Accreditation:* ATS. Part-time and evening/weekend programs available. *Degree requirements:* For master's, comprehensive exam, thesis optional; for doctorate, thesis/dissertation. *Entrance requirements:* For master's, GRE General Test or MAT, minimum GPA of 3.0. Electronic applications accepted. *Faculty research:* Fundamental morals, bioethics, social ethics, liturgical and sacramental theology, biblical studies.

Beacon University, Graduate Programs, Columbus, GA 31909. Offers cell church development (MAPM); counseling ministry (MAPM); military chaplaincy (MAPM); organizational leadership (MAPM); pastoral ministry (MAPM); theology (M Div, MABS). Part-time and evening/weekend programs available. Postbaccalaureate distance learning degree programs offered (minimal on-campus study). *Degree requirements:* For master's and M Div, comprehensive exam. *Entrance requirements:* For M Div, MAT or GRE or GMAT or MTE, official undergrad and/or transf.; for master's, MAT or GRE or NTE or GMAT, official undergrad and/or trsfr. Additional exam requirements/recommendations for international students: Required—TOEFL (minimum score 500 paper-based; 173 computer-based; 61 iBT); Recommended—IELTS (minimum score 6).

Bethany Theological Seminary, Graduate and Professional Programs, Richmond, IN 47374-4019. Offers biblical studies (MA Th); ministry studies (M Div); peace studies (M Div, MA Th); theological studies (MA Th, CATS); youth ministry (M Div). *Accreditation:* ACIPE; ATS. Part-time programs available. Postbaccalaureate distance learning degree programs offered (minimal on-campus study). *Degree requirements:* For master's, thesis. *Entrance requirements:* For M Div, letters of reference, minimum GPA of 2.75; for master's, letters of reference, minimum GPA of 3.0. Additional exam requirements/recommendations for international students: Required—TOEFL (minimum score 550 paper-based; 218 computer-based).

Bethel College, Division of Graduate Studies, Program in Christian Ministries, Mishawaka, IN 46545-5591. Offers M Min. Part-time and evening/weekend programs available. *Faculty:* 1 full-time (0 women), 7 part-time/adjunct (0 women). *Students:* 13 full-time (3 women), 47 part-time (17 women); includes 10 minority (9 African Americans, 1 Hispanic American), 1 international. 33 applicants, 88% accepted, 24 enrolled. In 2008, 17 master's awarded. *Degree requirements:* For master's, thesis or alternative. *Entrance requirements:* Additional exam requirements/recommendations for international students: Required—TOEFL (minimum score 540 paper-based; 207 computer-based). *Application deadline:* For fall admission, 5/1 for international students; for spring admission, 10/1 for international students. Applications are processed on a rolling basis. Application fee: $25. Electronic applications accepted. *Expenses:* Tuition: Full-time $6120; part-time $340 per credit hour. Tuition and fees vary according to program. *Financial support:* Career-related internships or fieldwork available. Financial award applicants required to submit FAFSA. *Unit head:* Dr. Gene Carpenter, Director, 574-257-3332, E-mail: carpeng@bethelcollege.edu. *Application contact:* Dr. John Dendiu, Advisor, 574-257-2675, Fax: 574-257-3385, E-mail: dendiuj@bethelcollege.edu.

Bethel Seminary, Graduate and Professional Programs, St. Paul, MN 55112-6998. Offers applied ministry (MA); biblical studies (MATS, Certificate); children's and family ministry (MACFM); Christian education (MACE); Christian thought (M Div, MACT); church leadership (D Min); community ministry leadership (MA, Certificate); congregation and family care (D Min); global and contextual studies (MA, MATS); historical studies (MATS); lay ministry (Certificate); marriage and family studies (M Div); marriage and family therapy (MAMFT, Certificate); pastoral ministries (M Div); spiritual formation (Certificate); theological studies (MATS, Certificate); transformational leadership (MATL); youth ministries (MACE). *Accreditation:* ACIPE; ATS (one or more programs are accredited). Part-time and evening/weekend programs available. Postbaccalaureate distance learning degree programs offered (minimal on-campus study). *Faculty:* 26 full-time (2 women), 93 part-time/adjunct (29 women). *Students:* 397 full-time (124 women), 707 part-time (299 women); includes 218 minority (123 African Americans, 1 American Indian/Alaska Native, 67 Asian Americans or Pacific Islanders, 27 Hispanic Americans), 14 international. Average age 36. 470 applicants, 90% accepted, 270 enrolled. In 2008, 63 first professional degrees, 101 master's, 10 doctorates awarded. *Degree requirements:* For master's, variable foreign language requirement, thesis (for some programs); for doctorate, thesis/dissertation; for M Div, one foreign language. *Entrance requirements:* For M Div, letters of reference; for master's, letters of reference, transcripts, personal statement; for doctorate, M Div, letters of reference, essays, organizational support. Additional exam requirements/recommendations for international students: Required—TOEFL (minimum score 550 paper-based; 213 computer-based). *Application deadline:* For fall admission, 8/1 priority date for domestic students, 3/1 for international students; for winter admission, 12/1 priority date for domestic students; for spring admission, 3/1 priority date for domestic students. Applications are processed on a rolling basis. Application fee: $20. Electronic applications accepted. *Financial support:* In 2008–09, 688 students received support, including 20 teaching assistantships; career-related internships or fieldwork, Federal Work-Study, scholarships/grants, and tuition waivers (full) also available. Financial award application deadline: 7/15; financial award applicants required to submit FAFSA. *Faculty research:* Nature of theology, ethics, biblical commentaries, nature of God, science and theology. *Unit head:* Dr. Leland Eliason, Executive Vice President and Provost, 651-638-6182. *Application contact:* Joseph V. Dworak, Director of Admissions, 651-638-6288, Fax: 651-638-6002, E-mail: j-dworak@bethel.edu.

Biblical Theological Seminary, Graduate and Professional Programs, Hatfield, PA 19440-2499. Offers advanced missional leadership (D Min); advanced pastoral studies (Certificate); biblical counseling (Certificate); biblical studies (MA, Certificate); counseling (MA); ministry (MA); missional theology (MA); theology (M Div); youth ministry (Certificate). *Accreditation:* ATS. Part-time programs available. Postbaccalaureate distance learning degree programs offered. *Degree requirements:* For M Div, thesis/dissertation. *Entrance requirements:* Additional exam requirements/recommendations for international students: Required—TOEFL (minimum score 550 paper-based; 213 computer-based). *Faculty research:* Old Testament narrative, Old Testament historiography, Hebrew syntax, parables, addictions.

Bob Jones University, Graduate Programs, Greenville, SC 29614. Offers accountancy (MS); Bible (MA); Bible translation (MA); Biblical studies (Certificate); broadcast management (MS); business administration (MBA); church history (MA, PhD); church ministries (MA); church music (MM); cinema and video production (MA); counseling (MS); curriculum and instruction (Ed D); divinity (M Div); dramatic production (MA); educational leadership (MS, Ed D, Ed S); elementary education (M Ed, MAT); English (M Ed, MA, MAT); fine arts (MA); graphic design (MA); history (M Ed, MA); illustration (MA); interpretative speech (MA); mathematics (M Ed, MAT); medical missions (Certificate); ministry (MM, D Min); multi-categorical special education (M Ed, MAT); music (M Ed); New Testament interpretation (PhD); Old Testament interpretation (PhD); orchestral instrument performance (MM); organ performance (MM); pastoral studies (MA); personnel services (MS, Ed S); piano pedagogy (MM); piano performance (MM); platform arts (MA); radio and television broadcasting (MS); rhetoric and public address (MA); secondary education (M Ed); studio art (MA); teaching Bible (MA); theology (MA, PhD); voice performance (MM); youth ministries (MA); M Div/MM.

Boston College, Graduate School of Arts and Sciences, School of Theology and Ministry, Chestnut Hill, MA 02467-3800. Offers church leadership (MA); divinity (M Div); pastoral ministry (MA), including Hispanic ministry, liturgy and worship, pastoral care and counseling, spirituality; religious education (MA, PhD); sacred theology (STD, STL); social justice/social ministry (MA); spiritual direction (MA); theological studies (MTS); theology (Th M, PhD); youth ministry (MA); MA/MA; MS/MA; MSW/MA. Part-time programs available. *Degree requirements:* For doctorate, one foreign language, thesis/dissertation. *Entrance requirements:* For doctorate, GRE. Additional exam requirements/recommendations for international students: Required—TOEFL (minimum score 550 paper-based; 213 computer-based). Electronic applications accepted. *Expenses:* Tuition: Part-time $1148 per credit. Required fees: $60. *Faculty research:* Philosophy and practice of religious education, pastoral psychology, liturgical and spiritual theology, spiritual formation for the practice of ministry.

Briercrest Seminary, Graduate Programs, Program in Christian Ministries, Caronport, SK S0H 0S0, Canada. Offers leadership (MA); marriage and family counseling (MA); missions (MA); pastoral counseling (MA); worship (MA); youth and family ministry (MA). Part-time programs available. *Degree requirements:* For master's, comprehensive exam, thesis optional. *Entrance requirements:* Additional exam requirements/recommendations for international students: Required—TOEFL (minimum score 550 paper-based; 213 computer-based).

Briercrest Seminary, Graduate Programs, Program in Theology, Caronport, SK S0H 0S0, Canada. Offers Biblical studies (M Div); leadership and management (M Div); New Testament (MATS); Old Testament (MATS); pastoral counseling (M Div); pastoral ministry (M Div); theological studies (M Div); theology (MATS); worship (M Div); youth and family ministry (M Div). *Accreditation:* ATS. Part-time programs available. *Degree requirements:* For master's, comprehensive exam, thesis optional. *Entrance requirements:* Additional exam requirements/recommendations for international students: Required—TOEFL (minimum score 550 paper-based; 213 computer-based).

Caldwell College, Graduate Studies, Program in Pastoral Ministry, Caldwell, NJ 07006-6195. Offers MA. Part-time and evening/weekend programs available. *Degree requirements:* For master's, thesis. *Entrance requirements:* For master's, minimum GPA of 3.0, 2 years of ministry experience. Additional exam requirements/recommendations for international students: Required—TOEFL (minimum score 580 paper-based; 237 computer-based). Electronic applications accepted.

California Baptist University, Program in Counseling Ministry, Riverside, CA 92504-3206. Offers MA. Part-time programs available. *Faculty:* 2 full-time (0 women). *Students:* 2 full-time (both women), 6 part-time (5 women); includes 4 minority (1 African American, 3 Hispanic Americans). 6 applicants, 50% accepted, 3 enrolled. In 2008, 4 master's awarded. *Degree requirements:* For master's, thesis or alternative. *Entrance requirements:* For master's, minimum undergraduate GPA of 2.75. Additional exam requirements/recommendations for international students: Required—TOEFL (minimum score 575 paper-based; 230 computer-based; 89 iBT). *Application deadline:* For fall admission, 8/1 priority date for domestic students, 7/1 priority date for international students; for spring admission, 12/1 priority date for domestic students, 10/15 priority date for international students. Applications are processed on a rolling basis. Application fee: $45. Electronic applications accepted. *Expenses:* Contact institution. *Financial support:* Federal Work-Study and scholarships/grants available. Support available to part-time students. Financial award applicants required to submit FAFSA. *Unit head:* Dr. Nathan Lewis, Director, 951-343-4348, Fax: 951-343-4569, E-mail: nlewis@calbaptist.edu. *Application contact:* Gail Ronveaux, Dean of Graduate Enrollment, 951-343-5045, Fax: 951-343-5095, E-mail: graduateadmissions@calbaptist.edu.

California Baptist University, Program in Counseling Psychology, Riverside, CA 92504-3206. Offers professional counseling (MS); professional ministry (MS). Part-time programs available. *Faculty:* 4 full-time (2 women), 4 part-time/adjunct (2 women). *Students:* 79 full-time (61 women), 54 part-time (42 women); includes 58 minority (14 African Americans, 1 American Indian/Alaska Native, 9 Asian Americans or Pacific Islanders, 34 Hispanic Americans), 3 international. 116 applicants, 54% accepted, 48 enrolled. In 2008, 45 master's awarded. *Degree requirements:* For master's, comprehensive exam, 24 hours (individual) or 50 hours (group) psychotherapy. *Entrance requirements:* For master's, Minnesota Multiphasic Personality Inventory, Myers-Briggs Type Inventory, course work in developmental psychology, theories of personality, and statistics; minimum undergraduate GPA of 2.75. Additional exam requirements/recommendations for international students: Required—TOEFL (minimum score 575 paper-based; 230 computer-based; 89 iBT). *Application deadline:* For fall admission, 9/1 for domestic students, 7/1 priority date for international students; for spring admission, 1/3 for domestic students, 10/15 priority date for international students. Applications are processed on a rolling basis. Application fee: $45. Electronic applications accepted. *Expenses:* Contact institution. *Financial support:* Career-related internships or fieldwork, Federal Work-Study, and scholarships/grants available. Support available to part-time students. Financial award applicants required to submit FAFSA. *Unit head:* Dr. Gary Collins, Director and Associate Dean, School of Business, 951-343-4304, Fax: 951-343-4569, E-mail: gcollins@calbaptist.edu. *Application contact:* Gail Ronveaux, Dean of Graduate Enrollment, 951-343-5045, Fax: 951-343-5095, E-mail: graduateadmissions@calbaptist.edu.

Calvary Bible College and Theological Seminary, Calvary Theological Seminary, Kansas City, MO 64147-1341. Offers Bible and theology (MS); Biblical counseling (MA); Biblical studies (MA); Christian ministry (MA); Christian studies (MS); Christian theology (MA); New Testament (MA); Old Testament (MA); pastoral studies (M Div). Part-time and evening/weekend programs available. *Faculty:* 3 full-time (0 women), 2 part-time/adjunct (0 women). *Students:* 21 full-time (7 women), 37 part-time (16 women); includes 5 African Americans, 4 Asian Americans or Pacific Islanders, 3 Hispanic Americans, 2 international. Average age 38. In 2008, 13 master's awarded. *Degree requirements:* For master's, one foreign language, comprehensive exam, thesis; for M Div, 2 foreign languages, comprehensive exam, thesis/dissertation. *Entrance requirements:* For M Div and master's, GRE, minimum GPA of 2.5, 50 semester hours of course work in liberal arts, BA or BS degree, doctrine agreement. Additional exam requirements/recommendations for international students: Required—TOEFL (minimum score 550 paper-based; 213 computer-based). *Application deadline:* For fall admission, 7/15 priority date for domestic and international students; for spring admission, 12/1 priority date for domestic and international students. Application fee: $25. *Financial support:* In 2008–09, 13 students received support. Scholarships/grants available. Financial award application deadline: 11/5. *Unit head:* Dr. Thomas Baurain, Academic Dean, 816-322-0110 Ext. 1502, Fax: 816-331-4474. *Application contact:* Bob Crank, Director of Admissions, 800-326-3960 Ext. 1326, Fax: 816-331-4474.

Capital Bible Seminary, Graduate and Professional Programs, Lanham, MD 20706-3599. Offers biblical studies (MA, Certificate); Christian counseling (MA); Christian counseling and discipleship (Certificate); ministry leadership (MA); theology (M Div, Th M). *Accreditation:* ATS (one or more programs are accredited). Part-time and evening/weekend programs available. *Degree requirements:* For master's, 2 foreign languages, comprehensive exam, thesis (for some programs); for M Div, 2 foreign languages, comprehensive exam. *Entrance requirements:* For M Div and master's, GRE General Test, Greek exam for those with 2 years of Greek, proficiency exam in theology, previous course work in Biblical studies. Additional exam requirements/recommendations for international students: Required—TOEFL (minimum score 550 paper-based; 213 computer-based). *Faculty research:* Dead Sea Scrolls, spiritual gifts, hermeneutics.

Cardinal Stritch University, College of Arts and Sciences, Department of Religious Studies, Milwaukee, WI 53217-3985. Offers lay ministries (MA); ministry (MA); religious studies (MA). Part-time and evening/weekend programs available. *Degree requirements:* For master's,

Pastoral Ministry and Counseling

Cardinal Stritch University *(continued)*
comprehensive exam, thesis, faculty recommendation, research project. *Entrance requirements:* For master's, interview, minimum GPA of 2.75.

Catholic Theological Union at Chicago, Graduate and Professional Programs, Chicago, IL 60615-5698. Offers biblical spirituality (Certificate); cross-cultural ministries (D Min); cross-cultural missions (Certificate); divinity (M Div); liturgical studies (Certificate); liturgy (D Min); pastoral studies (MAPS, Certificate); spiritual formation (Certificate); spirituality (D Min); theology (MA); M Div/MA; M Div/MSW; M Div/PhD. *Accreditation:* ACIPE; ATS (one or more programs are accredited). Part-time and evening/weekend programs available. *Degree requirements:* For master's, one foreign language, comprehensive exam (for some programs), thesis (for some programs); for doctorate, thesis/dissertation. *Entrance requirements:* For doctorate, master's degree, 5 years of active ministry. *Faculty research:* Doctrine, sacraments, ethics, Bible.

The Catholic University of America, School of Theology and Religious Studies, Washington, DC 20064. Offers M Div, STB, MA, MRE, D Min, PhD, STD, STL, MSLS/MA. *Accreditation:* ATS (one or more programs are accredited). Part-time programs available. Terminal master's awarded for partial completion of doctoral program. *Degree requirements:* For master's, comprehensive exam; for doctorate, comprehensive exam, thesis/dissertation; for first professional degree, one foreign language; for STL, one foreign language, comprehensive exam, thesis. *Entrance requirements:* For first professional degree and master's, GRE General Test, 3 letters of recommendation; for doctorate and STL, GRE, 3 letters of recommendation. Additional exam requirements/recommendations for international students: Required—TOEFL (minimum score 580 paper-based; 237 computer-based). Electronic applications accepted. *Faculty research:* Biblical studies, canon law, church history, liturgical studies, religion and religious education.

Chaminade University of Honolulu, Graduate Services, Program in Pastoral Leadership, Honolulu, HI 96816-1578. Offers MAPL. Part-time and evening/weekend programs available. Postbaccalaureate distance learning degree programs offered (minimal on-campus study). *Degree requirements:* For master's, internship or thesis. *Entrance requirements:* For master's, 2 letters of recommendation. Additional exam requirements/recommendations for international students: Required—TOEFL (minimum score 550 paper-based). Electronic applications accepted.

Chaminade University of Honolulu, Graduate Services, Program in Pastoral Theology, Honolulu, HI 96816-1578. Offers MPT. Part-time and evening/weekend programs available. Postbaccalaureate distance learning degree programs offered. *Degree requirements:* For master's, capstone course. *Entrance requirements:* For master's, 2 letters of recommendation. Additional exam requirements/recommendations for international students: Required—TOEFL (minimum score 550 paper-based). Electronic applications accepted.

Chicago Theological Seminary, Graduate and Professional Programs, Chicago, IL 60637-1507. Offers preaching (D Min); religion and health (D Min); religious studies (MA); spirituality and spiritual direction (D Min); theology (M Div); theology, ethics and the human sciences (PhD); M Div/MSW. *Accreditation:* ACIPE; ATS. Part-time programs available. *Faculty:* 13 full-time (5 women). *Students:* 71 full-time (32 women), 139 part-time (76 women); includes 54 minority (45 African Americans, 6 Asian Americans or Pacific Islanders, 3 Hispanic Americans), 33 international. *Degree requirements:* For master's, thesis; for doctorate, 2 foreign languages, comprehensive exam, thesis/dissertation; for M Div, thesis/dissertation. *Entrance requirements:* For doctorate, GRE General Test. Additional exam requirements/recommendations for international students: Required—TOEFL (minimum score 217 computer-based). *Application deadline:* For fall admission, 2/15 priority date for domestic and international students; for spring admission, 11/1 for domestic and international students. Application fee: $50. *Financial support:* Fellowships, institutionally sponsored loans, scholarships/grants, and tuition waivers (partial) available. Support available to part-time students. Financial award application deadline: 3/1; financial award applicants required to submit FAFSA. *Faculty research:* Bible, culture and hermeneutics, theology, gender and sexuality, black faith and life, spirituality and psychology, practical theology. Total annual research expenditures: $150,000. *Unit head:* Dr. Theodore W. Jennings, Acting Dean, 773-752-5757, Fax: 773-752-1903, E-mail: tjennings@ctschicago.edu. *Application contact:* Rev. Lin Sanford Keppert, Director of Admissions, Recruitment and Financial Aid, E-mail: lkeppert@ctschicago.edu.

Christian Theological Seminary, Graduate and Professional Programs, Indianapolis, IN 46208-3301. Offers marriage and family (MA); pastoral care and counseling (D Min); practical theology (D Min); psychotherapy and faith (MA); sacred theology (STM); specialized ministries (MA); theological studies (MTS); theology (M Div). *Accreditation:* AAMFT/COAMFTE (one or more programs are accredited); ACIPE; ATS. Part-time programs available. Terminal master's awarded for partial completion of doctoral program. *Degree requirements:* For master's, comprehensive exam (for some programs), thesis (for some programs); for doctorate, comprehensive exam, thesis/dissertation; for M Div, comprehensive exam, thesis/dissertation (for some programs), missionary and cross-cultural experience. *Entrance requirements:* For master's, GRE General Test, MAT; for doctorate, M Div or BD. Electronic applications accepted. *Faculty research:* Faith formation, peer learning post graduation

Christ the King Seminary, Graduate and Professional Programs, East Aurora, NY 14052. Offers divinity (M Div); pastoral ministry (MA); pastoral studies (Certificate); theology (MA). *Accreditation:* ATS. Part-time and evening/weekend programs available. *Degree requirements:* For master's, comprehensive exam, thesis; for M Div, comprehensive exam. *Entrance requirements:* For M Div and master's, previous course work in philosophy and religious studies.

Church of God Theological Seminary, Graduate and Professional Programs, Cleveland, TN 37320-3330. Offers counseling (MA); discipleship and Christian formations (MA); ministry (D Min); theology (M Div). *Accreditation:* ACIPE; ATS. Part-time programs available. *Degree requirements:* For M Div, 2 foreign languages, thesis/dissertation, internship. *Faculty research:* Biblical exegesis.

Cincinnati Christian University, Graduate School, Program in Counseling, Cincinnati, OH 45204-3200. Offers MAC. *Degree requirements:* For master's, thesis or alternative, integration paper. *Entrance requirements:* For master's, GRE General Test, interview, minimum undergraduate GPA of 3.0. Additional exam requirements/recommendations for international students: Required—TOEFL. Electronic applications accepted. *Expenses:* Contact institution.

Claremont School of Theology, Graduate and Professional Programs, Program in Ministry, Claremont, CA 91711-3199. Offers D Min. *Accreditation:* ACIPE. *Degree requirements:* For doctorate, thesis/dissertation. *Entrance requirements:* For doctorate, GRE General Test. Additional exam requirements/recommendations for international students: Required—TOEFL (minimum score 230 computer-based). Electronic applications accepted.

Collège Dominicain de Philosophie et de Théologie, Graduate Programs, Program in Pastoral Theology, Ottawa, ON K1R 7G3, Canada. Offers M Prof Past, M Th Past. Part-time and evening/weekend programs available. *Degree requirements:* For master's, thesis. *Entrance requirements:* For master's, bachelor in theology. *Faculty research:* Pastoral theology.

College of Mount St. Joseph, Graduate Program in Religious Studies, Cincinnati, OH 45233-1670. Offers spiritual and pastoral care (MA). Part-time and evening/weekend programs available. *Faculty:* 4 full-time (2 women). *Students:* 24 part-time (18 women); includes 2 minority (both African Americans). Average age 49. 10 applicants, 100% accepted, 2 enrolled. In 2008, 8 master's awarded. *Degree requirements:* For master's, comprehensive exam, integrating project. *Entrance requirements:* For master's, 3 letters of recommendation, interview, essay, minimum GPA of 2.7. Additional exam requirements/recommendations for international students: Required—TOEFL (minimum score 560 paper-based; 220 computer-based).

Application deadline: Applications are processed on a rolling basis. Application fee: $50. Electronic applications accepted. *Expenses:* Contact institution. *Financial support:* In 2008–09, 18 students received support. Career-related internships or fieldwork and scholarships/grants available. Support available to part-time students. Financial award application deadline: 6/1; financial award applicants required to submit FAFSA. *Faculty research:* Contextual/cultural/systematic theology, historical/spiritual theology, business/economics ethics, social justice, Biblical/cultural/pastoral theology. *Unit head:* Dr. John Trokan, Chair, 513-244-4272, Fax: 513-244-4222, E-mail: john_trokan@mail.msj.edu. *Application contact:* Marilyn Hoskins, Assistant Director of Admissions for Graduate Recruitment, 513-244-4723, Fax: 513-244-4629, E-mail: marilyn_hoskins@mail.msj.edu.

Columbia International University, Columbia Biblical Seminary and School of Missions, Columbia, SC 29230-3122. Offers academic ministries (M Div); bible exposition (M Div, MABE); biblical studies (Certificate); counseling ministries (Certificate); divinity (M Div); educational ministries (M Div, MAEM, Certificate); intercultural studies (M Div, MAIS, Certificate); leadership (D Min); leadership for evangelism/mobilization (MALM); member care (D Min); ministry (Certificate); missions (D Min); pastoral counseling and spiritual formation (M Div, MAPS); preaching (D Min); theology (MA). *Accreditation:* ATS (one or more programs are accredited). Part-time and evening/weekend programs available. *Degree requirements:* For master's, integrative seminar; for doctorate, comprehensive exam, thesis/dissertation; for M Div, internship. *Entrance requirements:* For master's, minimum GPA of 2.7; for doctorate, 3 years of ministerial experience, M Div. Additional exam requirements/recommendations for international students: Required—TOEFL. Electronic applications accepted.

Concordia University, Nebraska, Graduate Programs in Education, Program in Family Life Ministry, Seward, NE 68434-1599. Offers MS. Part-time and evening/weekend programs available. *Degree requirements:* For master's, thesis or alternative. *Entrance requirements:* For master's, GRE, MAT, or NTE, minimum GPA of 3.0, BS in education or equivalent.

Concordia University, St. Paul, College of Vocation and Ministry, St. Paul, MN 55104-5494. Offers Christian education (Certificate); Christian outreach (MA). Evening/weekend programs available. Postbaccalaureate distance learning degree programs offered (minimal on-campus study). *Faculty:* 1 full-time (0 women), 4 part-time/adjunct (1 woman). *Students:* 15 full-time (5 women), 4 part-time (3 women). Average age 32. In 2008, 2 master's, 10 other advanced degrees awarded. *Application deadline:* Applications are processed on a rolling basis. Application fee: $50. Electronic applications accepted. *Financial support:* Applicants required to submit FAFSA. *Unit head:* Dr. David Lumpp, Dean, 651-641-8217, E-mail: lumpp@csp.edu. *Application contact:* Kimberly Craig, Director of Graduate and Cohort Admission, 651-603-6223, Fax: 651-603-6320, E-mail: craig@csp.edu.

The Criswell College, Graduate School of the Bible, Dallas, TX 75246-1537. Offers biblical studies (M Div); Christian leadership (MA); counseling (MA); Jewish studies (MA); ministry (MA); theological and biblical studies (MA). Part-time programs available. *Degree requirements:* For master's, 2 foreign languages, thesis optional; for M Div, 2 foreign languages, thesis/dissertation optional. *Entrance requirements:* For M Div and master's, GRE General Test, minimum GPA of 2.5. Electronic applications accepted. *Faculty research:* Emphasis on biblical languages (Hebrew and Greek), expository preaching and evangelism in the local church.

Dallas Baptist University, College of Adult Education, Professional Development Program, Dallas, TX 75211-9299. Offers accounting (MA); church leadership (MA); counseling (MA); criminal justice (MA); English as a second language (MA); finance (MA); higher education (MA); leadership studies (MA); management (MA); management information systems (MA); marketing (MA); missions (MA). Part-time and evening/weekend programs available. *Faculty:* 68 full-time (30 women), 113 part-time/adjunct (47 women). *Students:* 10 full-time, 83 part-time. 30 applicants, 47% accepted. In 2008, 39 master's awarded. *Entrance requirements:* For master's, minimum GPA of 3.0. Additional exam requirements/recommendations for international students: Required—TOEFL, IELTS. Application fee: $25. *Expenses:* Tuition: Part-time $558 per credit hour. *Financial support:* Federal Work-Study, institutionally sponsored loans, scholarships/grants, and tuition waivers (full and partial) available. Support available to part-time students. Financial award applicants required to submit FAFSA. *Unit head:* Dr. John Tarwater, Acting Director, 214-333-6830, Fax: 214-333-5558, E-mail: graduate@dbu.edu. *Application contact:* Kit P. Montgomery, Director of Graduate Programs, 214-333-5242, Fax: 214-333-5579, E-mail: graduate@dbu.edu.

Dallas Baptist University, Gary Cook School of Leadership, Program in Christian Education, Dallas, TX 75211-9299. Offers adult ministry (MA); business ministry (MA); childhood ministry (MA); collegiate ministry (MA); communication ministry (MA); counseling ministry (MA); education ministry (MA); general ministry (MA); missions ministry (MA); student ministry (MA); worship ministry (MA). Part-time and evening/weekend programs available. *Faculty:* 68 full-time (30 women), 113 part-time/adjunct (47 women). *Students:* 13 full-time, 55 part-time. 45 applicants. In 2008, 22 master's awarded. *Entrance requirements:* For master's, minimum GPA of 3.0. Additional exam requirements/recommendations for international students: Required—TOEFL. *Application deadline:* Applications are processed on a rolling basis. Application fee: $25. Electronic applications accepted. *Expenses:* Tuition: Part-time $558 per credit hour. *Financial support:* Federal Work-Study, institutionally sponsored loans, scholarships/grants, and tuition waivers (full and partial) available. Support available to part-time students. Financial award applicants required to submit FAFSA. *Unit head:* Dr. Judy Morris, Director, 214-333-5246, Fax: 214-333-5115, E-mail: graduate@dbu.edu. *Application contact:* Kit P. Montgomery, Director of Graduate Programs, 214-333-5242, Fax: 214-333-5579, E-mail: graduate@dbu.edu.

Dallas Baptist University, Gary Cook School of Leadership, Program in Christian Education: Childhood Ministry, Dallas, TX 75211-9299. Offers MA. Part-time and evening/weekend programs available. *Faculty:* 68 full-time (30 women), 113 part-time/adjunct (47 women). *Students:* 4 full-time, 26 part-time. In 2008, 3 master's awarded. *Entrance requirements:* For master's, minimum GPA of 3.0. Additional exam requirements/recommendations for international students: Required—TOEFL, IELTS. Application fee: $25. *Expenses:* Tuition: Part-time $558 per credit hour. *Financial support:* Federal Work-Study, institutionally sponsored loans, scholarships/grants, and tuition waivers (full and partial) available. Support available to part-time students. Financial award applicants required to submit FAFSA. *Unit head:* Tommy Sanders, Director, 214-333-6851, Fax: 214-333-6955, E-mail: graduate@dbu.edu. *Application contact:* Kit P. Montgomery, Director of Graduate Programs, 214-333-5242, Fax: 214-333-5579, E-mail: graduate@dbu.edu.

Dallas Baptist University, Gary Cook School of Leadership, Program in Christian Education: Student Ministry, Dallas, TX 75211-9299. Offers MA. Part-time and evening/weekend programs available. *Faculty:* 68 full-time (30 women), 113 part-time/adjunct (47 women). *Students:* 2 full-time, 10 part-time. 3 applicants. In 2008, 2 master's awarded. *Entrance requirements:* For master's, minimum GPA of 3.0. Additional exam requirements/recommendations for international students: Required—TOEFL, IELTS. Application fee: $25. *Expenses:* Tuition: Part-time $558 per credit hour. *Financial support:* Federal Work-Study, institutionally sponsored loans, scholarships/grants, and tuition waivers (full and partial) available. Support available to part-time students. Financial award applicants required to submit FAFSA. *Unit head:* Dr. Dwayne Ulmer, Director, 214-333-6851, Fax: 214-333-6955, E-mail: graduate@dbu.edu. *Application contact:* Kit P. Montgomery, Director of Graduate Programs, 214-333-5242, Fax: 214-333-5579, E-mail: graduate@dbu.edu.

Dallas Baptist University, Gary Cook School of Leadership, Program in Global Leadership, Dallas, TX 75211-9299. Offers business communication (MA); Christian education/missions (MA); ESL (MA); general studies (MA); global studies (MA); international business (MA); missions (MA); worship/missions (MA). Part-time and evening/weekend programs available. *Faculty:* 68 full-time (30 women), 113 part-time/adjunct (47 women). *Students:* 11 full-time, 26 part-time. 15 applicants, 40% accepted. *Entrance requirements:* For master's, minimum GPA of 3.0. Additional exam requirements/recommendations for international students: Required—TOEFL, IELTS. Application fee: $25. *Expenses:* Tuition: Part-time $558 per credit hour. *Financial* *support:* Federal Work-Study, institutionally sponsored loans, scholarships/grants, and tuition waivers (full and partial) available. Support available to part-time students. Financial award applicants required to submit FAFSA. *Unit head:* Dr. Bob Garrett, Director, 214-333-5292, Fax: 214-333-6955, E-mail: graduate@dbu.edu. *Application contact:* Kit P. Montgomery, Director of Graduate Programs, 214-333-5242, Fax: 214-333-5579, E-mail: graduate@dbu.edu.

Dallas Baptist University, Gary Cook School of Leadership, Program in Worship Leadership, Dallas, TX 75211-9299. Offers MA. Part-time and evening/weekend programs available. *Faculty:* 68 full-time (30 women), 113 part-time/adjunct (47 women). *Students:* 16 full-time, 22 part-time. In 2008, 7 master's awarded. *Entrance requirements:* For master's, minimum GPA of 3.0. Additional exam requirements/recommendations for international students: Required—TOEFL, IELTS. Application fee: $25. *Expenses:* Tuition: Part-time $558 per credit hour. *Financial support:* Federal Work-Study, institutionally sponsored loans, scholarships/grants, and tuition waivers (full and partial) available. Support available to part-time students. Financial award applicants required to submit FAFSA. *Unit head:* Dr. Jim Lemons, Director, 214-333-5454, Fax: 214-333-6955, E-mail: graduate@dbu.edu. *Application contact:* Kit P. Montgomery, Director of Graduate Programs, 214-333-5242, Fax: 214-333-5579, E-mail: graduate@dbu.edu.

Dallas Theological Seminary, Graduate Programs, Dallas, TX 75204-6499. Offers academic ministries (Th M); Bible translation (Th M); biblical and theological studies (CGS); biblical counseling (MA, Th M); biblical exegesis and linguistics (MA); biblical exposition (PhD); biblical studies (MA); Christian education (MA, D Min); cross-cultural ministries (MA, Th M); educational leadership (Th M); evangelism and discipleship (Th M); interdisciplinary studies (Th M); media and communication (MA); media arts in ministry (Th M); ministry (D Min); New Testament studies (Th M, PhD); Old Testament studies (PhD); parachurch ministries (Th M); pastoral ministries (Th M); sacred theology (STM); theological studies (PhD); women's ministry (Th M). *Accreditation:* ATS (one or more programs are accredited). Part-time and evening/weekend programs available. *Degree requirements:* For master's, variable foreign language requirement, thesis (for some programs); for doctorate, 2 foreign languages, thesis/dissertation. *Entrance requirements:* Additional exam requirements/recommendations for international students: Required—TOEFL, TWE. *Application deadline:* For fall admission, 7/1 priority date for domestic students, 1/15 for international students; for winter admission, 11/1 priority date for domestic students; for spring admission, 11/1 priority date for domestic students. Applications are processed on a rolling basis. Application fee: $30. Electronic applications accepted. *Financial support:* Career-related internships or fieldwork, institutionally sponsored loans, scholarships/grants, and tuition waivers (full and partial) available. Financial award application deadline: 2/28. *Unit head:* Dr. Mark L. Bailey, President, 214-841-3676, Fax: 214-841-3565. *Application contact:* Josh Bleeker, Director of Admissions, 214-841-3661, Fax: 214-841-3664, E-mail: admissions@dts.edu.

Denver Seminary, Graduate and Professional Programs, Littleton, CO 80120. Offers apologetics (Certificate); biblical studies (MA); Christian formation and soul care (MA, Certificate); Christian studies (MA, Certificate); church and parachurch leadership (D Min); counseling licensure (MA); counseling ministry (MA); intercultural ministry (Certificate); leadership (MA, Certificate); marriage and family counseling (D Min); pastoral ministry (D Min); philosophy of religion (MA); spiritual guidance (Certificate); theology (M Div, Certificate); worship (Certificate); youth and family ministry (MA). *Accreditation:* ACA; ACIPE; ATS (one or more programs are accredited). Part-time and evening/weekend programs available. Postbaccalaureate distance learning degree programs offered. *Degree requirements:* For master's, 2 foreign languages, thesis (for some programs); for doctorate, 2 foreign languages, thesis/dissertation; for M Div, 2 foreign languages. *Entrance requirements:* For M Div, minimum undergraduate GPA of 2.5; for master's, minimum undergraduate GPA of 3.0; for doctorate, M Div, 3 years of ministry experience. Additional exam requirements/recommendations for international students: Required—TOEFL (minimum score 575 paper-based; 233 computer-based; 90 iBT). Electronic applications accepted.

Eastern Mennonite University, Eastern Mennonite Seminary, Harrisonburg, VA 22802-2462. Offers church leadership (MA); divinity (M Div); ministry studies (Certificate); online theological studies (Certificate); religion (MA); theological studies (Certificate). *Accreditation:* ATS. Part-time programs available. *Faculty:* 8 full-time (2 women), 8 part-time/adjunct (2 women). *Students:* 48 full-time (21 women), 30 part-time (10 women); includes 6 minority (5 African Americans, 1 Hispanic American), 12 international. Average age 40. 40 applicants, 100% accepted, 37 enrolled. In 2008, 15 first professional degrees, 9 master's awarded. *Degree requirements:* For master's, thesis (for some programs); for M Div, thesis/dissertation (for some programs), supervised field education. *Entrance requirements:* For M Div and master's, minimum GPA of 2.5. Additional exam requirements/recommendations for international students: Required—TOEFL (minimum score 550 paper-based; 213 computer-based). *Application deadline:* For fall admission, 6/15 priority date for domestic and international students; for winter admission, 11/15 priority date for domestic and international students; for spring admission, 3/15 priority date for domestic and international students. Applications are processed on a rolling basis. Application fee: $25. *Expenses:* Contact institution. *Financial support:* Application deadline: 6/30; *Faculty research:* Spiritual direction and 'culture of call"; leadership coaching: an approach to leadership in a culture of call; clarity of call in the probationary process for United Methodist clergy in Virginia; EMS women's experiences of culture of call efforts; practices of excellent and fruitful Mennonite pastoral ministry. Total annual research expenditures: $45,000. *Unit head:* Dr. Ervin R. Stutzman, Seminary Dean, 540-432-4261, Fax: 540-432-4444, E-mail: stutzerv@emu.edu. *Application contact:* Don A. Yoder, Director of Seminary and Graduate Admissions, 540-432-4257, Fax: 540-432-4598, E-mail: yoderda@emu.edu.

Eastern Mennonite University, Program in Counseling, Harrisonburg, VA 22802-2462. Offers MA, M Div/MA. *Accreditation:* ACA (one or more programs are accredited); ACIPE. Part-time programs available. *Faculty:* 3 full-time (2 women), 3 part-time/adjunct (2 women). *Students:* 25 full-time (18 women), 9 part-time (8 women); includes 2 minority (1 African American, 1 Asian American or Pacific Islander), 3 international. Average age 38. 28 applicants, 75% accepted, 17 enrolled. In 2008, 20 master's awarded. *Degree requirements:* For master's, practicum, internship. *Entrance requirements:* For master's, minimum GPA of 3.0. Additional exam requirements/recommendations for international students: Required—TOEFL (minimum score 550 paper-based). *Application deadline:* For fall admission, 3/1 for domestic students. Application fee: $25. *Expenses:* Contact institution. *Financial support:* In 2008–09, 7 students received support. Scholarships/grants available. Financial award application deadline: 6/30; financial award applicants required to submit FAFSA. *Faculty research:* Career and gender, empathy and consciousness, pastoral counseling, education models. *Unit head:* Dr. P. David Glanzer, Professor of Counselor Education, 540-432-4244, Fax: 540-432-4444, E-mail: glanzerd@emu.edu. *Application contact:* Brenda C. Fairweather, Administrative Assistant, 540-432-4243, Fax: 540-432-4444, E-mail: fairweat@emu.edu.

Eastern University, Palmer Theological Seminary, Program in Ministry, St. Davids, PA 19087-3696. Offers marriage and family (D Min). *Accreditation:* ACIPE. Part-time programs available. *Degree requirements:* For doctorate, thesis/dissertation. *Entrance requirements:* For doctorate, 3 years of experience, involvement in ministry, church endorsement. *Expenses:* Contact institution.

Ecumenical Theological Seminary, Program in Ministry, Detroit, MI 48201. Offers D Min. *Accreditation:* ACIPE.

Emmanuel School of Religion, Graduate and Professional Programs, Johnson City, TN 37601-9438. Offers Christian care and counseling (M Div); Christian doctrine (M Div); Christian education (M Div); Christian ministries (M Div); church history (M Div, MAR); ministry (D Min); New Testament (M Div, MAR); Old Testament (M Div, MAR); urban ministry (M Div); world mission (M Div). *Accreditation:* ACIPE; ATS. Part-time programs available. *Faculty:* 12 full-time (2 women), 2 part-time/adjunct (0 women). *Students:* 86 full-time (26 women), 42 part-time (10 women); includes 5 minority (4 African Americans, 1 Hispanic American), 14 international. Average age 32. 47 applicants, 98% accepted, 34 enrolled. In 2008, 16 first professional degrees, 6 master's, 2 doctorates awarded. *Degree requirements:* For master's, 2 foreign languages, thesis; for M Div, 2 foreign languages, thesis/dissertation or alternative. *Entrance requirements:* For doctorate, GRE General Test, Minnesota Multiphasic Personality Inventory, M Div or equivalent. *Application deadline:* For fall admission, 8/1 priority date for domestic students. Applications are processed on a rolling basis. Application fee: $25. *Expenses:* Tuition: Full-time $7800; part-time $325 per credit. Required fees: $122.50 per semester. Tuition and fees vary according to degree level and program. *Financial support:* In 2008–09, 90 students received support, including 10 teaching assistantships with partial tuition reimbursements available; career-related internships or fieldwork, institutionally sponsored loans, scholarships/grants, and tuition waivers (partial) also available. Support available to part-time students. Financial award application deadline: 4/1; financial award applicants required to submit FAFSA. *Faculty research:* Theology of Old Testament prophets, spiritual formation for Christian leaders, history of African churches and religions, social world of early Christianity, lay pastoral counseling. Total annual research expenditures: $12,000. *Unit head:* Dr. Rollin A Ramsaran, Dean and Professor of New Testament, 423-461-1524, Fax: 423-926-6198, E-mail: RamsaranR@esr.edu. *Application contact:* Shelley Gasser, Administrative Assistant for Admissions, 423-461-1535, Fax: 423-926-6198, E-mail: GasserS@esr.edu.

Evangelical Theological Seminary, Graduate and Professional Programs, Myerstown, PA 17067-1212. Offers divinity (M Div); marriage and family therapy (MA); ministry (Certificate); religion (MA). *Accreditation:* ATS (one or more programs are accredited). Part-time programs available. Postbaccalaureate distance learning degree programs offered (minimal on-campus study). *Degree requirements:* For master's, 2 foreign languages; for M Div, 2 foreign languages, ministry internship. *Entrance requirements:* For M Div and master's, minimum GPA of 2.5. Additional exam requirements/recommendations for international students: Required—TOEFL (minimum score 550 paper-based; 213 computer-based). *Faculty research:* Literary form and structure within the Hebrew and Greek scriptures, Wesley studies, esoteric biblical languages, the Mosaic law and the Christian, ethics.

Faith Baptist Bible College and Theological Seminary, Graduate Program, Ankeny, IA 50021. Offers biblical studies (MA); pastoral studies (M Div); pastoral training (MA); religion (MA); theological studies (MA). Part-time programs available. *Faculty:* 4 full-time (0 women), 7 part-time/adjunct (0 women). *Students:* 28 full-time (3 women), 28 part-time (2 women); includes 1 minority (Hispanic American), 1 international. Average age 29. In 2008, 9 first professional degrees, 12 master's awarded. *Degree requirements:* For master's, thesis or alternative; for M Div, 2 foreign languages. *Entrance requirements:* Additional exam requirements/recommendations for international students: Required—TOEFL (minimum score 550 paper-based; 197 computer-based). *Application deadline:* For fall admission, 8/1 priority date for domestic students, 8/1 for international students; for spring admission, 12/15 for domestic and international students. Applications are processed on a rolling basis. Application fee: $25. *Expenses:* Tuition: Full-time $10,228; part-time $392 per credit hour. Required fees: $95 per semester. One-time fee: $50. Tuition and fees vary according to class time and course load. *Financial support:* Career-related internships or fieldwork and scholarships/grants available. Support available to part-time students. Financial award application deadline: 3/1; financial award applicants required to submit FAFSA. *Faculty research:* Baptist theology, American church history. *Unit head:* Dr. Ernest Schmidt, Dean of Seminary, 515-964-0601, Fax: 514-964-1638, E-mail: schmidte@faith.edu. *Application contact:* Patrick Odle, Vice President of Enrollment, 888-FAITH4U, Fax: 515-964-1638, E-mail: odlep@faith.edu.

Fordham University, Graduate School of Religion and Religious Education, New York, NY 10458. Offers pastoral counseling and spiritual care (MA); pastoral ministry/spirituality/pastoral counseling (D Min); religion and religious education (MA); religious education (MS, PhD, PD); spiritual direction (Certificate). Part-time programs available. Terminal master's awarded for partial completion of doctoral program. *Degree requirements:* For master's, research paper; for doctorate, comprehensive exam, thesis/dissertation. *Entrance requirements:* For doctorate, MAT. Electronic applications accepted. *Expenses:* Contact institution. *Faculty research:* Spirituality and spiritual direction, pastoral care and counseling, adult family and community, growth and young adult.

Freed-Hardeman University, School of Biblical Studies, Program in Ministry, Henderson, TN 38340-2399. Offers M Min. Part-time programs available. *Faculty:* 10 full-time (0 women), 2 part-time/adjunct (0 women). *Students:* 2 full-time (0 women), 19 part-time (0 women); includes 2 minority (1 African American, 1 Asian American or Pacific Islander). Average age 35. 2 applicants, 100% accepted, 2 enrolled. In 2008, 12 master's awarded. *Degree requirements:* For master's, comprehensive exam, internship. *Entrance requirements:* For master's, GRE General Test or MAT. Additional exam requirements/recommendations for international students: Required—TOEFL (minimum score 500 paper-based; 173 computer-based). *Application deadline:* For fall admission, 8/1 priority date for domestic students; for spring admission, 12/1 for domestic students. Applications are processed on a rolling basis. Application fee: $35. *Expenses:* Tuition: Full-time $4284; part-time $357 per credit hour. Required fees: $16 per credit hour. *Financial support:* Career-related internships or fieldwork, Federal Work-Study, tuition waivers (partial), and unspecified assistantships available. Support available to part-time students. Financial award application deadline: 8/1; financial award applicants required to submit FAFSA. *Unit head:* Dr. Mark Blackwelder, Director of Graduate Studies, 731-989-6769, Fax: 731-989-6400, E-mail: mblackwelder@fhu.edu. *Application contact:* Dr. Samuel T. Jones, Vice President for Academics, 731-989-6004, Fax: 731-989-6945, E-mail: sjones@fhu.edu.

Fuller Theological Seminary, Graduate School of Theology, Pasadena, CA 91182. Offers Christian leadership (MACL); evangelism (MA); family life education (MA); ministry (M Div, D Min); pastoral ministry (MA); recovery ministry (MA); theology (MAT, Th M, PhD); worship music ministry (MA); worship, theology, and the arts (MA); youth, family, and culture (MA). M Div offered jointly with Denver Conservative Baptist Seminary. *Accreditation:* ACIPE; ATS (one or more programs are accredited). Part-time and evening/weekend programs available. *Degree requirements:* For doctorate, variable foreign language requirement, thesis/dissertation; for M Div, 2 foreign languages. *Entrance requirements:* For doctorate, GRE General Test. *Faculty research:* New Testament, Old Testament, systematic theology, history, practical theology.

Gannon University, School of Graduate Studies, College of Humanities, Education, and Social Sciences, School of Humanities, Program in Pastoral Studies, Erie, PA 16541-0001. Offers MA, Certificate. Part-time and evening/weekend programs available. *Students:* 2 full-time (both women), 9 part-time (6 women); includes 1 minority (Hispanic American). Average age 42. 5 applicants, 40% accepted, 2 enrolled. In 2008, 1 master's awarded. *Degree requirements:* For master's, comprehensive exam, thesis or alternative, research project; internship and written evaluation. *Entrance requirements:* For master's, interview; minimum 10 credits of course work in philosophy, religious studies, or theology. Additional exam requirements/recommendations for international students: Required—TOEFL (minimum score 500 paper-based; 173 computer-based). *Application deadline:* Applications are processed on a rolling basis. Application fee: $25. Electronic applications accepted. *Expenses:* Tuition: Full-time $13,050; part-time $725 per credit. Required fees: $502; $16 per credit. Tuition and fees vary according to course load, degree level, campus/location and program. *Financial support:* Career-related internships or fieldwork, scholarships/grants, and unspecified assistantships available. Financial award application deadline: 7/1; financial award applicants required to submit FAFSA. *Unit head:* Dr. Mary Anne Rivera, Director, 814-871-5646, E-mail: rivera006@gannon.edu. *Application contact:* Kara Morgan, Assistant Director of Graduate Admissions, 814-871-5831, Fax: 814-871-5827, E-mail: graduate@gannon.edu.

Gardner-Webb University, M. Christopher White School of Divinity, Boiling Springs, NC 28017. Offers Christian education (M Div); ministry (D Min); missiology (M Div); pastoral care and counseling (M Div); pastoral ministry (M Div); M Div/MA. *Accreditation:* ACIPE; ATS. Part-time programs available. *Degree requirements:* For M Div, 2 foreign languages. *Entrance requirements:* For M Div, minimum GPA of 2.0; for doctorate, minimum GPA of 2.75. *Expenses:* Contact institution. *Faculty research:* Jewish Christian dialogue, Islam.

Garrett-Evangelical Theological Seminary, Graduate and Professional Programs, Evanston, IL 60201-3298. Offers Bible and culture (PhD); Christian education (MA); Christian education and congregational studies (PhD); contemporary theology and culture (PhD); divinity (M Div);

Pastoral Ministry and Counseling

Garrett-Evangelical Theological Seminary (continued)
ethics, church, and society (MA); liturgical studies (PhD); ministry (D Min); music ministry (MA); pastoral care and counseling (MA); pastoral theology, personality, and culture (PhD); spiritual formation and evangelism (MA); theological studies (MTS); M Div/MSW. *Accreditation:* ACIPE; ATS (one or more programs are accredited). Part-time programs available. *Degree requirements:* For master's, thesis (for some programs); for doctorate, thesis/dissertation. *Entrance requirements:* For doctorate, GRE (PhD). Additional exam requirements/ recommendations for international students: Required—TOEFL (minimum score 560 paper-based; 230 computer-based). Electronic applications accepted.

General Theological Seminary, Graduate and Professional Programs, New York, NY 10011-4977. Offers Anglican studies (STM, Th D, Certificate); ascetical theology (Certificate); biblical studies (Certificate); congregational development (Certificate); divinity (M Div); historical and theological studies (Certificate); spiritual direction (MASD, STM, Certificate); theology (MA). *Accreditation:* ACIPE; ATS. Part-time and evening/weekend programs available. Terminal master's awarded for partial completion of doctoral program. *Degree requirements:* For master's, thesis; for doctorate, 2 foreign languages, thesis/dissertation. *Entrance requirements:* For M Div, GRE General Test, bishop's endorsement; for master's, GRE General Test; for doctorate, GRE, M Div or MA. Additional exam requirements/recommendations for international students: Required—TOEFL. *Faculty research:* Liturgy, New Testament, ethics, history, ecumenical relations.

George Fox University, George Fox Evangelical Seminary, Newberg, OR 97132-2697. Offers divinity (M Div); ministry (D Min), including global missional leadership, leadership and spiritual formation, leadership in the emerging culture; ministry leadership (MA); spiritual formation (MA); spiritual formation and discipleship (Certificate); theological studies (MA). *Accreditation:* ACIPE; ATS. Part-time and evening/weekend programs available. Postbaccalaureate distance learning degree programs offered (minimal on-campus study). *Faculty:* 7 full-time (2 women), 17 part-time/adjunct (7 women). *Students:* 51 full-time (6 women), 289 part-time (94 women); includes 27 minority (6 African Americans, 2 American Indian/Alaska Native, 15 Asian Americans or Pacific Islanders, 4 Hispanic Americans), 6 international. Average age 41. 134 applicants, 94% accepted, 97 enrolled. In 2008, 9 first professional degrees, 18 master's, 20 doctorates, 5 other advanced degrees awarded. *Degree requirements:* For master's, variable foreign language requirement, thesis optional, internship; for doctorate, thesis/dissertation. *Entrance requirements:* Additional exam requirements/recommendations for international students: Required—TOEFL (minimum score 550 paper-based; 213 computer-based; 80 iBT). *Application deadline:* For fall admission, 7/1 for domestic and international students; for spring admission, 11/1 for domestic and international students. Applications are processed on a rolling basis. Application fee: $40. Electronic applications accepted. *Expenses:* Contact institution. *Financial support:* In 2008–09, 33 students received support. Career-related internships or fieldwork and scholarships/grants available. Financial award application deadline: 5/1; financial award applicants required to submit FAFSA. *Unit head:* Dr. Chuck Conniry, Vice President and Dean, George Fox Evangelical Seminary, 503-554-6152, E-mail: cconniry@georgefox.edu. *Application contact:* Sheila Bartlett, Admissions Counselor, 800-631-0921, Fax: 503-554-6122, E-mail: sbartlett@georgefox.edu.

Georgian Court University, School of Arts and Humanities, Lakewood, NJ 08701-2697. Offers Catholic school leadership (Certificate); parish business management (Certificate); pastoral administration (Certificate); pastoral ministry (Certificate); religious education (Certificate); theology (MA, Certificate). Part-time and evening/weekend programs available. *Faculty:* 3 full-time (1 woman). *Students:* 23 part-time (18 women); includes 3 minority (1 African American, 1 Asian American or Pacific Islander, 1 Hispanic American). Average age 54. 7 applicants, 100% accepted, 5 enrolled. In 2008, 6 master's awarded. *Degree requirements:* For master's, thesis (for some programs). *Entrance requirements:* For master's, 3 letters of recommendation. Additional exam requirements/recommendations for international students: Required—TOEFL (minimum score 550 paper-based; 213 computer-based). *Application deadline:* For fall admission, 8/1 priority date for domestic students, 4/1 for international students; for spring admission, 1/1 priority date for domestic students, 7/1 for international students. Applications are processed on a rolling basis. Application fee: $40. Electronic applications accepted. *Expenses:* Tuition: Full-time $12,276; part-time $682 per credit. Required fees: $400 per year. Tuition and fees vary according to campus/location. *Financial support:* Scholarships/grants, health care benefits, and unspecified assistantships available. Financial award application deadline: 4/15; financial award applicants required to submit FAFSA. *Unit head:* Dr. Linda James, Dean, 732-987-2617, Fax: 732-987-2007. *Application contact:* Eugene Soltys, Director of Graduate Admissions, 732-987-2770, Fax: 732-987-2084, E-mail: graduateadmissions@georgian.edu.

Golden Gate Baptist Theological Seminary, Graduate and Professional Programs, Mill Valley, CA 94941-3197. Offers divinity (M Div); early childhood education (Certificate); education leadership (MAEL, Diploma); ministry (D Min); theological studies (MTS); theology (Th M); youth ministry (Certificate). *Accreditation:* ACIPE; ATS (one or more programs are accredited). Part-time and evening/weekend programs available. *Degree requirements:* For master's, thesis (for some programs); for doctorate, 2 foreign languages, thesis/dissertation; for M Div, 2 foreign languages. *Entrance requirements:* For doctorate, MAT. Additional exam requirements/ recommendations for international students: Required—TOEFL (minimum score 550 paper-based; 213 computer-based). Electronic applications accepted.

Gonzaga University, College of Arts and Sciences, Department of Religious Studies, Spokane, WA 99258. Offers pastoral ministry (MA); religious studies (MA); spirituality (MA). *Degree requirements:* For master's, comprehensive exam. *Entrance requirements:* For master's, GRE General Test or MAT, minimum GPA of 3.0. Additional exam requirements/recommendations for international students: Required—TOEFL.

Gordon-Conwell Theological Seminary, Graduate and Professional Programs, South Hamilton, MA 01982. Offers Biblical languages (MABL); church history (MACH); counseling (MACO); ministry (D Min); missions/evangelism (MAME); New Testament (MANT); Old Testament (MAOT); religion (MAR); theology (M Div, MATH, Th M, Th D). *Accreditation:* ACIPE; ATS (one or more programs are accredited). Part-time and evening/weekend programs available. *Degree requirements:* For master's, one foreign language, thesis optional; for doctorate, 2 foreign languages, thesis/dissertation; for M Div, 2 foreign languages. *Entrance requirements:* For M Div and master's, minimum GPA of 2.5; for doctorate, minimum GPA of 3.0.

Graceland University, Community of Christ Seminary, Independence, MO 64050. Offers Christian ministry (MACM); religion (MAR). Part-time programs available. Postbaccalaureate distance learning degree programs offered (minimal on-campus study). *Faculty:* 2 full-time (1 woman), 14 part-time/adjunct (6 women). *Students:* 13 full-time (5 women), 6 part-time (3 women); includes 1 minority (American Indian/Alaska Native), 1 international. Average age 43. 9 applicants, 78% accepted, 7 enrolled. In 2008, 10 master's awarded. *Degree requirements:* For master's, thesis optional, portfolio or thesis (for MAR); practicum (for MACM). *Entrance requirements:* For master's, minimum cumulative GPA of 3.0. *Application deadline:* For fall admission, 8/15 priority date for domestic students; for winter admission, 10/15 priority date for domestic students; for spring admission, 4/15 priority date for domestic students. Applications are processed on a rolling basis. Application fee: $50. *Expenses:* Contact institution. *Financial support:* Scholarships/grants available. Financial award application deadline: 12/15; financial award applicants required to submit FAFSA. *Faculty research:* Theology. *Unit head:* Dr. Don H. Compier, Dean, 800-833-0524 Ext. 4900, Fax: 816-833-2990, E-mail: dcompier@graceland.edu. *Application contact:* Judy K. Luffman, Executive Assistant, 816-833-0524 Ext. 4508, Fax: 816-833-2990, E-mail: luffman@graceland.edu.

Grace Theological Seminary, Graduate and Professional Programs, Winona Lake, IN 46590-9907. Offers biblical studies (Certificate); camp administration (MA); counseling (M Div); exegetical studies (MA); intercultural studies (M Div, MA); local church studies (MA); pastoral studies (M Div); theological studies (MA); theology (D Min, Diploma). *Accreditation:* ATS. Part-time programs available. Postbaccalaureate distance learning degree programs offered (no on-campus study). *Degree requirements:* For master's, thesis optional; for doctorate, 2 foreign languages, thesis/dissertation; for M Div, 2 foreign languages, thesis/dissertation optional. *Entrance requirements:* For M Div and master's, MAT, minimum GPA of 2.5. Electronic applications accepted. *Faculty research:* Biblical theology, language, and church ministries.

Grace University, College of Graduate Studies, Counseling Program, Omaha, NE 68108. Offers MA. *Entrance requirements:* For master's, minimum undergraduate GPA of 3.0.

Grand Rapids Theological Seminary of Cornerstone University, Graduate Programs, Grand Rapids, MI 49525-5897. Offers biblical counseling (MA); Biblical counseling (M Div); chaplaincy (M Div); Christian education (M Div, MA); intercultural studies (M Div, MA); New Testament (MA, Th M); Old Testament (MA, Th M); pastoral studies (M Div); systematic theology (MA); theology (Th M). *Accreditation:* ATS. Part-time programs available. Postbaccalaureate distance learning degree programs offered (minimal on-campus study). *Entrance requirements:* Additional exam requirements/recommendations for international students: Required—TOEFL (minimum score 577 paper-based; 233 computer-based; 90 iBT). Electronic applications accepted.

Greenville College, Program in Leadership and Ministry, Greenville, IL 62246-0159. Offers MA. Part-time programs available. *Degree requirements:* For master's, 6 hours of research/ practicum in applied ministry, minimum GPA of 3.0. *Entrance requirements:* For master's, 1 year of work experience in Christian ministry, interview. Additional exam requirements/ recommendations for international students: Required—TOEFL (minimum score 525 paper-based; 197 computer-based). Electronic applications accepted.

Hampton University, Graduate College, Department of Education, Program in Counseling, Hampton, VA 23668. Offers college student development (MA); community agency counseling (MA); pastoral counseling (MA); school counseling (MA). *Accreditation:* NCATE. Part-time and evening/weekend programs available. *Entrance requirements:* For master's, GRE General Test.

Harding University, College of Bible and Religion, Master of Ministry Program, Searcy, AR 72149-0001. Offers M Min. Part-time and evening/weekend programs available. Postbaccalaureate distance learning degree programs offered. *Faculty:* 6 part-time/adjunct (0 women). *Students:* 6 full-time (1 woman), 39 part-time (3 women); includes 4 minority (2 African Americans, 1 American Indian/Alaska Native, 1 Hispanic American), 1 international. Average age 36. 13 applicants, 100% accepted, 13 enrolled. In 2008, 6 master's awarded. *Degree requirements:* For master's, 3 practica (1 hour each), portfolio, capstone project. *Entrance requirements:* For master's, 16 hours course work in Bible, minimum GPA of 2.75. *Application deadline:* For fall admission, 8/1 priority date for domestic and international students; for spring admission, 12/1 priority date for domestic students, 12/15 priority date for international students. Applications are processed on a rolling basis. Application fee: $25. Electronic applications accepted. *Expenses:* Tuition: Full-time $9360; part-time $520 per credit hour. Required fees: $21 per credit hour. Tuition and fees vary according to course load and program. *Financial support:* In 2008–09, 43 students received support. Career-related internships or fieldwork, Federal Work-Study, scholarships/grants, and unspecified assistantships available. *Unit head:* Dr. Bill Richardson, Director/Associate Professor, 501-279-4252, Fax: 501-279-4081, E-mail: mmin@harding.edu. *Application contact:* Debbie Stewart, Information Contact, 501-279-4252, E-mail: dstewart@harding.edu.

Harding University Graduate School of Religion, Graduate Programs, Memphis, TN 38117-5499. Offers Christian ministry (MA); counseling (MA); ministry (M Div, D Min); religion (MA). *Accreditation:* ATS. Part-time programs available. Postbaccalaureate distance learning degree programs offered (minimal on-campus study). *Degree requirements:* For master's, variable foreign language requirement, thesis (for some programs); for doctorate, one foreign language, thesis/dissertation; for M Div, 2 foreign languages, thesis/dissertation optional. *Entrance requirements:* For M Div, GRE General Test (for graduates of non-accredited schools), minimum GPA of 2.5; for master's, minimum GPA of 2.7; for doctorate, minimum GPA of 3.0. Additional exam requirements/recommendations for international students: Required—TOEFL (minimum score 550 paper-based; 213 computer-based; 79 iBT). Electronic applications accepted.

Hardin-Simmons University, Graduate School, Logsdon School of Theology, Logsdon Seminary, Seminary Program in Family Ministry, Abilene, TX 79698-0001. Offers MA. Part-time programs available. *Faculty:* 3 full-time (1 woman). *Students:* 13 full-time (7 women), 12 part-time (5 women); includes 2 minority (1 American Indian/Alaska Native, 1 Hispanic American). Average age 29. 7 applicants, 100% accepted, 7 enrolled. In 2008, 5 master's awarded. *Degree requirements:* For master's, comprehensive exam, clinical experience, project. *Entrance requirements:* For master's, minimum undergraduate GPA of 3.0 in major, 2.7 overall; 6 hours of course work in psychology; interview; writing sample; 6 hours of course work in Old and New Testament; references. Additional exam requirements/recommendations for international students: Required—TOEFL (minimum score 555 paper-based; 213 computer-based; 75 iBT). *Application deadline:* For fall admission, 8/15 priority date for domestic students, 4/1 for international students; for spring admission, 1/5 priority date for domestic students, 9/1 for international students. Applications are processed on a rolling basis. Application fee: $50. *Expenses:* Tuition: Full-time $10,620; part-time $590 per credit hour. Required fees: $590; $110 per semester. Tuition and fees vary according to course load and degree level. *Financial support:* In 2008–09, 20 students received support, including 1 fellowship (averaging $1,800 per year); career-related internships or fieldwork and scholarships/grants also available. Support available to part-time students. Financial award application deadline: 6/30; financial award applicants required to submit FAFSA. *Unit head:* Dr. Randall Maurer, Director, 325-670-1599, Fax: 325-670-1406, E-mail: rmaurer@hsutx.edu. *Application contact:* Dr. Gary Stanlake, Dean of Graduate Studies, 325-670-1298, Fax: 325-670-1564, E-mail: gradoff@hsutx.edu.

Hartford Seminary, Graduate Programs, Hartford, CT 06105-2279. Offers black ministry (Certificate); Islamic studies (MA); ministerios Hispanos (Certificate); ministry (D Min); religious studies (MA); women's leadership institute (Certificate). *Accreditation:* ATS (one or more programs are accredited). Part-time and evening/weekend programs available. Postbaccalaureate distance learning degree programs offered (no on-campus study). *Degree requirements:* For master's, thesis optional, oral exam; for doctorate, thesis/dissertation, oral exam. *Entrance requirements:* For doctorate, experience in ministry, M Div. Additional exam requirements/recommendations for international students: Required—TOEFL (minimum score 550 paper-based; 213 computer-based; 80 iBT). *Faculty research:* Liturgy and social justice, professional leadership in ministry, congregational studies, Christian-Muslim relations, American religion.

Heritage Baptist College and Heritage Theological Seminary, Program in Theological Studies, Cambridge, ON N3C 3T2, Canada. Offers chaplaincy (M Div); counselling (M Div); general (M Div); ministry (D Min); pastoral (M Div); research (M Div); theological studies (MA, Certificate). *Accreditation:* ATS.

Heritage Christian University, Graduate Programs, Florence, AL 35630. Offers counseling (MM); Greek (MA); ministry (MM); New Testament (MA). *Degree requirements:* For master's, practicum (MM), major research paper (MA). *Entrance requirements:* For master's, MAT or GRE, bachelor's degree in Bible from an accredited college or university, minimum GPA of 2.75, 3 letters of recommendation.

Hillsdale Free Will Baptist College, Department of Bible Studies, Moore, OK 73160-1208. Offers ministry (MA). Part-time and evening/weekend programs available. *Degree requirements:* For master's, thesis optional. *Entrance requirements:* Additional exam requirements/ recommendations for international students: Recommended—TOEFL (minimum score 500 paper-based).

Holmes Institute, Graduate Program, Burbank, CA 91505. Offers consciousness studies (MS). *Faculty:* 50 part-time/adjunct (35 women). *Students:* Average age 40. 16 applicants,

100% accepted, 16 enrolled. *Degree requirements:* For master's, comprehensive exam, 1 colloquium, 2 spiritual retreats per year, internship, 2 spiritual conferences. *Entrance requirements:* For master's, 3 letters of recommendation, interview. *Application deadline:* Applications are processed on a rolling basis. Application fee: $100. *Expenses:* Tuition: Part-time $5966 per year.

Holy Names University, Graduate Division, Department of Counseling Psychology, Oakland, CA 94619-1699. Offers counseling psychology (MA); forensic psychology (MA, Certificate); pastoral counseling (MA, Certificate). Part-time and evening/weekend programs available. *Faculty:* 1 (woman) full-time, 9 part-time/adjunct (5 women). *Students:* 38 full-time (33 women), 13 part-time (12 women); includes 33 minority (25 African Americans, 2 Asian Americans or Pacific Islanders, 6 Hispanic Americans), 1 international. Average age 35. 22 applicants, 68% accepted, 11 enrolled. In 2008, 13 master's awarded. *Degree requirements:* For master's, comprehensive paper, seminars. *Entrance requirements:* For master's, minimum undergraduate GPA of 2.6 overall, 3.0 in major. Additional exam requirements/recommendations for international students: Required—TOEFL (minimum score 550 paper-based; 213 computer-based; 80 iBT). *Application deadline:* For fall admission, 8/1 priority date for domestic students, 8/1 for international students; for spring admission, 12/1 priority date for domestic students, 12/1 for international students. Applications are processed on a rolling basis. Application fee: $65. *Expenses:* Tuition: Full-time $6255; part-time $695 per unit. Required fees: $340. Tuition and fees vary according to course load, program, reciprocity agreements and student's religious affiliation. *Financial support:* In 2008–09, 38 students received support. Available to part-time students. Application deadline: 3/2; *Faculty research:* Cognitive psychology, anger management, grief and grief counseling, post-modernism and psychotherapy, spirituality and psychology. *Unit head:* Dr. Helen Shoemaker, Program Director, 510-436-1543, E-mail: shoemaker@hnu.edu. *Application contact:* 800-430-1321, Fax: 510-436-1325, E-mail: AdultEd@hnu.edu.

Holy Names University, Graduate Division, Program in Pastoral Ministries, Oakland, CA 94619-1699. Offers MA, Certificate. Part-time programs available. Postbaccalaureate distance learning degree programs offered (no on-campus study). *Faculty:* 3 part-time/adjunct (2 women). *Students:* 1 (woman) full-time, 38 part-time (27 women); includes 14 minority (1 African American, 2 Asian Americans or Pacific Islanders, 11 Hispanic Americans). Average age 50. 19 applicants, 84% accepted, 10 enrolled. In 2008, 7 master's, 8 other advanced degrees awarded. *Degree requirements:* For master's, ministry project. *Entrance requirements:* Additional exam requirements/recommendations for international students: Required—TOEFL (minimum score 550 paper-based; 213 computer-based; 80 iBT). *Application deadline:* For fall admission, 8/1 priority date for domestic and international students; for spring admission, 12/1 priority date for domestic and international students. Application fee: $65. *Expenses:* Tuition: Full-time $6255; part-time $695 per unit. Required fees: $340. Tuition and fees vary according to course load, program, reciprocity agreements and student's religious affiliation. *Financial support:* In 2008–09, 3 students received support. Applicants required to submit FAFSA. *Faculty research:* Ethics, cross-cultural management, faith development through liturgy, multi-cultural community building. *Unit head:* Dr. Robert Lassalle-Klein, Director, 510-436-1074. *Application contact:* Graduate Admissions Office, 800-430-1321, Fax: 510-436-1325, E-mail: AdultEd@hnu.edu.

Houston Baptist University, College of Education and Behavioral Sciences, Program in Christian Counseling, Houston, TX 77074-3298. Offers MACC. *Degree requirements:* For master's, comprehensive exam. *Entrance requirements:* For master's, GRE General Test, minimum GPA of 3.0. Additional exam requirements/recommendations for international students: Required—TOEFL (minimum score 550 paper-based; 213 computer-based).

Houston Graduate School of Theology, Graduate School, Houston, TX 77092. Offers counseling (MA); pastoral ministry (M Div, D Min); theology (MA). *Accreditation:* ATS (one or more programs are accredited). Part-time and evening/weekend programs available. *Degree requirements:* For master's, thesis (for some programs); for doctorate, thesis/dissertation; for M Div, thesis/dissertation optional. *Entrance requirements:* For doctorate, GRE General Test or MAT, M Div or equivalent. Additional exam requirements/recommendations for international students: Required—TOEFL (minimum score 550 paper-based; 213 computer-based). *Faculty research:* Hermeneutics, spirituality, religion of Eastern Europe.

Huntington University, Graduate School, Huntington, IN 46750-1299. Offers counseling (MA), including licensed mental health counselor; education (M Ed); ministry leadership (MA), including pastoral or discipling ministry; youth ministry leadership (MA). Part-time programs available. Postbaccalaureate distance learning degree programs offered (minimal on-campus study). *Faculty:* 4 full-time (0 women), 16 part-time/adjunct (4 women). *Students:* 9 full-time (5 women), 67 part-time (14 women); includes 2 minority (both African Americans), 2 international. Average age 39. 27 applicants, 89% accepted, 24 enrolled. In 2008, 4 master's awarded. *Degree requirements:* For master's, thesis. *Entrance requirements:* For master's, GRE (for counseling and education students only). Additional exam requirements/recommendations for international students: Required—TOEFL. *Application deadline:* For fall admission, 7/1 priority date for domestic and international students; for winter admission, 11/1 priority date for domestic and international students; for spring admission, 2/1 priority date for domestic and international students. Applications are processed on a rolling basis. Application fee: $20. Electronic applications accepted. *Expenses:* Tuition: Part-time $425 per credit hour. Tuition and fees vary according to program. *Financial support:* In 2008–09, 51 students received support. Scholarships/grants available. Support available to part-time students. Financial award application deadline: 8/1; financial award applicants required to submit FAFSA. *Faculty research:* Outreach, family ministry outreach, leadership, evangelism, youth ministry. *Unit head:* Dr. Steven Holtrop, Associate Dean for Graduate and Adult Studies, 260-359-4166, Fax: 260-359-4126, E-mail: sholtrop@huntington.edu. *Application contact:* Lori Garde, Program Coordinator, 260-359-4039, Fax: 260-359-4126, E-mail: lgarde@huntington.edu.

Iliff School of Theology, Graduate and Professional Programs, Denver, CO 80210-4798. Offers biblical studies (MA); church history (MA); religion (MA); religion and social change (MA); specialized ministry (MASM), including justice and peace, pastoral theology and care, religious leadership; theology (M Div, MTS, D Min, PhD), including Biblical studies (PhD), religion and psychological studies (PhD), religion and social change (PhD), theology, philosophy and culture (PhD); theology/ethics (MA). *Accreditation:* ACIPE; ATS. Part-time and evening/weekend programs available. *Degree requirements:* For master's, one foreign language, thesis (for some programs); for doctorate, 2 foreign languages, comprehensive exam, thesis/dissertation; for M Div, thesis/dissertation optional. *Entrance requirements:* For M Div, minimum GPA of 2.75, references; for master's, minimum GPA of 3.0, writing sample, references; for doctorate, GRE General Test, minimum GPA of 3.0, writing sample, letters of recommendation. Additional exam requirements/recommendations for international students: Required—TOEFL (minimum score 550 paper-based). Electronic applications accepted. *Faculty research:* Pastoral care, history, church music, contemporary church, biblical studies.

Indiana Wesleyan University, College of Graduate Studies, Wesleyan Seminary, Program in Ministry, Marion, IN 46953-4974. Offers ministerial leadership (MA); youth ministries (MA). Part-time programs available. Postbaccalaureate distance learning degree programs offered (minimal on-campus study). *Faculty:* 5 full-time (0 women), 8 part-time/adjunct (1 woman). *Students:* 130 full-time (30 women), 15 part-time (3 women); includes 24 minority (22 African Americans, 2 Hispanic Americans). In 2008, 39 master's awarded. *Degree requirements:* For master's, one foreign language, capstone practicum and/or project. *Entrance requirements:* Additional exam requirements/recommendations for international students: Required—TOEFL. *Application deadline:* Applications are processed on a rolling basis. Application fee: $25. Electronic applications accepted. *Expenses:* Contact institution. *Financial support:* In 2008–09, 1 research assistantship with full tuition reimbursement was awarded; career-related internships or fieldwork also available. Support available to part-time students. Financial award applicants required to submit FAFSA. *Faculty research:* History of worship innovation, history of New Testament afterlife traditions, second century mantanism, cross-cultural ministry, church health and growth, leadership in Christian organizations, managing change in the church, effective youth ministry, women in ministry, biblical hermeneutics. *Unit head:* Dr. Russ Gunsalus, Director of Graduate Studies in Ministry, 765-677-2259, Fax: 765-677-1456, E-mail: russ.gunsalus@indwes.edu. *Application contact:* Tom Leas, Director of Adult Enrollment Services, 800-895-0036, Fax: 765-677-2404, E-mail: graduate@indwes.edu.

Inter American University of Puerto Rico, Metropolitan Campus, Graduate Programs, Program in Pastoral Theology, San Juan, PR 00919-1293. Offers PhD.

International Baptist College, Program in Ministry, Tempe, AZ 85282. Offers M Min, D Min.

Iona College, School of Arts and Science, Department of Family and Pastoral Counseling, New Rochelle, NY 10801-1890. Offers family counseling (MS, Certificate); pastoral counseling (MS). Part-time and evening/weekend programs available. *Faculty:* 4 full-time (0 women), 2 part-time/adjunct (both women). *Students:* 30 full-time (23 women), 9 part-time (7 women); includes 10 minority (6 African Americans, 4 Hispanic Americans), 1 international. Average age 35. 38 applicants, 61% accepted, 10 enrolled. In 2008, 5 master's awarded. *Degree requirements:* For master's, thesis, project. *Entrance requirements:* For master's, draw-a-person test, sentence completion test, interview, minimum GPA of 3.0. *Application deadline:* Applications are processed on a rolling basis. Application fee: $50. Electronic applications accepted. *Expenses:* Contact institution. *Financial support:* Career-related internships or fieldwork, tuition waivers (partial), and unspecified assistantships available. Support available to part-time students. Financial award application deadline: 4/15; financial award applicants required to submit FAFSA. *Faculty research:* Marriage counseling. *Unit head:* Dr. Robert Burns, Chair, 914-633-2418, E-mail: rburns@iona.edu. *Application contact:* Veronica Jarek-Prinz, Director of Graduate Admissions, 914-633-2420, Fax: 914-633-2277, E-mail: vjarekprinz@iona.edu.

Jewish University of America, Graduate School, Abrams Institute of Pastoral Counseling, Skokie, IL 60077-3248. Offers counseling (MA); pastoral counseling (MPC, DPC). *Degree requirements:* For master's, thesis optional; for doctorate, one foreign language, thesis/dissertation. *Entrance requirements:* For master's and doctorate, interview.

John Brown University, Graduate Studies Division of Christian Ministry, Siloam Springs, AR 72761-2121. Offers leadership and ethics (MA); ministry leadership (MA); pastoral counseling (MA); youth ministry (MA). Part-time and evening/weekend programs available. *Faculty:* 4 part-time/adjunct (1 woman). *Students:* 27 full-time (19 women), 26 part-time (12 women); includes 10 minority (9 African Americans, 1 Hispanic American). Average age 37. In 2008, 2 master's awarded. *Entrance requirements:* For master's, GRE General Test, MAT, minimum GPA of 3.0. Additional exam requirements/recommendations for international students: Required—TOEFL (minimum score 550 paper-based; 173 computer-based). *Application deadline:* For fall admission, 8/11 priority date for domestic students; for spring admission, 1/12 priority date for domestic students. Applications are processed on a rolling basis. Application fee: $35 ($100 for international students). Electronic applications accepted. *Expenses:* Tuition: Full-time $7740; part-time $430 per credit hour. *Financial support:* Application deadline: 3/1. *Unit head:* Dr. Dan Lambert, Director, 479-524-7264, Fax: 479-238-8574, E-mail: dlambert@jbu.edu. *Application contact:* Dr. Dan Lambert, Director, 479-524-7264, Fax: 479-238-8574, E-mail: dlambert@jbu.edu.

The Johns Hopkins University, School of Education, Department of Counseling and Human Services, Baltimore, MD 21218-2699. Offers addictions counseling (Certificate); clinical community counseling (Certificate); clinical supervision (Certificate); contemporary trauma (Certificate); counseling (MS, CAGS); counseling at-risk youth (Certificate); organizational counseling (Certificate); play therapy (Certificate); spiritual and existential counseling and therapy (Certificate). Part-time and evening/weekend programs available. *Entrance requirements:* For master's, minimum GPA of 3.0, interview, resumé, letters of recommendation; for other advanced degree, master's or doctoral degree, interview, resumé, minimum GPA of 3.0, letters of recommendation. Additional exam requirements/recommendations for international students: Required—TOEFL (minimum score 600 paper-based; 250 computer-based; 100 iBT).

Knox Theological Seminary, Graduate Programs, Program in Ministry, Fort Lauderdale, FL 33308. Offers D Min. Part-time programs available. *Degree requirements:* For doctorate, thesis/dissertation. *Entrance requirements:* For doctorate, M Div or equivalent. Additional exam requirements/recommendations for international students: Required—TOEFL, TWE (minimum score 5).

Lancaster Bible College, Graduate School, Lancaster, PA 17608-3403. Offers Bible (MA); consulting resource teacher (M Ed); counseling (MA); ministry (MA); school counseling (M Ed). Part-time and evening/weekend programs available. *Degree requirements:* For master's, comprehensive exam (for some programs), thesis (for some programs). *Entrance requirements:* For master's, bachelor's degree with a minimum of 30 credits of course work in Bible, minimum undergraduate GPA of 3.0, interview. Additional exam requirements/recommendations for international students: Required—TOEFL.

La Salle University, School of Arts and Sciences, Program in Theological, Pastoral and Liturgical Studies, Philadelphia, PA 19141-1199. Offers pastoral studies (MA); religion (MA); theological studies (MA). Part-time and evening/weekend programs available. *Entrance requirements:* For master's, 26 credits in humanistic subjects, religion, theology, or ministry-related work.

La Sierra University, School of Religion, Riverside, CA 92515. Offers pastoral ministry (M Div); religion (MA); religious education (MA); religious studies (MA). *Accreditation:* ATS. Part-time programs available. *Degree requirements:* For master's, one foreign language, thesis or alternative. *Entrance requirements:* For master's, GRE General Test, minimum GPA of 3.0.

Liberty University, College of Arts and Sciences, Lynchburg, VA 24502. Offers counseling (MA); nursing (MSN); pastoral care and counseling (PhD); professional counseling (PhD). *Accreditation:* AACN. Part-time programs available. Postbaccalaureate distance learning degree programs offered (minimal on-campus study). *Degree requirements:* For master's, comprehensive exam (for some programs); for doctorate, comprehensive exam, thesis/dissertation. *Entrance requirements:* For master's, GRE General Test (MSN), minimum undergraduate GPA of 3.0; for doctorate, GRE General Test, minimum master's GPA of 3.25. Additional exam requirements/recommendations for international students: Required—TOEFL (minimum score 600 paper-based; 250 computer-based). Electronic applications accepted. *Expenses:* Tuition: Full-time $7286; part-time $1779 per semester. Required fees: $150 per semester. *Faculty research:* God concept and adult attachment, building marital strength, image of God and gender, breastfeeding behavior among adolescent mothers, osteoporosis.

Lincoln Christian Seminary, Graduate and Professional Programs, Lincoln, IL 62656-2167. Offers Bible and theology (MA); Bible translation (MA); counseling ministry (MA); divinity (M Div); leadership ministry (MA, D Min). MA in Bible translation offered jointly with Pioneer Bible Translators (Dallas, TX). *Accreditation:* ACIPE; ATS. Part-time programs available. *Degree requirements:* For master's, 2 foreign languages, thesis; for doctorate, thesis/dissertation; for M Div, 2 foreign languages. *Entrance requirements:* For M Div and master's, minimum GPA of 2.5; for doctorate, MDiv or equivalent. Additional exam requirements/recommendations for international students: Required—TOEFL (minimum score 550 paper-based; 213 computer-based). Electronic applications accepted.

Loma Linda University, Faculty of Religion, Program in Clinical Ministry, Loma Linda, CA 92350. Offers MA, Certificate. *Degree requirements:* For master's, comprehensive exam, thesis optional. *Entrance requirements:* For master's, baccalaureate degree, minimum 3.0 GPA. Additional exam requirements/recommendations for international students: Required—TOEFL. Electronic applications accepted.

Loras College, Graduate Division, Program in Theology and Ministry, Dubuque, IA 52004-0178. Offers ministry (MA); theology (MA). Part-time and evening/weekend programs available. *Degree requirements:* For master's, comprehensive exam (for some programs), thesis (for

Pastoral Ministry and Counseling

Loras College (continued)
some programs). *Entrance requirements:* For master's, bachelor's degree or undergraduate minor in religious studies or equivalent, minimum undergraduate GPA of 2.75.

Loyola Marymount University, College of Liberal Arts, Department of Theological Studies, Program in Pastoral Theology, Los Angeles, CA 90045-2659. Offers MA. Part-time and evening/weekend programs available. *Degree requirements:* For master's, one foreign language, comprehensive exam, thesis or alternative. *Entrance requirements:* For master's, GRE General Test. Additional exam requirements/recommendations for international students: Required—TOEFL. Electronic applications accepted.

Loyola University Chicago, Institute of Pastoral Studies, Program in Pastoral Counseling, Chicago, IL 60611-2196. Offers pastoral care and counseling (MA); pastoral counseling (MA, Certificate); M Div/MA. *Accreditation:* ACIPE. Part-time programs available. *Faculty:* 6 full-time (2 women), 12 part-time/adjunct (7 women). *Students:* 32 full-time (21 women), 22 part-time (20 women); includes 11 minority (8 African Americans, 2 Asian Americans or Pacific Islanders, 1 Hispanic American), 4 international. Average age 42. 24 applicants, 75% accepted, 13 enrolled. In 2008, 13 master's awarded. *Degree requirements:* For master's, thesis or alternative, integration project. *Application deadline:* For fall admission, 2/15 priority date for domestic students. Applications are processed on a rolling basis. Application fee: $50. Electronic applications accepted. *Expenses:* Tuition: Full-time $13,500; part-time $750 per credit hour. Required fees: $60 per semester. Full-time tuition and fees vary according to program. *Financial support:* In 2008–09, 7 students received support. Career-related internships or fieldwork, Federal Work-Study, and institutionally sponsored loans available. Support available to part-time students. Financial award application deadline: 3/1; financial award applicants required to submit FAFSA. *Faculty research:* Pastoral psychotherapy, enrichment outcome, marriage and family therapy, marriage and family spirituality, gender and ethnicity issues, theological anthropology. *Unit head:* Dr. Paul R. Giblin, Associate Professor, 312-915-7483, Fax: 312-915-7410, E-mail: pgibli@luc.edu. *Application contact:* Dr. Paul R. Giblin, Associate Professor, 312-915-7483, Fax: 312-915-7410, E-mail: pgibli@luc.edu.

Loyola University Chicago, Institute of Pastoral Studies, Program in Pastoral Studies, Chicago, IL 60611-2196. Offers MA. *Accreditation:* ACIPE. *Faculty:* 6 full-time (2 women). *Students:* 80 full-time (48 women), 69 part-time (46 women); includes 13 minority (6 African Americans, 1 Asian American or Pacific Islander, 6 Hispanic Americans), 6 international. Average age 43. 21 applicants, 90% accepted, 14 enrolled. In 2008, 39 master's awarded. *Application deadline:* For fall admission, 8/1 priority date for domestic students; for spring admission, 12/1 for domestic students. Applications are processed on a rolling basis. Application fee: $50. *Expenses:* Tuition: Full-time $13,500; part-time $750 per credit hour. Required fees: $60 per semester. Full-time tuition and fees vary according to program. *Financial support:* Career-related internships or fieldwork, Federal Work-Study, institutionally sponsored loans, and scholarships/grants available. Support available to part-time students. Financial award application deadline: 3/1. *Unit head:* Dr. Peter Gilmour, Director, 312-915-7400, Fax: 312-915-7410, E-mail: pgilmou@luc.edu. *Application contact:* Randy Gibbons, Administrative Assistant, 312-915-7450, Fax: 312-915-7410, E-mail: rgibbon@luc.edu.

Loyola University Maryland, Graduate Programs, College of Arts and Sciences, Department of Pastoral Counseling, Program in Pastoral Counseling, Baltimore, MD 21210-2699. Offers MS, PhD, CAS. Part-time and evening/weekend programs available. *Faculty:* 46 full-time (16 women), 35 part-time/adjunct (19 women). *Students:* 111 full-time (68 women), 239 part-time (177 women); includes 106 minority (91 African Americans, 1 American Indian/Alaska Native, 11 Asian Americans or Pacific Islanders, 3 Hispanic Americans). Average age 44. In 2008, 62 master's, 6 doctorates, 4 other advanced degrees awarded. *Entrance requirements:* For master's, doctorate, and CAS, GRE General Test, GRE Subject Test (recommended). Additional exam requirements/recommendations for international students: Required—TOEFL (minimum score 550 paper-based; 213 computer-based). *Application deadline:* Applications are processed on a rolling basis. Application fee: $50. *Financial support:* Research assistantships available. Financial award applicants required to submit FAFSA. *Unit head:* Dr. Danielle Lasure-Bryant, Director, 410-617-7606, E-mail: drlasurebryant@loyola.edu. *Application contact:* Dr. Danielle Lasure-Bryant, Director, 410-617-7606, E-mail: drlasurebryant@loyola.edu.

Loyola University Maryland, Graduate Programs, College of Arts and Sciences, Department of Pastoral Counseling, Program in Spiritual and Pastoral Care, Baltimore, MD 21210-2699. Offers MA. Part-time and evening/weekend programs available. *Faculty:* 46 full-time (16 women), 35 part-time/adjunct (19 women). *Students:* 111 full-time (68 women), 239 part-time (177 women); includes 106 minority (91 African Americans, 1 American Indian/Alaska Native, 11 Asian Americans or Pacific Islanders, 3 Hispanic Americans). Average age 46. In 2008, 62 master's awarded. *Entrance requirements:* For master's, GRE General Test, GRE Subject Test (recommended). Additional exam requirements/recommendations for international students: Required—TOEFL (minimum score 550 paper-based; 213 computer-based). *Application deadline:* For fall admission, 4/1 priority date for domestic students; for spring admission, 11/1 priority date for domestic students. Applications are processed on a rolling basis. Application fee: $50. *Financial support:* Applicants required to submit FAFSA. *Unit head:* Dr. Thomas E. Rodgerson, Director, 410-617-7635, E-mail: trodgerson@loyola.edu. *Application contact:* Dr. Thomas E. Rodgerson, Director, 410-617-7635, E-mail: trodgerson@loyola.edu.

Lutheran School of Theology at Chicago, Graduate and Professional Programs, Chicago, IL 60615-5199. Offers ministry (D Min); ministry, pastoral care, and counseling (D Min PCC); theological studies (MA, PhD); theology (M Div, Th M). *Accreditation:* ACIPE; ATS (one or more programs are accredited). Part-time programs available. Terminal master's awarded for partial completion of doctoral program. *Degree requirements:* For master's, variable foreign language requirement; for doctorate, variable foreign language requirement, thesis/dissertation. *Entrance requirements:* For master's, GRE (Th M), M Div or equivalent (Th M); for doctorate, GRE, M Div or equivalent, 3 years of professional experience (D Min, D Min PCC). Additional exam requirements/recommendations for international students: Required—TOEFL, TOEFL (Th M).

Lutheran Theological Seminary, Graduate and Professional Programs, Saskatoon, SK S7N 0X3, Canada. Offers Biblical studies (MTS); church history (MTS); ethics/church and society (MTS); history of Christianity (STM); New Testament (STM); Old Testament (STM); pastoral studies (STM); pastoral theology (MTS); systematic theology (MTS); systematic theology and philosophy of religion (STM); theology (M Div, D Div). *Accreditation:* ATS. Part-time programs available. *Degree requirements:* For master's, thesis; for M Div, Greek, Hebrew.

Lutheran Theological Seminary at Gettysburg, Graduate and Professional Programs, Gettysburg, PA 17325-1795. Offers divinity (M Div); ministerial studies (MAMS); outdoor ministry (MAR); parish ministry (D Min); theology (STM). *Accreditation:* ACIPE; ATS (one or more programs are accredited). Part-time programs available. Postbaccalaureate distance learning degree programs offered (no on-campus study). *Degree requirements:* For master's, thesis (for some programs); for M Div, one foreign language. Electronic applications accepted.

The Lutheran Theological Seminary at Philadelphia, Graduate School, Philadelphia, PA 19119-1794. Offers divinity (M Div); ministry (D Min); religion (MAR); social ministry (Certificate); theology (STM). *Accreditation:* ACIPE; ATS. Part-time and evening/weekend programs available. *Degree requirements:* For master's, one foreign language, comprehensive exam (for some programs), thesis (for some programs); for doctorate, thesis/dissertation; for M Div, 2 foreign languages. *Entrance requirements:* For M Div and master's, minimum undergraduate GPA of 2.8; for doctorate, minimum first professional GPA of 3.0. Additional exam requirements/recommendations for international students: Required—TOEFL (minimum score 550 paper-based; 213 computer-based), TWE. Electronic applications accepted.

Luther Rice University, Graduate Programs, Lithonia, GA 30038-2454. Offers Bible/theology (M Div); Christian education (M Div); Christian studies (MA); church ministry (D Min); counseling (M Div); discipleship counseling (MA); ministry (M Div, MA); missions/evangelism (M Div). Part-time programs available. Postbaccalaureate distance learning degree programs offered (no on-campus study). *Degree requirements:* For doctorate, thesis/dissertation. *Entrance requirements:* Additional exam requirements/recommendations for international students: Required—TOEFL (minimum score 500 paper-based; 173 computer-based).

Madonna University, Program in Religious Studies, Livonia, MI 48150-1173. Offers pastoral ministry (MA).

Malone University, Graduate Program in Christian Ministries, Canton, OH 44709-3897. Offers Christian leadership in sports ministry (MA); Christian ministries (MA); leadership in the Christian church (MA). Part-time and evening/weekend programs available. *Faculty:* 7 full-time (1 woman), 4 part-time/adjunct (0 women). *Students:* 3 full-time (1 woman), 29 part-time (10 women); includes 8 minority (7 African Americans, 1 American Indian/Alaska Native). Average age 37. In 2008, 10 master's awarded. *Entrance requirements:* For master's, minimum GPA of 3.0. Additional exam requirements/recommendations for international students: Required—TOEFL (minimum score 550 paper-based). *Application deadline:* Applications are processed on a rolling basis. Application fee: $25. *Expenses:* Contact institution. *Financial support:* Tuition waivers (partial) and unspecified assistantships available. Support available to part-time students. Financial award application deadline: 6/30. *Faculty research:* Pauline theology, history of biblical interpretation, Johannine epistles, miracles in the New Testament, God's judgment and love. *Unit head:* Dr. D. Nathan Phinney, Interim Director, 330-471-8194, Fax: 330-471-8477, E-mail: dphinney@malone.edu. *Application contact:* David L. Kleffman, Assistant Director of Enrollment, 330-471-8447, Fax: 330-471-8343, E-mail: dkleffman@malone.edu.

Maple Springs Baptist Bible College and Seminary, Graduate and Professional Programs, Capitol Heights, MD 20743. Offers biblical studies (MA, Certificate); Christian counseling (MA); church administration (MA); divinity (M Div); ministry (D Min); religious education (MRE).

Maranatha Baptist Bible College, Program in Biblical Counseling, Watertown, WI 53094. Offers MA. Part-time programs available. *Faculty:* 5 full-time (0 women), 2 part-time/adjunct (0 women). *Students:* 7 full-time (5 women), 5 part-time (3 women). Average age 24. 7 applicants, 100% accepted, 7 enrolled. In 2008, 2 master's awarded. *Application deadline:* Applications are processed on a rolling basis. Application fee: $50. *Expenses:* Tuition: Full-time $3840; part-time $240 per credit hour. Required fees: $20 per credit hour. *Financial support:* In 2008–09, 2 students received support. Scholarships/grants and tuition waivers (full and partial) available. Support available to part-time students. *Unit head:* Dr. Larry Oats, Dean of Maranatha Baptist Seminary, 920-206-2324, Fax: 920-261-9109, E-mail: loats@mbbc.edu. *Application contact:* Dr. Jim Harrison, Director of Admissions, 920-206-2327, Fax: 920-261-9109, E-mail: admissions@mbbc.edu.

Martin University, Graduate School of Urban Ministry, Indianapolis, IN 46218-3867. Offers urban ministry studies (MA). Part-time and evening/weekend programs available. *Degree requirements:* For master's, Greek, oral and written comprehensive exam or thesis. *Faculty research:* How to bridge the gap between black theology and the black church.

Marymount University, School of Education and Human Services, Program in Pastoral Counseling, Arlington, VA 22207-4299. Offers pastoral and spiritual care (MA); pastoral counseling (MA, Certificate). Part-time and evening/weekend programs available. *Students:* 7 full-time (6 women), 14 part-time (all women); includes 7 minority (all African Americans). Average age 38. 8 applicants, 100% accepted, 8 enrolled. In 2008, 2 master's awarded. *Degree requirements:* For master's, thesis or alternative. *Entrance requirements:* For master's, GRE, 2 letters of recommendation, interview, resumé, personal statement; for Certificate, master's degree in counseling. Additional exam requirements/recommendations for international students: Required—TOEFL (minimum score 600 paper-based; 250 computer-based; 100 iBT). *Application deadline:* For fall admission, 2/16 for domestic and international students. Application fee: $40. Electronic applications accepted. *Expenses:* Tuition: Full-time $12,420; part-time $690 per credit hour. Required fees: $126; $7 per credit hour. Tuition and fees vary according to degree level. *Financial support:* In 2008–09, 12 students received support; research assistantships with full tuition reimbursements available, career-related internships or fieldwork, Federal Work-Study, scholarships/grants, and unspecified assistantships available. Support available to part-time students. Financial award applicants required to submit FAFSA. *Unit head:* Dr. Charles Harris, Chair, 703-284-1664, Fax: 703-284-5708, E-mail: charles.harris@marymount.edu. *Application contact:* Francesca Reed, Director, Graduate Admissions, 703-284-5901, Fax: 703-527-3815, E-mail: grad.admissions@marymount.edu.

The Master's College and Seminary, The Master's Seminary, Santa Clarita, CA 91321-1200. Offers biblical counseling (MABC); New Testament (Th D); Old Testament (Th D); preaching (D Min); theology (M Div, M Th, Th D). Part-time programs available. *Degree requirements:* For master's, 2 foreign languages, thesis; for doctorate, 4 foreign languages, thesis/dissertation; for M Div, 2 foreign languages, thesis/dissertation. *Entrance requirements:* For M Div, minimum 2 years of college; for master's, minimum GPA of 2.75; for doctorate, Th M, minimum GPA of 3.5. Additional exam requirements/recommendations for international students: Required—TOEFL (minimum score 550 paper-based).

McCormick Theological Seminary, Graduate and Professional Programs, Chicago, IL 60615. Offers ministry (D Min); theological studies (MATS, Certificate); theology (M Div); M Div/MSW. *Accreditation:* ACIPE; ATS (one or more programs are accredited). Part-time and evening/weekend programs available. *Degree requirements:* For master's, thesis (for some programs); for doctorate, thesis/dissertation. *Entrance requirements:* For M Div and master's, minimum GPA of 3.0; for doctorate, M Div, minimum 3 years in pastorate. *Faculty research:* Faith formation, families, biblical literature, Dead Sea scrolls, women in antiquity.

McMaster University, McMaster Divinity College, Hamilton, ON L8S 4M2, Canada. Offers biblical studies (M Div); Biblical studies (MA, MTS, Diploma); Christian interpretation/history (M Div, MA, MTS, Diploma); Christian ministry (M Div, MA, MTS, Diploma); Christian Studies (Certificate); Christian theology (PhD). Affiliated with the Toronto School of Theology. *Accreditation:* ATS. Part-time programs available. *Degree requirements:* For master's, one foreign language, thesis optional; for doctorate, 3 foreign languages, comprehensive exam, thesis/dissertation; for other advanced degree, 2 foreign languages, thesis. *Entrance requirements:* For master's, minimum B average in undergraduate course work, 3 letters of reference; for doctorate, minimum B+ average in bachelor's and master's, appropriate modern/ancient language, interview; for other advanced degree, 6 units of related Biblical language, minimum B+ average in undergraduate course work, minimum 15 units of course work in related area of study, 3 letters of recommendation. Additional exam requirements/recommendations for international students: Required—TOEFL (minimum score 550 paper-based; 237 computer-based). *Faculty research:* Ethics, Biblical studies, language studies, church history, Christian ministry.

Meadville Lombard Theological School, Graduate and Professional Programs, Chicago, IL 60637-1602. Offers divinity (M Div); ministry (D Min); religion (MA); M Div/MSW. *Accreditation:* ACIPE; ATS. Part-time programs available. Postbaccalaureate distance learning degree programs offered (minimal on-campus study). *Entrance requirements:* For M Div and master's, bachelor's degree; for doctorate, bachelor's and masters degrees, 3 years of ministry.

Mennonite Brethren Biblical Seminary, School of Theology, Program in Christian Ministry, Fresno, CA 93727-5097. Offers MA. Part-time programs available. Postbaccalaureate distance learning degree programs offered (minimal on-campus study). *Entrance requirements:* Additional exam requirements/recommendations for international students: Required—TOEFL (minimum score 550 paper-based; 213 computer-based).

Midwestern Baptist Theological Seminary, Graduate and Professional Programs, Kansas City, MO 64118-4697. Offers Biblical archaeology (MA); Biblical languages (MA); Christian education (M Div, MACE); Christian foundations—lay ministry (Graduate Certificate); collegiate ministries (M Div); counseling (MA); educational ministry (D Ed Min); international church planting (M Div); ministry (M Div, D Min); North American church planting (M Div); sacred music (MCM); urban ministry (M Div); worship leadership (M Div); youth ministry (M Div). *Accreditation:* ATS. Part-time programs available. Postbaccalaureate distance learning degree programs offered (minimal on-campus study). *Degree requirements:* For doctorate, thesis/dissertation; for M Div, 2 foreign languages. *Entrance requirements:* For doctorate, MAT. Electronic applications accepted. *Faculty research:* Ministerial studies, Biblical and theological studies, missions, counseling.

Missouri Baptist University, Graduate Programs, St. Louis, MO 63141-8660. Offers business administration (MBA); Christian ministries (MACM); counseling (MAC); education (MSE); education administration (MEA); educational leadership (MSE, Ed S); teaching (MAT).

Moody Bible Institute, Graduate School, Chicago, IL 60610-3284. Offers biblical studies (MABS, Graduate Certificate); intercultural studies (MAIS, Graduate Certificate); ministry (M Div, M Min); spiritual formation and discipleship (MASF, Graduate Certificate); urban studies (MA, Graduate Certificate). Part-time programs available. *Degree requirements:* For master's, 2 foreign languages, fieldwork (MABS); colloquium, field research project (MA Min). *Entrance requirements:* For master's, 30 hours in Bible/theology, 2 years of ministry experience (MA Min).

Mount Marty College, Graduate Studies Division, Yankton, SD 57078-3724. Offers business administration (MBA); nurse anesthesia (MS); pastoral ministries (MPM). *Accreditation:* AANA/CANAEP (one or more programs are accredited). *Degree requirements:* For master's, thesis or alternative. *Entrance requirements:* For master's, GRE General Test, minimum GPA of 3.0. Electronic applications accepted. *Faculty research:* Clinical anesthesia, professional characteristics, motivations of applicants.

Neumann University, Program in Pastoral Counseling, Aston, PA 19014-1298. Offers pastoral counseling (MS, CAS); spiritual direction (CSD). Part-time and evening/weekend programs available. *Faculty:* 3 full-time (2 women), 7 part-time/adjunct (5 women). *Students:* 9 full-time (4 women), 101 part-time (78 women); includes 17 minority (10 African Americans, 1 American Indian/Alaska Native, 3 Asian Americans or Pacific Islanders, 3 Hispanic Americans). Average age 49. 50 applicants, 100% accepted, 45 enrolled. In 2008, 23 master's awarded. *Degree requirements:* For master's, clinical case study. *Entrance requirements:* Additional exam requirements/recommendations for international students: Required—TOEFL. *Application deadline:* Applications are processed on a rolling basis. Application fee: $50. *Financial support:* In 2008–09, 8 students received support. Available to part-time students. Application deadline: 3/15; *Faculty research:* Development of an integrated model of religion/psychology for remediation and prevention of emotional disturbance. *Unit head:* Dr. Leonard DiPaul, Executive Director, 610-558-5220, Fax: 610-459-1370, E-mail: dipall@neumann.edu. *Application contact:* Kittie D. Pain, Associate Director of Admissions, Graduate and Adult Programs, 610-558-5613, Fax: 610-558-5652, E-mail: paink@neumann.edu.

New Brunswick Theological Seminary, Graduate and Professional Programs, Program in Metro-Urban Ministry, New Brunswick, NJ 08901-1196. Offers theological studies (D Min). Part-time programs available. *Degree requirements:* For doctorate, thesis/dissertation. *Entrance requirements:* For doctorate, M Div. *Faculty research:* Urban-land use planning, theology of the city.

New Orleans Baptist Theological Seminary, Graduate and Professional Programs, Division of Pastoral Ministries, New Orleans, LA 70126-4858. Offers M Div, MAMFC, D Min, PhD. *Accreditation:* ACIPE. *Degree requirements:* For doctorate, thesis/dissertation; for M Div, project report. *Entrance requirements:* For master's and doctorate, GRE General Test.

The Nigerian Baptist Theological Seminary, Graduate Studies, Ogbomoso, Nigeria. Offers church music (M Div, M Th, Diploma); divinity (M Div); ministry (D Min); religious education (M Div, M Th, PhD); theological studies (MATS); theology (M Th, PhD). Part-time programs available. *Degree requirements:* For master's, thesis, 2 Nigerian languages; for M Div, thesis/dissertation (for some programs), 2 biblical languages; for Diploma, thesis or alternative.

Northern Baptist Theological Seminary, Graduate and Professional Programs, Lombard, IL 60148-5698. Offers Biblical studies (MA); Christian ministries (MACM); divinity (M Div); ministry (D Min); missional church (MA); theology (MA). *Accreditation:* ATS. Part-time programs available. *Faculty:* 6 full-time (1 woman), 30 part-time/adjunct (5 women). *Students:* 127 full-time (38 women), 20 part-time (13 women); includes 67 minority (51 African Americans, 12 Asian Americans or Pacific Islanders, 4 Hispanic Americans), 3 international. Average age 40. *Degree requirements:* For doctorate, thesis/dissertation; for M Div, field experience. *Entrance requirements:* For doctorate, 3 years in the ministry post-M Div. Additional exam requirements/recommendations for international students: Required—TOEFL. *Application deadline:* For fall admission, 9/1 priority date for domestic students, 2/1 priority date for international students; for winter admission, 12/1 priority date for domestic students; for spring admission, 3/1 priority date for domestic students. Applications are processed on a rolling basis. Application fee: $35. Electronic applications accepted. *Expenses:* Tuition: Full-time $15,800; part-time $440 per credit. Required fees: $100 per quarter. Tuition and fees vary according to degree level. *Financial support:* Career-related internships or fieldwork and scholarships/grants available. Support available to part-time students. Financial award application deadline: 9/1. *Faculty research:* Theology, worship studies, church history, evangelism, Bible. *Unit head:* Alistair Brown, Dean, 630-620-2103, Fax: 630-620-2190. *Application contact:* Greg Henson, Executive Director of External Relations, 630-620-2180, Fax: 630-620-2190, E-mail: admissions@seminary.edu.

North Greenville University, T. Walter Brashier Graduate School, Greer, SC 29651. Offers business administration (MBA); Christian ministry (MCM). Part-time and evening/weekend programs available. Postbaccalaureate distance learning degree programs offered (no on-campus study). *Faculty:* 3 full-time (1 woman), 9 part-time/adjunct (1 woman). *Students:* 51 full-time (21 women), 60 part-time (22 women); includes 17 minority (14 African Americans, 3 Hispanic Americans), 4 international. Average age 32. 135 applicants, 85% accepted, 111 enrolled. In 2008, 39 master's awarded. *Degree requirements:* For master's, comprehensive exam (for some programs), thesis or alternative, capstone course. *Entrance requirements:* For master's, GMAT, GRE, minimum GPA of 2.25 overall, 2.5 in major. Additional exam requirements/recommendations for international students: Required—TOEFL (minimum score 550 paper-based; 213 computer-based). *Application deadline:* For fall admission, 8/1 for domestic students, 6/1 for international students; for winter admission, 1/1 for domestic students, 10/1 for international students; for spring admission, 3/1 for domestic students, 1/1 for international students. Applications are processed on a rolling basis. Application fee: $30. Electronic applications accepted. *Expenses:* Tuition: Full-time $4500; part-time $750 per course. One-time fee: $150. *Financial support:* In 2008–09, 35 students received support. Federal Work-Study, institutionally sponsored loans, scholarships/grants, and tuition waivers (partial) available. Support available to part-time students. Financial award applicants required to submit FAFSA. *Faculty research:* Organizational behavior, church growth, homiletics, human resources, business strategy. *Unit head:* Dr. Joseph Samuel Isgett, Vice President for Graduate Studies, 864-877-3052, Fax: 864-877-1653, E-mail: sisgett@ngu.edu. *Application contact:* Tawana P. Scott, Director of Graduate Enrollment, 864-877-1598, Fax: 864-877-1653, E-mail: tscott@ngu.edu.

North Park Theological Seminary, Graduate and Professional Programs, Program in Christian Ministry, Chicago, IL 60625-4895. Offers MACM, MA/MBA, MA/MM.

North Park Theological Seminary, Graduate and Professional Programs, Program in Christian Studies, Chicago, IL 60625-4895. Offers adult ministry (Certificate); camping and retreat ministry (Certificate); children and family ministry (Certificate); Christian formation-all ages (Certificate); Christian spirituality (Certificate); faith and health (Certificate); justice ministry (Certificate); leadership and administration (Certificate); spiritual direction (Certificate); youth ministry (Certificate). *Accreditation:* ACIPE. Part-time programs available. *Entrance requirements:* For degree, minimum GPA of 2.5. Additional exam requirements/recommendations for international students: Required—TOEFL.

Northwest Nazarene University, Graduate Studies, Program in Religion, Nampa, ID 83686-5897. Offers Christian education (MA); missional leadership (MA); pastoral ministry (MA); religion (M Div); spiritual formation (MA). Part-time and evening/weekend programs available. Postbaccalaureate distance learning degree programs offered (no on-campus study). *Faculty:* 10 full-time (2 women), 24 part-time/adjunct (5 women). *Students:* 135 full-time (36 women), 11 part-time (5 women); includes 17 minority (8 African Americans, 1 American Indian/Alaska Native, 5 Asian Americans or Pacific Islanders, 3 Hispanic Americans). In 2008, 42 master's awarded. *Application deadline:* Applications are processed on a rolling basis. Application fee: $50. Electronic applications accepted. *Unit head:* Dr. Jay Akkerman, Director, Graduate Studies, 208-467-8437, Fax: 208-467-8252. *Application contact:* Jill Jones, Program Assistant, 208-467-8368, Fax: 208-467-8252, E-mail: jdjones@nnu.edu.

Notre Dame College, Graduate Studies, South Euclid, OH 44121-4293. Offers accounting (Certificate); creative critical thinking (M Ed); financial services management (Certificate); information systems (Certificate); learning disabilities (M Ed); management (Certificate); paralegal (Certificate); pastoral ministry (Certificate); reading (M Ed); teacher education (Certificate). Part-time and evening/weekend programs available. *Degree requirements:* For master's, thesis. *Entrance requirements:* For master's, GRE General Test, MAT, minimum GPA of 2.75, valid teaching certificate. *Faculty research:* Cognitive psychology, teaching critical thinking in the classroom.

Oakwood University, Program in Pastoral Studies, Huntsville, AL 35896. Offers MA. *Entrance requirements:* For master's, Biblical Literacy Entrance Test (BLET), minimum cumulative GPA of 2.5, 2 letters of recommendation, current resumé, 3 years of pastoral or local church leadership experience. Additional exam requirements/recommendations for international students: Required—TOEFL (minimum score 500 paper-based; 173 computer-based).

Oblate School of Theology, Graduate and Professional Programs, San Antonio, TX 78216-6693. Offers divinity (M Div); Hispanic ministry (D Min); pastoral ministry (MAP Min); pastoral studies (Certificate); spirituality (MA Sp); supervision (D Min), including clinical pastoral education, general supervision; theology (MA Th); M Div/MA Th. *Accreditation:* ACIPE; ATS (one or more programs are accredited). Part-time programs available. *Faculty:* 24 full-time (7 women), 6 part-time/adjunct (1 woman). *Students:* 91 full-time (5 women), 56 part-time (25 women); includes 62 minority (7 African Americans, 3 American Indian/Alaska Native, 13 Asian Americans or Pacific Islanders, 39 Hispanic Americans), 29 international. Average age 39. 33 applicants, 100% accepted, 33 enrolled. In 2008, 16 first professional degrees, 8 master's, 5 Certificates awarded. *Degree requirements:* For master's, thesis (for some programs), practicum; for doctorate, paper, practicum; for M Div, one foreign language, seminar. *Entrance requirements:* For M Div, MAT, interview, course work in philosophy and theology; for master's, MAT, interview, course work in theology or religious studies, minimum GPA of 2.5; for doctorate, M Div. Additional exam requirements/recommendations for international students: Required—TOEFL (minimum score 197 computer-based; 71 iBT). *Application deadline:* For fall admission, 6/15 priority date for domestic and international students; for spring admission, 12/30 for domestic and international students. Applications are processed on a rolling basis. Application fee: $45. *Expenses:* Tuition: Full-time $11,570; part-time $445 per credit hour. Required fees: $170 per semester. One-time fee: $85 full-time. Part-time tuition and fees vary according to course level and course load. *Financial support:* Scholarships/grants available. Support available to part-time students. Financial award application deadline: 8/1; financial award applicants required to submit FAFSA. *Unit head:* Sr. Elaine Brothers, Academic Dean, 210-341-1366, Fax: 214-341-4519, E-mail: ebrothers@ost.edu. *Application contact:* James Oberhausen, Director of Admission/Registrar, 210-341-1366 Ext. 212, Fax: 210-341-4519, E-mail: registrar@ost.edu.

Oklahoma Christian University, Graduate School of Theology, Oklahoma City, OK 73136-1100. Offers family life ministry (MA); ministry (M Div, MA); youth ministry (MA). Part-time programs available. Postbaccalaureate distance learning degree programs offered (minimal on-campus study). *Faculty:* 11 full-time (0 women). *Students:* 12 full-time (2 women), 30 part-time (4 women); includes 3 minority (2 African Americans, 1 American Indian/Alaska Native), 3 international. *Degree requirements:* For master's, one foreign language, comprehensive exam, field experience; for M Div, 2 foreign languages, comprehensive exam, field experience. *Entrance requirements:* For M Div and master's, minimum undergraduate GPA of 3.0. Additional exam requirements/recommendations for international students: Required—TOEFL (minimum score 550 paper-based; 213 computer-based). *Application deadline:* For fall admission, 8/15 priority date for domestic and international students; for spring admission, 1/3 priority date for domestic and international students. Applications are processed on a rolling basis. Application fee: $25. Electronic applications accepted. *Financial support:* Career-related internships or fieldwork, Federal Work-Study, scholarships/grants, and tuition waivers (partial) available. Support available to part-time students. Financial award application deadline: 3/1. *Faculty research:* Early marriage adjustment, new religions, Ethiopic language, church health, Hebrew rhetoric. *Unit head:* Dr. John Harrison, Chair, 405-425-5377, Fax: 405-425-5076, E-mail: john.harrison@oc.edu. *Application contact:* Dustin Crawford, Admissions Counselor, 405-425-5485, Fax: 405-425-5076, E-mail: dustin.crawford@oc.edu.

Oral Roberts University, School of Theology and Missions, Tulsa, OK 74171-0001. Offers biblical literature (MA), including advanced languages, Judaic-Christian studies; Christian counseling (MA), including marriage and family therapy; Christian education (MA); divinity (M Div); missions (MA); practical theology (MA); theological/historical studies (MA); theology (D Min). *Accreditation:* ATS; NASM. Part-time programs available. Postbaccalaureate distance learning degree programs offered (minimal on-campus study). *Degree requirements:* For master's, thesis (for some programs), practicum/internship; for doctorate, thesis/dissertation, applied research project; for M Div, one foreign language, field experience. *Entrance requirements:* For M Div and master's, GRE General Test or MAT, minimum GPA of 2.5; for doctorate, M Div, minimum GPA of 3.0, 3 years of full-time ministry experience. Additional exam requirements/recommendations for international students: Required—TOEFL (minimum score 500 paper-based; 213 computer-based; 79 iBT). Electronic applications accepted.

Ottawa University, Graduate Studies-Arizona, Program in Professional Counseling, Ottawa, KS 66067-3399. Offers Christian counseling (MA); expressive arts therapy (MA); marriage and family therapy (MA); treatment of trauma, abuse and deprivation (MA). Programs offered in Mesa, Phoenix, Tempe and West Valley, AZ. Part-time and evening/weekend programs available. Postbaccalaureate distance learning degree programs offered. *Degree requirements:* For master's, comprehensive exam, thesis or alternative, field experience, practicum. *Entrance requirements:* For master's, minimum undergraduate GPA of 3.0; course work in theories of personality, abnormal psychology, and human growth and development. Additional exam requirements/recommendations for international students: Required—TOEFL (minimum score 550 paper-based; 213 computer-based).

Philadelphia Biblical University, School of Church and Community Ministries, Langhorne, PA 19047-2990. Offers Christian counseling (MSCC). Part-time and evening/weekend programs available. *Faculty:* 4 full-time (1 woman), 9 part-time/adjunct (6 women). *Students:* 5 full-time (all women), 124 part-time (90 women); includes 38 minority (31 African Americans, 6 Asian Americans or Pacific Islanders, 1 Hispanic American). Average age 37. 77 applicants, 61% accepted, 38 enrolled. In 2008, 39 master's awarded. *Entrance requirements:* Additional exam requirements/recommendations for international students: Required—TOEFL (minimum score 550 paper-based; 213 computer-based). *Application deadline:* Applications are processed on a rolling basis. Application fee: $25. Electronic applications accepted. *Expenses:* Tuition: Full-time $9450; part-time $525 per credit. Required fees: $10; $10 per year. Tuition and fees vary according to program. *Financial support:* In 2008–09, 63 students received support. Scholarships/grants available. Support available to part-time students. Financial award applicants required to submit FAFSA. *Unit head:* Donald Cheyney, Dean, 215-702-4546, E-mail: dcheyney@pbu.edu. *Application contact:* Gwen Dorsey, Enrollment Counselor, Graduate Counseling, 800-572-2472, Fax: 215-702-4248, E-mail: gdorsey@pbu.edu.

Phillips Theological Seminary, Programs in Theology, Doctor of Ministry Program, Tulsa, OK 74116. Offers parish ministry (D Min); pastoral counseling (D Min); practices of ministry (D Min).

Pastoral Ministry and Counseling

Phillips Theological Seminary (continued)
Accreditation: ATS. Part-time programs available. *Degree requirements:* For doctorate, thesis/dissertation. *Entrance requirements:* For doctorate, M Div, minimum GPA of 3.0, 3 years of post-M Div pastoral experience. *Expenses:* Contact institution. *Faculty research:* Politics and theology, media and theology, ecology and theology.

Providence College and Theological Seminary, Theological Seminary, Otterburne, MB R0A 1G0, Canada. Offers children's ministry (Certificate); Christian studies (MA, Certificate); counseling (MA); cross-cultural discipleship (Certificate); divinity (M Div); educational studies (MA), including counseling psychology, educational ministries, student development, teaching English to speakers of other languages, training teachers of English to speakers of other languages; global studies (MA); lay counseling (Diploma); ministry (D Min); teaching English to speakers of other languages (Certificate); theological studies (MA); training teacher of English to speakers of other languages (Certificate); youth ministry (Certificate). *Accreditation:* ATS. Part-time programs available. *Degree requirements:* For master's, variable foreign language requirement, thesis (for some programs); for doctorate, thesis/dissertation; for M Div, 2 foreign languages, comprehensive exam, thesis/dissertation (for some programs). *Entrance requirements:* Additional exam requirements/recommendations for international students: Recommended—TOEFL (minimum score 550 paper-based; 213 computer-based). *Faculty research:* Studies in Isaiah, theology of sin.

Reformed Theological Seminary–Charlotte Campus, Graduate and Professional Programs, Charlotte, NC 28226-6318. Offers biblical studies (MA); ministry (M Div, D Min); theological studies (MA). Part-time programs available. *Degree requirements:* For master's, comprehensive exam; for doctorate, thesis/dissertation; for M Div, 2 foreign languages, comprehensive exam. *Entrance requirements:* For master's, minimum GPA of 2.6; for doctorate, minimum GPA of 3.0. Additional exam requirements/recommendations for international students: Required—TOEFL (minimum score 550 paper-based; 213 computer-based). Electronic applications accepted.

Reformed Theological Seminary–Jackson Campus, Graduate and Professional Programs, Jackson, MS 39209-3099. Offers Bible, theology, and missions (Certificate); biblical studies (MA); Christian education (M Div, MA); counseling (M Div); divinity (M Div, Diploma); marriage and family therapy (MA); ministry (D Min); missions (M Div, MA, D Min); New Testament (Th M); Old Testament (Th M); theological studies (MA); theology (Th M); M Div/MA. *Accreditation:* AAMFT/COAMFTE (one or more programs are accredited); ATS (one or more programs are accredited). *Degree requirements:* For master's, thesis (for some programs), fieldwork; for doctorate, 2 foreign languages, thesis/dissertation; for M Div, 2 foreign languages, thesis/dissertation (for some programs). *Entrance requirements:* For M Div and master's, minimum GPA of 2.6; for doctorate, minimum GPA of 3.0. Additional exam requirements/recommendations for international students: Required—TOEFL.

Reformed Theological Seminary–Orlando Campus, Graduate Program, Oviedo, FL 32765-7197. Offers biblical studies (MA); Christian thought (MA); counseling (MA); ministry (D Min); reformation studies (Th M); theological studies (MA); theology (M Div); MA/Certificate. Part-time programs available. Postbaccalaureate distance learning degree programs offered (minimal on-campus study). *Entrance requirements:* For M Div and master's, minimum GPA of 2.6. Electronic applications accepted.

Regent University, Graduate School, School of Divinity, Virginia Beach, VA 23464-9800. Offers Biblical studies (MA); leadership and renewal (D Min); missiology (M Div, MA); practical theology (M Div, MA); renewal studies (PhD); M Div/M Ed; M Div/MA; M Div/MBA; M Ed/MA; MBA/MA. *Accreditation:* ACIPE; ATS. Part-time programs available. Postbaccalaureate distance learning degree programs offered (minimal on-campus study). *Faculty:* 21 full-time (4 women), 24 part-time/adjunct (5 women). *Students:* 194 full-time (90 women), 391 part-time (164 women); includes 249 minority (217 African Americans, 3 American Indian/Alaska Native, 11 Asian Americans or Pacific Islanders, 18 Hispanic Americans), 19 international. Average age 38. 320 applicants, 65% accepted, 137 enrolled. In 2008, 39 first professional degrees, 36 master's, 29 doctorates awarded. *Degree requirements:* For master's, comprehensive exam, thesis or alternative, internship; for doctorate, thesis/dissertation or alternative; for M Div, internship. *Entrance requirements:* For M Div, GRE General Test or MAT, minimum undergraduate GPA of 3.0, minimum 3 years of ministry experience, transcripts, recommendations; for master's, GRE General Test or MAT, minimum undergraduate GPA of 2.75, writing sample, clergy recommendation, transcripts; for doctorate, M Div or theological master's degree; minimum graduate GPA of 3.5 (PhD), 3.0 (D Min); recommendations; writing sample; transcripts. Additional exam requirements/recommendations for international students: Required—TOEFL (minimum score 577 paper-based; 233 computer-based). *Application deadline:* For fall admission, 5/1 priority date for domestic students. Applications are processed on a rolling basis. Application fee: $50. Electronic applications accepted. *Expenses:* Contact institution. *Financial support:* Fellowships with full and partial tuition reimbursements, career-related internships or fieldwork, scholarships/grants, tuition waivers (full and partial), and unspecified assistantships available. Support available to part-time students. Financial award application deadline: 9/1; financial award applicants required to submit FAFSA. *Faculty research:* Greek and Hebrew, theology, spiritual formation, global missions and world Christianity, women's studies. *Unit head:* Dr. Michael Palmer, Dean, 757-352-4406, Fax: 757-352-4597, E-mail: mpalmer@regent.edu. *Application contact:* Matthew Chadwick, Director of Admissions, 800-373-5504, Fax: 757-352-4381, E-mail: admissions@regent.edu.

Regis College, Graduate and Professional Programs, Toronto, ON M4Y 2R5, Canada. Offers ministry (D Min); ministry and spirituality (MAMS); sacred theology (STB, STM, STD, STL); theological study (MTS); theology (M Div, MA, Th M, PhD, Th D); M Div/MA. *Accreditation:* ATS (one or more programs are accredited). *Faculty:* 15 full-time (4 women), 12 part-time/adjunct (2 women). *Students:* 88 full-time (30 women), 131 part-time (78 women); includes 74 minority (16 African Americans, 1 American Indian/Alaska Native, 48 Asian Americans or Pacific Islanders, 9 Hispanic Americans). Average age 45. 73 applicants, 88% accepted, 52 enrolled. In 2008, 10 first professional degrees, 13 master's, 5 other advanced degrees awarded. Terminal master's awarded for partial completion of doctoral program. *Degree requirements:* For master's, 2 foreign languages, thesis; for doctorate, 3 foreign languages, comprehensive exam, thesis/dissertation; for first professional degree, comprehensive exam. *Entrance requirements:* For first professional degree, minimum GPA of 3.0; for master's, minimum GPA of 3.3; for doctorate, minimum GPA of 3.7. Additional exam requirements/recommendations for international students: Required—TOEFL (minimum score 580 paper-based; 237 computer-based; 93 iBT), TWE (minimum score 5). *Application deadline:* For fall admission, 3/15 priority date for domestic and international students; for winter admission, 12/1 for domestic and international students; for spring admission, 3/15 for domestic and international students. Applications are processed on a rolling basis. Application fee: $25. *Financial support:* In 2008–09, 58 students received support. Career-related internships or fieldwork and scholarships/grants available. Support available to part-time students. Financial award application deadline: 3/15. *Unit head:* Dr. Gordon Rixon, Dean, 416-922-5474 Ext. 225, Fax: 416-922-2898, E-mail: gordon.rixon@utoronto.ca. *Application contact:* Elaine Chu, Registrar, 416-922-5474 Ext. 226, Fax: 416-922-2898, E-mail: regis.registrar@utoronto.ca.

Roberts Wesleyan College, Division of Social Sciences, Rochester, NY 14624-1997. Offers counseling in ministry (MA); school counseling (MS); school psychology (MS).

Sacred Heart Major Seminary, School of Theology, Detroit, MI 48206-1799. Offers pastoral studies (MAPS); theology (M Div, MA). *Accreditation:* ACIPE; ATS. Part-time and evening/weekend programs available. *Degree requirements:* For master's, one foreign language, thesis optional, integrating project; for M Div, integrating seminar. *Entrance requirements:* For M Div and master's, GRE, previous course work in philosophy and theology. *Faculty research:* Local church history, patristics, spirituality, religious education.

St. Ambrose University, College of Arts and Sciences, Program in Pastoral Studies, Davenport, IA 52803-2898. Offers MPS. Part-time programs available. *Faculty:* 1 (woman) full-time. *Students:* 2 part-time (1 woman). Average age 51. *Degree requirements:* For master's, integration project. *Entrance requirements:* For master's, minimum GPA of 2.6, prior pastoral experience, 9 credits of course work in theology. Additional exam requirements/recommendations for international students: Required—TOEFL. *Application deadline:* For fall admission, 8/15 priority date for domestic students; for winter admission, 12/15 priority date for domestic students; for spring admission, 1/1 priority date for domestic students. Applications are processed on a rolling basis. Application fee: $25. Electronic applications accepted. *Expenses:* Contact institution. *Financial support:* In 2008–09, 1 student received support. Career-related internships or fieldwork, scholarships/grants, and tuition waivers (partial) available. Financial award application deadline: 8/15; financial award applicants required to submit FAFSA. *Faculty research:* Theological education, ecclesiology, spirituality and liturgy, medical ethics. *Unit head:* Dr. Corinne M Winter, Director, 563-333-6442, Fax: 563-333-6243, E-mail: wintercorinnem@sau.edu. *Application contact:* Dr. Corinne M Winter, Director, 563-333-6442, Fax: 563-333-6243, E-mail: wintercorinnem@sau.edu.

St. Augustine's Seminary of Toronto, Graduate and Professional Programs, Scarborough, ON M1M 1M3, Canada. Offers divinity (M Div); lay ministry (Diploma); religious education (MRE); theological studies (MTS, Diploma). *Accreditation:* ATS. Part-time and evening/weekend programs available. *Degree requirements:* For M Div, comprehensive exam (for some programs), thesis/dissertation optional, field education. *Entrance requirements:* Course work in philosophy. Additional exam requirements/recommendations for international students: Required—TOEFL (minimum score 580 paper-based; 237 computer-based), TWE (minimum score 5).

Saint Bernard's School of Theology and Ministry, Graduate and Professional Programs, Rochester, NY 14618. Offers pastoral studies (MA, Certificate); theological studies (MA); theology (M Div). *Accreditation:* ATS (one or more programs are accredited). Part-time and evening/weekend programs available. *Degree requirements:* For master's, variable foreign language requirement, thesis (for some programs). *Entrance requirements:* For M Div, minimum GPA of 2.0; for master's, minimum GPA of 2.5.

Saint Francis Seminary, Graduate and Professional Programs, St. Francis, WI 53235-3795. Offers M Div, MAPS. *Accreditation:* ACIPE; ATS. Part-time programs available. *Degree requirements:* For master's, comprehensive exam; for M Div, thesis/dissertation. *Entrance requirements:* For M Div and master's, Otis IQ Test, Terman Concept Mastery Test, interview. Additional exam requirements/recommendations for international students: Required—TOEFL (minimum score 550 paper-based).

St. John's Seminary, Graduate and Professional Programs, Camarillo, CA 93012-2598. Offers divinity (M Div); pastoral ministry (MAPM); theology (MA). *Accreditation:* ATS. Part-time programs available. *Faculty:* 19 full-time (4 women), 8 part-time/adjunct (1 woman). *Students:* 69 full-time (0 women), 10 part-time (5 women); includes 46 minority (1 African American, 25 Asian Americans or Pacific Islanders, 20 Hispanic Americans), 11 international. Average age 34. 13 applicants, 100% accepted, 13 enrolled. In 2008, 17 first professional degrees, 6 master's awarded. *Degree requirements:* For master's, comprehensive exam (for some programs), thesis optional, comprehensive integration paper (MAPM); for M Div, parish internship. *Entrance requirements:* For M Div, GRE General Test, bishop's approbation; for master's, GRE General Test, minimum GPA of 3.5 (MA), 2.5 (MAPM). Additional exam requirements/recommendations for international students: Required—TOEFL (minimum score 550 paper-based; 213 computer-based; 79 iBT). *Application deadline:* For fall admission, 7/15 priority date for domestic students. Applications are processed on a rolling basis. Application fee: $0. Electronic applications accepted. *Expenses:* Tuition: Full-time $12,750; part-time $425 per unit. One-time fee: $3421 full-time; $25 part-time. Full-time tuition and fees vary according to course load and program. *Faculty research:* Biblical studies, moral theology, historical studies, systematic theology, spiritual theology. *Unit head:* Rev. Richard Benson, CM, Academic Dean, 805-482-2755, Fax: 805-482-3470, E-mail: rbensoncm@stjohnsem.edu. *Application contact:* Esme M. Takahashi, Registrar, 805-482-2755 Ext. 1014, Fax: 805-482-3470, E-mail: registrar-sjs@stjohnsem.edu.

St. John's University, St. John's College of Liberal Arts and Sciences, Department of Theology and Religious Studies, Queens, NY 11439. Offers pastoral ministry (Certificate); priestly studies (M Div); theology (MA, Certificate). *Accreditation:* ACIPE. Part-time and evening/weekend programs available. *Students:* 1 (woman) full-time, 43 part-time (23 women); includes 12 minority (6 African Americans, 1 Asian American or Pacific Islander, 5 Hispanic Americans), 10 international. Average age 47. 36 applicants, 67% accepted, 14 enrolled. In 2008, 1 first professional degree, 19 master's, 2 other advanced degrees awarded. *Degree requirements:* For master's, thesis optional; for M Div, thesis/dissertation optional. *Entrance requirements:* For master's, minimum GPA of 3.0. Additional exam requirements/recommendations for international students: Required—TOEFL (minimum score 500 paper-based; 173 computer-based; 61 iBT), IELTS (minimum score 5.5). *Application deadline:* For fall admission, 5/1 priority date for domestic and international students; for spring admission, 11/1 priority date for domestic and international students. Applications are processed on a rolling basis. Application fee: $70. Electronic applications accepted. *Expenses:* Tuition: Full-time $20,760; part-time $865 per credit. Required fees: $300; $150 per semester. Tuition and fees vary according to program. *Financial support:* Research assistantships, scholarships/grants available. Support available to part-time students. Financial award application deadline: 3/1; financial award applicants required to submit FAFSA. *Faculty research:* Systematic theology, moral theory, biblical studies, pastoral theology, church history. *Unit head:* Fr. Michael Whalen, Chair, 718-990-5431, E-mail: whalenm@stjohns.edu. *Application contact:* Kathleen Davis, Director of Graduate Admission, 718-990-2790, Fax: 718-990-5686, E-mail: gradhelp@stjohns.edu.

Saint John's University, Saint John's School of Theology and Seminary, Collegeville, MN 56321. Offers divinity (M Div); liturgical music (MA); liturgical studies (MA); pastoral ministry (MA); theology (MA), including church history, liturgy, monastic studies, scripture, spirituality, systematics; M Div/MA. *Accreditation:* ATS. Part-time programs available. Postbaccalaureate distance learning degree programs offered (no on-campus study). *Degree requirements:* For master's, one foreign language, comprehensive exam (for some programs), thesis (for some programs). *Entrance requirements:* For master's, GRE General Test or MAT. Electronic applications accepted. *Faculty research:* Religious education, biblical literature.

Saint Leo University, Graduate Pastoral Studies, Saint Leo, FL 33574-6665. Offers MA. Part-time and evening/weekend programs available. *Entrance requirements:* For master's, minimum GPA of 3.0, letter of recommendation. Additional exam requirements/recommendations for international students: Required—TOEFL (minimum score 550 paper-based; 213 computer-based). Electronic applications accepted. *Faculty research:* Ecclesiology and the Second Vatican Council, sacramental theology and the liturgical movement, Christian and Eastern religious traditions, Ecumenism, ministry and technology.

Saint Mary-of-the-Woods College, Program in Pastoral Theology, Saint Mary-of-the-Woods, IN 47876. Offers pastoral theology (MA); youth ministry (Graduate Certificate). Part-time and evening/weekend programs available. Postbaccalaureate distance learning degree programs offered (minimal on-campus study). *Degree requirements:* For master's, thesis, qualifying exam.

St. Mary's University, Graduate School, Department of Theology, San Antonio, TX 78228-8507. Offers pastoral ministry (MA); theology (MA); JD/MA. Part-time and evening/weekend programs available. Postbaccalaureate distance learning degree programs offered (no on-campus study). *Students:* 2 full-time (0 women), 36 part-time (21 women); includes 8 minority (all Hispanic Americans), 1 international. Average age 42. 15 applicants, 47% accepted, 7 enrolled. In 2008, 7 master's awarded. *Degree requirements:* For master's, comprehensive exam, practicum (pastoral administration). *Entrance requirements:* For master's, GRE General Test, MAT, 12 credit hours in theology/philosophy. Additional exam requirements/

recommendations for international students: Required—TOEFL (minimum score 550 paper-based; 213 computer-based; 80 iBT). *Application deadline:* For fall admission, 8/1 for domestic students. Applications are processed on a rolling basis. Application fee: $0. Electronic applications accepted. *Expenses:* Tuition: Full-time $12,006; part-time $667 per credit hour. Required fees: $440; $220 per semester. *Financial support:* In 2008–09, 2 students received support, including 1 fellowship (averaging $2,000 per year), 1 research assistantship (averaging $4,500 per year); career-related internships or fieldwork, Federal Work-Study, institutionally sponsored loans, scholarships/grants, health care benefits, and unspecified assistantships also available. Financial award application deadline: 3/31; financial award applicants required to submit FAFSA. *Faculty research:* Bioethics; perceptions of ministry; Marian doctrines and the contemporary church; Jaspers, peace, and justice. *Unit head:* Rev. Daniel Thompson, Director, 210-436-3310, E-mail: dthompson@stmarytx.edu. *Application contact:* Dr. Henry Flores, Dean of the Graduate School, 210-436-3101, Fax: 210-431-2220, E-mail: hflores@stmarytx.edu.

Saint Mary's University of Minnesota, Schools of Graduate and Professional Programs, Graduate School of Health and Human Services, Institute in Pastoral Ministries, Winona, MN 55987-1399. Offers Canon law (Certificate); pastoral administration (MA); pastoral ministries (MA).

Saint Paul University, Faculty of Canon Law, Ottawa, ON K1S 1C4, Canada. Offers canon law (MCL, JCD, PhD, Graduate Certificate, JCL); canonical practice (Graduate Certificate); ecclesiastical administration (Graduate Certificate). Part-time programs available. *Degree requirements:* For master's, one foreign language; for doctorate, one foreign language, comprehensive exam, thesis/dissertation; for other advanced degree, one foreign language, comprehensive exam (for some programs), comprehensive exam and seminar paper (JCL). *Entrance requirements:* For master's, appropriate bachelor's degree, 18 credits in theology; for doctorate, JCL or MCL; for other advanced degree, B Th or equivalent (JCL), appropriate bachelor's degree, 18 credits in theology. *Faculty research:* All questions related to Church law.

Saint Paul University, Faculty of Human Sciences, Program in Counseling and Spirituality, Ottawa, ON K1S 1C4, Canada. Offers individual or marital/couple counseling (MA); spiritual care (MA). Part-time programs available. *Degree requirements:* For master's, research project or thesis. *Entrance requirements:* For master's, honors BA in human sciences, minimum B average, 12 theology credits.

St. Petersburg Theological Seminary, Graduate Programs, St. Petersburg, FL 33708. Offers Biblical studies (MA); counseling (MA); divinity (M Div); education (MA); Judaic studies (MA); ministry (MA, D Min); religious teacher (MA). Part-time and evening/weekend programs available. Postbaccalaureate distance learning degree programs offered (minimal on-campus study). *Degree requirements:* For master's, thesis; for doctorate, thesis/dissertation. *Entrance requirements:* For M Div and master's, Bachelor degree; for doctorate, Master degree. Electronic applications accepted.

Saints Cyril and Methodius Seminary, Graduate and Professional Programs, Orchard Lake, MI 48324. Offers pastoral ministry (MAPM); religious education (MARE); theology (M Div, MA). *Accreditation:* ATS. Part-time programs available.

St. Stephen's College, Programs in Theology, Edmonton, AB T6G 2J6, Canada. Offers ministry (D Min); pastoral counseling (MA); social transformation ministry (MA); spirituality and liturgy (MA); theological studies (MTS); theology (M Th). Part-time and evening/weekend programs available. Postbaccalaureate distance learning degree programs offered (minimal on-campus study). Terminal master's awarded for partial completion of doctoral program. *Degree requirements:* For master's, thesis; for doctorate, thesis/dissertation. *Entrance requirements:* Additional exam requirements/recommendations for international students: Required—TOEFL. Electronic applications accepted. *Faculty research:* Methodology for theological education, practice and supervision for ministry.

St. Thomas University, School of Theology and Ministry, Institute for Pastoral Ministries, Miami Gardens, FL 33054-6459. Offers pastoral ministries (MA, Certificate); practical theology (PhD). Part-time and evening/weekend programs available. *Degree requirements:* For master's, comprehensive exam; for doctorate, comprehensive exam, thesis/dissertation. *Entrance requirements:* For master's, interview, minimum GPA of 3.0 or GRE; for doctorate, GRE, MA in theology. Additional exam requirements/recommendations for international students: Required—TOEFL (minimum score 550 paper-based; 213 computer-based; 79 iBT). Electronic applications accepted.

Santa Clara University, School of Education, Counseling Psychology, and Pastoral Ministries, Program in Pastoral Ministries, Program in Pastoral Liturgy, Santa Clara, CA 95053. Offers MA. Part-time and evening/weekend programs available. *Students:* 4 part-time (0 women); includes 1 minority (Hispanic American), 1 international. Average age 48. In 2008, 3 master's awarded. *Degree requirements:* For master's, comprehensive exam, thesis. *Entrance requirements:* Additional exam requirements/recommendations for international students: Required—TOEFL. *Application deadline:* Applications are processed on a rolling basis. *Expenses:* Contact institution. *Financial support:* Application deadline: 3/1; *Unit head:* Fr. Tom Powers, S.J., Director, 408-554-4322. *Application contact:* Fr. Tom Powers, S.J., Director, 408-554-4322.

Seattle University, School of Theology and Ministry, Program in Pastoral Counseling, Seattle, WA 98122-1090. Offers MA.

Seattle University, School of Theology and Ministry, Program in Pastoral Studies, Seattle, WA 98122-1090. Offers MAPS. Part-time and evening/weekend programs available. *Degree requirements:* For master's, project. *Entrance requirements:* For master's, interview, minimum GPA of 2.75, 2 years of experience in field.

Seminary of the Immaculate Conception, School of Theology, Huntington, NY 11743-1696. Offers pastoral studies (MA); theology (M Div, MA, D Min, Certificate). *Accreditation:* ATS (one or more programs are accredited). Part-time and evening/weekend programs available. *Degree requirements:* For master's, comprehensive exam; for doctorate, thesis/dissertation; for M Div, one foreign language, thesis/dissertation. *Entrance requirements:* For M Div, college degree in philosophy-theology; for master's, undergraduate degree; for doctorate, MA plus 30 credits or M Div; for Certificate, MA in theology.

Seminary of the Southwest, Graduate and Professional Programs, Austin, TX 78768-2247. Offers Anglican studies (Advanced Diploma); chaplaincy (MCPC); counseling (MAC); divinity (M Div); religion (MAR); spiritual formation (MAPM); theological studies (Advanced Diploma). *Accreditation:* ACIPE; ATS (one or more programs are accredited). Part-time and evening/weekend programs available. *Faculty:* 10 full-time (3 women), 31 part-time/adjunct (11 women). *Students:* 46 full-time (29 women), 31 part-time (23 women); includes 7 minority (4 African Americans, 1 Asian American or Pacific Islander, 2 Hispanic Americans), 2 international. Average age 46. 28 applicants, 96% accepted, 22 enrolled. In 2008, 23 first professional degrees, 13 master's, 5 other advanced degrees awarded. *Degree requirements:* For master's, thesis (for some programs). *Entrance requirements:* For M Div and master's, GRE, MAT, interview; for Advanced Diploma, interview. *Application deadline:* For fall admission, 7/1 for domestic students; for spring admission, 11/1 for domestic students. Applications are processed on a rolling basis. Application fee: $50. *Expenses:* Tuition: Full-time $13,150; part-time $390 per credit hour. One-time fee: $75 full-time; $20 part-time. *Financial support:* Career-related internships or fieldwork and scholarships/grants available. Support available to part-time students. Financial award application deadline: 6/17. *Unit head:* Very Rev. Douglas Travis, Dean and President, 512-472-4133 Ext. 307, Fax: 512-472-3098, E-mail: dtravis@ssw.edu. *Application contact:* Jennielle Strother, Director of Admissions, 512-472-4133 Ext. 375, Fax: 512-472-3098, E-mail: jstrother@ssw.edu.

Seton Hall University, Immaculate Conception Seminary School of Theology, South Orange, NJ 07079-2697. Offers pastoral ministry (M Div, MA); theology (MA). *Accreditation:* ACIPE; ATS (one or more programs are accredited). Part-time and evening/weekend programs available. *Degree requirements:* For master's, one foreign language, comprehensive exam, thesis, final project; for M Div, final project and seminar, field education, spiritual formation. *Entrance requirements:* For M Div, GRE, MAT; for master's, GRE General Test or MAT. Electronic applications accepted. *Expenses:* Contact institution.

Shasta Bible College, Program in Biblical Counseling, Redding, CA 96002. Offers biblical counseling and Christian family life education (MA). Part-time programs available. *Degree requirements:* For master's, comprehensive exam (for some programs), thesis or alternative. *Entrance requirements:* For master's, minimum GPA of 2.5. Additional exam requirements/recommendations for international students: Required—TOEFL (minimum score 550 paper-based; 213 computer-based).

Shasta Bible College, Program in Christian Ministry, Redding, CA 96002. Offers MA. Part-time programs available. Postbaccalaureate distance learning degree programs offered (minimal on-campus study). *Entrance requirements:* Additional exam requirements/recommendations for international students: Required—TOEFL (minimum score 550 paper-based; 213 computer-based).

Simpson University, A.W. Tozer Theological Seminary, Redding, CA 96003-8606. Offers Christian leadership (MA); Christian studies (MA); intercultural studies (MA); ministry (M Div). Part-time and evening/weekend programs available. Postbaccalaureate distance learning degree programs offered (minimal on-campus study). *Degree requirements:* For master's, student portfolio. *Entrance requirements:* For master's, GRE General Test (if undergraduate GPA is below 2.5), 2 letters of reference, Christian Experience statement. Additional exam requirements/recommendations for international students: Required—TOEFL. Electronic applications accepted. *Expenses:* Contact institution.

Sioux Falls Seminary, Graduate and Professional Programs, Professional Program in Pastoral Ministry, Sioux Falls, SD 57105-1599. Offers M Div. *Accreditation:* ACIPE. Part-time programs available. *Entrance requirements:* Minimum GPA of 2.5.

Sioux Falls Seminary, Graduate and Professional Programs, Program in Counseling, Sioux Falls, SD 57105-1599. Offers MA. Part-time programs available. *Entrance requirements:* For master's, minimum GPA of 2.5.

Southern Baptist Theological Seminary, Billy Graham School of Missions, Evangelism and Church Growth, Louisville, KY 40280-0004. Offers Christian mission/world religion (PhD); evangelism/church growth (PhD); ministry (D Min); missiology (MA, D Miss); missions, evangelism and church growth (M Div); religion (Th M); theological studies (MA). *Accreditation:* ATS. Part-time and evening/weekend programs available. Postbaccalaureate distance learning degree programs offered (minimal on-campus study). *Degree requirements:* For master's and M Div, 2 foreign languages; for doctorate, 4 foreign languages, thesis/dissertation. *Entrance requirements:* For doctorate, GRE General Test, MAT, field essay, M Div. Additional exam requirements/recommendations for international students: Required—TOEFL, TWE. *Faculty research:* Assimilation of church congregants, effective methodologies of evangelism, expectations of church members, spiritual warfare literature, formative church discipline.

Southern Baptist Theological Seminary, School of Leadership and Church Ministry, Louisville, KY 40280-0004. Offers advanced youth ministry (M Div); Christian education (M Div, MACE); leadership (Ed D); leadership and church ministry (PhD); ministry (D Ed Min); women's leadership (M Div); youth ministry (M Div, MAYM). Part-time programs available. Postbaccalaureate distance learning degree programs offered (minimal on-campus study). *Degree requirements:* For doctorate, thesis/dissertation; for M Div, 2 foreign languages. *Entrance requirements:* For doctorate, GRE General Test, field essay, interview, M Div or MACE. Additional exam requirements/recommendations for international students: Required—TWE. *Faculty research:* Gerontology, creative teaching methods, faith development in children, faith development in youth, transformational learning.

Southern Baptist Theological Seminary, School of Theology, Louisville, KY 40280-0004. Offers biblical and theological studies (M Div); biblical counseling (M Div, MA, D Min); biblical spirituality (D Min); Christian ministry (M Div); expository preaching (D Min); pastoral studies (M Div); theological studies (MA); theology (Th M, PhD); theology and arts (MA); theology and law (MA); worldview and apologetics (M Div). *Accreditation:* ATS. Part-time and evening/weekend programs available. Postbaccalaureate distance learning degree programs offered (minimal on-campus study). *Degree requirements:* For master's, 2 foreign languages, thesis; for doctorate, 4 foreign languages, thesis/dissertation; for M Div, 2 foreign languages. *Entrance requirements:* For master's, GRE General Test, MAT, M Div; for doctorate, GRE General Test, MAT, interview, M Div, field essay. Additional exam requirements/recommendations for international students: Required—TOEFL, TWE. *Faculty research:* Biblical studies, contemporary theology, church history, pastoral care, ministry/missions studies.

Southern Evangelical Seminary, Graduate School of Ministry and Missions, Matthews, NC 28105. Offers apologetics (Certificate); Christian education (MA); church ministry (MA, Certificate); divinity (Certificate), including apologetics (M Div, Certificate); Islamic studies (Certificate); theology (M Div), including apologetics (M Div, Certificate), Biblical studies; youth ministry (MA). Part-time and evening/weekend programs available. Postbaccalaureate distance learning degree programs offered. *Degree requirements:* For master's, thesis (for some programs); for M Div, one foreign language. *Entrance requirements:* Additional exam requirements/recommendations for international students: Required—TOEFL (minimum score 600 paper-based; 250 computer-based).

Southern Wesleyan University, Program in Christian Ministries, Central, SC 29630-1020. Offers M Min. Evening/weekend programs available. *Degree requirements:* For master's, paper. *Entrance requirements:* For master's, GRE General Test or MAT.

Southwestern Assemblies of God University, Thomas F. Harrison School of Graduate Studies, Program in Theological Studies, Waxahachie, TX 75165-5735. Offers Bible and theology (MS); Biblical studies (M Div); counseling (M Div); cross cultural missions (M Div); practical theology (M Div); theological studies (M Div). Postbaccalaureate distance learning degree programs offered. *Degree requirements:* For master's, comprehensive written and oral exams. *Entrance requirements:* For master's, GRE General Test, minimum GPA of 2.5. Electronic applications accepted.

Southwestern Christian University, Program in Ministry, Bethany, OK 73008-0340. Offers church planting (M Min); church revitalization and renewal (M Min); intercultural studies (M Min); leadership (M Min); life coaching (M Min); pastoral ministries (M Min); work place ministries (M Min). Part-time programs available. *Degree requirements:* For master's, thesis. *Entrance requirements:* For master's, minimum GPA of 2.5. Additional exam requirements/recommendations for international students: Required—TOEFL (minimum score 500 paper-based). Electronic applications accepted.

Southwestern College, Fifth-Year Graduate Programs, Winfield, KS 67156-2499. Offers leadership (MS); management (MBA); specialized ministries (MA). Part-time programs available. *Faculty:* 9 part-time/adjunct (4 women). *Students:* 20 full-time (7 women), 12 part-time (5 women); includes 10 minority (7 African Americans, 1 American Indian/Alaska Native, 2 Hispanic Americans), 1 international. Average age 24. 33 applicants, 94% accepted, 28 enrolled. In 2008, 15 master's awarded. *Degree requirements:* For master's, practicum (MS). *Entrance requirements:* For master's, baccalaureate degree, minimum GPA of 3.0. Additional exam requirements/recommendations for international students: Required—TOEFL (minimum score 550 paper-based). *Application deadline:* For fall admission, 8/24 priority date for domestic students; for spring admission, 12/1 priority date for domestic students. Applications are processed on a rolling basis. Application fee: $25. Electronic applications accepted. *Expenses:*

Pastoral Ministry and Counseling

Southwestern College (continued)
Tuition: Full-time $6970; part-time $387 per credit. Tuition and fees vary according to class time, course load, campus/location and program. *Financial support:* In 2008–09, 27 students received support. Federal Work-Study, tuition waivers (partial), and unspecified assistantships available. Financial award application deadline: 4/1; financial award applicants required to submit FAFSA. *Unit head:* Dr. James Sheppard, Vice President for Academic Affairs, 620-229-6227, Fax: 620-229-6224, E-mail: james.sheppard@sckans.edu. *Application contact:* Marla Sexson, Director of Admissions, 800-846-1543 Ext. 6364, Fax: 620-229-6344, E-mail: marla.sexson@sckans.edu.

Spring Arbor University, School of Arts and Sciences, Spring Arbor, MI 49283-9799. Offers communication (MA); spiritual formation and leadership (MA). Part-time programs available. Postbaccalaureate distance learning degree programs offered (no on-campus study). *Faculty:* 6 full-time (1 woman), 11 part-time/adjunct (5 women). *Students:* 104 full-time (64 women), 38 part-time (24 women); includes 8 minority (7 African Americans, 1 Hispanic American), 1 international. Average age 42. In 2008, 3 master's awarded. *Degree requirements:* For master's, thesis (for some programs). *Entrance requirements:* For master's, GRE (taken within the last 5 years), writing sample, 3 recommendations, personal goals statement. Additional exam requirements/recommendations for international students: Required—TOEFL (minimum score 550 paper-based; 220 computer-based). Application fee: $40. *Expenses:* Contact institution. *Financial support:* Applicants required to submit FAFSA. *Unit head:* Dr. Wally Metts, Chair of the Department of Communication, 517-750-1200 Ext. 1491, E-mail: wmetts@arbor.edu. *Application contact:* Dale Glinz, Lead Recruitment Specialist/Trainer, Graduate and Professional Studies, 517-750-6703, E-mail: dglinz@arbor.edu.

Trinity Baptist College, Graduate Programs, Jacksonville, FL 32221. Offers Bible (M Ed); Christian school administration (M Ed); classroom practices (M Ed); ministry (M Min); special education (M Ed). Postbaccalaureate distance learning degree programs offered. *Entrance requirements:* For master's, GRE (M Ed), 2 letters of recommendation; minimum GPA of 2.5 (M Min) or 3.0 (M Ed); computer proficiency.

Trinity Episcopal School for Ministry, Graduate Programs, Ambridge, PA 15003-2397. Offers Anglican studies (Diploma); basic Christian studies (Diploma); divinity (M Div); ministry (D Min); mission and evangelism (MAME, Diploma); religion (MAR); youth ministry (Diploma). *Accreditation:* ATS (one or more programs are accredited). Part-time programs available. *Degree requirements:* For master's, thesis optional; for doctorate, thesis/dissertation; for M Div, thesis/dissertation optional, Greek and Hebrew. *Entrance requirements:* Additional exam requirements/recommendations for international students: Required—TOEFL. *Faculty research:* Pauline Epistles, contemporary theology, history of Anglican liturgy, book of Ruth, biblical theology.

Trinity International University, Trinity Evangelical Divinity School, Deerfield, IL 60015-1284. Offers Biblical and Near Eastern archaeology and languages (MA); Christian studies (MA, Certificate); Christian thought (MA); church history (MA, Th M); congregational ministry: pastor-teacher (M Div); congregational ministry: team ministry (M Div); counseling ministries (MA); counseling psychology (MA); cross-cultural ministry (M Div); educational studies (PhD); evangelism (MA); history of Christianity in America (MA); intercultural studies (MA, PhD); leadership and ministry management (D Min); military chaplaincy (D Min); ministry (MA); mission and evangelism (Th M); missions and evangelism (D Min); New Testament (MA, Th M); Old Testament (Th M); Old Testament and Semitic languages (MA); pastoral care (M Div); pastoral care and counseling (D Min); pastoral counseling and psychology (Th M); pastoral theology (Th M); philosophy of religion (MA); preaching (D Min); religion (MA); research ministry (M Div); systematic theology (Th M); theological studies (PhD); urban ministry (MA). *Accreditation:* ATS (one or more programs are accredited). Part-time programs available. Postbaccalaureate distance learning degree programs offered (minimal on-campus study). *Degree requirements:* For master's, comprehensive exam, thesis, fieldwork; for doctorate, comprehensive exam (for some programs), thesis/dissertation; for M Div, 2 foreign languages, fieldwork; for Certificate, comprehensive exam, integrative papers. *Entrance requirements:* For M Div, GRE, MAT; for master's, GRE, MAT, minimum cumulative undergraduate GPA of 3.0; for doctorate, GRE, minimum cumulative graduate GPA of 3.2; for Certificate, GRE, MAT, minimum undergraduate GPA of 2.5. Additional exam requirements/recommendations for international students: Required—TOEFL (minimum score 580 paper-based; 237 computer-based), TWE (minimum score 4). Electronic applications accepted.

Trinity Western University, ACTS Seminaries, Langley, BC V2Y 1Y1, Canada. Offers Christian studies (MA); church ministries (MA); cross cultural ministries (MA); theology (M Div, M Th, MAMFT, MLE, MTS, D Min). *Accreditation:* ATS. Part-time programs available. *Degree requirements:* For master's, thesis (for some programs), internship. *Entrance requirements:* For master's, BA or equivalent; for doctorate, MDiv or equivalent. Additional exam requirements/recommendations for international students: Required—TOEFL. *Expenses:* Contact institution. *Faculty research:* Theology of leadership.

Tyndale University College & Seminary, Graduate Programs, Toronto, ON M2M 4B3, Canada. Offers Biblical studies (M Div); Christian foundations (MTS); Christian studies (Diploma); counseling (M Div); educational ministry (M Div); missions (M Div, Diploma); pastoral and Chinese ministry (M Div); pastoral ministry (M Div); Pentecostal studies (MTS); spiritual formation (M Div, Diploma); theological studies (M Div); theology (Th M); worship and liturgy (M Div, MTS); youth and family ministry (M Div). *Accreditation:* ATS. Part-time programs available. Postbaccalaureate distance learning degree programs offered (no on-campus study). *Degree requirements:* For M Div, one foreign language, thesis/dissertation optional. *Entrance requirements:* For M Div, master's, and Diploma, minimum C+ average in undergraduate course work. Additional exam requirements/recommendations for international students: Required—TOEFL (minimum score 570 paper-based; 230 computer-based), TWE (minimum score 5). Electronic applications accepted. *Faculty research:* Canadian church history, Chinese church history, Old Testament, counseling ministries (narrative therapy), world religions.

Union University, School of Christian Studies, Jackson, TN 38305-3697. Offers Christian studies (MCS); expository preaching (D Min).

United Theological Seminary of the Twin Cities, Graduate and Professional Programs, New Brighton, MN 55112-2598. Offers advanced theological studies (Diploma); justice and peace studies (M Div); leadership toward racial justice (MA, Certificate); Methodist studies (M Div, MA); ministry (D Min); ministry renewal and professional development (Certificate); pastoral care and counseling (M Div); religion and theology (MA); theological and religious studies (Certificate); theology and the arts (MA); urban ministry (MARL); women's studies: religion, theology and ministry (MA). *Accreditation:* ACIPE; ATS. Part-time and evening/weekend programs available. *Faculty:* 10 full-time (6 women), 24 part-time/adjunct (12 women). *Students:* 60 full-time (34 women), 93 part-time (60 women); includes 10 minority (5 African Americans, 1 American Indian/Alaska Native, 3 Asian Americans or Pacific Islanders, 1 Hispanic American), 1 international. Average age 47. 39 applicants, 100% accepted, 32 enrolled. In 2008, 21 first professional degrees, 9 master's awarded. *Degree requirements:* For master's, thesis; for doctorate, comprehensive exam, thesis/dissertation; for M Div, integrative notebook, spiritual chronicle. *Entrance requirements:* For M Div and master's, minimum GPA of 2.75; strong analytical, reflective thinking and writing skills; vocational and academic goals compatible with those of Seminary; for doctorate, M Div or equivalent, minimum GPA of 3.0, 3 years experience in professional ministry; for other advanced degree, BA or equivalent life experience; strong analytical, reflective thinking and writing skills (Certificate); proficiency in English language, previous study of theology at a theological school, recommendation of student's denomination (Diploma). Additional exam requirements/recommendations for international students: Required—TOEFL (minimum score 550 paper-based). *Application deadline:* For fall admission, 7/1 priority date for domestic students, 11/1 priority date for international students; for winter admission, 11/1 priority date for domestic students; for spring admission, 11/15 priority date for domestic students. Applications are processed on a rolling basis. Application fee: $50. *Expenses:* Tuition: Full-time $11,070; part-time $410 per credit hour. Required fees: $295; $135 per term. One-time fee: $25. Tuition and fees vary according to course load, degree level and program. *Financial support:* In 2008–09, 98 students received support. Career-related internships or fieldwork, institutionally sponsored loans, and scholarships/grants available. Support available to part-time students. Financial award application deadline: 5/1; financial award applicants required to submit FAFSA. *Unit head:* Dr. Richard D. Weis, Dean of the Seminary, 651-255-6108 Ext. 108, Fax: 651-633-4315, E-mail: rweis@unitedseminary.edu. *Application contact:* Rev. Glen Herrington-Hall, Director of Admissions, 651-255-6107 Ext. 107, Fax: 651-633-4315, E-mail: gherrington-hall@unitedseminary.edu.

University of Dallas, Braniff Graduate School of Liberal Arts, Institute for Religious and Pastoral Studies, Irving, TX 75062-4736. Offers MCSL, MPM, MRE, MTS. *Accreditation:* ACIPE. Part-time and evening/weekend programs available. Postbaccalaureate distance learning degree programs offered (no on-campus study). *Faculty research:* Scripture, pastoral theology, ecclesiology, systematic theology, theological anthropology.

University of Dayton, Graduate School, College of Arts and Sciences, Department of Religious Studies, Dayton, OH 45469-1300. Offers pastoral ministry (MA); theological studies (MA); theology (PhD). Part-time and evening/weekend programs available. *Faculty:* 19 full-time (5 women), 5 part-time/adjunct (1 woman). *Students:* 49 full-time (21 women), 20 part-time (14 women); includes 2 minority (1 Asian American or Pacific Islander, 1 Hispanic American), 2 international. Average age 32. 61 applicants, 72% accepted, 23 enrolled. In 2008, 13 master's, 1 doctorate awarded. Terminal master's awarded for partial completion of doctoral program. *Degree requirements:* For master's, thesis or alternative; for doctorate, 2 foreign languages, comprehensive exam, thesis/dissertation. *Entrance requirements:* For master's, minimum undergraduate GPA of 3.0, 3 letters of recommendation, personal statement, official transcript(s); for doctorate, GRE General Test (minimum score of 600 on verbal), minimum GPA of 3.5, academic writing sample, 3 letters of recommendation, personal statement, official transcript(s). Additional exam requirements/recommendations for international students: Required—TOEFL (minimum score 550 paper-based; 213 computer-based; 80 iBT). *Application deadline:* For fall admission, 3/1 priority date for domestic and international students; for winter admission, 7/1 priority date for international students; for spring admission, 1/1 priority date for international students. Applications are processed on a rolling basis. Application fee: $0 ($50 for international students). Electronic applications accepted. *Expenses:* Contact institution. *Financial support:* In 2008–09, 28 students received support, including 4 fellowships with full tuition reimbursements available (averaging $15,814 per year), 8 research assistantships with full tuition reimbursements available (averaging $9,457 per year), 16 teaching assistantships with full tuition reimbursements available (averaging $15,814 per year); career-related internships or fieldwork, institutionally sponsored loans, scholarships/grants, health care benefits, tuition waivers (full), and unspecified assistantships also available. Support available to part-time students. Financial award application deadline: 3/1; financial award applicants required to submit FAFSA. *Faculty research:* Practical/constructive theology, theological ethics, U.S. Catholic/Christian life and thought, methodologies in Biblical studies, religion and science. *Unit head:* Dr. Sandra Yocum, Chair, 937-229-4321, Fax: 937-229-4330, E-mail: sandra.yocum@notes.udayton.edu. *Application contact:* Angela Jones-Glukhov, Associate Director of Graduate Admissions, 937-229-4305, Fax: 937-229-4729, E-mail: jonesgas@notes.udayton.edu.

University of Portland, Graduate School, College of Arts and Sciences, Department of Theology, Portland, OR 97203-5798. Offers pastoral ministry (MA). *Students:* 20 part-time (12 women); includes 4 Asian Americans or Pacific Islanders, 2 Hispanic Americans. Average age 50. In 2008, 6 master's awarded. *Entrance requirements:* For master's, GRE or MAT, 3 letters of recommendation, minimum GPA of 3.0, statement of goals, official transcripts. Additional exam requirements/recommendations for international students: Required—TOEFL (minimum score 550 paper-based; 80 iBT), IELTS (minimum score 7). *Application deadline:* For fall admission, 7/15 priority date for domestic and international students. Application fee: $45. *Expenses:* Tuition: Full-time $7380; part-time $8.20 per credit hour. *Financial support:* Federal Work-Study and scholarships/grants available. Financial award application deadline: 3/1; financial award applicants required to submit FAFSA. *Unit head:* Dr. Matt Baasten, Head, 503-943-7160. *Application contact:* Dr. Mary Labarre, Director, 503-943-7365, E-mail: labarre@up.edu.

University of Puget Sound, Graduate Studies, School of Education, Program in Counseling, Tacoma, WA 98416. Offers mental health counseling (M Ed); pastoral counseling (M Ed); school counseling (M Ed). *Accreditation:* NCATE. Part-time and evening/weekend programs available. *Faculty:* 2 full-time (both women), 1 (woman) part-time/adjunct. *Students:* 1 (woman) full-time, 23 part-time (17 women); includes 1 minority (Hispanic American). Average age 30. 27 applicants, 59% accepted, 11 enrolled. In 2008, 8 master's awarded. *Entrance requirements:* For master's, GRE General Test, minimum GPA of 3.0. Additional exam requirements/recommendations for international students: Required—TOEFL (minimum score 550 paper-based; 213 computer-based; 80 iBT). *Application deadline:* For fall admission, 3/1 priority date for domestic and international students. Applications are processed on a rolling basis. Application fee: $75. Electronic applications accepted. *Expenses:* Contact institution. *Financial support:* In 2008–09, 1 student received support, including 1 teaching assistantship with tuition reimbursement available (averaging $14,204 per year); career-related internships or fieldwork and tuition waivers (full) also available. Financial award application deadline: 3/31; financial award applicants required to submit FAFSA. *Faculty research:* Cross-role professional preparation, suicide prevention. *Unit head:* Dr. John Woodward, Dean, 253-879-3375, E-mail: woodward@pugetsound.edu. *Application contact:* Dr. George H. Mills, Vice President for Enrollment, 253-879-3211, Fax: 253-879-3993, E-mail: admission@pugetsound.edu.

University of Saint Francis, Graduate School, Department of Psychology and Counseling, Fort Wayne, IN 46808-3994. Offers general psychology (MS); mental health counseling (MS); pastoral counseling (MS); school counseling (MS Ed). Part-time and evening/weekend programs available. *Entrance requirements:* For master's, interview, minimum undergraduate GPA of 3.0.

University of St. Michael's College, Faculty of Theology, Toronto, ON M5S 1J4, Canada. Offers Catholic leadership (MA); eastern Christian studies (Certificate, Diploma); religious education (Diploma); theological studies (Diploma); theology (M Div, MA, MRE, MTS, D Min, PhD, Th D); theology and ecology (Certificate); theology and Jewish studies (MA). *Accreditation:* ATS (one or more programs are accredited). Part-time programs available. *Degree requirements:* For master's, thesis (for some programs), 1 foreign language (MA), 2 foreign languages (Th M); for doctorate, 3 foreign languages, comprehensive exam, thesis/dissertation; for M Div, thesis/dissertation optional; for other advanced degree, thesis optional. *Entrance requirements:* For M Div and other advanced degree, minimum GPA of 2.7; for master's, M Div or BA, course work in an ancient or modern language, minimum GPA of 3.3; for doctorate, MA in theology, Th M, or M Div with thesis, minimum GPA of 3.7. Additional exam requirements/recommendations for international students: Required—TOEFL (minimum score 600 paper-based; 250 computer-based). Electronic applications accepted. *Faculty research:* Patristics, eastern Christianity, ecology and theology, ecumenism, Jewish Christian studies.

University of St. Thomas, Graduate Studies, Saint Paul Seminary School of Divinity, Program in Theology/Pastoral Studies, St. Paul, MN 55105-1096. Offers religious education (MARE); theology (MA). *Accreditation:* ACIPE; ATS. Part-time and evening/weekend programs available. *Degree requirements:* For master's, one foreign language, comprehensive exam, thesis or alternative. *Entrance requirements:* For master's, GRE, interview, 3 letters of recommendation. Additional exam requirements/recommendations for international students: Required—TOEFL (minimum score 550 paper-based; 213 computer-based). Electronic applications accepted. *Expenses:* Contact institution. *Faculty research:* Theological education.

University of South Africa, College of Human Sciences, Pretoria, South Africa. Offers adult education (M Ed); African languages (MA, PhD); African politics (MA, PhD); Afrikaans (MA, PhD); ancient history (MA, PhD); ancient Near Eastern studies (MA, PhD); anthropology (MA, PhD); applied linguistics (MA); Arabic (MA, PhD); archaeology (MA); art history (MA); Biblical archaeology (MA); Biblical studies (M Th, D Th, PhD); Christian spirituality (M Th, D Th);

church history (M Th, D Th); classical studies (MA, PhD); clinical psychology (MA); communication (MA, PhD); comparative education (M Ed, Ed D); consulting psychology (D Admin, D Com, PhD); curriculum studies (M Ed, Ed D); development studies (M Admin, MA, D Admin, PhD); didactics (M Ed, Ed D); education (M Tech); education management (M Ed, Ed D); educational psychology (M Ed); English (MA); environmental education (M Ed); French (MA, PhD); German (MA, PhD); Greek (MA); guidance and counseling (M Ed); health studies (MA, PhD), including health sciences education (MA), health services management (MA), medical and surgical nursing science (critical care general) (MA), midwifery and neonatal nursing science (MA), trauma and emergency care (MA); history (MA, PhD); history of education (Ed D); inclusive education (M Ed, Ed D); information and communications technology policy and regulation (MA); information science (MA, MIS, PhD); international politics (MA, PhD); Islamic studies (MA, PhD); Italian (MA, PhD); Judaica (MA, PhD); linguistics (MA, PhD); mathematical education (M Ed); mathematics education (MA); missiology (M Th, D Th); modern Hebrew (MA, PhD); musicology (MA, MMus, D Mus, PhD); natural science education (M Ed); New Testament (M Th, D Th); Old Testament (D Th); pastoral therapy (M Th, D Th); philosophy (MA); philosophy of education (M Ed, Ed D); politics (MA, PhD); Portuguese (MA, PhD); practical theology (M Th, D Th); psychology (MA, MS, PhD); psychology of education (M Ed, Ed D); public health (MA); religious studies (MA, D Th, PhD); Romance languages (MA); Russian (MA, PhD); Semitic languages (MA, PhD); social behavior studies in HIV/AIDS (MA); social science (mental health) (MA); social science in development studies (MA); social science in psychology (MA); social science in social work (MA); social science in sociology (MA); social work (MSW, DSW, PhD); socio-education (M Ed, Ed D); sociolinguistics (MA); sociology (MA, PhD); Spanish (MA, PhD); systematic theology (M Th, D Th); TESOL (teaching English to speakers of other languages) (MA); theological ethics (M Th, D Th); theory of literature (MA, PhD); urban ministries (D Th); urban ministry (M Th).

University of Trinity College, Faculty of Divinity, Toronto, ON M5S 1H8, Canada. Offers ministry (Diploma); ministry for church musicians (Diploma); theology (M Div, MTS, Th M, D Min, PhD, Th D, Diploma, L Th); M Div/MA. *Accreditation:* ATS. Part-time programs available. *Faculty:* 4 full-time (1 woman), 34 part-time/adjunct (7 women). *Students:* 51 full-time (19 women), 72 part-time (35 women). Average age 45. *Degree requirements:* For master's, 2 foreign languages, thesis (for some programs); for doctorate, 3 foreign languages, comprehensive exam, thesis/dissertation; for M Div, thesis/dissertation optional; for other advanced degree, thesis (for some programs). *Entrance requirements:* For M Div, interview; for master's, 1 language (modern or ancient), interview; for doctorate, 2 languages (modern and ancient). Additional exam requirements/recommendations for international students: Required—TOEFL, TWE. *Application deadline:* For fall admission, 3/31 priority date for domestic and international students; for winter admission, 12/31 for domestic and international students; for spring admission, 4/30 priority date for domestic and international students. Applications are processed on a rolling basis. *Application fee:* $0. Tuition and fees charges are reported in Canadian dollars. *Expenses:* Tuition: Full-time $5669 Canadian dollars; part-time $1889 Canadian dollars per course. Required fees: $400 Canadian dollars; $50 Canadian dollars per semester. Tuition and fees vary according to degree level. *Financial support:* Fellowships, teaching assistantships, career-related internships or fieldwork, institutionally sponsored loans, and bursaries available. Support available to part-time students. Financial award application deadline: 5/15. *Faculty research:* Interreligious dialogue, feminist theology, systematic theology, philosophy of religion, pastoral theology. *Unit head:* Dr. David Neelands, Dean, 416-978-7750, Fax: 416-978-4949, E-mail: divdean@trinity.utoronto.ca. *Application contact:* Rachel Richards, Administrative Assistant to the Dean, 416-978-2133, Fax: 416-978-4949, E-mail: divinity@trinity.utoronto.ca.

Warner Pacific College, Graduate Programs, Portland, OR 97215-4099. Offers biblical and theological studies (MA); biblical studies (M Rel); education (M Ed); management/organizational leadership (MS); pastoral ministries (M Rel); religion and ethics (M Rel); teaching (MA); theology (M Rel). Part-time programs available. *Degree requirements:* For master's, thesis or alternative, Presentation of Defense. *Entrance requirements:* For master's, interview, minimum GPA of 2.5, letters of recommendations. *Faculty research:* New Testament studies, nineteenth-century Wesleyan theology, preaching and church growth, Christian ethics.

Wayland Baptist University, Graduate Programs, Programs in Religion, Plainview, TX 79072-6998. Offers Christian ministry (MCM); religion (MA). Part-time and evening/weekend programs available. Postbaccalaureate distance learning degree programs offered (no on-campus study). *Faculty:* 6 full-time (1 woman), 1 part-time/adjunct (0 women). *Students:* 12 part-time (5 women); includes 3 minority (all African Americans). Average age 38. 10 applicants, 100% accepted, 2 enrolled. In 2008, 1 master's awarded. *Degree requirements:* For master's, comprehensive exam. *Entrance requirements:* For master's, GRE or MAT. Additional exam requirements/recommendations for international students: Required—TOEFL (minimum score 500 paper-based; 173 computer-based; 61 iBT). *Application deadline:* Applications are processed on a rolling basis. Application fee: $50. *Expenses:* Tuition: Full-time $310; part-time $310 per credit hour. Required fees: $782; $9 per credit hour. $60 per semester. *Financial support:* Federal Work-Study, institutionally sponsored loans, and scholarships/grants available. Support available to part-time students. Financial award application deadline: 5/1; financial award applicants required to submit FAFSA. *Unit head:* Dr. Paul Sadler, Chairman, 806-291-1160,

Fax: 806-291-1969, E-mail: sadlerp@wbu.edu. *Application contact:* Amanda Stanton, Graduate Studies, 806-291-3414, Fax: 806-291-1950, E-mail: stanton@wbu.edu.

Wesley Biblical Seminary, Graduate Programs, Jackson, MS 39206. Offers Biblical literature (MA); Christian studies (MA); evangelism (M Div); family life ministry (M Div); honors research (M Div); missions (M Div); pastoral ministry (M Div); teaching (M Div); theology (MA). *Accreditation:* ATS. Part-time programs available. *Degree requirements:* For master's, thesis. *Entrance requirements:* Additional exam requirements/recommendations for international students: Required—TOEFL. Electronic applications accepted. *Faculty research:* Patristics, missiology, culture, hermeneutics.

Western Seminary, Graduate Programs, Program in Counseling, Portland, OR 97215-3367. Offers counseling (MA, Certificate); pastoral counseling (M Div); M Div/MA. Part-time programs available. *Degree requirements:* For master's, practicum; for M Div, 2 foreign languages, practicum. *Expenses:* Contact institution.

Western Seminary, Graduate Programs, Program in Intercultural Studies, Portland, OR 97215-3367. Offers MA, D Miss, Certificate, G Dip. Part-time programs available. *Degree requirements:* For master's, practicum; for doctorate, 2 foreign languages, thesis/dissertation.

Western Seminary, Graduate Programs, Program in Specialized Ministry, Portland, OR 97215-3367. Offers children / youth at risk (MA); coaching (MA); evangelism and equipping (MA); pastoral care to women (MA); youth and family ministry (MA); youth ministry (MA). *Degree requirements:* For master's, practicum.

Western Seminary–Sacramento Campus, Graduate Programs, Sacramento, CA 95821. Offers exegetical theology (MA); marital and family therapy (MA); ministry (M Div); specialized ministry (MA). Postbaccalaureate distance learning degree programs offered. *Entrance requirements:* For M Div, minimum GPA of 2.5; for master's, minimum GPA of 3.0.

Western Seminary–San Jose Campus, Graduate Programs, Los Gatos, CA 95032-4520. Offers exegetical theology (MA); expositional ministry (M Div); marital and family therapy (MA); ministry (M Div); pastoral ministry (M Div); specialized ministry (MA). Postbaccalaureate distance learning degree programs offered. *Degree requirements:* For master's, 2 foreign languages; for M Div, 3 foreign languages. *Entrance requirements:* For M Div, minimum GPA of 2.5; for master's, minimum GPA of 3.0.

Westminster Theological Seminary, Graduate and Professional Programs, Philadelphia, PA 19118. Offers apologetics (Th M); Biblical and urban studies (Certificate); Biblical counseling (MA); biblical studies (MAR); Christian studies (Certificate); church history (Th M); counseling (M Div); general studies (M Div, MAR); hermeneutics and Bible interpretations (PhD); historical and theological studies (PhD); historical theology (Th M); New Testament (Th M); Old Testament (Th M); pastoral counseling (D Min); pastoral ministry (M Div, D Min); systematic theology (Th M); theological studies (MAR); urban missions (M Div, MA, MAR, D Min). *Accreditation:* ATS. Part-time programs available. Terminal master's awarded for partial completion of doctoral program. *Degree requirements:* For master's, thesis (for some programs); for doctorate, 4 foreign languages, comprehensive exam (for some programs), thesis/dissertation; for M Div, 2 foreign languages. *Entrance requirements:* For doctorate, GRE General Test. Additional exam requirements/recommendations for international students: Required—TOEFL, TWE.

Wheaton College, Graduate School, Department of Psychology, Wheaton, IL 60187-5593. Offers clinical psychology (MA, Psy D); counseling ministries (MA). *Accreditation:* APA (one or more programs are accredited). Terminal master's awarded for partial completion of doctoral program. *Degree requirements:* For master's, thesis or alternative; for doctorate, thesis/dissertation, internship. *Entrance requirements:* For master's, GRE General Test, 18 hours of course work in psychology; for doctorate, GRE General Test.

Wilfrid Laurier University, Waterloo Lutheran Seminary, Waterloo, ON N2L 3C5, Canada. Offers Christian ethics (M Th); divinity (M Div); homiletics (M Th); ministry (D Min); pastoral counseling (M Th); spirituality in a health care setting (Diploma); theological studies (MTS); theology (Diploma); M Div/MTS/MSW. *Accreditation:* ATS. Part-time programs available. *Degree requirements:* For master's, one foreign language, thesis (for some programs); for doctorate, thesis/dissertation; for M Div, one foreign language, thesis/dissertation. *Entrance requirements:* For M Div, denominational endorsement; for master's, M Div, 2 units of clinical pastoral education (M Th); for doctorate, M Div, 3 years of ministry experience, proficiency in a foreign language, basic training in clinical pastoral education. Additional exam requirements/recommendations for international students: Required—TOEFL (minimum score 573 paper-based; 230 computer-based; 89 iBT), IELTS (minimum score 7). Electronic applications accepted. *Expenses:* Contact institution. *Faculty research:* Biblical study, church history, systematic theology.

Xavier University of Louisiana, Graduate School, Institute for Black Catholic Studies, New Orleans, LA 70125-1098. Offers pastoral theology (Th M). Part-time programs available. *Degree requirements:* For master's, comprehensive exam, practicum. *Entrance requirements:* For master's, GRE General Test, MAT, minimum GPA of 2.5. Additional exam requirements/recommendations for international students: Required—TOEFL.

Religion

Amridge University, Graduate and Professional Programs, Montgomery, AL 36117. Offers behavioral leadership and management (MA); biblical studies (MA, PhD); family therapy (D Min); leadership and management (MS); marriage and family therapy (M Div, MA, PhD), including marriage and family therapy (PhD), professional counseling (PhD); ministerial leadership (M Div, MS); pastoral counseling (M Div, MS); practical theology (MA); professional counseling (M Div, MA); theology (M Div, D Min). *Accreditation:* ATS. Part-time and evening/weekend programs available. Postbaccalaureate distance learning degree programs offered (no on-campus study). *Faculty:* 44 full-time (9 women), 18 part-time/adjunct (7 women). *Students:* 131 full-time (61 women), 218 part-time (119 women); includes 174 minority (164 African Americans, 1 American Indian/Alaska Native, 1 Asian American or Pacific Islander, 8 Hispanic Americans). Average age 35. *Degree requirements:* For master's, one foreign language, comprehensive exam (for some programs), thesis (for some programs); for doctorate, comprehensive exam (for some programs), thesis/dissertation; for M Div, comprehensive exam (for some programs). *Entrance requirements:* For M Div, master's, and doctorate, GRE General Test or MAT. Additional exam requirements/recommendations for international students: Required—TOEFL. *Application deadline:* For fall admission, 9/1 priority date for domestic students; for spring admission, 1/1 priority date for domestic students. Applications are processed on a rolling basis. Application fee: $75. Electronic applications accepted. *Expenses:* Tuition: Full-time $9630; part-time $535 per semester hour. Required fees: $600 per term. Tuition and fees vary according to course load and degree level. *Financial support:* Federal Work-Study and scholarships/grants available. Support available to part-time students. Financial award applicants required to submit FAFSA. *Faculty research:* Homiletics, hermeneutics, ancient Near Eastern history. *Unit head:* Rick Johnson, Director of Enrollment Management, 800-351-4040 Ext. 7513, Fax: 334-387-3878, E-mail: rickjohnson@amridgeuniversity.edu. *Application contact:* Ora Davis, Admissions Officer, 334-387-3877 Ext. 7524, Fax: 334-387-3878, E-mail: oradavis@amridgeuniversity.edu.

Arizona State University, Graduate College, College of Liberal Arts and Sciences, Division of Humanities, Department of Religious Studies, Tempe, AZ 85287. Offers MA, PhD. *Degree requirements:* For master's, thesis or alternative. *Entrance requirements:* For master's, GRE.

Azusa Pacific University, Haggard School of Theology, Program in Christian Education, Azusa, CA 91702-7000. Offers MAR.

Baptist Bible College of Pennsylvania, Baptist Bible Seminary, Clarks Summit, PA 18411-1297. Offers biblical studies (PhD); church planting (M Div); global missions (M Div); military chaplaincy (M Div); ministry (M Min, D Min); pastor of church education (M Div); pastor of outreach (M Div); pastoral counseling (M Div); pastoral leadership (M Div); theology (M Div, Th M); youth pastor (M Div). Part-time and evening/weekend programs available. Postbaccalaureate distance learning degree programs offered (minimal on-campus study). Terminal master's awarded for partial completion of doctoral program. *Degree requirements:* For master's, 2 foreign languages, thesis; for doctorate, 2 foreign languages, comprehensive exam (for some programs), thesis/dissertation, oral exam; for M Div, 2 foreign languages, thesis/dissertation, oral exam. *Entrance requirements:* For doctorate, Greek and Hebrew entrance exams (PhD). Electronic applications accepted.

Baylor University, Graduate School, College of Arts and Sciences, Department of Religion, Waco, TX 76798. Offers MA, PhD. *Students:* 53 full-time (7 women), 7 part-time (3 women); includes 5 minority (1 American Indian/Alaska Native, 1 Asian American or Pacific Islander, 3 Hispanic Americans), 7 international. In 2008, 1 master's, 7 doctorates awarded. Terminal master's awarded for partial completion of doctoral program. *Degree requirements:* For master's, one foreign language, thesis; for doctorate, 2 foreign languages, thesis/dissertation. *Entrance requirements:* For master's and doctorate, GRE General Test. *Application deadline:* Applications are processed on a rolling basis. Application fee: $25. *Financial support:* Fellowships, research assistantships, teaching assistantships, Federal Work-Study, institutionally sponsored loans, and scholarships/grants available. *Unit head:* Dr. Bill Pitts, Graduate Program Director,

Religion

Baylor University (continued)
254-710-6321, Fax: 254-710-3740, E-mail: william_pitts@baylor.edu. *Application contact:* Judy Mills, Administrative Assistant, 254-710-3742, Fax: 254-710-3870, E-mail: judy_mills@baylor.edu.

Baylor University, Graduate School, College of Arts and Sciences, J. M. Dawson Institute of Church-State Studies, Waco, TX 76798. Offers MA, PhD. *Students:* 34 full-time (11 women), 4 part-time (2 women); includes 6 minority (1 American Indian/Alaska Native, 2 Asian Americans or Pacific Islanders, 3 Hispanic Americans), 6 international. In 2008, 6 master's, 4 doctorates awarded. *Degree requirements:* For master's, thesis, oral exam; for doctorate, one foreign language, thesis/dissertation, preliminary exams. *Entrance requirements:* For master's, GRE General Test; for doctorate, GRE General Test, MA or equivalent. *Application deadline:* For fall admission, 3/1 for domestic students. Applications are processed on a rolling basis. Application fee: $25. *Financial support:* Fellowships, research assistantships, teaching assistantships, Federal Work-Study and institutionally sponsored loans available. Financial award application deadline: 3/1. *Faculty research:* Religion and politics, religion and public education, religious freedom and international politics, First Amendment jurisprudence. *Unit head:* Dr. Christopher Marsh, Graduate Program Director, 254-710-4412, Fax: 254-710-1571, E-mail: chris_marsh@baylor.edu. *Application contact:* Suzanne Seller, Administrative Assistant, 254-710-1510, Fax: 254-710-1571, E-mail: suzanne_sellers@baylor.edu.

Bellarmine University, Bellarmine College of Arts and Sciences, Louisville, KY 40205-0671. Offers spirituality (MA). *Entrance requirements:* For master's, minimum GPA of 2.8, letter of recommendation, spirituality autobiography. Additional exam requirements/recommendations for international students: Required—TOEFL (minimum score 550 paper-based; 213 computer-based; 80 iBT). *Expenses:* Contact institution.

Bethany Theological Seminary, Graduate and Professional Programs, Richmond, IN 47374-4019. Offers biblical studies (MA Th); ministry studies (M Div); peace studies (M Div, MA Th); theological studies (MA Th, CATS); youth ministry (M Div). *Accreditation:* ACIPE; ATS. Part-time programs available. Postbaccalaureate distance learning degree programs offered (minimal on-campus study). *Degree requirements:* For master's, thesis. *Entrance requirements:* For M Div, letters of reference, minimum GPA of 2.75; for master's, letters of reference, minimum GPA of 3.0. Additional exam requirements/recommendations for international students: Required—TOEFL (minimum score 550 paper-based; 218 computer-based).

Bethesda Christian University, Graduate and Professional Programs, Anaheim, CA 92801. Offers biblical studies (MA); music (MA); theology (M Div). *Entrance requirements:* For M Div and master's, interview.

Beulah Heights University, Graduate School, Atlanta, GA 30316. Offers biblical studies (MA); leadership studies (MA). *Entrance requirements:* Additional exam requirements/recommendations for international students: Required—TOEFL (minimum score 500 paper-based). Electronic applications accepted.

Biola University, Talbot School of Theology, La Mirada, CA 90639-0001. Offers Bible exposition (MA); biblical and theological studies (MA); Christian education (MACE); Christian ministry and leadership (MA); divinity (M Div); education (PhD); ministry (MA Min); New Testament (MA); Old Testament (MA); philosophy of religion and ethics (MA); spiritual formation (MA); spiritual formation and soul care (MA); theology (MA, Th M, D Min). *Accreditation:* ATS. Part-time and evening/weekend programs available. *Degree requirements:* For master's, variable foreign language requirement, thesis or alternative; for doctorate, variable foreign language requirement, thesis/dissertation; for M Div, thesis/dissertation or alternative. *Entrance requirements:* For M Div, minimum GPA of 2.6; for master's, minimum undergraduate GPA of 3.0; for doctorate, minimum GPA of 3.25. Additional exam requirements/recommendations for international students: Required—TOEFL (minimum score 550 paper-based; 213 computer-based). *Faculty research:* Moral development; biological, medical, and social ethics; ancient Near Eastern historical philosophy.

Bob Jones University, Graduate Programs, Greenville, SC 29614. Offers accountancy (MS); Bible (MA); Bible translation (MA); Biblical studies (Certificate); broadcast management (MS); business administration (MBA); church history (MA, PhD); church ministries (MA); church music (MM); cinema and video production (MA); counseling (MS); curriculum and instruction (Ed D); divinity (M Div); dramatic production (MA); educational leadership (MS, Ed D, Ed S); elementary education (M Ed, MAT); English (M Ed, MA, MAT); fine arts (MA); graphic design (MA); history (M Ed, MA); illustration (MA); interpretative speech (MA); mathematics (M Ed, MAT); medical missions (Certificate); ministry (MM, D Min); multi-categorical special education (M Ed, MAT); music (M Ed); New Testament interpretation (PhD); Old Testament interpretation (PhD); orchestral instrument performance (MM); organ performance (MM); pastoral studies (MA); personnel services (MS, Ed S); piano pedagogy (MM); piano performance (MM); platform arts (MA); radio and television broadcasting (MS); rhetoric and public address (MA); secondary education (M Ed); studio art (MA); teaching Bible (MA); theology (MA, PhD); voice performance (MM); youth ministries (MA); M Div/MM.

Boston University, Graduate School of Arts and Sciences, Division of Religious and Theological Studies, Boston, MA 02215. Offers MA, PhD. Terminal master's awarded for partial completion of doctoral program. *Degree requirements:* For master's, one foreign language, comprehensive exam, thesis; for doctorate, 2 foreign languages, comprehensive exam, thesis/dissertation. *Entrance requirements:* For master's and doctorate, GRE General Test, 3 letters of recommendation, academic writing sample. Additional exam requirements/recommendations for international students: Required—TOEFL (minimum score 550 paper-based; 213 computer-based).

Briercrest Seminary, Graduate Programs, Program in Christian Ministries, Caronport, SK S0H 0S0, Canada. Offers leadership (MA); marriage and family counseling (MA); missions (MA); pastoral counseling (MA); worship (MA); youth and family ministry (MA). Part-time programs available. *Degree requirements:* For master's, comprehensive exam, thesis optional. *Entrance requirements:* Additional exam requirements/recommendations for international students: Required—TOEFL (minimum score 550 paper-based; 213 computer-based).

Briercrest Seminary, Graduate Programs, Program in Theology, Caronport, SK S0H 0S0, Canada. Offers Biblical studies (M Div); leadership and management (M Div); New Testament (MATS); Old Testament (MATS); pastoral counseling (M Div); pastoral ministry (M Div); theological studies (M Div); theology (MATS); worship (M Div); youth and family ministry (M Div). *Accreditation:* ATS. Part-time programs available. *Degree requirements:* For master's, comprehensive exam, thesis optional. *Entrance requirements:* Additional exam requirements/recommendations for international students: Required—TOEFL (minimum score 550 paper-based; 213 computer-based).

Brown University, Graduate School, Department of Religious Studies, Providence, RI 02912. Offers ancient Judaism (PhD); early Christianity (PhD); religion and critical thought (PhD); religion in the ancient Mediterranean (PhD); religion, culture, and comparison (PhD). *Degree requirements:* For doctorate, 2 foreign languages, thesis/dissertation. *Entrance requirements:* For doctorate, GRE General Test.

Bryn Athyn College of the New Church, Academy of the New Church Theological School, Bryn Athyn, PA 19009-0717. Offers divinity (M Div); religious studies (MA). Part-time programs available. Postbaccalaureate distance learning degree programs offered (minimal on-campus study). *Degree requirements:* For master's, thesis; for M Div, 3 foreign languages, thesis/dissertation. *Entrance requirements:* Additional exam requirements/recommendations for international students: Required—TOEFL.

California Institute of Integral Studies, Graduate Programs, School of Consciousness and Transformation, San Francisco, CA 94103. Offers cultural anthropology and social transformation (MA); East-West psychology (MA, PhD); integrative health studies (MA); philosophy and religion (MA, PhD), including Asian and comparative studies, philosophy, cosmology, and consciousness, women's spirituality, women's spirituality flex format; social and cultural anthropology (PhD); transformative leadership (MA); transformative studies (PhD). Part-time and evening/weekend programs available. Postbaccalaureate distance learning degree programs offered (minimal on-campus study). *Faculty:* 29 full-time, 32 part-time/adjunct. *Students:* 334 full-time (218 women), 126 part-time (77 women); includes 102 minority (39 African Americans, 4 American Indian/Alaska Native, 35 Asian Americans or Pacific Islanders, 24 Hispanic Americans), 1 international. Average age 37. 223 applicants, 78% accepted, 110 enrolled. In 2008, 93 master's, 30 doctorates awarded. Terminal master's awarded for partial completion of doctoral program. *Degree requirements:* For master's, comprehensive exam (for some programs), thesis optional; for doctorate, comprehensive exam, thesis/dissertation. *Entrance requirements:* For master's, minimum GPA of 3.0, letters of recommendation, writing sample; for doctorate, master's degree, minimum GPA of 3.0, letters of recommendation, writing sample. Additional exam requirements/recommendations for international students: Required—TOEFL. *Application deadline:* For fall admission, 2/1 priority date for domestic and international students; for spring admission, 10/15 priority date for domestic and international students. Applications are processed on a rolling basis. Application fee: $65. Electronic applications accepted. *Expenses:* Tuition: Part-time $815 per contact hour. Required fees: $270; $135 per semester. Tuition and fees vary according to degree level. *Financial support:* In 2008–09, 271 students received support; research assistantships, teaching assistantships, career-related internships or fieldwork, Federal Work-Study, institutionally sponsored loans, scholarships/grants, and tuition waivers (partial) available. Support available to part-time students. Financial award application deadline: 3/15; financial award applicants required to submit FAFSA. *Faculty research:* Altered states of consciousness, dreams, cosmology, postcolonial studies, integrative health studies. *Application contact:* Allyson Werner, Senior Admissions Counselor, 415-575-6155, Fax: 415-575-1268.

See Close-Up on page 347.

California State University, Long Beach, Graduate Studies, College of Liberal Arts, Department of Religious Studies, Long Beach, CA 90840. Offers MA. Part-time and evening/weekend programs available. *Faculty:* 4 full-time (1 woman). *Students:* 8 full-time (5 women), 15 part-time (6 women); includes 11 minority (1 African American, 1 Asian American or Pacific Islander, 9 Hispanic Americans). 13 applicants, 54% accepted, 7 enrolled. *Entrance requirements:* Additional exam requirements/recommendations for international students: Required—TOEFL. *Application deadline:* For fall admission, 3/15 for domestic students, 7/1 for international students; for spring admission, 12/1 for international students. Applications are processed on a rolling basis. Application fee: $55. Electronic applications accepted. *Expenses:* Tuition, nonresident: full-time $11,160; part-time $372 per unit. Required fees: $4100; $1261 per semester. *Financial support:* Application deadline: 3/2; *Unit head:* Dr. Carlos Piar, Chair, 562-985-5341, Fax: 562-985-5540, E-mail: crpiar@csulb.edu. *Application contact:* Dr. Carlos Piar, Graduate Advisor, 562-985-5341, Fax: 562-985-5540, E-mail: crpiar@csulb.edu.

Cardinal Stritch University, College of Arts and Sciences, Department of Religious Studies, Milwaukee, WI 53217-3985. Offers lay ministries (MA); ministry (MA); religious studies (MA). Part-time and evening/weekend programs available. *Degree requirements:* For master's, comprehensive exam, thesis, faculty recommendation, research project. *Entrance requirements:* For master's, interview, minimum GPA of 2.75.

The Catholic University of America, School of Arts and Sciences, Program in Early Christian Studies, Washington, DC 20064. Offers MA, PhD, Certificate. Part-time programs available. Terminal master's awarded for partial completion of doctoral program. *Degree requirements:* For master's, 2 foreign languages, comprehensive exam, thesis optional; for doctorate, 3 foreign languages, comprehensive exam, thesis/dissertation. *Entrance requirements:* For master's and doctorate, GRE General Test, 3 letters of recommendation. Additional exam requirements/recommendations for international students: Required—TOEFL (minimum score 580 paper-based; 237 computer-based). Electronic applications accepted. *Faculty research:* Greek, Latin, Semitic languages and civilization in late antiquity and early Middle Ages.

The Catholic University of America, School of Theology and Religious Studies, Washington, DC 20064. Offers M Div, STB, MA, MRE, D Min, PhD, STD, STL, MSLS/MA. *Accreditation:* ATS (one or more programs are accredited). Part-time programs available. Terminal master's awarded for partial completion of doctoral program. *Degree requirements:* For master's, comprehensive exam; for doctorate, comprehensive exam, thesis/dissertation; for first professional degree, one foreign language; for STL, one foreign language, comprehensive exam, thesis. *Entrance requirements:* For first professional degree and master's, GRE General Test, 3 letters of recommendation; for doctorate and STL, GRE, 3 letters of recommendation. Additional exam requirements/recommendations for international students: Required—TOEFL (minimum score 580 paper-based; 237 computer-based). Electronic applications accepted. *Faculty research:* Biblical studies, canon law, church history, liturgical studies, religion and religious education.

Chestnut Hill College, School of Graduate Studies, Department of Religious Studies and Philosophy, Philadelphia, PA 19118-2693. Offers holistic spirituality (MA); holistic spirituality and healthcare (MA); holistic spirituality and spiritual direction (MA); holistic spirituality/health care (CAS); spiritual direction (CAS); spirituality (CAS); supervision of spiritual directors (CAS). Part-time and evening/weekend programs available. *Faculty:* 5 full-time (4 women). *Students:* 23 part-time (22 women); includes 4 minority (all African Americans). Average age 51. 7 applicants, 29% accepted. In 2008, 7 master's awarded. *Degree requirements:* For master's, thesis optional, practicum (for spiritual direction and healthcare tracks). *Entrance requirements:* For master's, MAT or GRE, transcripts, letters of recommendation, statement of professional goals, writing sample. Additional exam requirements/recommendations for international students: Required—TOEFL (minimum score 500 paper-based; 213 computer-based). *Application deadline:* For fall admission, 7/17 priority date for domestic and international students; for spring admission, 12/15 priority date for domestic and international students. Applications are processed on a rolling basis. Application fee: $50. *Expenses:* Tuition: Part-time $510 per credit hour. *Faculty research:* Interfaith spiritual direction, supervisory issues for spiritual directors, ecclesial responsibility of reconciliation, globalization of the Magdalene laundry system, ethical issues at the end of life. *Unit head:* Dr. Marie Conn, Department Chair, 215-248-7044, Fax: 215-248-7155, E-mail: mconn@chc.edu. *Application contact:* Amy Boorse, Administrative Assistant, School of Graduate Studies Office, 215-248-7170, Fax: 215-248-7161, E-mail: gradadmissions@chc.edu.

Chicago Theological Seminary, Graduate and Professional Programs, Chicago, IL 60637-1507. Offers preaching (D Min); religion and health (D Min); religious studies (MA); spirituality and spiritual direction (D Min); theology (M Div); theology, ethics and the human sciences (PhD); M Div/MSW. *Accreditation:* ACIPE; ATS. Part-time programs available. *Faculty:* 13 full-time (5 women). *Students:* 71 full-time (32 women), 139 part-time (76 women); includes 54 minority (45 African Americans, 6 Asian Americans or Pacific Islanders, 3 Hispanic Americans), 33 international. *Degree requirements:* For master's, thesis; for doctorate, 2 foreign languages, comprehensive exam, thesis/dissertation; for M Div, thesis/dissertation. *Entrance requirements:* For doctorate, GRE General Test. Additional exam requirements/recommendations for international students: Required—TOEFL (minimum score 217 computer-based). *Application deadline:* For fall admission, 2/15 priority date for domestic and international students; for spring admission, 11/1 for domestic and international students. Application fee: $50. *Financial support:* Fellowships, institutionally sponsored loans, scholarships/grants, and tuition waivers (partial) available. Support available to part-time students. Financial award application deadline: 3/1; financial award applicants required to submit FAFSA. *Faculty research:* Bible, culture and hermeneutics, theology, gender and sexuality, black faith and life, spirituality and psychology, practical theology. Total annual research expenditures: $150,000. *Unit head:* Dr. Theodore W. Jennings, Acting Dean, 773-752-5757, Fax: 773-752-1903, E-mail: tjennings@ctschicago.edu. *Application contact:* Rev. Lin Sanford Keppert, Director of Admissions, Recruitment and Financial Aid, E-mail: lkeppert@ctschicago.edu.

Christian Brothers University, Graduate and Professional Studies, School of Arts, Memphis, TN 38104-5581. Offers Catholic studies (MACS); curriculum and instruction (M Ed); educational leadership (MSEL); teacher-leadership (M Ed); teaching (MAT). Part-time and evening/weekend programs available. *Faculty:* 6 full-time (5 women), 13 part-time/adjunct (7 women). *Students:* 45 full-time (35 women), 171 part-time (126 women); includes 66 minority (61 African Americans, 1 Asian American or Pacific Islander, 4 Hispanic Americans), 2 international. Average age 33. In 2008, 72 master's awarded. *Entrance requirements:* For master's, GRE, GMAT, Praxis II. *Application deadline:* Applications are processed on a rolling basis. Application fee: $25. *Expenses:* Contact institution. *Financial support:* Institutionally sponsored loans available. Support available to part-time students. *Unit head:* Dr. Marius Carriere, Dean, 901-321-3366, Fax: 901-321-4340, E-mail: mcarrier@cbu.edu. *Application contact:* Dr. Talana L. Vogel, Director, 901-321-4101, Fax: 901-321-3408, E-mail: tvogel@cbu.edu.

Christian Theological Seminary, Graduate and Professional Programs, Indianapolis, IN 46208-3301. Offers marriage and family (MA); pastoral care and counseling (D Min); practical theology (D Min); psychotherapy and faith (MA); sacred theology (STM); specialized ministries (MA); theological studies (MTS); theology (M Div). *Accreditation:* AAMFT/COAMFTE (one or more programs are accredited); ACIPE; ATS. Part-time programs available. Terminal master's awarded for partial completion of doctoral program. *Degree requirements:* For master's, comprehensive exam (for some programs), thesis (for some programs); for doctorate, comprehensive exam, thesis/dissertation; for M Div, comprehensive exam, thesis/dissertation (for some programs), missionary and cross-cultural experience. *Entrance requirements:* For master's, GRE General Test, MAT; for doctorate, M Div or BD. Electronic applications accepted. *Faculty research:* Faith formation, peer learning post graduation.

Cincinnati Christian University, Graduate School, Cincinnati, OH 45204-3200. Offers biblical studies (MA); church history (MA); counseling (MAC); divinity (M Div); ministry (M Min); practical ministries (MA); theological studies (MA). *Accreditation:* ATS. Part-time programs available. *Degree requirements:* For master's, thesis (for some programs); for M Div, 2 foreign languages, oral exam. *Entrance requirements:* For master's, GRE General Test. Additional exam requirements/recommendations for international students: Required—TOEFL. Electronic applications accepted.

Claremont Graduate University, Graduate Programs, School of Religion, Claremont, CA 91711-6160. Offers Hebrew Bible (MA, PhD); history of Christianity and religions of North America (MA, PhD); New Testament (MA, PhD); philosophy of religion and theology (MA, PhD); theology, ethics and culture (MA, PhD); women's studies in religion (MA, PhD); MA/PhD; MBA/PhD. Part-time programs available. *Faculty:* 7 full-time (2 women), 2 part-time/adjunct (0 women). *Students:* 231 full-time (96 women), 4 part-time (2 women); includes 32 minority (13 African Americans, 11 Asian Americans or Pacific Islanders, 8 Hispanic Americans), 29 international. Average age 37. In 2008, 13 master's, 16 doctorates awarded. Terminal master's awarded for partial completion of doctoral program. *Entrance requirements:* For master's and doctorate, GRE General Test. Additional exam requirements/recommendations for international students: Required—TOEFL (minimum score 550 paper-based; 213 computer-based; 80 iBT). *Application deadline:* For fall admission, 2/1 priority date for domestic students. Applications are processed on a rolling basis. Application fee: $60. Electronic applications accepted. *Expenses:* Tuition: Full-time $33,698; part-time $1465 per unit. Required fees: $310; $155 per semester. Tuition and fees vary according to program. *Financial support:* Fellowships, research assistantships, teaching assistantships, Federal Work-Study, institutionally sponsored loans, and scholarships/grants available. Support available to part-time students. Financial award application deadline: 2/15; financial award applicants required to submit FAFSA. *Unit head:* Karen Torjesen, Dean, 909-607-3214, Fax: 909-621-9587, E-mail: karen.torjesen@cgu.edu. *Application contact:* Brent Smith, Recruiter, 909-607-2653, Fax: 909-607-9587, E-mail: brent.smith@cgu.edu.

Claremont School of Theology, Graduate and Professional Programs, Program in Religion, Claremont, CA 91711-3199. Offers practical theology (PhD); religion and theology (MA); religious education (MARE). *Accreditation:* ACIPE; ATS. Terminal master's awarded for partial completion of doctoral program. *Degree requirements:* For master's, thesis; for doctorate, 2 foreign languages, thesis/dissertation. *Entrance requirements:* For doctorate, GRE General Test. Additional exam requirements/recommendations for international students: Required—TOEFL (minimum score 250 computer-based). Electronic applications accepted.

College of the Humanities and Sciences, Harrison Middleton University, Graduate Program, Tempe, AZ 85282. Offers education (MA, Ed D); humanities (MA); imaginative literature (MA); interdisciplinary studies (DA); jurisprudence (MA); natural science (MA); philosophy and religion (MA); social science (MA). Part-time and evening/weekend programs available. Postbaccalaureate distance learning degree programs offered (no on-campus study). Electronic applications accepted.

Columbia Union College, Program in Religion, Takoma Park, MD 20912-7796. Offers MAR.

Columbia University, Graduate School of Arts and Sciences, Division of Humanities, Department of Religion, New York, NY 10027. Offers M Phil, MA, PhD. *Degree requirements:* For master's, 2 foreign languages, thesis, oral and written exams; for doctorate, variable foreign language requirement, thesis/dissertation. *Entrance requirements:* For master's and doctorate, GRE General Test. Additional exam requirements/recommendations for international students: Required—TOEFL.

Concordia University, School of Graduate Studies, Faculty of Arts and Science, Department of Religion, Program in History and Philosophy of Religion, Montréal, QC H3G 1M8, Canada. Offers MA. *Degree requirements:* For master's, comprehensive exam, thesis optional. *Entrance requirements:* For master's, honors degree in religion or equivalent. *Faculty research:* Comparative ethics, social theory and political society, Judaic studies.

Concordia University, School of Graduate Studies, Faculty of Arts and Science, Department of Religion, Program in Religion, Montréal, QC H3G 1M8, Canada. Offers PhD. *Degree requirements:* For doctorate, one foreign language, comprehensive exam, thesis/dissertation.

Concordia University Chicago, College of Graduate and Innovative Programs, Program in Religion, River Forest, IL 60305-1499. Offers MA. Part-time and evening/weekend programs available. *Degree requirements:* For master's, comprehensive exam, thesis. *Entrance requirements:* For master's, minimum GPA of 2.9. Additional exam requirements/recommendations for international students: Required—TOEFL (minimum score 550 paper-based; 195 computer-based). Electronic applications accepted. *Faculty research:* Dead Sea Scrolls, cultural construction of gender in early modern Europe, Luther, Luther's theology of the cross, gospels of Mark and John.

Cornell University, Graduate School, Graduate Fields of Arts and Sciences, Field of Asian Religions, Ithaca, NY 14853-0001. Offers PhD. *Faculty:* 8 full-time (3 women). *Students:* 8 full-time (2 women), 2 international. Average age 33. 9 applicants, 33% accepted, 1 enrolled. In 2008, 1 doctorate awarded. *Degree requirements:* For doctorate, comprehensive exam, thesis/dissertation. *Entrance requirements:* For doctorate, GRE General Test, academic writing sample, 3 letters of recommendation. Additional exam requirements/recommendations for international students: Required—TOEFL (minimum score 600 paper-based; 250 computer-based; 77 iBT). *Application deadline:* For fall admission, 1/15 for domestic students. Application fee: $70. Electronic applications accepted. *Expenses:* Tuition: Full-time $29,500. Required fees: $70. Full-time tuition and fees vary according to degree level, program and student level. *Financial support:* In 2008–09, 5 students received support, including 4 fellowships with full tuition reimbursements available, 1 research assistantship with full tuition reimbursement available; teaching assistantships with full tuition reimbursements available, institutionally sponsored loans, scholarships/grants, health care benefits, and unspecified assistantships also available. *Unit head:* Director of Graduate Studies, 607-255-9099, Fax: 607-255-1345. *Application contact:* Graduate Field Assistant, 607-255-9099, Fax: 607-255-1345, E-mail: asian-religions@cornell.edu.

Denver Seminary, Graduate and Professional Programs, Littleton, CO 80120. Offers apologetics (Certificate); biblical studies (MA); Christian formation and soul care (MA, Certificate); Christian studies (MA, Certificate); church and parachurch leadership (D Min); counseling licensure (MA); counseling ministry (MA); intercultural ministry (Certificate); leadership (MA, Certificate); marriage and family counseling (D Min); pastoral ministry (D Min); philosophy of religion (MA); spiritual guidance (Certificate); theology (M Div, Certificate); worship (Certificate); youth and family ministry (MA). *Accreditation:* ACA; ACIPE; ATS (one or more programs are accredited). Part-time and evening/weekend programs available. Postbaccalaureate distance learning degree programs offered. *Degree requirements:* For master's, 2 foreign languages, thesis (for some programs); for doctorate, 2 foreign languages, thesis/dissertation; for M Div, 2 foreign languages. *Entrance requirements:* For M Div, minimum undergraduate GPA of 2.5; for master's, minimum undergraduate GPA of 3.0; for doctorate, M Div, 3 years of ministry experience. Additional exam requirements/recommendations for international students: Required—TOEFL (minimum score 575 paper-based; 233 computer-based; 90 iBT). Electronic applications accepted.

Drew University, Caspersen School of Graduate Studies, Program in Biblical Studies and Early Christianity, Madison, NJ 07940-1493. Offers religion in ancient Israel (MA, PhD); the New Testament and early Christianity (MA, PhD). Part-time programs available. Terminal master's awarded for partial completion of doctoral program. *Degree requirements:* For master's, one foreign language, thesis; for doctorate, 2 foreign languages, comprehensive exam, thesis/dissertation. *Entrance requirements:* For master's and doctorate, GRE General Test. *Faculty research:* Folk religions of ancient Israel, New Testament exegesis and apocrypha, Near East archaeology, Hebrew Bible.

Drew University, Caspersen School of Graduate Studies, Program in Liturgical Studies, Madison, NJ 07940-1493. Offers MA, PhD. Part-time programs available. Terminal master's awarded for partial completion of doctoral program. *Degree requirements:* For master's, one foreign language, thesis; for doctorate, 2 foreign languages, comprehensive exam, thesis/dissertation. *Entrance requirements:* For master's and doctorate, GRE General Test. *Faculty research:* Historical liturgical development, especially early Christian and Reformation; contemporary liturgical practice; homiletics.

Drew University, Caspersen School of Graduate Studies, Program in Religion and Society, Madison, NJ 07940-1493. Offers anthropology of religion (MA, PhD); Christian social ethics (MA, PhD); psychology and religion (MA, PhD); sociology of religion (MA, PhD). Part-time programs available. Terminal master's awarded for partial completion of doctoral program. *Degree requirements:* For master's, one foreign language, thesis; for doctorate, 2 foreign languages, comprehensive exam, thesis/dissertation. *Entrance requirements:* For master's and doctorate, GRE General Test. *Faculty research:* Liberation theory, feminist critique, social science critique of religion.

Drew University, Caspersen School of Graduate Studies, Program in Theological and Religious Studies, Madison, NJ 07940-1493. Offers historical studies (MA, PhD); Methodist studies (PhD); philosophy of religion (MA, PhD); systematic theology (MA, PhD); theological ethics (MA, PhD). *Accreditation:* ATS. Part-time programs available. Terminal master's awarded for partial completion of doctoral program. *Degree requirements:* For master's, one foreign language, thesis; for doctorate, 2 foreign languages, comprehensive exam, thesis/dissertation. *Entrance requirements:* For master's and doctorate, GRE General Test. *Faculty research:* History and theology of religion, postmodern theologies, patristics.

Drew University, Caspersen School of Graduate Studies, Program in Wesleyan and Methodist Studies, Madison, NJ 07940-1493. Offers MA, PhD. *Entrance requirements:* For master's and doctorate, GRE General Test. Additional exam requirements/recommendations for international students: Required—TOEFL, TWE.

Duke University, Graduate School, Department of Religion, Durham, NC 27708. Offers MA, PhD. Part-time programs available. Terminal master's awarded for partial completion of doctoral program. *Degree requirements:* For master's, one foreign language, thesis or alternative; for doctorate, 2 foreign languages, thesis/dissertation. *Entrance requirements:* For master's and doctorate, GRE General Test. Additional exam requirements/recommendations for international students: Required—TOEFL (minimum score 550 paper-based; 213 computer-based; 83 iBT), IELTS (minimum score 7). Electronic applications accepted.

Earlham School of Religion, Graduate Programs, Richmond, IN 47374-5360. Offers religion (MA); theology (M Div, M Min). *Accreditation:* ACIPE; ATS. Part-time programs available. Postbaccalaureate distance learning degree programs offered (minimal on-campus study). *Degree requirements:* For master's, one foreign language, comprehensive exam, thesis; for M Div, project. *Entrance requirements:* For M Div and master's, 3 references. Additional exam requirements/recommendations for international students: Required—TOEFL (minimum score 550 paper-based; 218 computer-based; 82 iBT). Electronic applications accepted. *Faculty research:* Digitizing Quaker texts, vital Quaker ministry.

Eastern Mennonite University, Eastern Mennonite Seminary, Harrisonburg, VA 22802-2462. Offers church leadership (MA); divinity (M Div); ministry studies (Certificate); online theological studies (Certificate); religion (MA); theological studies (Certificate). *Accreditation:* ATS. Part-time programs available. *Faculty:* 8 full-time (2 women), 8 part-time/adjunct (2 women). *Students:* 48 full-time (21 women), 30 part-time (10 women); includes 6 minority (5 African Americans, 1 Hispanic American), 12 international. Average age 40. 40 applicants, 100% accepted, 37 enrolled. In 2008, 15 first professional degrees, 9 master's awarded. *Degree requirements:* For master's, thesis (for some programs); for M Div, thesis/dissertation (for some programs), supervised field education. *Entrance requirements:* For M Div and master's, minimum GPA of 2.5. Additional exam requirements/recommendations for international students: Required—TOEFL (minimum score 550 paper-based; 213 computer-based). *Application deadline:* For fall admission, 6/15 priority date for domestic and international students; for winter admission, 11/15 priority date for domestic and international students; for spring admission, 3/15 priority date for domestic and international students. Applications are processed on a rolling basis. Application fee: $25. *Expenses:* Contact institution. *Financial support:* Application deadline: 6/30; *Faculty research:* Spiritual direction and 'culture of call"; leadership coaching: an approach to leadership in a culture of call; clarity of call in the probationary process for United Methodist clergy in Virginia; EMS women's experiences of culture of call efforts; practices of excellent and fruitful Mennonite pastoral ministry. Total annual research expenditures: $45,000. *Unit head:* Dr. Ervin R. Stutzman, Seminary Dean, 540-432-4261, Fax: 540-432-4444, E-mail: stutzerv@emu.edu. *Application contact:* Don A. Yoder, Director of Seminary and Graduate Admissions, 540-432-4257, Fax: 540-432-4598, E-mail: yoderda@emu.edu.

Edgewood College, Program in Religious Studies, Madison, WI 53711-1997. Offers MA. Part-time and evening/weekend programs available. *Students:* 1 (woman) full-time, 8 part-time (7 women); includes 2 minority (both Hispanic Americans). Average age 47. *Entrance requirements:* For master's, minimum GPA of 2.75, 2 letters of reference, personal statement. Additional exam requirements/recommendations for international students: Required—TOEFL (minimum score 213 computer-based). *Application deadline:* For fall admission, 8/24 for domestic students, 8/1 for international students; for spring admission, 1/10 for domestic students, 10/1 for international students. Applications are processed on a rolling basis. Application fee: $25. Electronic applications accepted. *Expenses:* Tuition: Part-time $655 per credit. *Financial support:* Career-related internships or fieldwork, institutionally sponsored loans, scholarships/grants, and tuition waivers (partial) available. *Faculty research:* Interpretation theory and New Testament, women and religion, theology and literature, Hebrew poetry. *Unit head:* Dr. John Leonard, Chairperson, 608-663-2823, Fax: 608-663-3291, E-mail: jleonard@edgewood.edu. *Application contact:* Paula O'Malley, Director of Graduate and Professional Studies, 608-663-2217, Fax: 608-663-3496, E-mail: gps@edgewood.edu.

Elms College, Religious Studies Department, Chicopee, MA 01013-2839. Offers MAAT. Part-time and evening/weekend programs available. *Faculty:* 2 full-time (1 woman), 2 part-time/adjunct (0 women). *Students:* 12 part-time (6 women). Average age 35. 1 applicant,

Religion

Elms College (continued)

100% accepted, 1 enrolled. In 2008, 7 degrees awarded. *Degree requirements:* For master's, thesis. *Entrance requirements:* For master's, minimum GPA of 3.0. Additional exam requirements/recommendations for international students: Required—TOEFL. *Application deadline:* For fall admission, 7/1 priority date for domestic students; for spring admission, 11/1 priority date for domestic students. Applications are processed on a rolling basis. Application fee: $30. *Expenses:* Tuition: Full-time $10,116; part-time $562 per credit. Required fees: $40; $20 per semester. *Financial support:* Tuition waivers (partial) available. Financial award application deadline: 4/15; financial award applicants required to submit FAFSA. *Unit head:* Dr. Martin Pion, Director of MALA/MAAT Programs, 413-265-3581, Fax: 413-594-3951, E-mail: pionm@elms.edu. *Application contact:* Dr. Martin Pion, Director of MALA/MAAT Programs, 413-265-3581, Fax: 413-594-3951, E-mail: pionm@elms.edu.

Emmanuel School of Religion, Graduate and Professional Programs, Johnson City, TN 37601-9438. Offers Christian care and counseling (M Div); Christian doctrine (M Div); Christian education (M Div); Christian ministries (M Div); church history (M Div, MAR); ministry (D Min); New Testament (M Div, MAR); Old Testament (M Div, MAR); urban ministry (M Div); world mission (M Div). *Accreditation:* ACIPE; ATS. Part-time programs available. *Faculty:* 12 full-time (2 women), 2 part-time/adjunct (0 women). *Students:* 86 full-time (26 women), 42 part-time (10 women); includes 5 minority (4 African Americans, 1 Hispanic American), 14 international. Average age 32. 47 applicants, 98% accepted, 34 enrolled. In 2008, 16 first professional degrees, 6 master's, 2 doctorates awarded. *Degree requirements:* For master's, 2 foreign languages, thesis; for M Div, 2 foreign languages, thesis/dissertation or alternative. *Entrance requirements:* For doctorate, GRE General Test, Minnesota Multiphasic Personality Inventory, M Div or equivalent. *Application deadline:* For fall admission, 8/1 priority date for domestic students. Applications are processed on a rolling basis. Application fee: $25. *Expenses:* Tuition: Full-time $7800; part-time $325 per credit. Required fees: $122.50 per semester. Tuition and fees vary according to degree level and program. *Financial support:* In 2008–09, 90 students received support, including 10 teaching assistantships with partial tuition reimbursements available; career-related internships or fieldwork, institutionally sponsored loans, scholarships/grants, and tuition waivers (partial) also available. Support available to part-time students. Financial award application deadline: 4/1; financial award applicants required to submit FAFSA. *Faculty research:* Theology of Old Testament prophets, spiritual formation for Christian leaders, history of African churches and religions, social world of early Christianity, lay pastoral counseling. Total annual research expenditures: $12,000. *Unit head:* Dr. Rollin A Ramsaran, Dean and Professor of New Testament, 423-461-1524, Fax: 423-926-6198, E-mail: RamsaranR@esr.edu. *Application contact:* Shelley Gasser, Administrative Assistant for Admissions, 423-461-1535, Fax: 423-926-6198, E-mail: GasserS@esr.edu.

Emory University, Graduate School of Arts and Sciences, Department of Comparative Literature, Atlanta, GA 30322-1100. Offers comparative literature (PhD); English (Certificate); French (Certificate); Middle Eastern studies (PhD); philosophy (Certificate); psychoanalytic studies (PhD); religion (PhD); Spanish (Certificate); women studies (Certificate). *Degree requirements:* For doctorate, 2 foreign languages, comprehensive exam, thesis/dissertation. *Entrance requirements:* For doctorate, GRE General Test, minimum GPA of 3.0. Additional exam requirements/recommendations for international students: Required—TOEFL. Electronic applications accepted. *Faculty research:* Literary theory, psychoanalysis trauma and testimony, literature and religion, literature and technology, literature and philosophy, politics and global culture, literature and aesthetics.

Emory University, Graduate School of Arts and Sciences, Division of Religion, Atlanta, GA 30322-1100. Offers PhD. *Degree requirements:* For doctorate, 2 foreign languages, comprehensive exam, thesis/dissertation. *Entrance requirements:* For doctorate, GRE General Test, minimum GPA of 3.0. Additional exam requirements/recommendations for international students: Required—TOEFL. Electronic applications accepted. *Faculty research:* Systematic and historical theology, biblical studies.

Evangelical Theological Seminary, Graduate and Professional Programs, Myerstown, PA 17067-1212. Offers divinity (M Div); marriage and family therapy (MA); ministry (Certificate); religion (MA). *Accreditation:* ATS (one or more programs are accredited). Part-time programs available. Postbaccalaureate distance learning degree programs offered (minimal on-campus study). *Degree requirements:* For master's, 2 foreign languages; for M Div, 2 foreign languages, ministry internship. *Entrance requirements:* For M Div and master's, minimum GPA of 2.5. Additional exam requirements/recommendations for international students: Required—TOEFL (minimum score 550 paper-based; 213 computer-based). *Faculty research:* Literary form and structure within the Hebrew and Greek scriptures, Wesley studies, esoteric biblical languages, the Mosaic law and the Christian, ethics.

Faith Baptist Bible College and Theological Seminary, Graduate Program, Ankeny, IA 50021. Offers biblical studies (MA); pastoral studies (M Div); pastoral training (MA); religion (MA); theological studies (MA). Part-time programs available. *Faculty:* 4 full-time (0 women), 7 part-time/adjunct (0 women). *Students:* 28 full-time (3 women), 28 part-time (2 women); includes 1 minority (Hispanic American), 1 international. Average age 29. In 2008, 9 first professional degrees, 12 master's awarded. *Degree requirements:* For master's, thesis or alternative; for M Div, 2 foreign languages. *Entrance requirements:* Additional exam requirements/recommendations for international students: Required—TOEFL (minimum score 550 paper-based; 197 computer-based). *Application deadline:* For fall admission, 8/1 priority date for domestic students, 8/1 for international students; for spring admission, 12/15 for domestic and international students. Applications are processed on a rolling basis. Application fee: $25. *Expenses:* Tuition: Full-time $10,228; part-time $392 per credit hour. Required fees: $95 per semester. One-time fee: $50. Tuition and fees vary according to class time and course load. *Financial support:* Career-related internships or fieldwork and scholarships/grants available. Support available to part-time students. Financial award application deadline: 3/1; financial award applicants required to submit FAFSA. *Faculty research:* Baptist theology, American church history. *Unit head:* Dr. Ernest Schmidt, Dean of Seminary, 515-964-0601, Fax: 514-964-1638, E-mail: schmidte@faith.edu. *Application contact:* Patrick Odle, Vice President of Enrollment, 888-FAITH4U, Fax: 515-964-1638, E-mail: odlep@faith.edu.

Florida International University, College of Arts and Sciences, Department of Religious Studies, Miami, FL 33199. Offers MA. Part-time and evening/weekend programs available. *Degree requirements:* For master's, thesis. *Entrance requirements:* For master's, GRE General Test, minimum GPA of 3.0, 2 letters of recommendation. Additional exam requirements/recommendations for international students: Required—TOEFL (minimum score 550 paper-based; 213 computer-based). Electronic applications accepted.

Florida State University, Graduate Studies, College of Arts and Sciences, Department of Religion, Tallahassee, FL 32306. Offers humanities (PhD), including religion; religion (MA, PhD). Part-time programs available. Terminal master's awarded for partial completion of doctoral program. *Degree requirements:* For master's, one foreign language, thesis (for some programs); for doctorate, 3 foreign languages, thesis/dissertation. *Entrance requirements:* For master's, GRE General Test, minimum GPA of 3.0; for doctorate, GRE General Test, MA in religion. Additional exam requirements/recommendations for international students: Required—TOEFL. Electronic applications accepted. *Faculty research:* Wisdom literature, Hindu goddesses, feminist theology and medical ethics, Tibetan Buddhism, religion and emotion.

Fordham University, Graduate School of Religion and Religious Education, New York, NY 10458. Offers pastoral counseling and spiritual care (MA); pastoral ministry/spirituality/pastoral counseling (D Min); religion and religious education (MA); religious education (MS, PhD, PD); spiritual direction (Certificate). Part-time programs available. Terminal master's awarded for partial completion of doctoral program. *Degree requirements:* For master's, research paper; for doctorate, comprehensive exam, thesis/dissertation. *Entrance requirements:* For doctorate, MAT. Electronic applications accepted. *Expenses:* Contact institution. *Faculty research:* Spirituality and spiritual direction, pastoral care and counseling, adult family and community, growth and young adult.

General Theological Seminary, Graduate and Professional Programs, New York, NY 10011-4977. Offers Anglican studies (STM, Th D, Certificate); ascetical theology (Certificate); biblical studies (Certificate); congregational development (Certificate); divinity (M Div); historical and theological studies (Certificate); spiritual direction (MASD, STM, Certificate); theology (MA). *Accreditation:* ACIPE; ATS. Part-time and evening/weekend programs available. Terminal master's awarded for partial completion of doctoral program. *Degree requirements:* For master's, thesis; for doctorate, 2 foreign languages, thesis/dissertation. *Entrance requirements:* For M Div, GRE General Test, bishop's endorsement; for master's, GRE General Test; for doctorate, GRE, M Div or MA. Additional exam requirements/recommendations for international students: Required—TOEFL. *Faculty research:* Liturgy, New Testament, ethics, history, ecumenical relations.

George Fox University, George Fox Evangelical Seminary, Newberg, OR 97132-2697. Offers divinity (M Div); ministry (D Min), including global missional leadership, leadership and spiritual formation, leadership in the emerging culture; ministry leadership (MA); spiritual formation (MA); spiritual formation and discipleship (Certificate); theological studies (MA). *Accreditation:* ACIPE; ATS. Part-time and evening/weekend programs available. Postbaccalaureate distance learning degree programs offered (minimal on-campus study). *Faculty:* 7 full-time (2 women), 17 part-time/adjunct (7 women). *Students:* 51 full-time (6 women), 289 part-time (94 women); includes 27 minority (6 African Americans, 2 American Indian/Alaska Native, 15 Asian Americans or Pacific Islanders, 4 Hispanic Americans), 6 international. Average age 41. 134 applicants, 94% accepted, 97 enrolled. In 2008, 9 first professional degrees, 18 master's, 20 doctorates, 5 other advanced degrees awarded. *Degree requirements:* For master's, variable foreign language requirement, thesis optional, internship; for doctorate, thesis/dissertation. *Entrance requirements:* Additional exam requirements/recommendations for international students: Required—TOEFL (minimum score 550 paper-based; 213 computer-based; 80 iBT). *Application deadline:* For fall admission, 7/1 for domestic and international students; for spring admission, 11/1 for domestic and international students. Applications are processed on a rolling basis. Application fee: $40. Electronic applications accepted. *Expenses:* Contact institution. *Financial support:* In 2008–09, 33 students received support. Career-related internships or fieldwork and scholarships/grants available. Financial award application deadline: 5/1; financial award applicants required to submit FAFSA. *Unit head:* Dr. Chuck Conniry, Vice President and Dean, George Fox Evangelical Seminary, 503-554-6152, E-mail: cconniry@georgefox.edu. *Application contact:* Sheila Bartlett, Admissions Counselor, 800-631-0921, Fax: 503-554-6122, E-mail: sbartlett@georgefox.edu.

George Mason University, College of Humanities and Social Sciences, Interdisciplinary Studies Program, Fairfax, VA 22030. Offers anthropology (MAIS); community college teaching (MAIS); folklore (MAIS); higher education (MAIS); individualized studies (MAIS); religion, cultures, and values (MAIS); video-based production (MAIS); women's studies (MAIS); zoo and aquarium leadership (MAIS). Part-time and evening/weekend programs available. *Degree requirements:* For master's, thesis optional. *Entrance requirements:* For master's, GRE, GMAT, or MAT, interview, minimum GPA of 3.0 in last 60 hours of course work. Electronic applications accepted.

Georgetown University, Graduate School of Arts and Sciences, School of Continuing Studies, Washington, DC 20057. Offers American studies (MALS); Catholic studies (MALS); classical civilizations (MALS); ethics and the professions (MALS); human resources management (MPS); humanities (MALS); individualized study (MALS); international affairs (MALS); Islam and Muslim-Christian relations (MALS); journalism (MPS); liberal studies (DLS); literature and society (MALS); medieval and early modern European studies (MALS); public relations (MPS); real estate (MPS); religious studies (MALS); social and public policy (MALS); sports industry management (MPS); the theory and practice of American democracy (MALS); visual culture (MALS). *Entrance requirements:* Additional exam requirements/recommendations for international students: Required—TOEFL.

The George Washington University, Columbian College of Arts and Sciences, Department of Religion, Washington, DC 20052. Offers Hinduism and Islam (MA). Part-time and evening/weekend programs available. *Faculty:* 5 full-time (1 woman), 10 part-time/adjunct (4 women). *Students:* 4 full-time (2 women), 2 part-time (1 woman), 3 international. Average age 27. 10 applicants, 30% accepted, 0 enrolled. In 2008, 4 master's awarded. *Degree requirements:* For master's, one foreign language, comprehensive exam, thesis. *Entrance requirements:* For master's, GRE General Test, interview, minimum GPA of 3.0. Additional exam requirements/recommendations for international students: Required—TOEFL (minimum score 550 paper-based; 213 computer-based; 80 iBT). *Application deadline:* For fall admission, 4/1 priority date for domestic students, 1/15 priority date for international students; for spring admission, 10/1 priority date for domestic students, 9/1 priority date for international students. Applications are processed on a rolling basis. Application fee: $60. Electronic applications accepted. *Financial support:* In 2008–09, 1 student received support. Federal Work-Study and tuition waivers available. *Unit head:* Dr. Alfred Hiltebeitel, Chair, 202-994-1674, Fax: 202-994-9379, E-mail: religion@gwu.edu. *Application contact:* Information Contact, 202-994-6325, Fax: 202-994-9379, E-mail: religion@gwu.edu.

Georgia State University, College of Arts and Sciences, Department of Religious Studies, Atlanta, GA 30303-3083. Offers MA. Part-time programs available. *Degree requirements:* For master's, thesis. *Entrance requirements:* For master's, GRE, 3 letters of recommendation, writing sample. Electronic applications accepted. *Faculty research:* Comparative religions; history of religions; religious ethics; comparative religious ritual; Islam, Judaism, and the Middle East.

Gonzaga University, College of Arts and Sciences, Department of Religious Studies, Spokane, WA 99258. Offers pastoral ministry (MA); religious studies (MA); spirituality (MA). *Degree requirements:* For master's, comprehensive exam. *Entrance requirements:* For master's, GRE General Test or MAT, minimum GPA of 3.0. Additional exam requirements/recommendations for international students: Required—TOEFL.

Gordon-Conwell Theological Seminary, Graduate and Professional Programs, South Hamilton, MA 01982. Offers Biblical languages (MABL); church history (MACH); counseling (MACO); ministry (D Min); missions/evangelism (MAME); New Testament (MANT); Old Testament (MAOT); religion (MAR); theology (M Div, MATH, Th M, Th D). *Accreditation:* ACIPE; ATS (one or more programs are accredited). Part-time and evening/weekend programs available. *Degree requirements:* For master's, one foreign language, thesis optional; for doctorate, 2 foreign languages, thesis/dissertation; for M Div, 2 foreign languages. *Entrance requirements:* For M Div and master's, minimum GPA of 2.5; for doctorate, minimum GPA of 3.0.

Graceland University, Community of Christ Seminary, Independence, MO 64050. Offers Christian ministry (MACM); religion (MAR). Part-time programs available. Postbaccalaureate distance learning degree programs offered (minimal on-campus study). *Faculty:* 2 full-time (1 woman), 14 part-time/adjunct (6 women). *Students:* 13 full-time (5 women), 6 part-time (3 women); includes 1 minority (American Indian/Alaska Native), 1 international. Average age 43. 9 applicants, 78% accepted, 7 enrolled. In 2008, 10 master's awarded. *Degree requirements:* For master's, thesis optional, portfolio or thesis (for MAR); practicum (for MACM). *Entrance requirements:* For master's, minimum cumulative GPA of 3.0. *Application deadline:* For fall admission, 8/15 priority date for domestic students; for winter admission, 10/15 priority date for domestic students; for spring admission, 4/15 priority date for domestic students. Applications are processed on a rolling basis. Application fee: $50. *Expenses:* Contact institution. *Financial support:* Scholarships/grants available. Financial award application deadline: 12/15; financial award applicants required to submit FAFSA. *Faculty research:* Theology. *Unit head:* Dr. Don H. Compier, Dean, 800-833-0524 Ext. 4900, Fax: 816-833-2990, E-mail: dcompier@graceland.edu. *Application contact:* Judy K. Luffman, Executive Assistant, 816-833-0524 Ext. 4508, Fax: 816-833-2990, E-mail: luffman@graceland.edu.

Graduate Theological Union, Graduate Programs, Berkeley, CA 94709-1212. Offers art and religion (MA, PhD); biblical languages (MA); biblical studies (Old and New Testament) (MA, PhD, Th D); Buddhist studies (MA); Christian spirituality (MA, PhD); cultural and historical studies of religions (MA, PhD); ethics and social theory (PhD); history (MA, PhD, Th D); homiletics (MA, PhD, Th D); interdisciplinary studies (PhD, Th D); Jewish studies (MA, PhD, Certificate); liturgical studies (MA, PhD, Th D); Near Eastern religions (PhD); Orthodox Christian studies (MA); Orthodox studies (Certificate); religion and psychology (MA, PhD); religion and society/ethics and social theory (MA); systematic and philosophical theology (MA, PhD, Th D); women's studies in religion (Certificate); MA/M Div. *Accreditation:* ATS. Terminal master's awarded for partial completion of doctoral program. *Degree requirements:* For master's, one foreign language, thesis; for doctorate, one foreign language, comprehensive exam, thesis/dissertation. *Entrance requirements:* For master's, GRE General Test; for doctorate, GRE General Test, MA or M Div. Additional exam requirements/recommendations for international students: Required—TOEFL. Electronic applications accepted.

Grand Rapids Theological Seminary of Cornerstone University, Graduate Programs, Grand Rapids, MI 49525-5897. Offers biblical counseling (MA); Biblical counseling (M Div); chaplaincy (M Div); Christian education (M Div, MA); intercultural studies (M Div, MA); New Testament (MA, Th M); Old Testament (MA, Th M); pastoral studies (M Div); systematic theology (MA); theology (Th M). *Accreditation:* ATS. Part-time programs available. Postbaccalaureate distance learning degree programs offered (minimal on-campus study). *Entrance requirements:* Additional exam requirements/recommendations for international students: Required—TOEFL (minimum score 577 paper-based; 233 computer-based; 90 iBT). Electronic applications accepted.

Harding University Graduate School of Religion, Graduate Programs, Memphis, TN 38117-5499. Offers Christian ministry (MA); counseling (MA); ministry (M Div, D Min); religion (MA). *Accreditation:* ATS. Part-time programs available. Postbaccalaureate distance learning degree programs offered (minimal on-campus study). *Degree requirements:* For master's, variable foreign language requirement, thesis (for some programs); for doctorate, one foreign language, thesis/dissertation; for M Div, 2 foreign languages, thesis/dissertation optional. *Entrance requirements:* For M Div, GRE General Test (for graduates of non-accredited schools), minimum GPA of 2.5; for master's, minimum GPA of 2.7; for doctorate, minimum GPA of 3.0. Additional exam requirements/recommendations for international students: Required—TOEFL (minimum score 550 paper-based; 213 computer-based; 79 iBT). Electronic applications accepted.

Hardin-Simmons University, Graduate School, Logsdon School of Theology, Program in Religion, Abilene, TX 79698-0001. Offers MA. Part-time programs available. *Faculty:* 12 full-time (0 women), 9 part-time/adjunct (1 woman). *Students:* 1 full-time (0 women), 5 part-time (1 woman). Average age 28. 4 applicants, 100% accepted, 2 enrolled. In 2008, 1 master's awarded. *Degree requirements:* For master's, one foreign language, comprehensive exam, thesis or alternative. *Entrance requirements:* For master's, minimum undergraduate GPA of 3.0 in major, 2.7 overall, 18 hours of course work in religious studies, interview. Additional exam requirements/recommendations for international students: Required—TOEFL (minimum score 550 paper-based; 213 computer-based; 75 iBT). *Application deadline:* For fall admission, 8/15 priority date for domestic students, 4/1 for international students; for spring admission, 1/5 priority date for domestic students, 9/1 for international students. Applications are processed on a rolling basis. Application fee: $50. *Expenses:* Tuition: Full-time $10,620; part-time $590 per credit hour. Required fees: $590; $110 per semester. Tuition and fees vary according to course load and degree level. *Financial support:* In 2008–09, 7 students received support; fellowships, scholarships/grants available. Support available to part-time students. Financial award application deadline: 6/30; financial award applicants required to submit FAFSA. *Faculty research:* Archaeology research in Christian origins, Hebrew grammar, history of Christian education, training of ministers into the twenty-first century, role of women in the Old Testament, contemporary ethical issues. *Unit head:* Dr. Travis Frampton, Director, 325-670-1270, Fax: 325-670-1406, E-mail: frampton@hsutx.edu. *Application contact:* Dr. Gary Stanlake, Dean of Graduate Studies, 325-670-1298, Fax: 325-670-1564, E-mail: gradoff@hsutx.edu.

Hartford Seminary, Graduate Programs, Hartford, CT 06105-2279. Offers black ministry (Certificate); Islamic studies (MA); ministerios Hispanos (Certificate); ministry (D Min); religious studies (MA); women's leadership institute (Certificate). *Accreditation:* ATS (one or more programs are accredited). Part-time and evening/weekend programs available. Postbaccalaureate distance learning degree programs offered (no on-campus study). *Degree requirements:* For master's, thesis optional, oral exam; for doctorate, thesis/dissertation, oral exam. *Entrance requirements:* For doctorate, experience in ministry, M Div. Additional exam requirements/recommendations for international students: Required—TOEFL (minimum score 550 paper-based; 213 computer-based; 80 iBT). *Faculty research:* Liturgy and social justice, professional leadership in ministry, congregational studies, Christian-Muslim relations, American religion.

Harvard University, Graduate School of Arts and Sciences, Committee on the Study of Religion, Cambridge, MA 02138. Offers PhD. *Degree requirements:* For doctorate, 2 foreign languages, thesis/dissertation. *Entrance requirements:* For doctorate, GRE General Test. Additional exam requirements/recommendations for international students: Required—TOEFL. *Expenses:* Tuition: Full-time $32,556. Required fees: $1426. Full-time tuition and fees vary according to program and student level.

Hebrew Union College–Jewish Institute of Religion, School of Graduate Studies, Cincinnati, OH 45220-2488. Offers Bible and the ancient Near East (M Phil, MA, PhD); Hebrew letters (DHL); history of biblical interpretation (M Phil, MA, PhD); Jewish and Christian studies in the Greco-Roman period (M Phil, PhD); Jewish and cognate studies (M Phil); Judaic and cognate studies (MA, PhD); modern Jewish history (M Phil, MA, PhD); philosophy and Jewish religious thought (M Phil, MA, PhD); rabbinics (M Phil, MA, PhD). Part-time programs available. Terminal master's awarded for partial completion of doctoral program. *Degree requirements:* For master's, one foreign language, thesis optional; for doctorate, 3 foreign languages, comprehensive exam, thesis/dissertation. *Entrance requirements:* For master's and doctorate, GRE General Test, knowledge of Hebrew. Additional exam requirements/recommendations for international students: Required—TOEFL. *Faculty research:* Aramaic lexicon translations, German-Jewish history, neo-Babylonian texts.

Heritage Christian University, Graduate Programs, Florence, AL 35630. Offers counseling (MM); Greek (MA); ministry (MM); New Testament (MA). *Degree requirements:* For master's, practicum (MM), major research paper (MA). *Entrance requirements:* For master's, MAT or GRE, bachelor's degree in Bible from an accredited college or university, minimum GPA of 2.75, 3 letters of recommendation.

Holy Names University, Graduate Division, Sophia Center in Culture and Spirituality, Oakland, CA 94619-1699. Offers MA, Certificate. *Faculty:* 2 full-time (0 women), 11 part-time/adjunct (5 women). *Students:* 9 full-time (7 women), 22 part-time (18 women); includes 2 minority (1 African American, 1 Hispanic American), 4 international. Average age 55. 18 applicants, 67% accepted, 8 enrolled. In 2008, 26 master's, 12 other advanced degrees awarded. *Degree requirements:* For master's, thesis or alternative. *Entrance requirements:* For master's, minimum undergraduate GPA of 2.6 overall, 3.0 in major. Additional exam requirements/recommendations for international students: Required—TOEFL. *Application deadline:* For fall admission, 8/1 priority date for domestic students, 8/1 for international students; for spring admission, 12/1 priority date for domestic students, 2/1 for international students. Applications are processed on a rolling basis. Application fee: $65. *Expenses:* Tuition: Full-time $6255; part-time $695 per unit. Required fees: $340. Tuition and fees vary according to course load, program, reciprocity agreements and student's religious affiliation. *Financial support:* In 2008–09, 20 students received support. Available to part-time students. Application deadline: 3/2; *Faculty research:* Medieval mystics, environmental justice, work and spirituality. *Unit head:* Dr. James Conlon, Program Director, 510-436-1046, E-mail: conlon@hnu.edu. *Application contact:* 800-430-1321, Fax: 510-436-1325, E-mail: AdultEd@hnu.edu.

Hope International University, School of Graduate Studies, Programs in Ministry, Fullerton, CA 92831-3138. Offers Christian leadership (MCM); church music (MA); church music (Korean track) (MCM); church planting (MCM); intercultural studies (MCM); worship (MCM). Part-time and evening/weekend programs available. Postbaccalaureate distance learning degree programs offered (minimal on-campus study). *Degree requirements:* For master's, thesis (for some programs), project. *Entrance requirements:* For master's, minimum GPA of 3.0, MCM program requires an undergraduate degree in music, application, official transcripts, 2 references, statement of purpose. Additional exam requirements/recommendations for international students: Required—TOEFL (minimum score 550 paper-based; 213 computer-based; 86 iBT); Recommended—IELTS (minimum score 6.5). Electronic applications accepted. *Expenses:* Contact institution. *Faculty research:* Church dynamics, growth methodologies.

Iliff School of Theology, Graduate and Professional Programs, Denver, CO 80210-4798. Offers biblical studies (MA); church history (MA); religion (MA); religion and social change (MA); specialized ministry (MASM), including justice and peace, pastoral theology and care, religions leadership; theology (M Div, MTS, D Min, PhD), including Biblical studies (PhD), religion and psychological studies (PhD), religion and social change (PhD), theology, philosophy and culture (PhD); theology/ethics (MA). *Accreditation:* ACIPE; ATS. Part-time and evening/weekend programs available. *Degree requirements:* For master's, one foreign language, thesis (for some programs); for doctorate, 2 foreign languages, comprehensive exam, thesis/dissertation; for M Div, thesis/dissertation optional. *Entrance requirements:* For M Div, minimum GPA of 2.75, references; for master's, minimum GPA of 3.0, writing sample, references; for doctorate, GRE General Test, minimum GPA of 3.0, writing sample, letters of recommendation. Additional exam requirements/recommendations for international students: Required—TOEFL (minimum score 550 paper-based). Electronic applications accepted. *Faculty research:* Pastoral care, history, church music, contemporary church, biblical studies.

Indiana University Bloomington, University Graduate School, College of Arts and Sciences, Department of Religious Studies, Bloomington, IN 47405-7005. Offers MA, PhD. Part-time programs available. *Faculty:* 7 full-time (2 women). *Students:* 17 full-time (8 women), 7 part-time (4 women); includes 4 minority (3 Asian Americans or Pacific Islanders, 1 Hispanic American), 4 international. Average age 31. 124 applicants, 9% accepted, 0 enrolled. In 2008, 3 master's, 1 doctorate awarded. Terminal master's awarded for partial completion of doctoral program. *Degree requirements:* For master's, variable foreign language requirement, thesis or alternative; for doctorate, 2 foreign languages, thesis/dissertation. *Entrance requirements:* For master's, GRE General Test; for doctorate, GRE, MA, writing sample. Additional exam requirements/recommendations for international students: Required—TOEFL. *Application deadline:* For fall admission, 1/15 priority date for domestic students, 12/15 for international students; for spring admission, 9/1 for domestic and international students. Application fee: $50 ($60 for international students). *Expenses:* Tuition, area resident: Part-time $291.97 per credit hour. Tuition, state resident: part-time $291.97 per credit hour. Tuition, nonresident: part-time $850.33 per credit hour. Required fees: $110 per semester. Tuition and fees vary according to course load and program. *Financial support:* In 2008–09, 14 students received support, including 2 fellowships with full tuition reimbursements available (averaging $15,000 per year), 12 teaching assistantships with full tuition reimbursements available (averaging $11,300 per year); research assistantships, Federal Work-Study and institutionally sponsored loans also available. Financial award application deadline: 2/1. *Unit head:* Prof. David Brakke, Chair, 812-855-3531, Fax: 812-855-4687, E-mail: dbrakke@indiana.edu. *Application contact:* Debra Melsheimer, Graduate Secretary, 812-855-3531, Fax: 812-855-4687, E-mail: dmelshei@indiana.edu.

The Jewish Theological Seminary, The Graduate School, New York, NY 10027-4649. Offers ancient Judaism (MA, DHL, PhD); Bible (MA, DHL, PhD); Jewish education (PhD); Jewish history (MA, DHL, PhD); Jewish literature (MA, DHL, PhD); Jewish philosophy (MA, DHL, PhD); liturgy (MA, DHL, PhD); medieval Jewish studies (MA, DHL, PhD); Midrash (MA, DHL, PhD); modern Jewish studies (MA, DHL, PhD); Talmud and rabbinics (MA, DHL, PhD); MA/MSW. *Accreditation:* ACIPE. Part-time programs available. *Faculty:* 60 full-time (19 women), 73 part-time/adjunct (39 women). *Students:* 91 full-time (49 women), 27 part-time (14 women), 15 international. Average age 37. 77 applicants, 68% accepted, 23 enrolled. In 2008, 23 master's, 3 doctorates awarded. Terminal master's awarded for partial completion of doctoral program. *Degree requirements:* For master's, one foreign language, comprehensive exam (for some programs), thesis (for some programs); for doctorate, 3 foreign languages, comprehensive exam (for some programs), thesis/dissertation. *Entrance requirements:* For master's, GRE or MAT, 3 letters of recommendation, writing sample; for doctorate, GRE or MAT, 3 letters of recommendation, writing research sample. Additional exam requirements/recommendations for international students: Required—TOEFL (minimum score 100 computer-based). *Application deadline:* For fall admission, 1/15 priority date for domestic students. Applications are processed on a rolling basis. Application fee: $50. *Expenses:* Tuition: Full-time $21,200; part-time $1000 per credit. Required fees: $400 per semester. Tuition and fees vary according to degree level, program and student level. *Financial support:* Fellowships, career-related internships or fieldwork and tuition waivers (full and partial) available. Support available to part-time students. Financial award application deadline: 3/1; financial award applicants required to submit FAFSA. *Unit head:* Dr. Stephen Garfinkel, Dean, 212-678-8024, Fax: 212-678-8947, E-mail: gradschool@jtsa.edu. *Application contact:* Abby Eisenberg, Director of Graduate School Admissions, 212-678-8032, Fax: 212-280-6022, E-mail: abeisenberg@jtsa.edu.

See Close-Up on page 529.

John Carroll University, Graduate School, Department of Religious Studies, University Heights, OH 44118-4581. Offers MA. Part-time and evening/weekend programs available. *Degree requirements:* For master's, comprehensive exam, thesis (for some programs), research essay or thesis, foreign language proficiency. *Entrance requirements:* For master's, GRE General Test or MAT, minimum 2.5 GPA. Additional exam requirements/recommendations for international students: Required—TOEFL. Electronic applications accepted. *Faculty research:* Ethics, women's studies, contemporary theology, Bible studies, Latin American theology.

Kentucky Christian University, Graduate School, Grayson, KY 41143-2205. Offers Christian leadership (MA); New Testament (MA). Part-time programs available. *Degree requirements:* For master's, comprehensive exam (for some programs), thesis optional. *Entrance requirements:* For master's, minimum cumulative GPA of 2.75 in major or 2.5 overall; 6 additional hours in Bible (for non-Biblical undergraduate majors). Additional exam requirements/recommendations for international students: Required—TOEFL (minimum score 550 paper-based; 213 computer-based). Electronic applications accepted.

Knox Theological Seminary, Graduate Programs, Program in Christianity and Culture, Fort Lauderdale, FL 33308. Offers MA. Part-time and evening/weekend programs available. *Entrance requirements:* Additional exam requirements/recommendations for international students: Required—TOEFL, TWE.

La Salle University, School of Arts and Sciences, Program in Theological, Pastoral and Liturgical Studies, Philadelphia, PA 19141-1199. Offers pastoral studies (MA); religion (MA); theological studies (MA). Part-time and evening/weekend programs available. *Entrance requirements:* For master's, 26 credits in humanistic subjects, religion, theology, or ministry-related work.

La Sierra University, School of Religion, Riverside, CA 92515. Offers pastoral ministry (M Div); religion (MA); religious education (MA); religious studies (MA). *Accreditation:* ATS. Part-time programs available. *Degree requirements:* For master's, one foreign language, thesis or alternative. *Entrance requirements:* For master's, GRE General Test, minimum GPA of 3.0.

Lee University, Program in Religion, Cleveland, TN 37320-3450. Offers biblical studies (MA); theological studies (MA); youth and family ministry (MA). Part-time programs available. *Faculty:* 10 full-time (3 women), 2 part-time/adjunct (0 women). *Students:* 11 full-time (6 women), 8

Religion

Lee University (continued)
part-time (4 women); includes 1 minority (American Indian/Alaska Native). Average age 25. 6 applicants, 100% accepted, 4 enrolled. In 2008, 11 master's awarded. *Degree requirements:* For master's, comprehensive exam, thesis. *Entrance requirements:* For master's, GRE or MAT, minimum GPA of 3.0, 2 letters of recommendation, interview. *Application deadline:* For fall admission, 4/1 priority date for domestic students; for spring admission, 10/1 priority date for domestic students. Applications are processed on a rolling basis. Application fee: $25. *Expenses:* Tuition: Full-time $10,824; part-time $451 per credit. Required fees: $270; $200 per semester. Tuition and fees vary according to course load and program. *Financial support:* Career-related internships or fieldwork, Federal Work-Study, institutionally sponsored loans, scholarships/grants, and unspecified assistantships available. Financial award application deadline: 3/1; financial award applicants required to submit FAFSA. *Faculty research:* Book of Isaiah, Gospel of Mark, school of St. Victor of 12th century, spirit Christology, people groups of New Testament and work. Total annual research expenditures: $3,000. *Unit head:* Dr. Michael Fuller, Director, 423-614-8338, E-mail: mfuller@leeuniversity.edu. *Application contact:* Vicki Glasscock, Graduate Admissions Director, 423-614-8059, E-mail: vglasscock@leeuniversity.edu.

Liberty University, Liberty Theological Seminary and Graduate School, Lynchburg, VA 24502. Offers religious studies (M Div, MA, MAR, MRE, D Min); theology (Th M). Part-time programs available. Postbaccalaureate distance learning degree programs offered (minimal on-campus study). *Degree requirements:* For master's, 2 foreign languages, thesis (for some programs); for doctorate, 2 foreign languages, thesis/dissertation. *Entrance requirements:* For M Div, minimum undergraduate GPA of 2.0; for master's, minimum undergraduate GPA of 2.0, 9 credit hours of course work in Greek, 9 credit hours of course work in Hebrew (Th M); for doctorate, GRE General Test or MAT. Additional exam requirements/recommendations for international students: Required—TOEFL (minimum score 550 paper-based; 213 computer-based). Electronic applications accepted. *Expenses:* Contact institution.

Lipscomb University, Hazelip School of Theology, Nashville, TN 37204-3951. Offers biblical studies (MA); Christian studies (MA); divinity (M Div); ministry (MA); New Testament (MA); Old Testament (MA); theological studies (MTS); theology (MA). *Accreditation:* ATS. Part-time and evening/weekend programs available. *Degree requirements:* For master's, 2 foreign languages, comprehensive exam (for some programs); for M Div, 2 foreign languages. *Entrance requirements:* For M Div and master's, 2 references. Additional exam requirements/recommendations for international students: Required—TOEFL (minimum score 570 paper-based; 230 computer-based). Electronic applications accepted. *Faculty research:* Status of Churches of Christ in foreign nations, Hebrew grammar, marriage and family.

Loma Linda University, Faculty of Religion, Program in Religion and Science, Loma Linda, CA 92350. Offers MA. *Degree requirements:* For master's, comprehensive exam, thesis optional. *Entrance requirements:* Additional exam requirements/recommendations for international students: Required—TOEFL. Electronic applications accepted.

Louisville Presbyterian Theological Seminary, Graduate and Professional Programs, Louisville, KY 40205-1798. Offers Bible (MAR); divinity (M Div); ministry (D Min); religious thought (MAR); theology (Th M); JD/M Div; M Div/MBA; M Div/MS; M Div/MSW. *Accreditation:* AAMFT/COAMFTE (one or more programs are accredited); ACIPE; ATS (one or more programs are accredited). Part-time programs available. *Degree requirements:* For master's, one foreign language; for doctorate, thesis/dissertation; for M Div, 2 foreign languages. *Entrance requirements:* For master's, interview; for doctorate, M Div. Additional exam requirements/recommendations for international students: Required—TOEFL (minimum score 550 paper-based; 213 computer-based). Electronic applications accepted.

Loyola University Chicago, Institute of Pastoral Studies, Chicago, IL 60611-2196. Offers divinity (M Div); pastoral counseling (MA, Certificate), including pastoral care and counseling (MA), pastoral counseling; pastoral studies (MA); religious education (MA, Certificate); social justice (MA, Certificate); spiritual direction (Certificate); spirituality (MA); M Div/MA; M Div/MSN; M Div/MSW. *Accreditation:* ACIPE. Part-time and evening/weekend programs available. *Faculty:* 6 full-time (1 woman), 33 part-time/adjunct (16 women). *Students:* 137 full-time (88 women), 111 part-time (79 women); includes 28 minority (18 African Americans, 3 Asian Americans or Pacific Islanders, 7 Hispanic Americans), 11 international. Average age 42. 105 applicants, 88% accepted, 64 enrolled. In 2008, 6 first professional degrees, 53 master's awarded. *Degree requirements:* For master's, thesis optional, project; for M Div, project. *Entrance requirements:* For master's, interview. Additional exam requirements/recommendations for international students: Required—TOEFL. *Application deadline:* Applications are processed on a rolling basis. Application fee: $50. Electronic applications accepted. *Expenses:* Contact institution. *Financial support:* In 2008–09, 84 students received support. Career-related internships or fieldwork, Federal Work-Study, institutionally sponsored loans, scholarships/grants, and tuition waivers (partial) available. Support available to part-time students. Financial award application deadline: 3/1; financial award applicants required to submit FAFSA. *Faculty research:* Catholic theology, skills of religious ministry, family ministries, spirituality and divorced men. *Unit head:* Dr. Robert A. Ludwig, Director, 312-915-7467, Fax: 312-915-7410, E-mail: rludwig@luc.edu. *Application contact:* Randy Gibbons, Administrative Assistant, 312-915-7450, Fax: 312-915-7410, E-mail: rgibbon@luc.edu.

Lutheran Theological Seminary, Graduate and Professional Programs, Saskatoon, SK S7N 0X3, Canada. Offers Biblical studies (MTS); church history (MTS); ethics/church and society (MTS); history of Christianity (STM); New Testament (STM); Old Testament (STM); pastoral studies (STM); pastoral theology (MTS); systematic theology (MTS); systematic theology and philosophy of religion (STM); theology (M Div, D Div). *Accreditation:* ATS. Part-time programs available. *Degree requirements:* For master's, thesis; for M Div, Greek, Hebrew.

Lutheran Theological Seminary at Gettysburg, Graduate and Professional Programs, Gettysburg, PA 17325-1795. Offers divinity (M Div); ministerial studies (MAMS); outdoor ministry (MAR); parish ministry (D Min); theology (STM). *Accreditation:* ACIPE; ATS (one or more programs are accredited). Part-time programs available. Postbaccalaureate distance learning degree programs offered (no on-campus study). *Degree requirements:* For master's, thesis (for some programs); for M Div, one foreign language. Electronic applications accepted.

The Lutheran Theological Seminary at Philadelphia, Graduate School, Philadelphia, PA 19119-1794. Offers divinity (M Div); ministry (D Min); religion (MAR); social ministry (Certificate); theology (STM). *Accreditation:* ACIPE; ATS. Part-time and evening/weekend programs available. *Degree requirements:* For master's, one foreign language, comprehensive exam (for some programs), thesis (for some programs); for doctorate, thesis/dissertation; for M Div, 2 foreign languages. *Entrance requirements:* For M Div and master's, minimum undergraduate GPA of 2.8; for doctorate, minimum first professional GPA of 3.0. Additional exam requirements/recommendations for international students: Required—TOEFL (minimum score 550 paper-based; 213 computer-based), TWE. Electronic applications accepted.

Mars Hill Graduate School, Graduate Programs, Seattle, WA 98121. Offers Christian studies (MA); counseling psychology (MA); divinity (MS). Part-time programs available. *Entrance requirements:* For master's, MAT.

McGill University, Faculty of Graduate and Postdoctoral Studies, Faculty of Religious Studies, Montréal, QC H3A 2T5, Canada. Offers MA, STM, PhD. *Accreditation:* ATS.

McMaster University, School of Graduate Studies, Faculty of Social Sciences, Department of Religious Studies, Hamilton, ON L8S 4M2, Canada. Offers MA, PhD. Part-time programs available. *Degree requirements:* For master's, one foreign language, thesis; for doctorate, 2 foreign languages, comprehensive exam, thesis/dissertation. *Entrance requirements:* For master's, minimum B+ average. Additional exam requirements/recommendations for international students: Required—TOEFL (minimum score 580 paper-based; 237 computer-based). *Faculty research:* Hellenistic Judaism, religious biographies in Asia, medieval India, synoptic gospels, ritual and belief systems.

Memorial University of Newfoundland, School of Graduate Studies, Department of Religious Studies, St. John's, NL A1C 5S7, Canada. Offers MA. Part-time programs available. *Degree requirements:* For master's, one foreign language, thesis. *Entrance requirements:* For master's, honors degree in religious studies or equivalent. Electronic applications accepted. *Faculty research:* Biblical studies, Christian thought and history, world religions, ethics, contemporary spirituality.

Miami University, Graduate School, College of Arts and Sciences, Department of Comparative Religion, Oxford, OH 45056. Offers MA. Part-time programs available. *Degree requirements:* For master's, one foreign language, thesis, final exam. *Entrance requirements:* For master's, minimum undergraduate GPA of 3.0 during previous 2 years or 2.75 overall. Additional exam requirements/recommendations for international students: Required—TOEFL (minimum score 550 paper-based; 213 computer-based), TWE (minimum score 4). Electronic applications accepted.

Michigan Theological Seminary, Graduate Programs, Plymouth, MI 48170. Offers Bible (Graduate Certificate); Christian education (MA); counseling psychology (MA); divinity (M Div); theological studies (MA). *Accreditation:* ATS. Part-time and evening/weekend programs available. *Degree requirements:* For master's, one foreign language, thesis; for M Div, 2 foreign languages. *Faculty research:* Judaism, cults, world religions.

Midwestern Baptist Theological Seminary, Graduate and Professional Programs, Kansas City, MO 64118-4697. Offers Biblical archaeology (MA); Biblical languages (MA); Christian education (M Div, MACE); Christian foundations—lay ministry (Graduate Certificate); collegiate ministries (M Div); counseling (MA); educational ministry (D Ed Min); international church planting (M Div); ministry (M Div, D Min); North American church planting (M Div); sacred music (MCM); urban ministry (M Div); worship leadership (M Div); youth ministry (M Div). *Accreditation:* ATS. Part-time programs available. Postbaccalaureate distance learning degree programs offered (minimal on-campus study). *Degree requirements:* For doctorate, thesis/dissertation; for M Div, 2 foreign languages. *Entrance requirements:* For doctorate, MAT. Electronic applications accepted. *Faculty research:* Ministerial studies, Biblical and theological studies, missions, counseling.

Missouri State University, Graduate College, College of Humanities and Public Affairs, Department of Religious Studies, Springfield, MO 65804-0094. Offers MA. Part-time programs available. *Faculty:* 11 full-time (3 women). *Students:* 6 full-time (2 women), 25 part-time (10 women); includes 1 minority (American Indian/Alaska Native). Average age 35. 12 applicants, 100% accepted, 7 enrolled. In 2008, 6 master's awarded. *Degree requirements:* For master's, one foreign language, comprehensive exam, thesis or alternative. *Entrance requirements:* For master's, GRE, minimum GPA of 3.2. Additional exam requirements/recommendations for international students: Required—TOEFL (minimum score 550 paper-based; 213 computer-based; 79 iBT). *Application deadline:* For fall admission, 7/20 priority date for domestic students, 5/1 for international students; for spring admission, 12/20 priority date for domestic students, 9/1 for international students. Applications are processed on a rolling basis. Application fee: $35 ($50 for international students). Electronic applications accepted. *Expenses:* Tuition, state resident: full-time $3852; part-time $214 per credit hour. Tuition, nonresident: full-time $7524; part-time $418 per credit hour. Required fees: $230 per semester. Tuition and fees vary according to course level and course load. *Financial support:* Federal Work-Study, scholarships/grants, and unspecified assistantships available. Financial award application deadline: 3/31; financial award applicants required to submit FAFSA. *Faculty research:* Apocalyptic literature, Protestantism in American Society, contemporary Hinduism, Christian history. *Unit head:* Dr. J. E. Llewellyn, Head, 417-836-5514, Fax: 417-836-4757. *Application contact:* Eric Eckert, Coordinator of Admissions and Recruitment, 417-836-5331, Fax: 417-836-6888, E-mail: ericeckert@missouristate.edu.

Mount St. Mary's College, Graduate Division, Program in Religious Studies, Los Angeles, CA 90049-1599. Offers MA. Part-time and evening/weekend programs available. *Degree requirements:* For master's, thesis. *Entrance requirements:* For master's, MAT, minimum GPA of 3.0. *Faculty research:* Scripture, systematics, ethics, religious education for Mexican-Americans.

Naropa University, Graduate Programs, Program in Indo-Tibetan Buddhism, Boulder, CO 80302-6697. Offers MA. *Faculty:* 6 full-time (2 women), 10 part-time/adjunct (5 women). *Students:* 2 full-time (5 women), 2 part-time (1 woman). Average age 36. 3 applicants, 67% accepted, 1 enrolled. In 2008, 5 master's awarded. *Degree requirements:* For master's, comprehensive exam, thesis. *Entrance requirements:* For master's, writing sample, interview (by phone or in-person), 3 letters of recommendation, letter of interest, resumé. Additional exam requirements/recommendations for international students: Required—TOEFL (minimum score 600 paper-based; 250 computer-based). *Application deadline:* For fall admission, 1/15 priority date for domestic and international students. Applications are processed on a rolling basis. Application fee: $60. Electronic applications accepted. *Expenses:* Tuition: Full-time $14,767; part-time $726 per credit hour. Required fees: $45 per term. *Financial support:* In 2008–09, 5 students received support, including 5 research assistantships with partial tuition reimbursements available (averaging $3,000 per year), 2 teaching assistantships with partial tuition reimbursements available (averaging $3,000 per year); career-related internships or fieldwork, Federal Work-Study, scholarships/grants, health care benefits, tuition waivers (partial), and unspecified assistantships also available. Support available to part-time students. Financial award application deadline: 3/1; financial award applicants required to submit FAFSA. *Unit head:* Phillip Stanley, Co-Chair, 303-245-4728. *Application contact:* Donna McIntyre, Assistant Director of Graduate Admissions, 303-546-3555, Fax: 303-546-3583, E-mail: donna@naropa.edu.

See Close-Up on page 1121.

Naropa University, Graduate Programs, Program in Indo-Tibetan Buddhism with Language, Boulder, CO 80302-6697. Offers MA. *Faculty:* 6 full-time (2 women), 10 part-time/adjunct (5 women). *Students:* 15 full-time (1 woman), 4 part-time (2 women); includes 3 minority (1 American Indian/Alaska Native, 1 Asian American or Pacific Islander, 1 Hispanic American), 1 international. Average age 32. 19 applicants, 84% accepted, 8 enrolled. In 2008, 5 master's awarded. *Degree requirements:* For master's, comprehensive exam, thesis. *Entrance requirements:* For master's, writing sample, interview (by phone or in-person), resumé, letter of interest, 3 letters of recommendation. Additional exam requirements/recommendations for international students: Required—TOEFL (minimum score 600 paper-based; 250 computer-based). *Application deadline:* For fall admission, 1/15 priority date for domestic and international students. Applications are processed on a rolling basis. Application fee: $60. Electronic applications accepted. *Expenses:* Tuition: Full-time $14,767; part-time $726 per credit hour. Required fees: $45 per term. *Financial support:* In 2008–09, 11 students received support, including 5 research assistantships with partial tuition reimbursements available (averaging $3,000 per year), 2 teaching assistantships with partial tuition reimbursements available (averaging $3,000 per year); career-related internships or fieldwork, Federal Work-Study, scholarships/grants, health care benefits, tuition waivers (partial), and unspecified assistantships also available. Support available to part-time students. Financial award application deadline: 3/1; financial award applicants required to submit FAFSA. *Unit head:* Roger Dorris, Co-Chair, 303-546-0937. *Application contact:* Donna McIntyre, Assistant Director of Admissions, 303-546-3555, Fax: 303-546-3583, E-mail: donna@naropa.edu.

See Close-Up on page 1121.

Naropa University, Graduate Programs, Program in Religious Studies, Boulder, CO 80302-6697. Offers MA. *Faculty:* 6 full-time (2 women), 10 part-time/adjunct (5 women). *Students:* 9 full-time (3 women), 3 part-time (2 women), 1 international. Average age 30. 8 applicants, 50% accepted, 2 enrolled. In 2008, 9 master's awarded. *Degree requirements:* For master's, thesis. *Entrance requirements:* For master's, interview (by phone or in-person), writing sample, letter of interest, resumé, 3 letters of recommendation. Additional exam requirements/recommendations for international students: Required—TOEFL (minimum score 600 paper-based; 250 computer-based). *Application deadline:* For fall admission, 1/15 priority date for domestic and international students. Applications are processed on a rolling basis. Application fee: $60. Electronic applications accepted. *Expenses:* Tuition: Full-time $14,767; part-time $726 per credit hour. Required fees: $45 per term. *Financial support:* In 2008–09, 9 students received support, including 1 research assistantship with partial tuition reimbursement available (averaging $3,000 per year), 1 teaching assistantship with partial tuition reimbursement available (averaging $3,000 per year); career-related internships or fieldwork, Federal Work-Study, scholarships/grants, health care benefits, tuition waivers (partial), and unspecified assistantships also available. Support available to part-time students. Financial award application deadline: 3/1; financial award applicants required to submit FAFSA. *Unit head:* Phillip Stanley, Co-Chair, 303-245-4728. *Application contact:* Donna McIntyre, Assistant Director of Admissions, 303-546-3555, Fax: 303-546-3583, E-mail: donna@naropa.edu.

See Close-Up on page 1121.

Naropa University, Graduate Programs, Program in Religious Studies with Language, Boulder, CO 80302-6697. Offers MA. *Faculty:* 6 full-time (2 women), 10 part-time/adjunct (5 women). *Students:* 4 full-time (3 women), 2 part-time (1 woman). Average age 26. 19 applicants, 58% accepted, 4 enrolled. In 2008, 2 master's awarded. *Degree requirements:* For master's, thesis. *Entrance requirements:* For master's, interview, writing sample, resumé, 3 letters of recommendation, letter of interest. Additional exam requirements/recommendations for international students: Required—TOEFL (minimum score 600 paper-based; 250 computer-based). *Application deadline:* For fall admission, 1/15 priority date for domestic and international students. Applications are processed on a rolling basis. Electronic applications accepted. *Expenses:* Tuition: Full-time $14,767; part-time $726 per credit hour. Required fees: $45 per term. *Financial support:* In 2008–09, 3 students received support, including research assistantships with partial tuition reimbursements available (averaging $3,000 per year), teaching assistantships with partial tuition reimbursements available (averaging $3,000 per year); career-related internships or fieldwork, Federal Work-Study, scholarships/grants, health care benefits, tuition waivers (partial), and unspecified assistantships also available. Support available to part-time students. Financial award application deadline: 3/1; financial award applicants required to submit FAFSA. *Unit head:* Dr. Roger Dorris, Co-Chair, 303-245-4730. *Application contact:* Donna McIntyre, Assistant Director of Admissions, 303-546-3555, E-mail: donna@naropa.edu.

See Close-Up on page 1121.

New Life Theological Seminary, Graduate Program, Charlotte, NC 28206-7901. Offers urban Christian ministry (MA), including Biblical studies, church planting, divinity, youth/music. Part-time and evening/weekend programs available. *Degree requirements:* For master's, thesis. Electronic applications accepted.

New York University, Graduate School of Arts and Science, Draper Interdisciplinary Program in Humanities and Social Thought, New York, NY 10012-1019. Offers humanities and social thought (MA); religion (Advanced Certificate); social theory (Advanced Certificate). Part-time programs available. *Degree requirements:* For master's, thesis, comprehensive exam or essay. *Entrance requirements:* For degree, master's degree. Additional exam requirements/recommendations for international students: Required—TOEFL. *Faculty research:* Art world, gender politics, global histories, literary cultures, the city.

New York University, Graduate School of Arts and Science, Program in Religious Studies, New York, NY 10012-1019. Offers MA. Part-time programs available. *Degree requirements:* For master's, one foreign language, thesis. *Entrance requirements:* For master's, GRE General Test. Additional exam requirements/recommendations for international students: Required—TOEFL. *Faculty research:* Biblical and rabbinic Judaism, New Testament and early Christianity, comparative mysticism, gender and embodiment, East Asian religions.

Northwest Nazarene University, Graduate Studies, Program in Religion, Nampa, ID 83686-5897. Offers Christian education (MA); missional leadership (MA); pastoral ministry (MA); religion (M Div); spiritual formation (MA). Part-time and evening/weekend programs available. Postbaccalaureate distance learning degree programs offered (no on-campus study). *Faculty:* 10 full-time (2 women), 24 part-time/adjunct (5 women). *Students:* 135 full-time (36 women), 11 part-time (5 women); includes 17 minority (8 African Americans, 1 American Indian/Alaska Native, 5 Asian Americans or Pacific Islanders, 3 Hispanic Americans). In 2008, 42 master's awarded. *Application deadline:* Applications are processed on a rolling basis. Application fee: $50. Electronic applications accepted. *Unit head:* Dr. Jay Akkerman, Director, Graduate Studies, 208-467-8437, Fax: 208-467-8252. *Application contact:* Jill Jones, Program Assistant, 208-467-8368, Fax: 208-467-8252, E-mail: jdjones@nnu.edu.

Oblate School of Theology, Graduate and Professional Programs, San Antonio, TX 78216-6693. Offers divinity (M Div); Hispanic ministry (D Min); pastoral ministry (MAP Min); pastoral studies (Certificate); spirituality (MA Sp); supervision (D Min), including clinical pastoral education, general supervision; theology (MA Th); M Div/MA Th. *Accreditation:* ACIPE; ATS (one or more programs are accredited). Part-time programs available. *Faculty:* 24 full-time (7 women), 6 part-time/adjunct (1 woman). *Students:* 91 full-time (5 women), 56 part-time (25 women); includes 62 minority (7 African Americans, 3 American Indian/Alaska Native, 13 Asian Americans or Pacific Islanders, 39 Hispanic Americans), 29 international. Average age 39. 33 applicants, 100% accepted, 33 enrolled. In 2008, 16 first professional degrees, 8 master's, 5 Certificates awarded. *Degree requirements:* For master's, thesis (for some programs), practicum; for doctorate, paper, practicum; for M Div, one foreign language, seminar. *Entrance requirements:* For M Div, MAT, interview, course work in philosophy and theology; for master's, MAT, interview, course work in theology or religious studies, minimum GPA of 2.5; for doctorate, M Div. Additional exam requirements/recommendations for international students: Required—TOEFL (minimum score 197 computer-based; 71 iBT). *Application deadline:* For fall admission, 6/15 priority date for domestic and international students; for spring admission, 12/30 for domestic and international students. Applications are processed on a rolling basis. Application fee: $45. *Expenses:* Tuition: Full-time $11,570; part-time $445 per credit hour. Required fees: $170 per semester. One-time fee: $85 full-time. Part-time tuition and fees vary according to course level and course load. *Financial support:* Scholarships/grants available. Support available to part-time students. Financial award application deadline: 8/1; financial award applicants required to submit FAFSA. *Unit head:* Sr. Elaine Brothers, Academic Dean, 210-341-1366, Fax: 214-341-4519, E-mail: ebrothers@ost.edu. *Application contact:* James Oberhausen, Director of Admission/Registrar, 210-341-1366 Ext. 212, Fax: 210-341-4519, E-mail: registrar@ost.edu.

Oklahoma City University, Wimberly School of Religion and Graduate Theological Center, Oklahoma City, OK 73106-1402. Offers M Rel, MAR. Part-time and evening/weekend programs available. *Degree requirements:* For master's, thesis. *Entrance requirements:* For master's, minimum GPA of 2.7. Additional exam requirements/recommendations for international students: Required—TOEFL. *Faculty research:* Biblical studies, church history, social ethics, world religions.

Olivet Nazarene University, Graduate School, Division of Religion, Bourbonnais, IL 60914-2271. Offers biblical literature (MA); religion (MA); theology (MA). Part-time programs available. *Degree requirements:* For master's, thesis or alternative.

Oxford Graduate School, Graduate Programs, Dayton, TN 37321-6736. Offers family life education (M Litt); organizational leadership in nonprofits (M Litt); religion and society (D Phil).

Pacific School of Religion, Graduate and Professional Programs, Berkeley, CA 94709-1323. Offers M Div, MA, MTS, D Min, PhD, Th D, CAPS, CMS, CSS, CTS. *Accreditation:* ACIPE; ATS (one or more programs are accredited). Part-time programs available. *Degree requirements:* For master's, one foreign language, thesis (for some programs); for doctorate, thesis/dissertation. *Entrance requirements:* For M Div and master's, minimum GPA of 3.0; for doctorate, M Div, minimum GPA of 3.0 (D Min); for other advanced degree, M Div, minimum GPA of 3.0 (CAPS). Additional exam requirements/recommendations for international students: Required—TOEFL (minimum score 550 paper-based; 213 computer-based). Electronic applications accepted. *Faculty research:* Medical ethics, gay/lesbian studies in religion, Asian-American religion, race, culture and theology, theology in context.

Pepperdine University, Seaver College, Division of Religion, Malibu, CA 90263. Offers ministry (MS); religion (M Div, MA). Part-time and evening/weekend programs available. *Degree requirements:* For master's, 2 foreign languages, thesis (for some programs). *Entrance requirements:* For master's, GRE General Test. Additional exam requirements/recommendations for international students: Required—TOEFL.

Point Loma Nazarene University, Graduate Studies, Program in Religion, San Diego, CA 92106-2899. Offers M Min, MA. Part-time programs available. Postbaccalaureate distance learning degree programs offered (minimal on-campus study). *Degree requirements:* For master's, thesis optional. *Entrance requirements:* For master's, GRE General Test, letters of recommendation, writing sample. *Faculty research:* Theology, Christian education, church administration.

Princeton Theological Seminary, Graduate and Professional Programs, Princeton, NJ 08542-0803. Offers M Div, MA, Th M, D Min, PhD. *Accreditation:* ACIPE; ATS. Part-time programs available. Terminal master's awarded for partial completion of doctoral program. *Degree requirements:* For doctorate, 2 foreign languages, thesis/dissertation, comprehensive exam (PhD), French and German. *Entrance requirements:* For doctorate, GRE General Test. Additional exam requirements/recommendations for international students: Required—TOEFL. Electronic applications accepted.

Princeton University, Graduate School, Department of Religion, Princeton, NJ 08544-1019. Offers PhD. *Degree requirements:* For doctorate, variable foreign language requirement, comprehensive exam, thesis/dissertation. *Entrance requirements:* For doctorate, GRE General Test. Additional exam requirements/recommendations for international students: Required—TOEFL (minimum score 600 paper-based; 250 computer-based). Electronic applications accepted.

Providence College, Graduate Studies, Department of Religious Studies, Providence, RI 02918. Offers biblical studies (MABS); early Christian studies (MA Th); St. Thomas Aquinas studies (MA Th, MTS). Part-time and evening/weekend programs available. *Faculty:* 8 full-time (2 women). *Students:* 4 full-time (1 woman), 22 part-time (9 women). Average age 42. 12 applicants, 100% accepted. In 2008, 7 master's awarded. *Degree requirements:* For master's, comprehensive exam, Greek and Hebrew (biblical studies). *Entrance requirements:* Additional exam requirements/recommendations for international students: Required—TOEFL (minimum score 550 paper-based; 213 computer-based; 80 iBT). *Application deadline:* For fall admission, 8/1 priority date for domestic and international students; for spring admission, 12/1 priority date for domestic and international students. Applications are processed on a rolling basis. Application fee: $55. *Expenses:* Tuition: Full-time $8991; part-time $333 per credit hour. One-time fee: $170. Tuition and fees vary according to program. *Financial support:* In 2008–09, 4 research assistantships with full tuition reimbursements (averaging $8,400 per year) were awarded; career-related internships or fieldwork and unspecified assistantships also available. Support available to part-time students. Financial award application deadline: 8/1; financial award applicants required to submit FAFSA. *Unit head:* Rev. Thomas McCreesh, OP, Director, 401-865-1150, Fax: 401-865-1830, E-mail: tmccrees@providence.edu. *Application contact:* Carol A. Daniels, Coordinator of Graduate Faculty and Administrative Services, 401-865-2247, Fax: 401-865-1147, E-mail: daniels@providence.edu.

Queen's University at Kingston, School of Graduate Studies and Research, Faculty of Arts and Sciences, Department of Religious Studies, Kingston, ON K7L 3N6, Canada. Offers MA. *Degree requirements:* For master's, one foreign language, essay. *Entrance requirements:* For master's, honors BA in religious studies or equivalent. Additional exam requirements/recommendations for international students: Required—TOEFL (minimum score 600 paper-based; 250 computer-based). *Faculty research:* Modernity, culture, feminism, world religions, traditions.

Reformed Theological Seminary–Charlotte Campus, Graduate and Professional Programs, Charlotte, NC 28226-6318. Offers biblical studies (MA); ministry (M Div, D Min); theological studies (MA). Part-time programs available. *Degree requirements:* For master's, comprehensive exam; for doctorate, thesis/dissertation; for M Div, 2 foreign languages, comprehensive exam. *Entrance requirements:* For master's, minimum GPA of 2.6; for doctorate, minimum GPA of 3.0. Additional exam requirements/recommendations for international students: Required—TOEFL (minimum score 550 paper-based; 213 computer-based). Electronic applications accepted.

Reformed Theological Seminary–Washington D.C., Graduate and Professional Programs, McLean, VA 22101. Offers bible (M Div); practical theology (M Div); religion (MA); theology (M Div). Part-time and evening/weekend programs available. *Degree requirements:* For master's, integrative paper. *Entrance requirements:* For master's, minimum undergraduate GPA of 2.6. Electronic applications accepted. *Faculty research:* Theology, biblical studies, cultural studies.

Rice University, Graduate Programs, School of Humanities, Department of Religious Studies, Houston, TX 77251-1892. Offers PhD. *Degree requirements:* For doctorate, 2 foreign languages, comprehensive exam, thesis/dissertation. *Entrance requirements:* For doctorate, GRE General Test, minimum GPA of 3.0, writing sample. Additional exam requirements/recommendations for international students: Required—TOEFL. Electronic applications accepted. *Faculty research:* Religion and contemporary cultures; scriptural interpretation; ethics and philosophy of religion; mysticism; psychology and religious practices.

Sacred Heart University, Graduate Programs, College of Arts and Sciences, Department of Philosophy and Religious Studies, Fairfield, CT 06825-1000. Offers religious studies (MA). Part-time programs available. *Degree requirements:* For master's, comprehensive exam. *Entrance requirements:* Additional exam requirements/recommendations for international students: Required—TOEFL (minimum score 550 paper-based; 213 computer-based). Electronic applications accepted. *Expenses:* Contact institution.

St. Charles Borromeo Seminary, Overbrook, Graduate and Professional Programs, Division of Religious Studies, Wynnewood, PA 19096. Offers MA. Part-time programs available. *Faculty:* 2 full-time (both women), 4 part-time/adjunct (1 woman). *Students:* 46 part-time (23 women); includes 5 minority (2 African Americans, 1 Asian American or Pacific Islander, 2 Hispanic Americans). Average age 44. 16 applicants, 100% accepted, 15 enrolled. In 2008, 18 master's awarded. *Degree requirements:* For master's, comprehensive exam. *Entrance requirements:* For master's, 18 undergraduate credits in theology and/or philosophy or the equivalent. *Application deadline:* For fall admission, 7/15 for domestic students, 3/15 for international students; for spring admission, 11/15 for domestic students. Applications are processed on a rolling basis. Application fee: $0. *Expenses:* Tuition: Full-time $14,705; part-time $1351 per course. *Unit head:* Dr. Carmina Magnuson Chapp, Academic Dean, 610-785-6287, Fax: 610-667-4122, E-mail: academicdtdscs@adphila.org. *Application contact:* Dr. Carmina Magnuson Chapp, Academic Dean, 610-785-6287, Fax: 610-667-4122, E-mail: academicdtdscs@adphila.org.

Saint John's Seminary, Graduate Programs, Brighton, MA 02135. Offers M Div, MA Th, MAM. *Accreditation:* ATS.

Santa Clara University, School of Education, Counseling Psychology, and Pastoral Ministries, Program in Pastoral Ministries, Program in Catechetics, Santa Clara, CA 95053. Offers MA. Part-time and evening/weekend programs available. *Students:* 10 part-time (5 women); includes 1 minority (Asian American or Pacific Islander), 2 international. Average age 44. 3 applicants, 67% accepted, 2 enrolled. In 2008, 7 master's awarded. *Degree requirements:* For master's, comprehensive exam, thesis. *Entrance requirements:* Additional exam requirements/recommendations for international students: Required—TOEFL. *Application deadline:* Applications are processed on a rolling basis. *Expenses:* Contact institution. *Financial support:*

Religion

Santa Clara University (continued)
Application deadline: 3/1; *Unit head:* Fr. Tom Powers, S.J., Director, 408-554-4322. *Application contact:* Fr. Tom Powers, S.J., Director, 408-554-4322.

Santa Clara University, School of Education, Counseling Psychology, and Pastoral Ministries, Program in Pastoral Ministries, Program in Spirituality, Santa Clara, CA 95053. Offers MA. Part-time and evening/weekend programs available. *Students:* 3 full-time (all women), 12 part-time (8 women); includes 4 minority (2 Asian Americans or Pacific Islanders, 2 Hispanic Americans), 1 international. Average age 43. 4 applicants, 100% accepted, 4 enrolled. In 2008, 5 master's awarded. *Degree requirements:* For master's, comprehensive exam, thesis. *Entrance requirements:* Additional exam requirements/recommendations for international students: Required—TOEFL. *Application deadline:* Applications are processed on a rolling basis. *Expenses:* Contact institution. *Financial support:* Application deadline: 3/1; *Unit head:* Fr. Tom Powers, S.J., Director, 408-554-4322. *Application contact:* Fr. Tom Powers, S.J., Director, 408-554-4322.

Seminary of the Southwest, Graduate and Professional Programs, Austin, TX 78768-2247. Offers Anglican studies (Advanced Diploma); chaplaincy (MCPC); counseling (MAC); divinity (M Div); religion (MAR); spiritual formation (MAPM); theological studies (Advanced Diploma). *Accreditation:* ACIPE; ATS (one or more programs are accredited). Part-time and evening/weekend programs available. *Faculty:* 10 full-time (3 women), 31 part-time/adjunct (11 women). *Students:* 46 full-time (29 women), 31 part-time (23 women); includes 7 minority (4 African Americans, 1 Asian American or Pacific Islander, 2 Hispanic Americans), 2 international. Average age 46. 28 applicants, 96% accepted, 22 enrolled. In 2008, 23 first professional degrees, 13 master's, 5 other advanced degrees awarded. *Degree requirements:* For master's, thesis (for some programs). *Entrance requirements:* For M Div and master's, GRE, MAT, interview; for Advanced Diploma, interview. *Application deadline:* For fall admission, 7/1 for domestic students; for spring admission, 11/1 for domestic students. Applications are processed on a rolling basis. Application fee: $50. *Expenses:* Tuition: Full-time $13,150; part-time $390 per credit hour. One-time fee: $75 full-time; $20 part-time. *Financial support:* Career-related internships or fieldwork and scholarships/grants available. Support available to part-time students. Financial award application deadline: 6/17. *Unit head:* Very Rev. Douglas Travis, Dean and President, 512-472-4133 Ext. 307, Fax: 512-472-3098, E-mail: dtravis@ssw.edu. *Application contact:* Jennielle Strother, Director of Admissions, 512-472-4133 Ext. 375, Fax: 512-472-3098, E-mail: jstrother@ssw.edu.

Seton Hall University, College of Arts and Sciences, Department of Jewish-Christian Studies, South Orange, NJ 07079-2697. Offers MA. Part-time and evening/weekend programs available. *Degree requirements:* For master's, one foreign language, thesis or alternative. Electronic applications accepted. *Faculty research:* Jewish-Christian issues, biblical studies, Holocaust studies.

See Close-Up on page 533.

Simpson University, A.W. Tozer Theological Seminary, Redding, CA 96003-8606. Offers Christian leadership (MA); Christian studies (MA); intercultural studies (MA); ministry (M Div). Part-time and evening/weekend programs available. Postbaccalaureate distance learning degree programs offered (minimal on-campus study). *Degree requirements:* For master's, student portfolio. *Entrance requirements:* For master's, GRE General Test (if undergraduate GPA is below 2.5), 2 letters of reference, Christian Experience statement. Additional exam requirements/recommendations for international students: Required—TOEFL. Electronic applications accepted. *Expenses:* Contact institution.

Sioux Falls Seminary, Graduate and Professional Programs, Program in Christian Leadership, Sioux Falls, SD 57105-1599. Offers MA.

Sioux Falls Seminary, Graduate and Professional Programs, Program in Religious Studies, Sioux Falls, SD 57105-1599. Offers MA. Part-time programs available. *Entrance requirements:* For master's, minimum GPA of 2.5.

Southern Adventist University, School of Religion, Collegedale, TN 37315-0370. Offers Biblical and theological studies (MA); church leadership and management (MA); church ministry and homiletics (MA); evangelism and world mission (MA); religious studies (MA). Summer program only. Part-time programs available. *Degree requirements:* For master's, comprehensive exam, thesis (for some programs). *Entrance requirements:* For master's, GRE. Additional exam requirements/recommendations for international students: Required—TOEFL (minimum score 550 paper-based). *Faculty research:* Biblical archaeology.

Southern Baptist Theological Seminary, Billy Graham School of Missions, Evangelism and Church Growth, Louisville, KY 40280-0004. Offers Christian mission/world religion (PhD); evangelism/church growth (PhD); ministry (D Min); missiology (MA, D Miss); missions, evangelism and church growth (M Div); religion (Th M); theological studies (MA). *Accreditation:* ATS. Part-time and evening/weekend programs available. Postbaccalaureate distance learning degree programs offered (minimal on-campus study). *Degree requirements:* For master's and M Div, 2 foreign languages; for doctorate, 4 foreign languages, thesis/dissertation. *Entrance requirements:* For doctorate, GRE General Test, MAT, field essay, M Div. Additional exam requirements/recommendations for international students: Required—TOEFL, TWE. *Faculty research:* Assimilation of church congregants, effective methodologies of evangelism, expectations of church members, spiritual warfare literature, formative church discipline.

Southern Baptist Theological Seminary, School of Church Music and Worship, Louisville, KY 40280-0004. Offers church music (M Div, MCM, MM); church music and worship (DMA, DMM); worship (M Div, MAW). *Accreditation:* NASM. *Degree requirements:* For master's, comprehensive exam; for doctorate, one foreign language, thesis/dissertation. *Entrance requirements:* For doctorate, GRE General Test, MAT, auditions. Additional exam requirements/recommendations for international students: Required—TOEFL, TWE. *Faculty research:* Baptist hymnody, church music drama, keyboard literature, impact of contemporary pop culture on church music.

Southern Baptist Theological Seminary, School of Theology, Louisville, KY 40280-0004. Offers biblical and theological studies (M Div); biblical counseling (M Div, MA, D Min); biblical spirituality (D Min); Christian ministry (M Div); expository preaching (D Min); pastoral studies (M Div); theological studies (MA); theology (Th M, PhD); theology and arts (MA); theology and law (MA); worldview and apologetics (M Div). *Accreditation:* ATS. Part-time and evening/weekend programs available. Postbaccalaureate distance learning degree programs offered (minimal on-campus study). *Degree requirements:* For master's, 2 foreign languages, thesis; for doctorate, 4 foreign languages, thesis/dissertation; for M Div, 2 foreign languages. *Entrance requirements:* For master's, GRE General Test, MAT, M Div; for doctorate, GRE General Test, MAT, interview, M Div, field essay. Additional exam requirements/recommendations for international students: Required—TOEFL, TWE. *Faculty research:* Biblical studies, contemporary theology, church history, pastoral care, ministry/missions studies.

Southern California Seminary, Graduate and Professional Programs, El Cajon, CA 92019. Offers biblical studies (MA); counseling psychology (MACP); psychology (Psy D); religious studies (MRS); theology (M Div). Part-time and evening/weekend programs available. Postbaccalaureate distance learning degree programs offered (minimal on-campus study). *Degree requirements:* For master's, thesis (for some programs); for doctorate, thesis/dissertation; for M Div, 2 foreign languages. *Entrance requirements:* For doctorate, master's degree in psychology. Additional exam requirements/recommendations for international students: Required—TOEFL (minimum score 550 paper-based). Electronic applications accepted.

Southern Evangelical Seminary, Graduate School of Ministry and Missions, Matthews, NC 28105. Offers apologetics (Certificate); Christian education (MA); church ministry (MA, Certificate); divinity (Certificate), including apologetics (M Div, Certificate); Islamic studies (Certificate); theology (M Div), including apologetics (M Div, Certificate), Biblical studies; youth ministry (MA). Part-time and evening/weekend programs available. Postbaccalaureate distance learning degree programs offered. *Degree requirements:* For master's, thesis (for some programs); for M Div, one foreign language. *Entrance requirements:* Additional exam requirements/recommendations for international students: Required—TOEFL (minimum score 600 paper-based; 250 computer-based).

Southern Evangelical Seminary, Veritas Graduate School of Apologetics and Counter-Cult Ministry, Matthews, NC 28105. Offers apologetics (MA, D Min, PhD, Certificate); Islamic studies (MA); Jewish studies (MA); philosophy (MA); religion (MA). *Accreditation:* ATS. Part-time and evening/weekend programs available. Postbaccalaureate distance learning degree programs offered (minimal on-campus study). *Degree requirements:* For master's, thesis optional; for doctorate, comprehensive exam (for some programs), thesis/dissertation. *Entrance requirements:* Additional exam requirements/recommendations for international students: Required—TOEFL (minimum score 600 paper-based; 250 computer-based).

Southern Methodist University, Dedman College, Graduate Program in Religious Studies, Dallas, TX 75275-0133. Offers MA, PhD. *Faculty:* 8 full-time (1 woman), 3 part-time/adjunct (1 woman). *Students:* 15 full-time (5 women), 17 part-time (6 women); includes 2 minority (1 African American, 1 American Indian/Alaska Native), 3 international. Average age 33. 70 applicants, 16% accepted, 6 enrolled. In 2008, 1 master's, 1 doctorate awarded. *Degree requirements:* For master's, one foreign language, thesis, oral exam, written exams; for doctorate, 2 foreign languages, thesis/dissertation, oral and written exams. *Entrance requirements:* For master's and doctorate, GRE General Test, minimum GPA of 3.0, course work in religion. Additional exam requirements/recommendations for international students: Required—TOEFL (minimum score 550 paper-based; 210 computer-based; 79 iBT). *Application deadline:* For fall admission, 1/15 for domestic and international students. Application fee: $75. Electronic applications accepted. *Financial support:* In 2008–09, 23 fellowships with full and partial tuition reimbursements (averaging $9,580 per year), 5 research assistantships with full and partial tuition reimbursements (averaging $2,500 per year), 6 teaching assistantships with full and partial tuition reimbursements (averaging $2,000 per year) were awarded; institutionally sponsored loans, scholarships/grants, and tuition waivers (full and partial) also available. Financial award application deadline: 2/1; financial award applicants required to submit FAFSA. *Faculty research:* Theology and ethics, Biblical studies, history of Christian doctrine, philosophy of religion. *Unit head:* Prof. Charles M. Wood, Director, 214-768-2432, Fax: 214-768-2117. *Application contact:* Lucy Cobbe, Assistant to Director of Graduate Program, 214-768-2432, Fax: 214-768-2117, E-mail: gradreli@mail.smu.edu.

Southern Nazarene University, Graduate College, Department of Philosophy and Religion, Bethany, OK 73008. Offers theology (MA). Part-time programs available. *Degree requirements:* For master's, one foreign language, thesis optional. *Entrance requirements:* For master's, GMAT, English proficiency exam, minimum GPA of 3.0 in last 60 hours/major, 2.7 overall.

Southwestern Assemblies of God University, Thomas F. Harrison School of Graduate Studies, Program in Theological Studies, Waxahachie, TX 75165-5735. Offers Bible and theology (MS); Biblical studies (M Div); counseling (M Div); cross cultural missions (M Div); practical theology (M Div); theological studies (M Div). Postbaccalaureate distance learning degree programs offered. *Degree requirements:* For master's, comprehensive written and oral exams. *Entrance requirements:* For master's, GRE General Test, minimum GPA of 2.5. Electronic applications accepted.

Stanford University, School of Humanities and Sciences, Department of Religious Studies, Stanford, CA 94305-9991. Offers MA, PhD. Terminal master's awarded for partial completion of doctoral program. *Degree requirements:* For master's, one foreign language, thesis optional; for doctorate, 2 foreign languages, thesis/dissertation, qualifying exam. *Entrance requirements:* For master's and doctorate, GRE General Test. Additional exam requirements/recommendations for international students: Required—TOEFL. Electronic applications accepted.

Syracuse University, Graduate School, College of Arts and Sciences, Program in Religion, Syracuse, NY 13244. Offers MA, PhD. Part-time programs available. Terminal master's awarded for partial completion of doctoral program. *Degree requirements:* For master's, one foreign language, comprehensive exam, thesis optional; for doctorate, 2 foreign languages, comprehensive exam, thesis/dissertation. *Entrance requirements:* For master's and doctorate, GRE General Test. Additional exam requirements/recommendations for international students: Required—TOEFL. Electronic applications accepted.

Taylor University, Master of Arts in Religious Studies Program, Upland, IN 46989-1001. Offers biblical studies (MA); world religions (MA). Part-time programs available. *Faculty:* 4 part-time/adjunct. *Students:* 5 part-time (1 woman); includes 1 African American. Average age 25. 3 applicants, 100% accepted, 3 enrolled. *Degree requirements:* For master's, thesis. *Application deadline:* Applications are processed on a rolling basis. *Expenses:* Contact institution. *Financial support:* In 2008–09, 2 students received support, including 3 fellowships (averaging $2,000 per year). Financial award applicants required to submit FAFSA. *Unit head:* Dr. Sheri Klouda, Graduate Chair, Master of Arts in Religious Studies, 765-998-4786, Fax: 765-998-4930, E-mail: shklouda@taylor.edu. *Application contact:* Kari Manganello, Program Assistant, 765-998-5148, Fax: 765-998-4930, E-mail: krmangane@taylor.edu.

Temple Baptist Seminary, Program in Theology, Chattanooga, TN 37404-3530. Offers biblical languages (M Div); Biblical studies (MABS); Christian education (MACE); English Bible û language tools (M Div); theology (MM, D Min). Part-time and evening/weekend programs available. Postbaccalaureate distance learning degree programs offered (minimal on-campus study). *Degree requirements:* For doctorate, thesis/dissertation; for M Div, proficiency in Greek and Hebrew. *Entrance requirements:* For doctorate, minimum GPA of 3.0, M Div.

Temple University, Graduate School, College of Liberal Arts, Department of Religion, Philadelphia, PA 19122-6096. Offers MA, PhD. Part-time programs available. *Degree requirements:* For doctorate, variable foreign language requirement, thesis/dissertation. *Entrance requirements:* For doctorate, GRE General Test, minimum GPA of 3.0. Additional exam requirements/recommendations for international students: Required—TOEFL (minimum score 550 paper-based; 213 computer-based; 79 iBT). Electronic applications accepted. *Faculty research:* Textural and historical origins; philosophy of religion and religious thought; religion, culture, and society.

Trevecca Nazarene University, Graduate Division, Graduate Religion Programs, Nashville, TN 37210-2877. Offers biblical studies (MA); preaching and practical theology (MA); systematic theology/historical theology (MA). Part-time programs available. *Faculty:* 4 full-time (0 women). *Students:* 29 full-time (3 women), 26 part-time (5 women); includes 8 minority (all African Americans), 1 international. Average age 35. In 2008, 5 master's awarded. *Degree requirements:* For master's, comprehensive exam, thesis optional. *Entrance requirements:* For master's, GRE General Test or MAT, minimum GPA of 2.7, 2 letters of recommendation, philosophy of ministry statement. Additional exam requirements/recommendations for international students: Required—TOEFL (minimum score 550 paper-based; 213 computer-based). *Application deadline:* Applications are processed on a rolling basis. Application fee: $25. Electronic applications accepted. *Expenses:* Contact institution. *Financial support:* Applicants required to submit FAFSA. *Unit head:* Dr. Tim Green, Dean/Director, 615-248-1378, Fax: 615-248-7417, E-mail: admissions_rel@trevecca.edu. *Application contact:* Sherry Crutchfield, Secretary, 615-248-1378, Fax: 615-248-7417, E-mail: admissions_rel@trevecca.edu.

Trinity Episcopal School for Ministry, Graduate Programs, Ambridge, PA 15003-2397. Offers Anglican studies (Diploma); basic Christian studies (Diploma); divinity (M Div); ministry (D Min); mission and evangelism (MAME, Diploma); religion (MAR); youth ministry (Diploma). *Accreditation:* ATS (one or more programs are accredited). Part-time programs available. *Degree requirements:* For master's, thesis optional; for doctorate, thesis/dissertation; for M Div, thesis/dissertation optional, Greek and Hebrew. *Entrance requirements:* Additional exam requirements/recommendations for international students: Required—TOEFL. *Faculty research:* Pauline Epistles, contemporary theology, history of Anglican liturgy, book of Ruth, biblical theology.

Trinity International University, South Florida Campus, Divinity School, Miami, FL 33132-1996. Offers MA, Certificate.

Union University, School of Christian Studies, Jackson, TN 38305-3697. Offers Christian studies (MCS); expository preaching (D Min).

United Theological Seminary of the Twin Cities, Graduate and Professional Programs, New Brighton, MN 55112-2598. Offers advanced theological studies (Diploma); justice and peace studies (M Div); leadership toward racial justice (MA, Certificate); Methodist studies (M Div, MA); ministry (D Min); ministry renewal and professional development (Certificate); pastoral care and counseling (M Div); religion and theology (MA); theological and religious studies (Certificate); theology and the arts (MA); urban ministry (MARL); women's studies: religion, theology and ministry (MA). *Accreditation:* ACIPE; ATS. Part-time and evening/weekend programs available. *Faculty:* 10 full-time (6 women), 24 part-time/adjunct (12 women). *Students:* 60 full-time (34 women), 93 part-time (60 women); includes 10 minority (5 African Americans, 1 American Indian/Alaska Native, 3 Asian Americans or Pacific Islanders, 1 Hispanic American), 1 international. Average age 47. 39 applicants, 100% accepted, 32 enrolled. In 2008, 21 first professional degrees, 9 master's awarded. *Degree requirements:* For master's, thesis; for doctorate, comprehensive exam, thesis/dissertation; for M Div, integrative notebook, spiritual chronicle. *Entrance requirements:* For M Div and master's, minimum GPA of 2.75; strong analytical, reflective thinking and writing skills; vocational and academic goals compatible with those of Seminary; for doctorate, M Div or equivalent, minimum GPA of 3.0, 3 years experience in professional ministry; for other advanced degree, BA or equivalent life experience; strong analytical, reflective thinking and writing skills (Certificate); proficiency in English language, previous study of theology at a theological school, recommendation of student's denomination (Diploma). Additional exam requirements/recommendations for international students: Required—TOEFL (minimum score 550 paper-based). *Application deadline:* For fall admission, 7/1 priority date for domestic students, 11/1 priority date for international students; for winter admission, 11/1 priority date for domestic students; for spring admission, 11/15 priority date for domestic students. Applications are processed on a rolling basis. Application fee: $50. *Expenses:* Tuition: Full-time $11,070; part-time $410 per credit hour. Required fees: $295; $135 per term. One-time fee: $25. Tuition and fees vary according to course load, degree level and program. *Financial support:* In 2008–09, 98 students received support. Career-related internships or fieldwork, institutionally sponsored loans, and scholarships/grants available. Support available to part-time students. Financial award application deadline: 5/1; financial award applicants required to submit FAFSA. *Unit head:* Dr. Richard D. Weis, Dean of the Seminary, 651-255-6108 Ext. 108, Fax: 651-633-4315, E-mail: rweis@unitedseminary.edu. *Application contact:* Rev. Glen Herrington-Hall, Director of Admissions, 651-255-6107 Ext. 107, Fax: 651-633-4315, E-mail: gherrington-hall@unitedseminary.edu.

Université de Sherbrooke, Faculty of Theology, Ethics and Philosophy, Sherbrooke, QC J1K 2R1, Canada. Offers applied ethics (Diploma); human science of religions (MA); intercultural training (Diploma); philosophy (MA, PhD); spiritual anthropology (Diploma); theology (MA, PhD, Diploma). Part-time and evening/weekend programs available. Postbaccalaureate distance learning degree programs offered. Terminal master's awarded for partial completion of doctoral program. *Entrance requirements:* For master's, bachelor's degree in related discipline; for doctorate, master's degree in related discipline. *Faculty research:* Faith and culture interrelation.

Université du Québec à Montréal, Graduate Programs, Program in Religious Sciences, Montréal, QC H3C 3P8, Canada. Offers MA, PhD. Part-time programs available. *Degree requirements:* For master's, thesis; for doctorate, thesis/dissertation. *Entrance requirements:* For master's, appropriate bachelor's degree or equivalent, proficiency in French; for doctorate, appropriate master's degree or equivalent, proficiency in French.

Université Laval, Faculty of Theology and Religious Sciences, Programs in Human Sciences of Religion, Québec, QC G1K 7P4, Canada. Offers MA, PhD. Terminal master's awarded for partial completion of doctoral program. *Degree requirements:* For master's, thesis (for some programs); for doctorate, comprehensive exam, thesis/dissertation. *Entrance requirements:* For master's, knowledge of French, comprehension of a second language; for doctorate, knowledge of French and English. Electronic applications accepted.

The University of British Columbia, Faculty of Arts and Faculty of Graduate Studies, Department of Classical, Near Eastern and Religious Studies, Program in Religious Studies, Vancouver, BC V6T 1Z1, Canada. Offers MA, PhD. Part-time programs available. *Degree requirements:* For master's, 2 foreign languages, comprehensive exam, thesis optional; for doctorate, 2 foreign languages, comprehensive exam, thesis/dissertation. *Entrance requirements:* For master's, upper second class standing; for doctorate, MA degree. Additional exam requirements/recommendations for international students: Required—TOEFL (minimum score 600 paper-based; 250 computer-based), IELTS. Electronic applications accepted. *Faculty research:* Hebrew Bible in ancient Near Eastern context, Christian scriptures in Greco-Roman context, mystical aspects of religion, the feminine in western traditions, modern Jewish experience.

The University of British Columbia, Faculty of Arts and Faculty of Graduate Studies, Department of Classical, Near Eastern and Religious Studies, Programmes in Classics, Vancouver, BC V6T 1Z1, Canada. Offers ancient culture, religion, and ethnicity (MA); classical and near eastern archaeology (MA); classics (MA, PhD). Part-time programs available. *Degree requirements:* For master's, 2 foreign languages, thesis or comprehensive exam; for doctorate, 2 foreign languages, comprehensive exam, thesis/dissertation. *Entrance requirements:* For master's, upper second class standing; for doctorate, MA degree. Additional exam requirements/recommendations for international students: Required—TOEFL (minimum score 600 paper-based; 250 computer-based), IELTS (minimum score 7.5). Electronic applications accepted. *Faculty research:* Classical archaeology, ancient historians, late antiquity, ancient prose fiction, epigraphy.

University of Calgary, Faculty of Graduate Studies, Faculty of Humanities, Department of Religious Studies, Calgary, AB T2N 1N4, Canada. Offers MA, PhD. Part-time programs available. *Degree requirements:* For master's, one foreign language, thesis; for doctorate, 2 foreign languages, thesis/dissertation, candidacy exam. *Entrance requirements:* For master's, minimum GPA of 3.3; for doctorate, minimum GPA of 3.5. Additional exam requirements/recommendations for international students: Required—TOEFL (minimum score 550 paper-based; 213 computer-based). *Faculty research:* Eastern religions, Western religions, nature of religion.

University of California, Berkeley, Graduate Division, College of Letters and Science, Department of Near Eastern Studies, Program in Near Eastern Religions, Berkeley, CA 94720-1500. Offers PhD. *Degree requirements:* For doctorate, 2 foreign languages, thesis/dissertation, qualifying exam. *Entrance requirements:* For doctorate, GRE General Test, MA or equivalent in Near Eastern studies or related field; minimum GPA of 3.0, 3 letters of recommendation.

University of California, Berkeley, Graduate Division, Group in Buddhist Studies, Berkeley, CA 94720-1500. Offers PhD. *Degree requirements:* For doctorate, 4 foreign languages, thesis/dissertation, dissertation defense, qualifying exam. *Entrance requirements:* For doctorate, GRE General Test, MA in Japanese, Chinese, or Sanskrit; minimum GPA of 3.0, 3 letters of recommendation. Electronic applications accepted.

University of California, Santa Barbara, Graduate Division, College of Letters and Sciences, Division of Humanities and Fine Arts, Department of Religious Studies, Santa Barbara, CA 93106-3130. Offers European Medieval studies (PhD); feminist studies (PhD); global studies (PhD); religous studies (MA, PhD); MA/PhD. *Faculty:* 18 full-time (8 women), 11 part-time/

adjunct (5 women). *Students:* 86 full-time (33 women). Average age 31. 151 applicants, 31% accepted, 17 enrolled. In 2008, 7 master's, 6 doctorates awarded. Terminal master's awarded for partial completion of doctoral program. *Degree requirements:* For master's, one foreign language, comprehensive exam (for some programs); thesis (for some programs); for doctorate, one foreign language, thesis/dissertation. *Entrance requirements:* For master's, GRE General Test; for doctorate, GRE General Test, MA in related field, 3 letters of recommendation, statement of purpose, personal achievements/contributions statement, resumé/curriculum vitae, transcripts for post-secondary institutions attended. Additional exam requirements/recommendations for international students: Required—TOEFL (paper: 550, computer: 213, IBT: 80) or IELTS (7). *Application deadline:* For fall admission, 12/1 for domestic and international students. Application fee: $70 ($90 for international students). Electronic applications accepted. *Expenses:* Tuition, nonresident: full-time $25,149. Required fees: $10,143. Full-time tuition and fees vary according to campus/location, reciprocity agreements and student level. *Financial support:* In 2008–09, 67 students received support, including 29 fellowships with full and partial tuition reimbursements available (averaging $12,600 per year), 5 research assistantships with full and partial tuition reimbursements available (averaging $7,900 per year), 46 teaching assistantships with partial tuition reimbursements available (averaging $8,400 per year); career-related internships or fieldwork, Federal Work-Study, institutionally sponsored loans, scholarships/grants, traineeships, health care benefits, tuition waivers (full and partial), and unspecified assistantships also available. Financial award application deadline: 12/1; financial award applicants required to submit FAFSA. *Faculty research:* Religion and politics, religion and violence, contemporary spirituality, religious traditions, theoretical approaches to the study of religion, area studies. *Unit head:* Prof. Catherine L. Albanese, Chair, 805-893-3564, Fax: 805-893-2059, E-mail: albanese@religion.ucsb.edu. *Application contact:* Sally J. Lombrozo, Graduate Program Assistant, 805-893-2744, Fax: 805-893-2059, E-mail: lombrozo@religion.ucsb.edu.

University of Chicago, Divinity School, Chicago, IL 60637-1513. Offers M Div, AM, AMRS, PhD, JD/M Div, JD/MA, JD/PhD, MPP/M Div, MSW/M Div. *Accreditation:* ATS (one or more programs are accredited). Part-time programs available. *Degree requirements:* For master's and M Div, one foreign language; for doctorate, 2 foreign languages, comprehensive exam, thesis/dissertation. *Entrance requirements:* For M Div, master's, and doctorate, GRE General Test. Additional exam requirements/recommendations for international students: Required—TOEFL (minimum score 600 paper-based; 250 computer-based). Electronic applications accepted. *Expenses:* Contact institution. *Faculty research:* Theology, history of religion, ethics, biblical studies, philosophy of religion.

University of Colorado at Boulder, Graduate School, College of Arts and Sciences, Department of Religious Studies, Boulder, CO 80309. Offers MA. *Degree requirements:* For master's, one foreign language, comprehensive exam, thesis. *Entrance requirements:* For master's, minimum undergraduate GPA of 2.75. *Faculty research:* Comparative studies in religion, methodologies in the study of religion, religion and dance, history of religions (including Hinduism, Buddhism and religions of China and Japan), Islam, Christianity.

University of Denver, Division of Arts, Humanities and Social Sciences, Department of Religious Studies, Denver, CO 80208. Offers MA. *Faculty:* 6 full-time (2 women). *Students:* 2 full-time (1 woman), 8 part-time (5 women), 2 international. Average age 29. In 2008, 6 master's awarded. *Entrance requirements:* For master's, GRE. *Application deadline:* Applications are processed on a rolling basis. Application fee: $50. Electronic applications accepted. *Unit head:* Dr. Ginette Ishimatsu, Chairperson, 303-871-2755. *Application contact:* Dr. Carl Raschke, Information Contact, 303-371-2749, E-mail: rlgs@du.edu.

University of Denver, Graduate Studies, Joint Program in Religious and Theological Studies, Denver, CO 80208. Offers PhD. Part-time programs available. *Students:* 42 full-time (17 women), 35 part-time (11 women); includes 10 minority (5 African Americans, 1 American Indian/Alaska Native, 2 Asian Americans or Pacific Islanders, 2 Hispanic Americans), 6 international. Average age 38. In 2008, 5 doctorates awarded. *Entrance requirements:* For doctorate, GRE. *Application deadline:* For fall admission, 1/15 for domestic students. Application fee: $50. *Unit head:* Dr. Frank Seeburger, Head, 303-871-2766. *Application contact:* Dr. Frank Seeburger, Head, 303-871-2766.

University of Detroit Mercy, College of Liberal Arts and Education, Department of Religious Studies, Detroit, MI 48221. Offers MA. *Degree requirements:* For master's, thesis or alternative. *Entrance requirements:* For master's, minimum GPA of 3.0. *Faculty research:* History of religions, textual studies (Old and New Testaments), ethical and cultural studies.

University of Florida, Graduate School, College of Liberal Arts and Sciences, Department of Religion, Gainesville, FL 32611. Offers religion (MA, PhD), including religion and nature (PhD), religion in the Americas (PhD), religions of Asia (PhD). Part-time programs available. *Degree requirements:* For master's, one foreign language, thesis. *Entrance requirements:* For master's, GRE General Test, minimum GPA of 3.0. Additional exam requirements/recommendations for international students: Required—TOEFL (minimum score 550 paper-based; 213 computer-based). Electronic applications accepted. *Faculty research:* Religion in America, Christian thought, Islam, religions of India, comparative religion.

University of Georgia, Graduate School, College of Arts and Sciences, Department of Religion, Athens, GA 30602. Offers MA. *Degree requirements:* For master's, one foreign language, thesis. *Entrance requirements:* For master's, GRE General Test. Electronic applications accepted.

University of Hawaii at Manoa, Graduate Division, Colleges of Arts and Sciences, College of Arts and Humanities, Department of Religion, Honolulu, HI 96822. Offers MA. Part-time programs available. *Degree requirements:* For master's, one foreign language, thesis optional. *Entrance requirements:* For master's, GRE General Test. Additional exam requirements/recommendations for international students: Required—TOEFL (minimum score 600 paper-based; 250 computer-based; 100 iBT), IELTS (minimum score 7). *Faculty research:* Buddhism, East Asian religion, South Asian religion, Polynesian religion, Western religions.

The University of Iowa, Graduate College, College of Liberal Arts and Sciences, Department of Religious Studies, Iowa City, IA 52242-1316. Offers MA, PhD, JD/MA. Terminal master's awarded for partial completion of doctoral program. *Degree requirements:* For master's, thesis optional, exam; for doctorate, comprehensive exam, thesis/dissertation. *Entrance requirements:* For master's and doctorate, GRE General Test, minimum GPA of 3.0. Additional exam requirements/recommendations for international students: Required—TOEFL (minimum score 550 paper-based; 213 computer-based; 81 iBT). Electronic applications accepted. *Faculty research:* Eastern and Western religion.

The University of Kansas, Graduate Studies, College of Liberal Arts and Sciences, Department of Religious Studies, Lawrence, KS 66045. Offers MA. Part-time programs available. *Faculty:* 10. *Students:* 13 full-time (7 women), 6 part-time (3 women); includes 2 minority (both African Americans). Average age 31. 7 applicants, 86% accepted, 2 enrolled. In 2008, 3 master's awarded. *Degree requirements:* For master's, comprehensive exam, thesis optional. *Entrance requirements:* For master's, minimum GPA of 3.0. Additional exam requirements/recommendations for international students: Required—TOEFL. *Application deadline:* For fall admission, 1/10 priority date for domestic and international students; for spring admission, 12/1 priority date for domestic and international students. Applications are processed on a rolling basis. Application fee: $45 ($55 for international students). Electronic applications accepted. *Expenses:* Tuition, area resident: Full-time $6122; part-time $255.10 per credit hour. Tuition, state resident: full-time $6122; part-time $255.10 per credit hour. Tuition, nonresident: full-time $14,629; part-time $609.55 per credit hour. Required fees: $847; $70.56 per credit hour. Tuition and fees vary according to course load and program. *Financial support:* Fellowships, teaching assistantships with full and partial tuition reimbursements, unspecified assistantships available. Financial award application deadline: 1/1. *Faculty research:* Judaism and Christianity, Islam, religions in Asia, methods and theories, American and Native American

Religion

The University of Kansas (continued)
religion. *Unit head:* Daniel B. Stevenson, Chair, 785-864-7258, Fax: 785-864-5205, E-mail: rstudies@ku.edu. *Application contact:* Paul Mirecki, Graduate Director, 785-864-7258, Fax: 785-864-5205, E-mail: pmirecki@ku.edu.

University of Lethbridge, School of Graduate Studies, Lethbridge, AB T1K 3M4, Canada. Offers accounting (MScM); addictions counseling (M Sc); agricultural biotechnology (M Sc); agricultural studies (M Sc, MA); anthropology (MA); archaeology (MA); art (MA); biochemistry (M Sc); biological sciences (M Sc); biomolecular science (PhD); biosystems and biodiversity (PhD); Canadian studies (MA); chemistry (M Sc); computer science (M Sc); computer science and geographical information science (M Sc); counseling psychology (M Ed); dramatic arts (MA); earth, space, and physical science (PhD); economics (MA); educational leadership (M Ed); English (MA); environmental science (M Sc); evolution and behavior (PhD); exercise science (M Sc); finance (MScM); French (MA); French/German (MA); French/Spanish (MA); general education (M Ed); general management (MScM); geography (M Sc, MA); German (MA); health sciences (M Sc, MA); history (MA); human resource management and labour relations (MScM); individualized multidisciplinary (M Sc, MA); information systems (MScM); international management (MScM); kinesiology (M Sc, MA); management (M Sc, MA); marketing (MScM); mathematics (M Sc); music (MA); Native American studies (MA); neuroscience (M Sc, PhD); new media (MA); nursing (M Sc); philosophy (MA); physics (M Sc); policy and strategy (MScM); political science (MA); psychology (M Sc, MA); religious studies (MA); sociology (MA); theoretical and computational science (PhD); urban and regional studies (MA). Part-time and evening/weekend programs available. *Degree requirements:* For doctorate, comprehensive exam, thesis/dissertation. *Entrance requirements:* For master's, GMAT (M Sc in management), bachelor's degree in related field, minimum GPA of 3.0 during previous 20 graded semester courses, 2 years teaching or related experience (M Ed); for doctorate, master's degree, minimum graduate GPA of 3.5. Additional exam requirements/recommendations for international students: Required—TOEFL. *Faculty research:* Movement and brain plasticity, gibberellin physiology, photosynthesis, carbon cycling, molecular properties of main-group ring components.

University of Manitoba, Faculty of Graduate Studies, Faculty of Arts, Department of Religion, Winnipeg, MB R3T 2N2, Canada. Offers MA, PhD. *Degree requirements:* For master's, one foreign language, thesis or alternative.

University of Minnesota, Twin Cities Campus, Graduate School, College of Liberal Arts, Department of Classical and Near Eastern Studies, Minneapolis, MN 55455-0213. Offers ancient and medieval art and archaeology (MA, PhD); classics (MA, PhD); Greek (MA, PhD); Latin (MA, PhD); religions in antiquity (MA). Part-time programs available. Terminal master's awarded for partial completion of doctoral program. *Degree requirements:* For master's, 2 foreign languages, comprehensive exam, thesis or alternative; for doctorate, variable foreign language requirement, comprehensive exam, thesis/dissertation. *Entrance requirements:* For master's and doctorate, GRE, 3 letters of recommendation, department application, writing sample, copies of transcripts, personal statement. Additional exam requirements/recommendations for international students: Required—TOEFL. Electronic applications accepted. *Faculty research:* Greek and Latin literature, archaeology, religions in antiquity, ancient Near East.

University of Missouri–Columbia, Graduate School, College of Arts and Sciences, Department of Religious Studies, Columbia, MO 65211. Offers MA. *Faculty:* 9 full-time (4 women), 1 (woman) part-time/adjunct. *Students:* 8 full-time (5 women), 3 part-time (1 woman). Average age 29. 15 applicants, 20% accepted, 3 enrolled. In 2008, 3 master's awarded. *Entrance requirements:* For master's, GRE General Test, minimum GPA of 3.0. Additional exam requirements/recommendations for international students: Required—TOEFL (minimum score 550 paper-based; 213 computer-based; 79 iBT). *Application deadline:* For fall admission, 2/1 priority date for domestic students. Application fee: $45 ($60 for international students). *Financial support:* Research assistantships, teaching assistantships, institutionally sponsored loans available. *Unit head:* Dr. Robert Baum, Department Chair, E-mail: baumr@missouri.edu. *Application contact:* Dr. Signe Cohen, Director of Graduate Studies, 573-882-4769, E-mail: cohens@missouri.edu.

University of Mobile, Graduate Programs, Program in Religious Studies, Mobile, AL 36613. Offers biblical/theological studies (MA); marriage and family counseling (MA). Part-time and evening/weekend programs available. *Faculty:* 5 full-time (0 women), 1 part-time/adjunct (0 women). *Students:* 16 full-time (14 women), 41 part-time (33 women); includes 25 minority (23 African Americans, 2 American Indian/Alaska Native). Average age 32. In 2008, 13 master's awarded. *Degree requirements:* For master's, one foreign language, comprehensive exam, thesis optional. *Entrance requirements:* For master's, GRE General Test. Additional exam requirements/recommendations for international students: Required—TOEFL (minimum score 550 paper-based; 213 computer-based; 80 iBT). *Application deadline:* For fall admission, 8/3 priority date for domestic students; for spring admission, 12/23 for domestic students. Applications are processed on a rolling basis. Application fee: $40 ($50 for international students). *Expenses:* Tuition: Full-time $7560; part-time $420 per credit hour. Required fees: $240; $120 per semester. *Financial support:* Federal Work-Study available. Support available to part-time students. Financial award application deadline: 8/1. *Unit head:* Dr. Cecil Taylor, Dean, School of Christian Studies, 251-442-2255, Fax: 251-442-2523, E-mail: ctaylor@mail.umobile.edu. *Application contact:* Tammy C. Eubanks, Administrative Assistant to Dean of Graduate Programs, 251-442-2270, Fax: 251-442-2523, E-mail: teubanks@umobile.edu.

The University of North Carolina at Chapel Hill, Graduate School, College of Arts and Sciences, Department of Religious Studies, Chapel Hill, NC 27599. Offers MA, PhD. *Degree requirements:* For master's, one foreign language, comprehensive exam, thesis; for doctorate, 2 foreign languages, comprehensive exam, thesis/dissertation. *Entrance requirements:* For master's and doctorate, GRE General Test, minimum GPA of 3.0. Additional exam requirements/recommendations for international students: Required—TOEFL. *Faculty research:* Religion.

The University of North Carolina at Charlotte, Graduate School, College of Arts and Sciences, Department of Religious Studies, Charlotte, NC 28223-0001. Offers MA. *Faculty:* 13 full-time (6 women). *Students:* 3 full-time (1 woman), 20 part-time (11 women); includes 1 minority (African American). Average age 33. 11 applicants, 91% accepted, 8 enrolled. In 2008, 1 master's awarded. *Entrance requirements:* For master's, GRE or MAT, 3 letters of reference. Additional exam requirements/recommendations for international students: Required—TOEFL (minimum score 557 paper-based; 220 computer-based). *Application deadline:* For fall admission, 7/15 for domestic students, 5/1 for international students; for spring admission, 11/15 for domestic students, 10/1 for international students. Applications are processed on a rolling basis. Application fee: $55. Electronic applications accepted. *Expenses:* Tuition, area resident: Full-time $2919; part-time $122 per credit hour. Tuition, state resident: full-time $2919; part-time $122 per credit hour. Tuition, nonresident: full-time $13,126; part-time $547 per credit hour. Required fees: $1779; $91 per credit hour. Tuition and fees vary according to program. *Financial support:* In 2008–09, 5 teaching assistantships (averaging $9,600 per year) were awarded; career-related internships or fieldwork, Federal Work-Study, institutionally sponsored loans, scholarships/grants, unspecified assistantships, and 2 administrative assistantships ($7,800 average) also available. Support available to part-time students. Financial award application deadline: 4/1; financial award applicants required to submit FAFSA. *Unit head:* Dr. James D. Tabor, Chair, 704-687-4598, Fax: 704-687-3002, E-mail: jdtabor@email.uncc.edu. *Application contact:* Kathy B. Giddings, Director of Graduate Admissions, 704-687-3366, Fax: 704-687-3279, E-mail: agidding@uncc.edu.

University of North Texas, Robert B. Toulouse School of Graduate Studies, College of Arts and Sciences, Department of Philosophy and Religion Studies, Denton, TX 76203. Offers philosophy (MA, PhD). *Degree requirements:* For master's, one foreign language, thesis or alternative. *Entrance requirements:* For master's, GRE General Test. Additional exam requirements/recommendations for international students: Required—proof of English language proficiency required for non-native English speakers; Recommended—TOEFL (minimum score 550 paper-based; 213 computer-based).

University of Notre Dame, Graduate School, College of Arts and Letters, Division of Humanities, Program in Early Christian Studies, Notre Dame, IN 46556. Offers MA. *Faculty:* 26 full-time (6 women). *Students:* 9 full-time (3 women), 1 international. 28 applicants, 18% accepted, 4 enrolled. In 2008, 1 master's awarded. *Degree requirements:* For master's, 3 foreign languages, comprehensive exam. *Entrance requirements:* For master's, GRE General Test. Additional exam requirements/recommendations for international students: Required—TOEFL (minimum score 600 paper-based; 250 computer-based; 80 iBT). *Application deadline:* For fall admission, 2/1 priority date for domestic students, 2/1 for international students. Application fee: $50. Electronic applications accepted. *Financial support:* Fellowships, research assistantships with full tuition reimbursements, teaching assistantships, tuition waivers (full) available. Financial award application deadline: 2/1. *Faculty research:* Early Christian theology, worship and scriptural interpretation; late antique and Byzantine history; art and culture; Greek and Latin literature. *Unit head:* Dr. Martin Bloomer, SJ, Director of Graduate Studies, 574-631-7195. *Application contact:* Dr. Barbara Turpin, Director of Graduate Admissions, 574-631-7706, Fax: 574-631-4183.

University of Ottawa, Faculty of Graduate and Postdoctoral Studies, Faculty of Arts, Department of Classics and Religious Studies, Ottawa, ON K1N 6N5, Canada. Offers classical studies (MA); religious studies (PhD). *Degree requirements:* For master's, comprehensive exam, thesis or alternative; for doctorate, comprehensive exam, thesis/dissertation. *Entrance requirements:* For master's, honors degree or equivalent, minimum B average; for doctorate, master's degree, minimum B+ average. Electronic applications accepted. *Faculty research:* Religions in Canada, including Amerindian and Inuit religions; religion and culture; late antiquity.

University of Pennsylvania, School of Arts and Sciences, Graduate Group in Religious Studies, Philadelphia, PA 19104. Offers PhD. *Degree requirements:* For doctorate, thesis/dissertation, approved specialty languages, preliminary and final exams. *Entrance requirements:* For doctorate, GRE. Additional exam requirements/recommendations for international students: Required—TOEFL. Electronic applications accepted. *Faculty research:* Judaism and Christianity (ancient, medieval, modern), Islam, Hinduism, Buddhism, modern religious thought.

University of Pittsburgh, School of Arts and Sciences, Cooperative Doctoral Program in Religion, Pittsburgh, PA 15260. Offers PhD. *Degree requirements:* For doctorate, 2 foreign languages, comprehensive exam, thesis/dissertation, preliminary exam. *Entrance requirements:* For doctorate, GRE General Test, sample of research or written work, 3 letters of recommendation, transcripts. Additional exam requirements/recommendations for international students: Required—TOEFL (minimum score 600 paper-based; 250 computer-based; 100 iBT). Electronic applications accepted. *Faculty research:* Contemporary Catholicism and religion in America, Buddhism and East Asian religions, philosophy and religion and religious thought and language, medieval to modern Jewish history, theories and methods in the study of religion.

University of Pittsburgh, School of Arts and Sciences, Department of Religious Studies, Pittsburgh, PA 15260. Offers MA. *Degree requirements:* For master's, comprehensive exam, thesis. *Entrance requirements:* For master's, GRE General Test, sample of written work, 3 letters of recommendation, transcripts. Additional exam requirements/recommendations for international students: Required—TOEFL (minimum score 600 paper-based; 250 computer-based; 100 iBT). Electronic applications accepted. *Faculty research:* Contemporary Catholicism and religion in America, Buddhism and East Asian religions, philosophy and religion and religious thought and language, Medieval to modern Jewish history, theories and methods in the study of religion.

University of Regina, Faculty of Graduate Studies and Research, Faculty of Arts, Department of Religious Studies, Regina, SK S4S 0A2, Canada. Offers MA, PhD. Part-time programs available. *Faculty:* 10 full-time (3 women), 2 part-time/adjunct (0 women). *Students:* 6 full-time (5 women), 4 part-time (1 woman). In 2008, 1 master's awarded. *Degree requirements:* For master's, thesis. *Entrance requirements:* Additional exam requirements/recommendations for international students: Required—TOEFL (minimum score 580 paper-based; 237 computer-based; 88 iBT). *Application deadline:* Applications are processed on a rolling basis. Application fee: $85 ($100 for international students). Electronic applications accepted. *Financial support:* In 2008–09, 1 fellowship (averaging $15,000 per year), 1 research assistantship (averaging $13,500 per year), 1 teaching assistantship (averaging $6,558 per year) were awarded; scholarships/grants also available. Financial award application deadline: 6/15. *Faculty research:* Christianity, Hinduism, Buddhism, Islam, Judaism. *Unit head:* Dr. Leona Anderson, Head, 306-585-4580, Fax: 306-585-4815, E-mail: leona.anderson@uregina.ca. *Application contact:* Dr. Leona Anderson, Head, 306-585-4580, Fax: 306-585-4815, E-mail: leona.anderson@uregina.ca.

University of St. Thomas, Graduate Studies, College of Arts and Sciences, Program in Catholic Studies, St. Paul, MN 55105-1096. Offers MA. Part-time and evening/weekend programs available. *Degree requirements:* For master's, thesis. *Entrance requirements:* For master's, bachelor's degree with minimum GPA of 3.0, writing sample, 3 letters of recommendation. Additional exam requirements/recommendations for international students: Required—TOEFL (minimum score 550 paper-based).

University of Saskatchewan, College of Graduate Studies and Research, College of Arts and Sciences, Department of Religious Studies and Anthropology, Saskatoon, SK S7N 5A2, Canada. Offers MA. *Degree requirements:* For master's, thesis. *Entrance requirements:* Additional exam requirements/recommendations for international students: Required—TOEFL.

University of South Africa, College of Human Sciences, Pretoria, South Africa. Offers adult education (M Ed); African languages (MA, PhD); African politics (MA, PhD); Afrikaans (MA, PhD); ancient history (MA, PhD); ancient Near Eastern studies (MA, PhD); anthropology (MA, PhD); applied linguistics (MA); Arabic (MA, PhD); archaeology (MA); art history (MA); Biblical archaeology (MA); Biblical studies (M Th, D Th, PhD); Christian spirituality (M Th, D Th); church history (M Th, D Th); classical studies (MA, PhD); clinical psychology (MA); communication (MA, PhD); comparative education (M Ed, Ed D); consulting psychology (D Admin, D Com, PhD); curriculum studies (M Ed, Ed D); development studies (M Admin, MA, D Admin, PhD); didactics (M Ed, Ed D); education (M Tech); education management (M Ed, Ed D); educational psychology (M Ed); English (MA); environmental education (M Ed); French (MA, PhD); German (MA, PhD); Greek (MA); guidance and counseling (M Ed); health studies (MA, PhD), including health sciences education (MA), health services management (MA), medical and surgical nursing science (critical care general) (MA), midwifery and neonatal nursing science (MA), trauma and emergency care (MA); history (MA, PhD); history of education (Ed D); inclusive education (M Ed, Ed D); information and communications technology policy and regulation (MA); information science (MA, MIS, PhD); international politics (MA, PhD); Islamic studies (MA, PhD); Italian (MA, PhD); Judaica (MA, PhD); linguistics (MA, PhD); mathematical education (M Ed); mathematics education (MA); missiology (M Th, D Th); modern Hebrew (MA, PhD); musicology (MA, MMus, D Mus, PhD); natural science education (M Ed); New Testament (M Th, D Th); Old Testament (D Th); pastoral therapy (M Th, D Th); philosophy (MA); philosophy of education (M Ed, Ed D); politics (MA, PhD); Portuguese (MA, PhD); practical theology (M Th, D Th); psychology (MA, MS, PhD); psychology of education (M Ed, Ed D); public health (MA); religious studies (MA, D Th, PhD); Romance languages (MA); Russian (MA, PhD); Semitic languages (MA, PhD); social behavior studies in HIV/AIDS (MA); social science (mental health) (MA); social science in development studies (MA); social science in psychology (MA); social science in social work (MA); social science in sociology (MA); social work (MSW, DSW, PhD); socio-education (M Ed, Ed D); sociolinguistics (MA); sociology (MA, PhD); Spanish (MA, PhD); systematic theology (M Th, D Th); TESOL (teaching English to speakers of other languages) (MA); theological ethics (M Th, D Th); theory of literature (MA, PhD); urban ministries (D Th); urban ministry (M Th).

University of South Carolina, The Graduate School, College of Arts and Sciences, Department of Religious Studies, Columbia, SC 29208. Offers MA. Part-time programs available. *Degree requirements:* For master's, one foreign language, comprehensive exam, thesis. *Entrance requirements:* For master's, GRE General Test or MAT. Additional exam requirements/recommendations for international students: Required—TOEFL. Electronic applications accepted. *Faculty research:* Biblical and Near Eastern studies, theology and religious thought, religion and culture, South Asian religions, Islamic studies.

University of Southern California, Graduate School, College of Letters, Arts and Sciences, School of Religion, Los Angeles, CA 90089. Offers social ethics (MA, PhD); JD/MA. Terminal master's awarded for partial completion of doctoral program. *Degree requirements:* For master's, thesis optional; for doctorate, one foreign language, thesis/dissertation. *Entrance requirements:* For master's and doctorate, GRE General Test. *Faculty research:* Religion in America, religions of immigrants, ancient Near Eastern archaeology and religion, religious pluralism, religion and popular culture, and religion and science.

University of South Florida, Graduate School, College of Arts and Sciences, Department of Religious Studies, Tampa, FL 33620-9951. Offers MA. Part-time and evening/weekend programs available. *Faculty:* 11 full-time (3 women), 1 part-time/adjunct (0 women). *Students:* 16 full-time (10 women), 13 part-time (7 women); includes 5 minority (1 African American, 1 Asian American or Pacific Islander, 3 Hispanic Americans). 22 applicants, 41% accepted, 6 enrolled. In 2008, 3 master's awarded. *Degree requirements:* For master's, comprehensive exam, thesis. *Entrance requirements:* For master's, GRE General Test, minimum GPA of 3.0 in last 60 hours. Additional exam requirements/recommendations for international students: Required—TOEFL (minimum score 550 paper-based; 213 computer-based). *Application deadline:* For fall admission, 2/15 priority date for domestic students, 1/2 priority date for international students; for spring admission, 10/15 priority date for domestic students, 6/1 priority date for international students. Applications are processed on a rolling basis. Application fee: $30. Electronic applications accepted. *Expenses:* Tuition, state resident: full-time $2624.40; part-time $291.60 per credit hour. Tuition, nonresident: full-time $7822; part-time $869.13 per credit hour. *Financial support:* Teaching assistantships with full tuition reimbursements, unspecified assistantships available. Financial award applicants required to submit FAFSA. *Faculty research:* Scripture and history of Judaism, Christianity, and Islam; religion and society; new religions; comparative religious ethics; narrative and religion. Total annual research expenditures: $16,060. *Unit head:* Mozella Mitchell, Chairperson, 813-974-1852, Fax: 813-974-1853, E-mail: mmitchel@cas.usf.edu. *Application contact:* Wei Zhang, Associate Professor, 813-974-1845, Fax: 813-974-1853, E-mail: wzhang5@cas.usf.edu.

The University of Tennessee, Graduate School, College of Arts and Sciences, Department of Philosophy, Knoxville, TN 37996. Offers medical ethics (MA, PhD); philosophy (MA, PhD); religious studies (MA). Part-time programs available. *Degree requirements:* For master's, thesis or alternative; for doctorate, one foreign language, thesis/dissertation. *Entrance requirements:* For master's and doctorate, GRE General Test, minimum GPA of 2.7. Additional exam requirements/recommendations for international students: Required—TOEFL. Electronic applications accepted. *Expenses:* Tuition, area resident: Part-time $348 per credit hour. Tuition, state resident: full-time $6262. Tuition, nonresident: full-time $18,920; part-time $1052 per credit hour. Required fees: $812; $36 per credit hour. Tuition and fees vary according to program.

University of the Incarnate Word, School of Graduate Studies and Research, College of Humanities, Arts, and Social Sciences, Program in Religious Studies, San Antonio, TX 78209-6397. Offers MA. Part-time programs available. *Faculty:* 1 (woman) full-time, 1 part-time/adjunct (0 women). *Students:* 15 part-time (10 women); includes 10 minority (2 African Americans, 8 Hispanic Americans), 1 international. Average age 40. In 2008, 5 master's awarded. *Degree requirements:* For master's, pastoral project. *Entrance requirements:* For master's, personal statement, recommendation letters, 12 credit hours related undergraduate coursework. Additional exam requirements/recommendations for international students: Required—TOEFL (minimum score 560 paper-based; 220 computer-based; 83 iBT). *Application deadline:* Applications are processed on a rolling basis. Application fee: $20. Electronic applications accepted. *Expenses:* Tuition: Full-time $11,520; part-time $640 per credit hour. Required fees: $1494; $83 per credit hour. One-time fee: $50. Tuition and fees vary according to degree level and program. *Financial support:* Federal Work-Study, scholarships/grants, and tuition waivers (partial) available. Financial award applicants required to submit FAFSA. *Unit head:* Sr. Eilish Ryan, Chair, 210-829-3871, Fax: 210-829-3880, E-mail: eryan@uiwtx.edu. *Application contact:* Andrea Cyterski-Acosta, Dean of Enrollment, 210-829-6005, Fax: 210-829-3921, E-mail: admis@uiwtx.edu.

University of the West, Department of Religious Studies, Rosemead, CA 91770. Offers Buddhist studies (MA, DBS); comparative religions (MA); religious studies (PhD). Part-time and evening/weekend programs available. *Degree requirements:* For master's, thesis or comprehensive exam, competency in language associated with Buddhist Canon literature; for doctorate, one foreign language, comprehensive exam, thesis/dissertation.

University of Toronto, School of Graduate Studies, Humanities Division, Centre for the Study of Religion, Toronto, ON M5S 1A1, Canada. Offers MA, PhD. Part-time programs available. *Degree requirements:* For master's, one foreign language, research paper, language requirement examination; for doctorate, 2 foreign languages, thesis/dissertation, language examinations, general examinations, oral examination. *Entrance requirements:* For master's, BA in religion or a related field; minimum A- average in final year, 3 letters of recommendation, resumé; for doctorate, MA in religion, minimum average of A- in MA courses with no individual grade below a B, 3 letters of recommendation, resumé, brief writing sample. Additional exam requirements/recommendations for international students: Required—TOEFL (minimum score 600 paper-based; 250 computer-based), TWE (minimum score 5).

University of Virginia, College and Graduate School of Arts and Sciences, Department of Religious Studies, Charlottesville, VA 22903. Offers MA, PhD. *Faculty:* 32 full-time (11 women), 1 part-time/adjunct (0 women). *Students:* 83 full-time (30 women); includes 5 minority (3 African Americans, 2 Asian Americans or Pacific Islanders), 5 international. Average age 32. 206 applicants, 30% accepted, 23 enrolled. In 2008, 10 master's, 9 doctorates awarded. *Degree requirements:* For master's, one foreign language, thesis optional; for doctorate, 2 foreign languages, comprehensive exam, thesis/dissertation. *Entrance requirements:* For master's and doctorate, GRE General Test, 3 letters of recommendation. Additional exam requirements/recommendations for international students: Required—TOEFL (minimum score 600 paper-based; 250 computer-based; 90 iBT), IELTS (minimum score 7). *Application deadline:* For fall admission, 12/3 for domestic and international students. Applications are processed on a rolling basis. Application fee: $60. Electronic applications accepted. *Expenses:* Tuition, area resident: Full-time $10,452. Tuition, state resident: full-time $10,452. Tuition, nonresident: full-time $20,010. Required fees: $2176. Part-time tuition and fees vary according to course load and program. *Financial support:* Fellowships, teaching assistantships available. Financial award applicants required to submit FAFSA. *Unit head:* Paul Groner, Chair, 434-924-6705, Fax: 434-924-1467. *Application contact:* Elizabeth Smith, E-mail: eas5x@virginia.edu.

University of Washington, Graduate School, College of Arts and Sciences, Department of Asian Languages and Literature, Seattle, WA 98195. Offers Buddhist studies (MA, PhD); Chinese language and literature (MA, PhD); Japanese language and literature (MA, PhD); Korean language and literature (MA, PhD); South Asian language and literature (MA, PhD). *Degree requirements:* For master's, 2 foreign languages, general exam, thesis or 2 research papers; for doctorate, 3 foreign languages, thesis/dissertation, general exam. *Entrance requirements:* For master's, GRE, minimum GPA of 3.0; for doctorate, GRE, master's degree in related field, minimum GPA of 3.0. Additional exam requirements/recommendations for international students: Required—TOEFL. Electronic applications accepted. *Faculty research:* Textual, linguistic, philological, and literary study of languages and literatures of Asia.

University of Washington, Graduate School, College of Arts and Sciences, Henry M. Jackson School of International Studies, Comparative Religion Program, Seattle, WA 98195. Offers MAIS. *Degree requirements:* For master's, 2 foreign languages. *Entrance requirements:* For master's, GRE General Test, minimum GPA of 3.0. Additional exam requirements/recommendations for international students: Required—TOEFL (minimum score 500 paper-based; 213 computer-based). Electronic applications accepted.

University of Waterloo, Graduate Studies, Faculty of Arts, Department of Religious Studies, Waterloo, ON N2L 3G1, Canada. Offers religious diversity in North America (PhD). *Degree requirements:* For doctorate, thesis/dissertation. *Entrance requirements:* Additional exam requirements/recommendations for international students: Required—TOEFL. Electronic applications accepted. *Faculty research:* Religious diversity in North America.

The University of Winnipeg, Graduate Studies, Department of Religious Studies, Winnipeg, MB R3B 2E9, Canada. Offers MA. Part-time programs available. *Faculty research:* Religion and culture, social ethics, religious liberalism, history of Canaanite and Israelite religion, literary criticism of the Hebrew Bible.

Vanderbilt University, Graduate School, Department of Religion, Nashville, TN 37240-1001. Offers MA, PhD. *Faculty:* 47 full-time (14 women). *Students:* 113 full-time (55 women), 1 part-time (0 women); includes 25 minority (18 African Americans, 1 American Indian/Alaska Native, 3 Asian Americans or Pacific Islanders, 3 Hispanic Americans), 12 international. Average age 35. 255 applicants, 12% accepted, 20 enrolled. In 2008, 13 master's, 9 doctorates awarded. *Degree requirements:* For master's, one foreign language, thesis; for doctorate, 2 foreign languages, thesis/dissertation, final and qualifying exams. *Entrance requirements:* For master's and doctorate, GRE General Test. Additional exam requirements/recommendations for international students: Required—TOEFL (minimum score 570 paper-based; 230 computer-based; 88 iBT). *Application deadline:* For fall admission, 1/15 for domestic and international students. Application fee: $0. Electronic applications accepted. *Financial support:* Fellowships with full and partial tuition reimbursements, teaching assistantships with full and partial tuition reimbursements, Federal Work-Study, institutionally sponsored loans, health care benefits, and tuition waivers (full and partial) available. Support available to part-time students. Financial award application deadline: 1/15; financial award applicants required to submit CSS PROFILE or FAFSA. *Faculty research:* Hebrew Bible, New Testament, church history, theology, ethics. *Unit head:* John S. McClure, Chair, 615-343-3977, Fax: 615-343-5449, E-mail: john.s.mcclure@vanderbilt.edu. *Application contact:* James P. Byrd, Director of Graduate Studies, 615-343-3977, Fax: 615-343-5449, E-mail: james.p.byrd@vanderbilt.edu.

Vanguard University of Southern California, Graduate Programs in Religion, Costa Mesa, CA 92626-9601. Offers leadership studies (MA); theological studies (MTS). Part-time and evening/weekend programs available. *Faculty:* 5 full-time (0 women), 1 part-time/adjunct (0 women). *Students:* 21 full-time (5 women), 54 part-time (17 women); includes 13 minority (1 African American, 1 American Indian/Alaska Native, 3 Asian Americans or Pacific Islanders, 8 Hispanic Americans), 2 international. Average age 38. 21 applicants, 57% accepted, 9 enrolled. *Degree requirements:* For master's, one foreign language, comprehensive exam, thesis (for some programs). *Entrance requirements:* For master's, minimum GPA of 3.0; course work in humanities, religion, and social sciences (MA); minimum GPA of 2.5 (MTS). Additional exam requirements/recommendations for international students: Required—TOEFL (minimum score 550 paper-based; 213 computer-based; 79 iBT). *Application deadline:* For fall admission, 4/1 priority date for domestic and international students; for spring admission, 10/1 priority date for domestic and international students. Applications are processed on a rolling basis. Application fee: $45. Electronic applications accepted. *Expenses:* Contact institution. *Financial support:* In 2008–09, 3 teaching assistantships (averaging $3,333 per year) were awarded; scholarships/grants, tuition waivers (partial), and unspecified assistantships also available. Financial award application deadline: 3/2. *Faculty research:* Apocalyptic literature, narrative theology, ecumenism and Pentecost. *Unit head:* Dr. Richard Israel, Associate Dean, 714-556-3610 Ext. 3223, Fax: 714-957-9317. *Application contact:* Angel McGee, Secretary, Graduate Program in Religion, 714-556-3610 Ext. 3237, Fax: 714-957-9317, E-mail: angel.mcgee@vanguard.edu.

Virginia University of Lynchburg, Graduate Programs, Lynchburg, VA 24501-6417. Offers Christian ministry (M Div).

Wake Forest University, Graduate School of Arts and Sciences, Department of Religion, Winston-Salem, NC 27109. Offers MA. *Accreditation:* ACIPE. Part-time programs available. *Degree requirements:* For master's, one foreign language, thesis. *Entrance requirements:* For master's, GRE General Test. Additional exam requirements/recommendations for international students: Required—TOEFL (minimum score 213 computer-based; 79 iBT). Electronic applications accepted. *Faculty research:* Christian origins, biblical archaeology, psychology and religion, religion and literature.

Warner Pacific College, Graduate Programs, Portland, OR 97215-4099. Offers biblical and theological studies (MA); biblical studies (M Rel); education (M Ed); management/organizational leadership (MS); pastoral ministries (M Rel); religion and ethics (M Rel); teaching (MA); theology (M Rel). Part-time programs available. *Degree requirements:* For master's, thesis or alternative, Presentation of Defense. *Entrance requirements:* For master's, interview, minimum GPA of 2.5, letters of recommendations. *Faculty research:* New Testament studies, nineteenth-century Wesleyan theology, preaching and church growth, Christian ethics.

Wayland Baptist University, Graduate Programs, Programs in Religion, Plainview, TX 79072-6998. Offers Christian ministry (MCM); religion (MA). Part-time and evening/weekend programs available. Postbaccalaureate distance learning degree programs offered (no on-campus study). *Faculty:* 6 full-time (1 woman), 1 part-time/adjunct (0 women). *Students:* 12 part-time (5 women); includes 3 minority (all African Americans). Average age 38. 10 applicants, 100% accepted, 2 enrolled. In 2008, 1 master's awarded. *Degree requirements:* For master's, comprehensive exam. *Entrance requirements:* For master's, GRE or MAT. Additional exam requirements/recommendations for international students: Required—TOEFL (minimum score 500 paper-based; 173 computer-based; 61 iBT). *Application deadline:* Applications are processed on a rolling basis. Application fee: $50. *Expenses:* Tuition: Full-time $310; part-time $310 per credit hour. Required fees: $782; $9 per credit hour. $60 per semester. *Financial support:* Federal Work-Study, institutionally sponsored loans, and scholarships/grants available. Support available to part-time students. Financial award application deadline: 5/1; financial award applicants required to submit FAFSA. *Unit head:* Dr. Paul Sadler, Chairman, 806-291-1160, Fax: 806-291-1969, E-mail: sadlerp@wbu.edu. *Application contact:* Amanda Stanton, Graduate Studies, 806-291-3414, Fax: 806-291-1950, E-mail: stanton@wbu.edu.

Western Michigan University, Graduate College, College of Arts and Sciences, Department of Comparative Religion, Kalamazoo, MI 49008-5202. Offers MA. *Degree requirements:* For master's, one foreign language, thesis optional, oral exam.

Western Seminary, Graduate Programs, Program in Biblical and Theological Studies, Portland, OR 97215-3367. Offers biblical and theological studies (MA, G Dip); biblical studies (Certificate); theology (Th M). *Accreditation:* ATS. Part-time programs available. *Degree requirements:* For master's, thesis or alternative, practicum.

Westminster Seminary California, Programs in Theology, Escondido, CA 92027-4128. Offers Biblical studies (MA); historical theology (MA); theological studies (M Div, MA). *Accreditation:* ATS. Part-time and evening/weekend programs available. *Degree requirements:* For master's, 2 foreign languages, thesis (for some programs); for M Div, 2 foreign languages, internship. *Entrance requirements:* For M Div and master's, 2 letters of reference. Additional exam requirements/recommendations for international students: Required—TOEFL (minimum score 570 paper-based; 230 computer-based; 89 iBT), TWE (minimum score 4.5). *Faculty research:* Neo-paganism, New Testament background, eschatology, Protestant scholasticism, Ezekiel.

Westminster Theological Seminary, Graduate and Professional Programs, Philadelphia, PA 19118. Offers apologetics (Th M); Biblical and urban studies (Certificate); Biblical counseling

Religion

Westminster Theological Seminary (continued)
(MA); biblical studies (MAR); Christian studies (Certificate); church history (Th M); counseling (M Div); general studies (M Div, MAR); hermeneutics and Bible interpretations (PhD); historical and theological studies (PhD); historical theology (Th M); New Testament (Th M); Old Testament (Th M); pastoral counseling (D Min); pastoral ministry (M Div, D Min); systematic theology (Th M); theological studies (MAR); urban missions (M Div, MA, MAR, D Min). *Accreditation:* ATS. Part-time programs available. Terminal master's awarded for partial completion of doctoral program. *Degree requirements:* For master's, thesis (for some programs); for doctorate, 4 foreign languages, comprehensive exam (for some programs), thesis/dissertation; for M Div, 2 foreign languages. *Entrance requirements:* For doctorate, GRE General Test. Additional exam requirements/recommendations for international students: Required—TOEFL, TWE.

Wheaton College, Graduate School, Department of Biblical and Theological Studies, Program in Religion in American Life, Wheaton, IL 60187-5593. Offers MA. Part-time programs available. *Degree requirements:* For master's, thesis optional. *Entrance requirements:* For master's, GRE General Test, MAT. Electronic applications accepted.

Wilfrid Laurier University, Faculty of Graduate Studies, Faculty of Arts, Department of Religion and Culture, Waterloo, ON N2L 3C5, Canada. Offers MA, PhD. *Degree requirements:* For master's, thesis optional; for doctorate, thesis/dissertation. *Entrance requirements:* For master's, honors BA or the equivalent in religious studies or other interdisciplinary social science or humanities program, minimum B average in overall undergraduate course work, B+ average in the undergraduate major; for doctorate, MA in religious studies, minimum A-

average. Additional exam requirements/recommendations for international students: Required—TOEFL (minimum score 230 computer-based; 89 iBT). Electronic applications accepted. *Faculty research:* Religious diversity in North America.

Wycliffe College, Division of Advanced Degree Studies, Toronto, ON M5S 1H7, Canada. Offers MA, Th M, D Min, PhD, Th D. *Accreditation:* ATS (one or more programs are accredited). Part-time programs available. Terminal master's awarded for partial completion of doctoral program. *Degree requirements:* For master's, 2 foreign languages, thesis (for some programs); for doctorate, 3 foreign languages, thesis/dissertation. *Entrance requirements:* Additional exam requirements/recommendations for international students: Required—TOEFL (minimum score 600 paper-based; 250 computer-based). *Expenses:* Contact institution. *Faculty research:* Old and New Testament, doctrine, ethics, philosophy, history.

Wycliffe College, Division of Basic Degree Studies, Toronto, ON M5S 1H7, Canada. Offers Christian Studies (Diploma); theology (M Div, M Rel, MTS). *Accreditation:* ATS. Part-time programs available. *Degree requirements:* For master's, one foreign language, thesis; for M Div, thesis/dissertation optional. *Entrance requirements:* Additional exam requirements/recommendations for international students: Required—TOEFL (minimum score 580 paper-based).

Yale University, Graduate School of Arts and Sciences, Department of Religious Studies, New Haven, CT 06520. Offers PhD. *Degree requirements:* For doctorate, 2 foreign languages, thesis/dissertation. *Entrance requirements:* For doctorate, GRE General Test.

Theology

Abilene Christian University, Graduate School, College of Biblical Studies, Graduate School of Theology, Program in Divinity, Abilene, TX 79699-9100. Offers M Div. *Accreditation:* ATS. *Students:* 40 full-time (6 women), 21 part-time (3 women); includes 3 minority (2 African Americans, 1 Hispanic American), 2 international. 22 applicants, 82% accepted, 12 enrolled. *Degree requirements:* For M Div, one foreign language, comprehensive exam. *Entrance requirements:* GMAT, GRE, or MAT. *Application deadline:* For fall admission, 4/1 priority date for domestic students; for spring admission, 11/1 for domestic students. Applications are processed on a rolling basis. Application fee: $40 ($45 for international students). Electronic applications accepted. *Expenses:* Tuition: Full-time $10,728; part-time $640 per hour. Required fees: $1090; $53.50 per hour. $10 per term. Tuition and fees vary according to campus/location. *Financial support:* In 2008–09, 30 students received support. Applicants required to submit FAFSA. *Unit head:* Dr. Tim Sensing, Graduate Advisor, 325-674-3792, Fax: 325-674-6180, E-mail: sensingt@acu.edu. *Application contact:* William Horn, Graduate Admissions Counselor, 325-674-2656, Fax: 325-674-6717, E-mail: gradinfo@acu.edu.

Abilene Christian University, Graduate School, College of Biblical Studies, Graduate School of Theology, Program in History and Theology, Abilene, TX 79699-9100. Offers MA. *Students:* 5 full-time (2 women), 6 part-time (0 women). 5 applicants, 100% accepted, 3 enrolled. In 2008, 2 master's awarded. *Degree requirements:* For master's, comprehensive exam, thesis. *Application deadline:* For fall admission, 4/1 priority date for domestic students; for spring admission, 11/1 for domestic students. Applications are processed on a rolling basis. Application fee: $40 ($45 for international students). Electronic applications accepted. *Expenses:* Tuition: Full-time $10,728; part-time $640 per hour. Required fees: $1090; $53.50 per hour. $10 per term. Tuition and fees vary according to campus/location. *Financial support:* In 2008–09, 7 students received support. Application deadline: 4/1; *Unit head:* Dr. Douglas Foster, Graduate Advisor, 325-674-3730, Fax: 325-674-6180, E-mail: foster@bible.acu.edu. *Application contact:* William Horn, Graduate Admissions Counselor, 325-674-2656, Fax: 325-674-6717, E-mail: gradinfo@acu.edu.

Abilene Christian University, Graduate School, College of Biblical Studies, Graduate School of Theology, Program in New Testament, Abilene, TX 79699-9100. Offers MA. *Accreditation:* ATS. *Students:* 2 full-time (1 woman), 2 part-time (0 women). In 2008, 1 master's awarded. *Degree requirements:* For master's, comprehensive exam, thesis. *Entrance requirements:* For master's, GRE General Test or MAT. *Application deadline:* For fall admission, 4/1 priority date for domestic students; for spring admission, 11/1 for domestic students. Applications are processed on a rolling basis. Application fee: $40 ($45 for international students). Electronic applications accepted. *Expenses:* Tuition: Full-time $10,728; part-time $640 per hour. Required fees: $1090; $53.50 per hour. $10 per term. Tuition and fees vary according to campus/location. *Financial support:* In 2008–09, 2 students received support. Application deadline: 4/1; *Unit head:* Dr. James Thompson, Graduate Advisor, 325-674-3781, Fax: 325-674-2417, E-mail: thompsonja@acu.edu. *Application contact:* William Horn, Graduate Admissions Counselor, 325-674-2656, Fax: 325-674-6717, E-mail: gradinfo@acu.edu.

Abilene Christian University, Graduate School, College of Biblical Studies, Graduate School of Theology, Program in Old Testament, Abilene, TX 79699-9100. Offers MA. *Students:* 2 full-time (both women). 3 applicants, 100% accepted, 0 enrolled. In 2008, 1 master's awarded. *Degree requirements:* For master's, comprehensive exam, thesis. *Application deadline:* For fall admission, 4/1 priority date for domestic students; for spring admission, 11/1 for domestic students. Applications are processed on a rolling basis. Application fee: $40 ($45 for international students). Electronic applications accepted. *Expenses:* Tuition: Full-time $10,728; part-time $640 per hour. Required fees: $1090; $53.50 per hour. $10 per term. Tuition and fees vary according to campus/location. *Financial support:* In 2008–09, 2 students received support. Application deadline: 4/1; *Unit head:* Dr. Mark Hamilton, Graduate Advisor, 325-674-3765, Fax: 325-674-6180, E-mail: wmh00c@acu.edu. *Application contact:* William Horn, Graduate Admissions Counselor, 325-674-2656, Fax: 325-674-6717, E-mail: gradinfo@acu.edu.

Acadia University, Divinity College, Wolfville, NS B4P 2R6, Canada. Offers divinity (M Div); theology (MA, D Min), including biblical studies (MA), church history (MA), theology (MA). *Accreditation:* ATS. Part-time programs available. *Faculty:* 12 full-time (2 women), 12 part-time/adjunct (1 woman). *Students:* 33 full-time (11 women), 28 part-time (4 women). Average age 43. In 2008, 32 master's, 6 doctorates awarded. *Degree requirements:* For master's, one foreign language, thesis (for some programs); for doctorate, one foreign language, comprehensive exam, thesis/dissertation. *Entrance requirements:* For M Div, minimum GPA of 2.0; for master's, minimum GPA of 3.0 (MA), (M Div); for doctorate, minimum GPA of 3.0, 3 years ministry experience. Additional exam requirements/recommendations for international students: Required—TOEFL. *Application deadline:* For fall admission, 6/30 priority date for domestic students, 4/1 priority date for international students; for spring admission, 4/30 priority date for domestic students. Applications are processed on a rolling basis. Application fee: $25. *Expenses:* Contact institution. *Financial support:* In 2008–09, 8 teaching assistantships (averaging $1,000 per year) were awarded; career-related internships or fieldwork, institutionally sponsored loans, and scholarships/grants also available. Support available to part-time students. Financial award application deadline: 8/12. *Faculty research:* Biblical canon, Jesus, Dead Sea Scrolls, Baptist studies, old testament–Septuagint. *Unit head:* Dr. Harry M. Gardner, President, 902-585-2212, Fax: 902-585-2233, E-mail: harry.gardner@acadiau.ca. *Application contact:* Shawna Peverill, Manager of Student Services, 902-585-2215, Fax: 902-585-2233, E-mail: shawna.peverill@acadiau.ca.

Alliance Theological Seminary, Graduate and Professional Programs, Nyack, NY 10960. Offers Christian ministry (MPS); counseling (MA); intercultural studies (MA); missions (MPS);

New Testament (MA); Old Testament (MA); theology (M Div); urban ministry (MPS). *Accreditation:* ATS. Part-time programs available. *Degree requirements:* For master's, comprehensive exam (for some programs), thesis optional, internships; for M Div, 2 foreign languages, internship. *Entrance requirements:* Proficiency in New Testament Greek, minimum GPA of 2.5 (undergraduate). Additional exam requirements/recommendations for international students: Required—TOEFL (minimum score 550 paper-based; 213 computer-based).

Ambrose University College, Ambrose Seminary, Calgary, AB T2P 3T5, Canada. Offers biblical/theological studies (MA); Chinese ministries (Certificate); Christian studies (Diploma); church education (M Div); intercultural ministries (M Div, MA, Certificate, Diploma); leadership and ministry (MA, Certificate, Diploma); pastoral ministries (M Div). *Accreditation:* ATS (one or more programs are accredited). Part-time programs available. *Degree requirements:* For master's, 2 foreign languages, internship; for M Div, one foreign language, internship. *Entrance requirements:* For master's, bachelor degree. Additional exam requirements/recommendations for international students: Required—TOEFL or IELTS. Electronic applications accepted. *Faculty research:* Evangelicalism and sociology, missiological trends, chaplaincy, intertestamental studies, postmodernism.

American Baptist Seminary of the West, Graduate and Professional Programs, Berkeley, CA 94704-3029. Offers community leadership (MA); theology (M Div, MA). *Accreditation:* ACIPE; ATS (one or more programs are accredited). Part-time and evening/weekend programs available. *Faculty:* 4 full-time (all women), 5 part-time/adjunct (0 women). *Students:* 50 full-time (29 women), 21 part-time (11 women); includes 50 minority (44 African Americans, 6 Asian Americans or Pacific Islanders), 13 international. *Entrance requirements:* For M Div, minimum GPA of 2.5; for master's, minimum GPA of 3.0. Additional exam requirements/recommendations for international students: Required—TOEFL (minimum score 550 paper-based; 250 computer-based). *Application deadline:* For fall admission, 4/15 priority date for domestic students, 4/15 for international students. Applications are processed on a rolling basis. Application fee: $25. Electronic applications accepted. *Expenses:* Tuition: Full-time $12,750; part-time $500 per credit. Required fees: $240 per semester. One-time fee: $250. Tuition and fees vary according to degree level. *Financial support:* Career-related internships or fieldwork, institutionally sponsored loans, scholarships/grants, tuition waivers (partial), and tuition discount available. Support available to part-time students. Financial award application deadline: 4/15; financial award applicants required to submit FAFSA. *Unit head:* Dr. Paul M. Martin, President for the Interim, 510-841-1905 Ext. 224, Fax: 510-841-2446, E-mail: pmartin@absw.edu. *Application contact:* Rev. Michelle M. Holmes, Vice President, 510-841-1905 Ext. 225, Fax: 510-841-2446, E-mail: mmholmes@absw.edu.

American Jewish University, Graduate School, Ziegler School of Rabbinic Studies, Bel Air, CA 90077-1599. Offers MARS. *Degree requirements:* For master's, one foreign language. *Entrance requirements:* For master's, GRE General Test, interview. Additional exam requirements/recommendations for international students: Required—TOEFL.

Amridge University, Graduate and Professional Programs, Montgomery, AL 36117. Offers behavioral leadership and management (MA); biblical studies (MA, PhD); family therapy (D Min); leadership and management (MS); marriage and family therapy (M Div, MA, PhD), including marriage and family therapy (PhD), professional counseling (PhD); ministerial leadership (M Div, MS); pastoral counseling (M Div, MS); practical theology (MA); professional counseling (M Div, MA); theology (M Div, D Min). *Accreditation:* ATS. Part-time and evening/weekend programs available. Postbaccalaureate distance learning degree programs offered (no on-campus study). *Faculty:* 44 full-time (9 women), 18 part-time/adjunct (7 women). *Students:* 131 full-time (61 women), 218 part-time (119 women); includes 174 minority (164 African Americans, 1 American Indian/Alaska Native, 1 Asian American or Pacific Islander, 8 Hispanic Americans). Average age 35. *Degree requirements:* For master's, one foreign language, comprehensive exam (for some programs), thesis (for some programs); for doctorate, comprehensive exam (for some programs), thesis/dissertation; for M Div, comprehensive exam (for some programs). *Entrance requirements:* For M Div, master's, and doctorate, GRE General Test or MAT. Additional exam requirements/recommendations for international students: Required—TOEFL. *Application deadline:* For fall admission, 9/1 priority date for domestic students; for spring admission, 1/1 priority date for domestic students. Applications are processed on a rolling basis. Application fee: $75. Electronic applications accepted. *Expenses:* Tuition: Full-time $9630; part-time $535 per semester hour. Required fees: $600 per term. Tuition and fees vary according to course load and degree level. *Financial support:* Federal Work-Study and scholarships/grants available. Support available to part-time students. Financial award applicants required to submit FAFSA. *Faculty research:* Homiletics, hermeneutics, ancient Near Eastern history. *Unit head:* Rick Johnson, Director of Enrollment Management, 800-351-4040 Ext. 7513, Fax: 334-387-3878, E-mail: rickjohnson@amridgeuniversity.edu. *Application contact:* Ora Davis, Admissions Officer, 334-387-3877 Ext. 7524, Fax: 334-387-3878, E-mail: oradavis@amridgeuniversity.edu.

Anderson University, School of Theology, Anderson, IN 46012-3495. Offers missions (MA); theology (M Div, MTS, D Min). *Accreditation:* ACIPE; ATS. Part-time programs available. *Degree requirements:* For master's, one foreign language, thesis, integrative senior seminar; for doctorate, thesis/dissertation; for M Div, thesis/dissertation (for some programs). *Faculty research:* Small-church/bivocational ministry, women in ministry.

Andover Newton Theological School, Graduate and Professional Programs, Newton Centre, MA 02459-2243. Offers divinity (M Div); general (MA); psychology and religion (MA); religious education (MA); research (MA); sacred theology (STM); theology (D Min); theology and the arts (MA). *Accreditation:* ACIPE; ATS. Part-time programs available. *Degree requirements:* For master's, comprehensive exam (for some programs), thesis (for some programs); for doctorate, comprehensive exam, thesis/dissertation. *Entrance requirements:* For doctorate, M Div or equivalent. Additional exam requirements/recommendations for international students: Required—TOEFL (minimum score 550 paper-based; 213 computer-based). Electronic applications accepted.

Andrews University, School of Graduate Studies, Seventh-day Adventist Theological Seminary, Berrien Springs, MI 49104. Offers ministry (M Div, D Min); pastoral ministry (MA); religious education (MA, Ed D, PhD, Ed S); theology (M Th, Th D); youth ministry (MA). *Accreditation:* ATS. *Faculty:* 35 full-time (3 women), 1 (woman) part-time/adjunct. *Students:* 377 full-time (63 women), 494 part-time (46 women); includes 336 minority (173 African Americans, 3 American Indian/Alaska Native, 43 Asian Americans or Pacific Islanders, 117 Hispanic Americans), 239 international. Average age 41. In 2008, 103 first professional degrees, 26 master's, 23 doctorates, 3 other advanced degrees awarded. *Degree requirements:* For master's, thesis optional; for doctorate, variable foreign language requirement, thesis/dissertation; for M Div, one foreign language, thesis/dissertation optional. *Entrance requirements:* For master's, GRE Subject Test, minimum GPA of 2.0. Additional exam requirements/recommendations for international students: Required—TOEFL (minimum score 550 paper-based). *Application deadline:* Applications are processed on a rolling basis. Application fee: $40. *Expenses:* Tuition: Full-time $18,360; part-time $765 per credit hour. Required fees: $476; $765 per credit hour. $238 per semester. Tuition and fees vary according to degree level. *Financial support:* Fellowships, research assistantships, teaching assistantships, career-related internships or fieldwork, Federal Work-Study, and institutionally sponsored loans available. *Unit head:* Dr. Denis Fortin, Dean, 269-471-3537. *Application contact:* Carolyn Hurst, Director, 800-253-2874, Fax: 269-471-6321.

Apex School of Theology, Graduate Programs, Durham, NC 27713. Offers M Div, MCE. *Faculty research:* Sociology, educational sciences, economics.

Aquinas Institute of Theology, Graduate and Professional Programs, St. Louis, MO 63108. Offers biblical studies (Certificate); health care mission (MAHCM); ministry (M Div); pastoral care (Certificate); pastoral ministry (MAPM); pastoral studies (MAPS); preaching (D Min); spiritual direction (Certificate); theology (M Div, MA); Thomistic studies (Certificate); M Div/MA; MAPS/MSW. *Accreditation:* ATS (one or more programs are accredited). Part-time and evening/weekend programs available. Postbaccalaureate distance learning degree programs offered (minimal on-campus study). *Faculty:* 17 full-time (10 women), 4 part-time/adjunct (2 women). *Students:* 74 full-time (25 women), 193 part-time (127 women); includes 37 minority (16 African Americans, 1 American Indian/Alaska Native, 10 Asian Americans or Pacific Islanders, 10 Hispanic Americans), 12 international. Average age 41. 76 applicants, 87% accepted, 56 enrolled. In 2008, 42 master's, 8 doctorates awarded. *Degree requirements:* For master's, one foreign language, comprehensive exam, thesis or major paper; for doctorate, thesis/dissertation. *Entrance requirements:* For M Div and master's, MAT; for doctorate, 3 years of ministerial experience, 6 hours of graduate course work in homiletics, M Div or the equivalent, minimum GPA of 3.0. Additional exam requirements/recommendations for international students: Required—TOEFL. *Application deadline:* For fall admission, 3/15 priority date for domestic and international students; for spring admission, 11/15 priority date for domestic and international students. Applications are processed on a rolling basis. Application fee: $50. *Expenses:* Tuition: Full-time $14,784; part-time $616 per credit hour. Required fees: $195 per semester. Tuition and fees vary according to course load. *Financial support:* Career-related internships or fieldwork, scholarships/grants, health care benefits, and tuition waivers (partial) available. Support available to part-time students. Financial award application deadline: 3/15; financial award applicants required to submit CSS PROFILE or FAFSA. *Faculty research:* Theology of preaching, hermeneutics, lay ecclesiastical ministry, pastoral and practical theology. *Unit head:* Fr. Gregory Heille, Academic Dean, 314-256-8800, Fax: 314-256-8888, E-mail: heille@ai.edu. *Application contact:* David Werthmann, Director of Admissions, 314-256-8806, Fax: 314-256-8888, E-mail: admissions@ai.edu.

Asbury Theological Seminary, Graduate and Professional Programs, Wilmore, KY 40390-1199. Offers MA, MAC, MACE, MACL, MAPC, MAXM, MAYM, Th M, D Miss, PhD, Certificate. *Accreditation:* ATS. Part-time programs available. Postbaccalaureate distance learning degree programs offered (minimal on-campus study). *Faculty:* 67 full-time (15 women), 74 part-time/adjunct (14 women). *Students:* 708 full-time (219 women), 852 part-time (263 women); includes 110 minority (59 African Americans, 10 American Indian/Alaska Native, 12 Asian Americans or Pacific Islanders, 29 Hispanic Americans), 156 international. Average age 25. 765 applicants, 75% accepted, 364 enrolled. In 2008, 95 master's, 15 doctorates, 38 other advanced degrees awarded. Terminal master's awarded for partial completion of doctoral program. *Degree requirements:* For master's, thesis (for some programs); for doctorate, thesis/dissertation, qualifying exam. *Entrance requirements:* For master's, minimum GPA of 2.75; for doctorate, minimum GPA of 3.0. Additional exam requirements/recommendations for international students: Required—TOEFL, IELTS. *Application deadline:* Applications are processed on a rolling basis. Application fee: $50. Electronic applications accepted. *Expenses:* Tuition: Full-time $12,474; part-time $462 per credit hour. Required fees: $50; $30 per year. Tuition and fees vary according to course level, course load, degree level, campus/location and program. *Financial support:* In 2008–09, 1,317 students received support. Career-related internships or fieldwork, Federal Work-Study, institutionally sponsored loans, and scholarships/grants available. Support available to part-time students. Financial award applicants required to submit FAFSA. *Unit head:* Dr. Leslie A. Andrews, Provost, 859-858-2206, Fax: 859-858-2025, E-mail: leslie.andrews@asburyseminary.edu. *Application contact:* Janelle Vernon, Admissions Director, 859-858-2211, Fax: 859-858-2287, E-mail: admissions.office@asburyseminary.edu.

Ashland Theological Seminary, Graduate Programs, Ashland, OH 44805. Offers biblical and theological studies (MA, MAR), including New Testament (MA), Old Testament (MA); Christian ministry (MAPT); Christian studies (Diploma); clinical pastoral counseling (MACPC); historical studies (MA); ministry (D Min); pastoral counseling (MAPC); pastoral ministry (M Div); theological studies (MA). *Accreditation:* ATS. Part-time programs available. *Degree requirements:* For master's, comprehensive exam (for some programs), thesis (for some programs); for doctorate, thesis/dissertation; for M Div, 2 foreign languages. *Entrance requirements:* For M Div, minimum GPA of 2.75; for master's, minimum undergraduate GPA of 2.75; for doctorate, M Div, minimum undergraduate GPA of 3.0. Additional exam requirements/recommendations for international students: Required—TOEFL (minimum score 550 paper-based). Electronic applications accepted. *Faculty research:* Semitic languages and linguistics, rhetorical and social-scientific criticism, Anabaptist studies, inner spiritual healing, African-American clergy in film and literature.

Assemblies of God Theological Seminary, Graduate and Professional Programs, Springfield, MO 65802. Offers biblical preaching (D Min); Christian ministries (MA); divinity (M Div); intercultural studies (D Miss, PhD); missional leadership (D Min); relief and development (D Miss); self-design study (D Min); women in leadership (D Min). *Accreditation:* ATS. Part-time and evening/weekend programs available. Postbaccalaureate distance learning degree programs offered (minimal on-campus study). *Faculty:* 16 full-time (3 women), 21 part-time/adjunct (4 women). *Students:* 220 full-time (69 women), 226 part-time (49 women); includes 49 minority (11 African Americans, 5 American Indian/Alaska Native, 11 Asian Americans or Pacific Islanders, 22 Hispanic Americans), 7 international. Average age 36. *Degree requirements:* For master's, analytical reflection paper or comprehensive exam; for doctorate, thesis/dissertation; for M Div, one foreign language, analytical reflection paper. *Entrance requirements:* For M Div, minimum GPA of 2.0; for master's, minimum GPA of 2.5; for doctorate, minimum GPA of 3.0. Additional exam requirements/recommendations for international students: Required—TOEFL (minimum score 550 paper-based; 213 computer-based; 80 iBT). *Application deadline:* For fall admission, 7/1 priority date for domestic students, 6/1 priority date for international students; for spring admission, 12/1 priority date for domestic students, 11/1 priority date for international students. Applications are processed on a rolling basis. Application fee: $35. Electronic applications accepted. *Financial support:* Career-related internships or fieldwork, Federal Work-Study, and scholarships/grants available. Support available to part-time students. Financial award application deadline: 7/15; financial award applicants required to submit FAFSA. *Unit head:* Stephen Lim, Academic Dean, 417-268-1000, Fax: 417-268-1001, E-mail: slim@agts.edu. *Application contact:* Stephen Lim, Academic Dean, 417-268-1000, Fax: 417-268-1001, E-mail: slim@agts.edu.

Associated Mennonite Biblical Seminary, Graduate and Professional Programs, Elkhart, IN 46517-1999. Offers Christian formation (MA); divinity (M Div); mission and evangelism (MA); peace studies (MA); theological studies (MA, Certificate). *Accreditation:* ACIPE; ATS. Part-time programs available. *Degree requirements:* For master's, comprehensive exam, thesis optional; for M Div, integration paper. *Entrance requirements:* For M Div, master's, and Certificate, 3 letters of reference. Additional exam requirements/recommendations for international students: Required—TOEFL (minimum score 550 paper-based; 213 computer-based). Electronic applications accepted. *Faculty research:* Biblical studies, theology, church history, church leadership.

The Athenaeum of Ohio, Graduate Programs, Cincinnati, OH 45230-5900. Offers biblical studies (MABS); divinity (M Div); lay ministry (Certificate); pastoral counseling (MAPC); pastoral ministry (MA); theology (MA Th); M Div/MA Th; M Div/MABS; M Div/MAPC. *Accreditation:* ATS (one or more programs are accredited). Part-time and evening/weekend programs available. *Degree requirements:* For master's, one foreign language, comprehensive exam (for some programs), thesis optional; for M Div, comprehensive exam.

Atlantic School of Theology, Graduate and Professional Programs, Halifax, NS B3H 3B5, Canada. Offers M Div, MTS, Graduate Certificate. *Accreditation:* ATS. Part-time programs available. Postbaccalaureate distance learning degree programs offered (minimal on-campus study). *Degree requirements:* For master's, thesis. *Entrance requirements:* For M Div, master's, and Graduate Certificate, minimum B average in undergraduate course work. *Faculty research:* Ethics and biology; death, dying and pastoral care; theology and the economy; adult education; John and anti-Judaism.

Austin Graduate School of Theology, Program in Theological Studies, Austin, TX 78705-5610. Offers MATS. Part-time programs available. *Degree requirements:* For master's, 2 foreign languages, comprehensive exam, faculty forums. *Entrance requirements:* For master's, 3 letters of reference. Additional exam requirements/recommendations for international students: Required—TOEFL (minimum score 550 paper-based). *Faculty research:* Revelation, synoptic problem, acadian, biblical archaeology, worship.

Austin Presbyterian Theological Seminary, Graduate and Professional Programs, Austin, TX 78705-5797. Offers divinity (M Div); ministry (D Min); theological studies (MA); M Div/MATS; M Div/MSSW. *Accreditation:* ACIPE; ATS. Part-time programs available. *Degree requirements:* For doctorate, thesis/dissertation; for M Div, Greek, Hebrew. *Entrance requirements:* References. Additional exam requirements/recommendations for international students: Required—TOEFL (minimum score 550 paper-based; 213 computer-based; 79 iBT). *Faculty research:* Mystical theology, religious pluralism, narrative preaching, social ethics, pastoral care and healing.

Ave Maria University, Graduate Programs, Ave Maria, FL 34142. Offers pastoral theology (MTS); theology (MA, PhD). Terminal master's awarded for partial completion of doctoral program. *Degree requirements:* For master's, one foreign language, thesis; for doctorate, 3 foreign languages, comprehensive exam, thesis/dissertation. *Entrance requirements:* For master's, GRE; for doctorate, GRE, M Div or equivalent; MA or MTS in religion, theology, or philosophy; bachelor's degree with strong background in religion, theology, and/or philosophy.

Ave Maria University, Institute for Pastoral Theology, Ave Maria, FL 34142. Offers MTS. Part-time and evening/weekend programs available.

Azusa Pacific University, Haggard School of Theology, Program in Ministry, Azusa, CA 91702-7000. Offers D Min.

Azusa Pacific University, Haggard School of Theology, Program in Non-Profit Leadership and Theology, Azusa, CA 91702-7000. Offers Christian non-profit leadership (MA).

Azusa Pacific University, Haggard School of Theology, Program in Religion: Biblical Studies, Azusa, CA 91702-7000. Offers MAR.

Azusa Pacific University, Haggard School of Theology, Program in Religion: Theology and Ethics, Azusa, CA 91702-7000. Offers MAR.

Bangor Theological Seminary, Professional Program, Bangor, ME 04401-4699. Offers M Div, MA, MTS, D Min. M Div not offered at Portland, ME campus. *Accreditation:* ACIPE; ATS. Part-time programs available. *Degree requirements:* For master's, thesis optional; for doctorate, project, report; for M Div, thesis/dissertation optional. *Entrance requirements:* For M Div and master's, Bachelor degree; for doctorate, M Div, 3 years in ministry. Additional exam requirements/recommendations for international students: Required—TOEFL (minimum score 550 paper-based; 213 computer-based; 80 iBT). *Faculty research:* Formation of the New Testament canon, critical pedagogy, history of theological education, human sexuality, the Isaiah Scroll.

Baptist Bible College, Graduate School of Theology, Springfield, MO 65803-3498. Offers biblical counseling (MA); biblical studies (MA); church ministry (MA); intercultural studies (MA); theology (M Div). Part-time programs available. *Degree requirements:* For master's, 2 foreign languages, thesis (for some programs); for M Div, 2 foreign languages, thesis/dissertation (for some programs). *Entrance requirements:* For master's, outcomes test. Electronic applications accepted.

Baptist Bible College of Pennsylvania, Baptist Bible Seminary, Clarks Summit, PA 18411-1297. Offers biblical studies (PhD); church planting (M Div); global missions (M Div); military chaplaincy (M Div); ministry (M Min, D Min); pastor of church education (M Div); pastor of outreach (M Div); pastoral counseling (M Div); pastoral leadership (M Div); theology (M Div, Th M); youth pastor (M Div). Part-time and evening/weekend programs available. Postbaccalaureate distance learning degree programs offered (minimal on-campus study). Terminal master's awarded for partial completion of doctoral program. *Degree requirements:* For master's, 2 foreign languages, thesis; for doctorate, 2 foreign languages, comprehensive exam (for some programs), thesis/dissertation, oral exam; for M Div, 2 foreign languages, thesis/dissertation, oral exam. *Entrance requirements:* For doctorate, Greek and Hebrew entrance exams (PhD). Electronic applications accepted.

Baptist Missionary Association Theological Seminary, Graduate and Professional Programs, Jacksonville, TX 75766-5407. Offers M Div, MAR. *Accreditation:* ATS. Part-time programs available. *Degree requirements:* For master's, thesis optional; for M Div, 2 foreign languages, thesis/dissertation optional. *Entrance requirements:* Additional exam requirements/recommendations for international students: Required—TOEFL (minimum score 550 paper-based; 213 computer-based). Electronic applications accepted. *Faculty research:* Education, Biblical studies.

Baptist Theological Seminary at Richmond, Graduate and Professional Program, Richmond, VA 23227. Offers children and family ministry (M Div); Christian education (M Div); church music (M Div); theology (D Min); youth and student ministry (M Div); M Div/MS; M Div/MSW. *Accreditation:* ATS. Part-time programs available. Postbaccalaureate distance learning degree programs offered (minimal on-campus study). *Degree requirements:* For doctorate, one foreign language, comprehensive exam, thesis/dissertation, field study, independent study; for M Div, one foreign language, comprehensive exam (for some programs), thesis/dissertation optional, mission immersion experience, internship. *Entrance requirements:* For doctorate, MAT, M Div, 3 years of full-time ministry experience. Additional exam requirements/recommendations for international students: Required—TOEFL (minimum score 481 paper-based; 213 computer-based). *Faculty research:* New Testament studies, Old Testament studies, pastoral care, church history, theology.

Theology

Barry University, School of Arts and Sciences, Department of Theology and Philosophy, Miami Shores, FL 33161-6695. Offers ministry (D Min); pastoral ministry for Hispanics (MA); pastoral theology (MA); practical theology (MA). *Accreditation:* ATS. Part-time and evening/weekend programs available. *Degree requirements:* For master's, comprehensive exam, thesis optional; for doctorate, thesis/dissertation. *Entrance requirements:* For master's, GRE General Test or MAT, minimum GPA of 3.0. Electronic applications accepted. *Faculty research:* Fundamental morals, bioethics, social ethics, liturgical and sacramental theology, biblical studies.

Baylor University, George W. Truett Seminary, Waco, TX 76798. Offers M Div, MTS, D Min, M Div/MM, M Div/MS Ed, M Div/MSW, MTS/MSW. *Accreditation:* ATS. *Faculty:* 17 full-time (3 women), 7 part-time/adjunct (1 woman). *Students:* 313 full-time (101 women), 93 part-time (23 women); includes 93 minority (52 African Americans, 2 American Indian/Alaska Native, 7 Asian Americans or Pacific Islanders, 32 Hispanic Americans), 26 international. Average age 29. 144 applicants, 94% accepted, 102 enrolled. In 2008, 70 first professional degrees, 6 master's, 1 doctorate awarded. *Degree requirements:* For M Div, Greek and Hebrew. *Entrance requirements:* For M Div, minimum GPA of 2.75; for doctorate, minimum M Div GPA of 3.0. Additional exam requirements/recommendations for international students: Required—TOEFL (minimum score 82 computer-based). *Application deadline:* For fall admission, 5/1 priority date for domestic students, 5/1 for international students; for spring admission, 11/1 priority date for domestic students, 11/1 for international students. Applications are processed on a rolling basis. Application fee: $35. *Expenses:* Contact institution. *Financial support:* In 2008–09, 207 students received support, including 1 research assistantship, 12 teaching assistantships; career-related internships or fieldwork, institutionally sponsored loans, scholarships/grants, tuition waivers (partial), and unspecified assistantships also available. Support available to part-time students. Financial award application deadline: 8/1; financial award applicants required to submit FAFSA. Total annual research expenditures: $10,000. *Unit head:* Dr. David E. Garland, Dean, 254-710-3755, Fax: 254-710-3753. *Application contact:* Dr. Grear Howard, Director of Student Services, 254-710-3755, Fax: 254-710-7233, E-mail: grear_howard@baylor.edu.

Beacon University, Graduate Programs, Columbus, GA 31909. Offers cell church development (MAPM); counseling ministry (MAPM); military chaplaincy (MAPM); organizational leadership (MAPM); pastoral ministry (MAPM); theology (M Div, MABS). Part-time and evening/weekend programs available. Postbaccalaureate distance learning degree programs offered (minimal on-campus study). *Degree requirements:* For master's and M Div, comprehensive exam. *Entrance requirements:* For M Div, MAT or GRE or GMAT or MTE, official undergrad and/or transf.; for master's, MAT or GRE or NTE or GMAT, official undergrad and/or trsfr. Additional exam requirements/recommendations for international students: Required—TOEFL (minimum score 500 paper-based; 173 computer-based; 61 iBT); Recommended—IELTS (minimum score 6).

Bethany Theological Seminary, Graduate and Professional Programs, Richmond, IN 47374-4019. Offers biblical studies (MA Th); ministry studies (M Div); peace studies (M Div, MA Th); theological studies (MA Th, CATS); youth ministry (M Div). *Accreditation:* ACIPE; ATS. Part-time programs available. Postbaccalaureate distance learning degree programs offered (minimal on-campus study). *Degree requirements:* For master's, thesis. *Entrance requirements:* For M Div, letters of reference, minimum GPA of 2.75; for master's, letters of reference, minimum GPA of 3.0. Additional exam requirements/recommendations for international students: Required—TOEFL (minimum score 550 paper-based; 218 computer-based).

Beth Benjamin Academy of Connecticut, Graduate and Professional Programs, Stamford, CT 06901-1202.

Bethel College, Division of Graduate Studies, Program in Theological Studies, Mishawaka, IN 46545-5591. Offers MATS. Part-time and evening/weekend programs available. *Faculty:* 1 full-time (0 women), 7 part-time/adjunct (0 women). *Students:* 4 full-time (0 women), 13 part-time (4 women); includes 2 minority (both African Americans). 7 applicants, 86% accepted, 4 enrolled. In 2008, 2 master's awarded. *Entrance requirements:* Additional exam requirements/recommendations for international students: Required—TOEFL (minimum score 540 paper-based; 207 computer-based). *Application deadline:* For fall admission, 5/1 for international students; for spring admission, 10/1 for international students. Applications are processed on a rolling basis. Application fee: $25. Electronic applications accepted. *Expenses:* Tuition: Full-time $6120; part-time $340 per credit hour. Tuition and fees vary according to program. *Financial support:* Career-related internships or fieldwork available. Financial award applicants required to submit FAFSA. *Unit head:* Dr. Eugene Carpenter, Director, 574-257-3332, E-mail: carpeng@bethelcollege.edu. *Application contact:* Dr. John Dendiu, Advisor, 574-257-2675, Fax: 574-257-3385, E-mail: dendiuj@bethelcollege.edu.

Bethel Seminary, Graduate and Professional Programs, St. Paul, MN 55112-6998. Offers applied ministry (MA); biblical studies (MATS, Certificate); children's and family ministry (MACFM); Christian education (MACE); Christian thought (M Div, MACT); church leadership (D Min); community ministry leadership (MA, Certificate); congregation and family care (D Min); global and contextual studies (MA, MATS); historical studies (MATS); lay ministry (Certificate); marriage and family studies (M Div); marriage and family therapy (MAMFT, Certificate); pastoral ministries (M Div); spiritual formation (Certificate); theological studies (MATS, Certificate); transformational leadership (MATL); youth ministries (MACE). *Accreditation:* ACIPE; ATS (one or more programs are accredited). Part-time and evening/weekend programs available. Postbaccalaureate distance learning degree programs offered (minimal on-campus study). *Faculty:* 26 full-time (2 women), 93 part-time/adjunct (29 women). *Students:* 397 full-time (124 women), 707 part-time (299 women); includes 218 minority (123 African Americans, 1 American Indian/Alaska Native, 67 Asian Americans or Pacific Islanders, 27 Hispanic Americans), 14 international. Average age 36. 470 applicants, 90% accepted, 270 enrolled. In 2008, 63 first professional degrees, 101 master's, 10 doctorates awarded. *Degree requirements:* For master's, variable foreign language requirement, thesis (for some programs); for doctorate, thesis/dissertation; for M Div, one foreign language. *Entrance requirements:* For M Div, letters of reference; for master's, letters of reference, transcripts, personal statement; for doctorate, M Div, letters of reference, essays, organizational support. Additional exam requirements/recommendations for international students: Required—TOEFL (minimum score 550 paper-based; 213 computer-based). *Application deadline:* For fall admission, 8/1 priority date for domestic students, 3/1 for international students; for winter admission, 12/1 priority date for domestic students; for spring admission, 3/1 priority date for domestic students. Applications are processed on a rolling basis. Application fee: $20. Electronic applications accepted. *Financial support:* In 2008–09, 688 students received support, including 20 teaching assistantships; career-related internships or fieldwork, Federal Work-Study, scholarships/grants, and tuition waivers (full) also available. Financial award application deadline: 7/15; financial award applicants required to submit FAFSA. *Faculty research:* Nature of theology, ethics, biblical commentaries, nature of God, science and theology. *Unit head:* Dr. Leland Eliason, Executive Vice President and Provost, 651-638-6182. *Application contact:* Joseph V. Dworak, Director of Admissions, 651-638-6288, Fax: 651-638-6002, E-mail: j-dworak@bethel.edu.

Bethesda Christian University, Graduate and Professional Programs, Anaheim, CA 92801. Offers biblical studies (MA); music (MA); theology (M Div). *Entrance requirements:* For M Div and master's, interview.

Beth HaMedrash Shaarei Yosher Institute, Graduate Programs, Brooklyn, NY 11204. *Accreditation:* AARTS.

Beth Hatalmud Rabbinical College, Graduate Programs, Brooklyn, NY 11214. *Accreditation:* AARTS.

Beth Medrash Govoha, Graduate Programs, Lakewood, NJ 08701-2797. *Accreditation:* AARTS.

Bethune-Cookman University, School of Graduate and Professional Studies, Daytona Beach, FL 32114-3099. Offers transformative leadership (MS). Postbaccalaureate distance learning degree programs offered (minimal on-campus study). *Degree requirements:* For master's,

thesis. *Entrance requirements:* For master's, GRE or MAT, minimum GPA of 2.75 in the last 60 semester hours; 3 letters of recommendation. Additional exam requirements/recommendations for international students: Required—TOEFL (minimum score 550 paper-based; 213 computer-based). Electronic applications accepted. *Faculty research:* Civic engagement, communication ethics, service learning in higher education women in leadership.

Bexley Hall Episcopal Seminary, Graduate Programs, Columbus, OH 43209-2325. Offers M Div, MA. *Accreditation:* ATS.

Biblical Theological Seminary, Graduate and Professional Programs, Hatfield, PA 19440-2499. Offers advanced missional leadership (D Min); advanced pastoral studies (Certificate); biblical counseling (Certificate); biblical studies (MA, Certificate); counseling (MA); ministry (MA); missional theology (MA); theology (M Div); youth ministry (Certificate). *Accreditation:* ATS. Part-time programs available. Postbaccalaureate distance learning degree programs offered. *Degree requirements:* For M Div, thesis/dissertation. *Entrance requirements:* Additional exam requirements/recommendations for international students: Required—TOEFL (minimum score 550 paper-based; 213 computer-based). *Faculty research:* Old Testament narrative, Old Testament historiography, Hebrew syntax, parables, addictions.

Biola University, School of Professional Studies, La Mirada, CA 90639-0001. Offers Christian apologetics (MA); organizational leadership (MA). Part-time and evening/weekend programs available. *Entrance requirements:* For master's, minimum undergraduate GPA of 3.0. Additional exam requirements/recommendations for international students: Required—TOEFL (minimum score 550 paper-based; 213 computer-based).

Biola University, Talbot School of Theology, La Mirada, CA 90639-0001. Offers Bible exposition (MA); biblical and theological studies (MA); Christian education (MACE); Christian ministry and leadership (MA); divinity (M Div); education (PhD); ministry (MA Min); New Testament (MA); Old Testament (MA); philosophy of religion and ethics (MA); spiritual formation (MA); spiritual formation and soul care (MA); theology (MA, Th M, D Min). *Accreditation:* ATS. Part-time and evening/weekend programs available. *Degree requirements:* For master's, variable foreign language requirement, thesis or alternative; for doctorate, variable foreign language requirement, thesis/dissertation; for M Div, thesis/dissertation or alternative. *Entrance requirements:* For M Div, minimum GPA of 2.6; for master's, minimum undergraduate GPA of 3.0; for doctorate, minimum GPA of 3.25. Additional exam requirements/recommendations for international students: Required—TOEFL (minimum score 550 paper-based; 213 computer-based). *Faculty research:* Moral development; biological, medical, and social ethics; ancient Near Eastern historical philosophy.

Blessed John XXIII National Seminary, School of Theology, Weston, MA 02493-2618. Offers M Div. *Accreditation:* ATS. *Faculty:* 9 full-time (0 women), 19 part-time/adjunct (3 women). *Students:* 60 full-time (0 women); includes 12 minority (3 African Americans, 1 American Indian/Alaska Native, 4 Asian Americans or Pacific Islanders, 4 Hispanic Americans). Average age 45. In 2008, 15 M Divs awarded. *Entrance requirements:* Bachelor's degree or equivalent in life experience. *Application deadline:* For fall admission, 7/15 priority date for domestic students. Applications are processed on a rolling basis. Application fee: $0. *Expenses:* Tuition: Full-time $21,500. *Financial support:* Career-related internships or fieldwork available. *Unit head:* Rev. Peter J. Uglietto, President and Rector, 781-899-5500, Fax: 781-891-9057, E-mail: rev.uglietto@blessedjohnxxiii.edu. *Application contact:* Rev. Peter J. Uglietto, President and Rector, 781-899-5500, Fax: 781-891-9057, E-mail: rev.uglietto@blessedjohnxxiii.edu.

Bob Jones University, Graduate Programs, Greenville, SC 29614. Offers accountancy (MS); Bible (MA); Bible translation (MA); Biblical studies (Certificate); broadcast management (MS); business administration (MBA); church history (MA, PhD); church ministries (MA); church music (MM); cinema and video production (MA); counseling (MS); curriculum and instruction (Ed D); divinity (M Div); dramatic production (MA); educational leadership (MS, Ed D, Ed S); elementary education (M Ed, MAT); English (M Ed, MA, MAT); fine arts (MA); graphic design (MA); history (M Ed, MA); illustration (MA); interpretative speech (MA); mathematics (M Ed, MAT); medical missions (Certificate); ministry (MM, D Min); multi-categorical special education (M Ed, MAT); music (M Ed); New Testament interpretation (PhD); Old Testament interpretation (PhD); orchestral instrument performance (MM); organ performance (MM); pastoral studies (MA); personnel services (MS, Ed S); piano pedagogy (MM); piano performance (MM); platform arts (MA); radio and television broadcasting (MS); rhetoric and public address (MA); secondary education (M Ed); studio art (MA); teaching Bible (MA); theology (MA, PhD); voice performance (MM); youth ministries (MA). M Div/MM.

Boston College, Graduate School of Arts and Sciences, Department of Theology, Chestnut Hill, MA 02467-3800. Offers PhD. *Accreditation:* ATS. Part-time programs available. Terminal master's awarded for partial completion of doctoral program. *Degree requirements:* For doctorate, thesis/dissertation. *Entrance requirements:* For doctorate, GRE General Test. Additional exam requirements/recommendations for international students: Required—TOEFL (minimum score 590 paper-based; 250 computer-based; 91 iBT). Electronic applications accepted. *Expenses:* Tuition: Part-time $1148 per credit. Required fees: $60. *Faculty research:* Roman Catholic theology, Christian social ethics, Bible, history of Christian life and thought.

Boston College, Graduate School of Arts and Sciences, School of Theology and Ministry, Chestnut Hill, MA 02467-3800. Offers church leadership (MA); divinity (M Div); pastoral ministry (MA), including Hispanic ministry, liturgy and worship, pastoral care and counseling, spirituality; religious education (MA, PhD); sacred theology (STD, STL); social justice/social ministry (MA); spiritual direction (MA); theological studies (MTS); theology (Th M, PhD); youth ministry (MA); MA/MA; MS/MA; MSW/MA. Part-time programs available. *Degree requirements:* For doctorate, one foreign language, thesis/dissertation. *Entrance requirements:* For doctorate, GRE. Additional exam requirements/recommendations for international students: Required—TOEFL (minimum score 550 paper-based; 213 computer-based). Electronic applications accepted. *Expenses:* Tuition: Part-time $1148 per credit. Required fees: $60. *Faculty research:* Philosophy and practice of religious education, pastoral psychology, liturgical and spiritual theology, spiritual formation for the practice of ministry.

Boston University, School of Theology, Boston, MA 02215. Offers M Div, MSM, MTS, STM, D Min, Th D, D Min/MSW, M Div/MSM, M Div/MSW, MTS/MSW. *Accreditation:* ACIPE; ATS. Part-time programs available. *Degree requirements:* For master's, comprehensive exam; for doctorate, 2 foreign languages, comprehensive exam, thesis/dissertation. *Entrance requirements:* For M Div and master's, GRE General Test or MAT, minimum GPA of 3.0; for doctorate, GRE General Test or MAT, minimum GPA of 3.3. Electronic applications accepted. *Expenses:* Contact institution. *Faculty research:* Israelite literature in its social and cultural context, New Testament literature in its social and cultural context, Reformation history, women in the church, social ethics.

Briercrest Seminary, Graduate Programs, Program in Theology, Caronport, SK S0H 0S0, Canada. Offers Biblical studies (M Div); leadership and management (M Div); New Testament (MATS); Old Testament (MATS); pastoral counseling (M Div); pastoral ministry (M Div); theological studies (M Div); theology (MATS); worship (M Div); youth and family ministry (M Div). *Accreditation:* ATS. Part-time programs available. *Degree requirements:* For master's, comprehensive exam, thesis optional. *Entrance requirements:* Additional exam requirements/recommendations for international students: Required—TOEFL (minimum score 550 paper-based; 213 computer-based).

Bryn Athyn College of the New Church, Academy of the New Church Theological School, Bryn Athyn, PA 19009-0717. Offers divinity (M Div); religious studies (MA). Part-time programs available. Postbaccalaureate distance learning degree programs offered (minimal on-campus study). *Degree requirements:* For master's, thesis; for M Div, 3 foreign languages, thesis/dissertation. *Entrance requirements:* Additional exam requirements/recommendations for international students: Required—TOEFL.

California Institute of Integral Studies, Graduate Programs, School of Consciousness and Transformation, San Francisco, CA 94103. Offers cultural anthropology and social transformation (MA); East-West psychology (MA, PhD); integrative health studies (MA); philosophy and religion (MA, PhD), including Asian and comparative studies, philosophy, cosmology, and consciousness, women's spirituality, women's spirituality flex format; social and cultural anthropology (PhD); transformative leadership (MA); transformative studies (PhD). Part-time and evening/weekend programs available. Postbaccalaureate distance learning degree programs offered (minimal on-campus study). *Faculty:* 29 full-time, 32 part-time/adjunct. *Students:* 334 full-time (218 women), 126 part-time (77 women); includes 102 minority (39 African Americans, 4 American Indian/Alaska Native, 35 Asian Americans or Pacific Islanders, 24 Hispanic Americans), 1 international. Average age 37. 223 applicants, 78% accepted, 110 enrolled. In 2008, 93 master's, 30 doctorates awarded. Terminal master's awarded for partial completion of doctoral program. *Degree requirements:* For master's, comprehensive exam (for some programs), thesis optional; for doctorate, comprehensive exam, thesis/dissertation. *Entrance requirements:* For master's, minimum GPA of 3.0, letters of recommendation, writing sample; for doctorate, master's degree, minimum GPA of 3.0, letters of recommendation, writing sample. Additional exam requirements/recommendations for international students: Required—TOEFL. *Application deadline:* For fall admission, 2/1 priority date for domestic and international students; for spring admission, 10/15 priority date for domestic and international students. Applications are processed on a rolling basis. Application fee: $65. Electronic applications accepted. *Expenses:* Tuition: Part-time $815 per contact hour. Required fees: $270; $135 per semester. Tuition and fees vary according to degree level. *Financial support:* In 2008–09, 271 students received support; research assistantships, teaching assistantships, career-related internships or fieldwork, Federal Work-Study, institutionally sponsored loans, scholarships/grants, and tuition waivers (partial) available. Support available to part-time students. Financial award application deadline: 3/15; financial award applicants required to submit FAFSA. *Faculty research:* Altered states of consciousness, dreams, cosmology, postcolonial studies, integrative health studies. *Application contact:* Allyson Werner, Senior Admissions Counselor, 415-575-6155, Fax: 415-575-1268.

See Close-Up on page 347.

Calvary Bible College and Theological Seminary, Calvary Theological Seminary, Kansas City, MO 64147-1341. Offers Bible and theology (MS); Biblical counseling (MA); Biblical studies (MA); Christian ministry (MA); Christian studies (MS); Christian theology (MA); New Testament (MA); Old Testament (MA); pastoral studies (M Div). Part-time and evening/weekend programs available. *Faculty:* 3 full-time (0 women), 2 part-time/adjunct (0 women). *Students:* 21 full-time (7 women), 37 part-time (16 women); includes 5 African Americans, 4 Asian Americans or Pacific Islanders, 3 Hispanic Americans, 2 international. Average age 38. In 2008, 13 master's awarded. *Degree requirements:* For master's, one foreign language, comprehensive exam, thesis; for M Div, 2 foreign languages, comprehensive exam, thesis/dissertation. *Entrance requirements:* For M Div and master's, GRE, minimum GPA of 2.5, 50 semester hours of course work in liberal arts, BA or BS degree, doctrine agreement. Additional exam requirements/recommendations for international students: Required—TOEFL (minimum score 550 paper-based; 213 computer-based). *Application deadline:* For fall admission, 7/15 priority date for domestic and international students; for spring admission, 12/1 priority date for domestic and international students. Application fee: $25. *Financial support:* In 2008–09, 13 students received support. Scholarships/grants available. Financial award application deadline: 11/5. *Unit head:* Dr. Thomas Baurain, Academic Dean, 816-322-0110 Ext. 1502, Fax: 816-331-4474. *Application contact:* Bob Crank, Director of Admissions, 800-326-3960 Ext. 1326, Fax: 816-331-4474.

Calvin Theological Seminary, Graduate and Professional Programs, Grand Rapids, MI 49546-4387. Offers divinity (M Div); educational ministry (MA); historical theology (PhD); missions: church growth (MA); philosophical and moral theology (PhD); systematic theology (PhD); theological studies (MTS); theology (Th M). *Accreditation:* ACIPE; ATS. Part-time programs available. *Degree requirements:* For master's, thesis (for some programs); for doctorate, 4 foreign languages, comprehensive exam, thesis/dissertation; for M Div, 2 foreign languages. *Entrance requirements:* For doctorate, GRE General Test, Hebrew, Greek, and a modern foreign language. Additional exam requirements/recommendations for international students: Required—TOEFL (minimum score 550 paper-based; 213 computer-based), TWE (minimum score 4). Electronic applications accepted. *Faculty research:* Recent Trinity theory, Christian anthropology, Proverbs, reformed confessions, Paul's view of law.

Campbellsville University, School of Theology, Campbellsville, KY 42718-2799. Offers theology (M Th). Part-time programs available. *Degree requirements:* For master's, comprehensive exam, thesis optional. *Entrance requirements:* For master's, GRE General Test, minimum GPA of 3.0 in major, minimum GPA of 2.75 overall, 18 hours of undergraduate coursework in Christian studies. Electronic applications accepted. *Expenses:* Tuition: Full-time $6570; part-time $365 per credit hour. Required fees: $60 per term. *Faculty research:* Clergy needing graduate theology education, trinity and Christian faith, Old Testament David narratives, leadership Principles on Christian University integration of Christian principles in counseling process.

Campbell University, Graduate and Professional Programs, Divinity School, Buies Creek, NC 27506. Offers Christian education (MA); divinity (M Div); ministry (D Min); M Div/MA; M Div/MBA. *Accreditation:* ATS. *Degree requirements:* For doctorate, final project. *Entrance requirements:* For master's, minimum GPA of 2.5; for doctorate, MAT, M Div, minimum graduate GPA of 3.0. Additional exam requirements/recommendations for international students: Required—TOEFL (minimum score 580 paper-based; 237 computer-based). *Expenses:* Contact institution. *Faculty research:* New Testament, theology, spiritual formation, Old Testament, Christian leadership.

Canadian Southern Baptist Seminary, Graduate Programs, Cochrane, AB T4C 2G1, Canada. Offers ministry (M Div); religious education (MRE). *Accreditation:* ATS. Part-time programs available. *Faculty:* 8 full-time (0 women), 3 part-time/adjunct (1 woman). *Students:* 22 full-time (4 women), 22 part-time (5 women); includes 9 minority (1 African American, 5 Asian Americans or Pacific Islanders, 3 Hispanic Americans), 12 international. Average age 30. *Entrance requirements:* Additional exam requirements/recommendations for international students: Required—TOEFL (minimum score 560 paper-based; 220 computer-based), IELTS (minimum score 6.5). *Application deadline:* For fall admission, 7/1 priority date for domestic and international students; for winter admission, 11/15 priority date for domestic and international students. Applications are processed on a rolling basis. Application fee: $50. Tuition charges are reported in Canadian dollars. *Expenses:* Tuition: Full-time $4800 Canadian dollars. Tuition and fees vary according to course load and campus/location. *Application contact:* Kathleen McNaughton, Registrar, 403-932-6622 Ext. 221, E-mail: registrar@csbs.ca.

Capital Bible Seminary, Graduate and Professional Programs, Lanham, MD 20706-3599. Offers biblical studies (MA, Certificate); Christian counseling (MA); Christian counseling and discipleship (Certificate); ministry leadership (MA); theology (M Div, Th M). *Accreditation:* ATS (one or more programs are accredited). Part-time and evening/weekend programs available. *Degree requirements:* For master's, 2 foreign languages, comprehensive exam, thesis (for some programs); for M Div, 2 foreign languages, comprehensive exam. *Entrance requirements:* For M Div and master's, GRE General Test, Greek exam for those with 2 years of Greek, proficiency exam in theology, previous course work in Biblical studies. Additional exam requirements/recommendations for international students: Required—TOEFL (minimum score 550 paper-based; 213 computer-based). *Faculty research:* Dead Sea Scrolls, spiritual gifts, hermeneutics.

Carey Theological College, Graduate Programs, Vancouver, BC V6T 1J6, Canada. Offers MPM, D Min. *Accreditation:* ATS. Part-time programs available. *Faculty:* 8 full-time (2 women), 17 part-time/adjunct (3 women). *Students:* 1 full-time (0 women), 103 part-time (23 women); includes 38 minority (1 African American, 31 Asian Americans or Pacific Islanders, 6 Hispanic Americans). Average age 45. 27 applicants, 78% accepted, 21 enrolled. In 2008, 8 master's, 5 doctorates awarded. *Degree requirements:* For doctorate, thesis/dissertation. *Entrance requirements:* For master's, undergraduate degree with minimum GPA of 2.7; for doctorate, M Div degree with minimum GPA of 3.5. Additional exam requirements/recommendations for international students: Required—TOEFL (minimum score 577 paper-based; 233 computer-based; 90 iBT). *Application deadline:* Applications are processed on a rolling basis. Application fee: $60. Electronic applications accepted. Tuition and fees charges are reported in Canadian dollars. *Expenses:* Tuition: Full-time $7500 Canadian dollars; part-time $250 Canadian dollars per credit. One-time fee: $350 Canadian dollars. *Financial support:* In 2008–09, 4 students received support. Scholarships/grants available. *Faculty research:* Missional church, new monasticism, women in leadership, spiritual formation, applied theology. *Unit head:* Dr. Barbara Mutch, Academic Vice President, 604-224-4308, Fax: 604-224-5014, E-mail: barmutch@careytheologicalcollege.ca. *Application contact:* Rev. Myrna Sears, Registrar, 604-224-4308, Fax: 604-224-5014, E-mail: msears@careytheologicalcollege.ca.

The Catholic Distance University, Graduate Programs, Hamilton, VA 20158. Offers religious studies (MRS); theology (MA). Part-time and evening/weekend programs available. Postbaccalaureate distance learning degree programs offered (no on-campus study). *Degree requirements:* For master's, comprehensive exam, capstone paper or project.

Catholic Theological Union at Chicago, Graduate and Professional Programs, Chicago, IL 60615-5698. Offers biblical spirituality (Certificate); cross-cultural ministries (D Min); cross-cultural missions (Certificate); divinity (M Div); liturgical studies (Certificate); liturgy (D Min); pastoral studies (MAPS, Certificate); spiritual formation (Certificate); spirituality (D Min); theology (MA); M Div/MA; M Div/MSW; M Div/PhD. *Accreditation:* ACIPE; ATS (one or more programs are accredited). Part-time and evening/weekend programs available. *Degree requirements:* For master's, one foreign language, comprehensive exam (for some programs), thesis (for some programs); for doctorate, thesis/dissertation. *Entrance requirements:* For doctorate, master's degree, 5 years of active ministry. *Faculty research:* Doctrine, sacraments, ethics, Bible.

The Catholic University of America, School of Canon Law, Washington, DC 20064. Offers JCD, JCL, JD/JCL. *Degree requirements:* For doctorate, 2 foreign languages, thesis/dissertation. *Entrance requirements:* For doctorate, GRE General Test, 2 letters of recommendation. Additional exam requirements/recommendations for international students: Required—TOEFL (minimum score 580 paper-based; 237 computer-based). Electronic applications accepted.

The Catholic University of America, School of Theology and Religious Studies, Washington, DC 20064. Offers M Div, STB, MA, MRE, D Min, PhD, STD, STL, MSLS/MA. *Accreditation:* ATS (one or more programs are accredited). Part-time programs available. Terminal master's awarded for partial completion of doctoral program. *Degree requirements:* For master's, comprehensive exam; for doctorate, comprehensive exam, thesis/dissertation; for first professional degree, one foreign language; for STL, one foreign language, comprehensive exam, thesis. *Entrance requirements:* For first professional degree and master's, GRE General Test, 3 letters of recommendation; for doctorate and STL, GRE, 3 letters of recommendation. Additional exam requirements/recommendations for international students: Required—TOEFL (minimum score 580 paper-based; 237 computer-based). Electronic applications accepted. *Faculty research:* Biblical studies, canon law, church history, liturgical studies, religion and religious education.

Central Baptist Theological Seminary, Graduate and Professional Programs, Shawnee, KS 66226. Offers missional church studies (MA); theological studies (MA); theology (M Div, Diploma). *Accreditation:* ACIPE; ATS (one or more programs are accredited). Part-time programs available. *Degree requirements:* For master's, thesis optional, MMPI, Myers-Briggs, Enneagram; for M Div, thesis/dissertation optional. *Entrance requirements:* For master's, accredited bachelor's degree with minimum GPA of 2.3. Additional exam requirements/recommendations for international students: Required—TOEFL (minimum score 547 paper-based; 210 computer-based; 77 iBT). Electronic applications accepted.

Central Baptist Theological Seminary of Virginia Beach, Graduate Programs, Virginia Beach, VA 23464. Offers M Div, MBS, Th M. *Entrance requirements:* For M Div, GRE, interview, M Div or equivalent from an accredited seminary, minimum cumulative GPA of 2.7, church endorsement, 4 recommendations; for master's, GRE, interview, minimum cumulative GPA of 2.4, church endorsement, 4 recommendations. Electronic applications accepted.

Central Yeshiva Tomchei Tmimim-Lubavitch, Graduate Programs, Brooklyn, NY 11230. *Accreditation:* AARTS.

Chaminade University of Honolulu, Graduate Services, Program in Pastoral Theology, Honolulu, HI 96816-1578. Offers MPT. Part-time and evening/weekend programs available. Postbaccalaureate distance learning degree programs offered. *Degree requirements:* For master's, capstone course. *Entrance requirements:* For master's, 2 letters of recommendation. Additional exam requirements/recommendations for international students: Required—TOEFL (minimum score 550 paper-based). Electronic applications accepted.

Chicago Theological Seminary, Graduate and Professional Programs, Chicago, IL 60637-1507. Offers preaching (D Min); religion and health (D Min); religious studies (MA); spirituality and spiritual direction (D Min); theology (M Div); theology, ethics and the human sciences (PhD); M Div/MSW. *Accreditation:* ACIPE; ATS. Part-time programs available. *Faculty:* 13 full-time (5 women). *Students:* 71 full-time (32 women), 139 part-time (76 women); includes 54 minority (45 African Americans, 6 Asian Americans or Pacific Islanders, 3 Hispanic Americans), 33 international. *Degree requirements:* For master's, thesis; for doctorate, 2 foreign languages, comprehensive exam, thesis/dissertation; for M Div, thesis/dissertation. *Entrance requirements:* For doctorate, GRE General Test. Additional exam requirements/recommendations for international students: Required—TOEFL (minimum score 217 computer-based). *Application deadline:* For fall admission, 2/15 priority date for domestic and international students; for spring admission, 11/1 for domestic and international students. Application fee: $50. *Financial support:* Fellowships, institutionally sponsored loans, scholarships/grants, and tuition waivers (partial) available. Support available to part-time students. Financial award application deadline: 3/1; financial award applicants required to submit FAFSA. *Faculty research:* Bible, culture and hermeneutics, theology, gender and sexuality, black faith and life, spirituality and psychology, practical theology. Total annual research expenditures: $150,000. *Unit head:* Dr. Theodore W. Jennings, Acting Dean, 773-752-5757, Fax: 773-752-1903, E-mail: tjennings@ctschicago.edu. *Application contact:* Rev. Lin Sanford Keppert, Director of Admissions, Recruitment and Financial Aid, E-mail: lkeppert@ctschicago.edu.

Christendom College, Notre Dame Graduate School, Front Royal, VA 22630-5103. Offers theological studies (MA). Part-time and evening/weekend programs available. *Degree requirements:* For master's, one foreign language, thesis or alternative. Electronic applications accepted.

Christian Theological Seminary, Graduate and Professional Programs, Indianapolis, IN 46208-3301. Offers marriage and family (MA); pastoral care and counseling (D Min); practical theology (D Min); psychotherapy and faith (MA); sacred theology (STM); specialized ministries (MA); theological studies (MTS); theology (M Div). *Accreditation:* AAMFT/COAMFTE (one or more programs are accredited); ACIPE; ATS. Part-time programs available. Terminal master's awarded for partial completion of doctoral program. *Degree requirements:* For master's, comprehensive exam (for some programs), thesis (for some programs); for doctorate, comprehensive exam, thesis/dissertation; for M Div, comprehensive exam, thesis/dissertation (for some programs), missionary and cross-cultural experience. *Entrance requirements:* For master's, GRE General Test, MAT; for doctorate, M Div or BD. Electronic applications accepted. *Faculty research:* Faith formation, peer learning post graduation.

Christ the King Seminary, Graduate and Professional Programs, East Aurora, NY 14052. Offers divinity (M Div); pastoral ministry (MA); pastoral studies (Certificate); theology (MA). *Accreditation:* ATS. Part-time and evening/weekend programs available. *Degree requirements:*

Theology

Christ the King Seminary (continued)
For master's, comprehensive exam, thesis; for M Div, comprehensive exam. *Entrance requirements:* For M Div and master's, previous course work in philosophy and religious studies.

Church Divinity School of the Pacific, Graduate and Professional Programs, Berkeley, CA 94709-1217. Offers M Div, MA, MTS, D Min, Certificate. *Accreditation:* ACIPE; ATS (one or more programs are accredited). Part-time programs available. *Degree requirements:* For master's, one foreign language, thesis; for doctorate, thesis/dissertation; for M Div, one foreign language. *Entrance requirements:* For M Div, master's, and Certificate, GRE General Test, letters of reference; for doctorate, letters of reference. Additional exam requirements/recommendations for international students: Required—TOEFL. Electronic applications accepted.

Church of God Theological Seminary, Graduate and Professional Programs, Cleveland, TN 37320-3330. Offers counseling (MA); discipleship and Christian formations (MA); ministry (D Min); theology (M Div). *Accreditation:* ACIPE; ATS. Part-time programs available. *Degree requirements:* For M Div, 2 foreign languages, thesis/dissertation, internship. *Faculty research:* Biblical exegesis.

Cincinnati Christian University, Graduate School, Cincinnati, OH 45204-3200. Offers biblical studies (MA); church history (MA); counseling (MAC); divinity (M Div); ministry (M Min); practical ministries (MA); theological studies (MA). *Accreditation:* ATS. Part-time programs available. *Degree requirements:* For master's, thesis (for some programs); for M Div, 2 foreign languages, oral exam. *Entrance requirements:* For master's, GRE General Test. Additional exam requirements/recommendations for international students: Required—TOEFL. Electronic applications accepted.

Claremont Graduate University, Graduate Programs, School of Religion, Claremont, CA 91711-6160. Offers Hebrew Bible (MA, PhD); history of Christianity and religions of North America (MA, PhD); New Testament (MA, PhD); philosophy of religion and theology (MA, PhD); theology, ethics and culture (MA, PhD); women's studies in religion (MA, PhD); MA/PhD; MBA/PhD. Part-time programs available. *Faculty:* 7 full-time (2 women), 2 part-time/adjunct (0 women). *Students:* 231 full-time (96 women), 4 part-time (2 women); includes 32 minority (13 African Americans, 11 Asian Americans or Pacific Islanders, 8 Hispanic Americans), 29 international. Average age 37. In 2008, 13 master's, 16 doctorates awarded. Terminal master's awarded for partial completion of doctoral program. *Entrance requirements:* For master's and doctorate, GRE General Test. Additional exam requirements/recommendations for international students: Required—TOEFL (minimum score 550 paper-based; 213 computer-based; 80 iBT). *Application deadline:* For fall admission, 2/1 priority date for domestic students. Applications are processed on a rolling basis. Application fee: $60. Electronic applications accepted. *Expenses:* Tuition: Full-time $33,698; part-time $1465 per unit. Required fees: $310; $155 per semester. Tuition and fees vary according to program. *Financial support:* Fellowships, research assistantships, teaching assistantships, Federal Work-Study, institutionally sponsored loans, and scholarships/grants available. Support available to part-time students. Financial award application deadline: 2/15; financial award applicants required to submit FAFSA. *Unit head:* Karen Torjesen, Dean, 909-607-3214, Fax: 909-621-9587, E-mail: karen.torjesen@cgu.edu. *Application contact:* Brent Smith, Recruiter, 909-607-2653, Fax: 909-607-9587, E-mail: brent.smith@cgu.edu.

Claremont School of Theology, Graduate and Professional Programs, Master of Divinity Program, Claremont, CA 91711-3199. Offers M Div. *Accreditation:* ACIPE; ATS. Part-time programs available. *Entrance requirements:* Additional exam requirements/recommendations for international students: Required—TOEFL (minimum score 230 computer-based). Electronic applications accepted.

Claremont School of Theology, Graduate and Professional Programs, Program in Religion, Claremont, CA 91711-3199. Offers practical theology (PhD); religion and theology (MA); religious education (MARE). *Accreditation:* ACIPE; ATS. Terminal master's awarded for partial completion of doctoral program. *Degree requirements:* For master's, thesis; for doctorate, 2 foreign languages, thesis/dissertation. *Entrance requirements:* For doctorate, GRE General Test. Additional exam requirements/recommendations for international students: Required—TOEFL (minimum score 250 computer-based). Electronic applications accepted.

Colgate Rochester Crozer Divinity School, Graduate and Professional Programs, Rochester, NY 14620-2530. Offers M Div, MA, D Min, Certificate. *Accreditation:* ACIPE; ATS (one or more programs are accredited). Part-time programs available. Postbaccalaureate distance learning degree programs offered (minimal on-campus study). *Faculty:* 8 full-time (4 women), 15 part-time/adjunct (7 women). *Students:* 69 full-time, 46 part-time; includes 36 minority (27 African Americans, 2 American Indian/Alaska Native, 4 Asian Americans or Pacific Islanders, 3 Hispanic Americans), 7 international. Average age 43. 46 applicants, 98% accepted, 37 enrolled. In 2008, 18 first professional degrees, 1 master's, 2 doctorates awarded. *Degree requirements:* For master's, thesis; for doctorate, thesis/dissertation; for M Div, supervised ministry year. *Entrance requirements:* For M Div and master's, BA/BS, personal statement; for doctorate, M Div, 3 years professional experience. Additional exam requirements/recommendations for international students: Required—TOEFL (minimum score 600 paper-based; 237 computer-based; 93 iBT). *Application deadline:* For fall admission, 7/1 priority date for domestic students, 3/1 for international students; for spring admission, 12/1 priority date for domestic students. Applications are processed on a rolling basis. Application fee: $35. *Expenses:* Tuition: Full-time $8670; part-time $482 per credit hour. Required fees: $155. Tuition and fees vary according to course load and student level. *Financial support:* In 2008–09, 49 students received support. Scholarships/grants available. Financial award application deadline: 9/1; financial award applicants required to submit FAFSA. *Faculty research:* Old Testament, New Testament, Christian ethics, black church studies, woman and gender studies. *Unit head:* Dr. Eugene C. Bay, President, 585-271-1320 Ext. 680, Fax: 585-271-8013. *Application contact:* Melissa M. Morral, Vice President for Enrollment Services, 585-340-9500, Fax: 585-340-9644, E-mail: mmorral@crcds.edu.

Collège Dominicain de Philosophie et de Théologie, Graduate Programs, Programs in Theology, Ottawa, ON K1R 7G3, Canada. Offers M Th, MA Th, PhD, Th D, L Th. Part-time and evening/weekend programs available. *Degree requirements:* For master's, 3 foreign languages, research paper; for doctorate, 3 foreign languages, thesis/dissertation, candidacy exam. *Entrance requirements:* For master's, B Th or the equivalent, minimum A- average in undergraduate course work; for doctorate, MA Th or equivalent, minimum A- average in graduate course work.

College of Emmanuel and St. Chad, Bachelor of Theology Program, Saskatoon, SK S7N 0W6, Canada. Offers B Th. Part-time programs available. Postbaccalaureate distance learning degree programs offered (minimal on-campus study). *Degree requirements:* For B Th, internship. *Entrance requirements:* 1 year of university level work or equivalent. Additional exam requirements/recommendations for international students: Required—TOEFL. *Faculty research:* Pauline studies, New Testament, ethics, congregational development, trauma and spirituality.

College of Emmanuel and St. Chad, Graduate Programs, Saskatoon, SK S7N 0W6, Canada. Offers M Div, MTS, STM. Part-time programs available. *Degree requirements:* For master's, thesis optional. *Entrance requirements:* For master's, M Div or MTS (STM). Additional exam requirements/recommendations for international students: Required—TOEFL. *Faculty research:* New Testament, systematics, Christian education, theology, ethics.

College of Mount St. Joseph, Graduate Program in Religious Studies, Cincinnati, OH 45233-1670. Offers spiritual and pastoral care (MA). Part-time and evening/weekend programs available. *Faculty:* 4 full-time (2 women). *Students:* 24 part-time (18 women); includes 2 minority (both African Americans). Average age 49. 10 applicants, 100% accepted, 2 enrolled. In 2008, 8 master's awarded. *Degree requirements:* For master's, comprehensive exam, integrating project. *Entrance requirements:* For master's, 3 letters of recommendation, interview, essay, minimum GPA of 2.7. Additional exam requirements/recommendations for international students: Required—TOEFL (minimum score 560 paper-based; 220 computer-based). *Application deadline:* Applications are processed on a rolling basis. Application fee: $50. Electronic applications accepted. *Expenses:* Contact institution. *Financial support:* In 2008–09, 18 students received support. Career-related internships or fieldwork and scholarships/grants available. Support available to part-time students. Financial award application deadline: 6/1; financial award applicants required to submit FAFSA. *Faculty research:* Contextual/cultural/systematic theology, historical/spiritual theology, business/economics ethics, social justice, Biblical/cultural/pastoral theology. *Unit head:* Dr. John Trokan, Chair, 513-244-4272, Fax: 513-244-4222, E-mail: john_trokan@mail.msj.edu. *Application contact:* Marilyn Hoskins, Assistant Director of Admissions for Graduate Recruitment, 513-244-4723, Fax: 513-244-4629, E-mail: marilyn_hoskins@mail.msj.edu.

College of Saint Elizabeth, Department of Theology, Morristown, NJ 07960-6989. Offers MA. Part-time and evening/weekend programs available. *Faculty:* 2 full-time (1 woman), 4 part-time/adjunct (1 woman). *Students:* 15 part-time (11 women), 1 international. Average age 54. 9 applicants, 78% accepted, 3 enrolled. In 2008, 4 master's awarded. *Degree requirements:* For master's, thesis or alternative, 3 essays, oral exam. *Entrance requirements:* For master's, interview, minimum GPA of 3.0. *Application deadline:* For fall admission, 3/1 priority date for domestic students; for spring admission, 9/1 for domestic students. Applications are processed on a rolling basis. Application fee: $35. Electronic applications accepted. *Expenses:* Tuition: Part-time $759 per credit. Required fees: $380 per semester. *Financial support:* Tuition waivers (partial) and unspecified assistantships available. Support available to part-time students. Financial award applicants required to submit FAFSA. *Unit head:* Sr. Kathleen Flanagan, Director of the Graduate Program in Theology, 973-290-4336, Fax: 973-290-4312, E-mail: kflanagan@cse.edu. *Application contact:* Donna Tatarka, Dean of Admission, 973-290-4705, Fax: 973-290-4710, E-mail: dtatarka@cse.edu.

Columbia International University, Columbia Biblical Seminary and School of Missions, Columbia, SC 29230-3122. Offers academic ministries (M Div); bible exposition (M Div, MABE); biblical studies (Certificate); counseling ministries (Certificate); divinity (M Div); educational ministries (M Div, MAEM, Certificate); intercultural studies (M Div, MAIS, Certificate); leadership (D Min); leadership for evangelism/mobilization (MALM); member care (D Min); ministry (Certificate); missions (D Min); pastoral counseling and spiritual formation (M Div, MAPS); preaching (D Min); theology (MA). *Accreditation:* ATS (one or more programs are accredited). Part-time and evening/weekend programs available. *Degree requirements:* For master's, integrative seminar; for doctorate, comprehensive exam, thesis/dissertation; for M Div, internship. *Entrance requirements:* For master's, minimum GPA of 2.7; for doctorate, 3 years of ministerial experience, M Div. Additional exam requirements/recommendations for international students: Required—TOEFL. Electronic applications accepted.

Columbia Theological Seminary, Graduate and Professional Programs, Decatur, GA 30031-0520. Offers M Div, MATS, Th M, D Min, Th D. *Accreditation:* ACIPE; ATS (one or more programs are accredited). Terminal master's awarded for partial completion of doctoral program. *Degree requirements:* For master's, thesis (for some programs); for doctorate, one foreign language, thesis/dissertation; for M Div, 2 foreign languages. *Entrance requirements:* For doctorate, M Div or equivalent, 3 years practice of ministry. Additional exam requirements/recommendations for international students: Required—TOEFL.

Concordia Lutheran Seminary, Graduate and Professional Programs, Edmonton, AB T5B 4E3, Canada. Offers M Div, Graduate Certificate. *Accreditation:* ATS (one or more programs are accredited). Part-time programs available. *Faculty:* 4 full-time (0 women), 4 part-time/adjunct (0 women). *Students:* 17 full-time (0 women), 5 part-time (1 woman); includes 2 minority (both Asian Americans or Pacific Islanders). Average age 31. *Degree requirements:* For M Div, 2 foreign languages, thesis/dissertation. *Entrance requirements:* GRE General Test, 1 year of Greek, 1 year of Hebrew, minimum GPA of 2.0. Additional exam requirements/recommendations for international students: Required—TOEFL. *Application deadline:* For fall admission, 4/1 priority date for domestic students; for winter admission, 10/30 priority date for domestic students. Application fee: $30 ($100 for international students). Tuition and fees charges are reported in Canadian dollars. *Expenses:* Tuition: Full-time $7200 Canadian dollars; part-time $200 Canadian dollars per credit hour. Required fees: $25 Canadian dollars per semester. One-time fee: $455 Canadian dollars full-time. *Financial support:* Scholarships/grants available. Financial award application deadline: 8/30. *Faculty research:* Lutheran Pietism, Christianity and culture, missiology, Christian worship, homiletics. *Application contact:* Jeffrey Nachtigall, Director of Admissions, 780-474-1468, Fax: 780-479-5067, E-mail: admissions@concordiasem.ab.ca.

Concordia Seminary, Graduate Programs, St. Louis, MO 63105-3199. Offers M Div, MA, STM, D Min, PhD, Certificate. *Accreditation:* ACIPE; ATS (one or more programs are accredited). Terminal master's awarded for partial completion of doctoral program. *Degree requirements:* For master's, 3 foreign languages, thesis optional; for doctorate, 4 foreign languages, thesis/dissertation; for M Div, 2 foreign languages, comprehensive exam (for some programs), thesis/dissertation (for some programs). *Entrance requirements:* For M Div, GRE General Test, previous course work in public speaking, Greek, Hebrew, Old Testament, New Testament, and Christian Doctrine; for master's and doctorate, GRE General Test, theological essay in English (foreign students only). Additional exam requirements/recommendations for international students: Required—TOEFL. *Faculty research:* Family counseling, educational administration, contemporary theology, pastoral office, humanism and education.

Concordia Theological Seminary, Graduate and Professional Programs, Fort Wayne, IN 46825-4996. Offers M Div, MA, STM, D Min, PhD. *Accreditation:* ATS. Part-time programs available. *Degree requirements:* For master's, 2 foreign languages, thesis, oral exam, language exam, comprehensive exam (STM); for doctorate, comprehensive exam, thesis/dissertation, oral exam; for M Div, one foreign language, 1 year of vicarage. *Entrance requirements:* GRE General Test, minimum GPA of 2.25.

Concordia University, School of Graduate Studies, Faculty of Arts and Science, Department of Theological Studies, Montréal, QC H3G 1M8, Canada. Offers MA. *Degree requirements:* For master's, one foreign language, research papers or thesis. *Entrance requirements:* For master's, minimum B average in theology. *Faculty research:* Interpretation theory, theological methodology.

Concordia University, School of Theology, Irvine, CA 92612-3299. Offers MA. Part-time programs available. *Degree requirements:* For master's, one foreign language, thesis. *Entrance requirements:* For master's, GRE, MAT. Additional exam requirements/recommendations for international students: Required—TOEFL (minimum score 550 paper-based; 213 computer-based).

Concordia University, St. Paul, College of Vocation and Ministry, St. Paul, MN 55104-5494. Offers Christian education (Certificate); Christian outreach (MA). Evening/weekend programs available. Postbaccalaureate distance learning degree programs offered (minimal on-campus study). *Faculty:* 1 full-time (0 women), 4 part-time/adjunct (1 woman). *Students:* 15 full-time (5 women), 4 part-time (3 women). Average age 32. In 2008, 2 master's, 10 other advanced degrees awarded. *Application deadline:* Applications are processed on a rolling basis. Application fee: $50. Electronic applications accepted. *Financial support:* Applicants required to submit FAFSA. *Unit head:* Dr. David Lumpp, Dean, 651-641-8217, E-mail: lumpp@csp.edu. *Application contact:* Kimberly Craig, Director of Graduate and Cohort Admission, 651-603-6223, Fax: 651-603-6320, E-mail: craig@csp.edu.

Covenant Theological Seminary, Graduate and Professional Programs, St. Louis, MO 63141-8697. Offers M Div, MA, MAC, MAEM, Th M, D Min, Certificate. *Accreditation:* ATS (one or more programs are accredited). Part-time and evening/weekend programs available. Postbaccalaureate distance learning degree programs offered (minimal on-campus study). *Faculty:* 23 full-time (0 women), 23 part-time/adjunct (8 women). *Students:* 375 full-time (67 women),

437 part-time (126 women); includes 97 minority (36 African Americans, 1 American Indian/Alaska Native, 46 Asian Americans or Pacific Islanders, 14 Hispanic Americans), 47 international. Average age 34. 269 applicants, 98% accepted, 198 enrolled. In 2008, 62 first professional degrees, 64 master's, 4 doctorates awarded. *Degree requirements:* For master's, 2 foreign languages, thesis (for some programs); for doctorate, 2 foreign languages, thesis/dissertation; for M Div and Certificate, 2 foreign languages. *Entrance requirements:* For doctorate and Certificate, M Div. Additional exam requirements/recommendations for international students: Required—TOEFL (minimum score 550 paper-based; 213 computer-based). *Application deadline:* Applications are processed on a rolling basis. Application fee: $50. Electronic applications accepted. *Expenses:* Tuition: Full-time $9720. *Financial support:* In 2008–09, 588 students received support. Career-related internships or fieldwork, institutionally sponsored loans, scholarships/grants, and tuition waivers (full and partial) available. Support available to part-time students. Financial award application deadline: 4/15; financial award applicants required to submit FAFSA. *Unit head:* Dr. Sean Lucas, Chief Academic Officer, 314-434-4044. *Application contact:* Jeremy Kicklighter, Director of Admissions, 314-434-4044, Fax: 314-434-4819, E-mail: admissions@covenantseminary.edu.

Creighton University, Graduate School, College of Arts and Sciences, Department of Theology, Omaha, NE 68178-0001. Offers Christian spirituality (MA); ministry (MA); theology (MA). Part-time and evening/weekend programs available. *Entrance requirements:* For master's, GRE General Test, 9 hours of theology coursework, 3 letters of recommendation. Additional exam requirements/recommendations for international students: Required—TOEFL (minimum score 550 paper-based; 213 computer-based; 80 iBT).

The Criswell College, Graduate School of the Bible, Dallas, TX 75246-1537. Offers biblical studies (M Div); Christian leadership (MA); counseling (MA); Jewish studies (MA); ministry (MA); theological and biblical studies (MA). Part-time programs available. *Degree requirements:* For master's, 2 foreign languages, thesis optional; for M Div, 2 foreign languages, thesis/dissertation optional. *Entrance requirements:* For M Div and master's, GRE General Test, minimum GPA of 2.5. Electronic applications accepted. *Faculty research:* Emphasis on biblical languages (Hebrew and Greek), expository preaching and evangelism in the local church.

Crown College, Graduate Studies, St. Bonifacius, MN 55375-9001. Offers Christian studies (MA); educational leadership (MA); intercultural leadership studies (MA); ministry leadership (MA); organizational leadership (MA). Part-time and evening/weekend programs available. Postbaccalaureate distance learning degree programs offered (no on-campus study). *Faculty:* 15 part-time/adjunct (4 women). *Students:* 94 full-time (32 women), 29 part-time (18 women); includes 17 minority (9 African Americans, 5 Asian Americans or Pacific Islanders, 3 Hispanic Americans). Average age 37. 75 applicants, 77% accepted, 43 enrolled. In 2008, 41 master's awarded. *Degree requirements:* For master's, thesis optional. *Entrance requirements:* For master's, 12 credits in foundational studies, minimum GPA of 2.5. Additional exam requirements/recommendations for international students: Required—TOEFL (minimum score 500 paper-based). *Application deadline:* For fall admission, 8/1 priority date for domestic students; for winter admission, 1/1 priority date for domestic students; for spring admission, 6/1 priority date for domestic students. Applications are processed on a rolling basis. Application fee: $20. *Expenses:* Tuition: Part-time $379 per credit. Required fees: $100 per term. *Financial support:* Scholarships/grants available. *Unit head:* Don Bouchard, Director of Adult and Graduate Studies, 952-446-4224, Fax: 952-416-4349, E-mail: grad@crown.edu. *Application contact:* Nate Erickson, Enrollment Coordinator, 952-446-4370, Fax: 952-446-4349, E-mail: grad@crown.edu.

Dallas Theological Seminary, Graduate Programs, Dallas, TX 75204-6499. Offers academic ministries (Th M); Bible translation (Th M); biblical and theological studies (CGS); biblical counseling (MA, Th M); biblical exegesis and linguistics (MA); biblical exposition (PhD); biblical studies (MA); Christian education (MA, D Min); cross-cultural ministries (MA, Th M); educational leadership (Th M); evangelism and discipleship (Th M); interdisciplinary studies (Th M); media and communication (MA); media arts in ministry (Th M); ministry (D Min); New Testament studies (Th M, PhD); Old Testament studies (PhD); parachurch ministries (Th M); pastoral ministries (Th M); sacred theology (STM); theological studies (PhD); women's ministry (Th M). *Accreditation:* ATS (one or more programs are accredited). Part-time and evening/weekend programs available. *Degree requirements:* For master's, variable foreign language requirement, thesis (for some programs); for doctorate, 2 foreign languages, thesis/dissertation. *Entrance requirements:* Additional exam requirements/recommendations for international students: Required—TOEFL, TWE. *Application deadline:* For fall admission, 7/1 priority date for domestic students, 1/15 for international students; for winter admission, 11/1 priority date for domestic students; for spring admission, 11/1 priority date for domestic students. Applications are processed on a rolling basis. Application fee: $30. Electronic applications accepted. *Financial support:* Career-related internships or fieldwork, institutionally sponsored loans, scholarships/grants, and tuition waivers (full and partial) available. Financial award application deadline: 2/28. *Unit head:* Dr. Mark L. Bailey, President, 214-841-3676, Fax: 214-841-3565. *Application contact:* Josh Bleeker, Director of Admissions, 214-841-3661, Fax: 214-841-3664, E-mail: admissions@dts.edu.

Darkei Noam Rabbinical College, Graduate Programs, Brooklyn, NY 11210.

Denver Seminary, Graduate and Professional Programs, Littleton, CO 80120. Offers apologetics (Certificate); biblical studies (MA); Christian formation and soul care (MA, Certificate); Christian studies (MA, Certificate); church and parachurch leadership (D Min); counseling licensure (MA); counseling ministry (MA); intercultural ministry (Certificate); leadership (MA, Certificate); marriage and family counseling (D Min); pastoral ministry (D Min); philosophy of religion (MA); spiritual guidance (Certificate); theology (M Div, Certificate); worship (Certificate); youth and family ministry (MA). *Accreditation:* ACA; ACIPE; ATS (one or more programs are accredited). Part-time and evening/weekend programs available. Postbaccalaureate distance learning degree programs offered. *Degree requirements:* For master's, 2 foreign languages, thesis (for some programs); for doctorate, 2 foreign languages, thesis/dissertation; for M Div, 2 foreign languages. *Entrance requirements:* For M Div, minimum undergraduate GPA of 2.5; for master's, minimum undergraduate GPA of 3.0; for doctorate, M Div, 3 years of ministry experience. Additional exam requirements/recommendations for international students: Required—TOEFL (minimum score 575 paper-based; 233 computer-based; 90 iBT). Electronic applications accepted.

Dominican House of Studies, Pontifical Faculty of the Immaculate Conception, Graduate and Professional Programs in Theology, Washington, DC 20017-1585. Offers moral theology (STL); sacred scripture (STL); systematic theology (STL); theology (STB, MA). *Accreditation:* ATS (one or more programs are accredited). Part-time programs available. *Faculty:* 10 full-time (1 woman), 9 part-time/adjunct (2 women). *Students:* 68 full-time (4 women), 9 part-time (3 women); includes 4 minority (1 Asian American or Pacific Islander, 3 Hispanic Americans), 24 international. Average age 32. 44 applicants, 95% accepted, 34 enrolled. In 2008, 1 first professional degree, 1 master's, 2 other advanced degrees awarded. *Degree requirements:* For master's, one foreign language, thesis, thesis defense; for first professional degree, 2 foreign languages, comprehensive exam; for STL, 3 foreign languages, comprehensive exam (for some programs), thesis (for some programs), lecture. *Entrance requirements:* For first professional degree, 18 credits of philosophy (36 for STB); reading knowledge of Latin; BA with minimum GPA of 3.0 (3.25 for STB); for master's, 18 credits of philosophy; reading knowledge of Latin; BA with minimum GPA of 3.0. Additional exam requirements/recommendations for international students: Required—TOEFL (minimum score 550 paper-based; 215 computer-based; 79 iBT). *Application deadline:* For fall admission, 7/1 priority date for domestic and international students; for spring admission, 12/1 priority date for domestic and international students. Applications are processed on a rolling basis. Application fee: $50. *Expenses:* Tuition: Full-time $13,680; part-time $570 per credit. Required fees: $50 per semester. *Financial support:* In 2008–09, 8 students received support. Career-related internships or fieldwork and Federal Work-Study available. Financial award application deadline: 6/30; financial award applicants required to submit FAFSA. *Faculty research:* Sacred scripture, moral theology, systematic theology, philosophy, languages. Total annual research expenditures:

$22,891. *Unit head:* Fr. Gabriel O'Donnell, OP, Academic Dean, 202-495-3832, Fax: 202-495-3873, E-mail: dean@dhs.edu. *Application contact:* Tobias John Nathe, Registrar, 202-495-3836, Fax: 202-495-3873, E-mail: registrar@dhs.edu.

Dominican School of Philosophy and Theology, Graduate Programs, Department of Theology, Berkeley, CA 94708. Offers M Div, Certificate, M Div/MA, MA/MA. *Accreditation:* ATS (one or more programs are accredited). Part-time programs available. *Entrance requirements:* Minimum GPA of 2.5. Additional exam requirements/recommendations for international students: Required—TOEFL (minimum score 550 paper-based; 68 computer-based). *Faculty research:* Literary and historical study of scripture, Christianity in late antiquity, homiletic theory, religion and art, Christology.

Drew University, Caspersen School of Graduate Studies, Program in Theological and Religious Studies, Madison, NJ 07940-1493. Offers historical studies (MA, PhD); Methodist studies (PhD); philosophy of religion (MA, PhD); systematic theology (MA, PhD); theological ethics (MA, PhD). *Accreditation:* ATS. Part-time programs available. Terminal master's awarded for partial completion of doctoral program. *Degree requirements:* For master's, one foreign language, thesis; for doctorate, 2 foreign languages, comprehensive exam, thesis/dissertation. *Entrance requirements:* For master's and doctorate, GRE General Test. *Faculty research:* History and theology of religion, postmodern theologies, patristics.

Drew University, Caspersen School of Graduate Studies, Program in Wesleyan and Methodist Studies, Madison, NJ 07940-1493. Offers MA, PhD. *Entrance requirements:* For master's and doctorate, GRE General Test. Additional exam requirements/recommendations for international students: Required—TOEFL, TWE.

Drew University, The Theological School, Madison, NJ 07940-1493. Offers M Div, MTS, STM, D Min, Certificate. *Accreditation:* ACIPE; ATS. Part-time programs available. Postbaccalaureate distance learning degree programs offered (minimal on-campus study). *Degree requirements:* For doctorate, thesis/dissertation. *Entrance requirements:* For M Div, 3 years professional ministry experience; for master's, minimum GPA of 3.0. Additional exam requirements/recommendations for international students: Required—TOEFL (minimum score 516 paper-based; 230 computer-based; 88 iBT), TWE. Electronic applications accepted. *Expenses:* Contact institution. *Faculty research:* Biblical studies, constructive theology, ecology and religion, gender and religion, race/ethnicity and religion.

Duke University, Divinity School, Durham, NC 27708-0586. Offers M Div, MTS, Th M, Th D, JD/MTS, M Div/MSW. *Accreditation:* ACIPE; ATS. Part-time programs available. *Degree requirements:* For master's, thesis optional; for doctorate, 2 foreign languages, thesis/dissertation; for M Div, field experience, spiritual formation, faculty evaluation. *Entrance requirements:* For M Div and master's, 5 letters of reference, 2 essays; for doctorate, GRE, 4 letters of reference, 2-page statement of purpose, one sample of academic writing. Additional exam requirements/recommendations for international students: Required—TOEFL (minimum score 580 paper-based; 237 computer-based; 93 iBT). Electronic applications accepted. *Expenses:* Contact institution. *Faculty research:* Biblical studies, historical church studies, theological studies, church ministry studies.

Duquesne University, Graduate School of Liberal Arts, Department of Theology, Pittsburgh, PA 15282-0001. Offers pastoral ministry (MA); religious education (MA); systematic theology (PhD); theology (MA). Part-time and evening/weekend programs available. *Faculty:* 13 full-time (4 women). *Students:* 67 full-time (30 women), 52 part-time (37 women); includes 4 minority (3 African Americans, 1 Asian American or Pacific Islander), 12 international. Average age 35. 28 applicants, 96% accepted, 22 enrolled. In 2008, 22 master's, 8 doctorates awarded. *Degree requirements:* For master's, comprehensive exam; for doctorate, 2 foreign languages, comprehensive exam, thesis/dissertation. *Entrance requirements:* For master's and doctorate, GRE General Test. Additional exam requirements/recommendations for international students: Required—TOEFL. *Application deadline:* For fall admission, 2/1 for domestic and international students. Application fee: $50. Electronic applications accepted. *Expenses:* Tuition: Part-time $819 per credit. Required fees: $78 per credit. Tuition and fees vary according to course load. *Financial support:* In 2008–09, 8 teaching assistantships with full tuition reimbursements (averaging $9,900 per year) were awarded; career-related internships or fieldwork, scholarships/grants, tuition waivers (partial), and unspecified assistantships also available. Support available to part-time students. Financial award application deadline: 5/1. *Unit head:* Dr. George Worgul, Chair, 412-396-6530. *Application contact:* Dr. Marie Baird, Director, 412-396-6000.

Earlham School of Religion, Graduate Programs, Richmond, IN 47374-5360. Offers religion (MA); theology (M Div, M Min). *Accreditation:* ACIPE; ATS. Part-time programs available. Postbaccalaureate distance learning degree programs offered (minimal on-campus study). *Degree requirements:* For master's, one foreign language, comprehensive exam, thesis; for M Div, project. *Entrance requirements:* For M Div and master's, 3 references. Additional exam requirements/recommendations for international students: Required—TOEFL (minimum score 550 paper-based; 218 computer-based; 82 iBT). Electronic applications accepted. *Faculty research:* Digitizing Quaker texts, vital Quaker ministry.

Eastern Mennonite University, Eastern Mennonite Seminary, Harrisonburg, VA 22802-2462. Offers church leadership (MA); divinity (M Div); ministry studies (Certificate); online theological studies (Certificate); religion (MA); theological studies (Certificate). *Accreditation:* ATS. Part-time programs available. *Faculty:* 8 full-time (2 women), 8 part-time/adjunct (2 women). *Students:* 48 full-time (21 women), 30 part-time (10 women); includes 6 minority (5 African Americans, 1 Hispanic American), 12 international. Average age 40. 40 applicants, 100% accepted, 37 enrolled. In 2008, 15 first professional degrees, 9 master's awarded. *Degree requirements:* For master's, thesis (for some programs); for M Div, thesis/dissertation (for some programs), supervised field education. *Entrance requirements:* For M Div and master's, minimum GPA of 2.5. Additional exam requirements/recommendations for international students: Required—TOEFL (minimum score 550 paper-based; 213 computer-based). *Application deadline:* For fall admission, 6/15 priority date for domestic and international students; for winter admission, 11/15 priority date for domestic and international students; for spring admission, 3/15 priority date for domestic and international students. Applications are processed on a rolling basis. Application fee: $25. *Expenses:* Contact institution. *Financial support:* Application deadline: 6/30; *Faculty research:* Spiritual direction and 'culture of call'; leadership coaching: an approach to leadership in a culture of call; clarity of call in the probationary process for United Methodist clergy in Virginia; EMS women's experiences of culture of call efforts; practices of excellent and fruitful Mennonite pastoral ministry. Total annual research expenditures: $45,000. *Unit head:* Dr. Ervin R. Stutzman, Seminary Dean, 540-432-4261, Fax: 540-432-4444, E-mail: stutzerv@emu.edu. *Application contact:* Don A. Yoder, Director of Seminary and Graduate Admissions, 540-432-4257, Fax: 540-432-4598, E-mail: yoderda@emu.edu.

Eastern University, Palmer Theological Seminary, Wynnewood, PA 19096-3430. Offers M Div, MTS, D Min, M Div/MBA, M Div/MSW. *Accreditation:* ACIPE; ATS; MSA/CIHE. Part-time and evening/weekend programs available. *Entrance requirements:* Additional exam requirements/recommendations for international students: Required—TOEFL.

Ecumenical Theological Seminary, Professional Program, Detroit, MI 48201. Offers M Div. *Accreditation:* ACIPE; ATS.

Eden Theological Seminary, Graduate and Professional Programs, St. Louis, MO 63119-3192. Offers M Div, MAPS, MTS, D Min. *Accreditation:* ACIPE; ATS. *Degree requirements:* For master's, comprehensive exam (for some programs), thesis (for some programs), 2 oral exams; for doctorate, professional essay, supervised in-service projects; for M Div, thesis/dissertation optional, 2 oral exams. *Entrance requirements:* For M Div and master's, interview, minimum GPA of 2.7; for doctorate, interview, minimum GPA of 3.0. Additional exam requirements/recommendations for international students: Required—TOEFL (minimum score 550 paper-based). Electronic applications accepted. *Faculty research:* Psalms, pastoral ethics, historical Jesus, leadership roles, congregational life.

Theology

Emmanuel School of Religion, Graduate and Professional Programs, Johnson City, TN 37601-9438. Offers Christian care and counseling (M Div); Christian doctrine (M Div); Christian education (M Div); Christian ministries (M Div); church history (M Div, MAR); ministry (D Min); New Testament (M Div, MAR); Old Testament (M Div, MAR); urban ministry (M Div); world mission (M Div). *Accreditation:* ACIPE; ATS. Part-time programs available. *Faculty:* 12 full-time (2 women), 2 part-time/adjunct (0 women). *Students:* 86 full-time (26 women), 42 part-time (10 women); includes 5 minority (4 African Americans, 1 Hispanic American), 14 international. Average age 32. 47 applicants, 98% accepted, 34 enrolled. In 2008, 16 first professional degrees, 6 master's, 2 doctorates awarded. *Degree requirements:* For master's, 2 foreign languages, thesis; for M Div, 2 foreign languages; thesis/dissertation or alternative. *Entrance requirements:* For doctorate, GRE General Test, Minnesota Multiphasic Personality Inventory, M Div or equivalent. *Application deadline:* For fall admission, 8/1 priority date for domestic students. Applications are processed on a rolling basis. Application fee: $25. *Expenses:* Tuition: Full-time $7800; part-time $325 per credit. Required fees: $122.50 per semester. Tuition and fees vary according to degree level and program. *Financial support:* In 2008–09, 90 students received support, including 10 teaching assistantships with partial tuition reimbursements available; career-related internships or fieldwork, institutionally sponsored loans, scholarships/grants, and tuition waivers (partial) also available. Support available to part-time students. Financial award application deadline: 4/1; financial award applicants required to submit FAFSA. *Faculty research:* Theology of Old Testament prophets, spiritual formation for Christian leaders, history of African churches and religions, social world of early Christianity, lay pastoral counseling. Total annual research expenditures: $12,000. *Unit head:* Dr. Rollin A Ramsaran, Dean and Professor of New Testament, 423-461-1524, Fax: 423-926-6198, E-mail: RamsaranR@esr.edu. *Application contact:* Shelley Gasser, Administrative Assistant for Admissions, 423-461-1535, Fax: 423-926-6198, E-mail: GasserS@esr.edu.

Emory University, Candler School of Theology, Atlanta, GA 30322-1100. Offers M Div, MTS, Th M, Th D, JD/M Div, JD/MTS, M Div/MBA. *Accreditation:* ACIPE; ATS. Part-time programs available. *Degree requirements:* For master's, thesis optional; for doctorate, thesis/dissertation; for M Div, thesis/dissertation optional. *Entrance requirements:* For M Div, minimum undergraduate GPA of 2.75; for master's, minimum undergraduate GPA of 3.0; for doctorate, M Div and 8 units of course work in clinical pastoral education. Additional exam requirements/recommendations for international students: Required—TOEFL (minimum score 213 computer-based). *Expenses:* Contact institution. *Faculty research:* Biblical studies, church history, ministry practice, pastoral care and ethics.

Episcopal Divinity School, Graduate and Professional Programs, Cambridge, MA 02138-3494. Offers M Div, MATS, D Min, CTS. *Accreditation:* ACIPE; ATS (one or more programs are accredited). Part-time programs available. *Degree requirements:* For master's, thesis optional; for doctorate, thesis/dissertation, project; for M Div, thesis/dissertation optional, fieldwork. *Entrance requirements:* For M Div and master's, GRE General Test or MAT, 2 interviews; for doctorate, 2 interviews, M Div or equivalent; for CTS, GRE General Test, MAT, or advanced degree; 2 interviews. Additional exam requirements/recommendations for international students: Required—TOEFL. *Faculty research:* Anglican, global, and ecumenical studies; congregational studies; feminist liberation theologies.

Erskine Theological Seminary, Graduate and Professional Programs, Due West, SC 29639-0668. Offers M Div, MACE, MACM, MAPM, MATS, MCM, D Min. *Accreditation:* ATS. Part-time and evening/weekend programs available. *Degree requirements:* For doctorate, thesis/dissertation; for M Div, 2 foreign languages. *Entrance requirements:* For master's, Myers Briggs Type Indicator, Taylor Johnson Temperament Analysis, Ministry Specialties Test (MACM), minimum GPA of 3.0, interview with committee (MACM); for doctorate, minimum GPA of 3.0 during M Div. Additional exam requirements/recommendations for international students: Required—TOEFL (minimum score 550 paper-based). Electronic applications accepted. *Faculty research:* Church administration, biblical studies.

Evangelical Seminary of Puerto Rico, Graduate and Professional Programs, San Juan, PR 00925-2207. Offers M Div, MAR, D Min. *Accreditation:* ATS. Part-time programs available. *Degree requirements:* For master's, comprehensive exam; for M Div, integration essay. *Entrance requirements:* For M Div, Admission Test for Graduate Studies, denominational endorsement; for master's, Admission Test for Graduate Studies; for doctorate, 3 years experience in ministry service. Additional exam requirements/recommendations for international students: Required—TOEFL, EXADEP. *Faculty research:* Protestantism in Puerto Rico.

Evangelical Theological Seminary, Graduate and Professional Programs, Myerstown, PA 17067-1212. Offers divinity (M Div); marriage and family therapy (MA); ministry (Certificate); religion (MA). *Accreditation:* ATS (one or more programs are accredited). Part-time programs available. Postbaccalaureate distance learning degree programs offered (minimal on-campus study). *Degree requirements:* For master's, 2 foreign languages; for M Div, 2 foreign languages, ministry internship. *Entrance requirements:* For M Div and master's, minimum GPA of 2.5. Additional exam requirements/recommendations for international students: Required—TOEFL (minimum score 550 paper-based; 213 computer-based). *Faculty research:* Literary form and structure within the Hebrew and Greek scriptures, Wesley studies, esoteric biblical languages, the Mosaic law and the Christian, ethics.

Faith Baptist Bible College and Theological Seminary, Graduate Program, Ankeny, IA 50021. Offers biblical studies (MA); pastoral studies (M Div); pastoral training (MA); religion (MA); theological studies (MA). Part-time programs available. *Faculty:* 4 full-time (0 women), 7 part-time/adjunct (0 women). *Students:* 28 full-time (3 women), 28 part-time (2 women); includes 1 minority (Hispanic American), 1 international. Average age 29. In 2008, 9 first professional degrees, 12 master's awarded. *Degree requirements:* For master's, thesis or alternative; for M Div, 2 foreign languages. *Entrance requirements:* Additional exam requirements/recommendations for international students: Required—TOEFL (minimum score 550 paper-based; 197 computer-based). *Application deadline:* For fall admission, 8/1 priority date for domestic students; 8/1 for international students; for spring admission, 12/15 for domestic and international students. Applications are processed on a rolling basis. Application fee: $25. *Expenses:* Tuition: Full-time $10,228; part-time $392 per credit hour. Required fees: $95 per semester. One-time fee: $50. Tuition and fees vary according to class time and course load. *Financial support:* Career-related internships or fieldwork and scholarships/grants available. Support available to part-time students. Financial award application deadline: 3/1; financial award applicants required to submit FAFSA. *Faculty research:* Baptist theology, American church history. *Unit head:* Dr. Ernest Schmidt, Dean of Seminary, 515-964-0601, Fax: 514-964-1638, E-mail: schmidte@faith.edu. *Application contact:* Patrick Odle, Vice President of Enrollment, 888-FAITH4U, Fax: 515-964-1638, E-mail: odlep@faith.edu.

Faith Evangelical Lutheran Seminary, Graduate and Professional Programs, Tacoma, WA 98407. Offers B Th, M Div, MCM, MTS, D Min. Part-time and evening/weekend programs available. Postbaccalaureate distance learning degree programs offered (minimal on-campus study). *Degree requirements:* For master's, thesis optional; for doctorate, thesis/dissertation; for first professional degree, thesis/dissertation (for some programs). *Entrance requirements:* For first professional degree and master's, minimum undergraduate GPA of 2.7; for doctorate, minimum graduate GPA of 3.0. Additional exam requirements/recommendations for international students: Required—TOEFL (minimum score 550 paper-based; 213 computer-based).

Fordham University, Graduate School of Arts and Sciences, Department of Theology, New York, NY 10458. Offers MA, PhD. Part-time and evening/weekend programs available. Terminal master's awarded for partial completion of doctoral program. *Degree requirements:* For master's, one foreign language, comprehensive exam; for doctorate, 2 foreign languages, comprehensive exam, thesis/dissertation. *Entrance requirements:* For master's and doctorate, GRE General Test. Additional exam requirements/recommendations for international students: Required—TOEFL (minimum score 650 paper-based; 280 computer-based). Electronic applications accepted. *Faculty research:* History of Christian tradition, contemporary systematic theology, theological/feminist ethics, American Catholicism, biblical exegesis and theology.

Franciscan School of Theology, Graduate and Professional Programs, Berkeley, CA 94709-1294. Offers M Div, MA, MAMC, MTS. *Accreditation:* ATS (one or more programs are accredited). Part-time programs available. *Degree requirements:* For master's, one foreign language, thesis. *Entrance requirements:* For master's, GRE General Test (MA). Additional exam requirements/recommendations for international students: Required—TOEFL (minimum score 550 paper-based; 213 computer-based). *Faculty research:* Church history, multicultural ministries, ethics and morality, catechesis, biblical studies.

Franciscan University of Steubenville, Graduate Programs, Department of Theology, Steubenville, OH 43952-1763. Offers theology and Christian ministry (MA). Part-time programs available. Postbaccalaureate distance learning degree programs offered (minimal on-campus study). *Degree requirements:* For master's, comprehensive exam. *Entrance requirements:* For master's, minimum undergraduate GPA of 3.0.

Freed-Hardeman University, School of Biblical Studies, Program in Divinity, Henderson, TN 38340-2399. Offers M Div. Part-time programs available. *Faculty:* 10 full-time (0 women), 1 part-time/adjunct (0 women). *Students:* 1 full-time (0 women), 12 part-time (0 women). Average age 31. 2 applicants, 100% accepted, 2 enrolled. *Entrance requirements:* Additional exam requirements/recommendations for international students: Required—TOEFL (minimum score 500 paper-based; 173 computer-based). *Application deadline:* For fall admission, 8/1 priority date for domestic students. Applications are processed on a rolling basis. Application fee: $35. *Expenses:* Tuition: Full-time $4284; part-time $357 per credit hour. Required fees: $16 per credit hour. *Financial support:* Career-related internships or fieldwork, Federal Work-Study, tuition waivers (partial), and unspecified assistantships available. Support available to part-time students. Financial award application deadline: 8/1; financial award applicants required to submit FAFSA. *Unit head:* Dr. Mark Blackwelder, Director of Graduate Studies, School of Biblical Studies, 731-989-6769, Fax: 731-989-6400, E-mail: mblackwelder@fhu.edu. *Application contact:* Dr. Samuel T. Jones, Vice President for Academics, 731-989-6004, Fax: 731-989-6945, E-mail: sjones@fhu.edu.

Freed-Hardeman University, School of Biblical Studies, Program in New Testament, Henderson, TN 38340-2399. Offers MA. Part-time programs available. *Faculty:* 10 full-time (0 women), 1 part-time/adjunct (0 women). *Students:* 9 full-time (0 women), 17 part-time (1 woman); includes 7 minority (1 American Indian/Alaska Native, 4 Asian Americans or Pacific Islanders, 2 Hispanic Americans). Average age 28. 4 applicants, 100% accepted, 4 enrolled. In 2008, 8 master's awarded. *Degree requirements:* For master's, one foreign language, comprehensive exam, thesis. *Entrance requirements:* For master's, GRE General Test or MAT. Additional exam requirements/recommendations for international students: Required—TOEFL (minimum score 500 paper-based; 173 computer-based). *Application deadline:* For fall admission, 8/1 priority date for domestic students; for spring admission, 12/1 for domestic students. Applications are processed on a rolling basis. Application fee: $35. *Expenses:* Tuition: Full-time $4284; part-time $357 per credit hour. Required fees: $16 per credit hour. *Financial support:* Career-related internships or fieldwork, Federal Work-Study, tuition waivers (partial), and unspecified assistantships available. Support available to part-time students. Financial award application deadline: 8/1; financial award applicants required to submit FAFSA. *Unit head:* Dr. Mark Blackwelder, Director of Graduate Studies, 731-989-6769, Fax: 731-989-6400, E-mail: mblackwelder@fhu.edu. *Application contact:* Dr. Samuel T. Jones, Vice President for Academics, 731-989-6004, Fax: 731-989-6945, E-mail: sjones@fhu.edu.

Friends University, Graduate School, Division of Science, Arts, and Education, Program in Christian Ministry, Wichita, KS 67213. Offers MACM. Evening/weekend programs available. *Entrance requirements:* Additional exam requirements/recommendations for international students: Required—TOEFL (minimum score 560 paper-based; 220 computer-based). Electronic applications accepted.

Fuller Theological Seminary, Graduate School of Theology, Pasadena, CA 91182. Offers Christian leadership (MACL); evangelism (MA); family life education (MA); ministry (M Div, D Min); pastoral ministry (MA); recovery ministry (MA); theology (MAT, Th M, PhD); worship music ministry (MA); worship, theology, and the arts (MA); youth, family, and culture (MA). M Div offered jointly with Denver Conservative Baptist Seminary. *Accreditation:* ACIPE; ATS (one or more programs are accredited). Part-time and evening/weekend programs available. *Degree requirements:* For doctorate, variable foreign language requirement, thesis/dissertation; for M Div, 2 foreign languages. *Entrance requirements:* For doctorate, GRE General Test. *Faculty research:* New Testament, Old Testament, systematic theology, history, practical theology.

Gardner-Webb University, M. Christopher White School of Divinity, Boiling Springs, NC 28017. Offers Christian education (M Div); ministry (D Min); missiology (M Div); pastoral care and counseling (M Div); pastoral ministry (M Div); M Div/MA. *Accreditation:* ACIPE; ATS. Part-time programs available. *Degree requirements:* For M Div, 2 foreign languages. *Entrance requirements:* For M Div, minimum GPA of 2.0; for doctorate, minimum GPA of 2.75. *Expenses:* Contact institution. *Faculty research:* Jewish Christian dialogue, Islam.

Garrett-Evangelical Theological Seminary, Graduate and Professional Programs, Evanston, IL 60201-3298. Offers Bible and culture (PhD); Christian education (MA); Christian education and congregational studies (PhD); contemporary theology and culture (PhD); divinity (M Div); ethics, church, and society (MA); liturgical studies (PhD); ministry (D Min); music ministry (MA); pastoral care and counseling (MA); pastoral theology, personality, and culture (PhD); spiritual formation and evangelism (MA); theological studies (MTS); M Div/MSW. *Accreditation:* ACIPE; ATS (one or more programs are accredited). Part-time programs available. *Degree requirements:* For master's, thesis (for some programs); for doctorate, thesis/dissertation. *Entrance requirements:* For doctorate, GRE (PhD). Additional exam requirements/recommendations for international students: Required—TOEFL (minimum score 560 paper-based; 230 computer-based). Electronic applications accepted.

General Theological Seminary, Graduate and Professional Programs, New York, NY 10011-4977. Offers Anglican studies (STM, Th D, Certificate); ascetical theology (Certificate); biblical studies (Certificate); congregational development (Certificate); divinity (M Div); historical and theological studies (Certificate); spiritual direction (MASD, STM, Certificate); theology (MA). *Accreditation:* ACIPE; ATS. Part-time and evening/weekend programs available. Terminal master's awarded for partial completion of doctoral program. *Degree requirements:* For master's, thesis; for doctorate, 2 foreign languages, thesis/dissertation. *Entrance requirements:* For M Div, GRE General Test, bishop's endorsement; for master's, GRE General Test; for doctorate, GRE, M Div or MA. Additional exam requirements/recommendations for international students: Required—TOEFL. *Faculty research:* Liturgy, New Testament, ethics, history, ecumenical relations.

George Fox University, George Fox Evangelical Seminary, Newberg, OR 97132-2697. Offers divinity (M Div); ministry (D Min), including global missional leadership, leadership and spiritual formation, leadership in the emerging culture; ministry leadership (MA); spiritual formation (MA); spiritual formation and discipleship (Certificate); theological studies (MA). *Accreditation:* ACIPE; ATS. Part-time and evening/weekend programs available. Postbaccalaureate distance learning degree programs offered (minimal on-campus study). *Faculty:* 7 full-time (2 women), 17 part-time/adjunct (7 women). *Students:* 51 full-time (6 women), 289 part-time (94 women); includes 27 minority (6 African Americans, 2 American Indian/Alaska Native, 15 Asian Americans or Pacific Islanders, 4 Hispanic Americans), 6 international. Average age 41. 134 applicants, 94% accepted, 97 enrolled. In 2008, 9 first professional degrees, 18 master's, 20 doctorates, 5 other advanced degrees awarded. *Degree requirements:* For master's, variable foreign language requirement, thesis optional, internship; for doctorate, thesis/dissertation. *Entrance requirements:* Additional exam requirements/recommendations for international students: Required—TOEFL (minimum score 550 paper-based; 213 computer-based; 80 iBT). *Application deadline:* For fall admission, 7/1 for domestic and international students; for spring admission, 11/1 for domestic and international students. Applications are processed on a rolling basis. Application fee: $40. Electronic applications accepted. *Expenses:* Contact institution. *Financial support:* In 2008–09, 33 students received support. Career-related internships or fieldwork and scholarships/grants available. Financial award application deadline: 5/1; financial award applicants required to submit FAFSA. *Unit head:* Dr. Chuck Conniry, Vice President and Dean, George Fox Evangelical Seminary, 503-554-6152, E-mail: cconniry@georgefox.edu. *Application contact:* Sheila Bartlett, Admissions Counselor, 800-631-0921, Fax: 503-554-6122, E-mail: sbartlett@georgefox.edu.

Georgetown University, Graduate School of Arts and Sciences, Department of Theology, Washington, DC 20057. Offers PhD.

Georgian Court University, School of Arts and Humanities, Lakewood, NJ 08701-2697. Offers Catholic school leadership (Certificate); parish business management (Certificate); pastoral administration (Certificate); pastoral ministry (Certificate); religious education (Certificate); theology (MA, Certificate). Part-time and evening/weekend programs available. *Faculty:* 3 full-time (1 woman). *Students:* 23 part-time (18 women); includes 3 minority (1 African American, 1 Asian American or Pacific Islander, 1 Hispanic American). Average age 54. 7 applicants, 100% accepted, 5 enrolled. In 2008, 6 master's awarded. *Degree requirements:* For master's, thesis (for some programs). *Entrance requirements:* For master's, 3 letters of recommendation. Additional exam requirements/recommendations for international students: Required—TOEFL (minimum score 550 paper-based; 213 computer-based). *Application deadline:* For fall admission, 8/1 priority date for domestic students, 4/1 for international students; for spring admission, 1/1 priority date for domestic students, 7/1 for international students. Applications are processed on a rolling basis. Application fee: $40. Electronic applications accepted. *Expenses:* Tuition: Full-time $12,276; part-time $682 per credit. Required fees: $400 per year. Tuition and fees vary according to campus/location. *Financial support:* Scholarships/grants, health care benefits, and unspecified assistantships available. Financial award application deadline: 4/15; financial award applicants required to submit FAFSA. *Unit head:* Dr. Linda James, Dean, 732-987-2617, Fax: 732-987-2007. *Application contact:* Eugene Soltys, Director of Graduate Admissions, 732-987-2770, Fax: 732-987-2084, E-mail: graduateadmissions@georgian.edu.

Global University, Graduate School of Theology, Springfield, MO 65804. Offers biblical studies (MA); divinity (M Div); ministerial studies (MA), including education, leadership, missions, New Testament, Old Testament. Part-time and evening/weekend programs available. Postbaccalaureate distance learning degree programs offered (no on-campus study). *Faculty:* 10 full-time (1 woman), 83 part-time/adjunct (10 women). *Students:* 200 full-time (27 women), 175 part-time (48 women); includes 250 minority (150 African Americans, 25 American Indian/Alaska Native, 50 Asian Americans or Pacific Islanders, 25 Hispanic Americans). Average age 49. 148 applicants, 94% accepted, 139 enrolled. In 2008, 1 first professional degree, 27 master's awarded. *Degree requirements:* For master's, thesis (for some programs). *Entrance requirements:* For M Div, minimum undergraduate GPA of 3.0; for master's, minimum undergraduate GPA of 3.0, 15 undergraduate credit hours of course work in Bible or theology. *Application deadline:* Applications are processed on a rolling basis. Application fee: $50. Electronic applications accepted. *Expenses:* Tuition: Full-time $3690; part-time $205 per credit hour. Required fees: $205 per credit hour. One-time fee: $50 full-time. *Faculty research:* Higher education, cross-cultural missions. *Unit head:* Dr. Carl Chrisner, Dean, 417-862-9533 Ext. 2237, Fax: 417-869-5623, E-mail: cchrisner@globaluniversity.edu. *Application contact:* Jody Patterson, Graduate Student Enrollment Representative, 417-862-9533 Ext. 2347, Fax: 417-862-0863, E-mail: gradenroll@globaluniversity.edu.

Golden Gate Baptist Theological Seminary, Graduate and Professional Programs, Mill Valley, CA 94941-3197. Offers divinity (M Div); early childhood education (Certificate); education leadership (MAEL, Diploma); ministry (D Min); theological studies (MTS); theology (Th M); youth ministry (Certificate). *Accreditation:* ACIPE; ATS (one or more programs are accredited). Part-time and evening/weekend programs available. *Degree requirements:* For master's, thesis (for some programs); for doctorate, 2 foreign languages, thesis/dissertation; for M Div, 2 foreign languages. *Entrance requirements:* For doctorate, MAT. Additional exam requirements/recommendations for international students: Required—TOEFL (minimum score 550 paper-based; 213 computer-based). Electronic applications accepted.

Gordon-Conwell Theological Seminary, Graduate and Professional Programs, South Hamilton, MA 01982. Offers Biblical languages (MABL); church history (MACH); counseling (MACO); ministry (D Min); missions/evangelism (MAME); New Testament (MANT); Old Testament (MAOT); religion (MAR); theology (M Div, MATH, Th M, Th D). *Accreditation:* ACIPE; ATS (one or more programs are accredited). Part-time and evening/weekend programs available. *Degree requirements:* For master's, one foreign language, thesis optional; for doctorate, 2 foreign languages, thesis/dissertation; for M Div, 2 foreign languages. *Entrance requirements:* For M Div and master's, minimum GPA of 2.5; for doctorate, minimum GPA of 3.0.

Grace Theological Seminary, Graduate and Professional Programs, Winona Lake, IN 46590-9907. Offers biblical studies (Certificate); camp administration (MA); counseling (M Div); exegetical studies (MA); intercultural studies (M Div, MA); local church studies (MA); pastoral studies (M Div); theological studies (MA); theology (D Min, Diploma). *Accreditation:* ATS. Part-time programs available. Postbaccalaureate distance learning degree programs offered (no on-campus study). *Degree requirements:* For master's, thesis optional; for doctorate, 2 foreign languages, thesis/dissertation; for M Div, 2 foreign languages, thesis/dissertation optional. *Entrance requirements:* For M Div and master's, MAT, minimum GPA of 2.5. Electronic applications accepted. *Faculty research:* Biblical theology, language, and church ministries.

Grace University, College of Graduate Studies, Bible Department, Omaha, NE 68108. Offers MA. *Degree requirements:* For master's, thesis optional. *Entrance requirements:* For master's, minimum undergraduate GPA of 3.0. Electronic applications accepted.

Graduate Theological Union, Graduate Programs, Berkeley, CA 94709-1212. Offers art and religion (MA, PhD); biblical languages (MA); biblical studies (Old and New Testament) (MA, PhD, Th D); Buddhist studies (MA); Christian spirituality (MA, PhD); cultural and historical studies of religions (MA, PhD); ethics and social theory (PhD); history (MA, PhD, Th D); homiletics (MA, PhD, Th D); interdisciplinary studies (PhD, Th D); Jewish studies (MA, PhD, Certificate); liturgical studies (MA, PhD, Th D); Near Eastern religions (PhD); Orthodox Christian studies (MA); Orthodox studies (Certificate); religion and psychology (MA, PhD); religion and society/ethics and social theory (MA); systematic and philosophical theology (MA, PhD, Th D); women's studies in religion (Certificate); MA/M Div. *Accreditation:* ATS. Terminal master's awarded for partial completion of doctoral program. *Degree requirements:* For master's, one foreign language, thesis; for doctorate, one foreign language, comprehensive exam, thesis/dissertation. *Entrance requirements:* For master's, GRE General Test; for doctorate, GRE General Test, MA or M Div. Additional exam requirements/recommendations for international students: Required—TOEFL. Electronic applications accepted.

Grand Rapids Theological Seminary of Cornerstone University, Graduate Programs, Grand Rapids, MI 49525-5897. Offers biblical counseling (MA); Biblical counseling (M Div); chaplaincy (M Div); Christian education (M Div, MA); intercultural studies (M Div, MA); New Testament (MA, Th M); Old Testament (MA, Th M); pastoral studies (M Div); systematic theology (MA); theology (Th M). *Accreditation:* ATS. Part-time programs available. Postbaccalaureate distance learning degree programs offered (minimal on-campus study). *Entrance requirements:* Additional exam requirements/recommendations for international students: Required—TOEFL (minimum score 577 paper-based; 233 computer-based; 90 iBT). Electronic applications accepted.

Harding University Graduate School of Religion, Graduate Programs, Memphis, TN 38117-5499. Offers Christian ministry (MA); counseling (MA); ministry (M Div, D Min); religion (MA). *Accreditation:* ATS. Part-time programs available. Postbaccalaureate distance learning degree programs offered (minimal on-campus study). *Degree requirements:* For master's, variable foreign language requirement, thesis (for some programs); for doctorate, one foreign language, thesis/dissertation; for M Div, 2 foreign languages, thesis/dissertation optional. *Entrance requirements:* For M Div, GRE General Test (for graduates of non-accredited schools), minimum GPA of 2.5; for master's, minimum GPA of 2.7; for doctorate, minimum GPA of 3.0. Additional exam requirements/recommendations for international students: Required—TOEFL (minimum score 550 paper-based; 213 computer-based; 79 iBT). Electronic applications accepted.

Hardin-Simmons University, Graduate School, Logsdon School of Theology, Abilene, TX 79698-0001. Offers M Div, MA. Part-time and evening/weekend programs available. *Faculty:* 15 full-time (1 woman), 9 part-time/adjunct (1 woman). *Students:* 74 full-time (20 women), 46 part-time (11 women); includes 12 minority (3 African Americans, 2 American Indian/Alaska Native, 7 Hispanic Americans). Average age 31. 35 applicants, 80% accepted, 23 enrolled. In 2008, 12 first professional degrees, 6 master's awarded. *Entrance requirements:* Additional exam requirements/recommendations for international students: Required—TOEFL (minimum score 550 paper-based; 213 computer-based; 75 iBT). *Application deadline:* For fall admission, 8/15 priority date for domestic students, 4/1 for international students; for spring admission, 1/5 priority date for domestic students, 9/1 for international students. Applications are processed on a rolling basis. Application fee: $50. *Expenses:* Tuition: Full-time $10,620; part-time $590 per credit hour. Required fees: $590; $110 per semester. Tuition and fees vary according to course load and degree level. *Financial support:* In 2008–09, 107 students received support, including 7 fellowships (averaging $1,686 per year); scholarships/grants also available. Support available to part-time students. Financial award application deadline: 6/30; financial award applicants required to submit FAFSA. *Unit head:* Dr. Thomas V. Brisco, Dean, 325-670-1266, Fax: 325-670-1406, E-mail: tbrisco@hsutx.edu. *Application contact:* Dr. Gary Stanlake, Dean of Graduate Studies, 325-670-1298, Fax: 325-670-1564, E-mail: gradoff@hsutx.edu.

Hardin-Simmons University, Graduate School, Logsdon School of Theology, Logsdon Seminary, Seminary Program in Theology, Abilene, TX 79698-0001. Offers M Div. *Accreditation:* ATS. Part-time programs available. *Faculty:* 12 full-time (0 women), 9 part-time/adjunct (1 woman). *Students:* 60 full-time (13 women), 29 part-time (5 women); includes 10 minority (3 African Americans, 1 American Indian/Alaska Native, 6 Hispanic Americans). Average age 32. 24 applicants, 71% accepted, 14 enrolled. In 2008, 12 M Divs awarded. *Degree requirements:* For M Div, 2 foreign languages, chapel/spiritual formations, colloquium, ministry retreat and formation conferences. *Entrance requirements:* Minimum GPA of 2.0, interview, 3 letters of recommendation. Additional exam requirements/recommendations for international students: Required—TOEFL (minimum score 550 paper-based; 213 computer-based; 75 iBT). *Application deadline:* For fall admission, 8/15 priority date for domestic students, 4/1 for international students; for spring admission, 1/5 priority date for domestic students, 9/1 for international students. Applications are processed on a rolling basis. Application fee: $50. *Expenses:* Tuition: Full-time $10,620; part-time $590 per credit hour. Required fees: $590; $110 per semester. Tuition and fees vary according to course load and degree level. *Financial support:* In 2008–09, 80 students received support, including 6 fellowships (averaging $1,667 per year); career-related internships or fieldwork and scholarships/grants also available. Support available to part-time students. Financial award application deadline: 6/30; financial award applicants required to submit FAFSA. *Faculty research:* Hebrew grammar, history of Christian education, training of ministers into the twenty-first century, role of women in Old Testament, contemporary ethical issues, Ricouer in contemporary theology. *Unit head:* Dr. Robert Ellis, Director, 325-670-5841, E-mail: rellis@hsutx.edu. *Application contact:* Dr. Gary Stanlake, Dean of Graduate Studies, 325-670-1298, Fax: 325-670-1564, E-mail: gradoff@hsutx.edu.

Hartford Seminary, Graduate Programs, Hartford, CT 06105-2279. Offers black ministry (Certificate); Islamic studies (MA); ministerios Hispanos (Certificate); ministry (D Min); religious studies (MA); women's leadership institute (Certificate). *Accreditation:* ATS (one or more programs are accredited). Part-time and evening/weekend programs available. Postbaccalaureate distance learning degree programs offered (no on-campus study). *Degree requirements:* For master's, thesis optional, oral exam; for doctorate, thesis/dissertation, oral exam. *Entrance requirements:* For doctorate, experience in ministry, M Div. Additional exam requirements/recommendations for international students: Required—TOEFL (minimum score 550 paper-based; 213 computer-based; 80 iBT). *Faculty research:* Liturgy and social justice, professional leadership in ministry, congregational studies, Christian-Muslim relations, American religion.

Harvard University, Harvard Divinity School, Cambridge, MA 02138. Offers M Div, MTS, Th M, PhD, Th D. PhD offered by Harvard Graduate School of Arts and Sciences. *Accreditation:* ACIPE; ATS. *Faculty:* 36 full-time (15 women), 81 part-time/adjunct (35 women). *Students:* 432 full-time (235 women); includes 78 minority (33 African Americans, 4 American Indian/Alaska Native, 20 Asian Americans or Pacific Islanders, 21 Hispanic Americans), 41 international. Average age 26. 677 applicants, 37% accepted, 161 enrolled. In 2008, 43 first professional degrees, 119 master's, 11 doctorates awarded. *Degree requirements:* For master's, one foreign language, thesis (for some programs); for doctorate, 3 foreign languages, comprehensive exam, thesis/dissertation; for M Div, one foreign language, thesis/dissertation, field education. *Entrance requirements:* For M Div, master's, and doctorate, GRE General Test. Additional exam requirements/recommendations for international students: Required—TOEFL (minimum score 600 paper-based; 250 computer-based; 100 iBT). *Application deadline:* For fall admission, 1/11 for domestic and international students. Application fee: $75. Electronic applications accepted. *Expenses:* Contact institution. *Financial support:* In 2008–09, 418 students received support, including 398 fellowships with tuition reimbursements available (averaging $21,469 per year); teaching assistantships, career-related internships or fieldwork, Federal Work-Study, and scholarships/grants also available. Support available to part-time students. Financial award application deadline: 2/1; financial award applicants required to submit FAFSA. *Faculty research:* Theology, women's studies, history, comparative religion. *Unit head:* William A. Graham, Dean, 917-495-4513, Fax: 617-496-8026. *Application contact:* Loida Feliz, Director of Admissions, 617-495-5796, Fax: 617-495-0345, E-mail: lfeliz@hds,harvard.edu.

Hebrew College, Rabbinical School, Newton Centre, MA 02459. Offers MA. *Entrance requirements:* For master's, interview. Additional exam requirements/recommendations for international students: Required—TOEFL.

Hebrew Theological College, Department of Talmud and Rabbinics, Skokie, IL 60077-3263. Offers Rabbi.

Hebrew Union College–Jewish Institute of Religion, Rabbinical School, New York, NY 10012-1186. Offers MAHL. *Degree requirements:* For MAHL, one foreign language, thesis/dissertation, fieldwork, sermons. *Entrance requirements:* GRE, language exam, minimum GPA of 3.0, minimum 2 years of college-level Hebrew. Additional exam requirements/recommendations for international students: Required—TOEFL. *Faculty research:* Philosophy and theology, Bible, Hebrew, pastoral care, history and Rabbinics.

Hebrew Union College–Jewish Institute of Religion, Rabbinic School, Cincinnati, OH 45220-2488. Offers MAHL. *Accreditation:* ACIPE. *Degree requirements:* For MAHL, one foreign language, thesis/dissertation. *Entrance requirements:* GRE General Test, Hebrew competency exam, interview, psychological test. *Faculty research:* Comprehensive Aramaic lexicon, four-volume history (German Jews and modern times).

Hebrew Union College–Jewish Institute of Religion, School of Graduate Studies, Program in Pastoral Counseling, New York, NY 10012-1186. Offers D Min. *Accreditation:* ACIPE. *Degree requirements:* For doctorate, thesis/dissertation. *Entrance requirements:* For doctorate, M Div (or higher), ordination/certification for ministry. Additional exam requirements/recommendations for international students: Required—TOEFL. *Expenses:* Contact institution. *Faculty research:* Philosophy and theology, Bible, Hebrew, pastoral care, history and Rabbinics.

Hebrew Union College–Jewish Institute of Religion, School of Rabbinical Studies, Los Angeles, CA 90007-3796. Offers MAHL. *Accreditation:* ACIPE. *Degree requirements:* For MAHL, one foreign language, thesis/dissertation, Hebrew. *Entrance requirements:* GRE General Test, interview, minimum undergraduate GPA of 3.0, 2 years of college-level Hebrew. Additional exam requirements/recommendations for international students: Required—TOEFL (minimum score 550 paper-based). Electronic applications accepted.

Theology

Heritage Baptist College and Heritage Theological Seminary, Program in Theological Studies, Cambridge, ON N3C 3T2, Canada. Offers chaplaincy (M Div); counselling (M Div); general (M Div); ministry (D Min); pastoral (M Div); research (M Div); theological studies (MA, Certificate). *Accreditation:* ATS.

Holy Apostles College and Seminary, Department of Theology, Cromwell, CT 06416-2005. Offers bioethics (MA, Certificate, Post Master's Certificate); church history (MA, Certificate, Post Master's Certificate); dogmatic theology (MA, Certificate, Post Master's Certificate); liturgical music (MA, Certificate, Post Master's Certificate); liturgy (MA, Certificate, Post Master's Certificate); moral theology (MA, Certificate, Post Master's Certificate); philosophical theology (MA, Certificate, Post Master's Certificate); religious education (MA, Certificate, Post Master's Certificate); sacred scripture (MA, Post Master's Certificate); sacred scriptures (Certificate); theology (M Div). Part-time and evening/weekend programs available. Postbaccalaureate distance learning degree programs offered (no on-campus study). *Degree requirements:* For master's, one foreign language, comprehensive exam, thesis optional; for other advanced degree, culminating paper. *Entrance requirements:* For M Div, interview; for master's, minimum undergraduate GPA of 3.0; for other advanced degree, minimum graduate GPA of 3.0. Electronic applications accepted. *Faculty research:* Roman Catholic theology, philosophy.

Holy Cross Greek Orthodox School of Theology, Theological Programs, Brookline, MA 02445-7496. Offers M Div, MTS, Th M. *Accreditation:* ATS. Part-time programs available. *Degree requirements:* For master's, 2 foreign languages, thesis (for some programs); for M Div, 2 foreign languages, thesis/dissertation (for some programs). *Entrance requirements:* For M Div and master's, GRE General Test, interview, written submission. Additional exam requirements/recommendations for international students: Required—TOEFL (minimum score 550 paper-based; 213 computer-based). *Faculty research:* Spirituality, liturgies, ecumenism, church history.

Hood Theological Seminary, Graduate and Professional Programs, Salisbury, NC 28144. Offers M Div, MTS, D Min. *Accreditation:* ATS. Evening/weekend programs available. *Degree requirements:* For master's, thesis optional; for doctorate, thesis/dissertation; for M Div, thesis/dissertation optional. *Faculty research:* Old Testament human sexuality, preaching and the vulnerable, socio-historical issues, Pauline studies, multiculturalism/African-American studies.

Houston Baptist University, College of Arts and Humanities, Program in Theological Studies, Houston, TX 77074-3298. Offers MATS. Part-time and evening/weekend programs available. *Degree requirements:* For master's, comprehensive exam. *Entrance requirements:* For master's, GRE General Test, 6 hours of course work in Greek or Hebrew (optional), interview, minimum GPA of 2.5. Additional exam requirements/recommendations for international students: Required—TOEFL (minimum score 550 paper-based; 213 computer-based). *Expenses:* Contact institution.

Houston Graduate School of Theology, Graduate School, Houston, TX 77092. Offers counseling (MA); pastoral ministry (M Div, D Min); theology (MA). *Accreditation:* ATS (one or more programs are accredited). Part-time and evening/weekend programs available. *Degree requirements:* For master's, thesis (for some programs); for doctorate, thesis/dissertation; for M Div, thesis/dissertation optional. *Entrance requirements:* For doctorate, GRE General Test or MAT, M Div or equivalent. Additional exam requirements/recommendations for international students: Required—TOEFL (minimum score 550 paper-based; 213 computer-based). *Faculty research:* Hermeneutics, spirituality, religion of Eastern Europe.

Howard University, School of Divinity, Washington, DC 20017. Offers M Div, MARS, D Min. *Accreditation:* ACIPE; ATS. Part-time and evening/weekend programs available. *Degree requirements:* For master's, thesis; for doctorate, thesis/dissertation; for M Div, thesis/dissertation optional. *Entrance requirements:* For M Div, minimum GPA of 2.0; for master's and doctorate, minimum GPA of 3.0. Electronic applications accepted. *Faculty research:* African-American religious experience, women in ministry, ecumenics, biblical studies.

Iliff School of Theology, Graduate and Professional Programs, Denver, CO 80210-4798. Offers biblical studies (MA); church history (MA); religion (MA); religion and social change (MA); specialized ministry (MASM), including justice and peace, pastoral theology and care, religious leadership; theology (M Div, MTS, D Min, PhD), including Biblical studies (PhD), religion and psychological studies (PhD), religion and social change (PhD), theology, philosophy and culture (PhD); theology/ethics (MA). *Accreditation:* ACIPE; ATS. Part-time and evening/weekend programs available. *Degree requirements:* For master's, one foreign language, thesis (for some programs); for doctorate, 2 foreign languages, comprehensive exam, thesis/dissertation; for M Div, thesis/dissertation optional. *Entrance requirements:* For M Div, minimum GPA of 2.75, references; for master's, minimum GPA of 3.0, writing sample, references; for doctorate, GRE General Test, minimum GPA of 3.0, writing sample, letters of recommendation. Additional exam requirements/recommendations for international students: Required—TOEFL (minimum score 550 paper-based). Electronic applications accepted. *Faculty research:* Pastoral care, history, church music, contemporary church, biblical studies.

Indiana Wesleyan University, College of Graduate Studies, Master of Divinity Program, Marion, IN 46953-4974. Offers M Div. Postbaccalaureate distance learning degree programs offered (minimal on-campus study). *Degree requirements:* For M Div, capstone. *Expenses:* Tuition: Full-time $7020; part-time $390 per credit hour. One-time fee: $290 full-time; $85 part-time. Full-time tuition and fees vary according to course load. *Unit head:* Nathan Lamb, Director, 800-895-0036 Ext. 2089, E-mail: nathan.lamb@indwes.edu. *Application contact:* David McMillan, Assistant Director of Enrollment Management, 765-677-2688, E-mail: david.mcmillan@indwes.edu.

Indiana Wesleyan University, College of Graduate Studies, Wesleyan Seminary, Program in Ministry, Marion, IN 46953-4974. Offers ministerial leadership (MA); youth ministries (MA). Part-time programs available. Postbaccalaureate distance learning degree programs offered (minimal on-campus study). *Faculty:* 5 full-time (0 women), 8 part-time/adjunct (1 woman). *Students:* 130 full-time (30 women), 15 part-time (3 women); includes 24 minority (22 African Americans, 2 Hispanic Americans). In 2008, 39 master's awarded. *Degree requirements:* For master's, one foreign language, capstone practicum and/or project. *Entrance requirements:* Additional exam requirements/recommendations for international students: Required—TOEFL. *Application deadline:* Applications are processed on a rolling basis. Application fee: $25. Electronic applications accepted. *Expenses:* Contact institution. *Financial support:* In 2008–09, 1 research assistantship with full tuition reimbursement was awarded; career-related internships or fieldwork also available. Support available to part-time students. Financial award applicants required to submit FAFSA. *Faculty research:* History of worship innovation, history of New Testament afterlife traditions, second century mantanism, cross-cultural ministry, church health and growth, leadership in Christian organizations, managing change in the church, effective youth ministry, women in ministry, biblical hermeneutics. *Unit head:* Dr. Russ Gunsalus, Director of Graduate Studies in Ministry, 765-677-2259, Fax: 765-677-1456, E-mail: russ.gunsalus@indwes.edu. *Application contact:* Tom Leas, Director of Adult Enrollment Services, 800-895-0036, Fax: 765-677-2404, E-mail: graduate@indwes.edu.

Institute for Christian Studies, Graduate Programs, Toronto, ON M5T 1R4, Canada. Offers education (M Phil F, PhD); history of philosophy (M Phil F, PhD); philosophical aesthetics (M Phil F, PhD); philosophy of religion (M Phil F, PhD); political theory (M Phil F, PhD); systematic philosophy (M Phil F, PhD); theology (M Phil F, PhD); worldview studies (MWS). Part-time programs available. Postbaccalaureate distance learning degree programs offered (minimal on-campus study). *Degree requirements:* For master's, one foreign language, thesis; for doctorate, 2 foreign languages, thesis/dissertation. *Entrance requirements:* For master's and doctorate, philosophy background. Additional exam requirements/recommendations for international students: Required—TOEFL (minimum score 600 paper-based; 250 computer-based). *Faculty research:* Human rights, anthropology of self, medieval discourse, gender and body, post-modern thought; biblical hermeneutics, creational aesthetics, ecumenism, epistemology, political theory and public policy, relational psychotherapy.

Inter American University of Puerto Rico, Metropolitan Campus, Graduate Programs, Program in Theological Studies, San Juan, PR 00919-1293. Offers PhD.

Interdenominational Theological Center, Graduate and Professional Programs, Atlanta, GA 30314-4112. Offers M Div, MACE, MACM, D Min, Th D, M Div/MACE, M Div/MACM, MACM/MACE. *Accreditation:* ACIPE; ATS (one or more programs are accredited). Part-time and evening/weekend programs available. Postbaccalaureate distance learning degree programs offered (minimal on-campus study). *Faculty:* 20 full-time (6 women), 33 part-time/adjunct (13 women). *Students:* 259 full-time (109 women), 167 part-time (71 women); includes 386 minority (384 African Americans, 2 Hispanic Americans), 17 international. Average age 40. 163 applicants, 83% accepted, 102 enrolled. In 2008, 80 first professional degrees, 4 master's, 5 doctorates awarded. *Degree requirements:* For doctorate, thesis/dissertation. *Entrance requirements:* For M Div, bachelor's degree; for doctorate, master's degree. *Application deadline:* For fall admission, 7/1 for domestic and international students; for spring admission, 11/3 for domestic and international students. Applications are processed on a rolling basis. Application fee: $50. *Expenses:* Tuition: Full-time $10,780; part-time $632 per credit. Required fees: $604; $632 per credit. *Financial support:* In 2008–09, 375 students received support, including 4 research assistantships; career-related internships or fieldwork and Federal Work-Study also available. Support available to part-time students. Financial award application deadline: 6/15; financial award applicants required to submit FAFSA. *Unit head:* Dr. Michael A. Battle, President, 404-527-7702, Fax: 404-527-7770, E-mail: mbattle@itc.edu. *Application contact:* Walter Cabassa, Office of Admission and Recruitment, 404-527-7792, E-mail: wcabassa@itc.edu.

International Baptist College, Program in Biblical Studies, Tempe, AZ 85282. Offers MA.

Jesuit School of Theology at Berkeley, Programs in Theology, Berkeley, CA 94709-1193. Offers M Div, MA, MABL, MTS, Th M, STD, STL, MA/M Div. *Accreditation:* ATS (one or more programs are accredited). Part-time programs available. *Degree requirements:* For master's, one foreign language, thesis; for doctorate, 2 foreign languages, comprehensive exam, thesis/dissertation; for M Div, comprehensive exam. *Entrance requirements:* For M Div, GRE, undergraduate course work in philosophy; for master's, GRE. Additional exam requirements/recommendations for international students: Required—TOEFL, TWE.

The Jewish Theological Seminary, The Graduate School, New York, NY 10027-4649. Offers ancient Judaism (MA, DHL, PhD); Bible (MA, DHL, PhD); Jewish education (PhD); Jewish history (MA, DHL, PhD); Jewish literature (MA, DHL, PhD); Jewish philosophy (MA, DHL, PhD); liturgy (MA, DHL, PhD); medieval Jewish studies (MA, DHL, PhD); Midrash (MA, DHL, PhD); modern Jewish studies (MA, DHL, PhD); Talmud and rabbinics (MA, DHL, PhD); MA/MSW. *Accreditation:* ACIPE. Part-time programs available. *Faculty:* 60 full-time (19 women), 73 part-time/adjunct (39 women). *Students:* 91 full-time (49 women), 27 part-time (14 women), 15 international. Average age 37. 77 applicants, 68% accepted, 23 enrolled. In 2008, 23 master's, 3 doctorates awarded. Terminal master's awarded for partial completion of doctoral program. *Degree requirements:* For master's, one foreign language, comprehensive exam (for some programs), thesis (for some programs); for doctorate, 3 foreign languages, comprehensive exam (for some programs), thesis/dissertation. *Entrance requirements:* For master's, GRE or MAT, 3 letters of recommendation, writing sample; for doctorate, GRE or MAT, 3 letters of recommendation, writing research sample. Additional exam requirements/recommendations for international students: Required—TOEFL (minimum score 100 computer-based). *Application deadline:* For fall admission, 1/15 priority date for domestic students. Applications are processed on a rolling basis. Application fee: $50. *Expenses:* Tuition: Full-time $21,200; part-time $1000 per credit. Required fees: $400 per semester. Tuition and fees vary according to degree level, program and student level. *Financial support:* Fellowships, career-related internships or fieldwork and tuition waivers (full and partial) available. Support available to part-time students. Financial award application deadline: 3/1; financial award applicants required to submit FAFSA. *Unit head:* Dr. Stephen Garfinkel, Dean, 212-678-8024, Fax: 212-678-8947, E-mail: gradschool@jtsa.edu. *Application contact:* Abby Eisenberg, Director of Graduate School Admissions, 212-678-8032, Fax: 212-280-6022, E-mail: abeisenberg@jtsa.edu.

See Close-Up on page 529.

The Jewish Theological Seminary, The Rabbinical School, New York, NY 10027-4649. Offers MA, Rabbi. *Accreditation:* ACIPE. *Faculty:* 60 full-time (19 women), 73 part-time/adjunct (39 women). *Students:* 120 full-time (43 women), 11 part-time (4 women); includes 1 minority (Hispanic American), 15 international. Average age 29. 50 applicants, 60% accepted, 24 enrolled. In 2008, 13 master's, 31 other advanced degrees awarded. *Degree requirements:* For master's and Rabbi, one foreign language, competency exams. *Entrance requirements:* For master's and Rabbi, GRE, interview, writing sample. Additional exam requirements/recommendations for international students: Required—TOEFL. *Application deadline:* For fall admission, 12/31 for domestic students. Applications are processed on a rolling basis. Application fee: $65. *Expenses:* Contact institution. *Financial support:* Fellowships, career-related internships or fieldwork available. Support available to part-time students. Financial award application deadline: 3/1; financial award applicants required to submit FAFSA. *Unit head:* Rabbi Daniel Nevins, Dean, 212-678-8907, E-mail: danevins@jtsa.edu. *Application contact:* Rabbi Marcus Schwartz, Director of Admission, 212-678-8818, Fax: 212-280-6022, E-mail: moschwartz@jtsa.edu.

See Close-Up on page 531.

Johnson Bible College, Program in New Testament, Knoxville, TN 37998-1001. Offers preaching (MA); research (MA). Part-time and evening/weekend programs available. Postbaccalaureate distance learning degree programs offered (no on-campus study). *Degree requirements:* For master's, one foreign language, comprehensive exam, thesis (for some programs). *Entrance requirements:* For master's, minimum GPA of 2.5. Additional exam requirements/recommendations for international students: Required—TOEFL.

Kehilath Yakov Rabbinical Seminary, Graduate Programs, Ossining, NY 10562. *Accreditation:* AARTS.

Kenrick-Glennon Seminary, Graduate and Professional Programs, St. Louis, MO 63119-4330. Offers M Div, MA. *Accreditation:* ATS. *Degree requirements:* For master's, thesis optional. *Entrance requirements:* MAT.

Kentucky Christian University, Graduate School, Grayson, KY 41143-2205. Offers Christian leadership (MA); New Testament (MA). Part-time programs available. *Degree requirements:* For master's, comprehensive exam (for some programs), thesis optional. *Entrance requirements:* For master's, minimum cumulative GPA of 2.75 in major or 2.5 overall; 6 additional hours in Bible (for non-Biblical undergraduate majors). Additional exam requirements/recommendations for international students: Required—TOEFL (minimum score 550 paper-based; 213 computer-based). Electronic applications accepted.

Knox College, College of Theology, Toronto, ON M5S 2E6, Canada. Offers M Div, MRE, MTS, Th M, D Min, Th D. Applicants for D Min, Th M, and Th D must apply to Toronto School of Theology. *Accreditation:* ATS. Part-time programs available. *Degree requirements:* For master's, one foreign language, thesis (for some programs); for doctorate, 2 foreign languages, thesis/dissertation. *Entrance requirements:* For doctorate, M Div. Additional exam requirements/recommendations for international students: Required—TOEFL (minimum score 580 paper-based; 237 computer-based), TWE (minimum score 5). *Faculty research:* Nineteenth century theologians.

Knox Theological Seminary, Graduate Programs, Program in Biblical Studies, Fort Lauderdale, FL 33308. Offers CBS. *Accreditation:* ATS. Part-time and evening/weekend programs available. *Entrance requirements:* Additional exam requirements/recommendations for international students: Required—TOEFL, TWE (minimum score 5).

Knox Theological Seminary, Graduate Programs, Program in Divinity, Fort Lauderdale, FL 33308. Offers M Div. *Accreditation:* ATS. Part-time and evening/weekend programs available.

Entrance requirements: Additional exam requirements/recommendations for international students: Required—TOEFL, TWE (minimum score 5).

Knox Theological Seminary, Graduate Programs, Program in New and Old Testament, Fort Lauderdale, FL 33308. Offers MBT. *Accreditation:* ATS. Part-time and evening/weekend programs available. *Degree requirements:* For master's, one foreign language, thesis. *Entrance requirements:* Additional exam requirements/recommendations for international students: Required—TOEFL, TWE (minimum score 5).

Kol Yaakov Torah Center, Graduate Program, Monsey, NY 10952-2954. Offers Advanced Rabbinic Degree. *Accreditation:* AARTS. Part-time and evening/weekend programs available. *Faculty research:* Talmud, Jewish law.

Lakeland College, Graduate Studies Division, Program in Theology, Sheboygan, WI 53082-0359. Offers MAT.

Lancaster Bible College, Graduate School, Lancaster, PA 17608-3403. Offers Bible (MA); consulting resource teacher (M Ed); counseling (MA); ministry (MA); school counseling (M Ed). Part-time and evening/weekend programs available. *Degree requirements:* For master's, comprehensive exam (for some programs), thesis (for some programs). *Entrance requirements:* For master's, bachelor's degree with a minimum of 30 credits of course work in Bible, minimum undergraduate GPA of 3.0, interview. Additional exam requirements/recommendations for international students: Required—TOEFL.

Lancaster Theological Seminary, Graduate and Professional Programs, Lancaster, PA 17603-2812. Offers biblical studies (M Div, MAR); church life and work (M Div, MAR); historical studies (M Div, MAR); integrated ministry studies (M Div, MAR); lay leadership (Certificate); theological studies (M Div, MAR); theology (D Min). *Accreditation:* ACIPE; ATS. *Degree requirements:* For doctorate, thesis/dissertation; for M Div, one foreign language.

La Salle University, School of Arts and Sciences, Program in Theological, Pastoral and Liturgical Studies, Philadelphia, PA 19141-1199. Offers pastoral studies (MA); religion (MA); theological studies (MA). Part-time and evening/weekend programs available. *Entrance requirements:* For master's, 26 credits in humanistic subjects, religion, theology, or ministry-related work.

Lee University, Program in Religion, Cleveland, TN 37320-3450. Offers biblical studies (MA); theological studies (MA); youth and family ministry (MA). Part-time programs available. *Faculty:* 10 full-time (3 women), 2 part-time/adjunct (0 women). *Students:* 11 full-time (6 women), 8 part-time (4 women); includes 1 minority (American Indian/Alaska Native). Average age 25. 6 applicants, 100% accepted, 4 enrolled. In 2008, 11 master's awarded. *Degree requirements:* For master's, comprehensive exam, thesis. *Entrance requirements:* For master's, GRE or MAT, minimum GPA of 3.0, 2 letters of recommendation, interview. *Application deadline:* For fall admission, 4/1 priority date for domestic students; for spring admission, 10/1 priority date for domestic students. Applications are processed on a rolling basis. Application fee: $25. *Expenses:* Tuition: Full-time $10,824; part-time $451 per credit. Required fees: $270; $200 per semester. Tuition and fees vary according to course load and program. *Financial support:* Career-related internships or fieldwork, Federal Work-Study, institutionally sponsored loans, scholarships/grants, and unspecified assistantships available. Financial award application deadline: 3/1; financial award applicants required to submit FAFSA. *Faculty research:* Book of Isaiah, Gospel of Mark, school of St. Victor of 12th century, spirit Christology, people groups of New Testament and work. Total annual research expenditures: $3,000. *Unit head:* Dr. Michael Fuller, Director, 423-614-8338, E-mail: mfuller@leeuniversity.edu. *Application contact:* Vicki Glasscock, Graduate Admissions Director, 423-614-8059, E-mail: vglasscock@leeuniversity.edu.

Lexington Theological Seminary, Graduate and Professional Programs, Lexington, KY 40508-3218. Offers M Div, MA, MAPS, D Min, M Div/MSW. *Accreditation:* ACIPE; ATS. Part-time and evening/weekend programs available. *Degree requirements:* For master's, thesis; for doctorate, thesis/dissertation. *Entrance requirements:* Additional exam requirements/recommendations for international students: Required—TOEFL (minimum score 600 paper-based; 250 computer-based). *Faculty research:* History of biblical interpretation, biblical apocalyptic, psalms, history of Stone-Campbell traditions.

Liberty University, Liberty Theological Seminary and Graduate School, Lynchburg, VA 24502. Offers religious studies (M Div, MA, MAR, MRE, D Min); theology (Th M). Part-time programs available. Postbaccalaureate distance learning degree programs offered (minimal on-campus study). *Degree requirements:* For master's, 2 foreign languages, thesis (for some programs); for doctorate, 2 foreign languages, thesis/dissertation. *Entrance requirements:* For M Div, minimum undergraduate GPA of 2.0; for master's, minimum undergraduate GPA of 2.0, 9 credit hours of course work in Greek, 9 credit hours of course work in Hebrew (Th M); for doctorate, GRE General Test or MAT. Additional exam requirements/recommendations for international students: Required—TOEFL (minimum score 550 paper-based; 213 computer-based). Electronic applications accepted. *Expenses:* Contact institution.

Lincoln Christian Seminary, Graduate and Professional Programs, Lincoln, IL 62656-2167. Offers Bible and theology (MA); Bible translation (MA); counseling ministry (MA); divinity (M Div); leadership ministry (MA, D Min). MA in Bible translation offered jointly with Pioneer Bible Translators (Dallas, TX). *Accreditation:* ACIPE; ATS. Part-time programs available. *Degree requirements:* For master's, 2 foreign languages, thesis; for doctorate, thesis/dissertation; for M Div, 2 foreign languages. *Entrance requirements:* For M Div and master's, minimum GPA of 2.5; for doctorate, MDiv or equivalent. Additional exam requirements/recommendations for international students: Required—TOEFL (minimum score 550 paper-based; 213 computer-based). Electronic applications accepted.

Lipscomb University, Hazelip School of Theology, Nashville, TN 37204-3951. Offers biblical studies (MA); Christian studies (MA); divinity (M Div); ministry (MA); New Testament (MA); Old Testament (MA); theological studies (MTS); theology (MA). *Accreditation:* ATS. Part-time and evening/weekend programs available. *Degree requirements:* For master's, 2 foreign languages, comprehensive exam (for some programs); for M Div, 2 foreign languages. *Entrance requirements:* For M Div and master's, 2 references. Additional exam requirements/recommendations for international students: Required—TOEFL (minimum score 570 paper-based; 230 computer-based). Electronic applications accepted. *Faculty research:* Status of Churches of Christ in foreign nations, Hebrew grammar, marriage and family.

Logos Evangelical Seminary, Graduate Programs, El Monte, CA 91731. Offers M Div, MA, Th M, D Min. *Accreditation:* ATS (one or more programs are accredited). Part-time programs available. *Degree requirements:* For master's, comprehensive exam, thesis; for doctorate, thesis/dissertation. *Entrance requirements:* For M Div, BA with a minimum GPA of 2.66, 2 recommendations, 3 years post-baptism; for master's, MA in biblical studies with a minimum GPA of 3.33, 1.5 year of a biblical language, 2 recommendations, 1 research paper; for doctorate, M Div with a minimum GPA of 3.0, 3 years ministry experience, 2 recommendations. Additional exam requirements/recommendations for international students: Required—TOEFL (minimum score 450 paper-based; 133 computer-based; 45 iBT). Electronic applications accepted. *Faculty research:* Asian-American hermaneutics, narrative theology, Biblical application on Song of Songs.

Loras College, Graduate Division, Program in Theology and Ministry, Dubuque, IA 52004-0178. Offers ministry (MA); theology (MA). Part-time and evening/weekend programs available. *Degree requirements:* For master's, comprehensive exam (for some programs), thesis (for some programs). *Entrance requirements:* For master's, bachelor's degree or undergraduate minor in religious studies or equivalent, minimum undergraduate GPA of 2.75.

Louisville Presbyterian Theological Seminary, Graduate and Professional Programs, Louisville, KY 40205-1798. Offers Bible (MAR); divinity (M Div); ministry (D Min); religious thought (MAR); theology (Th M); JD/M Div; M Div/MBA; M Div/MS; M Div/MSW. *Accreditation:* AAMFT/COAMFTE (one or more programs are accredited); ACIPE; ATS (one or more programs

are accredited). Part-time programs available. *Degree requirements:* For master's, one foreign language; for doctorate, thesis/dissertation; for M Div, 2 foreign languages. *Entrance requirements:* For master's, interview; for doctorate, M Div. Additional exam requirements/recommendations for international students: Required—TOEFL (minimum score 550 paper-based; 213 computer-based). Electronic applications accepted.

Loyola Marymount University, College of Liberal Arts, Department of Theological Studies, Program in Theology, Los Angeles, CA 90045-2659. Offers MA. *Accreditation:* ATS. *Degree requirements:* For master's, one foreign language, comprehensive exam, thesis or alternative. *Entrance requirements:* For master's, GRE General Test. Additional exam requirements/recommendations for international students: Required—TOEFL (minimum score 600 paper-based; 250 computer-based). Electronic applications accepted.

Loyola University Chicago, Graduate School, Department of Theology, Chicago, IL 60611-2196. Offers MA, PhD. Part-time and evening/weekend programs available. *Faculty:* 16 full-time (5 women). *Students:* 81 full-time (27 women), 4 part-time (2 women); includes 2 minority (1 African American, 1 Hispanic American), 11 international. Average age 34. 80 applicants, 54% accepted, 13 enrolled. In 2008, 7 master's, 9 doctorates awarded. Terminal master's awarded for partial completion of doctoral program. *Degree requirements:* For master's, comprehensive exam; for doctorate, 2 foreign languages, comprehensive exam, thesis/dissertation. *Entrance requirements:* For master's, GRE General Test, minimum GPA of 3.0, 9 hours of course work in theology; for doctorate, GRE General Test, minimum GPA of 3.0, master's degree or equivalent. Additional exam requirements/recommendations for international students: Required—TOEFL. *Application deadline:* For fall admission, 1/15 for domestic and international students; for spring admission, 12/1 for domestic and international students. Application fee: $50. Electronic applications accepted. *Expenses:* Tuition: Full-time $13,500; part-time $750 per credit hour. Required fees: $60 per semester. Full-time tuition and fees vary according to program. *Financial support:* In 2008–09, 12 students received support, including 12 research assistantships (averaging $14,000 per year); fellowships, teaching assistantships, institutionally sponsored loans also available. Financial award application deadline: 1/15; financial award applicants required to submit FAFSA. *Faculty research:* Systematics, historical theology, constructive theology, scripture, theological ethics. *Unit head:* Dr. Susan Ross, PhD, Department Chair, 773-508-2364, Fax: 773-508-2386, E-mail: sross@luc.edu. *Application contact:* Dr. Robert A. Divito, PhD, Graduate Program Director, 773-508-8453, Fax: 773-508-2386, E-mail: rdivito@luc.edu.

Loyola University Chicago, Institute of Pastoral Studies, Professional Program in Divinity, Chicago, IL 60611-2196. Offers M Div, M Div/MA, M Div/MSN, M Div/MSW. *Accreditation:* ACIPE. *Faculty:* 8 full-time (2 women), 26 part-time/adjunct (12 women). *Students:* 18 full-time (14 women), 12 part-time (7 women); includes 4 minority (all African Americans), 1 international. Average age 39. 16 applicants, 81% accepted, 7 enrolled. In 2008, 6 M Divs awarded. *Degree requirements:* For M Div, project. *Entrance requirements:* Minimum GPA of 3.0, 1 year of ministry experience. Additional exam requirements/recommendations for international students: Required—TOEFL. *Application deadline:* For fall admission, 8/1 priority date for domestic students; for spring admission, 12/1 priority date for domestic students. Applications are processed on a rolling basis. Application fee: $50. Electronic applications accepted. *Expenses:* Contact institution. *Financial support:* In 2008–09, 9 students received support. Career-related internships or fieldwork, Federal Work-Study, institutionally sponsored loans, and scholarships/grants available. Support available to part-time students. Financial award application deadline: 2/1; financial award applicants required to submit FAFSA. *Faculty research:* Women leadership development for professionals in ministry, religious memoirs, passing on the values of Jesus, justice. *Unit head:* Dr. Robert T. O'Gorman, Professor, 312-915-7485, Fax: 312-915-7410, E-mail: rogorma@luc.edu. *Application contact:* Randy Gibbons, Administrative Assistant, 312-915-7450, Fax: 312-915-7410, E-mail: rgibbon@luc.edu.

Loyola University Chicago, Institute of Pastoral Studies, Program in Pastoral Counseling, Chicago, IL 60611-2196. Offers pastoral care and counseling (MA); pastoral counseling (MA, Certificate); M Div/MA. *Accreditation:* ACIPE. Part-time programs available. *Faculty:* 6 full-time (2 women), 12 part-time/adjunct (7 women). *Students:* 32 full-time (21 women), 22 part-time (20 women); includes 11 minority (8 African Americans, 2 Asian Americans or Pacific Islanders, 1 Hispanic American), 4 international. Average age 42. 24 applicants, 75% accepted, 13 enrolled. In 2008, 13 master's awarded. *Degree requirements:* For master's, thesis or alternative, integration project. *Application deadline:* For fall admission, 2/15 priority date for domestic students. Applications are processed on a rolling basis. Application fee: $50. Electronic applications accepted. *Expenses:* Tuition: Full-time $13,500; part-time $750 per credit hour. Required fees: $60 per semester. Full-time tuition and fees vary according to program. *Financial support:* In 2008–09, 7 students received support. Career-related internships or fieldwork, Federal Work-Study, and institutionally sponsored loans available. Support available to part-time students. Financial award application deadline: 3/1; financial award applicants required to submit FAFSA. *Faculty research:* Pastoral psychotherapy, enrichment outcome, marriage and family therapy, marriage and family spirituality, gender and ethnicity issues, theological anthropology. *Unit head:* Dr. Paul R. Giblin, Associate Professor, 312-915-7483, Fax: 312-915-7410, E-mail: pgibli@luc.edu. *Application contact:* Dr. Paul R. Giblin, Associate Professor, 312-915-7483, Fax: 312-915-7410, E-mail: pgibli@luc.edu.

Loyola University New Orleans, College of Social Sciences, Loyola Institute for Ministry, New Orleans, LA 70118-6195. Offers pastoral studies (MPS); religious education (MRE); theology and ministry (Certificate). Part-time and evening/weekend programs available. Postbaccalaureate distance learning degree programs offered (no on-campus study). *Students:* 3 full-time (2 women), 284 part-time (207 women); includes 44 minority (8 African Americans, 1 American Indian/Alaska Native, 4 Asian Americans or Pacific Islanders, 31 Hispanic Americans), 4 international. Average age 48. 156 applicants, 96% accepted, 88 enrolled. In 2008, 78 master's, 1 other advanced degree awarded. *Entrance requirements:* For master's, minimum GPA of 2.5, resumé, 2 letters of recommendation, transcript, essay, work experience. Additional exam requirements/recommendations for international students: Required—TOEFL (minimum score 550 paper-based; 213 computer-based). *Application deadline:* Applications are processed on a rolling basis. Application fee: $20. Electronic applications accepted. *Expenses:* Tuition: Full-time $13,146; part-time $626 per credit hour. Required fees: $876; $229 per semester. *Financial support:* Career-related internships or fieldwork, scholarships/grants, health care benefits, tuition waivers (partial), and room and board assistance available. Support available to part-time students. Financial award application deadline: 5/1; financial award applicants required to submit FAFSA. *Faculty research:* Practical theology, ministry education, small Christian communities, religion and ecology, Christian spirituality. *Unit head:* Tom Ryan, PhD, Director, 504-865-2069, Fax: 504-865-2066, E-mail: tfryan@loyno.edu. *Application contact:* Cecelia M. Bennett, Associate Director, 504-865-3398, Fax: 504-865-2066, E-mail: abennett@loyno.edu.

Lubbock Christian University, Graduate Biblical Studies, Lubbock, TX 79407-2099. Offers Bible and ministry (MS); biblical interpretation (MA). Part-time programs available. *Degree requirements:* For master's, one foreign language, thesis (for some programs). *Entrance requirements:* For master's, GRE General Test or MAT. *Faculty research:* Commentary on John, commentary on First and Second Thessalonians, mission teams, church leadership, family systems.

Lutheran School of Theology at Chicago, Graduate and Professional Programs, Chicago, IL 60615-5199. Offers ministry (D Min); ministry, pastoral care, and counseling (D Min PCC); theological studies (MA, PhD); theology (M Div, Th M). *Accreditation:* ACIPE; ATS (one or more programs are accredited). Part-time programs available. Terminal master's awarded for partial completion of doctoral program. *Degree requirements:* For master's, variable foreign language requirement; for doctorate, variable foreign language requirement, thesis/dissertation. *Entrance requirements:* For master's, GRE (Th M), M Div or equivalent (Th M); for doctorate, GRE, M Div or equivalent, 3 years of professional experience (D Min, D Min PCC). Additional exam requirements/recommendations for international students: Required—TOEFL, TOEFL (Th M).

Theology

Lutheran Theological Seminary, Graduate and Professional Programs, Saskatoon, SK S7N 0X3, Canada. Offers Biblical studies (MTS); church history (MTS); ethics/church and society (MTS); history of Christianity (STM); New Testament (STM); Old Testament (STM); pastoral studies (STM); pastoral theology (MTS); systematic theology (MTS); systematic theology and philosophy of religion (STM); theology (M Div, D Div). *Accreditation:* ATS. Part-time programs available. *Degree requirements:* For master's, thesis; for M Div, Greek, Hebrew.

Lutheran Theological Seminary at Gettysburg, Graduate and Professional Programs, Gettysburg, PA 17325-1795. Offers divinity (M Div); ministerial studies (MAMS); outdoor ministry (MAR); parish ministry (D Min); theology (STM). *Accreditation:* ACIPE; ATS (one or more programs are accredited). Part-time programs available. Postbaccalaureate distance learning degree programs offered (no on-campus study). *Degree requirements:* For master's, thesis (for some programs); for M Div, one foreign language. Electronic applications accepted.

The Lutheran Theological Seminary at Philadelphia, Graduate School, Philadelphia, PA 19119-1794. Offers divinity (M Div); ministry (D Min); religion (MAR); social ministry (Certificate); theology (STM). *Accreditation:* ACIPE; ATS. Part-time and evening/weekend programs available. *Degree requirements:* For master's, one foreign language, comprehensive exam (for some programs), thesis (for some programs); for doctorate, thesis/dissertation; for M Div, 2 foreign languages. *Entrance requirements:* For M Div and master's, minimum undergraduate GPA of 2.8; for doctorate, minimum first professional GPA of 3.0. Additional exam requirements/recommendations for international students: Required—TOEFL (minimum score 550 paper-based; 213 computer-based), TWE. Electronic applications accepted.

Lutheran Theological Southern Seminary, Graduate and Professional Programs, Columbia, SC 29203. Offers M Div, MAR, STM, D Min. *Accreditation:* ACIPE; ATS. Part-time programs available. *Degree requirements:* For master's, comprehensive exam (for some programs), thesis (for some programs); for M Div, 2 foreign languages. *Faculty research:* Theology in 21st century, Biblical interpretation.

Luther Rice University, Graduate Programs, Lithonia, GA 30038-2454. Offers Bible/theology (M Div); Christian education (M Div); Christian studies (MA); church ministry (D Min); counseling (M Div); discipleship counseling (MA); ministry (M Div, MA); missions/evangelism (M Div). Part-time programs available. Postbaccalaureate distance learning degree programs offered (no on-campus study). *Degree requirements:* For doctorate, thesis/dissertation. *Entrance requirements:* Additional exam requirements/recommendations for international students: Required—TOEFL (minimum score 500 paper-based; 173 computer-based).

Luther Seminary, Graduate and Professional Programs, St. Paul, MN 55108-1445. Offers M Div, M Th, MA, MSM, D Min, PhD. *Accreditation:* ACIPE; ATS. *Degree requirements:* For master's, thesis or alternative; for doctorate, 2 foreign languages, thesis/dissertation; for M Div, 2 foreign languages, 1 year internship. *Entrance requirements:* For M Div, minimum GPA of 3.0; for master's, minimum GPA of 2.8; for doctorate, GRE General Test. Electronic applications accepted. *Faculty research:* Theology, psychology (pastoral care), church history, Bible, Islamic studies.

Machzikei Hadath Rabbinical College, Graduate Programs, Brooklyn, NY 11204-1805. Offers First Talmudic Degree. *Accreditation:* AARTS.

Madonna University, Program in Religious Studies, Livonia, MI 48150-1173. Offers pastoral ministry (MA).

Malone University, Graduate Program in Christian Ministries, Canton, OH 44709-3897. Offers Christian leadership in sports ministry (MA); Christian ministries (MA); leadership in the Christian church (MA). Part-time and evening/weekend programs available. *Faculty:* 7 full-time (1 woman), 4 part-time/adjunct (0 women). *Students:* 3 full-time (1 woman), 29 part-time (10 women); includes 8 minority (7 African Americans, 1 American Indian/Alaska Native). Average age 37. In 2008, 10 master's awarded. *Entrance requirements:* For master's, minimum GPA of 3.0. Additional exam requirements/recommendations for international students: Required—TOEFL (minimum score 550 paper-based). *Application deadline:* Applications are processed on a rolling basis. Application fee: $25. *Expenses:* Contact institution. *Financial support:* Tuition waivers (partial) and unspecified assistantships available. Support available to part-time students. Financial award application deadline: 6/30. *Faculty research:* Pauline theology, history of biblical interpretation, Johannine epistles, miracles in the New Testament, God's judgment and love. *Unit head:* Dr. D. Nathan Phinney, Interim Director, 330-471-8194, Fax: 330-471-8477, E-mail: dphinney@malone.edu. *Application contact:* David L. Kleffman, Assistant Director of Enrollment, 330-471-8447, Fax: 330-471-8343, E-mail: dkleffman@malone.edu.

Maple Springs Baptist Bible College and Seminary, Graduate and Professional Programs, Capitol Heights, MD 20743. Offers biblical studies (MA, Certificate); Christian counseling (MA); church administration (MA); divinity (M Div); ministry (D Min); religious education (MRE).

Maranatha Baptist Bible College, Program in Biblical Studies, Watertown, WI 53094. Offers MA. Part-time programs available. *Faculty:* 5 full-time (0 women), 2 part-time/adjunct (0 women). *Students:* 10 full-time (0 women), 9 part-time (0 women). Average age 27. 6 applicants, 100% accepted, 6 enrolled. In 2008, 8 master's awarded. *Degree requirements:* For master's, one foreign language, fieldwork. *Application deadline:* Applications are processed on a rolling basis. Application fee: $50. *Expenses:* Tuition: Full-time $3840; part-time $240 per credit hour. Required fees: $20 per credit hour. *Financial support:* In 2008–09, 8 students received support. Scholarships/grants and tuition waivers (full and partial) available. Support available to part-time students. *Faculty research:* Bible structure, counseling techniques, church history. *Unit head:* Dr. Larry Oats, Dean of Maranatha Baptist Seminary, 920-206-2324, Fax: 920-261-9109, E-mail: loats@mbbc.edu. *Application contact:* Dr. Jim Harrison, Director of Admissions, 920-206-2327, Fax: 920-261-9109, E-mail: admissions@mbbc.edu.

Maranatha Baptist Bible College, Program in Theology, Watertown, WI 53094. Offers MA. Part-time programs available. *Faculty:* 5 full-time (0 women), 2 part-time/adjunct (0 women). *Students:* 3 full-time (0 women), 2 part-time (0 women). Average age 27. In 2008, 1 master's awarded. *Expenses:* Tuition: Full-time $3840; part-time $240 per credit hour. Required fees: $20 per credit hour. *Unit head:* Dr. Larry Oats, Dean of Maranatha Baptist Seminary, 920-206-2324, Fax: 920-261-9109, E-mail: loats@mbbc.edu. *Application contact:* Dr. Jim Harrison, Director of Admissions, 920-206-2327, Fax: 920-261-9109, E-mail: admissions@mbbc.edu.

Marquette University, Graduate School, College of Arts and Sciences, Department of Theology, Milwaukee, WI 53201-1881. Offers ethics (PhD); historical theology (MA, PhD); religious studies (PhD), including scriptural theology (MA, PhD); systematic theology (MA, PhD); theology (MA), including scriptural theology (MA, PhD); theology and society (PhD). Part-time programs available. Terminal master's awarded for partial completion of doctoral program. *Degree requirements:* For master's, one foreign language, comprehensive exam, thesis or alternative; for doctorate, 2 foreign languages, thesis/dissertation, qualifying exam. *Entrance requirements:* For master's and doctorate, GRE General Test. Additional exam requirements/recommendations for international students: Required—TOEFL. *Faculty research:* Old Testament theology, New Testament theology, church history, Christian ethics.

Mars Hill Graduate School, Graduate Programs, Seattle, WA 98121. Offers Christian studies (MA); counseling psychology (MA); divinity (MS). Part-time programs available. *Entrance requirements:* For master's, MAT.

Marylhurst University, Department of Religious StudiesûApplied Theology Program, Marylhurst, OR 97036-0261. Offers applied theology (MA). Part-time and evening/weekend programs available. *Faculty:* 1 full-time (0 women), 9 part-time/adjunct (5 women). *Students:* 3 full-time (all women), 24 part-time (17 women). Average age 48. 6 applicants, 100% accepted, 6 enrolled. In 2008, 9 master's awarded. *Degree requirements:* For master's, thesis. *Entrance requirements:* For master's, MAT, resumé, 3 letters of recommendation, interview, autobiography, personal statement. Additional exam requirements/recommendations for international students: Recommended—TOEFL (minimum score 550 paper-based; 213 computer-based; 80 iBT). *Application deadline:* For fall admission, 6/30 priority date for domestic students, 6/30 for international students; for winter admission, 11/30 priority date for domestic students, 11/30 for international students; for spring admission, 3/30 priority date for domestic students, 3/30 for international students. Applications are processed on a rolling basis. Application fee: $40 ($50 for international students). Electronic applications accepted. *Expenses:* Tuition: Full-time $11,988; part-time $444 per quarter hour. Required fees: $297; $11 per quarter hour. *Financial support:* Fellowships, research assistantships, teaching assistantships, Federal Work-Study and scholarships/grants available. Support available to part-time students. Financial award applicants required to submit FAFSA. *Faculty research:* Pastoral care, scripture, world religions. *Unit head:* Dr. Jerry Roussell, Chair, 503-636-8141, Fax: 503-697-5597, E-mail: jroussell@marylhurst.edu. *Application contact:* Kathleen Schneff, Admissions Specialist, 800-634-9982 Ext. 3322, Fax: 503-635-6585, E-mail: admissions@marylhurst.edu.

Marylhurst University, Department of Religious StudiesûDivinity Program, Marylhurst, OR 97036-0261. Offers M Div. Part-time and evening/weekend programs available. *Faculty:* 1 full-time (0 women), 9 part-time/adjunct (5 women). *Students:* 11 full-time (9 women), 16 part-time (13 women). Average age 48. 9 applicants, 89% accepted, 8 enrolled. In 2008, 6 M Divs awarded. *Degree requirements:* For M Div, thesis/dissertation. *Entrance requirements:* MAT, resumé, 3 letters of recommendation, interview. Additional exam requirements/recommendations for international students: Required—TOEFL (minimum score 550 paper-based; 213 computer-based; 80 iBT). *Application deadline:* For fall admission, 6/30 for domestic students; for winter admission, 11/30 for domestic students; for spring admission, 3/30 for domestic students. Applications are processed on a rolling basis. Application fee: $40 ($50 for international students). Electronic applications accepted. *Expenses:* Tuition: Full-time $11,988; part-time $444 per quarter hour. Required fees: $297; $11 per quarter hour. *Financial support:* Fellowships, research assistantships, teaching assistantships, Federal Work-Study and scholarships/grants available. Support available to part-time students. Financial award applicants required to submit FAFSA. *Faculty research:* Scripture-biblical studies, theology, history, ministry, spirituality. *Unit head:* Dr. Jerry Roussell, Chair, 503-636-8141, Fax: 503-697-5597, E-mail: jroussell@marylhurst.edu. *Application contact:* Kathleen Schneff, Admissions Specialist, 800-634-9982 Ext. 3322, Fax: 503-635-6585, E-mail: admissions@marylhurst.edu.

The Master's College and Seminary, The Master's Seminary, Santa Clarita, CA 91321-1200. Offers biblical counseling (MABC); New Testament (Th D); Old Testament (Th D); preaching (D Min); theology (M Div, M Th, Th D). Part-time programs available. *Degree requirements:* For master's, 2 foreign languages, thesis; for doctorate, 4 foreign languages, thesis/dissertation; for M Div, 2 foreign languages, thesis/dissertation. *Entrance requirements:* For M Div, minimum 2 years of college; for master's, minimum GPA of 2.75; for doctorate, Th M, minimum GPA of 3.5. Additional exam requirements/recommendations for international students: Required—TOEFL (minimum score 550 paper-based).

McCormick Theological Seminary, Graduate and Professional Programs, Chicago, IL 60615. Offers ministry (D Min); theological studies (MATS, Certificate); theology (M Div); M Div/MSW. *Accreditation:* ACIPE; ATS (one or more programs are accredited). Part-time and evening/weekend programs available. *Degree requirements:* For master's, thesis (for some programs); for doctorate, thesis/dissertation. *Entrance requirements:* For M Div and master's, minimum GPA of 3.0; for doctorate, M Div, minimum 3 years in pastorate. *Faculty research:* Faith formation, families, biblical literature, Dead Sea scrolls, women in antiquity.

McGill University, Faculty of Graduate and Postdoctoral Studies, Faculty of Religious Studies, Montréal, QC H3A 2T5, Canada. Offers MA, STM, PhD. *Accreditation:* ATS.

McMaster University, McMaster Divinity College, Hamilton, ON L8S 4M2, Canada. Offers biblical studies (M Div); Biblical studies (MA, MTS, Diploma); Christian interpretation/history (M Div, MA, MTS, Diploma); Christian ministry (M Div, MA, MTS, Diploma); Christian Studies (Certificate); Christian theology (PhD). Affiliated with the Toronto School of Theology. *Accreditation:* ATS. Part-time programs available. *Degree requirements:* For master's, one foreign language, thesis optional; for doctorate, 3 foreign languages, comprehensive exam, thesis/dissertation; for other advanced degree, 2 foreign languages, thesis. *Entrance requirements:* For master's, minimum B average in undergraduate course work, 3 letters of reference; for doctorate, minimum B+ average in bachelor's and master's, appropriate modern/ancient language, interview; for other advanced degree, 6 units of related Biblical language, minimum B+ average in undergraduate course work, minimum 15 units of course work in related area of study, 3 letters of recommendation. Additional exam requirements/recommendations for international students: Required—TOEFL (minimum score 550 paper-based; 237 computer-based). *Faculty research:* Ethics, Biblical studies, language studies, church history, Christian ministry.

Meadville Lombard Theological School, Graduate and Professional Programs, Chicago, IL 60637-1602. Offers divinity (M Div); ministry (D Min); religion (MA); M Div/MSW. *Accreditation:* ACIPE; ATS. Part-time programs available. Postbaccalaureate distance learning degree programs offered (minimal on-campus study). *Entrance requirements:* For M Div and master's, bachelor's degree; for doctorate, bachelor's and masters degrees, 3 years of ministry.

Memphis Theological Seminary, Graduate and Professional Programs, Memphis, TN 38104-4395. Offers M Div, MAR, D Min. *Accreditation:* ATS. Part-time programs available. *Degree requirements:* For doctorate, thesis/dissertation. *Entrance requirements:* For doctorate, M Div, 3 years in ministry.

Mennonite Brethren Biblical Seminary, School of Theology, Program in Divinity, Fresno, CA 93727-5097. Offers M Div. *Accreditation:* ATS. *Degree requirements:* For M Div, one foreign language.

Mennonite Brethren Biblical Seminary, School of Theology, Programs in New Testament, Old Testament, and Theology, Fresno, CA 93727-5097. Offers New Testament (MA); Old Testament (MA); theology (MA). Part-time programs available. *Entrance requirements:* Additional exam requirements/recommendations for international students: Required—TOEFL (minimum score 550 paper-based; 213 computer-based).

Mercer University, Graduate Studies, Cecil B. Day Campus, James and Carolyn McAfee School of Theology, Macon, GA 31207-0003. Offers M Div, D Min. *Accreditation:* ATS. Part-time programs available. *Degree requirements:* For doctorate, thesis/dissertation, fieldwork, seminars; for M Div, 2 foreign languages. *Entrance requirements:* For M Div, letters of recommendation, minimum B+ average in undergraduate course work; for doctorate, MAT, minimum B+ average in undergraduate course work, letters of recommendation. *Expenses:* Contact institution. *Faculty research:* Biblical studies, Baptist heritage, Christian heritage, theology, pastoral care.

Mesivta of Eastern Parkway–Yeshiva Zichron Meilech, Graduate Programs, Brooklyn, NY 11218-5559. *Accreditation:* AARTS.

Mesivta Tifereth Jerusalem of America, Graduate Programs, New York, NY 10002-6301. *Accreditation:* AARTS.

Mesivta Torah Vodaath Rabbinical Seminary, Graduate Programs, Brooklyn, NY 11218-5299. *Accreditation:* AARTS.

Methodist Theological School in Ohio, Graduate and Professional Programs, Delaware, OH 43015-8004. Offers M Div, MACE, MACM, MTS, D Min, M Div/MACE, M Div/MACM, M Div/MTS. *Accreditation:* ACIPE; ATS. Part-time programs available. *Entrance requirements:* For master's, official transcripts, 3 letters of recommendation. Additional exam requirements/recommendations for international students: Required—TOEFL (minimum score 577 paper-based; 233 computer-based; 90 iBT).

Michigan Theological Seminary, Graduate Programs, Plymouth, MI 48170. Offers Bible (Graduate Certificate); Christian education (MA); counseling psychology (MA); divinity (M Div); theological studies (MA). *Accreditation:* ATS. Part-time and evening/weekend programs available.

Degree requirements: For master's, one foreign language, thesis; for M Div, 2 foreign languages. *Faculty research:* Judaism, cults, world religions.

Mid-America Baptist Theological Seminary, Graduate and Professional Programs, Cordova, TN 38016. Offers M Div, MACE, MCE, MM, D Min, PhD. *Degree requirements:* For doctorate, 4 foreign languages, thesis/dissertation; for M Div, 2 foreign languages. *Entrance requirements:* For doctorate, MAT. Additional exam requirements/recommendations for international students: Required—TOEFL (minimum score 600 paper-based; 250 computer-based). Electronic applications accepted.

Mid-America Baptist Theological Seminary Northeast Branch, Program in Theology, Schenectady, NY 12303-3463. Offers M Div. Part-time and evening/weekend programs available. *Degree requirements:* For M Div, 2 foreign languages. *Entrance requirements:* Additional exam requirements/recommendations for international students: Required—TOEFL. Electronic applications accepted.

Mid-America Reformed Seminary, Graduate Programs, Dyer, IN 46311. Offers M Div, MTS. *Accreditation:* ATS. *Degree requirements:* For M Div, comprehensive exam. *Entrance requirements:* Additional exam requirements/recommendations for international students: Required—TOEFL (minimum score 550 paper-based).

Midwestern Baptist Theological Seminary, Graduate and Professional Programs, Kansas City, MO 64118-4697. Offers Biblical archaeology (MA); Biblical languages (MA); Christian education (M Div, MACE); Christian foundations—lay ministry (Graduate Certificate); collegiate ministries (M Div); counseling (MA); educational ministry (D Ed Min); international church planting (M Div); ministry (M Div, D Min); North American church planting (M Div); sacred music (MCM); urban ministry (M Div); worship leadership (M Div); youth ministry (M Div). *Accreditation:* ATS. Part-time programs available. Postbaccalaureate distance learning degree programs offered (minimal on-campus study). *Degree requirements:* For doctorate, thesis/dissertation; for M Div, 2 foreign languages. *Entrance requirements:* For doctorate, MAT. Electronic applications accepted. *Faculty research:* Ministerial studies, Biblical and theological studies, missions, counseling.

Midwest University, Graduate Programs, Wentzville, MO 63385. Offers social work (DSW); teaching English to speakers of other languages (MA); theology (M Div, MA, D Min). Part-time programs available. Postbaccalaureate distance learning degree programs offered (minimal on-campus study). *Degree requirements:* For master's, thesis (for some programs); for doctorate, thesis/dissertation; for M Div, thesis/dissertation (for some programs). *Entrance requirements:* Additional exam requirements/recommendations for international students: Recommended—TOEFL (minimum score 550 paper-based).

Mirrer Yeshiva, Graduate Programs, Brooklyn, NY 11223-2010. *Accreditation:* AARTS.

Moody Bible Institute, Graduate School, Chicago, IL 60610-3284. Offers biblical studies (MABS, Graduate Certificate); intercultural studies (MAIS, Graduate Certificate); ministry (M Div, M Min); spiritual formation and discipleship (MASF, Graduate Certificate); urban studies (MA, Graduate Certificate). Part-time programs available. *Degree requirements:* For master's, 2 foreign languages, fieldwork (MABS); colloquium, field research project (MA Min). *Entrance requirements:* For master's, 30 hours in Bible/theology, 2 years of ministry experience (MA Min).

Moravian Theological Seminary, Graduate and Professional Programs, Bethlehem, PA 18018-6614. Offers M Div, MAPC, MATS. *Accreditation:* ACIPE; ATS (one or more programs are accredited). Part-time programs available. *Degree requirements:* For master's, thesis. *Entrance requirements:* Additional exam requirements/recommendations for international students: Required—TOEFL.

Mount Angel Seminary, Program in Theology, Saint Benedict, OR 97373. Offers M Div, MA. *Accreditation:* ACIPE; ATS. Part-time programs available. *Degree requirements:* For master's, thesis optional.

Mount St. Mary's University, Graduate Seminary, Emmitsburg, MD 21727-7799. Offers M Div, MA. *Accreditation:* ATS. *Faculty:* 10 full-time (0 women), 4 part-time/adjunct (2 women). *Students:* 143 full-time (0 women), 2 part-time (0 women); includes 11 minority (5 Asian Americans or Pacific Islanders, 6 Hispanic Americans), 13 international. Average age 30. 57 applicants, 74% accepted, 42 enrolled. In 2008, 36 first professional degrees, 10 master's awarded. *Degree requirements:* For master's, one foreign language, comprehensive exam, thesis, language proficiency exams. *Entrance requirements:* For M Div, 24 credits of course work in philosophy; for master's, 18 credits of course work in philosophy. Additional exam requirements/recommendations for international students: Required—TOEFL (minimum score 550 paper-based; 213 computer-based). *Application deadline:* For fall admission, 8/1 for domestic and international students. Application fee: $0. *Expenses:* Contact institution. *Financial support:* In 2008–09, 49 students received support. Career-related internships or fieldwork and scholarships/grants available. Financial award applicants required to submit FAFSA. *Faculty research:* Mariology, medical ethics, Old Testament translations, Carolingian church history, Patristic theology. *Unit head:* Rev. Steven P. Rohlfs, Vice President/Rector, 301-447-5295, Fax: 301-447-5636, E-mail: rohlfs@msmary.edu. *Application contact:* Susan Nield, Seminary Admissions, 301-447-7423, Fax: 301-447-7402, E-mail: Nield@msmary.edu.

Mount Vernon Nazarene University, Program in Ministry, Mount Vernon, OH 43050-9500. Offers M Min. Part-time and evening/weekend programs available. *Degree requirements:* For master's, project. *Faculty research:* Pastoral effectiveness and professional development.

Naropa University, Graduate Programs, Program in Divinity, Boulder, CO 80302-6697. Offers M Div. *Faculty:* 6 full-time (2 women), 10 part-time/adjunct (5 women). *Students:* 17 full-time (10 women), 5 part-time (all women); includes 2 minority (1 American Indian/Alaska Native, 1 Asian American or Pacific Islander), 1 international. Average age 37. 20 applicants, 85% accepted, 9 enrolled. *Entrance requirements:* In-person interview, writing sample. Additional exam requirements/recommendations for international students: Required—TOEFL (minimum score 600 paper-based; 250 computer-based). *Application deadline:* For fall admission, 1/15 priority date for domestic and international students. Applications are processed on a rolling basis. Application fee: $60. Electronic applications accepted. *Expenses:* Tuition: Full-time $14,767; part-time $726 per credit hour. Required fees: $45 per term. *Financial support:* In 2008–09, 15 students received support, including 3 research assistantships with partial tuition reimbursements available (averaging $3,000 per year), 3 teaching assistantships with partial tuition reimbursements available (averaging $3,000 per year); career-related internships or fieldwork, Federal Work-Study, scholarships/grants, health care benefits, tuition waivers (partial), and unspecified assistantships also available. Support available to part-time students. Financial award application deadline: 3/1; financial award applicants required to submit FAFSA. *Unit head:* Phillip Stanley, Co-Chair, 303-245-4728. *Application contact:* Donna McIntyre, Assistant Director of Graduate Admissions, 303-546-3555, Fax: 303-546-3583, E-mail: donna@naropa.edu.

See Close-Up on page 1121.

Nashotah House, School of Theology, Nashotah, WI 53058-9793. Offers M Div, MTS, STM, Certificate. *Accreditation:* ACIPE; ATS (one or more programs are accredited). Part-time programs available. *Degree requirements:* For master's, thesis optional; for M Div, 2 foreign languages, thesis/dissertation optional, clinical experience. *Entrance requirements:* For M Div, master's, and Certificate, GRE General Test or MAT, interview. Additional exam requirements/recommendations for international students: Required—TOEFL. *Faculty research:* Formation for parochial ministry, ancient Semitic epigraphy.

Nazarene Theological Seminary, Graduate and Professional Programs, Kansas City, MO 64131-1263. Offers Christian education (MA); intercultural studies (MA); theological studies (MA); theology (M Div, D Min). *Accreditation:* ACIPE; ATS. Part-time programs available. *Degree requirements:* For master's, comprehensive exam (for some programs), thesis (for some

programs); for doctorate, thesis/dissertation. *Entrance requirements:* Additional exam requirements/recommendations for international students: Required—TOEFL. Electronic applications accepted.

Ner Israel Rabbinical College, Graduate Programs, Baltimore, MD 21208. Offers MTL, DTL, Professional Certificate. *Accreditation:* AARTS.

Ner Israel Yeshiva College of Toronto, Graduate Programs, Thornhill, ON L4J 8A7, Canada. *Accreditation:* AARTS.

New Brunswick Theological Seminary, Graduate and Professional Programs, New Brunswick, NJ 08901-1196. Offers metro-urban ministry (D Min), including theological studies; theological studies (M Div, MA); M Div/MA. *Accreditation:* ACIPE; ATS. Part-time and evening/weekend programs available. *Degree requirements:* For master's, thesis optional. *Entrance requirements:* For M Div, minimum GPA of 2.0; for master's, minimum GPA of 3.0; for doctorate, M Div. Additional exam requirements/recommendations for international students: Required—TOEFL. Electronic applications accepted.

Newman Theological College, Theology Program, Edmonton, AB T6V 1H3, Canada. Offers M Div, M Th, MTS. *Accreditation:* ATS. Part-time programs available. *Degree requirements:* For master's, comprehensive exam, thesis; for M Div, comprehensive exam, thesis/dissertation. *Entrance requirements:* For M Div, bachelor's degree including 12 credits in philosophy; for master's, M Div. Additional exam requirements/recommendations for international students: Required—TOEFL (minimum score 560 paper-based; 220 computer-based).

New Orleans Baptist Theological Seminary, Graduate and Professional Programs, Division of Biblical Studies, New Orleans, LA 70126-4858. Offers MA. *Accreditation:* ACIPE; ATS.

New Orleans Baptist Theological Seminary, Graduate and Professional Programs, Division of Theological and Historical Studies, New Orleans, LA 70126-4858. Offers M Div, D Min, PhD. *Accreditation:* ACIPE; ATS (one or more programs are accredited). *Degree requirements:* For doctorate, thesis/dissertation. *Entrance requirements:* For doctorate, GRE General Test.

New York Theological Seminary, Graduate and Professional Programs, New York, NY 10115. Offers M Div, MPS, MSW, D Min. *Accreditation:* ACIPE; ATS (one or more programs are accredited). Part-time programs available. *Degree requirements:* For doctorate, thesis/dissertation; for M Div, thesis/dissertation, supervised ministry. *Entrance requirements:* For M Div, interview; for doctorate, M Div, 3 years of ministry experience, interview. Additional exam requirements/recommendations for international students: Required—TOEFL. *Faculty research:* Women in leadership; crime and punishment; church history; culture, politics and theology.

The Nigerian Baptist Theological Seminary, Graduate Studies, Ogbomoso, Nigeria. Offers church music (M Div, M Th, Diploma); divinity (M Div); ministry (D Min); religious education (M Div, M Th, PhD); theological studies (MATS); theology (M Th, PhD). Part-time programs available. *Degree requirements:* For master's, thesis, 2 Nigerian languages; for M Div, thesis/dissertation (for some programs), 2 biblical languages; for Diploma, thesis or alternative.

Northeastern Seminary at Roberts Wesleyan College, Graduate and Professional Programs, Rochester, NY 14624. Offers ministry (D Min); theological studies (MA); theology (M Div); M Div/MSW. *Accreditation:* ATS. Evening/weekend programs available. *Degree requirements:* For master's, thesis (for some programs); for doctorate, one foreign language, thesis/dissertation. *Entrance requirements:* For doctorate, M Div, 3 years of full-time ministry experience. Additional exam requirements/recommendations for international students: Required—TOEFL (minimum score 550 paper-based). Electronic applications accepted. *Faculty research:* Historical theology, spiritual formation, biblical theology, counseling education.

Northern Baptist Theological Seminary, Graduate and Professional Programs, Lombard, IL 60148-5698. Offers Biblical studies (MA); Christian ministries (MACM); divinity (M Div); ministry (D Min); missional church (MA); theology (MA). *Accreditation:* ATS. Part-time programs available. *Faculty:* 6 full-time (1 woman), 30 part-time/adjunct (5 women). *Students:* 127 full-time (38 women), 20 part-time (13 women); includes 67 minority (51 African Americans, 12 Asian Americans or Pacific Islanders, 4 Hispanic Americans), 3 international. Average age 40. *Degree requirements:* For doctorate, thesis/dissertation; for M Div, field experience. *Entrance requirements:* For doctorate, 3 years in the ministry post-M Div. Additional exam requirements/recommendations for international students: Required—TOEFL. *Application deadline:* For fall admission, 9/1 priority date for domestic students, 2/1 priority date for international students; for winter admission, 12/1 priority date for domestic students; for spring admission, 3/1 priority date for domestic students. Applications are processed on a rolling basis. Application fee: $35. Electronic applications accepted. *Expenses:* Tuition: Full-time $15,800; part-time $440 per credit. Required fees: $100 per quarter. Tuition and fees vary according to degree level. *Financial support:* Career-related internships or fieldwork and scholarships/grants available. Support available to part-time students. Financial award application deadline: 9/1. *Faculty research:* Theology, worship studies, church history, evangelism, Bible. *Unit head:* Alistair Brown, Dean, 630-620-2103, Fax: 630-620-2190. *Application contact:* Greg Henson, Executive Director of External Relations, 630-620-2180, Fax: 630-620-2190, E-mail: admissions@seminary.edu.

North Park Theological Seminary, Graduate and Professional Programs, Professional Program, Chicago, IL 60625-4895. Offers M Div, M Div/MBA, M Div/MM. *Accreditation:* ACIPE; ATS. Part-time programs available. *Degree requirements:* For M Div, 2 foreign languages. *Entrance requirements:* Minimum GPA of 2.5. Additional exam requirements/recommendations for international students: Required—TOEFL.

North Park Theological Seminary, Graduate and Professional Programs, Program in Christian Formation, Chicago, IL 60625-4895. Offers MA, MA/MM.

North Park Theological Seminary, Graduate and Professional Programs, Program in Preaching, Chicago, IL 60625-4895. Offers D Min. *Accreditation:* ACIPE; ATS. *Degree requirements:* For doctorate, thesis/dissertation. *Entrance requirements:* For doctorate, 3 years of preaching experience.

North Park Theological Seminary, Graduate and Professional Programs, Program in Theological Studies, Chicago, IL 60625-4895. Offers MATS, MATS/MBA, MATS/MM. *Accreditation:* ACIPE; ATS. Part-time programs available. *Degree requirements:* For master's, comprehensive exam or thesis. *Entrance requirements:* For master's, minimum GPA of 2.5. Additional exam requirements/recommendations for international students: Required—TOEFL.

Northwest Baptist Seminary, Programs in Theology, Tacoma, WA 98407. Offers M Div, M Min, MTS, STM, Th M, D Min, Certificate. Part-time and evening/weekend programs available. *Degree requirements:* For master's, thesis; for M Div, thesis/dissertation (for some programs). *Entrance requirements:* Greek placement exam. Additional exam requirements/recommendations for international students: Required—TOEFL (minimum score 550 paper-based; 213 computer-based), IELTS (minimum score 6).

Notre Dame Seminary, Graduate School of Theology, New Orleans, LA 70118-4391. Offers M Div, MA. *Accreditation:* ACIPE; ATS. Part-time programs available. *Degree requirements:* For master's, one foreign language, comprehensive exam, thesis. *Entrance requirements:* For M Div, GRE, previous course work in philosophy; for master's, GRE. Additional exam requirements/recommendations for international students: Required—TOEFL.

Oakland City University, Chapman Seminary, Oakland City, IN 47660-1099. Offers M Div, D Min. *Accreditation:* ATS. Part-time programs available. *Degree requirements:* For doctorate, thesis/dissertation. *Entrance requirements:* For M Div, GRE General Test, minimum GPA of 2.75 in undergraduate major or 2.5 overall; for doctorate, GRE, MAT, letters of recommendation. Additional exam requirements/recommendations for international students: Required—TOEFL. *Expenses:* Contact institution. *Faculty research:* Pastoral ministry, Christian education, missions.

Theology

Oblate School of Theology, Graduate and Professional Programs, San Antonio, TX 78216-6693. Offers divinity (M Div); Hispanic ministry (D Min); pastoral ministry (MAP Min); pastoral studies (Certificate); spirituality (MA Sp); supervision (D Min), including clinical pastoral education, general supervision; theology (MA Th); M Div/MA Th. *Accreditation:* ACIPE; ATS (one or more programs are accredited). Part-time programs available. *Faculty:* 24 full-time (7 women), 6 part-time/adjunct (1 woman). *Students:* 91 full-time (5 women), 56 part-time (25 women); includes 62 minority (7 African Americans, 3 American Indian/Alaska Native, 13 Asian Americans or Pacific Islanders, 39 Hispanic Americans), 29 international. Average age 39. 33 applicants, 100% accepted, 33 enrolled. In 2008, 16 first professional degrees, 8 master's, 5 Certificates awarded. *Degree requirements:* For master's, thesis (for some programs), practicum; for doctorate, paper, practicum; for M Div, one foreign language, seminar. *Entrance requirements:* For M Div, MAT, interview, course work in philosophy and theology; for master's, MAT, interview, course work in theology or religious studies, minimum GPA of 2.5; for doctorate, M Div. Additional exam requirements/recommendations for international students: Required—TOEFL (minimum score 197 computer-based; 71 iBT). *Application deadline:* For fall admission, 6/15 priority date for domestic and international students; for spring admission, 12/30 for domestic and international students. Applications are processed on a rolling basis. Application fee: $45. *Expenses:* Tuition: Full-time $11,570; part-time $445 per credit hour. Required fees: $170 per semester. One-time fee: $85 full-time. Part-time tuition and fees vary according to course level and course load. *Financial support:* Scholarships/grants available. Support available to part-time students. Financial award application deadline: 8/1; financial award applicants required to submit FAFSA. *Unit head:* Sr. Elaine Brothers, Academic Dean, 210-341-1366, Fax: 214-341-4519, E-mail: ebrothers@ost.edu. *Application contact:* James Oberhausen, Director of Admission/Registrar, 210-341-1366 Ext. 212, Fax: 210-341-4519, E-mail: registrar@ost.edu.

Ohio Dominican University, Graduate Programs, Division of Theology, Arts and Ideas, Columbus, OH 43219-2099. Offers theology (MA). Part-time and evening/weekend programs available. *Degree requirements:* For master's, thesis or alternative. *Entrance requirements:* For master's, 20 undergraduate semester hours of theology or the equivalent, 3 letters of recommendation, interview. Additional exam requirements/recommendations for international students: Required—TOEFL (minimum score 550 paper-based; 213 computer-based).

Ohr Hameir Theological Seminary, Graduate Programs, Peekskill, NY 10566. *Accreditation:* AARTS.

Oklahoma Christian University, Graduate School of Theology, Oklahoma City, OK 73136-1100. Offers family life ministry (MA); ministry (M Div, MA); youth ministry (MA). Part-time programs available. Postbaccalaureate distance learning degree programs offered (minimal on-campus study). *Faculty:* 11 full-time (0 women). *Students:* 12 full-time (2 women), 30 part-time (4 women); includes 3 minority (2 African Americans, 1 American Indian/Alaska Native), 3 international. *Degree requirements:* For master's, one foreign language, comprehensive exam, field experience; for M Div, 2 foreign languages, comprehensive exam, field experience. *Entrance requirements:* For M Div and master's, minimum undergraduate GPA of 3.0. Additional exam requirements/recommendations for international students: Required—TOEFL (minimum score 550 paper-based; 213 computer-based). *Application deadline:* For fall admission, 8/15 priority date for domestic and international students; for spring admission, 1/3 priority date for domestic and international students. Applications are processed on a rolling basis. Application fee: $25. Electronic applications accepted. *Financial support:* Career-related internships or fieldwork, Federal Work-Study, scholarships/grants, and tuition waivers (partial) available. Support available to part-time students. Financial award application deadline: 3/1. *Faculty research:* Early marriage adjustment, new religions, Ethiopic language, church health, Hebrew rhetoric. *Unit head:* Dr. John Harrison, Chair, 405-425-5377, Fax: 405-425-5076, E-mail: john.harrison@oc.edu. *Application contact:* Dustin Crawford, Admissions Counselor, 405-425-5485, Fax: 405-425-5076, E-mail: dustin.crawford@oc.edu.

Olivet Nazarene University, Graduate School, Department of Practical Ministries, Bourbonnais, IL 60914-2271. Offers MPM. Part-time programs available. *Degree requirements:* For master's, thesis or alternative.

Olivet Nazarene University, Graduate School, Division of Religion, Bourbonnais, IL 60914-2271. Offers biblical literature (MA); religion (MA); theology (MA). Part-time programs available. *Degree requirements:* For master's, thesis or alternative.

Oral Roberts University, School of Theology and Missions, Tulsa, OK 74171-0001. Offers biblical literature (MA), including advanced languages, Judaic-Christian studies; Christian counseling (MA), including marriage and family therapy; Christian education (MA); divinity (M Div); missions (MA); practical theology (MA); theological/historical studies (MA); theology (D Min). *Accreditation:* ATS; NASM. Part-time programs available. Postbaccalaureate distance learning degree programs offered (minimal on-campus study). *Degree requirements:* For master's, thesis (for some programs), practicum/internship; for doctorate, thesis/dissertation, applied research project; for M Div, one foreign language, field experience. *Entrance requirements:* For M Div and master's, GRE General Test or MAT, minimum GPA of 2.5; for doctorate, M Div, minimum GPA of 3.0, 3 years of full-time ministry experience. Additional exam requirements/recommendations for international students: Required—TOEFL (minimum score 500 paper-based; 213 computer-based; 79 iBT). Electronic applications accepted.

Pacific Lutheran Theological Seminary, Graduate and Professional Programs, Berkeley, CA 94708-1597. Offers M Div, MA, MCM, MTS, PhD, Th D, Certificate, M Div/MA. *Accreditation:* ACIPE; ATS (one or more programs are accredited). Part-time programs available. *Degree requirements:* For master's, variable foreign language requirement, thesis or alternative; for M Div, one foreign language. *Entrance requirements:* Minimum cumulative GPA of 2.5, two semesters of Greek. *Faculty research:* Theology and genetics, power and prayer, liturgy and ethics, Christianity and Confucianism, religion and abuse.

Pacific School of Religion, Graduate and Professional Programs, Berkeley, CA 94709-1323. Offers M Div, MA, MTS, D Min, PhD, Th D, CAPS, CMS, CSS, CTS. *Accreditation:* ACIPE; ATS (one or more programs are accredited). Part-time programs available. *Degree requirements:* For master's, one foreign language, thesis (for some programs); for doctorate, thesis/dissertation. *Entrance requirements:* For M Div and master's, minimum GPA of 3.0; for doctorate, M Div, minimum GPA of 3.0 (D Min); for other advanced degree, M Div, minimum GPA of 3.0 (CAPS). Additional exam requirements/recommendations for international students: Required—TOEFL (minimum score 550 paper-based; 213 computer-based). Electronic applications accepted. *Faculty research:* Medical ethics, gay/lesbian studies in religion, Asian-American religion, race, culture and theology, theology in context.

Payne Theological Seminary, Program in Theology, Wilberforce, OH 45384-3474. Offers M Div. *Accreditation:* ACIPE; ATS. Part-time and evening/weekend programs available. Postbaccalaureate distance learning degree programs offered (minimal on-campus study). *Degree requirements:* For M Div, 2 foreign languages, thesis/dissertation.

Philadelphia Biblical University, School of Biblical Studies, Langhorne, PA 19047-2990. Offers M Div, MSB. Part-time and evening/weekend programs available. *Faculty:* 5 full-time (0 women), 6 part-time/adjunct (0 women). *Students:* 18 full-time (2 women), 76 part-time (18 women); includes 33 minority (26 African Americans, 6 Asian Americans or Pacific Islanders, 1 Hispanic American), 3 international. Average age 39. 59 applicants, 47% accepted, 28 enrolled. In 2008, 1 M Div, 9 master's awarded. *Entrance requirements:* Additional exam requirements/recommendations for international students: Required—TOEFL (minimum score 550 paper-based; 213 computer-based). *Application deadline:* Applications are processed on a rolling basis. Application fee: $25. Electronic applications accepted. *Expenses:* Tuition: Full-time $9450; part-time $525 per credit. Required fees: $10; $10 per year. Tuition and fees vary according to program. *Financial support:* In 2008–09, 50 students received support. Scholarships/grants available. Support available to part-time students. Financial award applicants required to submit FAFSA. *Unit head:* Dr. O. Herbert Hirt, Dean, 215-702-4354, Fax: 215-702-4359, E-mail: bible@pbu.edu. *Application contact:* Binu Abraham, Assistant Director, Graduate Admissions, 800-572-2472, Fax: 215-702-4248, E-mail: babraham@pbu.edu.

Phillips Theological Seminary, Programs in Theology, Tulsa, OK 74116. Offers administration of church agencies (M Div); campus ministry (M Div); church-related social work (M Div); college and seminary teaching (M Div); global mission work (M Div); institutional chaplaincy (M Div); ministerial vocations in Christian education (M Div); ministry (D Min), including parish ministry, pastoral counseling, practices of ministry; ministry and culture (MAMC), including Christian education, congregational leadership, history and practice of Christian spirituality, theology, ethics, and culture; ministry of music (M Div); pastoral care and counseling (M Div); pastoral ministry (M Div); theological studies (MTS). *Accreditation:* ATS. Part-time programs available. Postbaccalaureate distance learning degree programs offered (minimal on-campus study). *Degree requirements:* For master's, thesis (for some programs); for doctorate, thesis/dissertation. *Entrance requirements:* For master's, minimum GPA of 2.5; for doctorate, M Div, minimum GPA of 3.0. *Faculty research:* Biblical studies, historical studies, theology and culture, practical theology, theology and film.

Piedmont Baptist College and Graduate School, Piedmont Baptist Graduate School, Winston-Salem, NC 27101-5197. Offers chaplaincy track (MABS); non-language track (MABS); PhD preparation track (MABS); theology (M Min, PhD). Part-time programs available. Postbaccalaureate distance learning degree programs offered (no on-campus study). *Degree requirements:* For master's, 2 foreign languages, comprehensive exam, thesis or alternative; for doctorate, 2 foreign languages, comprehensive exam. *Entrance requirements:* For master's, GRE General Test, BA/BS; for doctorate, Hebrew and Greek proficiency, MA. Electronic applications accepted. *Faculty research:* Theological and biblical studies.

Pittsburgh Theological Seminary, Graduate and Professional Programs, Pittsburgh, PA 15206-2596. Offers divinity (M Div); ministry (D Min); theology (MA, STM); JD/M Div; M Div/MS; M Div/MSW. *Accreditation:* ATS (one or more programs are accredited). Part-time and evening/weekend programs available. *Faculty:* 18 full-time (3 women), 8 part-time/adjunct (1 woman). *Students:* 254 full-time (87 women), 64 part-time (31 women); includes 52 minority (46 African Americans, 1 American Indian/Alaska Native, 4 Asian Americans or Pacific Islanders, 1 Hispanic American), 13 international. Average age 36. 135 applicants, 70% accepted, 78 enrolled. In 2008, 46 first professional degrees, 8 master's, 12 doctorates awarded. *Degree requirements:* For master's, comprehensive exam (for some programs), thesis (for some programs); for doctorate, thesis/dissertation; for M Div, one foreign language. *Entrance requirements:* For M Div and master's, bachelor's degree with minimum GPA of 2.7, interview, references; for doctorate, interview, references. Additional exam requirements/recommendations for international students: Required—TOEFL (minimum score 570 paper-based; 230 computer-based; 89 iBT). *Application deadline:* For fall admission, 6/31 priority date for domestic students, 12/1 for international students; for winter admission, 10/15 priority date for domestic students; for spring admission, 1/15 priority date for domestic students. Applications are processed on a rolling basis. Application fee: $40. *Expenses:* Tuition: Full-time $273; part-time $295 per credit. Required fees: $46 per term. *Financial support:* In 2008–09, 137 students received support. Career-related internships or fieldwork, scholarships/grants, and institutional work-study available. Financial award application deadline: 4/15; financial award applicants required to submit FAFSA. *Unit head:* Dr. Byron H. Jackson, Dean of Faculty and Vice President for Academic Affairs, 412-362-5610 Ext. 2118, Fax: 412-363-3260, E-mail: bjackson@pts.edu. *Application contact:* Sherry Sparks, Director of Admissions, 412-362-5610 Ext. 2115, Fax: 412-363-3260, E-mail: ssparks@pts.edu.

Pontifical Catholic University of Puerto Rico, College of Arts and Humanities, Department of Theology and Philosophy, Ponce, PR 00717-0777. Offers M Div.

Pontifical College Josephinum, School of Theology, Columbus, OH 43235-1498. Offers M Div, MA. *Accreditation:* ATS. Part-time programs available. *Faculty:* 17 full-time (1 woman), 5 part-time/adjunct (2 women). *Students:* 49 full-time (0 women), 2 part-time (0 women); includes 5 minority (2 Asian Americans or Pacific Islanders, 3 Hispanic Americans), 10 international. Average age 28. 16 applicants, 88% accepted, 14 enrolled. In 2008, 9 master's awarded. *Degree requirements:* For master's, 3 foreign languages, comprehensive exam, thesis; for M Div, 2 foreign languages, thesis/dissertation. *Entrance requirements:* For M Div, GRE General Test, 24 credit hours of course work in philosophy, 12 credit hours of course work in theology; for master's, GRE General Test, 15 credit hours of course work in philosophy, 6 credit hours of course work in scripture. Additional exam requirements/recommendations for international students: Required—TOEFL (minimum score 600 paper-based; 250 computer-based). *Application deadline:* For fall admission, 8/15 for domestic students. Applications are processed on a rolling basis. Application fee: $35. *Expenses:* Tuition: Full-time $20,053; part-time $630 per credit hour. Required fees: $707. *Financial support:* Career-related internships or fieldwork and Federal Work-Study available. Financial award application deadline: 8/15; financial award applicants required to submit FAFSA. *Unit head:* Rev. Msgr. Nevin Klingor, Vice Rector School of Theology, 614-885-5585, Fax: 614-885-2307, E-mail: nklinger@pcj.edu. *Application contact:* Dr. Perry Cahall, Director of Admissions, 614-885-5585, Fax: 614-885-2307, E-mail: pcahall@pcj.edu.

Princeton Theological Seminary, Graduate and Professional Programs, Princeton, NJ 08542-0803. Offers M Div, MA, Th M, D Min, PhD. *Accreditation:* ACIPE; ATS. Part-time programs available. Terminal master's awarded for partial completion of doctoral program. *Degree requirements:* For doctorate, 2 foreign languages, thesis/dissertation, comprehensive exam (PhD), French and German. *Entrance requirements:* For doctorate, GRE General Test. Additional exam requirements/recommendations for international students: Required—TOEFL. Electronic applications accepted.

The Protestant Episcopal Theological Seminary in Virginia, Graduate and Professional Programs, Alexandria, VA 22304. Offers M Div, MACE, MTS, D Min. *Accreditation:* ACIPE; ATS. Part-time programs available. *Degree requirements:* For master's, 2 foreign languages, thesis; for doctorate, thesis/dissertation. *Entrance requirements:* For M Div, master's, and doctorate, GRE General Test.

Providence College, Graduate Studies, Department of Religious Studies, Providence, RI 02918. Offers biblical studies (MABS); early Christian studies (MA Th); St. Thomas Aquinas studies (MA Th, MTS). Part-time and evening/weekend programs available. *Faculty:* 8 full-time (2 women). *Students:* 4 full-time (1 woman), 22 part-time (9 women). Average age 42. 12 applicants, 100% accepted. In 2008, 7 master's awarded. *Degree requirements:* For master's, comprehensive exam, Greek and Hebrew (biblical studies). *Entrance requirements:* Additional exam requirements/recommendations for international students: Required—TOEFL (minimum score 550 paper-based; 213 computer-based; 80 iBT). *Application deadline:* For fall admission, 8/1 priority date for domestic and international students; for spring admission, 12/1 priority date for domestic and international students. Applications are processed on a rolling basis. Application fee: $55. *Expenses:* Tuition: Full-time $8991; part-time $333 per credit hour. One-time fee: $170. Tuition and fees vary according to program. *Financial support:* In 2008–09, 4 research assistantships with full tuition reimbursements (averaging $8,400 per year) were awarded; career-related internships or fieldwork and unspecified assistantships also available. Support available to part-time students. Financial award application deadline: 8/1; financial award applicants required to submit FAFSA. *Unit head:* Rev. Thomas McCreesh, OP, Director, 401-865-1150, Fax: 401-865-1830, E-mail: tmccrees@providence.edu. *Application contact:* Carol A. Daniels, Coordinator of Graduate Faculty and Administrative Services, 401-865-2247, Fax: 401-865-1147, E-mail: daniels@providence.edu.

Providence College and Theological Seminary, Theological Seminary, Otterburne, MB R0A 1G0, Canada. Offers children's ministry (Certificate); Christian studies (MA, Certificate); counseling (MA); cross-cultural discipleship (Certificate); divinity (M Div); educational studies (MA), including counseling psychology, educational ministries, student development, teaching English to speakers of other languages, training teachers of English to speakers of other languages; global studies (MA); lay counseling (Diploma); ministry (D Min); teaching English to speakers of other languages (Certificate); theological studies (MA); training teacher of English to speakers of other languages (Certificate); youth ministry (Certificate). *Accreditation:* ATS. Part-time programs available. *Degree requirements:* For master's, variable foreign language requirement, thesis (for some programs); for doctorate, thesis/dissertation; for M Div, 2 foreign languages, comprehensive exam, thesis/dissertation (for some programs). *Entrance requirements:* Additional exam requirements/recommendations for international students: Recommended—TOEFL (minimum score 550 paper-based; 213 computer-based). *Faculty research:* Studies in Isaiah, theology of sin.

Queen's University at Kingston, Queen's Theological College, Kingston, ON K7L 3N6, Canada. Offers M Div, MTS, Certificate. *Accreditation:* ATS. Part-time programs available. *Degree requirements:* For master's, thesis (for some programs); for M Div, 2 foreign languages. *Entrance requirements:* For master's, minimum undergraduate B average. Additional exam requirements/recommendations for international students: Required—TOEFL (minimum score 580 paper-based). *Faculty research:* Early Christian group formations, pastoral care and spiritual direction, feminist theology, public religion, interpretation of Biblical texts using psychologies of shame and trauma.

Quincy University, Program in Theological Studies, Quincy, IL 62301-2699. Offers MTS. Part-time and evening/weekend programs available. In 2008, 1 master's awarded. *Entrance requirements:* For master's, MAT or GRE. Additional exam requirements/recommendations for international students: Required—TOEFL. *Application deadline:* Applications are processed on a rolling basis. Application fee: $25. Electronic applications accepted. *Expenses:* Tuition: Full-time $8400; part-time $350 per semester hour. Required fees: $15 per semester hour. Tuition and fees vary according to course load and program. *Financial support:* Applicants required to submit FAFSA. *Unit head:* Dr. Ed Maniscalco, Director, 217-228-5432 Ext. 3201, E-mail: manised@quincy.edu. *Application contact:* Jennifer O'Donnell, Coordinator of Adult Studies, 217-228-5404, Fax: 217-228-5479, E-mail: admissions@quincy.edu.

Rabbi Isaac Elchanan Theological Seminary, Graduate Program, New York, NY 10033-1807. Offers Certificate of Advanced Ordination, Certificate of Ordination. *Degree requirements:* For other advanced degree, one foreign language, comprehensive exam. *Entrance requirements:* For degree, oral exam, 2 interview, undergraduate major in Jewish studies or equivalent. *Faculty research:* Talmud, rabbinics.

Rabbinical Academy Mesivta Rabbi Chaim Berlin, Graduate Program, Brooklyn, NY 11230-4715. Offers Advanced Talmudic Degree, Second Talmudic Degree. *Accreditation:* AARTS. *Degree requirements:* For other advanced degree, 2 foreign languages. *Entrance requirements:* For degree, must be a graduate of a rabbinical school.

Rabbinical College Beth Shraga, Graduate Programs, Monsey, NY 10952-3035. *Accreditation:* AARTS.

Rabbinical College Bobover Yeshiva B'nei Zion, Graduate Programs, Brooklyn, NY 11219. *Accreditation:* AARTS.

Rabbinical College Ch'san Sofer, Graduate Programs, Brooklyn, NY 11204. *Accreditation:* AARTS.

Rabbinical College of Long Island, Graduate Programs, Long Beach, NY 11561-3305. *Accreditation:* AARTS.

Rabbinical Seminary M'kor Chaim, Graduate Programs, Brooklyn, NY 11219. *Accreditation:* AARTS.

Rabbinical Seminary of America, Graduate Programs, Flushing, NY 11367. School offers a master's and first professional degree. *Accreditation:* AARTS.

Reconstructionist Rabbinical College, Graduate Program, Wyncote, PA 19095-1898. Offers MAHL, MAJS, DHL, Certificate. Part-time programs available. *Degree requirements:* For master's, one foreign language, thesis (MAJS), completion of rabbinical program (MAHL); for doctorate and MAHL, one foreign language. *Entrance requirements:* For MAHL and doctorate, GRE General Test, placement examinations in Hebrew and Judaism; for master's, GRE General Test. *Faculty research:* Bible, Hebrew Semitic texts, contemporary Judaism.

Reformed Presbyterian Theological Seminary, Graduate and Professional Programs, Pittsburgh, PA 15208-2594. Offers M Div, MTS, D Min. *Accreditation:* ATS. Part-time and evening/weekend programs available. Electronic applications accepted. *Faculty research:* Prayer.

Reformed Theological Seminary–Charlotte Campus, Graduate and Professional Programs, Charlotte, NC 28226-6318. Offers biblical studies (MA); ministry (M Div, D Min); theological studies (MA). Part-time programs available. *Degree requirements:* For master's, comprehensive exam; for doctorate, thesis/dissertation; for M Div, 2 foreign languages, comprehensive exam. *Entrance requirements:* For master's, minimum GPA of 2.6; for doctorate, minimum GPA of 3.0. Additional exam requirements/recommendations for international students: Required—TOEFL (minimum score 550 paper-based; 213 computer-based). Electronic applications accepted.

Reformed Theological Seminary–Jackson Campus, Graduate and Professional Programs, Jackson, MS 39209-3099. Offers Bible, theology, and missions (Certificate); biblical studies (MA); Christian education (M Div, MA); counseling (M Div); divinity (M Div, Diploma); marriage and family therapy (MA); ministry (D Min); missions (M Div, MA, D Min); New Testament (Th M); Old Testament (Th M); theological studies (MA); theology (Th M); M Div/MA. *Accreditation:* AAMFT/COAMFTE (one or more programs are accredited); ATS (one or more programs are accredited). *Degree requirements:* For master's, thesis (for some programs), fieldwork; for doctorate, 2 foreign languages, thesis/dissertation; for M Div, 2 foreign languages, thesis/dissertation (for some programs). *Entrance requirements:* For M Div and master's, minimum GPA of 2.6; for doctorate, minimum GPA of 3.0. Additional exam requirements/recommendations for international students: Required—TOEFL.

Reformed Theological Seminary–Orlando Campus, Graduate Program, Oviedo, FL 32765-7197. Offers biblical studies (MA); Christian thought (MA); counseling (MA); ministry (D Min); reformation studies (Th M); theological studies (MA); theology (M Div); MA/Certificate. Part-time programs available. Postbaccalaureate distance learning degree programs offered (minimal on-campus study). *Entrance requirements:* For M Div and master's, minimum GPA of 2.6. Electronic applications accepted.

Reformed Theological Seminary–Washington D.C., Graduate and Professional Programs, McLean, VA 22101. Offers bible (M Div); practical theology (M Div); religion (MA); theology (M Div). Part-time and evening/weekend programs available. *Degree requirements:* For master's, integrative paper. *Entrance requirements:* For master's, minimum undergraduate GPA of 2.6. Electronic applications accepted. *Faculty research:* Theology, biblical studies, cultural studies.

Regent College, Program in Theology, Vancouver, BC V6T 2E4, Canada. Offers M Div, MCS, Th M, Dip CS. *Accreditation:* ATS (one or more programs are accredited). Part-time and evening/weekend programs available. *Faculty:* 21 full-time (4 women), 17 part-time/adjunct (6 women). *Students:* 269 full-time (92 women), 293 part-time (111 women); includes 166 minority (4 African Americans, 1 American Indian/Alaska Native, 152 Asian Americans or Pacific Islanders, 9 Hispanic Americans). Average age 33. 263 applicants, 86% accepted, 135 enrolled. In 2008, 46 first professional degrees, 96 master's, 61 Dip CSs awarded. *Degree requirements:* For master's, thesis (for some programs). *Entrance requirements:* For M Div and Dip CS, minimum GPA of 2.8; for master's, minimum GPA of 2.8 (MCS), 3.5 (Th M). Additional exam requirements/recommendations for international students: Required—TOEFL (minimum score 575 paper-based; 230 computer-based; 90 iBT), TWE (minimum score 5). *Application deadline:* For fall admission, 2/1 priority date for domestic students, 1/1 priority date for international students; for winter admission, 7/1 priority date for domestic and international students; for

spring admission, 2/1 priority date for domestic students, 1/1 priority date for international students. Application fee: $60 Canadian dollars. Tuition and fees charges are reported in Canadian dollars. *Expenses:* Tuition: Full-time $14,940 Canadian dollars; part-time $475 Canadian dollars per credit. Required fees: $475 Canadian dollars per credit. $135 Canadian dollars per term. One-time fee: $210.21 Canadian dollars. *Financial support:* In 2008–09, 71 students received support, including 150 teaching assistantships (averaging $2,500 per year); career-related internships or fieldwork, scholarships/grants, and health care benefits also available. Financial award application deadline: 3/1. *Faculty research:* Integration of theology with secular life, biblical studies. *Unit head:* Dr. Rod Wilson, President, 604-221-3318, Fax: 604-224-3097, E-mail: presidentsoffice@regent-college.edu. *Application contact:* Cindy Y. Aalders, Director of Admissions, 604-224-3245 Ext. 335, Fax: 604-224-3097, E-mail: admissions@regent-college.edu.

Regent University, Graduate School, School of Divinity, Virginia Beach, VA 23464-9800. Offers Biblical studies (MA); leadership and renewal (D Min); missiology (M Div, MA); practical theology (M Div, MA); renewal studies (PhD); M Div/M Ed; M Div/MA; M Div/MBA; M Ed/MA; MBA/MA. *Accreditation:* ACIPE; ATS. Part-time programs available. Postbaccalaureate distance learning degree programs offered (minimal on-campus study). *Faculty:* 21 full-time (4 women), 24 part-time/adjunct (5 women). *Students:* 194 full-time (90 women), 391 part-time (164 women); includes 249 minority (217 African Americans, 3 American Indian/Alaska Native, 11 Asian Americans or Pacific Islanders, 18 Hispanic Americans), 19 international. Average age 38. 320 applicants, 65% accepted, 137 enrolled. In 2008, 39 first professional degrees, 36 master's, 29 doctorates awarded. *Degree requirements:* For master's, comprehensive exam, thesis or alternative, internship; for doctorate, thesis/dissertation or alternative; for M Div, internship. *Entrance requirements:* For M Div, GRE General Test or MAT, minimum undergraduate GPA of 3.0, minimum 3 years of ministry experience, transcripts, recommendations; for master's, GRE General Test or MAT, minimum undergraduate GPA of 2.75, writing sample, clergy recommendation, transcripts; for doctorate, M Div or theological master's degree; minimum graduate GPA of 3.5 (PhD), 3.0 (D Min); recommendations; writing sample; transcripts. Additional exam requirements/recommendations for international students: Required—TOEFL (minimum score 577 paper-based; 233 computer-based). *Application deadline:* For fall admission, 5/1 priority date for domestic students. Applications are processed on a rolling basis. Application fee: $50. Electronic applications accepted. *Expenses:* Contact institution. *Financial support:* Fellowships with full and partial tuition reimbursements, career-related internships or fieldwork, scholarships/grants, tuition waivers (full and partial), and unspecified assistantships available. Support available to part-time students. Financial award application deadline: 9/1; financial award applicants required to submit FAFSA. *Faculty research:* Greek and Hebrew, theology, spiritual formation, global missions and world Christianity, women's studies. *Unit head:* Dr. Michael Palmer, Dean, 757-352-4406, Fax: 757-352-4597, E-mail: mpalmer@regent.edu. *Application contact:* Matthew Chadwick, Director of Admissions, 800-373-5504, Fax: 757-352-4381, E-mail: admissions@regent.edu.

Regis College, Graduate and Professional Programs, Toronto, ON M4Y 2R5, Canada. Offers ministry (D Min); ministry and spirituality (MAMS); sacred theology (STB, STM, STD, STL); theological study (MTS); theology (M Div, MA, Th M, PhD, Th D); M Div/MA. *Accreditation:* ATS (one or more programs are accredited). *Faculty:* 15 full-time (4 women), 12 part-time/adjunct (2 women). *Students:* 88 full-time (30 women), 131 part-time (78 women); includes 74 minority (16 African Americans, 1 American Indian/Alaska Native, 48 Asian Americans or Pacific Islanders, 9 Hispanic Americans). Average age 45. 73 applicants, 88% accepted, 52 enrolled. In 2008, 10 first professional degrees, 13 master's, 5 other advanced degrees awarded. Terminal master's awarded for partial completion of doctoral program. *Degree requirements:* For master's, 2 foreign languages, thesis; for doctorate, 3 foreign languages, comprehensive exam, thesis/dissertation; for first professional degree, comprehensive exam. *Entrance requirements:* For first professional degree, minimum GPA of 3.0; for master's, minimum GPA of 3.3; for doctorate, minimum GPA of 3.7. Additional exam requirements/recommendations for international students: Required—TOEFL (minimum score 580 paper-based; 237 computer-based; 93 iBT), TWE (minimum score 5). *Application deadline:* For fall admission, 3/15 priority date for domestic and international students; for winter admission, 12/1 for domestic and international students; for spring admission, 3/15 for domestic and international students. Applications are processed on a rolling basis. Application fee: $25. *Financial support:* In 2008–09, 58 students received support. Career-related internships or fieldwork and scholarships/grants available. Support available to part-time students. Financial award application deadline: 3/15. *Unit head:* Dr. Gordon Rixon, Dean, 416-922-5474 Ext. 225, Fax: 416-922-2898, E-mail: gordon.rixon@utoronto.ca. *Application contact:* Elaine Chu, Registrar, 416-922-5474 Ext. 226, Fax: 416-922-2898, E-mail: regis.registrar@utoronto.ca.

Sacred Heart Major Seminary, School of Theology, Detroit, MI 48206-1799. Offers pastoral studies (MAPS); theology (M Div, MA). *Accreditation:* ACIPE; ATS. Part-time and evening/weekend programs available. *Degree requirements:* For master's, one foreign language, thesis optional, integrating project; for M Div, integrating seminar. *Entrance requirements:* For M Div and master's, GRE, previous course work in philosophy and theology. *Faculty research:* Local church history, patristics, spirituality, religious education.

Sacred Heart School of Theology, Graduate and Professional Programs, Hales Corners, WI 53130-0429. Offers theology (M Div, MA). *Accreditation:* ACIPE; ATS. Part-time programs available. *Degree requirements:* For master's, essay or comprehensive exam; for M Div, integrating seminar. *Entrance requirements:* For master's, MAT, 6 hours of course work each in philosophy and theology, letter of recommendation.

St. Andrew's College in Winnipeg, Graduate Programs, Winnipeg, MB R3T 2M7, Canada. Offers M Div. *Degree requirements:* For M Div, one foreign language, thesis/dissertation. *Faculty research:* Church history, doctrine, liturgical theology.

St. Augustine's Seminary of Toronto, Graduate and Professional Programs, Scarborough, ON M1M 1M3, Canada. Offers divinity (M Div); lay ministry (Diploma); religious education (MRE); theological studies (MTS, Diploma). *Accreditation:* ATS. Part-time and evening/weekend programs available. *Degree requirements:* For M Div, comprehensive exam (for some programs), thesis/dissertation optional, field education. *Entrance requirements:* Course work in philosophy. Additional exam requirements/recommendations for international students: Required—TOEFL (minimum score 580 paper-based; 237 computer-based), TWE (minimum score 5).

Saint Bernard's School of Theology and Ministry, Graduate and Professional Programs, Rochester, NY 14618. Offers pastoral studies (MA, Certificate); theological studies (MA); theology (M Div). *Accreditation:* ATS (one or more programs are accredited). Part-time and evening/weekend programs available. *Degree requirements:* For master's, variable foreign language requirement, thesis (for some programs). *Entrance requirements:* For M Div, minimum GPA of 2.0; for master's, minimum GPA of 2.5.

St. Bonaventure University, School of Graduate Studies, School of Franciscan Studies, St. Bonaventure, NY 14778-2284. Offers MA, Adv C. Part-time programs available. *Degree requirements:* For master's, thesis optional, integration seminar and paper.

St. Catherine University, Graduate Programs, Program in Theology, St. Paul, MN 55105-1789. Offers MA. Part-time and evening/weekend programs available. *Degree requirements:* For master's, comprehensive exam, thesis (for some programs). *Entrance requirements:* For master's, MAT, minimum GPA of 3.0. Additional exam requirements/recommendations for international students: Required—Michigan English Language Assessment Battery or TOEFL (minimum paper-based score 600; computer 250; iBT 100). *Expenses:* Contact institution. *Faculty research:* Feminist scholarship, historical theology, symbols, rites of purification, spirituality.

St. Charles Borromeo Seminary, Overbrook, Graduate and Professional Programs, Division of Theology, Wynnewood, PA 19096. Offers M Div, MA. *Accreditation:* ATS. Part-time programs

Theology

St. Charles Borromeo Seminary, Overbrook (continued)

available. *Faculty:* 11 full-time (3 women), 10 part-time/adjunct (2 women). *Students:* 58 full-time (0 women); includes 3 minority (1 American Indian/Alaska Native, 2 Asian Americans or Pacific Islanders), 3 international. Average age 28. 27 applicants, 100% accepted, 27 enrolled. In 2008, 22 first professional degrees, 4 master's awarded. *Degree requirements:* For master's, comprehensive exam, research papers; for M Div, comprehensive exam. *Entrance requirements:* For M Div, previous course work in philosophy and theology; for master's, M Div. *Application deadline:* For fall admission, 7/15 for domestic students, 3/15 for international students; for spring admission, 11/15 for domestic students. Applications are processed on a rolling basis. Application fee: $0. *Expenses:* Tuition: Full-time $14,705; part-time $1351 per course. *Financial support:* Federal Work-Study and scholarships/grants available. *Unit head:* Rev. Robert A. Pesarchick, Academic Dean, 610-785-6204, Fax: 610-667-1422, E-mail: academicdcdscs@adphila.org. *Application contact:* Rev. David E. Diamond, Vice Rector, 610-785-6271, Fax: 610-617-9267, E-mail: frdd@adphila.org.

Saint Francis Seminary, Graduate and Professional Programs, St. Francis, WI 53235-3795. Offers M Div, MAPS. *Accreditation:* ACIPE; ATS. Part-time programs available. *Degree requirements:* For master's, comprehensive exam; for M Div, thesis/dissertation. *Entrance requirements:* For M Div and master's, Otis IQ Test, Terman Concept Mastery Test, interview. Additional exam requirements/recommendations for international students: Required—TOEFL (minimum score 550 paper-based).

St. John's Seminary, Graduate and Professional Programs, Camarillo, CA 93012-2598. Offers divinity (M Div); pastoral ministry (MAPM); theology (MA). *Accreditation:* ATS. Part-time programs available. *Faculty:* 19 full-time (4 women), 8 part-time/adjunct (1 woman). *Students:* 69 full-time (0 women), 10 part-time (5 women); includes 46 minority (1 African American, 25 Asian Americans or Pacific Islanders, 20 Hispanic Americans), 11 international. Average age 34. 13 applicants, 100% accepted, 13 enrolled. In 2008, 17 first professional degrees, 6 master's awarded. *Degree requirements:* For master's, comprehensive exam (for some programs), thesis optional, comprehensive integration paper (MAPM); for M Div, parish internship. *Entrance requirements:* For M Div, GRE General Test, bishop's approbation; for master's, GRE General Test, minimum GPA of 3.5 (MA), 2.5 (MAPM). Additional exam requirements/recommendations for international students: Required—TOEFL (minimum score 550 paper-based; 213 computer-based; 79 iBT). *Application deadline:* For fall admission, 7/15 priority date for domestic students. Applications are processed on a rolling basis. Application fee: $0. Electronic applications accepted. *Expenses:* Tuition: Full-time $12,750; part-time $425 per unit. One-time fee: $3421 full-time; $25 part-time. Full-time tuition and fees vary according to course load and program. *Faculty research:* Biblical studies, moral theology, historical studies, systematic theology, spiritual theology. *Unit head:* Rev. Richard Benson, CM, Academic Dean, 805-482-2755, Fax: 805-482-3470, E-mail: rbensoncm@stjohnsem.edu. *Application contact:* Esme M. Takahashi, Registrar, 805-482-2755 Ext. 1014, Fax: 805-482-3470, E-mail: registrar-sjs@stjohnsem.edu.

Saint John's Seminary, Graduate Programs, Brighton, MA 02135. Offers M Div, MA Th, MAM. *Accreditation:* ATS.

St. John's University, St. John's College of Liberal Arts and Sciences, Department of Theology and Religious Studies, Queens, NY 11439. Offers pastoral ministry (Certificate); priestly studies (M Div); theology (MA, Certificate). *Accreditation:* ACIPE. Part-time and evening/weekend programs available. *Students:* 1 (woman) full-time, 43 part-time (23 women); includes 12 minority (6 African Americans, 1 Asian American or Pacific Islander, 5 Hispanic Americans), 10 international. Average age 47. 36 applicants, 67% accepted, 14 enrolled. In 2008, 1 first professional degree, 19 master's, 2 other advanced degrees awarded. *Degree requirements:* For master's, thesis optional; for M Div, thesis/dissertation optional. *Entrance requirements:* For master's, minimum GPA of 3.0. Additional exam requirements/recommendations for international students: Required—TOEFL (minimum score 500 paper-based; 173 computer-based; 61 iBT), IELTS (minimum score 5.5). *Application deadline:* For fall admission, 5/1 priority date for domestic and international students; for spring admission, 11/1 priority date for domestic and international students. Applications are processed on a rolling basis. Application fee: $70. Electronic applications accepted. *Expenses:* Tuition: Full-time $20,760; part-time $865 per credit. Required fees: $300; $150 per semester. Tuition and fees vary according to program. *Financial support:* Research assistantships, scholarships/grants available. Support available to part-time students. Financial award application deadline: 3/1; financial award applicants required to submit FAFSA. *Faculty research:* Systematic theology, moral theory, biblical studies, pastoral theology, church history. *Unit head:* Fr. Michael Whalen, Chair, 718-990-5431, E-mail: whalenm@stjohns.edu. *Application contact:* Kathleen Davis, Director of Graduate Admission, 718-990-2790, Fax: 718-990-5686, E-mail: gradhelp@stjohns.edu.

Saint John's University, Saint John's School of Theology and Seminary, Collegeville, MN 56321. Offers divinity (M Div), liturgical music (MA); liturgical studies (MA); pastoral ministry (MA); theology (MA), including church history, liturgy, monastic studies, scripture, spirituality, systematics; M Div/MA. *Accreditation:* ATS. Part-time programs available. Postbaccalaureate distance learning degree programs offered (no on-campus study). *Degree requirements:* For master's, one foreign language, comprehensive exam (for some programs), thesis (for some programs). *Entrance requirements:* For master's, GRE General Test or MAT. Electronic applications accepted. *Faculty research:* Religious education, biblical literature.

St. Joseph's Seminary, Institute of Religious Studies, Yonkers, NY 10704. Offers MA. *Accreditation:* ATS. Part-time and evening/weekend programs available. *Degree requirements:* For master's, comprehensive exam. *Entrance requirements:* For master's, 18 hours in theology and/or philosophy. Electronic applications accepted. *Expenses:* Contact institution. *Faculty research:* Medical ethics, mystical theology of Karl Rahner, medieval church history.

St. Joseph's Seminary, Professional Program, Yonkers, NY 10704. Offers divinity (M Div); theology (MA). *Accreditation:* ATS. *Degree requirements:* For master's, one foreign language, thesis; for M Div, comprehensive exam. *Entrance requirements:* For M Div and master's, 27 credits in philosophy and 9 in theology.

Saint Louis University, Graduate School, College of Arts and Sciences and Graduate School, Department of Theological Studies, St. Louis, MO 63103-2097. Offers historical theology (MA, PhD); theology (MA). Part-time programs available. *Degree requirements:* For master's, comprehensive exam; for doctorate, 4 foreign languages, comprehensive exam, thesis/dissertation, preliminary exams. *Entrance requirements:* For master's and doctorate, GRE General Test, letters of recommendation, resumé, interview, transcripts, goal statement. Additional exam requirements/recommendations for international students: Required—TOEFL (minimum score 550 paper-based; 213 computer-based). Electronic applications accepted. *Faculty research:* Biblical and early church studies, medieval and renaissance studies, modern and American Christianity, comparative and interreligious studies, moral and ethical theology.

Saint Mary-of-the-Woods College, Program in Pastoral Theology, Saint Mary-of-the-Woods, IN 47876. Offers pastoral theology (MA); youth ministry (Graduate Certificate). Part-time and evening/weekend programs available. Postbaccalaureate distance learning degree programs offered (minimal on-campus study). *Degree requirements:* For master's, thesis, qualifying exam.

Saint Mary Seminary and Graduate School of Theology, School of Theology, Wickliffe, OH 44092-2527. Offers M Div, MA, D Min. *Accreditation:* ATS. Part-time programs available. *Degree requirements:* For master's, comprehensive exam, symposium; for doctorate, thesis/dissertation, final project, symposium; for M Div, one foreign language, evaluation by faculty for ordination. *Entrance requirements:* For M Div, GRE General Test, previous course work in religion and philosophy; for master's, GRE General Test, previous course work in religion; for doctorate, M Div or equivalent, 3 years in full-time ministry, interviews, ministry profile report. *Faculty research:* Pastoral ministry, theology of ministry, ecclesiology, American Catholics.

St. Mary's Seminary and University, Ecumenical Institute of Theology, Baltimore, MD 21210-1994. Offers church ministries (MA); theology (MA Th, Certificate). *Accreditation:* ACIPE; ATS. Part-time and evening/weekend programs available. *Degree requirements:* For master's, thesis or alternative, comprehensive exam or colloquium. *Expenses:* Contact institution. *Faculty research:* Scripture and ethics, theology and literature, early Christianity and Judaism, medical and social ethics.

Announcement: The Ecumenical Institute of Theology at St. Mary's Seminary and University offers part-time, accredited theological education for laypeople and clergy from all faith traditions. Students may pursue the M.A. in Theology program or the M.A. in Church Ministries program (with 7 different tracks), certificates in 6 areas, or the post-master's Certificate of Advanced Studies.

St. Mary's Seminary and University, School of Theology, Baltimore, MD 21210-1994. Offers M Div, STB, MA Th, STD, STL. *Accreditation:* ACIPE; ATS (one or more programs are accredited). Part-time programs available. Terminal master's awarded for partial completion of doctoral program. *Degree requirements:* For master's and first professional degree, comprehensive exam. *Entrance requirements:* For master's, Computerized Adaptive Placement Assessment and Support System.

St. Mary's University, Graduate School, Department of Theology, San Antonio, TX 78228-8507. Offers pastoral ministry (MA); theology (MA); JD/MA. Part-time and evening/weekend programs available. Postbaccalaureate distance learning degree programs offered (no on-campus study). *Students:* 2 full-time (0 women), 36 part-time (21 women); includes 8 minority (all Hispanic Americans), 1 international. Average age 42. 15 applicants, 47% accepted, 7 enrolled. In 2008, 7 master's awarded. *Degree requirements:* For master's, comprehensive exam, practicum (pastoral administration). *Entrance requirements:* For master's, GRE General Test, MAT, 12 credit hours in theology/philosophy. Additional exam requirements/recommendations for international students: Required—TOEFL (minimum score 550 paper-based; 213 computer-based; 80 iBT). *Application deadline:* For fall admission, 8/1 for domestic students. Applications are processed on a rolling basis. Application fee: $0. Electronic applications accepted. *Expenses:* Tuition: Full-time $12,006; part-time $667 per credit hour. Required fees: $440; $220 per semester. *Financial support:* In 2008–09, 2 students received support, including 1 fellowship (averaging $2,000 per year), 1 research assistantship (averaging $4,500 per year); career-related internships or fieldwork, Federal Work-Study, institutionally sponsored loans, scholarships/grants, health care benefits, and unspecified assistantships also available. Financial award application deadline: 3/31; financial award applicants required to submit FAFSA. *Faculty research:* Bioethics; perceptions of ministry; Marian doctrines and the contemporary church; Jaspers, peace, and justice. *Unit head:* Rev. Daniel Thompson, Director, 210-436-3310, E-mail: dthompson@stmarytx.edu. *Application contact:* Dr. Henry Flores, Dean of the Graduate School, 210-436-3101, Fax: 210-431-2220, E-mail: hflores@stmarytx.edu.

Saint Meinrad School of Theology, Professional Program, Saint Meinrad, IN 47577. Offers M Div. *Accreditation:* ACIPE; ATS. *Entrance requirements:* 30 credits in philosophy, 12 credits in theology. Additional exam requirements/recommendations for international students: Required—TOEFL (minimum score 550 paper-based).

Saint Meinrad School of Theology, Program in Catholic Philosophical Studies, Saint Meinrad, IN 47577. Offers MA. *Entrance requirements:* Additional exam requirements/recommendations for international students: Required—TOEFL (minimum score 550 paper-based).

Saint Meinrad School of Theology, Program in Catholic Thought and Life, Saint Meinrad, IN 47577. Offers MA. *Accreditation:* ACIPE; ATS. Part-time and evening/weekend programs available. *Degree requirements:* For master's, comprehensive exam.

Saint Meinrad School of Theology, Program in Theological Studies, Saint Meinrad, IN 47577. Offers MTS. *Accreditation:* ACIPE; ATS. Part-time and evening/weekend programs available. *Degree requirements:* For master's, thesis.

Saint Michael's College, Graduate Programs, Program in Theology and Pastoral Ministry, Colchester, VT 05439. Offers theology (MA, CAS, Certificate). Part-time and evening/weekend programs available. *Degree requirements:* For master's, thesis optional, 1 foreign language if thesis option selected. *Entrance requirements:* For master's, bachelor's degree in arts, science, philosophy, theology, or education; minimum GPA of 3.0; 24 hours of course work in theology and other humanistic disciplines. Additional exam requirements/recommendations for international students: Required—TOEFL (minimum score 550 paper-based; 213 computer-based; 80 iBT), IELTS (minimum score 6). Electronic applications accepted. *Expenses:* Contact institution.

St. Norbert College, Program in Theological Studies, De Pere, WI 54115-2099. Offers MTS. Part-time programs available. *Faculty:* 5 full-time (2 women), 3 part-time/adjunct (2 women). *Students:* 61 part-time (44 women); includes 7 minority (1 Asian American or Pacific Islander, 6 Hispanic Americans). 4 applicants, 125% accepted, 5 enrolled. In 2008, 4 master's awarded. *Degree requirements:* For master's, comprehensive exam, thesis. *Entrance requirements:* For master's, minimum of 8 credits of course work in theology/religious studies, BA degree from an accredited institution. *Application deadline:* Applications are processed on a rolling basis. Application fee: $50. Electronic applications accepted. *Expenses:* Tuition: Part-time $350 per credit hour. *Financial support:* In 2008–09, 9 students received support. Scholarships/grants available. Support available to part-time students. *Faculty research:* Practical theology, Holocaust, Rahner, women in the Bible and Christian ethics. *Unit head:* Dr. Howard Ebert, Director, 920-403-3956, Fax: 920-403-4086, E-mail: howard.ebert@snc.edu. *Application contact:* Dinah Grassel, Program Coordinator, 920-403-3957, Fax: 920-403-4086, E-mail: dinah.grassel@snc.edu.

St. Patrick's Seminary & University, School of Theology, Menlo Park, CA 94025-3596. Offers M Div, STB, MA. *Accreditation:* ATS (one or more programs are accredited). Part-time programs available. *Degree requirements:* For master's, comprehensive exam, thesis or alternative. *Entrance requirements:* For first professional degree, GRE General Test or MAT, minimum GPA of 2.0, interview; for master's, GRE General Test, minimum GPA of 3.0, interview. Additional exam requirements/recommendations for international students: Required—TOEFL (minimum score 550 paper-based; 215 computer-based; 80 iBT), TWE. *Faculty research:* Systematic theology, sacred scripture, moral theology, liturgy.

Saint Paul School of Theology, Graduate and Professional Programs, Kansas City, MO 64127-2440. Offers M Div, MA, MTS, D Min. *Accreditation:* ACIPE; ATS. Part-time programs available. *Degree requirements:* For doctorate, thesis/dissertation. *Entrance requirements:* For M Div and master's, minimum GPA of 2.75; for doctorate, minimum GPA of 3.0. Additional exam requirements/recommendations for international students: Required—TOEFL. *Faculty research:* Religion and aging; leadership development; feminist, African-American, and liberation theology; rural ministry; worship and the arts.

Saint Paul University, Faculty of Canon Law, Ottawa, ON K1S 1C4, Canada. Offers canon law (MCL, JCD, PhD, Graduate Certificate, JCL); canonical practice (Graduate Certificate); ecclesiastical administration (Graduate Certificate). Part-time programs available. *Degree requirements:* For master's, one foreign language; for doctorate, one foreign language, comprehensive exam, thesis/dissertation; for other advanced degree, one foreign language, comprehensive exam (for some programs), comprehensive exam and seminar paper (JCL). *Entrance requirements:* For master's, appropriate bachelor's degree, 18 credits in theology; for doctorate, JCL or MCL; for other advanced degree, B Th or equivalent (JCL), appropriate bachelor's degree, 18 credits in theology. *Faculty research:* All questions related to Church law.

Saint Paul University, Faculty of Human Sciences, Program in Counseling and Spirituality, Ottawa, ON K1S 1C4, Canada. Offers individual or marital/couple counseling (MA); spiritual care (MA). Part-time programs available. *Degree requirements:* For master's, research project or thesis. *Entrance requirements:* For master's, honors BA in human sciences, minimum B average, 12 theology credits.

Saint Paul University, Faculty of Theology, Ottawa, ON K1S 1C4, Canada. Offers MA Th, MP Th, MRE, D Min, D Th, PhD, L Th. *Degree requirements:* For master's and L Th, one foreign language; for doctorate, one foreign language, comprehensive exam, thesis/dissertation. *Entrance requirements:* For master's, B Th; for doctorate, MA Th, L Th, MP TH, M Div. *Faculty research:* Biblical studies, systematic and historical theology, ethics, spirituality, Eastern Christian studies, applied theology.

St. Petersburg Theological Seminary, Graduate Programs, St. Petersburg, FL 33708. Offers Biblical studies (MA); counseling (MA); divinity (M Div); education (MA); Judaic studies (MA); ministry (MA, D Min); religious teacher (MA). Part-time and evening/weekend programs available. Postbaccalaureate distance learning degree programs offered (minimal on-campus study). *Degree requirements:* For master's, thesis; for doctorate, thesis/dissertation. *Entrance requirements:* For M Div and master's, Bachelor degree; for doctorate, Master degree. Electronic applications accepted.

St. Peter's Seminary, Department of Theology, London, ON N6A 3Y1, Canada. Offers M Div, MTS. *Accreditation:* ATS.

Saints Cyril and Methodius Seminary, Graduate and Professional Programs, Orchard Lake, MI 48324. Offers pastoral ministry (MAPM); religious education (MARE); theology (M Div, MA). *Accreditation:* ATS. Part-time programs available.

St. Stephen's College, Programs in Theology, Edmonton, AB T6G 2J6, Canada. Offers ministry (D Min); pastoral counseling (MA); social transformation ministry (MA); spirituality and liturgy (MA); theological studies (MTS); theology (M Th). Part-time and evening/weekend programs available. Postbaccalaureate distance learning degree programs offered (minimal on-campus study). Terminal master's awarded for partial completion of doctoral program. *Degree requirements:* For master's, thesis; for doctorate, thesis/dissertation. *Entrance requirements:* Additional exam requirements/recommendations for international students: Required—TOEFL. Electronic applications accepted. *Faculty research:* Methodology for theological education, practice and supervision for ministry.

St. Thomas University, School of Theology and Ministry, Institute for Pastoral Ministries, Miami Gardens, FL 33054-6459. Offers pastoral ministries (MA, Certificate); practical theology (PhD). Part-time and evening/weekend programs available. *Degree requirements:* For master's, comprehensive exam; for doctorate, comprehensive exam, thesis/dissertation. *Entrance requirements:* For master's, interview, minimum GPA of 3.0 or GRE; for doctorate, GRE, MA in theology. Additional exam requirements/recommendations for international students: Required—TOEFL (minimum score 550 paper-based; 213 computer-based; 79 iBT). Electronic applications accepted.

St. Tikhon's Orthodox Theological Seminary, Divinity Program, South Canaan, PA 18459. Offers M Div. *Accreditation:* ATS. *Faculty:* 8 full-time (1 woman), 6 part-time/adjunct (0 women). *Students:* 48 full-time (0 women), 7 part-time (0 women); includes 3 minority (1 African American, 2 Hispanic Americans), 4 international. 35 applicants, 80% accepted, 28 enrolled. *Degree requirements:* For M Div, one foreign language, thesis/dissertation optional. *Entrance requirements:* Letters of recommendation. *Application deadline:* For fall admission, 7/30 for domestic students, 6/30 for international students. Applications are processed on a rolling basis. Application fee: $15. *Expenses:* Tuition: Full-time $85; part-time $85 per credit. Required fees: $100; $10 per semester. One-time fee: $100. *Financial support:* Fellowships with partial tuition reimbursements, career-related internships or fieldwork, institutionally sponsored loans, scholarships/grants, and tuition waivers (partial) available. *Faculty research:* Church history, patristics, scripture, spirituality. *Unit head:* Bp. Tikhon Mollard, Rector, 570-937-4411, Fax: 570-937-4139, E-mail: bp.tikhon@stots.edu. *Application contact:* Fr. Michael Dahulich, Dean and Director of Admissions, 570-937-4411 Ext. 113, Fax: 570-937-3100, E-mail: fr.michael@stots.edu.

Saint Vincent de Paul Regional Seminary, Graduate and Professional Programs, Boynton Beach, FL 33436-4899. Offers theology (M Div, MA Th). *Accreditation:* ATS. Part-time programs available. *Degree requirements:* For master's, comprehensive exam (for some programs), thesis optional; for M Div, one foreign language. *Entrance requirements:* For M Div and master's, GRE General Test, MAT. Additional exam requirements/recommendations for international students: Required—TOEFL.

Saint Vincent Seminary, School of Theology, Latrobe, PA 15650-2690. Offers M Div, MA. *Accreditation:* ATS. Part-time programs available. *Degree requirements:* For master's, one foreign language, comprehensive exam; for M Div, one foreign language. *Entrance requirements:* For M Div, minimum GPA of 2.5; for master's, minimum GPA of 3.0. Additional exam requirements/recommendations for international students: Required—TOEFL (minimum score 550 paper-based; 220 computer-based). Electronic applications accepted. *Faculty research:* Church history, preaching, psychology of religion, Biblical studies, moral theology.

St. Vladimir's Orthodox Theological Seminary, Graduate School of Theology, Crestwood, NY 10707-1699. Offers general theological studies (MA); liturgical music (MA); religious education (MA); theology (M Div, M Th, D Min); M Div/MA. MA in general theological studies, M Div offered jointly with St. Nersess Seminary. *Accreditation:* ATS. Part-time programs available. *Degree requirements:* For master's, one foreign language, thesis, fieldwork; for doctorate, thesis/dissertation, fieldwork; for M Div, one foreign language, thesis/dissertation, fieldwork. *Entrance requirements:* For doctorate, M Div, minimum GPA of 3.0. Additional exam requirements/recommendations for international students: Required—TOEFL (minimum score 250 computer-based).

Samford University, Beeson School of Divinity, Birmingham, AL 35229. Offers M Div, MTS, D Min, JD/M Div, JD/MTS, M Div/MBA, M Div/MM, M Div/MSE. *Accreditation:* ATS. *Faculty:* 18 full-time (3 women), 4 part-time/adjunct (0 women). *Students:* 174 full-time (32 women), 11 part-time (4 women); includes 28 minority (27 African Americans, 1 Hispanic American). Average age 31. 74 applicants, 73% accepted, 43 enrolled. In 2008, 46 first professional degrees, 11 master's, 8 doctorates awarded. *Degree requirements:* For master's, one foreign language, thesis optional; for doctorate, thesis/dissertation; for M Div, 2 foreign languages, thesis/dissertation optional, 4 internships (including 1 cross-cultural experience). *Entrance requirements:* For M Div and master's, minimum GPA of 2.5; for doctorate, minimum GPA of 3.0. Additional exam requirements/recommendations for international students: Required—TOEFL (minimum score 550 paper-based; 213 computer-based). *Application deadline:* For fall admission, 3/1 for domestic and international students; for spring admission, 10/1 for domestic and international students. Application fee: $25. Electronic applications accepted. *Expenses:* Contact institution. *Financial support:* In 2008–09, 158 students received support. Scholarships/grants and tuition waivers (full and partial) available. Financial award applicants required to submit FAFSA. *Faculty research:* New Testament theology, exegesis of Psalms, doctrinal preaching, history of Anglicanism, racial reconciliation. *Unit head:* Dr. Timothy George, Dean, 205-726-2632, E-mail: tfgeorge@samford.edu. *Application contact:* Dr. Timothy George, Dean, 205-726-2632, E-mail: tfgeorge@samford.edu.

San Francisco Theological Seminary, Graduate and Professional Programs, San Anselmo, CA 94960-2997. Offers M Div, MA, MATS, D Min, PhD, Th D, M Div/MA. *Accreditation:* ACIPE; ATS (one or more programs are accredited). Part-time programs available. *Degree requirements:* For master's, one foreign language, thesis (for some programs); for doctorate, thesis/dissertation; for M Div, one foreign language, internship. *Entrance requirements:* For master's, minimum GPA of 3.0; for doctorate, M Div. Additional exam requirements/recommendations for international students: Required—TOEFL.

Seabury-Western Theological Seminary, School of Theology, Evanston, IL 60201-2976. Offers advanced theological studies (Certificate); church music and liturgy (MTS); congregational

development (D Min); preaching (D Min); theological studies (MA); theology (M Div, L Th). D Min in congregational development offered in summer only. *Accreditation:* ACIPE; ATS (one or more programs are accredited). Part-time programs available. *Degree requirements:* For master's, thesis; for doctorate, thesis/dissertation; for other advanced degree, thesis (for some programs). *Entrance requirements:* For M Div and master's, interview, sample of written work. *Faculty research:* Liturgical interpretations of baptism, trinitarian theology, congregational development, post modern biblical criticism-Matthew.

Seattle University, School of Theology and Ministry, Program in Divinity, Seattle, WA 98122-1090. Offers M Div. *Accreditation:* ATS. Part-time and evening/weekend programs available. *Degree requirements:* For M Div, project. *Entrance requirements:* Interview, minimum GPA of 2.75.

Seattle University, School of Theology and Ministry, Program in Transforming Spirituality, Seattle, WA 98122-1090. Offers MATS, Certificate. *Accreditation:* ATS. Part-time and evening/weekend programs available. *Degree requirements:* For master's, project. *Entrance requirements:* For master's, interview, minimum GPA of 2.75.

Seminary of the Immaculate Conception, School of Theology, Huntington, NY 11743-1696. Offers pastoral studies (MA); theology (M Div, MA, D Min, Certificate). *Accreditation:* ATS (one or more programs are accredited). Part-time and evening/weekend programs available. *Degree requirements:* For master's, comprehensive exam; for doctorate, thesis/dissertation; for M Div, one foreign language, thesis/dissertation. *Entrance requirements:* For M Div, college degree in philosophy-theology; for master's, undergraduate degree; for doctorate, MA plus 30 credits or M Div; for Certificate, MA in theology.

Seminary of the Southwest, Graduate and Professional Programs, Austin, TX 78768-2247. Offers Anglican studies (Advanced Diploma); chaplaincy (MCPC); counseling (MAC); divinity (M Div); religion (MAR); spiritual formation (MAPM); theological studies (Advanced Diploma). *Accreditation:* ACIPE; ATS (one or more programs are accredited). Part-time and evening/weekend programs available. *Faculty:* 10 full-time (3 women), 31 part-time/adjunct (11 women). *Students:* 46 full-time (29 women), 31 part-time (23 women); includes 7 minority (4 African Americans, 1 Asian American or Pacific Islander, 2 Hispanic Americans), 2 international. Average age 46. 28 applicants, 96% accepted, 22 enrolled. In 2008, 23 first professional degrees, 13 master's, 5 other advanced degrees awarded. *Degree requirements:* For master's, thesis (for some programs). *Entrance requirements:* For M Div and master's, GRE, MAT, interview; for Advanced Diploma, interview. *Application deadline:* For fall admission, 7/1 for domestic students; for spring admission, 11/1 for domestic students. Applications are processed on a rolling basis. Application fee: $50. *Expenses:* Tuition: Full-time $13,150; part-time $390 per credit hour. One-time fee: $75 full-time; $20 part-time. *Financial support:* Career-related internships or fieldwork and scholarships/grants available. Support available to part-time students. Financial award application deadline: 6/17. *Unit head:* Very Rev. Douglas Travis, Dean and President, 512-472-4133 Ext. 307, Fax: 512-472-3098, E-mail: dtravis@ssw.edu. *Application contact:* Jennielle Strother, Director of Admissions, 512-472-4133 Ext. 375, Fax: 512-472-3098, E-mail: jstrother@ssw.edu.

Seton Hall University, Immaculate Conception Seminary School of Theology, South Orange, NJ 07079-2697. Offers pastoral ministry (M Div, MA); theology (MA). *Accreditation:* ACIPE; ATS (one or more programs are accredited). Part-time and evening/weekend programs available. *Degree requirements:* For master's, one foreign language, comprehensive exam, thesis, final project; for M Div, final project and seminar, field education, spiritual formation. *Entrance requirements:* For M Div, GRE, MAT; for master's, GRE General Test or MAT. Electronic applications accepted. *Expenses:* Contact institution.

Sewanee: The University of the South, School of Theology, Sewanee, TN 37383. Offers M Div, MA, STM, D Min. *Accreditation:* ACIPE; ATS. Part-time programs available. *Faculty:* 11 full-time (4 women), 11 part-time/adjunct (4 women). *Students:* 70 full-time (26 women), 9 part-time (7 women); includes 6 minority (5 African Americans, 1 Hispanic American), 1 international. Average age 44. 50 applicants, 72% accepted. In 2008, 28 first professional degrees, 3 master's, 5 doctorates awarded. *Degree requirements:* For master's, thesis; for doctorate, thesis/dissertation. *Entrance requirements:* For M Div, GRE General Test, interview; for master's, GRE General Test, M Div (STM); for doctorate, M Div. Additional exam requirements/recommendations for international students: Required—TOEFL (minimum score 550 paper-based). *Application deadline:* For fall admission, 4/1 priority date for domestic students, 4/1 for international students. Applications are processed on a rolling basis. Application fee: $25. *Expenses:* Tuition: Full-time $15,804; part-time $660 per credit hour. Required fees: $576. *Financial support:* Institutionally sponsored loans and scholarships/grants available. Support available to part-time students. Financial award application deadline: 5/1; financial award applicants required to submit FAFSA. *Unit head:* Very Rev. William S. Stafford, Dean, 931-598-1288, Fax: 931-598-1412, E-mail: wstafford@sewanee.edu. *Application contact:* Roslyn Dianne Weaver, Director of Admissions/Registrar, 931-598-1283, Fax: 931-598-1852, E-mail: rweaver@sewanee.edu.

Shaw University, Divinity School, Raleigh, NC 27601-2399. Offers M Div, MRE. *Accreditation:* ATS. Part-time and evening/weekend programs available. *Degree requirements:* For master's, thesis; for M Div, thesis/dissertation. *Entrance requirements:* For M Div and master's, letters of reference. Electronic applications accepted. *Faculty research:* HIV/AIDS awareness through faith-based curriculum, domestic abuse and violence prevention, pedagogy for non-traditional theology education, health disparities in the African-American community, technology and theological education.

Sh'or Yoshuv Rabbinical College, Graduate Programs, Far Rockaway, NY 11691-4002. *Accreditation:* AARTS.

Sioux Falls Seminary, Graduate and Professional Programs, Professional Program in Ministry, Sioux Falls, SD 57105-1599. Offers D Min. *Accreditation:* ACIPE. Part-time programs available. *Degree requirements:* For doctorate, thesis/dissertation. *Entrance requirements:* For doctorate, M Div, 3 years of ministry.

Sioux Falls Seminary, Graduate and Professional Programs, Program in Bible and Theology, Sioux Falls, SD 57105-1599. Offers MA. *Accreditation:* ACIPE; ATS. Part-time programs available. *Degree requirements:* For master's, 2 foreign languages, thesis or alternative. *Entrance requirements:* For master's, minimum GPA of 2.5.

Sioux Falls Seminary, Graduate and Professional Programs, Program in Theological Studies, Sioux Falls, SD 57105-1599. Offers Certificate.

Southeastern Baptist Theological Seminary, Graduate and Professional Programs, Wake Forest, NC 27588-1889. Offers advanced biblical studies (M Div); Christian education (M Div, MACE); Christian ethics (PhD); Christian ministry (M Div); Christian planting (M Div); church music (MACM); counseling (MACO); evangelism (PhD); language (M Div); ministry (D Min); New Testament (PhD); Old Testament (PhD); philosophy (PhD); theology (Th M, PhD); women's studies (M Div). *Accreditation:* ACIPE; ATS (one or more programs are accredited). *Degree requirements:* For master's, thesis (for some programs), oral exam; for doctorate, thesis/dissertation, fieldwork; for M Div, supervised ministry. *Entrance requirements:* For master's, Cooperative English Test, minimum GPA of 2.0, M Div or equivalent (Th M); for doctorate, GRE General Test or MAT, Cooperative English Test, M Div or equivalent, 3 years of professional experience.

Southern Adventist University, School of Religion, Collegedale, TN 37315-0370. Offers Biblical and theological studies (MA); church leadership and management (MA); church ministry and homiletics (MA); evangelism and world mission (MA); religious studies (MA). Summer program only. Part-time programs available. *Degree requirements:* For master's, comprehensive exam, thesis (for some programs). *Entrance requirements:* For master's, GRE. Additional

Theology

Southern Adventist University (continued)
exam requirements/recommendations for international students: Required—TOEFL (minimum score 550 paper-based). *Faculty research:* Biblical archaeology.

Southern Baptist Theological Seminary, Billy Graham School of Missions, Evangelism and Church Growth, Louisville, KY 40280-0004. Offers Christian mission/world religion (PhD); evangelism/church growth (PhD); ministry (D Min); missiology (MA, D Miss); missions, evangelism and church growth (M Div); religion (Th M); theological studies (MA). *Accreditation:* ATS. Part-time and evening/weekend programs available. Postbaccalaureate distance learning degree programs offered (minimal on-campus study). *Degree requirements:* For master's and M Div, 2 foreign languages; for doctorate, 4 foreign languages, thesis/dissertation. *Entrance requirements:* For doctorate, GRE General Test, MAT, field essay, M Div. Additional exam requirements/recommendations for international students: Required—TOEFL, TWE. *Faculty research:* Assimilation of church congregants, effective methodologies of evangelism, expectations of church members, spiritual warfare literature, formative church discipline.

Southern Baptist Theological Seminary, School of Theology, Louisville, KY 40280-0004. Offers biblical and theological studies (M Div); biblical counseling (M Div, MA, D Min); biblical spirituality (D Min); Christian ministry (M Div); expository preaching (D Min); pastoral studies (M Div); theological studies (MA); theology (Th M, PhD); theology and arts (MA); theology and law (MA); worldview and apologetics (M Div). *Accreditation:* ATS. Part-time and evening/weekend programs available. Postbaccalaureate distance learning degree programs offered (minimal on-campus study). *Degree requirements:* For master's, 2 foreign languages, thesis; for doctorate, 4 foreign languages, thesis/dissertation; for M Div, 2 foreign languages. *Entrance requirements:* For master's, GRE General Test, MAT, M Div; for doctorate, GRE General Test, MAT, interview, M Div, field essay. Additional exam requirements/recommendations for international students: Required—TOEFL, TWE. *Faculty research:* Biblical studies, contemporary theology, church history, pastoral care, ministry/missions studies.

Southern California Seminary, Graduate and Professional Programs, El Cajon, CA 92019. Offers biblical studies (MA); counseling psychology (MACP); psychology (Psy D); religious studies (MRS); theology (M Div). Part-time and evening/weekend programs available. Postbaccalaureate distance learning degree programs offered (minimal on-campus study). *Degree requirements:* For master's, thesis (for some programs); for doctorate, thesis/dissertation; for M Div, 2 foreign languages. *Entrance requirements:* For doctorate, master's degree in psychology. Additional exam requirements/recommendations for international students: Required—TOEFL (minimum score 550 paper-based). Electronic applications accepted.

Southern Evangelical Seminary, Graduate School of Ministry and Missions, Matthews, NC 28105. Offers apologetics (Certificate); Christian education (MA); church ministry (MA, Certificate); divinity (Certificate), including apologetics (M Div, Certificate); Islamic studies (Certificate); theology (M Div), including apologetics (M Div, Certificate), Biblical studies; youth ministry (MA). Part-time and evening/weekend programs available. Postbaccalaureate distance learning degree programs offered. *Degree requirements:* For master's, thesis (for some programs); for M Div, one foreign language. *Entrance requirements:* Additional exam requirements/recommendations for international students: Required—TOEFL (minimum score 600 paper-based; 250 computer-based).

Southern Evangelical Seminary, Veritas Graduate School of Apologetics and Counter-Cult Ministry, Matthews, NC 28105. Offers apologetics (MA, D Min, PhD, Certificate); Islamic studies (MA); Jewish studies (MA); philosophy (MA); religion (MA). *Accreditation:* ATS. Part-time and evening/weekend programs available. Postbaccalaureate distance learning degree programs offered (minimal on-campus study). *Degree requirements:* For master's, thesis optional; for doctorate, comprehensive exam (for some programs), thesis/dissertation. *Entrance requirements:* Additional exam requirements/recommendations for international students: Required—TOEFL (minimum score 600 paper-based; 250 computer-based).

Southern Methodist University, Perkins School of Theology, Dallas, TX 75275. Offers M Div, CMM, MSM, MTS, D Min. *Accreditation:* ACIPE; ATS. Part-time programs available. *Faculty:* 31 full-time (12 women), 13 part-time/adjunct (3 women). *Students:* 172 full-time (90 women), 192 part-time (109 women); includes 88 minority (60 African Americans, 2 American Indian/Alaska Native, 5 Asian Americans or Pacific Islanders, 21 Hispanic Americans), 6 international. Average age 39. 141 applicants, 77% accepted, 75 enrolled. In 2008, 68 first professional degrees, 29 master's, 15 doctorates awarded. *Degree requirements:* For master's, thesis (for some programs), internship; for doctorate, internship, oral exam, professional project; for M Div, internship. *Entrance requirements:* For M Div and master's, minimum GPA of 2.75; for doctorate, minimum graduate GPA of 3.0, M Div or equivalent, 3 years of ministry experience. Additional exam requirements/recommendations for international students: Required—TOEFL (minimum score 600 paper-based; 250 computer-based), TWE. *Application deadline:* For fall admission, 5/1 for domestic students, 12/15 for international students; for spring admission, 11/1 for domestic students. Applications are processed on a rolling basis. Application fee: $50. *Expenses:* Contact institution. *Financial support:* In 2008–09, 188 students received support, including 3 fellowships with full tuition reimbursements available (averaging $5,000 per year); career-related internships or fieldwork, Federal Work-Study, scholarships/grants, and minister's family tuition awards also available. Support available to part-time students. Financial award application deadline: 3/1; financial award applicants required to submit FAFSA. Total annual research expenditures: $271,008. *Unit head:* Dr. William B. Lawrence, Dean, 214-768-2534, Fax: 214-768-2966. *Application contact:* Rev. Herbert S. Coleman, Director, Recruitment and Admissions, 214-768-2139, Fax: 214-768-4245, E-mail: theology@smu.edu.

Southern Nazarene University, Graduate College, Department of Philosophy and Religion, Bethany, OK 73008. Offers theology (MA). Part-time programs available. *Degree requirements:* For master's, one foreign language, thesis optional. *Entrance requirements:* For master's, GMAT, English proficiency exam, minimum GPA of 3.0 in last 60 hours/major, 2.7 overall.

Southwestern Assemblies of God University, Thomas F. Harrison School of Graduate Studies, Program in Theological Studies, Waxahachie, TX 75165-5735. Offers Bible and theology (MS); Biblical studies (M Div); counseling (M Div); cross cultural missions (M Div); practical theology (M Div); theological studies (M Div). Postbaccalaureate distance learning degree programs offered. *Degree requirements:* For master's, comprehensive written and oral exams. *Entrance requirements:* For master's, GRE General Test, minimum GPA of 2.5. Electronic applications accepted.

Southwestern Baptist Theological Seminary, School of Theology, Fort Worth, TX 76122-0000. Offers M Div, MA Islamic, MA Miss, MA Th, Th M, D Min, PhD, SPTH. *Accreditation:* ACIPE; ATS (one or more programs are accredited). Part-time and evening/weekend programs available. Terminal master's awarded for partial completion of doctoral program. *Degree requirements:* For master's, 2 foreign languages, thesis (for some programs); for doctorate, 2 foreign languages, comprehensive exam, thesis/dissertation, oral exams; for M Div, 2 foreign languages, thesis/dissertation (for some programs). *Entrance requirements:* For doctorate, GRE, M Div or equivalent. Additional exam requirements/recommendations for international students: Required—TOEFL (minimum score 550 paper-based; 213 computer-based). Electronic applications accepted. *Faculty research:* Backgrounds to the New Testament, methods of teaching ancient Biblical languages, geography of the New Testament world, Baptist history.

Spring Arbor University, School of Arts and Sciences, Spring Arbor, MI 49283-9799. Offers communication (MA); spiritual formation and leadership (MA). Part-time programs available. Postbaccalaureate distance learning degree programs offered (no on-campus study). *Faculty:* 6 full-time (1 woman), 11 part-time/adjunct (5 women). *Students:* 104 full-time (64 women), 38 part-time (24 women); includes 8 minority (7 African Americans, 1 Hispanic American), 1 international. Average age 42. In 2008, 3 master's awarded. *Degree requirements:* For master's, thesis (for some programs). *Entrance requirements:* For master's, GRE (taken within the last 5 years), writing sample, 3 recommendations, personal goals statement. Additional exam requirements/recommendations for international students: Required—TOEFL (minimum score 550 paper-based; 220 computer-based). Application fee: $40. *Expenses:* Contact institution. *Financial support:* Applicants required to submit FAFSA. *Unit head:* Dr. Wally Metts, Chair of the Department of Communication, 517-750-1200 Ext. 1491, E-mail: wmetts@arbor.edu. *Application contact:* Dale Glinz, Lead Recruitment Specialist/Trainer, Graduate and Professional Studies, 517-750-6703, E-mail: dglinz@arbor.edu.

Spring Hill College, Graduate Programs, Program in Theology, Mobile, AL 36608-1791. Offers MA, MPS, MTS. Part-time and evening/weekend programs available. *Faculty:* 5 full-time (0 women), 4 part-time/adjunct (2 women). *Students:* 56 part-time (26 women); includes 13 minority (6 African Americans, 2 American Indian/Alaska Native, 1 Asian American or Pacific Islander, 4 Hispanic Americans). Average age 45. 45 applicants, 58% accepted, 10 enrolled. In 2008, 24 master's awarded. *Degree requirements:* For master's, variable foreign language requirement, comprehensive exam, thesis (for some programs). *Entrance requirements:* Additional exam requirements/recommendations for international students: Required—TOEFL (minimum score 550 paper-based; 213 computer-based; 80 iBT), IELTS (minimum score 6.5). *Application deadline:* For fall admission, 8/1 priority date for domestic and international students; for spring admission, 12/1 priority date for domestic and international students. Applications are processed on a rolling basis. Application fee: $25 ($35 for international students). Electronic applications accepted. *Expenses:* Tuition: Full-time $4860; part-time $270 per credit hour. Tuition and fees vary according to program. *Financial support:* In 2008–09, 20 students received support. Career-related internships or fieldwork, scholarships/grants, and loans available. Support available to part-time students. Financial award applicants required to submit FAFSA. *Unit head:* Dr. John B. Switzer, Director of Graduate Theology Programs, 251-380-4669, Fax: 251-460-2194, E-mail: jswitzer@shc.edu. *Application contact:* Donna B. Tarasavage, Director of Marketing and Recruiting, Graduate and Continuing Studies, 251-380-3094, Fax: 251-460-2190, E-mail: grad@shc.edu.

Starr King School for the Ministry, Professional Program, Berkeley, CA 94709-1209. Offers M Div. *Accreditation:* ACIPE; ATS.

Talmudic College of Florida, Program in Talmudic Law, Miami Beach, FL 33139. Offers MRE, Master of Talmudic Law, Doctor of Talmudic Law. *Accreditation:* AARTS. Terminal master's awarded for partial completion of doctoral program. *Degree requirements:* For master's, 2 foreign languages; for doctorate, 2 foreign languages, thesis/dissertation. *Entrance requirements:* For master's, oral exam, undergraduate Judaic studies degree; for doctorate, oral exam, Judaic studies degree.

Taylor College and Seminary, Graduate and Professional Programs, Edmonton, AB T6J 4T3, Canada. Offers Christian studies (Diploma); intercultural studies (MA, Diploma); theology (M Div, MTS). *Accreditation:* ATS. Part-time programs available. *Degree requirements:* For master's, comprehensive exam, thesis optional. *Entrance requirements:* Additional exam requirements/recommendations for international students: Required—TOEFL (minimum score 550 paper-based; 213 computer-based), IELTS (minimum score 6.5). *Faculty research:* Biblical studies, administration and organization, world religions.

Temple Baptist Seminary, Program in Theology, Chattanooga, TN 37404-3530. Offers biblical languages (M Div); Biblical studies (MABS); Christian education (MACE); English Bible û language tools (M Div); theology (MM, D Min). Part-time and evening/weekend programs available. Postbaccalaureate distance learning degree programs offered (minimal on-campus study). *Degree requirements:* For doctorate, thesis/dissertation; for M Div, proficiency in Greek and Hebrew. *Entrance requirements:* For doctorate, minimum GPA of 3.0, M Div.

Toronto School of Theology, Graduate Programs, Toronto, ON M5S 2C3, Canada. Offers M Div, M Mus, M Rel, MA, MAMS, MPS, MRE, MTS, Th M, D Min, PhD, Th D. Federation of seven Toronto-area theological colleges; basic degrees offered through the member colleges jointly with the University of Toronto. *Accreditation:* ATS. Postbaccalaureate distance learning degree programs offered (minimal on-campus study). *Faculty:* 102 full-time (24 women), 206 part-time/adjunct (64 women). *Students:* 680 full-time (250 women), 509 part-time (274 women). Average age 42. In 2008, 148 first professional degrees, 18 master's, 20 doctorates awarded. Terminal master's awarded for partial completion of doctoral program. *Degree requirements:* For master's, 2 foreign languages, thesis; for doctorate, 3 foreign languages, comprehensive exam, thesis/dissertation. *Entrance requirements:* For master's, language exams, minimum B+ average in undergraduate course work; for doctorate, language exams, first-class standing in master's program. Additional exam requirements/recommendations for international students: Required—TOEFL. *Application deadline:* For fall admission, 1/15 priority date for domestic and international students. Applications are processed on a rolling basis. Application fee: $100 Canadian dollars. Electronic applications accepted. *Financial support:* Career-related internships or fieldwork available. *Unit head:* Dr. Alan L. Hayes, Director, 416-978-7822, Fax: 416-978-7821, E-mail: alan.hayes@utoronto.ca. *Application contact:* Jonathan Weverink, Advanced Degree Administrator, 416-978-4050, Fax: 416-978-7821, E-mail: inquiries@tct.odu.

Trevecca Nazarene University, Graduate Division, Graduate Religion Programs, Nashville, TN 37210-2877. Offers biblical studies (MA); preaching and practical theology (MA); systematic theology/historical theology (MA). Part-time programs available. *Faculty:* 4 full-time (0 women). *Students:* 29 full-time (3 women), 26 part-time (5 women); includes 8 minority (all African Americans), 1 international. Average age 35. In 2008, 5 master's awarded. *Degree requirements:* For master's, comprehensive exam, thesis optional. *Entrance requirements:* For master's, GRE General Test or MAT, minimum GPA of 2.7, 2 letters of recommendation, philosophy of ministry statement. Additional exam requirements/recommendations for international students: Required—TOEFL (minimum score 550 paper-based; 213 computer-based). *Application deadline:* Applications are processed on a rolling basis. Application fee: $25. Electronic applications accepted. *Expenses:* Contact institution. *Financial support:* Applicants required to submit FAFSA. *Unit head:* Dr. Tim Green, Dean/Director, 615-248-1378, Fax: 615-248-7417, E-mail: admissions_rel@trevecca.edu. *Application contact:* Sherry Crutchfield, Secretary, 615-248-1378, Fax: 615-248-7417, E-mail: admissions_rel@trevecca.edu.

Trinity Episcopal School for Ministry, Graduate Programs, Ambridge, PA 15003-2397. Offers Anglican studies (Diploma); basic Christian studies (Diploma); divinity (M Div); ministry (D Min); mission and evangelism (MAME, Diploma); religion (MAR); youth ministry (Diploma). *Accreditation:* ATS (one or more programs are accredited). Part-time programs available. *Degree requirements:* For master's, thesis optional; for doctorate, thesis/dissertation; for M Div, thesis/dissertation optional, Greek and Hebrew. *Entrance requirements:* Additional exam requirements/recommendations for international students: Required—TOEFL. *Faculty research:* Pauline Epistles, contemporary theology, history of Anglican liturgy, book of Ruth, biblical theology.

Trinity International University, Trinity Evangelical Divinity School, Deerfield, IL 60015-1284. Offers Biblical and Near Eastern archaeology and languages (MA); Christian studies (MA, Certificate); Christian thought (MA); church history (MA, Th M); congregational ministry: pastor-teacher (M Div); congregational ministry: team ministry (M Div); counseling ministries (MA); counseling psychology (MA); cross-cultural ministry (M Div); educational studies (PhD); evangelism (MA); history of Christianity in America (MA); intercultural studies (MA, PhD); leadership and ministry management (D Min); military chaplaincy (D Min); ministry (MA); mission and evangelism (Th M); missions and evangelism (D Min); New Testament (MA, Th M); Old Testament (Th M); Old Testament and Semitic languages (MA); pastoral care (M Div); pastoral care and counseling (D Min); pastoral counseling and psychology (Th M); pastoral theology (Th M); philosophy of religion (MA); preaching (D Min); religion (MA); research ministry (M Div); systematic theology (Th M); theological studies (PhD); urban ministry (MA). *Accreditation:* ATS (one or more programs are accredited). Part-time programs available. Postbaccalaureate distance learning degree programs offered (minimal on-campus study). *Degree requirements:* For master's, comprehensive exam, thesis, fieldwork; for doctorate, comprehensive exam (for some programs), thesis/dissertation; for M Div, 2 foreign languages, fieldwork; for Certificate, comprehensive exam, integrative papers. *Entrance requirements:* For

M Div, GRE, MAT; for master's, GRE, MAT, minimum cumulative undergraduate GPA of 3.0; for doctorate, GRE, minimum cumulative graduate GPA of 3.2; for Certificate, GRE, MAT, minimum undergraduate GPA of 2.5. Additional exam requirements/recommendations for international students: Required—TOEFL (minimum score 580 paper-based; 237 computer-based), TWE (minimum score 4). Electronic applications accepted.

Trinity Lutheran Seminary, Graduate and Professional Programs, Columbus, OH 43209-2334. Offers church music (MA); divinity (M Div); lay ministry (MA); sacred theology (STM); theological studies (MTS); MSN/MTS; MTS/JD. *Accreditation:* ACIPE; ATS. Part-time programs available. *Degree requirements:* For master's, thesis (for some programs); for M Div, 2 foreign languages, internship. *Entrance requirements:* For master's, M Div or equivalent (STM). Additional exam requirements/recommendations for international students: Required—TOEFL (minimum score 500 paper-based).

Trinity Western University, ACTS Seminaries, Langley, BC V2Y 1Y1, Canada. Offers Christian studies (MA); church ministries (MA); cross cultural ministries (MA); theology (M Div, M Th, MAMFT, MLE, MTS, D Min). *Accreditation:* ATS. Part-time programs available. *Degree requirements:* For master's, thesis (for some programs), internship. *Entrance requirements:* For master's, BA or equivalent; for doctorate, MDiv or equivalent. Additional exam requirements/recommendations for international students: Required—TOEFL. *Expenses:* Contact institution. *Faculty research:* Theology of leadership.

Trinity Western University, Faculty of Graduate Studies, Program in Biblical Studies, Langley, BC V2Y 1Y1, Canada. Offers MA. *Accreditation:* ATS. Part-time programs available. *Degree requirements:* For master's, 2 foreign languages, thesis, 2 years Greek; 2 years Hebrew. *Entrance requirements:* For master's, minimum GPA of 3.0, degree in biblical studies, master of divinity or 42 hours Biblical Study credit. Additional exam requirements/recommendations for international students: Required—TOEFL (minimum score 600 paper-based; 250 computer-based). Electronic applications accepted. *Faculty research:* Intertestamental literature, Dead Sea Scrolls, Biblical literature, history of Jesus, ancient languages.

Tyndale University College & Seminary, Graduate Programs, Toronto, ON M2M 4B3, Canada. Offers Biblical studies (M Div); Christian foundations (MTS); Christian studies (Diploma); counseling (M Div); educational ministry (M Div); missions (M Div, Diploma); pastoral and Chinese ministry (M Div); pastoral ministry (M Div); Pentecostal studies (MTS); spiritual formation (M Div, Diploma); theological studies (M Div); theology (Th M); worship and liturgy (M Div, MTS); youth and family ministry (M Div). *Accreditation:* ATS. Part-time programs available. Postbaccalaureate distance learning degree programs offered (no on-campus study). *Degree requirements:* For M Div, one foreign language, thesis/dissertation optional. *Entrance requirements:* For M Div, master's, and Diploma, minimum C+ average in undergraduate course work. Additional exam requirements/recommendations for international students: Required—TOEFL (minimum score 570 paper-based; 230 computer-based), TWE (minimum score 5). Electronic applications accepted. *Faculty research:* Canadian church history, Chinese church history, Old Testament, counseling ministries (narrative therapy), world religions.

Unification Theological Seminary, Graduate Program, Main Campus, Barrytown, NY 12507. Offers M Div, MRE, D Min. Part-time programs available. *Faculty:* 7 full-time (2 women), 6 part-time/adjunct (1 woman). *Students:* 86 full-time (19 women), 13 part-time (1 woman); includes 25 minority (10 African Americans, 1 American Indian/Alaska Native, 12 Asian Americans or Pacific Islanders, 2 Hispanic Americans), 57 international. Average age 37. In 2008, 6 first professional degrees, 21 master's awarded. *Degree requirements:* For master's, one foreign language, project; for doctorate, thesis/dissertation; for M Div, one foreign language, thesis/dissertation. *Entrance requirements:* For M Div and master's, bachelor's degree; for doctorate, M Div or equivalency. Additional exam requirements/recommendations for international students: Required—TOEFL (minimum score 450 paper-based; 133 computer-based; 45 iBT). *Application deadline:* For fall admission, 8/15 priority date for domestic students; for spring admission, 1/15 priority date for domestic students. Applications are processed on a rolling basis. Application fee: $30. *Expenses:* Tuition: Full-time $10,250; part-time $410 per credit. Required fees: $127 per semester. Tuition and fees vary according to course load, degree level and campus/location. *Financial support:* In 2008–09, 99 students received support; teaching assistantships, career-related internships or fieldwork, institutionally sponsored loans, scholarships/grants, and tuition waivers (partial) available. Financial award applicants required to submit FAFSA. *Faculty research:* Church leadership, church history, world religions, ecumenism, interfaith peace building, service learning. *Unit head:* Dr. Kathy Winings, Academic Dean, 845-752-3000 Ext. 228, Fax: 845-752-3014, E-mail: academics@uts.edu. *Application contact:* Henry Christopher, Director of Admissions, 845-752-3000 Ext. 200, Fax: 845-752-3016, E-mail: admissions@uts.edu.

Unification Theological Seminary, Graduate Program, New York Extension, New York, NY 10036. Offers M Div, MRE. Part-time and evening/weekend programs available. *Faculty:* 4 full-time (1 woman), 10 part-time/adjunct (2 women). *Students:* 21 full-time (9 women), 53 part-time (27 women); includes 65 minority (56 African Americans, 2 American Indian/Alaska Native, 3 Asian Americans or Pacific Islanders, 4 Hispanic Americans), 4 international. Average age 41. In 2008, 3 first professional degrees, 4 master's awarded. *Degree requirements:* For master's, project; for M Div, thesis/dissertation. *Entrance requirements:* For M Div and master's, bachelor's degree. Additional exam requirements/recommendations for international students: Required—TOEFL (minimum score 450 paper-based; 133 computer-based). *Application deadline:* For fall admission, 8/15 priority date for domestic students; for spring admission, 1/15 priority date for domestic students. Applications are processed on a rolling basis. Application fee: $30. *Expenses:* Tuition: Full-time $10,250; part-time $410 per credit. Required fees: $127 per semester. Tuition and fees vary according to course load, degree level and campus/location. *Financial support:* In 2008–09, 74 students received support. Career-related internships or fieldwork, institutionally sponsored loans, scholarships/grants, and tuition waivers (partial) available. Financial award applicants required to submit FAFSA. *Unit head:* Dr. Lonnie McLeod, Dean of the Extension Center, 212-563-6647 Ext. 104, Fax: 212-563-6431, E-mail: LHOPEC@aol.com. *Application contact:* Rev. Leander Hardaway, Admissions Officer, 212-563-6647 Ext. 15, Fax: 212-563-6431, E-mail: lwhardaway@aol.com.

Union Theological Seminary and Presbyterian School of Christian Education, School of Theological Studies, Richmond, VA 23227-4597. Offers M Div, Th M, D Min, PhD, M Div/MA. *Accreditation:* ACIPE; ATS. Terminal master's awarded for partial completion of doctoral program. *Degree requirements:* For master's, oral and written exams; for doctorate, 2 foreign languages, comprehensive exam, thesis/dissertation; for M Div, 2 foreign languages. *Entrance requirements:* For doctorate, GRE General Test. Additional exam requirements/recommendations for international students: Required—TOEFL, TWE.

Union Theological Seminary in the City of New York, Graduate and Professional Programs, New York, NY 10027-5710. Offers M Div, MA, STM, Ed D, PhD, M Div/MSSW. *Accreditation:* ACIPE; ATS (one or more programs are accredited). Part-time programs available. *Degree requirements:* For master's, one foreign language, thesis; for doctorate, 2 foreign languages, thesis/dissertation; for M Div, one foreign language, thesis/dissertation. *Entrance requirements:* For doctorate, GRE General Test, sample of written work. *Faculty research:* American religious history, psychiatry and religion, Christian ethics, New Testament.

United Talmudical Seminary, Graduate Programs, Brooklyn, NY 11211-7900. *Accreditation:* AARTS.

United Theological Seminary, Graduate and Professional Programs, Trotwood, OH 45426. Offers M Div, MA, MATS, D Min, M Div/MA. *Accreditation:* ATS. Part-time and evening/weekend programs available. *Degree requirements:* For master's, thesis (for some programs), comprehensive evaluation; for doctorate, thesis/dissertation, final exam; for M Div, comprehensive evaluation. *Entrance requirements:* For M Div, minimum GPA of 2.5, 5 letters of recommendation, interview; for master's, minimum GPA of 2.5, interview, 5 letters of recommendation; for doctorate, minimum GPA of 3.0, 2 letters of recommendation, interview. Additional exam requirements/recommendations for international students: Required—TOEFL (minimum score 550 paper-based; 213 computer-based). *Application deadline:* For fall admission, 8/1 for domestic students, 1/15 for international students; for spring admission, 1/1 for domestic students. Applications are processed on a rolling basis. Application fee: $40. Electronic applications accepted. *Expenses:* Tuition: Full-time $9746; part-time $443 per hour. Required fees: $80 per semester. Tuition and fees vary according to course load. *Financial support:* In 2008–09, 87 students received support. Career-related internships or fieldwork, Federal Work-Study, and scholarships/grants available. Financial award application deadline: 4/1; financial award applicants required to submit CSS PROFILE or FAFSA. *Unit head:* Rev. Julie M. Hostetter, Director of Academic and Student Services, 937-529-2201 Ext. 330, Fax: 937-529-2292, E-mail: jhostetter@united.edu. *Application contact:* Linda Rice, Admissions Officer, 937-529-2201 Ext. 3307, Fax: 937-529-2292, E-mail: utsadmis@united.edu.

United Theological Seminary of the Twin Cities, Graduate and Professional Programs, New Brighton, MN 55112-2598. Offers advanced theological studies (Diploma); justice and peace studies (M Div); leadership toward racial justice (MA, Certificate); Methodist studies (M Div, MA); ministry (D Min); ministry renewal and professional development (Certificate); pastoral care and counseling (M Div); religion and theology (MA); theological and religious studies (Certificate); theology and the arts (MA); urban ministry (MARL); women's studies: religion, theology and ministry (MA). *Accreditation:* ACIPE; ATS. Part-time and evening/weekend programs available. *Faculty:* 10 full-time (6 women), 24 part-time/adjunct (12 women). *Students:* 60 full-time (34 women), 93 part-time (60 women); includes 10 minority (5 African Americans, 1 American Indian/Alaska Native, 3 Asian Americans or Pacific Islanders, 1 Hispanic American), 1 international. Average age 47. 39 applicants, 100% accepted, 32 enrolled. In 2008, 21 first professional degrees, 9 master's awarded. *Degree requirements:* For master's, thesis; for doctorate, comprehensive exam, thesis/dissertation; for M Div, integrative notebook, spiritual chronicle. *Entrance requirements:* For M Div and master's, minimum GPA of 2.75; strong analytical, reflective thinking and writing skills; vocational and academic goals compatible with those of Seminary; for doctorate, M Div or equivalent, minimum GPA of 3.0, 3 years experience in professional ministry; for other advanced degree, BA or equivalent life experience; strong analytical, reflective thinking and writing skills (Certificate); proficiency in English language, previous study of theology at a theological school, recommendation of student's denomination (Diploma). Additional exam requirements/recommendations for international students: Required—TOEFL (minimum score 550 paper-based). *Application deadline:* For fall admission, 7/1 priority date for domestic students, 11/1 priority date for international students; for winter admission, 11/1 priority date for domestic students; for spring admission, 11/15 priority date for domestic students. Applications are processed on a rolling basis. Application fee: $50. *Expenses:* Tuition: Full-time $11,070; part-time $410 per credit hour. Required fees: $295; $135 per term. One-time fee: $25. Tuition and fees vary according to course load, degree level and program. *Financial support:* In 2008–09, 98 students received support. Career-related internships or fieldwork, institutionally sponsored loans, and scholarships/grants available. Support available to part-time students. Financial award application deadline: 5/1; financial award applicants required to submit FAFSA. *Unit head:* Dr. Richard D. Weis, Dean of the Seminary, 651-255-6108 Ext. 108, Fax: 651-633-4315, E-mail: rweis@unitedseminary.edu. *Application contact:* Rev. Glen Herrington-Hall, Director of Admissions, 651-255-6107 Ext. 107, Fax: 651-633-4315, E-mail: gherrington-hall@unitedseminary.edu.

Université de Montréal, Faculty of Theology and Sciences of Religions, Montréal, QC H3C 3J7, Canada. Offers MA, D Th, PhD, Certificate, DESS, L Th. *Faculty:* 23 full-time (7 women), 5 part-time/adjunct (1 woman). *Students:* 83 full-time (20 women), 17 part-time (12 women). 74 applicants, 36% accepted, 24 enrolled. In 2008, 14 master's, 7 doctorates awarded. *Degree requirements:* For master's, one foreign language; for doctorate, 2 foreign languages, thesis/dissertation, general exam. *Application deadline:* For fall admission, 2/1 priority date for domestic students; for winter admission, 11/1 priority date for domestic students; for spring admission, 2/1 priority date for domestic students. Application fee: $100. Electronic applications accepted. *Financial support:* Research assistantships, teaching assistantships, institutionally sponsored loans and tuition waivers (partial) available. *Unit head:* Jean-Claude Breton, Dean, 514-343-7160, Fax: 514-343-5738, E-mail: jean-claude.breton@umontreal.ca. *Application contact:* Jean-Fran??ois Roussel, Associate Dean of Graduate Studies, 514-343-6840, Fax: 514-343-5738, E-mail: jean-francois.roussel@umontreal.ca.

Université de Sherbrooke, Faculty of Theology, Ethics and Philosophy, Sherbrooke, QC J1K 2R1, Canada. Offers applied ethics (Diploma); human science of religions (MA); intercultural training (Diploma); philosophy (MA, PhD); spiritual anthropology (Diploma); theology (MA, PhD, Diploma). Part-time and evening/weekend programs available. Postbaccalaureate distance learning degree programs offered. Terminal master's awarded for partial completion of doctoral program. *Entrance requirements:* For master's, bachelor's degree in related discipline; for doctorate, master's degree in related discipline. *Faculty research:* Faith and culture interrelation.

Université du Québec à Chicoutimi, Graduate Programs, Program in Theology (Pastoral Studies), Chicoutimi, QC G7H 2B1, Canada. Offers MA, PhD. Part-time programs available. *Degree requirements:* For doctorate, thesis/dissertation. *Entrance requirements:* For master's, appropriate bachelor's degree, proficiency in French; for doctorate, appropriate master's degree, proficiency in French.

Université Laval, Faculty of Theology and Religious Sciences, Program in Practical Theology, Québec, QC G1K 7P4, Canada. Offers D Th P. Part-time programs available. *Degree requirements:* For doctorate, comprehensive exam, thesis/dissertation. *Entrance requirements:* For doctorate, knowledge of French and English. Electronic applications accepted.

Université Laval, Faculty of Theology and Religious Sciences, Programs in Theology, Québec, QC G1K 7P4, Canada. Offers MA, PhD. Terminal master's awarded for partial completion of doctoral program. *Degree requirements:* For master's, thesis (for some programs); for doctorate, comprehensive exam, thesis/dissertation. *Entrance requirements:* For master's and doctorate, knowledge of French, comprehension of written English. Electronic applications accepted.

University of Chicago, Divinity School, Chicago, IL 60637-1513. Offers M Div, AM, AMRS, PhD, JD/M Div, JD/MA, JD/PhD, MPP/M Div, MSW/M Div. *Accreditation:* ATS (one or more programs are accredited). Part-time programs available. *Degree requirements:* For master's and M Div, one foreign language; for doctorate, 2 foreign languages, comprehensive exam, thesis/dissertation. *Entrance requirements:* For M Div, master's, and doctorate, GRE General Test. Additional exam requirements/recommendations for international students: Required—TOEFL (minimum score 600 paper-based; 250 computer-based). Electronic applications accepted. *Expenses:* Contact institution. *Faculty research:* Theology, history of religion, ethics, biblical studies, philosophy of religion.

University of Dallas, Braniff Graduate School of Liberal Arts, Department of Theology, Irving, TX 75062-4736. Offers M Th, MA. Part-time programs available. *Degree requirements:* For master's, one foreign language, comprehensive exam, thesis (for some programs). *Entrance requirements:* For master's, GRE General Test. *Faculty research:* Patristics, justice in the Old and New Testament, Pauline literature, Christology, theology of the Trinity.

University of Dayton, Graduate School, College of Arts and Sciences, Department of Religious Studies, Dayton, OH 45469-1300. Offers pastoral ministry (MA); theological studies (MA); theology (PhD). Part-time and evening/weekend programs available. *Faculty:* 19 full-time (5 women), 5 part-time/adjunct (1 woman). *Students:* 49 full-time (21 women), 20 part-time (14 women); includes 2 minority (1 Asian American or Pacific Islander, 1 Hispanic American), 2 international. Average age 32. 61 applicants, 72% accepted, 23 enrolled. In 2008, 13 master's, 1 doctorate awarded. Terminal master's awarded for partial completion of doctoral program. *Degree requirements:* For master's, thesis or alternative; for doctorate, 2 foreign languages, comprehensive exam, thesis/dissertation. *Entrance requirements:* For master's, minimum undergraduate GPA of 3.0, 3 letters of recommendation, personal statement, official transcript(s); for doctorate, GRE General Test (minimum score of 600 on verbal), minimum GPA of 3.5, academic writing sample, 3 letters of recommendation, personal statement, official transcript(s).

Theology

University of Dayton (continued)

Additional exam requirements/recommendations for international students: Required—TOEFL (minimum score 550 paper-based; 213 computer-based; 80 iBT). *Application deadline:* For fall admission, 3/1 priority date for domestic and international students; for winter admission, 7/1 priority date for international students; for spring admission, 1/1 priority date for international students. Applications are processed on a rolling basis. Application fee: $0 ($50 for international students). Electronic applications accepted. *Expenses:* Contact institution. *Financial support:* In 2008–09, 28 students received support, including 4 fellowships with full tuition reimbursements available (averaging $15,814 per year), 8 research assistantships with full tuition reimbursements available (averaging $9,457 per year), 16 teaching assistantships with full tuition reimbursements available (averaging $15,814 per year); career-related internships or fieldwork, institutionally sponsored loans, scholarships/grants, health care benefits, tuition waivers (full), and unspecified assistantships also available. Support available to part-time students. Financial award application deadline: 3/1; financial award applicants required to submit FAFSA. *Faculty research:* Practical/constructive theology, theological ethics, U.S. Catholic/Christian life and thought, methodologies in Biblical studies, religion and science. *Unit head:* Dr. Sandra Yocum, Chair, 937-229-4321, Fax: 937-229-4330, E-mail: sandra.yocum@notes.udayton.edu. *Application contact:* Angela Jones-Glukhov, Associate Director of Graduate Admissions, 937-229-4305, Fax: 937-229-4729, E-mail: jonesgas@notes.udayton.edu.

University of Denver, Graduate Studies, Joint Program in Religious and Theological Studies, Denver, CO 80208. Offers PhD. Part-time programs available. *Students:* 42 full-time (17 women), 35 part-time (11 women); includes 10 minority (5 African Americans, 1 American Indian/Alaska Native, 2 Asian Americans or Pacific Islanders, 2 Hispanic Americans), 6 international. Average age 38. In 2008, 5 doctorates awarded. *Entrance requirements:* For doctorate, GRE. *Application deadline:* For fall admission, 1/15 for domestic students. Application fee: $50. *Unit head:* Dr. Frank Seeburger, Head, 303-871-2766. *Application contact:* Dr. Frank Seeburger, Head, 303-871-2766.

University of Dubuque, Theological Seminary, Dubuque, IA 52001-5099. Offers M Div, MAR, D Min. *Accreditation:* ACIPE; ATS. Postbaccalaureate distance learning degree programs offered (minimal on-campus study). *Degree requirements:* For doctorate, thesis/dissertation. *Entrance requirements:* Additional exam requirements/recommendations for international students: Recommended—TOEFL (minimum score 550 paper-based; 220 computer-based; 80 iBT). *Faculty research:* Biblical archaeology, biblical theology, reformed history and theology, pastoral theology, homiletics.

University of Mobile, Graduate Programs, Program in Religious Studies, Mobile, AL 36613. Offers biblical/theological studies (MA); marriage and family counseling (MA). Part-time and evening/weekend programs available. *Faculty:* 5 full-time (0 women), 1 part-time/adjunct (0 women). *Students:* 16 full-time (14 women), 41 part-time (33 women); includes 25 minority (23 African Americans, 2 American Indian/Alaska Native). Average age 32. In 2008, 13 master's awarded. *Degree requirements:* For master's, one foreign language, comprehensive exam, thesis optional. *Entrance requirements:* For master's, GRE General Test. Additional exam requirements/recommendations for international students: Required—TOEFL (minimum score 550 paper-based; 213 computer-based; 80 iBT). *Application deadline:* For fall admission, 8/3 priority date for domestic students; for spring admission, 12/23 for domestic students. Applications are processed on a rolling basis. Application fee: $40 ($50 for international students). *Expenses:* Tuition: Full-time $7560; part-time $420 per credit hour. Required fees: $240; $120 per semester. *Financial support:* Federal Work-Study available. Support available to part-time students. Financial award application deadline: 8/1. *Unit head:* Dr. Cecil Taylor, Dean, School of Christian Studies, 251-442-2255, Fax: 251-442-2523, E-mail: ctaylor@mail.umobile.edu. *Application contact:* Tammy C. Eubanks, Administrative Assistant to Dean of Graduate Programs, 251-442-2270, Fax: 251-442-2523, E-mail: teubanks@umobile.edu.

University of Notre Dame, Graduate School, College of Arts and Letters, Division of Humanities, Department of Theology, Notre Dame, IN 46556. Offers M Div, MA, MSM, MTS, PhD. *Accreditation:* ACIPE; ATS. *Faculty:* 54 full-time (14 women), 3 part-time/adjunct (0 women). *Students:* 245 full-time (105 women), 9 part-time (4 women); includes 32 minority (2 African Americans, 10 Asian Americans or Pacific Islanders, 20 Hispanic Americans), 18 international. 404 applicants, 20% accepted, 65 enrolled. In 2008, 10 first professional degrees, 49 master's, 15 doctorates awarded. Terminal master's awarded for partial completion of doctoral program. *Degree requirements:* For master's, one foreign language, comprehensive exam, thesis or alternative; for doctorate, 3 foreign languages, comprehensive exam, thesis/dissertation, candidacy exam. *Entrance requirements:* For M Div, master's, and doctorate, GRE General Test. Additional exam requirements/recommendations for international students: Required—TOEFL (minimum score 600 paper-based; 250 computer-based; 80 iBT). *Application deadline:* For fall admission, 1/2 for domestic and international students. Application fee: $50. Electronic applications accepted. *Financial support:* Fellowships with full tuition reimbursements, research assistantships with full tuition reimbursements, teaching assistantships with full tuition reimbursements, tuition waivers (full) available. Financial award application deadline: 1/2. *Faculty research:* Liturgy, ethics, historical studies, biblical studies, systematic theology. *Unit head:* Dr. John Cavadini, Chair of Theology Department, 574-631-5732, E-mail: theodgs@nd.edu. *Application contact:* Dr. Barbara Turpin, Director of Graduate Admissions, 574-631-7706, Fax: 574-631-4183.

University of Saint Mary of the Lake–Mundelein Seminary, School of Theology, Mundelein, IL 60060. Offers M Div, STB, MA, D Min, Certificate, STL. *Accreditation:* ATS (one or more programs are accredited). *Faculty:* 45 full-time (5 women), 11 part-time/adjunct (1 woman). *Students:* 222 full-time (4 women); includes 10 minority (2 African Americans, 3 Asian Americans or Pacific Islanders, 5 Hispanic Americans), 78 international. Average age 30. 95 applicants, 75% accepted, 71 enrolled. In 2008, 38 first professional degrees, 1 master's, 1 doctorate, 10 other advanced degrees awarded. *Degree requirements:* For doctorate, thesis/dissertation; for first professional degree, thesis/dissertation (for some programs). *Entrance requirements:* For first professional degree, master's, doctorate, and other advanced degree, bachelor's degree. Additional exam requirements/recommendations for international students: Required—TOEFL. *Application deadline:* Applications are processed on a rolling basis. Application fee: $0. Electronic applications accepted. *Expenses:* Tuition: Full-time $18,087; part-time $480 per credit hour. Required fees: $250; $250. One-time fee: $50 full-time. *Financial support:* Career-related internships or fieldwork available. *Unit head:* Rev. Raymond J. Webb, Academic Dean, 847-566-6401. *Application contact:* Rev. Raymond J. Webb, Academic Dean, 847-566-6401.

University of St. Michael's College, Faculty of Theology, Toronto, ON M5S 1J4, Canada. Offers Catholic leadership (MA); eastern Christian studies (Certificate, Diploma); religious education (Diploma); theological studies (Diploma); theology (M Div, MA, MRE, MTS, D Min, PhD, Th D); theology and ecology (Certificate); theology and Jewish studies (MA). *Accreditation:* ATS (one or more programs are accredited). Part-time programs available. *Degree requirements:* For master's, thesis (for some programs), 1 foreign language (MA), 2 foreign languages (Th M); for doctorate, 3 foreign languages, comprehensive exam, thesis/dissertation; for M Div, thesis/dissertation optional; for other advanced degree, thesis optional. *Entrance requirements:* For M Div and other advanced degree, minimum GPA of 2.7; for master's, M Div or BA, course work in an ancient or modern language, minimum GPA of 3.3; for doctorate, MA in theology, Th M, or M Div with thesis, minimum GPA of 3.7. Additional exam requirements/recommendations for international students: Required—TOEFL (minimum score 600 paper-based; 250 computer-based). Electronic applications accepted. *Faculty research:* Patristics, eastern Christianity, ecology and theology, ecumenism, Jewish Christian studies.

University of St. Thomas, Graduate Studies, Saint Paul Seminary School of Divinity, Program in Divinity, St. Paul, MN 55105-1096. Offers M Div. *Accreditation:* ACIPE; ATS. Part-time programs available. *Entrance requirements:* MAT, interview, 3 letters of recommendation. Additional exam requirements/recommendations for international students: Required—TOEFL (minimum score 550 paper-based; 213 computer-based). *Faculty research:* Theological education.

University of St. Thomas, Graduate Studies, Saint Paul Seminary School of Divinity, Program in Theology/Pastoral Studies, St. Paul, MN 55105-1096. Offers religious education (MARE); theology (MA). *Accreditation:* ACIPE; ATS. Part-time and evening/weekend programs available. *Degree requirements:* For master's, one foreign language, comprehensive exam, thesis or alternative. *Entrance requirements:* For master's, GRE, interview, 3 letters of recommendation. Additional exam requirements/recommendations for international students: Required—TOEFL (minimum score 550 paper-based; 213 computer-based). Electronic applications accepted. *Expenses:* Contact institution. *Faculty research:* Theological education.

University of St. Thomas, School of Theology, Houston, TX 77006-4696. Offers M Div, MAPS, MAT. *Accreditation:* ACIPE; ATS. Part-time programs available. *Faculty:* 10 full-time (3 women), 7 part-time/adjunct (1 woman). *Students:* 85 full-time (9 women), 105 part-time (43 women); includes 41 minority (5 African Americans, 11 Asian Americans or Pacific Islanders, 25 Hispanic Americans), 20 international. Average age 40. 44 applicants, 86% accepted, 30 enrolled. In 2008, 19 M Divs, 29 master's awarded. *Degree requirements:* For master's, comprehensive exam (MAT). *Entrance requirements:* For M Div, minimum GPA of 2.0 in philosophy and theology; for master's, minimum GPA of 2.3 (MAPS); 3.0 in theology, philosophy, or religious studies (MAT). Additional exam requirements/recommendations for international students: Required—TOEFL (minimum score 550 paper-based; 213 computer-based). *Application deadline:* Applications are processed on a rolling basis. Application fee: $35. Electronic applications accepted. *Expenses:* Contact institution. *Financial support:* In 2008–09, 14 students received support. Federal Work-Study and scholarships/grants available. Support available to part-time students. Financial award application deadline: 3/1; financial award applicants required to submit FAFSA. *Unit head:* Dr. Sandra C. Magie, Dean, 713-686-4345 Ext. 242, Fax: 713-683-8673, E-mail: smagie@stthom.edu. *Application contact:* Connie Henry, Office Manager, 713-686-4345 Ext. 231, Fax: 713-683-8673, E-mail: henryc@stthom.edu.

University of San Francisco, College of Arts and Sciences, Department of Theology and Religious Studies, San Francisco, CA 94117-1080. Offers theology (MA). Part-time and evening/weekend programs available. *Degree requirements:* For master's, thesis or alternative. *Entrance requirements:* For master's, minimum GPA of 2.7. *Faculty research:* World religions, sacraments, psychology and religion, Bible, liberation theology, moral theology.

The University of Scranton, College of Graduate and Continuing Education, Program in Theology, Scranton, PA 18510. Offers MA. Part-time and evening/weekend programs available. *Faculty:* 14 full-time (5 women). *Students:* 1 full-time (0 women), 16 part-time (6 women); includes 1 minority (Hispanic American), 1 international. Average age 32. 9 applicants, 89% accepted. In 2008, 2 master's awarded. *Degree requirements:* For master's, thesis (for some programs), capstone experience. *Entrance requirements:* For master's, minimum GPA of 2.75. Additional exam requirements/recommendations for international students: Required—TOEFL (minimum score 500 paper-based; 173 computer-based), IELTS (minimum score 5.5). *Application deadline:* Applications are processed on a rolling basis. Application fee: $50. *Expenses:* Contact institution. *Financial support:* In 2008–09, 2 students received support, including 2 teaching assistantships with full tuition reimbursements available (averaging $3,300 per year); career-related internships or fieldwork, Federal Work-Study, and unspecified assistantships also available. Support available to part-time students. Financial award application deadline: 3/1. *Unit head:* Dr. Charles R. Pinches, Chair, 570-941-4302, Fax: 570-941-6369, E-mail: pinchesc1@scranton.edu. *Application contact:* Joseph M. Roback, Director of Admissions, 570-941-4385, Fax: 570-941-5928, E-mail: roback j2@scranton.edu.

University of South Africa, College of Human Sciences, Pretoria, South Africa. Offers adult education (M Ed); African languages (MA, PhD); African politics (MA, PhD); Afrikaans (MA, PhD); ancient history (MA, PhD); ancient Near Eastern studies (MA, PhD); anthropology (MA, PhD); applied linguistics (MA); Arabic (MA, PhD); archaeology (MA); art history (MA); Biblical archaeology (MA); Biblical studies (M Th, D Th, PhD); Christian spirituality (M Th, D Th); church history (M Th, D Th); classical studies (MA, PhD); clinical psychology (MA); communication (MA, PhD); comparative education (M Ed, Ed D); consulting psychology (D Admin, D Com, PhD); curriculum studies (M Ed, Ed D); development studies (M Admin, MA, D Admin, PhD); didactics (M Ed, Ed D); education (M Tech); education management (M Ed, Ed D); educational psychology (M Ed); English (MA); environmental education (M Ed); French (MA, PhD); German (MA, PhD); Greek (MA); guidance and counseling (M Ed); health studies (MA, PhD), including health sciences education (MA), health services management (MA), medical and surgical nursing science (critical care general) (MA), midwifery and neonatal nursing science (MA), trauma and emergency care (MA); history (MA, PhD); history of education (Ed D); inclusive education (M Ed, Ed D); information and communications technology policy and regulation (MA); information science (MA, MIS, PhD); international politics (MA, PhD); Islamic studies (MA, PhD); Italian (MA, PhD); Judaica (MA, PhD); linguistics (MA, PhD); mathematical education (M Ed); mathematics education (MA); missiology (M Th, D Th); modern Hebrew (MA, PhD); musicology (MA, MMus, D Mus, PhD); natural science education (M Ed); New Testament (M Th, D Th); Old Testament (D Th); pastoral therapy (M Th, D Th); philosophy (MA); philosophy of education (M Ed, Ed D); politics (MA, PhD); Portuguese (MA, PhD); practical theology (M Th, D Th); psychology (MA, MS, PhD); psychology of education (M Ed, Ed D); public health (MA); religious studies (MA, D Th, PhD); Romance languages (MA); Russian (MA, PhD); Semitic languages (MA, PhD); social behavior studies in HIV/AIDS (MA); social science (mental health) (MA); social science in development studies (MA); social science in psychology (MA); social science in social work (MA); social science in sociology (MA); social work (MSW, DSW, PhD); socio-education (M Ed, Ed D); sociolinguistics (MA); sociology (MA, PhD); Spanish (MA, PhD); systematic theology (M Th, D Th); TESOL (teaching English to speakers of other languages) (MA); theological ethics (M Th, D Th); theory of literature (MA, PhD); urban ministries (D Th); urban ministry (M Th).

University of Trinity College, Faculty of Divinity, Toronto, ON M5S 1H8, Canada. Offers ministry (Diploma); ministry for church musicians (Diploma); theology (M Div, MTS, Th M, D Min, PhD, Th D, Diploma, L Th); M Div/MA. *Accreditation:* ATS. Part-time programs available. *Faculty:* 4 full-time (1 woman), 34 part-time/adjunct (7 women). *Students:* 51 full-time (19 women), 72 part-time (35 women). Average age 45. *Degree requirements:* For master's, 2 foreign languages, thesis (for some programs); for doctorate, 3 foreign languages, comprehensive exam, thesis/dissertation; for M Div, thesis/dissertation optional; for other advanced degree, thesis (for some programs). *Entrance requirements:* For M Div, interview; for master's, 1 language (modern or ancient), interview; for doctorate, 2 languages (modern and ancient). Additional exam requirements/recommendations for international students: Required—TOEFL, TWE. *Application deadline:* For fall admission, 3/31 priority date for domestic and international students; for winter admission, 12/31 for domestic and international students; for spring admission, 4/30 priority date for domestic and international students. Applications are processed on a rolling basis. Application fee: $0. Tuition and fees charges are reported in Canadian dollars. *Expenses:* Tuition: Full-time $5669 Canadian dollars; part-time $1889 Canadian dollars per course. Required fees: $400 Canadian dollars; $50 Canadian dollars per semester. Tuition and fees vary according to degree level. *Financial support:* Fellowships, teaching assistantships, career-related internships or fieldwork, institutionally sponsored loans, and bursaries available. Support available to part-time students. Financial award application deadline: 5/15. *Faculty research:* Interreligious dialogue, feminist theology, systematic theology, philosophy of religion, pastoral theology. *Unit head:* Dr. David Neelands, Dean, 416-978-7750, Fax: 416-978-4949, E-mail: divdean@trinity.utoronto.ca. *Application contact:* Rachel Richards, Administrative Assistant to the Dean, 416-978-2133, Fax: 416-978-4949, E-mail: divinity@trinity.utoronto.ca.

The University of Winnipeg, Faculty of Theology, Winnipeg, MB R3B 2E9, Canada. Offers marriage and family therapy (MMFT, Certificate); sacred theology (STM); theology (M Div). *Accreditation:* AAMFT/COAMFTE; ATS. Part-time programs available. *Degree requirements:* For M Div, thesis/dissertation optional.

Ursuline College, School of Graduate Studies, Graduate Program in Ministry, Pepper Pike, OH 44124-4398. Offers MA. Part-time programs available. *Faculty:* 1 (woman) full-time, 1 (woman) part-time/adjunct. *Students:* 19 part-time (16 women); includes 3 minority (2 African

Americans, 1 Hispanic American). Average age 36. 3 applicants, 100% accepted, 2 enrolled. In 2008, 7 master's awarded. *Degree requirements:* For master's, thesis. *Entrance requirements:* For master's, minimum undergraduate GPA of 3.0, interview. Additional exam requirements/recommendations for international students: Required—TOEFL (minimum score 500 paper-based; 173 computer-based). *Application deadline:* For fall admission, 8/1 priority date for domestic students. Applications are processed on a rolling basis. Application fee: $25. *Expenses:* Contact institution. *Financial support:* In 2008–09, 15 students received support. Federal Work-Study available. Financial award application deadline: 3/1; financial award applicants required to submit FAFSA. *Unit head:* Dr. Linda Martin, Co-Director, 440-646-8191, Fax: 440-684-6088, E-mail: lmartin@ursuline.edu. *Application contact:* Lauren Anderson, Secretary, 440-646-8119, Fax: 440-684-6088, E-mail: gradsch@ursuline.edu.

Valparaiso University, Graduate Division, Program in Liberal Studies, Concentration in Theology, Valparaiso, IN 46383. Offers MALS, Post-Master's Certificate, JD/MALS. Part-time and evening/weekend programs available. *Entrance requirements:* For master's, minimum GPA of 3.0. Additional exam requirements/recommendations for international students: Required—TOEFL (minimum score 550 paper-based; 213 computer-based). *Application deadline:* Applications are processed on a rolling basis. Application fee: $30 ($50 for international students). Electronic applications accepted. *Financial support:* Available to part-time students. Applicants required to submit FAFSA. *Unit head:* Dr. David L. Rowland, Dean, Graduate Studies and Continuing Education, 219-464-5313, Fax: 219-464-5381, E-mail: David.Rowland@valpo.edu. *Application contact:* Jamie Haney, Coordinator of Recruitment Activities, 219-464-5313, Fax: 219-464-5381, E-mail: Jamie.Haney@valpo.edu.

Valparaiso University, Graduate Division, Program in Liberal Studies, Concentration in Theology and Ministry, Valparaiso, IN 46383. Offers MALS, Post-Master's Certificate. Part-time and evening/weekend programs available. *Students:* 1 (woman) part-time. Average age 35. *Entrance requirements:* For master's, minimum GPA of 3.0. Additional exam requirements/recommendations for international students: Required—TOEFL (minimum score 550 paper-based; 213 computer-based). *Application deadline:* Applications are processed on a rolling basis. Application fee: $30 ($50 for international students). Electronic applications accepted. *Financial support:* Available to part-time students. Applicants required to submit FAFSA. *Unit head:* Dr. David L. Rowland, Dean, Graduate Studies and Continuing Education, 219-464-5313, Fax: 219-464-5381, E-mail: David.Rowland@valpo.edu. *Application contact:* Jamie Haney, Coordinator of Recruitment Activities, 219-464-5313, Fax: 219-464-5381, E-mail: Jamie.Haney@valpo.edu.

Vancouver School of Theology, Graduate and Professional Programs, Vancouver, BC V6T 1L4, Canada. Offers spiritual direction (Graduate Diploma); theological studies (MATS); theology (M Div, Th M, Dip CS). *Accreditation:* ATS. Part-time programs available. *Degree requirements:* For master's, comprehensive exam (for some programs), thesis (for some programs); for M Div, thesis/dissertation (for some programs); for other advanced degree, one foreign language, thesis. *Entrance requirements:* Additional exam requirements/recommendations for international students: Required—TOEFL. Electronic applications accepted. *Faculty research:* Old Testament studies, pastoral theology, New Testament studies, field education, church history, systematic theology, spirituality.

Vanderbilt University, Divinity School, Nashville, TN 37240-1001. Offers M Div, MTS, JD/M Div, JD/MTS, MBA/M Div, MBA/MTS, MD/M Div, MD/MTS, MSN/M Div, MSN/MTS. *Accreditation:* ACIPE; ATS. Part-time programs available. *Entrance requirements:* Additional exam requirements/recommendations for international students: Required—TOEFL (minimum score 630 paper-based; 250 computer-based; 100 iBT). Electronic applications accepted. *Expenses:* Contact institution.

Vanguard University of Southern California, Graduate Programs in Religion, Costa Mesa, CA 92626-9601. Offers leadership studies (MA); theological studies (MTS). Part-time and evening/weekend programs available. *Faculty:* 5 full-time (0 women), 1 part-time/adjunct (0 women). *Students:* 21 full-time (5 women), 54 part-time (17 women); includes 13 minority (1 African American, 1 American Indian/Alaska Native, 3 Asian Americans or Pacific Islanders, 8 Hispanic Americans), 2 international. Average age 38. 21 applicants, 57% accepted, 9 enrolled. *Degree requirements:* For master's, one foreign language, comprehensive exam, thesis (for some programs). *Entrance requirements:* For master's, minimum GPA of 3.0; course work in humanities, religion, and social sciences (MA); minimum GPA of 2.5 (MTS). Additional exam requirements/recommendations for international students: Required—TOEFL (minimum score 550 paper-based; 213 computer-based; 79 iBT). *Application deadline:* For fall admission, 4/1 priority date for domestic and international students; for spring admission, 10/1 priority date for domestic and international students. Applications are processed on a rolling basis. Application fee: $45. Electronic applications accepted. *Expenses:* Contact institution. *Financial support:* In 2008–09, 3 teaching assistantships (averaging $3,333 per year) were awarded; scholarships/grants, tuition waivers (partial), and unspecified assistantships also available. Financial award application deadline: 3/2. *Faculty research:* Apocalyptic literature, narrative theology, ecumenism and Pentecost. *Unit head:* Dr. Richard Israel, Associate Dean, 714-556-3610 Ext. 3223, Fax: 714-957-9317. *Application contact:* Angel McGee, Secretary, Graduate Program in Religion, 714-556-3610 Ext. 3237, Fax: 714-957-9317, E-mail: angel.mcgee@vanguard.edu.

Victoria University, Emmanuel College, Toronto, ON M5S 1K7, Canada. Offers M Div, MA, MPS, MRE, MTS, Th M, D Min, PhD, Th D, Certificate, Diploma, L Th, M Div/MA, M Div/MPS, M Div/MRE. *Accreditation:* ATS. Part-time programs available. *Faculty:* 11 full-time (5 women), 9 part-time/adjunct (3 women). *Students:* 97 full-time (54 women), 52 part-time (34 women); includes 18 minority (2 African Americans, 1 American Indian/Alaska Native, 11 Asian Americans or Pacific Islanders, 4 Hispanic Americans), 7 international. Average age 42. 56 applicants, 88% accepted, 34 enrolled. In 2008, 18 first professional degrees, 2 master's, 3 doctorates, 3 other advanced degrees awarded. Terminal master's awarded for partial completion of doctoral program. *Degree requirements:* For master's, 2 foreign languages, thesis (for some programs); for doctorate, 2 foreign languages, thesis/dissertation; for M Div, one foreign language, thesis/dissertation optional. *Entrance requirements:* For M Div and other advanced degree, BA, B Sc; for master's, BA, BSc; for doctorate, M Div, MA, MTS, ThM. Additional exam requirements/recommendations for international students: Required—TOEFL (minimum score 600 paper-based; 250 computer-based; 100 iBT), IELTS (minimum score 7), TWE (minimum score 5). *Application deadline:* For fall admission, 6/30 for domestic students, 1/15 for international students; for winter admission, 11/30 for domestic students; for spring admission, 3/30 for domestic students. Application fee: $0. Electronic applications accepted. Tuition and fees charges are reported in Canadian dollars. *Expenses:* Tuition: Full-time $5670 Canadian dollars. Required fees: $325 Canadian dollars. One-time fee: $35 Canadian dollars full-time. *Financial support:* In 2008–09, 78 students received support, including 2 fellowships (averaging $11,000 per year), 13 teaching assistantships (averaging $11,000 per year); career-related internships or fieldwork and scholarships/grants also available. Support available to part-time students. Financial award application deadline: 5/30. *Faculty research:* New Testament and Old Testament hermeneutics, religious symbolism, Reformation, liberation theology, Canadian church history. *Unit head:* Dr. Mark G. Toulouse, Principal, 416-585-4540, Fax: 416-585-4516, E-mail: m.toulouse@utoronto.ca. *Application contact:* Wanda Chin, Registrar, 416-585-4538, Fax: 416-585-4516, E-mail: wanda.chin@utoronto.ca.

Villanova University, Graduate School of Liberal Arts and Sciences, Department of Theology, Villanova, PA 19085-1699. Offers MA. Part-time and evening/weekend programs available. *Faculty:* 5 full-time (2 women), 1 part-time/adjunct (0 women). *Students:* 13 full-time (6 women), 14 part-time (7 women); includes 3 minority (1 African American, 1 Asian American or Pacific Islander, 1 Hispanic American). Average age 31. 21 applicants, 100% accepted, 13 enrolled. In 2008, 10 master's awarded. *Degree requirements:* For master's, one foreign language, comprehensive exam, thesis optional. *Entrance requirements:* For master's, GRE, minimum GPA of 3.0. *Application deadline:* For fall admission, 8/1 for domestic and international students; for spring admission, 12/1 for domestic and international students. Applications are processed on a rolling basis. Application fee: $50. Electronic applications accepted. *Financial support:* Research assistantships, Federal Work-Study and scholarships/grants available. Financial award applicants required to submit FAFSA. *Unit head:* Dr. Bernard Prusak, Chair, 610-519-7423. *Application contact:* Dr. Gerald Long, Dean, Graduate School of Liberal Arts and Sciences, 610-519-7093, Fax: 610-519-7096.

Virginia Union University, School of Theology, Richmond, VA 23220-1170. Offers M Div, D Min. *Accreditation:* ACIPE; ATS. Part-time and evening/weekend programs available. *Entrance requirements:* Additional exam requirements/recommendations for international students: Required—TOEFL.

Walsh University, Graduate Studies, Program in Theology, North Canton, OH 44720-3396. Offers MA. *Faculty:* 1 full-time (0 women), 8 part-time/adjunct (4 women). *Students:* 21 part-time (14 women). Average age 48. 7 applicants, 86% accepted, 6 enrolled. *Degree requirements:* For master's, thesis (for some programs). *Entrance requirements:* For master's, MAT, minimum GPA of 3.0. *Application deadline:* For fall admission, 7/15 priority date for domestic students. Applications are processed on a rolling basis. Application fee: $25. Electronic applications accepted. *Expenses:* Tuition: Full-time $9450; part-time $525 per credit. Part-time tuition and fees vary according to course load and program. *Financial support:* In 2008–09, 6 students received support; research assistantships with tuition reimbursements available available. Financial award application deadline: 12/31. *Faculty research:* Service learning, agents of change, Biblical studies, Augustine's De Trinitate, religious identity, historical theology. *Unit head:* Dr. David Baxter, Dean of Instruction, 330-490-7045, Fax: 330-490-7287, E-mail: dbaxter@walsh.edu. *Application contact:* Angela Piverotto, Director of Graduate and Transfer Admissions, 830-490-7174, Fax: 330-490-7165, E-mail: apiverotto@walsh.edu.

Warner Pacific College, Graduate Programs, Portland, OR 97215-4099. Offers biblical and theological studies (MA); biblical studies (M Rel); education (M Ed); management/organizational leadership (MS); pastoral ministries (M Rel); religion and ethics (M Rel); teaching (MA); theology (M Rel). Part-time programs available. *Degree requirements:* For master's, thesis or alternative, Presentation of Defense. *Entrance requirements:* For master's, interview, minimum GPA of 2.5, letters of recommendations. *Faculty research:* New Testament studies, nineteenth-century Wesleyan theology, preaching and church growth, Christian ethics.

Wartburg Theological Seminary, Graduate and Professional Programs, Dubuque, IA 52004-5004. Offers diaconal ministry (MA); theology (M Div, MA, MATDE, STM). *Accreditation:* ACIPE; ATS. *Degree requirements:* For master's, thesis (for some programs); for M Div, thesis/dissertation optional. *Entrance requirements:* For M Div, minimum GPA of 2.5; for master's, minimum GPA of 3.0 (STM). Additional exam requirements/recommendations for international students: Required—TOEFL (minimum score 500 paper-based; 173 computer-based; 80 iBT). Electronic applications accepted.

Washington Theological Union, Graduate and Professional Programs, Washington, DC 20012. Offers M Div, MA, MAPS, MTS, D Min, M Div/MA. *Accreditation:* ACIPE; ATS. Part-time programs available. Postbaccalaureate distance learning degree programs offered. *Degree requirements:* For master's, one foreign language, comprehensive exam, thesis. *Entrance requirements:* For M Div, 18 hours of course work in philosophy; for master's, 18 hours of course work in philosophy and religious studies.

Wesley Biblical Seminary, Graduate Programs, Jackson, MS 39206. Offers Biblical literature (MA); Christian studies (MA); evangelism (M Div); family life ministry (M Div); honors research (M Div); missions (M Div); pastoral ministry (M Div); teaching (M Div); theology (MA). *Accreditation:* ATS. Part-time programs available. *Degree requirements:* For master's, thesis. *Entrance requirements:* Additional exam requirements/recommendations for international students: Required—TOEFL. Electronic applications accepted. *Faculty research:* Patristics, missiology, culture, hermeneutics.

Wesley Theological Seminary, Graduate and Professional Programs, Washington, DC 20016-5690. Offers M Div, MA, MTS, D Min, M Div/MA, M Div/MTS. *Accreditation:* ACIPE; ATS. Part-time programs available. *Degree requirements:* For master's, thesis; for doctorate, thesis/dissertation; for M Div, thesis/dissertation or alternative. *Entrance requirements:* For M Div and master's, minimum GPA of 2.7; for doctorate, minimum GPA of 3.0.

Western Seminary, Graduate Programs, Program in Biblical and Theological Studies, Portland, OR 97215-3367. Offers biblical and theological studies (MA, G Dip); biblical studies (Certificate); theology (Th M). *Accreditation:* ATS. Part-time programs available. *Degree requirements:* For master's, thesis or alternative, practicum.

Western Seminary–Sacramento Campus, Graduate Programs, Sacramento, CA 95821. Offers exegetical theology (MA); marital and family therapy (MA); ministry (M Div); specialized ministry (MA). Postbaccalaureate distance learning degree programs offered. *Entrance requirements:* For M Div, minimum GPA of 2.5; for master's, minimum GPA of 3.0.

Western Seminary–San Jose Campus, Graduate Programs, Los Gatos, CA 95032-4520. Offers exegetical theology (MA); expositional ministry (M Div); marital and family therapy (MA); ministry (M Div); pastoral ministry (M Div); specialized ministry (MA). Postbaccalaureate distance learning degree programs offered. *Degree requirements:* For master's, 2 foreign languages; for M Div, 3 foreign languages. *Entrance requirements:* For M Div, minimum GPA of 2.5; for master's, minimum GPA of 3.0.

Western Theological Seminary, Graduate and Professional Programs, Holland, MI 49423-3622. Offers M Div, M Th, D Min. *Accreditation:* ACIPE; ATS. Part-time programs available. Postbaccalaureate distance learning degree programs offered (minimal on-campus study). *Degree requirements:* For doctorate, 2 foreign languages, thesis/dissertation; for M Div, 2 foreign languages. *Entrance requirements:* For doctorate, 5 years of experience in the ministry (must be ordained). Additional exam requirements/recommendations for international students: Required—TOEFL.

Westminster Seminary California, Programs in Theology, Escondido, CA 92027-4128. Offers Biblical studies (MA); historical theology (MA); theological studies (M Div, MA). *Accreditation:* ATS. Part-time and evening/weekend programs available. *Degree requirements:* For master's, 2 foreign languages, thesis (for some programs); for M Div, 2 foreign languages, internship. *Entrance requirements:* For M Div and master's, 2 letters of reference. Additional exam requirements/recommendations for international students: Required—TOEFL (minimum score 570 paper-based; 230 computer-based; 89 iBT), TWE (minimum score 4.5). *Faculty research:* Neo-paganism, New Testament background, eschatology, Protestant scholasticism, Ezekiel.

Westminster Theological Seminary, Graduate and Professional Programs, Philadelphia, PA 19118. Offers apologetics (Th M); Biblical and urban studies (Certificate); Biblical counseling (MA); biblical studies (MAR); Christian studies (Certificate); church history (Th M); counseling (M Div); general studies (M Div, MAR); hermeneutics and Bible interpretations (PhD); historical and theological studies (PhD); historical theology (Th M); New Testament (Th M); Old Testament (Th M); pastoral counseling (D Min); pastoral ministry (M Div, D Min); systematic theology (Th M); theological studies (MAR); urban missions (M Div, MA, MAR, D Min). *Accreditation:* ATS. Part-time programs available. Terminal master's awarded for partial completion of doctoral program. *Degree requirements:* For master's, thesis (for some programs); for doctorate, 4 foreign languages, comprehensive exam (for some programs), thesis/dissertation; for M Div, 2 foreign languages. *Entrance requirements:* For doctorate, GRE General Test. Additional exam requirements/recommendations for international students: Required—TOEFL, TWE.

Wheaton College, Graduate School, Department of Biblical and Theological Studies, Program in Biblical and Theological Studies, Wheaton, IL 60187-5593. Offers PhD. *Degree requirements:* For doctorate, thesis/dissertation. *Entrance requirements:* For doctorate, GRE. Electronic applications accepted.

Wheaton College, Graduate School, Department of Biblical and Theological Studies, Program in Biblical Archaeology, Wheaton, IL 60187-5593. Offers MA. *Degree requirements:* For master's,

Theology

Wheaton College *(continued)*
thesis or alternative, semester of study in Israel. *Entrance requirements:* For master's, GRE General Test or MAT. Electronic applications accepted.

Wheaton College, Graduate School, Department of Biblical and Theological Studies, Program in Biblical Exegesis, Wheaton, IL 60187-5593. Offers MA. *Degree requirements:* For master's, 2 foreign languages, thesis or alternative. *Entrance requirements:* For master's, GRE General Test or MAT. Electronic applications accepted.

Wheaton College, Graduate School, Department of Biblical and Theological Studies, Program in Biblical Studies, Wheaton, IL 60187-5593. Offers MA. Part-time programs available. *Degree requirements:* For master's, one foreign language, thesis optional. *Entrance requirements:* For master's, GRE General Test, MAT. Electronic applications accepted.

Wheaton College, Graduate School, Department of Biblical and Theological Studies, Program in General History of Christianity, Wheaton, IL 60187-5593. Offers biblical and theological studies (MA). Part-time and evening/weekend programs available. *Degree requirements:* For master's, thesis optional. *Entrance requirements:* For master's, GRE General Test, MAT.

Wheaton College, Graduate School, Department of Biblical and Theological Studies, Program in Historical and Systematic Theology, Wheaton, IL 60187-5593. Offers biblical and theological studies (MA). Electronic applications accepted.

Wilfrid Laurier University, Waterloo Lutheran Seminary, Waterloo, ON N2L 3C5, Canada. Offers Christian ethics (M Th); divinity (M Div); homiletics (M Th); ministry (D Min); pastoral counseling (M Th); spirituality in a health care setting (Diploma); theological studies (MTS); theology (Diploma); M Div/MTS/MSW. *Accreditation:* ATS. Part-time programs available. *Degree requirements:* For master's, one foreign language, thesis (for some programs); for doctorate, thesis/dissertation; for M Div, one foreign language, thesis/dissertation. *Entrance requirements:* For M Div, denominational endorsement; for master's, M Div, 2 units of clinical pastoral education (M Th); for doctorate, M Div, 3 years of ministry experience, proficiency in a foreign language, basic training in clinical pastoral education. Additional exam requirements/recommendations for international students: Required—TOEFL (minimum score 573 paper-based; 230 computer-based; 89 iBT), IELTS (minimum score 7). Electronic applications accepted. *Expenses:* Contact institution. *Faculty research:* Biblical study, church history, systematic theology.

Winebrenner Theological Seminary, Graduate Programs, Findlay, OH 45840. Offers church development (MA); family ministry (MA); theological study (MA); theological/ministerial studies (D Min); theology/ministerial studies (M Div). *Accreditation:* ATS (one or more programs are accredited). Part-time and evening/weekend programs available. *Faculty:* 6 full-time (1 woman), 5 part-time/adjunct (2 women). *Students:* 50 full-time (14 women), 49 part-time (20 women); includes 9 minority (all African Americans), 3 international. Average age 38. 16 applicants, 94% accepted, 13 enrolled. In 2008, 10 first professional degrees, 10 master's awarded. *Degree requirements:* For master's, supervised ministry, theological summit; for doctorate, thesis/dissertation, research project; for M Div, 2 foreign languages, supervised ministry, theological summit. *Entrance requirements:* For M Div and master's, background check; for doctorate, 3 years of post-M Div full-time ministry, background check. Additional exam requirements/recommendations for international students: Required—TOEFL (minimum score 550 paper-based; 213 computer-based). *Application deadline:* For fall admission, 8/15 priority date for domestic students; for winter admission, 12/15 priority date for domestic students; for spring admission, 4/15 priority date for domestic students. Applications are processed on a rolling basis. Application fee: $25. Electronic applications accepted. *Expenses:* Tuition: Full-time $10,500; part-time $410 per credit hour. Required fees: $110 per trimester. *Financial support:* In 2008–09, 32 students received support. Institutionally sponsored loans, scholarships/grants, and tuition waivers (partial) available. Support available to part-time students. Financial award application deadline: 7/1; financial award applicants required to submit FAFSA. *Faculty research:* Biblical languages (Hebrew, Koine Greek), Christian counseling, spiritual formation, church history, ecclesiology. *Unit head:* Dr. M. John Nissley, Vice President for Academic Advancement, 419-434-4247, Fax: 419-434-4267, E-mail: jnissley@winebrenner.edu. *Application*

contact: Jim Wilder, Regional Coordinator, 419-434-4220, Fax: 419-434-4267, E-mail: admissions@winebrenner.edu.

Wycliffe College, Division of Advanced Degree Studies, Toronto, ON M5S 1H7, Canada. Offers MA, Th M, D Min, PhD, Th D. *Accreditation:* ATS (one or more programs are accredited). Part-time programs available. Terminal master's awarded for partial completion of doctoral program. *Degree requirements:* For master's, 2 foreign languages, thesis (for some programs); for doctorate, 3 foreign languages, thesis/dissertation. *Entrance requirements:* Additional exam requirements/recommendations for international students: Required—TOEFL (minimum score 600 paper-based; 250 computer-based). *Expenses:* Contact institution. *Faculty research:* Old and New Testament, doctrine, ethics, philosophy, history.

Wycliffe College, Division of Basic Degree Studies, Toronto, ON M5S 1H7, Canada. Offers Christian Studies (Diploma); theology (M Div, M Rel, MTS). *Accreditation:* ATS. Part-time programs available. *Degree requirements:* For master's, one foreign language, thesis; for M Div, thesis/dissertation optional. *Entrance requirements:* Additional exam requirements/recommendations for international students: Required—TOEFL (minimum score 580 paper-based).

Xavier University, College of Arts and Sciences, Department of Theology, Cincinnati, OH 45207. Offers MA. Part-time programs available. *Faculty:* 13 full-time (5 women). *Students:* 4 full-time (1 woman), 23 part-time (12 women). Average age 36. 11 applicants, 73% accepted, 7 enrolled. In 2008, 6 master's awarded. *Degree requirements:* For master's, thesis optional, final paper and defense. *Entrance requirements:* For master's, MAT or GRE, letters of recommendation, transcripts. Additional exam requirements/recommendations for international students: Required—TOEFL (minimum score 550 paper-based; 213 computer-based). *Application deadline:* Applications are processed on a rolling basis. Application fee: $35. Electronic applications accepted. Tuition and fees vary according to course load, degree level and program. *Financial support:* In 2008–09, 7 teaching assistantships with partial tuition reimbursements were awarded. Financial award applicants required to submit FAFSA. *Faculty research:* Scripture, ethics, constructive theology, historical theology. *Unit head:* Dr. Marie Giblin, Chair, 513-745-2021, Fax: 513-745-3215, E-mail: giblin@xavier.edu. *Application contact:* Dr. Marie Giblin, Chair, 513-745-2021, Fax: 513-745-3215, E-mail: giblin@xavier.edu.

Xavier University of Louisiana, Graduate School, Institute for Black Catholic Studies, New Orleans, LA 70125-1098. Offers pastoral theology (Th M). Part-time programs available. *Degree requirements:* For master's, comprehensive exam, practicum. *Entrance requirements:* For master's, GRE General Test, MAT, minimum GPA of 2.5. Additional exam requirements/recommendations for international students: Required—TOEFL.

Yale University, Divinity School, New Haven, CT 06511. Offers M Div, MAR, STM, JD/M Div, JD/MAR, M Div/MBA, M Div/MF, M Div/MSN, M Div/MSW, MAR/MF, MAR/MSN, MAR/MSW, MD/M Div, MD/MAR. *Accreditation:* ACIPE; ATS. Part-time programs available. *Entrance requirements:* Additional exam requirements/recommendations for international students: Required—IELTS (minimum score 7). Electronic applications accepted. *Expenses:* Contact institution.

Yeshiva Beth Moshe, Graduate Programs, Scranton, PA 18505-2124. Offers Second Talmudical Degree, Talmudic Fellow Degree. *Accreditation:* AARTS.

Yeshiva Karlin Stolin Rabbinical Institute, Graduate Programs, Brooklyn, NY 11204. Offers Advanced Rabbinical Degree. *Accreditation:* AARTS.

Yeshiva of Nitra Rabbinical College, Graduate Programs, Mount Kisco, NY 10549. *Accreditation:* AARTS.

Yeshiva Shaar Hatorah Talmudic Research Institute, Graduate Programs, Kew Gardens, NY 11418-1469. *Accreditation:* AARTS.

Yeshivath Zichron Moshe, Graduate Programs, South Fallsburg, NY 12779. Offers Advanced Talmudic Degree, Talmudic Scholar Degree. *Accreditation:* AARTS. Part-time programs available.

Yeshiva Toras Chaim Talmudical Seminary, Graduate Programs, Denver, CO 80204-1415.

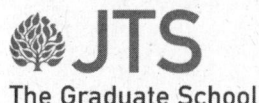
The Graduate School

THE JEWISH THEOLOGICAL SEMINARY

The Graduate School

Programs of Study

The Graduate School offers the most comprehensive program of advanced Jewish studies available in North America. Through specialized courses of study, students prepare to pursue careers in academia, Jewish art, or communal leadership. Programs of study leading to the M.A. and doctoral (D.H.L. and Ph.D.) degrees are offered in the following fields except as noted: ancient Judaism, Bible and ancient Semitic languages, interdepartmental studies (M.A. only), Jewish art and visual culture (M.A. only), Jewish history, Jewish literature, Jewish thought, Jewish women's studies (M.A. only), liturgy, medieval Jewish studies, midrash and scriptural interpretation, modern Jewish studies, and Talmud and Rabbinics. In addition, The Graduate School offers dual-degree programs with the Columbia University School of Social Work leading to the M.A./M.S.S.W. degrees and with Columbia University's School of International and Public Affairs leading to the M.A./M.P.A. degrees to prepare students to enter the field of communal service.

Research Facilities

The Library of The Jewish Theological Seminary houses the most complete collection of Judaica in the Western Hemisphere. With more than 380,000 volumes on open shelves, it is ideally suited for the research needs of graduate students. The Library's special collection, with more than 30,000 items, affords ample opportunities for original scholarship. Students also benefit from the library resources of neighboring Columbia University and Union Theological Seminary. M.A. and Ph.D. students also have access to the courses and facilities of several universities through a special consortial agreement.

Financial Aid

Financial aid based on need is available to U.S. and Canadian matriculated M.A. students in the form of scholarships, grants, and loans. There are also competitive merit awards available for outstanding M.A. candidates who apply by March 1. Moreover, some M.A. programs offer their own designated merit fellowships. Prospective Ph.D. students who complete their applications by January 2 are automatically considered for merit-based, five-year fellowships consisting of tuition, an annual stipend, pedagogic training, health insurance, and other benefits. Advanced doctoral students may be awarded teaching assistantships. Students may obtain information and applications for need-based aid from the Office of Financial Aid, 100 Schiff Building (212-678-8007; financialaid@jtsa.edu).

Cost of Study

For the 2008–09 academic year, tuition was $26,600 for full-time Ph.D. study and $21,200 for full-time M.A. study. Part-time students were charged $1000 per credit. In addition to tuition, a fee of $400 was charged per semester.

Living and Housing Costs

Residence hall rooms are available to single students at a cost of approximately $8800 to $9800 per academic year. Apartments of various sizes and costs are also available to married students. The housing application deadline for all new students entering the following fall semester is May 15. For more information, prospective students should contact the Office of Residence Life (212-678-8035; reslife@jtsa.edu).

Student Group

The Graduate School enrolled 175 students in fall 2008. Fifty-five percent of the students are women, and approximately 65 percent of all students receive financial aid.

Location

JTS is located on the vibrant Upper West Side of New York City. Its proximity to Columbia University, Teachers College, Union Theological Seminary, and the Manhattan School of Music puts The Graduate School in the heart of a dynamic academic community. Students are encouraged to explore the wealth of cultural activities New York City offers—from music and dance at Lincoln Center to theater on and off Broadway, from art at the Metropolitan and Whitney museums to the galleries in Chelsea and Williamsburg.

The Seminary

The Jewish Theological Seminary is a premier academic center consisting of five schools and a world-renowned library. Students flourish in an intellectual environment of warmth and creativity located in the heart of New York City's vibrant Jewish community. Academic departments of unparalleled range and depth offer a rich selection of courses in nearly every field of Judaic studies. Founded in 1886, its original mission was to preserve the knowledge and practice of Conservative Judaism. That mission has blossomed and expanded, and today JTS is a prestigious hub of Jewish learning. JTS grants undergraduate, graduate, and professional degrees through its schools; offers enriching programs for the Jewish community in the United States, Israel, and around the world; and enriches Jewish academic scholarship with its Hebraic and Judaic collection housed in The Library, the Western Hemisphere's most significant and outstanding repository of texts from the tenth century to the present.

Applying

Application for admission to degree programs should be made as early as possible. Although applications are accepted and reviewed all year, The Graduate School sets deadlines for those who wish to receive fellowship consideration (January 2 for Ph.D. applicants and March 1 for M.A. applicants). Ph.D. applicants must submit a $50 application fee; official college transcripts; three letters of academic reference; GRE or MAT scores; and a sample of academic research in the field of study, written in English. M.A. applicants must submit a $50 application fee; official college transcripts; three letters of reference, at least two of which must be academic; GRE or MAT scores; and a sample of written English. Applicants whose native language is other than English and who have not been educated at a college where English is the language of instruction should submit official scores of the Test of English as a Foreign Language (TOEFL) in lieu of the GRE or MAT. A minimum TOEFL score of 100 (Internet-based) is required. The Graduate School may also require nonnative English speakers to demonstrate oral/aural English proficiency; for details, students should contact the Admissions Office. For M.A. and doctoral programs, an interview with a members of the admissions committee and/or the department chair is recommended and may be required. Ph.D. candidates may begin their studies in the fall only, whereas M.A. candidates enter The Graduate School in either the fall or the spring. Students who wish to attend The Graduate School on a nonmatriculated basis may do so by submitting a nonmatriculated status application form, accompanied by a $35 application fee and an official college transcript indicating receipt of a B.A. degree. The Graduate School accepts nonmatriculated applications until one month prior to either the fall or spring semester. Two summer sessions are also available. The Graduate School is open to all men and women without regard to age, race, religion, sexual orientation, or national origin.

Correspondence and Information

The Graduate School
The Jewish Theological Seminary
3080 Broadway
Box 74
New York, New York 10027-4649
Phone: 212-678-8022
Fax: 212-280-6022
E-mail: gradschool@jtsa.edu
Web site: http://www.jtsa.edu/graduate

The Jewish Theological Seminary

THE FACULTY

Arnold Eisen, Chancellor.
Michael B. Greenbaum, Vice Chancellor.
Alan M. Cooper, Provost.
Stephen Garfinkel, Dean of The Graduate School and Dean of Academic Affairs.

Ancient Judaism Program
Stephen A. Geller, Professor.
Richard Kalmin, Professor and Program Adviser (fall 2008).
Seth Schwartz, Professor and Program Adviser (spring 2009).

Department of Bible and Ancient Semitic Languages
Alan M. Cooper, Professor.
Stephen A. Geller, Professor.
David Marcus, Professor.
Benjamin Sommer, Professor.
Robert Alan Harris, Associate Professor and Chair.
Stephen Garfinkel, Assistant Professor.
Walter Herzberg, Assistant Professor.
Amy Kalmanofsky, Assistant Professor.
Sharon Keller, Assistant Professor.
David Sperling, Adjunct Professor.
Elizabeth Bloch-Smith, Adjunct Associate Professor.
Miles Cohen, Adjunct Lecturer.

Department of Hebrew Language
Joel Roth, Chair.
Edna Nahshon, Associate Professor.
Nitza Krohn, Senior Lecturer.
Sarah Pelee, Lecturer.
Allon Pratt, Lecturer.
Shlomit Shraybom-Shivtiel, Adjunct Assistant Professor.

Interdepartmental Studies Program
Neil Danzig, Professor.
Edna Nahshon, Associate Professor.
Eitan Fishbane, Assistant Professor.
Maud Kozodoy, Assistant Professor and Program Adviser.

Jewish Art and Visual Culture Program
Vivian B. Mann, Adjunct Professor and Program Adviser.
Susan Chevlowe, Adjunct Assistant Professor.

Department of Jewish History
Daphna Canetti-Nisim, Schusterman Professor of Israel Studies.
David Fishman, Professor.
Ismar Schorsch, Professor.
Seth Schwartz, Professor.
Jack Wertheimer, Professor.
Benjamin R. Gampel, Associate Professor and Chair.
Shuly Rubin Schwartz, Associate Professor.
Stefanie Siegmund, Associate Professor.
Michael Stanislawski, Adjunct Professor.

Department of Jewish Literature
Alan Mintz, Professor and Chair (fall 2008).
David G. Roskies, Professor.
Raymond P. Scheindlin, Professor.
Barbara Mann, Associate Professor and Chair (spring 2009).
Debra Reed Blank, Assistant Professor.
Jeffrey Hoffman, Assistant Professor.
Maud Kozodoy, Assistant Professor.
Anne Lapidus Lerner, Assistant Professor.
Kenneth Berger, Adjunct Assistant Professor.

Department of Jewish Thought
Arnold Eisen, Professor.
Neil Gillman, Professor.
Alan Mittleman, Professor and Chair.
Eitan Fishbane, Assistant Professor.
Leonard Levin, Assistant Professor.
Richard Cohen, Adjunct Professor.
Alfredo Borodowski, Adjunct Assistant Professor.
Gordon Tucker, Adjunct Assistant Professor.

Jewish Professional Leadership: Jewish Studies and Social Work; Jewish Studies and Public Administration
Mayer Rabinowitz, Professor.
Aryeh Davidson, Assistant Professor.
Anne Lapidus Lerner, Assistant Professor.
Ilene Scholnick, Program Adviser.

Jewish Women's Studies Program
David C. Kraemer, Professor.
Stefanie Siegmund, Associate Professor and Program Adviser.
Barbara Mann, Associate Professor.
Anne Lapidus Lerner, Assistant Professor and Program Adviser.

Liturgy Program
Alan Mintz, Professor.
Raymond P. Scheindlin, Professor.
Eliezer Diamond, Associate Professor.
Boaz Tarsi, Associate Professor and Program Adviser.
Jeffrey Hoffman, Assistant Professor.

Medieval Jewish Studies Program
Raymond P. Scheindlin, Professor and Program Adviser (spring 2009).
Benjamin R. Gampel, Associate Professor and Program Adviser (fall 2008).
Robert Harris, Associate Professor.
Eitan Fishbane, Assistant Professor.
Evyatar Marienberg, Assistant Professor.

Midrash and Scriptural Interpretation Program
Alan M. Cooper, Professor.
Judith Hauptman, Professor.
David C. Kraemer, Professor.
Burton L. Visotzky, Professor and Program Adviser.
Robert Harris, Associate Professor.
Rachel Mikva, Assistant Professor.

Modern Jewish Studies Program
David Fishman, Professor and Program Adviser.
Alan Mintz, Professor.
David G. Roskies, Professor and Program Adviser.
Barbara Mann, Associate Professor.

Department of Talmud and Rabbinics
Neil Danzig, Professor.
Israel Francus, Professor.
Shamma Friedman, Professor.
Judith Hauptman, Professor and Chair.
Richard Kalmin, Professor.
David C. Kraemer, Professor.
Joel Roth, Professor.
Burton L. Visotzky, Professor.
Eliezer Diamond, Associate Professor.
Mayer E. Rabinowitz, Associate Professor.
Beth Berkowitz, Assistant Professor.
Marjorie Lehman, Assistant Professor.
Evyatar Marienberg, Assistant Professor.
Jonathan Milgram, Assistant Professor.
Jay Rovner, Adjunct Assistant Professor.

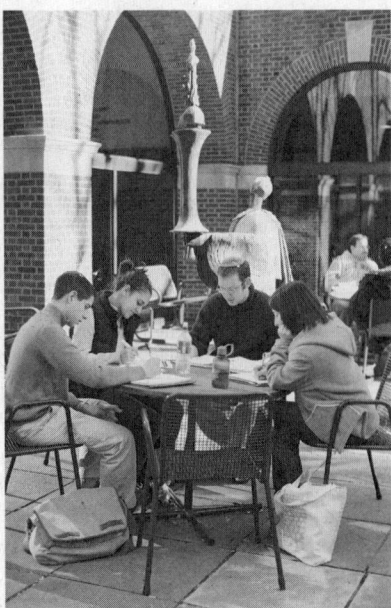

Students in the courtyard at The Jewish Theological Seminary.

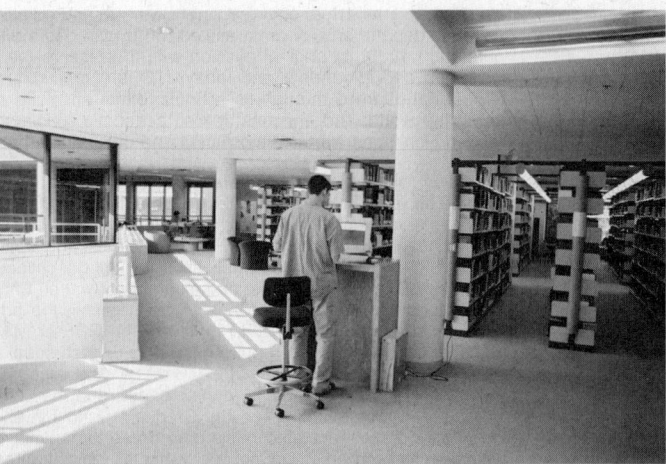

The Library of The Jewish Theological Seminary.

THE JEWISH THEOLOGICAL SEMINARY

The Rabbinical School

Program of Study

The Rabbinical School of The Jewish Theological Seminary (JTS) offers a five-year program of study and field experience that leads to rabbinical ordination under the auspices of the Conservative Movement. The third year is spent in Jerusalem at the Schechter Institute of Jewish Studies, JTS's Israeli affiliate. Through a consortium academia agreement, rabbinical students can enroll in courses at Union Theological Seminary and Hebrew Union College. A Master of Arts (M.A.) is earned during the program from the Graduate School or the William Davidson Graduate School of Jewish Education at JTS. Concentrations include Bible, rabbinics, Jewish history, Jewish women's studies, Jewish literature, liturgy, Midrash, Jewish education, and pastoral care.

The Mekhinah (preparatory) year program is for accepted candidates who need to acquire textual skills in the areas of Bible and Talmud.

Research Facilities

Rabbinical students regularly study in *havruta* (in pairs) in the Eisenfeld/Duker Beit Midrash. In addition, the library of The Jewish Theological Seminary houses the most complete collection of Judaica in the Western Hemisphere. With more than 340,000 volumes on open shelves, it is ideally suited for the research needs of graduate students. The library's special collection, with more than 30,000 items, affords ample opportunity for original scholarship. All students also benefit from the resources of neighboring Columbia University and Union Theological Seminary.

Financial Aid

The program at The Rabbinical School offers a significant number of merit-based fellowships. Applicants may obtain applications for merit-based fellowships directly from The Rabbinical School office. Candidates are encouraged to apply for the Wexner Graduate Fellowship from the Wexner Foundation.

Cost of Study

For the 2009–10 academic year, tuition is $11,300 per semester for full-time study. Part-time students are charged $1000 per credit.

Living and Housing Costs

Rooms and apartments (150 units) are available to single students at a cost of approximately $8000 per academic year. Apartments of various costs are available to married students. The housing application deadline for incoming students is May 12. For more information, students should contact the Office of Residence Life by calling 212-678-8035 or by sending an e-mail to reslife@jtsa.edu.

Student Group

In fall 2008, 152 students were enrolled in The Rabbinical School. Approximately 40 percent are women. A majority of students receive generous merit-based fellowships.

Location

JTS is located on the vibrant Upper West Side of New York City. Its proximity to Columbia University, Teachers College, Union Theological Seminary, and the Manhattan School of Music puts The Rabbinical School in the heart of a dynamic academic community. Students are encouraged to explore the wealth of cultural activities New York City offers—from music and dance at Lincoln Center to theater on and off Broadway, from art at the Metropolitan and Whitney museums to the galleries in SoHo and Greenwich Village.

The Seminary and The School

Founded in 1886, The Jewish Theological Seminary is the academic and spiritual center of Conservative Judaism worldwide. In 1904, it established The Jewish Museum. The New York campus includes five separate yet integrated schools: Albert A. List College of Jewish Studies, The Graduate School (the largest division), H. L. Miller Cantorial School and College of Jewish Music, The Rabbinical School, and William Davidson Graduate School of Jewish Education.

Applying

Applications for regular admission should be submitted by February 15 for the following fall. There is also an early action deadline of November 15. Applicants from outside the US should submit their materials by December 3. JTS does accept some late applications on case-by-case basis. A $50 application fee, application, essays, official college transcripts, three letters of recommendation, and GRE or LSAT scores are required. All candidates are considered for merit-based fellowships.

Correspondence and Information

Rabbi Mordecai Schwartz, Director of Admissions
The Rabbinical School
The Jewish Theological Seminary
3080 Broadway
New York, New York 10027-4649
Phone: 212-678-8818
E-mail: rabschool@jtsa.edu
Web site: http://www.jtsa.edu

The Jewish Theological Seminary

THE FACULTY AND THEIR RESEARCH

The Rabbinical School Administration

Daniel Nevins, Pearl Resnick Dean.
Lisa Gelber, Associate Dean and Rabbi of the Women's League Seminary Synagogue.
Mychal Springer, Associate Dean.
Mordecai Schwartz, Director of Admissions.
Jonathan Lipnick, Field Education Coordinator.

The Rabbinical School Faculty

Beth Berkowitz, Ph.D. (religious studies), Columbia. Rabbinic literature, Judaism and Christianity in late antiquity, ritual studies, theories and methods in the study of religion, cultural criticism.
Burton Cohen, Ph.D. (education), Chicago. Informal settings for Jewish education, preparation of teachers and principals for Jewish schools, teaching rabbinic literature to adults, use of computers in Jewish learning and educational research.
Miles B. Cohen, Ph.D. (hon.), Jewish Theological Seminary. Synagogue skills, such as chanting the Torah, Megillot, and prayers of the weekday, Shabbat, holiday services, and special life-cycle occasions; Hebrew grammar.
Alan Cooper, Ph.D. (religious studies), Yale. Linguistic structure of biblical poetry, the Bible.
Aryeh Davidson, Ph.D. (special education and developmental psychology), Columbia. Teacher preparation, leadership development, program evaluation, identity development of Jewish professionals.
Eliezer Diamond, Ph.D. (Talmud), Jewish Theological Seminary. Rabbinic literature; introductory, intermediate, and advanced Talmud study.
Arnold Eisen, Ph.D. (history of Jewish thought), Hebrew University. Jewish identity, revitalization of Jewish tradition, redefinition of the American Jewish community.
Shira Epstein, Ph.D. (curriculum and teaching), Columbia Teachers College. Gender and Jewish education, drama as pedagogy.
Eitan Fishbane, Ph.D., Brandeis. Near Eastern and Judaic studies, history and literature of Jewish mysticism.
David Fishman, Ph.D., Harvard. Modern Jewish history.
Shamma Friedman, Ph.D., Jewish Theological Seminary. Talmudic studies, including literary and conceptual development, stratification of the Talmudic sugya, linguistic studies in Hebrew and Aramaic, and the nature of variant readings of the Talmudic texts.
Benjamin Gampel, Ph.D. Columbia. Medieval and early modern Jewish history.
Stephen Garfinkel, Ph.D. (Middle East languages and cultures), Columbia. Early popular perceptions of Moses as a divine figure.
Stephen A. Geller, Ph.D., Harvard. Biblical literature, with special emphasis on the Book of Psalms, biblical poetry, and the prophets.
Neil Gillman, Ph.D., Columbia. Jewish philosophy.
Michael Greenbaum, Ph.D. (higher education administration), Columbia. Nonprofit management, leadership theory and practice, history of the Conservative Movement.
Robert Harris, Ph.D., Jewish Theological Seminary. Literature and commentary, particularly medieval Jewish biblical exegesis.
Judith Hauptman, Ph.D., Jewish Theological Seminary. Talmud, Talmudic research.
Barry Holtz, Ph.D., Brandeis. Classical texts, professional development for teachers, philosophy of Jewish education, current issues confronting Jewish education.
Carol Ingall, Ed.D., Boston University. Curriculum and instruction.
Richard Kalmin, Ph.D. Interpretation of rabbinic stories, ancient Jewish history, and the development of rabbinic literature.
Sharon Keller, Ph.D. (Hebrew and Judaic studies), NYU. Biblical literature, ancient Egyptian art, the Exodus, the afterlife, women's studies.
David Kraemer, Ph.D., Jewish Theological Seminary. Talmud and rabbinics.
Jeffrey Kress, Ph.D., Rutgers. Building Jewish values and identity by using principles of social and emotional learning to augment Jewish education.
Nitza Krohn. Hebrew language.
Marjorie Lehman, Ph.D., Columbia. Religion, Talmud and rabbinics.
Anne Lapidus Lerner, Ph.D., Harvard. Hebrew and American Jewish poetry, modern Jewish literature, portrayal of women in Jewish literature.
Michelle Lynn-Sachs, Ph.D., NYU. Educational leadership, congregational studies, sociology of education, sociology of religion.
Barbara Mann, Ph.D. (comparative literature), Berkeley. Israeli and Jewish literature, cultural studies, modern poetry, urban studies, literary modernism, fine arts.
Vivian Mann, Ph.D. Art history.
David Marcus, Ph.D., Columbia. Middle East languages and cultures; Bible and ancient languages, including Babylonian Aramaic and biblical Hebrew.
Evyatar Marienberg, Ph.D., École des Hautes Études en Sciences Sociale. Talmud, study of beliefs and practices of lay Jews and Christians from various periods.
Jonathan Milgram, Ph.D. (Talmud), Bar Ilan (Israel). Talmud criticism and medieval Jewish law.
Alan Mintz, Ph.D., Columbia. Hebrew literature and language.
Alan Mittleman, Ph.D., Temple. Jewish philosophy.
Edna Nahshon, Ph.D. (performance studies), NYU. Hebrew language.
Daniel Nevins, M.A., Jewish Theological Seminary. Homiletics.
Adina Ofek, Ph.D., Jewish Theological Seminary. Jewish education, Hebrew language.
Sarah Pelee, M.A. (educational counseling), Northwestern. Hebrew language.
Mayer Rabinowitz, Ph.D., Jewish Theological Seminary. Talmud and rabbinics.
Henry Rosenblum. Jewish music, hazzanut.
David Roskies, Ph.D. Brandeis. Jewish literature.
Joel Roth, Ph.D. (Talmud), Jewish Theological Seminary. Talmud and rabbinics.
Raymond Scheindlin, Ph.D., Columbia. Encounter of Hebrew and Arabic cultures in Spain, especially as embodied in the poetry of the two traditions.
Menahem Schmelzer, Ph.D. (Hebrew letters), Jewish Theological Seminary. Medieval Jewish literature.
Ismar Schorsch, Ph.D. (Jewish history), Columbia. Jewish history.
Seth Schwartz, Ph.D., (ancient history), Columbia. Jewish history.
Shuly Rubin Schwartz, Ph.D., Jewish Theological Seminary. American Jewish life, the Jewish family, Jewish women's studies.
Boaz Tarsi, Ph.D., Cornell. Theory of Ashkenazi liturgical music and the music theory of Western common-practice.
Burton Visotzky, Ph.D., Jewish Theological Seminary. Talmud and rabbinics.
Jack Wertheimer, Ph.D. Modern Jewish history, with a particular focus on the religious, communal, and organizational experiences of American Jews since World War II.

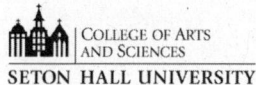
COLLEGE OF ARTS
AND SCIENCES
SETON HALL UNIVERSITY

SETON HALL UNIVERSITY

Department of Jewish-Christian Studies

Programs of Study	Seton Hall University's Graduate Department of Jewish-Christian Studies offers a Master of Arts (M.A.) degree and a certificate in Jewish-Christian studies, which cover all aspects of the historical relationships between Jews and Christians—their respective values and traditions. The programs serve as a model for eliminating prejudice through mutual understanding.
	Students working toward a degree normally gain an elementary knowledge of Hebrew early in the program, allowing them to enter the Hebrew mind-set of the writers. Courses provide critical study of foundational sources in their social world contexts, tracing how these traditions developed within diverse local settings. Students examine the religious, ethical, and social issues central for understanding Christians and Jews today against the background of anti-Semitism and the Holocaust.
	The Department requires that M.A. students choose from either of two programs of study—the thesis or the nonthesis option—in consultation with an adviser. Students in the thesis program complete 27 credits offered by the Department and 6 credits in the reading of Hebrew texts. An adviser's approval must be obtained for all courses chosen. Three credits must be completed in JCST 9001 Thesis (with the topic approved by the Thesis Committee). The thesis must make a contribution to continuing research in some aspect of Jewish-Christian studies. After consultation with the faculty members, students with a strong background in research may choose to do a more extensive investigation of an approved topic and produce a thesis for 6 credits (JCST 9002). Students in the nonthesis program complete 36 credits in Jewish-Christian studies, selecting courses with the approval of the Departmental adviser. Students must demonstrate a basic knowledge of biblical Hebrew.
	In the 12-credit Certificate in Jewish-Christian Studies program, students take a required class, Christian Jewish Encounter, and then select three other courses in consultation with the chair of the Department.
	For further details, students should see the Department's Web site at: http://www.shu.edu/academics/artsci/ma-jewish-christian-studies/index.cfm.
Research Facilities	The Institute of Judaeo-Christian Studies, founded in 1953, is primarily a center for research and publication. Its area of study is the Church's rootedness in Judaism and the relationship between the Church and the Jewish people through the ages. Its work includes an annual series of lectures, study days, and conferences. These are intended to inform the general public about various facets of Christian-Jewish relations.
	The Walsh Library, a state-of-the-art 155,000-square-foot building, houses 500,000 titles, 1,875 current periodicals, and an extensive collection of microform and other nonprint items that include videotapes, CD-ROM music, and other electronic media. Fahy Hall has twenty-eight classrooms, two TV studios, a Macintosh and IBM graphics lab, two classroom amphitheaters, and language and statistics labs. The recently renovated McNulty Hall has well-equipped science labs. Completed in 1997, Jubilee Hall, a six-story facility with 126,000 square feet of academic space, features high-tech classrooms with computer and multimedia capabilities.
Financial Aid	The H. Suzanne Jobert Scholarship Fund assists students pursuing the M.A. in Jewish-Christian Studies. Inquiries about this tuition scholarship may be made through the Department chair. The Sister Rose Thering Endowment for Jewish-Christian Studies, established in 1993 in honor of Sister Rose's work as an educator and advocate for improving relations between Christians and Jews, provides scholarships for teachers who want to learn more about promoting interreligious understanding and cooperation through education. Scholarships are available to teachers who wish to enroll as nonmatriculated students and take up to 12 credits to receive a certificate of completion.
Cost of Study	In 2009–10, tuition is $901 per credit. Full-time students pay $305 per semester in University and technology fees; part-time students pay $185.
Living and Housing Costs	Housing and living costs in South Orange and surrounding towns are comparable to most suburban cities, with studio and one-bedroom apartments renting for $750 to $1000 per month.
Student Group	Most students in the Jewish-Christian Studies degree and certificate programs are teachers in public, private, or parochial schools; education and ecumenical administrators; or clergy and seminarians. However, the programs also attract educational generalists who seek the means to explore Jewish and Christian studies for personal or career enrichment.
Location	Seton Hall is located on 58 acres in the village of South Orange, New Jersey, a suburban residential area 14 miles southwest of New York City. The town center is a 10-minute walk from the campus and features bookstores, coffee shops, and restaurants. The heart of midtown Manhattan is about 30 minutes away by train; students can take advantage of everything this exciting city has to offer while still living in a suburban area.
The University	Founded in 1856, Seton Hall is a private coeducational Catholic institution—the nation's oldest diocesan institution of higher education in the United States. With a total enrollment of about 10,000, including approximately 4,500 graduate students, the University comprises nine colleges and schools. Seton Hall is accredited by the Middle States Association of Colleges and Schools. Through the incorporation of technology into the curriculum, the College of Arts and Sciences seeks to enhance and enliven the learning environment. Rooted in tradition, yet looking to the future, the College offers a rich set of opportunities for intellectual discovery. Graduate students are guided by scholars and specialists toward the mastery of academic and professional areas.
Applying	In addition to the general University requirements for admission, the Department of Jewish-Christian Studies strongly recommends an interview or suitable correspondence with the Department chair to determine the objectives of the student in relation to the resources of the Department. Students must submit the completed application (available online at http://www.shu.edu/academics/artsci/apply-graduate.cfm), the $50 application fee, and transcripts from all previously attended universities and colleges. The deadlines for fall and spring admission are July 1 and November 1, respectively. Applications are processed on a rolling basis.
Correspondence and Information	The Rev. Lawrence Frizzell, Department Chair Department of Jewish-Christian Studies 240 Fahy Hall Seton Hall University 400 South Orange Avenue South Orange, New Jersey 07079 Phone: 973-761-9751 E-mail: jcst@shu.edu Web site: http://www.shu.edu/academics/artsci/ma-jewish-christian-studies/index.cfm

Seton Hall University

THE FACULTY AND THEIR RESEARCH

David M. Bossman, Professor and Director of the Sister Rose Thering Endowment; Ph.D., Saint Louis. Editor of the *Biblical Theology Bulletin* since 1981, Dr. Bossman applies cross-cultural analysis to the study of Christian and Jewish sources, contemporizing Jewish and Christian values and fostering cooperative partnerships. He is the founding director of the Sister Rose Thering Endowment for Jewish-Christian Studies.

Alan Brill, Associate Professor; Ph.D., Fordham. Teaches modern Jewish studies and is engaged in interfaith dialogue. Rabbi Brill holds a rabbinical degree from Yeshiva. He is the Cooperman-Ross Endowed Chair in Jewish-Christian Studies in Honor of Sister Rose Thering.

Asher Finkel, Professor; Ph.D., Tübingen (Germany). Postbiblical Judaism, Jewish thinkers, early Christianity. Rabbi Finkel holds a rabbinical degree from Yeshiva.

Lawrence Frizzell, Associate Professor, Chair of the Department of Jewish-Christian Studies, and Director of the Institute of Judaeo-Christian Studies; S.T.L., S.S.L., D.Phil., Oxford. Jewish literature of the Second Temple Period, Paul and John, Bible and liturgy.

John Morley, Faculty Emeritus, Religious Studies; Ph.D., NYU. The Holocaust: history and interpretation.

Section 13
Writing

This section contains a directory of institutions offering graduate work in writing, followed by in-depth entries submitted by institutions that chose to prepare detailed program descriptions. Additional information about programs listed in the directory but not augmented by an in-depth entry may be obtained by writing directly to the dean of a graduate school or chair of a department at the address given in the directory.

For programs offering related work, see also in this book *Communication* and *Media* and *Language and Literature*.

CONTENTS

Program Directories

Technical Writing   536
Writing   537

Close-Ups

Adelphi University   551

Carnegie Mellon University   553
Lesley University   555
The New School: A University   557
Southern Illinois University Carbondale   559

See also:

California College of the Arts—Art, Architecture,
    Design, and Writing   207
Columbia University—Film, Theater Arts, Visual Arts,
    and Writing   285
Naropa University—Graduate Studies   1121
Sarah Lawrence College—Fine Arts   289
School of the Art Institute of Chicago—Graduate
    Studies in Art   225
Seton Hall University—English   443

Technical Writing

Carnegie Mellon University, College of Humanities and Social Sciences, Department of English, Program in Professional Writing, Pittsburgh, PA 15213-3891. Offers editing and publishing (MAPW); policy and non-profit communication (MAPW); public and media relations / corporate communications (MAPW); science or healthcare communication (MAPW); technical writing (MAPW); writing for new media (MAPW); writing for print media (MAPW). Part-time programs available. *Entrance requirements:* For master's, GRE General Test. Additional exam requirements/recommendations for international students: Required—TOEFL, TWE.

See Close-Up on page 553.

Colorado State University, Graduate School, College of Liberal Arts, Department of Journalism and Technical Communication, Fort Collins, CO 80523-1785. Offers public communication and technology (MS, PhD); technical communication (MS). Part-time programs available. *Faculty:* 19 full-time (8 women). *Students:* 30 full-time (20 women), 32 part-time (25 women); includes 7 minority (1 American Indian/Alaska Native, 2 Asian Americans or Pacific Islanders, 4 Hispanic Americans), 7 international. Average age 34. 56 applicants, 68% accepted, 23 enrolled. In 2008, 13 master's awarded. *Degree requirements:* For master's, variable foreign language requirement, comprehensive exam (for some programs), thesis (for some programs); for doctorate, variable foreign language requirement, comprehensive exam (for some programs), thesis/dissertation (for some programs). *Entrance requirements:* For master's, GRE General Test, samples of written work, letters of recommendation, resumé or curriculum vitae, 3 writing/communication projects, bachelor's degree, statement of career plans; for doctorate, GRE General Test, master's degree, minimum GPA of 3.0, scholarly/professional work, letters of recommendation, statement of career plans, resumé. Additional exam requirements/recommendations for international students: Required—TOEFL (minimum score 600 paper-based; 250 computer-based). *Application deadline:* For fall admission, 2/15 priority date for domestic students, 12/15 priority date for international students; for spring admission, 6/15 priority date for domestic students. Applications are processed on a rolling basis. Application fee: $50. Electronic applications accepted. *Expenses:* Tuition, area resident: Full-time $5620; part-time $312.25 per credit. Tuition, state resident: full-time $5620; part-time $312.25 per credit. Tuition, nonresident: full-time $17,253; part-time $958.50 per credit. Required fees: $1449.56; $82.35 per credit. *Financial support:* In 2008–09, 18 students received support, including 18 teaching assistantships with partial tuition reimbursements available (averaging $7,912 per year); fellowships with partial tuition reimbursements available, research assistantships with full and partial tuition reimbursements available, career-related internships or fieldwork, Federal Work-Study, institutionally sponsored loans, scholarships/grants, traineeships, and unspecified assistantships also available. Support available to part-time students. Financial award application deadline: 3/1; financial award applicants required to submit FAFSA. *Faculty research:* Technical/science communication, public relations, health/risk communication, web/new media technologies, environmental communication. Total annual research expenditures: $314,040. *Unit head:* Dr. Greg Luft, Chair, 970-491-1979, Fax: 970-491-2908, E-mail: greg.luft@colostate.edu. *Application contact:* Craig Trumbo, Graduate Program Coordinator, 970-491-2077, Fax: 970-491-2908, E-mail: craig.trumbo@colostate.edu.

Drexel University, College of Arts and Sciences, Department of Culture and Communication, Philadelphia, PA 19104-2875. Offers communication (MS), including public communication, science communication, technical communication, publication management (MS). Part-time and evening/weekend programs available. *Degree requirements:* For master's, internship, professional portfolio. *Entrance requirements:* Additional exam requirements/recommendations for international students: Required—TOEFL. Electronic applications accepted. *Faculty research:* Science information and attitudes, science influence on literature, process of technical writing, document design, software documentation.

Fitchburg State College, Division of Graduate and Continuing Education, Program in Applied Communications, Fitchburg, MA 01420-2697. Offers applied communications (MS, Certificate); library media (MS); technical and professional writing (MS). Part-time and evening/weekend programs available. *Students:* 1 (woman) full-time, 6 part-time (4 women). Average age 40. 6 applicants, 100% accepted, 5 enrolled. In 2008, 3 master's awarded. *Entrance requirements:* For master's, GRE General Test or MAT, minimum 2 years of related experience, letters of recommendation, resumé. Additional exam requirements/recommendations for international students: Required—TOEFL (minimum score 550 paper-based; 213 computer-based; 79 iBT). *Application deadline:* Applications are processed on a rolling basis. Application fee: $25 ($50 for international students). *Expenses:* Tuition, state resident: full-time $3600; part-time $150 per credit. Tuition, nonresident: full-time $3600; part-time $150 per credit. Required fees: $109 per credit. *Financial support:* In 2008–09, research assistantships with partial tuition reimbursements (averaging $5,500 per year); Federal Work-Study, scholarships/grants, and unspecified assistantships also available. Support available to part-time students. Financial award application deadline: 3/1; financial award applicants required to submit FAFSA. *Unit head:* Dr. John Chetro-Szivos, Chair, 978-665-3261, Fax: 978-665-3658, E-mail: gce@fsc.edu. *Application contact:* Director of Admissions, 978-665-3144, Fax: 978-665-4540, E-mail: admissions@fsc.edu.

Illinois Institute of Technology, Graduate College, College of Science and Letters, Lewis Department of Humanities, Chicago, IL 60616-3793. Offers information architecture (MS); technical communication (PhD); technical communication and information design (MS). Part-time and evening/weekend programs available. *Faculty:* 17 full-time (6 women), 11 part-time/adjunct (4 women). *Students:* 9 full-time (5 women), 32 part-time (24 women); includes 13 minority (9 African Americans, 3 Asian Americans or Pacific Islanders, 1 Hispanic American), 6 international. Average age 34. 52 applicants, 44% accepted, 27 enrolled. In 2008, 9 master's, 2 doctorates awarded. *Degree requirements:* For master's, comprehensive exam, thesis or alternative, project; for doctorate, comprehensive exam, thesis/dissertation, qualifying exam. *Entrance requirements:* For master's, GRE General Test; for doctorate, GRE General Test, bachelor's degree in technical communication or other relevant field. Additional exam requirements/recommendations for international students: Required—TOEFL (minimum score 550 paper-based; 213 computer-based; 80 iBT). *Application deadline:* For fall admission, 5/1 for domestic and international students; for spring admission, 1/5 for domestic and international students. Applications are processed on a rolling basis. Application fee: $40. Electronic applications accepted. *Financial support:* In 2008–09, 15 teaching assistantships with partial tuition reimbursements (averaging $9,000 per year) were awarded; career-related internships or fieldwork, Federal Work-Study, institutionally sponsored loans, scholarships/grants, health care benefits, tuition waivers (partial), and unspecified assistantships also available. Support available to part-time students. Financial award applicants required to submit FAFSA. *Faculty research:* Discourse analysis, linguistics, readability, ethics in professions, instructional and document design, knowledge management, usability testing and evaluation, history and philosophy of science. Total annual research expenditures: $34,161. *Unit head:* Kathryn Riley, Professor and Chair, 312-567-3566, Fax: 312-567-5187, E-mail: riley@iit.edu. *Application contact:* Morgan Frederick, Assistant Director of Graduate Communications, 866-472-3448, Fax: 312-567-3138, E-mail: inquiry.grad@iit.edu.

James Madison University, The Graduate School, College of Arts and Letters, School of Writing, Rhetoric, and Technical Communication, Harrisonburg, VA 22807. Offers MA, MS. Part-time programs available. *Faculty:* 3 full-time (1 woman), 1 part-time/adjunct (0 women). *Students:* 14 full-time (11 women), 8 part-time (7 women); includes 2 minority (1 Asian American or Pacific Islander, 1 Hispanic American). Average age 27. In 2008, 5 master's awarded. *Degree requirements:* For master's, one foreign language, thesis, internship, practicum. *Entrance requirements:* For master's, GRE General Test, GRE Subject Test, TSC application dossier, 3 letters of recommendation, 20-30 page writing samples. Additional exam requirements/recommendations for international students: Required—TOEFL (minimum score 550 paper-based). *Application deadline:* For fall admission, 5/31 priority date for domestic students; for spring admission, 8/31 priority date for domestic students. Applications are processed on a rolling basis. Application fee: $55. Electronic applications accepted. *Expenses:* Tuition, area resident: Full-time $7008; part-time $292 per credit hour. Tuition, state resident: full-time $7008; part-time $292 per credit hour. Tuition, nonresident: full-time $20,352; part-time $848 per credit hour. *Financial support:* In 2008–09, 9 students received support, including 1 teaching assistantship with full tuition reimbursement available (averaging $8,664 per year); Federal Work-Study, unspecified assistantships, and 7 assistantships ($7,382), 1 service assistantship ($7,382) also available. Financial award application deadline: 3/1; financial award applicants required to submit FAFSA. *Unit head:* Dr. Shelley B Aley, Interim Director, 540-568-2334. *Application contact:* Lynette M. Bible, Director of Graduate Admissions, 540-568-6395, Fax: 540-568-7860, E-mail: biblelm@jmu.edu.

The Johns Hopkins University, Zanvyl Krieger School of Arts and Sciences, The Writing Seminars, Baltimore, MD 21218-2699. Offers fiction writing (MFA); poetry (MFA); science writing (MA). *Degree requirements:* For master's, one foreign language, thesis, foreign language exam (for MFA). *Entrance requirements:* For master's, GRE General Test, GRE Subject Test (recommended), foreign language exam, sample of written work, 3 letters of recommendation, official college transcripts, GRE scores, and goal statement. Additional exam requirements/recommendations for international students: Required—TOEFL (minimum score 600 paper-based; 250 computer-based). Electronic applications accepted. *Faculty research:* Film theory, literary criticism, contemporary fiction.

Laurentian University, School of Graduate Studies and Research, Programme in Science Communication, Sudbury, ON P3E 2C6, Canada. Offers G Dip.

Massachusetts Institute of Technology, School of Humanities, Arts, and Social Sciences, Program in Writing and Humanistic Studies, Graduate Program in Science Writing, Cambridge, MA 02139-4307. Offers SM. *Degree requirements:* For master's, thesis, internship. *Entrance requirements:* For master's, GRE General Test. Additional exam requirements/recommendations for international students: Required—TOEFL (minimum score 600 paper-based; 250 computer-based). Electronic applications accepted.

Metropolitan State University, College of Arts and Sciences, St. Paul, MN 55106-5000. Offers computer science (MS); liberal studies (MA); technical communication (MS). Part-time and evening/weekend programs available. *Entrance requirements:* For master's, BA/BS; 2.75 GPA; resumée. Additional exam requirements/recommendations for international students: Required—TOEFL (minimum score 550 paper-based; 213 computer-based). *Faculty research:* Computer security, software engineering, distributed systems, document design, diffusing of innovations, social issues and communication technology.

Miami University, Graduate School, College of Arts and Sciences, Department of English, Program in Technical and Scientific Communication, Oxford, OH 45056. Offers MTSC. Part-time programs available. *Degree requirements:* For master's, thesis, final exam. *Entrance requirements:* For master's, minimum undergraduate GPA of 3.0 during previous 2 years or 2.75 overall. Additional exam requirements/recommendations for international students: Required—TOEFL (minimum score 550 paper-based; 213 computer-based), TWE (minimum score 4). Electronic applications accepted.

Northern Arizona University, Graduate College, College of Arts and Letters, Department of English, Program in English, Flagstaff, AZ 86011. Offers creative writing (MA); general English (MA); literacy, technology and professional writing (MA); literature (MA); secondary English education (MA). *Degree requirements:* For master's, departmental qualifying exam. *Entrance requirements:* For master's, GRE General Test, GRE Subject Test.

Polytechnic Institute of NYU, Department of Humanities and Social Sciences, Major in Technical Writing and Specialized Journalism, Brooklyn, NY 11201-2990. Offers MS. *Degree requirements:* For master's, comprehensive exam (for some programs), thesis (for some programs). *Entrance requirements:* Additional exam requirements/recommendations for international students: Required—TOEFL (minimum score 550 paper-based; 213 computer-based); Recommended—IELTS (minimum score 6.5). Electronic applications accepted.

Regis University, College for Professional Studies, MA Program, Denver, CO 80221-1099. Offers criminology (MA); fine arts administration (Certificate); language and communication (MA); mediation (Certificate); psychology (MA); self-designed major (MA); social justice, peace, and reconciliation (Certificate); social science (MA); technical communication (Certificate). Program also offered in Henderson and Las Vegas (Summerlin), NV. Part-time and evening/weekend programs available. Postbaccalaureate distance learning degree programs offered (minimal on-campus study). *Degree requirements:* For master's, thesis, research project. *Entrance requirements:* For master's, resumé, recommendations, essays. Additional exam requirements/recommendations for international students: Required—TOEFL (minimum score 213 computer-based), TWE (minimum score 5). Electronic applications accepted. *Expenses:* Contact institution. *Faculty research:* Independent/nonresidential graduate study: new methods and models, adult learning and the capstone experience, Goal Setting, behavior of Adult students, Innovative Studies for Community Colleges.

Texas Tech University, Graduate School, College of Arts and Sciences, Department of English, Lubbock, TX 79409. Offers English (MA, PhD); technical communication (MA); technical communication and rhetoric (PhD). Part-time programs available. *Faculty:* 37 full-time (14 women), 3 part-time/adjunct (all women). *Students:* 100 full-time (37 women), 82 part-time (52 women); includes 19 minority (4 African Americans, 3 American Indian/Alaska Native, 6 Asian Americans or Pacific Islanders, 6 Hispanic Americans), 11 international. Average age 35. 188 applicants, 38% accepted, 33 enrolled. In 2008, 24 master's, 12 doctorates awarded. *Degree requirements:* For master's, one foreign language, thesis (for some programs); for doctorate, thesis/dissertation. *Entrance requirements:* For master's and doctorate, GRE General Test. Additional exam requirements/recommendations for international students: Required—TOEFL (minimum score 550 paper-based; 213 computer-based). *Application deadline:* For fall admission, 3/1 priority date for international students; for spring admission, 11/1 priority date for international students. Applications are processed on a rolling basis. Application fee: $50 ($60 for international students). Electronic applications accepted. *Expenses:* Tuition, area resident: Part-time $194 per credit hour. Tuition, state resident: full-time $4648; part-time $194 per credit hour. Tuition, nonresident: full-time $11,392; part-time $475 per credit hour. Required fees: $2206; $69 per credit hour. $389 per semester. *Financial support:* In 2008–09, 109 students received support, including 1 research assistantship with partial tuition reimbursement available (averaging $16,357 per year), 82 teaching assistantships with partial tuition reimbursements available (averaging $14,350 per year); Federal Work-Study and institutionally sponsored loans also available. Support available to part-time students. Financial award application deadline: 4/15; financial award applicants required to submit FAFSA. *Faculty research:* Computers and writing; technical communication and rhetoric; creative writing; nineteenth century studies; literature of social justice and the environment. Total annual research expenditures: $54,723. *Unit head:* Dr. Sam Dragga, Chair, 806-742-2501, Fax: 806-742-0989, E-mail: sam.dragga@ttu.edu. *Application contact:* Dr. Sean Grass, Director of Graduate Studies, 806-742-2501, Fax: 806-742-0989, E-mail: english.gradadvisor@ttu.edu.

The University of Alabama in Huntsville, School of Graduate Studies, College of Liberal Arts, Department of English, Huntsville, AL 35899. Offers English (MA); teaching of English to speakers of other languages (Certificate); technical communications (Certificate). Part-time and evening/weekend programs available. *Faculty:* 19 full-time (10 women). *Students:* 22 full-time (16 women), 43 part-time (34 women); includes 11 minority (8 African Americans, 1 American Indian/Alaska Native, 2 Hispanic Americans). Average age 32. 32 applicants, 75% accepted, 20 enrolled. In 2008, 20 master's, 7 other advanced degrees awarded. *Degree requirements:* For master's, one foreign language, comprehensive exam, thesis or alternative, oral and written exams. *Entrance requirements:* For master's and Certificate, GRE General

Test, minimum GPA of 3.0. Additional exam requirements/recommendations for international students: Required—TOEFL (minimum score 500 paper-based; 173 computer-based; 62 iBT). *Application deadline:* For fall admission, 7/15 for domestic students, 4/1 for international students; for spring admission, 11/30 for domestic students, 9/1 for international students. Applications are processed on a rolling basis. Application fee: $40 ($50 for international students). Electronic applications accepted. *Expenses:* Tuition, area resident: Full-time $5214; part-time $323 per credit hour. Tuition, state resident: full-time $5214; part-time $323 per credit hour. Tuition, nonresident: full-time $11,444; part-time $705 per credit hour. Required fees: $540; $120 per semester. Tuition and fees vary according to course load. *Financial support:* In 2008–09, 7 students received support, including 4 teaching assistantships with full and partial tuition reimbursements available (averaging $8,460 per year); career-related internships or fieldwork, Federal Work-Study, institutionally sponsored loans, scholarships/grants, health care benefits, and unspecified assistantships also available. Support available to part-time students. Financial award application deadline: 4/1; financial award applicants required to submit FAFSA. *Faculty research:* American and British literature, linguistics, technical writing, women's studies, rhetoric. *Unit head:* Dr. Rose Norman, Chair, 256-824-6320, Fax: 256-824-6949, E-mail: normanr@uah.edu. *Application contact:* Kathy Biggs, Graduate Studies Admissions Manager, 256-824-6199, Fax: 256-824-6405, E-mail: deangrad@uah.edu.

University of Arkansas at Little Rock, Graduate School, College of Arts, Humanities, and Social Science, Department of Rhetoric and Writing, Little Rock, AR 72204-1099. Offers professional and technical writing (MA). Part-time and evening/weekend programs available. *Degree requirements:* For master's, thesis or alternative, oral defense of final project. *Entrance requirements:* For master's, GRE, minimum GPA of 3.0, writing portfolio. *Faculty research:* Writing for industry, science, business, and government; composition and rhetorical theory; writing nonfiction; teaching of writing.

University of California, Santa Cruz, Division of Graduate Studies, Division of Physical and Biological Sciences, Program in Science Communication, Santa Cruz, CA 95064. Offers science illustration (Certificate); science writing (Certificate). *Entrance requirements:* For degree, GRE General Test, GRE Subject Test, bachelor's degree in science. Electronic applications accepted.

University of Central Florida, College of Arts and Humanities, Department of English, Orlando, FL 32816. Offers English (MA, MFA), including creative writing (MFA), English (MA); literature (MA); professional writing (Certificate); rhetoric and composition (MA); technical communication (MA); texts and technology (PhD). Part-time and evening/weekend programs available. *Faculty:* 68 full-time (39 women), 30 part-time/adjunct (1 woman). *Students:* 54 full-time (35 women), 67 part-time (42 women); includes 19 minority (5 African Americans, 3 Asian Americans or Pacific Islanders, 11 Hispanic Americans), 3 international. In 2008, 38 master's, 4 doctorates, 9 other advanced degrees awarded. *Degree requirements:* For master's, one foreign language, thesis or alternative. *Entrance requirements:* For master's, GRE General Test, minimum GPA of 3.0 in last 60 hours of course work. Additional exam requirements/recommendations for international students: Required—TOEFL. *Application deadline:* For fall admission, 6/15 for domestic students; for spring admission, 12/1 for domestic students. Application fee: $30. Electronic applications accepted. *Expenses:* Tuition, area resident: Full-time $6816; part-time $284 per credit. Tuition, state resident: full-time $6816; part-time $1076 per credit. Tuition, nonresident: full-time $25,824. Required fees: $216; $9 per credit. *Financial support:* In 2008–09, 6 fellowships with partial tuition reimbursements, 20 research assistantships with partial tuition reimbursements, 17 teaching assistantships with partial tuition reimbursements were awarded; career-related internships or fieldwork, Federal Work-Study, institutionally sponsored loans, tuition waivers (partial), and unspecified assistantships also available. Financial award application deadline: 3/1; financial award applicants required to submit FAFSA. *Unit head:* Dr. David Wallace, Chair, 407-823-1159, E-mail: dwallace@mail.ucf.edu. *Application contact:* Dr. David Wallace, Chair, 407-823-1159, E-mail: dwallace@mail.ucf.edu.

The University of North Carolina at Greensboro, Graduate School, College of Arts and Sciences, Department of English, Greensboro, NC 27412-5001. Offers creative writing (MFA); English (M Ed, MA, PhD, Certificate), including American literature (PhD), English (M Ed, MA), English literature (PhD), rhetoric and composition (PhD), technical writing (Certificate), women's studies (Certificate). *Degree requirements:* For master's, comprehensive exam; for doctorate, variable foreign language requirement, thesis/dissertation, preliminary exam. *Entrance requirements:* For master's, GRE General Test, minimum GPA of 3.0; for doctorate, GRE General Test, GRE Subject Test, critical writing sample, minimum GPA of 3.0. Additional exam requirements/recommendations for international students: Required—TOEFL. Electronic applications accepted.

University of North Texas, Robert B. Toulouse School of Graduate Studies, College of Arts and Sciences, Department of English, Denton, TX 76203. Offers creative writing (MA); English (MA, PhD); English as a second language (MA); linguistics (MA); Technical writing (MA). Terminal master's awarded for partial completion of doctoral program. *Degree requirements:* For master's, one foreign language, comprehensive exam, thesis optional; for doctorate, one foreign language, comprehensive exam, thesis/dissertation. *Entrance requirements:* For master's, GRE General Test, 3.0 GPA, personal statement, current vita/resumé, writing sample for creative writing program; for doctorate, GRE General Test, 3.5 GPA, 3 letters of recommendation, personal statement, writing sample. Additional exam requirements/recommendations for international students: Required—proof of English language proficiency required for non-native English speakers; Recommended—TOEFL (minimum score 550 paper-based; 213 computer-based). *Faculty research:* Creative writing, British and American literature, composition and rhetoric.

University of the Sciences in Philadelphia, College of Graduate Studies, Program in Biomedical Writing, Philadelphia, PA 19104-4495. Offers biomedical writing (MS); medical marketing writing (Certificate); regulatory affairs writing (Certificate). Part-time and evening/weekend programs available. Postbaccalaureate distance learning degree programs offered (minimal on-campus study). *Faculty:* 1 full-time (0 women), 6 part-time/adjunct (4 women). *Students:* 5 full-time (3 women), 35 part-time (27 women); includes 1 minority (Asian American or Pacific Islander). Average age 38. In 2008, 7 master's, 7 other advanced degrees awarded. *Entrance requirements:* For master's, GRE General Test. Additional exam requirements/recommendations for international students: Required—TOEFL, TWE. *Application deadline:* For fall admission, 5/1 for international students; for winter admission, 10/1 for international students; for spring admission, 3/1 for international students. Applications are processed on a rolling basis. Application fee: $50. *Expenses:* Contact institution. *Financial support:* In 2008–09, 7 students received support. Tuition waivers (partial) available. Support available to part-time students. Financial award application deadline: 5/1. *Faculty research:* History of medical writing and publishing, compliance, regulatory. *Unit head:* Dr. Susanna Dodgson, Director, 215-596-8512, E-mail: s.dodgso@usp.edu. *Application contact:* Joyce D'Angelo, Administrative Assistant, 215-596-8937, E-mail: j.dangel@usp.edu.

University of Waterloo, Graduate Studies, Faculty of Arts, Department of English, Language and Literature, Waterloo, ON N2L 3G1, Canada. Offers English language and literature (PhD); literary studies (MA); rhetoric and communication design (MA). Part-time programs available. *Degree requirements:* For master's, one foreign language, thesis optional; for doctorate, 2 foreign languages, thesis/dissertation. *Entrance requirements:* For master's, honors degree, minimum B+ average; for doctorate, master's degree, minimum A- average. Additional exam requirements/recommendations for international students: Required—TOEFL, TWE. Electronic applications accepted. *Faculty research:* Shakespeare, American literature, rhetoric, Romantics, moderns.

Writing

Abilene Christian University, Graduate School, College of Arts and Sciences, Department of English, Abilene, TX 79699-9100. Offers composition/rhetoric (MA); literature (MA); writing (MA). Part-time programs available. *Faculty:* 14 part-time/adjunct (5 women). *Students:* 11 full-time (7 women), 2 part-time (both women); includes 1 minority (Hispanic American), 1 international. 12 applicants, 50% accepted, 5 enrolled. In 2008, 6 master's awarded. *Degree requirements:* For master's, one foreign language, comprehensive exam, thesis optional. *Entrance requirements:* For master's, GRE General Test. *Application deadline:* For fall admission, 4/1 priority date for domestic students; for spring admission, 11/1 for domestic students. Applications are processed on a rolling basis. Application fee: $40 ($45 for international students). Electronic applications accepted. *Expenses:* Tuition: Full-time $10,728; part-time $640 per hour. Required fees: $1090; $53.50 per hour. $10 per term. Tuition and fees vary according to campus/location. *Financial support:* In 2008–09, 13 students received support; teaching assistantships, Federal Work-Study available. Support available to part-time students. Financial award application deadline: 4/1; financial award applicants required to submit FAFSA. *Faculty research:* Feminism, Shakespearean dimensions of new literature, poetic consciousness, deconstruction myths. *Unit head:* Dr. Dana McMichael, Graduate Adviser, 325-674-2253, Fax: 325-674-2408, E-mail: rankinw@acu.edu. *Application contact:* William Horn, Graduate Admissions Counselor, 325-674-2656, Fax: 325-674-6717, E-mail: gradinfo@acu.edu.

Adelphi University, Graduate School of Arts and Sciences, Program in Creative Writing, Garden City, NY 11530-0701. Offers MFA. Part-time and evening/weekend programs available. *Students:* 11 full-time (5 women), 15 part-time (12 women); includes 1 Asian American or Pacific Islander, 2 Hispanic Americans, 2 international. Average age 32. In 2008, 4 master's awarded. *Degree requirements:* For master's, thesis. *Entrance requirements:* For master's, 3 letters of reference, manuscript in chosen genre (poetry, fiction, playwriting). Additional exam requirements/recommendations for international students: Required—TOEFL (minimum score 550 paper-based; 213 computer-based; 80 iBT). *Application deadline:* For fall admission, 5/1 priority date for international students; for spring admission, 11/1 priority date for international students. Applications are processed on a rolling basis. Application fee: $50. Electronic applications accepted. *Expenses:* Tuition: Full-time $25,700; part-time $775 per credit hour. Required fees: $500. Tuition and fees vary according to course load, degree level, campus/location, program and student level. *Financial support:* Fellowships, Federal Work-Study available. *Unit head:* Judith Baumel, Director, 516-877-4031, E-mail: baumel@adelphi.edu. *Application contact:* Christine Murphy, Director of Admissions, 516-877-3050, Fax: 516-877-3039, E-mail: graduateadmissions@adelphi.edu.

See Close-Up on page 551.

American University, College of Arts and Sciences, Department of Literature, Program in Creative Writing, Washington, DC 20016-8047. Offers MFA. Part-time and evening/weekend programs available. *Students:* 33 full-time (22 women), 28 part-time (16 women); includes 6 minority (2 African Americans, 4 Hispanic Americans), 2 international. Average age 28. 147 applicants, 53% accepted, 20 enrolled. In 2008, 19 master's awarded. *Degree requirements:* For master's, comprehensive exam, thesis. *Entrance requirements:* For master's, GRE, sample of written work. Additional exam requirements/recommendations for international students: Required—TOEFL. *Application deadline:* For fall admission, 2/1 priority date for domestic students. Application fee: $80. *Expenses:* Tuition: Full-time $21,204; part-time $1178 per credit hour. Required fees: $380. Part-time tuition and fees vary according to course load and program. *Financial support:* Fellowships, research assistantships, teaching assistantships, career-related internships or fieldwork, institutionally sponsored loans, and tuition waivers (full and partial) available. Support available to part-time students. Financial award application deadline: 2/1. *Unit head:* Richard McCann, Co-Director, 202-885-2978, Fax: 202-885-2938. *Application contact:* Graduate Program Assistant.

Antioch University Los Angeles, Graduate Programs, Program in Creative Writing, Culver City, CA 90230. Offers creative writing (MFA); pedagogy of creative writing (Certificate). Postbaccalaureate distance learning degree programs offered (minimal on-campus study). *Degree requirements:* For master's, thesis. *Entrance requirements:* For master's, sample of written work. Additional exam requirements/recommendations for international students: Required—TOEFL. *Faculty research:* Creative nonfiction, fiction, poetry.

Antioch University McGregor, Graduate Programs, Individualized Liberal and Professional Studies Program, Yellow Springs, OH 45387-1609. Offers liberal and professional studies (MA), including counseling, creative writing, education, film studies, liberal studies, management, modern literature, psychology, theatre, visual arts. Part-time and evening/weekend programs available. Postbaccalaureate distance learning degree programs offered (minimal on-campus study). *Degree requirements:* For master's, thesis or alternative. *Entrance requirements:* For master's, resumé, 2 letters of reference. Electronic applications accepted. *Expenses:* Contact institution.

Arizona State University, Graduate College, College of Liberal Arts and Sciences, Division of Humanities, Department of English, Interdisciplinary Program in Creative Writing, Tempe, AZ 85287. Offers MFA. *Entrance requirements:* For master's, GRE.

Asbury College, Graduate Programs, Wilmore, KY 40390-1198. Offers biology: alternative certificate (MA Ed); chemistry: alternative certificate (MA Ed); English (Certificate); English as a second language (MA Ed); ESL (Certificate); French (Certificate); mathematics: alternative certificate (MA Ed); reading / writing (MA Ed); social studies (Certificate); Spanish (Certificate); special education (MA Ed); special education: alternative certificate (MA Ed). *Accreditation:* NCATE. Part-time programs available. *Degree requirements:* For master's, action research project, portfolio. *Entrance requirements:* For master's, PRAXIS/NTE, minimum GPA of 2.75, letters of recommendation. Additional exam requirements/recommendations for international students: Required—TOEFL (minimum score 550 paper-based).

Ashland University, College of Arts and Sciences, Program in Creative Writing, Ashland, OH 44805-3702. Offers MFA. Postbaccalaureate distance learning degree programs offered (minimal on-campus study). *Faculty:* 8 part-time/adjunct (5 women). *Students:* 26 full-time (19 women). Average age 36. *Degree requirements:* For master's, thesis. *Entrance requirements:* For master's, writing sample, minimum GPA of 2.75. *Application deadline:* For fall admission, 2/1 priority date for domestic students; for winter admission, 10/1 priority date for domestic students. Application fee: $30. *Expenses:* Tuition: Part-time $419 per credit hour. Tuition and fees vary according to degree level and program. *Financial support:* In 2008–09, 11 students received support. Career-related internships or fieldwork, Federal Work-Study, and institutionally sponsored loans available. *Unit head:* Dr. Stephen Haven, Director, MFA Program, 419-289-5979, E-mail: shaven@ashland.edu. *Application contact:* Sarah Marie Wells, Administrative Director, MFA Program, 419-289-5957, E-mail: swells@ashland.edu.

Writing

Ball State University, Graduate School, College of Sciences and Humanities, Department of English, Muncie, IN 47306-1099. Offers English (MA, PhD), including composition, creative writing (MA), general (MA), literature; linguistics (MA, PhD), including applied linguistics (PhD); linguistics and teaching English to speakers of other languages (MA); teaching English to speakers of other languages (MA). *Degree requirements:* For doctorate, variable foreign language requirement, thesis/dissertation. *Entrance requirements:* For master's, GRE General Test, writing sample; for doctorate, GRE General Test, GRE Subject Test, minimum graduate GPA of 3.2, writing sample. *Faculty research:* American literature; literary editing; Medieval, Renaissance, and eighteenth century British literature; rhetoric.

Belmont University, College of Arts and Sciences, Department of English, Nashville, TN 37212-3757. Offers literature (MA); writing (MA). Part-time and evening/weekend programs available. *Faculty:* 16 full-time (12 women). *Students:* 2 full-time (both women), 37 part-time (31 women); includes 3 minority (2 African Americans, 1 Hispanic American). Average age 28. 15 applicants, 80% accepted, 11 enrolled. In 2008, 10 master's awarded. *Degree requirements:* For master's, one foreign language, comprehensive exam (for some programs), thesis optional. *Entrance requirements:* For master's, GRE, letters of recommendation, writing sample. Additional exam requirements/recommendations for international students: Required—TOEFL. *Application deadline:* For fall admission, 8/1 for domestic students; for spring admission, 12/1 for domestic students. Applications are processed on a rolling basis. Application fee: $50. Electronic applications accepted. *Expenses:* Contact institution. *Financial support:* In 2008–09, 20 students received support. Federal Work-Study and scholarships/grants available. Financial award applicants required to submit FAFSA. *Faculty research:* Gender, autobiography, folklore, Shakespeare, editing. *Unit head:* Dr. James Wells, Director, 615-460-6239, Fax: 615-460-5720, E-mail: james.wells@mail.belmont.edu. *Application contact:* Dr. James Wells, Director, 615-460-6239, Fax: 615-460-5720, E-mail: james.wells@mail.belmont.edu.

Bennington College, Graduate Programs, The Bennington Writing Seminars, Bennington, VT 05201. Offers creative writing (MFA). Postbaccalaureate distance learning degree programs offered (minimal on-campus study). *Faculty:* 15 full-time (5 women), 6 part-time/adjunct (3 women). *Students:* 103 full-time (76 women); includes 6 minority (3 African Americans, 3 Hispanic Americans), 2 international. Average age 38. 165 applicants, 35% accepted, 28 enrolled. In 2008, 50 master's awarded. *Degree requirements:* For master's, thesis, collection of essays or poems, or collection of short stories and/or a novel. *Entrance requirements:* For master's, manuscript. *Application deadline:* For fall admission, 3/1 for domestic students; for spring admission, 9/1 for domestic students. Application fee: $60. *Expenses:* Contact institution. *Financial support:* In 2008–09, 6 students received support. Scholarships/grants available. Financial award application deadline: 4/1; financial award applicants required to submit FAFSA. *Unit head:* Sven Birkerts, Director, Writing Seminars, 802-440-4452, Fax: 802-440-4453, E-mail: writing@bennington.edu. *Application contact:* Victoria Clausi, Associate Director of Writing Seminars, 802-440-4454, Fax: 802-440-4453, E-mail: writing@bennington.edu.

Boise State University, Graduate College, College of Arts and Sciences, Department of English, Program in Creative Writing, Boise, ID 83725-0399. Offers MFA. *Degree requirements:* For master's, thesis. *Entrance requirements:* For master's, GRE General Test, minimum GPA of 3.0.

Boston University, Graduate School of Arts and Sciences, Creative Writing Program, Boston, MA 02215. Offers MFA.

Boston University, Graduate School of Arts and Sciences, Department of English, Boston, MA 02215. Offers creative writing (MA); English (MA, PhD). Terminal master's awarded for partial completion of doctoral program. *Degree requirements:* For master's, one foreign language, thesis; for doctorate, 2 foreign languages, comprehensive exam, thesis/dissertation, qualifying/oral exam. *Entrance requirements:* For master's and doctorate, GRE General Test, GRE Subject Test, sample of written work, 2 letters of recommendation. Additional exam requirements/recommendations for international students: Required—TOEFL (minimum score 550 paper-based; 213 computer-based).

Boston University, Graduate School of Arts and Sciences, Editorial Institute, Boston, MA 02215. Offers MA, PhD. *Degree requirements:* For master's, one foreign language, thesis; for doctorate, one foreign language, comprehensive exam, thesis/dissertation. *Entrance requirements:* For master's and doctorate, GRE General Test, thesis proposal, 3 letters of recommendation. Additional exam requirements/recommendations for international students: Required—TOEFL (minimum score 550 paper-based; 213 computer-based).

Bowling Green State University, Graduate College, College of Arts and Sciences, Department of English, Program in Creative Writing, Bowling Green, OH 43403. Offers fiction (MFA); poetry (MFA). Part-time programs available. *Degree requirements:* For master's, thesis or alternative. *Entrance requirements:* For master's, GRE General Test. Additional exam requirements/recommendations for international students: Required—TOEFL. Electronic applications accepted. *Faculty research:* Poetry, criticism, novels, translation, travel writing.

Bowling Green State University, Graduate College, College of Arts and Sciences, Department of English, Program in English, Bowling Green, OH 43403. Offers English (MA, PhD); literature (MA); rhetoric and writing (PhD); scientific and technical communication (MA). Part-time programs available. *Degree requirements:* For master's, thesis or alternative; for doctorate, comprehensive exam, thesis/dissertation, foreign language or proficiency in Old English. *Entrance requirements:* For master's and doctorate, GRE General Test. Additional exam requirements/recommendations for international students: Required—TOEFL. Electronic applications accepted. *Faculty research:* Postmodern literary theory, rhetorical theory, ethnic American literature, literature and culture, composition pedagogy.

Brooklyn College of the City University of New York, Division of Graduate Studies, Department of English, Program in Creative Writing, Brooklyn, NY 11210-2889. Offers fiction (MFA); playwriting (MFA); poetry (MFA). Part-time and evening/weekend programs available. *Students:* 9 full-time (8 women), 55 part-time (31 women); includes 10 minority (4 African Americans, 4 Asian Americans or Pacific Islanders, 2 Hispanic Americans). Average age 30. 362 applicants, 12% accepted, 25 enrolled. In 2008, 27 master's awarded. *Degree requirements:* For master's, comprehensive exam, thesis or alternative, 36 credits. *Entrance requirements:* For master's, 12 undergraduate advanced credits in English, writing sample, 2 letters of recommendation, manuscript. Additional exam requirements/recommendations for international students: Required—TOEFL. *Application deadline:* For fall admission, 2/1 for domestic and international students. Applications are processed on a rolling basis. Application fee: $125. Electronic applications accepted. *Expenses:* Tuition, state resident: full-time $7360; part-time $310 per credit hour. Tuition, nonresident: full-time $13,800; part-time $575 per credit hour. *Financial support:* Federal Work-Study, institutionally sponsored loans, and scholarships/grants available. Support available to part-time students. Financial award application deadline: 5/1; financial award applicants required to submit FAFSA. *Faculty research:* Postmodern fiction. *Unit head:* Dr. James Davis, Graduate Deputy Chairperson, 718-951-5195, E-mail: jcdavis@brooklyn.cuny.edu. *Application contact:* Hernan Sierra, Graduate Admissions Coordinator, 718-951-4536, Fax: 718-951-4506, E-mail: grads@brooklyn.cuny.edu.

Brown University, Graduate School, Department of English, Program in Nonfiction Writing, Providence, RI 02912. Offers MFA. *Degree requirements:* For master's, thesis. *Entrance requirements:* For master's, GRE General Test, GRE Subject Test.

California College of the Arts, Graduate Programs, Program in Writing, San Francisco, CA 94107. Offers MFA. *Degree requirements:* For master's, thesis, exhibit. *Entrance requirements:* For master's, appropriate bachelor's degree, portfolio. Additional exam requirements/recommendations for international students: Required—TOEFL (minimum score 600 paper-based; 250 computer-based). Electronic applications accepted.

See Close-Up on page 207.

California Institute of the Arts, School of Critical Studies, Valencia, CA 91355-2340. Offers writing (MFA, Adv C). *Entrance requirements:* For master's, portfolio. Additional exam requirements/recommendations for international students: Required—TOEFL.

California Institute of the Arts, School of Theatre, Valencia, CA 91355-2340. Offers acting (MFA, Adv C); design and technology (Adv C); directing (MFA); performing arts design and technology (MFA); theater management (MFA, Adv C); writing for performance (MFA). *Accreditation:* NAST. *Degree requirements:* For master's, thesis (for some programs), faculty review, performance or portfolio. *Entrance requirements:* For master's, audition or portfolio, interview. Additional exam requirements/recommendations for international students: Required—TOEFL. Electronic applications accepted.

California State University, Fresno, Division of Graduate Studies, College of Arts and Humanities, Department of English, Fresno, CA 93740-8027. Offers composition theory (MA); creative writing (MFA); literature (MA). Part-time and evening/weekend programs available. *Degree requirements:* For master's, one foreign language, thesis. *Entrance requirements:* For master's, GRE General Test, minimum GPA of 3.0, writing sample. Additional exam requirements/recommendations for international students: Required—TOEFL. Electronic applications accepted. *Faculty research:* American literature, Renaissance literature, foreign literature.

California State University, Long Beach, Graduate Studies, College of Liberal Arts, Department of English, Long Beach, CA 90840. Offers creative writing (MFA); English (MA). Part-time programs available. *Faculty:* 50 full-time (24 women), 78 part-time/adjunct (45 women). *Students:* 60 full-time (42 women), 114 part-time (78 women); includes 43 minority (5 African Americans, 1 American Indian/Alaska Native, 17 Asian Americans or Pacific Islanders, 20 Hispanic Americans). Average age 34. *Degree requirements:* For master's, one foreign language, comprehensive exam or thesis. *Entrance requirements:* For master's, GRE Subject Test, minimum GPA of 3.0 in English. *Application deadline:* For fall admission, 5/1 for domestic students. Applications are processed on a rolling basis. Application fee: $55. Electronic applications accepted. *Expenses:* Tuition, nonresident: full-time $11,160; part-time $372 per unit. Required fees: $4100; $1261 per semester. *Financial support:* Federal Work-Study, institutionally sponsored loans, and scholarships/grants available. Financial award application deadline: 3/2. *Faculty research:* English and American literature, literary theory, linguistics, rhetoric and composition. *Unit head:* Dr. Eileen S. Klink, Chair, 562-985-4223, Fax: 562-985-2369, E-mail: eklink@csulb.edu. *Application contact:* Dr. Beth Lau, Graduate Adviser, 562-985-42852, Fax: 562-985-4223, E-mail: blau@csulb.edu.

California State University, Long Beach, Graduate Studies, College of the Arts, Department of Theatre Arts, Long Beach, CA 90840. Offers acting (MFA); dramatic writing (MFA); technical theatre/design (MFA); theatre management (MFA); MBA/MFA. *Accreditation:* NAST. Part-time programs available. *Faculty:* 6 full-time (3 women), 3 part-time/adjunct (0 women). *Students:* 27 full-time (17 women), 12 part-time (7 women); includes 3 minority (all Asian Americans or Pacific Islanders), 5 international. Average age 32. 24 applicants, 29% accepted, 5 enrolled. *Degree requirements:* For master's, thesis or alternative. *Application deadline:* For fall admission, 7/1 for domestic students; for spring admission, 12/1 for domestic students. Applications are processed on a rolling basis. Application fee: $55. Electronic applications accepted. *Expenses:* Tuition, nonresident: full-time $11,160; part-time $372 per unit. Required fees: $4100; $1261 per semester. *Financial support:* Research assistantships, teaching assistantships, Federal Work-Study, institutionally sponsored loans, scholarships/grants, and traineeships available. Financial award application deadline: 3/2. *Unit head:* Dr. Joanne L. Gordon, Chair, 562-985-7891, Fax: 562-985-2263, E-mail: jgordon@csulb.edu. *Application contact:* Barbara Matthews, Graduate Adviser, 562-985-4042, Fax: 562-985-2263, E-mail: jmatthew@csulb.edu.

California State University, Northridge, Graduate Studies, College of Humanities, Department of English, Northridge, CA 91330. Offers creative writing (MA); literature (MA); rhetoric and composition theory (MA). Part-time and evening/weekend programs available. *Faculty:* 33 full-time (16 women), 71 part-time/adjunct (60 women). *Students:* 42 full-time (27 women), 133 part-time (96 women); includes 38 minority (4 African Americans, 1 American Indian/Alaska Native, 14 Asian Americans or Pacific Islanders, 19 Hispanic Americans). Average age 34. 114 applicants, 74% accepted, 51 enrolled. In 2008, 40 master's awarded. *Degree requirements:* For master's, thesis or alternative. *Entrance requirements:* For master's, writing proficiency test, GRE General Test or minimum GPA of 3.0. Additional exam requirements/recommendations for international students: Required—TOEFL. *Application deadline:* For fall admission, 11/30 for domestic students. Application fee: $55. *Financial support:* Teaching assistantships available. Financial award application deadline: 3/1. *Faculty research:* Reading improvement, professional writing, Dickens, Shaw, English as a second language. *Unit head:* Dr. George Uba, Chair, 818-677-3434, E-mail: george.uba@csun.edu. *Application contact:* Dr. Marjie Seagoe, Graduate Studies Secretary, 818-677-3433.

California State University, Sacramento, Graduate Studies, College of Arts and Letters, Department of English, Sacramento, CA 95819-6048. Offers creative writing (MA); teaching English to speakers of other languages (MA). Part-time programs available. *Degree requirements:* For master's, thesis, project, or comprehensive exam; writing proficiency exam. *Entrance requirements:* For master's, portfolio (creative writing); minimum GPA of 3.0 in English, 2.75 overall during previous 2 years. Additional exam requirements/recommendations for international students: Required—TOEFL. Electronic applications accepted. *Faculty research:* Teaching composition, remedial writing.

California State University, San Bernardino, Graduate Studies, College of Arts and Letters, Department of English, San Bernardino, CA 92407-2397. Offers creative writing (MFA); English composition (MA). Part-time and evening/weekend programs available. *Faculty:* 18 full-time (12 women), 1 (woman) part-time/adjunct. *Students:* 68 full-time (45 women), 48 part-time (35 women); includes 41 minority (14 African Americans, 1 American Indian/Alaska Native, 7 Asian Americans or Pacific Islanders, 19 Hispanic Americans), 1 international. Average age 36. 46 applicants, 63% accepted, 23 enrolled. In 2008, 28 master's awarded. *Degree requirements:* For master's, one foreign language, thesis. *Entrance requirements:* For master's, BA in English or linguistics, minimum GPA of 3.0. Additional exam requirements/recommendations for international students: Required—TOEFL. *Application deadline:* For fall admission, 8/31 priority date for domestic students. Application fee: $55. *Expenses:* Tuition, area resident: Full-time $1252; part-time $726 per quarter. Required fees: $334 per quarter. Tuition and fees vary according to degree level and student level. *Financial support:* Research assistantships, teaching assistantships, career-related internships or fieldwork, Federal Work-Study, institutionally sponsored loans, and writing center tutorships available. Support available to part-time students. Financial award application deadline: 3/1. *Faculty research:* Composition and literary theory, theatrical theory, creative writing, relationship between evaluating writing and teaching composition. *Unit head:* Dr. Juan Delgado, Chair, 909-537-5834, Fax: 909-537-7086, E-mail: jdelgado@csusb.edu. *Application contact:* Olivia Rosas, Director of Admissions, 909-537-7577, Fax: 909-537-7034, E-mail: orosas@csusb.edu.

California State University, San Marcos, College of Arts and Sciences, Program in Literature and Writing Studies, San Marcos, CA 92096-0001. Offers MA. Part-time and evening/weekend programs available. *Degree requirements:* For master's, one foreign language, thesis. *Entrance requirements:* For master's, GRE General Test, minimum GPA of 3.0, writing sample. *Faculty research:* Postcolonialism, feminism rhetoric, cultural studies, creative writing, critical theory.

California State University, Stanislaus, College of Humanities and Social Sciences, Department of English, Turlock, CA 95382. Offers English (MA); literature (MA); rhetoric and teaching of writing (MA); TESOL (MA, Certificate). Part-time programs available. *Degree requirements:* For master's, one foreign language, comprehensive exam, thesis. *Entrance requirements:* For master's, GRE General Test, minimum GPA of 3.0, 2 letters of reference, personal statement; for Certificate, minimum GPA of 3.0, 2 letters of reference. Additional exam requirements/recommendations for international students: Required—TOEFL (minimum score 550 paper-based; 213 computer-based), TWE (minimum score 4). Electronic applications accepted. *Faculty research:* Transnational literacies, Renaissance and Medieval literature, abolition writings and slave narratives, qualitative writing.

Carlow University, Humanities Division, Pittsburgh, PA 15213-3165. Offers creative writing (MFA), including fiction, nonfiction, poetry. Part-time and evening/weekend programs available. *Faculty:* 8 part-time/adjunct (4 women). *Students:* 30 part-time (27 women); includes 3 minority (all African Americans). Average age 41. In 2008, 8 master's awarded. *Degree requirements:* For master's, thesis or alternative. *Entrance requirements:* For master's, minimum GPA of 3.0, resumé, two essays, writing samples, two letters of recommendation. Additional exam requirements/recommendations for international students: Required—TOEFL (minimum score 550 paper-based; 213 computer-based). *Application deadline:* For fall admission, 6/15 priority date for domestic and international students; for spring admission, 11/15 priority date for domestic and international students. Applications are processed on a rolling basis. Application fee: $20. *Expenses:* Tuition: Part-time $700 per credit. *Financial support:* Career-related internships or fieldwork, Federal Work-Study, and scholarships/grants available. Support available to part-time students. Financial award application deadline: 4/1; financial award applicants required to submit FAFSA. *Unit head:* Ellie Wymard, PhD, Director of MFA Program, 412-578-6597, Fax: 412-578-8706, E-mail: wymardex@carlow.edu. *Application contact:* Jo Danhires, Administrative Assistant, Admissions, 412-578-6059, Fax: 412-578-6321, E-mail: gradstudies@carlow.edu.

Carnegie Mellon University, College of Humanities and Social Sciences, Department of English, Program in Professional Writing, Pittsburgh, PA 15213-3891. Offers editing and publishing (MAPW); policy and non-profit communication (MAPW); public and media relations / corporate communications (MAPW); science or healthcare communication (MAPW); technical writing (MAPW); writing for new media (MAPW); writing for print media (MAPW). Part-time programs available. *Entrance requirements:* For master's, GRE General Test. Additional exam requirements/recommendations for international students: Required—TOEFL, TWE.

See Close-Up on page 553.

Central Michigan University, College of Graduate Studies, College of Humanities and Social and Behavioral Sciences, Department of English Language and Literature, Mount Pleasant, MI 48859. Offers English composition and communication (MA); English language and literature (MA), including children's and young adult literature, creative writing, general concentration; teaching English to speakers of other languages (TESOL) (MA). Part-time and evening/weekend programs available. *Faculty:* 17 full-time (8 women), 11 part-time/adjunct (7 women). *Students:* 16 full-time (5 women), 53 part-time (32 women); includes 1 African American, 1 American Indian/Alaska Native, 2 Hispanic Americans, 8 international. Average age 32. *Degree requirements:* For master's, thesis or alternative. *Application deadline:* Applications are processed on a rolling basis. Application fee: $35 ($45 for international students). Electronic applications accepted. *Expenses:* Tuition, state resident: full-time $3717; part-time $413 per credit. Tuition, nonresident: full-time $6894; part-time $766 per credit. *Financial support:* Fellowships with tuition reimbursements, research assistantships with tuition reimbursements, teaching assistantships with tuition reimbursements, career-related internships or fieldwork, Federal Work-Study, unspecified assistantships, and out-of-state merit awards available. *Faculty research:* Composition theory, science fiction history and bibliography, children's and young adult literature, nineteenth century American literature, applied linguistics. *Unit head:* Dr. Marcia Taylor, Chairperson, 989-774-3171, Fax: 989-774-1271, E-mail: taylo1mm@cmich.edu. *Application contact:* Dr. Jeffrey A. Weinstock, Coordinator, Graduate Studies in English, 989-774-3101, Fax: 989-774-1271, E-mail: weins1ja@cmich.edu.

Chapman University, Graduate Studies, Wilkinson College of Humanities and Social Sciences, Department of English, Orange, CA 92866. Offers creative writing (MFA); English (MA). Part-time and evening/weekend programs available. *Faculty:* 18 full-time (8 women), 22 part-time/adjunct (10 women). *Students:* 40 full-time (21 women), 37 part-time (28 women); includes 7 minority (1 African American, 1 American Indian/Alaska Native, 3 Asian Americans or Pacific Islanders, 2 Hispanic Americans). Average age 30. 57 applicants, 67% accepted, 25 enrolled. In 2008, 28 master's awarded. *Degree requirements:* For master's, comprehensive exam (for some programs), thesis (for some programs). *Entrance requirements:* For master's, GRE or MAT, minimum undergraduate GPA of 2.5. Additional exam requirements/recommendations for international students: Required—TOEFL (minimum score 550 paper-based; 213 computer-based; 80 iBT). *Application deadline:* For fall admission, 5/1 priority date for domestic students. Applications are processed on a rolling basis. Application fee: $50. Electronic applications accepted. *Expenses:* Contact institution. *Financial support:* Fellowships, Federal Work-Study and scholarships/grants available. Financial award application deadline: 3/2; financial award applicants required to submit FAFSA. *Unit head:* Dr. Paul Gulino, Department Chair, 714-997-6750, E-mail: gulino@chapman.edu. *Application contact:* Priscilla Garcia Powers, Graduate Admission Counselor, 714-997-6711, E-mail: pgarcia@chapman.edu.

Chapman University, Graduate Studies, Wilkinson College of Humanities and Social Sciences, Program in Creative Writing, Orange, CA 92866. Offers MFA. Part-time and evening/weekend programs available. *Faculty:* 19 full-time (8 women), 19 part-time/adjunct (11 women). *Students:* 33 full-time (21 women), 25 part-time (13 women); includes 7 minority (1 African American, 2 Asian Americans or Pacific Islanders, 4 Hispanic Americans). Average age 29. 40 applicants, 80% accepted, 22 enrolled. In 2008, 19 master's awarded. *Degree requirements:* For master's, thesis, project. *Entrance requirements:* For master's, GRE General Test or MAT, minimum undergraduate GPA of 3.0, sample of creative writing. Additional exam requirements/recommendations for international students: Required—TOEFL (minimum score 550 paper-based). *Application deadline:* Applications are processed on a rolling basis. Application fee: $55. Electronic applications accepted. *Expenses:* Contact institution. *Financial support:* Fellowships, Federal Work-Study and scholarships/grants available. Financial award application deadline: 6/30; financial award applicants required to submit FAFSA. *Unit head:* Dr. Richard Ruppel, Chair, 714-997-6754, E-mail: ruppel@chapman.edu. *Application contact:* Jim Blaylock, Coordinator, 714-997-6750, E-mail: blaylock@chapman.edu.

Chatham University, Program in Writing, Pittsburgh, PA 15232-2826. Offers children's writing (MFA); fiction (MFA); non-fiction (MFA); poetry (MFA); professional writing (MPW); screenwriting (MFA). Part-time and evening/weekend programs available. Postbaccalaureate distance learning degree programs offered (minimal on-campus study). *Students:* 57 full-time (47 women), 88 part-time (67 women). Average age 33. 67 applicants, 85% accepted, 57 enrolled. In 2008, 43 master's awarded. *Entrance requirements:* For master's, minimum GPA of 3.0, writing sample, recommendation letters. Additional exam requirements/recommendations for international students: Required—TOEFL (minimum score 600 paper-based; 250 computer-based; 100 iBT), IELTS (minimum score 6.5), TWE. *Application deadline:* For fall admission, 3/15 priority date for domestic students, 5/1 priority date for international students; for spring admission, 10/15 priority date for domestic students, 10/1 priority date for international students. Applications are processed on a rolling basis. Application fee: $45. Electronic applications accepted. *Expenses:* Tuition: Part-time $686 per credit. Tuition and fees vary according to program. *Financial support:* Career-related internships or fieldwork available. Financial award applicants required to submit FAFSA. *Faculty research:* Ecopoetics; environment and culture; wilderness and literature; literature of exploration, exile, and home. *Unit head:* Dr. Sheryl St. Germain, Director, 412-365-1190, Fax: 412-365-1505, E-mail: sstgermain@chatham.edu. *Application contact:* Dory Perry, Associate Director of Graduate Admissions, 412-365-2758, Fax: 412-365-1609, E-mail: gradadmissions@chatham.edu.

Chicago State University, School of Graduate and Professional Studies, College of Arts and Sciences, Department of English, Chicago, IL 60628. Offers creative writing (MFA); English (MA). *Degree requirements:* For master's, comprehensive exam. *Entrance requirements:* For master's, minimum GPA of 2.75.

City College of the City University of New York, Graduate School, College of Liberal Arts and Science, Division of the Humanities and Arts, Department of English, Program in Creative Writing, New York, NY 10031-9198. Offers MA, MFA. *Degree requirements:* For master's, one

foreign language, comprehensive exam, thesis. *Entrance requirements:* For master's, GRE, minimum GPA of 3.0, 10-15 poems or 30-50 pages of fiction (short stories or novel excerpt). Additional exam requirements/recommendations for international students: Required—TOEFL (minimum score 600 paper-based; 250 computer-based).

Claremont Graduate University, Graduate Programs, School of Arts and Humanities, Department of English, Claremont, CA 91711-6160. Offers American studies (MA, PhD); critical theory (MA, PhD); early modern studies (MA, PhD); English (M Phil, MA, PhD); literary theory (PhD); literature (MA, PhD); literature and creative writing (MA); literature and film (MA); MBA/MA; MBA/PhD. Part-time programs available. *Faculty:* 2 full-time (1 woman), 2 part-time/adjunct (0 women). *Students:* 78 full-time (46 women), 12 part-time (9 women); includes 15 minority (1 African American, 2 American Indian/Alaska Native, 7 Asian Americans or Pacific Islanders, 5 Hispanic Americans), 2 international. Average age 35. In 2008, 9 master's, 11 doctorates awarded. *Entrance requirements:* For master's and doctorate, GRE General Test. Additional exam requirements/recommendations for international students: Required—TOEFL (minimum score 550 paper-based; 213 computer-based; 80 iBT). *Application deadline:* For fall admission, 2/1 priority date for domestic students. Applications are processed on a rolling basis. Application fee: $60. Electronic applications accepted. *Expenses:* Tuition: Full-time $33,698; part-time $1465 per unit. Required fees: $310; $155 per semester. Tuition and fees vary according to program. *Financial support:* Fellowships, Federal Work-Study, institutionally sponsored loans, and scholarships/grants available. Support available to part-time students. Financial award application deadline: 2/15; financial award applicants required to submit FAFSA. *Faculty research:* American, comparative, and English Renaissance literature; modernism; feminist literature and theory. *Unit head:* Wendy Martin, Chair, 909-621-8612, Fax: 909-607-1221, E-mail: wendy.martin@cgu.edu. *Application contact:* Justin Evans, Admissions Coordinator, 909-607-1278, Fax: 909-607-1221, E-mail: justin.evans@cgu.edu.

Clemson University, Graduate School, College of Architecture, Arts, and Humanities, Department of English, Program in Professional Communication, Clemson, SC 29634. Offers MA. Part-time programs available. *Students:* 32 full-time (22 women), 9 part-time (6 women); includes 4 minority (1 African American, 1 Asian American or Pacific Islander, 2 Hispanic Americans), 2 international. Average age 30. 34 applicants, 62% accepted, 15 enrolled. In 2008, 10 master's awarded. *Degree requirements:* For master's, one foreign language, thesis optional, oral exam. *Entrance requirements:* For master's, GRE General Test, minimum GPA of 3.0. Additional exam requirements/recommendations for international students: Required—TOEFL, IELTS. *Application deadline:* For fall admission, 6/1 priority date for domestic students, 4/15 for international students; for spring admission, 12/1 for domestic students, 9/15 for international students. Applications are processed on a rolling basis. Application fee: $55. Full-time tuition and fees vary according to program. *Financial support:* Research assistantships, teaching assistantships available. Financial award application deadline: 4/1; financial award applicants required to submit FAFSA. *Faculty research:* Usability testing, rhetoric, communication across the curriculum, intercultural communication. *Unit head:* Dr. Summer Taylor, Coordinator, 864-656-6689, Fax: 864-656-1345, E-mail: slsmith@clemson.edu. *Application contact:* Dr. Summer Taylor, Coordinator, 864-656-6689, Fax: 864-656-1345, E-mail: slsmith@clemson.edu.

Cleveland State University, College of Graduate Studies, College of Liberal Arts and Social Sciences, Department of English, Cleveland, OH 44115. Offers creative writing (MFA); English (MA). Part-time and evening/weekend programs available. *Faculty:* 19 full-time (8 women), 29 part-time/adjunct (13 women). *Students:* 22 full-time (14 women), 63 part-time (45 women); includes 10 minority (9 African Americans, 1 Asian American or Pacific Islander) 3 international. Average age 34. 43 applicants, 53% accepted, 14 enrolled. In 2008, 17 master's awarded. *Degree requirements:* For master's, comprehensive exam, thesis. *Entrance requirements:* For master's, minimum GPA of 2.75, undergraduate concentration in English, writing sample, portfolio. Additional exam requirements/recommendations for international students: Required—TOEFL (525 paper-based; 197 computer-based) or IELTS (6 paper-based). *Application deadline:* For fall admission, 7/18 priority date for domestic students, 5/15 for international students; for spring admission, 12/15 for domestic students, 11/1 for international students. Applications are processed on a rolling basis. Application fee: $30. Electronic applications accepted. *Financial support:* In 2008–09, 20 students received support, including 1 fellowship (averaging $1,000 per year), 5 research assistantships with full and partial tuition reimbursements available (averaging $3,480 per year), 7 teaching assistantships with full and partial tuition reimbursements available (averaging $3,480 per year); Federal Work-Study, institutionally sponsored loans, tuition waivers (full and partial), and unspecified assistantships also available. Support available to part-time students. Financial award application deadline: 2/15. *Faculty research:* Literary history and criticism, linguistics, literature. Total annual research expenditures: $5,000. *Unit head:* Dr. David M. Larson, Chairperson, 216-687-3951, Fax: 216-687-6943, E-mail: d.larson@csuohio.edu. *Application contact:* Dr. Jennifer M. Jeffers, Graduate Director, 216-687-3975, Fax: 216-687-6943, E-mail: j.m.jeffers53@csuohio.edu.

Colorado State University, Graduate School, College of Liberal Arts, Department of English, Fort Collins, CO 80523-1773. Offers creative writing (MFA); English (MA). Part-time programs available. *Faculty:* 30 full-time (19 women). *Students:* 104 full-time (65 women), 55 part-time (40 women); includes 15 minority (3 American Indian/Alaska Native, 4 Asian Americans or Pacific Islanders, 8 Hispanic Americans), 14 international. Average age 30. 276 applicants, 41% accepted, 53 enrolled. In 2008, 43 master's awarded. *Degree requirements:* For master's, variable foreign language requirement, comprehensive exam (for some programs), thesis (for some programs), exams. *Entrance requirements:* For master's, GRE, writing sample, BA/BS with minimum GPA of 3.0, letters of recommendation, statement of purpose. Additional exam requirements/recommendations for international students: Required—TOEFL (minimum score 550 paper-based), TOEFL paper-based score of 575 required for creative writing. *Application deadline:* For fall admission, 4/1 priority date for domestic students; for spring admission, 9/1 priority date for domestic students. Applications are processed on a rolling basis. Application fee: $50. Electronic applications accepted. *Expenses:* Tuition, area resident: Full-time $5620; part-time $312.25 per credit. Tuition, state resident: full-time $5620; part-time $312.25 per credit. Tuition, nonresident: full-time $17,253; part-time $958.50 per credit. Required fees: $1449.56; $82.35 per credit. *Financial support:* In 2008–09, 34 students received support, including 34 teaching assistantships with full tuition reimbursements available (averaging $12,313 per year); fellowships, research assistantships, career-related internships or fieldwork, Federal Work-Study, institutionally sponsored loans, scholarships/grants, traineeships, and unspecified assistantships also available. Support available to part-time students. Financial award application deadline: 5/1; financial award applicants required to submit FAFSA. *Faculty research:* Computers and writing, environmental writing, cultural studies, new historicism, performance and identity. Total annual research expenditures: $72,058. *Unit head:* Dr. Bruce Ronda, Chair, 970-491-6428, Fax: 970-491-5601, E-mail: bruce.ronda@colostate.edu. *Application contact:* Marnie Leonard, Administrative Assistant, 970-491-2403, Fax: 970-491-7541, E-mail: marnie.leonard@colostate.edu.

Columbia College Chicago, Graduate School, Department of Fiction Writing, Chicago, IL 60605-1996. Offers creative writing (MFA); teaching of writing (MA); MFA/MA. Part-time programs available. *Students:* 28 full-time (12 women), 47 part-time (28 women); includes 20 minority (11 African Americans, 1 American Indian/Alaska Native, 2 Asian Americans or Pacific Islanders, 6 Hispanic Americans), 1 international. Average age 33. 110 applicants, 13 enrolled. In 2008, 19 master's awarded. *Degree requirements:* For master's, thesis. *Entrance requirements:* For master's, minimum GPA of 3.0, work sample, thirty pages of manuscript in roughly equal amounts of fiction and expository prose. Additional exam requirements/recommendations for international students: Required—TOEFL (minimum score 550 paper-based; 213 computer-based). *Application deadline:* For fall admission, 2/1 priority date for domestic and international students. Applications are processed on a rolling basis. Application fee: $55. Electronic applications accepted. *Expenses:* Tuition: Full-time $15,992; part-time $633 per credit hour. *Financial support:* Fellowships, career-related internships or fieldwork, Federal Work-Study, and scholarships/grants available. Support available to part-time students. Financial award application deadline: 8/13; financial award applicants required to submit FAFSA. *Unit head:* Randall

Writing

Columbia College Chicago (continued)
Albers, Chairperson, 312-369-7616, Fax: 312-369-8043, E-mail: ralbers@colum.edu. *Application contact:* Keith Cleveland, Office of Provost/Senior Vice President, 312-369-7261, Fax: 312-369-8022, E-mail: kcleveland@colum.edu.

Columbia College Chicago, Graduate School, Program in Poetry, Chicago, IL 60605-1996. Offers MFA. Part-time programs available. *Students:* 20 full-time (11 women), 3 part-time (1 woman); includes 4 minority (3 African Americans, 1 Asian American or Pacific Islander). Average age 28. 14 applicants, 10 enrolled. In 2008, 10 master's awarded. *Degree requirements:* For master's, thesis. *Entrance requirements:* For master's, interview, writing sample, minimum GPA of 3.0. Additional exam requirements/recommendations for international students: Required—TOEFL (minimum score 550 paper-based; 213 computer-based). *Application deadline:* For fall admission, 2/2 for domestic and international students. Application fee: $55. Electronic applications accepted. *Expenses:* Tuition: Full-time $15,992; part-time $633 per credit hour. *Financial support:* Fellowships, Federal Work-Study and scholarships/grants available. Support available to part-time students. Financial award application deadline: 8/13; financial award applicants required to submit FAFSA. *Unit head:* Ken Daley, Department Chair, 312-369-8121, Fax: 312-369-8001, E-mail: kdaley@colum.edu. *Application contact:* Tony Trigilio, Director of the Graduate Program, 312-369-8138, Fax: 312-369-8001, E-mail: ttrigilio@colum.edu.

Columbia University, School of the Arts, Writing Division, New York, NY 10027. Offers fiction (MFA); nonfiction (MFA); poetry (MFA). *Degree requirements:* For master's, thesis. *Entrance requirements:* For master's, 3 letters of recommendation, writing sample. Additional exam requirements/recommendations for international students: Required—TOEFL (minimum score 600 paper-based; 250 computer-based). Electronic applications accepted.

See Close-Up on page 285.

Concordia University, School of Graduate Studies, Faculty of Arts and Science, Department of English, Program in Creative Writing, Montréal, QC H3G 1M8, Canada. Offers MA. *Degree requirements:* For master's, one foreign language, thesis. *Entrance requirements:* For master's, honors degree in English, minimum GPA of 3.3 in English literature, portfolio. *Faculty research:* Fiction, poetry, prose, drama.

Cornell University, Graduate School, Graduate Fields of Arts and Sciences, Field of English Language and Literature, Ithaca, NY 14853-0001. Offers African-American literature (PhD); American literature after 1865 (PhD); American literature to 1865 (PhD); American studies (PhD); colonial and postcolonial literature (PhD); creative writing (MFA); cultural studies (PhD); dramatic literature (PhD); English poetry (PhD); English Renaissance to 1660 (PhD); lesbian, bisexual, and gay literature studies (PhD); literary criticism and theory (PhD); nineteenth century (PhD); Old and Middle English (PhD); prose fiction (PhD); Restoration and eighteenth century (PhD); twentieth century (PhD); women's literature (PhD); MFA/PhD. *Faculty:* 54 full-time (27 women). *Students:* 100 full-time (53 women); includes 24 minority (8 African Americans, 4 American Indian/Alaska Native, 6 Asian Americans or Pacific Islanders, 6 Hispanic Americans), 14 international. Average age 29. 821 applicants, 6% accepted, 23 enrolled. In 2008, 19 master's, 12 doctorates awarded. Terminal master's awarded for partial completion of doctoral program. *Degree requirements:* For master's, one foreign language, thesis; for doctorate, one foreign language, comprehensive exam, thesis/dissertation, teaching experience. *Entrance requirements:* For master's, GRE General Test, 3 letters of recommendation, creative writing sample; for doctorate, GRE General Test, GRE Subject Test (English), 3 letters of recommendation, writing sample. Additional exam requirements/recommendations for international students: Required—TOEFL (minimum score 600 paper-based; 250 computer-based; 77 iBT). *Application deadline:* For fall admission, 1/10 for domestic students. Application fee: $70. Electronic applications accepted. *Expenses:* Tuition: Full-time $29,500. Required fees: $70. Full-time tuition and fees vary according to degree level, program and student level. *Financial support:* In 2008–09, 96 students received support, including 41 fellowships with full tuition reimbursements available, 1 research assistantship with full tuition reimbursement available, 54 teaching assistantships with full tuition reimbursements available; institutionally sponsored loans, scholarships/grants, health care benefits, tuition waivers (full and partial), and unspecified assistantships also available. Financial award applicants required to submit FAFSA. *Faculty research:* English and American literature, women's writing, ethnic and post-colonial literature, critical theory, medievalism. *Unit head:* Director of Graduate Studies, 607-255-7989, Fax: 607-255-6661. *Application contact:* Graduate Field Assistant, 607-255-7989, Fax: 607-255-6661, E-mail: english_grad@cornell.edu.

DePaul University, College of Liberal Arts and Sciences, Department of English, Program in Writing and Publishing, Chicago, IL 60604-2287. Offers MA. *Unit head:* Dr. William Fahrenbach, Chairperson, 773-325-1776, E-mail: bfahrenb@depaul.edu. *Application contact:* Dr. Lesley Kordecki, Director, 773-325-1786, Fax: 773-325-8607, E-mail: lkordeck@depaul.edu.

Eastern Kentucky University, The Graduate School, College of Arts and Sciences, Department of English and Theatre, Richmond, KY 40475-3102. Offers creative writing (MFA); English (MA). Part-time and evening/weekend programs available. *Degree requirements:* For master's, thesis optional. *Entrance requirements:* For master's, GRE General Test, minimum GPA of 2.5, minor in English with 3.0 GPA. *Faculty research:* Old English, Victorian studies, women's studies, rhetoric, popular culture, novel studies.

Eastern Michigan University, Graduate School, College of Arts and Sciences, Department of English Language and Literature, Program in Creative Writing, Ypsilanti, MI 48197. Offers MA. Part-time and evening/weekend programs available. Postbaccalaureate distance learning degree programs offered (minimal on-campus study). *Entrance requirements:* Additional exam requirements/recommendations for international students: Required—TOEFL.

Eastern Michigan University, Graduate School, College of Arts and Sciences, Department of English Language and Literature, Program in Teaching of Writing, Ypsilanti, MI 48197. Offers MA, Graduate Certificate.

Eastern Michigan University, Graduate School, College of Arts and Sciences, Department of English Language and Literature, Program in Written and Technical Communications, Ypsilanti, MI 48197. Offers technical communications (MA, Graduate Certificate); written communications (MA). Part-time and evening/weekend programs available. Postbaccalaureate distance learning degree programs offered (minimal on-campus study). *Entrance requirements:* Additional exam requirements/recommendations for international students: Required—TOEFL.

Eastern Washington University, Graduate Studies, College of Arts and Letters, Inland Northwest Center for Writers, Cheney, WA 99004-2431. Offers MFA. *Degree requirements:* For master's, comprehensive exam, thesis. *Entrance requirements:* For master's, GRE General Test, minimum GPA of 3.0, sample of written work.

Emerson College, Graduate Studies, School of the Arts, Department of Writing, Literature and Publishing, Program in Creative Writing, Boston, MA 02116-4624. Offers MFA. Part-time programs available. *Students:* 121 full-time (68 women), 29 part-time (20 women); includes 20 minority (4 African Americans, 1 American Indian/Alaska Native, 9 Asian Americans or Pacific Islanders, 6 Hispanic Americans), 1 international. Average age 28. 277 applicants, 50% accepted, 53 enrolled. In 2008, 39 master's awarded. *Entrance requirements:* For master's, GRE General Test, 15 page writing sample. Additional exam requirements/recommendations for international students: Required—TOEFL (minimum score 550 paper-based; 213 computer-based; 80 iBT), IELTS (minimum score 6.5). *Application deadline:* For fall admission, 1/5 for domestic and international students. Application fee: $60 ($75 for international students). Electronic applications accepted. *Expenses:* Tuition: Full-time $17,720; part-time $886 per credit. Required fees: $60 per year. One-time fee: $170. *Financial support:* In 2008–09, 30 students received support, including 9 fellowships with partial tuition reimbursements available (averaging $16,000 per year), 15 research assistantships with partial tuition reimbursements available (averaging $10,000 per year); career-related internships or fieldwork, Federal Work-Study, institutionally sponsored loans, scholarships/grants, and unspecified assistantships also available. Support available to part-time students. Financial award application deadline: 1/5; financial award applicants required to submit FAFSA. *Unit head:* Prof. Frederick Reiken, Graduate Program Director, 617-824-8750, E-mail: Frederick_Reiken@emerson.edu. *Application contact:* Office of Graduate Admission, 617-824-8610, Fax: 617-824-8614, E-mail: gradapp@emerson.edu.

Emerson College, Graduate Studies, School of the Arts, Department of Writing, Literature and Publishing, Program in Publishing and Writing, Boston, MA 02116-4624. Offers MA. Part-time programs available. *Students:* 85 full-time (75 women), 19 part-time (17 women); includes 11 minority (2 African Americans, 1 American Indian/Alaska Native, 4 Asian Americans or Pacific Islanders, 4 Hispanic Americans), 6 international. Average age 26. 182 applicants, 42% accepted, 47 enrolled. In 2008, 54 master's awarded. *Degree requirements:* For master's, thesis or alternative. *Entrance requirements:* For master's, GRE General Test, 15 page writing sample. Additional exam requirements/recommendations for international students: Required—TOEFL (minimum score 550 paper-based; 213 computer-based; 80 iBT), IELTS (minimum score 6.5). *Application deadline:* For fall admission, 1/5 for domestic and international students. Applications are processed on a rolling basis. Application fee: $60 ($75 for international students). Electronic applications accepted. *Expenses:* Tuition: Full-time $17,720; part-time $886 per credit. Required fees: $60 per year. One-time fee: $170. *Financial support:* In 2008–09, 27 students received support, including 3 fellowships with partial tuition reimbursements available (averaging $14,000 per year), 18 research assistantships with partial tuition reimbursements available (averaging $10,000 per year); career-related internships or fieldwork, Federal Work-Study, institutionally sponsored loans, scholarships/grants, and unspecified assistantships also available. Support available to part-time students. Financial award application deadline: 1/5; financial award applicants required to submit FAFSA. *Faculty research:* Publishing. *Unit head:* Prof. Lisa Diercks, Director, 617-824-8750, E-mail: Lisa_Diercks@emerson.edu. *Application contact:* Office of Graduate Admission, 617-824-8610, Fax: 617-824-8614, E-mail: gradapp@emerson.edu.

Fairfield University, College of Arts and Sciences, Fairfield, CT 06824-5195. Offers American studies (MA); communication (MA); creative writing (MFA); mathematics (MS). Part-time and evening/weekend programs available. *Faculty:* 46 full-time (20 women), 15 part-time/adjunct (7 women). *Students:* 6 full-time (1 woman), 53 part-time (26 women); includes 1 African American, 2 Hispanic Americans. Average age 41. 23 applicants, 78% accepted, 14 enrolled. In 2008, 36 master's awarded. *Degree requirements:* For master's, capstone research course. *Entrance requirements:* For master's, minimum GPA of 3.0, 2 letters of recommendation, resumé, essay. Additional exam requirements/recommendations for international students: Required—TOEFL (minimum score 550 paper-based; 213 computer-based; 80 iBT). *Application deadline:* For fall admission, 5/15 for international students; for spring admission, 10/15 for international students. Applications are processed on a rolling basis. Application fee: $60. Electronic applications accepted. *Expenses:* Tuition: Full-time $9450; part-time $525 per credit hour. Required fees: $25 per semester. Tuition and fees vary according to course load and program. *Financial support:* In 2008–09, 19 students received support. Unspecified assistantships available. Financial award applicants required to submit FAFSA. *Faculty research:* Non-commutative algebra, partial differential equations, writing (fiction, non-fiction and poetry), communication for social change, comparative media systems, negotiation and management. *Unit head:* Dr. Robbin Crabtree, Dean, 203-254-4000 Ext. 3263, Fax: 203-254-4119, E-mail: rcrabtree@fairfield.edu. *Application contact:* Marianne Gumpper, Director of Graduate and Continuing Studies Admissions, 203-254-4184, Fax: 203-254-4073, E-mail: gradadmis@fairfield.edu.

Fairleigh Dickinson University, College at Florham, Maxwell Becton College of Arts and Sciences, Department of English, Communication and Philosophy, Program in Creative Writing, Madison, NJ 07940-1099. Offers MFA. *Students:* 31 full-time (10 women), 9 part-time (2 women), 1 international. Average age 36. 43 applicants, 63% accepted, 11 enrolled. In 2008, 7 master's awarded. *Application deadline:* Applications are processed on a rolling basis. Application fee: $40. *Unit head:* Dr. Martin Green, Chairperson, 973-443-8712. *Application contact:* Susan Brooman, University Director, Graduate Admissions, 973-443-8905, Fax: 973-443-8088, E-mail: grad@fdu.edu.

Florida Atlantic University, Dorothy F. Schmidt College of Arts and Letters, Department of English, Boca Raton, FL 33431-0991. Offers British and American literature (MA); creative nonfiction (MFA); creative writing (MA); fiction (MFA); multicultural literatures and literacies (MA); poetry (MFA); science fiction and fantasy (MA); teaching English (MAT). Part-time programs available. *Faculty:* 49 full-time (24 women), 17 part-time/adjunct (7 women). *Students:* 51 full-time (28 women), 29 part-time (26 women); includes 16 minority (4 African Americans, 1 American Indian/Alaska Native, 2 Asian Americans or Pacific Islanders, 9 Hispanic Americans), 1 international. Average age 31. 53 applicants, 57% accepted, 16 enrolled. In 2008, 27 master's awarded. *Degree requirements:* For master's, one foreign language, thesis. *Entrance requirements:* For master's, GRE General Test, minimum GPA of 3.0, writing samples, 2 letters of recommendation. *Application deadline:* For fall admission, 3/1 for domestic students, 2/15 for international students; for spring admission, 11/1 for domestic students, 7/15 for international students. Applications are processed on a rolling basis. Application fee: $30. Electronic applications accepted. *Expenses:* Tuition, state resident: full-time $4867; part-time $270.40 per credit hour. Tuition, nonresident: full-time $16,486; part-time $915.87 per credit hour. *Financial support:* Fellowships, teaching assistantships with partial tuition reimbursements, Federal Work-Study and tuition waivers available. Support available to part-time students. Financial award application deadline: 3/1. *Faculty research:* African-American writers, critical theory, British American, Asian American. *Unit head:* Dr. Wenying Xu, Chair, 561-297-2065, Fax: 561-297-3807, E-mail: wxu@fau.edu. *Application contact:* Dr. Andrew Furman, Director of Graduate Studies, 561-297-3835, Fax: 561-297-3807, E-mail: afurman@fau.edu.

Florida International University, College of Arts and Sciences, Department of English, Program in Creative Writing, Miami, FL 33199. Offers MFA. Part-time and evening/weekend programs available. *Degree requirements:* For master's, thesis. *Entrance requirements:* For master's, GRE General Test, minimum GPA of 3.0 writing sample. Additional exam requirements/recommendations for international students: Required—TOEFL (minimum score 550 paper-based; 213 computer-based). Electronic applications accepted.

Florida State University, Graduate Studies, College of Arts and Sciences, Department of English, Tallahassee, FL 32306. Offers creative writing (MFA, PhD); literature (MA, PhD); rhetoric and composition (MA, PhD). Part-time programs available. *Degree requirements:* For master's, one foreign language, thesis or alternative; for doctorate, 2 foreign languages, thesis/dissertation. *Entrance requirements:* For master's, GRE General Test, GRE Subject Test (literature), sample of written work, 3 letters of recommendation; for doctorate, GRE General Test, sample of written work, 3 letters of recommendation. Electronic applications accepted. *Faculty research:* British literature, American literature, creative writing, rhetoric, multiethnic literature.

George Mason University, College of Humanities and Social Sciences, Department of English, Program in Creative Writing, Fairfax, VA 22030. Offers MFA. *Degree requirements:* For master's, one foreign language, thesis, exam or project. *Entrance requirements:* For master's, minimum GPA of 3.0 in last 60 hours, portfolio. Electronic applications accepted.

Georgia College & State University, Graduate School, School of Liberal Arts and Sciences, Department of English, Speech, and Journalism, Program in Creative Writing, Milledgeville, GA 31061. Offers MFA. *Degree requirements:* For master's, thesis. *Entrance requirements:* For master's, GRE or MAT, writing portfolio, letters of recommendation, official transcripts and statement of purpose. Additional exam requirements/recommendations for international students: Required—TOEFL.

Georgia State University, College of Arts and Sciences, Department of English, Program in Creative Writing, Atlanta, GA 30303-3083. Offers MA, MFA, PhD. *Degree requirements:* For master's, variable foreign language requirement, comprehensive exam, thesis; for doctorate, 2 foreign languages, comprehensive exam, thesis/dissertation. *Entrance requirements:* For master's and doctorate, GRE General Test, portfolio. Additional exam requirements/ recommendations for international students: Required—TOEFL. Electronic applications accepted.

Goddard College, Graduate Programs, Master of Fine Arts in Creative Writing Program, Plainfield, VT 05667-9432. Offers MFA. Program residency available in Plainfield, VT or Port Townsend, WA. Postbaccalaureate distance learning degree programs offered (minimal on-campus study). *Faculty:* 27 part-time/adjunct (19 women). *Students:* 164 full-time. Average age 38. 101 applicants, 62% accepted, 48 enrolled. *Degree requirements:* For master's, thesis, completed manuscript, teaching practicum, three critical papers, reading of 45 to 60 literary works. *Entrance requirements:* For master's, undergraduate degree, transcripts, three letters of recommendation, preliminary study plan and bibliography, creative writing sample or samples, current resumé. *Application deadline:* Applications are processed on a rolling basis. Application fee: $40. Electronic applications accepted. *Expenses:* Contact institution. *Financial support:* In 2008–09, 147 students received support. Applicants required to submit FAFSA. *Unit head:* Paul Selig, Director, 802-454-8311, Fax: 802-454-7835, E-mail: paul.selig@goddard.edu. *Application contact:* David DeLucca, Senior Admissions Counselor, 800-906-8312 Ext. 248, Fax: 802-454-1029, E-mail: david.delucca@goddard.edu.

Goucher College, Program in Creative Nonfiction, Baltimore, MD 21204-2794. Offers MFA. Part-time and evening/weekend programs available. Postbaccalaureate distance learning degree programs offered (minimal on-campus study). *Degree requirements:* For master's, manuscript, portfolio. *Entrance requirements:* For master's, writing sample. *Expenses:* Contact institution.

Hofstra University, College of Liberal Arts and Sciences, Department of English, Hempstead, NY 11549. Offers English and creative writing (MA); English literature (MA). Part-time programs available. *Faculty:* 12 full-time (7 women). *Students:* 16 full-time (9 women), 18 part-time (15 women); includes 1 minority (Hispanic American). Average age 31. 41 applicants, 73% accepted, 14 enrolled. In 2008, 15 master's awarded. *Degree requirements:* For master's, thesis optional. *Entrance requirements:* For master's, writing sample, essay, minimum GPA of 3.0 in literature courses. Additional exam requirements/recommendations for international students: Required—TOEFL (minimum score 550 paper-based; 213 computer-based; 80 iBT). *Application deadline:* Applications are processed on a rolling basis. Application fee: $60. Electronic applications accepted. *Expenses:* Tuition: Full-time $15,300; part-time $850 per credit. Required fees: $970; $165 per term. Tuition and fees vary according to program. *Financial support:* In 2008–09, 13 students received support, including 5 fellowships with full and partial tuition reimbursements available (averaging $2,605 per year), 1 research assistantship with full and partial tuition reimbursement available (averaging $14,220 per year); Federal Work-Study, institutionally sponsored loans, scholarships/grants, and tuition waivers (full and partial) also available. Support available to part-time students. Financial award applicants required to submit FAFSA. *Faculty research:* Herman Melville, disability studies, Early American literature, Queer Theory, twentieth century popular culture. *Unit head:* Dr. Joseph A. Fichtelberg, Chairperson, 516-463-5455, Fax: 516-463-6395, E-mail: engjaf@hofstra.edu. *Application contact:* Carol Drummer, Dean of Graduate Admissions, 516-463-4876, Fax: 516-463-4664, E-mail: gradstudent@hofstra.edu.

Hollins University, Graduate Programs, Program in Creative Writing, Roanoke, VA 24020-1603. Offers MFA. *Faculty:* 6 full-time (1 woman), 1 (woman) part-time/adjunct. *Students:* 24 full-time (15 women); includes 5 minority (4 African Americans, 1 Asian American or Pacific Islander). Average age 26. 182 applicants, 15% accepted, 13 enrolled. In 2008, 11 master's awarded. *Degree requirements:* For master's, comprehensive exam, thesis. *Entrance requirements:* For master's, manuscripts, 3 letters of recommendation. Additional exam requirements/recommendations for international students: Required—TOEFL (minimum score 550 paper-based; 213 computer-based; 79 iBT). *Application deadline:* For fall admission, 1/6 for domestic and international students. Application fee: $40. Electronic applications accepted. *Expenses:* Contact institution. *Financial support:* In 2008–09, 24 fellowships with full and partial tuition reimbursements (averaging $7,872 per year), 8 teaching assistantships (averaging $3,000 per year) were awarded; scholarships/grants and unspecified assistantships also available. Support available to part-time students. Financial award application deadline: 2/2; financial award applicants required to submit FAFSA. *Faculty research:* Poetry, fiction, creative nonfiction, literary criticism, literary theory. *Unit head:* Cathryn Hankla, Director, 540-362-6317, Fax: 540-362-6097, E-mail: creative.writing@hollins.edu. *Application contact:* Cathy S. Koon, Manager of Graduate Services, 540-362-6326, Fax: 540-362-6288, E-mail: ckoon@hollins.edu.

Hunter College of the City University of New York, Graduate School, School of Arts and Sciences, Department of English, Program in Creative Writing, New York, NY 10021-5085. Offers creative writing (MFA); fiction (MFA); nonfiction (MFA); poetry (MFA). Part-time and evening/weekend programs available. *Faculty:* 32 full-time (17 women). *Students:* 38 full-time (28 women). Average age 31. 305 applicants, 6% accepted, 18 enrolled. In 2008, 17 master's awarded. *Degree requirements:* For master's, thesis. *Entrance requirements:* For master's, creative writing manuscript (up to 10 pages of poetry or 25-30 pages of fiction or nonfiction); 500-word personal statement; nonfiction proposal (for nonfiction applicants only). *Application deadline:* For fall admission, 2/1 for domestic and international students. Application fee: $125. *Financial support:* In 2008–09, 18 students received support, including 12 fellowships (averaging $5,000 per year); Federal Work-Study and tuition waivers (partial) also available. Support available to part-time students. Financial award application deadline: 4/15. *Unit head:* Sue Nacey, Coordinator, 212-772-5164, Fax: 212-772-5076, E-mail: mfa@hunter.cuny.edu. *Application contact:* Elena Georgiou, Coordinator, 212-772-5164, Fax: 212-772-5076, E-mail: egeorgio@hunter.cuny.edu.

Illinois State University, Graduate School, College of Arts and Sciences, Department of English, Program in Writing, Normal, IL 61790-2200. Offers MA, MS. *Degree requirements:* For master's, comprehensive exam, internship or practicum. *Entrance requirements:* For master's, GRE General Test, minimum GPA of 3.0 in last 60 hours.

Indiana State University, School of Graduate Studies, College of Arts and Sciences, Department of English, Terre Haute, IN 47809-1401. Offers English teaching (MA); history (MA); literature (MA). Part-time and evening/weekend programs available. *Degree requirements:* For master's, one foreign language, thesis optional. *Entrance requirements:* For master's, minimum GPA of 2.75 in all English courses above freshman level. Additional exam requirements/ recommendations for international students: Required—TOEFL (minimum score 550 paper-based). Electronic applications accepted.

Indiana University Bloomington, University Graduate School, College of Arts and Sciences, Department of English, Bloomington, IN 47405-7000. Offers composition, literacy, and culture (PhD); creative writing (MA, MFA), including fiction, poetry; language (MA); literature (MA, PhD); writing (MA). Part-time programs available. *Faculty:* 51 full-time (23 women). *Students:* 180 full-time (115 women), 22 part-time (12 women); includes 25 minority (6 African Americans, 10 Asian Americans or Pacific Islanders, 9 Hispanic Americans), 10 international. Average age 30. 627 applicants, 11% accepted, 32 enrolled. In 2008, 27 master's, 11 doctorates awarded. Terminal master's awarded for partial completion of doctoral program. *Degree requirements:* For master's, one foreign language, thesis (for some programs); for doctorate, 2 foreign languages, thesis/dissertation, qualifying exam. *Entrance requirements:* For master's, GRE General Test, GRE Subject Test (for all but MFA and MA in creative writing), minimum GPA of 3.5; for doctorate, GRE General Test, GRE Subject Test, minimum GPA of 3.7. Additional exam requirements/recommendations for international students: Required—TOEFL. *Application deadline:* For fall admission, 1/15 priority date for domestic students, 12/15 for international students. Application fee: $50 ($60 for international students). Electronic applications accepted. *Expenses:* Tuition, area resident: Part-time $291.97 per credit hour. Tuition, state resident: part-time $291.97 per credit hour. Tuition, nonresident: part-time $850.33 per credit hour. Required fees: $110 per semester. Tuition and fees vary according to course load and program. *Financial support:* In 2008–09, 22 fellowships (averaging $14,337 per year), 1 research assistantship (averaging $7,500 per year), 136 teaching assistantships (averaging $13,000 per year) were awarded; career-related internships or fieldwork and health care benefits also available. Financial award application deadline: 2/1. *Unit head:* George Hutchinson, Chair, 812-855-8225, E-mail: gbhutchi@indiana.edu. *Application contact:* Patricia Ingham, Director of Admissions, 812-855-0521, Fax: 812-855-9535, E-mail: pingham@indiana.edu.

Indiana University of Pennsylvania, School of Graduate Studies and Research, College of Humanities and Social Sciences, Department of English, Program in Composition and Teaching English to Speakers of Other Languages, Indiana, PA 15705-1087. Offers composition and teaching English to speakers of other languages (PhD); teaching English (MAT); teaching English to speakers of other languages (MA). *Faculty:* 31 full-time (17 women). *Students:* 57 full-time (29 women), 145 part-time (98 women); includes 10 minority (4 African Americans, 1 American Indian/Alaska Native, 3 Asian Americans or Pacific Islanders, 2 Hispanic Americans), 72 international. Average age 37. 187 applicants, 34% accepted, 29 enrolled. In 2008, 20 master's, 12 doctorates awarded. *Degree requirements:* For master's, thesis optional; for doctorate, one foreign language, comprehensive exam, thesis/dissertation. *Entrance requirements:* For master's and doctorate, 2 letters of recommendation. Additional exam requirements/ recommendations for international students: Required—TOEFL. *Application deadline:* For fall admission, 7/1 priority date for domestic students; for spring admission, 11/1 for domestic students. Applications are processed on a rolling basis. Application fee: $30. *Expenses:* Tuition, area resident: Full-time $6430; part-time $357 per credit. Tuition, nonresident: full-time $10,288; part-time $572 per credit. Required fees: $1547.50; $107 per credit. $283 per year. *Financial support:* In 2008–09, 2 fellowships (averaging $2,666 per year), 19 research assistantships with full and partial tuition reimbursements (averaging $5,841 per year), 11 teaching assistantships with partial tuition reimbursements (averaging $12,355 per year) were awarded. Financial award application deadline: 3/15; financial award applicants required to submit FAFSA. *Unit head:* Dr. Ben Rafoth, Graduate Coordinator, 724-357-2272. *Application contact:* Dr. Ben Rafoth, Graduate Coordinator, 724-357-2272.

The Johns Hopkins University, Zanvyl Krieger School of Arts and Sciences, Advanced Academic Programs, Program in Writing, Washington, DC 20036. Offers MA. Part-time and evening/weekend programs available. *Degree requirements:* For master's, thesis. *Entrance requirements:* For master's, writing samples. Additional exam requirements/recommendations for international students: Required—TOEFL (minimum score 600 paper-based; 250 computer-based; 100 iBT).

The Johns Hopkins University, Zanvyl Krieger School of Arts and Sciences, The Writing Seminars, Baltimore, MD 21218-2699. Offers fiction writing (MFA); poetry (MFA); science writing (MA). *Degree requirements:* For master's, one foreign language, thesis, foreign language exam (for MFA). *Entrance requirements:* For master's, GRE General Test, GRE Subject Test (recommended), foreign language exam, sample of written work, 3 letters of recommendation, official college transcripts, GRE scores, and goal statement. Additional exam requirements/ recommendations for international students: Required—TOEFL (minimum score 600 paper-based; 250 computer-based). Electronic applications accepted. *Faculty research:* Film theory, literary criticism, contemporary fiction.

Kennesaw State University, College of Humanities and Social Sciences, Program in Professional Writing, Kennesaw, GA 30144-5591. Offers MAPW. Part-time and evening/weekend programs available. *Faculty:* 18 full-time (9 women), 2 part-time/adjunct (1 woman). *Students:* 29 full-time (22 women), 71 part-time (54 women); includes 16 minority (11 African Americans, 1 American Indian/Alaska Native, 1 Asian American or Pacific Islander, 3 Hispanic Americans), 1 international. Average age 34. 67 applicants, 70% accepted, 30 enrolled. In 2008, 27 master's awarded. *Entrance requirements:* For master's, GRE General Test, minimum GPA of 2.5, writing sample. Additional exam requirements/recommendations for international students: Required—TOEFL (minimum score 550 paper-based; 213 computer-based; 80 iBT), IELTS (minimum score 6). *Application deadline:* For fall admission, 3/1 for domestic and international students. Application fee: $60. Electronic applications accepted. *Expenses:* Tuition, area resident: Full-time $3668; part-time $153 per semester hour. Tuition, state resident: full-time $3668; part-time $153 per semester hour. Tuition, nonresident: full-time $14,670; part-time $612 per semester hour. Required fees: $948; $474 per semester. *Financial support:* In 2008–09, 2 research assistantships with full tuition reimbursements (averaging $15,000 per year) were awarded; Federal Work-Study also available. Support available to part-time students. Financial award application deadline: 6/15; financial award applicants required to submit FAFSA. *Unit head:* Dr. Jim Elledge, Director, 678-797-2039, E-mail: jellege1@kennesaw.edu. *Application contact:* Vilma Marquez, Admissions Counselor, 770-420-4377, Fax: 770-423-6885, E-mail: ksugrad@kennesaw.edu.

Kent State University, College of Arts and Sciences, Department of English, Kent, OH 44242-0001. Offers comparative literature (MA); creative writing (MFA); English (PhD); English for teachers (MA); literature and writing (MA); rhetoric and composition (PhD); teaching English as a second language (MA). Part-time programs available. Terminal master's awarded for partial completion of doctoral program. *Degree requirements:* For master's, one foreign language, thesis optional; for doctorate, one foreign language, thesis/dissertation, qualifying exams. *Entrance requirements:* For master's and doctorate, GRE General Test, writing sample, letters of recommendation. Additional exam requirements/recommendations for international students: Required—TOEFL (minimum score 600 paper-based). Electronic applications accepted. *Faculty research:* British and American literature, textual editing, rhetoric and composition, cultural studies, linguistic and critical theories.

La Sierra University, College of Arts and Sciences, Department of English and Communication, Riverside, CA 92515. Offers communication (MA), including public relations/ advertising, theory emphasis; English (MA), including literary emphasis, writing emphasis. Part-time programs available. *Degree requirements:* For master's, one foreign language. *Entrance requirements:* For master's, GRE General Test.

Lesley University, Graduate School of Arts and Social Sciences, Program in Creative Writing, Cambridge, MA 02138-2790. Offers MFA. Part-time programs available. Postbaccalaureate distance learning degree programs offered (minimal on-campus study). *Degree requirements:* For master's, intensive residency. *Entrance requirements:* For master's, writing sample. Additional exam requirements/recommendations for international students: Required—TOEFL (minimum score 550 paper-based; 213 computer-based; 80 iBT). *Expenses:* Contact institution.

See Close-Up on page 555.

Lindenwood University, Graduate Programs, College of Individualized Education, St. Charles, MO 63301-1695. Offers administration (MSA); business administration (MBA); communication (MS); communications (MA); criminal justice and administration (MS); gerontology (MA); health management (MS); human resource management (MS); information technology (MBA, Certificate); management (MSA); managing information technology (MS); marketing (MSA); writing (MFA). Part-time and evening/weekend programs available. *Faculty:* 14 full-time (7 women), 119 part-time/adjunct (50 women). *Students:* 750 full-time (489 women), 138 part-time (91 women); includes 196 minority (182 African Americans, 1 American Indian/Alaska Native, 5 Asian Americans or Pacific Islanders, 8 Hispanic Americans), 14 international. Average age 34. In 2008, 349 master's awarded. *Degree requirements:* For master's, thesis (for some programs), minimum GPA of 3.0, 1 colloquium per term. *Entrance requirements:* For master's, interview, minimum GPA of 3.0. Additional exam requirements/recommendations for international students: Required—TOEFL (minimum score 550 paper-based; 213 computer-based; 80 iBT). *Application deadline:* For fall admission, 9/30 priority date for domestic and international students; for winter admission, 12/30 priority date for domestic and international students; for spring admission, 3/30 priority date for domestic and international students. Applications are processed on a rolling basis. Application fee: $30 ($100 for international students). *Expenses:* Tuition: Full-time $12,700; part-time $360 per credit hour. *Financial support:* Career-related internships or fieldwork, institutionally sponsored loans, tuition waivers (partial), and unspecified assistantships available. Financial award application deadline: 6/30; financial award applicants required to submit FAFSA. *Unit head:* Dan Kemper, Dean of

Writing

Lindenwood University (continued)
Lindenwood College for Individual Education, 636-949-4501, Fax: 636-949-4505, E-mail: dkemper@lindenwood.edu. *Application contact:* Brett Barger, Dean of Evening Admissions and Extension Campuses, 636-949-4934, Fax: 636-949-4109, E-mail: adultadmissions@lindenwood.edu.

Long Island University, Brooklyn Campus, Richard L. Conolly College of Liberal Arts and Sciences, Department of English, Brooklyn, NY 11201-8423. Offers English literature (MA); professional and creative writing (MA); teaching of writing (MA). Part-time and evening/weekend programs available. *Degree requirements:* For master's, thesis or alternative. *Entrance requirements:* For master's, 2 letters of recommendation. Additional exam requirements/recommendations for international students: Required—TOEFL (minimum score 550 paper-based; 173 computer-based). Electronic applications accepted.

Longwood University, Office of Graduate Studies, Department of English and Modern Languages, Farmville, VA 23909. Offers 6-12 initial teaching/licensure (MA); creative writing (MA); English education and writing (MA); literature (MA). Part-time programs available. *Degree requirements:* For master's, comprehensive exam (for some programs), thesis (for some programs). *Entrance requirements:* For master's, minimum GPA of 2.75. Additional exam requirements/recommendations for international students: Required—TOEFL (minimum score 550 paper-based; 213 computer-based).

Louisiana State University and Agricultural and Mechanical College, Graduate School, College of Arts and Sciences, Department of English, Baton Rouge, LA 70803. Offers creative writing (MFA); English (MA, PhD). Part-time programs available. Terminal master's awarded for partial completion of doctoral program. *Degree requirements:* For master's, comprehensive exam; for doctorate, one foreign language, comprehensive exam, thesis/dissertation. *Entrance requirements:* For master's, GRE General Test, minimum GPA of 3.0; for doctorate, GRE General Test, GRE Subject Test, minimum GPA of 3.0. Additional exam requirements/recommendations for international students: Required—TOEFL (minimum score 550 paper-based; 213 computer-based; 79 iBT). Electronic applications accepted. *Faculty research:* American literature, British literature, cultural studies, rhetoric and composition, folklore.

Loyola Marymount University, School of Film and Television, Department of Screenwriting, Program in Screen Writing, Los Angeles, CA 90045-2659. Offers MFA. *Degree requirements:* For master's, thesis, project or script. *Entrance requirements:* For master's, GRE General Test, writing sample. Electronic applications accepted.

Manhattanville College, Graduate Programs, Humanities and Social Sciences Programs, Program in Writing, Purchase, NY 10577-2132. Offers MA. Part-time and evening/weekend programs available. *Degree requirements:* For master's, thesis. *Entrance requirements:* For master's, interview, 2 letters of recommendation. *Faculty research:* Published writers: fiction, poetry, essay.

Massachusetts Institute of Technology, School of Humanities, Arts, and Social Sciences, Program in Writing and Humanistic Studies, Graduate Program in Science Writing, Cambridge, MA 02139-4307. Offers SM. *Degree requirements:* For master's, thesis, internship. *Entrance requirements:* For master's, GRE General Test. Additional exam requirements/recommendations for international students: Required—TOEFL (minimum score 600 paper-based; 250 computer-based). Electronic applications accepted.

McNeese State University, Doré School of Graduate Studies, College of Liberal Arts, Department of English and Foreign Languages, Program in Creative Writing, Lake Charles, LA 70609. Offers MFA. Evening/weekend programs available. *Faculty:* 15 full-time (9 women). *Students:* 21 full-time (10 women); includes 2 minority (1 African American, 1 Asian American or Pacific Islander). In 2008, 4 master's awarded. *Degree requirements:* For master's, thesis, public reading. *Entrance requirements:* For master's, GRE, writing sample. *Application deadline:* For fall admission, 5/15 priority date for domestic and international students; for spring admission, 10/15 priority date for domestic and international students. Applications are processed on a rolling basis. Application fee: $20 ($30 for international students). *Expenses:* Tuition, area resident: Full-time $2386. Tuition, state resident: full-time $2386. Required fees: $885. Tuition and fees vary according to course load. *Financial support:* Teaching assistantships available. Financial award application deadline: 5/1. *Unit head:* Dr. Joe L. Cash, Head, 337-475-5326, Fax: 337-475-5327, E-mail: jcash@mcneese.edu. *Application contact:* Dr. George F. Mead, Interim Dean of Dore' School of Graduate Studies, 337-475-5396, Fax: 337-475-5397, E-mail: admissions@mcneese.edu.

Miami University, Graduate School, College of Arts and Sciences, Department of English, Oxford, OH 45056. Offers composition and rhetoric (MA, PhD); creative writing (MA); criticism (PhD); English and American literature and language (PhD); English education (MAT); library theory (PhD); literature (MA, MAT, PhD); technical and scientific communication (MTSC). Part-time programs available. *Degree requirements:* For master's, final exam; for doctorate, 2 foreign languages, comprehensive exam, thesis/dissertation, final exams. *Entrance requirements:* For master's, minimum undergraduate GPA of 3.0 during previous 2 years or 2.75 overall; for doctorate, GRE General Test, GRE Subject Test, minimum GPA of 2.75 (undergraduate), 3.0 (graduate). Additional exam requirements/recommendations for international students: Required—TOEFL (minimum score 550 paper-based; 213 computer-based), TWE (minimum score 4). Electronic applications accepted.

Michigan State University, The Graduate School, College of Arts and Letters, Program in Rhetoric and Writing, East Lansing, MI 48824. Offers critical studies in literacy and pedagogy (MA); digital rhetoric and professional writing (MA); rhetoric and writing (PhD). *Entrance requirements:* Additional exam requirements/recommendations for international students: Required—TOEFL. Electronic applications accepted. *Faculty research:* Rhetoric, writing and communication studies; media studies; technical communication, writing for digital environments.

Mills College, Graduate Studies, Department of English, Oakland, CA 94613-1000. Offers book art and creative writing (MFA); creative writing, poetry (MFA); creative writing, prose (MFA); English and American literature (MA). Part-time programs available. *Faculty:* 9 full-time (7 women), 24 part-time/adjunct (20 women). *Students:* 94 full-time (67 women), 7 part-time (6 women); includes 29 minority (13 African Americans, 8 Asian Americans or Pacific Islanders, 8 Hispanic Americans). Average age 30. 154 applicants, 86% accepted, 50 enrolled. In 2008, 37 master's awarded. *Degree requirements:* For master's, comprehensive exam, thesis. *Entrance requirements:* For master's, manuscript, writing sample. Additional exam requirements/recommendations for international students: Required—TOEFL. *Application deadline:* For fall admission, 2/1 priority date for domestic students; for spring admission, 11/1 for domestic students. Applications are processed on a rolling basis. Application fee: $50. Electronic applications accepted. *Expenses:* Tuition: Full-time $25,072; part-time $6272 per course. Required fees: $880. *Financial support:* In 2008–09, 86 students received support, including 83 fellowships (averaging $6,994 per year), 28 teaching assistantships with partial tuition reimbursements available (averaging $2,430 per year); scholarships/grants also available. Support available to part-time students. Financial award application deadline: 2/1; financial award applicants required to submit FAFSA. *Faculty research:* Creative writing, African-American literature, Victorian women writers, theories of sexuality, Shakespeare. *Unit head:* Dr. Cynthia Scheinberg, Chair, 510-430-2213, E-mail: cyns@mills.edu. *Application contact:* Marika Benko, Graduate Admission Specialist, 510-430-3309, Fax: 510-430-2159, E-mail: grad-studies@mills.edu.

Minnesota State University Mankato, College of Graduate Studies, College of Arts and Humanities, Department of English, Mankato, MN 56001. Offers creative writing (MFA); English (MA, MS); English literature (MA); teaching English (MS, MT); teaching English as a second language (MA, Certificate); technical communication (Certificate). Part-time programs available. *Students:* 36 full-time (20 women), 107 part-time (82 women). *Degree requirements:* For master's, one foreign language, comprehensive exam, thesis or alternative. *Entrance requirements:* For master's, minimum GPA of 3.0 during previous 2 years, writing sample (MFA). Additional exam requirements/recommendations for international students: Required—TOEFL. *Application deadline:* Applications are processed on a rolling basis. Application fee: $40. Electronic applications accepted. *Financial support:* Research assistantships with full tuition reimbursements, teaching assistantships with full tuition reimbursements, career-related internships or fieldwork, Federal Work-Study, and unspecified assistantships available. Financial award application deadline: 3/15; financial award applicants required to submit FAFSA. *Faculty research:* Keats and Christianity. *Unit head:* Dr. John Banschbach, Chairperson, 507-389-2117. *Application contact:* 507-389-2321, E-mail: grad@mnsu.edu.

Minnesota State University Moorhead, Graduate Studies, College of Arts and Humanities, Program in Creative Writing, Moorhead, MN 56563-0002. Offers MFA. Part-time programs available. *Degree requirements:* For master's, thesis, final manuscript, final oral exam. *Entrance requirements:* For master's, manuscript, minimum GPA of 2.75, 3 letters of recommendation. Additional exam requirements/recommendations for international students: Required—TOEFL (minimum score 550 paper-based; 213 computer-based). Electronic applications accepted.

Murray State University, College of Humanities and Fine Arts, Department of English and Philosophy, Program in Creative Writing, Murray, KY 42071. Offers MFA.

Naropa University, Graduate Programs, Program in Creative Writing, Boulder, CO 80302-6697. Offers MFA. Program is offered online only. Part-time and evening/weekend programs available. Postbaccalaureate distance learning degree programs offered (minimal on-campus study). *Faculty:* 10 full-time (5 women), 14 part-time/adjunct (11 women). *Students:* 4 full-time (3 women), 38 part-time (29 women); includes 5 minority (2 African Americans, 2 Asian Americans or Pacific Islanders, 1 Hispanic American). Average age 34. 29 applicants, 66% accepted, 10 enrolled. In 2008, 10 master's awarded. *Degree requirements:* For master's, manuscript. *Entrance requirements:* For master's, manuscript/writing sample; supplemental application, resumé, 3 letters of recommendation, letter of interest, technology check list. Additional exam requirements/recommendations for international students: Required—TOEFL (minimum score 600 paper-based; 250 computer-based). *Application deadline:* For fall admission, 1/15 priority date for domestic and international students; for spring admission, 10/15 for domestic students, 10/15 priority date for international students. Applications are processed on a rolling basis. Application fee: $60. Electronic applications accepted. *Expenses:* Tuition: Full-time $14,767; part-time $726 per credit hour. Required fees: $45 per term. *Financial support:* In 2008–09, 3 students received support, including research assistantships with partial tuition reimbursements available (averaging $3,000 per year), teaching assistantships with partial tuition reimbursements available (averaging $3,000 per year); career-related internships or fieldwork, Federal Work-Study, scholarships/grants, health care benefits, tuition waivers (partial), and unspecified assistantships also available. Support available to part-time students. Financial award application deadline: 3/1; financial award applicants required to submit FAFSA. *Unit head:* Junior Burke, Chair, 303-245-4820. *Application contact:* Kate Levene, Undergraduate and Graduate Admissions Counselor, 303-546-3572, Fax: 303-546-3583, E-mail: klevene@naropa.edu.

See Close-Up on page 1121.

Naropa University, Graduate Programs, Program in Writing and Poetics, Boulder, CO 80302-6697. Offers MFA. *Faculty:* 10 full-time (5 women), 14 part-time/adjunct (11 women). *Students:* 35 full-time (23 women), 6 part-time (2 women); includes 5 minority (2 African Americans, 2 Asian Americans or Pacific Islanders, 1 Hispanic American). Average age 30. 61 applicants, 64% accepted, 11 enrolled. In 2008, 29 master's awarded. *Degree requirements:* For master's, thesis. *Entrance requirements:* For master's, manuscript; supplemental application, resumé, 3 letters of recommendation, letter of interest. Additional exam requirements/recommendations for international students: Required—TOEFL (minimum score 600 paper-based; 250 computer-based). *Application deadline:* For fall admission, 1/15 priority date for domestic and international students; for spring admission, 10/15 priority date for domestic and international students. Applications are processed on a rolling basis. Application fee: $60. Electronic applications accepted. *Expenses:* Tuition: Full-time $14,767; part-time $726 per credit hour. Required fees: $45 per term. *Financial support:* In 2008–09, 32 students received support, including 5 research assistantships with partial tuition reimbursements available (averaging $2,500 per year), 3 teaching assistantships with partial tuition reimbursements available (averaging $2,500 per year); career-related internships or fieldwork, Federal Work-Study, scholarships/grants, health care benefits, tuition waivers (partial), and unspecified assistantships also available. Support available to part-time students. Financial award application deadline: 3/1; financial award applicants required to submit FAFSA. *Unit head:* Junior Burke, Chair, 303-245-4820. *Application contact:* Kate Levene, Admissions Counselor, 303-245-4657, Fax: 303-546-3583, E-mail: klevene@naropa.edu.

See Close-Up on page 1121.

National-Louis University, College of Arts and Sciences, Program in Written Communication, Chicago, IL 60603. Offers MS. Part-time programs available. *Students:* 1 full-time (0 women), 40 part-time (32 women); includes 18 minority (14 African Americans, 1 Asian American or Pacific Islander, 3 Hispanic Americans). Average age 35. In 2008, 5 master's awarded. *Degree requirements:* For master's, thesis. *Entrance requirements:* For master's, GRE, MAT, or Watson-Glaser Critical Thinking Appraisal, interview, minimum GPA of 3.0. *Application deadline:* Applications are processed on a rolling basis. *Financial support:* Federal Work-Study, institutionally sponsored loans, scholarships/grants, and tuition waivers available. Support available to part-time students. Financial award applicants required to submit FAFSA. *Unit head:* Steven Masello, Professor, 224-233-2247, Fax: 224-233-2247, E-mail: smasello@nl.edu. *Application contact:* Dr. Larry Poselli, Vice President of Enrollment and Student Services, 800-443-5522 Ext. 5718, Fax: 312-261-.3550, E-mail: larry.polselli@nl.edu.

National University, Academic Affairs, College of Letters and Sciences, Department of Art and Humanities, La Jolla, CA 92037-1011. Offers creative writing (MFA); English (MA); history (MA). Part-time and evening/weekend programs available. Postbaccalaureate distance learning degree programs offered (no on-campus study). *Faculty:* 19 full-time (6 women), 180 part-time/adjunct (92 women). *Students:* 208 full-time (153 women), 433 part-time (302 women); includes 137 minority (57 African Americans, 10 American Indian/Alaska Native, 19 Asian Americans or Pacific Islanders, 51 Hispanic Americans). Average age 38. 420 applicants, 100% accepted, 420 enrolled. In 2008, 152 master's awarded. *Degree requirements:* For master's, thesis (for some programs). *Entrance requirements:* For master's, interview, minimum GPA of 2.5. Additional exam requirements/recommendations for international students: Required—TOEFL (minimum score 550 paper-based; 213 computer-based; 79 iBT), IELTS (minimum score 6). *Application deadline:* Applications are processed on a rolling basis. Application fee: $60 ($65 for international students). Electronic applications accepted. *Expenses:* Tuition: Full-time $8694; part-time $322 per credit hour. Tuition and fees vary according to course load. *Financial support:* Career-related internships or fieldwork, institutionally sponsored loans, scholarships/grants, and tuition waivers (partial) available. Support available to part-time students. Financial award application deadline: 6/30; financial award applicants required to submit FAFSA. *Unit head:* Dr. Janet Baker, Chair, 858-642-8472, Fax: 858-642-8715, E-mail: jbaker@nu.edu. *Application contact:* Dominick Giovanniello, Associate Regional Dean—San Diego, 800-NAT-UNIV, Fax: 858-541-7792, E-mail: dgiovann@nu.edu.

New England College, Program in Creative Writing, Henniker, NH 03242-3293. Offers poetry (MFA). Part-time and evening/weekend programs available. Electronic applications accepted. *Faculty research:* Poetry collections.

New Mexico Highlands University, Graduate Studies, College of Arts and Sciences, Department of Humanities, Las Vegas, NM 87701. Offers English (MA), including creative writing, language, rhetoric and composition, literature. *Faculty:* 12 full-time (6 women). *Students:* 12 full-time (6 women), 4 part-time (3 women); includes 3 minority (all Hispanic Americans), 1 international. Average age 30. 10 applicants, 70% accepted, 5 enrolled. In 2008, 5 master's awarded. *Degree requirements:* For master's, comprehensive exam, thesis. *Entrance* *requirements:* For master's, minimum undergraduate GPA of 3.0. Additional exam requirements/recommendations for international students: Required—TOEFL (minimum score 540 paper-based; 207 computer-based). *Application deadline:* For fall admission, 8/1 priority date for domestic students. Applications are processed on a rolling basis. Application fee: $15. *Expenses:* Tuition, state resident: full-time $2880; part-time $120 per credit hour. Tuition, nonresident: full-time $4234; part-time $176 per credit hour. International tuition: $5645 full-time. One-time fee: $20. *Financial support:* In 2008–09, 8 students received support, including teaching assistantships with full and partial tuition reimbursements available (averaging $6,500 per year); career-related internships or fieldwork, Federal Work-Study, institutionally sponsored loans, scholarships/grants, tuition waivers (full and partial), and unspecified assistantships also available. Support available to part-time students. Financial award application deadline: 3/1; financial award applicants required to submit FAFSA. *Faculty research:* 20th century literature, life path writing in homeless shelters, native American philosophy, medieval intellectual and cultural history, creating pedagogical tools for teaching law. *Unit head:* Dr. Brandon Kempner, Department Head, 505-454-3286, E-mail: bkempner@nmhu.edu. *Application contact:* Diane Trujillo, Administrative Assistant, Graduate Studies, 505-454-3266, Fax: 505-426-2117, E-mail: dtrujillo@nmhu.edu.

New Mexico State University, Graduate School, College of Arts and Sciences, Department of English, Las Cruces, NM 88003-8001. Offers creative writing (MFA); English (MA); rhetoric and professional communication (PhD). Part-time programs available. *Faculty:* 20 full-time (12 women), 2 part-time/adjunct (0 women). *Students:* 73 full-time (39 women), 36 part-time (24 women); includes 15 minority (3 American Indian/Alaska Native, 12 Hispanic Americans), 9 international. Average age 32. 135 applicants, 41% accepted, 40 enrolled. In 2008, 25 master's, 2 doctorates awarded. *Degree requirements:* For master's, one foreign language, thesis (for some programs); for doctorate, comprehensive exam, thesis/dissertation, internship. *Entrance requirements:* For master's and doctorate, sample of written work. *Application deadline:* For fall admission, 2/1 for domestic and international students. Application fee: $30 ($50 for international students). Electronic applications accepted. *Expenses:* Tuition, area resident: Full-time $3890; part-time $212.85 per credit. Tuition, state resident: full-time $3890; part-time $212.85 per credit. Tuition, nonresident: full-time $13,916; part-time $630.55 per credit. Required fees: $1218; $609 per semester. *Financial support:* In 2008–09, 81 students received support, including 3 research assistantships (averaging $9,217 per year), 53 teaching assistantships (averaging $15,623 per year); fellowships, career-related internships or fieldwork, Federal Work-Study, institutionally sponsored loans, scholarships/grants, health care benefits, and unspecified assistantships also available. Financial award application deadline: 2/1; financial award applicants required to submit FAFSA. *Faculty research:* Composition research, history and theory of rhetoric, technical/professional communication, creative writing, English and American literature. *Unit head:* Dr. Elizabeth Schirmer, Head, 575-646-1733, Fax: 575-646-7725, E-mail: eschirme@nmsu.edu. *Application contact:* Dr. Elizabeth Schirmer, Director of Graduate Studies, 575-646-1733, E-mail: eschirme@nmsu.edu.

The New School: A University, The New School for General Studies, Program in Creative Writing, New York, NY 10011. Offers MFA. Evening/weekend programs available. *Faculty:* 2 full-time (1 woman), 27 part-time/adjunct (15 women). *Students:* 197 full-time (132 women), 5 part-time (3 women); includes 29 minority (8 African Americans, 10 Asian Americans or Pacific Islanders, 11 Hispanic Americans), 10 international. Average age 29. In 2008, 91 master's awarded. *Degree requirements:* For master's, thesis. *Entrance requirements:* For master's, portfolio. Additional exam requirements/recommendations for international students: Required—TOEFL (minimum score 600 paper-based; 250 computer-based; 100 iBT). *Application deadline:* For fall admission, 1/15 for domestic students. Applications are processed on a rolling basis. Application fee: $50. *Expenses:* Contact institution. *Financial support:* Research assistantships, teaching assistantships with partial tuition reimbursements, Federal Work-Study, scholarships/grants, and tuition waivers (partial) available. Financial award application deadline: 3/1; financial award applicants required to submit FAFSA. *Unit head:* Dr. Robert Polito, Director, 212-229-5611, Fax: 212-645-0661. *Application contact:* David Norris, Director of Admissions, 212-229-5630, Fax: 212-989-3887, E-mail: nsadmissions@newschool.edu.

See Close-Up on page 557.

New York University, Graduate School of Arts and Science, Department of English, Program in Creative Writing, New York, NY 10012-1019. Offers MA, MFA. Part-time and evening/weekend programs available. *Degree requirements:* For master's, one foreign language, thesis or alternative. *Entrance requirements:* For master's, GRE General Test, sample of written work. Additional exam requirements/recommendations for international students: Required—TOEFL. *Faculty research:* Fiction, poetry.

New York University, Tisch School of the Arts Asia, Singapore, NY 248923, Singapore. Offers animation and digital arts (MFA); dramatic writing (MFA); film production (MFA). *Entrance requirements:* Additional exam requirements/recommendations for international students: Required—TOEFL (minimum score 610 paper-based; 250 computer-based; 105 iBT). Electronic applications accepted.

New York University, Tisch School of the Arts, Rita and Burton Goldberg Department of Dramatic Writing, New York, NY 10012-1019. Offers MFA. *Degree requirements:* For master's, thesis, play or screenplay, internship. *Entrance requirements:* For master's, writing sample. Additional exam requirements/recommendations for international students: Required—TOEFL or IELTS. Electronic applications accepted. *Faculty research:* Craft of screenwriting film story analysis, production elements in film and theatre.

North Carolina State University, Graduate School, College of Humanities and Social Sciences, Department of English, Program in Creative Writing, Raleigh, NC 27695. Offers MFA. *Degree requirements:* For master's, thesis optional. *Entrance requirements:* For master's, GRE. Electronic applications accepted. *Faculty research:* Science fiction, Asian poetry, translation, Southern writers, satiric fiction.

Northeastern Illinois University, Graduate College, College of Arts and Sciences, Department of English, Programs in English, Chicago, IL 60625-4699. Offers composition/writing (MA); literature (MA). Part-time and evening/weekend programs available. *Degree requirements:* For master's, comprehensive exam, thesis optional, minimum GPA of 3.0. *Entrance requirements:* For master's, 30 hours of undergraduate course work in literature and composition (literature), BA in English or approval (composition/writing), minimum GPA of 2.75. Additional exam requirements/recommendations for international students: Required—TOEFL (minimum score 550 paper-based; 213 computer-based; 80 iBT). Electronic applications accepted. *Faculty research:* Arthurian literature, Southern American literature, rhetoric and theories of authorship.

Northern Arizona University, Graduate College, College of Arts and Letters, Department of English, Program in English, Flagstaff, AZ 86011. Offers creative writing (MA); general English (MA); literacy, technology and professional writing (MA); literature (MA); secondary English education (MA). *Degree requirements:* For master's, departmental qualifying exam. *Entrance requirements:* For master's, GRE General Test, GRE Subject Test.

Northern Michigan University, College of Graduate Studies, College of Arts and Sciences, Department of English, Marquette, MI 49855-5301. Offers creative writing (MFA); literature (MA); pedagogy (MA); writing (MA). Part-time programs available. *Degree requirements:* For master's, thesis or alternative. *Entrance requirements:* For master's, minimum GPA of 2.75.

Northwestern University, Medill School of Journalism, Evanston, IL 60208. Offers broadcast journalism (MSJ); integrated marketing communications (MSIMC), including advertising/sales promotion, direct database and e-commerce marketing, general studies, public relations; magazine publishing (MSJ); new media (MSJ); reporting and writing (MSJ). *Accreditation:* ACEJMC (one or more programs are accredited). *Entrance requirements:* For master's, GRE General Test, GMAT or LSAT (MSJ). Additional exam requirements/recommendations for international students: Required—TOEFL. Electronic applications accepted. *Expenses:* Contact institution. *Faculty research:* Web business journalism, cultural stereotypes, voter apathy, digital television.

Oklahoma City University, Petree College of Arts and Sciences, Program in Liberal Arts, Oklahoma City, OK 73106-1402. Offers art (MLA); general studies (MLA); leadership/management (MLA); literature (MLA); mass communications (MLA); philosophy (MLA); writing (MLA). Part-time and evening/weekend programs available. *Degree requirements:* For master's, comprehensive exam, thesis optional. *Entrance requirements:* Additional exam requirements/recommendations for international students: Required—TOEFL.

Oklahoma State University, College of Arts and Sciences, Department of English, Stillwater, OK 74078. Offers creative writing (MA); English (MFA); literature (PhD). *Faculty:* 52 full-time (30 women), 2 part-time/adjunct (both women). *Students:* 3 full-time (2 women), 131 part-time (77 women); includes 14 minority (4 African Americans, 6 American Indian/Alaska Native, 2 Asian Americans or Pacific Islanders, 2 Hispanic Americans), 19 international. Average age 32. 134 applicants, 40% accepted, 24 enrolled. In 2008, 16 master's, 6 doctorates awarded. *Degree requirements:* For master's, comprehensive exam, thesis; for doctorate, comprehensive exam, thesis/dissertation. *Entrance requirements:* For master's, GRE General Test, minimum GPA of 3.0, writing sample; for doctorate, GRE General Test, minimum GPA of 3.5, writing sample. Additional exam requirements/recommendations for international students: Required—TOEFL. *Application deadline:* For fall admission, 3/1 priority date for international students; for spring admission, 8/1 priority date for international students. Applications are processed on a rolling basis. Application fee: $40 ($75 for international students). Electronic applications accepted. *Expenses:* Tuition, state resident: full-time $3716.40; part-time $154.85 per credit hour. Tuition, nonresident: full-time $14,448; part-time $602 per credit hour. Required fees: $1772.40; $73.85 per credit hour. One-time fee: $50. Tuition and fees vary according to course load and campus/location. *Financial support:* In 2008–09, 5 research assistantships (averaging $10,399 per year), 79 teaching assistantships (averaging $14,715 per year) were awarded; career-related internships or fieldwork, Federal Work-Study, scholarships/grants, health care benefits, tuition waivers (partial), and unspecified assistantships also available. Support available to part-time students. Financial award application deadline: 3/1; financial award applicants required to submit FAFSA. *Faculty research:* American and British novel, poetry, and autobiography; Native American languages and literature; institutional history of American film, history, and adaptations; rhetoric and theories of human communication; learning strategies of second language learners. *Unit head:* Dr. Carol Moder, Head, 405-744-9474, Fax: 405-744-6326. *Application contact:* Dr. Gordon Emslie, Dean, 405-744-6368, Fax: 405-744-0355, E-mail: grad_i@okstate.edu.

Old Dominion University, College of Arts and Letters, Program in Creative Writing, Norfolk, VA 23529. Offers MFA. Part-time programs available. *Faculty:* 6 full-time (3 women), 1 part-time/adjunct. *Students:* 13 full-time (7 women), 10 part-time (7 women); includes 1 minority (African American). Average age 34. 44 applicants, 43% accepted, 6 enrolled. In 2008, 6 master's awarded. *Degree requirements:* For master's, comprehensive exam, thesis. *Entrance requirements:* For master's, GRE General Test, 24 hours previous course work in English, minimum B average, sample of written work. Additional exam requirements/recommendations for international students: Required—TOEFL. *Application deadline:* For fall admission, 2/15 for domestic students. Application fee: $40. Electronic applications accepted. *Expenses:* Tuition, area resident: Full-time $7704; part-time $321 per credit. Tuition, state resident: full-time $7704; part-time $321 per credit. Tuition, nonresident: full-time $19,104; part-time $796 per credit. Required fees: $99 per semester. One-time fee: $40. *Financial support:* In 2008–09, 13 students received support, including 2 fellowships with tuition reimbursements available (averaging $13,000 per year), 3 research assistantships with tuition reimbursements available (averaging $10,000 per year), 8 teaching assistantships with tuition reimbursements available (averaging $10,000 per year); scholarships/grants and unspecified assistantships also available. Financial award application deadline: 2/15. *Faculty research:* Literary fiction, nonfiction, poetry. Total annual research expenditures: $35,000. *Unit head:* Dr. Luisa Igloria, Graduate Program Director, 757-683-3929, Fax: 757-683-3241, E-mail: cwgpd@odu.edu. *Application contact:* Dr. Robert Wojtowicz, Associate Dean, 757-683-6077, Fax: 757-683-5746, E-mail: rwojtowi@odu.edu.

Otis College of Art and Design, Program in Writing, Los Angeles, CA 90045-9785. Offers MFA. *Faculty:* 1 full-time (0 women), 5 part-time/adjunct (1 woman). *Students:* 11 full-time (8 women), 13 part-time (7 women); includes 15 minority (3 African Americans, 7 Asian Americans or Pacific Islanders, 5 Hispanic Americans). Average age 34. 44 applicants, 61% accepted, 11 enrolled. In 2008, 6 master's awarded. *Degree requirements:* For master's, thesis. *Entrance requirements:* For master's, writing sample. *Application deadline:* For fall admission, 2/15 for domestic and international students. Application fee: $50. Electronic applications accepted. *Expenses:* Tuition: Full-time $30,464. Required fees: $700. *Financial support:* Federal Work-Study, scholarships/grants, and tuition waivers (partial) available. Financial award applicants required to submit FAFSA. *Unit head:* Paul Vangelisti, Chair, 310-665-6891, Fax: 310-665-6890, E-mail: pvangel@otis.edu. *Application contact:* Information Contact, 310-665-6820, Fax: 310-665-6821, E-mail: admissions@otis.edu.

Our Lady of the Lake University of San Antonio, College of Arts and Sciences, Program in English, San Antonio, TX 78207-4689. Offers English and communication arts (MA); English and literature (MA); English education (MA); writing (MA). Part-time and evening/weekend programs available. *Students:* 12 full-time (11 women), 7 part-time (all women); includes 14 minority (1 African American, 13 Hispanic Americans). Average age 31. In 2008, 15 master's awarded. *Degree requirements:* For master's, comprehensive exam, thesis optional. *Entrance requirements:* For master's, GRE General Test or MAT, minimum GPA of 3.0 in last 60 hours, 2.5 overall. Additional exam requirements/recommendations for international students: Required—TOEFL. *Application deadline:* Applications are processed on a rolling basis. Application fee: $25 ($50 for international students). Electronic applications accepted. *Expenses:* Tuition: Full-time $11,970; part-time $665 per credit hour. Required fees: $500; $250 per term. *Financial support:* Research assistantships, teaching assistantships, career-related internships or fieldwork, Federal Work-Study, institutionally sponsored loans, and tuition waivers (partial) available. Financial award application deadline: 4/15. *Faculty research:* Writing theory and research, contemporary Southern literature, popular culture, poetry, literature of the Southwest. *Unit head:* Dr. Leah Larson, Chair, 210-434-2387 Ext. 2260, E-mail: larsl@lake.ollusa.edu. *Application contact:* 210-434-6711, Fax: 210-431-4036, E-mail: gradadm@lake.ollusa.edu.

Pacific Lutheran University, Division of Graduate Studies, Division of Humanities, Tacoma, WA 98447. Offers creative writing (MFA). Offered during summer only. Part-time programs available. *Degree requirements:* For master's, thesis, final residency including teaching class. *Entrance requirements:* For master's, portfolio, book review. Additional exam requirements/recommendations for international students: Required—TOEFL. Electronic applications accepted. *Expenses:* Contact institution.

Penn State University Park, Graduate School, College of the Liberal Arts, Department of English, State College, University Park, PA 16802-1503. Offers MA, MFA, PhD.

Purdue University, Graduate School, College of Liberal Arts, Department of English, West Lafayette, IN 47907. Offers creative writing (MFA); literature (MA, PhD), including linguistics, literature and philosophy (PhD), rhetoric and composition, theory and cultural studies (PhD). Part-time programs available. *Degree requirements:* For master's, one foreign language; for doctorate, one foreign language, thesis/dissertation. *Entrance requirements:* For master's and doctorate, GRE General Test, sample of written work. Additional exam requirements/recommendations for international students: Required—TOEFL. Electronic applications accepted. *Faculty research:* Cultural studies, postmodern narrative, contemporary women writers, composition theory, slave narratives.

Writing

Queens College of the City University of New York, Division of Graduate Studies, Arts and Humanities Division, Department of English, Flushing, NY 11367-1597. Offers creative writing (MA); English language and literature (MA). Part-time and evening/weekend programs available. *Degree requirements:* For master's, one foreign language, thesis (for some programs), oral exam (English language and literature). *Entrance requirements:* For master's, manuscript (creative writing), minimum GPA of 3.0. Additional exam requirements/recommendations for international students: Required—TOEFL.

Queens University of Charlotte, College of Arts and Sciences, Charlotte, NC 28274-0002. Offers creative writing (MFA). Part-time programs available. Postbaccalaureate distance learning degree programs offered (minimal on-campus study). *Faculty:* 4 full-time (1 woman), 2 part-time/adjunct (1 woman). *Students:* 81 full-time (58 women), 1 part-time (0 women); includes 16 minority (12 African Americans, 2 Asian Americans or Pacific Islanders, 2 Hispanic Americans). 21 applicants, 95% accepted, 19 enrolled. In 2008, 46 master's awarded. *Application deadline:* Applications are processed on a rolling basis. Application fee: $45. Electronic applications accepted. *Unit head:* Dr. Betty J. Powell, Dean, 704-337-2463, Fax: 704-337-2325. *Application contact:* Melissa Marshall, MFA Coordinator, 704-337-2499, Fax: 704-337-2325.

Rhode Island College, School of Graduate Studies, Faculty of Arts and Sciences, Department of English, Providence, RI 02908-1991. Offers creative writing (MA); English (MA). Part-time and evening/weekend programs available. *Faculty:* 15 full-time (8 women). *Students:* 4 full-time (all women), 15 part-time (9 women); includes 1 minority (Asian American or Pacific Islander). Average age 36. In 2008, 7 master's awarded. *Degree requirements:* For master's, thesis (for some programs). *Entrance requirements:* For master's, GRE General Test, 3 letters of recommendation, interview. Additional exam requirements/recommendations for international students: Recommended—TOEFL (minimum score 550 paper-based; 213 computer-based; 79 iBT). *Application deadline:* For fall admission, 4/1 for domestic students; for spring admission, 11/1 for domestic students. Applications are processed on a rolling basis. Application fee: $50. *Expenses:* Tuition, area resident: Full-time $6816; part-time $284 per credit hour. Tuition, state resident: full-time $6816; part-time $284 per credit hour. Tuition, nonresident: full-time $13,920; part-time $580 per credit hour. Required fees: $454; $16 per credit. $68 per term. *Financial support:* Teaching assistantships with full tuition reimbursements, career-related internships or fieldwork, Federal Work-Study, scholarships/grants, health care benefits, and unspecified assistantships available. Support available to part-time students. Financial award application deadline: 5/15; financial award applicants required to submit FAFSA. *Unit head:* Dr. Maureen Reddy, Chair, 401-456-8028. *Application contact:* Graduate Studies, 401-456-8700.

Rivier College, School of Graduate Studies, Department of English, Nashua, NH 03060. Offers English (MA, MAT); writing and literature (MA); MA/MAT. Part-time and evening/weekend programs available. *Degree requirements:* For master's, comprehensive exam (for some programs). *Entrance requirements:* For master's, GRE Subject Test.

Roosevelt University, Graduate Division, College of Arts and Sciences, Department of Literature and Languages, Program in Creative Writing, Chicago, IL 60605-1394. Offers MFA. Part-time and evening/weekend programs available. *Students:* 13 full-time (9 women), 21 part-time (12 women); includes 4 minority (1 African American, 1 Asian American or Pacific Islander, 2 Hispanic Americans). Average age 31. 174 applicants, 22% accepted, 14 enrolled. In 2008, 9 master's awarded. *Application deadline:* For fall admission, 6/1 priority date for domestic students. Applications are processed on a rolling basis. Application fee: $25 ($35 for international students). *Expenses:* Tuition: Full-time $14,730; part-time $709 per credit. Required fees: $175 per semester. Tuition and fees vary according to course load and program. *Financial support:* Application deadline: 2/15. *Faculty research:* Poetry, fiction, nonfiction, script writing. *Unit head:* Janet Wondra, Head, 312-341-3670. *Application contact:* Joanne Canyon-Heller, Coordinator of Graduate Admission, 877-APPLY RU, Fax: 312-281-3356, E-mail: applyru@roosevelt.edu.

Rosemont College, Graduate School, Program in Creative Writing, Rosemont, PA 19010-1699. Offers MFA.

Rowan University, Graduate School, College of Communication, Program in Writing, Glassboro, NJ 08028-1701. Offers MA. Part-time and evening/weekend programs available. *Students:* 3 full-time (1 woman), 23 part-time (13 women); includes 3 minority (1 African American, 1 Asian American or Pacific Islander, 1 Hispanic American). Average age 33. 14 applicants, 79% accepted, 4 enrolled. In 2008, 11 master's awarded. *Degree requirements:* For master's, thesis. *Entrance requirements:* For master's, GRE. Additional exam requirements/recommendations for international students: Required—TOEFL. *Application deadline:* For fall admission, 10/15 for domestic students; for spring admission, 2/15 for domestic students. Application fee: $50. Electronic applications accepted. *Expenses:* Tuition, area resident: Full-time $10,624; part-time $590 per credit. Tuition, state resident: full-time $10,624; part-time $590 per credit. Tuition, nonresident: full-time $10,624; part-time $590 per credit. Required fees: $2258; $124.90 per credit. *Financial support:* Career-related internships or fieldwork, scholarships/grants, and health care benefits available. Support available to part-time students. *Unit head:* Dr. Mira Lalovic-Hand, Interim Associate Provost/Director of Graduate School, 856-256-5120, E-mail: Lalovic-hand@rowan.edu. *Application contact:* Karen Haynes, Graduate Coordinator, 856-256-4052, E-mail: Haynes@rowan.edu.

Rutgers, The State University of New Jersey, Camden, Graduate School of Arts and Sciences, Program in Creative Writing, Camden, NJ 08102-1401. Offers MFA. *Degree requirements:* For master's, thesis. *Entrance requirements:* For master's, GRE (for assistantships), 2 letters of recommendation, writing sample, statement of goals. Additional exam requirements/recommendations for international students: Required—TOEFL, IELTS. Electronic applications accepted. *Faculty research:* Poetry, fiction, nonfiction, short stories.

Rutgers, The State University of New Jersey, Newark, Graduate School, Program in Creative Writing, Newark, NJ 07102. Offers MFA. *Entrance requirements:* For master's, GRE, minimum undergraduate B average.

Rutgers, The State University of New Jersey, New Brunswick, Mason Gross School of the Arts, Department of Theater Arts, Piscataway, NJ 08854-8097. Offers acting (MFA); design (MFA); directing (MFA); playwriting (MFA); stage management (MFA). *Degree requirements:* For master's, thesis (for some programs), performance project. *Entrance requirements:* For master's, audition, interview, portfolio. Electronic applications accepted. *Faculty research:* Faculty of working professional.

Saint Joseph's University, College of Arts and Sciences, Program in Writing Studies, Philadelphia, PA 19131-1395. Offers MA. Part-time and evening/weekend programs available. *Students:* 1 full-time (0 women), 40 part-time (26 women); includes 6 minority (all African Americans), 1 international. Average age 30. In 2008, 22 master's awarded. *Entrance requirements:* For master's, 2 letters of recommendation, resumé, 2 writing samples, application, official transcripts, personal statement. Additional exam requirements/recommendations for international students: Required—TOEFL (minimum score 550 paper-based; 213 computer-based; 79 iBT). *Application deadline:* For fall admission, 7/15 priority date for domestic students, 4/15 priority date for international students; for winter admission, 1/15 priority date for international students; for spring admission, 11/15 priority date for domestic students, 10/15 priority date for international students. Applications are processed on a rolling basis. Application fee: $35. Electronic applications accepted. *Expenses:* Tuition: Part-time $745 per credit. Tuition and fees vary according to course load, degree level and program. *Financial support:* Unspecified assistantships available. Financial award applicants required to submit FAFSA. *Unit head:* Dr. Ann Green, Director, 610-660-1889, E-mail: agreen@sju.edu. *Application contact:* Coralee Dixon, Assistant Director of Graduate Admissions, 610-660-1102, Fax: 610-660-1224, E-mail: coralee.dixon@sju.edu.

Saint Mary's College of California, School of Liberal Arts, Program in Creative Writing, Moraga, CA 94575. Offers MFA. *Degree requirements:* For master's, thesis. *Entrance requirements:* For master's, sample of written work. *Faculty research:* Poetry, fiction, nonfiction.

Saint Xavier University, Graduate Studies, School of Arts and Sciences, Department of English, Chicago, IL 60655-3105. Offers English (CAS); literary studies (MA); teaching of writing (MA); writing pedagogy (CAS). Part-time and evening/weekend programs available. *Entrance requirements:* For master's, MAT or GRE, minimum GPA of 3.0.

Salisbury University, Graduate Division, Program in English, Salisbury, MD 21801-6837. Offers composition, language and rhetoric (MA); literature (MA); teaching English to speakers of other languages (MA). Part-time and evening/weekend programs available. *Faculty:* 19 full-time (7 women), 1 part-time/adjunct (0 women). *Students:* 11 full-time (8 women), 23 part-time (15 women); includes 3 minority (2 African Americans, 1 Hispanic American), 1 international. Average age 29. 21 applicants, 67% accepted, 10 enrolled. In 2008, 22 master's awarded. *Degree requirements:* For master's, comprehensive exam (for some programs), thesis optional. *Entrance requirements:* For master's, GRE General Test, MAT or PRAXIS, minimum GPA of 3.0, 2 letters of recommendation. Additional exam requirements/recommendations for international students: Required—TOEFL (minimum score 550 paper-based; 213 computer-based). *Application deadline:* For fall admission, 8/1 for domestic students; for spring admission, 1/1 for domestic students. Applications are processed on a rolling basis. Application fee: $45. Electronic applications accepted. *Expenses:* Tuition, area resident: Part-time $270 per credit hour. Tuition, state resident: part-time $270 per credit hour. Tuition, nonresident: part-time $566 per credit hour. Required fees: $52 per credit hour. *Financial support:* In 2008–09, 13 students received support, including 13 teaching assistantships with full tuition reimbursements available; career-related internships or fieldwork and scholarships/grants also available. Support available to part-time students. Financial award applicants required to submit FAFSA. *Faculty research:* Shakespeare, Keats, J. D. Salinger, Samuel Johnson, post colonial theory. *Unit head:* Dr. John D. Kalb, Graduate Program Director, 410-543-6049, Fax: 410-548-2142, E-mail: jdkalb@salisbury.edu. *Application contact:* Dr. John D. Kalb, Graduate Program Director, 410-543-6049, Fax: 410-548-2142, E-mail: jdkalb@salisbury.edu.

San Diego State University, Graduate and Research Affairs, College of Arts and Letters, Department of English and Comparative Literature, San Diego, CA 92182. Offers creative writing (MFA); English (MA). *Degree requirements:* For master's, one foreign language, comprehensive exam (for some programs), thesis (for some programs). *Entrance requirements:* For master's, GRE General Test, minimum GPA of 2.85, writing sample, 3 letters of recommendation. Additional exam requirements/recommendations for international students: Required—TOEFL. Electronic applications accepted.

San Diego State University, Graduate and Research Affairs, College of Arts and Letters, Department of Rhetoric and Writing, San Diego, CA 92182. Offers MA. Part-time programs available. *Degree requirements:* For master's, thesis. *Entrance requirements:* For master's, GRE General Test, writing sample, 3 letters of reference. Additional exam requirements/recommendations for international students: Required—TOEFL. Electronic applications accepted.

San Francisco State University, Division of Graduate Studies, College of Humanities, Department of Creative Writing, San Francisco, CA 94132-1722. Offers MA, MFA. Part-time programs available. *Degree requirements:* For master's, thesis.

San Jose State University, Graduate Studies and Research, College of Humanities and the Arts, Department of English and Comparative Literature, San Jose, CA 95192-0001. Offers creative writing (MFA); literature (MA); secondary English education (Certificate). *Degree requirements:* For master's, one foreign language, thesis or alternative. *Entrance requirements:* For master's, GRE. Additional exam requirements/recommendations for international students: Required—TOEFL. Electronic applications accepted.

Sarah Lawrence College, Graduate Studies, Program in Writing, Bronxville, NY 10708-5999. Offers creative non-fiction (MFA); fiction (MFA); poetry (MFA). Part-time programs available. *Faculty:* 43 part-time/adjunct (25 women). *Students:* 106 full-time (82 women), 48 part-time (41 women); includes 18 minority (6 African Americans, 6 Asian Americans or Pacific Islanders, 6 Hispanic Americans), 3 international. Average age 31. 352 applicants, 46% accepted, 72 enrolled. In 2008, 60 master's awarded. *Degree requirements:* For master's, thesis. *Entrance requirements:* For master's, sample of creative writing, minimum B average in undergraduate course work. Additional exam requirements/recommendations for international students: Required—TOEFL (minimum score 600 paper-based). *Application deadline:* For fall admission, 1/15 for domestic students. Application fee: $60. *Expenses:* Tuition: Full-time $26,544; part-time $1106 per credit. Required fees: $450. Tuition and fees vary according to program. *Financial support:* Fellowships, scholarships/grants and unspecified assistantships available. Support available to part-time students. Financial award application deadline: 3/1; financial award applicants required to submit CSS PROFILE or FAFSA. *Unit head:* Kate Johnson, Co-Director, 914-395-2373. *Application contact:* Susan Guma, Dean of Graduate Studies, 914-395-2373, E-mail: sguma@mail.slc.edu.

See Close-Up on page 289.

Savannah College of Art and Design, Graduate School, Program in Professional Writing, Savannah, GA 31402-3146. Offers MFA. Part-time programs available. *Degree requirements:* For master's, thesis. *Entrance requirements:* Additional exam requirements/recommendations for international students: Required—TOEFL (minimum score 450 paper-based; 133 computer-based). Electronic applications accepted. *Expenses:* Tuition: Full-time $28,215; part-time $3135 per course. One-time fee: $500.

School of the Art Institute of Chicago, Graduate Division, Program in Writing, Chicago, IL 60603-3103. Offers MFA, Certificate. *Entrance requirements:* Additional exam requirements/recommendations for international students: Required—TOEFL.

See Close-Up on page 225.

Seattle Pacific University, Masters of Fine Arts in Creative Writing Program, Seattle, WA 98119-1997. Offers MFA. Part-time programs available. *Faculty:* 1 full-time (0 women), 6 part-time/adjunct (4 women). *Students:* 22 part-time (13 women); includes 6 minority (2 African Americans, 2 Asian Americans or Pacific Islanders, 2 Hispanic Americans), 1 international. Average age 37. In 2008, 10 master's awarded. *Application deadline:* For fall admission, 2/15 for domestic students; for spring admission, 10/1 for domestic students. Application fee: $50. Electronic applications accepted. *Expenses:* Tuition: Full-time $659; part-time $659 per credit hour. One-time fee: $50. Tuition and fees vary according to program. *Financial support:* In 2008–09, 15 students received support. Applicants required to submit FAFSA. *Unit head:* Dr. Gregory Wolfe, Director, 206-281-2109, E-mail: gwolfe@spu.edu. *Application contact:* Grad Center The, 206-281-2091.

Seton Hall University, College of Arts and Sciences, Department of English, South Orange, NJ 07079-2697. Offers MA. Part-time and evening/weekend programs available. *Degree requirements:* For master's, one foreign language, comprehensive exam, thesis optional, research seminars. Electronic applications accepted. *Faculty research:* The essay, modern poetry, the novel, medieval poetry, Renaissance drama.

See Close-Up on page 443.

Seton Hill University, Program in Writing Popular Fiction, Greensburg, PA 15601. Offers MA. Part-time programs available. Postbaccalaureate distance learning degree programs offered (minimal on-campus study). *Degree requirements:* For master's, thesis or alternative. *Entrance requirements:* For master's, writing sample. Additional exam requirements/recommendations for international students: Required—TOEFL (minimum score 600 paper-based; 250 computer-based). Electronic applications accepted. *Faculty research:* Romance novels, science fiction novels, children's fiction, mystery, horror.

Sewanee: The University of the South, Sewanee School of Letters, Sewanee, TN 37383-1000. Offers American literature and English literature (MA); creative writing (MFA). Programs offered only during the summer. Part-time programs available. *Faculty:* 8 full-time (3 women).

Students: 36 full-time (20 women), 6 part-time (2 women); includes 3 minority (2 African Americans, 1 Asian American or Pacific Islander). Average age 31. 20 applicants, 95% accepted, 12 enrolled. *Degree requirements:* For master's, thesis (for some programs). *Entrance requirements:* For master's, writing sample, 2 letters of recommendation. *Application deadline:* For spring admission, 2/1 priority date for domestic and international students. Applications are processed on a rolling basis. Application fee: $40. Electronic applications accepted. *Expenses:* Contact institution. *Financial support:* Application deadline: 4/1; *Unit head:* Dr. John M Grammer, Director, 931-598-1483, Fax: 931-598-3303, E-mail: jgrammer@sewanee.edu. *Application contact:* Margaret D Binnicker, Coordinator, 931-598-1636, Fax: 931-598-3303, E-mail: mbinnick@sewanee.edu.

Slippery Rock University of Pennsylvania, Graduate Studies (Recruitment), College of Humanities, Fine and Performing Arts, Department of English, Slippery Rock, PA 16057-1383. Offers literature and composition (MA); professional writing (MA). Part-time and evening/weekend programs available. *Degree requirements:* For master's, comprehensive exam (for some programs), thesis (for some programs). *Entrance requirements:* For master's, GRE General Test, MAT, minimum GPA of 2.75. *Application deadline:* For fall admission, 7/1 priority date for domestic and international students; for spring admission, 11/1 priority date for domestic and international students. Applications are processed on a rolling basis. Application fee: $25. Electronic applications accepted. *Expenses:* Tuition, area resident: Full-time $6430; part-time $357 per credit. Tuition, state resident: full-time $6430; part-time $357 per credit. Tuition, nonresident: full-time $10,288; part-time $572 per credit. Required fees: $2062; $158 per credit. *Financial support:* Career-related internships or fieldwork, Federal Work-Study, scholarships/grants, and unspecified assistantships available. Support available to part-time students. Financial award application deadline: 5/1; financial award applicants required to submit FAFSA. *Unit head:* Dr. Joseph McCarren, Graduate Coordinator, 724-738-2868, Fax: 724-738-4829, E-mail: joseph.mccarren@sru.edu. *Application contact:* Angela Piverotto, Interim Director of Graduate Studies, 724-738-2051, Fax: 724-738-2146, E-mail: graduate.admissions@sru.edu.

Sonoma State University, School of Arts and Humanities, Department of English, Rohnert Park, CA 94928-3609. Offers American literature (MA); creative writing (MA); English literature (MA); world literature (MA). Part-time and evening/weekend programs available. *Degree requirements:* For master's, one foreign language, thesis or alternative. *Entrance requirements:* For master's, minimum GPA of 2.5. *Faculty research:* Women writers, international literature in English, literature of fantasy.

Southern Illinois University Carbondale, Graduate School, College of Liberal Arts, Department of English, Program in Creative Writing, Carbondale, IL 62901-4701. Offers MFA. *Degree requirements:* For master's, one foreign language, thesis. *Entrance requirements:* For master's, GRE General Test, GRE Subject Test, minimum GPA of 2.7. Additional exam requirements/recommendations for international students: Required—TOEFL.

See Close-Up on page 559.

Southern Illinois University Edwardsville, Graduate Studies and Research, College of Arts and Sciences, Department of English Language and Literature, Program in Creative Writing, Edwardsville, IL 62026-0001. Offers MA. Part-time programs available. *Students:* 4 full-time (all women), 10 part-time (7 women). Average age 26. 13 applicants, 69% accepted. In 2008, 4 master's awarded. *Degree requirements:* For master's, one foreign language, thesis. *Entrance requirements:* Additional exam requirements/recommendations for international students: Required—TOEFL (minimum score 550 paper-based; 213 computer-based; 79 iBT), IELTS (minimum score 6.5). *Application deadline:* For fall admission, 7/20 for domestic students, 6/1 for international students; for spring admission, 12/14 for domestic students, 10/1 for international students. Applications are processed on a rolling basis. Application fee: $30. Electronic applications accepted. *Expenses:* Tuition, area resident: Full-time $5838. Tuition, nonresident: full-time $14,596. Required fees: $1525. *Financial support:* Fellowships with full tuition reimbursements, research assistantships with full tuition reimbursements, teaching assistantships with full tuition reimbursements available. Financial award application deadline: 3/1; financial award applicants required to submit FAFSA. *Unit head:* Dr. Eileen Joy, Director, 618-650-3971, E-mail: ejoy@siue.edu. *Application contact:* Dr. Eileen Joy, Director, 618-650-3971, E-mail: ejoy@siue.edu.

Southern New Hampshire University, School of Liberal Arts, Manchester, NH 03106-1045. Offers clinical services for adults psychiatric disabilities (Certificate); clinical services for children and adolescents with psychiatric disabilities (Certificate); clinical services for persons with co-occurring substance abuse and psychiatric disabilities (Certificate); community mental health (MS); fiction writing (MFA); non-fiction writing (MFA); teaching English as a foreign language (MS). Part-time and evening/weekend programs available. *Degree requirements:* For master's, one foreign language, thesis. *Entrance requirements:* For master's, minimum GPA of 2.75: MS-TEFL, 3.0: MFA. Additional exam requirements/recommendations for international students: Required—TOEFL (minimum score 550 paper-based; 213 computer-based; 79 iBT), IELTS (minimum score 6.5), TWE (minimum score 5). Electronic applications accepted. *Expenses:* Contact institution. *Faculty research:* Action research, state of the art practice in behavioral health services, wraparound approaches to working with youth, learning styles.

Spalding University, Graduate Studies, College of Social Sciences and Humanities, Program in Writing, Louisville, KY 40203-2188. Offers MFA. Postbaccalaureate distance learning degree programs offered (minimal on-campus study). *Degree requirements:* For master's, thesis. *Entrance requirements:* For master's, writing sample, letters of recommendation. Additional exam requirements/recommendations for international students: Required—TOEFL (minimum score 535 paper-based; 203 computer-based). Electronic applications accepted. *Expenses:* Tuition: Full-time $11,340; part-time $630 per credit hour. Tuition and fees vary according to program. *Faculty research:* Fiction, creative nonfiction, poetry, writing for children, playwriting/screenwriting.

Stony Brook University, State University of New York, Stony Brook Southampton, Program in Writing and Literature, Stony Brook, NY 11794. Offers fiction (MFA); poetry (MFA); scientific writing (MFA), including environmental, medical, technological; scriptwriting (MFA). *Faculty:* 1 (woman) full-time, 12 part-time/adjunct (6 women). *Students:* 6 full-time (4 women), 27 part-time (19 women); includes 2 minority (1 African American, 1 Asian American or Pacific Islander). 29 applicants, 66% accepted. In 2008, 5 master's awarded. *Expenses:* Tuition, area resident: Full-time $7880; part-time $328 per credit hour. Tuition, state resident: full-time $7880; part-time $328 per credit hour. Tuition, nonresident: full-time $13,250; part-time $552 per credit hour. Required fees: $848. *Financial support:* In 2008–09, 6 teaching assistantships were awarded. *Unit head:* Dr. Robert Reeves, Director, 631-6325030, Fax: 631-6322576, E-mail: southamptonwriters@notes.cc.sunysb.edu. *Application contact:* Director of Graduate Admissions and Program Administration.

Syracuse University, Graduate School, College of Arts and Sciences, Program in Composition and Cultural Rhetoric, Syracuse, NY 13244. Offers PhD. *Entrance requirements:* For doctorate, GRE. Electronic applications accepted.

Syracuse University, Graduate School, College of Arts and Sciences, Program in Creative Writing, Syracuse, NY 13244. Offers MFA. *Degree requirements:* For master's, thesis. *Entrance requirements:* For master's, GRE General Test, sample of written work. Additional exam requirements/recommendations for international students: Required—TOEFL.

Temple University, Graduate School, College of Liberal Arts, Department of English, Program in Creative Writing, Philadelphia, PA 19122-6096. Offers MA. Part-time programs available. *Degree requirements:* For master's, comprehensive exam, manuscript. *Entrance requirements:* For master's, GRE General Test, minimum GPA of 3.0. Additional exam requirements/recommendations for international students: Required—TOEFL (minimum score 550 paper-based; 213 computer-based; 79 iBT). Electronic applications accepted. *Faculty research:* Poetry, fiction, cultural studies.

Texas State University–San Marcos, Graduate School, College of Liberal Arts, Department of English, Program in Creative Writing, San Marcos, TX 78666. Offers MFA. Part-time and evening/weekend programs available. *Degree requirements:* For master's, comprehensive exam, thesis. *Entrance requirements:* For master's, 24 hours of undergraduate course work in English (12 advanced) with minimum GPA of 3.25, 6 hours of course work in foreign language, minimum GPA of 2.75 in last 60 hours, writing portfolios. Additional exam requirements/recommendations for international students: Required—TOEFL (minimum score 550 paper-based; 213 computer-based). Electronic applications accepted.

Towson University, College of Graduate Studies and Research, Program in Professional Writing, Towson, MD 21252-0001. Offers MS. Part-time and evening/weekend programs available. *Degree requirements:* For master's, thesis optional, exam. *Entrance requirements:* For master's, sample of written work (obtain instructions from English dept), minimum GPA of 3.0, (2) letters of recommendation, official transcripts. Electronic applications accepted. *Faculty research:* Creative writing, essay writing, sociopsychological linguistics, interdisciplinary rhetoric, global communication.

Union Institute & University, Online MA Programs, Cincinnati, OH 45206-1925. Offers health and wellness (MA); history and culture (MA); leadership (MA); literature and writing (MA); psychology (MA). Part-time programs available. Postbaccalaureate distance learning degree programs offered (no on-campus study). *Degree requirements:* For master's, thesis. *Expenses:* Contact institution.

The University of Akron, Graduate School, Buchtel College of Arts and Sciences, Department of English, Akron, OH 44325. Offers composition (MA); creative writing (MFA); literature (MA). Part-time programs available. *Degree requirements:* For master's, thesis optional. *Entrance requirements:* For master's, BA in English, minimum GPA of 2.75, writing portfolio, letters of recommendation. Additional exam requirements/recommendations for international students: Required—TOEFL (minimum score 580 paper-based; 237 computer-based; 92 iBT). Electronic applications accepted. *Faculty research:* British and American literary studies, literary theory, creative writing, applied linguistics.

The University of Alabama, Graduate School, College of Arts and Sciences, Department of English, Tuscaloosa, AL 35487. Offers composition and rhetoric (PhD); creative writing (MFA), including fiction, poetry; literature (MA, PhD); rhetoric and composition (MA); teaching English as a second language (MATESOL). *Faculty:* 35 full-time (13 women). *Students:* 120 full-time (66 women), 16 part-time (12 women); includes 15 minority (8 African Americans, 2 American Indian/Alaska Native, 3 Asian Americans or Pacific Islanders, 2 Hispanic Americans), 5 international. Average age 28. 237 applicants, 20% accepted, 31 enrolled. In 2008, 21 master's, 2 doctorates awarded. *Degree requirements:* For master's, one foreign language, comprehensive exam, thesis (for some programs); for doctorate, 2 foreign languages, comprehensive exam, thesis/dissertation. *Entrance requirements:* For master's and doctorate, GRE, minimum GPA of 3.0, critical writing sample. Additional exam requirements/recommendations for international students: Required—TOEFL. *Application deadline:* For fall admission, 1/15 priority date for domestic students, 1/15 for international students. Application fee: $30. Electronic applications accepted. *Expenses:* Tuition, area resident: Full-time $6400. Tuition, state resident: full-time $6400. Tuition, nonresident: full-time $18,000. *Financial support:* In 2008–09, 7 fellowships with full tuition reimbursements (averaging $15,000 per year), 1 research assistantship (averaging $11,708 per year), 106 teaching assistantships with full tuition reimbursements (averaging $11,708 per year) were awarded; career-related internships or fieldwork, scholarships/grants, health care benefits, and unspecified assistantships also available. Financial award application deadline: 1/15. *Faculty research:* Critical theory; modern, Renaissance, and African-American literature. Total annual research expenditures: $8,282. *Unit head:* Dr. Catherine E. Davies, Director of Graduate Studies, 205-348-8499, E-mail: cdavies@bama.ua.edu. *Application contact:* Vernita W. James, Office Assistant II, 205-348-0766, Fax: 205-348-1388, E-mail: vwjames@bama.ua.edu.

University of Alaska Anchorage, College of Arts and Sciences, Program in Creative Writing and Literary Arts, Anchorage, AK 99508-8060. Offers MFA. Part-time programs available. *Degree requirements:* For master's, comprehensive exam, thesis or alternative. *Entrance requirements:* For master's, portfolio, minimum GPA of 3.0. Additional exam requirements/recommendations for international students: Required—TOEFL (minimum score 550 paper-based; 213 computer-based). *Faculty research:* Alaska Quarterly Review publications, feminist studies, ecocriticism and native writing, poetry.

University of Alaska Fairbanks, College of Liberal Arts, Department of English, Fairbanks, AK 99775-5720. Offers creative writing (MFA); literature (MA); MA/MFA. Part-time programs available. *Faculty:* 16 full-time (7 women), 2 part-time/adjunct (1 woman). *Students:* 33 full-time (14 women), 13 part-time (12 women); includes 5 minority (2 American Indian/Alaska Native, 2 Asian Americans or Pacific Islanders, 1 Hispanic American). Average age 32. 55 applicants, 51% accepted, 16 enrolled. In 2008, 3 master's awarded. *Degree requirements:* For master's, comprehensive exam, thesis or alternative, oral exams, oral defense. *Entrance requirements:* For master's, GRE General Test, academic writing sample. Additional exam requirements/recommendations for international students: Required—TOEFL (minimum score 550 paper-based; 213 computer-based; 80 iBT). *Application deadline:* For fall admission, 6/1 for domestic students, 3/1 for international students; for spring admission, 10/15 for domestic students, 9/1 for international students. Applications are processed on a rolling basis. Application fee: $60. Electronic applications accepted. *Expenses:* Tuition, area resident: Full-time $5418; part-time $301 per credit. Tuition, state resident: full-time $5418; part-time $301 per credit. Tuition, nonresident: full-time $11,070; part-time $615 per credit. Required fees: $849; $25 per credit. $78 per semester. Tuition and fees vary according to course load and reciprocity agreements. *Financial support:* In 2008–09, 1 research assistantship (averaging $13,330 per year), 26 teaching assistantships (averaging $11,844 per year) were awarded; fellowships, Federal Work-Study, scholarships/grants, health care benefits, and unspecified assistantships also available. Support available to part-time students. Financial award application deadline: 7/1; financial award applicants required to submit FAFSA. *Faculty research:* Traditional Alaskan native literature, British literature, pedagogy, American literature, rhetoric/composition history. *Unit head:* Dr. Cooper Burns, Department Chair, 907-474-7193, Fax: 907-474-5247, E-mail: faengl@uaf.edu. *Application contact:* Dr. Cooper Burns, Department Chair, 907-474-7193, Fax: 907-474-5247, E-mail: faengl@uaf.edu.

The University of Arizona, Graduate College, College of Humanities, Department of English, Program in Creative Writing, Tucson, AZ 85721. Offers MFA. *Entrance requirements:* For master's, minimum GPA of 3.0. Additional exam requirements/recommendations for international students: Required—TOEFL. Electronic applications accepted.

University of Arkansas, Graduate School, J. William Fulbright College of Arts and Sciences, Department of English, Program in Creative Writing, Fayetteville, AR 72701-1201. Offers MFA. *Degree requirements:* For master's, thesis.

University of Arkansas at Little Rock, Graduate School, College of Arts, Humanities, and Social Science, Department of Rhetoric and Writing, Little Rock, AR 72204-1099. Offers professional and technical writing (MA). Part-time and evening/weekend programs available. *Degree requirements:* For master's, thesis or alternative, oral defense of final project. *Entrance requirements:* For master's, GRE, minimum GPA of 3.0, writing portfolio. *Faculty research:* Writing for industry, science, business, and government; composition and rhetorical theory; writing nonfiction; teaching of writing.

University of Baltimore, Graduate School, The Yale Gordon College of Liberal Arts, Program in Creative Writing and Publishing Arts, Baltimore, MD 21201-5779. Offers MFA. Part-time and evening/weekend programs available. *Students:* 15 full-time (12 women), 36 part-time (25 women); includes 14 minority (9 African Americans, 1 American Indian/Alaska Native, 2 Asian Americans or Pacific Islanders, 2 Hispanic Americans). Average age 28. 77 applicants, 48% accepted, 27 enrolled. *Entrance requirements:* Additional exam requirements/recommendations

Writing

University of Baltimore (continued)

for international students: Required—TOEFL. *Application deadline:* For fall admission, 3/31 for domestic and international students. Application fee: $31. *Expenses:* Tuition, state resident: part-time $568 per credit. Tuition, nonresident: part-time $824 per credit. Required fees: $250 per semester. *Financial support:* In 2008–09, 3 students received support. Application deadline: 3/1; *Unit head:* Kendra Kopelke, Director, 410-837-6026, E-mail: kkopelke@ubalt.edu. *Application contact:* Kevin Nies, Executive Director, Office of Graduate Admission, 410-837-6565, E-mail: knies@ubalt.edu.

University of Baltimore, Graduate School, The Yale Gordon College of Liberal Arts, Program in Publications Design, Baltimore, MD 21201-5779. Offers MA. Part-time and evening/weekend programs available. *Faculty:* 6 full-time (3 women), 10 part-time/adjunct (6 women). *Students:* 30 full-time (20 women), 135 part-time (107 women); includes 46 minority (35 African Americans, 6 Asian Americans or Pacific Islanders, 5 Hispanic Americans), 5 international. Average age 30. 79 applicants, 62% accepted, 43 enrolled. In 2008, 39 master's awarded. *Degree requirements:* For master's, seminar project. *Entrance requirements:* For master's, minimum GPA of 3.0, portfolio, interview. Additional exam requirements/recommendations for international students: Required—TOEFL (minimum score 550 paper-based; 213 computer-based). *Application deadline:* For fall admission, 8/1 priority date for domestic students, 6/1 for international students; for spring admission, 12/15 for domestic students, 11/1 for international students. Applications are processed on a rolling basis. Application fee: $30. Electronic applications accepted. *Expenses:* Tuition, state resident: part-time $568 per credit. Tuition, nonresident: part-time $824 per credit. Required fees: $250 per semester. *Financial support:* In 2008–09, 9 research assistantships were awarded; fellowships, career-related internships or fieldwork and Federal Work-Study also available. Support available to part-time students. Financial award application deadline: 4/1; financial award applicants required to submit FAFSA. *Faculty research:* Communication theory, graphic design, media technology. *Unit head:* Dr. Stephanie Gibson, Director, Main Publications Design, 410-837-6050, E-mail: sgibson@ubalt.edu. *Application contact:* Kevin Nies, Assistant Director, Office of Graduate Admission, 410-837-6565, E-mail: knies@ubalt.edu.

The University of British Columbia, Faculty of Arts, Creative Writing Program, Vancouver, BC V6T 1Z1, Canada. Offers creative writing (MFA); creative writing and film (MFA); creative writing and theatre (MFA). Part-time programs available. Postbaccalaureate distance learning degree programs offered (minimal on-campus study). *Degree requirements:* For master's, thesis. *Entrance requirements:* For master's, sample of written work. Additional exam requirements/recommendations for international students: Required—TOEFL (minimum score 550 paper-based; 213 computer-based). Electronic applications accepted. *Expenses:* Contact institution. *Faculty research:* Writing of fiction; poetry, creative nonfiction, plays for stage, screen, television, radio, writing for children and translation, song lyrics and libretto.

The University of British Columbia, Faculty of Arts and Faculty of Graduate Studies, Department of Theatre and Film, Film Program, Vancouver, BC V6T 1Z1, Canada. Offers creative writing and film production (MFA); film production (MFA, Diploma); film studies (MA). *Degree requirements:* For master's, thesis (MA), thesis or project (MFA). *Entrance requirements:* For master's, bachelor's degree in film production or equivalent, BA in film studies. Additional exam requirements/recommendations for international students: Required—TOEFL (minimum score 600 paper-based). Electronic applications accepted. *Faculty research:* Film history, theory, criticism; producing; experimental film.

University of California, Davis, Graduate Studies, Program in English, Davis, CA 95616. Offers creative writing (MA); English (MA, PhD). Terminal master's awarded for partial completion of doctoral program. *Degree requirements:* For master's, one foreign language, thesis optional; for doctorate, 2 foreign languages, thesis/dissertation. *Entrance requirements:* For master's and doctorate, GRE General Test, GRE Subject Test, minimum GPA of 3.0, writing sample. Additional exam requirements/recommendations for international students: Required—TOEFL (minimum score 550 paper-based; 213 computer-based). Electronic applications accepted. *Faculty research:* Feminist theory, ethnic literature, literary theory, history of literature, literature of nature.

University of California, Irvine, Office of Graduate Studies, School of Humanities, Department of English and Comparative Literature, Program in Writing, Irvine, CA 92697. Offers creative writing (MFA), including fiction, poetry. *Degree requirements:* For master's, thesis. *Entrance requirements:* For master's, minimum GPA of 3.0, sample of written work. Electronic applications accepted.

University of California, Riverside, Graduate Division, Department of Creative Writing, Palm Desert, CA 92211. Offers creative writing and writing for the performing arts (MFA). Program also offered at Palm Desert Graduate Center. *Faculty:* 15 part-time/adjunct (5 women). *Students:* 58 part-time (36 women); includes 2 African Americans, 3 Asian Americans or Pacific Islanders, 4 Hispanic Americans. Average age 34. 25 applicants, 80% accepted, 10 enrolled. In 2008, 13 master's awarded. *Degree requirements:* For master's, thesis, final project. *Entrance requirements:* For master's, writing sample. Additional exam requirements/recommendations for international students: Required—TOEFL (minimum score 550 paper-based; 213 computer-based; 80 iBT). *Application deadline:* For fall admission, 8/1 for domestic students, 6/1 for international students; for winter admission, 11/1 for domestic students, 8/1 for international students; for spring admission, 2/1 for domestic students, 12/1 for international students. Applications are processed on a rolling basis. Application fee: $60 ($75 for international students). Electronic applications accepted. *Expenses:* Tuition, nonresident: full-time $4898. Required fees: $10,362. *Financial support:* In 2008–09, 1 fellowship with partial tuition reimbursement (averaging $12,000 per year) was awarded; research assistantships, teaching assistantships with partial tuition reimbursements. *Faculty research:* Non-fiction, playwriting, screenwriting, poetry, fiction. *Unit head:* Tod Goldberg, Administrative Director, 760-834-0928, Fax: 760-834-0800, E-mail: tod.goldberg@ucr.edu. *Application contact:* Michelle Harding, Program Representative, 760-834-0926, Fax: 760-834-0796, E-mail: michelle.harding@ucr.edu.

University of California, Santa Cruz, Division of Graduate Studies, Division of Social Sciences, Program in Social Documentation, Santa Cruz, CA 95064. Offers MA. *Entrance requirements:* For master's, writing sample, resumé or curriculum vitae, sample of documentary production work. Electronic applications accepted.

University of Central Florida, College of Arts and Humanities, Department of English, Program in English, Orlando, FL 32816. Offers creative writing (MFA); English (MA). *Students:* 31 full-time (21 women), 47 part-time (33 women); includes 15 minority (5 African Americans, 1 Asian American or Pacific Islander, 9 Hispanic Americans). In 2008, 38 master's awarded. *Expenses:* Tuition, area resident: Full-time $6816; part-time $284 per credit. Tuition, state resident: full-time $6816; part-time $1076 per credit. Tuition, nonresident: full-time $25,824. Required fees: $216; $9 per credit. *Financial support:* In 2008–09, 3 fellowships (averaging $8,500 per year), 13 research assistantships (averaging $5,000 per year), 11 teaching assistantships (averaging $5,600 per year) were awarded.

University of Central Oklahoma, College of Graduate Studies and Research, College of Liberal Arts, Department of English, Edmond, OK 73034-5209. Offers composition skills (MA); contemporary literature (MA); creative writing (MA); teaching English as a second language (MA); traditional studies (MA). Part-time programs available. *Degree requirements:* For master's, one foreign language. *Entrance requirements:* For master's, 24 hours of course work in English language and literature. Additional exam requirements/recommendations for international students: Required—TOEFL (minimum score 550 paper-based; 213 computer-based). Electronic applications accepted. *Faculty research:* John Milton, Harriet Beecher Stowe.

University of Colorado at Boulder, Graduate School, College of Arts and Sciences, Department of English, Boulder, CO 80309. Offers literature (MA, PhD), including creative writing (MA).

Part-time programs available. *Degree requirements:* For master's, one foreign language, comprehensive exam, thesis or alternative; for doctorate, 2 foreign languages, comprehensive exam, thesis/dissertation. *Entrance requirements:* For master's, GRE General Test, GRE Subject Test, minimum undergraduate GPA of 3.0; for doctorate, GRE General Test, GRE Subject Test. *Faculty research:* Creative writing (MA), language, critical theory, literature.

University of Florida, Graduate School, College of Liberal Arts and Sciences, Department of English, Gainesville, FL 32611. Offers creative writing (MFA); English (MA, PhD). *Degree requirements:* For master's, variable foreign language requirement, thesis or alternative; for doctorate, thesis/dissertation. *Entrance requirements:* For master's and doctorate, GRE General Test, minimum GPA of 3.0. Additional exam requirements/recommendations for international students: Required—TOEFL (minimum score 550 paper-based; 213 computer-based). Electronic applications accepted.

University of Georgia, Graduate School, College of Arts and Sciences, Department of English, Athens, GA 30602. Offers creative writing (MFA, PhD); English (MA, MAT, PhD). *Degree requirements:* For master's, one foreign language, thesis (MA); for doctorate, 2 foreign languages, thesis/dissertation. *Entrance requirements:* For master's and doctorate, GRE General Test. Additional exam requirements/recommendations for international students: Required—TWE. Electronic applications accepted.

University of Houston, College of Liberal Arts and Social Sciences, Department of English, Houston, TX 77204. Offers applied English linguistics (MA); English and American literature (MA, PhD); literature and creative writing (MA, MFA, PhD). Postbaccalaureate distance learning degree programs offered. *Faculty:* 21 full-time (10 women), 7 part-time/adjunct (3 women). *Students:* 78 full-time (35 women), 49 part-time (39 women); includes 21 minority (4 African Americans, 1 American Indian/Alaska Native, 10 Asian Americans or Pacific Islanders, 6 Hispanic Americans), 4 international. Average age 33. 197 applicants, 24% accepted, 22 enrolled. In 2008, 28 master's, 13 doctorates awarded. *Degree requirements:* For master's, one foreign language, thesis (for some programs); for doctorate, 2 foreign languages, comprehensive exam, thesis/dissertation. *Entrance requirements:* For master's, GRE General Test, GRE Subject Test, minimum GPA of 3.0 in last 60 hours of course work; for doctorate, GRE General Test, GRE Subject Test, writing sample. Additional exam requirements/recommendations for international students: Required—TOEFL. *Application deadline:* For fall admission, 1/1 priority date for domestic students. Applications are processed on a rolling basis. Application fee: $50. *Expenses:* Tuition, state resident: full-time $5164; part-time $287 per credit. Tuition, nonresident: full-time $10,222; part-time $568 per credit. *Financial support:* In 2008–09, 2 fellowships with full tuition reimbursements (averaging $7,100 per year), 68 teaching assistantships with full tuition reimbursements (averaging $12,250 per year) were awarded; career-related internships or fieldwork, Federal Work-Study, institutionally sponsored loans, scholarships/grants, health care benefits, and unspecified assistantships also available. Support available to part-time students. Financial award application deadline: 2/1. *Unit head:* Wyman Henderson, Chairperson, 713-743-3004, Fax: 713-743-3215, E-mail: whh@uh.edu. *Application contact:* Ruby Jones, Advising Assistant, 713-743-2941, Fax: 713-743-3215, E-mail: rjones@uh.edu.

University of Houston–Downtown, College of Humanities and Social Sciences, Department of English, Houston, TX 77002-1001. Offers professional writing and technical communication (MS). Part-time and evening/weekend programs available. *Faculty:* 11 full-time (7 women). *Students:* 3 full-time (2 women), 19 part-time (17 women); includes 10 minority (8 African Americans, 1 Asian American or Pacific Islander, 1 Hispanic American). Average age 37. 6 applicants, 83% accepted, 5 enrolled. In 2008, 4 master's awarded. *Degree requirements:* For master's, thesis optional, graduation portfolio with oral defense. *Entrance requirements:* For master's, GRE (including Analytical Writing section), personal application statement, resumé, writing sample, 3 letters of recommendation. Additional exam requirements/recommendations for international students: Required—TOEFL (minimum score 600 paper-based; 250 computer-based; 86 iBT). *Application deadline:* For fall admission, 3/15 for domestic and international students; for spring admission, 11/15 for domestic and international students. Application fee: $35 ($60 for international students). Electronic applications accepted. *Expenses:* Tuition, area resident: Full-time $3060; part-time $170 per credit hour. Tuition, state resident: full-time $3060; part-time $170 per credit hour. Tuition, nonresident: full-time $7488; part-time $416 per credit hour. International tuition: $7570 full-time. Required fees: $854; $307 per term. Tuition and fees vary according to course load. *Financial support:* Applicants required to submit FAFSA. *Faculty research:* Environmental rhetoric, instructional design, usability, assessment, presentation slides. *Unit head:* Dr. Robert Jarrett, Chair, 713-221-8013, Fax: 713-226-5205, E-mail: JarrettR@uhd.edu. *Application contact:* Dr. Ann Jennings, Coordinator of MS in Professional Writing and Technical Communication and Professor, Department of English, 713-221-8013, Fax: 713-226-5205, E-mail: mspwtc@uhd.edu.

University of Idaho, College of Graduate Studies, College of Letters, Arts and Social Sciences, Department of English, Program in Creative Writing, Moscow, ID 83844-2282. Offers MFA. *Students:* 29 full-time, 4 part-time. Average age 31. In 2008, 17 master's awarded. *Entrance requirements:* For master's, minimum GPA of 2.8. *Application deadline:* For fall admission, 8/1 for domestic students; for spring admission, 12/15 for domestic students. Application fee: $55 ($60 for international students). *Expenses:* Tuition, nonresident: full-time $10,080; part-time $336 per credit. Required fees: $5212; $267 per credit. Tuition and fees vary according to program. *Financial support:* Application deadline: 2/15. *Unit head:* Dr. Kurt Olsson, Chair, 208-883-6156. *Application contact:* Dr. Kurt Olsson, Chair, 208-883-6156.

University of Illinois at Chicago, Graduate College, College of Liberal Arts and Sciences, Department of English, Chicago, IL 60607-7128. Offers English (MA, PhD), including creative writing (PhD), English education (MA), English studies, writing (MA); linguistics (MA), including teaching English to speakers of other languages/applied linguistics. Part-time and evening/weekend programs available. *Degree requirements:* For doctorate, variable foreign language requirement, thesis/dissertation, written and oral exams. *Entrance requirements:* For master's, GRE General Test, GRE Subject Test; for doctorate, GRE General Test, GRE Subject Test, minimum GPA of 2.0. Additional exam requirements/recommendations for international students: Required—TOEFL. Electronic applications accepted. *Faculty research:* Literary history and theory.

University of Illinois at Urbana–Champaign, Graduate College, College of Liberal Arts and Sciences, Department of English, Champaign, IL 61820. Offers creative writing (MFA); English (MA, PhD). *Faculty:* 59 full-time (25 women), 2 part-time/adjunct (1 woman). *Students:* 88 full-time (63 women), 67 part-time (36 women); includes 12 minority (4 African Americans, 1 American Indian/Alaska Native, 5 Asian Americans or Pacific Islanders, 2 Hispanic Americans), 12 international. 361 applicants, 16% accepted, 26 enrolled. In 2008, 20 master's, 15 doctorates awarded. *Entrance requirements:* For master's, GRE General Test, GRE Subject Test, minimum GPA of 3.0; writing sample. Additional exam requirements/recommendations for international students: Required—TOEFL (minimum score 550 paper-based; 213 computer-based). *Application deadline:* Applications are processed on a rolling basis. Application fee: $60 ($75 for international students). Electronic applications accepted. *Financial support:* In 2008–09, 76 fellowships, 11 research assistantships, 124 teaching assistantships were awarded; tuition waivers (full and partial) also available. *Faculty research:* English and American literature, cultural studies and critical theory. *Unit head:* Perry Perry, Head, 217-333-2391, Fax: 217-333-4321, E-mail: cperry@illinois.edu. *Application contact:* Stephanie Shockey, Secretary, 217-244-3646, Fax: 217-333-4321, E-mail: shockey@illinois.edu.

The University of Iowa, Graduate College, College of Liberal Arts and Sciences, Department of English, Iowa City, IA 52242-1316. Offers English (PhD); literary criticism (PhD); literary history (PhD); literary studies (MA); nonfiction writing (MFA); rhetorical theory and stylistics (PhD); writer's workshop (MFA); JD/PhD. *Degree requirements:* For master's, thesis (for some programs), exam; for doctorate, comprehensive exam, thesis/dissertation. *Entrance requirements:* For master's and doctorate, GRE General Test, minimum GPA of 3.0. Additional exam requirements/recommendations for international students: Required—TOEFL (minimum score 640 paper-based; 273 computer-based; 112 iBT). Electronic applications accepted.

The University of Kansas, Graduate Studies, College of Liberal Arts and Sciences, Department of English, Lawrence, KS 66045. Offers creative writing (MFA); English (MA, PhD). Part-time programs available. *Faculty:* 37. *Students:* 92 full-time (61 women), 12 part-time (5 women); includes 9 minority (5 African Americans, 4 Hispanic Americans), 3 international. Average age 33. 166 applicants, 24% accepted, 21 enrolled. In 2008, 19 master's, 13 doctorates awarded. *Degree requirements:* For master's, one foreign language, comprehensive exam (for some programs), thesis or alternative; for doctorate, 2 foreign languages, comprehensive exam, thesis/dissertation. *Entrance requirements:* For master's and doctorate, GRE General Test, minimum GPA of 3.3. Additional exam requirements/recommendations for international students: Required—TOEFL. *Application deadline:* For fall admission, 1/1 priority date for domestic and international students. Applications are processed on a rolling basis. Application fee: $45 ($55 for international students). Electronic applications accepted. *Expenses:* Tuition, area resident: Full-time $6122; part-time $255.10 per credit hour. Tuition, state resident: full-time $6122; part-time $255.10 per credit hour. Tuition, nonresident: full-time $14,629; part-time $609.55 per credit hour. Required fees: $847; $70.56 per credit hour. Tuition and fees vary according to course load and program. *Financial support:* Fellowships, research assistantships, teaching assistantships with full and partial tuition reimbursements, unspecified assistantships available. Financial award application deadline: 1/1. *Faculty research:* African-American literature, 20th century American literature, Renaissance literature, creative writing. *Unit head:* Dorice Elliott, Chair, 785-864-4520, E-mail: delliott@ku.edu. *Application contact:* Joseph Harrington, Director of Graduate Studies, 785-864-4520, E-mail: j-harrington@ku.edu.

University of Louisiana at Lafayette, BI Moody III College of Business Administration MBA Program, College of Liberal Arts, Department of English, Lafayette, LA 70504. Offers British and American literature (MA), including creative writing, folklore, rhetoric; creative writing (PhD); literature (PhD); rhetoric (PhD). Part-time programs available. Terminal master's awarded for partial completion of doctoral program. *Degree requirements:* For master's, one foreign language, thesis or alternative; for doctorate, 2 foreign languages, comprehensive exam, thesis/dissertation. *Entrance requirements:* For master's, GRE General Test, minimum GPA of 2.75; for doctorate, GRE General Test, minimum GPA of 3.0. Additional exam requirements/recommendations for international students: Required—TOEFL (minimum score 550 paper-based; 213 computer-based). Electronic applications accepted. *Faculty research:* Composition theory, Southern literature, medieval literature.

University of Louisville, Graduate School, College of Arts and Sciences, Department of English, Program in English, Louisville, KY 40292. Offers creative writing (MA); literature (MA); rhetoric and composition (MA). Part-time and evening/weekend programs available. *Faculty:* 40 full-time (24 women). *Students:* 33 full-time (19 women), 29 part-time (18 women); includes 4 African Americans, 2 Asian Americans or Pacific Islanders, 1 international. Average age 28. 58 applicants, 95% accepted, 33 enrolled. In 2008, 16 master's awarded. *Degree requirements:* For master's, one foreign language, thesis or culminating project. *Entrance requirements:* For master's, GRE General Test, 10-15 page critical writing sample, 2 academic letters of recommendation, transcripts of all college work;. Additional exam requirements/recommendations for international students: Required—TOEFL (minimum score 600 paper-based; 210 computer-based; 100 iBT). *Application deadline:* For fall admission, 1/5 priority date for domestic and international students; for spring admission, 12/1 for domestic students. Applications are processed on a rolling basis. Application fee: $50. Electronic applications accepted. *Financial support:* In 2008–09, 19 students received support, including 18 teaching assistantships with full tuition reimbursements available (averaging $15,500 per year); health care benefits and unspecified assistantships also available. Financial award application deadline: 1/5. *Faculty research:* English literatures and cultures; American literatures and cultures; critical theory and cultural studies; rhetoric and composition; creative writing. Total annual research expenditures: $278,898. *Unit head:* Dr. Susan Griffin, Chair, 502-852-6801, Fax: 502-852-4182, E-mail: smgriff01@louisville.edu. *Application contact:* Libby Leggett, Director, Graduate Admissions, 502-852-3101, Fax: 502-852-6536, E-mail: gradadm@louisville.edu.

University of Maryland, College Park, Graduate Studies, College of Arts and Humanities, Department of English, Creative Writing Program, College Park, MD 20742. Offers MA, MFA, PhD. *Degree requirements:* For master's, thesis optional, written exam; for doctorate, one foreign language, oral and written exams. *Entrance requirements:* For master's, GRE General Test, minimum GPA of 3.5, writing sample, 3 letters of recommendation. Additional exam requirements/recommendations for international students: Required—TOEFL. Electronic applications accepted. *Faculty research:* Early British literature, American literature.

University of Massachusetts Amherst, Graduate School, College of Humanities and Fine Arts, Department of English, Amherst, MA 01003. Offers creative writing (MFA); English and American literature (MA, PhD). Part-time programs available. Terminal master's awarded for partial completion of doctoral program. *Degree requirements:* For master's, one foreign language, thesis optional; for doctorate, one foreign language, comprehensive exam, thesis/dissertation. *Entrance requirements:* For master's, GRE General Test, GRE Subject Test (MA), writing sample (MFA); for doctorate, GRE General Test, GRE Subject Test. Additional exam requirements/recommendations for international students: Required—TOEFL (minimum score 550 paper-based; 213 computer-based; 79 iBT), IELTS (minimum score 6.5). Electronic applications accepted. *Expenses:* Tuition, area resident: Full-time $2640. Tuition, nonresident: full-time $9936. One-time fee: $332 full-time. Tuition and fees vary according to course load.

University of Massachusetts Dartmouth, Graduate School, College of Arts and Sciences, Program in Professional Writing, North Dartmouth, MA 02747-2300. Offers MA, Post-baccalaureate Certificate. Part-time programs available. *Faculty:* 23 full-time (11 women), 39 part-time/adjunct (25 women). *Students:* 8 full-time (5 women), 19 part-time (14 women). Average age 36. 13 applicants, 92% accepted, 8 enrolled. In 2008, 9 master's awarded. *Degree requirements:* For master's, thesis. *Entrance requirements:* For master's, MAT or GRE, portfolio or writing sample (10-30 pages), 3 letters of recommendation. Additional exam requirements/recommendations for international students: Required—TOEFL (minimum score 500 paper-based). *Application deadline:* For fall admission, 4/1 for domestic students, 2/1 for international students; for spring admission, 11/1 for domestic students, 9/1 for international students. Application fee: $40 ($60 for international students). Electronic applications accepted. *Expenses:* Tuition, state resident: full-time $2071; part-time $86.29 per credit. Tuition, nonresident: full-time $8099; part-time $337.46 per credit. Required fees: $7946. Tuition and fees vary according to class time, course load and reciprocity agreements. *Financial support:* In 2008–09, 8 teaching assistantships with full tuition reimbursements (averaging $10,450 per year) were awarded; career-related internships or fieldwork, Federal Work-Study, and unspecified assistantships also available. Support available to part-time students. Financial award application deadline: 3/1; financial award applicants required to submit FAFSA. *Unit head:* Dr. Jerry Blitefield, Director, 508-910-6601, Fax: 508-999-9325, E-mail: jblitefield@umassd.edu. *Application contact:* Elan Turcotte-Shamski, Graduate Admissions Officer, 508-999-8604, Fax: 508-999-8183, E-mail: graduate@umassd.edu.

University of Memphis, Graduate School, College of Arts and Sciences, Department of English, Memphis, TN 38152. Offers creative writing (MFA); English (MA, Graduate Certificate); writing and language studies (PhD). Part-time programs available. *Faculty:* 36 full-time (17 women), 2 part-time/adjunct (both women). *Students:* 83 full-time (48 women), 112 part-time (90 women); includes 36 minority (33 African Americans, 2 Asian Americans or Pacific Islanders, 1 Hispanic American), 11 international. Average age 35. 100 applicants, 84% accepted, 27 enrolled. In 2008, 44 master's, 2 doctorates, 13 other advanced degrees awarded. Terminal master's awarded for partial completion of doctoral program. *Degree requirements:* For master's, one foreign language, comprehensive exam, thesis or alternative; for doctorate, 2 foreign languages, comprehensive exam, thesis/dissertation. *Entrance requirements:* For master's, GRE General Test or MAT, minimum GPA of 2.5; for doctorate, GRE General Test, minimum GPA of 3.0. *Application deadline:* For fall admission, 8/1 for domestic students; for spring

admission, 12/1 for domestic students. Applications are processed on a rolling basis. Application fee: $35 ($60 for international students). *Expenses:* Tuition, area resident: Full-time $6242; part-time $330 per credit hour. Tuition, state resident: full-time $6242; part-time $330 per credit hour. Tuition, nonresident: full-time $17,828; part-time $815 per credit hour. Required fees: $1156. *Financial support:* Research assistantships with full tuition reimbursements, teaching assistantships with full tuition reimbursements available. Financial award applicants required to submit FAFSA. *Faculty research:* American literature, cultural studies, ESL/linguistics, composition studies/professional writing. *Unit head:* Dr. Eric C. Link, Chair, 901-678-2651, Fax: 901-678-2226, E-mail: eclink@memphis.edu. *Application contact:* Dr. Verner D. Mitchell, Director, Graduate Studies, 901-678-3099, Fax: 901-678-2226, E-mail: vdmtchll@memphis.edu.

University of Miami, Graduate School, College of Arts and Sciences, Department of English, Coral Gables, FL 33124. Offers creative writing (MFA); English (MA, PhD). Part-time programs available. Terminal master's awarded for partial completion of doctoral program. *Degree requirements:* For master's, one foreign language, thesis optional; for doctorate, one foreign language, thesis/dissertation. *Entrance requirements:* For master's and doctorate, GRE General Test. Electronic applications accepted. *Faculty research:* Anglo-Irish literature, feminist criticism and theory, Caribbean literature, early modern literature and culture, postcolonial and ethnic studies.

University of Michigan, Horace H. Rackham School of Graduate Studies, College of Literature, Science, and the Arts, Department of English Language and Literature, Creative Writing Program, Ann Arbor, MI 48109. Offers MFA. *Degree requirements:* For master's, comprehensive exam, thesis. *Entrance requirements:* For master's, writing sample. Additional exam requirements/recommendations for international students: Required—TOEFL (minimum score 620 paper-based; 260 computer-based; 106 iBT). Electronic applications accepted. *Faculty research:* Prose, poetry.

University of Missouri–St. Louis, College of Arts and Sciences, Department of English, St. Louis, MO 63121. Offers American literature (MA); creative writing (MFA); English (MA); English literature (MA); linguistics (MA); teaching of writing (Graduate Certificate). Part-time and evening/weekend programs available. *Faculty:* 19 full-time (12 women), 1 part-time/adjunct (0 women). *Students:* 14 full-time (8 women), 98 part-time (71 women); includes 10 minority (8 African Americans, 1 Asian American or Pacific Islander, 1 Hispanic American). Average age 32. In 2008, 21 master's awarded. *Degree requirements:* For master's, thesis optional. *Entrance requirements:* For master's, writing sample. Additional exam requirements/recommendations for international students: Required—TOEFL (minimum score 550 paper-based; 213 computer-based). *Application deadline:* For fall admission, 7/1 priority date for domestic and international students; for spring admission, 12/1 priority date for domestic and international students. Applications are processed on a rolling basis. Application fee: $35 ($40 for international students). Electronic applications accepted. *Expenses:* Tuition, area resident: Full-time $5377; part-time $298.70 per credit hour. Tuition, nonresident: full-time $13,381; part-time $472.50 per credit hour. Required fees: $4078; $52 per credit hour. *Financial support:* In 2008–09, 2 research assistantships (averaging $9,000 per year), 4 teaching assistantships with full and partial tuition reimbursements (averaging $9,000 per year) were awarded. Financial award applicants required to submit FAFSA. *Faculty research:* Victorian literature, Shakespeare and Renaissance literature, eighteenth century literature, composition theory. *Unit head:* Dr. Frank Grady, Director of Graduate Studies, 314-516-5541, Fax: 314-516-5781, E-mail: fgrady@umsl.edu. *Application contact:* 314-516-5458, Fax: 314-516-5310, E-mail: gradadm@umsl.edu.

The University of Montana, Graduate School, College of Arts and Sciences, Department of English, Program in Creative Writing, Missoula, MT 59812-0002. Offers fiction (MFA); non-fiction (MFA); poetry (MFA). *Degree requirements:* For master's, final creative paper. *Entrance requirements:* For master's, GRE General Test, sample of written work. Additional exam requirements/recommendations for international students: Required—TOEFL. *Faculty research:* Fiction, poetry, nonfiction.

University of Nebraska at Kearney, College of Graduate Study, College of Fine Arts and Humanities, Department of English, Kearney, NE 68849-0001. Offers creative writing (MA); literature (MA). Part-time and evening/weekend programs available. *Degree requirements:* For master's, thesis optional. *Entrance requirements:* For master's, GRE General Test, writing samples. Additional exam requirements/recommendations for international students: Required—TOEFL (minimum score 550 paper-based; 213 computer-based). Electronic applications accepted. *Faculty research:* Narrative theory, popular culture, western and plains literature, women's studies, media studies.

University of Nebraska at Omaha, Graduate Studies and Research, College of Arts and Sciences, Department of English, Omaha, NE 68182. Offers advanced writing (Certificate); English (MA); teaching English to speakers of other languages (Certificate); technical communication (Certificate). Part-time and evening/weekend programs available. *Degree requirements:* For master's, comprehensive exam, thesis (for some programs). *Entrance requirements:* For master's, minimum GPA of 3.0, statement of purpose, 3 letters of recommendation, writing sample. Additional exam requirements/recommendations for international students: Required—TOEFL (minimum score 600 paper-based; 250 computer-based; 100 iBT). Electronic applications accepted.

University of Nebraska at Omaha, Graduate Studies and Research, Program in Writing, Omaha, NE 68182. Offers MFA. Postbaccalaureate distance learning degree programs offered (no on-campus study). *Degree requirements:* For master's, comprehensive exam. *Entrance requirements:* For master's, portfolio, letters of recommendation. Additional exam requirements/recommendations for international students: Required—TOEFL (minimum score 550 paper-based; 213 computer-based; 80 iBT). Electronic applications accepted.

University of Nebraska–Lincoln, Graduate College, College of Arts and Sciences, Department of English, Lincoln, NE 68588-0333. Offers composition and rhetoric (MA, PhD); creative writing (MA, PhD); literature studies (MA, PhD). *Faculty:* 39 full-time (23 women). *Students:* 77 full-time (57 women), 54 part-time (36 women); includes 5 minority (3 African Americans, 2 Hispanic Americans), 6 international. In 2008, 11 master's, 15 doctorates awarded. *Degree requirements:* For master's, thesis optional; for doctorate, one foreign language, comprehensive exam, thesis/dissertation. *Entrance requirements:* For master's, writing sample; for doctorate, GRE General Test, writing sample. Additional exam requirements/recommendations for international students: Required—TOEFL (minimum score 600 paper-based; 250 computer-based). *Application deadline:* For fall admission, 1/15 for domestic and international students. Application fee: $40. Electronic applications accepted. *Expenses:* Tuition, state resident: full-time $4275; part-time $237.50 per credit hour. Tuition, nonresident: full-time $11,525; part-time $640.25 per credit hour. Required fees: $1068; $10.35 per credit hour. $440.70 per semester. Tuition and fees vary according to course load and program. *Financial support:* Fellowships, research assistantships, teaching assistantships, Federal Work-Study, health care benefits, and unspecified assistantships available. Support available to part-time students. Financial award application deadline: 1/15. *Faculty research:* Creative writing, composition and rhetoric, women's studies, North American literature, medieval/Renaissance studies. *Unit head:* Dr. Linda Pratt, Chair, 402-472-3191, Fax: 402-472-1123. *Application contact:* Ginny Gross, Director of Graduate Admissions, 402-472-2878, Fax: 402-472-0589, E-mail: grad_admissions@unl.edu.

University of Nevada, Las Vegas, Graduate College, College of Liberal Arts, Department of English, Las Vegas, NV 89154-5011. Offers creative writing (MFA); English (MA, PhD). Part-time programs available. *Faculty:* 32 full-time (12 women), 5 part-time/adjunct (0 women). *Students:* 66 full-time (31 women), 21 part-time (14 women); includes 4 minority (1 Asian American or Pacific Islander, 3 Hispanic Americans), 4 international. Average age 35. 172 applicants, 23% accepted, 25 enrolled. In 2008, 16 master's, 3 doctorates awarded. *Degree requirements:* For master's, one foreign language, comprehensive exam, thesis (for some programs); for doctorate, 2 foreign languages, comprehensive exam, thesis/dissertation. *Entrance requirements:* For

Writing

University of Nevada, Las Vegas *(continued)*
master's, GRE General Test (Verbal); for doctorate, GRE General Test (Verbal and Subject). Additional exam requirements/recommendations for international students: Required—TOEFL (minimum score 550 paper-based; 213 computer-based; 80 iBT), IELTS (minimum score 7). *Application deadline:* For fall admission, 2/15 priority date for domestic and international students. Applications are processed on a rolling basis. Application fee: $60 ($75 for international students). Electronic applications accepted. *Expenses:* Tuition, state resident: full-time $1414; part-time $198 per credit. Tuition, nonresident: full-time $12,509; part-time $415.75 per credit. International tuition: $14,249 full-time. Required fees: $4 per credit. $252 per semester. Tuition and fees vary according to course load. *Financial support:* In 2008–09, 69 students received support, including 5 research assistantships with partial tuition reimbursements available (averaging $19,400 per year), 64 teaching assistantships with partial tuition reimbursements available (averaging $11,803 per year); institutionally sponsored loans, scholarships/grants, health care benefits, and unspecified assistantships also available. Financial award application deadline: 3/1. *Faculty research:* Contemporary poetry and fiction, Renaissance literature and Renaissance studies, Post-Structuralist literary theory and criticism, business and professional writing, 19th and 20th century British and American literature. *Unit head:* Dr. Richard Harp, Chair/Professor, 702-895-0919, Fax: 702-895-4801, E-mail: richard.harp@unlv.edu. *Application contact:* Graduate College Admissions Evaluator, 702-895-3320, Fax: 702-895-4180, E-mail: gradcollege@unlv.edu.

University of New Hampshire, Graduate School, College of Liberal Arts, Department of English, Durham, NH 03824. Offers English (MFA, PhD); English education (MST); language and linguistics (MA); literature (MA); writing (MA). Part-time programs available. *Faculty:* 35 full-time (18 women). *Students:* 50 full-time (29 women), 66 part-time (44 women); includes 6 minority (1 African American, 3 Asian Americans or Pacific Islanders, 2 Hispanic Americans), 5 international. Average age 34. 267 applicants, 44% accepted, 37 enrolled. In 2008, 33 master's, 1 doctorate awarded. *Degree requirements:* For master's, one foreign language; for doctorate, 2 foreign languages, thesis/dissertation. *Entrance requirements:* For master's, GRE General Test, sample of written work; for doctorate, GRE General Test, GRE Subject Test, sample of written work. Additional exam requirements/recommendations for international students: Required—TOEFL (minimum score 550 paper-based; 213 computer-based; 80 iBT). *Application deadline:* For fall admission, 2/15 priority date for domestic students, 2/15 for international students. Applications are processed on a rolling basis. Application fee: $60. Electronic applications accepted. *Expenses:* Tuition, area resident: Full-time $9720; part-time $540 per credit hour. Tuition, nonresident: full-time $23,200; part-time $954 per credit hour. Required fees: $1446; $361.50 per term. *Financial support:* In 2008–09, 58 students received support, including 3 fellowships, 1 research assistantship, 47 teaching assistantships; career-related internships or fieldwork, Federal Work-Study, scholarships/grants, and tuition waivers (full and partial) also available. Support available to part-time students. Financial award application deadline: 2/15. *Unit head:* Dr. Andrew Merton, Chairperson, 603-862-3963. *Application contact:* Sue Smith, Administrative Assistant, 603-862-3963, E-mail: engl.grad@unh.edu.

University of New Mexico, Graduate School, College of Arts and Sciences, Department of English, Albuquerque, NM 87131-2039. Offers creative writing (MFA); English (MA, PhD). Part-time programs available. *Degree requirements:* For master's, one foreign language, comprehensive exam (for some programs), thesis (for some programs), portfolio; for doctorate, 2 foreign languages, comprehensive exam, thesis/dissertation. *Entrance requirements:* For master's, GRE General Test, GRE Subject Test (literature MA), writing sample; for doctorate, GRE General Test, GRE Subject Test, writing sample. Electronic applications accepted. *Faculty research:* American literature, Native American literature, Chicana/o literature, British and Irish literature, creative writing, rhetoric and writing.

University of New Mexico, Graduate School, College of Arts and Sciences, Program in Creative Writing, Albuquerque, NM 87131-2039. Offers MFA. *Degree requirements:* For master's, comprehensive exam, thesis. *Entrance requirements:* For master's, writing sample. *Faculty research:* Creative writing, fiction, creative non-fiction, poetry.

University of New Mexico, Graduate School, College of Fine Arts, Department of Theatre and Dance, Albuquerque, NM 87131-2039. Offers dramatic writing (MFA); theater and dance (MA). *Accreditation:* NASD; NAST. *Degree requirements:* For master's, comprehensive exam (for some programs), thesis (for some programs). *Entrance requirements:* For master's, minimum GPA of 3.0, undergraduate major in theatre, dance or closely related field, 3 letters of recommendation, letter of intent. Electronic applications accepted. *Faculty research:* Theater education and outreach, choreography, dramatic writing, dance history/criticism.

The University of North Carolina at Greensboro, Graduate School, College of Arts and Sciences, Department of English, Program in Creative Writing, Greensboro, NC 27412-5001. Offers MFA. *Degree requirements:* For master's, comprehensive exam, thesis. *Entrance requirements:* For master's, GRE General Test, minimum GPA of 3.0, writing sample. Additional exam requirements/recommendations for international students: Required—TOEFL. Electronic applications accepted. *Faculty research:* Fiction, poetry, science fiction, film studies.

The University of North Carolina Wilmington, College of Arts and Sciences, Department of Creative Writing, Wilmington, NC 28403-3297. Offers MFA. Part-time programs available. *Faculty:* 14 full-time (6 women). *Students:* 44 full-time (28 women), 21 part-time (13 women); includes 1 minority (Hispanic American), 2 international. Average age 29. 299 applicants, 24% accepted, 25 enrolled. In 2008, 19 master's awarded. *Degree requirements:* For master's, comprehensive exam, thesis. *Entrance requirements:* For master's, Writing sample. Additional exam requirements/recommendations for international students: Required—TOEFL (minimum score 550 paper-based; 217 computer-based; 79 iBT), IELTS (minimum score 6.5). *Application deadline:* For fall admission, 3/1 for domestic students. Application fee: $60. *Expenses:* Tuition, area resident: Full-time $4838. Tuition, state resident: full-time $4838. Tuition, nonresident: full-time $14,898. Required fees: $969.38 per semester. Tuition and fees vary according to course load, campus/location and program. *Financial support:* In 2008–09, 16 teaching assistantships with full and partial tuition reimbursements (averaging $14,000 per year) were awarded; career-related internships or fieldwork and Federal Work-Study also available. Support available to part-time students. Financial award application deadline: 3/15. *Unit head:* Dr. Philip Gerard, Chair, 910-962-3329, Fax: 910-962-7461, E-mail: gerardp@uncw.edu. *Application contact:* Lisa Bertini, MFA program assistant, 910-962-3070, E-mail: bertinil@uncw.edu.

University of North Florida, College of Arts and Sciences, Department of English, Jacksonville, FL 32224-2645. Offers MA. Part-time and evening/weekend programs available. *Faculty:* 14 full-time (6 women). *Students:* 14 full-time (12 women), 48 part-time (40 women); includes 6 minority (3 African Americans, 3 Hispanic Americans), 1 international. Average age 32. 37 applicants, 57% accepted, 9 enrolled. In 2008, 23 master's awarded. *Degree requirements:* For master's, comprehensive exam, thesis optional. *Entrance requirements:* For master's, GRE General Test, minimum GPA of 3.0 in last 60 hours, writing sample. Additional exam requirements/recommendations for international students: Required—TOEFL (minimum score 500 paper-based; 173 computer-based). *Application deadline:* For fall admission, 7/6 priority date for domestic students, 5/1 for international students; for spring admission, 11/1 priority date for domestic students, 10/1 for international students. Applications are processed on a rolling basis. Application fee: $30. Electronic applications accepted. *Expenses:* Tuition, area resident: Full-time $5782.08; part-time $240.92 per credit hour. Tuition, state resident: full-time $5782.08; part-time $240.92 per credit hour. Tuition, nonresident: full-time $19,974; part-time $832.26 per credit hour. Required fees: $952.80; $39.70 per credit hour. *Financial support:* In 2008–09, 29 students received support; research assistantships, teaching assistantships, Federal Work-Study and tuition waivers (partial) available. Support available to part-time students. Financial award application deadline: 4/1; financial award applicants required to submit FAFSA. *Faculty research:* Genre, period, and individual author studies in British, American, and world literature; literary criticism and theory—psychological, new historical and cultural, deconstructive, feminist, narrative, mythic; film and popular culture; online poetry

publishing. *Unit head:* Dr. Samuel A. Kimball, Chair, 904-620-2273, Fax: 904-620-3940, E-mail: skimball@unf.edu. *Application contact:* Dr. Jason Mauro, Graduate Coordinator, 904-620-2273, Fax: 904-620-3940, E-mail: jmauro@unf.edu.

University of North Texas, Robert B. Toulouse School of Graduate Studies, College of Arts and Sciences, Department of English, Denton, TX 76203. Offers creative writing (MA); English (MA, PhD); English as a second language (MA); linguistics (MA); Technical writing (MA). Terminal master's awarded for partial completion of doctoral program. *Degree requirements:* For master's, one foreign language, comprehensive exam, thesis optional; for doctorate, one foreign language, comprehensive exam, thesis/dissertation. *Entrance requirements:* For master's, GRE General Test, 3.0 GPA, personal statement, current vita/resumé, writing sample for creative writing program; for doctorate, GRE General Test, 3.5 GPA, 3 letters of recommendation, personal statement, writing sample. Additional exam requirements/recommendations for international students: Required—proof of English language proficiency required for non-native English speakers; Recommended—TOEFL (minimum score 550 paper-based; 213 computer-based). *Faculty research:* Creative writing, British and American literature, composition and rhetoric.

University of Notre Dame, Graduate School, College of Arts and Letters, Division of Humanities, Department of English, Creative Writing Program, Notre Dame, IN 46556. Offers MFA. *Faculty:* 7 full-time (2 women), 2 part-time/adjunct (1 woman). *Students:* 23 full-time (12 women); includes 6 minority (1 American Indian/Alaska Native, 2 Asian Americans or Pacific Islanders, 3 Hispanic Americans), 2 international. 187 applicants, 14% accepted, 12 enrolled. In 2008, 11 master's awarded. *Degree requirements:* For master's, thesis. *Entrance requirements:* For master's, GRE General Test, minimum GPA of 3.0. Additional exam requirements/recommendations for international students: Required—TOEFL (minimum score 600 paper-based; 250 computer-based; 80 iBT). *Application deadline:* For fall admission, 1/2 for domestic and international students. Application fee: $50. Electronic applications accepted. *Financial support:* Fellowships with full tuition reimbursements, teaching assistantships with full tuition reimbursements, tuition waivers (full) available. Financial award application deadline: 1/2. *Faculty research:* Novels, stories, poetry. *Unit head:* Prof. Steven Tomasula, Director, 574-631-7526, E-mail: creativewriting@nd.edu. *Application contact:* Dr. Barbara Turpin, Director of Graduate Admissions, 574-631-7706, Fax: 574-631-4183.

University of Oklahoma, Graduate College, Gaylord College of Journalism and Mass Communication, Program in Journalism and Mass Communication, Norman, OK 73019-0390. Offers advertising and public relations (MA); information gathering and distribution (MA); mass communication management and policy (MA); professional writing (MA); telecommunication and new technology (MA). Part-time programs available. *Students:* 33 full-time (16 women), 34 part-time (18 women); includes 12 minority (4 African Americans, 4 American Indian/Alaska Native, 1 Asian American or Pacific Islander, 3 Hispanic Americans), 8 international. 28 applicants, 75% accepted, 14 enrolled. *Degree requirements:* For master's, thesis optional. *Entrance requirements:* For master's, GRE General Test, minimum GPA of 3.2, 9 hours of course work in journalism, course work in statistics. Additional exam requirements/recommendations for international students: Required—TOEFL (minimum score 600 paper-based; 250 computer-based), TWE (minimum score 5). *Application deadline:* For fall admission, 2/1 for domestic students, 4/1 for international students; for spring admission, 11/1 for domestic students, 9/1 for international students. Application fee: $40 ($90 for international students). Electronic applications accepted. *Expenses:* Tuition, state resident: full-time $3744; part-time $156 per credit hour. Tuition, nonresident: full-time $13,577; part-time $565.70 per credit hour. Required fees: $2415.40; $90.10 per credit hour. *Financial support:* In 2008–09, 25 students received support, including 2 fellowships (averaging $4,500 per year); career-related internships or fieldwork, scholarships/grants, health care benefits, and unspecified assistantships also available. *Faculty research:* Organizational management; rhetorical analysis; international public relations; digital production; normative theory. *Unit head:* Dr. Joe Foote, Dean, 405-325-2721, Fax: 405-325-7565, E-mail: jfoote@ou.edu. *Application contact:* Kelly Storm, Graduate Advisor, 405-325-2722, Fax: 405-325-7565, E-mail: kstorm@ou.edu.

University of Oklahoma, Graduate College, Gaylord College of Journalism and Mass Communication, Program in Professional Writing, Norman, OK 73019-0390. Offers MPW. Part-time programs available. *Students:* 7 full-time (5 women), 9 part-time (6 women); includes 2 minority (1 American Indian/Alaska Native, 1 Asian American or Pacific Islander). 4 applicants, 100% accepted, 3 enrolled. *Degree requirements:* For master's, project. *Entrance requirements:* For master's, GRE General Test, 2 letters of recommendation, resumé, writing sample. Additional exam requirements/recommendations for international students: Required—TOEFL (minimum score 600 paper-based; 250 computer-based), TWE (minimum score 5). *Application deadline:* For fall admission, 7/1 for domestic students, 4/1 for international students; for spring admission, 11/1 for domestic students, 9/1 for international students. Application fee: $40 ($90 for international students). Electronic applications accepted. *Expenses:* Tuition, state resident: full-time $3744; part-time $156 per credit hour. Tuition, nonresident: full-time $13,577; part-time $565.70 per credit hour. Required fees: $2415.40; $90.10 per credit hour. *Financial support:* In 2008–09, 6 students received support. Career-related internships or fieldwork, scholarships/grants, health care benefits, and unspecified assistantships available. Financial award applicants required to submit FAFSA. *Faculty research:* Creative writing; script writing; nonfiction. *Unit head:* Dr. Joe Foote, Dean, 405-325-2721, Fax: 405-325-7565, E-mail: jfoote@ou.edu. *Application contact:* Kelly Storm, Graduate Advisor, 405-325-2722, Fax: 405-325-7565, E-mail: kstorm@ou.edu.

University of Oregon, Graduate School, College of Arts and Sciences, Department of Creative Writing, Eugene, OR 97403. Offers MFA. *Degree requirements:* For master's, thesis, exam. *Entrance requirements:* For master's, minimum GPA of 3.0. Additional exam requirements/recommendations for international students: Required—TOEFL. *Faculty research:* Poetry, fiction, literary nonfiction.

University of Pennsylvania, Graduate School of Education, Division of Language in Education, Program in Reading, Writing, and Literacy, Philadelphia, PA 19104. Offers MS Ed, Ed D, PhD. Part-time programs available. *Degree requirements:* For master's, comprehensive exam; for doctorate, one foreign language, thesis/dissertation, preliminary exam. *Entrance requirements:* For master's and doctorate, GRE General Test or MAT. Additional exam requirements/recommendations for international students: Required—TOEFL. Electronic applications accepted. *Expenses:* Contact institution. *Faculty research:* Reading and writing relationships, classroom teachers as researchers, comprehension processes.

University of Pittsburgh, School of Arts and Sciences, Department of English, Pittsburgh, PA 15260. Offers cultural and critical studies (PhD); English (MA); writing (MFA). Part-time programs available. *Degree requirements:* For master's, one foreign language; for doctorate, 2 foreign languages, comprehensive exam, thesis/dissertation. *Entrance requirements:* For master's and doctorate, GRE General Test, writing sample. Additional exam requirements/recommendations for international students: Required—TOEFL. *Faculty research:* Cultural studies, literary history and theory, film, composition.

University of San Francisco, College of Arts and Sciences, Program in Writing, San Francisco, CA 94117-1080. Offers MFA. Part-time and evening/weekend programs available. *Degree requirements:* For master's, thesis. *Entrance requirements:* For master's, minimum GPA of 3.0, writing sample. *Faculty research:* Techniques of teaching the novel to writers, oral history.

University of South Carolina, The Graduate School, College of Arts and Sciences, Department of English Language and Literature, Columbia, SC 29208. Offers creative writing (MFA); English (MA, PhD); English education (MAT); MLIS/MA. MAT offered in cooperation with the College of Education. Part-time programs available. *Degree requirements:* For master's, one foreign language, comprehensive exam, thesis; for doctorate, 2 foreign languages, comprehensive exam, thesis/dissertation. *Entrance requirements:* For master's, GRE General Test (MFA), GRE Subject Test (MA, MAT), sample of written work; for doctorate, GRE General Test, GRE Subject Test, sample of written work. Additional exam requirements/recommendations for international students: Required—TOEFL. Electronic applications accepted. *Faculty research:* American literature, British literature, composition and rhetoric, linguistics, speech communication.

University of Southern California, Graduate School, College of Letters, Arts and Sciences, Department of English, Los Angeles, CA 90089. Offers English and American literature (MA, PhD); English literature and creative writing (PhD). Terminal master's awarded for partial completion of doctoral program. *Degree requirements:* For doctorate, one foreign language, thesis/dissertation. *Entrance requirements:* For doctorate, GRE General Test, GRE Subject Test. *Faculty research:* Creative writing and literature, early modern studies, gender and sexuality, narrative studies, poetry and poetics, media, film and popular culture.

University of Southern California, Graduate School, College of Letters, Arts and Sciences, Program in Professional Writing, Los Angeles, CA 90089. Offers MPW. Part-time and evening/weekend programs available. *Degree requirements:* For master's, thesis. *Entrance requirements:* For master's, GRE General Test. *Faculty research:* Screenplays, teleplays, fiction, non-fiction, plays, poetry, journalism and publishing, magazine and book publishing.

University of Southern Maine, College of Arts and Sciences, Program in Creative Writing, Portland, ME 04104. Offers MFA.

The University of Texas at Austin, Graduate School, College of Liberal Arts, Department of English, Austin, TX 78712-1111. Offers creative writing (MA); English (MA, PhD). Part-time programs available. Terminal master's awarded for partial completion of doctoral program. *Degree requirements:* For master's, 2 foreign languages; for doctorate, variable foreign language requirement. *Entrance requirements:* For master's and doctorate, GRE General Test. Electronic applications accepted.

The University of Texas at Austin, Graduate School, Program in Writing, Austin, TX 78712-1111. Offers MFA. Electronic applications accepted.

The University of Texas at El Paso, Graduate School, College of Liberal Arts, Department of Creative Writing, El Paso, TX 79968-0001. Offers creative writing in English (MFA); creative writing in Spanish (MFA). Part-time and evening/weekend programs available. *Degree requirements:* For master's, thesis. *Entrance requirements:* For master's, departmental exam (creative writing in Spanish), minimum GPA of 3.0. Additional exam requirements/recommendations for international students: Required—TOEFL. Electronic applications accepted.

The University of Texas at El Paso, Graduate School, College of Liberal Arts, Department of English, El Paso, TX 79968-0001. Offers English and American literature (MA); rhetoric and composition (PhD); rhetoric and writing studies (MA); teaching English (MAT). Part-time and evening/weekend programs available. *Degree requirements:* For master's, thesis optional. *Entrance requirements:* For master's, GRE General Test, minimum GPA of 3.0. Additional exam requirements/recommendations for international students: Required—TOEFL. Electronic applications accepted. *Faculty research:* Literature, creative writing, literary theory.

The University of Texas at San Antonio, College of Liberal and Fine Arts, Department of English, Classics and Philosophy, San Antonio, TX 78249-0617. Offers creative writing (Graduate Certificate); English (MA, PhD). Part-time and evening/weekend programs available. *Degree requirements:* For master's, comprehensive exam, thesis optional; for doctorate, comprehensive exam, thesis/dissertation. *Entrance requirements:* For master's, GRE General Test, minimum GPA of 3.3 on all upper division English courses; for doctorate, GRE General Test. Additional exam requirements/recommendations for international students: Required—TOEFL (minimum score 500 paper-based; 173 computer-based). Electronic applications accepted. *Faculty research:* English and American literature, linguistics.

University of the Sacred Heart, Graduate Programs, Department of Communication, San Juan, PR 00914-0383. Offers contemporary culture and media (MA); editing for media (MA); public relations (MA); publicity (MA); scriptwriting (MA). Part-time and evening/weekend programs available. *Degree requirements:* For master's, thesis.

University of the Sacred Heart, Graduate Programs, Program in Creative Writing, San Juan, PR 00914-0383. Offers MA.

The University of Toledo, College of Graduate Studies, College of Arts and Sciences, Department of English Language and Literature, Toledo, OH 43606-3390. Offers English as a second language (MA); literature (MA); teaching of writing (Certificate). Part-time programs available. *Degree requirements:* For master's, one foreign language. *Entrance requirements:* For master's, minimum GPA of 2.7. Electronic applications accepted. *Faculty research:* Literary criticism, linguistics, creative writing, folklore and cultural studies.

University of Utah, The Graduate School, College of Humanities, Department of English, Program in Creative Writing, Salt Lake City, UT 84112-1107. Offers MFA.

University of Victoria, Faculty of Graduate Studies, Faculty of Fine Arts, Department of Writing, Victoria, BC V8W 2Y2, Canada. Offers MFA. *Entrance requirements:* For master's, portfolio, 400-word statement of purpose, 2 letters of reference.

University of Virginia, College and Graduate School of Arts and Sciences, Department of English Language and Literature, Program in Creative Writing, Charlottesville, VA 22903. Offers MFA. *Students:* 27 full-time (13 women); includes 1 minority (Asian American or Pacific Islander), 1 international. Average age 27. 621 applicants, 2% accepted, 12 enrolled. In 2008, 10 master's awarded. *Degree requirements:* For master's, comprehensive exam, thesis. *Entrance requirements:* For master's, GRE General Test, writing sample. Additional exam requirements/recommendations for international students: Required—TOEFL (minimum score 600 paper-based; 250 computer-based; 90 iBT), IELTS (minimum score 7). *Application deadline:* For fall admission, 1/4 for domestic students. Application fee: $60. Electronic applications accepted. *Expenses:* Tuition, area resident: Full-time $10,452. Tuition, state resident: full-time $10,452. Tuition, nonresident: full-time $20,010. Required fees: $2176. Part-time tuition and fees vary according to course load and program. *Financial support:* Fellowships, teaching assistantships available. Financial award application deadline: 1/4; financial award applicants required to submit FAFSA. *Unit head:* Sydney Blair, Director, Creative Writing Program, E-mail: shb7f@virginia.edu. *Application contact:* Barbara Moriarty, Administrative Assistant, E-mail: bam9s@virginia.edu.

University of Washington, Graduate School, College of Arts and Sciences, Department of English, Seattle, WA 98195. Offers creative writing (MFA); English as a second language (MAT); English literature and language (MA, MAT, PhD). Part-time programs available. Terminal master's awarded for partial completion of doctoral program. *Degree requirements:* For master's, one foreign language, thesis (for some programs); for doctorate, one foreign language, thesis/dissertation. *Entrance requirements:* For master's, GRE General Test, GRE Subject Test (for English (MA, MAT) only), minimum GPA of 3.0; for doctorate, GRE General Test, GRE Subject Test. Additional exam requirements/recommendations for international students: Required—TOEFL. Electronic applications accepted. *Faculty research:* English and American literature, critical theory, creative writing, language theory.

University of West Florida, College of Arts and Sciences: Arts, Department of English and Foreign Languages, Pensacola, FL 32514-5750. Offers creative writing (MA); literature (MA). Part-time and evening/weekend programs available. *Faculty:* 7 full-time (2 women). *Students:* 7 full-time (4 women), 29 part-time (22 women); includes 4 minority (1 African American, 1 American Indian/Alaska Native, 2 Asian Americans or Pacific Islanders). Average age 31. 20 applicants, 80% accepted, 12 enrolled. In 2008, 2 master's awarded. *Degree requirements:* For master's, thesis. *Entrance requirements:* For master's, GRE General Test, minimum GPA of 3.0. Additional exam requirements/recommendations for international students: Required—TOEFL (minimum score 550 paper-based; 213 computer-based). *Application deadline:* For fall admission, 6/1 for domestic students, 5/15 for international students; for spring admission, 11/1 for domestic students, 10/1 for international students. Applications are processed on a rolling basis. Application fee: $30. *Expenses:* Tuition, state resident: full-time $6095; part-time $253.97 per credit hour. Tuition, nonresident: full-time $21,919; part-time $913.31 per credit hour. *Financial support:* In 2008–09, 6 research assistantships with partial tuition reimbursements (averaging $2,187 per year), 9 teaching assistantships with partial tuition reimbursements (averaging $4,556 per year) were awarded; scholarships/grants, tuition waivers (partial), and unspecified assistantships also available. Support available to part-time students. Financial award application deadline: 4/15; financial award applicants required to submit FAFSA. *Faculty research:* Faulkner, Shakespeare, American humor, women's studies, poetry. *Unit head:* Dr. Bob Yeager, Chairperson, 850-474-2923. *Application contact:* Terry McCray, Assistant Director of Graduate Admissions, 850-473-7718, Fax: 850-473-7714, E-mail: gradadmissions@uwf.edu.

University of Windsor, Faculty of Graduate Studies, Faculty of Arts and Social Sciences, Department of English Language, Literature and Creative Writing, Windsor, ON N9B 3P4, Canada. Offers English: creative writing and language and literature (MA); English: language and literature (MA). Part-time programs available. *Degree requirements:* For master's, thesis. *Entrance requirements:* For master's, minimum B average, portfolio. Additional exam requirements/recommendations for international students: Required—TOEFL (minimum score 600 paper-based; 250 computer-based). Electronic applications accepted. *Faculty research:* Use of gender-related terms in popular culture; international and Aboriginal literatures: expression of cultural identity; critical analysis of authors: Pope, Munroe, Lady Morgan, Orwell, Thomas; the 'feminine" voice in literature and contemporary culture.

University of Wisconsin–Madison, Graduate School, College of Letters and Science, Department of English, Madison, WI 53706-1380. Offers applied English linguistics (MA); composition and rhetoric (PhD); creative writing (MFA); English language and linguistics (PhD); literary studies (MA, PhD). *Degree requirements:* For doctorate, thesis/dissertation.

University of Wisconsin–Milwaukee, Graduate School, College of Letters and Sciences, Department of English, Milwaukee, WI 53201-0413. Offers creative writing (PhD); English (MA); linguistics (PhD); professional writing (PhD); professional writing and communication (Certificate); rhetoric and composition (PhD); MLIS/MA. *Faculty:* 40 full-time (19 women). *Students:* 107 full-time (64 women), 82 part-time (54 women); includes 13 minority (8 African Americans, 1 American Indian/Alaska Native, 2 Asian Americans or Pacific Islanders, 2 Hispanic Americans), 23 international. Average age 35. 187 applicants, 41% accepted, 34 enrolled. In 2008, 31 master's, 14 doctorates awarded. *Degree requirements:* For master's, thesis or alternative; for doctorate, one foreign language, thesis/dissertation. *Entrance requirements:* For master's, GRE General Test, GRE Subject Test; for doctorate, GRE. Additional exam requirements/recommendations for international students: Required—TOEFL (minimum score 550 paper-based; 79 iBT), IELTS (minimum score 6.5). *Application deadline:* For fall admission, 1/1 priority date for domestic students; for spring admission, 9/1 for domestic students. Applications are processed on a rolling basis. Application fee: $45 ($75 for international students). *Expenses:* Tuition, area resident: Full-time $7320; part-time $165 per credit. Tuition, state resident: full-time $7320; part-time $165 per credit. Tuition, nonresident: full-time $17,840; part-time $714 per credit. Tuition and fees vary according to campus/location, program and reciprocity agreements. *Financial support:* In 2008–09, 74 teaching assistantships were awarded; career-related internships or fieldwork and unspecified assistantships also available. Support available to part-time students. Financial award application deadline: 4/15. Total annual research expenditures: $53,677. *Unit head:* Tasha Oren, Representative, 414-229-2643, Fax: 414-229-2643, E-mail: tgoren@uwm.edu. *Application contact:* General Information Contact, 414-229-4982, Fax: 414-229-6967, E-mail: gradschool@uwm.edu.

University of Wyoming, Graduate School, College of Arts and Sciences, Department of English, Laramie, WY 82070. Offers creative writing (MFA); English (MA). Part-time programs available. *Faculty:* 28 full-time (14 women), 5 part-time/adjunct (3 women). *Students:* 35 full-time (17 women), 10 part-time (6 women); includes 1 minority (Hispanic American), 1 international. Average age 28. 72 applicants, 26% accepted, 13 enrolled. In 2008, 9 master's awarded. *Degree requirements:* For master's, thesis or alternative, internship. *Entrance requirements:* For master's, GRE General Test, minimum GPA of 3.0. *Application deadline:* For fall admission, 3/1 priority date for domestic students; for spring admission, 12/1 for domestic students. Applications are processed on a rolling basis. Application fee: $50. Electronic applications accepted. *Financial support:* In 2008–09, 14 teaching assistantships were awarded; institutionally sponsored loans also available. Financial award application deadline: 3/1. *Faculty research:* Literature and theory, creative writing, English as a second language, ethnic and women's studies, composition. *Unit head:* Dr. Peter Parolin, Department Chair, Professor, 307-766-6452, Fax: 307-766-3189, E-mail: parolin@uwyo.edu. *Application contact:* Rachel Michelle Ferrell, MFA in Creative Writing Program Coordinator, 307-766-2867, Fax: 307-766-2697, E-mail: cw@uwyo.edu.

Utah State University, School of Graduate Studies, College of Humanities, Arts and Social Sciences, Department of English, Logan, UT 84322. Offers American studies (MA, MS), including folklore, western American literature and culture; English (MA, MS), including literature and writing, technical writing. Part-time and evening/weekend programs available. *Degree requirements:* For master's, thesis or alternative. *Entrance requirements:* For master's, GRE General Test or MAT, minimum GPA of 3.0, recommendation letters, writing samples. Additional exam requirements/recommendations for international students: Required—TOEFL. *Faculty research:* Scottish enlightenment, material culture, composition theory, creative nonfiction, literary criticism.

Vanderbilt University, Graduate School, Program in Creative Writing, Nashville, TN 37240-1001. Offers MFA. *Faculty:* 10 full-time (6 women). *Students:* 9 full-time (4 women), 2 part-time (both women); includes 1 minority (African American). Average age 28. 104 applicants, 10% accepted, 6 enrolled. In 2008, 5 master's awarded. *Degree requirements:* For master's, comprehensive exam, thesis. *Entrance requirements:* For master's, GRE General Test, sample of written work. Additional exam requirements/recommendations for international students: Required—TOEFL (minimum score 570 paper-based; 230 computer-based; 88 iBT). *Application deadline:* For fall admission, 1/15 for domestic and international students. Application fee: $0. Electronic applications accepted. *Financial support:* Fellowships with full and partial tuition reimbursements, teaching assistantships with full and partial tuition reimbursements, Federal Work-Study, institutionally sponsored loans, and health care benefits available. Financial award application deadline: 1/15; financial award applicants required to submit CSS PROFILE or FAFSA. *Unit head:* Kate Daniels, PhD, Interim Director, 615-322-2618, E-mail: kate.daniels@vanderbilt.edu. *Application contact:* Margaret Quigley, MFA Graduate Assistant, 615-322-2765, E-mail: creativewriting@vanderbilt.edu.

Virginia Commonwealth University, Graduate School, College of Humanities and Sciences, Department of English, Program in Creative Writing, Richmond, VA 23284-9005. Offers fiction (MFA); fictional poetry (MFA); poetry (MFA). *Entrance requirements:* For master's, portfolio.

Virginia Commonwealth University, Graduate School, College of Humanities and Sciences, Department of English, Program in English, Richmond, VA 23284-9005. Offers literature (MA); writing and rhetoric (MA).

Warren Wilson College, MFA Program for Writers, Swannanoa, Asheville, NC 28815-9000. Offers MFA. Postbaccalaureate distance learning degree programs offered (minimal on-campus study). *Degree requirements:* For master's, thesis, public reading, teaching experience. *Entrance requirements:* For master's, manuscript of creative work. *Faculty research:* Analytic writing, creative and analytic study of literature.

Washington University in St. Louis, Graduate School of Arts and Sciences, Department of English and American Literature, Writing Program, St. Louis, MO 63130-4899. Offers MFAW. *Students:* 23 full-time (15 women); includes 4 minority (1 African American, 2 Asian Americans or Pacific Islanders, 1 Hispanic American), 2 international. 256 applicants, 5% accepted, 11 enrolled. In 2008, 11 master's awarded. *Degree requirements:* For master's, thesis or written

Writing

Washington University in St. Louis (continued)

exam. *Entrance requirements:* For master's, GRE General Test, sample of written work. *Application deadline:* For fall admission, 1/4 for domestic students. Application fee: $45. Electronic applications accepted. *Financial support:* Fellowships, teaching assistantships, career-related internships or fieldwork, Federal Work-Study, institutionally sponsored loans, and tuition waivers (full and partial) available. Support available to part-time students. Financial award application deadline: 1/15. *Unit head:* Dr. Kellie Wells, Coordinator, 314-935-5120. *Application contact:* Kathy Schneider, Academic Coordinator, 314-935-5120.

Wayne State University, College of Liberal Arts and Sciences, Department of English, Detroit, MI 48202. Offers comparative literature (MA); English (MA, PhD). *Degree requirements:* For master's, one foreign language, essay or thesis; for doctorate, one foreign language, thesis/dissertation. *Entrance requirements:* For master's, GRE General Test, minimum GPA of 3.25 in English, 3.0 overall, statement of purpose; references; sample essay; for doctorate, GRE General Test, GRE Subject Test, statement of purpose, references, sample essay. Additional exam requirements/recommendations for international students: Required—TOEFL (minimum score 550 paper-based; 213 computer-based); Recommended—TWE (minimum score 6). Electronic applications accepted. *Faculty research:* English and American literature, cultural studies, composition, linguistics, film.

Western Connecticut State University, Division of Graduate Studies, School of Arts and Sciences, Department of English, Danbury, CT 06810-6885. Offers English (MA); literature option (MA); TESOL option (MA); writing option (MA). Part-time programs available. *Faculty:* 5 full-time (2 women). *Students:* 8 full-time (5 women), 35 part-time (26 women); includes 6 minority (2 African Americans, 1 Asian American or Pacific Islander, 3 Hispanic Americans), 2 international. Average age 40. 23 applicants, 48% accepted, 11 enrolled. In 2008, 10 master's awarded. *Degree requirements:* For master's, thesis (for writing option), completion of program in 6 years with minimum cumulative GPA of 3.0. *Entrance requirements:* For master's, minimum GPA of 2.5, writing sample. *Application deadline:* For fall admission, 8/5 priority date for domestic students; for spring admission, 1/5 priority date for domestic students. Applications are processed on a rolling basis. Application fee: $50. *Expenses:* Tuition, state resident: full-time $4377; part-time $363 per credit. Tuition, nonresident: full-time $12,195; part-time $363 per credit. Required fees: $3574; $60 per credit. Part-time tuition and fees vary according to degree level and program. *Financial support:* Teaching assistantships, career-related internships or fieldwork available. Support available to part-time students. Financial award application deadline: 5/1; financial award applicants required to submit FAFSA. *Unit head:* Dr. Shouhua Qi, Co-Coordinator, 203-837-9048, Fax: 203-837-8525, E-mail: qis@wcsu.edu. *Application contact:* Chris Shankle, Associate Director of Graduate Studies, 203-837-9005, Fax: 203-837-8326, E-mail: shanklec@wcsu.edu.

Western Connecticut State University, Division of Graduate Studies, School of Arts and Sciences, Department of Writing, Linguistics, and Creative Process, Danbury, CT 06810-6885. Offers professional writing (MFA). Part-time programs available. *Faculty:* 5 full-time (1 woman), 35 part-time/adjunct (17 women). *Students:* 23 full-time (10 women), 15 part-time (10 women); includes 6 minority (4 African Americans, 1 American Indian/Alaska Native, 1 Asian American or Pacific Islander). Average age 37. 21 applicants, 67% accepted, 10 enrolled. In 2008, 13 master's awarded. *Degree requirements:* For master's, thesis, completion of program within 4 years with minimum cumulative GPA of 3.0, enrichment project that compliments course of study. *Entrance requirements:* For master's, 2 writing samples: a 20-50 page portfolio of previous writing; brief essay. *Application deadline:* For fall admission, 8/5 priority date for domestic students; for spring admission, 1/5 priority date for domestic students. Application fee: $50. *Expenses:* Contact institution. *Unit head:* Dr. Brian Clements, Associate Professor/MFA Coordinator, 203-837-8876, Fax: 636-246-7589, E-mail: clementsb@wcsu.edu. *Application contact:* Chris Shankle, Associate Director of Graduate Admissions, 203-837-9005, Fax: 203-837-8326, E-mail: shanklec@wcsu.edu.

Western Kentucky University, Graduate Studies, Potter College of Arts and Letters, Department of English, Bowling Green, KY 42101. Offers education (MA); English (MA Ed); literature (MA), including American literature, British literature, literary theory, women writers, world literature; teaching English as a second language (MA); writing (MA). Part-time and evening/weekend programs available. *Degree requirements:* For master's, comprehensive

exam, thesis optional, final exam. *Entrance requirements:* For master's, GRE General Test, minimum GPA of 2.75. Additional exam requirements/recommendations for international students: Required—TOEFL (minimum score 555 paper-based; 213 computer-based; 79 iBT). *Faculty research:* Improving writing, linking teacher knowledge and performance, Victorian women writers, Kentucky women writers, Kentucky poets.

Western Michigan University, Graduate College, College of Arts and Sciences, Department of English, Kalamazoo, MI 49008-5202. Offers creative writing (MFA); English (MA, PhD); English education (MA, PhD); professional writing (MA). *Degree requirements:* For master's, oral exams; for doctorate, one foreign language, thesis/dissertation, oral exam, written exams. *Entrance requirements:* For master's and doctorate, GRE General Test, GRE Subject Test.

Westminster College, Program in Professional Communication, Salt Lake City, UT 84105-3697. Offers MPC. Part-time and evening/weekend programs available. *Faculty:* 7 full-time (3 women), 4 part-time/adjunct (2 women). *Students:* 16 full-time (13 women), 53 part-time (40 women); includes 4 minority (1 American Indian/Alaska Native, 2 Asian Americans or Pacific Islanders, 1 Hispanic American), 2 international. Average age 33. 36 applicants, 83% accepted, 24 enrolled. In 2008, 15 master's awarded. *Degree requirements:* For master's, field project. *Entrance requirements:* For master's, personal resumé, sample of professional writing, application letter, official transcripts, baccalaureate information. Additional exam requirements/recommendations for international students: Required—TOEFL (minimum score 600 paper-based). *Application deadline:* For fall admission, 8/1 priority date for domestic students. Applications are processed on a rolling basis. Application fee: $40. Electronic applications accepted. *Expenses:* Tuition: Part-time $840 per credit hour. Tuition and fees vary according to course load and program. *Financial support:* In 2008–09, 32 students received support. Career-related internships or fieldwork and tuition reimbursement available. Support available to part-time students. Financial award applicants required to submit FAFSA. *Faculty research:* Critical communication pedagogy, sexuality and gender, autoethnography, regulation of broadcast indecency, hypertext theory. *Unit head:* Dr. Helen Hodgson, Director, 801-832-2821, Fax: 801-832-3102, E-mail: hhodgson@westminstercollege.edu. *Application contact:* Joel Bauman, Vice President of Enrollment Services, 801-832-2200, Fax: 801-832-3101, E-mail: admission@westminstercollege.edu.

West Virginia University, Eberly College of Arts and Sciences, Department of English, Program in Creative Writing, Morgantown, WV 26506. Offers MFA. Part-time and evening/weekend programs available.

Wichita State University, Graduate School, Fairmount College of Liberal Arts and Sciences, Department of English, Wichita, KS 67260. Offers creative writing (MA, MFA); English (MA, MFA). Part-time and evening/weekend programs available. *Degree requirements:* For master's, comprehensive exam. *Entrance requirements:* For master's, GRE, writing sample (MFA). Additional exam requirements/recommendations for international students: Required—TOEFL. Electronic applications accepted.

Wilkes University, College of Graduate and Professional Studies, College of Arts, Humanities and Social Sciences, Program in Creative Writing, Wilkes-Barre, PA 18766-0002. Offers MA, MFA. *Students:* 97 full-time (55 women), 10 part-time (4 women); includes 9 minority (4 African Americans, 2 American Indian/Alaska Native, 1 Asian American or Pacific Islander, 2 Hispanic Americans). Average age 39. In 2008, 27 master's awarded. *Entrance requirements:* Additional exam requirements/recommendations for international students: Required—TOEFL (minimum score 500 paper-based; 173 computer-based; 79 iBT). Application fee: $45. *Expenses:* Contact institution. *Financial support:* Application deadline: 3/1. *Unit head:* Dr. Bonnie Culver, Director, 570-408-4527, Fax: 570-408-7846, E-mail: bonnie.culver@wilkes.edu. *Application contact:* Kathleen Houlihan, Director of Graduate Studies, 570-408-3235, Fax: 570-408-7846, E-mail: kathleen.houlihan@wilkes.edu.

Wright State University, School of Graduate Studies, College of Liberal Arts, Department of English Language and Literatures, Dayton, OH 45435. Offers composition and rhetoric (MA); English (MA); literature (MA); teaching English to speakers of other languages (MA). *Degree requirements:* For master's, thesis optional, portfolio. *Entrance requirements:* For master's, 20 hours in upper-level English. Additional exam requirements/recommendations for international students: Required—TOEFL. *Faculty research:* American literature, world literature in English, applied linguistics, writing theory and pedagogy.

ADELPHI UNIVERSITY

College of the Arts and Sciences
Program in Creative Writing

Program of Study

The Master of Fine Arts (M.F.A.) in creative writing offers students the opportunity to specialize in three major genres—fiction, poetry, and playwriting. This cross-genre program is distinctive from the traditional two-genre M.F.A. programs in which students study either fiction or poetry. Its unique Professional Development Practicum introduces students to the professional and practical life of writers across many disciplines.

Taught by distinguished faculty members who have published extensively, the program prepares students for careers in writing, teaching, and/or more advanced graduate studies through training in creative writing, language and literary studies, research, and teaching. Most classes are seminars that are held in the evenings once a week, either from 4 to 6:30 p.m. or from 7 to 9:30 p.m. Students must complete 37 credits in a plan of study that includes writing workshops (16 credits) and literature classes (12 credits). Students must also complete an 4-credit thesis colloquium. The 1-credit Professional Development Practicum meets once a week in the spring semester of the first year. Through meetings with writers and agents, students learn firsthand about the professional life of a writer. They also learn the practical procedures of submitting a manuscript or applying for a grant. Students and their advisers determine the appropriate plan of study. A student thesis is required in all programs.

Research Facilities

The University's primary research holdings are at Swirbul Library and include 646,720 volumes (including bound periodicals and government publications), 805,545 items in microformats, 32,353 audiovisual items, 1,738 periodical subscriptions, and access to over 27,000 electronic journal titles. Online access is provided to more than 200 research databases.

Financial Aid

All applicants are eligible for financial aid and are automatically considered for one of six partial (one-half) tuition remissions. Second-year students and students entering with a previous M.A. degree are eligible for graduate teaching fellowships in the Department of English. There are also opportunities for work-study positions, for community service teaching grants, or for positions at the Writing Center and the Learning Center.

Cost of Study

For the 2008–09 academic year, the tuition rate was $830 per credit. University fees ranged from $200 to $400 per semester.

Living and Housing Costs

The University assists single and married students in finding suitable accommodations whenever possible. The cost of living is dependent upon location and the number of rooms rented.

Location

Located in historic Garden City, New York, 45 minutes from Manhattan and 20 minutes from Queens, Adelphi's 75-acre suburban campus is known for the beauty of its landscape and architecture. The campus is a short walk from the Long Island Rail Road and is convenient to New York's major airports and several major highways. Off-campus centers are located in Manhattan, Hauppauge, and Poughkeepsie.

The University and The College

Founded in 1896, Adelphi is a fully accredited, private university with more than 8,000 undergraduate, graduate, and returning-adult students in the arts and sciences, business, clinical psychology, education, nursing, and social work. Students come from thirty-six states and from forty-seven countries. *The Princeton Review* named Adelphi University a Best College in the Northeastern Region, and *Fiske Guide to Colleges* recognized Adelphi as a "Best Buy" in higher education for two years in a row. The University is the only private institution on Long Island and one of only twenty-six in the nation to earn this recognition.

Mindful of the cultural inheritance of the past, the College of Arts and Sciences encompasses those realms of inquiry that have characterized the modern pursuit of knowledge. The faculty members of the College place a high priority on their students' intellectual development in and out of the classroom and structure programs and opportunities to foster that growth. Students analyze original research or other creative work, develop firsthand facility with creative or research methodologies, undertake collaborative work with peers and mentors, engage in serious internships, and hone communicative skills.

Applying

A baccalaureate degree is required for admission (the degree does not have to be in English or literature). A student must submit the completed application form, the $50 application fee, official college transcripts, two letters of reference from people familiar with the student's writing, a personal statement (of no more than 1,000 words and about the student's writing life and goals), and a manuscript in one genre only (poetry, fiction, or playwriting). The application deadlines are January 15 for fall enrollment and September 15 for spring enrollment. After those dates, rolling admissions are made on a space-available basis.

Correspondence and Information

Judith Baumel, Director of the M.F.A. Program
Harvey Hall, Room 212
College of Arts and Sciences
Adelphi University
Garden City, New York 11530-0701
Phone: 516-877-4031
Fax: 516-877-3039
E-mail: baumel@adelphi.edu
Web site: http://academics.adelphi.edu/artsci/creativewriting/

Adelphi University

THE FACULTY AND THEIR RESEARCH

CREATIVE WRITING

Judith Baumel, Associate Professor; M.A., Johns Hopkins, 1978. Contemporary poetry.

Martha Cooley, Assistant Professor; B.A., Trinity, 1977. Creative writing, modern and contemporary American literature, world literatures in translation (particularly Italian).

Anton Dudley, Assistant Professor; M.F.A., NYU, 2001. Dramatic writing.

Kermit Frazier, Associate Professor; M.F.A., NYU, 1977; M.A., Syracuse, 1970. Playwriting, television writing, contemporary drama, African American drama, the literature of AIDS.

Jacqueline Jones LaMon, Assistant Professor; J.D., UCLA, 1987; M.F.A., Indiana, 2006.

Igor Webb, Professor; Ph.D., Stanford, 1971. The nineteenth-century novel. *The Short Prose Reader: Annotated Instructor's Edition*, 9th ed. (Boston: McGraw-Hill, 2000).

LITERATURE

Jennifer Fleischner, Professor; Ph.D., Columbia, 1988. Twentieth-century American literature. *Mrs. Lincoln and Mrs. Keckly: The Remarkable Story of the Friendship Between a First Lady and a Former Slave* (New York: Broadway Books, 2003).

Michael Matto, Assistant Professor; Ph.D., NYU, 1998. History of the English language, history of rhetoric, Old English literature and culture, theories of metaphor, history of subjectivity.

Christopher Mayo, Assistant Professor; Ph.D., Brandeis, 2004. Restoration and eighteenth-century British literature and culture. "'A Lord Among Wits': Lord Chesterfield and his Reception of Johnson's Letter." In *Johnsonian News Letter* 56(2):38–42, September 2005.

Adam McKeown, Assistant Professor; Ph.D., NYU, 2000. Shakespeare, early modern visual culture. "Looking at Britomart Looking at Pictures." In *Studies in English Literature* 45:43–64 (2005).

Lahney Preston-Matto, Assistant Professor; Ph.D., NYU, 2000. Twentieth-century medievalism, translation theory, gender, twentieth-century Irish poetry, cultural studies. "Staking in Tongues: Speech-Act as Weapon in *Buffy the Vampire Slayer*." In *Fighting the Forces: What's at Stake in Buffy the Vampire Slayer*, eds. R. V. Wilcox and D. Lavery (Lanham, MD: Rowman and Littlefield, 2002).

Susan Weisser, Professor; Ph.D., Columbia, 1987. The nineteenth-century novel, autobiography, romantic love and gender. Introduction and notes to Jane Austen's *Persuasion* (New York: Barnes & Noble Classics, 2003).

Peter West, Assistant Professor.

Carnegie Mellon

CARNEGIE MELLON UNIVERSITY

Department of English
Graduate Programs in Professional Writing and Communication Design

Programs of Study

The Department of English at Carnegie Mellon offers two graduate degree programs in professional communication: the Master of Arts in Professional Writing (MAPW) and, in conjunction with Carnegie Mellon's School of Design, the joint Master of Design in Communication Planning and Information Design (CPID). Both programs prepare students to directly enter the world of professional communication in print and electronic media and provide the balanced integration of theory, practice, and production needed in these fields The programs vary in the degree to which they emphasize the visual and verbal aspects of communication. The MAPW program foregrounds writing as its foundational skill while offering significant instruction in the complementary skill of visual design for print and electronic texts. The CPID program consistently foregrounds the creative potential of the interplay between words and images in traditional and interactive media and is unique in cross-training writers and designers in the same cohort. Students interested in the CPID program should contact the School of Design directly for detailed information on the program (phone: 412-268-2828).

The MAPW is a flexible and customizable program that prepares students for careers as technical and professional writers, communications specialists, and information designers and managers in a range of traditional and emerging fields. MAPW students study the basics of print and electronic communication in six foundations courses and then specialize through student-selected concentrations. The core curriculum includes professional and technical writing, grammar, style, rhetoric, graphic and document design, and organizational management. Electives and concentrations include technical writing (particularly for the software industry), communication design (including online and multimedia), corporate and business communications, journalism, editing, and science and health-care communications. There is also a concentration in investigative journalism through study abroad at Strathclyde University in Scotland during the third semester.

Students gain extensive experience in planning, creating, testing, and revising professional documents. Students develop important project management and interpersonal skills through work with clients and team-based projects. In addition, they are prepared to research and understand the communication needs and practices of organizations, to use the latest research in writing and document design, and to develop facility in mastering emerging technologies.

The MAPW program requires three semesters, or 40 credit hours, of course work plus a three- to six-month professional internship generally completed between the second and third semesters. The CPID program requires two years of course work and a master's thesis and project, completed during the second year.

Research Facilities

More than 400 UNIX, Macintosh, and Windows computers are available in public clusters on the Carnegie Mellon campus. In addition, the Department of English maintains a cluster reserved for MAPW and CPID students, with dedicated computers and desktop publishing equipment. This cluster is equipped with current software for word processing, page layout, drawing, imaging, and Web authoring. Cluster hardware features high-end Macintosh machines and a few Windows machines. Additional equipment includes laser printers and scanners. The English department's usability testing lab allows students to conduct user tests of software and print documents, capturing user performance with digital video for subsequent analysis and editing. Students also have access to Carnegie Mellon's on-site print shop, which provides a full range of printing services.

Financial Aid

All students accepted full-time into the MAPW program receive a scholarship that directly reduces tuition by a significant amount. Qualified MAPW applicants who apply by February 15 of each year may also be eligible for additional merit-based scholarship funds. Graduate student loans are available through Carnegie Mellon's Office of Financial Aid, and MAPW students may apply for research assistantships within the Department. Students applying to the CPID program should contact the School of Design (phone: 412-268-2828) for financial aid information.

Cost of Study

Fees and expenses for full-time graduate students in 2009–10 are tuition, $33,810; activity fees, $400; and books and supplies, about $500. Part-time students are charged tuition at a unit rate.

Living and Housing Costs

There is a wide range of affordable housing options close to the Carnegie Mellon campus. Housing costs in Pittsburgh are typically lower than those in other urban settings. Room and board for a single graduate student average around $7000 for a full year. Carnegie Mellon does not provide housing for graduate students.

Student Group

Carnegie Mellon is a national research university of about 10,000 students and 4,000 faculty, research, and administrative staff members. Students come from all fifty states and forty-eight other countries. Nine percent are members of ethnic minority groups; about 20 percent are international students. Of the 95 graduate students enrolled in the Department of English, about 35 are in the literary and cultural studies program, 29 in rhetoric, 32 in the MAPW program, and 15 in the Master of Design program. The ratio of men to women is approximately even.

Student Outcomes

The programs produce graduates who are resourceful, multidimensional professionals with strong career potential. Graduates typically seek communications-based careers in government, business, nonprofits, and industry. Recent graduates have moved directly into positions in organizations such as IBM, NIH, Apple, Ketchum, Bank of New York Mellon, Catapult, Google, Compunetix, Fitch Richardson-Smith, Alcoa, MediaSite, and SiegelGale.

Location

Pittsburgh, Pennsylvania, was rated the number one "Most Livable City" by *Places Rated Almanac* in 2007. The city offers good public transportation, a lively arts and theater scene, diverse outdoor recreation, and an appealing geographical setting. The University is in the Oakland section near Schenley Park, the Carnegie Museums, and the University of Pittsburgh and its medical center. Adjacent neighborhoods offer housing, local shopping, and interesting restaurants and coffee shops. New York City, Philadelphia, Toronto, and Washington, D.C., are all within driving distance.

The University and The Department

Carnegie Mellon comprises a diverse blend of academic disciplines, including nationally recognized programs in cognitive psychology, computer science, design, human-computer interaction, management and public policy, robotics, writing and rhetoric, and applied history. The English department offers undergraduate majors in English, creative writing, professional writing, and technical writing. Carnegie Mellon is recognized as one of the most-wired of U.S. campuses and a pioneer in the use of computing in education.

Applying

MAPW applicants should submit transcripts, three letters of recommendation, a statement of intent, writing samples, a resume, GRE scores, and a nonrefundable fee of $50. Applicants not educated in the United States, Canada, Great Britain, Australia, or New Zealand must also submit TOEFL scores. Interviews, either face-to-face or by telephone, may be required. Applications for the MAPW program are accepted on a rolling basis, with admission closing when enrollment goals are met. MAPW applicants should submit their materials as early as possible and no later than February 15 to be considered for financial aid beyond the usual tuition remission scholarship. Applicants for the CPID program should contact the School of Design (phone: 412-268-2828) for specific application instructions.

Correspondence and Information

MAPW
Director of Graduate Studies
Department of English
Carnegie Mellon University
Pittsburgh, Pennsylvania 15213
Phone: 412-268-2850
Fax: 412-268-7989
E-mail: info@english.hss.cmu.edu
Web site: http://english.cmu.edu

Anita Kulina Smith
CPID Graduate Program Coordinator
Phone: 412-268-6843
E-mail: grad-info@design.cmu.edu
Web site: http://www.design.cmu.edu/ (follow the program link)

Carnegie Mellon University

THE FACULTY AND THEIR RESEARCH

Marian Aguiar, Assistant Professor of English and Literary and Cultural Studies; Ph.D., Massachusetts. Postcolonial and modernism.

Jane Bernstein, Professor of English and Creative Writing; M.F.A., Columbia. Fiction, nonfiction, screenwriting.

Claudia Carlos, Assistant Professor of Rhetoric; Ph.D., Illinois at Urbana-Champaign. Style, argument theory and practice, history of rhetoric, rhetoric of indirection.

Gerald P. Costanzo, Professor of English and Creative Writing; M.A., M.A.T., Johns Hopkins. Poetry, literature.

James Daniels, Thomas S. Baker Professor of English and Creative Writing; M.F.A., Bowling Green State. Poetry, fiction.

Sharon Dilworth, Associate Professor of English and Creative Writing; M.F.A., Michigan. Fiction, screenwriting.

Linda Flower, Professor of English and Rhetoric; Ph.D., Rutgers. Environmental rhetoric, cognitive rhetoric, community literacy.

Terrance Hayes, Professor of Creative Writing; M.F.A., Pittsburgh. Poetry, contemporary literature.

Paul Hopper, Paul Mellon Distinguished Professor of the Humanities and Professor of Rhetoric and Linguistics; Ph.D., Texas. Grammar, discourse studies, linguistics.

Suguru Ishizaki, Associate Professor of Rhetoric and Visual Design; Ph.D., MIT. Visual and document design, writing and design for new media.

Barbara Johnstone, Professor of English and Rhetoric; Ph.D., Michigan. Discourse studies, sociolinguistics.

David S. Kaufer, Professor of English and Rhetoric and Head; Ph.D., Wisconsin. Argument theory, technology and writing, professional communication.

Alan Kennedy, Professor of English; Ph.D., Edinburgh. Modern and Victorian fiction, theories of fiction, poststructural and cultural theory.

Jon P. Klancher, Associate Professor of English; Ph.D., UCLA. Sociology of culture, history of critical theory, Victorian studies, history of the book.

Peggy Knapp, Professor of English; Ph.D., Pittsburgh. Medieval, Renaissance, early modern English studies.

Hilary Masters, Professor of English and Creative Writing; A.B., Brown. Fiction, essays.

Jane McCafferty, Associate Professor of Creative Writing; M.F.A., Pittsburgh. Fiction, magazine writing, literary nonfiction.

Christine Neuwirth, Professor of English and Human-Computer Interaction; Ph.D., Carnegie Mellon. Computer tools for reading and writing, policy arguments, collaborative writing, technical and professional communication, Web and multimedia design.

Kathleen Newman, Associate Professor of English; Ph.D., Yale. American studies, media studies.

Richard Purcell, Assistant Professor of English; Ph.D., Pittsburgh. African American literature, history of Western humanism.

Andreea Deciu Ritivoi, Associate Professor of Rhetoric; Ph.D., Minnesota. Intercultural communication, rhetoric of public policy, professional and technical communication.

Karen Rossi Schnakenberg, Teaching Professor of Rhetoric and Professional Writing; Ph.D., Carnegie Mellon. Technical and professional communication, pedagogy of writing, instructional design, history of writing instruction.

David R. Shumway, Professor of English and Literary and Cultural Studies; Ph.D., Indiana. Organization of power, history of the discipline of English, film and media studies.

Kristina Straub, Professor of English and Associate Head; Ph.D., Emory. Feminist theory, cultural studies, lesbian and gay history and theory, eighteenth-century studies.

Danielle Wetzel, Assistant Professor of Rhetoric and Writing; Ph.D., Carnegie Mellon. Discourse analysis, composition pedagogies and second-language writing.

Jeffrey Williams, Professor of English; Ph.D., SUNY at Stony Brook. History of English departments, critical history and theory, nineteenth-century literature.

James Wynn, Assistant Professor of English; Ph.D., Maryland. Rhetoric of science, professional communication, science writing.

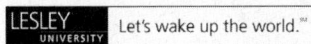

LESLEY UNIVERSITY

Master of Fine Arts in Creative Writing

Program of Study

The Master of Fine Arts (M.F.A.) in creative writing at Lesley University is a two-year, low-residency program in which students, under the guidance of a faculty mentor, design their own concentrations in fiction, nonfiction, poetry, writing for stage and screen, or writing for young people. A nine-day residency begins each semester with an invigorating program of seminars, workshops, readings, and individual conferences to develop the semester's program of study. Students then work independently during the semester under the direction of their faculty mentors—the program's flexibility allowing all participants to work from wherever they live.

Over a four-semester period, students attend four full residencies and take 12 credits per semester, as outlined in each semester's study-plan contract. Following the fourth semester—focused primarily on the creative thesis—graduating students spend a portion of a fifth residency to present a craft seminar, the final requirement for graduation. They may also give a reading from their creative thesis. Grades for each semester are pass-fail, accompanied by narrative evaluations by faculty mentors.

Lesley's M.F.A. in creative writing differs from other low-residency programs in a number of ways. The interdisciplinary component encourages students to expand their abilities as writers by widening their aesthetic experience and deepening their creative thinking. While the multigenre expertise of the M.F.A. faculty is the student's key resource, those with an interest in the visual arts have the opportunity to work with faculty members from the Art Institute of Boston at Lesley (AIB), and those seeking to integrate their writing with such disciplines as art therapy, psychology, and education have the resources of Lesley's Graduate School of Art and Social Sciences and the Lesley Seminars. The interdisciplinary component also offers opportunities for real-world literary experience, including paid and unpaid internships or assistantships in editing, publishing, and teaching at such organizations as Beacon Press; the Concord Poetry Center; David R. Godine, Publisher; Harvard Extension School; *Harvard Review;* the Horn Book; and Lesley University's Humanities Division and Academic Resource Center. Students also have the opportunity to participate in independent studies in an Art of the Author Interview project, book reviewing, magazine writing, photography, and writing the 10-minute play. Some students' interdisciplinary projects have led to full-time publishing jobs, paid teaching assistantships, professional Web sites, book publication, and publications in such journals as the *AWP Writer's Chronicle, Gettysburg Review, Harvard Review,* and *Massachusetts Review.*

Moreover, with its residencies taking place in Cambridge, Massachusetts, Lesley's program draws energy from one of the literary and historic capitals of the United States. Many of the core and visiting faculty members have thrived for years in this epicenter of writing and publishing. Their experiences make them uniquely astute advisers for student writers who need to understand the complexities and opportunities of contemporary literary culture.

Given these advantages, graduates of Lesley's M.F.A. Program in Creative Writing are equipped for new challenges as they continue to write, explore new genres and art forms, and participate in a serious community of writers and artists.

Research Facilities

Lesley University's Ludcke Library holds a working collection of books, periodicals, microfilm, microfiche, nonprint materials, and software resources that are readily available to students. The library provides Internet resources and database access to general and subject-specific resources that are appropriate to the subject focuses of the University. Through the Fenway Consortium, students can access thirteen other institutional libraries in the Boston-Cambridge area.

Financial Aid

A limited number of scholarships are available for students in the M.F.A. in creative writing program; however, the Financial Aid Office assists students as needed in obtaining various types of educational assistance, including Federal Pell Grants, Federal Stafford Student Loans, and Federal Perkins Loans. Some teaching assistantships are also available on a limited basis to M.F.A. candidates with other advanced degrees. In addition, funds from Lesley's Graduate Assistantship Program are available to M.F.A. students. Moreover, a senior teaching fellowship in the undergraduate Humanities Division is available every two years to a qualified Lesley M.F.A. alumnus or alumna.

Cost of Study

The flat tuition for the 2008–09 year was $7140 per semester for the program, plus a residency fee of $350 per residency session. A student requiring accommodations for the residency should plan on an additional cost of approximately $500 to $700 for each nine-day residency, plus the cost of travel to and from Boston.

Living and Housing Costs

For the summer residency, on-campus housing is available to nonlocal students in the M.F.A. in creative writing program. For the winter residency, the program's staff members help nonlocal students arrange housing at off-season rates. Information on local housing and assistance in obtaining housing are available upon request from the M.F.A. program's Assistant Director.

Student Group

The graduate on-campus and off-campus enrollment at Lesley University consists of more than 5,000 students who range in age from their mid-20s to their early 70s—in all stages of professional development. Students come from fifty states and thirty-two countries. Most are currently employed or have worked in the professional field of their choice and have returned to graduate school to enhance their training, learn new skills, or change careers.

Location

Lesley University is located in the historic city of Cambridge, Massachusetts, between Harvard University and Porter Squares in Cambridge, in the greater Boston metropolitan area. The Art Institute of Boston at Lesley University occupies a campus in Kenmore Square in Boston. The University is conveniently connected to downtown Boston by public transportation. Numerous historical sites and cultural attractions are easily accessed by train or bus or on foot, including theaters, museums, concerts, and professional sports events.

The University

Lesley University, founded in 1909 as a women's teaching college, continues its commitment to educating undergraduates while also offering graduate and Ph.D. programs in the fields of education, environmental studies, human services, counseling and psychology, and the arts. With today's student in mind, Lesley University has successfully pioneered a wide variety of flexible programs for adult learners that share a commitment to quality, innovation, and the integration of theory with practice.

Lesley offers degree programs for learners at all levels. The University also supports several centers and hosts a variety of academic and professional conferences and institutes. Lesley programs operate throughout Massachusetts and in twenty-three other states as well as at an affiliated site in Israel.

Applying

The deadline for applying for fall semester (residency in June/July) is March 1. The deadline for applying for spring semester (residency in January) is September 1. Applications are reviewed after these dates on a space-available basis.

A writing sample is a required part of the application. Applicants in fiction or creative nonfiction should submit approximately 20 double-spaced pages of prose. Applicants in poetry should submit up to 10 single-spaced pages of poetry. Applicants for writing for stage and screen should submit 15–20 double-spaced pages of script. Applicants in writing for young people should submit 15 double-spaced pages of Young Adult or Middle-Grade prose or two to three picture-book stories. Applicants must submit three copies of their writing sample with their application. If applying in more than one genre, applicants should submit three copies of the writing sample for each genre. Applicants should clearly indicate, on the title page of their writing samples, the genre to which they are applying.

Correspondence and Information

Office of Graduate and Adult Bachelor's Admissions
Lesley University
29 Everett Street
Cambridge, Massachusetts 02138-2790
Phone: 617-349-8300
     888.LESLEY.U (toll-free)
E-mail: info@lesley.edu
Web site: http://www.lesley.edu/oncampus

Lesley University

THE FACULTY AND THEIR RESEARCH

At the heart of the Lesley M.F.A. in creative writing program are its faculty mentors and visiting writers. Included among them are 2 former U.S. Poet Laureates; former fellows from the Mary Ingraham Bunting Institute of Radcliffe College; a recipient of the Commonwealth Prize for Poetry and Canada's Governor General's Award for Literature; winners of the Flannery O'Connor Award, Guggenheim fellowships, the Koret Foundation Book Prize, NEA fellowships, the Norma Farber First Book Award, the Parents' Choice Award, the Parenting's Reading Magic Award, Pushcart Prizes, Whiting awards, numerous state arts council awards, Ingram Merrill Foundation grants, and the PEN Discovery Award; and winners of, or nominees for, the National Book Award and the Pulitzer Prize. In addition, several books by the faculty mentors have been named "notable books" by the *Los Angeles Times*, the *New York Times*, and the *Washington Post*. Many faculty members have published their work in the *New York Times Magazine*, *The Atlantic Monthly*, *The New Yorker*, *The American Poetry Review*, *Antaeus*, *Paris Review*, *Smithsonian*, *Poetry*, *The Nation*, *Grand Street*, *Kenyon Review*, *Best American Poetry*, *The Best American Essays*, *Triquarterly*, and hundreds of other important journals and anthologies.

Faculty Mentors

Steven Cramer, Program Director. Poetry. Author of *Goodbye to the Orchard, Dialogue for the Left and Right Hand, The World Book*, and *The Eye That Desires to Look Upward*.

Anne Bernays. Fiction and Nonfiction. Author of nine novels, including *Growing Up Rich, Professor Romeo*, and *Trophy House*.

Brian Bouldrey. Fiction. Author of *Honorable Bandit: A Walk Across Corsica; Monster: Adventures in American Machismo; The Genius of Desire; Love, the Magician;* and *The Boom Economy*.

Jami Brandli, Writing for Stage and Screen. Author of published and produced plays *Normal, Moon Man, Flooding*, and *Looking for Bruce*.

Barry Brodsky, Writing for Stage and Screen. Author of published and produced plays and screenplays, including *All Other Nights, The Twelve-forty, The Surrender*, and *The Boys of Winter*.

Wayne Brown. Fiction, Nonfiction, and Poetry. Author of *Landscape with Heron: Stories and Remembrances, The Child of the Sea: Stories and Remembrances, Voyages* (poems), *Edna Manley: The Private Years*, and *On The Coast* (poems).

Jane Brox. Nonfiction. Author of *Clearing Land: Legacies of the American Farm, Five Thousand Days Like This One*, and *Here and Nowhere Else*.

Teresa Cader. Poetry. Author of *Guests* and *The Paper Wasp*.

Rafael Campo. Poetry. Author of *The Enemy; Landscape with Human Figure; The Other Man Was Me; What the Body Told; Diva; The Desire to Heal: A Doctor's Education in Empathy, Identity, and Poetry;* and *The Healing Art: A Doctor's Black Bag of Poetry*.

Leah Hager Cohen, Nonfiction and Poetry. Author of *Train Go Sorry: Inside a Deaf World; Glass, Paper , Beans: Revelations on the Nature and Value of Ordinary Things; Heat Lightening;* and *Heart, You Bully, You Punk*.

Pat Lowery Collins. Writing for Young People. Author of numerous works for children, including *The Fattening Hut, Schooner, Just Imagine, Signs and Wonders*, and *Come Out Come Out*. (http://www.patlowerycollins.com)

David Elliott. Writing for Young People. Author of *Evangeline Mudd and the Great Mink Escapade, Hazel Nutt, Mad Scientist, And Here's to You!, Evangeline Mudd and the Golden-haired Apes of the Ikkinasti Jungle, The Transmogrification of Roscoe Wizzle, Cool Crazy Crickets*, and *Cool Crazy Crickets to the Rescue*.

Thomas Sayers Ellis. Poetry. Author of *The Maverick Room, The Genuine Negro Hero*, and *Good Junk* and coeditor of *On the Verge: Emerging Poets and Artists*.

Tony Eprile. Fiction. Author of the novel *The Persistence of Memory* and *Temporary Sojourner and Other South African Stories*.

Laurie Foos. Fiction. Author of the novels *Ex Utero, Portrait of the Walrus by a Young Artist, Twinship, Bingo Under the Crucifix*, and *Before Elvis There Was Nothing*.

Susan Goodman. Writing for Young People. Author of *The Ultimate Field Trip* series and the *Brave Kids* series as well as *On This Spot: An Expedition Back Through Time; Choppers; The Truth About Poop; Skyscraper; All in Just One Cookie; Gee, Whiz! It's All About Pee;* and other books.

Marcie Hershman, Fiction and Nonfiction. Author of the novels *Tales of the Master Race* and *Safe in America* and the memoir *Speak to Me: Grief, Love and What Endures*.

Alexandra Johnson. Nonfiction. Author of *Leaving a Trace: On Keeping a Journal* and *The Hidden Writer: Diaries and the Creative Life*.

Rachel Kadish. Fiction and Nonfiction. Author of the novels *Tolstoy Lied: A Love Story* and *From a Sealed Room*.

Hester Kaplan. Fiction. Author of *The Edge of Marriage*, a short story collection and *Kinship Theory*, a novel.

Michael Lowenthal. Fiction. Author of the novels *Charity Girl, Avoidance*, and *The Same Embrace*.

William Lychack. Fiction. Author of the novel *The Wasp Eater* and *The Architect of Flowers*, a collection of stories.

Chris Lynch. Writing for Young People. Author of *Inexcusable; Free Will; Me, Dead Dad & Alcatraz; Shadow Boxer;* and *Slot Machine*.

Rachel Manley. Nonfiction. Author of *Slipstream: A Daughter Remembers* and *Drumblair: Memories of a Jamaican Childhood*.

Cate Marvin. Poetry. Author of *Fragment of the Head of a Queen* and *World's Tallest Disaster* and coeditor of *Legitimate Dangers: American Poets of the New Century*.

Kyoko Mori. Fiction and Nonfiction. Author of *Stone Field, True Arrow; Polite Lies: On Being a Woman Caught Between Cultures; The Dream of Water: A Memoir; One Bird; Fallout* (poems); and *Shizuko's Daughter*.

Spencer Reece, Poetry. Author of *The Clerk's Tale* and *Remembering James Merrill*.

Katherine Russell Rich, Nonfiction. Author of *The Red Devil* and *Unspeakable: Life in Another Language*.

Anita Riggio. Writing for Young People. Author and illustrator of *Smack Dab in the Middle, Beware the Brindlebeast, Secret Signs, A Moon in My Teacup*, and *Jitterbug*, a novel for middle-grade readers, as well as illustrator of *The Whispering Cloth* and other picture books.

Christina Shea. Fiction. Author of the novel *Moira's Crossing*.

Kate Snodgrass, Writing for Stage and Screen. Author of published and produced plays *Haiku; Que Sera, Sera;* and *Critics Circle* and produced plays *Observatory, The Glider*, and *How I Saw the Light*.

Janet Sylvester. Poetry. Author of *That Mulberry Wine, A Visitor at the Gate*, and *The Mark of Flesh*.

A. J. Verdelle. Fiction. Author of the novel *The Good Negress*.

Visiting Writers and Artists: A Selection

Ellen Driscoll, sculptor and installation artist, with numerous solo exhibitions, including New York City's Whitney Museum of American Art and the Contemporary Arts Center, Cincinnati. In 2001, she completed a major public commission, "As Above, So Below," for Grand Central Station.

Andre Dubus III, author of *House of Sand and Fog; Bluesman, The Cage Keeper and Other Stories;* and *We Don't Live Here Anymore*.

David Ferry, author of *No Country I Know: New and Selected Poems and Translation* and translator of *The Epistles of Horace, The Georgics of Virgil, Gilgamesh*, and *The Odes of Horace*.

Louise Glück, former Poet Laureate of the United States; winner of the Bollingen Prize, the Pulitzer Prize, and the National Book Critics Circle Award; and author of eleven collections—including *Averno, The Seven Ages, Vita Nova, Meadowlands, The Wild Iris, Ararat, The Triumph of Achilles, Descending Figure*, and *The House on Marshland*—as well as *Proofs and Theories: Essays on Poetry*.

Robie H. Harris, author of numerous books for young people, including *It's So Amazing! A Book About Eggs, Sperm, Birth, Babies, and Families; Happy Birth Day!; Don't Forget to Come Back; Goodbye, Mousie;* and *It's Perfectly Normal: Changing Bodies, Growing Up, Sex, and Sexual Health*.

Emily Hiestand, author of *Angela the Upside-Down Girl: and Other Domestic Travels* and *The Very Rich Hours: Travels in Orkney, Belize, the Everglades, and Greece;* also a highly regarded poet and photographer. (http://www.elementsboston.net/about/emily.htm)

Richard Hoffman, author of *Half the House: A Memoir* and *Without Paradise* (poems).

Marie Howe, author of *The Good Thief* (National Poetry Series winner, 1988) and *What the Living Do*.

Major Jackson, author of *Hoops* and *Leaving Saturn*.

Lois Lowry, award-winning author of numerous books for young readers, including *Messenger, The Silent Boy, Gathering Blue, The Giver, Looking Back: A Book of Memories*, and the *Anastasia Krupkik* series.

Gail Mazur, author of five poetry collections including *Nightfire, The Pose of Happiness, The Common, They Can't Take that Away from Me* (National Book Award finalist), and *Zeppo's First Wife: New and Selected Poems*.

Roland Merullo, author of the novels *Leaving Losapas; A Russian Requiem; Revere Beach Boulevard;* and *In Revere, in Those Days* as well as *Revere Beach Elegy: A Memoir of Home and Beyond* and *A Passion for Golf: In Pursuit of the Innermost Game*.

Sue Miller, author of six novels: *The Good Mother, Family Pictures, For Love, The Distinguished Guest, While I Was Gone*, and *The World Below* and the story collection, *Inventing the Abbotts*.

Leslea Newman, author of numerous books for children and adults, including *Hachiko Waits, Heather Has Two Mommies, A Letter to Harvey Milk*, and *Write from the Heart*.

Deborah Noyes, author of *When the Wolf Girls Came, Prudence and Moxie*, and *Red Butterfly* and editor of and contributor to the young adult fiction anthology, *Gothic! Ten Original Dark Tales*.

Tom Perrotta, author of the novels *Little Children, Joe College*, and *Election*.

Robert Pinsky, former Poet Laureate of the United States and author of twelve books of poetry, translation, and criticism, most recently *The Figured Wheel: New and Collected Poems, 1966–1996* and *Jersey Rain*.

David Rivard, author of the poetry collections *Torque, Wise Poison, Bewitched Playground*, and *Sugar Town*.

Lloyd Schwartz, Pulitzer Prize winner for music criticism; author of three books of poetry, *These People; Goodnight, Gracie;* and *Cairo Traffic;* and editor of *Elizabeth Bishop and Her Art*.

Maurice Sendak, renowned author and illustrator and winner of countless honors for his achievements, including the Hans Christian Andersen International Medal for his body of illustration work, the Laura Ingalls Wilder Award for his "substantial and lasting contribution to children's literature," and the National Medal of Arts, awarded by President Clinton.

Tom Sleigh, author of five books of poetry, *After One, Waking, The Chain, The Dreamhouse*, and *Far Side of the Earth*—a translation of Euripides' *Herakles*, and a play, *Rubber*.

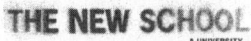

THE NEW SCHOOL: A UNIVERSITY

Graduate Writing Program

Program of Study

The New School has been a vital center for writing and writing instruction since 1931, when Gorham Munson, a Manhattan editor and influential member of Alfred Stieglitz's circle, introduced his workshop in creative writing. Since 1996, The New School has offered a Master of Fine Arts (M.F.A.) in creative writing, with concentrations in fiction, nonfiction, poetry, and writing for children. Founded by poet and biographer Robert Polito, the M.F.A. program marks the latest transformation in the University's commitment to creative writing. Both in the classroom and through the participation of distinguished visitors, the Graduate Writing Program aims to help students fully engage with the vibrant, diverse world of writing in New York City and beyond.

The M.F.A. program is a full-time course of study balancing writing workshops with seminars in the reading of literature. The program is designed to be completed in four semesters. During each of their first three terms, students enroll in one writing workshop (4 credits) in their area of concentration and one literature seminar (4 credits) and must participate in the Writer's Life Colloquium (1 credit). During their final term of residence, students continue to participate in the Writer's Life Colloquium but no longer enroll in writing workshops or literature seminars. Instead, they work closely with one or more New School writer-teacher advisers in independent study leading to the creation of a writing thesis (4 credits) and a literature project (4 credits), both within their area of concentration. Because of the intensive nature of the Graduate Writing Program, transfer credits are not accepted.

Research Facilities

The Raymond Fogelman Library contains books, standard references, pamphlets, and periodicals used by graduate students in all programs. Graduate students also have access to facilities of the Research Library Association of South Manhattan, which includes Cooper Union and New York University. It is one of the largest interuniversity library consortia in the country. Beyond the consortium are the rich resources of New York City, including 250 METRO member libraries and the public library system of the five boroughs. The University Computing Center is also available to students for their research and writing.

Financial Aid

M.F.A. students are eligible for state and federal grants and loans, and departmental scholarships are awarded to new and continuing students. The committee considers both merit and need in granting available funds. A University scholars' fund also allocates grants to incoming students from underrepresented groups. The University offers an extended payment plan that involves monthly billing throughout the year.

Cost of Study

Tuition for the 2009–10 academic year is $1220 per credit. A University services fee of $100 and a $15 student activities fee are charged each term. For more information, students should visit http://www.newschool.edu/tuition.

Living and Housing Costs

The University Housing Office maintains a comprehensive resource center with apartment listings. University-run apartments and residence halls are also available. The cost of housing, food, transportation, books, and living expenses averages $17,000 annually. For more information, students can visit http://www.newschool.edu/studentservices.

Student Group

M.F.A. students bring to the program a variety of academic backgrounds and types of professional experience. Many continue to work while attending the program. Sixty percent of the students are women; 23 percent are from underrepresented groups. The average age is 26 years. The program currently enrolls approximately 200 students.

Location

The New School writing program reflects the diversity and breadth of the writer's life in New York City. All writing workshops and literature seminar instructors are themselves published writers and experienced teachers, and guests from the city's vast publishing industry—including magazine and book editors, publishers, literary agents, and prominent teachers of writing—are invited to speak at dozens of events organized each semester.

The University

The New School is a leading university in New York City, offering distinguished programs in design, liberal arts, the performing arts, and social and political science, leading to seventy graduate and undergraduate degrees. To learn more, students should visit http://www.newschool.edu/degreeprograms. A privately supported institution, The New School is accredited by the Commission on Higher Education of the Middle States Association of Colleges and Schools and chartered as a university by the Regents of the State of New York.

The eight schools that make up The New School are The New School for General Studies, The New School for Social Research, Milano The New School for Management and Urban Policy, Parsons The New School for Design, Eugene Lang College The New School for Liberal Arts, Mannes College The New School for Music, The New School for Drama, and The New School for Jazz and Contemporary Music.

Applying

The Graduate Writing Program welcomes applications from aspiring writers of diverse academic backgrounds and life experiences. They must hold a bachelor's degree from an accredited college or university. Applications are reviewed by an admissions committee consisting of the director of the writing program and members of the faculty. The writing sample is the most important factor in this review, but letters of recommendation, academic transcripts, and the student's statement of purpose are all carefully evaluated. The deadline for fall admission is January 15. For more information and an application, students can visit http://www.writing.newschool.edu, attend an information session at The New School, or contact the Office of Admissions and Student Services.

Correspondence and Information

Graduate Writing Program
Office of Admissions and Student Services
The New School
66 West 12th Street, Room 401
New York, New York 10011

Phone: 212-229-5630
E-mail: nsadmissions@newschool.edu
Web site: http://www.newschool.edu/writing

The New School: A University

THE FACULTY

Many of America's most important poets, novelists, literary critics, and editors have been part of The New School's writing faculty, including Robert Frost, W. H. Auden, Robert Lowell, LeRoi Jones (Amiri Baraka), Frank O'Hara, Kenneth Koch, Kay Boyle, Marguerite Young, and Alfred Kazin.

Along with Robert Polito, director, and David Lehman, the current M.F.A. faculty includes Jeffery Renard Allen, Jonathan Ames, Susan Bell, Mark Bibbins, Susan Cheever, Jonathan Dee, Elaine Equi, David Gates, Vivian Gornick, Shelley Jackson, Zia Jaffrey, Joyce Johnson, Hettie Jones, James Lasdun, David Lehman, Suzannah Lessard, Philip Lopate, Honor Moore, Maggie Nelson, Sigrid Nunez, Dale Peck, Francine Prose, Liam Rector, Helen Schulman, Tor Seidler, Dani Shapiro, Prageeta Sharma, Laurie Sheck, Darcey Steinke, Benjamin Taylor, Abigail Thomas, Paul Violi, Sarah Weeks, Susan Wheeler, and Stephen Wright.

For a complete list of faculty members and courses, students should visit http://www.writing.newschool.edu/writing.

Southern™
Illinois University
Carbondale

SOUTHERN ILLINOIS UNIVERSITY CARBONDALE

Department of English
M.F.A. in Creative Writing

Programs of Study

The Master of Fine Arts (M.F.A.) in creative writing at Southern Illinois University Carbondale (SIUC) is a studio-academic program designed to assist talented students in developing their skills as poets or fiction writers. While the M.F.A. is the accepted credential for teachers of creative writing, the program gives primary emphasis to the development of students as writers. The fundamental elements of the program are writing workshops, in which students read and critique the writing of their peers under the guidance of a faculty writer, intensive tutorial work with the thesis director on the student's writing, and the study of the traditions, forms, and theories of literature from a writer's stance. The faculty members (3 poets and 3 fiction writers) work closely with the students and ensure that each student has exposure to a variety of styles and personalities from traditional to experimental. The small program size provides an excellent student-teacher ratio and encourages both formal and informal apprenticeship and tutorial relationships. While no academic program can promise to create writers, the M.F.A. program strives to provide committed, talented writers the guidance, instruction, support, and community that help them produce their best work. The M.F.A. in creative writing program requires satisfactory completion of 48 semester hours. M.F.A. students may elect to focus their studies in fiction or poetry or in a combination of the two genres.

Research Facilities

SIUC's Morris Library contains more than 2.5 million volumes, 3 million microfilms, and more than 12,000 current serial subscriptions. Library users have electronic access to a statewide automated catalog system and nearly 600 electronic data files and CD-ROM products via workstations located throughout the building. The library's special collections are extensive in areas pertinent to graduate students and research and include papers, manuscripts, letters, and research materials in American and British expatriate literature; twentieth-century philosophy, especially John Dewey and the Open Court press; the Irish literary renaissance; literary modernism, with an especially strong collection of James Joyce materials; and proletariat theater. The Humanities Library is particularly rich in both traditional and contemporary monographs and periodicals.

Financial Aid

SIUC offers a number of competitive fellowships to full-time graduate students. Awards are made by the Graduate School on the recommendation of the Graduate Studies Committee. For further information, students should contact the Graduate School. The deadline for applicants for fellowships is usually one month earlier than the deadline for graduate assistantships. Almost all M.F.A. students hold graduate assistantships that provide stipends for the academic year and full remission of tuition. The application deadline for admission with assistantship support is early February, with student notification before April 1.

Cost of Study

In-state graduate tuition is $328 per credit hour in 2009–10. Out-of-state tuition is 2.5 times the in-state tuition rate ($820 per credit hour). Graduate students with at least a 25 percent appointment as a graduate assistant receive a tuition scholarship. Fees vary from $589.03 (1 credit hour) to $1557.50 (12 credit hours). Students with a graduate assistantship receive a 50 percent reduction in the primary care medical fee. New graduate students from Arkansas, Indiana, Kentucky, Missouri, and Tennessee qualify for the alternate tuition rate, which is equivalent to the in-state graduate tuition rate.

Living and Housing Costs

For married couples, students with families, and single graduate students, the University has 690 efficiency and one-, two-, three-, and four-bedroom apartments that rent for $499 to $720 per month in 2009–10. Residence halls for single graduate students are also available, as are accessible residence hall rooms and apartments for students with disabilities.

Student Group

University enrollment exceeds 21,000, including more than 4,000 graduate students. Men and women come from all fifty states and more than 100 other countries. About 53 percent of the graduate students are women, 23 percent are international, and 13 percent are members of American minority groups.

Location

SIUC is 350 miles south of Chicago and 100 miles southeast of St. Louis. Nestled in rolling hills bordered by the Ohio and Mississippi Rivers and enhanced by a mild climate, the area has state parks, national forests and wildlife refuges, and large lakes for outdoor recreation. Cultural offerings include theater, opera, concerts, art exhibits, and cinema. Educational facilities for the families of students are excellent.

The University

Southern Illinois University Carbondale is a comprehensive public university with a variety of general and professional education programs. The University offers bachelor's, associate, master's, and doctoral degrees; the J.D. degree; and the M.D. degree. The University is fully accredited by the North Central Association of Colleges and Schools. The Graduate School has an essential role in the development and coordination of graduate instruction and research programs. The Graduate Council has academic responsibility for determining graduate standards, recommending new graduate programs and research centers, and establishing policies to facilitate the research effort. Southern Illinois University Carbondale is a state-funded university founded in 1869.

Applying

Applicants to the M.F.A. program must complete all forms in the application package, including a separate application for admission to the Graduate School, a nonrefundable processing fee of $40, three letters of recommendation, a statement of purpose, and a writing sample. International students must submit TOEFL scores and a statement showing sufficient financial support at the time of application. The minimum GPA for admission to SIUC's Graduate School is 2.7 (out of 4.0). Application materials for admission, including graduate assistantship support, are available from the Department of English. Application material is also available online at the Departmental Web site. Separate application forms for fellowships are available from the Graduate School.

Correspondence and Information

M.F.A. in Creative Writing Program
Department of English
Southern Illinois University Carbondale
Carbondale, Illinois 62901-4503

Phone: 618-453-6894
E-mail: gradengl@siu.edu
Web site: http://www.siu.edu/departments/English

Southern Illinois University Carbondale

THE FACULTY AND THEIR RESEARCH

Kent Haruf, Professor Emeritus; M.F.A., Iowa, 1973. Fiction writing.
Rodney Jones, Professor; M.F.A., North Carolina at Greensboro, 1973. Poetry writing.
Judy Jordan, Assistant Professor; M.F.A., Utah, 2000. Creative writing, poetry.
Allison E. Joseph, Associate Professor; M.F.A., Indiana, 1992. Poetry writing.
E. Beth Lordan, Professor and Assistant to the Chair; M.F.A., Cornell, 1987. Fiction writing.
Michael Magnuson, Associate Professor and Director of Creative Writing; M.F.A., Florida, 1997. Fiction writing.

ACADEMIC AND PROFESSIONAL PROGRAMS IN INTERDISCIPLINARY STUDIES

Section 14
Interdisciplinary Studies

This section contains a directory of institutions offering graduate work in interdisciplinary studies, followed by in-depth entries submitted by institutions that chose to prepare detailed program descriptions. Additional information about programs listed in the directory but not augmented by an in-depth entry may be obtained by writing directly to the dean of a graduate school or chair of a department at the address given in the directory.

For programs offering related work, see also in this book *Comparative and Interdisciplinary Arts, Humanities,* and *Social Sciences.*

CONTENTS

Program Directory

Interdisciplinary Studies   564

Close-Ups

Mountain State University   573
New York University   575

Interdisciplinary Studies

Alaska Pacific University, Graduate Programs, Liberal Studies Department, Self-Designed Programs, Anchorage, AK 99508-4672. Offers MA. Part-time and evening/weekend programs available. *Degree requirements:* For master's, thesis or project. *Entrance requirements:* For master's, MAT (preferred), GRE General Test or GMAT. *Expenses:* Contact institution.

Amberton University, Graduate School, Program in Professional Development, Garland, TX 75041-5595. Offers MA. *Entrance requirements:* For master's, minimum GPA of 3.0.

American University, College of Arts and Sciences, Interdisciplinary Programs, Washington, DC 20016-8001. Offers MA. *Students:* 2 part-time (1 woman), both international. Average age 29. 1 applicant, 0% accepted. In 2008, 3 master's awarded. Application fee: $80. *Expenses:* Tuition: Full-time $21,204; part-time $1178 per credit hour. Required fees: $380. Part-time tuition and fees vary according to course load and program.

Angelo State University, College of Graduate Studies, Program in Interdisciplinary Studies, San Angelo, TX 76909. Offers MA, MS. Part-time and evening/weekend programs available. *Students:* 1 full-time (0 women), 1 (woman) part-time. Average age 48. 2 applicants, 100% accepted, 1 enrolled. In 2008, 2 master's awarded. *Degree requirements:* For master's, comprehensive exam. *Entrance requirements:* For master's, GRE General Test. Additional exam requirements/recommendations for international students: Required—TOEFL or IELTS. *Application deadline:* For fall admission, 7/15 priority date for domestic students, 6/10 for international students; for spring admission, 12/1 priority date for domestic students, 11/1 for international students. Applications are processed on a rolling basis. Application fee: $25 ($50 for international students). Electronic applications accepted. *Financial support:* Federal Work-Study and scholarships/grants available. Support available to part-time students. Financial award application deadline: 3/1; financial award applicants required to submit FAFSA. *Unit head:* Dr. Brian J. May, Interim Dean of the College of Graduate Studies, 325-942-2169, Fax: 325-942-2194, E-mail: brian.may@angelo.edu. *Application contact:* Theresa Fortin, Graduate Admissions Assistant, 325-942-2169, Fax: 325-942-2194, E-mail: theresa.fortin@angelo.edu.

Antioch University New England, Graduate School, Department of Environmental Studies, Individualized Program, Keene, NH 03431-3552. Offers MS. *Degree requirements:* For master's, practicum, seminar, thesis or project. *Entrance requirements:* For master's, detailed proposal.

Arizona State University at the West campus, New College of Interdisciplinary Arts and Sciences, Phoenix, AZ 85069-7100. Offers interdisciplinary studies (MA); social justice and human rights (MA). Part-time and evening/weekend programs available. *Degree requirements:* For master's, applied project. *Entrance requirements:* For master's, GRE, letter of recommendation, writing sample, personal statement. Additional exam requirements/recommendations for international students: Required—TOEFL (minimum score 550 paper-based; 213 computer-based; 83 iBT), IELTS (minimum score 6.5). Electronic applications accepted.

Athabasca University, Centre for Integrated Studies, Athabasca, AB T9S 3A3, Canada. Offers adult education (MA); community studies (MA); cultural studies (MA); educational studies (MA); global change (MA); work, organization, and leadership (MA). Part-time and evening/weekend programs available. Postbaccalaureate distance learning degree programs offered (no on-campus study). *Faculty:* 8 full-time (3 women), 16 part-time/adjunct (13 women). *Students:* 651 part-time (467 women). Average age 36. 150 applicants, 87% accepted, 112 enrolled. In 2008, 39 master's awarded. *Degree requirements:* For master's, project. *Entrance requirements:* For master's, 3- or 4-year BA. Additional exam requirements/recommendations for international students: Required—TOEFL (minimum score 560 paper-based; 220 computer-based). *Application deadline:* For fall admission, 3/1 for domestic and international students; for winter admission, 10/1 for domestic and international students. Application fee: $65. Electronic applications accepted. Tuition and fees charges are reported in Canadian dollars. *Expenses:* Tuition, area resident: Full-time $13,255 Canadian dollars; part-time $1205 Canadian dollars per course. Tuition, state resident: full-time $13,255 Canadian dollars; part-time $1205 Canadian dollars per course. Tuition, nonresident: full-time $13,255 Canadian dollars; part-time $1205 Canadian dollars per course. International tuition: $15,455 Canadian dollars full-time. One-time fee: $280 Canadian dollars. *Faculty research:* Women's history, literature and culture studies, sustainable development, labor and education. *Unit head:* Dr. Michael Gismondi, Program Director, 780-675-6218, Fax: 780-675-6921, E-mail: mikeg@athabascau.ca. *Application contact:* Derek Stovin, Program Administrator, 780-675-6236, Fax: 780-675-6921, E-mail: dereks@athabascau.ca.

Baylor University, Graduate School, College of Arts and Sciences, J. M. Dawson Institute of Church-State Studies, Waco, TX 76798. Offers MA, PhD. *Students:* 34 full-time (11 women), 4 part-time (2 women); includes 6 minority (1 American Indian/Alaska Native, 2 Asian Americans or Pacific Islanders, 3 Hispanic Americans), 6 international. In 2008, 6 master's, 4 doctorates awarded. *Degree requirements:* For master's, thesis, oral exam; for doctorate, one foreign language, thesis/dissertation, preliminary exams. *Entrance requirements:* For master's, GRE General Test; for doctorate, GRE General Test, MA or equivalent. *Application deadline:* For fall admission, 3/1 for domestic students. Applications are processed on a rolling basis. Application fee: $25. *Financial support:* Fellowships, research assistantships, teaching assistantships, Federal Work-Study and institutionally sponsored loans available. Financial award application deadline: 3/1. *Faculty research:* Religion and politics, religion and public education, religious freedom and international politics, First Amendment jurisprudence. *Unit head:* Dr. Christopher Marsh, Graduate Program Director, 254-710-4412, Fax: 254-710-1571, E-mail: chris_marsh@baylor.edu. *Application contact:* Suzanne Seller, Administrative Assistant, 254-710-1510, Fax: 254-710-1571, E-mail: suzanne_sellers@baylor.edu.

Boise State University, Graduate College, College of Arts and Sciences, Program in Interdisciplinary Studies, Boise, ID 83725-0399. Offers MA, MS. Part-time programs available. *Degree requirements:* For master's, thesis. *Entrance requirements:* For master's, minimum GPA of 3.0. Electronic applications accepted.

Boston University, Metropolitan College (Continuing Education), Department of Liberal Studies, Boston, MA 02215. Offers interdisciplinary studies (MLA). Part-time and evening/weekend programs available. *Degree requirements:* For master's, thesis. *Entrance requirements:* For master's, interview. Additional exam requirements/recommendations for international students: Required—TOEFL (minimum score 560 paper-based). Electronic applications accepted. *Faculty research:* Arts and gastronomy.

Bowling Green State University, Graduate College, Interdisciplinary Studies, Bowling Green, OH 43403. Offers M Ed, MA, MS, PhD. Part-time programs available. *Degree requirements:* For master's, thesis or alternative; for doctorate, comprehensive exam, thesis/dissertation. *Entrance requirements:* For master's and doctorate, GRE General Test. Additional exam requirements/recommendations for international students: Required—TOEFL. Electronic applications accepted.

Buffalo State College, State University of New York, Graduate Studies and Research, Program in Multidisciplinary Studies, Buffalo, NY 14222-1095. Offers MA, MS. Part-time and evening/weekend programs available. *Degree requirements:* For master's, thesis or project. *Entrance requirements:* For master's, minimum GPA of 2.5. Additional exam requirements/recommendations for international students: Required—TOEFL (minimum score 550 paper-based; 213 computer-based).

California State University, Bakersfield, Division of Graduate Studies, Program in Interdisciplinary Studies, Bakersfield, CA 93311-1022. Offers MA. *Degree requirements:* For master's, thesis or project. *Entrance requirements:* For master's, minimum GPA of 3.0 in last 90 quarter units. Additional exam requirements/recommendations for international students: Required—TOEFL (minimum score 550 paper-based; 213 computer-based). *Faculty research:* Ethics, physical education and health.

California State University, Chico, Graduate School, Interdisciplinary Programs, Chico, CA 95929-0234. Offers interdisciplinary studies (MA, MS); science teaching (MS); simulation science (MS). Part-time programs available. *Degree requirements:* For master's, thesis or alternative, oral exam. *Entrance requirements:* For master's, GRE General Test or MAT, 3 letters of recommendation, purposed program plan, statement of purpose. Additional exam requirements/recommendations for international students: Required—TOEFL (minimum score 550 paper-based; 213 computer-based; 80 iBT), IELTS (minimum score 6.5).

California State University, East Bay, Academic Programs and Graduate Studies, Interdisciplinary Programs, Hayward, CA 94542-3000. Offers MA, MS, Certificate. Part-time programs available. *Degree requirements:* For master's, comprehensive exam, project or thesis. *Entrance requirements:* Additional exam requirements/recommendations for international students: Required—TOEFL (minimum score 550 paper-based; 213 computer-based). Electronic applications accepted.

California State University, Long Beach, Graduate Studies, Interdisciplinary Studies Program, Long Beach, CA 90840. Offers MA, MS. Part-time programs available. *Students:* 4 full-time (2 women), 4 part-time (3 women); includes 2 Hispanic Americans. Average age 39. *Degree requirements:* For master's, thesis. *Entrance requirements:* For master's, minimum undergraduate GPA of 3.0. *Application deadline:* For fall admission, 3/30 for domestic students. Applications are processed on a rolling basis. Application fee: $55. Electronic applications accepted. *Expenses:* Tuition, nonresident: full-time $11,160; part-time $372 per unit. Required fees: $4100; $1261 per semester. *Financial support:* Federal Work-Study, institutionally sponsored loans, and scholarships/grants available. Financial award application deadline: 3/2. *Unit head:* Dr. Cecile Lindsay, Director, 562-985-8225, Fax: 562-985-1680, E-mail: clindsay@csulb.edu. *Application contact:* Dr. Cecile Lindsay, Director, 562-985-8225, Fax: 562-985-1680, E-mail: clindsay@csulb.edu.

California State University, Monterey Bay, College of Science, Media Arts and Technology, School of Information Technology and Communication Design, Seaside, CA 93955-8001. Offers interdisciplinary studies (MA), including instructional science and technology; management and information technology (MA). *Faculty:* 2 full-time (1 woman), 4 part-time/adjunct (2 women). *Students:* 50 full-time (30 women), 16 part-time (12 women); includes 19 minority (1 African American, 12 Asian Americans or Pacific Islanders, 6 Hispanic Americans), 3 international. Average age 40. 55 applicants, 71% accepted, 31 enrolled. In 2008, 15 master's awarded. *Degree requirements:* For master's, capstone or thesis. *Entrance requirements:* For master's, GRE, 2 letters of recommendation, minimum GPA of 3.0, essay, transcript, statement of purpose, technology screening assessment. Additional exam requirements/recommendations for international students: Required—TOEFL (minimum score 550 paper-based; 213 computer-based; 71 iBT). *Application deadline:* For fall admission, 12/15 for domestic students; for spring admission, 3/1 for domestic students. Application fee: $55. Electronic applications accepted. *Expenses:* Tuition, state resident: full-time $3756; part-time $2178 per year. Tuition, nonresident: full-time $14,456; part-time $6246 per year. Required fees: $487; $244 per term. *Financial support:* In 2008–09, 18 students received support. Application deadline: 3/2; *Faculty research:* Electronic commerce, e-learning, knowledge management, international business, business and public policy. *Unit head:* Dr. Eric Y. Tao, Director, 831-582-4222, Fax: 831-582-4484, E-mail: eric_tao@csumb.edu. *Application contact:* Chris Khan, Program Coordinator, 831-582-4791, Fax: 831-582-4484, E-mail: chris_khan@csumb.edu.

California State University, Northridge, Graduate Studies, Interdisciplinary Studies, Northridge, CA 91330. Offers MA, MS. *Students:* 8 full-time (5 women), 23 part-time (14 women); includes 11 African Americans, 2 Asian Americans or Pacific Islanders, 3 Hispanic Americans, 2 international. Average age 40. In 2008, 5 master's awarded. *Entrance requirements:* For master's, GRE if cumulative undergraduate GPA below 3.0. Additional exam requirements/recommendations for international students: Required—TOEFL. *Application deadline:* For fall admission, 11/30 for domestic students. Application fee: $55. *Financial support:* Federal Work-Study available. Financial award application deadline: 3/1. *Unit head:* Hedy Carpenter, Associate Director of Graduate Programs, 818-677-2138. *Application contact:* Hedy Carpenter, Associate Director of Graduate Programs, 818-677-2138.

California State University, San Bernardino, Graduate Studies, Interdisciplinary Programs, San Bernardino, CA 92407-2397. Offers MA. Part-time and evening/weekend programs available. *Students:* 2 full-time (1 woman), 4 part-time (2 women). Average age 37. 10 applicants, 30% accepted, 2 enrolled. In 2008, 4 master's awarded. *Degree requirements:* For master's, thesis or alternative, advancement to candidacy. *Entrance requirements:* For master's, Graduate Entrance Writing Exam, minimum overall undergraduate GPA of 2.5; 3.0 in major. *Application deadline:* For fall admission, 8/31 priority date for domestic students. Application fee: $55. *Expenses:* Tuition, area resident: Full-time $1252; part-time $726 per quarter. Required fees: $334 per quarter. Tuition and fees vary according to degree level and student level. *Financial support:* Career-related internships or fieldwork, Federal Work-Study, and institutionally sponsored loans available. Support available to part-time students. Financial award application deadline: 3/1. *Unit head:* Dr. Sandra Kamusikiri, Dean of Graduate Studies, 909-537-5058, Fax: 909-537-7034, E-mail: skamusik@csusb.edu. *Application contact:* Olivia Rosas, Director of Admissions, 909-537-7577, Fax: 909-537-7034, E-mail: orosas@csusb.edu.

California State University, Stanislaus, Programs in Interdisciplinary Studies, Turlock, CA 95382. Offers MA, MS. Part-time and evening/weekend programs available. *Degree requirements:* For master's, thesis. *Entrance requirements:* For master's, GRE, minimum GPA of 3.0, personal statement. Electronic applications accepted.

Cambridge College, School of Education, Cambridge, MA 02138-5304. Offers art education (M Ed); autism spectrum disorders (M Ed); behavioral management (M Ed); early childhood teacher (M Ed); education specialist: curriculum and instruction (CAGS); educational leadership (Ed D); elementary teacher (M Ed); English as a second language (M Ed), general science (M Ed); health/family and consumer sciences (M Ed); history (M Ed); humane education (M Ed); individualized (M Ed); information technology literacy (M Ed); instructional technology (M Ed); interdisciplinary studies (M Ed); library teacher (M Ed); literacy education (M Ed); mathematics (M Ed); mathematics education (M Ed); middle school mathematics and science (M Ed); school administration (M Ed, CAGS); school guidance counselor (M Ed); school nurse education (M Ed); science (M Ed); science education (M Ed); special education administrator (CAGS); special education/moderate disabilities (M Ed); teaching skills and methodologies (M Ed); workforce education (M Ed). Part-time and evening/weekend programs available. Postbaccalaureate distance learning degree programs offered (minimal on-campus study). *Faculty:* 9 full-time (3 women), 461 part-time/adjunct (263 women). *Students:* 1,036 full-time (830 women), 1,191 part-time (928 women); includes 1,163 minority (802 African Americans, 6 American Indian/Alaska Native, 36 Asian Americans or Pacific Islanders, 319 Hispanic Americans), 17 international. Average age 37. 866 applicants, 77% accepted, 524 enrolled. In 2008, 927 master's, 11 doctorates, 223 CAGSs awarded. *Degree requirements:* For master's, thesis, internship/practicum; for doctorate, thesis/dissertation; for CAGS, thesis. *Entrance requirements:* For master's and CAGS, resumé, 2 professional references, health insurance, interview, essay, official transcripts; for doctorate, curriculum vitae or resumé for 5 years progressively responsible professional experience; 2 letters of recommendation; health insurance; interview; essay; official transcripts; portfolio of scholarly and professional work; qualifying assessment. Additional exam requirements/recommendations for international students: Required—TOEFL (minimum score 550 paper-based; 213 computer-based; 79 iBT). *Application deadline:* For fall admission, 9/8 priority date for domestic students; for winter admission, 1/8 for domestic students; for spring admission, 5/21 priority date for domestic students. Applications are processed on a rolling basis. Application fee: $30. Electronic applications accepted. *Expenses:* Tuition: Full-time $6960; part-time $435 per credit. One-time fee: $140 full-time. Tuition and fees vary according to degree level, campus/location and program.

Financial support: In 2008–09, 1,722 students received support. Career-related internships or fieldwork, Federal Work-Study, and scholarships/grants available. Financial award applicants required to submit FAFSA. *Faculty research:* Adult education, accelerated learning, mathematics education, brain compatible learning, special education and law. *Unit head:* Dr. Jo-Ann Testaverde, EdD, Acting Dean, 617-873-0187, Fax: 617-873-0222, E-mail: joann.testaverde@cambridgecollege.edu. *Application contact:* Robin Laskey, Associate Director of Admissions, 800-877-4723 Ext. 1141, E-mail: robin.laskey@cambridgecollege.edu.

Campbell University, Graduate and Professional Programs, School of Education, Buies Creek, NC 27506. Offers administration (MSA); community counseling (MA); elementary education (M Ed); English education (M Ed); interdisciplinary studies (M Ed); mathematics education (M Ed); middle grades education (M Ed); physical education (M Ed); school counseling (M Ed); secondary education (M Ed); social science education (M Ed). *Accreditation:* NCATE. Part-time and evening/weekend programs available. *Degree requirements:* For master's, comprehensive exam. *Entrance requirements:* For master's, GRE General Test, minimum GPA of 2.7. *Faculty research:* Spiritual values and wellness issues in counseling, stress and professional burnout among counselors, thinking strategies, leadership, adaptive technology.

Central Washington University, Graduate Studies, Research and Continuing Education, Individual Studies Program, Ellensburg, WA 98926. Offers M Ed, MA, MS. Part-time programs available. *Degree requirements:* For master's, thesis. *Entrance requirements:* For master's, GRE General Test, minimum GPA of 3.0. Additional exam requirements/recommendations for international students: Required—TOEFL (minimum score 550 paper-based; 213 computer-based; 79 iBT).

College of the Humanities and Sciences, Harrison Middleton University, Graduate Program, Tempe, AZ 85282. Offers education (MA, Ed D); humanities (MA); imaginative literature (MA); interdisciplinary studies (DA); jurisprudence (MA); natural science (MA); philosophy and religion (MA); social science (MA). Part-time and evening/weekend programs available. Postbaccalaureate distance learning degree programs offered (no on-campus study). Electronic applications accepted.

Columbia University, Graduate School of Arts and Sciences, Program in Liberal Studies, New York, NY 10027. Offers American studies (MA); East Asian studies (MA); human rights studies (MA); Islamic culture studies (MA); Jewish studies (MA); medieval studies (MA); modern European studies (MA); South Asian studies (MA). Part-time and evening/weekend programs available. *Degree requirements:* For master's, thesis.

Dalhousie University, Faculty of Graduate Studies, Interdisciplinary PhD Program, Halifax, NS B3H 4H6, Canada. Offers PhD. *Students:* 11 full-time (7 women). In 2008, 1 doctorate awarded. *Degree requirements:* For doctorate, thesis/dissertation. *Entrance requirements:* Additional exam requirements/recommendations for international students: Required—TOEFL, IELTS, 1 of the following 5 approved tests: TOEFL, IELTS, CANTEST, CAEL, Michigan English Language Assessment Battery. *Application deadline:* For fall admission, 6/1 for domestic students, 4/1 for international students; for winter admission, 10/31 for domestic students, 8/31 for international students; for spring admission, 2/28 for domestic students, 12/31 for international students. Applications are processed on a rolling basis. Application fee: $70. Electronic applications accepted. *Expenses:* Contact institution. *Financial support:* Fellowships available. *Unit head:* Dr. Bassett Raewyn, Graduate Coordinator, E-mail: idph@dal.ca. *Application contact:* Elizabeth Clark, Administrative Secretary, 902-494-8078, Fax: 902-494-8797, E-mail: elizabethclark@dal.ca.

Dallas Baptist University, College of Adult Education, Professional Development Program, Dallas, TX 75211-9299. Offers accounting (MA); church leadership (MA); counseling (MA); criminal justice (MA); English as a second language (MA); finance (MA); higher education (MA); leadership studies (MA); management (MA); management information systems (MA); marketing (MA); missions (MA). Part-time and evening/weekend programs available. *Faculty:* 68 full-time (30 women), 113 part-time/adjunct (47 women). *Students:* 10 full-time, 83 part-time. 30 applicants, 47% accepted. In 2008, 39 master's awarded. *Entrance requirements:* For master's, minimum GPA of 3.0. Additional exam requirements/recommendations for international students: Required—TOEFL, IELTS. Application fee: $25. *Expenses:* Tuition: Part-time $558 per credit hour. *Financial support:* Federal Work-Study, institutionally sponsored loans, scholarships/grants, and tuition waivers (full and partial) available. Support available to part-time students. Financial award applicants required to submit FAFSA. *Unit head:* Dr. John Tarwater, Acting Director, 214-333-6830, Fax: 214-333-5558, E-mail: graduate@dbu.edu. *Application contact:* Kit P. Montgomery, Director of Graduate Programs, 214-333-5242, Fax: 214-333-5579, E-mail: graduate@dbu.edu.

DePaul University, College of Liberal Arts and Sciences, Department of Interdisciplinary Studies, Chicago, IL 60614. Offers MA, MS. Part-time and evening/weekend programs available. *Students:* 17 full-time (12 women), 16 part-time (9 women); includes 10 minority (3 African Americans, 1 Asian American or Pacific Islander, 6 Hispanic Americans), 1 international. Average age 31. 10 applicants, 90% accepted. In 2008, 10 master's awarded. *Degree requirements:* For master's, thesis optional. *Application deadline:* Applications are processed on a rolling basis. Application fee: $25. *Unit head:* Dr. Fassil Demissie, Director, 773-325-7356, E-mail: fdemissie@depaul.edu. *Application contact:* Ann Spittle, Director of Graduate Admissions, 312-362-8300, Fax: 312-362-5749, E-mail: admitdpu@depaul.edu.

Drew University, Caspersen School of Graduate Studies, Program in Arts and Letters, Madison, NJ 07940-1493. Offers holocaust and genocide studies (Certificate); interdisciplinary studies (M Litt, D Litt). Part-time and evening/weekend programs available. Terminal master's awarded for partial completion of doctoral program. *Degree requirements:* For master's, thesis optional; for doctorate, thesis/dissertation. *Expenses:* Contact institution. *Faculty research:* Interdisciplinary studies across art, literature, music, philosophy, religion, and history.

Eastern Washington University, Graduate Studies, Interdisciplinary Studies, Cheney, WA 99004-2431. Offers MA, MS. *Degree requirements:* For master's, comprehensive exam, thesis or alternative. *Entrance requirements:* For master's, minimum GPA of 3.0.

Emory University, Graduate School of Arts and Sciences, Graduate Institute of Liberal Arts, Atlanta, GA 30322-1100. Offers PhD. *Degree requirements:* For doctorate, one foreign language, comprehensive exam, thesis/dissertation. *Entrance requirements:* For doctorate, GRE General Test. Electronic applications accepted. *Faculty research:* American cultural criticism, intellectual history, psychoanalysis, history of science, popular culture.

Fitchburg State College, Division of Graduate and Continuing Education, Program in Interdisciplinary Studies, Fitchburg, MA 01420-2697. Offers CAGS. Part-time and evening/weekend programs available. *Students:* 1 (woman) full-time, 47 part-time (35 women); includes 1 minority (Hispanic American), 1 international. Average age 43. 15 applicants, 100% accepted, 6 enrolled. In 2008, 23 CAGSs awarded. *Entrance requirements:* For degree, master's degree, letters of recommendation, resumé. Additional exam requirements/recommendations for international students: Required—TOEFL (minimum score 550 paper-based; 213 computer-based; 79 iBT). *Application deadline:* Applications are processed on a rolling basis. Application fee: $25 ($50 for international students). *Expenses:* Tuition, state resident: full-time $3600; part-time $150 per credit. Tuition, nonresident: full-time $3600; part-time $150 per credit. Required fees: $109 per credit. *Financial support:* In 2008–09, research assistantships with partial tuition reimbursements (averaging $5,500 per year); Federal Work-Study, scholarships/grants, and unspecified assistantships also available. Support available to part-time students. Financial award application deadline: 3/1; financial award applicants required to submit FAFSA. *Unit head:* Dr. Harry Semerjian, Chair, 978-665-3279, Fax: 978-665-3658, E-mail: gce@fsc.edu. *Application contact:* Director of Admissions, 978-665-3144, Fax: 978-665-4540, E-mail: admissions@fsc.edu.

Florida Gulf Coast University, College of Health Professions, Department of Health Sciences, Fort Myers, FL 33965-6565. Offers MS. Part-time and evening/weekend programs available. Postbaccalaureate distance learning degree programs offered (no on-campus study). *Faculty:* 42 full-time (33 women), 30 part-time/adjunct (20 women). *Students:* 24 full-time (16 women), 16 part-time (11 women); includes 6 minority (3 African Americans, 3 Hispanic Americans). Average age 37. 13 applicants, 100% accepted, 12 enrolled. In 2008, 9 master's awarded. *Degree requirements:* For master's, final project or thesis. *Entrance requirements:* For master's, GRE General Test or MAT, minimum GPA of 3.0. Additional exam requirements/recommendations for international students: Required—TOEFL (minimum score 550 paper-based; 213 computer-based). *Application deadline:* For fall admission, 7/1 priority date for domestic students; for spring admission, 11/15 for domestic students. Applications are processed on a rolling basis. Application fee: $30. Electronic applications accepted. *Financial support:* Career-related internships or fieldwork available. *Faculty research:* Health services administration, gerontology, therapeutic recreation, health professions education, exercise physiology. *Unit head:* Dr. Joan Glacken, Chair, 239-590-7498, Fax: 239-590-7474, E-mail: jglacken@fgcu.edu. *Application contact:* Dr. Joan Glacken, Chair, 239-590-7498, Fax: 239-590-7474, E-mail: jglacken@fgcu.edu.

Franklin Pierce University, Graduate Studies, Rindge, NH 03461-0060. Offers emerging network technology (Graduate Certificate); health practice management (MBA, Graduate Certificate); human resource management (MBA); human resources management (Graduate Certificate); information technology management (MS); leadership (MBA, DA); nursing (MS); physical therapy (DPT); sports facilities management (MS); teacher education (M Ed). *Accreditation:* APTA. Part-time and evening/weekend programs available. *Faculty:* 27 full-time (16 women), 18 part-time/adjunct (4 women). *Students:* 275 full-time (163 women), 223 part-time (141 women); includes 6 minority (1 African American, 2 Asian Americans or Pacific Islanders, 3 Hispanic Americans). Average age 38. *Entrance requirements:* For master's, minimum GPA of 2.5. Additional exam requirements/recommendations for international students: Required—TOEFL (minimum score 550 paper-based; 195 computer-based). *Application deadline:* Applications are processed on a rolling basis. Application fee: $0. Electronic applications accepted. Tuition and fees vary according to course load, degree level, campus/location and program. *Financial support:* Available to part-time students. Applicants required to submit FAFSA. *Unit head:* Dr. Robert G. Goddard, Assistant Dean, 603-899-4361, Fax: 603-229-4580, E-mail: goddardr@franklinpierce.edu. *Application contact:* 800-325-1090, Fax: 603-898-0827, E-mail: gpsadmin@franklinpierce.edu.

Fresno Pacific University, Graduate Programs, Individualized Study Program, Fresno, CA 93702-4709. Offers MA. Part-time and evening/weekend programs available. *Degree requirements:* For master's, thesis. *Entrance requirements:* For master's, GMAT, GRE General Test, or MAT, 2 writing samples, interview. Additional exam requirements/recommendations for international students: Required—TOEFL (minimum score 550 paper-based; 213 computer-based). Electronic applications accepted.

Frostburg State University, Graduate School, College of Education, Department of Educational Professions, Program in Interdisciplinary Education, Frostburg, MD 21532-1099. Offers M Ed. Part-time and evening/weekend programs available. *Degree requirements:* For master's, thesis or alternative. Electronic applications accepted.

George Mason University, College of Humanities and Social Sciences, Interdisciplinary Studies Program, Fairfax, VA 22030. Offers anthropology (MAIS); community college teaching (MAIS); folklore (MAIS); higher education (MAIS); individualized studies (MAIS); religion, cultures, and values (MAIS); video-based production (MAIS); women's studies (MAIS); zoo and aquarium leadership (MAIS). Part-time and evening/weekend programs available. *Degree requirements:* For master's, thesis optional. *Entrance requirements:* For master's, GRE, GMAT, or MAT, interview, minimum GPA of 3.0 in last 60 hours of course work. Electronic applications accepted.

Georgetown University, Graduate School of Arts and Sciences, School of Continuing Studies, Washington, DC 20057. Offers American studies (MALS); Catholic studies (MALS); classical civilizations (MALS); ethics and the professions (MALS); human resources management (MPS); humanities (MALS); individualized study (MALS); international affairs (MALS); Islam and Muslim-Christian relations (MALS); journalism (MPS); liberal studies (DLS); literature and society (MALS); medieval and early modern European studies (MALS); public relations (MPS); real estate (MPS); religious studies (MALS); social and public policy (MALS); sports industry management (MPS); the theory and practice of American democracy (MALS); visual culture (MALS). *Entrance requirements:* Additional exam requirements/recommendations for international students: Required—TOEFL.

Goddard College, Graduate Programs, Master of Arts in Individualized Studies Program, Plainfield, VT 05667-9432. Offers consciousness studies (MA); environmental studies (MA); transformative language arts (MA). Postbaccalaureate distance learning degree programs offered (minimal on-campus study). *Faculty:* 10 part-time/adjunct (6 women). *Students:* 43. Average age 37. 32 applicants, 78% accepted, 19 enrolled. *Degree requirements:* For master's, thesis. *Entrance requirements:* For master's, 3 letters of recommendation, study plan, bibliography, interview. *Application deadline:* Applications are processed on a rolling basis. Application fee: $40. Electronic applications accepted. *Expenses:* Contact institution. *Financial support:* In 2008–09, 39 students received support. Applicants required to submit FAFSA. *Unit head:* Prof. Ruth Farmer, Director, 802-454-8311, Fax: 802-454-7835, E-mail: ruth.farmer@goddard.edu. *Application contact:* Phillip Robertson, Admissions Counselor, 800-468-4888 Ext. 221, Fax: 802-454-1029, E-mail: phillip.robertson@goddard.edu.

Graduate School and University Center of the City University of New York, Graduate Studies, Interdisciplinary Studies, New York, NY 10016-4039. Offers language in social context (PhD); medieval studies (PhD); public policy (MA, PhD); urban studies (MA, PhD); women's studies (MA, PhD). Terminal master's awarded for partial completion of doctoral program. *Degree requirements:* For master's, thesis; for doctorate, comprehensive exam, thesis/dissertation. *Entrance requirements:* For master's and doctorate, GRE General Test.

Hodges University, Graduate Programs, Naples, FL 34119. Offers business administration (MBA); computer information technology (MS); criminal justice (MCJ); education (MPS); information systems management (MIS); interdisciplinary (MPS); law (MPS); management (MSM); professional studies (MPS); psychology (MPS); public administration (MPA). Part-time and evening/weekend programs available. Postbaccalaureate distance learning degree programs offered (no on-campus study). *Faculty:* 13 full-time (4 women), 3 part-time/adjunct (2 women). *Students:* 21 full-time (13 women), 210 part-time (138 women); includes 68 minority (33 African Americans, 2 Asian Americans or Pacific Islanders, 33 Hispanic Americans). Average age 36. In 2008, 82 master's awarded. *Degree requirements:* For master's, comprehensive exam (for some programs). *Entrance requirements:* For master's, in-house entrance exam. *Application deadline:* Applications are processed on a rolling basis. Application fee: $50. Electronic applications accepted. *Expenses:* Tuition: Full-time $16,200; part-time $600 per credit hour. Required fees: $570. *Financial support:* In 2008–09, 200 students received support. Federal Work-Study and scholarships/grants available. Financial award application deadline: 7/9; financial award applicants required to submit FAFSA. *Unit head:* Terry McMahan, President, 239-513-1122, Fax: 239-598-6253, E-mail: tmcmahan@hodges.edu. *Application contact:* Rita Lampus, Vice President of Student Enrollment Management, 239-513-1122, Fax: 239-598-6253, E-mail: rlampus@hodges.edu.

Hofstra University, College of Liberal Arts and Sciences, New College, Hempstead, NY 11549. Offers interdisciplinary studies (MA). Part-time and evening/weekend programs available. *Students:* 5 applicants, 40% accepted, 0 enrolled. In 2008, 2 master's awarded. *Degree requirements:* For master's, thesis. *Entrance requirements:* For master's, minimum undergraduate GPA of 3.0, bachelor's degree. Additional exam requirements/recommendations for international students: Required—TOEFL (minimum score 550 paper-based; 213 computer-based). *Application deadline:* Applications are processed on a rolling basis. Application fee: $60. Electronic applications accepted. *Expenses:* Contact institution. *Financial support:* Fellowships with full and partial tuition reimbursements, research assistantships with full and

Interdisciplinary Studies

Hofstra University (continued)
partial tuition reimbursements, Federal Work-Study, institutionally sponsored loans, scholarships/grants, tuition waivers (full and partial), and unspecified assistantships available. Support available to part-time students. Financial award applicants required to submit FAFSA. *Faculty research:* Anthropology, religion, ethics, human rights, literature, history. *Unit head:* Dr. Barry Nass, Vice Dean, 516-463-5820, Fax: 516-463-4832, E-mail: barry.n.nass@hofstra.edu. *Application contact:* Carol Drummer, Dean of Graduate Admissions, 516-463-4876, Fax: 516-463-4664, E-mail: gradstudent@hofstra.edu.

Hollins University, Graduate Programs, Program in Liberal Studies, Roanoke, VA 24020-1603. Offers humanities (MALS); interdisciplinary studies (MALS); justice and legal studies (MALS); liberal studies (CAS); social science (MALS); visual and performing arts (MALS). Part-time and evening/weekend programs available. *Faculty:* 6 full-time (1 woman), 7 part-time/adjunct (4 women). *Students:* 20 full-time (17 women), 78 part-time (56 women); includes 14 minority (13 African Americans, 1 Hispanic American), 1 international. Average age 39. 33 applicants, 85% accepted, 23 enrolled. In 2008, 42 master's awarded. *Degree requirements:* For master's, thesis. *Entrance requirements:* For master's, letters of recommendation, interview. Additional exam requirements/recommendations for international students: Required—TOEFL (minimum score 550 paper-based; 213 computer-based; 79 iBT). *Application deadline:* For fall admission, 7/1 priority date for domestic and international students; for spring admission, 12/10 priority date for domestic and international students. Applications are processed on a rolling basis. Application fee: $40. Electronic applications accepted. *Expenses:* Tuition: Full-time $26,720; part-time $590 per credit hour. Required fees: $280. *Financial support:* In 2008–09, 53 students received support, including 2 fellowships (averaging $1,189 per year); Federal Work-Study and scholarships/grants also available. Support available to part-time students. Financial award application deadline: 7/15; financial award applicants required to submit FAFSA. *Faculty research:* Elderly blacks, film, feminist economics, US voting patterns, Wagner, diversity. *Unit head:* Dr. Edward A. Lynch, Director, 540-362-6475, Fax: 540-362-6288, E-mail: elynch@hollins.edu. *Application contact:* Cathy S. Koon, Manager of Graduate Services, 540-362-6326, Fax: 540-362-6288, E-mail: ckoon@hollins.edu.

Idaho State University, Office of Graduate Studies, Department of Interdisciplinary Studies, Pocatello, ID 83209. Offers general interdisciplinary (M Ed, MA, MNS); waste management and environmental science (MS). Part-time programs available. *Faculty:* 2 full-time (1 woman). In 2008, 2 master's awarded. *Degree requirements:* For master's, comprehensive exam, thesis optional. *Entrance requirements:* For master's, GRE General Test or MAT, minimum GPA of 3.0. Additional exam requirements/recommendations for international students: Required—TOEFL (minimum score 550 paper-based; 213 computer-based; 80 iBT). *Application deadline:* For fall admission, 7/1 for domestic students, 6/1 for international students; for spring admission, 12/1 for domestic students, 11/1 for international students. Applications are processed on a rolling basis. Application fee: $55. *Expenses:* Tuition, area resident: Full-time $3114; part-time $276 per credit hour. Tuition, state resident: full-time $3114; part-time $276 per credit hour. Tuition, nonresident: full-time $12,318; part-time $404 per credit hour. Required fees: $2360. Tuition and fees vary according to course load and reciprocity agreements. *Financial support:* Career-related internships or fieldwork, Federal Work-Study, scholarships/grants, and unspecified assistantships available. Support available to part-time students. Financial award application deadline: 1/1; financial award applicants required to submit FAFSA. *Unit head:* Dr. Pamela Crowell, Vice President for Research, 208-282-2714, Fax: 208-282-4529. *Application contact:* Ellen Combs, Graduate School Technical Records Specialist, 208-282-2150, Fax: 208-282-4847.

Iowa State University of Science and Technology, Graduate College, Interdisciplinary Programs, Program in Interdisciplinary Graduate Studies, Ames, IA 50011. Offers MA, MS. *Students:* 22 full-time (13 women), 51 part-time (37 women); includes 19 minority (14 African Americans, 1 American Indian/Alaska Native, 4 Hispanic Americans), 13 international. 30 applicants, 90% accepted, 23 enrolled. In 2008, 20 master's awarded. *Degree requirements:* For master's, thesis or alternative. *Entrance requirements:* Additional exam requirements/recommendations for international students: Required—TOEFL (minimum score 550 paper-based; 79 iBT), IELTS (6.5) or TOEFL. *Application deadline:* For fall admission, 5/1 priority date for domestic and international students; for spring admission, 10/1 for domestic and international students. Application fee: $30 ($70 for international students). Electronic applications accepted. *Expenses:* Tuition, area resident: Full-time $6446; part-time $359 per credit. Tuition, state resident: full-time $6446; part-time $359 per credit. Tuition, nonresident: full-time $17,330; part-time $963 per credit. Required fees: $790; $249.25 per semester. Tuition and fees vary according to course load and program. *Financial support:* In 2008–09, 16 research assistantships with full and partial tuition reimbursements (averaging $12,150 per year), 5 teaching assistantships with full and partial tuition reimbursements (averaging $12,150 per year) were awarded; fellowships, scholarships/grants, health care benefits, and unspecified assistantships also available. *Unit head:* Chair, Supervisory Committee, 515-294-1170. *Application contact:* Linda Thorson, Information Contact, 515-294-1170, Fax: 515-294-3003, E-mail: grad_admissions@iastate.edu.

John F. Kennedy University, Graduate School of Holistic Studies, Department of Integral Studies, Program in Consciousness Studies, Pleasant Hill, CA 94523-4817. Offers MA. Part-time and evening/weekend programs available. *Degree requirements:* For master's, thesis or alternative. *Entrance requirements:* For master's, interview. Additional exam requirements/recommendations for international students: Required—TOEFL.

Lesley University, Graduate School of Arts and Social Sciences, Self-Designed Master's Program in Interdisciplinary Studies, Cambridge, MA 02138-2790. Offers individualized studies (MA); integrative holistic health (MA); women's studies (MA). Part-time and evening/weekend programs available. Postbaccalaureate distance learning degree programs offered (no on-campus study). *Entrance requirements:* For master's, 3 letters of recommendation. Additional exam requirements/recommendations for international students: Required—TOEFL (minimum score 550 paper-based; 213 computer-based; 80 iBT). *Expenses:* Tuition: Full-time $13,770; part-time $765 per credit hour. Required fees: $150. Tuition and fees vary according to course load, degree level, campus/location and program.

Long Island University, C.W. Post Campus, College of Liberal Arts and Sciences, Program in Interdisciplinary Studies, Brookville, NY 11548-1300. Offers MA, MS. Part-time and evening/weekend programs available. *Degree requirements:* For master's, thesis. *Entrance requirements:* For master's, minimum GPA of 3.0. Electronic applications accepted.

Marquette University, Graduate School, Interdisciplinary PhD Program, Milwaukee, WI 53201-1881. Offers PhD. *Degree requirements:* For doctorate, thesis/dissertation. *Entrance requirements:* For doctorate, GRE General Test. Additional exam requirements/recommendations for international students: Required—TOEFL.

Marylhurst University, Department of Interdisciplinary Studies, Marylhurst, OR 97036-0261. Offers MA. Part-time and evening/weekend programs available. *Faculty:* 2 full-time (both women), 2 part-time/adjunct (1 woman). *Students:* 1 (woman) full-time, 30 part-time (21 women); includes 1 minority (Hispanic American). Average age 47. 11 applicants, 82% accepted, 9 enrolled. In 2008, 10 master's awarded. *Degree requirements:* For master's, thesis. *Entrance requirements:* For master's, 2 letters of recommendation, writing sample, personal statement, interview. Additional exam requirements/recommendations for international students: Recommended—TOEFL (minimum score 550 paper-based; 213 computer-based; 80 iBT). *Application deadline:* Applications are processed on a rolling basis. Application fee: $40 ($50 for international students). Electronic applications accepted. *Expenses:* Tuition: Full-time $11,988; part-time $444 per quarter hour. Required fees: $297; $11 per quarter hour. *Financial support:* Federal Work-Study and scholarships/grants available. Support available to part-time students. Financial award applicants required to submit FAFSA. *Faculty research:* World religions, spirituality and literature, philosophy, humanities. *Unit head:* Dr. Debrah B. Bokowski, Chair, 503-636-8141, Fax: 503-697-5597, E-mail: dbokowski@marylhurst.edu. *Application contact:* Kathleen Schneff, Admissions Specialist, 800-634-9982 Ext. 3322, Fax: 503-635-6585, E-mail: admissions@marylhurst.edu.

Marywood University, Academic Affairs, Insalaco College of Creative Arts and Management, Department of Communication Arts, Program in Communication Arts, Scranton, PA 18509-1598. Offers corporate communication (Certificate); e-business (Certificate); health communication (Certificate); instructional technology (Certificate); interdisciplinary (MA); library science/information specialist (Certificate); media management (MA); production (MA).

Mills College, Graduate Studies, Program in Computer Science, Oakland, CA 94613-1000. Offers computer science (Certificate); interdisciplinary computer science (MA). Part-time programs available. *Faculty:* 6 full-time (5 women), 2 part-time/adjunct (1 woman). *Students:* 2 full-time (1 woman), 1 (woman) part-time; includes 1 minority (Asian American or Pacific Islander). Average age 34. 4 applicants, 100% accepted, 1 enrolled. *Degree requirements:* For master's, thesis. *Entrance requirements:* Additional exam requirements/recommendations for international students: Required—TOEFL. *Application deadline:* For fall admission, 2/1 priority date for domestic students; for spring admission, 11/1 for domestic students. Applications are processed on a rolling basis. Application fee: $50. Electronic applications accepted. *Expenses:* Tuition: Full-time $25,072; part-time $6272 per course. Required fees: $880. *Financial support:* Career-related internships or fieldwork and residence awards available. Financial award application deadline: 2/1; financial award applicants required to submit FAFSA. *Faculty research:* Dynamical systems, linear programming, theory of computer viruses, interface design, intelligent tutoring systems. *Unit head:* Susan S. Wang, Department Head, 510-430-2138, E-mail: wang@mills.edu. *Application contact:* Marika Benko, Director of Graduate Admissions, 510-430-2355, Fax: 510-430-2159, E-mail: rmcglaut@mills.edu.

Minnesota State University Mankato, College of Graduate Studies, Program in Cross-disciplinary Studies, Mankato, MN 56001. Offers MS. Part-time and evening/weekend programs available. *Students:* 1 full-time (0 women), 3 part-time (1 woman). *Degree requirements:* For master's, comprehensive exam, thesis or alternative. *Entrance requirements:* For master's, GRE General Test, minimum GPA of 3.0 during previous 2 years. Additional exam requirements/recommendations for international students: Required—TOEFL. *Application deadline:* For fall admission, 7/1 priority date for domestic students; for spring admission, 11/1 for domestic students. Applications are processed on a rolling basis. Application fee: $40. Electronic applications accepted. *Financial support:* Research assistantships with full tuition reimbursements, teaching assistantships with full tuition reimbursements, career-related internships or fieldwork, Federal Work-Study, and unspecified assistantships available. Support available to part-time students. Financial award application deadline: 3/15; financial award applicants required to submit FAFSA. *Unit head:* Chris Mickle, Graduate Coordinator, 507-389-2321. *Application contact:* 507-389-2321, E-mail: grad@mnsu.edu.

Montana State University–Billings, College of Education, Department of Educational Theory and Practice, Option in Interdisciplinary Studies, Billings, MT 59101-0298. Offers M Ed. *Degree requirements:* For master's, thesis or alternative. *Entrance requirements:* For master's, GRE General Test or MAT, minimum GPA of 3.0 (undergraduate), 3.25 (graduate).

Montana Tech of The University of Montana, Graduate School, Interdisciplinary Program, Butte, MT 59701-8997. Offers MS. Part-time programs available. *Students:* 3 full-time (2 women), 1 international. 2 applicants, 100% accepted, 2 enrolled. In 2008, 2 master's awarded. *Degree requirements:* For master's, comprehensive exam (for some programs), thesis optional. *Entrance requirements:* For master's, GRE General Test, minimum GPA 3.0. Additional exam requirements/recommendations for international students: Required—TOEFL (minimum score 525 paper-based; 195 computer-based; 71 iBT). *Application deadline:* For fall admission, 4/1 for domestic students, 3/1 priority date for international students; for spring admission, 10/1 for domestic students, 7/1 priority date for international students. Application fee: $30. *Expenses:* Tuition, state resident: full-time $4919; part-time $306 per credit. Tuition, nonresident: full-time $14,141; part-time $819 per credit. *Financial support:* In 2008–09, 3 teaching assistantships (averaging $5,509 per year) were awarded; research assistantships, career-related internships or fieldwork, tuition waivers (full and partial), and unspecified assistantships also available. *Unit head:* Dr. Joseph Figueira, Associate Vice Chancellor of Academic Affairs and Research/Dean of the Graduate School, 406-496-4456. *Application contact:* Cindy Dunstan, Administrator, Graduate School, 406-496-4304, Fax: 406-496-4710, E-mail: cdunstan@mtech.edu.

Mountain State University, Graduate Studies, Program in Interdisciplinary Studies, Beckley, WV 25802-9003. Offers MA, MS. Part-time and evening/weekend programs available. Postbaccalaureate distance learning degree programs offered (no on-campus study). *Faculty:* 9 full-time (3 women), 15 part-time/adjunct (6 women). *Students:* 32 full-time (20 women), 11 part-time (8 women); includes 7 minority (5 African Americans, 1 American Indian/Alaska Native, 1 Asian American or Pacific Islander), 1 international. Average age 38. 48 applicants, 67% accepted, 27 enrolled. In 2008, 5 master's awarded. *Degree requirements:* For master's, thesis or alternative. *Entrance requirements:* Additional exam requirements/recommendations for international students: Required—TOEFL (minimum score 550 paper-based; 213 computer-based); Recommended—IELTS (minimum score 6.5). *Application deadline:* For fall admission, 5/31 priority date for domestic and international students. Applications are processed on a rolling basis. Application fee: $25 ($50 for international students). Electronic applications accepted. *Expenses:* Tuition: Full-time $4020; part-time $335 per contact hour. *Financial support:* Federal Work-Study, scholarships/grants, and unspecified assistantships available. Support available to part-time students. Financial award applicants required to submit FAFSA. *Unit head:* Dr. Brian Holloway, Dean, School of Graduate Studies, 304-929-1690, Fax: 304-929-1637, E-mail: holloway@mountainstate.edu. *Application contact:* Dinah Rock, Coordinator of Graduate Academic Services, 304-929-1690, Fax: 304-929-1637, E-mail: drock@mountainstate.edu.

See Close-Up on page 573.

New Mexico State University, Graduate School, Interdisciplinary Program, Las Cruces, NM 88003-8001. Offers MA, MS, PhD. Part-time programs available. Postbaccalaureate distance learning degree programs offered (minimal on-campus study). *Faculty:* 1 full-time (0 women). *Students:* 40 full-time (21 women), 183 part-time (122 women); includes 97 minority (9 African Americans, 5 American Indian/Alaska Native, 3 Asian Americans or Pacific Islanders, 80 Hispanic Americans), 13 international. Average age 36. 259 applicants, 97% accepted, 176 enrolled. *Degree requirements:* For master's, comprehensive exam, thesis; for doctorate, comprehensive exam, thesis/dissertation. *Entrance requirements:* For master's, GRE General Test, minimum GPA of 2.5; for doctorate, GRE General Test, minimum GPA of 3.0. Additional exam requirements/recommendations for international students: Required—TOEFL (minimum score 550 paper-based; 213 computer-based; 79 iBT), IELTS. *Application deadline:* Applications are processed on a rolling basis. Application fee: $30 ($50 for international students). *Expenses:* Tuition, area resident: Full-time $3890; part-time $212.85 per credit. Tuition, state resident: full-time $3890; part-time $212.85 per credit. Tuition, nonresident: full-time $13,916; part-time $630.55 per credit. Required fees: $1218; $609 per semester. *Financial support:* In 2008–09, 5 students received support, including 2 research assistantships with full tuition reimbursements available (averaging $5,925 per year), 1 teaching assistantship with full tuition reimbursement available (averaging $17,289 per year); fellowships, career-related internships or fieldwork, Federal Work-Study, and health care benefits also available. Financial award application deadline: 3/1. *Faculty research:* Bioinformatics, molecular genetics, plant pathology. *Unit head:* Dr. Linda Lacey, Dean, 575-646-5746, Fax: 575-646-7721, E-mail: lacey@nmsu.edu. *Application contact:* Elena Luna, Coordinator, 575-646-3498, Fax: 575-646-7721, E-mail: rosluna@nmsu.edu.

New York University, Gallatin School of Individualized Study, New York, NY 10012-1019. Offers MA. Part-time programs available. *Degree requirements:* For master's, thesis. *Entrance requirements:* Additional exam requirements/recommendations for international students:

Required—TOEFL. *Expenses:* Contact institution. *Faculty research:* Arts and culture, gender studies, political and social thought, literature, classical studies.

See Close-Up on page 575.

Niagara University, Graduate Division of Arts and Sciences, Program in Interdisciplinary Studies, Niagara Falls, Niagara University, NY 14109. Offers MA. *Faculty:* 1 full-time (0 women). *Students:* 3 full-time (all women), 11 part-time (8 women); includes 2 minority (1 African American, 1 American Indian/Alaska Native), 1 international. Average age 35. In 2008, 2 master's awarded. *Application deadline:* For fall admission, 8/1 for domestic students. Applications are processed on a rolling basis. *Expenses:* Tuition: Full-time $12,330; part-time $685 per contact hour. Required fees: $25 per semester. Tuition and fees vary according to program. *Unit head:* Dr. Thomas A. Chambers, Director, Interdisciplinary Studies, 716-286-8091, E-mail: chambers@niagara.edu. *Application contact:* Dr. Talia Harmon, Director, 716-286-8093, Fax: 716-286-8061, E-mail: tharmon@niagara.edu.

Nova Southeastern University, Graduate School of Humanities and Social Sciences, Department of Multi-Disciplinary Studies, Fort Lauderdale, FL 33314-7796. Offers college student affairs (MS); college student personnel administration (Certificate); cross-disciplinary studies (MA); qualitative research (Certificate). Part-time programs available. Postbaccalaureate distance learning degree programs offered (no on-campus study). *Faculty:* 4 part-time/adjunct (2 women). *Students:* 24 full-time (15 women), 35 part-time (29 women); includes 24 minority (20 African Americans, 4 Hispanic Americans), 2 international. 45 applicants, 67% accepted, 30 enrolled. In 2008, 7 master's awarded. *Degree requirements:* For master's, comprehensive exam, thesis optional, portfolio. *Entrance requirements:* For master's, interview, minimum GPA of 3.0. Additional exam requirements/recommendations for international students: Required—TOEFL. *Application deadline:* For fall admission, 7/1 priority date for domestic and international students; for winter admission, 11/1 priority date for domestic and international students; for spring admission, 3/1 priority date for domestic and international students. Applications are processed on a rolling basis. Electronic applications accepted. *Financial support:* In 2008–09, 20 research assistantships with tuition reimbursements (averaging $15,600 per year) were awarded; career-related internships or fieldwork, Federal Work-Study, institutionally sponsored loans, and scholarships/grants also available. Financial award applicants required to submit CSS PROFILE. *Unit head:* Dr. Judith McKay, Senior Associate Dean, 954-262-3060, Fax: 954-262-3893, E-mail: mckayj@nsu.nova.edu. *Application contact:* Marcia Arango, Student Recruitment Coordinator, 954-262-3006, Fax: 954-262-3968, E-mail: marango@nsu.nova.edu.

The Ohio State University, Graduate School, College of Humanities, Department of Comparative Studies, Columbus, OH 43210. Offers MA, PhD. *Entrance requirements:* For master's and doctorate, GRE General Test. Additional exam requirements/recommendations for international students: Required—TOEFL (minimum score 600 paper-based; 250 computer-based). Electronic applications accepted.

Oregon State University, Graduate School, Program in Interdisciplinary Studies, Corvallis, OR 97331. Offers MAIS. Program focuses on three areas of study and must include at least one area of study in liberal arts. Part-time programs available. *Degree requirements:* For master's, thesis optional. *Entrance requirements:* For master's, minimum GPA of 3.0 in last 90 hours of course work. Additional exam requirements/recommendations for international students: Required—TOEFL.

Regis University, College for Professional Studies, MA Program, Denver, CO 80221-1099. Offers criminology (MA); fine arts administration (Certificate); language and communication (MA); mediation (Certificate); psychology (MA); self-designed major (MA); social justice, peace, and reconciliation (Certificate); social science (MA); technical communication (Certificate). Program also offered in Henderson and Las Vegas (Summerlin), NV. Part-time and evening/weekend programs available. Postbaccalaureate distance learning degree programs offered (minimal on-campus study). *Degree requirements:* For master's, thesis, research project. *Entrance requirements:* For master's, resumé, recommendations, essays. Additional exam requirements/recommendations for international students: Required—TOEFL (minimum score 213 computer-based), TWE (minimum score 5). Electronic applications accepted. *Expenses:* Contact institution. *Faculty research:* Independent/nonresidential graduate study: new methods and models, adult learning and the capstone experience, Goal Setting, behavior of Adult students, Innovative Studies for Community Colleges.

Rensselaer Polytechnic Institute, Graduate School, School of Science, Program in Multidisciplinary Science, Troy, NY 12180-3590. Offers MS, PhD. Part-time programs available. Terminal master's awarded for partial completion of doctoral program. *Degree requirements:* For master's, comprehensive exam (for some programs), thesis optional; for doctorate, comprehensive exam, thesis/dissertation. *Entrance requirements:* For master's and doctorate, GRE General Test. Additional exam requirements/recommendations for international students: Required—TOEFL. Electronic applications accepted. *Faculty research:* Bioinformatics, polymer science, biocomputation.

Rochester Institute of Technology, Graduate Enrollment Services, College of Applied Science and Technology, Center for Multidisciplinary Studies, Program in Professional Studies, Rochester, NY 14623-5603. Offers MS. *Entrance requirements:* For master's, minimum GPA of 3.0. Additional exam requirements/recommendations for international students: Required—TOEFL (minimum score 550 paper-based; 213 computer-based; 79 iBT).

Rosalind Franklin University of Medicine and Science, College of Health Professions, Department of Interprofessional Healthcare Studies, Interprofessional Healthcare Studies Program, North Chicago, IL 60064-3095. Offers D Sc, PhD.

Rutgers, The State University of New Jersey, New Brunswick, Graduate School, BioMaPS Institute for Quantitative Biology, Piscataway, NJ 08854-8097. Offers computational biology and molecular biophysics (PhD). *Degree requirements:* For doctorate, comprehensive exam, thesis/dissertation. *Entrance requirements:* For doctorate, GRE. Additional exam requirements/recommendations for international students: Required—TOEFL. Electronic applications accepted. *Faculty research:* Structural biology, systems biology, bioinformatics, translational medicine, genomics.

San Diego State University, Graduate and Research Affairs, Interdisciplinary Studies, San Diego, CA 92182. Offers MA, MS. Part-time programs available. *Degree requirements:* For master's, thesis. *Entrance requirements:* For master's, GRE General Test. Additional exam requirements/recommendations for international students: Required—TOEFL. Electronic applications accepted.

San Jose State University, Graduate Studies and Research, Graduate Studies Program, Program in Interdisciplinary Studies, San Jose, CA 95192-0001. Offers MA, MS. Electronic applications accepted.

Sarah Lawrence College, Graduate Studies, Individualized Study Program, Bronxville, NY 10708-5999. Offers MA. Part-time programs available. *Degree requirements:* For master's, thesis. *Application fee:* $60. *Expenses:* Tuition: Full-time $26,544; part-time $1106 per credit. Required fees: $450. Tuition and fees vary according to program. *Financial support:* Career-related internships or fieldwork, scholarships/grants, and unspecified assistantships available. Support available to part-time students. Financial award application deadline: 3/1; financial award applicants required to submit FAFSA. *Unit head:* Susan Guma, Dean of Graduate Studies, 914-395-2373, E-mail: sguma@mail.slc.edu. *Application contact:* Susan Guma, Dean of Graduate Studies, 914-395-2373, E-mail: sguma@mail.slc.edu.

Sonoma State University, Institute of Interdisciplinary Studies/Special Major, Rohnert Park, CA 94928-3609. Offers special major (MA, MS). Part-time programs available. *Degree requirements:* For master's, thesis or alternative. *Entrance requirements:* For master's, written English proficiency test, minimum GPA of 3.0 in last 60 hours.

Stanford University, School of Education, Program in Social Sciences, Policy, and Educational Practice, Stanford, CA 94305-9991. Offers administration and policy analysis (Ed D, PhD); anthropology of education (PhD); economics of education (PhD); educational linguistics (PhD); evaluation (MA), including interdisciplinary studies; higher education (PhD); history of education (PhD); interdisciplinary studies (PhD); international comparative education (MA, PhD); international education administration and policy analysis (MA); philosophy of education (PhD); policy analysis (MA); prospective principal's program (MA); sociology of education (PhD). *Degree requirements:* For master's, thesis (for some programs); for doctorate, thesis/dissertation. *Entrance requirements:* For master's and doctorate, GRE General Test. Electronic applications accepted.

State University of New York at Fredonia, Graduate Studies, Graduate Programs in Interdisciplinary Studies, Fredonia, NY 14063-1136. Offers MA, MS. Part-time and evening/weekend programs available. *Degree requirements:* For master's, thesis optional.

State University of New York at New Paltz, Graduate School, School of Fine and Performing Arts, Department of Fine Arts, New Paltz, NY 12561. Offers ceramics (MFA); interdisciplinary (MA); metal (MFA); painting/drawing (MFA); printmaking (MFA); sculpture (MFA). *Accreditation:* NASAD (one or more programs are accredited). Part-time and evening/weekend programs available. *Faculty:* 22 full-time (16 women), 7 part-time/adjunct (4 women). *Students:* 45 full-time (38 women), 16 part-time (11 women); includes 3 minority (2 Asian Americans or Pacific Islanders, 1 Hispanic American), 8 international. Average age 31. 91 applicants, 34% accepted, 22 enrolled. In 2008, 31 master's awarded. *Degree requirements:* For master's, thesis, portfolio, exhibit (MFA). *Entrance requirements:* For master's, minimum GPA of 3.0, portfolio. Additional exam requirements/recommendations for international students: Required—TOEFL (minimum score 550 paper-based; 213 computer-based; 80 iBT). *Application deadline:* For fall admission, 2/15 for domestic and international students. Applications are processed on a rolling basis. Application fee: $50. Electronic applications accepted. *Financial support:* In 2008–09, 13 students received support, including 3 fellowships (averaging $8,000 per year), 2 research assistantships with partial tuition reimbursements available (averaging $5,000 per year), 8 teaching assistantships with partial tuition reimbursements available (averaging $5,000 per year); Federal Work-Study, institutionally sponsored loans, scholarships/grants, traineeships, tuition waivers (full), and unspecified assistantships also available. Financial award application deadline: 8/11; financial award applicants required to submit FAFSA. *Unit head:* Prof. Myra Mimlitsch-Gray, Chair, 845-257-3833, E-mail: mimlitsm@newpaltz.edu. *Application contact:* Prof. Emily puthoffe@newpaltz.edu, Coordinator, 845-257-3834, E-mail: shiftana@newpaltz.edu.

Stephen F. Austin State University, Graduate School, College of Applied Arts and Science, Program in Interdisciplinary Studies, Nacogdoches, TX 75962. Offers MIS. Part-time programs available. *Degree requirements:* For master's, comprehensive exam, thesis optional. *Entrance requirements:* For master's, GRE General Test. Additional exam requirements/recommendations for international students: Required—TOEFL (minimum score 550 paper-based; 213 computer-based).

Teachers College, Columbia University, Graduate Faculty of Education, Interdisciplinary Programs, New York, NY 10027-6696. Offers Ed M, MA, Ed D. Part-time programs available. *Students:* 4 full-time (3 women), 25 part-time (11 women); includes 8 minority (4 African Americans, 2 Asian Americans or Pacific Islanders, 2 Hispanic Americans), 2 international. Average age 39. 3 applicants, 67% accepted, 1 enrolled. In 2008, 4 master's, 1 doctorate awarded. Terminal master's awarded for partial completion of doctoral program. *Degree requirements:* For doctorate, thesis/dissertation. *Application deadline:* For fall admission, 5/15 for domestic students. Application fee: $75. *Expenses:* Tuition: Full-time $26,040; part-time $1085 per credit. Required fees: $720. *Financial support:* Fellowships, career-related internships or fieldwork, Federal Work-Study, institutionally sponsored loans, and tuition waivers (full and partial) available. Support available to part-time students. Financial award application deadline: 2/1. *Unit head:* Susan Furhman, President, 212-678-3050. *Application contact:* Director of Admissions, 212-678-3083, Fax: 212-678-4171.

Texas A&M University–Texarkana, Graduate Studies and Research, College of Arts and Sciences and Education, Texarkana, TX 75505-5518. Offers adult education (MS); curriculum and instruction (MS); education (MS); educational administration (M Ed); English (MA); history (MS); instructional technology (MS); interdisciplinary studies (MS); special education (M Ed, MS). Part-time and evening/weekend programs available. *Degree requirements:* For master's, comprehensive exam (for some programs), thesis optional. *Entrance requirements:* For master's, minimum GPA of 2.5 on last 60 hours of bachelor's degree. Additional exam requirements/recommendations for international students: Required—TOEFL. Electronic applications accepted.

Texas State University–San Marcos, Graduate School, Interdisciplinary Studies in Political Science, San Marcos, TX 78666. Offers MAIS. *Degree requirements:* For master's, comprehensive exam.

Texas State University–San Marcos, Graduate School, Interdisciplinary Studies Program in Applied Sociology, San Marcos, TX 78666. Offers MAIS. Part-time and evening/weekend programs available. *Degree requirements:* For master's, comprehensive exam. *Entrance requirements:* For master's, 3.0 GPA on last 60 hrs. of undergraduate, 3 letters of reference, letter of intent. Additional exam requirements/recommendations for international students: Required—TOEFL (minimum score 550 paper-based; 213 computer-based). Electronic applications accepted.

Texas State University–San Marcos, Graduate School, Interdisciplinary Studies Program in Biology, San Marcos, TX 78666. Offers MSIS. *Degree requirements:* For master's, comprehensive exam.

Texas State University–San Marcos, Graduate School, Interdisciplinary Studies Program in Criminal Justice, San Marcos, TX 78666. Offers MSIS. Part-time and evening/weekend programs available. *Degree requirements:* For master's, comprehensive exam.

Texas State University–San Marcos, Graduate School, Interdisciplinary Studies Program in Educational Administration and Psychological Services, San Marcos, TX 78666. Offers MAIS. *Degree requirements:* For master's, comprehensive exam.

Texas State University–San Marcos, Graduate School, Interdisciplinary Studies Program in Elementary Mathematics, Science, and Technology, San Marcos, TX 78666. Offers MSIS. *Degree requirements:* For master's, comprehensive exam. *Entrance requirements:* Additional exam requirements/recommendations for international students: Required—TOEFL (minimum score 550 paper-based; 213 computer-based). Electronic applications accepted.

Texas State University–San Marcos, Graduate School, Interdisciplinary Studies Program in Health, Physical Education, and Recreation, San Marcos, TX 78666. Offers MAIS. Part-time and evening/weekend programs available. *Degree requirements:* For master's, comprehensive exam, thesis or alternative. *Entrance requirements:* For master's, GRE General Test, minimum GPA of 2.75 in last 60 hours of course work. Additional exam requirements/recommendations for international students: Required—TOEFL.

Texas State University–San Marcos, Graduate School, Interdisciplinary Studies Program in Modern Languages, San Marcos, TX 78666. Offers MAIS. *Degree requirements:* For master's, comprehensive exam.

Texas State University–San Marcos, Graduate School, Interdisciplinary Studies Program in Occupational Education, San Marcos, TX 78666. Offers MAIS, MSIS. *Degree requirements:* For master's, comprehensive exam. *Entrance requirements:* For master's, GPA 2.75 for undergraduate work, statement of personal goals. Additional exam requirements/recommendations for international students: Required—TOEFL (minimum score 550 paper-based; 213 computer-based).

Interdisciplinary Studies

Texas State University–San Marcos, Graduate School, Interdisciplinary Studies Program in Psychology, San Marcos, TX 78666. Offers MAIS. *Degree requirements:* For master's, comprehensive exam.

Texas Tech University, Graduate School, Program in Interdisciplinary Studies, Lubbock, TX 79409. Offers MA, MS. Part-time and evening/weekend programs available. *Faculty:* 2 full-time (1 woman). *Students:* 60 full-time (29 women), 56 part-time (37 women); includes 27 minority (7 African Americans, 2 American Indian/Alaska Native, 2 Asian Americans or Pacific Islanders, 16 Hispanic Americans), 14 international. Average age 32. 113 applicants, 88% accepted, 50 enrolled. In 2008, 15 master's awarded. *Degree requirements:* For master's, comprehensive exam, thesis or alternative. *Entrance requirements:* For master's, GRE General Test. Additional exam requirements/recommendations for international students: Required—TOEFL (minimum score 550 paper-based; 213 computer-based). *Application deadline:* For fall admission, 3/1 priority date for international students; for spring admission, 11/1 priority date for international students. Applications are processed on a rolling basis. Application fee: $50 ($60 for international students). Electronic applications accepted. *Expenses:* Tuition, area resident: Part-time $194 per credit hour. Tuition, state resident: full-time $4648; part-time $194 per credit hour. Tuition, nonresident: full-time $11,392; part-time $475 per credit hour. Required fees: $2206; $69 per credit hour. $389 per semester. *Financial support:* In 2008–09, 78 students received support; teaching assistantships with partial tuition reimbursements available, career-related internships or fieldwork, Federal Work-Study, and institutionally sponsored loans available. Support available to part-time students. Financial award application deadline: 4/15; financial award applicants required to submit FAFSA. *Faculty research:* Literature-short story, comparative literature. *Unit head:* Dr. Wendell Aycock, Associate Dean, 806-742-2781 Ext. 228, E-mail: wendell.aycock@ttu.edu. *Application contact:* Graduate Adviser, 806-742-2781 Ext. 228.

Trinity Western University, Faculty of Graduate Studies, Program in Interdisciplinary Humanities, Langley, BC V2Y 1Y1, Canada. Offers general humanities (MAIH); specialized (MAIH), including English, history, philosophy. Part-time and evening/weekend programs available. Postbaccalaureate distance learning degree programs offered (minimal on-campus study). *Degree requirements:* For master's, 36 semester hours. *Entrance requirements:* For master's, strong undergraduate degree in Humanities or English, History or Philosophy. *Faculty research:* Literary theory, gender, medieval and early modern literature, philosophy of religion, Thomas Merton's poetics.

Tulane University, School of Science and Engineering, Interdisciplinary PhD Program, New Orleans, LA 70118-5669. Offers PhD.

Union Institute & University, Online MA Programs, Cincinnati, OH 45206-1925. Offers health and wellness (MA); history and culture (MA); leadership (MA); literature and writing (MA); psychology (MA). Part-time programs available. Postbaccalaureate distance learning degree programs offered (no on-campus study). *Degree requirements:* For master's, thesis. *Expenses:* Contact institution.

Union Institute & University, PhD Program in Interdisciplinary Studies, Cincinnati, OH 45206-1925. Offers interdisciplinary studies (PhD), including ethical and creative leadership, humanities and society, public policy and social issues;). Individually-designed interdisciplinary programs. Postbaccalaureate distance learning degree programs offered (minimal on-campus study). *Degree requirements:* For doctorate, thesis/dissertation, internship, residency. *Entrance requirements:* For doctorate, master's degree, letters of recommendation, interview. *Faculty research:* Women's studies, adult education, spirituality.

The University of Alabama in Huntsville, School of Graduate Studies, Interdisciplinary Studies, Huntsville, AL 35899. Offers MS, PhD, Certificate. Part-time and evening/weekend programs available. *Faculty:* 77 full-time (10 women), 2 part-time/adjunct (0 women). *Students:* 35 full-time (17 women), 25 part-time (6 women); includes 12 minority (10 African Americans, 1 American Indian/Alaska Native, 1 Hispanic American), 22 international. Average age 31. 67 applicants, 31% accepted, 16 enrolled. In 2008, 2 master's, 4 doctorates, 13 other advanced degrees awarded. *Degree requirements:* For master's, comprehensive exam, thesis or alternative, oral and written exams; for doctorate, comprehensive exam, thesis/dissertation, oral and written exams. *Entrance requirements:* For master's and doctorate, GRE General Test, minimum GPA of 3.0; for Certificate, GMAT (score of at least 500), minimum AACSB index of 1080. Additional exam requirements/recommendations for international students: Required—TOEFL (minimum score 500 paper-based; 173 computer-based; 62 iBT). *Application deadline:* For fall admission, 7/15 for domestic students, 4/1 for international students; for spring admission, 11/30 for domestic students, 9/1 for international students. Applications are processed on a rolling basis. Application fee: $40 ($50 for international students). Electronic applications accepted. *Expenses:* Tuition, area resident: Full-time $5214; part-time $323 per credit hour. Tuition, state resident: full-time $5214; part-time $323 per credit hour. Tuition, nonresident: full-time $11,444; part-time $705 per credit hour. Required fees: $540; $120 per semester. Tuition and fees vary according to course load. *Financial support:* In 2008–09, 34 students received support, including 1 fellowship with full tuition reimbursement available (averaging $26,000 per year), 17 research assistantships with full and partial tuition reimbursements available (averaging $11,953 per year), 16 teaching assistantships with full and partial tuition reimbursements available (averaging $11,589 per year); career-related internships or fieldwork, Federal Work-Study, institutionally sponsored loans, scholarships/grants, health care benefits, and unspecified assistantships also available. Support available to part-time students. Financial award application deadline: 4/1; financial award applicants required to submit FAFSA. Total annual research expenditures: $1.5 million. *Unit head:* Dr. Debra Moriarity, Dean of Graduate Studies, 256-824-6002, Fax: 256-824-6405, E-mail: deangrad@uah.edu. *Application contact:* Kathy Biggs, Graduate Studies Admissions Manager, 256-824-6199, Fax: 256-824-6405, E-mail: deangrad@uah.edu.

University of Alaska Anchorage, College of Arts and Sciences, Program in Interdisciplinary Studies, Anchorage, AK 99508-8060. Offers MA, MS. Part-time programs available. *Entrance requirements:* For master's, GRE General Test, GRE Subject Test, minimum GPA of 3.0. Additional exam requirements/recommendations for international students: Required—TOEFL (minimum score 550 paper-based; 213 computer-based).

University of Alaska Fairbanks, Graduate School for Interdisciplinary Studies, Fairbanks, AK 99775-7560. Offers MA, MS, PhD. Part-time programs available. *Faculty:* 1 part-time/adjunct (0 women). *Students:* 2 full-time (both women), 1 part-time (0 women), 1 international. Average age 42. 3 applicants, 0% accepted.Terminal master's awarded for partial completion of doctoral program. *Degree requirements:* For master's, comprehensive exam (for some programs), thesis (for some programs); for doctorate, one foreign language, comprehensive exam, thesis/dissertation, oral defense, oral exam. *Entrance requirements:* For master's and doctorate, GRE General Test. Additional exam requirements/recommendations for international students: Required—TOEFL (minimum score 550 paper-based; 213 computer-based; 80 iBT). *Application deadline:* For fall admission, 6/1 for domestic students, 3/1 for international students; for spring admission, 10/15 for domestic students, 9/1 for international students. Applications are processed on a rolling basis. Application fee: $60. Electronic applications accepted. *Expenses:* Tuition, area resident: Full-time $5418; part-time $301 per credit. Tuition, state resident: full-time $5418; part-time $301 per credit. Tuition, nonresident: full-time $11,070; part-time $615 per credit. Required fees: $849; $25 per credit. $78 per semester. Tuition and fees vary according to course load and reciprocity agreements. *Financial support:* In 2008–09, 2 research assistantships (averaging $5,236 per year) were awarded; fellowships, teaching assistantships, career-related internships or fieldwork, Federal Work-Study, scholarships/grants, health care benefits, and unspecified assistantships also available. Support available to part-time students. Financial award application deadline: 2/15; financial award applicants required to submit FAFSA. *Unit head:* Lawrence Duffy, Interim Dean, 907-474-7716, Fax: 907-474-1984, E-mail: fyinds@uaf.edu. *Application contact:* Lawrence Duffy, Interim Dean, 907-474-7716, Fax: 907-474-1984, E-mail: fyinds@uaf.edu.

The University of Arizona, Graduate College, Graduate Interdisciplinary Programs, Tucson, AZ 85721. Offers American Indian studies (MA, PhD); applied mathematics (MS, PMS, PhD), including applied mathematics (MS, PhD), mathematical sciences (PMS); biomedical engineering (MS, PhD); cancer biology (PhD); genetics (MS, PhD); insect science (PhD); neuroscience (PhD); physiological sciences (PhD); second language acquisition and teaching (PhD); statistics (MS, PhD); JD/MA. Part-time programs available. *Entrance requirements:* Additional exam requirements/recommendations for international students: Required—TOEFL.

University of Arkansas, Graduate School, Interdisciplinary Program in Comparative Literature and Cultural Studies, Fayetteville, AR 72701-1201. Offers classical studies (MA); comparative literature (PhD). *Degree requirements:* For master's, one foreign language, comprehensive exam, thesis optional; for doctorate, 2 foreign languages, comprehensive exam, thesis/dissertation. *Entrance requirements:* For master's and doctorate, GRE General Test. *Faculty research:* Literary and cultural theory, cultural studies, postcolonial theory, gender studies, world literature.

University of Arkansas, Graduate School, Interdisciplinary Program in Environmental Dynamics, Fayetteville, AR 72701-1201. Offers PhD. *Degree requirements:* For doctorate, thesis/dissertation.

University of Central Florida, College of Graduate Studies, Program in Interdisciplinary Studies, Orlando, FL 32816. Offers MA, MS. *Students:* 10 full-time (7 women), 22 part-time (15 women); includes 7 minority (1 African American, 6 Hispanic Americans). In 2008, 14 master's awarded. *Degree requirements:* For master's, thesis or alternative. *Entrance requirements:* For master's, GRE General Test, minimum GPA of 3.0 in last 60 hours. Additional exam requirements/recommendations for international students: Required—TOEFL. Application fee: $30. Electronic applications accepted. *Expenses:* Tuition, area resident: Full-time $6816; part-time $284 per credit. Tuition, state resident: full-time $6816; part-time $1076 per credit. Tuition, nonresident: full-time $25,824. Required fees: $216; $9 per credit. *Financial support:* In 2008–09, 3 research assistantships (averaging $5,600 per year), 1 teaching assistantship (averaging $7,000 per year) were awarded; fellowships also available. *Unit head:* Dr. Michael Hampton, Director, 407-823-2136, E-mail: mhampton@mail.ucf.edu. *Application contact:* Dr. Michael Hampton, Director, 407-823-2136, E-mail: mhampton@mail.ucf.edu.

University of Chicago, Division of the Biological Sciences, The Interdisciplinary Scientist Training Program, Chicago, IL 60637-1513. Offers PhD. *Students:* 2 full-time (0 women). Average age 25. 7 applicants, 14% accepted, 1 enrolled. *Degree requirements:* For doctorate, thesis/dissertation, ethics class, 2 teaching assistantships. *Entrance requirements:* Additional exam requirements/recommendations for international students: Required—TOEFL (minimum score 600 paper-based; 250 computer-based; 104 iBT), IELTS (minimum score 7). *Application deadline:* For fall admission, 12/1 for domestic and international students. Application fee: $55. Electronic applications accepted. *Financial support:* In 2008–09, 2 students received support, including fellowships (averaging $29,053 per year), research assistantships (averaging $29,053 per year). Financial award applicants required to submit FAFSA. *Unit head:* Dr. Harinder Singh, Head, E-mail: hsingh@uchicago.edu. *Application contact:* Diane Hall, Student Contact, E-mail: djh8@uchicago.edu.

University of Cincinnati, Graduate School, McMicken College of Arts and Sciences, Interdisciplinary Studies Program, Cincinnati, OH 45221. Offers PhD. *Entrance requirements:* For doctorate, GRE General Test. Electronic applications accepted.

University of Houston–Victoria, School of Arts and Sciences, Program in Interdisciplinary Studies, Victoria, TX 77901-4450. Offers MAIS. Part-time and evening/weekend programs available. Postbaccalaureate distance learning degree programs offered (no on-campus study). *Degree requirements:* For master's, comprehensive exam or thesis. *Entrance requirements:* For master's, GRE General Test. Additional exam requirements/recommendations for international students: Required—TOEFL (minimum score 550 paper-based; 213 computer-based).

University of Idaho, College of Graduate Studies, Program in Interdisciplinary Studies, Moscow, ID 83844-2282. Offers MA, MS. *Faculty:* 4. *Students:* 1 full-time, 2 part-time. Average age 33. In 2008, 1 master's awarded. *Entrance requirements:* For master's, minimum GPA of 2.8. *Application deadline:* For fall admission, 8/1 for domestic students; for spring admission, 12/15 for domestic students. Application fee: $55 ($60 for international students). *Expenses:* Tuition, nonresident: full-time $10,080; part-time $336 per credit. Required fees: $5212; $267 per credit. Tuition and fees vary according to program. *Financial support:* Application deadline: 2/15. *Unit head:* Dr. Margrit von Braun, Dean of Graduate Studies, 208-885 Ext. 6243. *Application contact:* Dr. Margrit von Braun, Dean of Graduate Studies, 208-885 Ext. 6243.

University of Illinois at Springfield, Graduate Programs, College of Liberal Arts and Sciences, Individual Option Program, Springfield, IL 62703-5407. Offers MA. Part-time and evening/weekend programs available. *Faculty:* 5 full-time (3 women). *Students:* 5 full-time (4 women), 24 part-time (14 women); includes 5 minority (2 African Americans, 1 American Indian/Alaska Native, 1 Asian American or Pacific Islander, 1 Hispanic American). Average age 39. 19 applicants, 53% accepted, 9 enrolled. In 2008, 13 master's awarded. *Degree requirements:* For master's, project or thesis. *Entrance requirements:* For master's, application form, personal statement, two letters of reference, interview. Additional exam requirements/recommendations for international students: Required—TOEFL (minimum score 500 paper-based; 176 computer-based; 61 iBT). *Application deadline:* Applications are processed on a rolling basis. Application fee: $50 ($60 for international students). *Expenses:* Tuition, state resident: full-time $6144; part-time $256 per credit hour. Tuition, nonresident: full-time $13,980; part-time $582.50 per credit hour. Required fees: $1800. *Financial support:* In 2008–09, research assistantships with full tuition reimbursements (averaging $8,109 per year), teaching assistantships with full tuition reimbursements (averaging $8,109 per year) were awarded; career-related internships or fieldwork, Federal Work-Study, scholarships/grants, health care benefits, and unspecified assistantships also available. Support available to part-time students. Financial award application deadline: 11/15; financial award applicants required to submit FAFSA. *Unit head:* Dr. Annette Van Dyke, Program Administrator, 217-206-7420, Fax: 217-206-6217, E-mail: vandyke.annette@uis.edu. *Application contact:* Dr. Lynn Pardie, Office of Graduate Studies, 800-252-8533, Fax: 217-206-7623, E-mail: pardie.lynn@uis.edu.

The University of Kansas, University of Kansas Medical Center, School of Medicine, Interdisciplinary Graduate Program in Biomedical Sciences (IGPBS), Kansas City, KS 66160. Offers MA, MPH, MS, PhD, MD/MPH, MD/MS, MD/PhD. Part-time and evening/weekend programs available. *Students:* 17 full-time (10 women), 2 part-time (1 woman); includes 1 minority (Hispanic American), 8 international. Average age 24. 240 applicants, 20% accepted, 19 enrolled.Terminal master's awarded for partial completion of doctoral program. *Degree requirements:* For master's, thesis; for doctorate, comprehensive exam, thesis/dissertation. *Entrance requirements:* For master's and doctorate, GRE. Additional exam requirements/recommendations for international students: Required—TOEFL. *Application deadline:* For fall admission, 1/15 priority date for domestic and international students. Applications are processed on a rolling basis. Application fee: $0. Electronic applications accepted. *Expenses:* Tuition, area resident: Full-time $6122; part-time $255.10 per credit hour. Tuition, state resident: full-time $6122; part-time $255.10 per credit hour. Tuition, nonresident: full-time $14,629; part-time $609.55 per credit hour. Required fees: $847; $70.56 per credit hour. Tuition and fees vary according to course load and program. *Financial support:* In 2008–09, 1 student received support; fellowships with full tuition reimbursements available, research assistantships with full tuition reimbursements available, teaching assistantships with full tuition reimbursements available, Federal Work-Study available. Support available to part-time students. Financial award application deadline: 3/30; financial award applicants required to submit FAFSA. *Faculty research:* Cardiovascular biology, neurosciences, signal transduction and cancer biology, molecular biology and genetics, developmental biology. *Unit head:* Dr. Michael J. Werle,

Graduate Adviser, 913-588-7491, Fax: 913-588-2710, E-mail: mwerle@kumc.edu. *Application contact:* Miranda Rudloff, Coordinator, 913-588-2719, Fax: 913-588-5242, E-mail: mrudloff@kumc.edu.

University of Louisville, Graduate School, Interdisciplinary Studies, Louisville, KY 40292-0001. Offers MA, MS. *Students:* 11 full-time (8 women), 7 part-time (3 women); includes 3 African Americans, 2 Asian Americans or Pacific Islanders. Average age 33. *Degree requirements:* For master's, thesis. *Entrance requirements:* For master's, GRE General Test. *Application deadline:* Applications are processed on a rolling basis. Application fee: $50.

University of Maine, Graduate School, Interdisciplinary Doctoral Program, Orono, ME 04469. Offers PhD. Part-time and evening/weekend programs available. *Degree requirements:* For doctorate, comprehensive exam, thesis/dissertation. *Entrance requirements:* For doctorate, GRE General Test. Additional exam requirements/recommendations for international students: Required—TOEFL. Electronic applications accepted.

University of Manitoba, Faculty of Graduate Studies, Interdisciplinary Programs, Individual Interdisciplinary Programs, Winnipeg, MB R3T 2N2, Canada. Offers M Sc, MA, PhD.

University of Maryland, College Park, Graduate Studies, Interdepartmental Programs, College Park, MD 20742. Offers PhD, MA/MLS, MBA/MPM. *Entrance requirements:* For doctorate, GRE General Test. Additional exam requirements/recommendations for international students: Required—TOEFL. Electronic applications accepted.

University of Medicine and Dentistry of New Jersey, School of Health Related Professions, Department of Interdisciplinary Studies, Program in Health Sciences, Newark, NJ 07107-1709. Offers cardiopulmonary sciences (PhD); clinical laboratory sciences (PhD); health sciences (MS); interdisciplinary studies (PhD); nutrition (PhD); physical therapy/movement science (PhD). *Degree requirements:* For doctorate, thesis/dissertation. *Entrance requirements:* For doctorate, interview, writing sample. Additional exam requirements/recommendations for international students: Required—TOEFL. Electronic applications accepted.

University of Minnesota, Twin Cities Campus, Graduate School, College of Liberal Arts, Department of Cultural Studies and Comparative Literature, Program in Comparative Studies in Discourse and Society, Minneapolis, MN 55455-0213. Offers PhD. *Degree requirements:* For doctorate, 2 foreign languages, thesis/dissertation. *Entrance requirements:* For doctorate, GRE General Test, sample of written work. Additional exam requirements/recommendations for international students: Required—TOEFL. *Faculty research:* Cultural theory; music; architecture, space, and urbanism; body and gender; film and popular culture.

University of Missouri–Kansas City, School of Graduate Studies, Kansas City, MO 64110-2499. Offers interdisciplinary studies (PhD), including art history, cell biology and biophysics, chemistry, computer and electrical engineering, computer science and informatics, economics, education, engineering, English, entrepreneurship and innovation, geosciences, history, mathematics and statistics, molecular biology and biochemistry, music education, oral biology, pharmaceutical sciences, pharmacology, physics, political science, psychology, public affairs and administration, religious studies, social science consortium, sociology, telecommunications and computer networking, urban leadership and policy studies in education. Students select two or more subjects. *Students:* 112 full-time (45 women), 251 part-time (97 women); includes 17 minority (7 African Americans, 6 Asian Americans or Pacific Islanders, 4 Hispanic Americans), 163 international. Average age 35. 172 applicants, 40% accepted, 58 enrolled. In 2008, 32 doctorates awarded. *Degree requirements:* For doctorate, comprehensive exam, thesis/dissertation, residency. *Entrance requirements:* For doctorate, GRE General Test, minimum GPA of 2.75 (undergraduate), 3.0 (graduate). Additional exam requirements/recommendations for international students: Required—TOEFL (minimum score 550 paper-based; 213 computer-based; 80 iBT), TWE (minimum score 4). *Application deadline:* For fall admission, 1/15 priority date for domestic and international students. Applications are processed on a rolling basis. Application fee: $45 ($50 for international students). Electronic applications accepted. *Expenses:* Tuition, state resident: full-time $5376; part-time $298.70 per credit hour. Tuition, nonresident: full-time $13,882; part-time $771.20 per credit hour. Required fees: $640.28; $34.65 per contact hour. $30 per semester. Tuition and fees vary according to course load and program. *Financial support:* Fellowships with partial tuition reimbursements, research assistantships with partial tuition reimbursements, teaching assistantships with partial tuition reimbursements, career-related internships or fieldwork, Federal Work-Study, tuition waivers (partial), and unspecified assistantships available. Support available to part-time students. Financial award application deadline: 3/1; financial award applicants required to submit FAFSA. *Unit head:* Dr. Ronald MacQuarrie, Dean, 816-235-1301, Fax: 816-235-1310, E-mail: macquarrier@umkc.edu. *Application contact:* Qunicy Bennett Johnson, Administrative Assistant, 816-235-1559, Fax: 816-235-1310, E-mail: bennettq@umkc.edu.

The University of Montana, Graduate School, Program in Interdisciplinary Studies, Missoula, MT 59812-0002. Offers individual interdisciplinary programs (IIP) (PhD); interdisciplinary studies (MIS). *Degree requirements:* For doctorate, thesis/dissertation. *Entrance requirements:* For master's, GRE General Test. Additional exam requirements/recommendations for international students: Required—TOEFL.

University of New Brunswick Fredericton, School of Graduate Studies, Interdisciplinary Studies Program, Fredericton, NB E3B 5A3, Canada. Offers M IDST, PhD. *Faculty:* 27 full-time (17 women), 5 part-time/adjunct (2 women). *Students:* 30 full-time (22 women), 6 part-time (2 women). In 2008, 4 master's, 1 doctorate awarded. *Degree requirements:* For master's, thesis; for doctorate, comprehensive exam, thesis/dissertation. *Entrance requirements:* For master's, honors degree with A- average, minimum GPA of 3.5; for doctorate, master's degree with A-average, minimum GPA of 3.5. Application fee: $50 Canadian dollars. Tuition and fees charges are reported in Canadian dollars. *Expenses:* Tuition, area resident: Full-time $5562 Canadian dollars. Tuition, nonresident: full-time $9450 Canadian dollars. Required fees: $333 Canadian dollars. *Financial support:* In 2008–09, 4 fellowships, 13 research assistantships, 1 teaching assistantship were awarded. *Faculty research:* Support needs of young adults with cancer; risk analysis, cervical cancer; treatment of persons with disabilities; tourism strategy; farm-related injuries. *Unit head:* Dr. Linda Eyre, Assistant Dean of Graduate Studies, 506-447-3044, Fax: 506-453-4817, E-mail: gradidst@unb.ca. *Application contact:* Janet Amirault, Graduate Secretary, 506-458-7558, Fax: 506-453-4817, E-mail: jamiraul@unb.ca.

University of Northern British Columbia, Office of Graduate Studies, Prince George, BC V2N 4Z9, Canada. Offers business administration (Diploma); community health science (M Sc); disability management (MA); education (M Ed); first nations studies (MA); gender studies (MA); history (MA); interdisciplinary studies (MA); international studies (MA); mathematical, computer and physical sciences (M Sc); natural resources and environmental studies (M Sc, MA, MNRES, PhD); political science (MA); psychology (M Sc, PhD); social work (MSW). Part-time and evening/weekend programs available. Postbaccalaureate distance learning degree programs offered (no on-campus study). *Degree requirements:* For master's, thesis; for doctorate, thesis/dissertation. *Entrance requirements:* For master's, GRE, minimum B average in undergraduate course work; for doctorate, candidacy exam, minimum A average in graduate course work.

University of North Texas, Robert B. Toulouse School of Graduate Studies, Interdisciplinary Studies, Denton, TX 76203. Offers MA, MS. Part-time programs available. *Degree requirements:* For master's, comprehensive exam, thesis optional. *Entrance requirements:* For master's, GRE General Test, minimum GPA of 2.8, 3 letters of reference, personal statement, degree plan. Additional exam requirements/recommendations for international students: Required—proof of English language proficiency required for non-native English speakers; Recommended—TOEFL (minimum score 550 paper-based; 213 computer-based; 80 iBT).

University of Oklahoma, Graduate College, Program in Interdisciplinary Studies, Norman, OK 73019-0390. Offers MA, MS, PhD. Part-time and evening/weekend programs available. *Students:* 133 full-time (67 women), 412 part-time (158 women); includes 124 minority (55

African Americans, 10 American Indian/Alaska Native, 17 Asian Americans or Pacific Islanders, 42 Hispanic Americans), 13 international. 94 applicants, 98% accepted, 80 enrolled. In 2008, 132 master's, 4 doctorates awarded. *Entrance requirements:* Additional exam requirements/recommendations for international students: Recommended—TOEFL (minimum score 550 paper-based; 213 computer-based). *Application deadline:* For fall admission, 6/1 for domestic students, 4/1 for international students; for spring admission, 11/1 for domestic students, 9/1 for international students. Applications are processed on a rolling basis. Application fee: $40 ($90 for international students). Electronic applications accepted. *Expenses:* Tuition, state resident: full-time $3744; part-time $156 per credit hour. Tuition, nonresident: full-time $13,577; part-time $565.70 per credit hour. Required fees: $2415.40; $90.10 per credit hour. *Financial support:* In 2008–09, 33 students received support. Tuition waivers (full and partial) and unspecified assistantships available. Financial award applicants required to submit FAFSA. Total annual research expenditures: $40,011. *Unit head:* Lee Williams, Dean/Vice President of Research, 405-325-3811, Fax: 405-325-5346, E-mail: lwilliams@ou.edu. *Application contact:* Angela Castillo, Academic Counselor II, 405-325-3841, Fax: 405-325-5346, E-mail: acastillo@ou.edu.

University of Oregon, Graduate School, Interdisciplinary Program in Applied Information Management, Eugene, OR 97403. Offers MS. Part-time and evening/weekend programs available. *Degree requirements:* For master's, project. *Entrance requirements:* For master's, GMAT, GRE, or MAT. Additional exam requirements/recommendations for international students: Required—TOEFL. Electronic applications accepted. *Expenses:* Contact institution. *Faculty research:* Business management, information design.

University of Ottawa, Faculty of Graduate and Postdoctoral Studies, Interdisciplinary Programs, Ottawa, ON K1N 6N5, Canada. Offers e-business (Certificate); e-commerce (Certificate); finance (Certificate); health services and policies research (Diploma); population health (PhD); population health risk assessment and management (Certificate); public management and governance (Certificate); systems science (Certificate).

University of Pittsburgh, School of Medicine, Graduate Programs in Medicine, Interdisciplinary Biomedical Sciences Program, Pittsburgh, PA 15260. Offers PhD. *Degree requirements:* For doctorate, comprehensive exam, thesis/dissertation. *Entrance requirements:* For doctorate, GRE General Test, GRE Subject Test, minimum QPA of 3.0. Additional exam requirements/recommendations for international students: Required—TOEFL (minimum score 600 paper-based; 250 computer-based; 100 iBT), IELTS (minimum score 7). Electronic applications accepted. *Faculty research:* Biochemistry and molecular genetics, cell biology and molecular physiology, cellular and molecular pathology, immunology, molecular pharmacology.

The University of South Dakota, Graduate School, Interdisciplinary Studies Program, Vermillion, SD 57069-2390. Offers interdisciplinary studies (MA). Part-time programs available. Postbaccalaureate distance learning degree programs offered. *Degree requirements:* For master's, thesis or alternative. *Entrance requirements:* For master's, minimum GPA of 2.7; supplemental packet. Additional exam requirements/recommendations for international students: Required—TOEFL (minimum score 550 paper-based; 213 computer-based; 79 iBT). Electronic applications accepted.

The University of Texas at Arlington, Graduate School, School of Urban and Public Affairs, Department of Interdisciplinary Science, Arlington, TX 76019. Offers MA. Part-time and evening/weekend programs available. *Students:* 1 (woman) full-time, 16 part-time (10 women); includes 6 minority (1 African American, 1 American Indian/Alaska Native, 4 Hispanic Americans). 6 applicants, 100% accepted, 3 enrolled. *Entrance requirements:* For master's, GRE. Additional exam requirements/recommendations for international students: Required—TOEFL (minimum score 550 paper-based; 213 computer-based). *Application deadline:* For fall admission, 6/15 for domestic students. Application fee: $35 ($50 for international students). *Expenses:* Tuition, area resident: Full-time $6500. Tuition, state resident: full-time $6500. Tuition, nonresident: full-time $11,558. *Unit head:* Dr. Allen Repko, Director, 817-272-2338, E-mail: repko@uta.edu. *Application contact:* Dr. Allen Repko, Director, 817-272-2338, E-mail: repko@uta.edu.

The University of Texas at Brownsville, Graduate Studies, College of Liberal Arts, Department of English, Brownsville, TX 78520-4991. Offers English (MA); interdisciplinary studies (MAIS). Part-time and evening/weekend programs available. *Degree requirements:* For master's, comprehensive exam or thesis. *Entrance requirements:* For master's, GRE General Test. Additional exam requirements/recommendations for international students: Required—TOEFL. *Faculty research:* Sandra Cisneros, Nathaniel Hawthorne, Rodolfo Araya, Isabel Allende, linguistics.

The University of Texas at Brownsville, Graduate Studies, College of Liberal Arts, Department of Modern Languages, Brownsville, TX 78520-4991. Offers interdisciplinary studies (MAIS); Spanish (MA). Part-time and evening/weekend programs available. *Degree requirements:* For master's, comprehensive exam, thesis optional. *Entrance requirements:* For master's, GRE General Test, letters of recommendation, interview. Additional exam requirements/recommendations for international students: Required—TOEFL. *Faculty research:* Children's literature, Hispanic folklore, translation.

The University of Texas at Dallas, School of Interdisciplinary Studies, Richardson, TX 75083-0688. Offers interdisciplinary studies (MA). Part-time and evening/weekend programs available. *Faculty:* 3 full-time (2 women). *Students:* 13 full-time (10 women), 27 part-time (17 women); includes 15 minority (8 African Americans, 4 Asian Americans or Pacific Islanders, 3 Hispanic Americans). Average age 39. 24 applicants, 83% accepted, 15 enrolled. In 2008, 22 master's awarded. *Degree requirements:* For master's, research project, seminar. *Entrance requirements:* For master's, GRE General Test, minimum GPA of 3.0. Additional exam requirements/recommendations for international students: Required—TOEFL (minimum score 550 paper-based; 213 computer-based). *Application deadline:* For fall admission, 7/15 for domestic students, 5/1 priority date for international students; for spring admission, 11/15 for domestic students, 9/1 priority date for international students. Applications are processed on a rolling basis. Application fee: $50 ($100 for international students). Electronic applications accepted. *Expenses:* Tuition, area resident: full-time $8320. Tuition, state resident: full-time $8320. Tuition, nonresident: full-time $15,054. Part-time tuition and fees vary according to course load. *Financial support:* Fellowships, research assistantships, teaching assistantships with tuition reimbursements, career-related internships or fieldwork, Federal Work-Study, institutionally sponsored loans, and scholarships/grants available. Support available to part-time students. Financial award application deadline: 4/30; financial award applicants required to submit FAFSA. *Faculty research:* Biomedical ethics, history and philosophy of science, social control and regulation, national security, education policy. *Unit head:* Dr. George Fair, Dean, 972-883-2350, Fax: 972-883-2440, E-mail: gwfair@utdallas.edu. *Application contact:* Dr. Elizabeth Salter, Associate Dean, 972-883-2323, Fax: 972-883-2440, E-mail: emsalter@utdallas.edu.

The University of Texas at El Paso, Graduate School, College of Liberal Arts, Interdisciplinary Program in Liberal Arts, El Paso, TX 79968-0001. Offers MAIS. Part-time and evening/weekend programs available. *Degree requirements:* For master's, thesis or alternative. *Entrance requirements:* For master's, GRE General Test, minimum GPA of 3.0 in major. Additional exam requirements/recommendations for international students: Required—TOEFL. Electronic applications accepted.

The University of Texas at El Paso, Graduate School, College of Science, Interdisciplinary Studies Program, El Paso, TX 79968-0001. Offers MSIS. Part-time and evening/weekend programs available. *Degree requirements:* For master's, thesis optional. *Entrance requirements:* For master's, GRE General Test. Additional exam requirements/recommendations for international students: Required—TOEFL. Electronic applications accepted.

The University of Texas at San Antonio, College of Education and Human Development, Department of Interdisciplinary Learning and Teaching, San Antonio, TX 78249-0617. Offers curriculum and instruction (MA); early childhood education (MA); instructional technology

Interdisciplinary Studies

The University of Texas at San Antonio (continued)

(MA); reading (MA); special education (MA). Part-time and evening/weekend programs available. *Degree requirements:* For master's, comprehensive exam, thesis optional. *Entrance requirements:* For master's, GRE General Test. Additional exam requirements/recommendations for international students: Required—TOEFL (minimum score 500 paper-based; 173 computer-based). Electronic applications accepted. *Faculty research:* Early childhood, reading, special education, foundations, curriculum and instruction.

The University of Texas at Tyler, College of Arts and Sciences, Department of Biology, Tyler, TX 75799-0001. Offers biology (MS); interdisciplinary studies (MSIS). *Degree requirements:* For master's, comprehensive exam, thesis, oral qualifying exam, thesis defense. *Entrance requirements:* For master's, GRE General Test, GRE Subject Test, bachelor's degree in biology or equivalent. Additional exam requirements/recommendations for international students: Required—TOEFL (minimum score 79 computer-based). Electronic applications accepted. *Faculty research:* Phenotypic plasticity and heritability of life history traits, invertebrate ecology and genetics, systematics and phylogenetics of reptiles, hibernation physiology in turtles, landscape ecology, host-microbe interaction; outer membrane proteins in bacteria.

The University of Texas at Tyler, College of Arts and Sciences, Department of Literature and Languages, Tyler, TX 75799-0001. Offers English (MA); interdisciplinary studies (MAIS). Part-time and evening/weekend programs available. *Degree requirements:* For master's, one foreign language, comprehensive exam, thesis optional. *Entrance requirements:* For master's, GRE General Test, minimum GPA of 3.0, four semesters—or the equivalent—of one foreign language. Additional exam requirements/recommendations for international students: Required—TOEFL (minimum score 79 computer-based). Electronic applications accepted. *Faculty research:* Medieval and Tudor drama, Shakespeare, British Romanticism, British and Irish modernism, American realism, Greek drama, Nineteenth Century American literature.

The University of Texas at Tyler, College of Education and Psychology, Department of Psychology, Tyler, TX 75799-0001. Offers clinical psychology (MS), including neuropsychology, school psychology; counseling psychology (MA), including general, marriage and family; interdisciplinary studies (MSIS); school counseling (MA). Part-time and evening/weekend programs available. *Degree requirements:* For master's, comprehensive exam, thesis optional. *Entrance requirements:* For master's, GRE General Test, minimum GPA of 3.0. Additional exam requirements/recommendations for international students: Required—TOEFL (minimum score 79 computer-based). Electronic applications accepted. *Faculty research:* Neuropsychology, child abuse, psychometric properties of psychological instruments, maternal behavior, clinical practice issues, victimization of women, post-traumatic stress disorder.

The University of Texas at Tyler, College of Engineering and Computer Science, Department of Computer Science, Tyler, TX 75799-0001. Offers computer science (MS); interdisciplinary studies (MSIS). *Degree requirements:* For master's, comprehensive exam, thesis optional. *Entrance requirements:* For master's, GRE General Test, previous course work in data structures and computer organization, 6 hours of course work in calculus and statistics. Additional exam requirements/recommendations for international students: Required—TOEFL (minimum score 79 computer-based). Electronic applications accepted. *Faculty research:* Database design, software engineering, client-server architecture, visual programming, data mining, computer security, digital image processing, simulation and modeling, comp science education.

The University of Texas–Pan American, College of Arts and Humanities, Program in Interdisciplinary Studies, Edinburg, TX 78541-2999. Offers MAIS, MSIS. Part-time and evening/weekend programs available. *Degree requirements:* For master's, comprehensive exam, thesis or alternative. *Entrance requirements:* For master's, GRE General Test, minimum GPA of 3.0.

University of the Incarnate Word, School of Graduate Studies and Research, College of Humanities, Arts, and Social Sciences, Program in Multidisciplinary Studies, San Antonio, TX 78209-6397. Offers MA. Part-time and evening/weekend programs available. *Students:* 10 part-time (4 women); includes 3 minority (all Hispanic Americans). Average age 41. In 2008, 1 master's awarded. *Degree requirements:* For master's, thesis or alternative, capstone. *Entrance requirements:* For master's, GRE, MAT, GMAT. Additional exam requirements/recommendations for international students: Required—TOEFL (minimum score 560 paper-based; 220 computer-based; 83 iBT). *Application deadline:* Applications are processed on a rolling basis. Application fee: $20. Electronic applications accepted. *Expenses:* Tuition: Full-time $11,520; part-time $640 per credit hour. Required fees: $1494; $83 per credit hour. One-time fee: $50. Tuition and fees vary according to degree level and program. *Financial support:* Federal Work-Study and scholarships/grants available. Financial award applicants required to submit FAFSA. *Unit head:* Dr. Kevin Vichcales, Dean, School of Graduate Studies and Research. *Application contact:* Andrea Cyterski-Acosta, Dean of Enrollment, 210-829-6005, Fax: 210-829-3921, E-mail: admis@uiwtx.edu.

University of the Incarnate Word, School of Graduate Studies and Research, School of Mathematics, Science, and Engineering, Program in Multidisciplinary Sciences, San Antonio, TX 78209-6397. Offers MA. Part-time and evening/weekend programs available. *Students:* 19 part-time (13 women); includes 10 minority (1 African American, 1 American Indian/Alaska Native, 2 Asian Americans or Pacific Islanders, 6 Hispanic Americans). Average age 40. In 2008, 11 master's awarded. *Degree requirements:* For master's, capstone. *Entrance requirements:* For master's, GRE, BA or BS education with teaching certification and teaching experience. Additional exam requirements/recommendations for international students: Required—TOEFL (minimum score 560 paper-based; 220 computer-based; 83 iBT). *Application deadline:* Applications are processed on a rolling basis. Application fee: $20. Electronic applications accepted. *Expenses:* Tuition: Full-time $11,520; part-time $640 per credit hour. Required fees: $1494; $83 per credit hour. One-time fee: $50. Tuition and fees vary according to degree level and program. *Financial support:* Federal Work-Study and scholarships/grants available. Financial award applicants required to submit FAFSA. *Unit head:* Dr. Alakananda Chaudhuri, 210-829-3145, Fax: 210-829-3153, E-mail: alakanan@uiwtx.edu. *Application contact:* Andrea Cyterski-Acosta, Dean of Enrollment, 210-829-6005, Fax: 210-829-3921, E-mail: admis@uiwtx.edu.

University of Virginia, College and Graduate School of Arts and Sciences, Program in Art and Architectural History, Charlottesville, VA 22903. Offers MA, PhD. *Students:* 54 full-time (40 women); includes 1 minority (African American), 2 international. Average age 31. 52 applicants, 44% accepted, 11 enrolled. In 2008, 2 master's, 2 doctorates awarded. *Degree requirements:* For master's, one foreign language, comprehensive exam, thesis; for doctorate, 2 foreign languages, thesis/dissertation, oral exam. *Entrance requirements:* For master's and doctorate, GRE, 2 letters of recommendation. *Application deadline:* For fall admission, 12/7 for domestic and international students. Applications are processed on a rolling basis. Electronic applications accepted. *Expenses:* Tuition, area resident: Full-time $10,452. Tuition, state resident: full-time $10,452. Tuition, nonresident: full-time $20,010. Required fees: $2176. Part-time tuition and fees vary according to course load and program. *Financial support:* Application deadline: 12/7. *Unit head:* Lawrence O. Goedde, Chair, 434-924-6123, Fax: 434-924-3647, E-mail: artdept@virginia.edu. *Application contact:* Aaron Mills, Associate Dean of Graduate Academic Programs and Research, 434-924-6739, Fax: 434-924-6737, E-mail: grad-a-s@virginia.edu.

University of Washington, Tacoma, Graduate Programs, Tacoma, WA 98402-3100. Offers accounting (MBA); certified financial analyst (MBA); computing and software systems (MS); educational administrator (M Ed); interdisciplinary studies (MA); K-8 teacher education (M Ed); nursing (MN); professional certification (M Ed); secondary science education (M Ed); social work (MSW); special education (M Ed). Part-time and evening/weekend programs available. *Students:* 192 full-time (127 women), 329 part-time (260 women); includes 99 minority (22 African Americans, 6 American Indian/Alaska Native, 38 Asian Americans or Pacific Islanders, 33 Hispanic Americans). Average age 35. 324 applicants, 55% accepted, 132 enrolled. In 2008, 156 master's awarded. *Degree requirements:* For master's, comprehensive exam (for

some programs), thesis (for some programs), minimum GPA of 2.7 in all courses. *Entrance requirements:* For master's, GRE, GMAT, minimum GPA of 3.0 in last 90 graded credits. Additional exam requirements/recommendations for international students: Required—TOEFL (minimum score 580 paper-based; 237 computer-based; 70 iBT), MLT. *Application deadline:* For fall admission, 4/15 priority date for domestic and international students; for winter admission, 10/15 priority date for domestic and international students; for spring admission, 1/15 priority date for domestic and international students. Applications are processed on a rolling basis. Application fee: $65 ($75 for international students). Electronic applications accepted. *Expenses:* Tuition, area resident: Full-time $10,476; part-time $498 per credit. Tuition, state resident: full-time $10,476; part-time $498 per credit. Tuition, nonresident: full-time $22,947; part-time $1092 per credit. Tuition and fees vary according to course load, degree level and program. *Financial support:* Federal Work-Study, institutionally sponsored loans, and scholarships/grants available. Support available to part-time students. *Faculty research:* AIDS patient care (Social Work), impact of globalization on international urban areas (Urban Studies), water quality (Environmental Science), community based health care (Nursing), educational studies (Education). Total annual research expenditures: $550,000. *Unit head:* Dr. Patricia Spakes, Chancellor, 253-692-5646, E-mail: pspakes@u.washington.edu. *Application contact:* Joan Abe, Director, Graduate School, 253-543-5929, E-mail: uwgrad@u.washington.edu.

The University of Western Ontario, Faculty of Graduate Studies, Center for the Study of Theory and Criticism, London, ON N6A 5B8, Canada. Offers MA, PhD. *Degree requirements:* For master's, one foreign language, thesis; for doctorate, one foreign language, comprehensive exam, thesis/dissertation. *Entrance requirements:* For master's, honors degree or equivalent, minimum B+ average, 2 samples of written work; for doctorate, MA in humanitites or social sciences.

University of Wisconsin–Milwaukee, Graduate School, Program in Multidisciplinary Studies, Milwaukee, WI 53201-0413. Offers PhD. *Students:* 3 full-time (all women). Average age 42. In 2008, 1 doctorate awarded. *Degree requirements:* For doctorate, thesis/dissertation. *Application deadline:* For fall admission, 1/1 priority date for domestic students; for spring admission, 9/1 for domestic students. Applications are processed on a rolling basis. Application fee: $45 ($75 for international students). *Expenses:* Tuition, area resident: Full-time $7320; part-time $165 per credit. Tuition, state resident: full-time $7320; part-time $165 per credit. Tuition, nonresident: full-time $17,840; part-time $714 per credit. Tuition and fees vary according to campus/location, program and reciprocity agreements. *Financial support:* Career-related internships or fieldwork and unspecified assistantships available. Support available to part-time students. Financial award application deadline: 4/15. *Unit head:* Gwat-Yong Lie, Associate Professor, 414-229-4100, E-mail: gwatlie@uwm.edu. *Application contact:* Wendy Fall, Director of Student Services, 414-229-6569, Fax: 414-229-6967, E-mail: wendyf@uwm.edu.

Virginia Commonwealth University, Graduate School, Program in Interdisciplinary Studies, Richmond, VA 23284-9005. Offers MIS. Part-time programs available. *Degree requirements:* For master's, thesis optional. *Entrance requirements:* For master's, GRE General Test, minimum GPA of 2.8.

Virginia Polytechnic Institute and State University, Graduate School, College of Liberal Arts and Human Sciences, Program in Social, Political, Ethical and Cultural Thought, Blacksburg, VA 24061. Offers PhD, Graduate Certificate.

Virginia Polytechnic Institute and State University, Graduate School, Intercollege, Blacksburg, VA 24061. Offers MIT, MS, PhD. *Entrance requirements:* Additional exam requirements/recommendations for international students: Required—TOEFL. Electronic applications accepted.

Virginia State University, School of Graduate Studies, Research, and Outreach, Program in Interdisciplinary Studies, Petersburg, VA 23806-0001. Offers MIS. *Degree requirements:* For master's, thesis optional.

Washington State University, Graduate School, Individual Interdisciplinary Doctoral Program, Pullman, WA 99164. Offers PhD. *Degree requirements:* For doctorate, comprehensive exam, thesis/dissertation. *Entrance requirements:* For doctorate, minimum GPA of 3.5, master's degree from an accredited institution. Additional exam requirements/recommendations for international students: Required—TOEFL.

Wayland Baptist University, Graduate Programs, Program in Multidisciplinary Science, Plainview, TX 79072-6998. Offers MS. Part-time and evening/weekend programs available. *Faculty:* 10 full-time (2 women), 1 part-time/adjunct (0 women). *Students:* 11 part-time (10 women). Average age 38. In 2008, 2 master's awarded. *Degree requirements:* For master's, comprehensive exam. *Entrance requirements:* For master's, GRE or MAT. Additional exam requirements/recommendations for international students: Required—TOEFL (minimum score 500 paper-based; 173 computer-based; 61 iBT). *Application deadline:* Applications are processed on a rolling basis. Application fee: $50. *Expenses:* Tuition: Full-time $310; part-time $310 per credit hour. Required fees: $782; $9 per credit hour. $60 per semester. *Financial support:* Federal Work-Study, institutionally sponsored loans, and scholarships/grants available. Support available to part-time students. Financial award application deadline: 5/1; financial award applicants required to submit FAFSA. *Unit head:* Dr. Vaughn Ross, Chairman, Division of Mathematics and Science, 806-291-1115, Fax: 806-291-1968, E-mail: vross@wpu.edu. *Application contact:* Amanda Stanton, Graduate Studies, 806-291-3414, Fax: 806-291-1950, E-mail: stanton@wbu.edu.

Western Kentucky University, Graduate Studies, College of Education and Behavioral Sciences, Department of Special Instructional Programs, Bowling Green, KY 42101. Offers exceptional child education (MAE); interdisciplinary early child education (MAE); library media education (MS); literacy (MAE). Part-time and evening/weekend programs available. Post-baccalaureate distance learning degree programs offered (minimal on-campus study). *Degree requirements:* For master's, comprehensive exam. *Entrance requirements:* For master's, GRE General Test. Additional exam requirements/recommendations for international students: Required—TOEFL (minimum score 555 paper-based; 213 computer-based; 79 iBT). *Faculty research:* Teacher preparation in moderate/severe disabilities.

Western New Mexico University, Graduate Division, Interdisciplinary Studies, Silver City, NM 88062-0680. Offers MA. Part-time programs available. *Degree requirements:* For master's, comprehensive exam (for some programs), thesis optional. *Entrance requirements:* For master's, GRE General Test, GRE Subject Test, minimum GPA of 3.2 in last 64 hours of undergraduate study. Additional exam requirements/recommendations for international students: Required—TOEFL (minimum score 550 paper-based; 213 computer-based).

West Texas A&M University, Program in Interdisciplinary Studies, Canyon, TX 79016-0001. Offers MA, MS. Part-time and evening/weekend programs available. Postbaccalaureate distance learning degree programs offered (minimal on-campus study). *Degree requirements:* For master's, comprehensive exam, thesis or alternative. *Entrance requirements:* For master's, GRE General Test, interview with graduate Dean. Additional exam requirements/recommendations for international students: Required—TOEFL (minimum score 550 paper-based). Electronic applications accepted.

Worcester Polytechnic Institute, Graduate Studies and Research, Department of Social Science and Policy Studies, Worcester, MA 01609-2280. Offers interdisciplinary social science (PhD); system dynamics (MS, Graduate Certificate). Part-time and evening/weekend programs available. *Faculty:* 4 full-time (1 woman), 2 part-time/adjunct (0 women). *Students:* 17 part-time (5 women); includes 1 minority (African American), 4 international. Average age 40. 14 applicants, 57% accepted, 5 enrolled. In 2008, 1 master's awarded. *Entrance requirements:* For master's, GRE General Test, 3 letters of recommendation, statement of purpose. Additional exam requirements/recommendations for international students: Required—TOEFL (minimum score 550 paper-based; 213 computer-based; 79 iBT), IELTS (minimum score 6.5). *Application deadline:* For fall admission, 1/15 priority date for domestic students, 1/15 for international students; for spring admission, 10/15 priority date for domestic students, 10/15 for international

---

students. Applications are processed on a rolling basis. Application fee: $70. Electronic applications accepted. *Financial support:* Fellowships, research assistantships, teaching assistantships, career-related internships or fieldwork, institutionally sponsored loans, scholarships/grants, and unspecified assistantships available. Financial award application deadline: 1/15. *Faculty research:* Sustainable development, information economics, judgment and decision making, learning science, system dynamics, social simulation, political economys. Total annual research expenditures: $228,578. *Unit head:* Dr. James K. Doyle, Head, 508-831-5296, Fax: 508-831-5896, E-mail: doyle@wpi.edu. *Application contact:* Dr. Oleg Pavlov, Graduate Coordinator, 508-831-5296, Fax: 508-831-5896, E-mail: opavlov@wpi.edu.

Worcester Polytechnic Institute, Graduate Studies and Research, Programs in Interdisciplinary Studies, Worcester, MA 01609-2280. Offers bioscience administration (MS); impact engineering (MS); manufacturing engineering management (MS); power systems management (MS); social science (PhD); systems modeling (MS). Part-time and evening/weekend programs available. *Faculty:* 1 part-time/adjunct (0 women). *Students:* 7 full-time (4 women), 96 part-time (23 women); includes 8 minority (6 African Americans, 2 Hispanic Americans), 2 international. Average age 37. 69 applicants, 67% accepted, 25 enrolled. In 2008, 50 master's awarded. *Degree requirements:* For master's, thesis; for doctorate, comprehensive exam, thesis/

dissertation. *Entrance requirements:* For master's and doctorate, 3 letters of recommendation. Additional exam requirements/recommendations for international students: Required—TOEFL (minimum score 550 paper-based; 213 computer-based; 79 iBT), IELTS (minimum score 6.5). *Application deadline:* For fall admission, 1/15 priority date for domestic students; for spring admission, 10/15 priority date for domestic students. Application fee: $70. *Financial support:* Unspecified assistantships available. Financial award application deadline: 1/15. Total annual research expenditures: $64,780. *Unit head:* Dr. Fred J. Looft, Head, 508-831-5231, Fax: 508-831-5491, E-mail: fjlooft@wpi.edu. *Application contact:* Lynne Dougherty, Administrative Assistant, 508-831-5301, Fax: 508-831-5717, E-mail: grad@wpi.edu.

Wright State University, School of Graduate Studies, Interdisciplinary Programs, Program in Interdisciplinary Studies, Dayton, OH 45435. Offers MA, MS. *Degree requirements:* For master's, thesis optional. *Entrance requirements:* Additional exam requirements/recommendations for international students: Required—TOEFL.

York University, Faculty of Graduate Studies, Program in Interdisciplinary Studies, Toronto, ON M3J 1P3, Canada. Offers MA. Part-time programs available. *Degree requirements:* For master's, thesis or alternative. Electronic applications accepted.

MOUNTAIN STATE UNIVERSITY

Graduate Program in Interdisciplinary Studies

Mountain State University

Programs of Study	The Graduate Program in Interdisciplinary Studies at Mountain State University (MSU) is offered through the School of Graduate Studies. A graduate degree in interdisciplinary studies allows students to create programs of study incorporating the work of different domains of knowledge. It provides a useful approach for those whose interests fall between traditional areas. Students can integrate a variety of disciplines and incorporate fieldwork, directed research, mentored learning, and other forms of study.

The 36-semester-hour degree program is divided into three phases: methodology, content, and perspective.

In the methodology phase (3 hours), the student develops a detailed degree plan for proposal to the program. This proposal, based on the student's research, tells what he or she plans to learn in the content phase and details a plan to demonstrate that learning in the perspective phase.

Once the program has approved the degree plan, the student begins the content phase (25 hours). The content phase typically includes graduate-level courses, directed study, field experience and research, and a major project.

The culminating element in the degree program is the perspective project (8 hours) in which the student demonstrates mastery of the program content in a work featuring analysis, synthesis, and evaluation. The perspective project may be a traditional thesis; however, it may instead take the form of an extended written document or project.

Although students may structure their studies around different areas of specific interest, standardized curricula are provided for those who wish to pursue graduate study in selected fields: adult learning facilitation (M.A.), disability studies (M.S.), liberal studies (M.A.), psychology studies (M.A.), and social and behavioral studies (M.S.). These programs incorporate the University course work to fulfill the content phase of the program.

In addition to master's degree options, the Graduate Program in Interdisciplinary Studies offers four graduate certificates. Certificate programs are designed for those who wish to strengthen their workplace credentials or to pursue knowledge outside the structure of a degree program. Three 15-hour certificate programs are offered: cultures and social concepts, in which the student pursues interdisciplinary understanding of the relationship between cultural concepts and social movements; planning for success, which includes contexts for and strategies of management; and professional communication, which is a blend of written and Web presentation, grant writing, teaching, and training, all underpinned by a study of great presenters. The Graduate Program in Interdisciplinary Studies also offers an 18-credit-hour certificate in psychology studies.

Research Facilities

Learning resources include multimedia classrooms, computer laboratories, computer-assisted instruction, nursing and health assessment labs, and laboratories for the basic sciences. The Robert C. Byrd Learning Resource Center includes a student-centered library and media center. The collection comprises more than 95,000 titles, supplemented both by interlibrary loan and by extensive electronic resources, including ProQuest, CINAHL (Cumulative Index to Nursing and Allied Health Literature), Social Issues Resources Series (SIRS), EBSCOhost, Westlaw, Wilson Web, Newsbank, and Medline. Technology resources include state-of-the-art telecommunication links, equipment, and high-speed access and software.

Financial Aid

Eligible graduate students may qualify for Federal Stafford Student Loans. Prospective students must submit the Free Application for Federal Student Aid (FAFSA) for determination of eligibility. Most graduate students receive some sort of financial assistance.

Cost of Study

Tuition for 2009–10 is $335 per credit hour. Payment plans are available.

Living and Housing Costs

Many affordable housing opportunities are available in the neighborhoods surrounding the campus and in other nearby areas, which range from suburban to rural. Graduate students may also live on campus. Residence hall fees for 2009–10 are $1500 per semester for double occupancy and $2150 per semester for a private room (subject to availability). Students living on campus are required to purchase one of the University's meal plans.

Student Group

Mountain State University serves more than 8,000 students a year. Graduate enrollment and programming have grown steadily since the University's first graduate program was launched in 1998.

Location

Mountain State University's main campus is located near downtown Beckley, West Virginia, a small city that serves as a regional center for business, health care, education, and tourism in the heart of the southern West Virginia mountains. The Beckley area offers the quiet of a small town with a wealth of recreational and cultural opportunities. Nearby recreational opportunities include white-water rafting on the famed New and Gauley Rivers, skiing, hiking, biking, climbing and rappelling, and other outdoor pursuits. Beckley is an hour's drive from the state capital of Charleston and just a few hours from Pittsburgh, Pennsylvania; Washington, D.C.; and other eastern metropolitan areas.

The University

For seventy-five years, Mountain State University has been a leader in overcoming barriers to higher education and in offering academic programs that combine a liberal arts foundation with career-oriented studies. The University features innovative programming, flexible learning arrangements, well-qualified and deeply committed faculty members, and outstanding student services, all in a relaxed atmosphere.

Applying

Admission to the Graduate Program in Interdisciplinary Studies is open to students with a bachelor's degree from a regionally accredited college or university. There are no standardized test requirements, although on admission, a writing sample may be required for advising and assessment purposes. Students intending a psychology studies emphasis should refer to the online graduate catalog for additional admission requirements.

Applicants should submit a graduate application and arrange for official transcripts of all undergraduate studies and any graduate work to be sent directly to the School of Graduate Studies. Students can apply, enroll, and begin their studies at any time during the academic year.

Because of the individualized nature of the program, it is recommended that applicants discuss their educational goals with a program representative either before they apply or as soon as possible after acceptance.

Correspondence and Information

Mountain State University
Box 9003
Beckley, West Virginia 25802-9003
Phone: 304-929-INFO (4636)
866-FOR-MSU1 (866-367-6781) (toll-free)
E-mail: gomsu@mountainstate.edu
Web site: http://www.mountainstate.edu

Mountain State University

THE GRADUATE FACULTY

For information about faculty members, students should visit http://www.mountainstate.edu/majors/whystudy/gids/default.aspx.

NEW YORK UNIVERSITY

Gallatin School of Individualized Study

Program of Study

The Gallatin School offers an M.A. degree in individualized study. Working closely with a faculty adviser, self-motivated students have the opportunity to develop an individually tailored, interdisciplinary educational program. Students master an area of concentration that integrates study in several disciplines. For example, a student who is interested in the arts and community could combine courses in educational theater, arts administration, and sociology; a student with an interest in the cultural history of the United States might combine English with history and museum studies; a student with an interest in communications might develop a program to include course work in cinema studies, gender studies, and media ecology; and a student wishing to study the European Union might combine course work in politics, history, and social policy. A student's course of study is not limited to these examples. Students are encouraged to design a program according to their individual needs and interests. With the adviser, the student designs a 40-credit M.A. program consisting of course work and other options that may include independent study, tutorials, internships, and private lessons in the arts.

The course work is taken in the various graduate schools of NYU, such as the Graduate School of Arts and Science; the Stern School of Business; the Wagner Graduate School of Public Service; the Steinhardt School of Culture, Education, and Human Development; the School of Continuing and Professional Studies; the Silver School of Social Work; and the Tisch School of the Arts (selected courses). In addition to course work, independent study and tutorials allow students to pursue in-depth research, while internships and private lessons enable students to take advantage of the resources of New York City. The program requires 40 credits; students may apply for a maximum of 12 transfer credits and/or course-equivalency credits, which are based on previous work experience or training. A thesis is required and can be a traditional research paper, an applied project, or an artistic endeavor, such as a performance, a novel, or a work of visual art.

During the first year and a half, the curriculum for full-time students consists primarily of course work from the various schools of NYU along with independent study, tutorials, and internships (if desired). Students may attend on a full-time or part-time basis. Full-time students usually complete the program in 2 or 2½ years; part-time students generally complete the program in three to four years but are given up to six years.

Research Facilities

NYU's Bobst Library, one of the largest open-stack research libraries in the nation, houses nearly 3.9 million volumes, 41,000 journal subscriptions, and over 5 million microforms, and provides access to thousands of electronic resources on site and via the Internet. Bobst, the flagship of a nine-library, 5.1 million-volume system, offers specialized reference centers, providing students with wireless access, computer workstations and classrooms, study spaces, and 24-hour access. Included in the system are the Avery Fisher Center for Music and Media, the Fales Collection of English and American Literature, and the Tamiment Library for research in labor history and politics. Beyond Bobst, there is the Courant Institute of Mathematical Sciences library, focusing on mathematics and computer science; the Stephen Chan Library of Fine Arts at the Institute of Fine Arts, which houses collections in art history and archaeology; the Jack Brause Real Estate Library at the Real Estate Institute; and the Institute for the Study of the Ancient World library. Additional collections include the Frederick L. Ehrman Medical Library of NYU's School of Medicine, the Dental Center's Waldmann Memorial Library, and the School of Law's library.

In addition to dozens of other research centers, the following international cultural centers are available for student use: Casa Italiana Zerilli-Marimò, Glucksman Ireland House, Bronfman Center for Jewish Student Life, King Juan Carlos I of Spain Center, La Maison Française, Deutsches Haus, and Hagop Kevorkian Center.

The Grey Art Gallery, the University's fine arts museum, presents innovative exhibitions each year that encompass all aspects of the visual arts.

NYU's Information Technology Services (ITS) provides computer, network, telephone, and Internet services to students and the entire University. It connects people to their work and studies and to the information, training, and technical resources they need to achieve their goals. ITS supports the broad spectrum of University activities and technology services for students, in support of research, scholarship, and instruction.

Financial Aid

Scholarships, work-study opportunities, loans, and a deferred-payment plan are available. Financial aid is awarded on the basis of merit and demonstrated financial need to both full-time and part-time students. To be considered for a Gallatin Scholarship, students must submit the Free Application for Federal Student Aid (FAFSA). Resident assistantships and student employment are also available.

In 2008–09, 58 percent of graduate students received some form of aid; of those receiving aid, 75 percent received scholarships/grants, 82 percent received loans, and 6 percent received work-study. The range of scholarship/grant packages was $250–$57,473. The range of loan packages was $1312–$60,253.

In addition to the Gallatin Scholarship, other sources of financial support include the following: The Catherine B. Reynolds Program in Social Entrepreneurship at New York University, a comprehensive initiative designed to train the next generation of leaders in public service, offering 20 graduate fellowships each year (http://www.nyu.edu/reynolds); Foreign Language and Area Studies (FLAS) Fellowships, visit the Web site of one of these three designated National Resource Centers at NYU, Center for European and Mediterranean Studies (http://cems.as.nyu.edu/object/cems.grad.fellowships.html), The Hagop Kevorkian Center (http://www.nyu.edu/gsas/program/neareast/4_FLAS.html), or the Center for Latin American and Caribbean Studies (http://www.nyu.edu/gsas/program/latin/FLAS_PAGE.htm); Residential Education Assistantship Opportunities: Resident Assistants and Community Education Assistants (http://www.nyu.edu/residential.education/staff/studentselection/index.html); NYU America Reads/America Counts (http://www.steinhardt.nyu.edu/americareads); New York State Tuition Assistance Program (http://www.nyu.edu/financial.aid/tap.html); and part-time students and international students (http://www.nyu.edu/financial.aid).

Cost of Study

Tuition for the 2008–09 academic year at Gallatin was $1159 per credit per term, plus additional nonrefundable registration and services fees. Tuition is paid per credit, per term. The University offers a comprehensive health insurance benefit plan at $2170 per year. Full-time and international students are automatically enrolled in this plan unless they already have comparable coverage.

Living and Housing Costs

Graduate student housing at NYU provides the advantages of apartment-style living with the convenience, security, activities, and supportive environment of residence hall life. Several types of accommodations are offered to suit different preferences and budgets, including shared studios, double rooms in one- and two-bedroom apartments, and a limited number of private rooms in two- and three-person suites. Off-campus housing is also available at market rates. Meal plans are available but not required. For further information, students may visit http://www.nyu.edu/housing.

Student Group

There are approximately 200 graduate students in the Gallatin School. Half of the students are from the New York metropolitan area, while the other half comes from across the country as well as from international locations. Because of the diversity offered in the Gallatin School, students come from a wide range of undergraduate disciplines.

Student Outcomes

Because of the individualized nature of Gallatin, graduates embark on a wide variety of professions. In the arts, graduates include choreographers, artistic directors of dance and theater companies, performers, writers, arts administrators, curators, and museum directors. Graduates in the arts often remain in academia, teaching the arts at all levels, from elementary to university. In the field of finance, Gallatin graduates hold positions in such firms as Oppenheimer & Company, the Bank of America, and Citigroup. Others enter the fields of nutrition, psychotherapy, journalism, education, and communications, while many have obtained positions in government, social, and environmental agencies. Graduates have also entered Ph.D. programs in such areas as literature, sociology, cinema, performance studies, cultural studies, educational theater, history, music composition, and political science.

Location

NYU's Gallatin School is located in historic Greenwich Village, which is known for its small-scale, European style of living. NYU's campus is within minutes of Broadway and off-Broadway drama and dance, art galleries, coffeehouses, restaurants, clubs, bookstores, and world-renowned museums and libraries. The Jerome S. Coles Sports and Recreation Center and the Palladium Athletic Facility serve the recreational needs of all students.

The University

NYU is a private university, comprising fourteen schools and colleges. The University was founded in 1831 by Albert Gallatin, treasury secretary under Thomas Jefferson, and other prominent New Yorkers who believed that the place for a university was not in "the seclusion of cloistered halls but in the throbbing heart of a great city." In this spirit, the Gallatin School was founded in 1972.

Applying

Students may be admitted for the fall or spring semesters. In addition to official transcripts, two letters of recommendation and a statement of purpose are required.

Correspondence and Information

Director of Graduate Admissions
Gallatin School of Individualized Study
New York University
715 Broadway, 6th Floor
New York, New York 10003-6806
Phone: 212-998-7370
Web site: http://www.nyu.edu/info/gallatin09

New York University

THE FACULTY

Students in the Gallatin School take courses in the various graduate schools of New York University. Essentially, the entire graduate faculty of the University instructs Gallatin students. The following is a list of Gallatin faculty members.

Susanne Wofford, Ph.D., Yale. Dean, Gallatin School of Individualized Study. Shakespeare, Spenser, Renaissance and classical epic, comparative European drama, and narrative and literary theory.

Sinan Antoon, Ph.D., Harvard. Premodern Arab-Islamic culture and contemporary Arab culture and politics.

Gene Cittadino, Ph.D., Wisconsin. Understanding and interpreting the historical and present role of scientific knowledge in our culture, the interaction of science and cultural values in the shaping of environmental policy.

Nina Cornyetz, Ph.D., Columbia. Critical, literary, and filmic theory; intellectual history; gender and sexuality; cultural studies with a specialization in Japan.

Michael D. Dinwiddie, M.F.A., NYU. Cultural studies, African American theater history, dramatic writing, filmmaking, and ragtime music.

Stephen Duncombe, Ph.D., CUNY Graduate Center. Media and cultural studies, history of the mass and alternative media, intersection of culture and politics.

Sharon Friedman, Ph.D., NYU. Literary interpretation, feminist criticism, women dramatists, critical writing across the curriculum.

Lisa Goldfarb, Ph.D., CUNY Graduate Center. Comparative literature and writing, nineteenth- and twentieth-century European and American poetry and fiction, music and literature, philosophic questions in literature, literature and history of New York City.

Jean Graybeal, Ph.D., Syracuse. Philosophy and psychology of religion, phenomenology, feminist theory, the question of embodiment.

Karen Hornick, Ph.D., Columbia. Literature, media, philosophy, cultural history, writing.

Kristin Horton, M.F.A., Iowa. Directing, Shakespeare, new play development, theater and cross-cultural dialogue, reinventing the classics for the contemporary stage.

Steven Hutkins, Ph.D., NYU. Theme of place and literature: the places where we live and travel, the places that have been imagined by writers and philosophers.

Bradley Lewis, Ph.D., George Washington; M.D., Tennessee. Interface of medicine, humanities, cultural studies of science, disability studies.

Ritty Lukose, Ph.D., Chicago. Gender, globalization, and colonial, postcolonial, and diasporic modernities as they impact South Asia—particularly youth development, consumption, citizenship, politics, and gender and feminist issues.

Julie Malnig, Ph.D., NYU. Social and popular dance, the history of popular entertainments, performance art, feminist performance and criticism, performance writing.

Eve Meltzer, Ph.D., Berkeley. Contemporary art history, photography, material culture, and a range of philosophical and theoretical discourses, including psychoanalysis, structuralism, and phenomenology.

M. Bella Mirabella, Ph.D., Rutgers. Literature and culture of the Renaissance, including the ancient and medieval periods, with a focus on drama, theater, performance, and gender.

Ali Mirsepassi, Ph.D., American. Middle Eastern studies, social theory, sociology of religion, Islam and modernity, intellectual history, Iranian studies.

David Thornton Moore, Ed.D., Harvard. History of social thought and contemporary social issues, work reform and experiential learning, innovations in higher education.

Sara Murphy, Ph.D. NYU. Literature and philosophy, critical theory, feminist and gender studies, nineteenth-century literary cultures.

Kimberly Phillips-Fein, Ph.D., Columbia. American political, business, and labor history; history of economic thought; the role of business in the development of the modern conservative movement in the second half of the twentieth century; the role of economic ideas in the rise of conservatism.

Stacy Pies, Ph.D., CUNY, Graduate Center. Poetry, world literature—narrative across the disciplines and narrative theology, literary criticism, literature and philosophy, writing on cities and urbanism.

René Francisco Poitevin, Ph.D., California, Davis. Local labor markets, gentrification, race and ethnicity in the United States, geographic information systems.

Millery Polyné, Ph.D., Michigan–Ann Arbor. History of African American and Afro-Caribbean/Afro-Latino cultural, political, and economic initiatives in the nineteenth and twentieth centuries; cultural studies; dance; race and sports; jazz.

Laurin Raiken, M.A., Adelphi. Sociology and political economy of the arts; arts management and cultural policy; arts, community, and social change; Native American studies; the relationship between Kabbalah and art.

George Shulman, Ph.D., Berkeley. Political thought and American studies, political thought in Europe and the United States, tragic and biblical traditions.

Laura M. Slatkin, Ph.D., Harvard. Ancient Greek and Roman poetry—especially epic and drama, wisdom traditions in classical and Near Eastern antiquity, gender studies, anthropological approaches to the literature of the ancient Mediterranean world, cultural poetics.

Matthew Stanley, Ph.D., Harvard. History and philosophy of science.

Clyde R. Taylor, Ph.D., Wayne State. Politics of representation, vernacular modernisms, cinema and society, African American and African literature, cultural symbolism.

Jack (John Kuo Wei) Tchen, Ph.D., NYU. Cross-cultural and community studies; New York City history; Asians in the Americas; race, colonialism, and museums; dialogic theory; radical pedagogy.

Alejandro Velasco, Ph.D., Duke. History of modern Latin America, social movements, urban culture, democratization.

E. Frances White, Ph.D., Boston University. History of Africa and its diaspora; history of gender and sexuality; critical race theory.

A Gallatin professor talks with students.

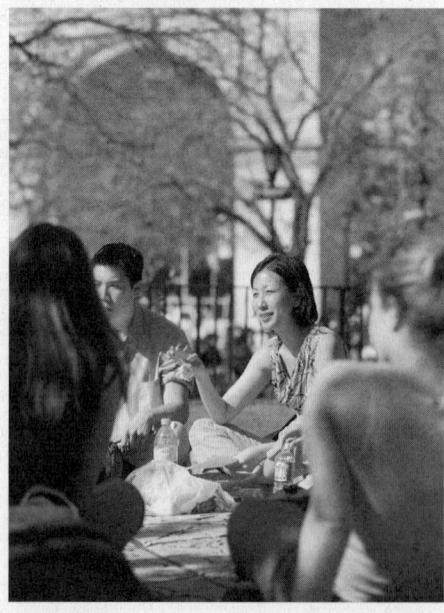

Gallatin students use Washington Square Park as an outdoor classroom.

ACADEMIC AND PROFESSIONAL
PROGRAMS IN THE SOCIAL SCIENCES

Section 15
Area and Cultural Studies

This section contains a directory of institutions offering graduate work in area and cultural studies, followed by in-depth entries submitted by institutions that chose to prepare detailed program descriptions. Additional information about programs listed in the directory but not augmented by an in-depth entry may be obtained by writing directly to the dean of a graduate school or chair of a department at the address given in the directory.

For programs offering related work, see also in this book *Geography, History, Language and Literature, Political Science and International Affairs,* and *Sociology, Anthropology, and Archaeology.*

CONTENTS

Program Directories

African-American Studies 580
African Studies 581
American Indian/Native American Studies 583
American Studies 584
Asian-American Studies 588
Asian Studies 588
Canadian Studies 593
Cultural Studies 594
East European and Russian Studies 596
Ethnic Studies 598
Folklore 598
Gender Studies 599
Hispanic Studies 600
Holocaust Studies 602
Jewish Studies 602
Latin American Studies 604
Near and Middle Eastern Studies 608
Northern Studies 611
Pacific Area/Pacific Rim Studies 611
Western European Studies 611
Women's Studies 613

Close-Ups

George Mason University 619
Sarah Lawrence College 621
Seton Hall University 623
Washington University in St. Louis 625

See also:

American University—International Service 861
California Institute of Integral Studies—Humanities 347
Central European University—Social Sciences and Humanities 349
The Jewish Theological Seminary—Graduate Studies 529
Seton Hall University—Jewish-Christian Studies 533
University of California, San Diego—International Relations and Pacific Studies 881

African-American Studies

Boston University, Graduate School of Arts and Sciences, Program in African American Studies, Boston, MA 02215. Offers MA. *Degree requirements:* For master's, one foreign language, comprehensive exam. *Entrance requirements:* For master's, GRE General Test, 2 letters of recommendation. Additional exam requirements/recommendations for international students: Required—TOEFL (minimum score 550 paper-based; 213 computer-based).

Carnegie Mellon University, College of Humanities and Social Sciences, Department of History, Pittsburgh, PA 15213-3891. Offers African and African-American diaspora (PhD); culture and power (PhD); gender and the family (PhD); history (MA, MS); history and policy (MA); labor and politics (PhD); science, technology, medicine and environment (PhD). Part-time programs available. *Degree requirements:* For doctorate, oral and written comprehensive exams, dissertation defense. *Entrance requirements:* For doctorate, GRE General Test. Additional exam requirements/recommendations for international students: Required—TOEFL. Electronic applications accepted. *Faculty research:* Anthropology and history, African American history, technology/environment, cultural history analysis.

Clark Atlanta University, School of Arts and Sciences, Department of African-American Studies, Atlanta, GA 30314. Offers MA, DAH. Part-time programs available. *Faculty:* 1 full-time (0 women), 1 (woman) part-time/adjunct. *Students:* 13 full-time (11 women), 18 part-time (13 women); includes 27 minority (all African Americans), 2 international. Average age 38. 9 applicants, 89% accepted, 3 enrolled. In 2008, 3 master's, 2 doctorates awarded. *Degree requirements:* For master's, one foreign language, thesis. *Entrance requirements:* For master's, GRE General Test, minimum GPA of 2.5. Additional exam requirements/recommendations for international students: Required—TOEFL (minimum score 500 paper-based; 173 computer-based). *Application deadline:* For fall admission, 4/1 for domestic and international students; for spring admission, 11/1 for domestic and international students. Applications are processed on a rolling basis. Application fee: $40 ($55 for international students). Electronic applications accepted. *Expenses:* Tuition: Full-time $12,240; part-time $680 per credit hour. Required fees: $710; $355 per semester. *Financial support:* Scholarships/grants available. Financial award application deadline: 4/30; financial award applicants required to submit FAFSA. *Unit head:* Dr. Josephine Bradley, Chairperson, 404-880-6810, E-mail: jbradley@cau.edu. *Application contact:* Michelle Clark-Davis, Graduate Program Admissions, 404-880-6605, E-mail: cauadmissions@cau.edu.

Clark Atlanta University, School of Arts and Sciences, Department of Africana Women's Studies, Atlanta, GA 30314. Offers MA, DAH. Part-time programs available. *Faculty:* 1 (woman) full-time, 1 part-time/adjunct (0 women). *Students:* 4 full-time (all women), 9 part-time (8 women); includes 12 minority (all African Americans), 1 international. Average age 34. 6 applicants, 67% accepted, 1 enrolled. In 2008, 2 master's, 4 doctorates awarded. *Degree requirements:* For master's, one foreign language, thesis; for doctorate, 2 foreign languages, thesis/dissertation. *Entrance requirements:* For master's, GRE General Test, minimum GPA of 2.5; for doctorate, GRE General Test, minimum graduate GPA of 3.0. Additional exam requirements/recommendations for international students: Required—TOEFL (minimum score 500 paper-based; 173 computer-based). *Application deadline:* For fall admission, 4/1 for domestic and international students; for spring admission, 11/1 for domestic and international students. Applications are processed on a rolling basis. Application fee: $40 ($55 for international students). Electronic applications accepted. *Expenses:* Tuition: Full-time $12,240; part-time $680 per credit hour. Required fees: $710; $355 per semester. *Financial support:* Scholarships/grants available. Financial award application deadline: 4/30; financial award applicants required to submit FAFSA. *Faculty research:* Concerns of women of African descent globally. *Unit head:* Dr. Josephine Bradley, Chairperson, 404-880-6810, E-mail: jbradley@cau.edu. *Application contact:* Michelle Clark-Davis, Graduate Program Admissions, 404-880-6605, E-mail: cauadmissions@cau.edu.

Columbia University, Graduate School of Arts and Sciences, Program in African-American Studies, New York, NY 10027. Offers MA. Part-time programs available.

Cornell University, Graduate School, Graduate Fields of Arts and Sciences, Field of African and African-American Studies, Ithaca, NY 14853-0001. Offers African studies (MPS); African-American studies (MPS). *Faculty:* 15 full-time (6 women). *Students:* 15 full-time (10 women); includes 13 minority (11 African Americans, 2 Hispanic Americans). Average age 29. 31 applicants, 29% accepted, 7 enrolled. In 2008, 4 master's awarded. *Degree requirements:* For master's, thesis. *Entrance requirements:* For master's, GRE General Test (recommended), 3 letters of recommendation. Additional exam requirements/recommendations for international students: Required—TOEFL (minimum score 550 paper-based; 213 computer-based; 77 iBT). *Application deadline:* For fall admission, 1/30 for domestic students. Application fee: $70. Electronic applications accepted. *Expenses:* Tuition: Full-time $29,500. Required fees: $70. Full-time tuition and fees vary according to degree level, program and student level. *Financial support:* In 2008–09, 14 students received support, including 7 fellowships with full tuition reimbursements available, 7 teaching assistantships with full tuition reimbursements available; research assistantships, institutionally sponsored loans, scholarships/grants, health care benefits, tuition waivers (full and partial), and unspecified assistantships also available. Financial award applicants required to submit FAFSA. *Faculty research:* African-American literature, art, cinema and theater; African-American politics and public policy; African history, politics and art; Caribbean politics and Africana Diaspora. *Unit head:* Director of Graduate Studies, 607-255-4625, Fax: 607-255-0784. *Application contact:* Graduate Field Assistant, 607-255-4625, Fax: 607-255-0784, E-mail: spt1@cornell.edu.

Cornell University, Graduate School, Graduate Fields of Arts and Sciences, Field of English Language and Literature, Ithaca, NY 14853-0001. Offers African-American literature (PhD); American literature after 1865 (PhD); American literature to 1865 (PhD); American studies (PhD); colonial and postcolonial literature (PhD); creative writing (MFA); cultural studies (PhD); dramatic literature (PhD); English poetry (PhD); English Renaissance to 1660 (PhD); lesbian, bisexual, and gay literature studies (PhD); literary criticism and theory (PhD); nineteenth century (PhD); Old and Middle English (PhD); prose fiction (PhD); Restoration and eighteenth century (PhD); twentieth century (PhD); women's literature (PhD); MFA/PhD. *Faculty:* 54 full-time (27 women). *Students:* 100 full-time (53 women); includes 24 minority (8 African Americans, 4 American Indian/Alaska Native, 6 Asian Americans or Pacific Islanders, 6 Hispanic Americans), 14 international. Average age 29. 821 applicants, 6% accepted, 23 enrolled. In 2008, 19 master's, 12 doctorates awarded. Terminal master's awarded for partial completion of doctoral program. *Degree requirements:* For master's, one foreign language, thesis; for doctorate, one foreign language, comprehensive exam, thesis/dissertation, teaching experience. *Entrance requirements:* For master's, GRE General Test, 3 letters of recommendation, creative writing sample; for doctorate, GRE General Test, GRE Subject Test (English), 3 letters of recommendation, writing sample. Additional exam requirements/recommendations for international students: Required—TOEFL (minimum score 600 paper-based; 250 computer-based; 77 iBT). *Application deadline:* For fall admission, 1/10 for domestic students. Application fee: $70. Electronic applications accepted. *Expenses:* Tuition: Full-time $29,500. Required fees: $70. Full-time tuition and fees vary according to degree level, program and student level. *Financial support:* In 2008–09, 96 students received support, including 41 fellowships with full tuition reimbursements available, 1 research assistantship with full tuition reimbursement available, 54 teaching assistantships with full tuition reimbursements available; institutionally sponsored loans, scholarships/grants, health care benefits, tuition waivers (full and partial), and unspecified assistantships also available. Financial award applicants required to submit FAFSA. *Faculty research:* English and American literature, women's writing, ethnic and post-colonial literature, critical theory, medievalism. *Unit head:* Director of Graduate Studies, 607-255-7989, Fax: 607-255-6661. *Application contact:* Graduate Field Assistant, 607-255-7989, Fax: 607-255-6661, E-mail: english_grad@cornell.edu.

Eastern Michigan University, Graduate School, College of Arts and Sciences, Department of African-American Studies, Ypsilanti, MI 48197. Offers Graduate Certificate.

Florida Agricultural and Mechanical University, Division of Graduate Studies, Research, and Continuing Education, College of Arts and Sciences, Division of History and Political Sciences, Program in Applied Social Science, Tallahassee, FL 32307-3200. Offers African American history (MASS); criminal justice (MASS); economics (MASS); history (MASS); political science (MASS); public administration (MASS); public management (MASS); social work (MASS); sociology (MASS). Part-time programs available. *Degree requirements:* For master's, thesis optional. *Entrance requirements:* For master's, GRE General Test, minimum GPA of 3.0. *Faculty research:* Southern history, black history, election trends, presidential history.

Harvard University, Graduate School of Arts and Sciences, Department of African and African American Studies, Cambridge, MA 02138. Offers PhD. *Expenses:* Tuition: Full-time $32,556. Required fees: $1426. Full-time tuition and fees vary according to program and student level.

Indiana University Bloomington, University Graduate School, College of Arts and Sciences, Department of African American and African Diaspora Studies, Bloomington, IN 47405-7000. Offers MA. Part-time programs available. *Faculty:* 3 full-time (1 woman). *Students:* 14 full-time (9 women), 4 part-time (3 women); includes 13 minority (all African Americans), 4 international. Average age 29. 17 applicants, 88% accepted, 9 enrolled. In 2008, 7 master's awarded. *Entrance requirements:* For master's, GRE, minimum GPA of 3.0. Additional exam requirements/recommendations for international students: Required—TOEFL. *Application deadline:* For fall admission, 1/15 priority date for domestic students, 12/15 for international students; for spring admission, 9/1 for domestic and international students. Applications are processed on a rolling basis. Application fee: $50 ($60 for international students). Electronic applications accepted. *Expenses:* Tuition, area resident: Part-time $291.97 per credit hour. Tuition, state resident: part-time $291.97 per credit hour. Tuition, nonresident: part-time $850.33 per credit hour. Required fees: $110 per semester. Tuition and fees vary according to course load and program. *Financial support:* Fellowships with tuition reimbursements, research assistantships with tuition reimbursements, teaching assistantships with tuition reimbursements available. *Unit head:* Dr. Valerie Grim, Chair, 812-855-3875. *Application contact:* Yunika Jackson, Department Secretary, 812-855-3875, E-mail: ytjackso@indiana.edu.

Michigan State University, The Graduate School, College of Arts and Letters, Program in African American and African Studies, East Lansing, MI 48824. Offers MA, PhD. *Entrance requirements:* Additional exam requirements/recommendations for international students: Required—TOEFL. Electronic applications accepted. *Faculty research:* Black American and diasporic studies, comparative communities of color.

Morgan State University, School of Graduate Studies, College of Liberal Arts, Department of History and Geography, Baltimore, MD 21251. Offers African-American studies (MA); history (MA, PhD). Part-time and evening/weekend programs available. *Degree requirements:* For master's, comprehensive exam, thesis; for doctorate, comprehensive exam, thesis/dissertation. *Entrance requirements:* For master's, minimum GPA of 2.5; for doctorate, GRE or MAT. Additional exam requirements/recommendations for international students: Required—TOEFL (minimum score 550 paper-based; 213 computer-based). *Faculty research:* Women's history, African diaspora history, urban history.

North Carolina Agricultural and Technical State University, Graduate School, College of Arts and Sciences, Department of English, Program in English and Afro-American Literature, Greensboro, NC 27411. Offers MA. Part-time and evening/weekend programs available. *Degree requirements:* For master's, comprehensive exam, qualifying exam. *Entrance requirements:* For master's, GRE General Test, minimum GPA of 3.0.

The Ohio State University, Graduate School, College of Humanities, Department of African-American and African Studies, Columbus, OH 43210. Offers MA. *Degree requirements:* For master's, comprehensive exam, internship or thesis. *Entrance requirements:* For master's, GRE General Test. Additional exam requirements/recommendations for international students: Required—TOEFL (minimum score 600 paper-based; 250 computer-based). Electronic applications accepted.

Rutgers, The State University of New Jersey, New Brunswick, Graduate School, Program in History, Piscataway, NJ 08854-8097. Offers African-American history (PhD); early American history (PhD); early modern European history (PhD); east Asian history (PhD); global and comparative history (PhD); history (PhD); history of diplomacy and foreign relations (PhD); history of technology, environment and health (PhD); history of the Atlantic cultures and African diaspora (PhD); Latin American history (PhD); medieval history (PhD); modern European history (PhD); nineteenth and twentieth century American history (PhD); women's and gender history (PhD). *Degree requirements:* For doctorate, thesis/dissertation. *Entrance requirements:* For doctorate, GRE General Test, sample of written work. Electronic applications accepted. *Faculty research:* American history, European history, Afro-American history, women's history, Latin American history.

Syracuse University, Graduate School, College of Arts and Sciences, Program in Pan-African Studies, Syracuse, NY 13244. Offers MA. *Entrance requirements:* For master's, GRE General Test. Additional exam requirements/recommendations for international students: Required—TOEFL. Electronic applications accepted.

Temple University, Graduate School, College of Liberal Arts, Department of African American Studies, Philadelphia, PA 19122-6096. Offers MA, PhD. Terminal master's awarded for partial completion of doctoral program. *Degree requirements:* For master's, comprehensive exam; for doctorate, one foreign language, thesis/dissertation, oral and written qualifying exams. *Entrance requirements:* For doctorate, MA in African American studies. Additional exam requirements/recommendations for international students: Required—TOEFL (minimum score 550 paper-based; 213 computer-based; 79 iBT). Electronic applications accepted. *Faculty research:* Afrocentric theory; African-American youth; centered drama, literature, and history; comparative analysis; South and West Africa; Nile Valley.

University at Albany, State University of New York, College of Arts and Sciences, Department of Africana Studies, Albany, NY 12222-0001. Offers African studies (MA); Afro-American studies (MA). Part-time and evening/weekend programs available. *Entrance requirements:* Additional exam requirements/recommendations for international students: Required—TOEFL (minimum score 550 paper-based; 213 computer-based). Electronic applications accepted. *Faculty research:* The black family, Afro-centricity in poetry, black women in U.S. literature, African economic development, African American history.

University of California, Berkeley, Graduate Division, College of Letters and Science, Department of African American Studies, Berkeley, CA 94720-1500. Offers PhD. *Degree requirements:* For doctorate, one foreign language, thesis/dissertation. *Entrance requirements:* For doctorate, minimum GPA of 3.0, 3 letters of recommendation. Additional exam requirements/recommendations for international students: Required—TOEFL (paper-based 570; computer-based 230) or IELTS (paper-based 7). *Faculty research:* Black influence on U.S. foreign policy, black intellectuals, ethnic space in urban society, representation in museums of African-Americans and British Americans during slavery.

University of California, Los Angeles, Graduate Division, College of Letters and Science, Program in Afro-American Studies, Los Angeles, CA 90095. Offers MA, MA/JD. *Students:* 28 full-time (18 women); includes 27 minority (25 African Americans, 2 Hispanic Americans). Average age 27. 41 applicants, 54% accepted, 11 enrolled. In 2008, 7 master's awarded. *Degree requirements:* For master's, one foreign language, comprehensive exam or thesis. *Entrance requirements:* For master's, GRE General Test, minimum GPA of 3.0, sample of written work. *Application deadline:* For fall admission, 12/15 for domestic and international students. Application fee: $60 ($80 for international students). Electronic applications accepted.

Expenses: Tuition, nonresident: full-time $14,694. Required fees: $9669.50. Full-time tuition and fees vary according to course load, degree level, program and student level. *Financial support:* In 2008–09, 26 fellowships with full and partial tuition reimbursements, 4 research assistantships with full and partial tuition reimbursements, 5 teaching assistantships with full and partial tuition reimbursements were awarded; Federal Work-Study, institutionally sponsored loans, scholarships/grants, health care benefits, tuition waivers (full and partial), and unspecified assistantships also available. Financial award application deadline: 3/1; financial award applicants required to submit FAFSA. *Unit head:* Brenda Stevenson, Chair, 310-825-7403. *Application contact:* Departmental Office, 310-825-9821, E-mail: idpstaff@bunche.ucla.edu.

The University of Iowa, Graduate College, College of Liberal Arts and Sciences, Program in African American World Studies, Iowa City, IA 52242-1316. Offers MA. *Degree requirements:* For master's, thesis optional, exam. *Entrance requirements:* For master's, GRE General Test, minimum GPA of 3.0. Additional exam requirements/recommendations for international students: Required—TOEFL (minimum score 550 paper-based; 213 computer-based; 81 iBT). Electronic applications accepted.

The University of Kansas, Graduate Studies, College of Liberal Arts and Sciences, Department of African and African-American Studies, Lawrence, KS 66045. Offers African and African-American studies (MA); African Studies (Graduate Certificate). *Faculty:* 10. *Degree requirements:* For master's, variable foreign language requirement, thesis or alternative. *Entrance requirements:* For master's, GRE, all academic transcripts, 3 letters of recommendation, personal statement of purpose, writing sample. Additional exam requirements/recommendations for international students: Required—TOEFL. *Application deadline:* For fall admission, 5/1 for domestic students. Applications are processed on a rolling basis. Application fee: $45 ($50 for international students). Electronic applications accepted. *Expenses:* Tuition, area resident: Full-time $6122; part-time $255.10 per credit hour. Tuition, state resident: full-time $6122; part-time $255.10 per credit hour. Tuition, nonresident: full-time $14,629; part-time $609.55 per credit hour. Required fees: $847; $70.56 per credit hour. Tuition and fees vary according to course load and program. *Faculty research:* African Theatre, YaKuur Culture, interracial communication, African development and urban planning, African literature, Muslim women in West Africa, identity formation in African and Disaporan settings, African American history, North African and Arab societies, civil rights. *Unit head:* Dr. Peter Ukpokodu, Chair, 785-864-3054, Fax: 785-864-5330, E-mail: afs@ku.edu. *Application contact:* Dr. Peter Ukpokodu, Chair, 785-864-3054, Fax: 785-864-5330, E-mail: afs@ku.edu.

University of Louisville, Graduate School, College of Arts and Sciences, Department of Pan-African Studies, Louisville, KY 40292. Offers African and Diaspora studies (MA); African-American studies (MA); MA/MSW; MSSW/MA. Part-time programs available. *Faculty:* 12 full-time (6 women). *Students:* 11 full-time (7 women), 7 part-time (6 women); includes 15 African Americans, 1 international. Average age 30. 11 applicants, 55% accepted, 5 enrolled. In 2008, 4 master's awarded. *Degree requirements:* For master's, comprehensive exam, thesis optional. *Entrance requirements:* For master's, GRE General Test. Additional exam requirements/recommendations for international students: Recommended—TOEFL (minimum score 550 paper-based; 213 computer-based; 79 iBT). *Application deadline:* For fall admission, 10/15 for domestic and international students; for spring admission, 3/15 for domestic and international students. Application fee: $50. Electronic applications accepted. *Financial support:* In 2008–09, 10 students received support, including 8 teaching assistantships with tuition reimbursements available (averaging $1,200 per year). Financial award applicants required to submit FAFSA. *Faculty research:* African popular culture, black male identity development, education and retention, contemporary politics in Nigeria, poverty in the Caribbean. *Unit head:* Dr. Theresa Rajack-Talley, Chair, 502-852-4192, Fax: 502-852-5954, E-mail: tatall01@gwise.louisville.edu. *Application contact:* Dr. Theresa Rajack-Talley, Acting Graduate Studies Director, 502-852-4192, Fax: 502-852-5954, E-mail: tatall01@louisville.edu.

University of Massachusetts Amherst, Graduate School, College of Humanities and Fine Arts, Department of Afro-American Studies, Amherst, MA 01003. Offers MA, PhD. Part-time programs available. Terminal master's awarded for partial completion of doctoral program. *Degree requirements:* For master's, thesis or alternative; for doctorate, comprehensive exam, thesis/dissertation. *Entrance requirements:* For doctorate, writing sample. Additional exam requirements/recommendations for international students: Required—TOEFL (minimum score 550 paper-based; 213 computer-based; 79 iBT), IELTS (minimum score 6.5). Electronic applications accepted. *Expenses:* Tuition, area resident: Full-time $2640. Tuition, nonresident: full-time $9936. One-time fee: $332 full-time. Tuition and fees vary according to course load.

University of Wisconsin–Madison, Graduate School, College of Letters and Science, Department of Afro-American Studies, Madison, WI 53706-1380. Offers MA. *Degree requirements:* For master's, thesis or alternative. *Entrance requirements:* For master's, bachelor's degree in related field, minimum GPA of 3.0. Additional exam requirements/recommendations for international students: Required—TOEFL. Electronic applications accepted. *Faculty research:* Afro American art, history, music, literature, and culture.

West Virginia University, Eberly College of Arts and Sciences, Department of History, Morgantown, WV 26506. Offers African history (MA, PhD); African-American history (MA, PhD); American history (MA, PhD); Appalachian/regional history (MA, PhD); East Asian history (MA, PhD); European history (MA, PhD); history of science and technology (MA, PhD); Latin American history (MA). Part-time programs available. *Degree requirements:* For master's, one foreign language, thesis (for some programs), oral exam, thesis defense; for doctorate, one foreign language, comprehensive exam, thesis/dissertation, dissertation defense. *Entrance requirements:* For master's, GRE General Test, minimum GPA of 3.0; for doctorate, GRE General Test. Additional exam requirements/recommendations for international students: Required—TOEFL (minimum score 550 paper-based), IELTS (minimum score 6.5). Electronic applications accepted. *Faculty research:* U.S., Appalachia, modern Europe, Africa, colonial and post-colonial societies.

Yale University, Graduate School of Arts and Sciences, Interdisciplinary Program in African-American Studies, New Haven, CT 06520. Offers PhD. *Entrance requirements:* For doctorate, GRE General Test.

African Studies

Boston University, Graduate School of Arts and Sciences, Department of International Relations, Boston, MA 02215. Offers African studies (Certificate); international relations (MA); international relations and environmental policy management (MA); international relations and international communication (MA); JD/MA; MBA/MA. *Degree requirements:* For master's, one foreign language, comprehensive exam, thesis. *Entrance requirements:* For master's, GRE General Test, 3 letters of recommendation; for Certificate, GRE General Test. Additional exam requirements/recommendations for international students: Required—TOEFL (minimum score 600 paper-based; 250 computer-based).

California State University, Long Beach, Graduate Studies, College of Liberal Arts, Department of History, Long Beach, CA 90840. Offers Africa and the Middle East (MA); ancient/Medieval Europe (MA); Asia (MA); Latin America (MA); modern Europe (MA); United States (MA); world (MA). Part-time and evening/weekend programs available. *Faculty:* 17 full-time (11 women), 2 part-time/adjunct (1 woman). *Students:* 9 full-time (4 women), 45 part-time (18 women); includes 15 minority (2 African Americans, 3 Asian Americans or Pacific Islanders, 10 Hispanic Americans), 1 international. Average age 35. 40 applicants, 50% accepted, 11 enrolled. *Degree requirements:* For master's, one foreign language, comprehensive exam or thesis. *Application deadline:* For fall admission, 3/1 for domestic students. Applications are processed on a rolling basis. Application fee: $55. Electronic applications accepted. *Expenses:* Tuition, nonresident: full-time $11,160; part-time $372 per unit. Required fees: $4100; $1261 per semester. *Financial support:* Research assistantships, Federal Work-Study, institutionally sponsored loans, and scholarships/grants available. Financial award application deadline: 3/2. *Faculty research:* All periods of European and American history, recent Asian and African history. *Unit head:* Dr. Nancy L Quam-Wickham, Graduate Advisor, 562-985-4431, Fax: 562-985-5431, E-mail: quamwick@csulb.edu. *Application contact:* Dr. Houri Berberian, Graduate Advisor, 562-985-4524, Fax: 562-985-4431, E-mail: hberber@csulb.edu.

Carnegie Mellon University, College of Humanities and Social Sciences, Department of History, Pittsburgh, PA 15213-3891. Offers African and African-American diaspora (PhD); culture and power (PhD); gender and the family (PhD); history (MA, MS); history and policy (MA); labor and politics (PhD); science, technology, medicine and environment (PhD). Part-time programs available. *Degree requirements:* For doctorate, oral and written comprehensive exams, dissertation defense. *Entrance requirements:* For doctorate, GRE General Test. Additional exam requirements/recommendations for international students: Required—TOEFL. Electronic applications accepted. *Faculty research:* Anthropology and history, African American history, technology/environment, cultural history analysis.

Claremont Graduate University, Graduate Programs, School of Arts and Humanities, Department of History, Claremont, CA 91711-6160. Offers Africana history (Certificate); American studies and U.S. history (MA, PhD); archival studies (MA); early modern studies (MA, PhD); European studies (MA, PhD); oral history (MA, PhD); MBA/MA; MBA/PhD. *Faculty:* 3 full-time (2 women). *Students:* 67 full-time (33 women), 8 part-time (3 women); includes 15 minority (1 African American, 3 Asian Americans or Pacific Islanders, 11 Hispanic Americans), 1 international. Average age 35. In 2008, 6 master's, 8 doctorates awarded. Terminal master's awarded for partial completion of doctoral program. *Entrance requirements:* For master's and doctorate, GRE General Test. Additional exam requirements/recommendations for international students: Required—TOEFL (minimum score 550 paper-based; 213 computer-based; 80 iBT). *Application deadline:* For fall admission, 2/1 priority date for domestic students. Applications are processed on a rolling basis. Application fee: $60. Electronic applications accepted. *Expenses:* Tuition: Full-time $33,698; part-time $1465 per unit. Required fees: $310; $155 per semester. Tuition and fees vary according to program. *Financial support:* Fellowships, research assistantships, Federal Work-Study, institutionally sponsored loans, and scholarships/grants available. Support available to part-time students. Financial award application deadline: 2/15; financial award applicants required to submit FAFSA. *Faculty research:* Intellectual and social history, cultural studies, gender studies, Western history, Chicano history. *Unit head:* Janet Farrell Brodie, Chair, 909-621-8880, Fax: 909-621-8609, E-mail: janet.brodie@cgu.edu. *Application contact:* Justin Evans, Admissions Coordinator, 909-607-1278, E-mail: justin.evans@cgu.edu.

Claremont Graduate University, Graduate Programs, School of Educational Studies, Claremont, CA 91711-6160. Offers Africana education (Certificate); education and policy (MA, PhD); higher education/student affairs (MA, PhD); human development (MA, PhD); public school administration (MA, PhD); quantitative evaluation (MA, PhD); special education (MA, PhD); teacher education (MA); teaching and learning (MA, PhD); urban leadership (PhD); MBA/PhD. Part-time programs available. *Faculty:* 19 full-time (13 women), 1 part-time/adjunct (0 women). *Students:* 267 full-time (190 women), 202 part-time (146 women); includes 204 minority (55 African Americans, 1 American Indian/Alaska Native, 43 Asian Americans or Pacific Islanders, 105 Hispanic Americans), 7 international. Average age 37. In 2008, 81 master's, 34 doctorates, 1 other advanced degree awarded. Terminal master's awarded for partial completion of doctoral program. *Entrance requirements:* For master's and doctorate, GRE General Test. Additional exam requirements/recommendations for international students: Required—TOEFL (minimum score 550 paper-based; 213 computer-based; 80 iBT). *Application deadline:* For fall admission, 2/1 priority date for domestic students. Applications are processed on a rolling basis. Application fee: $60. Electronic applications accepted. *Expenses:* Tuition: Full-time $33,698; part-time $1465 per unit. Required fees: $310; $155 per semester. Tuition and fees vary according to program. *Financial support:* Fellowships, research assistantships, Federal Work-Study, institutionally sponsored loans, and scholarships/grants available. Support available to part-time students. Financial award application deadline: 2/15; financial award applicants required to submit FAFSA. *Faculty research:* Education administration, K-12 and higher education, multicultural education, education policy, diversity in higher education, faculty issues. *Unit head:* Margaret Grogan, Dean, 909-621-8075, Fax: 909-621-8734, E-mail: margaret.grogan@cgu.edu. *Application contact:* Nicole Kouyoumdjian, Director of External Affairs, 909-607-8493, Fax: 909-621-8734, E-mail: nicole.kouyoumdjian@cgu.edu.

Columbia University, School of International and Public Affairs, Institute of African Studies, New York, NY 10027. Offers Certificate. Students must be enrolled in a separate graduate degree program at Columbia University. Electronic applications accepted.

Cornell University, Graduate School, Graduate Fields of Arts and Sciences, Field of African and African-American Studies, Ithaca, NY 14853-0001. Offers African studies (MPS); African-American studies (MPS). *Faculty:* 15 full-time (6 women). *Students:* 15 full-time (10 women); includes 13 minority (11 African Americans, 2 Hispanic Americans). Average age 29. 31 applicants, 29% accepted, 7 enrolled. In 2008, 4 master's awarded. *Degree requirements:* For master's, thesis. *Entrance requirements:* For master's, GRE General Test (recommended), 3 letters of recommendation. Additional exam requirements/recommendations for international students: Required—TOEFL (minimum score 550 paper-based; 213 computer-based; 77 iBT). *Application deadline:* For fall admission, 1/30 for domestic students. Application fee: $70. Electronic applications accepted. *Expenses:* Tuition: Full-time $29,500. Required fees: $70. Full-time tuition and fees vary according to degree level, program and student level. *Financial support:* In 2008–09, 14 students received support, including 7 fellowships with full tuition reimbursements available, 7 teaching assistantships with full tuition reimbursements available; research assistantships, institutionally sponsored loans, scholarships/grants, health care benefits, tuition waivers (full and partial), and unspecified assistantships also available. Financial award applicants required to submit FAFSA. *Faculty research:* African-American literature, art, cinema and theater; African-American politics and public policy; African history, politics and art; Caribbean politics and Africana Diaspora. *Unit head:* Director of Graduate Studies, 607-255-4625, Fax: 607-255-0784. *Application contact:* Graduate Field Assistant, 607-255-4625, Fax: 607-255-0784, E-mail: spt1@cornell.edu.

Cornell University, Graduate School, Graduate Fields of Arts and Sciences, Field of History, Ithaca, NY 14853-0001. Offers African history (MA, PhD); American history (MA, PhD); ancient history (MA, PhD); early modern European history (MA, PhD); English history (MA, PhD); French history (MA, PhD); German history (MA, PhD); history of science (MA, PhD); Latin American history (MA, PhD); medieval Chinese history (MA, PhD); medieval history (MA, PhD); modern Chinese history (MA, PhD); modern European history (MA, PhD); modern Japanese history (MA, PhD); premodern Islamic history (MA, PhD); premodern Japanese history (MA, PhD); Renaissance history (MA, PhD); Russian history (MA, PhD); Southeast Asian history (MA, PhD). *Faculty:* 54 full-time (14 women). *Students:* 65 full-time (35 women); includes 12 minority (4 African Americans, 3 Asian Americans or Pacific Islanders, 5 Hispanic

African Studies

Cornell University (continued)

Americans), 19 international. Average age 31. 205 applicants, 8% accepted, 11 enrolled. In 2008, 12 master's, 6 doctorates awarded. Terminal master's awarded for partial completion of doctoral program. *Degree requirements:* For master's, thesis; for doctorate, 2 foreign languages, comprehensive exam, thesis/dissertation, 1 year of teaching experience. *Entrance requirements:* For master's and doctorate, GRE General Test, writing sample, 3 letters of recommendation. Additional exam requirements/recommendations for international students: Required—TOEFL (minimum score 550 paper-based; 213 computer-based; 77 iBT). *Application deadline:* For fall admission, 1/15 for domestic students. Application fee: $70. Electronic applications accepted. *Expenses:* Tuition: Full-time $29,500. Required fees: $70. Full-time tuition and fees vary according to degree level, program and student level. *Financial support:* In 2008–09, 54 students received support, including 27 fellowships with full tuition reimbursements available, 3 research assistantships with full tuition reimbursements available, 24 teaching assistantships with full tuition reimbursements available; institutionally sponsored loans, scholarships/grants, health care benefits, tuition waivers (full and partial), and unspecified assistantships also available. Financial award applicants required to submit FAFSA. *Unit head:* Director of Graduate Studies, 607-255-6738, Fax: 607-255-0469. *Application contact:* Graduate Field Assistant, 607-255-6738, Fax: 607-255-0469, E-mail: history_grad_info@cornell.edu.

Florida International University, College of Arts and Sciences, Program in African-New World Studies, Miami, FL 33199. Offers MA. Part-time and evening/weekend programs available. *Degree requirements:* For master's, one foreign language, thesis optional. *Entrance requirements:* For master's, GRE General Test, minimum GPA of 3.0, letters of recommendation. Additional exam requirements/recommendations for international students: Required—TOEFL.

Harvard University, Graduate School of Arts and Sciences, Department of African and African American Studies, Cambridge, MA 02138. Offers PhD. *Expenses:* Tuition: Full-time $32,556. Required fees: $1426. Full-time tuition and fees vary according to program and student level.

Howard University, Graduate School, Department of African Studies, Washington, DC 20059-0002. Offers MA, PhD. Part-time programs available. *Degree requirements:* For master's, one foreign language, comprehensive exam, thesis, internship; for doctorate, 2 foreign languages, comprehensive exam, thesis/dissertation, field research for some. *Entrance requirements:* For master's, GRE General Test, minimum GPA of 3.0; for doctorate, GRE General Test, minimum GPA of 3.5. Electronic applications accepted. *Faculty research:* African literature and film, economics of Africa, international relations, public policy analysis, gender.

Indiana University Bloomington, University Graduate School, College of Arts and Sciences, African Studies Program, Bloomington, IN 47405-7000. Offers MA. *Students:* 1 (woman) full-time, 1 (woman) part-time; includes 1 minority (African American). Average age 28. 7 applicants, 43% accepted, 1 enrolled. In 2008, 1 master's awarded. Application fee: $50 ($60 for international students). *Expenses:* Tuition, area resident: Part-time $291.97 per credit hour. Tuition, state resident: part-time $291.97 per credit hour. Tuition, nonresident: part-time $850.33 per credit hour. Required fees: $110 per semester. Tuition and fees vary according to course load and program. *Unit head:* Dr. Samuel Obeng, Director, 812-855-8284, E-mail: sobeng@indiana.edu. *Application contact:* Sue Hanson, Graduate Secretary, 812-855-8284, E-mail: shanson@indiana.edu.

The Johns Hopkins University, Paul H. Nitze School of Advanced International Studies, Washington, DC 20036. Offers international development (Certificate); international public policy (MIPP); international relations (MA, PhD), including African studies (MA), American foreign policy (MA), Asian studies (MA), Canadian studies (MA), conflict management (MA), European studies (MA), global theory and history (MA), international development (MA), international law, and organizations (MA), international policy (MA), international relations (general) (MA), Latin American studies (MA), Middle East studies (MA), Russian and Eurasian studies (MA), strategic studies (MA); international studies (Certificate); JD/MA; MBA/MA; MHS/MA. Terminal master's awarded for partial completion of doctoral program. *Degree requirements:* For master's, one foreign language, 16 non-language courses (8 for MIPP), 2 core examinations, comprehensive oral exam, paper (for some programs); for doctorate, 2 foreign languages, thesis/dissertation, 3 comprehensive exams, defense. *Entrance requirements:* For master's, GMAT or GRE General Test, previous course work in economics, foreign language, undergraduate degree; for doctorate, GRE General Test, master's degree. Additional exam requirements/recommendations for international students: Required—TOEFL (minimum paper-based score of 600, computer-based 250, iBT 100) or IELTS (minimum 7.0). Electronic applications accepted. *Expenses:* Contact institution. *Faculty research:* Regional studies and functional fields of international relations, international economics, conflict management, global theory and history, international law and organizations, international policy, strategic studies.

Michigan State University, The Graduate School, College of Arts and Letters, Program in African American and African Studies, East Lansing, MI 48824. Offers MA, PhD. *Entrance requirements:* Additional exam requirements/recommendations for international students: Required—TOEFL. Electronic applications accepted. *Faculty research:* Black American and diasporic studies, comparative communities of color.

New York University, Graduate School of Arts and Science, Department of History, New York, NY 10012-1019. Offers African diaspora (PhD); African history (PhD); archival management and historical editing (Advanced Certificate); Atlantic history (PhD); French studies/history (PhD); Hebrew and Judaic studies/history (PhD); history (MA, PhD), including Europe (PhD), Latin American and the Caribbean (PhD), United States (PhD), women's history (MA); Middle Eastern history (MA); Middle Eastern studies/history (PhD); public history (Advanced Certificate); world history (MA); JD/MA; MA/Advanced Certificate. Part-time programs available. Terminal master's awarded for partial completion of doctoral program. *Degree requirements:* For master's, seminar paper; for doctorate, one foreign language, thesis/dissertation, oral and written exams; for Advanced Certificate, internship. *Entrance requirements:* For master's, GRE General Test, minimum GPA of 3.0, writing sample; for doctorate, GRE. Additional exam requirements/ recommendations for international students: Required—TOEFL. *Faculty research:* African, East Asian, Medieval, early modern, and modern European history; U.S. history; African and African diaspora; Latin American history; Atlantic World.

New York University, Graduate School of Arts and Science, Program in Africana Studies, New York, NY 10012-1019. Offers MA. *Degree requirements:* For master's, thesis or alternative. *Entrance requirements:* For master's, GRE, sample of written work. Additional exam requirements/recommendations for international students: Required—TOEFL. *Faculty research:* Pan-Africanism, black urban studies, film and literature of black diaspora, cultural politics and theory, politics of identity.

New York University, Graduate School of Arts and Science, Program in Museum Studies, New York, NY 10012-1019. Offers museum studies (MA, Advanced Certificate), including Africana studies (MA), Hebrew and Judaic studies (MA), Latin American and Caribbean studies (MA), Near Eastern studies (MA). Part-time and evening/weekend programs available. *Entrance requirements:* For degree, master's or PhD. *Faculty research:* Modern and contemporary art, history of museums and exhibitions, conservation of cultural materials, museum anthropology, ethnography.

Northwestern University, The Graduate School, Program of African Studies, Evanston, IL 60208. Offers Certificate. *Degree requirements:* For Certificate, one foreign language. *Faculty research:* Collapsing states in Africa, HIV/AIDS in Africa, Islam in Africa, African philosophy.

The Ohio State University, Graduate School, College of Humanities, Department of African-American and African Studies, Columbus, OH 43210. Offers MA. *Degree requirements:* For master's, comprehensive exam, internship or thesis. *Entrance requirements:* For master's,

GRE General Test. Additional exam requirements/recommendations for international students: Required—TOEFL (minimum score 600 paper-based; 250 computer-based). Electronic applications accepted.

Ohio University, Graduate College, Center for International Studies, Program in African Studies, Athens, OH 45701-2979. Offers MA. Part-time programs available. *Degree requirements:* For master's, one foreign language, thesis optional. *Entrance requirements:* For master's, GRE, minimum GPA of 3.0. Additional exam requirements/recommendations for international students: Required—TOEFL (minimum score 550 paper-based; 213 computer-based). *Faculty research:* African social sciences and the humanities.

Rutgers, The State University of New Jersey, New Brunswick, Graduate School, Program in History, Piscataway, NJ 08854-8097. Offers African-American history (PhD); early American history (PhD); early modern European history (PhD); east Asian history (PhD); global and comparative history (PhD); history (PhD); history of diplomacy and foreign relations (PhD); history of technology, environment and health (PhD); history of the Atlantic cultures and African diaspora (PhD); Latin American history (PhD); medieval history (PhD); modern European history (PhD); nineteenth and twentieth century American history (PhD); women's and gender history (PhD). *Degree requirements:* For doctorate, thesis/dissertation. *Entrance requirements:* For doctorate, GRE General Test, sample of written work. Electronic applications accepted. *Faculty research:* American history, European history, Afro-American history, women's history, Latin American history.

St. John's University, St. John's College of Liberal Arts and Sciences, Institute of Asian Studies, Queens, NY 11439. Offers Asian and African cultural studies (Adv C); Asian studies (Adv C); Chinese studies (MA, Adv C); East Asian culture studies (Adv C); East Asian studies (MA). Part-time and evening/weekend programs available. *Students:* 6 full-time (4 women), 5 part-time (3 women); includes 3 minority (2 Asian Americans or Pacific Islanders, 1 Hispanic American), 7 international. Average age 25. 13 applicants, 100% accepted, 4 enrolled. In 2008, 5 master's awarded. *Degree requirements:* For master's, one foreign language, comprehensive exam, thesis optional. *Entrance requirements:* For master's, 18 hours of course work in the field, minimum GPA of 3.0. Additional exam requirements/recommendations for international students: Required—TOEFL (minimum score 500 paper-based; 173 computer-based; 61 iBT), IELTS (minimum score 5.5). *Application deadline:* For fall admission, 5/1 priority date for domestic and international students; for spring admission, 11/1 priority date for domestic and international students. Applications are processed on a rolling basis. Application fee: $70. Electronic applications accepted. *Expenses:* Tuition: Full-time $20,760; part-time $865 per credit. Required fees: $300; $150 per semester. Tuition and fees vary according to program. *Financial support:* Research assistantships, scholarships/grants available. Support available to part-time students. Financial award application deadline: 3/1; financial award applicants required to submit FAFSA. *Faculty research:* East Asian philosophy and religion, Chinese language and literature, Japanese language, modern Japan, Chinese art and history. *Unit head:* Dr. Bernadette Li, Chair, 718-990-1657, E-mail: lib@stjohns.edu. *Application contact:* Kathleen Davis, Director of Graduate Admission, 718-990-2790, Fax: 718-990-5686, E-mail: gradhelp@stjohns.edu.

Stony Brook University, State University of New York, Graduate School, College of Arts and Sciences, Department of Africana Studies, Stony Brook, NY 11794-4340. Offers MA. *Degree requirements:* For master's, research thesis project, research seminar. *Entrance requirements:* For master's, GRE General Test, minimum GPA of 3.0, 3 letters of recommendation. *Expenses:* Tuition, area resident: Full-time $7880; part-time $328 per credit hour. Tuition, state resident: full-time $7880; part-time $328 per credit hour. Tuition, nonresident: full-time $13,250; part-time $552 per credit hour. Required fees: $848. *Unit head:* Floris Cash, Chairperson, 631-632-7472. *Application contact:* Anthony Hurley, Graduate Program Director, 631-632-1366.

Syracuse University, Graduate School, College of Arts and Sciences, Program in Pan-African Studies, Syracuse, NY 13244. Offers MA. *Entrance requirements:* For master's, GRE General Test. Additional exam requirements/recommendations for international students: Required—TOEFL. Electronic applications accepted.

University at Albany, State University of New York, College of Arts and Sciences, Department of Africana Studies, Albany, NY 12222-0001. Offers African studies (MA); Afro-American studies (MA). Part-time and evening/weekend programs available. *Entrance requirements:* Additional exam requirements/recommendations for international students: Required—TOEFL (minimum score 550 paper-based; 213 computer-based). Electronic applications accepted. *Faculty research:* The black family, Afro-centricity in poetry, black women in U.S. literature, African economic development, African American history.

University of California, Los Angeles, Graduate Division, College of Letters and Science, Program in African Studies, Los Angeles, CA 90095. Offers MA, MPH/MA. *Students:* 16 full-time (9 women); includes 7 minority (all African Americans), 1 international. Average age 27. 16 applicants, 75% accepted, 8 enrolled. In 2008, 1 master's awarded. *Degree requirements:* For master's, one foreign language, comprehensive exam or thesis. *Entrance requirements:* For master's, GRE General Test, minimum GPA of 3.0, sample of research writing. *Application deadline:* For fall admission, 12/15 for domestic and international students. Application fee: $60 ($80 for international students). Electronic applications accepted. *Expenses:* Tuition, nonresident: full-time $14,694. Required fees: $9669.50. Full-time tuition and fees vary according to course load, degree level, program and student level. *Financial support:* In 2008–09, 13 fellowships with full and partial tuition reimbursements, 6 research assistantships with full and partial tuition reimbursements, 8 teaching assistantships with full and partial tuition reimbursements were awarded; Federal Work-Study, institutionally sponsored loans, scholarships/grants, health care benefits, tuition waivers (full and partial), and unspecified assistantships also available. Financial award application deadline: 3/1; financial award applicants required to submit FAFSA. *Unit head:* Katrina Thompson, Chair, 310-206-6571. *Application contact:* Departmental Office, 310-206-6571, E-mail: idpgrads@international.ucla.edu.

University of Connecticut, Graduate School, College of Liberal Arts and Sciences, Field of International Studies, Program in African Studies, Storrs, CT 06269. Offers MA. *Degree requirements:* For master's, comprehensive exam. *Entrance requirements:* For master's, GRE General Test. Additional exam requirements/recommendations for international students: Required—TOEFL (minimum score 550 paper-based; 213 computer-based). Electronic applications accepted.

University of Florida, Graduate School, College of Liberal Arts and Sciences, Center for African Studies, Gainesville, FL 32611. Offers Certificate. Part-time programs available. *Faculty research:* Governance, human rights, African archaeology, southern African history, wildlife conservation and natural resources.

University of Illinois at Urbana–Champaign, Graduate College, College of Liberal Arts and Sciences, Center for African Studies, Champaign, IL 61820. Offers MA. *Students:* 10 full-time (8 women), 1 (woman) part-time; includes 5 minority (4 African Americans, 1 Hispanic American), 1 international. 15 applicants, 60% accepted, 3 enrolled. In 2008, 2 master's awarded. *Entrance requirements:* For master's, minimum GPA of 3.0. Additional exam requirements/ recommendations for international students: Required—TOEFL (minimum score 550 paper-based; 213 computer-based; 79 iBT). *Application deadline:* Applications are processed on a rolling basis. Application fee: $60 ($75 for international students). Electronic applications accepted. *Financial support:* In 2008–09, 9 fellowships, 1 teaching assistantship were awarded; research assistantships, tuition waivers (full and partial) also available. *Unit head:* Merle Bowen, Director, 217-333-6335, Fax: 217-244-2429, E-mail: bowen@illinois.edu. *Application contact:* Sue Swisher, Administrative Aide, 217-244-4713, Fax: 217-244-2429, E-mail: swisher@illinois.edu.

The University of Kansas, Graduate Studies, College of Liberal Arts and Sciences, Department of African and African-American Studies, Lawrence, KS 66045. Offers African and African-

American studies (MA); African Studies (Graduate Certificate). *Faculty:* 10. *Degree requirements:* For master's, variable foreign language requirement, thesis or alternative. *Entrance requirements:* For master's, GRE, all academic transcripts, 3 letters of recommendation, personal statement of purpose, writing sample. Additional exam requirements/recommendations for international students: Required—TOEFL. *Application deadline:* For fall admission, 5/1 for domestic students. Applications are processed on a rolling basis. Application fee: $45 ($50 for international students). Electronic applications accepted. *Expenses:* Tuition, area resident: Full-time $6122; part-time $255.10 per credit hour. Tuition, state resident: full-time $6122; part-time $255.10 per credit hour. Tuition, nonresident: full-time $14,629; part-time $609.55 per credit hour. Required fees: $847; $70.56 per credit hour. Tuition and fees vary according to course load and program. *Faculty research:* African Theatre, YaKuur Culture, interracial communication, African development and urban planning, African literature, Muslim women in West Africa, identity formation in African and Disaporan settings, African American history, North African and Arab societies, civil rights. *Unit head:* Dr. Peter Ukpokodu, Chair, 785-864-3054, Fax: 785-864-5330, E-mail: afs@ku.edu. *Application contact:* Dr. Peter Ukpokodu, Chair, 785-864-3054, Fax: 785-864-5330, E-mail: afs@ku.edu.

University of Louisville, Graduate School, College of Arts and Sciences, Department of Pan-African Studies, Louisville, KY 40292. Offers African and Diaspora studies (MA); African-American studies (MA); MA/MSW; MSSW/MA. Part-time programs available. *Faculty:* 12 full-time (6 women). *Students:* 11 full-time (7 women), 7 part-time (6 women); includes 15 African Americans, 1 international. Average age 30. 11 applicants, 55% accepted, 5 enrolled. In 2008, 4 master's awarded. *Degree requirements:* For master's, comprehensive exam, thesis optional. *Entrance requirements:* For master's, GRE General Test. Additional exam requirements/recommendations for international students: Recommended—TOEFL (minimum score 550 paper-based; 213 computer-based; 79 iBT). *Application deadline:* For fall admission, 10/15 for domestic and international students; for spring admission, 3/15 for domestic and international students. Application fee: $50. Electronic applications accepted. *Financial support:* In 2008–09, 10 students received support, including 8 teaching assistantships with tuition reimbursements available (averaging $1,200 per year). Financial award applicants required to submit FAFSA. *Faculty research:* African popular culture, black male identity development, education and retention, contemporary politics in Nigeria, poverty in the Caribbean. *Unit head:* Dr. Theresa Rajack-Talley, Chair, 502-852-4192, Fax: 502-852-5954, E-mail: tatall01@gwise.louisville.edu. *Application contact:* Dr. Theresa Rajack-Talley, Acting Graduate Studies Director, 502-852-4192, Fax: 502-852-5954, E-mail: tatall01@louisville.edu.

University of Pittsburgh, University Center for International Studies, Pittsburgh, PA 15260. Offers African studies (Certificate); Asian studies (Certificate); European Union studies (Certificate); global studies (Certificate); Latin American studies (Certificate); Russian and East European studies (Certificate); West European studies (Certificate).

University of South Florida, Graduate School, College of Arts and Sciences, Department of Africana Studies, Tampa, FL 33620-9951. Offers MLA. *Faculty:* 5 full-time (1 woman). *Students:* 3 applicants, 33% accepted, 1 enrolled. *Degree requirements:* For master's, comprehensive exam, thesis. *Entrance requirements:* For master's, GRE, 3 letters of recommendation. Additional exam requirements/recommendations for international students: Required—TOEFL (minimum score 550 paper-based; 213 computer-based). *Application deadline:* For fall admission, 2/15 for domestic students, 1/2 for international students; for spring admission, 10/15 for domestic students, 6/1 for international students. Application fee: $30. *Expenses:* Tuition, state resident: full-time $2624.40; part-time $291.60 per credit hour. Tuition, nonresident: full-time $7822; part-time $869.13 per credit hour. *Financial support:* Tuition waivers (full) available. Financial award applicants required to submit FAFSA. *Unit head:* Deborah Plant, Program Director, 813-974-4220, Fax: 813-974-2668, E-mail: plant@cas.usf.edu. *Application contact:* Deborah Plant, Program Director, 813-974-4220, Fax: 813-974-2668, E-mail: plant@cas.usf.edu.

The University of Texas at Austin, Graduate School, College of Liberal Arts, John L. Warfield Center for African and African American Studies, Austin, TX 78712-1111. Offers African Diaspora studies (MA, PhD). Part-time programs available. *Degree requirements:* For master's, one foreign language, thesis. *Entrance requirements:* For master's, GRE General Test. Electronic applications accepted.

University of Wisconsin–Madison, Graduate School, College of Letters and Science, Department of African Languages and Literature, Madison, WI 53706-1380. Offers MA, PhD. Part-time programs available. *Degree requirements:* For master's, one foreign language, thesis; for doctorate, 2 foreign languages, comprehensive exam, thesis/dissertation. *Entrance requirements:* For master's, BA in African language and literature; for doctorate, MA in African language and literature. Electronic applications accepted. *Faculty research:* Oral traditions, language pedagogy, stylistics, sociolinguistics, literary criticism.

University of Wisconsin–Madison, Graduate School, College of Letters and Science, Department of History, Madison, WI 53706-1380. Offers African history (MA, PhD); Central Asian history (MA, PhD); comparative world history (MA, PhD); East Asian history (MA, PhD); European history (MA, PhD); gender and women's history (MA, PhD); Latin American and Caribbean history (MA, PhD); Middle Eastern history (MA, PhD); South Asian history (MA, PhD); Southeast Asian history (MA, PhD); United States history (MA, PhD). Terminal master's awarded for partial completion of doctoral program. *Degree requirements:* For master's, thesis (for some programs); for doctorate, variable foreign language requirement, thesis/dissertation. *Entrance requirements:* For master's and doctorate, GRE General Test. Additional exam requirements/recommendations for international students: Required—Michigan English Language Assessment Battery or TOEFL. Electronic applications accepted. *Faculty research:* American, African, European, Asian, Latin American, and Middle Eastern history.

University of Wisconsin–Milwaukee, Graduate School, College of Letters and Sciences, Department of Africology, Milwaukee, WI 53201-0413. Offers PhD. *Faculty:* 9 full-time (5 women). *Degree requirements:* For doctorate, comprehensive exam. *Entrance requirements:* For doctorate, GRE General Test. Additional exam requirements/recommendations for international students: Required—TOEFL (minimum score 550 paper-based; 79 iBT), IELTS (minimum score 6.5). *Expenses:* Tuition, area resident: Full-time $7320; part-time $165 per credit. Tuition, state resident: full-time $7320; part-time $165 per credit. Tuition, nonresident: full-time $17,840; part-time $714 per credit. Tuition and fees vary according to campus/location, program and reciprocity agreements. *Financial support:* In 2008–09, 1 teaching assistantship was awarded. *Unit head:* Abera Gelan, Representative, 414-229-4155, E-mail: agelan@uwm.edu. *Application contact:* General Information Contact, 414-229-4982, Fax: 414-229-6967, E-mail: gradschool@uwm.edu.

West Virginia University, Eberly College of Arts and Sciences, Department of History, Morgantown, WV 26506. Offers African history (MA, PhD); African-American history (MA, PhD); American history (MA, PhD); Appalachian/regional history (MA, PhD); East Asian history (MA, PhD); European history (MA, PhD); history of science and technology (MA, PhD); Latin American history (MA). Part-time programs available. *Degree requirements:* For master's, one foreign language, thesis (for some programs), oral exam, thesis defense; for doctorate, one foreign language, comprehensive exam, thesis/dissertation, dissertation defense. *Entrance requirements:* For master's, GRE General Test, minimum GPA of 3.0; for doctorate, GRE General Test. Additional exam requirements/recommendations for international students: Required—TOEFL (minimum score 550 paper-based), IELTS (minimum score 6.5). Electronic applications accepted. *Faculty research:* U.S., Appalachia, modern Europe, Africa, colonial and post-colonial societies.

Yale University, Graduate School of Arts and Sciences, Interdisciplinary Program in African Studies, New Haven, CT 06520. Offers MA. *Degree requirements:* For master's, one foreign language, thesis. *Entrance requirements:* For master's, GRE General Test.

American Indian/Native American Studies

Central Michigan University, College of Graduate Studies, College of Humanities and Social and Behavioral Sciences, Program in Humanities, Mount Pleasant, MI 48859. Offers humanities (MA), including contemporary issues in the humanities: race, class, and gender, images and ideas of self, Native American issues in modern culture, popular culture studies, the rise of industrial society. Part-time and evening/weekend programs available. *Students:* 3 full-time (1 woman), 7 part-time (4 women). Average age 37. *Degree requirements:* For master's, thesis or alternative. *Application deadline:* Applications are processed on a rolling basis. Application fee: $35 ($45 for international students). Electronic applications accepted. *Expenses:* Tuition, state resident: full-time $3717; part-time $413 per credit. Tuition, nonresident: full-time $6894; part-time $766 per credit. *Financial support:* Fellowships with tuition reimbursements, Federal Work-Study, unspecified assistantships, and out-of-state merit awards available. *Faculty research:* Rise of industrial society; images and ideas of self; contemporary issues of race, class, and gender; popular culture; Native American issues in modern culture. *Unit head:* Dr. Ronald Primeau, Director, 989-774-3117, Fax: 989-774-7106, E-mail: ronald.r.primeau@cmich.edu. *Application contact:* Judith L. Prince, Director of Graduate Student Services, 989-774-1059, Fax: 989-774-1857, E-mail: judith.l.prince@cmich.edu.

Montana State University, College of Graduate Studies, College of Letters and Science, Department of Native American Studies, Bozeman, MT 59717. Offers MA. Part-time programs available. *Degree requirements:* For master's, comprehensive exam. *Entrance requirements:* For master's, GRE General Test. Additional exam requirements/recommendations for international students: Required—TOEFL (minimum score 550 paper-based; 213 computer-based). Electronic applications accepted. *Faculty research:* Ethnoecology, American Indian cultural studies, Federal Indian law and policy, indigenous political theory, American Indian literature.

Trent University, Graduate Studies, The Frost Centre for Canadian Studies and Indigenous Studies, Peterborough, ON K9J 7B8, Canada. Offers Canadian studies (PhD); Canadian studies and indigenous studies (MA). Part-time programs available. *Degree requirements:* For master's, thesis. *Entrance requirements:* For master's, honors degree. *Faculty research:* Native community-based socioeconomic development, environmental and social impact inventory, regional studies.

Trent University, Graduate Studies, Program in Indigenous Studies, Peterborough, ON K9J 7B8, Canada. Offers PhD. Part-time programs available. *Degree requirements:* For doctorate, thesis/dissertation. *Entrance requirements:* For doctorate, master's degree.

The University of Arizona, Graduate College, Graduate Interdisciplinary Programs, Graduate Interdisciplinary Program in American Indian Studies, Tucson, AZ 85721. Offers MA, PhD, JD/MA. Part-time programs available. *Degree requirements:* For master's, thesis; for doctorate, one foreign language, comprehensive exam, thesis/dissertation. *Entrance requirements:* For master's and doctorate, minimum GPA of 3.0. Additional exam requirements/recommendations for international students: Required—TOEFL. *Faculty research:* Indian law and policy, Indian societies, Indian language and literature, Indian education.

University of California, Davis, Graduate Studies, Program in Native American Studies, Davis, CA 95616. Offers MA, PhD. Terminal master's awarded for partial completion of doctoral program. *Degree requirements:* For master's, comprehensive exam (for some programs), thesis (for some programs); for doctorate, thesis/dissertation. *Entrance requirements:* For doctorate, GRE. Additional exam requirements/recommendations for international students: Required—TOEFL (minimum score 550 paper-based; 213 computer-based).

University of California, Los Angeles, Graduate Division, College of Letters and Science, Program in American Indian Studies, Los Angeles, CA 90095. Offers MA, JD/MA. *Students:* 21 full-time (12 women); includes 16 minority (15 American Indian/Alaska Native, 1 Hispanic American). Average age 28. 20 applicants, 50% accepted, 8 enrolled. In 2008, 7 master's awarded. *Degree requirements:* For master's, comprehensive exam or thesis. *Entrance requirements:* For master's, GRE General Test (recommended), minimum GPA of 3.0, sample of written work. *Application deadline:* For fall admission, 12/15 for domestic and international students. Application fee: $60 ($80 for international students). Electronic applications accepted. *Expenses:* Tuition, nonresident: full-time $14,694. Required fees: $9669.50. Full-time tuition and fees vary according to course load, degree level, program and student level. *Financial support:* In 2008–09, 16 fellowships with full and partial tuition reimbursements, 1 research assistantship with full and partial tuition reimbursement, 3 teaching assistantships with full and partial tuition reimbursements were awarded; Federal Work-Study, institutionally sponsored loans, scholarships/grants, health care benefits, tuition waivers (full and partial), and unspecified assistantships also available. Financial award application deadline: 3/1; financial award applicants required to submit FAFSA. *Unit head:* Dr. Felicia Hodge, Chair, 310-825-7315. *Application contact:* Departmental Office, 310-825-7315, E-mail: aisc@ucla.edu.

The University of Kansas, Graduate Studies, College of Liberal Arts and Sciences, Global Indigenous Nations Studies Program, Lawrence, KS 66045-7515. Offers MA, JD/MA. Part-time programs available. *Faculty:* 1 (woman) full-time, 3 part-time/adjunct (2 women). *Students:* 25 full-time (18 women); includes 19 minority (all American Indian/Alaska Native). Average age 35. 8 applicants, 100% accepted, 4 enrolled. In 2008, 10 master's awarded. *Degree requirements:* For master's, thesis or alternative. *Entrance requirements:* For master's, GRE, resumé, writing sample, minimum GPA of 3.0 (preferred), three recommendations, personal statement, original transcripts. Additional exam requirements/recommendations for international students: Required—TOEFL. *Application deadline:* For fall admission, 3/15 priority date for domestic and international students. Applications are processed on a rolling basis. Application fee: $45 ($50 for international students). Electronic applications accepted. *Expenses:* Tuition, area resident: Full-time $6122; part-time $255.10 per credit hour. Tuition, state resident: full-time $6122; part-time $255.10 per credit hour. Tuition, nonresident: full-time $14,629; part-time $609.55 per credit hour. Required fees: $847; $70.56 per credit hour. Tuition and fees vary according to course load and program. *Financial support:* In 2008–09, 10 students received support; fellowships, teaching assistantships, Federal Work-Study, institutionally sponsored loans, and scholarships/grants available. Support available to part-time students. Financial award application deadline: 3/15; financial award applicants required to submit FAFSA. *Faculty research:* American Indian history, religion, literature, law, languages, decolonization, sovereignty, pre-Columbian cultures of Latin America. *Unit head:* Dr. John Hoopes, Director, 785-864-2660, Fax: 785-864-0370, E-mail: indigenous@ku.edu. *Application contact:* Prof. Sharon O'Brien, Graduate Coordinator, 785-864-2660, Fax: 785-864-0370, E-mail: indigenous@ku.edu.

American Indian/Native American Studies

University of Lethbridge, School of Graduate Studies, Lethbridge, AB T1K 3M4, Canada. Offers accounting (MScM); addictions counseling (M Sc); agricultural biotechnology (M Sc); agricultural studies (M Sc, MA); anthropology (MA); archaeology (MA); art (MA); biochemistry (M Sc); biological sciences (M Sc); biomolecular science (PhD); biosystems and biodiversity (PhD); Canadian studies (MA); chemistry (M Sc); computer science (M Sc); computer science and geographical information science (M Sc); counseling psychology (M Ed); dramatic arts (MA); earth, space, and physical science (PhD); economics (MA); educational leadership (M Ed); English (MA); environmental science (M Sc); evolution and behavior (PhD); exercise science (M Sc); finance (MScM); French (MA); French/German (MA); French/Spanish (MA); general education (M Ed); general management (MScM); geography (M Sc, MA); German (MA); health sciences (M Sc, MA); history (MA); human resource management and labour relations (MScM); individualized multidisciplinary (M Sc, MA); information systems (MScM); international management (MScM); kinesiology (M Sc, MA); management (M Sc, MA); marketing (MScM); mathematics (M Sc); music (MA); Native American studies (MA); neuroscience (M Sc, PhD); new media (MA); nursing (M Sc); philosophy (MA); physics (M Sc); policy and strategy (MScM); political science (MA); psychology (M Sc, MA); religious studies (MA); sociology (MA); theoretical and computational science (PhD); urban and regional studies (MA). Part-time and evening/weekend programs available. *Degree requirements:* For doctorate, comprehensive exam, thesis/dissertation. *Entrance requirements:* For master's, GMAT (M Sc in management), bachelor's degree in related field, minimum GPA of 3.0 during previous 20 graded semester courses, 2 years teaching or related experience (M Ed); for doctorate, master's degree, minimum graduate GPA of 3.5. Additional exam requirements/recommendations for international students: Required—TOEFL. *Faculty research:* Movement and brain plasticity, gibberellin physiology, photosynthesis, carbon cycling, molecular properties of main-group ring components.

University of Manitoba, Faculty of Graduate Studies, Faculty of Arts, Department of Native Studies, Winnipeg, MB R3T 2N2, Canada. Offers MA.

University of Oklahoma, Graduate College, College of Arts and Sciences, Department of Native American Studies, Norman, OK 73019-0390. Offers MA. Part-time programs available. *Faculty:* 7 full-time (3 women), 1 (woman) part-time/adjunct. *Students:* 12 full-time (9 women), 4 part-time (3 women); includes 12 minority (all American Indian/Alaska Native). 8 applicants, 88% accepted, 4 enrolled. In 2008, 2 master's awarded. *Degree requirements:* For master's, thesis. *Entrance requirements:* For master's, minimum undergraduate GPA of 3.0, 3 letters of recommendation. *Application deadline:* For fall admission, 2/1 for domestic students, 4/1 for international students; for spring admission, 11/1 for domestic students, 9/1 for international students. Applications are processed on a rolling basis. Application fee: $40 ($90 for international students). Electronic applications accepted. *Expenses:* Tuition, state resident: full-time $3744; part-time $156 per credit hour. Tuition, nonresident: full-time $13,577; part-time $565.70 per credit hour. Required fees: $2415.40; $90.10 per credit hour. *Financial support:* In 2008–09, 16 students received support, including 8 teaching assistantships with partial tuition reimbursements available (averaging $10,000 per year); tuition waivers (partial) and unspecified assistantships also available. Financial award application deadline: 2/1; financial award applicants required to submit FAFSA. *Faculty research:* Indians, race and identity politics among Cherokees, American Indian contemporary literature, Seminoles, Native American women, American Indian history, ethics and value conflicts in archaeology, native American literature, aesthetic understanding of native American art. *Unit head:* Joe Watkins, Director, 405-325-2312, Fax: 405-325-0842, E-mail: jwatkins@ou.edu. *Application contact:* Barbara Hobson, Assistant Director, 405-325-2324, Fax: 405-325-0842, E-mail: bhobson@ou.edu.

University of Regina, Faculty of Graduate Studies and Research, Faculty of Arts, Program in Indigenous Studies, Regina, SK S4S 0A2, Canada. Offers MA. Offered as special case program. Part-time programs available. *Faculty:* 10 full-time (3 women). *Students:* 2 full-time (1 woman). 1 applicant, 0% accepted. In 2008, 1 master's awarded. *Degree requirements:* For master's, thesis. *Entrance requirements:* For master's, honors degree in Indian studies or related field. Additional exam requirements/recommendations for international students: Required—TOEFL (minimum score 580 paper-based; 237 computer-based; 88 iBT). *Application deadline:* For fall admission, 3/15 for domestic students. Application fee: $85 ($100 for international students). Electronic applications accepted. *Financial support:* Fellowships, research assistantships, teaching assistantships, scholarships/grants available. Financial award application deadline: 6/15. *Unit head:* Dr. David Miller, 790-5959 Ext. 3209, E-mail: dmiller@firstnationsuniversity.ca. *Application contact:* Dr. David Miller, 790-5959 Ext. 3209, E-mail: dmiller@firstnationsuniversity.ca.

American Studies

American University, School of International Service, Washington, DC 20016-8071. Offers comparative and regional studies (Certificate); cross-cultural communication (Certificate); development management (MS); ethics, peace, and global affairs (MA); European studies (Certificate); global environmental policy (MA, Certificate); international affairs (MA), including comparative and regional studies, environmental policy, international economic policy, international politics, natural resources and sustainable development, U.S. foreign policy; international communication (MA, Certificate); international development (MA, Certificate); international development management (Certificate); international economic policy (Certificate); international economic relations (Certificate); international media (MA); international peace and conflict resolution (MA, Certificate); international relations (PhD); international service (MIS); peace building (Certificate); the Americas (Certificate); United States foreign policy (Certificate); JD/MA. Part-time and evening/weekend programs available. *Faculty:* 70 full-time (28 women), 51 part-time/adjunct (20 women). *Students:* 519 full-time (317 women), 335 part-time (205 women); includes 157 minority (54 African Americans, 2 American Indian/Alaska Native, 45 Asian Americans or Pacific Islanders, 56 Hispanic Americans), 116 international. Average age 27. 1,901 applicants, 58% accepted, 277 enrolled. In 2008, 358 master's, 5 doctorates, 9 other advanced degrees awarded. Terminal master's awarded for partial completion of doctoral program. *Degree requirements:* For master's, one foreign language, comprehensive exam, thesis or alternative; for doctorate, one foreign language, comprehensive exam, thesis/dissertation, research practicum; for Certificate, minimum 15 credit hours related course work. *Entrance requirements:* For master's, GRE, 24 credits of course work in related social sciences, minimum GPA of 3.5, 2 letters of recommendation, bachelor's degree, resumé, statement of purpose; for doctorate, GRE, 2 letters of recommendation, 24 credits in related social sciences; for Certificate, bachelor's degree. Additional exam requirements/recommendations for international students: Required—TOEFL (minimum score 600 paper-based; 250 computer-based; 100 iBT). *Application deadline:* For fall admission, 1/15 priority date for domestic students; for spring admission, 10/1 priority date for domestic students. Applications are processed on a rolling basis. Application fee: $50. *Expenses:* Tuition: Full-time $21,204; part-time $1178 per credit hour. Required fees: $380. Part-time tuition and fees vary according to course load and program. *Financial support:* Career-related internships or fieldwork, Federal Work-Study, and institutionally sponsored loans available. Financial award application deadline: 1/15. *Faculty research:* International intellectual property, international environmental issues, international law and legal order, international telecommunications/technology, international sustainable development. *Unit head:* Dr. Louis W. Goodman, Dean, 202-885-1600, Fax: 202-885-2494. *Application contact:* Yasmin Quianzon, Director of Graduate Admissions and Financial Aid, 202-885-2496, Fax: 202-885-1109.

See Close-Up on page 861.

Appalachian State University, Cratis D. Williams Graduate School, Center for Appalachian Studies, Boone, NC 28608. Offers culture (MA); music (MA); sustainable development (MA). Part-time programs available. *Faculty:* 14 full-time (5 women). *Students:* 19 full-time (11 women), 5 part-time (3 women). 20 applicants, 90% accepted, 10 enrolled. In 2008, 6 master's awarded. *Degree requirements:* For master's, one foreign language, comprehensive exam, thesis optional. *Entrance requirements:* For master's, GRE General Test, 3 letters of recommendation. Additional exam requirements/recommendations for international students: Required—TOEFL (minimum score 570 paper-based; 230 computer-based; 79 iBT), IELTS (minimum score 6.5). *Application deadline:* For fall admission, 7/1 for domestic students, 2/1 for international students; for spring admission, 11/1 for domestic students, 7/1 for international students. Applications are processed on a rolling basis. Application fee: $50. Electronic applications accepted. *Expenses:* Tuition, area resident: Full-time $2600; part-time $700 per course. Tuition, state resident: full-time $2600; part-time $700 per course. Tuition, nonresident: full-time $5000; part-time $3300 per course. Required fees: $2150; $330 per course. Tuition and fees vary according to campus/location. *Financial support:* In 2008–09, 8 research assistantships (averaging $7,000 per year) were awarded; fellowships, teaching assistantships, career-related internships or fieldwork, Federal Work-Study, scholarships/grants, and unspecified assistantships also available. Financial award application deadline: 4/1; financial award applicants required to submit FAFSA. *Faculty research:* Appalachian culture, sustainable development, Appalachian music. Total annual research expenditures: $10,500. *Unit head:* Dr. Pat Beaver, Director, 828-262-2550, E-mail: beaverpd@appstate.edu. *Application contact:* Dr. Bruce Stewart, Graduate Program Director, 828-262-4858, E-mail: stewartbe1@appstate.edu.

Baylor University, Graduate School, College of Arts and Sciences, Program in American Studies, Waco, TX 76798. Offers MA. *Students:* 3 full-time (2 women), 1 (woman) part-time; includes 1 minority (African American), 1 international. In 2008, 1 master's awarded. *Degree requirements:* For master's, thesis, final oral exam. *Entrance requirements:* For master's, GRE General Test, 24 semester hours of course work in subjects with American content. *Application deadline:* For fall admission, 8/1 for domestic students. Applications are processed on a rolling basis. Application fee: $25. *Financial support:* Fellowships, Federal Work-Study and institutionally sponsored loans available. Financial award application deadline: 4/15. *Unit head:* Dr. Doug Ferdon, Graduate Program Director, 254-710-6350, Fax: 254-710-3600, E-mail: doug_ferdon@baylor.edu. *Application contact:* Margaret Kramer, Administrative Assistant, 254-710-4350, Fax: 254-710-3870, E-mail: margaret_kramer@baylor.edu.

Boston University, Graduate School of Arts and Sciences, Program in American and New England Studies, Boston, MA 02215. Offers PhD. *Degree requirements:* For doctorate, one foreign language, comprehensive exam, thesis/dissertation. *Entrance requirements:* For doctorate, GRE General Test, scholarly writing sample, 3 letters of recommendation. Additional exam requirements/recommendations for international students: Required—TOEFL (minimum score 550 paper-based; 213 computer-based).

Bowling Green State University, Graduate College, College of Arts and Sciences, American Culture Studies Program, Bowling Green, OH 43403. Offers MA, PhD. Part-time programs available. *Degree requirements:* For master's, thesis or alternative; for doctorate, comprehensive exam, thesis/dissertation. *Entrance requirements:* For master's and doctorate, GRE General Test. Additional exam requirements/recommendations for international students: Required—TOEFL. Electronic applications accepted. *Faculty research:* Race and ethnicity, gender, popular culture.

Bowling Green State University, Graduate College, College of Arts and Sciences, Department of Popular Culture, Bowling Green, OH 43403. Offers MA. Part-time programs available. *Degree requirements:* For master's, thesis or alternative. *Entrance requirements:* For master's, GRE General Test. Additional exam requirements/recommendations for international students: Required—TOEFL. Electronic applications accepted. *Faculty research:* Mass media (popular film, TV, and music); folklore/folklife; ritual, festival, celebration, and holidays; global, international, and popular culture; nineteenth century everyday life.

Brandeis University, Graduate School of Arts and Sciences, Department of History, Program in American History, Waltham, MA 02454-9110. Offers MA, PhD. Part-time programs available. Terminal master's awarded for partial completion of doctoral program. *Degree requirements:* For master's, one foreign language, thesis, colloquia, directed research, seminars; for doctorate, one foreign language, comprehensive exam, thesis/dissertation, colloquia, directed research, seminars. *Entrance requirements:* For master's and doctorate, GRE General Test, resumé, writing sample, letters of recommendation, statement of purpose. Additional exam requirements/recommendations for international students: Required—TOEFL (minimum score 600 paper-based; 250 computer-based; 100 iBT), IELTS (minimum score 7). Electronic applications accepted. *Faculty research:* American polity, social history, cultural, legal, colonial.

Brown University, Graduate School, Department of American Civilization, Providence, RI 02912. Offers American civilization (MA, PhD); public humanities (MA). *Degree requirements:* For doctorate, thesis/dissertation, preliminary exam.

California State University, Fullerton, Graduate Studies, College of Humanities and Social Sciences, Department of American Studies, Fullerton, CA 92834-9480. Offers MA. Part-time programs available. *Students:* 13 full-time (7 women), 35 part-time (24 women); includes 11 minority (6 Asian Americans or Pacific Islanders, 5 Hispanic Americans), 2 international. Average age 27. 34 applicants, 79% accepted, 18 enrolled. In 2008, 18 master's awarded. *Degree requirements:* For master's, comprehensive exam or thesis. *Entrance requirements:* For master's, minimum GPA of 3.0 in major, 2.5 in last 60 hours. Application fee: $55. Tuition and fees vary according to degree level. *Financial support:* Teaching assistantships, Federal Work-Study, institutionally sponsored loans, and scholarships/grants available. Support available to part-time students. Financial award application deadline: 3/1. *Unit head:* Dr. Jesse Battan, Chair, 657-278-2441. *Application contact:* Dr. John Ibson, Adviser, 657-278-3625.

California State University, Long Beach, Graduate Studies, College of Liberal Arts, Department of History, Long Beach, CA 90840. Offers Africa and the Middle East (MA); ancient/Medieval Europe (MA); Asia (MA); Latin America (MA); modern Europe (MA); United States (MA); world (MA). Part-time and evening/weekend programs available. *Faculty:* 17 full-time (11 women), 2 part-time/adjunct (1 woman). *Students:* 9 full-time (4 women), 45 part-time (18 women); includes 15 minority (2 African Americans, 3 Asian Americans or Pacific Islanders, 10 Hispanic Americans), 1 international. Average age 35. 40 applicants, 50% accepted, 11 enrolled. *Degree requirements:* For master's, one foreign language, comprehensive exam or thesis. *Application deadline:* For fall admission, 3/1 for domestic students. Applications are processed on a rolling basis. Application fee: $55. Electronic applications accepted. *Expenses:* Tuition, nonresident: full-time $11,160; part-time $372 per unit. Required fees: $4100; $1261 per semester. *Financial support:* Research assistantships, Federal Work-Study, institutionally sponsored loans, and scholarships/grants available. Financial award application deadline: 3/2. *Faculty research:* All periods of European and American history, recent Asian and African history. *Unit head:* Dr. Nancy L Quam-Wickham, Graduate Advisor, 562-985-4431, Fax: 562-985-5431, E-mail: quamwick@csulb.edu. *Application contact:* Dr. Houri Berberian, Graduate Advisor, 562-985-4524, Fax: 562-985-4431, E-mail: hberber@csulb.edu.

The Catholic University of America, School of Arts and Sciences, Department of History, Washington, DC 20064. Offers MA, PhD, JD/MA, MSLS/MA. Part-time programs available. *Degree requirements:* For master's, one foreign language, comprehensive exam, thesis or alternative; for doctorate, 2 foreign languages, comprehensive exam, thesis/dissertation, oral exams. *Entrance requirements:* For master's and doctorate, GRE General Test, 3 letters of recommendation. Additional exam requirements/recommendations for international students: Required—TOEFL (minimum score 580 paper-based; 237 computer-based). Electronic applications accepted. *Faculty research:* Medieval family law, U.S. liberalism, capitalism in Europe, Mexican rural society, urbanization in France.

Central Michigan University, College of Graduate Studies, College of Humanities and Social and Behavioral Sciences, Department of History, Mount Pleasant, MI 48859. Offers European history (Graduate Certificate); history (MA, PhD); modern history (Graduate Certificate); United States history (Graduate Certificate). Offered jointly with the University of Stratclyde, Scotland. Part-time programs available. *Faculty:* 15 full-time (5 women). *Students:* 22 full-time (8 women), 15 part-time (2 women); includes 1 Hispanic American. Average age 30. *Degree requirements:* For master's, thesis or alternative; for doctorate, comprehensive exam, thesis/dissertation. Application fee: $35 ($45 for international students). Electronic applications accepted. *Expenses:* Tuition, state resident: full-time $3717; part-time $413 per credit. Tuition, nonresident: full-time $6894; part-time $766 per credit. *Financial support:* Fellowships with tuition reimbursements, research assistantships with tuition reimbursements, teaching assistantships with tuition reimbursements, Federal Work-Study, unspecified assistantships, and out-of-state merit awards available. *Faculty research:* Colonial and revolutionary United States history, modern European history, Latin American and transatlantic history, transnational and comparative history, United States social history. *Unit head:* Dr. Timothy D. Hall, Chairperson, 989-773-3374, Fax: 989-774-1156, E-mail: hall1td@cmich.edu. *Application contact:* Dr. Timothy D. Hall, Chairperson, 989-773-3374, Fax: 989-774-1156, E-mail: hall1td@cmich.edu.

Claremont Graduate University, Graduate Programs, School of Arts and Humanities, Department of English, Claremont, CA 91711-6160. Offers American studies (MA, PhD); critical theory (MA, PhD); early modern studies (MA, PhD); English (M Phil, MA, PhD); literary theory (PhD); literature (MA, PhD); literature and creative writing (MA); literature and film (MA); MBA/MA; MBA/PhD. Part-time programs available. *Faculty:* 2 full-time (1 woman), 2 part-time/adjunct (0 women). *Students:* 78 full-time (46 women), 12 part-time (9 women); includes 15 minority (1 African American, 2 American Indian/Alaska Native, 7 Asian Americans or Pacific Islanders, 5 Hispanic Americans), 2 international. Average age 35. In 2008, 9 master's, 11 doctorates awarded. *Entrance requirements:* For master's and doctorate, GRE General Test. Additional exam requirements/recommendations for international students: Required—TOEFL (minimum score 550 paper-based; 213 computer-based; 80 iBT). *Application deadline:* For fall admission, 2/1 priority date for domestic students. Applications are processed on a rolling basis. Application fee: $60. Electronic applications accepted. *Expenses:* Tuition: Full-time $33,698; part-time $1465 per unit. Required fees: $310; $155 per semester. Tuition and fees vary according to program. *Financial support:* Fellowships, Federal Work-Study, institutionally sponsored loans, and scholarships/grants available. Support available to part-time students. Financial award application deadline: 2/15; financial award applicants required to submit FAFSA. *Faculty research:* American, comparative, and English Renaissance literature; modernism; feminist literature and theory. *Unit head:* Wendy Martin, Chair, 909-621-8612, Fax: 909-607-1221, E-mail: wendy.martin@cgu.edu. *Application contact:* Justin Evans, Admissions Coordinator, 909-607-1278, Fax: 909-607-1221, E-mail: justin.evans@cgu.edu.

Claremont Graduate University, Graduate Programs, School of Arts and Humanities, Department of History, Claremont, CA 91711-6160. Offers Africana history (Certificate); American studies and U.S. history (MA, PhD); archival studies (MA); early modern studies (MA, PhD); European studies (MA, PhD); oral history (MA, PhD); MBA/MA; MBA/PhD. *Faculty:* 3 full-time (2 women). *Students:* 67 full-time (33 women), 8 part-time (3 women); includes 15 minority (1 African American, 3 Asian Americans or Pacific Islanders, 11 Hispanic Americans), 1 international. Average age 35. In 2008, 6 master's, 8 doctorates awarded. Terminal master's awarded for partial completion of doctoral program. *Entrance requirements:* For master's and doctorate, GRE General Test. Additional exam requirements/recommendations for international students: Required—TOEFL (minimum score 550 paper-based; 213 computer-based; 80 iBT). *Application deadline:* For fall admission, 2/1 priority date for domestic students. Applications are processed on a rolling basis. Application fee: $60. Electronic applications accepted. *Expenses:* Tuition: Full-time $33,698; part-time $1465 per unit. Required fees: $310; $155 per semester. Tuition and fees vary according to program. *Financial support:* Fellowships, research assistantships, Federal Work-Study, institutionally sponsored loans, and scholarships/grants available. Support available to part-time students. Financial award application deadline: 2/15; financial award applicants required to submit FAFSA. *Faculty research:* Intellectual and social history, cultural studies, gender studies, Western history, Chicano history. *Unit head:* Janet Farrell Brodie, Chair, 909-621-8880, Fax: 909-621-8609, E-mail: janet.brodie@cgu.edu. *Application contact:* Justin Evans, Admissions Coordinator, 909-607-1278, E-mail: justin.evans@cgu.edu.

Clark University, Graduate School, Department of History, Program in American History, Worcester, MA 01610-1477. Offers PhD. *Students:* 10 full-time (4 women). 15 applicants, 60% accepted, 6 enrolled. *Application deadline:* For fall admission, 1/15 for domestic students. Application fee: $50. *Expenses:* Tuition: Full-time $34,900; part-time $1091 per credit hour. Required fees: $30. *Financial support:* In 2008–09, fellowships with full and partial tuition reimbursements (averaging $11,850 per year), research assistantships with full and partial tuition reimbursements (averaging $11,850 per year), teaching assistantships with full and partial tuition reimbursements (averaging $11,850 per year) were awarded. *Unit head:* Dr. Drew McCoy, Chair, 508-793-7288. *Application contact:* Diane Fenner, Academic Secretary, 508-793-7288, Fax: 508-793-8816, E-mail: history@clarku.edu.

The College of William and Mary, Faculty of Arts and Sciences, Program in American Studies, Williamsburg, VA 23187-8795. Offers MA, PhD, JD/MA. Part-time programs available. Terminal master's awarded for partial completion of doctoral program. *Degree requirements:* For master's, thesis; for doctorate, one foreign language, comprehensive exam, thesis/dissertation. *Entrance requirements:* For master's, BA Degree; for doctorate, MA Degree. Additional exam requirements/recommendations for international students: Required—TOEFL. Electronic applications accepted. *Expenses:* Tuition, state resident: full-time $6400; part-time $300 per credit hour. Tuition, nonresident: full-time $19,720; part-time $800 per credit hour. International tuition: $19,720 full-time. Required fees: $3860. *Faculty research:* Native American literature and environment, Guada canal and memory, 20th century African-American celebrity, African-American's relation to war, American religious nationalism.

Columbia University, Graduate School of Arts and Sciences, Program in Liberal Studies, New York, NY 10027. Offers American studies (MA); East Asian studies (MA); human rights studies (MA); Islamic culture studies (MA); Jewish studies (MA); medieval studies (MA); modern European studies (MA); South Asian studies (MA). Part-time and evening/weekend programs available. *Degree requirements:* For master's, thesis.

Cornell University, Graduate School, Graduate Fields of Arts and Sciences, Field of English Language and Literature, Ithaca, NY 14853-0001. Offers African-American literature (PhD); American literature after 1865 (PhD); American literature to 1865 (PhD); American studies (PhD); colonial and postcolonial literature (PhD); creative writing (MFA); cultural studies (PhD); dramatic literature (PhD); English poetry (PhD); English Renaissance to 1660 (PhD); lesbian, bisexual, and gay literature studies (PhD); literary criticism and theory (PhD); nineteenth century (PhD); Old and Middle English (PhD); prose fiction (PhD); Restoration and eighteenth century (PhD); twentieth century (PhD); women's literature (PhD); MFA/PhD. *Faculty:* 54 full-time (27 women). *Students:* 100 full-time (53 women); includes 24 minority (8 African Americans, 4 American Indian/Alaska Native, 6 Asian Americans or Pacific Islanders, 6 Hispanic Americans), 14 international. Average age 29. 821 applicants, 6% accepted, 23 enrolled. In 2008, 19 master's, 12 doctorates awarded. Terminal master's awarded for partial completion of doctoral program. *Degree requirements:* For master's, one foreign language, thesis; for doctorate, one foreign language, comprehensive exam, thesis/dissertation, teaching experience. *Entrance requirements:* For master's, GRE General Test, 3 letters of recommendation, creative writing sample; for doctorate, GRE General Test, GRE Subject Test (English), 3 letters of recommendation, writing sample. Additional exam requirements/recommendations for international students: Required—TOEFL (minimum score 600 paper-based; 250 computer-based; 77 iBT). *Application deadline:* For fall admission, 1/10 for domestic students. Application fee: $70. Electronic applications accepted. *Expenses:* Tuition: Full-time $29,500. Required fees: $70. Full-time tuition and fees vary according to degree level, program and student level. *Financial support:* In 2008–09, 96 students received support, including 41 fellowships with full tuition reimbursements available, 1 research assistantship with full tuition reimbursement available, 54 teaching assistantships with full tuition reimbursements available; institutionally sponsored loans, scholarships/grants, health care benefits, tuition waivers (full and partial), and unspecified assistantships also available. Financial award applicants required to submit FAFSA. *Faculty research:* English and American literature, women's writing, ethnic and post-colonial literature, critical theory, medievalism. *Unit head:* Director of Graduate Studies, 607-255-7989, Fax: 607-255-6661. *Application contact:* Graduate Field Assistant, 607-255-7989, Fax: 607-255-6661, E-mail: english_grad@cornell.edu.

Cornell University, Graduate School, Graduate Fields of Arts and Sciences, Field of History, Ithaca, NY 14853-0001. Offers African history (MA, PhD); American history (MA, PhD); ancient history (MA, PhD); early modern European history (MA, PhD); English history (MA, PhD); French history (MA, PhD); German history (MA, PhD); history of science (MA, PhD); Latin American history (MA, PhD); medieval Chinese history (MA, PhD); medieval history (MA, PhD); modern Chinese history (MA, PhD); modern European history (MA, PhD); modern Japanese history (MA, PhD); premodern Islamic history (MA, PhD); premodern Japanese history (MA, PhD); Renaissance history (MA, PhD); Russian history (MA, PhD); Southeast Asian history (MA, PhD). *Faculty:* 54 full-time (14 women). *Students:* 65 full-time (35 women); includes 12 minority (4 African Americans, 3 Asian Americans or Pacific Islanders, 5 Hispanic Americans), 19 international. Average age 31. 205 applicants, 8% accepted, 11 enrolled. In 2008, 12 master's, 6 doctorates awarded. Terminal master's awarded for partial completion of doctoral program. *Degree requirements:* For master's, thesis; for doctorate, 2 foreign languages, comprehensive exam, thesis/dissertation, 1 year of teaching experience. *Entrance requirements:* For master's and doctorate, GRE General Test, writing sample, 3 letters of recommendation. Additional exam requirements/recommendations for international students: Required—TOEFL (minimum score 550 paper-based; 213 computer-based; 77 iBT). *Application deadline:* For fall admission, 1/15 for domestic students. Application fee: $70. Electronic applications accepted. *Expenses:* Tuition: Full-time $29,500. Required fees: $70. Full-time tuition and fees vary according to degree level, program and student level. *Financial support:* In 2008–09, 54 students received support, including 27 fellowships with full tuition reimbursements available, 3 research assistantships with full tuition reimbursements available, 24 teaching assistantships with full tuition reimbursements available; institutionally sponsored loans, scholarships/grants, health care benefits, tuition waivers (full and partial), and unspecified assistantships also available. Financial award applicants required to submit FAFSA. *Unit head:* Director of Graduate Studies, 607-255-6738, Fax: 607-255-0469. *Application contact:* Graduate Field Assistant, 607-255-6738, Fax: 607-255-0469, E-mail: history_grad_info@cornell.edu.

Cornell University, Graduate School, Graduate Fields of Arts and Sciences, Field of History of Art and Archaeology, Ithaca, NY 14853. Offers American art (PhD); ancient art and archaeology (PhD); Asian art (PhD); baroque art (PhD); medieval art (PhD); modern art (PhD); Renaissance art (PhD); Southeast Asian art (PhD); theory and criticism (PhD). *Faculty:* 17 full-time (11 women). *Students:* 23 full-time (19 women); includes 4 minority (1 African American, 2 Asian Americans or Pacific Islanders, 1 Hispanic American), 7 international. Average age 33. 76 applicants, 8% accepted, 4 enrolled. In 2008, 1 doctorate awarded. *Degree requirements:* For doctorate, one foreign language, comprehensive exam, thesis/dissertation, general exams in 3 areas. *Entrance requirements:* For doctorate, GRE General Test, sample of written work, 3 letters of recommendation. Additional exam requirements/recommendations for international students: Required—TOEFL (minimum score 550 paper-based; 213 computer-based; 77 iBT). *Application deadline:* For fall admission, 1/15 for domestic students. Application fee: $70. Electronic applications accepted. *Expenses:* Tuition: Full-time $29,500. Required fees: $70. Full-time tuition and fees vary according to degree level, program and student level. *Financial support:* In 2008–09, 17 students received support, including 10 fellowships with full tuition reimbursements available, 1 research assistantship with full tuition reimbursement available, 6 teaching assistantships with full tuition reimbursements available; institutionally sponsored loans, scholarships/grants, health care benefits, tuition waivers (full and partial), and unspecified assistantships also available. Financial award applicants required to submit FAFSA. *Unit head:* Director of Graduate Studies, 607-255-4905, Fax: 607-255-0566, E-mail: art_history@cornell.edu. *Application contact:* Graduate Field Assistant, 607-255-4905, Fax: 607-255-0566, E-mail: art_history@cornell.edu.

Drake University, School of Education, Department of Teaching and Learning, Program in Secondary Education, Des Moines, IA 50311-4516. Offers art (MAT); biology (MAT); business (MAT); chemistry (MAT); English (MAT); general science (MAT); history-American (MAT); history-world (MAT); journalism (MAT); mathematics (MAT); physical science (MAT); physics (MAT); sociology (MAT); speech (MAT); speech communication (MAT); theatre (MAT). Part-time programs available. *Degree requirements:* For master's, comprehensive exam, thesis (for some programs), internships (for some programs). *Entrance requirements:* For master's, GRE General Test, MAT, or Drake Writing Assessment, resumé, 2 letters of recommendation. Additional exam requirements/recommendations for international students: Required—TOEFL (minimum score 550 paper-based; 213 computer-based). Electronic applications accepted. *Faculty research:* Counseling and rehabilitation, behavioral supports, inquiry-based science methods, teacher quality enhancement.

East Carolina University, Graduate School, Thomas Harriot College of Arts and Sciences, Department of History, Greenville, NC 27858-4353. Offers American history (MA); European history (MA); maritime history (MA). Part-time and evening/weekend programs available. *Degree requirements:* For master's, one foreign language, comprehensive exam, thesis. *Entrance requirements:* For master's, GRE General Test, GRE Subject Test. Additional exam requirements/recommendations for international students: Required—TOEFL.

Eastern Michigan University, Graduate School, College of Arts and Sciences, Department of History and Philosophy, Program in Social Science, Ypsilanti, MI 48197. Offers social science (MA, Graduate Certificate); social science and American culture (MLS). Part-time and evening/weekend programs available. Postbaccalaureate distance learning degree programs offered (minimal on-campus study). *Degree requirements:* For master's, thesis optional. *Entrance requirements:* Additional exam requirements/recommendations for international students: Required—TOEFL.

Emory & Henry College, Graduate Programs, Emory, VA 24327-0947. Offers American history (MA Ed); professional studies (M Ed); reading specialist (MA Ed). Part-time and evening/weekend programs available. *Entrance requirements:* For master's, GRE or PRAXIS I, recommendations, writing sample, official transcripts.

Fairfield University, College of Arts and Sciences, Fairfield, CT 06824-5195. Offers American studies (MA); communication (MA); creative writing (MFA); mathematics (MS). Part-time and evening/weekend programs available. *Faculty:* 46 full-time (20 women), 15 part-time/adjunct (7 women). *Students:* 6 full-time (1 woman), 53 part-time (26 women); includes 1 African American, 2 Hispanic Americans. Average age 41. 23 applicants, 78% accepted, 14 enrolled. In 2008, 36 master's awarded. *Degree requirements:* For master's, capstone research course. *Entrance requirements:* For master's, minimum GPA of 3.0, 2 letters of recommendation, resumé, essay. Additional exam requirements/recommendations for international students: Required—TOEFL (minimum score 550 paper-based; 213 computer-based; 80 iBT). *Application deadline:* For fall admission, 5/15 for international students; for spring admission, 10/15 for international students. Applications are processed on a rolling basis. Application fee: $60.

American Studies

Fairfield University (continued)
Electronic applications accepted. *Expenses:* Tuition: Full-time $9450; part-time $525 per credit hour. Required fees: $25 per semester. Tuition and fees vary according to course load and program. *Financial support:* In 2008–09, 19 students received support. Unspecified assistantships available. Financial award applicants required to submit FAFSA. *Faculty research:* Non-commutative algebra, partial differential equations, writing (fiction, non-fiction and poetry), communication for social change, comparative media systems, negotiation and management. *Unit head:* Dr. Robbin Crabtree, Dean, 203-254-4000 Ext. 3263, Fax: 203-254-4119, E-mail: rcrabtree@fairfield.edu. *Application contact:* Marianne Gumpper, Director of Graduate and Continuing Studies Admissions, 203-254-4184, Fax: 203-254-4073, E-mail: gradadmis@fairfield.edu.

Florida State University, Graduate Studies, College of Arts and Sciences, Department of Interdisciplinary Humanities, Program in American and Florida Studies, Tallahassee, FL 32306. Offers MA, Certificate. Part-time programs available. *Degree requirements:* For master's, one foreign language, thesis or alternative. *Entrance requirements:* For master's, GRE General Test, minimum GPA of 3.0. Electronic applications accepted. *Faculty research:* American intellectual history, religion in America, Hemingway, consumer culture, Florida history, Florida culture, development of communities.

Georgetown University, Graduate School of Arts and Sciences, School of Continuing Studies, Washington, DC 20057. Offers American studies (MALS); Catholic studies (MALS); classical civilizations (MALS); ethics and the professions (MALS); human resources management (MPS); humanities (MALS); individualized study (MALS); international affairs (MALS); Islam and Muslim-Christian relations (MALS); journalism (MPS); liberal studies (DLS); literature and society (MALS); medieval and early modern European studies (MALS); public relations (MPS); real estate (MPS); religious studies (MALS); social and public policy (MALS); sports industry management (MPS); the theory and practice of American democracy (MALS); visual culture (MALS). *Entrance requirements:* Additional exam requirements/recommendations for international students: Required—TOEFL.

The George Washington University, Columbian College of Arts and Sciences, Department of American Studies, Washington, DC 20052. Offers American studies (PhD); folklife (MA); historic preservation (MA); material culture (MA). Part-time and evening/weekend programs available. *Faculty:* 11 full-time (5 women), 3 part-time/adjunct (1 woman). *Students:* 18 full-time (11 women), 23 part-time (14 women); includes 5 minority (4 African Americans, 1 Hispanic American), 3 international. Average age 31. 116 applicants, 23% accepted, 8 enrolled. In 2008, 11 master's, 5 doctorates awarded. Terminal master's awarded for partial completion of doctoral program. *Degree requirements:* For master's, comprehensive exam; for doctorate, one foreign language, thesis/dissertation, general exam. *Entrance requirements:* For master's and doctorate, GRE General Test, minimum GPA of 3.0. Additional exam requirements/recommendations for international students: Required—TOEFL (minimum score 550 paper-based; 213 computer-based; 80 iBT). *Application deadline:* For fall admission, 1/15 priority date for domestic and international students; for spring admission, 10/1 for domestic students. Application fee: $60. *Financial support:* In 2008–09, 22 students received support; fellowships, research assistantships, teaching assistantships, career-related internships or fieldwork, Federal Work-Study, institutionally sponsored loans, and tuition waivers available. Financial award application deadline: 1/15. *Unit head:* James A Miller, Chair, 202-994-6743, E-mail: jam@gwu.edu. *Application contact:* Information Contact, 202-994-6070, Fax: 202-994-8651, E-mail: amst@gwu.edu.

Harvard University, Graduate School of Arts and Sciences, Committee on History of American Civilization, Cambridge, MA 02138. Offers PhD. *Degree requirements:* For doctorate, 2 foreign languages, thesis/dissertation. *Entrance requirements:* For doctorate, GRE General Test, GRE Subject Test (recommended). Additional exam requirements/recommendations for international students: Required—TOEFL. *Expenses:* Tuition: Full-time $32,556. Required fees: $1426. Full-time tuition and fees vary according to program and student level. *Faculty research:* American history, literature, and religion in the Colonial era; twentieth century American history, literature, and law; Southern literature, history, and sociology.

Lehigh University, College of Arts and Sciences, Program in American Studies, Bethlehem, PA 18015. Offers MA. Part-time programs available. *Students:* 8 full-time (6 women), 4 part-time (3 women), 1 international. Average age 31. 12 applicants, 58% accepted, 2 enrolled. In 2008, 5 master's awarded. *Degree requirements:* For master's, thesis. *Entrance requirements:* For master's, GRE. Additional exam requirements/recommendations for international students: Required—TOEFL. *Application deadline:* For fall admission, 7/15 for domestic and international students; for spring admission, 12/1 for domestic and international students. Application fee: $65. Electronic applications accepted. *Financial support:* In 2008–09, 1 fellowship with full tuition reimbursement was awarded; tuition waivers (full) and unspecified assistantships also available. *Unit head:* Prof. Edward Whitley, Director, 610-758-4745, Fax: 610-758-6554, E-mail: amstdgrad@lehigh.edu. *Application contact:* Mary T. Harnett, Coordinator, 610-758-4745, Fax: 610-758-6554, E-mail: amstdgrad@lehigh.edu.

Lindenwood University, Graduate Programs, School of Humanities, St. Charles, MO 63301-1695. Offers American studies (MA). Part-time programs available. *Faculty:* 4 full-time (2 women), 5 part-time/adjunct (1 woman). *Students:* 4 full-time (3 women). Average age 32. In 2008, 1 master's awarded. *Degree requirements:* For master's, minimum GPA of 3.0. *Entrance requirements:* For master's, minimum GPA of 2.5, essay, official transcripts, 2 letters of recommendation. Additional exam requirements/recommendations for international students: Required—TOEFL (minimum score 550 paper-based; 213 computer-based; 80 iBT). *Application deadline:* For fall admission, 8/30 priority date for domestic and international students; for spring admission, 12/30 for domestic students, 12/30 priority date for international students. Applications are processed on a rolling basis. Application fee: $30 ($100 for international students). Electronic applications accepted. *Expenses:* Tuition: Full-time $12,700; part-time $360 per credit hour. *Financial support:* Career-related internships or fieldwork, institutionally sponsored loans, tuition waivers (partial), and unspecified assistantships available. Financial award application deadline: 6/30; financial award applicants required to submit FAFSA. *Unit head:* Dr. Ana Schnellmann, Dean of Humanities, 636-949-4873, E-mail: aschnellmann@lindenwood.edu. *Application contact:* Brett Barger, Dean of Evening Admissions and Extension Campuses, 636-949-4934, Fax: 636-949-4109, E-mail: adultadmissions@lindenwood.edu.

Michigan State University, The Graduate School, College of Arts and Letters, Program in American Studies, East Lansing, MI 48824. Offers MA, PhD. *Entrance requirements:* Additional exam requirements/recommendations for international students: Required—TOEFL. Electronic applications accepted.

Mississippi State University, College of Arts and Sciences, Department of History, Mississippi State, MS 39762. Offers MA, PhD. Part-time programs available. *Degree requirements:* For master's, one foreign language, comprehensive exam, thesis optional; for doctorate, 2 foreign languages, thesis/dissertation, comprehensive oral and written exam. *Entrance requirements:* For master's, minimum GPA of 3.0; for doctorate, GRE General Test, writing sample, minimum graduate GPA of 3.0. Additional exam requirements/recommendations for international students: Required—TOEFL. *Faculty research:* U.S. political, diplomatic, military, social, and cultural history; modern Europe; Latin America; Asian history; African history.

Montana State University, College of Graduate Studies, Interdisciplinary Program in American Studies, Bozeman, MT 59717. Offers MA, PhD.

New Mexico Highlands University, Graduate Studies, College of Arts and Sciences, Program in Southwest Studies, Las Vegas, NM 87701. Offers anthropology (MA). Program is interdisciplinary. Part-time programs available. *Faculty:* 12 full-time (7 women). *Students:* 7 full-time (3 women), 8 part-time (5 women); includes 3 minority (all Hispanic Americans). Average age 37. 8 applicants, 75% accepted, 4 enrolled. In 2008, 2 master's awarded. *Degree requirements:* For master's, comprehensive exam, thesis or alternative. *Entrance requirements:* For master's, minimum undergraduate GPA of 3.0. Additional exam requirements/recommendations for international students: Required—TOEFL (minimum score 540 paper-based; 207 computer-based). *Application deadline:* For fall admission, 8/1 priority date for domestic students. Applications are processed on a rolling basis. Application fee: $15. *Expenses:* Tuition, state resident: full-time $2880; part-time $120 per credit hour. Tuition, nonresident: full-time $4234; part-time $176 per credit hour. International tuition: $5645 full-time. One-time fee: $20. *Financial support:* In 2008–09, 13 students received support, including teaching assistantships (averaging $6,500 per year); career-related internships or fieldwork, Federal Work-Study, institutionally sponsored loans, scholarships/grants, tuition waivers (full and partial), and unspecified assistantships also available. Support available to part-time students. Financial award application deadline: 3/1; financial award applicants required to submit FAFSA. *Application contact:* Diane Trujillo, Administrative Assistant, Graduate Studies, 505-454-3266, Fax: 505-426-2117, E-mail: dtrujillo@nmhu.edu.

New York University, Graduate School of Arts and Science, Program in American Studies, New York, NY 10012-1019. Offers MA, PhD. Part-time programs available. *Degree requirements:* For master's, one foreign language, thesis; for doctorate, 2 foreign languages, thesis/dissertation. *Entrance requirements:* For master's and doctorate, GRE General Test, writing sample. Additional exam requirements/recommendations for international students: Required—TOEFL. *Faculty research:* Cultural politics; race, gender, and sexuality studies; nationalism and transnationalism; science and technology; urban and suburban studies.

New York University, Graduate School of Arts and Science, Program in Irish and Irish American Studies, New York, NY 10012-1019. Offers MA. Part-time programs available. *Degree requirements:* For master's, one foreign language. *Entrance requirements:* For master's, GRE General Test. Additional exam requirements/recommendations for international students: Required—TOEFL.

Northeastern State University, Graduate College, College of Liberal Arts, Program in American Studies, Tahlequah, OK 74464-2399. Offers MA. Part-time and evening/weekend programs available. *Students:* 3 full-time (1 woman), 14 part-time (8 women); includes 4 minority (2 American Indian/Alaska Native, 2 Hispanic Americans). In 2008, 7 master's awarded. *Degree requirements:* For master's, thesis, written and oral examinations. *Entrance requirements:* For master's, GRE, minimum GPA of 2.5. Additional exam requirements/recommendations for international students: Required—TOEFL (minimum score 213 computer-based). *Application deadline:* For fall admission, 6/1 priority date for domestic students. Applications are processed on a rolling basis. Application fee: $0 ($25 for international students). Electronic applications accepted. *Financial support:* Teaching assistantships, Federal Work-Study available. Financial award application deadline: 3/1. *Unit head:* Dr. Chris Owen, Coordinator, 918-456-5511, Fax: 918-458-2390, E-mail: owen@nsuok.edu. *Application contact:* Margie Railey, Administrative Assistant, 918-456-5511 Ext. 2093, Fax: 918-458-2061, E-mail: railey@nsouk.edu.

Penn State Harrisburg, Graduate School, School of Humanities, Middletown, PA 17057-4898. Offers American studies (MA); humanities (MA). Evening/weekend programs available.

Pepperdine University, Seaver College, Humanities Division, Malibu, CA 90263. Offers American studies (MA); history (MA). *Degree requirements:* For master's, oral and written exams. *Entrance requirements:* For master's, GRE General Test, undergraduate major or 15 upper-division units in history. Additional exam requirements/recommendations for international students: Required—TOEFL.

Providence College, Graduate Studies, Department of History, Providence, RI 02918. Offers American history (MA); European history (MA). Part-time and evening/weekend programs available. *Faculty:* 11 full-time (3 women), 3 part-time/adjunct (0 women). *Students:* 17 full-time (9 women), 47 part-time (20 women), 1 international. Average age 31. 10 applicants, 100% accepted. In 2008, 26 master's awarded. *Degree requirements:* For master's, comprehensive exam, thesis optional. *Entrance requirements:* Additional exam requirements/recommendations for international students: Required—TOEFL (minimum score 550 paper-based; 213 computer-based; 80 iBT). *Application deadline:* For fall admission, 8/1 priority date for domestic and international students; for spring admission, 12/31 priority date for domestic students, 12/1 priority date for international students. Applications are processed on a rolling basis. Application fee: $55. *Expenses:* Tuition: Full-time $8991; part-time $333 per credit hour. One-time fee: $170. Tuition and fees vary according to program. *Financial support:* In 2008–09, 8 research assistantships with full tuition reimbursements (averaging $8,400 per year) were awarded; career-related internships or fieldwork, institutionally sponsored loans, and unspecified assistantships also available. Support available to part-time students. Financial award application deadline: 8/1; financial award applicants required to submit FAFSA. *Faculty research:* Modern Europe, American social and political history, Modern Ireland, Rhode Island, Eastern European history. *Unit head:* Dr. Paul O'Malley, Director of Graduate Program in History, 401-865-2193, Fax: 401-865-1193, E-mail: pomalley@providence.edu. *Application contact:* Phyllis S. Cardullo, Senior Administrative Coordinator, 401-865-2193, Fax: 401-865-1193, E-mail: pcardull@providence.edu.

Purdue University, Graduate School, College of Liberal Arts, Program in American Studies, West Lafayette, IN 47907. Offers MA, PhD. *Degree requirements:* For master's, essay; for doctorate, one foreign language, thesis/dissertation. *Entrance requirements:* For master's and doctorate, GRE General Test, sample of written work. Additional exam requirements/recommendations for international students: Required—TOEFL, TWE. Electronic applications accepted. *Faculty research:* American history, literature, politics, sociology, women's studies, African-American studies, mass culture.

Rutgers, The State University of New Jersey, Newark, Graduate School, Program in American Studies, Newark, NJ 07102. Offers MA, PhD. *Entrance requirements:* For master's and doctorate, GRE, minimum undergraduate B average.

Saint Louis University, Graduate School, College of Arts and Sciences and Graduate School, Department of American Studies, St. Louis, MO 63103-2097. Offers MA, MA-R, PhD. Part-time programs available. *Degree requirements:* For master's, thesis optional, comprehensive written and oral exams; for doctorate, one foreign language, comprehensive exam, thesis/dissertation, preliminary exams. *Entrance requirements:* For master's and doctorate, GRE General Test, letters of recommendation, resumé, goal statement, transcripts. Additional exam requirements/recommendations for international students: Required—TOEFL (minimum score 525 paper-based; 194 computer-based). Electronic applications accepted. *Faculty research:* Urban studies, American religion, intellectual history, southern culture, African-American literature.

State University of New York College at Cortland, Graduate Studies, School of Arts and Sciences, Program in American Civilization and Culture, Cortland, NY 13045. Offers CAS. Part-time and evening/weekend programs available. *Entrance requirements:* Additional exam requirements/recommendations for international students: Required—TOEFL.

Trinity College, Graduate Programs, Program in American Studies, Hartford, CT 06106-3100. Offers MA. Part-time and evening/weekend programs available. *Degree requirements:* For master's, thesis or alternative. *Entrance requirements:* For master's, minimum GPA of 3.0.

Universidad de las Américas–Puebla, Division of Graduate Studies, School of Social Sciences, Program in American Studies, Puebla, Mexico. Offers MA. Part-time and evening/weekend programs available. *Degree requirements:* For master's, one foreign language, thesis. *Faculty research:* NAFTA, technology, culture, politics and economics in NAFTA region.

University at Buffalo, the State University of New York, Graduate School, College of Arts and Sciences, Department of American Studies, Buffalo, NY 14260. Offers MA, PhD. Post-baccalaureate distance learning degree programs offered (minimal on-campus study). Terminal master's awarded for partial completion of doctoral program. *Degree requirements:* For master's, comprehensive exam, thesis (for some programs); for doctorate, comprehensive exam, thesis/dissertation. *Entrance requirements:* For master's, minimum GPA of 3.0; for doctorate, GRE, minimum GPA of 3.0. Additional exam requirements/recommendations for international students: Required—TOEFL (minimum score 550 paper-based; 213 computer-based). Electronic applications accepted. *Faculty research:* Native American studies, intercultural studies, indigenous people's studies, multiculturalism, border theory, cultural studies, American popular culture.

The University of Alabama, Graduate School, College of Arts and Sciences, Department of American Studies, Tuscaloosa, AL 35487. Offers MA. Part-time programs available. *Faculty:* 5 full-time (1 woman). *Students:* 12 full-time (6 women), 1 part-time (0 women); includes 2 minority (1 African American, 1 Asian American or Pacific Islander), 1 international. Average age 24. 13 applicants, 69% accepted, 5 enrolled. In 2008, 6 master's awarded. *Degree requirements:* For master's, comprehensive exam, thesis optional. *Entrance requirements:* For master's, GRE or MAT. Additional exam requirements/recommendations for international students: Required—TOEFL. *Application deadline:* For fall admission, 1/15 priority date for domestic and international students; for spring admission, 11/30 priority date for domestic and international students. Applications are processed on a rolling basis. Application fee: $30. Electronic applications accepted. *Expenses:* Tuition, area resident: Full-time $6400. Tuition, state resident: full-time $6400. Tuition, nonresident: full-time $18,000. *Financial support:* In 2008–09, 12 students received support, including 5 teaching assistantships with full tuition reimbursements available (averaging $10,291 per year); Federal Work-Study, tuition waivers (full), and unspecified assistantships also available. *Faculty research:* Social and cultural history, popular music, African-American arts, the South, women's history, Asian-American studies, sports, Latino Studies. *Unit head:* Dr. Lynne M. Adrian, Associate Professor, 205-348-5940, Fax: 205-348-9766, E-mail: ladrian@tenhoor.as.ua.edu. *Application contact:* Dr. Lynne M. Adrian, Associate Professor, 205-348-5940, Fax: 205-348-9766, E-mail: ladrian@tenhoor.as.ua.edu.

University of Central Oklahoma, College of Graduate Studies and Research, College of Liberal Arts, Department of History, Edmond, OK 73034-5209. Offers history (MA); museum studies (MA); social studies teaching (MA); Southwestern studies (MA). Part-time programs available. *Degree requirements:* For master's, thesis optional. *Entrance requirements:* Additional exam requirements/recommendations for international students: Required—TOEFL (minimum score 550 paper-based; 213 computer-based). Electronic applications accepted. *Faculty research:* China, Russia, civil war, American naval logistics.

University of Dallas, Braniff Graduate School of Liberal Arts, Program in American Studies, Irving, TX 75062-4736. Offers MAS. Part-time programs available. *Degree requirements:* For master's, comprehensive exam. *Entrance requirements:* For master's, GRE General Test. *Faculty research:* Shakespeare, Milton, Melville, Hawthorne, liberty and American literature.

University of Delaware, College of Arts and Sciences, Winterthur Program in Early American Culture, Newark, DE 19716. Offers MA. *Degree requirements:* For master's, thesis. *Entrance requirements:* For master's, GRE General Test, minimum GPA of 3.0. Electronic applications accepted. *Faculty research:* American material culture, American studies, decorative arts.

University of Hawaii at Manoa, Graduate Division, Colleges of Arts and Sciences, College of Arts and Humanities, Department of American Studies, Honolulu, HI 96822. Offers American studies (MA, PhD); historic preservation (Graduate Certificate); museum studies (Graduate Certificate). Part-time programs available. *Degree requirements:* For master's, comprehensive exam (for some programs), thesis (for some programs); for doctorate, comprehensive exam, thesis/dissertation. *Entrance requirements:* For master's and doctorate, GRE General Test. Additional exam requirements/recommendations for international students: Required—TOEFL (minimum score 600 paper-based; 250 computer-based; 100 iBT), IELTS (minimum score 7). *Faculty research:* Ethnicity and race, popular culture, historic preservation, arts and culture, international relations.

The University of Iowa, Graduate College, College of Liberal Arts and Sciences, Department of American Studies, Iowa City, IA 52242-1316. Offers MA, PhD. *Degree requirements:* For master's, thesis optional, exam; for doctorate, comprehensive exam, thesis/dissertation. *Entrance requirements:* For master's and doctorate, GRE General Test, minimum GPA of 3.0. Additional exam requirements/recommendations for international students: Required—TOEFL (minimum score 550 paper-based; 213 computer-based; 81 iBT). Electronic applications accepted.

The University of Kansas, Graduate Studies, College of Liberal Arts and Sciences, Program in American Studies, Lawrence, KS 66045. Offers MA, PhD, MUP/MA. Part-time programs available. *Faculty:* 10. *Students:* 41 full-time (24 women), 6 part-time (3 women); includes 6 minority (4 African Americans, 1 American Indian/Alaska Native, 1 Hispanic American), 12 international. Average age 35. 36 applicants, 39% accepted, 3 enrolled. In 2008, 4 master's, 5 doctorates awarded. Terminal master's awarded for partial completion of doctoral program. *Degree requirements:* For master's, thesis or alternative; for doctorate, 2 foreign languages, comprehensive exam, thesis/dissertation. *Entrance requirements:* For master's and doctorate, GRE General Test. Additional exam requirements/recommendations for international students: Required—TOEFL. *Application deadline:* For fall admission, 5/1 for domestic students. Applications are processed on a rolling basis. Application fee: $45 ($50 for international students). Electronic applications accepted. *Expenses:* Tuition, area resident: Full-time $6122; part-time $255.10 per credit hour. Tuition, state resident: full-time $6122; part-time $255.10 per credit hour. Tuition, nonresident: full-time $14,629; part-time $609.55 per credit hour. Required fees: $847; $70.56 per credit hour. Tuition and fees vary according to course load and program. *Financial support:* Fellowships with full tuition reimbursements, research assistantships with partial tuition reimbursements, teaching assistantships with full and partial tuition reimbursements, Federal Work-Study, scholarships/grants, health care benefits, and unspecified assistantships available. Financial award application deadline: 12/21. *Faculty research:* Transnational and global American studies of race, gender, class, religion, ethnicity, sexuality, jazz studies, public health and medicine; migration and immigration; Latino/a studies; African-American studies; Jewish studies; women's studies; oral history; ethnography. *Unit head:* Cheryl Lester, Director, 785-864-2309, Fax: 785-864-5772, E-mail: chlester@ku.edu. *Application contact:* Kay Isbell, Information Contact, 785-864-2306, Fax: 785-864-5772, E-mail: amerst@ku.edu.

University of Louisiana at Lafayette, BI Moody III College of Business Administration MBA Program, College of Liberal Arts, Department of Modern Languages, Program in Francophone Studies, Lafayette, LA 70504. Offers PhD. *Degree requirements:* For doctorate, 2 foreign languages, comprehensive exam, thesis/dissertation. *Entrance requirements:* For doctorate, GRE General Test, minimum GPA of 2.75. Additional exam requirements/recommendations for international students: Required—TOEFL (minimum score 550 paper-based; 213 computer-based). Electronic applications accepted. *Faculty research:* Louisiana folklore; eighteenth century French literature, contemporary criticism.

University of Maryland, College Park, Graduate Studies, College of Arts and Humanities, Department of American Studies, College Park, MD 20742. Offers MA, PhD. *Degree requirements:* For master's, thesis optional, thesis or scholarly paper and exam; for doctorate, thesis/dissertation, 3 comprehensive exams. *Entrance requirements:* For master's, GRE General Test, minimum GPA of 3.0, writing sample, 3 letters of recommendation; for doctorate, GRE General Test. Additional exam requirements/recommendations for international students: Required—TOEFL. Electronic applications accepted. *Faculty research:* Material culture, modes of culture, cultural movements, popular culture, ethnography.

University of Massachusetts Boston, Office of Graduate Studies, College of Liberal Arts, Program in American Studies, Boston, MA 02125-3393. Offers MA. Part-time and evening/weekend programs available. *Degree requirements:* For master's, thesis or capstone project. *Entrance requirements:* For master's, minimum GPA of 2.75. *Faculty research:* War in American culture, immigration history, Latin Americans, history of race and popular music, education and Asian Americans.

University of Michigan, Horace H. Rackham School of Graduate Studies, College of Literature, Science, and the Arts, Interdepartmental Program in American Culture, Ann Arbor, MI 48109. Offers AM, PhD. Terminal master's awarded for partial completion of doctoral program. *Degree requirements:* For doctorate, field and preliminary exams, oral defense of dissertation. *Entrance requirements:* For master's, GRE General Test; for doctorate, GRE General Test, sample of written work. Additional exam requirements/recommendations for international students: Required—TOEFL. Electronic applications accepted. *Faculty research:* Cultural studies; ethnic studies, American culture methodology, literature, history.

University of Michigan–Flint, Graduate Programs, Program in American Culture, Flint, MI 48502-1950. Offers MLS. Part-time programs available. *Faculty:* 3 full-time (2 women), 2 part-time/adjunct (0 women). *Students:* 6 full-time (3 women), 27 part-time (18 women); includes 5 minority (4 African Americans, 1 Hispanic American). Average age 42. 16 applicants, 94% accepted, 14 enrolled. In 2008, 22 master's awarded. *Degree requirements:* For master's, thesis or alternative. *Entrance requirements:* For master's, minimum GPA of 3.0, 24 undergraduate credits in humanities and social sciences. Additional exam requirements/recommendations for international students: Required—TOEFL (minimum score 560 paper-based; 220 computer-based; 84 iBT), IELTS (minimum score 6.5). *Application deadline:* For fall admission, 8/1 for domestic students, 5/1 for international students; for winter admission, 11/15 for domestic students, 9/1 for international students; for spring admission, 3/15 for domestic students, 1/1 for international students. Application fee: $55. Electronic applications accepted. *Expenses:* Tuition, area resident: Full-time $9973; part-time $415.50 per credit. Tuition, state resident: full-time $9973; part-time $415.50 per credit. Tuition, nonresident: full-time $14,960; part-time $623.30 per credit. Required fees: $368; $141 per term. Tuition and fees vary according to course level, course load, degree level and student level. *Financial support:* Federal Work-Study, scholarships/grants, and unspecified assistantships available. Support available to part-time students. Financial award application deadline: 6/1; financial award applicants required to submit FAFSA. *Unit head:* Dr. M Jan Furman, Director, 810-762-3285, E-mail: jfurman@umflint.edu. *Application contact:* Bradley T. Maki, Director of Graduate Admissions, 810-762-3171, Fax: 810-766-6789, E-mail: bmaki@umflint.edu.

University of Minnesota, Twin Cities Campus, Graduate School, College of Liberal Arts, Department of American Studies, Minneapolis, MN 55455-0213. Offers PhD. *Degree requirements:* For doctorate, one foreign language, comprehensive exam, thesis/dissertation. *Entrance requirements:* For doctorate, GRE General Test, sample of written work, 3 letters of recommendation. Additional exam requirements/recommendations for international students: Required—TOEFL (minimum score 550 paper-based; 213 computer-based). *Faculty research:* American Indian history, nationalism/transnationalism, gender and sexuality, race and ethnicity.

University of Mississippi, Graduate School, College of Liberal Arts, Interdisciplinary Program in Southern Studies, Oxford, University, MS 38677. Offers MA. *Entrance requirements:* For master's, GRE General Test, minimum GPA of 3.0. Additional exam requirements/recommendations for international students: Required—TOEFL. Electronic applications accepted.

University of New Mexico, Graduate School, College of Arts and Sciences, Department of American Studies, Albuquerque, NM 87131-2039. Offers MA, PhD. Part-time programs available. Terminal master's awarded for partial completion of doctoral program. *Degree requirements:* For master's, comprehensive exam (for some programs), thesis (for some programs); for doctorate, one foreign language, comprehensive exam, thesis/dissertation. *Entrance requirements:* For master's, BA in related field; for doctorate, MA in related field, complete dossier. Additional exam requirements/recommendations for international students: Required—TOEFL. Electronic applications accepted. *Faculty research:* Culture studies environment/science/technology, gender, race/class/ethnicity, popular culture, Southwest studies.

University of Southern California, Graduate School, College of Letters, Arts and Sciences, Department of American Studies and Ethnicity, Los Angeles, CA 90089. Offers PhD. Terminal master's awarded for partial completion of doctoral program. *Degree requirements:* For doctorate, one foreign language, thesis/dissertation. *Entrance requirements:* For doctorate, GRE. *Faculty research:* Race, ethnicity, culture, gender, sexuality.

University of Southern Maine, College of Arts and Sciences, Program in American and New England Studies, Portland, ME 04104-9300. Offers MA. Part-time and evening/weekend programs available. *Degree requirements:* For master's, thesis optional. *Entrance requirements:* For master's, GRE General Test or MAT. Additional exam requirements/recommendations for international students: Required—TOEFL. *Faculty research:* Social history, regional culture, landscape of literature, material culture, art and architecture.

University of South Florida, Graduate School, College of Arts and Sciences, Department of Humanities and American Studies, Tampa, FL 33620-9951. Offers American studies (MA); liberal arts (MLA). Part-time and evening/weekend programs available. *Faculty:* 5 full-time (2 women), 1 part-time/adjunct (0 women). *Students:* 32 full-time (18 women), 19 part-time (7 women); includes 11 minority (8 African Americans, 3 Hispanic Americans). 20 applicants, 55% accepted, 11 enrolled. In 2008, 7 master's awarded. *Degree requirements:* For master's, comprehensive exam, thesis. *Entrance requirements:* For master's, GRE General Test, minimum GPA of 3.0 in last 60 hours, academic writing sample. Additional exam requirements/recommendations for international students: Required—TOEFL (minimum score 550 paper-based; 213 computer-based). *Application deadline:* For fall admission, 2/15 priority date for domestic students, 1/2 for international students; for spring admission, 10/15 priority date for domestic students, 6/1 for international students. Application fee: $30. *Expenses:* Tuition, state resident: full-time $2624.40; part-time $291.60 per credit hour. Tuition, nonresident: full-time $7822; part-time $869.13 per credit hour. *Financial support:* In 2008–09, 4 teaching assistantships with tuition reimbursements were awarded; scholarships/grants also available. Financial award application deadline: 4/4. *Faculty research:* American South, American autobiography, material culture, critical theory, cultural studies. *Unit head:* Daniel Belgrad, Chairperson, 813-974-9388, Fax: 813-974-9409, E-mail: ams@cas.usf.edu. *Application contact:* Maria Cizmic, Program Director, 813-974-9388, Fax: 813-974-9409, E-mail: mcizmic@cas.usf.edu.

The University of Texas at Austin, Graduate School, College of Liberal Arts, Department of American Studies, Austin, TX 78712-1111. Offers MA, PhD. Part-time programs available. *Degree requirements:* For master's, thesis; for doctorate, one foreign language, thesis/dissertation, qualifying oral exam. *Entrance requirements:* For master's and doctorate, GRE General Test, minimum GPA of 3.5. Electronic applications accepted. *Faculty research:* Race, gender, and ethnicity; history of the American West; American design and archaeology; literary cultural history; religion and psychology in American culture.

University of Utah, The Graduate School, College of Humanities, Department of English, Salt Lake City, UT 84112-1107. Offers American studies (MA, PhD); British American literature (MA, PhD); creative writing (MFA, PhD); literature (PhD); rhetoric and composition (PhD). *Degree requirements:* For master's, one foreign language, thesis (for some programs), written exam; for doctorate, 2 foreign languages, comprehensive exam, thesis/dissertation. *Entrance requirements:* For master's and doctorate, GRE General Test, minimum GPA of 3.2. Additional exam requirements/recommendations for international students: Required—TOEFL (minimum score 500 paper-based; 173 computer-based; 120 iBT). Electronic applications accepted. *Faculty research:* Poetics and modern poetry, 19th and 20th century British and American literature, the American west, environmental studies, critical theory and race and gender studies.

University of Wisconsin–Madison, Graduate School, College of Letters and Science, Department of History, Madison, WI 53706-1380. Offers African history (MA, PhD); Central Asian history (MA, PhD); comparative world history (MA, PhD); East Asian history (MA, PhD); European history (MA, PhD); gender and women's history (MA, PhD); Latin American and Caribbean history (MA, PhD); Middle Eastern history (MA, PhD); South Asian history (MA, PhD); Southeast Asian history (MA, PhD); United States history (MA, PhD). Terminal master's awarded for partial completion of doctoral program. *Degree requirements:* For master's, thesis (for some programs); for doctorate, variable foreign language requirement, thesis/dissertation. *Entrance requirements:* For master's and doctorate, GRE General Test. Additional exam requirements/recommendations for international students: Required—Michigan English

American Studies

University of Wisconsin–Madison *(continued)*
Language Assessment Battery or TOEFL. Electronic applications accepted. *Faculty research:* American, African, European, Asian, Latin American, and Middle Eastern history.

University of Wyoming, Graduate School, College of Arts and Sciences, American Studies Program, Laramie, WY 82070. Offers MA. Part-time programs available. *Faculty:* 3 full-time (1 woman). *Students:* 15 full-time (10 women), 3 part-time (all women), 5 international. Average age 28. 9 applicants, 78% accepted, 7 enrolled. In 2008, 3 master's awarded. *Degree requirements:* For master's, thesis optional. *Entrance requirements:* For master's, GRE General Test, minimum GPA of 3.0. *Application deadline:* For fall admission, 4/1 priority date for domestic students. Applications are processed on a rolling basis. Application fee: $50. *Financial support:* In 2008–09, 10 research assistantships with tuition reimbursements, 7 teaching assistantships with tuition reimbursements were awarded; career-related internships or fieldwork, Federal Work-Study, and tuition waivers (partial) also available. Financial award application deadline: 3/1. *Faculty research:* Material culture, American culture, ethnicity, cultural environments, public culture. Total annual research expenditures: $25,000. *Unit head:* Dr. Eric Sandeen, Director, 307-766-3898. *Application contact:* Audrey C. Shalinsky, Associate Dean, 307-766-4106, Fax: 307-766-2697, E-mail: asdean@uwyo.edu.

Utah State University, School of Graduate Studies, College of Humanities, Arts and Social Sciences, Department of English and Department of History, Program in American Studies, Logan, UT 84322. Offers folklore (MA, MS); western American literature and culture (MA, MS). Part-time and evening/weekend programs available. *Degree requirements:* For master's, thesis or alternative. *Entrance requirements:* For master's, GRE General Test or MAT, minimum GPA of 3.0, 3 letters of recommendation, writing sample. Additional exam requirements/recommendations for international students: Required—TOEFL. *Faculty research:* Folklore and folklife, American culture, regional studies, material culture, Jewish folklore, Native American folklore.

Washington State University, Graduate School, College of Liberal Arts, Department of History, Pullman, WA 99164. Offers early and modern European history (MA, PhD); environmental history (MA, PhD); Latin American history (MA, PhD); modern East Asia history (MA, PhD); public history (MA, PhD); US history (MA, PhD); women's history (MA, PhD); world history (MA, PhD). Part-time programs available. *Degree requirements:* For master's, comprehensive exam (for some programs), thesis, oral exam; for doctorate, one foreign language, comprehensive exam, thesis/dissertation, oral and written exam. *Entrance requirements:* For master's, GRE General Test, minimum GPA of 3.3, language background

form, writing sample; for doctorate, GRE General Test, minimum GPA of 3.5, language background form, writing sample. Additional exam requirements/recommendations for international students: Required—TOEFL (minimum score 550 paper-based). Electronic applications accepted. *Faculty research:* Public, world, environmental, women and U.S. history.

Washington State University, Graduate School, College of Liberal Arts, Program in American Studies, Pullman, WA 99164. Offers ethnic studies (MA, PhD); feminist studies (MA, PhD); history (MA, PhD); literature (MA, PhD). *Degree requirements:* For master's, one foreign language, comprehensive exam (for some programs), thesis optional, oral exam; for doctorate, one foreign language, comprehensive exam (for some programs), thesis/dissertation, oral exam. *Entrance requirements:* For master's and doctorate, GRE General Test, minimum GPA of 3.0, writing sample, 3 letters of recommendation. Additional exam requirements/recommendations for international students: Required—TOEFL. *Faculty research:* The American West in multicultural perspective; nineteenth century historical, literary, and cultural studies; comparative American ethnic literatures and cultures; American cultures and the environment; American rhetoric.

West Virginia University, Eberly College of Arts and Sciences, Department of History, Morgantown, WV 26506. Offers African history (MA, PhD); African-American history (MA, PhD); American history (MA, PhD); Appalachian/regional history (MA, PhD); East Asian history (MA, PhD); European history (MA, PhD); history of science and technology (MA, PhD); Latin American history (MA). Part-time programs available. *Degree requirements:* For master's, one foreign language, thesis (for some programs), oral exam, thesis defense; for doctorate, one foreign language, comprehensive exam, thesis/dissertation, dissertation defense. *Entrance requirements:* For master's, GRE General Test, minimum GPA of 3.0; for doctorate, GRE General Test. Additional exam requirements/recommendations for international students: Required—TOEFL (minimum score 550 paper-based), IELTS (minimum score 6.5). Electronic applications accepted. *Faculty research:* U.S., Appalachia, modern Europe, Africa, colonial and post-colonial societies.

Wheaton College, Graduate School, Department of Biblical and Theological Studies, Program in Religion in American Life, Wheaton, IL 60187-5593. Offers MA. Part-time programs available. *Degree requirements:* For master's, thesis optional. *Entrance requirements:* For master's, GRE General Test, MAT. Electronic applications accepted.

Yale University, Graduate School of Arts and Sciences, Interdisciplinary Program in American Studies, New Haven, CT 06520. Offers PhD. *Degree requirements:* For doctorate, one foreign language, thesis/dissertation. *Entrance requirements:* For doctorate, GRE General Test.

Asian-American Studies

California State University, Long Beach, Graduate Studies, College of Liberal Arts, Department of Asian and Asian American Studies, Long Beach, CA 90840. Offers Asian American studies (Certificate); Asian studies (MA). Part-time programs available. *Faculty:* 8 full-time (5 women), 1 part-time/adjunct (0 women). *Students:* 9 full-time (6 women), 10 part-time (5 women); includes 11 minority (all Asian Americans or Pacific Islanders), 6 international. Average age 41. 12 applicants, 75% accepted, 5 enrolled. *Degree requirements:* For master's, one foreign language, comprehensive exam or thesis. *Application deadline:* For fall admission, 5/1 for domestic students. Applications are processed on a rolling basis. Application fee: $55. Electronic applications accepted. *Expenses:* Tuition, nonresident: full-time $11,160; part-time $372 per unit. Required fees: $4100; $1261 per semester. *Financial support:* Federal Work-Study, institutionally sponsored loans, and scholarships/grants available. Financial award application deadline: 3/2. *Faculty research:* South Asia, China, Japan, Southeast Asia, Asian-Americans in the U.S. *Unit head:* Dr. John N Tsuchida, Chair, 562-985-4645, Fax: 562-985-1535, E-mail: jtsuchid@csulb.edu. *Application contact:* Dr. Linda Maram, Graduate Advisor, 562-985-4822, Fax: 562-985-1535, E-mail: lnemaram@csulb.edu.

San Francisco State University, Division of Graduate Studies, College of Ethnic Studies, Program in Asian American Studies, San Francisco, CA 94132-1722. Offers MA.

University of California, Los Angeles, Graduate Division, College of Letters and Science, Program in Asian-American Studies, Los Angeles, CA 90095. Offers MA, MA/MPH, MA/MSW. *Students:* 13 full-time (10 women); includes 8 minority (7 Asian Americans or Pacific Islanders, 1 Hispanic American), 1 international. Average age 24. 29 applicants, 41% accepted, 7 enrolled. In 2008, 8 master's awarded. *Degree requirements:* For master's, one foreign language, comprehensive exam or thesis, research tool. *Entrance requirements:* For master's, minimum GPA of 3.0, sample of written work. *Application deadline:* For fall admission, 12/15 for domestic and international students. Application fee: $60 ($80 for international students). Electronic applications accepted. *Expenses:* Tuition, nonresident: full-time $14,694. Required fees: $9669.50. Full-time tuition and fees vary according to course load, degree level, program and student level. *Financial support:* In 2008–09, 18 fellowships with full and partial tuition reimbursements, 3 research assistantships with full and partial tuition reimbursements, 9 teaching assistantships with full and partial tuition reimbursements were awarded; Federal Work-Study, institutionally sponsored loans, scholarships/grants, health care benefits, tuition waivers (full and partial), and unspecified assistantships also available. Financial award application deadline: 3/1; financial award applicants required to submit FAFSA. *Unit head:* Dr. Lane Hirabayashi, Chair, 310-267-5592. *Application contact:* Departmental Office, 310-267-5592, E-mail: maprogram@asianam.ucla.edu.

Asian Studies

California Institute of Integral Studies, Graduate Programs, School of Consciousness and Transformation, San Francisco, CA 94103. Offers cultural anthropology and social transformation (MA); East-West psychology (MA, PhD); integrative health studies (MA); philosophy and religion (MA, PhD), including Asian and comparative studies, philosophy, cosmology, and consciousness, women's spirituality, women's spirituality flex format; social and cultural anthropology (PhD); transformative leadership (MA); transformative studies (PhD). Part-time and evening/weekend programs available. Postbaccalaureate distance learning degree programs offered (minimal on-campus study). *Faculty:* 29 full-time, 32 part-time/adjunct. *Students:* 334 full-time (218 women), 126 part-time (77 women); includes 102 minority (39 African Americans, 4 American Indian/Alaska Native, 35 Asian Americans or Pacific Islanders, 24 Hispanic Americans), 1 international. Average age 37. 223 applicants, 78% accepted, 110 enrolled. In 2008, 93 master's, 30 doctorates awarded. Terminal master's awarded for partial completion of doctoral program. *Degree requirements:* For master's, comprehensive exam (for some programs), thesis optional; for doctorate, comprehensive exam, thesis/dissertation. *Entrance requirements:* For master's, minimum GPA of 3.0, letters of recommendation, writing sample; for doctorate, master's degree, minimum GPA of 3.0, letters of recommendation, writing sample. Additional exam requirements/recommendations for international students: Required—TOEFL. *Application deadline:* For fall admission, 2/1 priority date for domestic and international students; for spring admission, 10/15 priority date for domestic and international students. Applications are processed on a rolling basis. Application fee: $65. Electronic applications accepted. *Expenses:* Tuition: Part-time $815 per contact hour. Required fees: $270; $135 per semester. Tuition and fees vary according to degree level. *Financial support:* In 2008–09, 271 students received support; research assistantships, teaching assistantships, career-related internships or fieldwork, Federal Work-Study, institutionally sponsored loans, scholarships/grants, and tuition waivers (partial) available. Support available to part-time students. Financial award application deadline: 3/15; financial award applicants required to submit FAFSA. *Faculty research:* Altered states of consciousness, dreams, cosmology, postcolonial studies, integrative health studies. *Application contact:* Allyson Werner, Senior Admissions Counselor, 415-575-6155, Fax: 415-575-1268.

See Close-Up on page 347.

California State University, Long Beach, Graduate Studies, College of Liberal Arts, Department of Asian and Asian American Studies, Long Beach, CA 90840. Offers Asian American studies (Certificate); Asian studies (MA). Part-time programs available. *Faculty:* 8 full-time (5 women),

1 part-time/adjunct (0 women). *Students:* 9 full-time (6 women), 10 part-time (5 women); includes 11 minority (all Asian Americans or Pacific Islanders), 6 international. Average age 41. 12 applicants, 75% accepted, 5 enrolled. *Degree requirements:* For master's, one foreign language, comprehensive exam or thesis. *Application deadline:* For fall admission, 5/1 for domestic students. Applications are processed on a rolling basis. Application fee: $55. Electronic applications accepted. *Expenses:* Tuition, nonresident: full-time $11,160; part-time $372 per unit. Required fees: $4100; $1261 per semester. *Financial support:* Federal Work-Study, institutionally sponsored loans, and scholarships/grants available. Financial award application deadline: 3/2. *Faculty research:* South Asia, China, Japan, Southeast Asia, Asian-Americans in the U.S. *Unit head:* Dr. John N Tsuchida, Chair, 562-985-4645, Fax: 562-985-1535, E-mail: jtsuchid@csulb.edu. *Application contact:* Dr. Linda Maram, Graduate Advisor, 562-985-4822, Fax: 562-985-1535, E-mail: lnemaram@csulb.edu.

California State University, Long Beach, Graduate Studies, College of Liberal Arts, Department of History, Long Beach, CA 90840. Offers Africa and the Middle East (MA); ancient/Medieval Europe (MA); Asia (MA); Latin America (MA); modern Europe (MA); United States (MA); world (MA). Part-time and evening/weekend programs available. *Faculty:* 17 full-time (11 women), 2 part-time/adjunct (1 woman). *Students:* 9 full-time (4 women), 45 part-time (18 women); includes 15 minority (2 African Americans, 3 Asian Americans or Pacific Islanders, 10 Hispanic Americans), 1 international. Average age 35. 40 applicants, 50% accepted, 11 enrolled. *Degree requirements:* For master's, one foreign language, comprehensive exam or thesis. *Application deadline:* For fall admission, 3/1 for domestic students. Applications are processed on a rolling basis. Application fee: $55. Electronic applications accepted. *Expenses:* Tuition, nonresident: full-time $11,160; part-time $372 per unit. Required fees: $4100; $1261 per semester. *Financial support:* Research assistantships, Federal Work-Study, institutionally sponsored loans, and scholarships/grants available. Financial award application deadline: 3/2. *Faculty research:* All periods of European and American history, recent Asian and African history. *Unit head:* Dr. Nancy L Quam-Wickham, Graduate Advisor, 562-985-4431, Fax: 562-985-5431, E-mail: quamwick@csulb.edu. *Application contact:* Dr. Houri Berberian, Graduate Advisor, 562-985-4524, Fax: 562-985-4431, E-mail: hberber@csulb.edu.

Columbia University, Graduate School of Arts and Sciences, Division of Humanities, Department of East Asian Languages and Cultures, New York, NY 10027. Offers East Asian languages and cultures (M Phil, MA, PhD); Oriental studies (M Phil, MA, PhD). *Degree requirements:* For master's, one foreign language, comprehensive exam, thesis; for doctorate,

2 foreign languages, thesis/dissertation. *Entrance requirements:* For master's and doctorate, GRE General Test. Additional exam requirements/recommendations for international students: Required—TOEFL.

Columbia University, Graduate School of Arts and Sciences, Division of Humanities, Department of Middle East Languages and Cultures, New York, NY 10027. Offers Hebrew language and literature (M Phil, MA, PhD); Middle Eastern languages and cultures (M Phil, MA, PhD); South Asian languages and cultures (M Phil, MA, PhD). Part-time programs available. *Degree requirements:* For master's, thesis, oral and written exams; for doctorate, 3 foreign languages, thesis/dissertation. *Entrance requirements:* For master's and doctorate, GRE General Test. Additional exam requirements/recommendations for international students: Required—TOEFL. *Faculty research:* Indo-Iranian, Turkish, central Asian, and Armenian studies; Arabic and ancient Semitics.

Columbia University, Graduate School of Arts and Sciences, Program in East Asian Regional Studies, New York, NY 10027. Offers MA. *Degree requirements:* For master's, 2 foreign languages. *Entrance requirements:* For master's, GRE General Test.

Columbia University, Graduate School of Arts and Sciences, Program in Liberal Studies, New York, NY 10027. Offers American studies (MA); East Asian studies (MA); human rights studies (MA); Islamic culture studies (MA); Jewish studies (MA); medieval studies (MA); modern European studies (MA); South Asian studies (MA). Part-time and evening/weekend programs available. *Degree requirements:* For master's, thesis.

Columbia University, School of International and Public Affairs, Southern Asian Institute, New York, NY 10027. Offers Certificate. Students must be enrolled in a separate graduate degree program at Columbia University. Electronic applications accepted.

Columbia University, School of International and Public Affairs, Weatherhead East Asian Institute, New York, NY 10027. Offers Asian studies (Certificate). Students must be enrolled in a separate graduate degree program at Columbia University. *Entrance requirements:* For degree, proficiency in East Asian language. Electronic applications accepted.

Cornell University, Graduate School, Graduate Fields of Arts and Sciences, Field of Asian Religions, Ithaca, NY 14853-0001. Offers PhD. *Faculty:* 8 full-time (3 women). *Students:* 8 full-time (2 women), 2 international. Average age 33. 9 applicants, 33% accepted, 1 enrolled. In 2008, 1 doctorate awarded. *Degree requirements:* For doctorate, comprehensive exam, thesis/dissertation. *Entrance requirements:* For doctorate, GRE General Test, academic writing sample, 3 letters of recommendation. Additional exam requirements/recommendations for international students: Required—TOEFL (minimum score 600 paper-based; 250 computer-based; 77 iBT). *Application deadline:* For fall admission, 1/15 for domestic students. Application fee: $70. Electronic applications accepted. *Expenses:* Tuition: Full-time $29,500. Required fees: $70. Full-time tuition and fees vary according to degree level, program and student level. *Financial support:* In 2008–09, 5 students received support, including 4 fellowships with full tuition reimbursements available, 1 research assistantship with full tuition reimbursement available; teaching assistantships with full tuition reimbursements available, institutionally sponsored loans, scholarships/grants, health care benefits, and unspecified assistantships also available. *Unit head:* Director of Graduate Studies, 607-255-9099, Fax: 607-255-1345. *Application contact:* Graduate Field Assistant, 607-255-9099, Fax: 607-255-1345, E-mail: asian-religions@cornell.edu.

Cornell University, Graduate School, Graduate Fields of Arts and Sciences, Field of Asian Studies, Ithaca, NY 14853-0001. Offers East Asian linguistics (MA); East Asian studies (MA); South Asian linguistics (MA); South Asian studies (MA); Southeast Asian linguistics (MA); Southeast Asian studies (MA). *Faculty:* 50 full-time (20 women). *Students:* 8 full-time (2 women); includes 4 minority (1 African American, 2 Asian Americans or Pacific Islanders, 1 Hispanic American), 3 international. Average age 31. 55 applicants, 29% accepted, 5 enrolled. In 2008, 3 master's awarded. *Degree requirements:* For master's, one foreign language, thesis. *Entrance requirements:* For master's, GRE General Test, 3 letters of recommendation. Additional exam requirements/recommendations for international students: Required—TOEFL (minimum score 550 paper-based; 213 computer-based; 77 iBT). *Application deadline:* Applications are processed on a rolling basis. Application fee: $70. Electronic applications accepted. *Expenses:* Tuition: Full-time $29,500. Required fees: $70. Full-time tuition and fees vary according to degree level, program and student level. *Financial support:* In 2008–09, 5 students received support, including 1 fellowship with full tuition reimbursement available, 4 research assistantships with full tuition reimbursements available; teaching assistantships with full tuition reimbursements available, institutionally sponsored loans, scholarships/grants, health care benefits, tuition waivers (full and partial), and unspecified assistantships also available. Financial award applicants required to submit FAFSA. *Faculty research:* East Asian studies, South Asian studies, Southeast Asian studies. *Unit head:* Director of Graduate Studies, 607-255-9099, Fax: 607-255-1345. *Application contact:* Graduate Field Assistant, 607-255-9099, Fax: 607-255-1345, E-mail: asian@cornell.edu.

Cornell University, Graduate School, Graduate Fields of Arts and Sciences, Field of East Asian Literature, Ithaca, NY 14853-0001. Offers Asian religions (MA, PhD); Chinese linguistics (MA, PhD); Chinese philology (MA, PhD); classical Chinese literature (MA, PhD); classical Japanese literature (MA, PhD); Japanese linguistics (MA, PhD); Korean literature (MA, PhD); modern Chinese literature (MA, PhD); modern Japanese literature (MA, PhD). *Faculty:* 14 full-time (6 women). *Students:* 18 full-time (9 women); includes 6 minority (all Asian Americans or Pacific Islanders), 9 international. Average age 34. 41 applicants, 7% accepted, 2 enrolled. In 2008, 2 master's, 3 doctorates awarded. *Degree requirements:* For master's, 2 foreign languages, thesis, teaching experience; for doctorate, 2 foreign languages, comprehensive exam, thesis/dissertation, teaching experience. *Entrance requirements:* For master's and doctorate, GRE General Test, 3 years of study in Chinese, Japanese, Korean, or Vietnamese, 3 letters of recommendation, academic writing sample. Additional exam requirements/recommendations for international students: Required—TOEFL (minimum score 600 paper-based; 250 computer-based; 77 iBT). *Application deadline:* For fall admission, 1/10 priority date for domestic students. Application fee: $70. Electronic applications accepted. *Expenses:* Tuition: Full-time $29,500. Required fees: $70. Full-time tuition and fees vary according to degree level, program and student level. *Financial support:* In 2008–09, 17 students received support, including 8 fellowships with full tuition reimbursements available, 2 research assistantships with full tuition reimbursements available, 7 teaching assistantships with full tuition reimbursements available; institutionally sponsored loans, scholarships/grants, health care benefits, tuition waivers (full and partial), and unspecified assistantships also available. Financial award applicants required to submit FAFSA. *Faculty research:* Vietnamese literature; Chinese literature, drama, and film; Japanese theater and literature; popular culture in East Asia; Korean literature; Asian linguistics. *Unit head:* Director of Graduate Studies, 607-255-9099. *Application contact:* Graduate Field Assistant, 607-255-9099, E-mail: east_asian_lit@cornell.edu.

Cornell University, Graduate School, Graduate Fields of Arts and Sciences, Field of History, Ithaca, NY 14853-0001. Offers African history (MA, PhD); American history (MA, PhD); ancient history (MA, PhD); early modern European history (MA, PhD); English history (MA, PhD); French history (MA, PhD); German history (MA, PhD); history of science (MA, PhD); Latin American history (MA, PhD); medieval Chinese history (MA, PhD); medieval history (MA, PhD); modern Chinese history (MA, PhD); modern European history (MA, PhD); modern Japanese history (MA, PhD); premodern Islamic history (MA, PhD); premodern Japanese history (MA, PhD); Renaissance history (MA, PhD); Russian history (MA, PhD); Southeast Asian history (MA, PhD). *Faculty:* 54 full-time (14 women). *Students:* 65 full-time (35 women); includes 12 minority (4 African Americans, 3 Asian Americans or Pacific Islanders, 5 Hispanic Americans), 19 international. Average age 31. 205 applicants, 8% accepted, 11 enrolled. In 2008, 12 master's, 6 doctorates awarded. Terminal master's awarded for partial completion of doctoral program. *Degree requirements:* For master's, thesis; for doctorate, 2 foreign languages, comprehensive exam, thesis/dissertation, 1 year of teaching experience. *Entrance requirements:* For master's and doctorate, GRE General Test, writing sample, 3 letters of recommendation.

Additional exam requirements/recommendations for international students: Required—TOEFL (minimum score 550 paper-based; 213 computer-based; 77 iBT). *Application deadline:* For fall admission, 1/15 for domestic students. Application fee: $70. Electronic applications accepted. *Expenses:* Tuition: Full-time $29,500. Required fees: $70. Full-time tuition and fees vary according to degree level, program and student level. *Financial support:* In 2008–09, 54 students received support, including 27 fellowships with full tuition reimbursements available, 3 research assistantships with full tuition reimbursements available, 24 teaching assistantships with full tuition reimbursements available; institutionally sponsored loans, scholarships/grants, health care benefits, tuition waivers (full and partial), and unspecified assistantships also available. Financial award applicants required to submit FAFSA. *Unit head:* Director of Graduate Studies, 607-255-6738, Fax: 607-255-0469. *Application contact:* Graduate Field Assistant, 607-255-6738, Fax: 607-255-0469, E-mail: history_grad_info@cornell.edu.

Cornell University, Graduate School, Graduate Fields of Arts and Sciences, Field of History of Art and Archaeology, Ithaca, NY 14853. Offers American art (PhD); ancient art and archaeology (PhD); Asian art (PhD); baroque art (PhD); medieval art (PhD); modern art (PhD); Renaissance art (PhD); Southeast Asian art (PhD); theory and criticism (PhD). *Faculty:* 17 full-time (11 women). *Students:* 23 full-time (19 women); includes 4 minority (1 African American, 2 Asian Americans or Pacific Islanders, 1 Hispanic American), 7 international. Average age 33. 76 applicants, 8% accepted, 4 enrolled. In 2008, 1 doctorate awarded. *Degree requirements:* For doctorate, one foreign language, comprehensive exam, thesis/dissertation, general exams in 3 areas. *Entrance requirements:* For doctorate, GRE General Test, sample of written work, 3 letters of recommendation. Additional exam requirements/recommendations for international students: Required—TOEFL (minimum score 550 paper-based; 213 computer-based; 77 iBT). *Application deadline:* For fall admission, 1/15 for domestic students. Application fee: $70. Electronic applications accepted. *Expenses:* Tuition: Full-time $29,500. Required fees: $70. Full-time tuition and fees vary according to degree level, program and student level. *Financial support:* In 2008–09, 17 students received support, including 10 fellowships with full tuition reimbursements available, 1 research assistantship with full tuition reimbursement available, 6 teaching assistantships with full tuition reimbursements available; institutionally sponsored loans, scholarships/grants, health care benefits, tuition waivers (full and partial), and unspecified assistantships also available. Financial award applicants required to submit FAFSA. *Unit head:* Director of Graduate Studies, 607-255-4905, Fax: 607-255-0566, E-mail: art_history@cornell.edu. *Application contact:* Graduate Field Assistant, 607-255-4905, Fax: 607-255-0566, E-mail: art_history@cornell.edu.

Cornell University, Graduate School, Graduate Fields of Arts and Sciences, Field of Linguistics, Ithaca, NY 14853-0001. Offers applied linguistics (MA, PhD); East Asian linguistics (MA, PhD); English linguistics (MA, PhD); general linguistics (MA, PhD); Germanic linguistics (MA, PhD); Indo-European linguistics (MA, PhD); phonetics (MA, PhD); phonological theory (MA, PhD); Romance linguistics (MA, PhD); second language acquisition (MA, PhD); semantics (MA, PhD); Slavic linguistics (MA, PhD); sociolinguistics (MA, PhD); South Asian linguistics (MA, PhD); Southeast Asian linguistics (MA, PhD); syntactic theory (MA, PhD). *Faculty:* 15 full-time (6 women). *Students:* 32 full-time (15 women); includes 1 minority (Hispanic American), 16 international. Average age 30. 93 applicants, 16% accepted, 7 enrolled. In 2008, 5 master's, 7 doctorates awarded. Terminal master's awarded for partial completion of doctoral program. *Degree requirements:* For master's, one foreign language, thesis; for doctorate, one foreign language, comprehensive exam, thesis/dissertation. *Entrance requirements:* For master's and doctorate, GRE General Test, 2 letters of recommendation. Additional exam requirements/recommendations for international students: Required—TOEFL (minimum score 600 paper-based; 250 computer-based; 77 iBT). *Application deadline:* For fall admission, 1/15 for domestic students. Application fee: $70. Electronic applications accepted. *Expenses:* Tuition: Full-time $29,500. Required fees: $70. Full-time tuition and fees vary according to degree level, program and student level. *Financial support:* In 2008–09, 32 students received support, including 11 fellowships with full tuition reimbursements available, 4 research assistantships with full tuition reimbursements available, 17 teaching assistantships with full tuition reimbursements available; institutionally sponsored loans, scholarships/grants, health care benefits, tuition waivers (full and partial), and unspecified assistantships also available. Financial award applicants required to submit FAFSA. *Faculty research:* Phonology and phonetics; syntax and semantics; historical linguistics; philosophy of language; language acquisition. *Unit head:* Director of Graduate Studies, 607-255-1105. *Application contact:* Graduate Field Assistant, 607-255-1105, E-mail: lingfield@cornell.edu.

Duke University, Graduate School, Department of East Asian Studies, Durham, NC 27708. Offers AM, Certificate. Part-time programs available. *Entrance requirements:* For master's, GRE General Test. Additional exam requirements/recommendations for international students: Required—TOEFL (minimum score 550 paper-based; 213 computer-based; 83 iBT), IELTS (minimum score 7). Electronic applications accepted.

Florida International University, College of Arts and Sciences, Program in Asian Studies, Miami, FL 33199. Offers MA. Part-time and evening/weekend programs available. *Degree requirements:* For master's, thesis. *Entrance requirements:* For master's, minimum GPA of 3.0, letters of recommendation. Additional exam requirements/recommendations for international students: Required—TOEFL (minimum score 550 paper-based; 213 computer-based). Electronic applications accepted.

Florida State University, Graduate Studies, College of Social Sciences, Program in Asian Studies, Tallahassee, FL 32306. Offers MA. Part-time programs available. *Degree requirements:* For master's, one foreign language, comprehensive exam, thesis optional. *Entrance requirements:* For master's, GRE General Test, minimum GPA of 3.0. Additional exam requirements/recommendations for international students: Required—TOEFL (minimum score 550 paper-based; 213 computer-based; 80 iBT). Electronic applications accepted. *Faculty research:* Art history of the Orient, Asian history and politics.

The George Washington University, Elliott School of International Affairs, Program in Asian Studies, Washington, DC 20052. Offers MA, JD/MA, MBA/MA, MPH/MA. Part-time and evening/weekend programs available. *Students:* 26 full-time (12 women), 8 part-time (3 women); includes 5 minority (3 Asian Americans or Pacific Islanders, 2 Hispanic Americans), 7 international. Average age 27. 98 applicants, 66% accepted, 18 enrolled. In 2008, 17 master's awarded. *Degree requirements:* For master's, one foreign language, capstone project. *Entrance requirements:* For master's, GRE General Test, 2 years (or the equivalent) of an approved Asian language. Additional exam requirements/recommendations for international students: Required—TOEFL. *Application deadline:* For fall admission, 2/1 for domestic students; for spring admission, 10/1 for domestic students. Application fee: $60. Electronic applications accepted. *Financial support:* In 2008–09, 7 students received support; fellowships with tuition reimbursements available, research assistantships with tuition reimbursements available, career-related internships or fieldwork, Federal Work-Study, institutionally sponsored loans, and tuition waivers (full) available. Financial award application deadline: 1/15; financial award applicants required to submit FAFSA. *Faculty research:* Sino-Soviet studies, Japanese-U.S. relations, Chinese foreign policy, economic development in China. *Unit head:* Elizabeth Chacko, Director, 202-994-5328, Fax: 202-994-2484, E-mail: echacko@gwu.edu. *Application contact:* Jeff V. Miles, Director of Graduate Admissions, 202-994-7050, Fax: 202-994-9537, E-mail: esiagrad@gwu.edu.

Harvard University, Graduate School of Arts and Sciences, Committee on Inner Asian and Altaic Studies, Cambridge, MA 02138. Offers PhD. *Degree requirements:* For doctorate, 2 foreign languages, thesis/dissertation, oral general exam. *Entrance requirements:* For doctorate, GRE General Test, proficiency in a related foreign language. Additional exam requirements/recommendations for international students: Required—TOEFL. *Expenses:* Tuition: Full-time $32,556. Required fees: $1426. Full-time tuition and fees vary according to program and student level.

Harvard University, Graduate School of Arts and Sciences, Committee on Regional Studies–East Asia, Cambridge, MA 02138. Offers Chinese studies (AM); Japanese studies

Asian Studies

Harvard University (continued)
(AM); Korean studies (AM); Mongolian studies (AM); Vietnamese studies (AM). *Degree requirements:* For master's, one foreign language, seminar paper. *Entrance requirements:* For master's, GRE General Test. Additional exam requirements/recommendations for international students: Required—TOEFL. *Expenses:* Tuition: Full-time $32,556. Required fees: $1426. Full-time tuition and fees vary according to program and student level.

Harvard University, Graduate School of Arts and Sciences, Department of Sanskrit and Indian Studies, Cambridge, MA 02138. Offers Indian philosophy (AM, PhD); Pali (AM, PhD); Sanskrit (AM, PhD); Tibetan (AM, PhD); Urdu (AM, PhD). Terminal master's awarded for partial completion of doctoral program. *Degree requirements:* For master's, 3 foreign languages; for doctorate, 3 foreign languages, thesis/dissertation. *Entrance requirements:* For master's, GRE General Test; for doctorate, GRE General Test, proficiency in French and German. Additional exam requirements/recommendations for international students: Required—TOEFL. *Expenses:* Tuition: Full-time $32,556. Required fees: $1426. Full-time tuition and fees vary according to program and student level.

Indiana University Bloomington, University Graduate School, College of Arts and Sciences, Department of Central Eurasian Studies, Bloomington, IN 47405-7000. Offers MA, PhD. *Faculty:* 11 full-time (0 women). *Students:* 37 full-time (10 women), 6 part-time (1 woman); includes 3 minority (1 American Indian/Alaska Native, 2 Asian Americans or Pacific Islanders), 10 international. Average age 31. 37 applicants, 81% accepted, 6 enrolled. In 2008, 16 master's, 1 doctorate awarded. Terminal master's awarded for partial completion of doctoral program. *Degree requirements:* For master's, one foreign language, thesis; for doctorate, 2 foreign languages, thesis/dissertation, qualifying exams. *Entrance requirements:* For master's, minimum GPA of 3.0, 2 years of a foreign language; for doctorate, minimum GPA of 3.5, 1 research language. Additional exam requirements/recommendations for international students: Required—TOEFL. *Application deadline:* For fall admission, 1/15 priority date for domestic students, 12/15 for international students; for spring admission, 9/1 priority date for domestic students, 9/1 for international students. Applications are processed on a rolling basis. Application fee: $50 ($60 for international students). Electronic applications accepted. *Expenses:* Tuition, area resident: Part-time $291.97 per credit hour. Tuition, state resident: part-time $291.97 per credit hour. Tuition, nonresident: part-time $850.33 per credit hour. Required fees: $110 per semester. Tuition and fees vary according to course load and program. *Financial support:* Fellowships with full tuition reimbursements, research assistantships with full tuition reimbursements, teaching assistantships with full tuition reimbursements, Federal Work-Study available. Financial award application deadline: 2/16. *Faculty research:* Central Asia, Hungarian civilization, Tibetan civilization, Turkish studies, Mongolian philology. *Unit head:* Christopher Atwood, Chair, 812-855-2233, E-mail: catwood@indiana.edu. *Application contact:* April Younger, Graduate Secretary, 812-855-2233, E-mail: ayounger@indiana.edu.

Indiana University Bloomington, University Graduate School, College of Arts and Sciences, Department of East Asian Languages and Cultures, Bloomington, IN 47405-7000. Offers Chinese (MA, PhD); East Asian languages and cultures (PhD); East Asian studies (MA); Japanese (MA, PhD); language pedagogy (MA). Part-time programs available. *Faculty:* 7 full-time (2 women). *Students:* 17 full-time (10 women), 11 part-time (7 women); includes 3 minority (1 African American, 1 Asian American or Pacific Islander, 1 Hispanic American), 7 international. Average age 33. 84 applicants, 30% accepted, 10 enrolled. In 2008, 6 master's, 1 doctorate awarded. *Degree requirements:* For master's, 2 foreign languages, thesis; for doctorate, 2 foreign languages, thesis/dissertation. *Entrance requirements:* Additional exam requirements/recommendations for international students: Required—TOEFL. *Application deadline:* For fall admission, 1/15 for domestic students, 12/15 for international students; for spring admission, 9/1 for domestic and international students. Applications are processed on a rolling basis. Application fee: $50 ($60 for international students). Electronic applications accepted. *Expenses:* Tuition, area resident: Part-time $291.97 per credit hour. Tuition, state resident: part-time $291.97 per credit hour. Tuition, nonresident: part-time $850.33 per credit hour. Required fees: $110 per semester. Tuition and fees vary according to course load and program. *Financial support:* Fellowships, teaching assistantships, Federal Work-Study and tuition waivers (full) available. Financial award application deadline: 3/1. *Faculty research:* Postwar/postmodern Japanese fiction, modern Chinese film and literature, classical Chinese literature and philosophy, Chinese and Japanese linguistics and pedagogy, East Asian politics. *Unit head:* Robert Eno, Chair, 812-855-0856, E-mail: eno@indiana.edu. *Application contact:* Edith Sarra, Director of Graduate Studies, 812-855-4031, Fax: 812-855-6402, E-mail: eserra@indiana.edu.

The Johns Hopkins University, Paul H. Nitze School of Advanced International Studies, Washington, DC 20036. Offers international development (Certificate); international public policy (MIPP); international relations (MA, PhD), including African studies (MA), American foreign policy (MA), Asian studies (MA), Canadian studies (MA), conflict management (MA), European studies (MA), global theory and history (MA), international development (MA), international law, and organizations (MA), international policy (MA), international relations (general) (MA), Latin American studies (MA), Middle East studies (MA), Russian and Eurasian studies (MA), strategic studies (MA); international studies (Certificate); JD/MA; MBA/MA; MHS/MA. Terminal master's awarded for partial completion of doctoral program. *Degree requirements:* For master's, one foreign language, 16 non-language courses (8 for MIPP), 2 core examinations, comprehensive oral exam, paper (for some programs); for doctorate, 2 foreign languages, thesis/dissertation, 3 comprehensive exams, defense. *Entrance requirements:* For master's, GMAT or GRE General Test, previous course work in economics, foreign language, undergraduate degree; for doctorate, GRE General Test, master's degree. Additional exam requirements/recommendations for international students: Required—TOEFL (minimum paper-based score of 600, computer-based 250, iBT 100) or IELTS (minimum 7.0). Electronic applications accepted. *Expenses:* Contact institution. *Faculty research:* Regional studies and functional fields of international relations, international economics, conflict management, global theory and history, international law and organizations, international policy, strategic studies.

Maharishi University of Management, Graduate Studies, Program in Maharishi Vedic Science, Fairfield, IA 52557. Offers MA, PhD. Evening/weekend programs available. *Degree requirements:* For master's, thesis; for doctorate, thesis/dissertation. *Entrance requirements:* For master's, minimum GPA of 3.0; for doctorate, GRE, minimum GPA of 3.0. Additional exam requirements/recommendations for international students: Required—TOEFL. *Faculty research:* Modern science and Vedic science, unification of knowledge, philosophy of science, Sanskrit.

McGill University, Faculty of Graduate and Postdoctoral Studies, Faculty of Arts, Department of East Asian Studies, Montréal, QC H3A 2T5, Canada. Offers MA, PhD.

New York University, Graduate School of Arts and Science, Department of East Asian Studies, New York, NY 10012-1019. Offers MA, PhD. Part-time programs available. *Degree requirements:* For master's and doctorate, one foreign language. *Entrance requirements:* For master's and doctorate, GRE General Test. Additional exam requirements/recommendations for international students: Required—TOEFL. Electronic applications accepted.

Ohio University, Graduate College, Center for International Studies, Program in Southeast Asian Studies, Athens, OH 45701-2979. Offers MA. *Degree requirements:* For master's, one foreign language, thesis optional. *Entrance requirements:* For master's, minimum GPA of 3.0. Additional exam requirements/recommendations for international students: Required—TOEFL (minimum score 550 paper-based; 213 computer-based). *Faculty research:* Indonesian and Malaysian: political, history, literature, media, Islam, and environmental problems.

Princeton University, Graduate School, Department of East Asian Studies, Princeton, NJ 08544-1019. Offers PhD. *Degree requirements:* For doctorate, 2 foreign languages, thesis/dissertation. *Entrance requirements:* For doctorate, GRE General Test, fluency in Japanese and/or Chinese. Additional exam requirements/recommendations for international students: Required—TOEFL (minimum score 600 paper-based; 250 computer-based). Electronic applications accepted. *Faculty research:* Modern and classical Japanese literature, premodern Chinese and Japanese history, Chinese narrative and poetry.

Rutgers, The State University of New Jersey, New Brunswick, Graduate School, Program in History, Piscataway, NJ 08854-8097. Offers African-American history (PhD); early American history (PhD); early modern European history (PhD); east Asian history (PhD); global and comparative history (PhD); history (PhD); history of diplomacy and foreign relations (PhD); history of technology, environment and health (PhD); history of the Atlantic cultures and African diaspora (PhD); Latin American history (PhD); medieval history (PhD); modern European history (PhD); nineteenth and twentieth century American history (PhD); women's and gender history (PhD). *Degree requirements:* For doctorate, thesis/dissertation. *Entrance requirements:* For doctorate, GRE General Test, sample of written work. Electronic applications accepted. *Faculty research:* American history, European history, Afro-American history, women's history, Latin American history.

St. John's College, Graduate Institute in Liberal Education, Program in Eastern Classics, Santa Fe, NM 87505-4599. Offers MA. Part-time and evening/weekend programs available. *Entrance requirements:* For master's, 2 letters of recommendation. Additional exam requirements/recommendations for international students: Required—TOEFL, TWE. *Expenses:* Contact institution.

St. John's University, St. John's College of Liberal Arts and Sciences, Institute of Asian Studies, Queens, NY 11439. Offers Asian and African cultural studies (Adv C); Asian studies (Adv C); Chinese studies (MA, Adv C); East Asian culture studies (Adv C); East Asian studies (MA). Part-time and evening/weekend programs available. *Students:* 6 full-time (4 women), 5 part-time (3 women); includes 3 minority (2 Asian Americans or Pacific Islanders, 1 Hispanic American), 7 international. Average age 25. 13 applicants, 100% accepted, 4 enrolled. In 2008, 5 master's awarded. *Degree requirements:* For master's, one foreign language, comprehensive exam, thesis optional. *Entrance requirements:* For master's, 18 hours of course work in the field, minimum GPA of 3.0. Additional exam requirements/recommendations for international students: Required—TOEFL (minimum score 500 paper-based; 173 computer-based; 61 iBT), IELTS (minimum score 5.5). *Application deadline:* For fall admission, 5/1 priority date for domestic and international students; for spring admission, 11/1 priority date for domestic and international students. Applications are processed on a rolling basis. Application fee: $70. Electronic applications accepted. *Expenses:* Tuition: Full-time $20,760; part-time $865 per credit. Required fees: $300; $150 per semester. Tuition and fees vary according to program. *Financial support:* Research assistantships, scholarships/grants available. Support available to part-time students. Financial award application deadline: 3/1; financial award applicants required to submit FAFSA. *Faculty research:* East Asian philosophy and religion, Chinese language and literature, Japanese language, modern Japan, Chinese art and history. *Unit head:* Dr. Bernadette Li, Chair, 718-990-1657, E-mail: lib@stjohns.edu. *Application contact:* Kathleen Davis, Director of Graduate Admission, 718-990-2790, Fax: 718-990-5686, E-mail: gradhelp@stjohns.edu.

San Diego State University, Graduate and Research Affairs, College of Arts and Letters, Center for Asian Studies, San Diego, CA 92182. Offers MA. *Degree requirements:* For master's, one foreign language, thesis. *Entrance requirements:* For master's, GRE General Test, 3 letters of reference, writing sample. Additional exam requirements/recommendations for international students: Required—TOEFL. Electronic applications accepted. *Faculty research:* Language acquisition process, social organization of Asia, economic development.

Seton Hall University, College of Arts and Sciences, Department of Asian Studies, South Orange, NJ 07079-2697. Offers MA. Part-time and evening/weekend programs available. *Degree requirements:* For master's, thesis optional. Electronic applications accepted. *Faculty research:* Modern Chinese history, contemporary Chinese politics, ancient Chinese history, Hinduism, Asian business, Japanese history.

See Close-Up on page 623.

Stanford University, School of Humanities and Sciences, Center for East Asian Studies, Stanford, CA 94305-9991. Offers MA. *Degree requirements:* For master's, one foreign language, thesis. *Entrance requirements:* For master's, GRE General Test. Additional exam requirements/recommendations for international students: Required—TOEFL. Electronic applications accepted.

United Theological Seminary of the Twin Cities, Graduate and Professional Programs, New Brighton, MN 55112-2598. Offers advanced theological studies (Diploma); justice and peace studies (M Div); leadership toward racial justice (MA, Certificate); Methodist studies (M Div, MA); ministry (D Min); ministry renewal and professional development (Certificate); pastoral care and counseling (M Div); religion and theology (MA); theological and religious studies (Certificate); theology and the arts (MA); urban ministry (MARL); women's studies: religion, theology and ministry (MA). *Accreditation:* ACIPE; ATS. Part-time and evening/weekend programs available. *Faculty:* 10 full-time (6 women), 24 part-time/adjunct (12 women). *Students:* 60 full-time (34 women), 93 part-time (60 women); includes 10 minority (5 African Americans, 1 American Indian/Alaska Native, 3 Asian Americans or Pacific Islanders, 1 Hispanic American), 1 international. Average age 47. 39 applicants, 100% accepted, 32 enrolled. In 2008, 21 first professional degrees, 9 master's awarded. *Degree requirements:* For master's, thesis; for doctorate, comprehensive exam, thesis/dissertation; for M Div, integrative notebook, spiritual chronicle. *Entrance requirements:* For M Div and master's, minimum GPA of 2.75; strong analytical, reflective thinking and writing skills; vocational and academic goals compatible with those of Seminary; for doctorate, M Div or equivalent, minimum GPA of 3.0, 3 years experience in professional ministry; for other advanced degree, BA or equivalent life experience; strong analytical, reflective thinking and writing skills (Certificate); proficiency in English language, previous study of theology at a theological school, recommendation of student's denomination (Diploma). Additional exam requirements/recommendations for international students: Required—TOEFL (minimum score 550 paper-based). *Application deadline:* For fall admission, 7/1 priority date for domestic students, 11/1 priority date for international students; for winter admission, 11/1 priority date for domestic students; for spring admission, 11/15 priority date for domestic students. Applications are processed on a rolling basis. Application fee: $50. *Expenses:* Tuition: Full-time $11,070; part-time $410 per credit hour. Required fees: $295; $135 per term. One-time fee: $25. Tuition and fees vary according to course load, degree level and program. *Financial support:* In 2008–09, 98 students received support. Career-related internships or fieldwork, institutionally sponsored loans, and scholarships/grants available. Support available to part-time students. Financial award application deadline: 5/1; financial award applicants required to submit FAFSA. *Unit head:* Dr. Richard D. Weis, Dean of the Seminary, 651-255-6108 Ext. 108, Fax: 651-633-4315, E-mail: rweis@unitedseminary.edu. *Application contact:* Rev. Glen Herrington-Hall, Director of Admissions, 651-255-6107 Ext. 107, Fax: 651-633-4315, E-mail: gherrington-hall@unitedseminary.edu.

University of Alberta, Faculty of Graduate Studies and Research, Department of East Asian Studies, Edmonton, AB T6G 2E1, Canada. Offers Chinese literature (MA); East Asian interdisciplinary studies (MA); Japanese literature (MA). Part-time programs available. *Degree requirements:* For master's, one foreign language, thesis. *Entrance requirements:* Additional exam requirements/recommendations for international students: Required—TOEFL. Electronic applications accepted. *Faculty research:* Classical Chinese poetry and poetics, Chinese philosophy, modern/contemporary Chinese literature, modern Japanese literature and culture, Japanese women's writing.

The University of Arizona, Graduate College, College of Humanities, Department of East Asian Studies, Tucson, AZ 85721. Offers MA, PhD. Part-time programs available. Terminal master's awarded for partial completion of doctoral program. *Degree requirements:* For master's, one foreign language; for doctorate, 2 foreign languages. *Entrance requirements:* For master's, GRE General Test, 2 letters of recommendation, minimum GPA of 3.0, statement of purpose; for doctorate, GRE General Test, 2 letters of recommendation, minimum GPA of 3.0, statement of purpose, writing sample. Additional exam requirements/recommendations for international students: Required—TOEFL (minimum score 550 paper-based). Electronic applications accepted. *Faculty research:* Chinese history, Chinese/Japanese linguistics, Chinese/Japanese literature, Chinese/Japanese religion.

The University of British Columbia, Faculty of Arts, Department of Asian Studies, Vancouver, BC V6T 1Z1, Canada. Offers MA, PhD. *Degree requirements:* For master's, one foreign language, thesis; for doctorate, 2 foreign languages, thesis/dissertation. *Entrance requirements:* For master's, BA degree; for doctorate, master's degree in Asian studies or equivalent. Additional exam requirements/recommendations for international students: Required—TOEFL (minimum score 570 paper-based; 230 computer-based; 85 iBT). Electronic applications accepted. *Faculty research:* Language; linguistics; literature; religion and philosophy; premodern history of China, Japan, Korea, South and South East Asia.

The University of British Columbia, Faculty of Graduate Studies, Institute of Asian Research, Vancouver, BC V6T 1Z1, Canada. Offers MAPPS. Part-time programs available. *Degree requirements:* For master's, thesis optional. *Entrance requirements:* Additional exam requirements/recommendations for international students: Required—TOEFL (minimum score 600 paper-based; 250 computer-based; 100 iBT), GRE (recommended). Electronic applications accepted. *Faculty research:* Social cohesion, globalization, social safety nets, research and development alliances, knowledge-based workshops.

University of California, Berkeley, Graduate Division, College of Letters and Science, Department of South and Southeast Asian Studies, Berkeley, CA 94720-1500. Offers Hindi (MA, PhD); Indonesian (MA, PhD); Sanskrit (MA, PhD); Tamil (MA, PhD). Terminal master's awarded for partial completion of doctoral program. *Degree requirements:* For master's, 2 foreign languages, thesis; for doctorate, 2 foreign languages, thesis/dissertation, oral qualifying exam. *Entrance requirements:* For master's and doctorate, GRE General Test, minimum GPA of 3.0, 3 letters of recommendation. Electronic applications accepted.

University of California, Berkeley, Graduate Division, Group in Asian Studies, Berkeley, CA 94720-1500. Offers Asian studies (PhD); East Asian studies (MA); Northeast Asian studies (MA); South Asian studies (MA); Southeast Asian studies (MA); JD/MA; MBA/MA; MJ/MA. *Degree requirements:* For master's, one foreign language, comprehensive exam or thesis; for doctorate, 2 foreign languages, thesis/dissertation, qualifying exam. *Entrance requirements:* For master's and doctorate, GRE General Test, minimum GPA of 3.0, 3 letters of recommendation.

University of California, Berkeley, Graduate Division, Group in Buddhist Studies, Berkeley, CA 94720-1500. Offers PhD. *Degree requirements:* For doctorate, 4 foreign languages, thesis/dissertation, dissertation defense, qualifying exam. *Entrance requirements:* For doctorate, GRE General Test, MA in Japanese, Chinese, or Sanskrit; minimum GPA of 3.0, 3 letters of recommendation. Electronic applications accepted.

University of California, Los Angeles, Graduate Division, College of Letters and Science, Department of Asian Languages and Cultures, Los Angeles, CA 90095. Offers MA, PhD. *Faculty:* 15. *Students:* 37 full-time (23 women); includes 11 minority (all Asian Americans or Pacific Islanders), 14 international. Average age 30. 54 applicants, 20% accepted, 8 enrolled. In 2008, 10 master's, 1 doctorate awarded. Terminal master's awarded for partial completion of doctoral program. *Degree requirements:* For master's, one foreign language, comprehensive exam or thesis; for doctorate, 2 foreign languages, thesis/dissertation, oral and written qualifying exams. *Entrance requirements:* For master's, GRE General Test, minimum GPA of 3.0, sample of written work; for doctorate, GRE General Test, minimum undergraduate GPA of 3.0, sample of research writing or thesis in English. Additional exam requirements/recommendations for international students: Required—TOEFL. *Application deadline:* For fall admission, 12/1 for domestic and international students. Application fee: $60 ($80 for international students). Electronic applications accepted. *Expenses:* Tuition, nonresident: full-time $14,694. Required fees: $9669.50. Full-time tuition and fees vary according to course load, degree level, program and student level. *Financial support:* In 2008–09, 49 fellowships with full and partial tuition reimbursements, 20 research assistantships with full and partial tuition reimbursements, 30 teaching assistantships with full and partial tuition reimbursements were awarded; Federal Work-Study, institutionally sponsored loans, scholarships/grants, health care benefits, tuition waivers (full and partial), and unspecified assistantships also available. Financial award application deadline: 3/1; financial award applicants required to submit FAFSA. *Unit head:* Dr. Lee Namhee, Chair, 310-794-2666. *Application contact:* Departmental Office, 310-206-8235, E-mail: alcgen@humnet.ucla.edu.

University of California, Los Angeles, Graduate Division, College of Letters and Science, Interdepartmental Program in East Asian Studies, Los Angeles, CA 90095. Offers MA. *Students:* 14 full-time (9 women); includes 9 minority (1 African American, 8 Asian Americans or Pacific Islanders), 3 international. Average age 27. 48 applicants, 63% accepted, 9 enrolled. In 2008, 4 master's awarded. *Degree requirements:* For master's, one foreign language, comprehensive exam. *Entrance requirements:* For master's, GRE General Test, minimum undergraduate GPA of 3.0. *Application deadline:* For fall admission, 12/15 for domestic and international students. Application fee: $60 ($80 for international students). Electronic applications accepted. *Expenses:* Tuition, nonresident: full-time $14,694. Required fees: $9669.50. Full-time tuition and fees vary according to course load, degree level, program and student level. *Financial support:* In 2008–09, 2 fellowships with full and partial tuition reimbursements, 1 research assistantship with full and partial tuition reimbursement, 2 teaching assistantships with full and partial tuition reimbursements were awarded; Federal Work-Study, institutionally sponsored loans, scholarships/grants, health care benefits, tuition waivers (full and partial), and unspecified assistantships also available. Financial award application deadline: 3/1; financial award applicants required to submit FAFSA. *Unit head:* David Schaberg, Director, 310-206-6571. *Application contact:* Program Office, 310-206-6571, E-mail: idgrads@international.ucla.edu.

University of California, Riverside, Graduate Division, Program in Southeast Asian Studies, Riverside, CA 92521-0102. Offers MA. *Degree requirements:* For master's, one foreign language, thesis. *Expenses:* Tuition, nonresident: full-time $4898. Required fees: $10,362. *Faculty research:* Southeast Asian texts, rituals and performance, music and technoculture, dance ethnography, ethnomusicology.

University of California, Santa Barbara, Graduate Division, College of Letters and Sciences, Division of Humanities and Fine Arts, Department of East Asian Languages and Cultural Studies, Santa Barbara, CA 93106-7075. Offers Asian Studies (MA), including Asian Studies, East Asian language and cultural studies; Asian studies (MA), including Asian Studies, East Asian language and cultural studies; East Asian language and cultural studies (PhD); MA/PhD. *Students:* 13 full-time (8 women). Average age 27. 76 applicants, 28% accepted, 6 enrolled. In 2008, 2 master's awarded. *Degree requirements:* For master's, one foreign language, thesis or alternative; for doctorate, 2 foreign languages, thesis/dissertation. *Entrance requirements:* For master's and doctorate, GRE, 3 letters of recommendation, statement of purpose, personal achievements/contributions statement, resumé/curriculum vitae, transcripts for post-secondary institutions attended. Additional exam requirements/recommendations for international students: Required—TOEFL (paper: 550, computer: 213, IBT: 80) or IELTS (7). *Application deadline:* For fall admission, 4/1 for domestic and international students. Application fee: $70 ($90 for international students). Electronic applications accepted. *Expenses:* Tuition, nonresident: full-time $25,149. Required fees: $10,143. Full-time tuition and fees vary according to campus/location, reciprocity agreements and student level. *Financial support:* In 2008–09, 10 students received support, including 5 fellowships with full and partial tuition reimbursements available (averaging $11,000 per year), 10 teaching assistantships with partial tuition reimbursements available (averaging $8,200 per year); Federal Work-Study, institutionally sponsored loans, scholarships/grants, health care benefits, and unspecified assistantships also available. Financial award application deadline: 12/15; financial award applicants required to submit FAFSA. *Faculty research:* Chinese literature, Chinese film, Japanese society, Japanese literature, East Asian cultural studies. *Unit head:* Dr. William Powell, Chair, 805-893-4455, Fax: 805-893-3011, E-mail: bpowell@religion.ucsb.edu. *Application contact:* Dr. Ronald Egan, Faculty Graduate Advisor, 805-893-3770, Fax: 805-893-3011, E-mail: ronegan@eastasian.ucsb.edu.

University of Chicago, Division of the Humanities, Department of East Asian Languages and Civilizations, Chicago, IL 60637-1513. Offers AM, PhD. Terminal master's awarded for partial completion of doctoral program. *Degree requirements:* For master's, one foreign language, thesis; for doctorate, 2 foreign languages, thesis/dissertation. *Entrance requirements:* For master's and doctorate, GRE General Test. Additional exam requirements/recommendations for international students: Required—TOEFL.

University of Chicago, Division of the Humanities, Department of South Asian Languages and Civilizations, Chicago, IL 60637-1513. Offers South Asian languages and civilizations (AM, PhD), including Bengali (PhD), Hindi (PhD), Sanskrit (PhD), Tamil (PhD), Urdu (PhD). Terminal master's awarded for partial completion of doctoral program. *Degree requirements:* For master's, one foreign language, thesis; for doctorate, 2 foreign languages, thesis/dissertation. *Entrance requirements:* For master's and doctorate, GRE General Test. Additional exam requirements/recommendations for international students: Required—TOEFL.

University of Colorado at Boulder, Graduate School, College of Arts and Sciences, Department of East Asian Languages and Civilizations, Boulder, CO 80309. Offers Chinese (MA, PhD); Japanese (MA, PhD). Part-time programs available. *Degree requirements:* For master's, comprehensive exam. *Entrance requirements:* For master's, BA in Chinese or Japanese, minimum undergraduate GPA of 3.0. Additional exam requirements/recommendations for international students: Required—TOEFL. *Faculty research:* Chinese and Japanese modern and classical literature, religions, linguistics, language pedagogy, pre-modern and contemporary fiction, sociolinguistics.

University of Hawaii at Manoa, Graduate Division, School of Pacific and Asian Studies, Program in Asian Studies, Concentration in Korean Studies, Honolulu, HI 96822. Offers Graduate Certificate. Part-time programs available. *Degree requirements:* For Graduate Certificate, one foreign language. *Entrance requirements:* For degree, GRE. Additional exam requirements/recommendations for international students: Required—TOEFL (minimum score 560 paper-based; 220 computer-based; 83 iBT), IELTS (minimum score 5).

University of Hawaii at Manoa, Graduate Division, School of Pacific and Asian Studies, Program in Asian Studies, Concentration in Southeast Asian Studies, Honolulu, HI 96822. Offers Graduate Certificate. Part-time programs available. *Degree requirements:* For Graduate Certificate, one foreign language. *Entrance requirements:* For degree, GRE. Additional exam requirements/recommendations for international students: Required—TOEFL (minimum score 560 paper-based; 220 computer-based; 83 iBT), IELTS (minimum score 5).

University of Illinois at Urbana–Champaign, Graduate College, College of Liberal Arts and Sciences, School of Literatures, Cultures and Linguistics, Department of East Asian Languages and Cultures, Champaign, IL 61820. Offers Asian studies (MA); East Asian languages and cultures (PhD). *Faculty:* 15 full-time (5 women), 1 (woman) part-time/adjunct. *Students:* 29 full-time (24 women), 8 part-time (all women); includes 2 minority (1 Asian American or Pacific Islander, 1 Hispanic American), 27 international. 76 applicants, 13% accepted, 9 enrolled. In 2008, 3 master's, 3 doctorates awarded. *Entrance requirements:* For master's, GRE General Test, minimum GPA of 3.0; writing sample; for doctorate, GRE, minimum GPA of 3.0; writing sample. Additional exam requirements/recommendations for international students: Required—TOEFL (minimum score 103 iBT). *Application deadline:* Applications are processed on a rolling basis. Application fee: $60 ($75 for international students). Electronic applications accepted. *Financial support:* In 2008–09, 10 fellowships, 1 research assistantship, 25 teaching assistantships were awarded; tuition waivers (full and partial) also available. *Unit head:* Karen Kelsky, Head, 217-244-9077, Fax: 217-244-2223, E-mail: kelsky@illinois.edu. *Application contact:* David Goodman, Director of Graduate Studies, 217-244-1432, Fax: 217-244-2223, E-mail: dgoodman@illinois.edu.

The University of Iowa, Graduate College, College of Liberal Arts and Sciences, Program in Asian Languages and Literature, Iowa City, IA 52242-1316. Offers MA. *Degree requirements:* For master's, thesis optional, exam. *Entrance requirements:* For master's, GRE General Test, minimum GPA of 3.0. Additional exam requirements/recommendations for international students: Required—TOEFL (minimum score 590 paper-based; 243 computer-based; 96 iBT). Electronic applications accepted.

The University of Kansas, Graduate Studies, College of Liberal Arts and Sciences, Department of East Asian Languages and Cultures, Lawrence, KS 66045. Offers MA, MBA/MA. Part-time programs available. *Faculty:* 7. *Students:* 11 full-time (5 women), 3 part-time (2 women); includes 1 minority (Asian American or Pacific Islander), 3 international. Average age 31. 17 applicants, 29% accepted, 3 enrolled. In 2008, 1 master's awarded. *Degree requirements:* For master's, one foreign language, thesis. *Entrance requirements:* For master's, GRE, 3 letters of recommendation, statement of purpose, writing sample. Additional exam requirements/recommendations for international students: Required—TOEFL. *Application deadline:* For fall admission, 5/1 priority date for domestic students, 5/1 for international students; for spring admission, 12/1 priority date for domestic students, 12/1 for international students. Applications are processed on a rolling basis. Application fee: $45 ($55 for international students). Electronic applications accepted. *Expenses:* Tuition, area resident: Full-time $6122; part-time $255.10 per credit hour. Tuition, state resident: full-time $6122; part-time $255.10 per credit hour. Tuition, nonresident: full-time $14,629; part-time $609.55 per credit hour. Required fees: $847; $70.56 per credit hour. Tuition and fees vary according to course load and program. *Financial support:* Fellowships, teaching assistantships with full and partial tuition reimbursements, unspecified assistantships available. Financial award application deadline: 2/1. *Faculty research:* Gender relations in literature, ancient Chinese law, visual culture of modern Japan, Japanese language pedagogy, Chinese paleography, Korean shamanism, folklore, traditional Chinese and Japanese literature, Chinese linguistics and language pedagogy. *Unit head:* Margaret Childs, Chair and Graduate Director, 785-864-3100, E-mail: mgchilds@ku.edu. *Application contact:* Georgia Damis, Administrative Specialist, 785-864-3100, Fax: 785-864-4298, E-mail: ealc@ku.edu.

University of Michigan, Horace H. Rackham School of Graduate Studies, College of Literature, Science, and the Arts, Center for Chinese Studies, Ann Arbor, MI 48109. Offers Asian studies: China (AM, Graduate Certificate); JD/AM; MBA/AM; MPP/AM. Part-time programs available. *Degree requirements:* For master's, one foreign language, thesis. *Entrance requirements:* For master's, GRE General Test. Additional exam requirements/recommendations for international students: Required—TOEFL. Electronic applications accepted. *Faculty research:* Economic reform in China, Chinese religion, history of late Imperial China, Chinese foreign policy, Chinese music and music history.

University of Michigan, Horace H. Rackham School of Graduate Studies, College of Literature, Science, and the Arts, Center for Japanese Studies, Ann Arbor, MI 48109. Offers AM, JD/AM, MBA/AM. Part-time programs available. *Degree requirements:* For master's, one foreign language, thesis or alternative. *Entrance requirements:* For master's, GRE General Test. Additional exam requirements/recommendations for international students: Required—TOEFL (minimum score 560 paper-based; 220 computer-based; 84 iBT). Electronic applications accepted. *Faculty research:* Japanese literature; Japanese history; Japanese linguistics and language pedagogy; gender and sexuality in Japan.

University of Michigan, Horace H. Rackham School of Graduate Studies, College of Literature, Science, and the Arts, Center for South Asian Studies, Ann Arbor, MI 48109. Offers MA, Certificate, MBA/MA. Part-time programs available. *Degree requirements:* For master's, one foreign language, thesis, 24 credits area studies; for Certificate, one foreign language, 15 credits area studies. *Entrance requirements:* For master's, GRE General Test, GMAT (MA/MBA), LSAT (law), 3 transcripts; for Certificate, GRE General Test, GMAT (MA/MBA), LSAT (law), 2 transcripts. Additional exam requirements/recommendations for international students: Required—TOEFL (minimum score 560 paper-based; 220 computer-based; 84 iBT). Electronic

Asian Studies

University of Michigan (continued)
applications accepted. *Faculty research:* History of Islam and South Asia; ethnicity and nationalism; global and transnational feminism; South Asian architecture and urbanism; mysticism and politics in Indian religions.

University of Michigan, Horace H. Rackham School of Graduate Studies, College of Literature, Science, and the Arts, Center for Southeast Asian Studies, Ann Arbor, MI 48109. Offers MA, Graduate Certificate, MBA/MA, MPP/MA. Part-time programs available. *Degree requirements:* For master's, one foreign language, thesis, 24 credits area studies; for Graduate Certificate, one foreign language, 15 credits area studies. *Entrance requirements:* For master's, GRE General Test, GMAT (MA/MBA), LSAT (dual degree law), 3 recommendations; transcripts; statement of purpose; for Graduate Certificate, GRE General Test, GMAT (MA/MBA), LSAT (dual degree law), 2 recommendations; transcripts; statement of purpose. Additional exam requirements/recommendations for international students: Required—TOEFL (minimum score 560 paper-based; 220 computer-based; 84 iBT). Electronic applications accepted. *Faculty research:* Modern Southeast Asia political economy and policy-making; media, ritual, and religion; technology and colonialism in Southeast Asia; urbanization in developing countries; modernity and mass culture in Southeast Asia.

University of Michigan, Horace H. Rackham School of Graduate Studies, College of Literature, Science, and the Arts, Department of Asian Languages and Cultures, Ann Arbor, MI 48109. Offers MA, PhD. Terminal master's awarded for partial completion of doctoral program. *Degree requirements:* For master's, variable foreign language requirement, thesis; for doctorate, 2 foreign languages, thesis/dissertation, oral defense of dissertation, preliminary exam. *Entrance requirements:* For master's and doctorate, GRE General Test. Additional exam requirements/recommendations for international students: Required—TOEFL (minimum score 600 paper-based; 250 computer-based). Electronic applications accepted. *Faculty research:* Literature, linguistics, religion, philosophy, music, cinema.

University of Minnesota, Twin Cities Campus, Graduate School, College of Liberal Arts, Department of Asian Languages and Literatures, Minneapolis, MN 55455-0213. Offers Asian literatures, cultures, and media (PhD). *Degree requirements:* For doctorate, comprehensive exam, thesis/dissertation. *Entrance requirements:* For doctorate, GRE, 3 letters of recommendation. Additional exam requirements/recommendations for international students: Required—TOEFL (minimum score 550 paper-based; 213 computer-based), IELTS (minimum score 6.5). Electronic applications accepted. *Faculty research:* Gender studies, post-colonial theory, poetics and poetic theory, film studies, post modernist thought.

University of Oregon, Graduate School, College of Arts and Sciences, Program in Asian Studies, Eugene, OR 97403. Offers MA. Part-time programs available. *Degree requirements:* For master's, one foreign language, thesis or alternative. *Entrance requirements:* For master's, GRE General Test. Additional exam requirements/recommendations for international students: Required—TOEFL. *Faculty research:* East and Southeast Asia, Pacific Islands.

University of Pennsylvania, School of Arts and Sciences, Graduate Group in East Asian Languages and Civilization, Philadelphia, PA 19104. Offers AM, PhD.

University of Pennsylvania, School of Arts and Sciences, Graduate Group in South Asian Regional Studies, Philadelphia, PA 19104. Offers AM, PhD. Terminal master's awarded for partial completion of doctoral program. *Degree requirements:* For master's, one foreign language, thesis, written exam; for doctorate, 3 foreign languages, thesis/dissertation, written exam. *Entrance requirements:* For master's, GRE General Test. Additional exam requirements/recommendations for international students: Required—TOEFL. Electronic applications accepted. *Faculty research:* South Asian linguistics, literature, and history; economic history.

University of Pittsburgh, School of Arts and Sciences, Department of East Asian Languages and Literatures, Pittsburgh, PA 15260. Offers East Asian studies (MA). Part-time programs available. *Degree requirements:* For master's, one foreign language, thesis, oral comprehensive exam. *Entrance requirements:* For master's, GRE General Test, 2 years of Chinese or Japanese, minimum QPA of 3.0. Additional exam requirements/recommendations for international students: Required—TOEFL (minimum score 600 paper-based). Electronic applications accepted. *Faculty research:* Chinese literature, film, and poetry; Japanese literature, film, and theater; Chinese society and culture; East Asian foreign policy, security studies, and economic history; Japanese performing arts and fine arts.

University of Pittsburgh, University Center for International Studies, Pittsburgh, PA 15260. Offers African studies (Certificate); Asian studies (Certificate); European Union studies (Certificate); global studies (Certificate); Latin American studies (Certificate); Russian and East European studies (Certificate); West European studies (Certificate).

University of San Francisco, College of Arts and Sciences, Program in Asia Pacific Studies, San Francisco, CA 94117-1080. Offers MA, MA/MBA. Part-time and evening/weekend programs available. *Degree requirements:* For master's, one foreign language, thesis. *Entrance requirements:* For master's, minimum GPA of 3.0. *Faculty research:* History of Christianity in China, U.S.-China policy, East Asian economies and political systems, sociolinguistic aspects of Japanese.

University of Southern California, Graduate School, College of Letters, Arts and Sciences, Department of East Asian Languages and Cultures, Los Angeles, CA 90089. Offers MA, PhD. *Degree requirements:* For master's, one foreign language, thesis; for doctorate, 2 foreign languages, thesis/dissertation. *Entrance requirements:* For master's and doctorate, GRE General Test. *Faculty research:* Premodern Chinese history, modern and classical Chinese literature, Japanese, Korea.

University of Southern California, Graduate School, College of Letters, Arts and Sciences, Department of East Asian Studies, Los Angeles, CA 90089. Offers MA, MBA/MA. Part-time programs available. *Degree requirements:* For master's, thesis. *Entrance requirements:* For master's, GRE General Test. *Faculty research:* China, Japan, Korea, film/cinema in East Asia, geography.

The University of Texas at Austin, Graduate School, College of Liberal Arts, Department of Asian Studies, Austin, TX 78712-1111. Offers Asian cultures and languages (MA, PhD); Asian studies (MA). Part-time programs available. *Degree requirements:* For master's, thesis; for doctorate, 3 foreign languages, thesis/dissertation. *Entrance requirements:* For master's and doctorate, GRE General Test. Electronic applications accepted. *Faculty research:* Modern Taiwanese fiction, modern Japanese literature, religious studies in South Asia during classical period.

University of Toronto, School of Graduate Studies, Humanities Division, Centre for South Asian Studies, Toronto, ON M5S 1A1, Canada. Offers MA, PhD. Students who wish to be admitted into the Collaborative Program in South Asian Studies must apply to one of the following units: anthropology, English, history, geography, political science (PhD only), religious studies, social work. Part-time programs available. *Degree requirements:* For master's, thesis optional; for doctorate, one foreign language, thesis/dissertation.

University of Toronto, School of Graduate Studies, Humanities Division, Department of East Asian Studies, Toronto, ON M5S 1A1, Canada. Offers MA, PhD. Part-time programs available. *Degree requirements:* For master's, thesis optional; for doctorate, 2 foreign languages, comprehensive exam, thesis/dissertation. *Entrance requirements:* For master's, writing sample, 2 letters of recommendation, BA in a specialist or East Asian studies program, minimum B+ average in final year; for doctorate, writing sample, 3 letters of recommendation, MA in East Asian studies. Additional exam requirements/recommendations for international students: Required—TOEFL (minimum score 600 paper-based), TWE (minimum score 5). Electronic applications accepted.

University of Utah, The Graduate School, College of Humanities, Asian Studies Program, Salt Lake City, UT 84112-1107. Offers MA.

University of Victoria, Faculty of Graduate Studies, Faculty of Humanities, Department of Pacific and Asian Studies, Victoria, BC V8W 2Y2, Canada. Offers MA. *Degree requirements:* For master's, thesis. *Entrance requirements:* For master's, minimum B+ average, writing sample. Additional exam requirements/recommendations for international students: Required—TOEFL (minimum score 575 paper-based; 233 computer-based), IELTS (minimum score 7). Electronic applications accepted. *Faculty research:* Culture, ethnicity and identity; economy and society; gender studies; languages and linguistics; literature.

University of Virginia, College and Graduate School of Arts and Sciences, Department of East Asian Languages, Literatures, and Cultures, Charlottesville, VA 22903. Offers East Asian studies (MA); MBA/MA. *Faculty:* 14 full-time (12 women), 1 (woman) part-time/adjunct. *Students:* 3 full-time (1 woman), 1 international. Average age 24. 15 applicants, 33% accepted, 2 enrolled. In 2008, 1 master's awarded. *Degree requirements:* For master's, one foreign language, comprehensive exam, thesis. *Entrance requirements:* For master's, GRE General Test, 2 letters of recommendation. Additional exam requirements/recommendations for international students: Required—TOEFL, IELTS. *Application deadline:* For fall admission, 1/15 for domestic and international students; for winter admission, 9/15 for domestic and international students. Applications are processed on a rolling basis. Application fee: $60. Electronic applications accepted. *Expenses:* Tuition, area resident: Full-time $10,452. Tuition, state resident: full-time $10,452. Tuition, nonresident: full-time $20,010. Required fees: $2176. Part-time tuition and fees vary according to course load and program. *Financial support:* Applicants required to submit FAFSA. *Unit head:* Daniel Lefkowitz, Chair, 434-924-7836, Fax: 434-924-6977, E-mail: eastasiacenter@virginia.edu. *Application contact:* Daniel Lefkowitz, Chair, 434-924-7836, Fax: 434-924-6977, E-mail: eastasiacenter@virginia.edu.

University of Washington, Graduate School, College of Arts and Sciences, Department of Asian Languages and Literature, Seattle, WA 98195. Offers Buddhist studies (MA, PhD); Chinese language and literature (MA, PhD); Japanese language and literature (MA, PhD); Korean language and literature (MA, PhD); South Asian language and literature (MA, PhD). *Degree requirements:* For master's, 2 foreign languages, general exam, thesis or 2 research papers; for doctorate, 3 foreign languages, thesis/dissertation, general exam. *Entrance requirements:* For master's, GRE, minimum GPA of 3.0; for doctorate, GRE, master's degree in related field, minimum GPA of 3.0. Additional exam requirements/recommendations for international students: Required—TOEFL. Electronic applications accepted. *Faculty research:* Textual, linguistic, philological, and literary study of languages and literatures of Asia.

University of Washington, Graduate School, College of Arts and Sciences, Henry M. Jackson School of International Studies, China Studies Program, Seattle, WA 98195. Offers MAIS. *Degree requirements:* For master's, one foreign language, thesis optional. *Entrance requirements:* For master's, GRE General Test, minimum GPA of 3.0. Additional exam requirements/recommendations for international students: Required—TOEFL (minimum score 500 paper-based; 213 computer-based). Electronic applications accepted.

University of Washington, Graduate School, College of Arts and Sciences, Henry M. Jackson School of International Studies, Japan Studies Program, Seattle, WA 98195. Offers MAIS. *Degree requirements:* For master's, one foreign language. *Entrance requirements:* For master's, GRE General Test, minimum GPA of 3.0. Additional exam requirements/recommendations for international students: Required—TOEFL (minimum score 500 paper-based; 213 computer-based). Electronic applications accepted.

University of Washington, Graduate School, College of Arts and Sciences, Henry M. Jackson School of International Studies, Korea Studies Program, Seattle, WA 98195. Offers MAIS. *Degree requirements:* For master's, one foreign language. *Entrance requirements:* For master's, GRE General Test, minimum GPA of 3.0. Additional exam requirements/recommendations for international students: Required—TOEFL (minimum score 500 paper-based; 213 computer-based). Electronic applications accepted.

University of Washington, Graduate School, College of Arts and Sciences, Henry M. Jackson School of International Studies, Russian, East European and Central Asian Studies Program, Seattle, WA 98195. Offers Central Asian studies (MAIS); East European studies (MAIS); Russian studies (MAIS). *Degree requirements:* For master's, one foreign language, thesis. *Entrance requirements:* For master's, GRE General Test, 2 years of relevant language, minimum GPA of 3.0. Additional exam requirements/recommendations for international students: Required—TOEFL (minimum score 500 paper-based; 213 computer-based). Electronic applications accepted.

University of Washington, Graduate School, College of Arts and Sciences, Henry M. Jackson School of International Studies, South Asian Studies Program, Seattle, WA 98195. Offers MAIS. *Degree requirements:* For master's, one foreign language, thesis optional. *Entrance requirements:* For master's, GRE General Test, minimum GPA of 3.0. Additional exam requirements/recommendations for international students: Required—TOEFL (minimum score 500 paper-based; 213 computer-based). Electronic applications accepted.

University of Wisconsin–Madison, Graduate School, College of Letters and Science, Center for Southeast Asian Studies, Madison, WI 53706. Offers MA. Part-time programs available. *Degree requirements:* For master's, one foreign language, oral defense of seminar paper. Electronic applications accepted. *Faculty research:* Economic development, censorship, political change, pedagogical developments in Indonesia, Philippine historical demography, environment photography.

University of Wisconsin–Madison, Graduate School, College of Letters and Science, Department of East Asian Languages and Literature, Madison, WI 53706-1380. Offers Chinese literature (MA, PhD); Chinese thought (MA, PhD); Japanese linguistics (MA, PhD); Japanese literature (MA, PhD). Part-time programs available. Terminal master's awarded for partial completion of doctoral program. *Degree requirements:* For master's, one foreign language, seminars, written exam; for doctorate, 3 foreign languages, thesis/dissertation, seminars, preliminary exams, oral exams. *Entrance requirements:* For master's, GRE General Test, BA or equivalent in major field; for doctorate, GRE General Test, MA or equivalent in major field. Electronic applications accepted. *Faculty research:* Modern and historical linguistics, literature, literary and cultural history.

University of Wisconsin–Madison, Graduate School, College of Letters and Science, Department of History, Madison, WI 53706-1380. Offers African history (MA, PhD); Central Asian history (MA, PhD); comparative world history (MA, PhD); East Asian history (MA, PhD); European history (MA, PhD); gender and women's history (MA, PhD); Latin American and Caribbean history (MA, PhD); Middle Eastern history (MA, PhD); South Asian history (MA, PhD); Southeast Asian history (MA, PhD); United States history (MA, PhD). Terminal master's awarded for partial completion of doctoral program. *Degree requirements:* For master's, thesis (for some programs); for doctorate, variable foreign language requirement, thesis/dissertation. *Entrance requirements:* For master's and doctorate, GRE General Test. Additional exam requirements/recommendations for international students: Required—Michigan English Language Assessment Battery or TOEFL. Electronic applications accepted. *Faculty research:* American, African, European, Asian, Latin American, and Middle Eastern history.

University of Wisconsin–Madison, Graduate School, College of Letters and Science, Department of Languages and Cultures of Asia, Madison, WI 53706-1380. Offers civilizations and cultures (PhD); languages and cultures of Asia (MA); languages and literatures (PhD); religions of Asia (PhD). Part-time programs available. Terminal master's awarded for partial completion of doctoral program. *Degree requirements:* For master's, one foreign language, thesis or alternative; for doctorate, 2 foreign languages, thesis/dissertation. *Entrance requirements:* For master's, minimum GPA of 3.0; for doctorate, minimum GPA of 3.25, master's degree. Electronic applications accepted. *Faculty research:* Literature, folklore, religion.

Valparaiso University, Graduate Division, Program in Chinese Studies, Valparaiso, IN 46383. Offers MA, JD/MA. Part-time and evening/weekend programs available. *Students:* 11 full-time (4 women), 6 part-time (4 women); includes 2 minority (both Asian Americans or Pacific Islanders), 1 international. Average age 28. In 2008, 2 master's awarded. *Entrance requirements:* For master's, minimum GPA of 3.0, Chinese language proficiency. Additional exam requirements/recommendations for international students: Required—TOEFL (minimum score 550 paper-based; 213 computer-based). *Application deadline:* Applications are processed on a rolling basis. Application fee: $30 ($50 for international students). Electronic applications accepted. *Financial support:* Scholarships/grants and unspecified assistantships available. Support available to part-time students. Financial award applicants required to submit FAFSA. *Unit head:* Dr. David L. Rowland, Dean, Graduate Studies and Continuing Education, 219-464-5313, Fax: 219-464-5381, E-mail: David.Rowland@valpo.edu. *Application contact:* Jamie Haney, Coordinator of Recruitment Activities, 219-464-5313, Fax: 219-464-5381, E-mail: Jamie.Haney@valpo.edu.

Washington State University, Graduate School, College of Liberal Arts, Department of History, Pullman, WA 99164. Offers early and modern European history (MA, PhD); environmental history (MA, PhD); Latin American history (MA, PhD); modern East Asia history (MA, PhD); public history (MA, PhD); US history (MA, PhD); women's history (MA, PhD); world history (MA, PhD). Part-time programs available. *Degree requirements:* For master's, comprehensive exam (for some programs), thesis, oral exam; for doctorate, one foreign language, comprehensive exam, thesis/dissertation, oral and written exam. *Entrance requirements:* For master's, GRE General Test, minimum GPA of 3.3, language background form, writing sample; for doctorate, GRE General Test, minimum GPA of 3.5, language background form, writing sample. Additional exam requirements/recommendations for international students: Required—TOEFL (minimum score 550 paper-based). Electronic applications accepted. *Faculty research:* Public, world, environmental, women and U.S. history.

Washington University in St. Louis, Graduate School of Arts and Sciences, Program in East Asian Studies, St. Louis, MO 63130-4899. Offers East Asian studies (MA); JD/MA. PhD offered through specific departments. *Students:* 16 full-time (8 women); includes 3 minority (1 American Indian/Alaska Native, 2 Asian Americans or Pacific Islanders), 6 international. 35 applicants, 26% accepted, 7 enrolled. In 2008, 6 master's awarded. *Entrance requirements:* For master's, GRE General Test. *Application deadline:* For fall admission, 1/15 priority date for domestic students. Application fee: $45. Electronic applications accepted. *Financial support:* Fellowships, research assistantships, teaching assistantships, tuition waivers available. Financial award application deadline: 1/15. *Unit head:* Dr. Letty Chen, Chairperson, 314-935-4448. *Application contact:* Assistant to the Dean, 314-935-6880, Fax: 314-935-4887.

See Close-Up on page 625.

West Virginia University, Eberly College of Arts and Sciences, Department of History, Morgantown, WV 26506. Offers African history (MA, PhD); African-American history (MA, PhD); American history (MA, PhD); Appalachian/regional history (MA, PhD); East Asian history (MA, PhD); European history (MA, PhD); history of science and technology (MA, PhD); Latin American history (MA). Part-time programs available. *Degree requirements:* For master's, one foreign language, thesis (for some programs), oral exam, thesis defense; for doctorate, one foreign language, comprehensive exam, thesis/dissertation, dissertation defense. *Entrance requirements:* For master's, GRE General Test, minimum GPA of 3.0; for doctorate, GRE General Test. Additional exam requirements/recommendations for international students: Required—TOEFL (minimum score 550 paper-based), IELTS (minimum score 6.5). Electronic applications accepted. *Faculty research:* U.S., Appalachia, modern Europe, Africa, colonial and post-colonial societies.

Yale University, Graduate School of Arts and Sciences, Program in East Asian Studies, New Haven, CT 06520. Offers MA. *Degree requirements:* For master's, one foreign language. *Entrance requirements:* For master's, GRE General Test.

Canadian Studies

Carleton University, Faculty of Graduate Studies, Faculty of Arts and Social Sciences, School of Canadian Studies, Ottawa, ON K1S 5B6, Canada. Offers MA, PhD. *Degree requirements:* For master's, one foreign language, thesis optional; for doctorate, one foreign language, thesis/dissertation. *Entrance requirements:* For master's, honors degree. Additional exam requirements/recommendations for international students: Required—TOEFL. Electronic applications accepted. *Faculty research:* Modern Canada, cultural studies, women's studies, aboriginal studies and the north, heritage conservation.

Collège universitaire de Saint-Boniface, Program in Canadian Studies, Saint-Boniface, MB R2H 0H7, Canada. Offers MA.

The Johns Hopkins University, Paul H. Nitze School of Advanced International Studies, Washington, DC 20036. Offers international development (Certificate); international public policy (MIPP); international relations (MA, PhD), including African studies (MA), American foreign policy (MA), Asian studies (MA), Canadian studies (MA), conflict management (MA), European studies (MA), global theory and history (MA), international development (MA), international law, and organizations (MA), international policy (MA), international relations (general) (MA), Latin American studies (MA), Middle East studies (MA), Russian and Eurasian studies (MA), strategic studies (MA); international studies (Certificate); JD/MA; MBA/MA; MHS/MA. Terminal master's awarded for partial completion of doctoral program. *Degree requirements:* For master's, one foreign language, 16 non-language courses (8 for MIPP), 2 core examinations, comprehensive oral exam, paper (for some programs); for doctorate, 2 foreign languages, thesis/dissertation, 3 comprehensive exams, defense. *Entrance requirements:* For master's, GMAT or GRE General Test, previous course work in economics, foreign language, undergraduate degree; for doctorate, GRE General Test, master's degree. Additional exam requirements/recommendations for international students: Required—TOEFL (minimum paper-based score of 600, computer-based 250, iBT 100) or IELTS (minimum 7.0). Electronic applications accepted. *Expenses:* Contact institution. *Faculty research:* Regional studies and functional fields of international relations, international economics, conflict management, global theory and history, international law and organizations, international policy, strategic studies.

Queen's University at Kingston, School of Graduate Studies and Research, Faculty of Arts and Sciences, Department of Political Studies, Kingston, ON K7L 3N6, Canada. Offers Canadian politics (PhD); comparative politics (PhD); gender and politics (PhD); international relations (PhD); political theory (PhD). *Degree requirements:* For master's, thesis or alternative; for doctorate, one foreign language, thesis/dissertation, qualifying exams. *Entrance requirements:* Additional exam requirements/recommendations for international students: Required—TOEFL (minimum score 600 paper-based; 250 computer-based). *Faculty research:* Canadian politics, comparative politics, political thought, international politics, women and politics.

Saint Mary's University, Faculty of Arts, Program in Atlantic Canada Studies, Halifax, NS B3H 3C3, Canada. Offers MA. Part-time and evening/weekend programs available. *Degree requirements:* For master's, thesis. *Entrance requirements:* For master's, honors degree. *Expenses:* Contact institution.

Trent University, Graduate Studies, The Frost Centre for Canadian Studies and Indigenous Studies, Peterborough, ON K9J 7B8, Canada. Offers Canadian studies (PhD); Canadian studies and indigenous studies (MA). Part-time programs available. *Degree requirements:* For master's, thesis. *Entrance requirements:* For master's, honors degree. *Faculty research:* Native community-based socioeconomic development, environmental and social impact inventory, regional studies.

Université de Sherbrooke, Faculty of Letters and Human Sciences, Department of Letters and Communications, Sherbrooke, QC J1K 2R1, Canada. Offers comparative Canadian literature (MA, PhD); French literature (MA, PhD); linguistics (MA); lit&erature de crèation (MA, PhD); theatre (MA). *Degree requirements:* For master's, thesis or alternative; for doctorate, thesis/dissertation. *Entrance requirements:* For master's, minimum GPA of 2.8; for doctorate, minimum GPA of 3.0.

Université du Québec à Chicoutimi, Graduate Programs, Program in Regional Studies, Chicoutimi, QC G7H 2B1, Canada. Offers MA. Part-time programs available. *Degree requirements:* For master's, thesis. *Entrance requirements:* For master's, appropriate bachelor's degree, proficiency in French.

University of Lethbridge, School of Graduate Studies, Lethbridge, AB T1K 3M4, Canada. Offers accounting (MScM); addictions counseling (M Sc); agricultural biotechnology (M Sc); agricultural studies (M Sc, MA); anthropology (MA); archaeology (MA); art (MA); biochemistry (M Sc); biological sciences (M Sc); biomolecular science (PhD); biosystems and biodiversity (PhD); Canadian studies (MA); chemistry (M Sc); computer science (M Sc); computer science and geographical information science (M Sc); counseling psychology (M Ed); dramatic arts (MA); earth, space, and physical science (PhD); economics (MA); educational leadership (M Ed); English (MA); environmental science (M Sc); evolution and behavior (PhD); exercise science (M Sc); finance (MScM); French (MA); French/German (MA); French/Spanish (MA); general education (M Ed); general management (MScM); geography (M Sc, MA); German (MA); health sciences (M Sc, MA); history (MA); human resource management and labour relations (MScM); individualized multidisciplinary (M Sc, MA); information systems (MScM); international management (MScM); kinesiology (M Sc, MA); management (M Sc, MA); marketing (MScM); mathematics (M Sc); music (MA); Native American studies (MA); neuroscience (M Sc, PhD); new media (MA); nursing (M Sc); philosophy (MA); physics (M Sc); policy and strategy (MScM); political science (MA); psychology (M Sc, MA); religious studies (MA); sociology (MA); theoretical and computational science (PhD); urban and regional studies (MA). Part-time and evening/weekend programs available. *Degree requirements:* For doctorate, comprehensive exam, thesis/dissertation. *Entrance requirements:* For master's, GMAT (M Sc in management), bachelor's degree in related field, minimum GPA of 3.0 during previous 20 graded semester courses, 2 years teaching or related experience (M Ed); for doctorate, master's degree, minimum graduate GPA of 3.5. Additional exam requirements/recommendations for international students: Required—TOEFL. *Faculty research:* Movement and brain plasticity, gibberellin physiology, photosynthesis, carbon cycling, molecular properties of main-group ring components.

University of Manitoba, Faculty of Graduate Studies, College Universitaire de Saint Boniface, Program in Canadian Studies, Winnipeg, MB R3T 2N2, Canada. Offers MA.

University of Ottawa, Faculty of Graduate and Postdoctoral Studies, Faculty of Arts, Institute of Canadian Studies, Ottawa, ON K1N 6N5, Canada. Offers economics (PhD); English (PhD); geography (PhD); history (PhD); lettres Françaises (PhD); linguistics (PhD); philosophy (PhD); political science (PhD); psychology (PhD); religious studies (PhD); translation studies (PhD). *Degree requirements:* For doctorate, comprehensive exam, thesis/dissertation.

University of Regina, Faculty of Graduate Studies and Research, Faculty of Arts, Canadian Plains Studies Program, Regina, SK S4S 0A2, Canada. Offers MA, PhD. Offered as special case program. Part-time programs available. *Faculty:* 1 full-time (0 women). *Students:* 3 full-time (1 woman), 1 part-time (0 women). In 2008, 1 doctorate awarded. *Degree requirements:* For master's, thesis; for doctorate, thesis/dissertation. *Entrance requirements:* Additional exam requirements/recommendations for international students: Required—TOEFL (minimum score 580 paper-based; 237 computer-based; 88 iBT). *Application deadline:* Applications are processed on a rolling basis. Application fee: $85 ($100 for international students). Electronic applications accepted. *Financial support:* Fellowships, research assistantships, teaching assistantships, scholarships/grants available. Financial award application deadline: 6/15. *Faculty research:* Prairie region. *Unit head:* Dr. Harry Diaz, Graduate Program Coordinator, 306-585-4758, Fax: 306-585-4699, E-mail: canadian.plains@uregina.ca. *Application contact:* Dr. Dongyan Blachford, Associate Dean, 306-585-5186, Fax: 306-337-2444, E-mail: dongyan.blachford@uregina.ca.

University of Saskatchewan, College of Graduate Studies and Research, College of Arts and Sciences, Department of Native Studies, Saskatoon, SK S7N 5A2, Canada. Offers MA, PhD. *Degree requirements:* For master's, thesis; for doctorate, thesis/dissertation. *Entrance requirements:* Additional exam requirements/recommendations for international students: Required—TOEFL.

Cultural Studies

Ambrose University College, Ambrose Seminary, Calgary, AB T2P 3T5, Canada. Offers biblical/theological studies (MA); Chinese ministries (Certificate); Christian studies (Diploma); church education (M Div); intercultural ministries (M Div, MA, Certificate, Diploma); leadership and ministry (MA, Certificate, Diploma); pastoral ministries (M Div). *Accreditation:* ATS (one or more programs are accredited). Part-time programs available. *Degree requirements:* For master's, 2 foreign languages, internship; for M Div, one foreign language, internship. *Entrance requirements:* For master's, bachelor degree. Additional exam requirements/recommendations for international students: Required—TOEFL or IELTS. Electronic applications accepted. *Faculty research:* Evangelicalism and sociology, missiological trends, chaplaincy, intertestamental studies, postmodernism.

American University, School of International Service, Washington, DC 20016-8071. Offers comparative and regional studies (Certificate); cross-cultural communication (Certificate); development management (MS); ethics, peace, and global affairs (MA); European studies (Certificate); global environmental policy (MA, Certificate); international affairs (MA), including comparative and regional studies, environmental policy, international economic policy, international politics, natural resources and sustainable development, U.S. foreign policy; international communication (MA, Certificate); international development (MA, Certificate); international development management (Certificate); international economic policy (Certificate); international economic relations (Certificate); international media (MA); international peace and conflict resolution (MA, Certificate); international relations (PhD); international service (MIS); peace building (Certificate); the Americas (Certificate); United States foreign policy (Certificate); JD/MA. Part-time and evening/weekend programs available. *Faculty:* 70 full-time (28 women), 51 part-time/adjunct (20 women). *Students:* 519 full-time (317 women), 335 part-time (205 women); includes 157 minority (54 African Americans, 2 American Indian/Alaska Native, 45 Asian Americans or Pacific Islanders, 56 Hispanic Americans), 116 international. Average age 27. 1,901 applicants, 58% accepted, 277 enrolled. In 2008, 358 master's, 5 doctorates, 9 other advanced degrees awarded. Terminal master's awarded for partial completion of doctoral program. *Degree requirements:* For master's, one foreign language, comprehensive exam, thesis or alternative; for doctorate, one foreign language, comprehensive exam, thesis/dissertation, research practicum; for Certificate, minimum 15 credit hours related course work. *Entrance requirements:* For master's, GRE, 24 credits of course work in related social sciences, minimum GPA of 3.5, 2 letters of recommendation, bachelor's degree, resumé, statement of purpose; for doctorate, GRE, 2 letters of recommendation, 24 credits in related social sciences; for Certificate, bachelor's degree. Additional exam requirements/recommendations for international students: Required—TOEFL (minimum score 600 paper-based; 250 computer-based; 100 iBT). *Application deadline:* For fall admission, 1/15 priority date for domestic students; for spring admission, 10/1 priority date for domestic students. Applications are processed on a rolling basis. Application fee: $50. *Expenses:* Tuition: Full-time $21,204; part-time $1178 per credit hour. Required fees: $380. Part-time tuition and fees vary according to course load and program. *Financial support:* Career-related internships or fieldwork, Federal Work-Study, and institutionally sponsored loans available. Financial award application deadline: 1/15. *Faculty research:* International intellectual property, international environmental issues, international law and legal order, international telecommunications/technology, international sustainable development. *Unit head:* Dr. Louis W. Goodman, Dean, 202-885-1600, Fax: 202-885-2494. *Application contact:* Yasmin Quianzon, Director of Graduate Admissions and Financial Aid, 202-885-2496, Fax: 202-885-1109.

See Close-Up on page 861.

Appalachian State University, Cratis D. Williams Graduate School, Center for Appalachian Studies, Boone, NC 28608. Offers culture (MA); music (MA); sustainable development (MA). Part-time programs available. *Faculty:* 14 full-time (5 women). *Students:* 19 full-time (11 women), 5 part-time (3 women). 20 applicants, 90% accepted, 10 enrolled. In 2008, 6 master's awarded. *Degree requirements:* For master's, one foreign language, comprehensive exam, thesis optional. *Entrance requirements:* For master's, GRE General Test, 3 letters of recommendation. Additional exam requirements/recommendations for international students: Required—TOEFL (minimum score 570 paper-based; 230 computer-based; 79 iBT), IELTS (minimum score 6.5). *Application deadline:* For fall admission, 7/1 for domestic students, 2/1 for international students; for spring admission, 11/1 for domestic students, 7/1 for international students. Applications are processed on a rolling basis. Application fee: $50. Electronic applications accepted. *Expenses:* Tuition, area resident: Full-time $2600; part-time $700 per course. Tuition, state resident: full-time $2600; part-time $700 per course. Tuition, nonresident: full-time $5000; part-time $3300 per course. Required fees: $2150; $330 per course. Tuition and fees vary according to campus/location. *Financial support:* In 2008–09, 8 research assistantships (averaging $7,000 per year) were awarded; fellowships, teaching assistantships, career-related internships or fieldwork, Federal Work-Study, scholarships/grants, and unspecified assistantships also available. Financial award application deadline: 4/1; financial award applicants required to submit FAFSA. *Faculty research:* Appalachian culture, sustainable development, Appalachian music. Total annual research expenditures: $10,500. *Unit head:* Dr. Pat Beaver, Director, 828-262-2550, E-mail: beaverpd@appstate.edu. *Application contact:* Dr. Bruce Stewart, Graduate Program Director, 828-262-4858, E-mail: stewartbe1@appstate.edu.

Arizona State University, Graduate College, College of Liberal Arts and Sciences, Division of Humanities, Program in Film and Media Studies, Tempe, AZ 85287. Offers American media and popular culture (MAS); film analysis (MLS); screenwriting (MAS).

Assemblies of God Theological Seminary, Graduate and Professional Programs, Springfield, MO 65802. Offers biblical preaching (D Min); Christian ministries (MA); divinity (M Div); intercultural studies (D Miss, PhD); missional leadership (D Min); relief and development (D Miss); self-design study (D Min); women in leadership (D Min). *Accreditation:* ATS. Part-time and evening/weekend programs available. Postbaccalaureate distance learning degree programs offered (minimal on-campus study). *Faculty:* 16 full-time (3 women), 21 part-time/adjunct (4 women). *Students:* 220 full-time (69 women), 226 part-time (49 women); includes 49 minority (11 African Americans, 5 American Indian/Alaska Native, 11 Asian Americans or Pacific Islanders, 22 Hispanic Americans), 7 international. Average age 36. *Degree requirements:* For master's, analytical reflection paper or comprehensive exam; for doctorate, thesis/dissertation; for M Div, one foreign language, analytical reflection paper. *Entrance requirements:* For M Div, minimum GPA of 2.0; for master's, minimum GPA of 2.5; for doctorate, minimum GPA of 3.0. Additional exam requirements/recommendations for international students: Required—TOEFL (minimum score 550 paper-based; 213 computer-based; 80 iBT). *Application deadline:* For fall admission, 7/1 priority date for domestic students, 6/1 priority date for international students; for spring admission, 12/1 priority date for domestic students, 11/1 priority date for international students. Applications are processed on a rolling basis. Application fee: $35. Electronic applications accepted. *Financial support:* Career-related internships or fieldwork, Federal Work-Study, and scholarships/grants available. Support available to part-time students. Financial award application deadline: 7/15; financial award applicants required to submit FAFSA. *Unit head:* Stephen Lim, Academic Dean, 417-268-1000, Fax: 417-268-1001, E-mail: slim@agts.edu. *Application contact:* Stephen Lim, Academic Dean, 417-268-1000, Fax: 417-268-1001, E-mail: slim@agts.edu.

Athabasca University, Centre for Integrated Studies, Athabasca, AB T9S 3A3, Canada. Offers adult education (MA); community studies (MA); cultural studies (MA); educational studies (MA); global change (MA); work, organization, and leadership (MA). Part-time and evening/weekend programs available. Postbaccalaureate distance learning degree programs offered (no on-campus study). *Faculty:* 8 full-time (3 women), 16 part-time/adjunct (13 women). *Students:* 651 part-time (467 women). Average age 36. 150 applicants, 87% accepted, 112 enrolled. In 2008, 39 master's awarded. *Degree requirements:* For master's, project. *Entrance requirements:* For master's, 3- or 4-year BA. Additional exam requirements/recommendations for international students: Required—TOEFL (minimum score 560 paper-based; 220 computer-based). *Application deadline:* For fall admission, 3/1 for domestic and international students; for winter admission, 10/1 for domestic and international students. Application fee: $65. Electronic applications accepted. Tuition and fees charges are reported in Canadian dollars. *Expenses:* Tuition, area resident: Full-time $13,255 Canadian dollars; part-time $1205 Canadian dollars per course. Tuition, state resident: full-time $13,255 Canadian dollars; part-time $1205 Canadian dollars per course. Tuition, nonresident: full-time $13,255 Canadian dollars; part-time $1205 Canadian dollars per course. International tuition: $15,455 Canadian dollars full-time. One-time fee: $280 Canadian dollars. *Faculty research:* Women's history, literature and culture studies, sustainable development, labor and education. *Unit head:* Dr. Michael Gismondi, Program Director, 780-675-6218, Fax: 780-675-6921, E-mail: mikeg@athabascau.ca. *Application contact:* Derek Stovin, Program Administrator, 780-675-6236, Fax: 780-675-6921, E-mail: dereks@athabascau.ca.

Baptist Bible College, Graduate School of Theology, Springfield, MO 65803-3498. Offers biblical counseling (MA); biblical studies (MA); church ministry (MA); intercultural studies (MA); theology (M Div). Part-time programs available. *Degree requirements:* For master's, 2 foreign languages, thesis (for some programs); for M Div, 2 foreign languages, thesis/dissertation (for some programs). *Entrance requirements:* For master's, outcomes test. Electronic applications accepted.

Biola University, School of Intercultural Studies, La Mirada, CA 90639-0001. Offers applied linguistics (MA); intercultural education (PhD); intercultural studies (MAICS); missiology (D Miss); missions (MA); teaching English to speakers of other languages (MA, Certificate). Part-time and evening/weekend programs available. Terminal master's awarded for partial completion of doctoral program. *Degree requirements:* For master's, one foreign language, comprehensive exam; for doctorate, one foreign language, comprehensive exam, thesis/dissertation. *Entrance requirements:* For master's, minimum undergraduate GPA of 3.0; for doctorate, MA, 3 years of ministry experience, minimum graduate GPA of 3.3. Additional exam requirements/recommendations for international students: Required—TOEFL (minimum score 550 paper-based; 213 computer-based). Electronic applications accepted.

Brandeis University, Graduate School of Arts and Sciences, Program in Cultural Production, Waltham, MA 02454-9110. Offers MA. Part-time programs available. *Entrance requirements:* For master's, GRE (recommended), statement of purpose, 2 letters of recommendation, official transcripts, resumé, portfolio/writing sample. Additional exam requirements/recommendations for international students: Required—TOEFL (minimum score 650 paper-based; 250 computer-based; 100 iBT), IELTS (minimum score 7). Electronic applications accepted.

Brock University, Faculty of Graduate Studies, Faculty of Social Sciences, Program in Popular Culture, St. Catharines, ON L2S 3A1, Canada. Offers MA. Part-time programs available. *Degree requirements:* For master's, thesis optional. *Entrance requirements:* For master's, honors BA. Additional exam requirements/recommendations for international students: Required—TOEFL (minimum score 550 paper-based; 213 computer-based; 80 iBT), IELTS (minimum score 6.5), TWE (minimum score 4). Electronic applications accepted. *Faculty research:* Film and television studies, popular music, historical aspects of popular culture, popular literature.

Carnegie Mellon University, College of Humanities and Social Sciences, Department of History, Pittsburgh, PA 15213-3891. Offers African and African-American diaspora (PhD); culture and power (PhD); gender and the family (PhD); history (MA, MS); history and policy (MA); labor and politics (PhD); science, technology, medicine and environment (PhD). Part-time programs available. *Degree requirements:* For doctorate, oral and written comprehensive exams, dissertation defense. *Entrance requirements:* For doctorate, GRE General Test. Additional exam requirements/recommendations for international students: Required—TOEFL. Electronic applications accepted. *Faculty research:* Anthropology and history, African American history, technology/environment, cultural history analysis.

The Catholic University of America, School of Architecture and Planning, Washington, DC 20064. Offers M Arch, M Arch Studies. Part-time programs available. *Degree requirements:* For master's, thesis. *Entrance requirements:* For master's, minimum GPA of 2.7, portfolio, 3 letters of recommendation. Additional exam requirements/recommendations for international students: Required—TOEFL (minimum score 500 paper-based; 173 computer-based). Electronic applications accepted. *Expenses:* Contact institution. *Faculty research:* Architectural history, sacred architecture, computers, technology, urban design, preservation.

Central Michigan University, College of Graduate Studies, College of Humanities and Social and Behavioral Sciences, Program in Humanities, Mount Pleasant, MI 48859. Offers humanities (MA), including contemporary issues in the humanities: race, class, and gender, images and ideas of self, Native American issues in modern culture, popular culture studies, the rise of industrial society. Part-time and evening/weekend programs available. *Students:* 3 full-time (1 woman), 7 part-time (4 women). Average age 37. *Degree requirements:* For master's, thesis or alternative. *Application deadline:* Applications are processed on a rolling basis. Application fee: $35 ($45 for international students). Electronic applications accepted. *Expenses:* Tuition, state resident: full-time $3717; part-time $413 per credit. Tuition, nonresident: full-time $6894; part-time $766 per credit. *Financial support:* Fellowships with tuition reimbursements, Federal Work-Study, unspecified assistantships, and out-of-state merit awards available. *Faculty research:* Rise of industrial society; images and ideas of self; contemporary issues of race, class, and gender; popular culture; Native American issues in modern culture. *Unit head:* Dr. Ronald Primeau, Director, 989-774-3117, Fax: 989-774-7106, E-mail: ronald.r.primeau@cmich.edu. *Application contact:* Judith L. Prince, Director of Graduate Student Services, 989-774-1059, Fax: 989-774-1857, E-mail: judith.l.prince@cmich.edu.

Chapman University, Graduate Studies, College of Educational Studies, Program in Education: Cultural and Curricular Studies, Orange, CA 92866. Offers PhD. *Faculty:* 19 full-time (13 women), 20 part-time/adjunct (12 women). *Students:* 8 full-time (6 women), 1 part-time (0 women); includes 5 minority (2 African Americans, 3 Hispanic Americans). Average age 34. 21 applicants, 43% accepted, 9 enrolled. *Degree requirements:* For doctorate, thesis/dissertation. *Expenses:* Tuition: Full-time $11,970; part-time $665 per credit. Required fees: $456; $456 per year. Tuition and fees vary according to course load, degree level and program. *Financial support:* Federal Work-Study and scholarships/grants available. *Unit head:* Dr. Joel Colbert, Director, 714-744-7076. *Application contact:* Rika Judd, Graduate Admission Counselor, 714-997-6786, Fax: 714-997-6713, E-mail: rjudd@chapman.edu.

Claremont Graduate University, Graduate Programs, School of Arts and Humanities, Department of Cultural Studies, Claremont, CA 91711-6160. Offers Africana studies (Certificate); cultural studies (MA, PhD); media studies (MA, PhD); museum studies (MA). Part-time programs available. *Faculty:* 2 full-time (1 woman). *Students:* 57 full-time (41 women), 10 part-time (5 women); includes 21 minority (11 African Americans, 5 Asian Americans or Pacific Islanders, 5 Hispanic Americans), 6 international. Average age 35. In 2008, 8 master's, 2 doctorates awarded. *Entrance requirements:* For master's and doctorate, GRE General Test. Additional exam requirements/recommendations for international students: Required—TOEFL (minimum score 550 paper-based; 213 computer-based; 80 iBT). *Application deadline:* For fall admission, 2/1 priority date for domestic students. Applications are processed on a rolling basis. Application fee: $60. Electronic applications accepted. *Expenses:* Tuition: Full-time $33,698; part-time $1465 per unit. Required fees: $310; $155 per semester. Tuition and fees vary according to program. *Financial support:* Fellowships, research assistantships, Federal Work-Study, institutionally sponsored loans, and scholarships/grants available. Support available to part-time students. Financial award application deadline: 2/15; financial award applicants required to submit FAFSA. *Unit head:* Eve Oishi, Chair, 909-607-7587, E-mail: eve.oishi@cgu.edu. *Application contact:* Justin Evans, Admissions Coordinator, 909-607-1278, Fax: 909-607-1221, E-mail: humanities@cgu.edu.

Columbia International University, Columbia Biblical Seminary and School of Missions, Columbia, SC 29230-3122. Offers academic ministries (M Div); bible exposition (M Div, MABE); biblical studies (Certificate); counseling ministries (Certificate); divinity (M Div); educational ministries (M Div, MAEM, Certificate); intercultural studies (M Div, MAIS, Certificate); leadership (D Min); leadership for evangelism/mobilization (MALM); member care (D Min); ministry (Certificate); missions (D Min); pastoral counseling and spiritual formation (M Div, MAPS); preaching (D Min); theology (MA). *Accreditation:* ATS (one or more programs are accredited). Part-time and evening/weekend programs available. *Degree requirements:* For master's, integrative seminar; for doctorate, comprehensive exam, thesis/dissertation; for M Div, internship. *Entrance requirements:* For master's, minimum GPA of 2.7; for doctorate, 3 years of ministerial experience, M Div. Additional exam requirements/recommendations for international students: Required—TOEFL. Electronic applications accepted.

Cornell University, Graduate School, Graduate Fields of Arts and Sciences, Field of English Language and Literature, Ithaca, NY 14853-0001. Offers African-American literature (PhD); American literature after 1865 (PhD); American literature to 1865 (PhD); American studies (PhD); colonial and postcolonial literature (PhD); creative writing (MFA); cultural studies (PhD); dramatic literature (PhD); English poetry (PhD); English Renaissance to 1660 (PhD); lesbian, bisexual, and gay literature studies (PhD); literary criticism and theory (PhD); nineteenth century (PhD); Old and Middle English (PhD); prose fiction (PhD); Restoration and eighteenth century (PhD); twentieth century (PhD); women's literature (PhD); MFA/PhD. *Faculty:* 54 full-time (27 women). *Students:* 100 full-time (53 women); includes 24 minority (8 African Americans, 4 American Indian/Alaska Native, 6 Asian Americans or Pacific Islanders, 6 Hispanic Americans), 14 international. Average age 29. 821 applicants, 6% accepted, 23 enrolled. In 2008, 19 master's, 12 doctorates awarded. Terminal master's awarded for partial completion of doctoral program. *Degree requirements:* For master's, one foreign language, thesis; for doctorate, one foreign language, comprehensive exam, thesis/dissertation, teaching experience. *Entrance requirements:* For master's, GRE General Test, 3 letters of recommendation, creative writing sample; for doctorate, GRE General Test, GRE Subject Test (English), 3 letters of recommendation, writing sample. Additional exam requirements/recommendations for international students: Required—TOEFL (minimum score 600 paper-based; 250 computer-based; 77 iBT). *Application deadline:* For fall admission, 1/10 for domestic students. Application fee: $70. Electronic applications accepted. *Expenses:* Tuition: Full-time $29,500. Required fees: $70. Full-time tuition and fees vary according to degree level, program and student level. *Financial support:* In 2008–09, 96 students received support, including 41 fellowships with full tuition reimbursements available, 1 research assistantship with full tuition reimbursement available, 54 teaching assistantships with full tuition reimbursements available; institutionally sponsored loans, scholarships/grants, health care benefits, tuition waivers (full and partial), and unspecified assistantships also available. Financial award applicants required to submit FAFSA. *Faculty research:* English and American literature, women's writing, ethnic and post-colonial literature, critical theory, medievalism. *Unit head:* Director of Graduate Studies, 607-255-7989, Fax: 607-255-6661. *Application contact:* Graduate Field Assistant, 607-255-7989, Fax: 607-255-6661, E-mail: english_grad@cornell.edu.

Eastern Michigan University, Graduate School, College of Education, Department of Teacher Education, Program in Culture and Diversity, Ypsilanti, MI 48197. Offers MA.

George Mason University, College of Humanities and Social Sciences, Program in Cultural Studies, Fairfax, VA 22030. Offers PhD. Part-time and evening/weekend programs available. *Degree requirements:* For doctorate, one foreign language, comprehensive exam, thesis/dissertation, foreign language exams. *Entrance requirements:* For doctorate, GRE General Test, sample of written work, MA or simultaneous application to related MA program at George Mason University. Additional exam requirements/recommendations for international students: Required—TOEFL. Electronic applications accepted.

See Close-Up on page 619.

Grace Theological Seminary, Graduate and Professional Programs, Winona Lake, IN 46590-9907. Offers biblical studies (Certificate); camp administration (MA); counseling (M Div); exegetical studies (MA); intercultural studies (M Div, MA); local church studies (MA); pastoral studies (M Div); theological studies (MA); theology (D Min, Diploma). *Accreditation:* ATS. Part-time programs available. Postbaccalaureate distance learning degree programs offered (no on-campus study). *Degree requirements:* For master's, thesis optional; for doctorate, 2 foreign languages, thesis/dissertation; for M Div, 2 foreign languages, thesis/dissertation optional. *Entrance requirements:* For M Div and master's, MAT, minimum GPA of 2.5. Electronic applications accepted. *Faculty research:* Biblical theology, language, and church ministries.

Graduate Theological Union, Graduate Programs, Berkeley, CA 94709-1212. Offers art and religion (MA, PhD); biblical languages (MA); biblical studies (Old and New Testament) (MA, PhD, Th D); Buddhist studies (MA); Christian spirituality (MA, PhD); cultural and historical studies of religions (MA, PhD); ethics and social theory (PhD); history (MA, PhD, Th D); homiletics (MA, PhD, Th D); interdisciplinary studies (PhD, Th D); Jewish studies (MA, PhD, Certificate); liturgical studies (MA, PhD, Th D); Near Eastern religions (PhD); Orthodox Christian studies (MA); Orthodox studies (Certificate); religion and psychology (MA, PhD); religion and society/ethics and social theory (MA); systematic and philosophical theology (MA, PhD, Th D); women's studies in religion (Certificate); MA/M Div. *Accreditation:* ATS. Terminal master's awarded for partial completion of doctoral program. *Degree requirements:* For master's, one foreign language, thesis; for doctorate, one foreign language, comprehensive exam, thesis/dissertation. *Entrance requirements:* For master's, GRE General Test; for doctorate, GRE General Test, MA or M Div. Additional exam requirements/recommendations for international students: Required—TOEFL. Electronic applications accepted.

Lewis & Clark College, Graduate School of Education and Counseling, Department of Counseling Psychology, Portland, OR 97219-7899. Offers addictions treatment (MA); counseling psychology (MA, MS); marriage, couple and family therapy (MA); psychological and cultural studies (MA); school psychology (MS, Ed S). Part-time and evening/weekend programs available. *Degree requirements:* For master's, thesis proposal (MS). *Entrance requirements:* For master's, GRE General Test, minimum undergraduate GPA of 2.75. Additional exam requirements/recommendations for international students: Required—TOEFL (minimum score 575 paper-based; 233 computer-based). Electronic applications accepted. *Faculty research:* Treatment of depression, substance abuse, child-family problems, health psychology, marital relations.

Maranatha Baptist Bible College, Program in Cross-Cultural Studies, Watertown, WI 53094. Offers MA. Part-time programs available. *Faculty:* 5 full-time (0 women), 2 part-time/adjunct (0 women). *Students:* 3 full-time (all women), 1 part-time (0 women). Average age 23. 3 applicants, 100% accepted, 3 enrolled. *Application deadline:* Applications are processed on a rolling basis. Application fee: $50. *Expenses:* Tuition: Full-time $3840; part-time $240 per credit hour. Required fees: $20 per credit hour. *Financial support:* Scholarships/grants and tuition waivers (full and partial) available. Support available to part-time students. *Unit head:* Dr. Larry Oats, Dean of Maranatha Baptist Seminary, 920-206-2324, Fax: 920-261-9109, E-mail: loats@mbbc.edu. *Application contact:* Dr. Jim Harrison, Director of Admissions, 920-206-2327, Fax: 920-261-9109, E-mail: admissions@mbbc.edu.

McMaster University, School of Graduate Studies, Faculty of Humanities, Department of English and Cultural Studies, Hamilton, ON L8S 4M2, Canada. Offers cultural studies and critical theory (MA); English (MA, PhD). Part-time programs available. *Degree requirements:* For master's, one foreign language, thesis; for doctorate, one foreign language, comprehensive exam, thesis/dissertation. *Entrance requirements:* For master's, honors degree, minimum B+ average in at least 6 full courses of English beyond year 1; for doctorate, MA; minimum A-average in two of three courses. Additional exam requirements/recommendations for international students: Required—TOEFL (minimum score 580 paper-based; 237 computer-based). *Faculty research:* Literary theory, feminist theory, literature of migration, Bakhting globalization.

New York University, Steinhardt School of Culture, Education and Human Development, New York, NY 10012-1019. Offers MA, MFA, MM, MPH, MS, DA, DPS, DPT, Ed D, PhD, Advanced Certificate. *Accreditation:* Teacher Education Accreditation Council. Part-time and evening/weekend programs available. *Degree requirements:* For doctorate, comprehensive exam (for some programs), thesis/dissertation. *Entrance requirements:* For doctorate, GRE General Test, interview. Additional exam requirements/recommendations for international students: Required—TOEFL. *Expenses:* Contact institution. *Faculty research:* Equity, urban adolescents, arts in education, globalization, community and public health.

St. Francis Xavier University, Graduate Studies, Department of Celtic Studies, Antigonish, NS B2G 2W5, Canada. Offers MA. *Degree requirements:* For master's, thesis. *Entrance requirements:* Additional exam requirements/recommendations for international students: Required—TOEFL (minimum score 580 paper-based; 236 computer-based). *Faculty research:* Scottish Gaelic in Nova Scotia.

San Francisco State University, Division of Graduate Studies, College of Behavioral and Social Sciences, Human Sexuality Studies Program, San Francisco, CA 94132-1722. Offers MA.

Simmons College, College of Arts and Sciences Graduate Studies, Program in Gender/Cultural Studies, Boston, MA 02115. Offers MA, MA/MAT, MA/MS. Part-time programs available. *Faculty:* 20 full-time (17 women), 1 part-time/adjunct (0 women). *Students:* 1 (woman) full-time, 26 part-time (all women); includes 7 minority (2 African Americans, 2 Asian Americans or Pacific Islanders, 3 Hispanic Americans). Average age 26. 43 applicants, 65% accepted, 15 enrolled. In 2008, 11 master's awarded. *Degree requirements:* For master's, project, thesis, internship, or fieldwork. *Entrance requirements:* For master's, academic writing sample. Additional exam requirements/recommendations for international students: Required—TOEFL (minimum score 600 paper-based; 250 computer-based; 100 iBT). *Application deadline:* For fall admission, 8/1 priority date for domestic and international students; for winter admission, 12/15 priority date for domestic and international students; for spring admission, 5/1 priority date for domestic and international students. Applications are processed on a rolling basis. Application fee: $35. Electronic applications accepted. *Financial support:* In 2008–09, 11 students received support, including 10 teaching assistantships (averaging $2,000 per year); research assistantships, scholarships/grants and unspecified assistantships also available. Financial award application deadline: 3/1; financial award applicants required to submit FAFSA. *Faculty research:* Obscenity, gender and media studies, gender and sexuality, race, postcolonialism. *Unit head:* Dr. Sarah Leonard, Director, 617-521-2254, Fax: 617-521-3090. *Application contact:* Kristen Haack, Director, Graduate Studies Admission, 617-521-2917, Fax: 617-521-3058, E-mail: gsa@simmons.edu.

Simpson University, A.W. Tozer Theological Seminary, Redding, CA 96003-8606. Offers Christian leadership (MA); Christian studies (MA); intercultural studies (MA); ministry (M Div). Part-time and evening/weekend programs available. Postbaccalaureate distance learning degree programs offered (minimal on-campus study). *Degree requirements:* For master's, student portfolio. *Entrance requirements:* For master's, GRE General Test (if undergraduate GPA is below 2.5), 2 letters of reference, Christian Experience statement. Additional exam requirements/recommendations for international students: Required—TOEFL. Electronic applications accepted. *Expenses:* Contact institution.

Southern Illinois University Carbondale, Graduate School, College of Liberal Arts, Department of Foreign Languages and Literatures, Carbondale, IL 62901-4701. Offers MA. Part-time programs available. *Degree requirements:* For master's, one foreign language, thesis. *Entrance requirements:* For master's, minimum GPA of 2.7. Additional exam requirements/recommendations for international students: Required—TOEFL. *Faculty research:* Bibliography, historical linguistics, language pedagogy, philology, commercial facets.

State University of New York at Binghamton, Graduate School, School of Arts and Sciences, Philosophy, Interpretation and Culture Program, Binghamton, NY 13902-6000. Offers MA, PhD. *Students:* 21 full-time (11 women), 32 part-time (13 women); includes 15 minority (7 African Americans, 2 Asian Americans or Pacific Islanders, 6 Hispanic Americans), 18 international. Average age 35. 40 applicants, 53% accepted, 10 enrolled. In 2008, 3 master's, 6 doctorates awarded. Application fee: $60. *Expenses:* Tuition, area resident: Full-time $6900; part-time $288 per credit. Tuition, state resident: full-time $6900; part-time $288 per credit. Tuition, nonresident: full-time $10,920; part-time $455 per credit. Required fees: $1130. Part-time tuition and fees vary according to course load, program and student level. *Financial support:* In 2008–09, 10 students received support, including 8 teaching assistantships with full tuition reimbursements available (averaging $14,500 per year); career-related internships or fieldwork, Federal Work-Study, institutionally sponsored loans, scholarships/grants, health care benefits, and unspecified assistantships also available. Financial award application deadline: 2/15; financial award applicants required to submit FAFSA. *Unit head:* Dr. William Haver, Director, 607-777-3827. *Application contact:* Victoria Williams, Recruiting and Admissions Coordinator, 607-777-2151, Fax: 607-777-2501, E-mail: vwilliam@binghamton.edu.

Stony Brook University, State University of New York, Graduate School, College of Arts and Sciences, Department of Comparative Literary and Cultural Studies, Stony Brook, NY 11794. Offers comparative literature (MA, PhD); cultural studies (PhD). Evening/weekend programs available. *Faculty:* 7 full-time (1 woman). *Students:* 35 full-time (21 women), 4 part-time (3 women); includes 6 minority (5 Asian Americans or Pacific Islanders, 1 Hispanic American), 17 international. Average age 30. 101 applicants, 19% accepted. In 2008, 1 master's, 1 doctorate awarded. Terminal master's awarded for partial completion of doctoral program. *Degree requirements:* For master's, 2 foreign languages, exam; for doctorate, 3 foreign languages, comprehensive exam, thesis/dissertation. *Entrance requirements:* For master's and doctorate, GRE General Test, minimum GPA of 3.5 in major, 3.0 overall. Additional exam requirements/recommendations for international students: Required—TOEFL. *Application deadline:* For fall admission, 1/15 for domestic students. Application fee: $60. *Expenses:* Tuition, area resident: Full-time $7880; part-time $328 per credit hour. Tuition, state resident: full-time $7880; part-time $328 per credit hour. Tuition, nonresident: full-time $13,250; part-time $552 per credit hour. Required fees: $848. *Financial support:* In 2008–09, 24 teaching assistantships were awarded; fellowships, research assistantships also available. *Faculty research:* Literary theory, interdisciplinary studies, literary history. *Unit head:* Prof. Krin Gabbard, Chairman, 631-632-7456. *Application contact:* Dr. Kent Marks, Assistant Dean, Admissions and Records, 631-632-4723, Fax: 631-632-7243, E-mail: kmarks@notes.cc.sunysb.edu.

Taylor College and Seminary, Graduate and Professional Programs, Edmonton, AB T6J 4T3, Canada. Offers Christian studies (Diploma); intercultural studies (MA, Diploma); theology (M Div, MTS). *Accreditation:* ATS. Part-time programs available. *Degree requirements:* For master's, comprehensive exam, thesis optional. *Entrance requirements:* Additional exam requirements/recommendations for international students: Required—TOEFL (minimum score 550 paper-based; 213 computer-based), IELTS (minimum score 6.5). *Faculty research:* Biblical studies, administration and organization, world religions.

Trent University, Graduate Studies, Program in Cultural Studies, Peterborough, ON K9J 7B8, Canada. Offers PhD.

Union Institute & University, Online MA Programs, Cincinnati, OH 45206-1925. Offers health and wellness (MA); history and culture (MA); leadership (MA); literature and writing (MA); psychology (MA). Part-time programs available. Postbaccalaureate distance learning degree programs offered (no on-campus study). *Degree requirements:* For master's, thesis. *Expenses:* Contact institution.

Union University, Institute for International and Intercultural Studies, Jackson, TN 38305-3697. Offers MAIS. Part-time and evening/weekend programs available. *Degree requirements:* For master's, capstone course. *Entrance requirements:* For master's, GRE, minimum undergraduate GPA of 3.0, 3 letters of reference. Additional exam requirements/recommendations for international students: Required—TOEFL (minimum score 560 paper-

Union University (continued)
based; 220 computer-based). Electronic applications accepted. *Faculty research:* International education, ethnographic field research, intercultural training for professionals and students, language and culture.

University of Alaska Fairbanks, College of Liberal Arts, Department of Alaska Native Studies, Fairbanks, AK 99775-6300. Offers cross cultural studies (MA). *Faculty:* 2 full-time (0 women), 2 part-time/adjunct (0 women). *Students:* 5 full-time (3 women), 5 part-time (3 women); includes 4 minority (all American Indian/Alaska Native). Average age 42. 6 applicants, 50% accepted, 2 enrolled. In 2008, 3 master's awarded. *Degree requirements:* For master's, comprehensive exam. *Entrance requirements:* Additional exam requirements/recommendations for international students: Required—TOEFL (minimum score 550 paper-based; 213 computer-based; 80 iBT). *Application deadline:* For fall admission, 6/1 for domestic students, 3/1 for international students; for spring admission, 10/15 for domestic students, 9/1 for international students. Applications are processed on a rolling basis. Application fee: $60. Electronic applications accepted. *Expenses:* Tuition, area resident: Full-time $5418; part-time $301 per credit. Tuition, state resident: full-time $5418; part-time $301 per credit. Tuition, nonresident: full-time $11,070; part-time $615 per credit. Required fees: $849; $25 per credit. $78 per semester. Tuition and fees vary according to course load and reciprocity agreements. *Financial support:* In 2008–09, 1 fellowship (averaging $13,500 per year) was awarded; research assistantships, teaching assistantships, Federal Work-Study, scholarships/grants, health care benefits, and unspecified assistantships also available. Support available to part-time students. Financial award application deadline: 7/1; financial award applicants required to submit FAFSA. *Faculty research:* Alaska native literature, oral traditions, history, law and policy; Alaska native cultures, art, native American religion and philosophy. *Unit head:* Dr. James K. Ruppert, Chair, 907-474-7181, Fax: 907-474-5666, E-mail: fngdb@uaf.edu. *Application contact:* Dr. James K. Ruppert, Chair, 907-474-7181, Fax: 907-474-5666, E-mail: fngdb@uaf.edu.

University of California, Davis, Graduate Studies, Graduate Group in Cultural Studies, Davis, CA 95616. Offers MA, PhD. *Degree requirements:* For master's, thesis; for doctorate, thesis/dissertation. *Entrance requirements:* For doctorate, GRE. Additional exam requirements/recommendations for international students: Required—TOEFL (minimum score 550 paper-based; 213 computer-based). Electronic applications accepted.

University of Hawaii at Manoa, Graduate Division, East-West Center, Honolulu, HI 96822. Offers international cultural studies (Graduate Certificate). Part-time programs available. *Entrance requirements:* For degree, GRE General Test. Additional exam requirements/recommendations for international students: Required—TOEFL (minimum score 540 paper-based; 207 computer-based; 76 iBT), IELTS (minimum score 5).

University of Houston–Clear Lake, School of Human Sciences and Humanities, Programs in Human Sciences, Houston, TX 77058-1098. Offers behavioral sciences (MA), including criminology, cross cultural studies, general psychology, sociology; clinical psychology (MA); criminology (MA); cross cultural studies (MA); family therapy (MA); fitness and human performance (MA); school psychology (MA). *Accreditation:* AAMFT/COAMFTE. Part-time and evening/weekend programs available. Postbaccalaureate distance learning degree programs offered (minimal on-campus study). *Degree requirements:* For master's, thesis or alternative. *Entrance requirements:* For master's, GRE General Test. Additional exam requirements/recommendations for international students: Required—TOEFL (minimum score 550 paper-based; 213 computer-based). Electronic applications accepted. *Faculty research:* Smoking cessation, adolescent sexuality, white collar crime, serial murder, human factors/human computer interaction.

University of Minnesota, Twin Cities Campus, Graduate School, College of Liberal Arts, Department of Cultural Studies and Comparative Literature, Program in Comparative Studies in Discourse and Society, Minneapolis, MN 55455-0213. Offers PhD. *Degree requirements:* For doctorate, 2 foreign languages, thesis/dissertation. *Entrance requirements:* For doctorate, GRE General Test, sample of written work. Additional exam requirements/recommendations for international students: Required—TOEFL. *Faculty research:* Cultural theory; music; architecture, space, and urbanism; body and gender; film and popular culture.

University of Pittsburgh, School of Arts and Sciences, Department of English, Pittsburgh, PA 15260. Offers cultural and critical studies (PhD); English (MA); writing (MFA). Part-time programs available. *Degree requirements:* For master's, one foreign language; for doctorate, 2 foreign languages, comprehensive exam, thesis/dissertation. *Entrance requirements:* For master's and doctorate, GRE General Test, writing sample. Additional exam requirements/recommendations for international students: Required—TOEFL. *Faculty research:* Cultural studies, literary history and theory, film, composition.

The University of Texas at San Antonio, College of Education and Human Development, Division of Bicultural-Bilingual Studies, San Antonio, TX 78249-0617. Offers bicultural-bilingual studies (MA); culture, literacy, and language (PhD); teaching English as a second language (MA). Part-time and evening/weekend programs available. *Degree requirements:* For master's, one foreign language, comprehensive exam, thesis optional; for doctorate, one foreign language, comprehensive exam, thesis/dissertation. *Entrance requirements:* For master's and doctorate, GRE General Test. Additional exam requirements/recommendations for international students: Required—TOEFL (minimum score 500 paper-based; 173 computer-based). Electronic applications accepted. *Faculty research:* Spanish-English bilingualism, cultural transmission in bilingual communities, literacy in bilingual settings, content-based ESL, second language acquisition in classroom contexts.

University of the Sacred Heart, Graduate Programs, Department of Communication, Program in Contemporary Culture and Means, San Juan, PR 00914-0383. Offers MA. *Degree requirements:* For master's, thesis.

Washington State University, Graduate School, College of Liberal Arts, Edward R. Murrow College of Communication, Pullman, WA 99164. Offers health communications (MA, PhD); intercultural and international communications (MA, PhD); media and society (MA, PhD); media process and effects (MA, PhD); organizational communications (MA, PhD). *Degree requirements:* For master's, comprehensive exam (for some programs), thesis optional, oral exam; for doctorate, comprehensive exam, thesis/dissertation. *Entrance requirements:* For master's, GRE General Test, minimum GPA of 3.25, 3 letters of recommendation; for doctorate, GRE General Test, minimum undergraduate GPA of 3.25, graduate 3.5; MA in communication; 3 letters of recommendation. Additional exam requirements/recommendations for international students: Required—TOEFL (minimum score 580 paper-based; 237 computer-based). Electronic applications accepted. *Faculty research:* Advocacy communication, mediated communication in decision making, communication technology policy and effects, multicultural and international psychology and physiology of communication.

Wheaton College, Graduate School, Department of Intercultural Studies, Wheaton, IL 60187-5593. Offers evangelism (MA); intercultural studies (MA); intercultural studies/teaching English as a second language (MA); missions (MA); teaching English as a second language (Certificate). Part-time programs available. *Degree requirements:* For master's, thesis or alternative. *Entrance requirements:* For master's, GRE General Test, MAT. Electronic applications accepted.

Wilfrid Laurier University, Faculty of Graduate Studies, Faculty of Arts, Cultural Analysis and Social Theory Program, Waterloo, ON N2L 3C5, Canada. Offers MA. *Entrance requirements:* For master's, honours BA in humanities, social science or interdisciplinary program with social theory, minimum B+ in final year of full-time study. Additional exam requirements/recommendations for international students: Required—TOEFL (minimum score 230 computer-based; 89 iBT). Electronic applications accepted. *Faculty research:* Globalization, identify and social movements, body politics: gender, sexuality and embodiment, cultural representation and social theory.

East European and Russian Studies

Boston College, Graduate School of Arts and Sciences, Department of Slavic and Eastern Languages, Program in Slavic Studies, Chestnut Hill, MA 02467-3800. Offers MA, MA/JD, MBA/MA. Part-time programs available. *Degree requirements:* For master's, 3 foreign languages, comprehensive exam, thesis or alternative. *Entrance requirements:* Additional exam requirements/recommendations for international students: Required—TOEFL (minimum score 550 paper-based; 213 computer-based). Electronic applications accepted. *Expenses:* Tuition: Part-time $1148 per credit. Required fees: $60.

Brown University, Graduate School, Department of Slavic Languages, Providence, RI 02912. Offers Russian language and literature (AM); Slavic languages (AM); Slavic studies (PhD). *Degree requirements:* For master's, one foreign language; for doctorate, 2 foreign languages, thesis/dissertation, preliminary exam.

Carleton University, Faculty of Graduate Studies, Faculty of Public Affairs and Management, Institute of European and Russian Studies, Ottawa, ON K1S 5B6, Canada. Offers European and European Union studies (MA); European integration studies (Diploma); Russian, Eurasian and transition studies (MA). *Degree requirements:* For master's, one foreign language, thesis optional. *Entrance requirements:* For master's, honors degree or equivalent; 2 years of Russian, German or other central east European language. Additional exam requirements/recommendations for international students: Required—TOEFL. *Faculty research:* East-West relations, minority rights in Russia and Eastern Europe.

Columbia University, Graduate School of Arts and Sciences, Program in Russian, Eurasian and East European Regional Studies, New York, NY 10027. Offers MA. Part-time programs available.

Columbia University, School of International and Public Affairs, The East Central Europe Center, New York, NY 10027. Offers Certificate. Students must be enrolled in a separate graduate degree program at Columbia University. Electronic applications accepted. *Faculty research:* Ethnic politics, modern East Central European history, post-Communist economic and political transitions, East Central European language and literature.

Columbia University, School of International and Public Affairs, The Harriman Institute, New York, NY 10027. Offers Certificate. Students must be enrolled in a separate graduate degree program at Columbia University. Part-time programs available. *Degree requirements:* For Certificate, one foreign language, thesis. *Entrance requirements:* For degree, minimum 2 years of Russian. Electronic applications accepted.

Cornell University, Graduate School, Graduate Fields of Arts and Sciences, Field of History, Ithaca, NY 14853-0001. Offers African history (MA, PhD); American history (MA, PhD); ancient history (MA, PhD); early modern European history (MA, PhD); English history (MA, PhD); French history (MA, PhD); German history (MA, PhD); history of science (MA, PhD); Latin American history (MA, PhD); medieval Chinese history (MA, PhD); medieval history (MA, PhD); modern Chinese history (MA, PhD); modern European history (MA, PhD); modern Japanese history (MA, PhD); premodern Islamic history (MA, PhD); premodern Japanese history (MA, PhD); Renaissance history (MA, PhD); Russian history (MA, PhD); Southeast Asian history (MA, PhD). *Faculty:* 54 full-time (14 women). *Students:* 65 full-time (35 women); includes 12 minority (4 African Americans, 3 Asian Americans or Pacific Islanders, 5 Hispanic Americans), 19 international. Average age 31. 205 applicants, 8% accepted, 11 enrolled. In 2008, 12 master's, 6 doctorates awarded. Terminal master's awarded for partial completion of doctoral program. *Degree requirements:* For master's, thesis; for doctorate, 2 foreign languages, comprehensive exam, thesis/dissertation, 1 year of teaching experience. *Entrance requirements:* For master's and doctorate, GRE General Test, writing sample, 3 letters of recommendation. Additional exam requirements/recommendations for international students: Required—TOEFL (minimum score 550 paper-based; 213 computer-based; 77 iBT). *Application deadline:* For fall admission, 1/15 for domestic students. Application fee: $70. Electronic applications accepted. *Expenses:* Tuition: Full-time $29,500. Required fees: $70. Full-time tuition and fees vary according to degree level, program and student level. *Financial support:* In 2008–09, 54 students received support, including 27 fellowships with full tuition reimbursements available, 3 research assistantships with full tuition reimbursements available, 24 teaching assistantships with full tuition reimbursements available; institutionally sponsored loans, scholarships/grants, health care benefits, tuition waivers (full and partial), and unspecified assistantships also available. Financial award applicants required to submit FAFSA. *Unit head:* Director of Graduate Studies, 607-255-6738, Fax: 607-255-0469. *Application contact:* Graduate Field Assistant, 607-255-6738, Fax: 607-255-0469, E-mail: history_grad_info@cornell.edu.

Florida State University, Graduate Studies, College of Social Sciences, Program in Russian and East European Studies, Tallahassee, FL 32306. Offers MA. Part-time programs available. *Degree requirements:* For master's, one foreign language, comprehensive exam, thesis optional. *Entrance requirements:* For master's, GRE General Test, minimum GPA of 3.0. Additional exam requirements/recommendations for international students: Required—TOEFL (minimum score 550 paper-based; 213 computer-based; 80 iBT). Electronic applications accepted.

Georgetown University, Graduate School of Arts and Sciences, Program in Russian and East European Studies, Washington, DC 20057. Offers MA, MA/JD, MA/PhD. *Degree requirements:* For master's, one foreign language, comprehensive exam, thesis optional. *Entrance requirements:* For master's, GRE General Test. Additional exam requirements/recommendations for international students: Required—TOEFL. *Faculty research:* East-West trade.

The George Washington University, Elliott School of International Affairs, Program in European and Eurasian Studies, Washington, DC 20052. Offers MA, JD/MA, MBA/MA. Part-time and evening/weekend programs available. *Students:* 12 full-time (7 women), 8 part-time (4 women), 1 international. Average age 26. 47 applicants, 68% accepted, 11 enrolled. In 2008, 18 master's awarded. *Degree requirements:* For master's, one foreign language, capstone project. *Entrance requirements:* For master's, GRE General Test, 2 years (or the equivalent) of a modern European language (or Russian), 2 semesters of introductory economics (macro or micro economics). Additional exam requirements/recommendations for international students: Required—TOEFL. *Application deadline:* For fall admission, 2/1 for domestic students; for spring admission, 10/1 for domestic students. Application fee: $60. Electronic applications accepted. *Financial support:* In 2008–09, 3 students received support; fellowships with tuition reimbursements available, research assistantships with tuition reimbursements available, career-related internships or fieldwork, Federal Work-Study, institutionally sponsored loans, and tuition waivers available. Financial award application deadline: 1/15; financial award applicants required to submit FAFSA. *Faculty research:* NATO, European economics, European history, European Union. *Unit head:* Hope Harrison, Director, 202-994-5439, Fax: 202-994-5436, E-mail: hopeharr@gwu.edu. *Application contact:* Jeff V. Miles, Director of Graduate Admissions, 202-994-7050, Fax: 202-994-9537, E-mail: esiagrad@gwu.edu.

Harvard University, Graduate School of Arts and Sciences, Committee on Regional Studies-Russia, Eastern Europe, and Central Asia, Cambridge, MA 02138. Offers AM. *Degree requirements:* For master's, one foreign language. *Entrance requirements:* For master's, GRE General Test. Additional exam requirements/recommendations for international students: Required—TOEFL. *Expenses:* Tuition: Full-time $32,556. Required fees: $1426. Full-time tuition and fees vary according to program and student level. *Faculty research:* Strategic policy, ethnography and demography of U.S.S.R., non-Russian nationality language training.

Indiana University Bloomington, University Graduate School, College of Arts and Sciences, Russian and East European Institute, Bloomington, IN 47405-7000. Offers MA, Certificate, MBA/MA, MIS/MA, MLS/MA, MPA/MA. Part-time programs available. *Students:* 18 full-time (10 women), 5 part-time (all women); includes 4 minority (2 Asian Americans or Pacific Islanders, 2 Hispanic Americans). Average age 27. 27 applicants, 56% accepted, 3 enrolled. In 2008, 11 master's awarded. *Degree requirements:* For master's, one foreign language, essay, proficiency and written exams; for Certificate, one foreign language, oral and proficiency exams. *Entrance requirements:* For master's, GRE General Test, minimum 2 years of college Russian (Russian area studies); for Certificate, GRE General Test. Additional exam requirements/recommendations for international students: Required—TOEFL. *Application deadline:* For fall admission, 1/15 priority date for domestic students, 12/15 for international students; for spring admission, 9/1 priority date for domestic students, 9/1 for international students. Applications are processed on a rolling basis. Application fee: $50 ($60 for international students). *Expenses:* Tuition, area resident: Part-time $291.97 per credit hour. Tuition, state resident: part-time $291.97 per credit hour. Tuition, nonresident: part-time $850.33 per credit hour. Required fees: $110 per semester. Tuition and fees vary according to course load and program. *Financial support:* Fellowships, research assistantships with full tuition reimbursements, teaching assistantships, career-related internships or fieldwork, Federal Work-Study, and institutionally sponsored loans available. Financial award application deadline: 2/15; financial award applicants required to submit FAFSA. *Faculty research:* Political and economic transition of former Soviet Union and Eastern Europe, Russian and Soviet history, Slavic literature and linguistics, education and mass media of former Soviet Union and Eastern Europe. *Unit head:* David Ransel, Director, 812-855-7309, Fax: 812-855-6411, E-mail: ransel@indiana.edu. *Application contact:* Marianne Davis, Administrative Secretary, 812-855-3869, Fax: 812-855-6411, E-mail: marwdavi@indiana.edu.

The Johns Hopkins University, Paul H. Nitze School of Advanced International Studies, Washington, DC 20036. Offers international development (Certificate); international public policy (MIPP); international relations (MA, PhD), including African studies (MA), American foreign policy (MA), Asian studies (MA), Canadian studies (MA), conflict management (MA), European studies (MA), global theory and history (MA), international development (MA), international law, and organizations (MA), international policy (MA), international relations (general) (MA), Latin American studies (MA), Middle East studies (MA), Russian and Eurasian studies (MA), strategic studies (MA); international studies (Certificate); JD/MA; MBA/MA; MHS/MA. Terminal master's awarded for partial completion of doctoral program. *Degree requirements:* For master's, one foreign language, 16 non-language courses (8 for MIPP), 2 core examinations, comprehensive oral exam, paper (for some programs); for doctorate, 2 foreign languages, thesis/dissertation, 3 comprehensive exams, defense. *Entrance requirements:* For master's, GMAT or GRE General Test, previous course work in economics, foreign language, undergraduate degree; for doctorate, GRE General Test, master's degree. Additional exam requirements/recommendations for international students: Required—TOEFL (minimum paper-based score of 600, computer-based 250, iBT 100) or IELTS (minimum 7.0). Electronic applications accepted. *Expenses:* Contact institution. *Faculty research:* Regional studies and functional fields of international relations, international economics, conflict management, global theory and history, international law and organizations, international policy, strategic studies.

La Salle University, School of Arts and Sciences, Central and Eastern European Studies Program, Philadelphia, PA 19141-1199. Offers MA. Part-time and evening/weekend programs available. *Degree requirements:* For master's, one foreign language, thesis or alternative. *Entrance requirements:* For master's, MAT. Additional exam requirements/recommendations for international students: Required—TOEFL. *Expenses:* Contact institution. *Faculty research:* Ukrainian culture, Russian studies, business in Central and Eastern European countries.

The Ohio State University, Graduate School, College of Humanities, Department of Slavic and East European Languages and Literatures, Program in Slavic and East European Studies, Columbus, OH 43210. Offers MA. *Degree requirements:* For master's, thesis optional. *Entrance requirements:* For master's, GRE General Test. Additional exam requirements/recommendations for international students: Required—TOEFL (paper-based 550; computer-based 213) or IELTS (7) or Michigan English Language Assessment Battery (82). Electronic applications accepted.

Stanford University, School of Humanities and Sciences, Center for Russian and East European Studies, Stanford, CA 94305-9991. Offers MA. *Degree requirements:* For master's, one foreign language. *Entrance requirements:* For master's, GRE General Test. Additional exam requirements/recommendations for international students: Required—TOEFL. Electronic applications accepted.

University of Alberta, Faculty of Graduate Studies and Research, Department of Modern Languages and Cultural Studies, Edmonton, AB T6G 2E1, Canada. Offers applied linguistics (Germanic, Romance, Slavic) (MA); French language, literatures and linguistics (PhD); French language, literatures, and linguistics (MA); Germanic languages, literatures and linguistics (PhD); Germanic languages, literatures, and linguistics (MA); Italian studies (MA); Slavic languages and literatures (Russian, Ukrainian) (MA, PhD); Slavic linguistics (Russian, Ukrainian) (MA, PhD); Spanish and Latin American studies (MA, PhD); Ukrainian folklore (MA, PhD). Part-time programs available. *Degree requirements:* For master's, one foreign language, thesis; for doctorate, 2 foreign languages, comprehensive exam, thesis/dissertation. *Entrance requirements:* For master's and doctorate, 1 language other than English. Additional exam requirements/recommendations for international students: Required—Michigan English Language Assessment Battery or TOEFL (paper score 550; computer score 213). Electronic applications accepted. *Faculty research:* Russian/Ukrainian studies; German studies; contemporary Latin American, French and Francophone studies; Italian studies.

The University of British Columbia, Faculty of Arts and Faculty of Graduate Studies, Department of Central, Eastern and Northern European Studies, Vancouver, BC V6T 1Z1, Canada. Offers Germanic studies (MA, PhD). Part-time programs available. *Degree requirements:* For master's, one foreign language, thesis optional, exam; for doctorate, comprehensive exam, thesis/dissertation. *Entrance requirements:* For master's, BA in German; for doctorate, MA in German. Additional exam requirements/recommendations for international students: Required—TOEFL (minimum score 550 paper-based; 213 computer-based). Electronic applications accepted. *Faculty research:* Second language acquisition, media theory, performance theory, gender studies, cultural studies.

University of Illinois at Urbana–Champaign, Graduate College, College of Liberal Arts and Sciences, Russian, East European and Eurasian Center, Champaign, IL 61820. Offers MA. *Students:* 10 full-time (1 woman). 20 applicants, 70% accepted, 6 enrolled. In 2008, 2 master's awarded. *Entrance requirements:* For master's, GRE, writing sample. Additional exam requirements/recommendations for international students: Required—TOEFL (minimum score 550 paper-based; 213 computer-based). *Application deadline:* Applications are processed on a rolling basis. Application fee: $60 ($75 for international students). Electronic applications accepted. *Financial support:* In 2008–09, 9 fellowships were awarded; research assistantships, teaching assistantships, tuition waivers (full and partial) also available. *Unit head:* Richard Tempest, Head, 217-244-4720, Fax: 217-333-7310, E-mail: rtempest@illinois.edu. *Application contact:* Merrily Shaw, Assistant to the Director, 217-244-4721, Fax: 217-333-1582, E-mail: mshaw2@illinois.edu.

The University of Kansas, Graduate Studies, College of Liberal Arts and Sciences, Center for Russian, East European and Eurasian Studies, Lawrence, KS 66045. Offers MA. Part-time programs available. *Faculty:* 45. *Students:* 7 full-time (2 women), 1 part-time (0 women). Average age 30. 15 applicants, 87% accepted, 4 enrolled. In 2008, 8 master's awarded. *Degree requirements:* For master's, one foreign language, comprehensive exam, interdisciplinary capstone seminar. *Entrance requirements:* For master's, GRE General Test, 3 letters of recommendation. Additional exam requirements/recommendations for international students: Required—TOEFL. *Application deadline:* For fall admission, 5/1 priority date for domestic students, 2/14 priority date for international students; for spring admission, 10/1 priority date for domestic students, 9/1 priority date for international students. Applications are processed on a rolling basis. Application fee: $45 ($55 for international students). Electronic applications accepted. *Expenses:* Tuition, area resident: Full-time $6122; part-time $255.10 per credit hour. Tuition, state resident: full-time $6122; part-time $255.10 per credit hour. Tuition, nonresident: full-time $14,629; part-time $609.55 per credit hour. Required fees: $847; $70.56 per credit hour. Tuition and fees vary according to course load and program. *Financial support:* In 2008–09, 8 fellowships with full tuition reimbursements, 2 research assistantships with full and partial tuition reimbursements were awarded; scholarships/grants and tuition waivers (partial) also available. Financial award application deadline: 1/31; financial award applicants required to submit FAFSA. *Faculty research:* Transition studies, Russian history and philosophy, Ukrainian and Russian domestic and foreign policies, Slavic languages and literatures, security policies in Central Asia and the Caucasus. *Unit head:* Dr. Edith Clowes, Director, 785-864-4236, Fax: 785-864-3800, E-mail: crees@ku.edu. *Application contact:* Dr. Eve Levin, Associate Director, 785-864-4236, Fax: 785-864-3800, E-mail: evelevin@ku.edu.

University of Michigan, Horace H. Rackham School of Graduate Studies, College of Literature, Science, and the Arts, Interdepartmental Program in Russian and East European Studies, Ann Arbor, MI 48109. Offers AM, Certificate, JD/AM, MBA/AM, MPP/AM. Part-time programs available. *Degree requirements:* For master's, one foreign language, thesis. *Entrance requirements:* For master's, GRE General Test. Additional exam requirements/recommendations for international students: Required—TOEFL. Electronic applications accepted.

The University of North Carolina at Chapel Hill, Graduate School, Curriculum in Russian and East European Studies, Chapel Hill, NC 27599. Offers MA. Part-time programs available. *Degree requirements:* For master's, one foreign language, thesis. *Entrance requirements:* For master's, GRE General Test. Additional exam requirements/recommendations for international students: Required—TOEFL. Electronic applications accepted. *Faculty research:* Language, area studies, social sciences, sciences, professional schools.

University of Pittsburgh, University Center for International Studies, Pittsburgh, PA 15260. Offers African studies (Certificate); Asian studies (Certificate); European Union studies (Certificate); global studies (Certificate); Latin American studies (Certificate); Russian and East European studies (Certificate); West European studies (Certificate).

University of Saskatchewan, College of Graduate Studies and Research, College of Arts and Sciences, Department of Languages and Linguistics, Saskatoon, SK S7N 5A2, Canada. Offers MA. *Degree requirements:* For master's, 2 foreign languages, thesis. *Entrance requirements:* Additional exam requirements/recommendations for international students: Required—TOEFL.

The University of Texas at Austin, Graduate School, College of Liberal Arts, Center for Russian, East European, and Eurasian Studies, Austin, TX 78712-1111. Offers MA, JD/MA, MBA/MA, MP Aff/MA. Part-time programs available. *Degree requirements:* For master's, one foreign language, report or thesis. *Entrance requirements:* For master's, GRE General Test, 3 years of formal language training or equivalent, minimum GPA of 3.0. Electronic applications accepted. *Faculty research:* East European gypsies, elite transformation and democracy in Eastern Europe, elite partisanship as an intervening variable in Russian politics, post-Soviet youth in Russia.

University of Toronto, School of Graduate Studies, Social Sciences Division, Centre for European, Russian and Eurasian Studies, Toronto, ON M5S 1A1, Canada. Offers MA. *Degree requirements:* For master's, one foreign language, language proficiency test. *Entrance requirements:* For master's, minimum B+ average in final year, coursework in Russian/East European subjects, 2 years of study in a relevant language.

University of Washington, Graduate School, College of Arts and Sciences, Henry M. Jackson School of International Studies, Russian, East European and Central Asian Studies Program, Seattle, WA 98195. Offers Central Asian studies (MAIS); East European studies (MAIS); Russian studies (MAIS). *Degree requirements:* For master's, one foreign language, thesis. *Entrance requirements:* For master's, GRE General Test, 2 years of relevant language, minimum GPA of 3.0. Additional exam requirements/recommendations for international students: Required—TOEFL (minimum score 500 paper-based; 213 computer-based). Electronic applications accepted.

Yale University, Graduate School of Arts and Sciences, Department of Slavic Languages and Literatures, New Haven, CT 06520. Offers medieval Slavic literature and philology (PhD); Polish literature (PhD); Russian literature (PhD); Slavic languages and literatures and film studies (PhD). *Degree requirements:* For doctorate, 3 foreign languages, thesis/dissertation. *Entrance requirements:* For doctorate, GRE General Test.

Yale University, Graduate School of Arts and Sciences, Program in Russian and East European Studies, New Haven, CT 06520. Offers MA. *Degree requirements:* For master's, 2 foreign languages. *Entrance requirements:* For master's, GRE General Test.

Ethnic Studies

Cornell University, Graduate School, Graduate Fields of Arts and Sciences, Field of Sociology, Ithaca, NY 14853-0001. Offers economy and society (MA, PhD); gender and life course (MA, PhD); methodology (MA, PhD); organizations (MA, PhD); policy analysis (MA, PhD); political sociology/social movements (MA, PhD); racial and ethnic relations (MA, PhD); social networks (MA, PhD); social psychology (MA, PhD); social stratification (MA, PhD). *Faculty:* 32 full-time (12 women). *Students:* 40 full-time (16 women); includes 8 minority (2 African Americans, 4 Asian Americans or Pacific Islanders, 2 Hispanic Americans), 10 international. Average age 31. 148 applicants, 7% accepted, 4 enrolled. In 2008, 1 master's, 7 doctorates awarded. Terminal master's awarded for partial completion of doctoral program. *Degree requirements:* For master's, thesis; for doctorate, thesis/dissertation, 1 year of teaching experience. *Entrance requirements:* For master's and doctorate, GRE General Test, 2 letters of recommendation, writing sample. Additional exam requirements/recommendations for international students: Required—TOEFL (minimum score 550 paper-based; 213 computer-based; 77 iBT). *Application deadline:* For fall admission, 1/15 for domestic students. Application fee: $70. Electronic applications accepted. *Expenses:* Tuition: Full-time $29,500. Required fees: $70. Full-time tuition and fees vary according to degree level, program and student level. *Financial support:* In 2008–09, 32 students received support, including 9 fellowships with full tuition reimbursements available, 8 research assistantships with full tuition reimbursements available, 15 teaching assistantships with full tuition reimbursements available; institutionally sponsored loans, scholarships/grants, health care benefits, tuition waivers (full and partial), and unspecified assistantships also available. Financial award applicants required to submit FAFSA. *Faculty research:* Comparative societal analysis, work and family, simulations, social class and mobility, racial segregation and inequality. *Unit head:* Director of Graduate Studies, 607-255-4266. *Application contact:* Graduate Field Assistant, 607-255-4266, E-mail: sociology@cornell.edu.

Minnesota State University Mankato, College of Graduate Studies, College of Social and Behavioral Sciences, Department of Ethnic Studies, Mankato, MN 56001. Offers MS. *Students:* 9 full-time (4 women), 9 part-time (3 women). *Application deadline:* For fall admission, 7/1 for domestic students, 5/1 for international students; for winter admission, 11/1 for domestic students; for spring admission, 10/1 for international students. Applications are processed on a rolling basis. Electronic applications accepted. *Unit head:* Dr. Kebba Darboe, Graduate Coordinator, 507-389-5014. *Application contact:* Dr. Kebba Darboe, Graduate Coordinator, 507-389-5014.

San Francisco State University, Division of Graduate Studies, College of Ethnic Studies, Program in Ethnic Studies, San Francisco, CA 94132-1722. Offers MA.

United Theological Seminary of the Twin Cities, Graduate and Professional Programs, New Brighton, MN 55112-2598. Offers advanced theological studies (Diploma); justice and peace studies (M Div); leadership toward racial justice (MA, Certificate); Methodist studies (M Div, MA); ministry (D Min); ministry renewal and professional development (Certificate); pastoral care and counseling (M Div); religion and theology (MA); theological and religious studies (Certificate); theology and the arts (MA); urban ministry (MARL); women's studies: religion, theology and ministry (MA). *Accreditation:* ACIPE; ATS. Part-time and evening/weekend programs available. *Faculty:* 10 full-time (6 women), 24 part-time/adjunct (12 women). *Students:* 60 full-time (34 women), 93 part-time (60 women); includes 10 minority (5 African Americans, 1 American Indian/Alaska Native, 3 Asian Americans or Pacific Islanders, 1 Hispanic American), 1 international. Average age 47. 39 applicants, 100% accepted, 32 enrolled. In 2008, 21 first professional degrees, 9 master's awarded. *Degree requirements:* For master's, thesis; for doctorate, comprehensive exam, thesis/dissertation; for M Div, integrative notebook, spiritual chronicle. *Entrance requirements:* For M Div and master's, minimum GPA of 2.75; strong analytical, reflective thinking and writing skills; vocational and academic goals compatible with those of Seminary; for doctorate, M Div or equivalent, minimum GPA of 3.0, 3 years experience in professional ministry; for other advanced degree, BA or equivalent life experience; strong analytical, reflective thinking and writing skills (Certificate); proficiency in English language, previous study of theology at a theological school, recommendation of student's denomination

(Diploma). Additional exam requirements/recommendations for international students: Required—TOEFL (minimum score 550 paper-based). *Application deadline:* For fall admission, 7/1 priority date for domestic students, 11/1 priority date for international students; for winter admission, 11/1 priority date for domestic students; for spring admission, 11/15 priority date for domestic students. Applications are processed on a rolling basis. Application fee: $50. *Expenses:* Tuition: Full-time $11,070; part-time $410 per credit hour. Required fees: $295; $135 per term. One-time fee: $25. Tuition and fees vary according to course load, degree level and program. *Financial support:* In 2008–09, 98 students received support. Career-related internships or fieldwork, institutionally sponsored loans, and scholarships/grants available. Support available to part-time students. Financial award application deadline: 5/1; financial award applicants required to submit FAFSA. *Unit head:* Dr. Richard D. Weis, Dean of the Seminary, 651-255-6108 Ext. 108, Fax: 651-633-4315, E-mail: rweis@unitedseminary.edu. *Application contact:* Rev. Glen Herrington-Hall, Director of Admissions, 651-255-6107 Ext. 107, Fax: 651-633-4315, E-mail: gherrington-hall@unitedseminary.edu.

Université Laval, Faculty of Letters, Department of History, Programs in Ethnology of French-Speaking People in North America, Québec, QC G1K 7P4, Canada. Offers MA, PhD. Terminal master's awarded for partial completion of doctoral program. *Degree requirements:* For master's, thesis; for doctorate, comprehensive exam, thesis/dissertation. *Entrance requirements:* For master's and doctorate, English exam (comprehension of written English), knowledge of French. Electronic applications accepted.

University of California, Berkeley, Graduate Division, Group in Ethnic Studies, Berkeley, CA 94720-1500. Offers PhD. *Degree requirements:* For doctorate, one foreign language, thesis/dissertation, qualifying exam. *Entrance requirements:* For doctorate, minimum GPA of 3.0, 3 letters of recommendation. *Faculty research:* Gender and race, Asian American visual art, racial theory and politics, Chicana/o literature and visual arts, history of Native North Americans.

University of California, Riverside, Graduate Division, Department of Ethnic Studies, Riverside, CA 92521. Offers PhD. *Faculty:* 12 full-time (4 women). *Students:* 46 applicants, 28% accepted, 4 enrolled. *Degree requirements:* For doctorate, variable foreign language requirement, comprehensive exam, thesis/dissertation. *Entrance requirements:* For doctorate, GRE, writing sample. Additional exam requirements/recommendations for international students: Required—TOEFL (minimum score 550 paper-based; 213 computer-based; 80 iBT). *Application deadline:* For fall admission, 5/1 for domestic students, 2/1 for international students. Applications are processed on a rolling basis. Application fee: $70 ($85 for international students). Electronic applications accepted. *Expenses:* Contact institution. *Financial support:* Applicants required to submit FAFSA. *Faculty research:* The political economy of race, class, gender, sexuality, cultural production, the state, law, criminal justice and grass roots responses. *Unit head:* Dr. Alfredo Mirande, Chair, 951-827-1012. *Application contact:* Andrea Gonzales, Graduate Program Coordinator, 951-827-1821, E-mail: andrea.gonzales@ucr.edu.

University of California, San Diego, Office of Graduate Studies, Department of Ethnic Studies, La Jolla, CA 92093. Offers MA, PhD. Electronic applications accepted.

Washington State University, Graduate School, College of Liberal Arts, Program in American Studies, Pullman, WA 99164. Offers ethnic studies (MA, PhD); feminist studies (MA, PhD); history (MA, PhD); literature (MA, PhD). *Degree requirements:* For master's, one foreign language, comprehensive exam (for some programs), thesis optional, oral exam; for doctorate, one foreign language, comprehensive exam (for some programs), thesis/dissertation, oral exam. *Entrance requirements:* For master's and doctorate, GRE General Test, minimum GPA of 3.0, writing sample, 3 letters of recommendation. Additional exam requirements/recommendations for international students: Required—TOEFL. *Faculty research:* The American West in multicultural perspective; nineteenth century historical, literary, and cultural studies; comparative American ethnic literatures and cultures; American cultures and the environment; American rhetoric.

Folklore

George Mason University, College of Humanities and Social Sciences, Interdisciplinary Studies Program, Fairfax, VA 22030. Offers anthropology (MAIS); community college teaching (MAIS); folklore (MAIS); higher education (MAIS); individualized studies (MAIS); religion, cultures, and values (MAIS); video-based production (MAIS); women's studies (MAIS); zoo and aquarium leadership (MAIS). Part-time and evening/weekend programs available. *Degree requirements:* For master's, thesis optional. *Entrance requirements:* For master's, GRE, GMAT, or MAT, interview, minimum GPA of 3.0 in last 60 hours of course work. Electronic applications accepted.

The George Washington University, Columbian College of Arts and Sciences, Department of American Studies, Washington, DC 20052. Offers American studies (PhD); folklife (MA); historic preservation (MA); material culture (MA). Part-time and evening/weekend programs available. *Faculty:* 11 full-time (5 women), 3 part-time/adjunct (1 woman). *Students:* 18 full-time (11 women), 23 part-time (14 women); includes 5 minority (4 African Americans, 1 Hispanic American), 3 international. Average age 31. 116 applicants, 23% accepted, 8 enrolled. In 2008, 11 master's, 5 doctorates awarded. Terminal master's awarded for partial completion of doctoral program. *Degree requirements:* For master's, comprehensive exam; for doctorate, one foreign language, thesis/dissertation, general exam. *Entrance requirements:* For master's and doctorate, GRE General Test, minimum GPA of 3.0. Additional exam requirements/recommendations for international students: Required—TOEFL (minimum score 550 paper-based; 213 computer-based; 80 iBT). *Application deadline:* For fall admission, 1/15 priority date for domestic and international students; for spring admission, 10/1 for domestic students. Application fee: $60. *Financial support:* In 2008–09, 22 students received support; fellowships, research assistantships, teaching assistantships, career-related internships or fieldwork, Federal Work-Study, institutionally sponsored loans, and tuition waivers available. Financial award application deadline: 1/15. *Unit head:* James A Miller, Chair, 202-994-6743, E-mail: jam@gwu.edu. *Application contact:* Information Contact, 202-994-6070, Fax: 202-994-8651, E-mail: amst@gwu.edu.

The George Washington University, Columbian College of Arts and Sciences, Department of Anthropology, Concentration in Folklife, Washington, DC 20052. Offers MA. In 2008, 1 master's awarded. *Degree requirements:* For master's, comprehensive exam, thesis or alternative. *Entrance requirements:* For master's, GRE General Test, minimum GPA of 3.0. *Application deadline:* For fall admission, 4/1 priority date for domestic and international students; for spring admission, 10/1 priority date for domestic and international students. Application fee: $60. *Financial support:* Fellowships, teaching assistantships available. Financial award application deadline: 2/1. *Unit head:* Dr. John Vlach, Director, 202-994-7318, E-mail: jmv@gwu.edu. *Application contact:* Information Contact, 202-994-6075, E-mail: anth@gwu.edu.

Indiana University Bloomington, University Graduate School, College of Arts and Sciences, Department of Folklore and Ethnomusicology, Bloomington, IN 47408-3890. Offers folklore (MA, PhD), including ethnomusicology. Part-time programs available. *Faculty:* 12 full-time (5 women), 11 part-time/adjunct (6 women). *Students:* 88 full-time (51 women), 25 part-time (20 women); includes 24 minority (12 African Americans, 1 American Indian/Alaska Native, 5 Asian Americans or Pacific Islanders, 6 Hispanic Americans), 21 international. Average age 34. 89 applicants, 40% accepted, 10 enrolled. In 2008, 6 master's, 7 doctorates awarded. *Degree requirements:* For master's, one foreign language, comprehensive exam, thesis or alternative; project or thesis; for doctorate, 2 foreign languages, comprehensive exam, thesis/dissertation. *Entrance requirements:* For master's and doctorate, GRE General Test, minimum GPA of 3.0. Additional exam requirements/recommendations for international students: Required—TOEFL (minimum score 550 paper-based; 213 computer-based; 79 iBT). *Application deadline:* For fall admission, 1/15 for domestic students, 12/1 for international students. Application fee: $50 ($60 for international students). Electronic applications accepted. *Expenses:* Tuition, area resident: Part-time $291.97 per credit hour. Tuition, state resident: part-time $291.97 per credit hour. Tuition, nonresident: part-time $850.33 per credit hour. Required fees: $110 per semester. Tuition and fees vary according to course load and program. *Financial support:* In 2008–09, 38 students received support, including 5 fellowships with full tuition reimbursements available (averaging $15,000 per year), 21 research assistantships with full tuition reimbursements available (averaging $11,000 per year), 12 teaching assistantships with full tuition reimbursements available (averaging $11,000 per year); Federal Work-Study and unspecified assistantships also available. Financial award application deadline: 3/1; financial award applicants required to submit FAFSA. *Faculty research:* Narrative, performance studies, material culture, popular culture, music. *Unit head:* Dr. Portia Maultsby, Chair, 812-855-0395, Fax: 812-855-4008, E-mail: maultsby@indiana.edu. *Application contact:* Christopher Roush, Graduate Secretary, 812-855-0389, Fax: 812-855-4008, E-mail: croush@indiana.edu.

Memorial University of Newfoundland, School of Graduate Studies, Department of Folklore, St. John's, NL A1C 5S7, Canada. Offers MA, PhD. Part-time programs available. *Degree requirements:* For master's, thesis optional; for doctorate, one foreign language, comprehensive exam, thesis/dissertation, oral thesis defense. *Entrance requirements:* For master's, 36 credit hours of course work in folklore, humanities, or social studies; honors degree; for doctorate, MA in folklore or related field. Electronic applications accepted. *Faculty research:* Narrative, folklife, belief theory, methodology, popular culture.

University of Alberta, Faculty of Graduate Studies and Research, Department of Modern Languages and Cultural Studies, Edmonton, AB T6G 2E1, Canada. Offers applied linguistics (Germanic, Romance, Slavic) (MA); French language, literatures and linguistics (PhD); French language, literatures, and linguistics (MA); Germanic languages, literatures and linguistics (PhD); Germanic languages, literatures, and linguistics (MA); Italian studies (MA); Slavic languages and literatures (Russian, Ukrainian) (MA, PhD); Slavic linguistics (Russian, Ukrainian) (MA, PhD); Spanish and Latin American studies (MA, PhD); Ukrainian folklore (MA, PhD). Part-time programs available. *Degree requirements:* For master's, one foreign language, thesis; for doctorate, 2 foreign languages, comprehensive exam, thesis/dissertation. *Entrance requirements:* For master's and doctorate, 1 language other than English. Additional exam requirements/recommendations for international students: Required—Michigan English Language Assessment Battery or TOEFL (paper score 550; computer score 213). Electronic applications accepted. *Faculty research:* Russian/Ukrainian studies; German studies; contemporary Latin American, French and Francophone studies; Italian studies.

University of California, Berkeley, Graduate Division, Group in Folklore, Berkeley, CA 94720-1500. Offers MA. *Entrance requirements:* For master's, GRE General Test, minimum GPA of 3.0, 3 letters of recommendation.

University of Louisiana at Lafayette, BI Moody III College of Business Administration MBA Program, College of Liberal Arts, Department of English, Lafayette, LA 70504. Offers British and American literature (MA), including creative writing, folklore, rhetoric; creative writing (PhD); literature (PhD); rhetoric (PhD). Part-time programs available. Terminal master's awarded for partial completion of doctoral program. *Degree requirements:* For master's, one foreign language, thesis or alternative; for doctorate, 2 foreign languages, comprehensive exam, thesis/dissertation. *Entrance requirements:* For master's, GRE General Test, minimum GPA of 2.75; for doctorate, GRE General Test, minimum GPA of 3.0. Additional exam requirements/recommendations for international students: Required—TOEFL (minimum score 550 paper-based; 213 computer-based). Electronic applications accepted. *Faculty research:* Composition theory, Southern literature, medieval literature.

The University of North Carolina at Chapel Hill, Graduate School, College of Arts and Sciences, Curriculum in Folklore, Chapel Hill, NC 27599. Offers MA. *Degree requirements:* For master's, one foreign language, comprehensive exam, thesis. *Entrance requirements:* For master's, GRE General Test, minimum GPA of 3.0, writing sample. Electronic applications accepted. *Faculty research:* Public folklore, politics of culture, folklore and feminist theory, belief and health systems, Southern culture.

University of Oregon, Graduate School, College of Arts and Sciences, Folklore Program, Eugene, OR 97403. Offers independent study: folklore (MA, MS). Part-time programs available. *Degree requirements:* For master's, one foreign language, project or thesis. *Entrance*

requirements: For master's, GRE General Test, minimum GPA of 3.0. Additional exam requirements/recommendations for international students: Required—TOEFL. *Faculty research:* American folklore, East European folklore, film and folklore, folk religion and belief, ballad.

The University of Texas at Austin, Graduate School, College of Liberal Arts, Department of Anthropology, Program in Folklore and Public Culture, Austin, TX 78712-1111. Offers MA, PhD. Part-time programs available. Terminal master's awarded for partial completion of doctoral program. *Degree requirements:* For master's, one foreign language, thesis, report; for doctorate, one foreign language, thesis/dissertation. *Entrance requirements:* For master's and doctorate, GRE General Test. Electronic applications accepted. *Faculty research:* Expressive culture, gender, genre, folklore and culture of British Isles, ethnography of speaking.

University of Wisconsin–Madison, Graduate School, College of Letters and Science, Department of Scandinavian Studies, Madison, WI 53706-1380. Offers area studies (MA); folklore (PhD); literature (MA, PhD); philology (PhD). Part-time programs available. *Degree requirements:* For master's, 2 foreign languages, exam; for doctorate, thesis/dissertation, exam. *Entrance requirements:* For master's, minimum GPA of 3.25; for doctorate, minimum GPA of 3.5. Electronic applications accepted. *Faculty research:* Historical fiction, Icelandic poetry, nineteenth-century literature, theater, gender studies, folklore.

Utah State University, School of Graduate Studies, College of Humanities, Arts and Social Sciences, Department of English and Department of History, Program in American Studies, Logan, UT 84322. Offers folklore (MA, MS); western American literature and culture (MA, MS). Part-time and evening/weekend programs available. *Degree requirements:* For master's, thesis or alternative. *Entrance requirements:* For master's, GRE General Test or MAT, minimum GPA of 3.0, 3 letters of recommendation, writing sample. Additional exam requirements/recommendations for international students: Required—TOEFL. *Faculty research:* Folklore and folklife, American culture, regional studies, material culture, Jewish folklore, Native American folklore.

Gender Studies

The American University in Cairo, Graduate Studies and Research, School of Humanities and Social Sciences, Program in Gender and Women's Studies, Cairo, Egypt. Offers gender and development (MA, Diploma); gender and justice (MA, Diploma); gender and women's studies in the Middle East and North Africa (MA, Diploma).

Arizona State University, Graduate College, College of Liberal Arts and Sciences, Division of Social Sciences, Women and Gender Studies Program, Tempe, AZ 85287. Offers gender studies (PhD).

Carnegie Mellon University, College of Humanities and Social Sciences, Department of History, Pittsburgh, PA 15213-3891. Offers African and African-American diaspora (PhD); culture and power (PhD); gender and the family (PhD); history (MA, MS); history and policy (MA); labor and politics (PhD); science, technology, medicine and environment (PhD). Part-time programs available. *Degree requirements:* For doctorate, oral and written comprehensive exams, dissertation defense. *Entrance requirements:* For doctorate, GRE General Test. Additional exam requirements/recommendations for international students: Required—TOEFL. Electronic applications accepted. *Faculty research:* Anthropology and history, African American history, technology/environment, cultural history analysis.

Central European University, Graduate Studies, School of Social Sciences and Humanities, Budapest, Hungary. Offers economics (MA, PhD); gender studies (MA, PhD); international relations and European studies (MA, PhD); mathematics and its applications (MS, PhD); medieval studies (MA, PhD); nationalism studies (MA, PhD); philosophy (MA, PhD); political science (MA, PhD); public policy (MA, PhD); sociology and social anthropology (MA, PhD). Terminal master's awarded for partial completion of doctoral program. *Degree requirements:* For master's, one foreign language, thesis; for doctorate, one foreign language, comprehensive exam, thesis/dissertation. *Entrance requirements:* For master's, CEU subject tests, interview; for doctorate, GRE, CEU subject test, interview. Additional exam requirements/recommendations for international students: Required—TOEFL (minimum score 570 paper-based; 230 computer-based). Electronic applications accepted. *Faculty research:* Civil society, fiscal decentralization, party politics, political philosophy (especially Liberalism, theory of Democracy).

See Close-Up on page 349.

Central Michigan University, College of Graduate Studies, College of Humanities and Social and Behavioral Sciences, Program in Humanities, Mount Pleasant, MI 48859. Offers humanities (MA), including contemporary issues in the humanities: race, class, and gender, images and ideas of self, Native American issues in modern culture, popular culture studies, the rise of industrial society. Part-time and evening/weekend programs available. *Students:* 3 full-time (1 woman), 7 part-time (4 women). Average age 37. *Degree requirements:* For master's, thesis or alternative. *Application deadline:* Applications are processed on a rolling basis. Application fee: $35 ($45 for international students). Electronic applications accepted. *Expenses:* Tuition, state resident: full-time $3717; part-time $413 per credit. Tuition, nonresident: full-time $6894; part-time $766 per credit. *Financial support:* Fellowships with tuition reimbursements, Federal Work-Study, unspecified assistantships, and out-of-state merit awards available. *Faculty research:* Rise of industrial society; images and ideas of self; contemporary issues of race, class, and gender; popular culture; Native American issues in modern culture. *Unit head:* Dr. Ronald Primeau, Director, 989-774-3117, Fax: 989-774-7106, E-mail: ronald.r.primeau@cmich.edu. *Application contact:* Judith L. Prince, Director of Graduate Student Services, 989-774-1059, Fax: 989-774-1857, E-mail: judith.l.prince@cmich.edu.

Cornell University, Graduate School, Graduate Fields of Arts and Sciences, Field of Sociology, Ithaca, NY 14853-0001. Offers economy and society (MA, PhD); gender and life course (MA, PhD); methodology (MA, PhD); organizations (MA, PhD); policy analysis (MA, PhD); political sociology/social movements (MA, PhD); racial and ethnic relations (MA, PhD); social networks (MA, PhD); social psychology (MA, PhD); social stratification (MA, PhD). *Faculty:* 32 full-time (12 women). *Students:* 40 full-time (16 women); includes 8 minority (2 African Americans, 4 Asian Americans or Pacific Islanders, 2 Hispanic Americans), 10 international. Average age 31. 148 applicants, 7% accepted, 4 enrolled. In 2008, 1 master's, 7 doctorates awarded. Terminal master's awarded for partial completion of doctoral program. *Degree requirements:* For master's, thesis; for doctorate, thesis/dissertation, 1 year of teaching experience. *Entrance requirements:* For master's and doctorate, GRE General Test, 2 letters of recommendation, writing sample. Additional exam requirements/recommendations for international students: Required—TOEFL (minimum score 550 paper-based; 213 computer-based; 77 iBT). *Application deadline:* For fall admission, 1/15 for domestic students. Application fee: $70. Electronic applications accepted. *Expenses:* Tuition: Full-time $29,500. Required fees: $70. Full-time tuition and fees vary according to degree level, program and student level. *Financial support:* In 2008–09, 32 students received support, including 9 fellowships with full tuition reimbursements available, 8 research assistantships with full tuition reimbursements available, 15 teaching assistantships with full tuition reimbursements available; institutionally sponsored loans, scholarships/grants, health care benefits, tuition waivers (full and partial), and unspecified assistantships also available. Financial award applicants required to submit FAFSA. *Faculty research:* Comparative societal analysis, work and family, simulations, social class and mobility,

racial segregation and inequality. *Unit head:* Director of Graduate Studies, 607-255-4266. *Application contact:* Graduate Field Assistant, 607-255-4266, E-mail: sociology@cornell.edu.

Eastern Michigan University, Graduate School, College of Arts and Sciences, Department of Women's and Gender Studies, Ypsilanti, MI 48197. Offers MLS. Part-time and evening/weekend programs available. Postbaccalaureate distance learning degree programs offered (minimal on-campus study). *Degree requirements:* For master's, thesis optional. *Entrance requirements:* Additional exam requirements/recommendations for international students: Required—TOEFL.

Indiana University Bloomington, University Graduate School, College of Arts and Sciences, Gender Studies Program, Bloomington, IN 47405-7000. Offers PhD. *Faculty:* 4 full-time (all women). *Students:* 18 full-time (15 women); includes 2 minority (1 American Indian/Alaska Native, 1 Hispanic American), 2 international. Average age 28. 76 applicants, 8% accepted, 4 enrolled. *Application deadline:* For fall admission, 1/12 priority date for domestic students, 12/1 priority date for international students. Application fee: $50 ($60 for international students). *Expenses:* Tuition, area resident: Part-time $291.97 per credit hour. Tuition, state resident: part-time $291.97 per credit hour. Tuition, nonresident: part-time $850.33 per credit hour. Required fees: $110 per semester. Tuition and fees vary according to course load and program. *Financial support:* Fellowships with tuition reimbursements, research assistantships with tuition reimbursements, teaching assistantships with tuition reimbursements available. *Unit head:* Helen Gremillion, Director of Graduate Studies, 812-855-0101, E-mail: hgremill@indiana.edu. *Application contact:* Nina Taylor, Graduate Secretary, 812-855-4848, E-mail: nitaylor@indiana.edu.

Indiana University–Purdue University Indianapolis, School of Liberal Arts, Department of Sociology, Indianapolis, IN 46202-2896. Offers family/gender studies (MA); medical sociology (MA); work/occupations (MA).

Memorial University of Newfoundland, School of Graduate Studies, Department of Sociology, St. John's, NL A1C 5S7, Canada. Offers gender (PhD); maritime sociology (PhD); sociology (M Phil, MA); work and development (PhD). Part-time programs available. *Degree requirements:* For master's, comprehensive exam, thesis optional, program journal (M Phil); for doctorate, one foreign language, comprehensive exam, thesis/dissertation, oral defense of thesis. *Entrance requirements:* For master's, 2nd class degree from university of recognized standing in area of study; for doctorate, MA, M Phil, or equivalent. Electronic applications accepted. *Faculty research:* Work and development, gender, maritime sociology.

Northwestern University, The Graduate School, Program in Gender Studies, Evanston, IL 60208. Offers PhD/Certificate. *Faculty research:* Anthropology, gender in Victorian period, autobiography, performance ethnographies, Slavic literature, women in the law.

Queen's University at Kingston, School of Graduate Studies and Research, Faculty of Arts and Sciences, Department of Political Studies, Kingston, ON K7L 3N6, Canada. Offers Canadian politics (PhD); comparative politics (PhD); gender and politics (PhD); international relations (PhD); political theory (PhD). *Degree requirements:* For master's, thesis or alternative; for doctorate, one foreign language, thesis/dissertation, qualifying exams. *Entrance requirements:* Additional exam requirements/recommendations for international students: Required—TOEFL (minimum score 600 paper-based; 250 computer-based). *Faculty research:* Canadian politics, comparative politics, political thought, international politics, women and politics.

Roosevelt University, Graduate Division, College of Arts and Sciences, Department of Literature and Languages, Program in Women's and Gender Studies, Chicago, IL 60605-1394. Offers MA, Certificate. Part-time and evening/weekend programs available. *Students:* 16 full-time (15 women), 5 part-time (all women); includes 1 minority (African American). Average age 32. 50 applicants, 48% accepted, 10 enrolled. In 2008, 8 master's awarded. *Degree requirements:* For master's, thesis. *Entrance requirements:* For master's, minimum GPA of 2.7. *Application deadline:* For fall admission, 6/1 priority date for domestic students. Applications are processed on a rolling basis. Application fee: $25 ($35 for international students). *Expenses:* Tuition: Full-time $14,730; part-time $709 per credit. Required fees: $175 per semester. Tuition and fees vary according to course load and program. *Financial support:* Application deadline: 2/15. *Faculty research:* Feminist economics; philosophy of feminism; race, class, and gender; women and art; women's history. *Unit head:* Ann Brigham, Head, 312-341-3725, Fax: 312-341-3680, E-mail: abrigham@roosevelt.edu. *Application contact:* Joanne Canyon-Heller, Coordinator of Graduate Admission, 877-APPLY RU, Fax: 312-281-3356, E-mail: applyru@roosevelt.edu.

Rutgers, The State University of New Jersey, New Brunswick, Graduate School, Program in Women's and Gender Studies, Piscataway, NJ 08854-8097. Offers MA, PhD. Part-time programs available. *Degree requirements:* For master's, thesis or alternative; for doctorate, comprehensive exam, thesis/dissertation. *Entrance requirements:* For master's and doctorate, GRE General Test, writing sample, 3 letters of recommendation. Additional exam requirements/recommendations for international students: Required—TOEFL. *Faculty research:* Feminist theory, gender and sexuality, global and cultural studies, women in history, literature, and politics, feminist politics.

Gender Studies

Simmons College, College of Arts and Sciences Graduate Studies, Program in Gender/Cultural Studies, Boston, MA 02115. Offers MA, MA/MAT, MA/MS. Part-time programs available. *Faculty:* 20 full-time (17 women), 1 part-time/adjunct (0 women). *Students:* 1 (woman) full-time, 26 part-time (all women); includes 7 minority (2 African Americans, 2 Asian Americans or Pacific Islanders, 3 Hispanic Americans). Average age 26. 43 applicants, 65% accepted, 15 enrolled. In 2008, 11 master's awarded. *Degree requirements:* For master's, project, thesis, internship, or fieldwork. *Entrance requirements:* For master's, academic writing sample. Additional exam requirements/recommendations for international students: Required—TOEFL (minimum score 600 paper-based; 250 computer-based; 100 iBT). *Application deadline:* For fall admission, 8/1 priority date for domestic and international students; for winter admission, 12/15 priority date for domestic and international students; for spring admission, 5/1 priority date for domestic and international students. Applications are processed on a rolling basis. Application fee: $35. Electronic applications accepted. *Financial support:* In 2008–09, 11 students received support, including 10 teaching assistantships (averaging $2,000 per year); research assistantships, scholarships/grants and unspecified assistantships also available. Financial award application deadline: 3/1; financial award applicants required to submit FAFSA. *Faculty research:* Obscenity, gender and media studies, gender and sexuality, race, postcolonialism. *Unit head:* Dr. Sarah Leonard, Director, 617-521-2254, Fax: 617-521-3090. *Application contact:* Kristen Haack, Director, Graduate Studies Admission, 617-521-2917, Fax: 617-521-3058, E-mail: gsa@simmons.edu.

University of Florida, Graduate School, College of Liberal Arts and Sciences, Center for Women's Studies and Gender Research, Gainesville, FL 32611. Offers gender and development (Graduate Certificate); women's studies (MA, MWS, Graduate Certificate); MA/JD; MA/MA.

The University of North Carolina at Greensboro, Graduate School, College of Arts and Sciences, Program in Women's and Gender Studies, Greensboro, NC 27412-5001. Offers MA, Certificate. Electronic applications accepted.

University of Northern British Columbia, Office of Graduate Studies, Prince George, BC V2N 4Z9, Canada. Offers business administration (Diploma); community health science (M Sc); disability management (MA); education (M Ed); first nations studies (MA); gender studies (MA); history (MA); interdisciplinary studies (MA); international studies (MA); mathematical, computer and physical sciences (M Sc); natural resources and environmental studies (M Sc, MA, MNRES, PhD); political science (MA); psychology (M Sc, PhD); social work (MSW). Part-time and evening/weekend programs available. Postbaccalaureate distance learning degree programs offered (no on-campus study). *Degree requirements:* For master's, thesis; for doctorate, thesis/dissertation. *Entrance requirements:* For master's, GRE, minimum B average in undergraduate course work; for doctorate, candidacy exam, minimum A average in graduate course work.

University of Northern Iowa, Graduate College, Program in Women's and Gender Studies, Cedar Falls, IA 50614. Offers MA. *Students:* 4 full-time (all women), 3 part-time (2 women); includes 1 minority (African American), 2 international. 7 applicants, 71% accepted, 2 enrolled. In 2008, 1 master's awarded. *Degree requirements:* For master's, comprehensive exam (for some programs), thesis or alternative. *Entrance requirements:* For master's, minimum GPA of 3.0. Additional exam requirements/recommendations for international students: Required—TOEFL (minimum score 500 paper-based; 180 computer-based; 61 iBT). *Application deadline:* Applications are processed on a rolling basis. Application fee: $30 ($50 for international students). Electronic applications accepted. *Expenses:* Tuition, state resident: full-time $6446. Tuition, nonresident: full-time $14,874. Required fees: $852. *Financial support:* Application deadline: 2/1. *Unit head:* Dr. Phyllis Baker, Head/Graduate Coordinator, 319-273-2109, Fax: 319-273-3053, E-mail: phyllis.baker@uni.edu. *Application contact:* Laurie S. Russell, Record Analyst, 319-273-2623, Fax: 319-273-6792, E-mail: laurie.russell@uni.edu.

University of Saskatchewan, College of Graduate Studies and Research, College of Arts and Sciences, Department of Women's and Gender Studies, Saskatoon, SK S7N 5A2, Canada. Offers MA, PhD. *Degree requirements:* For master's, thesis; for doctorate, thesis/dissertation. *Entrance requirements:* Additional exam requirements/recommendations for international students: Required—TOEFL.

Virginia Commonwealth University, Graduate School, College of Humanities and Sciences, Wilder School of Government and Public Affairs, Department of Sociology, Program in Gender Violence Intervention, Richmond, VA 23284-9005. Offers Certificate, MSW/Certificate.

Hispanic Studies

Brown University, Graduate School, Department of Hispanic Studies, Providence, RI 02912. Offers MA, PhD. *Degree requirements:* For master's, one foreign language, thesis; for doctorate, 2 foreign languages, thesis/dissertation, preliminary exam.

California State University, Los Angeles, Graduate Studies, College of Natural and Social Sciences, Department of Chicano Studies, Los Angeles, CA 90032-8530. Offers Mexican-American studies (MA). Part-time and evening/weekend programs available. *Faculty:* 3 full-time (2 women), 3 part-time/adjunct (1 woman). *Students:* 8 full-time (3 women), 15 part-time (11 women); includes 22 minority (2 African Americans, 20 Hispanic Americans), 1 international. Average age 32. 7 applicants, 100% accepted, 4 enrolled. In 2008, 2 master's awarded. *Degree requirements:* For master's, one foreign language, comprehensive exam or thesis. *Entrance requirements:* For master's, undergraduate major in Mexican-American studies or related area, 12 units in Chicano studies. Additional exam requirements/recommendations for international students: Required—TOEFL (minimum score 500 paper-based; 173 computer-based). *Application deadline:* For fall admission, 6/15 for domestic students, 5/1 for international students; for winter admission, 11/1 for domestic students, 9/1 for international students; for spring admission, 2/1 for domestic students, 10/1 for international students. Applications are processed on a rolling basis. Application fee: $55. Electronic applications accepted. *Expenses:* Tuition, nonresident: part-time $226 per credit. Required fees: $4019. *Financial support:* Career-related internships or fieldwork and Federal Work-Study available. Support available to part-time students. Financial award application deadline: 3/1. *Faculty research:* U.S.-Mexican relations, Chicano literature, community organization among Chicanos and Hispanics, Spanish language in the American Southwest. *Unit head:* Dr. Michael Soldatenko, Chair, 323-343-2400, Fax: 323-343-5609, E-mail: msoldat@calstatela.edu. *Application contact:* Dr. Jose L. Galvan, Dean of Graduate Studies, 323-343-3820, Fax: 323-343-5653, E-mail: jgalvan@cslanet.calstatela.edu.

California State University, Northridge, Graduate Studies, College of Humanities, Department of Chicana and Chicano Studies, Northridge, CA 91330. Offers MA. *Faculty:* 23 full-time (14 women), 38 part-time/adjunct (13 women). *Students:* 13 full-time (7 women), 27 part-time (15 women); includes 39 minority (all Hispanic Americans), 1 international. Average age 30. 29 applicants, 59% accepted, 16 enrolled. In 2008, 2 master's awarded. *Degree requirements:* For master's, thesis, project. *Entrance requirements:* Additional exam requirements/recommendations for international students: Required—TOEFL. *Application deadline:* For fall admission, 11/30 for domestic students. Application fee: $55. *Financial support:* Application deadline: 3/1. *Unit head:* Dr. David Rodriguez, Chair, 818-677-2734. *Application contact:* Dr. David Rodriguez, Chair, 818-677-2734.

Eastern Michigan University, Graduate School, College of Arts and Sciences, Department of Foreign Languages and Bilingual Studies, Program in Foreign Languages, Ypsilanti, MI 48197. Offers French (MA); German (MA); German for business (Graduate Certificate); Hispanic language and cultures (Graduate Certificate); Japanese business practices (Graduate Certificate); Spanish (MA). Part-time and evening/weekend programs available. Postbaccalaureate distance learning degree programs offered (minimal on-campus study). *Degree requirements:* For master's, one foreign language, thesis optional. *Entrance requirements:* Additional exam requirements/recommendations for international students: Required—TOEFL.

La Salle University, School of Arts and Sciences, Program in Bilingual/Bicultural Studies (Spanish), Philadelphia, PA 19141-1199. Offers MA. Part-time and evening/weekend programs available. *Degree requirements:* For master's, one foreign language, thesis or alternative, project. *Entrance requirements:* For master's, GRE or MAT. *Expenses:* Contact institution. *Faculty research:* Puerto Rican literature, cross-cultural communication, English as a second language methodology, Spanish language.

Louisiana State University and Agricultural and Mechanical College, Graduate School, College of Arts and Sciences, Department of Foreign Languages and Literatures, Baton Rouge, LA 70803. Offers Hispanic studies (MA). Part-time programs available. *Degree requirements:* For master's, 2 foreign languages, thesis optional. *Entrance requirements:* For master's, GRE General Test, minimum GPA of 3.0. Additional exam requirements/recommendations for international students: Required—TOEFL (minimum score 550 paper-based; 213 computer-based; 79 iBT). Electronic applications accepted. *Faculty research:* Hispanic cultural studies, linguistics, literary and cultural theory, peninsular and Latin American literature.

McGill University, Faculty of Graduate and Postdoctoral Studies, Faculty of Arts, Department of Hispanic Studies, Montréal, QC H3A 2T5, Canada. Offers MA, PhD.

Michigan State University, The Graduate School, College of Arts and Letters, Department of Spanish and Portuguese, East Lansing, MI 48824. Offers applied Spanish linguistics (MA); Hispanic cultural studies (PhD); Hispanic literatures (MA). *Entrance requirements:* Additional exam requirements/recommendations for international students: Required—TOEFL. Electronic applications accepted.

Pontifical Catholic University of Puerto Rico, College of Arts and Humanities, Department of Hispanic Studies, Ponce, PR 00717-0777. Offers grammar and writing (Professional Certificate); Hispanic studies (MA). Part-time and evening/weekend programs available. *Degree requirements:* For master's, variable foreign language requirement, comprehensive exam, thesis or alternative. *Entrance requirements:* For master's, GRE General Test, 2 letters of recommendation, interview, minimum GPA of 2.75. Electronic applications accepted.

Queen's University at Kingston, School of Graduate Studies and Research, Faculty of Arts and Sciences, Department of Spanish and Italian, Kingston, ON K7L 3N6, Canada. Offers Spanish language and literature (MA). Part-time programs available. *Degree requirements:* For master's, one foreign language, thesis. *Entrance requirements:* Additional exam requirements/recommendations for international students: Required—TOEFL. Electronic applications accepted. *Faculty research:* Golden Age, nineteenth- and twentieth-century Peninsular novel, literary theory, colonial Latin America, nineteenth-and-twentieth century Latin America.

St. Thomas University, School of Leadership Studies, Program in Hispanic Media, Miami Gardens, FL 33054-6459. Offers MA, Certificate. Part-time and evening/weekend programs available. *Degree requirements:* For master's, comprehensive exam. *Entrance requirements:* Additional exam requirements/recommendations for international students: Required—TOEFL (minimum score 550 paper-based; 213 computer-based; 79 iBT). Electronic applications accepted.

San Jose State University, Graduate Studies and Research, College of Social Sciences, Department of Mexican-American Studies, San Jose, CA 95192-0001. Offers MA. Electronic applications accepted.

Stony Brook University, State University of New York, Graduate School, College of Arts and Sciences, Department of Hispanic Languages and Literature, Stony Brook, NY 11794. Offers MA, PhD. Evening/weekend programs available. *Faculty:* 12 full-time (6 women). *Students:* 39 full-time (26 women), 15 part-time (11 women); includes 23 minority (1 African American, 22 Hispanic Americans), 16 international. Average age 33. 30 applicants, 53% accepted. In 2008, 6 master's, 4 doctorates awarded. *Degree requirements:* For master's, one foreign language, thesis or alternative; for doctorate, 2 foreign languages, thesis/dissertation. *Entrance requirements:* For master's, GRE General Test, BA in Spanish; for doctorate, GRE General Test, MA in Spanish. Additional exam requirements/recommendations for international students: Required—TOEFL. *Application deadline:* For fall admission, 1/15 for domestic students. Application fee: $60. *Expenses:* Contact institution. *Financial support:* In 2008–09, 22 teaching assistantships were awarded; fellowships, research assistantships, tuition waivers and unspecified assistantships also available. *Faculty research:* Spanish language and literature. *Unit head:* Dr. Victoriano Roncero-Lopez, Chair, 631-632-9669, E-mail: roncero@oponline.net. *Application contact:* Dr. Kathleen Vernon, Director of Graduate Studies, 631-632-9668, Fax: 631-632-9724, E-mail: kvernon@notes.cc.sunysb.edu.

Texas A&M International University, Office of Graduate Studies and Research, College of Arts and Sciences, Department of Language and Literature, Laredo, TX 78041-1900. Offers English (MA); Hispanic studies (PhD); Spanish (MA). *Entrance requirements:* For master's, GRE General Test. Additional exam requirements/recommendations for international students: Required—TOEFL (minimum score 550 paper-based; 213 computer-based).

Université de Montréal, Faculty of Arts and Sciences, Department of Literatures and Modern Languages, Montréal, QC H3C 3J7, Canada. Offers German literature (PhD); German studies (MA); Hispanic literature (PhD); Hispanic studies (MA); literature and cinema (PhD). *Faculty:* 14 full-time (6 women), 1 (woman) part-time/adjunct. *Students:* 22 full-time (15 women), 23 part-time (16 women). 42 applicants, 45% accepted, 15 enrolled. In 2008, 13 master's awarded. Terminal master's awarded for partial completion of doctoral program. *Degree requirements:* For master's, 2 foreign languages, thesis; for doctorate, 2 foreign languages, thesis/dissertation, general exam. *Application deadline:* For fall admission, 2/1 priority date for domestic students; for winter admission, 11/1 priority date for domestic students; for spring admission, 2/1 priority date for domestic students. Application fee: $100. Electronic applications accepted. *Financial support:* Teaching assistantships available. *Unit head:* Georges Bastin, Director, 514-343-7050, Fax: 514-343-2255, E-mail: georges.bastin@umontreal.ca. *Application contact:* Nikola von Merveldt, Responsible for German Studies Program, 514-343-5905, Fax: 514-343-2255, E-mail: n.von.merveldt@umontreal.ca.

University of Alberta, Faculty of Graduate Studies and Research, Department of Modern Languages and Cultural Studies, Edmonton, AB T6G 2E1, Canada. Offers applied linguistics (Germanic, Romance, Slavic) (MA); French language, literatures and linguistics (PhD); French language, literatures, and linguistics (MA); Germanic languages, literatures and linguistics (PhD); Germanic languages, literatures, and linguistics (MA); Italian studies (MA); Slavic languages and literatures (Russian, Ukrainian) (MA, PhD); Slavic linguistics (Russian, Ukrainian) (MA, PhD); Spanish and Latin American studies (MA, PhD); Ukrainian folklore (MA, PhD). Part-time programs available. *Degree requirements:* For master's, one foreign language, thesis; for doctorate, 2 foreign languages, comprehensive exam, thesis/dissertation. *Entrance requirements:* For master's and doctorate, 1 language other than English. Additional exam requirements/recommendations for international students: Required—Michigan English Language Assessment Battery or TOEFL (paper score 550; computer score 213). Electronic applications accepted. *Faculty research:* Russian/Ukrainian studies; German studies; contemporary Latin American, French and Francophone studies; Italian studies.

The University of British Columbia, Faculty of Arts and Faculty of Graduate Studies, Department of French, Hispanic and Italian Studies, Vancouver, BC V6T 1Z1, Canada. Offers French (MA, PhD); Hispanic studies (MA, PhD). Part-time programs available. *Degree requirements:* For master's, thesis optional; for doctorate, 2 foreign languages, comprehensive exam, thesis/dissertation. *Entrance requirements:* For master's, BA degree; for doctorate, MA degree. Additional exam requirements/recommendations for international students: Required—TOEFL (minimum score 550 paper-based; 213 computer-based; 80 iBT). Electronic applications accepted. *Faculty research:* Medieval and Renaissance literature, modern literature, romance philology and linguistics, cultural studies, women's literature.

University of California, Berkeley, Graduate Division, College of Letters and Science, Department of Hispanic Languages and Literature, Berkeley, CA 94720-1500. Offers PhD. *Degree requirements:* For doctorate, thesis/dissertation, qualifying exam. *Entrance requirements:* For doctorate, GRE General Test, minimum GPA of 3.0, 3 letters of recommendation. Additional exam requirements/recommendations for international students: Required—TOEFL (minimum score 570 paper-based; 230 computer-based).

University of California, Los Angeles, Graduate Division, College of Letters and Science, Department of Spanish and Portuguese, Program in Hispanic Languages and Literature, Los Angeles, CA 90095. Offers PhD. *Students:* 47 full-time (36 women); includes 21 minority (1 Asian American or Pacific Islander, 20 Hispanic Americans), 7 international. Average age 32. 30 applicants, 30% accepted, 8 enrolled. In 2008, 7 doctorates awarded. *Degree requirements:* For doctorate, 2 foreign languages, thesis/dissertation, oral and written exams. *Entrance requirements:* For doctorate, GRE General Test, minimum undergraduate GPA of 3.0, sample of written work (recommended), Master's degree. *Application deadline:* For fall admission, 12/31 for domestic and international students. Application fee: $60 ($80 for international students). Electronic applications accepted. *Expenses:* Tuition, nonresident: full-time $14,694. Required fees: $9669.50. Full-time tuition and fees vary according to course load, degree level, program and student level. *Financial support:* In 2008–09, 52 fellowships with full and partial tuition reimbursements, 12 research assistantships with full and partial tuition reimbursements, 42 teaching assistantships with full and partial tuition reimbursements were awarded; Federal Work-Study, institutionally sponsored loans, health care benefits, tuition waivers (full and partial), and unspecified assistantships also available. Financial award applicants required to submit FAFSA. *Unit head:* Dr. Ruiz Teofilo, Chair, 310-825-3194. *Application contact:* Departmental Office, 310-825-1036, E-mail: peinado@humnet.ucla.edu.

University of California, Riverside, Graduate Division, Department of Hispanic Studies, Riverside, CA 92521-0102. Offers Spanish (MA, PhD). *Faculty:* 8 full-time (3 women). *Students:* 23 full-time (14 women); includes 18 minority (all Hispanic Americans), 2 international. Average age 34. 14 applicants, 21% accepted, 3 enrolled. In 2008, 6 master's, 1 doctorate awarded. Terminal master's awarded for partial completion of doctoral program. *Degree requirements:* For master's, one foreign language, comprehensive exam; for doctorate, one foreign language, thesis/dissertation, qualifying exams, 1 quarter of teaching experience. *Entrance requirements:* For master's and doctorate, GRE General Test, minimum GPA of 3.2. Additional exam requirements/recommendations for international students: Required—TOEFL (minimum score 550 paper-based; 213 computer-based; 80 iBT). *Application deadline:* For fall admission, 1/5 for domestic students, 2/1 for international students; for winter admission, 9/1 for domestic students, 7/1 for international students; for spring admission, 12/1 for domestic students, 10/1 for international students. Applications are processed on a rolling basis. Application fee: $60 ($75 for international students). Electronic applications accepted. *Expenses:* Tuition, nonresident: full-time $4898. Required fees: $10,362. *Financial support:* In 2008–09, fellowships with tuition reimbursements (averaging $12,000 per year), teaching assistantships with tuition reimbursements (averaging $16,500 per year) were awarded; career-related internships or fieldwork, Federal Work-Study, institutionally sponsored loans, scholarships/grants, health care benefits, and tuition waivers (full and partial) also available. Financial award application deadline: 1/5; financial award applicants required to submit FAFSA. *Faculty research:* Spanish literature of sixteenth, seventeenth and twentieth century; pre-Columbian and colonial Latin American literature; nineteenth and twentieth century Latin American literature. *Unit head:* Dr. David E. Hevzberger, Chair, 951-827-5007 Ext. 11462, Fax: 951-827-2160, E-mail: david.herzberger@ucr.edu. *Application contact:* Dr. Benjamin Liu, Graduate Advisor, 951-827-1569, Fax: 951-827-2294, E-mail: clhsgrad@ucr.edu.

University of California, Santa Barbara, Graduate Division, College of Letters and Sciences, Division of Humanities and Fine Arts, Department of Spanish and Portuguese, Santa Barbara, CA 93106-4150. Offers Hispanic languages and literature (PhD), including applied linguistics, European Medieval studies, feminist studies, Hispanic languages and literature; Portuguese (MA); Spanish (MA); Spanish and Portuguese (MA); MA/PhD. Spanish Language Institute available during summer session. *Faculty:* 16 full-time (6 women). *Students:* 29 full-time (16 women). Average age 30. 46 applicants, 39% accepted, 9 enrolled. In 2008, 4 master's, 2 doctorates awarded. *Degree requirements:* For master's, 2 foreign languages, comprehensive exam (for some programs), thesis optional; for doctorate, 2 foreign languages, comprehensive exam, thesis/dissertation. *Entrance requirements:* For master's, GRE, 2 writing samples, undergraduate major in Spanish or equivalent, 3 letters of recommendation, statement of purpose, personal achievements/contributions statement, resumé/curriculum vitae, transcripts for post-secondary institutions attended; for doctorate, GRE, 2 writing samples, master's degree, 3 letters of recommendation, statement of purpose, personal achievements/contributions statement, resumé/curriculum vitae, transcripts for post-secondary institutions attended. Additional exam requirements/recommendations for international students: Required—TOEFL (minimum score 550 paper-based; 213 computer-based; 80 iBT), IELTS (minimum score 7), TOEFL or IELTS. *Application deadline:* For fall admission, 3/1 for domestic and international students; for winter admission, 11/1 for domestic and international students; for spring admission, 2/1 for domestic and international students. Application fee: $70 ($90 for international students). Electronic applications accepted. *Expenses:* Tuition, nonresident: full-time $25,149. Required fees: $10,143. Full-time tuition and fees vary according to campus/location, reciprocity agreements and student level. *Financial support:* In 2008–09, 30 students received support, including 9 fellowships with full and partial tuition reimbursements available (averaging $7,000 per year), 29 teaching assistantships with partial tuition reimbursements available (averaging $11,500 per year); career-related internships or fieldwork, Federal Work-Study, institutionally sponsored loans, scholarships/grants, health care benefits, tuition waivers (full and partial), and unspecified assistantships also available. Financial award application deadline: 1/7; financial award applicants required to submit FAFSA. *Faculty research:* 19th century Spanish and Portuguese literature, Spanish and Spanish American literature, 19th and 20th century Portuguese and Brazilian literatures, Hispanic Linguistics, Catalan language and culture. *Unit head:* Prof. Francisco A. Lomeli, Chair, 805-893-5715, Fax: 805-893-8341, E-mail: lomeli@spanport.ucsb.edu. *Application contact:* Carol Conley, Graduate Program Assistant, 805-893-3162, Fax: 805-893-8341, E-mail: cconley@spanport.ucsb.edu.

University of California, Santa Barbara, Graduate Division, College of Letters and Sciences, Division of Social Sciences, Department of Chicana and Chicano Studies, Santa Barbara, CA 93106-4120. Offers PhD, MA/PhD. *Faculty:* 9 full-time (5 women), 1 part-time/adjunct (0 women). *Students:* 20 full-time (10 women). Average age 30. 19 applicants, 32% accepted, 3 enrolled. *Degree requirements:* For doctorate, one foreign language, comprehensive exam, thesis/dissertation. *Entrance requirements:* For doctorate, GRE, writing sample, 3 letters of recommendation, statement of purpose, personal achievements/contributions statement, resumé/curriculum vitae, transcripts for post-secondary institutions attended. Additional exam requirements/recommendations for international students: Required—TOEFL (paper: 550, computer: 213, IBT: 80) or IELTS. *Application deadline:* For fall admission, 12/15 for domestic and international students. Application fee: $70 ($90 for international students). Electronic applications accepted. *Expenses:* Tuition, nonresident: full-time $25,149. Required fees: $10,143. Full-time tuition and fees vary according to campus/location, reciprocity agreements and student level. *Financial support:* In 2008–09, 19 students received support, including 12 fellowships with full and partial tuition reimbursements available (averaging $9,150 per year), 17 teaching assistantships with partial tuition reimbursements available (averaging $9,700 per year); career-related internships or fieldwork, Federal Work-Study, institutionally sponsored loans, scholarships/grants, health care benefits, tuition waivers (full and partial), and unspecified assistantships also available. Financial award application deadline: 12/15; financial award applicants required to submit FAFSA. *Faculty research:* Global, postcolonial and border studies; literature, culture and representation; political history and community; critical and cultural theory; gender and sexuality studies. *Unit head:* Dr. Juan Vincente Palerm, Chair, 805-893-3601, Fax: 805-893-4076, E-mail: palerm@anth.ucsb.edu. *Application contact:* Katherine G. Morales, Staff Graduate Advisor, 805-893-5269, Fax: 805-893-4076, E-mail: kmorales@chicst.ucsb.edu.

University of Illinois at Chicago, Graduate College, College of Liberal Arts and Sciences, Department of Spanish, French, Italian and Portuguese, Program in Hispanic Studies, Chicago, IL 60607-7128. Offers Hispanic linguistics (MA, PhD); Hispanic literary and cultural studies (MA, PhD). Part-time programs available. Terminal master's awarded for partial completion of doctoral program. *Degree requirements:* For master's, one foreign language, departmental qualifying exam. *Entrance requirements:* For master's, GRE General Test, minimum GPA of 2.75, undergraduate major in Spanish. Additional exam requirements/recommendations for international students: Required—TOEFL. Electronic applications accepted.

University of Kentucky, Graduate School, College of Arts and Sciences, Program in Hispanic Studies, Lexington, KY 40506-0032. Offers MA, PhD. *Degree requirements:* For master's, one foreign language, comprehensive exam, thesis optional; for doctorate, 2 foreign languages, comprehensive exam, thesis/dissertation. *Entrance requirements:* For master's, GRE General Test, minimum undergraduate GPA of 2.75; for doctorate, GRE General Test, minimum graduate GPA of 3.0. Additional exam requirements/recommendations for international students: Required—TOEFL (minimum score 550 paper-based; 213 computer-based). Electronic applications accepted. *Faculty research:* Hispanic linguistics, medieval Spanish literature and civilization, Renaissance and Golden Age literature and civilization, Spanish American literature and civilization.

University of Nevada, Las Vegas, Graduate College, College of Liberal Arts, Department of Foreign Languages, Las Vegas, NV 89154-5047. Offers Hispanic studies (MA); Spanish translation (Certificate). Part-time programs available. *Faculty:* 5 full-time (4 women). *Students:* 2 full-time (both women), 10 part-time (6 women); includes 7 minority (1 Asian American or Pacific Islander, 6 Hispanic Americans). Average age 40. 12 applicants, 50% accepted, 4 enrolled. In 2008, 3 master's, 1 other advanced degree awarded. *Degree requirements:* For master's and Certificate, one foreign language, comprehensive exam. *Entrance requirements:* Additional exam requirements/recommendations for international students: Required—TOEFL (minimum score 550 paper-based; 213 computer-based; 80 iBT), IELTS (minimum score 7). *Application deadline:* For fall admission, 8/1 priority date for domestic students, 5/1 for international students; for spring admission, 12/1 priority date for domestic students, 10/1 for international students. Applications are processed on a rolling basis. Application fee: $60 ($75 for international students). Electronic applications accepted. *Expenses:* Tuition, state resident: full-time $1414; part-time $198 per credit. Tuition, nonresident: full-time $12,509; part-time $415.75 per credit. International tuition: $14,249 full-time. Required fees: $4 per credit. $252 per semester. Tuition and fees vary according to course load. *Financial support:* In 2008–09, 2 students received support, including 2 teaching assistantships with partial tuition reimbursements available (averaging $10,000 per year); institutionally sponsored loans, scholarships/grants, health care benefits, and unspecified assistantships also available. Financial award application deadline: 3/1. *Faculty research:* Second language acquisition/Romance languages, Old French, sociolinguistics/Romance languages, Spanish poetry of the 20's and 30's, post-Spanish Civil War women's fiction. *Unit head:* Dr. Ralph Buechler, Chair/Associate Professor, 702-895-3546, Fax: 702-895-3431, E-mail: ralph.buechler@unlv.edu. *Application contact:* Graduate College Admissions Evaluator, 702-895-3320, Fax: 702-895-4180, E-mail: gradcollege@unlv.edu.

The University of North Carolina at Greensboro, Graduate School, College of Arts and Sciences, Department of Romance Languages, Program in Spanish, Greensboro, NC 27412-5001. Offers advanced Spanish language and Hispanic cultural studies (Certificate); Spanish (MA). *Degree requirements:* For master's, one foreign language, comprehensive exam, thesis or alternative. *Entrance requirements:* For master's, GRE General Test, 3-5 minute tape demonstrating foreign language proficiency, composition in Spanish, sample paper in English. Additional exam requirements/recommendations for international students: Required—TOEFL. Electronic applications accepted.

The University of North Carolina Wilmington, College of Arts and Sciences, Department of Foreign Languages and Literature, Wilmington, NC 28403-3297. Offers Hispanic studies (Graduate Certificate). Part-time programs available. Postbaccalaureate distance learning degree programs offered. *Faculty:* 17 full-time (10 women). *Students:* 7 part-time (6 women); includes 6 minority (all Hispanic Americans), 3 international. Average age 41. 13 applicants, 62% accepted, 5 enrolled. *Degree requirements:* For master's, one foreign language, comprehensive exam, thesis or alternative. *Entrance requirements:* For master's, GRE. Additional exam requirements/recommendations for international students: Required—TOEFL (minimum score 550 paper-based; 217 computer-based; 79 iBT), IELTS (minimum score 6.5). Application fee: $60. *Expenses:* Tuition, area resident: Full-time $4838. Tuition, state resident: full-time $4838. Tuition, nonresident: full-time $14,898. Required fees: $969.38 per semester. Tuition and fees vary according to course load, campus/location and program. *Financial support:* In 2008–09, 4 teaching assistantships with full and partial tuition reimbursements (averaging $9,500 per year) were awarded. *Unit head:* Dr. Raymond Burt, Chair, 910-962-4095, E-mail: burtr@uncw.edu. *Application contact:* Dr. R. Terry Mount, Graduate Coordinator, 910-962-3344, E-mail: mountt@uncw.edu.

University of Pittsburgh, School of Arts and Sciences, Department of Hispanic Languages and Literatures, Pittsburgh, PA 15260. Offers MA, PhD. Part-time programs available. Terminal master's awarded for partial completion of doctoral program. *Degree requirements:* For master's, one foreign language, comprehensive exam (for some programs), thesis or alternative, research paper; for doctorate, 2 foreign languages, comprehensive exam, thesis/dissertation. *Entrance requirements:* Additional exam requirements/recommendations for international students: Required—TOEFL (minimum score 550 paper-based; 213 computer-based; 80 iBT). Electronic applications accepted. *Faculty research:* Latin American, Luso-Brazilian, and peninsular literature; cultural theory; cultural studies; race, ethnicity, and post-colonial studies.

University of Puerto Rico, Mayagüez Campus, Graduate Studies, College of Arts and Sciences, Department of Hispanic Studies, Mayagüez, PR 00681-9000. Offers MA. Part-time programs available. *Degree requirements:* For master's, comprehensive exam, thesis. *Entrance requirements:* For master's, minimum GPA of 2.75, BA degree in Hispanic studies or its equivalent. *Faculty research:* Spanish literature, Hispanic-American literature, Puerto Rican literature, stylistics, linguistics.

University of Puerto Rico, Río Piedras, College of Humanities, Department of Hispanic Studies, San Juan, PR 00931-3300. Offers MA, PhD. Part-time programs available. *Degree requirements:* For master's, one foreign language, comprehensive exam, thesis; for doctorate, one foreign language, comprehensive exam, thesis/dissertation. *Entrance requirements:* For master's, PAEG or GRE, interview, minimum GPA of 3.0, letter of recommendation (2); for

Hispanic Studies

University of Puerto Rico, Río Piedras (continued)
doctorate, PAEG or GRE, interview, master's degree, minimum GPA of 3.0, letter of recommendation (2). *Faculty research:* Poetry of Luis Palés Matos, short stories in Puerto Rico, language in the social process, 'Decima Popular", Anglicism.

The University of Texas at Austin, Graduate School, College of Liberal Arts, Center for Mexican American Studies, Austin, TX 78712-1111. Offers MA.

University of Victoria, Faculty of Graduate Studies, Faculty of Humanities, Department of Hispanic and Italian Studies, Victoria, BC V8W 2Y2, Canada. Offers Hispanic and Italian studies (MA); Hispanic studies (MA). *Degree requirements:* For master's, one foreign language, comprehensive exam, thesis (for some programs). *Entrance requirements:* For master's, undergraduate major in Hispanic studies, minimum B+ average. Additional exam requirements/recommendations for international students: Required—TOEFL (minimum score 575 paper-based; 233 computer-based), IELTS (minimum score 7). Electronic applications accepted. *Faculty research:* Medieval/Renaissance Spanish and Italian literature, Golden Age literature, Latin American literature.

University of Washington, Graduate School, College of Arts and Sciences, Department of Romance Languages and Literature, Division of Spanish and Portuguese Studies, Seattle, WA 98195. Offers Hispanic literary and cultural studies (MA). *Degree requirements:* For master's, 2 foreign languages, thesis optional, exam. *Entrance requirements:* For master's, GRE General Test, minimum GPA of 3.0. Additional exam requirements/recommendations for international students: Required—TOEFL. Electronic applications accepted. *Faculty research:* Medieval through modern Spanish literature and film, Latin American literature, poetry and essay, pan-Hispanic ballad, Hispanic cultural studies, second language acquisition and applied linguistics.

Villanova University, Graduate School of Liberal Arts and Sciences, Department of Modern Languages and Literature, Villanova, PA 19085-1699. Offers Hispanic studies (MA). Part-time and evening/weekend programs available. *Faculty:* 3 full-time (1 woman). *Students:* 3 full-time (1 woman), 18 part-time (13 women); includes 12 minority (1 Asian American or Pacific Islander, 11 Hispanic Americans), 6 international. Average age 37. 9 applicants, 100% accepted, 6 enrolled. In 2008, 4 master's awarded. *Degree requirements:* For master's, one foreign language, comprehensive exam. *Entrance requirements:* For master's, minimum GPA of 3.0, writing sample in Spanish. Additional exam requirements/recommendations for international students: Required—TOEFL. *Application deadline:* For fall admission, 8/1 for domestic and international students; for spring admission, 12/1 for domestic and international students. Applications are processed on a rolling basis. Application fee: $50. Electronic applications accepted. *Financial support:* Teaching assistantships with tuition reimbursements, Federal Work-Study and scholarships/grants available. Financial award applicants required to submit FAFSA. *Unit head:* Silvia Nagy-Zekmi, Chair, 610-519-7478. *Application contact:* Dr. Gerald Long, Dean, Graduate School of Liberal Arts and Sciences, 610-519-7093, Fax: 610-519-7096.

Holocaust Studies

Clark University, Graduate School, Department of History, Program in Holocaust History, Worcester, MA 01610-1477. Offers PhD. *Students:* 8 full-time (5 women), 2 international. Average age 31. 27 applicants, 15% accepted, 3 enrolled. *Degree requirements:* For doctorate, thesis/dissertation. *Entrance requirements:* Additional exam requirements/recommendations for international students: Required—TOEFL. *Application deadline:* For fall admission, 1/15 for domestic students. Application fee: $50. *Expenses:* Tuition: Full-time $34,900; part-time $1091 per credit hour. Required fees: $30. *Financial support:* In 2008–09, fellowships with full and partial tuition reimbursements (averaging $11,850 per year), research assistantships with full and partial tuition reimbursements (averaging $11,850 per year), teaching assistantships with full and partial tuition reimbursements (averaging $11,850 per year) were awarded; tuition waivers (partial) also available. *Faculty research:* Jewish persecution, children and survivors, Germany's role in the holocaust. *Unit head:* Deborah Dwork, Professor, 508-421-3745. *Application contact:* Tatyana Macaulay, Program Officer, 508-793-7764, Fax: 508-793-8827, E-mail: chgs@clarku.edu.

Drew University, Caspersen School of Graduate Studies, Program in Arts and Letters, Madison, NJ 07940-1493. Offers holocaust and genocide studies (Certificate); interdisciplinary studies (M Litt, D Litt). Part-time and evening/weekend programs available. Terminal master's awarded for partial completion of doctoral program. *Degree requirements:* For master's, thesis optional; for doctorate, thesis/dissertation. *Expenses:* Contact institution. *Faculty research:* Interdisciplinary studies across art, literature, music, philosophy, religion, and history.

Gratz College, Graduate Programs, Program in Jewish Studies, Melrose Park, PA 19027. Offers classical studies (MA); Holocaust studies (Certificate); Jewish studies (MA, Certificate); modern studies (MA). Part-time programs available. Postbaccalaureate distance learning degree programs offered. *Degree requirements:* For master's, one foreign language, comprehensive exam, thesis optional.

Kean University, Nathan Weiss Graduate College, Program in Holocaust and Genocide Studies, Union, NJ 07083. Offers MA. Part-time and evening/weekend programs available. *Students:* 4 full-time (0 women), 14 part-time (10 women); includes 1 Hispanic American. Average age 36. 6 applicants, 100% accepted, 3 enrolled. In 2008, 1 master's awarded. *Degree requirements:* For master's, comprehensive exam, thesis. *Entrance requirements:* For master's, GRE General Test or MAT, minimum GPA of 3.0 or experience, 3 letters of recommendation, interview. *Application deadline:* For fall admission, 5/1 for domestic students; for spring admission, 11/1 for domestic students. Application fee: $60 ($150 for international students). Electronic applications accepted. *Expenses:* Tuition, state resident: full-time $10,128; part-time $422 per credit. Tuition, nonresident: full-time $13,728; part-time $572 per credit. Required fees: $2570; $107 per credit. Part-time tuition and fees vary according to course load, degree level and program. *Financial support:* In 2008–09, 1 research assistantship with full tuition reimbursement (averaging $3,217 per year) was awarded; unspecified assistantships also available. *Unit head:* Dr. Keith Nunes, Program Coordinator, 908-737-5987, E-mail: knunes@kean.edu. *Application contact:* Steven Koch, Pre-Admissions Coordinator, 908-737-4723, Fax: 908-737-5965, E-mail: grad-adm@kean.edu.

Laura and Alvin Siegal College of Judaic Studies, Graduate Programs, Beachwood, OH 44122-7116. Offers humanities (MA), including Holocaust studies; religious education (MAJS), including Jewish education, Judaic studies. Part-time and evening/weekend programs available. Postbaccalaureate distance learning degree programs offered (no on-campus study). *Degree requirements:* For master's, one foreign language, thesis. *Entrance requirements:* For master's, interview.

The Richard Stockton College of New Jersey, School of Graduate and Continuing Education, Program in Holocaust and Genocide Studies, Pomona, NJ 08240-0195. Offers MA. Part-time programs available. *Faculty:* 2 part-time/adjunct (1 woman). *Students:* 5 full-time (all women), 13 part-time (9 women); includes 4 minority (3 African Americans, 1 Asian American or Pacific Islander). Average age 32. 15 applicants, 93% accepted, 8 enrolled. In 2008, 11 master's awarded. *Degree requirements:* For master's, thesis optional. *Entrance requirements:* Additional exam requirements/recommendations for international students: Required—TOEFL. *Application deadline:* For fall admission, 8/1 for domestic and international students; for spring admission, 1/5 for domestic and international students. Applications are processed on a rolling basis. Application fee: $50. *Expenses:* Tuition, area resident: Full-time $8526; part-time $474 per credit. Tuition, state resident: full-time $8526; part-time $474 per credit. Tuition, nonresident: full-time $13,125; part-time $729 per course. Required fees: $2030; $113 per credit. *Financial support:* In 2008–09, 12 students received support, including 3 fellowships with partial tuition reimbursements available, 9 research assistantships with full tuition reimbursements available; career-related internships or fieldwork and unspecified assistantships also available. Financial award application deadline: 3/1; financial award applicants required to submit FAFSA. *Faculty research:* Women and the Holocaust, survivor perspectives, liberty and persecution. *Unit head:* Dr. Michael Hayse, Interim Director, 609-626-3404, Fax: 609-748-5541, E-mail: mahg@stockton.edu. *Application contact:* Alison Henry, Associate Director of Admissions, 609-652-4261, Fax: 609-626-5541, E-mail: admissions@stockton.edu.

Seton Hall University, College of Arts and Sciences, Department of Jewish-Christian Studies, South Orange, NJ 07079-2697. Offers MA. Part-time and evening/weekend programs available. *Degree requirements:* For master's, one foreign language, thesis or alternative. Electronic applications accepted. *Faculty research:* Jewish-Christian issues, biblical studies, Holocaust studies.

See Close-Up on page 533.

Seton Hill University, Program in Genocide and Holocaust Studies, Greensburg, PA 15601. Offers Certificate.

West Chester University of Pennsylvania, Office of Graduate Studies, College of Arts and Sciences, Department of History, West Chester, PA 19383. Offers history (M Ed, MA); holocaust and genocide studies (MA, Certificate); social studies/history (Teaching Certificate). Part-time and evening/weekend programs available. *Students:* 20 full-time (8 women), 34 part-time (16 women); includes 1 minority (African American). Average age 30. 38 applicants, 95% accepted, 21 enrolled. In 2008, 12 master's awarded. *Degree requirements:* For master's, thesis optional. *Entrance requirements:* For master's and other advanced degree, GMAT, GRE General Test, or MAT, statement of professional goals, writing sample, minimum GPA of 3.0 in history, three letters of recommendation. Additional exam requirements/recommendations for international students: Required—TOEFL (minimum score 550 paper-based; 213 computer-based; 80 iBT). *Application deadline:* For fall admission, 4/15 priority date for domestic students, 3/15 for international students; for spring admission, 10/15 for domestic students, 9/1 for international students. Applications are processed on a rolling basis. Application fee: $35. Electronic applications accepted. *Expenses:* Tuition, state resident: full-time $6430; part-time $357 per credit. Tuition, nonresident: full-time $10,288; part-time $572 per credit. Required fees: $652.50; $50 per credit. $67 per semester. *Financial support:* In 2008–09, 2 research assistantships with full and partial tuition reimbursements (averaging $5,000 per year) were awarded; unspecified assistantships also available. Support available to part-time students. Financial award application deadline: 2/15; financial award applicants required to submit FAFSA. *Faculty research:* Oral histories, siege of Leningrad. *Unit head:* Dr. Wayne Hanley, Chair, 610-436-2201, E-mail: whanley@wcupa.edu. *Application contact:* Dr. Jonathan Friedman, Director of the Holocaust/Genocide Education Center and Graduate Coordinator of Holocaust and Genocide Studies, 610-436-2972, E-mail: jfriedmans@wcupa.edu.

Jewish Studies

American Jewish University, Graduate School, Bel Air, CA 90077-1599. Offers MA Ed, MAJCS, MARS, MBA. Part-time and evening/weekend programs available. *Entrance requirements:* For master's, interview, minimum undergraduate GPA of 3.0. Additional exam requirements/recommendations for international students: Required—TOEFL.

American Jewish University, Graduate School, David Lieber School of Graduate Studies, Program in Jewish Communal Studies, Bel Air, CA 90077-1599. Offers MAJCS. *Degree requirements:* For master's, thesis. *Entrance requirements:* For master's, GMAT or GRE General Test, interview.

Baltimore Hebrew University, Peggy Meyerhoff Pearlstone School of Graduate Studies, Program in Jewish Communal Service, Baltimore, MD 21215-3996. Offers MAJCS. Part-time programs available. *Degree requirements:* For master's, one foreign language, thesis or alternative. *Entrance requirements:* Additional exam requirements/recommendations for international students: Required—TOEFL (minimum score 213 computer-based).

Baltimore Hebrew University, Peggy Meyerhoff Pearlstone School of Graduate Studies, Program in Jewish Education, Baltimore, MD 21215-3996. Offers MAJE. Part-time programs available. *Degree requirements:* For master's, one foreign language, thesis or alternative. *Entrance requirements:* For master's, minimum GPA of 3.0. Additional exam requirements/recommendations for international students: Required—TOEFL (minimum score 213 computer-based).

Baltimore Hebrew University, Peggy Meyerhoff Pearlstone School of Graduate Studies, Program in Jewish Studies, Baltimore, MD 21215-3996. Offers MAJS, PhD. Part-time programs available. Terminal master's awarded for partial completion of doctoral program. *Degree requirements:* For master's, one foreign language, comprehensive exam (for some programs), thesis or alternative; for doctorate, 3 foreign languages, comprehensive exam, thesis/dissertation. *Entrance requirements:* For master's, minimum GPA of 3.0; for doctorate, GRE General Test, minimum GPA of 3.5, master's thesis or equivalent. Additional exam requirements/recommendations for international students: Required—TOEFL.

Brandeis University, Graduate School of Arts and Sciences, Department of Near Eastern and Judaic Studies, Waltham, MA 02454-9110. Offers Near Eastern and Judaic studies (MA, PhD);

Near Eastern and Judaic studies and sociology (PhD); Near Eastern and Judaic studies and women's studies (MA); teaching of Hebrew (MAT). Part-time programs available. Terminal master's awarded for partial completion of doctoral program. *Degree requirements:* For master's, one foreign language, comprehensive exam, thesis or alternative; for doctorate, 3 foreign languages, comprehensive exam, thesis/dissertation. *Entrance requirements:* For master's and doctorate, GRE General Test (recommended), letters of recommendation, transcripts, statement of purpose. Additional exam requirements/recommendations for international students: Required—TOEFL (minimum score 600 paper-based; 250 computer-based; 100 iBT), IELTS (minimum score 7). Electronic applications accepted. *Faculty research:* Ancient Near East and Bible, philosophy, history, modern Middle East, Islamic studies.

Brandeis University, Graduate School of Arts and Sciences, Hornstein: The Jewish Professional Leadership Program, Waltham, MA 02454-9110. Offers MA/MA, MBA/MA, MPP/MA. Part-time programs available. *Entrance requirements:* Additional exam requirements/ recommendations for international students: Required—TOEFL (minimum score 600 paper-based; 250 computer-based; 100 iBT), IELTS (minimum score 7). Electronic applications accepted. *Faculty research:* Leadership, informal education, demography, Jewish identity, Israel-Diaspora relations.

Brooklyn College of the City University of New York, Division of Graduate Studies, Department of Judaic Studies, Brooklyn, NY 11210-2889. Offers MA. Part-time and evening/ weekend programs available. *Students:* 4 part-time (3 women). Average age 42. 4 applicants, 100% accepted, 4 enrolled. In 2008, 1 master's awarded. *Degree requirements:* For master's, 2 foreign languages, thesis or alternative, comprehensive exam or thesis. *Entrance requirements:* For master's, 18 upper-level credits in Judaic studies, interview, 2 letters of recommendation. Additional exam requirements/recommendations for international students: Required—TOEFL. *Application deadline:* For fall admission, 3/1 priority date for domestic students, 2/1 priority date for international students; for spring admission, 11/1 priority date for domestic students, 10/1 priority date for international students. Applications are processed on a rolling basis. Application fee: $125. Electronic applications accepted. *Expenses:* Tuition, state resident: full-time $7360; part-time $310 per credit hour. Tuition, nonresident: full-time $13,800; part-time $575 per credit hour. *Financial support:* Federal Work-Study, institutionally sponsored loans, and scholarships/grants available. Support available to part-time students. Financial award application deadline: 5/1; financial award applicants required to submit FAFSA. *Faculty research:* Biblical studies, Talmud and Midrash, modern Jewish history and thought. *Unit head:* Dr. Sara Reguer, Chairperson, 718-951-5229, Fax: 718-951-4703, E-mail: sreguer@brooklyn.cuny.edu. *Application contact:* Hernan Sierra, Graduate Admissions Coordinator, 718-951-4536, Fax: 718-951-4506, E-mail: grads@brooklyn.cuny.edu.

Brown University, Graduate School, Department of Religious Studies, Providence, RI 02912. Offers ancient Judaism (PhD); early Christianity (PhD); religion and critical thought (PhD); religion in the ancient Mediterranean (PhD); religion, culture, and comparison (PhD). *Degree requirements:* For doctorate, 2 foreign languages, thesis/dissertation. *Entrance requirements:* For doctorate, GRE General Test.

Columbia University, Graduate School of Arts and Sciences, Division of Humanities, Program in Jewish Studies, New York, NY 10027. Offers M Phil, MA, PhD. *Degree requirements:* For master's, variable foreign language requirement; for doctorate, variable foreign language requirement, thesis/dissertation. *Entrance requirements:* For master's and doctorate, GRE General Test. Additional exam requirements/recommendations for international students: Required—TOEFL. *Faculty research:* Jewish history, culture, and institutions; Hebrew, Yiddish, and Jewish languages and literatures; history of Jewish philosophy and religion.

Columbia University, Graduate School of Arts and Sciences, Interdepartmental Committee on Yiddish Studies, New York, NY 10027. Offers MA. Applicants must apply for admission to one of the participating departments: Germanic Languages, History, Middle East Languages and Cultures, Religion. *Entrance requirements:* For master's, high degree of proficiency in Yiddish.

Columbia University, Graduate School of Arts and Sciences, Program in Liberal Studies, New York, NY 10027. Offers American studies (MA); East Asian studies (MA); human rights studies (MA); Islamic culture studies (MA); Jewish studies (MA); medieval studies (MA); modern European studies (MA); South Asian studies (MA). Part-time and evening/weekend programs available. *Degree requirements:* For master's, thesis.

Concordia University, School of Graduate Studies, Faculty of Arts and Science, Department of Religion, Program in Judaic Studies, Montréal, QC H3G 1M8, Canada. Offers MA. *Degree requirements:* For master's, one foreign language, comprehensive exam, thesis optional. *Entrance requirements:* For master's, Hebrew exam, honors degree in Judaic studies or equivalent. Additional exam requirements/recommendations for international students: Required—TOEFL. *Faculty research:* Jewish religious reflections and modern philosophy of religion, Judaism and modernity, Judaism in late antiquity.

Cornell University, Graduate School, Graduate Fields of Arts and Sciences, Field of Near Eastern Studies, Ithaca, NY 14853-0001. Offers ancient Near Eastern studies (MA, PhD); Arabic and Islamic studies (MA, PhD); biblical studies (MA, PhD); Hebrew and Judaic studies (MA, PhD). *Faculty:* 16 full-time (5 women). *Students:* 5 full-time (2 women), 1 international. Average age 26. 28 applicants, 14% accepted, 2 enrolled.Terminal master's awarded for partial completion of doctoral program. *Degree requirements:* For master's, one foreign language, thesis; for doctorate, 2 foreign languages, comprehensive exam, thesis/dissertation. *Entrance requirements:* For master's and doctorate, GRE General Test, 2 years of 1 Near Eastern language, 3 letters of recommendation, writing sample. Additional exam requirements/ recommendations for international students: Required—TOEFL (minimum score 550 paper-based; 213 computer-based; 77 iBT). *Application deadline:* For fall admission, 2/1 for domestic students. Application fee: $70. Electronic applications accepted. *Expenses:* Tuition: Full-time $29,500. Required fees: $70. Full-time tuition and fees vary according to degree level, program and student level. *Financial support:* In 2008–09, 5 students received support, including 3 fellowships with full tuition reimbursements available, 2 teaching assistantships with full tuition reimbursements available; research assistantships with full tuition reimbursements available, institutionally sponsored loans, scholarships/grants, health care benefits, tuition waivers (full and partial), and unspecified assistantships also available. Financial award applicants required to submit FAFSA. *Faculty research:* Ancient Near East (including archeology), Hebrew and Judaic studies (including bible), early Christianity, Arabic and Islamic studies, modern Middle East. *Unit head:* Director of Graduate Studies, 607-255-1329, Fax: 607-255-6450. *Application contact:* Graduate Field Assistant, 607-255-1329, Fax: 607-255-6450, E-mail: neareastern@ cornell.edu.

The Criswell College, Graduate School of the Bible, Dallas, TX 75246-1537. Offers biblical studies (M Div); Christian leadership (MA); counseling (MA); Jewish studies (MA); ministry (MA); theological and biblical studies (MA). Part-time programs available. *Degree requirements:* For master's, 2 foreign languages, thesis optional; for M Div, 2 foreign languages, thesis/ dissertation optional. *Entrance requirements:* For M Div and master's, GRE General Test, minimum GPA of 2.5. Electronic applications accepted. *Faculty research:* Emphasis on biblical languages (Hebrew and Greek), expository preaching and evangelism in the local church.

Emory University, Graduate School of Arts and Sciences, Program in Jewish Studies, Atlanta, GA 30322-1100. Offers MA. *Degree requirements:* For master's, one foreign language, thesis optional. *Entrance requirements:* For master's, GRE General Test, 2 years of course work in Hebrew or equivalent, writing sample. Additional exam requirements/recommendations for international students: Required—TOEFL. Electronic applications accepted. *Faculty research:* Medieval Jewish history and culture, Hebrew language and linguistics, Jewish law, Jewish ethics, Holocaust studies.

Graduate Theological Union, Graduate Programs, Berkeley, CA 94709-1212. Offers art and religion (MA, PhD); biblical languages (MA); biblical studies (Old and New Testament) (MA, PhD, Th D); Buddhist studies (MA); Christian spirituality (MA, PhD); cultural and historical studies of religions (MA, PhD); ethics and social theory (PhD); history (MA, PhD, Th D); homiletics (MA, PhD, Th D); interdisciplinary studies (PhD, Th D); Jewish studies (MA, PhD, Certificate); liturgical studies (MA, PhD, Th D); Near Eastern religions (PhD); Orthodox Christian studies (MA); Orthodox studies (Certificate); religion and psychology (MA, PhD); religion and society/ethics and social theory (MA); systematic and philosophical theology (MA, PhD, Th D); women's studies in religion (Certificate); MA/M Div. *Accreditation:* ATS. Terminal master's awarded for partial completion of doctoral program. *Degree requirements:* For master's, one foreign language, thesis; for doctorate, one foreign language, comprehensive exam, thesis/ dissertation. *Entrance requirements:* For master's, GRE General Test; for doctorate, GRE General Test, MA or M Div. Additional exam requirements/recommendations for international students: Required—TOEFL. Electronic applications accepted.

Gratz College, Graduate Programs, Program in Jewish Studies, Melrose Park, PA 19027. Offers classical studies (MA); Holocaust studies (Certificate); Jewish studies (MA, Certificate); modern studies (MA). Part-time programs available. Postbaccalaureate distance learning degree programs offered. *Degree requirements:* For master's, one foreign language, comprehensive exam, thesis optional.

Harvard University, Graduate School of Arts and Sciences, Department of Near Eastern Languages and Civilizations, Cambridge, MA 02138. Offers Akkadian and Sumerian (AM, PhD); Arabic (AM, PhD); Armenian (AM, PhD); biblical history (AM, PhD); Hebrew (AM, PhD); Indo-Muslim culture (AM, PhD); Iranian (AM, PhD); Jewish history and literature (AM, PhD); Persian (AM, PhD); Semitic philology (AM, PhD); Syro-Palestinian archaeology (AM, PhD); Turkish (AM, PhD). *Degree requirements:* For doctorate, variable foreign language requirement, thesis/dissertation, general exams. *Entrance requirements:* For master's, GRE General Test; for doctorate, GRE General Test, proficiency in a Near Eastern language. Additional exam requirements/recommendations for international students: Required—TOEFL. *Expenses:* Tuition: Full-time $32,556. Required fees: $1426. Full-time tuition and fees vary according to program and student level.

Hebrew College, Cantor Educator Program, Newton Centre, MA 02459. Offers MJ Ed. *Entrance requirements:* For master's, GRE, interview. Additional exam requirements/recommendations for international students: Required—TOEFL.

Hebrew College, Program in Jewish Studies, Newton Centre, MA 02459. Offers Jewish liturgical music (Certificate); Jewish music education (Certificate); Jewish studies (MA). Part-time and evening/weekend programs available. Postbaccalaureate distance learning degree programs offered (minimal on-campus study). *Degree requirements:* For master's, one foreign language. *Entrance requirements:* For master's, GRE, interview. Additional exam requirements/ recommendations for international students: Required—TOEFL.

Hebrew Union College–Jewish Institute of Religion, Edgar F. Magnin School of Graduate Studies, Los Angeles, CA 90007-3796. Offers MAJS, DHL, DHS. Part-time programs available. Terminal master's awarded for partial completion of doctoral program. *Degree requirements:* For master's, one foreign language, thesis, Hebrew; for doctorate, one foreign language, thesis/dissertation, Hebrew. *Entrance requirements:* For master's, GRE General Test, Hebrew Language Test, interview, minimum undergraduate GPA of 3.0; for doctorate, GRE General Test, Hebrew Language Test, interview, minimum graduate GPA of 3.0. Additional exam requirements/recommendations for international students: Required—TOEFL (minimum score 550 paper-based). Electronic applications accepted.

Hebrew Union College–Jewish Institute of Religion, Rabbinic School, Cincinnati, OH 45220-2488. Offers MAHL. *Accreditation:* ACIPE. *Degree requirements:* For MAHL, one foreign language, thesis/dissertation. *Entrance requirements:* GRE General Test, Hebrew competency exam, interview, psychological test. *Faculty research:* Comprehensive Aramaic lexicon, four-volume history (German Jews and modern times).

Hebrew Union College–Jewish Institute of Religion, School of Graduate Studies, Cincinnati, OH 45220-2488. Offers Bible and the ancient Near East (M Phil, MA, PhD); Hebrew letters (DHL); history of biblical interpretation (M Phil, MA, PhD); Jewish and Christian studies in the Greco-Roman period (M Phil, PhD); Jewish and cognate studies (M Phil); Judaic and cognate studies (MA, PhD); modern Jewish history (M Phil, MA, PhD); philosophy and Jewish religious thought (M Phil, MA, PhD); rabbinics (M Phil, MA, PhD). Part-time programs available. Terminal master's awarded for partial completion of doctoral program. *Degree requirements:* For master's, one foreign language, thesis optional; for doctorate, 3 foreign languages, comprehensive exam, thesis/dissertation. *Entrance requirements:* For master's and doctorate, GRE General Test, knowledge of Hebrew. Additional exam requirements/recommendations for international students: Required—TOEFL. *Faculty research:* Aramaic lexicon translations, German-Jewish history, neo-Babylonian texts.

Hebrew Union College–Jewish Institute of Religion, School of Graduate Studies, Program in Judaic Studies, New York, NY 10012-1186. Offers MAJS. Part-time programs available. *Degree requirements:* For master's, one foreign language, thesis. *Entrance requirements:* For master's, GRE, minimum 2 years of college-level Hebrew. *Faculty research:* Philosophy and theology, Bible, Hebrew, history and Rabbinics.

The Jewish Theological Seminary, The Graduate School, New York, NY 10027-4649. Offers ancient Judaism (MA, DHL, PhD); Bible (MA, DHL, PhD); Jewish education (PhD); Jewish history (MA, DHL, PhD); Jewish literature (MA, DHL, PhD); Jewish philosophy (MA, DHL, PhD); liturgy (MA, DHL, PhD); medieval Jewish studies (MA, DHL, PhD); Midrash (MA, DHL, PhD); modern Jewish studies (MA, DHL, PhD); Talmud and rabbinics (MA, DHL, PhD); MA/MSW. *Accreditation:* ACIPE. Part-time programs available. *Faculty:* 60 full-time (19 women), 73 part-time/adjunct (39 women). *Students:* 91 full-time (49 women), 27 part-time (14 women), 15 international. Average age 37. 77 applicants, 68% accepted, 23 enrolled. In 2008, 23 master's, 3 doctorates awarded. Terminal master's awarded for partial completion of doctoral program. *Degree requirements:* For master's, one foreign language, comprehensive exam (for some programs), thesis (for some programs); for doctorate, 3 foreign languages, comprehensive exam (for some programs), thesis/dissertation. *Entrance requirements:* For master's, GRE or MAT, 3 letters of recommendation, writing sample; for doctorate, GRE or MAT, 3 letters of recommendation, writing research sample. Additional exam requirements/recommendations for international students: Required—TOEFL (minimum score 100 computer-based). *Application deadline:* For fall admission, 1/15 priority date for domestic students. Applications are processed on a rolling basis. Application fee: $50. *Expenses:* Tuition: Full-time $21,200; part-time $1000 per credit. Required fees: $400 per semester. Tuition and fees vary according to degree level, program and student level. *Financial support:* Fellowships, career-related internships or fieldwork and tuition waivers (full and partial) available. Support available to part-time students. Financial award application deadline: 3/1; financial award applicants required to submit FAFSA. *Unit head:* Dr. Stephen Garfinkel, Dean, 212-678-8024, Fax: 212-678-8947, E-mail: gradschool@ jtsa.edu. *Application contact:* Abby Eisenberg, Director of Graduate School Admissions, 212-678-8032, Fax: 212-280-6022, E-mail: abeisenberg@jtsa.edu.

See Close-Up on page 529.

The Jewish Theological Seminary, William Davidson Graduate School of Jewish Education, New York, NY 10027-4649. Offers MA, Ed D. Offered in conjunction with Rabbinical School; H. L. Miller Cantorial School and College of Jewish Music; Teacher's College, Columbia University; and Union Theological Seminary. Part-time programs available. Postbaccalaureate distance learning degree programs offered (minimal on-campus study). *Faculty:* 60 full-time (19 women), 73 part-time/adjunct (39 women). *Students:* 80 full-time (7 women), 26 part-time (18 women); includes 1 minority (Hispanic American), 10 international. Average age 35. 38 applicants, 92% accepted, 25 enrolled. In 2008, 35 master's, 1 doctorate awarded. *Degree requirements:* For master's, one foreign language, thesis optional; for doctorate, one foreign language, comprehensive exam, thesis/dissertation. *Entrance requirements:* For master's, GRE or MAT, 3 letters of recommendation; for doctorate, GRE or MAT, writing sample, 3 letters

Jewish Studies

The Jewish Theological Seminary *(continued)*
of recommendation. *Application deadline:* For fall admission, 7/15 priority date for domestic students. Applications are processed on a rolling basis. Application fee: $50. *Expenses:* Tuition: Full-time $21,200; part-time $1000 per credit. Required fees: $400 per semester. Tuition and fees vary according to degree level, program and student level. *Financial support:* Fellowships, career-related internships or fieldwork available. Financial award application deadline: 3/1. *Unit head:* Dr. Barry Holtz, Dean, 212-678-8030, Fax: 212-749-9085, E-mail: baholtz@jtsa.edu. *Application contact:* Abby Eisenberg, Director of Admissions, 212-678-8032, Fax: 212-280-6022, E-mail: abeisenberg@jtsa.edu.

Jewish University of America, Graduate School, Graduate Research Division, Skokie, IL 60077-3248. Offers Bible (MHL, DHL); Hebrew (MHL, DHL); history (MHL, DHL); Jewish studies (MHL, DHL); philosophy (MHL, DHL); rabbinics (MHL, DHL). Part-time programs available. *Degree requirements:* For doctorate, one foreign language, thesis/dissertation; for MHL, thesis/dissertation optional. *Entrance requirements:* For MHL and doctorate, interview.

Laura and Alvin Siegal College of Judaic Studies, Graduate Programs, Program in Religious Education, Beachwood, OH 44122-7116. Offers Jewish education (MAJS); Judaic studies (MAJS). Part-time and evening/weekend programs available. Postbaccalaureate distance learning degree programs offered (minimal on-campus study). *Degree requirements:* For master's, one foreign language, thesis. *Entrance requirements:* For master's, interview.

McGill University, Faculty of Graduate and Postdoctoral Studies, Faculty of Arts, Department of Jewish Studies, Montréal, QC H3A 2T5, Canada. Offers MA.

New York University, Graduate School of Arts and Science, Program in Museum Studies, New York, NY 10012-1019. Offers museum studies (MA, Advanced Certificate), including Africana studies (MA), Hebrew and Judaic studies (MA), Latin American and Caribbean studies (MA), Near Eastern studies (MA). Part-time and evening/weekend programs available. *Entrance requirements:* For degree, master's or PhD. *Faculty research:* Modern and contemporary art, history of museums and exhibitions, conservation of cultural materials, museum anthropology, ethnography.

New York University, Graduate School of Arts and Science, Skirball Department of Hebrew and Judaic Studies, New York, NY 10012-1019. Offers Hebrew and Judaic studies (MA, PhD); Hebrew and Judaic studies/museum studies (MA). Part-time programs available. Terminal master's awarded for partial completion of doctoral program. *Degree requirements:* For master's, 2 foreign languages, comprehensive exam, thesis optional; for doctorate, 4 foreign languages, comprehensive exam, thesis/dissertation. *Entrance requirements:* For master's, GRE General Test, minimum 2 years of undergraduate course work in Hebrew; for doctorate, GRE General Test. Additional exam requirements/recommendations for international students: Required—TOEFL. *Faculty research:* Post-biblical and Talmudic literature and history, mysticism, Bible and ancient Near East, medieval and modern Jewish history, medieval and modern Jewish philosophy.

New York University, Steinhardt School of Culture, Education and Human Development, Department of Humanities and Social Sciences in the Professions, Program in Education and Jewish Studies, New York, NY 10012-1019. Offers PhD. Part-time and evening/weekend programs available. *Degree requirements:* For doctorate, thesis/dissertation. *Entrance requirements:* For doctorate, GRE General Test, interview. Additional exam requirements/recommendations for international students: Required—TOEFL. *Faculty research:* Jewish education, educational history, Judaic studies.

St. Petersburg Theological Seminary, Graduate Programs, St. Petersburg, FL 33708. Offers Biblical studies (MA); counseling (MA); divinity (M Div); education (MA); Judaic studies (MA); ministry (MA, D Min); religious teacher (MA). Part-time and evening/weekend programs available. Postbaccalaureate distance learning degree programs offered (minimal on-campus study). *Degree requirements:* For master's, thesis; for doctorate, thesis/dissertation. *Entrance requirements:* For M Div and master's, Bachelor degree; for doctorate, Master degree. Electronic applications accepted.

Seton Hall University, College of Arts and Sciences, Department of Jewish-Christian Studies, South Orange, NJ 07079-2697. Offers MA. Part-time and evening/weekend programs available. *Degree requirements:* For master's, one foreign language, thesis or alternative. Electronic applications accepted. *Faculty research:* Jewish-Christian issues, biblical studies, Holocaust studies.

See Close-Up on page 533.

Southern Evangelical Seminary, Veritas Graduate School of Apologetics and Counter-Cult Ministry, Matthews, NC 28105. Offers apologetics (MA, D Min, PhD, Certificate); Islamic studies (MA); Jewish studies (MA); philosophy (MA); religion (MA). *Accreditation:* ATS. Part-time and evening/weekend programs available. Postbaccalaureate distance learning degree programs offered (minimal on-campus study). *Degree requirements:* For master's, thesis optional; for doctorate, comprehensive exam (for some programs), thesis/dissertation. *Entrance requirements:* Additional exam requirements/recommendations for international students: Required—TOEFL (minimum score 600 paper-based; 250 computer-based).

Spertus Institute of Jewish Studies, Graduate Programs, Program in Jewish Studies, Chicago, IL 60605-1901. Offers MAJS, MSJE, MSJS, DJS, DSJS. Part-time and evening/weekend programs available. Postbaccalaureate distance learning degree programs offered (minimal on-campus study). *Degree requirements:* For master's, one foreign language, thesis (for some programs); for doctorate, one foreign language, thesis/dissertation. *Entrance requirements:* For master's, interview, BAJS (MAJS); for doctorate, MAJS.

Telshe Yeshiva–Chicago, Graduate Program, Chicago, IL 60625-5598. Offers Second Talmudic Degree. *Accreditation:* AARTS.

Touro College, Graduate School of Jewish Studies, New York, NY 10010. Offers MA. Part-time programs available. *Degree requirements:* For master's, one foreign language, thesis. *Entrance requirements:* For master's, previous course work in Jewish studies, proficiency in Hebrew. *Faculty research:* Medieval and modern Jewish history, Jewish philosophy, holocaust studies, Jewish education.

University of California, Berkeley, Graduate Division, Program in Jewish Studies, Berkeley, CA 94720-1500. Offers PhD. *Entrance requirements:* For doctorate, GRE General Test, 3 letters of recommendation.

University of California, San Diego, Office of Graduate Studies, Department of History, La Jolla, CA 92093. Offers history (MA, PhD); Judaic studies (MA); science studies (PhD). *Degree requirements:* For doctorate, thesis/dissertation. *Entrance requirements:* For master's and doctorate, GRE General Test. Electronic applications accepted.

University of Connecticut, Graduate School, College of Liberal Arts and Sciences, Field of International Studies, Program in Judaic Studies, Storrs, CT 06269. Offers MA. *Entrance requirements:* Additional exam requirements/recommendations for international students: Required—TOEFL (minimum score 550 paper-based; 213 computer-based). Electronic applications accepted.

University of Maryland, College Park, Graduate Studies, College of Arts and Humanities, Program in Jewish Studies, College Park, MD 20742. Offers MA. *Degree requirements:* For master's, thesis or 2 major research papers. *Entrance requirements:* For master's, GRE General Test, 3 letters of recommendation, writing sample. Additional exam requirements/recommendations for international students: Required—TOEFL.

University of Michigan, Jean and Samuel Frankel Center for Judaic Studies, Ann Arbor, MI 48109. Offers MA, Graduate Certificate. Part-time programs available. *Degree requirements:* For master's, one foreign language, thesis, foreign language must be either Hebrew or Yiddish. *Entrance requirements:* For master's, GRE General Test; for Graduate Certificate, Admission to a U-M doctoral program. Additional exam requirements/recommendations for international students: Required—TOEFL (minimum score 540 paper-based; 220 computer-based). Electronic applications accepted. *Faculty research:* Jewish history (antique to modern); Jewish literature; Yiddish language and literature; Jewish cultural studies; Jewish political and social studies.

The University of Montana, Graduate School, School of Fine Arts, Department of Art, Missoula, MT 59812-0002. Offers fine arts (MA, MFA), including art (MA), art history (MA), ceramics (MFA), integrated arts and education (MA), media arts (MFA), painting and drawing (MFA), photography (MFA), printmaking (MFA), sculpture (MFA). *Accreditation:* NASAD (one or more programs are accredited). *Degree requirements:* For master's, thesis exhibit. *Entrance requirements:* For master's, GRE General Test, portfolio.

University of St. Michael's College, Faculty of Theology, Toronto, ON M5S 1J4, Canada. Offers Catholic leadership (MA); eastern Christian studies (Certificate, Diploma); religious education (Diploma); theological studies (Diploma); theology (M Div, MA, MRE, MTS, D Min, PhD, Th D); theology and ecology (Certificate); theology and Jewish studies (MA). *Accreditation:* ATS (one or more programs are accredited). Part-time programs available. *Degree requirements:* For master's, thesis (for some programs), 1 foreign language (MA), 2 foreign languages (Th M); for doctorate, 3 foreign languages, comprehensive exam, thesis/dissertation; for M Div, thesis/dissertation optional; for other advanced degree, thesis optional. *Entrance requirements:* For M Div and other advanced degree, minimum GPA of 2.7; for master's, M Div or BA, course work in an ancient or modern language, minimum GPA of 3.3; for doctorate, MA in theology, Th M, or M Div with thesis, minimum GPA of 3.7. Additional exam requirements/recommendations for international students: Required—TOEFL (minimum score 600 paper-based; 250 computer-based). Electronic applications accepted. *Faculty research:* Patristics, eastern Christianity, ecology and theology, ecumenism, Jewish Christian studies.

University of Wisconsin–Madison, Graduate School, College of Letters and Science, Department of Hebrew and Semitic Studies, Madison, WI 53706-1380. Offers MA, PhD. Terminal master's awarded for partial completion of doctoral program. *Degree requirements:* For master's, 2 foreign languages; for doctorate, thesis/dissertation. *Entrance requirements:* For master's and doctorate, GRE. Electronic applications accepted. *Faculty research:* Biblical language and literature, Northwest Semitic languages.

University of Wisconsin–Milwaukee, Graduate School, College of Letters and Sciences, Interdepartmental Program in Foreign Language and Literature, Milwaukee, WI 53201-0413. Offers classics and Hebrew studies (MAFLL); comparative literature (MAFLL); French and Italian (MAFLL); German (MAFLL); Slavic studies (MAFLL); translation (Certificate). Part-time programs available. *Faculty:* 39 full-time (17 women). *Students:* 32 full-time (25 women), 28 part-time (19 women); includes 5 minority (1 Asian American or Pacific Islander, 4 Hispanic Americans), 22 international. Average age 32. 51 applicants, 65% accepted, 26 enrolled. In 2008, 19 master's awarded. *Degree requirements:* For master's, 2 foreign languages, thesis or alternative. *Entrance requirements:* Additional exam requirements/recommendations for international students: Required—TOEFL (minimum score 550 paper-based; 79 iBT), IELTS (minimum score 6.5). *Application deadline:* For fall admission, 1/1 priority date for domestic students; for spring admission, 9/1 for domestic students. Applications are processed on a rolling basis. Application fee: $45 ($75 for international students). *Expenses:* Tuition, area resident: Full-time $7320; part-time $165 per credit. Tuition, state resident: full-time $7320; part-time $165 per credit. Tuition, nonresident: full-time $17,840; part-time $714 per credit. Tuition and fees vary according to campus/location, program and reciprocity agreements. *Financial support:* In 2008–09, 2 research assistantships, 35 teaching assistantships were awarded; career-related internships or fieldwork and unspecified assistantships also available. Support available to part-time students. Financial award application deadline: 4/15. Total annual research expenditures: $43,420. *Unit head:* Gabrielle Verdier, Representative, 414-229-3346, Fax: 414-229-2741, E-mail: verdier@uwm.edu. *Application contact:* General Information Contact, 414-229-4982, Fax: 414-229-6967, E-mail: gradschool@uwm.edu.

Yeshiva University, Bernard Revel Graduate School of Jewish Studies, New York, NY 10033-3201. Offers MA, PhD. Part-time programs available. Terminal master's awarded for partial completion of doctoral program. *Degree requirements:* For master's, comprehensive exam; for doctorate, 2 foreign languages, comprehensive exam, thesis/dissertation. *Entrance requirements:* For master's and doctorate, GRE General Test (recommended), reading knowledge of Hebrew, minimum GPA of 3.0. *Faculty research:* Bible, Jewish history, Jewish philosophy and mysticism, Talmud, Semitic languages.

Latin American Studies

American University, College of Arts and Sciences, Department of Language and Foreign Studies, Program in Spanish: Latin American Studies, Washington, DC 20016-8045. Offers Spanish: Latin American studies (MA); translation (Certificate). Part-time and evening/weekend programs available. *Students:* 17 full-time (13 women), 10 part-time (8 women); includes 9 minority (5 African Americans, 4 Hispanic Americans), 2 international. Average age 26. 23 applicants, 96% accepted, 7 enrolled. In 2008, 11 master's, 5 other advanced degrees awarded. *Degree requirements:* For master's, one foreign language, comprehensive exam, thesis or alternative, research requirement. *Entrance requirements:* For master's, GRE, bachelor's degree in language or equivalent, essay in Spanish, minimum GPA of 3.2, statement of purpose; for Certificate, bachelor's degree in Spanish or BA in any field plus Spanish proficiency. Additional exam requirements/recommendations for international students:

Required—TOEFL. *Application deadline:* For fall admission, 2/1 for domestic students; for spring admission, 10/1 for domestic students. Application fee: $80. *Expenses:* Tuition: Full-time $21,204; part-time $1178 per credit hour. Required fees: $380. Part-time tuition and fees vary according to course load and program. *Financial support:* Fellowships, career-related internships or fieldwork, Federal Work-Study, and institutionally sponsored loans available. Financial award application deadline: 2/1. *Faculty research:* Latin American culture, literature, and history; computer-aided instruction.

Arizona State University, Graduate College, College of Liberal Arts and Sciences, Division of Humanities, Department of History, Tempe, AZ 85287. Offers East/Southeast Asian history (MA, PhD); European history (MA, PhD); Latin American studies (MA, PhD); North American history (MA, PhD); public history (MA). *Degree requirements:* For master's, thesis or alternative;

for doctorate, 2 foreign languages, thesis/dissertation. *Entrance requirements:* For master's and doctorate, GRE.

Boricua College, Program in Latin American and Caribbean Studies (Brooklyn Campus), New York, NY 10032-1560. Offers MA. Evening/weekend programs available. *Degree requirements:* For master's, thesis, 40 credits. *Entrance requirements:* For master's, interview by the faculty, essay. Additional exam requirements/recommendations for international students: Required—Boricua College's exam.

Boricua College, Program in Latin American and Caribbean Studies (Manhattan Campus), New York, NY 10032-1560. Offers MA. Evening/weekend programs available. *Degree requirements:* For master's, thesis, 40 credits. *Entrance requirements:* For master's, interview by the faculty, essay. Additional exam requirements/recommendations for international students: Required—Boricua College's exam.

Brown University, Graduate School, Center for Portuguese and Brazilian Studies, Providence, RI 02912. Offers Brazilian studies (AM); Portuguese and Brazilian studies (AM, PhD); Portuguese Bilingual Education and Cross-Cultural Studies (AM); MA/PhD. *Degree requirements:* For doctorate, thesis/dissertation.

California State University, Long Beach, Graduate Studies, College of Liberal Arts, Department of History, Long Beach, CA 90840. Offers Africa and the Middle East (MA); ancient/Medieval Europe (MA); Asia (MA); Latin America (MA); modern Europe (MA); United States (MA); world (MA). Part-time and evening/weekend programs available. *Faculty:* 17 full-time (11 women), 2 part-time/adjunct (1 woman). *Students:* 9 full-time (4 women), 45 part-time (18 women); includes 15 minority (2 African Americans, 3 Asian Americans or Pacific Islanders, 10 Hispanic Americans), 1 international. Average age 35. 40 applicants, 50% accepted, 11 enrolled. *Degree requirements:* For master's, one foreign language, comprehensive exam or thesis. *Application deadline:* For fall admission, 3/1 for domestic students. Applications are processed on a rolling basis. Application fee: $55. Electronic applications accepted. *Expenses:* Tuition, nonresident: full-time $11,160; part-time $372 per unit. Required fees: $4100; $1261 per semester. *Financial support:* Research assistantships, Federal Work-Study, institutionally sponsored loans, and scholarships/grants available. Financial award application deadline: 3/2. *Faculty research:* All periods of European and American history, recent Asian and African history. *Unit head:* Dr. Nancy L Quam-Wickham, Graduate Advisor, 562-985-4431, Fax: 562-985-5431, E-mail: quamwick@csulb.edu. *Application contact:* Dr. Houri Berberian, Graduate Advisor, 562-985-4524, Fax: 562-985-4431, E-mail: hberber@csulb.edu.

California State University, Los Angeles, Graduate Studies, College of Natural and Social Sciences, Department of Latin American Studies, Los Angeles, CA 90032-8530. Offers MA. Part-time and evening/weekend programs available. *Faculty:* 1 full-time (0 women). *Students:* 17 full-time (10 women), 21 part-time (9 women); includes 28 minority (all Hispanic Americans), 1 international. Average age 32. 15 applicants, 100% accepted, 11 enrolled. In 2008, 4 master's awarded. *Degree requirements:* For master's, one foreign language, comprehensive exam, thesis. *Entrance requirements:* For master's, minimum GPA of 2.5. Additional exam requirements/recommendations for international students: Required—TOEFL (minimum score 500 paper-based; 173 computer-based). *Application deadline:* For fall admission, 6/15 for domestic students, 5/1 for international students; for winter admission, 11/1 for domestic students, 9/1 for international students; for spring admission, 2/1 for domestic students, 10/1 for international students. Applications are processed on a rolling basis. Application fee: $55. Electronic applications accepted. *Expenses:* Tuition, nonresident: part-time $226 per credit. Required fees: $4019. *Financial support:* Federal Work-Study available. Support available to part-time students. Financial award application deadline: 3/1. *Faculty research:* Central America, Cuba, Third World development, labor history, redemocratization. *Unit head:* Dr. Marjorie W. Bray, Coordinator, 323-343-2180, Fax: 323-343-5485, E-mail: mbray@calstatela.edu. *Application contact:* Dr. Jose L. Galvan, Dean of Graduate Studies, 323-343-3820, Fax: 323-343-5653, E-mail: jgalvan@cslanet.calstatela.edu.

Centro de Estudios Avanzados de Puerto Rico y el Caribe, Graduate Program in Puerto Rican and Caribbean Studies, Old San Juan, PR 00902-3970. Offers Puerto Rican and Caribbean history (MA, PhD); Puerto Rican and Caribbean literature (MA, PhD); Puerto Rican studies (MA). Part-time and evening/weekend programs available. *Degree requirements:* For master's, comprehensive exam, thesis; for doctorate, 2 foreign languages, comprehensive exam, thesis/dissertation. *Entrance requirements:* For master's and doctorate, interview. *Faculty research:* Literature, history, art, folklore, and culture of Puerto Rico and Caribbean countries.

Cleveland State University, College of Graduate Studies, College of Liberal Arts and Social Sciences, Department of Modern Languages, Cleveland, OH 44115. Offers French (M Ed); Spanish (M Ed, MA), including language and linguistics (MA), Latin American studies (MA), peninsular studies (MA), Spanish (MA). Part-time and evening/weekend programs available. *Faculty:* 12 full-time (9 women). *Students:* 7 full-time (6 women), 11 part-time (8 women); includes 7 minority (1 African American, 6 Hispanic Americans), 1 international. Average age 37. 11 applicants, 100% accepted, 8 enrolled. In 2008, 9 master's awarded. *Degree requirements:* For master's, one foreign language, comprehensive exam, thesis optional, study abroad. *Entrance requirements:* For master's, undergraduate major in Spanish or equivalent, essay in Spanish, writing sample. Additional exam requirements/recommendations for international students: Required—TOEFL (minimum score 525 paper-based; 197 computer-based). *Application deadline:* For fall admission, 7/25 priority date for domestic students; for spring admission, 12/15 priority date for domestic students. Applications are processed on a rolling basis. Application fee: $30. Electronic applications accepted. *Financial support:* In 2008–09, 6 students received support, including 6 teaching assistantships with full tuition reimbursements available (averaging $7,030 per year); Federal Work-Study also available. *Faculty research:* Second language acquisition, sociolinguistics, contemporary Spanish novel, Arabic diaspora in Latin America, border literature. *Unit head:* Dr. Tama L. Engelking, Chairperson, 216-523-7175, Fax: 216-687-4650, E-mail: t.engelking@csuohio.edu. *Application contact:* Dr. Antonio Medina-Rivera, Graduate Director, 216-523-7168, Fax: 216-687-4650, E-mail: a.medinarivera@csuohio.edu.

Columbia University, School of International and Public Affairs, Institute of Latin American Studies, New York, NY 10027. Offers Latin American and Caribbean studies (MA); Latin American studies (Certificate). Students must also be enrolled in a separate graduate degree program at Columbia University. *Degree requirements:* For master's, 2 foreign languages, thesis. Electronic applications accepted. *Faculty research:* Rights vs. efficiency in a globalized era, citizenship and governance in Latin America and Western Europe.

Cornell University, Graduate School, Graduate Fields of Arts and Sciences, Field of Archaeology, Ithaca, NY 14853-0001. Offers environmental archaeology (MA); historical archaeology (MA); Latin American archaeology (MA); medieval archaeology (MA); Mediterranean and Near Eastern archaeology (MA); Stone Age archaeology (MA). *Faculty:* 12 full-time (3 women). *Students:* 4 full-time (3 women). Average age 27. 10 applicants, 40% accepted, 2 enrolled. *Degree requirements:* For master's, one foreign language, thesis. *Entrance requirements:* For master's, GRE General Test, 3 letters of recommendation, sample of written work. Additional exam requirements/recommendations for international students: Required—TOEFL (minimum score 550 paper-based; 213 computer-based; 77 iBT). *Application deadline:* For fall admission, 1/15 for domestic students. Application fee: $70. Electronic applications accepted. *Expenses:* Tuition: Full-time $29,500. Required fees: $70. Full-time tuition and fees vary according to degree level, program and student level. *Financial support:* In 2008–09, 4 students received support, including 1 fellowship with full tuition reimbursement available, 1 research assistantship with full tuition reimbursement available, 2 teaching assistantships with full tuition reimbursements available; institutionally sponsored loans, scholarships/grants, health care benefits, tuition waivers (full and partial), and unspecified assistantships also available. Financial award applicants required to submit FAFSA. *Faculty research:* Anatolia, Lydia, Sardis, classical and Hellenistic Greece; science in archaeology; North American Indians; Stone Age Africa; Maya trade. *Unit head:* Director of Graduate Studies, 607-255-6768, E-mail: blj7@cornell.edu. *Application contact:* Graduate Field Assistant, 607-255-6768, E-mail: dsd6@cornell.edu.

Cornell University, Graduate School, Graduate Fields of Arts and Sciences, Field of History, Ithaca, NY 14853-0001. Offers African history (MA, PhD); American history (MA, PhD); ancient history (MA, PhD); early modern European history (MA, PhD); English history (MA, PhD); French history (MA, PhD); German history (MA, PhD); history of science (MA, PhD); Latin American history (MA, PhD); medieval Chinese history (MA, PhD); medieval history (MA, PhD); modern Chinese history (MA, PhD); modern European history (MA, PhD); modern Japanese history (MA, PhD); premodern Islamic history (MA, PhD); premodern Japanese history (MA, PhD); Renaissance history (MA, PhD); Russian history (MA, PhD); Southeast Asian history (MA, PhD). *Faculty:* 54 full-time (14 women). *Students:* 65 full-time (35 women); includes 12 minority (4 African Americans, 3 Asian Americans or Pacific Islanders, 5 Hispanic Americans), 19 international. Average age 31. 205 applicants, 8% accepted, 11 enrolled. In 2008, 12 master's, 6 doctorates awarded. Terminal master's awarded for partial completion of doctoral program. *Degree requirements:* For master's, thesis; for doctorate, 2 foreign languages, comprehensive exam, thesis/dissertation, 1 year of teaching experience. *Entrance requirements:* For master's and doctorate, GRE General Test, writing sample, 3 letters of recommendation. Additional exam requirements/recommendations for international students: Required—TOEFL (minimum score 550 paper-based; 213 computer-based; 77 iBT). *Application deadline:* For fall admission, 1/15 for domestic students. Application fee: $70. Electronic applications accepted. *Expenses:* Tuition: Full-time $29,500. Required fees: $70. Full-time tuition and fees vary according to degree level, program and student level. *Financial support:* In 2008–09, 54 students received support, including 27 fellowships with full tuition reimbursements available, 3 research assistantships with full tuition reimbursements available, 24 teaching assistantships with full tuition reimbursements available; institutionally sponsored loans, scholarships/grants, health care benefits, tuition waivers (full and partial), and unspecified assistantships also available. Financial award applicants required to submit FAFSA. *Unit head:* Director of Graduate Studies, 607-255-6738, Fax: 607-255-0469. *Application contact:* Graduate Field Assistant, 607-255-6738, Fax: 607-255-0469, E-mail: history_grad_info@cornell.edu.

Duke University, Graduate School, Center for Latin American and Caribbean Studies, Durham, NC 27708-0586. Offers Certificate. *Faculty research:* Political economy of development, social transformations in Central America, Colonial literature, history and fiscal policies, comparative Spanish-American literature and poetry.

Duke University, Graduate School, Department of History, Durham, NC 27708. Offers history (AM, PhD); Latin American studies (PhD); JD/AM; MD/PhD. *Degree requirements:* For doctorate, 2 foreign languages, thesis/dissertation. *Entrance requirements:* For doctorate, GRE General Test. Additional exam requirements/recommendations for international students: Required—TOEFL (minimum score 550 paper-based; 213 computer-based; 83 iBT), IELTS (minimum score 7). Electronic applications accepted.

Florida International University, College of Arts and Sciences, Latin American and Caribbean Studies Center, Miami, FL 33199. Offers MA. *Degree requirements:* For master's, one foreign language, thesis or alternative. *Entrance requirements:* For master's, GRE General Test, minimum GPA of 3.0, 3 letters of recommendation. Additional exam requirements/recommendations for international students: Required—TOEFL (minimum score 550 paper-based; 213 computer-based). Electronic applications accepted.

Fordham University, Graduate School of Arts and Sciences, Program in Latin American and Latino Studies, New York, NY 10458. Offers MA, Certificate. *Entrance requirements:* Additional exam requirements/recommendations for international students: Required—TOEFL (minimum score 650 paper-based; 280 computer-based). Electronic applications accepted. *Faculty research:* Latinos and Hollywood, Puerto Rican women and labor history, education and the state in El Salvador, Avant-garde literature in 20th century Latin America.

Georgetown University, Graduate School of Arts and Sciences, Center for Latin American Studies, Washington, DC 20057-1026. Offers MA, MA/JD, MA/PhD. *Degree requirements:* For master's, one foreign language, comprehensive exam, thesis optional. *Entrance requirements:* For master's, GRE General Test, minimum B average. Additional exam requirements/recommendations for international students: Required—TOEFL.

The George Washington University, Elliott School of International Affairs, Program in Latin American and Hemispheric Studies, Washington, DC 20052. Offers MA, JD/MA, MBA/MA. Part-time and evening/weekend programs available. *Students:* 17 full-time (12 women), 7 part-time (2 women); includes 6 minority (1 African American, 1 Asian American or Pacific Islander, 4 Hispanic Americans), 1 international. Average age 26. 43 applicants, 77% accepted, 9 enrolled. In 2008, 7 master's awarded. *Degree requirements:* For master's, one foreign language, capstone project. *Entrance requirements:* For master's, GRE General Test, 2 years (or the equivalent) of Spanish or Portuguese. Additional exam requirements/recommendations for international students: Required—TOEFL. *Application deadline:* For fall admission, 2/1 for domestic students; for spring admission, 10/1 for domestic students. Application fee: $60. Electronic applications accepted. *Financial support:* In 2008–09, 4 students received support; fellowships with tuition reimbursements available, research assistantships with tuition reimbursements available, career-related internships or fieldwork, Federal Work-Study, institutionally sponsored loans, and tuition waivers (full) available. Financial award application deadline: 1/15; financial award applicants required to submit FAFSA. *Faculty research:* Democracy and change in Andean nations, rural economic development, peasant cooperatives and political change. *Unit head:* Cynthia McClintock, Director, 202-994-6589, Fax: 202-994-7743, E-mail: mcclin@gwu.edu. *Application contact:* Jeff V. Miles, Director of Graduate Admissions, 202-994-7050, Fax: 202-994-9537, E-mail: esiagrad@gwu.edu.

Georgia State University, College of Arts and Sciences, Department of History, Atlanta, GA 30303-3083. Offers heritage preservation (MHP, Certificate); history (MA, PhD); Latin American studies (Certificate). Part-time and evening/weekend programs available. *Degree requirements:* For master's, one foreign language, comprehensive exam, thesis, exam; for doctorate, 2 foreign languages, comprehensive exam, thesis/dissertation, exam. *Entrance requirements:* For master's, GRE General Test; for doctorate, GRE General Test, sample of written work. Additional exam requirements/recommendations for international students: Required—TOEFL. Electronic applications accepted. *Faculty research:* Historic preservation, labor history, twentieth-century U.S. history, American South, world history.

Indiana University Bloomington, University Graduate School, College of Arts and Sciences, Center for Latin American and Caribbean Studies, Bloomington, IN 47405-7000. Offers MA, MBA/MA, MLS/MA, MPA/MA. Part-time programs available. *Students:* 9 full-time (5 women), 1 (woman) part-time; includes 3 minority (1 African American, 1 Asian American or Pacific Islander, 1 Hispanic American), 1 international. Average age 27. 24 applicants, 63% accepted, 6 enrolled. In 2008, 5 master's awarded. *Degree requirements:* For master's, one foreign language, oral and written exam. *Entrance requirements:* For master's, GRE General Test. Additional exam requirements/recommendations for international students: Required—TOEFL. *Application deadline:* For fall admission, 1/15 priority date for domestic students, 12/15 for international students; for spring admission, 9/1 priority date for domestic students, 9/1 for international students. Applications are processed on a rolling basis. Application fee: $50 ($60 for international students). *Expenses:* Tuition, area resident: Part-time $291.97 per credit hour. Tuition, state resident: part-time $291.97 per credit hour. Tuition, nonresident: part-time $850.33 per credit hour. Required fees: $110 per semester. Tuition and fees vary according to course load and program. *Financial support:* Fellowships with tuition reimbursements, research assistantships with tuition reimbursements, teaching assistantships with tuition reimbursements, career-related internships or fieldwork, Federal Work-Study, institutionally sponsored loans, scholarships/grants, and unspecified assistantships available. Financial award application deadline: 7/15; financial award applicants required to submit FAFSA. *Unit head:* Dr. Jeffrey

Latin American Studies

Indiana University Bloomington *(continued)*
Gould, Director, 812-855-9098, Fax: 812-855-5345, E-mail: gouldj@indiana.edu. *Application contact:* Amy Belcher, Information Contact, 812-855-9097, Fax: 812-855-5345, E-mail: clacs@indiana.edu.

The Johns Hopkins University, Paul H. Nitze School of Advanced International Studies, Washington, DC 20036. Offers international development (Certificate); international public policy (MIPP); international relations (MA, PhD), including African studies (MA), American foreign policy (MA), Asian studies (MA), Canadian studies (MA), conflict management (MA), European studies (MA), global theory and history (MA), international development (MA), international law, and organizations (MA), international policy (MA), international relations (general) (MA), Latin American studies (MA), Middle East studies (MA), Russian and Eurasian studies (MA), strategic studies (MA); international studies (Certificate); JD/MA; MBA/MA; MHS/MA. Terminal master's awarded for partial completion of doctoral program. *Degree requirements:* For master's, one foreign language, 16 non-language courses (8 for MIPP), 2 core examinations, comprehensive oral exam, paper (for some programs); for doctorate, 2 foreign languages, thesis/dissertation, 3 comprehensive exams, defense. *Entrance requirements:* For master's, GMAT or GRE General Test, previous course work in economics, foreign language, undergraduate degree; for doctorate, GRE General Test, master's degree. Additional exam requirements/recommendations for international students: Required—TOEFL (minimum paper-based score of 600, computer-based 250, iBT 100) or IELTS (minimum 7.0). Electronic applications accepted. *Expenses:* Contact institution. *Faculty research:* Regional studies and functional fields of international relations, international economics, conflict management, global theory and history, international law and organizations, international policy, strategic studies.

La Salle University, School of Arts and Sciences, Program in Bilingual/Bicultural Studies (Spanish), Philadelphia, PA 19141-1199. Offers MA. Part-time and evening/weekend programs available. *Degree requirements:* For master's, one foreign language, thesis or alternative, project. *Entrance requirements:* For master's, GRE or MAT. *Expenses:* Contact institution. *Faculty research:* Puerto Rican literature, cross-cultural communication, English as a second language methodology, Spanish language.

Michigan State University, The Graduate School, College of Social Science, Program in Chicano/Latino Studies, East Lansing, MI 48824. Offers PhD. *Entrance requirements:* Additional exam requirements/recommendations for international students: Required—TOEFL. Electronic applications accepted.

New York University, Graduate School of Arts and Science, Center for Latin American and Caribbean Studies, New York, NY 10012-1019. Offers MA, JD/MA. Part-time programs available. *Degree requirements:* For master's, one foreign language, thesis or alternative, major project. *Entrance requirements:* For master's, GRE General Test, knowledge of Portuguese or Spanish. Additional exam requirements/recommendations for international students: Required—TOEFL. *Faculty research:* Latin American politics, Caribbean societies, Andean history, political economy of cultural policies.

New York University, Graduate School of Arts and Science, Program in Museum Studies, New York, NY 10012-1019. Offers museum studies (MA, Advanced Certificate), including Africana studies (MA), Hebrew and Judaic studies (MA), Latin American and Caribbean studies (MA), Near Eastern studies (MA). Part-time and evening/weekend programs available. *Entrance requirements:* For degree, master's or PhD. *Faculty research:* Modern and contemporary art, history of museums and exhibitions, conservation of cultural materials, museum anthropology, ethnography.

Ohio University, Graduate College, Center for International Studies, Program in Latin American Studies, Athens, OH 45701-2979. Offers MA. Part-time programs available. *Degree requirements:* For master's, one foreign language, thesis optional. *Entrance requirements:* For master's, minimum GPA of 3.0. Additional exam requirements/recommendations for international students: Required—TOEFL (minimum score 550 paper-based; 213 computer-based). *Faculty research:* Central America, Ecuador, Brazil, transnational migration, microfinance.

San Diego State University, Graduate and Research Affairs, College of Arts and Letters, Center for Latin American Studies, San Diego, CA 92182. Offers MA, MBA/MA. *Degree requirements:* For master's, 2 foreign languages, thesis or alternative. *Entrance requirements:* For master's, GRE General Test, 3 letters of reference. Additional exam requirements/recommendations for international students: Required—TOEFL. Electronic applications accepted. *Faculty research:* Latin American politics and economics.

Simon Fraser University, Graduate Studies, Faculty of Arts and Social Sciences, Latin American Studies Program, Burnaby, BC V5A 1S6, Canada. Offers MA. *Degree requirements:* For master's, thesis. *Entrance requirements:* For master's, minimum GPA of 3.0. Additional exam requirements/recommendations for international students: Required—TOEFL or IELTS. *Faculty research:* Sociology theory, social and cultural anthropology, political sociology, religion and society, Canadian native people.

Tulane University, School of Liberal Arts, Roger Thayer Stone Center for Latin American Studies, New Orleans, LA 70118-5669. Offers MA, PhD, MBA/MA, MCL/MA. Terminal master's awarded for partial completion of doctoral program. *Degree requirements:* For master's, one foreign language, thesis optional; for doctorate, 2 foreign languages, thesis/dissertation. *Entrance requirements:* For master's, GRE General Test, minimum B average in undergraduate course work; for doctorate, GRE General Test. Additional exam requirements/recommendations for international students: Required—TOEFL. Electronic applications accepted.

University at Albany, State University of New York, College of Arts and Sciences, Latin American, Caribbean, and US Latino Studies, Albany, NY 12222-0001. Offers MA, Certificate. Part-time programs available. *Degree requirements:* For master's, thesis. *Entrance requirements:* For master's, ability to read and write Spanish. Additional exam requirements/recommendations for international students: Required—TOEFL (minimum score 550 paper-based; 213 computer-based). Electronic applications accepted. *Faculty research:* Meso-American anthropology, Latin American women's studies, Latinos in the U.S.

The University of Arizona, Graduate College, College of Social and Behavioral Sciences, Center for Latin American Studies, Tucson, AZ 85721. Offers MA. Part-time programs available. *Degree requirements:* For master's, 2 foreign languages, comprehensive exam, thesis optional. *Entrance requirements:* For master's, GRE, minimum GPA of 3.0, resumé or curriculum vitae, 2 letters of recommendation, statement of purpose. Additional exam requirements/recommendations for international students: Required—TOEFL (minimum score 550 paper-based). *Faculty research:* Comparative analyses of national identities and of democratization across Latin America, environmental problems and management along the U.S.—Mexican border, integration efforts along the Peru/Ecuador border, social justice issues in Guatemala.

University of California, Berkeley, Graduate Division, Group in Latin American Studies, Berkeley, CA 94720-1500. Offers MA, MJ/MA. *Degree requirements:* For master's, 2 foreign languages. *Entrance requirements:* For master's, GRE General Test, minimum GPA of 3.0, reading knowledge of Spanish or Portuguese, 3 letters of recommendation. Additional exam requirements/recommendations for international students: Required—TOEFL. Electronic applications accepted. *Faculty research:* Rural development, border communities, political economy, geography, history.

University of California, Los Angeles, Graduate Division, College of Letters and Science, Program in Latin American Studies, Los Angeles, CA 90095. Offers MA, M Ed/MA, MA/MA, MBA/MA, MLIS/MA, MPH/MA. *Students:* 27 full-time (20 women); includes 22 minority (1 African American, 1 Asian American or Pacific Islander, 20 Hispanic Americans). Average age 28. 44 applicants, 55% accepted, 8 enrolled. In 2008, 10 master's awarded. *Degree requirements:* For master's, 2 foreign languages, comprehensive exam or thesis. *Entrance requirements:* For master's, GRE General Test, minimum GPA of 3.0. *Application deadline:* For fall admission, 12/15 for domestic and international students. Application fee: $60 ($80 for international students). Electronic applications accepted. *Expenses:* Tuition, nonresident: full-time $14,694. Required fees: $9669.50. Full-time tuition and fees vary according to course load, degree level, program and student level. *Financial support:* In 2008–09, 11 fellowships with full and partial tuition reimbursements, 3 research assistantships with full and partial tuition reimbursements, 5 teaching assistantships with full and partial tuition reimbursements were awarded; Federal Work-Study, institutionally sponsored loans, scholarships/grants, health care benefits, tuition waivers (full and partial), and unspecified assistantships also available. Financial award application deadline: 3/1; financial award applicants required to submit FAFSA. *Unit head:* Dr. Kevin Terraciano, Chair, 310-206-6571. *Application contact:* Departmental Office, 310-206-6571, E-mail: idpgrads@international.ucla.edu.

University of California, San Diego, Office of Graduate Studies, Department of Political Science, Latin American Studies Program, La Jolla, CA 92093. Offers MA. *Entrance requirements:* For master's, GRE General Test, GRE Subject Test. Electronic applications accepted.

University of California, Santa Barbara, Graduate Division, College of Letters and Sciences, Division of Humanities and Fine Arts, Department of Spanish and Portuguese, Santa Barbara, CA 93106-4150. Offers Hispanic languages and literature (PhD), including applied linguistics, European Medieval studies, feminist studies, Hispanic languages and literature; Portuguese (MA); Spanish (MA); Spanish and Portuguese (MA); MA/PhD. Spanish Language Institute available during summer session. *Faculty:* 16 full-time (6 women). *Students:* 29 full-time (16 women). Average age 30. 46 applicants, 39% accepted, 9 enrolled. In 2008, 4 master's, 2 doctorates awarded. *Degree requirements:* For master's, 2 foreign languages, comprehensive exam (for some programs), thesis optional; for doctorate, 2 foreign languages, comprehensive exam, thesis/dissertation. *Entrance requirements:* For master's, GRE, 2 writing samples, undergraduate major in Spanish or equivalent, 3 letters of recommendation, statement of purpose, personal achievements/contributions statement, resumé/curriculum vitae, transcripts for post-secondary institutions attended; for doctorate, GRE, 2 writing samples, master's degree, 3 letters of recommendation, statement of purpose, personal achievements/contributions statement, resumé/curriculum vitae, transcripts for post-secondary institutions attended. Additional exam requirements/recommendations for international students: Required—TOEFL (minimum score 550 paper-based; 213 computer-based; 80 iBT), IELTS (minimum score 7), TOEFL or IELTS. *Application deadline:* For fall admission, 3/1 for domestic and international students; for winter admission, 11/1 for domestic and international students; for spring admission, 2/1 for domestic and international students. Application fee: $70 ($90 for international students). Electronic applications accepted. *Expenses:* Tuition, nonresident: full-time $25,149. Required fees: $10,143. Full-time tuition and fees vary according to campus/location, reciprocity agreements and student level. *Financial support:* In 2008–09, 30 students received support, including 9 fellowships with full and partial tuition reimbursements available (averaging $7,000 per year), 29 teaching assistantships with partial tuition reimbursements available (averaging $11,500 per year); career-related internships or fieldwork, Federal Work-Study, institutionally sponsored loans, scholarships/grants, health care benefits, tuition waivers (full and partial), and unspecified assistantships also available. Financial award application deadline: 1/7; financial award applicants required to submit FAFSA. *Faculty research:* 19th century Spanish and Portuguese literature, Spanish and Spanish American literature, 19th and 20th century Portuguese and Brazilian literatures, Hispanic Linguistics, Catalan language and culture. *Unit head:* Prof. Francisco A. Lomeli, Chair, 805-893-5715, Fax: 805-893-8341, E-mail: lomeli@spanport.ucsb.edu. *Application contact:* Carol Conley, Graduate Program Assistant, 805-893-3162, Fax: 805-893-8341, E-mail: cconley@spanport.ucsb.edu.

University of California, Santa Barbara, Graduate Division, College of Letters and Sciences, Division of Humanities and Fine Arts, Program in Latin American and Iberian Studies, Santa Barbara, CA 93106-4150. Offers MA. *Faculty:* 56 part-time/adjunct (26 women). *Students:* 10 full-time (4 women). Average age 33. 23 applicants, 65% accepted, 4 enrolled. In 2008, 8 master's awarded. *Degree requirements:* For master's, one foreign language, comprehensive exam (for some programs), thesis. *Entrance requirements:* For master's, GRE, 2 writing samples, BA, 3 letters of recommendation, statement of purpose, personal achievements/contributions statement, resumé/curriculum vitae, transcripts for post-secondary institutions attended. Additional exam requirements/recommendations for international students: Required—TOEFL (minimum score 550 paper-based; 213 computer-based; 80 iBT), IELTS (minimum score 7), TOEFL or IELTS. *Application deadline:* For fall admission, 5/1 for domestic and international students. Applications are processed on a rolling basis. Application fee: $70 ($90 for international students). Electronic applications accepted. *Expenses:* Tuition, nonresident: full-time $25,149. Required fees: $10,143. Full-time tuition and fees vary according to campus/location, reciprocity agreements and student level. *Financial support:* In 2008–09, 6 students received support, including 5 fellowships with full and partial tuition reimbursements available (averaging $9,900 per year), 3 teaching assistantships with partial tuition reimbursements available (averaging $10,000 per year); Federal Work-Study, institutionally sponsored loans, scholarships/grants, and health care benefits also available. Financial award application deadline: 1/15; financial award applicants required to submit FAFSA. *Faculty research:* Political science, anthropology, history, sociology, Portuguese. *Unit head:* Prof. Kathleen Bruhn, Director, 805-893-2999, Fax: 805-893-8341, E-mail: laisdirector@spanport.ucsb.edu. *Application contact:* Carol Conley, Graduate Program Assistant, 805-893-3162, Fax: 805-893-8341, E-mail: cconley@spanport.ucsb.edu.

University of Central Florida, College of Sciences, Department of Sociology, Orlando, FL 32816. Offers applied sociology (MA); domestic violence (MA); Maya studies (Certificate); sociology (PhD). Part-time and evening/weekend programs available. *Faculty:* 17 full-time (11 women), 4 part-time/adjunct (1 woman). *Students:* 44 full-time (35 women), 31 part-time (21 women); includes 19 minority (9 African Americans, 10 Hispanic Americans). In 2008, 4 master's, 1 doctorate, 3 other advanced degrees awarded. *Degree requirements:* For master's, comprehensive written exam or thesis. *Entrance requirements:* For master's, GRE General Test, minimum GPA of 3.0 in last 60 hours of course work. Additional exam requirements/recommendations for international students: Required—TOEFL. *Application deadline:* For fall admission, 7/15 for domestic students; for spring admission, 12/1 for domestic students. Application fee: $30. Electronic applications accepted. *Expenses:* Tuition, area resident: Full-time $6816; part-time $284 per credit. Tuition, state resident: full-time $6816; part-time $1076 per credit. Tuition, nonresident: full-time $25,824. Required fees: $216; $9 per credit. *Financial support:* In 2008–09, 7 fellowships with partial tuition reimbursements (averaging $10,800 per year), 8 research assistantships with partial tuition reimbursements (averaging $10,400 per year), 25 teaching assistantships with partial tuition reimbursements (averaging $9,600 per year) were awarded; career-related internships or fieldwork, Federal Work-Study, institutionally sponsored loans, tuition waivers (partial), and unspecified assistantships also available. Financial award application deadline: 3/1; financial award applicants required to submit FAFSA. *Faculty research:* Religious subcultures, attitudes toward abortion, population, sport research, stratification. *Unit head:* Dr. Jay Corzine, Chair, 407-823-2227, Fax: 407-823-5156, E-mail: hcorzine@mail.ucf.edu. *Application contact:* Dr. Jay Corzine, Chair, 407-823-2227, Fax: 407-823-5156, E-mail: hcorzine@mail.ucf.edu.

University of Chicago, Division of Social Sciences and Division of the Humanities, Latin American and Caribbean Studies Program, Chicago, IL 60637-1513. Offers AM, MBA/AM. *Degree requirements:* For master's, one foreign language, thesis. *Entrance requirements:* For master's, GRE General Test. Additional exam requirements/recommendations for international students: Required—TOEFL. Electronic applications accepted.

University of Connecticut, Graduate School, College of Liberal Arts and Sciences, Field of International Studies, Program in Latin American Studies, Storrs, CT 06269. Offers MA. *Degree requirements:* For master's, comprehensive exam. *Entrance requirements:* For master's, GRE General Test. Additional exam requirements/recommendations for international students: Required—TOEFL (minimum score 550 paper-based; 213 computer-based). Electronic applications accepted.

University of Florida, Graduate School, College of Liberal Arts and Sciences, Center for Latin American Studies, Gainesville, FL 32611. Offers MA, Certificate, JD/MA. Part-time programs available. *Degree requirements:* For master's, thesis. *Entrance requirements:* For master's, GRE General Test, minimum GPA of 3.0. Additional exam requirements/recommendations for international students: Required—TOEFL (minimum score 550 paper-based; 213 computer-based). Electronic applications accepted. *Faculty research:* Tropical conservation and development; ethnicity in the Americas, Brazil, and Cuba; North American Free Trade Agreement.

University of Illinois at Urbana–Champaign, Graduate College, College of Liberal Arts and Sciences, Center for Latin American and Caribbean Studies, Champaign, IL 61820. Offers Latin American studies (MA). *Students:* 8 full-time (5 women), 1 (woman) part-time; includes 6 minority (1 African American, 1 Asian American or Pacific Islander, 4 Hispanic Americans). 14 applicants, 79% accepted, 4 enrolled. *Entrance requirements:* For master's, GRE, minimum GPA of 3.0; writing sample. Additional exam requirements/recommendations for international students: Required—TOEFL (minimum score 550 paper-based; 213 computer-based). *Application deadline:* Applications are processed on a rolling basis. Application fee: $60 ($75 for international students). Electronic applications accepted. *Financial support:* In 2008–09, 5 fellowships, 2 teaching assistantships were awarded; research assistantships, tuition waivers (full and partial) also available. *Unit head:* Nils Jacobson, Director, 217-333-3182, Fax: 217-244-7333, E-mail: njacobse@illinois.edu. *Application contact:* Angelina Cotler, Associate Director, 217-244-2790, Fax: 217-244-7333, E-mail: cotler@illinois.edu.

The University of Kansas, Graduate Studies, College of Liberal Arts and Sciences, Center of Latin American Studies, Lawrence, KS 66045. Offers Brazilian studies (Graduate Certificate); Central American and Mexican studies (Graduate Certificate); Latin American studies (MA). Part-time programs available. *Faculty:* 31. *Students:* 11 full-time (6 women), 2 part-time (1 woman); includes 2 minority (both Hispanic Americans), 1 international. Average age 29. 6 applicants, 33% accepted, 1 enrolled. In 2008, 4 master's awarded. *Degree requirements:* For master's, 2 foreign languages, comprehensive exam, thesis optional. *Entrance requirements:* For master's, GRE, minimum GPA of 3.0, references, writing sample. Additional exam requirements/recommendations for international students: Required—TOEFL. *Application deadline:* For spring admission, 2/1 priority date for domestic and international students. Applications are processed on a rolling basis. Application fee: $45 ($50 for international students). Electronic applications accepted. *Expenses:* Tuition, area resident: Full-time $6122; part-time $255.10 per credit hour. Tuition, state resident: full-time $6122; part-time $255.10 per credit hour. Tuition, nonresident: full-time $14,629; part-time $609.55 per credit hour. Required fees: $847; $70.56 per credit hour. Tuition and fees vary according to course load and program. *Financial support:* Fellowships with full tuition reimbursements, research assistantships with full and partial tuition reimbursements, teaching assistantships with full and partial tuition reimbursements, scholarships/grants and unspecified assistantships available. Financial award application deadline: 2/1. *Faculty research:* Democracy, ethnicity, literature, environment, gender. *Unit head:* Peter Herlihy, Graduate Advisor, 785-864-4213, Fax: 785-864-3800, E-mail: herlihy@ku.edu. *Application contact:* Judy Farmer, Office Manager, 785-864-4213, Fax: 785-864-3800, E-mail: jfarmer@ku.edu.

University of Massachusetts Dartmouth, Graduate School, College of Arts and Sciences, Department of Portuguese, North Dartmouth, MA 02747-2300. Offers Luso-Afro-Brazilian studies (PhD); Portuguese (MA). Part-time programs available. *Faculty:* 6 full-time (2 women), 1 part-time/adjunct (0 women). *Students:* 10 full-time (6 women), 11 part-time (6 women); includes 6 minority (1 African American, 1 Asian American or Pacific Islander, 4 Hispanic Americans), 2 international. Average age 34. 5 applicants, 100% accepted, 2 enrolled. In 2008, 1 master's awarded. *Degree requirements:* For master's, comprehensive exam (for some programs). *Entrance requirements:* For master's, GRE (recommended), 10-page writing sample; for doctorate, GRE. Additional exam requirements/recommendations for international students: Required—TOEFL (minimum score 500 paper-based). *Application deadline:* For fall admission, 4/20 priority date for domestic students, 2/20 priority date for international students; for spring admission, 11/15 priority date for domestic students, 9/15 priority date for international students. Applications are processed on a rolling basis. Application fee: $40 ($60 for international students). Electronic applications accepted. *Expenses:* Tuition, state resident: full-time $2071; part-time $86.29 per credit. Tuition, nonresident: full-time $8099; part-time $337.46 per credit. Required fees: $7946. Tuition and fees vary according to class time, course load and reciprocity agreements. *Financial support:* In 2008–09, 2 research assistantships with full tuition reimbursements (averaging $17,025 per year), 8 teaching assistantships with full tuition reimbursements (averaging $16,000 per year) were awarded. Financial award application deadline: 3/1; financial award applicants required to submit FAFSA. *Unit head:* Victor J Mendes, Director, Graduate Studies, 508-999-8338, Fax: 508-999-9272, E-mail: vmendes@umassd.edu. *Application contact:* Elan Turcotte-Shamski, Graduate Admissions Officer, 508-999-8604, Fax: 508-999-8183, E-mail: graduate@umassd.edu.

University of Miami, Graduate School, College of Arts and Sciences, Department of Latin American and Caribbean Studies, Coral Gables, FL 33124. Offers Latin American studies (MA). Part-time programs available. *Degree requirements:* For master's, comprehensive exam (for some programs), thesis, linguistic competency in Spanish or Portuguese, reading competency in a second Latin American language. *Entrance requirements:* For master's, GRE, 3 letters of recommendation. Additional exam requirements/recommendations for international students: Required—TOEFL. Electronic applications accepted. *Faculty research:* Literary, media, religious, visual and cultural studies, environment and tourism studies, US-Latin American Relations and drug trafficking, migration, globalization, and social movements, democratization, regime transitions, and citizenship.

University of New Mexico, Graduate School, College of Arts and Sciences, Committee on Latin American Studies, Albuquerque, NM 87131-2039. Offers MA, PhD, JD/MA, MBA/MA, MCRP/MA, MSN/MA. *Degree requirements:* For master's, one foreign language, comprehensive exam (for some programs), thesis (for some programs); for doctorate, 2 foreign languages, comprehensive exam, thesis/dissertation. *Entrance requirements:* For master's, GRE General Test, intermediate competence in Spanish, Portuguese or indigenous Latin American Language, background in LAS-related coursework; for doctorate, GRE General Test, master's degree in related field, one Latin American language. Additional exam requirements/recommendations for international students: Required—TOEFL. Electronic applications accepted.

The University of North Carolina at Chapel Hill, Graduate School, College of Arts and Sciences, Department of Political Science, Chapel Hill, NC 27599. Offers Latin American studies (Certificate); political science (MA, PhD); trans-Atlantic studies (MA). *Degree requirements:* For master's, comprehensive exam; for doctorate, one foreign language, comprehensive exam, thesis/dissertation. *Entrance requirements:* For master's and doctorate, GRE General Test, minimum GPA of 3.0 recommended. Electronic applications accepted.

The University of North Carolina at Charlotte, Graduate School, College of Arts and Sciences, Department of Languages and Culture Studies, Charlotte, NC 28223-0001. Offers Latin American studies (MA); Spanish (MA). Part-time and evening/weekend programs available. *Faculty:* 22 full-time (12 women), 1 part-time/adjunct (0 women). *Students:* 13 full-time (11 women), 19 part-time (12 women); includes 13 minority (4 African Americans, 9 Hispanic Americans). Average age 28. 26 applicants, 92% accepted, 18 enrolled. In 2008, 13 master's awarded. *Degree requirements:* For master's, thesis optional. *Entrance requirements:* For master's, GRE, 3 letters of reference, minimum GPA of 2.75. Additional exam requirements/recommendations for international students: Required—TOEFL (minimum score 557 paper-based; 220 computer-based). *Application deadline:* For fall admission, 7/15 for domestic students, 5/1 for international students; for spring admission, 11/15 for domestic students, 10/1 for international students. Applications are processed on a rolling basis. Application fee: $55. Electronic applications accepted. *Expenses:* Tuition, area resident: Full-time $2919; part-time $122 per credit hour. Tuition, state resident: full-time $2919; part-time $122 per credit hour. Tuition, nonresident: full-time $13,126; part-time $547 per credit hour. Required fees: $1779; $91 per credit hour. Tuition and fees vary according to program. *Financial support:* In 2008–09, 4 teaching assistantships (averaging $6,250 per year) were awarded; career-related internships or fieldwork, Federal Work-Study, institutionally sponsored loans, scholarships/grants, unspecified assistantships, and 3 administrative assistantships ($9,667 average) also available. Support available to part-time students. Financial award application deadline: 4/1; financial award applicants required to submit FAFSA. *Faculty research:* Twentieth and twenty-first century Spanish literature, Central American literature, Caribbean literature, Mexican literature, literature of the Southern Cone. *Unit head:* Robert L. Reimer, Chair, 704-687-8767, Fax: 704-687-3496. *Application contact:* Kathy B. Giddings, Director of Graduate Admissions, 704-687-3366, Fax: 704-687-3279, E-mail: agidding@uncc.edu.

University of Notre Dame, Graduate School, College of Arts and Letters, Division of Humanities, Department of Romance Languages and Literatures, Notre Dame, IN 46556. Offers French and Francophone studies (MA); Iberian and Latin American studies (MA); Italian studies (MA); Romance literatures (MA). *Faculty:* 25 full-time (10 women), 4 part-time/adjunct (all women). *Students:* 17 full-time (12 women); includes 4 minority (all Hispanic Americans), 2 international. 30 applicants, 47% accepted, 11 enrolled. In 2008, 11 master's awarded. *Degree requirements:* For master's, 2 foreign languages, comprehensive exam, thesis optional. *Entrance requirements:* For master's, GRE General Test, BA in target language. Additional exam requirements/recommendations for international students: Required—TOEFL (minimum score 600 paper-based; 250 computer-based; 80 iBT). *Application deadline:* For fall admission, 2/1 priority date for domestic students, 2/1 for international students. Application fee: $50. Electronic applications accepted. *Financial support:* Teaching assistantships with full tuition reimbursements, tuition waivers (full) available. Financial award application deadline: 2/1. *Faculty research:* Literature of discovery and exploration, modern literature, literary criticism, medieval literature, feminist critical theory. *Unit head:* Dr. John Welle, Director of Graduate Studies, 574-631-6887, E-mail: al.romland.1@nd.edu. *Application contact:* Dr. Barbara Turpin, Director of Graduate Admissions, 574-631-7706, Fax: 574-631-4183.

University of Pittsburgh, University Center for International Studies, Pittsburgh, PA 15260. Offers African studies (Certificate); Asian studies (Certificate); European Union studies (Certificate); global studies (Certificate); Latin American studies (Certificate); Russian and East European studies (Certificate); West European studies (Certificate).

University of South Florida, Graduate School, College of Arts and Sciences, Department of Government and International Affairs, Tampa, FL 33620-9951. Offers Latin American Caribbean and Latino Studies (MA); political science (MA); public administration (MPA). Part-time and evening/weekend programs available. *Faculty:* 18 full-time (3 women), 1 (woman) part-time/adjunct. *Students:* 33 full-time (21 women), 98 part-time (50 women); includes 39 minority (20 African Americans, 5 Asian Americans or Pacific Islanders, 14 Hispanic Americans), 6 international. 81 applicants, 62% accepted, 29 enrolled. In 2008, 27 master's awarded. *Degree requirements:* For master's, comprehensive exam, thesis; for doctorate, comprehensive exam, thesis/dissertation. *Entrance requirements:* For master's, GRE (minimum score: 470 verbal, 470 quantitative), minimum GPA of 3.0 in last 60 hours of course work. Additional exam requirements/recommendations for international students: Required—TOEFL (minimum score 550 paper-based; 213 computer-based). *Application deadline:* For fall admission, 2/15 for domestic students; for spring admission, 10/15 for domestic students. Applications are processed on a rolling basis. Application fee: $30. Electronic applications accepted. *Expenses:* Tuition, state resident: full-time $2624.40; part-time $291.60 per credit hour. Tuition, nonresident: full-time $7822; part-time $869.13 per credit hour. *Financial support:* Scholarships/grants and unspecified assistantships available. Financial award application deadline: 4/1. *Unit head:* Dr. Mohsen Milani, Chairperson, 813-974-2384, Fax: 813-974-0832, E-mail: milani@chuma1.cas.usf.edu. *Application contact:* Dr. Stephen Tauber, Graduate Coordinator, 813-974-0781, Fax: 813-974-0832, E-mail: stauber@chuma1.cas.usf.edu.

University of South Florida, Graduate School, College of Arts and Sciences, Institute for the Study of Latin America and the Caribbean, Tampa, FL 33620-9951. Offers Cuban studies (Graduate Certificate); Latin American and Caribbean studies (Graduate Certificate); Latin American, Caribbean and Latino studies (MA). *Students:* 9 full-time (5 women), 9 part-time (4 women); includes 9 minority (2 African Americans, 1 Asian American or Pacific Islander, 6 Hispanic Americans), 2 international. 12 applicants, 83% accepted, 7 enrolled. In 2008, 5 master's awarded. *Degree requirements:* For master's, comprehensive exam, thesis. *Entrance requirements:* For master's, GPA 3.0. Additional exam requirements/recommendations for international students: Required—TOEFL (minimum score 550 paper-based; 213 computer-based). *Application deadline:* For fall admission, 2/15 priority date for domestic students, 1/2 for international students; for spring admission, 10/15 priority date for domestic students, 6/1 for international students. Application fee: $30. *Expenses:* Tuition, state resident: full-time $2624.40; part-time $291.60 per credit hour. Tuition, nonresident: full-time $7822; part-time $869.13 per credit hour. *Unit head:* Nina Thompson, Director, 813-974-3547, Fax: 813-974-4075, E-mail: nina@cas.usf.edu. *Application contact:* Nina Thompson, Director, 813-974-3547, Fax: 813-974-4075, E-mail: nina@cas.usf.edu.

The University of Texas at Austin, Graduate School, College of Liberal Arts, Teresa Lozano Long Institute of Latin American Studies, Austin, TX 78712-1111. Offers MA, PhD, JD/MA, MBA/MA, MP Aff/MA, MSCRP/MA. *Entrance requirements:* For master's and doctorate, GRE General Test.

University of Wisconsin–Madison, Graduate School, College of Letters and Science, Department of History, Madison, WI 53706-1380. Offers African history (MA, PhD); Central Asian history (MA, PhD); comparative world history (MA, PhD); East Asian history (MA, PhD); European history (MA, PhD); gender and women's history (MA, PhD); Latin American and Caribbean history (MA, PhD); Middle Eastern history (MA, PhD); South Asian history (MA, PhD); Southeast Asian history (MA, PhD); United States history (MA, PhD). Terminal master's awarded for partial completion of doctoral program. *Degree requirements:* For master's, thesis (for some programs); for doctorate, variable foreign language requirement, thesis/dissertation. *Entrance requirements:* For master's and doctorate, GRE General Test. Additional exam requirements/recommendations for international students: Required—Michigan English Language Assessment Battery or TOEFL. Electronic applications accepted. *Faculty research:* American, African, European, Asian, Latin American, and Middle Eastern history.

University of Wisconsin–Madison, Graduate School, College of Letters and Science, Latin American, Caribbean and Iberian Studies Program, Madison, WI 53706-1380. Offers MA, MA/JD. *Degree requirements:* For master's, 2 foreign languages, thesis. *Entrance requirements:* For master's, minimum GPA of 3.0. Electronic applications accepted. *Faculty research:* Development, gender, social movements, cultural studies, history.

Vanderbilt University, Graduate School, Program in Latin American Studies, Nashville, TN 37240-1001. Offers MA, LL M/MA, MBA/MA. *Students:* 12 full-time (6 women), 1 part-time (0 women); includes 4 minority (1 African American, 3 Hispanic Americans), 2 international. Average age 27. 25 applicants, 20% accepted, 4 enrolled. In 2008, 7 master's awarded. *Degree requirements:* For master's, 2 foreign languages, thesis or alternative. *Entrance requirements:* For master's, GRE General Test. Additional exam requirements/recommendations for international students: Required—TOEFL (minimum score 570 paper-based; 230 computer-based; 88 iBT). *Application deadline:* For fall admission, 1/15 for domestic and international students. Application fee: $0. Electronic applications accepted. *Financial support:* Teaching assistantships with full tuition reimbursements, Federal Work-Study, institutionally sponsored loans, and health care benefits available. Financial award application deadline: 1/15; financial award applicants required to submit CSS PROFILE or FAFSA. *Faculty research:* Latin American and Iberian studies, anthropology, history, Spanish and Portuguese, social and political science. *Unit head:* Edward Fischer, PhD, Director, 615-322-2527, Fax: 615-322-2305, E-mail: edward.f.fischer@vanderbilt.edu. *Application contact:* Frank Robinson, PhD, Associate Director, 615-322-2527, Fax: 615-322-2305, E-mail: william.f.robinson@vanderbilt.edu.

West Virginia University, Eberly College of Arts and Sciences, Department of History, Morgantown, WV 26506. Offers African history (MA, PhD); African-American history (MA,

Latin American Studies

West Virginia University (continued)
PhD); American history (MA, PhD); Appalachian/regional history (MA, PhD); East Asian history (MA, PhD); European history (MA, PhD); history of science and technology (MA, PhD); Latin American history (MA). Part-time programs available. *Degree requirements:* For master's, one foreign language, thesis (for some programs), oral exam, thesis defense; for doctorate, one foreign language, comprehensive exam, thesis/dissertation, dissertation defense. *Entrance requirements:* For master's, GRE General Test, minimum GPA of 3.0; for doctorate, GRE General Test. Additional exam requirements/recommendations for international students: Required—TOEFL (minimum score 550 paper-based), IELTS (minimum score 6.5). Electronic applications accepted. *Faculty research:* U.S., Appalachia, modern Europe, Africa, colonial and post-colonial societies.

Yale University, Graduate School of Arts and Sciences, Department of Spanish and Portuguese, New Haven, CT 06520. Offers Latin American literature (PhD); Luso-Brazilian and Spanish/Spanish American literatures (PhD); Spanish peninsular literature (PhD). Terminal master's awarded for partial completion of doctoral program. *Degree requirements:* For doctorate, 3 foreign languages, thesis/dissertation. *Entrance requirements:* For doctorate, GRE General Test.

Near and Middle Eastern Studies

The American University in Cairo, Graduate Studies and Research, School of Humanities and Social Sciences, Department of Arabic Studies, Cairo, Egypt. Offers Arab language and literature (MA); Islamic art and architecture (MA); Islamic studies (Diploma); Middle East studies (MA, Diploma); Middle Eastern history (MA). Part-time programs available. *Degree requirements:* For master's, thesis optional, proficiency in French or German. *Entrance requirements:* Additional exam requirements/recommendations for international students: Required—English entrance exam and/or TOEFL. Electronic applications accepted. *Faculty research:* History of early Islam, Ayubbid, and Mamluk periods; nineteenth- and twentieth-century Middle East Islamic jurisprudence; contemporary Arabic literary criticism.

The American University in Cairo, Graduate Studies and Research, School of Humanities and Social Sciences, Department of Sociology, Anthropology, Psychology, and Egyptology, Cairo, Egypt. Offers sociology and anthropology (MA). *Degree requirements:* For master's, one foreign language, thesis. *Entrance requirements:* Additional exam requirements/recommendations for international students: Required—English entrance exam and/or TOEFL. Electronic applications accepted. *Faculty research:* Development, gender, sociopolitical economic formulations, social science indigenization, Arab world.

American University of Beirut, Graduate Programs, Faculty of Arts and Sciences, Beirut, Lebanon. Offers anthropology (MA); Arabic language and literature (MA); archaeology (MA); biology (MS); chemistry (MS); computer science (MS); economics (MA); education (MA); English language (MA); English literature (MA); environmental policy planning (MSES); financial economics (MAFE); geology (MS); history (MA); mathematics (MA, MS); Middle Eastern studies (MA); philosophy (MA); physics (MS); political studies (MA); psychology (MA); public administration (MA); sociology (MA); statistics (MA, MS). Part-time programs available. *Degree requirements:* For master's, one foreign language, comprehensive exam, thesis (for some programs). *Entrance requirements:* For master's, GRE, letter of recommendation. Additional exam requirements/recommendations for international students: Required—TOEFL (minimum score 600 paper-based; 250 computer-based; 100 iBT), IELTS (minimum score 7.5). *Faculty research:* String theory and supergravity; computer graphics; algebra and number theory; popular Arabic literature; marine and freshwater biology; integrating science, math and technology.

The American University of Paris, Graduate Programs, Paris, France. Offers finance (MSF); global communications (MAGC); international affairs, conflict resolution and civil society development (MA); Middle Eastern and Islamic studies (MA); public administration (MPA). *Degree requirements:* For master's, thesis. *Entrance requirements:* For master's, minimum undergraduate GPA of 3.0.

Brandeis University, Graduate School of Arts and Sciences, Department of Near Eastern and Judaic Studies, Waltham, MA 02454-9110. Offers Near Eastern and Judaic studies (MA, PhD); Near Eastern and Judaic studies and sociology (PhD); Near Eastern and Judaic studies and women's studies (MA); teaching of Hebrew (MAT). Part-time programs available. Terminal master's awarded for partial completion of doctoral program. *Degree requirements:* For master's, one foreign language, comprehensive exam, thesis or alternative; for doctorate, 3 foreign languages, comprehensive exam, thesis/dissertation. *Entrance requirements:* For master's and doctorate, GRE General Test (recommended), letters of recommendation, transcripts, statement of purpose. Additional exam requirements/recommendations for international students: Required—TOEFL (minimum score 600 paper-based; 250 computer-based; 100 iBT), IELTS (minimum score 7). Electronic applications accepted. *Faculty research:* Ancient Near East and Bible, philosophy, history, modern Middle East, Islamic studies.

California State University, Long Beach, Graduate Studies, College of Liberal Arts, Department of History, Long Beach, CA 90840. Offers Africa and the Middle East (MA); ancient/Medieval Europe (MA); Asia (MA); Latin America (MA); modern Europe (MA); United States (MA); world (MA). Part-time and evening/weekend programs available. *Faculty:* 17 full-time (11 women), 2 part-time/adjunct (1 woman). *Students:* 9 full-time (4 women), 45 part-time (18 women); includes 15 minority (2 African Americans, 3 Asian Americans or Pacific Islanders, 10 Hispanic Americans), 1 international. Average age 35. 40 applicants, 50% accepted, 11 enrolled. *Degree requirements:* For master's, one foreign language, comprehensive exam or thesis. *Application deadline:* For fall admission, 3/1 for domestic students. Applications are processed on a rolling basis. Application fee: $55. Electronic applications accepted. *Expenses:* Tuition, nonresident: full-time $11,160; part-time $372 per unit. Required fees: $4100; $1261 per semester. *Financial support:* Research assistantships, Federal Work-Study, institutionally sponsored loans, and scholarships/grants available. Financial award application deadline: 3/2. *Faculty research:* All periods of European and American history, recent Asian and African history. *Unit head:* Dr. Nancy L Quam-Wickham, Graduate Advisor, 562-985-4431, Fax: 562-985-5431, E-mail: quamwick@csulb.edu. *Application contact:* Dr. Houri Berberian, Graduate Advisor, 562-985-4524, Fax: 562-985-4431, E-mail: hberber@csulb.edu.

The Catholic University of America, School of Arts and Sciences, Department of Semitic and Egyptian Languages and Literature, Washington, DC 20064. Offers MA, PhD. *Degree requirements:* For master's, 2 foreign languages, comprehensive exam, thesis or alternative; for doctorate, 2 foreign languages, comprehensive exam, thesis/dissertation. *Entrance requirements:* For master's and doctorate, GRE General Test, 3 letters of recommendation. Additional exam requirements/recommendations for international students: Required—TOEFL (minimum score 580 paper-based; 237 computer-based). Electronic applications accepted. *Faculty research:* Christian history and literature of the Near East, Hebrew Bible.

Columbia University, Graduate School of Arts and Sciences, Division of Humanities, Department of Middle East Languages and Cultures, New York, NY 10027. Offers Hebrew language and literature (M Phil, MA, PhD); Middle Eastern languages and cultures (M Phil, MA, PhD); South Asian languages and cultures (M Phil, MA, PhD). Part-time programs available. *Degree requirements:* For master's, thesis, oral and written exams; for doctorate, 3 foreign languages, thesis/dissertation. *Entrance requirements:* For master's and doctorate, GRE General Test. Additional exam requirements/recommendations for international students: Required—TOEFL. *Faculty research:* Indo-Iranian, Turkish, central Asian, and Armenian studies; Arabic and ancient Semitics.

Columbia University, Graduate School of Arts and Sciences, Program in Liberal Studies, New York, NY 10027. Offers American studies (MA); East Asian studies (MA); human rights studies (MA); Islamic culture studies (MA); Jewish studies (MA); medieval studies (MA); modern European studies (MA); South Asian studies (MA). Part-time and evening/weekend programs available. *Degree requirements:* For master's, thesis.

Columbia University, School of International and Public Affairs, Middle East Institute, New York, NY 10027. Offers Certificate. Students must also be enrolled in a separate graduate degree program at Columbia University. Electronic applications accepted.

Cornell University, Graduate School, Graduate Fields of Arts and Sciences, Field of Archaeology, Ithaca, NY 14853-0001. Offers environmental archaeology (MA); historical archaeology (MA); Latin American archaeology (MA); medieval archaeology (MA); Mediterranean and Near Eastern archaeology (MA); Stone Age archaeology (MA). *Faculty:* 12 full-time (3 women). *Students:* 4 full-time (3 women). Average age 27. 10 applicants, 40% accepted, 2 enrolled. *Degree requirements:* For master's, one foreign language, thesis. *Entrance requirements:* For master's, GRE General Test, 3 letters of recommendation, sample of written work. Additional exam requirements/recommendations for international students: Required—TOEFL (minimum score 550 paper-based; 213 computer-based; 77 iBT). *Application deadline:* For fall admission, 1/15 for domestic students. Application fee: $70. Electronic applications accepted. *Expenses:* Tuition: Full-time $29,500. Required fees: $70. Full-time tuition and fees vary according to degree level, program and student level. *Financial support:* In 2008–09, 4 students received support, including 1 fellowship with full tuition reimbursement available, 1 research assistantship with full tuition reimbursement available, 2 teaching assistantships with full tuition reimbursements available; institutionally sponsored loans, scholarships/grants, health care benefits, tuition waivers (full and partial), and unspecified assistantships also available. Financial award applicants required to submit FAFSA. *Faculty research:* Anatolia, Lydia, Sardis, classical and Hellenistic Greece; science in archaeology; North American Indians; Stone Age Africa; Maya trade. *Unit head:* Director of Graduate Studies, 607-255-6768, E-mail: blj7@cornell.edu. *Application contact:* Graduate Field Assistant, 607-255-6768, E-mail: dsd6@cornell.edu.

Cornell University, Graduate School, Graduate Fields of Arts and Sciences, Field of History, Ithaca, NY 14853-0001. Offers African history (MA, PhD); American history (MA, PhD); ancient history (MA, PhD); early modern European history (MA, PhD); English history (MA, PhD); French history (MA, PhD); German history (MA, PhD); history of science (MA, PhD); Latin American history (MA, PhD); medieval Chinese history (MA, PhD); medieval history (MA, PhD); modern Chinese history (MA, PhD); modern European history (MA, PhD); modern Japanese history (MA, PhD); premodern Islamic history (MA, PhD); premodern Japanese history (MA, PhD); Renaissance history (MA, PhD); Russian history (MA, PhD); Southeast Asian history (MA, PhD). *Faculty:* 54 full-time (14 women). *Students:* 65 full-time (35 women); includes 12 minority (4 African Americans, 3 Asian Americans or Pacific Islanders, 5 Hispanic Americans), 19 international. Average age 31. 205 applicants, 8% accepted, 11 enrolled. In 2008, 12 master's, 6 doctorates awarded. Terminal master's awarded for partial completion of doctoral program. *Degree requirements:* For master's, thesis; for doctorate, 2 foreign languages, comprehensive exam, thesis/dissertation, 1 year of teaching experience. *Entrance requirements:* For master's and doctorate, GRE General Test, writing sample, 3 letters of recommendation. Additional exam requirements/recommendations for international students: Required—TOEFL (minimum score 550 paper-based; 213 computer-based; 77 iBT). *Application deadline:* For fall admission, 1/15 for domestic students. Application fee: $70. Electronic applications accepted. *Expenses:* Tuition: Full-time $29,500. Required fees: $70. Full-time tuition and fees vary according to degree level, program and student level. *Financial support:* In 2008–09, 54 students received support, including 27 fellowships with full tuition reimbursements available, 3 research assistantships with full tuition reimbursements available, 24 teaching assistantships with full tuition reimbursements available; institutionally sponsored loans, scholarships/grants, health care benefits, tuition waivers (full and partial), and unspecified assistantships also available. Financial award applicants required to submit FAFSA. *Unit head:* Director of Graduate Studies, 607-255-6738, Fax: 607-255-0469. *Application contact:* Graduate Field Assistant, 607-255-6738, Fax: 607-255-0469, E-mail: history_grad_info@cornell.edu.

Cornell University, Graduate School, Graduate Fields of Arts and Sciences, Field of Near Eastern Studies, Ithaca, NY 14853-0001. Offers ancient Near Eastern studies (MA, PhD); Arabic and Islamic studies (MA, PhD); biblical studies (MA, PhD); Hebrew and Judaic studies (MA, PhD). *Faculty:* 16 full-time (5 women). *Students:* 5 full-time (2 women), 1 international. Average age 26. 28 applicants, 14% accepted, 2 enrolled.Terminal master's awarded for partial completion of doctoral program. *Degree requirements:* For master's, one foreign language, thesis; for doctorate, 2 foreign languages, comprehensive exam, thesis/dissertation. *Entrance requirements:* For master's and doctorate, GRE General Test, 2 years of 1 Near Eastern language, 3 letters of recommendation, writing sample. Additional exam requirements/recommendations for international students: Required—TOEFL (minimum score 550 paper-based; 213 computer-based; 77 iBT). *Application deadline:* For fall admission, 2/1 for domestic students. Application fee: $70. Electronic applications accepted. *Expenses:* Tuition: Full-time $29,500. Required fees: $70. Full-time tuition and fees vary according to degree level, program and student level. *Financial support:* In 2008–09, 5 students received support, including 3 fellowships with full tuition reimbursements available, 2 teaching assistantships with full tuition reimbursements available; research assistantships with full tuition reimbursements available, institutionally sponsored loans, scholarships/grants, health care benefits, tuition waivers (full and partial), and unspecified assistantships also available. Financial award applicants required to submit FAFSA. *Faculty research:* Ancient Near East (including archeology), Hebrew and Judaic studies (including bible), early Christianity, Arabic and Islamic studies, modern Middle East. *Unit head:* Director of Graduate Studies, 607-255-1329, Fax: 607-255-6450. *Application contact:* Graduate Field Assistant, 607-255-1329, Fax: 607-255-6450, E-mail: neareastern@cornell.edu.

Drew University, Caspersen School of Graduate Studies, Program in Biblical Studies and Early Christianity, Madison, NJ 07940-1493. Offers religion in ancient Israel (MA, PhD); the New Testament and early Christianity (MA, PhD). Part-time programs available. Terminal master's awarded for partial completion of doctoral program. *Degree requirements:* For master's, one foreign language, thesis; for doctorate, 2 foreign languages, comprehensive exam, thesis/dissertation. *Entrance requirements:* For master's and doctorate, GRE General Test. *Faculty research:* Folk religions of ancient Israel, New Testament exegesis and apocrypha, Near East archaeology, Hebrew Bible.

Emory University, Graduate School of Arts and Sciences, Department of Comparative Literature, Atlanta, GA 30322-1100. Offers comparative literature (PhD); English (Certificate); French (Certificate); Middle Eastern studies (PhD); philosophy (Certificate); psychoanalytic studies (PhD); religion (PhD); Spanish (Certificate); women studies (Certificate). *Degree requirements:* For doctorate, 2 foreign languages, comprehensive exam, thesis/dissertation. *Entrance requirements:* For doctorate, GRE General Test, minimum GPA of 3.0. Additional exam requirements/recommendations for international students: Required—TOEFL. Electronic applications accepted. *Faculty research:* Literary theory, psychoanalysis trauma and testimony, literature and religion, literature and technology, literature and philosophy, politics and global culture, literature and aesthetics.

Georgetown University, Graduate School of Arts and Sciences, The Center for Contemporary Arab Studies, Washington, DC 20057. Offers MA, Certificate, MA/JD, MA/PhD. *Degree requirements:* For master's, one foreign language, comprehensive exam, proficiency in Arabic. *Entrance requirements:* For master's, GRE, minimum GPA of 3.0. Additional exam requirements/recommendations for international students: Required—TOEFL. *Faculty research:* Contemporary Arab world.

Georgetown University, Graduate School of Arts and Sciences, Department of Arabic and Islamic Studies, Washington, DC 20057. Offers Arabic area studies (PhD); Islamic studies (MA, PhD); linguistics (MA, PhD). *Degree requirements:* For master's, comprehensive exam, research project; for doctorate, one foreign language, comprehensive exam, thesis/dissertation. *Entrance requirements:* Additional exam requirements/recommendations for international students: Required—TOEFL.

The George Washington University, Elliott School of International Affairs, Program in Middle East Studies, Washington, DC 20052. Offers MA. *Students:* 27 full-time (14 women), 9 part-time (2 women); includes 2 minority (1 African American, 1 Asian American or Pacific Islander), 1 international. Average age 25. 106 applicants, 61% accepted, 23 enrolled. *Application deadline:* For fall admission, 2/1 for domestic students; for spring admission, 10/1 for domestic students. *Financial support:* In 2008–09, 7 students received support. Tuition waivers available. Financial award application deadline: 1/15. *Unit head:* Nathan J. Brown, Director, 202-994-2123, Fax: 202-994-5477, E-mail: nbrown@gwu.edu. *Application contact:* Jeff V. Miles, Director of Graduate Admissions, 202-994-7050, Fax: 202-994-9537, E-mail: esiagrad@gwu.edu.

Harvard University, Graduate School of Arts and Sciences, Committee on Middle Eastern Studies, Cambridge, MA 02138. Offers anthropology and Middle Eastern studies (PhD); economics and Middle Eastern studies (PhD); fine arts and Middle Eastern studies (PhD); history and Middle Eastern studies (PhD); regional studies–Middle East (AM). Terminal master's awarded for partial completion of doctoral program. *Degree requirements:* For master's, one foreign language; for doctorate, 2 foreign languages, thesis/dissertation. *Entrance requirements:* For master's, GRE General Test; for doctorate, GRE General Test, 1 year of course work in Middle Eastern regional studies, proficiency in a related language. Additional exam requirements/recommendations for international students: Required—TOEFL. *Expenses:* Tuition: Full-time $32,556. Required fees: $1426. Full-time tuition and fees vary according to program and student level.

Harvard University, Graduate School of Arts and Sciences, Department of Near Eastern Languages and Civilizations, Cambridge, MA 02138. Offers Akkadian and Sumerian (AM, PhD); Arabic (AM, PhD); Armenian (AM, PhD); biblical history (AM, PhD); Hebrew (AM, PhD); Indo-Muslim culture (AM, PhD); Iranian (AM, PhD); Jewish history and literature (AM, PhD); Persian (AM, PhD); Semitic philology (AM, PhD); Syro-Palestinian archaeology (AM, PhD); Turkish (AM, PhD). *Degree requirements:* For doctorate, variable foreign language requirement, thesis/dissertation, general exams. *Entrance requirements:* For master's, GRE General Test; for doctorate, GRE General Test, proficiency in a Near Eastern language. Additional exam requirements/recommendations for international students: Required—TOEFL. *Expenses:* Tuition: Full-time $32,556. Required fees: $1426. Full-time tuition and fees vary according to program and student level.

Hebrew Union College–Jewish Institute of Religion, School of Graduate Studies, Cincinnati, OH 45220-2488. Offers Bible and the ancient Near East (M Phil, MA, PhD); Hebrew letters (DHL); history of biblical interpretation (M Phil, MA, PhD); Jewish and Christian studies in the Greco-Roman period (M Phil, PhD); Jewish and cognate studies (M Phil); Judaic and cognate studies (MA, PhD); modern Jewish history (M Phil, MA, PhD); philosophy and Jewish religious thought (M Phil, MA, PhD); rabbinics (M Phil, MA, PhD). Part-time programs available. Terminal master's awarded for partial completion of doctoral program. *Degree requirements:* For master's, one foreign language, thesis optional; for doctorate, 3 foreign languages, comprehensive exam, thesis/dissertation. *Entrance requirements:* For master's and doctorate, GRE General Test, knowledge of Hebrew. Additional exam requirements/recommendations for international students: Required—TOEFL. *Faculty research:* Aramaic lexicon translations, German-Jewish history, neo-Babylonian texts.

The Johns Hopkins University, Paul H. Nitze School of Advanced International Studies, Washington, DC 20036. Offers international development (Certificate); international public policy (MIPP); international relations (MA, PhD), including African studies (MA), American foreign policy (MA), Asian studies (MA), Canadian studies (MA), conflict management (MA), European studies (MA), global theory and history (MA), international development (MA), international law, and organizations (MA), international policy (MA), international relations (general) (MA), Latin American studies (MA), Middle East studies (MA), Russian and Eurasian studies (MA), strategic studies (MA); international studies (Certificate); JD/MA; MBA/MA; MHS/MA. Terminal master's awarded for partial completion of doctoral program. *Degree requirements:* For master's, one foreign language, 16 non-language courses (8 for MIPP), 2 core examinations, comprehensive oral exam, paper (for some programs); for doctorate, 2 foreign languages, thesis/dissertation, 3 comprehensive exams, defense. *Entrance requirements:* For master's, GMAT or GRE General Test, previous course work in economics, foreign language, undergraduate degree; for doctorate, GRE General Test, master's degree. Additional exam requirements/recommendations for international students: Required—TOEFL (minimum paper-based score of 600, computer-based 250, iBT 100) or IELTS (minimum 7.0). Electronic applications accepted. *Expenses:* Contact institution. *Faculty research:* Regional studies and functional fields of international relations, international economics, conflict management, global theory and history, international law and organizations, international policy, strategic studies.

The Johns Hopkins University, Zanvyl Krieger School of Arts and Sciences, Department of Near Eastern Studies, Baltimore, MD 21218-2699. Offers PhD. Part-time programs available. *Degree requirements:* For doctorate, 2 foreign languages, comprehensive exam, thesis/dissertation. *Entrance requirements:* Additional exam requirements/recommendations for international students: Required—TOEFL (minimum score 600 paper-based; 250 computer-based). Electronic applications accepted. *Faculty research:* Egyptology, Assyriology, religions of ancient Israel and Syria, ancient and biblical law, demotic Egyptian.

McGill University, Faculty of Graduate and Postdoctoral Studies, Faculty of Arts, Institute of Islamic Studies, Montréal, QC H3A 2T5, Canada. Offers MA, PhD, Diploma.

New York University, Graduate School of Arts and Science, Hagop Kevorkian Center for Near Eastern Studies, Department of Middle Eastern and Islamic Studies, New York, NY 10012-1019. Offers Middle Eastern and Islamic studies (MA, PhD); Middle Eastern and Islamic studies/history (PhD). Part-time programs available. Terminal master's awarded for partial completion of doctoral program. *Degree requirements:* For master's, 2 foreign languages, thesis; for doctorate, 4 foreign languages, comprehensive exam, thesis/dissertation. *Entrance requirements:* For master's and doctorate, GRE General Test. Additional exam requirements/recommendations for international students: Required—TOEFL. *Faculty research:* Middle Eastern history, Arabic/Persian/Turkish language and literature, cultures and societies of Middle East, Islamic studies.

New York University, Graduate School of Arts and Science, Hagop Kevorkian Center for Near Eastern Studies, Program in Near Eastern Studies, New York, NY 10012-1019. Offers Near Eastern studies (MA); Near Eastern studies (museum studies) (MA); Near Eastern studies/journalism (MA). Part-time programs available. *Degree requirements:* For master's, one foreign language, thesis. *Entrance requirements:* For master's, GRE General Test. Additional exam requirements/recommendations for international students: Required—TOEFL. *Faculty research:* Politics, political economy, anthropology, history and culture of the Middle East.

New York University, Graduate School of Arts and Science, Program in Museum Studies, New York, NY 10012-1019. Offers museum studies (MA, Advanced Certificate), including Africana studies (MA), Hebrew and Judaic studies (MA), Latin American and Caribbean studies (MA), Near Eastern studies (MA). Part-time and evening/weekend programs available. *Entrance requirements:* For degree, master's or PhD. *Faculty research:* Modern and contemporary art, history of museums and exhibitions, conservation of cultural materials, museum anthropology, ethnography.

Princeton University, Graduate School, Department of Near Eastern Studies, Princeton, NJ 08544-1019. Offers MA, PhD. *Degree requirements:* For master's, one foreign language, thesis; for doctorate, 2 foreign languages, thesis/dissertation. *Entrance requirements:* For master's and doctorate, GRE General Test. Additional exam requirements/recommendations for international students: Required—TOEFL. Electronic applications accepted.

Regent University, Graduate School, Robertson School of Government, Virginia Beach, VA 23464. Offers health care policy and administration (MA); international politics (MA); law and public policy (MA); Mid-East Politics (MA); political leadership and management (MA); political management (MA); public administration (MA); public policy (MA); terrorism and homeland defense (MA); world economies and political development (MA); JD/MA; M Div/MA; M Ed/MA; MBA/MA. Part-time and evening/weekend programs available. Postbaccalaureate distance learning degree programs offered (minimal on-campus study). *Faculty:* 6 full-time (1 woman), 11 part-time/adjunct (1 woman). *Students:* 60 full-time (33 women), 69 part-time (34 women); includes 29 minority (22 African Americans, 1 Asian American or Pacific Islander, 6 Hispanic Americans), 3 international. Average age 30. 136 applicants, 54% accepted, 54 enrolled. In 2008, 48 master's awarded. *Degree requirements:* For master's, thesis optional, internship. *Entrance requirements:* For master's, GRE General Test or LSAT, minimum undergraduate GPA of 3.0, writing sample, resumé, interview, references, transcripts. Additional exam requirements/recommendations for international students: Required—TOEFL (minimum score 577 paper-based; 233 computer-based). *Application deadline:* For fall admission, 5/1 priority date for domestic students; for spring admission, 11/1 priority date for domestic students. Applications are processed on a rolling basis. Application fee: $50. Electronic applications accepted. *Expenses:* Contact institution. *Financial support:* Career-related internships or fieldwork, scholarships/grants, tuition waivers (full and partial), and unspecified assistantships available. Support available to part-time students. Financial award application deadline: 9/1; financial award applicants required to submit FAFSA. *Faculty research:* Education reform, political character issues, social capital concerns, administrative ethics, Biblical law and public policy. *Unit head:* Dr. Charles W. Dunn, Dean, 757-352-4322, Fax: 757-352-4643, E-mail: cwdunn@regent.edu. *Application contact:* Matthew Chadwick, Director of Admissions, 800-373-5504, Fax: 757-352-4381, E-mail: admissions@regent.edu.

SIT Graduate Institute, Graduate Programs, Program in Global Management (Oman), Brattleboro, VT 05302-0676. Offers MGM. Program offered in the Sultanate of Oman. Part-time programs available. *Degree requirements:* For master's, capstone project. *Entrance requirements:* For master's, 1,000-1,500 word essay. Additional exam requirements/recommendations for international students: Required—TOEFL (minimum score of 550 paper-based, 213 computer-based, 79 iBT) or IELTS (minimum score of 6.0).

Southern Evangelical Seminary, Veritas Graduate School of Apologetics and Counter-Cult Ministry, Matthews, NC 28105. Offers apologetics (MA, D Min, PhD, Certificate); Islamic studies (MA); Jewish studies (MA); philosophy (MA); religion (MA). *Accreditation:* ATS. Part-time and evening/weekend programs available. Postbaccalaureate distance learning degree programs offered (minimal on-campus study). *Degree requirements:* For master's, thesis optional; for doctorate, comprehensive exam (for some programs), thesis/dissertation. *Entrance requirements:* Additional exam requirements/recommendations for international students: Required—TOEFL (minimum score 600 paper-based; 250 computer-based).

The University of Arizona, Graduate College, College of Social and Behavioral Sciences, Department of Near Eastern Studies, Tucson, AZ 85721. Offers MA, PhD. Part-time and evening/weekend programs available. Terminal master's awarded for partial completion of doctoral program. *Degree requirements:* For master's, one foreign language; for doctorate, 3 foreign languages, thesis/dissertation. *Entrance requirements:* For master's and doctorate, GRE General Test, minimum GPA of 3.0, statement of purpose, curriculum vitae, writing sample. Additional exam requirements/recommendations for international students: Required—TOEFL (minimum score 550 paper-based; 213 computer-based). Electronic applications accepted.

University of California, Berkeley, Graduate Division, College of Letters and Science, Department of Near Eastern Studies, Program in Near Eastern Religions, Berkeley, CA 94720-1500. Offers PhD. *Degree requirements:* For doctorate, 2 foreign languages, thesis/dissertation, qualifying exam. *Entrance requirements:* For doctorate, GRE General Test, MA or equivalent in Near Eastern studies or related field; minimum GPA of 3.0, 3 letters of recommendation.

University of California, Berkeley, Graduate Division, College of Letters and Science, Department of Near Eastern Studies, Program in Near Eastern Studies, Berkeley, CA 94720-1500. Offers MA, PhD. *Degree requirements:* For doctorate, 2 foreign languages, thesis/dissertation, qualifying exam. *Entrance requirements:* For master's and doctorate, GRE General Test, minimum GPA of 3.0, 3 letters of recommendation.

University of California, Los Angeles, Graduate Division, College of Letters and Science, Department of Near Eastern Languages and Cultures, Los Angeles, CA 90034. Offers MA, PhD. *Students:* 46 full-time (21 women); includes 3 minority (1 Asian American or Pacific Islander, 2 Hispanic Americans), 1 international. Average age 28. 60 applicants, 35% accepted, 7 enrolled. In 2008, 4 master's, 2 doctorates awarded. *Degree requirements:* For master's, one foreign language, comprehensive exam; for doctorate, 2 foreign languages, thesis/dissertation, oral and written qualifying exams. *Entrance requirements:* For master's and doctorate, GRE General Test, minimum GPA of 3.25, sample of written work recommended. Additional exam requirements/recommendations for international students: Required—TOEFL. *Application deadline:* For fall admission, 12/1 for domestic and international students. Application fee: $60 ($80 for international students). Electronic applications accepted. *Expenses:* Tuition, nonresident: full-time $14,694. Required fees: $9669.50. Full-time tuition and fees vary according to course load, degree level, program and student level. *Financial support:* In 2008–09, 29 fellowships with full and partial tuition reimbursements, 24 research assistantships with full and partial tuition reimbursements, 21 teaching assistantships with full and partial tuition reimbursements were awarded; Federal Work-Study, institutionally sponsored loans, scholarships/grants, health care benefits, tuition waivers (full and partial), and unspecified assistantships also available. Financial award application deadline: 3/1; financial award applicants required to submit FAFSA. *Unit head:* Dr. Elizabeth Carter, Chair, 310-206-5474. *Application contact:* Departmental Office, 310-825-4165, E-mail: nreast@humnet.ucla.edu.

University of California, Los Angeles, Graduate Division, College of Letters and Science, Program in Indo-European Studies, Los Angeles, CA 90095. Offers PhD. *Students:* 11 full-time (4 women), 3 international. Average age 26. 13 applicants, 46% accepted, 3 enrolled. In 2008, 2 doctorates awarded. *Degree requirements:* For doctorate, 2 foreign languages, thesis/dissertation, oral and written qualifying exams. *Entrance requirements:* For doctorate, minimum undergraduate GPA of 3.0, writing sample, competency in Classical Latin. *Application deadline:* For fall admission, 1/15 for domestic and international students. Application fee: $60 ($80 for international students). Electronic applications accepted. *Expenses:* Tuition, nonresident: full-time $14,694. Required fees: $9669.50. Full-time tuition and fees vary according to course load, degree level, program and student level. *Financial support:* In 2008–09, 6 fellowships with full

Near and Middle Eastern Studies

University of California, Los Angeles (continued)
and partial tuition reimbursements, 8 research assistantships with full and partial tuition reimbursements, 4 teaching assistantships with full and partial tuition reimbursements were awarded; Federal Work-Study, institutionally sponsored loans, scholarships/grants, health care benefits, tuition waivers (full and partial), and unspecified assistantships also available. Financial award application deadline: 3/1; financial award applicants required to submit FAFSA. *Unit head:* Dr. Stephanie Jamison, Chair, 310-206-1590. *Application contact:* Departmental Office, 310-206-1590, E-mail: dabugheida@humnet.ucla.edu.

University of California, Los Angeles, Graduate Division, College of Letters and Science, Program in Islamic Studies, Los Angeles, CA 90095. Offers MA, PhD, MPH/MA. *Students:* 22 full-time (7 women); includes 3 minority (2 African Americans, 1 Hispanic American), 4 international. Average age 32. 36 applicants, 47% accepted, 10 enrolled. In 2008, 1 doctorate awarded. *Degree requirements:* For master's, one foreign language, comprehensive exam; for doctorate, 2 foreign languages, thesis/dissertation, oral and written qualifying exams. *Entrance requirements:* For master's, GRE General Test, minimum GPA of 3.0; for doctorate, GRE General Test, minimum undergraduate GPA of 3.0, Masters degree, advanced level proficiency in Arabic. *Application deadline:* For fall admission, 12/15 for domestic students. Application fee: $60 ($80 for international students). Electronic applications accepted. *Expenses:* Tuition, nonresident: full-time $14,694. Required fees: $9669.50. Full-time tuition and fees vary according to course load, degree level, program and student level. *Financial support:* In 2008–09, 7 fellowships with full and partial tuition reimbursements, 6 research assistantships with full and partial tuition reimbursements, 9 teaching assistantships with full and partial tuition reimbursements were awarded; Federal Work-Study, institutionally sponsored loans, scholarships/grants, health care benefits, tuition waivers (full and partial), and unspecified assistantships also available. Financial award application deadline: 3/1; financial award applicants required to submit FAFSA. *Unit head:* Dr. Michael Morony, Chair, 310-206-6571. *Application contact:* Departmental Office, 310-206-6571, E-mail: idpgrads@international.ucla.edu.

University of Chicago, Division of Social Sciences and Division of the Humanities, Middle Eastern Studies Program, Chicago, IL 60637-1513. Offers AM, MBA/AM, MPP/AM. *Degree requirements:* For master's, one foreign language, thesis. *Entrance requirements:* For master's, GRE General Test. Additional exam requirements/recommendations for international students: Required—TOEFL. Electronic applications accepted.

University of Chicago, Division of the Humanities, Department of Near Eastern Languages and Civilizations, Chicago, IL 60637-1513. Offers AM, PhD. Terminal master's awarded for partial completion of doctoral program. *Degree requirements:* For master's, one foreign language, comprehensive exam, thesis; for doctorate, 2 foreign languages, comprehensive exam, thesis/dissertation. *Entrance requirements:* For master's and doctorate, GRE General Test. Additional exam requirements/recommendations for international students: Required—TOEFL.

The University of Kansas, Graduate Studies, College of Liberal Arts and Sciences, Center for Russian, East European and Eurasian Studies, Lawrence, KS 66045. Offers MA. Part-time programs available. *Faculty:* 45. *Students:* 7 full-time (2 women), 1 part-time (0 women). Average age 30. 15 applicants, 87% accepted, 4 enrolled. In 2008, 8 master's awarded. *Degree requirements:* For master's, one foreign language, comprehensive exam, interdisciplinary capstone seminar. *Entrance requirements:* For master's, GRE General Test, 3 letters of recommendation. Additional exam requirements/recommendations for international students: Required—TOEFL. *Application deadline:* For fall admission, 5/1 priority date for domestic students, 2/14 priority date for international students; for spring admission, 10/1 priority date for domestic students, 9/1 priority date for international students. Applications are processed on a rolling basis. Application fee: $45 ($55 for international students). Electronic applications accepted. *Expenses:* Tuition, area resident: Full-time $6122; part-time $255.10 per credit hour. Tuition, state resident: full-time $6122; part-time $255.10 per credit hour. Tuition, nonresident: full-time $14,629; part-time $609.55 per credit hour. Required fees: $847; $70.56 per credit hour. Tuition and fees vary according to course load and program. *Financial support:* In 2008–09, 8 fellowships with full tuition reimbursements, 2 research assistantships with full and partial tuition reimbursements were awarded; scholarships/grants and tuition waivers (partial) also available. Financial award application deadline: 1/31; financial award applicants required to submit FAFSA. *Faculty research:* Transition studies, Russian history and philosophy, Ukrainian and Russian domestic and foreign policies, Slavic languages and literatures, security policies in Central Asia and the Caucasus. *Unit head:* Dr. Edith Clowes, Director, 785-864-4236, Fax: 785-864-3800, E-mail: crees@ku.edu. *Application contact:* Dr. Eve Levin, Associate Director, 785-864-4236, Fax: 785-864-3800, E-mail: evelevin@ku.edu.

University of Michigan, Horace H. Rackham School of Graduate Studies, College of Literature, Science, and the Arts, Department of Near Eastern Studies, Ann Arbor, MI 48109. Offers ancient Israel/Hebrew Bible (AM, PhD); Arabic (AM, PhD); Armenian (AM, PhD); early Christian studies (AM, PhD); Egyptology (AM, PhD); Hebrew (AM, PhD); Islamic studies (AM, PhD); Mesopotamian and ancient Near Eastern studies (AM, PhD); Persian (AM, PhD); teaching of Arabic as a foreign Language (AM); Turkish (AM, PhD). Part-time programs available. Terminal master's awarded for partial completion of doctoral program. *Degree requirements:* For master's, 2 foreign languages; for doctorate, 4 foreign languages, oral defense of dissertation, preliminary exam. *Entrance requirements:* For master's, GRE General Test; for doctorate, GRE General Test, master's degree. Additional exam requirements/recommendations for international students: Required—TOEFL (minimum score 560 paper-based; 220 computer-based; 84 iBT). *Faculty research:* Middle and Near Eastern literatures, languages, cultures from ancient times to the present.

University of Michigan, Horace H. Rackham School of Graduate Studies, Interdepartmental Program in Modern Middle Eastern and North African Studies, Ann Arbor, MI 48109. Offers AM, JD/AM, MBA/AM, MPH/AM. *Degree requirements:* For master's, one foreign language, thesis or alternative. *Entrance requirements:* For master's, GRE General Test. Additional exam requirements/recommendations for international students: Required—TOEFL. Electronic applications accepted. *Faculty research:* Middle east and north Africa.

University of Pennsylvania, School of Arts and Sciences, Graduate Group in Near Eastern Languages and Civilization, Philadelphia, PA 19104. Offers AM, PhD.

University of South Africa, College of Human Sciences, Pretoria, South Africa. Offers adult education (M Ed); African languages (MA, PhD); African politics (MA, PhD); Afrikaans (MA, PhD); ancient history (MA, PhD); ancient Near Eastern studies (MA, PhD); anthropology (MA, PhD); applied linguistics (MA); Arabic (MA, PhD); archaeology (MA); art history (MA); Biblical archaeology (MA); Biblical studies (M Th, D Th, PhD); Christian spirituality (M Th, D Th); church history (M Th, D Th); classical studies (MA, PhD); clinical psychology (MA); communication (MA, PhD); comparative education (M Ed, Ed D); consulting psychology (D Admin, D Com, PhD); curriculum studies (M Ed, Ed D); development studies (M Admin, MA, D Admin, PhD); didactics (M Ed, Ed D); education (M Tech); education management (M Ed, Ed D); educational psychology (M Ed); English (MA); environmental education (M Ed); French (MA, PhD); German (MA, PhD); Greek (MA); guidance and counseling (M Ed); health studies (MA, PhD), including health sciences education (MA), health services management (MA), medical and surgical nursing science (critical care general) (MA), midwifery and neonatal nursing science (MA), trauma and emergency care (MA); history (MA, PhD); history of education (Ed D); inclusive education (M Ed, Ed D); information and communications technology policy and regulation (MA); information science (MA, MIS, PhD); international politics (MA, PhD); Islamic studies (MA, PhD); Italian (MA, PhD); Judaica (MA, PhD); linguistics (MA, PhD); mathematical education (M Ed); mathematics education (MA); missiology (M Th, D Th); modern Hebrew (MA, PhD); musicology (MA, MMus, D Mus, PhD); natural science education (M Ed); New Testament (M Th, D Th); Old Testament (D Th); pastoral therapy (M Th, D Th); philosophy (MA); philosophy of education (M Ed, Ed D); politics (MA, PhD); Portuguese (MA, PhD); practical theology (M Th, D Th); psychology (MA, MS, PhD); psychology of education (M Ed, Ed D); public health (MA); religious studies (MA, D Th, PhD); Romance languages (MA); Russian (MA, PhD); Semitic languages (MA, PhD); social behavior studies in HIV/AIDS (MA); social science (mental health) (MA); social science in development studies (MA); social science in psychology (MA); social science in social work (MA); social science in sociology (MA); social work (MSW, DSW, PhD); socio-education (M Ed, Ed D); sociolinguistics (MA); sociology (MA, PhD); Spanish (MA, PhD); systematic theology (M Th, D Th); TESOL (teaching English to speakers of other languages) (MA); theological ethics (M Th, D Th); theory of literature (MA, PhD); urban ministries (D Th); urban ministry (M Th).

The University of Texas at Austin, Graduate School, College of Liberal Arts, Center for Middle Eastern Studies, Austin, TX 78712-1111. Offers MA, JD/MA, MBA/MA, MLIS/MA, MP Aff/MA. *Degree requirements:* For master's, one foreign language, thesis optional. *Entrance requirements:* For master's, GRE General Test. Electronic applications accepted.

The University of Texas at Austin, Graduate School, College of Liberal Arts, Department of Middle Eastern Studies, Austin, TX 78712-1111. Offers Arabic (MA, PhD); Hebrew (MA). *Degree requirements:* For master's, one foreign language, comprehensive exam, thesis; for doctorate, 2 foreign languages, comprehensive exam, thesis/dissertation. *Entrance requirements:* For master's and doctorate, GRE General Test. Additional exam requirements/recommendations for international students: Required—TOEFL. Electronic applications accepted. *Faculty research:* Islamic studies, Persian language and literature, Hebrew language, Jewish studies, Arabic literature and language.

University of Toronto, School of Graduate Studies, Humanities Division, Department of Near and Middle Eastern Civilizations, Toronto, ON M5S 1A1, Canada. Offers MA, PhD. Part-time programs available. *Degree requirements:* For master's, thesis optional; for doctorate, 2 foreign languages, thesis/dissertation, language proficiency exams. *Entrance requirements:* For master's, BA in relevant area, minimum B+ average in final year, prior coursework in ancient Near Eastern or Islamic civilizations, 2 letters of reference; for doctorate, MA in relevant area with a minimum A– average, 2 letters of reference. Additional exam requirements/recommendations for international students: Required—TOEFL (minimum score 580 paper-based; 237 computer-based), TWE (minimum score 5).

University of Utah, The Graduate School, College of Humanities, Program in Middle East Studies, Salt Lake City, UT 84112-1107. Offers anthropology (MA); Arabic (MA, PhD); Arabic and linguistics (MA, PhD); Hebrew (MA); history (MA, PhD); Persian (MA, PhD); political science (MA, PhD); Turkish (MA). Terminal master's awarded for partial completion of doctoral program. *Degree requirements:* For master's, 2 foreign languages, comprehensive exam, thesis optional; for doctorate, 3 foreign languages, comprehensive exam, thesis/dissertation. *Entrance requirements:* For master's, GRE General Test, minimum GPA of 3.2; for doctorate, GRE General Test, MA in Middle East studies or equivalent, minimum GPA of 3.2. Additional exam requirements/recommendations for international students: Required—TOEFL (minimum score 580 paper-based; 237 computer-based; 92 iBT). *Faculty research:* Arabic literature and linguistics, Islamic studies, Middle East history, political science, Judaic studies.

University of Washington, Graduate School, College of Arts and Sciences, Department of Near Eastern Languages and Civilization, Seattle, WA 98195. Offers MA. *Degree requirements:* For master's, 2 foreign languages, exams. *Entrance requirements:* For master's, GRE, minimum GPA of 3.0. Additional exam requirements/recommendations for international students: Required—TOEFL. Electronic applications accepted. *Faculty research:* Arabic, Hebrew, Persian, and Turkish literature; Islamic civilization and religion; Central Asian Turkic language and literature; Hebrew Bible and ancient Near East; ancient Christianity.

University of Washington, Graduate School, College of Arts and Sciences, Henry M. Jackson School of International Studies, Middle Eastern Studies Program, Seattle, WA 98195. Offers MAIS. *Degree requirements:* For master's, one foreign language, thesis optional. *Entrance requirements:* For master's, GRE Geheral Test, minimum GPA of 3.0. Additional exam requirements/recommendations for international students: Required—TOEFL (minimum score 500 paper-based; 213 computer-based). Electronic applications accepted.

University of Washington, Graduate School, Interdisciplinary Program in Near and Middle Eastern Studies, Seattle, WA 98195. Offers PhD. *Degree requirements:* For doctorate, 3 foreign languages, thesis/dissertation. *Entrance requirements:* For doctorate, GRE General Test, minimum GPA of 3.0. Additional exam requirements/recommendations for international students: Required—TOEFL. Electronic applications accepted.

University of Waterloo, Graduate Studies, Faculty of Arts, Department of Classical Studies, Waterloo, ON N2L 3G1, Canada. Offers ancient Mediterranean cultures (MA). *Degree requirements:* For master's, one foreign language. *Entrance requirements:* For master's, BA, B+. *Faculty research:* Ancient history, philosophy, anthropology, religion, culture.

University of Wisconsin–Madison, Graduate School, College of Letters and Science, Department of History, Madison, WI 53706-1380. Offers African history (MA, PhD); Central Asian history (MA, PhD); comparative world history (MA, PhD); East Asian history (MA, PhD); European history (MA, PhD); gender and women's history (MA, PhD); Latin American and Caribbean history (MA, PhD); Middle Eastern history (MA, PhD); South Asian history (MA, PhD); Southeast Asian history (MA, PhD); United States history (MA, PhD). Terminal master's awarded for partial completion of doctoral program. *Degree requirements:* For master's, thesis (for some programs); for doctorate, variable foreign language requirement, thesis/dissertation. *Entrance requirements:* For master's and doctorate, GRE General Test. Additional exam requirements/recommendations for international students: Required—Michigan English Language Assessment Battery or TOEFL. Electronic applications accepted. *Faculty research:* American, African, European, Asian, Latin American, and Middle Eastern history.

Wayne State University, College of Liberal Arts and Sciences, Department of Classical and Modern Languages, Literatures, and Cultures, Program in Near Eastern and Asian Studies, Detroit, MI 48202. Offers language learning (MA); Near Eastern studies (MA). *Degree requirements:* For master's, one foreign language. *Entrance requirements:* For master's, GRE General Test. Additional exam requirements/recommendations for international students: Required—TOEFL (minimum score 550 paper-based; 213 computer-based); Recommended—TWE (minimum score 6). Electronic applications accepted. *Faculty research:* Modern Middle East history, Arabic language and culture studies, Chinese linguistics, Islamic studies, Judaic studies.

Yale University, Graduate School of Arts and Sciences, Department of Near Eastern Languages and Civilizations, New Haven, CT 06520. Offers Arabic and Islamic studies (MA, PhD); archaeology of the ancient Near East (MA, PhD); Assyriology (MA, PhD); Egyptology (MA, PhD); Graeco-Arabic studies (MA, PhD); Northwest Semitic, Bible, comparative Semitics (MA, PhD). *Degree requirements:* For doctorate, 2 foreign languages, thesis/dissertation. *Entrance requirements:* For doctorate, GRE General Test.

Northern Studies

University of Alaska Fairbanks, College of Liberal Arts, Department of Northern Studies, Fairbanks, AK 99775-6460. Offers environmental politics and policy (MA); Northern history (MA). Part-time programs available. *Faculty:* 7 full-time (3 women), 2 part-time/adjunct (both women). *Students:* 18 full-time (8 women), 18 part-time (12 women); includes 2 minority (1 African American, 1 American Indian/Alaska Native), 5 international. Average age 34. 24 applicants, 50% accepted, 11 enrolled. In 2008, 5 master's awarded. *Degree requirements:* For master's, comprehensive exam, thesis or alternative. *Entrance requirements:* Additional exam requirements/recommendations for international students: Required—TOEFL (minimum score 550 paper-based; 213 computer-based; 80 iBT). *Application deadline:* For fall admission, 6/1 for domestic students, 3/1 for international students; for spring admission, 10/15 for domestic students, 9/1 for international students. Applications are processed on a rolling basis. Application fee: $60. Electronic applications accepted. *Expenses:* Tuition, area resident: Full-time $5418; part-time $301 per credit. Tuition, state resident: full-time $5418; part-time $301 per credit. Tuition, nonresident: full-time $11,070; part-time $615 per credit. Required fees: $849; $25 per credit. $78 per semester. Tuition and fees vary according to course load and reciprocity agreements. *Financial support:* In 2008–09, 3 research assistantships (averaging $7,517 per year), 11 teaching assistantships (averaging $7,671 per year) were awarded; fellowships, career-related internships or fieldwork, Federal Work-Study, scholarships/grants, health care benefits, and unspecified assistantships also available. Support available to part-time students. Financial award application deadline: 1/1; financial award applicants required to submit FAFSA. *Faculty research:* Canadian history, environmental history, Native Alaskan history and art, fetal alcohol syndrome. *Unit head:* Dr. Judith S. Kleinfeld, Co-Director, 907-474-7126, Fax: 907-474-5817, E-mail: fynors@uaf.edu. *Application contact:* Dr. Judith S. Kleinfeld, Co-Director, 907-474-7126, Fax: 907-474-5817, E-mail: fynors@uaf.edu.

University of Manitoba, Faculty of Graduate Studies, Faculty of Arts, Department of Icelandic Language and Literature, Winnipeg, MB R3T 2N2, Canada. Offers MA.

Pacific Area/Pacific Rim Studies

University of California, San Diego, Office of Graduate Studies, Graduate School of International Relations and Pacific Studies, La Jolla, CA 92093-0520. Offers economics and international affairs (PhD); Pacific international affairs (MPIA); political science and international affairs (PhD). *Degree requirements:* For master's, one foreign language; for doctorate, thesis/dissertation. *Entrance requirements:* For master's, GMAT or GRE General Test; for doctorate, GRE General Test. Additional exam requirements/recommendations for international students: Required—TOEFL (minimum score 550 paper-based; 213 computer-based). Electronic applications accepted. *Faculty research:* Pacific Rim as system and placement in global relations; studies in international economics, management and finance; analysis of patterns of policymaking in countries of the Pacific.

See Close-Up on page 881.

University of Guam, Office of Graduate Studies, College of Liberal Arts and Social Sciences, Micronesian Studies Program, Mangilao, GU 96923. Offers MA. *Degree requirements:* For master's, thesis. *Entrance requirements:* For master's, GRE General Test. Additional exam requirements/recommendations for international students: Required—TOEFL. *Faculty research:* Adolescent suicide in Micronesia, history of Micronesia, traditional agriculture in the Pacific, Micronesian languages, health and cultural practices.

University of Hawaii at Manoa, Graduate Division, School of Pacific and Asian Studies, Program in Pacific Island Studies, Honolulu, HI 96822. Offers MA, Graduate Certificate. Part-time programs available. *Degree requirements:* For master's, thesis optional. *Entrance requirements:* Additional exam requirements/recommendations for international students: Required—TOEFL (minimum score 580 paper-based; 237 computer-based; 92 iBT), IELTS (minimum score 5).

University of San Francisco, College of Arts and Sciences, Program in Asia Pacific Studies, San Francisco, CA 94117-1080. Offers MA, MA/MBA. Part-time and evening/weekend programs available. *Degree requirements:* For master's, one foreign language, thesis. *Entrance requirements:* For master's, minimum GPA of 3.0. *Faculty research:* History of Christianity in China, U.S.-China policy, East Asian economies and political systems, sociolinguistic aspects of Japanese.

University of Victoria, Faculty of Graduate Studies, Faculty of Humanities, Department of Pacific and Asian Studies, Victoria, BC V8W 2Y2, Canada. Offers MA. *Degree requirements:* For master's, thesis. *Entrance requirements:* For master's, minimum B+ average, writing sample. Additional exam requirements/recommendations for international students: Required—TOEFL (minimum score 575 paper-based; 233 computer-based), IELTS (minimum score 7). Electronic applications accepted. *Faculty research:* Culture, ethnicity and identity; economy and society; gender studies; languages and linguistics; literature.

Western European Studies

American University, School of International Service, Washington, DC 20016-8071. Offers comparative and regional studies (Certificate); cross-cultural communication (Certificate); development management (MS); ethics, peace, and global affairs (MA); European studies (Certificate); global environmental policy (MA, Certificate); international affairs (MA), including comparative and regional studies, environmental policy, international economic policy, international politics, natural resources and sustainable development, U.S. foreign policy; international communication (MA, Certificate); international development (MA, Certificate); international development management (Certificate); international economic policy (Certificate); international economic relations (Certificate); international media (MA); international peace and conflict resolution (MA, Certificate); international relations (PhD); international service (MIS); peace building (Certificate); the Americas (Certificate); United States foreign policy (Certificate); JD/MA. Part-time and evening/weekend programs available. *Faculty:* 70 full-time (28 women), 51 part-time/adjunct (20 women). *Students:* 519 full-time (317 women), 335 part-time (205 women); includes 157 minority (54 African Americans, 2 American Indian/Alaska Native, 45 Asian Americans or Pacific Islanders, 56 Hispanic Americans), 116 international. Average age 27. 1,901 applicants, 58% accepted, 277 enrolled. In 2008, 358 master's, 5 doctorates, 9 other advanced degrees awarded. Terminal master's awarded for partial completion of doctoral program. *Degree requirements:* For master's, one foreign language, comprehensive exam, thesis or alternative; for doctorate, one foreign language, comprehensive exam, thesis/dissertation, research practicum; for Certificate, minimum 15 credit hours related course work. *Entrance requirements:* For master's, GRE, 24 credits of course work in related social sciences, minimum GPA of 3.5, 2 letters of recommendation, bachelor's degree, resumé, statement of purpose; for doctorate, GRE, 2 letters of recommendation, 24 credits in related social sciences; for Certificate, bachelor's degree. Additional exam requirements/recommendations for international students: Required—TOEFL (minimum score 600 paper-based; 250 computer-based; 100 iBT). *Application deadline:* For fall admission, 1/15 priority date for domestic students; for spring admission, 10/1 priority date for domestic students. Applications are processed on a rolling basis. Application fee: $50. *Expenses:* Tuition: Full-time $21,204; part-time $1178 per credit hour. Required fees: $380. Part-time tuition and fees vary according to course load and program. *Financial support:* Career-related internships or fieldwork, Federal Work-Study, and institutionally sponsored loans available. Financial award application deadline: 1/15. *Faculty research:* International intellectual property, international environmental issues, international law and legal order, international telecommunications/technology, international sustainable development. *Unit head:* Dr. Louis W. Goodman, Dean, 202-885-1600, Fax: 202-885-2494. *Application contact:* Yasmin Quianzon, Director of Graduate Admissions and Financial Aid, 202-885-2496, Fax: 202-885-1109.

See Close-Up on page 861.

Boston College, Graduate School of Arts and Sciences, Department of History, Chestnut Hill, MA 02467-3800. Offers European national studies (MA); history (MA, PhD); medieval studies (MA). Terminal master's awarded for partial completion of doctoral program. *Degree requirements:* For master's, one foreign language, comprehensive exam, thesis optional; for doctorate, 2 foreign languages, comprehensive exam, thesis/dissertation. *Entrance requirements:* For master's and doctorate, GRE General Test, writing sample. Additional exam requirements/recommendations for international students: Required—TOEFL (minimum score 590 paper-based; 250 computer-based; 91 iBT). Electronic applications accepted. *Expenses:* Tuition: Part-time $1148 per credit. Required fees: $60. *Faculty research:* Modern and early modern European, U.S., Russian, and Soviet history; European and U.S. intellectual history.

Brown University, Graduate School, Center for Portuguese and Brazilian Studies, Providence, RI 02912. Offers Brazilian studies (AM); Portuguese and Brazilian studies (AM, PhD); Portuguese Bilingual Education and Cross-Cultural Studies (AM); MA/PhD. *Degree requirements:* For doctorate, thesis/dissertation.

California State University, Long Beach, Graduate Studies, College of Liberal Arts, Department of History, Long Beach, CA 90840. Offers Africa and the Middle East (MA); ancient/Medieval Europe (MA); Asia (MA); Latin America (MA); modern Europe (MA); United States (MA); world (MA). Part-time and evening/weekend programs available. *Faculty:* 17 full-time (11 women), 2 part-time/adjunct (1 woman). *Students:* 9 full-time (4 women), 45 part-time (18 women); includes 15 minority (2 African Americans, 3 Asian Americans or Pacific Islanders, 10 Hispanic Americans), 1 international. Average age 35. 40 applicants, 50% accepted, 11 enrolled. *Degree requirements:* For master's, one foreign language, comprehensive exam or thesis. *Application deadline:* For fall admission, 3/1 for domestic students. Applications are processed on a rolling basis. Application fee: $55. Electronic applications accepted. *Expenses:* Tuition, nonresident: full-time $11,160; part-time $372 per unit. Required fees: $4100; $1261 per semester. *Financial support:* Research assistantships, Federal Work-Study, institutionally sponsored loans, and scholarships/grants available. Financial award application deadline: 3/2. *Faculty research:* All periods of European and American history, recent Asian and African history. *Unit head:* Dr. Nancy L Quam-Wickham, Graduate Advisor, 562-985-4431, Fax: 562-985-5431, E-mail: quamwick@csulb.edu. *Application contact:* Dr. Houri Berberian, Graduate Advisor, 562-985-4524, Fax: 562-985-4431, E-mail: hberber@csulb.edu.

Carleton University, Faculty of Graduate Studies, Faculty of Public Affairs and Management, Institute of European and Russian Studies, Ottawa, ON K1S 5B6, Canada. Offers European and European Union studies (MA); European integration studies (Diploma); Russian, Eurasian and transition studies (MA). *Degree requirements:* For master's, one foreign language, thesis optional. *Entrance requirements:* For master's, honors degree or equivalent; 2 years of Russian, German or other central east European language. Additional exam requirements/recommendations for international students: Required—TOEFL. *Faculty research:* East-West relations, minority rights in Russia and Eastern Europe.

The Catholic University of America, School of Arts and Sciences, Department of History, Washington, DC 20064. Offers MA, PhD, JD/MA, MSLS/MA. Part-time programs available. *Degree requirements:* For master's, one foreign language, comprehensive exam, thesis or alternative; for doctorate, 2 foreign languages, comprehensive exam, thesis/dissertation, oral exams. *Entrance requirements:* For master's and doctorate, GRE General Test, 3 letters of recommendation. Additional exam requirements/recommendations for international students: Required—TOEFL (minimum score 580 paper-based; 237 computer-based). Electronic applications accepted. *Faculty research:* Medieval family law, U.S. liberalism, capitalism in Europe, Mexican rural society, urbanization in France.

The Catholic University of America, School of Arts and Sciences, Program in Irish Studies, Washington, DC 20064. Offers MA. Part-time programs available. *Degree requirements:* For master's, one foreign language, comprehensive exam. *Entrance requirements:* For master's, GRE General Test, 3 letters of recommendation, writing sample. Additional exam requirements/recommendations for international students: Required—TOEFL (minimum score 580 paper-based; 237 computer-based). Electronic applications accepted. *Faculty research:* Eighteenth and nineteenth century Irish literature, contemporary Irish literature, Irish language, Irish politics, Irish American history.

Central Michigan University, College of Graduate Studies, College of Humanities and Social and Behavioral Sciences, Department of History, Mount Pleasant, MI 48859. Offers European history (Graduate Certificate); history (MA, PhD); modern history (Graduate Certificate); United States history (Graduate Certificate). Offered jointly with the University of Stratclyde, Scotland. Part-time programs available. *Faculty:* 15 full-time (5 women). *Students:* 22 full-time (8 women), 15 part-time (2 women); includes 1 Hispanic American. Average age 30. *Degree requirements:* For master's, thesis or alternative; for doctorate, comprehensive exam, thesis/dissertation. Application fee: $35 ($45 for international students). Electronic applications accepted. *Expenses:*

Western European Studies

Central Michigan University (continued)

Tuition, state resident: full-time $3717; part-time $413 per credit. Tuition, nonresident: full-time $6894; part-time $766 per credit. *Financial support:* Fellowships with tuition reimbursements, research assistantships with tuition reimbursements, teaching assistantships with tuition reimbursements, Federal Work-Study, unspecified assistantships, and out-of-state merit awards available. *Faculty research:* Colonial and revolutionary United States history, modern European history, Latin American and transatlantic history, transnational and comparative history, United States social history. *Unit head:* Dr. Timothy D. Hall, Chairperson, 989-773-3374, Fax: 989-774-1156, E-mail: hall1td@cmich.edu. *Application contact:* Dr. Timothy D. Hall, Chairperson, 989-773-3374, Fax: 989-774-1156, E-mail: hall1td@cmich.edu.

Claremont Graduate University, Graduate Programs, School of Arts and Humanities, Department of History, Claremont, CA 91711-6160. Offers Africana history (Certificate); American studies and U.S. history (MA, PhD); archival studies (MA); early modern studies (MA, PhD); European studies (MA, PhD); oral history (MA, PhD); MBA/MA; MBA/PhD. *Faculty:* 3 full-time (2 women). *Students:* 67 full-time (33 women), 8 part-time (3 women); includes 15 minority (1 African American, 3 Asian Americans or Pacific Islanders, 11 Hispanic Americans), 1 international. Average age 35. In 2008, 6 master's, 8 doctorates awarded. Terminal master's awarded for partial completion of doctoral program. *Entrance requirements:* For master's and doctorate, GRE General Test. Additional exam requirements/recommendations for international students: Required—TOEFL (minimum score 550 paper-based; 213 computer-based; 80 iBT). *Application deadline:* For fall admission, 2/1 priority date for domestic students. Applications are processed on a rolling basis. Application fee: $60. Electronic applications accepted. *Expenses:* Tuition: Full-time $33,698; part-time $1465 per unit. Required fees: $310; $155 per semester. Tuition and fees vary according to program. *Financial support:* Fellowships, research assistantships, Federal Work-Study, institutionally sponsored loans, and scholarships/grants available. Support available to part-time students. Financial award application deadline: 2/15; financial award applicants required to submit FAFSA. *Faculty research:* Intellectual and social history, cultural studies, gender studies, Western history, Chicano history. *Unit head:* Janet Farrell Brodie, Chair, 909-621-8880, Fax: 909-621-8609, E-mail: janet.brodie@cgu.edu. *Application contact:* Justin Evans, Admissions Coordinator, 909-607-1278, E-mail: justin.evans@cgu.edu.

Columbia University, Graduate School of Arts and Sciences, Program in Liberal Studies, New York, NY 10027. Offers American studies (MA); East Asian studies (MA); human rights studies (MA); Islamic culture studies (MA); Jewish studies (MA); medieval studies (MA); modern European studies (MA); South Asian studies (MA). Part-time and evening/weekend programs available. *Degree requirements:* For master's, thesis.

Columbia University, School of International and Public Affairs, Institute for the Study of Europe, New York, NY 10027. Offers Certificate. Students must be enrolled in a separate graduate degree program at Columbia University. Electronic applications accepted.

Cornell University, Graduate School, Graduate Fields of Arts and Sciences, Field of History, Ithaca, NY 14853-0001. Offers African history (MA, PhD); American history (MA, PhD); ancient history (MA, PhD); early modern European history (MA, PhD); English history (MA, PhD); French history (MA, PhD); German history (MA, PhD); history of science (MA, PhD); Latin American history (MA, PhD); medieval Chinese history (MA, PhD); medieval history (MA, PhD); modern Chinese history (MA, PhD); modern European history (MA, PhD); modern Japanese history (MA, PhD); premodern Islamic history (MA, PhD); premodern Japanese history (MA, PhD); Renaissance history (MA, PhD); Russian history (MA, PhD); Southeast Asian history (MA, PhD). *Faculty:* 54 full-time (14 women). *Students:* 65 full-time (35 women); includes 12 minority (4 African Americans, 3 Asian Americans or Pacific Islanders, 5 Hispanic Americans), 19 international. Average age 31. 205 applicants, 8% accepted, 11 enrolled. In 2008, 12 master's, 6 doctorates awarded. Terminal master's awarded for partial completion of doctoral program. *Degree requirements:* For master's, thesis; for doctorate, 2 foreign languages, comprehensive exam, thesis/dissertation, 1 year of teaching experience. *Entrance requirements:* For master's and doctorate, GRE General Test, writing sample, 3 letters of recommendation. Additional exam requirements/recommendations for international students: Required—TOEFL (minimum score 550 paper-based; 213 computer-based; 77 iBT). *Application deadline:* For fall admission, 1/15 for domestic students. Application fee: $70. Electronic applications accepted. *Expenses:* Tuition: Full-time $29,500. Required fees: $70. Full-time tuition and fees vary according to degree level, program and student level. *Financial support:* In 2008–09, 54 students received support, including 27 fellowships with full tuition reimbursements available, 3 research assistantships with full tuition reimbursements available, 24 teaching assistantships with full tuition reimbursements available; institutionally sponsored loans, scholarships/grants, health care benefits, tuition waivers (full and partial), and unspecified assistantships also available. Financial award applicants required to submit FAFSA. *Unit head:* Director of Graduate Studies, 607-255-6738, Fax: 607-255-0469. *Application contact:* Graduate Field Assistant, 607-255-6738, Fax: 607-255-0469, E-mail: history_grad_info@cornell.edu.

East Carolina University, Graduate School, Thomas Harriot College of Arts and Sciences, Department of History, Greenville, NC 27858-4353. Offers American history (MA); European history (MA); maritime history (MA). Part-time and evening/weekend programs available. *Degree requirements:* For master's, one foreign language, comprehensive exam, thesis. *Entrance requirements:* For master's, GRE General Test, GRE Subject Test. Additional exam requirements/recommendations for international students: Required—TOEFL.

Georgetown University, Graduate School of Arts and Sciences, BMW Center for German and European Studies, Washington, DC 20057. Offers MA, MA/JD, MA/PhD. *Degree requirements:* For master's, 2 foreign languages, comprehensive exam. *Entrance requirements:* For master's, GRE General Test. Additional exam requirements/recommendations for international students: Required—TOEFL. *Faculty research:* Trans-Atlantic relations, European Union, German and European Studies.

The George Washington University, Elliott School of International Affairs, Program in European and Eurasian Studies, Washington, DC 20052. Offers MA, JD/MA, MBA/MA. Part-time and evening/weekend programs available. *Students:* 12 full-time (7 women), 8 part-time (4 women), 1 international. Average age 26. 47 applicants, 68% accepted, 11 enrolled. In 2008, 18 master's awarded. *Degree requirements:* For master's, one foreign language, capstone project. *Entrance requirements:* For master's, GRE General Test, 2 years (or the equivalent) of a modern European language (or Russian), 2 semesters of introductory economics (macro or micro economics). Additional exam requirements/recommendations for international students: Required—TOEFL. *Application deadline:* For fall admission, 2/1 for domestic students; for spring admission, 10/1 for domestic students. Application fee: $60. Electronic applications accepted. *Financial support:* In 2008–09, 3 students received support; fellowships with tuition reimbursements available, research assistantships with tuition reimbursements available, career-related internships or fieldwork, Federal Work-Study, institutionally sponsored loans, and tuition waivers available. Financial award application deadline: 1/15; financial award applicants required to submit FAFSA. *Faculty research:* NATO, European economics, European history, European Union. *Unit head:* Hope Harrison, Director, 202-994-5439, Fax: 202-994-5436, E-mail: hopeharr@gwu.edu. *Application contact:* Jeff V. Miles, Director of Graduate Admissions, 202-994-7050, Fax: 202-994-9537, E-mail: esiagrad@gwu.edu.

Indiana University Bloomington, University Graduate School, College of Arts and Sciences, Department of West European Studies, Bloomington, IN 47405-7000. Offers MA. *Faculty:* 1 full-time (0 women). *Students:* 5 full-time (3 women), 3 part-time (2 women), 1 international. Average age 30. 8 applicants, 75% accepted, 3 enrolled. In 2008, 1 master's awarded. *Degree requirements:* For master's, 2 foreign languages, thesis. *Entrance requirements:* For master's, GRE General Test. Additional exam requirements/recommendations for international students: Required—TOEFL. *Application deadline:* For fall admission, 1/15 priority date for domestic students, 12/15 for international students; for spring admission, 9/1 priority date for domestic students, 9/1 for international students. Applications are processed on a rolling basis. Application

fee: $50 ($60 for international students). *Expenses:* Tuition, area resident: Part-time $291.97 per credit hour. Tuition, state resident: part-time $291.97 per credit hour. Tuition, nonresident: part-time $850.33 per credit hour. Required fees: $110 per semester. Tuition and fees vary according to course load and program. *Financial support:* Fellowships with full tuition reimbursements, research assistantships with full tuition reimbursements, teaching assistantships with partial tuition reimbursements available. *Faculty research:* European integration, economics of Europe, European union, European culture and identity, expansion of European union. *Unit head:* Dr. Patricia McManus, Director, 812-855-3280, E-mail: pmcmanus@indiana.edu. *Application contact:* Deborah Piston-Hatlen, Associate Director, 812-855-3280, Fax: 812-855-7695, E-mail: weur@indiana.edu.

The Johns Hopkins University, Paul H. Nitze School of Advanced International Studies, Washington, DC 20036. Offers international development (Certificate); international public policy (MIPP); international relations (MA, PhD), including African studies (MA), American foreign policy (MA), Asian studies (MA), Canadian studies (MA), conflict management (MA), European studies (MA), global theory and history (MA), international development (MA), international law, and organizations (MA), international policy (MA), international relations (general) (MA), Latin American studies (MA), Middle East studies (MA), Russian and Eurasian studies (MA), strategic studies (MA); international studies (Certificate); JD/MA; MBA/MA; MHS/MA. Terminal master's awarded for partial completion of doctoral program. *Degree requirements:* For master's, one foreign language, 16 non-language courses (8 for MIPP), 2 core examinations, comprehensive oral exam, paper (for some programs); for doctorate, 2 foreign languages, thesis/dissertation, 3 comprehensive exams, defense. *Entrance requirements:* For master's, GMAT or GRE General Test, previous course work in economics, foreign language, undergraduate degree; for doctorate, GRE General Test, master's degree. Additional exam requirements/recommendations for international students: Required—TOEFL (minimum paper-based score of 600, computer-based 250, iBT 100) or IELTS (minimum 7.0). Electronic applications accepted. *Expenses:* Contact institution. *Faculty research:* Regional studies and functional fields of international relations, international economics, conflict management, global theory and history, international law and organizations, international policy, strategic studies.

Mississippi State University, College of Arts and Sciences, Department of History, Mississippi State, MS 39762. Offers MA, PhD. Part-time programs available. *Degree requirements:* For master's, one foreign language, comprehensive exam, thesis optional; for doctorate, 2 foreign languages, thesis/dissertation, comprehensive oral and written exam. *Entrance requirements:* For master's, minimum GPA of 3.0; for doctorate, GRE General Test, writing sample, minimum graduate GPA of 3.0. Additional exam requirements/recommendations for international students: Required—TOEFL. *Faculty research:* U.S. political, diplomatic, military, social, and cultural history; modern Europe; Latin America; Asian history; African history.

New York University, Graduate School of Arts and Science, Center for European Studies, New York, NY 10012-1019. Offers MA. *Entrance requirements:* For master's, GRE General Test. Additional exam requirements/recommendations for international students: Required—TOEFL. Electronic applications accepted. *Faculty research:* Xenophobia, migration, and identity politics in Europe; European Union and political economy; Central Eastern Europe.

San Diego State University, Graduate and Research Affairs, College of Arts and Letters, Department of European Studies, San Diego, CA 92182. Offers MA. *Degree requirements:* For master's, one foreign language. *Entrance requirements:* For master's, GRE General Test. Additional exam requirements/recommendations for international students: Required—TOEFL. Electronic applications accepted.

The University of British Columbia, Faculty of Graduate Studies, Institute for European Studies, Vancouver, BC V6T 1Z1, Canada. Offers MA.

University of Connecticut, Graduate School, College of Liberal Arts and Sciences, Field of International Studies, Program in European Studies, Storrs, CT 06269. Offers MA. *Degree requirements:* For master's, comprehensive exam. *Entrance requirements:* For master's, GRE General Test. Additional exam requirements/recommendations for international students: Required—TOEFL (minimum score 550 paper-based; 213 computer-based). Electronic applications accepted.

University of Connecticut, Graduate School, College of Liberal Arts and Sciences, Field of International Studies, Program in Italian History and Culture, Storrs, CT 06269. Offers MA. *Entrance requirements:* Additional exam requirements/recommendations for international students: Required—TOEFL (minimum score 550 paper-based; 213 computer-based). Electronic applications accepted.

University of Guelph, Graduate Program Services, College of Arts, School of Languages and Literatures, Program in European Studies, Guelph, ON N1G 2W1, Canada. Offers MA. *Degree requirements:* For master's, six semester courses, research paper. *Entrance requirements:* For master's, curriculum vitae, letter of intent, writing sample, 2 letters of recommendation, transcript.

University of Nevada, Reno, Graduate School, Interdisciplinary Program in Basque Studies, Reno, NV 89557. Offers PhD. *Faculty:* 5 full-time (2 women). *Students:* 2 full-time (both women), 2 part-time (1 woman); includes 1 minority (Hispanic American), 2 international. Average age 38. 1 applicant, 100% accepted, 1 enrolled. In 2008, 2 doctorates awarded. *Degree requirements:* For doctorate, thesis/dissertation. *Entrance requirements:* For doctorate, GRE General Test, master's degree in related field, minimum GPA of 3.0. Additional exam requirements/recommendations for international students: Required—TOEFL (minimum score 500 paper-based; 173 computer-based; 61 iBT), IELTS (minimum score 6), TOFEL or IELTS. *Application deadline:* For fall admission, 3/1 priority date for domestic and international students; for spring admission, 11/1 priority date for domestic and international students. Applications are processed on a rolling basis. Application fee: $60 ($95 for international students). Electronic applications accepted. *Expenses:* Tuition, state resident: full-time $1710; part-time $1140 per semester. Tuition, nonresident: full-time $7115. Required fees: $158 per semester. *Financial support:* In 2008–09, 2 research assistantships with partial tuition reimbursements (averaging $14,000 per year) were awarded; teaching assistantships, Federal Work-Study, institutionally sponsored loans, scholarships/grants, health care benefits, and unspecified assistantships also available. Financial award application deadline: 3/1; financial award applicants required to submit FAFSA. *Faculty research:* Ethnic groups, Basque society, migration studies, symbolic anthropology, terrorism. *Unit head:* Dr. Sandra Ott, Graduate Programs Director, 775-682-5573, E-mail: sott@unr.edu. *Application contact:* Michele Sandberg, Application Contact, 775-784-7026, Fax: 775-784-6064, E-mail: gradschool@unr.edu.

University of Pittsburgh, University Center for International Studies, Pittsburgh, PA 15260. Offers African studies (Certificate); Asian studies (Certificate); European Union studies (Certificate); global studies (Certificate); Latin American studies (Certificate); Russian and East European studies (Certificate); West European studies (Certificate).

Washington State University, Graduate School, College of Liberal Arts, Department of History, Pullman, WA 99164. Offers early and modern European history (MA, PhD); environmental history (MA, PhD); Latin American history (MA, PhD); modern East Asia history (MA, PhD); public history (MA, PhD); US history (MA, PhD); women's history (MA, PhD); world history (MA, PhD). Part-time programs available. *Degree requirements:* For master's, comprehensive exam (for some programs), thesis, oral exam; for doctorate, one foreign language, comprehensive exam, thesis/dissertation, oral and written exam. *Entrance requirements:* For master's, GRE General Test, minimum GPA of 3.3, language background form, writing sample; for doctorate, GRE General Test, minimum GPA of 3.5, language background form, writing sample. Additional exam requirements/recommendations for international students: Required—TOEFL (minimum score 550 paper-based). Electronic applications accepted. *Faculty research:* Public, world, environmental, women and U.S. history.

Women's Studies

The American University in Cairo, Graduate Studies and Research, School of Humanities and Social Sciences, Program in Gender and Women's Studies, Cairo, Egypt. Offers gender and development (MA, Diploma); gender and justice (MA, Diploma); gender and women's studies in the Middle East and North Africa (MA, Diploma).

Assemblies of God Theological Seminary, Graduate and Professional Programs, Springfield, MO 65802. Offers biblical preaching (D Min); Christian ministries (MA); divinity (M Div); intercultural studies (D Miss, PhD); missional leadership (D Min); relief and development (D Miss); self-design study (D Min); women in leadership (D Min). *Accreditation:* ATS. Part-time and evening/weekend programs available. Postbaccalaureate distance learning degree programs offered (minimal on-campus study). *Faculty:* 16 full-time (3 women), 21 part-time/adjunct (4 women). *Students:* 220 full-time (69 women), 226 part-time (49 women); includes 49 minority (11 African Americans, 5 American Indian/Alaska Native, 11 Asian Americans or Pacific Islanders, 22 Hispanic Americans), 7 international. Average age 36. *Degree requirements:* For master's, analytical reflection paper or comprehensive exam; for doctorate, thesis/dissertation; for M Div, one foreign language, analytical reflection paper. *Entrance requirements:* For M Div, minimum GPA of 2.0; for master's, minimum GPA of 2.5; for doctorate, minimum GPA of 3.0. Additional exam requirements/recommendations for international students: Required—TOEFL (minimum score 550 paper-based; 213 computer-based; 80 iBT). *Application deadline:* For fall admission, 7/1 priority date for domestic students, 6/1 priority date for international students; for spring admission, 12/1 priority date for domestic students, 11/1 priority date for international students. Applications are processed on a rolling basis. Application fee: $35. Electronic applications accepted. *Financial support:* Career-related internships or fieldwork, Federal Work-Study, and scholarships/grants available. Support available to part-time students. Financial award application deadline: 7/15; financial award applicants required to submit FAFSA. *Unit head:* Stephen Lim, Academic Dean, 417-268-1000, Fax: 417-268-1001, E-mail: slim@agts.edu. *Application contact:* Stephen Lim, Academic Dean, 417-268-1000, Fax: 417-268-1001, E-mail: slim@agts.edu.

Brandeis University, Graduate School of Arts and Sciences, Joint Degree Programs in Women's and Gender Studies, Waltham, MA 02454-9110. Offers anthropology and women's and gender studies (MA); English and women's and gender studies (MA); music and women's and gender studies (MA); Near Eastern and Judaic studies and women's and gender studies (MA); sociology and women's and gender studies (MA); sustainable international development and women's/gender studies (MA). Part-time programs available. *Degree requirements:* For master's, thesis. *Entrance requirements:* For master's, GRE, sample of written work, resumé. Additional exam requirements/recommendations for international students: Required—TOEFL (minimum score 600 paper-based; 250 computer-based; 100 iBT), IELTS (minimum score 7). Electronic applications accepted.

California Institute of Integral Studies, Graduate Programs, School of Consciousness and Transformation, San Francisco, CA 94103. Offers cultural anthropology and social transformation (MA); East-West psychology (MA, PhD); integrative health studies (MA); philosophy and religion (MA, PhD), including Asian and comparative studies, philosophy, cosmology, and consciousness, women's spirituality, women's spirituality flex format; social and cultural anthropology (PhD); transformative leadership (MA); transformative studies (PhD). Part-time and evening/weekend programs available. Postbaccalaureate distance learning degree programs offered (minimal on-campus study). *Faculty:* 29 full-time, 32 part-time/adjunct. *Students:* 334 full-time (218 women), 126 part-time (77 women); includes 102 minority (39 African Americans, 4 American Indian/Alaska Native, 35 Asian Americans or Pacific Islanders, 24 Hispanic Americans), 1 international. Average age 37. 223 applicants, 78% accepted, 110 enrolled. In 2008, 93 master's, 30 doctorates awarded. Terminal master's awarded for partial completion of doctoral program. *Degree requirements:* For master's, comprehensive exam (for some programs), thesis optional; for doctorate, comprehensive exam, thesis/dissertation. *Entrance requirements:* For master's, minimum GPA of 3.0, letters of recommendation, writing sample; for doctorate, master's degree, minimum GPA of 3.0, letters of recommendation, writing sample. Additional exam requirements/recommendations for international students: Required—TOEFL. *Application deadline:* For fall admission, 2/1 priority date for domestic and international students; for spring admission, 10/15 priority date for domestic and international students. Applications are processed on a rolling basis. Application fee: $65. Electronic applications accepted. *Expenses:* Tuition: Part-time $815 per contact hour. Required fees: $270; $135 per semester. Tuition and fees vary according to degree level. *Financial support:* In 2008–09, 271 students received support; research assistantships, teaching assistantships, career-related internships or fieldwork, Federal Work-Study, institutionally sponsored loans, scholarships/grants, and tuition waivers (partial) available. Support available to part-time students. Financial award application deadline: 3/15; financial award applicants required to submit FAFSA. *Faculty research:* Altered states of consciousness, dreams, cosmology, postcolonial studies, integrative health studies. *Application contact:* Allyson Werner, Senior Admissions Counselor, 415-575-6155, Fax: 415-575-1268.

See Close-Up on page 347.

Claremont Graduate University, Graduate Programs, School of Arts and Humanities, Program in Applied Women's Studies, Claremont, CA 91711-6160. Offers MA. *Faculty:* 1 (woman) full-time. *Students:* 12 full-time (all women), 4 part-time (all women); includes 4 minority (2 African Americans, 1 Asian American or Pacific Islander, 1 Hispanic American). Average age 28. In 2008, 5 master's awarded. *Entrance requirements:* For master's, GRE General Test. Additional exam requirements/recommendations for international students: Required—TOEFL (minimum score 550 paper-based; 213 computer-based; 80 iBT). *Application deadline:* For fall admission, 2/1 priority date for domestic students. Applications are processed on a rolling basis. Application fee: $60. Electronic applications accepted. *Expenses:* Tuition: Full-time $33,698; part-time $1465 per unit. Required fees: $310; $155 per semester. Tuition and fees vary according to program. *Financial support:* Fellowships, research assistantships, teaching assistantships, Federal Work-Study, institutionally sponsored loans, and scholarships/grants available. Support available to part-time students. Financial award application deadline: 2/15; financial award applicants required to submit FAFSA. *Unit head:* Linda Perkins, Director, 909-621-8696, E-mail: linda.perkins@cgu.edu. *Application contact:* Justin Evans, Admissions Coordinator, 909-607-1278, Fax: 909-607-1221, E-mail: humanities@cgu.edu.

Claremont Graduate University, Graduate Programs, School of Religion, Claremont, CA 91711-6160. Offers Hebrew Bible (MA, PhD); history of Christianity and religions of North America (MA, PhD); New Testament (MA, PhD); philosophy of religion and theology (MA, PhD); theology, ethics and culture (MA, PhD); women's studies in religion (MA, PhD); MA/PhD; MBA/PhD. Part-time programs available. *Faculty:* 7 full-time (2 women), 2 part-time/adjunct (0 women). *Students:* 231 full-time (96 women), 4 part-time (2 women); includes 32 minority (13 African Americans, 11 Asian Americans or Pacific Islanders, 8 Hispanic Americans), 29 international. Average age 37. In 2008, 13 master's, 16 doctorates awarded. Terminal master's awarded for partial completion of doctoral program. *Entrance requirements:* For master's and doctorate, GRE General Test. Additional exam requirements/recommendations for international students: Required—TOEFL (minimum score 550 paper-based; 213 computer-based; 80 iBT). *Application deadline:* For fall admission, 2/1 priority date for domestic students. Applications are processed on a rolling basis. Application fee: $60. Electronic applications accepted. *Expenses:* Tuition: Full-time $33,698; part-time $1465 per unit. Required fees: $310; $155 per semester. Tuition and fees vary according to program. *Financial support:* Fellowships, research assistantships, teaching assistantships, Federal Work-Study, institutionally sponsored loans, and scholarships/grants available. Support available to part-time students. Financial award application deadline: 2/15; financial award applicants required to submit FAFSA. *Unit head:* Karen Torjesen, Dean, 909-607-3214, Fax: 909-621-9587, E-mail: karen.torjesen@cgu.edu. *Application contact:* Brent Smith, Recruiter, 909-607-2653, Fax: 909-607-9587, E-mail: brent.smith@cgu.edu.

Clark Atlanta University, School of Arts and Sciences, Department of Africana Women's Studies, Atlanta, GA 30314. Offers MA, DAH. Part-time programs available. *Faculty:* 1 (woman) full-time, 1 part-time/adjunct (0 women). *Students:* 4 full-time (all women), 9 part-time (8 women); includes 12 minority (all African Americans), 1 international. Average age 34. 6 applicants, 67% accepted, 1 enrolled. In 2008, 2 master's, 4 doctorates awarded. *Degree requirements:* For master's, one foreign language, thesis; for doctorate, 2 foreign languages, thesis/dissertation. *Entrance requirements:* For master's, GRE General Test, minimum GPA of 2.5; for doctorate, GRE General Test, minimum graduate GPA of 3.0. Additional exam requirements/recommendations for international students: Required—TOEFL (minimum score 500 paper-based; 173 computer-based). *Application deadline:* For fall admission, 4/1 for domestic and international students; for spring admission, 11/1 for domestic and international students. Applications are processed on a rolling basis. Application fee: $40 ($55 for international students). Electronic applications accepted. *Expenses:* Tuition: Full-time $12,240; part-time $680 per credit hour. Required fees: $710; $355 per semester. *Financial support:* Scholarships/grants available. Financial award application deadline: 4/30; financial award applicants required to submit FAFSA. *Faculty research:* Concerns of women of African descent globally. *Unit head:* Dr. Josephine Bradley, Chairperson, 404-880-6810, E-mail: jbradley@cau.edu. *Application contact:* Michelle Clark-Davis, Graduate Program Admissions, 404-880-6605, E-mail: cauadmissions@cau.edu.

Cornell University, Graduate School, Graduate Fields of Arts and Sciences, Field of English Language and Literature, Ithaca, NY 14853-0001. Offers African-American literature (PhD); American literature after 1865 (PhD); American literature to 1865 (PhD); American studies (PhD); colonial and postcolonial literature (PhD); creative writing (MFA); cultural studies (PhD); dramatic literature (PhD); English poetry (PhD); English Renaissance to 1660 (PhD); lesbian, bisexual, and gay literature studies (PhD); literary criticism and theory (PhD); nineteenth century (PhD); Old and Middle English (PhD); prose fiction (PhD); Restoration and eighteenth century (PhD); twentieth century (PhD); women's literature (PhD); MFA/PhD. *Faculty:* 54 full-time (27 women). *Students:* 100 full-time (53 women); includes 24 minority (8 African Americans, 4 American Indian/Alaska Native, 6 Asian Americans or Pacific Islanders, 6 Hispanic Americans), 14 international. Average age 29. 821 applicants, 6% accepted, 23 enrolled. In 2008, 19 master's, 12 doctorates awarded. Terminal master's awarded for partial completion of doctoral program. *Degree requirements:* For master's, one foreign language, thesis; for doctorate, one foreign language, comprehensive exam, thesis/dissertation, teaching experience. *Entrance requirements:* For master's, GRE General Test, 3 letters of recommendation, creative writing sample; for doctorate, GRE General Test, GRE Subject Test (English), 3 letters of recommendation, writing sample. Additional exam requirements/recommendations for international students: Required—TOEFL (minimum score 600 paper-based; 250 computer-based; 77 iBT). *Application deadline:* For fall admission, 1/10 for domestic students. Application fee: $70. Electronic applications accepted. *Expenses:* Tuition: Full-time $29,500. Required fees: $70. Full-time tuition and fees vary according to degree level, program and student level. *Financial support:* In 2008–09, 96 students received support, including 41 fellowships with full tuition reimbursements available, 1 research assistantship with full tuition reimbursement available, 54 teaching assistantships with full tuition reimbursements available; institutionally sponsored loans, scholarships/grants, health care benefits, tuition waivers (full and partial), and unspecified assistantships also available. Financial award applicants required to submit FAFSA. *Faculty research:* English and American literature, women's writing, ethnic and post-colonial literature, critical theory, medievalism. *Unit head:* Director of Graduate Studies, 607-255-7989, Fax: 607-255-6661. *Application contact:* Graduate Field Assistant, 607-255-7989, Fax: 607-255-6661, E-mail: english_grad@cornell.edu.

Drew University, Caspersen School of Graduate Studies, Women's Studies Program, Madison, NJ 07940-1493. Offers MA. *Degree requirements:* For master's, one foreign language, thesis. *Entrance requirements:* For master's, GRE General Test. *Faculty research:* Feminist theory, feminist literature, gender analysis, social theory and religion.

Duke University, Graduate School, Women's Studies Program, Durham, NC 27708-0586. Offers Certificate. *Faculty research:* History of women's studies, feminist pedagogy, higher education, women's health, race/class/gender and sexual orientation.

Eastern Michigan University, Graduate School, College of Arts and Sciences, Department of Women's and Gender Studies, Ypsilanti, MI 48197. Offers MLS. Part-time and evening/weekend programs available. Postbaccalaureate distance learning degree programs offered (minimal on-campus study). *Degree requirements:* For master's, thesis optional. *Entrance requirements:* Additional exam requirements/recommendations for international students: Required—TOEFL.

Emory University, Graduate School of Arts and Sciences, Department of Comparative Literature, Atlanta, GA 30322-1100. Offers comparative literature (PhD); English (Certificate); French (Certificate); Middle Eastern studies (PhD); philosophy (Certificate); psychoanalytic studies (PhD); religion (PhD); Spanish (Certificate); women studies (Certificate). *Degree requirements:* For doctorate, 2 foreign languages, comprehensive exam, thesis/dissertation. *Entrance requirements:* For doctorate, GRE General Test, minimum GPA of 3.0. Additional exam requirements/recommendations for international students: Required—TOEFL. Electronic applications accepted. *Faculty research:* Literary theory, psychoanalysis trauma and testimony, literature and religion, literature and technology, literature and philosophy, politics and global culture, literature and aesthetics.

Emory University, Graduate School of Arts and Sciences, Department of Spanish and Portuguese, Atlanta, GA 30322-1100. Offers comparative literature (Certificate); film studies (Certificate); Spanish (PhD); women's studies (Certificate). *Degree requirements:* For doctorate, 2 foreign languages, comprehensive exam, thesis/dissertation. *Entrance requirements:* For doctorate, GRE General Test. Additional exam requirements/recommendations for international students: Required—TOEFL. Electronic applications accepted. *Faculty research:* Spanish literature, Spanish-American literature, literary theory, criticism, cultural studies.

Emory University, Graduate School of Arts and Sciences, Department of Women's Studies, Atlanta, GA 30322-1100. Offers PhD. *Degree requirements:* For doctorate, comprehensive exam, thesis/dissertation. *Entrance requirements:* For doctorate, GRE General Test, writing sample. Additional exam requirements/recommendations for international students: Required—TOEFL. Electronic applications accepted. *Faculty research:* Feminist theory, women's literature, African-American literature, gender in cross-cultural perspective, public policy and globalization.

Florida Atlantic University, Dorothy F. Schmidt College of Arts and Letters, Women's Studies Center, Boca Raton, FL 33431-0991. Offers MA, Certificate. *Faculty:* 2 full-time (both women), 1 (woman) part-time/adjunct. *Students:* 5 full-time (4 women), 4 part-time (all women); includes 1 minority (Hispanic American). Average age 31. 8 applicants, 25% accepted, 1 enrolled. In 2008, 3 master's awarded. *Degree requirements:* For master's, comprehensive exam, thesis or alternative. *Entrance requirements:* For master's, GRE General Test, minimum GPA of 3.0. *Application deadline:* For fall admission, 7/1 for domestic students, 2/15 for international students; for spring admission, 11/1 for domestic students, 7/15 for international students. Applications are processed on a rolling basis. Application fee: $30. *Expenses:* Tuition, state resident: full-time $4867; part-time $270.40 per credit hour. Tuition, nonresident: full-time $16,486; part-time $915.87 per credit hour. *Financial support:* Fellowships with full and partial tuition reimbursements, teaching assistantships with full and partial tuition reimbursements, career-related internships or fieldwork, Federal Work-Study, institutionally sponsored loans, scholarships/grants, and unspecified assistantships available. Support available to part-time students. *Faculty research:* Women and science/technology, feminist theory, violence against women, women and international development, feminist medical anthropology. *Unit head:* Dr. Josephine Beoku-Betts, Director, 561-297-3865, Fax: 561-297-2127. *Application contact:* Dr. Jane Caputi, Professor, 561-297-2056, Fax: 561-297-2127, E-mail: jcaputi@fau.edu.

Women's Studies

George Mason University, College of Humanities and Social Sciences, Interdisciplinary Studies Program, Fairfax, VA 22030. Offers anthropology (MAIS); community college teaching (MAIS); folklore (MAIS); higher education (MAIS); individualized studies (MAIS); religion, cultures, and values (MAIS); video-based production (MAIS); women's studies (MAIS); zoo and aquarium leadership (MAIS). Part-time and evening/weekend programs available. *Degree requirements:* For master's, thesis optional. *Entrance requirements:* For master's, GRE, GMAT, or MAT, interview, minimum GPA of 3.0 in last 60 hours of course work. Electronic applications accepted.

The George Washington University, Columbian College of Arts and Sciences, Department of Women's Studies, Washington, DC 20052. Offers MA, Certificate. Part-time and evening/weekend programs available. *Faculty:* 1 (woman) full-time, 3 part-time/adjunct (all women). *Students:* 15 full-time (14 women), 20 part-time (19 women); includes 4 minority (2 African Americans, 1 Asian American or Pacific Islander, 1 Hispanic American), 1 international. Average age 27. 21 applicants, 95% accepted, 9 enrolled. In 2008, 11 master's awarded. *Degree requirements:* For master's, comprehensive exam, thesis or alternative. *Entrance requirements:* For master's, GRE General Test, minimum GPA of 3.0. Additional exam requirements/recommendations for international students: Required—TOEFL (minimum score 550 paper-based; 213 computer-based; 80 iBT). *Application deadline:* For fall admission, 4/1 priority date for domestic students, 1/15 priority date for international students; for spring admission, 10/1 priority date for domestic students, 9/1 priority date for international students. Applications are processed on a rolling basis. Application fee: $60. Electronic applications accepted. *Financial support:* In 2008–09, 2 students received support; fellowships with tuition reimbursements available, teaching assistantships with tuition reimbursements available, Federal Work-Study, institutionally sponsored loans, and tuition waivers available. Financial award application deadline: 1/15. *Unit head:* Dr. Daniel Moshenberg, Director, 202-994-9086, Fax: 202-994-7249. *Application contact:* Information Contact, 202-994-6942, Fax: 202-994-2249, E-mail: wstu@gwu.edu.

The George Washington University, Columbian College of Arts and Sciences, Trachtenberg School of Public Policy and Public Administration, Washington, DC 20052. Offers public administration (MPA), including budget and public finance, federal policy, politics, and management, international development management, managing public organizations, managing state and local governments, nonprofit management, policy analysis and evaluation, public administration, public-private policy and management; public policy (MA, MPP), including environmental and resource policy (MA), philosophy and social policy (MA), women's studies (MA); public policy and administration (PhD); JD/MPP; MPA/JD; PhD/MPP. Part-time and evening/weekend programs available. *Faculty:* 19 full-time (8 women), 12 part-time/adjunct (3 women). *Students:* 82 full-time (57 women), 130 part-time (80 women); includes 28 minority (9 African Americans, 1 American Indian/Alaska Native, 10 Asian Americans or Pacific Islanders, 8 Hispanic Americans), 28 international. Average age 31. 225 applicants, 38% accepted, 31 enrolled. In 2008, 64 master's, 7 doctorates awarded. *Degree requirements:* For doctorate, thesis/dissertation, general exam. *Entrance requirements:* For master's, GRE General Test, minimum GPA of 3.0; for doctorate, GRE General Test, interview, minimum GPA of 3.0. Additional exam requirements/recommendations for international students: Required—TOEFL (minimum score 600 paper-based; 250 computer-based; 100 iBT). *Application deadline:* For fall admission, 1/15 priority date for domestic and international students; for spring admission, 10/1 priority date for domestic students, 9/1 priority date for international students. Applications are processed on a rolling basis. Application fee: $60. Electronic applications accepted. *Financial support:* In 2008–09, 87 students received support; fellowships, teaching assistantships, institutionally sponsored loans and tuition waivers available. Financial award application deadline: 1/15. *Unit head:* Dr. Joseph J. Cordes, Director, 202-994-5826, Fax: 202-994-8913, E-mail: cordes@gwu.edu. *Application contact:* Information Contact, 202-994-8500, Fax: 202-994-8913, E-mail: pubpol@gwu.edu.

The George Washington University, Columbian College of Arts and Sciences, Trachtenberg School of Public Policy and Public Administration, Interdisciplinary Programs in Public Policy, Program in Women's Studies, Washington, DC 20052. Offers MA. Part-time and evening/weekend programs available. *Students:* 2 full-time (both women), 9 part-time (8 women). Average age 26. 12 applicants, 67% accepted, 5 enrolled. In 2008, 9 master's awarded. *Degree requirements:* For master's, comprehensive exam. *Entrance requirements:* For master's, GRE General Test, minimum GPA of 3.0. Additional exam requirements/recommendations for international students: Required—TOEFL (minimum score 600 paper-based; 250 computer-based; 100 iBT). *Application deadline:* For fall admission, 4/1 priority date for domestic and international students; for spring admission, 10/1 priority date for domestic students, 9/1 priority date for international students. Applications are processed on a rolling basis. Application fee: $60. Electronic applications accepted. *Financial support:* In 2008–09, 4 students received support; fellowships with tuition reimbursements available, teaching assistantships with tuition reimbursements available, tuition waivers available. Financial award application deadline: 1/15. *Unit head:* Prof. Daniel Moshenberg, Director, 202-994-9086, E-mail: dym@gwu.edu. *Application contact:* Information Contact, 202-994-6942, Fax: 202-994-7249, E-mail: wstu@gwu.edu.

Georgia State University, College of Arts and Sciences, Women's Studies Institute, Atlanta, GA 30303-3083. Offers MA. Part-time programs available. *Degree requirements:* For master's, one foreign language, comprehensive exam, thesis, portfolio. *Entrance requirements:* For master's, GRE General Test. Additional exam requirements/recommendations for international students: Required—TOEFL. Electronic applications accepted. *Faculty research:* Globalization and gender, womanism, culture and gender, black feminist thought, feminist theory.

Graduate School and University Center of the City University of New York, Graduate Studies, Interdisciplinary Studies, New York, NY 10016-4039. Offers language in social context (PhD); medieval studies (PhD); public policy (MA, PhD); urban studies (MA, PhD); women's studies (MA, PhD). Terminal master's awarded for partial completion of doctoral program. *Degree requirements:* For master's, thesis; for doctorate, comprehensive exam, thesis/dissertation. *Entrance requirements:* For master's and doctorate, GRE General Test.

Graduate Theological Union, Graduate Programs, Berkeley, CA 94709-1212. Offers art and religion (MA, PhD); biblical languages (MA); biblical studies (Old and New Testament) (MA, PhD, Th D); Buddhist studies (MA); Christian spirituality (MA, PhD); cultural and historical studies of religions (MA, PhD); ethics and social theory (PhD); history (MA, PhD, Th D); homiletics (MA, PhD, Th D); interdisciplinary studies (PhD, Th D); Jewish studies (MA, PhD, Certificate); liturgical studies (MA, PhD, Th D); Near Eastern religions (PhD); Orthodox Christian studies (MA); Orthodox studies (Certificate); religion and psychology (MA, PhD); religion and society/ethics and social theory (MA); systematic and philosophical theology (MA, PhD, Th D); women's studies in religion (Certificate); MA/M Div. *Accreditation:* ATS. Terminal master's awarded for partial completion of doctoral program. *Degree requirements:* For master's, one foreign language, thesis; for doctorate, one foreign language, comprehensive exam, thesis/dissertation. *Entrance requirements:* For master's, GRE General Test; for doctorate, GRE General Test, MA or M Div. Additional exam requirements/recommendations for international students: Required—TOEFL. Electronic applications accepted.

Institute of Transpersonal Psychology, Residential Programs, Palo Alto, CA 94303. Offers clinical psychology (PhD); counseling psychology (MA); transpersonal psychology (MA, PhD); women's spirituality (PhD). Part-time and evening/weekend programs available. *Faculty:* 17 full-time (9 women), 31 part-time/adjunct (18 women). *Students:* 268 full-time (189 women), 40 part-time (31 women); includes 53 minority (9 African Americans, 3 American Indian/Alaska Native, 21 Asian Americans or Pacific Islanders, 20 Hispanic Americans), 14 international. Average age 38. 168 applicants, 52% accepted, 56 enrolled. In 2008, 47 master's, 16 doctorates awarded. Terminal master's awarded for partial completion of doctoral program. *Degree requirements:* For doctorate, thesis/dissertation. *Entrance requirements:* For master's and doctorate, bachelor's degree. *Application deadline:* For fall admission, 2/15 priority date for domestic students. Applications are processed on a rolling basis. Application fee: $55. *Expenses:* Tuition: Full-time $24,543; part-time $577 per unit. Tuition and fees vary according to degree level. *Financial support:* In 2008–09, 178 students received support; teaching assistantships, career-related internships or fieldwork, Federal Work-Study, and scholarships/grants available. Support available to part-time students. Financial award application deadline: 7/1; financial award applicants required to submit FAFSA. *Unit head:* Dr. Paul Roy, Academic Vice President, 650-493-4430 Ext. 243, Fax: 650-493-6835, E-mail: proy@itp.edu. *Application contact:* 650-493-4430 Ext. 16, Fax: 650-493-6835, E-mail: itpinfo@itp.edu.

Lakehead University, Graduate Studies, Department of History, Thunder Bay, ON P7B 5E1, Canada. Offers gerontology (MA); history (MA); women's studies (MA). Part-time programs available. *Degree requirements:* For master's, one foreign language, thesis. *Entrance requirements:* For master's, minimum B average. Additional exam requirements/recommendations for international students: Required—TOEFL. Tuition charges are reported in Canadian dollars. *Expenses:* Tuition, area resident: Full-time $6500 Canadian dollars. International tuition: $13,700 Canadian dollars full-time. *Faculty research:* Canadian history, British history, Russian/German history, women's studies.

Lakehead University, Graduate Studies, Faculty of Education, Thunder Bay, ON P7B 5E1, Canada. Offers educational studies (PhD); gerontology (M Ed); women's studies (M Ed). Part-time and evening/weekend programs available. *Degree requirements:* For master's, project or thesis. *Entrance requirements:* For master's, minimum B average. Additional exam requirements/recommendations for international students: Required—TOEFL. Tuition charges are reported in Canadian dollars. *Expenses:* Tuition, area resident: Full-time $6500 Canadian dollars. International tuition: $13,700 Canadian dollars full-time. *Faculty research:* Art education, AIDS education, language arts education, gerontology, women's studies.

Lakehead University, Graduate Studies, Faculty of Social Sciences and Humanities, Department of English, Thunder Bay, ON P7B 5E1, Canada. Offers English (MA); women's studies (MA). Part-time and evening/weekend programs available. *Degree requirements:* For master's, one foreign language, thesis optional. *Entrance requirements:* For master's, minimum B average. Additional exam requirements/recommendations for international students: Required—TOEFL. Tuition charges are reported in Canadian dollars. *Expenses:* Tuition, area resident: Full-time $6500 Canadian dollars. International tuition: $13,700 Canadian dollars full-time. *Faculty research:* Rhetoric and literary studies, children's literature, nineteenth- and twentieth-century American literature, modern literature, women's studies.

Lakehead University, Graduate Studies, Faculty of Social Sciences and Humanities, Department of Sociology, Thunder Bay, ON P7B 5E1, Canada. Offers gerontology (MA); health services and policy research (MA); sociology (MA); women's studies (MA). Part-time and evening/weekend programs available. *Degree requirements:* For master's, research project or thesis. *Entrance requirements:* For master's, minimum B average. Additional exam requirements/recommendations for international students: Required—TOEFL. Tuition charges are reported in Canadian dollars. *Expenses:* Tuition, area resident: Full-time $6500 Canadian dollars. International tuition: $13,700 Canadian dollars full-time. *Faculty research:* Sociology of medicine, cultural and social change, health human resources, gerontology, women's studies.

Lakehead University, Graduate Studies, School of Social Work, Thunder Bay, ON P7B 5E1, Canada. Offers gerontology (MSW); social work (MSW); women's studies (MSW). Part-time programs available. *Degree requirements:* For master's, thesis or project. *Entrance requirements:* For master's, minimum B average. Additional exam requirements/recommendations for international students: Required—TOEFL. Tuition charges are reported in Canadian dollars. *Expenses:* Tuition, area resident: Full-time $6500 Canadian dollars. International tuition: $13,700 Canadian dollars full-time. *Faculty research:* Clinical psychology, social work and practice theory, long-term care, health care for frail elderly, women's studies.

Lakehead University, Graduate Studies, Women's Studies Collaborative Program, Thunder Bay, ON P7B 5E1, Canada. Offers M Ed, MA, MSW. Part-time programs available. *Degree requirements:* For master's, thesis (for some programs). *Entrance requirements:* Additional exam requirements/recommendations for international students: Required—TOEFL. Tuition charges are reported in Canadian dollars. *Expenses:* Tuition, area resident: Full-time $6500 Canadian dollars. International tuition: $13,700 Canadian dollars full-time. *Faculty research:* Feminist thought, feminist pedagogy, women of literature, Canadian women's history, well-being of women.

Lesley University, Graduate School of Arts and Social Sciences, Self-Designed Master's Program in Interdisciplinary Studies, Cambridge, MA 02138-2790. Offers individualized studies (MA); integrative holistic health (MA); women's studies (MA). Part-time and evening/weekend programs available. Postbaccalaureate distance learning degree programs offered (no on-campus study). *Entrance requirements:* For master's, 3 letters of recommendation. Additional exam requirements/recommendations for international students: Required—TOEFL (minimum score 550 paper-based; 213 computer-based; 80 iBT). *Expenses:* Tuition: Full-time $13,770; part-time $765 per credit hour. Required fees: $150. Tuition and fees vary according to course load, degree level, campus/location and program.

Memorial University of Newfoundland, School of Graduate Studies, Interdisciplinary Program in Women's Studies, St. John's, NL A1C 5S7, Canada. Offers MWS.

Minnesota State University Mankato, College of Graduate Studies, College of Social and Behavioral Sciences, Department of Women's Studies, Mankato, MN 56001. Offers MS, Certificate. Part-time programs available. *Students:* 4 full-time (3 women), 4 part-time (3 women). *Degree requirements:* For master's, comprehensive exam, thesis or alternative. *Entrance requirements:* For master's, minimum GPA of 3.0 during previous 2 years of course work. Additional exam requirements/recommendations for international students: Required—TOEFL. *Application deadline:* For fall admission, 7/1 priority date for domestic students; for spring admission, 11/1 for domestic students. Applications are processed on a rolling basis. Application fee: $40. *Financial support:* Research assistantships, teaching assistantships with full tuition reimbursements, career-related internships or fieldwork, Federal Work-Study, institutionally sponsored loans, and unspecified assistantships available. Support available to part-time students. Financial award application deadline: 3/15; financial award applicants required to submit FAFSA. *Unit head:* Dr. Maria Bevacqua, Chairperson, 507-389-2077. *Application contact:* 507-389-2321, E-mail: grad@mnsu.edu.

Mount Saint Vincent University, Graduate Programs, Department of Women's Studies, Halifax, NS B3M 2J6, Canada. Offers MA. Part-time programs available. *Degree requirements:* For master's, thesis. Electronic applications accepted.

The Ohio State University, Graduate School, College of Humanities, Department of Women's Studies, Columbus, OH 43210. Offers MA, PhD. *Degree requirements:* For master's, thesis optional. *Entrance requirements:* Additional exam requirements/recommendations for international students: Required—TOEFL (minimum score 600 paper-based; 250 computer-based). Electronic applications accepted.

Old Dominion University, College of Arts and Letters, Graduate Programs in International Studies, Norfolk, VA 23529. Offers conflict and cooperation (PhD), including women's studies certificate; U.S. foreign policy (MA), including modeling and simulation certificate. Part-time programs available. *Faculty:* 14 full-time (3 women). *Students:* 40 full-time (16 women), 34 part-time (15 women); includes 6 minority (2 African Americans, 1 Asian American or Pacific Islander, 3 Hispanic Americans), 24 international. Average age 32. 99 applicants, 54% accepted, 30 enrolled. In 2008, 10 master's, 5 doctorates awarded. Terminal master's awarded for partial completion of doctoral program. *Degree requirements:* For master's, one foreign language, comprehensive exam, thesis optional; for doctorate, one foreign language, comprehensive exam, thesis/dissertation. *Entrance requirements:* For master's, GRE General Test, sample of written work, 2 letters of recommendation; for doctorate, GRE General Test, sample of written work, 3 letters of recommendation. Additional exam requirements/recommendations for international students: Required—TOEFL (minimum score 570 paper-based; 230 computer-based). *Application deadline:* For fall admission, 3/15 for domestic students, 2/15 for international students; for spring admission, 10/15 for domestic and international students. Application fee: $40. Electronic applications accepted. *Expenses:* Tuition, area resident: Full-time $7704; part-time $321 per credit. Tuition, state resident: full-time $7704; part-time $321 per credit. Tuition, nonresident: full-time $19,104; part-time $796 per credit. Required fees: $99 per semester. One-time fee: $40. *Financial support:* In 2008–09, 20 students received support, including 2 fellowships (averaging $13,000 per year), 9 research assistantships with tuition reimbursements available (averaging $11,000 per year), 9 teaching assistantships with tuition reimbursements available (averaging $11,000 per year); career-related internships or fieldwork, institutionally sponsored loans, scholarships/grants, and unspecified assistantships also available. Support available to part-time students. Financial award application deadline: 2/15; financial award applicants required to submit FAFSA. *Faculty research:* U.S. foreign policy, international security, transatlantic and transpacific relations, transnational issues, IPE and development. Total annual research expenditures: $330,391. *Unit head:* Dr. Regina Karp, Graduate Program Director, 757-683-5700, Fax: 757-683-5701, E-mail: rkarp@odu.edu. *Application contact:* Dr. Angelica Huizar, 757-683-3988, Fax: 757-683-5701, E-mail: ahuizar@odu.edu.

Queen's University at Kingston, School of Graduate Studies and Research, Faculty of Arts and Sciences, Department of Sociology, Kingston, ON K7L 3N6, Canada. Offers communication and Information technology (MA, PhD); feminist sociology (MA, PhD); socio-legal studies (MA, PhD); sociological theory (MA, PhD). Part-time programs available. *Degree requirements:* For master's, thesis; for doctorate, comprehensive exam, thesis/dissertation. *Entrance requirements:* For master's, honors bachelors degree in sociology; for doctorate, honors bachelors degree, masters degree in sociology. Additional exam requirements/recommendations for international students: Required—TOEFL. *Faculty research:* Social change and modernization, social control, deviance and criminology, surveillance.

Roosevelt University, Graduate Division, College of Arts and Sciences, Department of Literature and Languages, Program in Women's and Gender Studies, Chicago, IL 60605-1394. Offers MA, Certificate. Part-time and evening/weekend programs available. *Students:* 16 full-time (15 women), 5 part-time (all women); includes 1 minority (African American). Average age 32. 50 applicants, 48% accepted, 10 enrolled. In 2008, 8 master's awarded. *Degree requirements:* For master's, thesis. *Entrance requirements:* For master's, minimum GPA of 2.7. *Application deadline:* For fall admission, 6/1 priority date for domestic students. Applications are processed on a rolling basis. Application fee: $25 ($35 for international students). *Expenses:* Tuition: Full-time $14,730; part-time $709 per credit. Required fees: $175 per semester. Tuition and fees vary according to course load and program. *Financial support:* Application deadline: 2/15. *Faculty research:* Feminist economics; philosophy of feminism; race, class, and gender; women and art; women's history. *Unit head:* Ann Brigham, Head, 312-341-3725, Fax: 312-341-3680, E-mail: abrigham@roosevelt.edu. *Application contact:* Joanne Canyon-Heller, Coordinator of Graduate Admission, 877-APPLY RU, Fax: 312-281-3356, E-mail: applyru@roosevelt.edu.

Rutgers, The State University of New Jersey, New Brunswick, Graduate School, Department of Political Science, Piscataway, NJ 08854-8097. Offers American politics (PhD); comparative politics (PhD); international relations (PhD); political theory (PhD); public law (PhD); women and politics (PhD). *Degree requirements:* For doctorate, one foreign language, comprehensive exam, thesis/dissertation. *Entrance requirements:* For doctorate, GRE General Test. Additional exam requirements/recommendations for international students: Required—TOEFL.

Rutgers, The State University of New Jersey, New Brunswick, Graduate School, Program in Women's and Gender Studies, Piscataway, NJ 08854-8097. Offers MA, PhD. Part-time programs available. *Degree requirements:* For master's, thesis or alternative; for doctorate, comprehensive exam, thesis/dissertation. *Entrance requirements:* For master's and doctorate, GRE General Test, writing sample, 3 letters of recommendation. Additional exam requirements/recommendations for international students: Required—TOEFL. *Faculty research:* Feminist theory, gender and sexuality, global and cultural studies, women in history, literature, and politics, feminist politics.

Saint Mary's University, Faculty of Arts, Program in Women and Gender Studies, Halifax, NS B3H 3C3, Canada. Offers MA. Part-time programs available. *Degree requirements:* For master's, thesis. *Entrance requirements:* For master's, honors degree.

San Diego State University, Graduate and Research Affairs, College of Arts and Letters, Department of Women's Studies, San Diego, CA 92182. Offers MA. *Entrance requirements:* For master's, GRE General Test, 2 letters of reference. Additional exam requirements/recommendations for international students: Required—TOEFL. Electronic applications accepted.

San Francisco State University, Division of Graduate Studies, College of Humanities, Department of Women Studies, San Francisco, CA 94132-1722. Offers MA. Part-time and evening/weekend programs available.

Sarah Lawrence College, Graduate Studies, Program in Women's History, Bronxville, NY 10708-5999. Offers MA. Part-time programs available. *Faculty:* 9 part-time/adjunct (8 women). *Students:* 26 full-time (25 women), 4 part-time (all women); includes 7 minority (2 African Americans, 2 Asian Americans or Pacific Islanders, 3 Hispanic Americans), 1 international. Average age 27. 48 applicants, 85% accepted, 18 enrolled. In 2008, 8 master's awarded. *Degree requirements:* For master's, thesis. *Entrance requirements:* For master's, previous course work in history, minimum B average in undergraduate course work. Additional exam requirements/recommendations for international students: Required—TOEFL (minimum score 600 paper-based). *Application deadline:* For fall admission, 2/1 priority date for domestic students. Applications are processed on a rolling basis. Application fee: $60. *Expenses:* Tuition: Full-time $26,544; part-time $1106 per credit. Required fees: $450. Tuition and fees vary according to program. *Financial support:* Fellowships, career-related internships or fieldwork available. Support available to part-time students. Financial award application deadline: 3/1; financial award applicants required to submit CSS PROFILE or FAFSA. *Unit head:* Priscilla Murolo, Director, 914-395-2405. *Application contact:* Susan Guma, Dean of Graduate Studies, 914-395-2373, E-mail: sguma@mail.slc.edu.

See Close-Up on page 621.

Simon Fraser University, Graduate Studies, Faculty of Arts and Social Sciences, Department of Women's Studies, Burnaby, BC V5A 1S6, Canada. Offers MA, PhD. *Degree requirements:* For master's, thesis or alternative. *Entrance requirements:* For master's, minimum GPA of 3.8. Additional exam requirements/recommendations for international students: Required—TOEFL or IELTS. *Faculty research:* Theory development, disability, economics, globalization.

Southeastern Baptist Theological Seminary, Graduate and Professional Programs, Wake Forest, NC 27588-1889. Offers advanced biblical studies (M Div); Christian education (M Div, MACE); Christian ethics (PhD); Christian ministry (M Div); Christian planting (M Div); church music (MACM); counseling (MACO); evangelism (PhD); language (M Div); ministry (D Min); New Testament (PhD); Old Testament (PhD); philosophy (PhD); theology (Th M, PhD); women's studies (M Div). *Accreditation:* ACIPE; ATS (one or more programs are accredited). *Degree requirements:* For master's, thesis (for some programs), oral exam; for doctorate, thesis/dissertation, fieldwork; for M Div, supervised ministry. *Entrance requirements:* For master's, Cooperative English Test, minimum GPA of 2.0, M Div or equivalent (Th M); for doctorate, GRE General Test or MAT, Cooperative English Test, M Div or equivalent, 3 years of professional experience.

Southern Connecticut State University, School of Graduate Studies, School of Arts and Sciences, Program in Women's Studies, New Haven, CT 06515-1355. Offers MA. Part-time and evening/weekend programs available. *Degree requirements:* For master's, thesis or alternative. *Entrance requirements:* For master's, interview. Electronic applications accepted.

Suffolk University, College of Arts and Sciences, Program in Women's Health, Boston, MA 02108-2770. Offers MA. *Entrance requirements:* For master's, statement of professional goals, official transcripts, 2 letters of recommendation, resumé. Additional exam requirements/recommendations for international students: Required—TOEFL (minimum score 550 paper-based; 213 computer-based; 80 iBT). Electronic applications accepted. *Expenses:* Contact institution.

Texas Woman's University, Graduate School, College of Arts and Sciences, Program in Women's Studies, Denton, TX 76201. Offers MA. *Students:* 11 full-time (all women), 17 part-time (all women); includes 10 minority (4 African Americans, 1 American Indian/Alaska Native, 5 Hispanic Americans), 1 international. Average age 31. In 2008, 10 master's awarded. *Degree requirements:* For master's, thesis. *Entrance requirements:* For master's, 2 letters of reference, personal essay. Additional exam requirements/recommendations for international students: Required—TOEFL (minimum score 550 paper-based; 213 computer-based; 79 iBT). *Application deadline:* For fall admission, 4/1 for international students; for spring admission, 8/1 for international students. Applications are processed on a rolling basis. Application fee: $30 ($50 for international students). Electronic applications accepted. *Expenses:* Tuition, state resident: full-time $3564; part-time $198 per semester hour. Tuition, nonresident: full-time $8622; part-time $479 per semester hour. Required fees: $1158; $64 per semester hour. Tuition and fees vary according to course load. *Financial support:* In 2008–09, 9 research assistantships (averaging $10,440 per year), 4 teaching assistantships (averaging $10,440 per year) were awarded; career-related internships or fieldwork, Federal Work-Study, institutionally sponsored loans, scholarships/grants, traineeships, health care benefits, and unspecified assistantships also available. Support available to part-time students. Financial award application deadline: 3/1; financial award applicants required to submit FAFSA. *Faculty research:* Feminism and religion, family violence, feminist theory, women of color, feminist ethics. *Unit head:* Dr. Claire L. Sahlin, Director, 940-898-2119, Fax: 940-898-2101, E-mail: csahlin@twu.edu. *Application contact:* Samuel Wheeler, Assistant Director of Admissions, 940-898-3188, Fax: 940-898-3081, E-mail: wheelersr@twu.edu.

Towson University, College of Graduate Studies and Research, Program in Women's Studies, Towson, MD 21252-0001. Offers MS, Certificate. *Degree requirements:* For master's, thesis optional. *Entrance requirements:* For master's, minimum GPA of 3.0, 9 credits of course work in women's studies and/or the social sciences. Electronic applications accepted. *Faculty research:* Gender and international relations, health, economics, violence against women, public policy.

United Theological Seminary of the Twin Cities, Graduate and Professional Programs, New Brighton, MN 55112-2598. Offers advanced theological studies (Diploma); justice and peace studies (M Div); leadership toward racial justice (MA, Certificate); Methodist studies (M Div, MA); ministry (D Min); ministry renewal and professional development (Certificate); pastoral care and counseling (M Div); religion and theology (MA); theological and religious studies (Certificate); theology and the arts (MA); urban ministry (MARL); women's studies: religion, theology and ministry (MA). *Accreditation:* ACIPE; ATS. Part-time and evening/weekend programs available. *Faculty:* 10 full-time (6 women), 24 part-time/adjunct (12 women). *Students:* 60 full-time (34 women), 93 part-time (60 women); includes 10 minority (5 African Americans, 1 American Indian/Alaska Native, 3 Asian Americans or Pacific Islanders, 1 Hispanic American), 1 international. Average age 47. 39 applicants, 100% accepted, 32 enrolled. In 2008, 21 first professional degrees, 9 master's awarded. *Degree requirements:* For master's, thesis; for doctorate, comprehensive exam, thesis/dissertation; for M Div, integrative notebook, spiritual chronicle. *Entrance requirements:* For M Div and master's, minimum GPA of 2.75; strong analytical, reflective thinking and writing skills; vocational and academic goals compatible with those of Seminary; for doctorate, M Div or equivalent, minimum GPA of 3.0, 3 years experience in professional ministry; for other advanced degree, BA or equivalent life experience; strong analytical, reflective thinking and writing skills (Certificate); proficiency in English language; previous study of theology at a theological school, recommendation of student's denomination (Diploma). Additional exam requirements/recommendations for international students: Required—TOEFL (minimum score 550 paper-based). *Application deadline:* For fall admission, 7/1 priority date for domestic students, 11/1 priority date for international students; for winter admission, 11/1 priority date for domestic students; for spring admission, 11/15 priority date for domestic students. Applications are processed on a rolling basis. Application fee: $50. *Expenses:* Tuition: Full-time $11,070; part-time $410 per credit hour. Required fees: $295; $135 per term. One-time fee: $25. Tuition and fees vary according to course load, degree level and program. *Financial support:* In 2008–09, 98 students received support. Career-related internships or fieldwork, institutionally sponsored loans, and scholarships/grants available. Support available to part-time students. Financial award application deadline: 5/1; financial award applicants required to submit FAFSA. *Unit head:* Dr. Richard D. Weis, Dean of the Seminary, 651-255-6108 Ext. 108, Fax: 651-633-4315, E-mail: rweis@unitedseminary.edu. *Application contact:* Rev. Glen Herrington-Hall, Director of Admissions, 651-255-6107 Ext. 107, Fax: 651-633-4315, E-mail: gherrington-hall@unitedseminary.edu.

Université Laval, Faculty of Social Sciences, Program in Feminist Studies, Québec, QC G1K 7P4, Canada. Offers Diploma. Part-time programs available. *Entrance requirements:* For degree, knowledge of French, comprehension of written English. Electronic applications accepted.

University at Albany, State University of New York, College of Arts and Sciences, Department of Women's Studies, Albany, NY 12222-0001. Offers MA, DA. *Entrance requirements:* Additional exam requirements/recommendations for international students: Required—TOEFL (minimum score 550 paper-based; 213 computer-based). Electronic applications accepted. *Faculty research:* Feminist pedagogy, lesbian and gay studies, women in the African diaspora, women's health policy, literature of feminism.

The University of Alabama, Graduate School, College of Arts and Sciences, Department of Women's Studies, Tuscaloosa, AL 35487. Offers MA. *Faculty:* 4 full-time (all women). *Students:* 12 full-time (all women), 1 (woman) part-time; includes 2 minority (both African Americans). Average age 27. 10 applicants, 70% accepted, 6 enrolled. In 2008, 2 master's awarded. *Degree requirements:* For master's, comprehensive exam, thesis. *Entrance requirements:* For master's, MAT or GRE. Additional exam requirements/recommendations for international students: Required—TOEFL. *Application deadline:* For fall admission, 3/7 priority date for domestic students, 3/7 for international students. Application fee: $30. Electronic applications accepted. *Expenses:* Tuition, area resident: Full-time $6400. Tuition, state resident: full-time $6400. Tuition, nonresident: full-time $18,000. *Financial support:* In 2008–09, 6 students received support, including 3 research assistantships with tuition reimbursements available (averaging $10,908 per year), 3 teaching assistantships with tuition reimbursements available (averaging $10,908 per year); health care benefits and unspecified assistantships also available. Financial award application deadline: 4/1. *Faculty research:* Feminist theory, domestic violence, women's health, women in baseball, women in films. Total annual research expenditures: $12,926. *Unit head:* Dr. Ida M. Johnson, Chair, 205-348-8462, Fax: 205-348-3584, E-mail: ijohnson@bama.ua.edu. *Application contact:* Dr. Carol Pierman, Director of Graduate Studies, 205-348-9841, Fax: 205-348-3584, E-mail: cpierman@bama.ua.edu.

The University of Arizona, Graduate College, College of Social and Behavioral Sciences, Department of Women's Studies, Tucson, AZ 85721. Offers MA, PhD. Part-time programs available. *Degree requirements:* For master's, thesis/project. *Entrance requirements:* For master's and doctorate, GRE, minimum GPA of 3.0, 3 letters of recommendation. Additional exam requirements/recommendations for international students: Required—TOEFL (minimum score 600 paper-based; 250 computer-based). Electronic applications accepted. *Faculty research:* Gender race and border studies, sexuality and the body, gender health and science, cultural representation and theory, public policy and social movements.

University of California, Los Angeles, Graduate Division, College of Letters and Science, Program in Women's Studies, Los Angeles, CA 90095. Offers MA, PhD. *Students:* 23 full-time (all women); includes 9 minority (3 African Americans, 1 American Indian/Alaska Native, 2

Women's Studies

University of California, Los Angeles (continued)
Asian Americans or Pacific Islanders, 3 Hispanic Americans). Average age 30. 47 applicants, 26% accepted, 3 enrolled. In 2008, 7 master's, 1 doctorate awarded. Terminal master's awarded for partial completion of doctoral program. *Degree requirements:* For master's, comprehensive exam or thesis; for doctorate, one foreign language, thesis/dissertation, written and oral exams. *Entrance requirements:* For master's, GRE General Test, Degree objective must be Ph.D; for doctorate, GRE General Test, minimum undergraduate GPA of 3.0. *Application deadline:* For fall admission, 12/15 for domestic and international students. Application fee: $60 ($80 for international students). Electronic applications accepted. *Expenses:* Tuition, nonresident: full-time $14,694. Required fees: $9669.50. Full-time tuition and fees vary according to course load, degree level, program and student level. *Financial support:* In 2008–09, 29 fellowships with full and partial tuition reimbursements, 12 research assistantships with full and partial tuition reimbursements, 14 teaching assistantships with full and partial tuition reimbursements were awarded; Federal Work-Study, institutionally sponsored loans, scholarships/grants, health care benefits, tuition waivers (full and partial), and unspecified assistantships also available. Financial award applicants required to submit FAFSA. *Unit head:* Dr. Christine Littleton, Chair, 310-206-8101. *Application contact:* Department Office, 310-206-8101, E-mail: women@women.ucla.edu.

University of California, Santa Barbara, Graduate Division, College of Letters and Sciences, Division of Humanities and Fine Arts, Department of English, Santa Barbara, CA 93106-3170. Offers English (PhD); feminist studies (PhD); global studies (PhD); MA/PhD. *Faculty:* 26 full-time (13 women), 17 part-time/adjunct (12 women). *Students:* 81 full-time (43 women). Average age 30. 151 applicants, 19% accepted, 13 enrolled. In 2008, 12 doctorates awarded. Terminal master's awarded for partial completion of doctoral program. *Degree requirements:* For doctorate, one foreign language, comprehensive exam, thesis/dissertation. *Entrance requirements:* For doctorate, GRE General Test, GRE Subject Test (literature), sample of written work, 3 letters of recommendation, statement of purpose, personal achievements/contributions statement, resumé/curriculum vitae, transcripts for post-secondary institutions attended. Additional exam requirements/recommendations for international students: Required—TOEFL (paper: 550, computer: 213, IBT: 80) or IELTS (7). *Application deadline:* For fall admission, 12/15 for domestic and international students. Application fee: $70 ($90 for international students). Electronic applications accepted. *Expenses:* Tuition, nonresident: full-time $25,149. Required fees: $10,143. Full-time tuition and fees vary according to campus/location, reciprocity agreements and student level. *Financial support:* In 2008–09, 70 students received support, including 32 fellowships with full and partial tuition reimbursements available (averaging $10,800 per year), 6 research assistantships with full and partial tuition reimbursements available (averaging $4,200 per year), 54 teaching assistantships with partial tuition reimbursements available (averaging $10,800 per year); Federal Work-Study, institutionally sponsored loans, scholarships/grants, health care benefits, tuition waivers (full and partial), and unspecified assistantships also available. Financial award application deadline: 12/15; financial award applicants required to submit FAFSA. *Faculty research:* Renaissance literature, 18th century literature, American literature, race and ethnic studies, literature and theory of technology/media/information. *Unit head:* Prof. Alan Liu, Chair, 805-893-3478, Fax: 805-893-4622, E-mail: ayliu@english.ucsb.edu. *Application contact:* Chelsea Houdyshell, Staff Graduate Advisor, 805-893-2639, Fax: 805-893-4622, E-mail: chelsea@english.ucsb.edu.

University of California, Santa Barbara, Graduate Division, College of Letters and Sciences, Division of Humanities and Fine Arts, Department of French and Italian, Santa Barbara, CA 93106-4140. Offers French (MA, MABL, PhD), including applied linguistics (PhD), European Medieval studies (PhD), feminist studies (PhD), French (MABL, PhD); MA/PhD. French Language Institute available during summer sessions. *Faculty:* 21 full-time (12 women). *Students:* 11 full-time (7 women). Average age 31. 16 applicants, 63% accepted, 3 enrolled. In 2008, 1 master's, 5 doctorates awarded. Terminal master's awarded for partial completion of doctoral program. *Degree requirements:* For master's, 2 foreign languages, comprehensive exam; for doctorate, 2 foreign languages, comprehensive exam, thesis/dissertation. *Entrance requirements:* For master's, GRE, sample of written work, tape of spoken French, BA or the equivalent, 3 letters of recommendation, statement of purpose, personal achievements/contributions statement, resumé/curriculum vitae, transcripts for post-secondary institutions attended; for doctorate, GRE, sample of written work, tape of spoken French, MA or the equivalent, 3 letters of recommendation, statement of purpose, personal achievements/contributions statement, resumé/curriculum vitae, transcripts for post-secondary institutions attended. Additional exam requirements/recommendations for international students: Required—TOEFL (paper: 550, computer: 213, IBT: 80) or IELTS (7). *Application deadline:* For fall admission, 5/1 for domestic and international students; for winter admission, 10/1 for domestic and international students; for spring admission, 1/15 for domestic and international students. Application fee: $70 ($90 for international students). Electronic applications accepted. *Expenses:* Tuition, nonresident: full-time $25,149. Required fees: $10,143. Full-time tuition and fees vary according to campus/location, reciprocity agreements and student level. *Financial support:* In 2008–09, 11 students received support, including 5 fellowships with full and partial tuition reimbursements available (averaging $8,100 per year), 11 teaching assistantships with partial tuition reimbursements available (averaging $11,400 per year); career-related internships or fieldwork, Federal Work-Study, institutionally sponsored loans, scholarships/grants, traineeships, health care benefits, tuition waivers (full and partial), and unspecified assistantships also available. Financial award applicants required to submit FAFSA. *Faculty research:* French and Francophone studies, comparative literature, second language acquisition, applied linguistics, performance studies, feminist and gender studies. Total annual research expenditures: $2,500. *Unit head:* Prof. Jon Snyder, Chair, 805-893-2220, Fax: 805-893-8826, E-mail: snyder@frit.ucsb.edu. *Application contact:* Rosa Pinter, Graduate Staff Advisor, 805-893-3398, Fax: 805-893-8826, E-mail: pinter@frit.ucsb.edu.

University of California, Santa Barbara, Graduate Division, College of Letters and Sciences, Division of Humanities and Fine Arts, Department of Germanic, Slavic, and Semitic Studies, Santa Barbara, CA 93106-4130. Offers Germanic languages and literature (MA, PhD), including applied linguistics (PhD), feminist studies (PhD); MA/PhD. *Faculty:* 7 full-time (4 women). *Students:* 2 full-time (0 women). Average age 31. 6 applicants, 50% accepted, 1 enrolled. In 2008, 1 master's awarded. Terminal master's awarded for partial completion of doctoral program. *Degree requirements:* For master's, 2 foreign languages, comprehensive exam, thesis; for doctorate, 3 foreign languages, comprehensive exam, thesis/dissertation. *Entrance requirements:* For master's and doctorate, GRE. Additional exam requirements/recommendations for international students: Required—TOEFL (minimum score 550 paper-based; 213 computer-based; 80 iBT), IELTS (minimum score 7), TOEFL or IELTS. *Application deadline:* For fall admission, 12/31 priority date for domestic students, 5/1 priority date for international students; for winter admission, 11/1 priority date for domestic and international students; for spring admission, 2/1 priority date for domestic and international students. Applications are processed on a rolling basis. Application fee: $70 ($90 for international students). Electronic applications accepted. *Expenses:* Tuition, nonresident: full-time $25,149. Required fees: $10,143. Full-time tuition and fees vary according to campus/location, reciprocity agreements and student level. *Financial support:* In 2008–09, 2 students received support, including 2 fellowships with full and partial tuition reimbursements available (averaging $10,100 per year), 1 teaching assistantship with partial tuition reimbursement available (averaging $11,600 per year); Federal Work-Study, institutionally sponsored loans, scholarships/grants, health care benefits, and tuition waivers (full and partial) also available. Financial award application deadline: 12/31; financial award applicants required to submit FAFSA. *Faculty research:* Critical theory, media technology, psychoanalysis, German romanticism, Goethe. *Unit head:* Prof. Elisabeth Weber, Chair, 805-893-3527, Fax: 805-893-2374, E-mail: weber@gss.ucsb.edu. *Application contact:* Sierra Gray, Graduate Program Assistant, 805-893-2131, Fax: 805-893-2374, E-mail: sierra@gss.ucsb.edu.

University of California, Santa Barbara, Graduate Division, College of Letters and Sciences, Division of Humanities and Fine Arts, Department of History, Santa Barbara, CA 93106-9410. Offers feminist studies (PhD); global studies (PhD); public history (PhD); MA/PhD. *Faculty:* 40 full-time (17 women), 11 part-time/adjunct (6 women). *Students:* 120 full-time (62 women). Average age 34. 130 applicants, 38% accepted, 22 enrolled. In 2008, 9 doctorates awarded. Terminal master's awarded for partial completion of doctoral program. *Degree requirements:* For doctorate, comprehensive exam, thesis/dissertation, one or more languages depending on field of study. *Entrance requirements:* For doctorate, GRE, 3 letters of recommendation, statement of purpose, personal achievements/contributions statement, resumé/curriculum vitae, transcripts for post-secondary institutions attended. Additional exam requirements/recommendations for international students: Required—TOEFL (minimum score 550 paper-based; 213 computer-based; 80 iBT), IELTS (minimum score 7), TOEFL or IELTS. *Application deadline:* For fall admission, 12/5 for domestic and international students. Application fee: $70 ($90 for international students). Electronic applications accepted. *Expenses:* Tuition, nonresident: full-time $25,149. Required fees: $10,143. Full-time tuition and fees vary according to campus/location, reciprocity agreements and student level. *Financial support:* In 2008–09, 94 students received support, including 53 fellowships with full and partial tuition reimbursements available (averaging $8,600 per year), 2 research assistantships with full and partial tuition reimbursements available (averaging $7,400 per year), 70 teaching assistantships with partial tuition reimbursements available (averaging $9,400 per year); Federal Work-Study, institutionally sponsored loans, scholarships/grants, traineeships, health care benefits, tuition waivers (full and partial), and unspecified assistantships also available. Financial award application deadline: 12/5; financial award applicants required to submit FAFSA. *Faculty research:* Europe, U. S., Latin America, Africa, Middle East, East Asia. *Unit head:* Kenneth J. Moure, Chair, 805-893-2993, Fax: 805-893-8795, E-mail: moure@history.ucrb.edu. *Application contact:* Prof. Sharon Farmer, Director of Graduate Studies, 805-893-2543, Fax: 805-893-8795, E-mail: farmer@history.ucsb.edu.

University of California, Santa Barbara, Graduate Division, College of Letters and Sciences, Division of Humanities and Fine Arts, Department of Music, Santa Barbara, CA 93106-6070. Offers brass (MM); composition (MA, PhD); conducting (MM, DMA); ethnomusicology (MA, PhD); feminist studies (PhD); keyboard (MM, DMA); musicology (MA, PhD); piano accompanying (MM); strings (MM, DMA); theory (MA, PhD); voice (MM, DMA); woodwinds (MM); MA/PhD; MM/DMA. *Faculty:* 28 full-time (6 women), 17 part-time/adjunct (6 women). *Students:* 71 full-time (34 women). Average age 30. 103 applicants, 31% accepted, 24 enrolled. In 2008, 13 master's, 11 doctorates awarded. Terminal master's awarded for partial completion of doctoral program. *Degree requirements:* For master's, variable foreign language requirement, comprehensive exam (for some programs), thesis (for some programs); for doctorate, variable foreign language requirement, comprehensive exam, thesis/dissertation. *Entrance requirements:* For master's, GRE, tape/audition, media (performance), portfolio (composition), writing sample, 3 letters of recommendation, statement of purpose, personal achievements/contributions statement, resumé/curriculum vitae, transcripts for post-secondary institutions attended; for doctorate, tape/audition (DMA), media (performance), portfolio (composition), writing sample, 3 letters of recommendation, statement of purpose, personal achievements/contributions statement, resumé/curriculum vitae, transcripts for post-secondary institutions attended. Additional exam requirements/recommendations for international students: Required—TOEFL (paper: 550, computer: 213, IBT: 80) or IELTS (7). Application fee: $70 ($90 for international students). Electronic applications accepted. *Expenses:* Tuition, nonresident: full-time $25,149. Required fees: $10,143. Full-time tuition and fees vary according to campus/location, reciprocity agreements and student level. *Financial support:* In 2008–09, 62 students received support, including 31 fellowships with full and partial tuition reimbursements available (averaging $7,700 per year), 2 research assistantships with full and partial tuition reimbursements available (averaging $6,200 per year), 42 teaching assistantships with partial tuition reimbursements available (averaging $8,500 per year); Federal Work-Study, institutionally sponsored loans, scholarships/grants, health care benefits, tuition waivers (full and partial), and unspecified assistantships also available. Financial award applicants required to submit FAFSA. *Faculty research:* Music theory, ethnomusicology, musicology, music performance, music composition. *Unit head:* Dr. Paul Berkowitz, Chair, Fax: 805-893-7194, E-mail: berkowit@music.ucsb.edu. *Application contact:* David L. Holmes, Student Affairs Officer, 805-893-4603, Fax: 805-893-7194, E-mail: dholmes@music.ucsb.edu.

University of California, Santa Barbara, Graduate Division, College of Letters and Sciences, Division of Humanities and Fine Arts, Department of Religious Studies, Santa Barbara, CA 93106-3130. Offers European Medieval studies (PhD); feminist studies (PhD); global studies (PhD); religous studies (MA, PhD); MA/PhD. *Faculty:* 18 full-time (8 women), 11 part-time/adjunct (5 women). *Students:* 86 full-time (33 women). Average age 31. 151 applicants, 31% accepted, 17 enrolled. In 2008, 7 master's, 6 doctorates awarded. Terminal master's awarded for partial completion of doctoral program. *Degree requirements:* For master's, one foreign language, comprehensive exam (for some programs), thesis (for some programs); for doctorate, one foreign language, thesis/dissertation. *Entrance requirements:* For master's, GRE General Test; for doctorate, GRE General Test, MA in related field, 3 letters of recommendation, statement of purpose, personal achievements/contributions statement, resumé/curriculum vitae, transcripts for post-secondary institutions attended. Additional exam requirements/recommendations for international students: Required—TOEFL (paper: 550, computer: 213, IBT: 80) or IELTS (7). *Application deadline:* For fall admission, 12/1 for domestic and international students. Application fee: $70 ($90 for international students). Electronic applications accepted. *Expenses:* Tuition, nonresident: full-time $25,149. Required fees: $10,143. Full-time tuition and fees vary according to campus/location, reciprocity agreements and student level. *Financial support:* In 2008–09, 67 students received support, including 29 fellowships with full and partial tuition reimbursements available (averaging $12,600 per year), 5 research assistantships with full and partial tuition reimbursements available (averaging $7,900 per year), 46 teaching assistantships with partial tuition reimbursements available (averaging $8,400 per year); career-related internships or fieldwork, Federal Work-Study, institutionally sponsored loans, scholarships/grants, traineeships, health care benefits, tuition waivers (full and partial), and unspecified assistantships also available. Financial award application deadline: 12/1; financial award applicants required to submit FAFSA. *Faculty research:* Religion and politics, religion and violence, contemporary spirituality, religious traditions, theoretical approaches to the study of religion, area studies. *Unit head:* Prof. Catherine L. Albanese, Chair, 805-893-3564, Fax: 805-893-2059, E-mail: albanese@religion.ucsb.edu. *Application contact:* Sally J. Lombrozo, Graduate Program Assistant, 805-893-2744, Fax: 805-893-2059, E-mail: lombrozo@religion.ucsb.edu.

University of California, Santa Barbara, Graduate Division, College of Letters and Sciences, Division of Humanities and Fine Arts, Department of Spanish and Portuguese, Santa Barbara, CA 93106-4150. Offers Hispanic languages and literature (PhD), including applied linguistics, European Medieval studies, feminist studies, Hispanic languages and literature; Portuguese (MA); Spanish (MA); Spanish and Portuguese (MA); MA/PhD. Spanish Language Institute available during summer session. *Faculty:* 16 full-time (6 women). *Students:* 29 full-time (16 women). Average age 30. 46 applicants, 39% accepted, 9 enrolled. In 2008, 4 master's, 2 doctorates awarded. *Degree requirements:* For master's, 2 foreign languages, comprehensive exam (for some programs), thesis optional; for doctorate, 2 foreign languages, comprehensive exam, thesis/dissertation. *Entrance requirements:* For master's, GRE, 2 writing samples, undergraduate major in Spanish or equivalent, 3 letters of recommendation, statement of purpose, personal achievements/contributions statement, resumé/curriculum vitae, transcripts for post-secondary institutions attended; for doctorate, GRE, 2 writing samples, master's degree, 3 letters of recommendation, statement of purpose, personal achievements/contributions statement, resumé/curriculum vitae, transcripts for post-secondary institutions attended. Additional exam requirements/recommendations for international students: Required—TOEFL (minimum score 550 paper-based; 213 computer-based; 80 iBT), IELTS (minimum score 7), TOEFL or IELTS. *Application deadline:* For fall admission, 3/1 for domestic and international students; for winter admission, 11/1 for domestic and international students; for spring admission, 2/1 for domestic and international students. Application fee: $70 ($90 for international students). Electronic applications accepted. *Expenses:* Tuition, nonresident: full-time $25,149. Required fees: $10,143. Full-time tuition and fees vary according to campus/location, reciprocity agreements and student level. *Financial support:* In 2008–09, 30 students received support, including

9 fellowships with full and partial tuition reimbursements available (averaging $7,000 per year), 29 teaching assistantships with partial tuition reimbursements available (averaging $11,500 per year); career-related internships or fieldwork, Federal Work-Study, institutionally sponsored loans, scholarships/grants, health care benefits, tuition waivers (full and partial), and unspecified assistantships also available. Financial award application deadline: 1/7; financial award applicants required to submit FAFSA. *Faculty research:* 19th century Spanish and Portuguese literature, Spanish and Spanish American literature, 19th and 20th century Portuguese and Brazilian literatures, Hispanic Linguistics, Catalan language and culture. *Unit head:* Prof. Francisco A. Lomeli, Chair, 805-893-5715, Fax: 805-893-8341, E-mail: lomeli@spanport.ucsb.edu. *Application contact:* Carol Conley, Graduate Program Assistant, 805-893-3162, Fax: 805-893-8341, E-mail: cconley@spanport.ucsb.edu.

University of California, Santa Barbara, Graduate Division, College of Letters and Sciences, Division of Humanities and Fine Arts, Department of Theatre and Dance, Santa Barbara, CA 93106-7060. Offers theater studies (MA, PhD), including European Medieval studies (PhD), feminist studies (PhD), theater studies (PhD); MA/PhD. *Faculty:* 7 full-time (3 women), 1 (woman) part-time/adjunct. *Students:* 22 full-time (15 women). Average age 33. 22 applicants, 36% accepted, 5 enrolled. In 2008, 3 master's, 5 doctorates awarded. Terminal master's awarded for partial completion of doctoral program. *Degree requirements:* For master's, variable foreign language requirement, comprehensive exam, thesis; for doctorate, one foreign language, comprehensive exam, thesis/dissertation. *Entrance requirements:* For master's and doctorate, GRE, sample of written work, 3 letters of recommendation, statement of purpose, personal achievements/contributions statement, resumé/curriculum vitae, transcripts for post-secondary institutions attended. Additional exam requirements/recommendations for international students: Required—TOEFL (paper: 550, computer: 213, IBT: 80) or IELTS (7). *Application deadline:* For fall admission, 1/5 for domestic and international students. Application fee: $70 ($90 for international students). Electronic applications accepted. *Expenses:* Tuition, nonresident: full-time $25,149. Required fees: $10,143. Full-time tuition and fees vary according to campus/location, reciprocity agreements and student level. *Financial support:* In 2008-09, 23 students received support, including 13 fellowships with full and partial tuition reimbursements available (averaging $11,600 per year), 29 teaching assistantships with partial tuition reimbursements available (averaging $11,500 per year); Federal Work-Study, scholarships/grants, traineeships, health care benefits, and unspecified assistantships also available. Support available to part-time students. Financial award application deadline: 1/5; financial award applicants required to submit FAFSA. *Faculty research:* Spanish/Latin American drama, performance studies and European theatre history, East Asian and Russian studies, playwriting, Medieval theatre. *Unit head:* Prof. Simon Williams, Chair, 805-893-5515, Fax: 805-893-7029, E-mail: williams@theaterdance.ucsb.edu. *Application contact:* Mary Tench, Graduate Program Assistant, 805-893-3147, Fax: 805-893-7029, E-mail: mtench@theaterdance.ucsb.edu.

University of California, Santa Barbara, Graduate Division, College of Letters and Sciences, Division of Humanities and Fine Arts, Program in Comparative Literature, Santa Barbara, CA 93106-4130. Offers comparative literature (PhD); East Asian literatures (PhD); feminist studies (PhD); MA/PhD. *Faculty:* 56 full-time (24 women). *Students:* 24 full-time (18 women). Average age 29. 43 applicants, 40% accepted, 5 enrolled. In 2008, 5 doctorates awarded. Terminal master's awarded for partial completion of doctoral program. *Degree requirements:* For doctorate, 2 foreign languages, comprehensive exam, thesis/dissertation. *Entrance requirements:* For doctorate, GRE. Additional exam requirements/recommendations for international students: Required—TOEFL (paper: 550, computer: 213, IBT: 80) or IELTS (7). *Application deadline:* For fall admission, 12/15 for domestic and international students. Application fee: $70 ($90 for international students). Electronic applications accepted. *Expenses:* Tuition, nonresident: full-time $25,149. Required fees: $10,143. Full-time tuition and fees vary according to campus/location, reciprocity agreements and student level. *Financial support:* In 2008-09, 24 students received support, including 15 fellowships with full and partial tuition reimbursements available (averaging $6,900 per year), 1 research assistantship (averaging $10,600 per year), 18 teaching assistantships with partial tuition reimbursements available (averaging $10,400 per year); Federal Work-Study, institutionally sponsored loans, scholarships/grants, health care benefits, and tuition waivers (full and partial) also available. Financial award application deadline: 12/15; financial award applicants required to submit FAFSA. *Faculty research:* Media studies, literary theory, cultural studies, early-modern and modern literature, critical theory. *Unit head:* Prof. Elisabeth Weber, Chair, 805-893-3527, Fax: 805-893-2374, E-mail: weber@gss.ucsb.edu. *Application contact:* Sierra Gray, Graduate Program Assistant, 805-893-2131, Fax: 805-893-2374, E-mail: sierra@gss.ucsb.edu.

University of California, Santa Barbara, Graduate Division, College of Letters and Sciences, Division of Social Sciences, Department of Feminist Studies, Santa Barbara, CA 93106-7110. Offers MA, PhD, MA/PhD. *Entrance requirements:* For master's and doctorate, GRE, writing sample, 3 letters of recommendation, statement of purpose, personal achievements/contributions statement, resumé/curriculum vitae, transcripts for post-secondary institutions attended. Additional exam requirements/recommendations for international students: Required—TOEFL (paper: 550, computer: 213, IBT: 80) or IELTS. *Application deadline:* For fall admission, 12/15 for domestic and international students. Application fee: $70 ($90 for international students). Electronic applications accepted. *Expenses:* Tuition, nonresident: full-time $25,149. Required fees: $10,143. Full-time tuition and fees vary according to campus/location, reciprocity agreements and student level. *Unit head:* Eileen Boris, Chair, 805-893-8444, E-mail: boris@femst.ucsb.edu. *Application contact:* Christina Toy, Graduate Admissions Officer, 805-893-4330, Fax: 805-893-8676, E-mail: christina@femst.ucsb.edu.

University of California, Santa Barbara, Graduate Division, College of Letters and Sciences, Division of Social Sciences, Department of Political Science, Santa Barbara, CA 93106-9420. Offers political science (MA); women's studies (PhD); MA/PhD. Part-time programs available. *Faculty:* 22 full-time (10 women), 5 part-time/adjunct (2 women). *Students:* 51 full-time (22 women). Average age 30. 94 applicants, 32% accepted, 7 enrolled. In 2008, 9 master's, 4 doctorates awarded. Terminal master's awarded for partial completion of doctoral program. *Degree requirements:* For master's, comprehensive exam (for some programs), thesis optional; for doctorate, one foreign language, comprehensive exam, thesis/dissertation. *Entrance requirements:* For master's, GRE General Test, bachelor's degree with minimum GPA of 3.0, 3 letters of recommendation, statement of purpose, personal achievements/contributions statement, resumé/curriculum vitae, transcripts for post-secondary institutions attended; for doctorate, GRE General Test, master's degree with minimum GPA of 3.0, 3 letters of recommendation, statement of purpose, personal achievements/contributions statement, resumé/curriculum vitae, transcripts for post-secondary institutions attended. Additional exam requirements/recommendations for international students: Required—TOEFL (minimum score 600 paper-based; 250 computer-based; 100 iBT), TOEFL or IELTS. *Application deadline:* For fall admission, 1/1 priority date for domestic and international students. Application fee: $70 ($90 for international students). Electronic applications accepted. *Expenses:* Tuition, nonresident: full-time $25,149. Required fees: $10,143. Full-time tuition and fees vary according to campus/location, reciprocity agreements and student level. *Financial support:* In 2008-09, 43 students received support, including 25 fellowships with full tuition reimbursements available (averaging $8,200 per year), 42 teaching assistantships with partial tuition reimbursements available (averaging $8,900 per year); Federal Work-Study, institutionally sponsored loans, scholarships/grants, and health care benefits also available. Financial award applicants required to submit FAFSA. *Faculty research:* American politics, comparative politics, international relations, political theory, methodology. *Unit head:* Dr. John Woolley, Chair, 805-893-3432, Fax: 805-893-3309, E-mail: woolley@polsci.ucsb.edu. *Application contact:* Linda James, Staff Graduate Advisor, 805-893-3626, Fax: 805-893-3309, E-mail: james@polsci.ucsb.edu.

University of California, Santa Barbara, Graduate Division, College of Letters and Sciences, Division of Social Sciences, Department of Sociology, Santa Barbara, CA 93106-9430. Offers global studies (PhD); human development (PhD); language, interaction and social organization (PhD); technology and society (PhD); women's studies (PhD); MA/PhD. *Faculty:* 35 full-time (14 women). *Students:* 77 full-time (50 women). Average age 30. 155 applicants, 9% accepted, 8 enrolled. In 2008, 10 doctorates awarded. Terminal master's awarded for partial completion

of doctoral program. *Degree requirements:* For doctorate, comprehensive exam, thesis/dissertation. *Entrance requirements:* For doctorate, GRE General Test, sample of written work, 3 letters of recommendation, statement of purpose, personal achievements/contributions statement, resumé/curriculum vitae, transcripts for post-secondary institutions attended. Additional exam requirements/recommendations for international students: Required—TOEFL (minimum score 550 paper-based; 213 computer-based; 80 iBT), TOEFL or IELTS. *Application deadline:* For fall admission, 12/10 for domestic students. Application fee: $70 ($90 for international students). Electronic applications accepted. *Expenses:* Tuition, nonresident: full-time $25,149. Required fees: $10,143. Full-time tuition and fees vary according to campus/location, reciprocity agreements and student level. *Financial support:* In 2008-09, 69 students received support, including 50 fellowships with full tuition reimbursements available (averaging $7,900 per year), 6 research assistantships with full and partial tuition reimbursements available (averaging $2,600 per year), 53 teaching assistantships with partial tuition reimbursements available (averaging $9,200 per year); career-related internships or fieldwork, Federal Work-Study, institutionally sponsored loans, scholarships/grants, health care benefits, and unspecified assistantships also available. Financial award applicants required to submit FAFSA. *Faculty research:* Conversation analysis, social movements, human sexuality, urban sociology, race and ethnic relations. *Unit head:* Prof. Verta Taylor, Chair, 805-893-3118, Fax: 805-893-3324, E-mail: grad-soc@soc.ucsb.edu. *Application contact:* Ra Thea, Graduate Staff Advisor, 805-893-3328, Fax: 805-893-3324, E-mail: grad-soc@soc.ucsb.edu.

University of Cincinnati, Graduate School, McMicken College of Arts and Sciences, Department of Women's Studies, Cincinnati, OH 45221. Offers MA, Certificate, MA/JD. Part-time programs available. *Degree requirements:* For master's, comprehensive exam, final paper/project. *Entrance requirements:* For master's, GRE General Test, Undergraduate degree transcripts, 3 letters of recommendation, completed application. Additional exam requirements/recommendations for international students: Required—TOEFL (minimum score 600 paper-based), IELTS (minimum score 6.5). Electronic applications accepted. *Faculty research:* Feminist legal, sexuality, international political economy, Latin American, cultural/literary and environmental studies.

University of Florida, Graduate School, College of Liberal Arts and Sciences, Center for Women's Studies and Gender Research, Gainesville, FL 32611. Offers gender and development (Graduate Certificate); women's studies (MA, MWS, Graduate Certificate); MA/JD; MA/MA.

University of Georgia, Graduate School, College of Arts and Sciences, Institute for Women's Studies, Athens, GA 30602. Offers Certificate.

University of Hawaii at Manoa, Graduate Division, Colleges of Arts and Sciences, College of Social Sciences, Advanced Women's Studies Program, Honolulu, HI 96822. Offers Graduate Certificate. Part-time programs available. *Entrance requirements:* Additional exam requirements/recommendations for international students: Required—TOEFL (minimum score 500 paper-based; 173 computer-based; 61 iBT), IELTS (minimum score 5).

The University of Iowa, Graduate College, College of Liberal Arts and Sciences, Department of Women's Studies, Iowa City, IA 52242-1316. Offers PhD. *Degree requirements:* For doctorate, comprehensive exam, thesis/dissertation. *Entrance requirements:* For doctorate, GRE General Test, minimum GPA of 3.0. Additional exam requirements/recommendations for international students: Required—TOEFL (minimum score 550 paper-based; 213 computer-based; 81 iBT). Electronic applications accepted.

University of Louisville, Graduate School, College of Arts and Sciences, Department of Women's and Gender Studies, Louisville, KY 40292-0001. Offers MA, Certificate, MSSW/MA. Part-time programs available. *Faculty:* 5 full-time (all women), 7 part-time/adjunct (6 women). *Students:* 11 full-time (10 women), 5 part-time (4 women); includes 3 African Americans, 1 international. Average age 30. 6 applicants, 100% accepted, 6 enrolled. In 2008, 2 master's awarded. *Entrance requirements:* For master's, GRE, writing sample, personal statement. Electronic applications accepted. *Financial support:* In 2008-09, 13 students received support, including 1 teaching assistantship (averaging $12,000 per year). Financial award application deadline: 5/15; financial award applicants required to submit FAFSA. *Unit head:* Nancy M. Theriot, Chairperson, 502-852-8160, Fax: 502-852-4421, E-mail: nancyt@louisville.edu. *Application contact:* Libby Leggett, Director, Graduate Admissions, 502-852-3101, Fax: 502-852-6536, E-mail: gradadm@louisville.edu.

University of Maryland, Baltimore County, Graduate School, College of Arts, Humanities and Social Sciences, Program in Gender and Women's Studies, Baltimore, MD 21250. Offers Postbaccalaureate Certificate. Part-time and evening/weekend programs available. *Students:* 1 (woman) part-time; includes African American. Average age 25. 1 applicant, 100% accepted, 1 enrolled. In 2008, 1 Postbaccalaureate Certificate awarded. *Entrance requirements:* For degree, BA. *Application deadline:* Applications are processed on a rolling basis. Application fee: $50. Electronic applications accepted. *Financial support:* In 2008-09, 1 teaching assistantship with partial tuition reimbursement (averaging $7,500 per year) was awarded; health care benefits also available. *Faculty research:* Feminist theory, reproductive and sexual politics, U.S. women's history. *Unit head:* Dr. Carole McCann, Director and Associate Professor of Gender and Women's Studies, 410-455-2161, E-mail: gwst@umbc.edu. *Application contact:* Dr. Carole McCann, Director and Associate Professor of Gender and Women's Studies, 410-455-2161, E-mail: gwst@umbc.edu.

University of Maryland, College Park, Graduate Studies, College of Arts and Humanities, Department of Women's Studies, College Park, MD 20742. Offers MA, PhD. *Degree requirements:* For master's, thesis or alternative; for doctorate, one foreign language, thesis/dissertation or alternative. *Entrance requirements:* For master's, GRE General Test, writing sample, 3 letters of recommendation. Additional exam requirements/recommendations for international students: Required—TOEFL. *Faculty research:* Gender roles, national and global diversity, sexuality.

University of Massachusetts Boston, Office of Graduate Studies, Division of Continuing Education and John W. McCormack Graduate School of Policy Studies, Program in Women in Politics and Government, Boston, MA 02125-3393. Offers Certificate. Part-time and evening/weekend programs available. *Degree requirements:* For Certificate, practicum, final project. *Entrance requirements:* For degree, interview, minimum GPA of 2.75.

University of Massachusetts Boston, Office of Graduate Studies, John W. McCormack Graduate School of Policy Studies, Boston, MA 02125-3393. Offers gerontology (MA, MS, PhD, Certificate), including gerontology (MS, PhD, Certificate), gerontology research (MA); management in aging services (MA); public affairs (MS); public policy (PhD); women in politics and government (Certificate). Certificate program in women in politics and government offered jointly with Division of Continuing Education. Part-time and evening/weekend programs available. *Degree requirements:* For doctorate, thesis/dissertation; for Certificate, practicum, final project. *Entrance requirements:* For doctorate, GRE General Test; for Certificate, interview, minimum GPA of 2.5.

University of Michigan, Horace H. Rackham School of Graduate Studies, College of Literature, Science, and the Arts, Department of Women's Studies, Ann Arbor, MI 48109. Offers English and women's studies (PhD); history and women's studies (PhD); lesbian, gay, bisexual, transgender, queer (LGBTQ) studies (Certificate); psychology and women's studies (PhD); sociology and women's studies (PhD); women's studies (Certificate). *Degree requirements:* For doctorate, variable foreign language requirement, thesis/dissertation. *Entrance requirements:* For doctorate, GRE General Test, previous undergraduate course work in women's studies. Electronic applications accepted. *Faculty research:* Gender issues; LGBTQ studies; sexuality; women and science; global feminism.

University of Minnesota, Twin Cities Campus, Graduate School, College of Liberal Arts, Department of Gender, Women, and Sexuality Studies, Minneapolis, MN 55455-0213. Offers feminist studies (PhD). *Degree requirements:* For doctorate, comprehensive exam, thesis/dissertation. *Entrance requirements:* For doctorate, GRE. Additional exam requirements/

Women's Studies

University of Minnesota, Twin Cities Campus (continued)
recommendations for international students: Required—TOEFL (minimum score 550 paper-based). Electronic applications accepted. *Faculty research:* Transnational feminist theories, critical development theory, feminist postcolonialisms, feminist science studies and studying of health, literature, Asian diasporas, sexuality and queer theory.

University of Nevada, Las Vegas, Graduate College, College of Liberal Arts, Women's Studies Department, Las Vegas, NV 89154-5055. Offers Womens Studies (Certificate). *Faculty:* 4 full-time (all women). *Students:* 3 part-time (all women). Average age 32. 6 applicants, 83% accepted, 5 enrolled. In 2008, 2 Certificates awarded. *Entrance requirements:* Additional exam requirements/recommendations for international students: Required—TOEFL (minimum score 550 paper-based; 213 computer-based; 80 iBT), IELTS (minimum score 7). *Application deadline:* For fall admission, 6/15 priority date for domestic students, 5/1 for international students; for spring admission, 11/15 priority date for domestic students, 10/1 for international students. Applications are processed on a rolling basis. Application fee: $60 ($75 for international students). Electronic applications accepted. *Expenses:* Tuition, state resident: full-time $1414; part-time $198 per credit. Tuition, nonresident: full-time $12,509; part-time $415.75 per credit. International tuition: $14,249 full-time. Required fees: $4 per credit. $252 per semester. Tuition and fees vary according to course load. *Financial support:* In 2008–09, 2 students received support, including 2 research assistantships with partial tuition reimbursements available (averaging $10,000 per year); institutionally sponsored loans, scholarships/grants, health care benefits, and unspecified assistantships also available. Financial award application deadline: 3/1. *Faculty research:* Transnational feminism; intersection of gender, race, class and sexuality; sexuality studies; Chicana/Latina feminism; gender and development. *Unit head:* Dr. S Charusheela, Chair/Associate Professor, 702-895-0467, Fax: 702-895-0850, E-mail: s.charusheela@unlv.edu. *Application contact:* Graduate College Admissions Evaluator, 702-895-3320, Fax: 702-895-4180, E-mail: gradcollege@unlv.edu.

University of New Mexico, Graduate School, College of Arts and Sciences, Program in Women Studies, Albuquerque, NM 87131-2039. Offers Graduate Certificate. *Degree requirements:* For Graduate Certificate, thesis. *Entrance requirements:* For degree, must be enrolled in degree-granting program before acceptance for Graduate Certification in Women Studies.

The University of North Carolina at Greensboro, Graduate School, College of Arts and Sciences, Department of English, Greensboro, NC 27412-5001. Offers creative writing (MFA); English (M Ed, MA, PhD, Certificate), including American literature (PhD), English (M Ed, MA), English literature (PhD), rhetoric and composition (PhD), technical writing (Certificate), women's studies (Certificate). *Degree requirements:* For master's, comprehensive exam; for doctorate, variable foreign language requirement, thesis/dissertation, preliminary exam. *Entrance requirements:* For master's, GRE General Test, minimum GPA of 3.0; for doctorate, GRE General Test, GRE Subject Test, critical writing sample, minimum GPA of 3.0. Additional exam requirements/recommendations for international students: Required—TOEFL. Electronic applications accepted.

The University of North Carolina at Greensboro, Graduate School, College of Arts and Sciences, Program in Women's and Gender Studies, Greensboro, NC 27412-5001. Offers MA, Certificate. Electronic applications accepted.

University of Northern Iowa, Graduate College, Program in Women's and Gender Studies, Cedar Falls, IA 50614. Offers MA. *Students:* 4 full-time (all women), 3 part-time (2 women); includes 1 minority (African American), 2 international. 7 applicants, 71% accepted, 2 enrolled. In 2008, 1 master's awarded. *Degree requirements:* For master's, comprehensive exam (for some programs), thesis or alternative. *Entrance requirements:* For master's, minimum GPA of 3.0. Additional exam requirements/recommendations for international students: Required—TOEFL (minimum score 500 paper-based; 180 computer-based; 61 iBT). *Application deadline:* Applications are processed on a rolling basis. Application fee: $30 ($50 for international students). Electronic applications accepted. *Expenses:* Tuition, state resident: full-time $6446. Tuition, nonresident: full-time $14,874. Required fees: $852. *Financial support:* Application deadline: 2/1. *Unit head:* Dr. Phyllis Baker, Head/Graduate Coordinator, 319-273-2109, Fax: 319-273-3053, E-mail: phyllis.baker@uni.edu. *Application contact:* Laurie S. Russell, Record Analyst, 319-273-2623, Fax: 319-273-6792, E-mail: laurie.russell@uni.edu.

University of Ottawa, Faculty of Graduate and Postdoctoral Studies, Faculty of Social Sciences, Institute of Women's Studies, Ottawa, ON K1N 6N5, Canada. Offers criminology (MA, MCA); education (MA); English (MA); history (MA); human kinetics (MA); law (LL M); lettres Françaises (MA); nursing (M Sc); pastoral studies (MA); political science (MA); religious studies (MA); sociology (MA). *Degree requirements:* For master's, thesis or alternative.

University of Pittsburgh, School of Arts and Sciences, Program in Women's Studies, Pittsburgh, PA 15260. Offers Doctoral Certificate, Master's Certificate. Part-time programs available. Electronic applications accepted. *Faculty research:* Global feminisms; gender and interpersonal violence; race and gender studies; representation and gender in media, arts, and literature; concepts of the body.

University of Regina, Faculty of Graduate Studies and Research, Faculty of Arts, Department of Women's Studies, Regina, SK S4S 0A2, Canada. Offers MA. Offered as a special case program. Part-time programs available. *Faculty:* 2 full-time (both women). *Students:* 1 (woman) full-time, 1 (woman) part-time. 1 applicant, 100% accepted. *Degree requirements:* For master's, thesis. *Entrance requirements:* Additional exam requirements/recommendations for international students: Required—TOEFL (minimum score 580 paper-based; 237 computer-based; 88 iBT). *Application deadline:* Applications are processed on a rolling basis. Application fee: $85 ($100 for international students). Electronic applications accepted. *Financial support:* Fellowships, research assistantships, teaching assistantships, scholarships/grants available. Financial award application deadline: 6/15. *Unit head:* Dr. Wendee Kubik, Graduate Program Coordinator, 306-585-4668, E-mail: wendee.kubik@uregina.ca. *Application contact:* Dr. Dongyan Blachford, Associate Dean, 306-585-5186, Fax: 306-337-2444, E-mail: dongyan.blachford@uregina.ca.

University of Saskatchewan, College of Graduate Studies and Research, College of Arts and Sciences, Department of Women's and Gender Studies, Saskatoon, SK S7N 5A2, Canada. Offers MA, PhD. *Degree requirements:* For master's, thesis; for doctorate, thesis/dissertation.

Entrance requirements: Additional exam requirements/recommendations for international students: Required—TOEFL.

University of South Carolina, The Graduate School, College of Arts and Sciences, Program in Women's Studies, Columbia, SC 29208. Offers Certificate. Part-time programs available. *Entrance requirements:* For degree, GRE General Test or MAT. Additional exam requirements/recommendations for international students: Required—TOEFL. Electronic applications accepted. *Faculty research:* Health; pedagogy; intersection of race, class, gender; public policy; politics of culture and representations, feminist political economics.

University of South Florida, Graduate School, College of Arts and Sciences, Department of Women's Studies, Tampa, FL 33620-9951. Offers MA. Part-time programs available. *Faculty:* 3 full-time (2 women). *Students:* 5 full-time (all women), 1 (woman) part-time; includes 1 minority (African American). 11 applicants, 55% accepted, 1 enrolled. In 2008, 5 master's awarded. *Degree requirements:* For master's, comprehensive exam, thesis (for some programs), thesis or internship. *Entrance requirements:* For master's, GRE General Test, 3 letters of reference, writing sample, minimum GPA 3.0 in last 60 hours. Additional exam requirements/recommendations for international students: Required—TOEFL (minimum score 550 paper-based; 213 computer-based). *Application deadline:* For fall admission, 2/15 for domestic students, 1/2 for international students; for spring admission, 10/15 for domestic students, 6/1 for international students. Applications are processed on a rolling basis. Application fee: $30. *Expenses:* Tuition, state resident: full-time $2624.40; part-time $291.60 per credit hour. Tuition, nonresident: full-time $7822; part-time $869.13 per credit hour. *Financial support:* In 2008–09, 7 students received support; fellowships with full tuition reimbursements available, teaching assistantships with full tuition reimbursements available available. Financial award application deadline: 3/1. Total annual research expenditures: $9,023. *Unit head:* Dr. Kim Vaz, Chairperson, 813-974-0985, Fax: 813-974-0336, E-mail: vaz@cas.usf.edu. *Application contact:* Earles Jenifer, Graduate Director, 813-974-5520, Fax: 813-974-0336, E-mail: jlearles@mail.usf.edu.

University of Washington, Graduate School, College of Arts and Sciences, Department of Women Studies, Seattle, WA 98195. Offers PhD. Terminal master's awarded for partial completion of doctoral program. *Degree requirements:* For doctorate, one foreign language, thesis/dissertation, exam. *Entrance requirements:* For doctorate, GRE General Test. Additional exam requirements/recommendations for international students: Required—TOEFL. Electronic applications accepted. *Faculty research:* Women's history in U.S. and China; Native American ethnography and identity; women, science, and technology; political economy of development, feminism and nationalism.

University of Wisconsin–Madison, Graduate School, College of Letters and Science, Department of History, Madison, WI 53706-1380. Offers African history (MA, PhD); Central Asian history (MA, PhD); comparative world history (MA, PhD); East Asian history (MA, PhD); European history (MA, PhD); gender and women's history (MA, PhD); Latin American and Caribbean history (MA, PhD); Middle Eastern history (MA, PhD); South Asian history (MA, PhD); Southeast Asian history (MA, PhD); United States history (MA, PhD). Terminal master's awarded for partial completion of doctoral program. *Degree requirements:* For master's, thesis (for some programs); for doctorate, variable foreign language requirement, thesis/dissertation. *Entrance requirements:* For master's and doctorate, GRE General Test. Additional exam requirements/recommendations for international students: Required—Michigan English Language Assessment Battery or TOEFL. Electronic applications accepted. *Faculty research:* American, African, European, Asian, Latin American, and Middle Eastern history.

Washington State University, Graduate School, College of Liberal Arts, Program in American Studies, Pullman, WA 99164. Offers ethnic studies (MA, PhD); feminist studies (MA, PhD); history (MA, PhD); literature (MA, PhD). *Degree requirements:* For master's, one foreign language, comprehensive exam (for some programs), thesis optional, oral exam; for doctorate, one foreign language, comprehensive exam (for some programs), thesis/dissertation, oral exam. *Entrance requirements:* For master's and doctorate, GRE General Test, minimum GPA of 3.0, writing sample, 3 letters of recommendation. Additional exam requirements/recommendations for international students: Required—TOEFL. *Faculty research:* The American West in multicultural perspective; nineteenth century historical, literary, and cultural studies; comparative American ethnic literatures and cultures; American cultures and the environment; American rhetoric.

West Chester University of Pennsylvania, Office of Graduate Studies, College of Arts and Sciences, Department of Women's Studies, West Chester, PA 19383. Offers leadership for women (MSA, Certificate). Part-time and evening/weekend programs available. *Students:* 1 (woman) full-time, 1 (woman) part-time; includes 1 minority (African American). Average age 24. 1 applicant, 100% accepted, 1 enrolled. In 2008, 1 master's awarded. *Degree requirements:* For master's, comprehensive exam. *Entrance requirements:* For master's, GMAT, GRE General Test, or MAT, interview, statement of professional goals, resumé, two letters of reference. Additional exam requirements/recommendations for international students: Required—TOEFL (minimum score 550 paper-based; 213 computer-based; 80 iBT). *Application deadline:* For fall admission, 4/15 priority date for domestic students, 3/15 for international students; for spring admission, 10/15 for domestic students, 9/1 for international students. Applications are processed on a rolling basis. Application fee: $35. Electronic applications accepted. *Expenses:* Tuition, state resident: full-time $6430; part-time $357 per credit. Tuition, nonresident: full-time $10,288; part-time $572 per credit. Required fees: $652.50; $50 per credit. $67 per semester. *Financial support:* In 2008–09, research assistantships with full and partial tuition reimbursements (averaging $5,000 per year); unspecified assistantships also available. Support available to part-time students. Financial award application deadline: 2/15; financial award applicants required to submit FAFSA. *Unit head:* Dr. Jen Bacon, Director, 610-436-2464, E-mail: jbacon@wcupa.edu. *Application contact:* Dr. Lorraine Bernotsky, Graduate Coordinator, 610-738-0576, E-mail: lbernotsky@wcupa.edu.

Western Seminary, Graduate Programs, Program in Specialized Ministry, Portland, OR 97215-3367. Offers children / youth at risk (MA); coaching (MA); evangelism and equipping (MA); pastoral care to women (MA); youth and family ministry (MA); youth ministry (MA). *Degree requirements:* For master's, practicum.

York University, Faculty of Graduate Studies, Faculty of Arts, Program in Women's Studies, Toronto, ON M3J 1P3, Canada. Offers MA, PhD. *Degree requirements:* For master's, thesis or alternative; for doctorate, comprehensive exam, thesis/dissertation. Electronic applications accepted.

GEORGE MASON UNIVERSITY

College of Arts and Sciences
Ph.D. Program in Cultural Studies

Program of Study

Cultural studies is a new field of scholarly inquiry, emerging in the second half of the twentieth century. Broadly speaking, cultural studies analyzes the production and circulation of meanings in objects of all kinds, including representations in mass media as well as oppositional subcultures, industrial products as well as practices of performance and display. Although cultural studies draws freely on theory and methods from more traditional disciplines (anthropology, history, literary theory, philosophy, political economy, and sociology), it responds to questions not immediately answerable by conventional means. That is, it seeks to account for everyday cultural objects under conditions constrained by power and defined by contestation, conflict, and change. Unlike traditional disciplines, cultural studies also implies social self-reflection, an awareness that the scholar and his or her scholarship are themselves very much caught up in the political currents and in the global circulation of meanings being studied. Finally, cultural studies both draws on and produces the key strands of contemporary cultural theory: semiotics, deconstruction, dialogics, poststructuralism, and neo-Marxism.

The first of its kind at the doctoral level in the United States, the Program in Cultural Studies at George Mason draws on faculty members from ten different departments, programs, and institutes. As a center for advanced graduate training, it is a research-oriented program. The course of study consists of 48 credit hours beyond the M.A. The core curriculum (18 credits) includes an introduction to cultural studies and a research methods course, as well as courses on political economy, gender/sexuality, critical race studies, science/technology, social institutions, and visual/performance culture. The field specializations (18 credit hours) involve intensive research and work in two areas of cultural studies scholarship. Fields of specialization, chosen by the student and crafted under the guidance of faculty advisers, point logically toward the dissertation (12 credit hours) and other forms of professional development. The Colloquium Series, an intellectual centerpiece of the program, is organized by faculty members and students and forms the basis for one of the required core courses. The Colloquium brings to the campus distinguished outside scholars from diverse backgrounds and perspectives to broaden the discussion of issues and debates relevant to contemporary research in cultural studies.

Research Facilities

The University library, which houses more than 600,000 volumes, is pioneering electronic global access to research materials. Every building on campus is linked by a fiber-optics network, and students also have use of state-of-the-art multimedia computer labs and facilities, including a virtual reality lab. The Washington Regional Library Consortium gives students access to 4 million volumes.

Financial Aid

Fellowship aid, teaching and research assistantships, and tuition remission are available to qualified applicants.

Cost of Study

Tuition is $371 per credit hour for in-state students and $929.50 per credit hour for out-of-state students. The normal full-time load is 9 credit hours per semester. Fees are $60 per year.

Living and Housing Costs

Room and board costs for students living on campus average $4840 per year. Housing for graduate students is extremely limited. Most students live off campus. The cost of living is comparable to that in other large northeastern urban areas.

Student Group

Sixty-three students (many are part-time) come from diverse backgrounds and with diverse career plans. The University's total enrollment is 30,000 and growing each year.

Location

The University's main campus in northern Virginia covers nearly 600 wooded acres. Nearby Washington, D.C., offers students access to some of the world's great cultural institutions. Students are entitled to participate in seminars and internships and to use archives and collections at institutions such as the Folger Shakespeare Library, the Smithsonian, and the Library of Congress.

The University and The Program

A young, dynamic institution, George Mason has become known for the development of innovative interdisciplinary programs. The Program in Cultural Studies fits naturally with the University's strengths in information technology, public policy, history and new media, and the arts.

Applying

Students with M.A. degrees in relevant fields are eligible to apply to the Program in Cultural Studies. Students with only a bachelor's degree must apply to an M.A. program in one of the following departments: English, sociology, history, philosophy, foreign languages and literatures, or economics, all of which have established feeder tracks in cultural studies. Students with only a bachelor's degree may apply simultaneously to the Program in Cultural Studies. All applicants must submit grade transcripts, a statement of interest, a writing sample, scores on the General Test of the Graduate Record Examinations, and three academic letters of reference. The statement of interest should include an account of the applicant's intellectual interests as these have been shaped in general studies. It should also provide a general overview of the course of graduate study and in the doctoral dissertation. Applicants who are not native English speakers should also submit TOEFL scores. Students may apply for either full-time or part-time status. The application deadline is January 15.

Correspondence and Information

Roger N. Lancaster, Director
Program in Cultural Studies
MSN 5E4
George Mason University
Fairfax, Virginia 22030-4444
Phone: 703-993-2851
Fax: 703-993-2852
E-mail: cultural@gmu.edu
Web site: http://culturalstudies.gmu.edu/

Applicants should send materials to:
Graduate Admissions Office
MSN 2D2
George Mason University
4400 University Drive
Fairfax, Virginia 22030

George Mason University

THE FACULTY AND THEIR RESEARCH

Denise Albanese, Ph.D., Stanford. Early modern literature and culture, colonialism, early scientific modernity.
Amal Amireh, Ph.D., Boston University. English.
Debra Bergoffen, Ph.D., Georgetown. Feminist theory, women's studies.
Amy Best, Ph.D., Syracuse. Sociology and anthropology.
Andrew Bickford, Ph.D., Rutgers. Sociology and anthropology.
Johanna Bockman, Ph.D., California, San Diego. Global affairs.
Lorraine Brown, Ph.D., Maryland, College Park. Nineteenth- and twentieth-century contemporary drama, focusing on gender and museum studies; American and European studies.
Zofia Burr, Ph.D., Cornell. Twentieth-century poetry, poetic theory, women's studies.
Jack Censer, Dean, College of Humanities and Social Sciences; Ph.D., Johns Hopkins. French history, press and public opinion, political traditions.
Michael Chang, Ph.D., California, San Diego. History and art history.
Dina Copelman, Ph.D., Princeton. European and women's history.
Rick Davis, College of Visual and Performing Arts; Ph.D., Yale.
Marion Deshmukh, Ph.D., Columbia. German and European cultural, intellectual, and art history.
Sheila ffolliott, Ph.D., Pennsylvania. Art collecting and patronage; gender, with focus on queenship images and museum display.
Joel Foreman, Ph.D., George Washington. Online writing instruction systems.
John Foster, Ph.D., Yale. Postmodernism, modes of narrative, comparative literature.
Wayne Froman, Ph.D., Fordham. Hermeneutics, post-Heideggerian French philosophical thought, phenomenology.
Cynthia Fuchs, Ph.D., Pennsylvania. Gender studies, TV and film, postmodern theory.
Timothy Gibson, Ph.D., Simon Fraser. Communication.
Paula Gilbert, Ph.D., Columbia. Gender and women's studies, comparative literature.
Michele Greet, Ph.D., NYU. History and art history.
Gregory Guagnano, Ph.D., California, Davis. Environmental sociology, evolutionary theory.
Hugh Gusterson, Ph.D., Stanford. Sociology and anthropology.
Nancy Weiss Hanrahan, Ph.D., New School for Social Research. Sociology of music, cultural criticism.
Devon Hodges, Ph.D., SUNY at Buffalo. Feminist theory, early modern culture.
Mack Holt, Ph.D., Emory. Popular political culture, Reformation, European history.
Lois Horton, Ph.D., Brandeis. Social history, urban sociology, social welfare policy.
Mark Jacobs, Ph.D., Chicago. Sociological theory, juvenile justice, sociology of culture.
Rosemary Jann, Ph.D., Northwestern. Literary theory, historiography, British fiction and poetry.
Kristin Johnsen-Neshati, M.F.A., Yale. Russian drama, Shakespeare, women playwrights.
Deborah Kaplan, Ph.D., Brandeis. Women's studies, gender studies, performance theory.
Timothy Kaposy, Ph.D., McMaster. Cultural studies.
Matthew Karush, Ph.D., Chicago. History and art history.
David Kaufmann, Ph.D., Yale. Critical theory, contemporary poetry, eighteenth-century and Romantic literature and intellectual history.
Roger Lancaster, Director, Cultural Studies Program; Ph.D., Berkeley. Marxism and critical theory; gender, sexuality, and lesbigay studies; Latin America.
Alison Landsberg, Ph.D., Chicago. English, history, American literature and culture, immigration and mass culture 1890–1935, commemoration and public history in twentieth-century America, film theory and spectatorship.
Jennifer Leeman, Ph.D., Georgetown. Modern and classical languages.
Cynthia Lont, Ph.D., Iowa. Mass communication theory, women and media, women's music and culture.
Peter Mandaville, Co-Director, Center for Global Studies; Ph.D., Kent (England).
Robert Matz, Ph.D., Johns Hopkins. Early modern culture, history of literature, cultural theory.
Char Miller, Ph.D., Johns Hopkins. Public and international affairs.
John O'Connor, Ph.D., Virginia. Collaborative online writing, fiction and nonfiction hypertext, the effects of multimedia on writing.
Michael O'Malley, Ph.D., Berkeley. Nineteenth-century U.S. social and cultural history.
Ann Palkovich, Ph.D., Northwestern. Complex adaptive systems, construction of meaning in material culture.
Lisa M. Rabin, Ph.D., Yale. Spanish-American literature, with emphasis on poetry and the Colonial period; comparative literature; interdisciplinary studies of literature and art; literary theory; women's studies.
John Radner, Ph.D., Harvard. Eighteenth-century British literature, autobiography, utopian literature and practice.
Janine Ricouart, Ph.D., California, Davis. Gay and lesbian studies, Canadian/Quebec studies, women's studies.
Jeanette Roan, Ph.D., Rochester. English.
Karen Rosenblum, Ph.D., Colorado. Sex and gender studies, deviance, language.
Mark Sample, Ph.D., Pennsylvania. English.
Jessica Scarlata, Ph.D., Rutgers. English.
Linda Seligmann, Ph.D., Illinois at Urbana-Champaign. Political economy, anthropological theory and methods, language and culture, Latin America.
Debra Shutika, Ph.D., Pennsylvania. English.
Paul Smith, Ph.D., Kent (England). Theory and pedagogy of cultural studies, modernist poetry, gender studies.
Suzanne E. Smith, Ph.D., Yale. African-American history, twentieth century versus cultural history, film studies.
Peter Stearns, Provost of George Mason University; Ph.D., Harvard. Social history.
Jeffrey Stewart, Ph.D., Yale. U.S. cultural history, history of the 1920s and 1930s, African-American culture.
Ellen Todd, Ph.D., Stanford. Issues of representation, gender, and spectatorship in American art from the Civil War to the present.
Toni-Michelle Travis, Ph.D., Chicago. Public and international affairs, government, African-American studies.
Steven Vallas, Ph.D., Rutgers. Sociology and anthropology.
Alok Yadov, Ph.D., Cornell. Colonial and post-Colonial studies, nations and nationalism, early modern studies.
Margaret Yocom, Ph.D., Massachusetts. Folklore, construction of race and gender, English drama.
Rosemarie Zagarri, Ph.D., Yale. Colonial and Revolutionary America, political and cultural history.

SARAH LAWRENCE COLLEGE

Women's History

Program of Study	Founded in 1972, the Sarah Lawrence master's program in women's history was the first in the nation to offer graduate study in this field. The intellectually challenging program introduces students to the rapidly expanding historical literature on women, feminist theory in its relation to women's history, and research methods and resources in the field.
	The program features small seminars, close collaborative work with faculty members, focused and intense immersion in the literature of the field, and immediate research in primary sources. Courses address the impact of gender, social class, race, ethnicity, and sexual orientation on women's experiences in culture and society. While concentrating their efforts on historical issues, students may also pursue related topics in women's studies that are available across the curriculum.
	The major emphasis of the program is United States women's history, but interdisciplinary and cross-cultural work is encouraged.
	The program, which leads to the Master of Arts degree in women's history, requires two years of study and completion of 36 course credits (24 credits in the first year, 12 in the second). All students write a thesis during their second year.
	A joint-degree program in women's history and law is offered in cooperation with Pace University Law School. Students in this program can pursue study leading to a master's degree in women's history and a J.D. By taking courses that are acceptable for transfer credit in each of the schools involved, and through careful course planning, the joint-degree student can complete both degrees in four years of full-time study. This program can also be completed on a part-time basis.
Research Facilities	The College's facilities include classrooms, laboratories, and a computer center; a modern library with 202,265 books and 880 periodicals, which is linked by computer to more than 6,000 other libraries; the Performing Arts Center; a music building, including a music library; and a state-of-the-art sports complex.
Financial Aid	Graduate students are welcome to apply for financial aid. There are two required forms for U.S. citizens (and other federally eligible students) and one form for international students. U.S. citizens should complete the Free Application for Federal Student Aid (FAFSA) and the Financial Aid PROFILE. International students may use the College's International Application for Financial Aid. There are links to all three forms at http://www.sarahlawrence.edu/finaid. March 1 is the College's preferential filing date. It is important that all applicants for financial aid complete either the PROFILE or the international application for aid at the same time as their application for admission. All financial aid is awarded on the basis of need. Students who complete the appropriate forms in a timely manner are automatically considered for all aid resources administered by Sarah Lawrence College. Grants (gift aid) and student loans comprise the two elements of a Sarah Lawrence financial aid package. Every federally eligible aid recipient is offered a student loan. Students are not required to accept the loan in order to receive Sarah Lawrence College gift aid. International students are advised to investigate financing opportunities offered by their government or private institutions. Detailed descriptions and a thorough explanation of financial aid procedures are available in *Financing Your Graduate Education at Sarah Lawrence College*, published and updated by the Office of Graduate Studies. A copy of the booklet is mailed to all students who apply to a graduate studies program.
Cost of Study	For more information about program costs, prospective students should visit http://www.slc.edu/student-accounts/Graduate_Tuition_and_Costs.php.
Living and Housing Costs	Estimated expenses for off-campus housing and food are $16,320 per year.
Student Group	Sarah Lawrence attracts students who seek a creative education within the rigorous discipline of women's history. Work in history trains students in advanced research, writing, and presentation skills applicable to almost any field. Graduates of the program have pursued more advanced work in history and in other social science fields; museum, library, and archival work; teaching; educational administration; public policy; international affairs; law; and advocacy work.
	The student body of the entire Sarah Lawrence graduate studies program is diverse, with about 300 students ranging in age from 22 to 55. Students in the women's history program come from across the country and often have extensive work experience.
Location	The College is situated in the Bronxville/Yonkers suburban community in southern Westchester County, just 15 miles north of midtown Manhattan in New York City. Main roads and a commuter railroad make it possible to reach the city in about 30 minutes, enabling students to take advantage of the social, cultural, and intellectual resources of New York.
The College	Founded in 1926, Sarah Lawrence is a small liberal arts college for men and women. It is a lively community of students, scholars, and artists, offering outstanding programs on the graduate level. The College is nationally renowned for its unique academic structure, which combines small classes with individual student-faculty conferences.
Applying	Applicants for graduate studies must have received a B.A. or an equivalent degree from an accredited college or university. Applicants should write to the College address, giving a brief summary of their educational and professional background, and reason for seeking the master's degree. Applicants are asked to complete an application form and to furnish transcripts of all undergraduate work; two letters of recommendation, preferably from former teachers; and a sample of their best academic writing. GRE scores are not required. Applicants are encouraged to visit the campus and to meet with students, faculty members, and the director of graduate studies. For deadline information, please see our Web site at http://www.slc.edu/graduate/index.html.
	To qualify for the joint program, students must apply separately to each school. Financial aid applications also must be made to each school. (Students may receive financial aid from only one school per semester.) Prospective students can apply online at https://data.slc.edu/graduate/index.php.
Correspondence and Information	Susan Guma Dean of Graduate Studies Sarah Lawrence College Bronxville, New York 10709-5999 Phone: 914-395-2371 Fax: 914-395-2664 E-mail: grad@sarahlawrence.edu Web site: http://www.sarahlawrence.edu

Sarah Lawrence College

THE FACULTY AND THEIR RESEARCH

Priscilla Murolo, Director; Ph.D., Yale. U.S. labor history.
Tara James, Associate Director; M.A., Sarah Lawrence.
Eileen Ka-may Cheng, Ph.D., Yale. Nineteenth-century America, with a focus on intellectual and political history.
Rachel Cohen, A.B., Harvard. Writing/creative nonfiction.
Lyde Cullen Sizer, Ph.D., Brown. Women's literary cultures, American popular culture, the American Civil War.
K. Komozi Woodard, Ph.D., Pennsylvania. African American history and culture, with emphasis on the black freedom movement, American urban history, and ghetto formation.

Affiliate Faculty

Julie Abraham, Lesbian and gay studies.
Bella Brodzki, Literature.
Isabelle de Sena, Spanish/literature.
Mary Dillard, History.
Arnold Krupat, Literature.
Chikwenye Ogunyemi, Literature.
David Peritz, Political science.
Mary Porter, Anthropology.
Marilyn Power, Economics.
Kasturi Ray, Global studies
Sandra Robinson, Asian studies.
Judith Rodenbeck, Art history.
Shahnaz Rouse, Sociology.
Barbara Schecter, Psychology.
Pauline Watts, History.
Matilde Zimmermann, History.

Students visiting a cemetery as part of their course work.

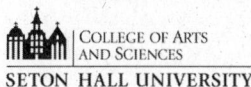

SETON HALL UNIVERSITY

Department of Asian Studies

Programs of Study

The Department of Asian Studies offers graduate courses leading to the Master of Arts (M.A.) degree. The Department also offers a dual master's degree program—the M.A. in Asian Studies/M.A. in Diplomacy and International Relations—with the John C. Whitehead School of Diplomacy and International Relations. The major program provides students with training in the languages and cultures of Asia, leading to careers in government, international services, research, teaching, or business as well as advanced graduate study. Languages offered by the Department are Chinese (Mandarin) and Japanese. Area courses cover the civilizations and affairs of Asia, with emphasis on China, India, and Japan.

M.A. students can complete either 39 credits of course work or 36 credits and a thesis. Core courses total 21 credits; the remaining credits are electives. The 60-credit dual M.A. program requires that students complete 45 credits in core courses (including 18 credits in diplomacy and international relations, 12 credits in traditional East Asia, and 6 credits in modern and contemporary East Asia), 3 credits in free electives, and 9 credits in research and practicum.

The Department of Asian Studies offers a track in Teaching Chinese Language and Culture. The program prepares students to meet the Chinese content area requirement for a New Jersey Certificate of Eligibility (CE). The curriculum includes courses in the Chinese language, literature, theory, civilization, Chinese linguistics, applied linguistics, and teaching methods. Upon successful completion of 39 credits, students receive a Master of Arts in Asian studies and are eligible to enter a New Jersey State Department of Education alternate route program. On completion of the alternate route program, students receive a New Jersey Certificate as teacher of Chinese.

For further information about graduate programs in Asian Studies, students should visit the Web site at http://www.shu.edu/academics/artsci/ma-asian-studies/index.cfm.

Research Facilities

In cooperation with the Asia Center, the Department conducts research on Asia, sponsors conferences, conducts summer institutes, and has an impressive program of publication.

The Language Resource Center (LRC) in the College of Arts and Sciences houses the theater-style Screening Room and a state-of-the-art computer workstation area. All computers have keyboards installed in a number of languages, including Arabic, Chinese, and Japanese, and have Internet access, video recording and editing software, and connections to a VCR/DVD combo for viewing. The LRC provides DVDs, videos, and other media in Arabic, Chinese, English, French, German, Italian, Japanese, Spanish, Russian, and other languages and offers self-paced language learning materials for Seton Hall community members who wish to study a language on their own.

The Walsh Library, a state-of-the-art 155,000-square-foot building, houses 500,000 titles, 1,875 current periodicals, and an extensive collection of microform and other nonprint items that include videotapes, CD-ROM music, and other electronic media. Fahy Hall has twenty-eight classrooms, two TV studios, a Macintosh and IBM graphics lab, two classroom amphitheaters, and language and statistics labs. The recently renovated McNulty Hall has well-equipped science labs. Completed in 1997, Jubilee Hall, a six-story facility with 126,000 square feet of academic space, features high-tech classrooms with computer and multimedia capabilities and the Center for Securities Trading and Analysis, commonly referred to as the Trading Room.

Financial Aid

Each year the Department normally awards teaching assistantships to a limited number of qualified graduate students majoring in Asian studies. Full-time teaching assistants receive a monthly stipend for ten months (September–June) in addition to a waiver of the University's tuition (up to 12 credits per semester). Half-time teaching assistants receive half of the stipend and tuition remission for half of their credit hours. During the appointment period, teaching assistants are solely responsible for their travel expenses, room and board, and all other expenses of a personal nature. For general financial aid information, as well as information on graduate assistantships and teaching assistantships and their respective applications, students should visit http://www.shu.edu/applying/graduate/grad-finaid.cfm.

Cost of Study

In 2009–10, tuition is $901 per credit. Full-time students pay $305 per semester in University and technology fees; part-time students pay $185.

Living and Housing Costs

Housing and living costs in South Orange and surrounding towns are comparable to most suburban cities, with studio and one-bedroom apartments renting for $750 to $1000 per month.

Location

Seton Hall is located on 58 acres in the village of South Orange, New Jersey, a suburban residential area 14 miles southwest of New York City. The town center is a 10-minute walk from the campus and features bookstores, coffee shops, and restaurants. The heart of midtown Manhattan is about 30 minutes away by train; students can take advantage of everything this exciting city has to offer while still living in a suburban area.

The University and The Department

Founded in 1856, Seton Hall is a private coeducational Catholic institution—the nation's oldest diocesan institution of higher education in the United States. With a total enrollment of about 10,000, including approximately 4,500 graduate students, the University comprises nine colleges and schools. Seton Hall is accredited by the Middle States Association of Colleges and Schools. Through the incorporation of technology into the curriculum, the College of Arts and Sciences seeks to enhance and enliven the learning environment. Rooted in tradition, yet looking to the future, the College offers a rich set of opportunities for intellectual discovery. Graduate students are guided by scholars and specialists toward the mastery of academic and professional areas.

The Department of Asian Studies at Seton Hall University has long been recognized as a pioneer and leader in the field of Asian studies. Recently, the *Fiske Guide to Colleges*, published by the *New York Times*, cited the Department for excellence in the quality of its faculty and programs. The Department has a more-than-fifty-year tradition in Asian studies. It views itself and its achievements as a clear sign of Seton Hall's dedication to international studies. Purely by chance, when the name Seton Hall University is rendered into Chinese, it translates as "The West-East University." This coincidence proved true when Seton Hall became one of the first American universities to develop exchanges with Asian universities.

Applying

In addition to the general University requirements for admission to graduate studies, candidates should show a strong background in Asian studies or in one of the disciplines in which the Department offers courses. Students must submit the completed application (available online at http://www.shu.edu/academics/artsci/apply-graduate.cfm), the $50 application fee, a resume, a statement of purpose, two letters of recommendation, and transcripts from all previously attended universities or colleges. For the dual master's degree program, students must apply independently to each degree program, preferably indicating at the time of application that they intend to follow the joint Asian studies/diplomacy program when admitted. The deadlines for fall and spring admission are July 1 and November 1, respectively. Applications are processed on a rolling basis.

For the track in Teaching Chinese and Culture, all candidates are required to demonstrate a strong proficiency in both English and Chinese. Nonnative speakers of Chinese are required to take the Hanyu Shuiping Kaoshi (HSK), a national standard Chinese language proficiency test. International students and those who have received their baccalaureate degrees from universities outside the United States are required to submit official TOEFL scores.

Correspondence and Information

Dr. Shigeru Osuka, Director of Graduate Studies
Department of Asian Studies
Fahy Hall 211
Seton Hall University
400 South Orange Avenue
South Orange, New Jersey 07079
Phone: 973-275-2712
Fax: 973-761-9596
E-mail: osukashi@shu.edu
Web site: http://www.shu.edu/academics/artsci/ma-asian-studies/index.cfm

Seton Hall University

THE FACULTY AND THEIR RESEARCH

Full-time Faculty

Deborah Brown, Associate Professor and Undergraduate Adviser; Ph.D., Drew. Asian religions, modern and contemporary Asian history and politics.

Dongdong Chen, Assistant Professor, Chinese Program Director; Ph.D., McGill. Linguistics, language acquisition, Chinese language.

Edwin Pak-wah Leung, Professor and Chair; Ph.D., California, Santa Barbara. Modern Asian, modern Chinese history and politics, international politics and business.

Michael Linderman, Assistant Professor; Ph.D., Pennsylvania.

Shigeru Osuka, Associate Professor, Japanese Program Director, and Director of Graduate Studies; Ed.D., Hawaii. Japanese language, Japanese history, Asian religions, Buddhist studies, Japanese religions.

Adjunct Faculty

Fen-Dow Chu, Ph.D., MIT. Traditional Chinese history.

Claire Diab, M.A., Seton Hall. Asian religions and culture.

Hwa-Soon Meyer, Ed.D., Columbia. Korean history and culture, ethno music and dance, Korean language.

Hiroko Ogino, B.A., Tsuda Women's College. Japanese language and culture.

Mei Zhao, Ph.D., Suzhou. Chinese language and literature.

WASHINGTON UNIVERSITY IN ST. LOUIS

Programs in East Asian Studies

Program of Study

Washington University in St. Louis has trained East Asian specialists for careers in scholarship, diplomacy, law, and business for more than forty years. The University has a nationally distinguished faculty and an innovative curriculum in East Asian cultures, business, and law. Because admission to the graduate programs is selective and classes are small, students receive a high degree of individual training. There is considerable latitude in designing programs of study to meet personal and professional objectives.

The Master of Arts (M.A.) degree in East Asian studies offers advanced interdisciplinary training in Chinese or Japanese studies. Major areas of focus include literature, political economy, law, gender, intellectual history, and business organization. The program begins with the core seminar in East Asian Studies, which introduces students to rigorous methodological and analytical tools and approaches, and concludes with a series of exit examinations in the students' chosen fields. Normally requiring three semesters to complete, students may extend their program to allow further language training, overseas study, internships, or thesis writing.

The joint J.D./M.A. program in law and East Asian studies offers an integrated curriculum, combining the School of Law's regular program and strengths in East Asian legal studies with the interdisciplinary East Asian studies program. Coordinated Master of Arts and Master of Business Administration degrees (M.A./M.B.A.) are also available. Students typically complete the J.D./M.A. in seven to eight semesters and the M.A./M.B.A. in six.

Advanced study in East Asia is available through graduate exchange arrangements with major Chinese, Japanese, and Korean institutions and through University language programs in Japan, the People's Republic of China, and Taiwan.

Research Facilities

The East Asian Library contains 145,300 volumes of books and bound periodicals in Chinese, Japanese, and Korean. The Law Library has a major collection on Chinese law, which now includes most Chinese primary legal materials (statutes and cases), supplemented with legal encyclopedias, major law treatises, and monograph series, and it is preparing for a substantial expansion of the Japanese law collection, with a particular emphasis on commercial law. The John M. Olin Library collection includes approximately 21,000 volumes on East Asian subjects in Western languages as well as more than 400 serial holdings on East Asia in Western languages. A member of the OCLC online cataloging system, the Olin Library has access to library holdings in East Asian studies across the country. The East Asian Library terminal has Chinese, Japanese, and Korean capability.

Financial Aid

Most students receive full- or partial-tuition scholarships. Fellowships, Washington University Fellowships, and Spencer T. Olin Fellowships for Women are awarded on a competitive basis. Teaching assistantships are normally reserved for advanced students.

Cost of Study

Graduate tuition for students enrolled in Washington University Graduate School of Arts and Sciences was $36,200 for 18 to 24 units in the academic year 2008–09.

Living and Housing Costs

Living expenses during the 2008–09 academic year were approximately $16,780, including books and medical insurance.

Student Group

In 2008–09, 12 students were pursuing the M.A. in East Asian studies, the joint J.D./M.A., or the joint M.A./M.B.A. The student community also includes East Asian specialists pursuing Ph.D. degrees in such programs as Chinese/Japanese and comparative literature, history, anthropology, and political science.

Student Outcomes

Many M.A. graduates of the programs in East Asian Studies continue for advanced degrees in academe or professional schools. Others report careers in international banking, education, nonprofit organizations, or government service. Graduates of the J.D./M.A. program serve as associates with firms in New York, Chicago, Taipei, Beijing, Tokyo, and Hong Kong; international tax consultants; assistant district attorneys; and as professors with international law schools. M.B.A./M.A. graduates have accepted offers from worldwide electronics companies and other renowned corporations with postings in East Asia.

Location

St. Louis, a metropolitan area of more than 2.5 million, enhances the excellence and innovation of Washington University's international studies. More than 300 firms, including ten Fortune 500 companies, are actively engaged in East Asian business. The city also offers a network of international cultural institutions, including the St. Louis Symphony Orchestra, the Saint Louis Art Museum, the Opera Theatre of St. Louis, the Missouri Botanical Garden (with special Japanese and Chinese gardens), a recently renovated riverfront area, and many fine ethnic restaurants.

The University

Founded in 1853, Washington University is an independent institution dedicated to excellence in graduate and professional education. The East Asian studies programs are located on the 168-acre Danforth Campus, within a few minutes walk of the main library, the East Asian Library, the John M. Olin School of Business, the School of Law, the Center for Political Economy, and other facilities. Graduate students also have access to the East Asian faculty members at the University of Missouri–St. Louis.

Applying

Candidates are required to have their college transcripts and their scores on the Graduate Record Examinations sent to program office. Students whose native language is not English are required to send an official copy of their TOEFL results. Applicants to the joint J.D./M.A. and M.A./M.B.A. programs apply for admission to both East Asian Studies and the relevant professional school.

Correspondence and Information

East Asian Studies
Campus Box 1088
McMillan Hall, Room 244
Washington University in St. Louis
1 Brookings Drive
St. Louis, Missouri 63130-4899
Phone: 314-935-4448
Fax: 314-935-5485
E-mail: eas@artsci.wustl.edu
Web site: http://eastasian.artsci.wustl.edu/

Washington University in St. Louis

THE FACULTY AND THEIR RESEARCH

Art History
Gwen Bennett. Chinese Neolithic period archaeology.

History
Steven Miles. Modern Chinese history.
Lori Watt. Modern Japanese history.

Languages and Literatures
Hiroo Aridome. Japanese language.
Letty Lingchei Chen. Modern Chinese literature.
Rebecca Copeland. Modern Japanese literature.
Beata Grant. Chinese literature and religious studies.
Shino Hayashi. Japanese language.
Robert E. Hegel. Chinese vernacular fiction and drama.
M. Mimi Kim. Korean language.
Pauline Chen Lee. Chinese religion and culture.
Xia Liang. Chinese language.
Chun-ying Lin. Chinese language.
Marvin H. Marcus. Modern Japanese literature.
Virginia Marcus. Japanese language.
Robert E. Morrell (Emeritus). Japanese literature and Buddhism.
Judy Zhijun Mu. Chinese language.
Jamie Newhard. Premodern Japanese literature.
Wei Wang. Chinese language.
Fengtao Wu. Chinese language.

Law
John O. Haley. Comparative law, litigation, Japanese law.
Charles McManis. Intellectual property law in East Asia.
Carl Minzner. Chinese law and politics.

Performing Arts
Mary Jean Cowell. Japanese theater and dance.

Section 16
Communication and Media

This section contains a directory of institutions offering graduate work in communication and media, followed by in-depth entries submitted by institutions that chose to prepare detailed program descriptions. Additional information about programs listed in the directory but not augmented by an in-depth entry may be obtained by writing directly to the dean of a graduate school or chair of a department at the address given in the directory.

For programs offering related work, see also in this book *Film, Television, and Video; Language and Literature;* and *Psychology and Counseling.* In the other guides in this series:

Graduate Programs in Engineering & Applied Sciences

See *Computer Science and Information Technology* and *Telecommunications*

Graduate Programs in Business, Education, Health, Information Studies, Law & Social Work

See *Advertising and Public Relations*

CONTENTS

Program Directories

Communication—General	628
Arts Journalism	646
Broadcast Journalism	646
Corporate and Organizational Communication	646
Health Communication	651
Internet and Interactive Multimedia	652
Journalism	654
Mass Communication	659
Media Studies	664
Publishing	669
Rhetoric	670
Speech and Interpersonal Communication	674
Technical Communication	678

Announcements

Indiana University Bloomington	632
Syracuse University	638

Close-Ups

American University	681
Boston University	683
Columbia University	685
CUNY Graduate School of Journalism	687
Hawai'i Pacific University	689
The New School: A University	691
Point Park University	693
Quinnipiac University	695
Seton Hall University	697
Southern Illinois University Carbondale	
Mass Communication and Media Arts (M.F.A.)	699
Mass Communication and Media Arts (Ph.D.)	701
Speech Communication	703
Syracuse University	705
University of Denver	707
University of Southern California	709

See also:

American University—International Service	861
Carnegie Mellon University—Professional Writing and Communication Design	553
The New School: A University—International Affairs	873
Pratt Institute—Art and Design	219
Savannah College of Art and Design—Art and Design	223
School of the Art Institute of Chicago—Graduate Studies in Art	225
Southern Illinois University Carbondale—English	445

Communication—General

Abilene Christian University, Graduate School, College of Arts and Sciences, Department of Communication, Program in Communication, Abilene, TX 79699-9100. Offers MA. Part-time programs available. *Faculty:* 7 part-time/adjunct (2 women). *Students:* 13 full-time (9 women), 7 part-time (5 women); includes 1 minority (African American), 7 international. 15 applicants, 87% accepted, 8 enrolled. In 2008, 11 master's awarded. *Degree requirements:* For master's, one foreign language, comprehensive exam, thesis optional. *Entrance requirements:* For master's, GRE General Test. Additional exam requirements/recommendations for international students: Required—TOEFL (minimum score 213 computer-based). *Application deadline:* For fall admission, 4/1 priority date for domestic students; for spring admission, 11/1 for domestic students. Applications are processed on a rolling basis. Application fee: $40 ($45 for international students). Electronic applications accepted. *Expenses:* Tuition: Full-time $10,728; part-time $640 per hour. Required fees: $1090; $53.50 per hour. $10 per term. Tuition and fees vary according to campus/location. *Financial support:* In 2008–09, 17 students received support; teaching assistantships, Federal Work-Study available. Support available to part-time students. Financial award application deadline: 4/1; financial award applicants required to submit FAFSA. *Faculty research:* Intercultural communication, family communication, forensics, organizational communication. *Unit head:* Dr. Paul Lakey, Graduate Adviser, 325-674-2292, Fax: 325-674-6966, E-mail: lakeyp@acu.edu. *Application contact:* William Horn, Graduate Admissions Counselor, 325-674-2656, Fax: 325-674-6717, E-mail: gradinfo@acu.edu.

American University, School of Communication, Washington, DC 20016-8001. Offers MA, MFA. *Accreditation:* ACEJMC (one or more programs are accredited). Part-time and evening/weekend programs available. *Faculty:* 42 full-time (18 women), 15 part-time/adjunct. *Students:* 126 full-time (75 women), 199 part-time (126 women); includes 76 minority (49 African Americans, 14 Asian Americans or Pacific Islanders, 13 Hispanic Americans), 29 international. Average age 27. 506 applicants, 66% accepted, 177 enrolled. In 2008, 159 master's awarded. *Degree requirements:* For master's, comprehensive exam, thesis or alternative. *Entrance requirements:* For master's, GRE General Test. Additional exam requirements/recommendations for international students: Required—TOEFL (minimum score 600 paper-based; 260 computer-based; 100 iBT), IELTS (minimum score 7). *Application deadline:* For fall admission, 2/1 priority date for domestic students, 4/1 priority date for international students; for spring admission, 11/15 for domestic students. Applications are processed on a rolling basis. Application fee: $50. Electronic applications accepted. *Expenses:* Tuition: Full-time $21,204; part-time $1178 per credit hour. Required fees: $380. Part-time tuition and fees vary according to course load and program. *Financial support:* In 2008–09, 64 students received support, including 6 fellowships with partial tuition reimbursements available (averaging $23,000 per year), 15 research assistantships with partial tuition reimbursements available (averaging $18,000 per year), 15 teaching assistantships with partial tuition reimbursements available (averaging $18,000 per year); career-related internships or fieldwork, Federal Work-Study, institutionally sponsored loans, scholarships/grants, and tuition waivers (partial) also available. Financial award application deadline: 2/1; financial award applicants required to submit FAFSA. *Faculty research:* New communication technology, documentaries and public broadcasting, litigation and public relations, dissident media, race and gender and the media, international journalism and human rights, social media. *Unit head:* Dean Larry Kirkman, Dean, 202-885-2058, Fax: 202-885-2099, E-mail: larry@american.edu. *Application contact:* Sharmeen Ahsan-Bracciale, Graduate Admissions Office, 202-885-2040, Fax: 202-885-2019, E-mail: sharmeen@american.edu.

See Close-Up on page 681.

The American University in Cairo, Graduate Studies and Research, School of Business, Economics and Communication, Department of Journalism and Mass Communication, Cairo, Egypt. Offers journalism and mass communication (MA); television and digital journalism (MA). Part-time programs available. *Degree requirements:* For master's, thesis (for some programs). *Entrance requirements:* For master's, English entrance exam, GMAT. Electronic applications accepted. *Faculty research:* Mass media and national development/censorship, intercultural photo communication, comparative journalism/television.

The American University of Paris, Graduate Programs, Paris, France. Offers finance (MSF); global communications (MAGC); international affairs, conflict resolution and civil society development (MA); Middle Eastern and Islamic studies (MA); public administration (MPA). *Degree requirements:* For master's, thesis. *Entrance requirements:* For master's, minimum undergraduate GPA of 3.0.

Andrews University, School of Graduate Studies, College of Arts and Sciences, Interdisciplinary Studies in Communication Program, Berrien Springs, MI 49104. Offers MA. In 2008, 3 master's awarded. *Application deadline:* Applications are processed on a rolling basis. Application fee: $43. *Expenses:* Tuition: Full-time $18,360; part-time $765 per credit hour. Required fees: $476; $765 per credit hour. $238 per semester. Tuition and fees vary according to degree level. *Unit head:* Dr. Janice Y. Watson, Area Coordinator, 269-471-3126. *Application contact:* Carolyn Hurst, Supervisor of Graduate Admission, 800-253-2874, Fax: 269-471-3228, E-mail: graduate@andrews.edu.

Angelo State University, College of Graduate Studies, College of Liberal and Fine Arts, Department of Communications, Drama, and Journalism, San Angelo, TX 76909. Offers communication systems management (MA). Part-time and evening/weekend programs available. *Faculty:* 2 full-time (0 women). *Students:* 8 full-time (4 women), 2 part-time (1 woman); includes 3 minority (all Hispanic Americans). Average age 44. 4 applicants, 100% accepted, 2 enrolled. *Degree requirements:* For master's, comprehensive exam, thesis optional. *Entrance requirements:* For master's, GRE General Test. Additional exam requirements/recommendations for international students: Required—TOEFL or IELTS. *Application deadline:* For fall admission, 7/15 priority date for domestic students, 6/10 for international students; for spring admission, 12/1 priority date for domestic students, 11/1 for international students. Applications are processed on a rolling basis. Application fee: $40 ($50 for international students). Electronic applications accepted. *Financial support:* In 2008–09, 5 students received support, including 3 teaching assistantships (averaging $10,251 per year); career-related internships or fieldwork, Federal Work-Study, scholarships/grants, and unspecified assistantships also available. Support available to part-time students. Financial award application deadline: 3/1; financial award applicants required to submit FAFSA. *Unit head:* Dr. June H. Smith, Department Head, 325-942-2031 Ext. 228, E-mail: june.smith@angelo.edu. *Application contact:* Dr. Lana Marlow, Graduate Advisor, 325-942-2032 Ext. 356, E-mail: lana.marlow@angelo.edu.

Arizona State University, Graduate College, College of Liberal Arts and Sciences, Division of Social Sciences, Hugh Downs School of Human Communication, Tempe, AZ 85287. Offers communication (MA, PhD). *Degree requirements:* For master's, thesis or alternative; for doctorate, thesis/dissertation.

Arizona State University at the West campus, College of Human Services, Department of Communication Studies, Phoenix, AZ 85069-7100. Offers communication (MA). Part-time and evening/weekend programs available. *Degree requirements:* For master's, comprehensive exams or thesis. *Entrance requirements:* For master's, GRE if GPA below 3.0 in last 60 hours of undergraduate study, 2 letters of recommendation, minimum GPA of 3.0 in last 2 years of undergraduate study, personal statement, writing sample of scholarly work. Additional exam requirements/recommendations for international students: Required—TOEFL (minimum score 550 paper-based; 213 computer-based; 83 iBT), IELTS (minimum score 6.5). Electronic applications accepted. *Faculty research:* Research regarding various ways in which communication shapes social contexts, constructs people's realities, and constitutes human relationships.

Arkansas State University, Graduate School, College of Communications, Jonesboro, State University, AR 72467. Offers MA, MSMC, SCCT. Part-time programs available. *Faculty:* 13 full-time (5 women), 1 part-time/adjunct (0 women). *Students:* 20 full-time (14 women), 19 part-time (7 women); includes 15 minority (all African Americans), 9 international. Average age 28. 34 applicants, 94% accepted, 20 enrolled. In 2008, 10 master's awarded. *Degree requirements:* For master's, one foreign language, comprehensive exam, thesis or alternative. *Entrance requirements:* For master's, GRE General Test, appropriate bachelor's degree, letters of reference, official transcript; for SCCT, interview, master's degree, official transcript. Additional exam requirements/recommendations for international students: Required—TOEFL (minimum score 550 paper-based; 213 computer-based; 79 iBT), IELTS (minimum score 6). *Application deadline:* For fall admission, 7/15 for domestic students, 7/1 for international students; for spring admission, 12/1 for domestic students, 11/13 for international students. Applications are processed on a rolling basis. Application fee: $30 ($40 for international students). Electronic applications accepted. *Expenses:* Tuition, state resident: full-time $3744; part-time $208 per credit hour. Tuition, nonresident: full-time $9540; part-time $530 per credit hour. International tuition: $7938 full-time. Required fees: $896; $47 per credit hour. $25 per term. One-time fee: $50. Tuition and fees vary according to course load and program. *Financial support:* In 2008–09, 15 students received support. Career-related internships or fieldwork, scholarships/grants, and unspecified assistantships available. Financial award application deadline: 7/1; financial award applicants required to submit FAFSA. *Faculty research:* Audience analysis, agenda setting, nonverbal communication, media ethics, political advertising. Total annual research expenditures: $48,913. *Unit head:* Dr. Russell Shain, Dean, 870-972-2468, Fax: 870-972-3856, E-mail: rshain@astate.edu. *Application contact:* Dr. Andrew Sustich, Dean of the Graduate School, 870-972-3029, Fax: 870-972-3857, E-mail: sustich@astate.edu.

Arkansas Tech University, Graduate School, School of Liberal and Fine Arts, Russellville, AR 72801. Offers communication (MLA); English (M Ed, MA); fine arts (MLA); history (MA); multi-media journalism (MA); social science (MLA); social studies (M Ed); Spanish (MA, MLA); teaching English as a second language (MA, MLA). Part-time programs available. *Students:* 40 full-time (31 women), 81 part-time (60 women); includes 10 minority (3 African Americans, 2 American Indian/Alaska Native, 2 Asian Americans or Pacific Islanders, 3 Hispanic Americans), 19 international. Average age 33. In 2008, 70 master's awarded. *Degree requirements:* For master's, project. *Entrance requirements:* For master's, GRE General Test or MAT. Additional exam requirements/recommendations for international students: Required—TOEFL (minimum score 500 paper-based; 173 computer-based; 61 iBT). *Application deadline:* For fall admission, 3/1 priority date for domestic students, 5/1 priority date for international students; for winter admission, 10/1 priority date for international students; for spring admission, 10/1 priority date for domestic and international students. Applications are processed on a rolling basis. Application fee: $0 ($30 for international students). Electronic applications accepted. *Expenses:* Tuition, state resident: full-time $1575; part-time $175 per credit hour. Tuition, nonresident: full-time $3150; part-time $350 per credit hour. Tuition and fees vary according to course load. *Financial support:* In 2008–09, teaching assistantships with full tuition reimbursements (averaging $4,000 per year); career-related internships or fieldwork, Federal Work-Study, scholarships/grants, health care benefits, and unspecified assistantships also available. Support available to part-time students. Financial award application deadline: 4/15; financial award applicants required to submit FAFSA. *Unit head:* Dr. Georgena Duncan, Dean, 479-968-0266, Fax: 479-968-0275, E-mail: georgena.duncan@atu.edu. *Application contact:* Dr. Eldon G. Clary, Dean of Graduate School, 479-968-0398, Fax: 479-964-0542, E-mail: graduate.school@atu.edu.

Auburn University, Graduate School, College of Liberal Arts, Department of Communication and Journalism, Auburn University, AL 36849. Offers communication (MA); mass communications (MA). Part-time programs available. *Faculty:* 25 full-time (13 women), 7 part-time/adjunct (3 women). *Students:* 19 full-time (11 women), 7 part-time (5 women); includes 3 minority (all African Americans), 2 international. Average age 28. 23 applicants, 65% accepted, 10 enrolled. In 2008, 4 master's awarded. *Degree requirements:* For master's, thesis (for some programs). *Entrance requirements:* For master's, GRE General Test. *Application deadline:* For fall admission, 7/7 for domestic students; for spring admission, 11/24 for domestic students. Applications are processed on a rolling basis. Application fee: $25 ($50 for international students). Electronic applications accepted. *Expenses:* Tuition, area resident: Full-time $5880; part-time $243 per credit hour. Tuition, state resident: full-time $5880; part-time $243 per credit hour. Tuition, nonresident: full-time $17,640; part-time $729 per credit hour. International tuition: $17,846 full-time. Required fees: $620. Tuition and fees vary according to program and reciprocity agreements. *Financial support:* Teaching assistantships, Federal Work-Study available. Support available to part-time students. Financial award application deadline: 3/15. *Unit head:* Dr. Mary Helen Brown, Acting Chair, 334-844-2727. *Application contact:* Dr. George Flowers, Dean of the Graduate School, 334-844-2125.

Austin Peay State University, College of Graduate Studies, College of Arts and Letters, Department of Communication, Clarksville, TN 37044. Offers communication arts (MA). Part-time and evening/weekend programs available. Postbaccalaureate distance learning degree programs offered (no on-campus study). *Faculty:* 12 full-time (5 women), 4 part-time/adjunct (3 women). *Students:* 15 full-time (10 women), 74 part-time (49 women); includes 23 minority (19 African Americans, 2 Asian Americans or Pacific Islanders, 2 Hispanic Americans). Average age 32. 30 applicants, 100% accepted, 27 enrolled. In 2008, 19 master's awarded. *Degree requirements:* For master's, comprehensive exam, thesis (for some programs). *Entrance requirements:* For master's, GRE General Test, 3 letters of recommendation, bachelor's degree. Additional exam requirements/recommendations for international students: Required—TOEFL (minimum score 500 paper-based; 173 computer-based). *Application deadline:* For fall admission, 7/27 priority date for domestic students; for spring admission, 12/17 priority date for domestic students. Applications are processed on a rolling basis. Application fee: $25. Electronic applications accepted. *Expenses:* Tuition, area resident: Full-time $5772; part-time $305 per credit hour. Tuition, state resident: full-time $5772; part-time $305 per credit hour. Tuition, nonresident: full-time $16,664; part-time $778 per credit hour. Required fees: $1224. *Financial support:* In 2008–09, 7 research assistantships with full tuition reimbursements (averaging $6,996 per year) were awarded; career-related internships or fieldwork, Federal Work-Study, institutionally sponsored loans, scholarships/grants, and unspecified assistantships also available. Support available to part-time students. Financial award application deadline: 3/1; financial award applicants required to submit FAFSA. *Unit head:* Dr. Mike Gotcher, Chair, 931-221-7378, Fax: 931-221-7265, E-mail: comm@apsu.edu. *Application contact:* Dr. Charles Pinder, Dean, College of Graduate Studies, 931-221-7414, Fax: 931-221-7641, E-mail: pinderc@apsu.edu.

Ball State University, Graduate School, College of Communication, Information, and Media, Muncie, IN 47306-1099. Offers MA, MS.

Barry University, School of Arts and Sciences, Department of Communication, Miami Shores, FL 33161-6695. Offers broadcasting (Certificate); communication (MA), including broadcast communication, public relations and corporate communications; organizational communication (MS). Part-time and evening/weekend programs available. *Degree requirements:* For master's, thesis (for some programs). *Entrance requirements:* For master's, GRE General Test, MAT, minimum GPA of 3.0. Electronic applications accepted. *Faculty research:* Organizational communication, broadcast communication, intercultural communication, advertising, leadership.

Baylor University, Graduate School, College of Arts and Sciences, Department of Communication Studies, Waco, TX 76798. Offers MA. Part-time programs available. *Students:* 15 full-time (6 women), 3 part-time (1 woman); includes 2 minority (1 Asian American or Pacific Islander, 1 Hispanic American), 1 international. Average age 22. In 2008, 5 master's awarded. *Degree requirements:* For master's, thesis or alternative. *Entrance requirements:* For master's, GRE General Test. *Application deadline:* For fall admission, 8/1 for domestic students. Applications are processed on a rolling basis. Application fee: $25. *Financial support:* In 2008–09, 12 teaching assistantships were awarded; career-related internships or fieldwork, Federal Work-Study, institutionally sponsored loans, and scholarships/grants also available. Financial award application deadline: 4/1. *Faculty research:* Rhetoric and debate, organizational communication, media studies, new technology. *Unit head:* Dr. Mark Morman, Graduate Program Director,

254-710-1621, E-mail: mark_morman@baylor.edu. *Application contact:* Marilyn Spivey, Administrative Assistant, 254-710-1621, Fax: 254-710-3870, E-mail: marilyn_spivey@baylor.edu.

Bellarmine University, School of Communication, Louisville, KY 40205-0671. Offers MA, MS.

Bethel University, Graduate School, Department of Communication Studies, St. Paul, MN 55112-6999. Offers communication (MA); post-secondary teaching (Certificate). Evening/weekend programs available. *Degree requirements:* For master's, comprehensive exam, thesis. *Entrance requirements:* For master's, MAT, interview, minimum GPA of 3.0, course work in communication and statistics, references. Additional exam requirements/recommendations for international students: Required—TOEFL (minimum score 550 paper-based; 213 computer-based). Electronic applications accepted.

Boise State University, Graduate College, College of Social Sciences and Public Affairs, Department of Communication, Boise, ID 83725-0399. Offers MA. Part-time programs available. *Degree requirements:* For master's, thesis. *Entrance requirements:* For master's, minimum GPA of 3.0, writing sample. Electronic applications accepted.

Boston University, College of Communication, Boston, MA 02215. Offers MFA, MS, JD/MS, MBA/MS. Part-time programs available. *Degree requirements:* For master's, thesis. *Entrance requirements:* For master's, GRE General Test. Additional exam requirements/recommendations for international students: Required—TOEFL. Electronic applications accepted.

See Close-Up on page 683.

Bowling Green State University, Graduate College, College of Arts and Sciences, School of Communication Studies, Bowling Green, OH 43403. Offers MA, PhD. Part-time programs available. Terminal master's awarded for partial completion of doctoral program. *Degree requirements:* For master's, thesis or alternative; for doctorate, comprehensive exam, thesis/dissertation. *Entrance requirements:* For master's and doctorate, GRE General Test. Additional exam requirements/recommendations for international students: Required—TOEFL. Electronic applications accepted.

Brandeis University, Rabb School of Continuing Studies, Division of Graduate Professional Studies, Virtual Team Management and Communication Program, Waltham, MA 02454-9110. Offers Graduate Certificate. Part-time and evening/weekend programs available. Post-baccalaureate distance learning degree programs offered (no on-campus study). *Entrance requirements:* For degree, resumé, official transcripts, recommendations. Additional exam requirements/recommendations for international students: Recommended—TOEFL (minimum score 600 paper-based; 250 computer-based; 100 iBT). Electronic applications accepted.

Brigham Young University, Graduate Studies, College of Fine Arts and Communications, Department of Communications, Provo, UT 84602. Offers mass communications (MA). *Faculty:* 17 full-time (3 women). *Students:* 7 full-time (6 women), 36 part-time (20 women); includes 5 minority (1 African American, 1 American Indian/Alaska Native, 3 Hispanic Americans). Average age 29. 33 applicants, 52% accepted, 9 enrolled. In 2008, 10 master's awarded. *Degree requirements:* For master's, comprehensive exam, thesis. *Entrance requirements:* For master's, GRE, minimum GPA of 3.0 in last 60 hours of course work. Additional exam requirements/recommendations for international students: Required—TOEFL (minimum score 580 paper-based; 237 computer-based; 85 iBT). *Application deadline:* For fall admission, 2/28 for domestic and international students. Application fee: $50. Electronic applications accepted. *Expenses:* Tuition: Full-time $5160; part-time $287 per credit hour. Tuition and fees vary according to program and student's religious affiliation. *Financial support:* In 2008–09, 22 students received support, including 25 research assistantships with full and partial tuition reimbursements available (averaging $4,307 per year), 10 teaching assistantships with full and partial tuition reimbursements available (averaging $4,657 per year); career-related internships or fieldwork, institutionally sponsored loans, scholarships/grants, unspecified assistantships, and supplementary awards also available. Financial award application deadline: 5/15; financial award applicants required to submit FAFSA. *Faculty research:* Ethics, international, magazine, newspaper, media effects. *Unit head:* Dr. Bradley L. Rawlins, Chair, 801-422-2997, Fax: 801-422-0160, E-mail: comms_secretary@byu.edu. *Application contact:* Dr. Steven R. Thomsen, Graduate Coordinator, 801-422-2078, Fax: 801-422-0160, E-mail: steven_thomsen@byu.edu.

California State University, Chico, Graduate School, College of Communication and Education, Department of Communication Arts and Sciences, Program in Communication Studies, Chico, CA 95929-0722. Offers MA. *Degree requirements:* For master's, thesis. *Entrance requirements:* Additional exam requirements/recommendations for international students: Required—TOEFL (minimum score 550 paper-based; 213 computer-based; 80 iBT), IELTS (minimum score 6.5). Electronic applications accepted.

California State University, East Bay, Academic Programs and Graduate Studies, College of Letters, Arts, and Social Sciences, Department of Communication, Hayward, CA 94542-3000. Offers MA. Part-time programs available. *Degree requirements:* For master's, comprehensive exam, thesis optional, project or thesis. *Entrance requirements:* For master's, GRE, minimum GPA of 3.0 in field. Additional exam requirements/recommendations for international students: Required—TOEFL (minimum score 550 paper-based; 213 computer-based). Electronic applications accepted.

California State University, Fresno, Division of Graduate Studies, College of Arts and Humanities, Department of Communication, Fresno, CA 93740-8027. Offers MA. Part-time and evening/weekend programs available. *Degree requirements:* For master's, thesis or alternative. *Entrance requirements:* For master's, GRE General Test, minimum GPA of 3.1. Additional exam requirements/recommendations for international students: Required—TOEFL. Electronic applications accepted. *Faculty research:* Learning styles, education, critical thinking.

California State University, Fullerton, Graduate Studies, College of Communications, Department of Communications, Fullerton, CA 92834-9480. Offers communications—advertising (MA); communications—entertainment and tourism (MA); communications—journalism (MA); communications—public relations (MA). Part-time programs available. *Students:* 21 full-time (17 women), 38 part-time (32 women); includes 18 minority (1 African American, 6 Asian Americans or Pacific Islanders, 11 Hispanic Americans), 9 international. Average age 29. 94 applicants, 38% accepted, 13 enrolled. In 2008, 33 master's awarded. *Degree requirements:* For master's, project or thesis. *Entrance requirements:* For master's, GRE General Test. Application fee: $55. Tuition and fees vary according to degree level. *Financial support:* Teaching assistantships, career-related internships or fieldwork, Federal Work-Study, institutionally sponsored loans, and scholarships/grants available. Support available to part-time students. Financial award application deadline: 3/1. *Unit head:* Dr. Tony Fellow, Chair, 657-278-3517. *Application contact:* Coordinator, 657-278-3832.

California State University, Long Beach, Graduate Studies, College of Liberal Arts, Department of Communication Studies, Long Beach, CA 90840. Offers MA. Part-time programs available. *Faculty:* 7 full-time (all women). *Students:* 66 full-time (63 women), 32 part-time (all women); includes 10 minority (2 African Americans, 1 American Indian/Alaska Native, 3 Asian Americans or Pacific Islanders, 4 Hispanic Americans), 1 international. Average age 30. 64 applicants, 20% accepted, 11 enrolled. *Degree requirements:* For master's, comprehensive exam or thesis. *Entrance requirements:* For master's, GRE. *Application deadline:* For fall admission, 2/27 for domestic students. Applications are processed on a rolling basis. Application fee: $55. Electronic applications accepted. *Expenses:* Tuition, nonresident: full-time $11,160; part-time $372 per unit. Required fees: $4100; $1261 per semester. *Financial support:* Federal Work-Study, institutionally sponsored loans, and scholarships/grants available. Financial award application deadline: 3/2. *Faculty research:* Rhetoric, public address, communication theory, interpersonal communication, intercultural communication. *Unit head:* Dr. Sharon Downey, Chair, 562-985-4301, Fax: 562-985-4259, E-mail: shadowney@csulb.edu. *Application contact:* Dr. Ann Johnson, Graduate Adviser, 562-985-9190, Fax: 562-985-4259, E-mail: ajohnso7@csulb.edu.

California State University, Los Angeles, Graduate Studies, College of Arts and Letters, Department of Communication Studies, Los Angeles, CA 90032-8530. Offers speech communication (MA); television, film and theatre (MFA). Part-time and evening/weekend programs available. *Faculty:* 12 full-time (3 women). *Students:* 64 full-time (37 women), 40 part-time (32 women); includes 47 minority (15 African Americans, 1 American Indian/Alaska Native, 13 Asian Americans or Pacific Islanders, 18 Hispanic Americans), 18 international. Average age 30. 88 applicants, 92% accepted, 47 enrolled. In 2008, 8 master's awarded. *Degree requirements:* For master's, comprehensive exam or thesis. *Entrance requirements:* For master's, minimum GPA of 2.75 in last 90 units of course work. Additional exam requirements/recommendations for international students: Required—TOEFL (minimum score 500 paper-based; 173 computer-based). *Application deadline:* For fall admission, 6/15 for domestic students, 5/1 for international students; for winter admission, 11/1 for domestic students, 9/1 for international students; for spring admission, 2/1 for domestic students, 10/1 for international students. Applications are processed on a rolling basis. Application fee: $55. Electronic applications accepted. *Expenses:* Tuition, nonresident: part-time $226 per credit. Required fees: $4019. *Financial support:* Career-related internships or fieldwork and Federal Work-Study available. Support available to part-time students. Financial award application deadline: 3/1. *Faculty research:* Organizational, interpersonal, intercultural, and instructional communication; rhetorical theories. *Unit head:* Dr. John Ramirez, Chair, 323-343-4200, Fax: 323-343-6467, E-mail: jramire4@calstatela.edu. *Application contact:* Dr. Jose L. Galvan, Dean of Graduate Studies, 323-343-3820, Fax: 323-343-5653, E-mail: jgalvan@cslanet.calstatela.edu.

California State University, Northridge, Graduate Studies, College of Arts, Media, and Communication, Northridge, CA 91330. Offers MA, MFA, MM. Part-time and evening/weekend programs available. *Faculty:* 87 full-time (39 women), 177 part-time/adjunct (64 women). *Students:* 108 full-time (65 women), 154 part-time (108 women); includes 61 minority (11 African Americans, 1 American Indian/Alaska Native, 16 Asian Americans or Pacific Islanders, 33 Hispanic Americans), 20 international. Average age 33. 376 applicants, 44% accepted, 103 enrolled. In 2008, 69 master's awarded. *Entrance requirements:* Additional exam requirements/recommendations for international students: Required—TOEFL. *Application deadline:* For fall admission, 11/30 for domestic students. Application fee: $55. *Financial support:* Teaching assistantships, career-related internships or fieldwork, Federal Work-Study, and unspecified assistantships available. Support available to part-time students. Financial award application deadline: 3/1. *Unit head:* Robert Bucker, Dean, 818-677-2246, E-mail: robert.bucker@csun.edu. *Application contact:* Robert Bucker, Dean, 818-677-2246, E-mail: robert.bucker@csun.edu.

California State University, Sacramento, Graduate Studies, College of Arts and Letters, Department of Communication Studies, Sacramento, CA 95819-6048. Offers MA. Part-time programs available. *Degree requirements:* For master's, thesis or alternative, writing proficiency exam. *Entrance requirements:* For master's, minimum GPA of 3.25 during previous 2 years. Additional exam requirements/recommendations for international students: Required—TOEFL. Electronic applications accepted.

California State University, San Bernardino, Graduate Studies, College of Arts and Letters, Department of Communication Studies, San Bernardino, CA 92407-2397. Offers communication studies (MA); integrated marketing communication (MA). *Faculty:* 7 full-time (6 women), 1 part-time/adjunct (0 women). *Students:* 30 full-time (23 women), 17 part-time (15 women); includes 17 minority (6 African Americans, 11 Hispanic Americans), 12 international. Average age 29. 74 applicants, 34% accepted, 20 enrolled. In 2008, 17 master's awarded. *Degree requirements:* For master's, comprehensive exam, advancement to candidacy. *Entrance requirements:* Additional exam requirements/recommendations for international students: Required—TOEFL. *Application deadline:* For fall admission, 8/31 priority date for domestic students. Application fee: $55. *Expenses:* Tuition, area resident: Full-time $1252; part-time $726 per quarter. Required fees: $334 per quarter. Tuition and fees vary according to degree level and student level. *Unit head:* Dr. Mo Bahk, Chair, 909-537-5820, Fax: 909-537-7009, E-mail: mbahk@csusb.edu. *Application contact:* Olivia Rosas, Director of Admissions, 909-537-7577, Fax: 909-537-7034, E-mail: orosas@csusb.edu.

Carleton University, Faculty of Graduate Studies, Faculty of Public Affairs and Management, School of Journalism and Communication, Program in Communication, Ottawa, ON K1S 5B6, Canada. Offers MA, PhD. *Degree requirements:* For master's, thesis optional; for doctorate, comprehensive exam, thesis/dissertation. *Entrance requirements:* For master's, honors degree. Additional exam requirements/recommendations for international students: Required—TOEFL. *Faculty research:* History of communication and media systems, communication/information technologies and society, communication and social relations, communication policy and political economy.

Carnegie Mellon University, College of Fine Arts, School of Design, Program in Communication Planning and Information Design, Pittsburgh, PA 15213-3891. Offers M Des. Part-time programs available. *Degree requirements:* For master's, thesis. *Entrance requirements:* For master's, GRE, portfolio of relevant work. Additional exam requirements/recommendations for international students: Required—TOEFL (minimum score 600 paper-based). *Faculty research:* Dynamic information design, communication design, systems design, strategic planning, kinetic typography and emotion.

Carnegie Mellon University, College of Humanities and Social Sciences, Department of English, Pittsburgh, PA 15213-3891. Offers communication planning and design (M Des); literary and cultural studies (MA, PhD); professional writing (MAPW), including editing and publishing, policy and non-profit communication, public and media relations / corporate communications, science or healthcare communication, technical writing, writing for new media, writing for print media; rhetoric (MA, PhD). Part-time programs available. Terminal master's awarded for partial completion of doctoral program. *Degree requirements:* For doctorate, 2 foreign languages, comprehensive exam, thesis/dissertation. *Entrance requirements:* For master's and doctorate, GRE General Test. Additional exam requirements/recommendations for international students: Required—TOEFL, TWE. *Faculty research:* Cognitive processes in discourse with emphasis on writing, testing, and evaluation.

Central Connecticut State University, School of Graduate Studies, School of Arts and Sciences, Department of Communication, New Britain, CT 06050-4010. Offers organizational communication (MS); public relations/promotions (Certificate). Part-time and evening/weekend programs available. *Faculty:* 13 full-time (4 women), 9 part-time/adjunct (3 women). *Students:* 5 full-time (3 women), 22 part-time (15 women); includes 5 minority (2 African Americans, 1 Asian American or Pacific Islander, 2 Hispanic Americans), 1 international. Average age 29. 21 applicants, 43% accepted, 6 enrolled. In 2008, 11 master's, 1 other advanced degree awarded. *Degree requirements:* For master's, comprehensive exam, thesis or alternative. *Entrance requirements:* For master's, minimum undergraduate GPA of 3.0, essay. Additional exam requirements/recommendations for international students: Required—TOEFL. *Application deadline:* For fall admission, 7/1 for domestic students; for spring admission, 12/1 for domestic students. Applications are processed on a rolling basis. Application fee: $50. Electronic applications accepted. *Expenses:* Tuition, area resident: Full-time $4377; part-time $420 per credit. Tuition, state resident: full-time $6566; part-time $420 per credit. Tuition, nonresident: full-time $12,195; part-time $420 per credit. Required fees: $3462. One-time fee: $62 part-time. *Financial support:* In 2008–09, 2 students received support, including 2 research assistantships; career-related internships or fieldwork, Federal Work-Study, scholarships/grants, and unspecified assistantships also available. Support available to part-time students. Financial award application deadline: 3/1; financial award applicants required to submit FAFSA. *Faculty research:* Organizational communication, mass communication, intercultural communication, political communication, information management. *Unit head:* Dr. Serafin Mendez-Mendez, Chair, 860-832-2690. *Application contact:* Dr. Serafin Mendez-Mendez, Chair, 860-832-2690.

Central Michigan University, College of Graduate Studies, College of Communication and Fine Arts, Department of Communication and Dramatic Arts, Mount Pleasant, MI 48859. Offers interpersonal and public communication (MA), including communication and dramatic arts.

Communication—General

Central Michigan University (continued)
Part-time programs available. *Faculty:* 14 full-time (8 women). *Students:* 19 full-time (14 women), 22 part-time (18 women); includes 2 African Americans, 1 American Indian/Alaska Native, 1 international. Average age 28. *Degree requirements:* For master's, thesis. *Application deadline:* For fall admission, 3/15 for domestic and international students; for winter admission, 10/15 for domestic and international students; for spring admission, 10/15 for domestic and international students. Applications are processed on a rolling basis. Application fee: $35 ($45 for international students). Electronic applications accepted. *Expenses:* Tuition, state resident: full-time $3717; part-time $413 per credit. Tuition, nonresident: full-time $6894; part-time $766 per credit. *Financial support:* Fellowships with tuition reimbursements, teaching assistantships with tuition reimbursements, career-related internships or fieldwork, Federal Work-Study, unspecified assistantships, and out-of-state merit awards available. *Faculty research:* Communication theory, interpersonal/nonverbal communication, organizational communication, family and interpersonal communication, political communication. *Unit head:* Dr. Neil Vanderpool, Chairperson, 989-774-3177, Fax: 989-774-2498, E-mail: vande2n@cmich.edu. *Application contact:* Dr. Lesley Withers, Graduate Program Coordinator, 989-774-6673, Fax: 989-774-2498, E-mail: withe1la@cmich.edu.

Clarion University of Pennsylvania, Office of Research and Graduate Studies, College of Arts and Sciences, Department of Mass Media Arts, Journalism, and Communication Studies, Clarion, PA 16214. Offers MS. Part-time programs available. *Degree requirements:* For master's, comprehensive exam, thesis or alternative. *Entrance requirements:* For master's, minimum QPA of 3.0. Additional exam requirements/recommendations for international students: Required—TOEFL (minimum score 600 paper-based; 250 computer-based; 100 iBT). Electronic applications accepted.

Clark University, Graduate School, College of Professional and Continuing Education, Program in Professional Communication, Worcester, MA 01610-1477. Offers MSPC. *Students:* 19 full-time (15 women), 22 part-time (13 women); includes 3 minority (1 African American, 1 American Indian/Alaska Native, 1 Hispanic American), 9 international. Average age 30. 12 applicants, 100% accepted, 12 enrolled. In 2008, 33 master's awarded. *Degree requirements:* For master's, thesis optional. *Application deadline:* Applications are processed on a rolling basis. Application fee: $50. Electronic applications accepted. *Expenses:* Tuition: Full-time $34,900; part-time $1091 per credit hour. Required fees: $30. *Unit head:* Max E. Hess, Director of Graduate Studies, 508-793-7217, Fax: 508-793-7232. *Application contact:* Julia Parent, Director of Marketing, Communications, and Admissions, 508-793-7217, Fax: 508-793-7232, E-mail: jparent@clarku.edu.

Clemson University, Graduate School, College of Architecture, Arts, and Humanities, Department of English, Program in Professional Communication, Clemson, SC 29634. Offers MA. Part-time programs available. *Students:* 32 full-time (22 women), 9 part-time (6 women); includes 4 minority (1 African American, 1 Asian American or Pacific Islander, 2 Hispanic Americans), 2 international. Average age 30. 34 applicants, 62% accepted, 15 enrolled. In 2008, 10 master's awarded. *Degree requirements:* For master's, one foreign language, thesis optional, oral exam. *Entrance requirements:* For master's, GRE General Test, minimum GPA of 3.0. Additional exam requirements/recommendations for international students: Required—TOEFL, IELTS. *Application deadline:* For fall admission, 6/1 priority date for domestic students, 4/15 for international students; for spring admission, 12/1 for domestic students, 9/15 for international students. Applications are processed on a rolling basis. Application fee: $55. Full-time tuition and fees vary according to program. *Financial support:* Research assistantships, teaching assistantships available. Financial award application deadline: 4/1; financial award applicants required to submit FAFSA. *Faculty research:* Usability testing, rhetoric, communication across the curriculum, intercultural communication. *Unit head:* Dr. Summer Taylor, Coordinator, 864-656-6689, Fax: 864-656-1345, E-mail: slsmith@clemson.edu. *Application contact:* Dr. Summer Taylor, Coordinator, 864-656-6689, Fax: 864-656-1345, E-mail: slsmith@clemson.edu.

Clemson University, Graduate School, College of Architecture, Arts, and Humanities, Department of English, Program in Rhetorics, Communication and Information Design, Clemson, SC 29634. Offers PhD. *Students:* 22 full-time (10 women), 2 part-time (1 woman); includes 4 minority (3 African Americans, 1 Asian American or Pacific Islander), 4 international. Average age 36. 19 applicants, 37% accepted, 6 enrolled. In 2008, 1 doctorate awarded. *Degree requirements:* For doctorate, thesis/dissertation (for some programs). *Entrance requirements:* For doctorate, GRE, master's degree in English, communications studies, art, professional communication or related field; portfolio; 3 letters of reference; minimum graduate GPA of 3.5. Additional exam requirements/recommendations for international students: Required—TOEFL (minimum score 550 paper-based; 213 computer-based). *Application deadline:* For fall admission, 2/1 priority date for domestic students, 4/15 for international students. Application fee: $55. Full-time tuition and fees vary according to program. *Financial support:* Teaching assistantships available. *Unit head:* Dr. Victor Vitanza, Coordinator, 864-656-6411, Fax: 864-656-0599, E-mail: sophist@clemson.edu. *Application contact:* Dr. Victor Vitanza, Coordinator, 864-656-6411, Fax: 864-656-0599, E-mail: sophist@clemson.edu.

Clemson University, Graduate School, College of Business and Behavioral Science, Department of Graphic Communications, Clemson, SC 29634. Offers MS. *Faculty:* 6 full-time (1 woman), 4 part-time/adjunct (2 women). *Students:* 8 full-time (3 women), 2 part-time (both women); includes 1 minority (African American), 2 international. Average age 28. 6 applicants, 67% accepted, 2 enrolled. In 2008, 6 master's awarded. *Entrance requirements:* For master's, GRE General Test. Additional exam requirements/recommendations for international students: Required—TOEFL. *Application deadline:* For fall admission, 4/15 for international students; for spring admission, 9/15 for international students. Application fee: $55. Full-time tuition and fees vary according to program. *Financial support:* In 2008–09, 8 teaching assistantships (averaging $6,918 per year) were awarded; research assistantships. Financial award applicants required to submit FAFSA. *Unit head:* Dr. Samuel T. Ingram, Chair, 864-656-3447. *Application contact:* Nancy Leininger, 864-656-3447, Fax: 864-656-5344, E-mail: lnancy@clemson.edu.

Cleveland State University, College of Graduate Studies, College of Liberal Arts and Social Sciences, School of Communication, Cleveland, OH 44115. Offers applied communication theory and methodology (MA); culture, communication and health care (Certificate). Part-time and evening/weekend programs available. *Faculty:* 11 full-time (5 women). *Students:* 18 full-time (14 women), 8 part-time (6 women); includes 1 minority (African American), 4 international. Average age 30. 25 applicants, 44% accepted, 9 enrolled. In 2008, 14 master's awarded. *Degree requirements:* For master's, variable foreign language requirement, comprehensive exam (for some programs), thesis optional, thesis, project, comprehensive exam, or collaborative project. *Entrance requirements:* For master's, GRE or MAT, minimum undergraduate GPA of 2.75, 2 letters of recommendation. Additional exam requirements/recommendations for international students: Required—TOEFL (minimum score 525 paper-based; 197 computer-based). *Application deadline:* For fall admission, 8/25 priority date for domestic students, 5/15 priority date for international students; for spring admission, 1/14 priority date for domestic students, 11/1 priority date for international students. Applications are processed on a rolling basis. Application fee: $30. Electronic applications accepted. *Financial support:* In 2008–09, 14 students received support, including 5 research assistantships with full and partial tuition reimbursements available (averaging $11,000 per year), 9 teaching assistantships with full and partial tuition reimbursements available (averaging $11,000 per year); tuition waivers (full) and unspecified assistantships also available. Financial award application deadline: 8/1. *Faculty research:* Interpersonal, organizational, and mass communication; health communication. *Unit head:* Dr. Richard M. Perloff, Director, 216-687-4631, Fax: 216-687-5435, E-mail: r.perloff@csuohio.edu. *Application contact:* Dr. Richard M. Perloff, Director, 216-687-4631, Fax: 216-687-5435, E-mail: r.perloff@csuohio.edu.

The College at Brockport, State University of New York, School of Arts and Performance, Department of Communication, Brockport, NY 14420-2997. Offers MA. Part-time and evening/weekend programs available. *Degree requirements:* For master's, thesis or alternative, research project. *Entrance requirements:* For master's, minimum GPA of 3.0, letters of recommendation. Additional exam requirements/recommendations for international students: Required—TOEFL (minimum score 550 paper-based; 213 computer-based; 79 iBT). *Faculty research:* Organizational communication, rhetorical theory and criticism, media theory and criticism, interpersonal communication, communication theory.

College of Charleston, Graduate School, School of Humanities and Social Sciences, Program in Communication, Charleston, SC 29424-0001. Offers MA. Part-time and evening/weekend programs available. *Faculty:* 20 full-time (10 women). *Students:* 12 full-time (10 women), 15 part-time (13 women); includes 3 minority (1 African American, 1 American Indian/Alaska Native, 1 Asian American or Pacific Islander), 1 international. Average age 27. 22 applicants, 45% accepted, 9 enrolled. *Degree requirements:* For master's, comprehensive exam or thesis. *Entrance requirements:* For master's, GRE, writing sample; 2 letters of recommendation; minimum GPA of 2.75 overall, 3.0 in major. Additional exam requirements/recommendations for international students: Required—TOEFL. *Application deadline:* For fall admission, 4/1 for domestic students; for spring admission, 11/1 for domestic students. Applications are processed on a rolling basis. Application fee: $45. Electronic applications accepted. *Expenses:* Tuition, area resident: Full-time $6624; part-time $368 per credit hour. Tuition, state resident: full-time $6624; part-time $368 per credit hour. Tuition, nonresident: full-time $16,074; part-time $893 per credit hour. Required fees: $30; $30 per course. One-time fee: $45. *Financial support:* Research assistantships, teaching assistantships, career-related internships or fieldwork, scholarships/grants, and unspecified assistantships available. Financial award applicants required to submit FAFSA. *Unit head:* Dr. Vincent Benigni, Director, 844-983-7854, E-mail: fergusond@cofc.edu. *Application contact:* Susan Hallatt, Director of Graduate Admissions, 843-953-5614, Fax: 843-953-1434, E-mail: hallatts@cofc.edu.

The College of New Rochelle, Graduate School, Division of Art and Communication Studies, Program in Communication Studies, New Rochelle, NY 10805-2308. Offers MS, Certificate. Part-time and evening/weekend programs available. *Degree requirements:* For master's, thesis or alternative. *Entrance requirements:* For master's, GRE General Test, interview, minimum GPA of 3.0. Additional exam requirements/recommendations for international students: Required—TOEFL.

College of Notre Dame of Maryland, Graduate Studies, Program in Contemporary Communication, Baltimore, MD 21210-2476. Offers MA. Part-time and evening/weekend programs available. *Degree requirements:* For master's, thesis optional. *Entrance requirements:* For master's, minimum GPA of 3.0. Additional exam requirements/recommendations for international students: Required—TOEFL (minimum score 500 paper-based; 173 computer-based; 61 iBT). Electronic applications accepted.

Columbia University, Graduate School of Business, Doctoral Program in Business, New York, NY 10027. Offers business (PhD), including accounting, decision, risk, and operations, finance and economics, management, marketing. *Accreditation:* AACSB. *Degree requirements:* For doctorate, comprehensive exam, thesis/dissertation, major field exam, research paper, thesis proposal. *Entrance requirements:* For doctorate, GMAT or GRE (finance), 2 letters of reference, resumé. Additional exam requirements/recommendations for international students: Required—TOEFL. Electronic applications accepted. *Expenses:* Contact institution.

Columbia University, Graduate School of Business, MBA Program, New York, NY 10027. Offers accounting (MBA); decision, risk, and operations (MBA); entrepreneurship (MBA); finance and economics (MBA); human resource management (MBA); international business (MBA); management/leadership (MBA); marketing (MBA); media (MBA); real estate (MBA); social enterprise (MBA); DDS/MBA; JD/MBA; MBA/MIA; MBA/MPH; MBA/MS; MD/MBA. *Entrance requirements:* For master's, GMAT, 2 letters of recommendation, official transcripts, essay, personal statement, completed application. Additional exam requirements/recommendations for international students: Required—TOEFL. Electronic applications accepted.

Concordia University, School of Graduate Studies, Faculty of Arts and Science, Department of Communication Studies, Montréal, QC H3G 1M8, Canada. Offers communication (PhD); communication studies (Diploma); media studies (MA). *Degree requirements:* For master's, thesis optional; for doctorate, one foreign language, comprehensive exam, thesis/dissertation, research practicum, seminar. *Entrance requirements:* For master's, bachelor's degree in communications, 2 years of media-related experience; for doctorate, MA in communications. *Faculty research:* Communication and development, organizational communication, cultural studies, rhetoric, future studies.

Cornell University, Graduate School, Graduate Fields of Agriculture and Life Sciences, Field of Communication, Ithaca, NY 14853-0001. Offers communication (MPS, MS, PhD); communication research methods (MS, PhD); international communication (MS, PhD); science and environmental communication (MS, PhD); social psychology of communication (MS, PhD); uses and effects of communication (MS, PhD). *Faculty:* 20 full-time (8 women). *Students:* 31 full-time (20 women); includes 4 minority (2 Asian Americans or Pacific Islanders, 2 Hispanic Americans), 12 international. Average age 30. 158 applicants, 15% accepted, 11 enrolled. In 2008, 10 master's, 1 doctorate awarded. *Degree requirements:* For master's, thesis (MS); for doctorate, comprehensive exam, thesis/dissertation. *Entrance requirements:* For master's and doctorate, GRE General Test, 3 letters of recommendation. Additional exam requirements/recommendations for international students: Required—TOEFL (minimum score 600 paper-based; 250 computer-based; 100 iBT). *Application deadline:* For fall admission, 1/15 for domestic students. Application fee: $70. Electronic applications accepted. *Expenses:* Tuition: Full-time $29,500. Required fees: $70. Full-time tuition and fees vary according to degree level, program and student level. *Financial support:* In 2008–09, 28 students received support, including 3 fellowships with full tuition reimbursements available, 6 research assistantships with full tuition reimbursements available, 19 teaching assistantships with full tuition reimbursements available; institutionally sponsored loans, scholarships/grants, health care benefits, tuition waivers (full and partial), and unspecified assistantships also available. Financial award applicants required to submit FAFSA. *Faculty research:* Mass communication, communication technologies, science and environmental communication. *Unit head:* Director of Graduate Studies, 607-255-2112. *Application contact:* Graduate Field Assistant, 607-255-2112, E-mail: commgrad@cornell.edu.

DePaul University, College of Communication, Chicago, IL 60614. Offers journalism (MA); media, culture and society (MA); organizational and multicultural communication (MA); public relations and advertising (MA). Part-time and evening/weekend programs available. *Faculty:* 31 full-time (17 women), 15 part-time/adjunct (7 women). *Students:* 135 full-time (106 women), 43 part-time (35 women); includes 49 minority (25 African Americans, 7 Asian Americans or Pacific Islanders, 17 Hispanic Americans), 8 international. Average age 29. 242 applicants, 47% accepted, 68 enrolled. In 2008, 64 master's awarded. *Degree requirements:* For master's, comprehensive exam (for some programs), final exam or thesis/project. *Entrance requirements:* For master's, GRE General Test (public relations and advertising), minimum GPA of 3.0, writing sample, essay, letters of recommendation, resumé. Additional exam requirements/recommendations for international students: Required—TOEFL (minimum score 590 paper-based; 245 computer-based; 96 iBT). Application fee: $40. Electronic applications accepted. *Financial support:* In 2008–09, 8 students received support, including 4 research assistantships with partial tuition reimbursements available, 2 teaching assistantships with full tuition reimbursements available (averaging $12,000 per year); fellowships with full tuition reimbursements available, career-related internships or fieldwork, scholarships/grants, and tuition waivers (partial) also available. Support available to part-time students. Financial award applicants required to submit FAFSA. *Faculty research:* Intercultural communication, corporate culture, diversity in the working place, organizational socialization, critical cultural studies. *Unit head:* Dr. Jacqueline Taylor, Dean, 773-325-7216, Fax: 773-325-7584, E-mail: jtaylor@depaul.edu. *Application contact:* Ann Spittle, Director of Graduate Admission, 773-325-8369, Fax: 773-325-2395, E-mail: aspittle@depaul.edu.

DeVry University, Keller Graduate School of Management, Oakbrook Terrace, IL 60181. Offers accounting and financial management (MAFM); business administration (MBA); human resources management (MHRM); information systems management (MISM); network and communications management (MNCM); project management (MPM); public administration (MPA).

Drake University, School of Journalism and Mass Communication, Communication Leadership Program, Des Moines, IA 50311-4516. Offers MCL. *Degree requirements:* For master's, comprehensive exam (for some programs), thesis (for some programs), internships (for some programs).

Drexel University, College of Arts and Sciences, Department of Culture and Communication, Philadelphia, PA 19104-2875. Offers communication (MS), including public communication, science communication, technical communication; publication management (MS). Part-time and evening/weekend programs available. *Degree requirements:* For master's, internship, professional portfolio. *Entrance requirements:* Additional exam requirements/recommendations for international students: Required—TOEFL. Electronic applications accepted. *Faculty research:* Science information and attitudes, science influence on literature, process of technical writing, document design, software documentation.

Drury University, Program in Communication, Springfield, MO 65802. Offers MA. Part-time and evening/weekend programs available. *Entrance requirements:* For master's, GMAT or MAT. Additional exam requirements/recommendations for international students: Required—TOEFL. Electronic applications accepted. *Expenses:* Contact institution.

Duquesne University, Graduate School of Liberal Arts, Department of Communication and Rhetorical Studies, Pittsburgh, PA 15282-0001. Offers communication (MA); rhetoric (PhD). Part-time and evening/weekend programs available. *Faculty:* 6 full-time (3 women), 5 part-time/adjunct (3 women). *Students:* 78 full-time (44 women), 46 part-time (30 women); includes 4 minority (3 African Americans, 1 Hispanic American), 11 international. Average age 27. 38 applicants, 100% accepted, 33 enrolled. In 2008, 19 master's, 9 doctorates awarded. *Degree requirements:* For master's, thesis optional, practicum; for doctorate, 2 foreign languages, comprehensive exam, thesis/dissertation. *Entrance requirements:* For master's, GRE General Test, MAT or GMAT; for doctorate, GRE General Test. Additional exam requirements/recommendations for international students: Required—TOEFL. *Application deadline:* For fall admission, 2/1 priority date for domestic and international students; for spring admission, 11/1 priority date for domestic and international students. Applications are processed on a rolling basis. Application fee: $50. Electronic applications accepted. *Expenses:* Tuition: Part-time $819 per credit. Required fees: $78 per credit. Tuition and fees vary according to course load. *Financial support:* In 2008–09, 9 research assistantships with full tuition reimbursements (averaging $9,000 per year), 10 teaching assistantships with full tuition reimbursements (averaging $13,000 per year) were awarded; career-related internships or fieldwork, Federal Work-Study, institutionally sponsored loans, scholarships/grants, tuition waivers (full and partial), and unspecified assistantships also available. Financial award application deadline: 5/1. *Unit head:* Dr. Ronald Arnett, Chair, 412-396-5076. *Application contact:* Dr. Janie Fritz, Director, 412-396-6460.

Eastern Michigan University, Graduate School, College of Arts and Sciences, Department of Communication and Theatre Arts, Program in Communication, Ypsilanti, MI 48197. Offers MA. Part-time and evening/weekend programs available. Postbaccalaureate distance learning degree programs offered (minimal on-campus study). *Degree requirements:* For master's, thesis or alternative. *Entrance requirements:* Additional exam requirements/recommendations for international students: Required—TOEFL.

Eastern New Mexico University, Graduate School, College of Liberal Arts and Sciences, Department of Communicative Arts and Sciences, Portales, NM 88130. Offers MA. Part-time programs available. Postbaccalaureate distance learning degree programs offered (minimal on-campus study). *Degree requirements:* For master's, comprehensive exam, thesis optional. *Entrance requirements:* For master's, minimum GPA of 2.5. Electronic applications accepted. *Faculty research:* Radio and television production.

Eastern Washington University, Graduate Studies, College of Social and Behavioral Sciences, Department of Communication Studies, Cheney, WA 99004-2431. Offers MSC. Part-time and evening/weekend programs available. *Degree requirements:* For master's, comprehensive exam, thesis or alternative. *Entrance requirements:* For master's, GRE General Test, minimum GPA of 3.0.

East Tennessee State University, School of Graduate Studies, College of Arts and Sciences, Department of Communication, Johnson City, TN 37614. Offers MA. *Entrance requirements:* For master's, GRE. Additional exam requirements/recommendations for international students: Required—TOEFL (minimum score 550 paper-based; 213 computer-based). *Faculty research:* Political communications, visual communication, depictions of gender and ethnicity in print and online media and online corporate media, presidential rhetoric and newspaper coverage of presidential speeches.

Edinboro University of Pennsylvania, Graduate Studies and Research, School of Liberal Arts, Department of Communications and Media Studies, Edinboro, PA 16444. Offers MA. Part-time and evening/weekend programs available. *Faculty:* 4 full-time (1 woman). *Students:* 33 full-time (22 women), 12 part-time (8 women); includes 5 minority (3 African Americans, 1 Asian American or Pacific Islander, 1 Hispanic American), 3 international. Average age 29. In 2008, 20 master's awarded. *Degree requirements:* For master's, thesis or alternative, competency exam. *Entrance requirements:* For master's, GRE or MAT, minimum QPA of 2.5. *Application deadline:* Applications are processed on a rolling basis. Application fee: $30. Electronic applications accepted. *Expenses:* Tuition, state resident: full-time $6430; part-time $357 per credit. Tuition, nonresident: full-time $8038; part-time $572 per credit. International tuition: $15,171.58 full-time. Required fees: $2113; $60 per credit. Tuition and fees vary according to course load. *Financial support:* In 2008–09, 10 research assistantships with full and partial tuition reimbursements (averaging $3,850 per year) were awarded; career-related internships or fieldwork, Federal Work-Study, scholarships/grants, and unspecified assistantships also available. Support available to part-time students. Financial award application deadline: 2/15; financial award applicants required to submit FAFSA. *Unit head:* Dr. Andrew Smith, Program Head, 814-732-2165, E-mail: arsmith@edinboro.edu. *Application contact:* Dr. Andrew Smith, Program Head, 814-732-2165, E-mail: arsmith@edinboro.edu.

Emerson College, Graduate Studies, School of Communication, Department of Communication Studies, Boston, MA 02116-4624. Offers communication management (MA). Part-time programs available. *Students:* 42 full-time (34 women), 9 part-time (7 women); includes 6 minority (1 African American, 1 American Indian/Alaska Native, 4 Asian Americans or Pacific Islanders), 15 international. Average age 26. 41 applicants, 85% accepted, 17 enrolled. In 2008, 26 master's awarded. *Entrance requirements:* For master's, GMAT or GRE General Test. Additional exam requirements/recommendations for international students: Required—TOEFL (minimum score 550 paper-based; 213 computer-based; 80 iBT), IELTS (minimum score 6.5). *Application deadline:* For fall admission, 3/1 for domestic students, 5/1 for international students; for spring admission, 11/1 for domestic and international students. Applications are processed on a rolling basis. Application fee: $60 ($75 for international students). Electronic applications accepted. *Expenses:* Tuition: Full-time $17,720; part-time $886 per credit. Required fees: $60 per year. One-time fee: $170. *Financial support:* In 2008–09, 10 students received support, including 2 fellowships (averaging $14,000 per year), 6 research assistantships (averaging $10,000 per year); career-related internships or fieldwork, Federal Work-Study, institutionally sponsored loans, scholarships/grants, and unspecified assistantships also available. Support available to part-time students. Financial award application deadline: 3/1. *Unit head:* Prof. Linda Gallant, Graduate Program Director, 617-824-8491, E-mail: Linda_Gallant@emerson.edu. *Application contact:* Office of Graduate Admission, 617-824-8610, Fax: 617-824-8614, E-mail: gradapp@emerson.edu.

Fairfield University, College of Arts and Sciences, Fairfield, CT 06824-5195. Offers American studies (MA); communication (MA); creative writing (MFA); mathematics (MS). Part-time and evening/weekend programs available. *Faculty:* 46 full-time (20 women), 15 part-time/adjunct (7 women). *Students:* 6 full-time (1 woman), 53 part-time (26 women); includes 1 African American, 2 Hispanic Americans. Average age 41. 23 applicants, 78% accepted, 14 enrolled. In 2008, 36 master's awarded. *Degree requirements:* For master's, capstone research course. *Entrance requirements:* For master's, minimum GPA of 3.0, 2 letters of recommendation, resumé, essay. Additional exam requirements/recommendations for international students: Required—TOEFL (minimum score 550 paper-based; 213 computer-based; 80 iBT). *Application deadline:* For fall admission, 5/15 for international students; for spring admission, 10/15 for international students. Applications are processed on a rolling basis. Application fee: $60. Electronic applications accepted. *Expenses:* Tuition: Full-time $9450; part-time $525 per credit hour. Required fees: $25 per semester. Tuition and fees vary according to course load and program. *Financial support:* In 2008–09, 19 students received support. Unspecified assistantships available. Financial award applicants required to submit FAFSA. *Faculty research:* Non-commutative algebra, partial differential equations, writing (fiction, non-fiction and poetry), communication for social change, comparative media systems, negotiation and management. *Unit head:* Dr. Robbin Crabtree, Dean, 203-254-4000 Ext. 3263, Fax: 203-254-4119, E-mail: rcrabtree@fairfield.edu. *Application contact:* Marianne Gumpper, Director of Graduate and Continuing Studies Admissions, 203-254-4184, Fax: 203-254-4073, E-mail: gradadmis@fairfield.edu.

Fairleigh Dickinson University, Metropolitan Campus, University College: Arts, Sciences, and Professional Studies, School of Art and Media Studies, Program in Media and Communications, Teaneck, NJ 07666-1914. Offers MA. *Students:* 6 full-time (5 women), 12 part-time (7 women), 5 international. Average age 31. 15 applicants, 67% accepted, 7 enrolled. In 2008, 4 master's awarded. Application fee: $40. *Application contact:* Susan Brooman, University Director of Graduate Admissions, 201-692-2554, Fax: 201-692-2560, E-mail: globaleducation@fdu.edu.

Fitchburg State College, Division of Graduate and Continuing Education, Program in Applied Communications, Fitchburg, MA 01420-2697. Offers applied communications (MS, Certificate); library media (MS); technical and professional writing (MS). Part-time and evening/weekend programs available. *Students:* 1 (woman) full-time, 6 part-time (4 women). Average age 40. 6 applicants, 100% accepted, 5 enrolled. In 2008, 3 master's awarded. *Entrance requirements:* For master's, GRE General Test or MAT, minimum 2 years of related experience, letters of recommendation, resumé. Additional exam requirements/recommendations for international students: Required—TOEFL (minimum score 550 paper-based; 213 computer-based; 79 iBT). *Application deadline:* Applications are processed on a rolling basis. Application fee: $25 ($50 for international students). *Expenses:* Tuition, state resident: full-time $3600; part-time $150 per credit. Tuition, nonresident: full-time $3600; part-time $150 per credit. Required fees: $109 per credit. *Financial support:* In 2008–09, research assistantships with partial tuition reimbursements (averaging $5,500 per year); Federal Work-Study, scholarships/grants, and unspecified assistantships also available. Support available to part-time students. Financial award application deadline: 3/1; financial award applicants required to submit FAFSA. *Unit head:* Dr. John Chetro-Szivos, Chair, 978-665-3261, Fax: 978-665-3658, E-mail: gce@fsc.edu. *Application contact:* Director of Admissions, 978-665-3144, Fax: 978-665-4540, E-mail: admissions@fsc.edu.

Florida Atlantic University, Dorothy F. Schmidt College of Arts and Letters, School of Communication and Multimedia Studies, Boca Raton, FL 33431-0991. Offers communication studies (MA); film and video (Certificate); film studies (MA); multimedia journalism studies (MA). Part-time programs available. *Faculty:* 21 full-time (10 women), 14 part-time/adjunct (3 women). *Students:* 15 full-time (11 women), 10 part-time (5 women); includes 2 minority (1 Asian American or Pacific Islander, 1 Hispanic American), 3 international. Average age 29. 35 applicants, 37% accepted, 7 enrolled. In 2008, 8 master's awarded. *Degree requirements:* For master's, one foreign language, comprehensive exam (for some programs), thesis (for some programs). *Entrance requirements:* For master's, GRE General Test, minimum GPA of 3.0. *Application deadline:* For fall admission, 7/1 priority date for domestic students, 4/1 for international students; for spring admission, 11/1 for domestic students, 10/1 for international students. Applications are processed on a rolling basis. Application fee: $30. Electronic applications accepted. *Expenses:* Tuition, state resident: full-time $4867; part-time $270.40 per credit hour. Tuition, nonresident: full-time $16,486; part-time $915.87 per credit hour. *Financial support:* Teaching assistantships with partial tuition reimbursements, Federal Work-Study and institutionally sponsored loans available. Support available to part-time students. Financial award application deadline: 3/1. *Faculty research:* Cultural studies, gender studies, film, communication theory, journalism, new media. *Unit head:* Dr. Susan S. Reilly, Director, 561-297-1095, Fax: 561-297-2615, E-mail: sreilly@fau.edu. *Application contact:* Dr. Eric M. Freedman, Graduate Coordinator, 561-297-2534, Fax: 561-297-2615, E-mail: efreedma@fau.edu.

Florida Institute of Technology, Graduate Programs, College of Psychology and Liberal Arts, Department of Humanities and Communication, Melbourne, FL 32901-6975. Offers communication (MS). Part-time and evening/weekend programs available. *Degree requirements:* For master's, comprehensive exam (for some programs), thesis (for some programs). *Entrance requirements:* For master's, GRE General Test, minimum GPA of 3.0, 2 letters of recommendation, writing sample. Additional exam requirements/recommendations for international students: Required—TOEFL (minimum score 550 paper-based; 213 computer-based). Electronic applications accepted. *Expenses:* Tuition: Part-time $980 per credit hour. *Faculty research:* Communication of astronomy in the 17th century, persuasion and patronage in 17th century work, technical and cross-cultural communication.

Florida State University, Graduate Studies, College of Communication, Department of Communication, Tallahassee, FL 32306. Offers corporate and public communication (MA, MS); integrated marketing communication (MA, MS); mass communication (PhD); media and communication studies (MA, MS); speech communication (PhD). Part-time programs available. *Degree requirements:* For master's, thesis (for some programs); for doctorate, comprehensive exam, thesis/dissertation. *Entrance requirements:* For master's, GRE General Test, minimum GPA of 3.0; for doctorate, GRE General Test, minimum GPA of 3.3 in graduate course work. Additional exam requirements/recommendations for international students: Required—TOEFL (minimum score 600 paper-based; 250 computer-based; 100 iBT). *Faculty research:* Communication technology and policy, marketing communication, communication content and effect, new communication/information technologies.

Fordham University, Graduate School of Arts and Sciences, Department of Communication and Media Studies, New York, NY 10458. Offers public communications (MA). Part-time and evening/weekend programs available. *Degree requirements:* For master's, thesis, internship. *Entrance requirements:* For master's, GRE General Test. Additional exam requirements/recommendations for international students: Required—TOEFL (minimum score 600 paper-based; 250 computer-based). Electronic applications accepted.

Fort Hays State University, Graduate School, College of Arts and Sciences, Department of Communication, Hays, KS 67601-4099. Offers MS. Part-time programs available. *Degree requirements:* For master's, comprehensive exam, thesis optional. *Entrance requirements:* Additional exam requirements/recommendations for international students: Required—TOEFL (minimum score 550 paper-based; 213 computer-based). Electronic applications accepted. *Faculty research:* Listening skills development, oral sensory motor skills, speech, reading, articulation in preschool children.

George Mason University, College of Humanities and Social Sciences, Program in Communications, Fairfax, VA 22030. Offers MA, PhD. *Entrance requirements:* For master's, GRE or MAT, minimum GPA of 3.0 in last 60 undergraduate hours, 3 letters of recommendation.

Communication—General

Georgetown University, Graduate School of Arts and Sciences, Program in Communication, Culture, and Technology, Washington, DC 20057. Offers MA. Part-time and evening/weekend programs available. *Degree requirements:* For master's, thesis (for some programs). *Entrance requirements:* For master's, GRE General Test, 3 letters of recommendation, writing sample. Additional exam requirements/recommendations for international students: Required—TOEFL (minimum score 600 paper-based; 250 computer-based). Electronic applications accepted.

The George Washington University, Elliott School of International Affairs, Program in Global Communication, Washington, DC 20052. Offers MA. *Students:* 4 full-time (3 women), 5 part-time (all women); includes 1 minority (Hispanic American), 1 international. Average age 26. 21 applicants, 67% accepted, 7 enrolled. *Application deadline:* For fall admission, 2/1 for domestic students; for spring admission, 10/1 for domestic students. *Financial support:* Application deadline: 1/15. *Unit head:* Sean Aday, Director, 202-994-4220, Fax: 202-994-5806, E-mail: seanaday@gwu.edu. *Application contact:* Jeff V. Miles, Director of Graduate Admissions, 202-994-7050, Fax: 202-994-9537, E-mail: esiagrad@gwu.edu.

Georgia State University, College of Arts and Sciences, Department of Communication, Atlanta, GA 30303-3083. Offers film/video/digital imaging (MA); human communication and social influence (MA); mass communication (MA); moving image studies (PhD); public communication (PhD). Part-time programs available. *Degree requirements:* For master's, one foreign language, thesis or alternative; for doctorate, comprehensive exam, thesis/dissertation. *Entrance requirements:* For master's and doctorate, GRE General Test. Additional exam requirements/recommendations for international students: Required—TOEFL (minimum score 80 computer-based). Electronic applications accepted. *Faculty research:* Critical/cultural studies, rhetoric studies, film/media studies, mass communications/journalism, audience studies.

Gonzaga University, School of Professional Studies, Program in Communication and Leadership Studies, Spokane, WA 99258. Offers MA. Postbaccalaureate distance learning degree programs offered.

Governors State University, College of Arts and Sciences, Program in Communication and Training, University Park, IL 60466-0975. Offers communication studies (MA); instructional and training technology (MA); media communication (MA). Part-time and evening/weekend programs available. *Degree requirements:* For master's, thesis or alternative.

Grand Valley State University, College of Liberal Arts and Sciences, School of Communications, Allendale, MI 49401-9403. Offers MS. Part-time and evening/weekend programs available. *Faculty:* 3 full-time (1 woman), 2 part-time/adjunct (0 women). *Students:* 14 full-time (12 women), 37 part-time (23 women); includes 13 minority (8 African Americans, 2 Asian Americans or Pacific Islanders, 3 Hispanic Americans), 5 international. Average age 31. 17 applicants, 88% accepted, 10 enrolled. In 2008, 25 master's awarded. *Degree requirements:* For master's, thesis or alternative. *Entrance requirements:* For master's, minimum GPA of 3.0 in last 60 hours, 2 letters of recommendation. Additional exam requirements/recommendations for international students: Required—TOEFL (minimum score 550 paper-based; 213 computer-based). *Application deadline:* For fall admission, 8/15 priority date for domestic students; for winter admission, 12/15 priority date for domestic students; for spring admission, 4/15 priority date for domestic students. Applications are processed on a rolling basis. Application fee: $30. Electronic applications accepted. *Financial support:* In 2008–09, 5 research assistantships with tuition reimbursements (averaging $8,000 per year) were awarded; career-related internships or fieldwork, Federal Work-Study, and institutionally sponsored loans also available. Support available to part-time students. Financial award application deadline: 4/15. *Faculty research:* Communication technology, databases, organizational communication, systems theory, public relations and advertising. *Unit head:* Dr. Alex Nesterenko, Director, 616-331-3668, Fax: 616-895-2700, E-mail: nesterea@gvsu.edu. *Application contact:* Dr. William Michael Pritchard, Coordinator, 616-331-3668, Fax: 616-331-2700, E-mail: pritchmi@gvsu.edu.

Harvard University, Extension School, Cambridge, MA 02138-3722. Offers applied sciences (CAS); biotechnology (ALM); educational technologies (ALM); educational technology (CET); English for graduate and professional studies (DGP); environmental management (ALM, CEM); information technology (ALM); journalism (ALM); liberal arts (ALM); management (ALM, CM); mathematics for teaching (ALM); museum studies (ALM); premedical studies (Diploma); publication and communication (CPC). Part-time and evening/weekend programs available. *Degree requirements:* For master's, thesis. *Entrance requirements:* For master's, 3 completed graduate courses with grade of B or higher. Additional exam requirements/recommendations for international students: Required—TOEFL (minimum score 600 paper-based; 250 computer-based), TWE (minimum score 5). *Expenses:* Contact institution.

Hawai'i Pacific University, College of Communication, Honolulu, HI 96813. Offers MA. Part-time and evening/weekend programs available. *Faculty:* 11 full-time (4 women), 3 part-time/adjunct (1 woman). *Students:* 66 full-time (47 women), 51 part-time (33 women); includes 35 minority (7 African Americans, 2 American Indian/Alaska Native, 23 Asian Americans or Pacific Islanders, 3 Hispanic Americans), 40 international. Average age 28. 75 applicants, 81% accepted, 29 enrolled. In 2008, 36 master's awarded. *Degree requirements:* For master's, thesis. *Entrance requirements:* Additional exam requirements/recommendations for international students: Recommended—TOEFL (minimum score 550 paper-based; 213 computer-based; 80 iBT), TWE (minimum score 5). *Application deadline:* For fall admission, 2/15 priority date for domestic students; for spring admission, 10/15 priority date for domestic students. Applications are processed on a rolling basis. Application fee: $50. Electronic applications accepted. *Expenses:* Tuition: Full-time $10,800; part-time $600 per credit. *Financial support:* In 2008–09, 65 students received support. Career-related internships or fieldwork, Federal Work-Study, scholarships/grants, and unspecified assistantships available. Support available to part-time students. Financial award application deadline: 3/1; financial award applicants required to submit FAFSA. *Unit head:* Dr. Steven Combs, Dean, 808-544-0828, Fax: 808-544-0835, E-mail: scombs@hpu.edu. *Application contact:* Danny Lam, Assistant Director of Graduate Admissions, 808-544-1135, Fax: 808-544-0280, E-mail: graduate@hpu.edu.

See Close-Up on page 689.

Hofstra University, School of Communication, Hempstead, NY 11549. Offers MA, MFA. Part-time and evening/weekend programs available. *Faculty:* 10 full-time (5 women), 5 part-time/adjunct (2 women). *Students:* 26 full-time (11 women), 29 part-time (18 women); includes 13 minority (7 African Americans, 3 Asian Americans or Pacific Islanders, 3 Hispanic Americans), 1 international. Average age 28. 56 applicants, 93% accepted, 25 enrolled. In 2008, 6 master's awarded. *Degree requirements:* For master's, comprehensive exam (for some programs), thesis (for some programs). *Entrance requirements:* For master's, letters of recommendation, interview. Additional exam requirements/recommendations for international students: Required—TOEFL (minimum score 550 paper-based; 213 computer-based; 80 iBT). *Application deadline:* Applications are processed on a rolling basis. Application fee: $60. Electronic applications accepted. *Expenses:* Tuition: Full-time $15,300; part-time $850 per credit. Required fees: $970; $165 per term. Tuition and fees vary according to program. *Financial support:* In 2008–09, 28 students received support, including 4 fellowships with full and partial tuition reimbursements available (averaging $3,325 per year), 2 research assistantships with full and partial tuition reimbursements available (averaging $9,480 per year); Federal Work-Study, institutionally sponsored loans, scholarships/grants, tuition waivers (full and partial), and unspecified assistantships also available. Support available to part-time students. Financial award applicants required to submit FAFSA. *Faculty research:* Public deliberation, rhetoric and labor, nonfiction media production or documentary film, community journalism, journalism history. *Unit head:* Dr. Cliff Jernigan, Acting Dean, 516-463-5214, Fax: 516-463-4866, E-mail: avfczj@hofstra.edu. *Application contact:* Carol Drummer, Dean of Graduate Admissions, 516-463-4876, Fax: 516-463-4664, E-mail: gradstudent@hofstra.edu.

Howard University, School of Communications, Washington, DC 20059-0002. Offers MA, MFA, MS, PhD. Part-time and evening/weekend programs available. Terminal master's awarded for partial completion of doctoral program. *Degree requirements:* For master's, comprehensive exam (for some programs), thesis optional; for doctorate, one foreign language, comprehensive exam, thesis/dissertation. *Entrance requirements:* For master's, GRE General Test, minimum GPA of 3.0; for doctorate, GRE General Test, minimum GPA of 3.2. Additional exam requirements/recommendations for international students: Required—TOEFL. Electronic applications accepted. *Expenses:* Contact institution. *Faculty research:* Communication disorders, intercultural communication, communication skills, race and media.

Illinois Institute of Technology, Graduate College, College of Science and Letters, Lewis Department of Humanities, Chicago, IL 60616-3793. Offers information architecture (MS); technical communication (PhD); technical communication and information design (MS). Part-time and evening/weekend programs available. *Faculty:* 17 full-time (6 women), 11 part-time/adjunct (4 women). *Students:* 9 full-time (5 women), 32 part-time (24 women); includes 13 minority (9 African Americans, 3 Asian Americans or Pacific Islanders, 1 Hispanic American), 6 international. Average age 34. 52 applicants, 44% accepted, 27 enrolled. In 2008, 9 master's, 2 doctorates awarded. *Degree requirements:* For master's, comprehensive exam, thesis or alternative, project; for doctorate, comprehensive exam, thesis/dissertation, qualifying exam. *Entrance requirements:* For master's, GRE General Test; for doctorate, GRE General Test, bachelor's degree in technical communication or other relevant field. Additional exam requirements/recommendations for international students: Required—TOEFL (minimum score 550 paper-based; 213 computer-based; 80 iBT). *Application deadline:* For fall admission, 5/1 for domestic and international students; for spring admission, 1/5 for domestic and international students. Applications are processed on a rolling basis. Application fee: $40. Electronic applications accepted. *Financial support:* In 2008–09, 15 teaching assistantships with partial tuition reimbursements (averaging $9,000 per year) were awarded; career-related internships or fieldwork, Federal Work-Study, institutionally sponsored loans, scholarships/grants, health care benefits, tuition waivers (partial), and unspecified assistantships also available. Support available to part-time students. Financial award applicants required to submit FAFSA. *Faculty research:* Discourse analysis, linguistics, readability, ethics in professions, instructional and document design, knowledge management, usability testing and evaluation, history and philosophy of science. Total annual research expenditures: $34,161. *Unit head:* Kathryn Riley, Professor and Chair, 312-567-3566, Fax: 312-567-5187, E-mail: riley@iit.edu. *Application contact:* Morgan Frederick, Assistant Director of Graduate Communications, 866-472-3448, Fax: 312-567-3138, E-mail: inquiry.grad@iit.edu.

Illinois State University, Graduate School, College of Arts and Sciences, School of Communication, Normal, IL 61790-2200. Offers MA, MS. *Degree requirements:* For master's, thesis or alternative. *Entrance requirements:* For master's, GRE General Test, minimum GPA of 2.8 in last 60 hours of course work. Additional exam requirements/recommendations for international students: Required—TOEFL. *Faculty research:* Corporation for public broadcasting, FY2007, community service grant for WGLT-FM, Illinois public broadcasting grant FY2007 for WGLT-FM; WGLT digital conversion fund.

Indiana State University, School of Graduate Studies, College of Arts and Sciences, Department of Communication, Terre Haute, IN 47809-1401. Offers communication studies (MA, MS); radio, television and film (MA, MS). Part-time programs available. *Degree requirements:* For master's, thesis (for some programs), oral and written exam. *Entrance requirements:* For master's, GRE General Test. Additional exam requirements/recommendations for international students: Required—TOEFL. *Faculty research:* Women in media, communication apprehension, media history.

Indiana University Bloomington, University Graduate School, College of Arts and Sciences, Department of Telecommunications, Bloomington, IN 47405-7000. Offers mass communications (PhD); telecommunications (MA, MS). *Faculty:* 11 full-time (4 women). *Students:* 69 full-time (31 women); includes 8 minority (5 African Americans, 2 Asian Americans or Pacific Islanders, 1 Hispanic American), 38 international. Average age 31. 52 applicants, 52% accepted, 17 enrolled. In 2008, 17 master's, 8 doctorates awarded. Terminal master's awarded for partial completion of doctoral program. *Degree requirements:* For master's, thesis (for some programs); for doctorate, thesis/dissertation. *Entrance requirements:* For master's and doctorate, GRE General Test. Additional exam requirements/recommendations for international students: Required—TOEFL. *Application deadline:* For fall admission, 1/15 priority date for domestic students, 12/15 for international students. Applications are processed on a rolling basis. Application fee: $50 ($60 for international students). *Expenses:* Tuition, area resident: Part-time $291.97 per credit hour. Tuition, state resident: part-time $291.97 per credit hour. Tuition, nonresident: part-time $850.33 per credit hour. Required fees: $110 per semester. Tuition and fees vary according to course load and program. *Financial support:* Fellowships, research assistantships, teaching assistantships, tuition waivers (full) available. *Faculty research:* Media processes and effects, media law and policy, media management, media design and production. *Unit head:* Tamera Theodore, Graduate Secretary, 812-855-2017, E-mail: ttheodor@indiana.edu. *Application contact:* Tamera Theodore, Graduate Secretary, 812-855-2017, E-mail: ttheodor@indiana.edu.

Announcement: Our goal is to train media experts. The MS degree prepares students for careers in production (games, other interactive media) or management. MA and PhD degrees prepare students for careers in media research as media consultants or academics. The PhD program is ranked among the top 12 in the country. The department offers state-of-the-art teaching, research, and production facilities. Funding is available for all three degrees. Visit www.indiana.edu/~telecom/index.html.

Indiana University of Pennsylvania, School of Graduate Studies and Research, College of Education and Educational Technology, Department of Communications Media, Indiana, PA 15705-1087. Offers adult education and communications technology (MA); communications media and instructional technology (PhD). *Faculty:* 5 full-time (0 women). *Students:* 8 full-time (2 women), 13 part-time (7 women); includes 2 minority (1 African American, 1 Asian American or Pacific Islander), 1 international. Average age 34. 33 applicants, 64% accepted, 21 enrolled. *Expenses:* Tuition, area resident: Full-time $6430; part-time $357 per credit. Tuition, nonresident: full-time $10,288; part-time $572 per credit. Required fees: $1547.50; $107 per credit. $283 per year. *Financial support:* In 2008–09, 4 research assistantships (averaging $5,801 per year), 3 teaching assistantships (averaging $20,909 per year) were awarded. *Unit head:* Dr. Mark Piwinsky, Chairperson, 724-357-3954, Fax: 724-357-5503, E-mail: Mark.Piwinsky@iup.edu. *Application contact:* Dr. Edward Nardi, Associate Dean, 724-357-2480, Fax: 724-357-5595, E-mail: ewnardi@iup.edu.

Indiana University–Purdue University Fort Wayne, College of Arts and Sciences, Department of Communication, Fort Wayne, IN 46805-1499. Offers professional communication (MA, MS). Part-time programs available. *Faculty:* 8 full-time (4 women), 1 (woman) part-time/adjunct. *Students:* 6 full-time (3 women), 16 part-time (9 women); includes 2 minority (both African Americans), 1 international. Average age 33. 12 applicants, 100% accepted, 9 enrolled. In 2008, 14 master's awarded. *Degree requirements:* For master's, oral exam. *Entrance requirements:* For master's, GRE General Test, minimum GPA of 3.0. Additional exam requirements/recommendations for international students: Required—TOEFL (minimum score 550 paper-based; 213 computer-based; 77 iBT). *Application deadline:* For fall admission, 2/15 priority date for domestic and international students; for spring admission, 9/15 priority date for domestic and international students. Applications are processed on a rolling basis. Application fee: $55. Electronic applications accepted. *Expenses:* Tuition, area resident: Full-time $4376; part-time $243 per credit. Tuition, state resident: full-time $4376; part-time $243 per credit. Tuition, nonresident: full-time $10,337; part-time $574 per credit. Required fees: $503; $27.95 per credit. Tuition and fees vary according to course load. *Financial support:* In 2008–09, 7 teaching assistantships with partial tuition reimbursements (averaging $12,740 per year) were awarded; scholarships/grants also available. Support available to part-time students. Financial award application deadline: 3/1; financial award applicants required to submit FAFSA. *Faculty research:* Displacing race, New York ethnic slum films. *Unit head:* Dr. Marcia Dixson, Chair and Associate Professor, 260-481-6558, Fax: 260-481-6183, E-mail: dixson@po.ipfw.edu. *Application* *contact:* Dr. Steven Carr, Graduate Program Director, 260-481-6545, Fax: 260-481-6183, E-mail: carr@ipfw.edu.

Instituto Tecnológico y de Estudios Superiores de Monterrey, Campus Ciudad Obregón, Programs in Education, Program in Communications, Ciudad Obregón, Mexico. Offers ME.

Instituto Tecnológico y de Estudios Superiores de Monterrey, Campus Monterrey, Graduate and Research Division, Program in Natural and Social Sciences, Monterrey, Mexico. Offers biotechnology (MS); chemistry (MS, PhD); communications (MS); education (MA). Part-time programs available. *Degree requirements:* For master's, one foreign language, thesis; for doctorate, one foreign language, thesis/dissertation. *Entrance requirements:* For master's, EXADEP; for doctorate, EXADEP, master's degree in related field. Additional exam requirements/recommendations for international students: Required—TOEFL. *Faculty research:* Cultural industries, mineral substances, bioremediation, food processing, CQ in industrial chemical processing.

International University in Geneva, Master of Arts in Media and Communication Program, Geneva, Switzerland. Offers luxury management (MA); marketing (MA). *Faculty:* 9 full-time (2 women), 23 part-time/adjunct (11 women). *Students:* 7 full-time (all women); includes 1 Asian American or Pacific Islander, 1 Hispanic American. Average age 31. 30 applicants, 53% accepted, 7 enrolled. In 2008, 1 master's awarded. *Degree requirements:* For master's, comprehensive exam. *Entrance requirements:* Additional exam requirements/recommendations for international students: Required—TOEFL. *Application deadline:* For fall admission, 7/31 priority date for domestic students, 7/1 priority date for international students; for winter admission, 11/2 priority date for domestic students, 10/9 priority date for international students; for spring admission, 2/12 priority date for domestic students, 1/22 priority date for international students. Applications are processed on a rolling basis. Application fee: $150. Electronic applications accepted. *Unit head:* Dr. Leonid Androuchko, Unit Coordinator, 41-22710-7110, Fax: 41-22710-7111, E-mail: info@iun.ch. *Application contact:* Uliana Horler, Admissions Officer, 41-22710-7110, Fax: 41-22710-7111, E-mail: master@iun.ch.

Ithaca College, Division of Graduate and Professional Studies, Roy H. Park School of Communications, Program in Communications, Ithaca, NY 14850-7020. Offers MS. Part-time programs available. *Faculty:* 6 full-time (1 woman). *Students:* 22 full-time (16 women), 10 part-time (7 women); includes 1 minority (African American), 8 international. Average age 28. 39 applicants, 74% accepted, 16 enrolled. In 2008, 20 master's awarded. *Degree requirements:* For master's, comprehensive exam (for some programs), thesis optional. *Entrance requirements:* For master's, minimum GPA of 3.0. Additional exam requirements/recommendations for international students: Required—TOEFL (minimum score 550 paper-based; 213 computer-based; 80 iBT). *Application deadline:* For fall admission, 7/1 for domestic and international students; for spring admission, 12/1 for domestic and international students. Applications are processed on a rolling basis. Application fee: $40. Electronic applications accepted. *Expenses:* Tuition: Full-time $18,090; part-time $603 per hour. *Financial support:* In 2008–09, 27 students received support, including 18 teaching assistantships (averaging $7,360 per year); career-related internships or fieldwork, Federal Work-Study, scholarships/grants, and unspecified assistantships also available. Support available to part-time students. Financial award application deadline: 3/1; financial award applicants required to submit FAFSA. *Faculty research:* Corporate communication systems, technology in the workforce, crises and diversity, social marketing, instructional design. *Unit head:* Dr. Howard Kalman, Chairperson of the Graduate Programs in Communications, 607-274-3527, Fax: 607-274-1263, E-mail: gps@ithaca.edu. *Application contact:* Rob Gearhart, Interim Dean, Graduate and Professional Studies, 607-274-3527, Fax: 607-274-1263, E-mail: gps@ithaca.edu.

The Johns Hopkins University, Zanvyl Krieger School of Arts and Sciences, Advanced Academic Programs, Program in Communication in Contemporary Society, Washington, DC 20036. Offers MA, MA/MBA. Part-time and evening/weekend programs available. *Degree requirements:* For master's, thesis. *Entrance requirements:* For master's, minimum GPA of 3.0, strong writing skills. Additional exam requirements/recommendations for international students: Required—TOEFL (minimum score 250 computer-based; 100 iBT). Electronic applications accepted.

Kansas State University, Graduate School, College of Arts and Sciences, Department of Communication Studies, Theatre and Dance, Manhattan, KS 66505. Offers rhetoric/communication (MA); theatre (MA). *Faculty:* 16 full-time (8 women). *Students:* 30 full-time (24 women), 7 part-time (2 women); includes 4 minority (1 African American, 1 American Indian/Alaska Native, 1 Asian American or Pacific Islander, 1 Hispanic American), 1 international. Average age 27. 11 applicants, 100% accepted, 7 enrolled. In 2008, 12 master's awarded. *Degree requirements:* For master's, thesis or alternative. *Entrance requirements:* For master's, GRE General Test (recommended), minimum GPA of 3.0. Additional exam requirements/recommendations for international students: Required—TOEFL. *Application deadline:* For fall admission, 3/1 for domestic students, 2/1 priority date for international students; for spring admission, 10/1 for domestic students, 8/1 priority date for international students. Applications are processed on a rolling basis. Application fee: $30 ($55 for international students). *Expenses:* Tuition, area resident: Full-time $6466; part-time $269.40 per credit hour. Tuition, state resident: full-time $6466; part-time $269.40 per credit hour. Tuition, nonresident: full-time $14,874; part-time $619.75 per credit hour. Required fees: $673; $23.40 per credit hour. Tuition and fees vary according to campus/location. *Financial support:* In 2008–09, 27 teaching assistantships with full tuition reimbursements (averaging $10,111 per year) were awarded; career-related internships or fieldwork, institutionally sponsored loans, and scholarships/grants also available. Support available to part-time students. Financial award application deadline: 3/1; financial award applicants required to submit FAFSA. *Faculty research:* Drama therapy, directing, costume design, scenic design, and technical theatre mechanics and safety. *Unit head:* Charles Griffin, Head, 785-532-6860, Fax: 785-532-3714, E-mail: charlieg@ksu.edu. *Application contact:* William Schenck-Hamlin, Director, 785-532-6861, Fax: 785-532-3714, E-mail: billsh@ksu.edu.

Kean University, College of Humanities and Social Sciences, Program in Communication Studies, Union, NJ 07083. Offers MA. Part-time and evening/weekend programs available. *Faculty:* 7 full-time (3 women). *Students:* 8 full-time (7 women), 9 part-time (8 women); includes 4 African Americans, 1 Asian American or Pacific Islander, 3 Hispanic Americans, 4 international. Average age 30. 11 applicants, 45% accepted, 4 enrolled. In 2008, 5 master's awarded. *Degree requirements:* For master's, comprehensive exam, thesis optional. *Entrance requirements:* For master's, GRE General Test, minimum GPA of 3.0, 3 letters of recommendation, interview, personal statement/essay. *Application deadline:* For fall admission, 5/1 for domestic students; for spring admission, 11/1 for domestic students. Application fee: $60 ($150 for international students). Electronic applications accepted. *Expenses:* Tuition, state resident: full-time $10,128; part-time $422 per credit. Tuition, nonresident: full-time $13,728; part-time $572 per credit. Required fees: $2570; $107 per credit. Part-time tuition and fees vary according to course load, degree level and program. *Financial support:* In 2008–09, 4 research assistantships with full tuition reimbursements (averaging $3,217 per year) were awarded; unspecified assistantships also available. *Unit head:* Dr. Wenli Yuan, Program Coordinator, 908-737-0441, E-mail: wyuan@kean.edu. *Application contact:* Steven Koch, Pre-Admissions Coordinator, 908-737-4723, Fax: 908-737-5965, E-mail: grad-adm@kean.edu.

Kent State University, College of Communication and Information, School of Communication Studies, Kent, OH 44242-0001. Offers MA, PhD. *Degree requirements:* For master's, thesis optional; for doctorate, variable foreign language requirement, thesis/dissertation. *Entrance requirements:* For master's and doctorate, GRE General Test, minimum GPA of 3.0. Additional exam requirements/recommendations for international students: Required—TOEFL (minimum score 600 paper-based), TWE (minimum score 5). Electronic applications accepted. *Faculty research:* Interpersonal communication, organizational communication, mass communication, new technologies and communication.

Lasell College, Graduate and Professional Studies in Communication, Newton, MA 02466-2709. Offers integrated marketing communication (MSC, Graduate Certificate); public relations (MSC, Graduate Certificate). Part-time and evening/weekend programs available. Postbaccalaureate distance learning degree programs offered (minimal on-campus study). *Entrance requirements:* For master's and Graduate Certificate, bachelor's degree from an accredited institution. Additional exam requirements/recommendations for international students: Required—TOEFL (minimum score 550 paper-based; 213 computer-based; 79 iBT), IELTS (minimum score 6). *Application deadline:* For fall admission, 8/30 priority date for domestic and international students; for winter admission, 11/30 priority date for domestic and international students; for spring admission, 12/30 priority date for domestic and international students. Applications are processed on a rolling basis. Application fee: $40. Electronic applications accepted. *Expenses:* Tuition: Full-time $4500; part-time $500 per credit hour. Required fees: $55 per term. *Financial support:* Institutionally sponsored loans available. Support available to part-time students. Financial award application deadline: 8/30; financial award applicants required to submit FAFSA. *Unit head:* Dr. Janice Barrett, Chair, Department of Communication, 617-243-2400, E-mail: gradinfo@lasell.edu. *Application contact:* Adrienne Franciosi, Director of Graduate Admission, 617-243-2400, Fax: 617-243-2450, E-mail: gradinfo@lasell.edu.

La Sierra University, College of Arts and Sciences, Department of English and Communication, Riverside, CA 92515. Offers communication (MA), including public relations/advertising, theory emphasis; English (MA), including literary emphasis, writing emphasis. Part-time programs available. *Degree requirements:* For master's, one foreign language. *Entrance requirements:* For master's, GRE General Test.

Liberty University, School of Communications, Lynchburg, VA 24502. Offers MA. Part-time programs available. *Degree requirements:* For master's, thesis. *Entrance requirements:* For master's, minimum undergraduate GPA of 3.0, 2 faculty recommendations, 1 pastoral recommendation. Additional exam requirements/recommendations for international students: Required—TOEFL (minimum score 600 paper-based; 250 computer-based). Electronic applications accepted. *Expenses:* Tuition: Full-time $7286; part-time $1779 per semester. Required fees: $150 per semester.

Lindenwood University, Graduate Programs, College of Individualized Education, St. Charles, MO 63301-1695. Offers administration (MSA); business administration (MBA); communication (MS); communications (MA); criminal justice and administration (MS); gerontology (MA); health management (MS); human resource management (MS); information technology (MBA, Certificate); management (MSA); managing information technology (MS); marketing (MSA); writing (MFA). Part-time and evening/weekend programs available. *Faculty:* 14 full-time (7 women), 119 part-time/adjunct (50 women). *Students:* 750 full-time (489 women), 138 part-time (91 women); includes 196 minority (182 African Americans, 1 American Indian/Alaska Native, 5 Asian Americans or Pacific Islanders, 8 Hispanic Americans), 14 international. Average age 34. In 2008, 349 master's awarded. *Degree requirements:* For master's, thesis (for some programs), minimum GPA of 3.0, 1 colloquium per term. *Entrance requirements:* For master's, interview, minimum GPA of 3.0. Additional exam requirements/recommendations for international students: Required—TOEFL (minimum score 550 paper-based; 213 computer-based; 80 iBT). *Application deadline:* For fall admission, 9/30 priority date for domestic and international students; for winter admission, 12/30 priority date for domestic and international students; for spring admission, 3/30 priority date for domestic and international students. Applications are processed on a rolling basis. Application fee: $30 ($100 for international students). *Expenses:* Tuition: Full-time $12,700; part-time $360 per credit hour. *Financial support:* Career-related internships or fieldwork, institutionally sponsored loans, tuition waivers (partial), and unspecified assistantships available. Financial award application deadline: 6/30; financial award applicants required to submit FAFSA. *Unit head:* Dan Kemper, Dean of Lindenwood College for Individual Education, 636-949-4501, Fax: 636-949-4505, E-mail: dkemper@lindenwood.edu. *Application contact:* Brett Barger, Dean of Evening Admissions and Extension Campuses, 636-949-4934, Fax: 636-949-4109, E-mail: adultadmissions@lindenwood.edu.

Louisiana State University and Agricultural and Mechanical College, Graduate School, College of Arts and Sciences, Department of Communication Studies, Baton Rouge, LA 70803. Offers MA, PhD. *Degree requirements:* For master's, thesis; for doctorate, one foreign language, thesis/dissertation. *Entrance requirements:* For master's and doctorate, GRE General Test, minimum GPA of 3.0. Additional exam requirements/recommendations for international students: Required—TOEFL (minimum score 550 paper-based; 213 computer-based; 79 iBT). Electronic applications accepted. *Faculty research:* Rhetorical theory and criticism, performance studies, interpersonal communication.

Marquette University, Graduate School, College of Communication, Milwaukee, WI 53201-1881. Offers advertising and public relations (MA); broadcasting and electronic communications (MA); communications studies (MA); journalism (MA); mass communications (MA); religious communications (MA); science, health and environmental communications (MA). *Accreditation:* ACEJMC. Part-time and evening/weekend programs available. *Degree requirements:* For master's, comprehensive exam. *Entrance requirements:* For master's, GRE. Additional exam requirements/recommendations for international students: Required—TOEFL. *Faculty research:* Urban journalism, gender and communication, intercultural communication, religious communication.

Marshall University, Academic Affairs Division, College of Liberal Arts, Department of Communication Studies, Huntington, WV 25755. Offers MA. *Degree requirements:* For master's, thesis optional.

Marywood University, Academic Affairs, Insalaco College of Creative Arts and Management, Department of Communication Arts, Program in Communication Arts, Scranton, PA 18509-1598. Offers corporate communication (Certificate); e-business (Certificate); health communication (Certificate); instructional technology (Certificate); interdisciplinary (MA); library science/information specialist (Certificate); media management (MA); production (MA).

McGill University, Faculty of Graduate and Postdoctoral Studies, Faculty of Arts, Department of Art History and Communication Studies, Montréal, QC H3A 2T5, Canada. Offers MA, PhD.

Miami University, Graduate School, College of Arts and Sciences, Department of Communication, Oxford, OH 45056. Offers mass communication (MA); speech communication (MA). Part-time programs available. *Degree requirements:* For master's, final exam. *Entrance requirements:* For master's, minimum undergraduate GPA of 3.0 during previous 2 years or 2.75 overall. Additional exam requirements/recommendations for international students: Required—TOEFL (minimum score 550 paper-based; 213 computer-based), TWE (minimum score 4). Electronic applications accepted.

Michigan State University, The Graduate School, College of Communication Arts and Sciences, Department of Communication, East Lansing, MI 48824. Offers MA, PhD. *Entrance requirements:* Additional exam requirements/recommendations for international students: Required—TOEFL (minimum score 580 paper-based; 237 computer-based). Electronic applications accepted.

Mississippi College, Graduate School, College of Arts and Sciences, School of Christian Studies and the Arts, Department of Communication, Clinton, MS 39058. Offers applied communication (MSC); public relations and corporate communication (MSC). Part-time programs available. *Degree requirements:* For master's, comprehensive exam, thesis optional. *Entrance requirements:* For master's, GRE or NTE, minimum GPA of 2.5. Additional exam requirements/recommendations for international students: Recommended—IELTS. Electronic applications accepted.

Missouri State University, Graduate College, College of Arts and Letters, Department of Communication and Mass Media, Springfield, MO 65804-0094. Offers MA. Part-time programs available. *Faculty:* 11 full-time (6 women). *Students:* 24 full-time (15 women), 21 part-time (14

Communication—General

Missouri State University (continued)
women); includes 2 minority (1 African American, 1 Hispanic American), 1 international. Average age 28. 24 applicants, 100% accepted, 14 enrolled. In 2008, 16 master's awarded. *Degree requirements:* For master's, comprehensive exam, thesis or alternative. *Entrance requirements:* For master's, GRE General Test, minimum GPA of 3.0. Additional exam requirements/recommendations for international students: Required—TOEFL (minimum score 550 paper-based; 213 computer-based; 79 iBT). *Application deadline:* For fall admission, 7/20 for domestic students, 5/1 for international students; for spring admission, 12/20 for domestic students, 9/1 for international students. Applications are processed on a rolling basis. Application fee: $35 ($50 for international students). Electronic applications accepted. *Expenses:* Tuition, state resident: full-time $3852; part-time $214 per credit hour. Tuition, nonresident: full-time $7524; part-time $418 per credit hour. Required fees: $230 per semester. Tuition and fees vary according to course level and course load. *Financial support:* In 2008–09, 1 research assistantship with full tuition reimbursement (averaging $7,340 per year), 15 teaching assistantships with full tuition reimbursements (averaging $7,340 per year) were awarded; career-related internships or fieldwork, Federal Work-Study, institutionally sponsored loans, scholarships/grants, and unspecified assistantships also available. Support available to part-time students. Financial award application deadline: 3/31; financial award applicants required to submit FAFSA. *Faculty research:* Conflict resolution, media analysis, intercultural communication, rhetorical criticism. *Unit head:* Dr. Kelly McNeilis, Head, 417-836-4423, Fax: 417-836-4774, E-mail: communication@missouristate.edu. *Application contact:* Eric Eckert, Coordinator of Graduate Admissions and Recruitment, 417-836-5331, Fax: 417-836-6888, E-mail: ericeckert@missouristate.edu.

Missouri State University, Graduate College, Interdisciplinary Program in Administrative Studies, Springfield, MO 65804-0094. Offers applied communication (MS); criminal justice (MS); environmental management (MS); project management (MS); sports management (MS). Part-time and evening/weekend programs available. Postbaccalaureate distance learning degree programs offered (no on-campus study). *Students:* 16 full-time (9 women), 56 part-time (25 women); includes 7 minority (4 African Americans, 2 Asian Americans or Pacific Islanders, 1 Hispanic American). Average age 34. 16 applicants, 100% accepted, 12 enrolled. In 2008, 33 master's awarded. *Degree requirements:* For master's, comprehensive exam, thesis or alternative. *Entrance requirements:* For master's, GRE, GMAT, 3 years of work experience. Additional exam requirements/recommendations for international students: Required—TOEFL (minimum score 550 paper-based; 213 computer-based; 79 iBT). *Application deadline:* For fall admission, 7/20 priority date for domestic students; for spring admission, 12/20 priority date for domestic students. Applications are processed on a rolling basis. Application fee: $35 ($50 for international students). Electronic applications accepted. *Expenses:* Tuition, state resident: full-time $3852; part-time $214 per credit hour. Tuition, nonresident: full-time $7524; part-time $418 per credit hour. Required fees: $230 per semester. Tuition and fees vary according to course level and course load. *Financial support:* In 2008–09, 4 teaching assistantships with full tuition reimbursements (averaging $8,535 per year) were awarded; career-related internships or fieldwork, Federal Work-Study, institutionally sponsored loans, scholarships/grants, and unspecified assistantships also available. Support available to part-time students. Financial award application deadline: 3/31; financial award applicants required to submit FAFSA. *Unit head:* John Bourhis, Director, 417-836-6390, E-mail: johnbourhis@missouristate.edu. *Application contact:* Eric Eckert, Coordinator of Graduate Admissions and Recruitment, 417-836-5331, Fax: 417-836-6888, E-mail: ericeckert@missouristate.edu.

Monmouth University, Graduate School, Department of Corporate and Public Communication, West Long Branch, NJ 07764-1898. Offers corporate and public communication (MA); human resources communication (Certificate); media studies (Certificate); public relations (Certificate). *Faculty:* 9 full-time (5 women). *Students:* 5 full-time (3 women), 40 part-time (28 women); includes 8 minority (4 African Americans, 1 Asian American or Pacific Islander, 3 Hispanic Americans), 3 international. Average age 32. 19 applicants, 95% accepted, 10 enrolled. In 2008, 14 master's awarded. *Degree requirements:* For master's, comprehensive exam, project. *Entrance requirements:* For master's, GRE, minimum GPA of 3.0 in major, 2.75 overall. Additional exam requirements/recommendations for international students: Required—TOEFL (minimum score 550 paper-based; 213 computer-based; 79 iBT), IELTS (minimum score 5), Michigan English Language Assessment Battery (minimum score: 77), Cambridge A, B, C. *Application deadline:* For fall admission, 7/15 priority date for domestic students, 6/1 for international students; for spring admission, 11/15 priority date for domestic students, 11/1 for international students. Applications are processed on a rolling basis. Application fee: $50. Electronic applications accepted. *Expenses:* Tuition: Full-time $13,914; part-time $773 per credit. Required fees: $628; $157 per semester. *Financial support:* In 2008–09, 26 students received support, including 23 fellowships (averaging $1,142 per year), 5 research assistantships (averaging $4,794 per year); scholarships/grants and unspecified assistantships also available. Support available to part-time students. Financial award application deadline: 3/1; financial award applicants required to submit FAFSA. *Faculty research:* Service learning, history of television, feminism and the media, executive communication, public relations pedagogy. *Unit head:* Dr. Eleanor Novek, Program Director, 732-263-5449, Fax: 732-571-3609, E-mail: enovek@monmouth.edu. *Application contact:* Kevin Roane, Director, Office of Graduate Admission, 732-571-3452, Fax: 732-263-5123, E-mail: gradadm@monmouth.edu.

Montana State University–Billings, College of Arts and Sciences, Department of Communication and Theater, Billings, MT 59101-0298. Offers public relations (MS). Part-time programs available. Postbaccalaureate distance learning degree programs offered. *Degree requirements:* For master's, thesis optional. *Entrance requirements:* For master's, GRE General Test, minimum undergraduate GPA of 3.0, 3 letters of recommendation.

Montclair State University, The Office of Graduate Admissions and Support Services, School of the Arts, Department of Communication Studies, Montclair, NJ 07043-1624. Offers organizational communication (MA); public relations (MA); speech communication (MA). Part-time and evening/weekend programs available. *Faculty:* 6 full-time (2 women), 36 part-time/adjunct (18 women). *Students:* 9 full-time (7 women), 20 part-time (15 women); includes 6 minority (4 African Americans, 2 Hispanic Americans), 2 international. Average age 30. 29 applicants, 38% accepted, 8 enrolled. In 2008, 7 master's awarded. *Degree requirements:* For master's, comprehensive exam. *Entrance requirements:* For master's, GRE General Test, minimum GPA of 3.0; undergraduate degree or work in theatre, oral interpretation, speech communication, media, or broadcasting; 2 letters of recommendation. Additional exam requirements/recommendations for international students: Required—TOEFL (minimum score 83 computer-based). *Application deadline:* For fall admission, 6/1 for international students; for spring admission, 10/1 for international students. Applications are processed on a rolling basis. Application fee: $60. Electronic applications accepted. *Financial support:* In 2008–09, 1 research assistantship with full tuition reimbursement (averaging $7,000 per year) was awarded; Federal Work-Study, scholarships/grants, and unspecified assistantships also available. Support available to part-time students. Financial award application deadline: 3/1; financial award applicants required to submit FAFSA. *Unit head:* Dr. Harry Haines, Chair, 973-655-4200. *Application contact:* Amy Aiello, Associate Director of Admissions, 973-655-5147, Fax: 973-655-7869, E-mail: graduate.school@montclair.edu.

Morehead State University, Graduate Programs, Caudill College of Humanities, Department of Communication and Theatre, Morehead, KY 40351. Offers communication (MA). Part-time and evening/weekend programs available. *Faculty:* 6 full-time (1 woman). *Students:* 14 full-time (8 women), 12 part-time (7 women); includes 3 minority (2 African Americans, 1 Hispanic American), 4 international. Average age 29. 10 applicants, 90% accepted, 7 enrolled. In 2008, 10 master's awarded. *Degree requirements:* For master's, comprehensive exam, thesis optional. *Entrance requirements:* For master's, GRE General Test, sample of written work. Additional exam requirements/recommendations for international students: Required—TOEFL (minimum score 500 paper-based; 173 computer-based). *Application deadline:* For fall admission, 8/1 priority date for domestic and international students; for spring admission, 12/1 priority date for domestic and international students. Applications are processed on a rolling basis. Application

fee: $30 ($55 for international students). *Expenses:* Tuition, area resident: Full-time $6084; part-time $338 per credit hour. Tuition, state resident: full-time $6084; part-time $338 per credit hour. Tuition, nonresident: full-time $15,804; part-time $878 per credit hour. *Financial support:* In 2008–09, 6 teaching assistantships (averaging $6,000 per year) were awarded; career-related internships or fieldwork, Federal Work-Study, and unspecified assistantships also available. Financial award application deadline: 4/1; financial award applicants required to submit FAFSA. *Faculty research:* Mass media effects, organizational communications, advertising/public relations. *Unit head:* Dr. Robert Willenbrink, Chair, 606-783-2134, Fax: 606-783-2457, E-mail: r.willenbrink@moreheadstate.edu. *Application contact:* Michelle Barber, Graduate Admissions Counselor, 606-783-2039, Fax: 606-783-5061, E-mail: m.barber@moreheadstate.edu.

National University, Academic Affairs, School of Media and Communication, La Jolla, CA 92037-1011. Offers MA, MFA, MS. Part-time and evening/weekend programs available. Postbaccalaureate distance learning degree programs offered (no on-campus study). *Faculty:* 14 full-time (6 women), 85 part-time/adjunct (29 women). *Students:* 70 full-time (26 women), 153 part-time (70 women); includes 71 minority (31 African Americans, 1 American Indian/Alaska Native, 13 Asian Americans or Pacific Islanders, 26 Hispanic Americans). Average age 39. 138 applicants, 100% accepted, 138 enrolled. In 2008, 62 master's awarded. *Degree requirements:* For master's, thesis (for some programs). *Entrance requirements:* For master's, interview, minimum GPA of 2.5. Additional exam requirements/recommendations for international students: Required—TOEFL (minimum score 550 paper-based; 213 computer-based; 79 iBT), IELTS (minimum score 6). *Application deadline:* Applications are processed on a rolling basis. Application fee: $60 ($65 for international students). Electronic applications accepted. *Expenses:* Tuition: Full-time $8694; part-time $322 per credit hour. Tuition and fees vary according to course load. *Financial support:* Career-related internships or fieldwork, institutionally sponsored loans, scholarships/grants, and tuition waivers (partial) available. Support available to part-time students. Financial award application deadline: 6/30; financial award applicants required to submit FAFSA. *Faculty research:* Digital media/film/journalism. *Unit head:* Karla Berry, Dean, 858-309-3442, Fax: 858-309-3450, E-mail: kberry@nu.edu. *Application contact:* Dominick Giovanniello, Associate Regional Dean—San Diego, 800-NAT-UNIV, Fax: 858-541-7792, E-mail: dgiovann@nu.edu.

New Mexico State University, Graduate School, College of Arts and Sciences, Department of Communication Studies, Las Cruces, NM 88003-8001. Offers MA. Part-time programs available. *Faculty:* 5 full-time (2 women). *Students:* 25 full-time (18 women), 9 part-time (6 women); includes 13 minority (3 African Americans, 10 Hispanic Americans), 4 international. Average age 31. 30 applicants, 90% accepted, 18 enrolled. In 2008, 11 master's awarded. *Degree requirements:* For master's, comprehensive exam (for some programs), thesis (for some programs). *Entrance requirements:* For master's, minimum GPA of 3.0. *Application deadline:* For fall admission, 7/1 priority date for domestic students; for spring admission, 4/1 priority date for domestic students. Applications are processed on a rolling basis. Application fee: $30 ($50 for international students). Electronic applications accepted. *Expenses:* Tuition, area resident: Full-time $3890; part-time $212.85 per credit. Tuition, state resident: full-time $3890; part-time $212.85 per credit. Tuition, nonresident: full-time $13,916; part-time $630.55 per credit. Required fees: $1218; $609 per semester. *Financial support:* In 2008–09, 26 students received support, including 17 teaching assistantships with partial tuition reimbursements available (averaging $13,913 per year); fellowships, research assistantships, Federal Work-Study and health care benefits also available. Financial award application deadline: 3/1. *Faculty research:* Interpersonal, organizational, intercultural, political, and health communication. *Unit head:* Dr. Anne P. Hubbell, Head, 575-646-2801, Fax: 575-646-1603, E-mail: ahubbell@nmsu.edu. *Application contact:* Elena Luna, Coordinator, 575-646-3498, Fax: 575-646-7721, E-mail: rosluna@nmsu.edu.

The New School: A University, The New School for General Studies, Program in Media Studies, New York, NY 10011. Offers communication theory (MA); media studies (MA). Part-time and evening/weekend programs available. *Faculty:* 19 full-time (8 women), 44 part-time/adjunct (16 women). *Students:* 203 full-time (131 women), 272 part-time (180 women); includes 101 minority (31 African Americans, 3 American Indian/Alaska Native, 28 Asian Americans or Pacific Islanders, 39 Hispanic Americans), 72 international. Average age 30. In 2008, 143 master's awarded. *Degree requirements:* For master's, thesis optional. *Entrance requirements:* For master's, interview. Additional exam requirements/recommendations for international students: Required—TOEFL (minimum score 600 paper-based; 250 computer-based; 100 iBT). *Application deadline:* For fall admission, 4/15 for domestic students; for spring admission, 10/15 for domestic students. Applications are processed on a rolling basis. Application fee: $50. *Expenses:* Tuition: Full-time $27,144; part-time $1508 per credit. Required fees: $355 per semester. *Financial support:* Fellowships, research assistantships, teaching assistantships, Federal Work-Study, scholarships/grants, and tuition waivers (partial) available. Financial award application deadline: 3/1; financial award applicants required to submit FAFSA. *Faculty research:* Effect of technology on society, effect of US media on international affairs, effect of media on corporate affairs. *Unit head:* Dr. Peter L. Haratonik, Interim Chair, Media Studies and Film, 212-229-8903, Fax: 212-465-0661, E-mail: haraton@newschool.edu. *Application contact:* David Norris, Director of Admissions, 212-229-5630, Fax: 212-989-3887, E-mail: nsadmissions@newschool.edu.

See Close-Up on page 691.

New York Institute of Technology, Graduate Division, School of Arts and Sciences, Program in Communication Arts, Old Westbury, NY 11568-8000. Offers MA. Part-time and evening/weekend programs available. *Students:* 85 full-time (62 women), 88 part-time (56 women); includes 33 minority (13 African Americans, 8 Asian Americans or Pacific Islanders, 12 Hispanic Americans), 65 international. Average age 31. In 2008, 107 master's awarded. *Degree requirements:* For master's, thesis or alternative. *Entrance requirements:* For master's, minimum QPA of 2.85. Additional exam requirements/recommendations for international students: Required—TOEFL (minimum score 550 paper-based; 213 computer-based). *Application deadline:* For fall admission, 7/1 priority date for domestic students; for spring admission, 12/1 priority date for domestic students. Applications are processed on a rolling basis. Application fee: $50. Electronic applications accepted. *Expenses:* Tuition: Part-time $783 per credit. *Financial support:* Research assistantships with partial tuition reimbursements, career-related internships or fieldwork, Federal Work-Study, institutionally sponsored loans, tuition waivers (partial), and unspecified assistantships available. Support available to part-time students. Financial award applicants required to submit FAFSA. *Faculty research:* Distance learning technology, computer animation, intercultural communication, multimedia technology. *Unit head:* Dr. Dena Winokur, Director, 212-261-1636, Fax: 516-686-7736, E-mail: dwinokur@nyit.edu. *Application contact:* Dr. Jacquelyn Nealon, Vice President for Enrollment Services, 516-686-7925, Fax: 516-686-7597, E-mail: jnealon@nyit.edu.

New York University, Steinhardt School of Culture, Education and Human Development, Department of Media, Culture and Communication, New York, NY 10012-1019. Offers media ecology/culture and communication (PhD); media, culture, and communication (MA). Part-time and evening/weekend programs available. *Entrance requirements:* Additional exam requirements/recommendations for international students: Required—TOEFL. *Faculty research:* Digital media, intercultural communication, race and politics, media criticism, media literacy.

Norfolk State University, School of Graduate Studies, School of Liberal Arts, Department of Media and Communication, Norfolk, VA 23504. Offers MA. Part-time programs available. *Degree requirements:* For master's, thesis. *Entrance requirements:* For master's, GRE, minimum GPA of 2.5, letters of recommendation. Additional exam requirements/recommendations for international students: Required—TOEFL.

North Carolina State University, Graduate School, College of Humanities and Social Sciences, Department of Communication, Raleigh, NC 27695. Offers MS. Part-time programs available. *Degree requirements:* For master's, thesis optional. *Entrance requirements:* For master's, GRE, minimum undergraduate GPA of 3.0 during last 60 hours. Electronic applications accepted. *Faculty research:* Instructional communication, political communication, organizational conflict management, intercultural communication, communication technology.

North Dakota State University, College of Graduate and Interdisciplinary Studies, College of Arts, Humanities and Social Sciences, Department of Communication, Fargo, ND 58105. Offers communication (PhD); mass communication (MA, MS); speech communication (MA, MS). Part-time programs available. Postbaccalaureate distance learning degree programs offered (no on-campus study). *Faculty:* 11 full-time (5 women), 3 part-time/adjunct (1 woman). *Students:* 38 full-time (25 women), 23 part-time (17 women); includes 4 minority (1 African American, 2 Asian Americans or Pacific Islanders, 1 Hispanic American), 3 international. Average age 27. 62 applicants, 40% accepted, 19 enrolled. In 2008, 15 master's, 8 doctorates awarded. Terminal master's awarded for partial completion of doctoral program. *Degree requirements:* For master's, thesis (for some programs); for doctorate, comprehensive exam, thesis/dissertation, 2-3 publications referred before comps. *Entrance requirements:* For master's, GRE, minimum undergraduate GPA of 3.25; for doctorate, GRE, minimum undergraduate GPA of 3.5. Additional exam requirements/recommendations for international students: Required—TOEFL (minimum score 600 paper-based; 250 computer-based; 100 iBT), IELTS (minimum score 7). *Application deadline:* For fall admission, 2/15 priority date for domestic students; for winter admission, 10/15 priority date for domestic students. Applications are processed on a rolling basis. Application fee: $45 ($60 for international students). Electronic applications accepted. *Financial support:* In 2008–09, 38 students received support, including 1 fellowship with full tuition reimbursement available (averaging $16,000 per year), 10 research assistantships with full tuition reimbursements available (averaging $12,000 per year), 10 teaching assistantships with full tuition reimbursements available (averaging $8,100 per year); career-related internships or fieldwork, Federal Work-Study, institutionally sponsored loans, tuition waivers (full), and unspecified assistantships also available. Financial award application deadline: 2/1. *Faculty research:* Communication and rhetorical theory, organizational communication, broadcast and print journalism, international communication, public relations and advertising. Total annual research expenditures: $148,496. *Unit head:* Dr. Paul E. Nelson, Chair, 701-231-7705, Fax: 701-231-7784, E-mail: paul.nelson.1@ndsu.edu. *Application contact:* Dr. Judy C. Pearson, Director of Graduate Studies, 701-231-6551, Fax: 701-231-1074, E-mail: judy.pearson@ndsu.edu.

Northeastern State University, Graduate College, College of Liberal Arts, Department of Communication, Tahlequah, OK 74464-2399. Offers MA. Part-time and evening/weekend programs available. *Students:* 6 full-time (3 women), 11 part-time (10 women); includes 4 minority (all American Indian/Alaska Native). In 2008, 8 master's awarded. *Degree requirements:* For master's, comprehensive exam. *Entrance requirements:* For master's, GRE, MAT, minimum GPA of 2.5. Additional exam requirements/recommendations for international students: Required—TOEFL (minimum score 213 computer-based). *Application deadline:* For fall admission, 6/1 priority date for domestic students. Applications are processed on a rolling basis. Application fee: $0 ($25 for international students). Electronic applications accepted. *Financial support:* Teaching assistantships, Federal Work-Study available. Financial award application deadline: 3/1. *Unit head:* Dr. Mike Chanselar, Chair, 918-456-5511 Ext. 3600, Fax: 918-458-2348. *Application contact:* Margie Railey, Administrative Assistant, 918-456-5511 Ext. 2093, Fax: 918-458-2061, E-mail: railey@nsouk.edu.

Northern Arizona University, Graduate College, College of Social and Behavioral Sciences, School of Communication, Flagstaff, AZ 86011. Offers applied communication (MA).

Northern Illinois University, Graduate School, College of Liberal Arts and Sciences, Department of Communication, De Kalb, IL 60115-2854. Offers communication studies (MA). Part-time programs available. *Degree requirements:* For master's, comprehensive exam, thesis optional. *Entrance requirements:* For master's, GRE General Test, minimum GPA of 2.75. Additional exam requirements/recommendations for international students: Required—TOEFL (minimum score 550 paper-based; 213 computer-based). Electronic applications accepted. *Faculty research:* Journalism, history film studies, rhetoric or criticism, globalization, mass media law.

Northern Kentucky University, Office of Graduate Programs, College of Informatics, Program in Communication, Highland Heights, KY 41099. Offers MA. Part-time and evening/weekend programs available. Postbaccalaureate distance learning degree programs offered (minimal on-campus study). *Students:* 11 full-time (9 women), 36 part-time (27 women); includes 5 minority (3 African Americans, 2 Asian Americans or Pacific Islanders), 1 international. Average age 30. 27 applicants, 81% accepted, 16 enrolled. In 2008, 12 master's awarded. *Degree requirements:* For master's, thesis (for some programs). *Entrance requirements:* For master's, GRE, minimum GPA of 3.0, 3 letters of recommendation, 500-word statement of interest. Additional exam requirements/recommendations for international students: Required—TOEFL (minimum score 550 paper-based; 213 computer-based; 79 iBT), Michigan Test may be substituted only if taken at NKU (minimu score of 80); Recommended—IELTS (minimum score 6.5). *Application deadline:* For fall admission, 2/28 priority date for domestic students, 6/1 for international students; for spring admission, 10/31 priority date for domestic students, 10/1 for international students. Applications are processed on a rolling basis. Application fee: $40. Electronic applications accepted. *Expenses:* Tuition, area resident: Full-time $6642. Tuition, state resident: full-time $6642. Tuition, nonresident: full-time $11,682. *Financial support:* Unspecified assistantships available. Financial award applicants required to submit FAFSA. *Faculty research:* Organizational and professional communication, relational/interpersonal communication, communication teaching and pedagogy, documentary studies, public relations. *Unit head:* Dr. Cady Short-Thompson, Program Director, 859-572-6614, Fax: 859-572-5378, E-mail: shorthomp@nku.edu. *Application contact:* Dr. Peg Griffin, Director of Graduate Programs, 859-572-6934, Fax: 859-572-6670, E-mail: griffinp@nku.edu.

Northwestern University, The Graduate School, School of Communication, Department of Communication Studies, Evanston, IL 60208. Offers communication studies (MA, PhD); communication systems strategy and management (MSC); managerial communication (MSC). MA and PhD admissions and degrees offered through The Graduate School. Terminal master's awarded for partial completion of doctoral program. *Degree requirements:* For doctorate, thesis/dissertation. *Entrance requirements:* For master's and doctorate, GRE General Test. Additional exam requirements/recommendations for international students: Required—TOEFL. Electronic applications accepted.

The Ohio State University, Graduate School, College of Social and Behavioral Sciences, School of Communication, Program in Communication, Columbus, OH 43210. Offers MA, PhD. *Degree requirements:* For doctorate, thesis/dissertation. *Entrance requirements:* For master's and doctorate, GRE General Test. Additional exam requirements/recommendations for international students: Required—TOEFL (minimum score 620 paper-based; 250 computer-based). Electronic applications accepted.

The Ohio State University, Graduate School, College of Social and Behavioral Sciences, School of Communication, Program in Journalism and Communication, Columbus, OH 43210. Offers MA. *Entrance requirements:* For master's, GRE General Test. Electronic applications accepted.

Ohio University, Graduate College, Scripps College of Communication, Athens, OH 45701-2979. Offers MA, MCTP, MS, PhD. Part-time programs available. *Degree requirements:* For master's, comprehensive exam (for some programs); for doctorate, comprehensive exam, thesis/dissertation. *Entrance requirements:* For master's and doctorate, GRE General Test. Additional exam requirements/recommendations for international students: Required—TOEFL. Electronic applications accepted. *Expenses:* Contact institution. *Faculty research:* Health communication, organizational communication, mass communication, media studies, international communication.

Our Lady of the Lake University of San Antonio, College of Arts and Sciences, Program in English, San Antonio, TX 78207-4689. Offers English and communication arts (MA); English and literature (MA); English education (MA); writing (MA). Part-time and evening/weekend programs available. *Students:* 12 full-time (11 women), 7 part-time (all women); includes 14 minority (1 African American, 13 Hispanic Americans). Average age 31. In 2008, 15 master's awarded. *Degree requirements:* For master's, comprehensive exam, thesis optional. *Entrance requirements:* For master's, GRE General Test or MAT, minimum GPA of 3.0 in last 60 hours, 2.5 overall. Additional exam requirements/recommendations for international students: Required—TOEFL. *Application deadline:* Applications are processed on a rolling basis. Application fee: $25 ($50 for international students). Electronic applications accepted. *Expenses:* Tuition: Full-time $11,970; part-time $665 per credit hour. Required fees: $500; $250 per term. *Financial support:* Research assistantships, teaching assistantships, career-related internships or fieldwork, Federal Work-Study, institutionally sponsored loans, and tuition waivers (partial) available. Financial award application deadline: 4/15. *Faculty research:* Writing theory and research, contemporary Southern literature, popular culture, poetry, literature of the Southwest. *Unit head:* Dr. Leah Larson, Chair, 210-434-2387 Ext. 2260, E-mail: larsl@lake.ollusa.edu. *Application contact:* 210-434-6711, Fax: 210-431-4036, E-mail: gradadm@lake.ollusa.edu.

Penn State University Park, Graduate School, College of Communications, State College, University Park, PA 16802-1503. Offers MA, PhD. *Accreditation:* ACEJMC (one or more programs are accredited). *Entrance requirements:* For master's and doctorate, GRE General Test. Additional exam requirements/recommendations for international students: Required—TOEFL (minimum score 550 paper-based; 213 computer-based; 80 iBT). Electronic applications accepted.

Penn State University Park, Graduate School, College of the Liberal Arts, Department of Communication Arts and Sciences, State College, University Park, PA 16802-1503. Offers MA, PhD.

Pepperdine University, Seaver College, Division of Communication, Malibu, CA 90263. Offers MA. Part-time programs available. *Degree requirements:* For master's, thesis or alternative. *Entrance requirements:* For master's, GRE General Test, bachelor's degree in communication or related field. Additional exam requirements/recommendations for international students: Required—TOEFL.

Pittsburg State University, Graduate School, College of Arts and Sciences, Department of Communication, Pittsburg, KS 66762. Offers applied communication (MA); communication education (MA); theatre (MA). *Degree requirements:* For master's, thesis or alternative.

Point Park University, School of Arts and Sciences, Department of Journalism and Mass Communication, Pittsburgh, PA 15222-1984. Offers MA. Part-time and evening/weekend programs available. *Faculty:* 9 full-time, 13 part-time/adjunct. *Students:* 35 full-time (27 women), 47 part-time (36 women); includes 13 minority (11 African Americans, 1 American Indian/Alaska Native, 1 Asian American or Pacific Islander), 3 international. Average age 27. 101 applicants, 56% accepted, 36 enrolled. In 2008, 24 master's awarded. *Degree requirements:* For master's, comprehensive exam (for some programs), thesis or alternative. *Entrance requirements:* For master's, GRE (if GPA below 2.75), minimum GPA of 2.75, 2 letters of recommendation; 500 word statement of intent. Additional exam requirements/recommendations for international students: Required—TOEFL. *Application deadline:* Applications are processed on a rolling basis. Application fee: $30. Electronic applications accepted. *Expenses:* Tuition: Full-time $11,880; part-time $660 per credit. Required fees: $486; $27 per credit. *Financial support:* In 2008–09, 6 students received support, including 6 research assistantships with full tuition reimbursements available (averaging $5,400 per year); career-related internships or fieldwork, Federal Work-Study, and scholarships/grants also available. Support available to part-time students. Financial award application deadline: 5/1; financial award applicants required to submit FAFSA. *Unit head:* Helen Fallon, Chair, 412-392-3982, E-mail: hfallon@pointpark.edu. *Application contact:* Emily R. Quidetto, Recruiter/Counselor, 412-392-4794, Fax: 412-392-6164, E-mail: equidetto@pointpark.edu.

See Close-Up on page 693.

Polytechnic Institute of NYU, Department of Electrical and Computer Engineering, Major in Wireless Communications, Brooklyn, NY 11201-2990. Offers Certificate. *Entrance requirements:* Additional exam requirements/recommendations for international students: Required—TOEFL (minimum score 550 paper-based; 213 computer-based); Recommended—IELTS (minimum score 6.5). Electronic applications accepted.

Purdue University, Graduate School, College of Liberal Arts, Department of Communication, West Lafayette, IN 47907. Offers MA, MS, PhD. *Degree requirements:* For master's, comprehensive exams or thesis; for doctorate, thesis/dissertation. *Entrance requirements:* For master's, GRE General Test, writing sample; for doctorate, GRE General Test, master's degree, writing sample. Additional exam requirements/recommendations for international students: Required—TOEFL, TWE. Electronic applications accepted. *Faculty research:* Interpersonal communication, mass communication, organizational communication, public affairs and issue management, rhetorical studies.

Purdue University Calumet, Graduate School, School of Liberal Arts and Social Sciences, Department of Communication and Creative Arts, Hammond, IN 46323-2094. Offers communication (MA). Part-time and evening/weekend programs available. *Degree requirements:* For master's, comprehensive exam, thesis optional, thesis or extended course work. *Entrance requirements:* For master's, minimum GPA of 3.0. Additional exam requirements/recommendations for international students: Required—TOEFL. Electronic applications accepted. *Faculty research:* International communication, gender studies, political rhetoric, media effects, media accountability.

Queen's University at Kingston, School of Graduate Studies and Research, Faculty of Arts and Sciences, Department of Sociology, Kingston, ON K7L 3N6, Canada. Offers communication and Information technology (MA, PhD); feminist sociology (MA, PhD); socio-legal studies (MA, PhD); sociological theory (MA, PhD). Part-time programs available. *Degree requirements:* For master's, thesis; for doctorate, comprehensive exam, thesis/dissertation. *Entrance requirements:* For master's, honors bachelors degree in sociology; for doctorate, honors bachelors degree, masters degree in sociology. Additional exam requirements/recommendations for international students: Required—TOEFL. *Faculty research:* Social change and modernization, social control, deviance and criminology, surveillance.

Quinnipiac University, School of Communications, Hamden, CT 06518-1940. Offers MS. Part-time and evening/weekend programs available. *Faculty:* 9 full-time (2 women), 14 part-time/adjunct (3 women). *Students:* 44 full-time (24 women), 62 part-time (38 women); includes 17 minority (10 African Americans, 1 Asian American or Pacific Islander, 6 Hispanic Americans), 1 international. Average age 29. 61 applicants, 95% accepted, 42 enrolled. In 2008, 43 master's awarded. *Entrance requirements:* For master's, minimum GPA of 2.8, portfolio or writing sample. Additional exam requirements/recommendations for international students: Required—TOEFL (minimum score 575 paper-based; 233 computer-based; 90 iBT), IELTS (minimum score 6.5). *Application deadline:* For fall admission, 7/30 priority date for domestic students, 4/30 priority date for international students; for spring admission, 12/15 priority date for domestic students, 9/15 priority date for international students. Applications are processed on a rolling basis. Application fee: $45. Electronic applications accepted. *Expenses:* Tuition: Full-time $14,600; part-time $730 per credit. Required fees: $630; $30 per credit. *Financial support:* In 2008–09, 1 fellowship with full tuition reimbursement was awarded; career-related internships or fieldwork, tuition waivers (partial), and unspecified assistantships also available. Support available to part-time students. Financial award application deadline: 4/15; financial award applicants required to submit FAFSA. *Unit head:* Graduate Admissions Office, 800-462-1944, Fax: 203-582-3443, E-mail: graduate@quinnipiac.edu. *Application contact:* Scott Farber, Information Contact, E-mail: graduate@quinnipiac.edu.

See Close-Up on page 695.

Communication—General

Regent University, Graduate School, School of Communication and the Arts, Virginia Beach, VA 23464-9800. Offers acting (MFA); acting and directing (MFA); cinema arts/television arts (MA); communication (MA, PhD); digital media (MA); directing for cinema/TV (MA); journalism (MA); producing for cinema/TV (MA); script and screenwriting (MFA); theatre (MA). Part-time programs available. Postbaccalaureate distance learning degree programs offered (minimal on-campus study). *Faculty:* 26 full-time (3 women), 15 part-time/adjunct (3 women). *Students:* 136 full-time (77 women), 163 part-time (90 women); includes 83 minority (59 African Americans, 3 American Indian/Alaska Native, 5 Asian Americans or Pacific Islanders, 16 Hispanic Americans), 15 international. Average age 32. 230 applicants, 63% accepted, 102 enrolled. In 2008, 53 master's, 16 doctorates awarded. *Degree requirements:* For master's, thesis or alternative; for doctorate, thesis/dissertation. *Entrance requirements:* For master's, GRE General Test or MAT, minimum undergraduate GPA of 3.0, writing sample, computer literacy survey, recommendation, resumé, interview, audition (MFA programs); for doctorate, GRE General Test, minimum graduate GPA of 3.0, writing sample, computer literacy survey, recommendation, interview, transcripts. Additional exam requirements/recommendations for international students: Required—TOEFL (minimum score 577 paper-based; 233 computer-based). *Application deadline:* For fall admission, 3/1 priority date for domestic students; for spring admission, 10/1 priority date for domestic students. Applications are processed on a rolling basis. Application fee: $50. Electronic applications accepted. *Expenses:* Contact institution. *Financial support:* Fellowships with full and partial tuition reimbursements, career-related internships or fieldwork, scholarships/grants, tuition waivers (full and partial), and unspecified assistantships available. Support available to part-time students. Financial award application deadline: 9/1; financial award applicants required to submit FAFSA. *Faculty research:* Southern gospel music, education and entertainment, celebrities and the media, journalism and ethics, C. S. Lewis. *Unit head:* Michael Patrick, Dean, 757-352-4970, Fax: 757-352-4279, E-mail: michpat@regent.edu. *Application contact:* Matthew Chadwick, Director of Admissions, 800-373-5504, Fax: 757-352-4381, E-mail: admissions@regent.edu.

Regis University, College for Professional Studies, MA Program, Denver, CO 80221-1099. Offers criminology (MA); fine arts administration (Certificate); language and communication (MA); mediation (Certificate); psychology (MA); self-designed major (MA); social justice, peace, and reconciliation (Certificate); social science (MA); technical communication (Certificate). Program also offered in Henderson and Las Vegas (Summerlin), NV. Part-time and evening/weekend programs available. Postbaccalaureate distance learning degree programs offered (minimal on-campus study). *Degree requirements:* For master's, thesis, research project. *Entrance requirements:* For master's, resumé, recommendations, essays. Additional exam requirements/recommendations for international students: Required—TOEFL (minimum score 213 computer-based), TWE (minimum score 5). Electronic applications accepted. *Expenses:* Contact institution. *Faculty research:* Independent/nonresidential graduate study: new methods and models, adult learning and the capstone experience, Goal Setting, behavior of Adult students, Innovative Studies for Community Colleges.

Rensselaer Polytechnic Institute, Graduate School, School of Humanities and Social Sciences, Department of Language, Literature, and Communication, Troy, NY 12180-3590. Offers communication and rhetoric (MS, PhD); human-computer interaction (MS); technical communication (MS). Part-time programs available. Postbaccalaureate distance learning degree programs offered (minimal on-campus study). Terminal master's awarded for partial completion of doctoral program. *Degree requirements:* For master's, thesis optional; for doctorate, comprehensive exam, thesis/dissertation. *Entrance requirements:* For master's, GRE General Test, resumé; for doctorate, GRE General Test, writing sample, resumé or curriculum vitae. Additional exam requirements/recommendations for international students: Required—TOEFL (minimum score 570 paper-based; 230 computer-based). Electronic applications accepted. *Faculty research:* Human-computer interaction, virtual institutions/communities, media design, theory and culture, usability, digital and visual rhetoric.

Rochester Institute of Technology, Graduate Enrollment Services, College of Imaging Arts and Sciences, School of Print Media, Rochester, NY 14623-5603. Offers print media (MS). *Entrance requirements:* For master's, minimum GPA of 3.0. Additional exam requirements/recommendations for international students: Required—TOEFL (minimum score 550 paper-based; 213 computer-based; 79 iBT).

Rochester Institute of Technology, Graduate Enrollment Services, College of Liberal Arts, Department of Communications, Program in Communication and Media Technologies, Rochester, NY 14623-5603. Offers MS. *Degree requirements:* For master's, thesis. *Entrance requirements:* For master's, minimum GPA of 3.0, writing sample. Additional exam requirements/recommendations for international students: Required—TOEFL (minimum score 600 paper-based; 250 computer-based; 100 iBT). Electronic applications accepted.

Roosevelt University, Graduate Division, College of Arts and Sciences, Department of Communication, Chicago, IL 60605-1394. Offers integrated marketing communications (MSIMC); journalism (MSJ). Part-time and evening/weekend programs available. *Students:* 80 full-time (62 women), 156 part-time (124 women); includes 96 minority (76 African Americans, 4 American Indian/Alaska Native, 7 Asian Americans or Pacific Islanders, 9 Hispanic Americans), 24 international. Average age 30. 470 applicants, 94% accepted, 91 enrolled. In 2008, 81 master's awarded. *Application deadline:* For fall admission, 6/1 priority date for domestic students. Applications are processed on a rolling basis. Application fee: $25 ($35 for international students). *Expenses:* Tuition: Full-time $14,730; part-time $709 per credit. Required fees: $175 per semester. Tuition and fees vary according to course load and program. *Financial support:* Research assistantships, career-related internships or fieldwork and Federal Work-Study available. Financial award application deadline: 2/15. *Unit head:* Linda Jones, Chair, 312-281-3230. *Application contact:* Joanne Canyon-Heller, Coordinator of Graduate Admission, 877-APPLY RU, Fax: 312-281-3356, E-mail: applyru@roosevelt.edu.

Rutgers, The State University of New Jersey, New Brunswick, School of Communication, Information and Library Studies, Program in Communication, Library and Information Science and Media Studies, Piscataway, NJ 08854-8097. Offers PhD. Part-time programs available. *Degree requirements:* For doctorate, comprehensive exam, thesis/dissertation, qualifying exams. *Entrance requirements:* For doctorate, GRE General Test, proficiency in statistics. Additional exam requirements/recommendations for international students: Required—TOEFL (minimum score 600 paper-based; 250 computer-based). Electronic applications accepted. *Faculty research:* Information science, media studies.

Saginaw Valley State University, College of Arts and Behavioral Sciences, Program in Communication and Digital Media Design, University Center, MI 48710. Offers MA. Part-time and evening/weekend programs available. *Students:* 19 full-time (10 women), 22 part-time (13 women); includes 4 minority (2 African Americans, 1 Asian American or Pacific Islander, 1 Hispanic American), 16 international. Average age 31. 23 applicants, 91% accepted, 14 enrolled. In 2008, 17 master's awarded. *Degree requirements:* For master's, thesis. *Entrance requirements:* For master's, minimum GPA of 2.75. Additional exam requirements/recommendations for international students: Required—TOEFL. *Application deadline:* Applications are processed on a rolling basis. Application fee: $25. Electronic applications accepted. *Expenses:* Tuition, state resident: full-time $8620; part-time $359.15 per credit hour. Tuition, nonresident: full-time $16,526; part-time $688.60 per credit hour. Required fees: $350.40; $14.60 per credit hour. Tuition and fees vary according to campus/location. *Financial support:* Federal Work-Study and scholarships/grants available. Support available to part-time students. Financial award application deadline: 4/1; financial award applicants required to submit FAFSA. *Unit head:* Dr. Steve Erickson, Program Coordinator/Professor of Theatre, 989-964-4147, E-mail: erickson@svsu.edu. *Application contact:* Dr. Steve Erickson, Program Coordinator/Professor of Theatre, 989-964-4147, E-mail: erickson@svsu.edu.

St. John's University, St. John's College of Liberal Arts and Sciences, Department of Speech, Communication Sciences and Theatre, Queens, NY 11439. Offers MA, Au D, Advanced Diploma. *Accreditation:* ASHA. Evening/weekend programs available. *Students:* 40 full-time (37 women), 118 part-time (111 women); includes 29 minority (10 African Americans, 8 Asian Americans or Pacific Islanders, 11 Hispanic Americans), 1 international. Average age 27. 405 applicants, 22% accepted, 38 enrolled. In 2008, 44 master's awarded. *Degree requirements:* For master's, comprehensive exam, thesis optional, internship. *Entrance requirements:* For master's, minimum GPA of 3.0. Additional exam requirements/recommendations for international students: Required—TOEFL (minimum score 500 paper-based; 173 computer-based; 61 iBT), IELTS (minimum score 5.5). *Application deadline:* For fall admission, 2/1 for domestic students, 5/1 priority date for international students; for spring admission, 10/1 for domestic students, 11/1 priority date for international students. Applications are processed on a rolling basis. Application fee: $70. Electronic applications accepted. *Expenses:* Contact institution. *Financial support:* Research assistantships, career-related internships or fieldwork and scholarships/grants available. Support available to part-time students. Financial award application deadline: 3/1; financial award applicants required to submit FAFSA. *Faculty research:* Bilingualism and adult and child language disorders, dysphagia speech motor control, electrophysiological measurement of hearing, central auditory processing disorders and auditory habilitation and rehabilitation. *Unit head:* Dr. Fredericka Bell-Berti, Chair, 718-990-6450, E-mail: bellf@stjohns.edu. *Application contact:* Kathleen Davis, Director of Graduate Admission, 718-990-2790, Fax: 718-990-5686, E-mail: gradhelp@stjohns.edu.

Saint Louis University, Graduate School, College of Arts and Sciences and Graduate School, Department of Communication, St. Louis, MO 63103-2097. Offers MA, MA-R. Part-time programs available. *Degree requirements:* For master's, thesis (for some programs), comprehensive oral and written exams. *Entrance requirements:* For master's, GRE General Test, letters of recommendation, resumé, interview, transcripts, goal statement. Additional exam requirements/recommendations for international students: Required—TOEFL (minimum score 525 paper-based; 194 computer-based). Electronic applications accepted. *Faculty research:* Media studies, organizational communication, dialogue, intercultural communication, qualitative research methods.

St. Mary's University, Graduate School, Department of English and Communication Studies, Program in Communication Studies, San Antonio, TX 78228-8507. Offers MA. Part-time programs available. Postbaccalaureate distance learning degree programs offered (minimal on-campus study). *Faculty:* 3 full-time (0 women), 1 part-time/adjunct (0 women). *Students:* 9 full-time (7 women), 19 part-time (13 women); includes 18 minority (4 African Americans, 14 Hispanic Americans), 1 international. Average age 32. 10 applicants, 80% accepted, 8 enrolled. *Degree requirements:* For master's, comprehensive exam. *Entrance requirements:* For master's, GRE General Test, MAT. Additional exam requirements/recommendations for international students: Required—TOEFL (minimum score 550 paper-based; 213 computer-based; 80 iBT). *Application deadline:* For fall admission, 8/1 priority date for domestic students. Applications are processed on a rolling basis. Application fee: $0. Electronic applications accepted. *Expenses:* Tuition: Full-time $12,006; part-time $667 per credit hour. Required fees: $440; $220 per semester. *Financial support:* In 2008–09, 4 students received support, including 3 fellowships (averaging $2,500 per year), 1 research assistantship (averaging $4,500 per year); career-related internships or fieldwork, Federal Work-Study, institutionally sponsored loans, scholarships/grants, and health care benefits also available. Financial award application deadline: 3/31; financial award applicants required to submit FAFSA. *Faculty research:* Persuasion and negotiation, group dynamics, language and communication, business communication, organizational communication. *Unit head:* Dr. Elijah Akhahenda, Director, 210-436-3107. *Application contact:* Dr. Henry Flores, Dean of the Graduate School, 210-436-3101, Fax: 210-431-2220, E-mail: hflores@stmarytx.edu.

St. Thomas University, School of Leadership Studies, Miami Gardens, FL 33054-6459. Offers MA, MPS, MS, Ed D, Certificate. Part-time and evening/weekend programs available. *Entrance requirements:* Additional exam requirements/recommendations for international students: Required—TOEFL (minimum score 550 paper-based; 213 computer-based; 79 iBT).

San Diego State University, Graduate and Research Affairs, College of Professional Studies and Fine Arts, School of Communication, San Diego, CA 92182. Offers advertising and public relations (MA); critical-cultural studies (MA); interaction studies (MA); intercultural and international studies (MA); new media studies (MA); news and information studies (MA); telecommunications and media management (MA). *Degree requirements:* For master's, thesis. *Entrance requirements:* For master's, GRE General Test, 3 letters of recommendation. Additional exam requirements/recommendations for international students: Required—TOEFL. Electronic applications accepted.

San Jose State University, Graduate Studies and Research, College of Social Sciences, Department of Communication Studies, San Jose, CA 95192-0001. Offers MA. *Degree requirements:* For master's, comprehensive exam, thesis or alternative, project. *Entrance requirements:* For master's, minimum GPA of 3.0. Electronic applications accepted.

Seton Hall University, College of Arts and Sciences, Department of Communication, South Orange, NJ 07079-2697. Offers corporate and public communication (MA); strategic communication and leadership (MA). Part-time and evening/weekend programs available. Postbaccalaureate distance learning degree programs offered (minimal on-campus study). *Entrance requirements:* For master's, GRE or GMAT, minimum GPA of 3.0. Electronic applications accepted. *Faculty research:* Managerial communication, communication consulting, communication and development.

See Close-Up on page 697.

Shippensburg University of Pennsylvania, School of Graduate Studies, College of Arts and Sciences, Department of Communication/Journalism, Shippensburg, PA 17257-2299. Offers communication studies (MS). Part-time and evening/weekend programs available. *Faculty:* 7 full-time (3 women). *Students:* 9 full-time (5 women), 21 part-time (15 women); includes 2 minority (both African Americans). Average age 30. 20 applicants, 80% accepted, 9 enrolled. In 2008, 11 master's awarded. *Degree requirements:* For master's, thesis optional, 6-credit thesis option or 3-credit professional project, candidacy. *Entrance requirements:* For master's, GRE or MAT (if GPA is below 2.75), 3 professional references, 400-500 word essay, resumé. Additional exam requirements/recommendations for international students: Required—TOEFL (minimum score 580 paper-based; 237 computer-based), Recommended—IELTS (minimum score 6). *Application deadline:* For fall admission, 3/1 for international students; for spring admission, 7/1 for international students. Applications are processed on a rolling basis. Application fee: $30. Electronic applications accepted. *Expenses:* Contact institution. *Financial support:* In 2008–09, 9 research assistantships with full tuition reimbursements (averaging $5,000 per year) were awarded; career-related internships or fieldwork, scholarships/grants, unspecified assistantships, and resident hall directors, student payroll positions also available. Support available to part-time students. Financial award application deadline: 3/1; financial award applicants required to submit FAFSA. *Unit head:* Dr. Ted Carlin, Chairperson, 717-477-1521, Fax: 717-477-4013, E-mail: ejcarl@ship.edu. *Application contact:* Renee Payne, Associate Dean of Graduate Admissions, 717-477-1231, Fax: 717-477-4016, E-mail: rmpayn@ship.edu.

Shippensburg University of Pennsylvania, School of Graduate Studies, College of Arts and Sciences, Department of Sociology and Anthropology, Shippensburg, PA 17257-2299. Offers organizational development and leadership (MS), including business, communications, education, environmental management, higher education, historical administration, individual and organizational development, public organizations, social structures and organizations. Part-time and evening/weekend programs available. *Faculty:* 4 full-time (3 women). *Students:* 12 full-time (2 women), 30 part-time (21 women); includes 5 minority (4 African Americans, 1 Asian American or Pacific Islander), 3 international. Average age 31. 39 applicants, 79% accepted, 17 enrolled. In 2008, 13 master's awarded. *Degree requirements:* For master's, capstone experience. *Entrance requirements:* For master's, interview (if GPA less than 2.75), resumé, goals statement. Additional exam requirements/recommendations for international students: Required—TOEFL (minimum score 560 paper-based; 220 computer-based); Recommended—IELTS (minimum score 6). *Application deadline:* For fall admission, 3/1 for international students; for spring admission, 7/1 for international students. Applications are processed on a rolling basis. Application fee: $30. Electronic applications accepted. *Expenses:* Tuition, state resident: full-time $6430; part-time $357 per credit. Tuition, nonresident: full-time $10,288; part-time $572 per credit. Required fees: $1127; $38 per credit. One-time fee: $44 part-time. *Financial support:* In 2008–09, 8 research assistantships with full tuition reimbursements (averaging $5,000 per year) were awarded; career-related internships or fieldwork, scholarships/grants, unspecified assistantships, and resident hall directors, student payroll positions also available. Support available to part-time students. Financial award applicants required to submit FAFSA. *Unit head:* Dr. Barbara Denison, Chairperson, 717-477-1735, Fax: 717-477-4011, E-mail: bjdeni@ship.edu. *Application contact:* Renee Payne, Associate Dean of Graduate Admissions, 717-477-1231, Fax: 717-477-4016, E-mail: rmpayn@ship.edu.

Simon Fraser University, Graduate Studies, Faculty of Applied Sciences, School of Communication, Burnaby, BC V5A 1S6, Canada. Offers MA, PhD. *Degree requirements:* For master's, thesis optional; for doctorate, thesis/dissertation. *Entrance requirements:* For master's, minimum GPA of 3.0; for doctorate, minimum GPA of 3.5. Additional exam requirements/recommendations for international students: Required—TOEFL or IELTS. Electronic applications accepted. *Faculty research:* Theory and methodology, policy studies in communication media and telecommunication, international development, journalism studies, telelearning and telework.

South Dakota State University, Graduate School, College of Arts and Science, Department of Journalism and Mass Communication, Brookings, SD 57007. Offers communication studies and journalism (MS). Part-time and evening/weekend programs available. *Faculty:* 4 full-time (2 women). *Students:* 6 full-time (0 women), 19 part-time (13 women); includes 1 minority (African American). 18 applicants, 94% accepted, 17 enrolled. In 2008, 6 master's awarded. *Degree requirements:* For master's, thesis, oral exam. *Entrance requirements:* Additional exam requirements/recommendations for international students: Required—TOEFL (minimum score 550 paper-based; 213 computer-based; 79 iBT). *Application deadline:* For fall admission, 4/15 priority date for international students; for spring admission, 8/15 priority date for international students. Applications are processed on a rolling basis. Application fee: $35. *Faculty research:* Mass communication applications. *Unit head:* Dr. Mary Arnold, Head, 605-688-4171, Fax: 605-688-5034, E-mail: mary.arnold@sdstate.edu. *Application contact:* Lyle D. Olson, Graduate Coordinator, 605-688-6516, Fax: 605-688-5034, E-mail: lyle.olson@sdstate.edu.

Southeastern Louisiana University, College of Arts, Humanities and Social Sciences, Department of Communication, Hammond, LA 70402. Offers organizational communication (MA). Part-time and evening/weekend programs available. *Faculty:* 2 full-time (1 woman). *Students:* 10 full-time (7 women), 26 part-time (19 women); includes 5 minority (all African Americans), 2 international. Average age 29. 19 applicants, 100% accepted, 14 enrolled. In 2008, 8 master's awarded. *Degree requirements:* For master's, comprehensive exam. *Entrance requirements:* For master's, GRE General Test (800 or better), bachelor's degree in communication or related field, minimum GPA of 3.0. Additional exam requirements/recommendations for international students: Required—TOEFL (minimum score 500 paper-based; 173 computer-based; 61 iBT). *Application deadline:* For fall admission, 7/15 priority date for domestic students, 6/1 priority date for international students; for spring admission, 12/1 priority date for domestic students, 10/1 priority date for international students. Applications are processed on a rolling basis. Application fee: $20 ($30 for international students). Electronic applications accepted. *Expenses:* Tuition, area resident: Full-time $2376. Tuition, state resident: full-time $2376. Tuition, nonresident: full-time $6876. Required fees: $1105. *Financial support:* In 2008–09, 5 students received support, including 4 research assistantships with full tuition reimbursements available (averaging $10,100 per year), 1 teaching assistantship with full tuition reimbursement available (averaging $10,100 per year); career-related internships or fieldwork, Federal Work-Study, institutionally sponsored loans, unspecified assistantships, and administrative assistantships also available. Support available to part-time students. Financial award application deadline: 5/1; financial award applicants required to submit FAFSA. *Faculty research:* Cross cultural communication in multi-national organizations, health communication among women, leadership communication, new media in organizations, crisis communication in organizations. *Unit head:* Dr. Karen Fontenot, Department Head, 985-549-2105, Fax: 985-549-5014, E-mail: kfontenot@selu.edu. *Application contact:* Sandra Meyers, Graduate Admissions Analyst, 985-549-2066, Fax: 985-549-5632, E-mail: admissions@selu.edu.

Southern Illinois University Carbondale, Graduate School, College of Mass Communication and Media Arts, Carbondale, IL 62901-4701. Offers MA, MFA, PhD, MBA/MA. Part-time programs available. *Degree requirements:* For doctorate, thesis/dissertation. *Entrance requirements:* For doctorate, GRE General Test, minimum GPA of 3.25. Additional exam requirements/recommendations for international students: Required—TOEFL.

See Close-Ups on pages 699 and 701.

Southern Methodist University, Meadows School of the Arts, Division of Communication Arts, Dallas, TX 75275. Offers MA. Part-time and evening/weekend programs available. *Faculty:* 9 full-time (3 women), 6 part-time/adjunct (1 woman). *Students:* 12 full-time (7 women), 1 part-time (0 women); includes 2 minority (1 American Indian/Alaska Native, 1 Hispanic American), 5 international. Average age 30. 9 applicants, 78% accepted, 4 enrolled. In 2008, 6 master's awarded. *Degree requirements:* For master's, thesis or alternative. *Entrance requirements:* For master's, GRE General Test, minimum undergraduate GPA of 3.0 in major field during last 2 years. Additional exam requirements/recommendations for international students: Required—TOEFL (minimum score 550 paper-based; 213 computer-based; 80 iBT). *Application deadline:* For fall admission, 3/1 priority date for domestic and international students. Application fee: $75. *Financial support:* In 2008–09, 7 students received support, including 7 teaching assistantships (averaging $6,500 per year); research assistantships, scholarships/grants, tuition waivers (full), and unspecified assistantships also available. Financial award application deadline: 3/15. *Faculty research:* Digital sound, new technology, film and gender study, popular film and TV genres, Asian cinema. Total annual research expenditures: $10,000. *Unit head:* Rick Worland, Chair, 214-768-3708, Fax: 214-768-2784, E-mail: rworland@smu.edu. *Application contact:* Jean Cherry, Director of Graduate Admissions and Records, 214-768-3765, Fax: 214-768-3272, E-mail: jcherry@smu.edu.

Southern Polytechnic State University, School of Arts and Sciences, Department of English, Technical Communication, and Media Arts, Marietta, GA 30060-2896. Offers communications management (Graduate Certificate); content development (Graduate Certificate); information design and communication (MS); instructional design (Graduate Certificate); technical and professional communication (Graduate Certificate); visual communication and graphics (Graduate Certificate). Part-time and evening/weekend programs available. Postbaccalaureate distance learning degree programs offered (minimal on-campus study). *Faculty:* 4 full-time (3 women), 1 part-time/adjunct. *Students:* 5 full-time (4 women), 38 part-time (25 women); includes 13 minority (12 African Americans, 1 Hispanic American), 3 international. Average age 38. 38 applicants, 68% accepted, 23 enrolled. In 2008, 10 master's awarded. *Degree requirements:* For master's, thesis optional, 36 hours completed through thesis option (6 hours), internship option (6 hours) or advanced coursework option (6 hours); for Graduate Certificate, thesis optional, 18 hours completed through thesis option (6 hours), internship option (6 hours) or advanced coursework option (6 hours). *Entrance requirements:* For master's, GRE, statement of purpose, writing sample, professional recommendations, proctored essay; for Graduate Certificate, statement of purpose, writing sample, professional recommendations, proctored essay. Additional exam requirements/recommendations for international students: Required—TOEFL (minimum score 550 paper-based; 213 computer-based; 79 iBT), IELTS (minimum score 6.5). *Application deadline:* For fall admission, 5/1 priority date for domestic students, 7/1 priority date for international students; for spring admission, 9/1 priority date for domestic students, 11/1 priority date for international students. Applications are processed on a rolling basis. Application fee: $20. Electronic applications accepted. *Expenses:* Tuition, area resident: Full-time $2752; part-time $172 per semester hour. Tuition, state resident: full-time $2752; part-time $172 per semester hour. Tuition, nonresident: full-time $10,992; part-time $687 per semester hour. Required fees: $365 per semester. *Financial support:* In 2008–09, 14 students received support, including 1 research assistantship with full tuition reimbursement available (averaging $4,000 per year); career-related internships or fieldwork, Federal Work-Study, scholarships/grants, and unspecified assistantships also available. Support available to part-time students. Financial award application deadline: 5/1; financial award applicants required to submit FAFSA. *Faculty research:* Usability, user-centered design, instructional design, information architecture, information design. *Unit head:* Dr. Mark Nunes, Chair, 678-915-7202, Fax: 678-915-7425, E-mail: mnunes@spsu.edu. *Application contact:* Nikki Palamiotis, Director of Graduate Studies, 678-915-4276, Fax: 678-915-7292, E-mail: npalamio@spsu.edu.

Southern Utah University, College of Humanities and Social Sciences, Program in Communication, Cedar City, UT 84720-2498. Offers MA. Electronic applications accepted.

Spalding University, Graduate Studies, College of Business and Communication, Louisville, KY 40203-2188. Offers business communication (MS). Part-time and evening/weekend programs available. *Degree requirements:* For master's, project. *Entrance requirements:* For master's, GRE or GMAT, writing sample, interview, letters of recommendation. Additional exam requirements/recommendations for international students: Required—TOEFL (minimum score 535 paper-based; 203 computer-based). Electronic applications accepted. *Expenses:* Tuition: Full-time $11,340; part-time $630 per credit hour. Tuition and fees vary according to program. *Faculty research:* Curriculum development, consumer behavior, interdisciplinary pedagogy.

Spring Arbor University, School of Arts and Sciences, Spring Arbor, MI 49283-9799. Offers communication (MA); spiritual formation and leadership (MA). Part-time programs available. Postbaccalaureate distance learning degree programs offered (no on-campus study). *Faculty:* 6 full-time (1 woman), 11 part-time/adjunct (5 women). *Students:* 104 full-time (64 women), 38 part-time (24 women); includes 8 minority (7 African Americans, 1 Hispanic American), 1 international. Average age 42. In 2008, 3 master's awarded. *Degree requirements:* For master's, thesis (for some programs). *Entrance requirements:* For master's, GRE (taken within the last 5 years), writing sample, 3 recommendations, personal goals statement. Additional exam requirements/recommendations for international students: Required—TOEFL (minimum score 550 paper-based; 220 computer-based). Application fee: $40. *Expenses:* Contact institution. *Financial support:* Applicants required to submit FAFSA. *Unit head:* Dr. Wally Metts, Chair of the Department of Communication, 517-750-1200 Ext. 1491, E-mail: wmetts@arbor.edu. *Application contact:* Dale Glinz, Lead Recruitment Specialist/Trainer, Graduate and Professional Studies, 517-750-6703, E-mail: dglinz@arbor.edu.

Stanford University, School of Humanities and Sciences, Department of Communication, Stanford, CA 94305-9991. Offers communication (journalism specialization) (MA); communication theory and research (PhD). *Degree requirements:* For master's, thesis, project; for doctorate, thesis/dissertation, qualifying examination, area examination, 2 projects. *Entrance requirements:* For master's and doctorate, GRE General Test. Additional exam requirements/recommendations for international students: Required—TOEFL (minimum score 600 paper-based; 250 computer-based). Electronic applications accepted.

State University of New York College at Potsdam, School of Arts and Sciences, Department of English and Communication, Potsdam, NY 13676. Offers English and communication (MA). Part-time and evening/weekend programs available. *Faculty:* 6 full-time (3 women), 1 (woman) part-time/adjunct. *Students:* 14 full-time (7 women), 9 part-time (7 women), 1 international. 13 applicants, 77% accepted, 8 enrolled. In 2008, 6 master's awarded. *Degree requirements:* For master's, one foreign language, thesis or alternative. *Entrance requirements:* For master's, minimum GPA of 3.0 in last 60 hours of undergraduate course work. Additional exam requirements/recommendations for international students: Required—TOEFL (minimum score 550 paper-based; 213 computer-based; 80 iBT), IELTS (minimum score 6). *Application deadline:* For fall admission, 4/1 priority date for domestic and international students; for spring admission, 10/15 priority date for domestic and international students. Applications are processed on a rolling basis. Application fee: $50. *Expenses:* Tuition, state resident: full-time $7390; part-time $328 per credit hour. Tuition, nonresident: full-time $12,085; part-time $552 per credit hour. Required fees: $952; $43.70 per credit hour. *Financial support:* In 2008–09, 1 student received support; teaching assistantships with full tuition reimbursements available, Federal Work-Study and unspecified assistantships available. Support available to part-time students. Financial award application deadline: 3/1; financial award applicants required to submit FAFSA. *Unit head:* Dr. Lisa Wilson, Director of Graduate Studies, English and Communication, 315-267-2004, Fax: 315-267-3256, E-mail: wilsonlm@potsdam.edu. *Application contact:* Peter Cutler, Graduate Admissions Counselor, 315-267-3154, Fax: 315-267-4802, E-mail: cutlerpj@potsdam.edu.

State University of New York College of Environmental Science and Forestry, Program in Environmental Science, Syracuse, NY 13210-2779. Offers environmental and community land planning (MPS, MS, PhD); environmental and natural resources policy (PhD); environmental communication and participatory processes (MPS, MS, PhD); environmental policy and democratic processes (MPS, MS, PhD); environmental systems and risk management (MPS, MS, PhD); water and wetland resource studies (MPS, MS, PhD). Part-time programs available. *Degree requirements:* For master's, thesis (for some programs); for doctorate, comprehensive exam, thesis/dissertation. *Entrance requirements:* For master's and doctorate, GRE General Test, minimum GPA of 3.0. Additional exam requirements/recommendations for international students: Required—TOEFL (minimum score 550 paper-based; 213 computer-based; 80 iBT), IELTS (minimum score 6). *Faculty research:* Environmental education/communications, water resources, land resources, waste management.

Stephen F. Austin State University, Graduate School, College of Applied Arts and Science, Department of Communication, Nacogdoches, TX 75962. Offers communication (MA); mass communication (MA). Part-time programs available. *Degree requirements:* For master's, comprehensive exam, thesis optional. *Entrance requirements:* For master's, GRE General Test. Additional exam requirements/recommendations for international students: Required—TOEFL (minimum score 550 paper-based; 213 computer-based).

Stevens Institute of Technology, Graduate School, Charles V. Schaefer Jr. School of Engineering, Department of Electrical and Computer Engineering, Program in Electrical Engineering, Hoboken, NJ 07030. Offers computer architecture and digital system design (M Eng); electrical engineering (PhD); microelectronics and photonics science and technology (M Eng); signal processing for communications (M Eng); telecommunications systems engineering (M Eng); wireless communications (M Eng, Certificate). *Degree requirements:* For master's, thesis optional; for doctorate, variable foreign language requirement, thesis/dissertation. *Entrance requirements:* For master's, doctorate, and Certificate, GRE. Additional exam requirements/recommendations for international students: Required—TOEFL. Electronic applications accepted.

Suffolk University, College of Arts and Sciences, Department of Communication, Boston, MA 02108-2770. Offers communication studies (MAC); integrated marketing communication (MAC); organizational communication (MAC); public relations and advertising (MAC). Part-time and evening/weekend programs available. *Degree requirements:* For master's, thesis optional. *Entrance requirements:* For master's, GRE General Test, MAT, or GMAT, statement of professional goals, official transcripts, 2 letters of recommendation, resumé. Additional exam requirements/recommendations for international students: Required—TOEFL (minimum score 550 paper-based; 213 computer-based; 80 iBT). Electronic applications accepted. *Expenses:* Contact institution. *Faculty research:* New media and new markets for advertising, First Amendment issues with the Internet, gender and intercultural communication, organizational development.

Syracuse University, Graduate School, College of Visual and Performing Arts, Program in Communication and Rhetorical Studies, Syracuse, NY 13244. Offers MA, MS. Part-time programs available. *Entrance requirements:* For master's, GRE General Test, writing sample. Additional exam requirements/recommendations for international students: Required—TOEFL. Electronic applications accepted.

Communication—General

Syracuse University, Graduate School, S. I. Newhouse School of Public Communications, Syracuse, NY 13244. Offers MA, MS, PhD, JD/MA, JD/MS, MS/MA. *Accreditation:* ACEJMC (one or more programs are accredited). Postbaccalaureate distance learning degree programs offered (minimal on-campus study). *Degree requirements:* For master's, comprehensive exam (for some programs); for doctorate, thesis/dissertation, qualifying exams. *Entrance requirements:* For master's and doctorate, GRE General Test. Additional exam requirements/recommendations for international students: Required—TOEFL (minimum score 600 paper-based; 250 computer-based; 100 iBT), IELTS (minimum score 7). Electronic applications accepted. *Faculty research:* Media convergence, political reporting, interactive multimedia, popular television, advertising effectiveness.

Announcement: We have recently launched our redesigned Web site at newhouse.syr.edu. It incorporates information about our ten professional master's programs as well as details on admissions, financial aid, and other University resources. The Web site also includes information session dates, recent alumni profiles, and examples of student work.

See Close-Up on page 705.

Teachers College, Columbia University, Graduate Faculty of Education, Department of Math, Science and Technology, Program in Communications, New York, NY 10027-6696. Offers Ed M, MA, Ed D. Part-time and evening/weekend programs available. *Faculty:* 24 part-time/adjunct. *Students:* 10 full-time (7 women), 38 part-time (28 women); includes 10 minority (4 African Americans, 4 Asian Americans or Pacific Islanders, 2 Hispanic Americans), 6 international. Average age 34. 25 applicants, 60% accepted, 9 enrolled. In 2008, 7 master's, 2 doctorates awarded. Terminal master's awarded for partial completion of doctoral program. *Degree requirements:* For doctorate, thesis/dissertation. *Entrance requirements:* For doctorate, GRE General Test or MAT. *Application deadline:* For fall admission, 5/15 for domestic students; for spring admission, 12/1 for domestic students. Application fee: $75. *Expenses:* Tuition: Full-time $26,040; part-time $1085 per credit. Required fees: $720. *Financial support:* Career-related internships or fieldwork, Federal Work-Study, institutionally sponsored loans, and tuition waivers (full and partial) available. Support available to part-time students. Financial award application deadline: 2/1. *Faculty research:* Television and youth, application of digital technology to education reform. *Unit head:* Dr. O. Roger Anderson, Chair, 212-678-3405. *Application contact:* Deanna Ghozati, Assistant Director of Admission, 212-678-4018, Fax: 212-678-4171, E-mail: ghozati@tc.edu.

Temple University, Graduate School, School of Communications and Theater, Philadelphia, PA 19122-6096. Offers MA, MFA, MJ, MS, PhD. Part-time and evening/weekend programs available. *Degree requirements:* For doctorate, one foreign language, thesis/dissertation. *Entrance requirements:* For master's, minimum GPA of 3.0; for doctorate, GRE General Test, minimum GPA of 3.0. Additional exam requirements/recommendations for international students: Required—TOEFL (minimum score 550 paper-based; 213 computer-based; 79 iBT). Electronic applications accepted.

Temple University, Health Sciences Center and Graduate School, College of Health Professions, Department of Communication Sciences, Philadelphia, PA 19122-6096. Offers communication sciences (PhD); linguistics (MA); speech-language-hearing (MA). *Accreditation:* ASHA. Part-time and evening/weekend programs available. *Degree requirements:* For doctorate, thesis/dissertation. *Entrance requirements:* For master's and doctorate, GRE General Test, minimum GPA of 3.0. Additional exam requirements/recommendations for international students: Required—TOEFL (minimum score 550 paper-based; 213 computer-based; 79 iBT). Electronic applications accepted. *Faculty research:* Fluency, infants and families, multilingual/multicultural communication, geriatrics, conflict process, language, health communication.

Texas A&M University, College of Liberal Arts, Department of Communication, College Station, TX 77843. Offers MA, PhD. *Faculty:* 15. *Students:* 47 full-time (31 women), 31 part-time (19 women); includes 12 minority (4 African Americans, 1 Asian American or Pacific Islander, 7 Hispanic Americans), 13 international. Average age 27. In 2008, 6 master's, 7 doctorates awarded. *Degree requirements:* For master's, thesis or alternative; for doctorate, thesis/dissertation. *Entrance requirements:* For master's, GRE General Test. Additional exam requirements/recommendations for international students: Required—TOEFL. *Application deadline:* For fall admission, 2/15 priority date for domestic students; for spring admission, 10/15 for domestic students. Applications are processed on a rolling basis. Application fee: $50 ($75 for international students). Electronic applications accepted. *Expenses:* Tuition, area resident: Full-time $3838.50. Tuition, state resident: full-time $3838.50. Tuition, nonresident: full-time $8897. Required fees: $2359.60. *Financial support:* In 2008–09, fellowships with partial tuition reimbursements (averaging $12,000 per year), research assistantships with partial tuition reimbursements (averaging $11,000 per year), teaching assistantships with partial tuition reimbursements (averaging $11,000 per year) were awarded; institutionally sponsored loans also available. Financial award application deadline: 2/1; financial award applicants required to submit FAFSA. *Faculty research:* Rhetoric and public affairs, communication and health, communication and organizations. *Unit head:* Dr. Richard L. Street, Head, 979-845-0209, E-mail: r-street@tamu.edu. *Application contact:* Barbara F. Sharf, Director of Graduate Studies, 979-845-0625, Fax: 979-845-6594, E-mail: bsharf@tamu.edu.

Texas Southern University, Tavis Smiley School of Communication, Houston, TX 77004-4584. Offers MA. Part-time programs available. *Faculty:* 4 full-time (2 women). *Students:* 15 full-time (11 women), 34 part-time (22 women); includes 46 African Americans, 1 Hispanic American, 2 international. Average age 30. 16 applicants, 100% accepted, 13 enrolled. In 2008, 15 master's awarded. *Degree requirements:* For master's, comprehensive exam, thesis. *Entrance requirements:* For master's, GRE General Test, minimum GPA of 2.5. Additional exam requirements/recommendations for international students: Required—TOEFL. *Application deadline:* For fall admission, 7/15 priority date for domestic students. Applications are processed on a rolling basis. Application fee: $50 ($75 for international students). *Expenses:* Tuition, area resident: Full-time $1912; part-time $96 per credit hour. Tuition, state resident: full-time $1912; part-time $96 per credit hour. Tuition, nonresident: full-time $6302; part-time $343 per credit hour. Required fees: $3542. *Financial support:* Fellowships, research assistantships, teaching assistantships, career-related internships or fieldwork, Federal Work-Study, and institutionally sponsored loans available. Financial award application deadline: 5/1. *Unit head:* Dr. James Ward, Dean, 713-313-7740, E-mail: ward_jw@tsu.edu. *Application contact:* Dr. Louis Browne, Graduate Adviser, 713-313-7024.

Texas State University–San Marcos, Graduate School, College of Fine Arts and Communication, San Marcos, TX 78666. Offers MA, MFA, MM. Part-time and evening/weekend programs available. *Degree requirements:* For master's, comprehensive exam. *Entrance requirements:* For master's, GRE General Test (for some programs), minimum GPA of 2.75 in last 60 hours of course work. Additional exam requirements/recommendations for international students: Required—TOEFL (minimum score 550 paper-based; 213 computer-based). Electronic applications accepted.

Texas State University–San Marcos, Graduate School, College of Fine Arts and Communication, Department of Communication Studies, Program in Communication Studies, San Marcos, TX 78666. Offers MA. Part-time and evening/weekend programs available. *Degree requirements:* For master's, comprehensive exam. *Entrance requirements:* For master's, minimum GPA of 3.0 in last 60 hours. Additional exam requirements/recommendations for international students: Required—TOEFL (minimum score 550 paper-based; 213 computer-based). Electronic applications accepted. *Faculty research:* Speech education, rhetoric and criticism, interpersonal and group communication, communication theory, rhetoric of Sojourner Truth.

Texas Tech University, Graduate School, College of Arts and Sciences, Department of Communication Studies, Lubbock, TX 79409. Offers MA. Part-time programs available. *Faculty:* 8 full-time (3 women). *Students:* 16 full-time (11 women), 6 part-time (4 women); includes 7 minority (1 African American, 1 Asian American or Pacific Islander, 5 Hispanic Americans), 2 international. Average age 26. 18 applicants, 28% accepted, 4 enrolled. In 2008, 6 master's awarded. *Degree requirements:* For master's, thesis. *Entrance requirements:* For master's, GRE General Test. Additional exam requirements/recommendations for international students: Required—TOEFL (minimum score 550 paper-based; 213 computer-based). *Application deadline:* For fall admission, 3/1 priority date for international students; for spring admission, 11/1 priority date for international students. Applications are processed on a rolling basis. Application fee: $50 ($60 for international students). Electronic applications accepted. *Expenses:* Tuition, area resident: Part-time $194 per credit hour. Tuition, state resident: full-time $4648; part-time $194 per credit hour. Tuition, nonresident: full-time $11,392; part-time $475 per credit hour. Required fees: $2206; $69 per credit hour. $389 per semester. *Financial support:* In 2008–09, 22 students received support, including 17 teaching assistantships with partial tuition reimbursements available (averaging $10,259 per year); research assistantships with partial tuition reimbursements available, Federal Work-Study and institutionally sponsored loans also available. Support available to part-time students. Financial award application deadline: 4/15; financial award applicants required to submit FAFSA. *Faculty research:* Computer mediated communication, intercultural communication, health communication, interpersonal communication, family communication. *Unit head:* Dr. Patrick C. Hughes, Chair, 806-742-3911, Fax: 806-742-1025, E-mail: patrick.hughes@ttu.edu. *Application contact:* Dr. Juliann Scholl, Graduate Director, 806-742-1675, Fax: 806-742-1025, E-mail: juliann.scholl@ttu.edu.

Towson University, College of Graduate Studies and Research, Program in Communications Management, Towson, MD 21252-0001. Offers MS. *Degree requirements:* For master's, thesis. *Entrance requirements:* For master's, 24 credits in mass communications, public relations and/or advertising, writing and statistics; professional experience; minimum GPA of 3.0. Electronic applications accepted.

Towson University, College of Graduate Studies and Research, Program in Strategic Public Relations and Integrated Communications, Towson, MD 21252-0001. Offers Certificate. Evening/weekend programs available. Postbaccalaureate distance learning degree programs offered (no on-campus study). *Entrance requirements:* For degree, 24 credits in related course work, minimum GPA of 3.0. Electronic applications accepted.

Trinity International University, Trinity Graduate School, Deerfield, IL 60015-1284. Offers bioethics (MA); communication and culture (MA); counseling psychology (MA); instructional leadership (M Ed); teaching (MA). Part-time and evening/weekend programs available. Postbaccalaureate distance learning degree programs offered (minimal on-campus study). *Degree requirements:* For master's, comprehensive exam. *Entrance requirements:* For master's, GRE General Test or MAT, minimum undergraduate GPA of 3.0. Additional exam requirements/recommendations for international students: Required—TOEFL (minimum score 580 paper-based; 237 computer-based), TWE (minimum score 4). Electronic applications accepted.

Trinity (Washington) University, School of Professional Studies, Washington, DC 20017-1094. Offers business administration (MBA); communication (MA); international security studies (MA); organizational management (MSA), including federal program management, human resource management, nonprofit management, organizational development, public and community health. Part-time and evening/weekend programs available. *Degree requirements:* For master's, thesis (for some programs), capstone project (MSA). *Entrance requirements:* For master's, minimum GPA of 2.5. Additional exam requirements/recommendations for international students: Required—TOEFL (minimum score 550 paper-based; 213 computer-based).

Troy University, Graduate School, College of Communication and Fine Arts, Troy, AL 36082. Offers MS. *Degree requirements:* For master's, comprehensive exam, thesis optional. *Entrance requirements:* For master's, GRE, MAT, or GMAT. Additional exam requirements/recommendations for international students: Required—TOEFL (minimum score 523 paper-based; 200 computer-based).

Université de Montréal, Faculty of Arts and Sciences, Department of Communication, Montréal, QC H3C 3J7, Canada. Offers communication (PhD); communication in changing organizations (Certificate); communication sciences (M Sc). *Faculty:* 17 full-time (8 women), 4 part-time/adjunct (2 women). *Students:* 37 full-time (26 women), 76 part-time (45 women). 145 applicants, 28% accepted, 37 enrolled. In 2008, 28 master's, 1 doctorate awarded. *Degree requirements:* For master's, thesis; for doctorate, one foreign language, thesis/dissertation, general exam. *Entrance requirements:* For doctorate, proficiency in French. *Application deadline:* For fall admission, 2/1 priority date for domestic students; for winter admission, 11/1 priority date for domestic students; for spring admission, 2/1 priority date for domestic students. Application fee: $100. Electronic applications accepted. *Financial support:* Fellowships, research assistantships, teaching assistantships, career-related internships or fieldwork available. *Faculty research:* Mass media/new communication technologies, organizational communication. *Unit head:* Francois Cooren, Director, 514-343-7819, Fax: 514-343-2298, E-mail: f.cooren@umontreal.ca. *Application contact:* Micheline Frenete, Responsible for the M Sc, 514-343-2056, E-mail: micheline.frenette@umontreal.ca.

Université du Québec à Montréal, Graduate Programs, Program in Communications, Montréal, QC H3C 3P8, Canada. Offers MA, PhD. Part-time programs available. *Degree requirements:* For master's, thesis; for doctorate, thesis/dissertation. *Entrance requirements:* For master's, appropriate bachelor's degree or equivalent, proficiency in French; for doctorate, appropriate master's degree or equivalent, proficiency in French.

Université du Québec à Trois-Rivières, Graduate Programs, Program in Social Communication, Trois-Rivières, QC G9A 5H7, Canada. Offers MA, DESS.

University at Albany, State University of New York, College of Arts and Sciences, Department of Communication, Albany, NY 12222-0001. Offers communication (MA); sociology and communication (PhD). Part-time programs available. *Degree requirements:* For master's, comprehensive exam, thesis or alternative; for doctorate, comprehensive exam, thesis/dissertation. *Entrance requirements:* For master's, minimum GPA of 3.0; for doctorate, GRE, minimum GPA of 3.0. Additional exam requirements/recommendations for international students: Required—TOEFL (minimum score 550 paper-based; 213 computer-based). Electronic applications accepted. *Faculty research:* Language and social interaction, campaign communication, media agenda-setting, high-speed management, organizational boundary-spanning.

University at Buffalo, the State University of New York, Graduate School, College of Arts and Sciences, Department of Communication, Buffalo, NY 14260. Offers MA, PhD. Part-time programs available. Terminal master's awarded for partial completion of doctoral program. *Degree requirements:* For master's, thesis; for doctorate, comprehensive exam, thesis/dissertation. *Entrance requirements:* For master's and doctorate, GRE General Test, minimum GPA of 3.0. Additional exam requirements/recommendations for international students: Required—TOEFL (minimum score 600 paper-based; 250 computer-based); Recommended—TWE. Electronic applications accepted. *Faculty research:* Technology, health, international, interpersonal.

The University of Akron, Graduate School, College of Fine and Applied Arts, School of Communication, Akron, OH 44325. Offers MA. Part-time and evening/weekend programs available. *Degree requirements:* For master's, thesis optional, thesis, project or written comprehensive exam. *Entrance requirements:* For master's, undergraduate major in communication or related area, minimum GPA of 2.75. Additional exam requirements/recommendations for international students: Required—TOEFL (minimum score 550 paper-based; 213 computer-based; 79 iBT). Electronic applications accepted. *Faculty research:* Communications theory, business and organization communications, criticism of communications, film and video studies, interpersonal and intercultural communications.

The University of Alabama, Graduate School, College of Communication and Information Sciences, Tuscaloosa, AL 35487. Offers MA, MFA, MLIS, PhD. *Accreditation:* ACEJMC (one or more programs are accredited at the [master's] level). *Faculty:* 51 full-time (21 women), 4 part-time/adjunct (3 women). *Students:* 195 full-time (132 women), 196 part-time (150 women); includes 39 minority (23 African Americans, 3 American Indian/Alaska Native, 6 Asian Americans or Pacific Islanders, 7 Hispanic Americans), 22 international. Average age 31. 472 applicants, 49% accepted, 87 enrolled. In 2008, 148 master's, 6 doctorates awarded. *Degree requirements:* For master's, comprehensive exam, thesis or alternative; for doctorate, comprehensive exam, thesis/dissertation. *Entrance requirements:* For master's, GRE; for doctorate, GRE, minimum graduate GPA of 3.0, master's degree. Additional exam requirements/recommendations for international students: Required—TOEFL (minimum score 600 paper-based; 250 computer-based). *Application deadline:* For fall admission, 2/15 priority date for domestic and international students; for winter admission, 11/1 priority date for international students; for spring admission, 11/1 priority date for domestic students. Applications are processed on a rolling basis. Application fee: $30. Electronic applications accepted. *Expenses:* Tuition, area resident: Full-time $6400. Tuition, state resident: full-time $6400. Tuition, nonresident: full-time $18,000. *Financial support:* In 2008–09, 78 students received support, including 3 fellowships with tuition reimbursements available (averaging $15,000 per year), 34 research assistantships with tuition reimbursements available (averaging $13,045 per year), 38 teaching assistantships with tuition reimbursements available (averaging $13,045 per year); career-related internships or fieldwork, Federal Work-Study, institutionally sponsored loans, and health care benefits also available. Financial award application deadline: 2/15. *Faculty research:* Media research, broadcast policy and law, political communication, media management, political advertising. Total annual research expenditures: $1.1 million. *Unit head:* Dr. Jennings Bryant, Associate Dean for Graduate Studies, 205-348-8593, Fax: 205-348-6774. *Application contact:* Diane Shaddix, Information Contact, 205-348-8593, Fax: 205-348-6774, E-mail: dshaddix@bama.ua.edu.

The University of Alabama at Birmingham, School of Arts and Humanities, Department of Communication Studies, Birmingham, AL 35294. Offers communication management (MA).

University of Alaska Fairbanks, College of Liberal Arts, Department of Communications, Fairbanks, AK 99775-5680. Offers professional communications (MA). Part-time programs available. *Faculty:* 4 full-time (3 women). *Students:* 10 full-time (8 women), 5 part-time (4 women); includes 3 minority (1 African American, 1 Asian American or Pacific Islander, 1 Hispanic American), 2 international. Average age 31. 15 applicants, 73% accepted, 10 enrolled. In 2008, 6 master's awarded. *Degree requirements:* For master's, comprehensive exam, thesis, oral defense. *Entrance requirements:* Additional exam requirements/recommendations for international students: Required—TOEFL (minimum score 550 paper-based; 213 computer-based; 80 iBT). *Application deadline:* For fall admission, 6/1 for domestic students, 3/1 for international students; for spring admission, 10/15 for domestic students, 9/1 for international students. Applications are processed on a rolling basis. Application fee: $60. Electronic applications accepted. *Expenses:* Tuition, area resident: Full-time $5418; part-time $301 per credit. Tuition, state resident: full-time $5418; part-time $301 per credit. Tuition, nonresident: full-time $11,070; part-time $615 per credit. Required fees: $849; $25 per credit. $78 per semester. Tuition and fees vary according to course load and reciprocity agreements. *Financial support:* In 2008–09, 10 teaching assistantships (averaging $12,006 per year) were awarded; fellowships, Federal Work-Study, scholarships/grants, tuition waivers, and unspecified assistantships also available. Support available to part-time students. Financial award application deadline: 7/1; financial award applicants required to submit FAFSA. *Faculty research:* Interpersonal communications, health communications, intercultural communications, politeness and face management in conversation, gender communication. *Unit head:* Dr. Robert Arundale, Department Chair, 907-474-6591, Fax: 907-474-5858, E-mail: fycomm@uaf.edu. *Application contact:* Dr. Robert Arundale, Department Chair, 907-474-6591, Fax: 907-474-5858, E-mail: fycomm@uaf.edu.

University of Alberta, Faculty of Extension, Edmonton, AB T6G 2E1, Canada. Offers communications and technology (MA).

University of Alberta, Faculty of Graduate Studies and Research, Program in Communications and Technology, Edmonton, AB T6G 2E1, Canada. Offers MACT.

The University of Arizona, Graduate College, College of Social and Behavioral Sciences, Department of Communication, Tucson, AZ 85721. Offers MA, PhD. Part-time programs available. Terminal master's awarded for partial completion of doctoral program. *Degree requirements:* For master's, thesis optional; for doctorate, comprehensive exam, thesis/dissertation. *Entrance requirements:* For master's, GRE General Test, minimum GPA of 3.25, writing sample; for doctorate, GRE General Test, minimum GPA of 3.5, writing sample. Additional exam requirements/recommendations for international students: Required—TOEFL (minimum score 550 paper-based; 213 computer-based). Electronic applications accepted. *Faculty research:* Health communication, new communication techologies.

University of Arkansas, Graduate School, J. William Fulbright College of Arts and Sciences, Department of Communication, Fayetteville, AR 72701-1201. Offers MA. Part-time programs available. *Degree requirements:* For master's, thesis. *Entrance requirements:* For master's, GRE General Test.

University of Calgary, Faculty of Graduate Studies, Faculty of Communication and Culture, Calgary, AB T2N 1N4, Canada. Offers MA, MCS, PhD. Part-time and evening/weekend programs available. *Degree requirements:* For master's, thesis, project (MCS), thesis (MA); for doctorate, thesis/dissertation. *Entrance requirements:* For master's, minimum GPA of 3.0; for doctorate, master's degree, minimum GPA of 3.0, BA degree, min GPA of 3.0. Additional exam requirements/recommendations for international students: Required—TOEFL (minimum score 600 paper-based; 250 computer-based); Recommended—IELTS (minimum score 8). Electronic applications accepted. *Faculty research:* Science communications, structuration theory, organizational communication, communication theory, media law.

University of California, Davis, Graduate Studies, Program in Communication, Davis, CA 95616. Offers MA. *Degree requirements:* For master's, comprehensive exam (for some programs), thesis (for some programs). *Entrance requirements:* For master's, GRE. Additional exam requirements/recommendations for international students: Required—TOEFL (minimum score 550 paper-based; 213 computer-based).

University of California, San Diego, Office of Graduate Studies, Department of Communication, La Jolla, CA 92093. Offers MA, PhD. *Entrance requirements:* For doctorate, GRE General Test. Electronic applications accepted.

University of California, San Diego, Office of Graduate Studies, Interdisciplinary Program in Cognitive Science, La Jolla, CA 92093. Offers cognitive science/anthropology (PhD); cognitive science/communication (PhD); cognitive science/computer science and engineering (PhD); cognitive science/linguistics (PhD); cognitive science/neuroscience (PhD); cognitive science/philosophy (PhD); cognitive science/psychology (PhD); cognitive science/sociology (PhD). Admissions offered through affiliated departments. *Degree requirements:* For doctorate, thesis/dissertation. *Entrance requirements:* For doctorate, GRE General Test, acceptance into one of the 8 participating departments. *Faculty research:* Language and cognition, philosophy of mind, visual perception, biological anthropology, sociolinguistics.

University of California, Santa Barbara, Graduate Division, College of Letters and Sciences, Division of Social Sciences, Department of Communication, Santa Barbara, CA 93106-4020. Offers human development (PhD); MA/PhD. *Faculty:* 20 full-time (8 women), 1 part-time/adjunct (0 women). *Students:* 38 full-time (26 women). Average age 28. 155 applicants, 12% accepted, 10 enrolled. In 2008, 2 doctorates awarded. *Degree requirements:* For doctorate, comprehensive exam, thesis/dissertation. *Entrance requirements:* For doctorate, GRE General Test, 3 letters of recommendation, statement of purpose, personal achievements/contributions statement, resumé/curriculum vitae, transcripts for post-secondary institutions attended. Additional exam requirements/recommendations for international students: Required—TOEFL (minimum score 600 paper-based; 213 computer-based; 80 iBT), TOEFL or IELTS. *Application deadline:* For fall admission, 1/1 for domestic and international students. Application fee: $70 ($90 for international students). Electronic applications accepted. *Expenses:* Tuition, nonresident: full-time $25,149. Required fees: $10,143. Full-time tuition and fees vary according to campus/location, reciprocity agreements and student level. *Financial support:* In 2008–09, 38 students received support, including 38 fellowships with full and partial tuition reimbursements available (averaging $5,500 per year), 5 research assistantships with full and partial tuition reimbursements available (averaging $7,800 per year), 34 teaching assistantships with partial tuition reimbursements available (averaging $11,000 per year); Federal Work-Study, institutionally sponsored loans, scholarships/grants, health care benefits, tuition waivers (full and partial), and unspecified assistantships also available. Financial award application deadline: 1/1; financial award applicants required to submit FAFSA. *Faculty research:* Interpersonal communication, organizational communication, media communication, political communication, intrapersonal communication. Total annual research expenditures: $100,000. *Unit head:* Prof. Michael Stohl, Chair, 805-893-7935, Fax: 805-893-7102, E-mail: mstohl@comm.ucsb.edu. *Application contact:* Nancy Siris-Rawls, Graduate Program Assistant, 805-893-3046, Fax: 805-893-7102, E-mail: nsiris@comm.ucsb.edu.

University of California, Santa Cruz, Division of Graduate Studies, Division of Physical and Biological Sciences, Program in Science Communication, Santa Cruz, CA 95064. Offers science illustration (Certificate); science writing (Certificate). *Entrance requirements:* For degree, GRE General Test, GRE Subject Test, bachelor's degree in science. Electronic applications accepted.

University of Central Florida, College of Sciences, Nicholson School of Communication, Orlando, FL 32816. Offers business communication (MA); interpersonal communication (MA); mass communication (MA). Part-time and evening/weekend programs available. *Faculty:* 41 full-time (18 women), 36 part-time/adjunct (18 women). *Students:* 44 full-time (39 women), 28 part-time (25 women); includes 15 minority (6 African Americans, 3 Asian Americans or Pacific Islanders, 6 Hispanic Americans), 9 international. In 2008, 29 master's awarded. *Degree requirements:* For master's, thesis or comprehensive exam. *Entrance requirements:* For master's, GRE General Test, minimum GPA of 3.0 in last 60 hours of course work. Additional exam requirements/recommendations for international students: Required—TOEFL. *Application deadline:* For fall admission, 7/15 for domestic students; for spring admission, 12/7 for domestic students. Application fee: $30. Electronic applications accepted. *Expenses:* Tuition, area resident: Full-time $6816; part-time $284 per credit. Tuition, state resident: full-time $6816; part-time $1076 per credit. Tuition, nonresident: full-time $25,824. Required fees: $216; $9 per credit. *Financial support:* In 2008–09, 2 fellowships with partial tuition reimbursements (averaging $10,000 per year), 4 research assistantships with partial tuition reimbursements (averaging $4,400 per year), 16 teaching assistantships with partial tuition reimbursements (averaging $6,400 per year) were awarded; career-related internships or fieldwork, Federal Work-Study, institutionally sponsored loans, tuition waivers (partial), and unspecified assistantships also available. Financial award application deadline: 3/1; financial award applicants required to submit FAFSA. *Faculty research:* Persuasion, communication apprehension, nonverbal communication, conflict resolution. *Unit head:* Dr. Robert Chandler, Director, 407-823-2683, Fax: 407-823-5216, E-mail: rcchandl@mail.ucf.edu. *Application contact:* Dr. Robert Chandler, Director, 407-823-2683, Fax: 407-823-5216, E-mail: rcchandl@mail.ucf.edu.

University of Central Missouri, The Graduate School, College of Arts, Humanities and Social Sciences, Department of Communication, Warrensburg, MO 64093. Offers communication (MA); speech communication (MA). Part-time programs available. *Degree requirements:* For master's, comprehensive exam, internship, research papers or thesis. *Entrance requirements:* For master's, minimum GPA of 2.5. Additional exam requirements/recommendations for international students: Required—TOEFL (minimum score 500 paper-based; 173 computer-based).

University of Cincinnati, Graduate School, McMicken College of Arts and Sciences, Department of Communication, Cincinnati, OH 45221. Offers MA. Part-time programs available. *Degree requirements:* For master's, comprehensive exam, thesis or alternative. *Entrance requirements:* For master's, GRE General Test, undergraduate course work in communication. Additional exam requirements/recommendations for international students: Required—TOEFL. Electronic applications accepted. *Faculty research:* Political communication, health communication, organizational communication, interpersonal communication.

University of Colorado at Boulder, Graduate School, College of Arts and Sciences, Department of Communication, Boulder, CO 80309. Offers MA, PhD. *Degree requirements:* For master's, comprehensive exam, thesis optional; for doctorate, comprehensive exam, thesis/dissertation. *Entrance requirements:* For master's and doctorate, GRE General Test, minimum undergraduate GPA of 3.2. *Faculty research:* Organizational communication, computer-mediated communication and new technology, critical cultural studies, rhetoric and civil discourse, interpersonal communication, language and social interaction.

University of Colorado at Boulder, Graduate School, School of Journalism and Mass Communication, Boulder, CO 80309. Offers communication (PhD), including media studies; mass communication research (MA); newsgathering (MA). *Accreditation:* ACEJMC (one or more programs are accredited). Part-time programs available. *Degree requirements:* For master's, comprehensive exam, thesis or alternative; for doctorate, comprehensive exam, thesis/dissertation. *Entrance requirements:* For master's, GRE General Test, minimum undergraduate GPA of 2.75; for doctorate, GRE General Test, minimum undergraduate GPA of 3.2, 3.5 graduate. *Faculty research:* Writing on science and the environment, mass communication and public opinion, minority representation in the media, media and culture.

University of Colorado at Colorado Springs, Graduate School, College of Letters, Arts and Sciences, Department of Communications, Colorado Springs, CO 80933-7150. Offers MA. Part-time programs available. *Faculty:* 8 full-time (6 women). *Students:* 24 full-time (16 women), 13 part-time (8 women); includes 7 minority (5 African Americans, 2 Hispanic Americans), 1 international. Average age 31. 19 applicants, 100% accepted, 15 enrolled. In 2008, 14 master's awarded. *Degree requirements:* For master's, thesis optional. *Entrance requirements:* For master's, GRE General Test. *Financial support:* Teaching assistantships, career-related internships or fieldwork, Federal Work-Study, and institutionally sponsored loans available. Support available to part-time students. *Faculty research:* Organizational communication, interpersonal communication, communication education, oral communication, cultural diversity. *Unit head:* Dr. David Nelson, Chair, 719-255-4129, Fax: 719-255-4030, E-mail: drnelson@uccs.edu. *Application contact:* Debbie MacDonald, Program Assistant, 719-255-4114, Fax: 719-255-4030, E-mail: knorris@uccs.edu.

University of Colorado Denver, College of Liberal Arts and Sciences, Department of Communication, Denver, CO 80217-3364. Offers communication (MA); interactive media (Certificate); public relations (Certificate); technical and professional communication (Certificate); technical communication (MS); usability testing and interface design (Certificate). Part-time and evening/weekend programs available. *Degree requirements:* For master's, comprehensive exam, thesis or alternative. *Entrance requirements:* For master's, GRE General Test. Additional exam requirements/recommendations for international students: Required—TOEFL (minimum score 525 paper-based; 197 computer-based). Electronic applications accepted.

University of Connecticut, Graduate School, College of Liberal Arts and Sciences, Department of Communication Sciences, Storrs, CT 06269. Offers communication sciences (MA, Au D, PhD), including audiology (Au D, PhD), communication processes (MA), communication processes and marketing communication (PhD), speech-language pathology (MA, PhD); Au D/PhD. *Accreditation:* ASHA (one or more programs are accredited). Terminal master's awarded for partial completion of doctoral program. *Degree requirements:* For master's, comprehensive exam; for doctorate, thesis/dissertation. *Entrance requirements:* For master's and doctorate, GRE General Test. Additional exam requirements/recommendations for international students: Required—TOEFL (minimum score 550 paper-based; 213 computer-based). Electronic applications accepted.

Communication—General

University of Connecticut, Graduate School, College of Liberal Arts and Sciences, Department of Communication Sciences, Field of Communication Sciences, Program in Communication Processes, Storrs, CT 06269. Offers MA. *Degree requirements:* For master's, comprehensive exam. *Entrance requirements:* For master's, GRE General Test. Additional exam requirements/recommendations for international students: Required—TOEFL (minimum score 550 paper-based; 213 computer-based). Electronic applications accepted.

University of Dayton, Graduate School, College of Arts and Sciences, Department of Communication, Dayton, OH 45469-1300. Offers MA. Part-time and evening/weekend programs available. *Faculty:* 8 full-time (5 women), 1 part-time/adjunct (0 women). *Students:* 16 full-time (14 women), 2 part-time (both women); includes 3 minority (2 African Americans, 1 Asian American or Pacific Islander), 2 international. Average age 28. 35 applicants, 60% accepted, 11 enrolled. In 2008, 11 master's awarded. *Degree requirements:* For master's, comprehensive exam, thesis optional. *Entrance requirements:* For master's, GRE General Test, minimum undergraduate GPA of 3.0. Additional exam requirements/recommendations for international students: Required—TOEFL (minimum score 550 paper-based; 213 computer-based; 80 iBT). *Application deadline:* For fall admission, 3/1 priority date for domestic and international students; for winter admission, 7/1 priority date for international students; for spring admission, 1/1 priority date for international students. Applications are processed on a rolling basis. Application fee: $0 ($50 for international students). Electronic applications accepted. *Expenses:* Tuition: Full-time $6950; part-time $1737.50 per semester. Required fees: $25 per semester. Tuition and fees vary according to course level, course load, degree level and program. *Financial support:* In 2008–09, 8 teaching assistantships with full tuition reimbursements (averaging $9,517 per year) were awarded; career-related internships or fieldwork, institutionally sponsored loans, health care benefits, and unspecified assistantships also available. Support available to part-time students. Financial award applicants required to submit FAFSA. *Faculty research:* Health communication, organizational communication, mass communication. *Unit head:* Dr. Jon Hess, Chair, 937-229-2028, E-mail: jonathan.hess@notes.udayton.edu. *Application contact:* Angela Jones-Glukhov, Associate Director of Graduate Admissions, 937-229-4305, Fax: 937-229-4729, E-mail: jonesgas@notes.udayton.edu.

University of Delaware, College of Arts and Sciences, Department of Communication, Newark, DE 19716. Offers MA. Part-time and evening/weekend programs available. *Degree requirements:* For master's, comprehensive exam (for some programs), thesis (for some programs). *Entrance requirements:* For master's, GRE General Test, minimum GPA of 3.0. Additional exam requirements/recommendations for international students: Required—TOEFL (minimum score 600 paper-based; 270 computer-based). Electronic applications accepted. *Faculty research:* Politics and the media, online social interaction technologies, mass communication law, media and the perceptions of reality, the role of communication in public opinion processes, small group research, communication during resource dilemmas.

University of Denver, Division of Arts, Humanities and Social Sciences, School of Communication, Denver, CO 80208. Offers MA, MS, PhD. Part-time programs available. *Faculty:* 23 full-time (15 women), 7 part-time/adjunct (3 women). *Students:* 63 full-time (46 women), 58 part-time (44 women); includes 14 minority (4 African Americans, 2 Asian Americans or Pacific Islanders, 8 Hispanic Americans), 11 international. Average age 29. In 2008, 34 master's, 8 doctorates awarded. *Degree requirements:* For doctorate, one foreign language, thesis/dissertation. *Entrance requirements:* For master's, GRE General Test. Additional exam requirements/recommendations for international students: Required—TOEFL, TWE. *Application deadline:* Applications are processed on a rolling basis. Application fee: $50. Electronic applications accepted. *Financial support:* Career-related internships or fieldwork, Federal Work-Study, institutionally sponsored loans, and scholarships/grants available. Support available to part-time students. *Unit head:* Chairperson. *Application contact:* Information Contact, 303-871-2166, E-mail: mcomadm@du.edu.

See Close-Up on page 707.

University of Denver, University College, Denver, CO 80208. Offers applied communication (MAS, MPS, Certificate); computer information systems (MAS, Certificate); environmental policy and management (MAS, Certificate); geographic information systems (MAS, Certificate); human resource administration (MPS, Certificate); knowledge and information technologies (MAS); liberal studies (MLS, Certificate); modern languages (MLS, Certificate); organizational leadership (MPS, Certificate); security management (Certificate); technology management (MAS, Certificate), including 21st century strategic management (MAS), international markets (MAS), project management (MAS), research and development management (MAS); telecommunications (MAS, Certificate), including broadband (MAS), telecommunications management and policy (MAS), telecommunications technology (MAS), wireless networks (MAS). Part-time and evening/weekend programs available. Postbaccalaureate distance learning degree programs offered (no on-campus study). *Faculty:* 137 part-time/adjunct (55 women). *Students:* 28 full-time (15 women), 699 part-time (401 women); includes 129 minority (54 African Americans, 8 American Indian/Alaska Native, 22 Asian Americans or Pacific Islanders, 45 Hispanic Americans), 4 international. Average age 36. 845 applicants, 96% accepted, 326 enrolled. In 2008, 221 master's, 3 Certificates awarded. *Entrance requirements:* Additional exam requirements/recommendations for international students: Required—TOEFL (minimum score 550 paper-based; 213 computer-based). *Application deadline:* Applications are processed on a rolling basis. Application fee: $75. Electronic applications accepted. *Expenses:* Contact institution. *Financial support:* Applicants required to submit FAFSA. *Unit head:* Dr. James Davis, Dean, 303-871-2291, Fax: 303-871-4047, E-mail: jdavis@du.edu. *Application contact:* Information Contact, 303-871-3155.

University of Dubuque, Program in Communication, Dubuque, IA 52001-5099. Offers information technologies communication (MAC); leadership and management (MAC); strategic and corporate communication (MAC). Part-time and evening/weekend programs available. *Degree requirements:* For master's, thesis optional. *Entrance requirements:* For master's, GRE, minimum GPA of 2.5, 3 recommendations. Additional exam requirements/recommendations for international students: Required—TOEFL (minimum score 550 paper-based; 213 computer-based). Electronic applications accepted. *Faculty research:* Intercultural communication, management communication.

University of Florida, Graduate School, College of Journalism and Communications, Gainesville, FL 32611. Offers advertising (M Adv); journalism (MAMC); mass communication (MAMC, PhD); public relations (MAMC); telecommunication (MAMC); JD/MAMC; JD/PhD. *Accreditation:* ACEJMC (one or more programs are accredited). Part-time programs available. Terminal master's awarded for partial completion of doctoral program. *Degree requirements:* For master's, thesis optional; for doctorate, thesis/dissertation. *Entrance requirements:* For master's and doctorate, GRE General Test, minimum GPA of 3.0. Additional exam requirements/recommendations for international students: Required—TOEFL (minimum score 550 paper-based; 213 computer-based). Electronic applications accepted. *Faculty research:* Public opinion, law and policy, regulation, environmental communication, international communication.

University of Georgia, Graduate School, Grady School of Journalism and Mass Communication, Athens, GA 30602. Offers journalism and mass communication (MA); mass communication (PhD). *Accreditation:* ACEJMC (one or more programs are accredited). *Degree requirements:* For master's, comprehensive exam, thesis (MA); for doctorate, comprehensive exam, thesis/dissertation. *Entrance requirements:* For master's and doctorate, GRE General Test. Additional exam requirements/recommendations for international students: Required—TOEFL, TWE (PhD). Electronic applications accepted.

University of Hartford, College of Arts and Sciences, Program in Communication, West Hartford, CT 06117-1599. Offers MA. Part-time and evening/weekend programs available. *Degree requirements:* For master's, comprehensive exam, thesis optional. *Entrance requirements:* For master's, GRE, 3 letters of recommendation. Additional exam requirements/recommendations for international students: Required—TOEFL (minimum score 550 paper-based; 213 computer-based). Electronic applications accepted. *Expenses:* Contact institution. *Faculty research:* Communication reticence, relational communication, media literacy, journalism history, media audience attitude and behavior.

University of Hawaii at Manoa, Graduate Division, Colleges of Arts and Sciences, College of Social Sciences, School of Communications, Program in Communication, Honolulu, HI 96822. Offers MA. Part-time programs available. *Degree requirements:* For master's, thesis optional. *Entrance requirements:* Additional exam requirements/recommendations for international students: Required—TOEFL (minimum score 600 paper-based; 250 computer-based; 100 iBT), IELTS (minimum score 7).

University of Houston, College of Liberal Arts and Social Sciences, School of Communication, Houston, TX 77204. Offers mass communication studies (MA); public relations studies (MA); speech communication (MA). Part-time and evening/weekend programs available. *Faculty:* 7 full-time (4 women), 2 part-time/adjunct (0 women). *Students:* 29 full-time (25 women), 62 part-time (52 women); includes 32 minority (19 African Americans, 2 Asian Americans or Pacific Islanders, 11 Hispanic Americans), 13 international. Average age 29. 46 applicants, 85% accepted, 20 enrolled. In 2008, 20 master's awarded. *Entrance requirements:* For master's, GRE General Test, minimum GPA of 3.0 in last 60 hours of course work. *Application deadline:* For fall admission, 7/3 priority date for domestic students. Applications are processed on a rolling basis. Application fee: $25 ($75 for international students). *Expenses:* Tuition, state resident: full-time $5164; part-time $287 per credit. Tuition, nonresident: full-time $10,222; part-time $568 per credit. *Financial support:* In 2008–09, 2 fellowships with full tuition reimbursements (averaging $9,950 per year), 6 teaching assistantships with full tuition reimbursements (averaging $9,950 per year) were awarded; career-related internships or fieldwork, Federal Work-Study, institutionally sponsored loans, scholarships/grants, health care benefits, and unspecified assistantships also available. Support available to part-time students. Financial award application deadline: 2/1. *Faculty research:* Risk communication, relationship development, critical studies, corporate communication. *Unit head:* Beth Olson, Chairperson, 713-743-2873, Fax: 713-743-2876, E-mail: bolson@uh.edu. *Application contact:* Angela Parrish, Graduate Coordinator, 713-743-2873, Fax: 713-743-2876, E-mail: aparrish@bayou.uh.edu.

University of Illinois at Chicago, Graduate College, College of Liberal Arts and Sciences, Department of Communication, Chicago, IL 60607-7128. Offers MA, PhD. Evening/weekend programs available. *Degree requirements:* For master's, thesis. *Entrance requirements:* For master's, GRE General Test, minimum GPA of 3.0 in last 90 hours. Additional exam requirements/recommendations for international students: Required—TOEFL. Electronic applications accepted. *Faculty research:* Organizational, political, and interpersonal communication; public relations.

University of Illinois at Springfield, Graduate Programs, College of Liberal Arts and Sciences, Program in Communication, Springfield, IL 62703-5407. Offers MA. Part-time and evening/weekend programs available. *Faculty:* 10 full-time (6 women), 3 part-time/adjunct (2 women). *Students:* 17 full-time (9 women), 18 part-time (11 women); includes 3 minority (all African Americans), 1 international. Average age 30. 27 applicants, 52% accepted, 13 enrolled. In 2008, 20 master's awarded. *Degree requirements:* For master's, comprehensive exam, thesis, or project. *Entrance requirements:* For master's, UIS Graduate Admission Writing Exam, departmental writing proficiency exam, minimum undergraduate GPA of 3.0. Additional exam requirements/recommendations for international students: Required—TOEFL (minimum score 580 paper-based). *Application deadline:* Applications are processed on a rolling basis. Application fee: $50 ($60 for international students). Electronic applications accepted. *Expenses:* Tuition, state resident: full-time $6144; part-time $256 per credit hour. Tuition, nonresident: full-time $13,980; part-time $582.50 per credit hour. Required fees: $1800. *Financial support:* In 2008–09, research assistantships with full tuition reimbursements (averaging $8,109 per year), teaching assistantships with full tuition reimbursements (averaging $8,109 per year) were awarded; career-related internships or fieldwork, Federal Work-Study, scholarships/grants, health care benefits, and unspecified assistantships also available. Support available to part-time students. Financial award application deadline: 11/15; financial award applicants required to submit FAFSA. *Unit head:* Dr. Mary Bohlen, Program Administrator, 217-206-7362, Fax: 217-206-6217. *Application contact:* Dr. Lynn Pardie, Office of Graduate Studies, 800-252-8533, Fax: 217-206-7623, E-mail: pardie.lynn@uis.edu.

University of Illinois at Urbana–Champaign, Graduate College, College of Liberal Arts and Sciences, Department of Communication, Champaign, IL 61820. Offers communication (MA). *Faculty:* 24 full-time (11 women). *Students:* 39 full-time (27 women), 22 part-time (11 women); includes 9 minority (3 African Americans, 3 Asian Americans or Pacific Islanders, 3 Hispanic Americans), 1 international. 106 applicants, 22% accepted, 12 enrolled. In 2008, 7 master's, 5 doctorates awarded. *Entrance requirements:* For master's and doctorate, GRE, minimum GPA of 3.0; writing sample. Additional exam requirements/recommendations for international students: Required—TOEFL (minimum score 611 paper-based; 245 computer-based; 103 iBT). *Application deadline:* Applications are processed on a rolling basis. Application fee: $60 ($75 for international students). Electronic applications accepted. *Financial support:* In 2008–09, 2 fellowships, 13 research assistantships, 54 teaching assistantships were awarded; tuition waivers (full and partial) also available. *Unit head:* Dale Brashers, Head, 217-333-2683, Fax: 217-244-1598, E-mail: dbrasher@illinois.edu. *Application contact:* Mary Strum, Graduate Program Secretary, 217-333-2683, Fax: 217-244-1598, E-mail: strum@illinois.edu.

University of Illinois at Urbana–Champaign, Graduate College, College of Media, Institute of Communications Research, Champaign, IL 61820. Offers communications and media (PhD). *Faculty:* 10 full-time (4 women). *Students:* 39 full-time (20 women), 11 part-time (7 women); includes 12 minority (4 African Americans, 3 Asian Americans or Pacific Islanders, 5 Hispanic Americans), 18 international. 126 applicants, 6% accepted, 7 enrolled. In 2008, 10 doctorates awarded. *Entrance requirements:* For doctorate, GRE General Test, minimum GPA of 3.0. Additional exam requirements/recommendations for international students: Required—TOEFL (minimum score 550 paper-based). *Application deadline:* Applications are processed on a rolling basis. Application fee: $60 ($75 for international students). Electronic applications accepted. *Financial support:* In 2008–09, 15 fellowships, 16 research assistantships, 32 teaching assistantships were awarded; tuition waivers (full and partial) also available. *Faculty research:* Feminist cultural studies, media technology, international communications, Latino studies, economics of media. *Unit head:* Clifford Christians, Director, 217-333-1549, Fax: 217-244-7695, E-mail: cchrstns@illinois.edu. *Application contact:* Bonnie Howard, Administrative Secretary, 217-333-7860, Fax: 217-333-7695, E-mail: bbhoward@illinois.edu.

The University of Iowa, Graduate College, College of Liberal Arts and Sciences, Department of Communication Studies, Iowa City, IA 52242-1316. Offers communication research (MA, PhD); rhetorical studies (MA, PhD). *Degree requirements:* For master's, thesis optional, exam; for doctorate, comprehensive exam, thesis/dissertation. *Entrance requirements:* For master's and doctorate, GRE General Test, minimum GPA of 3.0. Additional exam requirements/recommendations for international students: Required—TOEFL (minimum score 550 paper-based; 213 computer-based; 81 iBT). Electronic applications accepted.

The University of Kansas, Graduate Studies, College of Liberal Arts and Sciences, Department of Communication Studies, Lawrence, KS 66045-7574. Offers MA, PhD. Evening/weekend programs available. *Faculty:* 21. *Students:* 59 full-time (37 women), 23 part-time (15 women); includes 3 minority (2 African Americans, 1 Asian American or Pacific Islander), 13 international. Average age 32. 94 applicants, 41% accepted, 21 enrolled. In 2008, 13 master's, 6 doctorates awarded. *Degree requirements:* For master's, comprehensive exam (for some programs), thesis or alternative; for doctorate, comprehensive exam, thesis/dissertation. *Entrance requirements:* For master's, GRE General Test, minimum GPA of 3.1; for doctorate, GRE General Test, minimum GPA of 3.2 (undergraduate), 3.6 (graduate). Additional exam requirements/recommendations for international students: Required—TOEFL. *Application deadline:* For fall admission, 1/15 priority date for domestic students, 1/15 for international students; for spring admission, 11/15 for domestic and international students. Applications are processed on a rolling basis. Application fee: $45 ($55 for international students). Electronic applications accepted. *Expenses:* Tuition, area resident: Full-time $6122; part-time $255.10 per credit hour. Tuition, state resident: full-time $6122; part-time $255.10 per credit hour.

Tuition, nonresident: full-time $14,629; part-time $609.55 per credit hour. Required fees: $847; $70.56 per credit hour. Tuition and fees vary according to course load and program. *Financial support:* Fellowships with tuition reimbursements, research assistantships, teaching assistantships with full and partial tuition reimbursements, unspecified assistantships available. Financial award application deadline: 1/15. *Faculty research:* Rhetoric, organizational communication, political communication, interpersonal communication, new technology. *Unit head:* Dr. Robert C. Rowland, Chair, 785-864-3633, Fax: 785-864-5203, E-mail: rrowland@ku.edu. *Application contact:* Dr. Beth Innocenti, Graduate Director, 785-864-9018, Fax: 785-864-5203, E-mail: bimanole@ku.edu.

University of Kentucky, Graduate School, College of Communications and Information Studies, Program in Communication, Lexington, KY 40506-0032. Offers MA, PhD. *Degree requirements:* For master's, comprehensive exam, thesis optional; for doctorate, comprehensive exam, thesis/dissertation. *Entrance requirements:* For master's, GRE General Test, minimum undergraduate GPA of 2.75; for doctorate, GRE General Test, minimum graduate GPA of 3.0, minimum undergraduate GPA of 2.75. Additional exam requirements/recommendations for international students: Required—TOEFL (minimum score 550 paper-based; 213 computer-based). Electronic applications accepted. *Faculty research:* Public service campaigns, health communication, mass media law and public policy, political communication, international and intercultural communication.

University of Louisiana at Lafayette, BI Moody III College of Business Administration MBA Program, College of Liberal Arts, Department of Communication, Lafayette, LA 70504. Offers mass communications (MS). Part-time programs available. *Degree requirements:* For master's, thesis optional. *Entrance requirements:* For master's, GRE General Test, minimum GPA of 2.75. Additional exam requirements/recommendations for international students: Required—TOEFL (minimum score 550 paper-based; 213 computer-based). Electronic applications accepted. *Faculty research:* Mass media problems, issues and ethics, mass communication, historical studies, conflict of interest and law and ethics in journalism, contemporary issues and trends in publications.

University of Louisiana at Monroe, Graduate School, College of Arts and Sciences, Department of Communication, Monroe, LA 71209-0001. Offers MA. *Faculty:* 5 full-time (3 women). *Students:* 12 full-time (6 women), 7 part-time (6 women); includes 4 African Americans, 2 international. Average age 27. In 2008, 6 master's awarded. *Degree requirements:* For master's, thesis. *Entrance requirements:* For master's, GRE (minimum verbal and quantitative score: 900), minimum GPA of 2.5. Additional exam requirements/recommendations for international students: Required—TOEFL (minimum score 500 paper-based; 173 computer-based; 61 iBT). *Application deadline:* For fall admission, 8/22 priority date for domestic students, 7/1 for international students; for winter admission, 12/12 priority date for domestic students; for spring admission, 1/17 priority date for domestic students, 11/1 for international students. Applications are processed on a rolling basis. Application fee: $20 ($30 for international students). Electronic applications accepted. *Expenses:* Tuition, area resident: Full-time $2403; part-time $1202 per semester. Tuition, state resident: full-time $2403; part-time $1202 per semester. Tuition, nonresident: full-time $2403; part-time $1202 per semester. International tuition: $8352 full-time. Required fees: $1239.40; $141 per credit hour. *Financial support:* In 2008–09, 3 teaching assistantships with full tuition reimbursements (averaging $2,500 per year) were awarded; research assistantships, career-related internships or fieldwork, Federal Work-Study, and unspecified assistantships also available. Financial award application deadline: 4/1; financial award applicants required to submit FAFSA. *Faculty research:* Interactive media, rhetoric progress, interpersonal, journalism history, gender/multicultural issues, forensics. *Unit head:* Dr. Carl L. Thameling, Interim Head, 318-342-1406, Fax: 318-342-1422, E-mail: thameling@ulm.edu. *Application contact:* Dr. Lesli K Pace, Graduate Coordinator, 318-342-1165, Fax: 318-342-1422, E-mail: pace@ulm.edu.

University of Maine, Graduate School, College of Liberal Arts and Sciences, Department of Communication and Journalism, Orono, ME 04469. Offers communication (MA). Part-time programs available. *Degree requirements:* For master's, thesis or alternative. *Entrance requirements:* For master's, GRE General Test. Additional exam requirements/recommendations for international students: Required—TOEFL. Electronic applications accepted. *Faculty research:* Rhetorical theory, semiotics, discourse analysis, gender and communication, children's talk/communication disorders.

University of Maryland, Baltimore County, Graduate School, College of Arts, Humanities and Social Sciences, Department of Modern Languages and Linguistics, Program in Intercultural Communication, Baltimore, MD 21250. Offers MA. Part-time and evening/weekend programs available. *Faculty:* 18 full-time (6 women), 3 part-time/adjunct (2 women). *Students:* 19 full-time (17 women), 17 part-time (12 women); includes 5 minority (1 African American, 2 Asian Americans or Pacific Islanders, 2 Hispanic Americans), 10 international. 25 applicants, 64% accepted, 12 enrolled. In 2008, 18 master's awarded. *Degree requirements:* For master's, one foreign language, comprehensive exam (for some programs), thesis (for some programs). *Entrance requirements:* For master's, GRE General Test, minimum GPA of 3.0, 3 letters of recommendation, self-evaluation and statement of support, resumé. Additional exam requirements/recommendations for international students: Required—TOEFL (minimum score 213 computer-based). *Application deadline:* For fall admission, 1/31 for domestic and international students. Applications are processed on a rolling basis. Application fee: $45. Electronic applications accepted. *Financial support:* In 2008–09, 8 students received support, including 4 teaching assistantships with full tuition reimbursements available (averaging $11,324 per year); tuition waivers also available. Financial award applicants required to submit FAFSA. *Faculty research:* Comparative television research-cross-cultural; cultural studies; social developments in Latin America; intercultural communication; French civilization and cultural studies; language, gender and sexuality; sociolinguistics; African linguistics; immigrants in U. S. and Latin American societies. *Unit head:* Dr. Edward Larkey, Director, 410-455-2104, Fax: 410-455-1025, E-mail: larkey@umbc.edu. *Application contact:* Dr. Edward Larkey, Director, 410-455-2104, Fax: 410-455-1025, E-mail: larkey@umbc.edu.

University of Maryland, College Park, Graduate Studies, College of Arts and Humanities, Department of Communication, College Park, MD 20742. Offers MA, PhD. *Degree requirements:* For master's, thesis optional; for doctorate, comprehensive exam, thesis/dissertation. *Entrance requirements:* For master's, GRE General Test, minimum GPA of 3.0, sample of scholarly writing, 3 letters of recommendation; for doctorate, GRE General Test. Additional exam requirements/recommendations for international students: Required—TOEFL. Electronic applications accepted. *Faculty research:* Health communication, interpersonal communication, persuasion, intercultural communication, contemporary rhetoric theory.

University of Massachusetts Amherst, Graduate School, College of Social and Behavioral Sciences, Department of Communication, Amherst, MA 01003. Offers MA, PhD. Part-time programs available. Terminal master's awarded for partial completion of doctoral program. *Degree requirements:* For master's, thesis or alternative; for doctorate, comprehensive exam, thesis/dissertation. *Entrance requirements:* For master's and doctorate, GRE General Test, 3 letters of recommendation. Additional exam requirements/recommendations for international students: Required—TOEFL (minimum score 550 paper-based; 213 computer-based; 79 iBT), IELTS (minimum score 6.5). Electronic applications accepted. *Expenses:* Tuition, area resident: Full-time $2640. Tuition, nonresident: full-time $9936. One-time fee: $332 full-time. Tuition and fees vary according to course load.

University of Memphis, Graduate School, College of Communication and Fine Arts, Department of Communication, Memphis, TN 38152. Offers communication (MA); communication arts (PhD); film and video production (MA). Part-time programs available. *Faculty:* 10 full-time (4 women). *Students:* 28 full-time (15 women), 17 part-time (9 women); includes 7 minority (all African Americans), 1 international. Average age 36. 24 applicants, 79% accepted, 12 enrolled. In 2008, 7 master's, 7 doctorates awarded. *Degree requirements:* For master's, comprehensive exam, thesis or alternative; for doctorate, comprehensive exam, thesis/dissertation. *Entrance requirements:* For master's and doctorate, GRE General Test. Additional exam requirements/recommendations for international students: Required—TOEFL (minimum score 550 paper-based; 210 computer-based). *Application deadline:* For fall admission, 8/1 for domestic students. Application fee: $35 ($60 for international students). *Expenses:* Tuition, area resident: Full-time $6242; part-time $330 per credit hour. Tuition, state resident: full-time $6242; part-time $330 per credit hour. Tuition, nonresident: full-time $17,828; part-time $815 per credit hour. Required fees: $1156. *Financial support:* Research assistantships with full tuition reimbursements, teaching assistantships with full tuition reimbursements, unspecified assistantships available. Financial award applicants required to submit FAFSA. *Faculty research:* Rhetoric, media studies, applied communication (health communication). *Unit head:* Dr. Mike Leff, Chair, 901-678-2565, Fax: 901-678-4331, E-mail: m_leff@bellsouth.net. *Application contact:* Dr. Sandra Sarkela, Coordinator of Graduate Studies, 901-678-3173, Fax: 901-678-4331, E-mail: ssarkela@memphis.edu.

University of Miami, Graduate School, School of Communication, Coral Gables, FL 33124. Offers communication (PhD); communication studies (MA); film studies (MA, PhD); motion pictures (MFA), including production, producing, and screenwriting; print journalism (MA); public relations (MA); Spanish language journalism (MA); television broadcast journalism (MA). *Accreditation:* ACEJMC. Part-time programs available. *Degree requirements:* For master's, comprehensive exam (for some programs), thesis (for some programs); for doctorate, comprehensive exam, thesis/dissertation. *Entrance requirements:* For master's, GRE General Test; for doctorate, GRE General Test, master's thesis or scholarly research. Additional exam requirements/recommendations for international students: Required—TOEFL (minimum score 600 paper-based; 250 computer-based; 100 iBT). Electronic applications accepted. *Faculty research:* Communication studies, mass communication, international/interpersonal communication, film studies, journalism.

University of Michigan, Horace H. Rackham School of Graduate Studies, College of Literature, Science, and the Arts, Department of Communication Studies, Ann Arbor, MI 48104-2523. Offers PhD. *Degree requirements:* For doctorate, comprehensive exam, thesis/dissertation. *Entrance requirements:* For doctorate, GRE. Additional exam requirements/recommendations for international students: Required—TOEFL (minimum score 560 paper-based; 220 computer-based; 84 iBT). Electronic applications accepted. *Faculty research:* Political communication; media, culture and society; media effects; race, gender, and the media; new media, media law and policy.

University of Minnesota, Twin Cities Campus, Graduate School, College of Design, Department of Design, Housing, and Apparel, Minneapolis, MN 55455-0213. Offers apparel (MA, MS, PhD); design communication (MA, MS, PhD); housing studies (MA, MS, PhD, Postbaccalaureate Certificate); interactive design (MFA); interior design (MA, MS, PhD). Part-time programs available. *Degree requirements:* For master's and Postbaccalaureate Certificate, comprehensive exam, thesis (for some programs); for doctorate, comprehensive exam, thesis/dissertation. *Entrance requirements:* For master's, GRE General Test, minimum GPA of 3.0 (preferred), portfolio, 3 letters of recommendation; for doctorate, GRE General Test, minimum GPA of 3.0 (preferred), portfolio, 3 letters of recommendation, writing sample; for Postbaccalaureate Certificate, GRE General Test, minimum GPA of 3.0 (preferred). Additional exam requirements/recommendations for international students: Required—TOEFL (minimum score 550 paper-based; 213 computer-based; 79 iBT). Electronic applications accepted. *Faculty research:* Housing policy and community development; consumer behavior; interactive design; design history; social, cultural, and behavioral issues related to designed environments.

University of Minnesota, Twin Cities Campus, Graduate School, College of Liberal Arts, Department of Communication Studies, Minneapolis, MN 55455-0213. Offers MA, PhD. *Degree requirements:* For master's, thesis or alternative; for doctorate, thesis/dissertation. *Entrance requirements:* For master's, GRE General Test, minimum GPA of 3.0; for doctorate, GRE General Test, minimum graduate GPA of 3.5. Additional exam requirements/recommendations for international students: Required—TOEFL. Electronic applications accepted. *Faculty research:* Rhetorical studies, communication theory, media studies, gender and communication, public address.

University of Missouri–Columbia, Graduate School, College of Arts and Sciences, Department of Communication, Columbia, MO 65211. Offers MA, PhD. *Faculty:* 11 full-time (6 women). *Students:* 22 full-time (13 women), 18 part-time (13 women); includes 4 minority (2 African Americans, 1 Asian American or Pacific Islander, 1 Hispanic American), 4 international. Average age 30. 88 applicants, 17% accepted, 8 enrolled. In 2008, 1 master's, 10 doctorates awarded. Terminal master's awarded for partial completion of doctoral program. *Degree requirements:* For doctorate, thesis/dissertation. *Entrance requirements:* For master's and doctorate, GRE General Test, minimum GPA of 3.0. Additional exam requirements/recommendations for international students: Required—TOEFL (minimum score 600 paper-based; 250 computer-based; 100 iBT). *Application deadline:* For fall admission, 2/15 priority date for domestic students. Applications are processed on a rolling basis. Application fee: $45 ($60 for international students). *Financial support:* Fellowships, research assistantships, teaching assistantships, institutionally sponsored loans available. *Unit head:* Dr. Mike Kramer, Department Chair, 573-882-6980, E-mail: kramerm@missouri.edu. *Application contact:* Martha Crump, Administrative Assistant, 573-882-4432, E-mail: crumpm@missouri.edu.

University of Missouri–St. Louis, College of Fine Arts and Communication, Department of Communication, St. Louis, MO 63121. Offers MA. Part-time and evening/weekend programs available. *Faculty:* 7 full-time (5 women). *Students:* 8 full-time (7 women), 16 part-time (12 women); includes 1 minority (African American), 4 international. Average age 29. In 2008, 6 master's awarded. *Entrance requirements:* For master's, 3 letters of recommendation. Additional exam requirements/recommendations for international students: Required—TOEFL (minimum score 600 paper-based; 233 computer-based). *Application deadline:* For fall admission, 7/15 for domestic and international students; for spring admission, 12/1 for domestic and international students. Application fee: $35 ($40 for international students). Electronic applications accepted. *Expenses:* Tuition, area resident: Full-time $5377; part-time $298.70 per credit hour. Tuition, nonresident: full-time $13,381; part-time $472.50 per credit hour. Required fees: $4078; $52 per credit hour. *Financial support:* In 2008–09, 5 teaching assistantships (averaging $12,000 per year) were awarded. Financial award application deadline: 4/1; financial award applicants required to submit FAFSA. *Faculty research:* Theory and methodology: intercultural, interpersonal, and mass organizational. *Unit head:* Dr. Alice Hall, Director of Graduate Studies, 314-516-5485, Fax: 314-516-5816, E-mail: halla@umsl.edu. *Application contact:* 314-516-5458, Fax: 314-516-6996, E-mail: gradadm@umsl.edu.

The University of Montana, Graduate School, College of Arts and Sciences, Department of Communication Studies, Missoula, MT 59812-0002. Offers MA. *Degree requirements:* For master's, thesis (for some programs). *Entrance requirements:* For master's, GRE General Test. Additional exam requirements/recommendations for international students: Required—TOEFL (minimum score 525 paper-based; 197 computer-based). *Faculty research:* Conflict management, organizational communication, language, personal relationships, rhetoric.

University of Nebraska at Omaha, Graduate Studies and Research, College of Communication, Fine Arts and Media, School of Communication, Omaha, NE 68182. Offers MA. Part-time and evening/weekend programs available. *Degree requirements:* For master's, comprehensive exam, thesis (for some programs). *Entrance requirements:* For master's, minimum GPA of 3.25, essay, 15 undergraduate communication courses. Additional exam requirements/recommendations for international students: Required—TOEFL (minimum score 550 paper-based; 213 computer-based; 80 iBT). Electronic applications accepted.

University of Nebraska–Lincoln, Graduate College, College of Arts and Sciences, Department of Communication Studies, Lincoln, NE 68588. Offers instructional communication (MA, PhD); interpersonal communication (MA, PhD); marketing, communication studies, and advertising (MA, PhD); organizational communication (MA, PhD); rhetoric and culture (MA, PhD). *Faculty:* 7 full-time (4 women). *Students:* 23 full-time (15 women), 9 part-time (8 women); includes 1 minority (Asian American or Pacific Islander), 1 international. Average age 35. In 2008, 2

Communication—General

University of Nebraska–Lincoln (continued)
master's, 2 doctorates awarded. *Degree requirements:* For master's, thesis optional; for doctorate, comprehensive exam, thesis/dissertation. *Entrance requirements:* For master's and doctorate, GRE General Test, writing sample. Additional exam requirements/recommendations for international students: Required—TOEFL (minimum score 600 paper-based; 250 computer-based). *Application deadline:* For fall admission, 1/15 for domestic and international students. Applications are processed on a rolling basis. Application fee: $40. Electronic applications accepted. *Expenses:* Tuition, state resident: full-time $4275; part-time $237.50 per credit hour. Tuition, nonresident: full-time $11,525; part-time $640.25 per credit hour. Required fees: $1068; $10.35 per credit hour. $440.70 per semester. Tuition and fees vary according to course load and program. *Financial support:* Fellowships, research assistantships, teaching assistantships, Federal Work-Study, health care benefits, and unspecified assistantships available. Support available to part-time students. Financial award application deadline: 1/15. *Faculty research:* Message strategies, gender communication, political communication, organizational communication, instructional communication. *Unit head:* Dr. William Seiler, Chair, 402-472-2069. *Application contact:* Ginny Gross, Director of Graduate Admissions, 402-472-2878, Fax: 402-472-0589, E-mail: grad_admissions@unl.edu.

University of Nevada, Las Vegas, Graduate College, Greenspun College of Urban Affairs, Department of Communication Studies, Las Vegas, NV 89154-4052. Offers MA. Part-time programs available. *Faculty:* 9 full-time (4 women). *Students:* 15 full-time (9 women), 4 part-time (3 women); includes 5 minority (2 African Americans, 3 Hispanic Americans). Average age 31. 16 applicants, 75% accepted, 7 enrolled. In 2008, 6 master's awarded. *Degree requirements:* For master's, comprehensive exam (for some programs), thesis (for some programs). *Entrance requirements:* For master's, GRE General Test. Additional exam requirements/recommendations for international students: Required—TOEFL (minimum score 550 paper-based; 213 computer-based; 80 iBT), IELTS (minimum score 7). *Application deadline:* For fall admission, 1/15 priority date for domestic and international students. Applications are processed on a rolling basis. Application fee: $60 ($75 for international students). Electronic applications accepted. *Expenses:* Tuition, state resident: full-time $1414; part-time $198 per credit. Tuition, nonresident: full-time $12,509; part-time $415.75 per credit. International tuition: $14,249 full-time. Required fees: $4 per credit. $252 per semester. Tuition and fees vary according to course load. *Financial support:* In 2008–09, 13 students received support, including 13 teaching assistantships with partial tuition reimbursements available (averaging $10,000 per year); institutionally sponsored loans, scholarships/grants, health care benefits, and unspecified assistantships also available. Financial award application deadline: 3/1. *Faculty research:* Rhetoric (public influence), interpersonal communication. *Unit head:* Dr. Tom Burkholder, Chair/Associate Professor, 702-895-5125, Fax: 702-895-4805, E-mail: tom.burkholder@unlv.edu. *Application contact:* Graduate College Admissions Evaluator, 702-895-3320, Fax: 702-895-4180, E-mail: gradcollege@unlv.edu.

University of New Mexico, Graduate School, College of Arts and Sciences, Department of Communication and Journalism, Albuquerque, NM 87131-2039. Offers communication (MA, PhD). Part-time programs available. *Degree requirements:* For master's, comprehensive exam (for some programs), thesis (for some programs), 30 hour class work and 6 hour thesis or project, or 36 hours class work and comprehensive exam; for doctorate, 2 foreign languages, comprehensive exam, thesis/dissertation. *Entrance requirements:* For master's and doctorate, GRE General Test, letters of recommendation, writing sample, letter of intent, vita, transcripts, application fee. Additional exam requirements/recommendations for international students: Required—TOEFL (minimum score 550 paper-based; 213 computer-based). Electronic applications accepted. *Faculty research:* Interpersonal/organizational communication, rhetoric, mass communication, intercultural communication, health communication.

The University of North Carolina at Chapel Hill, Graduate School, College of Arts and Sciences, Department of Communication Studies, Chapel Hill, NC 27599. Offers MA, PhD. *Degree requirements:* For master's, comprehensive exam, thesis; for doctorate, thesis/dissertation. *Entrance requirements:* For master's and doctorate, GRE General Test, minimum GPA of 3.0. Electronic applications accepted.

The University of North Carolina at Charlotte, Graduate School, College of Arts and Sciences, Department of Communication Studies, Charlotte, NC 28223-0001. Offers MA. Part-time and evening/weekend programs available. *Faculty:* 12 full-time (5 women). *Students:* 11 full-time (7 women), 14 part-time (11 women); includes 1 African American, 4 international. Average age 27. 31 applicants, 45% accepted, 7 enrolled. In 2008, 5 master's awarded. *Degree requirements:* For master's, thesis or alternative. *Entrance requirements:* For master's, GRE General Test, minimum GPA of 2.75 overall. Additional exam requirements/recommendations for international students: Required—TOEFL (minimum score 557 paper-based; 220 computer-based). *Application deadline:* For fall admission, 3/15 for domestic students, 5/1 for international students; for spring admission, 11/15 for domestic students, 10/1 for international students. Applications are processed on a rolling basis. Application fee: $55. Electronic applications accepted. *Expenses:* Tuition, area resident: Full-time $2919; part-time $122 per credit hour. Tuition, state resident: full-time $2919; part-time $122 per credit hour. Tuition, nonresident: full-time $13,126; part-time $547 per credit hour. Required fees: $1779; $91 per credit hour. Tuition and fees vary according to program. *Financial support:* In 2008–09, 1 research assistantship (averaging $4,000 per year), 12 teaching assistantships (averaging $10,287 per year) were awarded; career-related internships or fieldwork, Federal Work-Study, institutionally sponsored loans, scholarships/grants, unspecified assistantships, and 1 administrative assistantship ($9,000) also available. Support available to part-time students. Financial award application deadline: 4/1; financial award applicants required to submit FAFSA. *Faculty research:* Health literacy, systems of care and mental illness, the communication of emotions in gendered workplaces, international constructs of public relations managerial responsibilities, sports culture and the construction of social contracts, African American oratory. *Unit head:* Dr. Richard W. Leeman, Chair, 704-687-4005, Fax: 704-687-6900, E-mail: rwleeman@email.uncc.edu. *Application contact:* Kathy B. Giddings, Director of Graduate Admissions, 704-687-3366, Fax: 704-687-3279, E-mail: agidding@uncc.edu.

The University of North Carolina at Greensboro, Graduate School, College of Arts and Sciences, Department of Communication, Greensboro, NC 27412-5001. Offers communication studies (MA). Part-time programs available. *Degree requirements:* For master's, thesis or alternative. *Entrance requirements:* For master's, GRE General Test, MAT, or PRAXIS. Additional exam requirements/recommendations for international students: Required—TOEFL. Electronic applications accepted.

University of North Dakota, Graduate School, College of Arts and Sciences, School of Communication, Grand Forks, ND 58202. Offers MA, PhD. Part-time programs available. *Degree requirements:* For master's, comprehensive exam, thesis or alternative; for doctorate, thesis/dissertation. *Entrance requirements:* For master's and doctorate, GRE General Test, minimum GPA of 3.0. Additional exam requirements/recommendations for international students: Required—TOEFL (minimum score 550 paper-based; 213 computer-based; 79 iBT), IELTS (minimum score 6.5). Electronic applications accepted. *Faculty research:* Communication technologies, mass communication in diverse society, acculturation and socialization functions.

University of Northern Colorado, Graduate School, College of Humanities and Social Sciences, School of Communication, Program in Communication Studies, Greeley, CO 80639. Offers MA. Part-time programs available. *Faculty:* 4 full-time (1 woman). *Students:* 10 full-time (7 women), 9 part-time (7 women), 2 international. Average age 32. 12 applicants, 92% accepted, 5 enrolled. In 2008, 13 master's awarded. *Degree requirements:* For master's, comprehensive exam, thesis or alternative. *Entrance requirements:* For master's, GRE General Test, 3 letters of recommendation. *Application deadline:* Applications are processed on a rolling basis. Application fee: $50 ($60 for international students). Electronic applications accepted. *Expenses:* Tuition, state resident: full-time $4370; part-time $242.75 per credit hour. Tuition, nonresident: full-time $12,366; part-time $687 per credit hour. Required fees: $664.20; $36.90 per credit hour. *Financial support:* In 2008–09, 6 teaching assistantships (averaging $7,884 per year) were awarded; research assistantships. Financial award application deadline: 3/1; financial award applicants required to submit FAFSA. *Unit head:* Dr. James Keaton, Program Coordinator, 970-351-2045, Fax: 970-351-2336. *Application contact:* Linda Sisson, Graduate Student Admission Coordinator, 970-351-1807, Fax: 970-351-2371, E-mail: linda.sisson@unco.edu.

University of Northern Iowa, Graduate College, College of Humanities and Fine Arts, Department of Communication Studies, Cedar Falls, IA 50614. Offers MA. Part-time and evening/weekend programs available. *Students:* 26 full-time (17 women), 19 part-time (16 women); includes 10 minority (8 African Americans, 2 Hispanic Americans), 9 international. 37 applicants, 62% accepted, 9 enrolled. In 2008, 20 master's awarded. *Degree requirements:* For master's, comprehensive exam, thesis or alternative. *Entrance requirements:* For master's, minimum GPA of 3.0. Additional exam requirements/recommendations for international students: Required—TOEFL (minimum score 500 paper-based; 180 computer-based; 61 iBT). *Application deadline:* For fall admission, 8/1 priority date for domestic students. Applications are processed on a rolling basis. Application fee: $30 ($50 for international students). Electronic applications accepted. *Expenses:* Tuition, state resident: full-time $6446. Tuition, nonresident: full-time $14,874. Required fees: $852. *Financial support:* Career-related internships or fieldwork, Federal Work-Study, scholarships/grants, and tuition waivers (full and partial) available. Support available to part-time students. Financial award application deadline: 2/1. *Unit head:* Dr. John Fritch, Head, 319-273-2217, Fax: 319-273-7356, E-mail: john.fritch@uni.edu. *Application contact:* Laurie S. Russell, Record Analyst, 319-273-2623, Fax: 319-273-6792, E-mail: laurie.russell@uni.edu.

University of North Texas, Robert B. Toulouse School of Graduate Studies, College of Arts and Sciences, Department of Communication Studies, Denton, TX 76203. Offers MA, MS. Part-time programs available. *Degree requirements:* For master's, one foreign language, comprehensive exam, thesis optional, internship or problem in lieu of thesis. *Entrance requirements:* For master's, GRE General Test, letter of application, statement of purpose, vital resumé, transcripts. Additional exam requirements/recommendations for international students: Required—proof of English language proficiency required for non-native English speakers; Recommended—TOEFL (minimum score 550 paper-based; 213 computer-based). *Faculty research:* Rhetoric, performance studies, interpersonal communication, organizational communication, health communication.

University of Oklahoma, Graduate College, College of Arts and Sciences, Department of Communication, Norman, OK 73019. Offers MA, PhD. Postbaccalaureate distance learning degree programs offered (no on-campus study). *Faculty:* 16 full-time (7 women), 3 part-time/adjunct (0 women). *Students:* 46 full-time (30 women), 48 part-time (24 women); includes 16 minority (8 African Americans, 1 American Indian/Alaska Native, 4 Asian Americans or Pacific Islanders, 3 Hispanic Americans), 14 international. 65 applicants, 54% accepted, 13 enrolled. In 2008, 11 master's, 3 doctorates awarded. Terminal master's awarded for partial completion of doctoral program. *Degree requirements:* For master's, comprehensive exam, thesis or alternative; for doctorate, thesis/dissertation, general exam. *Entrance requirements:* For master's, GRE General Test, minimum undergraduate GPA of 3.0; for doctorate, GRE General Test, minimum graduate GPA of 3.5. Additional exam requirements/recommendations for international students: Required—TOEFL (minimum score 550 paper-based; 213 computer-based). *Application deadline:* For fall admission, 4/1 priority date for domestic students, 4/1 for international students; for spring admission, 11/1 for domestic students, 9/1 for international students. Applications are processed on a rolling basis. Application fee: $40 ($90 for international students). Electronic applications accepted. *Expenses:* Tuition, state resident: full-time $3744; part-time $156 per credit hour. Tuition, nonresident: full-time $13,577; part-time $565.70 per credit hour. Required fees: $2415.40; $90.10 per credit hour. *Financial support:* In 2008–09, 31 students received support, including 2 fellowships (averaging $3,000 per year), 1 research assistantship with partial tuition reimbursement available (averaging $19,350 per year), 32 teaching assistantships with partial tuition reimbursements available (averaging $12,197 per year); Federal Work-Study, scholarships/grants, tuition waivers (partial), and unspecified assistantships also available. Support available to part-time students. Financial award applicants required to submit FAFSA. *Faculty research:* Health communication, political, social influence, intercultural communication, interpersonal communication. Total annual research expenditures: $232,768. *Unit head:* Dr. Kevin Wright, Assistant Chair, 405-325-3111, Fax: 405-325-7625, E-mail: kbwright@ou.edu. *Application contact:* Amy Johnson, Graduate Liaison, 405-325-2561, Fax: 405-325-7625, E-mail: amyjj@ou.edu.

University of Oregon, Graduate School, School of Journalism and Communication, Eugene, OR 97403. Offers MA, MS, PhD. *Accreditation:* ACEJMC (one or more programs are accredited); ASHA. Part-time programs available. *Degree requirements:* For master's, thesis or alternative. *Entrance requirements:* For master's, GRE General Test; for doctorate, master's degree. *Faculty research:* Impact of mass communication, media technology, media accountability, craft attitudes, media economics.

University of Ottawa, Faculty of Graduate and Postdoctoral Studies, Faculty of Arts, Department of Communication, Ottawa, ON K1N 6N5, Canada. Offers MA. Electronic applications accepted. *Faculty research:* Media studies, organizational communications.

University of Pennsylvania, Annenberg School for Communication, Philadelphia, PA 19104. Offers PhD. *Degree requirements:* For doctorate, thesis/dissertation. *Entrance requirements:* For doctorate, GRE General Test. Electronic applications accepted.

University of Pittsburgh, School of Arts and Sciences, Department of Communication, Pittsburgh, PA 15260. Offers MA, PhD. *Degree requirements:* For master's, comprehensive exam, thesis optional; for doctorate, comprehensive exam, thesis/dissertation. *Entrance requirements:* For master's and doctorate, GRE General Test, sample of written work. Additional exam requirements/recommendations for international students: Required—TOEFL (minimum score 550 paper-based; 213 computer-based; 80 iBT). Electronic applications accepted. *Faculty research:* Media and cultural studies, public argument and discourse, rhetoric of science, history, criticism and theory of rhetoric.

University of Portland, Graduate School, College of Arts and Sciences, Department of Communication Studies, Portland, OR 97203-5798. Offers communication (MA); management communication (MS). Part-time and evening/weekend programs available. *Faculty:* 7 full-time (2 women), 1 part-time/adjunct (0 women). *Students:* 2 full-time (both women), 9 part-time (7 women); includes 1 American Indian/Alaska Native, 1 Asian American or Pacific Islander, 2 international. Average age 27. In 2008, 4 master's awarded. *Degree requirements:* For master's, thesis optional. *Entrance requirements:* For master's, GRE General Test, minimum GPA of 3.25, 3 letters of recommendation, resumé, statement of goals, official transcripts. Additional exam requirements/recommendations for international students: Required—TOEFL (minimum score 600 paper-based; 100 iBT), IELTS (minimum score 7.5). *Application deadline:* For fall admission, 7/15 priority date for domestic and international students; for spring admission, 12/15 priority date for domestic and international students. Applications are processed on a rolling basis. Application fee: $50. *Expenses:* Tuition: Full-time $7380; part-time $8.20 per credit hour. *Financial support:* Career-related internships or fieldwork, Federal Work-Study, scholarships/grants, and tuition waivers (partial) available. Financial award application deadline: 3/1; financial award applicants required to submit FAFSA. *Unit head:* Dr. Jeffrey Kerssen-Griep, Director, 503-943-7167, E-mail: kerssen@up.edu. *Application contact:* Chris James Olinger, Administrative Assistant, 503-943-7107, Fax: 503-943-7315, E-mail: olingerc@up.edu.

University of Rhode Island, Graduate School, College of Arts and Sciences, Department of Communication Studies, Kingston, RI 02881. Offers MA. *Expenses:* Tuition, state resident: full-time $8024; part-time $446 per credit. Tuition, nonresident: full-time $21,046; part-time $1169 per credit. Required fees: $1056; $26 per credit. $30 per semester. One-time fee: $95 part-time. *Unit head:* Dr. Lynne Derbyshire, Chair, 401-874-4732, E-mail: derbyshire@uri.edu.

Application contact: Harold D. Bibb, Associate Dean of the Graduate School, 401-874-2262, Fax: 401-874-5491.

University of South Africa, College of Human Sciences, Pretoria, South Africa. Offers adult education (M Ed); African languages (MA, PhD); African politics (MA, PhD); Afrikaans (MA, PhD); ancient history (MA, PhD); ancient Near Eastern studies (MA, PhD); anthropology (MA, PhD); applied linguistics (MA); Arabic (MA, PhD); archaeology (MA); art history (MA); Biblical archaeology (MA); Biblical studies (M Th, D Th, PhD); Christian spirituality (M Th, D Th); church history (M Th, D Th); classical studies (MA, PhD); clinical psychology (MA); communication (MA, PhD); comparative education (M Ed, Ed D); consulting psychology (D Admin, D Com, PhD); curriculum studies (M Ed, Ed D); development studies (M Admin, MA, D Admin, PhD); didactics (M Ed, Ed D); education (M Tech); education management (M Ed, Ed D); educational psychology (M Ed); English (MA); environmental education (M Ed); French (MA, PhD); German (MA, PhD); Greek (MA); guidance and counseling (M Ed); health studies (MA, PhD), including health sciences education (MA), health services management (MA), medical and surgical nursing science (critical care general) (MA), midwifery and neonatal nursing science (MA), trauma and emergency care (MA); history (MA, PhD); history of education (Ed D); inclusive education (M Ed, Ed D); information and communications technology policy and regulation (MA); information science (MA, MIS, PhD); international politics (MA, PhD); Islamic studies (MA, PhD); Italian (MA, PhD); Judaica (MA, PhD); linguistics (MA, PhD); mathematical education (M Ed); mathematics education (MA); missiology (M Th, D Th); modern Hebrew (MA, PhD); musicology (MA, MMus, D Mus, PhD); natural science education (M Ed); New Testament (M Th, D Th); Old Testament (D Th); pastoral therapy (M Th, D Th); philosophy (MA); philosophy of education (M Ed, Ed D); politics (MA, PhD); Portuguese (MA, PhD); practical theology (M Th, D Th); psychology (MA, MS, PhD); psychology of education (M Ed, Ed D); public health (MA); religious studies (MA, D Th, PhD); Romance languages (MA); Russian (MA, PhD); Semitic languages (MA, PhD); social behavior studies in HIV/AIDS (MA); social science (mental health) (MA); social science in development studies (MA); social science in psychology (MA); social science in social work (MA); social science in sociology (MA); social work (MSW, DSW, PhD); socio-education (M Ed, Ed D); sociolinguistics (MA); sociology (MA, PhD); Spanish (MA, PhD); systematic theology (M Th, D Th); TESOL (teaching English to speakers of other languages) (MA); theological ethics (M Th, D Th); theory of literature (MA, PhD); urban ministries (D Th); urban ministry (M Th).

University of South Alabama, Graduate School, College of Arts and Sciences, Department of Communication, Mobile, AL 36688-0002. Offers MA. *Faculty:* 9 full-time (4 women). *Students:* 21 full-time (13 women), 22 part-time (16 women); includes 7 minority (5 African Americans, 2 American Indian/Alaska Native), 4 international. 23 applicants, 43% accepted, 8 enrolled. In 2008, 6 master's awarded. *Degree requirements:* For master's, comprehensive exam, thesis optional. *Entrance requirements:* For master's, GRE, GMAT, minimum GPA of 3.0, BA in communication or 36 semester hours. *Application deadline:* For fall admission, 7/15 priority date for domestic students, 6/15 priority date for international students; for spring admission, 12/1 priority date for domestic students, 11/1 priority date for international students. Applications are processed on a rolling basis. Application fee: $35. *Expenses:* Tuition, area resident: Full-time $4656. Tuition, nonresident: full-time $9312. Required fees: $1102. *Financial support:* Research assistantships available. Financial award application deadline: 4/1. *Unit head:* Dr. Gerald Wilson, Chair, 251-380-2800. *Application contact:* Dr. Gerald Wilson, Chair, 251-380-2800.

The University of South Dakota, Graduate School, College of Arts and Sciences, Department of Communication Studies, Vermillion, SD 57069-2390. Offers MA. Part-time programs available. *Degree requirements:* For master's, comprehensive exam (for some programs), thesis (for some programs). *Entrance requirements:* For master's, minimum GPA of 2.7. Additional exam requirements/recommendations for international students: Required—TOEFL (minimum score 575 paper-based; 213 computer-based; 79 iBT). Electronic applications accepted. *Faculty research:* Male/female communication, interpersonal communication, relational communication, rhetoric and public address, organizational communication.

University of Southern California, Graduate School, Annenberg School for Communication, Los Angeles, CA 90089. Offers MA, MCM, MPD, PhD, JD/MCM, MA/M Sc, MCM/MAJCS. Part-time and evening/weekend programs available. Terminal master's awarded for partial completion of doctoral program. *Degree requirements:* For master's, comprehensive exam; for doctorate, thesis/dissertation. *Entrance requirements:* For master's, GRE General Test or GMAT, resumé, writing samples, letters of recommendation, statement of purpose; for doctorate, GRE General Test, resumé, writing samples, letters of recommendation, statement of purpose, interest survey. Additional exam requirements/recommendations for international students: Required—TOEFL (minimum score 280 computer-based; 114 iBT). Electronic applications accepted.

See Close-Up on page 709.

University of Southern California, Graduate School, Annenberg School for Communication, School of Communication, Program in Communication, Los Angeles, CA 90089. Offers communication (MA, PhD), including interpersonal and social dynamics (PhD), mass communication, technology, and public policy (PhD), organizational communication (PhD), rhetorical and cultural studies (PhD). *Degree requirements:* For doctorate, thesis/dissertation. *Entrance requirements:* For master's and doctorate, GRE General Test, resumé, writing samples, 3 letters of recommendation, interest survey questionnaire, statement of purpose. Additional exam requirements/recommendations for international students: Required—TOEFL (minimum score 280 computer-based; 115 iBT); Recommended—TWE. Electronic applications accepted. *Faculty research:* Computer-mediated communication, public health campaigns, communication democracy and the public sphere, new communication technologies in organizations, communication and community.

See Close-Up on page 709.

University of Southern California, Graduate School, Annenberg School for Communication, School of Communication, Program in Global Communication, Los Angeles, CA 90089. Offers MA/M Sc. Program offered jointly with London School of Economics. *Entrance requirements:* Additional exam requirements/recommendations for international students: Required—TOEFL (minimum score 280 computer-based; 114 iBT). Electronic applications accepted. *Faculty research:* New technology, audience analysis, globalization, entertainment industry, integrated communication.

See Close-Up on page 709.

University of South Florida, Graduate School, College of Arts and Sciences, Department of Communication, Tampa, FL 33620-9951. Offers MA, PhD. Part-time and evening/weekend programs available. *Faculty:* 15 full-time (9 women). *Students:* 36 full-time (24 women), 21 part-time (13 women); includes 11 minority (7 African Americans, 1 Asian American or Pacific Islander, 3 Hispanic Americans), 2 international. 82 applicants, 30% accepted, 9 enrolled. In 2008, 9 master's, 7 doctorates awarded. *Degree requirements:* For master's, comprehensive exam, thesis (for some programs); for doctorate, comprehensive exam, thesis/dissertation. *Entrance requirements:* For master's, GRE General Test or GMAT, minimum GPA of 3.0. Additional exam requirements/recommendations for international students: Required—TOEFL (minimum score 550 paper-based; 213 computer-based). *Application deadline:* For fall admission, 2/15 priority date for domestic students, 1/2 priority date for international students; for spring admission, 11/1 priority date for domestic students, 6/1 priority date for international students. Applications are processed on a rolling basis. Application fee: $30. Electronic applications accepted. *Expenses:* Tuition, state resident: full-time $2624.40; part-time $291.60 per credit hour. Tuition, nonresident: full-time $7822; part-time $869.13 per credit hour. *Financial support:* Career-related internships or fieldwork, Federal Work-Study, and institutionally sponsored loans available. Support available to part-time students. Financial award application deadline: 2/1; financial award applicants required to submit FAFSA. *Faculty research:* Organizational processes, gender relations, media criticism, interpersonal relations, health communication. *Unit head:* Dr. Kenneth Cissna, Chairperson, 813-974-6820, Fax: 813-974-6817, E-mail: kcissna@.cas.usf.edu. *Application contact:* Stacy Holman-Jones, Program Director, 813-974-6827, Fax: 813-974-6817, E-mail: holmanjo@cas.usf.edu.

The University of Tennessee, Graduate School, College of Communication and Information, Knoxville, TN 37996. Offers advertising (MS, PhD); broadcasting (MS, PhD); communications (MS, PhD); information sciences (MS, PhD); journalism (MS, PhD); public relations (MS, PhD); speech communication (MS, PhD). *Accreditation:* ACEJMC (one or more programs are accredited at the [master's] level). Part-time and evening/weekend programs available. Postbaccalaureate distance learning degree programs offered (no on-campus study). *Degree requirements:* For master's, thesis or alternative; for doctorate, thesis/dissertation. *Entrance requirements:* For master's and doctorate, GRE General Test, minimum GPA of 2.7. Additional exam requirements/recommendations for international students: Required—TOEFL. Electronic applications accepted. *Expenses:* Tuition, area resident: Part-time $348 per credit hour. Tuition, state resident: full-time $6262. Tuition, nonresident: full-time $18,920; part-time $1052 per credit hour. Required fees: $812; $36 per credit hour. Tuition and fees vary according to program.

The University of Texas at Arlington, Graduate School, College of Liberal Arts, Department of Communication, Arlington, TX 76019. Offers MA. Part-time and evening/weekend programs available. *Faculty:* 5 full-time (3 women). *Students:* 3 full-time (2 women), 20 part-time (19 women); includes 5 minority (2 African Americans, 3 Hispanic Americans), 2 international. 34 applicants, 38% accepted, 7 enrolled. In 2008, 16 master's awarded. *Degree requirements:* For master's, comprehensive exam (for some programs), thesis or alternative. *Entrance requirements:* For master's, GRE General Test. Additional exam requirements/recommendations for international students: Required—TOEFL (minimum score 550 paper-based; 213 computer-based). Application fee: $35 ($50 for international students). *Expenses:* Tuition, area resident: Full-time $6500. Tuition, state resident: full-time $6500. Tuition, nonresident: full-time $11,558. *Financial support:* In 2008–09, 2 research assistantships (averaging $7,200 per year), 1 teaching assistantship (averaging $2,500 per year) were awarded. *Unit head:* Dr. Charla Markham-Shaw, Chair, 817-272-2163, E-mail: markham@uta.edu. *Application contact:* Dr. Tom Christie, Graduate Advisor, 817-272-2163, E-mail: christie@uta.edu.

The University of Texas at Austin, Graduate School, College of Communication, Austin, TX 78712-1111. Offers MA, MFA, Au D, PhD, MBA/MA, MP Aff/MA. Part-time programs available. *Entrance requirements:* For master's and doctorate, GRE General Test. Electronic applications accepted.

The University of Texas at Dallas, School of Behavioral and Brain Sciences, Program in Communication Sciences and Disorders, Richardson, TX 75083-0688. Offers communication disorders (MS); communication sciences (PhD). Part-time and evening/weekend programs available. *Faculty:* 19 full-time (10 women), 10 part-time/adjunct (9 women). *Students:* 191 full-time (186 women), 11 part-time (10 women); includes 27 minority (4 African Americans, 1 American Indian/Alaska Native, 10 Asian Americans or Pacific Islanders, 12 Hispanic Americans), 5 international. Average age 27. 238 applicants, 46% accepted, 70 enrolled. In 2008, 102 master's, 4 doctorates awarded. *Degree requirements:* For doctorate, thesis/dissertation. *Entrance requirements:* For master's and doctorate, GRE General Test, minimum GPA of 3.0 in upper-level course work in field. Additional exam requirements/recommendations for international students: Required—TOEFL (minimum score 550 paper-based; 213 computer-based). *Application deadline:* For fall admission, 7/15 for domestic students, 5/1 priority date for international students; for spring admission, 11/15 for domestic students, 9/1 priority date for international students. Applications are processed on a rolling basis. Application fee: $50 ($100 for international students). Electronic applications accepted. *Expenses:* Tuition, area resident: Full-time $8320. Tuition, state resident: full-time $8320. Tuition, nonresident: full-time $15,054. Part-time tuition and fees vary according to course load. *Financial support:* In 2008–09, 4 research assistantships with tuition reimbursements (averaging $17,565 per year), 9 teaching assistantships with tuition reimbursements (averaging $11,495 per year) were awarded; fellowships, Federal Work-Study, institutionally sponsored loans, scholarships/grants, and unspecified assistantships also available. Support available to part-time students. Financial award application deadline: 4/30; financial award applicants required to submit FAFSA. *Faculty research:* Speech perception, auditory processing, language acquisition by young children, language development. *Unit head:* Dr. Robert D. Stillman, Program Head, 972-883-3106, Fax: 972-883-3022, E-mail: stillman@utdallas.edu. *Application contact:* Dr. Robert D. Stillman, Program Head, 972-883-3106, Fax: 972-883-3022, E-mail: stillman@utdallas.edu.

The University of Texas at El Paso, Graduate School, College of Liberal Arts, Department of Communication, El Paso, TX 79968-0001. Offers MA. Part-time and evening/weekend programs available. *Degree requirements:* For master's, thesis optional. *Entrance requirements:* For master's, GRE General Test, minimum GPA of 3.0. Additional exam requirements/recommendations for international students: Required—TOEFL. Electronic applications accepted. *Faculty research:* Cross-cultural communication, information media, telecommunication technology, trans-border communication, human communication.

The University of Texas at San Antonio, College of Liberal and Fine Arts, Department of Communication, San Antonio, TX 78249-0617. Offers MA. Part-time and evening/weekend programs available. *Entrance requirements:* Additional exam requirements/recommendations for international students: Required—TOEFL (minimum score 500 paper-based; 173 computer-based). Electronic applications accepted.

The University of Texas at Tyler, College of Arts and Sciences, Department of Communication, Tyler, TX 75799-0001. Offers communication (MA); interdisciplinary studies (MAIS, MSIS). Part-time programs available. *Degree requirements:* For master's, comprehensive exam. *Entrance requirements:* For master's, GRE General Test, minimum GPA of 2.5. Additional exam requirements/recommendations for international students: Required—TOEFL (minimum score 79 computer-based). Electronic applications accepted. *Faculty research:* Organizational communication, feminist criticism, religions communication, mass media.

The University of Texas–Pan American, College of Arts and Humanities, Department of Communications, Edinburg, TX 78541-2999. Offers communication (MA); theatre (MA). *Accreditation:* NAST. Part-time and evening/weekend programs available. *Degree requirements:* For master's, comprehensive exam, thesis or alternative. *Entrance requirements:* For master's, minimum GPA of 3.0. Additional exam requirements/recommendations for international students: Required—TOEFL. *Faculty research:* Rhetorical theory, intercultural and mass communication, American theatre, multicultural theatre and drama, television and film.

University of the Incarnate Word, School of Graduate Studies and Research, H-E-B School of Business and Administration, Programs in Administration, San Antonio, TX 78209-6397. Offers adult education (MAA); applied administration (MAA); communication arts (MAA); healthcare administration (MAA); instructional technology (MAA); international business (Certificate); nutrition (MAA); organizational development (MAA, Certificate); project management (Certificate); sports management (MAA). Part-time and evening/weekend programs available. Postbaccalaureate distance learning degree programs offered (no on-campus study). *Students:* 23 full-time (13 women), 144 part-time (103 women); includes 98 minority (17 African Americans, 3 Asian Americans or Pacific Islanders, 78 Hispanic Americans), 9 international. Average age 34. In 2008, 63 master's awarded. *Degree requirements:* For master's, capstone. *Entrance requirements:* For master's, GRE, GMAT. Additional exam requirements/recommendations for international students: Required—TOEFL (minimum score 560 paper-based; 220 computer-based; 83 iBT). *Application deadline:* Applications are processed on a rolling basis. Application fee: $20. Electronic applications accepted. *Expenses:* Tuition: Full-time $11,520; part-time $640 per credit hour. Required fees: $1494; $83 per credit hour. One-time fee: $50. Tuition and fees vary according to degree level and program. *Financial support:* Federal Work-Study and scholarships/grants available. Financial award applicants required to submit FAFSA. *Unit head:* Dr. Dan Dominguez, MAA Director, 210-829-3180, Fax: 210-805-3564, E-mail: domingue@

Communication—General

University of the Incarnate Word (continued)
uiwtx.edu. *Application contact:* Andrea Cyterski-Acosta, Dean of Enrollment, 210-829-6005, Fax: 210-829-3921, E-mail: admis@uiwtx.edu.

University of the Incarnate Word, School of Graduate Studies and Research, School of Interactive Media and Design, Program in Communication Arts, San Antonio, TX 78209-6397. Offers communication arts (MA); instructional technology (MA). Part-time and evening/weekend programs available. *Faculty:* 3 full-time (1 woman), 2 part-time/adjunct (0 women). *Students:* 8 full-time (6 women), 27 part-time (11 women); includes 23 minority (2 African Americans, 21 Hispanic Americans), 4 international. Average age 32. In 2008, 5 master's awarded. *Degree requirements:* For master's, thesis or alternative, capstone. *Entrance requirements:* For master's, GMAT, GRE General Test, interview, writing sample. Additional exam requirements/recommendations for international students: Required—TOEFL (minimum score 560 paper-based; 220 computer-based; 83 iBT). *Application deadline:* Applications are processed on a rolling basis. Application fee: $20. Electronic applications accepted. *Expenses:* Tuition: Full-time $11,520; part-time $640 per credit hour. Required fees: $1494; $83 per credit hour. One-time fee: $50. Tuition and fees vary according to degree level and program. *Financial support:* Federal Work-Study and scholarships/grants available. Financial award applicants required to submit FAFSA. *Unit head:* Dr. Valerie Greenberg, 210-829-3891, Fax: 210-829-3196, E-mail: greenber@uiwtx.edu. *Application contact:* Andrea Cyterski-Acosta, Dean of Enrollment, 210-829-6005, Fax: 210-829-3921, E-mail: admis@uiwtx.edu.

University of the Pacific, College of the Pacific, Department of Communication, Stockton, CA 95211-0197. Offers MA. *Faculty:* 9 full-time (2 women), 2 part-time/adjunct (1 woman). *Students:* 3 full-time (2 women), 20 part-time (15 women); includes 5 minority (2 African Americans, 2 Asian Americans or Pacific Islanders, 1 Hispanic American), 1 international. Average age 28. 35 applicants, 46% accepted, 12 enrolled. In 2008, 3 master's awarded. *Degree requirements:* For master's, thesis. *Entrance requirements:* For master's, GRE General Test. Additional exam requirements/recommendations for international students: Required—TOEFL (minimum score 475 paper-based; 150 computer-based). *Application deadline:* For fall admission, 3/1 priority date for domestic students; for spring admission, 10/1 for domestic students. Applications are processed on a rolling basis. Application fee: $75. *Expenses:* Tuition: Full-time $30,380; part-time $950 per unit. Required fees: $300. *Financial support:* In 2008–09, 8 teaching assistantships were awarded. Support available to part-time students. Financial award application deadline: 3/1; financial award applicants required to submit FAFSA. *Unit head:* Dr. Qingwen Dong, Chairman, 209-946-2505, E-mail: qdong@pacific.edu. *Application contact:* Information Contact, 209-946-2261.

University of the Sacred Heart, Graduate Programs, Department of Communication, San Juan, PR 00914-0383. Offers contemporary culture and media (MA); editing for media (MA); public relations (MA); publicity (MA); scriptwriting (MA). Part-time and evening/weekend programs available. *Degree requirements:* For master's, thesis.

The University of Toledo, College of Graduate Studies, College of Arts and Sciences, Department of Communications, Toledo, OH 43606-3390. Offers communication studies (Certificate).

University of Utah, The Graduate School, College of Humanities, Department of Communication, Salt Lake City, UT 84112-1107. Offers M Phil, MA, MS, PhD. Part-time programs available. *Degree requirements:* For master's, thesis or alternative; for doctorate, comprehensive exam, thesis/dissertation. *Entrance requirements:* For master's and doctorate, GRE General Test, minimum GPA of 3.0. Additional exam requirements/recommendations for international students: Required—TOEFL (minimum score 500 paper-based; 173 computer-based). Electronic applications accepted. *Faculty research:* Communication theory and history, rhetoric, mass communications, journalism, public address and forensics.

University of Vermont, Graduate College, College of Arts and Sciences, Department of Communication Sciences, Burlington, VT 05405. Offers MS. *Accreditation:* ASHA. *Students:* 28 (27 women); includes 1 minority (Asian American or Pacific Islander). 78 applicants, 37% accepted, 12 enrolled. In 2008, 7 master's awarded. *Entrance requirements:* For master's, GRE General Test. Additional exam requirements/recommendations for international students: Required—TOEFL (minimum score 550 paper-based; 213 computer-based; 80 iBT). *Application deadline:* For fall admission, 2/1 for domestic students. Application fee: $40. Electronic applications accepted. *Expenses:* Tuition, state resident: part-time $488 per credit. Tuition, nonresident: part-time $1232 per credit. *Financial support:* Fellowships available. Financial award application deadline: 3/1. *Unit head:* Prof. P. Prelock, Chair, 802-656-3861. *Application contact:* Prof. Barry Guitar, Coordinator, 802-656-3861.

University of Washington, Graduate School, College of Arts and Sciences, Department of Communication, Seattle, WA 98195. Offers MA, MC, PhD. Part-time programs available. Terminal master's awarded for partial completion of doctoral program. *Degree requirements:* For master's, thesis, project (MC); for doctorate, thesis/dissertation. *Entrance requirements:* For master's and doctorate, GRE, minimum GPA of 3.0, writing sample. Additional exam requirements/recommendations for international students: Required—TOEFL. Electronic applications accepted. *Faculty research:* Communication and culture, communication technology and society, international communication, political communication, rhetoric and critical studies.

University of Washington, Graduate School, College of Arts and Sciences, School of Art, Division of Design, Seattle, WA 98195. Offers industrial design (MFA); visual communication design (MFA).

University of West Florida, College of Arts and Sciences: Arts, Department of Communication Arts, Pensacola, FL 32514-5750. Offers MA. Part-time and evening/weekend programs available. *Faculty:* 1 (woman) full-time. *Students:* 9 full-time (7 women), 13 part-time (12 women); includes 4 minority (3 African Americans, 1 Hispanic American), 1 international. Average age 31. 12 applicants, 75% accepted, 9 enrolled. In 2008, 6 master's awarded. *Degree requirements:* For master's, thesis or alternative. *Entrance requirements:* For master's, GRE General Test, minimum GPA of 3.0. Additional exam requirements/recommendations for international students: Required—TOEFL (minimum score 550 paper-based; 213 computer-based). *Application deadline:* For fall admission, 6/1 for domestic students, 5/15 for international students; for spring admission, 11/1 for domestic students, 10/1 for international students. Applications are processed on a rolling basis. Application fee: $30. *Expenses:* Tuition, state resident: full-time $6095; part-time $253.97 per credit hour. Tuition, nonresident: full-time $21,919; part-time $913.31 per credit hour. *Financial support:* In 2008–09, 4 teaching assistantships with partial tuition reimbursements (averaging $1,888 per year) were awarded; career-related internships or fieldwork, Federal Work-Study, and scholarships/grants also available. Support available to part-time students. Financial award application deadline: 4/15; financial award applicants required to submit FAFSA. *Faculty research:* Equity studies. *Unit head:* Dr. Bruce M. Swain, Chairperson, 850-474-3278. *Application contact:* Terry McCray, Assistant Director of Graduate Admissions, 850-473-7718, Fax: 850-473-7714, E-mail: gradadmissions@uwf.edu.

University of Windsor, Faculty of Graduate Studies, Faculty of Arts and Social Sciences, Department of Communication Studies, Windsor, ON N9B 3P4, Canada. Offers communication and social justice (MA). *Degree requirements:* For master's, thesis. *Entrance requirements:* For master's, writing sample/media production or multimedia portfolio, minimum B average. Additional exam requirements/recommendations for international students: Required—TOEFL (minimum score 600 paper-based; 250 computer-based). Electronic applications accepted. *Faculty research:* Sociology of news, media ownership and control, communication networks and social movements, issues of media representation.

University of Wisconsin–Madison, Graduate School, College of Letters and Science, Department of Communication Arts, Madison, WI 53706-1380. Offers communication science (MA, PhD); film (MA, PhD); media and cultural studies (MA, PhD); rhetoric (MA, PhD). Terminal master's awarded for partial completion of doctoral program. *Degree requirements:* For master's, one foreign language, thesis (for some programs); for doctorate, one foreign language, thesis/dissertation. *Entrance requirements:* For master's and doctorate, GRE General Test, minimum GPA of 3.5. Electronic applications accepted.

University of Wisconsin–Madison, Graduate School, College of Letters and Science, School of Journalism and Mass Communication, Madison, WI 53706-1380. Offers family and consumer journalism (PhD); journalism and mass communication (MA); mass communication (PhD). Part-time programs available. *Degree requirements:* For master's, thesis (for some programs); for doctorate, thesis/dissertation. *Entrance requirements:* For master's, GRE General Test, minimum GPA of 3.0; for doctorate, GRE General Test, minimum GPA of 3.5. Additional exam requirements/recommendations for international students: Required—TOEFL. Electronic applications accepted. *Faculty research:* International/development communication; strategic mass communication; mass communication and the individual; science, technology, and environment communication; mass communication and societal institutions.

University of Wisconsin–Milwaukee, Graduate School, College of Letters and Sciences, Department of Communication, Milwaukee, WI 53201-0413. Offers communication (MA, PhD); rhetorical leadership (Certificate). Part-time programs available. *Faculty:* 17 full-time (10 women). *Students:* 17 full-time (14 women), 34 part-time (26 women); includes 4 minority (2 American Indian/Alaska Native, 2 Hispanic Americans), 7 international. Average age 29. 80 applicants, 70% accepted, 32 enrolled. In 2008, 19 master's awarded. *Degree requirements:* For master's, thesis or alternative; for doctorate, comprehensive exam. *Entrance requirements:* For master's, GRE General Test, minimum GPA of 3.0. Additional exam requirements/recommendations for international students: Required—TOEFL (minimum score 550 paper-based; 79 iBT), IELTS (minimum score 6). *Application deadline:* For fall admission, 1/1 priority date for domestic students; for spring admission, 9/1 for domestic students. Applications are processed on a rolling basis. Application fee: $45 ($75 for international students). *Expenses:* Tuition, area resident: Full-time $7320; part-time $165 per credit. Tuition, state resident: full-time $7320; part-time $165 per credit. Tuition, nonresident: full-time $17,840; part-time $714 per credit. Tuition and fees vary according to campus/location, program and reciprocity agreements. *Financial support:* In 2008–09, 30 teaching assistantships were awarded; career-related internships or fieldwork and unspecified assistantships also available. Support available to part-time students. Financial award application deadline: 4/15. *Unit head:* Mike Allen, Representative, 414-229-4261, Fax: 414-229-3859. *Application contact:* General Information Contact, 414-229-4982, Fax: 414-229-6967, E-mail: gradschool@uwm.edu.

University of Wisconsin–Stevens Point, College of Fine Arts and Communication, Division of Communication, Stevens Point, WI 54481-3897. Offers interpersonal communication (MA); mass communication (MA); organizational communication (MA); public relations (MA). Part-time programs available. *Students:* 7 full-time (3 women), 19 part-time (11 women). *Degree requirements:* For master's, thesis or alternative. *Entrance requirements:* For master's, GRE. Additional exam requirements/recommendations for international students: Required—TOEFL (minimum score 575 paper-based). *Application deadline:* For fall admission, 3/1 priority date for domestic students. Applications are processed on a rolling basis. Application fee: $45. *Expenses:* Tuition, state resident: full-time $7410. Tuition, nonresident: full-time $17,756. Full-time tuition and fees vary according to reciprocity agreements. *Financial support:* In 2008–09, 9 teaching assistantships were awarded; career-related internships or fieldwork, Federal Work-Study, institutionally sponsored loans, and unspecified assistantships also available. Support available to part-time students. Financial award application deadline: 5/1; financial award applicants required to submit FAFSA. *Faculty research:* Communication theory and research, film history. *Unit head:* Dr. James Haney, Chair, 715-346-3409, E-mail: jhaney@uwsp.edu. *Application contact:* Dr. Chris Sadler, Graduate Coordinator, 715-346-3898, E-mail: csadler@uwsp.edu.

University of Wisconsin–Superior, Graduate Division, Department of Communicating Arts, Superior, WI 54880-4500. Offers mass communication (MA); speech communication (MA); theater (MA). Part-time programs available. *Degree requirements:* For master's, comprehensive exam, thesis or alternative, position paper or project. *Entrance requirements:* For master's, minimum GPA of 2.75. *Faculty research:* Multimedia technology, ethics in journalism, diversity, electronic portfolio assessment.

University of Wisconsin–Whitewater, School of Graduate Studies, College of Arts and Communications, Department of Communication, Whitewater, WI 53190-1790. Offers corporate communication (MS); mass communication (MS). Part-time and evening/weekend programs available. Postbaccalaureate distance learning degree programs offered (no on-campus study). *Degree requirements:* For master's, thesis or alternative. *Entrance requirements:* For master's, 2 letters of recommendation. Additional exam requirements/recommendations for international students: Required—TOEFL (minimum score 550 paper-based; 213 computer-based). Electronic applications accepted.

University of Wyoming, Graduate School, College of Arts and Sciences, Department of Communication and Journalism, Laramie, WY 82070. Offers communication (MA). Part-time programs available. *Faculty:* 14 full-time (5 women). *Students:* 18 full-time (13 women), 15 part-time (11 women); includes 2 minority (1 American Indian/Alaska Native, 1 Asian American or Pacific Islander), 5 international. Average age 29. 21 applicants, 67% accepted, 9 enrolled. In 2008, 10 master's awarded. *Degree requirements:* For master's, thesis. *Entrance requirements:* For master's, GRE General Test, minimum GPA of 3.0. *Application deadline:* For fall admission, 6/1 priority date for domestic students. Applications are processed on a rolling basis. Application fee: $50. *Financial support:* In 2008–09, 8 teaching assistantships with full tuition reimbursements (averaging $10,062 per year) were awarded; career-related internships or fieldwork, Federal Work-Study, and institutionally sponsored loans also available. Financial award application deadline: 3/1. *Faculty research:* Personal relations, nonverbal behavior, media management, communication technology, conversation analysis. *Unit head:* Dr. Ken L. Smith, Chair, 307-766-6273, Fax: 307-766-3812. *Application contact:* Dr. Michael Brown, Director of Graduate Studies, 307-766-3822, Fax: 307-766-3812, E-mail: mrbrown@uwyo.edu.

Utah State University, School of Graduate Studies, College of Humanities, Arts and Social Sciences, Department of Journalism and Communication, Logan, UT 84322. Offers MA, MS. Part-time programs available. *Degree requirements:* For master's, comprehensive exam, thesis. *Entrance requirements:* For master's, GRE General Test or MAT, minimum GPA of 3.0. Additional exam requirements/recommendations for international students: Required—TOEFL. Electronic applications accepted. *Faculty research:* Race and gender and media, history of censorship, internet design and advertising, technology gap.

Villanova University, Graduate School of Liberal Arts and Sciences, Department of Communication, Villanova, PA 19085-1699. Offers MA. Part-time and evening/weekend programs available. *Faculty:* 6 full-time (0 women). *Students:* 21 full-time (15 women), 36 part-time (27 women); includes 11 minority (7 African Americans, 3 Asian Americans or Pacific Islanders, 1 Hispanic American), 2 international. Average age 28. 20 applicants, 45% accepted, 6 enrolled. In 2008, 10 master's awarded. *Degree requirements:* For master's, comprehensive exam (for some programs), thesis optional. *Entrance requirements:* For master's, GRE or GMAT, minimum GPA of 3.0, writing sample, personal essay. Additional exam requirements/recommendations for international students: Required—TOEFL. *Application deadline:* For fall admission, 4/15 for domestic students, 5/1 for international students; for spring admission, 11/15 for domestic students, 12/1 for international students. Applications are processed on a rolling basis. Application fee: $50. Electronic applications accepted. *Financial support:* Research assistantships, Federal Work-Study available. Financial award applicants required to submit FAFSA. *Unit head:* Dr. Emory Woodard, Director of Graduate Studies in Communication, 610-519-4780. *Application contact:* Dr. Gerald Long, Dean, Graduate School of Liberal Arts and Sciences, 610-519-7093, Fax: 610-519-7096.

Virginia Commonwealth University, Graduate School, College of Humanities and Sciences, School of Mass Communications, Program in Media, Art, and Text, Richmond, VA 23284-9005.

Offers PhD. *Entrance requirements:* For doctorate, GRE, MA, MAE, or MFA in appropriate field of study (English, art history, studio art, poetry, mass communications); 3 letters of recommendation.

Virginia Polytechnic Institute and State University, Graduate School, College of Liberal Arts and Human Sciences, Department of Communication, Blacksburg, VA 24061. Offers MA. *Entrance requirements:* Additional exam requirements/recommendations for international students: Required—TOEFL (minimum score 600 paper-based; 250 computer-based). Electronic applications accepted.

Wake Forest University, Graduate School of Arts and Sciences, Department of Communication, Winston-Salem, NC 27109. Offers speech communication (MA). Part-time programs available. *Degree requirements:* For master's, one foreign language, thesis. *Entrance requirements:* For master's, GRE General Test, writing sample. Additional exam requirements/recommendations for international students: Required—TOEFL (minimum score 213 computer-based; 79 iBT). Electronic applications accepted.

Washington State University, Graduate School, College of Liberal Arts, Edward R. Murrow College of Communication, Pullman, WA 99164. Offers health communications (MA, PhD); intercultural and international communications (MA, PhD); media and society (MA, PhD); media process and effects (MA, PhD); organizational communications (MA, PhD). *Degree requirements:* For master's, comprehensive exam (for some programs), thesis optional, oral exam; for doctorate, comprehensive exam, thesis/dissertation. *Entrance requirements:* For master's, GRE General Test, minimum GPA of 3.25, 3 letters of recommendation; for doctorate, GRE General Test, minimum undergraduate GPA of 3.25, graduate 3.5; MA in communication; 3 letters of recommendation. Additional exam requirements/recommendations for international students: Required—TOEFL (minimum score 580 paper-based; 237 computer-based). Electronic applications accepted. *Faculty research:* Advocacy communication, mediated communication in decision making, communication technology policy and effects, multicultural and international psychology and physiology of communication.

Wayne State College, School of Education and Counseling, Department of Educational Foundations and Leadership, Program in Curriculum and Instruction, Wayne, NE 68787. Offers alternative education (MSE); business and information technology education (MSE); communication arts education (MSE); early childhood education (MSE); elementary education (MSE); English as a second language (MSE); English education (MSE); family and consumer sciences education (MSE); industrial technology and vocational education (MSE); learning communities (MSE); mathematics education (MSE); music education (MSE); science education (MSE); social science education (MSE). *Accreditation:* NCATE. Part-time and evening/weekend programs available. *Degree requirements:* For master's, comprehensive exam, thesis optional. *Entrance requirements:* For master's, GRE General Test. Additional exam requirements/recommendations for international students: Required—TOEFL (minimum score 550 paper-based; 213 computer-based).

Wayne State University, College of Fine, Performing and Communication Arts, Department of Communication, Detroit, MI 48202. Offers communication studies (MA, PhD); public relations and organizational communication (MA); radio-TV-film (MA, PhD); speech communication (MA, PhD). *Degree requirements:* For master's, thesis, essay, or comprehensive exam; for doctorate, thesis/dissertation. *Entrance requirements:* For master's, minimum GPA of 3.0, personal statement; sample of academic writing; for doctorate, GRE, minimum GPA of 3.3, MA; letters of recommendation; personal statement; sample of written scholarship. Additional exam requirements/recommendations for international students: Required—TOEFL (minimum score 550 paper-based; 213 computer-based); Recommended—TWE (minimum score 6). Electronic applications accepted. *Faculty research:* Rhetorical theory and criticism; mass media theory and research; argumentation; organizational communication; risk and crisis communication; interpersonal, family, and health communication.

Webster University, School of Communications, St. Louis, MO 63119-3194. Offers MA. Part-time and evening/weekend programs available. Postbaccalaureate distance learning degree programs offered. *Entrance requirements:* For master's, 36 hours of graduate course work.

West Chester University of Pennsylvania, Office of Graduate Studies, College of Arts and Sciences, Department of Communication Studies, West Chester, PA 19383. Offers communication studies (MA). Part-time and evening/weekend programs available. *Students:* 8 full-time (6 women), 11 part-time (9 women); includes 4 minority (3 African Americans, 1 Asian American or Pacific Islander). Average age 29. 23 applicants, 83% accepted, 11 enrolled. In 2008, 6 master's awarded. *Degree requirements:* For master's, comprehensive exam, thesis optional. *Entrance requirements:* For master's, GRE or MAT, writing sample, minimum GPA of 3.0 in major, three letters of reference, goals statement. Additional exam requirements/recommendations for international students: Required—TOEFL (minimum score 550 paper-based; 213 computer-based; 80 iBT). *Application deadline:* For fall admission, 4/15 priority date for domestic students, 3/15 for international students; for spring admission, 10/15 for domestic students, 9/1 for international students. Applications are processed on a rolling basis. Application fee: $35. Electronic applications accepted. *Expenses:* Tuition, state resident: full-time $6430; part-time $357 per credit. Tuition, nonresident: full-time $10,288; part-time $572 per credit. Required fees: $652.50; $50 per credit. $67 per semester. *Financial support:* In 2008–09, 1 research assistantship with partial tuition reimbursement (averaging $5,000 per year) was awarded; unspecified assistantships also available. Support available to part-time students. Financial award application deadline: 2/15; financial award applicants required to submit FAFSA. *Faculty research:* Documentary of the Dalai Lama. *Unit head:* Dr. Timothy Brown, Chair, 610-436-2500, E-mail: tbrown@wcupa.edu. *Application contact:* Dr. Jack Orr, Graduate Coordinator, 610-436-2870, E-mail: jorr@wcupa.edu.

Western Illinois University, School of Graduate Studies, College of Fine Arts and Communication, Department of Communication, Macomb, IL 61455-1390. Offers MA. Part-time programs available. *Students:* 13 full-time (10 women), 10 part-time (6 women); includes 2 minority (1 African American, 1 Hispanic American), 3 international. Average age 27. 12 applicants, 92% accepted. In 2008, 3 master's awarded. *Degree requirements:* For master's, comprehensive exam (for some programs), thesis or alternative. *Entrance requirements:* Additional exam requirements/recommendations for international students: Required—TOEFL (minimum score 580 paper-based; 237 computer-based; 92 iBT). *Application deadline:* Applications are processed on a rolling basis. Application fee: $30. Electronic applications accepted. *Expenses:* Tuition, state resident: full-time $5696; part-time $237.34 per credit hour. Tuition, nonresident: full-time $11,392; part-time $474.68 per credit hour. Required fees: $1453; $60.55 per credit hour. *Financial support:* In 2008–09, 16 students received support, including 10 research assistantships with full tuition reimbursements available (averaging $7,040 per year), 6 teaching assistantships with full tuition reimbursements available (averaging $8,120 per year). Financial award applicants required to submit FAFSA. *Unit head:* Dr. Roberta Davilla, Chairperson, 309-298-1507. *Application contact:* Evelyn Hoing, Assistant Director of Graduate Studies, 309-298-1806, Fax: 309-298-2345, E-mail: grad-office@wiu.edu.

Western Kentucky University, Graduate Studies, Potter College of Arts and Letters, Department of Communication, Bowling Green, KY 42101. Offers communication (MA). Part-time and evening/weekend programs available. *Degree requirements:* For master's, comprehensive exam, thesis optional, final exam. *Entrance requirements:* For master's, GRE General Test, minimum GPA of 2.75. Additional exam requirements/recommendations for international students: Required—TOEFL (minimum score 555 paper-based; 213 computer-based; 79 iBT). *Faculty research:* Public rhetoric and public address organization communication, teamwork in communication, intercultural crisis communication.

Western Michigan University, Graduate College, College of Arts and Sciences, Department of Communication, Kalamazoo, MI 49008-5202. Offers MA.

Westminster College, Program in Professional Communication, Salt Lake City, UT 84105-3697. Offers MPC. Part-time and evening/weekend programs available. *Faculty:* 7 full-time (3 women), 4 part-time/adjunct (2 women). *Students:* 16 full-time (13 women), 53 part-time (40 women); includes 4 minority (1 American Indian/Alaska Native, 2 Asian Americans or Pacific Islanders, 1 Hispanic American), 2 international. Average age 33. 36 applicants, 83% accepted, 24 enrolled. In 2008, 15 master's awarded. *Degree requirements:* For master's, field project. *Entrance requirements:* For master's, personal resumé, sample of professional writing, application letter, official transcripts, baccalaureate information. Additional exam requirements/recommendations for international students: Required—TOEFL (minimum score 600 paper-based). *Application deadline:* For fall admission, 8/1 priority date for domestic students. Applications are processed on a rolling basis. Application fee: $40. Electronic applications accepted. *Expenses:* Tuition: Part-time $840 per credit hour. Tuition and fees vary according to course load and program. *Financial support:* In 2008–09, 32 students received support. Career-related internships or fieldwork and tuition reimbursement available. Support available to part-time students. Financial award applicants required to submit FAFSA. *Faculty research:* Critical communication pedagogy, sexuality and gender, autoethnography, regulation of broadcast indecency, hypertext theory. *Unit head:* Dr. Helen Hodgson, Director, 801-832-2821, Fax: 801-832-3102, E-mail: hhodgson@westminstercollege.edu. *Application contact:* Joel Bauman, Vice President of Enrollment Services, 801-832-2200, Fax: 801-832-3101, E-mail: admission@westminstercollege.edu.

West Texas A&M University, College of Fine Arts and Humanities, Department of Art, Communication, and Theater, Program in Communication, Canyon, TX 79016-0001. Offers MA. Part-time programs available. *Degree requirements:* For master's, comprehensive exam, thesis optional. *Entrance requirements:* For master's, GRE General Test, 24 hours of undergraduate communications courses, 1 letter of recommendation, interview with communication advisor. Additional exam requirements/recommendations for international students: Required—TOEFL (minimum score 550 paper-based). Electronic applications accepted. *Faculty research:* Comparison student learning in basic public speaking in traditional versus online format, impact of supervisor immediacy and power on organizational outcomes, storytelling, gender, nonverbal.

West Virginia University, Eberly College of Arts and Sciences, Department of Communication Studies, Morgantown, WV 26506. Offers communication in instruction (MA); communication studies (PhD); communication theory and research (MA); corporate and organizational communication (MA). Part-time programs available. *Degree requirements:* For master's, comprehensive exam (for some programs), thesis (for some programs); for doctorate, comprehensive exam, thesis/dissertation. *Entrance requirements:* For master's and doctorate, minimum GPA of 3.0. Additional exam requirements/recommendations for international students: Required—TOEFL. Electronic applications accepted. *Faculty research:* Instructional communication, interpersonal communication, health communication, influence, instructional communication, social influence.

West Virginia University, Perley Isaac Reed School of Journalism, Program in Integrated Marketing Communications, Morgantown, WV 26506. Offers MS. Part-time programs available. Postbaccalaureate distance learning degree programs offered (no on-campus study). *Entrance requirements:* For master's, GRE or GMAT. Additional exam requirements/recommendations for international students: Required—TOEFL.

Wichita State University, Graduate School, Fairmount College of Liberal Arts and Sciences, Elliot School of Communication, Wichita, KS 67260. Offers MA. Part-time programs available. *Degree requirements:* For master's, comprehensive exam, research project or thesis. *Entrance requirements:* For master's, GRE. Additional exam requirements/recommendations for international students: Required—TOEFL. Electronic applications accepted. *Faculty research:* Classical roots of rhetoric, gender and communication, communication perspective on suicide, small group communications, theatre studies.

Wilfrid Laurier University, Faculty of Graduate Studies, Faculty of Arts, Department of Communication Studies, Waterloo, ON N2L 3C5, Canada. Offers MA. *Degree requirements:* For master's, thesis optional. *Entrance requirements:* For master's, honours BA in communication studies or a cognate discipline from an approved university with a minimum B+ overall in last two years of study and in undergraduate major. Additional exam requirements/recommendations for international students: Required—TOEFL (minimum score 230 computer-based; 89 iBT). Electronic applications accepted. *Faculty research:* Visual communication and culture, media, technology and culture.

William Paterson University of New Jersey, College of the Arts and Communication, Program in Communication and Media Studies, Wayne, NJ 07470-8420. Offers MA. *Degree requirements:* For master's, comprehensive exam. *Entrance requirements:* For master's, GRE General Test or MAT, minimum GPA of 2.75. Electronic applications accepted. *Faculty research:* Cable television, intercultural communication.

York University, Faculty of Graduate Studies, Program in Communication and Culture, Toronto, ON M3J 1P3, Canada. Offers MA, PhD. *Degree requirements:* For master's, thesis or alternative; for doctorate, comprehensive exam, thesis/dissertation. Electronic applications accepted.

Arts Journalism

School of the Art Institute of Chicago, Graduate Division, Program in New Arts Journalism, Chicago, IL 60603-3103. Offers MA. *Entrance requirements:* Additional exam requirements/recommendations for international students: Required—TOEFL, IELTS.

See Close-Up on page 225.

Syracuse University, Graduate School, S. I. Newhouse School of Public Communications, Program in Arts Journalism, Syracuse, NY 13244. Offers MA. *Entrance requirements:* For master's, GRE General Test. Additional exam requirements/recommendations for international students: Required—TOEFL (minimum score 600 paper-based; 250 computer-based). Electronic applications accepted.

Broadcast Journalism

American University, School of Communication, Program in Journalism and Public Affairs, Washington, DC 20016-8001. Offers broadcast journalism (MA), including economic journalism, international journalism, public policy journalism; print journalism (MA), including economic journalism, international journalism, public policy journalism. *Accreditation:* ACEJMC. Part-time and evening/weekend programs available. *Faculty:* 13 full-time (5 women), 4 part-time/adjunct (all women). *Students:* 24 full-time (16 women); includes 10 minority (7 African Americans, 3 Asian Americans or Pacific Islanders), 10 international. 190 applicants, 63% accepted, 35 enrolled. In 2008, 40 master's awarded. *Degree requirements:* For master's, comprehensive exam, thesis or alternative. *Entrance requirements:* For master's, GRE General Test. Additional exam requirements/recommendations for international students: Required—TOEFL (minimum score 600 paper-based; 250 computer-based). *Application deadline:* For fall admission, 2/1 priority date for domestic students, 4/1 priority date for international students. Applications are processed on a rolling basis. Application fee: $50. Electronic applications accepted. *Expenses:* Tuition: Full-time $21,204; part-time $1178 per credit hour. Required fees: $380. Part-time tuition and fees vary according to course load and program. *Financial support:* In 2008–09, 3 fellowships with partial tuition reimbursements (averaging $27,000 per year), 14 research assistantships with tuition reimbursements (averaging $7,000 per year), 3 teaching assistantships with tuition reimbursements (averaging $7,000 per year) were awarded; career-related internships or fieldwork, Federal Work-Study, institutionally sponsored loans, scholarships/grants, tuition waivers (partial), and unspecified assistantships also available. Financial award application deadline: 2/1. *Faculty research:* Government and media effects of journalistic practices and policies, race and gender and the media, investigative reporting, computer assisted reporting. *Unit head:* Wendell Cochran, Division Director, 202-885-2072. *Application contact:* Sharmeen Ahsan-Bracciale, Graduate Admissions Office, 202-885-2040, Fax: 202-885-2019, E-mail: sharmeen@american.edu.

See Close-Up on page 681.

The American University in Cairo, Graduate Studies and Research, School of Business, Economics and Communication, Department of Journalism and Mass Communication, Cairo, Egypt. Offers journalism and mass communication (MA); television and digital journalism (MA). Part-time programs available. *Degree requirements:* For master's, thesis (for some programs). *Entrance requirements:* For master's, English entrance exam, GMAT. Electronic applications accepted. *Faculty research:* Mass media and national development/censorship, intercultural photo communication, comparative journalism/television.

Boston University, College of Communication, Department of Journalism, Boston, MA 02215. Offers broadcast journalism (MS); business and economics journalism (MS); photo journalism (MS); print journalism (MS); science journalism (MS). *Degree requirements:* For master's, thesis. *Entrance requirements:* For master's, GRE General Test, sample of written work. Additional exam requirements/recommendations for international students: Required—TOEFL. Electronic applications accepted.

See Close-Up on page 683.

Emerson College, Graduate Studies, School of Communication, Department of Journalism, Boston, MA 02116-4624. Offers print/multimedia journalism, broadcast journalism, integrated journalism (MA), including broadcast journalism, integrated journalism, print/multimedia journalism. Part-time programs available. *Students:* 64 full-time (39 women), 7 part-time (6 women); includes 9 minority (2 African Americans, 3 Asian Americans or Pacific Islanders, 4 Hispanic Americans), 10 international. Average age 26. 107 applicants, 76% accepted, 32 enrolled. In 2008, 21 master's awarded. *Entrance requirements:* For master's, GRE General Test. Additional exam requirements/recommendations for international students: Required—TOEFL (minimum score 550 paper-based; 213 computer-based; 80 iBT), IELTS (minimum score 6.5). *Application deadline:* For fall admission, 3/1 priority date for domestic students, 5/1 priority date for international students; for spring admission, 11/1 priority date for domestic students. Applications are processed on a rolling basis. Application fee: $60 ($75 for international students). Electronic applications accepted. *Expenses:* Tuition: Full-time $17,720;

part-time $886 per credit. Required fees: $60 per year. One-time fee: $170. *Financial support:* In 2008–09, 16 students received support, including 4 fellowships with partial tuition reimbursements available (averaging $14,000 per year), 7 research assistantships with partial tuition reimbursements available (averaging $10,000 per year); career-related internships or fieldwork, Federal Work-Study, institutionally sponsored loans, scholarships/grants, and unspecified assistantships also available. Support available to part-time students. Financial award application deadline: 3/1; financial award applicants required to submit FAFSA. *Faculty research:* Journalism. *Unit head:* Prof. Janet Kolodzy, Acting Chair, 617-824-8805, E-mail: Janet_Kolodzy@emerson.edu. *Application contact:* Office of Graduate Admission, 617-824-8610, Fax: 617-824-8614, E-mail: gradapp@emerson.edu.

Northwestern University, Medill School of Journalism, Evanston, IL 60208. Offers broadcast journalism (MSJ); integrated marketing communications (MSIMC), including advertising/sales promotion, direct database and e-commerce marketing, general studies, public relations; magazine publishing (MSJ); new media (MSJ); reporting and writing (MSJ). *Accreditation:* ACEJMC (one or more programs are accredited). *Entrance requirements:* For master's, GRE General Test, GMAT or LSAT (MSJ). Additional exam requirements/recommendations for international students: Required—TOEFL. Electronic applications accepted. *Expenses:* Contact institution. *Faculty research:* Web business journalism, cultural stereotypes, voter apathy, digital television.

Syracuse University, Graduate School, S. I. Newhouse School of Public Communications, Program in Broadcast Journalism, Syracuse, NY 13244. Offers MS. *Degree requirements:* For master's, capstone course. *Entrance requirements:* For master's, GRE General Test. Additional exam requirements/recommendations for international students: Required—TOEFL.

See Close-Up on page 705.

University of Maryland, College Park, Graduate Studies, Phillip Merrill College of Journalism, College Park, MD 20742. Offers broadcast journalism (MA); journalism (MA); journalism and media studies (PhD); online news (MA); public affairs reporting (MA). *Accreditation:* ACEJMC (one or more programs are accredited). Part-time and evening/weekend programs available. *Degree requirements:* For doctorate, thesis/dissertation, preliminary written and oral comprehensive exams. *Entrance requirements:* For master's and doctorate, GRE General Test, minimum GPA of 3.0, 3 letters of recommendation. Additional exam requirements/recommendations for international students: Required—TOEFL. Electronic applications accepted. *Faculty research:* Mass communication theory, specialized journalism, new telecommunication technologies, press integration.

University of Miami, Graduate School, School of Communication, Coral Gables, FL 33124. Offers communication (PhD); communication studies (MA); film studies (MA, PhD); motion pictures (MFA), including production, producing, and screenwriting; print journalism (MA); public relations (MA); Spanish language journalism (MA); television broadcast journalism (MA). *Accreditation:* ACEJMC. Part-time programs available. *Degree requirements:* For master's, comprehensive exam (for some programs), thesis (for some programs); for doctorate, comprehensive exam, thesis/dissertation. *Entrance requirements:* For master's, GRE General Test; for doctorate, GRE General Test, master's thesis or scholarly research. Additional exam requirements/recommendations for international students: Required—TOEFL (minimum score 600 paper-based; 250 computer-based; 100 iBT). Electronic applications accepted. *Faculty research:* Communication studies, mass communication, international/interpersonal communication, film studies, journalism.

University of Southern California, Graduate School, Annenberg School for Communication, School of Journalism, Program in Broadcast Journalism, Los Angeles, CA 90089. Offers MA. *Degree requirements:* For master's, comprehensive exam. *Entrance requirements:* For master's, GRE General Test, resumé, writing samples, letters of recommendation, statement of purpose. Additional exam requirements/recommendations for international students: Required—TOEFL (minimum score 280 computer-based; 114 iBT). Electronic applications accepted.

See Close-Up on page 709.

Corporate and Organizational Communication

The American University of Athens, The School of Graduate Studies, Athens, Greece. Offers biomedical sciences (MS); business (MBA); business communication (MA); computer sciences (MS); engineering and applied sciences (MS); politics and policy making (MA); systems engineering (MS); telecommunications (MS). *Entrance requirements:* For master's, University Degree/Resum&e, 2 recommendation letters/TOEFL score 550. Additional exam requirements/recommendations for international students: Required—TOEFL (minimum score 550 paper-based; 213 computer-based). *Faculty research:* Nanotechnology, environmental sciences, rock mechanics, human skin studies, Monte Carlo algorithms and software.

Antioch University Seattle, Graduate Programs, Center for Creative Change, Seattle, WA 98121-1814. Offers environment and community (MA); management (MS); organizational psychology (MA); strategic communications (MA); whole system design (MA). Evening/weekend programs available. Electronic applications accepted. *Expenses:* Contact institution.

Barry University, School of Arts and Sciences, Department of Communication, Miami Shores, FL 33161-6695. Offers broadcasting (Certificate); communication (MA), including broadcast communication, public relations and corporate communications; organizational communication (MS). Part-time and evening/weekend programs available. *Degree requirements:* For master's, thesis (for some programs). *Entrance requirements:* For master's, GRE General Test, MAT, minimum GPA of 3.0. Electronic applications accepted. *Faculty research:* Organizational communication, broadcast communication, intercultural communication, advertising, leadership.

Bernard M. Baruch College of the City University of New York, Weissman School of Arts and Sciences, Program in Corporate Communication, New York, NY 10010-5585. Offers MA.

Bowie State University, Graduate Programs, Program in Organizational Communication, Bowie, MD 20715-9465. Offers MA, Certificate. Part-time and evening/weekend programs

available. *Degree requirements:* For master's, comprehensive exam, thesis optional, research paper. *Entrance requirements:* For master's, minimum GPA of 2.5. Electronic applications accepted. *Faculty research:* International telecommunications, developmental communications.

California State University, San Bernardino, Graduate Studies, College of Arts and Letters, Department of Communication Studies, San Bernardino, CA 92407-2397. Offers communication studies (MA); integrated marketing communication (MA). *Faculty:* 7 full-time (6 women), 1 part-time/adjunct (0 women). *Students:* 30 full-time (23 women), 17 part-time (15 women); includes 17 minority (6 African Americans, 11 Hispanic Americans), 12 international. Average age 29. 74 applicants, 34% accepted, 20 enrolled. In 2008, 17 master's awarded. *Degree requirements:* For master's, comprehensive exam, advancement to candidacy. *Entrance requirements:* Additional exam requirements/recommendations for international students: Required—TOEFL. *Application deadline:* For fall admission, 8/31 priority date for domestic students. Application fee: $55. *Expenses:* Tuition, area resident: Full-time $1252; part-time $726 per quarter. Required fees: $334 per quarter. Tuition and fees vary according to degree level and student level. *Unit head:* Dr. Mo Bahk, Chair, 909-537-5820, Fax: 909-537-7009, E-mail: mbahk@csusb.edu. *Application contact:* Olivia Rosas, Director of Admissions, 909-537-7577, Fax: 909-537-7034, E-mail: orosas@csusb.edu.

Canisius College, Graduate Division, College of Arts and Sciences, Department of Communication and Leadership, Buffalo, NY 14208-1098. Offers MS. Part-time and evening/weekend programs available. *Faculty:* 10 full-time (4 women). *Students:* 5 full-time (2 women), 38 part-time (30 women); includes 8 minority (4 African Americans, 1 Asian American or Pacific Islander, 3 Hispanic Americans), 1 international. Average age 32. In 2008, 15 master's awarded. *Degree requirements:* For master's, thesis. *Entrance requirements:* For master's, GRE General Test or GMAT. *Application deadline:* For fall admission, 7/15 priority date for domestic students;

for spring admission, 4/15 priority date for domestic students. Applications are processed on a rolling basis. Application fee: $25. Electronic applications accepted. *Expenses:* Tuition: Full-time $33,750; part-time $680 per credit hour. Required fees: $18.50 per credit hour. *Financial support:* In 2008–09, 1 research assistantship with tuition reimbursement was awarded. *Unit head:* Dr. Rosanne L. Hartman, Director, 716-888-2589, Fax: 716-888-3118, E-mail: hartmanr@canisius.edu. *Application contact:* Dr. Rosanne L. Hartman, Director, Communication and Leadership, 716-888-2589, Fax: 716-888-3118, E-mail: hartmanr@canisius.edu.

Carnegie Mellon University, College of Humanities and Social Sciences, Department of English, Program in Professional Writing, Pittsburgh, PA 15213-3891. Offers editing and publishing (MAPW); policy and non-profit communication (MAPW); public and media relations / corporate communications (MAPW); science or healthcare communication (MAPW); technical writing (MAPW); writing for new media (MAPW); writing for print media (MAPW). Part-time programs available. *Entrance requirements:* For master's, GRE General Test. Additional exam requirements/recommendations for international students: Required—TOEFL, TWE.

See Close-Up on page 553.

Central Connecticut State University, School of Graduate Studies, School of Arts and Sciences, Department of Communication, New Britain, CT 06050-4010. Offers organizational communication (MS); public relations/promotions (Certificate). Part-time and evening/weekend programs available. *Faculty:* 13 full-time (4 women), 9 part-time/adjunct (3 women). *Students:* 5 full-time (3 women), 22 part-time (15 women); includes 5 minority (2 African Americans, 1 Asian American or Pacific Islander, 2 Hispanic Americans), 1 international. Average age 29. 21 applicants, 43% accepted, 6 enrolled. In 2008, 11 master's, 1 other advanced degree awarded. *Degree requirements:* For master's, comprehensive exam, thesis or alternative. *Entrance requirements:* For master's, minimum undergraduate GPA of 3.0, essay. Additional exam requirements/recommendations for international students: Required—TOEFL. *Application deadline:* For fall admission, 7/1 for domestic students; for spring admission, 12/1 for domestic students. Applications are processed on a rolling basis. Application fee: $50. Electronic applications accepted. *Expenses:* Tuition, area resident: Full-time $4377; part-time $420 per credit. Tuition, state resident: full-time $6566; part-time $420 per credit. Tuition, nonresident: full-time $12,195; part-time $420 per credit. Required fees: $3462. One-time fee: $62 part-time. *Financial support:* In 2008–09, 2 students received support, including 2 research assistantships; career-related internships or fieldwork, Federal Work-Study, scholarships/grants, and unspecified assistantships also available. Support available to part-time students. Financial award application deadline: 3/1; financial award applicants required to submit FAFSA. *Faculty research:* Organizational communication, mass communication, intercultural communication, political communication, information management. *Unit head:* Dr. Serafin Mendez-Mendez, Chair, 860-832-2690. *Application contact:* Dr. Serafin Mendez-Mendez, Chair, 860-832-2690.

Central Michigan University, College of Graduate Studies, Interdisciplinary Administration Programs, Mount Pleasant, MI 48859. Offers acquisitions administration (MSA, Graduate Certificate); general administration (MSA, Graduate Certificate); health services administration (MSA, Graduate Certificate); human resource administration (Graduate Certificate); human resources administration (MSA); information resource management (MSA, Graduate Certificate); international administration (MSA, Graduate Certificate); leadership (MSA); organizational communication (MSA, Graduate Certificate); public administration (MSA, Graduate Certificate); recreation and park administration (MSA); sport administration (MSA). *Accreditation:* AACSB. Part-time and evening/weekend programs available. Postbaccalaureate distance learning degree programs offered (no on-campus study). *Students:* 60 full-time (27 women), 61 part-time (35 women); includes 23 minority (16 African Americans, 3 American Indian/Alaska Native, 2 Asian Americans or Pacific Islanders, 2 Hispanic Americans), 29 international. Average age 29. *Degree requirements:* For master's, thesis or alternative. *Entrance requirements:* For master's, bachelor's degree with minimum GPA of 2.7. *Application deadline:* Applications are processed on a rolling basis. Application fee: $35 ($45 for international students). Electronic applications accepted. *Expenses:* Tuition, state resident: full-time $3717; part-time $413 per credit. Tuition, nonresident: full-time $6894; part-time $766 per credit. *Financial support:* Fellowships with tuition reimbursements, career-related internships or fieldwork, Federal Work-Study, unspecified assistantships, and out-of-state merit awards available. *Faculty research:* Interdisciplinary studies in acquisitions administration, health services administration, sport administration, recreation and park administration, and international administration. *Unit head:* Dr. Nana Korash, Director, 989-774-6525, Fax: 989-774-2575, E-mail: msa@cmich.edu. *Application contact:* Denise Schafer, Coordinator, 989-774-4373, Fax: 989-774-2575, E-mail: schaf1dr@cmich.edu.

College of Charleston, Graduate School, School of Humanities and Social Sciences, Program in Organizational and Corporate Communication, Charleston, SC 29424-0001. Offers Certificate. *Faculty:* 20 full-time (10 women). *Students:* 4 part-time (2 women); includes 2 minority (both African Americans). Average age 30. 5 applicants, 40% accepted, 0 enrolled. In 2008, 4 Certificates awarded. *Entrance requirements:* For degree, minimum GPA of 2.5. Additional exam requirements/recommendations for international students: Required—TOEFL. *Application deadline:* For fall admission, 4/1 for domestic students; for spring admission, 11/1 for domestic students. Application fee: $45. Electronic applications accepted. *Expenses:* Tuition, area resident: Full-time $6624; part-time $368 per credit hour. Tuition, state resident: full-time $6624; part-time $368 per credit hour. Tuition, nonresident: full-time $16,074; part-time $893 per credit hour. Required fees: $30; $30 per course. One-time fee: $45. *Unit head:* Dr. Vincent Benigni, Director, 844-983-7017, E-mail: benigniv@cofc.edu. *Application contact:* Susan Hallatt, Director of Graduate Admissions, 843-953-5614, Fax: 843-953-1434, E-mail: hallatts@cofc.edu.

Columbia University, Graduate School of Business, MBA Program, New York, NY 10027. Offers accounting (MBA); decision, risk, and operations (MBA); entrepreneurship (MBA); finance and economics (MBA); human resource management (MBA); international business (MBA); management/leadership (MBA); marketing (MBA); media (MBA); real estate (MBA); social enterprise (MBA); DDS/MBA; JD/MBA; MBA/MIA; MBA/MPH; MBA/MS; MD/MBA. *Entrance requirements:* For master's, GMAT, 2 letters of recommendation, official transcripts, essay, personal statement, completed application. Additional exam requirements/recommendations for international students: Required—TOEFL. Electronic applications accepted.

Columbia University, School of Continuing Education, Program in Strategic Communications, New York, NY 10027. Offers MS. Part-time and evening/weekend programs available. *Degree requirements:* For master's, 36 credits. *Entrance requirements:* For master's, BA/BS 3.0 GPA. Additional exam requirements/recommendations for international students: Required—American Language Program (ALP) placement test. Electronic applications accepted. *Faculty research:* Marketing communications, public relations, crisis management.

Concordia University Wisconsin, Graduate Programs, School of Business and Legal Studies, MBA Program, Mequon, WI 53097-2402. Offers finance (MBA); health care administration (MBA); human resource management (MBA); international business (MBA); international business-bilingual English/Chinese (MBA); management (MBA); management information systems (MBA); managerial communications (MBA); marketing (MBA); public administration (MBA); risk management (MBA). Postbaccalaureate distance learning degree programs offered (minimal on-campus study). *Degree requirements:* For master's, comprehensive exam, thesis or alternative. *Entrance requirements:* Additional exam requirements/recommendations for international students: Required—TOEFL. *Expenses:* Contact institution.

Dallas Baptist University, College of Business, Business Administration Program, Dallas, TX 75211-9299. Offers accounting (MBA); business communication (MBA); conflict resolution management (MBA); e-business (MBA); entrepreneurship (MBA); finance (MBA); health care management (MBA); international business (MBA); leading the non-profit organization (MBA); management (MBA); management information systems (MBA); marketing (MBA); project management (MBA); technology and engineering management (MBA). *Accreditation:* ACBSP. Part-time and evening/weekend programs available. *Faculty:* 68 full-time (30 women), 113 part-time/adjunct (47 women). *Students:* 157 full-time, 353 part-time. 294 applicants, 56% accepted, 143 enrolled. In 2008, 155 master's awarded. *Entrance requirements:* For master's, GMAT, minimum GPA of 3.0. Additional exam requirements/recommendations for international students: Required—TOEFL, IELTS. *Application deadline:* Applications are processed on a rolling basis. Application fee: $25. Electronic applications accepted. *Expenses:* Tuition: Part-time $558 per credit hour. *Financial support:* Federal Work-Study, institutionally sponsored loans, scholarships/grants, and tuition waivers (full and partial) available. Support available to part-time students. Financial award applicants required to submit FAFSA. *Faculty research:* Sports management, services marketing, retailing, strategic management, financial planning/investments. *Unit head:* Dr. Sandra S. Reid, Director, 214-333-5280, Fax: 214-333-5293, E-mail: graduate@dbu.edu. *Application contact:* Kit P. Montgomery, Director of Graduate Programs, 214-333-5242, Fax: 214-333-5579, E-mail: graduate@dbu.edu.

Dallas Baptist University, College of Business, Management Program, Dallas, TX 75211-9299. Offers business communication (MA); conflict resolution management (MA); general management (MA); health care management (MA); human resource management (MA); performance management (MA). Part-time and evening/weekend programs available. *Faculty:* 68 full-time (30 women), 113 part-time/adjunct (47 women). *Students:* 14 full-time, 106 part-time. In 2008, 60 master's awarded. *Entrance requirements:* For master's, GRE General Test, minimum GPA of 3.0. Additional exam requirements/recommendations for international students: Required—TOEFL, IELTS. *Application deadline:* Applications are processed on a rolling basis. Application fee: $25. Electronic applications accepted. *Expenses:* Tuition: Part-time $558 per credit hour. *Financial support:* Federal Work-Study, institutionally sponsored loans, scholarships/grants, and tuition waivers (full and partial) available. Support available to part-time students. Financial award applicants required to submit FAFSA. *Faculty research:* Organizational behavior, conflict personalities. *Unit head:* Joanne Hix, Director, 214-333-5793, Fax: 214-333-5293, E-mail: graduate@dbu.edu. *Application contact:* Kit P. Montgomery, Director of Graduate Programs, 214-333-5242, Fax: 214-333-5579, E-mail: graduate@dbu.edu.

Dallas Baptist University, Gary Cook School of Leadership, Program in Global Leadership, Dallas, TX 75211-9299. Offers business communication (MA); Christian education/missions (MA); ESL (MA); general studies (MA); global studies (MA); international business (MA); missions (MA); worship/missions (MA). Part-time and evening/weekend programs available. *Faculty:* 68 full-time (30 women), 113 part-time/adjunct (47 women). *Students:* 11 full-time, 26 part-time. 15 applicants, 40% accepted. *Entrance requirements:* For master's, minimum GPA of 3.0. Additional exam requirements/recommendations for international students: Required—TOEFL, IELTS. Application fee: $25. *Expenses:* Tuition: Part-time $558 per credit hour. *Financial support:* Federal Work-Study, institutionally sponsored loans, scholarships/grants, and tuition waivers (full and partial) available. Support available to part-time students. Financial award applicants required to submit FAFSA. *Unit head:* Dr. Bob Garrett, Director, 214-333-5292, Fax: 214-333-6955, E-mail: graduate@dbu.edu. *Application contact:* Kit P. Montgomery, Director of Graduate Programs, 214-333-5242, Fax: 214-333-5579, E-mail: graduate@dbu.edu.

DePaul University, College of Communication, Chicago, IL 60614. Offers journalism (MA); media, culture and society (MA); organizational and multicultural communication (MA); public relations and advertising (MA). Part-time and evening/weekend programs available. *Faculty:* 31 full-time (17 women), 15 part-time/adjunct (7 women). *Students:* 135 full-time (106 women), 43 part-time (35 women); includes 49 minority (25 African Americans, 7 Asian Americans or Pacific Islanders, 17 Hispanic Americans), 8 international. Average age 29. 242 applicants, 47% accepted, 68 enrolled. In 2008, 64 master's awarded. *Degree requirements:* For master's, comprehensive exam (for some programs), final exam or thesis/project. *Entrance requirements:* For master's, GRE General Test (public relations and advertising), minimum GPA of 3.0, writing sample, essay, letters of recommendation, resumé. Additional exam requirements/recommendations for international students: Required—TOEFL (minimum score 590 paper-based; 245 computer-based; 96 iBT). Application fee: $40. Electronic applications accepted. *Financial support:* In 2008–09, 8 students received support, including 4 research assistantships with partial tuition reimbursements available, 2 teaching assistantships with full tuition reimbursements available (averaging $12,000 per year); fellowships with full tuition reimbursements available, career-related internships or fieldwork, scholarships/grants, and tuition waivers (partial) also available. Support available to part-time students. Financial award applicants required to submit FAFSA. *Faculty research:* Intercultural communication, corporate culture, diversity in the working place, organizational socialization, critical cultural studies. *Unit head:* Dr. Jacqueline Taylor, Dean, 773-325-7216, Fax: 773-325-7584, E-mail: jtaylor@depaul.edu. *Application contact:* Ann Spittle, Director of Graduate Admission, 773-325-8369, Fax: 773-325-2395, E-mail: aspittle@depaul.edu.

Drexel University, College of Arts and Sciences, Department of Culture and Communication, Program in Communication, Philadelphia, PA 19104-2875. Offers public communication (MS); science communication (MS); technical communication (MS). Part-time and evening/weekend programs available. *Degree requirements:* For master's, internship, professional portfolio. *Entrance requirements:* For master's, GRE or minimum GPA of 3.0. Additional exam requirements/recommendations for international students: Required—TOEFL. Electronic applications accepted.

Emerson College, Graduate Studies, School of Communication, Department of Communication Studies, Program in Communication Management, Boston, MA 02116-4624. Offers MA. Part-time programs available. *Students:* 42 full-time (34 women), 9 part-time (7 women); includes 6 minority (1 African American, 1 American Indian/Alaska Native, 4 Asian Americans or Pacific Islanders), 15 international. Average age 26. 41 applicants, 85% accepted, 17 enrolled. In 2008, 26 master's awarded. *Entrance requirements:* For master's, GMAT or GRE General Test. Additional exam requirements/recommendations for international students: Required—TOEFL (minimum score 550 paper-based; 213 computer-based; 80 iBT), IELTS (minimum score 6.5). *Application deadline:* For fall admission, 3/1 priority date for domestic students, 5/1 priority date for international students; for spring admission, 11/1 priority date for domestic students. Applications are processed on a rolling basis. Application fee: $60 ($75 for international students). Electronic applications accepted. *Expenses:* Tuition: Full-time $17,720; part-time $886 per credit. Required fees: $60 per year. One-time fee: $170. *Financial support:* In 2008–09, 10 students received support, including 2 fellowships with partial tuition reimbursements available (averaging $14,000 per year), 6 research assistantships with partial tuition reimbursements available (averaging $10,000 per year); career-related internships or fieldwork, Federal Work-Study, institutionally sponsored loans, scholarships/grants, and unspecified assistantships also available. Support available to part-time students. Financial award application deadline: 3/1; financial award applicants required to submit FAFSA. *Faculty research:* Organizational management, corporate and organizational communication. *Unit head:* Prof. Linda Gallant, Graduate Program Director, 617-824-8491, E-mail: Linda_Gallant@emerson.edu. *Application contact:* Office of Graduate Admission, 617-824-8610, Fax: 617-824-8614, E-mail: gradapp@emerson.edu.

Fairleigh Dickinson University, College at Florham, Maxwell Becton College of Arts and Sciences, Department of English, Communication and Philosophy, Program in Corporate and Organizational Communication, Madison, NJ 07940-1099. Offers MA, MA/MBA. *Students:* 9 full-time (6 women), 34 part-time (24 women), 3 international. Average age 30. 14 applicants, 86% accepted, 10 enrolled. In 2008, 12 master's awarded. *Entrance requirements:* For master's, GRE General Test. *Application deadline:* Applications are processed on a rolling basis. Application fee: $40. *Application contact:* Susan Brooman, University Director, Graduate Admissions, 973-443-8905, Fax: 973-443-8088, E-mail: grad@fdu.edu.

Florida State University, Graduate Studies, College of Communication, Department of Communication, Tallahassee, FL 32306. Offers corporate and public communication (MA, MS); integrated marketing communication (MA, MS); mass communication (PhD); media and communication studies (MA, MS); speech communication (PhD). Part-time programs available. *Degree requirements:* For master's, thesis (for some programs); for doctorate, comprehensive exam, thesis/dissertation. *Entrance requirements:* For master's, GRE General Test, minimum

Corporate and Organizational Communication

Florida State University (continued)
GPA of 3.0; for doctorate, GRE General Test, minimum GPA of 3.3 in graduate course work. Additional exam requirements/recommendations for international students: Required—TOEFL (minimum score 600 paper-based; 250 computer-based; 100 iBT). *Faculty research:* Communication technology and policy, marketing communication, communication content and effect, new communication/information technologies.

Fordham University, Graduate School of Business Administration, New York, NY 10023. Offers accounting (MBA); communications and media management (MBA); executive business administration (EMBA); finance (MBA, MS); information systems (MBA, MS); management systems (MBA); marketing (MBA); media management (MS); taxation (MS); taxation and accounting (MTA);); JD/MBA; MBA/MIM; MS/MBA. *Accreditation:* AACSB. Part-time and evening/weekend programs available. *Entrance requirements:* For master's, GMAT, official undergraduate transcripts, 2 letters of recommendation, resumé, personal statement. Additional exam requirements/recommendations for international students: Required—TOEFL (minimum score 600 paper-based; 250 computer-based; 100 iBT). Electronic applications accepted. *Expenses:* Contact institution.

Franklin University, Marketing and Communications Program, Columbus, OH 43215-5399. Offers MS. Part-time and evening/weekend programs available. *Faculty:* 12 part-time/adjunct (2 women). *Students:* 84 full-time (61 women), 9 part-time (7 women); includes 23 minority (18 African Americans, 2 Asian Americans or Pacific Islanders, 3 Hispanic Americans), 4 international. Average age 34. 29 applicants, 93% accepted, 21 enrolled. In 2008, 51 master's awarded. *Degree requirements:* For master's, thesis or alternative. *Entrance requirements:* For master's, minimum undergraduate GPA of 2.75, undergraduate course work in marketing and statistics. Additional exam requirements/recommendations for international students: Required—TOEFL (minimum score 600 paper-based; 232 computer-based). *Application deadline:* For fall admission, 8/15 priority date for domestic students; for winter admission, 12/20 priority date for domestic students; for spring admission, 4/4 priority date for domestic students. Applications are processed on a rolling basis. Application fee: $30. Electronic applications accepted. *Expenses:* Tuition: Full-time $7470; part-time $450 per credit hour. *Financial support:* In 2008–09, 84 students received support. Application deadline: 6/30. *Unit head:* Dr. Doug Ross, Program Chair, 614-947-6149. *Application contact:* Graduate Services Office, 614-797-4700, Fax: 614-224-7723, E-mail: gradschl@franklin.edu.

HEC Montreal, School of Business Administration, Diploma Programs in Administration, Program in Marketing Communication, Montréal, QC H3T 2A7, Canada. Offers Diploma. All courses are given in French. Program offered on part-time basis only. Part-time programs available. *Students:* 78 part-time (60 women). 108 applicants, 34% accepted, 32 enrolled. In 2008, 28 Diplomas awarded. *Degree requirements:* For Diploma, one foreign language. *Entrance requirements:* For degree, relevant work experience, letters of recommendation. *Application deadline:* For fall admission, 4/15 for domestic and international students. Application fee: $76 Canadian dollars. Electronic applications accepted. Tuition and fees charges are reported in Canadian dollars. *Expenses:* Tuition, area resident: Part-time $62.27 Canadian dollars per credit. Tuition, state resident: full-time $2241.72 Canadian dollars; part-time $179.28 Canadian dollars per credit. Tuition, nonresident: full-time $6454 Canadian dollars; part-time $419.77 Canadian dollars per credit. International tuition: $15,111.72 Canadian dollars full-time. Required fees: $1218.75 Canadian dollars; $28.25 Canadian dollars per credit. $88 Canadian dollars per term. Tuition and fees vary according to degree level and program. *Financial support:* Scholarships/grants available. *Unit head:* Louise Cote, Director, 514-340-6205, Fax: 514-340-5640, E-mail: louise.cote@hec.ca. *Application contact:* Francine Blais, Administrative Director, 514-340-6112, Fax: 514-340-6411, E-mail: francine.blais@hec.ca.

Howard University, School of Communications, Department of Communication and Culture, Washington, DC 20059-0002. Offers intercultural communication (MA, PhD); organizational communication (MA, PhD). Offered through the Graduate School of Arts and Sciences. Part-time programs available. Terminal master's awarded for partial completion of doctoral program. *Degree requirements:* For master's, comprehensive exam or thesis; for doctorate, one foreign language, comprehensive exam, thesis/dissertation. *Entrance requirements:* For master's, English proficiency exam, GRE General Test, minimum GPA of 3.0; for doctorate, English proficiency exam, GRE General Test, master's degree in related field, minimum GPA of 3.5. Additional exam requirements/recommendations for international students: Required—TOEFL. *Faculty research:* Media effects, black discourse, development communication, African-American organizations.

Illinois Institute of Technology, Stuart School of Business, Program in Marketing Communication, Chicago, IL 60616-3793. Offers MS, JD/MS, MBA/MS. Part-time and evening/weekend programs available. *Faculty:* 2 full-time (0 women), 5 part-time/adjunct (2 women). *Students:* 32 full-time (23 women), 7 part-time (3 women); includes 1 minority (Asian American or Pacific Islander), 33 international. Average age 26. 91 applicants, 52% accepted, 12 enrolled. In 2008, 17 master's awarded. *Entrance requirements:* For master's, GMAT or GRE General Test. Additional exam requirements/recommendations for international students: Required—TOEFL (minimum score 600 paper-based; 250 computer-based; 100 iBT). *Application deadline:* For fall admission, 5/1 for domestic and international students; for spring admission, 1/5 for domestic and international students. Applications are processed on a rolling basis. Application fee: $75. Electronic applications accepted. *Expenses:* Contact institution. *Financial support:* Career-related internships or fieldwork, Federal Work-Study, institutionally sponsored loans, scholarships/grants, traineeships, health care benefits, and tuition waivers (partial) available. Support available to part-time students. Financial award applicants required to submit FAFSA. *Unit head:* Sanford Bredine, Associate Director and Senior Lecturer, 312-906-6540, Fax: 312-906-6549, E-mail: bredine@stuart.itt.edu. *Application contact:* Sanford Bredine, Associate Director and Senior Lecturer, 312-906-6540, Fax: 312-906-6549, E-mail: bredine@stuart.itt.edu.

Iowa State University of Science and Technology, Graduate College, College of Liberal Arts and Sciences, Department of English, Ames, IA 50011. Offers English (MA); rhetoric and professional communication (PhD). *Faculty:* 51 full-time (25 women), 10 part-time/adjunct (7 women). *Students:* 89 full-time (57 women), 34 part-time (22 women); includes 4 minority (1 African American, 3 Hispanic Americans), 28 international. 106 applicants, 58% accepted, 37 enrolled. In 2008, 31 master's awarded. *Degree requirements:* For master's, thesis or alternative; for doctorate, thesis/dissertation. *Entrance requirements:* For master's, GRE General Test, sample of written work, resumé, portfolio in creative writing; for doctorate, GRE General Test, sample of written work, resumé. Additional exam requirements/recommendations for international students: Required—TOEFL (minimum score 600 paper-based; 100 iBT), IELTS (7.0) or TOEFL. *Application deadline:* For fall admission, 1/5 priority date for domestic and international students. Application fee: $30 ($70 for international students). Electronic applications accepted. *Expenses:* Tuition, area resident: Full-time $6446; part-time $359 per credit. Tuition, state resident: full-time $6446; part-time $359 per credit. Tuition, nonresident: full-time $17,330; part-time $963 per credit. Required fees: $790; $249.25 per semester. Tuition and fees vary according to course load and program. *Financial support:* In 2008–09, 14 research assistantships with full and partial tuition reimbursements (averaging $16,308 per year), 79 teaching assistantships with full and partial tuition reimbursements (averaging $16,308 per year) were awarded; fellowships, scholarships/grants, health care benefits, and unspecified assistantships also available. *Faculty research:* Creative writing, literature, rhetoric, composition and professional communication, teaching English as a second language, applied linguistics. *Unit head:* Dr. Charles Kostelnick, Chair, 515-294-2477, Fax: 515-294-2125, E-mail: englgrad@iastate.edu. *Application contact:* Dr. Constance Post, Director of Graduate Education, 515-294-3175, E-mail: englgrad@iastate.edu.

John Carroll University, Graduate School, Department of Communications Management, University Heights, OH 44118-4581. Offers MA. Part-time and evening/weekend programs available. *Degree requirements:* For master's, comprehensive exam, thesis or project. *Entrance requirements:* For master's, GRE General Test, minimum GPA of 3.0. Additional exam requirements/recommendations for international students: Required—TOEFL. Electronic applications accepted. *Faculty research:* Communication law, media ethics, international studies, international broadcasting, media history.

Jones International University, School of Business, Centennial, CO 80112. Offers accounting (MBA); business communication (MABC); entrepreneurship (MABC, MBA); finance (MBA); global enterprise management (MBA); health care management (MBA); information security management (MBA); information technology management (MBA); leadership and influence (MABC); leading the customer-driven organization (MABC); negotiation and conflict management (MBA); project management (MABC, MBA). Program only offered online. Part-time and evening/weekend programs available. Postbaccalaureate distance learning degree programs offered (no on-campus study). *Degree requirements:* For master's, capstone project. *Entrance requirements:* For master's, minimum cumulative GPA of 2.5. Additional exam requirements/recommendations for international students: Recommended—TOEFL (minimum score 550 paper-based; 213 computer-based). Electronic applications accepted.

La Salle University, School of Arts and Sciences, Program in Professional Communication, Philadelphia, PA 19141-1199. Offers MA. Part-time and evening/weekend programs available. *Degree requirements:* For master's, exam or project. *Entrance requirements:* For master's, GRE or MAT. *Expenses:* Contact institution.

Lasell College, Graduate and Professional Studies in Communication, Newton, MA 02466-2709. Offers integrated marketing communication (MSC, Graduate Certificate); public relations (MSC, Graduate Certificate). Part-time and evening/weekend programs available. Postbaccalaureate distance learning degree programs offered (minimal on-campus study). *Entrance requirements:* For master's and Graduate Certificate, bachelor's degree from an accredited institution. Additional exam requirements/recommendations for international students: Required—TOEFL (minimum score 550 paper-based; 213 computer-based; 79 iBT), IELTS (minimum score 6). *Application deadline:* For fall admission, 8/30 priority date for domestic and international students; for winter admission, 11/30 priority date for domestic and international students; for spring admission, 12/30 priority date for domestic and international students. Applications are processed on a rolling basis. Application fee: $40. Electronic applications accepted. *Expenses:* Tuition: Full-time $4500; part-time $500 per credit hour. Required fees: $55 per term. *Financial support:* Institutionally sponsored loans available. Support available to part-time students. Financial award application deadline: 8/30; financial award applicants required to submit FAFSA. *Unit head:* Dr. Janice Barrett, Chair, Department of Communication, 617-243-2400, E-mail: gradinfo@lasell.edu. *Application contact:* Adrienne Franciosi, Director of Graduate Admission, 617-243-2400, Fax: 617-243-2450, E-mail: gradinfo@lasell.edu.

Loyola University Chicago, Graduate School of Business, Marketing Department, Chicago, IL 60611-2196. Offers integrated marketing communications (MS); marketing (MSIMC). Part-time and evening/weekend programs available. *Entrance requirements:* For master's, GMAT, letters of recommendation, personal statement. Additional exam requirements/recommendations for international students: Required—TOEFL (minimum score 550 paper-based; 213 computer-based; 80 iBT). Electronic applications accepted. *Expenses:* Contact institution. *Faculty research:* Web performance metrics, new venture marketing strategies over consumption, benefit segmentation strategies.

Manhattanville College, Graduate Programs, Humanities and Social Sciences Programs, Program in Management Communications, Purchase, NY 10577-2132. Offers MS. Part-time programs available. *Entrance requirements:* For master's, 2 letters of recommendation, interview.

Marietta College, Program in Corporate Media, Marietta, OH 45750-4000. Offers MCM. *Faculty:* 5 full-time (4 women), 2 part-time/adjunct (0 women). *Students:* 10 full-time (6 women), 8 part-time (3 women). *Unit head:* Marilee Morrow, Director, 740-376-4828, E-mail: marilee.morrow@marietta.edu. *Application contact:* Cathy J. Brown, Director of Graduate and Continuing Studies, 740-376-4740, Fax: 740-376-4423, E-mail: ce@marietta.edu.

Marist College, Graduate Programs, School of Communication and the Arts, Poughkeepsie, NY 12601-1387. Offers organizational communication and leadership (MA). Part-time programs available. Postbaccalaureate distance learning degree programs offered (no on-campus study). *Degree requirements:* For master's, thesis or comprehensive exam. *Entrance requirements:* For master's, GRE, minimum undergraduate GPA of 3.0, resumé, 3 letters of recommendation, transcript, statement of purpose. Additional exam requirements/recommendations for international students: Required—TOEFL (minimum score 550 paper-based; 213 computer-based; 80 iBT); Recommended—IELTS (minimum score 6.5). Electronic applications accepted.

Marywood University, Academic Affairs, Insalaco College of Creative Arts and Management, Department of Communication Arts, Program in Communication Arts, Scranton, PA 18509-1598. Offers corporate communication (Certificate); e-business (Certificate); health communication (Certificate); instructional technology (Certificate); interdisciplinary (MA); library science/information specialist (Certificate); media management (MA); production (MA).

Marywood University, Academic Affairs, Insalaco College of Creative Arts and Management, Department of Communication Arts, Program in Information Sciences, Scranton, PA 18509-1598. Offers corporate communication (MS); e-business (MS); health communication (MS); instructional technology (MS); library science/information science (MS).

Metropolitan College of New York, Program in Media Management, New York, NY 10013. Offers MBA. Evening/weekend programs available. *Degree requirements:* For master's, thesis, 10 day study abroad. *Entrance requirements:* For master's, GMAT or GRE, appropriate work experience, interview, minimum GPA of 2.7. Additional exam requirements/recommendations for international students: Required—TOEFL (minimum score 600 paper-based; 220 computer-based). Electronic applications accepted. *Expenses:* Contact institution.

Mississippi College, Graduate School, College of Arts and Sciences, School of Christian Studies and the Arts, Department of Communication, Clinton, MS 39058. Offers applied communication (MSC); public relations and corporate communication (MSC). Part-time programs available. *Degree requirements:* For master's, comprehensive exam, thesis optional. *Entrance requirements:* For master's, GRE or NTE, minimum GPA of 2.5. Additional exam requirements/recommendations for international students: Recommended—IELTS. Electronic applications accepted.

Monmouth University, Graduate School, Department of Corporate and Public Communication, West Long Branch, NJ 07764-1898. Offers corporate and public communication (MA); human resources communication (Certificate); media studies (Certificate); public relations (Certificate). *Faculty:* 9 full-time (5 women). *Students:* 5 full-time (3 women), 40 part-time (28 women); includes 8 minority (4 African Americans, 1 Asian American or Pacific Islander, 3 Hispanic Americans), 3 international. Average age 32. 19 applicants, 95% accepted, 10 enrolled. In 2008, 14 master's awarded. *Degree requirements:* For master's, comprehensive exam, project. *Entrance requirements:* For master's, GRE, minimum GPA of 3.0 in major, 2.75 overall. Additional exam requirements/recommendations for international students: Required—TOEFL (minimum score 550 paper-based; 213 computer-based; 79 iBT), IELTS (minimum score 5), Michigan English Language Assessment Battery (minimum score: 77), Cambridge A, B, C. *Application deadline:* For fall admission, 7/15 priority date for domestic students, 6/1 for international students; for spring admission, 11/15 priority date for domestic students, 11/1 for international students. Applications are processed on a rolling basis. Application fee: $50. Electronic applications accepted. *Expenses:* Tuition: Full-time $13,914; part-time $773 per credit. Required fees: $628; $157 per semester. *Financial support:* In 2008–09, 26 students received support, including 23 fellowships (averaging $1,142 per year), 5 research assistantships (averaging $4,794 per year); scholarships/grants and unspecified assistantships also available. Support available to part-time students. Financial award application deadline: 3/1; financial award applicants required to submit FAFSA. *Faculty research:* Service learning, history of television, feminism and the media, executive communication, public relations pedagogy. *Unit head:* Dr. Eleanor Novek, Program Director, 732-263-5449, Fax: 732-571-

3609, E-mail: enovek@monmouth.edu. *Application contact:* Kevin Roane, Director, Office of Graduate Admission, 732-571-3452, Fax: 732-263-5123, E-mail: gradadm@monmouth.edu.

Montclair State University, The Office of Graduate Admissions and Support Services, School of the Arts, Department of Communication Studies, Montclair, NJ 07043-1624. Offers organizational communication (MA); public relations (MA); speech communication (MA). Part-time and evening/weekend programs available. *Faculty:* 6 full-time (2 women), 36 part-time/adjunct (18 women). *Students:* 9 full-time (7 women), 20 part-time (15 women); includes 6 minority (4 African Americans, 2 Hispanic Americans), 2 international. Average age 30. 29 applicants, 38% accepted, 8 enrolled. In 2008, 7 master's awarded. *Degree requirements:* For master's, comprehensive exam. *Entrance requirements:* For master's, GRE General Test, minimum GPA of 3.0; undergraduate degree or work in theatre, oral interpretation, speech communication, media, or broadcasting; 2 letters of recommendation. Additional exam requirements/recommendations for international students: Required—TOEFL (minimum score 83 computer-based). *Application deadline:* For fall admission, 6/1 for international students; for spring admission, 10/1 for international students. Applications are processed on a rolling basis. Application fee: $60. Electronic applications accepted. *Financial support:* In 2008–09, 1 research assistantship with full tuition reimbursement (averaging $7,000 per year) was awarded; Federal Work-Study, scholarships/grants, and unspecified assistantships also available. Support available to part-time students. Financial award application deadline: 3/1; financial award applicants required to submit FAFSA. *Unit head:* Dr. Harry Haines, Chair, 973-655-4200. *Application contact:* Amy Aiello, Associate Director of Admissions, 973-655-5147, Fax: 973-655-7869, E-mail: graduate.school@montclair.edu.

Murray State University, College of Business and Public Affairs, Program in Organizational Communication, Murray, KY 42071. Offers MA, MS. Part-time programs available. *Degree requirements:* For master's, thesis (for some programs). *Entrance requirements:* For master's, minimum GPA of 2.5 for conditional admittance, 3.0 for unconditional admittance. Additional exam requirements/recommendations for international students: Required—TOEFL (minimum score 550 paper-based; 213 computer-based). *Faculty research:* Organizational learning, organizational culture, leadership, health communication, personality.

National University, Academic Affairs, School of Media and Communication, Department of Communication, La Jolla, CA 92037-1011. Offers strategic communication (MA). Part-time and evening/weekend programs available. Postbaccalaureate distance learning degree programs offered (no on-campus study). *Faculty:* 5 full-time (2 women), 24 part-time/adjunct (15 women). *Students:* 12 full-time (4 women); includes 3 African Americans, 2 Asian Americans or Pacific Islanders, 1 Hispanic American. 20 applicants, 100% accepted, 20 enrolled. In 2008, 3 master's awarded. *Degree requirements:* For master's, thesis. *Entrance requirements:* Additional exam requirements/recommendations for international students: Required—TOEFL (minimum score 550 paper-based; 213 computer-based; 79 iBT), IELTS (minimum score 6). *Application deadline:* For fall admission, 6/30 for international students. Applications are processed on a rolling basis. Application fee: $60 ($65 for international students). Electronic applications accepted. *Expenses:* Tuition: Full-time $8694; part-time $322 per credit hour. Tuition and fees vary according to course load. *Financial support:* Application deadline: 6/30; *Unit head:* Dr. Joan Vas Tassel, Dean, 858-309-3446, Fax: 858-309-3450, E-mail: jvantassel@nu.edu. *Application contact:* Dominick Giovanniello, Associate Regional Dean—San Diego, 800-NAT-UNIV, Fax: 858-541-7792, E-mail: dgiovann@nu.edu.

New Mexico State University, Graduate School, College of Arts and Sciences, Department of English, Las Cruces, NM 88003-8001. Offers creative writing (MFA); English (MA); rhetoric and professional communication (PhD). Part-time programs available. *Faculty:* 20 full-time (12 women), 2 part-time/adjunct (0 women). *Students:* 73 full-time (39 women), 36 part-time (24 women); includes 15 minority (3 American Indian/Alaska Native, 12 Hispanic Americans), 9 international. Average age 32. 135 applicants, 41% accepted, 40 enrolled. In 2008, 25 master's, 2 doctorates awarded. *Degree requirements:* For master's, one foreign language, thesis (for some programs); for doctorate, comprehensive exam, thesis/dissertation, internship. *Entrance requirements:* For master's and doctorate, sample of written work. *Application deadline:* For fall admission, 2/1 for domestic and international students. Application fee: $30 ($50 for international students). Electronic applications accepted. *Expenses:* Tuition, area resident: Full-time $3890; part-time $212.85 per credit. Tuition, state resident: full-time $3890; part-time $212.85 per credit. Tuition, nonresident: full-time $13,916; part-time $630.55 per credit. Required fees: $1218; $609 per semester. *Financial support:* In 2008–09, 81 students received support, including 3 research assistantships (averaging $9,217 per year), 53 teaching assistantships (averaging $15,623 per year); fellowships, career-related internships or fieldwork, Federal Work-Study, institutionally sponsored loans, scholarships/grants, health care benefits, and unspecified assistantships also available. Financial award application deadline: 2/1; financial award applicants required to submit FAFSA. *Faculty research:* Composition research, history and theory of rhetoric, technical/professional communication, creative writing, English and American literature. *Unit head:* Dr. Elizabeth Schirmer, Head, 575-646-1733, Fax: 575-646-7725, E-mail: eschirme@nmsu.edu. *Application contact:* Dr. Elizabeth Schirmer, Director of Graduate Studies, 575-646-1733, E-mail: eschirme@nmsu.edu.

New York University, School of Continuing and Professional Studies, Division of Programs in Business, Program in Public Relations and Corporate Communications, New York, NY 10012-1019. Offers MS. Part-time and evening/weekend programs available. *Degree requirements:* For master's, capstone project. *Entrance requirements:* For master's, GRE General Test or GMAT (for recent graduates), related work experience, 2 letters of recommendation, resumé, essay. Additional exam requirements/recommendations for international students: Required—TOEFL (minimum score 600 paper-based; 250 computer-based; 100 iBT), TWE. Electronic applications accepted.

Northwestern University, The Graduate School, School of Communication, Department of Communication Studies, Managerial Communication Program, Evanston, IL 60208. Offers MSC. *Entrance requirements:* For master's, GRE General Test.

Northwestern University, Medill School of Journalism, Integrated Marketing Communications Program, Evanston, IL 60208. Offers advertising/sales promotion (MSIMC); direct database and e-commerce marketing (MSIMC); general studies (MSIMC); public relations (MSIMC). Part-time programs available. *Entrance requirements:* For master's, GRE General Test or GMAT, full-time work experience (preferred). Additional exam requirements/recommendations for international students: Required—TOEFL. Electronic applications accepted. *Faculty research:* Data mining, business to business marketing, values in advertising, political advertising.

Oklahoma City University, Meinders School of Business, Program in Business Administration, Oklahoma City, OK 73106-1402. Offers finance (MBA); health administration (MBA); information technology (MBA); integrated marketing communications (MBA); international business (MBA); marketing (MBA); JD/MBA. *Accreditation:* ACBSP. Part-time and evening/weekend programs available. *Degree requirements:* For master's, comprehensive exam. *Entrance requirements:* For master's, minimum GPA of 2.5. Additional exam requirements/recommendations for international students: Required—TOEFL (minimum score 510 paper-based). *Faculty research:* Management information systems, international business strategies.

Queens University of Charlotte, School of Communication, Charlotte, NC 28274-0002. Offers organizational and strategic communication (MA). Part-time and evening/weekend programs available. *Faculty:* 2 full-time (1 woman), 3 part-time/adjunct (all women). *Students:* 2 full-time (1 woman), 27 part-time (23 women); includes 10 minority (4 African Americans, 2 Asian Americans or Pacific Islanders, 4 Hispanic Americans), 4 international. Average age 28. 11 applicants, 73% accepted, 7 enrolled. In 2008, 9 master's awarded. *Degree requirements:* For master's, capstone course. *Entrance requirements:* Additional exam requirements/recommendations for international students: Required—TOEFL. Application fee: $40. *Expenses:* Contact institution. *Financial support:* In 2008–09, 5 fellowships were awarded. *Unit head:* Van King, Dean, 704-337-2397, Fax: 704-688-2767. *Application contact:* Gilda McGee, Assistant Director, Graduate Admissions, 704-337-2313, Fax: 704-337-2403.

Radford University, College of Graduate and Professional Studies, College of Humanities and Behavioral Sciences, School of Communication, Radford, VA 24142. Offers corporate and professional communication (MS). Part-time and evening/weekend programs available. *Faculty:* 10 full-time (5 women). *Students:* 11 full-time (5 women), 14 part-time (6 women); includes 2 minority (both Hispanic Americans), 2 international. Average age 31. 19 applicants, 84% accepted, 8 enrolled. In 2008, 7 master's awarded. *Degree requirements:* For master's, comprehensive exam, thesis optional. *Entrance requirements:* For master's, GRE, minimum GPA of 2.75; short essay; 3 letters of reference. Additional exam requirements/recommendations for international students: Required—TOEFL (minimum score 550 paper-based; 213 computer-based; 79 iBT). *Application deadline:* For fall admission, 2/1 priority date for domestic students, 12/1 for international students; for spring admission, 9/1 for domestic students, 7/1 for international students. Applications are processed on a rolling basis. Application fee: $40. Electronic applications accepted. *Expenses:* Tuition, area resident: Full-time $4845; part-time $202 per credit. Tuition, state resident: full-time $4845; part-time $202 per credit. Tuition, nonresident: full-time $11,483; part-time $478 per credit. Required fees: $2349; $98 per credit. *Financial support:* In 2008–09, 15 students received support, including 5 research assistantships with partial tuition reimbursements available (averaging $8,000 per year), 5 teaching assistantships with partial tuition reimbursements available (averaging $8,700 per year); career-related internships or fieldwork, Federal Work-Study, institutionally sponsored loans, and scholarships/grants also available. Financial award application deadline: 3/1; financial award applicants required to submit FAFSA. *Unit head:* Dr. Lynn M Zoch, Director, 540-831-6553, Fax: 540-831-5883, E-mail: lzoch@radford.edu. *Application contact:* Graduate Admissions, 540-831-5431, Fax: 540-831-6061, E-mail: gradcollege@radford.edu.

Regis College, Department of Organizational and Professional Communication, Weston, MA 02493. Offers MS. Part-time and evening/weekend programs available. *Faculty:* 1 (woman) full-time, 3 part-time/adjunct (1 woman). *Students:* 12 part-time (all women); includes 2 minority (1 Asian American or Pacific Islander, 1 Hispanic American). Average age 34. 5 applicants, 100% accepted, 5 enrolled. In 2008, 13 master's awarded. *Degree requirements:* For master's, thesis. *Entrance requirements:* For master's, GRE or MAT. Additional exam requirements/recommendations for international students: Required—TOEFL (minimum score 550 paper-based; 213 computer-based). *Application deadline:* Applications are processed on a rolling basis. Application fee: $50. *Expenses:* Tuition: Part-time $676 per credit. *Financial support:* In 2008–09, 9 students received support. Scholarships/grants available. Financial award applicants required to submit FAFSA. *Unit head:* Dr. Joan Murray, Director, 781-768-7416, Fax: 781-768-7159, E-mail: joan.murray@regiscollege.edu. *Application contact:* Christine Petherick, Administrative Coordinator, Graduate Admission, 866-438-7344, Fax: 781-768-7071, E-mail: christine.petherick@regiscollege.edu.

Roosevelt University, Graduate Division, College of Arts and Sciences, Department of Communication, Program in Integrated Marketing Communications, Chicago, IL 60605-1394. Offers MSIMC. Part-time and evening/weekend programs available. *Students:* 61 full-time (48 women), 121 part-time (98 women); includes 68 minority (57 African Americans, 1 American Indian/Alaska Native, 4 Asian Americans or Pacific Islanders, 6 Hispanic Americans), 23 international. Average age 30. 270 applicants, 64% accepted, 64 enrolled. In 2008, 65 master's awarded. *Application deadline:* For fall admission, 6/1 priority date for domestic students. Applications are processed on a rolling basis. Application fee: $25 ($35 for international students). *Expenses:* Tuition: Full-time $14,730; part-time $709 per credit. Required fees: $175 per semester. Tuition and fees vary according to course load and program. *Financial support:* In 2008–09, 1 research assistantship was awarded; career-related internships or fieldwork and Federal Work-Study also available. Financial award application deadline: 2/15. *Faculty research:* Print journalism, urban high school journalism. *Application contact:* Joanne Canyon-Heller, Coordinator of Graduate Admission, 877-APPLY RU, Fax: 312-281-3356, E-mail: applyru@roosevelt.edu.

Schiller International University, Graduate Programs, London, Program in Communications, London, United Kingdom. Offers business communication (MA).

Seton Hall University, College of Arts and Sciences, Department of Communication, South Orange, NJ 07079-2697. Offers corporate and public communication (MA); strategic communication and leadership (MA). Part-time and evening/weekend programs available. Postbaccalaureate distance learning degree programs offered (minimal on-campus study). *Entrance requirements:* For master's, GRE or GMAT, minimum GPA of 3.0. Electronic applications accepted. *Faculty research:* Managerial communication, communication consulting, communication and development.

See Close-Up on page 697.

Simmons College, College of Arts and Sciences Graduate Studies, Program in Communications Management, Boston, MA 02115. Offers MS, MS/MA. Part-time programs available. *Faculty:* 12 part-time/adjunct (6 women). *Students:* 4 full-time (3 women), 73 part-time (66 women); includes 15 minority (9 African Americans, 2 Asian Americans or Pacific Islanders, 4 Hispanic Americans). Average age 30. 44 applicants, 84% accepted, 22 enrolled. In 2008, 29 master's awarded. *Degree requirements:* For master's, applied learning project. *Entrance requirements:* For master's, GRE General Test, MAT, or GMAT, 2 years of professional experience. Additional exam requirements/recommendations for international students: Required—TOEFL (minimum score 600 paper-based; 250 computer-based; 100 iBT). *Application deadline:* For fall admission, 8/1 priority date for domestic and international students; for winter admission, 12/15 priority date for domestic and international students; for spring admission, 5/1 priority date for domestic and international students. Applications are processed on a rolling basis. Application fee: $35. Electronic applications accepted. *Financial support:* In 2008–09, 11 students received support. Career-related internships or fieldwork, scholarships/grants, and unspecified assistantships available. Financial award application deadline: 3/1; financial award applicants required to submit FAFSA. *Faculty research:* Diversity in organizations, organizational communications, communications technologies, motivational communication. *Unit head:* Joan C. Abrams, Director, Assistant Professor, 617-521-2845, Fax: 617-521-3149, E-mail: abrams@simmons.edu. *Application contact:* Kristen Haack, Director, Graduate Studies Admission, 617-521-2917, Fax: 617-521-3058, E-mail: gsa@simmons.edu.

Southern Illinois University Edwardsville, Graduate Studies and Research, College of Arts and Sciences, Department of Speech Communication, Program in Corporate and Organizational Communication, Edwardsville, IL 62026-0001. Offers Postbaccalaureate Certificate. Part-time programs available. *Students:* 1 (woman) part-time. Average age 26. 8 applicants, 0% accepted. *Entrance requirements:* Additional exam requirements/recommendations for international students: Required—TOEFL (minimum score 550 paper-based; 213 computer-based; 79 iBT), IELTS (minimum score 6.5). *Application deadline:* For fall admission, 7/20 for domestic students, 6/1 for international students; for spring admission, 12/14 for domestic students, 10/1 for international students. Applications are processed on a rolling basis. Application fee: $30. Electronic applications accepted. *Expenses:* Tuition, area resident: Full-time $5838. Tuition, nonresident: full-time $14,596. Required fees: $1525. *Financial support:* Fellowships with full tuition reimbursements, research assistantships with full tuition reimbursements, teaching assistantships with full tuition reimbursements available. Financial award application deadline: 3/1; financial award applicants required to submit FAFSA. *Unit head:* Dr. Wai Hsien Cheah, Director, 618-650-5016, E-mail: wcheah@siue.edu. *Application contact:* Dr. Wai Hsien Cheah, Director, 618-650-5016, E-mail: wcheah@siue.edu.

Southern Polytechnic State University, School of Arts and Sciences, Department of English, Technical Communication, and Media Arts, Marietta, GA 30060-2896. Offers communications management (Graduate Certificate); content development (Graduate Certificate); information design and communication (MS); instructional design (Graduate Certificate); technical and professional communication (Graduate Certificate); visual communication and graphics (Graduate Certificate). Part-time and evening/weekend programs available. Postbaccalaureate distance learning degree programs offered (minimal on-campus study). *Faculty:* 4 full-time (3 women), 1 part-time/adjunct. *Students:* 5 full-time (4 women), 38 part-time (25 women); includes 13 minority (12 African Americans, 1 Hispanic American), 3 international. Average

Corporate and Organizational Communication

Southern Polytechnic State University (continued)
age 38. 38 applicants, 68% accepted, 23 enrolled. In 2008, 10 master's awarded. *Degree requirements:* For master's, thesis optional, 36 hours completed through thesis option (6 hours), internship option (6 hours) or advanced coursework option (6 hours); for Graduate Certificate, thesis optional, 18 hours completed through thesis option (6 hours), internship option (6 hours) or advanced coursework option (6 hours). *Entrance requirements:* For master's, GRE, statement of purpose, writing sample, professional recommendations, proctored essay; for Graduate Certificate, statement of purpose, writing sample, professional recommendations, proctored essay. Additional exam requirements/recommendations for international students: Required—TOEFL (minimum score 550 paper-based; 213 computer-based; 79 iBT), IELTS (minimum score 6.5). *Application deadline:* For fall admission, 5/1 priority date for domestic students, 7/1 priority date for international students; for spring admission, 9/1 priority date for domestic students, 11/1 priority date for international students. Applications are processed on a rolling basis. Application fee: $20. Electronic applications accepted. *Expenses:* Tuition, area resident: Full-time $2752; part-time $172 per semester hour. Tuition, state resident: full-time $2752; part-time $172 per semester hour. Tuition, nonresident: full-time $10,992; part-time $687 per semester hour. Required fees: $365 per semester. *Financial support:* In 2008–09, 14 students received support, including 1 research assistantship with full tuition reimbursement available (averaging $4,000 per year); career-related internships or fieldwork, Federal Work-Study, scholarships/grants, and unspecified assistantships also available. Support available to part-time students. Financial award application deadline: 5/1; financial award applicants required to submit FAFSA. *Faculty research:* Usability, user-centered design, instructional design, information architecture, information design. *Unit head:* Dr. Mark Nunes, Chair, 678-915-7202, Fax: 678-915-7425, E-mail: mnunes@spsu.edu. *Application contact:* Nikki Palamiotis, Director of Graduate Studies, 678-915-4276, Fax: 678-915-7292, E-mail: npalamio@spsu.edu.

Spalding University, Graduate Studies, College of Business and Communication, Louisville, KY 40203-2188. Offers business communication (MS). Part-time and evening/weekend programs available. *Degree requirements:* For master's, project. *Entrance requirements:* For master's, GRE or GMAT, writing sample, interview, letters of recommendation. Additional exam requirements/recommendations for international students: Required—TOEFL (minimum score 535 paper-based; 203 computer-based). Electronic applications accepted. *Expenses:* Tuition: Full-time $11,340; part-time $630 per credit hour. Tuition and fees vary according to program. *Faculty research:* Curriculum development, consumer behavior, interdisciplinary pedagogy.

Stevens Institute of Technology, Graduate School, Wesley J. Howe School of Technology Management, Program in Professional Communications, Hoboken, NJ 07030. Offers Certificate.

Suffolk University, College of Arts and Sciences, Department of Communication, Boston, MA 02108-2770. Offers communication studies (MAC); integrated marketing communication (MAC); organizational communication (MAC); public relations and advertising (MAC). Part-time and evening/weekend programs available. *Degree requirements:* For master's, thesis optional. *Entrance requirements:* For master's, GRE General Test, MAT, or GMAT, statement of professional goals, official transcripts, 2 letters of recommendation, resumé. Additional exam requirements/recommendations for international students: Required—TOEFL (minimum score 550 paper-based; 213 computer-based; 80 iBT). Electronic applications accepted. *Expenses:* Contact institution. *Faculty research:* New media and new markets for advertising, First Amendment issues with the Internet, gender and intercultural communication, organizational development.

Temple University, Graduate School, School of Communications and Theater, Department of Strategic and Organizational Communication, Philadelphia, PA 19122-6096. Offers communication management (MS); mass media and communication (PhD). *Entrance requirements:* Additional exam requirements/recommendations for international students: Required—TOEFL (minimum score 550 paper-based; 213 computer-based; 79 iBT).

Towson University, College of Graduate Studies and Research, Program in Communications Management, Towson, MD 21252-0001. Offers MS. *Degree requirements:* For master's, thesis. *Entrance requirements:* For master's, 24 credits in mass communications, public relations and/or advertising, writing and statistics; professional experience; minimum GPA of 3.0. Electronic applications accepted.

Universidad Autonoma de Guadalajara, Graduate Programs, Guadalajara, Mexico. Offers advertising and corporate communications (MA); architecture (M Arch); business (MBA); computational science (MCC); education (Ed M, Ed D); English-Spanish translation (MA); fiscal law (MA); international business (MIB); international corporate law (LL M); internet technologies (MS); labor health (MS); manufacturing systems (MMS); market research (MBA); philosophy (MA, PhD); quality systems (MQS); renewable energy (MS); teaching mathematics (MA).

University of Alaska Fairbanks, College of Liberal Arts, Department of Communications, Fairbanks, AK 99775-5680. Offers professional communications (MA). Part-time programs available. *Faculty:* 4 full-time (3 women). *Students:* 10 full-time (8 women), 5 part-time (4 women); includes 3 minority (1 African American, 1 Asian American or Pacific Islander, 1 Hispanic American), 2 international. Average age 31. 15 applicants, 73% accepted, 10 enrolled. In 2008, 6 master's awarded. *Degree requirements:* For master's, comprehensive exam, thesis, oral defense. *Entrance requirements:* Additional exam requirements/recommendations for international students: Required—TOEFL (minimum score 550 paper-based; 213 computer-based; 80 iBT). *Application deadline:* For fall admission, 6/1 for domestic students, 3/1 for international students; for spring admission, 10/15 for domestic students, 9/1 for international students. Applications are processed on a rolling basis. Application fee: $60. Electronic applications accepted. *Expenses:* Tuition, area resident: Full-time $5418; part-time $301 per credit. Tuition, state resident: full-time $5418; part-time $301 per credit. Tuition, nonresident: full-time $11,070; part-time $615 per credit. Required fees: $849; $25 per credit. $78 per semester. Tuition and fees vary according to course load and reciprocity agreements. *Financial support:* In 2008–09, 10 teaching assistantships (averaging $12,006 per year) were awarded; fellowships, Federal Work-Study, scholarships/grants, tuition waivers, and unspecified assistantships also available. Support available to part-time students. Financial award application deadline: 7/1; financial award applicants required to submit FAFSA. *Faculty research:* Interpersonal communications, health communications, intercultural communications, politeness and face management in conversation, gender communication. *Unit head:* Dr. Robert Arundale, Department Chair, 907-474-6591, Fax: 907-474-5858, E-mail: fycomm@uaf.edu. *Application contact:* Dr. Robert Arundale, Department Chair, 907-474-6591, Fax: 907-474-5858, E-mail: fycomm@uaf.edu.

University of Central Florida, College of Sciences, Nicholson School of Communication, Orlando, FL 32816. Offers business communication (MA); interpersonal communication (MA); mass communication (MA). Part-time and evening/weekend programs available. *Faculty:* 41 full-time (18 women), 36 part-time/adjunct (18 women). *Students:* 44 full-time (39 women), 28 part-time (25 women); includes 15 minority (6 African Americans, 3 Asian Americans or Pacific Islanders, 6 Hispanic Americans), 9 international. In 2008, 29 master's awarded. *Degree requirements:* For master's, thesis or comprehensive exam. *Entrance requirements:* For master's, GRE General Test, minimum GPA of 3.0 in last 60 hours of course work. Additional exam requirements/recommendations for international students: Required—TOEFL. *Application deadline:* For fall admission, 7/15 for domestic students; for spring admission, 12/7 for domestic students. Application fee: $30. Electronic applications accepted. *Expenses:* Tuition, area resident: Full-time $6816; part-time $284 per credit. Tuition, state resident: full-time $6816; part-time $1076 per credit. Tuition, nonresident: full-time $25,824. Required fees: $216; $9 per credit. *Financial support:* In 2008–09, 2 fellowships with partial tuition reimbursements (averaging $10,000 per year), 4 research assistantships with partial tuition reimbursements (averaging $4,400 per year), 16 teaching assistantships with partial tuition reimbursements (averaging $6,400 per year) were awarded; career-related internships or fieldwork, Federal Work-Study, institutionally sponsored loans, tuition waivers (partial), and unspecified assistantships also available. Financial award application deadline: 3/1; financial award applicants required to submit FAFSA. *Faculty research:* Persuasion, communication apprehension, nonverbal communication, conflict resolution. *Unit head:* Dr. Robert Chandler, Director, 407-823-2683, Fax: 407-823-5216, E-mail: rcchandl@mail.ucf.edu. *Application contact:* Dr. Robert Chandler, Director, 407-823-2683, Fax: 407-823-5216, E-mail: rcchandl@mail.ucf.edu.

University of Connecticut, Graduate School, College of Liberal Arts and Sciences, Department of Communication Sciences, Storrs, CT 06269. Offers communication sciences (MA, Au D, PhD), including audiology (Au D, PhD), communication processes (MA), communication processes and marketing communication (PhD), speech-language pathology (MA, PhD); Au D/PhD. *Accreditation:* ASHA (one or more programs are accredited). Terminal master's awarded for partial completion of doctoral program. *Degree requirements:* For master's, comprehensive exam; for doctorate, thesis/dissertation. *Entrance requirements:* For master's and doctorate, GRE General Test. Additional exam requirements/recommendations for international students: Required—TOEFL (minimum score 550 paper-based; 213 computer-based). Electronic applications accepted.

University of Connecticut, Graduate School, College of Liberal Arts and Sciences, Department of Communication Sciences, Field of Communication Sciences, Program in Communication Processes and Marketing Communication, Storrs, CT 06269. Offers PhD. *Degree requirements:* For doctorate, thesis/dissertation. *Entrance requirements:* For doctorate, GMAT or GRE General Test. Additional exam requirements/recommendations for international students: Required—TOEFL (minimum score 550 paper-based; 213 computer-based). Electronic applications accepted.

University of Nebraska–Lincoln, Graduate College, College of Arts and Sciences, Department of Communication Studies, Lincoln, NE 68588. Offers instructional communication (MA, PhD); interpersonal communication (MA, PhD); marketing, communication studies, and advertising (MA, PhD); organizational communication (MA, PhD); rhetoric and culture (MA, PhD). *Faculty:* 7 full-time (4 women). *Students:* 23 full-time (15 women), 9 part-time (8 women); includes 1 minority (Asian American or Pacific Islander), 1 international. Average age 35. In 2008, 2 master's, 2 doctorates awarded. *Degree requirements:* For master's, thesis optional; for doctorate, comprehensive exam, thesis/dissertation. *Entrance requirements:* For master's and doctorate, GRE General Test, writing sample. Additional exam requirements/recommendations for international students: Required—TOEFL (minimum score 600 paper-based; 250 computer-based). *Application deadline:* For fall admission, 1/15 for domestic and international students. Applications are processed on a rolling basis. Application fee: $40. Electronic applications accepted. *Expenses:* Tuition, state resident: full-time $4275; part-time $237.50 per credit hour. Tuition, nonresident: full-time $11,525; part-time $640.25 per credit hour. Required fees: $1068; $10.35 per credit hour. $440.70 per semester. Tuition and fees vary according to course load and program. *Financial support:* Fellowships, research assistantships, teaching assistantships, Federal Work-Study, health care benefits, and unspecified assistantships available. Support available to part-time students. Financial award application deadline: 1/15. *Faculty research:* Message strategies, gender communication, political communication, organizational communication, instructional communication. *Unit head:* Dr. William Seiler, Chair, 402-472-2069. *Application contact:* Ginny Gross, Director of Graduate Admissions, 402-472-2878, Fax: 402-472-0589, E-mail: grad_admissions@unl.edu.

University of Portland, Graduate School, College of Arts and Sciences, Department of Communication Studies, Portland, OR 97203-5798. Offers communication (MA); management communication (MS). Part-time and evening/weekend programs available. *Faculty:* 7 full-time (2 women), 1 part-time/adjunct (0 women). *Students:* 2 full-time (both women), 9 part-time (7 women); includes 1 American Indian/Alaska Native, 1 Asian American or Pacific Islander, 2 international. Average age 27. In 2008, 4 master's awarded. *Degree requirements:* For master's, thesis optional. *Entrance requirements:* For master's, GRE General Test, minimum GPA of 3.25, 3 letters of recommendation, resumé, statement of goals, official transcripts. Additional exam requirements/recommendations for international students: Required—TOEFL (minimum score 600 paper-based; 100 iBT), IELTS (minimum score 7.5). *Application deadline:* For fall admission, 7/15 priority date for domestic and international students; for spring admission, 12/15 priority date for domestic and international students. Applications are processed on a rolling basis. Application fee: $50. *Expenses:* Tuition: Full-time $7380; part-time $8.20 per credit hour. *Financial support:* Career-related internships or fieldwork, Federal Work-Study, scholarships/grants, and tuition waivers (partial) available. Financial award application deadline: 3/1; financial award applicants required to submit FAFSA. *Unit head:* Dr. Jeffrey Kerssen-Griep, Director, 503-943-7167, E-mail: kerssen@up.edu. *Application contact:* Chris James Olinger, Administrative Assistant, 503-943-7107, Fax: 503-943-7315, E-mail: olingerc@up.edu.

University of St. Thomas, Graduate Studies, Opus College of Business, Program in Business Communication, St. Paul, MN 55105-1096. Offers MBC. Part-time and evening/weekend programs available. *Degree requirements:* For master's, thesis, final project. *Entrance requirements:* For master's, GMAT or GRE. Additional exam requirements/recommendations for international students: Required—TOEFL. Electronic applications accepted. *Expenses:* Contact institution. *Faculty research:* Communication technology.

University of Southern California, Graduate School, Annenberg School for Communication, School of Communication, Program in Communication, Los Angeles, CA 90089. Offers communication (MA, PhD), including interpersonal and social dynamics (PhD), mass communication, technology, and public policy (PhD), organizational communication (PhD), rhetorical and cultural studies (PhD). *Degree requirements:* For doctorate, thesis/dissertation. *Entrance requirements:* For master's and doctorate, GRE General Test, resumé, writing samples, 3 letters of recommendation, interest survey questionnaire, statement of purpose. Additional exam requirements/recommendations for international students: Required—TOEFL (minimum score 280 computer-based; 115 iBT); Recommended—TWE. Electronic applications accepted. *Faculty research:* Computer-mediated communication, public health campaigns, communication democracy and the public sphere, new communication technologies in organizations, communication and community.

See Close-Up on page 709.

University of Southern California, Graduate School, Annenberg School for Communication, School of Communication, Program in Communication Management, Los Angeles, CA 90089. Offers MCM, JD/MCM, MCM/MAJCS. Part-time and evening/weekend programs available. *Degree requirements:* For master's, professional project. *Entrance requirements:* For master's, GRE General Test or GMAT, resumé, writing samples, recommendation letters, statement of purpose. Additional exam requirements/recommendations for international students: Required—TOEFL (minimum score 280 computer-based; 114 iBT). Electronic applications accepted. *Faculty research:* Global communication, communication law and policy, entertainment management, marketing communication, strategic and corporate communication management.

See Close-Up on page 709.

University of Wisconsin–Stevens Point, College of Fine Arts and Communication, Division of Communication, Stevens Point, WI 54481-3897. Offers interpersonal communication (MA); mass communication (MA); organizational communication (MA); public relations (MA). Part-time programs available. *Students:* 7 full-time (3 women), 19 part-time (11 women). *Degree requirements:* For master's, thesis or alternative. *Entrance requirements:* For master's, GRE. Additional exam requirements/recommendations for international students: Required—TOEFL (minimum score 575 paper-based). *Application deadline:* For fall admission, 3/1 priority date for domestic students. Applications are processed on a rolling basis. Application fee: $45. *Expenses:* Tuition, state resident: full-time $7410. Tuition, nonresident: full-time $17,756. Full-time tuition and fees vary according to reciprocity agreements. *Financial support:* In 2008–09, 9 teaching assistantships were awarded; career-related internships or fieldwork, Federal Work-Study, institutionally sponsored loans, and unspecified assistantships also available. Support available to part-time students. Financial award application deadline: 5/1;

financial award applicants required to submit FAFSA. *Faculty research:* Communication theory and research, film history. *Unit head:* Dr. James Haney, Chair, 715-346-3409, E-mail: jhaney@uwsp.edu. *Application contact:* Dr. Chris Sadler, Graduate Coordinator, 715-346-3898, E-mail: csadler@uwsp.edu.

University of Wisconsin–Whitewater, School of Graduate Studies, College of Arts and Communications, Department of Communication, Whitewater, WI 53190-1790. Offers corporate communication (MS); mass communication (MS). Part-time and evening/weekend programs available. Postbaccalaureate distance learning degree programs offered (no on-campus study). *Degree requirements:* For master's, thesis or alternative. *Entrance requirements:* For master's, 2 letters of recommendation. Additional exam requirements/recommendations for international students: Required—TOEFL (minimum score 550 paper-based; 213 computer-based). Electronic applications accepted.

Washington State University, Graduate School, College of Liberal Arts, Edward R. Murrow College of Communication, Pullman, WA 99164. Offers health communications (MA, PhD); intercultural and international communications (MA, PhD); media and society (MA, PhD); media process and effects (MA, PhD); organizational communications (MA, PhD). *Degree requirements:* For master's, comprehensive exam (for some programs), thesis optional, oral exam; for doctorate, comprehensive exam, thesis/dissertation. *Entrance requirements:* For master's, GRE General Test, minimum GPA of 3.25, 3 letters of recommendation; for doctorate, GRE General Test, minimum undergraduate GPA of 3.25, graduate 3.5; MA in communication; 3 letters of recommendation. Additional exam requirements/recommendations for international students: Required—TOEFL (minimum score 580 paper-based; 237 computer-based). Electronic applications accepted. *Faculty research:* Advocacy communication, mediated communication in decision making, communication technology policy and effects, multicultural and international psychology and physiology of communication.

Wayne State University, College of Fine, Performing and Communication Arts, Department of Communication, Detroit, MI 48202. Offers communication studies (MA, PhD); public relations and organizational communication (MA); radio-TV-film (MA, PhD); speech communication (MA, PhD). *Degree requirements:* For master's, thesis, essay, or comprehensive exam; for doctorate, thesis/dissertation. *Entrance requirements:* For master's, minimum GPA of 3.0, personal statement; sample of academic writing; for doctorate, GRE, minimum GPA of 3.3, MA; letters of recommendation; personal statement; sample of written scholarship. Additional exam requirements/recommendations for international students: Required—TOEFL (minimum score 550 paper-based; 213 computer-based); Recommended—TWE (minimum score 6). Electronic applications accepted. *Faculty research:* Rhetorical theory and criticism; mass media theory and research; argumentation; organizational communication; risk and crisis communication; interpersonal, family, and health communication.

Webster University, School of Communications, Program in Communications Management, St. Louis, MO 63119-3194. Offers MA.

Western Michigan University, Graduate College, College of Arts and Sciences, Department of Communication, Kalamazoo, MI 49008-5202. Offers MA.

West Virginia University, Eberly College of Arts and Sciences, Department of Communication Studies, Morgantown, WV 26506. Offers communication in instruction (MA); communication studies (PhD); communication theory and research (MA); corporate and organizational communication (MA). Part-time programs available. *Degree requirements:* For master's, comprehensive exam (for some programs), thesis (for some programs); for doctorate, comprehensive exam, thesis/dissertation. *Entrance requirements:* For master's and doctorate, minimum GPA of 3.0. Additional exam requirements/recommendations for international students: Required—TOEFL. Electronic applications accepted. *Faculty research:* Instructional communication, interpersonal communication, health communication, influence, instructional communication, social influence.

Health Communication

Boston University, Metropolitan College (Continuing Education), Program in Health Communication, Boston, MA 02215. Offers MS.

Chapman University, Graduate Studies, Schmid College of Science, Health Communication Program, Orange, CA 92866. Offers MS. Part-time and evening/weekend programs available. *Faculty:* 6 full-time (4 women), 5 part-time/adjunct (1 woman). *Students:* 5 full-time (4 women), 2 part-time (both women); includes 3 minority (2 African Americans, 1 Asian American or Pacific Islander), 1 international. Average age 35. 7 applicants, 100% accepted, 7 enrolled. *Entrance requirements:* For master's, GRE, minimum undergraduate GPA of 3.0. Additional exam requirements/recommendations for international students: Required—TOEFL (minimum score 550 paper-based; 213 computer-based; 80 iBT). *Application deadline:* Applications are processed on a rolling basis. Application fee: $50. Electronic applications accepted. *Expenses:* Tuition: Full-time $11,970; part-time $665 per credit. Required fees: $456; $456 per year. Tuition and fees vary according to course load, degree level and program. *Financial support:* Fellowships, Federal Work-Study and scholarships/grants available. Financial award application deadline: 6/30; financial award applicants required to submit FAFSA. *Unit head:* Dr. Lisa Sparks, Interim Dean, 714-997-6703, E-mail: sparks@chapman.edu. *Application contact:* Saundra Hoover, Director of Graduate Admissions, 714-997-6786, Fax: 714-997-6713, E-mail: shoover@chapman.edu.

Cleveland State University, College of Graduate Studies, College of Liberal Arts and Social Sciences, School of Communication, Cleveland, OH 44115. Offers applied communication theory and methodology (MA); culture, communication and health care (Certificate). Part-time and evening/weekend programs available. *Faculty:* 11 full-time (5 women). *Students:* 18 full-time (14 women), 8 part-time (6 women); includes 1 minority (African American), 4 international. Average age 30. 25 applicants, 44% accepted, 9 enrolled. In 2008, 14 master's awarded. *Degree requirements:* For master's, variable foreign language requirement, comprehensive exam (for some programs), thesis optional, thesis, project, comprehensive exam, or collaborative project. *Entrance requirements:* For master's, GRE or MAT, minimum undergraduate GPA of 2.75, 2 letters of recommendation. Additional exam requirements/recommendations for international students: Required—TOEFL (minimum score 525 paper-based; 197 computer-based). *Application deadline:* For fall admission, 8/25 priority date for domestic students, 5/15 priority date for international students; for spring admission, 1/14 priority date for domestic students, 11/1 priority date for international students. Applications are processed on a rolling basis. Application fee: $30. Electronic applications accepted. *Financial support:* In 2008–09, 14 students received support, including 5 research assistantships with full and partial tuition reimbursements available (averaging $11,000 per year), 9 teaching assistantships with full and partial tuition reimbursements available (averaging $11,000 per year); tuition waivers (full) and unspecified assistantships also available. Financial award application deadline: 8/1. *Faculty research:* Interpersonal, organizational, and mass communication; health communication. *Unit head:* Dr. Richard M. Perloff, Director, 216-687-4631, Fax: 216-687-5435, E-mail: r.perloff@csuohio.edu. *Application contact:* Dr. Richard M. Perloff, Director, 216-687-4631, Fax: 216-687-5435, E-mail: r.perloff@csuohio.edu.

East Carolina University, Graduate School, College of Fine Arts and Communication, School of Communication, Greenville, NC 27858-4353. Offers health communication (MA). *Entrance requirements:* For master's, GRE.

Emerson College, Graduate Studies, School of Communication, Department of Marketing Communication, Program in Health Communication, Boston, MA 02116-4624. Offers MA. Part-time programs available. *Students:* 36 full-time (33 women), 3 part-time (all women); includes 3 minority (1 Asian American or Pacific Islander, 2 Hispanic Americans), 1 international. Average age 25. 64 applicants, 66% accepted, 21 enrolled. In 2008, 19 master's awarded. *Entrance requirements:* For master's, GMAT or GRE General Test. Additional exam requirements/recommendations for international students: Required—TOEFL (minimum score 550 paper-based; 213 computer-based; 80 iBT), IELTS (minimum score 6.5). *Application deadline:* For fall admission, 6/1 priority date for domestic students, 5/1 for international students; for spring admission, 11/1 priority date for domestic students, 11/1 for international students. Applications are processed on a rolling basis. Application fee: $60 ($75 for international students). Electronic applications accepted. *Expenses:* Tuition: Full-time $17,720; part-time $886 per credit. Required fees: $60 per year. One-time fee: $170. *Financial support:* In 2008–09, 10 students received support, including 2 fellowships with partial tuition reimbursements available (averaging $14,000 per year), 8 research assistantships with partial tuition reimbursements available (averaging $10,000 per year); career-related internships or fieldwork, Federal Work-Study, institutionally sponsored loans, scholarships/grants, and unspecified assistantships also available. Support available to part-time students. Financial award application deadline: 3/1; financial award applicants required to submit CSS PROFILE or FAFSA. *Faculty research:* Health promotion, health communications. *Unit head:* Dr. Timothy Edgar, Director, 617-824-8492, E-mail: Timothy_Edgar@emerson.edu. *Application contact:* Office of Graduate Admission, 617-824-8610, Fax: 617-824-8614, E-mail: gradapp@emerson.edu.

The George Washington University, School of Public Health and Health Services, Department of Prevention and Community Health, Washington, DC 20052. Offers community-oriented primary care (MPH); health promotion (MPH); maternal and child health (MPH); public health communication and marketing (MPH). *Accreditation:* CEPH. *Faculty:* 17 full-time (9 women), 19 part-time/adjunct (11 women). *Students:* 390 applicants, 54% accepted, 40 enrolled. In 2008, 14 master's awarded. *Entrance requirements:* For master's, GRE or GMAT, 2 letters of recommendation, resumé. Additional exam requirements/recommendations for international students: Required—TOEFL. *Application deadline:* For fall admission, 4/15 for domestic and international students; for spring admission, 11/1 for domestic and international students. Application fee: $60. *Financial support:* Tuition waivers available. Financial award application deadline: 2/15. *Unit head:* Ayman El-Mohandes, Chair, 202-416-0415, Fax: 202-416-0433, E-mail: sphaxe@gwumc.edu. *Application contact:* Jane Smith, 202-994-0248, Fax: 202-994-3773, E-mail: sphhsinfo@gwumc.edu.

Marquette University, Graduate School, College of Communication, Milwaukee, WI 53201-1881. Offers advertising and public relations (MA); broadcasting and electronic communications (MA); communications studies (MA); journalism (MA); mass communications (MA); religious communications (MA); science, health and environmental communications (MA). *Accreditation:* ACEJMC. Part-time and evening/weekend programs available. *Degree requirements:* For master's, comprehensive exam. *Entrance requirements:* For master's, GRE. Additional exam requirements/recommendations for international students: Required—TOEFL. *Faculty research:* Urban journalism, gender and communication, intercultural communication, religious communication.

Marywood University, Academic Affairs, Insalaco College of Creative Arts and Management, Department of Communication Arts, Program in Communication Arts, Scranton, PA 18509-1598. Offers corporate communication (Certificate); e-business (Certificate); health communication (Certificate); instructional technology (Certificate); interdisciplinary (MA); library science/information specialist (Certificate); media management (MA); production (MA).

Marywood University, Academic Affairs, Insalaco College of Creative Arts and Management, Department of Communication Arts, Program in Information Sciences, Scranton, PA 18509-1598. Offers corporate communication (MS); e-business (MS); health communication (MS); instructional technology (MS); library science/information science (MS).

Michigan State University, The Graduate School, College of Communication Arts and Sciences, Program in Health Communication, East Lansing, MI 48824. Offers MA. *Entrance requirements:* Additional exam requirements/recommendations for international students: Required—TOEFL. Electronic applications accepted. *Faculty research:* Mass communication and public health, health communication for diverse populations, descriptive and analytical epidemiology.

Tufts University, School of Medicine, Public Health and Professional Degree Programs, Boston, MA 02111. Offers biomedical sciences (MS); health communication (MS); pain research, education and policy (MS); public health (MPH). *Accreditation:* CEPH (one or more programs are accredited). Part-time and evening/weekend programs available. *Degree requirements:* For master's, thesis (for some programs). *Entrance requirements:* For master's, GRE General Test. Additional exam requirements/recommendations for international students: Required—TOEFL. Electronic applications accepted. *Expenses:* Contact institution. *Faculty research:* Environmental and occupational health, nutrition, epidemiology, health communication, health services management and policy.

Tulane University, School of Public Health and Tropical Medicine, Department of Community Health Sciences, Program in Health Education and Communication, New Orleans, LA 70118-5669. Offers MPH. *Accreditation:* CEPH. *Degree requirements:* For master's, comprehensive exam. *Entrance requirements:* For master's, GRE General Test. Additional exam requirements/recommendations for international students: Required—TOEFL.

University of Florida, Graduate School, College of Health and Human Performance, Department of Health Education and Behavior, Gainesville, FL 32611. Offers health behavior (PhD); health communication (Graduate Certificate); health education and behavior (MS). *Accreditation:* NCATE (one or more programs are accredited). Part-time programs available. Terminal master's awarded for partial completion of doctoral program. *Degree requirements:* For master's, thesis (for some programs); for doctorate, thesis/dissertation. *Entrance requirements:* For master's and doctorate, GRE General Test, minimum GPA of 3.0. Additional exam requirements/recommendations for international students: Required—TOEFL (minimum score 550 paper-based; 213 computer-based). Electronic applications accepted. *Faculty research:* Adolescent health, human sexuality and HIV/AIDS, substance use, nutrition.

University of Southern California, Keck School of Medicine and Graduate School, Graduate Programs in Medicine, Department of Preventive Medicine, Master of Public Health Program, Los Angeles, CA 90089. Offers biometry/epidemiology (MPH); health communication (MPH); health promotion (MPH); preventive nutrition (MPH). *Accreditation:* CEPH. Part-time programs available. *Degree requirements:* For master's, practicum, final report, oral presentation. *Entrance requirements:* For master's, GRE General Test, MCAT, GMAT, DAT, minimum GPA of 3.0. Additional exam requirements/recommendations for international students: Required—TOEFL (minimum score 600 paper-based; 250 computer-based; 100 iBT). Electronic applications

Health Communication

University of Southern California (continued)
accepted. *Faculty research:* Substance abuse prevention, cancer and heart disease prevention, mass media and health communication research, health promotion, treatment compliance.

Washington State University, Graduate School, College of Liberal Arts, Edward R. Murrow College of Communication, Pullman, WA 99164. Offers health communications (MA, PhD); intercultural and international communications (MA, PhD); media and society (MA, PhD); media process and effects (MA, PhD); organizational communications (MA, PhD). *Degree requirements:* For master's, comprehensive exam (for some programs), thesis optional, oral exam; for doctorate, comprehensive exam, thesis/dissertation. *Entrance requirements:* For master's, GRE General Test, minimum GPA of 3.25, 3 letters of recommendation; for doctorate, GRE General Test, minimum undergraduate GPA of 3.25, graduate 3.5; MA in communication; 3 letters of recommendation. Additional exam requirements/recommendations for international students: Required—TOEFL (minimum score 580 paper-based; 237 computer-based). Electronic applications accepted. *Faculty research:* Advocacy communication, mediated communication in decision making, communication technology policy and effects, multicultural and international psychology and physiology of communication.

Internet and Interactive Multimedia

Academy of Art University, Graduate Program, School of Multimedia Communications, San Francisco, CA 94105-3410. Offers MA. Part-time and evening/weekend programs available. *Faculty:* 2 full-time (1 woman). *Students:* 1 (woman) full-time, 6 part-time (4 women); includes 2 minority (1 Asian American or Pacific Islander, 1 Hispanic American). Average age 30. 7 applicants. *Degree requirements:* For master's, final review. *Application deadline:* For fall admission, 9/7 for domestic and international students; for spring admission, 2/2 for domestic and international students. Applications are processed on a rolling basis. Application fee: $100 ($500 for international students). Electronic applications accepted. *Expenses:* Tuition: Full-time $18,400; part-time $770 per term. Tuition and fees vary according to program. *Financial support:* Career-related internships or fieldwork and Federal Work-Study available. Support available to part-time students. Financial award applicants required to submit FAFSA. *Unit head:* Jan Yanehiro, 800-544-ARTS, E-mail: info@academyart.edu. *Application contact:* Jan Yanehiro, 800-544-ARTS, E-mail: info@academyart.edu.

Alfred University, Graduate School, New York State College of Ceramics, School of Art and Design, Alfred, NY 14802-1205. Offers ceramic art (MFA); electronic integrated arts (MFA); glass art (MFA); sculpture (MFA). *Accreditation:* NASAD. *Degree requirements:* For master's, exhibit. *Entrance requirements:* For master's, portfolio. Additional exam requirements/recommendations for international students: Required—TOEFL (minimum score 550 paper-based; 213 computer-based; 80 iBT), IELTS (minimum score 6). Electronic applications accepted. *Faculty research:* Ceramic sculpture, functional ceramics, wood, mixed media, hot and cold glass.

Brooklyn College of the City University of New York, Division of Graduate Studies, Program in Performance and Interactive Media Arts, Brooklyn, NY 11210-2889. Offers MFA, CAS. *Students:* 8 full-time (4 women), 10 part-time (6 women); includes 4 minority (2 African Americans, 2 Hispanic Americans), 2 international. Average age 33. 13 applicants, 62% accepted, 8 enrolled. In 2008, 5 master's, 1 other advanced degree awarded. *Entrance requirements:* For master's, 2 letters of recommendation, resumé, portfolio, interview; for CAS, 2 letters of recommendation. Additional exam requirements/recommendations for international students: Required—TOEFL (minimum score 500 paper-based; 173 computer-based; 61 iBT). *Application deadline:* For fall admission, 2/15 priority date for domestic students, 2/1 priority date for international students. Applications are processed on a rolling basis. Application fee: $125. Electronic applications accepted. *Expenses:* Tuition, state resident: full-time $7360; part-time $310 per credit hour. Tuition, nonresident: full-time $13,800; part-time $575 per credit hour. *Financial support:* Application deadline: 5/1. *Unit head:* Dr. John Jannone, Director, E-mail: jannone brooklyn.cuny.edu. *Application contact:* Hernan Sierra, Graduate Admissions Coordinator, 718-951-4536, Fax: 718-951-4506, E-mail: grads@brooklyn.cuny.edu.

California State University, East Bay, Academic Programs and Graduate Studies, Multimedia Program, Hayward, CA 94542-3000. Offers MA. *Entrance requirements:* For master's, minimum GPA of 2.5. Additional exam requirements/recommendations for international students: Required—TOEFL (minimum score 550 paper-based; 213 computer-based).

Concordia University, School of Graduate Studies, Faculty of Engineering and Computer Science, Concordia Institute for Information Systems Engineering (CIISE), Montréal, QC H3G 1M8, Canada. Offers 3D graphics and game development (Certificate); information systems security (M Eng, MA Sc); quality systems engineering (M Eng, MA Sc); service engineering and network management (Certificate).

DePaul University, College of Computing and Digital Media, Chicago, IL 60604. Offers business information technology (MS); computational finance (MS); computer game development (MS); computer graphics and motion technology (MS); computer science (MS, PhD); computer, information and network security (MS), including applied technology; digital cinema (MFA, MS), including information technology project management (MS); e-commerce technology (MS); human-computer interaction (MS); information systems (MS); information technology (MA); information technology project management (MS); software engineering (MS); telecommunications systems (MS); JD/MS. Part-time and evening/weekend programs available. Postbaccalaureate distance learning degree programs offered (no on-campus study). *Faculty:* 76 full-time (15 women), 182 part-time/adjunct (43 women). *Students:* 966 full-time (254 women), 932 part-time (217 women); includes 429 minority (194 African Americans, 3 American Indian/Alaska Native, 149 Asian Americans or Pacific Islanders, 83 Hispanic Americans), 395 international. Average age 31. 930 applicants, 73% accepted, 319 enrolled. In 2008, 444 master's, 4 doctorates awarded. *Degree requirements:* For master's, thesis (for some programs); for doctorate, comprehensive exam, thesis/dissertation. *Entrance requirements:* For master's, GRE or GMAT (MS in computational finance), bachelor's degree; for doctorate, GRE, master's degree in computer science. Additional exam requirements/recommendations for international students: Required—TOEFL (minimum score 550 paper-based; 213 computer-based), IELTS (minimum score 6.5). *Application deadline:* For fall admission, 8/15 priority date for domestic students, 6/1 priority date for international students; for winter admission, 2/15 priority date for domestic students, 9/15 priority date for international students; for spring admission, 3/1 priority date for domestic students, 12/15 priority date for international students. Applications are processed on a rolling basis. Application fee: $25. Electronic applications accepted. *Expenses:* Contact institution. *Financial support:* In 2008–09, 69 students received support, including 2 fellowships with full tuition reimbursements available (averaging $18,000 per year), 75 teaching assistantships with full and partial tuition reimbursements available (averaging $5,780 per year); research assistantships, Federal Work-Study, scholarships/grants, tuition waivers (full and partial), and unspecified assistantships also available. Support available to part-time students. Financial award application deadline: 4/30; financial award applicants required to submit FAFSA. *Faculty research:* Bioinformatics, visual computing, graphics and animation, high performance and scientific computing, databases. Total annual research expenditures: $790,000. *Unit head:* Dr. David Miller, Dean, 312-362-8381, Fax: 312-362-5185. *Application contact:* Dr. Liz Friedman, Assistant Dean of Student Services, 312-362-8714, Fax: 312-362-5327, E-mail: efriedm2@cdm.depaul.edu.

Duquesne University, Graduate School of Liberal Arts, Program in Multimedia Technology, Pittsburgh, PA 15282-0001. Offers MS, Certificate. Part-time and evening/weekend programs available. *Faculty:* 10 full-time (1 woman), 3 part-time/adjunct (0 women). *Students:* 42 full-time (21 women), 27 part-time (13 women); includes 1 minority (Hispanic American), 5 international. Average age 22. 22 applicants, 95% accepted, 19 enrolled. In 2008, 14 master's awarded. *Entrance requirements:* For master's, MAT or GRE General Test, portfolio. Additional exam requirements/recommendations for international students: Required—TOEFL. *Application deadline:* For fall admission, 8/1 for domestic students, 5/1 for international students; for spring admission, 11/1 for domestic students. Applications are processed on a rolling basis. Application fee: $50. Electronic applications accepted. *Expenses:* Tuition: Part-time $819 per credit. Required fees: $78 per credit. Tuition and fees vary according to course load. *Financial support:* In 2008–09, 1 research assistantship with full tuition reimbursement (averaging $8,400 per year) was awarded; Federal Work-Study also available. Support available to part-time students. Financial award application deadline: 5/1. *Unit head:* Dr. John Shepherd, Director, 412-396-5772. *Application contact:* Linda L. Rendulic, Assistant to the Dean, 412-396-6400, Fax: 412-396-5265, E-mail: rendulic@duq.edu.

Elon University, Program in Interactive Media, Elon, NC 27244-2010. Offers MA. *Degree requirements:* For master's, 6-hour capstone. *Entrance requirements:* For master's, GRE. Additional exam requirements/recommendations for international students: Required—TOEFL (minimum score 550 paper-based; 213 computer-based; 79 iBT). *Application deadline:* For fall admission, 5/1 priority date for domestic students. Applications are processed on a rolling basis. Application fee: $50. Electronic applications accepted. *Unit head:* Dr. David Alan Copeland, Director, 336-278-5662, Fax: 336-278-5734, E-mail: dcopeland@elon.edu. *Application contact:* Art Fadde, Director of Graduate Admissions, 800-334-8448 Ext. 3, Fax: 336-278-7699, E-mail: afadde@elon.edu.

Full Sail University, Program in Education Media Design and Technology, Winter Park, FL 32792-7437. Offers MS. Postbaccalaureate distance learning degree programs offered (no on-campus study). *Entrance requirements:* Additional exam requirements/recommendations for international students: Required—TOEFL (minimum score 550 paper-based; 213 computer-based; 79 iBT).

Full Sail University, Program in Game Design, Winter Park, FL 32792-7437. Offers MS.

Georgetown University, Graduate School of Arts and Sciences, Program in Communication, Culture, and Technology, Washington, DC 20057. Offers MA. Part-time and evening/weekend programs available. *Degree requirements:* For master's, thesis (for some programs). *Entrance requirements:* For master's, GRE General Test, 3 letters of recommendation, writing sample. Additional exam requirements/recommendations for international students: Required—TOEFL (minimum score 600 paper-based; 250 computer-based). Electronic applications accepted.

Georgia Institute of Technology, Graduate Studies and Research, Ivan Allen College of Policy and International Affairs, School of Literature, Communication and Culture, Atlanta, GA 30332-0001. Offers digital media (MS, PhD); human computer interaction (MSHCI). *Degree requirements:* For master's, thesis or alternative. *Entrance requirements:* Additional exam requirements/recommendations for international students: Required—TOEFL. Electronic applications accepted. *Faculty research:* New media studies.

Indiana University–Purdue University Indianapolis, School of Informatics, Indianapolis, IN 46202-2896. Offers informatics (PhD); media arts and science (MS). Part-time and evening/weekend programs available. *Degree requirements:* For master's, multimedia project. *Entrance requirements:* For master's, minimum undergraduate GPA of 3.0, graduate 3.2; interview; portfolio; BA with demonstrated media arts skills. Additional exam requirements/recommendations for international students: Required—TOEFL.

Long Island University, C.W. Post Campus, School of Visual and Performing Arts, Department of Theatre, Film, Dance and Arts Management, Brookville, NY 11548-1300. Offers interactive multimedia (MA); theatre (MA). Part-time and evening/weekend programs available. *Degree requirements:* For master's, thesis. *Entrance requirements:* For master's, placement exam. Electronic applications accepted. *Faculty research:* Playwriting, intercultural dance and theatre, translation, Suzuki, set and costume design.

Marlboro College, Graduate Center, Program in Internet Engineering, Brattleboro, VT 05301. Offers MS. Part-time and evening/weekend programs available. Postbaccalaureate distance learning degree programs offered (minimal on-campus study). *Degree requirements:* For master's, capstone project. *Entrance requirements:* For master's, 2 letters of recommendation, transcripts, letter of intent. Electronic applications accepted.

Marlboro College, Graduate Center, Program in Teaching with Technology, Brattleboro, VT 05301. Offers MAT. Part-time and evening/weekend programs available. Postbaccalaureate distance learning degree programs offered (minimal on-campus study). *Degree requirements:* For master's, capstone project. *Entrance requirements:* For master's, 2 letters of recommendation, transcripts, letter of intent. Electronic applications accepted.

National University, Academic Affairs, School of Media and Communication, Department of Media, La Jolla, CA 92037-1011. Offers digital cinema (MFA); educational and instructional technology (MS); video game production and design (MFA). Part-time and evening/weekend programs available. Postbaccalaureate distance learning degree programs offered (no on-campus study). *Faculty:* 9 full-time (3 women), 61 part-time/adjunct (20 women). *Students:* 70 full-time (26 women), 141 part-time (62 women); includes 64 minority (28 African Americans, 1 American Indian/Alaska Native, 10 Asian Americans or Pacific Islanders, 25 Hispanic Americans). Average age 39. 118 applicants, 100% accepted, 118 enrolled. In 2008, 58 master's awarded. *Degree requirements:* For master's, thesis. *Entrance requirements:* For master's, interview, minimum GPA of 2.5. Additional exam requirements/recommendations for international students: Required—TOEFL (minimum score 550 paper-based; 213 computer-based; 79 iBT), IELTS (minimum score 6). *Application deadline:* Applications are processed on a rolling basis. Application fee: $60 ($65 for international students). Electronic applications accepted. *Expenses:* Tuition: Full-time $8694; part-time $322 per credit hour. Tuition and fees vary according to course load. *Financial support:* Career-related internships or fieldwork, institutionally sponsored loans, scholarships/grants, and tuition waivers (partial) available. Support available to part-time students. Financial award application deadline: 6/30; financial award applicants required to submit FAFSA. *Unit head:* Dr. Timothy Langdell, Department Chair, 310-662-2149, Fax: 858-309-3450, E-mail: tlangdell@nu.edu. *Application contact:* Dominick Giovanniello, Associate Regional Dean—San Diego, 800-NAT-UNIV, Fax: 858-541-7792, E-mail: dgiovann@nu.edu.

New Mexico Highlands University, Graduate Studies, College of Arts and Sciences, Program in Media Arts and Computer Science, Las Vegas, NM 87701. Offers media arts and computer science (MS). *Faculty:* 3 full-time (0 women). *Students:* 18 full-time (7 women), 9 part-time (2 women); includes 8 minority (1 African American, 1 Asian American or Pacific Islander, 6 Hispanic Americans), 11 international. Average age 30. 16 applicants, 69% accepted, 4 enrolled. In 2008, 9 master's awarded. *Degree requirements:* For master's, comprehensive exam, thesis. *Entrance requirements:* For master's, minimum undergraduate GPA of 3.0. Additional exam requirements/recommendations for international students: Required—TOEFL (minimum score 540 paper-based; 270 computer-based). Application fee: $15. *Expenses:* Tuition, state resident: full-time $2880; part-time $120 per credit hour. Tuition, nonresident: full-time $4234; part-time $176 per credit hour. International tuition: $5645 full-time. One-time fee: $20. *Financial support:* In 2008–09, 10 students received support, including teaching assistantships (averaging $7,200 per year); career-related internships or fieldwork, Federal Work-Study, institutionally sponsored loans, scholarships/grants, tuition waivers (full and partial), and unspecified assistantships also available. Support available to part-time students. Financial award application deadline: 3/1; financial award applicants required to submit FAFSA. *Faculty research:* Advanced digital compositing, photographic installations and exhibition design, pattern recognition, parallel and distributed computing, computer security education. *Unit head:* Dr. Hossein Tahani, Department Head of Computer Science, 505-426-2121, E-mail: htahani@nmhu.edu. *Application contact:* Diane Trujillo, Administrative Assistant for Graduate Studies, 505-454-3266, Fax: 505-426-2117, E-mail: dtrujillo@nmhu.edu.

New York University, Tisch School of the Arts, Interactive Telecommunications Program, New York, NY 10012-1019. Offers MPS. *Degree requirements:* For master's, thesis. *Entrance requirements:* Additional exam requirements/recommendations for international students: Required—TOEFL (minimum score 600 paper-based; 250 computer-based; 100 iBT), IELTS. Electronic applications accepted. *Faculty research:* Interactive narrative/storytelling, interactive media, web technology, physical computing, ubiquitous computing.

Polytechnic Institute of NYU, Department of Humanities and Social Sciences, Major in Integrated Digital Media, Brooklyn, NY 11201-2990. Offers MS, Graduate Certificate.

Pratt Institute, School of Art and Design, Program in Digital Arts, Brooklyn, NY 11205-3899. Offers digital arts (MFA); MS/MFA. *Accreditation:* NASAD. Part-time programs available. *Faculty:* 6 full-time (1 woman), 17 part-time/adjunct (8 women). *Students:* 73 full-time (37 women); includes 8 minority (2 African Americans, 3 Asian Americans or Pacific Islanders, 3 Hispanic Americans), 37 international. Average age 29. 124 applicants, 28% accepted, 15 enrolled. In 2008, 10 master's awarded. *Degree requirements:* For master's, thesis, exhibit. *Entrance requirements:* For. master's, portfolio or video tape, bachelor's degree, transcripts, letters of recommendation, statement. Additional exam requirements/recommendations for international students: Required—TOEFL (minimum score 550 paper-based; 213 computer-based). *Application deadline:* For fall admission, 2/1 for domestic and international students; for spring admission, 10/1 for domestic and international students. Applications are processed on a rolling basis. Application fee: $50 ($90 for international students). Electronic applications accepted. *Expenses:* Tuition: Full-time $20,412; part-time $1134 per credit. Required fees: $1190; $1190 per year. *Financial support:* Career-related internships or fieldwork, Federal Work-Study, institutionally sponsored loans, scholarships/grants, health care benefits, and unspecified assistantships available. Support available to part-time students. Financial award application deadline: 2/1; financial award applicants required to submit FAFSA. *Unit head:* Peter Patchen, Chair, 718-636-3693, E-mail: ppatchen@pratt.edu. *Application contact:* Young Hah, Director of Graduate Admissions, 718-636-3683, Fax: 718-399-4242, E-mail: yhah@pratt.edu.

See Close-Up on page 219.

Quinnipiac University, School of Communications, Program in Interactive Communications, Hamden, CT 06518-1940. Offers MS. Part-time and evening/weekend programs available. *Faculty:* 7 full-time (2 women), 6 part-time/adjunct (0 women). *Students:* 18 full-time (10 women), 34 part-time (18 women); includes 9 minority (4 African Americans, 1 Asian American or Pacific Islander, 4 Hispanic Americans). Average age 30. 26 applicants, 92% accepted, 19 enrolled. In 2008, 19 master's awarded. *Entrance requirements:* For master's, minimum GPA of 2.8, portfolio or writing sample. Additional exam requirements/recommendations for international students: Required—TOEFL (minimum score 575 paper-based; 233 computer-based; 90 iBT), IELTS (minimum score 6.5). *Application deadline:* For fall admission, 7/30 priority date for domestic students, 4/30 priority date for international students; for spring admission, 12/15 priority date for domestic students, 9/15 priority date for international students. Applications are processed on a rolling basis. Application fee: $45. Electronic applications accepted. *Expenses:* Tuition: Full-time $14,600; part-time $730 per credit. Required fees: $630; $30 per credit. *Financial support:* Tuition waivers (partial) and unspecified assistantships available. Support available to part-time students. Financial award application deadline: 4/15; financial award applicants required to submit FAFSA. *Faculty research:* Technology and democracy, the role of computing in social change. *Unit head:* Richard Hanley, Director, 203-582-8439, Fax: 203-582-5310, E-mail: rich.hanley@quinnipiac.edu. *Application contact:* Scott Farber, Director of Graduate Admissions, 800-462-1944, Fax: 203-582-3443, E-mail: scott.farber@quinnipiac.edu.

See Close-Up on page 695.

Robert Morris University, Graduate Studies, School of Communications and Information Systems, Moon Township, PA 15108-1189. Offers communication and information systems (MS); competitive intelligence systems (MS); information security and assurance (MS); information systems and communications (D Sc); information systems management (MS); information technology project management (MS); Internet information systems (MS); organizational studies (MS). Part-time and evening/weekend programs available. *Faculty:* 26 full-time (9 women), 9 part-time/adjunct (2 women). *Students:* 248 part-time (79 women); includes 49 minority (32 African Americans, 14 Asian Americans or Pacific Islanders, 3 Hispanic Americans), 19 international. Average age 33. 95 applicants, 94% accepted, 66 enrolled. In 2008, 160 master's, 9 doctorates awarded. *Degree requirements:* For doctorate, thesis/dissertation. *Entrance requirements:* For doctorate, employer letter of endorsement, interview. Additional exam requirements/recommendations for international students: Required—TOEFL (minimum score 550 paper-based; 213 computer-based; 79 iBT). *Application deadline:* For fall admission, 7/1 priority date for domestic and international students; for spring admission, 11/1 priority date for domestic and international students. Applications are processed on a rolling basis. Application fee: $35. Electronic applications accepted. *Expenses:* Contact institution. *Financial support:* Research assistantships with partial tuition reimbursements, institutionally sponsored loans and unspecified assistantships available. Support available to part-time students. Financial award application deadline: 5/1. *Unit head:* Dr. Barbara J. Levine, Acting Dean, 412-397-2591, Fax: 412-397-2481, E-mail: levine@rmu.edu. *Application contact:* Edward J. Lamm, Assistant Dean, Graduate Admissions, 412-397-5200, Fax: 412-397-2425, E-mail: graduateadmissions@rmu.edu.

Rochester Institute of Technology, Graduate Enrollment Services, Golisano College of Computing and Information Sciences, Department of Information Technology, Program in Game Design and Development, Rochester, NY 14623-5603. Offers MS. *Entrance requirements:* Additional exam requirements/recommendations for international students: Required—TOEFL (minimum score 570 paper-based; 230 computer-based; 88 iBT).

Rochester Institute of Technology, Graduate Enrollment Services, Golisano College of Computing and Information Sciences, Department of Information Technology, Program in Interactive Multimedia Development, Rochester, NY 14623-5603. Offers AC. *Entrance requirements:* For degree, GRE, minimum GPA of 3.0. Additional exam requirements/recommendations for international students: Required—TOEFL (minimum score 570 paper-based; 230 computer-based; 88 iBT).

Sacred Heart University, Graduate Programs, College of Arts and Sciences, Department of Computer Science and Information Technology, Fairfield, CT 06825-1000. Offers computer science (MS); database (CPS); information technology (MS, CPS); information technology and network security (CPS); interactive multimedia (CPS); Web development (CPS). Part-time and evening/weekend programs available. *Degree requirements:* For master's, thesis optional. *Entrance requirements:* Additional exam requirements/recommendations for international

students: Required—TOEFL (minimum score 550 paper-based; 213 computer-based). Electronic applications accepted. *Faculty research:* Contemporary market software.

San Diego State University, Graduate and Research Affairs, College of Professional Studies and Fine Arts, School of Communication, San Diego, CA 92182. Offers advertising and public relations (MA); critical-cultural studies (MA); interaction studies (MA); intercultural and international studies (MA); new media studies (MA); news and information studies (MA); telecommunications and media management (MA). *Degree requirements:* For master's, thesis. *Entrance requirements:* For master's, GRE General Test, 3 letters of recommendation. Additional exam requirements/recommendations for international students: Required—TOEFL. Electronic applications accepted.

Savannah College of Art and Design, Graduate School, Program in Interactive Design and Game Development, Savannah, GA 31402-3146. Offers MA, MFA. Part-time programs available. *Degree requirements:* For master's, thesis, internships. *Entrance requirements:* For master's, interview, portfolio. Additional exam requirements/recommendations for international students: Required—TOEFL (minimum score 450 paper-based; 133 computer-based). Electronic applications accepted. *Expenses:* Tuition: Full-time $28,215; part-time $3135 per course. One-time fee: $500.

School of Visual Arts, Graduate Programs, Program in Photography, Video and Related Media, New York, NY 10010-3994. Offers MFA. *Accreditation:* NASAD. *Degree requirements:* For master's, final review, project or thesis. *Entrance requirements:* For master's, portfolio. Additional exam requirements/recommendations for international students: Required—TOEFL (minimum score 550 paper-based; 213 computer-based; 79 iBT). Electronic applications accepted.

Simon Fraser University, Graduate Studies, Faculty of Applied Sciences, School of Interactive Arts and Technology, Surrey, BC V3T 2W1, Canada. Offers information technology (M Sc, PhD); interactive arts (M Sc, PhD). *Degree requirements:* For master's, thesis; for doctorate, comprehensive exam, thesis/dissertation. *Entrance requirements:* For master's, 2 references, curriculum vitae; for doctorate, 3 references, curriculum vitae, minimum GPA of 3.0. Additional exam requirements/recommendations for international students: Required—TOEFL (minimum score 570 paper-based; 230 computer-based), TWE (minimum score 5). Electronic applications accepted.

Southern Polytechnic State University, School of Arts and Sciences, Department of English, Technical Communication, and Media Arts, Marietta, GA 30060-2896. Offers communications management (Graduate Certificate); content development (Graduate Certificate); information design and communication (MS); instructional design (Graduate Certificate); technical and professional communication (Graduate Certificate); visual communication and graphics (Graduate Certificate). Part-time and evening/weekend programs available. Postbaccalaureate distance learning degree programs offered (minimal on-campus study). *Faculty:* 4 full-time (3 women), 1 part-time/adjunct. *Students:* 5 full-time (4 women), 38 part-time (25 women); includes 13 minority (12 African Americans, 1 Hispanic American), 3 international. Average age 38. 38 applicants, 68% accepted, 23 enrolled. In 2008, 10 master's awarded. *Degree requirements:* For master's, thesis optional, 36 hours completed through thesis option (6 hours), internship option (6 hours) or advanced coursework option (6 hours); for Graduate Certificate, thesis optional, 18 hours completed through thesis option (6 hours), internship option (6 hours) or advanced coursework option (6 hours). *Entrance requirements:* For master's, GRE, statement of purpose, writing sample, professional recommendations, proctored essay; for Graduate Certificate, statement of purpose, writing sample, professional recommendations, proctored essay. Additional exam requirements/recommendations for international students: Required—TOEFL (minimum score 550 paper-based; 213 computer-based; 79 iBT), IELTS (minimum score 6.5). *Application deadline:* For fall admission, 5/1 priority date for domestic students, 7/1 priority date for international students; for spring admission, 9/1 priority date for domestic students, 11/1 priority date for international students. Applications are processed on a rolling basis. Application fee: $20. Electronic applications accepted. *Expenses:* Tuition, area resident: Full-time $2752; part-time $172 per semester hour. Tuition, state resident: full-time $2752; part-time $172 per semester hour. Tuition, nonresident: full-time $10,992; part-time $687 per semester hour. Required fees: $365 per semester. *Financial support:* In 2008–09, 14 students received support, including 1 research assistantship with full tuition reimbursement available (averaging $4,000 per year); career-related internships or fieldwork, Federal Work-Study, scholarships/grants, and unspecified assistantships also available. Support available to part-time students. Financial award application deadline: 5/1; financial award applicants required to submit FAFSA. *Faculty research:* Usability, user-centered design, instructional design, information architecture, information design. *Unit head:* Dr. Mark Nunes, Chair, 678-915-7202, Fax: 678-915-7425, E-mail: mnunes@spsu.edu. *Application contact:* Nikki Palamiotis, Director of Graduate Studies, 678-915-4276, Fax: 678-915-7292, E-mail: npalamio@spsu.edu.

Stevens Institute of Technology, Graduate School, Charles V. Schaefer Jr. School of Engineering, Department of Computer Science, Hoboken, NJ 07030. Offers computer graphics (Certificate); computer science (MS, PhD); computer systems (Certificate); database management systems (Certificate); distributed systems (Certificate); elements of computer science (Certificate); enterprise computing (Certificate); enterprise security and information assurance (Certificate); health informatics (Certificate); multimedia experience and management (Certificate); networks and systems administration (Certificate); security and privacy (Certificate); service oriented computing (Certificate); software design (Certificate); theoretical computer science (Certificate). Part-time and evening/weekend programs available. Terminal master's awarded for partial completion of doctoral program. *Degree requirements:* For master's, thesis optional; for doctorate, variable foreign language requirement, comprehensive exam, thesis/dissertation. *Entrance requirements:* For master's and doctorate, GRE, minimum GPA of 3.0. Additional exam requirements/recommendations for international students: Required—TOEFL. Electronic applications accepted. *Faculty research:* Semantics, reliability theory, programming language, cyber security.

Towson University, College of Graduate Studies and Research, Program in Applied Information Technology, Towson, MD 21252-0001. Offers applied information technology (D Sc); database management (Certificate); information security and assurance (Certificate); information systems management (Certificate); Internet application development (Certificate); networking technologies (Certificate); software engineering (Certificate). *Entrance requirements:* For doctorate, minimum GPA 3.0, letter of intent, resumé, 2 letters of recommendation, personal assessment forms, official transcripts. Additional exam requirements/recommendations for international students: Required—TOEFL (minimum score 550 paper-based). Electronic applications accepted.

Towson University, College of Graduate Studies and Research, Program in Interactive Media Design, Towson, MD 21252-0001. Offers Certificate. Postbaccalaureate distance learning degree programs offered (no on-campus study). *Entrance requirements:* For degree, minimum GPA of 3.0, resumé, letter of intent, BA in art education or coursework, professional experience in graphic design or art education. Additional exam requirements/recommendations for international students: Required—TOEFL (minimum score 550 paper-based).

Towson University, College of Graduate Studies and Research, Program in Internet Application Development, Towson, MD 21252-0001. Offers Certificate. Part-time and evening/weekend programs available. Electronic applications accepted.

Universidad Autonoma de Guadalajara, Graduate Programs, Guadalajara, Mexico. Offers advertising and corporate communications (MA); architecture (M Arch); business (MBA); computational science (MCC); education (Ed M, Ed D); English-Spanish translation (MA); fiscal law (MA); international business (MIB); international corporate law (LL M); internet technologies (MS); labor health (MS); manufacturing systems (MMS); market research (MBA); philosophy (MA, PhD); quality systems (MQS); renewable energy (MS); teaching mathematics (MA).

Internet and Interactive Multimedia

University of Advancing Technology, Master of Science Program in Technology, Tempe, AZ 85283-1042. Offers advancing computer science (MS); emerging technologies (MS); game production and management (MS); information assurance (MS); technology leadership (MS). *Faculty:* 10 full-time (2 women), 1 part-time/adjunct (0 women). *Students:* 13 full-time (3 women), 4 part-time (2 women). Average age 25. In 2008, 5 master's awarded. *Degree requirements:* For master's, thesis or alternative, project or thesis. *Entrance requirements:* Additional exam requirements/recommendations for international students: Required—TOEFL (minimum score 550 paper-based). *Application deadline:* For fall admission, 8/15 priority date for domestic students, 7/15 priority date for international students; for winter admission, 12/15 priority date for domestic students, 11/15 priority date for international students; for spring admission, 4/1 priority date for domestic students, 3/1 priority date for international students. Applications are processed on a rolling basis. Application fee: $100 ($250 for international students). Electronic applications accepted. *Expenses:* Tuition: Full-time $16,200. *Financial support:* Career-related internships or fieldwork, Federal Work-Study, and scholarships/grants available. Financial award applicants required to submit FAFSA. *Faculty research:* Artificial intelligence, fractals, organizational management. *Unit head:* Kathleen Dunley, Dean of Graduate Education, 602-383-8283, Fax: 602-383-8222, E-mail: kdunley@uat.edu. *Application contact:* Information Contact, 800-658-5744, Fax: 602-383-8222.

University of Central Florida, College of Arts and Humanities, Division of Film and Digital Media, Orlando, FL 32816. Offers entrepreneurial digital cinema (MFA); interactive entertainment (MS); visual language and interactive media (MA, MFA). *Faculty:* 28 full-time (10 women), 7 part-time/adjunct (3 women). *Students:* 72 full-time (13 women), 42 part-time (6 women); includes 28 minority (10 African Americans, 2 Asian Americans or Pacific Islanders, 16 Hispanic Americans), 6 international. In 2008, 59 master's awarded. *Expenses:* Tuition, area resident: Full-time $6816; part-time $284 per credit. Tuition, state resident: full-time $6816; part-time $1076 per credit. Tuition, nonresident: full-time $25,824. Required fees: $216; $9 per credit. *Financial support:* In 2008–09, 2 fellowships (averaging $10,000 per year), 2 research assistantships (averaging $5,480 per year), 13 teaching assistantships (averaging $7,100 per year) were awarded. *Unit head:* Dr. Jose Maunez-Cuadra, Interim Chair, 407-823-6100, E-mail: jmaunez@mail.ucf.edu. *Application contact:* Dr. Jose Maunez-Cuadra, Interim Chair, 407-823-6100, E-mail: jmaunez@mail.ucf.edu.

University of Florida, Graduate School, College of Fine Arts, School of Art and Art History, Gainesville, FL 32611. Offers art (MFA), including ceramics, creative photography, drawing, electronic intermedia, graphic design, painting, printmaking, sculpture; art education (MA); art history (MA, PhD); digital arts and sciences (MA); museology (museum studies) (MA). *Accreditation:* NASAD. *Degree requirements:* For master's, variable foreign language requirement, project or thesis (MFA). *Entrance requirements:* For master's, portfolio (MFA), writing sample (MA), GRE General Test or minimum GPA of 3.0. Additional exam requirements/recommendations for international students: Required—TOEFL (minimum score 550 paper-based; 213 computer-based). Electronic applications accepted. *Faculty research:* Studio production, art historical studies of style context.

University of Georgia, Graduate School, Terry College of Business, Program in Internet Technology, Athens, GA 30602. Offers MIT.

University of Miami, Graduate School, College of Arts and Sciences, Department of Art and Art History, Coral Gables, FL 33124. Offers art history (MA); ceramics/glass (MFA); graphic design/multimedia (MFA); painting (MFA); photography/digital imaging (MFA); printmaking (MFA); sculpture (MFA). Part-time programs available. *Degree requirements:* For master's, variable foreign language requirement, thesis, exhibit (MFA), comprehensive exam (MA). *Entrance requirements:* For master's, GRE General Test (MA), research paper (MA), slide portfolio (MFA), artist statement (MFA). Additional exam requirements/recommendations for international students: Required—TOEFL. Electronic applications accepted. *Faculty research:* Installation art, public art.

University of Phoenix–Madison Campus, College of Graduate Business and Management, Madison, WI 53718-2416. Offers accounting (MBA); business and management (MBA); e-business (MBA); global management (MBA); human resources management (MBA, MM); management (MM); marketing (MBA); public administration (MBA).

University of San Francisco, College of Arts and Sciences, Department of Computer Science, Program in Web Science, San Francisco, CA 94117-1080. Offers MS.

University of Southern California, Graduate School, Annenberg School for Communication, School of Journalism, Program in Online Journalism, Los Angeles, CA 90089. Offers MA. Part-time programs available. *Degree requirements:* For master's, comprehensive exam, thesis. *Entrance requirements:* For master's, GRE General Test, resumé, writing samples, letters of recommendation, statement of purpose. Additional exam requirements/recommendations for international students: Required—TOEFL (minimum score 280 computer-based; 114 iBT). Electronic applications accepted.

See Close-Up on page 709.

University of Southern California, Graduate School, School of Cinematic Arts, Division of Interactive Media, Los Angeles, CA 90089. Offers interactive media (MFA). *Degree requirements:* For master's, thesis. *Entrance requirements:* For master's, GRE. *Faculty research:* Mobile media, game design innovation, immersive media.

University of Southern California, Graduate School, School of Engineering, Department of Computer Science, Los Angeles, CA 90089. Offers computer networks (MS); computer science (MS, PhD); multimedia and creative technologies (MS); robotics and automation (MS); software engineering (MS). Part-time programs available. Postbaccalaureate distance learning degree programs offered. Terminal master's awarded for partial completion of doctoral program. *Degree requirements:* For doctorate, thesis/dissertation. *Entrance requirements:* For master's and doctorate, GRE General Test. *Faculty research:* Neural computation, molecular composition, multi-media and virtual reality, databases.

University of Southern California, Graduate School, School of Engineering, Department of Electrical Engineering and Department of Computer Science, Program in Multimedia and Creative Technologies, Los Angeles, CA 90089. Offers MS. Part-time programs available. Postbaccalaureate distance learning degree programs offered. Terminal master's awarded for partial completion of doctoral program. *Degree requirements:* For master's, thesis optional. *Entrance requirements:* For master's, GRE General Test.

Virginia Commonwealth University, Graduate School, School of the Arts, Department of Graphic Design, Richmond, VA 23284-9005. Offers design/visual communications (MFA); interior environment (MFA); photography and film (MFA). *Accreditation:* NASAD. *Degree requirements:* For master's, thesis, exhibition. *Entrance requirements:* For master's, portfolio. *Faculty research:* Film, photography, interior environments, visual communication.

Western Illinois University, School of Graduate Studies, College of Education and Human Services, Department of Instructional Design and Technology, Macomb, IL 61455-1390. Offers distance learning (Certificate); graphic applications (Certificate); instructional design and technology (MS); multimedia (Certificate); technology integration in education (Certificate); training development (Certificate). Part-time programs available. Postbaccalaureate distance learning degree programs offered (no on-campus study). *Students:* 22 full-time (11 women), 61 part-time (42 women); includes 8 minority (7 African Americans, 1 Hispanic American), 5 international. Average age 38. 22 applicants, 82% accepted. In 2008, 31 master's, 4 other advanced degrees awarded. *Degree requirements:* For master's, thesis or alternative. *Entrance requirements:* Additional exam requirements/recommendations for international students: Required—TOEFL (minimum score 550 paper-based; 213 computer-based; 80 iBT). *Application deadline:* Applications are processed on a rolling basis. Application fee: $30. Electronic applications accepted. *Expenses:* Tuition, state resident: full-time $5696; part-time $237.34 per credit hour. Tuition, nonresident: full-time $11,392; part-time $474.68 per credit hour. Required fees: $1453; $60.55 per credit hour. *Financial support:* In 2008–09, 13 students received support, including 11 research assistantships with full tuition reimbursements available (averaging $7,040 per year), 2 teaching assistantships with full tuition reimbursements available (averaging $8,120 per year). Financial award applicants required to submit FAFSA. *Unit head:* Dr. Hoyet Hemphill, Chairperson, 309-298-1952. *Application contact:* Evelyn Hoing, Assistant Director of Graduate Studies, 309-298-1806, Fax: 309-298-2345, E-mail: grad-office@wiu.edu.

Wilmington University, Division of Information Technology and Advanced Communications, New Castle, DE 19720-6491. Offers corporate training (MS); information assurance (MS); information systems technologies (MS); Internet web design (MS); management information systems (MS). Part-time and evening/weekend programs available. *Entrance requirements:* Additional exam requirements/recommendations for international students: Required—TOEFL (minimum score 500 paper-based; 173 computer-based). Electronic applications accepted.

Journalism

American University, School of Communication, Program in Journalism and Public Affairs, Washington, DC 20016-8001. Offers broadcast journalism (MA), including economic journalism, international journalism, public policy journalism; print journalism (MA), including economic journalism, international journalism, public policy journalism. *Accreditation:* ACEJMC. Part-time and evening/weekend programs available. *Faculty:* 13 full-time (5 women), 4 part-time/adjunct (all women). *Students:* 24 full-time (16 women); includes 10 minority (7 African Americans, 3 Asian Americans or Pacific Islanders), 10 international. 190 applicants, 63% accepted, 35 enrolled. In 2008, 40 master's awarded. *Degree requirements:* For master's, comprehensive exam, thesis or alternative. *Entrance requirements:* For master's, GRE General Test. Additional exam requirements/recommendations for international students: Required—TOEFL (minimum score 600 paper-based; 250 computer-based). *Application deadline:* For fall admission, 2/1 priority date for domestic students, 4/1 priority date for international students. Applications are processed on a rolling basis. Application fee: $50. Electronic applications accepted. *Expenses:* Tuition: Full-time $21,204; part-time $1178 per credit hour. Required fees: $380. Part-time tuition and fees vary according to course load and program. *Financial support:* In 2008–09, 3 fellowships with partial tuition reimbursements (averaging $27,000 per year), 14 research assistantships with tuition reimbursements (averaging $7,000 per year), 3 teaching assistantships with tuition reimbursements (averaging $7,000 per year) were awarded; career-related internships or fieldwork, Federal Work-Study, institutionally sponsored loans, scholarships/grants, tuition waivers (partial), and unspecified assistantships also available. Financial award application deadline: 2/1. *Faculty research:* Government and media effects of journalistic practices and policies, race and gender and the media, investigative reporting, computer assisted reporting. *Unit head:* Wendell Cochran, Division Director, 202-885-2072. *Application contact:* Sharmeen Ahsan-Bracciale, Graduate Admissions Office, 202-885-2040, Fax: 202-885-2019, E-mail: sharmeen@american.edu.

See Close-Up on page 681.

American University, School of Communication, Weekend Programs in Communication, Washington, DC 20016-8001. Offers interactive journalism (MA); news media studies (MA); producing for film and video (MA); public communication (MA). *Accreditation:* ACEJMC. Part-time and evening/weekend programs available. *Faculty:* 5 part-time/adjunct (2 women). *Students:* 112 part-time (75 women). 137 applicants, 61% accepted, 61 enrolled. In 2008, 15 master's awarded. *Degree requirements:* For master's, comprehensive exam, thesis or alternative. *Entrance requirements:* Additional exam requirements/recommendations for international students: Required—TOEFL (minimum score 600 paper-based; 250 computer-based). *Application deadline:* For fall admission, 8/1 for domestic students. Applications are processed on a rolling basis. Application fee: $50. Electronic applications accepted. *Expenses:* Tuition: Full-time $21,204; part-time $1178 per credit hour. Required fees: $380. Part-time tuition and

fees vary according to course load and program. *Financial support:* In 2008–09, 3 fellowships (averaging $3,500 per year) were awarded; institutionally sponsored loans also available. *Unit head:* Wendell Cochran, Journalism Weekend Program Director, 202-885-2075, E-mail: cochran@american.edu. *Application contact:* Sharmeen Ahsan-Bracciale, Graduate Admissions Office, 202-885-2040, Fax: 202-885-2019, E-mail: sharmeen@american.edu.

See Close-Up on page 681.

The American University in Cairo, Graduate Studies and Research, School of Business, Economics and Communication, Department of Journalism and Mass Communication, Cairo, Egypt. Offers journalism and mass communication (MA); television and digital journalism (MA). Part-time programs available. *Degree requirements:* For master's, thesis (for some programs). *Entrance requirements:* For master's, English entrance exam, GMAT. Electronic applications accepted. *Faculty research:* Mass media and national development/censorship, intercultural photo communication, comparative journalism/television.

Angelo State University, College of Graduate Studies, College of Liberal and Fine Arts, Department of Communications, Drama, and Journalism, San Angelo, TX 76909. Offers communication systems management (MA). Part-time and evening/weekend programs available. *Faculty:* 2 full-time (0 women). *Students:* 8 full-time (4 women), 2 part-time (1 woman); includes 3 minority (all Hispanic Americans). Average age 44. 4 applicants, 100% accepted, 2 enrolled. *Degree requirements:* For master's, comprehensive exam, thesis optional. *Entrance requirements:* For master's, GRE General Test. Additional exam requirements/recommendations for international students: Required—TOEFL or IELTS. *Application deadline:* For fall admission, 7/15 priority date for domestic students, 6/10 for international students; for spring admission, 12/1 priority date for domestic students, 11/1 for international students. Applications are processed on a rolling basis. Application fee: $40 ($50 for international students). Electronic applications accepted. *Financial support:* In 2008–09, 5 students received support, including 3 teaching assistantships (averaging $10,251 per year); career-related internships or fieldwork, Federal Work-Study, scholarships/grants, and unspecified assistantships also available. Support available to part-time students. Financial award application deadline: 3/1; financial award applicants required to submit FAFSA. *Unit head:* Dr. June H. Smith, Department Head, 325-942-2031 Ext. 228, E-mail: june.smith@angelo.edu. *Application contact:* Dr. Lana Marlow, Graduate Advisor, 325-942-2032 Ext. 356, E-mail: lana.marlow@angelo.edu.

Arizona State University at the Downtown Phoenix Campus, Walter Cronkite School of Journalism and Mass Communication, Phoenix, AZ 85004. Offers MMC. *Accreditation:* ACEJMC. *Degree requirements:* For master's, 36 credit hours (includes class work and a professional immersion experience). *Entrance requirements:* For master's, GRE, minimum GPA of 3.0 in the last 60 semester hours or 90 quarter hours of undergraduate coursework; official transcripts; resumé and/or biographical sketch; 350- to 500-word personal statement; 3 letters of recommendation. Additional exam requirements/recommendations for international students: Required—TOEFL. Electronic applications accepted.

Arkansas State University, Graduate School, College of Communications, Department of Journalism, Jonesboro, State University, AR 72467. Offers MSMC. Part-time programs available. *Faculty:* 4 full-time (2 women), 1 part-time/adjunct (0 women). *Students:* 6 full-time (4 women), 3 part-time (1 woman); includes 2 minority (both African Americans), 3 international. Average age 24. 11 applicants, 91% accepted, 3 enrolled. In 2008, 1 master's awarded. *Degree requirements:* For master's, comprehensive exam, thesis or alternative. *Entrance requirements:* For master's, GRE General Test, appropriate bachelor's degree, letters of reference, recommendations, official transcript, written statement of purpose. Additional exam requirements/recommendations for international students: Required—TOEFL (minimum score 550 paper-based; 213 computer-based; 79 iBT), IELTS (minimum score 6). *Application deadline:* For fall admission, 7/15 for domestic students, 7/1 for international students; for spring admission, 12/1 for domestic students, 11/13 for international students. Applications are processed on a rolling basis. Application fee: $30 ($40 for international students). Electronic applications accepted. *Expenses:* Tuition, state resident: full-time $3744; part-time $208 per credit hour. Tuition, nonresident: full-time $9540; part-time $530 per credit hour. International tuition: $7938 full-time. Required fees: $896; $47 per credit hour. $25 per term. One-time fee: $50. Tuition and fees vary according to course load and program. *Financial support:* In 2008–09, 4 students received support. Career-related internships or fieldwork, scholarships/grants, and unspecified assistantships available. Financial award application deadline: 7/1; financial award applicants required to submit FAFSA. *Faculty research:* Campus press issues, communication and culture, digital pre-press workflow, editing specialized publications, media ethics in decision making. *Unit head:* Dr. Joel Gambill, Chair, 870-972-3075, Fax: 870-972-3321, E-mail: jgambil@astate.edu. *Application contact:* Dr. Andrew Sustich, Dean of the Graduate School, 870-972-3029, Fax: 870-972-3857, E-mail: sustich@astate.edu.

Arkansas Tech University, Graduate School, School of Liberal and Fine Arts, Russellville, AR 72801. Offers communication (MLA); English (M Ed, MA); fine arts (MLA); history (MA); multi-media journalism (MA); social science (MLA); social studies (M Ed); Spanish (MA, MLA); teaching English as a second language (MA, MLA). Part-time programs available. *Students:* 40 full-time (31 women), 81 part-time (60 women); includes 10 minority (3 African Americans, 2 American Indian/Alaska Native, 2 Asian Americans or Pacific Islanders, 3 Hispanic Americans), 19 international. Average age 33. In 2008, 70 master's awarded. *Degree requirements:* For master's, project. *Entrance requirements:* For master's, GRE General Test or MAT. Additional exam requirements/recommendations for international students: Required—TOEFL (minimum score 500 paper-based; 173 computer-based; 61 iBT). *Application deadline:* For fall admission, 3/1 priority date for domestic students, 5/1 priority date for international students; for winter admission, 10/1 priority date for international students; for spring admission, 10/1 priority date for domestic and international students. Applications are processed on a rolling basis. Application fee: $0 ($30 for international students). Electronic applications accepted. *Expenses:* Tuition, state resident: full-time $1575; part-time $175 per credit hour. Tuition, nonresident: full-time $3150; part-time $350 per credit hour. Tuition and fees vary according to course load. *Financial support:* In 2008–09, teaching assistantships with full tuition reimbursements (averaging $4,000 per year); career-related internships or fieldwork, Federal Work-Study, scholarships/grants, health care benefits, and unspecified assistantships also available. Support available to part-time students. Financial award application deadline: 4/15; financial award applicants required to submit FAFSA. *Unit head:* Dr. Georgena Duncan, Dean, 479-968-0266, Fax: 479-968-0275, E-mail: georgena.duncan@atu.edu. *Application contact:* Dr. Eldon G. Clary, Dean of Graduate School, 479-968-0398, Fax: 479-964-0542, E-mail: graduate.school@atu.edu.

Ball State University, Graduate School, College of Communication, Information, and Media, Department of Journalism, Muncie, IN 47306-1099. Offers journalism (MA); public relations (MA). *Entrance requirements:* For master's, resumé. *Faculty research:* Image studies, readership surveys, audience perception studies.

Baylor University, Graduate School, College of Arts and Sciences, Department of Journalism, Waco, TX 76798. Offers international journalism (MIJ); journalism (MA). *Students:* 11 full-time (9 women), 6 part-time (5 women); includes 2 minority (1 Asian American or Pacific Islander, 1 Hispanic American), 3 international. Average age 24. In 2008, 7 master's awarded. *Degree requirements:* For master's, proficiency in 1 foreign language (MIJ). *Entrance requirements:* For master's, GRE General Test. *Application deadline:* Applications are processed on a rolling basis. Application fee: $25. *Financial support:* Research assistantships, teaching assistantships, career-related internships or fieldwork, Federal Work-Study, and institutionally sponsored loans available. Support available to part-time students. *Faculty research:* International politics, mass media and society, journalism history, editing practices. *Unit head:* Dr. Amanda Sturgill, Graduate Program Director, 254-710-6322, Fax: 254-710-3363, E-mail: amanda_sturgill@baylor.edu. *Application contact:* Jan Loosier, Administrative Assistant, 254-710-3261, Fax: 254-710-3870, E-mail: jan_loosier@baylor.edu.

Bob Jones University, Graduate Programs, Greenville, SC 29614. Offers accountancy (MS); Bible (MA); Bible translation (MA); Biblical studies (Certificate); broadcast management (MS); business administration (MBA); church history (MA, PhD); church ministries (MA); church music (MM); cinema and video production (MA); counseling (MS); curriculum and instruction (Ed D); divinity (M Div); dramatic production (MA); educational leadership (MS, Ed D, Ed S); elementary education (M Ed, MAT); English (M Ed, MA, MAT); fine arts (MA); graphic design (MA); history (M Ed, MA); illustration (MA); interpretative speech (MA); mathematics (M Ed, MAT); medical missions (Certificate); ministry (MM, D Min); multi-categorical special education (M Ed, MAT); music (M Ed); New Testament interpretation (PhD); Old Testament interpretation (PhD); orchestral instrument performance (MM); organ performance (MM); pastoral studies (MA); personnel services (MS, Ed S); piano pedagogy (MM); piano performance (MM); platform arts (MA); radio and television broadcasting (MS); rhetoric and public address (MA); secondary education (M Ed); studio art (MA); teaching Bible (MA); theology (MA, PhD); voice performance (MM); youth ministries (MA); M Div/MM.

Boston University, College of Communication, Department of Journalism, Boston, MA 02215. Offers broadcast journalism (MS); business and economics journalism (MS); photo journalism (MS); print journalism (MS); science journalism (MS). *Degree requirements:* For master's, thesis. *Entrance requirements:* For master's, GRE General Test, sample of written work. Additional exam requirements/recommendations for international students: Required—TOEFL. Electronic applications accepted.

See Close-Up on page 683.

California State University, Fresno, Division of Graduate Studies, College of Arts and Humanities, Department of Mass Communication and Journalism, Fresno, CA 93740-8027. Offers MA. Part-time and evening/weekend programs available. *Degree requirements:* For master's, thesis. *Entrance requirements:* For master's, GRE General Test, minimum GPA of 3.0. Additional exam requirements/recommendations for international students: Required—TOEFL. Electronic applications accepted.

California State University, Fullerton, Graduate Studies, College of Communications, Department of Communications, Fullerton, CA 92834-9480. Offers communications—advertising (MA); communications—entertainment and tourism (MA); communications—journalism (MA); communications—public relations (MA). Part-time programs available. *Students:* 21 full-time (17 women), 38 part-time (32 women); includes 18 minority (1 African American, 6 Asian Americans or Pacific Islanders, 11 Hispanic Americans), 9 international. Average age 29. 94 applicants, 38% accepted, 13 enrolled. In 2008, 33 master's awarded. *Degree requirements:* For master's, project or thesis. *Entrance requirements:* For master's, GRE General Test. Application fee: $55. Tuition and fees vary according to degree level. *Financial support:* Teaching assistantships, career-related internships or fieldwork, Federal Work-Study, institutionally sponsored loans, and scholarships/grants available. Support available to part-time students. Financial award application deadline: 3/1. *Unit head:* Dr. Tony Fellow, Chair, 657-278-3517. *Application contact:* Coordinator, 657-278-3832.

California State University, Northridge, Graduate Studies, College of Arts, Media, and Communication, Department of Journalism, Northridge, CA 91330. Offers mass communication (MA). Part-time and evening/weekend programs available. *Faculty:* 13 full-time (7 women), 14 part-time/adjunct (4 women). *Students:* 11 full-time (8 women), 30 part-time (26 women); includes 14 minority (3 African Americans, 3 Asian Americans or Pacific Islanders, 8 Hispanic Americans), 3 international. Average age 30. 55 applicants, 49% accepted, 18 enrolled. In 2008, 13 master's awarded. *Degree requirements:* For master's, thesis. *Entrance requirements:* For master's, GRE General Test. Additional exam requirements/recommendations for international students: Required—TOEFL. *Application deadline:* For fall admission, 11/30 for domestic students. Application fee: $55. *Financial support:* Career-related internships or fieldwork and Federal Work-Study available. Financial award application deadline: 3/1. *Unit head:* Dr. Kent Kirkton, Chair, 818-677-3135, E-mail: kent.kirkton@csun.edu. *Application contact:* Dr. Kent Kirkton, Chair, 818-677-3135, E-mail: kent.kirkton@csun.edu.

Carleton University, Faculty of Graduate Studies, Faculty of Public Affairs and Management, School of Journalism and Communication, Ottawa, ON K1S 5B6, Canada. Offers communication (MA, PhD); journalism (MJ). *Degree requirements:* For master's, thesis optional; for doctorate, comprehensive exam, thesis/dissertation. *Entrance requirements:* For master's, honors degree. Additional exam requirements/recommendations for international students: Required—TOEFL. *Faculty research:* Specialized print reporting, broadcast journalism, journalism studies.

Columbia College Chicago, Graduate School, Department of Journalism, Chicago, IL 60605-1996. Offers public affairs journalism (MA). *Students:* 27 full-time (19 women), 8 part-time (7 women); includes 15 minority (11 African Americans, 4 Hispanic Americans), 1 international. Average age 27. 26 applicants, 7 enrolled. In 2008, 9 master's awarded. *Degree requirements:* For master's, thesis. *Entrance requirements:* For master's, interview, minimum GPA of 3.0, writing sample. Additional exam requirements/recommendations for international students: Required—TOEFL (minimum score 550 paper-based; 213 computer-based). *Application deadline:* For fall admission, 1/15 for domestic and international students. Application fee: $55. Electronic applications accepted. *Expenses:* Tuition: Full-time $15,992; part-time $633 per credit hour. *Financial support:* Fellowships, career-related internships or fieldwork, Federal Work-Study, and scholarships/grants available. Support available to part-time students. Financial award application deadline: 8/13; financial award applicants required to submit FAFSA. *Unit head:* Nancy Day, Chairperson, 312-344-7089, Fax: 312-369-8059, E-mail: nday@colum.edu. *Application contact:* Keith Cleveland, Office of Provost/Senior Vice President, 312-369-7261, Fax: 312-369-8022, E-mail: kcleveland@colum.edu.

Columbia University, Graduate School of Journalism, New York, NY 10027. Offers MA, MS, PhD, JD/MS, MIA/MS, MS/MBA. *Accreditation:* ACEJMC. Part-time programs available. *Degree requirements:* For master's, thesis; for doctorate, thesis/dissertation. *Entrance requirements:* For master's, writing test, 2-3 samples of journalistic work, minimum typing speed of 50 words per minute; for doctorate, GRE. Additional exam requirements/recommendations for international students: Required—TOEFL. *Expenses:* Contact institution. *Faculty research:* International communication, communication technologies, ethics in journalism, journalism history.

See Close-Up on page 685.

Concordia University, School of Graduate Studies, Faculty of Arts and Science, Department of Journalism, Montréal, QC H3G 1M8, Canada. Offers Diploma. *Degree requirements:* For Diploma, one foreign language. *Entrance requirements:* Additional exam requirements/recommendations for international students: Required—departmental English test or TOEFL.

CUNY Graduate School of Journalism, Graduate Program, New York, NY 10036. Offers MA. *Degree requirements:* For master's, internship, final or capstone project. *Entrance requirements:* For master's, GRE, 3 letters of recommendation, resumé. Additional exam requirements/recommendations for international students: Required—TOEFL (minimum score 260 computer-based; 105 iBT). Electronic applications accepted.

See Close-Up on page 687.

DePaul University, College of Communication, Chicago, IL 60614. Offers journalism (MA); media, culture and society (MA); organizational and multicultural communication (MA); public relations and advertising (MA). Part-time and evening/weekend programs available. *Faculty:* 31 full-time (17 women), 15 part-time/adjunct (7 women). *Students:* 135 full-time (106 women), 43 part-time (35 women); includes 49 minority (25 African Americans, 7 Asian Americans or Pacific Islanders, 17 Hispanic Americans), 8 international. Average age 29. 242 applicants, 47% accepted, 68 enrolled. In 2008, 64 master's awarded. *Degree requirements:* For master's, comprehensive exam (for some programs), final exam or thesis/project. *Entrance requirements:* For master's, GRE General Test (public relations and advertising), minimum GPA of 3.0, writing sample, essay, letters of recommendation, resumé. Additional exam requirements/recommendations for international students: Required—TOEFL (minimum score 590 paper-based; 245 computer-based; 96 iBT). Application fee: $40. Electronic applications accepted. *Financial support:* In 2008–09, 8 students received support, including 4 research assistantships with partial tuition reimbursements available, 2 teaching assistantships with full tuition reimbursements available (averaging $12,000 per year); fellowships with full tuition reimbursements available, career-related internships or fieldwork, scholarships/grants, and tuition waivers (partial) also available. Support available to part-time students. Financial award applicants required to submit FAFSA. *Faculty research:* Intercultural communication, corporate culture, diversity in the working place, organizational socialization, critical cultural studies. *Unit head:* Dr. Jacqueline Taylor, Dean, 773-325-7216, Fax: 773-325-7584, E-mail: jtaylor@depaul.edu. *Application contact:* Ann Spittle, Director of Graduate Admission, 773-325-8369, Fax: 773-325-2395, E-mail: aspittle@depaul.edu.

Drake University, School of Education, Department of Teaching and Learning, Program in Secondary Education, Des Moines, IA 50311-4516. Offers art (MAT); biology (MAT); business (MAT); chemistry (MAT); English (MAT); general science (MAT); history-American (MAT); history-world (MAT); journalism (MAT); mathematics (MAT); physical science (MAT); physics (MAT); sociology (MAT); speech (MAT); speech communication (MAT); theatre (MAT). Part-time programs available. *Degree requirements:* For master's, comprehensive exam, thesis (for some programs), internships (for some programs). *Entrance requirements:* For master's, GRE General Test, MAT, or Drake Writing Assessment, resumé, 2 letters of recommendation. Additional exam requirements/recommendations for international students: Required—TOEFL (minimum score 550 paper-based; 213 computer-based). Electronic applications accepted. *Faculty research:* Counseling and rehabilitation, behavioral supports, inquiry-based science methods, teacher quality enhancement.

Drexel University, School of Journalism, Philadelphia, PA 19104-2875. Offers MA. *Entrance requirements:* Additional exam requirements/recommendations for international students: Required—TOEFL.

Emerson College, Graduate Studies, School of Communication, Department of Journalism, Boston, MA 02116-4624. Offers print/multimedia journalism, broadcast journalism, integrated journalism (MA), including broadcast journalism, integrated journalism, print/multimedia journalism. Part-time programs available. *Students:* 64 full-time (39 women), 7 part-time (6 women); includes 9 minority (2 African Americans, 3 Asian Americans or Pacific Islanders, 4 Hispanic Americans), 10 international. Average age 26. 107 applicants, 76% accepted, 32 enrolled. In 2008, 21 master's awarded. *Entrance requirements:* For master's, GRE General Test. Additional exam requirements/recommendations for international students: Required—TOEFL (minimum score 550 paper-based; 213 computer-based; 80 iBT), IELTS (minimum score 6.5). *Application deadline:* For fall admission, 3/1 priority date for domestic students, 5/1

Journalism

Emerson College (continued)
priority date for international students; for spring admission, 11/1 priority date for domestic students. Applications are processed on a rolling basis. Application fee: $60 ($75 for international students). Electronic applications accepted. *Expenses:* Tuition: Full-time $17,720; part-time $886 per credit. Required fees: $60 per year. One-time fee: $170. *Financial support:* In 2008–09, 16 students received support, including 4 fellowships with partial tuition reimbursements available (averaging $14,000 per year), 7 research assistantships with partial tuition reimbursements available (averaging $10,000 per year); career-related internships or fieldwork, Federal Work-Study, institutionally sponsored loans, scholarships/grants, and unspecified assistantships also available. Support available to part-time students. Financial award application deadline: 3/1; financial award applicants required to submit FAFSA. *Faculty research:* Journalism. *Unit head:* Prof. Janet Kolodzy, Acting Chair, 617-824-8805, E-mail: Janet_Kolodzy@emerson.edu. *Application contact:* Office of Graduate Admission, 617-824-8610, Fax: 617-824-8614, E-mail: gradapp@emerson.edu.

Florida Agricultural and Mechanical University, Division of Graduate Studies, Research, and Continuing Education, School of Journalism and Graphic Communication, Tallahassee, FL 32307-3200. Offers journalism (MS). *Degree requirements:* For master's, comprehensive exam, thesis (for some programs). *Entrance requirements:* For master's, GRE General Test, minimum GPA of 3.0. Additional exam requirements/recommendations for international students: Required—TOEFL.

Florida Atlantic University, Dorothy F. Schmidt College of Arts and Letters, School of Communication and Multimedia Studies, Boca Raton, FL 33431-0991. Offers communication studies (MA); film and video (Certificate); film studies (MA); multimedia journalism studies (MA). Part-time programs available. *Faculty:* 21 full-time (10 women), 14 part-time/adjunct (3 women). *Students:* 15 full-time (11 women), 10 part-time (5 women); includes 2 minority (1 Asian American or Pacific Islander, 1 Hispanic American), 3 international. Average age 29. 35 applicants, 37% accepted, 7 enrolled. In 2008, 8 master's awarded. *Degree requirements:* For master's, one foreign language, comprehensive exam (for some programs), thesis (for some programs). *Entrance requirements:* For master's, GRE General Test, minimum GPA of 3.0. *Application deadline:* For fall admission, 7/1 priority date for domestic students, 4/1 for international students; for spring admission, 11/1 for domestic students, 10/1 for international students. Applications are processed on a rolling basis. Application fee: $30. Electronic applications accepted. *Expenses:* Tuition, state resident: full-time $4867; part-time $270.40 per credit hour. Tuition, nonresident: full-time $16,486; part-time $915.87 per credit hour. *Financial support:* Teaching assistantships with partial tuition reimbursements, Federal Work-Study and institutionally sponsored loans available. Support available to part-time students. Financial award application deadline: 3/1. *Faculty research:* Cultural studies, gender studies, film, communication theory, journalism, new media. *Unit head:* Dr. Susan S. Reilly, Director, 561-297-1095, Fax: 561-297-2615, E-mail: sreilly@fau.edu. *Application contact:* Dr. Eric M. Freedman, Graduate Coordinator, 561-297-2534, Fax: 561-297-2615, E-mail: efreedma@fau.edu.

Georgetown University, Graduate School of Arts and Sciences, School of Continuing Studies, Washington, DC 20057. Offers American studies (MALS); Catholic studies (MALS); classical civilizations (MALS); ethics and the professions (MALS); human resources management (MPS); humanities (MALS); individualized study (MALS); international affairs (MALS); Islam and Muslim-Christian relations (MALS); journalism (MPS); liberal studies (DLS); literature and society (MALS); medieval and early modern European studies (MALS); public relations (MPS); real estate (MPS); religious studies (MALS); social and public policy (MALS); sports industry management (MPS); the theory and practice of American democracy (MALS); visual culture (MALS). *Entrance requirements:* Additional exam requirements/recommendations for international students: Required—TOEFL.

Harvard University, Extension School, Cambridge, MA 02138-3722. Offers applied sciences (CAS); biotechnology (ALM); educational technologies (ALM); educational technology (CET); English for graduate and professional studies (DGP); environmental management (ALM, CEM); information technology (ALM); journalism (ALM); liberal arts (ALM); management (ALM, CM); mathematics for teaching (ALM); museum studies (ALM); premedical studies (Diploma); publication and communication (CPC). Part-time and evening/weekend programs available. *Degree requirements:* For master's, thesis. *Entrance requirements:* For master's, 3 completed graduate courses with grade of B or higher. Additional exam requirements/recommendations for international students: Required—TOEFL (minimum score 600 paper-based; 250 computer-based), TWE (minimum score 5). *Expenses:* Contact institution.

Hofstra University, School of Communication, Department of Journalism, Media Studies, and Public Relations, Hempstead, NY 11549. Offers journalism (MA). Part-time and evening/weekend programs available. *Faculty:* 4 full-time (2 women), 4 part-time/adjunct (1 woman). *Students:* 12 full-time (4 women), 13 part-time (10 women); includes 2 minority (1 African American, 1 Hispanic American). Average age 28. 24 applicants, 92% accepted, 11 enrolled. *Degree requirements:* For master's, thesis. *Entrance requirements:* For master's, minimum GPA of 2.75; bachelor's degree. Additional exam requirements/recommendations for international students: Required—TOEFL (minimum score 550 paper-based; 213 computer-based; 80 iBT). *Application deadline:* Applications are processed on a rolling basis. Application fee: $60. Electronic applications accepted. *Expenses:* Tuition: Full-time $15,300; part-time $850 per credit. Required fees: $970; $165 per term. Tuition and fees vary according to program. *Financial support:* In 2008–09, 13 students received support, including 1 fellowship with full and partial tuition reimbursement available (averaging $3,000 per year); research assistantships with full and partial tuition reimbursements available, Federal Work-Study, institutionally sponsored loans, scholarships/grants, tuition waivers (full and partial), and unspecified assistantships also available. Support available to part-time students. Financial award applicants required to submit FAFSA. *Faculty research:* Media ecology, media literacy, environmental and health journalism, the future of news, cultural issues and social justice refuting, RTNDA/Hofstra University Annual Survey. *Unit head:* Dr. Kristal Zook, Director, 516-463-4304, E-mail: jrnkzb@hofstra.edu. *Application contact:* Carol Drummer, Dean of Graduate Admissions, 516-463-4876, Fax: 516-463-4664, E-mail: gradstudent@hofstra.edu.

Indiana University Bloomington, School of Journalism, Bloomington, IN 47405-7000. Offers journalism (MA, MAT); mass communication (PhD); MA/JD; MA/MA. *Faculty:* 11 full-time (5 women). *Students:* 61 full-time (32 women), 15 part-time (8 women); includes 6 minority (2 African Americans, 3 Asian Americans or Pacific Islanders, 1 Hispanic American), 23 international. Average age 30. 132 applicants, 73% accepted, 45 enrolled. In 2008, 20 master's, 5 doctorates awarded. Terminal master's awarded for partial completion of doctoral program. *Degree requirements:* For master's, thesis (for some programs); for doctorate, thesis/dissertation. *Entrance requirements:* For master's and doctorate, GRE General Test. Additional exam requirements/recommendations for international students: Required—TOEFL. *Application deadline:* For fall admission, 1/15 priority date for domestic students; for spring admission, 9/1 priority date for domestic students. Applications are processed on a rolling basis. Application fee: $50 ($60 for international students). *Expenses:* Tuition, area resident: Part-time $291.97 per credit hour. Tuition, state resident: part-time $291.97 per credit hour. Tuition, nonresident: part-time $850.33 per credit hour. Required fees: $110 per semester. Tuition and fees vary according to course load and program. *Financial support:* Fellowships, research assistantships with full tuition reimbursements, teaching assistantships with partial tuition reimbursements, career-related internships or fieldwork, Federal Work-Study, institutionally sponsored loans, and tuition waivers (full) available. Financial award application deadline: 1/15. *Faculty research:* Political communication, international communication, communication history, communication law, visual communication. Total annual research expenditures: $165,185. *Unit head:* Bradley Hamm, Dean, 812-855-9247. *Application contact:* Amy Reynolds, Associate Dean of Graduate Studies, 812-855-8111.

Iona College, School of Arts and Science, Department of Mass Communication, New Rochelle, NY 10801-1890. Offers journalism (MS); public relations (MA). *Accreditation:* ACEJMC (one or

more programs are accredited). Part-time and evening/weekend programs available. *Faculty:* 6 full-time (1 woman), 7 part-time/adjunct (3 women). *Students:* 6 full-time (all women), 32 part-time (25 women); includes 5 minority (2 African Americans, 3 Hispanic Americans), 2 international. Average age 28. 37 applicants, 35% accepted, 10 enrolled. In 2008, 12 master's awarded. *Degree requirements:* For master's, comprehensive exam or thesis. *Entrance requirements:* For master's, GRE General Test, minimum GPA of 3.0. Additional exam requirements/recommendations for international students: Required—TOEFL (minimum score 550 paper-based; 213 computer-based). *Application deadline:* Applications are processed on a rolling basis. Application fee: $50. Electronic applications accepted. *Expenses:* Contact institution. *Financial support:* Career-related internships or fieldwork, tuition waivers (partial), and unspecified assistantships available. Support available to part-time students. Financial award application deadline: 4/15; financial award applicants required to submit FAFSA. *Faculty research:* Media ecology, new media, corporate communication, media images, organizational learning in public relations. *Unit head:* Br. Raymond Smith, Chair, 914-633-2354, E-mail: rrsmith@iona.edu. *Application contact:* Veronica Jarek-Prinz, Director of Graduate Admissions, 914-633-2420, Fax: 914-633-2277, E-mail: vjarekprinz@iona.edu.

Iowa State University of Science and Technology, Graduate College, College of Liberal Arts and Sciences, Greenlee School of Journalism and Mass Communication, Ames, IA 50011. Offers MS. *Faculty:* 19 full-time (5 women). *Students:* 22 full-time (15 women), 21 part-time (14 women); includes 5 minority (1 African American, 1 Asian American or Pacific Islander, 3 Hispanic Americans), 20 international. 41 applicants, 66% accepted, 17 enrolled. In 2008, 9 master's awarded. *Degree requirements:* For master's, thesis or alternative. *Entrance requirements:* For master's, GRE General Test. Additional exam requirements/recommendations for international students: Required—TOEFL (minimum score 570 paper-based; 88 iBT), IELTS (6.5) or TOEFL. *Application deadline:* For fall admission, 4/1 priority date for domestic and international students; for spring admission, 11/1 priority date for domestic and international students. Applications are processed on a rolling basis. Application fee: $30 ($70 for international students). Electronic applications accepted. *Expenses:* Tuition, area resident: Full-time $6446; part-time $359 per credit. Tuition, state resident: full-time $6446; part-time $359 per credit. Tuition, nonresident: full-time $17,330; part-time $963 per credit. Required fees: $790; $249.25 per semester. Tuition and fees vary according to course load and program. *Financial support:* In 2008–09, 17 research assistantships with full and partial tuition reimbursements (averaging $12,150 per year), 1 teaching assistantship with partial tuition reimbursement (averaging $12,150 per year) were awarded; fellowships, scholarships/grants, health care benefits, and unspecified assistantships also available. *Unit head:* Dr. Michael Bugeja, Chair, 515-294-0481, Fax: 515-294-5108, E-mail: greenlee@iastate.edu. *Application contact:* Dr. Eric Abbott, Director of Graduate Education, 515-294-0492, E-mail: masscomm@iastate.edu.

Kent State University, College of Communication and Information, School of Journalism and Mass Communication, Kent, OH 44242-0001. Offers MA. Part-time programs available. *Degree requirements:* For master's, thesis optional. *Entrance requirements:* For master's, GRE General Test, minimum GPA of 3.0. Additional exam requirements/recommendations for international students: Recommended—TOEFL (minimum score 600 paper-based; 250 computer-based). Electronic applications accepted. *Faculty research:* Electronic tablet newspapers, accuracy and ethics in broadcast news, internet credibility, First Amendment, HDTV.

Marquette University, Graduate School, College of Communication, Milwaukee, WI 53201-1881. Offers advertising and public relations (MA); broadcasting and electronic communications (MA); communications studies (MA); journalism (MA); mass communications (MA); religious communications (MA); science, health and environmental communications (MA). *Accreditation:* ACEJMC. Part-time and evening/weekend programs available. *Degree requirements:* For master's, comprehensive exam. *Entrance requirements:* For master's, GRE. Additional exam requirements/recommendations for international students: Required—TOEFL. *Faculty research:* Urban journalism, gender and communication, intercultural communication, religious communication.

Marshall University, Academic Affairs Division, School of Journalism and Mass Communications, Huntington, WV 25755. Offers MAJ. *Accreditation:* ACEJMC. *Degree requirements:* For master's, thesis optional. *Entrance requirements:* For master's, GRE General Test.

Michigan State University, The Graduate School, College of Communication Arts and Sciences, School of Journalism, East Lansing, MI 48824. Offers MA. *Entrance requirements:* Additional exam requirements/recommendations for international students: Required—TOEFL. Electronic applications accepted.

New York University, Graduate School of Arts and Science, Department of Biology, New York, NY 10012-1019. Offers biology (PhD); biomedical journalism (MS); cancer and molecular biology (PhD); computational biology (PhD); computers in biological research (MS); developmental genetics (PhD); general biology (MS); immunology and microbiology (PhD); molecular genetics (PhD); neurobiology (PhD); oral biology (MS); plant biology (PhD); recombinant DNA technology (MS); MS/MBA. Part-time programs available. Terminal master's awarded for partial completion of doctoral program. *Degree requirements:* For master's, thesis or alternative, qualifying paper; for doctorate, comprehensive exam, thesis/dissertation. *Entrance requirements:* For master's, GRE General Test; for doctorate, GRE General Test, GRE Subject Test. Additional exam requirements/recommendations for international students: Required—TOEFL. *Faculty research:* Genomics, molecular and cell biology, development and molecular genetics, molecular evolution of plants and animals.

New York University, Graduate School of Arts and Science, Department of Journalism, New York, NY 10012-1019. Offers biomedical journalism (MS); cultural reporting and criticism (MA); French studies/journalism (MA); journalism (MA); Latin American and Caribbean studies/journalism (MA); Near Eastern studies/journalism (MA); science and environmental reporting (Advanced Certificate); MA/Advanced Certificate. *Accreditation:* ACEJMC. Part-time programs available. *Degree requirements:* For master's, written projects. *Entrance requirements:* For master's, GRE General Test, sample of written work. Additional exam requirements/recommendations for international students: Required—TOEFL. *Faculty research:* Newspaper, magazine, and broadcast journalism; business and financial reporting; media studies.

Northeastern University, College of Arts and Sciences, School of Journalism, Boston, MA 02115-5096. Offers MA. Part-time and evening/weekend programs available. *Degree requirements:* For master's, thesis (for some programs). *Entrance requirements:* For master's, GRE General Test, minimum GPA of 3.0. Electronic applications accepted. *Faculty research:* Online journalism, broadcast news, foreign reporting, presidential debates, sporting society.

Northwestern University, Medill School of Journalism, Evanston, IL 60208. Offers broadcast journalism (MSJ); integrated marketing communications (MSIMC), including advertising/sales promotion, direct database and e-commerce marketing, general studies, public relations; magazine publishing (MSJ); new media (MSJ); reporting and writing (MSJ). *Accreditation:* ACEJMC (one or more programs are accredited). *Entrance requirements:* For master's, GRE General Test, GMAT or LSAT (MSJ). Additional exam requirements/recommendations for international students: Required—TOEFL. Electronic applications accepted. *Expenses:* Contact institution. *Faculty research:* Web business journalism, cultural stereotypes, voter apathy, digital television.

The Ohio State University, Graduate School, College of Social and Behavioral Sciences, School of Communication, Program in Journalism and Communication, Columbus, OH 43210. Offers MA. *Entrance requirements:* For master's, GRE General Test. Electronic applications accepted.

Ohio University, Graduate College, Scripps College of Communication, E.W. Scripps School of Journalism, Athens, OH 45701-2979. Offers MS, PhD. *Accreditation:* ACEJMC (one or more programs are accredited). Part-time programs available. *Degree requirements:* For master's, thesis or alternative; for doctorate, comprehensive exam, thesis/dissertation. *Entrance* *requirements:* For master's and doctorate, GRE General Test, minimum GPA of 3.0. Additional exam requirements/recommendations for international students: Required—TOEFL (minimum score 600 paper-based; 250 computer-based; 100 iBT). Electronic applications accepted. *Faculty research:* Newspaper, magazine, broadcasting, public relations, advertising.

Point Park University, School of Arts and Sciences, Department of Journalism and Mass Communication, Pittsburgh, PA 15222-1984. Offers MA. Part-time and evening/weekend programs available. *Faculty:* 9 full-time, 13 part-time/adjunct. *Students:* 35 full-time (27 women), 47 part-time (36 women); includes 13 minority (11 African Americans, 1 American Indian/Alaska Native, 1 Asian American or Pacific Islander), 3 international. Average age 27. 101 applicants, 56% accepted, 36 enrolled. In 2008, 24 master's awarded. *Degree requirements:* For master's, comprehensive exam (for some programs), thesis or alternative. *Entrance requirements:* For master's, GRE (if GPA below 2.75), minimum GPA of 2.75, 2 letters of recommendation; 500 word statement of intent. Additional exam requirements/recommendations for international students: Required—TOEFL. *Application deadline:* Applications are processed on a rolling basis. Application fee: $30. Electronic applications accepted. *Expenses:* Tuition: Full-time $11,880; part-time $660 per credit. Required fees: $486; $27 per credit. *Financial support:* In 2008–09, 6 students received support, including 6 research assistantships with full tuition reimbursements available (averaging $5,400 per year); career-related internships or fieldwork, Federal Work-Study, and scholarships/grants also available. Support available to part-time students. Financial award application deadline: 5/1; financial award applicants required to submit FAFSA. *Unit head:* Helen Fallon, Chair, 412-392-3982, E-mail: hfallon@pointpark.edu. *Application contact:* Emily R. Quidetto, Recruiter/Counselor, 412-392-4794, Fax: 412-392-6164, E-mail: equidetto@pointpark.edu.

See Close-Up on page 693.

Polytechnic Institute of NYU, Department of Humanities and Social Sciences, Major in Technical Writing and Specialized Journalism, Brooklyn, NY 11201-2990. Offers MS. *Degree requirements:* For master's, comprehensive exam (for some programs), thesis (for some programs). *Entrance requirements:* Additional exam requirements/recommendations for international students: Required—TOEFL (minimum score 550 paper-based; 213 computer-based); Recommended—IELTS (minimum score 6.5). Electronic applications accepted.

Quinnipiac University, School of Communications, Program in Journalism, Hamden, CT 06518-1940. Offers MS. Part-time and evening/weekend programs available. *Faculty:* 5 full-time (1 woman), 9 part-time/adjunct (3 women). *Students:* 26 full-time (14 women), 28 part-time (20 women); includes 9 minority (6 African Americans, 3 Hispanic Americans), 1 international. Average age 27. 35 applicants, 97% accepted, 23 enrolled. In 2008, 24 master's awarded. *Degree requirements:* For master's, project. *Entrance requirements:* For master's, minimum GPA of 2.8, portfolio or writing sample. Additional exam requirements/recommendations for international students: Required—TOEFL (minimum score 575 paper-based; 233 computer-based; 90 iBT), IELTS (minimum score 6.5). *Application deadline:* For fall admission, 7/30 priority date for domestic students, 4/30 priority date for international students; for spring admission, 12/15 priority date for domestic students, 9/15 priority date for international students. Applications are processed on a rolling basis. Application fee: $45. Electronic applications accepted. *Expenses:* Tuition: Full-time $14,600; part-time $730 per credit. Required fees: $630; $30 per credit. *Financial support:* In 2008–09, 1 fellowship with full tuition reimbursement was awarded; career-related internships or fieldwork and unspecified assistantships also available. Support available to part-time students. Financial award application deadline: 4/15; financial award applicants required to submit FAFSA. *Faculty research:* Journalism history, media representation, media and politics, media influence. *Unit head:* Richard Hanley, Director, 203-582-8439, Fax: 203-582-5310, E-mail: rich.hanley@quinnipiac.edu. *Application contact:* Scott Farber, Director of Graduate Admissions, 800-462-1944, Fax: 203-582-3443, E-mail: scott.farber@quinnipiac.edu.

See Close-Up on page 695.

Regent University, Graduate School, School of Communication and the Arts, Virginia Beach, VA 23464-9800. Offers acting (MFA); acting and directing (MFA); cinema arts/television arts (MA); communication (MA, PhD); digital media (MA); directing for cinema/TV (MA); journalism (MA); producing for cinema/TV (MA); script and screenwriting (MFA); theatre (MA). Part-time programs available. Postbaccalaureate distance learning degree programs offered (minimal on-campus study). *Faculty:* 26 full-time (3 women), 15 part-time/adjunct (3 women). *Students:* 136 full-time (77 women), 163 part-time (90 women); includes 83 minority (59 African Americans, 3 American Indian/Alaska Native, 5 Asian Americans or Pacific Islanders, 16 Hispanic Americans), 15 international. Average age 32. 230 applicants, 63% accepted, 102 enrolled. In 2008, 53 master's, 16 doctorates awarded. *Degree requirements:* For master's, thesis or alternative; for doctorate, thesis/dissertation. *Entrance requirements:* For master's, GRE General Test or MAT, minimum undergraduate GPA of 3.0, writing sample, computer literacy survey, recommendation, resumé, interview, audition (MFA programs); for doctorate, GRE General Test, minimum graduate GPA of 3.0, writing sample, computer literacy survey, recommendation, interview, transcripts. Additional exam requirements/recommendations for international students: Required—TOEFL (minimum score 577 paper-based; 233 computer-based). *Application deadline:* For fall admission, 3/1 priority date for domestic students; for spring admission, 10/1 priority date for domestic students. Applications are processed on a rolling basis. Application fee: $50. Electronic applications accepted. *Expenses:* Contact institution. *Financial support:* Fellowships with full and partial tuition reimbursements, career-related internships or fieldwork, scholarships/grants, tuition waivers (full and partial), and unspecified assistantships available. Support available to part-time students. Financial award application deadline: 9/1; financial award applicants required to submit FAFSA. *Faculty research:* Southern gospel music, education and entertainment, celebrities and the media, journalism and ethics, C. S. Lewis. *Unit head:* Michael Patrick, Dean, 757-352-4970, Fax: 757-352-4279, E-mail: michpat@regent.edu. *Application contact:* Matthew Chadwick, Director of Admissions, 800-373-5504, Fax: 757-352-4381, E-mail: admissions@regent.edu.

Roosevelt University, Graduate Division, College of Arts and Sciences, Department of Communication, Program in Journalism, Chicago, IL 60605-1394. Offers MSJ. Part-time and evening/weekend programs available. *Students:* 19 full-time (14 women), 31 part-time (26 women); includes 19 African Americans, 3 Asian Americans or Pacific Islanders, 3 Hispanic Americans, 1 international. Average age 30. 100 applicants, 58% accepted, 14 enrolled. In 2008, 16 master's awarded. *Application deadline:* For fall admission, 6/1 priority date for domestic students. Applications are processed on a rolling basis. Application fee: $25 ($35 for international students). *Expenses:* Tuition: Full-time $14,730; part-time $709 per credit. Required fees: $175 per semester. Tuition and fees vary according to course load and program. *Financial support:* Application deadline: 2/15. *Application contact:* Joanne Canyon-Heller, Coordinator of Graduate Admission, 877-APPLY RU, Fax: 312-281-3356, E-mail: applyru@roosevelt.edu.

School of the Art Institute of Chicago, Graduate Division, Program in New Arts Journalism, Chicago, IL 60603-3103. Offers MA. *Entrance requirements:* Additional exam requirements/recommendations for international students: Required—TOEFL, IELTS.

See Close-Up on page 225.

South Dakota State University, Graduate School, College of Arts and Science, Department of Journalism and Mass Communication, Brookings, SD 57007. Offers communication studies and journalism (MS). Part-time and evening/weekend programs available. *Faculty:* 4 full-time (2 women). *Students:* 6 full-time (0 women), 19 part-time (13 women); includes 1 minority (African American). 18 applicants, 94% accepted, 17 enrolled. In 2008, 6 master's awarded. *Degree requirements:* For master's, thesis, oral exam. *Entrance requirements:* Additional exam requirements/recommendations for international students: Required—TOEFL (minimum score 550 paper-based; 213 computer-based; 79 iBT). *Application deadline:* For fall admission, 4/15 priority date for international students; for spring admission, 8/15 priority date for international students. Applications are processed on a rolling basis. Application fee: $35. *Faculty research:* Mass communication applications. *Unit head:* Dr. Mary Arnold, Head, 605-688-4171, Fax: 605-688-5034, E-mail: mary.arnold@sdstate.edu. *Application contact:* Lyle D. Olson, Graduate Coordinator, 605-688-6516, Fax: 605-688-5034, E-mail: lyle.olson@sdstate.edu.

Southern Illinois University Carbondale, Graduate School, College of Mass Communication and Media Arts, Department of Journalism, Carbondale, IL 62901-4701. Offers PhD.

Stanford University, School of Humanities and Sciences, Department of Communication, Stanford, CA 94305-9991. Offers communication (journalism specialization) (MA); communication theory and research (PhD). *Degree requirements:* For master's, thesis, project; for doctorate, thesis/dissertation, qualifying examination, area examination, 2 projects. *Entrance requirements:* For master's and doctorate, GRE General Test. Additional exam requirements/recommendations for international students: Required—TOEFL (minimum score 600 paper-based; 250 computer-based). Electronic applications accepted.

Syracuse University, Graduate School, S. I. Newhouse School of Public Communications, Program in Arts Journalism, Syracuse, NY 13244. Offers MA. *Entrance requirements:* For master's, GRE General Test. Additional exam requirements/recommendations for international students: Required—TOEFL (minimum score 600 paper-based; 250 computer-based). Electronic applications accepted.

Syracuse University, Graduate School, S. I. Newhouse School of Public Communications, Program in Broadcast Journalism, Syracuse, NY 13244. Offers MS. *Degree requirements:* For master's, capstone course. *Entrance requirements:* For master's, GRE General Test. Additional exam requirements/recommendations for international students: Required—TOEFL.

See Close-Up on page 705.

Syracuse University, Graduate School, S. I. Newhouse School of Public Communications, Program in Magazine, Newspaper and Online Journalism, Syracuse, NY 13244. Offers MA. *Degree requirements:* For master's, capstone course. *Entrance requirements:* For master's, GRE General Test. Additional exam requirements/recommendations for international students: Required—TOEFL (minimum score 600 paper-based; 250 computer-based). Electronic applications accepted.

See Close-Up on page 705.

Temple University, Graduate School, School of Communications and Theater, Department of Journalism, Philadelphia, PA 19122-6096. Offers MJ. Part-time programs available. *Degree requirements:* For master's, written exam. *Entrance requirements:* For master's, GRE General Test, minimum GPA of 3.0. Additional exam requirements/recommendations for international students: Required—TOEFL (minimum score 550 paper-based; 213 computer-based; 79 iBT). Electronic applications accepted. *Faculty research:* Journalism history, advertising research, media law, media institutions.

Texas Christian University, College of Communication, Schieffer School of Journalism, Fort Worth, TX 76129-0002. Offers advertising/public relations (MS); news-editorial (MS). Part-time and evening/weekend programs available. *Degree requirements:* For master's, thesis, written exam. *Entrance requirements:* For master's, GRE General Test. Additional exam requirements/recommendations for international students: Required—TOEFL. *Application deadline:* For fall admission, 3/1 for domestic students; for spring admission, 12/1 for domestic students. Applications are processed on a rolling basis. Application fee: $0. *Expenses:* Tuition: Full-time $17,640. *Financial support:* Application deadline: 3/1. *Unit head:* Dr. John Tisdale, Director, 817-257-6554, E-mail: j.tisdale@tcu.edu. *Application contact:* Dr. John Tisdale, Director, 817-257-6554, E-mail: j.tisdale@tcu.edu.

Université Laval, Faculty of Letters, Department of Information and Communication, Program in International Journalism, Québec, QC G1K 7P4, Canada. Offers Diploma. Offered jointly with École Supérieure De Journalisme De Lille (France). *Entrance requirements:* For degree, English exam, French exam, test on international current events, interview, knowledge of French, knowledge of English. Electronic applications accepted.

The University of Alabama, Graduate School, College of Communication and Information Sciences, Department of Journalism, Tuscaloosa, AL 35487-0172. Offers MA. *Faculty:* 9 full-time (2 women), 1 (woman) part-time/adjunct. *Students:* 20 full-time (14 women), 4 part-time (3 women); includes 4 minority (all African Americans). Average age 24. 34 applicants, 71% accepted, 15 enrolled. In 2008, 9 master's awarded. Terminal master's awarded for partial completion of doctoral program. *Degree requirements:* For master's, comprehensive exam (for some programs), thesis or alternative. *Entrance requirements:* For master's, GRE or MAT, minimum GPA of 3.0. Additional exam requirements/recommendations for international students: Required—TOEFL (minimum score 600 paper-based; 250 computer-based). *Application deadline:* For fall admission, 3/1 priority date for domestic and international students; for spring admission, 11/1 priority date for domestic and international students. Applications are processed on a rolling basis. Application fee: $30. Electronic applications accepted. *Expenses:* Tuition, area resident: Full-time $6400. Tuition, state resident: full-time $6400. Tuition, nonresident: full-time $18,000. *Financial support:* In 2008–09, 7 students received support, including 4 research assistantships with full tuition reimbursements available (averaging $11,000 per year), 3 teaching assistantships with full tuition reimbursements available (averaging $11,000 per year); fellowships, career-related internships or fieldwork, Federal Work-Study, institutionally sponsored loans, scholarships/grants, health care benefits, and unspecified assistantships also available. Financial award application deadline: 2/15. *Faculty research:* Journalistic processes and practices, media effects, history, law, and mass communication theory. Total annual research expenditures: $424,561. *Unit head:* Dr. Jennifer Greer, Chair, 205-348-6304, Fax: 205-348-2780, E-mail: jdgreer@ua.edu. *Application contact:* Dr. Wilson Lowrey, Graduate Coordinator, 205-348-8608, Fax: 205-348-2780, E-mail: wlowrey@ua.edu.

University of Arkansas, Graduate School, J. William Fulbright College of Arts and Sciences, Department of Journalism, Fayetteville, AR 72701-1201. Offers MA.

University of Arkansas at Little Rock, Graduate School, College of Professional Studies, School of Mass Communication, Little Rock, AR 72204-1099. Offers journalism (MA). Part-time and evening/weekend programs available. *Degree requirements:* For master's, comprehensive exam, thesis optional. *Entrance requirements:* For master's, GRE General Test, minimum GPA of 2.7. *Faculty research:* Theory and practice of mass communication, social role of the mass media.

The University of British Columbia, Faculty of Arts and Faculty of Graduate Studies, The School of Journalism, Vancouver, BC V6T 1Z1, Canada. Offers MJ. *Degree requirements:* For master's, thesis. *Entrance requirements:* For master's, portfolio, resumé with cover letter, letters of reference, transcripts. Additional exam requirements/recommendations for international students: Required—TOEFL (minimum score 615 paper-based; 260 computer-based). Electronic applications accepted. *Expenses:* Contact institution. *Faculty research:* New media, media coverage, journalistic ethics, audiences, investigative journalism.

University of California, Berkeley, Graduate Division, Graduate School of Journalism, Berkeley, CA 94720-1500. Offers MJ, JD/MJ, MJ/MA. *Accreditation:* ACEJMC. *Degree requirements:* For master's, project. *Entrance requirements:* For master's, GRE General Test, 3 work samples, minimum GPA of 3.0, 3 letters of recommendation. Additional exam requirements/recommendations for international students: Required—TOEFL (minimum score 600 paper-based; 250 computer-based). *Faculty research:* Documentary, new media, print (newspaper and magazine), broadcast (television and radio), photography.

University of Colorado at Boulder, Graduate School, School of Journalism and Mass Communication, Boulder, CO 80309. Offers communication (PhD), including media studies; mass communication research (MA); newsgathering (MA). *Accreditation:* ACEJMC (one or more programs are accredited). Part-time programs available. *Degree requirements:* For master's, comprehensive exam, thesis or alternative; for doctorate, comprehensive exam,

Journalism

University of Colorado at Boulder (continued)

thesis/dissertation. *Entrance requirements:* For master's, GRE General Test, minimum undergraduate GPA of 2.75; for doctorate, GRE General Test, minimum undergraduate GPA of 3.2, 3.5 graduate. *Faculty research:* Writing on science and the environment, mass communication and public opinion, minority representation in the media, media and culture.

University of Florida, Graduate School, College of Journalism and Communications, Department of Journalism, Gainesville, FL 32611. Offers MAMC. *Degree requirements:* For master's, thesis optional. *Entrance requirements:* For master's, GRE General Test, minimum GPA of 3.0. Additional exam requirements/recommendations for international students: Required—TOEFL (minimum score 550 paper-based; 213 computer-based).

University of Georgia, Graduate School, Grady School of Journalism and Mass Communication, Athens, GA 30602. Offers journalism and mass communication (MA); mass communication (PhD). *Accreditation:* ACEJMC (one or more programs are accredited). *Degree requirements:* For master's, comprehensive exam, thesis (MA); for doctorate, comprehensive exam, thesis/dissertation. *Entrance requirements:* For master's and doctorate, GRE General Test. Additional exam requirements/recommendations for international students: Required—TOEFL, TWE (PhD). Electronic applications accepted.

University of Illinois at Springfield, Graduate Programs, College of Public Affairs and Administration, Public Affairs Reporting Program, Springfield, IL 62703-5407. Offers MA. Part-time and evening/weekend programs available. *Faculty:* 1 full-time (0 women). *Students:* 19 full-time (8 women); includes 3 minority (2 Asian Americans or Pacific Islanders, 1 Hispanic American). Average age 25. 25 applicants, 76% accepted, 19 enrolled. In 2008, 19 master's awarded. *Degree requirements:* For master's, internship, professional portfolio. *Entrance requirements:* For master's, literacy/competency writing test, interview, written work sample, narrative statement describing qualifications, three letters of reference. Additional exam requirements/recommendations for international students: Required—TOEFL (minimum score 500 paper-based; 176 computer-based; 61 iBT). Application fee: $50 ($60 for international students). Electronic applications accepted. *Expenses:* Tuition, state resident: full-time $6144; part-time $256 per credit hour. Tuition, nonresident: full-time $13,980; part-time $582.50 per credit hour. Required fees: $1800. *Financial support:* Career-related internships or fieldwork, Federal Work-Study, scholarships/grants, and health care benefits available. Support available to part-time students. Financial award application deadline: 11/15; financial award applicants required to submit FAFSA. *Unit head:* Dr. Charles Wheeler, Director, 217-206-6535, Fax: 217-206-7807, E-mail: wheeler.charles@uis.edu. *Application contact:* Dr. Lynn Pardie, Office of Graduate Studies, 800-252-8533, Fax: 217-206-7623, E-mail: pardie.lynn@uis.edu.

University of Illinois at Urbana–Champaign, Graduate College, College of Media, Department of Journalism, Champaign, IL 61820. Offers MS, MS/JD, MS/MBA. *Accreditation:* ACEJMC. *Faculty:* 13 full-time (3 women), 1 part-time/adjunct (0 women). *Students:* 18 full-time (11 women), 8 part-time (3 women); includes 3 minority (all African Americans), 4 international. 74 applicants, 23% accepted, 14 enrolled. In 2008, 21 master's awarded. *Entrance requirements:* For master's, GRE, minimum GPA of 3.0. Additional exam requirements/recommendations for international students: Required—TOEFL (minimum score 600 paper-based; 250 computer-based). *Application deadline:* Applications are processed on a rolling basis. Application fee: $60 ($75 for international students). Electronic applications accepted. *Financial support:* In 2008–09, 1 fellowship, 12 research assistantships, 11 teaching assistantships were awarded; tuition waivers (full and partial) also available. *Unit head:* Walter Harrington, Head, 217-333-0709, Fax: 217-333-7931, E-mail: wharring@illinois.edu. *Application contact:* Diana King-Schwanke, Secretary, 217-333-0709, Fax: 217-333-7931, E-mail: dking6@illinois.edu.

The University of Iowa, Graduate College, College of Liberal Arts and Sciences, School of Journalism and Mass Communication, Program in Professional Journalism, Iowa City, IA 52242-1316. Offers MA, JD/MA. *Accreditation:* ACEJMC. *Degree requirements:* For master's, thesis optional, exam. *Entrance requirements:* For master's, GRE General Test, minimum GPA of 3.0. Additional exam requirements/recommendations for international students: Required—TOEFL (minimum score 570 paper-based; 230 computer-based; 89 iBT). Electronic applications accepted. *Faculty research:* Verbal and visual aspects of historical, legal, social, and cross-cultural communication.

The University of Kansas, Graduate Studies, School of Journalism and Mass Communications, Lawrence, KS 66045. Offers journalism (MS). *Accreditation:* ACEJMC. Part-time programs available. *Faculty:* 23 full-time (8 women), 7 part-time/adjunct (4 women). *Students:* 42 full-time (25 women), 48 part-time (37 women); includes 10 minority (3 African Americans, 3 American Indian/Alaska Native, 1 Asian American or Pacific Islander, 3 Hispanic Americans), 11 international. Average age 30. 51 applicants, 82% accepted, 26 enrolled. In 2008, 13 master's awarded. *Degree requirements:* For master's, comprehensive exam, thesis. *Entrance requirements:* For master's, GRE General Test, minimum GPA of 3.0. Additional exam requirements/recommendations for international students: Required—TOEFL or IELTS. *Application deadline:* For fall admission, 2/1 for domestic and international students; for spring admission, 11/1 for domestic and international students. Application fee: $45 ($50 for international students). Electronic applications accepted. *Expenses:* Tuition, area resident: Full-time $6122; part-time $255.10 per credit hour. Tuition, state resident: full-time $6122; part-time $255.10 per credit hour. Tuition, nonresident: full-time $14,629; part-time $609.55 per credit hour. Required fees: $847; $70.56 per credit hour. Tuition and fees vary according to course load and program. *Financial support:* Fellowships, research assistantships, teaching assistantships with full and partial tuition reimbursements, career-related internships or fieldwork, scholarships/grants, and unspecified assistantships available. Support available to part-time students. Financial award application deadline: 2/1; financial award applicants required to submit FAFSA. *Faculty research:* Advertising, creativity, media economics, public relations, press law, online journalism, political journalism, marketing communication, new media, visual communication. *Unit head:* Ann Brill, Dean, 785-864-4755, Fax: 785-864-4396, E-mail: abrill@ku.edu. *Application contact:* Cindy Nesvarba, Graduate Records Coordinator, 785-864-7649, Fax: 785-864-5318, E-mail: cnesvarb@ku.edu.

University of Maryland, College Park, Graduate Studies, Phillip Merrill College of Journalism, College Park, MD 20742. Offers broadcast journalism (MA); journalism (MA); journalism and media studies (PhD); online news (MA); public affairs reporting (MA). *Accreditation:* ACEJMC (one or more programs are accredited). Part-time and evening/weekend programs available. *Degree requirements:* For doctorate, thesis/dissertation, preliminary written and oral comprehensive exams. *Entrance requirements:* For master's and doctorate, GRE General Test, minimum GPA of 3.0, 3 letters of recommendation. Additional exam requirements/recommendations for international students: Required—TOEFL. Electronic applications accepted. *Faculty research:* Mass communication theory, specialized journalism, new telecommunication technologies, press integration.

University of Memphis, Graduate School, College of Communication and Fine Arts, Department of Journalism, Memphis, TN 38152. Offers general journalism (MA); journalism administration (MA). *Accreditation:* ACEJMC. Postbaccalaureate distance learning degree programs offered (no on-campus study). *Faculty:* 5 full-time (2 women), 2 part-time/adjunct (1 woman). *Students:* 15 full-time (13 women), 27 part-time (17 women); includes 7 minority (6 African Americans, 1 Hispanic American). Average age 31. 26 applicants, 69% accepted, 10 enrolled. In 2008, 18 master's awarded. *Degree requirements:* For master's, comprehensive exam. *Entrance requirements:* For master's, GRE General Test, MAT. *Application deadline:* For fall admission, 8/1 for domestic students; for spring admission, 12/1 for domestic students. Applications are processed on a rolling basis. Application fee: $35 ($60 for international students). *Expenses:* Tuition, area resident: Full-time $6242; part-time $330 per credit hour. Tuition, state resident: full-time $6242; part-time $330 per credit hour. Tuition, nonresident: full-time $17,828; part-time $815 per credit hour. Required fees: $1156. *Financial support:* Research assistantships, teaching assistantships, scholarships/grants available. Support available to part-time students. Financial award applicants required to submit FAFSA. *Faculty research:* Spirit of libel law, statistical software packages, college yearbooks, computer-assisted grammar project, newspaper in education. *Unit head:* Dr. David Arant, Chair, 901-678-2401, Fax: 901-678-4287, E-mail: darant@memphis.edu. *Application contact:* Dr. Rick Fischer, Coordinator of Graduate Studies, 901-678-2853, Fax: 901-678-4287, E-mail: rfischer@memphis.edu.

University of Miami, Graduate School, School of Communication, Coral Gables, FL 33124. Offers communication (PhD); communication studies (MA); film studies (MA, PhD); motion pictures (MFA), including production, producing, and screenwriting; print journalism (MA); public relations (MA); Spanish language journalism (MA); television broadcast journalism (MA). *Accreditation:* ACEJMC. Part-time programs available. *Degree requirements:* For master's, comprehensive exam (for some programs), thesis (for some programs); for doctorate, comprehensive exam, thesis/dissertation. *Entrance requirements:* For master's, GRE General Test; for doctorate, GRE General Test, master's thesis or scholarly research. Additional exam requirements/recommendations for international students: Required—TOEFL (minimum score 600 paper-based; 250 computer-based; 100 iBT). Electronic applications accepted. *Faculty research:* Communication studies, mass communication, international/interpersonal communication, film studies, journalism.

University of Mississippi, Graduate School, College of Liberal Arts, Department of Journalism, Oxford, University, MS 38677. Offers MA. *Degree requirements:* For master's, thesis. *Entrance requirements:* For master's, GRE General Test, minimum GPA of 3.0. Additional exam requirements/recommendations for international students: Required—TOEFL. Electronic applications accepted.

University of Missouri–Columbia, Graduate School, School of Journalism, Columbia, MO 65211. Offers MA, PhD. *Accreditation:* ACEJMC (one or more programs are accredited). Part-time programs available. *Faculty:* 68 full-time (32 women), 6 part-time/adjunct (1 woman). *Students:* 174 full-time (115 women), 119 part-time (78 women); includes 26 minority (6 African Americans, 2 American Indian/Alaska Native, 5 Asian Americans or Pacific Islanders, 13 Hispanic Americans), 62 international. Average age 30. 283 applicants, 42% accepted, 96 enrolled. In 2008, 91 master's, 10 doctorates awarded. Terminal master's awarded for partial completion of doctoral program. *Degree requirements:* For master's, thesis (for some programs); for doctorate, 2 foreign languages, thesis/dissertation. *Entrance requirements:* For master's and doctorate, GRE General Test, minimum GPA of 3.0. Additional exam requirements/recommendations for international students: Required—TOEFL (minimum score 600 paper-based; 250 computer-based; 100 iBT). *Application deadline:* For fall admission, 2/1 priority date for domestic students; for winter admission, 9/1 priority date for domestic students. Applications are processed on a rolling basis. Application fee: $45 ($60 for international students). *Financial support:* Fellowships, research assistantships, teaching assistantships, career-related internships or fieldwork and institutionally sponsored loans available. *Unit head:* Dr. Esther Thorson, Associate Dean, 573-882-9590, E-mail: thorsone@missouri.edu. *Application contact:* Ginny Cowell, 573-882-4852, E-mail: cowellvj@missouri.edu.

The University of Montana, Graduate School, School of Journalism, Missoula, MT 59812-0002. Offers MA. *Accreditation:* ACEJMC. *Degree requirements:* For master's, thesis or alternative, professional project. *Entrance requirements:* For master's, GRE, statement, essay. Additional exam requirements/recommendations for international students: Required—TOEFL (minimum score 580 paper-based). Electronic applications accepted. *Faculty research:* Native American issues, natural resources, public affairs, economy, photojournalism, multimedia, media law.

University of Nebraska–Lincoln, Graduate College, College of Journalism and Mass Communications, Lincoln, NE 68588. Offers marketing, communication and advertising (MA); professional journalism (MA). Postbaccalaureate distance learning degree programs offered (no on-campus study). *Faculty:* 17 full-time (7 women). *Students:* 22 full-time (12 women), 48 part-time (21 women); includes 4 minority (2 American Indian/Alaska Native, 1 Asian American or Pacific Islander, 1 Hispanic American), 4 international. Average age 33. In 2008, 23 master's awarded. *Degree requirements:* For master's, thesis. *Entrance requirements:* For master's, samples of work. Additional exam requirements/recommendations for international students: Required—TOEFL (minimum score 600 paper-based; 250 computer-based). *Application deadline:* For fall admission, 3/15 for domestic students, 3/1 for international students; for spring admission, 10/15 for domestic students. Applications are processed on a rolling basis. Application fee: $40. Electronic applications accepted. *Expenses:* Tuition, state resident: full-time $4275; part-time $237.50 per credit hour. Tuition, nonresident: full-time $11,525; part-time $640.25 per credit hour. Required fees: $1068; $10.35 per credit hour. $440.70 per semester. Tuition and fees vary according to course load and program. *Financial support:* Fellowships, research assistantships, teaching assistantships, Federal Work-Study, health care benefits, and unspecified assistantships available. Financial award application deadline: 2/15. *Faculty research:* Interactive media and the Internet, community newspapers, children's radio, advertising involvement, telecommunications policy. *Unit head:* Dr. Will Norton, Dean, 402-472-3041. *Application contact:* Ginny Gross, Director of Graduate Admissions, 402-472-2878, Fax: 402-472-0589, E-mail: grad_admissions@unl.edu.

University of Nevada, Las Vegas, Graduate College, Greenspun College of Urban Affairs, School of Journalism and Media Studies, Las Vegas, NV 89154-5007. Offers MA. *Faculty:* 11 full-time (3 women). *Students:* 13 full-time (7 women), 11 part-time (8 women); includes 3 minority (1 African American, 2 Hispanic Americans), 2 international. Average age 29. 31 applicants, 77% accepted, 11 enrolled. In 2008, 7 master's awarded. *Entrance requirements:* For master's, GRE General Test. Additional exam requirements/recommendations for international students: Required—TOEFL (minimum score 550 paper-based; 213 computer-based; 80 iBT), IELTS (minimum score 7). *Application deadline:* For fall admission, 3/15 priority date for domestic and international students. Applications are processed on a rolling basis. Application fee: $60 ($75 for international students). Electronic applications accepted. *Expenses:* Tuition, state resident: full-time $1414; part-time $198 per credit. Tuition, nonresident: full-time $12,509; part-time $415.75 per credit. International tuition: $14,249 full-time. Required fees: $4 per credit. $252 per semester. Tuition and fees vary according to course load. *Financial support:* In 2008–09, 8 students received support, including 4 research assistantships with partial tuition reimbursements available (averaging $10,000 per year), 4 teaching assistantships with partial tuition reimbursements available (averaging $10,000 per year); institutionally sponsored loans, scholarships/grants, health care benefits, and unspecified assistantships also available. Financial award application deadline: 3/1. *Faculty research:* Journalism and media studies. *Unit head:* Dr. Ardyth Sohn, Director/Professor, 702-895-3270, Fax: 702-895-5189, E-mail: ardyth.sohn@unlv.edu. *Application contact:* Graduate College Admissions Evaluator, 702-895-3320, Fax: 702-895-4180, E-mail: gradcollege@unlv.edu.

University of Nevada, Reno, Graduate School, Donald W. Reynolds School of Journalism, Reno, NV 89557. Offers MA. *Accreditation:* ACEJMC. *Faculty:* 5 full-time (1 woman). *Students:* 8 full-time (5 women), 2 part-time (both women); includes 2 minority (1 Asian American or Pacific Islander, 1 Hispanic American), 1 international. Average age 36. 16 applicants, 69% accepted, 11 enrolled. In 2008, 8 master's awarded. *Degree requirements:* For master's, thesis. *Entrance requirements:* For master's, GRE General Test, minimum GPA of 2.75. Additional exam requirements/recommendations for international students: Required—TOEFL (minimum score 500 paper-based; 173 computer-based; 61 iBT), IELTS (minimum score 6), TOFEL or IELTS. *Application deadline:* For fall admission, 3/15 priority date for domestic and international students; for spring admission, 12/1 priority date for domestic and international students. Applications are processed on a rolling basis. Application fee: $60 ($95 for international students). Electronic applications accepted. *Expenses:* Tuition, state resident: full-time $1710; part-time $1140 per semester. Tuition, nonresident: full-time $7115. Required fees: $158 per semester. *Financial support:* In 2008–09, 4 research assistantships with partial tuition reimbursements (averaging $14,000 per year), 2 teaching assistantships with partial tuition reimbursements (averaging $14,000 per year) were awarded; Federal Work-Study, institutionally sponsored loans, scholarships/grants, health care benefits, and unspecified assistantships also available. Financial award application deadline: 3/1; financial award applicants required to submit FAFSA. *Faculty research:* Interactive environmental journalism. Total annual research expenditures: $122,561. *Unit head:* Dr. Donica Mensing, Graduate Program Director, 775-784-4187, E-mail: dmensing@unr.edu. *Application contact:* Michele Sandberg, Application Contact, 775-784-7026, Fax: 775-784-6064, E-mail: gradschool@unr.edu.

University of North Texas, Robert B. Toulouse School of Graduate Studies, College of Arts and Sciences, Department of Journalism, Denton, TX 76203. Offers journalism (MA, MJ); narrative journalism (Graduate Certificate). *Accreditation:* ACEJMC (one or more programs are accredited). Part-time programs available. *Degree requirements:* For master's, variable foreign language requirement, comprehensive exam, thesis or alternative. *Entrance requirements:* For master's, GRE General Test, GPC in lieu of verbal GRE, porfolio. Additional exam requirements/recommendations for international students: Recommended—TOEFL (minimum score 550 paper-based; 213 computer-based). *Faculty research:* Mass communication theory, public relations, advertising, mass communication technology, journalism ethics.

University of Oklahoma, Graduate College, Gaylord College of Journalism and Mass Communication, Program in Journalism and Mass Communication, Norman, OK 73019-0390. Offers advertising and public relations (MA); information gathering and distribution (MA); mass communication management and policy (MA); professional writing (MA); telecommunication and new technology (MA). Part-time programs available. *Students:* 33 full-time (16 women), 34 part-time (18 women); includes 12 minority (4 African Americans, 4 American Indian/Alaska Native, 1 Asian American or Pacific Islander, 3 Hispanic Americans), 8 international. 28 applicants, 75% accepted, 14 enrolled. *Degree requirements:* For master's, thesis optional. *Entrance requirements:* For master's, GRE General Test, minimum GPA of 3.2, 9 hours of course work in journalism, course work in statistics. Additional exam requirements/recommendations for international students: Required—TOEFL (minimum score 600 paper-based; 250 computer-based), TWE (minimum score 5). *Application deadline:* For fall admission, 2/1 for domestic students, 4/1 for international students; for spring admission, 11/1 for domestic students, 9/1 for international students. Application fee: $40 ($90 for international students). Electronic applications accepted. *Expenses:* Tuition, state resident: full-time $3744; part-time $156 per credit hour. Tuition, nonresident: full-time $13,577; part-time $565.70 per credit hour. Required fees: $2415.40; $90.10 per credit hour. *Financial support:* In 2008–09, 25 students received support, including 2 fellowships (averaging $4,500 per year); career-related internships or fieldwork, scholarships/grants, health care benefits, and unspecified assistantships also available. *Faculty research:* Organizational management; rhetorical analysis; international public relations; digital production; normative theory. *Unit head:* Dr. Joe Foote, Dean, 405-325-2721, Fax: 405-325-7565, E-mail: jfoote@ou.edu. *Application contact:* Kelly Storm, Graduate Advisor, 405-325-2722, Fax: 405-325-7565, E-mail: kstorm@ou.edu.

University of Oregon, Graduate School, School of Journalism and Communication, Eugene, OR 97403. Offers MA, MS, PhD. *Accreditation:* ACEJMC (one or more programs are accredited); ASHA. Part-time programs available. *Degree requirements:* For master's, thesis or alternative. *Entrance requirements:* For master's, GRE General Test; for doctorate, master's degree. *Faculty research:* Impact of mass communication, media technology, media accountability, craft attitudes, media economics.

University of South Carolina, The Graduate School, College of Mass Communications and Information Studies, School of Journalism and Mass Communications, Columbia, SC 29208. Offers MA, MMC, PhD. *Accreditation:* ACEJMC (one or more programs are accredited). Part-time programs available. *Degree requirements:* For master's, comprehensive exam, thesis (for some programs); for doctorate, one foreign language, comprehensive exam, thesis/dissertation. *Entrance requirements:* For master's and doctorate, GRE General Test, minimum GPA of 3.0. Additional exam requirements/recommendations for international students: Required—TOEFL (minimum score 600 paper-based; 250 computer-based; 75 iBT). Electronic applications accepted. *Faculty research:* Ethics, communications law, international communications, science/health/environmental/risk communications, convergent media.

University of Southern California, Graduate School, Annenberg School for Communication, School of Journalism, Program in Broadcast Journalism, Los Angeles, CA 90089. Offers MA. *Degree requirements:* For master's, comprehensive exam. *Entrance requirements:* For master's, GRE General Test, resumé, writing samples, letters of recommendation, statement of purpose. Additional exam requirements/recommendations for international students: Required—TOEFL (minimum score 280 computer-based; 114 iBT). Electronic applications accepted.

See Close-Up on page 709.

University of Southern California, Graduate School, Annenberg School for Communication, School of Journalism, Program in Print Journalism, Los Angeles, CA 90089. Offers MA. *Degree requirements:* For master's, comprehensive exam. *Entrance requirements:* For master's, GRE General Test, resumé, writing samples, letters of recommendation. Additional exam requirements/recommendations for international students: Required—TOEFL (minimum score 280 computer-based; 114 iBT). Electronic applications accepted.

See Close-Up on page 709.

University of Southern California, Graduate School, Annenberg School for Communication, School of Journalism, Program in Specialized Journalism, Los Angeles, CA 90089. Offers MA. *Degree requirements:* For master's, thesis. *Entrance requirements:* For master's, GRE General Test, resumé, professional work samples, letters of recommendation, statement of purpose. Additional exam requirements/recommendations for international students: Required—TOEFL (minimum score 280 computer-based; 114 iBT). Electronic applications accepted.

See Close-Up on page 709.

The University of Tennessee, Graduate School, College of Communication and Information, Knoxville, TN 37996. Offers advertising (MS, PhD); broadcasting (MS, PhD); communications (MS, PhD); information sciences (MS, PhD); journalism (MS, PhD); public relations (MS, PhD); speech communication (MS, PhD). *Accreditation:* ACEJMC (one or more programs are accredited at the [master's] level). Part-time and evening/weekend programs available. Postbaccalaureate distance learning degree programs offered (no on-campus study). *Degree requirements:* For master's, thesis or alternative; for doctorate, thesis/dissertation. *Entrance requirements:* For master's and doctorate, GRE General Test, minimum GPA of 2.7. Additional exam requirements/recommendations for international students: Required—TOEFL. Electronic applications accepted. *Expenses:* Tuition, area resident: Part-time $348 per credit hour. Tuition, state resident: full-time $6262. Tuition, nonresident: full-time $18,920; part-time $1052 per credit hour. Required fees: $812; $36 per credit hour. Tuition and fees vary according to program.

The University of Texas at Austin, Graduate School, College of Communication, School of Journalism, Austin, TX 78712-1111. Offers MA, PhD. Part-time programs available. *Degree requirements:* For master's, thesis; for doctorate, one foreign language, thesis/dissertation. *Entrance requirements:* For master's and doctorate, GRE General Test. Electronic applications accepted. *Faculty research:* Politics of race, gender, and sexuality; visual ethics; media law and ethics; national television violence study; agenda setting and public opinion.

The University of Western Ontario, Faculty of Graduate Studies, Faculty of Information and Media Studies, Program in Journalism, London, ON N6A 5B8, Canada. Offers MA. *Degree requirements:* For master's, internship. *Entrance requirements:* For master's, honors degree, minimum B average during previous 2 years of course work. Additional exam requirements/recommendations for international students: Required—TOEFL (minimum score 640 paper-based; 273 computer-based), TWE (minimum score 5). Electronic applications accepted.

University of Wisconsin–Madison, Graduate School, College of Agricultural and Life Sciences, Department of Life Sciences Communication, Madison, WI 53706-1380. Offers life sciences communication (MPS, MS); mass communication (PhD). *Degree requirements:* For doctorate, thesis/dissertation.

University of Wisconsin–Madison, Graduate School, College of Letters and Science, School of Journalism and Mass Communication, Program in Journalism and Mass Communication, Madison, WI 53706-1380. Offers MA.

Virginia Commonwealth University, Graduate School, College of Humanities and Sciences, School of Mass Communications, Program in Mass Communications, Richmond, VA 23284-9005. Offers scholastic journalism (MS); strategic public relations (MS). *Degree requirements:* For master's, comprehensive exam, thesis optional. *Entrance requirements:* For master's, GRE General Test.

West Virginia University, Perley Isaac Reed School of Journalism, Morgantown, WV 26506. Offers integrated marketing communications (MS); journalism (MSJ). MS program taught exclusively online. Part-time programs available. Postbaccalaureate distance learning degree programs offered (no on-campus study). *Degree requirements:* For master's, thesis or alternative. *Entrance requirements:* For master's, GRE General Test, minimum GPA of 3.0, writing samples. Additional exam requirements/recommendations for international students: Required—TOEFL. Electronic applications accepted. *Faculty research:* History, law, and women in media; press management; public opinion; advertising effectiveness; international advertising.

Mass Communication

American University, School of Communication, Program in International Media, Washington, DC 20016-8001. Offers MA. *Students:* 4 full-time (all women), 1 (woman) part-time. *Degree requirements:* For master's, one foreign language, comprehensive exam. *Entrance requirements:* For master's, GRE, bachelor's degree with minimum cumulative GPA of 3.3, 2 letters of reference. Additional exam requirements/recommendations for international students: Required—TOEFL. *Application deadline:* For fall admission, 6/1 for domestic students. Applications are processed on a rolling basis. *Expenses:* Tuition: Full-time $21,204; part-time $1178 per credit hour. Required fees: $380. Part-time tuition and fees vary according to course load and program. *Unit head:* Prof. Larry Kirkman, Dean, 202-885-2058, Fax: 202-885-2099, E-mail: larry@american.edu. *Application contact:* Sharmeen Ahsan-Bracciale, Graduate Admissions Office, 202-885-2040, Fax: 202-885-2019, E-mail: sharmeen@american.edu.

American University, School of Communication, Program in Public Communication, Washington, DC 20016-8001. Offers MA. *Accreditation:* ACEJMC. Part-time and evening/weekend programs available. *Faculty:* 11 full-time (6 women), 6 part-time/adjunct (2 women). *Students:* 45 full-time (32 women), 13 part-time (12 women); includes 6 African Americans, 3 Asian Americans or Pacific Islanders, 2 Hispanic Americans, 5 international. 153 applicants, 68% accepted, 43 enrolled. In 2008, 61 master's awarded. *Degree requirements:* For master's, comprehensive exam, thesis or alternative. *Entrance requirements:* For master's, GRE General Test. Additional exam requirements/recommendations for international students: Required—TOEFL (minimum score 600 paper-based; 250 computer-based). *Application deadline:* For fall admission, 2/1 priority date for domestic students, 4/1 priority date for international students. Applications are processed on a rolling basis. Application fee: $50. Electronic applications accepted. *Expenses:* Tuition: Full-time $21,204; part-time $1178 per credit hour. Required fees: $380. Part-time tuition and fees vary according to course load and program. *Financial support:* In 2008–09, 10 research assistantships with partial tuition reimbursements (averaging $11,000 per year), 2 teaching assistantships with partial tuition reimbursements (averaging $11,000 per year) were awarded; career-related internships or fieldwork, Federal Work-Study, institutionally sponsored loans, scholarships/grants, and tuition waivers (partial) also available. Financial award application deadline: 2/1. *Faculty research:* Litigation and public relations, cross-cultural and intercultural communication, statistical public relations, African-Americans and women in public communication, international public relations. *Unit head:* Leonard Steinhorn, Director, Public Communication Division, 202-885-2031, E-mail: lsteinh@american.edu. *Application contact:* Sharmeen Ahsan-Bracciale, Graduate Admissions Office, 202-885-2040, Fax: 202-885-2019, E-mail: sharmeen@american.edu.

See Close-Up on page 681.

American University, School of Communication, Weekend Programs in Communication, Washington, DC 20016-8001. Offers interactive journalism (MA); news media studies (MA); producing for film and video (MA); public communication (MA). *Accreditation:* ACEJMC. Part-time and evening/weekend programs available. *Faculty:* 5 part-time/adjunct (2 women). *Students:* 112 part-time (75 women). 137 applicants, 61% accepted, 61 enrolled. In 2008, 15 master's awarded. *Degree requirements:* For master's, comprehensive exam, thesis or alternative. *Entrance requirements:* Additional exam requirements/recommendations for international students: Required—TOEFL (minimum score 600 paper-based; 250 computer-based). *Application deadline:* For fall admission, 8/1 for domestic students. Applications are processed on a rolling basis. Application fee: $50. Electronic applications accepted. *Expenses:* Tuition: Full-time $21,204; part-time $1178 per credit hour. Required fees: $380. Part-time tuition and fees vary according to course load and program. *Financial support:* In 2008–09, 3 fellowships (averaging $3,500 per year) were awarded; institutionally sponsored loans also available. *Unit head:* Wendell Cochran, Journalism Weekend Program Director, 202-885-2075, E-mail: cochran@american.edu. *Application contact:* Sharmeen Ahsan-Bracciale, Graduate Admissions Office, 202-885-2040, Fax: 202-885-2019, E-mail: sharmeen@american.edu.

See Close-Up on page 681.

American University, School of International Service, Washington, DC 20016-8071. Offers comparative and regional studies (Certificate); cross-cultural communication (Certificate); development management (MS); ethics, peace, and global affairs (MA); European studies (Certificate); global environmental policy (MA, Certificate); international affairs (MA), including comparative and regional studies, environmental policy, international economic policy, international politics, natural resources and sustainable development, U.S. foreign policy; international communication (MA, Certificate); international development (MA, Certificate); international development management (Certificate); international economic policy (Certificate); international economic relations (Certificate); international media (MA); international peace and conflict resolution (MA, Certificate); international relations (PhD); international service (MIS); peace building (Certificate); the Americas (Certificate); United States foreign policy (Certificate); JD/MA. Part-time and evening/weekend programs available. *Faculty:* 70 full-time

Mass Communication

American University (continued)
(28 women), 51 part-time/adjunct (20 women). *Students:* 519 full-time (317 women), 335 part-time (205 women); includes 157 minority (54 African Americans, 2 American Indian/Alaska Native, 45 Asian Americans or Pacific Islanders, 56 Hispanic Americans), 116 international. Average age 27. 1,901 applicants, 58% accepted, 277 enrolled. In 2008, 358 master's, 5 doctorates, 9 other advanced degrees awarded. Terminal master's awarded for partial completion of doctoral program. *Degree requirements:* For master's, one foreign language, comprehensive exam, thesis or alternative; for doctorate, one foreign language, comprehensive exam, thesis/dissertation, research practicum; for Certificate, minimum 15 credit hours related course work. *Entrance requirements:* For master's, GRE, 24 credits of course work in related social sciences, minimum GPA of 3.5, 2 letters of recommendation, bachelor's degree, resumé, statement of purpose; for doctorate, GRE, 2 letters of recommendation, 24 credits in related social sciences; for Certificate, bachelor's degree. Additional exam requirements/recommendations for international students: Required—TOEFL (minimum score 600 paper-based; 250 computer-based; 100 iBT). *Application deadline:* For fall admission, 1/15 priority date for domestic students; for spring admission, 10/1 priority date for domestic students. Applications are processed on a rolling basis. Application fee: $50. *Expenses:* Tuition: Full-time $21,204; part-time $1178 per credit hour. Required fees: $380. Part-time tuition and fees vary according to course load and program. *Financial support:* Career-related internships or fieldwork, Federal Work-Study, and institutionally sponsored loans available. Financial award application deadline: 1/15. *Faculty research:* International intellectual property, international environmental issues, international law and legal order, international telecommunications/technology, international sustainable development. *Unit head:* Dr. Louis W. Goodman, Dean, 202-885-1600, Fax: 202-885-2494. *Application contact:* Yasmin Quianzon, Director of Graduate Admissions and Financial Aid, 202-885-2496, Fax: 202-885-1109.

See Close-Up on page 861.

The American University in Cairo, Graduate Studies and Research, School of Business, Economics and Communication, Department of Journalism and Mass Communication, Cairo, Egypt. Offers journalism and mass communication (MA); television and digital journalism (MA). Part-time programs available. *Degree requirements:* For master's, thesis (for some programs). *Entrance requirements:* For master's, English entrance exam, GMAT. Electronic applications accepted. *Faculty research:* Mass media and national development/censorship, intercultural photo communication, comparative journalism/television.

Arizona State University at the Downtown Phoenix Campus, Walter Cronkite School of Journalism and Mass Communication, Phoenix, AZ 85004. Offers MMC. *Accreditation:* ACEJMC. *Degree requirements:* For master's, 36 credit hours (includes class work and a professional immersion experience). *Entrance requirements:* For master's, GRE, minimum GPA of 3.0 in the last 60 semester hours or 90 quarter hours of undergraduate coursework; official transcripts; resumé and/or biographical sketch; 350- to 500-word personal statement; 3 letters of recommendation. Additional exam requirements/recommendations for international students: Required—TOEFL. Electronic applications accepted.

Auburn University, Graduate School, College of Liberal Arts, Department of Communication and Journalism, Auburn University, AL 36849. Offers communication (MA); mass communications (MA). Part-time programs available. *Faculty:* 25 full-time (13 women), 7 part-time/adjunct (3 women). *Students:* 19 full-time (11 women), 7 part-time (5 women); includes 3 minority (all African Americans), 2 international. Average age 28. 23 applicants, 65% accepted, 10 enrolled. In 2008, 4 master's awarded. *Degree requirements:* For master's, thesis (for some programs). *Entrance requirements:* For master's, GRE General Test. *Application deadline:* For fall admission, 7/7 for domestic students; for spring admission, 11/24 for domestic students. Applications are processed on a rolling basis. Application fee: $25 ($50 for international students). Electronic applications accepted. *Expenses:* Tuition, area resident: Full-time $5880; part-time $243 per credit hour. Tuition, state resident: full-time $5880; part-time $243 per credit hour. Tuition, nonresident: full-time $17,640; part-time $729 per credit hour. International tuition: $17,846 full-time. Required fees: $620. Tuition and fees vary according to program and reciprocity agreements. *Financial support:* Teaching assistantships, Federal Work-Study available. Support available to part-time students. Financial award application deadline: 3/15. *Unit head:* Dr. Mary Helen Brown, Acting Chair, 334-844-2727. *Application contact:* Dr. George Flowers, Dean of the Graduate School, 334-844-2125.

Boston University, College of Communication, Department of Mass Communication, Advertising, and Public Relations, Boston, MA 02215. Offers advertising (MS); communication research (MS); communication studies (MS); public relations (MS); JD/MS. *Degree requirements:* For master's, thesis. *Entrance requirements:* For master's, GRE General Test, samples of written work. Additional exam requirements/recommendations for international students: Required—TOEFL. Electronic applications accepted.

See Close-Up on page 683.

Brigham Young University, Graduate Studies, College of Fine Arts and Communications, Department of Communications, Provo, UT 84602. Offers mass communications (MA). *Faculty:* 17 full-time (3 women). *Students:* 7 full-time (6 women), 36 part-time (20 women); includes 5 minority (1 African American, 1 American Indian/Alaska Native, 3 Hispanic Americans). Average age 29. 33 applicants, 52% accepted, 9 enrolled. In 2008, 10 master's awarded. *Degree requirements:* For master's, comprehensive exam, thesis. *Entrance requirements:* For master's, GRE, minimum GPA of 3.0 in last 60 hours of course work. Additional exam requirements/recommendations for international students: Required—TOEFL (minimum score 580 paper-based; 237 computer-based; 85 iBT). *Application deadline:* For fall admission, 2/28 for domestic and international students. Application fee: $50. Electronic applications accepted. *Expenses:* Tuition: Full-time $5160; part-time $287 per credit hour. Tuition and fees vary according to program and student's religious affiliation. *Financial support:* In 2008–09, 22 students received support, including 25 research assistantships with full and partial tuition reimbursements available (averaging $4,307 per year), 10 teaching assistantships with full and partial tuition reimbursements available (averaging $4,657 per year); career-related internships or fieldwork, institutionally sponsored loans, scholarships/grants, unspecified assistantships, and supplementary awards also available. Financial award application deadline: 5/15; financial award applicants required to submit FAFSA. *Faculty research:* Ethics, international, magazine, newspaper, media effects. *Unit head:* Dr. Bradley L. Rawlins, Chair, 801-422-2997, Fax: 801-422-0160, E-mail: comms_secretary@byu.edu. *Application contact:* Dr. Steven R. Thomsen, Graduate Coordinator, 801-422-2078, Fax: 801-422-0160, E-mail: steven_thomsen@byu.edu.

California State University, Fresno, Division of Graduate Studies, College of Arts and Humanities, Department of Mass Communication and Journalism, Fresno, CA 93740-8027. Offers MA. Part-time and evening/weekend programs available. *Degree requirements:* For master's, thesis. *Entrance requirements:* For master's, GRE General Test, minimum GPA of 3.0. Additional exam requirements/recommendations for international students: Required—TOEFL. Electronic applications accepted.

California State University, Northridge, Graduate Studies, College of Arts, Media, and Communication, Department of Journalism, Northridge, CA 91330. Offers mass communication (MA). Part-time and evening/weekend programs available. *Faculty:* 13 full-time (7 women), 14 part-time/adjunct (4 women). *Students:* 11 full-time (8 women), 30 part-time (26 women); includes 14 minority (3 African Americans, 3 Asian Americans or Pacific Islanders, 8 Hispanic Americans), 3 international. Average age 30. 55 applicants, 49% accepted, 18 enrolled. In 2008, 13 master's awarded. *Degree requirements:* For master's, thesis. *Entrance requirements:* For master's, GRE General Test. Additional exam requirements/recommendations for international students: Required—TOEFL. *Application deadline:* For fall admission, 11/30 for domestic students. Application fee: $55. *Financial support:* Career-related internships or fieldwork and Federal Work-Study available. Financial award application deadline: 3/1. *Unit head:* Dr. Kent Kirkton, Chair, 818-677-3135, E-mail: kent.kirkton@csun.edu. *Application contact:* Dr. Kent Kirkton, Chair, 818-677-3135, E-mail: kent.kirkton@csun.edu.

Central Michigan University, College of Graduate Studies, College of Communication and Fine Arts, Department of Communication and Dramatic Arts, Concentration in Interpersonal and Public Communication, Mount Pleasant, MI 48859. Offers MA. Part-time programs available. *Faculty:* 14 full-time (8 women). *Students:* 19 full-time (14 women), 22 part-time (18 women); includes 2 African Americans, 1 American Indian/Alaska Native, 1 international. Average age 28. *Degree requirements:* For master's, thesis. *Entrance requirements:* For master's, minimum GPA of 3.0 in last 60 hours of undergraduate study and in last 15 hours of communication courses or other courses approved by department. *Application deadline:* For fall admission, 3/15 for domestic and international students; for winter admission, 10/15 for domestic and international students; for spring admission, 10/15 for domestic and international students. Application fee: $35 ($45 for international students). Electronic applications accepted. *Expenses:* Tuition, state resident: full-time $3717; part-time $413 per credit. Tuition, nonresident: full-time $6894; part-time $766 per credit. *Financial support:* Fellowships with tuition reimbursements, teaching assistantships with tuition reimbursements, career-related internships or fieldwork, Federal Work-Study, unspecified assistantships, and out-of-state merit awards available. *Faculty research:* Communication theory, interpersonal/nonverbal communication, organizational communication, family and interpersonal communication, political communication. *Unit head:* Dr. Neil Vanderpool, Chairperson, 989-774-3177, Fax: 989-774-2498, E-mail: vande2nj@cmich.edu. *Application contact:* Dr. Lesley Withers, Graduate Program Coordinator, 989-774-6673, Fax: 989-774-2498, E-mail: withe1la@cmich.edu.

The College of Saint Rose, Graduate Studies, School of Arts and Humanities, Department of Public Communications, Albany, NY 12203-1419. Offers MA. Part-time and evening/weekend programs available. *Degree requirements:* For master's, final project or thesis. *Entrance requirements:* For master's, minimum undergraduate GPA of 3.0, 2 writing samples. Additional exam requirements/recommendations for international students: Required—TOEFL (minimum score 550 paper-based; 213 computer-based). Electronic applications accepted.

Colorado State University, Graduate School, College of Liberal Arts, Department of Journalism and Technical Communication, Fort Collins, CO 80523-1785. Offers public communication and technology (MS, PhD); technical communication (MS). Part-time programs available. *Faculty:* 19 full-time (8 women). *Students:* 30 full-time (20 women), 32 part-time (25 women); includes 7 minority (1 American Indian/Alaska Native, 2 Asian Americans or Pacific Islanders, 4 Hispanic Americans), 7 international. Average age 34. 56 applicants, 68% accepted, 23 enrolled. In 2008, 13 master's awarded. *Degree requirements:* For master's, variable foreign language requirement, comprehensive exam (for some programs), thesis (for some programs); for doctorate, variable foreign language requirement, comprehensive exam (for some programs), thesis/dissertation (for some programs). *Entrance requirements:* For master's, GRE General Test, samples of written work, letters of recommendation, resumé or curriculum vitae, 3 writing/communication projects, bachelor's degree, statement of career plans; for doctorate, GRE General Test, master's degree, minimum GPA of 3.0, scholarly/professional work, letters of recommendation, statement of career plans, resumé. Additional exam requirements/recommendations for international students: Required—TOEFL (minimum score 600 paper-based; 250 computer-based). *Application deadline:* For fall admission, 2/15 priority date for domestic students, 12/15 priority date for international students; for spring admission, 6/15 priority date for domestic students. Applications are processed on a rolling basis. Application fee: $50. Electronic applications accepted. *Expenses:* Tuition, area resident: Full-time $5620; part-time $312.25 per credit. Tuition, state resident: full-time $5620; part-time $312.25 per credit. Tuition, nonresident: full-time $17,253; part-time $958.50 per credit. Required fees: $1449.56; $82.35 per credit. *Financial support:* In 2008–09, 18 students received support, including 18 teaching assistantships with partial tuition reimbursements available (averaging $7,912 per year); fellowships with partial tuition reimbursements available, research assistantships with full and partial tuition reimbursements available, career-related internships or fieldwork, Federal Work-Study, institutionally sponsored loans, scholarships/grants, traineeships, and unspecified assistantships also available. Support available to part-time students. Financial award application deadline: 3/1; financial award applicants required to submit FAFSA. *Faculty research:* Technical/science communication, public relations, health/risk communication, web/new media technologies, environmental communication. Total annual research expenditures: $314,040. *Unit head:* Dr. Greg Luft, Chair, 970-491-1979, Fax: 970-491-2908, E-mail: greg.luft@colostate.edu. *Application contact:* Craig Trumbo, Graduate Program Coordinator, 970-491-2077, Fax: 970-491-2908, E-mail: craig.trumbo@colostate.edu.

Drexel University, College of Arts and Sciences, Department of Culture and Communication, Program in Communication, Philadelphia, PA 19104-2875. Offers public communication (MS); science communication (MS); technical communication (MS). Part-time and evening/weekend programs available. *Degree requirements:* For master's, internship, professional portfolio. *Entrance requirements:* For master's, GRE or minimum GPA of 3.0. Additional exam requirements/recommendations for international students: Required—TOEFL. Electronic applications accepted.

Florida International University, School of Journalism and Mass Communication, Miami, FL 33199. Offers mass communication (MS). *Accreditation:* ACEJMC. Part-time and evening/weekend programs available. *Degree requirements:* For master's, thesis optional. *Entrance requirements:* For master's, minimum GPA of 3.0, essay, resumé. Additional exam requirements/recommendations for international students: Required—TOEFL. *Faculty research:* Post-Hurricane Andrew population studies, Central American journalism, employment discrimination.

Florida State University, Graduate Studies, College of Communication, Department of Communication, Tallahassee, FL 32306. Offers corporate and public communication (MA, MS); integrated marketing communication (MA, MS); mass communication (PhD); media and communication studies (MA, MS); speech communication (PhD). Part-time programs available. *Degree requirements:* For master's, thesis (for some programs); for doctorate, comprehensive exam, thesis/dissertation. *Entrance requirements:* For master's, GRE General Test, minimum GPA of 3.0; for doctorate, GRE General Test, minimum GPA of 3.3 in graduate course work. Additional exam requirements/recommendations for international students: Required—TOEFL (minimum score 600 paper-based; 250 computer-based; 100 iBT). *Faculty research:* Communication technology and policy, marketing communication, communication content and effect, new communication/information technologies.

Fordham University, Graduate School of Arts and Sciences, Department of Communication and Media Studies, New York, NY 10458. Offers public communications (MA). Part-time and evening/weekend programs available. *Degree requirements:* For master's, thesis, internship. *Entrance requirements:* For master's, GRE General Test. Additional exam requirements/recommendations for international students: Required—TOEFL (minimum score 600 paper-based; 250 computer-based). Electronic applications accepted.

The George Washington University, Columbian College of Arts and Sciences, School of Media and Public Affairs, Washington, DC 20052. Offers MA. *Faculty:* 24 full-time (7 women), 13 part-time/adjunct (2 women). *Students:* 12 full-time (8 women), 3 part-time (2 women); includes 2 minority (1 Asian American or Pacific Islander, 1 Hispanic American), 1 international. Average age 26. 94 applicants, 27% accepted, 9 enrolled. In 2008, 12 master's awarded. *Degree requirements:* For master's, thesis optional. *Entrance requirements:* For master's, GRE General Test. Additional exam requirements/recommendations for international students: Required—TOEFL (minimum score 550 paper-based; 213 computer-based; 80 iBT). *Application deadline:* For fall admission, 4/1 priority date for domestic students, 1/15 priority date for international students; for spring admission, 10/1 priority date for domestic students, 9/1 priority date for international students. Applications are processed on a rolling basis. Application fee: $60. Electronic applications accepted. *Financial support:* In 2008–09, fellowships with tuition reimbursements (averaging $10,000 per year), teaching assistantships with tuition reimbursements (averaging $5,000 per year) were awarded. Financial award application deadline: 1/15. *Unit head:* Lee W. Huebner, Director, 202-994-6227, E-mail: huebner@gwu.edu. *Application contact:* Information Contact, 202-994-6227, Fax: 202-994-5806, E-mail: smpa@gwu.edu.

Georgia State University, College of Arts and Sciences, Department of Communication, Atlanta, GA 30303-3083. Offers film/video/digital imaging (MA); human communication and social influence (MA); mass communication (MA); moving image studies (PhD); public communication (PhD). Part-time programs available. *Degree requirements:* For master's, one foreign language, thesis or alternative; for doctorate, comprehensive exam, thesis/dissertation. *Entrance requirements:* For master's and doctorate, GRE General Test. Additional exam requirements/recommendations for international students: Required—TOEFL (minimum score 80 computer-based). Electronic applications accepted. *Faculty research:* Critical/cultural studies, rhetoric studies, film/media studies, mass communications/journalism, audience studies.

Grambling State University, School of Graduate Studies and Research, College of Professional Studies, Program in Mass Communication, Grambling, LA 71245. Offers MA. *Accreditation:* ACEJMC. Part-time programs available. *Faculty:* 6 full-time (2 women). *Students:* 9 full-time (6 women), 3 part-time (2 women); includes 11 minority (10 African Americans, 1 Hispanic American), 1 international. Average age 29. In 2008, 7 master's awarded. *Degree requirements:* For master's, comprehensive exam, thesis optional. *Entrance requirements:* For master's, GRE, minimum GPA of 2.5 on last degree. Additional exam requirements/recommendations for international students: Required—TOEFL (minimum score 500 paper-based; 173 computer-based; 61 iBT). *Application deadline:* For fall admission, 7/1 for domestic and international students; for spring admission, 12/1 for domestic and international students. Applications are processed on a rolling basis. Application fee: $20 ($30 for international students). Electronic applications accepted. *Expenses:* Tuition, area resident: Full-time $3637; part-time $134 per credit hour. Tuition, nonresident: full-time $7651; part-time $134 per credit hour. Required fees: $1225; $134 per credit hour. $430 per semester. *Financial support:* In 2008–09, 1 research assistantship (averaging $6,500 per year) was awarded; career-related internships or fieldwork, health care benefits, tuition waivers (full and partial), and unspecified assistantships also available. Financial award application deadline: 5/31; financial award applicants required to submit FAFSA. *Unit head:* Dr. Martin Adu, Acting Department Head, 318-274-2189, Fax: 318-274-3194, E-mail: edum@gram.edu. *Application contact:* Katina Crowe, Special Assistant to Associate Vice President/Dean, 318-274-2158, Fax: 318-274-7373, E-mail: croweks@gram.edu.

Howard University, School of Communications, Division of Mass Communication and Media Studies, Washington, DC 20059-0002. Offers mass communication (MA, PhD); media studies (MA, PhD). Part-time and evening/weekend programs available. *Degree requirements:* For master's, comprehensive exam (for some programs), thesis optional; for doctorate, one foreign language, comprehensive exam, thesis/dissertation. *Entrance requirements:* For master's, GRE, minimum GPA of 3.0; for doctorate, GRE, minimum graduate GPA of 3.5. Additional exam requirements/recommendations for international students: Required—TOEFL. Electronic applications accepted. *Faculty research:* Advertising, public relations, journalism new media.

Indiana University Bloomington, School of Journalism, Bloomington, IN 47405-7000. Offers journalism (MA, MAT); mass communication (PhD); MA/JD; MA/MA. *Faculty:* 11 full-time (5 women). *Students:* 61 full-time (32 women), 15 part-time (8 women); includes 6 minority (2 African Americans, 3 Asian Americans or Pacific Islanders, 1 Hispanic American), 23 international. Average age 30. 132 applicants, 73% accepted, 45 enrolled. In 2008, 20 master's, 5 doctorates awarded. Terminal master's awarded for partial completion of doctoral program. *Degree requirements:* For master's, thesis (for some programs); for doctorate, thesis/dissertation. *Entrance requirements:* For master's and doctorate, GRE General Test. Additional exam requirements/recommendations for international students: Required—TOEFL. *Application deadline:* For fall admission, 1/15 priority date for domestic students; for spring admission, 9/1 priority date for domestic students. Applications are processed on a rolling basis. Application fee: $50 ($60 for international students). *Expenses:* Tuition, area resident: Part-time $291.97 per credit hour. Tuition, state resident: part-time $291.97 per credit hour. Tuition, nonresident: part-time $850.33 per credit hour. Required fees: $110 per semester. Tuition and fees vary according to course load and program. *Financial support:* Fellowships, research assistantships with full tuition reimbursements, teaching assistantships with partial tuition reimbursements, career-related internships or fieldwork, Federal Work-Study, institutionally sponsored loans, and tuition waivers (full) available. Financial award application deadline: 1/15. *Faculty research:* Political communication, international communication, communication history, communication law, visual communication. Total annual research expenditures: $165,185. *Unit head:* Bradley Hamm, Dean, 812-855-9247. *Application contact:* Amy Reynolds, Associate Dean of Graduate Studies, 812-855-8111.

Indiana University Bloomington, University Graduate School, College of Arts and Sciences, Department of Telecommunications, Program in Mass Communications, Bloomington, IN 47405-7000. Offers PhD. *Faculty:* 18 full-time (5 women). *Students:* 35 full-time (17 women); includes 1 minority (African American), 26 international. Average age 35. 23 applicants, 26% accepted, 4 enrolled. In 2008, 8 doctorates awarded. *Degree requirements:* For doctorate, comprehensive exam, thesis/dissertation. *Entrance requirements:* For doctorate, GRE General Test, minimum graduate GPA of 3.5, 3 letters of recommendation. Additional exam requirements/recommendations for international students: Required—TOEFL (minimum score 600 paper-based; 250 computer-based; 100 iBT). *Application deadline:* For fall admission, 1/15 priority date for domestic students, 12/15 priority date for international students. Applications are processed on a rolling basis. Application fee: $50 ($60 for international students). Electronic applications accepted. *Expenses:* Tuition, area resident: Part-time $291.97 per credit hour. Tuition, state resident: part-time $291.97 per credit hour. Tuition, nonresident: part-time $850.33 per credit hour. Required fees: $110 per semester. Tuition and fees vary according to course load and program. *Financial support:* In 2008–09, 14 students received support, including 5 research assistantships with full tuition reimbursements available (averaging $11,869 per year), 9 teaching assistantships with full tuition reimbursements available (averaging $11,869 per year); scholarships/grants and health care benefits also available. Financial award application deadline: 1/15. *Faculty research:* Media management, media psychology, telecommunications law and policy, media processes and effects, media design and production (e.g., video games, virtual worlds, documentary, multi-media art). Total annual research expenditures: $152,000. *Unit head:* Tamera Theodore, Graduate Program Administrator, 812-855-2017, Fax: 812-855-7955, E-mail: ttheodor@indiana.edu. *Application contact:* Tamera Theodore, Graduate Program Administrator, 812-855-2017, Fax: 812-855-7955, E-mail: ttheodor@indiana.edu.

Iona College, School of Arts and Science, Department of Mass Communication, New Rochelle, NY 10801-1890. Offers journalism (MS); public relations (MA). *Accreditation:* ACEJMC (one or more programs are accredited). Part-time and evening/weekend programs available. *Faculty:* 6 full-time (1 woman), 7 part-time/adjunct (3 women). *Students:* 6 full-time (all women), 32 part-time (25 women); includes 5 minority (2 African Americans, 3 Hispanic Americans), 2 international. Average age 28. 37 applicants, 35% accepted, 10 enrolled. In 2008, 12 master's awarded. *Degree requirements:* For master's, comprehensive exam or thesis. *Entrance requirements:* For master's, GRE General Test, minimum GPA of 3.0. Additional exam requirements/recommendations for international students: Required—TOEFL (minimum score 550 paper-based; 213 computer-based). *Application deadline:* Applications are processed on a rolling basis. Application fee: $50. Electronic applications accepted. *Expenses:* Contact institution. *Financial support:* Career-related internships or fieldwork, tuition waivers (partial), and unspecified assistantships available. Support available to part-time students. Financial award application deadline: 4/15; financial award applicants required to submit FAFSA. *Faculty research:* Media ecology, new media, corporate communication, media images, organizational learning in public relations. *Unit head:* Br. Raymond Smith, Chair, 914-633-2354, E-mail: rrsmith@iona.edu. *Application contact:* Veronica Jarek-Prinz, Director of Graduate Admissions, 914-633-2420, Fax: 914-633-2277, E-mail: vjarekprinz@iona.edu.

Iowa State University of Science and Technology, Graduate College, College of Liberal Arts and Sciences, Greenlee School of Journalism and Mass Communication, Ames, IA 50011. Offers MS. *Faculty:* 19 full-time (5 women). *Students:* 22 full-time (15 women), 21 part-time (14 women); includes 5 minority (1 African American, 1 Asian American or Pacific Islander, 3 Hispanic Americans), 20 international. 41 applicants, 66% accepted, 17 enrolled. In 2008, 9 master's awarded. *Degree requirements:* For master's, thesis or alternative. *Entrance requirements:* For master's, GRE General Test. Additional exam requirements/recommendations for international students: Required—TOEFL (minimum score 570 paper-based; 88 iBT), IELTS (6.5) or TOEFL. *Application deadline:* For fall admission, 4/1 priority date for domestic and international students; for spring admission, 11/1 priority date for domestic and international students. Applications are processed on a rolling basis. Application fee: $30 ($70 for international students). Electronic applications accepted. *Expenses:* Tuition, area resident: Full-time $6446; part-time $359 per credit. Tuition, state resident: full-time $6446; part-time $359 per credit. Tuition, nonresident: full-time $17,330; part-time $963 per credit. Required fees: $790; $249.25 per semester. Tuition and fees vary according to course load and program. *Financial support:* In 2008–09, 17 research assistantships with full and partial tuition reimbursements (averaging $12,150 per year), 1 teaching assistantship with partial tuition reimbursement (averaging $12,150 per year) were awarded; fellowships, scholarships/grants, health care benefits, and unspecified assistantships also available. *Unit head:* Dr. Michael Bugeja, Chair, 515-294-0481, Fax: 515-294-5108, E-mail: greenlee@iastate.edu. *Application contact:* Dr. Eric Abbott, Director of Graduate Education, 515-294-0492, E-mail: masscomm@iastate.edu.

Jackson State University, Graduate School, School of Liberal Arts, Department of Mass Communications, Jackson, MS 39217. Offers MS. Part-time and evening/weekend programs available. *Degree requirements:* For master's, comprehensive exam, thesis optional. *Entrance requirements:* For master's, GRE General Test. Additional exam requirements/recommendations for international students: Required—TOEFL.

Kansas State University, Graduate School, College of Arts and Sciences, A. Q. Miller School of Journalism and Mass Communications, Manhattan, KS 66506. Offers mass communications (MS). Part-time programs available. *Faculty:* 13 full-time (5 women). *Students:* 14 full-time (11 women), 5 part-time (4 women); includes 2 minority (both African Americans), 8 international. Average age 28. 16 applicants, 94% accepted, 9 enrolled. In 2008, 9 master's awarded. *Degree requirements:* For master's, thesis or alternative. *Entrance requirements:* For master's, GRE General Test, minimum GPA of 3.0. Additional exam requirements/recommendations for international students: Required—TOEFL (minimum score 600 paper-based). *Application deadline:* For fall admission, 2/1 priority date for domestic students; for spring admission, 7/1 priority date for domestic students. Applications are processed on a rolling basis. Application fee: $30 ($55 for international students). Electronic applications accepted. *Expenses:* Tuition, area resident: Full-time $6466; part-time $269.40 per credit hour. Tuition, state resident: full-time $6466; part-time $269.40 per credit hour. Tuition, nonresident: full-time $14,874; part-time $619.75 per credit hour. Required fees: $673; $23.40 per credit hour. Tuition and fees vary according to campus/location. *Financial support:* In 2008–09, 1 research assistantship (averaging $13,205 per year), 9 teaching assistantships with full tuition reimbursements (averaging $7,730 per year) were awarded; career-related internships or fieldwork, institutionally sponsored loans, and scholarships/grants also available. Support available to part-time students. Financial award application deadline: 3/10; financial award applicants required to submit FAFSA. *Faculty research:* Synergistic effects of integrated marketing communications; risk and hazard communication; leadership in media coverage; political communication; advertising psycholinguistic effects. Total annual research expenditures: $131,644. *Unit head:* Angela Powers, Head, 785-532-3955, Fax: 785-532-5484, E-mail: apowers@ksu.edu. *Application contact:* Hyun-Seung Jin, Director, 785-532-3959, Fax: 785-532-5484, E-mail: hsjin@ksu.edu.

Kent State University, College of Communication and Information, School of Journalism and Mass Communication, Kent, OH 44242-0001. Offers MA. Part-time programs available. *Degree requirements:* For master's, thesis optional. *Entrance requirements:* For master's, GRE General Test, minimum GPA of 3.0. Additional exam requirements/recommendations for international students: Recommended—TOEFL (minimum score 600 paper-based; 250 computer-based). Electronic applications accepted. *Faculty research:* Electronic tablet newspapers, accuracy and ethics in broadcast news, internet credibility, First Amendment, HDTV.

Louisiana State University and Agricultural and Mechanical College, Graduate School, Manship School of Mass Communication, Baton Rouge, LA 70803. Offers MMC, PhD. *Accreditation:* ACEJMC. Part-time programs available. Postbaccalaureate distance learning degree programs offered (minimal on-campus study). *Degree requirements:* For master's, thesis. *Entrance requirements:* For master's, GRE General Test, minimum GPA of 3.0. Additional exam requirements/recommendations for international students: Required—TOEFL (minimum score 550 paper-based; 213 computer-based; 79 iBT). Electronic applications accepted. *Faculty research:* Media effects, political communication, new media technologies, persuasive communication, journalism processes and practice.

Lynn University, College of Business and Management, Boca Raton, FL 33431-5598. Offers aviation management (MBA); financial valuation and investment management (MBA); global leadership (PhD); hospitality management (MBA); international business (MBA); marketing (MBA); mass communication and media management (MBA); sports and athletics administration (MBA). Part-time and evening/weekend programs available. Postbaccalaureate distance learning degree programs offered. *Degree requirements:* For master's, project; for doctorate, thesis/dissertation, qualifying paper. *Entrance requirements:* For master's, GMAT or GRE, minimum undergraduate GPA of 3.0, resumé, 2 letters of recommendation; for doctorate, GRE or GMAT, minimum graduate GPA of 3.25, resumé, 2 letters of recommendation. Additional exam requirements/recommendations for international students: Required—TOEFL (minimum score 550 paper-based; 213 computer-based). Electronic applications accepted. *Faculty research:* Labor relations, dynamic balance in leisure-time skills, ethics in athletics, hotel development.

Lynn University, Eugene M. and Christine E. Lynn College of International Communication, Boca Raton, FL 33431-5598. Offers mass communication (MS). Part-time and evening/weekend programs available. *Entrance requirements:* For master's, GRE, resumé, 2 letters of recommendation, minimum GPA of 3.0. Additional exam requirements/recommendations for international students: Required—TOEFL (minimum score 550 paper-based; 213 computer-based).

Marquette University, Graduate School, College of Communication, Milwaukee, WI 53201-1881. Offers advertising and public relations (MA); broadcasting and electronic communications (MA); communications studies (MA); journalism (MA); mass communications (MA); religious communications (MA); science, health and environmental communications (MA). *Accreditation:* ACEJMC. Part-time and evening/weekend programs available. *Degree requirements:* For master's, comprehensive exam. *Entrance requirements:* For master's, GRE. Additional exam requirements/recommendations for international students: Required—TOEFL. *Faculty research:* Urban journalism, gender and communication, intercultural communication, religious communication.

Marshall University, Academic Affairs Division, School of Journalism and Mass Communications, Huntington, WV 25755. Offers MAJ. *Accreditation:* ACEJMC. *Degree requirements:* For master's, thesis optional. *Entrance requirements:* For master's, GRE General Test.

Miami University, Graduate School, College of Arts and Sciences, Department of Communication, Program in Mass Communication, Oxford, OH 45056. Offers MA. Part-time programs available. *Degree requirements:* For master's, final exam. *Entrance requirements:* For master's, minimum undergraduate GPA of 3.0 during previous 2 years or 2.75 overall. Additional exam requirements/recommendations for international students: Required—TOEFL (minimum score 550 paper-based; 213 computer-based), TWE (minimum score 4). Electronic applications accepted.

Middle Tennessee State University, College of Graduate Studies, College of Mass Communication, Studies in Mass Communication, Murfreesboro, TN 37132. Offers MS. Part-time and evening/weekend programs available. Postbaccalaureate distance learning degree programs offered. *Degree requirements:* For master's, comprehensive exam, thesis optional. *Entrance requirements:* For master's, GRE. Additional exam requirements/recommendations for inter-

Mass Communication

Middle Tennessee State University (continued)
national students: Required—TOEFL (paper-based 525; computer-based 195; IBT 71) or IELTS (6.0). *Faculty research:* Ethics of digital media, communication administration, international media issues.

Murray State University, College of Business and Public Affairs, Program in Mass Communications, Murray, KY 42071. Offers MA, MS. Part-time programs available. *Entrance requirements:* Additional exam requirements/recommendations for international students: Required—TOEFL (minimum score 550 paper-based; 213 computer-based). *Faculty research:* AH media on the Internet, visual communication and learning, persuasion, media framing, history of radio and wireless technology.

The New School: A University, The New School for General Studies, Program in International Affairs, New York, NY 10011. Offers global management, trade, and finance (MA, MS); international development (MA, MS); international media and communication (MA, MS); international politics and diplomacy (MA, MS); service, civic, and non-profit management (MS). Part-time programs available. *Faculty:* 10 full-time (6 women), 26 part-time/adjunct (11 women). *Students:* 198 full-time (142 women), 147 part-time (92 women); includes 77 minority (25 African Americans, 19 Asian Americans or Pacific Islanders, 33 Hispanic Americans), 63 international. Average age 30. In 2008, 86 master's awarded. *Entrance requirements:* Additional exam requirements/recommendations for international students: Required—TOEFL (minimum score 600 paper-based; 250 computer-based; 100 iBT). *Application deadline:* For fall admission, 4/15 for domestic students; for spring admission, 10/15 for domestic students. Application fee: $50. *Expenses:* Tuition: Full-time $27,144; part-time $1508 per credit. Required fees: $355 per semester. *Financial support:* Fellowships with partial tuition reimbursements, research assistantships, teaching assistantships with partial tuition reimbursements, career-related internships or fieldwork, Federal Work-Study, scholarships/grants, tuition waivers (partial), and unspecified assistantships available. Support available to part-time students. Financial award application deadline: 3/1; financial award applicants required to submit FAFSA. *Unit head:* Dr. Michael Cohen, Director, 212-206-3524, Fax: 212-645-0661, E-mail: cohenm2@newschool.edu. *Application contact:* David Norris, Director of Admissions, 212-229-5630, Fax: 212-989-3887, E-mail: nsadmissions@newschool.edu.

See Close-Up on page 873.

North Dakota State University, College of Graduate and Interdisciplinary Studies, College of Arts, Humanities and Social Sciences, Department of Communication, Fargo, ND 58105. Offers communication (PhD); mass communication (MA, MS); speech communication (MA, MS). Part-time programs available. Postbaccalaureate distance learning degree programs offered (no on-campus study). *Faculty:* 11 full-time (5 women), 3 part-time/adjunct (1 woman). *Students:* 38 full-time (25 women), 23 part-time (17 women); includes 4 minority (1 African American, 2 Asian Americans or Pacific Islanders, 1 Hispanic American), 3 international. Average age 27. 62 applicants, 40% accepted, 19 enrolled. In 2008, 15 master's, 8 doctorates awarded. Terminal master's awarded for partial completion of doctoral program. *Degree requirements:* For master's, thesis (for some programs); for doctorate, comprehensive exam, thesis/dissertation, 2-3 publications referred before comps. *Entrance requirements:* For master's, GRE, minimum undergraduate GPA of 3.25; for doctorate, GRE, minimum undergraduate GPA of 3.5. Additional exam requirements/recommendations for international students: Required—TOEFL (minimum score 600 paper-based; 250 computer-based; 100 iBT), IELTS (minimum score 7). *Application deadline:* For fall admission, 2/15 priority date for domestic students; for winter admission, 10/15 priority date for domestic students. Applications are processed on a rolling basis. Application fee: $45 ($60 for international students). Electronic applications accepted. *Financial support:* In 2008–09, 38 students received support, including 1 fellowship with full tuition reimbursement available (averaging $16,000 per year), 10 research assistantships with full tuition reimbursements available (averaging $12,000 per year), 10 teaching assistantships with full tuition reimbursements available (averaging $8,100 per year); career-related internships or fieldwork, Federal Work-Study, institutionally sponsored loans, tuition waivers (full), and unspecified assistantships also available. Financial award application deadline: 2/1. *Faculty research:* Communication and rhetorical theory, organizational communication, broadcast and print journalism, international communication, public relations and advertising. Total annual research expenditures: $148,496. *Unit head:* Dr. Paul E. Nelson, Chair, 701-231-7705, Fax: 701-231-7784, E-mail: paul.nelson.1@ndsu.edu. *Application contact:* Dr. Judy C. Pearson, Director of Graduate Studies, 701-231-6551, Fax: 701-231-1074, E-mail: judy.pearson@ndsu.edu.

Oklahoma City University, Petree College of Arts and Sciences, Program in Liberal Arts, Oklahoma City, OK 73106-1402. Offers art (MLA); general studies (MLA); leadership/management (MLA); literature (MLA); mass communications (MLA); philosophy (MLA); writing (MLA). Part-time and evening/weekend programs available. *Degree requirements:* For master's, comprehensive exam, thesis optional. *Entrance requirements:* Additional exam requirements/recommendations for international students: Required—TOEFL.

Oklahoma State University, College of Arts and Sciences, School of Journalism and Broadcasting, Stillwater, OK 74078. Offers mass communication (MS). *Faculty:* 18 full-time (5 women), 3 part-time/adjunct (1 woman). *Students:* 9 full-time (7 women), 19 part-time (6 women); includes 2 minority (both American Indian/Alaska Native), 3 international. Average age 30. 28 applicants, 57% accepted, 11 enrolled. In 2008, 6 master's awarded. *Degree requirements:* For master's, thesis, project/creative component. *Entrance requirements:* For master's, GRE, minimum GPA of 3.0. Additional exam requirements/recommendations for international students: Required—TOEFL. *Application deadline:* For fall admission, 3/1 priority date for international students; for spring admission, 8/1 priority date for international students. Applications are processed on a rolling basis. Application fee: $40 ($75 for international students). Electronic applications accepted. *Expenses:* Tuition, state resident: full-time $3716.40; part-time $154.85 per credit hour. Tuition, nonresident: full-time $14,448; part-time $602 per credit hour. Required fees: $1772.40; $73.85 per credit hour. One-time fee: $50. Tuition and fees vary according to course load and campus/location. *Financial support:* In 2008–09, 4 teaching assistantships (averaging $11,655 per year) were awarded; career-related internships or fieldwork, Federal Work-Study, scholarships/grants, health care benefits, tuition waivers (partial), and unspecified assistantships also available. Support available to part-time students. Financial award application deadline: 3/1; financial award applicants required to submit FAFSA. *Unit head:* Dr. Derina Holtzhausen, Director, 405-744-6354, Fax: 405-744-7104. *Application contact:* Dr. Gordon Emslie, Dean, 405-744-6368, Fax: 405-744-0355, E-mail: grad_i@okstate.edu.

Penn State University Park, Graduate School, Intercollege Graduate Programs, State College, University Park, PA 16802-1503. Offers acoustics (M Eng, MS, PhD); bioengineering (MS, PhD); ecology (MS, PhD); environmental pollution control (MEPC, MS); genetics (MS, PhD); integrative biosciences (MS, PhD), including integrative biosciences; mass communications (PhD); nutrition (MS, PhD), including nutrition; physiology (MS, PhD); plant physiology (MS, PhD); quality and manufacturing management (MMM). *Entrance requirements:* Additional exam requirements/recommendations for international students: Required—TOEFL (minimum score 550 paper-based; 213 computer-based; 80 iBT). Electronic applications accepted.

Point Park University, School of Arts and Sciences, Department of Journalism and Mass Communication, Pittsburgh, PA 15222-1984. Offers MA. Part-time and evening/weekend programs available. *Faculty:* 9 full-time, 13 part-time/adjunct. *Students:* 35 full-time (27 women), 47 part-time (36 women); includes 13 minority (11 African Americans, 1 American Indian/Alaska Native, 1 Asian American or Pacific Islander), 3 international. Average age 27. 101 applicants, 56% accepted, 36 enrolled. In 2008, 24 master's awarded. *Degree requirements:* For master's, comprehensive exam (for some programs), thesis or alternative. *Entrance requirements:* For master's, GRE (if GPA below 2.75), minimum GPA of 2.75, 2 letters of recommendation; 500 word statement of intent. Additional exam requirements/recommendations for international students: Required—TOEFL. *Application deadline:* Applications are processed on a rolling basis. Application fee: $30. Electronic applications accepted. *Expenses:* Tuition: Full-time $11,880; part-time $660 per credit. Required fees: $486; $27 per credit. *Financial support:* In 2008–09, 6 students received support, including 6 research assistantships with full tuition reimbursements available (averaging $5,400 per year); career-related internships or fieldwork, Federal Work-Study, and scholarships/grants also available. Support available to part-time students. Financial award application deadline: 5/1; financial award applicants required to submit FAFSA. *Unit head:* Helen Fallon, Chair, 412-392-3982, E-mail: hfallon@pointpark.edu. *Application contact:* Emily R. Quidetto, Recruiter/Counselor, 412-392-4794, Fax: 412-392-6164, E-mail: equidetto@pointpark.edu.

See Close-Up on page 693.

St. Cloud State University, School of Graduate Studies, College of Fine Arts and Humanities, Department of Mass Communication, St. Cloud, MN 56301-4498. Offers MS. *Accreditation:* ACEJMC. *Degree requirements:* For master's, thesis or alternative. *Entrance requirements:* For master's, GRE General Test, minimum GPA of 2.75. Additional exam requirements/recommendations for international students: Required—Michigan English Language Assessment Battery; Recommended—TOEFL (minimum score 550 paper-based; 213 computer-based), IELTS (minimum score 6.5). Electronic applications accepted.

San Jose State University, Graduate Studies and Research, College of Applied Sciences and Arts, School of Journalism and Mass Communications, San Jose, CA 95192-0001. Offers mass communications (MS). *Accreditation:* ACEJMC. Part-time programs available. *Degree requirements:* For master's, thesis or alternative. *Entrance requirements:* For master's, GRE, minimum GPA of 3.0. Electronic applications accepted. *Faculty research:* Communications theory, mass media effects, public relations, international communications.

Southern Illinois University Carbondale, Graduate School, College of Mass Communication and Media Arts, Department of Mass Communication and Media Arts, Carbondale, IL 62901-4701. Offers MA, MFA.

Southern Illinois University Edwardsville, Graduate Studies and Research, College of Arts and Sciences, Department of Mass Communications, Program in Mass Communications, Edwardsville, IL 62026-0001. Offers MS. Part-time programs available. *Students:* 8 full-time (7 women), 18 part-time (14 women); includes 8 minority (7 African Americans, 1 American Indian/Alaska Native), 2 international. Average age 26. 23 applicants, 48% accepted. In 2008, 7 master's awarded. *Degree requirements:* For master's, comprehensive exam (for some programs), thesis (for some programs). *Entrance requirements:* Additional exam requirements/recommendations for international students: Required—TOEFL (minimum score 550 paper-based; 213 computer-based; 79 iBT), IELTS (minimum score 6.5). *Application deadline:* For fall admission, 7/20 for domestic students, 6/1 for international students; for spring admission, 12/14 for domestic students, 10/1 for international students. Applications are processed on a rolling basis. Application fee: $30. Electronic applications accepted. *Expenses:* Tuition, area resident: Full-time $5838. Tuition, nonresident: full-time $14,596. Required fees: $1525. *Financial support:* In 2008–09, 1 research assistantship with full tuition reimbursement (averaging $8,064 per year), 8 teaching assistantships with full tuition reimbursements (averaging $8,064 per year) were awarded; fellowships with full tuition reimbursements also available. Financial award application deadline: 3/1; financial award applicants required to submit FAFSA. *Unit head:* Dr. Gary Hicks, Director, 618-650-2242, E-mail: ghicks@siue.edu. *Application contact:* Dr. Gary Hicks, Director, 618-650-2242, E-mail: ghicks@siue.edu.

Southern University and Agricultural and Mechanical College, Graduate School, College of Arts and Humanities, Department of Mass Communications, Baton Rouge, LA 70813. Offers MA. *Accreditation:* ACEJMC. *Degree requirements:* For master's, comprehensive exam, thesis. *Entrance requirements:* For master's, GRE General Test. Additional exam requirements/recommendations for international students: Required—TOEFL (minimum score 525 paper-based; 193 computer-based). *Faculty research:* Photojournalism, textbook on broadcast.

Stephen F. Austin State University, Graduate School, College of Applied Arts and Science, Department of Communication, Nacogdoches, TX 75962. Offers communication (MA); mass communication (MA). Part-time programs available. *Degree requirements:* For master's, comprehensive exam, thesis optional. *Entrance requirements:* For master's, GRE General Test. Additional exam requirements/recommendations for international students: Required—TOEFL (minimum score 550 paper-based; 213 computer-based).

Syracuse University, Graduate School, S. I. Newhouse School of Public Communications, Program in Communications Management, Syracuse, NY 13244. Offers MS. Postbaccalaureate distance learning degree programs offered. *Degree requirements:* For master's, comprehensive exam, internship. *Entrance requirements:* For master's, GRE General Test. Additional exam requirements/recommendations for international students: Required—TOEFL. Electronic applications accepted.

See Close-Up on page 705.

Syracuse University, Graduate School, S. I. Newhouse School of Public Communications, Program in Mass Communications, Syracuse, NY 13244. Offers PhD. *Degree requirements:* For doctorate, thesis/dissertation, qualifying exams. *Entrance requirements:* For doctorate, GRE General Test. Additional exam requirements/recommendations for international students: Required—TOEFL. Electronic applications accepted.

See Close-Up on page 705.

Temple University, Graduate School, School of Communications and Theater, Department of Strategic and Organizational Communication, Program in Mass Media and Communication, Philadelphia, PA 19122-6096. Offers PhD. Part-time programs available. *Degree requirements:* For doctorate, one foreign language, thesis/dissertation. *Entrance requirements:* For doctorate, GRE General Test, minimum GPA of 3.0, sample of written work. Additional exam requirements/recommendations for international students: Required—TOEFL (minimum score 550 paper-based; 213 computer-based; 79 iBT). Electronic applications accepted. *Faculty research:* Aesthetics and criticism, media institutions, social theory and processes.

Texas State University–San Marcos, Graduate School, College of Fine Arts and Communication, School of Journalism and Mass Communication, San Marcos, TX 78666. Offers MA. *Degree requirements:* For master's, comprehensive exam, thesis or alternative. *Entrance requirements:* For master's, GRE General Test, departmental grammar test, minimum GPA of 3.0 in last 60 hours of course work. Additional exam requirements/recommendations for international students: Required—TOEFL (minimum score 550 paper-based; 213 computer-based). Electronic applications accepted.

Texas Tech University, Graduate School, College of Mass Communications, Lubbock, TX 79409. Offers MA, PhD. Part-time programs available. *Faculty:* 13 full-time (3 women), 1 part-time/adjunct (0 women). *Students:* 28 full-time (15 women), 8 part-time (4 women); includes 4 minority (1 American Indian/Alaska Native, 3 Hispanic Americans), 6 international. Average age 32. 56 applicants, 41% accepted, 9 enrolled. In 2008, 13 master's, 3 doctorates awarded. *Degree requirements:* For master's, thesis or alternative; for doctorate, thesis/dissertation. *Entrance requirements:* For master's, GRE General Test. Additional exam requirements/recommendations for international students: Required—TOEFL (minimum score 550 paper-based; 213 computer-based). *Application deadline:* For fall admission, 3/1 priority date for international students; for spring admission, 11/1 priority date for international students. Applications are processed on a rolling basis. Application fee: $50 ($60 for international students). Electronic applications accepted. *Expenses:* Tuition, area resident: Part-time $194 per credit hour. Tuition, state resident: full-time $4648; part-time $194 per credit hour. Tuition, nonresident: full-time $11,392; part-time $475 per credit hour. Required fees: $2206; $69 per credit hour. $389 per semester. *Financial support:* In 2008–09, 38 students received support, including 14 teaching assistantships with partial tuition reimbursements available (averaging $17,742 per year); research assistantships with partial tuition reimbursements available, Federal

Work-Study and institutionally sponsored loans also available. Support available to part-time students. Financial award application deadline: 4/15; financial award applicants required to submit FAFSA. *Faculty research:* Contemporary media use and structure; Hispanic media; characteristics of public relations spokesperson credibility; psychological measures of advertising effectiveness; media law. Total annual research expenditures: $65,656. *Unit head:* Dr. Jerry C. Hudson, Dean, 806-742-3385 Ext. 224, Fax: 806-742-1085, E-mail: jerry.hudson@ttu.edu. *Application contact:* Dr. Coy Callison, Associate Dean of Graduate Studies, 806-742-3385 Ext. 235, Fax: 806-742-1085, E-mail: coy.callison@ttu.edu.

Université Laval, Faculty of Letters, Department of Information and Communication, Program in Public Communication, Québec, QC G1K 7P4, Canada. Offers MA, PhD. Part-time programs available. *Degree requirements:* For master's, thesis (for some programs). *Entrance requirements:* For master's, knowledge of French, knowledge of English. Electronic applications accepted.

The University of Alabama, Graduate School, College of Communication and Information Sciences, Program in Mass Communications, Tuscaloosa, AL 35487. Offers PhD. *Students:* 44 full-time (22 women), 12 part-time (9 women); includes 2 minority (both African Americans), 14 international. Average age 34. 41 applicants, 54% accepted, 10 enrolled. In 2008, 6 doctorates awarded. Application fee: $30. *Expenses:* Tuition, area resident: Full-time $6400. Tuition, state resident: full-time $6400. Tuition, nonresident: full-time $18,000. *Unit head:* Dr. Jennings Bryant, Associate Dean for Graduate Studies, 205-348-8593, Fax: 205-348-6774. *Application contact:* Diane Shaddix, Information Contact, 205-348-8593, Fax: 205-348-6774, E-mail: dshaddix@bama.ua.edu.

University of Arkansas at Little Rock, Graduate School, College of Professional Studies, School of Mass Communication, Little Rock, AR 72204-1099. Offers journalism (MA). Part-time and evening/weekend programs available. *Degree requirements:* For master's, comprehensive exam, thesis optional. *Entrance requirements:* For master's, GRE General Test, minimum GPA of 2.7. *Faculty research:* Theory and practice of mass communication, social role of the mass media.

University of Central Florida, College of Sciences, Nicholson School of Communication, Orlando, FL 32816. Offers business communication (MA); interpersonal communication (MA); mass communication (MA). Part-time and evening/weekend programs available. *Faculty:* 41 full-time (18 women), 36 part-time/adjunct (18 women). *Students:* 44 full-time (39 women), 28 part-time (25 women); includes 15 minority (6 African Americans, 3 Asian Americans or Pacific Islanders, 6 Hispanic Americans), 9 international. In 2008, 29 master's awarded. *Degree requirements:* For master's, thesis or comprehensive exam. *Entrance requirements:* For master's, GRE General Test, minimum GPA of 3.0 in last 60 hours of course work. Additional exam requirements/recommendations for international students: Required—TOEFL. *Application deadline:* For fall admission, 7/15 for domestic students; for spring admission, 12/7 for domestic students. Application fee: $30. Electronic applications accepted. *Expenses:* Tuition, area resident: Full-time $6816; part-time $284 per credit. Tuition, state resident: full-time $6816; part-time $1076 per credit. Tuition, nonresident: full-time $25,824. Required fees: $216; $9 per credit. *Financial support:* In 2008–09, 2 fellowships with partial tuition reimbursements (averaging $10,000 per year), 4 research assistantships with partial tuition reimbursements (averaging $4,400 per year), 16 teaching assistantships with partial tuition reimbursements (averaging $6,400 per year) were awarded; career-related internships or fieldwork, Federal Work-Study, institutionally sponsored loans, tuition waivers (partial), and unspecified assistantships also available. Financial award application deadline: 3/1; financial award applicants required to submit FAFSA. *Faculty research:* Persuasion, communication apprehension, nonverbal communication, conflict resolution. *Unit head:* Dr. Robert Chandler, Director, 407-823-2683, Fax: 407-823-5216, E-mail: rcchandl@mail.ucf.edu. *Application contact:* Dr. Robert Chandler, Director, 407-823-2683, Fax: 407-823-5216, E-mail: rcchandl@mail.ucf.edu.

University of Central Missouri, The Graduate School, College of Arts, Humanities and Social Sciences, Department of Communication, Warrensburg, MO 64093. Offers communication (MA); speech communication (MA). Part-time programs available. *Degree requirements:* For master's, comprehensive exam, internship, research papers or thesis. *Entrance requirements:* For master's, minimum GPA of 2.5. Additional exam requirements/recommendations for international students: Required—TOEFL (minimum score 500 paper-based; 173 computer-based).

University of Colorado at Boulder, Graduate School, School of Journalism and Mass Communication, Boulder, CO 80309. Offers communication (PhD), including media studies; mass communication research (MA); newsgathering (MA). *Accreditation:* ACEJMC (one or more programs are accredited). Part-time programs available. *Degree requirements:* For master's, comprehensive exam, thesis or alternative; for doctorate, comprehensive exam, thesis/dissertation. *Entrance requirements:* For master's, GRE General Test, minimum undergraduate GPA of 2.75; for doctorate, GRE General Test, minimum undergraduate GPA of 3.2, 3.5 graduate. *Faculty research:* Writing on science and the environment, mass communication and public opinion, minority representation in the media, media and culture.

University of Denver, Division of Arts, Humanities and Social Sciences, School of Communication, Department of Mass Communications, Denver, CO 80208. Offers advertising management (MS); digital media studies (MA); mass communications (MA); public relations (MS); video production (MA). Part-time programs available. *Faculty:* 14 full-time (8 women), 4 part-time/adjunct (1 woman). *Students:* 3 full-time (1 woman), 42 part-time (30 women); includes 7 minority (1 African American, 6 Hispanic Americans), 3 international. Average age 27. In 2008, 17 master's awarded. *Degree requirements:* For master's, thesis (for some programs). *Entrance requirements:* For master's, GRE General Test. Additional exam requirements/recommendations for international students: Required—TOEFL, TWE. *Application deadline:* Applications are processed on a rolling basis. Application fee: $50. Electronic applications accepted. *Financial support:* In 2008–09, 4 research assistantships with full and partial tuition reimbursements (averaging $9,000 per year), 7 teaching assistantships with full and partial tuition reimbursements (averaging $10,000 per year) were awarded; career-related internships or fieldwork, Federal Work-Study, institutionally sponsored loans, and scholarships/grants also available. Support available to part-time students. Financial award application deadline: 3/1; financial award applicants required to submit FAFSA. *Faculty research:* Youth and civic engagement. Total annual research expenditures: $162,000. *Unit head:* Dr. Diane Waldman, Chair, 303-871-2008. *Application contact:* Information Contact, 303-871-2008, E-mail: mcom@du.edu.

See Close-Up on page 707.

University of Florida, Graduate School, College of Journalism and Communications, Gainesville, FL 32611. Offers advertising (M Adv); journalism (MAMC); mass communication (MAMC, PhD); public relations (MAMC); telecommunication (MAMC); JD/MAMC; JD/PhD. *Accreditation:* ACEJMC (one or more programs are accredited). Part-time programs available. Terminal master's awarded for partial completion of doctoral program. *Degree requirements:* For master's, thesis optional; for doctorate, thesis/dissertation. *Entrance requirements:* For master's and doctorate, GRE General Test, minimum GPA of 3.0. Additional exam requirements/recommendations for international students: Required—TOEFL (minimum score 550 paper-based; 213 computer-based). Electronic applications accepted. *Faculty research:* Public opinion, law and policy, regulation, environmental communication, international communication.

University of Georgia, Graduate School, Grady School of Journalism and Mass Communication, Athens, GA 30602. Offers journalism and mass communication (MA); mass communication (PhD). *Accreditation:* ACEJMC (one or more programs are accredited). *Degree requirements:* For master's, comprehensive exam, thesis (MA); for doctorate, comprehensive exam, thesis/dissertation. *Entrance requirements:* For master's and doctorate, GRE General Test. Additional exam requirements/recommendations for international students: Required—TOEFL, TWE (PhD). Electronic applications accepted.

University of Houston, College of Liberal Arts and Social Sciences, School of Communication, Houston, TX 77204. Offers mass communication studies (MA); public relations studies (MA); speech communication (MA). Part-time and evening/weekend programs available. *Faculty:* 7 full-time (4 women), 2 part-time/adjunct (0 women). *Students:* 29 full-time (25 women), 62 part-time (52 women); includes 32 minority (19 African Americans, 2 Asian Americans or Pacific Islanders, 11 Hispanic Americans), 13 international. Average age 29. 46 applicants, 85% accepted, 20 enrolled. In 2008, 20 master's awarded. *Entrance requirements:* For master's, GRE General Test, minimum GPA of 3.0 in last 60 hours of course work. *Application deadline:* For fall admission, 7/3 priority date for domestic students. Applications are processed on a rolling basis. Application fee: $25 ($75 for international students). *Expenses:* Tuition, state resident: full-time $5164; part-time $287 per credit. Tuition, nonresident: full-time $10,222; part-time $568 per credit. *Financial support:* In 2008–09, 2 fellowships with full tuition reimbursements (averaging $9,950 per year), 6 teaching assistantships with full tuition reimbursements (averaging $9,950 per year) were awarded; career-related internships or fieldwork, Federal Work-Study, institutionally sponsored loans, scholarships/grants, health care benefits, and unspecified assistantships also available. Support available to part-time students. Financial award application deadline: 2/1. *Faculty research:* Risk communication, relationship development, critical studies, corporate communication. *Unit head:* Beth Olson, Chairperson, 713-743-2873, Fax: 713-743-2876, E-mail: bolson@uh.edu. *Application contact:* Angela Parrish, Graduate Coordinator, 713-743-2873, Fax: 713-743-2876, E-mail: aparrish@bayou.uh.edu.

The University of Iowa, Graduate College, College of Liberal Arts and Sciences, School of Journalism and Mass Communication, Iowa City, IA 52242-1316. Offers mass communication (PhD); media communication (MA); professional journalism (MA); JD/MA. *Accreditation:* ACEJMC (one or more programs are accredited). *Degree requirements:* For master's, thesis optional, exam; for doctorate, comprehensive exam, thesis/dissertation. *Entrance requirements:* For master's and doctorate, GRE General Test, minimum GPA of 3.0. Additional exam requirements/recommendations for international students: Required—TOEFL (minimum score 570 paper-based; 230 computer-based; 89 iBT). Electronic applications accepted. *Faculty research:* Verbal and visual aspects of historical, legal, social, and cross-cultural communication.

University of Louisiana at Lafayette, BI Moody III College of Business Administration MBA Program, College of Liberal Arts, Department of Communication, Lafayette, LA 70504. Offers mass communications (MS). Part-time programs available. *Degree requirements:* For master's, thesis optional. *Entrance requirements:* For master's, GRE General Test, minimum GPA of 2.75. Additional exam requirements/recommendations for international students: Required—TOEFL (minimum score 550 paper-based; 213 computer-based). Electronic applications accepted. *Faculty research:* Mass media problems, issues and ethics, mass communication, historical studies, conflict of interest and law and ethics in journalism, contemporary issues and trends in publications.

University of Michigan, Horace H. Rackham School of Graduate Studies, College of Literature, Science, and the Arts, Department of Communication Studies, Ann Arbor, MI 48104-2523. Offers PhD. *Degree requirements:* For doctorate, comprehensive exam, thesis/dissertation. *Entrance requirements:* For doctorate, GRE. Additional exam requirements/recommendations for international students: Required—TOEFL (minimum score 560 paper-based; 220 computer-based; 84 iBT). Electronic applications accepted. *Faculty research:* Political communication; media, culture and society; media effects; race, gender, and the media; new media, media law and policy.

University of Minnesota, Twin Cities Campus, Graduate School, College of Liberal Arts, School of Journalism and Mass Communication, Minneapolis, MN 55455-0213. Offers health journalism (professional program) (MA); mass communication (MA, PhD); strategic communication (professional program) (MA). *Degree requirements:* For master's, thesis; for doctorate, comprehensive exam, thesis/dissertation. *Entrance requirements:* For master's and doctorate, GRE, letters of recommendation, minimum undergraduate GPA of 3.0, writing sample. Additional exam requirements/recommendations for international students: Required—TOEFL. *Faculty research:* Communication law, regulation, and ethics; history; mass media effects; new media, health communication.

University of Nebraska–Lincoln, Graduate College, College of Journalism and Mass Communications, Lincoln, NE 68588. Offers marketing, communication and advertising (MA); professional journalism (MA). Postbaccalaureate distance learning degree programs offered (no on-campus study). *Faculty:* 17 full-time (7 women). *Students:* 22 full-time (12 women), 48 part-time (21 women); includes 4 minority (2 American Indian/Alaska Native, 1 Asian American or Pacific Islander, 1 Hispanic American), 4 international. Average age 33. In 2008, 23 master's awarded. *Degree requirements:* For master's, thesis. *Entrance requirements:* For master's, samples of work. Additional exam requirements/recommendations for international students: Required—TOEFL (minimum score 600 paper-based; 250 computer-based). *Application deadline:* For fall admission, 3/15 for domestic students, 3/1 for international students; for spring admission, 10/15 for domestic students. Applications are processed on a rolling basis. Application fee: $40. Electronic applications accepted. *Expenses:* Tuition, state resident: full-time $4275; part-time $237.50 per credit hour. Tuition, nonresident: full-time $11,525; part-time $640.25 per credit hour. Required fees: $1068; $10.35 per credit hour. $440.70 per semester. Tuition and fees vary according to course load and program. *Financial support:* Fellowships, research assistantships, teaching assistantships, Federal Work-Study, health care benefits, and unspecified assistantships available. Financial award application deadline: 2/15. *Faculty research:* Interactive media and the Internet, community newspapers, children's radio, advertising involvement, telecommunications policy. *Unit head:* Dr. Will Norton, Dean, 402-472-3041. *Application contact:* Ginny Gross, Director of Graduate Admissions, 402-472-2878, Fax: 402-472-0589, E-mail: grad_admissions@unl.edu.

The University of North Carolina at Chapel Hill, Graduate School, School of Journalism and Mass Communication, Chapel Hill, NC 27599. Offers mass communication (MA, PhD). *Accreditation:* ACEJMC (one or more programs are accredited). Part-time programs available. *Degree requirements:* For master's, comprehensive exam, thesis; for doctorate, comprehensive exam, thesis/dissertation. *Entrance requirements:* For master's and doctorate, GRE General Test, minimum GPA of 3.0. Additional exam requirements/recommendations for international students: Required—TOEFL (minimum score 620 paper-based; 260 computer-based; 105 iBT). Electronic applications accepted. *Expenses:* Contact institution. *Faculty research:* Media processes and production, legal and regulatory issues, media effects, media history.

University of Oklahoma, Graduate College, Gaylord College of Journalism and Mass Communication, Program in Journalism and Mass Communication, Norman, OK 73019-0390. Offers advertising and public relations (MA); information gathering and distribution (MA); mass communication management and policy (MA); professional writing (MA); telecommunication and new technology (MA). Part-time programs available. *Students:* 33 full-time (16 women), 34 part-time (18 women); includes 12 minority (4 African Americans, 4 American Indian/Alaska Native, 1 Asian American or Pacific Islander, 3 Hispanic Americans), 8 international. 28 applicants, 75% accepted, 14 enrolled. *Degree requirements:* For master's, thesis optional. *Entrance requirements:* For master's, GRE General Test, minimum GPA of 3.2, 9 hours of course work in journalism, course work in statistics. Additional exam requirements/recommendations for international students: Required—TOEFL (minimum score 600 paper-based; 250 computer-based), TWE (minimum score 5). *Application deadline:* For fall admission, 2/1 for domestic students, 4/1 for international students; for spring admission, 11/1 for domestic students, 9/1 for international students. Application fee: $40 ($90 for international students). Electronic applications accepted. *Expenses:* Tuition, state resident: full-time $3744; part-time $156 per credit hour. Tuition, nonresident: full-time $13,577; part-time $565.70 per credit hour. Required fees: $2415.40; $90.10 per credit hour. *Financial support:* In 2008–09, 25 students received support, including 2 fellowships (averaging $4,500 per year); career-related internships or fieldwork, scholarships/grants, health care benefits, and unspecified assistantships also available. *Faculty research:* Organizational management; rhetorical analysis; international public relations; digital production; normative theory. *Unit head:* Dr. Joe Foote, Dean, 405-325-

Mass Communication

University of Oklahoma (continued)
2721, Fax: 405-325-7565, E-mail: jfoote@ou.edu. *Application contact:* Kelly Storm, Graduate Advisor, 405-325-2722, Fax: 405-325-7565, E-mail: kstorm@ou.edu.

University of Puerto Rico, Río Piedras, School of Communication, San Juan, PR 00931-3300. Offers MA. Part-time programs available. *Degree requirements:* For master's, comprehensive exam, thesis. *Entrance requirements:* For master's, GRE, PAEG, minimum GPA of 3.0, 2 letters of recommendation, interview.

University of Southern California, Graduate School, Annenberg School for Communication, School of Communication, Program in Communication, Los Angeles, CA 90089. Offers communication (MA, PhD), including interpersonal and social dynamics (PhD), mass communication, technology, and public policy (PhD), organizational communication (PhD), rhetorical and cultural studies (PhD). *Degree requirements:* For doctorate, thesis/dissertation. *Entrance requirements:* For master's and doctorate, GRE General Test, resumé, writing samples, 3 letters of recommendation, interest survey questionnaire, statement of purpose. Additional exam requirements/recommendations for international students: Required—TOEFL (minimum score 280 computer-based; 115 iBT); Recommended—TWE. Electronic applications accepted. *Faculty research:* Computer-mediated communication, public health campaigns, communication democracy and the public sphere, new communication technologies in organizations, communication and community.

See Close-Up on page 709.

University of Southern Mississippi, Graduate School, College of Arts and Letters, School of Mass Communication and Journalism, Hattiesburg, MS 39406-0001. Offers mass communication (MA, MS, PhD); public relations (MS). *Faculty:* 9 full-time (2 women), 3 part-time/adjunct (1 woman). *Students:* 37 full-time (27 women), 42 part-time (33 women); includes 18 minority (17 African Americans, 1 Asian American or Pacific Islander), 4 international. Average age 34. 32 applicants, 84% accepted, 21 enrolled. In 2008, 22 master's, 4 doctorates awarded. *Degree requirements:* For master's, comprehensive exam, thesis optional; for doctorate, comprehensive exam, thesis/dissertation. *Entrance requirements:* For master's, GRE General Test, minimum GPA of 3.0 in field of study, 2.75 in last 2 years; for doctorate, GRE General Test, minimum GPA of 3.5. Additional exam requirements/recommendations for international students: Required—TOEFL. *Application deadline:* For fall admission, 3/1 priority date for domestic students, 3/1 for international students. Applications are processed on a rolling basis. Application fee: $30. *Financial support:* In 2008–09, 18 students received support, including 12 teaching assistantships with full tuition reimbursements available (averaging $8,000 per year); fellowships with full tuition reimbursements available, research assistantships with full tuition reimbursements available, career-related internships or fieldwork, Federal Work-Study, and unspecified assistantships also available. Financial award application deadline: 3/15; financial award applicants required to submit FAFSA. *Unit head:* Dr. Christopher Campbell, Director, 601-266-5650, Fax: 601-266-4263. *Application contact:* Dr. Fei Xue, Graduate Coordinator, 601-266-5652, Fax: 601-266-6473, E-mail: fei.xue@usm.edu.

University of South Florida, Graduate School, College of Arts and Sciences, School of Mass Communications, Tampa, FL 33620-9951. Offers MA. *Accreditation:* ACEJMC. Part-time and evening/weekend programs available. *Faculty:* 8 full-time (3 women). *Students:* 26 full-time (all women), 19 part-time (12 women); includes 9 minority (5 African Americans, 4 Hispanic Americans), 6 international. 37 applicants, 46% accepted, 11 enrolled. In 2008, 16 master's awarded. *Degree requirements:* For master's, comprehensive exam, thesis. *Entrance requirements:* For master's, GRE General Test, minimum GPA of 3.0 in last 60 hours of course work. Additional exam requirements/recommendations for international students: Required—TOEFL (minimum score 550 paper-based; 213 computer-based). *Application deadline:* For fall admission, 2/15 for domestic students, 1/2 for international students; for spring admission, 10/15 for domestic students, 6/1 for international students. Application fee: $30. Electronic applications accepted. *Expenses:* Tuition, state resident: full-time $2624.40; part-time $291.60 per credit hour. Tuition, nonresident: full-time $7822; part-time $869.13 per credit hour. *Financial support:* Application deadline: 2/28. *Faculty research:* First Amendment analysis, civic journalism, public opinion, media ethics, public relation management. Total annual research expenditures: $87,468. *Unit head:* Dr. Edward Jay Friedlander, Chairperson, 813-974-6461, Fax: 813-974-2592, E-mail: efriedla@luna.cas.usf.edu. *Application contact:* Derina Holtzhausen, Application Contact, 813-974-6800, Fax: 813-974-2592, E-mail: dgiktzga@.cas.usf.edu.

University of Wisconsin–Madison, Graduate School, College of Letters and Science, School of Journalism and Mass Communication, Program in Journalism and Mass Communication, Madison, WI 53706-1380. Offers MA.

University of Wisconsin–Madison, Graduate School, College of Letters and Science, School of Journalism and Mass Communication, Program in Mass Communication, Madison, WI 53706-1380. Offers PhD. *Degree requirements:* For doctorate, thesis/dissertation.

University of Wisconsin–Stevens Point, College of Fine Arts and Communication, Division of Communication, Stevens Point, WI 54481-3897. Offers interpersonal communication (MA); mass communication (MA); organizational communication (MA); public relations (MA). Part-time programs available. *Students:* 7 full-time (3 women), 19 part-time (11 women). *Degree requirements:* For master's, thesis or alternative. *Entrance requirements:* For master's, GRE. Additional exam requirements/recommendations for international students: Required—TOEFL (minimum score 575 paper-based). *Application deadline:* For fall admission, 3/1 priority date for domestic students. Applications are processed on a rolling basis. Application fee: $45. *Expenses:* Tuition, state resident: full-time $7410. Tuition, nonresident: full-time $17,756. Full-time tuition and fees vary according to reciprocity agreements. *Financial support:* In 2008–09, 9 teaching assistantships were awarded; career-related internships or fieldwork, Federal Work-Study, institutionally sponsored loans, and unspecified assistantships also available. Support available to part-time students. Financial award application deadline: 5/1; financial award applicants required to submit FAFSA. *Faculty research:* Communication theory and research, film history. *Unit head:* Dr. James Haney, Chair, 715-346-3409, E-mail: jhaney@uwsp.edu. *Application contact:* Dr. Chris Sadler, Graduate Coordinator, 715-346-3898, E-mail: csadler@uwsp.edu.

University of Wisconsin–Superior, Graduate Division, Department of Communicating Arts, Superior, WI 54880-4500. Offers mass communication (MA); speech communication (MA); theater (MA). Part-time programs available. *Degree requirements:* For master's, comprehensive exam, thesis or alternative, position paper or project. *Entrance requirements:* For master's, minimum GPA of 2.75. *Faculty research:* Multimedia technology, ethics in journalism, diversity, electronic portfolio assessment.

University of Wisconsin–Whitewater, School of Graduate Studies, College of Arts and Communications, Department of Communication, Whitewater, WI 53190-1790. Offers corporate communication (MS); mass communication (MS). Part-time and evening/weekend programs available. Postbaccalaureate distance learning degree programs offered (no on-campus study). *Degree requirements:* For master's, thesis or alternative. *Entrance requirements:* For master's, 2 letters of recommendation. Additional exam requirements/recommendations for international students: Required—TOEFL (minimum score 550 paper-based; 213 computer-based). Electronic applications accepted.

Virginia Commonwealth University, Graduate School, College of Humanities and Sciences, School of Mass Communications, Program in Mass Communications, Richmond, VA 23284-9005. Offers scholastic journalism (MS); strategic public relations (MS). *Degree requirements:* For master's, comprehensive exam, thesis optional. *Entrance requirements:* For master's, GRE General Test.

Media Studies

American University, School of Communication, Film and Electronic Media Program, Washington, DC 20016-8001. Offers MFA. *Faculty:* 14 full-time (6 women). *Students:* 34 full-time (16 women), 39 part-time (19 women). 51 applicants, 73% accepted, 22 enrolled. In 2008, 141 master's awarded. *Degree requirements:* For master's, comprehensive exam, thesis or alternative. *Entrance requirements:* For master's, GRE General Test. Additional exam requirements/recommendations for international students: Required—TOEFL (minimum score 600 paper-based; 250 computer-based). *Application deadline:* For fall admission, 2/1 priority date for domestic and international students; for spring admission, 11/15 for domestic and international students. Applications are processed on a rolling basis. Application fee: $50. Electronic applications accepted. *Expenses:* Tuition: Full-time $21,204; part-time $1178 per credit hour. Required fees: $380. Part-time tuition and fees vary according to course load and program. *Financial support:* In 2008–09, 10 students received support, including 2 fellowships with partial tuition reimbursements available (averaging $13,000 per year), 2 research assistantships with partial tuition reimbursements available (averaging $11,000 per year), 4 teaching assistantships with partial tuition reimbursements available (averaging $11,000 per year); career-related internships or fieldwork, Federal Work-Study, institutionally sponsored loans, scholarships/grants, tuition waivers (partial), and unspecified assistantships also available. Financial award application deadline: 2/1. *Faculty research:* Documentary film production, social media, media and public policy, visual literacy, new technology. *Unit head:* Prof. John Douglass, Director, Film and Media Arts Division, 202-885-2045, Fax: 202-885-2019, E-mail: jdougla@american.edu. *Application contact:* Sharmeen Ahsan-Bracciale, Graduate Admissions Office, 202-885-2040, Fax: 202-885-2019, E-mail: sharmeen@american.edu.

Arizona State University, Graduate College, College of Liberal Arts and Sciences, Division of Humanities, Program in Film and Media Studies, Tempe, AZ 85287. Offers American media and popular culture (MAS); film analysis (MLS); screenwriting (MAS).

Arkansas State University, Graduate School, College of Communications, Department of Radio-Television, Jonesboro, State University, AR 72467. Offers MSMC. Part-time programs available. *Faculty:* 4 full-time (1 woman). *Students:* 10 full-time (8 women), 8 part-time (2 women); includes 11 minority (all African Americans), 4 international. Average age 29. 12 applicants, 100% accepted, 10 enrolled. In 2008, 2 master's awarded. *Degree requirements:* For master's, comprehensive exam, thesis or alternative. *Entrance requirements:* For master's, GRE General Test, appropriate bachelor's degree, letters of reference, recommendations, official transcript, written statement of purpose. Additional exam requirements/recommendations for international students: Required—TOEFL (minimum score 550 paper-based; 213 computer-based; 79 iBT), IELTS (minimum score 6). *Application deadline:* For fall admission, 7/15 for domestic students, 7/1 for international students; for spring admission, 12/1 for domestic students, 11/13 for international students. Applications are processed on a rolling basis. Application fee: $30 ($40 for international students). Electronic applications accepted. *Expenses:* Tuition, state resident: full-time $3744; part-time $208 per credit hour. Tuition, nonresident: full-time $9540; part-time $530 per credit hour. International tuition: $7938 full-time. Required fees: $896; $47 per credit hour. $25 per term. One-time fee: $50. Tuition and fees vary according to course load and program. *Financial support:* In 2008–09, 7 students received support. Career-related internships or fieldwork, scholarships/grants, and unspecified assistantships available. Financial award application deadline: 7/1; financial award applicants required to submit FAFSA. *Faculty research:* Cable and alternative technologies, development communications, Freedom of Information Act, public radio, role of media in national integration. *Unit head:* Dr. Osabuohien Amienyi, Chair, 870-972-3070, Fax: 870-972-2997, E-mail: osami@astate.edu. *Application contact:* Dr. Andrew Sustich, Dean of the Graduate School, 870-972-3029, Fax: 870-972-3857, E-mail: sustich@astate.edu.

Bob Jones University, Graduate Programs, Greenville, SC 29614. Offers accountancy (MS); Bible (MA); Bible translation (MA); Biblical studies (Certificate); broadcast management (MS); business administration (MBA); church history (MA, PhD); church ministries (MA); church music (MM); cinema and video production (MA); counseling (MS); curriculum and instruction (Ed D); divinity (M Div); dramatic production (MA); educational leadership (MS, Ed D, Ed S); elementary education (M Ed, MAT); English (M Ed, MA, MAT); fine arts (MA); graphic design (MA); history (M Ed, MA); illustration (MA); interpretative speech (MA); mathematics (M Ed, MAT); medical missions (Certificate); ministry (MM, D Min); multi-categorical special education (M Ed, MAT); music (M Ed); New Testament interpretation (PhD); Old Testament interpretation (PhD); orchestral instrument performance (MM); organ performance (MM); pastoral studies (MA); personnel services (MS, Ed S); piano pedagogy (MM); piano performance (MM); platform arts (MA); radio and television broadcasting (MS); rhetoric and public address (MA); secondary education (M Ed); studio art (MA); teaching Bible (MA); theology (MA, PhD); voice performance (MM); youth ministries (MA); M Div/MM.

Boston University, College of Communication, Department of Film and Television, Boston, MA 02215. Offers film production (MFA); film studies (MFA); screenwriting (MFA); television (MS); television management (MS); MBA/MS. *Degree requirements:* For master's, thesis. *Entrance requirements:* For master's, GMAT (MS in television management), GRE General Test, sample of written or creative work. Additional exam requirements/recommendations for international students: Required—TOEFL. Electronic applications accepted.

See Close-Up on page 683.

California State University, Fullerton, Graduate Studies, College of Communications, Department of Communications, Fullerton, CA 92834-9480. Offers communications—advertising (MA); communications—entertainment and tourism (MA); communications—journalism (MA); communications—public relations (MA). Part-time programs available. *Students:* 21 full-time (17 women), 38 part-time (32 women); includes 18 minority (1 African American, 6 Asian Americans or Pacific Islanders, 11 Hispanic Americans), 9 international. Average age 29. 94 applicants, 38% accepted, 13 enrolled. In 2008, 33 master's awarded. *Degree requirements:* For master's, project or thesis. *Entrance requirements:* For master's, GRE General Test. Application fee: $55. Tuition and fees vary according to degree level. *Financial support:* Teaching assistantships, career-related internships or fieldwork, Federal Work-Study, institutionally sponsored loans, and scholarships/grants available. Support available to part-time students. Financial award application deadline: 3/1. *Unit head:* Dr. Tony Fellow, Chair, 657-278-3517. *Application contact:* Coordinator, 657-278-3832.

Carnegie Mellon University, School of Computer Science and College of Fine Arts, Program in Entertainment Technology, Pittsburgh, PA 15213-3891. Offers MET.

Central Michigan University, College of Graduate Studies, College of Communication and Fine Arts, School of Broadcasting and Cinematic Arts, Mount Pleasant, MI 48859. Offers electronic media management (MA); electronic media studies (MA); film theory and criticism (MA); media production (MA). Part-time programs available. *Faculty:* 12 full-time (2 women). *Students:* 23 (8 women); includes 1 African American, 1 Asian American or Pacific Islander, 1 Hispanic American. Average age 26. *Degree requirements:* For master's, thesis or alternative. *Entrance requirements:* For master's, undergraduate degree in broadcasting, film studies, or an associated discipline with minimum GPA of 2.7. *Application deadline:* Applications are processed on a rolling basis. Application fee: $35 ($45 for international students). Electronic applications accepted. *Expenses:* Tuition, state resident: full-time $3717; part-time $413 per credit. Tuition, nonresident: full-time $6894; part-time $766 per credit. *Financial support:* Fellowships with tuition reimbursements, teaching assistantships with tuition reimbursements, career-related internships or fieldwork, Federal Work-Study, unspecified assistantships, and out-of-state merit awards available. Financial award application deadline: 3/7. *Faculty research:* Multimedia production, film history and criticism, writing and promotions, international broadcasting and media systems, history of American broadcasting. *Unit head:* Dr. Peter B. Orlik, Chairperson, 989-774-3851, Fax: 989-774-2426, E-mail: peter.b.orlik@cmich.edu. *Application contact:* Dr. Patricia Williamson, Graduate Program Coordinator, 989-774-2561, Fax: 989-774-2426, E-mail: willi1pa@cmich.edu.

City College of the City University of New York, Graduate School, College of Liberal Arts and Science, Division of the Humanities and Arts, Department of Media Arts Production, New York, NY 10031-9198. Offers MFA. *Entrance requirements:* For master's, videotape portfolio. Additional exam requirements/recommendations for international students: Required—TOEFL (minimum score 575 paper-based; 233 computer-based).

Claremont Graduate University, Graduate Programs, School of Arts and Humanities, Department of Cultural Studies, Claremont, CA 91711-6160. Offers Africana studies (Certificate); cultural studies (MA, PhD); media studies (MA, PhD); museum studies (MA). Part-time programs available. *Faculty:* 2 full-time (1 woman). *Students:* 57 full-time (41 women), 10 part-time (5 women); includes 21 minority (11 African Americans, 5 Asian Americans or Pacific Islanders, 5 Hispanic Americans), 6 international. Average age 35. In 2008, 8 master's, 2 doctorates awarded. *Entrance requirements:* For master's and doctorate, GRE General Test. Additional exam requirements/recommendations for international students: Required—TOEFL (minimum score 550 paper-based; 213 computer-based; 80 iBT). *Application deadline:* For fall admission, 2/1 priority date for domestic students. Applications are processed on a rolling basis. Application fee: $60. Electronic applications accepted. *Expenses:* Tuition: Full-time $33,698; part-time $1465 per unit. Required fees: $310; $155 per semester. Tuition and fees vary according to program. *Financial support:* Fellowships, research assistantships, Federal Work-Study, institutionally sponsored loans, and scholarships/grants available. Support available to part-time students. Financial award application deadline: 2/15; financial award applicants required to submit FAFSA. *Unit head:* Eve Oishi, Chair, 909-607-7587, E-mail: eve.oishi@cgu.edu. *Application contact:* Justin Evans, Admissions Coordinator, 909-607-1278, Fax: 909-607-1221, E-mail: humanities@cgu.edu.

College of Staten Island of the City University of New York, Graduate Programs, Program in Cinema and Media Studies, Staten Island, NY 10314-6600. Offers MA. Part-time and evening/weekend programs available. *Faculty:* 5 full-time (2 women). *Students:* 15 part-time (7 women); includes 1 minority (Asian American or Pacific Islander), 5 international. Average age 31. 13 applicants, 54% accepted, 5 enrolled. In 2008, 4 master's awarded. *Degree requirements:* For master's, comprehensive exam, thesis optional, written thesis; original film, media or production thesis or written examination; 36 credits in cinema and media studies courses. *Entrance requirements:* For master's, bachelor's degree, 10-12 page critical writing sample on film or media topic, 3 letters of recommendation, 1-2 page statement of purpose. Additional exam requirements/recommendations for international students: Required—TOEFL (minimum score 550 paper-based; 213 computer-based; 79 iBT). *Application deadline:* For fall admission, 4/19 priority date for domestic and international students; for spring admission, 11/16 for domestic and international students. Applications are processed on a rolling basis. Application fee: $125. Electronic applications accepted. *Expenses:* Tuition, area resident: Full-time $6400; part-time $270 per credit. Tuition, nonresident: full-time $12,000; part-time $500 per credit. Required fees: $378; $113 per semester. *Financial support:* In 2008–09, 1 student received support, including 4 teaching assistantships (averaging $1,250 per year); career-related internships or fieldwork, Federal Work-Study, and scholarships/grants also available. Support available to part-time students. Financial award application deadline: 4/1; financial award applicants required to submit CSS PROFILE or FAFSA. *Unit head:* Dr. Matthew Solomon, Coordinator/Associate Professor, 718-982-2548, E-mail: cinemamasters@mail.csi.cuny.edu. *Application contact:* Sasha Spence, Assistant Director of Graduate Recruitment and Admissions, 718-982-2699, Fax: 718-982-2500, E-mail: spence@mail.csi.cuny.edu.

Columbia College Chicago, Graduate School, Department of Arts, Entertainment and Media Management, Chicago, IL 60605-1996. Offers arts, entertainment and media management (MA), including media management, music business management, performing arts management, visual arts management. Evening/weekend programs available. *Students:* 117 full-time (84 women), 46 part-time (31 women); includes 51 minority (34 African Americans, 1 American Indian/Alaska Native, 4 Asian Americans or Pacific Islanders, 12 Hispanic Americans), 9 international. Average age 27. 247 applicants, 24% accepted, 53 enrolled. In 2008, 52 master's awarded. *Degree requirements:* For master's, thesis, internship. *Entrance requirements:* For master's, self-assessment essay. Additional exam requirements/recommendations for international students: Required—TOEFL (minimum score 550 paper-based; 213 computer-based). *Application deadline:* For fall admission, 2/2 for domestic and international students. Application fee: $55. Electronic applications accepted. *Expenses:* Tuition: Full-time $15,992; part-time $633 per credit hour. *Financial support:* Fellowships, career-related internships or fieldwork, Federal Work-Study, and scholarships/grants available. Support available to part-time students. Financial award application deadline: 8/13; financial award applicants required to submit FAFSA. *Unit head:* Dr. J. Dennis Rich, Chairperson, 312-369-7652, Fax: 312-369-8063, E-mail: drich@colum.edu. *Application contact:* Keith Cleveland, Office of Provost/Senior Vice President, 312-363-7261, Fax: 312-369-8047, E-mail: kcleveland@colum.edu.

Concordia University, School of Graduate Studies, Faculty of Arts and Science, Department of Communication Studies, Montréal, QC H3G 1M8, Canada. Offers communication (PhD); communication studies (Diploma); media studies (MA). *Degree requirements:* For master's, thesis optional; for doctorate, one foreign language, comprehensive exam, thesis/dissertation, research practicum, seminar. *Entrance requirements:* For master's, bachelor's degree in communications, 2 years of media-related experience; for doctorate, MA in communications. *Faculty research:* Communication and development, organizational communication, cultural studies, rhetoric, future studies.

Concordia University, School of Graduate Studies, Faculty of Fine Arts, Department of Studio Arts, Montréal, QC H3G 1M8, Canada. Offers studio arts (MFA), including film production, open media, painting, photography, print media, sculpture, ceramics and fibers. *Degree requirements:* For master's, thesis or alternative. *Entrance requirements:* For master's, portfolio.

Dallas Theological Seminary, Graduate Programs, Dallas, TX 75204-6499. Offers academic ministries (Th M); Bible translation (Th M); biblical and theological studies (CGS); biblical counseling (MA, Th M); biblical exegesis and linguistics (MA); biblical exposition (PhD); biblical studies (MA); Christian education (MA, D Min); cross-cultural ministries (MA, Th M); educational leadership (Th M); evangelism and discipleship (Th M); interdisciplinary studies (Th M); media and communication (MA); media arts in ministry (Th M); ministry (D Min); New Testament studies (Th M, PhD); Old Testament studies (PhD); parachurch ministries (Th M); pastoral ministries (Th M); sacred theology (STM); theological studies (PhD); women's ministry (Th M). *Accreditation:* ATS (one or more programs are accredited). Part-time and evening/weekend programs available. *Degree requirements:* For master's, variable foreign language requirement, thesis (for some programs); for doctorate, 2 foreign languages, thesis/dissertation. *Entrance requirements:* Additional exam requirements/recommendations for international students: Required—TOEFL, TWE. *Application deadline:* For fall admission, 7/1 priority date for domestic students, 1/15 for international students; for winter admission, 11/1 priority date for domestic students; for spring admission, 11/1 priority date for domestic students. Applications are processed on a rolling basis. Application fee: $30. Electronic applications accepted. *Financial support:* Career-related internships or fieldwork, institutionally sponsored loans, scholarships/grants, and tuition waivers (full and partial) available. Financial award application deadline: 2/28. *Unit head:* Dr. Mark L. Bailey, President, 214-841-3676, Fax: 214-841-3565. *Application contact:* Josh Bleeker, Director of Admissions, 214-841-3661, Fax: 214-841-3664, E-mail: admissions@dts.edu.

DePaul University, College of Communication, Chicago, IL 60614. Offers journalism (MA); media, culture and society (MA); organizational and multicultural communication (MA); public relations and advertising (MA). Part-time and evening/weekend programs available. *Faculty:* 31 full-time (17 women), 15 part-time/adjunct (7 women). *Students:* 135 full-time (106 women), 43 part-time (35 women); includes 49 minority (25 African Americans, 7 Asian Americans or Pacific Islanders, 17 Hispanic Americans), 8 international. Average age 29. 242 applicants, 47% accepted, 68 enrolled. In 2008, 64 master's awarded. *Degree requirements:* For master's, comprehensive exam (for some programs), final exam or thesis/project. *Entrance requirements:* For master's, GRE General Test (public relations and advertising), minimum GPA of 3.0, writing sample, essay, letters of recommendation, resumé. Additional exam requirements/recommendations for international students: Required—TOEFL (minimum score 590 paper-based; 245 computer-based; 96 iBT). Application fee: $40. Electronic applications accepted. *Financial support:* In 2008–09, 8 students received support, including 4 research assistantships with partial tuition reimbursements available, 2 teaching assistantships with full tuition reimbursements available (averaging $12,000 per year); fellowships with full tuition reimbursements available, career-related internships or fieldwork, scholarships/grants, and tuition waivers (partial) also available. Support available to part-time students. Financial award applicants required to submit FAFSA. *Faculty research:* Intercultural communication, corporate culture, diversity in the working place, organizational socialization, critical cultural studies. *Unit head:* Dr. Jacqueline Taylor, Dean, 773-325-7216, Fax: 773-325-7584, E-mail: jtaylor@depaul.edu. *Application contact:* Ann Spittle, Director of Graduate Admission, 773-325-8369, Fax: 773-325-2395, E-mail: aspittle@depaul.edu.

Digital Media Arts College, Graduate Programs, Boca Raton, FL 33431. Offers graphic design (MFA); special FX animation (MFA).

Drexel University, College of Media Arts and Design, Department of Design, Philadelphia, PA 19104-2875. Offers digital media (MS); fashion design (MS); interior design (MS); television management (MS); MS/MBA. *Degree requirements:* For master's, thesis. *Entrance requirements:* For master's, interview. Additional exam requirements/recommendations for international students: Required—TOEFL. Electronic applications accepted.

Edinboro University of Pennsylvania, Graduate Studies and Research, School of Liberal Arts, Department of Communications and Media Studies, Edinboro, PA 16444. Offers MA. Part-time and evening/weekend programs available. *Faculty:* 4 full-time (1 woman). *Students:* 33 full-time (22 women), 12 part-time (8 women); includes 5 minority (3 African Americans, 1 Asian American or Pacific Islander, 1 Hispanic American), 3 international. Average age 29. In 2008, 20 master's awarded. *Degree requirements:* For master's, thesis or alternative, competency exam. *Entrance requirements:* For master's, GRE or MAT, minimum QPA of 2.5. *Application deadline:* Applications are processed on a rolling basis. Application fee: $30. Electronic applications accepted. *Expenses:* Tuition, state resident: full-time $6430; part-time $357 per credit. Tuition, nonresident: full-time $8038; part-time $572 per credit. International tuition: $15,171.58 full-time. Required fees: $2113; $60 per credit. Tuition and fees vary according to course load. *Financial support:* In 2008–09, 10 research assistantships with full and partial tuition reimbursements (averaging $3,850 per year) were awarded; career-related internships or fieldwork, Federal Work-Study, scholarships/grants, and unspecified assistantships also available. Support available to part-time students. Financial award application deadline: 2/15; financial award applicants required to submit FAFSA. *Unit head:* Dr. Andrew Smith, Program Head, 814-732-2165, E-mail: arsmith@edinboro.edu. *Application contact:* Dr. Andrew Smith, Program Head, 814-732-2165, E-mail: arsmith@edinboro.edu.

Emerson College, Graduate Studies, School of the Arts, Department of Visual and Media Arts, Program in Media Art, Boston, MA 02116-4624. Offers MFA. Part-time and evening/weekend programs available. *Students:* 93 full-time (46 women), 37 part-time (14 women); includes 14 minority (4 African Americans, 1 American Indian/Alaska Native, 5 Asian Americans or Pacific Islanders, 4 Hispanic Americans), 16 international. Average age 29. 110 applicants, 65% accepted, 33 enrolled. In 2008, 49 master's awarded. *Degree requirements:* For master's, comprehensive exam, thesis or alternative. *Entrance requirements:* For master's, GRE General Test. Additional exam requirements/recommendations for international students: Required—TOEFL (minimum score 550 paper-based; 213 computer-based; 80 iBT), IELTS (minimum score 6.5). *Application deadline:* For fall admission, 6/1 priority date for domestic students, 5/1 for international students; for spring admission, 11/1 priority date for domestic students, 11/1 for international students. Applications are processed on a rolling basis. Application fee: $60 ($75 for international students). Electronic applications accepted. *Expenses:* Tuition: Full-time $17,720; part-time $886 per credit. Required fees: $60 per year. One-time fee: $170. *Financial support:* In 2008–09, 19 students received support, including 1 fellowship with partial tuition reimbursement available (averaging $14,000 per year), 16 research assistantships with partial tuition reimbursements available (averaging $10,000 per year); teaching assistantships with partial tuition reimbursements available, career-related internships or fieldwork, Federal Work-Study, institutionally sponsored loans, scholarships/grants, and unspecified assistantships also available. Support available to part-time students. Financial award application deadline: 3/1; financial award applicants required to submit CSS PROFILE or FAFSA. *Faculty research:* Media studies. *Unit head:* Prof. Jan Roberts-Breslin, Graduate Program Director, 617-824-8800, E-mail: Jan_Roberts_Breslin@emerson.edu. *Application contact:* Office of Graduate Admission, 617-824-8610, Fax: 617-824-8614, E-mail: gradapp@emerson.edu.

Fairleigh Dickinson University, Metropolitan Campus, University College: Arts, Sciences, and Professional Studies, School of Art and Media Studies, Program in Media and Communications, Teaneck, NJ 07666-1914. Offers MA. *Students:* 6 full-time (5 women), 12 part-time (7 women), 5 international. Average age 31. 15 applicants, 67% accepted, 7 enrolled. In 2008, 4 master's awarded. Application fee: $40. *Application contact:* Susan Brooman, University Director of Graduate Admissions, 201-692-2554, Fax: 201-692-2560, E-mail: globaleducation@fdu.edu.

Florida State University, Graduate Studies, College of Communication, Department of Communication, Tallahassee, FL 32306. Offers corporate and public communication (MA, MS); integrated marketing communication (MA, MS); mass communication (PhD); media and communication studies (MA, MS); speech communication (PhD). Part-time programs available. *Degree requirements:* For master's, thesis (for some programs); for doctorate, comprehensive exam, thesis/dissertation. *Entrance requirements:* For master's, GRE General Test, minimum GPA of 3.0; for doctorate, GRE General Test, minimum GPA of 3.3 in graduate course work. Additional exam requirements/recommendations for international students: Required—TOEFL (minimum score 600 paper-based; 250 computer-based; 100 iBT). *Faculty research:* Communication technology and policy, marketing communication, communication content and effect, new communication/information technologies.

Fordham University, Graduate School of Business Administration, New York, NY 10023. Offers accounting (MBA); communications and media management (MBA); executive business administration (EMBA); finance (MBA, MS); information systems (MBA, MS); management systems (MBA); marketing (MBA); media management (MS); taxation (MS); taxation and accounting (MTA);); JD/MBA; MBA/MIM; MS/MBA. *Accreditation:* AACSB. Part-time and evening/weekend programs available. *Entrance requirements:* For master's, GMAT, official undergraduate transcripts, 2 letters of recommendation, resumé, personal statement. Additional exam requirements/recommendations for international students: Required—TOEFL (minimum

Media Studies

Fordham University (continued)

score 600 paper-based; 250 computer-based; 100 iBT). Electronic applications accepted. *Expenses:* Contact institution.

Full Sail University, Program in Media Design, Winter Park, FL 32792-7437. Offers MFA. Postbaccalaureate distance learning degree programs offered.

Georgetown University, Graduate School of Arts and Sciences, School of Continuing Studies, Washington, DC 20057. Offers American studies (MALS); Catholic studies (MALS); classical civilizations (MALS); ethics and the professions (MALS); human resources management (MPS); humanities (MALS); individualized study (MALS); international affairs (MALS); Islam and Muslim-Christian relations (MALS); journalism (MPS); liberal studies (DLS); literature and society (MALS); medieval and early modern European studies (MALS); public relations (MPS); real estate (MPS); religious studies (MALS); social and public policy (MALS); sports industry management (MPS); the theory and practice of American democracy (MALS); visual culture (MALS). *Entrance requirements:* Additional exam requirements/recommendations for international students: Required—TOEFL.

Governors State University, College of Arts and Sciences, Program in Communication and Training, University Park, IL 60466-0975. Offers communication studies (MA); instructional and training technology (MA); media communication (MA). Part-time and evening/weekend programs available. *Degree requirements:* For master's, thesis or alternative.

Howard University, School of Communications, Division of Mass Communication and Media Studies, Washington, DC 20059-0002. Offers mass communication (MA, PhD); media studies (MA, PhD). Part-time and evening/weekend programs available. *Degree requirements:* For master's, comprehensive exam (for some programs), thesis optional; for doctorate, one foreign language, comprehensive exam, thesis/dissertation. *Entrance requirements:* For master's, GRE, minimum GPA of 3.0; for doctorate, GRE, minimum graduate GPA of 3.5. Additional exam requirements/recommendations for international students: Required—TOEFL. Electronic applications accepted. *Faculty research:* Advertising, public relations, journalism new media.

Hunter College of the City University of New York, Graduate School, School of Arts and Sciences, Department of Film and Media Studies, Program in Integrated Media Arts, New York, NY 10021-5085. Offers MA, MFA. Part-time and evening/weekend programs available. *Faculty:* 8 full-time (4 women), 2 part-time/adjunct (1 woman). *Students:* 13 full-time (10 women), 60 part-time (36 women); includes 9 minority (1 African American, 2 Asian Americans or Pacific Islanders, 6 Hispanic Americans). Average age 33. 78 applicants, 55% accepted, 26 enrolled. In 2008, 18 master's awarded. *Entrance requirements:* For master's, GRE General Test, 3 letters of recommendation, portfolio of media works, minimum GPA of 3.0. Additional exam requirements/recommendations for international students: Required—TOEFL, TWE. *Application deadline:* For fall admission, 2/1 for domestic students. Application fee: $125. *Financial support:* Federal Work-Study and tuition waivers (partial) available. Support available to part-time students. *Faculty research:* Nonfiction production, Internet as medium, public interest journalism, social and historical roots of media arts. *Unit head:* Kelly Anderson, Deputy Chair, 212-772-6008. *Application contact:* Mary Flanagan, New Media Advisor, 212-650-3219, E-mail: maryflanagan@hunter.cuny.edu.

Indiana State University, School of Graduate Studies, College of Arts and Sciences, Department of Communication, Terre Haute, IN 47809-1401. Offers communication studies (MA, MS); radio, television and film (MA, MS). Part-time programs available. *Degree requirements:* For master's, thesis (for some programs), oral and written exam. *Entrance requirements:* For master's, GRE General Test. Additional exam requirements/recommendations for international students: Required—TOEFL. *Faculty research:* Women in media, communication apprehension, media history.

Indiana University Bloomington, University Graduate School, College of Arts and Sciences, Department of Communication and Culture, Bloomington, IN 47405-7000. Offers film and media studies (PhD); performance and ethnography (PhD); rhetoric and public culture (PhD). *Faculty:* 24 full-time (12 women). *Students:* 81 full-time (45 women); includes 11 minority (2 African Americans, 1 American Indian/Alaska Native, 2 Asian Americans or Pacific Islanders, 6 Hispanic Americans), 10 international. Average age 32. 163 applicants, 20% accepted, 16 enrolled. In 2008, 5 master's, 11 doctorates awarded. *Degree requirements:* For master's, comprehensive exam; for doctorate, one foreign language, comprehensive exam, thesis/dissertation, student teaching. *Entrance requirements:* For master's and doctorate, GRE General Test (recommended), minimum GPA of 3.0, 3 letters of recommendation, writing sample. Additional exam requirements/recommendations for international students: Required—TOEFL (minimum score 550 paper-based; 213 computer-based). *Application deadline:* For winter admission, 1/1 for domestic students, 12/1 for international students. Application fee: $50 ($60 for international students). Electronic applications accepted. *Expenses:* Tuition, area resident: Part-time $291.97 per credit hour. Tuition, state resident: part-time $291.97 per credit hour. Tuition, nonresident: part-time $850.33 per credit hour. Required fees: $110 per semester. Tuition and fees vary according to course load and program. *Financial support:* In 2008–09, 65 students received support, including 4 fellowships with full tuition reimbursements available (averaging $18,000 per year), 61 teaching assistantships with full tuition reimbursements available (averaging $12,961 per year). Financial award application deadline: 4/15. *Faculty research:* Rhetoric and public culture, film and media studies, performance ethnography. *Unit head:* Prof. Gregory A. Waller, Chair, 812-855-2367, Fax: 812-855-6014, E-mail: cmcl@indiana.edu. *Application contact:* Kathy P. Teige, Graduate Secretary, 812-855-6389, Fax: 812-855-6014, E-mail: kteige@indiana.edu.

Indiana University of Pennsylvania, School of Graduate Studies and Research, College of Education and Educational Technology, Department of Communications Media, Indiana, PA 15705-1087. Offers adult education and communications technology (MA); communications media and instructional technology (PhD). *Faculty:* 5 full-time (0 women). *Students:* 8 full-time (2 women), 13 part-time (7 women); includes 2 minority (1 African American, 1 Asian American or Pacific Islander), 1 international. Average age 34. 33 applicants, 64% accepted, 21 enrolled. *Expenses:* Tuition, area resident: Full-time $6430; part-time $357 per credit. Tuition, nonresident: full-time $10,288; part-time $572 per credit. Required fees: $1547.50; $107 per credit. $283 per year. *Financial support:* In 2008–09, 4 research assistantships (averaging $5,801 per year), 3 teaching assistantships (averaging $20,909 per year) were awarded. *Unit head:* Dr. Mark Piwinsky, Chairperson, 724-357-3954, Fax: 724-357-5503, E-mail: Mark.Piwinsky@iup.edu. *Application contact:* Dr. Edward Nardi, Associate Dean, 724-357-2480, Fax: 724-357-5595, E-mail: ewnardi@iup.edu.

International University in Geneva, Master of Arts in Media and Communication Program, Geneva, Switzerland. Offers luxury management (MA); marketing (MA). *Faculty:* 9 full-time (2 women), 23 part-time/adjunct (11 women). *Students:* 7 full-time (all women); includes 1 Asian American or Pacific Islander, 1 Hispanic American. Average age 31. 30 applicants, 53% accepted, 7 enrolled. In 2008, 1 master's awarded. *Degree requirements:* For master's, comprehensive exam. *Entrance requirements:* Additional exam requirements/recommendations for international students: Required—TOEFL. *Application deadline:* For fall admission, 7/31 priority date for domestic students, 7/1 priority date for international students; for winter admission, 11/2 priority date for domestic students, 10/9 priority date for international students; for spring admission, 2/12 priority date for domestic students, 1/22 priority date for international students. Applications are processed on a rolling basis. Application fee: $150. Electronic applications accepted. *Unit head:* Dr. Leonid Androuchko, Unit Coordinator, 41-22710-7110, Fax: 41-22710-7111, E-mail: info@iun.ch. *Application contact:* Uliana Horler, Admissions Officer, 41-22710-7110, Fax: 41-22710-7111, E-mail: master@iun.ch.

Kutztown University of Pennsylvania, College of Graduate Studies and Extended Learning, College of Liberal Arts and Sciences, Program in Electronic Media, Kutztown, PA 19530-0730. Offers MS. Part-time and evening/weekend programs available. *Faculty:* 4 full-time (2 women). *Students:* 5 full-time (1 woman), 9 part-time (3 women), 2 international. Average age 28. 7 applicants, 86% accepted, 4 enrolled. In 2008, 4 master's awarded. *Degree requirements:* For master's, thesis. *Entrance requirements:* For master's, GRE General Test. Additional exam requirements/recommendations for international students: Required—TOEFL. *Application deadline:* For fall admission, 8/15 priority date for domestic and international students; for spring admission, 12/15 priority date for domestic and international students. Applications are processed on a rolling basis. Application fee: $35. Electronic applications accepted. *Expenses:* Tuition, area resident: Full-time $6430; part-time $357 per credit. Tuition, state resident: full-time $6430; part-time $357 per credit. Tuition, nonresident: full-time $10,288; part-time $572 per credit. Required fees: $1360; $72 per credit. $67 per semester. *Financial support:* Career-related internships or fieldwork, Federal Work-Study, scholarships/grants, and unspecified assistantships available. Financial award application deadline: 3/1; financial award applicants required to submit FAFSA. *Unit head:* Dr. Joseph Chuk, Chairperson, 610-683-4492, Fax: 610-683-4659, E-mail: chuk@kutztown.edu. *Application contact:* Dr. Linda Matthews, Interim Dean of Graduate Studies, 610-683-4201, Fax: 610-683-1393, E-mail: graduate@kutztown.edu.

Louisiana State University and Agricultural and Mechanical College, Graduate School, Manship School of Mass Communication, Baton Rouge, LA 70803. Offers MMC, PhD. *Accreditation:* ACEJMC. Part-time programs available. Postbaccalaureate distance learning degree programs offered (minimal on-campus study). *Degree requirements:* For master's, thesis. *Entrance requirements:* For master's, GRE General Test, minimum GPA of 3.0. Additional exam requirements/recommendations for international students: Required—TOEFL (minimum score 550 paper-based; 213 computer-based; 79 iBT). Electronic applications accepted. *Faculty research:* Media effects, political communication, new media technologies, persuasive communication, journalism processes and practice.

Lynn University, College of Business and Management, Boca Raton, FL 33431-5598. Offers aviation management (MBA); financial valuation and investment management (MBA); global leadership (PhD); hospitality management (MBA); international business (MBA); marketing (MBA); mass communication and media management (MBA); sports and athletics administration (MBA). Part-time and evening/weekend programs available. Postbaccalaureate distance learning degree programs offered. *Degree requirements:* For master's, project; for doctorate, thesis/dissertation, qualifying paper. *Entrance requirements:* For master's, GMAT or GRE, minimum undergraduate GPA of 3.0, resumé, 2 letters of recommendation; for doctorate, GRE or GMAT, minimum graduate GPA of 3.25, resumé, 2 letters of recommendation. Additional exam requirements/recommendations for international students: Required—TOEFL (minimum score 550 paper-based; 213 computer-based). Electronic applications accepted. *Faculty research:* Labor relations, dynamic balance in leisure-time skills, ethics in athletics, hotel development.

Marquette University, Graduate School, College of Communication, Milwaukee, WI 53201-1881. Offers advertising and public relations (MA); broadcasting and electronic communications (MA); communications studies (MA); journalism (MA); mass communications (MA); religious communications (MA); science, health and environmental communications (MA). *Accreditation:* ACEJMC. Part-time and evening/weekend programs available. *Degree requirements:* For master's, comprehensive exam. *Entrance requirements:* For master's, GRE. Additional exam requirements/recommendations for international students: Required—TOEFL. *Faculty research:* Urban journalism, gender and communication, intercultural communication, religious communication.

Marywood University, Academic Affairs, Insalaco College of Creative Arts and Management, Department of Communication Arts, Program in Communication Arts, Scranton, PA 18509-1598. Offers corporate communication (Certificate); e-business (Certificate); health communication (Certificate); instructional technology (Certificate); interdisciplinary (MA); library science/information specialist (Certificate); media management (MA); production (MA).

Massachusetts Institute of Technology, School of Architecture and Planning, Program in Media Arts and Sciences, Cambridge, MA 02139-4307. Offers media arts and sciences (SM, PhD); media technology (SM). Terminal master's awarded for partial completion of doctoral program. *Degree requirements:* For master's, thesis; for doctorate, comprehensive exam, thesis/dissertation. *Entrance requirements:* Additional exam requirements/recommendations for international students: Required—TOEFL (minimum score 600 paper-based; 250 computer-based). Electronic applications accepted. *Faculty research:* Human machine interaction; communications technologies; new media technologies; physical computing; learning and creativity.

Massachusetts Institute of Technology, School of Humanities, Arts, and Social Sciences, Program in Comparative Media Studies, Cambridge, MA 02139-4307. Offers SM. *Degree requirements:* For master's, thesis. *Entrance requirements:* For master's, GRE General Test. Additional exam requirements/recommendations for international students: Required—TOEFL (minimum score 577 paper-based; 233 computer-based). Electronic applications accepted. *Faculty research:* Convergence Culture; New Media Literacies; Games and Education; Civic Media; Media History.

Metropolitan College of New York, Program in Media Management, New York, NY 10013. Offers MBA. Evening/weekend programs available. *Degree requirements:* For master's, thesis, 10 day study abroad. *Entrance requirements:* For master's, GMAT or GRE, appropriate work experience, interview, minimum GPA of 2.7. Additional exam requirements/recommendations for international students: Required—TOEFL (minimum score 600 paper-based; 220 computer-based). Electronic applications accepted. *Expenses:* Contact institution.

Michigan State University, The Graduate School, College of Communication Arts and Sciences, Department of Telecommunication, Information Studies, and Media, East Lansing, MI 48824. Offers MA. *Entrance requirements:* Additional exam requirements/recommendations for international students: Required—TOEFL. Electronic applications accepted.

Michigan State University, The Graduate School, College of Communication Arts and Sciences, Program in Communication Arts and Sciences–Media and Information Studies, East Lansing, MI 48824. Offers PhD. *Entrance requirements:* Additional exam requirements/recommendations for international students: Required—TOEFL. Electronic applications accepted. *Faculty research:* Mass media, comparative media.

Monmouth University, Graduate School, Department of Corporate and Public Communication, West Long Branch, NJ 07764-1898. Offers corporate and public communication (MA); human resources communication (Certificate); media studies (Certificate); public relations (Certificate). *Faculty:* 9 full-time (5 women). *Students:* 5 full-time (3 women), 40 part-time (28 women); includes 8 minority (4 African Americans, 1 Asian American or Pacific Islander, 3 Hispanic Americans), 3 international. Average age 32. 19 applicants, 95% accepted, 10 enrolled. In 2008, 14 master's awarded. *Degree requirements:* For master's, comprehensive exam, project. *Entrance requirements:* For master's, GRE, minimum GPA of 3.0 in major, 2.75 overall. Additional exam requirements/recommendations for international students: Required—TOEFL (minimum score 550 paper-based; 213 computer-based; 79 iBT), IELTS (minimum score 5), Michigan English Language Assessment Battery (minimum score: 77), Cambridge A, B, C. *Application deadline:* For fall admission, 7/15 priority date for domestic students, 6/1 for international students; for spring admission, 11/15 priority date for domestic students, 11/1 for international students. Applications are processed on a rolling basis. Application fee: $50. Electronic applications accepted. *Expenses:* Tuition: Full-time $13,914; part-time $773 per credit. Required fees: $628; $157 per semester. *Financial support:* In 2008–09, 26 students received support, including 23 fellowships (averaging $1,142 per year), 5 research assistantships (averaging $4,794 per year); scholarships/grants and unspecified assistantships also available. Support available to part-time students. Financial award application deadline: 3/1; financial award applicants required to submit FAFSA. *Faculty research:* Service learning, history of television, feminism and the media, executive communication, public relations pedagogy. *Unit head:* Dr. Eleanor Novek, Program Director, 732-263-5449, Fax: 732-571-3609, E-mail: enovek@monmouth.edu. *Application contact:* Kevin Roane, Director, Office of Graduate Admission, 732-571-3452, Fax: 732-263-5123, E-mail: gradadm@monmouth.edu.

National University, Academic Affairs, School of Media and Communication, Department of Media, La Jolla, CA 92037-1011. Offers digital cinema (MFA); educational and instructional technology (MS); video game production and design (MFA). Part-time and evening/weekend programs available. Postbaccalaureate distance learning degree programs offered (no on-campus study). *Faculty:* 9 full-time (3 women), 61 part-time/adjunct (20 women). *Students:* 70 full-time (26 women), 141 part-time (62 women); includes 64 minority (28 African Americans, 1 American Indian/Alaska Native, 10 Asian Americans or Pacific Islanders, 25 Hispanic Americans). Average age 39. 118 applicants, 100% accepted, 118 enrolled. In 2008, 58 master's awarded. *Degree requirements:* For master's, thesis. *Entrance requirements:* For master's, interview, minimum GPA of 2.5. Additional exam requirements/recommendations for international students: Required—TOEFL (minimum score 550 paper-based; 213 computer-based; 79 iBT), IELTS (minimum score 6). *Application deadline:* Applications are processed on a rolling basis. Application fee: $60 ($65 for international students). Electronic applications accepted. *Expenses:* Tuition: Full-time $8694; part-time $322 per credit hour. Tuition and fees vary according to course load. *Financial support:* Career-related internships or fieldwork, institutionally sponsored loans, scholarships/grants, and tuition waivers (partial) available. Support available to part-time students. Financial award application deadline: 6/30; financial award applicants required to submit FAFSA. *Unit head:* Dr. Timothy Langdell, Department Chair, 310-662-2149, Fax: 858-309-3450, E-mail: tlangdell@nu.edu. *Application contact:* Dominick Giovanniello, Associate Regional Dean—San Diego, 800-NAT-UNIV, Fax: 858-541-7792, E-mail: dgiovann@nu.edu.

New Mexico Highlands University, Graduate Studies, College of Arts and Sciences, Program in Media Arts and Computer Science, Las Vegas, NM 87701. Offers media arts and computer science (MS). *Faculty:* 3 full-time (0 women). *Students:* 18 full-time (7 women), 9 part-time (2 women); includes 8 minority (1 African American, 1 Asian American or Pacific Islander, 6 Hispanic Americans), 11 international. Average age 30. 16 applicants, 69% accepted, 4 enrolled. In 2008, 9 master's awarded. *Degree requirements:* For master's, comprehensive exam, thesis. *Entrance requirements:* For master's, minimum undergraduate GPA of 3.0. Additional exam requirements/recommendations for international students: Required—TOEFL (minimum score 540 paper-based; 270 computer-based). Application fee: $15. *Expenses:* Tuition, state resident: full-time $2880; part-time $120 per credit hour. Tuition, nonresident: full-time $4234; part-time $176 per credit hour. International tuition: $5645 full-time. One-time fee: $20. *Financial support:* In 2008–09, 10 students received support, including teaching assistantships (averaging $7,200 per year); career-related internships or fieldwork, Federal Work-Study, institutionally sponsored loans, scholarships/grants, tuition waivers (full and partial), and unspecified assistantships also available. Support available to part-time students. Financial award application deadline: 3/1; financial award applicants required to submit FAFSA. *Faculty research:* Advanced digital compositing, photographic installations and exhibition design, pattern recognition, parallel and distributed computing, computer security education. *Unit head:* Dr. Hossein Tahani, Department Head of Computer Science, 505-426-2121, E-mail: htahani@nmhu.edu. *Application contact:* Diane Trujillo, Administrative Assistant for Graduate Studies, 505-454-3266, Fax: 505-426-2117, E-mail: dtrujillo@nmhu.edu.

The New School: A University, The New School for General Studies, Program in Media Studies, New York, NY 10011. Offers communication theory (MA); media studies (MA). Part-time and evening/weekend programs available. *Faculty:* 19 full-time (8 women), 44 part-time/adjunct (16 women). *Students:* 203 full-time (131 women), 272 part-time (180 women); includes 101 minority (31 African Americans, 3 American Indian/Alaska Native, 28 Asian Americans or Pacific Islanders, 39 Hispanic Americans), 72 international. Average age 30. In 2008, 143 master's awarded. *Degree requirements:* For master's, thesis optional. *Entrance requirements:* For master's, interview. Additional exam requirements/recommendations for international students: Required—TOEFL (minimum score 600 paper-based; 250 computer-based; 100 iBT). *Application deadline:* For fall admission, 4/15 for domestic students; for spring admission, 10/15 for domestic students. Applications are processed on a rolling basis. Application fee: $50. *Expenses:* Tuition: Full-time $27,144; part-time $1508 per credit. Required fees: $355 per semester. *Financial support:* Fellowships, research assistantships, teaching assistantships, Federal Work-Study, scholarships/grants, and tuition waivers (partial) available. Financial award application deadline: 3/1; financial award applicants required to submit FAFSA. *Faculty research:* Effect of technology on society, effect of US media on international affairs, effect of media on corporate affairs. *Unit head:* Dr. Peter L. Haratonik, Interim Chair, Media Studies and Film, 212-229-8903, Fax: 212-465-0661, E-mail: haraton@newschool.edu. *Application contact:* David Norris, Director of Admissions, 212-229-5630, Fax: 212-989-3887, E-mail: nsadmissions@newschool.edu.

See Close-Up on page 691.

New York University, Graduate School of Arts and Science, Department of Anthropology, Program in Culture and Media, New York, NY 10012-1019. Offers MA/Advanced Certificate, PhD/Advanced Certificate. Awarded with MA or PhD in anthropology. *Entrance requirements:* Additional exam requirements/recommendations for international students: Required—TOEFL. *Faculty research:* Critical history of ethnographic film, ethnography of media, indigenous media, politics of reproduction and disability, social movements.

New York University, Steinhardt School of Culture, Education and Human Development, Department of Media, Culture and Communication, New York, NY 10012-1019. Offers media ecology/culture and communication (PhD); media, culture, and communication (MA). Part-time and evening/weekend programs available. *Entrance requirements:* Additional exam requirements/recommendations for international students: Required—TOEFL. *Faculty research:* Digital media, intercultural communication, race and politics, media criticism, media literacy.

Norfolk State University, School of Graduate Studies, School of Liberal Arts, Department of Media and Communication, Norfolk, VA 23504. Offers MA. Part-time programs available. *Degree requirements:* For master's, thesis. *Entrance requirements:* For master's, GRE, minimum GPA of 2.5, letters of recommendation. Additional exam requirements/recommendations for international students: Required—TOEFL.

Northwestern University, The Graduate School, School of Communication, Department of Radio/Television/Film, Evanston, IL 60208. Offers MA, MFA, PhD. Admissions and degrees offered through The Graduate School. Part-time programs available. Terminal master's awarded for partial completion of doctoral program. *Degree requirements:* For master's, comprehensive exam or thesis; for doctorate, thesis/dissertation, qualifying exam. *Entrance requirements:* For master's and doctorate, GRE General Test. Additional exam requirements/recommendations for international students: Required—TOEFL. Electronic applications accepted. *Faculty research:* Art and new media, media theory and criticism, gender, media history, documentary.

Northwestern University, Medill School of Journalism, Evanston, IL 60208. Offers broadcast journalism (MSJ); integrated marketing communications (MSIMC), including advertising/sales promotion, direct database and e-commerce marketing, general studies, public relations; magazine publishing (MSJ); new media (MSJ); reporting and writing (MSJ). *Accreditation:* ACEJMC (one or more programs are accredited). *Entrance requirements:* For master's, GRE General Test, GMAT or LSAT (MSJ). Additional exam requirements/recommendations for international students: Required—TOEFL. Electronic applications accepted. *Expenses:* Contact institution. *Faculty research:* Web business journalism, cultural stereotypes, voter apathy, digital television.

Ohio University, Graduate College, Scripps College of Communication, School of Media Arts and Studies, Athens, OH 45701-2979. Offers mass communication (PhD); media arts and studies (MA). *Degree requirements:* For master's, comprehensive exam, thesis or alternative; for doctorate, comprehensive exam, thesis/dissertation. *Entrance requirements:* For master's, GRE General Test or MAT, minimum GPA of 3.0; for doctorate, GRE General Test or MAT. Additional exam requirements/recommendations for international students: Required—TOEFL (minimum score 600 paper-based; 250 computer-based). *Faculty research:* Children's media, international media, policy and regulation, new technologies, cultural studies.

Ohio University, Graduate College, Scripps College of Communication, School of Visual Communication, Athens, OH 45701-2979. Offers MA. *Accreditation:* NASAD. *Entrance requirements:* For master's, minimum GPA of 2.5, portfolio. Additional exam requirements/recommendations for international students: Required—TOEFL (minimum score 600 paper-based; 250 computer-based). Electronic applications accepted. *Faculty research:* Photographic communication (photojournalism, multimedia, and documentary), photographic illustration (product, editorial, architectural), multimedia (planning and design), media management.

Rochester Institute of Technology, Graduate Enrollment Services, College of Liberal Arts, Department of Communications, Program in Communication and Media Technologies, Rochester, NY 14623-5603. Offers MS. *Degree requirements:* For master's, thesis. *Entrance requirements:* For master's, minimum GPA of 3.0, writing sample. Additional exam requirements/recommendations for international students: Required—TOEFL (minimum score 600 paper-based; 250 computer-based; 100 iBT). Electronic applications accepted.

Saginaw Valley State University, College of Arts and Behavioral Sciences, Program in Communication and Digital Media Design, University Center, MI 48710. Offers MA. Part-time and evening/weekend programs available. *Students:* 19 full-time (10 women), 22 part-time (13 women); includes 4 minority (2 African Americans, 1 Asian American or Pacific Islander, 1 Hispanic American), 16 international. Average age 31. 23 applicants, 91% accepted, 14 enrolled. In 2008, 17 master's awarded. *Degree requirements:* For master's, thesis. *Entrance requirements:* For master's, minimum GPA of 2.75. Additional exam requirements/recommendations for international students: Required—TOEFL. *Application deadline:* Applications are processed on a rolling basis. Application fee: $25. Electronic applications accepted. *Expenses:* Tuition, state resident: full-time $8620; part-time $359.15 per credit hour. Tuition, nonresident: full-time $16,526; part-time $688.60 per credit hour. Required fees: $350.40; $14.60 per credit hour. Tuition and fees vary according to campus/location. *Financial support:* Federal Work-Study and scholarships/grants available. Support available to part-time students. Financial award application deadline: 4/1; financial award applicants required to submit FAFSA. *Unit head:* Dr. Steve Erickson, Program Coordinator/Professor of Theatre, 989-964-4147, E-mail: erickson@svsu.edu. *Application contact:* Dr. Steve Erickson, Program Coordinator/Professor of Theatre, 989-964-4147, E-mail: erickson@svsu.edu.

San Diego State University, Graduate and Research Affairs, College of Professional Studies and Fine Arts, School of Communication, San Diego, CA 92182. Offers advertising and public relations (MA); critical-cultural studies (MA); interaction studies (MA); intercultural and international studies (MA); new media studies (MA); news and information studies (MA); telecommunications and media management (MA). *Degree requirements:* For master's, thesis. *Entrance requirements:* For master's, GRE General Test, 3 letters of recommendation. Additional exam requirements/recommendations for international students: Required—TOEFL. Electronic applications accepted.

San Diego State University, Graduate and Research Affairs, College of Professional Studies and Fine Arts, School of Theater, Television and Film, Program in Television, Film, and New Media Production, San Diego, CA 92182. Offers MA. *Entrance requirements:* For master's, GRE General Test, 3 letters of recommendation, resumé, sample reel, influential book list, influential films list, hobby list. Additional exam requirements/recommendations for international students: Required—TOEFL. Electronic applications accepted. *Faculty research:* Experimental film and television programs, documentary film, television research and production.

San Francisco State University, Division of Graduate Studies, College of Creative Arts, Department of Broadcast and Electronic Communication Arts, San Francisco, CA 94132-1722. Offers radio and television (MA).

Savannah College of Art and Design, Graduate School, Program in Broadcast Design, Savannah, GA 31402-3146. Offers MA, MFA. Part-time programs available. *Degree requirements:* For master's, thesis, internships. *Entrance requirements:* For master's, interview, portfolio. Additional exam requirements/recommendations for international students: Required—TOEFL (minimum score 450 paper-based; 133 computer-based). Electronic applications accepted. *Expenses:* Tuition: Full-time $28,215; part-time $3135 per course. One-time fee: $500.

Savannah College of Art and Design, Graduate School, Program in Performing Arts, Savannah, GA 31402-3146. Offers MA, MFA. *Degree requirements:* For master's, thesis, internship. *Entrance requirements:* For master's, audition, interview. Additional exam requirements/recommendations for international students: Required—TOEFL (minimum score 450 paper-based; 133 computer-based). Electronic applications accepted. *Expenses:* Tuition: Full-time $28,215; part-time $3135 per course. One-time fee: $500.

See Close-Up on page 223.

Southern Illinois University Carbondale, Graduate School, College of Mass Communication and Media Arts, Department of Mass Communication and Media Arts, Carbondale, IL 62901-4701. Offers MA, MFA.

Southern Illinois University Carbondale, Graduate School, College of Mass Communication and Media Arts, Department of Professional Media and Media Management Studies, Carbondale, IL 62901-4701. Offers MA.

Southern Illinois University Carbondale, Graduate School, College of Mass Communication and Media Arts, Program in Media Theory and Research, Carbondale, IL 62901-4701. Offers MA.

Southern Illinois University Edwardsville, Graduate Studies and Research, College of Arts and Sciences, Department of Mass Communications, Program in Media Literacy, Edwardsville, IL 62026-0001. Offers Postbaccalaureate Certificate. Part-time programs available. *Students:* 1 applicant, 0% accepted. *Entrance requirements:* Additional exam requirements/recommendations for international students: Required—TOEFL (minimum score 550 paper-based; 213 computer-based; 79 iBT), IELTS (minimum score 6.5). *Application deadline:* For fall admission, 7/20 for domestic students, 6/1 for international students; for spring admission, 12/14 for domestic students, 10/1 for international students. Applications are processed on a rolling basis. Application fee: $30. Electronic applications accepted. *Expenses:* Tuition, area resident: Full-time $5838. Tuition, nonresident: full-time $14,596. Required fees: $1525. *Financial support:* Fellowships with full tuition reimbursements, research assistantships with full tuition reimbursements, teaching assistantships with full tuition reimbursements available. Financial award application deadline: 3/1; financial award applicants required to submit FAFSA. *Unit head:* Dr. Gary Hicks, Director, 618-650-2242, E-mail: ghicks@siue.edu. *Application contact:* Dr. Gary Hicks, Director, 618-650-2242, E-mail: ghicks@siue.edu.

Syracuse University, Graduate School, S. I. Newhouse School of Public Communications, Program in Media Management, Syracuse, NY 13244. Offers MS. *Degree requirements:* For master's, thesis optional, capstone course. *Entrance requirements:* For master's, GRE General Test or GMAT. Additional exam requirements/recommendations for international students: Required—TOEFL (minimum score 600 paper-based; 250 computer-based). Electronic applications accepted.

See Close-Up on page 705.

Syracuse University, Graduate School, S. I. Newhouse School of Public Communications, Program in Media Studies, Syracuse, NY 13244. Offers MA. *Degree requirements:* For master's, thesis. *Entrance requirements:* For master's, GRE General Test. Additional exam requirements/recommendations for international students: Required—TOEFL (minimum score 600 paper-based; 250 computer-based). Electronic applications accepted.

Syracuse University, Graduate School, S. I. Newhouse School of Public Communications, Program in Television, Radio, and Film, Syracuse, NY 13244. Offers MA. *Degree requirements:* For master's, comprehensive exam. *Entrance requirements:* For master's, GRE General Test.

Media Studies

Syracuse University (continued)
Additional exam requirements/recommendations for international students: Required—TOEFL (minimum score 600 paper-based; 250 computer-based). Electronic applications accepted.

See Close-Up on page 705.

Temple University, Graduate School, School of Communications and Theater, Department of Broadcasting, Telecommunications and Mass Media, Philadelphia, PA 19122-6096. Offers MA. Part-time programs available. *Degree requirements:* For master's, thesis optional, written exam. *Entrance requirements:* For master's, GRE General Test, minimum GPA of 3.0. Additional exam requirements/recommendations for international students: Required—TOEFL (minimum score 550 paper-based; 213 computer-based; 79 iBT). Electronic applications accepted. *Faculty research:* Media institutions, international communications, communication policy, media theory.

Temple University, Graduate School, School of Communications and Theater, Department of Strategic and Organizational Communication, Program in Mass Media and Communication, Philadelphia, PA 19122-6096. Offers PhD. Part-time programs available. *Degree requirements:* For doctorate, one foreign language, thesis/dissertation. *Entrance requirements:* For doctorate, GRE General Test, minimum GPA of 3.0, sample of written work. Additional exam requirements/recommendations for international students: Required—TOEFL (minimum score 550 paper-based; 213 computer-based; 79 iBT). Electronic applications accepted. *Faculty research:* Aesthetics and criticism, media institutions, social theory and processes.

University at Buffalo, the State University of New York, Graduate School, College of Arts and Sciences, Department of Media Study, Buffalo, NY 14260. Offers humanities (film studies concentration) (MA); media arts production (MFA); new media design (Certificate); M Arch/MFA. Part-time programs available. *Degree requirements:* For master's, thesis. *Entrance requirements:* For master's, portfolio. Additional exam requirements/recommendations for international students: Required—TOEFL (minimum score 550 paper-based; 213 computer-based), SPEAK (for those awarded assistantships). Electronic applications accepted. *Faculty research:* Digital arts, video, documentary, film, virtual reality, digital poetics, locative media.

The University of Alabama, Graduate School, College of Communication and Information Sciences, Department of Telecommunication and Film, Tuscaloosa, AL 35487-0152. Offers MA. *Faculty:* 8 full-time (2 women). *Students:* 8 full-time (6 women), 1 part-time (0 women); includes 1 minority (Hispanic American), 2 international. Average age 24. 7 applicants, 71% accepted, 3 enrolled. In 2008, 2 master's awarded. Terminal master's awarded for partial completion of doctoral program. *Degree requirements:* For master's, comprehensive exam, thesis or alternative. *Entrance requirements:* For master's, GRE, minimum GPA of 3.0. Additional exam requirements/recommendations for international students: Required—TOEFL (minimum score 600 paper-based; 79 iBT). *Application deadline:* For fall admission, 2/15 priority date for domestic students; for spring admission, 11/1 for domestic students. Applications are processed on a rolling basis. Application fee: $30. Electronic applications accepted. *Expenses:* Tuition, area resident: Full-time $6400. Tuition, state resident: full-time $6400. Tuition, nonresident: full-time $18,000. *Financial support:* In 2008–09, 6 students received support, including 2 research assistantships with tuition reimbursements available (averaging $9,825 per year), 2 teaching assistantships with tuition reimbursements available (averaging $9,825 per year); institutionally sponsored loans also available. Financial award application deadline: 2/15. *Faculty research:* Entertainment theory, news and public affairs, effects of telecommunications, management. Total annual research expenditures: $595,298. *Unit head:* Dr. Gary A. Copeland, Chair, 205-348-6350, Fax: 205-348-5162, E-mail: copeland@ua.edu. *Application contact:* Dr. Shuhua Zhou, Graduate Coordinator, 205-348-8653, Fax: 205-348-5162, E-mail: szhou@bama.ua.edu.

The University of Arizona, Graduate College, College of Fine Arts, School of Media Arts, Tucson, AZ 85721. Offers MA. Part-time programs available. *Degree requirements:* For master's, comprehensive exam. *Entrance requirements:* For master's, GRE, minimum GPA of 3.0. Additional exam requirements/recommendations for international students: Required—TOEFL (minimum score 550 paper-based). Electronic applications accepted.

University of California, Santa Barbara, Graduate Division, College of Letters and Sciences, Division of Humanities and Fine Arts, Department of Media Arts and Technology, Santa Barbara, CA 93106-6065. Offers electronic music and sound design (MA); media arts and technology (PhD); multimedia engineering (MS); visual and spatial arts (MA). *Faculty:* 33 full-time (3 women). *Students:* 29 full-time (3 women). Average age 30. 55 applicants, 33% accepted, 8 enrolled. In 2008, 5 master's awarded. Terminal master's awarded for partial completion of doctoral program. *Degree requirements:* For master's, comprehensive exam, thesis; for doctorate, comprehensive exam, thesis/dissertation. *Entrance requirements:* For master's and doctorate, GRE, portfolios; programming language and calculus-based math (expertise in 1 discipline and experience in another); 3 letters of recommendation; statement of purpose; personal achievements/contributions statement; resumé/curriculum vitae; transcripts for post-secondary institutions attended. Additional exam requirements/recommendations for international students: Required—TOEFL (minimum score 550 paper-based; 213 computer-based; 80 iBT), IELTS (minimum score 7), TOEFL or IELTS. *Application deadline:* For fall admission, 1/15 for domestic and international students. Application fee: $70 ($90 for international students). Electronic applications accepted. *Expenses:* Tuition, nonresident: full-time $25,149. Required fees: $10,143. Full-time tuition and fees vary according to campus/location, reciprocity agreements and student level. *Financial support:* In 2008–09, 23 students received support, including 10 fellowships with full and partial tuition reimbursements available (averaging $4,800 per year), 6 research assistantships with full and partial tuition reimbursements available (averaging $8,300 per year), 18 teaching assistantships with partial tuition reimbursements available (averaging $7,300 per year); career-related internships or fieldwork, Federal Work-Study, institutionally sponsored loans, scholarships/grants, health care benefits, tuition waivers (full and partial), and unspecified assistantships also available. Financial award application deadline: 1/15; financial award applicants required to submit FAFSA. *Faculty research:* Electronic music and sound design: computer music and algorithmic composition, computer generated music, human-computer cooperation in music, design and synthesis of new sounds, sonic diffusion, 3D spatial sound; interactive art: installations, generative and algorithmic art, immersive art environments, computational photography; visualization; transarchitecture, multimedia signal processing, human-computer interaction, multimedia systems. *Unit head:* Prof. Matthew A. Turk, Chair, 805-893-4236, Fax: 805-893-2930, E-mail: mturk@cs.ucsb.edu. *Application contact:* Diane E. Harden, Graduate Program Assistant, 805-893-2887, Fax: 805-893-2930, E-mail: diane@mat.ucsb.edu.

University of Chicago, Division of the Humanities, Committee on Cinema and Media Studies, Chicago, IL 60637-1513. Offers AM, PhD. *Degree requirements:* For master's, one foreign language, thesis; for doctorate, 2 foreign languages, thesis/dissertation.

University of Colorado at Boulder, ATLAS Institute (Alliance for Technology, Learning, and Society), Boulder, CO 80309. Offers technology, media, and society (PhD). *Faculty research:* Evaluation of the Dissector Tool based on the visible Human Data Project, assessing student outcomes for SENCER (an NSF-sponsored program using civic engagement to increase the interest and learning in undergraduate science at over 300 U.S. universities).

University of Colorado at Boulder, Graduate School, School of Journalism and Mass Communication, Program in Communication, Boulder, CO 80309. Offers media studies (PhD). *Entrance requirements:* For doctorate, GRE General Test, minimum undergraduate GPA of 3.25. Additional exam requirements/recommendations for international students: Required—TOEFL.

University of Denver, Division of Arts, Humanities and Social Sciences, School of Communication, Department of Mass Communications, Denver, CO 80208. Offers advertising management (MS); digital media studies (MA); mass communications (MA); public relations (MS); video production (MA). Part-time programs available. *Faculty:* 14 full-time (8 women), 4 part-time/adjunct (1 woman). *Students:* 3 full-time (1 woman), 42 part-time (30 women); includes 7 minority (1 African American, 6 Hispanic Americans), 3 international. Average age 27. In 2008, 17 master's awarded. *Degree requirements:* For master's, thesis (for some programs). *Entrance requirements:* For master's, GRE General Test. Additional exam requirements/recommendations for international students: Required—TOEFL, TWE. *Application deadline:* Applications are processed on a rolling basis. Application fee: $50. Electronic applications accepted. *Financial support:* In 2008–09, 4 research assistantships with full and partial tuition reimbursements (averaging $9,000 per year), 7 teaching assistantships with full and partial tuition reimbursements (averaging $10,000 per year) were awarded; career-related internships or fieldwork, Federal Work-Study, institutionally sponsored loans, and scholarships/grants also available. Support available to part-time students. Financial award application deadline: 3/1; financial award applicants required to submit FAFSA. *Faculty research:* Youth and civic engagement. Total annual research expenditures: $162,000. *Unit head:* Dr. Diane Waldman, Chair, 303-871-2008. *Application contact:* Information Contact, 303-871-2008, E-mail: mcom@du.edu.

See Close-Up on page 707.

University of Florida, Graduate School, College of Journalism and Communications, Department of Telecommunication, Gainesville, FL 32611. Offers MAMC. *Degree requirements:* For master's, thesis optional. *Entrance requirements:* For master's, GRE General Test, minimum GPA of 3.0.

University of Illinois at Urbana–Champaign, Graduate College, College of Media, Institute of Communications Research, Champaign, IL 61820. Offers communications and media (PhD). *Faculty:* 10 full-time (4 women). *Students:* 39 full-time (20 women), 11 part-time (7 women); includes 12 minority (4 African Americans, 3 Asian Americans or Pacific Islanders, 5 Hispanic Americans), 18 international. 126 applicants, 6% accepted, 7 enrolled. In 2008, 10 doctorates awarded. *Entrance requirements:* For doctorate, GRE General Test, minimum GPA of 3.0. Additional exam requirements/recommendations for international students: Required—TOEFL (minimum score 550 paper-based). *Application deadline:* Applications are processed on a rolling basis. Application fee: $60 ($75 for international students). Electronic applications accepted. *Financial support:* In 2008–09, 15 fellowships, 16 research assistantships, 32 teaching assistantships were awarded; tuition waivers (full and partial) also available. *Faculty research:* Feminist cultural studies, media technology, international communications, Latino studies, economics of media. *Unit head:* Clifford Christians, Director, 217-333-1549, Fax: 217-244-7695, E-mail: cchrstns@illinois.edu. *Application contact:* Bonnie Howard, Administrative Secretary, 217-333-7860, Fax: 217-333-7695, E-mail: bbhoward@illinois.edu.

The University of Iowa, Graduate College, College of Liberal Arts and Sciences, School of Journalism and Mass Communication, Iowa City, IA 52242-1316. Offers mass communication (PhD); media communication (MA); professional journalism (MA); JD/MA. *Accreditation:* ACEJMC (one or more programs are accredited). *Degree requirements:* For master's, thesis optional, exam; for doctorate, comprehensive exam, thesis/dissertation. *Entrance requirements:* For master's and doctorate, GRE General Test, minimum GPA of 3.0. Additional exam requirements/recommendations for international students: Required—TOEFL (minimum score 570 paper-based; 230 computer-based; 89 iBT). Electronic applications accepted. *Faculty research:* Verbal and visual aspects of historical, legal, social, and cross-cultural communication.

University of Lethbridge, School of Graduate Studies, Lethbridge, AB T1K 3M4, Canada. Offers accounting (MScM); addictions counseling (M Sc); agricultural biotechnology (M Sc); agricultural studies (M Sc, MA); anthropology (MA); archaeology (MA); art (MA); biochemistry (M Sc); biological sciences (M Sc); biomolecular science (PhD); biosystems and biodiversity (PhD); Canadian studies (MA); chemistry (M Sc); computer science (M Sc); computer science and geographical information science (M Sc); counseling psychology (M Ed); dramatic arts (MA); earth, space, and physical science (PhD); economics (MA); educational leadership (M Ed); English (MA); environmental science (M Sc); evolution and behavior (PhD); exercise science (M Sc); finance (MScM); French (MA); French/German (MA); French/Spanish (MA); general education (M Ed); general management (MScM); geography (M Sc, MA); German (MA); health sciences (M Sc, MA); history (MA); human resource management and labour relations (MScM); individualized multidisciplinary (M Sc, MA); information systems (MScM); international management (MScM); kinesiology (M Sc, MA); management (M Sc, MA); marketing (MScM); mathematics (M Sc); music (MA); Native American studies (MA); neuroscience (M Sc, PhD); new media (MA); nursing (M Sc); philosophy (MA); physics (M Sc); policy and strategy (MScM); political science (MA); psychology (M Sc, MA); religious studies (MA); sociology (MA); theoretical and computational science (PhD); urban and regional studies (MA). Part-time and evening/weekend programs available. *Degree requirements:* For doctorate, comprehensive exam, thesis/dissertation. *Entrance requirements:* For master's, GMAT (M Sc in management), bachelor's degree in related field, minimum GPA of 3.0 during previous 20 graded semester courses, 2 years teaching or related experience (M Ed); for doctorate, master's degree, minimum graduate GPA of 3.5. Additional exam requirements/recommendations for international students: Required—TOEFL. *Faculty research:* Movement and brain plasticity, gibberellin physiology, photosynthesis, carbon cycling, molecular properties of main-group ring components.

University of Maryland, College Park, Graduate Studies, Phillip Merrill College of Journalism, College Park, MD 20742. Offers broadcast journalism (MA); journalism (MA); journalism and media studies (PhD); online news (MA); public affairs reporting (MA). *Accreditation:* ACEJMC (one or more programs are accredited). Part-time and evening/weekend programs available. *Degree requirements:* For doctorate, thesis/dissertation, preliminary written and oral comprehensive exams. *Entrance requirements:* For master's and doctorate, GRE General Test, minimum GPA of 3.0, 3 letters of recommendation. Additional exam requirements/recommendations for international students: Required—TOEFL. Electronic applications accepted. *Faculty research:* Mass communication theory, specialized journalism, new telecommunication technologies, press integration.

University of Michigan, Horace H. Rackham School of Graduate Studies, The School of Music, Theatre, and Dance, Program in Media Arts, Ann Arbor, MI 48109. Offers MA. *Entrance requirements:* For master's, GRE, portfolio. Additional exam requirements/recommendations for international students: Required—TOEFL (minimum score 600 paper-based; 250 computer-based).

University of Nevada, Las Vegas, Graduate College, Greenspun College of Urban Affairs, School of Journalism and Media Studies, Las Vegas, NV 89154-5007. Offers MA. *Faculty:* 11 full-time (3 women). *Students:* 13 full-time (7 women), 11 part-time (8 women); includes 3 minority (1 African American, 2 Hispanic Americans), 2 international. Average age 29. 31 applicants, 77% accepted, 11 enrolled. In 2008, 7 master's awarded. *Entrance requirements:* For master's, GRE General Test. Additional exam requirements/recommendations for international students: Required—TOEFL (minimum score 550 paper-based; 213 computer-based; 80 iBT), IELTS (minimum score 7). *Application deadline:* For fall admission, 3/15 priority date for domestic and international students. Applications are processed on a rolling basis. Application fee: $60 ($75 for international students). Electronic applications accepted. *Expenses:* Tuition, state resident: full-time $1414; part-time $198 per credit. Tuition, nonresident: full-time $12,509; part-time $415.75 per credit. International tuition: $14,249 full-time. Required fees: $4 per credit. $252 per semester. Tuition and fees vary according to course load. *Financial support:* In 2008–09, 8 students received support, including 4 research assistantships with partial tuition reimbursements available (averaging $10,000 per year), 4 teaching assistantships with partial tuition reimbursements available (averaging $10,000 per year); institutionally sponsored loans, scholarships/grants, health care benefits, and unspecified assistantships also available. Financial award application deadline: 3/1. *Faculty research:* Journalism and media studies. *Unit head:* Dr. Ardyth Sohn, Director/Professor, 702-895-3270, Fax: 702-895-5189, E-mail: ardyth.sohn@unlv.edu. *Application contact:* Graduate College Admissions Evaluator, 702-895-3320, Fax: 702-895-4180, E-mail: gradcollege@unlv.edu.

The University of North Carolina at Greensboro, Graduate School, College of Arts and Sciences, Department of Broadcasting and Cinema, Greensboro, NC 27412-5001. Offers film and video production (MFA).

University of South Carolina, The Graduate School, College of Arts and Sciences, Department of Art, Division of Media Arts, Columbia, SC 29208. Offers MMA. *Degree requirements:* For master's, thesis. *Entrance requirements:* For master's, GRE General Test, interview, portfolio. Additional exam requirements/recommendations for international students: Required—TOEFL. Electronic applications accepted. *Faculty research:* Three dimensional imaging, script writing.

University of Southern California, Graduate School, Annenberg School for Communication, School of Communication, Program in Communication Management, Los Angeles, CA 90089. Offers MCM, JD/MCM, MCM/MAJCS. Part-time and evening/weekend programs available. *Degree requirements:* For master's, professional project. *Entrance requirements:* For master's, GRE General Test or GMAT, resumé, writing samples, recommendation letters, statement of purpose. Additional exam requirements/recommendations for international students: Required—TOEFL (minimum score 280 computer-based; 114 iBT). Electronic applications accepted. *Faculty research:* Global communication, communication law and policy, entertainment management, marketing communication, strategic and corporate communication management.

See Close-Up on page 709.

University of Southern California, Graduate School, Annenberg School for Communication, School of Journalism, Program in Broadcast Journalism, Los Angeles, CA 90089. Offers MA. *Degree requirements:* For master's, comprehensive exam. *Entrance requirements:* For master's, GRE General Test, resumé, writing samples, letters of recommendation, statement of purpose. Additional exam requirements/recommendations for international students: Required—TOEFL (minimum score 280 computer-based; 114 iBT). Electronic applications accepted.

See Close-Up on page 709.

University of Southern California, Graduate School, School of Cinematic Arts, Division of Animation and Digital Arts, Los Angeles, CA 90089. Offers film, video, and computer animation (MFA); media arts and practice (PhD). *Degree requirements:* For master's, thesis; for doctorate, thesis/dissertation. *Entrance requirements:* For master's and doctorate, GRE. *Faculty research:* Science visualization, visual effects, experimental animation, documentary visualization, motion graphics.

The University of Tennessee, Graduate School, College of Communication and Information, Knoxville, TN 37996. Offers advertising (MS, PhD); broadcasting (MS, PhD); communications (MS, PhD); information sciences (MS, PhD); journalism (MS, PhD); public relations (MS, PhD); speech communication (MS, PhD). *Accreditation:* ACEJMC (one or more programs are accredited at the [master's] level). Part-time and evening/weekend programs available. Post-baccalaureate distance learning degree programs offered (no on-campus study). *Degree requirements:* For master's, thesis or alternative; for doctorate, thesis/dissertation. *Entrance requirements:* For master's and doctorate, GRE General Test, minimum GPA of 2.7. Additional exam requirements/recommendations for international students: Required—TOEFL. Electronic applications accepted. *Expenses:* Tuition, area resident: Part-time $348 per credit hour. Tuition, state resident: full-time $6262. Tuition, nonresident: full-time $18,920; part-time $1052 per credit hour. Required fees: $812; $36 per credit hour. Tuition and fees vary according to program.

The University of Texas at Austin, Graduate School, College of Communication, Department of Radio-Television-Film, Austin, TX 78712-1111. Offers film and video production (MFA); radio-television-film (MA, PhD); screenwriting (MFA). *Degree requirements:* For master's, thesis (for some programs); for doctorate, thesis/dissertation. *Entrance requirements:* For master's and doctorate, GRE General Test. Electronic applications accepted. *Faculty research:* International communication, film studies, media and culture, telecommunication and new media, gender and sexuality.

The University of Western Ontario, Faculty of Graduate Studies, Faculty of Information and Media Studies, Programs in Media Studies, London, ON N6A 5B8, Canada. Offers MA, PhD. Part-time programs available. *Degree requirements:* For master's, thesis; for doctorate, comprehensive exam, thesis/dissertation. *Entrance requirements:* For master's, 2 letters of reference; for doctorate, MA in media studies, communications or related field. Additional exam requirements/recommendations for international students: Required—TOEFL (minimum score 625 paper-based), TWE (minimum score 5). Electronic applications accepted. *Faculty research:* Media cultures, media industries, media technologies.

University of Wisconsin–Madison, Graduate School, College of Letters and Science, Department of Communication Arts, Madison, WI 53706-1380. Offers communication science (MA, PhD); film (MA, PhD); media and cultural studies (MA, PhD); rhetoric (MA, PhD). Terminal master's awarded for partial completion of doctoral program. *Degree requirements:* For master's, one foreign language, thesis (for some programs); for doctorate, one foreign language, thesis/dissertation. *Entrance requirements:* For master's and doctorate, GRE General Test, minimum GPA of 3.5. Electronic applications accepted.

University of Wisconsin–Milwaukee, Graduate School, College of Letters and Sciences, Department of Media Studies, Milwaukee, WI 53201-0413. Offers media studies (MA); rhetorical leadership (Certificate). Part-time programs available. *Faculty:* 10 full-time (4 women). *Students:* 11 full-time (10 women), 16 part-time (8 women); includes 2 minority (both African Americans), 5 international. Average age 29. 34 applicants, 71% accepted, 11 enrolled. In 2008, 10 master's awarded. *Degree requirements:* For master's, thesis or alternative. *Entrance requirements:* For master's, GRE General Test, minimum GPA of 3.0. Additional exam requirements/recommendations for international students: Required—TOEFL (minimum score 550 paper-based; 79 iBT), IELTS (minimum score 6.5). *Application deadline:* For fall admission, 1/1 priority date for domestic students; for spring admission, 9/1 for domestic students. Applications are processed on a rolling basis. Application fee: $45 ($75 for international students). *Expenses:* Tuition, area resident: Full-time $7320; part-time $165 per credit. Tuition, state resident: full-time $7320; part-time $165 per credit. Tuition, nonresident: full-time $17,840; part-time $714 per credit. Tuition and fees vary according to campus/location, program and reciprocity agreements. *Financial support:* In 2008–09, 20 teaching assistantships were awarded; career-related internships or fieldwork and unspecified assistantships also available. Support available to part-time students. Financial award application deadline: 4/15. Total annual research expenditures: $3,617. *Unit head:* David Allen, Representative, 414-229-4619, Fax: 414-229-2411, E-mail: dsallen@uwm.edu. *Application contact:* General Information Contact, 414-229-4982, Fax: 414-229-6967, E-mail: gradschool@uwm.edu.

Virginia Commonwealth University, Graduate School, College of Humanities and Sciences, School of Mass Communications, Program in Media, Art, and Text, Richmond, VA 23284-9005. Offers PhD. *Entrance requirements:* For doctorate, GRE, MA, MAE, or MFA in appropriate field of study (English, art history, studio art, poetry, mass communications); 3 letters of recommendation.

Washington State University, Graduate School, College of Liberal Arts, Edward R. Murrow College of Communication, Pullman, WA 99164. Offers health communications (MA, PhD); intercultural and international communications (MA, PhD); media and society (MA, PhD); media process and effects (MA, PhD); organizational communications (MA, PhD). *Degree requirements:* For master's, comprehensive exam (for some programs), thesis optional, oral exam; for doctorate, comprehensive exam, thesis/dissertation. *Entrance requirements:* For master's, GRE General Test, minimum GPA of 3.25, 3 letters of recommendation; for doctorate, GRE General Test, minimum undergraduate GPA of 3.25, graduate 3.5; MA in communication; 3 letters of recommendation. Additional exam requirements/recommendations for international students: Required—TOEFL (minimum score 580 paper-based; 237 computer-based). Electronic applications accepted. *Faculty research:* Advocacy communication, mediated communication in decision making, communication technology policy and effects, multicultural and international psychology and physiology of communication.

Wayne State University, College of Fine, Performing and Communication Arts, Department of Communication, Detroit, MI 48202. Offers communication studies (MA, PhD); public relations and organizational communication (MA); radio-TV-film (MA, PhD); speech communication (MA, PhD). *Degree requirements:* For master's, thesis, essay, or comprehensive exam; for doctorate, thesis/dissertation. *Entrance requirements:* For master's, minimum GPA of 3.0, personal statement; sample of academic writing; for doctorate, GRE, minimum GPA of 3.3, MA; letters of recommendation; personal statement; sample of written scholarship. Additional exam requirements/recommendations for international students: Required—TOEFL (minimum score 550 paper-based; 213 computer-based); Recommended—TWE (minimum score 6). Electronic applications accepted. *Faculty research:* Rhetorical theory and criticism; mass media theory and research; argumentation; organizational communication; risk and crisis communication; interpersonal, family, and health communication.

Webster University, School of Communications, Program in Media Communications, St. Louis, MO 63119-3194. Offers MA.

Webster University, School of Communications, Program in Media Literacy, St. Louis, MO 63119-3194. Offers MA.

West Virginia State University, Graduate Programs, Program in Media Studies, Institute, WV 25112-1000. Offers MA. *Entrance requirements:* For master's, GRE, minimum GPA of 3.0, letters of recommendation. Additional exam requirements/recommendations for international students: Required—TOEFL (minimum score 550 paper-based).

William Paterson University of New Jersey, College of the Arts and Communication, Program in Communication and Media Studies, Wayne, NJ 07470-8420. Offers MA. *Degree requirements:* For master's, comprehensive exam. *Entrance requirements:* For master's, GRE General Test or MAT, minimum GPA of 2.75. Electronic applications accepted. *Faculty research:* Cable television, intercultural communication.

Publishing

Carnegie Mellon University, College of Humanities and Social Sciences, Department of English, Program in Professional Writing, Pittsburgh, PA 15213-3891. Offers editing and publishing (MAPW); policy and non-profit communication (MAPW); public and media relations / corporate communications (MAPW); science or healthcare communication (MAPW); technical writing (MAPW); writing for new media (MAPW); writing for print media (MAPW). Part-time programs available. *Entrance requirements:* For master's, GRE General Test. Additional exam requirements/recommendations for international students: Required—TOEFL, TWE.

See Close-Up on page 553.

DePaul University, College of Liberal Arts and Sciences, Department of English, Program in Writing and Publishing, Chicago, IL 60604-2287. Offers MA. *Unit head:* Dr. William Fahrenbach, Chairperson, 773-325-1776, E-mail: bfahrenb@depaul.edu. *Application contact:* Dr. Lesley Kordecki, Director, 773-325-1786, Fax: 773-325-8607, E-mail: lkordeck@depaul.edu.

Drexel University, College of Arts and Sciences, Department of Culture and Communication, Program in Publication Management, Philadelphia, PA 19104-2875. Offers MS. Part-time and evening/weekend programs available. *Degree requirements:* For master's, research project. *Entrance requirements:* Additional exam requirements/recommendations for international students: Required—TOEFL. Electronic applications accepted.

Drexel University, College of Media Arts and Design, Philadelphia, PA 19104-2875. Offers design (MS), including digital media, fashion design, interior design, television management; media arts (MS); performing arts (MS), including arts administration; MS/MBA. *Accreditation:* NASAD. Part-time and evening/weekend programs available. *Entrance requirements:* For master's, interview. Additional exam requirements/recommendations for international students: Required—TOEFL. Electronic applications accepted. *Expenses:* Contact institution.

Emerson College, Graduate Studies, School of the Arts, Department of Writing, Literature and Publishing, Program in Publishing and Writing, Boston, MA 02116-4624. Offers MA. Part-time programs available. *Students:* 85 full-time (75 women), 19 part-time (17 women); includes 11 minority (2 African Americans, 1 American Indian/Alaska Native, 4 Asian Americans or Pacific Islanders, 4 Hispanic Americans), 6 international. Average age 26. 182 applicants, 42% accepted, 47 enrolled. In 2008, 54 master's awarded. *Degree requirements:* For master's, thesis or alternative. *Entrance requirements:* For master's, GRE General Test, 15 page writing sample. Additional exam requirements/recommendations for international students: Required—TOEFL (minimum score 550 paper-based; 213 computer-based; 80 iBT), IELTS (minimum score 6.5). *Application deadline:* For fall admission, 1/5 for domestic and international students. Applications are processed on a rolling basis. Application fee: $60 ($75 for international students). Electronic applications accepted. *Expenses:* Tuition: Full-time $17,720; part-time $886 per credit. Required fees: $60 per year. One-time fee: $170. *Financial support:* In 2008–09, 27 students received support, including 3 fellowships with partial tuition reimbursements available (averaging $14,000 per year), 18 research assistantships with partial tuition reimbursements available (averaging $10,000 per year); career-related internships or fieldwork, Federal Work-Study, institutionally sponsored loans, scholarships/grants, and unspecified assistantships also available. Support available to part-time students. Financial award application deadline: 1/5; financial award applicants required to submit FAFSA. *Faculty research:* Publishing. *Unit head:* Prof. Lisa Diercks, Director, 617-824-8750, E-mail: Lisa_Diercks@emerson.edu. *Application contact:* Office of Graduate Admission, 617-824-8610, Fax: 617-824-8614, E-mail: gradapp@emerson.edu.

The George Washington University, College of Professional Studies, Program in Publishing, Washington, DC 20052. Offers MPS. Program offered at Alexandria, VA education center. *Students:* Average age 34. 57 applicants, 82% accepted, 27 enrolled. In 2008, 26 master's awarded. *Entrance requirements:* For master's, minimum cumulative GPA of 3.0. *Application deadline:* For fall admission, 4/1 for domestic and international students. Electronic applications accepted. *Unit head:* Dr. Arnold Grossblatt, Director, 202-994-7220, E-mail: arnieg@gwu.edu. *Application contact:* Kristin Williams, Asst VP Grad&Spec Enrlmnt Mgmt, 202-994-0467, Fax: 202-994-0371, E-mail: ksw@gwu.edu.

New York University, School of Continuing and Professional Studies, Division for Media Industry Studies and Design, Center for Publishing, New York, NY 10012-1019. Offers MS.

Publishing

New York University (continued)
Part-time and evening/weekend programs available. *Degree requirements:* For master's, thesis. *Entrance requirements:* For master's, GMAT or GRE General Test for recent graduates, work experience, 2 letters of recommendation, resumé, essay. Additional exam requirements/recommendations for international students: Required—TOEFL (minimum score 600 paper-based; 250 computer-based; 100 iBT), TWE. Electronic applications accepted. *Faculty research:* Special marketing and distribution channels.

Northwestern University, Medill School of Journalism, Evanston, IL 60208. Offers broadcast journalism (MSJ); integrated marketing communications (MSIMC), including advertising/sales promotion, direct database and e-commerce marketing, general studies, public relations; magazine publishing (MSJ); new media (MSJ); reporting and writing (MSJ). *Accreditation:* ACEJMC (one or more programs are accredited). *Entrance requirements:* For master's, GRE General Test, GMAT or LSAT (MSJ). Additional exam requirements/recommendations for international students: Required—TOEFL. Electronic applications accepted. *Expenses:* Contact institution. *Faculty research:* Web business journalism, cultural stereotypes, voter apathy, digital television.

Pace University, Dyson College of Arts and Sciences, Program in Publishing, New York, NY 10038. Offers MS. Part-time and evening/weekend programs available. Postbaccalaureate distance learning degree programs offered. *Degree requirements:* For master's, internship or thesis. *Entrance requirements:* For master's, GRE General Test. Electronic applications accepted.

Rosemont College, Graduate School, Program in English and Publishing and English Literature, Rosemont, PA 19010-1699. Offers English and publishing (MA); English literature (MA). Part-time programs available. *Degree requirements:* For master's, comprehensive exam (for some programs), thesis. *Entrance requirements:* For master's, Baccalaureat Degree 3.0 college GPA, statement of purpose, 3 letters of recommendation. Additional exam requirements/recommendations for international students: Required—TOEFL. Electronic applications accepted.

Simon Fraser University, Graduate Studies, Faculty of Arts and Social Sciences, Canadian Centre for Studies in Publishing, Burnaby, BC V5A 1S6, Canada. Offers M Pub. *Degree requirements:* For master's, internship, project report. *Entrance requirements:* For master's, minimum GPA of 3.0. Additional exam requirements/recommendations for international students: Required—TWE, TOEFL or IELTS. *Expenses:* Contact institution. *Faculty research:* History of publishing, electronic publishing, editing, multimedia, publication design.

University of Baltimore, Graduate School, The Yale Gordon College of Liberal Arts, Program in Creative Writing and Publishing Arts, Baltimore, MD 21201-5779. Offers MFA. Part-time and evening/weekend programs available. *Students:* 15 full-time (12 women), 36 part-time (25 women); includes 14 minority (9 African Americans, 1 American Indian/Alaska Native, 2 Asian Americans or Pacific Islanders, 2 Hispanic Americans). Average age 28. 77 applicants, 48% accepted, 27 enrolled. *Entrance requirements:* Additional exam requirements/recommendations for international students: Required—TOEFL. *Application deadline:* For fall admission, 3/31 for domestic and international students. Application fee: $31. *Expenses:* Tuition, state resident: part-time $568 per credit. Tuition, nonresident: part-time $824 per credit. Required fees: $250 per semester. *Financial support:* In 2008–09, 3 students received support. Application deadline: 3/1; *Unit head:* Kendra Kopelke, Director, 410-837-6026, E-mail: kkopelke@ubalt.edu. *Application contact:* Kevin Nies, Executive Director, Office of Graduate Admission, 410-837-6565, E-mail: knies@ubalt.edu.

University of Baltimore, Graduate School, The Yale Gordon College of Liberal Arts, Program in Publications Design, Baltimore, MD 21201-5779. Offers MA. Part-time and evening/weekend programs available. *Faculty:* 6 full-time (3 women), 10 part-time/adjunct (6 women). *Students:* 30 full-time (20 women), 135 part-time (107 women); includes 46 minority (35 African Americans, 6 Asian Americans or Pacific Islanders, 5 Hispanic Americans), 5 international. Average age 30. 79 applicants, 62% accepted, 43 enrolled. In 2008, 39 master's awarded. *Degree requirements:* For master's, seminar project. *Entrance requirements:* For master's, minimum GPA of 3.0, portfolio, interview. Additional exam requirements/recommendations for international students: Required—TOEFL (minimum score 550 paper-based; 213 computer-based). *Application deadline:* For fall admission, 8/1 priority date for domestic students, 6/1 for international students; for spring admission, 12/15 for domestic students, 11/1 for international students. Applications are processed on a rolling basis. Application fee: $30. Electronic applications accepted. *Expenses:* Tuition, state resident: part-time $568 per credit. Tuition, nonresident: part-time $824 per credit. Required fees: $250 per semester. *Financial support:* In 2008–09, 9 research assistantships were awarded; fellowships, career-related internships or fieldwork and Federal Work-Study also available. Support available to part-time students. Financial award application deadline: 4/1; financial award applicants required to submit FAFSA. *Faculty research:* Communication theory, graphic design, media technology. *Unit head:* Dr. Stephanie Gibson, Director, Main Publications Design, 410-837-6050, E-mail: sgibson@ubalt.edu. *Application contact:* Kevin Nies, Assistant Director, Office of Graduate Admission, 410-837-6565, E-mail: knies@ubalt.edu.

Rhetoric

Abilene Christian University, Graduate School, College of Arts and Sciences, Department of English, Abilene, TX 79699-9100. Offers composition/rhetoric (MA); literature (MA); writing (MA). Part-time programs available. *Faculty:* 14 part-time/adjunct (5 women). *Students:* 11 full-time (7 women), 2 part-time (both women); includes 1 minority (Hispanic American), 1 international. 12 applicants, 50% accepted, 5 enrolled. In 2008, 6 master's awarded. *Degree requirements:* For master's, one foreign language, comprehensive exam, thesis optional. *Entrance requirements:* For master's, GRE General Test. *Application deadline:* For fall admission, 4/1 priority date for domestic students; for spring admission, 11/1 for domestic students. Applications are processed on a rolling basis. Application fee: $40 ($45 for international students). Electronic applications accepted. *Expenses:* Tuition: Full-time $10,728; part-time $640 per hour. Required fees: $1090; $53.50 per hour. $10 per term. Tuition and fees vary according to campus/location. *Financial support:* In 2008–09, 13 students received support; teaching assistantships, Federal Work-Study available. Support available to part-time students. Financial award application deadline: 4/1; financial award applicants required to submit FAFSA. *Faculty research:* Feminism, Shakespearean dimensions of new literature, poetic consciousness, deconstruction myths. *Unit head:* Dr. Dana McMichael, Graduate Adviser, 325-674-2253, Fax: 325-674-2408, E-mail: rankinw@acu.edu. *Application contact:* William Horn, Graduate Admissions Counselor, 325-674-2656, Fax: 325-674-6717, E-mail: gradinfo@acu.edu.

Ball State University, Graduate School, College of Communication, Information, and Media, Department of Communication Studies, Muncie, IN 47306-1099. Offers speech, public address, forensics, and rhetoric (MA). *Entrance requirements:* For master's, GRE General Test.

Bob Jones University, Graduate Programs, Greenville, SC 29614. Offers accountancy (MS); Bible (MA); Bible translation (MA); Biblical studies (Certificate); broadcast management (MS); business administration (MBA); church history (MA, PhD); church ministries (MA); church music (MM); cinema and video production (MA); counseling (MS); curriculum and instruction (Ed D); divinity (M Div); dramatic production (MA); educational leadership (MS, Ed D, Ed S); elementary education (M Ed, MAT); English (M Ed, MA, MAT); fine arts (MA); graphic design (MA); history (M Ed, MA); illustration (MA); interpretative speech (MA); mathematics (M Ed, MAT); medical missions (Certificate); ministry (MM, D Min); multi-categorical special education (M Ed, MAT); music (M Ed); New Testament interpretation (PhD); Old Testament interpretation (PhD); orchestral instrument performance (MM); organ performance (MM); pastoral studies (MA); personnel services (MS, Ed S); piano pedagogy (MM); piano performance (MM); platform arts (MA); radio and television broadcasting (MS); rhetoric and public address (MA); secondary education (M Ed); studio art (MA); teaching Bible (MA); theology (MA, PhD); voice performance (MM); youth ministries (MA); M Div/MM.

Bowling Green State University, Graduate College, College of Arts and Sciences, Department of English, Program in English, Bowling Green, OH 43403. Offers English (MA, PhD); literature (MA); rhetoric and writing (PhD); scientific and technical communication (MA). Part-time programs available. *Degree requirements:* For master's, thesis or alternative; for doctorate, comprehensive exam, thesis/dissertation, foreign language or proficiency in Old English. *Entrance requirements:* For master's and doctorate, GRE General Test. Additional exam requirements/recommendations for international students: Required—TOEFL. Electronic applications accepted. *Faculty research:* Postmodern literary theory, rhetorical theory, ethnic American literature, literature and culture, composition pedagogy.

California State University, Dominguez Hills, College of Arts and Humanities, Department of English, Carson, CA 90747-0001. Offers English (MA); rhetoric and composition (Certificate); teaching English as a second language (Certificate). Part-time and evening/weekend programs available. *Faculty:* 15 full-time (5 women). *Students:* 27 full-time (15 women), 52 part-time (32 women); includes 38 minority (11 African Americans, 6 Asian Americans or Pacific Islanders, 21 Hispanic Americans), 3 international. Average age 36. 46 applicants, 87% accepted, 25 enrolled. In 2008, 28 master's awarded. *Degree requirements:* For master's, comprehensive exam (for some programs), thesis or alternative. *Entrance requirements:* For master's, minimum GPA of 3.0 in last 60 units. Additional exam requirements/recommendations for international students: Required—TOEFL (minimum score 550 paper-based; 213 computer-based). *Application deadline:* Applications are processed on a rolling basis. Application fee: $55. Electronic applications accepted. *Expenses:* Tuition, nonresident: part-time $339 per unit. Required fees: $1300 per semester. *Faculty research:* Gender studies, transnationalism, discourse analysis, visual culture, Shakespeare. *Unit head:* Dr. Helen Oesterheld, Chair, 310-243-3322, E-mail: hoesterheld@csudh.edu. *Application contact:* 310-243-3600.

California State University, Northridge, Graduate Studies, College of Humanities, Department of English, Northridge, CA 91330. Offers creative writing (MA); literature (MA); rhetoric and composition theory (MA). Part-time and evening/weekend programs available. *Faculty:* 33 full-time (16 women), 71 part-time/adjunct (60 women). *Students:* 42 full-time (27 women), 133 part-time (96 women); includes 38 minority (4 African Americans, 1 American Indian/Alaska Native, 14 Asian Americans or Pacific Islanders, 19 Hispanic Americans). Average age 34. 114 applicants, 74% accepted, 51 enrolled. In 2008, 40 master's awarded. *Degree requirements:* For master's, thesis or alternative. *Entrance requirements:* For master's, writing proficiency test, GRE General Test or minimum GPA of 3.0. Additional exam requirements/recommendations for international students: Required—TOEFL. *Application deadline:* For fall admission, 11/30 for domestic students. Application fee: $55. *Financial support:* Teaching assistantships available. Financial award application deadline: 3/1. *Faculty research:* Reading improvement, professional writing, Dickens, Shaw, English as a second language. *Unit head:* Dr. George Uba, Chair, 818-677-3434, E-mail: george.uba@csun.edu. *Application contact:* Dr. Marjie Seagoe, Graduate Studies Secretary, 818-677-3433.

California State University, Stanislaus, College of Humanities and Social Sciences, Department of English, Turlock, CA 95382. Offers English (MA); literature (MA); rhetoric and teaching of writing (MA); TESOL (MA, Certificate). Part-time programs available. *Degree requirements:* For master's, one foreign language, comprehensive exam, thesis. *Entrance requirements:* For master's, GRE General Test, minimum GPA of 3.0, 2 letters of reference, personal statement; for Certificate, minimum GPA of 3.0, 2 letters of reference. Additional exam requirements/recommendations for international students: Required—TOEFL (minimum score 550 paper-based; 213 computer-based), TWE (minimum score 4). Electronic applications accepted. *Faculty research:* Transnational literacies, Renaissance and Medieval literature, abolition writings and slave narratives, qualitative writing.

Carnegie Mellon University, College of Humanities and Social Sciences, Department of English, Pittsburgh, PA 15213-3891. Offers communication planning and design (M Des); literary and cultural studies (MA, PhD); professional writing (MAPW), including editing and publishing, policy and non-profit communication, public and media relations / corporate communications, science or healthcare communication, technical writing, writing for new media, writing for print media; rhetoric (MA, PhD). Part-time programs available. Terminal master's awarded for partial completion of doctoral program. *Degree requirements:* For doctorate, 2 foreign languages, comprehensive exam, thesis/dissertation. *Entrance requirements:* For master's and doctorate, GRE General Test. Additional exam requirements/recommendations for international students: Required—TOEFL, TWE. *Faculty research:* Cognitive processes in discourse with emphasis on writing, testing, and evaluation.

The Catholic University of America, School of Arts and Sciences, Department of English Language and Literature, Washington, DC 20064. Offers English language and literature (MA, PhD); rhetoric (MA, PhD); MSLS/MA. Part-time and evening/weekend programs available. Terminal master's awarded for partial completion of doctoral program. *Degree requirements:* For master's, one foreign language, comprehensive exam, thesis or alternative; for doctorate, 2 foreign languages, comprehensive exam, thesis/dissertation. *Entrance requirements:* For master's and doctorate, GRE General Test, 3 letters of recommendation, writing sample. Additional exam requirements/recommendations for international students: Required—TOEFL (minimum score 580 paper-based; 237 computer-based). Electronic applications accepted. *Faculty research:* Medieval literature, theory and history of rhetoric, modern Irish literature, religion and literature, English and American drama.

Clemson University, Graduate School, College of Architecture, Arts, and Humanities, Department of English, Program in Rhetorics, Communication and Information Design, Clemson, SC 29634. Offers PhD. *Students:* 22 full-time (10 women), 2 part-time (1 woman); includes 4 minority (3 African Americans, 1 Asian American or Pacific Islander), 4 international. Average age 36. 19 applicants, 37% accepted, 6 enrolled. In 2008, 1 doctorate awarded. *Degree requirements:* For doctorate, thesis/dissertation (for some programs). *Entrance requirements:* For doctorate, GRE, master's degree in English, communications studies, art, professional communication or related field; portfolio; 3 letters of reference; minimum graduate GPA of 3.5. Additional exam requirements/recommendations for international students: Required—TOEFL (minimum score 550 paper-based; 213 computer-based). *Application deadline:* For fall admission, 2/1 priority date for domestic students, 4/15 for international students. Application fee: $55. Full-time tuition and fees vary according to program. *Financial support:* Teaching assistantships available. *Unit head:* Dr. Victor Vitanza, Coordinator, 864-656-6411, Fax: 864-656-0599, E-mail: sophist@clemson.edu. *Application contact:* Dr. Victor Vitanza, Coordinator, 864-656-6411, Fax: 864-656-0599, E-mail: sophist@clemson.edu.

Duquesne University, Graduate School of Liberal Arts, Department of Communication and Rhetorical Studies, Pittsburgh, PA 15282-0001. Offers communication (MA); rhetoric (PhD).

Part-time and evening/weekend programs available. *Faculty:* 6 full-time (3 women), 5 part-time/adjunct (3 women). *Students:* 78 full-time (44 women), 46 part-time (30 women); includes 4 minority (3 African Americans, 1 Hispanic American), 11 international. Average age 27. 38 applicants, 100% accepted, 33 enrolled. In 2008, 19 master's, 9 doctorates awarded. *Degree requirements:* For master's, thesis optional, practicum; for doctorate, 2 foreign languages, comprehensive exam, thesis/dissertation. *Entrance requirements:* For master's, GRE General Test, MAT or GMAT; for doctorate, GRE General Test. Additional exam requirements/recommendations for international students: Required—TOEFL. *Application deadline:* For fall admission, 2/1 priority date for domestic and international students; for spring admission, 11/1 priority date for domestic and international students. Applications are processed on a rolling basis. Application fee: $50. Electronic applications accepted. *Expenses:* Tuition: Part-time $819 per credit. Required fees: $78 per credit. Tuition and fees vary according to course load. *Financial support:* In 2008–09, 9 research assistantships with full tuition reimbursements (averaging $9,000 per year), 10 teaching assistantships with full tuition reimbursements (averaging $13,000 per year) were awarded; career-related internships or fieldwork, Federal Work-Study, institutionally sponsored loans, scholarships/grants, tuition waivers (full and partial), and unspecified assistantships also available. Financial award application deadline: 5/1. *Unit head:* Dr. Ronald Arnett, Chair, 412-396-5076. *Application contact:* Dr. Janie Fritz, Director, 412-396-6460.

Eastern Washington University, Graduate Studies, College of Arts and Letters, Department of English, Cheney, WA 99004-2431. Offers literature (MA); rhetoric, composition, and technical communication (MA); teaching English as a second language (MA). *Degree requirements:* For master's, comprehensive exam, thesis or alternative. *Entrance requirements:* For master's, GRE General Test, minimum GPA of 3.0.

Florida State University, Graduate Studies, College of Arts and Sciences, Department of English, Tallahassee, FL 32306. Offers creative writing (MFA, PhD); literature (MA, PhD); rhetoric and composition (MA, PhD). Part-time programs available. *Degree requirements:* For master's, one foreign language, thesis or alternative; for doctorate, 2 foreign languages, thesis/dissertation. *Entrance requirements:* For master's, GRE General Test, GRE Subject Test (literature), sample of written work, 3 letters of recommendation; for doctorate, GRE General Test, sample of written work, 3 letters of recommendation. Electronic applications accepted. *Faculty research:* British literature, American literature, creative writing, rhetoric, multiethnic literature.

Georgia State University, College of Arts and Sciences, Department of English, Atlanta, GA 30303-3083. Offers creative writing (MA, MFA, PhD); English (MA, PhD); fiction (MFA); literary studies and composition (MA, PhD); poetry (MFA); rhetoric (MA, PhD). Part-time and evening/weekend programs available. *Degree requirements:* For master's, one foreign language, thesis; for doctorate, 2 foreign languages, comprehensive exam, thesis/dissertation, exam. *Entrance requirements:* For master's and doctorate, GRE General Test. Additional exam requirements/recommendations for international students: Required—TOEFL. Electronic applications accepted. *Faculty research:* Literary biography, folklore, Southern literature, medieval literature.

Hofstra University, School of Communication, Department of Speech Communication, Rhetoric, and Performance Studies, Hempstead, NY 11549. Offers speech communication and rhetorical studies (MA), including speech communication and rhetorical studies. Part-time and evening/weekend programs available. *Faculty:* 4 full-time (2 women). *Students:* 8 full-time (5 women), 13 part-time (7 women); includes 9 minority (6 African Americans, 2 Asian Americans or Pacific Islanders, 1 Hispanic American), 1 international. Average age 28. 14 applicants, 93% accepted, 8 enrolled. In 2008, 6 master's awarded. *Degree requirements:* For master's, thesis. *Entrance requirements:* For master's, 2 letters of recommendation, interview. Additional exam requirements/recommendations for international students: Required—TOEFL (minimum score 550 paper-based; 213 computer-based; 80 iBT). *Application deadline:* Applications are processed on a rolling basis. Application fee: $60. Electronic applications accepted. *Expenses:* Tuition: Full-time $15,300; part-time $850 per credit. Required fees: $970; $165 per term. Tuition and fees vary according to program. *Financial support:* In 2008–09, 12 students received support, including 1 fellowship with full and partial tuition reimbursement available (averaging $3,500 per year), 2 research assistantships with full and partial tuition reimbursements available (averaging $9,480 per year); Federal Work-Study, institutionally sponsored loans, scholarships/grants, tuition waivers (full and partial), and unspecified assistantships also available. Support available to part-time students. Financial award applicants required to submit FAFSA. *Faculty research:* Performance of race and gender, public deliberation, public memory, civic engagement and political participation, popular culture. *Unit head:* Dr. Maryanne Trasciatti, Chairperson, 516-463-7141, E-mail: sphmat@hofstra.edu. *Application contact:* Carol Drummer, Dean of Graduate Admissions, 516-463-4876, Fax: 516-463-4664, E-mail: gradstudent@hofstra.edu.

Idaho State University, Office of Graduate Studies, College of Arts and Sciences, Department of Communication and Rhetorical Studies, Pocatello, ID 83209. Offers communication and rhetorical studies (MA). Part-time programs available. *Faculty:* 4 full-time (1 woman). *Students:* 8 full-time (4 women), 4 part-time (2 women); includes 2 minority (both Hispanic Americans), 2 international. Average age 32. In 2008, 3 master's awarded. *Degree requirements:* For master's, comprehensive exam, thesis (for some programs). *Entrance requirements:* For master's, GRE General Test, minimum GPA of 3.0 in all upper level courses. Additional exam requirements/recommendations for international students: Required—TOEFL (minimum score 550 paper-based; 213 computer-based; 80 iBT). *Application deadline:* For fall admission, 7/1 for domestic students, 6/1 for international students; for spring admission, 12/1 for domestic students, 11/1 for international students. Applications are processed on a rolling basis. Application fee: $55. Electronic applications accepted. *Expenses:* Tuition, area resident: Full-time $3114; part-time $276 per credit hour. Tuition, state resident: full-time $3114; part-time $276 per credit hour. Tuition, nonresident: full-time $12,318; part-time $404 per credit hour. Required fees: $2360. Tuition and fees vary according to course load and reciprocity agreements. *Financial support:* In 2008–09, 3 teaching assistantships with full and partial tuition reimbursements (averaging $9,401 per year) were awarded; career-related internships or fieldwork, Federal Work-Study, institutionally sponsored loans, scholarships/grants, health care benefits, and unspecified assistantships also available. Support available to part-time students. Financial award application deadline: 1/1; financial award applicants required to submit FAFSA. *Faculty research:* Metaphor and cognition in organizational groups and teams; rhetorical criticism of contemporary culture, including music, film, television, and advertising; communication pedagogy; the effect of language on organizational identification and commitment; risk communication and crisis communication. *Unit head:* Dr. James DiSanza, Chairman, 208-282-3395, Fax: 208-282-4598, E-mail: disajame@isu.edu. *Application contact:* Ellen Combs, Graduate School Technical Records Specialist, 208-282-2150, Fax: 208-282-4847, E-mail: combelle@isu.edu.

Indiana University Bloomington, University Graduate School, College of Arts and Sciences, Department of Communication and Culture, Bloomington, IN 47405-7000. Offers film and media studies (PhD); performance and ethnography (PhD); rhetoric and public culture (PhD). *Faculty:* 24 full-time (12 women). *Students:* 81 full-time (45 women); includes 11 minority (2 African Americans, 1 American Indian/Alaska Native, 2 Asian Americans or Pacific Islanders, 6 Hispanic Americans), 10 international. Average age 32. 163 applicants, 20% accepted, 16 enrolled. In 2008, 5 master's, 11 doctorates awarded. *Degree requirements:* For master's, comprehensive exam; for doctorate, one foreign language, comprehensive exam, thesis/dissertation, student teaching. *Entrance requirements:* For master's and doctorate, GRE General Test (recommended), minimum GPA of 3.0, 3 letters of recommendation, writing sample. Additional exam requirements/recommendations for international students: Required—TOEFL (minimum score 550 paper-based; 213 computer-based). *Application deadline:* For winter admission, 1/1 for domestic students, 12/1 for international students. Application fee: $50 ($60 for international students). Electronic applications accepted. *Expenses:* Tuition, area resident: Part-time $291.97 per credit hour. Tuition, state resident: part-time $291.97 per credit hour. Tuition, nonresident: part-time $850.33 per credit hour. Required fees: $110 per semester. Tuition and fees vary according to course load and program. *Financial support:* In 2008–09, 65 students received support, including 4 fellowships with full tuition reimbursements available (averaging $18,000 per year), 61 teaching assistantships with full tuition reimbursements available (averaging $12,961 per year). Financial award application deadline: 4/15. *Faculty research:* Rhetoric and public culture, film and media studies, performance ethnography. *Unit head:* Prof. Gregory A. Waller, Chair, 812-855-2367, Fax: 812-855-6014, E-mail: cmcl@indiana.edu. *Application contact:* Kathy P. Teige, Graduate Secretary, 812-855-6389, Fax: 812-855-6014, E-mail: kteige@indiana.edu.

Indiana University of Pennsylvania, School of Graduate Studies and Research, College of Humanities and Social Sciences, Department of English, Indiana, PA 15705-1087. Offers composition and teaching English to speakers of other languages (MA, MAT, PhD), including composition and teaching English to speakers of other languages (PhD), teaching English (MAT), teaching English to speakers of other languages (MA); literature and criticism (MA, PhD), including generalist (MA), literature (MA), literature and criticism (PhD); rhetoric and linguistics (PhD). Part-time programs available. *Faculty:* 31 full-time (17 women). *Students:* 132 full-time (69 women), 241 part-time (155 women); includes 20 minority (12 African Americans, 1 American Indian/Alaska Native, 4 Asian Americans or Pacific Islanders, 3 Hispanic Americans), 105 international. Average age 36. 320 applicants, 39% accepted, 73 enrolled. In 2008, 40 master's, 28 doctorates awarded. *Degree requirements:* For master's, thesis optional; for doctorate, one foreign language, comprehensive exam, thesis/dissertation. *Entrance requirements:* For master's and doctorate, 2 letters of recommendation. Additional exam requirements/recommendations for international students: Required—TOEFL. *Application deadline:* For fall admission, 7/1 priority date for domestic students; for spring admission, 11/1 for domestic students. Applications are processed on a rolling basis. Application fee: $30. *Expenses:* Tuition, area resident: Full-time $6430; part-time $357 per credit. Tuition, nonresident: full-time $10,288; part-time $572 per credit. Required fees: $1547.50; $107 per credit. $283 per year. *Financial support:* In 2008–09, 7 fellowships (averaging $2,000 per year), 41 research assistantships with full and partial tuition reimbursements (averaging $5,808 per year), 22 teaching assistantships with partial tuition reimbursements (averaging $12,355 per year) were awarded. Financial award application deadline: 3/15; financial award applicants required to submit FAFSA. *Unit head:* Dr. Gail I. Berlin, Chairperson, 724-357-2261, E-mail: ivy@iup.edu. *Application contact:* Dr. Gail I. Berlin, Chairperson, 724-357-2261, E-mail: ivy@iup.edu.

Iowa State University of Science and Technology, Graduate College, College of Liberal Arts and Sciences, Department of English, Ames, IA 50011. Offers English (MA); rhetoric and professional communication (PhD). *Faculty:* 51 full-time (25 women), 10 part-time/adjunct (7 women). *Students:* 89 full-time (57 women), 34 part-time (22 women); includes 4 minority (1 African American, 3 Hispanic Americans), 28 international. 106 applicants, 58% accepted, 37 enrolled. In 2008, 31 master's awarded. *Degree requirements:* For master's, thesis or alternative; for doctorate, thesis/dissertation. *Entrance requirements:* For master's, GRE General Test, sample of written work, resumé, portfolio in creative writing; for doctorate, GRE General Test, sample of written work, resumé. Additional exam requirements/recommendations for international students: Required—TOEFL (minimum score 600 paper-based; 100 iBT), IELTS (7.0) or TOEFL. *Application deadline:* For fall admission, 1/5 priority date for domestic and international students. Application fee: $30 ($70 for international students). Electronic applications accepted. *Expenses:* Tuition, area resident: Full-time $6446; part-time $359 per credit. Tuition, state resident: full-time $6446; part-time $359 per credit. Tuition, nonresident: full-time $17,330; part-time $963 per credit. Required fees: $790; $249.25 per semester. Tuition and fees vary according to course load and program. *Financial support:* In 2008–09, 14 research assistantships with full and partial tuition reimbursements (averaging $16,308 per year), 79 teaching assistantships with full and partial tuition reimbursements (averaging $16,308 per year) were awarded; fellowships, scholarships/grants, health care benefits, and unspecified assistantships also available. *Faculty research:* Creative writing, literature, rhetoric, composition and professional communication, teaching English as a second language, applied linguistics. *Unit head:* Dr. Charles Kostelnick, Chair, 515-294-2477, Fax: 515-294-2125, E-mail: englgrad@iastate.edu. *Application contact:* Dr. Constance Post, Director of Graduate Education, 515-294-3175, E-mail: englgrad@iastate.edu.

Kansas State University, Graduate School, College of Arts and Sciences, Department of Communication Studies, Theatre and Dance, Manhattan, KS 66505. Offers rhetoric/communication (MA); theatre (MA). *Faculty:* 16 full-time (8 women). *Students:* 30 full-time (24 women), 7 part-time (2 women); includes 4 minority (1 African American, 1 American Indian/Alaska Native, 1 Asian American or Pacific Islander, 1 Hispanic American), 1 international. Average age 27. 11 applicants, 100% accepted, 7 enrolled. In 2008, 12 master's awarded. *Degree requirements:* For master's, thesis or alternative. *Entrance requirements:* For master's, GRE General Test (recommended), minimum GPA of 3.0. Additional exam requirements/recommendations for international students: Required—TOEFL. *Application deadline:* For fall admission, 3/1 for domestic students, 2/1 priority date for international students; for spring admission, 10/1 for domestic students, 8/1 priority date for international students. Applications are processed on a rolling basis. Application fee: $30 ($55 for international students). *Expenses:* Tuition, area resident: Full-time $6466; part-time $269.40 per credit hour. Tuition, state resident: full-time $6466; part-time $269.40 per credit hour. Tuition, nonresident: full-time $14,874; part-time $619.75 per credit hour. Required fees: $673; $23.40 per credit hour. Tuition and fees vary according to campus/location. *Financial support:* In 2008–09, 27 teaching assistantships with full tuition reimbursements (averaging $10,111 per year) were awarded; career-related internships or fieldwork, institutionally sponsored loans, and scholarships/grants also available. Support available to part-time students. Financial award application deadline: 3/1; financial award applicants required to submit FAFSA. *Faculty research:* Drama therapy, directing, costume design, scenic design, and technical theatre mechanics and safety. *Unit head:* Charles Griffin, Head, 785-532-6860, Fax: 785-532-3714, E-mail: charlieg@ksu.edu. *Application contact:* William Schenck-Hamlin, Director, 785-532-6861, Fax: 785-532-3714, E-mail: billsh@ksu.edu.

Kent State University, College of Arts and Sciences, Department of English, Kent, OH 44242-0001. Offers comparative literature (MA); creative writing (MFA); English (PhD); English for teachers (MA); literature and writing (MA); rhetoric and composition (PhD); teaching English as a second language (MA). Part-time programs available. Terminal master's awarded for partial completion of doctoral program. *Degree requirements:* For master's, one foreign language, thesis optional; for doctorate, one foreign language, thesis/dissertation, qualifying exams. *Entrance requirements:* For master's and doctorate, GRE General Test, writing sample, letters of recommendation. Additional exam requirements/recommendations for international students: Required—TOEFL (minimum score 600 paper-based). Electronic applications accepted. *Faculty research:* British and American literature, textual editing, rhetoric and composition, cultural studies, linguistic and critical theories.

Miami University, Graduate School, College of Arts and Sciences, Department of English, Oxford, OH 45056. Offers composition and rhetoric (MA, PhD); creative writing (MA); criticism (PhD); English and American literature and language (PhD); English education (MAT); library theory (PhD); literature (MA, MAT, PhD); technical and scientific communication (MTSC). Part-time programs available. *Degree requirements:* For master's, final exam; for doctorate, 2 foreign languages, comprehensive exam, thesis/dissertation, final exams. *Entrance requirements:* For master's, minimum undergraduate GPA of 3.0 during previous 2 years or 2.75 overall; for doctorate, GRE General Test, GRE Subject Test, minimum GPA of 2.75 (undergraduate), 3.0 (graduate). Additional exam requirements/recommendations for international students: Required—TOEFL (minimum score 550 paper-based; 213 computer-based), TWE (minimum score 4). Electronic applications accepted.

Michigan State University, The Graduate School, College of Arts and Letters, Program in Rhetoric and Writing, East Lansing, MI 48824. Offers critical studies in literacy and pedagogy (MA); digital rhetoric and professional writing (MA); rhetoric and writing (PhD). *Entrance requirements:* Additional exam requirements/recommendations for international students: Required—TOEFL. Electronic applications accepted. *Faculty research:* Rhetoric, writing and communication studies; media studies; technical communication, writing for digital environments.

Rhetoric

Michigan Technological University, Graduate School, College of Sciences and Arts, Department of Humanities, Program in Rhetoric and Technical Communication, Houghton, MI 49931-1295. Offers MS, PhD. Part-time programs available. Terminal master's awarded for partial completion of doctoral program. *Degree requirements:* For master's, comprehensive exam; for doctorate, one foreign language, comprehensive exam, thesis/dissertation. *Entrance requirements:* Additional exam requirements/recommendations for international students: Required—TOEFL (minimum score 600 paper-based; 250 computer-based). Electronic applications accepted.

New Mexico Highlands University, Graduate Studies, College of Arts and Sciences, Department of Humanities, Las Vegas, NM 87701. Offers English (MA), including creative writing, language, rhetoric and composition, literature. *Faculty:* 12 full-time (6 women). *Students:* 12 full-time (6 women), 4 part-time (3 women); includes 3 minority (all Hispanic Americans), 1 international. Average age 30. 10 applicants, 70% accepted, 5 enrolled. In 2008, 5 master's awarded. *Degree requirements:* For master's, comprehensive exam, thesis. *Entrance requirements:* For master's, minimum undergraduate GPA of 3.0. Additional exam requirements/recommendations for international students: Required—TOEFL (minimum score 540 paper-based; 207 computer-based). *Application deadline:* For fall admission, 8/1 priority date for domestic students. Applications are processed on a rolling basis. Application fee: $15. *Expenses:* Tuition, state resident: full-time $2880; part-time $120 per credit hour. Tuition, nonresident: full-time $4234; part-time $176 per credit hour. International tuition: $5645 full-time. One-time fee: $20. *Financial support:* In 2008–09, 8 students received support, including teaching assistantships with full and partial tuition reimbursements available (averaging $6,500 per year); career-related internships or fieldwork, Federal Work-Study, institutionally sponsored loans, scholarships/grants, tuition waivers (full and partial), and unspecified assistantships also available. Support available to part-time students. Financial award application deadline: 3/1; financial award applicants required to submit FAFSA. *Faculty research:* 20th century literature, life path writing in homeless shelters, native American philosophy, medieval intellectual and cultural history, creating pedagogical tools for teaching law. *Unit head:* Dr. Brandon Kempner, Department Head, 505-454-3286, E-mail: bkempner@nmhu.edu. *Application contact:* Diane Trujillo, Administrative Assistant, Graduate Studies, 505-454-3266, Fax: 505-426-2117, E-mail: dtrujillo@nmhu.edu.

New Mexico State University, Graduate School, College of Arts and Sciences, Department of English, Las Cruces, NM 88003-8001. Offers creative writing (MFA); English (MA); rhetoric and professional communication (PhD). Part-time programs available. *Faculty:* 20 full-time (12 women), 2 part-time/adjunct (0 women). *Students:* 73 full-time (39 women), 36 part-time (24 women); includes 15 minority (3 American Indian/Alaska Native, 12 Hispanic Americans), 9 international. Average age 32. 135 applicants, 41% accepted, 40 enrolled. In 2008, 25 master's, 2 doctorates awarded. *Degree requirements:* For master's, one foreign language, thesis (for some programs); for doctorate, comprehensive exam, thesis/dissertation, internship. *Entrance requirements:* For master's and doctorate, sample of written work. *Application deadline:* For fall admission, 2/1 for domestic and international students. Application fee: $30 ($50 for international students). Electronic applications accepted. *Expenses:* Tuition, area resident: Full-time $3890; part-time $212.85 per credit. Tuition, state resident: full-time $3890; part-time $212.85 per credit. Tuition, nonresident: full-time $13,916; part-time $630.55 per credit. Required fees: $1218; $609 per semester. *Financial support:* In 2008–09, 81 students received support, including 3 research assistantships (averaging $9,217 per year), 53 teaching assistantships (averaging $15,623 per year); fellowships, career-related internships or fieldwork, Federal Work-Study, institutionally sponsored loans, scholarships/grants, health care benefits, and unspecified assistantships also available. Financial award application deadline: 2/1; financial award applicants required to submit FAFSA. *Faculty research:* Composition research, history and theory of rhetoric, technical/professional communication, creative writing, English and American literature. *Unit head:* Dr. Elizabeth Schirmer, Head, 575-646-1733, Fax: 575-646-7725, E-mail: eschirme@nmsu.edu. *Application contact:* Dr. Elizabeth Schirmer, Director of Graduate Studies, 575-646-1733, E-mail: eschirme@nmsu.edu.

North Carolina State University, Graduate School, College of Humanities and Social Sciences, Program in Communication, Rhetoric, and Digital Media, Raleigh, NC 27695. Offers PhD.

Rensselaer Polytechnic Institute, Graduate School, School of Humanities and Social Sciences, Department of Language, Literature, and Communication, Programs in Communication and Rhetoric, Troy, NY 12180-3590. Offers MS, PhD. Terminal master's awarded for partial completion of doctoral program. *Degree requirements:* For master's, thesis optional; for doctorate, comprehensive exam, thesis/dissertation. *Entrance requirements:* For master's, GRE General Test, resumé; for doctorate, GRE General Test, writing sample, resumé or curriculum vitae. Additional exam requirements/recommendations for international students: Required—TOEFL (minimum score 570 paper-based; 230 computer-based). Electronic applications accepted. *Faculty research:* Human-computer interaction, media design and theory, rhetoric and culture, virtual institutions/communities, usability.

San Diego State University, Graduate and Research Affairs, College of Arts and Letters, Department of Rhetoric and Writing, San Diego, CA 92182. Offers MA. Part-time programs available. *Degree requirements:* For master's, thesis. *Entrance requirements:* For master's, GRE General Test, writing sample, 3 letters of reference. Additional exam requirements/recommendations for international students: Required—TOEFL. Electronic applications accepted.

Southern Illinois University Carbondale, Graduate School, College of Liberal Arts, Department of English, Carbondale, IL 62901-4701. Offers composition (MA, PhD), including composition, literature, rhetoric; creative writing (MFA). *Degree requirements:* For master's, one foreign language, thesis; for doctorate, 2 foreign languages, thesis/dissertation. *Entrance requirements:* For master's, GRE General Test, GRE Subject Test, minimum GPA of 2.7; for doctorate, GRE General Test, GRE Subject Test, minimum GPA of 3.25. Additional exam requirements/recommendations for international students: Required—TOEFL. *Faculty research:* British literature, English literature, modern Continental literature, literary criticism and theory, film studies, Irish studies.

See Close-Up on page 445.

Syracuse University, Graduate School, College of Arts and Sciences, Program in Composition and Cultural Rhetoric, Syracuse, NY 13244. Offers PhD. *Entrance requirements:* For doctorate, GRE. Electronic applications accepted.

Syracuse University, Graduate School, College of Visual and Performing Arts, Program in Communication and Rhetorical Studies, Syracuse, NY 13244. Offers MA, MS. Part-time programs available. *Entrance requirements:* For master's, GRE General Test, writing sample. Additional exam requirements/recommendations for international students: Required—TOEFL. Electronic applications accepted.

Texas State University–San Marcos, Graduate School, College of Liberal Arts, Department of English, Program in Rhetoric and Composition, San Marcos, TX 78666. Offers MA. Part-time programs available. *Entrance requirements:* For master's, 3.25 in a minimum of 24 hours of undergrad English, 6 hours foreign language. Additional exam requirements/recommendations for international students: Required—TOEFL (minimum score 550 paper-based; 213 computer-based). Electronic applications accepted.

Texas Tech University, Graduate School, College of Arts and Sciences, Department of English, Lubbock, TX 79409. Offers English (MA, PhD); technical communication (MA); technical communication and rhetoric (PhD). Part-time programs available. *Faculty:* 37 full-time (14 women), 3 part-time/adjunct (all women). *Students:* 100 full-time (37 women), 82 part-time (52 women); includes 19 minority (4 African Americans, 3 American Indian/Alaska Native, 6 Asian Americans or Pacific Islanders, 6 Hispanic Americans), 11 international. Average age 35. 188 applicants, 38% accepted, 33 enrolled. In 2008, 24 master's, 12 doctorates awarded. *Degree requirements:* For master's, one foreign language, thesis (for some programs); for doctorate, thesis/dissertation. *Entrance requirements:* For master's and doctorate, GRE General Test. Additional exam requirements/recommendations for international students: Required—TOEFL (minimum score 550 paper-based; 213 computer-based). *Application deadline:* For fall admission, 3/1 priority date for international students; for spring admission, 11/1 priority date for international students. Applications are processed on a rolling basis. Application fee: $50 ($60 for international students). Electronic applications accepted. *Expenses:* Tuition, area resident: Part-time $194 per credit hour. Tuition, state resident: full-time $4648; part-time $194 per credit hour. Tuition, nonresident: full-time $11,392; part-time $475 per credit hour. Required fees: $2206; $69 per credit hour. $389 per semester. *Financial support:* In 2008–09, 109 students received support, including 1 research assistantship with partial tuition reimbursement available (averaging $16,357 per year), 82 teaching assistantships with partial tuition reimbursements available (averaging $14,350 per year); Federal Work-Study and institutionally sponsored loans also available. Support available to part-time students. Financial award application deadline: 4/15; financial award applicants required to submit FAFSA. *Faculty research:* Computers and writing; technical communication and rhetoric; creative writing; nineteenth century studies; literature of social justice and the environment. Total annual research expenditures: $54,723. *Unit head:* Dr. Sam Dragga, Chair, 806-742-2501, Fax: 806-742-0989, E-mail: sam.dragga@ttu.edu. *Application contact:* Dr. Sean Grass, Director of Graduate Studies, 806-742-2501, Fax: 806-742-0989, E-mail: english.gradadvisor@ttu.edu.

Texas Woman's University, Graduate School, College of Arts and Sciences, Department of English, Speech, and Foreign Languages, Denton, TX 76201. Offers English (MA); rhetoric (PhD). Part-time programs available. *Faculty:* 11 full-time (6 women), 4 part-time/adjunct (2 women). *Students:* 10 full-time (all women), 49 part-time (43 women); includes 10 minority (4 African Americans, 1 American Indian/Alaska Native, 2 Asian Americans or Pacific Islanders, 3 Hispanic Americans), 1 international. Average age 37. In 2008, 8 master's, 4 doctorates awarded. *Degree requirements:* For master's, one foreign language, comprehensive exam, thesis; for doctorate, 2 foreign languages, comprehensive exam, thesis/dissertation. *Entrance requirements:* For master's, GRE General Test (minimum score: Verbal 500, Quantitative 350), 3 letters of reference, interview, minimum GPA of 3.0; for doctorate, GRE General Test, writing sample, 3 letters of reference, interview, minimum GPA of 3.0 on previous upper-division and graduate work. Additional exam requirements/recommendations for international students: Recommended—TOEFL (minimum score 600 paper-based; 213 computer-based; 79 iBT). *Application deadline:* For fall admission, 4/1 for international students; for spring admission, 8/1 for international students. Applications are processed on a rolling basis. Application fee: $30 ($50 for international students). Electronic applications accepted. *Expenses:* Tuition, state resident: full-time $3564; part-time $198 per semester hour. Tuition, nonresident: full-time $8622; part-time $479 per semester hour. Required fees: $1158; $64 per semester hour. Tuition and fees vary according to course load. *Financial support:* In 2008–09, 19 research assistantships (averaging $10,530 per year), 14 teaching assistantships (averaging $10,530 per year) were awarded; career-related internships or fieldwork, Federal Work-Study, institutionally sponsored loans, scholarships/grants, traineeships, health care benefits, and unspecified assistantships also available. Support available to part-time students. Financial award application deadline: 3/1; financial award applicants required to submit FAFSA. *Faculty research:* British and American literature, rhetoric: historical and applied, composition studies and technology, literary theory and criticism, women's literature and feminist rhetoric. *Unit head:* Dr. Bruce Krajewski, Chair, 940-898-2324, Fax: 940-898-2297, E-mail: gwest@twu.edu. *Application contact:* Samuel Wheeler, Assistant Director of Admissions, 940-898-3188, Fax: 940-898-3081, E-mail: wheelersr@twu.edu.

The University of Alabama, Graduate School, College of Arts and Sciences, Department of English, Tuscaloosa, AL 35487. Offers composition and rhetoric (PhD); creative writing (MFA), including fiction, poetry; literature (MA, PhD); rhetoric and composition (MA); teaching English as a second language (MATESOL). *Faculty:* 35 full-time (13 women). *Students:* 120 full-time (66 women), 16 part-time (12 women); includes 15 minority (8 African Americans, 2 American Indian/Alaska Native, 3 Asian Americans or Pacific Islanders, 2 Hispanic Americans), 5 international. Average age 28. 237 applicants, 20% accepted, 31 enrolled. In 2008, 21 master's, 2 doctorates awarded. *Degree requirements:* For master's, one foreign language, comprehensive exam, thesis (for some programs); for doctorate, 2 foreign languages, comprehensive exam, thesis/dissertation. *Entrance requirements:* For master's and doctorate, GRE, minimum GPA of 3.0, critical writing sample. Additional exam requirements/recommendations for international students: Required—TOEFL. *Application deadline:* For fall admission, 1/15 priority date for domestic students, 1/15 for international students. Application fee: $30. Electronic applications accepted. *Expenses:* Tuition, area resident: Full-time $6400. Tuition, state resident: full-time $6400. Tuition, nonresident: full-time $18,000. *Financial support:* In 2008–09, 7 fellowships with full tuition reimbursements (averaging $15,000 per year), 1 research assistantship (averaging $11,708 per year), 106 teaching assistantships with full tuition reimbursements (averaging $11,708 per year) were awarded; career-related internships or fieldwork, scholarships/grants, health care benefits, and unspecified assistantships also available. Financial award application deadline: 1/15. *Faculty research:* Critical theory; modern, Renaissance, and African-American literature. Total annual research expenditures: $8,282. *Unit head:* Dr. Catherine E. Davies, Director of Graduate Studies, 205-348-8499, E-mail: cdavies@bama.ua.edu. *Application contact:* Vernita W. James, Office Assistant II, 205-348-0766, Fax: 205-348-1388, E-mail: vwjames@bama.ua.edu.

The University of Arizona, Graduate College, College of Humanities, Department of English, Rhetoric, Composition and the Teaching of English Program, Tucson, AZ 85721. Offers MA, PhD. *Degree requirements:* For master's, one foreign language, comprehensive exam; for doctorate, one foreign language, comprehensive exam, thesis/dissertation. *Entrance requirements:* For master's, GRE, 3 letters of recommendation, minimum GPA of 3.0, statement of purpose, writing sample. Additional exam requirements/recommendations for international students: Required—TOEFL (minimum score 550 paper-based). Electronic applications accepted.

University of Arkansas at Little Rock, Graduate School, College of Arts, Humanities, and Social Science, Department of Rhetoric and Writing, Little Rock, AR 72204-1099. Offers professional and technical writing (MA). Part-time and evening/weekend programs available. *Degree requirements:* For master's, thesis or alternative, oral defense of final project. *Entrance requirements:* For master's, GRE, minimum GPA of 3.0, writing portfolio. *Faculty research:* Writing for industry, science, business, and government; composition and rhetorical theory; writing nonfiction; teaching of writing.

University of California, Berkeley, Graduate Division, College of Letters and Science, Department of Rhetoric, Berkeley, CA 94720-1500. Offers PhD. *Degree requirements:* For doctorate, 2 foreign languages, thesis/dissertation, qualifying exam. *Entrance requirements:* For doctorate, GRE General Test, minimum GPA of 3.0, 3 letters of recommendation. *Faculty research:* History and theory of rhetoric, public discourse (law, politics, and science), literature and philosophy, film.

The University of Iowa, Graduate College, College of Liberal Arts and Sciences, Department of Communication Studies, Iowa City, IA 52242-1316. Offers communication research (MA, PhD); rhetorical studies (MA, PhD). *Degree requirements:* For master's, thesis optional, exam; for doctorate, comprehensive exam, thesis/dissertation. *Entrance requirements:* For master's and doctorate, GRE General Test, minimum GPA of 3.0. Additional exam requirements/recommendations for international students: Required—TOEFL (minimum score 550 paper-based; 213 computer-based; 81 iBT). Electronic applications accepted.

The University of Iowa, Graduate College, College of Liberal Arts and Sciences, Department of English, Iowa City, IA 52242-1316. Offers English (PhD); literary criticism (PhD); literary history (PhD); literary studies (MA); nonfiction writing (MFA); rhetorical theory and stylistics (PhD); writer's workshop (MFA); JD/PhD. *Degree requirements:* For master's, thesis (for some programs), exam; for doctorate, comprehensive exam, thesis/dissertation. *Entrance requirements:* For master's and doctorate, GRE General Test, minimum GPA of 3.0. Additional exam requirements/recommendations for international students: Required—TOEFL (minimum score 640 paper-based; 273 computer-based; 112 iBT). Electronic applications accepted.

University of Louisiana at Lafayette, BI Moody III College of Business Administration MBA Program, College of Liberal Arts, Department of English, Lafayette, LA 70504. Offers British and American literature (MA), including creative writing, folklore, rhetoric; creative writing (PhD); literature (PhD); rhetoric (PhD). Part-time programs available. Terminal master's awarded for partial completion of doctoral program. *Degree requirements:* For master's, one foreign language, thesis or alternative; for doctorate, 2 foreign languages, comprehensive exam, thesis/dissertation. *Entrance requirements:* For master's, GRE General Test, minimum GPA of 2.75; for doctorate, GRE General Test, minimum GPA of 3.0. Additional exam requirements/recommendations for international students: Required—TOEFL (minimum score 550 paper-based; 213 computer-based). Electronic applications accepted. *Faculty research:* Composition theory, Southern literature, medieval literature.

University of Louisville, Graduate School, College of Arts and Sciences, Department of English, Program in English, Louisville, KY 40292. Offers creative writing (MA); literature (MA); rhetoric and composition (MA). Part-time and evening/weekend programs available. *Faculty:* 40 full-time (24 women). *Students:* 33 full-time (19 women), 29 part-time (18 women); includes 4 African Americans, 2 Asian Americans or Pacific Islanders, 1 international. Average age 28. 58 applicants, 95% accepted, 33 enrolled. In 2008, 16 master's awarded. *Degree requirements:* For master's, one foreign language, thesis or culminating project. *Entrance requirements:* For master's, GRE General Test, 10-15 page critical writing sample, 2 academic letters of recommendation, transcripts of all college work;. Additional exam requirements/recommendations for international students: Required—TOEFL (minimum score 600 paper-based; 210 computer-based; 100 iBT). *Application deadline:* For fall admission, 1/5 priority date for domestic and international students; for spring admission, 12/1 for domestic students. Applications are processed on a rolling basis. Application fee: $50. Electronic applications accepted. *Financial support:* In 2008–09, 19 students received support, including 18 teaching assistantships with full tuition reimbursements available (averaging $15,500 per year); health care benefits and unspecified assistantships also available. Financial award application deadline: 1/5. *Faculty research:* English literatures and cultures; American literatures and cultures; critical theory and cultural studies; rhetoric and composition; creative writing. Total annual research expenditures: $278,898. *Unit head:* Dr. Susan Griffin, Chair, 502-852-6801, Fax: 502-852-4182, E-mail: smgriff01@louisville.edu. *Application contact:* Libby Leggett, Director, Graduate Admissions, 502-852-3101, Fax: 502-852-6536, E-mail: gradadm@louisville.edu.

University of Louisville, Graduate School, College of Arts and Sciences, Department of English, Program in English Rhetoric and Composition, Louisville, KY 40292. Offers rhetoric and composition (PhD). Part-time programs available. *Faculty:* 40 full-time (24 women). *Students:* 39 full-time (21 women), 3 part-time (2 women); includes 5 African Americans, 3 international. Average age 34. 33 applicants, 33% accepted, 8 enrolled. In 2008, 4 doctorates awarded. *Degree requirements:* For doctorate, 2 foreign languages, comprehensive exam, thesis/dissertation. *Entrance requirements:* For doctorate, GRE General Test, 15-20 page critical writing sample, 1000-word statement of professional goals, 3 academic letters of recommendation, application for graduate teaching assistantship (resumé + statement of teaching philosophy), transcripts of all college work. Additional exam requirements/recommendations for international students: Required—TOEFL (minimum score 600 paper-based; 210 computer-based; 100 iBT). *Application deadline:* For fall admission, 1/5 priority date for domestic and international students. Application fee: $50. Electronic applications accepted. *Financial support:* In 2008–09, 28 students received support, including 4 fellowships with full tuition reimbursements available (averaging $19,992 per year), 4 teaching assistantships with full tuition reimbursements available (averaging $19,992 per year); health care benefits and fellowships, teaching assistantships also available. Financial award application deadline: 1/5. *Faculty research:* Literacy studies, including global literacies; cultural studies; historical rhetoric; composition studies; rhetorical theory. *Unit head:* Dr. Susan Griffin, Chair, 502-852-6801, Fax: 502-852-4182, E-mail: smgriff01@louisville.edu. *Application contact:* Libby Leggett, Director, Graduate Admissions, 502-852-3108, Fax: 502-852-3111, E-mail: gradadm@louisville.edu.

University of Nebraska–Lincoln, Graduate College, College of Arts and Sciences, Department of Communication Studies, Lincoln, NE 68588. Offers instructional communication (MA, PhD); interpersonal communication (MA, PhD); marketing, communication studies, and advertising (MA, PhD); organizational communication (MA, PhD); rhetoric and culture (MA, PhD). *Faculty:* 7 full-time (4 women). *Students:* 23 full-time (15 women), 9 part-time (8 women); includes 1 minority (Asian American or Pacific Islander), 1 international. Average age 35. In 2008, 2 master's, 2 doctorates awarded. *Degree requirements:* For master's, thesis optional; for doctorate, comprehensive exam, thesis/dissertation. *Entrance requirements:* For master's and doctorate, GRE General Test, writing sample. Additional exam requirements/recommendations for international students: Required—TOEFL (minimum score 600 paper-based; 250 computer-based). *Application deadline:* For fall admission, 1/15 for domestic and international students. Applications are processed on a rolling basis. Application fee: $40. Electronic applications accepted. *Expenses:* Tuition, state resident: full-time $4275; part-time $237.50 per credit hour. Tuition, nonresident: full-time $11,525; part-time $640.25 per credit hour. Required fees: $1068; $10.35 per credit hour. $440.70 per semester. Tuition and fees vary according to course load and program. *Financial support:* Fellowships, research assistantships, teaching assistantships, Federal Work-Study, health care benefits, and unspecified assistantships available. Support available to part-time students. Financial award application deadline: 1/15. *Faculty research:* Message strategies, gender communication, political communication, organizational communication, instructional communication. *Unit head:* Dr. William Seiler, Chair, 402-472-2069. *Application contact:* Ginny Gross, Director of Graduate Admissions, 402-472-2878, Fax: 402-472-0589, E-mail: grad_admissions@unl.edu.

University of Nebraska–Lincoln, Graduate College, College of Arts and Sciences, Department of English, Lincoln, NE 68588-0333. Offers composition and rhetoric (MA, PhD); creative writing (MA, PhD); literature studies (MA, PhD). *Faculty:* 39 full-time (23 women). *Students:* 77 full-time (57 women), 54 part-time (36 women); includes 5 minority (3 African Americans, 2 Hispanic Americans), 6 international. In 2008, 11 master's, 15 doctorates awarded. *Degree requirements:* For master's, thesis optional; for doctorate, one foreign language, comprehensive exam, thesis/dissertation. *Entrance requirements:* For master's, writing sample; for doctorate, GRE General Test, writing sample. Additional exam requirements/recommendations for international students: Required—TOEFL (minimum score 600 paper-based; 250 computer-based). *Application deadline:* For fall admission, 1/15 for domestic and international students. Application fee: $40. Electronic applications accepted. *Expenses:* Tuition, state resident: full-time $4275; part-time $237.50 per credit hour. Tuition, nonresident: full-time $11,525; part-time $640.25 per credit hour. Required fees: $1068; $10.35 per credit hour. $440.70 per semester. Tuition and fees vary according to course load and program. *Financial support:* Fellowships, research assistantships, teaching assistantships, Federal Work-Study, health care benefits, and unspecified assistantships available. Support available to part-time students. Financial award application deadline: 1/15. *Faculty research:* Creative writing, composition and rhetoric, women's studies, North American literature, medieval/Renaissance studies. *Unit head:* Dr. Linda Pratt, Chair, 402-472-3191, Fax: 402-472-1123. *Application contact:* Ginny Gross, Director of Graduate Admissions, 402-472-2878, Fax: 402-472-0589, E-mail: grad_admissions@unl.edu.

The University of North Carolina at Greensboro, Graduate School, College of Arts and Sciences, Department of English, Program in English, Greensboro, NC 27412-5001. Offers American literature (PhD); English (M Ed, MA); English literature (PhD); rhetoric and composition (PhD). *Degree requirements:* For master's, comprehensive exam, thesis or alternative; for doctorate, variable foreign language requirement, thesis/dissertation, preliminary exam. *Entrance requirements:* For master's, GRE General Test, GRE Subject Test, minimum GPA of 3.0; for doctorate, GRE General Test, GRE Subject Test, critical writing sample, minimum GPA of 3.0. Additional exam requirements/recommendations for international students: Required—TOEFL. Electronic applications accepted.

The University of Texas at El Paso, Graduate School, College of Liberal Arts, Department of English, El Paso, TX 79968-0001. Offers English and American literature (MA); rhetoric and composition (PhD); rhetoric and writing studies (MA); teaching English (MAT). Part-time and evening/weekend programs available. *Degree requirements:* For master's, thesis optional. *Entrance requirements:* For master's, GRE General Test, minimum GPA of 3.0. Additional exam requirements/recommendations for international students: Required—TOEFL. Electronic applications accepted. *Faculty research:* Literature, creative writing, literary theory.

University of Utah, The Graduate School, College of Humanities, Department of English, Salt Lake City, UT 84112-1107. Offers American studies (MA, PhD); British American literature (MA, PhD); creative writing (MFA, PhD); literature (PhD); rhetoric and composition (PhD). *Degree requirements:* For master's, one foreign language, thesis (for some programs), written exam; for doctorate, 2 foreign languages, comprehensive exam, thesis/dissertation. *Entrance requirements:* For master's and doctorate, GRE General Test, minimum GPA of 3.2. Additional exam requirements/recommendations for international students: Required—TOEFL (minimum score 500 paper-based; 173 computer-based; 120 iBT). Electronic applications accepted. *Faculty research:* Poetics and modern poetry, 19th and 20th century British and American literature, the American west, environmental studies, critical theory and race and gender studies.

University of Wisconsin–Madison, Graduate School, College of Letters and Science, Department of Communication Arts, Madison, WI 53706-1380. Offers communication science (MA, PhD); film (MA, PhD); media and cultural studies (MA, PhD); rhetoric (MA, PhD). Terminal master's awarded for partial completion of doctoral program. *Degree requirements:* For master's, one foreign language, thesis (for some programs); for doctorate, one foreign language, thesis/dissertation. *Entrance requirements:* For master's and doctorate, GRE General Test, minimum GPA of 3.5. Electronic applications accepted.

University of Wisconsin–Milwaukee, Graduate School, College of Letters and Sciences, Department of Communication, Milwaukee, WI 53201-0413. Offers communication (MA, PhD); rhetorical leadership (Certificate). Part-time programs available. *Faculty:* 17 full-time (10 women). *Students:* 17 full-time (14 women), 34 part-time (26 women); includes 4 minority (2 American Indian/Alaska Native, 2 Hispanic Americans), 7 international. Average age 29. 80 applicants, 70% accepted, 32 enrolled. In 2008, 19 master's awarded. *Degree requirements:* For master's, thesis or alternative; for doctorate, comprehensive exam. *Entrance requirements:* For master's, GRE General Test, minimum GPA of 3.0. Additional exam requirements/recommendations for international students: Required—TOEFL (minimum score 550 paper-based; 79 iBT), IELTS (minimum score 6). *Application deadline:* For fall admission, 1/1 priority date for domestic students; for spring admission, 9/1 for domestic students. Applications are processed on a rolling basis. Application fee: $45 ($75 for international students). *Expenses:* Tuition, area resident: Full-time $7320; part-time $165 per credit. Tuition, state resident: full-time $7320; part-time $165 per credit. Tuition, nonresident: full-time $17,840; part-time $714 per credit. Tuition and fees vary according to campus/location, program and reciprocity agreements. *Financial support:* In 2008–09, 30 teaching assistantships were awarded; career-related internships or fieldwork and unspecified assistantships also available. Support available to part-time students. Financial award application deadline: 4/15. *Unit head:* Mike Allen, Representative, 414-229-4261, Fax: 414-229-3859. *Application contact:* General Information Contact, 414-229-4982, Fax: 414-229-6967, E-mail: gradschool@uwm.edu.

University of Wisconsin–Milwaukee, Graduate School, College of Letters and Sciences, Department of English, Milwaukee, WI 53201-0413. Offers creative writing (PhD); English (MA); linguistics (PhD); professional writing (PhD); professional writing and communication (Certificate); rhetoric and composition (PhD); MLIS/MA. *Faculty:* 40 full-time (19 women). *Students:* 107 full-time (64 women), 82 part-time (54 women); includes 13 minority (8 African Americans, 1 American Indian/Alaska Native, 2 Asian Americans or Pacific Islanders, 2 Hispanic Americans), 23 international. Average age 35. 187 applicants, 41% accepted, 34 enrolled. In 2008, 31 master's, 14 doctorates awarded. *Degree requirements:* For master's, thesis or alternative; for doctorate, one foreign language, thesis/dissertation. *Entrance requirements:* For master's, GRE General Test, GRE Subject Test; for doctorate, GRE. Additional exam requirements/recommendations for international students: Required—TOEFL (minimum score 550 paper-based; 79 iBT), IELTS (minimum score 6.5). *Application deadline:* For fall admission, 1/1 priority date for domestic students; for spring admission, 9/1 for domestic students. Applications are processed on a rolling basis. Application fee: $45 ($75 for international students). *Expenses:* Tuition, area resident: Full-time $7320; part-time $165 per credit. Tuition, state resident: full-time $7320; part-time $165 per credit. Tuition, nonresident: full-time $17,840; part-time $714 per credit. Tuition and fees vary according to campus/location, program and reciprocity agreements. *Financial support:* In 2008–09, 74 teaching assistantships were awarded; career-related internships or fieldwork and unspecified assistantships also available. Support available to part-time students. Financial award application deadline: 4/15. Total annual research expenditures: $53,677. *Unit head:* Tasha Oren, Representative, 414-229-2643, Fax: 414-229-2643, E-mail: tgoren@uwm.edu. *Application contact:* General Information Contact, 414-229-4982, Fax: 414-229-6967, E-mail: gradschool@uwm.edu.

Virginia Commonwealth University, Graduate School, College of Humanities and Sciences, Department of English, Program in English, Richmond, VA 23284-9005. Offers literature (MA); writing and rhetoric (MA).

Wright State University, School of Graduate Studies, College of Liberal Arts, Department of English Language and Literatures, Dayton, OH 45435. Offers composition and rhetoric (MA); English (MA); literature (MA); teaching English to speakers of other languages (MA). *Degree requirements:* For master's, thesis optional, portfolio. *Entrance requirements:* For master's, 20 hours in upper-level English. Additional exam requirements/recommendations for international students: Required—TOEFL. *Faculty research:* American literature, world literature in English, applied linguistics, writing theory and pedagogy.

Speech and Interpersonal Communication

Arizona State University, Graduate College, College of Liberal Arts and Sciences, Division of Social Sciences, Hugh Downs School of Human Communication, Tempe, AZ 85287. Offers communication (MA, PhD). *Degree requirements:* For master's, thesis or alternative; for doctorate, thesis/dissertation.

Arkansas State University, Graduate School, College of Communications, Department of Communication Studies, Jonesboro, State University, AR 72467. Offers communication studies and theatre arts (MA); communication studies and theatre arts education (SCCT). Part-time programs available. *Faculty:* 5 full-time (2 women). *Students:* 4 full-time (2 women), 8 part-time (4 women); includes 2 minority (both African Americans), 2 international. Average age 29. 11 applicants, 91% accepted, 7 enrolled. In 2008, 7 master's awarded. *Degree requirements:* For master's, one foreign language, comprehensive exam, thesis or alternative. *Entrance requirements:* For master's, GRE General Test, appropriate bachelor's degree, writing sample, letter of recommendation, official transcript; for SCCT, GRE or MAT, appropriate master's degree, interview, official transcript. Additional exam requirements/recommendations for international students: Required—TOEFL (minimum score 550 paper-based; 213 computer-based; 79 iBT), IELTS (minimum score 6). *Application deadline:* For fall admission, 7/15 for domestic students, 7/1 for international students; for spring admission, 12/1 for domestic students, 11/13 for international students. Applications are processed on a rolling basis. Application fee: $30 ($40 for international students). Electronic applications accepted. *Expenses:* Tuition, state resident: full-time $3744; part-time $208 per credit hour. Tuition, nonresident: full-time $9540; part-time $530 per credit hour. International tuition: $7938 full-time. Required fees: $896; $47 per credit hour. $25 per term. One-time fee: $50. Tuition and fees vary according to course load and program. *Financial support:* In 2008–09, 4 students received support; teaching assistantships, career-related internships or fieldwork, scholarships/grants, and unspecified assistantships available. Financial award application deadline: 7/1; financial award applicants required to submit FAFSA. *Faculty research:* Business and professional speech development, communication consulting, speech communication, interpersonal communication, organizational training and development. *Unit head:* Dr. Thomas Bagland, Chair, 870-972-3091, Fax: 870-972-3856, E-mail: tbaglan@astate.edu. *Application contact:* Dr. Andrew Sustich, Dean of the Graduate School, 870-972-3029, Fax: 870-972-3857, E-mail: sustich@astate.edu.

Ball State University, Graduate School, College of Communication, Information, and Media, Department of Communication Studies, Muncie, IN 47306-1099. Offers speech, public address, forensics, and rhetoric (MA). *Entrance requirements:* For master's, GRE General Test.

Bob Jones University, Graduate Programs, Greenville, SC 29614. Offers accountancy (MS); Bible (MA); Bible translation (MA); Biblical studies (Certificate); broadcast management (MS); business administration (MBA); church history (MA, PhD); church ministries (MA); church music (MM); cinema and video production (MA); counseling (MS); curriculum and instruction (Ed D); divinity (M Div); dramatic production (MA); educational leadership (MS, Ed D, Ed S); elementary education (M Ed, MAT); English (M Ed, MA, MAT); fine arts (MA); graphic design (MA); history (M Ed, MA); illustration (MA); interpretative speech (MA); mathematics (M Ed, MAT); medical missions (Certificate); ministry (MM, D Min); multi-categorical special education (M Ed, MAT); music (M Ed); New Testament interpretation (PhD); Old Testament interpretation (PhD); orchestral instrument performance (MM); organ performance (MM); pastoral studies (MA); personnel services (MS, Ed S); piano pedagogy (MM); piano performance (MM); platform arts (MA); radio and television broadcasting (MS); rhetoric and public address (MA); secondary education (M Ed); studio art (MA); teaching Bible (MA); theology (MA, PhD); voice performance (MM); youth ministries (MA); M Div/MM.

Bowling Green State University, Graduate College, College of Arts and Sciences, School of Communication Studies, Program of Communication Studies, Bowling Green, OH 43403. Offers MA, PhD. Terminal master's awarded for partial completion of doctoral program. *Degree requirements:* For master's, thesis or alternative; for doctorate, comprehensive exam, thesis/dissertation. *Entrance requirements:* For master's and doctorate, GRE General Test. Additional exam requirements/recommendations for international students: Required—TOEFL. Electronic applications accepted. *Faculty research:* Rhetorical theory and criticism, culture and communication, interpersonal/organizational communication.

Brooklyn College of the City University of New York, Division of Graduate Studies, Department of Speech Communication Arts and Sciences, Brooklyn, NY 11210-2889. Offers audiology (Au D); speech (MA), including public communication; speech and hearing sciences (PhD); speech pathology (MS). The department offers courses at Brooklyn College that are creditable towards the CUNY doctoral degree (with permission of the executive officer of the doctoral program); MS in speech pathology has fall admissions only. *Accreditation:* ASHA (one or more programs are accredited). Part-time programs available. *Students:* 32 full-time (31 women), 60 part-time (58 women); includes 9 minority (2 African Americans, 1 Asian American or Pacific Islander, 6 Hispanic Americans), 5 international. Average age 28. 259 applicants, 32% accepted, 34 enrolled. In 2008, 34 master's awarded. Terminal master's awarded for partial completion of doctoral program. *Degree requirements:* For master's, comprehensive exam, NTE. *Entrance requirements:* For master's, GRE, minimum GPA of 3.0, interview, essay. *Expenses:* Tuition, state resident: full-time $7360; part-time $310 per credit hour. Tuition, nonresident: full-time $13,800; part-time $575 per credit hour. *Financial support:* Career-related internships or fieldwork, Federal Work-Study, institutionally sponsored loans, scholarships/grants, and traineeships available. Support available to part-time students. Financial award application deadline: 5/1; financial award applicants required to submit FAFSA. *Faculty research:* Language and learning disorders, aphasia, auditory disorders, public and business communication, voice and fluency disorders. *Unit head:* Dr. Michele Emmer, Chairperson, 718-951-5225, Fax: 718-951-4167, E-mail: memmer@brooklyn.cuny.edu. *Application contact:* Hernan Sierra, Graduate Admissions Coordinator, 718-951-4536, Fax: 718-951-4506, E-mail: grads@brooklyn.cuny.edu.

California State University, Fullerton, Graduate Studies, College of Communications, Department of Human Communications, Fullerton, CA 92834-9480. Offers communicative disorders (MA); speech communication (MA). *Accreditation:* ASHA. Part-time programs available. *Students:* 76 full-time (68 women), 44 part-time (37 women); includes 40 minority (6 African Americans, 9 Asian Americans or Pacific Islanders, 25 Hispanic Americans), 5 international. Average age 30. 249 applicants, 16% accepted, 37 enrolled. In 2008, 37 master's awarded. *Degree requirements:* For master's, comprehensive exam, thesis or alternative. *Entrance requirements:* For master's, minimum GPA of 3.0 in major. Application fee: $55. Tuition and fees vary according to degree level. *Financial support:* Teaching assistantships, career-related internships or fieldwork, Federal Work-Study, institutionally sponsored loans, and scholarships/grants available. Support available to part-time students. Financial award application deadline: 3/1. *Faculty research:* Speech therapy. *Unit head:* Dr. John Reinard, Chair, 657-278-3617. *Application contact:* Dr. John Reinard, Chair, 657-278-3617.

California State University, Fullerton, Graduate Studies, College of Humanities and Social Sciences, Program in Linguistics, Fullerton, CA 92834-9480. Offers analysis of specific language structures (MA); anthropological linguistics (MA); applied linguistics (MA); communication and semantics (MA); disorders of communication (MA); experimental phonetics (MA). Part-time programs available. *Students:* 14 full-time (8 women), 6 part-time (5 women); includes 2 minority (both Hispanic Americans), 10 international. Average age 32. 19 applicants, 68% accepted, 6 enrolled. In 2008, 9 master's awarded. *Degree requirements:* For master's, one foreign language, thesis or alternative, project. *Entrance requirements:* For master's, minimum GPA of 3.0, undergraduate major in linguistics or related field. Application fee: $55. Tuition and fees vary according to degree level. *Financial support:* Career-related internships or fieldwork, Federal Work-Study, institutionally sponsored loans, and scholarships/grants available. Support available to part-time students. Financial award application deadline: 3/1. *Unit head:* Dr. Franz Muller-Gotama, Adviser, 657-278-2441. *Application contact:* Dr. Franz Muller-Gotama, Adviser, 657-278-2441.

California State University, Los Angeles, Graduate Studies, College of Arts and Letters, Department of Communication Studies, Los Angeles, CA 90032-8530. Offers speech communication (MA); television, film and theatre (MFA). Part-time and evening/weekend programs available. *Faculty:* 12 full-time (3 women). *Students:* 64 full-time (37 women), 40 part-time (32 women); includes 47 minority (15 African Americans, 1 American Indian/Alaska Native, 13 Asian Americans or Pacific Islanders, 18 Hispanic Americans), 18 international. Average age 30. 88 applicants, 92% accepted, 47 enrolled. In 2008, 8 master's awarded. *Degree requirements:* For master's, comprehensive exam or thesis. *Entrance requirements:* For master's, minimum GPA of 2.75 in last 90 units of course work. Additional exam requirements/recommendations for international students: Required—TOEFL (minimum score 500 paper-based; 173 computer-based). *Application deadline:* For fall admission, 6/15 for domestic students, 5/1 for international students; for winter admission, 11/1 for domestic students, 9/1 for international students; for spring admission, 2/1 for domestic students, 10/1 for international students. Applications are processed on a rolling basis. Application fee: $55. Electronic applications accepted. *Expenses:* Tuition, nonresident: part-time $226 per credit. Required fees: $4019. *Financial support:* Career-related internships or fieldwork and Federal Work-Study available. Support available to part-time students. Financial award application deadline: 3/1. *Faculty research:* Organizational, interpersonal, intercultural, and instructional communication; rhetorical theories. *Unit head:* Dr. John Ramirez, Chair, 323-343-4200, Fax: 323-343-6467, E-mail: jramire4@calstatela.edu. *Application contact:* Dr. Jose L. Galvan, Dean of Graduate Studies, 323-343-3820, Fax: 323-343-5653, E-mail: jgalvan@cslanet.calstatela.edu.

California State University, Northridge, Graduate Studies, College of Arts, Media, and Communication, Department of Communication Studies, Northridge, CA 91330. Offers MA. *Faculty:* 9 full-time (5 women), 18 part-time/adjunct (12 women). *Students:* 21 full-time (17 women), 25 part-time (21 women); includes 1 African American, 3 Asian Americans or Pacific Islanders, 8 Hispanic Americans, 4 international. Average age 29. 66 applicants, 52% accepted, 16 enrolled. In 2008, 19 master's awarded. *Entrance requirements:* For master's, GRE General Test. Additional exam requirements/recommendations for international students: Required—TOEFL. *Application deadline:* For fall admission, 11/30 for domestic students. Application fee: $55. *Financial support:* Teaching assistantships available. Financial award application deadline: 3/1. *Unit head:* Dr. Bernardo Attias, Chair, 818-677-2853. *Application contact:* Dr. Bernardo Attias, Chair, 818-677-2853.

Central Michigan University, College of Graduate Studies, College of Communication and Fine Arts, Department of Communication and Dramatic Arts, Concentration in Interpersonal and Public Communication, Mount Pleasant, MI 48859. Offers MA. Part-time programs available. *Faculty:* 14 full-time (8 women). *Students:* 19 full-time (14 women), 22 part-time (18 women); includes 2 African Americans, 1 American Indian/Alaska Native, 1 international. Average age 28. *Degree requirements:* For master's, thesis. *Entrance requirements:* For master's, minimum GPA of 3.0 in last 60 hours of undergraduate study and in last 15 hours of communication courses or other courses approved by department. *Application deadline:* For fall admission, 3/15 for domestic and international students; for winter admission, 10/15 for domestic and international students; for spring admission, 10/15 for domestic and international students. Application fee: $35 ($45 for international students). Electronic applications accepted. *Expenses:* Tuition, state resident: full-time $3717; part-time $413 per credit. Tuition, nonresident: full-time $6894; part-time $766 per credit. *Financial support:* Fellowships with tuition reimbursements, teaching assistantships with tuition reimbursements, career-related internships or fieldwork, Federal Work-Study, unspecified assistantships, and out-of-state merit awards available. *Faculty research:* Communication theory, interpersonal/nonverbal communication, organizational communication, family and interpersonal communication, political communication. *Unit head:* Dr. Neil Vanderpool, Chairperson, 989-774-3177, Fax: 989-774-2498, E-mail: vande2nj@cmich.edu. *Application contact:* Dr. Lesley Withers, Graduate Program Coordinator, 989-774-6673, Fax: 989-774-2498, E-mail: withe1la@cmich.edu.

Colorado State University, Graduate School, College of Liberal Arts, Department of Communication Studies, Fort Collins, CO 80523-1783. Offers MA. *Faculty:* 14 full-time (5 women), 1 part-time/adjunct (0 women). *Students:* 25 full-time (20 women), 5 part-time (3 women); includes 2 minority (both Hispanic Americans). Average age 25. 32 applicants, 75% accepted, 14 enrolled. *Entrance requirements:* For master's, GRE General Test, minimum GPA of 3.0; writing sample, letters of recommendation, statement of goals. Additional exam requirements/recommendations for international students: Required—TOEFL (minimum score 550 paper-based; 230 computer-based). *Application deadline:* For fall admission, 1/31 priority date for domestic and international students. Applications are processed on a rolling basis. Application fee: $50. Electronic applications accepted. *Expenses:* Tuition, area resident: Full-time $5620; part-time $312.25 per credit. Tuition, state resident: full-time $5620; part-time $312.25 per credit. Tuition, nonresident: full-time $17,253; part-time $958.50 per credit. Required fees: $1449.56; $82.35 per credit. *Financial support:* In 2008–09, 21 students received support, including 21 teaching assistantships with full and partial tuition reimbursements available (averaging $12,111 per year); scholarships/grants and unspecified assistantships also available. Financial award application deadline: 3/1; financial award applicants required to submit FAFSA. *Faculty research:* Rhetorical theory and criticism, media and popular culture, intercultural communication, freedom of speech, communication theory. Total annual research expenditures: $29,370. *Unit head:* Dr. Sue Pendell, Head, 970-491-6140, Fax: 970-491-2160, E-mail: sue.pendell@colostate.edu. *Application contact:* Dr. Greg Dickinson, Director of Graduate Studies, 970-491-6893, Fax: 970-491-2160, E-mail: greg.dickinson@colostate.edu.

Drake University, School of Education, Department of Teaching and Learning, Program in Secondary Education, Des Moines, IA 50311-4516. Offers art (MAT); biology (MAT); business (MAT); chemistry (MAT); English (MAT); general science (MAT); history-American (MAT); history-world (MAT); journalism (MAT); mathematics (MAT); physical science (MAT); physics (MAT); sociology (MAT); speech (MAT); speech communication (MAT); theatre (MAT). Part-time programs available. *Degree requirements:* For master's, comprehensive exam, thesis (for some programs), internships (for some programs). *Entrance requirements:* For master's, GRE General Test, MAT, or Drake Writing Assessment, resumé, 2 letters of recommendation. Additional exam requirements/recommendations for international students: Required—TOEFL (minimum score 550 paper-based; 213 computer-based). Electronic applications accepted. *Faculty research:* Counseling and rehabilitation, behavioral supports, inquiry-based science methods, teacher quality enhancement.

Eastern Illinois University, Graduate School, College of Arts and Humanities, Department of Communication Studies, Charleston, IL 61920-3099. Offers MA. Part-time programs available. *Degree requirements:* For master's, major paper.

Florida State University, Graduate Studies, College of Communication, Department of Communication, Tallahassee, FL 32306. Offers corporate and public communication (MA, MS); integrated marketing communication (MA, MS); mass communication (PhD); media and communication studies (MA, MS); speech communication (PhD). Part-time programs available. *Degree requirements:* For master's, thesis (for some programs); for doctorate, comprehensive exam, thesis/dissertation. *Entrance requirements:* For master's, GRE General Test, minimum GPA of 3.0; for doctorate, GRE General Test, minimum GPA of 3.3 in graduate course work. Additional exam requirements/recommendations for international students: Required—TOEFL (minimum score 600 paper-based; 250 computer-based; 100 iBT). *Faculty research:* Communication technology and policy, marketing communication, communication content and effect, new communication/information technologies.

Georgia State University, College of Arts and Sciences, Department of Communication, Atlanta, GA 30303-3083. Offers film/video/digital imaging (MA); human communication and social influence (MA); mass communication (MA); moving image studies (PhD); public communication (PhD). Part-time programs available. *Degree requirements:* For master's, one foreign language, thesis or alternative; for doctorate, comprehensive exam, thesis/dissertation. *Entrance requirements:* For master's and doctorate, GRE General Test. Additional exam requirements/recommendations for international students: Required—TOEFL (minimum score 80 computer-based). Electronic applications accepted. *Faculty research:* Critical/cultural studies, rhetoric studies, film/media studies, mass communications/journalism, audience studies.

Hofstra University, School of Communication, Department of Speech Communication, Rhetoric, and Performance Studies, Hempstead, NY 11549. Offers speech communication and rhetorical studies (MA), including speech communication and rhetorical studies. Part-time and evening/weekend programs available. *Faculty:* 4 full-time (2 women). *Students:* 8 full-time (5 women), 13 part-time (7 women); includes 9 minority (6 African Americans, 2 Asian Americans or Pacific Islanders, 1 Hispanic American), 1 international. Average age 28. 14 applicants, 93% accepted, 8 enrolled. In 2008, 6 master's awarded. *Degree requirements:* For master's, thesis. *Entrance requirements:* For master's, 2 letters of recommendation, interview. Additional exam requirements/recommendations for international students: Required—TOEFL (minimum score 550 paper-based; 213 computer-based; 80 iBT). *Application deadline:* Applications are processed on a rolling basis. Application fee: $60. Electronic applications accepted. *Expenses:* Tuition: Full-time $15,300; part-time $850 per credit. Required fees: $970; $165 per term. Tuition and fees vary according to program. *Financial support:* In 2008–09, 12 students received support, including 1 fellowship with full and partial tuition reimbursement available (averaging $3,500 per year), 2 research assistantships with full and partial tuition reimbursements available (averaging $9,480 per year); Federal Work-Study, institutionally sponsored loans, scholarships/grants, tuition waivers (full and partial), and unspecified assistantships also available. Support available to part-time students. Financial award applicants required to submit FAFSA. *Faculty research:* Performance of race and gender, public deliberation, public memory, civic engagement and political participation, popular culture. *Unit head:* Dr. Maryanne Trasciatti, Chairperson, 516-463-7141, E-mail: sphmat@hofstra.edu. *Application contact:* Carol Drummer, Dean of Graduate Admissions, 516-463-4876, Fax: 516-463-4664, E-mail: gradstudent@hofstra.edu.

Idaho State University, Office of Graduate Studies, College of Arts and Sciences, Department of Communication and Rhetorical Studies, Pocatello, ID 83209. Offers communication and rhetorical studies (MA). Part-time programs available. *Faculty:* 4 full-time (1 woman). *Students:* 8 full-time (4 women), 4 part-time (2 women); includes 2 minority (both Hispanic Americans), 2 international. Average age 32. In 2008, 3 master's awarded. *Degree requirements:* For master's, comprehensive exam, thesis (for some programs). *Entrance requirements:* For master's, GRE General Test, minimum GPA of 3.0 in all upper level courses. Additional exam requirements/recommendations for international students: Required—TOEFL (minimum score 550 paper-based; 213 computer-based; 80 iBT). *Application deadline:* For fall admission, 7/1 for domestic students, 6/1 for international students; for spring admission, 12/1 for domestic students, 11/1 for international students. Applications are processed on a rolling basis. Application fee: $55. Electronic applications accepted. *Expenses:* Tuition, area resident: Full-time $3114; part-time $276 per credit hour. Tuition, state resident: full-time $3114; part-time $276 per credit hour. Tuition, nonresident: full-time $12,318; part-time $404 per credit hour. Required fees: $2360. Tuition and fees vary according to course load and reciprocity agreements. *Financial support:* In 2008–09, 3 teaching assistantships with full and partial tuition reimbursements (averaging $9,401 per year) were awarded; career-related internships or fieldwork, Federal Work-Study, institutionally sponsored loans, scholarships/grants, health care benefits, and unspecified assistantships also available. Support available to part-time students. Financial award application deadline: 1/1; financial award applicants required to submit FAFSA. *Faculty research:* Metaphor and cognition in organizational groups and teams; rhetorical criticism of contemporary culture, including music, film, television, and advertising; communication pedagogy; the effect of language on organizational identification and commitment; risk communication and crisis communication. *Unit head:* Dr. James DiSanza, Chairman, 208-282-3395, Fax: 208-282-4598, E-mail: disajame@isu.edu. *Application contact:* Ellen Combs, Graduate School Technical Records Specialist, 208-282-2150, Fax: 208-282-4847, E-mail: combelle@isu.edu.

Indiana University Bloomington, University Graduate School, College of Arts and Sciences, Department of Communication and Culture, Bloomington, IN 47405-7000. Offers film and media studies (PhD); performance and ethnography (PhD); rhetoric and public culture (PhD). *Faculty:* 24 full-time (12 women). *Students:* 81 full-time (45 women); includes 11 minority (2 African Americans, 1 American Indian/Alaska Native, 2 Asian Americans or Pacific Islanders, 6 Hispanic Americans), 10 international. Average age 32. 163 applicants, 20% accepted, 16 enrolled. In 2008, 5 master's, 11 doctorates awarded. *Degree requirements:* For master's, comprehensive exam; for doctorate, one foreign language, comprehensive exam, thesis/dissertation, student teaching. *Entrance requirements:* For master's and doctorate, GRE General Test (recommended), minimum GPA of 3.0, 3 letters of recommendation, writing sample. Additional exam requirements/recommendations for international students: Required—TOEFL (minimum score 550 paper-based; 213 computer-based). *Application deadline:* For winter admission, 1/1 for domestic students, 12/1 for international students. Application fee: $50 ($60 for international students). Electronic applications accepted. *Expenses:* Tuition, area resident: Part-time $291.97 per credit hour. Tuition, state resident: part-time $291.97 per credit hour. Tuition, nonresident: part-time $850.33 per credit hour. Required fees: $110 per semester. Tuition and fees vary according to course load and program. *Financial support:* In 2008–09, 65 students received support, including 4 fellowships with full tuition reimbursements available (averaging $18,000 per year), 61 teaching assistantships with full tuition reimbursements available (averaging $12,961 per year). Financial award application deadline: 4/15. *Faculty research:* Rhetoric and public culture, film and media studies, performance ethnography. *Unit head:* Prof. Gregory A. Waller, Chair, 812-855-2367, Fax: 812-855-6014, E-mail: cmcl@indiana.edu. *Application contact:* Kathy P. Teige, Graduate Secretary, 812-855-6389, Fax: 812-855-6014, E-mail: kteige@indiana.edu.

Kansas State University, Graduate School, College of Arts and Sciences, Department of Communication Studies, Theatre and Dance, Manhattan, KS 66505. Offers rhetoric/communication (MA); theatre (MA). *Faculty:* 16 full-time (8 women). *Students:* 30 full-time (24 women), 7 part-time (2 women); includes 4 minority (1 African American, 1 American Indian/Alaska Native, 1 Asian American or Pacific Islander, 1 Hispanic American), 1 international. Average age 27. 11 applicants, 100% accepted, 7 enrolled. In 2008, 12 master's awarded. *Degree requirements:* For master's, thesis or alternative. *Entrance requirements:* For master's, GRE General Test (recommended), minimum GPA of 3.0. Additional exam requirements/recommendations for international students: Required—TOEFL. *Application deadline:* For fall admission, 3/1 for domestic students, 2/1 priority date for international students; for spring admission, 10/1 for domestic students, 8/1 priority date for international students. Applications are processed on a rolling basis. Application fee: $30 ($55 for international students). *Expenses:* Tuition, area resident: Full-time $6466; part-time $269.40 per credit hour. Tuition, state resident: full-time $6466; part-time $269.40 per credit hour. Tuition, nonresident: full-time $14,874; part-time $619.75 per credit hour. Required fees: $673; $23.40 per credit hour. Tuition and fees vary according to campus/location. *Financial support:* In 2008–09, 27 teaching assistantships with full tuition reimbursements (averaging $10,111 per year) were awarded; career-related internships or fieldwork, institutionally sponsored loans, and scholarships/grants also available. Support available to part-time students. Financial award application deadline: 3/1; financial award applicants required to submit FAFSA. *Faculty research:* Drama therapy, directing, costume design, scenic design, and technical theatre mechanics and safety. *Unit head:* Charles Griffin, Head, 785-532-6860, Fax: 785-532-3714, E-mail: charlieg@ksu.edu. *Application contact:* William Schenck-Hamlin, Director, 785-532-6861, Fax: 785-532-3714, E-mail: billsh@ksu.edu.

Louisiana Tech University, Graduate School, College of Liberal Arts, Department of Speech, Ruston, LA 71272. Offers speech (MA); speech pathology and audiology (MA). *Accreditation:* ASHA. *Degree requirements:* For master's, thesis or alternative. *Entrance requirements:* For master's, GRE General Test.

Marquette University, Graduate School, College of Communication, Milwaukee, WI 53201-1881. Offers advertising and public relations (MA); broadcasting and electronic communications (MA); communications studies (MA); journalism (MA); mass communications (MA); religious communications (MA); science, health and environmental communications (MA). *Accreditation:* ACEJMC. Part-time and evening/weekend programs available. *Degree requirements:* For master's, comprehensive exam. *Entrance requirements:* For master's, GRE. Additional exam requirements/recommendations for international students: Required—TOEFL. *Faculty research:* Urban journalism, gender and communication, intercultural communication, religious communication.

Miami University, Graduate School, College of Arts and Sciences, Department of Communication, Program in Speech Communication, Oxford, OH 45056. Offers MA. Part-time programs available. *Degree requirements:* For master's, final exam. *Entrance requirements:* For master's, minimum undergraduate GPA of 3.0 during previous 2 years or 2.75 overall. Additional exam requirements/recommendations for international students: Required—TOEFL (minimum score 550 paper-based; 213 computer-based), TWE (minimum score 4). Electronic applications accepted.

Minnesota State University Mankato, College of Graduate Studies, College of Arts and Humanities, Department of Speech Communication, Mankato, MN 56001. Offers forensics (MFA); speech communication (MA, MS, MT). *Students:* 13 full-time (10 women), 17 part-time (9 women). *Degree requirements:* For master's, one foreign language, comprehensive exam, thesis. *Entrance requirements:* For master's, minimum GPA of 3.0 during previous 2 years, writing sample. *Application deadline:* For fall admission, 7/1 priority date for domestic students, 5/1 for international students; for spring admission, 11/1 for domestic students, 10/1 for international students. Applications are processed on a rolling basis. Application fee: $40. Electronic applications accepted. *Financial support:* Research assistantships, teaching assistantships with full tuition reimbursements, career-related internships or fieldwork, Federal Work-Study, and institutionally sponsored loans available. Support available to part-time students. Financial award application deadline: 3/15; financial award applicants required to submit FAFSA. *Unit head:* Dr. Daniel Cronn-Mills, Chairperson, 507-389-2213. *Application contact:* 507-389-2321, E-mail: grad@mnsu.edu.

Montclair State University, The Office of Graduate Admissions and Support Services, School of the Arts, Department of Communication Studies, Montclair, NJ 07043-1624. Offers organizational communication (MA); public relations (MA); speech communication (MA). Part-time and evening/weekend programs available. *Faculty:* 6 full-time (2 women), 36 part-time/adjunct (18 women). *Students:* 9 full-time (7 women), 20 part-time (15 women); includes 6 minority (4 African Americans, 2 Hispanic Americans), 2 international. Average age 30. 29 applicants, 38% accepted, 8 enrolled. In 2008, 7 master's awarded. *Degree requirements:* For master's, comprehensive exam. *Entrance requirements:* For master's, GRE General Test, minimum GPA of 3.0; undergraduate degree or work in theatre, oral interpretation, speech communication, media, or broadcasting; 2 letters of recommendation. Additional exam requirements/recommendations for international students: Required—TOEFL (minimum score 83 computer-based). *Application deadline:* For fall admission, 6/1 for international students; for spring admission, 10/1 for international students. Applications are processed on a rolling basis. Application fee: $60. Electronic applications accepted. *Financial support:* In 2008–09, 1 research assistantship with full tuition reimbursement (averaging $7,000 per year) was awarded; Federal Work-Study, scholarships/grants, and unspecified assistantships also available. Support available to part-time students. Financial award application deadline: 3/1; financial award applicants required to submit FAFSA. *Unit head:* Dr. Harry Haines, Chair, 973-655-4200. *Application contact:* Amy Aiello, Associate Director of Admissions, 973-655-5147, Fax: 973-655-7869, E-mail: graduate.school@montclair.edu.

New York University, Steinhardt School of Culture, Education and Human Development, Department of Media, Culture and Communication, New York, NY 10012-1019. Offers media ecology/culture and communication (PhD); media, culture, and communication (MA). Part-time and evening/weekend programs available. *Entrance requirements:* Additional exam requirements/recommendations for international students: Required—TOEFL. *Faculty research:* Digital media, intercultural communication, race and politics, media criticism, media literacy.

North Dakota State University, College of Graduate and Interdisciplinary Studies, College of Arts, Humanities and Social Sciences, Department of Communication, Fargo, ND 58105. Offers communication (PhD); mass communication (MA, MS); speech communication (MA, MS). Part-time programs available. Postbaccalaureate distance learning degree programs offered (no on-campus study). *Faculty:* 11 full-time (5 women), 3 part-time/adjunct (1 woman). *Students:* 38 full-time (25 women), 23 part-time (17 women); includes 4 minority (1 African American, 2 Asian Americans or Pacific Islanders, 1 Hispanic American), 3 international. Average age 27. 62 applicants, 40% accepted, 19 enrolled. In 2008, 15 master's, 8 doctorates awarded. Terminal master's awarded for partial completion of doctoral program. *Degree requirements:* For master's, thesis (for some programs); for doctorate, comprehensive exam, thesis/dissertation, 2-3 publications referred before comps. *Entrance requirements:* For master's, GRE, minimum undergraduate GPA of 3.25; for doctorate, GRE, minimum undergraduate GPA of 3.5. Additional exam requirements/recommendations for international students: Required—TOEFL (minimum score 600 paper-based; 250 computer-based; 100 iBT), IELTS (minimum score 7). *Application deadline:* For fall admission, 2/15 priority date for domestic students; for winter admission, 10/15 priority date for domestic students. Applications are processed on a rolling basis. Application fee: $45 ($60 for international students). Electronic applications accepted. *Financial support:* In 2008–09, 38 students received support, including 1 fellowship with full tuition reimbursement available (averaging $16,000 per year), 10 research assistantships with full tuition reimbursements available (averaging $12,000 per year), 10 teaching assistantships with full tuition reimbursements available (averaging $8,100 per year); career-related internships or fieldwork, Federal Work-Study, institutionally sponsored loans, tuition waivers (full), and unspecified assistantships also available. Financial award application deadline: 2/1. *Faculty research:* Communication and rhetorical theory, organizational communication, broadcast and print journalism, international communication, public relations and advertising. Total annual research expenditures: $148,496. *Unit head:* Dr. Paul E. Nelson, Chair, 701-231-7705, Fax: 701-231-7784, E-mail: paul.nelson.1@ndsu.edu. *Application contact:* Dr. Judy C. Pearson, Director of Graduate Studies, 701-231-6551, Fax: 701-231-1074, E-mail: judy.pearson@ndsu.edu.

Northeastern Illinois University, Graduate College, College of Arts and Sciences, Department of Communication, Media and Theatre, Program in Communication, Media and Theatre, Chicago, IL 60625-4699. Offers MA. Part-time and evening/weekend programs available. *Degree requirements:* For master's, comprehensive exam, oral exams, thesis or 3 term papers; minimum GPA of 3.0. *Entrance requirements:* For master's, 15 undergraduate hours in speech and performing arts, minimum GPA of 2.75. Additional exam requirements/recommendations for international students: Required—TOEFL (minimum score 550 paper-based; 213 computer-based; 80 iBT). Electronic applications accepted. *Faculty research:* Creative drama, family communication, fine arts and general education, playwriting techniques, interpersonal communications.

Northeastern University, Bouvé College of Health Sciences Graduate School, Department of Speech-Language Pathology and Audiology, Program in Audiology, Boston, MA 02115-5096. Offers Au D. *Entrance requirements:* For doctorate, GRE, minimum 3.2 GPA.

Northwestern University, The Graduate School, School of Communication, Department of Performance Studies, Evanston, IL 60208. Offers MA, PhD. Admissions and degrees offered through The Graduate School. Part-time programs available. Terminal master's awarded for partial completion of doctoral program. *Degree requirements:* For master's, recital; for doctorate, one foreign language, thesis/dissertation, recital. *Entrance requirements:* For master's and doctorate, GRE General Test. Additional exam requirements/recommendations for international students: Required—TOEFL. *Faculty research:* Adaptation/performance of literature, ethnography of performance, critical cultural studies, performance theory, intercultural performance, gender studies.

Speech and Interpersonal Communication

Ohio University, Graduate College, Scripps College of Communication, School of Communication Studies, Athens, OH 45701-2979. Offers PhD. *Degree requirements:* For doctorate, comprehensive exam, thesis/dissertation. *Entrance requirements:* For doctorate, GRE General Test, minimum GPA of 3.0. Additional exam requirements/recommendations for international students: Required—TOEFL. Electronic applications accepted. *Faculty research:* Rhetoric and public culture, relating and organizing, health communication.

Portland State University, Graduate Studies, College of Liberal Arts and Sciences, Department of Communication, Portland, OR 97207-0751. Offers general speech communication (MA, MS, Certificate). Part-time programs available. *Faculty:* 10 full-time (7 women), 10 part-time/adjunct (8 women). *Students:* 19 full-time (16 women), 10 part-time (7 women); includes 5 minority (4 Asian Americans or Pacific Islanders, 1 Hispanic American), 6 international. Average age 31. 28 applicants, 68% accepted, 15 enrolled. In 2008, 8 master's awarded. *Degree requirements:* For master's, thesis. *Entrance requirements:* For master's, GRE General Test, minimum GPA of 3.0 in upper-division course work or 2.75 overall, 3 letters of recommendation. Additional exam requirements/recommendations for international students: Required—TOEFL (minimum score 550 paper-based; 213 computer-based). *Application deadline:* For fall admission, 3/1 for domestic and international students. Application fee: $50. *Expenses:* Tuition, area resident: Full-time $8763; part-time $179 per credit hour. Tuition, state resident: full-time $8763; part-time $298 per credit hour. Tuition, nonresident: full-time $12,981; part-time $426 per credit hour. Required fees: $1242. One-time fee: $250. Tuition and fees vary according to course load and program. *Financial support:* In 2008–09, 1 research assistantship with full tuition reimbursement (averaging $6,372 per year), 9 teaching assistantships with full tuition reimbursements (averaging $6,042 per year) were awarded; career-related internships or fieldwork, Federal Work-Study, scholarships/grants, and unspecified assistantships also available. Support available to part-time students. Financial award application deadline: 3/1; financial award applicants required to submit FAFSA. *Unit head:* Cynthia Coleman, Chair, 503-725-5384, Fax: 503-725-5385, E-mail: morganbk@pdx.edu. *Application contact:* Kathleen Morgan, Office Coordinator, 503-725-5384, Fax: 503-725-5385, E-mail: morganbk@pdx.edu.

Rensselaer Polytechnic Institute, Graduate School, School of Humanities and Social Sciences, Department of Language, Literature, and Communication, Programs in Communication and Rhetoric, Troy, NY 12180-3590. Offers MS, PhD. Terminal master's awarded for partial completion of doctoral program. *Degree requirements:* For master's, thesis optional; for doctorate, comprehensive exam, thesis/dissertation. *Entrance requirements:* For master's, GRE General Test, resumé; for doctorate, GRE General Test, writing sample, resumé or curriculum vitae. Additional exam requirements/recommendations for international students: Required—TOEFL (minimum score 570 paper-based; 230 computer-based). Electronic applications accepted. *Faculty research:* Human-computer interaction, media design and theory, rhetoric and culture, virtual institutions/communities, usability.

San Francisco State University, Division of Graduate Studies, College of Humanities, Department of Communication Studies, San Francisco, CA 94132-1722. Offers MA. Part-time programs available.

San Jose State University, Graduate Studies and Research, College of Social Sciences, Department of History, San Jose, CA 95192-0001. Offers history (MA); history education (MA). *Degree requirements:* For master's, comprehensive exam, thesis or alternative. *Entrance requirements:* For master's, bachelor's degree or 15 units of course work in history, minimum GPA of 3.0. Electronic applications accepted.

Seton Hall University, School of Health and Medical Sciences, Program in Speech-Language Pathology, South Orange, NJ 07079-2697. Offers MS. *Entrance requirements:* For master's, GRE, bachelor's degree, clinical experience; minimum GPA of 3.0, undergraduate preprofessional coursework in communication sciences and disorders. Electronic applications accepted. *Faculty research:* Child language disorders, motor speech control, voice disorders, dysphagia, early intervention/teaming.

Southern Illinois University Carbondale, Graduate School, College of Liberal Arts, Department of Speech Communication, Carbondale, IL 62901-4701. Offers speech communication (MA, MS, PhD); speech/theater (PhD). *Degree requirements:* For master's, one foreign language, thesis or alternative; for doctorate, one foreign language, thesis/dissertation. *Entrance requirements:* For master's, GRE General Test or MAT, minimum GPA of 2.7; for doctorate, GRE General Test or MAT, minimum GPA of 3.25. Additional exam requirements/recommendations for international students: Required—TOEFL.

See Close-Up on page 703.

Southern Illinois University Edwardsville, Graduate Studies and Research, College of Arts and Sciences, Department of Speech Communication, Program in Speech Communication, Edwardsville, IL 62026-0001. Offers MA. Part-time and evening/weekend programs available. *Students:* 16 full-time (13 women), 9 part-time (8 women); includes 6 minority (5 African Americans, 1 Asian American or Pacific Islander). Average age 26. 19 applicants, 63% accepted. In 2008, 7 master's awarded. *Degree requirements:* For master's, thesis or alternative, final exam. *Entrance requirements:* Additional exam requirements/recommendations for international students: Required—TOEFL (minimum score 550 paper-based; 213 computer-based; 79 iBT), IELTS (minimum score 6.5). *Application deadline:* For fall admission, 7/20 for domestic students, 6/1 for international students; for spring admission, 12/14 for domestic students, 10/1 for international students. Applications are processed on a rolling basis. Application fee: $30. Electronic applications accepted. *Expenses:* Tuition, area resident: Full-time $5838. Tuition, nonresident: full-time $14,596. Required fees: $1525. *Financial support:* In 2008–09, 1 fellowship with full tuition reimbursement (averaging $8,370 per year), 13 teaching assistantships with full tuition reimbursements (averaging $8,064 per year) were awarded; research assistantships with full tuition reimbursements. Financial award application deadline: 3/1; financial award applicants required to submit FAFSA. *Unit head:* Dr. Wai Hsien Cheah, Director, 618-650-5016, E-mail: wcheah@siue.edu. *Application contact:* Dr. Wai Hsien Cheah, Director, 618-650-5016, E-mail: wcheah@siue.edu.

Texas A&M University–Commerce, Graduate School, College of Arts and Sciences, Department of Communication and Theatre, Commerce, TX 75429-3011. Offers theatre (MA, MS). Part-time programs available. *Degree requirements:* For master's, comprehensive exam, thesis (for some programs). *Entrance requirements:* For master's, GRE General Test. Electronic applications accepted. *Faculty research:* Theater history.

Texas Christian University, College of Communication, Department of Communication Studies, Fort Worth, TX 76129-0002. Offers communication in human relations (MS). Part-time and evening/weekend programs available. *Entrance requirements:* For master's, GRE General Test. Additional exam requirements/recommendations for international students: Required—TOEFL. *Application deadline:* For fall admission, 3/1 for domestic students; for spring admission, 12/1 for domestic students. Applications are processed on a rolling basis. Application fee: $0. *Expenses:* Tuition: Full-time $17,640. *Financial support:* Unspecified assistantships available. Financial award application deadline: 3/1. *Unit head:* Dr. Paul King, Chairperson, 817-257-7610, E-mail: p.king@tcu.edu. *Application contact:* Dr. John Burton, Director of Graduate Studies, 817-257-7603, Fax: 817-257-7703, E-mail: j.burton@tcu.edu.

The University of Alabama, Graduate School, College of Communication and Information Sciences, Department of Communication Studies, Tuscaloosa, AL 35487. Offers MA. *Faculty:* 9 full-time (6 women). *Students:* 20 full-time (10 women), 2 part-time (both women); includes 6 minority (4 African Americans, 1 American Indian/Alaska Native, 1 Hispanic American), 2 international. Average age 23. 32 applicants, 69% accepted, 11 enrolled. In 2008, 7 master's awarded. *Degree requirements:* For master's, comprehensive exam (for some programs), thesis optional, research colloquium presentation, final practicum report. *Entrance requirements:* For master's, GRE. Additional exam requirements/recommendations for international students: Required—TOEFL (minimum score 550 paper-based; 213 computer-based). *Application deadline:* For fall admission, 5/1 for domestic and international students; for spring admission, 11/1 for domestic and international students. Applications are processed on a rolling basis. Application fee: $30. Electronic applications accepted. *Expenses:* Tuition, area resident: Full-time $6400. Tuition, state resident: full-time $6400. Tuition, nonresident: full-time $18,000. *Financial support:* In 2008–09, 7 students received support, including 1 research assistantship with full tuition reimbursement available (averaging $10,908 per year), 6 teaching assistantships with full tuition reimbursements available (averaging $10,908 per year); career-related internships or fieldwork and health care benefits also available. Financial award application deadline: 5/1. *Faculty research:* Rhetorical theory, organizational communication, communication theory. Total annual research expenditures: $6,191. *Unit head:* Dr. Beth S. Bennett, Chair and Associate Professor, 205-348-5997, Fax: 205-348-8080, E-mail: bbennett@bama.ua.edu. *Application contact:* Dr. Tom Harris, Graduate Coordinator and Professor, 205-348-5997, Fax: 205-348-8080, E-mail: tharris@ua.edu.

University of Arkansas at Little Rock, Graduate School, College of Professional Studies, Department of Speech Communication, Little Rock, AR 72204-1099. Offers applied communication studies (MA). Part-time and evening/weekend programs available. *Degree requirements:* For master's, comprehensive exam, internship, paper, or thesis. *Entrance requirements:* For master's, GRE General Test, MAT, minimum GPA of 2.7. *Faculty research:* Communication theory and applications, managerial communication, human resource training and development, relational communication.

University of California, Santa Barbara, Graduate Division, College of Letters and Sciences, Division of Humanities and Fine Arts, Department of Linguistics, Santa Barbara, CA 93106-3100. Offers applied linguistics (PhD); cognitive science (PhD); human development (PhD); language, interaction, and social organizations (PhD); MA/PhD. *Faculty:* 23 full-time (12 women). *Students:* 25 full-time (14 women). Average age 32. 63 applicants, 17% accepted, 5 enrolled. In 2008, 5 doctorates awarded. *Degree requirements:* For doctorate, one foreign language, comprehensive exam, thesis/dissertation, 48 units of coursework, minimum GPA of 3.7. *Entrance requirements:* For doctorate, GRE, 3 letters of recommendation, statement of purpose, personal achievements/contributions statement, resumé/curriculum vitae, transcripts for post-secondary institutions attended. Additional exam requirements/recommendations for international students: Required—TOEFL (minimum score 550 paper-based; 213 computer-based; 80 iBT), IELTS (minimum score 7), TOEFL or IELTS. *Application deadline:* For fall admission, 12/1 priority date for domestic and international students. Application fee: $70 ($90 for international students). Electronic applications accepted. *Expenses:* Tuition, nonresident: full-time $25,149. Required fees: $10,143. Full-time tuition and fees vary according to campus/location, reciprocity agreements and student level. *Financial support:* In 2008–09, 24 students received support, including 19 fellowships with full and partial tuition reimbursements available (averaging $12,400 per year), 1 research assistantship with full and partial tuition reimbursement available (averaging $3,000 per year), 13 teaching assistantships with partial tuition reimbursements available (averaging $5,600 per year); Federal Work-Study, institutionally sponsored loans, scholarships/grants, health care benefits, and unspecified assistantships also available. Financial award application deadline: 12/1; financial award applicants required to submit FAFSA. *Faculty research:* Language, race and subcultural identities among California teenagers; language acquisition, psycholinguisticss; language documentation, fieldwork; syntax of nominalization in 5 Tibeto-Burman languages; perceptual correlates of syllable weight. *Unit head:* Prof. Patricia M. Clancy, Chair, 805-893-8658, Fax: 805-893-7769, E-mail: pclancy@linguistics.ucsb.edu. *Application contact:* Mary Rae Staton, Graduate Program Assistant, 805-893-3776, Fax: 805-893-7769, E-mail: staton@linguistics.ucsb.edu.

University of California, Santa Barbara, Graduate Division, College of Letters and Sciences, Division of Social Sciences, Department of Sociology, Santa Barbara, CA 93106-9430. Offers global studies (PhD); human development (PhD); language, interaction and social organization (PhD); technology and society (PhD); women's studies (PhD); MA/PhD. *Faculty:* 35 full-time (14 women). *Students:* 77 full-time (50 women). Average age 30. 155 applicants, 9% accepted, 8 enrolled. In 2008, 10 doctorates awarded. Terminal master's awarded for partial completion of doctoral program. *Degree requirements:* For doctorate, comprehensive exam, thesis/dissertation. *Entrance requirements:* For doctorate, GRE General Test, sample of written work, 3 letters of recommendation, statement of purpose, personal achievements/contributions statement, resumé/curriculum vitae, transcripts for post-secondary institutions attended. Additional exam requirements/recommendations for international students: Required—TOEFL (minimum score 550 paper-based; 213 computer-based; 80 iBT), TOEFL or IELTS. *Application deadline:* For fall admission, 12/10 for domestic students. Application fee: $70 ($90 for international students). Electronic applications accepted. *Expenses:* Tuition, nonresident: full-time $25,149. Required fees: $10,143. Full-time tuition and fees vary according to campus/location, reciprocity agreements and student level. *Financial support:* In 2008–09, 69 students received support, including 50 fellowships with full tuition reimbursements available (averaging $7,900 per year), 6 research assistantships with full and partial tuition reimbursements available (averaging $2,600 per year), 53 teaching assistantships with partial tuition reimbursements available (averaging $9,200 per year); career-related internships or fieldwork, Federal Work-Study, institutionally sponsored loans, scholarships/grants, health care benefits, and unspecified assistantships also available. Financial award applicants required to submit FAFSA. *Faculty research:* Conversation analysis, social movements, human sexuality, urban sociology, race and ethnic relations. *Unit head:* Prof. Verta Taylor, Chair, 805-893-3118, Fax: 805-893-3324, E-mail: grad-soc@soc.ucsb.edu. *Application contact:* Ra Thea, Graduate Staff Advisor, 805-893-3328, Fax: 805-893-3324, E-mail: grad-soc@soc.ucsb.edu.

University of Central Florida, College of Sciences, Nicholson School of Communication, Orlando, FL 32816. Offers business communication (MA); interpersonal communication (MA); mass communication (MA). Part-time and evening/weekend programs available. *Faculty:* 41 full-time (18 women), 36 part-time/adjunct (18 women). *Students:* 44 full-time (39 women), 28 part-time (25 women); includes 15 minority (6 African Americans, 3 Asian Americans or Pacific Islanders, 6 Hispanic Americans), 9 international. In 2008, 29 master's awarded. *Degree requirements:* For master's, thesis or comprehensive exam. *Entrance requirements:* For master's, GRE General Test, minimum GPA of 3.0 in last 60 hours of course work. Additional exam requirements/recommendations for international students: Required—TOEFL. *Application deadline:* For fall admission, 7/15 for domestic students; for spring admission, 12/7 for domestic students. Application fee: $30. Electronic applications accepted. *Expenses:* Tuition, area resident: Full-time $6816; part-time $284 per credit. Tuition, state resident: full-time $6816; part-time $1076 per credit. Tuition, nonresident: full-time $25,824. Required fees: $216; $9 per credit. *Financial support:* In 2008–09, 2 fellowships with partial tuition reimbursements (averaging $10,000 per year), 4 research assistantships with partial tuition reimbursements (averaging $4,400 per year), 16 teaching assistantships with partial tuition reimbursements (averaging $6,400 per year) were awarded; career-related internships or fieldwork, Federal Work-Study, institutionally sponsored loans, tuition waivers (partial), and unspecified assistantships also available. Financial award application deadline: 3/1; financial award applicants required to submit FAFSA. *Faculty research:* Persuasion, communication apprehension, nonverbal communication, conflict resolution. *Unit head:* Dr. Robert Chandler, Director, 407-823-2683, Fax: 407-823-5216, E-mail: rcchandl@mail.ucf.edu. *Application contact:* Dr. Robert Chandler, Director, 407-823-2683, Fax: 407-823-5216, E-mail: rcchandl@mail.ucf.edu.

University of Central Missouri, The Graduate School, College of Arts, Humanities and Social Sciences, Department of Communication, Warrensburg, MO 64093. Offers communication (MA); speech communication (MA). Part-time programs available. *Degree requirements:* For master's, comprehensive exam, internship, research papers or thesis. *Entrance requirements:* For master's, minimum GPA of 2.5. Additional exam requirements/recommendations for international students: Required—TOEFL (minimum score 500 paper-based; 173 computer-based).

University of Central Missouri, The Graduate School, College of Health and Human Services, Department of Communication Disorders, Warrensburg, MO 64093. Offers speech pathology and audiology (MS). Part-time programs available. *Degree requirements:* For master's, project, research paper, or thesis; observation (25 hours); clinical practicum (350 hours); National

Examination in Speech Pathology and Audiology (NESPA) exam. *Entrance requirements:* For master's, GRE, minimum GPA of 3.0, clinical practicum. Additional exam requirements/recommendations for international students: Required—TOEFL (minimum score 500 paper-based; 173 computer-based). *Faculty research:* Motor Speech disorders, Autism Intervention, Pediatric Swallowing Disorders, Adult Swallowing Disorders, Clinical Supervision.

University of Denver, Division of Arts, Humanities and Social Sciences, School of Communication, Department of Human Communication Studies, Denver, CO 80208. Offers MA, PhD. Part-time programs available. *Faculty:* 9 full-time (7 women), 3 part-time/adjunct (2 women). *Students:* 31 full-time (20 women), 4 part-time (3 women); includes 5 minority (2 African Americans, 2 Asian Americans or Pacific Islanders, 1 Hispanic American), 4 international. Average age 33. In 2008, 4 master's, 8 doctorates awarded. *Degree requirements:* For master's, comprehensive exam or thesis; for doctorate, one foreign language, thesis/dissertation. *Entrance requirements:* For master's and doctorate, GRE General Test. Additional exam requirements/recommendations for international students: Required—TOEFL, TWE. *Application deadline:* Applications are processed on a rolling basis. Application fee: $50. *Financial support:* In 2008–09, 30 students received support, including 15 teaching assistantships with full and partial tuition reimbursements available (averaging $12,500 per year); career-related internships or fieldwork, Federal Work-Study, institutionally sponsored loans, and scholarships/grants also available. Support available to part-time students. Financial award application deadline: 2/10; financial award applicants required to submit FAFSA. *Faculty research:* Successful community collaborative efforts, long-term marriages, cross-ethnic friendships, public dialogue about environmental risk, women's international cooperation. *Unit head:* Dr. Roy Wood, Chair, 303-871-2385. *Application contact:* Information Contact, 303-871-2385, E-mail: hcom@du.edu.

See Close-Up on page 707.

University of Georgia, Graduate School, College of Arts and Sciences, Department of Speech Communication, Athens, GA 30602. Offers MA, PhD. *Degree requirements:* For master's, thesis; for doctorate, one foreign language, thesis/dissertation. *Entrance requirements:* For master's and doctorate, GRE General Test. Electronic applications accepted.

University of Hawaii at Manoa, Graduate Division, Colleges of Arts and Sciences, College of Arts and Humanities, Department of Speech, Honolulu, HI 96822. Offers MA. Part-time programs available. *Degree requirements:* For master's, thesis optional. *Entrance requirements:* For master's, GRE General Test. Additional exam requirements/recommendations for international students: Required—TOEFL (minimum score 600 paper-based; 250 computer-based; 100 iBT), IELTS (minimum score 7). *Faculty research:* Social influence, relational management, message processing, intercultural communication.

University of Houston, College of Liberal Arts and Social Sciences, School of Communication, Houston, TX 77204. Offers mass communication studies (MA); public relations studies (MA); speech communication (MA). Part-time and evening/weekend programs available. *Faculty:* 7 full-time (4 women), 2 part-time/adjunct (0 women). *Students:* 29 full-time (25 women), 62 part-time (52 women); includes 32 minority (19 African Americans, 2 Asian Americans or Pacific Islanders, 11 Hispanic Americans), 13 international. Average age 29. 46 applicants, 85% accepted, 20 enrolled. In 2008, 20 master's awarded. *Entrance requirements:* For master's, GRE General Test, minimum GPA of 3.0 in last 60 hours of course work. *Application deadline:* For fall admission, 7/3 priority date for domestic students. Applications are processed on a rolling basis. Application fee: $25 ($75 for international students). *Expenses:* Tuition, state resident: full-time $5164; part-time $287 per credit. Tuition, nonresident: full-time $10,222; part-time $568 per credit. *Financial support:* In 2008–09, 2 fellowships with full tuition reimbursements (averaging $9,950 per year), 6 teaching assistantships with full tuition reimbursements (averaging $9,950 per year) were awarded; career-related internships or fieldwork, Federal Work-Study, institutionally sponsored loans, scholarships/grants, health care benefits, and unspecified assistantships also available. Support available to part-time students. Financial award application deadline: 2/1. *Faculty research:* Risk communication, relationship development, critical studies, corporate communication. *Unit head:* Beth Olson, Chairperson, 713-743-2873, Fax: 713-743-2876, E-mail: bolson@uh.edu. *Application contact:* Angela Parrish, Graduate Coordinator, 713-743-2873, Fax: 713-743-2876, E-mail: aparrish@bayou.uh.edu.

University of Maryland, College Park, Graduate Studies, College of Behavioral and Social Sciences, Department of Hearing and Speech Sciences, College Park, MD 20742. Offers audiology (MA, PhD); hearing and speech sciences (Au D); language pathology (MA, PhD); neuroscience (PhD); speech (MA, PhD). *Accreditation:* ASHA (one or more programs are accredited). *Degree requirements:* For master's, thesis optional; for doctorate, thesis/dissertation, written and oral exams. *Entrance requirements:* For master's, GRE General Test, minimum GPA of 3.5, 3 letters of recommendation; for doctorate, GRE General Test, minimum GPA of 3.5. Additional exam requirements/recommendations for international students: Required—TOEFL. Electronic applications accepted. *Faculty research:* Speech perception, language acquisition, bilingualism, hearing loss.

University of Nebraska–Lincoln, Graduate College, College of Arts and Sciences, Department of Communication Studies, Lincoln, NE 68588. Offers instructional communication (MA, PhD); interpersonal communication (MA, PhD); marketing, communication studies, and advertising (MA, PhD); organizational communication (MA, PhD); rhetoric and culture (MA, PhD). *Faculty:* 7 full-time (4 women). *Students:* 23 full-time (15 women), 9 part-time (8 women); includes 1 minority (Asian American or Pacific Islander), 1 international. Average age 35. In 2008, 2 master's, 2 doctorates awarded. *Degree requirements:* For master's, thesis optional; for doctorate, comprehensive exam, thesis/dissertation. *Entrance requirements:* For master's and doctorate, GRE General Test, writing sample. Additional exam requirements/recommendations for international students: Required—TOEFL (minimum score 600 paper-based; 250 computer-based). *Application deadline:* For fall admission, 1/15 for domestic and international students. Applications are processed on a rolling basis. Application fee: $40. Electronic applications accepted. *Expenses:* Tuition, state resident: full-time $4275; part-time $237.50 per credit hour. Tuition, nonresident: full-time $11,525; part-time $640.25 per credit hour. Required fees: $1068; $10.35 per credit hour. $440.70 per semester. Tuition and fees vary according to course load and program. *Financial support:* Fellowships, research assistantships, teaching assistantships, Federal Work-Study, health care benefits, and unspecified assistantships available. Support available to part-time students. Financial award application deadline: 1/15. *Faculty research:* Message strategies, gender communication, political communication, organizational communication, instructional communication. *Unit head:* Dr. William Seiler, Chair, 402-472-2069. *Application contact:* Ginny Gross, Director of Graduate Admissions, 402-472-2878, Fax: 402-472-0589, E-mail: grad_admissions@unl.edu.

University of Nevada, Reno, Graduate School, College of Liberal Arts, Department of Speech Communications, Reno, NV 89557. Offers MA. *Faculty:* 3 full-time (1 woman). *Students:* 5 full-time (3 women), 2 part-time (both women); includes 1 minority (Hispanic American). Average age 30. 7 applicants, 29% accepted, 2 enrolled. In 2008, 2 master's awarded. *Degree requirements:* For master's, thesis optional. *Entrance requirements:* For master's, GRE General Test, minimum GPA of 2.75. Additional exam requirements/recommendations for international students: Required—TOEFL (minimum score 500 paper-based; 173 computer-based; 61 iBT), IELTS (minimum score 6), TOFEL or IELTS. *Application deadline:* For fall admission, 3/1 priority date for domestic and international students; for spring admission, 11/1 priority date for domestic and international students. Applications are processed on a rolling basis. Application fee: $60 ($95 for international students). Electronic applications accepted. *Expenses:* Tuition, state resident: full-time $1710; part-time $1140 per semester. Tuition, nonresident: full-time $7115. Required fees: $158 per semester. *Financial support:* In 2008–09, 5 teaching assistantships with partial tuition reimbursements (averaging $14,000 per year) were awarded; Federal Work-Study, institutionally sponsored loans, scholarships/grants, health care benefits, and unspecified assistantships also available. Financial award application deadline: 3/1; financial award applicants required to submit FAFSA. *Faculty research:* Rhetorical theory and criticism; communications/sex roles; judicial, legal, contextual, and behavioral approaches to com-

munication theory. *Unit head:* Dr. Gwen Hullman, Graduate Program Director, 775-784-4854, E-mail: gwenh@unr.edu. *Application contact:* Michele Sandberg, Application Contact, 775-784-7026, Fax: 775-784-6064, E-mail: gradschool@unr.edu.

University of South Carolina, The Graduate School, College of Education, Department of Instruction and Teacher Education, Program in Secondary Education, Columbia, SC 29208. Offers art education (IMA, MAT); business education (IMA, MAT); English (MAT); foreign language (MAT); health education (MAT); mathematics (MAT); science (IMA, MAT); secondary (Ed D); secondary education (MT, PhD); social studies (MAT); theatre and speech (MAT). IMA and MT offered jointly with the subject areas. *Accreditation:* NCATE. *Degree requirements:* For master's, comprehensive exam, thesis (for some programs), foreign language (MA); for doctorate, one foreign language, comprehensive exam, thesis/dissertation. *Entrance requirements:* For master's, GRE General Test or MAT, teaching certificate (IMA, M Ed), interview; for doctorate, GRE General Test or MAT, interview. *Faculty research:* Middle school programs, professional development, school collaboration.

University of Southern California, Graduate School, Annenberg School for Communication, School of Communication, Program in Communication, Los Angeles, CA 90089. Offers communication (MA, PhD), including interpersonal and social dynamics (PhD), mass communication, technology, and public policy (PhD), organizational communication (PhD), rhetorical and cultural studies (PhD). *Degree requirements:* For doctorate, thesis/dissertation. *Entrance requirements:* For master's and doctorate, GRE General Test, resumé, writing samples, 3 letters of recommendation, interest survey questionnaire, statement of purpose. Additional exam requirements/recommendations for international students: Required—TOEFL (minimum score 280 computer-based; 115 iBT); Recommended—TWE. Electronic applications accepted. *Faculty research:* Computer-mediated communication, public health campaigns, communication democracy and the public sphere, new communication technologies in organizations, communication and community.

See Close-Up on page 709.

University of Southern Mississippi, Graduate School, College of Arts and Letters, Department of Speech Communication, Hattiesburg, MS 39406-0001. Offers MA, MS, PhD. *Faculty:* 8 full-time (2 women). *Students:* 13 full-time (6 women), 13 part-time (8 women); includes 2 minority (1 African American, 1 Hispanic American), 1 international. Average age 32. 17 applicants, 76% accepted, 11 enrolled. In 2008, 2 master's, 5 doctorates awarded. *Degree requirements:* For master's, comprehensive exam, thesis optional; for doctorate, comprehensive exam, thesis/dissertation. *Entrance requirements:* For master's, GRE General Test, minimum GPA of 3.0 last 60 hours, 3.0 in major; for doctorate, GRE General Test, minimum GPA of 3.5. Additional exam requirements/recommendations for international students: Required—TOEFL. *Application deadline:* For fall admission, 3/1 priority date for domestic students, 3/1 for international students. Application fee: $30. *Financial support:* In 2008–09, 1 fellowship with full tuition reimbursement (averaging $12,000 per year), 8 teaching assistantships with full tuition reimbursements (averaging $13,500 per year) were awarded; research assistantships, Federal Work-Study, scholarships/grants, and unspecified assistantships also available. Financial award application deadline: 3/15; financial award applicants required to submit FAFSA. *Faculty research:* Persuasion and social influence, interpersonal communication, organizational communication, political communication, crisis communication. *Unit head:* Dr. Charles Tardy, Chair, 601-266-4271, Fax: 601-266-4275. *Application contact:* Dr. Lawrence Hosman, Graduate Coordinator, 601-266-4271, Fax: 601-266-4275.

The University of Tennessee, Graduate School, College of Communication and Information, Knoxville, TN 37996. Offers advertising (MS, PhD); broadcasting (MS, PhD); communications (MS, PhD); information sciences (MS, PhD); journalism (MS, PhD); public relations (MS, PhD); speech communication (MS, PhD). *Accreditation:* ACEJMC (one or more programs are accredited at the [master's] level). Part-time and evening/weekend programs available. Post-baccalaureate distance learning degree programs offered (no on-campus study). *Degree requirements:* For master's, thesis or alternative; for doctorate, thesis/dissertation. *Entrance requirements:* For master's and doctorate, GRE General Test, minimum GPA of 2.7. Additional exam requirements/recommendations for international students: Required—TOEFL. Electronic applications accepted. *Expenses:* Tuition, area resident: Part-time $348 per credit hour. Tuition, state resident: full-time $6262. Tuition, nonresident: full-time $18,920; part-time $1052 per credit hour. Required fees: $812; $36 per credit hour. Tuition and fees vary according to program.

University of Wisconsin–Madison, Graduate School, College of Letters and Science, Department of Communicative Disorders, Madison, WI 53706-1380. Offers normal aspects of speech, language and hearing (MS, PhD); speech-language pathology (MS, PhD); MS/PhD. *Accreditation:* ASHA (one or more programs are accredited). *Degree requirements:* For doctorate, thesis/dissertation. *Entrance requirements:* For master's and doctorate, GRE. Electronic applications accepted. *Faculty research:* Language disorders in children and adults, disorders of speech production, intelligibility, fluency, hearing impairment, deafness.

University of Wisconsin–Stevens Point, College of Fine Arts and Communication, Division of Communication, Stevens Point, WI 54481-3897. Offers interpersonal communication (MA); mass communication (MA); organizational communication (MA); public relations (MA). Part-time programs available. *Students:* 7 full-time (3 women), 19 part-time (11 women). *Degree requirements:* For master's, thesis or alternative. *Entrance requirements:* For master's, GRE. Additional exam requirements/recommendations for international students: Required—TOEFL (minimum score 575 paper-based). *Application deadline:* For fall admission, 3/1 priority date for domestic students. Applications are processed on a rolling basis. Application fee: $45. *Expenses:* Tuition, state resident: full-time $7410. Tuition, nonresident: full-time $17,756. Full-time tuition and fees vary according to reciprocity agreements. *Financial support:* In 2008–09, 9 teaching assistantships were awarded; career-related internships or fieldwork, Federal Work-Study, institutionally sponsored loans, and unspecified assistantships also available. Support available to part-time students. Financial award application deadline: 5/1; financial award applicants required to submit FAFSA. *Faculty research:* Communication theory and research, film history. *Unit head:* Dr. James Haney, Chair, 715-346-3409, E-mail: jhaney@uwsp.edu. *Application contact:* Dr. Chris Sadler, Graduate Coordinator, 715-346-3898, E-mail: csadler@uwsp.edu.

University of Wisconsin–Superior, Graduate Division, Department of Communicating Arts, Superior, WI 54880-4500. Offers mass communication (MA); speech communication (MA); theater (MA). Part-time programs available. *Degree requirements:* For master's, comprehensive exam, thesis or alternative, position paper or project. *Entrance requirements:* For master's, minimum GPA of 2.75. *Faculty research:* Multimedia technology, ethics in journalism, diversity, electronic portfolio assessment.

Wake Forest University, Graduate School of Arts and Sciences, Department of Communication, Winston-Salem, NC 27109. Offers speech communication (MA). Part-time programs available. *Degree requirements:* For master's, one foreign language, thesis. *Entrance requirements:* For master's, GRE General Test, writing sample. Additional exam requirements/recommendations for international students: Required—TOEFL (minimum score 213 computer-based; 79 iBT). Electronic applications accepted.

Washington University in St. Louis, School of Medicine, Program in Audiology and Communication Sciences, St Louis, MO 63110. Offers audiology (Au D); deaf education (MS); speech and hearing sciences (PhD). *Accreditation:* ASHA (one or more programs are accredited). *Degree requirements:* For master's, comprehensive exam, thesis, independent study project, oral exam; for doctorate, comprehensive exam, thesis/dissertation, capstone project, oral exam. *Entrance requirements:* For master's, GRE General Test, minimum B average in undergraduate course work; for doctorate, GRE General Test, minimum B average. Additional exam requirements/recommendations for international students: Required—TOEFL (minimum score 600 paper-based; 250 computer-based; 100 iBT). Electronic applications accepted.

Speech and Interpersonal Communication

Washington University in St. Louis *(continued)*
Expenses: Contact institution. *Faculty research:* Sensory aids, noise, speech perception, biological deafness, audiology.

Wayne State University, College of Fine, Performing and Communication Arts, Department of Communication, Detroit, MI 48202. Offers communication studies (MA, PhD); public relations and organizational communication (MA); radio-TV-film (MA, PhD); speech communication (MA, PhD). *Degree requirements:* For master's, thesis, essay, or comprehensive exam; for doctorate, thesis/dissertation. *Entrance requirements:* For master's, minimum GPA of 3.0, personal statement; sample of academic writing; for doctorate, GRE, minimum GPA of 3.3, MA; letters of recommendation; personal statement; sample of written scholarship. Additional exam requirements/recommendations for international students: Required—TOEFL (minimum score 550 paper-based); 213 computer-based); Recommended—TWE (minimum score 6). Electronic applications accepted. *Faculty research:* Rhetorical theory and criticism; mass media theory and research; argumentation; organizational communication; risk and crisis communication; interpersonal, family, and health communication.

Technical Communication

Boise State University, Graduate College, College of Arts and Sciences, Department of English, Program in Technical Communication, Boise, ID 83725-0399. Offers MA. Part-time programs available. *Degree requirements:* For master's, thesis. *Entrance requirements:* For master's, minimum GPA of 3.0. Electronic applications accepted.

Bowling Green State University, Graduate College, College of Arts and Sciences, Department of English, Program in English, Bowling Green, OH 43403. Offers English (MA, PhD); literature (MA); rhetoric and writing (PhD); scientific and technical communication (MA). Part-time programs available. *Degree requirements:* For master's, thesis or alternative; for doctorate, comprehensive exam, thesis/dissertation, foreign language or proficiency in Old English. *Entrance requirements:* For master's and doctorate, GRE General Test. Additional exam requirements/recommendations for international students: Required—TOEFL. Electronic applications accepted. *Faculty research:* Postmodern literary theory, rhetorical theory, ethnic American literature, literature and culture, composition pedagogy.

Colorado State University, Graduate School, College of Liberal Arts, Department of Journalism and Technical Communication, Fort Collins, CO 80523-1785. Offers public communication and technology (MS, PhD); technical communication (MS). Part-time programs available. *Faculty:* 19 full-time (8 women). *Students:* 30 full-time (20 women), 32 part-time (25 women); includes 7 minority (1 American Indian/Alaska Native, 2 Asian Americans or Pacific Islanders, 4 Hispanic Americans), 7 international. Average age 34. 56 applicants, 68% accepted, 23 enrolled. In 2008, 13 master's awarded. *Degree requirements:* For master's, variable foreign language requirement, comprehensive exam (for some programs), thesis (for some programs); for doctorate, variable foreign language requirement, comprehensive exam (for some programs), thesis/dissertation (for some programs). *Entrance requirements:* For master's, GRE General Test, samples of written work, letters of recommendation, resumé or curriculum vitae, 3 writing/communication projects, bachelor's degree, statement of career plans; for doctorate, GRE General Test, master's degree, minimum GPA of 3.0, scholarly/professional work, letters of recommendation, statement of career plans, resumé. Additional exam requirements/recommendations for international students: Required—TOEFL (minimum score 600 paper-based; 250 computer-based). *Application deadline:* For fall admission, 2/15 priority date for domestic students, 12/15 priority date for international students; for spring admission, 6/15 priority date for domestic students. Applications are processed on a rolling basis. Application fee: $50. Electronic applications accepted. *Expenses:* Tuition, area resident: Full-time $5620; part-time $312.25 per credit. Tuition, state resident: full-time $5620; part-time $312.25 per credit. Tuition, nonresident: full-time $17,253; part-time $958.50 per credit. Required fees: $1449.56; $82.35 per credit. *Financial support:* In 2008–09, 18 students received support, including 18 teaching assistantships with partial tuition reimbursements available (averaging $7,912 per year); fellowships with partial tuition reimbursements available, research assistantships with full and partial tuition reimbursements available, career-related internships or fieldwork, Federal Work-Study, institutionally sponsored loans, scholarships/grants, traineeships, and unspecified assistantships also available. Support available to part-time students. Financial award application deadline: 3/1; financial award applicants required to submit FAFSA. *Faculty research:* Technical/science communication, public relations, health/risk communication, web/new media technologies, environmental communication. Total annual research expenditures: $314,040. *Unit head:* Dr. Greg Luft, Chair, 970-491-1979, Fax: 970-491-2908, E-mail: greg.luft@colostate.edu. *Application contact:* Craig Trumbo, Graduate Program Coordinator, 970-491-2077, Fax: 970-491-2908, E-mail: craig.trumbo@colostate.edu.

Drexel University, College of Arts and Sciences, Department of Culture and Communication, Program in Communication, Philadelphia, PA 19104-2875. Offers public communication (MS); science communication (MS); technical communication (MS). Part-time and evening/weekend programs available. *Degree requirements:* For master's, internship, professional portfolio. *Entrance requirements:* For master's, GRE or minimum GPA of 3.0. Additional exam requirements/recommendations for international students: Required—TOEFL. Electronic applications accepted.

Eastern Michigan University, Graduate School, College of Arts and Sciences, Department of English Language and Literature, Program in Written and Technical Communications, Ypsilanti, MI 48197. Offers technical communications (MA, Graduate Certificate); written communications (MA). Part-time and evening/weekend programs available. Postbaccalaureate distance learning degree programs offered (minimal on-campus study). *Entrance requirements:* Additional exam requirements/recommendations for international students: Required—TOEFL.

Eastern Washington University, Graduate Studies, College of Arts and Letters, Department of English, Cheney, WA 99004-2431. Offers literature (MA); rhetoric, composition, and technical communication (MA); teaching English as a second language (MA). *Degree requirements:* For master's, comprehensive exam, thesis or alternative. *Entrance requirements:* For master's, GRE General Test, minimum GPA of 3.0.

Harvard University, Graduate School of Education, Master's Programs in Education, Cambridge, MA 02138. Offers arts in education (Ed M); education policy and management (Ed M); higher education (Ed M); human development and psychology (Ed M); international education policy (Ed M); language and literacy (Ed M); learning and teaching (Ed M); mid-career mathematics and science (teaching certificate) (Ed M); mind brain and education (Ed M); risk and prevention (Ed M); school leadership (Ed M); special studies (Ed M); teaching and curriculum (teaching certificate) (Ed M); technology innovation and education (Ed M). Part-time programs available. *Faculty:* 61 full-time (29 women), 40 part-time/adjunct (24 women). *Students:* 504 full-time (403 women), 66 part-time (53 women); includes 129 minority (40 African Americans, 1 American Indian/Alaska Native, 59 Asian Americans or Pacific Islanders, 29 Hispanic Americans), 84 international. Average age 28. 1,255 applicants, 59% accepted, 533 enrolled. In 2008, 610 master's awarded. *Entrance requirements:* For master's, GRE General Test, 3 letters of recommendation, official transcripts, statement of purpose. Additional exam requirements/recommendations for international students: Required—TOEFL (minimum score 600 paper-based; 250 computer-based; 100 iBT), TWE (minimum score 5). *Application deadline:* For fall admission, 1/5 for domestic and international students. Application fee: $85. Electronic applications accepted. *Expenses:* Contact institution. *Financial support:* In 2008–09, 336 students received support, including 30 fellowships with full and partial tuition reimbursements available (averaging $15,975 per year); career-related internships or fieldwork, Federal Work-Study, institutionally sponsored loans, scholarships/grants, health care benefits, tuition waivers (full and partial), and unspecified assistantships also available. Support available to part-time students. Financial award application deadline: 2/1; financial award applicants required to submit FAFSA. *Faculty research:* Learning and development; educational leadership and organizations; educational policy analysis. Total annual research expenditures: $14.7

million. *Unit head:* Jennifer L. Petrallia, Assistant Dean for Master's Studies, 617-495-8445. *Application contact:* Information Contact, 617-495-3414, Fax: 617-496-3577, E-mail: gseadmissions@harvard.edu.

Lawrence Technological University, College of Arts and Sciences, Southfield, MI 48075-1058. Offers computer science (MS); educational technology (MET); science education (MSE); technical communication (MS). Part-time and evening/weekend programs available. *Faculty:* 14 full-time (6 women), 14 part-time/adjunct (4 women). *Students:* 2 full-time (0 women), 90 part-time (53 women); includes 11 minority (5 African Americans, 6 Asian Americans or Pacific Islanders), 18 international. Average age 30. 86 applicants, 78% accepted, 21 enrolled. In 2008, 35 master's awarded. *Degree requirements:* For master's, thesis (for some programs). *Entrance requirements:* For master's, GRE. Additional exam requirements/recommendations for international students: Required—TOEFL (minimum score 550 paper-based; 213 computer-based; 79 iBT). *Application deadline:* For fall admission, 8/1 priority date for domestic students, 6/1 for international students; for winter admission, 12/1 priority date for domestic students, 10/1 for international students; for spring admission, 5/1 priority date for domestic students, 3/1 for international students. Applications are processed on a rolling basis. Application fee: $50. Electronic applications accepted. *Expenses:* Tuition: Part-time $763 per credit hour. Required fees: $115 per semester. Tuition and fees vary according to course level, degree level, campus/location and program. *Financial support:* Federal Work-Study available. Financial award application deadline: 4/1; financial award applicants required to submit FAFSA. *Unit head:* Dr. Hsiao-Ping Moore, Dean, 248-204-3500, Fax: 248-204-3518, E-mail: scidean@ltu.edu. *Application contact:* Jane Rohrback, Director of Admissions, 248-204-3160, Fax: 248-204-3188, E-mail: admissions@ltu.edu.

Michigan Technological University, Graduate School, College of Sciences and Arts, Department of Humanities, Program in Rhetoric and Technical Communication, Houghton, MI 49931-1295. Offers MS, PhD. Part-time programs available. Terminal master's awarded for partial completion of doctoral program. *Degree requirements:* For master's, comprehensive exam; for doctorate, one foreign language, comprehensive exam, thesis/dissertation. *Entrance requirements:* Additional exam requirements/recommendations for international students: Required—TOEFL (minimum score 600 paper-based; 250 computer-based). Electronic applications accepted.

Minnesota State University Mankato, College of Graduate Studies, College of Arts and Humanities, Department of English, Mankato, MN 56001. Offers creative writing (MFA); English (MA, MS); English literature (MA); teaching English (MS, MT); teaching English as a second language (MA, Certificate); technical communication (Certificate). Part-time programs available. *Students:* 36 full-time (20 women), 107 part-time (82 women). *Degree requirements:* For master's, one foreign language, comprehensive exam, thesis or alternative. *Entrance requirements:* For master's, minimum GPA of 3.0 during previous 2 years, writing sample (MFA). Additional exam requirements/recommendations for international students: Required—TOEFL. *Application deadline:* Applications are processed on a rolling basis. Application fee: $40. Electronic applications accepted. *Financial support:* Research assistantships with full tuition reimbursements, teaching assistantships with full tuition reimbursements, career-related internships or fieldwork, Federal Work-Study, and unspecified assistantships available. Financial award application deadline: 3/15; financial award applicants required to submit FAFSA. *Faculty research:* Keats and Christianity. *Unit head:* Dr. John Banschbach, Chairperson, 507-389-2117. *Application contact:* 507-389-2321, E-mail: grad@mnsu.edu.

Montana Tech of The University of Montana, Graduate School, Department of Technical Communication, Butte, MT 59701-8997. Offers MS. Part-time programs available. *Faculty:* 5 full-time (2 women), 1 (woman) part-time/adjunct. *Students:* 4 full-time (all women), 6 part-time (5 women). 3 applicants, 100% accepted, 2 enrolled. *Degree requirements:* For master's, project or thesis. *Entrance requirements:* For master's, GRE General Test, minimum GPA of 3.0. Additional exam requirements/recommendations for international students: Required—TOEFL (minimum score 525 paper-based; 195 computer-based; 71 iBT). *Application deadline:* For fall admission, 4/1 priority date for domestic students, 3/1 priority date for international students; for spring admission, 10/1 priority date for domestic students, 7/1 priority date for international students. Applications are processed on a rolling basis. Application fee: $30. Electronic applications accepted. *Expenses:* Tuition, state resident: full-time $4919; part-time $306 per credit. Tuition, nonresident: full-time $14,141; part-time $819 per credit. *Financial support:* In 2008–09, 8 students received support, including 5 teaching assistantships with partial tuition reimbursements available (averaging $6,400 per year); research assistantships with partial tuition reimbursements available, career-related internships or fieldwork, tuition waivers (partial), and unspecified assistantships also available. Financial award application deadline: 4/1; financial award applicants required to submit FAFSA. *Faculty research:* Environmental concerns and the Big Hole River, history of Butte mining, African studies, multicultural communications. *Unit head:* Dr. Henrietta Shirk, Head, 406-496-4297, Fax: 406-496-4510, E-mail: hshirk@mtech.edu. *Application contact:* Cindy Dunstan, Administrator, Graduate School, 406-496-4304, Fax: 406-496-4710, E-mail: cdunstan@mtech.edu.

New Jersey Institute of Technology, Office of Graduate Studies, College of Science and Liberal Arts, Department of Humanities and Social Sciences, Program in Professional and Technical Communication, Newark, NJ 07102. Offers MS. Part-time and evening/weekend programs available. Terminal master's awarded for partial completion of doctoral program. *Degree requirements:* For master's, thesis or alternative. *Entrance requirements:* For master's, GRE General Test. Additional exam requirements/recommendations for international students: Required—TOEFL (minimum score 550 paper-based; 213 computer-based). Electronic applications accepted. *Expenses:* Tuition, area resident: Full-time $13,780; part-time $750 per credit. Tuition, state resident: full-time $13,780; part-time $750 per credit. Tuition, nonresident: full-time $19,580; part-time $1033 per credit. Required fees: $1956; $197 per credit. *Faculty research:* Technology transfer, global sustainability, technology policy, professional ethics.

North Carolina State University, Graduate School, College of Humanities and Social Sciences, Department of English, Program in Technical Communication, Raleigh, NC 27695. Offers MS. *Degree requirements:* For master's, thesis optional. *Entrance requirements:* For master's, GRE General Test. Electronic applications accepted. *Faculty research:* Workplace writing, organizational socialization and power, integrated and multimedia documentation systems, technical communication management, usability testing theories.

Polytechnic Institute of NYU, Department of Humanities and Social Sciences, Major in Technical Communication, Brooklyn, NY 11201-2990. Offers Graduate Certificate. *Entrance requirements:* Additional exam requirements/recommendations for international students:

Technical Communication

Required—TOEFL (minimum score 550 paper-based; 213 computer-based); Recommended—IELTS (minimum score 6.5). Electronic applications accepted.

Rensselaer Polytechnic Institute, Graduate School, School of Humanities and Social Sciences, Department of Language, Literature, and Communication, Program in Technical Communication, Troy, NY 12180-3590. Offers MS. Part-time programs available. *Degree requirements:* For master's, thesis optional. *Entrance requirements:* For master's, GRE General Test, resumé. Additional exam requirements/recommendations for international students: Required—TOEFL (minimum score 570 paper-based; 230 computer-based). Electronic applications accepted. *Faculty research:* Human-computer interaction, media design, theory and culture, teaching and learning in the virtual classroom, usability.

Rochester Institute of Technology, Graduate Enrollment Services, College of Applied Science and Technology, Center for Multidisciplinary Studies, Program in Technical Information Design, Rochester, NY 14623-5603. Offers AC. *Entrance requirements:* Additional exam requirements/recommendations for international students: Required—TOEFL (minimum score 550 paper-based; 213 computer-based; 79 iBT). Electronic applications accepted.

Southern Polytechnic State University, School of Arts and Sciences, Department of English, Technical Communication, and Media Arts, Marietta, GA 30060-2896. Offers communications management (Graduate Certificate); content development (Graduate Certificate); information design and communication (MS); instructional design (Graduate Certificate); technical and professional communication (Graduate Certificate); visual communication and graphics (Graduate Certificate). Part-time and evening/weekend programs available. Postbaccalaureate distance learning degree programs offered (minimal on-campus study). *Faculty:* 4 full-time (3 women), 1 part-time/adjunct. *Students:* 5 full-time (4 women), 38 part-time (25 women); includes 13 minority (12 African Americans, 1 Hispanic American), 3 international. Average age 38. 38 applicants, 68% accepted, 23 enrolled. In 2008, 10 master's awarded. *Degree requirements:* For master's, thesis optional, 36 hours completed through thesis option (6 hours), internship option (6 hours) or advanced coursework option (6 hours); for Graduate Certificate, thesis optional, 18 hours completed through thesis option (6 hours), internship option (6 hours) or advanced coursework option (6 hours). *Entrance requirements:* For master's, GRE, statement of purpose, writing sample, professional recommendations, proctored essay; for Graduate Certificate, statement of purpose, writing sample, professional recommendations, proctored essay. Additional exam requirements/recommendations for international students: Required—TOEFL (minimum score 550 paper-based; 213 computer-based; 79 iBT), IELTS (minimum score 6.5). *Application deadline:* For fall admission, 5/1 priority date for domestic students, 7/1 priority date for international students; for spring admission, 9/1 priority date for domestic students, 11/1 priority date for international students. Applications are processed on a rolling basis. Application fee: $20. Electronic applications accepted. *Expenses:* Tuition, area resident: Full-time $2752; part-time $172 per semester hour. Tuition, state resident: full-time $2752; part-time $172 per semester hour. Tuition, nonresident: full-time $10,992; part-time $687 per semester hour. Required fees: $365 per semester. *Financial support:* In 2008–09, 14 students received support, including 1 research assistantship with full tuition reimbursement available (averaging $4,000 per year); career-related internships or fieldwork, Federal Work-Study, scholarships/grants, and unspecified assistantships also available. Support available to part-time students. Financial award application deadline: 5/1; financial award applicants required to submit FAFSA. *Faculty research:* Usability, user-centered design, instructional design, information architecture, information design. *Unit head:* Dr. Mark Nunes, Chair, 678-915-7202, Fax: 678-915-7425, E-mail: mnunes@spsu.edu. *Application contact:* Nikki Palamiotis, Director of Graduate Studies, 678-915-4276, Fax: 678-915-7292, E-mail: npalamio@spsu.edu.

Texas State University–San Marcos, Graduate School, College of Liberal Arts, Department of English, Program in Technical Communication, San Marcos, TX 78666. Offers MA. *Degree requirements:* For master's, comprehensive exam, thesis or alternative. *Entrance requirements:* For master's, minimum GPA of 2.75 in last 60 hours of course work, portfolio. Additional exam requirements/recommendations for international students: Required—TOEFL (minimum score 550 paper-based; 213 computer-based). Electronic applications accepted.

University of Colorado Denver, College of Liberal Arts and Sciences, Department of Communication, Denver, CO 80217-3364. Offers communication (MA); interactive media (Certificate); public relations (Certificate); technical and professional communication (Certificate); technical communication (MS); usability testing and interface design (Certificate). Part-time and evening/weekend programs available. *Degree requirements:* For master's, comprehensive exam, thesis or alternative. *Entrance requirements:* For master's, GRE General Test. Additional exam requirements/recommendations for international students: Required—TOEFL (minimum score 525 paper-based; 197 computer-based). Electronic applications accepted.

University of Houston–Downtown, College of Humanities and Social Sciences, Department of English, Houston, TX 77002-1001. Offers professional writing and technical communication (MS). Part-time and evening/weekend programs available. *Faculty:* 11 full-time (7 women). *Students:* 3 full-time (2 women), 19 part-time (17 women); includes 10 minority (8 African Americans, 1 Asian American or Pacific Islander, 1 Hispanic American). Average age 37. 6 applicants, 83% accepted, 5 enrolled. In 2008, 4 master's awarded. *Degree requirements:* For master's, thesis optional, graduation portfolio with oral defense. *Entrance requirements:* For master's, GRE (including Analytical Writing section), personal application statement, resumé, writing sample, 3 letters of recommendation. Additional exam requirements/recommendations for international students: Required—TOEFL (minimum score 600 paper-based; 250 computer-based; 86 iBT). *Application deadline:* For fall admission, 3/15 for domestic and international students; for spring admission, 11/15 for domestic and international students. Application fee: $35 ($60 for international students). Electronic applications accepted. *Expenses:* Tuition, area resident: Tuition, area resident: full-time $3060; part-time $170 per credit hour. Tuition, state resident: full-time $3060; part-time $170 per credit hour. Tuition, nonresident: full-time $7488; part-time $416 per credit hour. International tuition: $7570 full-time. Required fees: $854; $307 per term. Tuition and fees vary according to course load. *Financial support:* Applicants required to submit FAFSA. *Faculty research:* Environmental rhetoric, instructional design, usability, assessment, presentation slides. *Unit head:* Dr. Robert Jarrett, Chair, 713-221-8013, Fax: 713-226-5205, E-mail: JarrettR@uhd.edu. *Application contact:* Dr. Ann Jennings, Coordinator of MS in Professional Writing and Technical Communication and Professor, Department of English, 713-221-8013, Fax: 713-226-5205, E-mail: mspwtc@uhd.edu.

University of Nebraska at Omaha, Graduate Studies and Research, College of Arts and Sciences, Department of English, Omaha, NE 68182. Offers advanced writing (Certificate); English (MA); teaching English to speakers of other languages (Certificate); technical communication (Certificate). Part-time and evening/weekend programs available. *Degree requirements:* For master's, comprehensive exam, thesis (for some programs). *Entrance requirements:* For master's, minimum GPA of 3.0, statement of purpose, 3 letters of recommendation, writing sample. Additional exam requirements/recommendations for international students: Required—TOEFL (minimum score 600 paper-based; 250 computer-based; 100 iBT). Electronic applications accepted.

University of Washington, Graduate School, College of Engineering, Department of Technical Communication, Seattle, WA 98195. Offers MSTC, PhD. Part-time and evening/weekend programs available. *Degree requirements:* For master's, thesis or alternative; for doctorate, comprehensive exam, thesis/dissertation. *Entrance requirements:* For master's, GRE General Test, minimum GPA of 3.0; for doctorate, GRE, minimum GPA of 3.0. Additional exam requirements/recommendations for international students: Required—TOEFL. Electronic applications accepted. *Faculty research:* Communication design, user interface design and usability, new media design, science news writing, comprehension processes.

AMERICAN UNIVERSITY

School of Communication

Programs of Study	American University's School of Communication (SOC) is a laboratory for professional education, communication research, and innovative production in journalism, film and media arts, and public communication, working across media platforms and with a focus on public affairs and public service. SOC offers graduate programs that prepare students for careers in traditional and emerging media. Students work closely with faculty in small, laboratory environments while pursuing professional opportunities in Washington, D.C.'s world-class media organizations, including Discovery Communications, National Geographic, *USA Today,* and *washingtonpost.com.* Most SOC faculty are practitioners who have won Oscars, Emmys, lifetime achievement awards, and other professional honors. A committed group of alumni also works with students individually in a unique mentoring program. All graduate programs emphasize writing, hands-on learning, and analysis of the social, legal, and economic challenges shaping today's communication industry. SOC offers five full-time and three weekend master's degree programs. The full-time programs include the Master of Arts (M.A.) in journalism and public affairs (33 hours), with tracks in broadcast and print journalism and concentrations in economic, international, and public policy journalism; the M.A. in public communication (30 hours), with concentrations in arts, government, political, and public interest communication as well as corporate and international public relations; the M.A. in film and video (36 hours), with concentrations in film and video production, screenwriting, multimedia, and film history, theory, and criticism; the Master of Fine Arts (M.F.A.) in film and electronic media, a terminal degree that allows students to pursue collegiate-level teaching careers; and the M.A. in international media (45 hours), a joint program with the School of International Service that offers a combination of theory, research, and professional production skills to provide a global media advantage. The weekend M.A. programs for working professionals include interactive journalism, public communication, and producing for film and video. Students move through the programs with a cohort of fellow students who meet every Saturday for twenty months.
Research Facilities	The SOC Friedheim Journalism Center (FJC) features two fully networked computer classrooms, each with twenty Macs configured for computer-assisted research and reporting, multimedia and Web authoring, and page layout and design. The FJC also contains a third, smaller lab with Mac and Windows computers for students' research, writing, and rich-media authoring. The School has three fully equipped Mac-based computer labs, all featuring state-of-the-art software applications for graphics production, digital imaging and compositing, layout and design, Web authoring, and digital video editing. A 109-seat theater is equipped with multiformat video projection and interactive videoconferencing capabilities. There are traditional black-and-white photographic darkroom facilities; small-, medium-, and large-format film cameras; high-quality digital scanning equipment; photo-quality color inkjet printing; and a growing collection of professional digital cameras, all dedicated for exclusive SOC-student use. A separate facility, the Media Production Center, houses a 40-foot by 40-foot, three-camera color television studio; the fully networked Ed Bliss Broadcast Newsroom; three digital audio studios; a large multiuse classroom; a field production equipment check-out facility; and ten digital video postproduction suites for Avid and Final Cut Pro editing.
Financial Aid	SOC offers merit-based financial aid awards on a competitive basis in all of its full-time graduate programs. Awards vary and may consist of tuition remission, stipend, teaching assistant or research assistant position, or a combination. In 2008–09, about 30 percent of SOC graduate students received merit-based financial aid. In addition to SOC-sponsored merit awards, the Journalism Division also offers prestigious fellowships in collaboration with the Center for Public Integrity, Bureau of National Affairs, and *USA Today.* American University offers need-based financial aid to students who qualify by filing the Free Application for Federal Student Aid (FAFSA) form.
Cost of Study	For the 2009–10 academic year, graduate tuition is $1237 per credit hour. Students may anticipate a 4 percent increase in tuition in each academic year. Full-time graduate study is considered to be at least 9 hours each semester; students in the full-time journalism and public communication programs usually complete 12 hours per semester. Special fees are charged for thesis processing, activities, and maintaining matriculation (if the student is not registered for courses). Courses requiring the use of production equipment or computer facilities typically incur additional lab fees.
Living and Housing Costs	Although many graduate students live off campus, the University has some graduate dormitory rooms and apartments available. The Off-Campus Housing Office maintains a referral file of rooms and apartments. Housing costs in Washington, D.C., are comparable to those in other major metropolitan areas.
Student Group	The SOC enrolls approximately 350 students in its graduate programs, divided more or less evenly among its full-time and weekend programs. Approximately 65 percent of the graduate students are women, 26 percent are members of minority groups, and 11 percent are international. All of the programs emphasize a strong liberal arts education as a requirement for admission, and none requires students to have majored in communication as undergraduates. Consequently, students selected in the competitive admission process come from diverse educational and professional backgrounds. Many students have worked professionally, and all have shown evidence of their professional and academic commitment.
Location	The School of Communication takes full advantage of the rich professional opportunities of Washington, D.C., as the nation's media capital as well as one of its largest production markets. Nationally recognized journalists, filmmakers, and public relations executives regularly serve as guest lecturers and adjunct professors. The city also offers the cultural resources of the Smithsonian Institution, the National Gallery of Art, the Kennedy Center for the Performing Arts, and the Library of Congress, plus a thriving artistic community of galleries and clubs.
The University and The School	Founded in 1893, American University (AU) is located on an 84-acre site in a residential area of northwest Washington that is accessible by Metro, the region's subway system. As a member of the Consortium of Universities of the Washington Metropolitan Area, AU offers its degree candidates the option of taking courses at other consortium universities for residence credit. SOC has educated communication professionals for forty years. Its journalism and public communication programs are accredited by the Accrediting Council for Education in Journalism and Mass Communications (ACEJMC), and its program in film and media arts is one of only fourteen U.S. programs accepted for membership in CILECT, the International Association of Film and Television Schools. The School's faculty members and alumni are working professionals who constitute a valuable network for graduating students seeking career advancement. SOC is home to the Center for Social Media, Investigative Reporting Workshop, J-Lab: Institute for Interactive Journalism, Center for Environmental Filmmaking, and Foreign Correspondence Network.
Applying	Applicants must have earned a minimum GPA of 3.0 during their last 60 credits (two years) of undergraduate study for application to all graduate programs, except the M.A. in international media, which requires a minimum GPA of 3.3 in the last 60 credits of undergraduate study. In addition, a 1,000-word statement of purpose, two letters of recommendation, a completed SOC graduate application form, and an application fee of $50 are required. Recommendations should be submitted on professional letterhead with a business card attached. International students who have learned English as a second language are required to score a minimum of 600 on the paper-based version, 250 on the computer-based version, or 100 on the Internet-based version of the TOEFL. SOC also accepts the IELTS exam for English proficiency from students with a minimum score of 7.0. All applicants for the full-time programs are required to take the GRE. The application deadline for fall admission into all full-time programs is June 1 (February 1 for merit award consideration). The film and video program admits students in the spring semester, with an application deadline of November 15. Weekend programs' priority deadline for applications is June 1; however, applications are accepted on a rolling admissions basis until the start of the fall semester in mid-August. Applications for financial aid should be submitted before February 1.
Correspondence and Information	Office of Graduate Programs School of Communication American University 4400 Massachusetts Avenue, NW Washington, D.C. 20016-8017 Phone: 202-885-2040 E-mail: gradcomm@american.edu Web site: http://www.soc.american.edu

American University

THE FACULTY

Larry Kirkman, Professor and Dean; M.A.T., Harvard.
Laird B. Anderson, Professor Emeritus; M.A., American. Journalism.
Patricia Aufderheide, Professor; Ph.D., Minnesota. Film and Media Arts.
Randall Blair, Associate Professor and Director, Weekend Producing for Film and Video Program; M.A., American. Film and Media Arts.
Kyle Brannon, Assistant Professor; M.F.A., American. Film and Electronic Media.
W. Joseph Campbell, Professor; Ph.D., North Carolina. Journalism.
Angie Chuang, Assistant Professor; M.A., Stanford. English Literature.
Wendell Cochran, Associate Professor; M.A., Missouri. Journalism.
John Doolittle, Associate Professor; Ph.D., Wisconsin–Madison. Journalism.
John Douglass, Associate Professor and Director, Film and Media Arts Division; M.A., American. Film and Media Arts.
Amy Eisman, Director, Writing Programs and Interactive Journalism Program; M.A., American. Journalism.
Larry Engel, Professor; M.F.A., Columbia. Film and Media Arts.
Wendy Melillo Farrill, Assistant Professor; M.A., Johns Hopkins. History, M.A., American. International Communication.
Lauren Feldman, Assistant Professor; Ph.D., Pennsylvania. Communication.
William Gentile, Artist-in-Residence; M.A., Ohio State.
Joseph Graf, Assistant Professor; M.A., Ohio State. Public Communication.
Jane Hall, Associate Professor; M.S.J., Columbia. Journalism.
Darrell Hayes, Assistant Professor and Director, Weekend Public Communication Program; M.A., Oklahoma. Public Communication.
Amy Hendrick, M.F.A., American. Film and Electronic Media.
Jerry Hendrix, Professor Emeritus; Ph.D., LSU. Public Communication.
Maria Ivancin, Assistant Professor; M.B.A., Illinois. Public Communication.
Leena Jayaswal, Associate Professor; M.F.A., Maryland Institute, College of Art. Film and Media Arts.
David Johnson, Assistant Professor; M.A., Texas A&M. Nautical Archaeology and Anthropology.
Iris Krasnow, Assistant Professor; M.A., Georgetown. Washington Journalism Semester.
Pallavi Kumar, Assistant Professor; M.A., Georgetown. Communication.
Charles Lewis, Professor; M.A., Johns Hopkins. Journalism.
Dotty Lynch, Executive-in-Residence; M.A., Fordham. Public Communication.
Brigid Maher, Assistant Professor; M.F.A., Northwestern. Film and Media Arts.
Sarah Menke-Fish, Assistant Professor; M.A., American. Film and Media Arts.
Kathryn Montgomery, Professor; Ph.D., UCLA. Public Communication.
Claudia Myers, Assistant Professor; M.F.A. Columbia. Film.
Matthew Nisbet, Assistant Professor; Ph.D., Cornell. Public Communication.
Jill Olmsted, Associate Professor and Director, Journalism Division; M.A., American. Journalism.
Chris Palmer, Distinguished-Film-Producer-in-Residence; M.A., Harvard. Film and Media Arts.
Lynne Perri, Journalist-in-Residence; M.S., Northwestern. Journalism.
Gemma Puglisi, Assistant Professor; M.A., Catholic University. Public Communication.
Rose Ann Robertson, Associate Dean; M.S., Southern Illinois. Journalism.
Rick Rockwell, Associate Professor; M.A., USC. Journalism.
Chris Simpson, Professor; M.A., Maryland. Journalism.
Rick Stack, Associate Professor; J.D., Missouri. Public Communication.
Leonard Steinhorn, Professor and Director, Public Communication Division; M.A., Johns Hopkins. Public Communication.
Margaret Stogner, Assistant Professor; M.A., Stanford. Film and Media Arts.
Rodger Streitmatter, Professor; Ph.D., American. Journalism.
John Watson, Associate Professor; J.D., Rutgers; Ph.D., North Carolina. Journalism.
Russell Williams, Artist-in-Residence; B.A., American. Film and Media Arts.
Lewis Wolfson, Professor Emeritus; M.S.J., Columbia; M.A., Harvard. Journalism.
Joanne Yamauchi, Professor Emeritus; Ph.D., Northwestern. Public Communication.
Rhonda Zaharna, Associate Professor; Ed.D., Columbia. Public Communication.
Anne Zelle, Professor Emeritus; M.A., Pius XII (Italy). Film and Media Arts.

BOSTON UNIVERSITY

College of Communication

Programs of Study	The College has three graduate departments: Film and Television; Mass Communication, Advertising, and Public Relations; and Journalism. Master of Science degree programs are available in the major fields of advertising, broadcast journalism, business and economics journalism, journalism, mass communication, public relations, science journalism, television, and media ventures. A Master of Fine Arts is offered in the areas of film production, film studies, and screenwriting. The College also offers the following dual-degree programs: J.D./M.S. in mass communication and M.B.A./M.S. in media ventures.
	The programs usually require three to four semesters of work. In several sequences, a creative project may be elected in place of a thesis. In the Department of Mass Communication, Advertising, and Public Relations, students may take a comprehensive exam in place of a thesis. A number of elective courses make up degree requirements within each program.
	Summer internships are encouraged in all programs. Few summer courses are offered. Degree candidates must complete their work in seven years from the date of first course registration, or they may be required to satisfy additional requirements.
Research Facilities	The College provides opportunities for students to participate actively in ongoing research projects through part-time work and assistantships in the Communication Research Center, a research division organized to accept projects that have academic merit, do not compete directly with available commercial research facilities, and are in keeping with the objectives of the College. Physical facilities include a city room with an Associated Press wire service drop and a copy desk; VDTs; photo labs with fully equipped digital darkrooms; Ezratti HD Lab, recording, and broadcast facilities; Final Cut Studio; AVID editing suites; a closed-circuit TV center; complete film facilities; seminar rooms; and a reading room. The College has several computer labs and a state-of-the-art multimedia lab with both PCs and Macs. The University's Mugar Library has a substantial communication collection.
Financial Aid	The University offers various financial aid options to qualified students. These programs include merit scholarships ranging from $1000 to full tuition, the Federal Work-Study Program, and Federal Stafford Loans. Graduate assistantships are available through the individual departments. The stipends for scholarships and assistantships ranged from $1000 to $6000 per semester in 2008–09. Various loan programs and part-time jobs are also available. Students are urged to use their own initiative in finding support, since the resources of the graduate programs are limited; possible sources of aid include state agencies and private organizations. Library references and online searches are helpful information sources.
Cost of Study	Tuition was $36,540 for the 2008–09 academic year.
Living and Housing Costs	Most graduate students are advised to seek off-campus housing. Limited on-campus graduate housing is available. The cost for room and board is estimated to be about $12,000 for the nine-month academic year. The University maintains apartments for married full-time graduate students and their families.
Student Group	Of the 338 full- and part-time graduate students enrolling in fall 2009, 173 were returning to continue their studies, while 165 were beginning programs. There were several international students in the entering group, and many domestic students were from outside New England. Women make up 75 percent of the graduate class. Alumni of the College are found throughout the United States and in many other countries, practicing their communication skills in media, government, industry, social institutions, education, and private business.
Location	Boston, the largest city in New England and one of the largest media markets in the U.S., is a seaport whose character results from a rich blend of historical heritage, active cultural life, and contemporary growth in technology, medicine, and business. Greater Boston, with more than fifty colleges and universities, remains an unrivaled center of learning. Within the city's compact center are the Boston Common and the Public Garden, Faneuil Hall Marketplace, art galleries, Chinatown, and the Freedom Trail, along which are some of the most important landmarks in U.S. history. Admission to the Museum of Fine Arts is free for University students. The Boston Symphony Orchestra, the Opera Company of Boston, and many fine chamber and jazz groups offer annual seasons, as do dance and theater companies. Boston is the home of the New England Patriots, the Red Sox, the Celtics, and the Bruins.
The University and The College	Boston University is an independent, coeducational, nonsectarian university with an enrollment of about 29,000 full-time students and a faculty of more than 2,500. Its academic diversity meets the needs of one of the largest bodies of scholars in the world. Incorporated in 1869, the University today provides students with the advantages of a large, contemporary educational complex while maintaining many traditional priorities. Its sixteen schools and colleges respond to students' occupational needs and the increasingly specialized demands they face in the modern world. The main campus, on the south bank of the Charles River, occupies 64 acres just west of downtown Boston. The University's Medical Center is in the city's south end.
	The College of Communication was founded in 1947 to provide professional education in public relations, journalism, broadcasting, and film. Graduate programs have been offered since the founding of the College. An integral part of the central campus, the College has its own building, lending a small-college atmosphere to its programs. The University is accredited by the New England Association of Schools and Colleges.
Applying	Applicants must have a bachelor's degree from an accredited college or university. Various majors are acceptable, but a strong background in social science and the humanities is considered desirable. Scores on the GRE General Test must be filed. M.B.A./M.S. media ventures students must file scores on the GMAT. Students applying to the J.D./M.S. in mass communication program must take the LSAT. International students must file TOEFL, in addition to the GRE scores; there are minimum score requirements, which can be found on the College's admissions Web site (http://www.bu.edu/com/grad/admission). Consideration is given to academic performance, test scores, recommendations, writing samples, and evidence of motivation in respect to the selected major. Applications with credentials must be received at the College of Communication by February 1. Early applications are encouraged. Incomplete applications cannot be reviewed. Online applications are preferred; applications may be submitted online at http://www.bu.edu/com/grad.
Correspondence and Information	Graduate Services College of Communication Boston University 640 Commonwealth Avenue Boston, Massachusetts 02215 Phone: 617-353-3481 800-992-6514 (toll-free) Fax: 617-358-0399 E-mail: comgrad@bu.edu Web site: http://www.bu.edu/com/grad

Boston University

THE FACULTY AND AREAS OF CONCENTRATION

The names of the full-time faculty members are listed below in conjunction with the department in which their major responsibilities lie. Many faculty members teach in several programs. The entire faculty teaches in both the undergraduate and graduate curricula of the College. In addition to possessing excellent academic credentials, most faculty members have had extensive experience as practitioners in their areas of specialization. The Dean ad interim of the College is Tobe L. Berkovitz, B.F.A., M.A., Ph.D. (theater arts, speech communication).

DEPARTMENT OF FILM AND TELEVISION. Paul Schneider, M.F.A., Chairman; John Bernstein, B.A., Ph.D. (film); Raymond Carney, Ph.D. (American studies); Mary Jane Doherty, M.S. (visual studies); Roy Grundmann, Ph.D. (critical studies); Samuel Kauffmann, M.S. (film production); John R. Kelly, Ph.D. (radio, film, and television); Frederick Lewis, M.A. (creative writing); Charles Merzbacher, M.F.A. (film production); Cathy Perron, M.S. (mass communication); Geoffrey Poister, Ph.D. (social science); Garland Waller, M.S. (broadcast journalism).

Film Production. Mary Jane Doherty, Director. This two-year program provides thorough, hands-on training in all aspects of film production: scriptwriting, directing, cinematography, postproduction, and distribution. The emphasis is on narrative filmmaking. The curriculum includes courses in critical studies of film masterworks.

Screenwriting. John Bernstein, Director. This two-year program emphasizes a non-formulaic approach to screenwriting and requires students to understand and practice the art of screenwriting, to learn the fundamentals of dramatic production, to understand various models of film structure and film history, and to comprehend the role of the storyteller and the place of the screenplay in the dramatic tradition.

Film Studies. Roy Grundmann, Director. This two-year program prepares students to work as critics, historians, scholars, teachers, librarians, archivists, programmers, or exhibitors. Film studies majors, under faculty supervision, may pursue a variety of critical approaches to film.

Media Ventures. Cathy Perron, Director. This three-semester program is for students who have decided to pursue media careers in various telecommunications industries. There is also a five-semester dual-degree program in conjunction with the Graduate School of Management.

Television Production. Cathy Perron, Director. This three-semester program combines hands-on production experience with courses in the history and social impact of television and in television management to prepare students for careers in production, management, programming, marketing, teaching, and criticism.

DEPARTMENT OF JOURNALISM. Lou Ureneck, B.A. (English), Chair; Fred Bayles, B.S. (journalism); Keith Botsford, A.M.; Chris Daly, M.A. (American history); Anne Donohue, M.S. (broadcast journalism), M.A. (international relations); Jonathan Klarfeld, A.B. (English); H. Joachim Maitre, Ph.D. (literature); Robert Manoff, M.C.P. (urban studies); Elizabeth Mehren, M.J.; Sasha Norkin, M.S.; Safoura Rafeizadeh, M.F.A. (graphic design); Caryl Rivers, M.S. (journalism); Ellen Ruppel Shell, B.A. (biology); Frank H. Shorr, M.S. (broadcasting and film); Peter Smith, B.S.; Peter Southwick, B.A. (government); Douglas Starr, M.S. (science reporting); Susan Walker, B.A.; Mitchell Zuckoff, M.A. (journalism).

Journalism. Jonathan Klarfeld, Director. The program in journalism provides qualified students with an in-depth understanding of the press in its various aspects—its editorial and economic functions, its relation to other social institutions, and its limitations and responsibilities. Competence in research in mass communication problems is one area of emphasis. Another is proficiency in reporting, writing and editing, and other professional practices that prepare graduates for employment in the field. Graduate students may elect the traditional research thesis or a reporting project in a specialized area, designed for publication in the form of magazine articles or as an extended newspaper series.

Broadcast Journalism. Sasha Norkin, Director. The program provides a working knowledge of the organization and structure of broadcasting and its relationship to government, mastery of the techniques of television and radio newswriting, and a survey of the varied aspects of television news programming.

Business and Economics Journalism. Lou Ureneck, Director. This program combines journalism training with instruction in business and economics. Core courses include an introduction to business and economics reporting, advanced business writing, international business and economics reporting, and investigative techniques.

Science Journalism. Douglas Starr and Ellen Ruppel Shell, Co-Directors. This program prepares students to work as reporters, writers, and editors for scientific, engineering, or business newspapers and magazines. Students are also exposed to basic courses in audiovisual subjects, broadcast journalism, and publication management and may select advanced courses and directed-study projects in these professional areas. The three-semester, 48-credit program includes internships of the student's choice with various organizations, including a science news service, scientific and engineering newspapers and magazines, and scientific, industrial, and business institutions. In conjunction with their internships or course work, students also usually prepare a major science communication project for professional production or publication.

DEPARTMENT OF MASS COMMUNICATION, ADVERTISING, AND PUBLIC RELATIONS. T. Barton Carter, J.D. (law), Chair; Judith Austin, B.F.A.; Tobe Berkovitz, Ph.D. (theater arts, speech communication); Christopher Cakebread, Ph.D. (mass communication); John Carroll, A.B. (Latin, Greek, and English); Carolyn Clark, M.S. (marketing); Dorothy Clark, M.S. (mass communication); Jo Doherty, M.S. (mass communication); Edward Downes, M.S. (journalism); Michel Elasmar, Ph.D. (mass communication); Thomas Fauls, M.S. (advertising); Hyun-Yeul Lee, Ph.D.; Joyce Macario, M.F.A. (graphic design); Peter Morrissey, B.S. (communication); Patrice Oppliger, Ph.D.; Susan Parenio, M.A. (English literature); John Verret, B.A. (economics); Tammy Vigil, Ph.D. (communication studies); H. Denis Wu, Ph.D.

Advertising. The M.S. in advertising at Boston University is designed to prepare students to work in advertising agencies, media companies, and other marketing communications organizations. Some are prepared for doctoral-level studies. All students must take courses that provide a broad understanding of the advertising industry and of the role of communication in contemporary society. In addition, they focus on developing advertising campaigns or research skills. Students may choose one of three tracks: management track, creative track, or thesis track. The management track prepares students for careers in account management, media, account planning, or advertising research. The creative track prepares students for careers in art direction or copywriting. The thesis track prepares students for careers in marketing research or education.

Mass Communication. The mass communication program is designed to cover the broad range of professional communications studies and industries without specializing in any one area and to provide students with a strong understanding of communications theory, processes, and application, along with basic writing and media skills. Through this generalist approach, students are prepared to practice in such professional areas as advertising agencies, newspapers, publishing houses, television and radio stations, and nonprofit and government agencies. The program incorporates policy, planning, and management studies.

Public Relations. The program in public relations is designed to provide professional instruction for qualified students seeking careers in public relations for business, government, and nonprofit organizations. The program has three foundations: the theory and process of communication, the administrative and policy sciences, and research findings in communication and the social sciences. These foundations are interconnected by a body of knowledge drawn from the liberal arts, particularly the social sciences, and applied to the practical decisions and programs of public relations.

The Journalism School
Columbia University

COLUMBIA UNIVERSITY

The Graduate School of Journalism

Programs of Study

The School offers two intensive master's degrees for students who are pursuing a professional career in journalism and a traditional doctoral program in journalism and communication.

The ten-month Master of Science (M.S.) program offers aspiring and experienced journalists the opportunity to study the skills, the art, and the ethics of journalism by reporting and writing stories that range from short news pieces to complex narrative features. Students learn how to think critically and deeply, to be both ethical and street smart, working with New York City as their laboratory. Students may choose from one of four specializations: newspaper, magazine, broadcast, or digital media. A flexible part-time M.S. program, which begins in late May, is available for students who want to work while continuing their education.

Applicants interested in investigative reporting may apply to the Toni Stabile Center for Investigative Journalism, a sub-specialization of the M.S. program. The Stabile Center is dedicated to training students interested in pursuing distinguished careers in investigative journalism. Candidates for the Master of Science degree are able to pursue this specialization, which is platform-neutral and is taken in addition to the traditional M.S. concentrations of broadcast, newspaper, magazine, and digital media. In order to graduate with a specialization in investigative journalism, students must apply to the program as part of their application for admission to the School and then take all four courses offered by the Stabile Center.

The Master of Arts (M.A.) program is a nine-month program designed for experienced journalists who would like to deepen their knowledge of journalism while focusing in on a particular subject area: politics, science, business, or the arts. M.A. student leaders are challenged to create new ways of telling stories based on a deeper understanding of difficult subjects. Students work closely with journalism school professors as well as professors from other academic departments at the university. The program is available full-time only, and runs from August to May.

The Ph.D. program draws upon the resources of Columbia University in a multi-disciplinary approach to the study of communications. Students craft individual courses of study from the wide array of departments and divisions at the university. In addition to the journalism school, these include the departments of political science and sociology; the professional schools of business and law; and Teachers College.

Dual-degree programs are offered with the School of Law, the School of Business, the School of International and Public Affairs, the Graduate School of Arts and Sciences' program in Earth and Environmental Sciences, and the Scripps Howard Program in Religion. Columbia also offers a joint degree program with the School of Journalism at Sciences Po in Paris.

Research Facilities

The Roone Arledge Broadcast Lab, a state-of-the-art facility with up-to-date nonlinear video editing, audio editing, and computer labs, is the backbone of the School's physical plant. Students also do their own research on LexisNexis, Dow Jones News/Retrieval, and Bloomberg. The School, as part of a university community of 28,000 students and faculty members, has libraries with more than 6 million volumes and a computer center for academic research projects.

Financial Aid

All admissions decisions are need-blind. The Graduate School of Journalism offers approximately $3.5 million annually in fellowships and scholarships to students who demonstrate high academic achievement, financial need, and exceptional promise for leading careers in journalism. Through its Student Financial Planning Office, Columbia works with each student to ease the cost of attendance through a combination of scholarships and need-based programs, including grants and federal and private loans. Each year, about 95 percent of the graduate students are assisted through educational loans totaling more than $6 million. All applicants requiring financial aid must fill out a Journalism School Scholarship Aid Form. In addition to that form, all domestic applicants must fill out a FAFSA. Students should visit the Web site for details. Students in the part-time program may apply for student loans, provided they enroll for a minimum of 6 credits.

Cost of Study

In 2009–10, tuition and fees total $48,610 for the M.S. program and $43,948 for the M.A. and Ph.D. programs. Students in the part-time program pay on a per-point basis. The cost of a point in 2009–10 is $1430.

Living and Housing Costs

In 2009–10, rooms in graduate residence halls for single students range from $8000 to $18,000 per academic year, depending on the size of the apartment, the number of students sharing it, and whether it is furnished. Single rooms off campus start at approximately $900 per month; apartments, at $1100. Single-room rates at International House, which accommodates 500 graduate students, range from $7500 to $13,000 per academic year. Apartment rates at International House range from $1000 to $2000 per month. With travel and telephone expenses, the yearly cost of living for a single student usually ranges from $20,000 to $25,000.

Student Group

Students at the School represent a diverse range of interests and aspirations. There are currently 438 students enrolled—256 full-time M.S. students, 110 part-time M.S. students, 47 M.A. students, and 25 Ph.D. students.

Location

The students' laboratory is New York City—one of the world's great news and media centers, where students report, write, edit, photograph, and present the news.

The University and The School

Founded in 1754 as King's College, Columbia University in the city of New York is the fifth oldest institution of higher learning in the United States and today is one of the world's leading academic and research institutions. The School of Journalism opened in 1912 as an undergraduate institution but since 1935 has operated exclusively at the graduate level. The University awards the Pulitzer Prizes in Journalism and Letters while the Journalism School administers the Alfred I. duPont–Columbia University Awards in Broadcast Journalism, the Maria Moors Cabot Prizes for Latin American reporting, the National Magazine Awards, the John Chancellor Award, the John B. Oakes Award for Environmental Reporting, and the Lukas Book Project. The School also publishes the *Columbia Journalism Review.* The Saul and Janice Poliak Center for the Study of First Amendment Issues was established and endowed in 1983 and the George T. Delacorte Center for Magazine Journalism in 1985. The School's 9,451 alumni include scores of publishers, top-ranking editors, foreign correspondents, reporters, and broadcasters.

Applying

The School accepts majors in all disciplines. Emphasis is on academic excellence in a substantive course of study, initiative, curiosity, a passion for journalism, and professional promise. All M.S. applicants are required to take a writing test that helps the admission committee assess their breadth of knowledge and use of English. The GRE is required for the Ph.D. application but not for the M.S. or M.A. programs. Applications must be filed with the $100 application fee. Application deadlines can be found at the School's Web site (http://www.journalism.columbia.edu). Decisions are posted electronically on or before April 1. The School uses an online application only. Students may check the admission Web site for updates and the recruitment schedule.

All dual-degree applicants must submit an application to the appropriate school in addition to the journalism application.

Correspondence and Information

The Graduate School of Journalism
Columbia University
2950 Broadway, Room 203
New York, New York 10027
Phone: 212-854-8608
Fax: 212-854-2352
E-mail: admissions@jrn.columbia.edu
Web site: http://www.journalism.columbia.edu

Columbia University

THE FACULTY

Nicholas Lemann, Henry R. Luce Professor and Dean; B.A., Harvard. Former managing editor, the *Washington Monthly;* associate editor, executive editor, *Texas Monthly;* national staff reporter, the *Washington Post;* national correspondent, the *Atlantic Monthly;* staff writer, the *New Yorker;* author of several books, including *The Last Battle of the Civil War* (2006), *The Big Test: The Secret History of the American Meritocracy* (1999), and *The Promised Land: The Great Black Migration and How It Changed America* (1991).

Helen Benedict, Professor of Journalism; M.S., Berkeley. Reporter, *Weekly News* (London); managing editor, *New Wings;* reporter, the *Independent* and the *Gazette* (California); freelance writer; author, *The Lonely Soldier: The Private War of Women Serving in Iraq,* published a piece in March 2007 on the sexual assault of women soldiers, which won the James Aronson Award for Social Justice Journalism *(Salon)*. Her other nonfiction books include *Virgin or Vamp: How the Press Covers Sex Crimes* (1992), *Portraits in Print* (1991), and *Recovery: How to Survive Sexual Assault* (1985, 1994). Her novels include *The Opposite of Love* (2007), *The Sailor's Wife* (2000), *Bad Angel* (1996, 1997), and *A World Like This* (1990).

Ann Cooper, Professor of Professional Practice, Coordinator, Broadcast Program; B.S., Iowa State. Award-winning journalist and foreign correspondent with more than twenty-five years of radio and print reporting experience, including more than ten years as NPR's (first) Moscow bureau chief; former executive director, Committee to Protect Journalists; winner of a duPont-Columbia Award for Broadcast Journalism.

Sheila Coronel, Professor of Professional Practice and Director, Stabile Center for Investigative Journalism; M.S., London School of Economics. Former executive director, Philippine Center for Investigative Journalism; reporter, the *New York Times,* the *Guardian* (London), and the *Manila Chronicle;* author of more than a dozen books, including *The Rulemakers: How the Wealthy and Well-Born Dominate Congress* (2004), *The Memory of Dances* (2002), *Edsa 2: A Nation in Revolt* (2001), and *Coups, Cults and Cannibals* (a collection of reportage, 1993).

June Cross, Associate Professor; B.A., Harvard. Former fellow at Carnegie Mellon University's School of Urban and Public Affairs and the W.E.B. DuBois Institute for Afro-American Studies at Harvard; producer, *This Far by Faith,* a six-part PBS series on the African-American religious experience; reporter, PBS's *Frontline, CBS News,* and PBS's *MacNeil/Lehrer NewsHour.* Emmy Award winner for the *NewsHour* on the U.S. invasion of Grenada, 1983; and *Secret Daughter,* an autobiographical film, 1997; duPont–Columbia Award for Excellence in Broadcast Journalism, 1995. She is the author of a memoir, *Secret Daughter* (2006).

John Dinges, Associate Professor of Journalism; M.A., Stanford. Reporter, copy editor, the *Des Moines Register* and the *Tribune;* special correspondent, assistant editor (foreign desk), the *Washington Post;* editor and writer, World Bank's *Urban Edge;* foreign editor, managing editor for news, editorial director, National Public Radio; winner, Maria Moors Cabot Prize for excellence in Latin American reporting; juror, Alfred I. duPont–Columbia University Awards; author, *The Condor Years: How Pinochet and His Allies Brought Terrorism to Three Continents* (2004); editor and coauthor, *Sound Reporting* (1992); editor, *Independence and Integrity: A Guidebook for Public Radio Journalism* (1995), *Our Man in Panama: The Shrewd Rise and Brutal Fall of Manuel Noriega* (1990), and *Assassination on Embassy Row* (1980).

Thomas Edsall, Joseph Pulitzer II and Edith Pulitzer Moore Professor of Journalism; B.A., Boston University. Reporter, the *Washington Post;* correspondent, the *New Republic* and the *National Journal;* reported for the *Baltimore Sun* and the *Providence Journal.* Contributor to *American Prospect,* the *Atlantic Monthly, Civilization, Dissent, Harper's,* the *Nation,* the *New Republic,* the *New York Review of Books,* and *Washington Monthly.* TV and radio commentator for CNN, CSPAN, MSNBC, PBS, FOX, and NPR. Author *Building Red America* (2006); *Chain Reaction: The Impact of Race, Rights, and Taxes on American Politics* (2005); *Power and Money: Writing About Politics* (1988); and *The New Politics of Inequality* (1984).

Samuel G. Freedman, Professor of Journalism; B.A., Wisconsin. Reporter, Bridgewater (New Jersey) *Courier-News;* reporter, *Chicago Tribune's Suburban Trib;* reporter, the *New York Times;* contributor, *Rolling Stone, Salon,* and the *New York Times;* contributing correspondent, *PBS Religion & Ethics NewsWeekly;* member, *USA Today* Board of Contributors; adjunct professor of theater, Columbia University School of the Arts; winner, numerous literary awards; author, *Who She Was: My Search for My Mother's Life (2005); Jew vs. Jew: The Struggle for the Soul of American Jewry* (2000), *The Inheritance: How Three Families and America Moved from Roosevelt to Reagan and Beyond* (1996), *Upon This Rock: The Miracles of a Black Church* (1993), and *Small Victories: The Real World of a Teacher, Her Students and Their High School* (1990).

Howard French, Associate Professor of Journalism; B.A., Massachusetts Amherst. French-English translator in Abidjan, Ivory Coast in the early 1980s, taught English literature at the University of Ivory Coast. From 1990 to 2008, the *New York Times'* bureau chief for Central America and the Caribbean, West Africa, Japan and the Koreas, and China in Shanghai. Twice nominated for the Pulitzer Prize, recipient of two Overseas Press Club Awards, and the Grantham Environmental Award, among others. Author of *A Continent for the Taking: The Tragedy and Hope of Africa* (2004). His work has appeared in the *Nation;* the *New York Review of Books; Transition; Rolling Stone;* the *New York Times Magazine;* the *Chronicle of Higher Education;* the *Crisis* and *Travel and Leisure.* As a documentary photographer, his work *Disappearing Shanghai* has been displayed in Asia, Europe, and North America.

Todd Gitlin, Professor of Journalism and Sociology; Ph.D., Berkeley. Contributing writer, *Mother Jones;* winner, numerous literary awards; member, editorial board, *Dissent and the American Scholar;* author, *Letters to a Young Activist* (2003); *Media Unlimited: How the Torrent of Images and Sounds Overwhelms Our Lives* (2002); *Sacrifice* (1999); *The Twilight of Common Dreams: Why America Is Wracked by Culture Wars* (1995); *The Murder of Albert Einstein* (1992); *Watching Television* (editor, 1987); *The Sixties: Years of Hope, Days of Rage* (1987); *Inside Prime Time* (1983); *The Whole World Is Watching: Mass Media in the Making and Unmaking of the Left* (1981); *Busy Being Born* (1974); and *Uptown: Poor Whites in Chicago* (1970).

Ari L. Goldman, Professor of Journalism; M.S., Columbia. Reporter and religion correspondent, the *New York Times;* director, Scripps Howard Program in Religion, Journalism and the Spiritual Life; author, *Living a Year of Kaddish* (2003), *Being Jewish* (2000), and *The Search for God at Harvard* (1991).

David Hajdu, Associate Professor of Journalism. Columnist, the *New Republic;* contributor, the *Atlantic Monthly,* the *New Yorker,* the *New York Review of Books,* the *New York Times Magazine,* and *Vanity Fair;* general editor, *Entertainment Weekly;* editor-at-large, New York Times Magazine Group; editor-in-chief, *Video Review.* Author of several books, including *The Ten-Cent Plague: The Great Comic-Book Scare and How It Changed America* (2008); *Positively 4th Street: The Lives and Times of Joan Baez, Bob Dylan, Mimi Baez Farina and Richard Farina* (2001); and *Lush Life: A Biography of Billy Strayhorn* (1996); the last two were finalists for the National Book Critics Circle Award.

LynNell Hancock, Associate Professor of Journalism; M.A., M.S., Columbia. Former assistant editor, Pantheon Books; freelance writer; staff writer, the *Village Voice;* education reporter, the *Daily News* (New York); education editor, *Newsweek;* former director, Prudential Fellowship for Children and the News; National Advisory Board member, Journalism Fellowships in Child and Family Policy; steering committee member, Institute for Child and Family Policy, Columbia University; contributor, *The Public Assault on America's Children: Poverty, Violence and Juvenile Injustice;* author, *Prairie Fires* (2007) and *Hands to Work: The Stories of Three Families Racing the Welfare Clock* (2002).

Marguerite Holloway, Assistant Professor and Director, Science and Environmental Journalism; M.S., Columbia. Codirector of the dual-degree earth and environmental sciences journalism program; contributing editor, *Scientific American;* reporter, *Medical Tribune;* freelance writer, the *Village Voice, Mother Jones, Discover,* the *New York Times, Natural History,* and *Wired.*

Stephen D. Isaacs, Professor of Journalism; B.A., Harvard. Reporter and editor, *Louisville Times* (Kentucky); reporter, the *Economist,* the *Guardian;* copy editor, reporter, city editor, metropolitan editor, Sunday magazine editor, New York bureau chief, national correspondent, the *Washington Post;* director, *Los Angeles Times/Washington Post* News Service; editor and senior vice president, the *Minneapolis Star;* producer, CBS News; producer and consultant, David Hartman; chairman, Private Network Productions; author, *Jews and American Politics* (1974).

Michael Janeway, Professor of Journalism and the Arts; B.A., Harvard. Reporter, *Newsday* and *Newsweek;* associate editor, *New Leader Magazine;* assistant editor, associate editor, managing editor, executive editor, the *Atlantic Monthly;* special assistant to Secretary of State Cyrus Vance; assistant managing editor, managing editor, editor in chief, the *Boston Globe;* executive editor, Trade and Reference Division, Houghton Mifflin Co.; author, *Republic of Denial: Press, Politics, and Public Life* (1999); coeditor, contributor, *A Story of Our Time: American Politics and the Press in an Era of Loss* (1999) and *Who We Are: An Atlantic Chronicle of the United States and Vietnam* (1968).

David A. Klatell, Professor of Professional Practice and Chair of International Studies; M.S., Boston University. Former news writer, producer, executive producer, WCVB-TV (Boston); senior producer, White House television pool; international station development, *New York Times* Television; consultant, international television news network development, Sweden and Portugal; former chair of the jury, Alfred I. duPont–Columbia University Awards in Broadcast Journalism; associate editor, *Encyclopedia of International Media and Communication;* contributor to the *Washington Post Sunday Magazine* and the *New York Times;* coauthor, *Inside Big-Time Sports* (1996) and *Sports for Sale, Television Money and the Fans* (1988).

Dale Maharidge, Associate Professor. 1988 Nieman Fellow, Harvard. Reporter, the *Cleveland Plain Dealer* and the *Sacramento Bee;* contributor, *Rolling Stone, George,* the *Nation, Mother Jones,* and the *New York Times.* Author, *Journey to Nowhere: The Saga of the New Underclass* (1985), inspired Bruce Springsteen to write two songs. *And Their Children After Them* (1989), won the Pulitzer Prize for nonfiction in 1990. Other books include *Denison, Iowa: Searching for the Soul of America Through the Secrets of a Midwest Town* (2005); *Homeland* (2004); *The Coming White Minority: California, Multiculturalism & the Nation's Future* (1996, 1999); *The Last Great American Hobo* (1993); and *Yosemite: A Landscape of Life* (1990).

Sylvia Nasar, John S. and James L. Knight Professor of Business Journalism; M.A., NYU. Research scientist, the Institute for Economic Analysis (1977–80); economist, Scientists Institute for Public Information and Control Data Corporation (1981–82); writer, *Fortune* magazine (1983–89); columnist, *U.S. News & World Report* (1990); reporter, the *New York Times* (1991–99); judge, National Book Award and Overseas Press Club Journalism Awards; author, *A Beautiful Mind,* winner of the 1998 National Book Critics Circle Award for Biography and finalist, Pulitzer Prize for Biography.

Victor Navasky, Delacorte Professor of Journalism and Director of the George Delacorte Center for Magazine Journalism; LL.B., Yale. Founder, editor, publisher, *Monocle;* editor, the *New York Times Magazine;* columnist, the *New York Times Book Review;* editor, publisher, editorial director, the *Nation;* author, *A Matter of Opinion* (which won the George Polk Book Award in 2005), *Naming Names* (which won a national Book Award in 1982), and *Kennedy Justice* (1971).

Mirta Ojito, Assistant Professor; M.A., Columbia. Reporter, the *Miami Herald, El Nuevo Herald,* and the *New York Times;* shared Pulitzer Prize for national reporting (2001) and received the American Society of Newspaper Editors' writing award for best foreign reporting (1999); author, *Finding Mañana: A Memoir of a Cuban Exodus* (2005).

Addie Rimmer, Associate Professor of Professional Practice; M.S., Columbia. Reporter, National News Council; Commodity News Services; copy editor, the *Miami Herald* and the *Wall Street Journal;* assistant managing editor, deputy features editor, *Press-Telegram* (Long Beach, California); editor and vice president, the *News* (Boca Raton, Florida); executive editor and vice president, *Daily Camera;* deputy managing editor/news, *Detroit Free Press.*

Michael Schudson, Professor of Journalism; Ph.D., Harvard. Author, *Why Democracies Need an Unlovable Press* (2008); *The Sociology of News* (2003); *The Good Citizen: A History of American CIVIC Life* (1998); *The Power of News* (1995); *Advertising, the Uneasy Persuasion* (1985); *Discovering the News: A Social History of American Newspapers (1978);* books concerning the history and sociology of the American news media, advertising, popular culture, Watergate, and cultural memory; former Guggenheim fellow; resident fellow at the Center for Advanced Study in the Behavioral Sciences, Palo Alto; and a MacArthur Foundation "genius" fellow. In 2004, he received the Murray Edelman distinguished career award from the political communication section of the American Political Science Association and the International Communication Association. Schudson's articles have appeared in *Columbia Journalism Review, Wilson Quarterly,* and the *American Prospect,* and he has published op-eds in the *New York Times, Washington Post, Los Angeles Times, Newsday,* the *Financial Times,* and the *San Diego Union.*

Michael Shapiro, Assistant Professor of Journalism; M.A., Missouri. Former reporter, Bridgewater (New Jersey) *Courier-News* and *Chicago Tribune's Suburban Trib;* associate editor, *Collector-Investor;* contributor to the *New York Times Magazine,* the *New Yorker, Esquire, Sports Illustrated, New York,* and the *Wall Street Journal;* author, *Bottom of the Ninth: Branch Rickey, Casey Stengel, and the Daring Scheme to Save Baseball From Itself;* (2009); *Solomon's Sword* (1999); *Who Will Teach for America?* (1993); *The Shadow in the Sun: A Korean Year of Love and Sorrow* (1990); and *Japan: In the Land of the Brokenhearted* (1989).

Alisa Solomon, Associate Professor and Director, Arts & Culture, M.A. Program; Ph.D., Yale. Staff writer at the *Village Voice;* contributor, the *Nation,* the *Forward,* and the *New York Times;* contributor of theater commentaries, WNYC; contributing editor, *Beyond the Pale: Radical Jewish Culture and Politics* (WBAI); author, *Re-dressing the Canon: Essays on Theatre and Gender* (1997); editor of three anthologies: *Wrestling with Zion: Progressive Jewish-American Responses to the Israeli-Palestinian Conflict* (with Tony Kushner), *Theater and Social Change* (Theater, 31:3), and *The Queerest Art: Essays on Lesbian and Gay Theater* (with Framji Minwalla).

Sreenath Sreenivasan, Professor of Professional Practice and Dean of Student Affairs; M.S., Columbia. Directs the digital media department at the School; worked as a journalist in India and Fiji; writes for the *New York Times, Popular Science, Time Digital,* and *BusinessWeek;* cofounder, the South Asian Journalists Association; founding administrator, Online Journalism Awards; technology reporter on air, WNBC, New York; formerly on-air technology reporter, WABC, New York.

James B. Stewart, Bloomberg Professor of Business and Economic Journalism; J.D., Harvard. Associate, Cravath, Swaine & Moore; reporter, executive editor, *American Lawyer;* reporter, *Page One;* editor, the *Wall Street Journal;* contributor, the *New Yorker;* editor at large, *Smart Money;* winner, Pulitzer Prize for explanatory journalism (1988); author, *DisneyWar* (2005), *Follow the Story* (1998), *Blood Sport* (1996), *Den of Thieves* (1991), *The Prosecutors* (1987), and *The Partners* (1984).

Alexander Stille, San Paolo Professor of International Journalism; M.S., Columbia. Contributor, the *New York Times, La Republica,* the *New Yorker,* the *New York Review of Books,* the *New York Times Magazine,* the *Atlantic Monthly,* and the *New Republic;* correspondent, *U.S. News & World Report,* the *Boston Globe,* and the *Toronto Globe and Mail;* winner of numerous literary awards; awarded a Guggenheim Foundation Fellowship in 2008; author, *The Sack of Rome: How a Beautiful European Country with a Fabled History and a Storied Culture Was Taken Over by a Man Named Silvio Berlusconi* (2006), *The Future of the Past* (2002), *Excellent Cadavers: The Mafia and the Death of the First Italian Republic* (1995), and *Benevolence and Betrayal: Five Italian Jewish Families Under Fascism* (1991).

Duy Lin Tu, Assistant Professor of Professional Practice and New Media Coordinator; M.S. Columbia. Co-founder and creative director, Resolution Seven, a commercial documentary and DVD studio; worked at ABC News, London and with MTV, CBS News, and the Food Network.

Richard Wald, Fred Friendly Professor of Journalism. Former vice president, ABC News; worked for the *Herald Tribune,* the *Washington Post,* NBC News, and the *Times-Mirror* (Los Angeles).

Jonathan Weiner, Professor of Journalism; M.A., Harvard. Writes for the *New Yorker,* the *New York Times Magazine,* and the *New Republic;* author, *His Brother's Keeper: A Story from the Edge of Medicine* (2004), chosen as one of the most notable books of the year by the *New York Times; Time, Love, Memory: A Great Biologist and His Quest for the Origins of Behavior* (1999), winner of the National Book Critics Circle Award; and *The Beak of the Finch* (1994), winner of the Pulitzer Prize for Nonfiction. In 2000 and 2001, he served as Rockefeller University's first Writer in Residence; awarded a Guggenheim Foundation Fellowship in 2008.

Other Faculty Members

Josh M. Friedman, Rhoda Lipton, Laura Muha, Robin Reisig, Andie Tucher.

Professors Emeriti

W. Phillips Davison, Osborn Elliott, John Foster Jr., Kenneth Goldstein, Luther Jackson, Penn T. Kimball, Joan Konner, Melvin Mencher, Donald Shanor, Seymour Topping, Frederick T. C. Yu.

Visiting and Special Faculty Members

Floyd Abrams, Sig Gissler, Frank Moretti, Arlene Morgan, Terri Thompson, Betsy West.

Members of the Adjunct Faculty

A list of adjunct faculty members can be found at http://www.journalism.columbia.edu/faculty/.

CUNY GRADUATE SCHOOL OF JOURNALISM

Master of Arts in Journalism

Programs of Study

The Master of Arts degree in journalism at CUNY's Graduate School of Journalism is an intensive, full-time, three-semester program designed to prepare students for a career in journalism. Required courses in the first and second semesters provide a solid grounding in reporting and writing skills needed by all journalists. In the second semester, students select a media track—print (newspaper or magazine), broadcast (radio or TV), or interactive—in which they want to hone their skills. However, all students get a broad introduction to all media platforms, so they are prepared to work in the converged newsroom of the future. Students also choose a subject-matter concentration—arts/culture, business/economics, health/medicine, international reporting, or urban affairs—allowing them to practice deeper reporting skills that can be applied to any beat, even as they develop an expertise in one area. Beyond the core reporting and writing instruction, required courses in the 45-credit program include legal and ethical issues, research techniques, and fundamentals of interactive media. Students have some flexibility in tailoring their course of study to their particular interests and goals.

To graduate, each student must complete a capstone project, which may be a significant print piece, broadcast project, or major Web site package. Students also participate in an 8–10 week paid summer internship between their second and third semesters to give them experience in a working newsroom and to strengthen their resume.

Between the first and second semesters, the School offers optional enrichment seminars in its January Academy. Examples include a workshop on freelance writing, an introduction to sports reporting, or workshops in computer-assisted reporting or broadcast editing. The School's Web-based NYCity News Service provides the opportunity for all students to have their work distributed to professional media outlets for usage. Broadcast students also can have their work distributed through CUNY-TV, a 24-hour cable TV station that reaches 2 million viewers.

Classes are small and instruction is personalized. The faculty includes veteran journalists, including 3 Pulitzer prize winners, as well as professionals working in newsrooms across the city who have chosen to share their expertise with the next generation of journalists.

Research Facilities

The CUNY Graduate School of Journalism's new state-of-the-art facility includes an 80-seat wireless newsroom, digital television and radio studios, editing suites equipped with Final Cut Pro editing software, wireless classrooms that can reach out anywhere in the world, a lecture hall, student café, and student lounges. Students learn on the latest technology and are able to borrow a broad array of audio, video, and photography equipment to carry out their assignments.

A library/research center houses a collection of 2,000 volumes, more than 40 periodical titles, sixty electronic journals, and databases focused on journalism. All electronic material can be accessed by students at the School or at home over the Internet. Through CUNY's university-wide library resources, students and faculty members have access to another 4 million items. The Research Center offers students interlibrary loan privileges as well as research instruction.

Financial Aid

More than 80 percent of the students receive a tuition scholarship from the school, ranging from $1000 to $11,320 over three semesters. These need- and merit-based scholarships funded by supporters of the School include the Arthur "Punch" Sulzberger Scholarship, News Corporation Scholarship, Himan Brown Scholarship, Connie Chung and Maury Povich Scholarship, Daniel Schorr Scholarship, Julius Barnathan Scholarship, and the Irving Rosenthal Scholarship. Many of these scholarship funds provide assistance to multiple students in each academic year.

Approximately 75 percent of students have opted to take advantage of federal student loans to cover their living costs while at School. Many students also qualify for federal work-study programs that pay students to work at the School while pursuing their degree. Many students continue to work while in School, but the School cautions against trying to work more than 12 hours per week.

To be considered for a need-based scholarship from the School of Journalism, students must submit the Application for Financial Assistance and the Free Application for Federal Student Aid (FAFSA) by February 1 (can be filed online). To qualify for federal loan funding, students are asked to complete the FAFSA by February 1.

Cost of Study

The tuition for New York State residents is $3200 per semester. Tuition for the entire three-semester program is $9600, plus fees of $1720, bringing the three-semester total for tuition and fees to $11,320.

The tuition for non–New York State residents is $500 per credit. Assuming 15 credits per semester, the tuition is $7500 per semester. Out-of-state residents who are U.S. citizens or permanent residents may qualify for in-state tuition in their third semester, if they become legal residents of New York State. If so, tuition for the entire three-semester program is $18,200 plus fees of $1720, bringing the three-semester total for tuition and fees to $19,920.

For international students, tuition for the entire three-semester program is $22,500, plus fees of $1720, bringing the three-semester total for tuition and fees to $24,220.

Living and Housing Costs

Estimated costs for room and board are about $8000 for an academic year. To minimize housing costs, many students live in the four boroughs outside Manhattan and share an apartment. Virtually all use public transportation. For those wishing to live in Manhattan, a number of rooms are reserved for graduate journalism students at the CUNY City College Towers dormitory. For more information, students should contact Chris Clarke at cclarke@capstonemail.com or by phone at 917-507-0055. That office can also provide information about other housing options and connect students interested in sharing housing.

Student Group

There are currently 49 students enrolled in the program; 42 percent are members of minority groups, and 68 percent are women. The average age is 26. Students come from a variety of backgrounds: from the journalism profession, from other professions, and straight from an undergraduate school. Although some had never written a journalistic article before, all demonstrated an ability to write and think, a deep curiosity about the world, and a strong interest in making journalism their profession.

Location

The CUNY Graduate School of Journalism is housed at 219 West 40th Street, a block from Times Square, in the former home of the legendary *New York Herald Tribune*. Located in the heart of the media capital of the world, the School is within a short walking distance of many of the nation's largest media companies. The new headquarters for *The New York Times* is next door.

The School and The University

The CUNY Graduate School of Journalism opened in August 2006 under the leadership of Stephen Shepard, who served as editor of *BusinessWeek* for more than twenty years. The School's Board of Advisors includes David Westin, president of ABC News; Richard Stengel, managing editor of *Time;* Mortimer Zuckerman, chairman and publisher of the *New York Daily News* and *U.S. News & World Report;* Mark Whitaker, senior vice president, NBC News; Norman Pearlstine, former editor of the *Wall Street Journal;* Rosanna Rosada, publisher of *El Diario/La Prensa;* Merrill Brown, former editor-in-chief of MSNBC.com and a new media consultant; Matthew Winkler, editor-in-chief of *Bloomberg News;* and Michael Oreskes, editor of the *International Herald Tribune*.

The Graduate School of Journalism operates under the aegis of the CUNY Graduate Center and is one of twenty institutions that comprise the City University of New York, the nation's largest urban university. The CUNY Graduate Center administers thirty doctoral and six master's programs as well as twenty-eight research institutes. The University's origins date back to 1847 to the Free Academy, which grew into City College. Throughout its history, the University has maintained a commitment to academic excellence and to providing access and opportunity to students from diverse ethnic and geographic backgrounds.

Applying

Applications are accepted for the fall semester only. A four-year undergraduate degree is required of all applicants, including international students. International applicants are defined as those who hold or intend to apply for a nonimmigrant visa. They must have the equivalent of a U.S. undergraduate degree and a minimum grade-point average of 3.0 (B) to be considered for admission. In addition to the Graduate Record Exam (GRE), all international applicants are required to take the Test of English as a Foreign Language (TOEFL), including its writing component, the TWE. The deadline for all applications is January 2. The School uses an online application that can be accessed on its Web site. Students may mail supporting application materials to Graduate School of Journalism, Office of Admissions, The Graduate Center, 365 Fifth Avenue, New York, New York 10016-4309.

Correspondence and Information

CUNY Graduate School of Journalism
219 West 40th Street
New York, New York 10018
Phone: 646-758-7700
E-mail: admissions@journalism.cuny.edu
Web site: http://www.journalism.cuny.edu

CUNY Graduate School of Journalism

THE FACULTY

Eric Alterman, Professor; Ph.D., Stanford. Senior fellow at the Center for American Progress; an award-winning author, widely published both in print and other media; writer of *The Nation*'s "Liberal Media" column and MSNBC.com's "Altercation" weblog.

Sarah Bartlett, Professor and Director of the Urban and Business Reporting Programs; M. Phil., Sussex (England). Editor-in-Chief of Oxygen Media; Assistant Managing Editor at *BusinessWeek;* former reporter at *Fortune* and *The New York Times;* author of two books; host of U$A Inc., a weekly show on finance on CUNY-TV.

Roslyn Bernstein, Professor; Ph.D., NYU. Founder of the journalism and business journalism programs at Baruch College; founder and publisher of *Dollars and $ense,* the Baruch College business review.

Jere Hester, Associate Professor and Director of NYCity News Service; B.A., NYU. City Editor of the *New York Daily News;* Editor-in-Chief, *Downtown Express.*

Ruth Hochberger, Editor in Residence; J.D., Boston College. Editor-in-Chief of the *New York Law Journal,* member of the New York Bar, criminal defense lawyer for the Legal Aid Society in Manhattan.

Lonnie Isabel, Associate Professor; B.A., Amherst. Deputy Managing Editor of *Newsday* responsible for supervising the national, foreign, state, Washington, health, and science staffs; Assistant Managing Editor and National Editor of *Newsday.*

Jeff Jarvis, Associate Professor and Director of the Interactive Media Program; B.A., Northwestern. Author of the Buzzmachine.com Web log; new-media columnist and consultant for *The Guardian* in London; President of Advance.net, the online arm of Advance Publications; creator and Managing Editor of *Entertainment Weekly;* critic and Development Editor *TV Guide;* Associate Publisher and Sunday Editor, *New York Daily News.*

Sandeep Junnarkar, Associate Professor; M.S., Columbia. Co-producer of Lives in Focus, a multimedia Web site that features stories on under-reported issues; New York Bureau Chief of CNET News.com; Web producer for New York Times on the Web; recognized by the Society of American Business Editors and Writers for online reporting.

Frederick Kaufman, Associate Professor; Ph.D., CUNY Graduate Center. Magazine journalist published in *The New York Times Sunday Magazine, The New York Times Sunday Book Review, New York Magazine, Harper's, The New Yorker, Gentleman's Quarterly, Interview, Spin, Spy, Aperture, Allure, Publisher's Weekly, The Village Voice Literary Supplement,* and other publications.

Glenn Lewis, Associate Professor; M.A., CUNY, City College. Magazine journalist published in *Publishers Weekly, Car & Driver, US, Seventeen, Family Weekly, Library Journal,* and the *Philadelphia Inquirer;* author of children's book series; co-founder of Book Smart, Inc.; expert commentator on media for Channel 5 News.

Trudy Lieberman, Director of Health/Medicine Reporting Program; B.A., Kansas. Director of the Center for Consumer Health Choices at Consumers Union, contributing editor to the *Columbia Journalism Review* and *The Nation,* consumer writer at the *Detroit Free Press,* author of five nonfiction books.

Anthony Mancini, Professor; B.A., Fordham. Widely published writer of fiction and nonfiction; began journalism career at the *New York Post;* contributed articles to numerous newspapers and magazines, including *The New York Times,* the *Washington Post, New York,* and *Travel & Leisure;* author of seven novels.

Heath Meriwether, Distinguished Writing Coach; M.A., Harvard. Publisher and Executive Editor of the *Detroit Free Press;* Executive Editor, Managing Editor, and reporter for the *Miami Herald.*

Margot Mifflin, Assistant Professor and Interim Director of the Arts/Culture Program; M.A., NYU. Contributing editor at *Elle;* freelance writer on art, pop culture, books, and women's issues published in *The New York Times, Salon.com, The Village Voice, The New Yorker,* and several women's magazines; author of two nonfiction books.

Paul Moses, Professor; M.F.A., Massachusetts Amherst. City Editor at *Newsday*'s New York City edition; lead writer on a New York *Newsday* team that won the Pulitzer Prize for Spot News Reporting; winner of the Silurians' award for breaking news coverage in 1992; Brooklyn Editor, City Hall Bureau Chief, and National Religion Writer during seventeen years at *Newsday.*

Linda Prout, Professor and Director of the Broadcast Program; M.S., Columbia. Writer and producer for PBS and the Bravo Network; Station Director for Harlem Community Radio; producer of award-winning series for television and video including *The Kids' Chronicle* and *WomanSource;* reporter for several print publications including *Newsday, Newsweek,* and the *Star-Ledger.*

Geanne Rosenberg, Associate Professor; M.S., J.D., Columbia. Journalist specializing in coverage of legal, regulatory, and business issues; published in *Columbia Journalism Review, The New York Times, The National Law Journal, Editor and Publisher Magazine, Investor's Business Daily,* and many other newspapers and magazines.

Stephen B. Shepard, Professor and Dean of the Graduate School of Journalism; M.S., Columbia. Editor-in-Chief of *Business Week,* the largest business magazine in the world, for twenty years; Senior Editor for National Affairs at *Newsweek* and editor of the *Saturday Review;* co-founder and Director of Columbia University's Knight-Bagehot Fellowship in Economic and Business Journalism.

Bernard Stein, Professor; B.A., Columbia. Editor and co-publisher of the *Riverdale Press,* an award-winning weekly community newspaper in the Bronx that has won more than 300 state and national awards for excellence; winner of the Pulitzer Prize for editorial writing in 1998.

Steven Strasser, Associate Professor; M.A., Columbia. Managing Editor, National Affairs Editor and senior writer for *Newsweek International;* Moscow Correspondent, Hong Kong Bureau Chief, and Asia Editor for *Newsweek;* recipient of three Overseas Press Club awards; editor of three nonfiction books.

Wayne Svoboda, Associate Professor and Director of the Print Program; M.S., Columbia; M.S., London School of Economics. East Coast Correspondent for *Time* magazine; Africa Editor at *The Economist;* freelance reporter for publications including the *Wall Street Journal* and *Institutional Investor;* Fulbright Scholar who has taught in Russia and the Czech Republic.

Judith Watson, Associate Professor and Associate Dean; B.A., Pomona. New York Bureau Chief of United Press International; New York State Editor and Albany Capitol Bureau Chief, UPI; Director, *Hoosier in Washington* news service; reporter for *The Frankfort Times.*

Scotti Williston, Senior Producer in Residence. Reporter for WPIX-TV, NY; TV producer in the U.S., Europe, the Middle East, Africa, Russia, and China; Cairo Bureau Chief and Rome Bureau Chief for CBS News; producer for CBS Sunday Morning; independent producer and consultant for NBC News, National Hellenic Radio (NYC), and WNET/PBS (NYC).

Adjunct Faculty

Rose Marie Arce, senior producer for CNN.

Michael Arena, former investigative reporter for *Newsday* who shared the Pulitzer Prize for Spot News reporting.

Russell Chun, freelance art and multimedia developer.

Greg David, Editor-in-Chief, *Crain's New York Business.*

David Diaz, veteran TV correspondent for WCBS and WNBC TV.

James Estrin, senior staff photographer for *The New York Times.*

Beth Fertig, senior reporter for WNYC radio.

George Freeman, Vice President and Assistant General Counsel for *The New York Times.*

Timothy Harper, freelance writer and editor with extensive reporting experience around the globe.

Jennifer Johnson Hicks, assistant news editor at The Wall Street Journal Online who oversees breaking news and production for the Web site in the evenings.

Mona Houck, staff editor on the national desk for *The New York Times.*

Susan Kuhn, former associate editor at *Forbes.*

Andrew W. Lehren, reporter at *The New York Times* specializing in computer-assisted reporting.

Rebecca Leung, former freelancer at the *Los Angeles Times* and former producer for CBS News, TheStreet.com, ABC News, and CNET.

Robert B. Levine, freelance journalist who covers music and pop culture for *The New York Times, Fortune,* and many other publications.

David Lewis, president of a documentary production company, former associate producer for *60 Minutes.*

Anne Mintz, Director of Knowledge Management at *Forbes.*

Alan Mirabella, senior editor at Bloomberg News in New York.

Barbara Oliver, Director of News Research for *The New York Times.*

Ivan Oransky, Deputy Editor of *The Scientist: Magazine of the Life Sciences.*

Eric Owles, senior online producer for *The New York Times.*

Tina Pamintuan, media producer and freelance writer, former NPR producer.

Garry Pierre-Pierre, editor and publisher of the *Haitian Times.*

Barbara Raab, senior writer and producer for NBC News.

Laura Sanders, reporter and senior editor at *Forbes* for twenty years.

John Schiumo, host of "The Call" for NY1.

Jan Simpson, former assistant managing editor at *Time* magazine in the Society/Life section.

Jack Styczynski, freelance sports feature writer and researcher for NBC News, *The New York Times,* and *People* magazine.

John Smock, photojournalist for SIPA, a photo agency with offices in New York and in Paris, and the Associated Press.

Indrani Sen, freelance magazine writer, former reporter for *Newsday.*

Dody Tsiantar, freelance magazine writer, veteran reporter for *Time.*

Rob Williams, reporter for *The Star-Ledger,* covering seven communities in Morris County and writing about development, the immigration debate, and related topics.

HAWAI'I PACIFIC UNIVERSITY

College of Communication

Program of Study

The Master of Arts in communication program (M.A./COM) provides students with an interdisciplinary approach integrating skills, theory, and knowledge. Students completing this Hawai'i Pacific University (HPU) program are prepared for careers ranging across the spectrum of business, marketing, advertising, mass media, public relations, entertainment, broadcast or print journalism, the Internet, or education. Technology is emphasized in each course so that graduates are prepared for rapid change in communication industries.

The M.A./COM requires a minimum of 39 semester hours of graduate work composed of 18 semester hours of core courses, 15 semester hours of electives, and 6 semester hours of writing a professional paper, project, or thesis. Assignments and internships use a pragmatic approach to develop marketable skills. Students apply what they learn in the classroom to actual problems faced by organizations and businesses.

Research Facilities

To support graduate studies, HPU's Meader and Atherton Libraries hold over 110,000 bound volumes, 350,000 microfiche items, and periodical subscriptions to 1,500 print titles and 30,000 electronic journals. Databases of public and state university libraries, legislative information, and business-oriented statistical data are also available in the library or online. Students can access HPU's library databases, course information, their academic information, and an e-mail account through Pipeline, the university's internal Web site for students. The University's accessible on-campus computer center houses more than 100 computers with specialized software to support graduate academic programs. HPU also provides free Wi-Fi so students can access Pipeline resources anywhere on campus using laptops. A significant number of online courses are available as well.

Financial Aid

The University participates in all federal financial aid programs designated for graduate students. These programs provide aid in the form of subsidized (need-based) and unsubsidized (non-need-based) Federal Stafford Student Loans. Through these loans, funds may be available to cover the student's entire cost of education. To apply for aid, students must submit the Free Application for Federal Student Aid (FAFSA) beginning January 1. Mailing of student award letters usually begins by the end of March. The University also offers several institutional scholarships and assistantships to new full-time, degree-seeking students. The Trustees' Scholar Program provides a 50 percent tuition waiver for two semesters; the Deans' Scholarship Program, a 20 percent tuition waiver for one semester; and the International Scholar Program, a 20 to 50 percent tuition waiver. Graduate assistantships, which give students a 50 percent tuition waiver for one semester, are also available. Priority consideration is given to those students who apply by the deadline.

Cost of Study

Tuition for graduate students enrolled in fall and spring semesters is determined on a per-credit basis; full-time status for a graduate student is 9 credits. Tuition for the optional winter and summer sessions is also determined on a per-credit basis. The estimated minimum funds needed for a nine-month academic year (September to May) based on 2009–10 school-year expenses is $25,739. For the 2009–10 academic year, full-time tuition is $11,880 for most graduate degree programs. Books, supplies, and transportation cost $1,885, and health insurance costs $880.

Living and Housing Costs

Most graduate students live in off-campus housing. The cost of living in off-campus apartments is approximately $11,094 for a double-occupancy room.

Student Group

University enrollment currently stands at more than 8,200. HPU is one of the most culturally diverse universities in America with students from all 50 U.S. states and more than 100 countries.

Location

Hawai'i Pacific University combines the excitement of an urban, downtown campus with the serenity of a residential campus and a pristine marine institute. The main campus is ideally located in downtown Honolulu, the business and financial center of the Pacific. Eight miles away, situated on 135 acres in Kaneohe, the windward Hawai'i Loa campus is the site of environmental sciences, marine biology, nursing, oceanography, and several liberal arts programs. The third campus, The Oceanic Institute, an affiliate of HPU, is an applied aquaculture research facility located on a 56-acre site at Makapu'u Point on the windward coast of Oahu, Hawaii. Students can travel between the three sites using the convenient HPU shuttle service. There are also eight military campus programs located at Pearl Harbor, Barbers Point, Hickam Air Force Base, Schofield Barracks, Fort Shafter, Tripler Army Medical Center, Kaneohe Marine Corps Air Station, and Camp Smith.

The University

HPU is a private, nonprofit university with approximately 8,200 students. Founded in 1965, HPU prides itself on maintaining strong academic programs, small class sizes, individual attention to students, and a diverse faculty and student population. HPU is recognized as a "Best in the West" college by the *Princeton Review* and a "Best Buy" by *Barron's* business magazine. HPU offers more than fifty acclaimed undergraduate programs and twelve distinguished graduate programs. The University has a faculty of more than 500, a student-faculty ratio of 18:1, and an average class size of 20. A wide range of counseling and other student support services are available. There are more than seventy student organizations on campus, including the Graduate Student Organization.

Applying

Students must have a baccalaureate degree from an accredited college or university in the United States or an equivalent degree from another country. Applicants should complete and forward a graduate admissions application, send in the $50 nonrefundable application fee, have official transcripts sent from all colleges or universities previously attended, and forward two letters of recommendation. A personal statement about the applicant's academic and career goals is required; submitting a resume is optional. Applicants who have taken the Graduate Record Examination (GRE) should have their scores sent directly to the Graduate Admissions Office. International students should submit scores of a recognized English proficiency test such as TOEFL. Admissions decisions are made on a rolling basis, and applicants are notified between one and two weeks after all documents have been submitted. Applicants are encouraged to submit their applications online.

Correspondence and Information

Graduate Admissions
Hawai'i Pacific University
1164 Bishop Street, #911
Honolulu, Hawaii 96813
Phone: 808-544-1135
    866-GRAD-HPU (toll-free)
Fax: 808-544-0280
E-mail: graduate@hpu.edu
Web site: http://www.hpu.edu/hpumacom

Hawai'i Pacific University

THE FACULTY

John N. Barnum, Associate Professor of Communication; Ph.D., Texas at Austin.
Peter Britos, Associate Professor of Communication; Ph.D., USC.
Dale Burke, Instructor of Communication; D.Min., Ancilla Domini College.
Brian Cannon, Assistant Professor of Communication; Ph.D., Regent University (Virginia).
Katherine Clarke, Instructor of Communication; M.A., Denver.
Thomas Dowd, Instructor of Communication; M.A., California State, Northridge.
Steven Combs, Professor of Communication; Ph.D., USC.
Matthew George, Assistant Professor of Communication; Ph.D., Berkley.
John P. Hart, Professor of Communication; Ph.D., Kansas.
Serena Hashimoto, Associate Professor of Communication; Ph.D., European Graduate School (Switzerland).
Lowell Ing, Assistant Professor of Communication; M.F.A., CUNY, City College.
Anne Kennedy, Assistant Professor of Communication; Ph.D., Bowling Green State.
Laurence LeDoux, Assistant Professor of Communication; D.A., Oregon.
Marianne Luken, Instructor of Communication; M.I.A., School for International Training.
Malia Smith, Instructor of Communication; M.A., Hawai'i Pacific.
Penny Pence Smith, Assistant Professor of Communication; Ph.D., North Carolina at Chapel Hill.
Lewis Trusty, Instructor of Communication; M.A., USC.
James D. Whitfield, Professor of Communication; Ed.D., Texas Tech.
John Windrow, Instructor of Journalism; M.A., Missouri–Columbia.
Yanjun Zhao, Assistant Professor of Organizational Change; Ph.D., Nebraska–Lincoln.

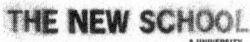

THE NEW SCHOOL: A UNIVERSITY

Department of Media Studies and Film
Master of Arts in Media Studies

Program of Study

The Master of Arts program in the Department of Media Studies and Film at The New School provides a theoretical and practical course of study for both filmmakers and those interested in exploring other types of media.

The program is highly individualized, and the curriculum includes production classes in video, audio, film, and multimedia technologies as well as academic seminars in communications theory. Students also have the option to complete their degree online through classes offered by The New School. Most students attend part-time and complete the degree in approximately three years. The thesis option requires 36 credits, and the nonthesis option requires 39 credits. In addition, the Department offers a 12-credit graduate certificate in media management; recently, it launched a one-year graduate certificate program in documentary media studies—the only one of its kind in New York City.

Media studies graduates use their degrees to enhance their current careers or build new ones in a broad spectrum of fields such as marketing, public relations, and nonprofit management. Many stay in the world of academia, pursuing Ph.D.'s or working as university professors. Still others work in creative fields as artists, filmmakers, designers, and more.

Research Facilities

The Raymond Fogelman Library at The New School contains books, standard references, pamphlets, and periodicals essential to the media studies program. Matriculated students may also use the Elmer Holmes Bobst Library at New York University and the Cooper Union Library, which are members, with The New School, of the Research Library Association of South Manhattan.

Students in the media studies program have access to Macintosh and PCs in the University Computing Center. They may also use the Knowledge Union multimedia lab, which offers state-of-the-art capabilities for multimedia production, including multimedia classrooms equipped for computer, video, and sound presentation; video and audio editing stations and suites; a large open lab with PowerMac, Windows, and Silicon Graphics workstations; and an equipment center. In addition, students often work with faculty members on research and production projects at off-campus sites throughout the New York metropolitan area.

Financial Aid

Nearly half of the full-time and part-time students in the media studies program receive financial aid, ranging from small awards to full scholarships. The Awards Committee considers both merit and need in granting available funds. The New School also offers an extended payment plan that involves monthly billing throughout the semester.

Cost of Study

Tuition for the 2009–10 academic year is $1124 per credit. A $100 University services fee, a $15 divisional fee, and a $5 student senate fee are charged each term. For more information, students should visit http://www.newschool.edu/tuition.

Living and Housing Costs

The University Housing Office maintains a comprehensive resource center with apartment listings. University apartments and residence halls are also available. The cost of housing, food, transportation, and living expenses averages $17,000 annually. More information is available online at http://www.newschool.edu/studentservices.

Student Group

Students in the media studies program are a diverse and creative group—a third come from outside the United States, a third are members of underrepresented groups, and more than half are women. Many students are already professionals and work in media-related jobs while attending the program.

Location

New York City is the communications capital of the world, and the media studies program takes full advantage of what the city has to offer. Broadcast television stations, cable operations, corporate communications facilities, and film, video, and audio production companies provide professional internship opportunities in research, and students also attend special events with media professionals each semester. In addition, students are encouraged to explore the numerous communications activities available only in New York City.

The School and The Department

Parsons is part of The New School, a leading university in New York City offering distinguished programs in design, liberal arts, the performing arts, and social and political science, leading to seventy graduate and undergraduate degrees. To learn more, students should visit http://www.newschool.edu/degreeprograms. A privately supported institution, The New School is accredited by the Commission on Higher Education of the Middle States Association of Colleges and Schools and chartered as a university by the Regents of the State of New York.

The guiding mission of the Department of Media Studies and Film at The New School is to help students develop a critical understanding of the mediated culture in which we live and master the skills needed to produce media messages in a variety of forms and genres. Since it was established at The New School in 1975, the program has been committed to strengthening the connection between media theory and practice. Today, in a world defined by rapidly changing information and communications technologies, it remains open to innovation and embraces all forms of media. The media studies program aims to prepare students for success in a competitive marketplace while educating them to be humane and thoughtful citizens in an increasingly mediated world. For more information about the program, prospective students should visit http://www.newschool.edu/mediastudies.

Applying

An applicant to the Media Studies program must hold a bachelor's degree from an accredited college or university. Applications from students in all academic disciplines are invited. A completed application, an application fee, a statement of purpose, official transcripts of all undergraduate and graduate studies, and one academic and one professional letter of recommendation should be submitted to the Media Studies Admissions Office by the stated application deadline. A personal interview may be required of all applicants. This interview may be waived or conducted by telephone under special circumstances. It is the responsibility of the applicant to ensure the receipt of admissions materials by the announced deadline. The application deadline for fall admission is February 15; the application deadline for spring admission is October 15.

To request a catalog and/or an application form, students should visit http://www.mediastudies.newschool.edu or contact the Office of Admissions.

Correspondence and Information

Office of Admissions
The New School
66 West 12th Street, Room 401
New York, New York 10011

Phone: 212-229-5630
E-mail: nsadmissions@newschool.edu
Web site: http://www.newschool.edu/mediastudies

The New School: A University

THE FACULTY

Core Faculty

Deirdre Boyle, M.A., Antioch (Ohio). Video historian, media critic, consultant, and programmer; author of *Subject to Change: Guerrilla Television Revisited, Video Preservation,* and *Video Classics.*

Paolo Carpignano, D.Lett., Rome. Author of *Crisis and Workers' Organization* and *The Formation of the Mass Worker in the USA* as well as numerous articles on international communications.

Sumita Chakravarty, Ph.D., Lucknow (India); Ph.D., Illinois at Urbana-Champaign. Author of *National Identity in Indian Popular Cinema;* articles in the *Quarterly Review of Film and Video, Cine-Tracts, South Asia Bulletin,* and *World Film Directors.*

Elizabeth Ellsworth, Ph.D., Wisconsin. Author of *Teaching Positions: Difference, Pedagogy, and the Power of Address;* architecture and media studies to address issues of time, space, and place in mediated learning environments.

Peter L. Haratonik, M.A., NYU. Acting chair, New School Department of Media Studies and Film; former director, Film/Video/Broadcasting, NYU; chair, Communication Arts Department; director, Television Institute, Hofstra University; past president of the Association of Communication Administration; author and consultant.

Jae Ho Kang, Ph.D., Cambridge. Former Alexander von Humboldt Research Fellow, Institute for Social Research at University of Frankfurt (Germany); social theory of media and mass culture, critical theory of art and technology; new media and political communications.

Lawrence (Kit) Laybourne, M.A., UCLA. A founder of the media studies program and head of animation and special projects at Oxygen Media; created the signature course, Foundations of Media Design.

Shannon Mattern, Ph.D., NYU. Author of *Public Places, Info Spaces: Creating the Modern Urban Library;* relationships between media and spatial theory and practice.

Diane Mitchell, M.F.A., Michigan State. Multimedia producer and designer; artist; awards include NEA, NYSCA, and NYCH grants and industry awards in multimedia production for Fortune 500 companies and the United Nations.

Vlad Nikolic, M.A., New School. Award-winning filmmaker and director for film and TV; films include *The End of the Millennium, Cut, Serendipity,* and the feature documentary *The City.*

Raphael Parra, B.A., CUNY, Hunter. Laureate, University of the Andes (Venezuela); professional AVID editor; owner and senior editor at Timeline Film and Video, a postproduction facility.

Paul Ryan, B.A., NYU. Author of articles in *Leonardo, Afterimage, Millennium, Terra Nova,* and *Semiotica,* among others; author of *Cybernetics of the Sacred* and *Video Mind, Earth Mind;* video art shown internationally and at the Museum of Modern Art.

Barry Salmon, M.A., New School. Composer of scores for numerous films as well as music for dance, theater, radio, and video art; performing and recording guitarist and record and CD producer.

Part-Time Faculty

For a current listing of courses and part-time faculty members, students should visit the Department's Web site at http://www.newschool.edu/mediastudies.

POINT PARK UNIVERSITY

Master of Arts in Journalism and Mass Communication

Program of Study

The graduate program in journalism and mass communication at Point Park University leads to the Master of Arts (M.A.) degree. The program admits students with a variety of undergraduate and professional backgrounds. The Point Park M.A. program, with opportunities such as working with the Innocence Institute of Western Pennsylvania and a news service tied to the *Pittsburgh Tribune-Review,* is exceptionally well designed for professionals already working, and planning to continue to work, for mass communication employers. Other admitted students plan to enter a doctoral program, or a mass communication profession for the first time.

Full-time students may easily complete the program within two calendar years, and extraordinarily motivated students may complete the program in one calendar year. Courses are offered during three semesters: fall, spring, and summer. Part-time students, who traditionally compose the bulk of the graduate student body, may complete the program within three years. Writing a master's thesis is optional but highly recommended for students planning to pursue any doctoral degree.

The 36-credit program includes a core of four courses; up to three may be waived, based on courses in previous undergraduate programs, and/or relevant work experience, and replaced with electives. At least one course taken outside the School of Communication in a related area is required. Two courses are for independent student research, including a thesis option. All students will complete six to nine electives that allow a student to design their own significant concentrations in public relations, print journalism, television broadcasting (in a state-of-the-art TV studio and control room), and/or advertising. Students may petition for up to 9 credits (three courses) of graduate work at another institution to be accepted as transfer credits.

Research Facilities

The University's library is located in the University Center, a gloriously renovated historic building. The combined holdings number about 125,000 monographs, 16,640 periodical subscriptions, 37 online databases, 650 audio and videocassettes, and a total microform count of 20,000 volumes. The online catalog, wireless Internet access, and printers are available throughout the building.

Students are able to borrow material not held within the system and have it delivered to the University Center through the various interlibrary loan programs.

The library's journalism and mass communication collection, which is the most extensive in western Pennsylvania and the second largest in the state, exceeds those of most research universities in Pennsylvania and other states.

Financial Aid

Students may apply for financial aid, which is granted on the basis of need, and for various state and federal loans. International applicants may seek loans and scholarships from a number of home-country and international agencies.

The School of Communication offers five graduate assistantships, including one working with the international scholarly journal *Journalism & Mass Communication Educator.* The assistant must be a full-time student in the program and be able to work in the School of Communication a minimum of 20 hours per week during fall and spring semesters.

Cost of Study

Tuition and fees for 2008–09 were $660 per credit. The cost of books and supplies averaged $350 per term.

Living and Housing Costs

Housing is available in the University's residence halls. The cost in 2008–09 was typically $4500 per term. Apartments are available to students within a short travel distance on Pittsburgh's effective mass transit system. A variety of meal plans are available at the campus student cafeteria.

Student Group

Enrollment in the graduate program in fall 2008 was nearly 90. Many were full-time. Most were employed full-time in the communications industry or elsewhere. Generally, a small contingent of international students adds an exciting multicultural flavor to the classes, which seldom exceed 15 students. For example, during 2008–09, the program hosted Fulbright students from Iraq and Russia, and other international students from countries such as Kenya and India.

Location

Pittsburgh is the nation's thirteenth-largest metropolitan area. In 2007, it was named the most livable city in the United States separately by *The Economist* magazine and by the *Places Rated Almanac* (Rand McNally method). Newspapers, radio and TV stations, and public relations and advertising agencies are within easy walking distance of the campus. The location is excellent for challenging graduate-level internships. Frequent association with professionals in the classroom, internships, part-time jobs, and freelancing often leads to full-time employment immediately after graduation.

The University

Point Park University is located in the Golden Triangle of downtown Pittsburgh. Founded in 1960, it has grown from a small business school to a four-year institution with graduate programs in journalism and mass communication, curriculum and instruction, engineering management, business administration, educational administration, criminal justice administration, acting/theater, and organizational leadership. It is accredited by the Middle States Association of Colleges and Schools and is a member of the Pittsburgh Council on Higher Education.

Applying

Applicants for the M.A. program must take the GRE if their undergraduate GPA falls below 2.75 overall and/or under 3.0 in their undergraduate major. Those whose first language is not English must take the TOEFL and the TWE. Students may be admitted for the fall, spring, or summer term.

Correspondence and Information

Point Park University
201 Wood Street
Pittsburgh, Pennsylvania 15222-1984
Phone: 412-392-3808
      800-321-0129 (toll-free)
Fax: 412-392-6164
E-mail: ptenroll@pointpark.edu
Web site: http://www.pointpark.edu

Point Park University

THE FACULTY

In addition to the full-time faculty members listed below, the program utilizes qualified professionals who represent organizations engaged in the mass communication concentrations of the M.A. program.

Dane S. Claussen, Director; Ph.D., Georgia.
David J. Fabilli, M.A., Youngstown State.
Helen M. Fallon, M.A., Duquesne.
Heather Starr Fiedler, Ph.D., Nova Southeastern.
Jan Getz, M.A., Miami (Ohio).
Steven Hallock, Ph.D., Ohio.
Anthony J. Moretti, Ph.D., Ohio.
William R. "Bill" Moushey Jr., M.S., Point Park.
Robert O'Gara, M.L.S., Duquesne.
Christopher Rolinson, M.A., Point Park.
Johan Yssel, Ph.D., South Africa.

QUINNIPIAC UNIVERSITY
School of Communications

Programs of Study	The Quinnipiac University School of Communications offers 36-credit Master of Science degree programs in journalism, interactive communications, and public relations. The Graduate Journalism Program prepares students for careers as reporters and editors in print, broadcast, and interactive journalism. Through a balance of courses in both beginning and advanced reportorial skills and analysis of the role of the media, students learn how to report, produce, and analyze news. The program welcomes both qualified students who do not have journalism experience and working journalists who want to upgrade or polish existing skills.
	The Graduate Program in Interactive Communications is based on the study of interactivity and the practical techniques of creating, distributing, and managing information and ideas for interactive news, strategic communications, entertainment, and information services. Through a balance of courses in digital media, content development, and analysis, students learn how to plan and create content and to think strategically across media platforms. Students who successfully complete the program are positioned to find career enhancement and fulfillment as content producers and content managers in the interactive space for companies and institutions.
	The Graduate Program in Public Relations offers students the opportunity to pursue an advanced degree in a highly competitive and growing field. The program is designed for early- to mid-career professionals interested in advancing their careers in public relations and/or transitioning into public relations from complementary fields such as finance, law, health care, technology, human resources, journalism, and marketing. Graduates of the program will be qualified to work as public relations specialists in both the public sector and private sector with expertise and skills applicable to corporate, non-profit, and government institutions. Students will study the conceptual and theoretical foundations of public relations, learn how to conduct and analyze public relations research and evaluation, and hone their skills in contemporary public relations practices and techniques. The program stresses professional competence, global consciousness, and professional and social responsibility.
	To receive the M.S. degree, students must complete 36 credits with at least a 3.0 average. A 3-credit capstone masterwork experience is required. Students can meet this requirement in the form of a master's project—such as an investigative magazine piece or an interactive narrative presentation—or a thesis that advances knowledge of the field. In addition to traditional course work, students can enroll in an internship. Graduate students have held internships at global, regional, and local media companies, including Fox News, Subway, ESPN, and the Tribune Company.
Research Facilities	The Ed McMahon Mass Communications Center houses the media production facilities for the School of Communications. Exceeding even the current capability of many broadcast stations in the world, the School of Communications' fully digital, high-definition studio offers students training in state-of-the-art production. Not since the introduction of color television in the early 1960s has there been such a monumental change in the quality of television images. Quinnipiac stands at the leading edge of this development, as it is among the first schools in the United States to provide high-definition production capabilities for its students. Sony HDC 910 12-bit HD multiformat studio cameras output 1080i for dazzling resolution and detail. Standard definition is available when required. The fully digital signal path through a Sony MVS 8000A HD/SD production switcher featuring multiple channels of digital video effects preserves pristine picture quality. All video is recorded digitally; video and audio are recorded directly to high-capacity Grass Valley Group HD/SD video servers or, for those productions requiring tape, a new Sony HDWS-2000 HDCAM studio recorder. The studio floor is large (30 feet by 40 feet, with a 16-foot-high grid) and equipped with industry-standard Mole-Richardson lighting units, grip equipment, and ample accessories for any style production. In the field, students shoot digital video with a variety of cameras, including three-chip professional-grade units. A remote equipment room provides students with all the accessories, lighting equipment, and tools needed to produce broadcast-quality audio and video on remote. The center's digital postproduction facilities feature Apple's Final Cut Pro HD. For graphics and animation, a number of high-end applications such as Adobe After Effects, Photoshop, and Discreet Combustion, are available. The McMahon Center also offers an audio production studio loaded with Digidesign's industry-standard Pro Tools software. A wide range of tools for radio production and soundtrack design are available. In addition, a comfortable, twenty-six-seat theater-style screening room with high-quality video projection and five-channel surround sound is available for classes and workshops. Students also have access to a fully equipped computer lab for interactive media production for work both in and out of class. The News Technology Center features the Associated Press ENPS newsroom automation software.
Financial Aid	Several avenues are available to help both full- and part-time students fund their education. Students may be eligible for Federal Stafford Student Loans. Several students each year are awarded graduate assistantships that partially cover tuition. Graduate assistantships are available for full- and part-time students and are renewable.
Cost of Study	Tuition in 2009–10 is $770 per credit hour. In addition, part-time students pay a $30-per-credit student fee, and full-time students pay $315 per semester in student fees.
Living and Housing Costs	Privately owned housing is available near the campus. Students can contact the Office of Residential Life or visit the University's Web site for information about off-campus housing.
Student Group	The Graduate Journalism Program has an active enrollment of 60 full- and part-time students. Some have extensive work experience; others are entering the workforce. The Graduate Program in Interactive Communications has an active enrollment of 50 full- and part-time students. Applicants come from every region in the United States as well as from Canada, Mexico, and other countries. The Graduate Public Relations Program is new for 2009–10.
Location	Quinnipiac University is located on a beautiful campus in Hamden, Connecticut, a suburb of New Haven. It is approximately 30 minutes from Hartford, 1½ hours from New York City, and 2 hours from Boston.
The University and The School	Quinnipiac University is nationally recognized as one of the leading centers for higher learning in the Northeast and is consistently ranked among the best master's-level universities in the North in *U.S. News & World Report's Guide to America's Best Colleges*. All programs have integrated computer technology into academic and campus life, and Quinnipiac has been recognized in *Yahoo! Internet Life* for its achievements in technology. Quinnipiac was ranked ninth in *PC Magazine*'s 2007 Top Wired Colleges. The University enrolls about 6,800 students and offers a full range of undergraduate and graduate programs through the School of Health Sciences, the School of Communications, the School of Business, the College of Arts and Sciences, Quinnipiac Online, and the School of Law.
	Quinnipiac University's School of Communications is one of the most highly regarded centers in the Northeast for superior education in journalism and the diverse fields of communication and public relations. By closely integrating professional experiences with a faculty of experts and an outstanding facility, the School thoroughly prepares professionals for rewarding careers in communications.
Applying	Admission to the graduate communications programs is selective and based on undergraduate performance, experience in the field (either as a student or professional), and professional recommendations. Individuals who hold undergraduate degrees in communications, the liberal arts and humanities, computer sciences, graphic design, and other interdisciplinary and professional disciplines are welcome to apply. Students must submit the required application form, the application fee, all college/university transcripts, a resume, and two recommendations. Applicants to each program must submit a portfolio sample, such as an article, videotapes, or an undergraduate paper, and a personal statement. The GRE is required for the Graduate Public Relations Program only.
Correspondence and Information	Office of Graduate Admissions Quinnipiac University 275 Mount Carmel Avenue Hamden, Connecticut 06518 Phone: 203-582-8672 800-462-1944 (toll-free) Fax: 203-582-3443 E-mail: graduate@quinnipiac.edu Web site: http://www.quinnipiac.edu/graduatestudies

Quinnipiac University

THE FULL-TIME FACULTY

Lou Adler (M.S., Purdue; J.D., Quinnipiac) is an Associate Professor of Communications. He is a veteran radio and television broadcaster with many years in both on-air and administrative positions with CBS, WOR, and WINS Radio. He joined the staff of WCBS radio when it became an all-news operation and later was elevated to Director of News Operations and Programs for Newsradio-880. He specializes in teaching the techniques of broadcast radio/TV news writing. His publications include articles in *Mass Media and Society and the Communicator,* the journal of the Radio-Television News Directors Association.

Edward Alwood (Ph.D., North Carolina) is an Associate Professor of Journalism. His research specialty concentrates on journalism history, particularly the early Cold War era of the 1940s and 1950s, and news coverage of minorities. His Ph.D. dissertation focused on communists in the press and received the prestigious Nafziger-White Dissertation Award from the Association of Educators in Journalism and Mass Communication. He is the author of the 1996 book *Straight News: Gays, Lesbians, and the News Media.* He worked for fourteen years as a news reporter at several television outlets, including the Washington bureau of CNN.

Lisa M. Burns (M.A., Duquesne) is an Assistant Professor of Media Studies. Her research interests include political communication, gender and the media, and journalism history with a focus on First Ladies and the media. Most recently, she contributed a chapter titled "A Forgotten First Lady: A Rhetorical Reassessment of Ellen Axson Wilson" to *Inventing Their Voices: The Rhetoric of American First Ladies of the Twentieth Century.* A former journalist, Lisa worked as a reporter, producer, and anchor at WDUQ FM 90.5, an NPR affiliate, and KQV 1410 AM, an all-news station, both of which are located in Pittsburgh, Pennsylvania. She covered news and sports, winning several state Associated Press awards.

Margarita Diaz (M.A., New School) is an Assistant Professor of Journalism. She was one of the founding editors of *El Daily News,* the first fully bilingual English-Spanish daily newspaper in the United States. In the 1990s she was an entertainment editor and writer at the *New York Daily News,* where she focused on film, television, and popular music coverage. Diaz has taught journalism at Hunter College and film studies at Barnard College.

Kathy Fitzpatrick (J.D., SMU) is Professor and Director of Graduate Studies for the public relations program. She has more than twenty years experience as a public relations educator. Her research focuses on legal and ethical issues in public relations, crisis management, and public diplomacy.

Alexander M. C. Halavais (Ph.D., Washington, Seattle), Assistant Professor of Communications, is a social architect interested in ways of helping form a culture of creativity, freedom, and justice. He formerly directed a master's program in informatics at the University at Buffalo (SUNY) and was Research Director for the New Media Research Lab at the University of Washington. He has worked in marketing for a large financial services firm, designed simulations for NASA, and worked as a public school teacher in Japan and as a budget analyst and planner in city government. Alex has published articles and book chapters on the role of computing in social change, particularly in journalism, politics, education, and geography. He has also edited an anthology of writings on cyberpornography and society.

Rich Hanley (M.A., Wesleyan) is an Assistant Professor of Journalism and the Graduate Program Director of Journalism and Interactive Communications. A journalist and producer, writer, and director of documentaries and Web sites, Hanley has worked for more than twenty-five years in the media profession, including a stint at *Time* magazine. His views on current events, the Internet, and pop culture are frequently sought by global and national media. Hanley teaches primarily in the Interactive Communications Graduate Program.

Paul Janensch (M.S., Columbia) an Associate Professor of Communications, spent thirty years as a news professional before joining the Quinnipiac faculty. A top editor of several newspapers, he was president of the Associated Press Managing Editors and served as a Pulitzer Prize competition juror. He has covered crime in Chicago, civil-rights marches in the South, and the Congressional debate over Vietnam in Washington. He has also traveled to Russia and China as a newspaper consultant and media expert. He writes the weekly Professor News column about news media issues for the *Hartford Courant* and records a weekly commentary for the five stations of WNPR Connecticut Public Radio.

Sharon Kleinman (Ph.D., Cornell) is an Associate Professor of Communications and Chair of the Department of Media Studies and Public Relations. She studies the history and social implications of communication technologies, popular culture, and issues concerning online and real-life communities. Her publications include articles in the *Journal of American and Comparative Cultures, Science Communication,* the *Journal of Women and Minorities in Science and Engineering,* and the *Journal of Technology in Human Services* as well as numerous essays in edited books, including biographies of notable scientists and historical essays on communication technologies.

Alexander Laskin (Ph.D., Florida) is an Assistant Professor of Public Relations. His research focuses on investor relations and international communications. He also has experience in strategic marketing services and research methods.

Sean Patrick Lyons (M.S., Columbia) is an Assistant Professor of Communications and a member of the Department of Journalism and Media Production. He has worked as a reporter for the *Boston Globe,* the *Waterbury* (Connecticut) *Republican-American,* the *Palm Beach Post,* and the *Providence Journal.* He has won a Society of Professional Journalists national public service medal and the Livingston Award, among other national awards.

Phillip Simon (M.A.L.S., Wesleyan) is an Assistant Professor and Director of the Department of Communications and Interactive Communications Graduate Program. He has extensive experience at Yale University in program design for Web-based educational and training programs, Web design, Web application design, and media graphics. He also has experience in documentary and art-related video and audio production.

Hillary Fussell Sisco (M.S., Radford) is an Assistant Professor of Public Relations. Her research focuses on crisis communication within nonprofit organizations and the application of public relations theory.

Vicki Todd (Ed.D., Texas Tech) is an Assistant Professor of Public Relations. Her research focuses on public relations education assessment, pedagogy, and student writing skills. She also has experience in creating advertising campaigns.

Antoaneta Vanc (Ph.D., Tennessee, Knoxville) is an Assistant Professor of Public Relations. Her research focuses on international and intercultural public relations, public diplomacy, and international communications. She has experience in public relations and communications in the office of the President of Romania.

Kurt Wise (Ph.D., Maryland, College Park) is an Associate Professor of Public Relations. His research focuses on the relationship between health care organizations and their strategic publics. He also has significant experience in public relations in both the public and private business sector.

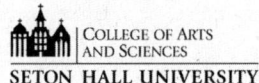

COLLEGE OF ARTS
AND SCIENCES
SETON HALL UNIVERSITY

SETON HALL UNIVERSITY

Department of Communication

Programs of Study

The Department of Communication offers three Master of Arts degrees—an onsite program in strategic communication, an online program in strategic communication and leadership, and another online program in corporate and professional communication. These programs of study are designed to serve the needs of the manager, executive, or professional communicator working in the public or private sector. Further details about the programs can be found at http://www.shu.edu/academics/artsci/graduate-communication-programs.cfm.

The **Master of Arts in Strategic Communication** (MASC) program offers students academically challenging courses that provide insight and practical strategies to help them succeed in the rapidly changing world. The program uniquely develops the critical skills of communication and leadership in ways that can be immediately applied in practice. Faculty members are experienced practitioners who bring extensive and diverse leadership experience to the classroom. Students are challenged to think creatively, apply state-of-the-art technology, and sharpen their leadership skills in a dynamic, small-classroom environment. The 36-credit program is designed to meet the professional needs of each student and can be completed in fifteen to twenty months. Courses are offered on a flexible evening, online, or weekend class schedule. The multidisciplinary program includes such topics as organizational communication, change management/management strategies, strategic communication and leadership, effective presentation skills, communication research, crisis management, group communication, cross-cultural communication, media relations, and public relations.

The **Master of Arts in Strategic Communication and Leadership** (MASCL) program has been designed to meet the needs of today's busy professional. Through a highly interactive online curriculum that allows for significant discussion of strategies and solutions to current issues in effective leadership and communication, the program provides an opportunity to network and study with colleagues and experts in specialized disciplines. Using state-of-the-art online learning technologies, this rigorous program is aimed at providing the high-potential individual with an opportunity to earn a Seton Hall University degree in a convenient cohort-based format. The MASCL requires 36 credits and takes twenty months to complete.

The **Master of Arts in Corporate and Professional Communication** (MACPC) has been designed for those students who want to improve their professional communication skills as well as those who want to improve their personal communication, leadership, critical thinking, and teaming skills. The program attracts a diverse group of students whose backgrounds in corporate, government, and nonprofit sectors in the United States and abroad contribute to the overall learning experience. Telecommunications, health care, entertainment, and pharmaceuticals are some of the many industries that are represented by students within the program. The 33-credit program is designed to meet the professional needs of each student. Courses are offered using an online modality, which allows students to pursue an advanced degree while working. The program can be completed in fifteen to twenty months.

Research Facilities

The Walsh Library, a state-of-the-art 155,000-square-foot building, houses 500,000 titles, 1,875 current periodicals, and an extensive collection of microform and other nonprint items that include videotapes, CD-ROM music, and other electronic media. Fahy Hall has twenty-eight classrooms, two TV studios, a Macintosh and IBM graphics lab, two classroom amphitheaters, and language and statistics labs. The recently redesigned McNulty Hall has well-equipped science labs. Completed in 1997, Jubilee Hall, a six-story facility with 126,000 square feet of academic space, features high-tech classrooms with computer and multimedia capabilities.

Financial Aid

Federal aid is available through fellowships, traineeships, and loans. The Office of Financial Aid, through the Educational Opportunity Office, offers Educational Opportunity Fund (EOF) grants to those who document eligibility. Direct federal student loans are also available through the Office of Financial Aid to students enrolled at least half-time.

A limited number of competitive graduate assistantships are available through the Department and through the University. Further details about financial aid and graduate assistantships are available at http://www.shu.edu/applying/graduate/grad-finaid.cfm.

Cost of Study

In 2009–10, tuition is $901 per credit. Full-time students pay $305 per semester in University and technology fees; part-time students pay $185.

Living and Housing Costs

Housing and living costs in South Orange and surrounding towns are comparable to most suburban cities, with studio and one-bedroom apartments renting for $750 to $1000 per month.

Student Group

Seton Hall University has about 4,500 graduate students. The Communication graduate programs attract a diverse group of students whose backgrounds in corporate, government, and nonprofit sectors in the United States and abroad contribute to the overall learning experience. Telecommunications, health care, entertainment, and pharmaceuticals are some of the many industries that are represented by students within the program.

Location

Seton Hall is located on 58 acres in the village of South Orange, New Jersey, a suburban residential area 14 miles southwest of New York City. The town center is a 10-minute walk from the campus and features bookstores, coffee shops, and restaurants. The heart of midtown Manhattan is just 30 minutes away by train. Known as the capital of finance, fashion, art, and entertainment, New York City offers the best of everything.

The University and The College

Founded in 1856, Seton Hall is a private coeducational Catholic institution—the nation's oldest diocesan institution of higher education in the United States. With a total enrollment of about 10,000, the University comprises nine colleges and schools. Seton Hall is accredited by the Middle States Association of Colleges and Schools. Through the incorporation of technology into the curriculum, the College of Arts and Sciences seeks to enhance and enliven the learning environment. Rooted in tradition yet looking to the future, the College offers a rich set of opportunities for intellectual discovery. Graduate students are guided by scholars and specialists toward the mastery of academic and professional areas.

Applying

Students must submit the completed application (available online at http://www.shu.edu/academics/artsci/apply-graduate.cfm), a $50 application fee, transcripts from all previously attended universities and colleges, GRE or MAT scores, three letters of recommendation, and a career goals essay/personal statement. Professionals with five or more years of work experience do not need to provide standardized test scores. The deadlines for fall and spring admission are July 1 and November 1, respectively. Applications are processed on a rolling basis.

Correspondence and Information

Dr. Richard Dool, Director
Graduate Communication Program
AS 222
Seton Hall University
400 South Orange Avenue
South Orange, New Jersey 07079

Phone: 973-761-9490
Fax: 973-761-9234
E-mail: communication@shu.edu
        doolrich@shu.edu
Web site: http://www.shu.edu/academics/artsci/graduate-
          communication-programs.cfm

Seton Hall University

THE FACULTY AND THEIR RESEARCH

Communication faculty members combine practical media experience with academic preparation. Each curricular area combines faculty members with impressive professional records and those with doctoral degrees for a blend of the academic and practical. With faculty members concentrating on specialized areas within the Department, students have the opportunity to work closely with their professors in laboratories and extracurricular programs and projects. This fosters one-to-one student-instructor contact, which is a hallmark of a communication education at Seton Hall.

Richard Dool, Assistant Professor; D.Mgt., Maryland. Dr. Dool has eighteen years of experience as a CEO of both public and private software firms and has managed companies in the United Kingdom, India, Australia, France, and Hong Kong. He is the author of *Enervative Change: The Impact of Change Management Initiatives on Job Satisfaction.* He has also authored articles related to online learning.

Patricia P. Kuchon, Professor; Ph.D., CUNY. For the past thirty-eight years, Dr. Kuchon has successfully served as a communication resource to students, corporate, and nonprofit agencies in the areas of gender communication, effective presentation skills, and the language of leadership. Her background in communication and psychology position her as an expert in personal and interpersonal communication effectiveness and diversity training. Dr. Kuchon is a licensed speech-language pathologist, holds a doctorate in communication sciences, and has been interviewed on a number of television and radio programs. Her professional experience includes working with Fortune 500 businesses, hospital and health-care systems, public and private schools, and hundreds of individuals including CEOs, physicians, politicians, sales persons, teachers, and television personalities who wish to become more effective speakers, leaders, and promoters of diversity in their workplaces.

Monsignor Dennis Mahon, Associate Professor; Ph.D., Syracuse. Msgr. Mahon served as Vice-Chancellor for Planning at Seton Hall from 1986 to 1995 and was the Vice President for Development at Catholic University of America from 1995 to 1997. In addition, Msgr. Mahon was the Executive Director of Catholic Community Services from 1997 to 2001 at Seton Hall.

Peter Reader, Associate Professor and Chair; M.F.A., Wisconsin–Madison. Theatrical design. Reader directs and designs plays for the Seton Hall Theatre. He has taught at Seton Hall since 1985.

Catherine Zizik, Associate Professor; M.F.A., George Washington. Speech and interpersonal communication. Zizik directs Seton Hall's award-winning forensics team.

Laura Iandiorio, Adjunct Professor; M.A., Rutgers. Professor Iandiorio is a copywriter and communications consultant, with close to twenty years of business writing experience that spans corporate, agency, nonprofit, and consultancy fields. Before starting Iandiorio Consulting, she worked in the communications departments for Dun & Bradstreet and the New Jersey State Bar Association. She specializes in business-to-business writing and serves as an adjunct professor for Seton Hall University and previously for Rutgers University.

Kenneth Mizrach, Adjunct Professor; M.A., Michigan. Professor Mizrach is a seasoned chief executive officer of the VA New Jersey Health Care System and has an impeccable track record as an organizational builder with strong leadership, strategic, and analytical skills.

SOUTHERN ILLINOIS UNIVERSITY CARBONDALE

College of Mass Communication and Media Arts
M.F.A. Program

Program of Study	The interdisciplinary Master of Fine Arts (M.F.A.) degree provides substantial advanced study for a small number of highly talented individuals. The program emphasizes the artistic development of the individual student and the creation of high-quality artistic works in photography, film, video, sound, new media, and interdisciplinary media. Course work in production, criticism, theory, history, and combined media studies emphasizes the interwoven character of traditional and contemporary approaches and technologies in the twenty-first-century.
Research Facilities	Southern Illinois University Carbondale has been designated as a New Media Center. State-of-the-art interactive multimedia labs, extensive facilities for audio, film, new media, photography, graphics, and video production, are available. Students have the opportunity to plan and organize the annual international Big Muddy Film Festival or Visiting Arts program. There are opportunities to work with WSIU Public Broadcasting, which operates two PBS-affiliated television stations and two NPR-affiliated FM radio stations. Students may also choose to become involved with the off-campus Big Muddy Independent Media Center, Carbondale's community radio station, and the town's emerging public access TV channel. The College also houses the Global Media Research Center, which brings together communication with other disciplines and draws in academic colleagues nationally and internationally, to study and evaluate global media operations and trends. The extensive holdings and wide array of bibliographic and instructional support services offered by Southern Illinois University Carbondale's Morris Library place it among the foremost research institutions. The library holds memberships in the Association of Research Libraries and the Center of Research Libraries in Chicago.
Financial Aid	Financial support that includes a stipend and a tuition waiver is available. The College provides three years of assistantship funding. A number of fellowship, assistantship, and scholarship opportunities, including those for traditionally underserved populations, are also available at the University level.
Cost of Study	In-state graduate tuition is $328 per credit hour in 2009–10. Out-of-state tuition is 2.5 times the in-state tuition rate ($820 per credit hour). Graduate students with at least a 25 percent appointment as a graduate assistant receive a tuition scholarship. Fees vary from $589.03 (1 credit hour) to $1557.50 (12 credit hours). Students with a graduate assistantship receive a 50 percent reduction in the primary care medical fee. New graduate students from Arkansas, Indiana, Kentucky, Missouri, and Tennessee qualify for the alternate tuition rate, which is equivalent to the in-state graduate tuition rate.
Living and Housing Costs	For married couples, students with families, and single graduate students, the University has 690 efficiency and one-, two-, three-, and four-bedroom apartments that rent for $499 to $720 per month in 2009–10. Residence halls for single graduate students are also available, as are accessible residence hall rooms and apartments for students with disabilities.
Student Group	In 2006–07, there were 25 graduate students in the College's M.F.A. program. The Graduate School has more than 3,644 students and 526 registered professional students.
Location	Carbondale is approximately 100 miles southeast of St. Louis, Missouri. Immediately south of Carbondale begins some of the most rugged and picturesque terrain in Illinois. Within 20 miles of the campus are two state parks and four recreational lakes, and much of the area is a part of the 240,000-acre Shawnee National Forest.
The University	Southern Illinois University Carbondale is a state-funded university founded in 1869. The Department of Cinema and Photography, the School of Journalism, and the Department of Radio-Television are in the College of Mass Communication and Media Arts, located in the Communications Building on the west side of the campus. WSIU Public Broadcasting provides hands-on experience for students.
Applying	Prospective students must present evidence of exceptional talent and/or potential in one or two media pursuits in the degree program and have a minimum GPA of 3.0. This evidence ordinarily consists of a portfolio of photographs or digitally generated art works, one or more films, videos, sound works, multimedia productions, Web art projects, or other evidence of artistic potential as well as a supporting letter of intent. A campus visit and interviews with faculty members are recommended, particularly for applicants with minimal course work in the field. Applications should be received at the Mass Communication and Media Arts graduate office by January 2 for admission consideration.
Correspondence and Information	Director of Graduate Studies College of Mass Communication and Media Arts Southern Illinois University Carbondale Carbondale, Illinois 62901-6606 Phone: 618-452-5120 Fax: 618-453-7714 E-mail: mcmagrad@siu.edu Web site: http://mcma.siu.edu

Southern Illinois University Carbondale

THE FACULTY AND THEIR INTERESTS

Department of Cinema and Photography

Lilly A. Boruszkowski, Associate Professor; M.F.A., Northwestern, 1979. Cinema production, postproduction sound, editing, documentary and experimental film.

Cade Bursell, Assistant Professor; M.F.A., San Francisco State, 2002. Cinema.

Susan Felleman, Associate Professor; Ph.D., CUNY Graduate Center, 1993. History and theory of film in relation to art, classical and contemporary Hollywood cinema, European "art" film, surrealism, psychoanalytic and feminist theory.

Sarah Kanouse, Assistant Professor; M.F.A., Illinois at Urbana-Champaign, 2004. Public space, media art, cultural geography, labor history, urban and rural relationships, art and activism.

Jyotsna Kapur, Associate Professor; Ph.D., Northwestern, 1998. Feminist and Marxist analysis of media, globalization, children's film and consumer culture, documentary and ethnographic film, the German and Japanese new wave and Indian cinema.

Gary P. Kolb, Professor and Interim Dean; M.F.A., Ohio, 1977. Photography and digital arts.

Fern Logan, Associate Professor; M.F.A., Art Institute of Chicago, 1993. Photography, digital applications and alternative processes.

Antonio Martinez, Assistant Professor; M.F.A., East Carolina, 2005. Digital imaging, alternative printing processes, multimedia installation, class and racial identity.

Daniel Overturf, Associate Professor; M.F.A., Southern Illinois Carbondale, 1983. Photography.

Jan Peterson Roddy, Associate Professor; M.F.A., Illinois, 1987. Photo/digital production, media arts, image and word, art/politics/spirituality, race, class, gender, sexuality in media, rural U.S. culture.

R. William Rowley, Associate Professor; M.F.A., Iowa, 1974. Digital and analog film production and postproduction techniques, experimental filmmaking, observational documentary, intermedia arts.

Deborah Tudor, Associate Professor and Chair; Ph.D., Northwestern, 1992. British cinema, Australian cinema, war and cinema, digital cinema, sports, the documentary.

Dru Vratil, Associate Professor; M.F.A., Iowa, 1998; Screenwriting.

Department of Radio-Television

Lisa Brooten, Assistant Professor; Ph.D., Ohio, 2002. Media and globalization, gender, social movements, political communication, interpretive/critical research methods, ethnography.

David Burns, Assistant Professor; M.F.A., Parsons, 2001. 2-D and 3-D digital imaging and animation.

John Downing, Professor and Director, Global Media Research Center; Ph.D., London School of Economics, 1974. International communication; alternative media and social movements; racism, ethnicity, and media; media and cultural history.

John Hocheimer, Professor and Chair; Ph.D., Stanford, 1986. Community radio, global media, media studies pedagogy, media history, spirituality and education, popular music.

Phylis Johnson, Associate Professor; Ph.D., Southern Illinois Carbondale, 2003. Sound production and performance acoustic ecology and sound culture, radio drama, oral literacy, media education.

Wago Kreider, Assistant Professor; M.F.A., Rutgers, 2006. Independent filmmaking, broadcast television production, media studies.

Novotny Lawrence, Assistant Professor; Ph.D., Kansas, 2004. African American representations in film and television, Japanese animation, Hindi cinema, film history, genre theory.

Sarah Lewison, Assistant Professor; M.F.A., California, San Diego, 2007. Video, media studies.

Eileen Meehan, Professor; Ph.D., Illinois at Urbana-Champaign, 1983. Political economy of the media, cultural studies, mass communications history, critical communications research.

Howard Motyl, Assistant Professor; Film and video production, the documentary.

Jay Needham, Assistant Professor; California Institute of the Arts, 1989. Video, film, digital audio production, electroacoustic music.

Manjunath Pendakur, Professor; Ph.D., Simon Fraser, 1980. Cultural imperialism, U.S. and Canadian film industries, India's film and television industries, media and public policy issues, the New World Information Order debate, globalization issues.

Jake Podber, Assistant Professor; Ph.D., Ohio, 2001. Media studies, oral history, cultural studies, Appalachian studies, media history.

Jan Thompson, Associate Professor; M.G.S., Roosevelt, 1988. Video production, documentary and sports production.

Paul Torre, Assistant Professor; Ph.D., South Carolina, 2006. Electronic media management, TV, film, critical studies, media management, international media market, relationships between Hollywood studios and German media companies.

School of Journalism

Linda Correll, Assistant Professor; M.A., CUNY, Hunter, 2007. Advertising, creativity in advertising.

Shahira Fahmy, Assistant Professor; Ph.D., Missouri–Columbia, 2003. New media, international communication, visual analysis.

William Freivogel, Associate Professor and Director; J.D., Washington (St. Louis), 2001. Journalism, law.

Katherine Frith, Associate Professor; Ed.D. candidate, Amherst. International advertising, copywriting, advertising and society.

Laura Hlavach, Assistant Professor; J.D., Texas, 1985. Libel, open meetings/open records acts, copyrights, twenty-first-century news writing and reporting, pedagogical constructivism.

Walter B. Jaehnig, Associate Professor and Director; Ph.D., Essex (England), 1974. Media ethics, media theory and philosophy, political violence reporting.

Michael Lawrence, University Professor of Journalism; B.A., Knox (Illinois), 1964. Former press secretary to the governor of Illinois, public policy.

Xigen Li, Assistant Professor; Ph.D., Michigan, 1999. News media and the Internet, impact of technology on mass media, theory of influence on news content, international news and media systems, news media and U.S.-China relations, China's news media.

Dennis Lowry, Professor; Ph.D., Iowa, 1972. Social issues in advertising, communication research methods, content analysis.

Cinzia Padovani, Assistant Professor; Ph.D., Colorado at Boulder, 1999. Historical approaches to political economy, public service broadcasting, international communication, social movements and the media.

Jyotika Ramaprasad, Associate Professor; Ph.D., Southern Illinois Carbondale, 1984. Communication and social change, global journalists, international communication, international advertising/consumer behavior.

SOUTHERN ILLINOIS UNIVERSITY CARBONDALE

College of Mass Communication and Media Arts
Ph.D. Program

Program of Study
The College-wide Ph.D. program engages students in the analysis of the fundamentals of media and communication, whether social, economic, political, cultural, historical, legal/regulatory, or international. Its firm grounding in conceptual and methodological debates is designed to educate researchers and instructors who make significant contributions to the field of media analysis, policies, and practices.

Research Facilities
The extensive holdings and wide array of bibliographic and instructional support services offered by Southern Illinois University Carbondale's Morris Library place it among the foremost research institutions. The library holds memberships in the Association of Research Libraries and the Center of Research Libraries in Chicago. The College is home to the Global Media Research Center, which brings together communication with other disciplines and draws in academic colleagues nationally and internationally, to study and evaluate global media operations and trends. The College also houses the New Media Center, extensive labs and studios for interactive multimedia development, film, audio, video, graphics, photography production, and the Communication Resource Center. Students committed to combining media analysis with practice have further opportunities to work with WSIU Public Broadcasting, which operates two PBS-affiliated television stations and two NPR-affiliated FM radio stations. They may also choose to become involved with the College's Big Muddy International Independent Film Festival, Visiting Artists Series, the off-campus Big Muddy Independent Media Center, Carbondale's community radio station, and the town's emerging public access TV channel.

Financial Aid
Financial support that includes a stipend and a tuition waiver is available. The College provides four years of assistantship funding. A number of fellowship, assistantship, and scholarship opportunities, including those for traditionally underserved populations, are also available at the University level.

Cost of Study
In-state graduate tuition is $328 per credit hour in 2009–10. Out-of-state tuition is 2.5 times the in-state tuition rate ($820 per credit hour). Graduate students with at least a 25 percent appointment as a graduate assistant receive a tuition scholarship. Fees vary from $589.03 (1 credit hour) to $1557.50 (12 credit hours). Students with a graduate assistantship receive a 50 percent reduction in the primary care medical fee. New graduate students from Arkansas, Indiana, Kentucky, Missouri, and Tennessee qualify for the alternate tuition rate, which is equivalent to the in-state graduate tuition rate.

Living and Housing Costs
For married couples, students with families, and single graduate students, the University has 690 efficiency and one-, two-, three-, and four-bedroom apartments that rent for $499 to $720 per month in 2009–10. Residence halls for single graduate students are also available, as are accessible residence hall rooms and apartments for students with disabilities.

Student Group
In 2006–07, there were 37 graduate students in the College's Ph.D. program. The graduate school has more than 3,644 students and 526 registered professional students.

Location
Carbondale is approximately 100 miles southeast of St. Louis, Missouri. Immediately south of Carbondale begins some of the most rugged and picturesque terrain in Illinois. Within 20 miles of the campus are two state parks and four recreational lakes, and much of the area is a part of the 240,000-acre Shawnee National Forest.

The University and the College
Southern Illinois University Carbondale is a state-funded university founded in 1869. The Department of Cinema and Photography, the Department of Radio-Television, and the School of Journalism are in the College of Mass Communication and Media Arts, located in the Communications Building on the west side of the campus. WSIU Public Broadcasting, also located in the Communications Building, provides hands-on experience for students.

Applying
Students applying to the Ph.D. program are required to have a 3.25 GPA and submit three letters of recommendation and GRE scores. Typically, those admitted score a minimum of 550 verbal and 450 quantitative on the GRE. International students are required to take the TOEFL exam and score 600 or above. Applications should be received in the MCMA graduate office by December 1.

Correspondence and Information
Director of Graduate Studies
College of Mass Communication and Media Arts
Southern Illinois University Carbondale
Carbondale, Illinois 62901-6606

Phone: 618-453-5120
Fax: 618-453-7714
Web site: http://mcmagrad.siu.edu

Southern Illinois University Carbondale

THE FACULTY

Department of Cinema and Photography

Lilly A. Boruszkowski, Associate Professor; M.F.A., Northwestern, 1979. Cinema production, post-production sound, editing, documentary and experimental film.

Cade Bursell, Assistant Professor; M.F.A., San Francisco State, 2002. Cinema.

Susan Felleman, Associate Professor; Ph.D., CUNY, 1993. History and theory of film in relation to art, classical and contemporary Hollywood cinema, European "art" film, surrealism, psychoanalytic and feminist theory.

Sarah Kanouse, Assistant Professor; M.F.A., Illinois at Urbana-Champaign, 2004. Public space, media art, cultural geography, labor history, urban and rural relationships, art and activism.

Jyotsna Kapur, Associate Professor; Ph.D., Northwestern, 1998. Feminist and Marxist analysis of media, globalization, children's film and consumer culture, documentary and ethnographic film, the German and Japanese new wave and Indian cinema.

Gary Kolb, Professor and Interim Dean; M.F.A., Ohio, 1977. Photography and digital arts.

Fern Logan, Associate Professor; M.F.A., Art Institute of Chicago, 1993. Photographer with special interest in digital applications and alternative processes.

Antonio Martinez, Assistant Professor; M.F.A., East Carolina, 2005. Digital imaging, alternative printing processes, multimedia installation, class and racial identity.

Daniel Overturf, Associate Professor; M.F.A., Southern Illinois at Carbondale, 1983. Photography.

Jan Peterson Roddy, Associate Professor; M.F.A., Illinois, 1987. Photo/digital production, media arts, image and word, art/politics/spirituality, race, class, gender, sexuality in media, rural U.S. culture.

R. William Rowley, Associate Professor and Chair; M.F.A., Iowa, 1974. Digital and analog film production and postproduction techniques, experimental filmmaking, observational documentary, intermedia arts.

Deborah Tudor, Associate Professor and Chair; Ph.D., Northwestern, 1992. British cinema, Australian cinema, war and cinema, digital cinema, sports, the documentary.

Dru Vratil, Associate Professor; M.F.A., Iowa, 1998. Screenwriting.

Department of Radio-Television

Lisa Brooten, Assistant Professor; Ph.D., Ohio, 2002. Media and globalization, gender, social movements, political communication, interpretive/critical research methods, ethnography.

David Burns, Assistant Professor; M.F.A., Parsons, 2001. 2-D and 3-D digital imaging and animation.

John Downing, Professor and Director, Global Media Research Center; Ph.D., London School of Economics, 1974. International communication; alternative media and social movements; racism, ethnicity, and media; media and cultural history.

John Hocheimer, Professor and Chair; Ph.D., Stanford, 1986. Community radio, global media, media studies pedagogy, media history, spirituality and education, popular music.

Phylis Johnson, Associate Professor; Ph.D., Southern Illinois Carbondale, 2003. Sound production and performance, acoustic ecology and sound culture, radio drama, oral literacy, media education.

Wago Kreider, Assistant Professor; M.F.A., Rutgers, 2006. Independent filmmaking, broadcast television production, media studies.

Novotny Lawrence, Assistant Professor; Ph.D., Kansas, 2004. African American representations in film and television, Japanese animation, Hindi cinema, film history, genre theory.

Sarah Lewison, Assistant Professor; M.F.A., California, San Diego, 2007. Video, media studies.

Eileen Meehan, Professor; Ph.D., Illinois at Urbana-Champaign, 1983. Political economy of the media, cultural studies, mass communications history, critical communications research.

Howard Motyl, Assistant Professor; Film and video production, the documentary.

Jay Needham, Assistant Professor; M.F.A., California Institute of the Arts, 1989. Video, film, digital audio production, electroacoustic music.

Manjunath Pendakur, Professor; Ph.D., Simon Fraser, 1980. Cultural imperialism, U.S. and Canadian film industries, India's film and television industries, media and public policy issues, the New World Information Order debate, globalization issues.

Jake Podber, Assistant Professor; Ph.D., Ohio, 2001. Media studies, oral history, cultural studies, Appalachian studies, media history.

Jan Thompson, Associate Professor; M.G.S., Roosevelt, 1988. Video production, documentary, sports production.

Paul Torre, Assistant Professor; Ph.D., South Carolina, 2006. Electronic media management, TV, film, critical studies, media management, international media market, relationships between Hollywood studios and German media companies.

School of Journalism

Linda Correll, Assistant Professor; M.A., CUNY, Hunter, 2007. Advertising, creativity in advertising.

Shahira Fahmy, Assistant Professor; Ph.D., Missouri–Columbia, 2003. New media, international communication, visual analysis.

William Freivogel, Associate Professor and Director; J.D., Washington (St. Louis), 2001. Journalism, law.

Katherine Frith, Associate Professor; Ed.D. candidate, Amherst. International advertising, copywriting, advertising and society.

Laura Hlavach, Assistant Professor; J.D., Texas, 1985. Libel, open meetings/open records acts, copyrights, twenty-first-century news writing and reporting, pedagogical constructivism.

Walter B. Jaehnig, Associate Professor and Director; Ph.D., Essex (England), 1974. Media ethics, media theory and philosophy, political violence reporting.

Michael Lawrence, University Professor of Journalism; B.A., Knox (Illinois), 1964. Public policy, former press secretary to the governor of Illinois.

Xigen Li, Assistant Professor; Ph.D., Michigan, 1999. News media and the Internet, impact of technology on mass media, theory of influence on news content, international news and media systems, news media and U.S.-China relations, China's news media.

Dennis Lowry, Professor; Ph.D., Iowa, 1972. Social issues in advertising, communication research methods, content analysis.

Cinzia Padovani, Assistant Professor; Ph.D., Colorado at Boulder, 1999. Historical approaches to political economy, public service broadcasting, international communication, social movements and the media.

Jyotika Ramaprasad, Associate Professor; Ph.D., Southern Illinois Carbondale, 1984. Communication and social change, global journalists, international communication, international advertising/consumer behavior.

SOUTHERN ILLINOIS UNIVERSITY CARBONDALE

Department of Speech Communication
Ph.D. Program

Program of Study

Doctoral graduate students elect to specialize in one of six concentrations: communication pedagogy; intercultural communication; interpersonal communication; performance studies; gender, sexuality, and communication; and rhetoric and philosophy of communication. Additional course work is also available in cultural studies, language and social interaction, organizational communication, public address, public relations, and semiotics. The Department of Speech Communication at Southern Illinois University Carbondale (SIUC) offers programs of study leading to the Master of Arts and Doctor of Philosophy degrees.

Graduate study in communication pedagogy focuses on teaching communication within the discipline and communication principles in a variety of instructional contexts. Communication pedagogy reflects interests across graduate areas, featuring topics such as communication, pedagogy and subjectivity, teaching as performance, feminist pedagogy, critical communication pedagogy, queer pedagogy, and intersectionality.

Graduate study in intercultural communication emphasizes theory and praxis, examining both U.S. national and international cultures with a focus on intercultural and intracultural communication. Courses are taught emphasizing intercultural communication in the classroom as well as in business and training settings. Students in this area can expect to explore issues of identity and intersectionality; language, discourse, and politics of representation; as well as globalization and postcoloniality as they relate to the study of culture and communication.

Interpersonal communication focuses on descriptive, naturalistic approaches to studying everyday interaction. Two primary approaches to interpersonal communication within the Department are conversation analysis and ethnography of communication. Related topics include language behavior, performance in everyday life, ethnographic fieldwork, interpersonal conflict, narrative, and social construction of gender and identity.

Graduate study in performance studies combines an interest in theory and praxis. Performance studies reflects interests in performance as a way of knowing, including historical and theoretical approaches to performance, literary criticism, performance criticism, and gender and performance, as well as interest in performing literature, performance art, and performance composition.

Graduate study in rhetoric and philosophy of communication focuses on phenomenology of composition, reflecting interest in hermeneutic and semiotic phenomenological orientations; philosophy of rhetoric, reflecting interests in argumentation theory, gender studies, philosophy of rhetoric, and cultural studies; and rhetorical studies, reflecting interests in classical and contemporary rhetorical theory.

Research Facilities

The Department offers extensive production opportunities in its performance laboratory, the Marion Kleinau Theatre, a listening laboratory for work in conversation analysis, and a computer laboratory.

Financial Aid

Most students hold graduate assistantships that provide competitive monthly stipends for the academic year as well as tuition waivers throughout the calendar year. As assistants, most students teach two sections of the Introduction to Oral Communication course each semester. Others work with the debate program, the Marion Kleinau Theatre, or the Public Relations Student Society of America or as research assistants. The University also offers a number of highly competitive fellowships, based upon academic accomplishments, letters of recommendation, GRE scores, and potential for success in graduate study. The deadline for applying for financial aid is February 1.

Cost of Study

In-state graduate tuition is $328 per credit hour in 2009–10. Out-of-state tuition is 2.5 times the in-state tuition rate ($820 per credit hour). Graduate students with at least a 25 percent appointment as a graduate assistant receive a tuition scholarship. Fees vary from $589.03 (1 credit hour) to $1557.50 (12 credit hours). Students with a graduate assistantship receive a 50 percent reduction in the primary care medical fee. New graduate students from Arkansas, Indiana, Kentucky, Missouri, and Tennessee qualify for the alternate tuition rate, which is equivalent to the in-state graduate tuition rate.

Living and Housing Costs

For married couples, students with families, and single graduate students, the University has 690 efficiency and one-, two-, three-, and four-bedroom apartments that rent for $499 to $720 per month in 2009–10. Residence halls for single graduate students are also available, as are accessible residence hall rooms and apartments for students with disabilities.

Student Group

The Department sponsors the Speech Communication Organization (SCO). This organization is made up of graduate student members whose purpose is to enhance professional development. In addition, SCO sponsors and plans various social events that include the sharing of peer scholarship and a brown bag discussion series.

Location

SIUC is 350 miles south of Chicago and 100 miles southeast of St. Louis. Nestled in rolling hills bordered by the Ohio and Mississippi Rivers and enhanced by a mild climate, the area has state parks, national forests and wildlife refuges, and large lakes for outdoor recreation. Cultural offerings include theater, opera, concerts, art exhibits, and cinema. Educational facilities for the families of students are excellent.

The University

Southern Illinois University Carbondale is a comprehensive public university with a variety of general and professional education programs. The University offers bachelor's and associate degrees, master's and doctoral degrees, the J.D. degree, and the M.D. degree. The University is fully accredited by the North Central Association of Colleges and Schools. The Graduate School has an essential role in the development and coordination of graduate instruction and research programs. The Graduate Council has academic responsibility for determining graduate standards, recommending new graduate programs and research centers, and establishing policies to facilitate the research effort.

Applying

Applications should be requested from the address given below. Each application must include a completed Departmental and Graduate School application form, three letters of recommendation, official transcripts from all colleges and universities previously attended, a personal statement of career goals, and GRE scores. The deadline for application is February 1 for the following fall. All materials should be sent directly to the Department of Speech Communication.

Correspondence and Information

Ronald J. Pelias
Director of Graduate Studies
Department of Speech Communication
Southern Illinois University
Carbondale, Illinois 62901-6605

Phone: 618-453-2291
Fax: 618-453-2812
E-mail: rpelias@siu.edu
Web site: http:/speechcommunication.siuc.edu/

Southern Illinois University Carbondale

THE FACULTY AND THEIR RESEARCH

Residing in the College of Liberal Arts, the Department of Speech Communication has a faculty that is active in regional, national, and international professional communication organizations. As a community of scholars, the faculty sustains a rich diversity of methodological, theoretical, and philosophical interest. The faculty members believe that their mission is to excel in teaching, research, and service. Working with approximately 200 undergraduate majors and more than 65 in-residence graduate students, the faculty members create an environment that fosters opportunity, possibility, and creativity.

Nilanjana R. Bardhan, Associate Professor; Ph.D., Ohio, 1998. Public relations, organizational communication, intercultural/international communication, media criticism, health communication.

Bryan Crow, Associate Professor; Ph.D., Iowa, 1982. Interpersonal communication, conversation analysis, relational pragmatics, language acquisition.

Suzanne Daughton, Associate Professor; Ph.D., Texas, 1991. Rhetorical theory and criticism, political communication, communication and gender, metaphor and narrative in rhetorical discourse.

Craig Gingrich-Philbrook, Associate Professor; Ph.D., Southern Illinois, 1994. Performance studies, performance art, queer theory, Continental philosophy, psychoanalysis, literary theory.

Todd Graham, Director of Debate; Ph.D., Arizona State, 2000. Interpersonal communication, humor studies, qualitative research methods, argumentation theory and practice.

Jonathan M. Gray, Associate Professor; Ph.D., LSU, 1999. Rhetorical theory and criticism, popular culture, communication pedagogy, folklore, cultural studies, performance.

Rachel Alicia Griffin, Assistant Professor; Ph.D., Denver, 2008. Intercultural communication, critical race theory, gender violence, critical pedagogy.

Ronald J. Pelias, Professor; Ph.D., Illinois, 1979. Performance studies, performance methodologies and criticism, performance composition, performative writing, performance art.

Elyse L. Pineau, Associate Professor; Ph.D., Northwestern, 1990. Performance studies, autobiography, performance methodologies, performance and gender, communication pedagogy.

Ross Singer, Assistant Professor; Ph.D., Bowling Green State, 2008. Organizational rhetoric, environmental rhetoric, rhetorical theory and criticism.

Miriam Sobre-Denton, Assistant Professor; Ph.D., Arizona State, 2009. Intercultural communication, language and culture, qualitative methods, identity and cross-cultural adaptation.

Nathan Stucky, Professor; Ph.D., Texas, 1988. Performance studies, narrative theory, conversation analysis, ethnographic performance, performance criticism.

Satoshi Toyosaki, Assistant Professor; Ph.D., Southern Illinois Carbondale, 2005. Intercultural/international communication, cultural studies, cultural identity performance.

John T. Warren, Associate Professor; Ph.D., Southern Illinois Carbondale, 2001. Communication pedagogy, critical/cultural studies, ethnographic methods, sexuality and gender studies.

SYRACUSE UNIVERSITY

S. I. Newhouse School of Public Communications

Programs of Study

The Newhouse School offers programs leading to three graduate degrees: Master of Arts (M.A.), Master of Science (M.S.), and Doctor of Philosophy (Ph.D.). Candidates for the M.A. and M.S. degrees can major in advertising; arts journalism; broadcast journalism; documentary film and history; magazine, newspaper, and online journalism; photography; media studies; new media; public relations; or television-radio-film. A master's program in media management leading to an M.S. degree is offered jointly by the Newhouse School and the Whitman School of Management. A course of study in public diplomacy leading to an M.S. degree in public relations and an M.A. degree in international relations is offered jointly by the Newhouse School and the Maxwell School of Citizenship and Public Affairs. A Doctor of Philosophy is offered in mass communications. Newhouse also offers an interdisciplinary distance learning degree program for experienced public relations practitioners, leading to an M.S. in communications management.

Generally, the resident professional master's programs are completed in one calendar year and 36 credits are required. However, 36 to 42 credits are required for media management, 40 credits for broadcast journalism, 39 credits for documentary film and history, 33 credits for photography, and a total of 58 credits for the public diplomacy course of study. Most students complete their studies by taking capstone courses. Television-radio-film students take comprehensive examinations, media studies students write theses, and photography students either write theses or complete special projects. In public relations, students either take a capstone course with a comprehensive examination or write theses.

The Ph.D. program in mass communications involves three years of academic work beyond the master's degree. Students must take a minimum of 60 credits beyond the master's level. A research dissertation is required of all doctoral candidates.

Research Facilities

Opportunities are available for Newhouse students to assist members of the faculty with research projects. The School has several research areas, including the Bleier Center for Television and Popular Culture, the Carnegie Legal Reporting Program, the Center for Digital Literacy, the Knight Chair in Political Reporting, and the Tully Center for Free Speech. In addition, students have access to the Transactional Records Access Clearinghouse (TRAC), a center devoted to assisting the news media in analyzing government documents through the use of computers. TRAC, which has an office complex at the School, is the leading research center for investigating and implementing new computer-assisted reporting techniques.

Financial Aid

There are University-wide competitions for McNair Fellowships and African American Fellowships. Newhouse annually awards two Turner Diversity Fellowships and two Newhouse Foundation Fellowships for Minorities. Both awards offer full tuition benefits as well as yearlong job placement after graduation. Several $10,000 Liu Foundation Multicultural Scholarships are awarded each year. The School awards a number of partial scholarships ranging from $5000 to $15,000. Instructional associates spend from 5 to 20 hours per week helping faculty members with classes or labs. They are paid $13 an hour and also receive partial-tuition scholarships. Need-based financial aid in the form of federal loans is also available.

Cost of Study

Tuition for graduate students is $1069 per credit for the 2008–09 academic year. Program fees range from $225 to $1050. Doctoral students are provided with a full-tuition scholarship and a stipend for work in teaching or research.

Living and Housing Costs

In 2008–09, University housing for single graduate students sharing an apartment costs approximately $9500 for the calendar year. There are also numerous apartment complexes and rental houses that graduate students choose to live in. Many are within walking distance or on the bus line. Dependent on a number of factors, rent ranges from approximately $400 per month to $1000 per month.

Student Group

Each year, students with a variety of backgrounds are considered for admission to the graduate programs. A previous communications degree is not required. Programs are competitive, and admitted students typically have academic records and GRE scores well above average. Approximately 240 new students are enrolled each year, the majority of whom study full-time. About 15 percent of the graduate student population is international, and the male-female ratio is about 40:60.

Student Outcomes

The Newhouse School has a wide and varied alumni base. Many graduates are recognized as leaders in the various fields of public communications. The School operates a Career Development Center to assist students and alumni with career opportunities. A computerized Career Advisory Network has been established to provide an online database of alumni contacts in businesses throughout the world. Recruiters frequently conduct interviews at the Newhouse School, and current job listings are circulated regularly.

Location

SU is located in the city of Syracuse, the geographic center of New York State. Syracuse combines all the amenities of a major urban area with small-town charm and an affordable cost of living. The metropolitan area is home to more than half a million people who take advantage of an active social scene and the region's natural recreational resources. The city also offers students many opportunities to gain practical experience in the various fields of communications.

The University and The School

Syracuse University was founded in 1870 by the United Methodist Church, with assistance from the city of Syracuse. Privately endowed, coeducational, and nonsectarian, the University has grown from an original enrollment of 41 students to an overall enrollment of 19,082, which includes 5,926 graduate students. A member of both the Association of American Universities and the Council of Graduate Schools, Syracuse University is considered one of the nation's major institutions of higher learning. The Newhouse School is fully accredited by the Accrediting Council on Education in Journalism and Mass Communications and has an enrollment of approximately 1,800 undergraduate and 275 graduate students.

Applying

A complete application includes official transcripts, three letters of recommendation, personal statement, resume, GRE scores (TOEFL scores, if applicable), and an application form. Applications should be submitted online at https://apply.embark.com/grad/syracuse/. Except for media studies, Newhouse master's programs are designed for students to begin study in early July. To apply for merit aid, students need only check the appropriate boxes on the application form. The deadline for master's programs admission and merit aid is February 1. Doctoral program applications are due by December 10.

Correspondence and Information

Graduate Records Office
S. I. Newhouse School of Public Communications
215 University Place
Syracuse, New York 13244-2100
Phone: 315-443-4039
Fax: 315-443-1834
E-mail: pcgrad@syr.edu
Web site: http://newhousemasters.syr.edu/

Syracuse University

THE FACULTY

Administration
Lorraine E. Branham, Dean.
Amy Falkner, Associate Dean for Academic Affairs.
Carla V. Lloyd, Associate Dean of Scholarly and Creative Activity.
Rosanna Grassi, Associate Dean for Student Affairs.
Joel Kaplan, Associate Dean for Professional Graduate Studies.
Carol M. Liebler, Director of the Doctoral Program.
Lynn M. Vanderhoek, Assistant Dean for Advancement.
Karen McGee, Assistant Dean for Student Affairs.

Advertising
James Tsao, Professor and Chair; Ph.D., Temple. Advertising strategy, international advertising, Internet advertising.
Amy Falkner, Associate Professor; M.A., Syracuse. Media planning, advertising to gay and lesbian markets.
Carla V. Lloyd, Associate Professor; Ph.D., Syracuse. Advertising media, copywriting.
Ed Russell, Assistant Professor; M.S., Northwestern. Advertising strategies, campaigns.
Brian Sheehan, Associate Professor; M.A., Loyola Marymount. Advertising management, digital media.

Broadcast Journalism
Dona Hayes, Associate Professor and Chair; M.S., Syracuse. Broadcast news writing, reporting, production.
Hubert Brown, Associate Professor; M.A., Nebraska–Lincoln. Political reporting, writing.
Michael E. Cremedas, Associate Professor; Ph.D., Florida. Writing, reporting, production management.
Frank Currier, Professor of Practice; M.A., Missouri–Columbia. Radio news reporting, producing.
Barbara Croll Fought, Associate Professor; J.D., Detroit. Broadcast news writing, reporting.
E. Robert Lissit, Associate Professor; M.S., Northwestern. Broadcast news writing, producing.
John Nicholson, Professor of Practice; B.S., Syracuse. Broadcast reporting.
Donald C. Torrance, Associate Professor; B.A., Alfred. Broadcast news writing, production.
Chris Tuohey, Assistant Professor; M.A., Ohio State. Broadcast news reporting.

Communications
Hubert Brown, Associate Professor and Chair; M.A., Nebraska–Lincoln. Political reporting, writing.
Courtney Barclay, Assistant Professor; Ph.D., Florida. Media law, online political communications, freedom of information.
Makana Chock, Assistant Professor; Ph.D., Cornell. Communications theory.
Bradley W. Gorham, Associate Professor; Ph.D., Wisconsin–Madison. Media and society, media effects.
Roy Gutterman, Visiting Professor; J.D., Syracuse. Communications law.
Carol M. Liebler, Associate Professor; Ph.D., Wisconsin–Madison. Communications theory, methodology.
David M. Rubin, Professor; Ph.D., Stanford. Communications law, media ethics, mass media and government.
Jay B. Wright, Professor; Ph.D., Syracuse. Communications law, ethics.

Magazine
Melissa Chessher, Associate Professor and Chair; M.A., Baylor. Magazine writing, editing.
Harriet Brown, Assistant Professor; M.F.A., Brooklyn. Magazine editing, science and medical journalism.
William A. Glavin Jr., Professor; M.S., Columbia. Magazine writing, editing.
Robert E. Lloyd, Associate Professor; M.A., Syracuse. Newswriting and reporting, media and society.
Mark J. Obbie, Assistant Professor; M.A., Missouri–Columbia. Magazine article writing and editing.

Newspaper
Steve Davis, Associate Professor and Chair; B.J., Missouri–Columbia. Newswriting, reporting, impact of the Internet on politics.
Lorraine E. Branham, Professor; B.A., Temple. Ethics, diversity and media.
Joan A. Deppa, Associate Professor; Ph.D., Michigan State. Newswriting, reporting, computer graphics.
Elizabeth Lynne Flocke, Professor; Ph.D., Missouri–Columbia. Newswriting, communications law.
Joel Kaplan, Associate Professor; M.S., Illinois; M.S.L., Yale. Newswriting, investigative reporting, communications law.
Johanna Keller, Director, Goldring Program; M.A., Antioch. Cultural journalism, arts criticism.
C. Marshall Matlock, Associate Professor; M.A., Central Michigan. Newswriting, newspaper design.

Gustav Niebuhr, Professor of Practice; M.A., Oxford. Religious journalism.
Nancy W. Sharp, Professor; M.S.Sc., Syracuse. Newswriting, reporting.
Francis Ward, Associate Professor; M.A., Syracuse. Newswriting, reporting.

Public Relations
Brenda J. Wrigley, Associate Professor and Chair; Ph.D., Syracuse. Gender and public relations, diversity issues.
Shannon Bowen, Associate Professor; Ph.D., Maryland. Ethics in corporate issues management, media ethics and terrorism, PR pedagogy.
Dennis F. Kinsey, Associate Professor; Ph.D., Stanford. Public relations theory, research.
Robert M. Kucharavy, Professor of Practice; M.A.L.A., Clark. Public relations management.
Kathryn E. Lee, Adjunct Professor; M.S., Syracuse. Public relations writing.
Maria P. Russell, Professor; M.A., Syracuse. Public relations management.
F. William Smullen III, Adjunct Professor; M.A., Syracuse. Government public relations, national security issues.
Nancy Snow, Associate Professor; Ph.D., American. Communication theories of public relations, brand marketing.
Sean (Sung-Un) Yang, Assistant Professor; Ph.D., Maryland. Public relations research, organization-public relationships.

Television-Radio-Film
Michael Schoonmaker, Chair; Ph.D., Syracuse. Television production, writing, media education.
Richard Breyer, Professor; M.A., NYU. Television production, documentary writing, production.
Bud Carey, Associate Professor; B.S., San Diego. Television industry, broadcast sales and promotion.
Fiona Chew, Associate Professor; Ph.D., Washington (Seattle). Television research.
Richard Dubin, Professor of Practice. Television writing, producing, and directing.
Larry Elin, Associate Professor; B.S., Syracuse. Television production, interactive media.
Tula Goenka, Assistant Professor; M.S., Syracuse. Television production, writing.
Sharon R. Hollenback, Professor; Ph.D., Texas at Austin. Television writing, media and society.
Patricia H. Longstaff, Associate Professor; M.P.A., Harvard; J.D., Iowa. Communications law, new technologies.
Peter K. Moller, Professor; M.A., Pennsylvania. Television production, writing.
Douglas Quin, Associate Professor; Ph.D., Union (Ohio). Film sound, exhibit media design, acoustic ecology, bioacoustics.
Evan S. Smith, Associate Professor; M.S., Syracuse. Film business, scriptwriting.
Robert J. Thompson, Professor; Ph.D., Northwestern. Television criticism, production.
Roosevelt R. Wright Jr., Associate Professor; Ph.D., Syracuse. Radio programming, management.

Visual and Interactive Communications
Anthony R. Golden, Associate Professor and Chair; Ph.D., Syracuse. Advertising and illustration photography.
Ken Harper, Assistant Professor; B.A., Western Kentucky. Multimedia content management systems.
Gregory Hedges, Visiting Professor; M.S., Syracuse. Graphic design, Web and multimedia production, typography.
Stephen M. Masiclat, Associate Professor; M.P.S., Cornell. Graphics, multimedia, Web design.
Lawrence Mason Jr., Professor; Ph.D., Syracuse. Communications and society, photojournalism, multimedia.
Bruce Strong, Associate Professor; M.A., Ohio. Photojournalism, multimedia storytelling.
David C. Sutherland, Associate Professor; M.A., Western Kentucky. Photojournalism, graphics.
Sherri A. Taylor, Coordinator, Scholastic Journalism Program; B.A., Baylor. Graphics.

Endowed Research Chairs
George A. Comstock, S. I. Newhouse Professor of Public Communications; Ph.D., Stanford. Mass communication, psychology of the behavioral effects of entertainment, communications theory.
Charlotte Grimes, Knight Chair in Political Reporting; B.S., East Carolina. Media and politics, political reporting, journalism ethics.
Pamela J. Shoemaker, John Ben Snow Professor of Public Communications; Ph.D., Wisconsin–Madison. Communications theory and research, gatekeeping, news content.

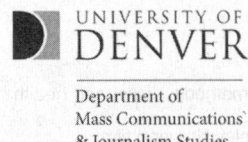

Department of
Mass Communications
& Journalism Studies

UNIVERSITY OF DENVER
School of Communication

Programs of Study

The University of Denver offers several graduate degrees in the Department of Mass Communications and Journalism Studies. They include the Master of Arts in mass communications (student-designed emphasis), the Master of Arts in mass communications (video production emphasis), and the Master of Science in public relations. In addition, the University offers the following interdisciplinary programs: the Master of Arts in international and intercultural communication (offered in conjunction with the Josef Korbel School of International Studies), the Master of Science in advertising management (offered in conjunction with the Daniels College of Business), and the Master of Arts in digital media studies (offered in partnership with the School of Art and Art History and the Department of Computer Science). Students can also choose from two combined degree options: the Master of Science in advertising management and Master of Science in public relations; and the Master of Science in public relations and Master of Arts in video production.

Research Facilities

On-campus facilities include a state-of-the-art video production studio; Digital DV and HD, HI-8, and nonlinear computer video editing suites; and extensive field production equipment. The department provides the latest technology in its computer labs. Students also have access to the research network housed in Penrose Library and Westminster Law Library. In addition, study rooms, computer labs, carrels, and duplication facilities are also available. Students also have access to other nearby major university libraries in the Rocky Mountain Front Range area.

Financial Aid

Financial aid opportunities include both merit-based and need-based options. Merit-based opportunities consist of fellowships, grants, teaching and research assistantships, and Dean's Tuition Scholarship credits. A special minority fellowship is available for the Ph.D. program. Need-based options include work-study positions and loans. Teaching assistantships include a monetary stipend and tuition waivers. Financial aid requests should be completed as close to the application deadline as possible.

Cost of Study

The cost of tuition for the 2009–10 academic year is $961 per quarter credit. Full-time student status is a minimum of 8 hours per quarter. Tuition for students carrying 12 to 18 hours per quarter is $11,532. The cost of books is approximately $1500 per year. Health fees are $420 per year.

Living and Housing Costs

Room and board range between $6000 and $9600 for on- and off-campus housing. Personal costs are approximately $2800.

Student Group

For the 2008–09 academic year, the number of graduate students enrolled in the Department of Mass Communications and Journalism Studies was 48. Graduate students span a wide range of demographic characteristics, backgrounds, and goals. More than half of the students receive some form of financial aid.

Location

Denver is the cultural and commercial center of the Rocky Mountain area. The area is a leading center for new communication technologies and methodologies worldwide, with a wide variety of communication industries and institutions. Students can continue their graduate education surrounded by the breathtaking beauty of the Rocky Mountains.

The University and The School

The Department of Mass Communications and Journalism Studies was founded in 1933 and has a rich tradition of offering programs with advanced intellectual and theoretical foundations provided by faculty who are committed to offering leading-edge communication theory and practice. There are currently 17 full-time faculty members in the department. The department has an outstanding teaching faculty, which is committed to ensuring that students get the best education possible. In addition, the School has some of the finest communication scholars in the world. Overall, the faculty's dedication, creativity, and openness to change and innovation have been responsible for the development of one of the most dynamic programs at the University of Denver.

Applying

All individuals applying to the graduate programs in the Department of Mass Communications and Journalism Studies need to supply the following specific information and data: official transcripts from each institution from which the applicant received academic credit and the GRE, which is required for both Ph.D. and master's degree applicants and for both domestic and international students. Applicants must also submit a one-page statement of purpose and three letters of recommendation. International students are required to take the Test of English as a Foreign Language (TOEFL) or the International English Language Testing System (IELTS) test for all programs. Some programs require international students to take the Test of Written English (TWE). International students applying for teaching assistantships must also take the Test of Spoken English (TSE). Students are not admitted to a degree program without having demonstrated competency in the English language.

Application deadlines for graduate programs vary. For more details, students should check the University of Denver Web site. Students are encouraged to apply for fall entrance, though occasionally they are admitted during winter or spring quarters.

Correspondence and Information

For more information, students should contact the following at the University of Denver, Denver, Colorado 80208 or visit the Web site at http://www.du.edu/mcom.

For the M.A. in mass communications or the M.S. in public relations or advertising management:
Lynn Schofield Clark, Director of Graduate Studies
Department of Mass Communications and Journalism
E-mail: mcom@du.edu

For the M.A. in international and intercultural communication:
Margaret Thompson, Director
International and Intercultural Communication Program
E-mail: iic@du.edu

For the M.A. in digital media studies:
Trace Reddell, Director
Digital Media Studies
E-mail: treddell@du.edu

University of Denver

THE FACULTY AND THEIR RESEARCH

Renee Botta, Associate Professor; Ph.D., Wisconsin–Madison, 1998. Media effects, audience behavior, quantitative research methods, social and health communication.

Rodney Buxton, Associate Professor; Ph.D., Texas at Austin, 1992. Critical/qualitative analysis, scriptwriting, and directing for television and film.

Lynn Clark, Associate Professor; Ph.D., Colorado at Boulder, 2005. Journalism, new media, religion and media, popular culture.

Christopher D. Coleman, Assistant Professor; M.F.A., Buffalo, SUNY. Digital media technology, digital foundations, combined media, digital animation.

Christof Demont-Heinrich, Assistant Professor; Ph.D., Colorado at Boulder, 2005. Newswriting and reporting, transnational and national identity, media discourse, linguistic and cultural dimensions of globalization, Web design.

Bill Depper, Assistant Professor; M.F.A., Iowa, 1988. Digital media studies.

Tony Gault, Associate Professor; M.F.A., Iowa, 1994. Scriptwriting, media production, media analysis.

Cathy A. Grieve, Assistant Professor and Director of Internships; Ph.D., Denver, 1979. Public relations, media effects.

Elizabeth Henry, Lecturer; Ph.D., Iowa, 2000. Film criticism, media history, public relations, literary journalism.

Nadia Kaneva, Assistant Professor; Ph.D., Colorado at Boulder, 2007. Culture and communication, public relations, globalization, online learning.

Trace Reddell, Assistant Professor; Ph.D., Colorado at Boulder, 1997. Web development, media theory, digital audio production.

Adrienne Russell, Assistant Professor; Ph.D., Indiana Bloomington, 2001. Digital media theory, new media, media controversies, journalism.

Ania Savage, Lecturer; M.S., Columbia, 1964. Domestic and international journalism, public relations.

Sheila Schroeder, Assistant Professor; Ph.D., Indiana, 1999. Qualitative research, video production, television criticism, sports and media.

Derigan Silver, Assistant Professor; Ph.D., North Carolina at Chapel Hill, 2008. First Amendment theory and law, government secrecy, media law, Internet law and policy.

Margaret Thompson, Associate Professor; Ph.D., Wisconsin–Madison, 1989. International communication, media effects, audience behavior, quantitative research methods.

Diane Waldman, Associate Professor; Ph.D., Wisconsin–Madison, 1981. Communication theory, qualitative research methods, film history and criticism.

Roy V. Wood, Professor; Ph.D., Denver, 1965. Organizational communication, research methods, public deliberation and ethics.

UNIVERSITY OF SOUTHERN CALIFORNIA
Annenberg School for Communication
School of Journalism
School of Communication

Programs In Communication, Journalism, Public Diplomacy, and Public Relations

Programs of Study

Through the School of Journalism and the School of Communication, the University of Southern California (USC) Annenberg School for Communication offers master's degrees in communication, communication management, global communication, journalism, public diplomacy, and strategic public relations and a Ph.D. in communication.

The School of Journalism, accredited by the Accrediting Council on Education of Journalism and Mass Communication (ACEJMC), places innovative multiplatform storytelling, pioneering digital and social networking opportunities, experimentation, and entrepreneurialism at the center of all that is taught. The School emphasizes hands-on training, writing, ethics, and professional practice. In the traditional two-year journalism programs, an innovative core curriculum teaches newswriting, reporting, and production across three media platforms. After completing the core curriculum, students concentrate on advanced course work. Student involvement is found in Neon Tommy, an online digital news site, *Annenberg TV News,* the award-winning day-of-air broadcasting operation; *Impact,* an outlet for long-form storytelling; and *Annenberg Radio News,* the day-of-air radio broadcast. The strategic public relations program equips students with the skills to succeed in agency, corporate, and nonprofit work. In the summer after the first year, students in journalism and strategic public relations may study and intern in Cape Town, Hong Kong, or London. In the nine-month specialized journalism programs, students focus on journalism leadership and decision making while completing graduate course work in academic disciplines outside of journalism. In the specialized journalism (the arts) program, art practitioners and artists learn how to write for publications while advancing their academic exposure to the arts.

The School of Communication offers five master's degrees. Communication management students concentrate their studies in one of seven tracks: entertainment management, health and social change communication, marketing communication, information and communication technologies, international communication, organizational and strategic corporate communication, and communication law and policy. In addition, post-master's degree certificate programs are offered in the same tracks. Through the Charles Annenberg Weingarten Program on Online Communities (APOC), students explore the effects, impact, implementation, and management of social networking in different areas of society and business.

Global communication students live and study in two dynamic, multicultural media capitals of the world—first in London at the London School of Economics and Political Science (LSE) and the second year in Los Angeles at USC Annenberg.

Public diplomacy students study the impact of private activities—from popular culture to fashion to sports to news—on the national interests of organizations, corporations, and governments worldwide. As part of the degree program, students complete a summer field experience in the United States or abroad after completing their first year. In addition to the two-year program, a one-year master's degree is offered for mid-career professionals with five years or more of experience in public diplomacy, international relations, or international communication.

Students in the M.A. and Ph.D. programs in communication focus their critical studies of inquiry through concentrations in health and interpersonal communication; information and society; media, culture, and community; organizational communication; and rhetoric and political communication. Students acquire and demonstrate humanistic and behavioral knowledge of communication while acquiring the skills requisite to scholarly research in the discipline.

Research Facilities

The School is home to the Norman Lear Center for Entertainment Research, the Center for the Digital Future, and the Annenberg Center for Online Communities. It is also a partner with the Annenberg Center and the Schools of Cinema/Television and Engineering in USC's Integrated Media Systems Center, the nation's only university-based multimedia research center, which is funded by the National Science Foundation and the USC Center on Public Diplomacy (in partnership with the College of Letters, Arts, and Sciences).

The Strategic Public Relations Center plays a leading role in bridging the substantial gap between the public relations profession and the academic community that studies it. A host of centers affiliated with the School of Journalism may be explored on the USC Annenberg Web site.

Financial Aid

Merit scholarships for master's degree students in communication management, journalism, public diplomacy, and strategic public relations are awarded competitively based on the graduate admission application. All U.S. citizens and permanent residents are encouraged to apply for need-based federal financial aid. International students are eligible for merit scholarship consideration, and are required to submit a confidential statement of financial support. Ph.D. students receive full support for five years.

Cost of Study

For the 2009–10 academic year, the estimated cost for a full-time master's degree student (tuition and fees) is $26,534 and the estimated cost for a Ph.D. student is $31,730. The costs of housing, board, books, supplies, and personal expenses vary. For part-time graduate student estimates, please refer to the USC financial aid Web site at http://www.usc.edu/admission/fa/applying_receiving/graduates/costs/html.

Living and Housing Costs

USC maintains a number of apartment buildings for graduate students only. Housing applications are sent to admitted students only. Rates for privately owned apartments near USC and elsewhere in greater Los Angeles are comparable to those in other large metropolitan areas. For more information on University housing options and rates, prospective students should visit http://www.housing.usc.edu.

Student Group

USC Annenberg enrolls approximately 560 graduate students. Thirty percent are international students. Some students enter the programs directly after earning the bachelor's degree; however, the majority of students have had some professional experience. The majority of Ph.D. students have completed a master's degree before enrolling at USC Annenberg. Most communication management students work or intern during the day, and many attend school part-time. Other master's degree and Ph.D. students attend daytime and evening classes. Graduate student organizations are active in this vibrant student-centered community.

Student Outcomes

School of Journalism graduates work at many of the nation's leading media and public relations organizations, such as ABC, CBS, NBC, CNN, Ketchum Public Relations, Manning Selvage & Lee, Weber Shandwick Worldwide, Ogilvy & Mather, EXPN, C-SPAN, CNBC, KMEX, Telemundo, KWHY, AOL, varity.com, LATimes.com, eCompanies, WashingtonPost.com, and the Associated Press. Communication management and global communication program graduates pursue careers in marketing communications and public relations, mass media, multimedia and interactive media management, media research and analysis, entertainment management, telecommunications, law and public policy, corporate communications, nonprofit management, and consulting. Graduates work at firms such as Warner Bros., FOXSports.com, GameSpot.com, AOL, McKinsey, KPMG, Nestlé USA, DIRECTV, MGM, Pacific Bell, and ABC TV.

The majority of Ph.D. graduates pursue careers in academia at such institutions as Georgetown University, Johns Hopkins University, Michigan State University, North Carolina State University, Northwestern University, City University of Hong Kong, Tokyo University, and the Universities of Illinois, Indiana, Texas at Austin, and Wisconsin. Ph.D. graduates also work in research, strategic analysis, and consulting with firms such as NuStats, the Pacific Telesis Group, Jet Propulsion Laboratory, and Frank Magid Associates.

Location

Los Angeles is a world capital of communication, entertainment, and multimedia. Many opportunities exist to contact and interact with alumni and other professionals and senior management, and for research in such areas as interactive media, radio/television/film, telecommunications, information systems, public and government policy, corporate communication, and marketing.

The School

Home to approximately 1,996 graduate and undergraduate students and 183 full-time faculty members, the USC Annenberg School is poised to tackle questions of our times with strategies and alternatives that serve the public good. The School's vibrant, intellectual community is enhanced by having Los Angeles as a neighborhood laboratory, providing critical exposure to new ideas, hands-on learning experiences, and professional opportunities. USC Annenberg offers professional academic advising, career development services, international programs, and a host of speaking series to compliment classroom instruction.

Applying

All applicants must complete the online USC Graduate Admission Application with required supplemental materials, including a professional resume, a statement of purpose, writing samples or scholarly writing, and letters of recommendation. Graduate Record Examinations (GRE) General Test scores are required for admission to all graduate degree programs, with two exceptions: the GRE is not required for admissions to the global communication degree program, and the GMAT is accepted in lieu of the GRE for admission to the communication management degree program. Proof of English language proficiency is required if the student's native language or language of instruction for their bachelor's degree is not English. Students must refer to the USC Annenberg Web site for graduate admission application guidelines for instructions.

In addition to the online USC graduate admission application, applicants to the M.A./M.Sc. in global communication program must complete the online LSE application.

Correspondence and Information

Admissions Office
Annenberg School for Communication
University of Southern California
3502 Watt Way, Suite 140
Los Angeles, California 90089-0281
Phone: 213-821-0770
Web site: http://www.annenberg.usc.edu/

University of Southern California

THE FACULTY AND THEIR RESEARCH

School of Journalism

Daniel H. Birman, M.A., Lecturer. Nonfiction/documentary producer, executive producer for USC Annenberg's *Impact.*

Laura Castañeda, M.A., Associate Professor of Professional Practice. Former AP reporter, business reporter, coeditor, coauthor.

William Celis, M.S., Associate Professor. Author of *Battle Rock: The Struggle Over a One-Room School in America's Vanishing West.* Former education correspondent, reporter, columnist.

Serena Cha, M.S., Director and Faculty Adviser, Annenberg TV News. Former TV producer.

Dana Chinn, M.B.A., Lecturer. Senior consultant, Media Insight Group.

Mike Chinoy, M.S., Visiting Professor. CNN's former senior Asia correspondent and bureau chief in Hong Kong and Beijing. Received duPont-Columbia, Peabody, and Emmy Awards for coverage of 1989 Tiananmen Square protests in China.

K. C. Cole, B.A., Professor. Science writer, columnist, editor, writer, author of seven books, including *The Universe and the Teacup: The Mathematics of Truth and Beauty.*

Marc Cooper, Lecturer and Associate Director, USC Annenberg Institute for Justice and Journalism. Senior editor, contributing editor, contributing writer, author of three nonfiction books, codirects the News21 project.

Norman Corwin, B.A., Visiting Professor and Writer-in-Residence. Radio/television dramatist and writer of five stage plays and nineteen books.

Geoffrey Cowan, L.L.B., University Professor and Annenberg Family Chair in Communication Leadership. Communication law attorney, Emmy Award–winning producer, playwright, newspaper columnist.

Ed Cray, B.A., Professor. Journalist, author of eighteen books.

Patricia Dean, M.S., Professor of Professional Practice and Associate Director, School of Journalism. Former senior executive producer and television program director, consumer investigative news producer, and news show and investigative unit producer. Codirects the News21 project.

Jennifer Floto, M.A., Associate Professor of Professional Practice. Former vice president/creative director of Ketchum Public Relations, former vice president/group manager for Manning Selvage & Lee, Los Angeles.

Félix Gutiérrez, Ph.D., Professor. Former senior vice president of Freedom Forum and Newseum, author/coauthor of five books and more than fifty scholarly articles and book chapters on Latinos and other racial/ethnic groups.

Jay T. Harris, B.A., Professor and Wallis Annenberg Chair in Journalism and Democracy. Formerly chairman and publisher of the *San Jose Mercury News;* vice president of operations for Knight-Ridder Inc.; executive editor, *Philadelphia Daily News;* national correspondent and columnist.

Robert Hernandez, B.A., Assistant Professor of Professional Practice. Formerly senior news director of development of the *Seattle Times*; Web designer and consultant for El Salvador's largest daily newspaper site, *La Prensa Gráfica*, Web producer for the *San Francisco Chronicle* and online editor of the *San Francisco Examiner*.

Henry Jenkins, Ph.D., Provost's Professor of Communication, Journalism, and Cinematic Arts. Research: role of journalism in the digital age, new media technologies in educational settings, transmedia storytelling.

Jonathan Kotler, J.D., Associate Professor. Attorney, coauthor, former dean of USC Graduate School.

Josh Kun, Ph.D., Berkeley, Associate Professor. Author, director of the Popular Music Project at Norman Lear Center. Research: music, popular culture, U.S.-Mexico border, race.

Andrew Lih, M.S., Visiting Professor. New media researcher, consultant, former video and multimedia journalist for *Wall Street Journal Online* and author of *The Wikipedia Revolution: How a Bunch of Nobodies Created the World's Greatest Encyclopedia.*

Judy Muller, B.A., Associate Professor. Commentator, author, former *ABC News* correspondent and *CBS News* correspondent and radio anchor.

Bryce Nelson, M. Phil., Professor. Former reporter, spokesman for Christopher Commission, and Director of School of Journalism.

Geneva Overholser, M.S., Director, School of Journalism. Award-winning journalist and media scholar, former editor, syndicated columnist, coeditor.

Tim Page, B.A., Visiting Professor. Chief music critic and culture writer for the *Washington Post,* Grammy Award nominee, author, winner of Pulitzer Prize in Criticism (1997).

Michael Parks, B.A., Professor and Director, School of Journalism. Former editor, executive vice president, vice president of Times Mirror Co., bureau chief, winner of Pulitzer Prize in International Reporting (1987).

Larry Pryor, M.S., Associate Professor. Founding editor of *Online Journalism Review;* former *Los Angeles Times* Web-site editor and newspaper writer, editor, and reporter. Research: New media topics.

Richard Reeves, M.E., Lecturer. Author of eleven books, syndicated columnist, former chief correspondent, national editor, magazine columnist, chief political correspondent.

Joe Saltzman, M.S., Professor. News and documentary writer/reporter/producer, author, director of the Image of the Journalist in Popular Culture project.

Stacy Scholder, B.A. Associate Director, *Annenberg TV News.* Former television producer, executive producer, news producer.

Philip Seib, J.D., Professor. Author of numerous books, coeditor. Research: international communication issues related to new media technologies, democratization, war, terrorism.

Willa Seidenberg, B.A., Lecturer and Director, *Annenberg Radio News.* Former radio reporter, anchor, producer, TV news writer, coauthor.

Erna Smith, B.A. Author of several studies on race and the media, former reporter, editor, and copy editor at several newspapers. Research: diversity issues in journalism, journalism education.

Roberto Suro, M.S., Professor and Director, Master of Arts in Specialized Journalism Program. Newspaper print journalist in foreign, domestic, and Washington coverage; author; founding director, Pew Hispanic Center. Research: Hispanic population.

Jerry Swerling, M.S., Professor of Professional Practice and Director, Strategic Public Relations Center. Principal of Swerling & Associates, Communications Management and Organizational Consulting.

Sandy Tolan, Associate Professor. Radio and print journalist, author, producer of radio documentaries and features.

Diane Winston, Ph.D., Associate Professor and Knight Chair in Media and Religion. Author, columnist, coeditor. Former newspaper reporter, television news writer, independent documentary filmmaker.

School of Communication

Jonathan D. Aronson, Ph.D., Professor. Cofounded Annenberg Research Network on International Communication. Research: communications policy, globalization, and international trade and trade negotiations. Former director, USC School of International Relations.

Sandra Ball-Rokeach, Ph.D., Associate Professor and Associate Dean for Faculty Affairs. Rockefeller and Fulbright Fellow. On editorial boards of a number of journals, coeditor of *Communication Research.* Research: transformation of urban communities.

Sarah Banet-Weiser, Ph.D., Associate Professor. Author and coeditor. Research: popular culture, media and consumer culture, with a focus on race, gender, and citizenship.

François Bar, Ph.D., Associate Professor and Director, Annenberg Research Network on International Communication. Research: continuing evolution of communication networks, including their deployment, regulation, and business use.

Daniela Baroffio-Bota, Ph.D., Senior Lecturer. Research: how feminism, U.S. militarism, and race in post-9/11 portrayals of female soldiers both consolidate traditional national ideologies and offer potential for resistance against patriarchal systems.

Manuel Castells, Ph.D., Professor and Wallis Annenberg Chair in Communication Technology and Society. Research: relationship between mass media, communication networks, and political power.

Peter Clarke, Ph.D., Professor. Author and former dean. Research: communication and health behavior; programs to improve the public's well-being, especially among underserved groups.

Michael J. Cody, Ph.D., Professor. Author and editor. Research: interpersonal communication and persuasion.

Jeffrey Cole, Ph.D., Research Professor and Director, Annenberg Center for the Digital Future. Research: effects of media policy, violence, and computer and Internet technology on all aspects of society. Founder/director of the twenty-country World Internet Project.

Geoffrey Cowan, L.L.B., University Professor and Annenberg Family Chair in Communication Leadership. Former director, *Voice of America;* communication law attorney; Emmy Award–winning producer, playwright, and newspaper columnist.

Nicholas Cull, Ph.D., Professor and Director, Master of Public Diplomacy Program. Author of numerous articles, including *Selling War,* one of *Choice* magazine's 10-best academic books of 1995.

Daniel Durbin, Ph.D., Senior Lecturer. Research: rhetoric of sports, health, fitness, nutrition, and medicine; promotion of health, fitness, and medicine in popular-press advertising.

Robeson Taj P. Frazier, Ph.D., Assistant Professor. Research: race and ethnicity, comparative political economy, popular culture, sport, globalization, transnationalism and internationalism.

Janet Fulk, Ph.D., Professor. Author. Research: impact of communication systems on collaboration and knowledge distribution across boundaries of space, time, team, organization, and nation.

G. Thomas Goodnight, Ph.D., Professor and Director, Doctoral Studies. Deliberation and postwar society, science communication, argument and aesthetics, public discourse.

Jerrold Green, Ph.D., Research Professor. Formerly with the RAND Corporation, a partner in Best-Associates, a merchant banking firm.

Larry Gross, Ph.D., Professor and Director, School of Communication. Author and editor. Research: media and culture, art and communication, visual communication, media portrayals of minorities.

Thomas A. Hollihan, Ph.D., Professor. Research: arguments that shape public policy and political discourse; including issues of citizenship and community in the postmodern age.

Andrea B. Hollingshead, Ph.D., Associate Professor. Research: strategic communication, knowledge sharing, social influence, decision making in teams and online communities.

Colleen Keough, Ph.D., Clinical Associate Professor. Strategic planning and financial management workshops in Central and Eastern Europe. Research: role of communications in conflict management.

Josh Kun, Ph.D., Associate Professor. Author of *Audiotopia;* directs the Popular Music Project at the Norman Lear Center. Research: music, popular culture, U.S.-Mexico border, race.

Randall Lake, Ph.D., Associate Professor. Writer. Research: contemporary rhetorical theory and practice, particularly political and public argumentation.

Ben Lee, Ph.D., Senior Lecturer. Sociologist and statistician. Research: human behavior in financial markets.

Kwan Min Lee, Ph.D., Assistant Professor. Author of "hot paper" in social sciences. Research: sociopsychological effects of new information and communication technologies, including human-computer and human-robot interaction.

Doe Mayer, Professor and Mary Pickford Chair, School of Cinematic Arts. Coauthor of *Creative Filmmaking From the Inside Out.* Research: practical international application of communication campaign strategies and designs for social issues and health-defined organizations.

Margaret McLaughlin, Ph.D., Professor. Key investigator at Integrated Media Systems Center. Research: use of virtual environments in delivery of health and social services.

Lynn C. Miller, Ph.D., Professor. Research: use of multidisciplinary approaches to create intelligent agents and virtual worlds for testing communication theory and enhancing health and educational outcomes.

Peter R. Monge, Ph.D., Professor. Coauthor and editor. Research: communication networks in a variety of social contexts, ecology of communication processes within organizational communities.

Sheila T. Murphy, Ph.D., Associate Professor. Research: relationship between emotion and cognition and their relative influence on judgments and beliefs, decision making, information processing, agenda setting, politics.

Stephen O'Leary, Ph.D., Associate Professor. Author. Research: religious communication, rhetorical theory, criticism.

Patricia Riley, Ph.D., Associate Professor and Director, M.A./M.Sc. in Global Communication Program. Author and consultant. Research: organizational communication, organizational politics, culture change, knowledge management.

Robert Scheer, Clinical Professor. Journalist and nationally syndicated columnist, author, editor, radio host.

Kenneth K. Sereno, Ph.D., Associate Professor. Research: communication theory, persuasion, interpersonal and family communication, humor's role in intimate relationships, effect of "clicker" technology in the classroom.

Christopher Smith, Ph.D., Senior Lecturer and Director, Johnson Communication Leadership Center. Research: modern financial markets and their impact on everyday culture, pop culture, entertainment's role in public diplomacy, convergence trends in media industries.

Stacy Smith, Ph.D., Associate Professor. Research: children's reactions to mass media, including developmental differences in emotional and cognitive processing; content patterns and effects of the media on youth.

Gordon Stables, Ph.D., Clinical Professor. Research: rhetoric and argumentation, policy debate and forensics, public debate surrounding the global war on terrorism.

Susan Resnick West, Ph.D. Author on performance appraisal, management of professional employees, and evaluation of strategic change efforts. Research: leadership, employee development, and evaluation to enable strategic change;

Dmitri Williams, Ph.D., Assistant Professor. Research: social and economic impacts of new media, with particular emphasis on video games and the Internet.

Ernest J. Wilson III, Ph.D., Professor and Walter Annenberg Chair in Communication. Research: politics of global sustainable innovation in high-tech industries, network inequality, China-Africa relations, and the role of culture in U.S. national security policy.

Section 17
Conflict Resolution and Mediation/Peace Studies

This section contains a directory of institutions offering graduate work in conflict resolution and mediation/peace studies. Additional information about programs listed in the directory may be obtained by writing directly to the dean of a graduate school or chair of a department at the address given in the directory.

For programs offering related work, see also in this book *Political Science and International Affairs* and *Public, Regional, and Industrial Affairs.* In another guide in this series:
Graduate Programs in Business, Education, Health, Information Studies, Law & Social Work
See *Business Administration and Management* and *Law*

CONTENTS

Program Directory
Conflict Resolution and Mediation/Peace Studies   712

Close-Ups

See:
American University—International Service   861
Tufts University—Law and Diplomacy   879

Conflict Resolution and Mediation/Peace Studies

Abilene Christian University, Graduate School, College of Arts and Sciences, Department of Conflict Resolution, Abilene, TX 79699-9100. Offers conflict resolution (Certificate); conflict resolution and reconciliation (MA). *Faculty:* 2 full-time (0 women), 3 part-time/adjunct (1 woman). *Students:* 15 full-time (6 women), 40 part-time (27 women); includes 3 minority (1 African American, 2 Hispanic Americans). 47 applicants, 87% accepted, 27 enrolled. In 2008, 21 other advanced degrees awarded. *Application deadline:* For fall admission, 4/1 priority date for domestic students; for spring admission, 10/1 for domestic students. Applications are processed on a rolling basis. Application fee: $40 ($45 for international students). Electronic applications accepted. *Expenses:* Tuition: Full-time $10,728; part-time $640 per hour. Required fees: $1090; $53.50 per hour. $10 per term. Tuition and fees vary according to campus/location. *Financial support:* In 2008–09, 42 students received support. Applicants required to submit FAFSA. *Unit head:* Dr. Joe L. Cope, Graduate Adviser, 325-674-2015, Fax: 325-674-6966, E-mail: copej@acu.edu. *Application contact:* William Horn, Graduate Admissions Counselor, 325-674-2656, Fax: 325-674-6717, E-mail: gradinfo@acu.edu.

American Public University System, AMU/APU Graduate Programs, Charles Town, WV 25414. Offers air warfare (MA Military Studies); American Revolution (MA Military Studies); business administration (MBA); Civil War (MA Military Studies); criminal justice (MA); defense management (MA Military Studies); emergency and disaster management (MA); environmental policy and management (MS); fire science management (MA); global engagement (MA); history (MA); homeland security (MA); humanities (MA); intelligence (MA Military Studies, MA Strategic Intelligence); international peace and conflict resolution (MA); international relations and conflict resolution (MA); joint warfare (MA Military Studies); land warfare international perspective (MA Military Studies); management (MA); military history (MA); military leadership (MA Military Studies); national security studies (MA); naval warfare international (MA Military Studies); naval warfare US (MA Military Studies); political science (MA); public administration (MA); public health (MA); security management (MA); space studies (MS); special ops/LIC (MA Military Studies); sports management (MA); transportation and logistics management (MA); transportation management (MA); unconventional warfare (MA Military Studies); World War II (MA Military Studies). Programs offered via distance learning only. Part-time and evening/weekend programs available. Postbaccalaureate distance learning degree programs offered (no on-campus study). *Degree requirements:* For master's, comprehensive exam. *Entrance requirements:* For master's, bachelor's degree or equivalent, minimum GPA of 2.7 in last 60 hours of course work. Electronic applications accepted. *Faculty research:* Military history, criminal justice, management performance, national security.

American University, School of International Service, Washington, DC 20016-8071. Offers comparative and regional studies (Certificate); cross-cultural communication (Certificate); development management (MS); ethics, peace, and global affairs (MA); European studies (Certificate); global environmental policy (MA, Certificate); international affairs (MA), including comparative and regional studies, environmental policy, international economic policy, international politics, natural resources and sustainable development, U.S. foreign policy; international communication (MA, Certificate); international development (MA, Certificate); international development management (Certificate); international economic policy (Certificate); international economic relations (Certificate); international media (MA); international peace and conflict resolution (MA, Certificate); international relations (PhD); international service (MIS); peace building (Certificate); the Americas (Certificate); United States foreign policy (Certificate); JD/MA. Part-time and evening/weekend programs available. *Faculty:* 70 full-time (28 women), 51 part-time/adjunct (20 women). *Students:* 519 full-time (317 women), 335 part-time (205 women); includes 157 minority (54 African Americans, 2 American Indian/Alaska Native, 45 Asian Americans or Pacific Islanders, 56 Hispanic Americans), 116 international. Average age 27. 1,901 applicants, 68% accepted, 277 enrolled. In 2008, 350 master's, 5 doctorates, 9 other advanced degrees awarded. Terminal master's awarded for partial completion of doctoral program. *Degree requirements:* For master's, one foreign language, comprehensive exam, thesis or alternative; for doctorate, one foreign language, comprehensive exam, thesis/dissertation, research practicum; for Certificate, minimum 15 credit hours related course work. *Entrance requirements:* For master's, GRE, 24 credits of course work in related social sciences, minimum GPA of 3.5, 2 letters of recommendation, bachelor's degree, resumé, statement of purpose; for doctorate, GRE, 2 letters of recommendation, 24 credits in related social sciences; for Certificate, bachelor's degree. Additional exam requirements/recommendations for international students: Required—TOEFL (minimum score 600 paper-based; 250 computer-based; 100 iBT). *Application deadline:* For fall admission, 1/15 priority date for domestic students; for spring admission, 10/1 priority date for domestic students. Applications are processed on a rolling basis. Application fee: $50. *Expenses:* Tuition: Full-time $21,204; part-time $1178 per credit hour. Required fees: $380. Part-time tuition and fees vary according to course load and program. *Financial support:* Career-related internships or fieldwork, Federal Work-Study, and institutionally sponsored loans available. Financial award application deadline: 1/15. *Faculty research:* International intellectual property, international environmental issues, international law and legal order, international telecommunications/technology, international sustainable development. *Unit head:* Dr. Louis W. Goodman, Dean, 202-885-1600, Fax: 202-885-2494. *Application contact:* Yasmin Quianzon, Director of Graduate Admissions and Financial Aid, 202-885-2496, Fax: 202-885-1109.

See Close-Up on page 861.

The American University of Paris, Graduate Programs, Paris, France. Offers finance (MSF); global communications (MAGC); international affairs, conflict resolution and civil society development (MA); Middle Eastern and Islamic studies (MA); public administration (MPA). *Degree requirements:* For master's, thesis. *Entrance requirements:* For master's, minimum undergraduate GPA of 3.0.

Antioch University McGregor, Graduate Programs, Program in Conflict Resolution, Yellow Springs, OH 45387-1609. Offers MA. Part-time and evening/weekend programs available. Postbaccalaureate distance learning degree programs offered (minimal on-campus study). *Degree requirements:* For master's, thesis or alternative. *Entrance requirements:* For master's, resumé, 2 letters of reference. Electronic applications accepted. *Expenses:* Contact institution.

Arcadia University, Graduate Studies, Program in International Peace and Conflict Management, Glenside, PA 19038-3295. Offers MAIPCR. Part-time and evening/weekend programs available. *Degree requirements:* For master's, one foreign language. *Entrance requirements:* For master's, GRE. Additional exam requirements/recommendations for international students: Required—TOEFL. *Expenses:* Contact institution.

Associated Mennonite Biblical Seminary, Graduate and Professional Programs, Elkhart, IN 46517-1999. Offers Christian formation (MA); divinity (M Div); mission and evangelism (MA); peace studies (MA); theological studies (MA, Certificate). *Accreditation:* ACIPE; ATS. Part-time programs available. *Degree requirements:* For master's, comprehensive exam, thesis optional; for M Div, integration paper. *Entrance requirements:* For M Div, master's, and Certificate, 3 letters of reference. Additional exam requirements/recommendations for international students: Required—TOEFL (minimum score 550 paper-based; 213 computer-based). Electronic applications accepted. *Faculty research:* Biblical studies, theology, church history, church leadership.

Baker University, School of Professional and Graduate Studies, Program in Conflict Management and Dispute Resolution, Baldwin City, KS 66006-0065. Offers MA. Part-time and evening/weekend programs available. *Students:* 9 full-time (6 women), 26 part-time (20 women); includes 8 minority (all African Americans). Average age 45. In 2008, 14 master's awarded. *Entrance requirements:* Additional exam requirements/recommendations for international students: Required—TOEFL (minimum score 600 paper-based; 250 computer-based). Application fee: $20. *Expenses:* Tuition: Full-time $9265; part-time $300 per credit hour. One-time fee: $2535 full-time. Tuition and fees vary according to course load, degree level and program. *Financial support:* Applicants required to submit FAFSA. *Unit head:* Dr. Marvin L. Hunt, Vice President and Dean, 913-491-4432, Fax: 913-491-0470, E-mail: marvin.hunt@bakeru.edu. *Application contact:* Assistant Dean for Instruction and Curriculum.

Bethany Theological Seminary, Graduate and Professional Programs, Richmond, IN 47374-4019. Offers biblical studies (MA Th); ministry studies (M Div); peace studies (M Div, MA Th); theological studies (MA Th, CATS); youth ministry (M Div). *Accreditation:* ACIPE; ATS. Part-time programs available. Postbaccalaureate distance learning degree programs offered (minimal on-campus study). *Degree requirements:* For master's, thesis. *Entrance requirements:* For M Div, letters of reference, minimum GPA of 2.75; for master's, letters of reference, minimum GPA of 3.0. Additional exam requirements/recommendations for international students: Required—TOEFL (minimum score 550 paper-based; 218 computer-based).

Brandeis University, Graduate School of Arts and Sciences, Program in Coexistence and Conflict, Waltham, MA 02454-9110. Offers MA, MA/MA. *Degree requirements:* For master's, thesis, internship. *Entrance requirements:* For master's, 3 letters of recommendation, curriculum vitae, resumé. Additional exam requirements/recommendations for international students: Required—TOEFL (minimum score 600 paper-based; 250 computer-based; 100 iBT); Recommended—IELTS (minimum score 7). Electronic applications accepted.

Brandeis University, Graduate School of Arts and Sciences, Program in Coexistence and Conflict and Sustainable International Development, Waltham, MA 02454-9110. Offers MA/MA.

California State University, Dominguez Hills, College of Arts and Humanities, Program in Negotiation, Conflict Resolution and Peacebuilding, Carson, CA 90747-0001. Offers MA. Part-time and evening/weekend programs available. Postbaccalaureate distance learning degree programs offered (no on-campus study). *Faculty:* 5 full-time (3 women). *Students:* 31 full-time (20 women), 177 part-time (106 women); includes 79 minority (29 African Americans, 12 Asian Americans or Pacific Islanders, 38 Hispanic Americans), 8 international. Average age 40. 172 applicants, 73% accepted, 56 enrolled. In 2008, 47 master's awarded. *Degree requirements:* For master's, portfolio. *Entrance requirements:* For master's, minimum GPA of 3.2, 3 letters of recommendation. *Application deadline:* For fall admission, 5/1 for domestic and international students; for spring admission, 12/1 for domestic and international students. Application fee: $55. Electronic applications accepted. *Expenses:* Tuition, nonresident: part-time $339 per unit. Required fees: $1300 per semester. *Faculty research:* Ethnic conflict, mediator ethics, teacher training, global conflict resolution (including role of ombuds), optimal multicultural process. *Unit head:* Dr. A. Marco Turk, Professor and Director, 310-243-3237, Fax: 310-516-4268, E-mail: amturk@csudh.edu. *Application contact:* Penny Ann LaBaun, Administrative Coordinator, 310-243-3237, Fax: 310-516-4268, E-mail: plabaun@csudh.edu.

Cambridge College, School of Management, Cambridge, MA 02138-5304. Offers business negotiation and conflict resolution (M Mgt); general business (M Mgt); health care informatics (M Mgt); healthcare management (M Mgt); leadership in human organizational dynamics (M Mgt); non-profit and public organization management (M Mgt); small business development (M Mgt); technology management (M Mgt). Part-time and evening/weekend programs available. *Faculty:* 4 full-time (3 women), 170 part-time/adjunct (130 women). *Students:* 422 full-time (255 women), 226 part-time (144 women); includes 258 minority (160 African Americans, 1 American Indian/Alaska Native, 40 Asian Americans or Pacific Islanders, 57 Hispanic Americans), 70 international. Average age 39. 229 applicants, 77% accepted, 134 enrolled. In 2008, 253 master's awarded. *Degree requirements:* For master's, thesis, core courses, seminars. *Entrance requirements:* For master's, resumé, health insurance, interview, essay, official transcripts. Additional exam requirements/recommendations for international students: Required—TOEFL (minimum score 550 paper-based; 213 computer-based; 79 iBT); Recommended—IELTS (minimum score 6). *Application deadline:* Applications are processed on a rolling basis. Application fee: $30. *Expenses:* Contact institution. *Financial support:* In 2008–09, 324 students received support. Federal Work-Study and scholarships/grants available. Financial award applicants required to submit FAFSA. *Faculty research:* Negotiation, mediation and conflict resolution; leadership; management of diverse organizations; case studies and simulation methodologies for management education. *Unit head:* Dr. Mary Ann Joseph, PhD, Acting Dean, 617-873-0127, Fax: 617-873-0673, E-mail: maryann.joseph@cambridgecollege.edu. *Application contact:* Jessie Haigh, Admissions Counselor, 617-873-0285, Fax: 617-873-0673, E-mail: jessie.haigh@cambridgecollege.edu.

Carleton University, Faculty of Graduate Studies, Faculty of Public Affairs and Management, Department of Law, Ottawa, ON K1S 5B6, Canada. Offers conflict resolution (Certificate); legal studies (MA). *Degree requirements:* For master's, thesis. *Entrance requirements:* For master's, honors degree. Additional exam requirements/recommendations for international students: Required—TOEFL. *Faculty research:* Legal and social theory; women, law, and gender relations; law, crime, and social order; political economy of law; international law.

Chaminade University of Honolulu, Graduate Services, Program in Education, Honolulu, HI 96816-1578. Offers social science via peace education (M Ed). Part-time and evening/weekend programs available. Postbaccalaureate distance learning degree programs offered (minimal on-campus study). *Degree requirements:* For master's, thesis or alternative. *Entrance requirements:* For master's, minimum GPA of 2.75, 3 letters of recommendation. Additional exam requirements/recommendations for international students: Required—TOEFL (minimum score 550 paper-based). *Faculty research:* Peace and curriculum education.

Colorado Technical University Colorado Springs, Graduate Studies, Program in Management, Colorado Springs, CO 80907-3896. Offers accounting (MBA, MSA); business administration (MBA); finance (MBA); human resources management (MBA); logistics/supply chain management (MBA); management (DM); marketing (MBA); mediation and dispute resolution (MBA); operations management (MBA); project management (MBA); technology management (MBA). Part-time and evening/weekend programs available. Postbaccalaureate distance learning degree programs offered. *Degree requirements:* For master's, thesis or alternative; for doctorate, thesis/dissertation. *Entrance requirements:* For doctorate, minimum graduate GPA of 3.0, 5 years of related work experience. *Faculty research:* Sexual harassment, performance evaluation, critical thinking.

Colorado Technical University Denver, Programs in Business Administration and Management, Greenwood Village, CO 80111. Offers accounting (MBA); business administration (MBA); business administration and management (EMBA); finance (MBA); human resource management (MBA); marketing (MBA); mediation and dispute resolution (MBA); operations management (MBA); project management (MBA); technology management (MBA). Part-time and evening/weekend programs available. *Degree requirements:* For master's, thesis or alternative. *Entrance requirements:* For master's, minimum undergraduate GPA of 3.0, resumé.

Columbia College, Graduate Programs, Department of Human Relations, Columbia, SC 29203-5998. Offers human behavior and conflict management (MA); interpersonal relations/conflict management (Certificate); organizational behavior/conflict management (Certificate). Part-time and evening/weekend programs available. Postbaccalaureate distance learning degree programs offered (minimal on-campus study). *Faculty:* 1 (woman) full-time, 3 part-time/adjunct (2 women). *Students:* 30 part-time (28 women); includes 17 minority (all African Americans). Average age 40. 40 applicants, 95% accepted, 25 enrolled. In 2008, 21 master's awarded.

Degree requirements: For master's, thesis, practicum. *Entrance requirements:* For master's, GRE General Test, MAT, 2 letters of recommendation, valid teaching certificate, minimum GPA of 3.2. Additional exam requirements/recommendations for international students: Required—TOEFL. *Application deadline:* For fall admission, 7/15 priority date for domestic students, 7/15 for international students. Applications are processed on a rolling basis. Application fee: $50. Electronic applications accepted. *Expenses:* Contact institution. *Financial support:* Available to part-time students. Application deadline: 7/1; *Faculty research:* Envisioning and the resolution of conflict, environmental conflict resolution, crisis negotiation. *Unit head:* Dr. Elaine Ferraro, Chair, 803-786-3687, Fax: 803-786-3790, E-mail: eferraro@colacoll.edu. *Application contact:* Carolyn Emeneker, Director of Graduate School and Evening College Admissions, 803-786-3766, Fax: 803-786-3674, E-mail: emeneker@colacoll.edu.

Columbia University, School of Continuing Education, Program in Negotiation and Conflict Resolution, New York, NY 10027. Offers MS. Part-time programs available. *Entrance requirements:* For master's, 2 letters of recommendation, professional resumé. Electronic applications accepted.

Cornell University, Graduate School, Graduate Fields of Architecture, Art and Planning, Field of Regional Science, Ithaca, NY 14853-0001. Offers environmental studies (MA, MS, PhD); international spatial problems (MA, MS, PhD); location theory (MA, MS, PhD); multiregional economic analysis (MA, MS, PhD); peace science (MA, MS, PhD); planning methods (MA, MS, PhD); urban and regional economics (MA, MS, PhD). *Faculty:* 17 full-time (5 women). *Students:* 22 full-time (10 women); includes 2 minority (1 African American, 1 Asian American or Pacific Islander), 19 international. Average age 33. 18 applicants, 67% accepted, 3 enrolled. In 2008, 3 master's, 2 doctorates awarded. Terminal master's awarded for partial completion of doctoral program. *Degree requirements:* For master's, thesis; for doctorate, comprehensive exam, thesis/dissertation. *Entrance requirements:* For master's and doctorate, GRE General Test, 2 letters of recommendation. Additional exam requirements/recommendations for international students: Required—TOEFL (minimum score 600 paper-based; 250 computer-based; 77 iBT). *Application deadline:* For fall admission, 1/15 priority date for domestic students. Application fee: $70. Electronic applications accepted. *Expenses:* Tuition: Full-time $29,500. Required fees: $70. Full-time tuition and fees vary according to degree level, program and student level. *Financial support:* In 2008–09, 7 students received support, including 2 research assistantships with full tuition reimbursements available, 5 teaching assistantships with full tuition reimbursements available; fellowships with full tuition reimbursements available, institutionally sponsored loans, scholarships/grants, health care benefits, tuition waivers (full and partial), and unspecified assistantships also available. Financial award applicants required to submit FAFSA. *Faculty research:* Urban and regional growth, spatial economics, formation of spatial patterns by socioeconomic systems, non-linear dynamics and complex systems, environmental-economic systems. *Unit head:* Director of Graduate Studies, 607-255-6848, Fax: 607-255-1971. *Application contact:* Graduate Field Assistant, 607-255-6848, Fax: 607-255-1971, E-mail: regsci@cornell.edu.

Creighton University, School of Law, Program in Negotiation and Dispute Resolution, Omaha, NE 68178-0001. Offers MS, Certificate. Part-time and evening/weekend programs available. Postbaccalaureate distance learning degree programs offered (minimal on-campus study). *Degree requirements:* For master's, thesis or alternative, practicum. *Entrance requirements:* Additional exam requirements/recommendations for international students: Required—TOEFL. Electronic applications accepted. *Faculty research:* Nationalism/identity and conflict; health care collaboration; complex adaptive items and conflict engagement; history, memory and conflict; culture and conflict.

Dallas Baptist University, College of Business, Business Administration Program, Dallas, TX 75211-9299. Offers accounting (MBA); business communication (MBA); conflict resolution management (MBA); e-business (MBA); entrepreneurship (MBA); finance (MBA); health care management (MBA); international business (MBA); leading the non-profit organization (MBA); management (MBA); management information systems (MBA); marketing (MBA); project management (MBA); technology and engineering management (MBA). *Accreditation:* ACBSP. Part-time and evening/weekend programs available. *Faculty:* 68 full-time (30 women), 113 part-time/adjunct (47 women). *Students:* 157 full-time, 353 part-time. 294 applicants, 56% accepted, 143 enrolled. In 2008, 155 master's awarded. *Entrance requirements:* For master's, GMAT, minimum GPA of 3.0. Additional exam requirements/recommendations for international students: Required—TOEFL, IELTS. *Application deadline:* Applications are processed on a rolling basis. Application fee: $25. Electronic applications accepted. *Expenses:* Tuition: Part-time $558 per credit hour. *Financial support:* Federal Work-Study, institutionally sponsored loans, scholarships/grants, and tuition waivers (full and partial) available. Support available to part-time students. Financial award applicants required to submit FAFSA. *Faculty research:* Sports management, services marketing, retailing, strategic management, financial planning/investments. *Unit head:* Dr. Sandra S. Reid, Director, 214-333-5280, Fax: 214-333-5293, E-mail: graduate@dbu.edu. *Application contact:* Kit P. Montgomery, Director of Graduate Programs, 214-333-5242, Fax: 214-333-5579, E-mail: graduate@dbu.edu.

Dallas Baptist University, College of Business, Management Program, Dallas, TX 75211-9299. Offers business communication (MA); conflict resolution management (MA); general management (MA); health care management (MA); human resource management (MA); performance management (MA). Part-time and evening/weekend programs available. *Faculty:* 68 full-time (30 women), 113 part-time/adjunct (47 women). *Students:* 14 full-time, 106 part-time. In 2008, 60 master's awarded. *Entrance requirements:* For master's, GRE General Test, minimum GPA of 3.0. Additional exam requirements/recommendations for international students: Required—TOEFL, IELTS. *Application deadline:* Applications are processed on a rolling basis. Application fee: $25. Electronic applications accepted. *Expenses:* Tuition: Part-time $558 per credit hour. *Financial support:* Federal Work-Study, institutionally sponsored loans, scholarships/grants, and tuition waivers (full and partial) available. Support available to part-time students. Financial award applicants required to submit FAFSA. *Faculty research:* Organizational behavior, conflict personalities. *Unit head:* Joanne Hix, Director, 214-333-5793, Fax: 214-333-5293, E-mail: graduate@dbu.edu. *Application contact:* Kit P. Montgomery, Director of Graduate Programs, 214-333-5242, Fax: 214-333-5579, E-mail: graduate@dbu.edu.

Duquesne University, Graduate School of Liberal Arts, Graduate Center for Social and Public Policy, Pittsburgh, PA 15282-1750. Offers conflict resolution and peace studies (Certificate); social and public policy (MA, Certificate). Programs are a collaboration between the Departments of Political Science and Sociology. Part-time and evening/weekend programs available. *Faculty:* 15 full-time (3 women), 1 (woman) part-time/adjunct. *Students:* 37 full-time (25 women), 12 part-time (9 women); includes 1 minority (African American), 7 international. Average age 27. 29 applicants, 90% accepted, 18 enrolled. In 2008, 9 master's awarded. *Degree requirements:* For master's, thesis. *Entrance requirements:* For master's, GRE General Test. Additional exam requirements/recommendations for international students: Required—TOEFL. *Application deadline:* For fall admission, 4/30 priority date for domestic and international students; for spring admission, 11/1 priority date for domestic and international students. Applications are processed on a rolling basis. Application fee: $50. Electronic applications accepted. *Expenses:* Tuition: Part-time $819 per credit. Required fees: $78 per credit. Tuition and fees vary according to course load. *Financial support:* In 2008–09, 20 students received support, including 12 research assistantships with full and partial tuition reimbursements available (averaging $9,000 per year), 4 teaching assistantships with full and partial tuition reimbursements available (averaging $9,000 per year); career-related internships or fieldwork, institutionally sponsored loans, scholarships/grants, tuition waivers (full and partial), and unspecified assistantships also available. Support available to part-time students. Financial award application deadline: 5/1. *Faculty research:* Program evaluation, environmental policy, criminal justice policy, health care policy. Total annual research expenditures: $30,000. *Unit head:* Dr. Joseph Yenerall, Director, 412-396-6485, Fax: 412-396-5265, E-mail: socialpolicy@duq.edu. *Application contact:* Linda L. Rendulic, Assistant to the Dean, 412-396-6400, Fax: 412-396-5265, E-mail: rendulic@duq.edu.

Eastern Mennonite University, Program in Conflict Transformation, Harrisonburg, VA 22802-2462. Offers MA, Graduate Certificate. Part-time programs available. *Faculty:* 7 full-time (2 women), 3 part-time/adjunct (1 woman). *Students:* 40 full-time (28 women), 12 part-time (5 women); includes 1 minority (African American), 7 international. Average age 37. *Degree requirements:* For master's, practicum. *Entrance requirements:* For master's, minimum undergraduate GPA of 2.75. Additional exam requirements/recommendations for international students: Required—TOEFL (minimum score 550 paper-based; 213 computer-based). *Application deadline:* For fall admission, 2/15 priority date for domestic and international students. Applications are processed on a rolling basis. Application fee: $25. Electronic applications accepted. *Expenses:* Contact institution. *Financial support:* In 2008–09, 4 students received support. Scholarships/grants available. Financial award application deadline: 6/30; financial award applicants required to submit FAFSA. *Faculty research:* Restorative justice, negotiation, security in an age of terror, trauma recovery, development, peace building. Total annual research expenditures: $30,000. *Unit head:* Dr. David Brubaker, Academic Director, 540-432-4423, Fax: 540-432-4449, E-mail: david.brubaker@emu.edu. *Application contact:* Janelle Myers-Benner, Administrative Assistant, 540-432-4986, Fax: 540-432-4449, E-mail: bennerj@emu.edu.

Florida International University, College of Education, Department of Educational Leadership and Policy Studies, Program in Conflict Resolution and Consensus Building, Miami, FL 33199. Offers Certificate. Part-time and evening/weekend programs available. *Entrance requirements:* Additional exam requirements/recommendations for international students: Required—TOEFL (minimum score 550 paper-based; 213 computer-based; 80 iBT), IELTS (minimum score 6.3). Electronic applications accepted. *Faculty research:* Workforce housing, labor conditions, labor organizations, workforce development.

Fresno Pacific University, Graduate Programs, Program in Peacemaking and Conflict Studies, Fresno, CA 93702-4709. Offers MA. Part-time and evening/weekend programs available. *Degree requirements:* For master's, thesis. *Entrance requirements:* For master's, GMAT, MAT, GRE, interview, 2 writing samples. Additional exam requirements/recommendations for international students: Required—TOEFL (minimum score 550 paper-based; 213 computer-based). Electronic applications accepted.

George Mason University, Institute for Conflict Analysis and Resolution, Fairfax, VA 22030. Offers MS, PhD. Part-time and evening/weekend programs available. *Degree requirements:* For master's, thesis optional; for doctorate, one foreign language, comprehensive exam, thesis/dissertation, oral defense of dissertation. *Entrance requirements:* For master's, 3 recommendation letters; for doctorate, sample of written work, 2 recommendation letters. Additional exam requirements/recommendations for international students: Required—TOEFL (minimum score 575 paper-based; 230 computer-based; 88 iBT). Electronic applications accepted. *Faculty research:* Preventive diplomacy, conflict/dispute resolution, peace/security, political violence, international terrorism.

George Mason University, School of Public Policy, Program in Peace Operations, Fairfax, VA 22030. Offers MNPS. Part-time programs available. *Degree requirements:* For master's, thesis or alternative. *Entrance requirements:* For master's, minimum undergraduate GPA of 3.0, 2 letters of recommendation, resumé, goals statement. Additional exam requirements/recommendations for international students: Required—TOEFL. Electronic applications accepted. *Expenses:* Contact institution.

Georgetown University, Graduate School of Arts and Sciences, Department of Government, Program in Conflict Resolution, Washington, DC 20057. Offers MA.

Georgetown University, Graduate School of Arts and Sciences, Edmund A. Walsh School of Foreign Service, Center for Peace and Security Studies, Washington, DC 20057. Offers security studies (MA); MA/JD; MA/PhD.

Hult International Business School, Program in International Relations—Hult London Campus, Cambridge, MA 02141. Offers conflict resolution (MA); diplomacy (MA); international public law (MA); international relations (MA); Middle East international security (MA); politics (MA); security studies (MA); terrorism (MA); U.S. foreign policy (MA). Part-time programs available. *Entrance requirements:* Additional exam requirements/recommendations for international students: Required—TOEFL (minimum score 580 paper-based; 237 computer-based), TWE (minimum score 5). Electronic applications accepted. *Faculty research:* American foreign politics, Middle East, security studies.

The Johns Hopkins University, Paul H. Nitze School of Advanced International Studies, Washington, DC 20036. Offers international development (Certificate); international public policy (MIPP); international relations (MA, PhD), including African studies (MA), American foreign policy (MA), Asian studies (MA), Canadian studies (MA), conflict management (MA), European studies (MA), global theory and history (MA), international development (MA), international law, and organizations (MA), international policy (MA), international relations (general) (MA), Latin American studies (MA), Middle East studies (MA), Russian and Eurasian studies (MA), strategic studies (MA); international studies (Certificate); JD/MA; MBA/MA; MHS/MA. Terminal master's awarded for partial completion of doctoral program. *Degree requirements:* For master's, one foreign language, 16 non-language courses (8 for MIPP), 2 core examinations, comprehensive oral exam, paper (for some programs); for doctorate, 2 foreign languages, thesis/dissertation, 3 comprehensive exams, defense. *Entrance requirements:* For master's, GMAT or GRE General Test, previous course work in economics, foreign language, undergraduate degree; for doctorate, GRE General Test, master's degree. Additional exam requirements/recommendations for international students: Required—TOEFL (minimum paper-based score of 600, computer-based 250, iBT 100) or IELTS (minimum 7.0). Electronic applications accepted. *Expenses:* Contact institution. *Faculty research:* Regional studies and functional fields of international relations, international economics, conflict management, global theory and history, international law and organizations, international policy, strategic studies.

Jones International University, School of Business, Centennial, CO 80112. Offers accounting (MBA); business communication (MABC); entrepreneurship (MABC, MBA); finance (MBA); global enterprise management (MBA); health care management (MBA); information security management (MBA); information technology management (MBA); leadership and influence (MABC); leading the customer-driven organization (MABC); negotiation and conflict management (MBA); project management (MABC, MBA). Program only offered online. Part-time and evening/weekend programs available. Postbaccalaureate distance learning degree programs offered (no on-campus study). *Degree requirements:* For master's, capstone project. *Entrance requirements:* For master's, minimum cumulative GPA of 2.5. Additional exam requirements/recommendations for international students: Recommended—TOEFL (minimum score 550 paper-based; 213 computer-based). Electronic applications accepted.

Kennesaw State University, College of Humanities and Social Sciences, Program in Conflict Management, Kennesaw, GA 30144-5591. Offers MSCM. Evening/weekend programs available. *Faculty:* 6 full-time (3 women). *Students:* 54 full-time (34 women); includes 15 minority (12 African Americans, 2 American Indian/Alaska Native, 1 Asian American or Pacific Islander), 4 international. Average age 39. 48 applicants, 71% accepted, 27 enrolled. In 2008, 27 master's awarded. *Entrance requirements:* For master's, GMAT, GRE, LSAT. Additional exam requirements/recommendations for international students: Required—TOEFL (minimum score 550 paper-based; 213 computer-based; 80 iBT), IELTS (minimum score 6). *Application deadline:* For fall admission, 6/1 for domestic and international students. Applications are processed on a rolling basis. Application fee: $60. Electronic applications accepted. *Expenses:* Tuition, area resident: Full-time $3668; part-time $153 per semester hour. Tuition, state resident: full-time $3668; part-time $153 per semester hour. Tuition, nonresident: full-time $14,670; part-time $612 per semester hour. Required fees: $948; $474 per semester. *Financial support:* In 2008–09, 1 research assistantship with full tuition reimbursement (averaging $15,000 per year) was awarded; Federal Work-Study and unspecified assistantships also available. Support available to part-time students. Financial award application deadline: 6/15; financial award

Conflict Resolution and Mediation/Peace Studies

Kennesaw State University (continued)

applicants required to submit FAFSA. *Unit head:* Dr. Linda Johnston, Director, 770-423-6299, Fax: 770-423-6312, E-mail: ljohnsto@kennesaw.edu. *Application contact:* Vilma Marquez, Admissions Counselor, 770-420-4377, Fax: 770-423-6885, E-mail: ksugrad@kennesaw.edu.

Lipscomb University, Institute for Conflict Management, Nashville, TN 37204-3951. Offers MA, Certificate. Part-time and evening/weekend programs available. *Degree requirements:* For master's, completion of externship. *Entrance requirements:* For master's, GRE, GMAT, LSAT or equivalent, 3 years work experience. *Expenses:* Contact institution.

Lipscomb University, MBA Program, Nashville, TN 37204-3951. Offers accounting (MBA); business administration (general) (MBA); conflict management (MBA); financial services (MBA); healthcare management (MBA); leadership (MBA); nonprofit management (MBA); sustainable practice (MBA). *Accreditation:* ACBSP. Part-time and evening/weekend programs available. *Entrance requirements:* For master's, GMAT, interview, 2 references, resumé. Additional exam requirements/recommendations for international students: Required—TOEFL (minimum score 570 paper-based; 230 computer-based). Electronic applications accepted. *Expenses:* Contact institution. *Faculty research:* Impact of spirituality on organization commitment; leadership; psychological empowerment; training.

Montclair State University, The Office of Graduate Admissions and Support Services, College of Humanities and Social Sciences, Department of Justice Studies, Montclair, NJ 07043-1624. Offers conflict management in the workplace (Certificate); dispute resolution (MA); governance, compliance and regulation (MA); intellectual property (MA); law and governance (MA); legal management, information and technology (MA); paralegal studies (Certificate). Part-time and evening/weekend programs available. *Faculty:* 9 full-time (7 women), 18 part-time/adjunct (9 women). *Students:* 7 full-time (3 women), 27 part-time (18 women); includes 12 minority (10 African Americans, 1 Asian American or Pacific Islander, 1 Hispanic American), 1 international. Average age 31. 15 applicants, 80% accepted, 10 enrolled. In 2008, 6 master's, 14 other advanced degrees awarded. *Degree requirements:* For master's, comprehensive exam, thesis or alternative. *Entrance requirements:* For master's, GRE General Test, minimum undergraduate GPA of 2.75, 2 letters of recommendation; for Certificate, 2 letters of recommendation. Additional exam requirements/recommendations for international students: Required—TOEFL (minimum score 83 computer-based). *Application deadline:* For fall admission, 6/1 for international students; for spring admission, 10/1 for international students. Applications are processed on a rolling basis. Application fee: $60. Electronic applications accepted. *Financial support:* Research assistantships with full tuition reimbursements, Federal Work-Study, scholarships/grants, and unspecified assistantships available. Support available to part-time students. Financial award application deadline: 3/1. *Unit head:* Dr. Norma Connolly, Chairperson, 973-655-4152, E-mail: connolyn@mail.montclair.edu. *Application contact:* Prof. Jack Baldwin-LeClair, Adviser, 973-655-4000, E-mail: leclairj@mail.montclair.edu.

National Defense University, College of International Security Affairs, Washington, DC 20319-5066. Offers strategic security studies (MA), including conflict management, counterterrorism, homeland defense/ security, international security studies. Part-time and evening/weekend programs available. *Faculty:* 13 full-time (3 women), 14 part-time/adjunct (2 women). *Students:* 33 full-time (2 women), 305 part-time (75 women). Average age 30. 133 applicants, 100% accepted, 133 enrolled. In 2008, 39 master's awarded. *Degree requirements:* For master's, thesis. *Entrance requirements:* Additional exam requirements/recommendations for international students: Required—TOEFL. *Unit head:* Dr. R. Joseph DeSutter, Director, 202-685-3871. *Application contact:* Dr. R. Joseph DeSutter, Director, 202-685-3871.

National University, Academic Affairs, College of Letters and Sciences, Department of Professional Studies, La Jolla, CA 92037-1011. Offers forensic science (MFS), including criminalistics and investigation; public administration (MPA), including alternative dispute resolution, human resource management, organizational leadership, public finance. Part-time and evening/weekend programs available. Postbaccalaureate distance learning degree programs offered (no on-campus study). *Faculty:* 9 full-time (3 women), 134 part-time/adjunct (31 women). *Students:* 126 full-time (67 women), 195 part-time (103 women); includes 137 minority (56 African Americans, 26 Asian Americans or Pacific Islanders, 55 Hispanic Americans), 2 international. Average age 38. 241 applicants, 100% accepted, 241 enrolled. In 2008, 104 master's awarded. *Degree requirements:* For master's, thesis. *Entrance requirements:* For master's, interview, minimum GPA of 2.5. Additional exam requirements/recommendations for international students: Required—TOEFL (minimum score 550 paper-based; 213 computer-based; 79 iBT), IELTS (minimum score 6). *Application deadline:* Applications are processed on a rolling basis. Application fee: $60 ($65 for international students). Electronic applications accepted. *Expenses:* Tuition: Full-time $8694; part-time $322 per credit hour. Tuition and fees vary according to course load. *Financial support:* Career-related internships or fieldwork, institutionally sponsored loans, scholarships/grants, and tuition waivers (partial) available. Support available to part-time students. Financial award application deadline: 6/30; financial award applicants required to submit FAFSA. *Unit head:* Chandrika M. Kelso, Associate Professor and Chair, 858-642-8433, Fax: 858-642-8715, E-mail: ckelso@nu.edu. *Application contact:* Dominick Giovanniello, Associate Regional Dean—San Diego, 800-NAT-UNIV, Fax: 858-541-7792, E-mail: dgiovann@nu.edu.

National University, Academic Affairs, School of Business and Management, Department of Leadership and Business Administration, La Jolla, CA 92037-1011. Offers alternative dispute resolution (MBA); e-business (MBA); financial management (MBA); human resource management (MBA); human resources management (MA); international business (MBA); knowledge management (MS); marketing (MBA); organizational leadership (MBA, MS); technology management (MBA). Part-time and evening/weekend programs available. Postbaccalaureate distance learning degree programs offered (no on-campus study). *Faculty:* 4 full-time (2 women), 40 part-time/adjunct (16 women). *Students:* 126 full-time (81 women), 172 part-time (105 women); includes 144 minority (62 African Americans, 3 American Indian/Alaska Native, 25 Asian Americans or Pacific Islanders, 54 Hispanic Americans), 7 international. Average age 38. 194 applicants, 100% accepted, 194 enrolled. In 2008, 62 master's awarded. *Degree requirements:* For master's, thesis. *Entrance requirements:* For master's, interview, minimum GPA of 2.5. Additional exam requirements/recommendations for international students: Required—TOEFL (minimum score 550 paper-based; 213 computer-based; 79 iBT), IELTS (minimum score 6). *Application deadline:* Applications are processed on a rolling basis. Application fee: $60 ($65 for international students). Electronic applications accepted. *Expenses:* Tuition: Full-time $8694; part-time $322 per credit hour. Tuition and fees vary according to course load. *Financial support:* Career-related internships or fieldwork, institutionally sponsored loans, scholarships/grants, and tuition waivers (partial) available. Support available to part-time students. Financial award application deadline: 6/30; financial award applicants required to submit FAFSA. *Unit head:* Dr. George Drops, Chair and Professor, 858-642-8438, Fax: 858-642-8406, E-mail: gdrops@nu.edu. *Application contact:* Dominick Giovanniello, Associate Regional Dean—San Diego, 800-NAT-UNIV, Fax: 858-541-7792, E-mail: dgiovann@nu.edu.

Norwich University, School of Graduate Studies, Program in Diplomacy, Northfield, VT 05663. Offers international commerce (MA); international conflict management (MA); international terrorism (MA). Evening/weekend programs available. *Faculty:* 1 full-time (0 women), 15 part-time/adjunct (3 women). *Students:* 156 full-time (50 women); includes 49 minority (9 African Americans, 8 American Indian/Alaska Native, 5 Asian Americans or Pacific Islanders, 27 Hispanic Americans), 2 international. Average age 33. 353 applicants, 95% accepted, 301 enrolled. In 2008, 145 master's awarded. *Degree requirements:* For master's, comprehensive exam, thesis optional. *Entrance requirements:* For master's, minimum undergraduate GPA of 2.75. Additional exam requirements/recommendations for international students: Required—TOEFL. *Application deadline:* For fall admission, 8/10 for domestic and international students; for winter admission, 11/7 for domestic and international students; for spring admission, 2/6 for domestic and international students. Application fee: $50. Electronic applications accepted. *Expenses:* Tuition: Full-time $8000. Full-time tuition and fees vary according to degree level and program. *Financial support:* Scholarships/grants available. Financial award applicants required to submit FAFSA. *Unit head:* Dr. Hal Kearsley, Program Director, 802-485-2730, E-mail: hkearsley@norwich.edu. *Application contact:* Fianna Verret, Administrative Director, 802-485-2783, Fax: 802-485-2533, E-mail: fverret@norwich.edu.

Nova Southeastern University, Graduate School of Humanities and Social Sciences, Department of Conflict Analysis and Resolution, Doctor of Conflict Analysis and Resolution Program, Fort Lauderdale, FL 33314-7796. Offers PhD, PhD/JD. Part-time and evening/weekend programs available. Postbaccalaureate distance learning degree programs offered (minimal on-campus study). *Faculty:* 11 full-time (7 women), 10 part-time/adjunct (4 women). *Students:* 97 full-time (58 women), 103 part-time (62 women); includes 100 minority (76 African Americans, 2 American Indian/Alaska Native, 3 Asian Americans or Pacific Islanders, 19 Hispanic Americans), 18 international. 75 applicants, 92% accepted, 38 enrolled. In 2008, 5 doctorates awarded. *Degree requirements:* For doctorate, comprehensive exam, thesis/dissertation, qualifying exam. *Entrance requirements:* For doctorate, interview, minimum GPA of 3.0. Additional exam requirements/recommendations for international students: Required—TOEFL. *Application deadline:* For fall admission, 7/1 priority date for domestic and international students; for winter admission, 11/1 priority date for domestic and international students; for spring admission, 5/1 priority date for domestic students, 3/1 priority date for international students. Applications are processed on a rolling basis. Application fee: $50. Electronic applications accepted. *Financial support:* In 2008–09, 144 students received support, including 7 research assistantships with partial tuition reimbursements available (averaging $15,600 per year), 3 teaching assistantships; career-related internships or fieldwork, Federal Work-Study, scholarships/grants, and unspecified assistantships also available. Financial award application deadline: 4/1; financial award applicants required to submit CSS PROFILE. *Faculty research:* International conflict, violence prevention, facilitation and mediation, communication and conflict. *Application contact:* Marcia Arango, Student Recruitment Coordinator, 954-262-3006, Fax: 954-262-3968, E-mail: marango@nsu.nova.edu.

Nova Southeastern University, Graduate School of Humanities and Social Sciences, Department of Conflict Analysis and Resolution, Master's Program in Conflict Analysis and Resolution, Fort Lauderdale, FL 33314-7796. Offers MS, JD/MS. Part-time and evening/weekend programs available. Postbaccalaureate distance learning degree programs offered (minimal on-campus study). *Faculty:* 11 full-time (7 women), 10 part-time/adjunct (4 women). *Students:* 17 full-time (11 women), 49 part-time (42 women); includes 42 minority (26 African Americans, 1 Asian American or Pacific Islander, 15 Hispanic Americans), 2 international. 67 applicants, 63% accepted, 40 enrolled. In 2008, 28 master's awarded. *Degree requirements:* For master's, comprehensive exam, thesis optional. *Entrance requirements:* For master's, interview, minimum GPA of 3.0, writing sample. Additional exam requirements/recommendations for international students: Required—TOEFL. Application fee: $50. *Faculty research:* International conflict, violence prevention, communication and conflict facilitation, mediation. *Unit head:* Dr. Marcia Sweedler, Interim Chair, 954-262-3019, Fax: 954-262-3968, E-mail: msweedle@nova.edu. *Application contact:* Marcia Arango, Student Recruitment Coordinator, 954-262-3006, Fax: 954-262-3968, E-mail: marango@nsu.nova.edu.

Old Dominion University, College of Arts and Letters, Graduate Programs in International Studies, Norfolk, VA 23529. Offers conflict and cooperation (PhD), including women's studies certificate; U.S. foreign policy (MA), including modeling and simulation certificate. Part-time programs available. *Faculty:* 14 full-time (3 women). *Students:* 40 full-time (16 women), 34 part-time (15 women); includes 6 minority (2 African Americans, 1 Asian American or Pacific Islander, 3 Hispanic Americans), 24 international. Average age 32. 99 applicants, 54% accepted, 30 enrolled. In 2008, 10 master's, 5 doctorates awarded. Terminal master's awarded for partial completion of doctoral program. *Degree requirements:* For master's, one foreign language, comprehensive exam, thesis optional; for doctorate, one foreign language, comprehensive exam, thesis/dissertation. *Entrance requirements:* For master's, GRE General Test, sample of written work, 2 letters of recommendation; for doctorate, GRE General Test, sample of written work, 3 letters of recommendation. Additional exam requirements/recommendations for international students: Required—TOEFL (minimum score 570 paper-based; 230 computer-based). *Application deadline:* For fall admission, 3/15 for domestic students, 2/15 for international students; for spring admission, 10/15 for domestic and international students. Application fee: $40. Electronic applications accepted. *Expenses:* Tuition, area resident: Full-time $7704; part-time $321 per credit. Tuition, state resident: full-time $7704; part-time $321 per credit. Tuition, nonresident: full-time $19,104; part-time $796 per credit. Required fees: $99 per semester. One-time fee: $40. *Financial support:* In 2008–09, 20 students received support, including 2 fellowships (averaging $13,000 per year), 9 research assistantships with tuition reimbursements available (averaging $11,000 per year), 9 teaching assistantships with tuition reimbursements available (averaging $11,000 per year); career-related internships or fieldwork, institutionally sponsored loans, scholarships/grants, and unspecified assistantships also available. Support available to part-time students. Financial award application deadline: 2/15; financial award applicants required to submit FAFSA. *Faculty research:* U.S. foreign policy, international security, transatlantic and transpacific relations, transnational issues, IPE and development. Total annual research expenditures: $330,391. *Unit head:* Dr. Regina Karp, Graduate Program Director, 757-683-5700, Fax: 757-683-5701, E-mail: rkarp@odu.edu. *Application contact:* Dr. Angelica Huizar, 757-683-3988, Fax: 757-683-5701, E-mail: ahuizar@odu.edu.

Pepperdine University, School of Law, Program in Dispute Resolution, Malibu, CA 90263. Offers LL M, MDR. *Degree requirements:* For master's, thesis. *Entrance requirements:* For master's, GRE General Test or LSAT. *Expenses:* Contact institution.

Portland State University, Graduate Studies, College of Liberal Arts and Sciences, Program in Conflict Resolution, Portland, OR 97207-0751. Offers MA, MS. *Faculty:* 6 full-time (2 women), 3 part-time/adjunct (2 women). *Students:* 45 full-time (27 women), 66 part-time (46 women); includes 14 minority (9 African Americans, 1 American Indian/Alaska Native, 1 Asian American or Pacific Islander, 3 Hispanic Americans), 7 international. Average age 37. 34 applicants, 82% accepted, 21 enrolled. In 2008, 17 master's awarded. *Degree requirements:* For master's, thesis or alternative, practicum. *Entrance requirements:* For master's, 3 letters of recommendation. Additional exam requirements/recommendations for international students: Required—TOEFL (minimum score 550 paper-based; 213 computer-based). *Application deadline:* For fall admission, 4/1 for domestic students, 3/1 for international students; for winter admission, 9/1 for domestic students, 8/1 for international students; for spring admission, 11/1 for domestic and international students. *Expenses:* Tuition, area resident: Full-time $8763; part-time $179 per credit hour. Tuition, state resident: full-time $8763; part-time $298 per credit hour. Tuition, nonresident: full-time $12,981; part-time $426 per credit hour. Required fees: $1242. One-time fee: $250. Tuition and fees vary according to course load and program. *Financial support:* In 2008–09, 1 teaching assistantship with full tuition reimbursement (averaging $7,716 per year) was awarded; Federal Work-Study also available. Total annual research expenditures: $9,551. *Unit head:* Dr. Robert Gould, Director, 503-725-9175, E-mail: gouldr@pdx.edu. *Application contact:* Stephen Jahnke, Program Administrator, 503-725-9175, E-mail: jahnkes@pdx.edu.

Regis University, College for Professional Studies, MA Program, Denver, CO 80221-1099. Offers criminology (MA); fine arts administration (Certificate); language and communication (MA); mediation (Certificate); psychology (MA); self-designed major (MA); social justice, peace, and reconciliation (Certificate); social science (MA); technical communication (Certificate). Program also offered in Henderson and Las Vegas (Summerlin), NV. Part-time and evening/weekend programs available. Postbaccalaureate distance learning degree programs offered (minimal on-campus study). *Degree requirements:* For master's, thesis, research project. *Entrance requirements:* For master's, resumé, recommendations, essays. Additional exam requirements/recommendations for international students: Required—TOEFL (minimum score 213 computer-based), TWE (minimum score 5). Electronic applications accepted. *Expenses:* Contact institution. *Faculty research:* Independent/nonresidential graduate study: new methods and models, adult learning and the capstone experience, Goal Setting, behavior of Adult students, Innovative Studies for Community Colleges.

Royal Roads University, Graduate Studies, Peace and Conflict Studies Program, Victoria, BC V9B 5Y2, Canada. Offers conflict analysis (G Dip); conflict analysis and management (MA); disaster and emergency management (MA); human security and peacebuilding (MA). Postbaccalaureate distance learning degree programs offered (minimal on-campus study). *Degree requirements:* For master's, thesis. *Entrance requirements:* For master's, 5-7 years of related work experience. Additional exam requirements/recommendations for international students: Required—TOEFL (paper-based 570; computer-based 233) or IELTS (paper-based 7) (recommended). Electronic applications accepted. *Faculty research:* Conflict analysis, ethno-political conflict reconciliation, international relations, displaced persons.

St. Edward's University, School of Education, Program in Teaching, Austin, TX 78704. Offers curriculum leadership (Certificate); instructional technology (Certificate); mentoring and supervision (Certificate); sports management (Certificate); teaching (MA), including conflict resolution, initial teacher certification, liberal arts, organization development and training, sports management, teacher leadership. Part-time and evening/weekend programs available. *Students:* 7 full-time (4 women), 33 part-time (20 women); includes 9 minority (2 African Americans, 7 Hispanic Americans), 1 international. Average age 30. 21 applicants, 67% accepted, 10 enrolled. In 2008, 4 master's awarded. *Degree requirements:* For master's, minimum 24 resident hours. *Entrance requirements:* For master's, GRE General Test, minimum GPA of 3.0 in last 60 hours or 2.75 overall. Additional exam requirements/recommendations for international students: Required—TOEFL (minimum score 550 paper-based; 213 computer-based; 79 iBT). *Application deadline:* For fall admission, 8/1 for domestic students, 7/1 for international students; for spring admission, 12/1 for domestic students, 11/1 for international students. Applications are processed on a rolling basis. Application fee: $45 ($50 for international students). Electronic applications accepted. *Expenses:* Tuition: Full-time $13,752; part-time $764 per credit hour. Required fees: $50 per semester. Full-time tuition and fees vary according to course load and program. *Financial support:* In 2008–09, 4 students received support. Scholarships/grants available. *Unit head:* Dr. David Hollier, Director, 512-448-8666, Fax: 512-428-1372, E-mail: davidh@stedwards.edu. *Application contact:* Kay L. Arnold, Graduate Admissions Coordinator, 512-233-1636, Fax: 512-428-1032, E-mail: kayla@stedwards.edu.

St. Edward's University, School of Management and Business, Program in Human Services, Austin, TX 78704. Offers administration (Certificate); conflict resolution (Certificate); family mediation (Certificate); human services (MA), including administration, conflict resolution, human resource management, organization development and training, social and psychological services; mediation (Certificate); organization development and training (Certificate). Part-time and evening/weekend programs available. *Students:* 2 full-time (both women), 53 part-time (42 women); includes 23 minority (5 African Americans, 2 Asian Americans or Pacific Islanders, 16 Hispanic Americans). Average age 33. 21 applicants, 90% accepted, 16 enrolled. In 2008, 22 master's awarded. *Degree requirements:* For master's, minimum 24 resident hours. *Entrance requirements:* For master's, GRE General Test, GMAT, minimum GPA of 2.75 in last 60 hours of course work. Additional exam requirements/recommendations for international students: Required—TOEFL (minimum score 550 paper-based; 213 computer-based; 79 iBT). *Application deadline:* For fall admission, 8/1 for domestic students, 7/1 for international students; for spring admission, 12/1 for domestic students, 11/1 for international students. Applications are processed on a rolling basis. Application fee: $45 ($50 for international students). Electronic applications accepted. *Expenses:* Tuition: Full-time $13,752; part-time $764 per credit hour. Required fees: $50 per semester. Full-time tuition and fees vary according to course load and program. *Financial support:* In 2008–09, 2 students received support. Scholarships/grants available. *Faculty research:* Leadership development, organizational management, public policy. *Unit head:* Dr. Constance D Porter, Director, 512-416-5827, Fax: 512-448-8492, E-mail: constanp@stedwards.edu. *Application contact:* Kay L. Arnold, Graduate Admissions Coordinator, 512-233-1636, Fax: 512-428-1032, E-mail: kayla@stedwards.edu.

Saint Paul University, Faculty of Human Sciences, Program in Conflict Studies, Ottawa, ON K1S 1C4, Canada. Offers MA. Part-time programs available. *Entrance requirements:* For master's, H=honors BA, B average.

SIT Graduate Institute, Graduate Programs, Master's Programs in Intercultural Service, Leadership, and Management, Program in Conflict Transformation, Brattleboro, VT 05302-0676. Offers MA.

Southern Methodist University, Annette Caldwell Simmons School of Education and Human Development, Department of Dispute Resolution and Counseling, Dallas, TX 75275. Offers counseling (MS); dispute resolution (MA, Certificate). Part-time programs available. *Faculty:* 6 full-time (2 women), 24 part-time/adjunct (10 women). *Students:* 9 full-time (7 women), 203 part-time (148 women); includes 41 minority (15 African Americans, 2 American Indian/Alaska Native, 7 Asian Americans or Pacific Islanders, 17 Hispanic Americans), 5 international. Average age 34. 103 applicants, 50% accepted, 46 enrolled. In 2008, 47 master's, 10 other advanced degrees awarded. *Degree requirements:* For master's, minimum GPA of 3.0, practica experience; two internships (for counseling). *Entrance requirements:* For master's, minimum undergraduate GPA of 2.75 (for dispute resolution), 3.0 (for counseling); essay, 3 letters of recommendation. Additional exam requirements/recommendations for international students: Required—TOEFL. *Application deadline:* For fall admission, 5/1 for domestic students; for spring admission, 12/1 for domestic students. Applications are processed on a rolling basis. Application fee: $75. Electronic applications accepted. *Unit head:* Dr. Tony Picchioni, Ph.D, Department Chair, 972-473-3408, Fax: 972-473-3425. *Application contact:* Cynthia McIntyre, Program Manager, 972-473-3431, Fax: 972-473-3425, E-mail: adr@smu.edu or counselingmaster@smu.edu.

Sullivan University, School of Business, Louisville, KY 40205. Offers business administration (MBA); collaborative leadership (MSCL); conflict management (MSCM); dispute resolution (MSDR); executive business administration (EMBA); human resource leadership (MSHRL); information technology (MSMIT); management and information technology (MBIT); pharmacy (Pharm D). Part-time programs available. Postbaccalaureate distance learning degree programs offered (no on-campus study). *Faculty:* 13 full-time (7 women), 11 part-time/adjunct (4 women). *Students:* 291 full-time (188 women), 319 part-time (211 women); includes 181 minority (143 African Americans, 1 American Indian/Alaska Native, 31 Asian Americans or Pacific Islanders, 6 Hispanic Americans), 9 international. In 2008, 126 master's awarded. *Entrance requirements:* Additional exam requirements/recommendations for international students: Required—TOEFL. *Application deadline:* Applications are processed on a rolling basis. Application fee: $100. *Unit head:* Dr. Eric S Harter, Dean of Graduate School, 502-456-6504, Fax: 502-456-0040, E-mail: eharter@sullivan.edu. *Application contact:* Beverly Horsley, Admissions Officer, 502-456-6505, Fax: 502-456-0040, E-mail: bhorsley@sullivan.edu.

Syracuse University, Graduate School, Maxwell School of Citizenship and Public Affairs, Program in Conflict Resolution, Syracuse, NY 13244.

Tufts University, Fletcher School of Law and Diplomacy, Medford, MA 02155. Offers LL M, MA, MAHA, MALD, MIB, PhD, DVM/MA, JD/MALD, MALD/MA, MALD/MBA, MALD/MS, MD/MA. Postbaccalaureate distance learning degree programs offered (minimal on-campus study). *Degree requirements:* For master's, one foreign language, thesis; for doctorate, one foreign language, comprehensive exam, thesis/dissertation, dissertation defense. *Entrance requirements:* For master's and doctorate, GMAT or GRE General Test. Additional exam requirements/recommendations for international students: Required—TOEFL (minimum score 600 paper-based; 250 computer-based; 100 iBT), IELTS (minimum score 7). Electronic applications accepted. *Expenses:* Contact institution. *Faculty research:* Negotiation and conflict resolution, international organizations, international business and economic law, security studies, development economics.

See Close-Up on page 879.

TUI University, College of Business Administration, Program in Business Administration, Cypress, CA 90630. Offers business administration (PhD); conflict and negotiation management (MBA); criminal justice administration (MBA); entrepreneurship (MBA); finance (MBA); general management (MBA); human resource management (MBA); information technology management (MBA); international business (MBA); logistics management (MBA); public management (MBA); strategic leadership (MBA). Part-time and evening/weekend programs available. Postbaccalaureate distance learning degree programs offered (no on-campus study). *Degree requirements:* For doctorate, comprehensive exam, thesis/dissertation, defense of dissertation. *Entrance requirements:* For master's, minimum GPA of 2.5 (students with GPA 3.0 or greater may transfer up to 30% of graduate level credits); for doctorate, minimum GPA of 3.4, curriculum vitae, course work in research methods or statistics. Additional exam requirements/recommendations for international students: Required—TOEFL. Electronic applications accepted.

United Theological Seminary of the Twin Cities, Graduate and Professional Programs, New Brighton, MN 55112-2598. Offers advanced theological studies (Diploma); justice and peace studies (M Div); leadership toward racial justice (MA, Certificate); Methodist studies (M Div, MA); ministry (D Min); ministry renewal and professional development (Certificate); pastoral care and counseling (M Div); religion and theology (MA); theological and religious studies (Certificate); theology and the arts (MA); urban ministry (MARL); women's studies: religion, theology and ministry (MA). *Accreditation:* ACIPE; ATS. Part-time and evening/weekend programs available. *Faculty:* 10 full-time (6 women), 24 part-time/adjunct (12 women). *Students:* 60 full-time (34 women), 93 part-time (60 women); includes 10 minority (5 African Americans, 1 American Indian/Alaska Native, 3 Asian Americans or Pacific Islanders, 1 Hispanic American), 1 international. Average age 47. 39 applicants, 100% accepted, 32 enrolled. In 2008, 21 first professional degrees, 9 master's awarded. *Degree requirements:* For master's, thesis; for doctorate, comprehensive exam, thesis/dissertation; for M Div, integrative notebook, spiritual chronicle. *Entrance requirements:* For M Div and master's, minimum GPA of 2.75; strong analytical, reflective thinking and writing skills; vocational and academic goals compatible with those of Seminary; for doctorate, M Div or equivalent, minimum GPA of 3.0, 3 years experience in professional ministry; for other advanced degree, BA or equivalent life experience; strong analytical, reflective thinking and writing skills (Certificate); proficiency in English language, previous study of theology at a theological school, recommendation of student's denomination (Diploma). Additional exam requirements/recommendations for international students: Required—TOEFL (minimum score 550 paper-based). *Application deadline:* For fall admission, 7/1 priority date for domestic students, 11/1 priority date for international students; for winter admission, 11/1 priority date for domestic students; for spring admission, 11/15 priority date for domestic students. Applications are processed on a rolling basis. Application fee: $50. *Expenses:* Tuition: Full-time $11,070; part-time $410 per credit hour. Required fees: $295; $135 per term. One-time fee: $25. Tuition and fees vary according to course load, degree level and program. *Financial support:* In 2008–09, 98 students received support. Career-related internships or fieldwork, institutionally sponsored loans, and scholarships/grants available. Support available to part-time students. Financial award application deadline: 5/1; financial award applicants required to submit FAFSA. *Unit head:* Dr. Richard D. Weis, Dean of the Seminary, 651-255-6108 Ext. 108, Fax: 651-633-4315, E-mail: rweis@unitedseminary.edu. *Application contact:* Rev. Glen Herrington-Hall, Director of Admissions, 651-255-6107 Ext. 107, Fax: 651-633-4315, E-mail: gherrington-hall@unitedseminary.edu.

Université de Sherbrooke, Faculty of Law, Sherbrooke, QC J1K 2R1, Canada. Offers alternative dispute resolution (LL M, Diploma); biotechnology (LL B); business administration (LL B); business law (Diploma); health law (LL M, Diploma); law (LL B, LL D); legal management (Diploma); notarial law (DDN); transnational law (Diploma). Part-time and evening/weekend programs available. *Degree requirements:* For master's, thesis; for other advanced degree, one foreign language. *Entrance requirements:* For master's and other advanced degree, LL B. Electronic applications accepted.

University of Arkansas at Little Rock, Graduate School, College of Professional Studies, Program in Conflict Mediation, Little Rock, AR 72204-1099. Offers Graduate Certificate.

University of Baltimore, Graduate School, The Yale Gordon College of Liberal Arts, Program in Negotiations and Conflict Management, Baltimore, MD 21201-5779. Offers negotiations and conflict management (MS). Part-time and evening/weekend programs available. *Faculty:* 4 full-time (2 women), 2 part-time/adjunct (1 woman). *Students:* 21 full-time (18 women), 48 part-time (35 women); includes 36 minority (30 African Americans, 3 Asian Americans or Pacific Islanders, 3 Hispanic Americans), 3 international. Average age 34. 58 applicants, 50% accepted, 22 enrolled. In 2008, 19 master's awarded. *Degree requirements:* For master's, thesis optional, internship. *Entrance requirements:* For master's, minimum GPA of 3.0. Additional exam requirements/recommendations for international students: Required—TOEFL (minimum score 550 paper-based; 213 computer-based). *Application deadline:* For fall admission, 8/1 for domestic students, 6/1 for international students; for spring admission, 12/1 for domestic students, 11/1 for international students. Application fee: $30. Electronic applications accepted. *Expenses:* Tuition, state resident: part-time $568 per credit. Tuition, nonresident: part-time $824 per credit. Required fees: $250 per semester. *Financial support:* In 2008–09, 1 research assistantship with full and partial tuition reimbursement was awarded. Financial award application deadline: 4/1; financial award applicants required to submit FAFSA. *Faculty research:* Communication and conflict, conflict management systems theory. Total annual research expenditures: $38,500. *Unit head:* Dr. Johannes Botes, Director, 410-837-5326, E-mail: jbotes@ubalt.edu. *Application contact:* Kevin Nies, Assistant Director, Office of Graduate Admission, 410-837-6565, E-mail: knies@ubalt.edu.

University of Bridgeport, International College, Bridgeport, CT 06604. Offers global development and peace (MA). Part-time and evening/weekend programs available. *Faculty:* 7 full-time (4 women), 8 part-time/adjunct (3 women). *Students:* 12 full-time (7 women), 3 part-time (2 women); includes 3 minority (all African Americans), 7 international. Average age 28. 28 applicants, 75% accepted, 11 enrolled. *Degree requirements:* For master's, thesis. *Entrance requirements:* Additional exam requirements/recommendations for international students: Recommended—TOEFL (minimum score 550 paper-based; 213 computer-based; 80 iBT), IELTS (minimum score 6.5). *Application deadline:* For fall admission, 8/1 priority date for domestic and international students; for spring admission, 12/1 priority date for domestic and international students. Application fee: $40 ($35 for international students). *Expenses:* Tuition: Full-time $19,820; part-time $595 per credit hour. Required fees: $75 per semester. *Unit head:* Dr. Thomas J Ward, Dean, 203-576-4966, Fax: 203-4967, E-mail: ward@bridgeport.edu. *Application contact:* Barbara L Maryak, Vice President of Enrollment Management, 203-576-4552, Fax: 203-576-4941, E-mail: admit@bridgeport.edu.

University of Denver, Graduate Studies, Conflict Resolution Institute, Denver, CO 80208. Offers MA. Part-time programs available. *Faculty:* 1 (woman) full-time, 2 part-time/adjunct (1 woman). *Students:* 13 full-time (7 women), 10 part-time (6 women); includes 4 minority (1 African American, 1 Asian American or Pacific Islander, 2 Hispanic Americans). Average age 27. In 2008, 5 master's awarded. *Degree requirements:* For master's, thesis, internship. *Entrance requirements:* For master's, GRE, GMAT, or LSAT, 3 letters of recommendation, personal statement. Additional exam requirements/recommendations for international students: Required—TOEFL. *Application deadline:* For fall admission, 2/15 priority date for domestic students; for winter admission, 11/1 priority date for domestic students; for spring admission, 1/15 priority date for domestic students. Applications are processed on a rolling basis. Application fee: $50. Electronic applications accepted. *Financial support:* Career-related internships or fieldwork, Federal Work-Study, scholarships/grants, and tuition waivers (partial) available. Financial award application deadline: 2/15; financial award applicants required to submit FAFSA. *Unit head:* Dr. Karen Feste, Director, 303-871-6477, E-mail: kfeste@du.edu. *Application contact:* Information Contact, 303-871-6477, E-mail: cri@du.edu.

University of Hawaii at Manoa, Graduate Division, Colleges of Arts and Sciences, College of Social Sciences, Spark M. Matsunaga Institute for Peace, Honolulu, HI 96822. Offers conflict resolution (Graduate Certificate). Part-time programs available. *Entrance requirements:* For degree, GRE General Test. Additional exam requirements/recommendations for international

Conflict Resolution and Mediation/Peace Studies

University of Hawaii at Manoa (continued)
students: Required—TOEFL (minimum score 540 paper-based; 207 computer-based; 76 iBT), IELTS (minimum score 5).

University of Massachusetts Amherst, Graduate School, College of Social and Behavioral Sciences, Department of Psychology, Amherst, MA 01003. Offers clinical psychology (MS, PhD); cognitive psychology (MS, PhD); developmental science (MS, PhD); psychology of peace and violence (MS, PhD); social psychology (MS, PhD). *Accreditation:* APA (one or more programs are accredited). Terminal master's awarded for partial completion of doctoral program. *Degree requirements:* For master's, thesis; for doctorate, comprehensive exam, thesis/dissertation. *Entrance requirements:* For master's and doctorate, GRE General Test, 3 letters of recommendation. Additional exam requirements/recommendations for international students: Required—TOEFL (minimum score 550 paper-based; 213 computer-based; 79 iBT), IELTS (minimum score 6.5). Electronic applications accepted. *Expenses:* Tuition, area resident: Full-time $2640. Tuition, nonresident: full-time $9936. One-time fee: $332 full-time. Tuition and fees vary according to course load.

University of Massachusetts Boston, Office of Graduate Studies, College of Public and Community Service, Program in Dispute Resolution, Boston, MA 02125-3393. Offers MA, Certificate. MA program accepts applications for fall admission only; Certificate program accepts applications for spring admission only. *Degree requirements:* For master's, practicum, final project. *Entrance requirements:* For master's, MAT or GRE, minimum GPA of 2.75; for Certificate, minimum GPA of 2.75. *Faculty research:* Mediation and negotiation, justice and conflict, cross-cultural mediation, environmental fairness, dispute resolution theory and ethics.

University of Missouri–Columbia, Graduate School and School of Law, Program in Dispute Resolution, Columbia, MO 65211. Offers LL M. *Students:* 4 full-time (0 women), 6 part-time (2 women), 1 international. Average age 46. 24 applicants, 54% accepted, 4 enrolled. In 2008, 15 master's awarded. *Entrance requirements:* Additional exam requirements/recommendations for international students: Required—TOEFL (minimum score 600 paper-based; 250 computer-based; 100 iBT). *Application deadline:* For fall admission, 1/1 priority date for domestic students. Application fee: $45 ($60 for international students). *Financial support:* Fellowships, research assistantships, teaching assistantships, institutionally sponsored loans available. *Unit head:* Dr. John Lande, Director, 573-882-3914, E-mail: landej@missouri.edu. *Application contact:* Karen Neylon, 573-882-2020, E-mail: neylonk@missouri.edu.

University of Missouri–St. Louis, College of Arts and Sciences, Department of Sociology, St. Louis, MO 63121. Offers advanced social perspective (MA); community conflict intervention (MA); program design and evaluation research (MA); social policy planning and administration (MA). Part-time and evening/weekend programs available. *Faculty:* 3 full-time (all women), 1 part-time/adjunct (0 women). *Students:* 6 full-time (3 women), 8 part-time (5 women); includes 2 minority (both African Americans), 1 international. Average age 34. In 2008, 7 master's awarded. *Degree requirements:* For master's, thesis optional. *Entrance requirements:* For master's, 2 letters of recommendation. Additional exam requirements/recommendations for international students: Required—TOEFL (minimum score 550 paper-based; 213 computer-based). *Application deadline:* For fall admission, 7/1 priority date for domestic and international students; for spring admission, 12/1 priority date for domestic and international students. Applications are processed on a rolling basis. Application fee: $35 ($40 for international students). Electronic applications accepted. *Expenses:* Tuition, area resident: Full-time $5377; part-time $298.70 per credit hour. Tuition, nonresident: full-time $13,381; part-time $472.50 per credit hour. Required fees: $4078; $52 per credit hour. *Financial support:* In 2008–09, 3 teaching assistantships with full and partial tuition reimbursements (averaging $7,870 per year) were awarded; career-related internships or fieldwork also available. Support available to part-time students. Financial award applicants required to submit FAFSA. *Faculty research:* Deviance, conflict intervention, minority groups, stratification, social psychology. *Unit head:* Dr. Chicako Usui, Chairperson, 314-516-6366. *Application contact:* 314-516-5458, Fax: 314-516-6996, E-mail: gradadm@umsl.edu.

University of New Brunswick Fredericton, School of Graduate Studies, Policy Studies Program, Fredericton, NB E3B 5A3, Canada. Offers people, property and alternative dispute resolution (M Phil); philosophy politics and economics (M Phil); sustainable development (M Phil). *Faculty:* 6 full-time (2 women), 13 part-time/adjunct (2 women). *Students:* 16 full-time (9 women), 4 part-time (3 women). In 2008, 3 master's awarded. *Entrance requirements:* For master's, minimum GPA of 3.5, BA. Additional exam requirements/recommendations for international students: Required—TOEFL (minimum score 600 paper-based), TWE (minimum score 5). Application fee: $50 Canadian dollars. Tuition and fees charges are reported in Canadian dollars. *Expenses:* Tuition, area resident: Full-time $5562 Canadian dollars. Tuition, nonresident: full-time $9450 Canadian dollars. Required fees: $333 Canadian dollars. *Financial support:* In 2008–09, 4 research assistantships, 1 teaching assistantship were awarded. *Unit head:* Dr. Linda Eyre, Dean of Graduate Studies, 506-447-3044, Fax: 506-453-4817, E-mail: gradidst@unb.ca. *Application contact:* Janet Amurault, Graduate Secretary, 506-458-7558, Fax: 506-453-4817, E-mail: jamiraul@unb.ca.

The University of North Carolina at Greensboro, Graduate School, Program in Conflict Resolution, Greensboro, NC 27412-5001. Offers MA, Certificate. Electronic applications accepted.

University of Notre Dame, Graduate School, College of Arts and Letters, Division of Social Science, Joan B. Kroc Institute for International Peace Studies, Notre Dame, IN 46556. Offers MA, PhD. *Faculty:* 38 full-time (11 women). *Students:* 41 full-time (27 women); includes 1 minority (Asian American or Pacific Islander), 30 international. 248 applicants, 10% accepted, 21 enrolled. In 2008, 19 master's awarded. *Degree requirements:* For master's, one foreign language, comprehensive exam, thesis optional; for doctorate, one foreign language, comprehensive exam, thesis/dissertation. *Entrance requirements:* For master's, GRE General Test. Additional exam requirements/recommendations for international students: Required—TOEFL (minimum score 600 paper-based; 250 computer-based; 80 iBT). *Application deadline:* For fall admission, 1/5 for domestic and international students. Application fee: $50. Electronic applications accepted. *Financial support:* Fellowships with full tuition reimbursements, research assistantships, teaching assistantships, career-related internships or fieldwork, scholarships/grants, health care benefits, and tuition waivers (full) available. Financial award application deadline: 1/5. *Faculty research:* The role of international norms and institutions in peacemaking; the impact of religious, philosophical, and cultural influences on peace; the dynamics of intergroup conflict and conflict transformation; the promotion of social, economic, and environmental justice. *Unit head:* Dr. Jaleh Dashti-Gibson, Director of Graduate Studies, 574-631-4371, E-mail: kroc-admissions@nd.edu. *Application contact:* Dr. Barbara Turpin, Director of Graduate Admissions, 574-631-7706, Fax: 574-631-4183.

University of Pittsburgh, Graduate School of Public and International Affairs, International Affairs Division, Program in Human Security, Pittsburgh, PA 15260. Offers MPIA. Part-time and evening/weekend programs available. *Degree requirements:* For master's, thesis optional, internship, capstone seminar. *Entrance requirements:* For master's, GRE General Test, 3 letters of recommendation, resumé, minimum GPA of 3.2. Additional exam requirements/

recommendations for international students: Required—TOEFL (minimum score 550 paper-based; 213 computer-based; 80 iBT), TWE (minimum score 4); Recommended—IELTS (minimum score 7). *Faculty research:* Human rights, human trafficking, threats to civilian populations, child soldiers.

University of San Diego, Joan B. Kroc School of Peace Studies, San Diego, CA 92110-2492. Offers peace and justice studies (MA). *Faculty:* 1 (woman) full-time. *Students:* 14 full-time (11 women), 4 international. Average age 27. 49 applicants, 59% accepted, 14 enrolled. In 2008, 10 master's awarded. *Degree requirements:* For master's, capstone project. *Entrance requirements:* For master's, GRE General Test, minimum GPA of 3.0. Additional exam requirements/recommendations for international students: Required—TOEFL (minimum score 580 paper-based; 237 computer-based; 83 iBT), TWE. *Application deadline:* For fall admission, 2/15 for domestic and international students. Application fee: $45. Electronic applications accepted. *Expenses:* Tuition: Full-time $19,710; part-time $1129 per unit. Required fees: $154. Full-time tuition and fees vary according to course load and degree level. *Financial support:* In 2008–09, 14 students received support, including 9 fellowships; career-related internships or fieldwork, Federal Work-Study, institutionally sponsored loans, scholarships/grants, and unspecified assistantships also available. Support available to part-time students. Financial award application deadline: 4/1; financial award applicants required to submit FAFSA. *Faculty research:* Conflict analysis and resolution. *Unit head:* Fr. William Headley, Dean, E-mail: wheadley@sandiego.edu. *Application contact:* Dr. John Mosby, Associate Director of Graduate Admissions, 619-260-4524, Fax: 619-260-4158, E-mail: grads@sandiego.edu.

University of the Sacred Heart, Graduate Programs, Program in Systems of Justice, San Juan, PR 00914-0383. Offers human rights and anti-discriminatory processes (MASJ); mediation and transformation of conflicts (MASJ).

University of Victoria, Faculty of Graduate Studies, Faculty of Human and Social Development, School of Public Administration, Victoria, BC V8W 2Y2, Canada. Offers dispute resolution (MADR); public administration (MPA, PhD); MPA/LL B. Part-time and evening/weekend programs available. Postbaccalaureate distance learning degree programs offered. *Degree requirements:* For master's, thesis (for some programs), report; for doctorate, thesis/dissertation, candidacy exam. *Entrance requirements:* For master's, GMAT or GRE General Test, professional resumé; for doctorate, GMAT or GRE General Test. Additional exam requirements/recommendations for international students: Required—TOEFL (minimum score 610 paper-based; 255 computer-based). Electronic applications accepted. *Faculty research:* Policy analysis, local government, performance management, energy markets, labor markets.

University of Wisconsin–Milwaukee, Graduate School, College of Letters and Sciences, Interdepartmental Program in Human Resources and Labor Relations, Milwaukee, WI 53201-0413. Offers human resources and labor relations (MHRLR); international human resources and labor relations (Certificate); mediation and negotiation (Certificate). Part-time programs available. *Faculty:* 17 full-time (7 women). *Students:* 14 full-time (10 women), 44 part-time (34 women); includes 12 minority (5 African Americans, 2 Asian Americans or Pacific Islanders, 5 Hispanic Americans), 2 international. Average age 32. 44 applicants, 41% accepted, 11 enrolled. In 2008, 20 master's awarded. *Entrance requirements:* For master's, GMAT or GRE General Test. Additional exam requirements/recommendations for international students: Required—TOEFL (minimum score 550 paper-based; 79 iBT), IELTS (minimum score 6.5). *Application deadline:* For fall admission, 1/1 priority date for domestic students; for spring admission, 9/1 for domestic students. Applications are processed on a rolling basis. Application fee: $45 ($75 for international students). *Expenses:* Tuition, area resident: Full-time $7320; part-time $165 per credit. Tuition, state resident: full-time $7320; part-time $165 per credit. Tuition, nonresident: full-time $17,840; part-time $714 per credit. Tuition and fees vary according to campus/location, program and reciprocity agreements. *Financial support:* Career-related internships or fieldwork available. Support available to part-time students. Financial award application deadline: 4/15. *Unit head:* Susan M. Donohue-Davies, Representative, 414-299-4009, Fax: 414-229-5915, E-mail: suedono@uwm.edu. *Application contact:* General Information Contact, 414-229-4982, Fax: 414-229-6967, E-mail: gradschool@uwm.edu.

Walden University, Graduate Programs, School of Public Policy and Administration, Minneapolis, MN 55401. Offers general public policy and administration (MPA); government management (Certificate); health policy (MPA); homeland security policy (MPA); interdisciplinary policy studies (MPA); law and public policy (MPA); local government management for sustainable communities (MPA); nonprofit management (Certificate); nonprofit management and leadership (MPA, MS); policy analysis (MPA); public management and leadership (MPA); public policy and administration (PhD), including criminal justice, health services, homeland security policy and coordination, international nongovernmental organizations, knowledge management, nonprofit management and leadership, public management and leadership, public policy, public safety management; terrorism, mediation, and peace (MPA). Part-time and evening/weekend programs available. Postbaccalaureate distance learning degree programs offered (minimal on-campus study). *Faculty:* 2 full-time, 55 part-time/adjunct. *Students:* 1,285 full-time (794 women), 144 part-time (96 women); includes 657 minority (591 African Americans, 8 American Indian/Alaska Native, 17 Asian Americans or Pacific Islanders, 41 Hispanic Americans), 20 international. Average age 39. 727 applicants, 54% accepted, 284 enrolled. In 2008, 101 master's, 6 doctorates awarded. *Degree requirements:* For doctorate, thesis/dissertation, residency. *Entrance requirements:* For master's, bachelor's degree or equivalent in related field, minimum GPA of 2.5, two references, goal statement, official transcripts, access to computer and Internet; for doctorate, master's degree or equivalent in related field, minimum GPA of 3.0, three years related professional/academic experience, two references, goal statement, official transcripts, access to computer and Internet. Additional exam requirements/recommendations for international students: Required—TOEFL (minimum score 550 paper-based; 213 computer-based), IELTS (minimum score 6.5), TOEFL, IELTS, or Michigan English Language Assessment Battery (minimum score 82). *Application deadline:* Applications are processed on a rolling basis. Application fee: $50. Electronic applications accepted. *Expenses:* Tuition: Full-time $12,877; part-time $520 per credit. Required fees: $1230. Tuition and fees vary according to course load, degree level and program. *Financial support:* In 2008–09, 3 students received support; fellowships with tuition reimbursements available, Federal Work-Study, scholarships/grants, unspecified assistantships, and family tuition reduction; active duty/veteran tuition reduction; group tuition reduction; interest-free payment plans available. Support available to part-time students. Financial award applicants required to submit FAFSA. *Unit head:* Dr. Mark Gordon, Interim Associate Dean, 800-925-3368. *Application contact:* Jennifer Hall, 866-4-WALDEN, E-mail: info@waldenu.edu.

Wayne State University, College of Fine, Performing and Communication Arts, Interdisciplinary Program in Dispute Resolution, Detroit, MI 48202. Offers MADR, Certificate, JD/MADR. *Entrance requirements:* For master's, GMAT, GRE General Test, or LSAT. Additional exam requirements/recommendations for international students: Required—TOEFL (minimum score 550 paper-based; 213 computer-based); Recommended—TWE (minimum score 6). Electronic applications accepted. *Faculty research:* Conflict resolution in higher education; workplace conflict and aggression; cultural diversity; domestic violence; intervention policies of major powers and small states.

Section 18
Criminology and Forensics

This section contains a directory of institutions offering graduate work in criminology and forensics, followed by in-depth entries submitted by institutions that chose to prepare detailed program descriptions. Additional information about programs listed in the directory but not augmented by an in-depth entry may be obtained by writing directly to the dean of a graduate school or chair of a department at the address given in the directory.

For programs offering related work, see also in this book *Political Science and International Affairs, Psychology and Counseling,* and *Sociology, Anthropology, and Archaeology.* In another guide in this series:

Graduate Programs in Business, Education, Health, Information Studies, Law & Social Work
See *Law* and *Social Work*

CONTENTS

Program Directories
Criminal Justice and Criminology — 718
Forensic Sciences — 736

Announcement
Roger Williams University — 726

Close-Ups
Michigan State University — 739
Nova Southeastern University — 741
Roger Williams University — 743

See also:
Alliant International University–Irvine—Forensic Psychology — 1055
Indiana University–Purdue University Indianapolis—Public Affairs — 1221
University of Pittsburgh—Public and International Affairs — 1243

Criminal Justice and Criminology

Albany State University, College of Arts and Humanities, Department of History, Political Science and Public Administration, Albany, GA 31705-2717. Offers community and economic development (MPA); criminal justice (MPA); fiscal management (MPA); general management (MPA); health administration and policy (MPA); human resources management (MPA); public policy (MPA); water resource management and policy (MPA). *Accreditation:* NASPAA. Part-time programs available. *Faculty:* 5 full-time (2 women). *Students:* 10 full-time (8 women), 42 part-time (29 women); includes 50 minority (49 African Americans, 1 Asian American or Pacific Islander). Average age 35. In 2008, 12 master's awarded. *Degree requirements:* For master's, comprehensive exam, thesis. *Entrance requirements:* For master's, GRE General Test, minimum GPA of 2.5. *Application deadline:* For fall admission, 4/15 for domestic and international students; for spring admission, 11/15 for domestic and international students. Applications are processed on a rolling basis. Application fee: $20. Electronic applications accepted. *Expenses:* Tuition, area resident: Full-time $4296; part-time $154 per semester hour. Tuition, state resident: full-time $4296; part-time $154 per semester hour. Tuition, nonresident: full-time $15,338; part-time $614 per semester hour. Required fees: $306 per semester. Tuition and fees vary according to course load. *Financial support:* Tuition waivers available. Financial award application deadline: 4/1; financial award applicants required to submit FAFSA. *Faculty research:* Transportation, urban affairs, political economy. *Unit head:* Dr. Rita Henry-Brown, Chair, 229-430-4870, Fax: 229-430-7895, E-mail: rita.brown@asurams.edu. *Application contact:* Diane P. Frink, Graduate Admission Counselor, 229-430-5118, Fax: 229-430-6398, E-mail: diane.frink@asurams.edu.

Albany State University, College of Sciences and Health Professions, Department of Criminal Justice and Forensic Science, Albany, GA 31705-2717. Offers criminal justice (MS). Part-time programs available. *Faculty:* 7 full-time (1 woman), 2 part-time/adjunct (0 women). *Students:* 22 full-time (14 women), 22 part-time (14 women); includes 43 minority (42 African Americans, 1 Asian American or Pacific Islander). Average age 28. In 2008, 2 master's awarded. *Degree requirements:* For master's, comprehensive exam. *Entrance requirements:* For master's, GRE General Test, minimum GPA of 2.5. *Application deadline:* For fall admission, 4/15 for domestic and international students; for spring admission, 11/15 for domestic and international students. Applications are processed on a rolling basis. Application fee: $20. Electronic applications accepted. *Expenses:* Tuition, area resident: Full-time $4296; part-time $154 per semester hour. Tuition, state resident: full-time $4296; part-time $154 per semester hour. Tuition, nonresident: full-time $15,338; part-time $614 per semester hour. Required fees: $306 per semester. Tuition and fees vary according to course load. *Financial support:* Application deadline: 4/1; *Faculty research:* Criminal alcoholic program, prevention of juvenile delinquency, police selection, constitutional issues. *Unit head:* Dr. Charles Ochie, Chair, 229-430-4864, Fax: 229-430-1676, E-mail: charles.ochie@asurams.edu. *Application contact:* Diane P. Frink, Graduate School Counselor, 229-430-5118, Fax: 229-430-6398, E-mail: diane.frink@asurams.edu.

American Public University System, AMU/APU Graduate Programs, Charles Town, WV 25414. Offers air warfare (MA Military Studies); American Revolution (MA Military Studies); business administration (MBA); Civil War (MA Military Studies); criminal justice (MA); defense management (MA Military Studies); emergency and disaster management (MA); environmental policy and management (MS); fire science management (MA); global engagement (MA); history (MA); homeland security (MA); humanities (MA); intelligence (MA Military Studies, MA Strategic Intelligence); international peace and conflict resolution (MA); international relations and conflict resolution (MA); joint warfare (MA Military Studies); land warfare international perspective (MA Military Studies); management (MA); military history (MA); military leadership (MA Military Studies); national security studies (MA); naval warfare international (MA Military Studies); naval warfare US (MA Military Studies); political science (MA); public administration (MA); public health (MA); security management (MA); space studies (MS); special ops/LIC (MA Military Studies); sports management (MA); transportation and logistics management (MA); transportation management (MA); unconventional warfare (MA Military Studies); World War II (MA Military Studies). Programs offered via distance learning only. Part time and evening/weekend programs available. Postbaccalaureate distance learning degree programs offered (no on-campus study). *Degree requirements:* For master's, comprehensive exam. *Entrance requirements:* For master's, bachelor's degree or equivalent, minimum GPA of 2.7 in last 60 hours of course work. Electronic applications accepted. *Faculty research:* Military history, criminal justice, management performance, national security.

American University, School of Public Affairs, Department of Justice, Law and Society, Washington, DC 20016-8043. Offers MS, PhD, JD/MS. Part-time and evening/weekend programs available. *Faculty:* 21 full-time (10 women), 13 part-time/adjunct (5 women). *Students:* 35 full-time (25 women), 27 part-time (19 women); includes 10 minority (6 African Americans, 2 Asian Americans or Pacific Islanders, 2 Hispanic Americans). Average age 27. 74 applicants, 72% accepted, 22 enrolled. In 2008, 28 master's, 3 doctorates awarded. *Degree requirements:* For master's, comprehensive exam, research requirement; for doctorate, comprehensive exam, thesis/dissertation. *Entrance requirements:* For master's, GRE, statement of purpose; 2 recommendations; for doctorate, GRE, minimum GPA of 3.2. Additional exam requirements/recommendations for international students: Required—TOEFL. *Application deadline:* For fall admission, 2/1 for domestic students; for spring admission, 11/1 for domestic students. Application fee: $55. *Expenses:* Tuition: Full-time $21,204; part-time $1178 per credit hour. Required fees: $380. Part-time tuition and fees vary according to course load and program. *Financial support:* Fellowships, research assistantships, teaching assistantships, career-related internships or fieldwork, Federal Work-Study, institutionally sponsored loans, and tuition waivers (full and partial) available. Financial award application deadline: 2/1. *Faculty research:* Mental health, court management. *Unit head:* Dr. Diedre Golash, Chair, 202-885-2955, E-mail: dgolash@american.edu. *Application contact:* Dr. Diedre Golash, Chair, 202-885-2955, E-mail: dgolash@american.edu.

American University of Puerto Rico, Program in Criminal Justice, Bayamón, PR 00960-2037. Offers MA.

Anderson University, Command College, Anderson, SC 29621-4035. Offers MA. Postbaccalaureate distance learning degree programs offered. *Entrance requirements:* For master's, minimum undergraduate GPA of 2.75, five years experience working in criminal justice field, resumé, goals statement.

Andrew Jackson University, Jeffrey D. Rubenstein College of Criminal Justice, Program in Criminal Justice, Birmingham, AL 35244. Offers MS. Part-time and evening/weekend programs available. Postbaccalaureate distance learning degree programs offered (no on-campus study). *Entrance requirements:* For master's, course work in calculus, statistics. Additional exam requirements/recommendations for international students: Required—TOEFL (minimum score 550 paper-based; 213 computer-based).

Anna Maria College, Graduate Division, Program in Criminal Justice, Paxton, MA 01612. Offers criminal justice (MS). Part-time and evening/weekend programs available. *Faculty:* 6 full-time (1 woman), 3 part-time/adjunct (2 women). *Students:* 25 full-time (12 women), 33 part-time (5 women); includes 4 minority (1 African American, 3 Hispanic Americans). Average age 32. In 2008, 16 master's awarded. *Degree requirements:* For master's, capstone project or thesis. *Entrance requirements:* For master's, bachelor's degree in related field, minimum GPA of 2.7. Additional exam requirements/recommendations for international students: Required—TOEFL (minimum score 500 paper-based). *Application deadline:* For fall admission, 3/1 priority date for domestic and international students; for spring admission, 11/1 priority date for domestic and international students. Applications are processed on a rolling basis. Application fee: $40. Electronic applications accepted. *Expenses:* Tuition: Part-time $1400 per course. *Financial support:* Applicants required to submit FAFSA. *Unit head:* Patricia Gavin, Director, 508-849-3377, Fax: 508-849-3343, E-mail: pgavin@annamaria.edu. *Application contact:* Dennis

Braun, Director, Graduate Studies and Continuing Education, 508-849-3293, Fax: 508-819-3362, E-mail: dbraun@annamaria.edu.

Anna Maria College, Graduate Division, Program in Justice Administration, Paxton, MA 01612. Offers MS. Part-time and evening/weekend programs available. *Faculty:* 5 part-time/adjunct (0 women). *Students:* 21 part-time (11 women); includes 3 minority (2 African Americans, 1 Hispanic American). Average age 35. In 2008, 14 master's awarded. *Degree requirements:* For master's, capstone project. *Entrance requirements:* Additional exam requirements/recommendations for international students: Required—TOEFL (minimum score 500 paper-based). *Application deadline:* For fall admission, 3/1 for domestic students; for spring admission, 11/1 for domestic students. Applications are processed on a rolling basis. Application fee: $40. Electronic applications accepted. *Expenses:* Tuition: Part-time $1400 per course. *Unit head:* Patricia Gavin, Director, 508-849-3377, Fax: 508-849-3343, E-mail: pgavin@annamaria.edu. *Application contact:* Dennis Braun, Director, Graduate Studies and Continuing Education, 508-849-3293, Fax: 508-819-3362, E-mail: dbraun@annamaria.edu.

Anna Maria College, Graduate Division, Program in Security Management, Paxton, MA 01612. Offers MA. *Degree requirements:* For master's, thesis. *Expenses:* Tuition: Part-time $1400 per course. *Unit head:* Dennis Braun, Director, Graduate Studies and Continuing Education, 508-849-3293, Fax: 508-819-3362, E-mail: dbraun@annamaria.edu. *Application contact:* Dennis Braun, Director, Graduate Studies and Continuing Education, 508-849-3293, Fax: 508-819-3362, E-mail: dbraun@annamaria.edu.

Appalachian State University, Cratis D. Williams Graduate School, Department of Government and Justice Studies, Boone, NC 28608. Offers criminal justice (MS); political science (MA), including American government, international relations; public administration (MPA), including public management, town, city and county management. Part-time programs available. Postbaccalaureate distance learning degree programs offered (no on-campus study). *Faculty:* 27 full-time (5 women), 12 part-time/adjunct (1 woman). *Students:* 70 full-time (29 women), 51 part-time (14 women); includes 9 minority (7 African Americans, 1 American Indian/Alaska Native, 1 Asian American or Pacific Islander), 4 international. 60 applicants, 92% accepted, 32 enrolled. In 2008, 58 master's awarded. *Degree requirements:* For master's, variable foreign language requirement, comprehensive exam, thesis optional. *Entrance requirements:* For master's, GRE General Test, 3 letters of recommendation. Additional exam requirements/recommendations for international students: Required—TOEFL (minimum score 570 paper-based; 230 computer-based; 79 iBT), IELTS (minimum score 6.5). *Application deadline:* For fall admission, 7/1 for domestic students, 2/1 for international students; for spring admission, 11/1 for domestic students, 7/1 for international students. Applications are processed on a rolling basis. Application fee: $50. Electronic applications accepted. *Expenses:* Tuition, area resident: Full-time $2600; part-time $700 per course. Tuition, state resident: full-time $2600; part-time $700 per course. Tuition, nonresident: full-time $5000; part-time $3300 per course. Required fees: $2150; $330 per course. Tuition and fees vary according to campus/location. *Financial support:* In 2008–09, 35 research assistantships (averaging $7,500 per year) were awarded; fellowships, teaching assistantships, career-related internships or fieldwork, Federal Work-Study, scholarships/grants, and unspecified assistantships also available. Financial award application deadline: 4/1; financial award applicants required to submit FAFSA. *Faculty research:* Campaign finance, emerging democracies, bureaucratic politics, judicial behavior, administration of justice. Total annual research expenditures: $8,500. *Unit head:* Dr. Brian Ellison, Chairperson, 828-262-3085, E-mail: ellisonba@appstate.edu. *Application contact:* Sandy Krause, Director of Admissions and Recruiting, 828-262-2130, Fax: 828-262-2709, E-mail: krausesl@appstate.edu.

Arizona State University at the West campus, College of Human Services, School of Criminology and Criminal Justice, Phoenix, AZ 85069-7100. Offers criminal justice (MA); criminology and criminal justice (MS, PhD). Part-time and evening/weekend programs available. *Degree requirements:* For master's, policy analysis project; for doctorate, thesis/dissertation. *Entrance requirements:* For master's, GRE (MS), 2 letters of recommendation, minimum 3.0 GPA, personal statement; for doctorate, GRE, 2 letters of recommendation, personal statement, resumé. Additional exam requirements/recommendations for international students: Required—TOEFL (minimum score 550 paper-based; 213 computer-based; 83 iBT). Electronic applications accepted.

Arkansas State University, Graduate School, College of Humanities and Social Sciences, Department of Criminology, Sociology, and Geography, Jonesboro, State University, AR 72467. Offers criminal justice (MA, Certificate); sociology (MA); sociology education (SCCT). Part-time programs available. *Faculty:* 7 full-time (4 women). *Students:* 8 full-time (6 women), 24 part-time (16 women); includes 12 minority (all African Americans), 1 international. Average age 32. 22 applicants, 77% accepted, 7 enrolled. In 2008, 10 master's awarded. *Degree requirements:* For master's, one foreign language, comprehensive exam, thesis or alternative; for other advanced degree, comprehensive exam. *Entrance requirements:* For master's, GRE General Test or MAT, appropriate bachelor's degree, official transcript, letters of recommendation, statement of purpose; for other advanced degree, GRE General Test or MAT, interview, master's degree, official transcript. Additional exam requirements/recommendations for international students: Required—TOEFL (minimum score 550 paper-based; 213 computer-based; 79 iBT), IELTS (minimum score 6). *Application deadline:* For fall admission, 7/15 for domestic students, 7/1 for international students; for spring admission, 12/1 for domestic students, 11/13 for international students. Applications are processed on a rolling basis. Application fee: $30 ($40 for international students). Electronic applications accepted. *Expenses:* Tuition, state resident: full-time $3744; part-time $208 per credit hour. Tuition, nonresident: full-time $9540; part-time $530 per credit hour. International tuition: $7938 full-time. Required fees: $896; $47 per credit hour. $25 per term. One-time fee: $50. Tuition and fees vary according to course load and program. *Financial support:* In 2008–09, 6 students received support. Career-related internships or fieldwork, scholarships/grants, and unspecified assistantships available. Financial award application deadline: 7/1; financial award applicants required to submit FAFSA. *Faculty research:* Land use—rural and recreational, resource management, climate change, peopling of the New World, gender, family, sexuality issues. *Unit head:* Dr. Anthony Troy Adams, Chair, 870-972-3705, Fax: 870-972-3694, E-mail: aadams@astate.edu. *Application contact:* Dr. Andrew Sustich, Dean of the Graduate School, 870-972-3029, Fax: 870-972-3857, E-mail: sustich@astate.edu.

Armstrong Atlantic State University, School of Graduate Studies, Program in Criminal Justice, Savannah, GA 31419-1997. Offers MS. Part-time and evening/weekend programs available. *Degree requirements:* For master's, comprehensive exam, thesis optional. *Entrance requirements:* For master's, GRE General Test or MAT, minimum GPA of 2.5, 2 letters of recommendation. Additional exam requirements/recommendations for international students: Required—TOEFL (minimum score 523 paper-based; 193 computer-based). Electronic applications accepted.

Auburn University Montgomery, School of Sciences, Department of Justice and Public Safety, Montgomery, AL 36124-4023. Offers MSJPS. Part-time and evening/weekend programs available. *Faculty:* 4 full-time (0 women), 4 part-time/adjunct (0 women). *Students:* 20 full-time (10 women), 41 part-time (24 women); includes 33 minority (32 African Americans, 1 American Indian/Alaska Native). Average age 34. In 2008, 38 master's awarded. *Degree requirements:* For master's, comprehensive exam, thesis optional. *Entrance requirements:* For master's, GRE General Test or MAT. *Application deadline:* Applications are processed on a rolling basis. Application fee: $25. Electronic applications accepted. *Expenses:* Tuition, state resident: full-time $5088; part-time $212 per credit. Tuition, nonresident: full-time $15,264; part-time $636 per credit. Required fees: $234. *Financial support:* Career-related internships or fieldwork and scholarships/grants available. Support available to part-time students. Financial award application deadline: 3/1; financial award applicants required to submit FAFSA. *Faculty research:*

Law enforcement, corrections, juvenile justice. *Unit head:* Dr. Gloria McPherson, Head, 334-244-3692, Fax: 334-244-3244, E-mail: gmcphers@mail.aum.edu. *Application contact:* Dr. Glen Ray, Acting Graduate Coordinator, 334-244-3590, Fax: 334-244-3826, E-mail: gray@mail.aum.edu.

Bayamón Central University, Graduate Programs, Program in Business Administration, Bayamón, PR 00960-1725. Offers accounting (MBA); finance (MBA); general business (MBA); management (MBA); management of security and protection (MBA); marketing (MBA). Part-time and evening/weekend programs available. *Degree requirements:* For master's, comprehensive exam (for some programs). *Entrance requirements:* For master's, EXADEP, bachelor's degree in business or related field.

Bellevue University, Graduate School, Bellevue, NE 68005-3098. Offers acquisition and contract management (MS); business administration (MBA); clinical counseling (MS); computer information systems (MS); healthcare administration (MA, MHA, MS), including healthcare administration (MHA), human services (MA, MS); human capital management (MS, PhD); instructional design and development (MS); leadership (MA); management (MA); management information systems (MS); organizational performance (MS); public administration (MPA); public health (MPH); security management (MS). Part-time and evening/weekend programs available. Postbaccalaureate distance learning degree programs offered (no on-campus study). *Degree requirements:* For master's, thesis or project. *Entrance requirements:* For master's, minimum GPA of 2.5 in last 60 hours. Additional exam requirements/recommendations for international students: Required—TOEFL (minimum score 538 paper-based; 200 computer-based).

Boise State University, Graduate College, College of Social Sciences and Public Affairs, Program in Criminal Justice Administration, Boise, ID 83725-0399. Offers MA. *Degree requirements:* For master's, thesis. *Entrance requirements:* For master's, minimum GPA of 3.0. Electronic applications accepted.

Boston University, Metropolitan College (Continuing Education), Department of Applied Social Sciences, Program in Criminal Justice, Boston, MA 02215. Offers MCJ. Part-time and evening/weekend programs available. Postbaccalaureate distance learning degree programs offered (no on-campus study). *Degree requirements:* For master's, comprehensive exam. *Entrance requirements:* Additional exam requirements/recommendations for international students: Required—TOEFL; Recommended—IELTS. Electronic applications accepted. *Faculty research:* Criminal justice administration and planning, criminology, police, corrections, collective violence, juvenile issues.

Bowling Green State University, Graduate College, College of Health and Human Services, Program in Criminal Justice, Bowling Green, OH 43403. Offers MSCJ. Part-time and evening/weekend programs available. Postbaccalaureate distance learning degree programs offered (no on-campus study). *Degree requirements:* For master's, thesis or alternative. *Entrance requirements:* For master's, GRE General Test. Additional exam requirements/recommendations for international students: Required—TOEFL. Electronic applications accepted.

Bridgewater State College, School of Graduate Studies, School of Arts and Sciences, Department of Sociology, Program in Criminal Justice, Bridgewater, MA 02325-0001. Offers MS. *Entrance requirements:* For master's, GRE General Test.

Buffalo State College, State University of New York, Graduate Studies and Research, Faculty of Applied Science and Education, Department of Criminal Justice, Buffalo, NY 14222-1095. Offers MS. Part-time and evening/weekend programs available. *Degree requirements:* For master's, comprehensive exam, project. *Entrance requirements:* For master's, minimum GPA of 3.0. Additional exam requirements/recommendations for international students: Required—TOEFL (minimum score 550 paper-based; 213 computer-based).

California State University, Fresno, Division of Graduate Studies, College of Social Sciences, Department of Criminology, Fresno, CA 93740-8027. Offers MS. Part-time and evening/weekend programs available. *Degree requirements:* For master's, thesis or alternative. *Entrance requirements:* For master's, GRE General Test, minimum GPA of 3.0. Additional exam requirements/recommendations for international students: Required—TOEFL. Electronic applications accepted. *Faculty research:* Substance abuse, gangs vs. law enforcement, needs of female offenders, battered women, crime victims.

California State University, Long Beach, Graduate Studies, College of Health and Human Services, Department of Criminal Justice, Long Beach, CA 90840. Offers MS. Part-time programs available. *Faculty:* 8 full-time (3 women), 5 part-time/adjunct (1 woman). *Students:* 26 full-time (20 women), 38 part-time (26 women); includes 40 minority (7 African Americans, 10 Asian Americans or Pacific Islanders, 23 Hispanic Americans), 2 international. Average age 29. 118 applicants, 58% accepted, 22 enrolled. *Degree requirements:* For master's, comprehensive course or thesis. *Entrance requirements:* For master's, minimum GPA of 3.0. *Application deadline:* For fall admission, 5/1 for domestic students. Applications are processed on a rolling basis. Application fee: $55. Electronic applications accepted. *Expenses:* Tuition, nonresident: full-time $11,160; part-time $372 per unit. Required fees: $4100; $1261 per semester. *Financial support:* Federal Work-Study, institutionally sponsored loans, and scholarships/grants available. Financial award application deadline: 3/2. *Unit head:* Dr. Henry F Fradella, Chair, 562-985-4738, Fax: 562-985-8086, E-mail: hfradell@csulb.edu. *Application contact:* Dr. Connie Ireland, Graduate Advisor, 562-985-8711, Fax: 562-985-8086, E-mail: cireland@csulb.edu.

California State University, Los Angeles, Graduate Studies, College of Health and Human Services, Department of Criminal Justice and Criminalistics, Los Angeles, CA 90032-8530. Offers criminal justice (MS); criminalistics (MS). Part-time and evening/weekend programs available. *Faculty:* 4 full-time (3 women), 1 part-time/adjunct (0 women). *Students:* 24 full-time (19 women), 29 part-time (20 women); includes 29 minority (11 Asian Americans or Pacific Islanders, 18 Hispanic Americans), 1 international. Average age 27. 43 applicants, 100% accepted, 20 enrolled. In 2008, 12 master's awarded. *Degree requirements:* For master's, thesis. *Entrance requirements:* For master's, minimum GPA of 2.75. Additional exam requirements/recommendations for international students: Required—TOEFL (minimum score 500 paper-based; 173 computer-based). *Application deadline:* For fall admission, 6/15 for domestic students, 5/1 for international students; for winter admission, 11/1 for domestic students, 9/1 for international students; for spring admission, 2/1 for domestic students, 10/1 for international students. Applications are processed on a rolling basis. Application fee: $55. *Expenses:* Tuition, nonresident: part-time $226 per credit. Required fees: $4019. *Financial support:* Federal Work-Study available. Support available to part-time students. Financial award application deadline: 3/1. *Unit head:* Dr. Joseph L. Peterson, Head, 323-343-4610, Fax: 323-343-4646, E-mail: joseph.peterson@calstatela.edu. *Application contact:* Dr. Jose L. Galvan, Dean of Graduate Studies, 323-343-3820, Fax: 323-343-5653, E-mail: jgalvan@cslanet.calstatela.edu.

California State University, Sacramento, Graduate Studies, College of Health and Human Services, Division of Criminal Justice, Sacramento, CA 95819-6048. Offers MS. Part-time programs available. *Degree requirements:* For master's, thesis or alternative, writing proficiency exam. *Entrance requirements:* For master's, BA in criminal justice or equivalent, minimum GPA of 2.5 during previous 2 years of course work. Additional exam requirements/recommendations for international students: Required—TOEFL. Electronic applications accepted.

California State University, San Bernardino, Graduate Studies, College of Social and Behavioral Sciences, Department of Criminal Justice, San Bernardino, CA 92407-2397. Offers MA. Part-time programs available. *Faculty:* 8 full-time (5 women), 2 part-time/adjunct (0 women). *Students:* 11 full-time (7 women), 20 part-time (9 women); includes 12 minority (2 African Americans, 2 Asian Americans or Pacific Islanders, 8 Hispanic Americans), 1 international. Average age 32. 42 applicants, 50% accepted, 18 enrolled. In 2008, 12 master's awarded. *Degree requirements:* For master's, thesis optional, comprehensive exam or thesis; advancement to candidacy. *Entrance requirements:* For master's, GRE General Test, minimum GPA of 3.0. *Application deadline:* For fall admission, 9/1 priority date for domestic students. Applications are processed on a rolling basis. Application fee: $55. *Expenses:* Tuition, area resident: Full-time $1252; part-time $726 per quarter. Required fees: $334 per quarter. Tuition and fees vary according to degree level and student level. *Financial support:* Research assistantships, career-related internships or fieldwork, Federal Work-Study, and institutionally sponsored loans available. Support available to part-time students. *Faculty research:* Crime seriousness, fear of crime, victimization, corrections management, crime correlates. *Unit head:* Dr. Larry Gaines, Chair, 909-537-5508, Fax: 909-537-7025, E-mail: lgaines@csusb.edu. *Application contact:* Olivia Rosas, Director of Admissions, 909-537-7577, Fax: 909-537-7034, E-mail: orosas@csusb.edu.

California State University, Stanislaus, College of Humanities and Social Sciences, Department of Criminal Justice, Turlock, CA 95382. Offers MA. Part-time programs available. *Degree requirements:* For master's, thesis optional. *Entrance requirements:* For master's, 3.0 minimum GPA, 3 letters of reference, personal statement. *Faculty research:* Police gerontology services, hate crimes, juvenile justice, masculinities and modern society, nutrition and criminal behavior.

California University of Pennsylvania, School of Graduate Studies and Research, College of Liberal Arts, Department of Sociology/Criminal Justice, California, PA 15419-1394. Offers social science—criminal justice (MA). Part-time and evening/weekend programs available. *Degree requirements:* For master's, comprehensive exam, thesis optional. *Entrance requirements:* For master's, MAT, minimum GPA of 3.0. Additional exam requirements/recommendations for international students: Required—TOEFL (minimum score 550 paper-based; 213 computer-based; 80 iBT). Electronic applications accepted. *Faculty research:* Ethics and law, ethics in police practice, law and morality, police policy, St. Thomas Aquinas and crime.

Calumet College of Saint Joseph, Program in Public Safety Administration, Whiting, IN 46394-2195. Offers MS.

Capella University, School of Human Services, Minneapolis, MN 55402. Offers addictions counseling (Certificate); counseling studies (MS, PhD); criminal justice (MS, PhD, Certificate); diversity studies (Certificate); general human services (MS, PhD); health care administration (MS, PhD, Certificate); management of nonprofit agencies (MS, PhD, Certificate); marital, couple and family counseling/therapy (MS); marriage and family services (Certificate); mental health counseling (MS); professional counseling (Certificate); social and community services (MS, PhD, Certificate). Part-time and evening/weekend programs available. Postbaccalaureate distance learning degree programs offered (minimal on-campus study). Terminal master's awarded for partial completion of doctoral program. *Degree requirements:* For master's, thesis optional, integrative project; for doctorate, comprehensive exam, thesis/dissertation. *Entrance requirements:* Additional exam requirements/recommendations for international students: Required—TOEFL (minimum score 550 paper-based; 213 computer-based), TWE (minimum score 4). Electronic applications accepted. *Faculty research:* Compulsive and addictive behaviors, substance abuse, assessment of psychopathology and neuropsychology.

Caribbean University, Graduate School, Bayamón, PR 00960-0493. Offers administration and supervision (MA Ed); criminal justice (MA); curriculum and instruction (MA Ed), including elementary education, English education, history education, mathematics education, primary education, science education, Spanish education; education (PhD); gerontology (MSN); human resources (MBA); museology, archiving and art history (MA Ed); neonatal pediatrics (MSN); physical education (MA Ed); special education (MA Ed). *Entrance requirements:* For master's, interview, minimum GPA of 2.5.

Carnegie Mellon University, H. John Heinz III College, School of Information Systems and Management, Program in Information Security Policy and Management, Pittsburgh, PA 15213-3891. Offers MSISPM.

Central Connecticut State University, School of Graduate Studies, School of Arts and Sciences, Department of Criminology and Criminal Justice, New Britain, CT 06050-4010. Offers criminal justice (MS). Part-time and evening/weekend programs available. *Faculty:* 11 full-time (4 women), 16 part-time/adjunct (2 women). *Students:* 6 full-time (2 women), 30 part-time (18 women); includes 8 minority (4 African Americans, 4 Hispanic Americans). Average age 32. 29 applicants, 66% accepted, 9 enrolled. In 2008, 8 master's awarded. *Degree requirements:* For master's, comprehensive exam, thesis or alternative. *Entrance requirements:* For master's, minimum undergraduate GPA of 3.0, essay. Additional exam requirements/recommendations for international students: Required—TOEFL. *Application deadline:* For fall admission, 5/1 for domestic students; for spring admission, 12/1 for domestic students. Applications are processed on a rolling basis. Application fee: $50. Electronic applications accepted. *Expenses:* Tuition, area resident: Full-time $4377; part-time $420 per credit. Tuition, state resident: full-time $6566; part-time $420 per credit. Tuition, nonresident: full-time $12,195; part-time $420 per credit. Required fees: $3462. One-time fee: $62 part-time. *Financial support:* In 2008–09, 3 students received support, including 2 research assistantships; career-related internships or fieldwork, Federal Work-Study, scholarships/grants, and unspecified assistantships also available. Support available to part-time students. Financial award application deadline: 3/1; financial award applicants required to submit FAFSA. *Unit head:* Dr. Raymond Tafrate, Chair, 860-832-3005. *Application contact:* Dr. Raymond Tafrate, Chair, 860-832-3005.

Chaminade University of Honolulu, Graduate Services, Program in Criminal Justice Administration, Honolulu, HI 96816-1578. Offers criminal justice administration (MSCJA); homeland security (Certificate). Part-time and evening/weekend programs available. Postbaccalaureate distance learning degree programs offered (no on-campus study). *Degree requirements:* For master's, thesis optional. *Entrance requirements:* For master's, minimum undergraduate GPA of 3.0, 3 letters of recommendation. Additional exam requirements/recommendations for international students: Required—TOEFL (minimum score 550 paper-based). Electronic applications accepted. *Faculty research:* Penology, juvenile delinquency, multicultural and ethnic diversity in criminology, law enforcement administration and training, homeland security.

Charleston Southern University, Department of Criminal Justice, Charleston, SC 29423-8087. Offers MSCJ. Part-time and evening/weekend programs available. *Faculty:* 2 full-time (both women), 1 part-time/adjunct. *Students:* 6 full-time (2 women), 20 part-time (13 women); includes 8 minority (7 African Americans, 1 Hispanic American), 1 international. Average age 31. 18 applicants, 72% accepted, 12 enrolled. *Degree requirements:* For master's, comprehensive exam, thesis optional. *Entrance requirements:* For master's, GRE or MAT, bachelor's degree in criminal justice. Additional exam requirements/recommendations for international students: Required—TOEFL (minimum score 550 paper-based; 213 computer-based; 79 iBT). *Application deadline:* Applications are processed on a rolling basis. Application fee: $30. *Expenses:* Tuition: Full-time $8832; part-time $368 per credit hour. Required fees: $30. One-time fee: $30. Tuition and fees vary according to course load and program. *Financial support:* Research assistantships with full tuition reimbursements available. Financial award application deadline: 4/15; financial award applicants required to submit FAFSA. *Unit head:* Dr. Jacqueline Fish, Chair, 843-863-7131, Fax: 843-863-7198, E-mail: jfish@csuniv.edu. *Application contact:* Alison Harrison, Graduate Enrollment Counselor, 843-863-7534, Fax: 843-863-7070, E-mail: aharrison@csuniv.edu.

Chicago State University, School of Graduate and Professional Studies, College of Arts and Sciences, Department of Criminal Justice, Chicago, IL 60628. Offers MS. Part-time and evening/weekend programs available. *Entrance requirements:* For master's, minimum GPA of 2.75. *Faculty research:* Gang crime.

Clark Atlanta University, School of Arts and Sciences, Department of Criminal Justice, Atlanta, GA 30314. Offers MA. Part-time programs available. *Faculty:* 4 full-time (0 women). *Students:* 4 full-time (all women), 3 part-time (2 women); includes 5 minority (all African Americans), 1 international. Average age 26. 3 applicants, 67% accepted, 1 enrolled. In 2008,

Criminal Justice and Criminology

Clark Atlanta University (continued)

3 master's awarded. *Degree requirements:* For master's, one foreign language, thesis. *Entrance requirements:* For master's, GRE General Test, minimum GPA of 2.5. Additional exam requirements/recommendations for international students: Required—TOEFL (minimum score 500 paper-based; 173 computer-based). *Application deadline:* For fall admission, 4/1 for domestic and international students; for spring admission, 11/1 for domestic and international students. Applications are processed on a rolling basis. Application fee: $40 ($55 for international students). *Expenses:* Tuition: Full-time $12,240; part-time $680 per credit hour. Required fees: $710; $355 per semester. *Financial support:* Fellowships, research assistantships, career-related internships or fieldwork, Federal Work-Study, scholarships/grants, and unspecified assistantships available. Support available to part-time students. Financial award application deadline: 4/30; financial award applicants required to submit FAFSA. *Faculty research:* Race and crime, black ex-offenders in the labor market. *Unit head:* Dr. Sandra Taylor, Chairperson, 404-880-8681, E-mail: staylor@cau.edu. *Application contact:* Michelle Clark-Davis, Graduate Program Admissions, 404-880-6605, E-mail: cauadmissions@cau.edu.

Colorado Technical University Colorado Springs, Graduate Studies, Program in Criminal Justice, Colorado Springs, CO 80907-3896. Offers MSM. Postbaccalaureate distance learning degree programs offered.

Colorado Technical University Denver, Program in Computer Science, Greenwood Village, CO 80111. Offers computer systems security (MSCS); database systems (MSCS); software engineering (MSCS). Part-time and evening/weekend programs available. *Degree requirements:* For master's, thesis or alternative. *Entrance requirements:* For master's, minimum undergraduate GPA of 3.0, resumé.

Colorado Technical University Sioux Falls, Program in Criminal Justice, Sioux Falls, SD 57108. Offers MSM.

Columbia College, Master of Science in Criminal Justice Program, Columbia, MO 65216-0002. Offers MSCJ. Evening/weekend programs available. Postbaccalaureate distance learning degree programs offered (no on-campus study). *Faculty:* 3 full-time (0 women), 6 part-time/adjunct (3 women). *Students:* 86 full-time (38 women); includes 24 minority (17 African Americans, 1 American Indian/Alaska Native, 1 Asian American or Pacific Islander, 5 Hispanic Americans). Average age 35. 46 applicants, 70% accepted, 15 enrolled. In 2008, 14 master's awarded. *Degree requirements:* For master's, final exams, culminating experience (intensive writing seminar). *Entrance requirements:* For master's, minimum cumulative GPA of 3.0. Additional exam requirements/recommendations for international students: Required—TOEFL (minimum score 500 paper-based; 173 computer-based; 61 iBT). *Application deadline:* For fall admission, 8/1 priority date for domestic and international students; for spring admission, 12/15 priority date for domestic and international students. Applications are processed on a rolling basis. Application fee: $55. Electronic applications accepted. *Expenses:* Tuition: Full-time $3420; part-time $285 per semester hour. Full-time tuition and fees vary according to campus/location. *Financial support:* In 2008–09, 53 students received support. Federal Work-Study and scholarships/grants available. Financial award applicants required to submit FAFSA. *Faculty research:* Organized crime, policing in America. *Unit head:* Dr. Joseph Carrier, MSCJ Graduate Program Coordinator, 573-875-7275, Fax: 573-876-4493, E-mail: jjcarrier@ccis.edu. *Application contact:* Samantha White, Director of Admissions, 573-875-7352, Fax: 573-875-7506, E-mail: sjwhite@ccis.edu.

Columbia Southern University, College of Safety and Emergency Services, Orange Beach, AL 36561. Offers criminal justice (MS); environmental management (MS); occupational safety and health (MS); occupational safety and health/environmental management (MS). Part-time and evening/weekend programs available. Postbaccalaureate distance learning degree programs offered (no on-campus study). *Entrance requirements:* For master's, Bachelor's Degree from accredited/approved institution. Additional exam requirements/recommendations for international students: Required—TOEFL. Electronic applications accepted.

Columbus State University, Graduate Studies, College of Arts and Letters, Program in Public Administration, Columbus, GA 31907-5645. Offers justice administration (MPA). Part-time and evening/weekend programs available. *Faculty:* 7 full-time (2 women), 13 part-time/adjunct (0 women). *Students:* 117 full-time (51 women), 226 part-time (76 women); includes 106 minority (99 African Americans, 2 American Indian/Alaska Native, 2 Asian Americans or Pacific Islanders, 3 Hispanic Americans), 1 international. Average age 36. 85 applicants, 76% accepted, 57 enrolled. In 2008, 114 master's awarded. *Degree requirements:* For master's, comprehensive exam. *Entrance requirements:* For master's, GRE General Test, GMAT, MAT. Additional exam requirements/recommendations for international students: Required—TOEFL (minimum score 550 paper-based; 213 computer-based). *Application deadline:* For fall admission, 5/1 priority date for domestic students, 5/1 for international students; for spring admission, 11/1 for domestic and international students. Applications are processed on a rolling basis. Application fee: $25. Electronic applications accepted. *Expenses:* Tuition, area resident: Full-time $3410; part-time $143 per credit hour. Tuition, state resident: full-time $3411; part-time $143 per credit hour. Tuition, nonresident: full-time $13,634; part-time $569 per credit hour. Required fees: $1348. *Financial support:* In 2008–09, 82 students received support, including 8 research assistantships with partial tuition reimbursements available (averaging $3,000 per year); career-related internships or fieldwork, Federal Work-Study, institutionally sponsored loans, scholarships/grants, tuition waivers (full), and unspecified assistantships also available. Support available to part-time students. Financial award application deadline: 5/1; financial award applicants required to submit FAFSA. *Unit head:* Dr. William Chappell, Program Director, 706-568-2055, E-mail: chappell_william@colstate.edu. *Application contact:* Katie Thornton, Graduate Admissions Specialist, 706-568-2035, Fax: 706-568-2462, E-mail: thornton_katie@colstate.edu.

Concordia University, St. Paul, College of Business and Organizational Leadership, St. Paul, MN 55104-5494. Offers business and organizational leadership (MBA); criminal justice leadership (MA); human resources management (MA); organizational management (MA). *Accreditation:* ACBSP. Evening/weekend programs available. Postbaccalaureate distance learning degree programs offered (minimal on-campus study). *Faculty:* 12 full-time (6 women), 26 part-time/adjunct (10 women). *Students:* 267 full-time (161 women), 11 part-time (3 women); includes 35 minority (22 African Americans, 10 Asian Americans or Pacific Islanders, 3 Hispanic Americans), 5 international. Average age 33. In 2008, 110 master's awarded. *Application deadline:* Applications are processed on a rolling basis. Application fee: $50. Electronic applications accepted. *Financial support:* Applicants required to submit FAFSA. *Unit head:* Dr. Bruce Corrie, Dean, 651-641-8226, Fax: 651-641-8807, E-mail: corrie@csp.edu. *Application contact:* Kimberly Craig, Director of Graduate and Cohort Admission, 651-603-6223, Fax: 651-603-6320, E-mail: craig@csp.edu.

Coppin State University, Division of Graduate Studies, Division of Arts and Sciences, Department of Criminal Justice and Law Enforcement, Baltimore, MD 21216-3698. Offers criminal justice (MS). Part-time and evening/weekend programs available. *Degree requirements:* For master's, thesis optional. *Entrance requirements:* For master's, GRE, minimum GPA of 3.0.

Curry College, Division of Continuing Education and Graduate Studies, Program in Criminal Justice, Milton, MA 02186-9984. Offers MA. Part-time and evening/weekend programs available. *Degree requirements:* For master's, thesis. *Entrance requirements:* For master's, MAT or GRE, resumé, recommendations, interview, written statement. Additional exam requirements/recommendations for international students: Required—TOEFL (minimum score 550 paper-based; 213 computer-based; 80 iBT). *Expenses:* Contact institution.

Dallas Baptist University, College of Adult Education, Professional Development Program, Dallas, TX 75211-9299. Offers accounting (MA); church leadership (MA); counseling (MA); criminal justice (MA); English as a second language (MA); finance (MA); higher education (MA); leadership studies (MA); management (MA); management information systems (MA); marketing (MA); missions (MA). Part-time and evening/weekend programs available. *Faculty:* 68 full-time (30 women), 113 part-time/adjunct (47 women). *Students:* 10 full-time, 83 part-time. 30 applicants, 47% accepted. In 2008, 39 master's awarded. *Entrance requirements:* For master's, minimum GPA of 3.0. Additional exam requirements/recommendations for international students: Required—TOEFL, IELTS. Application fee: $25. *Expenses:* Tuition: Part-time $558 per credit hour. *Financial support:* Federal Work-Study, institutionally sponsored loans, scholarships/grants, and tuition waivers (full and partial) available. Support available to part-time students. Financial award applicants required to submit FAFSA. *Unit head:* Dr. John Tarwater, Acting Director, 214-333-6830, Fax: 214-333-5558, E-mail: graduate@dbu.edu. *Application contact:* Kit P. Montgomery, Director of Graduate Programs, 214-333-5242, Fax: 214-333-5579, E-mail: graduate@dbu.edu.

Defiance College, Program in Business Administration, Defiance, OH 43512-1610. Offers criminal justice (MBA); health care (MBA); leadership (MBA). Part-time and evening/weekend programs available. *Degree requirements:* For master's, thesis. *Entrance requirements:* For master's, minimum GPA of 2.5.

Delta State University, Graduate Programs, College of Arts and Sciences, Division of Social Sciences, Program in Criminal Justice, Cleveland, MS 38733-0001. Offers MSCJ. Part-time programs available. Postbaccalaureate distance learning degree programs offered. *Degree requirements:* For master's, thesis or alternative.

DeSales University, Graduate Division, Program in Criminal Justice, Center Valley, PA 18034-9568. Offers MACJ. Part-time and evening/weekend programs available. Postbaccalaureate distance learning degree programs offered (no on-campus study). *Students:* 32 part-time. Application fee: $35. *Expenses:* Tuition: Full-time $16,720. Required fees: $800. Tuition and fees vary according to program. *Unit head:* Dr. Patrick McGrain, Director, 610-282-1100 Ext. 1584, E-mail: patrick.mcgrain@desales.edu. *Application contact:* Colleen Petrick, Secretary, Social Science Department, 610-212-1100 Ext. 1466, Fax: 610-282-0787, E-mail: colleen.petrick@desales.edu.

Drury University, Program in Criminology/Criminal Justice, Springfield, MO 65802. Offers criminal justice (MS); criminology (MA). Part-time and evening/weekend programs available. *Degree requirements:* For master's, thesis (for some programs). *Entrance requirements:* For master's, GMAT or MAT. Additional exam requirements/recommendations for international students: Required—TOEFL. Electronic applications accepted. *Expenses:* Contact institution. *Faculty research:* Gangs, fear of crime, social justice, social change and law, drug laws in Iran.

East Carolina University, Graduate School, College of Human Ecology, Department of Criminal Justice, Greenville, NC 27858-4353. Offers MS. Part-time and evening/weekend programs available. Postbaccalaureate distance learning degree programs offered (no on-campus study). *Degree requirements:* For master's, thesis, internship. *Entrance requirements:* For master's, GRE or MAT, bachelor's degree in criminal justice or related field. Additional exam requirements/recommendations for international students: Required—TOEFL. *Faculty research:* Corrections, policing, international criminal justice, terrorism.

East Central University, School of Graduate Studies, Department of Human Resources, Ada, OK 74820-6899. Offers administration (MSHR); counseling (MSHR); criminal justice (MSHR); rehabilitation counseling (MSHR). *Accreditation:* CORE. Part-time and evening/weekend programs available. *Degree requirements:* For master's, thesis optional. *Entrance requirements:* For master's, GRE General Test, MAT, minimum GPA of 2.5. Electronic applications accepted.

Eastern Kentucky University, The Graduate School, College of Justice and Safety, Program in Correctional and Juvenile Justice Studies, Richmond, KY 40475-3102. Offers MS. *Degree requirements:* For master's, comprehensive exam (for some programs), thesis (for some programs). *Entrance requirements:* For master's, GRE.

Eastern Kentucky University, The Graduate School, College of Justice and Safety, Program in Criminal Justice and Police Studies, Richmond, KY 40475-3102. Offers criminal justice (MS); criminal justice education (MS); police studies (MS). Part-time programs available. *Degree requirements:* For master's, thesis optional. *Entrance requirements:* For master's, GRE General Test, minimum GPA of 3.0.

Eastern Kentucky University, The Graduate School, College of Justice and Safety, Program in Loss Prevention and Safety, Richmond, KY 40475-3102. Offers MS. *Entrance requirements:* For master's, GRE.

Eastern Michigan University, Graduate School, College of Arts and Sciences, Department of Sociology, Anthropology and Criminology, Program in Criminology and Criminal Justice, Ypsilanti, MI 48197. Offers MA.

Eastern Michigan University, Graduate School, College of Technology, School of Technology Studies, Ypsilanti, MI 48197. Offers apparel, textile merchandising (MS); career, technical and workforce education (MS); hotel and restaurant management (MS, Graduate Certificate); information security (MLS, Graduate Certificate); legal administration (Graduate Certificate); technology studies (MLS, MS), including interdisciplinary technology (MLS), technology studies (MS). Part-time and evening/weekend programs available. Postbaccalaureate distance learning degree programs offered (minimal on-campus study). *Degree requirements:* For master's, thesis optional. *Entrance requirements:* For master's, GRE General Test. Additional exam requirements/recommendations for international students: Required—TOEFL.

East Tennessee State University, School of Graduate Studies, College of Arts and Sciences, Department of Criminal Justice and Criminology, Johnson City, TN 37614. Offers MA. Part-time and evening/weekend programs available. *Degree requirements:* For master's, thesis or alternative. *Entrance requirements:* For master's, GRE General Test, minimum GPA of 3.0. Additional exam requirements/recommendations for international students: Required—TOEFL (minimum score 550 paper-based; 213 computer-based). *Faculty research:* Prisonization, peacemaking, sentencing decisions, family violence and sexual violence, juvenile justice.

Everest University, Graduate Programs, Jacksonville, FL 32256. Offers business (MBA); criminal justice (MS).

Everest University, Program in Criminal Justice, Tampa, FL 33619. Offers MS. Part-time and evening/weekend programs available. Postbaccalaureate distance learning degree programs offered (minimal on-campus study). *Faculty:* 2 part-time/adjunct (both women). *Students:* 3 full-time (all women), 127 part-time (103 women); includes 67 minority (59 African Americans, 1 American Indian/Alaska Native, 1 Asian American or Pacific Islander, 6 Hispanic Americans). Average age 37. In 2008, 11 master's awarded. *Degree requirements:* For master's, thesis optional, externship, research practicum. *Entrance requirements:* Additional exam requirements/recommendations for international students: Required—TOEFL (minimum score 550 paper-based; 213 computer-based). *Application deadline:* Applications are processed on a rolling basis. Application fee: $25. *Expenses:* Tuition: Full-time $16,160; part-time $505 per credit hour. One-time fee: $45 full-time. *Financial support:* Federal Work-Study, institutionally sponsored loans, and scholarships/grants available. *Unit head:* Jim Pingel, Chair, 813-621-0041 Ext. 148, Fax: 813-623-5769, E-mail: JPingel@cci.edu. *Application contact:* Shandretta Pointer, Admissions Office, 813-621-0041 Ext. 106, Fax: 813-628-0919, E-mail: spointer@cci.edu.

Everest University, Program in Criminal Justice, Lakeland, FL 33801. Offers MS.

Everest University, Program in Criminal Justice, Pompano Beach, FL 33062. Offers MS.

Fairmont State University, Graduate Studies, Program in Criminal Justice, Fairmont, WV 26554. Offers MS. *Degree requirements:* For master's, thesis or comprehensive exam. *Entrance requirements:* For master's, GRE, minimum GPA of 3.0.

Fayetteville State University, Graduate School, Program in Criminal Justice, Fayetteville, NC 28301-4298. Offers MA.

Ferris State University, College of Education and Human Services, School of Criminal Justice, Big Rapids, MI 49307. Offers criminal justice administration (MS). Part-time programs available. *Degree requirements:* For master's, comprehensive exam, thesis optional. *Entrance requirements:* For master's, bachelor's degree in criminal justice or related field, minimum GPA of 3.0. Additional exam requirements/recommendations for international students: Required—TOEFL. Electronic applications accepted. *Faculty research:* Policy enactment, health and safety issues, criminological theory, juvenile justice, policy techniques, problem based learning.

Fitchburg State College, Division of Graduate and Continuing Education, Program in Criminal Justice, Fitchburg, MA 01420-2697. Offers MS. Part-time and evening/weekend programs available. *Entrance requirements:* For master's, GRE General Test or MAT, letters of recommendation, resumé. Additional exam requirements/recommendations for international students: Required—TOEFL (minimum score 550 paper-based; 213 computer-based; 79 iBT). *Application deadline:* Applications are processed on a rolling basis. Application fee: $25 ($50 for international students). *Expenses:* Tuition, state resident: full-time $3600; part-time $150 per credit. Tuition, nonresident: full-time $3600; part-time $150 per credit. Required fees: $109 per credit. *Financial support:* In 2008–09, research assistantships with partial tuition reimbursements (averaging $5,500 per year); Federal Work-Study, scholarships/grants, and unspecified assistantships also available. Support available to part-time students. Financial award application deadline: 3/1; financial award applicants required to submit FAFSA. *Unit head:* Dr. Richard Wiebe, Chair, 978-665-3356, Fax: 978-554-3658, E-mail: gce@fsc.edu. *Application contact:* Director of Admissions, 978-665-3144, Fax: 978-665-4540, E-mail: admissions@fsc.edu.

Florida Agricultural and Mechanical University, Division of Graduate Studies, Research, and Continuing Education, College of Arts and Sciences, Division of History and Political Sciences, Program in Applied Social Science, Tallahassee, FL 32307-3200. Offers African American history (MASS); criminal justice (MASS); economics (MASS); history (MASS); political science (MASS); public administration (MASS); public management (MASS); social work (MASS); sociology (MASS). Part-time programs available. *Degree requirements:* For master's, thesis optional. *Entrance requirements:* For master's, GRE General Test, minimum GPA of 3.0. *Faculty research:* Southern history, black history, election trends, presidential history.

Florida Atlantic University, College of Architecture, Urban and Public Affairs, School of Criminology and Criminal Justice, Boca Raton, FL 33431-0991. Offers MS. Part-time and evening/weekend programs available. Postbaccalaureate distance learning degree programs offered. *Faculty:* 13 full-time (4 women), 16 part-time/adjunct (2 women). *Students:* 5 full-time (1 woman), 15 part-time (8 women); includes 5 minority (2 African Americans, 3 Hispanic Americans), 1 international. Average age 31. 33 applicants, 42% accepted, 11 enrolled. In 2008, 10 master's awarded. *Degree requirements:* For master's, thesis optional. *Entrance requirements:* For master's, GRE General Test, minimum GPA of 3.0, undergraduate course work in statistics and criminology. Additional exam requirements/recommendations for international students: Required—TOEFL (minimum score 550 paper-based; 213 computer-based). *Application deadline:* For fall admission, 7/1 priority date for domestic students, 2/15 for international students; for spring admission, 11/1 priority date for domestic students, 7/15 for international students. Applications are processed on a rolling basis. Application fee: $30. Electronic applications accepted. *Expenses:* Tuition, state resident: full-time $4867; part-time $270.40 per credit hour. Tuition, nonresident: full-time $16,486; part-time $915.87 per credit hour. *Financial support:* Research assistantships with partial tuition reimbursements, institutionally sponsored loans, scholarships/grants, and unspecified assistantships available. Financial award application deadline: 4/1. *Faculty research:* Restorative, justice corrections, logic modeling, criminal justice management, crime causation. *Unit head:* Dr. Gordon Bazemore, Chair, 561-297-3240. *Application contact:* Dr. Mara Schiff, Graduate Program Coordinator, 954-762-5638, Fax: 954-762-5673, E-mail: mschiff@fau.edu.

Florida Gulf Coast University, College of Professional Studies, Program in Criminal Justice Studies, Fort Myers, FL 33965-6565. Offers MS. *Faculty:* 32 full-time (11 women), 29 part-time/adjunct (12 women). *Students:* 8 part-time (4 women); includes 4 minority (1 African American, 3 Hispanic Americans). Average age 26. 10 applicants, 70% accepted, 6 enrolled. *Entrance requirements:* For master's, GRE General Test, minimum GPA of 3.0. Additional exam requirements/recommendations for international students: Required—TOEFL (minimum score 550 paper-based; 213 computer-based). *Application deadline:* For fall admission, 3/1 for domestic students; for spring admission, 11/1 for domestic students. Applications are processed on a rolling basis. Application fee: $30. Electronic applications accepted. *Unit head:* Tony Barringer, Chair, 239-590-7849, E-mail: tbarring@fgcu.edu. *Application contact:* Tony Barringer, Chair, 239-590-7849, E-mail: tbarring@fgcu.edu.

Florida Gulf Coast University, College of Professional Studies, Program in Public Administration, Fort Myers, FL 33965-6565. Offers criminal justice (MPA); environmental policy (MPA); general public administration (MPA); management (MPA). Part-time programs available. *Faculty:* 32 full-time (11 women), 29 part-time/adjunct (12 women). *Students:* 49 full-time (30 women), 19 part-time (12 women); includes 13 minority (4 African Americans, 2 Asian Americans or Pacific Islanders, 7 Hispanic Americans). Average age 35. 34 applicants, 68% accepted, 19 enrolled. In 2008, 14 master's awarded. *Entrance requirements:* For master's, GRE General Test, MAT, minimum GPA of 3.0. Additional exam requirements/recommendations for international students: Required—TOEFL (minimum score 550 paper-based; 213 computer-based). *Application deadline:* For fall admission, 7/1 priority date for domestic students; for spring admission, 11/15 for domestic students. Applications are processed on a rolling basis. Application fee: $30. Electronic applications accepted. *Financial support:* In 2008–09, 5 research assistantships were awarded; career-related internships or fieldwork and tuition waivers (full and partial) also available. Support available to part-time students. *Faculty research:* Personnel, public policy, public finance, housing policy. *Unit head:* Terry Busson, Chair, 239-590-7704, E-mail: tbusson@fgcu.edu. *Application contact:* Roger Green, Information Contact, 239-590-7838, Fax: 239-590-7846.

Florida International University, College of Social Work, Justice and Public Affairs, School of Criminal Justice, Miami, FL 33199. Offers MS. Part-time and evening/weekend programs available. *Degree requirements:* For master's, thesis optional. *Entrance requirements:* For master's, minimum GPA of 3.0, letters of recommendation. Additional exam requirements/recommendations for international students: Required—TOEFL (minimum score 550 paper-based; 213 computer-based). Electronic applications accepted.

Florida State University, Graduate Studies, College of Criminology and Criminal Justice, Tallahassee, FL 32306. Offers MA, MSC, PhD, MPA/MSC, MS/MSW. Part-time and evening/weekend programs available. Postbaccalaureate distance learning degree programs offered (no on-campus study). *Degree requirements:* For master's, thesis optional; for doctorate, comprehensive exam, thesis/dissertation. *Entrance requirements:* For master's, GRE General Test; for doctorate, GRE General Test, area paper or thesis. Additional exam requirements/recommendations for international students: Required—TOEFL (minimum score 600 paper-based; 260 computer-based; 100 iBT). Electronic applications accepted. *Faculty research:* Criminological theory, criminal justice administration and planning, criminal justice evaluation, law and social control.

George Mason University, College of Humanities and Social Sciences, Administration of Justice Department, Fairfax, VA 22030.

The George Washington University, Columbian College of Arts and Sciences, Department of Forensic Sciences, Washington, DC 20052. Offers crime scene investigation (MFS); forensic chemistry (MFS); forensic molecular biology (MFS); forensic toxicology (MFS); high-technology crime investigation (MFS); security management (MFS). High-technology crime investigation and security management programs offered in Arlington, VA. Part-time and evening/weekend programs available. *Faculty:* 6 full-time (1 woman), 25 part-time/adjunct (6 women). *Students:* 98 full-time (71 women), 58 part-time (31 women); includes 26 minority (10 African Americans, 1 American Indian/Alaska Native, 12 Asian Americans or Pacific Islanders, 3 Hispanic Americans), 8 international. Average age 27. 155 applicants, 65% accepted, 48 enrolled. In 2008, 96 master's awarded. *Degree requirements:* For master's, comprehensive exam. *Entrance requirements:* For master's, GRE General Test, minimum GPA of 3.0. Additional exam requirements/recommendations for international students: Required—TOEFL (minimum score 550 paper-based; 213 computer-based; 80 iBT). *Application deadline:* For fall admission, 1/16 priority date for international students; for spring admission, 10/1 priority date for domestic students, 9/1 priority date for international students. Applications are processed on a rolling basis. Application fee: $60. Electronic applications accepted. *Financial support:* In 2008–09, 19 students received support; fellowships with partial tuition reimbursements available, Federal Work-Study and tuition waivers available. *Unit head:* Dr. Walter F. Rowe, Chair, 202-994-1469, E-mail: wfrowe@gwu.edu. *Application contact:* Dr. Walter F. Rowe, Chair, 202-994-1469, E-mail: wfrowe@gwu.edu.

The George Washington University, Columbian College of Arts and Sciences, Department of Sociology, Program in Criminology, Washington, DC 20052. Offers MA. *Students:* 3 full-time (all women), 2 part-time (both women); includes 1 minority (Hispanic American). Average age 24. 22 applicants, 50% accepted, 2 enrolled. *Degree requirements:* For master's, comprehensive exam. *Entrance requirements:* For master's, GRE General Test, minimum GPA of 3.0. Additional exam requirements/recommendations for international students: Required—TOEFL (minimum score 550 paper-based; 213 computer-based). *Application deadline:* For fall admission, 4/1 priority date for domestic and international students; for spring admission, 10/1 priority date for domestic and international students. Applications are processed on a rolling basis. Application fee: $60. Electronic applications accepted. *Financial support:* In 2008–09, fellowships with full tuition reimbursements (averaging $10,000 per year), teaching assistantships (averaging $5,000 per year) were awarded. Financial award application deadline: 2/1. *Unit head:* Ronald Weitzer, Director, 202-994-6895. *Application contact:* Information Contact, 202-994-6345, Fax: 202-994-3239, E-mail: soc@gwu.edu.

Georgia College & State University, Graduate School, School of Liberal Arts and Sciences, Department of Government and Sociology, Program in Criminal Justice, Milledgeville, GA 31061. Offers MS. *Degree requirements:* For master's, thesis optional, capstone project. *Entrance requirements:* For master's, GRE, 3 letters of recommendation. Additional exam requirements/recommendations for international students: Required—TOEFL.

Georgia State University, College of Health and Human Sciences, Department of Criminal Justice, Atlanta, GA 30303-3083. Offers MS, PhD. Part-time and evening/weekend programs available. *Degree requirements:* For master's, thesis optional, capstone seminar (optional). *Entrance requirements:* For master's, GRE General Test. Additional exam requirements/recommendations for international students: Required—TOEFL (minimum score 550 paper-based; 213 computer-based). Electronic applications accepted. *Faculty research:* Violence against women, social support and adolescent crime, agencies and assault victims, minority trust of police, active offender crime and minority status.

Graduate School and University Center of the City University of New York, Graduate Studies, Program in Criminal Justice, New York, NY 10016-4039. Offers PhD. *Degree requirements:* For doctorate, one foreign language, thesis/dissertation. *Entrance requirements:* For doctorate, GRE General Test, writing sample. Additional exam requirements/recommendations for international students: Required—TOEFL. Electronic applications accepted.

Grambling State University, School of Graduate Studies and Research, College of Professional Studies, Program in Criminal Justice, Grambling, LA 71245. Offers MS. Part-time programs available. *Faculty:* 6 full-time (3 women), 2 part-time/adjunct (0 women). *Students:* 62 full-time (44 women), 24 part-time (17 women); includes 78 minority (77 African Americans, 1 Hispanic American), 5 international. Average age 34. In 2008, 12 master's awarded. *Degree requirements:* For master's, comprehensive exam, thesis optional. *Entrance requirements:* For master's, GRE, minimum GPA of 2.5 on last degree and in four core courses. Additional exam requirements/recommendations for international students: Required—TOEFL (minimum score 500 paper-based; 173 computer-based; 61 iBT). *Application deadline:* For fall admission, 7/1 for domestic and international students; for spring admission, 12/1 for domestic and international students. Applications are processed on a rolling basis. Application fee: $20 ($30 for international students). Electronic applications accepted. *Expenses:* Tuition, area resident: Full-time $3637; part-time $134 per credit hour. Tuition, nonresident: full-time $7651; part-time $134 per credit hour. Required fees: $1225; $134 per credit hour. $430 per semester. *Financial support:* In 2008–09, 8 research assistantships (averaging $3,557 per year) were awarded; health care benefits, tuition waivers (full and partial), and unspecified assistantships also available. Financial award application deadline: 5/31; financial award applicants required to submit FAFSA. *Faculty research:* Corrections, terrorism, delinquency, complex organizations, post-modern theory. *Unit head:* Dr. Mahendra Singh, Department Head, Criminal Justice, 318-274-2526, Fax: 318-274-3101, E-mail: singhm@gram.edu. *Application contact:* Dr. Joyce Montgomery, Coordinator, 318-274-2876, Fax: 318-274-3101, E-mail: montgomeryj@gram.edu.

Grand Valley State University, College of Community and Public Service, School of Criminal Justice, Allendale, MI 49401-9403. Offers MS. Part-time and evening/weekend programs available. *Faculty:* 6 full-time (4 women). *Students:* 11 full-time (9 women), 8 part-time (5 women); includes 2 minority (both American Indian/Alaska Native), 1 international. Average age 27. 11 applicants, 73% accepted, 6 enrolled. In 2008, 5 master's awarded. *Degree requirements:* For master's, thesis or alternative. *Entrance requirements:* For master's, minimum GPA of 3.0. Additional exam requirements/recommendations for international students: Required—TOEFL. *Application deadline:* For fall admission, 7/30 priority date for domestic students; for winter admission, 12/10 priority date for domestic students; for spring admission, 4/10 priority date for domestic students. Application fee: $30. *Financial support:* In 2008–09, 12 students received support, including 1 research assistantship with full tuition reimbursement available (averaging $8,000 per year); career-related internships or fieldwork, Federal Work-Study, scholarships/grants, and unspecified assistantships also available. Support available to part-time students. Financial award application deadline: 5/1. *Faculty research:* Correctional administration, juvenile justice issues/gangs, women's issues, leadership, program/policy evaluation. *Unit head:* Dr. William Crawley, Director, 616-331-7143, Fax: 616-331-7155, E-mail: crawleyw@gvsu.edu. *Application contact:* Dr. Debra Ross, Information Contact, 616-331-7150, Fax: 616-331-7155, E-mail: rossd@gvsu.edu.

Hodges University, Graduate Programs, Naples, FL 34119. Offers business administration (MBA); computer information technology (MS); criminal justice (MCJ); education (MPS); information systems management (MIS); interdisciplinary (MPS); law (MPS); management (MSM); professional studies (MPS); psychology (MPS); public administration (MPA). Part-time and evening/weekend programs available. Postbaccalaureate distance learning degree programs offered (no on-campus study). *Faculty:* 13 full-time (4 women), 3 part-time/adjunct (2 women). *Students:* 21 full-time (13 women), 210 part-time (138 women); includes 68 minority (33 African Americans, 2 Asian Americans or Pacific Islanders, 33 Hispanic Americans). Average age 36. In 2008, 82 master's awarded. *Degree requirements:* For master's, comprehensive exam (for some programs). *Entrance requirements:* For master's, in-house entrance exam. *Application deadline:* Applications are processed on a rolling basis. Application fee: $50. Electronic applications accepted. *Expenses:* Tuition: Full-time $16,200; part-time $600 per credit hour. Required fees: $570. *Financial support:* In 2008–09, 200 students received support. Federal Work-Study and scholarships/grants available. Financial award application deadline: 7/9; financial award applicants required to submit FAFSA. *Unit head:* Terry McMahan, President, 239-513-1122, Fax: 239-598-6253, E-mail: tmcmahan@hodges.edu. *Application contact:* Rita Lampus, Vice President of Student Enrollment Management, 239-513-1122, Fax: 239-598-6253, E-mail: rlampus@hodges.edu.

Holy Family University, Graduate School, School of Arts and Sciences, Philadelphia, PA 19114-2094. Offers counseling psychology (MS); criminal justice (MA). Part-time and evening/weekend programs available. *Faculty:* 1 full-time (0 women), 4 part-time/adjunct (2 women). *Students:* 34 full-time (26 women), 122 part-time (98 women); includes 26 minority (13 African Americans, 3 Asian Americans or Pacific Islanders, 10 Hispanic Americans), 1 international.

Criminal Justice and Criminology

Holy Family University (continued)
Average age 30. 72 applicants, 61% accepted, 35 enrolled. In 2008, 4 master's awarded. *Degree requirements:* For master's, comprehensive exam, thesis optional. *Entrance requirements:* For master's, MAT, interview, minimum GPA of 3.0. *Application deadline:* For fall admission, 7/1 priority date for domestic students; for winter admission, 11/1 for domestic students. Applications are processed on a rolling basis. Application fee: $25. *Expenses:* Tuition: Part-time $555 per credit. Required fees: $85 per semester. One-time fee: $25 part-time. *Financial support:* Research assistantships with full and partial tuition reimbursements, Federal Work-Study available. Support available to part-time students. Financial award application deadline: 2/15; financial award applicants required to submit FAFSA. *Unit head:* Dr. Regina Hobaugh, Dean of the School of Arts and Sciences, 267-341-3278, Fax: 215-827-0492, E-mail: hobaugh@holyfamily.edu. *Application contact:* Gidget Marie Montelibans, Graduate Admissions Counselor, 267-341-3558, Fax: 215-637-1478, E-mail: gmontelibano@holyfamily.edu.

Husson University, School of Graduate and Professional Studies, Program in Criminal Justice Administration, Bangor, ME 04401-2999. Offers MS.

Illinois State University, Graduate School, College of Applied Science and Technology, Department of Criminal Justice Sciences, Normal, IL 61790-2200. Offers MA, MS. *Degree requirements:* For master's, thesis or alternative. *Entrance requirements:* For master's, GRE General Test, minimum GPA of 2.6 in last 60 hours of course work. *Faculty research:* Graduate practicum for victim assistance and advocacy, graduate practicum in adult probation cases, graduate practicum in youth intervention program.

Indiana State University, School of Graduate Studies, College of Arts and Sciences, Department of Criminology and Criminal Justice, Terre Haute, IN 47809-1401. Offers MA, MS. Part-time programs available. Postbaccalaureate distance learning degree programs offered (no on-campus study). *Degree requirements:* For master's, thesis (for some programs). *Entrance requirements:* For master's, minimum GPA of 2.75 in undergraduate work, 3.0 in previous graduate work. Additional exam requirements/recommendations for international students: Required—TOEFL (minimum score 550 paper-based). Electronic applications accepted. *Faculty research:* Violent crime, rape attitudes, classification of offenders, substance abuse, domestic violence.

Indiana University Bloomington, University Graduate School, College of Arts and Sciences, Department of Criminal Justice, Bloomington, IN 47405. Offers criminal justice (MA, PhD); criminology (MA, PhD); cross-cultural perspectives of crime and justice (MA, PhD); law and society (MA, PhD); psychology and the law (MA). Part-time programs available. *Faculty:* 15 full-time (5 women). *Students:* 41 full-time (23 women), 1 (woman) part-time; includes 5 minority (2 African Americans, 2 American Indian/Alaska Native, 1 Hispanic American), 5 international. Average age 31. 22 applicants, 64% accepted, 6 enrolled. In 2008, 4 master's awarded. Terminal master's awarded for partial completion of doctoral program. *Degree requirements:* For master's, thesis optional; for doctorate, thesis/dissertation, foreign language or research practicum. *Entrance requirements:* For master's and doctorate, GRE General Test. Additional exam requirements/recommendations for international students: Required—TOEFL (minimum score 600 paper-based; 250 computer-based; 100 iBT). *Application deadline:* For fall admission, 1/15 for domestic students, 12/1 for international students. Application fee: $55 ($65 for international students). Electronic applications accepted. *Expenses:* Contact institution. *Financial support:* In 2008–09, 1 fellowship with full tuition reimbursement (averaging $25,000 per year), 2 research assistantships with full tuition reimbursements (averaging $11,721 per year), 24 teaching assistantships with full tuition reimbursements (averaging $11,721 per year) were awarded; Federal Work-Study, health care benefits, tuition waivers (full), and unspecified assistantships also available. Financial award application deadline: 1/15. *Faculty research:* Violence, crime, juveniles, psychology and law, cross-cultural studies. *Unit head:* Roger J.R. Levesque, JD, PhD, Chair, 812-856-1210, E-mail: rlevesqu@indiana.edu. *Application contact:* Ruth Cord, Graduate Secretary, 812-856-4675, Fax: 812-855-5522, E-mail: rkapusti@indiana.edu.

Indiana University Northwest, School of Public and Environmental Affairs, Gary, IN 46408-1197. Offers criminal justice (MPA); environmental affairs (Graduate Certificate); health services administration (MPA); human services administration (MPA); nonprofit management (Graduate Certificate); public management (MPA, Graduate Certificate). *Accreditation:* NASPAA (one or more programs are accredited). Part-time programs available. *Entrance requirements:* For master's, GRE General Test or GMAT, letters of recommendation. *Faculty research:* Employment in income security policies, evidence in criminal justice, equal employment law, social welfare policy and welfare reform, public finance in developing countries.

Indiana University of Pennsylvania, School of Graduate Studies and Research, College of Health and Human Services, Department of Criminology, Doctoral Program in Criminology, Indiana, PA 15705-1087. Offers PhD. Part-time programs available. *Faculty:* 16 full-time (8 women). *Students:* 15 full-time (7 women), 39 part-time (23 women); includes 2 minority (both African Americans), 7 international. Average age 33. 23 applicants, 39% accepted, 6 enrolled. In 2008, 10 doctorates awarded. *Degree requirements:* For doctorate, one foreign language, comprehensive exam, thesis/dissertation. *Entrance requirements:* For doctorate, GRE, 3 letters of recommendation, writing sample, interview. Additional exam requirements/recommendations for international students: Required—TOEFL. *Application deadline:* For fall admission, 7/1 priority date for domestic students; for spring admission, 11/1 for domestic students. Applications are processed on a rolling basis. Application fee: $30. *Expenses:* Tuition, area resident: Full-time $6430; part-time $357 per credit. Tuition, nonresident: full-time $10,288; part-time $572 per credit. Required fees: $1547.50; $107 per credit. $283 per year. *Financial support:* In 2008–09, 3 fellowships (averaging $2,000 per year), 13 research assistantships with full and partial tuition reimbursements (averaging $5,998 per year), 4 teaching assistantships with partial tuition reimbursements (averaging $18,295 per year) were awarded; Federal Work-Study also available. Support available to part-time students. Financial award application deadline: 3/15; financial award applicants required to submit FAFSA. *Unit head:* Dr. Jennifer Roberts, Graduate Coordinator, 724-357-5933, E-mail: Jennifer.Roberts@iup.edu. *Application contact:* Dr. Jacqueline Beck, Associate Dean, 724-357-2560, E-mail: jbeck@iup.edu.

Indiana University of Pennsylvania, School of Graduate Studies and Research, College of Health and Human Services, Department of Criminology, Master's Program in Criminology, Indiana, PA 15705-1087. Offers MA. Part-time and evening/weekend programs available. *Faculty:* 16 full-time (8 women). *Students:* 45 full-time (20 women), 50 part-time (27 women); includes 7 minority (2 African Americans, 1 American Indian/Alaska Native, 1 Asian American or Pacific Islander, 3 Hispanic Americans), 2 international. Average age 29. 69 applicants, 72% accepted, 46 enrolled. In 2008, 42 master's awarded. *Degree requirements:* For master's, thesis optional. *Entrance requirements:* For master's, 2 letters of recommendation. Additional exam requirements/recommendations for international students: Required—TOEFL. *Application deadline:* For fall admission, 7/1 priority date for domestic students; for spring admission, 11/1 for domestic students. Applications are processed on a rolling basis. Application fee: $30. *Expenses:* Tuition, area resident: Full-time $6430; part-time $357 per credit. Tuition, nonresident: full-time $10,288; part-time $572 per credit. Required fees: $1547.50; $107 per credit. $283 per year. *Financial support:* In 2008–09, 11 research assistantships with full and partial tuition reimbursements (averaging $2,650 per year) were awarded; fellowships, Federal Work-Study also available. Support available to part-time students. Financial award application deadline: 3/15; financial award applicants required to submit FAFSA. *Unit head:* Dr. Shannon Phaneuf, Graduate Coordinator, 724-357-5977, E-mail: Shannon.Phaneuf@iup.edu. *Application contact:* Dr. Jacqueline Beck, Associate Dean, 724-357-2560, E-mail: jbeck@iup.edu.

Indiana University–Purdue University Indianapolis, School of Public and Environmental Affairs, Indianapolis, IN 46202-2896. Offers health administration (MHA); public affairs (MPA), including criminal justice, environmental management, nonprofit management, policy analysis, public management; JD/MHA; MBA/MHA; MLS/NMC; MLS/PMC; MSN/MHA. *Accreditation:* CAHME (one or more programs are accredited). Part-time and evening/weekend programs available. *Entrance requirements:* For master's, GRE General Test, minimum GPA of 3.0 (preferred). Additional exam requirements/recommendations for international students: Required—TOEFL. *Faculty research:* Economic development, water and air quality, ethics, financing, organization design and structure.

See Close-Up on page 1221.

Inter American University of Puerto Rico, Aguadilla Campus, Graduate School, Aguadilla, PR 00605. Offers counseling psychology with an emphasis in family (MS); criminal justice (MA); educative management and leadership (MA); elementary education (MA); industrial mangement (MBA); marketing (MBA). Part-time and evening/weekend programs available. *Degree requirements:* For master's, comprehensive exam. *Entrance requirements:* For master's, EXADEP, 2 letters of recommendation, minimum GPA of 2.5. Electronic applications accepted.

Inter American University of Puerto Rico, Metropolitan Campus, Graduate Programs, Program in Criminal Justice, San Juan, PR 00919-1293. Offers MA. Part-time and evening/weekend programs available. *Degree requirements:* For master's, comprehensive exam. *Entrance requirements:* For master's, GRE or EXADEP, interview. Electronic applications accepted.

Inter American University of Puerto Rico, Ponce Campus, Graduate School, Mercedita, PR 00715-1602. Offers accounting (MBA); biology (M Ed); chemistry (M Ed); criminal justice (MA); elementary education (M Ed); English as a Second Language (M Ed); finance (MBA); history (M Ed); human resources (MBA); marketing (MBA); mathematics (M Ed); Spanish (M Ed). *Entrance requirements:* For master's, minimum GPA of 2.5.

Iona College, School of Arts and Science, Program in Criminal Justice, New Rochelle, NY 10801-1890. Offers MS. Part-time and evening/weekend programs available. *Faculty:* 5 full-time (1 woman), 4 part-time/adjunct (0 women). *Students:* 1 (woman) full-time, 31 part-time (17 women); includes 9 minority (6 African Americans, 3 Hispanic Americans). Average age 31. 12 applicants, 92% accepted, 5 enrolled. In 2008, 12 master's awarded. *Degree requirements:* For master's, thesis. *Entrance requirements:* For master's, minimum GPA of 2.75. Additional exam requirements/recommendations for international students: Required—TOEFL (minimum score 550 paper-based; 213 computer-based). *Application deadline:* Applications are processed on a rolling basis. Application fee: $50. Electronic applications accepted. *Expenses:* Tuition: Part-time $755 per credit. Required fees: $175 per term. *Financial support:* Unspecified assistantships available. Financial award application deadline: 4/15; financial award applicants required to submit FAFSA. *Faculty research:* Police administration, victimology and criminal justice program evaluation. *Unit head:* Dr. Paul O'Connell, Chair, 914-633-2111, E-mail: poconnell@iona.edu. *Application contact:* Veronica Jarek-Prinz, Director of Graduate Admissions, 914-633-2420, Fax: 914-633-2277, E-mail: vjarekprinz@iona.edu.

Jackson State University, Graduate School, School of Liberal Arts, Center for Urban Affairs/Criminology and Justice Services, Jackson, MS 39217. Offers criminology and justice service (MA). Part-time and evening/weekend programs available. *Degree requirements:* For master's, comprehensive exam, thesis optional. *Entrance requirements:* For master's, GRE General Test. Additional exam requirements/recommendations for international students: Required—TOEFL.

Jacksonville State University, College of Graduate Studies and Continuing Education, College of Arts and Sciences, Department of Criminal Justice, Jacksonville, AL 36265-1602. Offers MS. Part-time and evening/weekend programs available. *Faculty:* 4 full-time (1 woman). *Students:* 9 full-time (4 women), 18 part-time (12 women); includes 12 minority (all African Americans), 1 international. Average age 29. 9 applicants, 67% accepted, 6 enrolled. In 2008, 10 master's awarded. *Degree requirements:* For master's, comprehensive exam, thesis (for some programs). *Entrance requirements:* For master's, GRE General Test or MAT. *Application deadline:* Applications are processed on a rolling basis. Application fee: $30. Electronic applications accepted. *Expenses:* Tuition, area resident: Full-time $4560; part-time $225 per credit hour. Tuition, state resident: full-time $4560; part-time $450 per credit hour. Tuition, nonresident: full-time $9120; part-time $450 per credit hour. *Financial support:* In 2008–09, 27 students received support. Available to part-time students. Application deadline: 4/1; *Unit head:* Richard Kania, Head, 256-782-5339, E-mail: rkania@jsu.edu. *Application contact:* Dr. Jean Pugliese, Associate Dean, 256-782-5329, Fax: 256-782-5321, E-mail: pugliese@jsu.edu.

John Jay College of Criminal Justice of the City University of New York, Graduate Studies, Program in Protection Management, New York, NY 10019-1093. Offers MS. Part-time and evening/weekend programs available. *Degree requirements:* For master's, thesis or alternative. *Entrance requirements:* For master's, minimum B average. Additional exam requirements/recommendations for international students: Required—TOEFL (minimum score 500 paper-based; 173 computer-based).

John Jay College of Criminal Justice of the City University of New York, Graduate Studies, Programs in Criminal Justice, New York, NY 10019-1093. Offers criminal justice (MA, PhD); criminology and deviance (PhD); forensic psychology (PhD); forensic science (PhD); law and philosophy (PhD); organizational behavior (PhD); public policy (PhD). Part-time and evening/weekend programs available. Terminal master's awarded for partial completion of doctoral program. *Degree requirements:* For master's, thesis or alternative; for doctorate, one foreign language, thesis/dissertation. *Entrance requirements:* For master's, GRE General Test, minimum B average; for doctorate, GRE General Test. Additional exam requirements/recommendations for international students: Required—TOEFL (minimum score 500 paper-based; 173 computer-based).

The Johns Hopkins University, School of Education, Division of Public Safety Leadership, Baltimore, MD 21218-2699. Offers homeland security (MS); intelligence analysis (MS); management (MS). Part-time and evening/weekend programs available. *Entrance requirements:* For master's, minimum GPA of 3.0, interview, resumé, letters of recommendation. Additional exam requirements/recommendations for international students: Required—TOEFL (minimum score 600 paper-based; 250 computer-based; 100 iBT). *Faculty research:* Ethics and integrity, counter terrorism, school safety, Homeland Security, identity theft.

Kaplan University–Davenport Campus, School of Criminal Justice, Davenport, IA 52807-2095. Offers corrections (MSCJ); global issues in criminal justice (MSCJ); law (MSCJ); leadership and executive management (MSCJ); policing (MSCJ). Part-time and evening/weekend programs available. Postbaccalaureate distance learning degree programs offered (no on-campus study). *Entrance requirements:* Additional exam requirements/recommendations for international students: Required—TOEFL (minimum score 550 paper-based; 218 computer-based; 80 iBT). Electronic applications accepted.

Kean University, College of Business and Public Administration, Program in Criminal Justice, Union, NJ 07083. Offers MA. Part-time and evening/weekend programs available. *Faculty:* 6 full-time (2 women). *Degree requirements:* For master's, thesis. *Entrance requirements:* For master's, GRE (minimum Analytic Writing score of 3.5), 3 reference letters, minimum GPA of 3.0, writing sample. *Application deadline:* For fall admission, 5/1 for domestic students; for spring admission, 11/1 for domestic students. Application fee: $60 ($150 for international students). Electronic applications accepted. *Expenses:* Tuition, state resident: full-time $10,128; part-time $422 per credit. Tuition, nonresident: full-time $13,728; part-time $572 per credit. Required fees: $2570; $107 per credit. Part-time tuition and fees vary according to course load, degree level and program. *Financial support:* In 2008–09, research assistantships with full tuition reimbursements (averaging $3,217 per year); unspecified assistantships also available. *Unit head:* Dr. Vanessa Garcia, Program Coordinator, 908-737-4302, E-mail: vgarcia@kean.edu. *Application contact:* Steven Koch, Pre-Admissions Coordinator, 908-737-4723, Fax: 908-737-5965, E-mail: grad-adm@kean.edu.

Keiser University, Program in Criminal Justice, Fort Lauderdale, FL 33309. Offers MA. Part-time programs available. Postbaccalaureate distance learning degree programs offered (no on-campus study). *Faculty:* 1 (woman) full-time, 5 part-time/adjunct (all women). *Students:* 8 full-time (5 women), 14 part-time (9 women); includes 8 minority (5 African Americans, 1 American Indian/Alaska Native, 2 Hispanic Americans). Average age 36. 19 applicants, 89% accepted, 13 enrolled. *Entrance requirements:* For master's, minimum GPA of 2.7 from an accredited college or university. Additional exam requirements/recommendations for international students: Required—TOEFL. *Application deadline:* Applications are processed on a rolling basis. Application fee: $50. Electronic applications accepted. *Expenses:* Tuition: Full-time $21,108; part-time $586 per credit hour. Required fees: $1800; $587 per credit hour. One-time fee: $195. *Financial support:* In 2008–09, 18 students received support. Federal Work-Study available. Financial award applicants required to submit FAFSA. *Unit head:* Dr. Sara Malmstrom, PhD, Dean of the Graduate School, 954-318-1620. *Application contact:* Manuel Christiansen, Associate Director of Admissions, 954-318-1620 Ext. 309, E-mail: mchristiansen@keiseruniversity.edu.

Kent State University, College of Arts and Sciences, Department of Justice Studies, Kent, OH 44242-0001. Offers MA. Part-time and evening/weekend programs available. *Degree requirements:* For master's, comprehensive exam, thesis optional. *Entrance requirements:* For master's, minimum GPA of 2.75. Additional exam requirements/recommendations for international students: Required—TOEFL. Electronic applications accepted. *Faculty research:* School violence, community policing.

Keuka College, Program in Criminal Justice Administration, Keuka Park, NY 14478-0098. Offers MS. Part-time and evening/weekend programs available. *Faculty:* 6 part-time/adjunct (2 women). *Students:* 9 full-time (6 women), 18 part-time (9 women); includes 8 minority (5 African Americans, 2 Asian Americans or Pacific Islanders, 1 Hispanic American). 89 applicants, 100% accepted, 80 enrolled. In 2008, 9 master's awarded. *Application deadline:* For fall admission, 8/15 for domestic students; for winter admission, 12/15 for domestic students; for spring admission, 4/15 for domestic students. Application fee: $30. *Expenses:* Contact institution. *Unit head:* Dr. Tom Tremer, Program Director, 315-279-5672, E-mail: ttremer@mail.keuka.edu. *Application contact:* Claudine Ninestine, Director of Admissions, 315-279-5413, Fax: 315-279-5386, E-mail: admissions@mail.keuka.edu.

Lamar University, College of Graduate Studies, College of Arts and Sciences, Department of Sociology, Social Work, and Criminal Justice, Beaumont, TX 77710. Offers applied criminology (MS). Part-time programs available. *Faculty:* 3 full-time (0 women). *Students:* 5 full-time (3 women), 3 part-time (1 woman); includes 3 minority (2 African Americans, 1 Hispanic American). Average age 29. 17 applicants, 18% accepted, 1 enrolled. In 2008, 4 master's awarded. *Degree requirements:* For master's, thesis or alternative, applied projects. *Entrance requirements:* For master's, GRE General Test. Additional exam requirements/recommendations for international students: Required—TOEFL. *Application deadline:* For fall admission, 8/1 priority date for domestic students; for spring admission, 12/1 priority date for domestic students. Applications are processed on a rolling basis. Application fee: $25 ($50 for international students). *Expenses:* Tuition, state resident: full-time $5000; part-time $195 per credit. Tuition, nonresident: full-time $12,376; part-time $476 per credit. Required fees: $1570. *Financial support:* In 2008–09, 3 fellowships with partial tuition reimbursements (averaging $1,000 per year) were awarded; career-related internships or fieldwork, Federal Work-Study, and scholarships/grants also available. Support available to part-time students. Financial award application deadline: 4/1; financial award applicants required to submit FAFSA. *Faculty research:* Corrections, planning and evaluations, juveniles, terrorism, Mexican criminal justice. *Unit head:* Dr. Li-Chen J. Ma, Chair, 409-880-8545, Fax: 409-880-2324, E-mail: lma@lamar.edu. *Application contact:* Dr. J. Rick Altemose, Graduate Program Director, 409-880-8549, Fax: 409-880-2324, E-mail: altemosejr@hal.lamar.edu.

Lewis University, College of Arts and Sciences, Program in Criminal/Social Justice, Romeoville, IL 60446. Offers criminal/social justice (MS). Part-time and evening/weekend programs available. *Students:* 13 full-time (7 women), 105 part-time (46 women); includes 44 minority (24 African Americans, 2 Asian Americans or Pacific Islanders, 18 Hispanic Americans). Average age 32. In 2008, 41 master's awarded. *Entrance requirements:* For master's, bachelor's degree or a minimum of 12 related hours in criminal/social justice, 2 letters of recommendation, minimum GPA of 3.0, interview. Additional exam requirements/recommendations for international students: Required—TOEFL (minimum score 550 paper-based; 213 computer-based). *Application deadline:* For fall admission, 5/1 priority date for international students; for spring admission, 11/15 priority date for international students. Applications are processed on a rolling basis. Application fee: $40. Electronic applications accepted. *Financial support:* Federal Work-Study, scholarships/grants, tuition waivers (full and partial), and unspecified assistantships available. Financial award application deadline: 5/1; financial award applicants required to submit FAFSA. *Faculty research:* Community policing, management, terrorism, biological warfare, drugs. *Unit head:* Dr. Calvin Edwards, Chair of Justice, Law and Public Safety Studies, 815-838-0500, Fax: 815-836-5870, E-mail: koloshsa@lewisu.edu. *Application contact:* Sarah Wiegman, Coordinator, 815-838-0500 Ext. 5686, Fax: 815-836-5870, E-mail: wiegmasa@lewisu.edu.

Lincoln University, School of Graduate Studies and Continuing Education, College of Liberal Arts, Education and Journalism, Department of Social and Behavioral Sciences, Jefferson City, MO 65102. Offers history (MA); social science (MA), including history, political science, sociology; sociology (MA); sociology/criminal justice (MA). Part-time and evening/weekend programs available. *Faculty:* 11 full-time (4 women), 4 part-time/adjunct (2 women). *Students:* 6 full-time (3 women), 21 part-time (11 women); includes 8 minority (all African Americans), 5 international. Average age 33. 13 applicants, 100% accepted, 9 enrolled. In 2008, 14 master's awarded. *Degree requirements:* For master's, comprehensive exam, thesis optional. *Entrance requirements:* For master's, GRE General Test or MAT, 15 undergraduate hours of course work in social science including 6 hours upper-division, with 9 hours in the area of concentration. Additional exam requirements/recommendations for international students: Required—TOEFL (minimum score 500 paper-based; 173 computer-based; 61 iBT). *Application deadline:* For fall admission, 7/1 priority date for domestic and international students; for spring admission, 12/1 priority date for domestic and international students. Applications are processed on a rolling basis. Application fee: $20. *Expenses:* Tuition, area resident: Full-time $4185; part-time $232.50 per credit hour. Tuition, nonresident: full-time $7767; part-time $431.50 per credit hour. Required fees: $270; $15 per credit hour. $252.50 per semester. One-time fee: $20. Tuition and fees vary according to course load. *Financial support:* Federal Work-Study and scholarships/grants available. Financial award application deadline: 4/1; financial award applicants required to submit FAFSA. *Faculty research:* Suicide prevention. *Unit head:* Dr. Debra F. Greene, Department Head, 573-681-5145, Fax: 573-681-5150, E-mail: greened@lincolnu.edu. *Application contact:* Irasema Steck, Administrative Assistant, 573-681-5247, Fax: 573-681-5106, E-mail: gradschool@lincolnu.edu.

Lindenwood University, Graduate Programs, College of Individualized Education, St. Charles, MO 63301-1695. Offers administration (MSA); business administration (MBA); communication (MS); communications (MA); criminal justice and administration (MS); gerontology (MA); health management (MS); human resource management (MS); information technology (MBA, Certificate); management (MSA); managing information technology (MS); marketing (MSA); writing (MFA). Part-time and evening/weekend programs available. *Faculty:* 14 full-time (7 women), 119 part-time/adjunct (50 women). *Students:* 750 full-time (489 women), 138 part-time (91 women); includes 196 minority (182 African Americans, 1 American Indian/Alaska Native, 5 Asian Americans or Pacific Islanders, 8 Hispanic Americans), 14 international. Average age 34. In 2008, 349 master's awarded. *Degree requirements:* For master's, thesis (for some programs), minimum GPA of 3.0, 1 colloquium per term. *Entrance requirements:* For master's, interview, minimum GPA of 3.0. Additional exam requirements/recommendations for international students: Required—TOEFL (minimum score 550 paper-based; 213 computer-based; 80 iBT). *Application deadline:* For fall admission, 9/30 priority date for domestic and international students; for winter admission, 12/30 priority date for domestic and international students; for spring admission, 3/30 priority date for domestic and international students. Applications are processed on a rolling basis. Application fee: $30 ($100 for international students). *Expenses:* Tuition: Full-time $12,700; part-time $360 per credit hour. *Financial support:* Career-related internships or fieldwork, institutionally sponsored loans, tuition waivers (partial), and unspecified assistantships available. Financial award application deadline: 6/30; financial award applicants required to submit FAFSA. *Unit head:* Dan Kemper, Dean of Lindenwood College for Individual Education, 636-949-4501, Fax: 636-949-4505, E-mail: dkemper@lindenwood.edu. *Application contact:* Brett Barger, Dean of Evening Admissions and Extension Campuses, 636-949-4934, Fax: 636-949-4109, E-mail: adultadmissions@lindenwood.edu.

Long Island University, Brentwood Campus, School of Public Service, Brentwood, NY 11717. Offers criminal justice (MS). Part-time and evening/weekend programs available.

Long Island University, C.W. Post Campus, College of Management, Department of Criminal Justice, Brookville, NY 11548-1300. Offers criminal justice (MS); fraud examination (MS); security administration (MS). Part-time and evening/weekend programs available. *Degree requirements:* For master's, thesis. *Entrance requirements:* For master's, minimum GPA of 3.0, background in criminal justice. Electronic applications accepted. *Faculty research:* Crime statistics, terrorism, women and law, policing.

Longwood University, Office of Graduate Studies, Department of Sociology, Anthropology, and Criminal Justice Studies, Farmville, VA 23909. Offers criminal justice (MS). Part-time and evening/weekend programs available. *Degree requirements:* For master's, comprehensive exam (for some programs), thesis (for some programs). *Entrance requirements:* For master's, minimum GPA of 2.75. Additional exam requirements/recommendations for international students: Required—TOEFL (minimum score 550 paper-based; 213 computer-based).

Loyola University Chicago, Graduate School, Department of Criminal Justice, Chicago, IL 60611-2196. Offers MA. Part-time and evening/weekend programs available. *Faculty:* 8 full-time (1 woman), 12 part-time/adjunct (1 woman). *Students:* 16 full-time (10 women), 22 part-time (11 women); includes 9 minority (5 African Americans, 4 Hispanic Americans). Average age 29. 23 applicants, 87% accepted, 14 enrolled. In 2008, 16 master's awarded. *Degree requirements:* For master's, comprehensive exam, thesis or alternative, field practicum. *Entrance requirements:* For master's, GRE, minimum GPA of 3.0. Additional exam requirements/recommendations for international students: Required—TOEFL (minimum score 550 paper-based; 213 computer-based). *Application deadline:* For fall admission, 6/15 priority date for domestic students; for spring admission, 12/1 for domestic students. Applications are processed on a rolling basis. Application fee: $50. Electronic applications accepted. *Expenses:* Tuition: Full-time $13,500; part-time $750 per credit hour. Required fees: $60 per semester. Full-time tuition and fees vary according to program. *Financial support:* In 2008–09, 3 students received support, including research assistantships with partial tuition reimbursements available (averaging $7,800 per year); career-related internships or fieldwork, scholarships/grants, and tuition waivers (full and partial) also available. Financial award application deadline: 2/1; financial award applicants required to submit FAFSA. *Faculty research:* Crime and delinquency causation, effectiveness and efficiency of criminal justice system. Total annual research expenditures: $120,000. *Unit head:* Dr. David Olson, Chair, 312-915-7563, Fax: 312-915-7650, E-mail: dolson1@luc.edu. *Application contact:* Dr. Gad Bensinger, Graduate Program Director, 312-915-7568, Fax: 312-915-8593, E-mail: gbesin@luc.edu.

Loyola University New Orleans, College of Social Sciences, Program in Criminal Justice, New Orleans, LA 70118-6195. Offers MCJ. Part-time and evening/weekend programs available. *Students:* 7 full-time (5 women), 21 part-time (14 women); includes 10 minority (8 African Americans, 2 Hispanic Americans). Average age 29. 19 applicants, 100% accepted, 17 enrolled. In 2008, 5 master's awarded. *Degree requirements:* For master's, comprehensive exam, research and practicum. *Entrance requirements:* For master's, GRE, resumé, interview, letters of recommendation, transcript, essay, work experience. Additional exam requirements/recommendations for international students: Required—TOEFL (minimum score 550 paper-based; 213 computer-based). *Application deadline:* For fall admission, 8/1 priority date for domestic and international students; for spring admission, 1/5 priority date for domestic and international students. Applications are processed on a rolling basis. Application fee: $20. Electronic applications accepted. *Expenses:* Contact institution. *Financial support:* In 2008–09, 4 research assistantships (averaging $4,000 per year) were awarded; scholarships/grants and unspecified assistantships also available. Financial award application deadline: 5/1; financial award applicants required to submit FAFSA. *Unit head:* William E. Thornton, PhD, Chair, Department of Criminal Justice, 504-865-2134, Fax: 504-865-3883, E-mail: thornton@loyno.edu. *Application contact:* David M. Aplin, Assistant to the Director, 504-865-3323, Fax: 504-865-3883, E-mail: daplin@loyno.edu.

Lynn University, College of Arts and Sciences, Boca Raton, FL 33431-5598. Offers applied psychology (MS); criminal justice administration (MS); emergency planning and administration (MS, Certificate). Part-time and evening/weekend programs available. Postbaccalaureate distance learning degree programs offered. *Entrance requirements:* For master's, GRE, resumé, 2 letters of recommendation, minimum undergraduate GPA of 3.0. Additional exam requirements/recommendations for international students: Required—TOEFL (minimum score 550 paper-based; 213 computer-based). *Faculty research:* Terrorism, criminological theory, corrections, emergency planning.

Madonna University, School of Business, Livonia, MI 48150-1173. Offers business administration (MBA); international business (MSBA); leadership studies (MSBA); leadership studies in criminal justice (MSBA); quality and operations management (MSBA). Part-time and evening/weekend programs available. Postbaccalaureate distance learning degree programs offered (minimal on-campus study). *Degree requirements:* For master's, thesis (for some programs), foreign language proficiency (international business). *Entrance requirements:* For master's, GMAT, GRE General Test, minimum GPA of 3.0. Electronic applications accepted. *Faculty research:* Management, women in management, future studies.

Marshall University, Academic Affairs Division, College of Liberal Arts, Department of Criminal Justice, Huntington, WV 25755. Offers MS. Evening/weekend programs available. *Degree requirements:* For master's, thesis optional. *Entrance requirements:* For master's, GRE General Test.

Marywood University, Academic Affairs, College of Health and Human Services, Department of Nursing and Public Administration, Program in Public Administration, Scranton, PA 18509-1598. Offers criminal justice (MPA); public administration (MPA); MPA/MSW. *Degree requirements:* For master's, thesis or alternative, internship/practicum. *Entrance requirements:* Additional exam requirements/recommendations for international students: Required—TOEFL (minimum score 550 paper-based; 213 computer-based). Electronic applications accepted.

Marywood University, Academic Affairs, College of Liberal Arts and Sciences, Department of Social Sciences, Program in Criminal Justice, Scranton, PA 18509-1598. Offers MS.

Mercyhurst College, Graduate Program, Program in Administration of Justice, Erie, PA 16546. Offers administration of justice (MS). Part-time and evening/weekend programs available. *Degree requirements:* For master's, thesis optional. *Entrance requirements:* For master's, GRE General Test, MAT, or minimum GPA of 3.0. Additional exam requirements/recommendations for international students: Required—TOEFL. Electronic applications accepted. *Faculty research:* Research methods, criminal justice administration, juvenile justice.

Mercyhurst College, Graduate Program, Program in Applied Intelligence, Erie, PA 16546. Offers MS, Certificate. *Entrance requirements:* For master's, GRE or MAT, interview. Additional exam requirements/recommendations for international students: Required—TOEFL. Electronic applications accepted.

Methodist University, School of Graduate Studies, Program in Justice Administration, Fayetteville, NC 28311-1498. Offers MJA.

Criminal Justice and Criminology

Michigan State University, The Graduate School, College of Social Science, School of Criminal Justice, East Lansing, MI 48824. Offers criminal justice (MS, PhD); forensic science (MS); law enforcement intelligence and analysis (MS). Postbaccalaureate distance learning degree programs offered. *Entrance requirements:* Additional exam requirements/recommendations for international students: Required—TOEFL. Electronic applications accepted.

See Close-Up on page 739.

Middle Tennessee State University, College of Graduate Studies, College of Education and Behavioral Science, Department of Criminal Justice Administration, Murfreesboro, TN 37132. Offers MCJ. Part-time and evening/weekend programs available. Postbaccalaureate distance learning degree programs offered. *Degree requirements:* For master's, one foreign language, comprehensive exam, thesis. *Entrance requirements:* For master's, GRE or MAT. Additional exam requirements/recommendations for international students: Required—TOEFL (paper-based 525; computer-based 195; IBT 71) or IELTS (6.0). Electronic applications accepted.

Midwestern State University, Graduate Studies, College of Health Sciences and Human Services, Program in Health Services and Public Administration, Wichita Falls, TX 76308. Offers health services administration (MHA); public administration (MPA); public administration (administrative justice) (MPA); public administration (health services administration) with certificate (MPA); public administration (health services) (MPA). Part-time and evening/weekend programs available. *Degree requirements:* For master's, comprehensive exam, thesis. *Entrance requirements:* For master's, GRE. Additional exam requirements/recommendations for international students: Required—TOEFL (minimum score 550 paper-based; 213 computer-based). Electronic applications accepted.

Minot State University, Graduate School, Program in Criminal Justice, Minot, ND 58707-0002. Offers MS. *Faculty:* 7 part-time/adjunct (1 woman). *Students:* 10 part-time (7 women); includes 2 minority (1 African American, 1 American Indian/Alaska Native). Average age 32. In 2008, 2 master's awarded. *Degree requirements:* For master's, comprehensive exam, thesis. *Entrance requirements:* For master's, GRE General Test, bachelor's degree minor in criminal justice or related field, minimum GPA of 3.0. Additional exam requirements/recommendations for international students: Required—TOEFL. *Application deadline:* Applications are processed on a rolling basis. Application fee: $35. *Expenses:* Tuition, area resident: Full-time $5527; part-time $230.30 per credit hour. Tuition, state resident: full-time $8291; part-time $345.45 per credit hour. Tuition, nonresident: full-time $14,758; part-time $614.90 per credit hour. Required fees: $865; $36.03 per credit hour. Tuition and fees vary according to course load and reciprocity agreements. *Financial support:* In 2008–09, 2 research assistantships with partial tuition reimbursements (averaging $2,500 per year) were awarded; career-related internships or fieldwork, institutionally sponsored loans, scholarships/grants, traineeships, tuition waivers (partial), and unspecified assistantships also available. Support available to part-time students. Financial award application deadline: 4/1. *Faculty research:* Sentencing, white-collar/organizational crime, juveniles, gender issues, policy analysis. *Unit head:* Dr. Harry Hoffman, Graduate Program Coordinator, 701-858-3284. *Application contact:* Dr. Harry Hoffman, Graduate Program Coordinator, 701-858-3284.

Mississippi College, Graduate School, College of Arts and Sciences, School of Humanities and Social Sciences, Department of History and Political Science, Clinton, MS 39058. Offers administration of justice (MSS); history (M Ed, MA, MSS); paralegal studies (Certificate); political science (MSS); social sciences (M Ed, MSS). Part-time programs available. *Degree requirements:* For master's, one foreign language, comprehensive exam, thesis (for some programs). *Entrance requirements:* For master's, GRE or NTE, minimum GPA of 2.5. Additional exam requirements/recommendations for international students: Recommended—IELTS. Electronic applications accepted.

Mississippi Valley State University, Department of Criminal Justice and Social Work, Itta Bena, MS 38941-1400. Offers criminal justice (MS). Part-time and evening/weekend programs available. *Degree requirements:* For master's, thesis optional. *Entrance requirements:* For master's, minimum GPA of 2.5. Electronic applications accepted. *Faculty research:* Police in the criminal justice system, the United States and international terrorism.

Missouri Southern State University, Program in Criminal Justice Administration, Joplin, MO 64801-1595. Offers MS. Postbaccalaureate distance learning degree programs offered. *Degree requirements:* For master's, thesis optional. *Entrance requirements:* For master's, minimum undergraduate GPA of 2.5.

Missouri State University, Graduate College, College of Humanities and Public Affairs, Department of Sociology, Anthropology, and Criminology, Springfield, MO 65804-0094. Offers criminology (MS). Part-time programs available. *Faculty:* 14 full-time (4 women). *Students:* 27 full-time (18 women), 11 part-time (7 women); includes 3 minority (1 African American, 1 Asian American or Pacific Islander, 1 Hispanic American). Average age 26. 19 applicants, 95% accepted, 16 enrolled. In 2008, 2 master's awarded. *Degree requirements:* For master's, comprehensive exam. *Entrance requirements:* For master's, GRE, minimum GPA of 3.0. Additional exam requirements/recommendations for international students: Required—TOEFL (minimum score 550 paper-based; 213 computer-based; 79 iBT). *Application deadline:* For fall admission, 7/20 priority date for domestic students, 5/1 for international students; for spring admission, 12/20 priority date for domestic students, 9/1 for international students. Applications are processed on a rolling basis. Application fee: $35 ($50 for international students). Electronic applications accepted. *Expenses:* Tuition, state resident: full-time $3852; part-time $214 per credit hour. Tuition, nonresident: full-time $7524; part-time $418 per credit hour. Required fees: $230 per semester. Tuition and fees vary according to course level and course load. *Financial support:* In 2008–09, 1 research assistantship with full tuition reimbursement (averaging $7,340 per year) was awarded; Federal Work-Study, institutionally sponsored loans, scholarships/grants, and unspecified assistantships also available. Financial award application deadline: 3/31; financial award applicants required to submit FAFSA. *Faculty research:* Youth delinquency, social theory, linguistic anthropology, forensic anthropology, Homeland Security. *Unit head:* Dr. Karl Kunkel, Head, 417-836-5640, Fax: 417-836-6416, E-mail: karlkunkel@missouristate.edu. *Application contact:* Eric Eckert, Coordinator of Admissions and Recruitment, 417-836-5331, Fax: 417-836-6888, E-mail: ericeckert@missouristate.edu.

Missouri State University, Graduate College, Interdisciplinary Program in Administrative Studies, Springfield, MO 65804-0094. Offers applied communication (MS); criminal justice (MS); environmental management (MS); project management (MS); sports management (MS). Part-time and evening/weekend programs available. Postbaccalaureate distance learning degree programs offered (no on-campus study). *Students:* 16 full-time (9 women), 56 part-time (25 women); includes 7 minority (4 African Americans, 2 Asian Americans or Pacific Islanders, 1 Hispanic American). Average age 34. 16 applicants, 100% accepted, 12 enrolled. In 2008, 33 master's awarded. *Degree requirements:* For master's, comprehensive exam, thesis or alternative. *Entrance requirements:* For master's, GRE, GMAT, 3 years of work experience. Additional exam requirements/recommendations for international students: Required—TOEFL (minimum score 550 paper-based; 213 computer-based; 79 iBT). *Application deadline:* For fall admission, 7/20 priority date for domestic students; for spring admission, 12/20 priority date for domestic students. Applications are processed on a rolling basis. Application fee: $35 ($50 for international students). Electronic applications accepted. *Expenses:* Tuition, state resident: full-time $3852; part-time $214 per credit hour. Tuition, nonresident: full-time $7524; part-time $418 per credit hour. Required fees: $230 per semester. Tuition and fees vary according to course level and course load. *Financial support:* In 2008–09, 4 teaching assistantships with full tuition reimbursements (averaging $8,535 per year) were awarded; career-related internships or fieldwork, Federal Work-Study, institutionally sponsored loans, scholarships/grants, and unspecified assistantships also available. Support available to part-time students. Financial award application deadline: 3/31; financial award applicants required to submit FAFSA. *Unit head:* John Bourhis, Director, 417-836-6390, E-mail: johnbourhis@missouristate.edu. *Application contact:* Eric Eckert, Coordinator of Graduate Admissions and Recruitment, 417-836-5331, Fax: 417-836-6888, E-mail: ericeckert@missouristate.edu.

Monmouth University, Graduate School, Department of Criminal Justice, West Long Branch, NJ 07764-1898. Offers criminal justice administration (MA, Certificate). Part-time and evening/weekend programs available. *Faculty:* 4 full-time (0 women), 3 part-time/adjunct (2 women). *Students:* 8 full-time (4 women), 23 part-time (14 women); includes 6 minority (3 African Americans, 1 Asian American or Pacific Islander, 2 Hispanic Americans), 1 international. Average age 30. 21 applicants, 95% accepted, 10 enrolled. In 2008, 20 master's awarded. *Degree requirements:* For master's, comprehensive exam, thesis or alternative. *Entrance requirements:* For master's, minimum GPA of 3.0 in major, 2.5 overall. Additional exam requirements/recommendations for international students: Required—TOEFL (minimum score 550 paper-based; 213 computer-based; 79 iBT), IELTS (minimum score 5), Michigan English Language Assessment Battery (minimum score: 77), Cambridge A, B, C. *Application deadline:* For fall admission, 7/15 priority date for domestic students, 6/1 for international students; for spring admission, 11/15 priority date for domestic students, 11/1 for international students. Applications are processed on a rolling basis. Application fee: $50. Electronic applications accepted. *Expenses:* Tuition: Full-time $13,914; part-time $773 per credit. Required fees: $628; $157 per semester. *Financial support:* In 2008–09, 15 students received support, including 13 fellowships (averaging $1,495 per year), 3 research assistantships (averaging $7,704 per year); career-related internships or fieldwork, scholarships/grants, tuition waivers (full and partial), and unspecified assistantships also available. Support available to part-time students. Financial award application deadline: 3/1; financial award applicants required to submit FAFSA. *Faculty research:* Violent crimes, criminal pathology, terrorism, computer crime, comparative CJ systems. *Unit head:* Dr. Gregory Coram, Director, 732-571-3448, Fax: 732-263-5148, E-mail: coram@monmouth.edu. *Application contact:* Kevin Roane, Director, Office of Graduate Admission, 732-571-3452, Fax: 732-263-5123, E-mail: gradadm@monmouth.edu.

Morehead State University, Graduate Programs, Caudill College of Humanities, Department of Sociology, Social Work and Criminology, Morehead, KY 40351. Offers criminology (MA); general sociology (MA); gerontology (MA). Part-time and evening/weekend programs available. *Faculty:* 7 full-time (4 women), 4 part-time/adjunct (1 woman). *Students:* 9 full-time (7 women), 18 part-time (12 women); includes 1 minority (African American). Average age 30. 20 applicants, 55% accepted, 7 enrolled. In 2008, 4 master's awarded. *Degree requirements:* For master's, comprehensive exam, thesis optional. *Entrance requirements:* For master's, GRE General Test, minimum GPA of 3.0 in sociology, 2.5 overall; 18 hours of course work in sociology, writing sample. Additional exam requirements/recommendations for international students: Required—TOEFL (minimum score 500 paper-based; 173 computer-based). *Application deadline:* For fall admission, 8/1 priority date for domestic and international students; for spring admission, 12/1 priority date for domestic and international students. Applications are processed on a rolling basis. Application fee: $30 ($55 for international students). Electronic applications accepted. *Expenses:* Tuition, area resident: Full-time $6084; part-time $338 per credit hour. Tuition, state resident: full-time $6084; part-time $338 per credit hour. Tuition, nonresident: full-time $15,804; part-time $878 per credit hour. *Financial support:* In 2008–09, 5 teaching assistantships (averaging $6,000 per year) were awarded; career-related internships or fieldwork, Federal Work-Study, and unspecified assistantships also available. Financial award application deadline: 4/1; financial award applicants required to submit FAFSA. *Faculty research:* Death and dying; aging, drinking, and drugs; economic development; adult children of alcoholics. *Unit head:* Dr. Clarenda Phillips, Department Chair, 606-783-2656, Fax: 606-783-5027, E-mail: r.bylund@moreheadstate.edu. *Application contact:* Michelle Barber, Graduate Admissions Counselor, 606-783-2039, Fax: 606-783-5061, E-mail: m.barber@moreheadstate.edu.

Mountain State University, Graduate Studies, Program in Criminal Justice Administration, Beckley, WV 25802-9003. Offers MCJA. Part-time and evening/weekend programs available. Postbaccalaureate distance learning degree programs offered (no on-campus study). *Faculty:* 7 full-time (2 women), 10 part-time/adjunct (4 women). *Students:* 12 full-time (8 women), 2 part-time (both women); includes 5 minority (all African Americans). Average age 41. 36 applicants, 69% accepted, 17 enrolled. In 2008, 7 master's awarded. *Degree requirements:* For master's, thesis or alternative. *Entrance requirements:* Additional exam requirements/recommendations for international students: Required—TOEFL (minimum score 550 paper-based; 213 computer-based); Recommended—IELTS (minimum score 6.5). *Application deadline:* For fall admission, 5/31 priority date for domestic and international students. Applications are processed on a rolling basis. Application fee: $25 ($50 for international students). Electronic applications accepted. *Expenses:* Tuition: Full-time $4020; part-time $335 per contact hour. *Financial support:* Federal Work-Study, scholarships/grants, and unspecified assistantships available. Support available to part-time students. Financial award applicants required to submit FAFSA. *Unit head:* Dr. Brian Holloway, Dean, School of Graduate Studies, 304-929-1690, Fax: 304-929-1637, E-mail: holloway@mountainstate.edu. *Application contact:* Dinah Rock, Coordinator of Graduate Academic Services, 304-929-1690, Fax: 304-929-1637, E-mail: drock@mountainstate.edu.

Mount Aloysius College, Program in Correctional Administration, Cresson, PA 16630-1999. Offers MA. *Entrance requirements:* For master's, GRE General Test.

National University, Academic Affairs, College of Letters and Sciences, Department of Professional Studies, La Jolla, CA 92037-1011. Offers forensic science (MFS), including criminalistics and investigation; public administration (MPA), including alternative dispute resolution, human resource management, organizational leadership, public finance. Part-time and evening/weekend programs available. Postbaccalaureate distance learning degree programs offered (no on-campus study). *Faculty:* 9 full-time (3 women), 134 part-time/adjunct (31 women). *Students:* 126 full-time (67 women), 195 part-time (103 women); includes 137 minority (56 African Americans, 26 Asian Americans or Pacific Islanders, 55 Hispanic Americans), 2 international. Average age 38. 241 applicants, 100% accepted, 241 enrolled. In 2008, 104 master's awarded. *Degree requirements:* For master's, thesis. *Entrance requirements:* For master's, interview, minimum GPA of 2.5. Additional exam requirements/recommendations for international students: Required—TOEFL (minimum score 550 paper-based; 213 computer-based; 79 iBT), IELTS (minimum score 6). *Application deadline:* Applications are processed on a rolling basis. Application fee: $60 ($65 for international students). Electronic applications accepted. *Expenses:* Tuition: Full-time $8694; part-time $322 per credit hour. Tuition and fees vary according to course load. *Financial support:* Career-related internships or fieldwork, institutionally sponsored loans, scholarships/grants, and tuition waivers (partial) available. Support available to part-time students. Financial award application deadline: 6/30; financial award applicants required to submit FAFSA. *Unit head:* Chandrika M. Kelso, Associate Professor and Chair, 858-642-8433, Fax: 858-642-8715, E-mail: ckelso@nu.edu. *Application contact:* Dominick Giovanniello, Associate Regional Dean—San Diego, 800-NAT-UNIV, Fax: 858-541-7792, E-mail: dgiovann@nu.edu.

New Jersey City University, Graduate Studies and Continuing Education, College of Professional Studies, Department of Criminal Justice, Jersey City, NJ 07305-1597. Offers criminal justice (MS); law enforcement (MS). Part-time and evening/weekend programs available. *Degree requirements:* For master's, thesis or alternative. *Entrance requirements:* For master's, GRE General Test or MAT. Additional exam requirements/recommendations for international students: Required—TOEFL.

New Mexico State University, Graduate School, College of Arts and Sciences, Department of Criminal Justice, Las Cruces, NM 88003-8001. Offers MCJ. Part-time and evening/weekend programs available. Postbaccalaureate distance learning degree programs offered (no on-campus study). *Faculty:* 8 full-time (4 women), 3 part-time/adjunct (2 women). *Students:* 45 full-time (29 women), 58 part-time (26 women); includes 40 minority (2 African Americans, 4 American Indian/Alaska Native, 3 Asian Americans or Pacific Islanders, 31 Hispanic Americans), 5 international. Average age 31. 52 applicants, 92% accepted, 35 enrolled. In 2008, 26 master's awarded. *Degree requirements:* For master's, comprehensive exam, thesis optional, oral and written exams. *Entrance requirements:* For master's, minimum GPA of 3.0. *Application* *deadline:* For fall admission, 4/1 priority date for domestic students; for spring admission, 11/1 priority date for domestic students. Applications are processed on a rolling basis. Application fee: $30 ($50 for international students). Electronic applications accepted. *Expenses:* Tuition, area resident: Full-time $3890; part-time $212.85 per credit. Tuition, state resident: full-time $3890; part-time $212.85 per credit. Tuition, nonresident: full-time $13,916; part-time $630.55 per credit. Required fees: $1218; $609 per semester. *Financial support:* In 2008–09, 14 students received support, including 1 research assistantship with partial tuition reimbursement available (averaging $15,800 per year), 10 teaching assistantships with partial tuition reimbursements available (averaging $12,838 per year); fellowships with partial tuition reimbursements available, career-related internships or fieldwork, health care benefits, and unspecified assistantships also available. Financial award application deadline: 4/1. *Faculty research:* Juvenile justice, jails and prison administration, courts and legal decision making, victim studies, policy and evaluation research. *Unit head:* Dr. James R. Maupin, Head, 575-646-3316, Fax: 575-646-2827, E-mail: jmaupin@nmsu.edu. *Application contact:* James Maupin, Professor, 575-646-3316, Fax: 575-646-2827, E-mail: jmaupin@nmsu.edu.

Niagara University, Graduate Division of Arts and Sciences, Department of Criminal Justice, Niagara Falls, Niagara University, NY 14109. Offers criminal justice administration (MS). *Faculty:* 6 full-time (2 women). *Students:* 18 full-time (13 women), 12 part-time (6 women); includes 1 minority (African American), 1 international. Average age 27. In 2008, 26 master's awarded. *Entrance requirements:* For master's, GRE. Additional exam requirements/recommendations for international students: Required—TOEFL. *Application deadline:* For fall admission, 8/1 for domestic students. Applications are processed on a rolling basis. Application fee: $30. *Expenses:* Tuition: Full-time $12,330; part-time $685 per contact hour. Required fees: $25 per semester. Tuition and fees vary according to program. *Financial support:* Fellowships, career-related internships or fieldwork and Federal Work-Study available. Support available to part-time students. *Unit head:* Dr. Talia Harmon, Director, 716-286-8093, Fax: 716-286-8061, E-mail: tharmon@niagara.edu. *Application contact:* Dr. Talia Harmon, Director, 716-286-8093, Fax: 716-286-8061, E-mail: tharmon@niagara.edu.

Nichols College, Graduate Program in Business Administration, Dudley, MA 01571-5000. Offers business administration (MBA, MOL); security management (MBA); sport management (MBA). Part-time and evening/weekend programs available. Postbaccalaureate distance learning degree programs offered (no on-campus study). *Faculty:* 33 part-time/adjunct (8 women). *Students:* 45 full-time (18 women), 229 part-time (117 women); includes 21 minority (11 African Americans, 5 Asian Americans or Pacific Islanders, 5 Hispanic Americans), 1 international. Average age 34. 310 applicants, 38% accepted, 42 enrolled. In 2008, 72 master's awarded. *Degree requirements:* For master's, minimum of 36 credits. *Entrance requirements:* For master's, official transcripts, 2 letters of recommendation, personal statement. Additional exam requirements/recommendations for international students: Required—TOEFL (minimum score 500 paper-based; 213 computer-based). *Application deadline:* Applications are processed on a rolling basis. Application fee: $25. Electronic applications accepted. *Expenses:* Tuition: Part-time $540 per credit. *Financial support:* Career-related internships or fieldwork available. Support available to part-time students. Financial award applicants required to submit FAFSA. *Unit head:* Laurie Albert, Dean, Graduate and Professional Studies, 508-213-2440, Fax: 800-243-3844, E-mail: laurie.albert@nichols.edu. *Application contact:* Nora Luquer, Assistant Director of Enrollment Services, 508-213-2295, Fax: 800-243-3844, E-mail: nora.luquer@nichols.edu.

Norfolk State University, School of Graduate Studies, School of Liberal Arts, Department of Sociology, Program in Criminal Justice, Norfolk, VA 23504. Offers MA.

North Carolina Central University, Division of Academic Affairs, College of Behavioral and Social Sciences, Department of Criminal Justice, Durham, NC 27707-3129. Offers MS. Part-time and evening/weekend programs available. *Degree requirements:* For master's, one foreign language, comprehensive exam, thesis or alternative. *Entrance requirements:* For master's, GRE, minimum GPA of 3.0 in major, 2.5 overall. Additional exam requirements/recommendations for international students: Required—TOEFL.

North Dakota State University, College of Graduate and Interdisciplinary Studies, College of Arts, Humanities and Social Sciences, Department of Criminal Justice and Political Science, Fargo, ND 58105. Offers criminal justice (MS, PhD). Part-time programs available. *Faculty:* 3 full-time (1 woman). *Students:* 11 full-time (8 women), 3 part-time (1 woman); includes 1 minority (Hispanic American), 1 international. Average age 25. 6 applicants, 67% accepted, 2 enrolled. In 2008, 1 master's awarded. Terminal master's awarded for partial completion of doctoral program. *Degree requirements:* For master's, thesis (for some programs); for doctorate, comprehensive exam, thesis/dissertation. *Entrance requirements:* For master's, minimum GPA of 3.0 in last 60 credit hours, approved bachelor's degree, course work in research methods and statistics; for doctorate, GRE General Test, minimum GPA of 3.0 over last 60 credit hours, 3 letters of recommendation. Additional exam requirements/recommendations for international students: Required—TOEFL (minimum score 525 paper-based; 197 computer-based; 71 iBT). *Application deadline:* For spring admission, 4/1 priority date for domestic students, 4/1 for international students. Applications are processed on a rolling basis. Application fee: $45 ($60 for international students). *Financial support:* In 2008–09, 6 research assistantships with tuition reimbursements (averaging $12,000 per year), 3 teaching assistantships with tuition reimbursements (averaging $6,000 per year) were awarded; career-related internships or fieldwork, institutionally sponsored loans, tuition waivers (full), and unspecified assistantships also available. Financial award application deadline: 4/1. *Faculty research:* Corrections, policing, drugs and crime, gender and crime, criminology. Total annual research expenditures: $150,000. *Unit head:* Dr. Kevin Thompson, Chair, 701-231-8938, Fax: 701-231-5877, E-mail: kevin.thompson@ndsu.edu. *Application contact:* Dr. Kevin Thompson, Chair, 701-231-8938, Fax: 701-231-5877, E-mail: kevin.thompson@ndsu.edu.

Northeastern State University, Graduate College, College of Liberal Arts, Program in Criminal Justice and Legal Studies, Tahlequah, OK 74464-2399. Offers criminal justice (MS). Part-time and evening/weekend programs available. *Students:* 19 full-time (9 women), 17 part-time (14 women); includes 17 minority (5 African Americans, 11 American Indian/Alaska Native, 1 Hispanic American). In 2008, 6 master's awarded. *Degree requirements:* For master's, thesis optional, oral exam. *Entrance requirements:* For master's, MAT or GRE, minimum GPA of 2.5. Additional exam requirements/recommendations for international students: Required—TOEFL (minimum score 213 computer-based). *Application deadline:* For fall admission, 6/1 priority date for domestic students. Applications are processed on a rolling basis. Application fee: $0 ($25 for international students). Electronic applications accepted. *Financial support:* Teaching assistantships, Federal Work-Study available. Financial award application deadline: 3/1. *Unit head:* Dr. Frank Zeigler, JD, Chair, 918-449-6595 Ext. 0, E-mail: zeigler@nsuok.edu. *Application contact:* Margie Railey, Administrative Assistant, 918-456-5511 Ext. 2093, Fax: 918-458-2061, E-mail: railey@nsouk.edu.

Northeastern University, College of Criminal Justice, Boston, MA 02115-5096. Offers MS, PhD. Part-time and evening/weekend programs available. *Degree requirements:* For master's, comprehensive exam, thesis optional. *Entrance requirements:* For master's and doctorate, GRE General Test. Additional exam requirements/recommendations for international students: Required—TOEFL. Electronic applications accepted. *Faculty research:* Juvenile justice, victimology, serial and mass murder, private security, criminology corrections, race and crime.

Northern Arizona University, Graduate College, College of Social and Behavioral Sciences, Department of Criminology and Criminal Justice, Flagstaff, AZ 86011. Offers applied criminology (MS); criminal justice policy and planning (Certificate). *Degree requirements:* For master's, thesis.

Northern Michigan University, College of Graduate Studies, College of Professional Studies, Department of Criminal Justice, Marquette, MI 49855-5301. Offers MS. Part-time and evening/weekend programs available. *Entrance requirements:* For master's, minimum GPA of 3.0.

Norwich University, School of Graduate Studies, Program in Justice Administration, Northfield, VT 05663. Offers corrections administration (MJA); justice administration (MJA); law administration (MJA). Evening/weekend programs available. *Faculty:* 7 part-time/adjunct (3 women). *Students:* 49 full-time (22 women); includes 8 minority (4 African Americans, 1 American Indian/Alaska Native, 2 Asian Americans or Pacific Islanders, 1 Hispanic American). Average age 36. 56 applicants, 95% accepted, 49 enrolled. In 2008, 49 master's awarded. *Entrance requirements:* For master's, minimum GPA of 2.75. Additional exam requirements/recommendations for international students: Required—TOEFL (minimum score 550 paper-based; 212 computer-based; 83 iBT). *Application deadline:* For fall admission, 8/10 for domestic and international students; for winter admission, 11/7 for domestic and international students; for spring admission, 2/6 for domestic and international students. Application fee: $50. Electronic applications accepted. *Expenses:* Tuition: Full-time $8000. Full-time tuition and fees vary according to degree level and program. *Financial support:* Scholarships/grants available. Financial award applicants required to submit FAFSA. *Unit head:* Donal Hartman, JD, Program Director, 802-485-2730, E-mail: dhartman@norwich.edu. *Application contact:* Chris Ormsby, Administrative Director, 802-485-2730, Fax: 802-485-2533, E-mail: cormsby@norwich.edu.

Nova Southeastern University, Criminal Justice Institute, Program in Criminal Justice, Fort Lauderdale, FL 33314-7796. Offers MS. *Faculty:* 41 part-time/adjunct (7 women). *Students:* 12 full-time (9 women), 145 part-time (90 women); includes 91 minority (62 African Americans, 2 American Indian/Alaska Native, 1 Asian American or Pacific Islander, 26 Hispanic Americans). 41 applicants, 73% accepted, 30 enrolled. In 2008, 50 master's awarded. *Degree requirements:* For master's, comprehensive exam (for some programs), thesis optional. *Entrance requirements:* For master's, 3 letters of recommendation, minimum GPA of 2.5. *Application deadline:* For fall admission, 7/8 for domestic students; for winter admission, 1/8 for domestic students; for spring admission, 3/8 for domestic students. Application fee: $50. *Financial support:* Applicants required to submit FAFSA. *Unit head:* Dr. Tammy Kushner, Director, 954-262-7001, Fax: 954-937-7005, E-mail: kushner@nova.edu. *Application contact:* Russell Garner, Administrative Assistant, 954-262-7001, E-mail: cji@nova.edu.

See Close-Up on page 741.

Oklahoma City University, Petree College of Arts and Sciences, Division of Sociology and Justice Studies, Oklahoma City, OK 73106-1402. Offers criminal justice (MCJ). Part-time and evening/weekend programs available. *Degree requirements:* For master's, thesis optional. *Entrance requirements:* For master's, minimum GPA of 3.0. Additional exam requirements/recommendations for international students: Required—TOEFL. *Expenses:* Contact institution. *Faculty research:* Victims, police, corrections, security, women and crime.

Old Dominion University, College of Arts and Letters, Program in Criminology and Criminal Justice, Norfolk, VA 23529. Offers PhD. Part-time and evening/weekend programs available. *Faculty:* 16 full-time (11 women). *Students:* 11 full-time (6 women), 1 part-time (0 women); includes 1 minority (Asian American or Pacific Islander). Average age 34. 14 applicants, 57% accepted, 5 enrolled. *Degree requirements:* For doctorate, comprehensive exam, thesis/dissertation, 48 credit hours. *Entrance requirements:* For doctorate, GRE General Test, MA; minimum graduate GPA of 3.25; theory, methods, and statistics graduate coursework; letters of reference; writing sample. Additional exam requirements/recommendations for international students: Required—TOEFL. *Application deadline:* For fall admission, 2/15 for domestic and international students. Application fee: $40. Electronic applications accepted. *Expenses:* Tuition, area resident: Full-time $7704; part-time $321 per credit. Tuition, state resident: full-time $7704; part-time $321 per credit. Tuition, nonresident: full-time $19,104; part-time $796 per credit. Required fees: $99 per semester. One-time fee: $40. *Financial support:* In 2008–09, 7 students received support, including 3 fellowships with full tuition reimbursements available (averaging $15,000 per year), 4 teaching assistantships with full tuition reimbursements available (averaging $15,000 per year). Financial award application deadline: 2/15. *Faculty research:* Inequality, crime and justice; domestic violence; community justice; criminological theory; methods; policing; courts and corrections; state crime. *Unit head:* Dr. Mona Danner, Graduate Program Director, 757-683-5931, Fax: 757-683-5634, E-mail: mdanner@odu.edu. *Application contact:* Dr. Robert Wojtowicz, Associate Dean, 757-683-6077, Fax: 757-683-5746, E-mail: rwojtowi@odu.edu.

Penn State Harrisburg, Graduate School, School of Public Affairs, Middletown, PA 17057-4898. Offers criminal justice (MA); health administration (MHA); public administration (MPA); public affairs (PhD); MPA/JD.

Penn State University Park, Graduate School, College of the Liberal Arts, Department of Sociology, State College, University Park, PA 16802-1503. Offers crime, law, and justice (MA, PhD); sociology (MA, PhD).

Point Park University, School of Arts and Sciences, Department of Criminal Justice and Intelligence Studies, Pittsburgh, PA 15222-1984. Offers criminal justice administration (MS). Evening/weekend programs available. *Faculty:* 4 full-time, 4 part-time/adjunct. *Students:* 31 full-time (24 women); includes 20 minority (19 African Americans, 1 Hispanic American). Average age 33. 65 applicants, 45% accepted, 20 enrolled. In 2008, 19 master's awarded. *Degree requirements:* For master's, comprehensive exam (for some programs), thesis or alternative. *Entrance requirements:* For master's, minimum GPA of 2.75, resumé, 2 letters of recommendation, statement of purpose. Additional exam requirements/recommendations for international students: Required—TOEFL. *Application deadline:* Applications are processed on a rolling basis. Application fee: $30. Electronic applications accepted. *Expenses:* Tuition: Full-time $11,880; part-time $660 per credit. Required fees: $486; $27 per credit. *Financial support:* In 2008–09, 2 students received support, including 2 teaching assistantships with full tuition reimbursements available (averaging $6,400 per year); Federal Work-Study and scholarships/grants also available. Support available to part-time students. Financial award application deadline: 5/1; financial award applicants required to submit FAFSA. *Unit head:* Dr. Lorelei Stein, Program Director, 412-392-3858, Fax: 412-392-3925, E-mail: lstein@pointpark.edu. *Application contact:* Lynn Ribar, Associate Director of Graduate and Adult Enrollment, 412-392-3908, Fax: 412-392-6164, E-mail: lrlbar@polntpark.edu.

Polytechnic Institute of NYU, Department of Computer and Information Science, Brooklyn, NY 11201-2990. Offers computer science (MS, PhD); cyber security (Graduate Certificate); software engineering (Graduate Certificate). Part-time and evening/weekend programs available. *Degree requirements:* For master's, comprehensive exam (for some programs), thesis (for some programs); for doctorate, comprehensive exam, thesis/dissertation. *Entrance requirements:* For master's, BA or BS in computer science, mathematics, science, or engineering; working knowledge of a high-level program; for doctorate, GRE General Test, GRE Subject Test, qualifying exam, BA or BS in science, engineering, or management; MS or 1 year of graduate course work. Additional exam requirements/recommendations for international students: Required—TOEFL (minimum score 550 paper-based; 213 computer-based); Recommended—IELTS (minimum score 6.5). Electronic applications accepted.

Pontifical Catholic University of Puerto Rico, Institute of Graduate Studies in Behavioral Science and Community Affairs, Program in Criminology, Ponce, PR 00717-0777. Offers MA. Part-time and evening/weekend programs available. *Degree requirements:* For master's, thesis. *Entrance requirements:* For master's, EXADEP, 3 letters of recommendation, interview, minimum GPA of 2.75.

Pontificia Universidad Catolica Madre y Maestra, Graduate School, Santiago, Dominican Republic. Offers administration (M Adm); architecture of interiors (M Arch); architecture of tourist lodgings (M Arch); banking and financial management (M Mgmt); civil law (LL M); construction administration (ME); corporate business law (LL M); criminal procedure law (LL M); environmental engineering (ME, MEE); finance (M Mgmt); human resources (EMBA); international business (M Mgmt); labor law and Social Security (LL M); logistics management (ME); marketing (M Mgmt); renewable energy (ME). *Entrance requirements:* For master's, curriculum vitae, interview.

Criminal Justice and Criminology

Portland State University, Graduate Studies, College of Urban and Public Affairs, Hatfield School of Government, Division of Criminology and Criminal Justice, Portland, OR 97207-0751. Offers MS, PhD. Part-time programs available. *Faculty:* 11 full-time (6 women), 11 part-time/adjunct (3 women). *Students:* 21 full-time (15 women), 4 part-time (3 women); includes 4 minority (2 African Americans, 2 Hispanic Americans). Average age 29. 16 applicants, 88% accepted, 10 enrolled. In 2008, 11 master's awarded. *Degree requirements:* For master's, thesis or alternative, comprehensive oral exam; for doctorate, comprehensive exam, thesis/dissertation, residency. *Entrance requirements:* For master's, minimum GPA of 3.0 in upper-division course work or 2.75 overall; for doctorate, GRE General Test. Additional exam requirements/recommendations for international students: Required—TOEFL (minimum score 550 paper-based; 213 computer-based). *Application deadline:* For fall admission, 3/15 priority date for domestic students, 3/1 priority date for international students. Application fee: $50. *Expenses:* Tuition, area resident: Full-time $8763; part-time $179 per credit hour. Tuition, state resident: full-time $8763; part-time $298 per credit hour. Tuition, nonresident: full-time $12,981; part-time $426 per credit hour. Required fees: $1242. One-time fee: $250. Tuition and fees vary according to course load and program. *Financial support:* In 2008–09, 5 teaching assistantships with full tuition reimbursements (averaging $8,445 per year) were awarded; research assistantships with full tuition reimbursements, career-related internships or fieldwork, Federal Work-Study, scholarships/grants, and unspecified assistantships also available. Support available to part-time students. Financial award application deadline: 3/1; financial award applicants required to submit FAFSA. *Faculty research:* History of criminal justice, mental health issues, international terrorism, offender assessment, domestic violence. Total annual research expenditures: $532,682. *Unit head:* Dr. Brian C. Renauer, Chair, 503-725-4014, Fax: 503-725-5199, E-mail: renauer@pdx.edu. *Application contact:* Rod Johnson, Admissions Officer, 503-725-4044, Fax: 503-725-5199, E-mail: rod@pdx.edu.

Radford University, College of Graduate and Professional Studies, College of Humanities and Behavioral Sciences, Department of Criminal Justice, Radford, VA 24142. Offers MA, MS. Part-time programs available. *Faculty:* 10 full-time (5 women). *Students:* 26 full-time (15 women), 11 part-time (7 women); includes 1 minority (African American), 1 international. Average age 28. 18 applicants, 78% accepted, 12 enrolled. In 2008, 21 master's awarded. *Degree requirements:* For master's, comprehensive exam, thesis optional. *Entrance requirements:* For master's, GRE, minimum GPA of 2.9; 2 letters of reference; original writing sample. Additional exam requirements/recommendations for international students: Required—TOEFL (minimum score 550 paper-based; 213 computer-based; 79 iBT). *Application deadline:* For fall admission, 3/1 priority date for domestic students, 12/1 for international students; for spring admission, 10/1 for domestic students, 7/1 for international students. Applications are processed on a rolling basis. Application fee: $40. Electronic applications accepted. *Expenses:* Tuition, area resident: Full-time $4845; part-time $202 per credit. Tuition, state resident: full-time $4845; part-time $202 per credit. Tuition, nonresident: full-time $11,483; part-time $478 per credit. Required fees: $2349; $98 per credit. *Financial support:* In 2008–09, 24 students received support, including 17 research assistantships with partial tuition reimbursements available (averaging $8,000 per year); career-related internships or fieldwork, Federal Work-Study, institutionally sponsored loans, scholarships/grants, and unspecified assistantships also available. Financial award application deadline: 3/1; financial award applicants required to submit FAFSA. *Faculty research:* Capital punishment, crime mapping and analysis, elder abuse, guns and gun control, rural crime. *Unit head:* Dr. Mary Atwell, Chair, 540-831-6339, Fax: 540-831-6075, E-mail: matwell@radford.edu. *Application contact:* Graduate Admissions, 540-831-6431, Fax: 540-831-6061, E-mail: gradcollege@radford.edu.

Regis University, College for Professional Studies, MA Program, Denver, CO 80221-1099. Offers criminology (MA); fine arts administration (Certificate); language and communication (MA); mediation (Certificate); psychology (MA); self-designed major (MA); social justice, peace, and reconciliation (Certificate); social science (MA); technical communication (Certificate). Program also offered in Henderson and Las Vegas (Summerlin), NV. Part-time and evening/weekend programs available. Postbaccalaureate distance learning degree programs offered (minimal on-campus study). *Degree requirements:* For master's, thesis, research project. *Entrance requirements:* For master's, resumé, recommendations, essays. Additional exam requirements/recommendations for international students: Required—TOEFL (minimum score 213 computer-based), TWE (minimum score 5). Electronic applications accepted. *Expenses:* Contact institution. *Faculty research:* Independent/nonresidential graduate study: new methods and models, adult learning and the capstone experience, Goal Setting, behavior of Adult students, Innovative Studies for Community Colleges.

The Richard Stockton College of New Jersey, School of Graduate and Continuing Education, Program in Criminal Justice, Pomona, NJ 08240-0195. Offers MA. Part-time and evening/weekend programs available. *Faculty:* 5 full-time (2 women). *Students:* 13 full-time (6 women), 22 part-time (10 women); includes 3 minority (2 African Americans, 1 Hispanic American). Average age 26. 21 applicants, 71% accepted, 12 enrolled. In 2008, 1 master's awarded. *Degree requirements:* For master's, comprehensive exam (for some programs), thesis, student portfolio project. *Entrance requirements:* For master's, GRE General Test, minimum GPA of 3.0. Additional exam requirements/recommendations for international students: Required—TOEFL. *Application deadline:* For fall admission, 8/1 for international students; for spring admission, 1/5 for domestic and international students. Application fee: $50. *Expenses:* Tuition, area resident: Full-time $8526; part-time $474 per credit. Tuition, state resident: full-time $8526; part-time $474 per credit. Tuition, nonresident: full-time $13,125; part-time $729 per course. Required fees: $2030; $113 per credit. *Financial support:* In 2008–09, 6 students received support, including 6 research assistantships with partial tuition reimbursements available; fellowships, career-related internships or fieldwork, scholarships/grants, and unspecified assistantships also available. Financial award application deadline: 3/1; financial award applicants required to submit FAFSA. *Faculty research:* Homeland security, forensic psychology, corrections, sex crimes, violent crimes. *Unit head:* Dr. Christine Tartaro, Director, 609-626-6035, E-mail: christine.tartaro@stockton.edu. *Application contact:* John Iacovelli, Dean of Enrollment Management, 866-RSC-2885, Fax: 609-748-5541, E-mail: admissions@stockton.edu.

Roger Williams University, School of Justice Studies, Bristol, RI 02809. Offers criminal justice (MS). Part-time and evening/weekend programs available. *Faculty:* 7 full-time (5 women). *Students:* 8 full-time (4 women), 41 part-time (14 women); includes 1 minority (African American). Average age 31. 17 applicants, 76% accepted, 10 enrolled. In 2008, 20 master's awarded. *Degree requirements:* For master's, comprehensive exam, thesis optional. *Entrance requirements:* For master's, Personal Statement, 2 Letters of Recommendation, Transcripts. Additional exam requirements/recommendations for international students: Recommended—IELTS. *Application deadline:* Applications are processed on a rolling basis. Application fee: $50. Electronic applications accepted. *Expenses:* Contact institution. *Financial support:* In 2008–09, 11 students received support. Application deadline: 6/15; *Unit head:* Dr. Stephanie Manzi, Dean, 401-254-3715, Fax: 401-254-3431, E-mail: smanzi@rwu.edu. *Application contact:* Lori Vales, Graduate Admission Coordinator, 401-254-6600, Fax: 401-254-3557, E-mail: gradadmit@rwu.edu.

Announcement: At the Roger Williams University School of Justice Studies, internationally known faculty members instill in students the tools to formulate policy and serve as administrators at agencies across the justice system. The school offers two graduate degrees: a master's in criminal justice and a joint master's/Juris Doctor degree with the Roger Williams University School of Law. For more information, visit www.rwu.edu/admission/graduate.

See Close-Up on page 743.

Rowan University, Graduate School, College of Liberal Arts and Sciences, Program in Criminal Justice, Glassboro, NJ 08028-1701. Offers MA. Part-time and evening/weekend programs available. *Students:* 7 full-time (2 women), 7 part-time (2 women); includes 2 minority (both Hispanic Americans). Average age 25. 13 applicants, 54% accepted, 5 enrolled. *Degree requirements:* For master's, thesis. *Entrance requirements:* For master's, GRE. Additional exam requirements/recommendations for international students: Required—TOEFL. *Application deadline:* Applications are processed on a rolling basis. Application fee: $50. Electronic applications accepted. *Expenses:* Tuition, area resident: Full-time $10,624; part-time $590 per credit. Tuition, state resident: full-time $10,624; part-time $590 per credit. Tuition, nonresident: full-time $10,624; part-time $590 per credit. Required fees: $2258; $124.90 per credit. *Financial support:* Career-related internships or fieldwork, scholarships/grants, health care benefits, and unspecified assistantships available. *Unit head:* Dr. Mira Lalovic-Hand, Interim Associate Provost/Director of Graduate School, 856-256-5120, E-mail: Lalovic-hand@rowan.edu. *Application contact:* Karen Haynes, Graduate Coordinator, 856-256-4052, Fax: 856-256-4436, E-mail: Haynes@rowan.edu.

Rutgers, The State University of New Jersey, Camden, Graduate School of Arts and Sciences, Program in Criminal Justice, Camden, NJ 08102-1401. Offers MA, MPA/MA. Part-time and evening/weekend programs available. *Degree requirements:* For master's, comprehensive exam, thesis optional. *Entrance requirements:* For master's, GRE, 3 letters of recommendation, statement of goals. Additional exam requirements/recommendations for international students: Required—TOEFL, IELTS. Electronic applications accepted. *Faculty research:* Criminal justice policy, public management, children in criminal justice system, violence, gender and crime.

Rutgers, The State University of New Jersey, Newark, Graduate School, School of Criminal Justice, Program in Criminal Justice, Newark, NJ 07102. Offers PhD. *Entrance requirements:* For doctorate, GRE, minimum undergraduate B average.

Sacred Heart University, Graduate Programs, College of Arts and Sciences, Department of Criminal Justice, Fairfield, CT 06825-1000. Offers MA. Part-time programs available. *Degree requirements:* For master's, thesis optional. *Entrance requirements:* Additional exam requirements/recommendations for international students: Required—TOEFL (minimum score 550 paper-based; 213 computer-based). Electronic applications accepted.

Sage Graduate School, Graduate School, Department of Sociology and Criminal Justice, Troy, NY 12180-4115. Offers forensic mental health (MS, Certificate). *Faculty:* 2 part-time/adjunct (both women). *Students:* 3 full-time (all women), 14 part-time (13 women); includes 2 minority (both African Americans). Average age 28. 32 applicants, 69% accepted, 12 enrolled. *Entrance requirements:* Additional exam requirements/recommendations for international students: Required—TOEFL (minimum score 550 paper-based; 213 computer-based). *Expenses:* Tuition: Full-time $10,080; part-time $560 per credit hour. *Unit head:* Dr. Maureen McLeod, Chair, 518-244-2211, E-mail: mcleom@sage.edu. *Application contact:* Wendy D. Diefendorf, Director of Graduate and Adult Admission, 518-244-2443, Fax: 518-244-6880, E-mail: diefew@sage.edu.

St. Ambrose University, College of Arts and Sciences, Program in Criminal Justice, Davenport, IA 52803-2898. Offers criminal justice (MCJ); juvenile justice education (MCJ). Part-time and evening/weekend programs available. *Faculty:* 3 full-time (1 woman), 3 part-time/adjunct (0 women). *Students:* 7 full-time (3 women), 18 part-time (8 women); includes 7 minority (2 African Americans, 2 American Indian/Alaska Native, 3 Hispanic Americans), 1 international. Average age 32. 13 applicants, 62% accepted, 6 enrolled. In 2008, 20 master's awarded. *Degree requirements:* For master's, thesis (for some programs), practicum or project. *Entrance requirements:* For master's, 2 years of work experience, 2 letters of recommendation, personal interview. Additional exam requirements/recommendations for international students: Required—TOEFL. *Application deadline:* For fall admission, 8/15 priority date for domestic students, 8/15 for international students; for spring admission, 11/1 for domestic and international students. Applications are processed on a rolling basis. Application fee: $25. Electronic applications accepted. *Expenses:* Tuition: Full-time $672; part-time $672 per contact hour. Tuition and fees vary according to degree level, program and reciprocity agreements. *Financial support:* In 2008–09, 17 students received support, including 3 research assistantships with partial tuition reimbursements available (averaging $2,670 per year); career-related internships or fieldwork, scholarships/grants, and unspecified assistantships also available. Financial award application deadline: 3/15; financial award applicants required to submit FAFSA. *Faculty research:* Community policing. *Unit head:* Dr. Christopher C Barnum, Acting Head, 563-333-6157, Fax: 563-333-6243, E-mail: barnumchristopherC@sau.edu. *Application contact:* Vivian F Force, Administrative Assistant, 563-333-6166, Fax: 563-333-6243, E-mail: forcevivianf@sau.edu.

St. Cloud State University, School of Graduate Studies, College of Social Sciences, Department of Criminal Justice, St. Cloud, MN 56301-4498. Offers criminal justice administration (MS); criminal justice counseling (MS); public safety executive leadership (MS). Part-time programs available. Postbaccalaureate distance learning degree programs offered (minimal on-campus study). *Degree requirements:* For master's, thesis or alternative. *Entrance requirements:* For master's, GRE General Test, minimum GPA of 2.75. Additional exam requirements/recommendations for international students: Required—Michigan English Language Assessment Battery; Recommended—TOEFL (minimum score 550 paper-based; 213 computer-based), IELTS (minimum score 6.5). Electronic applications accepted.

St. John's University, St. John's College of Liberal Arts and Sciences, Department of Sociology and Anthropology, Queens, NY 11439. Offers criminology and justice (MA); sociology (MA). Part-time and evening/weekend programs available. *Students:* 10 full-time (5 women), 49 part-time (28 women); includes 33 minority (14 African Americans, 8 Asian Americans or Pacific Islanders, 11 Hispanic Americans), 3 international. Average age 27. 68 applicants, 65% accepted, 22 enrolled. In 2008, 30 master's awarded. *Degree requirements:* For master's, comprehensive exam, thesis optional. *Entrance requirements:* For master's, 18 undergraduate credits in social services, minimum GPA of 3.0. Additional exam requirements/recommendations for international students: Required—TOEFL (minimum score 500 paper-based; 173 computer-based; 61 iBT), IELTS (minimum score 5.5). *Application deadline:* For fall admission, 5/1 priority date for domestic and international students; for spring admission, 11/1 priority date for domestic and international students. Applications are processed on a rolling basis. Application fee: $70. Electronic applications accepted. *Expenses:* Tuition: Full-time $20,760; part-time $865 per credit. Required fees: $300; $150 per semester. Tuition and fees vary according to program. *Financial support:* Research assistantships, career-related internships or fieldwork and scholarships/grants available. Support available to part-time students. Financial award application deadline: 3/1; financial award applicants required to submit FAFSA. *Faculty research:* Global black power movement, poverty, domestic violence and human trafficking, female juvenile violence, media and race. *Unit head:* Dr. Dawn Esposito, Chair, 718-990-5667, E-mail: espositd@stjohns.edu. *Application contact:* Kathleen Davis, Director of Graduate Admission, 718-990-2790, Fax: 718-990-5686, E-mail: gradhelp@stjohns.edu.

Saint Joseph's University, College of Arts and Sciences, Department of Criminal Justice, Philadelphia, PA 19131-1395. Offers administration/police executive (MS); behavior analysis (MS, Post-Master's Certificate); criminal justice (MS, Post-Master's Certificate); criminology (MS); federal law (MS); intelligence and crime (MS); probation, parole, and corrections (MS). Part-time and evening/weekend programs available. Postbaccalaureate distance learning degree programs offered. *Students:* 2 full-time (1 woman), 178 part-time (107 women); includes 56 minority (49 African Americans, 1 Asian American or Pacific Islander, 6 Hispanic Americans), 2 international. Average age 33. In 2008, 118 master's awarded. *Degree requirements:* For master's, thesis. *Entrance requirements:* For master's, GRE General Test or minimum GPA of 3.0, 2 letters of recommendation, personal statement, application, official transcripts. Additional exam requirements/recommendations for international students: Required—TOEFL (minimum score 550 paper-based; 213 computer-based; 79 iBT). *Application deadline:* For fall admission, 7/15 priority date for domestic students, 4/15 for international students; for winter admission, 1/15 for international students; for spring admission, 11/15 priority date for domestic students, 10/15 for international students. Applications are processed on a rolling basis. Application fee: $35. Electronic applications accepted. *Expenses:* Tuition: Part-time $745 per credit. Tuition and fees vary according to course load, degree level and program. *Financial support:* Career-related internships or fieldwork and unspecified assistantships available. Financial award applicants required to submit FAFSA. *Unit head:* Patricia Griffin, Director, 610-660-1294,

E-mail: pgriffin@sju.edu. *Application contact:* Coralee Dixon, Assistant Director of Graduate Admissions, 610-660-1102, Fax: 610-660-1224, E-mail: coralee.dixon@sju.edu.

Saint Leo University, Graduate Business Studies, Saint Leo, FL 33574-6665. Offers accounting (MBA); business (MBA); criminal justice (MBA); health services management (MBA); human resource administration (MBA); information security management (MBA); sport business (MBA). Part-time and evening/weekend programs available. Postbaccalaureate distance learning degree programs offered (no on-campus study). *Degree requirements:* For master's, thesis. *Entrance requirements:* For master's, GMAT, 5 years of professional work experience, resumé, 2 letters of recommendation. Additional exam requirements/recommendations for international students: Required—TOEFL (minimum score 550 paper-based; 213 computer-based). Electronic applications accepted. *Expenses:* Contact institution.

Saint Leo University, Graduate Studies in Criminal Justice, Saint Leo, FL 33574-6665. Offers criminal justice (MS); critical incident management (MS). Part-time and evening/weekend programs available. Postbaccalaureate distance learning degree programs offered (no on-campus study). *Entrance requirements:* For master's, minimum GPA of 3.0. Additional exam requirements/recommendations for international students: Required—TOEFL (minimum score 550 paper-based; 213 computer-based). Electronic applications accepted.

Saint Mary's University, Faculty of Arts, Program in Criminology, Halifax, NS B3H 3C3, Canada. Offers MA. Part-time programs available. *Degree requirements:* For master's, thesis. *Entrance requirements:* For master's, honors degree, minimum QPA of 3.33. *Expenses:* Contact institution.

St. Thomas University, School of Business, Department of Management, Miami Gardens, FL 33054-6459. Offers accounting (MBA); general management (MSM, Certificate); health management (MBA, MSM, Certificate); human resource management (MBA, MSM, Certificate); international business (MBA, MIB, MSM, Certificate); justice administration (MSM, Certificate); management accounting (MSM, Certificate); public management (MSM, Certificate); sports administration (MS). Part-time and evening/weekend programs available. *Degree requirements:* For master's, comprehensive exam. *Entrance requirements:* For master's, interview, minimum GPA of 3.0 or GMAT. Additional exam requirements/recommendations for international students: Required—TOEFL (minimum score 550 paper-based; 213 computer-based; 79 iBT). Electronic applications accepted.

Salem State College, School of Graduate Studies, Program in Criminal Justice, Salem, MA 01970-5353. Offers MS. Part-time and evening/weekend programs available. *Students:* 1 (woman) full-time, 9 part-time (4 women). Average age 26. In 2008, 5 master's awarded. Application fee: $35. *Unit head:* Kristen Kuehnle, Associate Professor, 978-542-6321, E-mail: kkuehnle@salemstate.edu. *Application contact:* Dr. Marc Glasser, Dean of the Graduate School, 978-542-6323, Fax: 978-542-7215.

Salve Regina University, Graduate Studies, Programs in Administration of Justice, Newport, RI 02840-4192. Offers justice and homeland security (MS); law enforcement leadership (MS). Part-time and evening/weekend programs available. *Faculty:* 2 full-time (0 women), 9 part-time/adjunct (1 woman). *Students:* 21 full-time (5 women), 30 part-time (5 women); includes 2 minority (1 African American, 1 Hispanic American). Average age 30. 16 applicants, 63% accepted, 8 enrolled. In 2008, 13 master's awarded. *Entrance requirements:* For master's, GMAT, GRE General Test, or MAT. Additional exam requirements/recommendations for international students: Required—TOEFL (minimum score 600 paper-based; 250 computer-based; 100 iBT). *Application deadline:* For fall admission, 3/5 priority date for domestic students, 3/15 priority date for international students; for spring admission, 9/15 priority date for domestic students, 9/5 priority date for international students. Applications are processed on a rolling basis. Application fee: $60. Electronic applications accepted. *Expenses:* Tuition: Part-time $395 per credit. Required fees: $40 per term. Tuition and fees vary according to degree level. *Financial support:* Career-related internships or fieldwork and Federal Work-Study available. Support available to part-time students. Financial award application deadline: 3/1; financial award applicants required to submit FAFSA. *Unit head:* Dr. Daniel Knight, Director, 401-341-3255, E-mail: knightd@salve.edu. *Application contact:* Kelly Alverson, Graduate Admissions Counselor, 401-341-2153, Fax: 401-341-2973, E-mail: kelly.alverson@salve.edu.

Sam Houston State University, College of Criminal Justice, Huntsville, TX 77341. Offers criminal justice (MS, PhD); criminal justice and criminology (MA); criminal justice management (MS); forensic science (MS); security studies (MS); victim services management (MS). *Faculty:* 25 full-time (4 women), 1 part-time/adjunct (0 women). *Students:* 76 full-time (40 women), 119 part-time (53 women); includes 26 minority (6 African Americans, 1 American Indian/Alaska Native, 5 Asian Americans or Pacific Islanders, 14 Hispanic Americans), 45 international. Average age 32. 102 applicants, 73% accepted, 67 enrolled. In 2008, 34 master's, 15 doctorates awarded. *Degree requirements:* For master's, thesis (for some programs); for doctorate, comprehensive exam, thesis/dissertation. *Entrance requirements:* For master's, GRE General Test; for doctorate, GRE General Test, master's degree. Additional exam requirements/recommendations for international students: Required—TOEFL (minimum score 550 paper-based; 213 computer-based; 79 iBT). *Application deadline:* For fall admission, 8/1 for domestic students; for spring admission, 12/1 for domestic students. Applications are processed on a rolling basis. Application fee: $20. *Expenses:* Tuition, state resident: full-time $3564; part-time $198 per credit hour. Tuition, nonresident: full-time $8622; part-time $479 per credit hour. Required fees: $1290. Tuition and fees vary according to course load and campus/location. *Financial support:* Fellowships, research assistantships, teaching assistantships, career-related internships or fieldwork, Federal Work-Study, institutionally sponsored loans, and unspecified assistantships available. Support available to part-time students. Financial award application deadline: 5/31; financial award applicants required to submit FAFSA. *Unit head:* Dr. Vincent Webb, Dean, 936-294-1632, Fax: 936-294-1653, E-mail: vwebb@shsu.edu. *Application contact:* Doris Powell-Pratt, Advisor, 936-294-3637, Fax: 936-294-4055, E-mail: icc_dcp@shsu.edu.

San Diego State University, Graduate and Research Affairs, College of Professional Studies and Fine Arts, School of Public Affairs, Program in Criminal Justice Administration, San Diego, CA 92182. Offers MPA. Part-time programs available. *Entrance requirements:* For master's, GRE General Test, 2 letters of reference. Additional exam requirements/recommendations for international students: Required—TOEFL. Electronic applications accepted.

San Diego State University, Graduate and Research Affairs, College of Professional Studies and Fine Arts, School of Public Affairs, Program in Criminal Justice and Criminology, San Diego, CA 92182. Offers MS. *Entrance requirements:* For master's, GRE General Test, 2 letters of reference. Additional exam requirements/recommendations for international students: Required—TOEFL. Electronic applications accepted.

San Jose State University, Graduate Studies and Research, College of Applied Sciences and Arts, Department of Justice Studies, San Jose, CA 95192-0001. Offers MS. Part-time programs available. *Degree requirements:* For master's, thesis or alternative. *Entrance requirements:* For master's, GRE or LSAT, minimum GPA of 3.0. Additional exam requirements/recommendations for international students: Required—TOEFL. Electronic applications accepted. *Faculty research:* Employee stress, interagency cooperation, prison industries, application of death penalty sentences, sucrose ingestion and delinquency.

Seattle University, College of Arts and Sciences, Department of Criminal Justice, Seattle, WA 98122-1090. Offers MACJ.

Shippensburg University of Pennsylvania, School of Graduate Studies, College of Education and Human Services, Department of Criminal Justice, Shippensburg, PA 17257-2299. Offers administration of justice (MS), including juvenile justice. Part-time and evening/weekend programs available. *Faculty:* 9 full-time (4 women). *Students:* 7 full-time (2 women), 49 part-time (28 women); includes 11 minority (8 African Americans, 1 American Indian/Alaska Native, 1 Asian American or Pacific Islander, 1 Hispanic American). Average age 30. 32 applicants, 88% accepted, 20 enrolled. In 2008, 24 master's awarded. *Degree requirements:* For master's, thesis optional, internship, practicum, or thesis. *Entrance requirements:* For master's, GRE or MAT (if GPA is below 2.75). Additional exam requirements/recommendations for international students: Required—TOEFL (minimum score 560 paper-based; 220 computer-based); Recommended—IELTS (minimum score 6). *Application deadline:* For fall admission, 3/1 for international students; for spring admission, 7/1 for international students. Applications are processed on a rolling basis. Application fee: $30. Electronic applications accepted. *Expenses:* Tuition, state resident: full-time $6430; part-time $357 per credit. Tuition, nonresident: full-time $10,288; part-time $572 per credit. Required fees: $1127; $38 per credit. One-time fee: $44 part-time. *Financial support:* In 2008–09, 3 research assistantships with full tuition reimbursements (averaging $5,000 per year) were awarded; career-related internships or fieldwork, scholarships/grants, unspecified assistantships, and resident hall directors, student payroll positions also available. Support available to part-time students. Financial award application deadline: 3/1; financial award applicants required to submit FAFSA. *Unit head:* Dr. John Lemmon, Chairperson, 717-477-1558, Fax: 717-477-4087, E-mail: jhlemm@ship.edu. *Application contact:* Renee Payne, Associate Dean of Graduate Admissions, 717-477-1231, Fax: 717-477-4016, E-mail: rmpayn@ship.edu.

Simon Fraser University, Graduate Studies, Faculty of Arts and Social Sciences, School of Criminology, Burnaby, BC V5A 1S6, Canada. Offers MA, PhD. *Degree requirements:* For master's, thesis; for doctorate, thesis/dissertation. *Entrance requirements:* For master's, minimum GPA of 3.0; for doctorate, minimum GPA of 3.5. Additional exam requirements/recommendations for international students: Required—TOEFL or IELTS. *Faculty research:* Media and crime, feminist jurisprudence, policy evaluation, penology, terrorism.

Southeast Missouri State University, School of Graduate Studies, Department of Criminal Justice and Sociology, Cape Girardeau, MO 63701-4799. Offers MS. Part-time and evening/weekend programs available. *Faculty:* 5 full-time (0 women). *Students:* 8 full-time (6 women), 41 part-time (24 women); includes 7 minority (4 African Americans, 1 American Indian/Alaska Native, 2 Hispanic Americans). Average age 32. 45 applicants, 93% accepted. In 2008, 6 master's awarded. *Degree requirements:* For master's, comprehensive exam (for some programs), thesis or alternative. *Entrance requirements:* For master's, minimum undergraduate GPA of 2.5. Additional exam requirements/recommendations for international students: Required—TOEFL (minimum score 550 paper-based; 213 computer-based); Recommended—IELTS (minimum score 6). *Application deadline:* For fall admission, 8/1 for domestic students, 7/1 for international students; for spring admission, 11/21 for domestic students, 11/1 for international students. Applications are processed on a rolling basis. Application fee: $25 ($100 for international students). Electronic applications accepted. *Expenses:* Tuition, area resident: Part-time $213.30 per credit hour. Tuition, state resident: part-time $213.30 per credit hour. Tuition, nonresident: part-time $393.30 per credit hour. Required fees: $23.70 per credit hour. *Financial support:* In 2008–09, 6 students received support, including 3 research assistantships with full tuition reimbursements available (averaging $7,600 per year), 3 teaching assistantships with full tuition reimbursements available (averaging $7,600 per year); unspecified assistantships also available. Financial award applicants required to submit FAFSA. *Unit head:* Dr. John Wade, Chairperson and Program Coordinator, 573-651-2541, E-mail: jwade@semo.edu. *Application contact:* Marsha L. Arant, Senior Administrative Assistant, School of Graduate Studies, 573-651-2192, Fax: 573-651-2001, E-mail: marant@semo.edu.

Southern Illinois University Carbondale, Graduate School, College of Liberal Arts, Administration of Justice Program, Carbondale, IL 62901-4701. Offers MA. *Degree requirements:* For master's, thesis optional. *Entrance requirements:* For master's, GRE General Test, minimum GPA of 2.7. Additional exam requirements/recommendations for international students: Required—TOEFL. *Faculty research:* Corrections, criminology, law enforcement, crime prevention, victims of crime.

Southern University and Agricultural and Mechanical College, Graduate School, Nelson Mandela School of Public Policy and Urban Affairs, Department of Criminal Justice, Baton Rouge, LA 70813. Offers MS. *Entrance requirements:* Additional exam requirements/recommendations for international students: Required—TOEFL (minimum score 525 paper-based; 193 computer-based).

Southwestern College, Professional Studies Programs, Wichita, KS 67207. Offers business administration (MBA); leadership (MS); management (MS); security administration (MS); specialized ministries (MA). Part-time and evening/weekend programs available. Postbaccalaureate distance learning degree programs offered (minimal on-campus study). *Faculty:* 2 full-time (0 women), 25 part-time/adjunct (12 women). *Students:* 100 full-time (36 women), 84 part-time (40 women); includes 27 minority (17 African Americans, 1 Asian American or Pacific Islander, 9 Hispanic Americans). Average age 37. 48 applicants, 100% accepted, 39 enrolled. In 2008, 64 master's awarded. *Degree requirements:* For master's, practicum/capstone project. *Entrance requirements:* For master's, baccalaureate degree; minimum GPA of 2.5, 3.0 for MBA. *Application deadline:* Applications are processed on a rolling basis. Application fee: $0. Electronic applications accepted. *Expenses:* Tuition: Full-time $6970; part-time $387 per credit. Tuition and fees vary according to class time, course load, campus/location and program. *Financial support:* In 2008–09, 133 students received support. Tuition waivers (partial) and unspecified assistantships available. Financial award application deadline: 4/1; financial award applicants required to submit FAFSA. *Unit head:* Gail Cullen, Director of Academic Affairs, 888-684-5335 Ext. 203, Fax: 316-688-5218, E-mail: gail.cullen@sckans.edu. *Application contact:* Gail Cullen, Director of Academic Affairs, 888-684-5335 Ext. 203, Fax: 316-688-5218, E-mail: gail.cullen@sckans.edu.

Suffolk University, College of Arts and Sciences, Program in Crime and Justice Studies, Boston, MA 02108-2770. Offers MSCJS, MSCJS/JD, MSCJS/MPA, MSCJS/MSMHC. Part-time programs available. *Entrance requirements:* For master's, statement of professional goals, official transcripts, 2 letters of recommendation, resumé. Additional exam requirements/recommendations for international students: Required—TOEFL (minimum score 550 paper-based; 213 computer-based; 80 iBT). Electronic applications accepted. *Expenses:* Contact institution. *Faculty research:* Restorative justice, anti-gang initiative, healthcare for female ex-offenders, violence against women, juvenile justice and the courts.

Sul Ross State University, School of Professional Studies, Department of Criminal Justice, Alpine, TX 79832. Offers MS. *Entrance requirements:* For master's, GRE General Test, minimum GPA of 2.5 in last 60 hours of undergraduate work.

Tarleton State University, College of Graduate Studies, College of Liberal and Fine Arts, Department of Social Work, Sociology, and Criminal Justice, Stephenville, TX 76402. Offers criminal justice (MCJ). Part-time and evening/weekend programs available. *Faculty:* 6 full-time (2 women). *Students:* 5 full-time (2 women), 6 part-time (4 women); includes 4 minority (3 African Americans, 1 Hispanic American). Average age 32. 9 applicants, 67% accepted, 3 enrolled. In 2008, 10 master's awarded. *Degree requirements:* For master's, comprehensive exam (for some programs), thesis optional. *Entrance requirements:* For master's, GRE General Test, minimum GPA of 3.0. Additional exam requirements/recommendations for international students: Required—TOEFL (minimum score 550 paper-based; 213 computer-based; 80 iBT). *Application deadline:* For fall admission, 8/5 priority date for domestic students; for spring admission, 12/1 for domestic students. Applications are processed on a rolling basis. Application fee: $30 ($130 for international students). Electronic applications accepted. *Expenses:* Tuition, area resident: Full-time $2853; part-time $158.50 per credit hour. Tuition, state resident: full-time $2853; part-time $158.50 per credit hour. Tuition, nonresident: full-time $7551; part-time $419.50 per credit hour. Required fees: $1040; $42 per credit hour. $124 per semester. Tuition and fees vary according to course load and campus/location. *Financial support:* In 2008–09, 1 research assistantship (averaging $12,000 per year) was awarded; career-related internships or fieldwork and Federal Work-Study also available. Support available to part-time students. Financial award application deadline: 5/1; financial award applicants required to submit FAFSA. *Unit head:* Kelli Styron, Department Head and Associate Professor, 254-968-9024, Fax: 254-

Criminal Justice and Criminology

Tarleton State University *(continued)*
968-9288, E-mail: styron@tarleton.edu. *Application contact:* Information Contact, 254-968-9104, Fax: 254-968-9670, E-mail: gradoffice@tarleton.edu.

Temple University, Graduate School, College of Liberal Arts, Department of Criminal Justice, Philadelphia, PA 19122-6096. Offers MA, PhD. Part-time programs available. Terminal master's awarded for partial completion of doctoral program. *Degree requirements:* For master's, thesis optional; for doctorate, thesis/dissertation, qualifying exams. *Entrance requirements:* For master's, GRE General Test, minimum GPA of 3.0; for doctorate, GRE General Test. Additional exam requirements/recommendations for international students: Required—TOEFL (minimum score 550 paper-based; 213 computer-based; 79 iBT). Electronic applications accepted. *Faculty research:* Criminal justice policy formulation, courts, correctional alternatives, community crime prevention, juvenile justice.

Tennessee State University, The School of Graduate Studies and Research, College of Arts and Sciences, Department of Criminal Justice, Nashville, TN 37209-1561. Offers MCJ. *Faculty:* 3 full-time (1 woman), 3 part-time/adjunct (2 women). *Students:* 2 full-time (both women), 40 part-time (27 women); includes 30 minority (all African Americans). Average age 32. 35 applicants, 60% accepted, 14 enrolled. In 2008, 1 master's awarded. *Degree requirements:* For master's, thesis. *Entrance requirements:* For master's, GRE General Test or MAT. *Application deadline:* For fall admission, 4/1 priority date for domestic and international students. Applications are processed on a rolling basis. Application fee: $25. Electronic applications accepted. *Financial support:* Unspecified assistantships available. *Unit head:* Dr. Deborah Burris-Kitchen, Head, 615-963-5571, E-mail: dburrisp-kitchen@tnstate.edu. *Application contact:* Deborah Chisom, Director of Graduate Admissions, 615-963-5962, Fax: 615-963-5963, E-mail: dchiscom@tnstate.edu.

Texas A&M International University, Office of Graduate Studies and Research, College of Arts and Sciences, Department of Behavioral, Applied Sciences, and Criminal Justice, Laredo, TX 78041-1900. Offers counseling psychology (MACP); criminal justice (MS); psychology (MS); sociology (MA). *Degree requirements:* For master's, thesis (for some programs). *Entrance requirements:* For master's, GRE General Test. Additional exam requirements/recommendations for international students: Required—TOEFL (minimum score 550 paper-based; 213 computer-based).

Texas Southern University, Graduate School, School of Public Affairs, Program in Administration of Justice, Houston, TX 77004-4584. Offers MS, PhD. *Faculty:* 3 full-time (0 women), 1 (woman) part-time/adjunct. *Students:* 15 full-time (5 women), 14 part-time (7 women); includes 23 African Americans, 1 Asian American or Pacific Islander, 2 Hispanic Americans, 2 international. Average age 38. 25 applicants, 92% accepted, 22 enrolled. Application fee: $50 ($75 for international students). *Expenses:* Tuition, area resident: Full-time $1912; part-time $96 per credit hour. Tuition, state resident: full-time $1912; part-time $96 per credit hour. Tuition, nonresident: full-time $6302; part-time $343 per credit hour. Required fees: $3542. *Financial support:* In 2008–09, 1 research assistantship (averaging $14,000 per year) was awarded; teaching assistantships. *Unit head:* Dr. Daniel Abeyie, Chair, 713-313-4808, E-mail: georgesabeyide@tsu.edu. *Application contact:* Pinkie Cotton, Administrative Assistant, 713-313-7311, E-mail: cotton_pe@tsu.edu.

Texas State University–San Marcos, Graduate School, College of Applied Arts, Department of Criminal Justice, San Marcos, TX 78666. Offers MSCJ. Part-time and evening/weekend programs available. *Degree requirements:* For master's, comprehensive exam. *Entrance requirements:* For master's, minimum GPA of 2.75 in last 60 hours of course work. Additional exam requirements/recommendations for international students: Required—TOEFL (minimum score 550 paper-based; 213 computer-based). Electronic applications accepted. *Faculty research:* Workplace violence, ethics, psychological profiling, tactical law enforcement, comparative justice systems.

Texas State University–San Marcos, Graduate School, Interdisciplinary Studies Program in Criminal Justice, San Marcos, TX 78666. Offers MSIS. Part-time and evening/weekend programs available. *Degree requirements:* For master's, comprehensive exam.

Tiffin University, Program in Business Administration, Tiffin, OH 44883-2161. Offers general management (MBA); leadership (MBA); safety and security management (MBA); sports management (MBA). *Accreditation:* ACBSP. Part-time and evening/weekend programs available. Postbaccalaureate distance learning degree programs offered (no on-campus study). *Entrance requirements:* For master's, minimum undergraduate GPA of 2.5, work experience. Additional exam requirements/recommendations for international students: Required—TOEFL (minimum score 550 paper-based; 213 computer-based). Electronic applications accepted. *Faculty research:* Small business, executive development operations, research and statistical analysis, market research, management information systems.

Tiffin University, Program in Criminal Justice, Tiffin, OH 44883-2161. Offers crime analysis (MSCJ); criminal behavior (MSCJ); forensic psychology (MSCJ); homeland security administration (MSCJ); justice administration (MSCJ). Part-time and evening/weekend programs available. Postbaccalaureate distance learning degree programs offered (no on-campus study). *Degree requirements:* For master's, thesis optional. *Entrance requirements:* For master's, minimum undergraduate GPA of 2.5, work experience. Additional exam requirements/recommendations for international students: Required—TOEFL (minimum score 550 paper-based; 213 computer-based). Electronic applications accepted. *Faculty research:* Terrorism, intelligence, homeland security, guns and crime.

Trine University, Program in Criminal Justice, Angola, IN 46703-1764. Offers MS.

Troy University, Graduate School, College of Arts and Sciences, Program in Criminal Justice, Troy, AL 36082. Offers administration of criminal justice (MS). Part-time and evening/weekend programs available. *Degree requirements:* For master's, comprehensive exam, thesis optional. *Entrance requirements:* For master's, GRE General Test, MAT, minimum GPA of 2.5. Additional exam requirements/recommendations for international students: Required—TOEFL (minimum score 523 paper-based; 200 computer-based). Electronic applications accepted. *Faculty research:* Crime victims, criminal justice personnel issues, disability issues in criminal justice.

TUI University, College of Business Administration, Program in Business Administration, Cypress, CA 90630. Offers business administration (PhD); conflict and negotiation management (MBA); criminal justice administration (MBA); entrepreneurship (MBA); finance (MBA); general management (MBA); human resource management (MBA); information technology management (MBA); international business (MBA); logistics management (MBA); public management (MBA); strategic leadership (MBA). Part-time and evening/weekend programs available. Postbaccalaureate distance learning degree programs offered (no on-campus study). *Degree requirements:* For doctorate, comprehensive exam, thesis/dissertation, defense of dissertation. *Entrance requirements:* For master's, minimum GPA of 2.5 (students with GPA 3.0 or greater may transfer up to 30% of graduate level credits); for doctorate, minimum GPA of 3.4, curriculum vitae, course work in research methods or statistics. Additional exam requirements/recommendations for international students: Required—TOEFL. Electronic applications accepted.

Universidad del Este, Graduate School, Carolina, PR 00983. Offers accounting (MBA); adult education (M Ed); agribusiness (MBA); bilingual education (M Ed); criminal justice and criminology (MA); early education (M Ed); elementary education (M Ed); human resources (MBA); information and virtual business technology (MBA); information security management (MBA); management (MBA); public policy (MPA); social work (MA), including clinical social work; special education (M Ed); strategic leadership (MBA); teaching English (M Ed); teaching Spanish (M Ed).

Universidad del Turabo, Graduate Programs, School of Social Sciences and Humanities, Programs in Public Affairs, Program in Criminal Justice Studies, Gurabo, PR 00778-3030. Offers MPA. *Entrance requirements:* For master's, GRE, EXADEP, interview.

Université de Montréal, Faculty of Arts and Sciences, School of Criminology, Montréal, QC H3C 3J7, Canada. Offers M Sc, PhD. *Faculty:* 24 full-time (6 women). *Students:* 69 full-time (56 women), 132 part-time (102 women). 143 applicants, 48% accepted, 62 enrolled. In 2008, 28 master's, 5 doctorates awarded. Terminal master's awarded for partial completion of doctoral program. *Degree requirements:* For master's, thesis; for doctorate, thesis/dissertation, general exam. *Entrance requirements:* For master's, B Sc in criminology or the equivalent; for doctorate, M Sc in criminology or equivalent. *Application deadline:* For fall admission, 2/1 for domestic students. Applications are processed on a rolling basis. Application fee: $100. Electronic applications accepted. *Financial support:* Fellowships, research assistantships, teaching assistantships, career-related internships or fieldwork available. Financial award application deadline: 3/15. *Faculty research:* Criminal behavior, criminality, prison population, victims of crime, female offender. *Unit head:* Marie-Marthe Cousineau, Chairman, 514-343-7322, Fax: 514-343-5650, E-mail: mm.cousineau@umontreal.ca. *Application contact:* Jo-Anne Wemmers, Graduate Student Affairs for the M Sc, 514-343-6111 Ext. 4864, Fax: 514-343-5650, E-mail: jo-anne.m.wemmers@umontreal.ca.

University at Albany, State University of New York, School of Criminal Justice, Albany, NY 12222-0001. Offers MA, PhD, MSW/MA. Part-time programs available. *Degree requirements:* For doctorate, thesis/dissertation. *Entrance requirements:* For master's and doctorate, GRE General Test. Additional exam requirements/recommendations for international students: Required—TOEFL (minimum score 550 paper-based; 213 computer-based). Electronic applications accepted. *Faculty research:* Causes of delinquency, comparative policing, world crime data, correctional policy, family violence.

The University of Alabama, Graduate School, College of Arts and Sciences, Department of Criminal Justice, Tuscaloosa, AL 35487. Offers MS. Part-time programs available. *Faculty:* 7 full-time (5 women). *Students:* 20 full-time (14 women), 7 part-time (5 women); includes 8 minority (6 African Americans, 1 Asian American or Pacific Islander, 1 Hispanic American). Average age 26. 23 applicants, 83% accepted, 13 enrolled. In 2008, 2 master's awarded. *Degree requirements:* For master's, comprehensive exam, thesis optional, thesis or policy and practice course. *Entrance requirements:* For master's, GRE. Additional exam requirements/recommendations for international students: Required—TOEFL. *Application deadline:* For fall admission, 3/1 priority date for domestic and international students; for winter admission, 11/1 priority date for domestic and international students. Applications are processed on a rolling basis. Application fee: $30. Electronic applications accepted. *Expenses:* Tuition, area resident: Full-time $6400. Tuition, state resident: full-time $6400. Tuition, nonresident: full-time $18,000. *Financial support:* In 2008–09, 1 fellowship (averaging $1,500 per year), 11 teaching assistantships with partial tuition reimbursements (averaging $5,145 per year) were awarded; institutionally sponsored loans, health care benefits, and unspecified assistantships also available. Financial award application deadline: 3/15. *Faculty research:* Domestic violence, AIDS research, youth and violence, gender crime, drugs and alcohol abuse, crime prevention. Total annual research expenditures: $13,562. *Unit head:* Dr. Ida Johnson, PhD, Interim Chair and Professor, 205-348-7795, Fax: 205-348-7178, E-mail: ijohnson@ua.edu. *Application contact:* Dr. David R. Forde, Professor, 205-348-7795, Fax: 205-348-7178, E-mail: drforde@ua.edu.

The University of Alabama at Birmingham, School of Social and Behavioral Sciences, Department of Justice Sciences, Birmingham, AL 35294. Offers criminal justice (MSCJ); forensic science (MSFS). Evening/weekend programs available. *Degree requirements:* For master's, thesis or alternative. *Entrance requirements:* For master's, GRE General Test or MAT. Electronic applications accepted.

The University of Alabama in Huntsville, School of Graduate Studies, Interdisciplinary Studies, Interdisciplinary Program in Information Assurance, Huntsville, AL 35899. Offers information assurance and cybersecurity (Certificate). Part-time and evening/weekend programs available. *Faculty:* 2 full-time (0 women), 2 part-time/adjunct (0 women). *Students:* 1 full-time (0 women), 13 part-time (3 women); includes 4 minority (2 African Americans, 1 American Indian/Alaska Native, 1 Hispanic American). Average age 38. 12 applicants, 67% accepted, 7 enrolled. In 2008, 12 Certificates awarded. *Entrance requirements:* For degree, GMAT, minimum GPA of 3.0. Additional exam requirements/recommendations for international students: Required—TOEFL (minimum score 550 paper-based; 213 computer-based; 62 iBT). *Application deadline:* For fall admission, 7/15 for domestic students, 4/1 for international students; for spring admission, 11/30 for domestic students, 9/1 for international students. Applications are processed on a rolling basis. Application fee: $40 ($50 for international students). Electronic applications accepted. *Expenses:* Tuition, area resident: Full-time $5214; part-time $323 per credit hour. Tuition, state resident: full-time $5214; part-time $323 per credit hour. Tuition, nonresident: full-time $11,444; part-time $705 per credit hour. Required fees: $540; $120 per semester. Tuition and fees vary according to course load. *Financial support:* Career-related internships or fieldwork, Federal Work-Study, institutionally sponsored loans, scholarships/grants, health care benefits, and unspecified assistantships available. Support available to part-time students. Financial award application deadline: 4/1; financial award applicants required to submit FAFSA. *Unit head:* Dr. Debra Moriarity, Dean of Graduate Studies, 256-824-6002, Fax: 256-824-6405, E-mail: deangrad@uah.edu. *Application contact:* Dr. Brent Wren, College of Business Administration Director of Graduate Programs, 256-824-6681, Fax: 256-824-7572, E-mail: brent.wren@uah.edu.

University of Alaska Fairbanks, College of Liberal Arts, Department of Justice, Fairbanks, AK 99775-6120. Offers MA. Part-time programs available. Postbaccalaureate distance learning degree programs offered (no on-campus study). *Faculty:* 1 full-time (0 women). *Students:* 18 part-time (8 women); includes 3 minority (2 American Indian/Alaska Native, 1 Hispanic American). Average age 36. 11 applicants, 91% accepted, 9 enrolled. In 2008, 7 master's awarded. *Degree requirements:* For master's, comprehensive exam, thesis or alternative, oral defense. *Entrance requirements:* Additional exam requirements/recommendations for international students: Required—TOEFL (minimum score 550 paper-based; 213 computer-based; 80 iBT). *Application deadline:* For fall admission, 6/1 for domestic students, 3/1 for international students; for spring admission, 10/15 for domestic students, 9/1 for international students. Applications are processed on a rolling basis. Application fee: $60. Electronic applications accepted. *Expenses:* Tuition, area resident: Full-time $5418; part-time $301 per credit. Tuition, state resident: full-time $5418; part-time $301 per credit. Tuition, nonresident: full-time $11,070; part-time $615 per credit. Required fees: $849; $25 per credit. $78 per semester. Tuition and fees vary according to course load and reciprocity agreements. *Financial support:* Federal Work-Study, scholarships/grants, and health care benefits available. Support available to part-time students. Financial award application deadline: 7/1; financial award applicants required to submit FAFSA. *Faculty research:* Substantive and procedural law, native Alaskans imprisoned in the Alaska State Department of Corrections, school violence, substance abuse in juveniles, community justice. *Unit head:* Dr. David M. Blurton, Department Chair, 907-474-5500, Fax: 907-474-6510, E-mail: fyjust@uaf.edu. *Application contact:* Dr. David M. Blurton, Department Chair, 907-474-5500, Fax: 907-474-6510, E-mail: fyjust@uaf.edu.

University of Alberta, Faculty of Graduate Studies and Research, Department of Sociology, Edmonton, AB T6G 2E1, Canada. Offers criminal justice (MA); demography (MA, PhD); sociology (MA, PhD). Part-time programs available. *Degree requirements:* For master's, thesis (for some programs); for doctorate, thesis/dissertation. *Faculty research:* Criminology, knowledge and culture, methods and theory, population studies, stratification.

University of Arkansas at Little Rock, Graduate School, College of Professional Studies, Department of Criminal Justice, Little Rock, AR 72204-1099. Offers MA, MS. MS program is by distance education. Part-time and evening/weekend programs available. *Degree requirements:* For master's, thesis defense or written comprehensive exam. *Entrance requirements:* For master's, GRE General Test or MAT, interview, minimum GPA of 2.75. *Faculty research:* Dissemination and analysis of behavioral science knowledge, leadership and managerial skills, philosophy of individual rights and humane treatment.

University of Baltimore, Graduate School, The Yale Gordon College of Liberal Arts, Division of Criminology, Criminal Justice, and Social Policy, Baltimore, MD 21201-5779. Offers criminal justice (MS); JD/MS. Part-time and evening/weekend programs available. *Faculty:* 5 full-time (1 woman), 7 part-time/adjunct (1 woman). *Students:* 9 full-time (7 women), 61 part-time (43 women); includes 37 minority (36 African Americans, 1 Asian American or Pacific Islander), 2 international. Average age 28. 77 applicants, 48% accepted, 27 enrolled. In 2008, 19 master's awarded. *Degree requirements:* For master's, thesis or alternative. *Entrance requirements:* For master's, interview, minimum GPA of 2.8. Additional exam requirements/recommendations for international students: Required—TOEFL (minimum score 550 paper-based; 213 computer-based). *Application deadline:* For fall admission, 8/1 priority date for domestic students, 6/1 for international students; for spring admission, 12/1 for domestic students, 11/1 for international students. Applications are processed on a rolling basis. Application fee: $30. Electronic applications accepted. *Expenses:* Tuition, state resident: part-time $568 per credit. Tuition, nonresident: part-time $824 per credit. Required fees: $250 per semester. *Financial support:* In 2008–09, 8 research assistantships were awarded; fellowships, career-related internships or fieldwork and Federal Work-Study also available. Support available to part-time students. Financial award application deadline: 4/1; financial award applicants required to submit FAFSA. *Faculty research:* Drugs and violence, police and community policing, women and crime, victimization, correction in community. Total annual research expenditures: $2 million. *Unit head:* Dr. Heather Pfeifer, Program Director, 410-837-5292, E-mail: hpfeifer@ubalt.edu. *Application contact:* Kevin Nies, Assistant Director, Office of Graduate Admission, 410-837-6565, E-mail: knies@ubalt.edu.

University of California, Irvine, Office of Graduate Studies, School of Social Ecology, Department of Criminology, Law and Society, Irvine, CA 92697. Offers MAS, PhD. *Degree requirements:* For doctorate, thesis/dissertation, research project. *Entrance requirements:* For master's and doctorate, GRE General Test, minimum GPA of 3.0. Additional exam requirements/recommendations for international students: Required—TOEFL (minimum score 550 paper-based; 213 computer-based). Electronic applications accepted. *Faculty research:* White-collar and corporate crime; immigration, the poor, homelessness, and governmental regulation; sentencing, community corrections, and diversion; mathematical and scientific evidence in jury trials; legal and criminological theory development.

University of Central Florida, College of Health and Public Affairs, Department of Criminal Justice and Legal Studies, Orlando, FL 32816. Offers corrections leadership (Certificate); crime analysis (Certificate); criminal justice (MS); juvenile justice leadership (Certificate); police leadership (Certificate). Part-time and evening/weekend programs available. *Faculty:* 35 full-time (13 women), 37 part-time/adjunct (6 women). *Students:* 51 full-time (37 women), 109 part-time (54 women); includes 44 minority (22 African Americans, 7 Asian Americans or Pacific Islanders, 15 Hispanic Americans), 2 international. In 2008, 91 master's, 29 other advanced degrees awarded. *Degree requirements:* For master's, thesis or alternative. *Entrance requirements:* For master's, GRE General Test, minimum GPA of 3.0. Additional exam requirements/recommendations for international students: Required—TOEFL. *Application deadline:* For fall admission, 7/15 for domestic students; for spring admission, 4/15 for domestic students. Electronic applications accepted. *Expenses:* Tuition, area resident: Full-time $6816; part-time $284 per credit. Tuition, state resident: full-time $6816; part-time $1076 per credit. Tuition, nonresident: full-time $25,824. Required fees: $216; $9 per credit. *Financial support:* In 2008–09, 4 fellowships with partial tuition reimbursements (averaging $10,000 per year), 5 research assistantships with partial tuition reimbursements (averaging $6,400 per year) were awarded; teaching assistantships with partial tuition reimbursements, career-related internships or fieldwork, Federal Work-Study, institutionally sponsored loans, tuition waivers (partial), and unspecified assistantships also available. Financial award application deadline: 3/1; financial award applicants required to submit FAFSA. *Unit head:* Dr. Robert Langworthy, Chair, 407-823-5929, E-mail: rlangwor@mail.ucf.edu. *Application contact:* Dr. Robert Langworthy, Chair, 407-823-5929, E-mail: rlangwor@mail.ucf.edu.

University of Central Missouri, The Graduate School, College of Health and Human Services, Department of Criminal Justice, Warrensburg, MO 64093. Offers criminal justice (MS), including administration of justice, administration/corrections, administrative/juvenile justices, corrections. Part-time programs available. *Degree requirements:* For master's, thesis or comprehensive exam. *Entrance requirements:* For master's, GRE General Test, minimum GPA of 2.75, 15 hours of course work in criminal justice. Additional exam requirements/recommendations for international students: Required—TOEFL (minimum score 500 paper-based; 173 computer-based). *Faculty research:* Restorative justice, sexual assault and the criminal justice system, police accountability, evaluation and court house shootings, juvenile justice, correctional reentry initiative, crime.

University of Central Missouri, The Graduate School, College of Health and Human Services, Department of Safety Sciences, Warrensburg, MO 64093. Offers fire science (MS); human services/public services (Ed S); industrial hygiene (MS); industrial safety management (MS); loss control (MS); occupational safety management (MS); public safety (MS); security (MS); transportation safety (MS). *Accreditation:* ABET (one or more programs are accredited). Part-time programs available. *Degree requirements:* For master's, comprehensive exam. *Entrance requirements:* For master's, GRE General Test, minimum GPA of 2.5, 15 hours of course work in related area; for Ed S, master's degree in related field. Additional exam requirements/recommendations for international students: Required—TOEFL (minimum score 500 paper-based; 173 computer-based).

University of Central Oklahoma, College of Graduate Studies and Research, College of Liberal Arts, Department of Sociology, Criminal Justice and Substance Abuse Studies, Edmond, OK 73034-5209. Offers criminal justice management and administration (MA). Part-time programs available. *Entrance requirements:* Additional exam requirements/recommendations for international students: Required—TOEFL (minimum score 550 paper-based; 213 computer-based). Electronic applications accepted. *Faculty research:* Gender issues, violent offenders.

University of Cincinnati, Graduate School, College of Education, Criminal Justice, and Human Services, Division of Criminal Justice, Cincinnati, OH 45221. Offers MS, PhD. Part-time programs available. Postbaccalaureate distance learning degree programs offered (no on-campus study). *Degree requirements:* For master's, thesis or alternative; for doctorate, thesis/dissertation. *Entrance requirements:* For master's, GRE or MAT, minimum GPA of 3.0; for doctorate, minimum GPA of 3.5. Additional exam requirements/recommendations for international students: Required—TOEFL (minimum score 550 paper-based), OEPT 3. Electronic applications accepted.

University of Colorado at Colorado Springs, Graduate School, Graduate School of Public Affairs, Colorado Springs, CO 80933-7150. Offers criminal justice (MCJ); public administration (MPA). Part-time and evening/weekend programs available. *Faculty:* 3 full-time (1 woman), 25 part-time/adjunct (15 women). *Students:* 40 full-time (23 women), 38 part-time (23 women); includes 10 minority (2 Asian Americans or Pacific Islanders, 8 Hispanic Americans). Average age 35. 34 applicants, 91% accepted, 24 enrolled. In 2008, 32 master's awarded. *Degree requirements:* For master's, internship (if no experience), capstone project. *Entrance requirements:* For master's, GRE General Test, GMAT, LSAT, minimum GPA of 3.0. *Application deadline:* For fall admission, 6/1 priority date for domestic students; for spring admission, 11/1 for domestic students. Applications are processed on a rolling basis. Application fee: $60 ($75 for international students). *Expenses:* Contact institution. *Financial support:* Career-related internships or fieldwork and Federal Work-Study available. Support available to part-time students. *Unit head:* Dr. Terry Schwartz, Dean, 719-255-4047, Fax: 719-255-4183, E-mail: tschwart@uccs.edu. *Application contact:* Mary Lou Kartis, Program Assistant, 719-255-4182, Fax: 719-255-4183, E-mail: mkartis@uccs.edu.

University of Colorado Denver, Graduate School of Public Affairs, Program in Criminal Justice, Denver, CO 80217-3364. Offers MCJ. Part-time and evening/weekend programs available. *Degree requirements:* For master's, comprehensive exam, thesis optional. *Entrance requirements:* For master's, GRE General Test, minimum GPA of 3.0. Additional exam requirements/recommendations for international students: Required—TOEFL (minimum score 500 paper-based).

University of Delaware, College of Arts and Sciences, Department of Sociology and Criminology, Newark, DE 19716. Offers criminology (MA, PhD); sociology (MA, PhD). *Degree requirements:* For master's, thesis; for doctorate, comprehensive exam, thesis/dissertation. *Entrance requirements:* For master's and doctorate, GRE, 3 letters of recommendation. Additional exam requirements/recommendations for international students: Required—TOEFL. Electronic applications accepted. *Faculty research:* Sex and gender, criminology/deviance, theory, methods, collective behavior.

University of Denver, University College, Denver, CO 80208. Offers applied communication (MAS, MPS, Certificate); computer information systems (MAS, Certificate); environmental policy and management (MAS, Certificate); geographic information systems (MAS, Certificate); human resource administration (MPS, Certificate); knowledge and information technologies (MAS); liberal studies (MLS, Certificate); modern languages (MLS, Certificate); organizational leadership (MPS, Certificate); security management (Certificate); technology management (MAS, Certificate), including 21st century strategic management (MAS), international markets (MAS), project management (MAS), research and development management (MAS); telecommunications (MAS, Certificate), including broadband (MAS), telecommunications management and policy (MAS), telecommunications technology (MAS), wireless networks (MAS). Part-time and evening/weekend programs available. Postbaccalaureate distance learning degree programs offered (no on-campus study). *Faculty:* 137 part-time/adjunct (55 women). *Students:* 28 full-time (15 women), 699 part-time (401 women); includes 129 minority (54 African Americans, 8 American Indian/Alaska Native, 22 Asian Americans or Pacific Islanders, 45 Hispanic Americans), 4 international. Average age 36. 845 applicants, 96% accepted, 326 enrolled. In 2008, 221 master's, 3 Certificates awarded. *Entrance requirements:* Additional exam requirements/recommendations for international students: Required—TOEFL (minimum score 550 paper-based; 213 computer-based). *Application deadline:* Applications are processed on a rolling basis. Application fee: $75. Electronic applications accepted. *Expenses:* Contact institution. *Financial support:* Applicants required to submit FAFSA. *Unit head:* Dr. James Davis, Dean, 303-871-2291, Fax: 303-871-4047, E-mail: jdavis@du.edu. *Application contact:* Information Contact, 303-871-3155.

University of Detroit Mercy, College of Liberal Arts and Education, Department of Criminal Justice and Human Services, Program in Criminal Justice Studies, Detroit, MI 48221. Offers MA. Part-time and evening/weekend programs available. *Degree requirements:* For master's, thesis or alternative. *Entrance requirements:* For master's, minimum GPA of 2.75. *Faculty research:* Socialization and social control, law and correction practices.

University of Detroit Mercy, College of Liberal Arts and Education, Department of Criminal Justice and Human Services, Program in Security Administration, Detroit, MI 48221. Offers MS. Part-time and evening/weekend programs available. *Degree requirements:* For master's, thesis or alternative. *Entrance requirements:* For master's, minimum GPA of 2.75. *Faculty research:* Physical information and personnel security.

University of Florida, Graduate School, College of Liberal Arts and Sciences, Department of Criminology, Law and Society, Gainesville, FL 32611. Offers criminology and law (MA, PhD); MA/JD; MA/PhD.

University of Great Falls, Graduate Studies, Program in Criminal Justice, Great Falls, MT 59405. Offers MSM. Part-time and evening/weekend programs available. *Degree requirements:* For master's, thesis optional. *Entrance requirements:* For master's, GRE General Test or MAT, 3 letters of recommendation. Additional exam requirements/recommendations for international students: Required—TOEFL (minimum score 500 paper-based; 205 computer-based). Electronic applications accepted. *Faculty research:* Delinquency, domestic violence law.

University of Guelph, Graduate Program Services, College of Social and Applied Human Sciences, Department of Criminology and Criminal Justice Policy, Guelph, ON N1G 2W1, Canada. Offers MA. *Degree requirements:* For master's, thesis or major paper. *Entrance requirements:* For master's, minimum B+ average during previous 2 years of coursework. Electronic applications accepted.

University of Guelph, Graduate Program Services, College of Social and Applied Human Sciences, Department of Sociology and Anthropology, Guelph, ON N1G 2W1, Canada. Offers anthropology (MA); crime and criminal justice policy (MA); sociology (MA, PhD). *Degree requirements:* For master's, thesis or major paper; for doctorate, comprehensive exam, thesis/dissertation. *Entrance requirements:* For master's, minimum B+ average during previous 2 years of course work, honors BA or equivalent; for doctorate, must have an MA in Sociology, must have 80% or higher in graduate level studies. Additional exam requirements/recommendations for international students: Required—TOEFL (minimum score 550 paper-based; 213 computer-based; 89 iBT), IELTS (minimum score 6.5), TOEFL or IELTS. Electronic applications accepted. *Faculty research:* Rural and development sociology; education, employment, and the workplace; race, ethnicity, and native studies; criminology and deviance; social psychology.

University of Houston–Clear Lake, School of Human Sciences and Humanities, Programs in Human Sciences, Houston, TX 77058-1098. Offers behavioral sciences (MA), including criminology, cross cultural studies, general psychology, sociology; clinical psychology (MA); criminology (MA); cross cultural studies (MA); family therapy (MA); fitness and human performance (MA); school psychology (MA). *Accreditation:* AAMFT/COAMFTE. Part-time and evening/weekend programs available. Postbaccalaureate distance learning degree programs offered (minimal on-campus study). *Degree requirements:* For master's, thesis or alternative. *Entrance requirements:* For master's, GRE General Test. Additional exam requirements/recommendations for international students: Required—TOEFL (minimum score 550 paper-based; 213 computer-based). Electronic applications accepted. *Faculty research:* Smoking cessation, adolescent sexuality, white collar crime, serial murder, human factors/human computer interaction.

University of Houston–Downtown, College of Public Service, Department of Criminal Justice, Houston, TX 77002-1001. Offers MS. Part-time and evening/weekend programs available. *Faculty:* 6 full-time (2 women). *Students:* 8 full-time (2 women), 53 part-time (27 women); includes 32 minority (13 African Americans, 2 Asian Americans or Pacific Islanders, 17 Hispanic Americans), 4 international. Average age 35. 27 applicants, 85% accepted, 19 enrolled. In 2008, 8 master's awarded. *Degree requirements:* For master's, thesis optional, thesis or project. *Entrance requirements:* For master's, GRE, MAT or GMAT, personal statement, 3 letters of recommendation. Additional exam requirements/recommendations for international students: Required—TOEFL (minimum score 550 paper-based; 213 computer-based; 79 iBT). *Application deadline:* For fall admission, 8/1 for domestic and international students; for spring admission, 11/15 for domestic and international students. Applications are processed on a rolling basis. Application fee: $35 ($60 for international students). Electronic applications accepted. *Expenses:* Tuition, area resident: Full-time $3060; part-time $170 per credit hour. Tuition, state resident: full-time $3060; part-time $170 per credit hour. Tuition, nonresident: full-time $7488; part-time $416 per credit hour. International tuition: $7570 full-time. Required fees: $854; $307 per term. Tuition and fees vary according to course load. *Financial support:* Federal Work-Study and scholarships/grants available. Financial award applicants required to submit FAFSA. *Faculty research:* Criminal justice education, issues in law enforcement, issues in security, adult probation, legal issues in prisons. *Unit head:* Dr. Clete Snell, Chair, 713-221-8943, Fax: 713-221-2726, E-mail: SnellC@uhd.edu. *Application contact:* Dr. Mark Kellar, Associate Professor and Graduate Coordinator, 713-221-8194, Fax: 713-226-5274, E-mail: kellarm@uhd.edu.

University of Houston–Downtown, College of Public Service, Master of Security Management for Executives Program, Houston, TX 77002-1001. Offers MSM. Part-time and evening/weekend programs available. *Faculty:* 4 full-time (2 women), 3 part-time/adjunct (0 women). *Students:* 26 full-time (3 women); includes 5 minority (4 African Americans, 1 Hispanic American). Average age 42. 19 applicants, 100% accepted, 15 enrolled. In 2008, 4 master's

Criminal Justice and Criminology

University of Houston–Downtown (continued)
awarded. *Degree requirements:* For master's, capstone project. *Entrance requirements:* For master's, letter of intent, 3 letters of recommendation from supervisors indicating probability of applicant's success in program, proof of three years of paid work experience with supervisory or managerial responsibilities. Additional exam requirements/recommendations for international students: Required—TOEFL (minimum score 550 paper-based; 213 computer-based; 80 iBT). *Application deadline:* For fall admission, 8/1 for domestic students, 5/1 for international students. Applications are processed on a rolling basis. Application fee: $35 ($60 for international students). Electronic applications accepted. *Expenses:* Tuition, area resident: Full-time $3060; part-time $170 per credit hour. Tuition, state resident: full-time $3060; part-time $170 per credit hour. Tuition, nonresident: full-time $7488; part-time $416 per credit hour. International tuition: $7570 full-time. Required fees: $854; $307 per term. Tuition and fees vary according to course load. *Financial support:* Federal Work-Study available. Financial award applicants required to submit FAFSA. *Unit head:* Dr. Beth Pelz, Dean, College of Public Service, 713-221-8194, Fax: 713-226-5274, E-mail: pelzb@uhd.edu. *Application contact:* Louis Evans, Assistant Dean, College of Public Service, 713-221-8194, Fax: 713-226-5274, E-mail: evansl@uhd.edu.

University of Illinois at Chicago, Graduate College, College of Liberal Arts and Sciences, Department of Criminal Justice, Chicago, IL 60607-7128. Offers MA, PhD. Evening/weekend programs available. *Degree requirements:* For master's, thesis. *Entrance requirements:* For master's, GRE General Test, minimum GPA of 3.0. Additional exam requirements/recommendations for international students: Required—TOEFL. Electronic applications accepted. *Faculty research:* Sentencing probation, police and court use of scientific evidence, community mediation and conflict resolution.

University of Louisiana at Monroe, Graduate School, College of Arts and Sciences, Program in Criminal Justice, Monroe, LA 71209-0001. Offers MA. Part-time and evening/weekend programs available. *Faculty:* 4 full-time (0 women). *Students:* 13 full-time (8 women), 14 part-time (8 women); includes 11 minority (all African Americans). Average age 28. In 2008, 5 master's awarded. *Degree requirements:* For master's, thesis (for some programs). *Entrance requirements:* For master's, GRE General Test, minimum GPA of 2.5. Additional exam requirements/recommendations for international students: Required—TOEFL (minimum score 500 paper-based; 173 computer-based; 61 iBT). *Application deadline:* For fall admission, 8/22 priority date for domestic students, 7/1 for international students; for winter admission, 12/12 priority date for domestic students; for spring admission, 1/17 for domestic students, 11/1 for international students. Applications are processed on a rolling basis. Application fee: $20 ($30 for international students). Electronic applications accepted. *Expenses:* Tuition, area resident: Full-time $2403; part-time $1202 per semester. Tuition, state resident: full-time $2403; part-time $1202 per semester. Tuition, nonresident: full-time $2403; part-time $1202 per semester. International tuition: $8352 full-time. Required fees: $1239.40; $141 per credit hour. *Financial support:* In 2008–09, 4 research assistantships with full tuition reimbursements (averaging $2,500 per year) were awarded; career-related internships or fieldwork, Federal Work-Study, and unspecified assistantships also available. Financial award application deadline: 4/1; financial award applicants required to submit FAFSA. *Unit head:* Dr. Robert D Hanser, Department Head, 318-342-1440, Fax: 318-342-1431, E-mail: hanser@ulm.edu. *Application contact:* Dr. Robert D Hanser, Department Head, 318-342-1440, Fax: 318-342-1431, E-mail: hanser@ulm.edu.

University of Louisville, Graduate School, College of Arts and Sciences, Department of Justice Administration, Louisville, KY 40292. Offers MS. Part-time and evening/weekend programs available. Postbaccalaureate distance learning degree programs offered (no on-campus study). *Faculty:* 13 full-time (4 women), 5 part-time/adjunct (2 women). *Students:* 15 full-time (11 women), 46 part-time (21 women); includes 7 African Americans, 2 American Indian/Alaska Native, 1 Asian American or Pacific Islander. Average age 34. 32 applicants, 81% accepted, 24 enrolled. In 2008, 23 master's awarded. *Degree requirements:* For master's, comprehensive exam (for some programs), thesis (for some programs), professional paper. *Entrance requirements:* For master's, GRE General Test, two letters of recommendation, and personal statement. Additional exam requirements/recommendations for international students: Required—TOEFL (minimum score 550 paper-based; 213 computer-based; 79 iBT). *Application deadline:* For fall admission, 7/1 priority date for domestic and international students; for spring admission, 11/15 priority date for domestic and international students. Applications are processed on a rolling basis. Application fee: $50. Electronic applications accepted. *Financial support:* In 2008–09, 5 students received support, including 5 research assistantships with full tuition reimbursements available (averaging $12,000 per year); health care benefits also available. Financial award application deadline: 8/1; financial award applicants required to submit FAFSA. *Faculty research:* Applied research, program evaluation and policy analysis in criminal justice; juvenile sex offender research; theoretical criminology; crime analysis; organizational and leadership management. Total annual research expenditures: $137,442. *Unit head:* Dr. Deborah G. Keeling, Chair, 502-852-6567, Fax: 502-852-0065, E-mail: dgwilson@louisville.edu. *Application contact:* Libby Leggett, Director, Graduate Admissions, 502-852-3101, Fax: 502-852-6536, E-mail: gradadm@louisville.edu.

University of Management and Technology, Program in Criminal Justice, Arlington, VA 22209. Offers MS.

University of Maryland, College Park, Graduate Studies, College of Behavioral and Social Sciences, Department of Criminology and Criminal Justice, College Park, MD 20742. Offers MA, PhD, JD/MA. Part-time and evening/weekend programs available. Terminal master's awarded for partial completion of doctoral program. *Degree requirements:* For master's, comprehensive exam, thesis optional; for doctorate, comprehensive exam, thesis/dissertation. *Entrance requirements:* For master's, GRE General Test, minimum GPA of 3.0, 3 letters of recommendation; for doctorate, GRE General Test. Additional exam requirements/recommendations for international students: Required—TOEFL. Electronic applications accepted. *Faculty research:* Theory, crime prevention, death penalty, criminal justice technology, policy.

University of Maryland Eastern Shore, Graduate Programs, Department of Criminal Justice, Princess Anne, MD 21853-1299. Offers criminology and criminal justice (MS). Part-time and evening/weekend programs available. *Degree requirements:* For master's, comprehensive exam, thesis optional. *Entrance requirements:* For master's, GRE General Test, interview. Additional exam requirements/recommendations for international students: Required—TOEFL (minimum score 213 computer-based; 80 iBT).

University of Massachusetts Lowell, College of Arts and Sciences, Department of Criminal Justice and Criminology, Lowell, MA 01854-2881. Offers MA. Part-time and evening/weekend programs available. *Degree requirements:* For master's, thesis optional. *Entrance requirements:* For master's, GRE General Test or MAT. Electronic applications accepted. *Faculty research:* Family violence, criminal justice management, corrections, policing, delinquency.

University of Memphis, Graduate School, College of Arts and Sciences, School of Urban Affairs and Public Policy, Department of Criminology and Criminal Justice, Memphis, TN 38152. Offers MA. Part-time programs available. *Faculty:* 5 full-time (2 women). *Students:* 9 full-time (5 women), 3 part-time (1 woman); includes 4 minority (all African Americans). Average age 30. 5 applicants, 100% accepted, 5 enrolled. In 2008, 4 master's awarded. *Degree requirements:* For master's, comprehensive exam, thesis optional. *Entrance requirements:* For master's, GRE General Test, minimum GPA of 3.0. *Application deadline:* For fall admission, 6/1 for domestic students; for spring admission, 11/1 for domestic students. Application fee: $35 ($60 for international students). *Expenses:* Tuition, area resident: Full-time $6242; part-time $330 per credit hour. Tuition, state resident: full-time $6242; part-time $330 per credit hour. Tuition, nonresident: full-time $17,828; part-time $815 per credit hour. Required fees: $1156. *Financial support:* Research assistantships with full tuition reimbursements, teaching assistantships with full tuition reimbursements, career-related internships or fieldwork, institutionally sponsored loans, and tuition waivers (partial) available. Financial award applicants required to submit FAFSA. *Faculty research:* Violence, crime prevention, crime analysis, survey research, crisis intervention. *Unit head:* Prof. W. Randolph, Dupont, Chair, 901-678-2737, Fax: 901-678-5279, E-mail: rdupont@memphis.edu. *Application contact:* Dr. K.B. Turner, Coordinator of Graduate Studies, 901-678-2737, Fax: 901-678-5279, E-mail: kbturner@memphis.edu.

University of Minnesota, Duluth, Graduate School, College of Liberal Arts, Department of Sociology/Anthropology, Program in Criminology, Duluth, MN 55812-2496. Offers MA. Part-time and evening/weekend programs available. *Degree requirements:* For master's, thesis or alternative. *Entrance requirements:* For master's, minimum GPA of 3.0, letter of recommendation, personal statement. Additional exam requirements/recommendations for international students: Required—TOEFL. *Faculty research:* Restorative justice, juvenile delinquency, social justice, program evaluation.

University of Missouri–Kansas City, College of Arts and Sciences, Department of Criminal Justice and Criminology, Kansas City, MO 64110-2499. Offers MS. Part-time and evening/weekend programs available. *Faculty:* 21 full-time (12 women), 1 (woman) part-time/adjunct. *Students:* 5 full-time (4 women), 25 part-time (20 women); includes 7 minority (5 African Americans, 1 Asian American or Pacific Islander, 1 Hispanic American). Average age 27. 11 applicants, 82% accepted, 8 enrolled. In 2008, 3 master's awarded. *Degree requirements:* For master's, thesis optional. *Entrance requirements:* For master's, GRE, minimum GPA of 3.0 in major, 2.7 overall. Additional exam requirements/recommendations for international students: Required—TOEFL (minimum score 550 paper-based; 213 computer-based; 80 iBT). *Application deadline:* For fall admission, 3/1 for domestic and international students; for spring admission, 11/1 for domestic and international students. Applications are processed on a rolling basis. Application fee: $45 ($50 for international students). Electronic applications accepted. *Expenses:* Tuition, state resident: full-time $5376; part-time $298.70 per credit hour. Tuition, nonresident: full-time $13,882; part-time $771.20 per credit hour. Required fees: $640.28; $34.65 per contact hour. $30 per semester. Tuition and fees vary according to course load and program. *Financial support:* In 2008–09, 4 teaching assistantships with full and partial tuition reimbursements (averaging $12,000 per year) were awarded; research assistantships with full tuition reimbursements, career-related internships or fieldwork, Federal Work-Study, institutionally sponsored loans, and tuition waivers (partial) also available. Support available to part-time students. Financial award application deadline: 3/1; financial award applicants required to submit FAFSA. *Faculty research:* Death penalty, community corrections, urban community and neighborhoods. Total annual research expenditures: $64,426. *Unit head:* Dr. Ken Novak, Chair, 816-235-1599, Fax: 816-235-5193, E-mail: novakk@umkc.edu. *Application contact:* Dr. Wayne L. Lucas, Graduate Advisor, 816-235-1598, Fax: 816-235-5193, E-mail: lucasw@umkc.edu.

University of Missouri–St. Louis, College of Arts and Sciences, Department of Criminology and Criminal Justice, St. Louis, MO 63121. Offers MA, PhD. *Faculty:* 15 full-time (7 women), 1 part-time/adjunct (0 women). *Students:* 30 full-time (20 women), 24 part-time (15 women); includes 5 minority (4 African Americans, 1 Hispanic American), 3 international. Average age 29. In 2008, 13 master's, 4 doctorates awarded. *Degree requirements:* For doctorate, thesis/dissertation. *Entrance requirements:* For doctorate, GRE General Test, writing sample, 3 letters of recommendation. Additional exam requirements/recommendations for international students: Required—TOEFL (minimum score 550 paper-based; 213 computer-based). *Application deadline:* For fall admission, 4/1 priority date for domestic and international students. Applications are processed on a rolling basis. Application fee: $35 ($40 for international students). Electronic applications accepted. *Expenses:* Tuition, area resident: Full-time $5377; part-time $298.70 per credit hour. Tuition, nonresident: full-time $13,381; part-time $472.50 per credit hour. Required fees: $4078; $52 per credit hour. *Financial support:* In 2008–09, 16 research assistantships with full and partial tuition reimbursements (averaging $14,000 per year), 4 teaching assistantships with full and partial tuition reimbursements (averaging $13,500 per year) were awarded; fellowships with full tuition reimbursements, career-related internships or fieldwork also available. Financial award applicants required to submit FAFSA. *Faculty research:* Crime control, criminological theory, juvenile delinquency, violence, drugs. *Unit head:* Dr. Richard Wright, Director of Graduate Studies, 314-516-5031, Fax: 314-516-5048, E-mail: surfer@umsl.edu. *Application contact:* 314-516-5458, Fax: 314-516-6996, E-mail: gradadm@umsl.edu.

The University of Montana, Graduate School, College of Arts and Sciences, Department of Sociology, Missoula, MT 59812-0002. Offers criminology (MA); rural and environmental change (MA); sociology (MA). *Entrance requirements:* For master's, GRE General Test. Additional exam requirements/recommendations for international students: Required—TOEFL. *Faculty research:* Housing, homelessness, hunger, infant mortality, work safety.

University of Nebraska at Omaha, Graduate Studies and Research, College of Public Affairs and Community Service, Department of Criminal Justice, Omaha, NE 68182. Offers MA, MS, PhD. Part-time and evening/weekend programs available. Terminal master's awarded for partial completion of doctoral program. *Degree requirements:* For master's, comprehensive exam, thesis (for some programs); for doctorate, comprehensive exam, thesis/dissertation. *Entrance requirements:* For master's, GRE General Test or MAT, previous course work in criminal justice, statistics, and research methods; minimum GPA of 3.0; for doctorate, GRE General Test, letters of recommendation, statement of intent. Additional exam requirements/recommendations for international students: Required—TOEFL (minimum score 550 paper-based; 213 computer-based; 80 iBT). Electronic applications accepted.

University of Nevada, Las Vegas, Graduate College, Greenspun College of Urban Affairs, Department of Criminal Justice, Las Vegas, NV 89154-5009. Offers MA. Part-time programs available. *Faculty:* 12 full-time (5 women). *Students:* 20 full-time (17 women), 18 part-time (10 women); includes 8 minority (4 African Americans, 2 Asian Americans or Pacific Islanders, 2 Hispanic Americans). Average age 29. 57 applicants, 54% accepted, 17 enrolled. In 2008, 11 master's awarded. *Degree requirements:* For master's, comprehensive exam (for some programs), thesis (for some programs). *Entrance requirements:* Additional exam requirements/recommendations for international students: Required—TOEFL (minimum score 550 paper-based; 213 computer-based; 80 iBT), IELTS (minimum score 7). *Application deadline:* For fall admission, 2/1 priority date for domestic and international students. Applications are processed on a rolling basis. Application fee: $60 ($75 for international students). Electronic applications accepted. *Expenses:* Tuition, state resident: full-time $1414; part-time $198 per credit. Tuition, nonresident: full-time $12,509; part-time $415.75 per credit. International tuition: $14,249 full-time. Required fees: $4 per credit. $252 per semester. Tuition and fees vary according to course load. *Financial support:* In 2008–09, 8 students received support, including 8 teaching assistantships with partial tuition reimbursements available (averaging $10,000 per year); research assistantships with partial tuition reimbursements available, institutionally sponsored loans, scholarships/grants, health care benefits, and unspecified assistantships also available. Financial award application deadline: 3/1. *Unit head:* Dr. Joel Lieberman, Chair/Associate Professor, 702-895-0013, Fax: 702-895-0252, E-mail: joel.lieberman@unlv.edu. *Application contact:* Graduate College Admissions Evaluator, 702-895-3320, Fax: 702-895-4180, E-mail: gradcollege@unlv.edu.

University of Nevada, Reno, Graduate School, College of Liberal Arts, School of Social Research and Justice Studies, Department of Criminal Justice, Reno, NV 89557. Offers MA. *Faculty:* 8 full-time (2 women). *Students:* 8 full-time (5 women), 10 part-time (9 women); includes 3 minority (2 African Americans, 1 Asian American or Pacific Islander). Average age 33. 10 applicants, 60% accepted, 5 enrolled. In 2008, 4 master's awarded. *Degree requirements:* For master's, comprehensive exam, thesis optional. *Entrance requirements:* For master's, GRE or LSAT, undergraduate degree in criminal justice with minimum GPA of 3.0. Additional exam requirements/recommendations for international students: Required—TOEFL (minimum score 500 paper-based; 173 computer-based; 61 iBT), IELTS (minimum score 6), TOFEL or IELTS. *Application deadline:* For fall admission, 3/31 for domestic students, 3/31 priority date for international students. Applications are processed on a rolling basis. Application fee: $60 ($95 for international students). Electronic applications accepted. *Expenses:* Tuition, state resident: full-time $1710; part-time $1140 per semester. Tuition, nonresident: full-time $7115. Required fees: $158 per semester. *Financial support:* In 2008–09, 2 teaching assistantships with partial tuition reimbursements (averaging $14,000 per year) were awarded; Federal Work-Study, institutionally sponsored loans, scholarships/grants, health care benefits, and unspecified assistantships also available. Financial award application deadline: 3/1; financial award applicants required to submit FAFSA. *Faculty research:* Criminal justice system, social policy interaction. *Unit head:* Dr. Timothy Griffin, Graduate Program Director, 775-784-9114, E-mail: tgriffin@unr.edu. *Application contact:* Michele Sandberg, Application Contact, 775-784-7026, Fax: 775-784-6064, E-mail: gradschool@unr.edu.

University of Nevada, Reno, Graduate School, College of Liberal Arts, School of Social Research and Justice Studies, Program in Justice Management, Reno, NV 89557. Offers MJM. Part-time programs available. Postbaccalaureate distance learning degree programs offered (no on-campus study). *Faculty:* 17 full-time (4 women). *Students:* 5 full-time (4 women), 52 part-time (29 women); includes 3 African Americans, 1 American Indian/Alaska Native, 5 Hispanic Americans. Average age 39. 38 applicants, 71% accepted, 17 enrolled. In 2008, 9 master's awarded. *Degree requirements:* For master's, thesis optional. *Entrance requirements:* For master's, minimum GPA of 2.75. Additional exam requirements/recommendations for international students: Required—TOEFL (minimum score 500 paper-based; 173 computer-based; 61 iBT), IELTS (minimum score 6), TOFEL or IELTS. *Application deadline:* Applications are processed on a rolling basis. Application fee: $0 ($95 for international students). Electronic applications accepted. *Expenses:* Tuition, state resident: full-time $1710; part-time $1140 per semester. Tuition, nonresident: full-time $7115. Required fees: $158 per semester. *Financial support:* Federal Work-Study, institutionally sponsored loans, scholarships/grants, health care benefits, and unspecified assistantships available. Financial award application deadline: 3/1; financial award applicants required to submit FAFSA. *Faculty research:* Justice administration, adult justice management, juvenile justice management. *Unit head:* Jane Robinson, Graduate Director, 775-784-6270, E-mail: justmgmt@unr.nevada.edu. *Application contact:* Michele Sandberg, Application Contact, 775-784-7026, Fax: 775-784-6064, E-mail: gradschool@unr.edu.

University of New Haven, Graduate School, Henry C. Lee College of Criminal Justice and Forensic Sciences, Program in Criminal Justice, West Haven, CT 06516-1916. Offers correctional counseling (MS); criminal justice management (MS); security management (MS). Part-time and evening/weekend programs available. *Faculty:* 3 full-time (0 women), 8 part-time/adjunct (1 woman). *Students:* 28 full-time (25 women), 29 part-time (20 women); includes 17 minority (10 African Americans, 2 Asian Americans or Pacific Islanders, 5 Hispanic Americans), 1 international. Average age 27. 66 applicants, 71% accepted, 28 enrolled. In 2008, 35 master's awarded. *Degree requirements:* For master's, thesis or alternative. *Entrance requirements:* Additional exam requirements/recommendations for international students: Required—TOEFL (minimum score 520 paper-based; 190 computer-based; 70 iBT), IELTS (minimum score 5.5). *Application deadline:* For fall admission, 5/31 for international students; for winter admission, 10/15 for international students; for spring admission, 1/15 for international students. Applications are processed on a rolling basis. Application fee: $50. *Expenses:* Tuition: Full-time $15,075; part-time $670 per credit. Required fees: $240; $45 per trimester. Tuition and fees vary according to course load and program. *Financial support:* Research assistantships with partial tuition reimbursements, teaching assistantships with partial tuition reimbursements, career-related internships or fieldwork, Federal Work-Study, scholarships/grants, tuition waivers, and unspecified assistantships available. Support available to part-time students. Financial award applicants required to submit FAFSA. *Unit head:* Dr. James J Cassidy, Coordinator, 203-932-7374. *Application contact:* Eloise Gormley, Director of Graduate Admissions, 203-932-7449, Fax: 203-932-7137, E-mail: gradinfo@newhaven.edu.

University of New Mexico, Robert O. Anderson Graduate School of Management, Albuquerque, NM 87131-2039. Offers accounting (M Acc, MBA), including accounting, tax accounting (MBA); financial, international and technology management (MBA), including financial management, international management, international management in Latin America, management of technology; marketing, information and decision sciences (MBA), including information assurance, management information systems, marketing management, operations management; organizational studies (MBA), including human resources management, policy and planning; JD/MBA; MBA/MA; MBA/MEME. *Accreditation:* AACSB. Part-time and evening/weekend programs available. *Entrance requirements:* For master's, GMAT. Additional exam requirements/recommendations for international students: Required—TOEFL (minimum score 550 paper-based; 213 computer-based). *Faculty research:* Organizational and social aspects of accounting, entrepreneurial learning, information requirements analysis, product disposition and replacement.

University of North Alabama, College of Arts and Sciences, Department of Social Work and Criminal Justice, Florence, AL 35632-0001. Offers criminal justice (MSCJ). Part-time and evening/weekend programs available. *Faculty:* 3 part-time/adjunct (0 women). *Students:* 9 full-time (6 women), 8 part-time (6 women); includes 5 minority (all African Americans). Average age 33. In 2008, 6 master's awarded. *Entrance requirements:* For master's, GRE General Test, MAT. *Application deadline:* For fall admission, 7/1 priority date for domestic students; for spring admission, 12/1 for domestic students. Applications are processed on a rolling basis. Application fee: $25. Electronic applications accepted. *Expenses:* Tuition, area resident: Full-time $4704; part-time $196 per credit hour. Tuition, state resident: full-time $4704; part-time $196 per credit hour. Tuition, nonresident: full-time $9408; part-time $392 per credit hour. Required fees: $882. Tuition and fees vary according to course load and program. *Unit head:* Dr. Joy Borah, Chair, 256-765-4531, E-mail: jsborah@una.edu. *Application contact:* Kim Mauldin, Director of Admissions, 256-765-4608, Fax: 256-765-4960, E-mail: komauldin@una.edu.

The University of North Carolina at Charlotte, Graduate School, College of Arts and Sciences, Department of Criminal Justice, Charlotte, NC 28223-0001. Offers MS. Part-time and evening/weekend programs available. *Faculty:* 14 full-time (7 women). *Students:* 10 full-time (4 women), 14 part-time (11 women). Average age 27. 26 applicants, 54% accepted, 9 enrolled. In 2008, 11 master's awarded. *Degree requirements:* For master's, thesis or comprehensive exam. *Entrance requirements:* For master's, GRE General Test or MAT, minimum GPA of 3.0 in undergraduate major, 2.75 overall. Additional exam requirements/recommendations for international students: Required—TOEFL (minimum score 557 paper-based; 220 computer-based). *Application deadline:* For fall admission, 7/1 for domestic students, 5/1 for international students; for spring admission, 11/1 for domestic students, 10/1 for international students. Applications are processed on a rolling basis. Application fee: $55. Electronic applications accepted. *Expenses:* Tuition, area resident: Full-time $2919; part-time $122 per credit hour. Tuition, state resident: full-time $2919; part-time $122 per credit hour. Tuition, nonresident: full-time $13,126; part-time $547 per credit hour. Required fees: $1779; $91 per credit hour. Tuition and fees vary according to program. *Financial support:* In 2008–09, 6 teaching assistantships (averaging $7,767 per year) were awarded; career-related internships or fieldwork, Federal Work-Study, institutionally sponsored loans, scholarships/grants, unspecified assistantships, and 4 administrative assistantships ($9,895 average) also available. Support available to part-time students. Financial award application deadline: 4/1; financial award applicants required to submit FAFSA. *Faculty research:* Social psychology, terrorism, and identity; diminished capacity mitigation in death penalty proceedings; effects of prenatal problems, family functioning, and neighborhood disadvantage in predicting violent offending; dynamic nature of the drug use/serious violence relationship; Chinese birth cohort: criminological implications. *Unit head:* Dr. Vivian B. Lord, Chair, 704-687-2562, Fax: 704-687-3349, E-mail: vblord@email.uncc.edu. *Application contact:* Kathy B. Giddings, Director of Graduate Admissions, 704-687-3366, Fax: 704-687-3279, E-mail: agidding@uncc.edu.

The University of North Carolina at Greensboro, Graduate School, College of Arts and Sciences, Department of Sociology, Greensboro, NC 27412-5001. Offers criminology (MA); sociology (MA). Part-time programs available. *Degree requirements:* For master's, comprehensive exam, thesis. *Entrance requirements:* For master's, GRE General Test. Additional exam requirements/recommendations for international students: Required—TOEFL. Electronic applications accepted.

The University of North Carolina Wilmington, College of Arts and Sciences, Department of Sociology and Criminology, Wilmington, NC 28403-3297. Offers criminology (MA); public sociology (MA). *Students:* 11 full-time (9 women), 7 part-time (all women). Average age 29. 24 applicants, 42% accepted, 7 enrolled. *Degree requirements:* For master's, comprehensive exam, thesis or alternative, thesis or internship. *Entrance requirements:* Additional exam requirements/recommendations for international students: Required—TOEFL (minimum score 550 paper-based; 217 computer-based; 79 iBT), IELTS (minimum score 6.5). *Application deadline:* For fall admission, 6/15 for domestic students. Application fee: $60. Electronic applications accepted. *Expenses:* Tuition, area resident: Full-time $4838. Tuition, state resident: full-time $4838. Tuition, nonresident: full-time $14,898. Required fees: $969.38 per semester. Tuition and fees vary according to course load, campus/location and program. *Financial support:* In 2008–09, 5 teaching assistantships with full and partial tuition reimbursements (averaging $9,500 per year) were awarded; unspecified assistantships also available. *Unit head:* Dr. Kimberly J. Cook, Chair, 910-962-3785, E-mail: cookk@uncw.edu. *Application contact:* Dr. Michael Maum, Graduate Coordinator, E-mail: maumm@uncw.edu.

University of North Dakota, Graduate School, College of Arts and Sciences, Program in Criminal Justice, Grand Forks, ND 58202. Offers PhD. Part-time programs available. *Entrance requirements:* For doctorate, GRE General Test. Additional exam requirements/recommendations for international students: Required—TOEFL (minimum score 550 paper-based; 213 computer-based; 79 iBT), IELTS (minimum score 6.5). Electronic applications accepted.

University of Northern Iowa, Graduate College, College of Social and Behavioral Sciences, Department of Sociology, Anthropology and Criminology, Cedar Falls, IA 50614. Offers criminology (MA); sociology (MA). Part-time and evening/weekend programs available. *Students:* 12 full-time (9 women), 2 part-time (both women); includes 1 minority (American Indian/Alaska Native). 30 applicants, 30% accepted, 7 enrolled. In 2008, 3 master's awarded. *Degree requirements:* For master's, thesis. *Entrance requirements:* For master's, minimum GPA of 3.0. Additional exam requirements/recommendations for international students: Required—TOEFL (minimum score 500 paper-based; 180 computer-based; 61 iBT). *Application deadline:* For fall admission, 8/1 priority date for domestic students. Applications are processed on a rolling basis. Application fee: $30 ($50 for international students). Electronic applications accepted. *Expenses:* Tuition, state resident: full-time $6446. Tuition, nonresident: full-time $14,874. Required fees: $852. *Financial support:* Career-related internships or fieldwork, Federal Work-Study, scholarships/grants, and tuition waivers (full and partial) available. Support available to part-time students. Financial award application deadline: 2/1. *Unit head:* Dr. Kent Sandstrom, Head, 319-273-2786, Fax: 319-273-7104, E-mail: kent.sandstrom@uni.edu. *Application contact:* Laurie S. Russell, Record Analyst, 319-273-2623, Fax: 319-273-6792, E-mail: laurie.russell@uni.edu.

University of North Florida, College of Arts and Sciences, Department of Criminology and Criminal Justice, Jacksonville, FL 32224-2645. Offers criminal justice (MSCJ). *Faculty:* 8 full-time (5 women). *Students:* 10 full-time (6 women), 15 part-time (12 women); includes 7 minority (3 African Americans, 1 Asian American or Pacific Islander, 3 Hispanic Americans), 3 international. Average age 29. 17 applicants, 59% accepted, 8 enrolled. In 2008, 9 master's awarded. *Degree requirements:* For master's, comprehensive exam, thesis optional. *Entrance requirements:* For master's, GRE General Test, minimum GPA of 3.0 in last 60 hours, letters of recommendation. Additional exam requirements/recommendations for international students: Required—TOEFL (minimum score 500 paper-based; 173 computer-based). *Application deadline:* For fall admission, 7/1 priority date for domestic students, 5/1 for international students; for spring admission, 11/1 priority date for domestic students, 10/1 for international students. Applications are processed on a rolling basis. Application fee: $30. Electronic applications accepted. *Expenses:* Tuition, area resident: Full-time $5782.08; part-time $240.92 per credit hour. Tuition, state resident: full-time $5782.08; part-time $240.92 per credit hour. Tuition, nonresident: full-time $19,974; part-time $832.26 per credit hour. Required fees: $952.80; $39.70 per credit hour. *Financial support:* In 2008–09, 6 students received support, including 1 teaching assistantship (averaging $6,000 per year). Financial award application deadline: 4/1; financial award applicants required to submit FAFSA. *Unit head:* Dr. Michael Hallett, Chair, 904-620-2850, E-mail: mhallett@unf.edu. *Application contact:* Kiersten Jarvis, Graduate Coordinator, The Graduate School, 904-620-1360, Fax: 904-620-1362, E-mail: kiersten.jarvis@unf.edu.

University of North Texas, Robert B. Toulouse School of Graduate Studies, College of Public Affairs and Community Service, Department of Criminal Justice, Denton, TX 76203. Offers MS. Part-time and evening/weekend programs available. *Degree requirements:* For master's, comprehensive exam, thesis optional, students can choose either option. *Entrance requirements:* For master's, GRE General Test, personal statement. Additional exam requirements/recommendations for international students: Required—proof of English language proficiency required for non-native English speakers; Recommended—TOEFL (minimum score 550 paper-based; 213 computer-based). *Faculty research:* Law enforcement administration/strategy, juvenile justice/delinquency, violent crime/victimization, terrorism correction administration/issues, capital punishment, criminalistics.

University of Ottawa, Faculty of Graduate and Postdoctoral Studies, Faculty of Social Sciences, Department of Criminology, Ottawa, ON K1N 6N5, Canada. Offers MA, MCA, PhD. *Degree requirements:* For master's, thesis or alternative. *Entrance requirements:* For master's, honors bachelor's degree or equivalent, minimum B average. Electronic applications accepted. *Faculty research:* Creation and reform of criminal policies in Canada.

University of Pennsylvania, School of Arts and Sciences, Graduate Group in Criminology, Philadelphia, PA 19104. Offers MA, MS, PhD.

University of Phoenix, The Artemis School, College of Health and Human Services, Phoenix, AZ 85034-7209. Offers administration of justice and security (MS); community counseling (MSC); education (MHA); family nurse practitioner (MSN); gerontology (MHA); health administration (MHA); health care education (MSN); health care management (MBA, MSN); informatics (MHA); marriage, family, and child therapy (MSC); nursing (MSN); nursing for nurse practitioners (MSN); psychology (MS); MSN/MBA; MSN/MHA. *Accreditation:* AACN. Evening/weekend programs available. Postbaccalaureate distance learning degree programs offered. *Degree requirements:* For master's, thesis (for some programs). *Entrance requirements:* For master's, 3 years of work experience, minimum undergraduate GPA of 2.5, RN license. Additional exam requirements/recommendations for international students: Required—TOEFL (minimum score 550 paper-based; 213 computer-based; 79 iBT). Electronic applications accepted.

University of Phoenix–Atlanta Campus, The Artemis School, College of Health and Human Services, Sandy Springs, GA 30350-4153. Offers administration of justice and security (MS); health administration (MHA); health care management (MBA); nursing (MSN); nursing/health care education (MSN); MSN/MBA; MSN/MHA. Evening/weekend programs available. Postbaccalaureate distance learning degree programs offered. *Degree requirements:* For master's, thesis (for some programs). *Entrance requirements:* For master's, minimum undergraduate GPA of 2.5, 3 years of work experience. Additional exam requirements/recommendations for international students: Required—TOEFL (minimum score 550 paper-based; 213 computer-based; 79 iBT). Electronic applications accepted.

University of Phoenix–Augusta Campus, College of Social and Behavioral Science, Augusta, GA 30909-4583. Offers administration of justice and security (MS).

University of Phoenix–Austin Campus, College of Social and Behavioral Science, Austin, TX 78759. Offers administration of justice and security (MS); psychology (MS). Postbaccalaureate distance learning degree programs offered.

Criminal Justice and Criminology

University of Phoenix–Bay Area Campus, The Artemis School, College of Health and Human Services, Pleasanton, CA 94588-3677. Offers administration of justice and security (MS); family nurse practitioner (MSN); health care management (MBA); marriage, family and child therapy (MSC); nursing (MSN); nursing/health care education (MSN); MSN/MBA. Evening/weekend programs available. Postbaccalaureate distance learning degree programs offered (no on-campus study). *Degree requirements:* For master's, thesis (for some programs). *Entrance requirements:* For master's, minimum undergraduate GPA of 2.5, 3 years of work experience, RN license. Additional exam requirements/recommendations for international students: Required—TOEFL (minimum score 550 paper-based; 213 computer-based; 79 iBT). Electronic applications accepted.

University of Phoenix–Birmingham Campus, College of Social and Behavioral Science, Birmingham, AL 35244. Offers administration of justice and security (MS); psychology (MS).

University of Phoenix–Chattanooga Campus, College of Social and Behavioral Science, Chattanooga, TN 37421-3707. Offers administration of justice and security (MS); psychology (MSP). Postbaccalaureate distance learning degree programs offered.

University of Phoenix–Cheyenne Campus, College of Social and Behavioral Science, Cheyenne, WY 82009. Offers administration of justice and security (MS); psychology (MS). Postbaccalaureate distance learning degree programs offered.

University of Phoenix–Cincinnati Campus, The Artemis School, College of Health and Human Services, West Chester, OH 45069-4875. Offers administration of justice and security (MS); health care management (MBA); nursing (MSN); psychology (MS). Evening/weekend programs available. Postbaccalaureate distance learning degree programs offered. *Degree requirements:* For master's, thesis (for some programs). *Entrance requirements:* For master's, minimum undergraduate GPA of 2.5, 3 years of work experience. Additional exam requirements/recommendations for international students: Required—TOEFL (minimum score 550 paper-based; 79 iBT). Electronic applications accepted.

University of Phoenix–Cleveland Campus, The Artemis School, College of Health and Human Services, Independence, OH 44131-2194. Offers administration of justice and security (MS); health care management (MBA); nursing (MSN); psychology (MS). Evening/weekend programs available. Postbaccalaureate distance learning degree programs offered. *Degree requirements:* For master's, thesis (for some programs). *Entrance requirements:* For master's, minimum undergraduate GPA of 2.5, 3 years of work experience. Additional exam requirements/recommendations for international students: Required—TOEFL (minimum score 550 paper-based; 213 computer-based; 79 iBT). Electronic applications accepted.

University of Phoenix–Columbus Georgia Campus, The Artemis School, College of Health and Human Services, Columbus, GA 31904-6321. Offers administration of justice and security (MS); health administration (MHA); health care management (MBA); nursing (MSN). Postbaccalaureate distance learning degree programs offered. *Degree requirements:* For master's, thesis (for some programs). *Entrance requirements:* For master's, minimum undergraduate GPA of 2.5, 3 years of work experience. Additional exam requirements/recommendations for international students: Required—TOEFL (minimum score 550 paper-based; 213 computer-based; 79 iBT). Electronic applications accepted.

University of Phoenix–Columbus Ohio Campus, The Artemis School, College of Health and Human Services, Columbus, OH 43240-4032. Offers administration of justice and security (MS); health care management (MBA); nursing (MSN); psychology (MS). Evening/weekend programs available. Postbaccalaureate distance learning degree programs offered. *Degree requirements:* For master's, thesis (for some programs). *Entrance requirements:* For master's, minimum undergraduate GPA of 2.5, 3 years work experience. Additional exam requirements/recommendations for international students: Required—TOEFL (minimum score 550 paper-based; 213 computer-based; 79 iBT). Electronic applications accepted.

University of Phoenix–Dallas Campus, The Artemis School, College of Health and Human Services, Dallas, TX 75251-2009. Offers administration of justice and security (MS); health administration (MHA); health care management (MBA); psychology (MS). Postbaccalaureate distance learning degree programs offered. *Degree requirements:* For master's, thesis (for some programs). *Entrance requirements:* For master's, minimum undergraduate GPA of 2.5, 3 years of work experience. Additional exam requirements/recommendations for international students: Required—TOEFL (minimum score 550 paper-based; 213 computer-based; 79 iBT). Electronic applications accepted.

University of Phoenix–Denver Campus, The Artemis School, College of Health and Human Services, Lone Tree, CO 80124-5453. Offers administration of justice and security (MS); community counseling (MSC); health administration (MHA); health care management (MBA); marriage, family and child therapy (MSC); nursing (MSN); psychology (MS); MSN/MBA; MSN/MHA. Evening/weekend programs available. Postbaccalaureate distance learning degree programs offered. *Degree requirements:* For master's, thesis (for some programs). *Entrance requirements:* For master's, minimum undergraduate GPA of 2.5, 3 years work experience, RN license. Additional exam requirements/recommendations for international students: Required—TOEFL (minimum score 550 paper-based; 213 computer-based; 79 iBT). Electronic applications accepted.

University of Phoenix–Des Moines Campus, College of Social and Behavioral Science, Des Moines, IA 50266. Offers administration of justice and security (MS). Postbaccalaureate distance learning degree programs offered.

University of Phoenix–Harrisburg Campus, College of Social and Behavioral Science, Harrisburg, PA 17112. Offers administration of justice and security (MS); psychology (MS). Postbaccalaureate distance learning degree programs offered.

University of Phoenix–Hawaii Campus, The Artemis School, College of Health and Human Services, Honolulu, HI 96813-4317. Offers administration of justice and security (MS); community counseling (MSC); education (MHA); family nurse practitioner (MSN); gerontology (MHA); health administration (MHA); health care management (MBA); marriage, family and child therapy (MSC); nursing (MSN); nursing/health care education (MSN); psychology (MS); MSN/MBA. Evening/weekend programs available. *Degree requirements:* For master's, thesis (for some programs). *Entrance requirements:* For master's, minimum undergraduate GPA of 2.5, 3 years of work experience, RN license. Additional exam requirements/recommendations for international students: Required—TOEFL (minimum score 550 paper-based; 213 computer-based; 79 iBT). Electronic applications accepted.

University of Phoenix–Houston Campus, The Artemis School, College of Health and Human Services, Houston, TX 77079-2004. Offers administration of justice and security (MS); health administration (MHA); health care management (MBA); psychology (MS). Postbaccalaureate distance learning degree programs offered. *Degree requirements:* For master's, thesis (for some programs). *Entrance requirements:* For master's, minimum undergraduate GPA of 2.5, 3 years of work experience. Additional exam requirements/recommendations for international students: Required—TOEFL (minimum score 550 paper-based; 213 computer-based; 79 iBT). Electronic applications accepted.

University of Phoenix–Idaho Campus, The Artemis School, College of Health and Human Services, Meridian, ID 83642-3014. Offers administration of justice and security (MS); health administration (MHA); health care management (MBA); nursing (MSN); nursing/health care education (MSN); psychology (MS); MSN/MBA. Evening/weekend programs available. Postbaccalaureate distance learning degree programs offered. *Degree requirements:* For master's, thesis (for some programs). *Entrance requirements:* For master's, minimum undergraduate GPA of 2.5, 3 years of work experience. Additional exam requirements/recommendations for international students: Required—TOEFL (minimum score 550 paper-based; 213 computer-based). Electronic applications accepted.

University of Phoenix–Indianapolis Campus, The Artemis School, College of Health and Human Services, Indianapolis, IN 46250-932. Offers administration of justice and security (MS); health administration (MHA); health care management (MBA); nursing (MSN); nursing/health care education (MSN); psychology (MS); MSN/MBA; MSN/MHA. Evening/weekend programs available. Postbaccalaureate distance learning degree programs offered. *Degree requirements:* For master's, thesis. *Entrance requirements:* For master's, 3 years work experience, minimum undergraduate GPA of 2.5. Additional exam requirements/recommendations for international students: Required—TOEFL (minimum score 500 paper-based; 213 computer-based). Electronic applications accepted.

University of Phoenix–Jersey City Campus, College of Social and Behavioral Science, Jersey City, NJ 07310. Offers administration of justice and security (MS); psychology (MS). Postbaccalaureate distance learning degree programs offered.

University of Phoenix–Kansas City Campus, The Artemis School, College of Health and Human Services, Kansas City, MO 64131-4517. Offers administration of justice and security (MS); community counseling (MSC); health administration (MHA); health care management (MBA); nursing (MSN); MSN/MBA. Evening/weekend programs available. Postbaccalaureate distance learning degree programs offered. *Degree requirements:* For master's, thesis (for some programs). *Entrance requirements:* For master's, 3 years work experience, minimum undergraduate GPA or 2.5. Additional exam requirements/recommendations for international students: Required—TOEFL (minimum score 550 paper-based; 213 computer-based).

University of Phoenix–Las Vegas Campus, The Artemis School, College of Health and Human Services, Las Vegas, NV 89128. Offers administration of justice and security (MS); health administration (MHA); health care management (MBA); marriage, family, and child therapy (MSC); mental health counseling (MSC); nursing (MSN); nursing/health care education (MSN); psychology (MS); MSN/MBA; MSN/MHA. Postbaccalaureate distance learning degree programs offered. *Entrance requirements:* For master's, minimum undergraduate GPA of 2.5, 3 years of work experience. Additional exam requirements/recommendations for international students: Required—TOEFL (minimum score 550 paper-based; 213 computer-based; 79 iBT). Electronic applications accepted.

University of Phoenix–Louisiana Campus, The Artemis School, College of Health and Human Services, Metairie, LA 70001-2082. Offers administration of justice and security (MS); health administration (MHA); health care management (MBA); nursing (MSN); psychology (MS); MSN/MBA. Evening/weekend programs available. Postbaccalaureate distance learning degree programs offered (no on-campus study). *Degree requirements:* For master's, thesis (for some programs). *Entrance requirements:* For master's, minimum undergraduate GPA of 2.5, 3 years work experience, RN license. Additional exam requirements/recommendations for international students: Required—TOEFL (minimum score 550 paper-based; 213 computer-based; 79 iBT). Electronic applications accepted.

University of Phoenix–Maryland Campus, The Artemis School, College of Health and Human Services, Columbia, MD 21045-5424. Offers administration of justice and security (MS); health administration (MHA); health care education (MSN); health care management (MBA); nursing (MSN); psychology (MS); MSN/MBA; MSN/MHA. Evening/weekend programs available. *Degree requirements:* For master's, thesis (for some programs). *Entrance requirements:* For master's, minimum undergraduate GPA of 2.5, 3 years work experience. Additional exam requirements/recommendations for international students: Required—TOEFL (minimum score 550 paper-based; 213 computer-based; 79 iBT). Electronic applications accepted.

University of Phoenix–Memphis Campus, College of Social and Behavioral Science, Cordova, TN 38018. Offers administration of justice and security (MS).

University of Phoenix–Metro Detroit Campus, The Artemis School, College of Health and Human Services, Southfield, MI 48076. Offers administration of justice and security (MS); health administration (MHA); health care education (MSN); health care management (MBA); nursing (MSN); MSN/MBA. Evening/weekend programs available. *Degree requirements:* For master's, thesis (for some programs). *Entrance requirements:* For master's, minimum undergraduate GPA of 2.5, 3 years of work experience, RN license. Additional exam requirements/recommendations for international students: Required—TOEFL (minimum score 550 paper-based; 213 computer-based; 79 iBT). Electronic applications accepted.

University of Phoenix–New Mexico Campus, The Artemis School, College of Health and Human Services, Albuquerque, NM 87109-4645. Offers administration of justice and security (MS); health administration (MHA); health care education (MSN); health care management (MBA); marriage and family therapy (MSC); nursing (MSN); psychology (MS); MSN/MBA. Evening/weekend programs available. *Degree requirements:* For master's, thesis (for some programs). *Entrance requirements:* For master's, minimum undergraduate GPA of 2.5, 3 years of work experience, RN license. Additional exam requirements/recommendations for international students: Required—TOEFL (minimum score 550 paper-based; 213 computer-based; 79 iBT). Electronic applications accepted.

University of Phoenix–Northern Nevada Campus, College of Social and Behavioral Science, Reno, NV 89511. Offers administration of justice and security (MS); marriage, family and child therapy (MSC); psychology (MS); school counseling (MSC).

University of Phoenix–Northern Virginia Campus, College of Social and Behavioral Science, Reston, VA 20190. Offers administration of justice and security (MS).

University of Phoenix–Northwest Arkansas Campus, College of Social and Behavioral Science, Rogers, AR 72756-9615. Offers administration of justice and security (MS).

University of Phoenix–Oklahoma City Campus, College of Health and Human Services, Oklahoma City, OK 73116-8244. Offers administration of justice and security (MS); health care management (MBA); nursing (MSN); psychology (MS).

University of Phoenix–Omaha Campus, College of Social and Behavioral Science, Omaha, NE 68154-5240. Offers administration of justice and security (MS).

University of Phoenix–Oregon Campus, The Artemis School, College of Health and Human Services, Tigard, OR 97223. Offers administration of justice and security (MS); health administration (MHA); health care management (MBA); nursing (MSN); psychology (MS); MSN/MBA. Evening/weekend programs available. *Degree requirements:* For master's, thesis (for some programs). *Entrance requirements:* For master's, minimum undergraduate GPA of 2.5, 3 years of work experience, current RN license (nursing). Additional exam requirements/recommendations for international students: Required—TOEFL (minimum score 550 paper-based; 213 computer-based; 79 iBT). Electronic applications accepted.

University of Phoenix–Philadelphia Campus, The Artemis School, College of Health and Human Services, Wayne, PA 19087-2121. Offers administration of justice and security (MS); health administration (MHA); health care education (MSN); health care management (MBA); nursing (MSN); psychology (MS); MSN/MBA. Evening/weekend programs available. *Degree requirements:* For master's, thesis (for some programs). *Entrance requirements:* For master's, minimum undergraduate GPA of 2.5, 3 years work experience. Additional exam requirements/recommendations for international students: Required—TOEFL (minimum score 550 paper-based; 213 computer-based; 79 iBT). Electronic applications accepted.

University of Phoenix–Pittsburgh Campus, The Artemis School, College of Health and Human Services, Pittsburgh, PA 15276. Offers administration of justice and security (MS); health administration (MHA); health care education (MSN); health care management (MBA); nursing (MSN); psychology (MS); MSN/MBA; MSN/MHA. Evening/weekend programs available. *Degree requirements:* For master's, thesis (for some programs). *Entrance requirements:* For master's, minimum undergraduate GPA of 2.5, 3 years work experience, current RN license (nursing). Additional exam requirements/recommendations for international students: Required—TOEFL (minimum score 550 paper-based; 213 computer-based; 79 iBT). Electronic applications accepted.

University of Phoenix–Renton Learning Center, College of Social and Behavioral Science, Renton, WA 98005. Offers administration of justice and security (MS).

University of Phoenix–Richmond Campus, The Artemis School, College of Health and Human Services, Richmond, VA 23230. Offers administration of justice and security (MS); health administration (MHA); health care education (MSN); health care management (MBA); nursing (MSN); psychology (MS); MSN/MBA; MSN/MHA. Evening/weekend programs available. *Degree requirements:* For master's, thesis (for some programs). *Entrance requirements:* For master's, minimum undergraduate GPA of 2.5, 3 years work experience, current RN license for nursing programs. Additional exam requirements/recommendations for international students: Required—TOEFL (minimum score 500 paper-based; 213 computer-based; 79 iBT). Electronic applications accepted.

University of Phoenix–Sacramento Valley Campus, The Artemis School, College of Health and Human Services, Sacramento, CA 95833-3632. Offers administration of justice and security (MS); community counseling (MSC); family nurse practitioner (MSN); health administration (MHA); health care education (MSN); health care management (MBA); marriage, family and child counseling (MSC); nursing (MSN); psychology (MS); MSN/MBA. Evening/weekend programs available. *Degree requirements:* For master's, thesis (for some programs). *Entrance requirements:* For master's, RN license, minimum undergraduate GPA of 2.5, 3 years work experience. Additional exam requirements/recommendations for international students: Required—TOEFL (minimum score 550 paper-based; 213 computer-based; 79 iBT). Electronic applications accepted.

University of Phoenix–St. Louis Campus, The Artemis School, College of Health and Human Services, St. Louis, MO 63043-4828. Offers administration of justice and security (MS); health administration (MHA); health care management (MBA); nursing (MSN); MSN/MBA; MSN/MHA. Evening/weekend programs available. *Degree requirements:* For master's, thesis (for some programs). *Entrance requirements:* For master's, minimum undergraduate GPA of 2.5, 3 years work experience. Additional exam requirements/recommendations for international students: Required—TOEFL (minimum score 550 paper-based; 213 computer-based; 79 iBT). Electronic applications accepted.

University of Phoenix–San Antonio Campus, College of Social and Behavioral Science, San Antonio, TX 78230. Offers administration of justice and security (MS); psychology (MS).

University of Phoenix–San Diego Campus, The Artemis School, College of Health and Human Services, San Diego, CA 92123. Offers administration of justice and security (MS); health care education (MSN); health care management (MBA); marriage, family and child counseling (MSC); marriage, family and child therapy (MSC); nursing (MSN); MSN/MBA. Evening/weekend programs available. *Degree requirements:* For master's, thesis (for some programs). *Entrance requirements:* For master's, minimum undergraduate GPA of 2.5, 3 years work experience, RN license. Additional exam requirements/recommendations for international students: Required—TOEFL (minimum score 550 paper-based; 213 computer-based; 79 iBT). Electronic applications accepted.

University of Phoenix–Savannah Campus, College of Social and Behavioral Science, Savannah, GA 31405-7400. Offers administration of justice and security (MS).

University of Phoenix–Southern Arizona Campus, The Artemis School, College of Health and Human Services, Tucson, AZ 85711. Offers administration of justice and security (MS); family nurse practitioner (MSN, Certificate); health administration (MHA); health care management (MBA); marriage, family and child therapy (MSC); nursing (MSN); psychology (MS). Evening/weekend programs available. *Degree requirements:* For master's, thesis (for some programs). *Entrance requirements:* For master's, minimum undergraduate GPA of 2.5, 3 years of work experience, RN license. Additional exam requirements/recommendations for international students: Required—TOEFL (minimum score 550 paper-based; 213 computer-based; 79 iBT). Electronic applications accepted.

University of Phoenix–Southern California Campus, The Artemis School, College of Health and Human Services, Costa Mesa, CA 92626. Offers administration of justice and security (MS); family nurse practitioner (MSN, Certificate); health administration (MHA); health care education (MSN); health care management (MBA); marriage, family and child therapy (MSC); nursing (MSN); psychology (MS); MSN/MBA; MSN/MHA. Evening/weekend programs available. *Degree requirements:* For master's, thesis (for some programs). *Entrance requirements:* For master's, minimum undergraduate GPA of 2.5, 3 years work experience, RN license. Additional exam requirements/recommendations for international students: Required—TOEFL (minimum score 550 paper-based; 213 computer-based; 79 iBT). Electronic applications accepted.

University of Phoenix–Southern Colorado Campus, The Artemis School, College of Health and Human Services, Colorado Springs, CO 80919-2335. Offers administration of justice and security (MS); community counseling (MSC); education (MHA); gerontology (MHA); health administration (MHA); health care management (MBA); marriage, family and child therapy (MSC); nursing (MSN); psychology (MS); MSN/MBA. Evening/weekend programs available. *Degree requirements:* For master's, thesis (for some programs). *Entrance requirements:* For master's, minimum undergraduate GPA of 2.5, 3 years of work experience, RN license. Additional exam requirements/recommendations for international students: Required—TOEFL (minimum score 550 paper-based; 213 computer-based; 79 iBT). Electronic applications accepted.

University of Phoenix–Springfield Campus, College of Social and Behavioral Science, Springfield, MO 65804-7211. Offers administration of justice and security (MS).

University of Phoenix–Tulsa Campus, College of Health and Human Services, Tulsa, OK 74146-3801. Offers administration of justice and security (MS); health care management (MBA); nursing (MSN); psychology (MS).

University of Pittsburgh, Graduate School of Public and International Affairs, Doctoral Program in Public and International Affairs, Pittsburgh, PA 15260. Offers development policy (PhD); foreign and security policy (PhD); international political economy (PhD); public administration (PhD); public policy (PhD). *Accreditation:* NASPAA. Part-time programs available. *Degree requirements:* For doctorate, comprehensive exam, thesis/dissertation. *Entrance requirements:* For doctorate, GRE, 3 letters of recommendation, resumé, minimum GPA of 3.0, writing sample. Additional exam requirements/recommendations for international students: Required—TOEFL (minimum score 600 paper-based; 250 computer-based; 100 iBT), TWE (minimum score 4); Recommended—IELTS (minimum score 7). Electronic applications accepted. *Faculty research:* International political economy, international development, public administration, public policy, foreign policy, international security policy.

See Close-Up on page 1243.

University of Regina, Faculty of Graduate Studies and Research, Faculty of Arts, Department of Justice Studies, Regina, SK S4S 0A2, Canada. Offers human justice (MA); justice studies (MA); police studies (MA). *Faculty:* 3 full-time (1 woman), 3 part-time/adjunct (1 woman). *Students:* 7 full-time (5 women), 12 part-time (5 women). 13 applicants, 38% accepted. In 2008, 1 master's awarded. *Degree requirements:* For master's, thesis. *Entrance requirements:* Additional exam requirements/recommendations for international students: Required—TOEFL (minimum score 580 paper-based; 237 computer-based; 88 iBT). *Application deadline:* For fall admission, 3/31 for domestic students. Application fee: $85 ($100 for international students). Electronic applications accepted. *Financial support:* In 2008–09, 2 fellowships (averaging $15,000 per year), 1 research assistantship (averaging $13,500 per year), 1 teaching assistantship (averaging $6,558 per year) were awarded. *Unit head:* Dr. Jim Mulvale, Head, 306-585-4237, E-mail: jim.mulvale@uregina.ca. *Application contact:* Dr. Annette Desmerais, Program Coordinator, 306-585-5066, E-mail: annette.desamarais@uregina.ca.

University of South Africa, College of Law, Pretoria, South Africa. Offers correctional services management (M Tech); criminology (MA, PhD); law (LL M, LL D); penology (MA, PhD); police science (MA, PhD); policing (M Tech); security risk management (M Tech); social science in criminology (MA).

University of South Carolina, The Graduate School, College of Arts and Sciences, Department of Criminology and Criminal Justice, Columbia, SC 29208. Offers MA, PhD, JD/MA. Part-time and evening/weekend programs available. *Degree requirements:* For master's, comprehensive exam, thesis; for doctorate, comprehensive exam, thesis/dissertation. *Entrance requirements:* For master's and doctorate, GRE. Additional exam requirements/recommendations for international students: Required—TOEFL. Electronic applications accepted. *Faculty research:* Juvenile delinquency, substance abuse, policy development, minority issues, law enforcement services.

University of Southern Mississippi, Graduate School, College of Science and Technology, Department of Administration of Justice, Hattiesburg, MS 39406-0001. Offers administration of justice (PhD); corrections (MA, MS); juvenile justice (MA, MS); law enforcement (MA, MS). Part-time programs available. *Faculty:* 9 full-time (3 women), 1 part-time/adjunct (0 women). *Students:* 13 full-time (9 women), 31 part-time (21 women); includes 12 minority (11 African Americans, 1 Hispanic American), 2 international. Average age 34. 23 applicants, 39% accepted, 6 enrolled. In 2008, 6 master's, 1 doctorate awarded. *Degree requirements:* For master's, comprehensive exam, thesis; for doctorate, comprehensive exam, thesis/dissertation. *Entrance requirements:* For master's, GRE General Test, minimum GPA of 2.75 in last 2 years, 3.0 in field of study; for doctorate, GRE General Test, minimum GPA of 3.5. Additional exam requirements/recommendations for international students: Required—TOEFL. *Application deadline:* For fall admission, 3/15 priority date for domestic students, 3/15 for international students. Applications are processed on a rolling basis. Application fee: $30. *Financial support:* In 2008–09, 2 research assistantships with full tuition reimbursements (averaging $7,000 per year), 9 teaching assistantships with full tuition reimbursements (averaging $8,000 per year) were awarded; career-related internships or fieldwork, Federal Work-Study, and institutionally sponsored loans also available. Financial award application deadline: 3/15; financial award applicants required to submit FAFSA. *Faculty research:* Crime in the family, police training models, humanities and criminal justice. *Unit head:* Dr. Lisa Nored, Chair, 601-266-4509, Fax: 601-266-4391. *Application contact:* Tera Wright, Manager of Graduate Admissions, 601-266-4509, Fax: 601-266-4391.

University of South Florida, Graduate School, College of Arts and Sciences, Department of Criminology, Tampa, FL 33620-9951. Offers criminal justice administration (MA); criminology (MA, PhD). *Faculty:* 14 full-time (5 women), 2 part-time/adjunct (0 women). In 2008, 35 master's awarded. *Degree requirements:* For master's, comprehensive exam, thesis (for some programs); for doctorate, comprehensive exam, thesis/dissertation. *Entrance requirements:* For master's, GRE General Test (criminology), 3 letters of recommendation, statement of purpose, writing sample, GPA 3.0; for doctorate, GRE General Test, 3 letters of recommendation, statement of purpose, writing sample. Additional exam requirements/recommendations for international students: Required—TOEFL (minimum score 550 paper-based; 213 computer-based). *Application deadline:* For fall admission, 2/15 for domestic students, 1/2 for international students; for spring admission, 9/30 for domestic students, 6/1 for international students. Application fee: $30. Electronic applications accepted. *Expenses:* Tuition, state resident: full-time $2624.40; part-time $291.60 per credit hour. Tuition, nonresident: full-time $7822; part-time $869.13 per credit hour. *Financial support:* In 2008–09, 10 students received support; fellowships with full tuition reimbursements available, research assistantships with partial tuition reimbursements available, teaching assistantships with partial tuition reimbursements available, scholarships/grants available. *Faculty research:* Criminal theory, drug abuse, violence, policing. Total annual research expenditures: $464,006. *Unit head:* Dr. Thomas Mieczkowski, Chairperson, 813-974-8281, Fax: 813-974-2803, E-mail: mieczkow@cas.usf.edu. *Application contact:* Lorie Fridell, Program Director, 813-974-6862, Fax: 813-974-2803, E-mail: lfridell@cas.usf.edu.

The University of Tennessee, Graduate School, College of Arts and Sciences, Department of Sociology, Knoxville, TN 37996. Offers criminology (MA, PhD); energy, environment, and resource policy (MA, PhD); political economy (MA, PhD). Part-time programs available. *Degree requirements:* For master's, thesis or alternative; for doctorate, thesis/dissertation. *Entrance requirements:* For master's, GRE General Test, minimum GPA of 3.0; for doctorate, GRE General Test, minimum GPA of 3.5. Additional exam requirements/recommendations for international students: Required—TOEFL. Electronic applications accepted. *Expenses:* Tuition, area resident: Part-time $348 per credit hour. Tuition, state resident: full-time $6262. Tuition, nonresident: full-time $18,920; part-time $1052 per credit hour. Required fees: $812; $36 per credit hour. Tuition and fees vary according to program.

The University of Tennessee at Chattanooga, Graduate School, College of Arts and Sciences, Department of Criminal Justice, Chattanooga, TN 37403. Offers MSCJ. Part-time and evening/weekend programs available. *Faculty:* 5 full-time (2 women). *Students:* 10 full-time (7 women), 12 part-time (5 women); includes 4 minority (all African Americans). Average age 29. 13 applicants, 77% accepted, 5 enrolled. In 2008, 14 master's awarded. *Degree requirements:* For master's, thesis (for some programs), qualifying exams, internship. *Entrance requirements:* For master's, GRE General Test or MAT. Additional exam requirements/recommendations for international students: Required—TOEFL (minimum score 550 paper-based; 213 computer-based; 79 iBT); Recommended—IELTS (minimum score 6). *Application deadline:* For fall admission, 8/1 priority date for domestic students, 6/1 for international students; for spring admission, 12/1 priority date for domestic students, 10/1 for international students. Applications are processed on a rolling basis. Application fee: $30 ($35 for international students). Electronic applications accepted. *Expenses:* Tuition, area resident: Full-time $6150; part-time $281 per credit hour. Tuition, nonresident: full-time $16,710; part-time $867 per credit hour. Required fees: $1100; $128 per credit hour. $550 per semester. *Financial support:* In 2008–09, 5 fellowships with full and partial tuition reimbursements (averaging $4,950 per year) were awarded; career-related internships or fieldwork, Federal Work-Study, institutionally sponsored loans, scholarships/grants, tuition waivers (partial), and unspecified assistantships also available. Support available to part-time students. Financial award application deadline: 4/1; financial award applicants required to submit FAFSA. *Faculty research:* Violence against women, crime prevention, police accountability, criminal justice privatization, public policy. *Unit head:* Dr. Helen M. Eigenberg, Chair, 423-425-4135, Fax: 423-425-2228, E-mail: helen-eigenberg@utc.edu. *Application contact:* Dr. Stephanie Bellar, Dean of Graduate Studies, 423-425-4666, Fax: 423-425-5223, E-mail: stephanie-bellar@utc.edu.

The University of Texas at Arlington, Graduate School, College of Liberal Arts, Department of Criminology and Criminal Justice, Arlington, TX 76019. Offers MA. Part-time and evening/weekend programs available. *Faculty:* 6 full-time (1 woman). *Students:* 12 full-time (10 women), 35 part-time (23 women); includes 17 minority (10 African Americans, 1 American Indian/Alaska Native, 6 Hispanic Americans). 30 applicants, 90% accepted, 17 enrolled. In 2008, 17 master's awarded. *Degree requirements:* For master's, comprehensive exam, thesis or alternative. *Entrance requirements:* For master's, GRE General Test, minimum GPA of 3.0 in last 60 hours of undergraduate course work, 3 letters of recommendation. Additional exam requirements/recommendations for international students: Required—TOEFL (minimum score 550 paper-based; 213 computer-based). *Application deadline:* For fall admission, 6/16 for domestic students. Applications are processed on a rolling basis. Application fee: $35 ($50 for international students). *Expenses:* Tuition, area resident: Full-time $6500. Tuition, state resident: full-time $6500. Tuition, nonresident: full-time $11,558. *Financial support:* Career-related internships or fieldwork available. Financial award application deadline: 6/1; financial award applicants required to submit FAFSA. *Unit head:* Dr. Alejandro del Carmen, Chair, 817-272-3318, Fax:

Criminal Justice and Criminology

The University of Texas at Arlington (continued)
817-272-5673, E-mail: adelcarmen@uta.edu. *Application contact:* Dr. Alejandro del Carmen, Chair, 817-272-3318, Fax: 817-272-5673, E-mail: adelcarmen@uta.edu.

The University of Texas at Dallas, School of Economic, Political and Policy Sciences, Program in Criminology, Richardson, TX 75083-0688. Offers MS, PhD. Part-time and evening/weekend programs available. *Faculty:* 8 full-time (2 women). *Students:* 23 full-time (14 women), 23 part-time (12 women); includes 11 minority (8 African Americans, 2 Asian Americans or Pacific Islanders, 1 Hispanic American). Average age 33. 17 applicants, 94% accepted, 9 enrolled. In 2008, 2 master's, 3 doctorates awarded. *Degree requirements:* For master's, thesis; for doctorate, thesis/dissertation. *Entrance requirements:* For master's and doctorate, GRE General Test, minimum GPA of 3.0 in upper-level course work in field. Additional exam requirements/recommendations for international students: Required—TOEFL (minimum score 550 paper-based; 213 computer-based). *Application deadline:* For fall admission, 7/15 for domestic students, 5/1 priority date for international students; for spring admission, 11/15 for domestic students, 9/1 priority date for international students. Applications are processed on a rolling basis. Application fee: $50 ($100 for international students). Electronic applications accepted. *Expenses:* Tuition, area resident: Full-time $8320. Tuition, state resident: full-time $8320. Tuition, nonresident: full-time $15,054. Part-time tuition and fees vary according to course load. *Financial support:* In 2008–09, 1 research assistantship (averaging $13,337 per year), 7 teaching assistantships (averaging $11,186 per year) were awarded; career-related internships or fieldwork, Federal Work-Study, institutionally sponsored loans, scholarships/grants, and unspecified assistantships also available. Support available to part-time students. Financial award application deadline: 4/30; financial award applicants required to submit FAFSA. *Unit head:* Dr. James W. Marquart, Program Head, 972-883-4948, Fax: 972-883-2735, E-mail: marquart@utdallas.edu. *Application contact:* Dr. Bruce A. Jacobs, Associate Program Head, 972-883-4557, Fax: 972-883-2735, E-mail: Bruce.Jacobs@utdallas.edu.

The University of Texas at San Antonio, College of Public Policy, Department of Criminal Justice, San Antonio, TX 78249-0617. Offers justice policy (MS). Part-time and evening/weekend programs available. *Degree requirements:* For master's, comprehensive exam, thesis optional. *Entrance requirements:* For master's, GRE General Test, minimum GPA of 3.0 on last 60 hours. Additional exam requirements/recommendations for international students: Required—TOEFL (minimum score 500 paper-based; 173 computer-based). Electronic applications accepted.

The University of Texas at Tyler, College of Arts and Sciences, Department of Social Sciences, Tyler, TX 75799-0001. Offers criminal justice (MS); public administration (MPA); sociology (MS). Part-time and evening/weekend programs available. *Degree requirements:* For master's, comprehensive exam, thesis optional. *Entrance requirements:* For master's, GRE General Test, minimum GPA of 3.0. Additional exam requirements/recommendations for international students: Required—TOEFL (minimum score 79 computer-based). *Faculty research:* Urban segregation, minority business, violent crime, gender discrimination.

The University of Texas of the Permian Basin, Office of Graduate Studies, College of Arts and Sciences, Department of Social Sciences, Program in Criminal Justice Administration, Odessa, TX 79762-0001. Offers MS. Part-time and evening/weekend programs available. *Degree requirements:* For master's, comprehensive exam (for some programs), thesis (for some programs). *Entrance requirements:* For master's, GRE General Test, 3 letters of recommendation. Additional exam requirements/recommendations for international students: Required—TOEFL (minimum score 550 paper-based; 213 computer-based).

The University of Texas–Pan American, College of Social and Behavioral Sciences, Department of Criminal Justice, Edinburg, TX 78541-2999. Offers MS. Part-time and evening/weekend programs available. Postbaccalaureate distance learning degree programs offered (no on-campus study). *Degree requirements:* For master's, comprehensive exam, thesis optional, applied project or thesis. *Entrance requirements:* For master's, minimum GPA of 2.75. *Faculty research:* Comparative criminal justice systems, death penalty, community policing, Hispanic women.

University of the Fraser Valley, Graduate Studies, Abbotsford, BC V2S 7M8, Canada. Offers criminal justice (MA). Evening/weekend programs available. *Degree requirements:* For master's, thesis optional, major research paper. *Entrance requirements:* For master's, bachelor's degree and work experience in related field. Additional exam requirements/recommendations for international students: Required—LPI exam; Recommended—TOEFL (minimum score 88 iBT), IELTS (minimum score 6.5), TWE. Electronic applications accepted. *Expenses:* Contact institution. *Faculty research:* Human trafficking, illegal drug trade, criminal justice, criminology, safe schools.

University of the Pacific, McGeorge School of Law, Sacramento, CA 95817. Offers advocacy (JD); advocacy practice and teaching (LL M); criminal justice (JD); intellectual property (JD); international legal studies (JD); international water resources law (LL M, JSD); law (JD); public law and policy (JD); public policy and law (LL M); tax (JD); transnational business practice (LL M); JD/MBA; JD/MPPA. *Accreditation:* ABA. Part-time and evening/weekend programs available. *Faculty:* 55 full-time (22 women), 73 part-time/adjunct (34 women). *Students:* 620 full-time (304 women), 396 part-time (194 women); includes 271 minority (33 African Americans, 14 American Indian/Alaska Native, 134 Asian Americans or Pacific Islanders, 90 Hispanic Americans). Average age 24. 2,627 applicants, 41% accepted. In 2008, 301 JDs, 49 master's awarded. *Degree requirements:* For master's, thesis (for some programs); for doctorate, thesis/dissertation. *Entrance requirements:* For JD, LSAT; for master's, JD; for doctorate, LL M. Additional exam requirements/recommendations for international students: Required—TOEFL (minimum score 600 paper-based; 250 computer-based; 100 iBT). *Application deadline:* For fall admission, 3/15 priority date for domestic students. Applications are processed on a rolling basis. Application fee: $50. Electronic applications accepted. *Expenses:* Contact institution. *Financial support:* In 2008–09, 925 students received support, including 9 fellowships, 76 research assistantships (averaging $1,961 per year); career-related internships or fieldwork, Federal Work-Study, institutionally sponsored loans, and scholarships/grants also available. Support available to part-time students. Financial award applicants required to submit FAFSA. *Faculty research:* International Legal Studies, Public Policy & Law, Advocacy, Intellectual Property Law, Taxation, & Criminal Law. *Unit head:* Elizabeth Rindskopf Parker, Dean, 916-739-7151, E-mail: elizabeth@uop.edu. *Application contact:* 916-739-7105, Fax: 916-739-7134, E-mail: admissionsmcgeorge@uop.edu.

The University of Toledo, College of Graduate Studies, College of Health Science and Human Service, Division of Human Services, Department of Criminal Justice, Toledo, OH 43606-3390. Offers criminal justice (MA); juvenile justice (Certificate); severe behavioral spectrum (Certificate).

University of Toronto, School of Graduate Studies, Social Sciences Division, Centre for Criminology, Toronto, ON M5S 1A1, Canada. Offers MA, PhD. Part-time programs available. *Degree requirements:* For master's, research paper (optional); for doctorate, comprehensive exam, thesis/dissertation. *Entrance requirements:* For master's, 2 letters of reference, bachelor's degree in social science or humanities, minimum B+ average in last 2 years of undergraduate study; for doctorate, 2 letters of reference, MA in criminology or equivalent, minimum A– average. Additional exam requirements/recommendations for international students: Required—TOEFL (minimum score 580 paper-based; 237 computer-based), TWE (minimum score 5).

University of West Florida, College of Professional Studies, Program in Administration, Pensacola, FL 32514-5750. Offers acquisition and contract administration (MSA); biomedical/pharmaceutical (MSA); criminal justice administration (MSA); education leadership (MSA); healthcare administration (MSA); nursing administration (MSA); public administration (MSA). Part-time and evening/weekend programs available. Postbaccalaureate distance learning degree programs offered (no on-campus study). *Students:* 31 full-time (22 women), 135 part-time (72 women); includes 50 minority (32 African Americans, 3 American Indian/Alaska Native, 4 Asian Americans or Pacific Islanders, 11 Hispanic Americans), 1 international. Average age 33. 102 applicants, 63% accepted, 52 enrolled. In 2008, 51 master's awarded. *Entrance requirements:* For master's, GRE General Test, minimum GPA of 3.0. Additional exam requirements/recommendations for international students: Required—TOEFL (minimum score 550 paper-based; 213 computer-based). *Application deadline:* For fall admission, 6/1 for domestic students, 5/15 for international students; for spring admission, 11/1 for domestic students, 10/1 for international students. Applications are processed on a rolling basis. Application fee: $30. *Expenses:* Tuition, state resident: full-time $6095; part-time $253.97 per credit hour. Tuition, nonresident: full-time $21,919; part-time $913.31 per credit hour. *Financial support:* In 2008–09, 7 fellowships (averaging $291 per year) were awarded; career-related internships or fieldwork, scholarships/grants, and unspecified assistantships also available. Support available to part-time students. Financial award application deadline: 4/15; financial award applicants required to submit FAFSA. *Unit head:* Dr. Karen Rasmussen, Chairperson, 850-474-2301, Fax: 850-474-2804. *Application contact:* Terry McCray, Assistant Director of Graduate Admissions, 850-473-7718, Fax: 850-473-7714, E-mail: gradadmissions@uwf.edu.

University of West Georgia, Graduate School, College of Arts and Sciences, Department of Sociology and Criminology, Program in Criminology, Carrollton, GA 30118. Offers MA. *Students:* 3 full-time (0 women); includes 1 African American, 1 Hispanic American. *Expenses:* Tuition, state resident: full-time $2844; part-time $158 per semester hour. Tuition, nonresident: full-time $11,340; part-time $630 per semester hour. Required fees: $1120; $41.56 per semester hour. $186 per semester. Tuition and fees vary according to course load. *Unit head:* Dr. N. Jane McCandless, Chair, 678-839-6505, Fax: 678-839-6506, E-mail: jmccandl@westga.edu. *Application contact:* Dr. Charles W. Clark, Interim Dean, 678-839-6508, E-mail: cclark@westga.edu.

University of Windsor, Faculty of Graduate Studies, Faculty of Arts and Social Sciences, Department of Sociology and Anthropology, Windsor, ON N9B 3P4, Canada. Offers criminology (MA); sociology (MA); sociology-social justice (PhD). Part-time programs available. *Degree requirements:* For master's, thesis; for doctorate, comprehensive exam, thesis/dissertation. *Entrance requirements:* For master's, minimum B+ average; for doctorate, writing sample, minimum B+ average. Additional exam requirements/recommendations for international students: Required—TOEFL (minimum score 560 paper-based; 220 computer-based). Electronic applications accepted. *Faculty research:* Power and social change; criminology/deviance; social psychology; comparative development; race and ethnic relations; family, sex, and gender, social justice.

University of Wisconsin–Milwaukee, Graduate School, School of Social Welfare, Department of Criminal Justice, Milwaukee, WI 53201-0413. Offers administration (MS); corrections (MS); law enforcement (MS). Part-time programs available. *Faculty:* 7 full-time (2 women). *Students:* 16 full-time (8 women), 15 part-time (9 women); includes 6 minority (4 African Americans, 1 American Indian/Alaska Native, 1 Hispanic American). Average age 28. 16 applicants, 56% accepted, 6 enrolled. In 2008, 11 master's awarded. *Degree requirements:* For master's, thesis or alternative. *Entrance requirements:* For master's, GRE General Test, MAT. Additional exam requirements/recommendations for international students: Required—TOEFL (minimum score 550 paper-based; 79 iBT), IELTS (minimum score 6.5). *Application deadline:* For fall admission, 1/1 priority date for domestic students; for spring admission, 9/1 for domestic students. Applications are processed on a rolling basis. Application fee: $45 ($75 for international students). *Expenses:* Tuition, area resident: Full-time $7320; part-time $165 per credit. Tuition, state resident: full-time $7320; part-time $165 per credit. Tuition, nonresident: full-time $17,840; part-time $714 per credit. Tuition and fees vary according to campus/location, program and reciprocity agreements. *Financial support:* In 2008–09, 4 teaching assistantships were awarded; career-related internships or fieldwork and unspecified assistantships also available. Support available to part-time students. Financial award application deadline: 4/15. Total annual research expenditures: $55,755. *Unit head:* Steven Brandl, Representative, 414-229-5443, Fax: 414-229-5311, E-mail: sgb@uwm.edu. *Application contact:* General Information Contact, 414-229-4982, Fax: 414-229-6967, E-mail: gradschool@uwm.edu.

University of Wisconsin–Platteville, School of Graduate Studies, Distance Learning Center, Online Master of Science in Criminal Justice Program, Platteville, WI 53818-3099. Offers MS. Part-time and evening/weekend programs available. Postbaccalaureate distance learning degree programs offered (no on-campus study). *Students:* 2 full-time (both women), 62 part-time (28 women); includes 5 minority (2 African Americans, 1 American Indian/Alaska Native, 2 Hispanic Americans), 1 international. 28 applicants, 61% accepted. In 2008, 18 master's awarded. *Degree requirements:* For master's, thesis or alternative. *Entrance requirements:* Additional exam requirements/recommendations for international students: Required—TOEFL (minimum score 500 paper-based; 173 computer-based). *Application deadline:* For fall admission, 7/1 priority date for domestic students; for spring admission, 11/1 priority date for domestic students. Applications are processed on a rolling basis. Application fee: $56. Electronic applications accepted. *Expenses:* Contact institution. *Financial support:* Scholarships/grants available. Support available to part-time students. *Unit head:* Dr. Cheryl Banachowski-Fuller, Coordinator, 608-342-1652, Fax: 608-342-1986, E-mail: banachoc@uwplatt.edu. *Application contact:* 608-342-1652, Fax: 608-342-1986, E-mail: criminaljstc@uwplatt.edu.

Upper Iowa University, Online Master's Programs, Fayette, IA 52142-1857. Offers accounting (MBA); corporate financial management (MBA); global business (MBA); health and human services (MPA); homeland security (MPA); human resources management (MBA); justice administration (MPA); organizational development (MBA); public personnel management (MPA); quality management (MBA). MBA also available at Madison, Wisconsin campus. Part-time programs available. Postbaccalaureate distance learning degree programs offered (no on-campus study). *Degree requirements:* For master's, research project. *Entrance requirements:* For master's, GMAT, GRE, or minimum GPA of 2.7 during last 60 hours. Additional exam requirements/recommendations for international students: Required—TOEFL (minimum score 570 paper-based; 230 computer-based). Electronic applications accepted. *Faculty research:* Total quality management, CQI, teams, organization culture and climate, management.

Utica College, Program in Economic Crime and Fraud Management, Utica, NY 13502-4892. Offers MBA. Part-time and evening/weekend programs available. Postbaccalaureate distance learning degree programs offered (minimal on-campus study). *Faculty:* 7 full-time (0 women). *Students:* 1 (woman) full-time, 85 part-time (44 women); includes 9 minority (5 African Americans, 1 Asian American or Pacific Islander, 3 Hispanic Americans), 4 international. Average age 40. In 2008, 47 master's awarded. *Entrance requirements:* For master's, BS, minimum GPA of 3.0. Additional exam requirements/recommendations for international students: Required—TOEFL (minimum score 525 paper-based; 195 computer-based). *Application deadline:* Applications are processed on a rolling basis. Application fee: $50. Electronic applications accepted. *Expenses:* Contact institution. *Financial support:* Career-related internships or fieldwork, scholarships/grants, tuition waivers (partial), and unspecified assistantships available. Support available to part-time students. Financial award application deadline: 3/15; financial award applicants required to submit FAFSA. *Unit head:* Dr. R. Bruce McBride, Director of Economic Crime Graduate Programs, 315-792-3808, E-mail: rmcbride@utica.edu. *Application contact:* John D. Rowe, Director of Graduate Admissions, 315-792-3824, Fax: 315-792-3003, E-mail: jrowe@utica.edu.

Utica College, Program in Economic Crime Management, Utica, NY 13502-4892. Offers MS. Part-time programs available. Postbaccalaureate distance learning degree programs offered (minimal on-campus study). *Faculty:* 4 full-time (0 women). *Students:* 1 (woman) full-time, 122 part-time (74 women); includes 20 minority (8 African Americans, 5 American Indian/Alaska Native, 1 Asian American or Pacific Islander, 6 Hispanic Americans), 2 international. Average age 37. In 2008, 17 master's awarded. *Degree requirements:* For master's, thesis. *Entrance requirements:* For master's, BS, minimum GPA of 3.0. Additional exam requirements/recommendations for international students: Required—TOEFL (minimum score 525 paper-based; 195 computer-based). *Application deadline:* Applications are processed on a rolling basis. Application fee: $50. Electronic applications accepted. *Expenses:* Contact institution.

Financial support: Career-related internships or fieldwork, scholarships/grants, tuition waivers (partial), and unspecified assistantships available. Support available to part-time students. Financial award application deadline: 3/15; financial award applicants required to submit FAFSA. *Unit head:* Dr. R. Bruce McBride, Director of Economic Crime Graduate Programs, 315-792-3808, E-mail: rmcbride@utica.edu. *Application contact:* John D. Rowe, Director of Graduate Admissions, 315-792-3824, Fax: 315-792-3003, E-mail: jrowe@utica.edu.

Valdosta State University, Graduate School, College of Arts and Sciences, Department of Sociology, Anthropology, and Criminal Justice, Valdosta, GA 31698. Offers criminal justice (MS); marriage and family therapy (MS); sociology (MS). *Accreditation:* AAMFT/COAMFTE. Part-time and evening/weekend programs available. *Faculty:* 19 full-time (7 women). *Students:* 3 full-time (2 women), 9 part-time (6 women); includes 4 minority (all African Americans). Average age 27. 7 applicants, 57% accepted, 2 enrolled. In 2008, 29 master's awarded. *Degree requirements:* For master's, thesis or alternative, comprehensive written and/or oral exams. *Entrance requirements:* For master's, GRE General Test or MAT (sociology, marriage and family therapy), minimum GPA of 2.5. Additional exam requirements/recommendations for international students: Required—TOEFL (minimum score 523 paper-based; 193 computer-based). *Application deadline:* For fall admission, 7/1 for domestic and international students; for spring admission, 11/15 for domestic and international students. Applications are processed on a rolling basis. Application fee: $40. Electronic applications accepted. *Financial support:* In 2008–09, 5 students received support, including 5 research assistantships with full tuition reimbursements available (averaging $2,452 per year); career-related internships or fieldwork, institutionally sponsored loans, scholarships/grants, and unspecified assistantships also available. Support available to part-time students. Financial award application deadline: 7/1; financial award applicants required to submit FAFSA. *Faculty research:* Police-civilian ride-along project. *Unit head:* Dr. Mike Capece, Acting Head, 229-333-5943, Fax: 229-333-5492. *Application contact:* Rebecca Waters, Coordinator of Graduate Admissions, 229-333-5694, Fax: 229-245-3853, E-mail: rlwaters@valdosta.edu.

Villanova University, Graduate School of Liberal Arts and Sciences, Graduate Program in Criminology, Law and Society, Villanova, PA 19085-1699. Offers MA. Part-time and evening/weekend programs available. *Faculty:* 4 full-time (1 woman). *Students:* 11 full-time (8 women), 2 part-time (both women); includes 3 minority (all African Americans). Average age 27. 12 applicants, 67% accepted, 5 enrolled. In 2008, 10 master's awarded. *Degree requirements:* For master's, comprehensive exam (for some programs), thesis (for some programs). *Entrance requirements:* For master's, GRE General Test, minimum GPA of 3.0. Additional exam requirements/recommendations for international students: Required—TOEFL. *Application deadline:* For fall admission, 8/1 for domestic and international students; for spring admission, 12/1 for domestic and international students. Applications are processed on a rolling basis. Application fee: $50. Electronic applications accepted. *Financial support:* Research assistantships, career-related internships or fieldwork, Federal Work-Study, scholarships/grants, and unspecified assistantships available. Financial award applicants required to submit FAFSA. *Unit head:* Dr. Lance Hannon, Director, 610-519-4776. *Application contact:* Dr. Gerald Long, Dean, Graduate School of Liberal Arts and Sciences, 610-519-7093, Fax: 610-519-7096.

Virginia College at Birmingham, Virginia College Online, Birmingham, AL 35209. Offers business administration (MBA); criminal justice (MCJ); cybersecurity (MC). Part-time and evening/weekend programs available. Postbaccalaureate distance learning degree programs offered (no on-campus study). *Financial support:* Applicants required to submit FAFSA. *Unit head:* Stan Banks, President, Virginia College Online, 877-207-1933, E-mail: vcoadm@vc.edu. *Application contact:* Hugh Jensen, Director of Admissions, 877-207-1933, E-mail: vcoadm@vc.edu.

Virginia Commonwealth University, Graduate School, College of Humanities and Sciences, Wilder School of Government and Public Affairs, Department of Criminal Justice, Richmond, VA 23284-9005. Offers MS, CCJA. Part-time and evening/weekend programs available. *Degree requirements:* For master's, thesis or comprehensive exam. *Entrance requirements:* For master's, GRE General Test, minimum GPA of 2.7.

Walden University, Graduate Programs, School of Counseling and Social Service, Minneapolis, MN 55401. Offers human services (PhD), including clinical social work, counseling, criminal justice, family studies and intervention strategies, general program in human services, human services administration, self-designed program in human services, social policy analysis and planning; mental health counseling (MS). Part-time and evening/weekend programs available. Postbaccalaureate distance learning degree programs offered (minimal on-campus study). *Faculty:* 6 full-time, 76 part-time/adjunct. *Students:* 1,235 full-time (1,026 women), 129 part-time (111 women); includes 595 minority (505 African Americans, 21 American Indian/Alaska Native, 16 Asian Americans or Pacific Islanders, 53 Hispanic Americans), 18 international. Average age 39. 724 applicants, 50% accepted, 250 enrolled. In 2008, 12 master's, 5 doctorates awarded. *Degree requirements:* For master's, thesis optional, residency; for doctorate, thesis/dissertation, residency. *Entrance requirements:* For master's, bachelor's degree or equivalent in related field, minimum GPA of 2.5, two references, goal statement, official transcripts, computer and Internet access; for doctorate, master's degree or equivalent in related field, minimum GPA of 3.0, three years related professional/academic experience, two references, goal statement, official transcripts, computer and Internet access. Additional exam requirements/recommendations for international students: Required—TOEFL (minimum score 550 paper-based; 213 computer-based), IELTS (minimum score 6.5), TOEFL, IELTS, or Michigan English Language Assessment Battery (minimum score 82). *Application deadline:* Applications are processed on a rolling basis. Application fee: $50. Electronic applications accepted. *Expenses:* Tuition: Full-time $12,877; part-time $520 per credit. Required fees: $1230. Tuition and fees vary according to course load, degree level and program. *Financial support:* Fellowships, Federal Work-Study, scholarships/grants, unspecified assistantships, and family tuition reduction; active duty/veteran tuition reduction; group tuition reduction; interest-free payment plans available. Support available to part-time students. Financial award applicants required to submit FAFSA. *Unit head:* Dr. Savitri Dixon-Saxon, Associate Dean, 800-925-3368. *Application contact:* Jennifer Hall, Director of Enrollment, 866-4-WALDEN, E-mail: info@waldenu.edu.

Walden University, Graduate Programs, School of Public Policy and Administration, Minneapolis, MN 55401. Offers general public policy and administration (MPA); government management (Certificate); health policy (MPA); homeland security policy (MPA); interdisciplinary policy studies (MPA); law and public policy (MPA); local government management for sustainable communities (MPA); nonprofit management (Certificate); nonprofit management and leadership (MPA, MS); policy analysis (MPA); public management and leadership (MPA); public policy and administration (PhD), including criminal justice, health services, homeland security policy and coordination, international nongovernmental organizations, knowledge management, nonprofit management and leadership, public management and leadership, public policy, public safety management; terrorism, mediation, and peace (MPA). Part-time and evening/weekend programs available. Postbaccalaureate distance learning degree programs offered (minimal on-campus study). *Faculty:* 2 full-time, 55 part-time/adjunct. *Students:* 1,285 full-time (794 women), 144 part-time (96 women); includes 657 minority (591 African Americans, 8 American Indian/Alaska Native, 17 Asian Americans or Pacific Islanders, 41 Hispanic Americans), 20 international. Average age 39. 727 applicants, 54% accepted, 284 enrolled. In 2008, 101 master's, 6 doctorates awarded. *Degree requirements:* For doctorate, thesis/dissertation, residency. *Entrance requirements:* For master's, bachelor's degree or equivalent in related field, minimum GPA of 2.5, two references, goal statement, official transcripts, access to computer and Internet; for doctorate, master's degree or equivalent in related field, minimum GPA of 3.0, three years related professional/academic experience, two references, goal statement, official transcripts, access to computer and Internet. Additional exam requirements/recommendations for international students: Required—TOEFL (minimum score 550 paper-based; 213 computer-based), IELTS (minimum score 6.5), TOEFL, IELTS, or Michigan English Language Assessment Battery (minimum score 82). *Application deadline:* Applications are processed on a rolling basis. Application fee: $50. Electronic applications accepted. *Expenses:* Tuition: Full-time $12,877; part-time $520 per credit. Required fees: $1230. Tuition and fees

vary according to course load, degree level and program. *Financial support:* In 2008–09, 3 students received support; fellowships with tuition reimbursements available, Federal Work-Study, scholarships/grants, unspecified assistantships, and family tuition reduction; active duty/veteran tuition reduction; group tuition reduction; interest-free payment plans available. Support available to part-time students. Financial award applicants required to submit FAFSA. *Unit head:* Dr. Mark Gordon, Interim Associate Dean, 800-925-3368. *Application contact:* Jennifer Hall, 866-4-WALDEN, E-mail: info@waldenu.edu.

Washburn University, School of Applied Studies, Department of Criminal Justice, Topeka, KS 66621. Offers MCJ. Part-time and evening/weekend programs available. Postbaccalaureate distance learning degree programs offered (minimal on-campus study). *Degree requirements:* For master's, thesis. *Entrance requirements:* For master's, GRE, 3 letters of reference. Electronic applications accepted. *Faculty research:* Practitioner behavior, police management and training, field and institutional correction administration, terrorism, police training, sex slaves.

Washington State University, Graduate School, College of Liberal Arts, Department of Political Science, Program in Criminal Justice, Pullman, WA 99164. Offers MA, PhD. *Degree requirements:* For master's, comprehensive exam (for some programs), thesis, oral exam; for doctorate, comprehensive exam, thesis/dissertation, oral or written exam. *Entrance requirements:* For master's, GRE General Test, minimum GPA of 3.0; for doctorate, GRE General Test, minimum GPA of 3.5. Electronic applications accepted. *Faculty research:* Community policing, community justice, corrections policy, crime prevention policy, criminal justice management.

Washington State University Spokane, Graduate Programs, Program in Criminal Justice, Spokane, WA 99210-1495. Offers MA, PhD. *Degree requirements:* For master's, comprehensive exam, thesis (for some programs); for doctorate, comprehensive exam, thesis/dissertation. *Entrance requirements:* For master's, GRE, minimum GPA of 3.0. Additional exam requirements/recommendations for international students: Required—TOEFL (minimum score 550 paper-based). *Faculty research:* Community oriented policing, crime, criminology theory, jury system, judicial evaluations, police performance.

Wayland Baptist University, Graduate Programs, Program in Counseling, Plainview, TX 79072-6998. Offers counseling (MA); government administration (MPA); homeland security (MPA); justice administration (MPA). Part-time and evening/weekend programs available. Postbaccalaureate distance learning degree programs offered. *Faculty:* 8 full-time (2 women). *Students:* 2 full-time (both women), 105 part-time (81 women); includes 27 minority (3 African Americans, 2 American Indian/Alaska Native, 2 Asian Americans or Pacific Islanders, 20 Hispanic Americans). Average age 34. 39 applicants, 95% accepted, 19 enrolled. In 2008, 34 master's awarded. *Degree requirements:* For master's, comprehensive exam. *Entrance requirements:* For master's, GRE, MAT. Application fee: $50. *Expenses:* Tuition: Full-time $310; part-time $310 per credit hour. Required fees: $782; $9 per credit hour. $60 per semester. *Financial support:* Federal Work-Study, institutionally sponsored loans, and scholarships/grants available. Support available to part-time students. Financial award application deadline: 5/1; financial award applicants required to submit FAFSA. *Unit head:* Dr. Estelle Owens, Chairman, 806-291-1171, Fax: 806-291-1972, E-mail: owensest@wbu.edu. *Application contact:* Amanda Stanton, Graduate Studies, 806-291-3414, Fax: 806-291-1950, E-mail: stanton@wbu.edu.

Wayne State University, College of Liberal Arts and Sciences, Department of Criminal Justice, Detroit, MI 48202. Offers MS. *Degree requirements:* For master's, comprehensive exam, essay. *Entrance requirements:* For master's, GRE if GPA is between 2.75 and 2.99, minimum GPA of 3.0 (resumé and writing sample if less than 3.0), 2 letters of recommendation, personal statement. Additional exam requirements/recommendations for international students: Required—TOEFL (minimum score 550 paper-based; 213 computer-based); Recommended—TWE (minimum score 6). Electronic applications accepted. *Faculty research:* Criminology, juvenile delinquency & justice, law, policing, corrections, social deviance.

Wayne State University, College of Liberal Arts and Sciences, Department of Political Science, Program in Public Administration, Detroit, MI 48202. Offers criminal justice (MPA); public administration (MPA). *Accreditation:* NASPAA. Evening/weekend programs available. *Entrance requirements:* For master's, GRE General Test. Additional exam requirements/recommendations for international students: Required—TOEFL (minimum score 550 paper-based; 213 computer-based); Recommended—TWE (minimum score 6). Electronic applications accepted. *Faculty research:* Urban politics, urban education, state administration.

Webber International University, Graduate School of Business, Babson Park, FL 33827-0096. Offers accounting (MBA); management (MBA); security management (MBA); sports management (MBA). Part-time and evening/weekend programs available. *Degree requirements:* For master's, thesis or alternative. *Entrance requirements:* For master's, previous course work in financial and managerial accounting. Additional exam requirements/recommendations for international students: Required—TOEFL. *Faculty research:* Finance strategy, market research, investments, intranet.

Webster University, School of Business and Technology, Department of Business, St. Louis, MO 63119-3194. Offers business (MA); business and organizational security management (MBA); computer resources and information management (MBA); environmental management (MBA); finance (MA, MBA); health services management (MBA); human resources development (MBA); human resources management (MBA); international business (MA, MBA); management and leadership (MBA); marketing (MBA); procurement and acquisitions management (MBA); telecommunications management (MBA). Part-time and evening/weekend programs available. Postbaccalaureate distance learning degree programs offered (no on-campus study).

Webster University, School of Business and Technology, Department of Management, St. Louis, MO 63119-3194. Offers business and organizational security management (MA); computer resources and information management (MA); environmental management (MS); health care management (MA); health services management (MA); human resources development (MA); human resources management (MA); management (DM); management and leadership (MA); marketing (MA); procurement and acquisitions management (MA); public administration (MA); quality management (MA); space systems operations management (MS); telecommunications management (MA). Part-time and evening/weekend programs available. Postbaccalaureate distance learning degree programs offered (no on-campus study). *Degree requirements:* For doctorate, thesis/dissertation, written exam. *Entrance requirements:* For doctorate, GMAT, 3 years of work experience, MBA.

West Chester University of Pennsylvania, Office of Graduate Studies, College of Business and Public Affairs, Department of Criminal Justice, West Chester, PA 19383. Offers criminal justice (MS). Part-time and evening/weekend programs available. *Students:* 20 full-time (8 women), 12 part-time (9 women); includes 7 minority (5 African Americans, 1 Asian American or Pacific Islander, 1 Hispanic American). Average age 26. 29 applicants, 90% accepted, 18 enrolled. In 2008, 12 master's awarded. *Degree requirements:* For master's, minimum GPA of 3.0, independent research project. *Entrance requirements:* For master's, MAT. Additional exam requirements/recommendations for international students: Required—TOEFL (minimum score 550 paper-based; 213 computer-based; 80 iBT). *Application deadline:* For fall admission, 4/15 priority date for domestic students, 3/15 for international students; for spring admission, 10/15 for domestic students, 9/1 for international students. Applications are processed on a rolling basis. Application fee: $35. Electronic applications accepted. *Expenses:* Tuition, state resident: full-time $6430; part-time $357 per credit. Tuition, nonresident: full-time $10,288; part-time $572 per credit. Required fees: $652.50; $50 per credit. $67 per semester. *Financial support:* In 2008–09, 2 research assistantships with full and partial tuition reimbursements (averaging $5,000 per year) were awarded; unspecified assistantships also available. Support available to part-time students. Financial award application deadline: 2/15; financial award applicants required to submit FAFSA. *Faculty research:* Criminal law, criminal procedure, constitutional interpretation. *Unit head:* Dr. Mary P. Brewster, Chair and Graduate Coordinator, 610-436-

Criminal Justice and Criminology

West Chester University of Pennsylvania (continued)
2630, E-mail: mbrewster@wcupa.edu. *Application contact:* Dr. Mary P. Brewster, Chair and Graduate Coordinator, 610-436-2630, E-mail: mbrewster@wcupa.edu.

Western Connecticut State University, Division of Graduate Studies, Ancell School of Business, Program in Justice Administration, Danbury, CT 06810-6885. Offers MS. Part-time programs available. *Faculty:* 6 full-time (0 women), 1 part-time/adjunct (0 women). *Students:* 2 full-time (0 women), 9 part-time (4 women); includes 1 minority (African American), 1 international. Average age 29. 4 applicants, 25% accepted, 1 enrolled. In 2008, 8 master's awarded. *Degree requirements:* For master's, comprehensive exam or research project; completion of program within 6 years with minimum cumulative GPA of 3.0. *Entrance requirements:* For master's, GMAT, GRE, LSAT, or MAT. *Application deadline:* For fall admission, 8/5 priority date for domestic students; for spring admission, 1/5 priority date for domestic students. Applications are processed on a rolling basis. Application fee: $50. *Expenses:* Tuition, state resident: full-time $4377; part-time $363 per credit. Tuition, nonresident: full-time $12,195; part-time $363 per credit. Required fees: $3574; $60 per credit. Part-time tuition and fees vary according to degree level and program. *Financial support:* Fellowships, career-related internships or fieldwork available. Support available to part-time students. Financial award application deadline: 5/1; financial award applicants required to submit FAFSA. *Unit head:* Dr. Anthony G. Markert, Assistant Professor, 203-837-8469, Fax: 203-837-8527, E-mail: markerta@wcsu.edu. *Application contact:* Chris Shankle, Associate Director of Graduate Admissions, 203-837-9005, Fax: 203-837-8326, E-mail: shanklec@wcsu.edu.

Western Illinois University, School of Graduate Studies, College of Education and Human Services, School of Law Enforcement and Justice Administration, Macomb, IL 61455-1390. Offers law enforcement and justice administration (MA); police executive administration (Certificate). Part-time programs available. *Students:* 43 full-time (15 women), 62 part-time (24 women); includes 14 minority (10 African Americans, 1 American Indian/Alaska Native, 1 Asian American or Pacific Islander, 2 Hispanic Americans), 1 international. Average age 29. 49 applicants, 86% accepted. In 2008, 31 master's, 7 other advanced degrees awarded. *Degree requirements:* For master's, thesis or alternative. *Entrance requirements:* For master's, GRE or MAT, minimum GPA of 3.0. Additional exam requirements/recommendations for international students: Required—TOEFL (minimum score 520 paper-based; 190 computer-based; 68 iBT). *Application deadline:* Applications are processed on a rolling basis. Application fee: $30. Electronic applications accepted. *Expenses:* Tuition, state resident: full-time $5696; part-time $237.34 per credit hour. Tuition, nonresident: full-time $11,392; part-time $474.68 per credit hour. Required fees: $1453; $60.55 per credit hour. *Financial support:* In 2008–09, 11 students received support, including 11 research assistantships with full tuition reimbursements available (averaging $7,040 per year). Financial award applicants required to submit FAFSA. *Unit head:* Dr. Darrell Ross, Chairperson, 309-298-1038. *Application contact:* Evelyn Hoing, Assistant Director of Graduate Studies, 309-298-1806, Fax: 309-298-2345, E-mail: grad-office@wiu.edu.

Western Oregon University, Graduate Programs, College of Liberal Arts and Sciences, Division of Social Science, Monmouth, OR 97361-1394. Offers criminal justice (MA, MS). Part-time and evening/weekend programs available. *Degree requirements:* For master's, thesis optional, written exams. *Entrance requirements:* For master's, minimum GPA of 3.0. Additional exam requirements/recommendations for international students: Required—TOEFL (minimum score 550 paper-based; 213 computer-based; 79 iBT), IELTS (minimum score 6.5). *Faculty research:* Prison to community transition of adult felons, community justice, restorative justice, parole and probation.

Westfield State College, Division of Graduate and Continuing Education, Department of Criminal Justice, Westfield, MA 01086. Offers MS. Part-time and evening/weekend programs available. *Faculty:* 4 full-time (2 women). *Students:* 9 full-time (2 women), 33 part-time (13 women); includes 4 minority (1 Asian American or Pacific Islander, 3 Hispanic Americans). Average age 32. In 2008, 19 master's awarded. *Degree requirements:* For master's, comprehensive exam, thesis (for some programs). *Entrance requirements:* For master's, GRE General Test or MAT, minimum undergraduate GPA of 2.7. *Application deadline:* Applications are processed on a rolling basis. Application fee: $30. *Financial support:* In 2008–09, 1 research assistantship with tuition reimbursement (averaging $1,600 per year) was awarded; career-related internships or fieldwork, Federal Work-Study, and tuition waivers (full and partial) also available. Support available to part-time students. Financial award application deadline: 4/1; financial award applicants required to submit CSS PROFILE. *Unit head:* Dr. Judith McDonald, Director, 413-572-5309 Ext. 5634. *Application contact:* Michelle Janke, Admissions Coordinator, 413-572-8022, Fax: 413-572-5227, E-mail: mjanke@wsc.ma.edu.

West Texas A&M University, College of Education and Social Sciences, Department of History and Political Science, Program in Criminal Justice, Canyon, TX 79016-0001. Offers MA. Part-time and evening/weekend programs available. *Degree requirements:* For master's, comprehensive exam, thesis optional. *Entrance requirements:* For master's, GRE General Test. Additional exam requirements/recommendations for international students: Required—TOEFL (minimum score 550 paper-based). Electronic applications accepted. *Faculty research:* Racial profiling, changing nature of prisons, campus police and parking services.

Wichita State University, Graduate School, Fairmount College of Liberal Arts and Sciences, School of Community Affairs, Wichita, KS 67260. Offers criminal justice (MA); gerontology (MA). Part-time programs available. Electronic applications accepted.

Widener University, College of Arts and Sciences, Program in Criminal Justice, Chester, PA 19013-5792. Offers MA, Psy D/MA. Part-time and evening/weekend programs available. *Faculty:* 1 full-time (0 women), 2 part-time/adjunct (0 women). *Students:* 1 full-time (0 women), 13 part-time (10 women); includes 3 minority (2 African Americans, 1 Asian American or Pacific Islander). Average age 31. 21 applicants, 90% accepted. In 2008, 1 master's awarded. *Degree requirements:* For master's, project. *Entrance requirements:* For master's, interview, minimum undergraduate GPA of 3.0. *Application deadline:* For fall admission, 3/1 priority date for domestic students. Applications are processed on a rolling basis. Application fee: $25 ($300 for international students). *Expenses:* Contact institution. *Financial support:* Career-related internships or fieldwork and institutionally sponsored loans available. Support available to part-time students. Financial award application deadline: 5/1. *Faculty research:* Criminal law and procedure, corrections, domestic violence. *Unit head:* Dr. William E. Harver, Director, 610-499-4554, Fax: 510-499-4605, E-mail: william.e.harver@widener.edu. *Application contact:* Christine M. Weist, Assistant to Associate Provost for Graduate Studies, 610-499-4351, Fax: 610-499-4277, E-mail: christine.m.weist@widener.edu.

Wilmington University, Division of Behavioral Science, New Castle, DE 19720-6491. Offers administration of human services (MS); administration of justice (MS); community counseling (MS). *Accreditation:* ACA. Part-time and evening/weekend programs available. *Entrance requirements:* Additional exam requirements/recommendations for international students: Required—TOEFL (minimum score 500 paper-based; 173 computer-based). Electronic applications accepted.

Wright State University, School of Graduate Studies, College of Liberal Arts, Program in Applied Behavioral Science, Dayton, OH 45435. Offers criminal justice and social problems (MA); international and comparative politics (MA). *Degree requirements:* For master's, thesis optional. *Entrance requirements:* Additional exam requirements/recommendations for international students: Required—TOEFL. *Faculty research:* Training and development, criminal justice and social problems, community systems, human factors, industrial/organizational psychology.

Xavier University, College of Social Sciences, Health and Education, Department of Criminal Justice, Cincinnati, OH 45207. Offers MS. Part-time and evening/weekend programs available. *Faculty:* 3 full-time (1 woman), 1 part-time/adjunct (0 women). *Students:* 7 full-time (4 women), 17 part-time (10 women); includes 2 minority (both African Americans), 1 international. Average age 29. 16 applicants, 94% accepted, 8 enrolled. In 2008, 11 master's awarded. *Degree requirements:* For master's, comprehensive exam, thesis or alternative. *Entrance requirements:* For master's, MAT, GRE, or LSAT, minimum GPA of 2.7. Additional exam requirements/recommendations for international students: Required—TOEFL (minimum score 550 paper-based; 213 computer-based). *Application deadline:* For fall admission, 8/15 priority date for domestic students. Applications are processed on a rolling basis. Application fee: $35. Electronic applications accepted. Tuition and fees vary according to course load, degree level and program. *Financial support:* Career-related internships or fieldwork, scholarships/grants, and unspecified assistantships available. Support available to part-time students. Financial award applicants required to submit FAFSA. *Faculty research:* Women and crime, gun violence, homicide, crime policy, policing. *Unit head:* Dr. Y. Gail Hurst, Chair, 513-745-1070, Fax: 513-745-3220, E-mail: hurst@xavier.edu. *Application contact:* Roger Bosse, Interim Director of Graduate Studies, 513-745-3357, Fax: 513-745-1048, E-mail: bosse@xavier.edu.

Youngstown State University, Graduate School, Bitonte College of Health and Human Services, Department of Criminal Justice, Youngstown, OH 44555-0001. Offers MS. Part-time and evening/weekend programs available. *Degree requirements:* For master's, thesis optional. *Entrance requirements:* For master's, minimum GPA of 2.7. Additional exam requirements/recommendations for international students: Required—TOEFL. *Faculty research:* Police human resource allocation, police administration, computerized test development, criminal law.

Forensic Sciences

Alliant International University–Irvine, Center for Forensic Studies, Irvine, CA 92612. Offers Psy D.

See Close-Up on page 1055.

Arcadia University, Graduate Studies, Program in Forensic Science, Glenside, PA 19038-3295. Offers MSFS.

Boston University, School of Medicine, Program in Biomedical Forensics, Boston, MA 02215. Offers MS. Part-time and evening/weekend programs available. Postbaccalaureate distance learning degree programs offered (minimal on-campus study). *Degree requirements:* For master's, thesis. *Entrance requirements:* For master's, GRE. Additional exam requirements/recommendations for international students: Required—TOEFL. Electronic applications accepted.

Cedar Crest College, Program in Forensic Science, Allentown, PA 18104-6196. Offers MS. *Degree requirements:* For master's, thesis, completion of coursework with a minimum GPA of 3.0. *Entrance requirements:* For master's, GRE. Electronic applications accepted. *Expenses:* Contact institution. *Faculty research:* Geotyping of low copy number DNA, presumétive and conformatory testing of GHB and GBL.

Chaminade University of Honolulu, Graduate Services, Program in Forensic Science, Honolulu, HI 96816-1578. Offers MSFS. Part-time programs available. *Degree requirements:* For master's, comprehensive exam, thesis or alternative. *Entrance requirements:* For master's, GRE, 2 letters of recommendation. Additional exam requirements/recommendations for international students: Required—TOEFL (minimum score 550 paper-based; 250 computer-based).

Duquesne University, Bayer School of Natural and Environmental Sciences, Program in Forensic Science and Law, Pittsburgh, PA 15282-0001. Offers MS. Part-time programs available. *Faculty:* 2 full-time (1 woman), 7 part-time/adjunct (5 women). *Students:* 26 full-time (20 women); includes 1 minority (African American), 1 international. Average age 23. 26 applicants, 100% accepted, 26 enrolled. In 2008, 29 master's awarded. *Degree requirements:* For master's, comprehensive exam. *Entrance requirements:* For master's, SAT or ACT, official transcripts, 1 recommendation form, personal essay. *Application deadline:* For fall admission, 7/1 for domestic and international students. Applications are processed on a rolling basis. Application fee: $50. Electronic applications accepted. *Expenses:* Tuition: Part-time $819 per credit. Required fees: $78 per credit. Tuition and fees vary according to course load. *Financial support:* Fellowships,

research assistantships, teaching assistantships, career-related internships or fieldwork available. Financial award application deadline: 5/1. *Faculty research:* Extraction protocols, mass spectrometry, synthetic fiber analysis, synthetic polymer characterization, trace analysis. *Unit head:* Dr. Federick W. Fochtman, Director, 412-396-6373, E-mail: fochtman@duq.edu. *Application contact:* Val Lijewski, Academic Advisor, 412-396-1084, Fax: 412-396-1402, E-mail: lijewskski@duq.edu.

Florida Gulf Coast University, College of Professional Studies, Program in Criminal Forensic Studies, Fort Myers, FL 33965-6565. Offers MS. *Faculty:* 32 full-time (11 women), 29 part-time/adjunct (12 women). *Students:* 32 full-time (27 women), 14 part-time (10 women); includes 5 minority (2 African Americans, 3 Hispanic Americans), 2 international. Average age 26. 26 applicants, 65% accepted, 13 enrolled. In 2008, 1 master's awarded. *Entrance requirements:* For master's, GRE General Test, minimum GPA 3.0. Additional exam requirements/recommendations for international students: Required—TOEFL (minimum score 550 paper-based; 213 computer-based). *Application deadline:* For fall admission, 4/1 for domestic students; for spring admission, 11/15 for domestic students. Applications are processed on a rolling basis. Application fee: $30. Electronic applications accepted. *Financial support:* Research assistantships, career-related internships or fieldwork and tuition waivers (full and partial) available. Support available to part-time students. *Unit head:* Dr. Kenneth Millar, Dean, 239-590-7724, Fax: 239-590-7846, E-mail: kmillar@fgcu.edu. *Application contact:* Dr. Kenneth Millar, Dean, 239-590-7724, Fax: 239-590-7846, E-mail: kmillar@fgcu.edu.

Florida International University, College of Arts and Sciences, Department of Chemistry, Miami, FL 33199. Offers chemistry (MS, PhD); forensic science (MS). Part-time and evening/weekend programs available. *Degree requirements:* For master's, thesis; for doctorate, comprehensive exam, thesis/dissertation. *Entrance requirements:* For master's and doctorate, GRE General Test, minimum GPA of 3.0. Additional exam requirements/recommendations for international students: Required—TOEFL (minimum score 550 paper-based; 213 computer-based). Electronic applications accepted. *Faculty research:* Organic synthesis and reaction catalysis, environmental chemistry, molecular beam studies, organic geochemistry, bioinorganic and organometallic chemistry.

Florida International University, College of Arts and Sciences, Program in Forensic Science, Miami, FL 33199. Offers MS. *Entrance requirements:* For master's, GRE, minimum GPA of 3.0, 3 letters of recommendation. Additional exam requirements/recommendations for international students: Required—TOEFL (minimum score 550 paper-based; 213 computer-based). Electronic applications accepted.

George Mason University, Volgenau School of Information Technology and Engineering, Department of Electrical and Computer Engineering, Fairfax, VA 22030. Offers communications and networking (Certificate); computer engineering (MS); computer forensics (MS); electrical and computer engineering (PhD); electrical engineering (MS); signal processing (Certificate); VLSI design/manufacturing (Certificate). Part-time and evening/weekend programs available. *Degree requirements:* For master's, thesis optional; for doctorate, thesis/dissertation, comprehensive oral and written exams. *Entrance requirements:* For master's, GMAT or GRE General Test, bachelor's degree in electrical engineering or related field, minimum GPA of 3.0 in last 60 hours of course work. Additional exam requirements/recommendations for international students: Required—TOEFL. Electronic applications accepted. *Faculty research:* Communication networks, signal processing, system failure diagnosis, multiprocessors, material processing using microwave energy.

The George Washington University, Columbian College of Arts and Sciences, Department of Forensic Sciences, Washington, DC 20052. Offers crime scene investigation (MFS); forensic chemistry (MFS); forensic molecular biology (MFS); forensic toxicology (MFS); high-technology crime investigation (MFS); security management (MFS). High-technology crime investigation and security management programs offered in Arlington, VA. Part-time and evening/weekend programs available. *Faculty:* 6 full-time (1 woman), 25 part-time/adjunct (6 women). *Students:* 98 full-time (71 women), 58 part-time (31 women); includes 26 minority (10 African Americans, 1 American Indian/Alaska Native, 12 Asian Americans or Pacific Islanders, 3 Hispanic Americans), 8 international. Average age 27. 155 applicants, 65% accepted, 48 enrolled. In 2008, 96 master's awarded. *Degree requirements:* For master's, comprehensive exam. *Entrance requirements:* For master's, GRE General Test, minimum GPA of 3.0. Additional exam requirements/recommendations for international students: Required—TOEFL (minimum score 550 paper-based; 213 computer-based; 80 iBT). *Application deadline:* For fall admission, 1/16 priority date for international students; for spring admission, 10/1 priority date for domestic students, 9/1 priority date for international students. Applications are processed on a rolling basis. Application fee: $60. Electronic applications accepted. *Financial support:* In 2008–09, 19 students received support; fellowships with partial tuition reimbursements available, Federal Work-Study and tuition waivers available. *Unit head:* Dr. Walter F. Rowe, Chair, 202-994-1469, E-mail: wfrowe@gwu.edu. *Application contact:* Dr. Walter F. Rowe, Chair, 202-994-1469, E-mail: wfrowe@gwu.edu.

John Jay College of Criminal Justice of the City University of New York, Graduate Studies, Program in Forensic Computing, New York, NY 10019-1093. Offers MS. Part-time and evening/weekend programs available. *Degree requirements:* For master's, thesis or alternative. *Entrance requirements:* For master's, GRE General Test, minimum B average. Additional exam requirements/recommendations for international students: Required—TOEFL (minimum score 500 paper-based; 173 computer-based).

John Jay College of Criminal Justice of the City University of New York, Graduate Studies, Program in Forensic Science, New York, NY 10019-1093. Offers MS. Part-time and evening/weekend programs available. *Degree requirements:* For master's, thesis. *Entrance requirements:* For master's, GRE, minimum B average. Additional exam requirements/recommendations for international students: Required—TOEFL (minimum score 500 paper-based; 173 computer-based).

John Jay College of Criminal Justice of the City University of New York, Graduate Studies, Programs in Criminal Justice, New York, NY 10019-1093. Offers criminal justice (MA, PhD); criminology and deviance (PhD); forensic psychology (PhD); forensic science (PhD); law and philosophy (PhD); organizational behavior (PhD); public policy (PhD). Part-time and evening/weekend programs available. Terminal master's awarded for partial completion of doctoral program. *Degree requirements:* For master's, thesis or alternative; for doctorate, one foreign language, thesis/dissertation. *Entrance requirements:* For master's, GRE General Test, minimum B average; for doctorate, GRE General Test. Additional exam requirements/recommendations for international students: Required—TOEFL (minimum score 500 paper-based; 173 computer-based).

McGill University, Faculty of Graduate and Postdoctoral Studies, Faculty of Dentistry, Montréal, QC H3A 2T5, Canada. Offers forensic dentistry (Certificate); oral and maxillofacial surgery (M Sc, PhD).

Mercyhurst College, Graduate Program, Program in Forensic and Biological Anthropology, Erie, PA 16546. Offers MS. *Entrance requirements:* For master's, GRE or MAT, undergraduate degree in related field, interview. Additional exam requirements/recommendations for international students: Required—TOEFL.

Michigan State University, The Graduate School, College of Social Science, School of Criminal Justice, East Lansing, MI 48824. Offers criminal justice (MS, PhD); forensic science (MS); law enforcement intelligence and analysis (MS). Postbaccalaureate distance learning degree programs offered. *Entrance requirements:* Additional exam requirements/recommendations for international students: Required—TOEFL. Electronic applications accepted.

See Close-Up on page 739.

National University, Academic Affairs, College of Letters and Sciences, Department of Professional Studies, La Jolla, CA 92037-1011. Offers forensic science (MFS), including criminalistics and investigation; public administration (MPA), including alternative dispute resolution, human resource management, organizational leadership, public finance. Part-time and evening/weekend programs available. Postbaccalaureate distance learning degree programs offered (no on-campus study). *Faculty:* 9 full-time (3 women), 134 part-time/adjunct (31 women). *Students:* 126 full-time (67 women), 195 part-time (103 women); includes 137 minority (56 African Americans, 26 Asian Americans or Pacific Islanders, 55 Hispanic Americans), 2 international. Average age 38. 241 applicants, 100% accepted, 241 enrolled. In 2008, 104 master's awarded. *Degree requirements:* For master's, thesis. *Entrance requirements:* For master's, interview, minimum GPA of 2.5. Additional exam requirements/recommendations for international students: Required—TOEFL (minimum score 550 paper-based; 213 computer-based; 79 iBT), IELTS (minimum score 6). *Application deadline:* Applications are processed on a rolling basis. Application fee: $60 ($65 for international students). Electronic applications accepted. *Expenses:* Tuition: Full-time $8694; part-time $322 per credit hour. Tuition and fees vary according to course load. *Financial support:* Career-related internships or fieldwork, institutionally sponsored loans, scholarships/grants, and tuition waivers (partial) available. Support available to part-time students. Financial award application deadline: 6/30; financial award applicants required to submit FAFSA. *Unit head:* Chandrika M. Kelso, Associate Professor and Chair, 858-642-8433, Fax: 858-642-8715, E-mail: ckelso@nu.edu. *Application contact:* Dominick Giovanniello, Associate Regional Dean—San Diego, 800-NAT-UNIV, Fax: 858-541-7792, E-mail: dgiovann@nu.edu.

Nebraska Wesleyan University, University College, Program in Forensic Science, Lincoln, NE 68504-2796. Offers MFS. Part-time and evening/weekend programs available.

Oklahoma State University Center for Health Sciences, Graduate Program in Forensic Sciences, Tulsa, OK 74107-1898. Offers forensic DNA/molecular biology (MS); forensic examination of questioned documents (MFSA, Certificate); forensic pathology (MS); forensic psychology (MS); forensic sciences (MFSA); forensic toxicology (MS). Part-time and evening/weekend programs available. Postbaccalaureate distance learning degree programs offered (no on-campus study). *Degree requirements:* For master's, comprehensive exam (for some programs), thesis (for some programs). *Entrance requirements:* For master's, MAT (MFSA) or GRE General Test, professional experience (MFSA). Additional exam requirements/recommendations for international students: Required—TOEFL (minimum score 600 paper-based; 250 computer-based), TWE (minimum score 5). *Faculty research:* DNA typing, DNA polymorphism, identification through DNA, disease transmission, forensic dentistry, neurotoxicity of HIV, forensic toxicology method development, toxin detection and characterization.

Pace University, Dyson College of Arts and Sciences, Program in Forensic Science, New York, NY 10038. Offers MS. *Entrance requirements:* Additional exam requirements/recommendations for international students: Required—TOEFL. Electronic applications accepted.

Philadelphia College of Osteopathic Medicine, Graduate and Professional Programs, Program in Forensic Medicine, Philadelphia, PA 19131-1694. Offers MS. *Entrance requirements:* For master's, minimum GPA of 3.0; coursework in biology, chemistry, anatomy and physiology.

Sam Houston State University, College of Criminal Justice, Huntsville, TX 77341. Offers criminal justice (MS, PhD); criminal justice and criminology (MA); criminal justice management (MS); forensic science (MS); security studies (MS); victim services management (MS). *Faculty:* 25 full-time (4 women), 1 part-time/adjunct (0 women). *Students:* 76 full-time (40 women), 119 part-time (53 women); includes 26 minority (6 African Americans, 1 American Indian/Alaska Native, 5 Asian Americans or Pacific Islanders, 14 Hispanic Americans), 45 international. Average age 32. 102 applicants, 73% accepted, 67 enrolled. In 2008, 34 master's, 15 doctorates awarded. *Degree requirements:* For master's, thesis (for some programs); for doctorate, comprehensive exam, thesis/dissertation. *Entrance requirements:* For master's, GRE General Test; for doctorate, GRE General Test, master's degree. Additional exam requirements/recommendations for international students: Required—TOEFL (minimum score 550 paper-based; 213 computer-based; 79 iBT). *Application deadline:* For fall admission, 8/1 for domestic students; for spring admission, 12/1 for domestic students. Applications are processed on a rolling basis. Application fee: $20. *Expenses:* Tuition, state resident: full-time $3564; part-time $198 per credit hour. Tuition, nonresident: full-time $8622; part-time $479 per credit hour. Required fees: $1290. Tuition and fees vary according to course load and campus/location. *Financial support:* Fellowships, research assistantships, teaching assistantships, career-related internships or fieldwork, Federal Work-Study, institutionally sponsored loans, and unspecified assistantships available. Support available to part-time students. Financial award application deadline: 5/31; financial award applicants required to submit FAFSA. *Unit head:* Dr. Vincent Webb, Dean, 936-294-1632, Fax: 936-294-1653, E-mail: vwebb@shsu.edu. *Application contact:* Doris Powell-Pratt, Advisor, 936-294-3637, Fax: 936-294-4055, E-mail: icc_dcp@shsu.edu.

Southeast Missouri State University, School of Graduate Studies, Department of Chemistry, Cape Girardeau, MO 63701-4799. Offers applied chemistry (MNS), including forensic chemistry. Part-time programs available. *Faculty:* 8 full-time (0 women). *Students:* 5 full-time (all women), 4 part-time (1 woman); includes 1 minority (Asian American or Pacific Islander). Average age 27. 16 applicants, 94% accepted. In 2008, 3 master's awarded. *Degree requirements:* For master's, comprehensive exam (for some programs), thesis (for some programs). *Entrance requirements:* For master's, GRE General Test, minimum GPA of 2.75 for last 30 semester hours of undergraduate science or math courses; 2 letters of recommendation; completed courses with associated labs in organic chemistry, analytical chemistry, chemistry instrumentation or quantitative analysis, and physical chemistry. Additional exam requirements/recommendations for international students: Required—TOEFL (minimum score 550 paper-based; 213 computer-based); Recommended—IELTS (minimum score 6). *Application deadline:* For fall admission, 8/1 for domestic students, 7/1 for international students; for spring admission, 11/21 for domestic students, 11/1 for international students. Applications are processed on a rolling basis. Application fee: $25 ($100 for international students). Electronic applications accepted. *Expenses:* Tuition, area resident: Part-time $213.30 per credit hour. Tuition, state resident: part-time $213.30 per credit hour. Tuition, nonresident: part-time $393.30 per credit hour. Required fees: $23.70 per credit hour. *Financial support:* In 2008–09, 8 students received support, including 1 research assistantship with full tuition reimbursement available, 7 teaching assistantships with full tuition reimbursements available (averaging $7,600 per year); unspecified assistantships also available. Financial award applicants required to submit FAFSA. *Faculty research:* Crystallography, trace metal detection, electrochemistry of metalloporphyrins, organic reactions with supported reagents, synthesis of molecules of biological interest. *Unit head:* Dr. Philip W. Crawford, Chairperson and Professor, 573-651-2166, Fax: 573-986-6433, E-mail: pcrawford@semo.edu. *Application contact:* Marsha L. Arant, Senior Administrative Assistant, School of Graduate Studies, 573-651-2192, Fax: 573-651-2001, E-mail: marant@semo.edu.

Southern Utah University, College of Science, Program in Forensic Science, Cedar City, UT 84720-2498. Offers MS. Electronic applications accepted.

Stevenson University, Graduate and Professional Studies Programs, Program in Forensic Science, Stevenson, MD 21153. Offers MS. Partnership program with Maryland State Police Forensic Sciences Division. *Students:* 16 full-time (14 women), 7 part-time (5 women); includes 1 African American, 2 Asian Americans or Pacific Islanders, 1 Hispanic American. In 2008, 5 master's awarded. *Entrance requirements:* For master's, bachelor's degree in chemistry, biology, physics, or a related science with a minimum cumulative and science/math GPA of 3.2; course/lab work in general biology, general chemistry, organic chemistry, physics, cell biology, molecular genetics, analytical chemistry, instrumental analysis, human anatomy and physiology, biotechniques, and biochemistry. *Expenses:* Tuition: Part-time $495 per credit. Required fees: $75 per term. *Application contact:* Nichole Metzger, Enrollment Counselor, 443-352-4417, E-mail: nmetzger@stevenson.edu.

Stevenson University, Graduate and Professional Studies Programs, Program in Forensic Studies, Stevenson, MD 21153. Offers forensic accounting (MS); forensic legal professional (MS); information technology (MS); interdisciplinary track (MS); investigations (MS). Postbaccalaureate distance learning degree programs offered (minimal on-campus study). *Students:* 39 full-time (28 women), 140 part-time (99 women); includes 50 African Americans, 7 Hispanic Americans. Average age 33. In 2008, 51 master's awarded. *Degree requirements:* For master's, capstone course. *Expenses:* Tuition: Part-time $495 per credit. Required fees: $75 per term. *Application contact:* Nichole Metzger, Enrollment Counselor, 443-352-4417, E-mail: nmetzger@stevenson.edu.

Syracuse University, Graduate School, College of Arts and Sciences, Program in Forensic Science, Syracuse, NY 13244. Offers MFS. Part-time programs available.

Towson University, College of Graduate Studies and Research, Program in Forensic Science, Towson, MD 21252-0001. Offers MS. *Entrance requirements:* For master's, minimum GPA 3.0 for full admission, Bachelor's in chemistry or forensic chemistry or related field.

Universidad del Turabo, Graduate Programs, School of Social Sciences and Humanities, Programs in Public Affairs, Program in Forensic Science, Gurabo, PR 00778-3030. Offers MSS.

University at Albany, State University of New York, College of Arts and Sciences, Department of Biological Sciences, Albany, NY 12222-0001. Offers biodiversity, conservation, and policy (MS); ecology, evolution, and behavior (MS, PhD); forensic molecular biology (MS); molecular, cellular, developmental, and neural biology (MS, PhD). *Degree requirements:* For master's, one foreign language; for doctorate, one foreign language, thesis/dissertation. *Entrance requirements:* For master's and doctorate, GRE General Test. Additional exam requirements/recommendations for international students: Required—TOEFL (minimum score 550 paper-based; 213 computer-based). Electronic applications accepted. *Faculty research:* Interferon, neural development, RNA self-splicing, behavioral ecology, DNA repair enzymes.

The University of Alabama at Birmingham, School of Social and Behavioral Sciences, Department of Justice Sciences, Birmingham, AL 35294. Offers criminal justice (MSCJ); forensic science (MSFS). Evening/weekend programs available. *Degree requirements:* For master's, thesis or alternative. *Entrance requirements:* For master's, GRE General Test or MAT. Electronic applications accepted.

University of California, Davis, Graduate Studies, Graduate Group in Forensic Science, Davis, CA 95616. Offers MS. *Degree requirements:* For master's, thesis. *Entrance requirements:* Additional exam requirements/recommendations for international students: Required—TOEFL

Forensic Sciences

University of California, Davis (continued)
(minimum score 550 paper-based; 213 computer-based), IELTS (minimum score 7). Electronic applications accepted.

University of Central Florida, College of Engineering and Computer Science, Interdisciplinary Program in Digital Forensics, Orlando, FL 32816. Offers MS. *Students:* 10 full-time (2 women), 22 part-time (4 women); includes 4 minority (1 African American, 2 Asian Americans or Pacific Islanders, 1 Hispanic American). *Degree requirements:* For master's, thesis optional. *Application deadline:* For fall admission, 7/15 for domestic students; for spring admission, 12/1 for domestic students. *Expenses:* Tuition, area resident: Full-time $6816; part-time $284 per credit. Tuition, state resident: full-time $6816; part-time $1076 per credit. Tuition, nonresident: full-time $25,824. Required fees: $216; $9 per credit. *Financial support:* In 2008–09, 1 research assistantship (averaging $18,000 per year) was awarded. *Unit head:* Dr. Sheau-Dong Lang, Program Coordinator, 407-823-2474, Fax: 407-823-5419, E-mail: lang@eecs.ucf.edu. *Application contact:* Dr. Sheau-Dong Lang, Program Coordinator, 407-823-2474, Fax: 407-823-5419, E-mail: lang@eecs.ucf.edu.

University of Central Florida, College of Engineering and Computer Science, School of Electrical Engineering and Computer Science, Orlando, FL 32816. Offers computer engineering (MS Cp E, PhD), including computer engineering; computer science (MS, PhD); digital forensics (MS); electrical engineering (MSEE, PhD, Certificate), including communications systems (Certificate), electrical engineering (MSEE, PhD), electronic circuits (Certificate). Part-time and evening/weekend programs available. *Faculty:* 59 full-time (5 women), 7 part-time/adjunct (0 women). *Students:* 308 full-time (57 women), 194 part-time (26 women); includes 74 minority (11 African Americans, 33 Asian Americans or Pacific Islanders, 30 Hispanic Americans), 201 international. In 2008, 167 master's, 48 doctorates awarded. *Degree requirements:* For master's, thesis or alternative; for doctorate, thesis/dissertation, departmental qualifying exam, candidacy exam. *Entrance requirements:* For master's, GRE General Test, minimum GPA of 3.0 in last 60 hours; for doctorate, GRE General Test, minimum GPA of 3.5 in last 60 hours. Additional exam requirements/recommendations for international students: Required—TOEFL. *Application deadline:* For fall admission, 7/15 priority date for domestic students; for spring admission, 12/1 priority date for domestic students. Application fee: $30. Electronic applications accepted. *Expenses:* Tuition, area resident: Full-time $6816; part-time $284 per credit. Tuition, state resident: full-time $6816; part-time $1076 per credit. Tuition, nonresident: full-time $25,824. Required fees: $216; $9 per credit. *Financial support:* In 2008–09, 31 fellowships with partial tuition reimbursements (averaging $9,500 per year), 165 research assistantships with partial tuition reimbursements (averaging $12,000 per year), 49 teaching assistantships with partial tuition reimbursements (averaging $8,300 per year) were awarded; career-related internships or fieldwork, Federal Work-Study, institutionally sponsored loans, tuition waivers (partial), and unspecified assistantships also available. Financial award application deadline: 3/1; financial award applicants required to submit FAFSA. *Faculty research:* Communication theory, solid-state devices, electromagnetics, electro-optics, digital signal processing. *Unit head:* Dr. Issa Batarseh, Director, 407-823-0189, Fax: 407-823-5419, E-mail: batarseh@mail.ucf.edu. *Application contact:* Dr. Issa Batarseh, Director, 407-823-0189, Fax: 407-823-5419, E-mail: batarseh@mail.ucf.edu.

University of Central Florida, College of Health and Public Affairs, Department of Criminal Justice and Legal Studies, Orlando, FL 32816. Offers corrections leadership (Certificate); crime analysis (Certificate); criminal justice (MS); juvenile justice leadership (Certificate); police leadership (Certificate). Part-time and evening/weekend programs available. *Faculty:* 35 full-time (13 women), 37 part-time/adjunct (6 women). *Students:* 51 full-time (37 women), 109 part-time (54 women); includes 44 minority (22 African Americans, 7 Asian Americans or Pacific Islanders, 15 Hispanic Americans), 2 international. In 2008, 91 master's, 29 other advanced degrees awarded. *Degree requirements:* For master's, thesis or alternative. *Entrance requirements:* For master's, GRE General Test, minimum GPA of 3.0. Additional exam requirements/recommendations for international students: Required—TOEFL. *Application deadline:* For fall admission, 7/15 for domestic students; for spring admission, 4/15 for domestic students. Electronic applications accepted. *Expenses:* Tuition, area resident: Full-time $6816; part-time $284 per credit. Tuition, state resident: full-time $6816; part-time $1076 per credit. Tuition, nonresident: full-time $25,824. Required fees: $216; $9 per credit. *Financial support:* In 2008–09, 4 fellowships with partial tuition reimbursements (averaging $10,000 per year), 5 research assistantships with partial tuition reimbursements (averaging $6,400 per year) were awarded; teaching assistantships with partial tuition reimbursements, career-related internships or fieldwork, Federal Work-Study, institutionally sponsored loans, tuition waivers (partial), and unspecified assistantships also available. Financial award application deadline: 3/1; financial award applicants required to submit FAFSA. *Unit head:* Dr. Robert Langworthy, Chair, 407-823-5929, E-mail: rlangwor@mail.ucf.edu. *Application contact:* Dr. Robert Langworthy, Chair, 407-823-5929, E-mail: rlangwor@mail.ucf.edu.

University of Central Florida, College of Sciences, Department of Chemistry, Orlando, FL 32816. Offers chemistry (MS, PhD); computer forensics (Certificate); forensic analysis (MS); forensic biochemistry (MS); industrial chemistry (MS). Part-time and evening/weekend programs available. *Faculty:* 24 full-time (1 woman), 5 part-time/adjunct (0 women). *Students:* 74 full-time (29 women), 44 part-time (13 women); includes 21 minority (5 African Americans, 4 Asian Americans or Pacific Islanders, 12 Hispanic Americans), 41 international. In 2008, 5 master's, 3 doctorates, 12 other advanced degrees awarded. *Degree requirements:* For master's, thesis, final exam. *Entrance requirements:* For master's, GRE General Test, minimum GPA of 3.0 in last 60 hours. Additional exam requirements/recommendations for international students: Required—TOEFL. *Application deadline:* For fall admission, 7/15 for domestic students; for spring admission, 12/1 for domestic students. Application fee: $30. Electronic applications accepted. *Expenses:* Tuition, area resident: Full-time $6816; part-time $284 per credit. Tuition, state resident: full-time $6816; part-time $1076 per credit. Tuition, nonresident: full-time $25,824. Required fees: $216; $9 per credit. *Financial support:* In 2008–09, 7 fellowships with partial tuition reimbursements (averaging $15,200 per year), 38 research assistantships with partial tuition reimbursements (averaging $9,000 per year), 39 teaching assistantships with partial tuition reimbursements (averaging $11,200 per year) were awarded; career-related internships or fieldwork, Federal Work-Study, institutionally sponsored loans, tuition waivers (partial), and unspecified assistantships also available. Financial award application deadline: 3/1; financial award applicants required to submit FAFSA. *Faculty research:* Physical and synthetic organic chemistry, lasers, polymers, biochemical action of pesticides, environmental analysis. *Unit head:* Dr. Kevin D. Belfield, Chair, 407-823-2246, Fax: 407-823-2252, E-mail: kbelfield@mail.ucf.edu. *Application contact:* Dr. Kevin D. Belfield, Chair, 407-823-2246, Fax: 407-823-2252, E-mail: kbelfield@mail.ucf.edu.

University of Florida, College of Pharmacy, Programs in Forensic Science, Gainesville, FL 32611. Offers forensic DNA and serology (MS, Certificate); forensic drug chemistry (MS, Certificate); forensic toxicology (MS, Certificate).

University of Illinois at Chicago, College of Pharmacy and Graduate College, Graduate Programs in Pharmacy, Program in Forensic Science, Chicago, IL 60607-7128. Offers MS. *Degree requirements:* For master's, thesis. *Entrance requirements:* For master's, GRE General Test. Additional exam requirements/recommendations for international students: Required—TOEFL. *Faculty research:* Interpretation of physical evidence, utilization of physical evidence, analytical toxicology of controlled substances, automated fingerprint systems, dye and ink characterizations.

University of Nevada, Las Vegas, Graduate College, Greenspun College of Urban Affairs, School of Social Work, Las Vegas, NV 89154-5032. Offers forensic social work (Advanced Certificate); social work (MSW); MSW/JD. *Accreditation:* CSWE. *Faculty:* 14 full-time (11 women). *Students:* 116 full-time (97 women), 66 part-time (51 women); includes 57 minority (24 African Americans, 1 American Indian/Alaska Native, 8 Asian Americans or Pacific Islanders, 24 Hispanic Americans), 1 international. Average age 33. 185 applicants, 61% accepted, 74 enrolled. In 2008, 66 master's, 3 other advanced degrees awarded. *Degree requirements:* For master's, comprehensive exam, thesis optional. *Entrance requirements:* Additional exam requirements/recommendations for international students: Required—TOEFL (minimum score 550 paper-based; 231 computer-based; 80 iBT), IELTS (minimum score 7). *Application deadline:* For fall admission, 2/1 priority date for domestic and international students. Applications are processed on a rolling basis. Application fee: $60 ($75 for international students). Electronic applications accepted. *Expenses:* Tuition, state resident: full-time $1414; part-time $198 per credit. Tuition, nonresident: full-time $12,509; part-time $415.75 per credit. International tuition: $14,249 full-time. Required fees: $4 per credit. $252 per semester. Tuition and fees vary according to course load. *Financial support:* In 2008–09, 4 students received support, including 4 teaching assistantships with partial tuition reimbursements available (averaging $10,000 per year); institutionally sponsored loans, scholarships/grants, health care benefits, and unspecified assistantships also available. Financial award application deadline: 3/1. *Faculty research:* Direct practice, management and community practice, child welfare. *Unit head:* Dr. Joanne Thompson, Director/Professor, 702-895-0521, Fax: 702-895-4079, E-mail: joanne.thompson@unlv.edu. *Application contact:* Graduate College Admissions Evaluator, 702-895-3320, Fax: 702-895-4180, E-mail: gradcollege@unlv.edu.

University of New Haven, Graduate School, Henry C. Lee College of Criminal Justice and Forensic Sciences, Program in Forensic Science, West Haven, CT 06516-1916. Offers advanced investigation (MS); criminalistics (MS); forensic science (MS). Part-time and evening/weekend programs available. *Faculty:* 5 full-time (1 woman), 2 part-time/adjunct (0 women). *Students:* 73 full-time (61 women), 15 part-time (7 women); includes 18 minority (9 African Americans, 1 American Indian/Alaska Native, 2 Asian Americans or Pacific Islanders, 6 Hispanic Americans), 1 international. Average age 26. 128 applicants, 77% accepted, 50 enrolled. In 2008, 29 master's awarded. *Degree requirements:* For master's, thesis or alternative. *Entrance requirements:* For master's, GRE. Additional exam requirements/recommendations for international students: Required—TOEFL (minimum score 520 paper-based; 190 computer-based; 70 iBT); Recommended—IELTS (minimum score 5.5). *Application deadline:* For fall admission, 5/31 for international students; for winter admission, 10/15 for international students; for spring admission, 1/15 for international students. Applications are processed on a rolling basis. Application fee: $50. *Expenses:* Tuition: Full-time $15,075; part-time $670 per credit. Required fees: $240; $45 per trimester. Tuition and fees vary according to course load and program. *Financial support:* Research assistantships with partial tuition reimbursements, teaching assistantships with partial tuition reimbursements, career-related internships or fieldwork, Federal Work-Study, scholarships/grants, tuition waivers, and unspecified assistantships available. Support available to part-time students. Financial award applicants required to submit FAFSA. *Unit head:* Dr. Timothy M Palmbach, Coordinator, 203-932-7116. *Application contact:* Dr. Timothy M Palmbach, Coordinator, 203-932-7116.

University of North Texas Health Science Center at Fort Worth, Graduate School of Biomedical Sciences, Fort Worth, TX 76107-2699. Offers anatomy and cell biology (MS, PhD); biochemistry and molecular biology (MS, PhD); biomedical sciences (MS, PhD); biotechnology (MS); forensic genetics (MS); integrative physiology (MS, PhD); medical science (MS); microbiology and immunology (MS, PhD); pharmacology (MS, PhD); science education (MS); DO/MS; DO/PhD. Terminal master's awarded for partial completion of doctoral program. *Degree requirements:* For master's, thesis; for doctorate, thesis/dissertation. *Entrance requirements:* For master's and doctorate, GRE General Test. Additional exam requirements/recommendations for international students: Required—TOEFL. *Expenses:* Contact institution. *Faculty research:* Alzheimer's disease, aging, eye diseases, cancer, cardiovascular disease.

University of Rhode Island, Graduate School, College of Arts and Sciences, Department of Computer Science and Statistics, Kingston, RI 02881. Offers applied mathematics (PhD), including computer science, statistics; computer science (MS, PhD); digital forensics (Graduate Certificate); statistics (MS). In 2008, 4 master's awarded. *Degree requirements:* For master's, thesis optional; for doctorate, one foreign language, thesis/dissertation. *Entrance requirements:* For master's, GRE Subject Test. *Application deadline:* Applications are processed on a rolling basis. Application fee: $35. *Expenses:* Tuition, state resident: full-time $8024; part-time $446 per credit. Tuition, nonresident: full-time $21,046; part-time $1169 per credit. Required fees: $1056; $26 per credit. $30 per semester. One-time fee: $95 part-time. *Financial support:* Unspecified assistantships available. *Unit head:* Dr. James Kowalski, Chair, 401-874-2510, E-mail: kowalski@cs.uri.edu. *Application contact:* Harold D. Bibb, Associate Dean of the Graduate School, 401-874-2262, Fax: 401-874-5491.

Virginia Commonwealth University, Graduate School, College of Humanities and Sciences, Department of Forensic Science, Richmond, VA 23284-9005. Offers MS.

West Virginia University, Eberly College of Arts and Sciences, Department of Biology, Morgantown, WV 26506. Offers cell and molecular biology (MS, PhD); environmental and evolutionary biology (MS, PhD); forensic biology (MS, PhD); genomic biology (MS, PhD); neurobiology (MS, PhD). Terminal master's awarded for partial completion of doctoral program. *Degree requirements:* For master's, thesis, final exam; for doctorate, thesis/dissertation, preliminary and final exams. *Entrance requirements:* For master's, GRE General Test, GRE Subject Test, minimum GPA of 3.0; for doctorate, GRE General Test, minimum GPA of 3.0. Additional exam requirements/recommendations for international students: Required—TOEFL. *Faculty research:* Environmental biology, genetic engineering, developmental biology, global change, biodiversity.

MICHIGAN STATE UNIVERSITY

School of Criminal Justice

Programs of Study	The School of Criminal Justice at Michigan State University (MSU) offers the Master of Science and Doctor of Philosophy in criminal justice.
	The master's degree requires a minimum of 30 semester hours. Students may elect to complete a thesis or a policy paper. The program is designed for those wishing to strengthen leadership and management skills in law enforcement, corrections, and delinquency prevention and for those applying to a research-oriented Ph.D. program in criminal justice. A specialization in security management, which provides a multidisciplinary educational experience for students interested in private and government security, is offered. A forensic science master's degree, combining science and criminal justice, is available for individuals with a bachelor's degree in natural science. The forensic program has a 38-credit requirement and students must complete a thesis.
	The School of Criminal Justice also offers the Master of Science in criminal justice through the Internet. This program, geared towards professionals, includes specializations in security management and judicial administration. The School also offers Internet-based Homeland Security, Intelligence Analysis, Security Management, and International Focus Graduate Certificate Programs.
	The Ph.D. program provides a strong foundation for students who wish to pursue careers in research and teaching. The program consists of core courses and electives in criminal justice and a cognate area, which may be in social science or a focus area that reflects individual interests such as race and ethnicity, gender, organizational theory, labor and industrial relations, urban studies, or Latino studies. A quantitative research component is required. A guidance committee assists students individually with the development of their program, based on individual educational backgrounds and career objectives.
Research Facilities	A computer laboratory is available to students, with IBM workstations and relevant databases for research and management issues. The available software and training include those associated with several statistical packages, such as SPSS for Windows and SAS, and alternative software systems for databases, graphics, spreadsheets, word processing, and desktop publishing. The University library is among the nation's largest, with more than 4 million volumes, 5 million items on microfilm and microfiche, and approximately 28,000 serial subscriptions.
	Computing facilities at MSU include more than fifty microcomputer laboratories across the campus, several of which are available 24 hours a day during the week. Multiple services for the University community are available, including statistical consulting and a computer store that sells equipment at an academic discount. E-mail accounts are free for all students and faculty and staff members.
	The School formally collaborates with the National Criminal Justice Data Archive, which provides numerous opportunities for research and advanced methodological courses. In addition, the School and MSU have established many international partnerships offering unique opportunities for global scholarship.
Financial Aid	Graduate assistantships at the master's and doctoral levels are available on a competitive basis. To be considered for an assistantship, students must be admitted to the criminal justice program with regular status. Stipends for 2008–09 ranged from $648 to $2142 per month. The assistantships require that the student work 10 to 30 hours per week on research projects and teaching. In addition, all assistantships provide a tuition award of 18 credits per academic year, a waiver of out-of-state tuition, and health insurance.
Cost of Study	Tuition for the 2008–09 academic year was $439.25 per credit hour for in-state students and $903.50 per credit hour for out-of-state students. Fees, including registration and technology support fees, totaled $466.
Living and Housing Costs	Housing for graduate students is available both on and off campus and varies in cost. The area market average for room and board is $6000 per academic year. Health insurance is available through the University.
Student Group	The School has an enrollment of approximately 650 undergraduates, 125 master's students, and 35 doctoral students. In fall 2008, 44 percent of master's students were women, 12 percent were members of minority groups, and 9 percent were international students; 33 percent of the doctoral candidates were women, 16 percent were members of minority groups, and 22 percent were international students.
Location	Located on the banks of the Red Cedar River, the nation's first land-grant university is situated on one of the most beautiful campuses in the country. The 5,198-acre East Lansing campus, an arboretum park with four designated natural areas, has received many national awards for its beauty and wealth of plant life. Lansing, the state capital, is only 2 miles from the campus and provides ready access to public agencies and businesses for students who seek research and practicum sites. With a population of 400,000, the metropolitan Lansing area offers diverse cultural and recreational activities. The Great Lakes, Detroit, and Ontario are all within 90 miles, and housing is attractive and affordable.
The University	Founded in 1855, MSU is one of the leading institutions of higher education in the United States. The University ranks among the fifteen largest in the nation, and has a total enrollment of approximately 43,366 students. More than 7,900 students are enrolled in graduate programs.
	Academic programs are directed by faculty members with national and international reputations. Faculty members at MSU work closely with graduate students and take pride in meeting the academic needs of individual students.
Applying	Applications for admission that are not submitted online must be accompanied by the application fee. Prospective doctoral students' applications are reviewed once each year. To ensure full consideration for the Ph.D. program, application materials, including scores from the GRE General Test, must be received by January 10. For master's degree applicants, all application materials, including scores from the GRE General Test, must be received by February 1 for the fall semester and September 1 for the spring semester. All application materials should be sent to the School of Criminal Justice.
Correspondence and Information	School of Criminal Justice 560 Baker Hall Michigan State University East Lansing, Michigan 48824-1118 Phone: 517-353-7133 E-mail: burrier@msu.edu Web site: http://www.criminaljustice.msu.edu

Michigan State University

THE FACULTY

Timothy Bynum, Professor; Ph.D., Florida State. Evaluation, research design, law enforcement, corrections policy analysis.

David Carter, Professor; Ph.D., Sam Houston State. Police management/policy, computer crime, law enforcement intelligence.

Soma Chaudhuri, Assistant Professor; Ph.D., Vanderbilt. Deviant behavior and social behavior.

Steve Chermak, Associate Professor; Ph.D., SUNY at Albany. Presentation of crime in media, terrorism, evaluating criminal justice interventions.

Jennifer Cobbina, Assistant Professor; Ph.D. Missouri. Corrections.

Charles Corley, Associate Professor; Ph.D., Bowling Green State. Delinquency causation and control, management of correctional programs.

Christina DeJong, Associate Professor; Ph.D., Maryland College Park. Gender, race, and crime; research methodology; sentencing.

Steven Dow, Associate Professor; Ph.D., Michigan; J.D., Ohio State. Law and politics.

David Foran, Associate Professor; Ph.D., Michigan. Forensic biology.

Carole Gibbs, Assistant Professor; Ph.D., Maryland, College Park. Criminological theory, corporate crime, gender/race/class and crime, environmental justice.

Meredith Gore, Assistant Professor; Ph.D. Cornell. Environmental management, environmental risk and governance.

Vincent Hoffman, Associate Professor; Ph.D., Michigan State. Adult and juvenile corrections.

Thomas Holt, Assistant Professor; Ph.D., Missouri. Cybersecurity.

John Hudzik, Professor; Ph.D., Michigan State. Planning and budgeting, courts, manpower.

Sanja Kutnjak Ivkovich, Associate Professor; Ph.D., Delaware; J.D., Harvard. Police deviance, judicial behavior and issues in global crime.

Christopher Maxwell, Assistant Professor; Ph.D., Rutgers. Crime prevention programs, criminal justice processing of intimate violence and hate-motivated crimes.

Sheila Royo Maxwell, Associate Professor; Ph.D., Rutgers. Drug treatment and control, community corrections, juvenile crime.

Edmund McGarrell, Professor and Director; Ph.D., SUNY at Albany. Communities and crime, strategic responses, restorative justice.

Christopher Melde, Assistant Professor; Ph.D., Missouri. Evaluation research, perceptions of crime, juvenile delinquency/victimization, corrections, criminological theory, research methods.

Merry Morash, Professor; Ph.D., Maryland College Park. Gender and crime, criminological theory and methods.

Mahesh Nalla, Professor; Ph.D., SUNY at Albany. Traditional/nontraditional policing, security management, comparative criminal justice.

Louie Rivers, Assistant Professor; Ph.D., Ohio State. Environmental risk perception and decision making.

Christopher Smith, Professor; Ph.D., Connecticut; J.D., Tennessee. Courts, criminal procedure, corrections law.

Jesenia Pizarro Terrill, Assistant Professor; Ph.D., Rutgers. Social ecology of violent crime, homicide victimization and perpetration, corrections policy, international and transnational crime.

William Terrill, Associate Professor; Ph.D., Rutgers. Policing, use of force.

Ruth Waddell Smith, Assistant Professor; Ph.D., Strathclyde. Forensic chemistry.

April Zeoli, Assistant Professor; Ph.D. Johns Hopkins. Intimate partner and youth violence.

NOVA SOUTHEASTERN UNIVERSITY

Criminal Justice Institute
Master of Science Degree in Criminal Justice

Program of Study	The Master of Science degree in criminal justice is offered online through the Criminal Justice Institute at Nova Southeastern University (NSU). Graduate students participate in a program that challenges them to examine and understand complex theory and issues surrounding criminal behavior, prevention, and intervention at the local, state, and federal levels. The program design begins with core courses that establish a foundation of knowledge, which is then augmented by several specialty tracks. These concentrations allow students to focus their studies in a particular area of interest and develop the advanced analytical skills necessary to become effective researchers and criminal justice professionals.
	Courses are offered during four terms: fall, winter, spring, and summer. The total number of credits required to successfully complete the master's program is 36, including five core courses, ten specialization courses, and two elective courses. A typical student's time commitment is approximately 1½ years, averaging two courses per semester.
	Through online technology, students from agencies and professional environments all over the world share the classroom. For the past forty years, Nova Southeastern University has been a leader in innovative educational delivery. Online learning is immediate and intensely interactive. It allows learning to reach beyond traditional boundaries and promotes a spirited exchange of knowledge, experience, and perspective. Students are able to collaborate with professionals who are actively involved in criminal justice agencies and form close bonds with their peers as well as with their professors, who serve as valued guides and mentors. The instructors are experts in their respective fields and guide their students in developing the skills necessary to reach their goals, including teaching, research, and professional employment in the criminal justice field.
Research Facilities	Nova Southeastern University has a complete library located on the main campus. It is accessible to all students in the master's degree program. The online format of the program enables students to conduct online research through the Internet and research service providers. The library has the capacity to house 1.4 million volumes of reference materials, making it the largest in Florida. The University Computing Center provides data processing facilities and services to meet the instructional, research, and administrative needs of the University and is available to qualified students for computer-oriented course work.
Financial Aid	Nova Southeastern University's Office of Student Financial Assistance administers comprehensive federal, state, institutional, and private financial aid programs. Students interested in receiving a financial aid packet should contact the Office of Student Financial Assistance at 954-262-3380 or 800-806-3680 (toll-free) or via the Internet at http://www.nova.edu/cwis/finaid. Because normal application processing takes six to eight weeks, and sometimes as many as twelve weeks, it is recommended that students apply for financial aid well in advance of the date funds will be needed. Awards are made only for the academic year. Applications are generally available each January for the following academic year. Nova Southeastern University offers scholarships, Federal Stafford Student Loans, Federal Perkins Loans, and Federal Work-Study Program positions for students who meet eligibility requirements.
Cost of Study	Tuition is $520 per credit hour. There is a registration fee of $50 per semester, and books and supplies cost $80–$200 per course. The application for degree fee is $75. Fees are subject to change without notice.
Living and Housing Costs	Students enrolled in the Master of Science degree program in criminal justice are enrolled online from around the world.
Student Group	While some students have an interest in pursuing a master's degree in this field without prior experience, most students enrolled in the program are employed in some capacity in the criminal justice field.
Location	The main campus of Nova Southeastern University is located on a 300-acre site in Fort Lauderdale, Florida. Fort Lauderdale is part of Broward County, a principal coastal area in south Florida and a rapidly growing community for business, industrial, electronics, and computer opportunities. NSU is 10 miles inland from the Atlantic Ocean and is easily accessible from major highways, including I-75, I-95, I-595, the Sawgrass Expressway, and Florida's Turnpike. The climate is subtropical and has an average year-round temperature of 75 degrees. Natural areas for outdoor activities such as sailing, fishing, golf, tennis, and swimming are easily and quickly accessible from the University. With tourism as a major industry, Fort Lauderdale provides some of the best in shopping, dining, and cultural offerings, which include concerts, opera, ballet, museums, theater, and professional sporting events.
The University and The Institute	Nova Southeastern University is an independent, nonsectarian, fully accredited, coeducational university chartered by the state of Florida in 1964. As an acknowledged leader in field-based degree programs, NSU offers courses of study leading to bachelor's, master's, educational specialist, and doctoral degrees. Undergraduate and graduate programs are offered in allied health (physical therapy, physician assistant studies, and occupational therapy), business, computer sciences, criminal justice, dental medicine, education, law, marine medicine, medical education, optometry, osteopathic medicine, pharmacy, psychology, public administration, and social sciences. NSU has a total enrollment of more than 23,520 students, including over 5,220 undergraduates.
	The Institute was established in 2001 to provide a supportive academic and professional environment for faculty members and students studying criminal justice.
Applying	To be admitted to the program, applicants must complete all parts of the admissions application form; submit an official transcript for each postsecondary school attended; provide a personal statement 150 to 300 words in length, indicating their goals in pursing a criminal justice degree at the graduate level; provide three letters of recommendation; and include a nonrefundable $50 application fee.
Correspondence and Information	Enrollment Processing Services (EPS) Attention: Criminal Justice Institute Nova Southeastern University 3301 College Avenue P.O. Box 299000 Fort Lauderdale, Florida 33329-9905 Phone: 954-262-7001 800-541-NOVA (6682; toll-free) E-mail: cji@nova.edu Web site: http://www.cji.nova.edu

Nova Southeastern University

THE FACULTY AND THEIR RESEARCH

Catherine Arcabascio, Professor and CJI Course Director; J.D., Boston College, 1987. Co-Founder and Director of the Florida Innocence Project.

Richard Beauchamp, Adjunct Professor; J.D., Stetson, 1984. Practices in the areas of insurance, real estate, commercial, and construction litigation and nursing home/health-care litigation.

Warren Brown, Adjunct Assistant Professor and Detective; Ph.D., Nova Southeastern, 2000; certified law enforcement officer. Conflict resolution, cultural diversity, defense tactics, hostage negotiation, drug abuse resistance education, gang resistance, investigation and interrogations.

Johnny Burris, Law School Professor and CJI Course Director; LL.M., Columbia, 1984. Criminal procedure, constitutional law, administrative law.

Frank De Piano, University Professor, Vice President of Academic Affairs, Chair, and CJI Course Director; Ph.D., South Carolina, 1980. Clinical psychology.

James Nardozzi, Adjunct Assistant Professor and Deputy Chief of Police; D.P.A., Nova Southeastern, 2003; certified law enforcement officer. Police administration and management, criminal investigation, white-collar crime, criminal justice.

Irving Rosenbaum, Vice Chancellor and Provost, Health Professions, and CJI Course Director; D.P.A., Nova Southeastern, 1984. Town administrator, city manager, consultant, research analyst, management analyst.

Rae Shearn, Esq., Adjunct Professor; former division chief prosecutor for Janet Reno. Currently, Shearn practices criminal defense in state and federal courts in the area of white-collar crime, complex RICO prosecutions, narcotic offenses, death-penalty litigation, and criminal defense for all other criminal prosecution.

Vincent Van Hasselt, Professor, CJI Course Director, and Interim Associate Dean, Center for Psychological Studies; Ph.D., Pittsburgh, 1979; certified law enforcement officer. Interpersonal violence, police psychology, criminal investigative analysis (psychological profiling), apprehension, interviewing and interrogation techniques, behavioral criminology.

George Yacoubian, Adjunct Assistant Professor and Director of Research; Ph.D., Madison, 2001. Drug treatment, drug prevention, drug-testing technology, genocide.

ROGER WILLIAMS UNIVERSITY

School of Justice Studies

Programs of Study

Today's criminal justice system professional faces an increasingly complex society. The School of Justice Studies at Roger Williams University (RWU) is aware of the growing need for competent, well-rounded individuals who can rise to these challenges. Because of this, RWU offers two graduate degree programs in criminal justice: the Master of Science degree program in criminal justice and the joint Master of Science/Juris Doctor (M.S./J.D.) degree. These degree programs prepare graduates to formulate justice system policy and serve effectively as administrators of U.S. justice system agencies.

Criminal justice graduate students will be exposed to both the theory and practice of the justice system. They will explore the fields of criminology, examining the nature and causes of crime, and justice system management, which focuses on modern administrative theory, legal issues in personnel administration, and the management of criminal justice agencies. Students with a strong interest in the legal aspects of criminal justice may enroll in the accelerated dual-degree program with the School of Law. A Roger Williams graduate education is all about the individual. Many evening classes are available for students working as professionals in criminal justice or the legal field. Conferences, seminars, and training sessions are available to students through a partnership with the University's Justice System Training and Research Institute. Graduate students in the criminal justice program often present research papers at national and local conferences.

Research Facilities

A robust research library is integral to graduate study. The Learning Commons at the Roger Williams University Library offers a wide array of instructional resources for the students. It is an improved model for research—a one-stop shop for instructional technology, traditional, and database research—that provides students access to myriad research resources. The University's state-of-the-art computer laboratories allow student access to the latest word and statistical processing software packages available, including full Internet access. The University's expansive library houses approximately 2,000 volumes and hundreds of films and other nonprint materials related to the U.S. justice system. Master's degree candidates also have access to the LexisNexis network and Westlaw as well as the RWU Law Library. In addition, the University is a member of the Helin Consortium, which gives students access to more than a million volumes of printed material. Quiet study space and group research areas are also available.

Financial Aid

Financing a graduate education can be challenging, especially in these trying economic times. Roger Williams University recognizes that some students may need financial assistance to meet the cost of higher education. Students with financial need may be able to receive funds from federal loan programs. Students with fully accepted status who maintain a minimum of 6 credits per semester are eligible to receive loans that cover the cost of graduate education. In order to be considered for the federal loan programs, students must submit the Free Application for Federal Student Aid (FAFSA), which is available from the Office of Financial Aid or at http://www.fafsa.gov.

Cost of Study

The 2008–09 graduate tuition was $639 per credit. Each 3-credit course cost $1917. Some additional fees may apply. Tuition information for the 2009–10 academic year is available at http://financialaid.rwu.edu.

Living and Housing Costs

University housing is available for graduate students. However, it is not guaranteed and the majority of graduate students seek a variety of off-campus housing options. In 2008–09, the average cost for on-campus graduate housing was $7313 per academic year. For more information about off-campus housing, visit http://housing.rwu.edu and click the "off-campus living" tab.

Student Group

The criminal justice graduate program is a unique blend of student voices and perspectives, including current local and state police officers, justice system professionals, and aspiring law enforcement students. Part-time study is available for students who are working professionals.

Location

Roger Williams University is located in Bristol, Rhode Island, a seaside town that is home to antique stores, gourmet restaurants, ice cream shops, and spas. The campus is less than 30 minutes by bus from Providence, Rhode Island's capital and largest city, which is packed with museums, coffee shops, the Providence Place Mall, live music, and much more. Providence is also a regional transportation hub, with an international airport and both bus and train stations. Also less than 30 minutes away from campus is Newport, home of famous beaches, shopping, festivals, and open markets.

The University and The School

Roger Williams University is a 52-year-old independent, coeducational liberal arts university that has quickly established itself as a leader in higher education. A dynamic educational environment in which students live and learn to be global citizens, the University is committed to its mantra of "Learning to bridge the world."

With thirty-nine academic programs and a robust array of co-curricular activities available on its waterfront campus in historic Bristol, Rhode Island, RWU looks to a set of core values in fulfilling its mission to prepare students for life as twenty-first century citizen-scholars. Over the past decade, the institution has achieved unprecedented academic and financial successes. In 2008, *U.S. News & World Report* named Roger Williams the eighth-ranked baccalaureate college in the north.

The School of Justice Studies offers both undergraduate and graduate degrees. SJS faculty members are regionally, nationally, and internationally known and the majority holds Ph.D.s in criminal justice, sociology, psychology, or a closely related field. Many also hold the Juris Doctor in addition to their doctorate. Complementing the traditional curriculum is the School's partnership with the Justice System Training and Research Institute (JSTRI). The Institute serves as a national model for integrating current research methodologies and state-of-the-art technology with the programmatic needs of the justice system. RWU's relationship with the JSTRI affords students additional learning and training experiences, as well as networking opportunities with criminal justice professionals.

Applying

Roger Williams University and the School of Justice Studies seek well-rounded students with leadership potential and a demonstrated commitment to education and academic achievement. Admission requirements include a bachelor's degree from an accredited institution, official transcripts of all previous undergraduate and graduate course work, a personal statement discussing relevant past experiences and career goals, two letters of recommendation attesting to the candidate's potential to complete graduate work, and a completed application form signed and accompanied by the $50 application fee. Entrance exams are not required, but applicants with a cumulative undergraduate grade point average below 3.0 are strongly encouraged to take either the GRE or MAT. Students interested in the Master of Science in Criminal Justice/Juris Doctor joint degree must apply separately to both the graduate program in the School of Justice Studies and the Juris Doctor program in the School of Law. They may submit their LSAT scores with both applications.

Applications are accepted in both paper and electronic form.

Correspondence and Information

Jason Pina
Dean of Continuing Studies and Graduate Admission
Roger Williams University
One Old Ferry Road
Bristol, Rhode Island 02809

Phone: 888-674-8479 (toll-free)
E-mail: gradadmit@rwu.edu
Web site: http://www.rwu.edu

Roger Williams University

THE FACULTY

Stephanie P. Manzi, Dean; Ph.D., Maryland.
Julie Coon, Assistant Professor of Criminal Justice; Ph.D., Cincinnati.
Kathleen M. Dunn, Professor; J.D., Boston University; Ph.D., Brown.
Robert P. Engvall, Professor of Criminal Justice; J.D., Ph.D., Iowa.
Jeffrey A. Jenkins, Associate Professor of Criminal Justice; J.D., New Mexico; Ed.D., Rutgers.
Christopher Menton, Associate Professor of Criminal Justice; Ed.D., Boston University.
Melissa Russano, Assistant Professor of Criminal Justice; Ph.D., Florida International.
Yolanda M. Scott, Associate Professor of Criminal Justice; Ph.D., Kentucky.
Sean Varano, Assistant Professor of Criminal Justice; J.D., Roger Williams; Ph.D., Michigan State.

Section 19
Economics

This section contains a directory of institutions offering graduate work in economics, followed by in-depth entries submitted by institutions that chose to prepare detailed program descriptions. Additional information about programs listed in the directory but not augmented by an in-depth entry may be obtained by writing directly to the dean of a graduate school or chair of a department at the address given in the directory.

For programs offering related work, see also in this book *Family and Consumer Sciences, Political Science and International Affairs,* and *Public, Regional, and Industrial Affairs.* In the other guides in this series:

Graduate Programs in the Physical Sciences, Mathematics, Agricultural Sciences, the Environment & Natural Resources
See *Agricultural and Food Sciences* and *Mathematical Sciences*
Graduate Programs in Engineering & Applied Sciences
See *Computer Science and Information Technology; Geological, Mineral/Mining, and Petroleum Engineering;* and *Industrial Engineering*
Graduate Programs in Business, Education, Health, Information Studies, Law & Social Work
See *Business Administration and Management*

CONTENTS

Program Directories

Agricultural Economics and Agribusiness 746
Applied Economics 750
Economic Development 752
Economics 755
International Economics 773
Mineral Economics 773

Announcement and Display

University of California, Riverside 765
Washington University in St. Louis 772

Close-Ups

Southern Illinois University Carbondale 775
Suffolk University 777
University of Illinois at Urbana–Champaign 779
University of New Hampshire 781
The University of Texas at Dallas 783

See also:

Central European University—Social Sciences and Humanities 349
Fordham University—International Political Economy and Development 865
The New School: A University—Political and Social Science 1251
University of California, San Diego—International Relations and Pacific Studies 881
University of Pittsburgh—Public and International Affairs 1243

Agricultural Economics and Agribusiness

Alabama Agricultural and Mechanical University, School of Graduate Studies, School of Agricultural and Environmental Sciences, Department of Agribusiness, Huntsville, AL 35811. Offers MS. Part-time programs available. *Students:* 6 full-time (5 women), 5 part-time (1 woman); includes 10 minority (all African Americans), 1 international. In 2008, 2 master's awarded. *Degree requirements:* For master's, thesis (for some programs). *Entrance requirements:* For master's, GRE General Test. Additional exam requirements/recommendations for international students: Required—TOEFL (minimum score 500 paper-based; 173 computer-based; 61 iBT). *Application deadline:* For fall admission, 5/1 priority date for domestic students. Applications are processed on a rolling basis. Application fee: $25. Electronic applications accepted. *Expenses:* Tuition, area resident: Full-time $3924; part-time $2616 per term. Tuition, nonresident: part-time $5234 per year. International tuition: $7848 full-time. Required fees: $198; $396 per credit hour. $2841 per term. One-time fee: $8498 full-time; $5682 part-time. Full-time tuition and fees vary according to program. *Financial support:* In 2008–09, fellowships with tuition reimbursements (averaging $15,000 per year), research assistantships with tuition reimbursements (averaging $10,000 per year) were awarded. Financial award application deadline: 4/1. *Faculty research:* Farm economics. *Unit head:* Dr. Willie J. Cheatham, Chair, 256-372-5410. *Application contact:* Dr. Caula Beyl, Dean, School of Graduate Studies, 256-372-5266, Fax: 256-372-5269, E-mail: caula.beyl@aamu.edu.

Alcorn State University, School of Graduate Studies, School of Agriculture and Applied Science, Alcorn State, MS 39096-7500. Offers agricultural economics (MS Ag); agronomy (MS Ag); animal science (MS Ag). *Degree requirements:* For master's, thesis optional. *Faculty research:* Aquatic systems, dairy herd improvement, fruit production, alternative farming practices.

American University of Beirut, Graduate Programs, Faculty of Agricultural and Food Sciences, Beirut, Lebanon. Offers agricultural economics (MS); animal sciences (MS); ecosystem management (MSES); food technology (MS); irrigation (MS); mechanization (MS); nutrition (MS); plant protection (MS); plant science (MS); poultry science (MS); soils (MS). Part-time programs available. *Degree requirements:* For master's, one foreign language, comprehensive exam, thesis (for some programs). *Entrance requirements:* For master's, letter of recommendation. Additional exam requirements/recommendations for international students: Required—TOEFL (minimum score 600 paper-based; 250 computer-based; 100 iBT), IELTS (minimum score 7.5). *Faculty research:* Sustainable animal systems/agriculture; natural resource management; community nutrition, obesity and food safety; integrated pest management; ecosystem management.

Arizona State University, Graduate College, W.P. Carey School of Business, Program in Business Administration, Tempe, AZ 85287. Offers agribusiness (PhD); business administration (MBA); finance (MBA, PhD); health sector management (MBA); information systems (PhD); management (MBA, PhD); marketing (MBA, PhD); supply chain management (MBA, PhD); JD/MBA; MBA/M Arch; MBA/MHSM. *Accreditation:* AACSB. *Degree requirements:* For master's, thesis optional; for doctorate, thesis/dissertation. *Entrance requirements:* For master's, GMAT.

Arizona State University at the Polytechnic Campus, Morrison School of Management and Agribusiness, Mesa, AZ 85212. Offers agribusiness (MS). Part-time and evening/weekend programs available. *Degree requirements:* For master's, thesis, oral defense. *Entrance requirements:* For master's, GMAT, GRE General Test, MAT, minimum GPA of 3.0, 3 letters of recommendation, resumé. Additional exam requirements/recommendations for international students: Required—TOEFL (minimum score 550 paper-based; 213 computer-based); Recommended—TWE. Electronic applications accepted. *Faculty research:* Agribusiness marketing, management and financial structuring.

Auburn University, Graduate School, College of Agriculture, Department of Agricultural Economics and Rural Sociology, Auburn University, AL 36849. Offers agricultural economics (M Ag, MS); applied economics (PhD). Part-time programs available. *Faculty:* 18 full-time (4 women). *Students:* 26 full-time (10 women), 6 part-time (1 woman); includes 4 minority (3 African Americans, 1 Asian American or Pacific Islander), 21 international. Average age 32. 36 applicants, 44% accepted, 7 enrolled. In 2008, 4 master's, 4 doctorates awarded. *Degree requirements:* For master's, thesis (for some programs); for doctorate, thesis/dissertation. *Entrance requirements:* For master's and doctorate, GRE General Test. *Application deadline:* For fall admission, 7/7 for domestic students; for spring admission, 11/24 for domestic students. Applications are processed on a rolling basis. Application fee: $25 ($50 for international students). Electronic applications accepted. *Expenses:* Tuition, area resident: Full-time $5880; part-time $243 per credit hour. Tuition, state resident: full-time $5880; part-time $243 per credit hour. Tuition, nonresident: full-time $17,640; part-time $729 per credit hour. International tuition: $17,846 full-time. Required fees: $620. Tuition and fees vary according to program and reciprocity agreements. *Financial support:* Research assistantships, teaching assistantships, Federal Work-Study available. Support available to part-time students. Financial award application deadline: 3/15. *Faculty research:* Farm management, agricultural marketing, production economics, resource economics, agricultural finance. *Unit head:* Dr. Curtis M. Jolly, Chair, 334-844-4800. *Application contact:* Dr. George Flowers, Dean of the Graduate School, 334-844-2125.

California Polytechnic State University, San Luis Obispo, College of Agriculture, Food and Environmental Sciences, Department of Agribusiness, San Luis Obispo, CA 93407. Offers MS. Part-time programs available. *Faculty:* 2 full-time (1 woman). *Students:* 3 full-time (1 woman), 3 part-time (2 women). Average age 28. 5 applicants, 80% accepted, 3 enrolled. *Degree requirements:* For master's, comprehensive exam, thesis. *Entrance requirements:* For master's, GRE General Test, minimum GPA of 2.75 in last 90 quarter units of course work. Additional exam requirements/recommendations for international students: Required—TOEFL (minimum score 550 paper-based; 213 computer-based), Either TOEFL or IELTS is acceptable. *Application deadline:* For fall admission, 7/1 for domestic students, 11/30 for international students; for winter admission, 11/1 for domestic students, 6/30 for international students; for spring admission, 2/1 for domestic students. Applications are processed on a rolling basis. Application fee: $55. Electronic applications accepted. *Expenses:* Tuition, nonresident: full-time $10,170; part-time $226 per unit. Required fees: $5751; $1265 per quarter. *Financial support:* Fellowships, research assistantships, teaching assistantships, career-related internships or fieldwork, Federal Work-Study, institutionally sponsored loans, scholarships/grants, and unspecified assistantships available. Support available to part-time students. Financial award application deadline: 3/2; financial award applicants required to submit FAFSA. *Unit head:* Dr. James Ahern, Graduate Coordinator, 805-756-5030, Fax: 805-756-5040, E-mail: jahern@calpoly.edu. *Application contact:* Dr. Mark Shelton, Associate Dean/Graduate Coordinator, 805-756-2161, Fax: 805-756-6577, E-mail: mshelton@calpoly.edu.

Colorado State University, Graduate School, College of Agricultural Sciences, Department of Agricultural and Resource Economics, Fort Collins, CO 80523-1172. Offers MS, PhD. Part-time programs available. *Faculty:* 17 full-time (3 women), 1 part-time/adjunct (0 women). *Students:* 26 full-time (13 women), 12 part-time (4 women); includes 2 minority (1 American Indian/Alaska Native, 1 Asian American or Pacific Islander), 9 international. Average age 29. 37 applicants, 81% accepted, 11 enrolled. In 2008, 4 master's, 3 doctorates awarded. Terminal master's awarded for partial completion of doctoral program. *Degree requirements:* For master's, thesis; for doctorate, comprehensive exam, thesis/dissertation. *Entrance requirements:* For master's and doctorate, GRE General Test, minimum GPA of 3.0, bachelor's degree, 3 letters of recommendation, statement of purpose. Additional exam requirements/recommendations for international students: Required—TOEFL (minimum score 550 paper-based; 213 computer-based; 80 iBT), IELTS (minimum score 6). Application fee: $50. Electronic applications accepted. *Expenses:* Tuition, area resident: Full-time $5620; part-time $312.25 per credit. Tuition, state resident: full-time $5620; part-time $312.25 per credit. Tuition, nonresident: full-time $17,253; part-time $958.50 per credit. Required fees: $1449.56; $82.35 per credit. *Financial support:* In 2008–09, 22 students received support, including 17 research assistantships with full tuition reimbursements available (averaging $13,319 per year), 5 teaching assistantships with full tuition reimbursements available (averaging $12,518 per year); fellowships with partial tuition reimbursements available, unspecified assistantships and fellowships (first year) also available. *Faculty research:* Agricultural production economics, marketing and agribusiness economics, international development, natural resource economics, environmental economics. Total annual research expenditures: $1.7 million. *Unit head:* Stephen P. Davies, Chair, 970-491-6955, Fax: 970-491-2067, E-mail: stephen.davies@colostate.edu. *Application contact:* Barbara A. Brown, Program Assistant, 970-491-6955, Fax: 970-491-2067, E-mail: barbara.brown@colostate.edu.

Cornell University, Graduate School, Graduate Fields of Agriculture and Life Sciences, Field of Applied Economics and Management, Ithaca, NY 14853-0001. Offers agricultural economics (MPS, MS, PhD), including agricultural finance, applied econometrics and quantitative analysis, economics of development, farm management and production economics (MPS), marketing and food distribution (MPS), public policy analysis (MPS); resource economics (MPS, MS, PhD), including environmental economics, environmental management (MPS), resource economics. *Faculty:* 46 full-time (6 women). *Students:* 81 full-time (34 women); includes 4 minority (1 African American, 1 American Indian/Alaska Native, 1 Asian American or Pacific Islander, 1 Hispanic American), 55 international. Average age 30. 243 applicants, 34% accepted, 26 enrolled. In 2008, 11 master's, 9 doctorates awarded. Terminal master's awarded for partial completion of doctoral program. *Degree requirements:* For master's, thesis (MS); for doctorate, comprehensive exam, thesis/dissertation. *Entrance requirements:* For master's and doctorate, GRE General Test, 2 letters of recommendation. Additional exam requirements/recommendations for international students: Required—TOEFL (minimum score 550 paper-based; 213 computer-based; 77 iBT). *Application deadline:* For fall admission, 1/15 priority date for domestic students. Application fee: $70. Electronic applications accepted. *Expenses:* Tuition: Full-time $29,500. Required fees: $70. Full-time tuition and fees vary according to degree level, program and student level. *Financial support:* In 2008–09, 43 students received support, including 6 fellowships with full tuition reimbursements available, 13 research assistantships with full tuition reimbursements available, 24 teaching assistantships with full tuition reimbursements available; institutionally sponsored loans, scholarships/grants, health care benefits, tuition waivers (full and partial), and unspecified assistantships also available. Financial award applicants required to submit FAFSA. *Faculty research:* Production economics, international economic development and trade, farm management and finance, resource and environmental economics, agricultural marketing and policy. *Unit head:* Director of Graduate Studies, 607-255-8048, Fax: 607-255-9984, E-mail: aegrad@cornell.edu. *Application contact:* Graduate Field Assistant, 607-255-8048, Fax: 607-255-9984, E-mail: aegrad@cornell.edu.

Cornell University, Graduate School, Graduate Fields of Agriculture and Life Sciences, Field of International Agriculture and Rural Development, Ithaca, NY 14853-0001. Offers international agriculture and development (MPS). *Faculty:* 46 full-time (9 women). *Students:* 35 full-time (11 women); includes 3 minority (1 American Indian/Alaska Native, 2 Asian Americans or Pacific Islanders), 4 international. Average age 31. 27 applicants, 59% accepted, 9 enrolled. In 2008, 6 master's awarded. *Degree requirements:* For master's, project paper. *Entrance requirements:* For master's, GRE General Test (recommended), 2 years of development experience, 2 letters of recommendation. Additional exam requirements/recommendations for international students: Required—TOEFL (minimum score 550 paper-based; 213 computer-based; 77 iBT). *Application deadline:* For fall admission, 3/1 for domestic students. Application fee: $70. Electronic applications accepted. *Expenses:* Tuition: Full-time $29,500. Required fees: $70. Full-time tuition and fees vary according to degree level, program and student level. *Financial support:* In 2008–09, 4 students received support, including 1 research assistantship with full tuition reimbursement available, 3 teaching assistantships with full tuition reimbursements available; fellowships with full tuition reimbursements available, institutionally sponsored loans, scholarships/grants, health care benefits, tuition waivers (full and partial), and unspecified assistantships also available. Financial award applicants required to submit FAFSA. *Unit head:* Director of Graduate Studies, 607-255-3037, Fax: 607-255-1005. *Application contact:* Graduate Field Assistant, 607-255-3035, Fax: 607-255-1005, E-mail: mpsiard@cornell.edu.

Delaware Valley College, Program in Food and Agribusiness, Doylestown, PA 18901-2697. Offers MBA. *Entrance requirements:* For master's, GMAT or undergraduate GPA greater than 3.0. *Expenses:* Contact institution.

Florida Agricultural and Mechanical University, Division of Graduate Studies, Research, and Continuing Education, College of Engineering Science, Technology, and Agriculture, Division of Agricultural Sciences, Tallahassee, FL 32307-3200. Offers agribusiness (MS); animal science (MS); engineering technology (MS); entomology (MS); food science (MS); international programs (MS); plant science (MS). *Degree requirements:* For master's, thesis. *Entrance requirements:* For master's, GRE General Test, minimum GPA of 3.0. Additional exam requirements/recommendations for international students: Required—TOEFL (minimum score 500 paper-based).

Illinois State University, Graduate School, College of Applied Science and Technology, Department of Agriculture, Normal, IL 61790-2200. Offers agribusiness (MS). *Degree requirements:* For master's, thesis optional. *Entrance requirements:* For master's, GRE General Test, minimum GPA of 3.0 in last 60 hours. *Faculty research:* Engineering-economic system models for rural ethanol production facilities, development and evaluation of a propane-fueled, production scale, on-site thermal destruction system C-FAR 2007; field scale evaluation and technology transfer of economically, ecologically systems; sound liquid swine manure treatment and application.

Instituto Centroamericano de Administración de Empresas, Graduate Programs, La Garita, Costa Rica. Offers agribusiness (MIAM); business administration (EMBA); economics and finance (MBA); industry and technology (MBA); sustainable development (MBA). *Degree requirements:* For master's, comprehensive exam, essay. *Entrance requirements:* For master's, GMAT or GRE, fluency in Spanish, interview, letters of recommendation, minimum 1 year of work experience. Electronic applications accepted. *Faculty research:* Competitiveness, production.

Iowa State University of Science and Technology, Graduate College, College of Liberal Arts and Sciences, Department of Economics and College of Agriculture, Program in Agricultural Economics, Ames, IA 50011. Offers MS, PhD. *Faculty:* 26 full-time (2 women), 3 part-time/adjunct (all women). *Students:* 35 full-time (12 women), 10 part-time (5 women); includes 1 minority (Asian American or Pacific Islander), 33 international. 54 applicants, 31% accepted, 5 enrolled. In 2008, 7 master's, 1 doctorate awarded. *Degree requirements:* For master's, thesis or alternative; for doctorate, thesis/dissertation. *Entrance requirements:* For master's and doctorate, GRE General Test. Additional exam requirements/recommendations for international students: Required—TOEFL (minimum score 570 paper-based; 88 iBT), IELTS (6.5) or TOEFL. *Application deadline:* For fall admission, 1/20 priority date for domestic and international students. Application fee: $30 ($70 for international students). Electronic applications accepted. *Expenses:* Tuition, area resident: Full-time $6446; part-time $359 per credit. Tuition, state resident: full-time $6446; part-time $359 per credit. Tuition, nonresident: full-time $17,330; part-time $963 per credit. Required fees: $790; $249.25 per semester. Tuition and fees vary according to course load and program. *Financial support:* In 2008–09, 19 research assistantships with full and partial tuition reimbursements (averaging $14,400 per year), 23 teaching assistantships with full and partial tuition reimbursements (averaging $15,030 per year) were awarded; fellowships, scholarships/grants, health care benefits, and unspecified assistantships also available. *Unit head:* Section Leader, 515-294-2702. *Application contact:* Dr. John Schroeter, Information Contact, 515-294-2702, E-mail: grad@econ.iastate.edu.

Kansas State University, Graduate School, College of Agriculture, Department of Agricultural Economics, Manhattan, KS 66506. Offers MAB, MS, PhD. Part-time programs available.

Postbaccalaureate distance learning degree programs offered (minimal on-campus study). *Faculty:* 26 full-time (1 woman), 1 part-time/adjunct (0 women). *Students:* 26 full-time (13 women), 8 part-time (4 women); includes 2 minority (both African Americans), 6 international. Average age 25. 48 applicants, 81% accepted, 14 enrolled. In 2008, 34 master's, 2 doctorates awarded. Terminal master's awarded for partial completion of doctoral program. *Degree requirements:* For master's, thesis or alternative, oral exam; for doctorate, thesis/dissertation, preliminary exams. *Entrance requirements:* For master's and doctorate, GRE General Test. Additional exam requirements/recommendations for international students: Required—TOEFL (minimum score 550 paper-based; 213 computer-based). *Application deadline:* For fall admission, 2/1 priority date for domestic students; for spring admission, 10/1 for domestic students. Applications are processed on a rolling basis. Application fee: $30 ($55 for international students). Electronic applications accepted. *Expenses:* Tuition, area resident: Full-time $6466; part-time $269.40 per credit hour. Tuition, state resident: full-time $6466; part-time $269.40 per credit hour. Tuition, nonresident: full-time $14,874; part-time $619.75 per credit hour. Required fees: $673; $23.40 per credit hour. Tuition and fees vary according to campus/location. *Financial support:* In 2008–09, 11 fellowships (averaging $22,500 per year), 26 research assistantships (averaging $18,004 per year), 6 teaching assistantships with partial tuition reimbursements (averaging $15,488 per year) were awarded; Federal Work-Study, institutionally sponsored loans, and scholarships/grants also available. Support available to part-time students. Financial award application deadline: 3/1; financial award applicants required to submit FAFSA. *Faculty research:* Livestock marketing, biofuels research, natural resources, agribusiness industry, and international development and trade. Total annual research expenditures: $1.7 million. *Unit head:* Allen Featherstone, Head, 785-532-4441, Fax: 785-532-6925, E-mail: afeather@ksu.edu. *Application contact:* Dr. John Crespi, Director, 785-532-3357, Fax: 785-532-6925, E-mail: jcrespi@agecon.ksu.edu.

Louisiana State University and Agricultural and Mechanical College, Graduate School, College of Agriculture, Department of Agricultural Economics and Agribusiness, Baton Rouge, LA 70803. Offers MS, PhD. *Degree requirements:* For master's, thesis (for some programs); for doctorate, thesis/dissertation. *Entrance requirements:* For master's and doctorate, GRE General Test, minimum GPA of 3.0. Additional exam requirements/recommendations for international students: Required—TOEFL (minimum score 550 paper-based; 213 computer-based; 79 iBT). Electronic applications accepted. *Faculty research:* Natural and environmental economics, agribusiness, marketing, production economics, community economics, rural development.

McGill University, Faculty of Graduate and Postdoctoral Studies, Faculty of Agricultural and Environmental Sciences, Department of Agricultural Economics, Montréal, QC H3A 2T5, Canada. Offers M Sc.

Michigan State University, The Graduate School, College of Agriculture and Natural Resources, Department of Agricultural, Food, and Resource Economics, East Lansing, MI 48824. Offers agricultural economics (MS, PhD). *Entrance requirements:* Additional exam requirements/recommendations for international students: Required—TOEFL (minimum score 550 paper-based; 213 computer-based), Michigan State University ELT (85), Michigan ELAB (83). Electronic applications accepted.

Mississippi State University, College of Agriculture and Life Sciences, Department of Agricultural Economics, Mississippi State, MS 39762. Offers agribusiness management (MABM); agricultural economics (PhD). Part-time programs available. *Degree requirements:* For master's, thesis (for some programs), comprehensive oral or written exam, thesis defense; for doctorate, thesis/dissertation, qualifying written exam, research exam. *Entrance requirements:* For master's, GRE, GMAT, minimum GPA of 3.0; for doctorate, GRE, minimum GPA of 3.0. Additional exam requirements/recommendations for international students: Required—TOEFL. Electronic applications accepted. *Faculty research:* Production economics, policy, resource economics, international trade, agribusiness management.

Montana State University, College of Graduate Studies, College of Agriculture, Department of Agricultural Economics and Economics, Bozeman, MT 59717. Offers applied economics (MS). Part-time programs available. *Degree requirements:* For master's, comprehensive exam. *Entrance requirements:* For master's, GRE General Test. Additional exam requirements/recommendations for international students: Required—TOEFL (minimum score 550 paper-based; 213 computer-based). Electronic applications accepted. *Faculty research:* Agricultural production, agricultural marketing/finance, governance (private and public), natural resource management.

New Mexico State University, Graduate School, College of Agriculture, Consumer and Environmental Sciences, Department of Agricultural Economics and Agricultural Business, Las Cruces, NM 88003-8001. Offers agribusiness (M Ag, MBA); agricultural economics (MS); economics (MA). Part-time programs available. *Faculty:* 5 full-time (1 woman), 1 part-time/adjunct (0 women). *Students:* 18 full-time (8 women), 7 part-time (4 women); includes 4 minority (1 African American, 1 American Indian/Alaska Native, 1 Asian American or Pacific Islander, 1 Hispanic American), 6 international. Average age 25. 12 applicants, 75% accepted, 5 enrolled. In 2008, 9 master's awarded. *Degree requirements:* For master's, thesis (for some programs). *Entrance requirements:* For master's, previous course work in intermediate microeconomics, intermediate macroeconomics, college-level calculus, statistics. Additional exam requirements/recommendations for international students: Required—TOEFL. *Application deadline:* For fall admission, 7/1 priority date for domestic and international students; for spring admission, 11/1 priority date for domestic and international students. Applications are processed on a rolling basis. Application fee: $30 ($50 for international students). Electronic applications accepted. *Expenses:* Tuition, area resident: Full-time $3890; part-time $212.85 per credit. Tuition, state resident: full-time $3890; part-time $212.85 per credit. Tuition, nonresident: full-time $13,916; part-time $630.55 per credit. Required fees: $1218; $609 per semester. *Financial support:* In 2008–09, 5 students received support, including 9 research assistantships (averaging $16,217 per year), 5 teaching assistantships (averaging $11,060 per year); career-related internships or fieldwork and health care benefits also available. Financial award application deadline: 3/1. *Faculty research:* Natural resource policy, production economics and farm/ranch management, agribusiness and marketing, international marketing and trade, agricultural risk management. *Unit head:* Dr. Terry Crawford, Head, 575-646-3215, Fax: 575-646-3808, E-mail: crawford@nmsu.edu. *Application contact:* Dr. L. Allen Torell, Professor, 575-646-4732, Fax: 575-646-3808, E-mail: atorell@nmsu.edu.

North Carolina Agricultural and Technical State University, Graduate School, School of Agriculture and Environmental Sciences, Department of Agribusiness, Applied Economics, and Agriscience Education, Greensboro, NC 27411. Offers agricultural economics (MS); agricultural education (MS). *Accreditation:* NCATE. Part-time and evening/weekend programs available. *Degree requirements:* For master's, comprehensive exam, thesis or alternative, qualifying exam. *Entrance requirements:* For master's, GRE General Test, minimum GPA of 3.0. *Faculty research:* Aid for small farmers, agricultural technology resources, labor force mobility, agrology.

North Carolina State University, Graduate School, College of Agriculture and Life Sciences, Program in Agricultural and Resource Economics, Raleigh, NC 27695. Offers MS. Part-time programs available. *Degree requirements:* For master's, thesis. *Entrance requirements:* Additional exam requirements/recommendations for international students: Required—TOEFL. Electronic applications accepted. *Faculty research:* Resource economics, international economics, labor economics, econometrics, environmental economics.

North Dakota State University, College of Graduate and Interdisciplinary Studies, College of Agriculture, Food Systems, and Natural Resources, Department of Agribusiness and Applied Economics, Fargo, ND 58105. Offers agribusiness and applied economics (MS); international agribusiness (MS); natural resource management (MS). Part-time programs available. *Faculty:* 16 full-time (3 women), 5 part-time/adjunct (1 woman). *Students:* 16 full-time (5 women), 2 part-time (0 women); includes 3 African Americans, 4 Asian Americans or Pacific Islanders, 1 Hispanic American. Average age 24. 28 applicants, 68% accepted, 12 enrolled. In 2008, 13 master's awarded. *Degree requirements:* For master's, thesis. *Entrance requirements:* For master's, minimum GPA of 3.0. Additional exam requirements/recommendations for international students: Required—TOEFL (minimum score 525 paper-based; 225 computer-based; 71 iBT). *Application deadline:* For fall admission, 2/1 priority date for domestic students, 3/1 priority date for international students. Applications are processed on a rolling basis. Application fee: $45 ($60 for international students). Electronic applications accepted. *Financial support:* In 2008–09, 8 research assistantships with tuition reimbursements (averaging $14,520 per year) were awarded; Federal Work-Study and institutionally sponsored loans also available. Financial award application deadline: 4/15. *Faculty research:* Agribusiness, transportation, marketing, microeconomics, trade. Total annual research expenditures: $1 million. *Unit head:* Dr. Thomas I. Wahl, Chair, 701-231-7470, Fax: 701-231-7400. *Application contact:* Dr. Thomas I. Wahl, Chair, 701-231-7470, Fax: 701-231-7400.

Northwest Missouri State University, Graduate School, Melvin and Valorie Booth College of Business and Professional Studies, Department of Agriculture, Program in Agricultural Economics, Maryville, MO 64468-6001. Offers MBA. *Degree requirements:* For master's, comprehensive exam. *Entrance requirements:* For master's, GMAT, minimum GPA of 2.5. Additional exam requirements/recommendations for international students: Required—TOEFL (minimum score 550 paper-based; 213 computer-based).

The Ohio State University, Graduate School, College of Food, Agricultural, and Environmental Sciences, Department of Agricultural, Environmental, and Development Economics, Columbus, OH 43210. Offers agricultural economics and rural sociology (MS, PhD). *Degree requirements:* For master's, thesis optional; for doctorate, thesis/dissertation. *Entrance requirements:* For master's and doctorate, GRE General Test. Additional exam requirements/recommendations for international students: Required—TOEFL (paper-based 550; computer-based 213) or IELTS (7) or Michigan English Language Assessment Battery (92). Electronic applications accepted.

Oklahoma State University, College of Agricultural Science and Natural Resources, Department of Agricultural Economics, Stillwater, OK 74078. Offers M Ag, MS, PhD. *Faculty:* 36 full-time (7 women). *Students:* 43 full-time (14 women), 21 part-time (9 women); includes 6 minority (3 American Indian/Alaska Native, 1 Asian American or Pacific Islander, 2 Hispanic Americans), 35 international. Average age 29. 87 applicants, 46% accepted, 18 enrolled. In 2008, 15 master's, 7 doctorates awarded. *Degree requirements:* For master's, thesis or report, oral exam; for doctorate, comprehensive exam, thesis/dissertation. *Entrance requirements:* For master's and doctorate, GRE or GMAT. Additional exam requirements/recommendations for international students: Required—TOEFL. *Application deadline:* For fall admission, 3/1 priority date for international students; for spring admission, 8/1 priority date for international students. Applications are processed on a rolling basis. Application fee: $40 ($75 for international students). Electronic applications accepted. *Expenses:* Tuition, state resident: full-time $3716.40; part-time $154.85 per credit hour. Tuition, nonresident: full-time $14,448; part-time $602 per credit hour. Required fees: $1772.40; $73.85 per credit hour. One-time fee: $50. Tuition and fees vary according to course load and campus/location. *Financial support:* In 2008–09, 42 research assistantships (averaging $13,795 per year), 5 teaching assistantships (averaging $16,406 per year) were awarded; career-related internships or fieldwork, Federal Work-Study, scholarships/grants, health care benefits, tuition waivers (partial), and unspecified assistantships also available. Support available to part-time students. Financial award application deadline: 3/1; financial award applicants required to submit FAFSA. *Faculty research:* Marketing and agribusiness, production and farm management, policy and natural resources, community and rural development, international trade and development. *Unit head:* Dr. Mike Woods, Head, 405-744-6161, Fax: 405-744-8210. *Application contact:* Dr. Gordon Emslie, Dean, 405-744-6368, Fax: 405-744-0355, E-mail: grad_i@okstate.edu.

Oregon State University, Graduate School, College of Agricultural Sciences, Department of Agricultural and Resource Economics, Corvallis, OR 97331. Offers agricultural and resource economics (M Agr, MAIS, MS, PhD); economics (MS, PhD). MS and PhD in economics offered through the University Graduate Faculty of Economics. Part-time programs available. Terminal master's awarded for partial completion of doctoral program. *Degree requirements:* For master's, thesis (for some programs); for doctorate, thesis/dissertation. *Entrance requirements:* For master's and doctorate, GRE General Test, minimum GPA of 3.0 in last 90 hours. Additional exam requirements/recommendations for international students: Required—TOEFL. *Faculty research:* Marine economics, environmental economics, effects of global climate change on agriculture, efficiency of agricultural markets, analysis of aquaculture development.

Penn State University Park, Graduate School, College of Agricultural Sciences, Department of Agricultural Economics and Rural Sociology, State College, University Park, PA 16802-1503. Offers agricultural, environmental and regional economics (M Agr, MS, PhD); rural sociology (M Agr, MS, PhD).

Prairie View A&M University, College of Agriculture and Human Sciences, Prairie View, TX 77446-0519. Offers agricultural economics (MS); animal sciences (MS); interdisciplinary human sciences (MS); soil science (MS). Part-time and evening/weekend programs available. *Degree requirements:* For master's, comprehensive exam, thesis (for some programs), field placement. *Entrance requirements:* For master's, GRE General Test, minimum GPA of 2.45. Additional exam requirements/recommendations for international students: Required—TOEFL (minimum score 550 paper-based). *Faculty research:* Domestic violence prevention, water quality, food growth regulators, wetland dynamics, biochemistry, poultry disaster, obesity and nutrition, family therapy.

Purdue University, Graduate School, College of Agriculture, Department of Agricultural Economics, West Lafayette, IN 47907. Offers agricultural economics (MS, PhD); food and agricultural business (EMBA). Part-time programs available. Terminal master's awarded for partial completion of doctoral program. *Degree requirements:* For master's, thesis (for some programs); for doctorate, thesis/dissertation. *Entrance requirements:* For master's and doctorate, GRE General Test. Additional exam requirements/recommendations for international students: Required—TOEFL, TWE (minimum score 4). Electronic applications accepted. *Faculty research:* Marketing, international trade, policy and development, production, resources.

Rutgers, The State University of New Jersey, New Brunswick, Graduate School, Program in Food and Business Economics, Piscataway, NJ 08854-8097. Offers MS. *Degree requirements:* For master's, comprehensive exam, thesis or alternative. *Entrance requirements:* Additional exam requirements/recommendations for international students: Required—TOEFL. Electronic applications accepted. *Faculty research:* Science policy, land use, nutrition policy, food industry, international development.

South Carolina State University, School of Graduate Studies, Department of Accounting, Agribusiness and Economics, Orangeburg, SC 29117-0001. Offers agribusiness (MS); agribusiness and entrepreneurship (MBA). Part-time and evening/weekend programs available. *Faculty:* 4 full-time (1 woman). *Students:* 8 full-time (5 women), 3 part-time (1 woman); includes 10 minority (6 African Americans, 3 Asian Americans or Pacific Islanders, 1 Hispanic American), 1 international. Average age 28. 12 applicants, 100% accepted, 8 enrolled. In 2008, 3 master's awarded. *Degree requirements:* For master's, comprehensive exam, business plan. *Entrance requirements:* For master's, GMAT, minimum GPA of 2.8. Additional exam requirements/recommendations for international students: Required—TOEFL. *Application deadline:* For fall admission, 6/15 for domestic and international students; for spring admission, 11/1 for domestic and international students. Applications are processed on a rolling basis. Application fee: $25. Electronic applications accepted. *Expenses:* Tuition, state resident: full-time $7806; part-time $434 per credit hour. Tuition, nonresident: full-time $15,298; part-time $850 per credit hour. *Financial support:* In 2008–09, 4 fellowships (averaging $5,542 per year) were awarded; research assistantships, career-related internships or fieldwork, Federal Work-Study, institutionally sponsored loans, and unspecified assistantships also available. Financial

Agricultural Economics and Agribusiness

South Carolina State University (continued)

award application deadline: 6/1. *Faculty research:* Small farm income and profitability, agricultural credit, aquaculture, low-input sustainable agriculture, rural development. *Unit head:* Dr. Barbara Adams, Chair, 803-536-8121, Fax: 803-533-3689, E-mail: badams@scsu.edu. *Application contact:* Dr. Stacey Settle, MBA Director, 803-536-8300, Fax: 803-516-4651, E-mail: ssettle@scsu.edu.

Southern Illinois University Carbondale, Graduate School, College of Agriculture, Department of Agribusiness Economics, Carbondale, IL 62901-4701. Offers MS, MBA/MS. Part-time programs available. *Degree requirements:* For master's, thesis. *Entrance requirements:* For master's, minimum GPA of 2.7. Additional exam requirements/recommendations for international students: Required—TOEFL. *Faculty research:* Agricultural finance and credit, agribusiness management, resource use, rural area economic development, marketing and price analysis.

Texas A&M University, College of Agriculture and Life Sciences, Department of Agricultural Economics, College Station, TX 77843. Offers MAB, MS, PhD. Part-time programs available. *Faculty:* 29. *Students:* 142 full-time (58 women), 15 part-time (4 women); includes 10 minority (3 African Americans, 3 Asian Americans or Pacific Islanders, 4 Hispanic Americans), 83 international. Average age 29. In 2008, 14 master's, 8 doctorates awarded. Terminal master's awarded for partial completion of doctoral program. *Degree requirements:* For master's, comprehensive exam (for some programs), thesis (for some programs); for doctorate, comprehensive exam, thesis/dissertation. *Entrance requirements:* For master's and doctorate, GRE General Test. Additional exam requirements/recommendations for international students: Required—TOEFL. *Application deadline:* For fall admission, 3/1 for domestic students; for spring admission, 8/1 for domestic students. Applications are processed on a rolling basis. Application fee: $50 ($75 for international students). Electronic applications accepted. *Expenses:* Tuition, area resident: Full-time $3838.50. Tuition, state resident: full-time $3838.50. Tuition, nonresident: full-time $8897. Required fees: $2359.60. *Financial support:* Fellowships, research assistantships, teaching assistantships, career-related internships or fieldwork, Federal Work-Study, institutionally sponsored loans, and unspecified assistantships available. Financial award application deadline: 3/1; financial award applicants required to submit FAFSA. *Faculty research:* Production economics, agricultural finance, resources, marketing and policy, agribusiness. *Unit head:* A. Gene Nelson, Head, 979-845-2116, Fax: 979-862-1563, E-mail: nelsong@tamu.edu. *Application contact:* Vicki L. Heard, Graduate Admissions Supervisor, 979-845-5222, Fax: 979-862-1563, E-mail: vheard@tamu.edu.

Texas A&M University–Kingsville, College of Graduate Studies, College of Agriculture and Home Economics, Program in Agribusiness, Kingsville, TX 78363. Offers MS. *Degree requirements:* For master's, comprehensive exam, thesis or alternative. *Entrance requirements:* For master's, GRE General Test, minimum GPA of 3.0. Additional exam requirements/recommendations for international students: Required—TOEFL.

Texas Tech University, Graduate School, College of Agricultural Sciences and Natural Resources, Department of Agricultural and Applied Economics, Lubbock, TX 79409. Offers agribusiness (MAB); agricultural and applied economics (MS, PhD); JD/MS. Part-time programs available. *Faculty:* 12 full-time (0 women). *Students:* 30 full-time (10 women), 5 part-time (2 women); includes 4 minority (2 Asian Americans or Pacific Islanders, 2 Hispanic Americans), 15 international. Average age 29. 48 applicants, 69% accepted, 15 enrolled. In 2008, 2 master's, 3 doctorates awarded. *Degree requirements:* For master's, thesis or alternative; for doctorate, thesis/dissertation. *Entrance requirements:* For master's and doctorate, GRE General Test. Additional exam requirements/recommendations for international students: Required—TOEFL (minimum score 550 paper-based; 213 computer-based). *Application deadline:* For fall admission, 3/1 priority date for international students; for spring admission, 11/1 priority date for international students. Applications are processed on a rolling basis. Application fee: $50 ($60 for international students). Electronic applications accepted. *Expenses:* Tuition, area resident: Part-time $194 per credit hour. Tuition, state resident: full-time $4648; part-time $194 per credit hour. Tuition, nonresident: full-time $11,392; part-time $475 per credit hour. Required fees: $2206; $69 per credit hour. $389 per semester. *Financial support:* In 2008–09, 26 students received support, including 22 research assistantships with partial tuition reimbursements available (averaging $12,939 per year), 2 teaching assistantships with partial tuition reimbursements available (averaging $13,770 per year); Federal Work-Study and institutionally sponsored loans also available. Support available to part-time students. Financial award application deadline: 4/15; financial award applicants required to submit FAFSA. *Faculty research:* Economics of the United States cotton and textile industries, natural resource management in semi-arid climates, commodity policy analysis, international trade in agricultural products, agribusiness analysis. Total annual research expenditures: $1 million. *Unit head:* Dr. Eduardo Segarra, Chair, 806-742-2821, Fax: 806-742-1099, E-mail: eduardo.segarra@ttu.edu. *Application contact:* Dr. Tom Knight, Graduate Adviser, 806-742-2821, Fax: 806-742-1099, E-mail: tom.knight@ttu.edu.

Texas Tech University, Jerry S. Rawls College of Business Administration, Programs in Business Administration, Lubbock, TX 79409. Offers agricultural business (MBA); business administration (IMBA); entrepreneurship (MBA); finance (MBA); general business (MBA); health organization management (MBA); international business (MBA); management and leadership skills (MBA); management information systems (MBA); marketing (MBA); statistics (MBA); JD/MBA; MBA/M Arch; MBA/MA; MBA/MD; MBA/MS. Part-time and evening/weekend programs available. *Faculty:* 58 full-time (8 women), 3 part-time/adjunct (0 women). *Students:* 46 full-time (10 women), 416 part-time (147 women); includes 81 minority (18 African Americans, 7 American Indian/Alaska Native, 12 Asian Americans or Pacific Islanders, 44 Hispanic Americans), 44 international. Average age 28. 410 applicants, 88% accepted, 283 enrolled. In 2008, 195 master's awarded. *Degree requirements:* For master's, capstone course. *Entrance requirements:* For master's, GMAT, holistic review of academic credentials. Additional exam requirements/recommendations for international students: Required—TOEFL (minimum score 550 paper-based; 213 computer-based; 79 iBT). *Application deadline:* For fall admission, 7/1 priority date for domestic students, 3/1 priority date for international students; for spring admission, 11/1 priority date for domestic students, 9/1 priority date for international students. Applications are processed on a rolling basis. Application fee: $50 ($60 for international students). Electronic applications accepted. *Expenses:* Tuition, area resident: Part-time $194 per credit hour. Tuition, state resident: full-time $4648; part-time $194 per credit hour. Tuition, nonresident: full-time $11,392; part-time $475 per credit hour. Required fees: $2206; $69 per credit hour. $389 per semester. *Financial support:* In 2008–09, 11 research assistantships (averaging $8,000 per year) were awarded; teaching assistantships, career-related internships or fieldwork, Federal Work-Study, scholarships/grants, health care benefits, and unspecified assistantships also available. Support available to part-time students. Financial award applicants required to submit FAFSA. *Unit head:* Dr. W. Jay Conover, Director, 806-742-1546, Fax: 806-742-3958, E-mail: jay.conover@ttu.edu. *Application contact:* Cynthia D. Barnes, Director, Graduate Services Center, 806-742-3184, Fax: 806-742-3958, E-mail: ba_grad@ttu.edu.

Tropical Agriculture Research and Higher Education Center, Graduate School, Turrialba, Costa Rica. Offers agribusiness management (MS); agroforestry systems (PhD); ecological agriculture (MS); environmental socioeconomics (MS); forestry in tropical and subtropical zones (PhD); integrated watershed management (MS); management and conservation of tropical rainforests and biodiversity (MS); tropical agriculture (PhD); tropical agroforestry (MS). *Entrance requirements:* For master's, GRE, 2 years of related professional experience, letters of recommendation; for doctorate, GRE, 4 letters of recommendation, letter of support from employing organization, master's degree in agronomy, biological sciences, forestry, natural resources or related field. Additional exam requirements/recommendations for international students: Required—TOEFL (minimum score 550 paper-based; 213 computer-based). Electronic applications accepted. *Faculty research:* Biodiversity in fragmented landscapes, ecosystem management, integrated pest management, environmental livestock production, biotechnology carbon balances in diverse land uses.

Tuskegee University, Graduate Programs, College of Agricultural, Environmental and Natural Sciences, Department of Agricultural Sciences, Program in Agricultural and Resource Economics, Tuskegee, AL 36088. Offers MS. *Faculty:* 13 full-time (1 woman), 2 part-time/adjunct (1 woman). *Students:* 11 full-time (9 women), 3 part-time (1 woman); includes 9 minority (all African Americans), 5 international. Average age 32. In 2008, 3 master's awarded. *Degree requirements:* For master's, thesis. *Entrance requirements:* For master's, GRE General Test. Additional exam requirements/recommendations for international students: Required—TOEFL (minimum score 500 paper-based; 69 computer-based). *Application deadline:* For fall admission, 7/15 for domestic students. Applications are processed on a rolling basis. Application fee: $25 ($35 for international students). *Expenses:* Tuition: Full-time $14,740; part-time $473 per credit hour. *Financial support:* Application deadline: 4/15. *Unit head:* Dr. P. K. Biswas, Head, 334-727-8446. *Application contact:* Dr. Robert L. Laney, Vice President/Director of Admissions and Enrollment Management, 334-727-8580, Fax: 334-727-5750, E-mail: planey@tuskegee.edu.

Universidad del Este, Graduate School, Carolina, PR 00983. Offers accounting (MBA); adult education (M Ed); agribusiness (MBA); bilingual education (M Ed); criminal justice and criminology (MA); early education (M Ed); elementary education (M Ed); human resources (MBA); information and virtual business technology (MBA); information security management (MBA); management (MBA); public policy (MPA); social work (MA), including clinical social work; special education (M Ed); strategic leadership (MBA); teaching English (M Ed); teaching Spanish (M Ed).

Université Laval, Faculty of Agricultural and Food Sciences, Department of Agricultural Economics and Consumer Sciences, Program in Agricultural Economics, Québec, QC G1K 7P4, Canada. Offers M Sc. Part-time programs available. *Degree requirements:* For master's, thesis (for some programs). *Entrance requirements:* For master's, knowledge of French. Electronic applications accepted.

University of Alberta, Faculty of Graduate Studies and Research, Department of Rural Economy, Edmonton, AB T6G 2E1, Canada. Offers agricultural economics (M Ag, M Sc, PhD); forest economics (M Ag, M Sc, PhD); rural sociology (M Ag, M Sc); MBA/M Ag. Part-time programs available. *Degree requirements:* For doctorate, thesis/dissertation. *Entrance requirements:* Additional exam requirements/recommendations for international students: Required—TOEFL. *Faculty research:* Agroforestry, development, extension education, marketing and trade, natural resources and environment, policy, production economics.

The University of Arizona, Graduate College, College of Agriculture and Life Sciences, Department of Agricultural and Resource Economics, Tucson, AZ 85721. Offers MS. *Degree requirements:* For master's, thesis or alternative. *Entrance requirements:* For master's, GRE General Test, 3 letters of recommendation, minimum GPA of 3.0, statement of purpose. Additional exam requirements/recommendations for international students: Required—TOEFL. *Faculty research:* Natural resources, international development trade, production and marketing, agricultural policy, rural development.

University of Arkansas, Graduate School, Dale Bumpers College of Agricultural, Food and Life Sciences, Department of Agricultural Economics, Fayetteville, AR 72701-1201. Offers MS. *Degree requirements:* For master's, thesis optional.

The University of British Columbia, Faculty of Graduate Studies, Faculty of Land and Food Systems, Agricultural Economics Program, Vancouver, BC V6T 1Z1, Canada. Offers M Sc. Part-time programs available. *Degree requirements:* For master's, thesis. *Entrance requirements:* Additional exam requirements/recommendations for international students: Required—TOEFL (minimum score 577 paper-based; 233 computer-based; 90 iBT), IELTS (minimum score 6.5). Electronic applications accepted. *Faculty research:* International development, natural resources and environmental economics, marketing and trade, agribusiness, food market analysis, applied econometrics.

University of California, Berkeley, Graduate Division, College of Natural Resources, Department of Agricultural and Resource Economics, Berkeley, CA 94720-1500. Offers PhD. *Degree requirements:* For doctorate, thesis/dissertation, qualifying exam. *Entrance requirements:* For doctorate, GRE General Test, minimum GPA of 3.0, 3 letters of recommendation. *Faculty research:* Agricultural economics and policy, environmental and resource economics and policy, international agricultural development and trade.

University of California, Davis, Graduate Studies, Program in Agricultural and Resource Economics, Davis, CA 95616. Offers MS, PhD, MBA/MS. Terminal master's awarded for partial completion of doctoral program. *Degree requirements:* For master's, thesis optional; for doctorate, thesis/dissertation. *Entrance requirements:* For master's, GRE General Test, minimum GPA of 3.0; for doctorate, GRE General Test, minimum GPA of 3.3. Additional exam requirements/recommendations for international students: Required—TOEFL (minimum score 550 paper-based; 213 computer-based). Electronic applications accepted. *Faculty research:* Applied microeconomics, international trade, development, econometrics, environmental economics.

University of California, Santa Barbara, Graduate Division, Donald Bren School of Environmental Science and Management, Santa Barbara, CA 93106-5131. Offers MESM, PhD. *Faculty:* 18 full-time (4 women), 24 part-time/adjunct (7 women). *Students:* 187 full-time (112 women); includes 21 minority (1 African American, 1 American Indian/Alaska Native, 11 Asian Americans or Pacific Islanders, 8 Hispanic Americans), 15 international. Average age 27. 335 applicants, 61% accepted, 89 enrolled. In 2008, 63 master's, 8 doctorates awarded. *Degree requirements:* For master's, thesis optional, group project as student thesis; for doctorate, comprehensive exam, thesis/dissertation. *Entrance requirements:* For master's and doctorate, GRE, 3 letters of recommendation, statement of purpose, personal achievements/contributions statement, resumé/curriculum vitae, transcripts for post-secondary institutions attended. Additional exam requirements/recommendations for international students: Required—TOEFL (minimum score 550 paper-based; 213 computer-based; 80 iBT), IELTS (minimum score 7), TOEFL or IELTS. *Application deadline:* For fall admission, 1/10 priority date for domestic and international students. Application fee: $70 ($90 for international students). Electronic applications accepted. *Expenses:* Tuition, nonresident: full-time $25,149. Required fees: $10,143. Full-time tuition and fees vary according to campus/location, reciprocity agreements and student level. *Financial support:* In 2008–09, 68 students received support, including 44 fellowships with full and partial tuition reimbursements available (averaging $8,400 per year), 20 research assistantships with full and partial tuition reimbursements available (averaging $6,600 per year), 28 teaching assistantships with partial tuition reimbursements available (averaging $6,900 per year); career-related internships or fieldwork, Federal Work-Study, institutionally sponsored loans, scholarships/grants, health care benefits, and unspecified assistantships also available. Financial award application deadline: 12/15; financial award applicants required to submit FAFSA. *Faculty research:* Ecological processes, environmental politics and policy, sustainability, conservation science and planning, water resources management. *Unit head:* Dr. John Melack, Acting Dean, 805-893-3879, Fax: 805-893-6113, E-mail: melack@bren.ucsb.edu. *Application contact:* Kristen Robinson, Graduate Program Advisor, 805-893-7611, Fax: 805-893-6113, E-mail: gradasst@bren.ucsb.edu.

University of Connecticut, Graduate School, College of Agriculture and Natural Resources, Department of Agricultural and Resource Economics, Field of Agricultural and Resource Economics, Storrs, CT 06269. Offers MS, PhD. Terminal master's awarded for partial completion of doctoral program. *Degree requirements:* For master's, comprehensive exam; for doctorate, thesis/dissertation. *Entrance requirements:* For master's and doctorate, GRE General Test. Additional exam requirements/recommendations for international students: Required—TOEFL (minimum score 550 paper-based; 213 computer-based). Electronic applications accepted.

University of Delaware, College of Agriculture and Natural Resources, Department of Food and Resource Economics, Newark, DE 19716. Offers agricultural economics (MS); agriculture and technical education (MA); bioresources engineering (MS). Part-time programs available. *Degree requirements:* For master's, thesis. *Entrance requirements:* For master's, GRE General

Test, 3 letters of recommendation. Additional exam requirements/recommendations for international students: Required—TOEFL (minimum score 550 paper-based; 213 computer-based). Electronic applications accepted. *Faculty research:* Experimental economics, environmental and resource economics, land use, law and economics.

University of Florida, Graduate School, College of Agricultural and Life Sciences, Department of Food and Resource Economics, Gainesville, FL 32611. Offers MAB, MS, PhD. *Degree requirements:* For master's, thesis optional; for doctorate, thesis/dissertation. *Entrance requirements:* For master's and doctorate, GRE General Test, minimum GPA of 3.0. Additional exam requirements/recommendations for international students: Required—TOEFL. Electronic applications accepted. *Faculty research:* Agribusiness management, production, environmental economics, international trade, economic development.

University of Georgia, Graduate School, College of Agricultural and Environmental Sciences, Department of Agricultural and Applied Economics, Athens, GA 30602. Offers agricultural economics (MAE, MS, PhD); environmental economics (MS). *Degree requirements:* For master's, thesis (MS); for doctorate, thesis/dissertation. *Entrance requirements:* For master's and doctorate, GRE General Test. Electronic applications accepted.

University of Guelph, Graduate Program Services, College of Management and Economics, MBA Program, Guelph, ON N1G 2W1, Canada. Offers food and agribusiness management (MBA); hospitality and tourism management (MBA). Part-time and evening/weekend programs available. Postbaccalaureate distance learning degree programs offered (minimal on-campus study). *Entrance requirements:* For master's, minimum B-average, minimum of 3 years of relevant work experience. Additional exam requirements/recommendations for international students: Required—TOEFL (minimum score 550 paper-based; 213 computer-based). Electronic applications accepted. *Faculty research:* Marketing, operations management, business policy, financial management, organizational behavior.

University of Guelph, Graduate Program Services, Ontario Agricultural College, Department of Food, Agricultural and Resource Economics, Guelph, ON N1G 2W1, Canada. Offers agricultural economics (M Sc, PhD); collaborative international development studies (MA/M Sc); MA/M Sc. Part-time programs available. *Degree requirements:* For master's, thesis; for doctorate, comprehensive exam, thesis/dissertation. *Entrance requirements:* For master's, minimum B- average during previous 2 years of course work; for doctorate, minimum B standing in recognized master's degree. Additional exam requirements/recommendations for international students: Required—TOEFL (minimum score 550 paper-based; 213 computer-based), IELTS (minimum score 6.5). Electronic applications accepted. *Faculty research:* Agricultural policy, agribusiness, environmental economics, agricultural marketing, production economics.

University of Idaho, College of Graduate Studies, College of Agricultural and Life Sciences, Department of Agricultural Economics and Rural Sociology, Moscow, ID 83844-2282. Offers agricultural economics (MS); applied economics (MS), including agribusiness emphasis, agricultural economics emphasis. *Faculty:* 9 full-time, 2 part-time/adjunct. *Students:* 10 full-time, 3 part-time. Average age 29. In 2008, 6 master's awarded. *Entrance requirements:* For master's, minimum GPA of 2.8. *Application deadline:* For fall admission, 8/1 for domestic students; for spring admission, 12/15 for domestic students. Application fee: $55 ($60 for international students). *Expenses:* Tuition, nonresident: full-time $10,080; part-time $336 per credit. Required fees: $5212; $267 per credit. Tuition and fees vary according to program. *Financial support:* Research assistantships, teaching assistantships available. Financial award application deadline: 2/15. *Faculty research:* Crops: potatoes, blue grass; livestock: beef, dairy; rural and community development; natural resources and the environment; farm and ranch management. *Unit head:* Dr. Larry W Van Tassell, Department Head, 208-885-7869, Fax: 208-885-5759. *Application contact:* Dr. Larry W Van Tassell, Department Head, 208-885-7869, Fax: 208-885-5759.

University of Illinois at Urbana–Champaign, Graduate College, College of Agricultural, Consumer and Environmental Sciences, Department of Agricultural and Consumer Economics, Champaign, IL 61820. Offers MS, PhD. *Faculty:* 33 full-time (9 women), 2 part-time/adjunct (both women). *Students:* 59 full-time (28 women), 15 part-time (6 women); includes 8 minority (2 African Americans, 3 Asian Americans or Pacific Islanders, 3 Hispanic Americans), 41 international. 81 applicants, 40% accepted, 21 enrolled. In 2008, 9 master's, 12 doctorates awarded. *Entrance requirements:* For master's, GRE, minimum GPA of 3.0; for doctorate, GRE, writing sample. Additional exam requirements/recommendations for international students: Required—TOEFL (minimum score 570 paper-based; 230 computer-based; 88 iBT), IELTS (minimum score 6.5), TOEFL or IELTS. *Application deadline:* Applications are processed on a rolling basis. Application fee: $60 ($75 for international students). Electronic applications accepted. *Financial support:* In 2008–09, 17 fellowships, 41 research assistantships, 25 teaching assistantships were awarded; tuition waivers (full and partial) also available. *Unit head:* Robert J. Hauser, Head, 217-333-8859, Fax: 217-333-5538, E-mail: r-hauser@illinois.edu. *Application contact:* Linda Foste, Administrative Assistant, 217-333-1830, Fax: 217-244-7088, E-mail: l-foste@illinois.edu.

University of Kentucky, Graduate School, College of Agriculture, Program in Agricultural Economics, Lexington, KY 40546-0276. Offers MS, PhD. *Degree requirements:* For master's, comprehensive exam, thesis optional; for doctorate, comprehensive exam, thesis/dissertation. *Entrance requirements:* For master's, GRE General Test, minimum undergraduate GPA of 2.75; for doctorate, GRE General Test, minimum graduate GPA of 3.0. Additional exam requirements/recommendations for international students: Required—TOEFL (minimum score 550 paper-based; 213 computer-based). Electronic applications accepted. *Faculty research:* Food and agricultural marketing, agricultural and food policy, natural resources and environment, rural economic development.

University of Maine, Graduate School, College of Natural Sciences, Forestry, and Agriculture, Department of Resource Economics and Policy, Orono, ME 04469. Offers resource economics and policy (MS); resource utilization (MS). Part-time programs available. *Degree requirements:* For master's, thesis (for some programs). *Entrance requirements:* For master's, GRE General Test. Additional exam requirements/recommendations for international students: Required—TOEFL. Electronic applications accepted. *Faculty research:* International trade, agricultural marketing, nonmarketing valuation, livestock health economics.

University of Manitoba, Faculty of Graduate Studies, Faculty of Agricultural and Food Sciences, Department of Agribusiness and Agricultural Economics, Winnipeg, MB R3T 2N2, Canada. Offers agribusiness (M Sc, PhD). *Degree requirements:* For master's, thesis or alternative; for doctorate, thesis/dissertation.

University of Maryland, College Park, Graduate Studies, College of Agriculture and Natural Resources, Department of Agricultural and Resource Economics, College Park, MD 20742. Offers agriculture economics (MS, PhD); resource economics (MS, PhD). Part-time and evening/weekend programs available. *Degree requirements:* For master's, variable foreign language requirement, thesis optional, oral exam; for doctorate, variable foreign language requirement, oral dissertation defense. *Entrance requirements:* For master's, GRE General Test, minimum GPA of 3.0, course work in microeconomics and calculus, 3 letters of recommendation; for doctorate, GRE General Test. Additional exam requirements/recommendations for international students: Required—TOEFL. Electronic applications accepted. *Faculty research:* Agricultural development, international trade, agricultural marketing, econometrics, farm management and production economics.

University of Massachusetts Amherst, Graduate School, College of Natural Resources and the Environment, Department of Resource Economics, Amherst, MA 01003. Offers MS, PhD. Part-time programs available. Terminal master's awarded for partial completion of doctoral program. *Degree requirements:* For master's, thesis or alternative; for doctorate, comprehensive exam, thesis/dissertation. *Entrance requirements:* For master's and doctorate, GRE General Test. Additional exam requirements/recommendations for international students: Required—

TOEFL (minimum score 550 paper-based; 213 computer-based; 79 iBT), IELTS (minimum score 6.5). Electronic applications accepted. *Expenses:* Tuition, area resident: Full-time $2640. Tuition, nonresident: full-time $9936. One-time fee: $332 full-time. Tuition and fees vary according to course load.

University of Missouri–Columbia, Graduate School, College of Agriculture, Food and Natural Resources, Department of Agricultural Economics, Columbia, MO 65211. Offers MS, PhD. *Faculty:* 27 full-time (5 women), 1 (woman) part-time/adjunct. *Students:* 20 full-time (8 women), 22 part-time (5 women); includes 4 minority (1 African American, 1 American Indian/Alaska Native, 2 Asian Americans or Pacific Islanders), 21 international. Average age 30. 47 applicants, 40% accepted, 11 enrolled. In 2008, 5 master's, 4 doctorates awarded. *Degree requirements:* For doctorate, thesis/dissertation. *Entrance requirements:* For master's and doctorate, GRE General Test, minimum GPA of 3.0. Additional exam requirements/recommendations for international students: Required—TOEFL (minimum score 600 paper-based; 205 computer-based). *Application deadline:* For fall admission, 3/1 priority date for domestic students; for winter admission, 10/1 for domestic students. Applications are processed on a rolling basis. Application fee: $45 ($60 for international students). *Financial support:* Research assistantships, teaching assistantships, institutionally sponsored loans available. *Unit head:* Dr. Michael Monson, Department Chair, E-mail: monsonm@missouri.edu. *Application contact:* Dr. Michael Monson, Department Chair, E-mail: monsonm@missouri.edu.

University of Nevada, Reno, Graduate School, College of Agriculture, Biotechnology and Natural Resources, Department of Resource Economics, Reno, NV 89557. Offers MS, PhD. *Faculty:* 13 full-time (4 women). *Students:* 17 full-time (10 women), 4 part-time (3 women), 10 international. Average age 33. 20 applicants, 80% accepted, 8 enrolled. In 2008, 4 master's, 2 doctorates awarded. Terminal master's awarded for partial completion of doctoral program. *Degree requirements:* For master's, thesis optional; for doctorate, thesis/dissertation. *Entrance requirements:* For master's, GRE General Test, minimum GPA of 2.75; for doctorate, GRE General Test, minimum GPA of 3.0. Additional exam requirements/recommendations for international students: Required—TOEFL (minimum score 500 paper-based; 173 computer-based; 61 iBT), IELTS (minimum score 6), TOFEL or IELTS. *Application deadline:* For fall admission, 3/1 priority date for domestic and international students; for spring admission, 11/1 priority date for domestic and international students. Applications are processed on a rolling basis. Application fee: $60 ($95 for international students). Electronic applications accepted. *Expenses:* Tuition, state resident: full-time $1710; part-time $1140 per semester. Tuition, nonresident: full-time $7115. Required fees: $158 per semester. *Financial support:* In 2008–09, 17 research assistantships with partial tuition reimbursements (averaging $20,000 per year) were awarded; Federal Work-Study, institutionally sponsored loans, scholarships/grants, health care benefits, and unspecified assistantships also available. Financial award application deadline: 3/1; financial award applicants required to submit FAFSA. *Faculty research:* Econometrics, environmental valuation, natural resource and environmental policy analysis, public lands management. Total annual research expenditures: $929,363. *Unit head:* Dr. Kim Rollins, Graduate Program Director, 775-784-1677, E-mail: krollins@cabnr.unr.edu. *Application contact:* Michele Sandberg, Application Contact, 775-784-7026, Fax: 775-784-6064, E-mail: gradschool@unr.edu.

University of Puerto Rico, Mayagüez Campus, Graduate Studies, College of Agricultural Sciences, Department of Agricultural Economics, Mayagüez, PR 00681-9000. Offers MS. Part-time programs available. *Degree requirements:* For master's, comprehensive exam, thesis. *Entrance requirements:* For master's, bachelor's degree in agricultural economics or its equivalent. *Faculty research:* Farm management, agricultural development, agrimarketing, natural resource economics.

University of Saskatchewan, College of Graduate Studies and Research, College of Agriculture, Department of Agricultural Economics, Saskatoon, SK S7N 5A2, Canada. Offers M Ag, M Sc, MA, PhD. *Degree requirements:* For master's, thesis; for doctorate, thesis/dissertation. *Entrance requirements:* Additional exam requirements/recommendations for international students: Required—TOEFL.

University of Saskatchewan, College of Graduate Studies and Research, Edwards School of Business, Program in Business Administration, Saskatoon, SK S7N 5A2, Canada. Offers agribusiness management (MBA); biotechnology management (MBA); health services management (MBA); indigenous management (MBA); international business management (MBA).

University of Vermont, Graduate College, College of Agriculture and Life Sciences, Department of Community Development and Applied Economics, Burlington, VT 05405. Offers community development and applied economics (MS); public administration (MPA). *Students:* 23 (12 women), 1 international. 26 applicants, 65% accepted, 6 enrolled. In 2008, 6 master's awarded. *Degree requirements:* For master's, thesis. *Entrance requirements:* For master's, GRE General Test. Additional exam requirements/recommendations for international students: Required—TOEFL (minimum score 550 paper-based; 213 computer-based; 80 iBT). *Application deadline:* For fall admission, 4/1 priority date for domestic students; for spring admission, 11/15 for domestic students. Applications are processed on a rolling basis. Application fee: $40. Electronic applications accepted. *Expenses:* Tuition, state resident: part-time $488 per credit. Tuition, nonresident: part-time $1232 per credit. *Financial support:* Fellowships, research assistantships, teaching assistantships, career-related internships or fieldwork available. Financial award application deadline: 3/1. *Faculty research:* Agricultural production and marketing. *Unit head:* Dr. J. Kolodinsky, Chairperson, 802-656-2001. *Application contact:* Dr. J. Kolodinsky, Chairperson, 802-656-2001.

University of Wisconsin–Madison, Graduate School, College of Agricultural and Life Sciences, Department of Agricultural and Applied Economics, Madison, WI 53706-1380. Offers MA, MS, PhD. Part-time programs available. *Degree requirements:* For doctorate, thesis/dissertation, preliminary exams. *Entrance requirements:* For master's and doctorate, GRE General Test. Additional exam requirements/recommendations for international students: Required—TOEFL. Electronic applications accepted. *Faculty research:* Environmental and resource economics, international development, state and local economics, food systems, markets and trade.

University of Wyoming, Graduate School, College of Agriculture, Department of Agricultural and Applied Economics, Laramie, WY 82070. Offers MS. Part-time programs available. *Faculty:* 12 full-time (2 women), 2 part-time/adjunct (1 woman). *Students:* 9 full-time (4 women), 5 part-time (1 woman), 2 international. Average age 27. 9 applicants, 67% accepted, 6 enrolled. In 2008, 2 master's awarded. *Degree requirements:* For master's, thesis (for some programs). *Entrance requirements:* For master's, GRE General Test, minimum GPA of 3.0. Additional exam requirements/recommendations for international students: Required—TOEFL. *Application deadline:* For fall admission, 2/15 priority date for domestic students, 2/1 for international students; for spring admission, 10/1 priority date for domestic students. Applications are processed on a rolling basis. Application fee: $50. Electronic applications accepted. *Financial support:* In 2008–09, 9 research assistantships with tuition reimbursements (averaging $11,072 per year) were awarded; career-related internships or fieldwork, Federal Work-Study, and institutionally sponsored loans also available. Financial award application deadline: 2/1; financial award applicants required to submit FAFSA. *Faculty research:* Farm management, agricultural markets, water economics, community development, agricultural business. Total annual research expenditures: $250,000. *Unit head:* Dr. Roger H. Coupal, Interim Department Head, 307-766-2386, Fax: 307-766-5544, E-mail: coupal@uwyo.edu. *Application contact:* Michell Anderson, Graduate Admissions Coordinator, 307-766-2287, Fax: 307-766-2374, E-mail: manders2@uwyo.edu.

Virginia Polytechnic Institute and State University, Graduate School, College of Agriculture and Life Sciences, Department of Agricultural and Applied Economics, Blacksburg, VA 24061. Offers agribusiness (MS); agricultural economics (MS, PhD); applied economics (MS); developmental and international economics (PhD); econometrics (PhD); macro and micro economics (PhD); markets and industrial organizations (PhD); public and regional/urban

Agricultural Economics and Agribusiness

Virginia Polytechnic Institute and State University *(continued)*
economics (PhD); resource and environmental economics (PhD). *Entrance requirements:* For master's and doctorate, GRE General Test. Additional exam requirements/recommendations for international students: Required—TOEFL (minimum score 575 paper-based; 231 computer-based). Electronic applications accepted. *Faculty research:* Rural development.

Washington State University, Graduate School, College of Agricultural, Human, and Natural Resource Sciences, School of Economic Sciences, Pullman, WA 99164. Offers agribusiness (MA, Certificate); agricultural economics (MA, PhD); applied economics (MA); economics (MA, PhD, Certificate), including applied economics (MA), economics (MA, PhD), international business economics (Certificate). Terminal master's awarded for partial completion of doctoral program. *Degree requirements:* For master's, comprehensive exam (for some programs), thesis (for some programs), oral exam; for doctorate, comprehensive exam, thesis/dissertation, oral exam, written exam, qualifying exams. *Entrance requirements:* For master's and doctorate, minimum GPA of 3.0, 3 letters of recommendation. Additional exam requirements/recommendations for international students: Required—TOEFL (minimum score 550 paper-based; 213 computer-based). Electronic applications accepted. *Faculty research:* Marketing, natural resources, production economics.

West Texas A&M University, College of Agriculture, Nursing, and Natural Sciences, Division of Agriculture, Emphasis in Agricultural Business and Economics, Canyon, TX 79016-0001. Offers MS. Part-time programs available. *Degree requirements:* For master's, comprehensive exam, thesis optional. *Entrance requirements:* For master's, GRE General Test. Additional exam requirements/recommendations for international students: Required—TOEFL (minimum

score 550 paper-based). Electronic applications accepted. *Faculty research:* Utilizing expected revenue in selecting optimal marketing alternatives for fixed resource cow/calf operators in the Texas panhandle.

West Virginia University, Davis College of Agriculture, Forestry and Consumer Sciences, Division of Resource Management and Sustainable Development, Program in Agricultural and Resource Economics, Morgantown, WV 26506. Offers MS. Part-time programs available. *Degree requirements:* For master's, thesis optional. *Entrance requirements:* For master's, GRE General Test, minimum GPA of 2.5, 1 calculus course. Additional exam requirements/recommendations for international students: Required—TOEFL. *Faculty research:* Agricultural production and marketing, rural development, mineral and energy economics, economic development.

William Woods University, Graduate and Adult Studies, Fulton, MO 65251-1098. Offers administration (Ed S); agriculture (MBA); athletic/activities administration (M Ed); curriculum and instruction (M Ed); curriculum leadership (Ed S); elementary administration (M Ed); health management (MBA); human resources (MBA); principalship (Ed S); secondary administration (M Ed); special education director (M Ed). Evening/weekend programs available. *Degree requirements:* For master's, capstone course (MBA), action research (M Ed); for Ed S, field experience. *Entrance requirements:* For master's, 2 recommendations, resumé, BA/BS; teaching certification (M Ed); course work in economics and accounting (MBA); for Ed S, M Ed, 2 letters of recommendation, resumé, teaching certification. Additional exam requirements/recommendations for international students: Required—TOEFL (minimum score 550 paper-based). Electronic applications accepted.

Applied Economics

American University, College of Arts and Sciences, Department of Economics, Washington, DC 20016-8029. Offers applied microeconomics (Certificate); economics (MA, PhD); international economic relations (Certificate). Part-time and evening/weekend programs available. *Faculty:* 23 full-time (10 women), 1 part-time/adjunct (0 women). *Students:* 56 full-time (23 women), 71 part-time (31 women); includes 12 minority (8 African Americans, 1 Asian American or Pacific Islander, 3 Hispanic Americans), 60 international. Average age 30. 149 applicants, 62% accepted, 24 enrolled. In 2008, 23 master's, 9 doctorates awarded. Terminal master's awarded for partial completion of doctoral program. *Degree requirements:* For master's, comprehensive exam, thesis or alternative; for doctorate, comprehensive exam, thesis/dissertation, 2 research seminars, field requirement. *Entrance requirements:* For master's and doctorate, GRE; for Certificate, bachelor's degree. Additional exam requirements/recommendations for international students: Required—TOEFL. *Application deadline:* For spring admission, 10/1 for domestic students. Applications are processed on a rolling basis. Application fee: $80. *Expenses:* Tuition: Full-time $21,204; part-time $1178 per credit hour. Required fees: $380. Part-time tuition and fees vary according to course load and program. *Financial support:* Fellowships, research assistantships with full and partial tuition reimbursements, teaching assistantships with full and partial tuition reimbursements, career-related internships or fieldwork, Federal Work-Study, institutionally sponsored loans, and tuition waivers (full and partial) available. Financial award application deadline: 2/1. *Faculty research:* Political economy, development, labor, gender. *Unit head:* Robert A. Blecker, Chair, 202-885-3767, Fax: 202-885-3790, E-mail: blecker@american.edu. *Application contact:* Kathleen Clowery, Director of Graduate Admissions, 202-885 Ext. 3621, Fax: 202-885-1505, E-mail: clowery@american.edu.

Auburn University, Graduate School, College of Agriculture, Department of Agricultural Economics and Rural Sociology, Auburn University, AL 36849. Offers agricultural economics (M Ag, MS); applied economics (PhD). Part-time programs available. *Faculty:* 18 full-time (4 women). *Students:* 26 full-time (10 women), 6 part-time (1 woman); includes 4 minority (3 African Americans, 1 Asian American or Pacific Islander), 21 international. Average age 32. 36 applicants, 44% accepted, 7 enrolled. In 2008, 4 master's, 4 doctorates awarded. *Degree requirements:* For master's, thesis (for some programs); for doctorate, thesis/dissertation. *Entrance requirements:* For master's and doctorate, GRE General Test. *Application deadline:* For fall admission, 7/7 for domestic students; for spring admission, 11/24 for domestic students. Applications are processed on a rolling basis. Application fee: $25 ($50 for international students). Electronic applications accepted. *Expenses:* Tuition, area resident: Full-time $5880; part-time $243 per credit hour. Tuition, state resident: full-time $5880; part-time $243 per credit hour. Tuition, nonresident: full-time $17,640; part-time $729 per credit hour. International tuition: $17,846 full-time. Required fees: $620. Tuition and fees vary according to program and reciprocity agreements. *Financial support:* Research assistantships, teaching assistantships, Federal Work-Study available. Support available to part-time students. Financial award application deadline: 3/15. *Faculty research:* Farm management, agricultural marketing, production economics, resource economics, agricultural finance. *Unit head:* Dr. Curtis M. Jolly, Chair, 334-844-4800. *Application contact:* Dr. George Flowers, Dean of the Graduate School, 334-844-2125.

Buffalo State College, State University of New York, Graduate Studies and Research, Faculty of Natural and Social Sciences, Department of Economics and Finance, Buffalo, NY 14222-1095. Offers applied economics (MA). *Degree requirements:* For master's, project. *Entrance requirements:* Additional exam requirements/recommendations for international students: Required—TOEFL (minimum score 550 paper-based; 213 computer-based).

Clemson University, Graduate School, College of Business and Behavioral Science, Department of Economics, Clemson, SC 29634. Offers applied economics (PhD); economics (MA). *Faculty:* 19 full-time (1 woman), 4 part-time/adjunct (0 women). *Students:* 78 full-time (33 women), 13 part-time (5 women); includes 7 minority (3 African Americans, 1 Asian American or Pacific Islander, 3 Hispanic Americans), 40 international. Average age 29. 119 applicants, 54% accepted, 32 enrolled. In 2008, 7 master's, 10 doctorates awarded. *Degree requirements:* For doctorate, thesis/dissertation. *Entrance requirements:* For master's and doctorate, GRE General Test. Additional exam requirements/recommendations for international students: Required—TOEFL. *Application deadline:* For fall admission, 6/1 for domestic students, 4/15 for international students; for spring admission, 9/15 for international students. Application fee: $55. Full-time tuition and fees vary according to program. *Financial support:* In 2008–09, 5 fellowships (averaging $6,200 per year), 7 research assistantships (averaging $13,854 per year), 57 teaching assistantships (averaging $14,429 per year) were awarded. Financial award applicants required to submit FAFSA. *Faculty research:* Applied price theory, financial economics, industrial economics, labor economics, monetary economics. Total annual research expenditures: $485,950. *Unit head:* Dr. Raymond Sauer, Interim Chair, 864-656-3969, Fax: 864-656-4192, E-mail: sauerr@clemson.edu. *Application contact:* Dr. Michael T Maloney, Director of Graduate Programs, 864-656-3430, Fax: 864-656-4192, E-mail: maloney@clemson.edu.

Cornell University, Graduate School, Graduate Fields of Arts and Sciences, Field of Economics, Ithaca, NY 14853-0001. Offers applied economics (PhD); basic analytical economics (PhD); econometrics and economic statistics (PhD); economic development and planning (PhD); economic theory (PhD); industrial organization and control (PhD); international economics (PhD); labor economics (PhD); monetary and macroeconomics (PhD); public finance (PhD). *Faculty:* 76 full-time (12 women). *Students:* 98 full-time (39 women); includes 6 minority (1

African American, 3 Asian Americans or Pacific Islanders, 2 Hispanic Americans), 54 international. Average age 29. 563 applicants, 14% accepted, 16 enrolled. In 2008, 16 doctorates awarded. *Degree requirements:* For doctorate, comprehensive exam, thesis/dissertation. *Entrance requirements:* For doctorate, GRE General Test, 3 letters of recommendation. Additional exam requirements/recommendations for international students: Required—TOEFL (minimum score 550 paper-based; 213 computer-based; 77 iBT). *Application deadline:* For fall admission, 1/15 priority date for domestic students. Application fee: $70. Electronic applications accepted. *Expenses:* Tuition: Full-time $29,500. Required fees: $70. Full-time tuition and fees vary according to degree level, program and student level. *Financial support:* In 2008–09, 81 students received support, including 18 fellowships with full tuition reimbursements available, 18 research assistantships with full tuition reimbursements available, 45 teaching assistantships with full tuition reimbursements available; institutionally sponsored loans, scholarships/grants, health care benefits, tuition waivers (full and partial), and unspecified assistantships also available. Financial award applicants required to submit FAFSA. *Faculty research:* Learning and games, economics of education, political economy, transfer payments, time series and nonparametrics. *Unit head:* Director of Graduate Studies, 607-255-4893, Fax: 607-255-2818. *Application contact:* Graduate Field Assistant, 607-255-4893, Fax: 607-255-2818, E-mail: econ_phd@cornell.edu.

Eastern Michigan University, Graduate School, College of Arts and Sciences, Department of Economics, Ypsilanti, MI 48197. Offers applied economics (MA); economics (MA); health economics (MA); international economics and development (MA); trade and development (MA). Part-time and evening/weekend programs available. Postbaccalaureate distance learning degree programs offered (minimal on-campus study). *Degree requirements:* For master's, thesis or alternative. *Entrance requirements:* Additional exam requirements/recommendations for international students: Required—TOEFL.

Georgia Southern University, Jack N. Averitt College of Graduate Studies, College of Business Administration, School of Economic Development, Program in Applied Economics, Statesboro, GA 30460. Offers MS. Program is held online. *Students:* 10 part-time (5 women); includes 2 minority (1 African American, 1 Hispanic American), 1 international. Average age 32. 26 applicants, 77% accepted, 10 enrolled. *Entrance requirements:* For master's, GRE or GMAT, minimum GPA of 3.0. Additional exam requirements/recommendations for international students: Required—TOEFL (minimum score 550 paper-based; 213 computer-based; 80 iBT). *Application deadline:* For fall admission, 3/1 priority date for domestic and international students; for spring admission, 10/1 priority date for domestic students, 10/1 for international students. Applications are processed on a rolling basis. Electronic applications accepted. *Expenses:* Tuition, area resident: Full-time $3840; part-time $160 per semester hour. Tuition, state resident: full-time $3840; part-time $160 per semester hour. Tuition, nonresident: full-time $15,336; part-time $639 per semester hour. Required fees: $1152. *Unit head:* Dr. Ron Shiffler, Dean, 912-478-5106, Fax: 912-478-0292, E-mail: shiffler@georgiasouthern.edu. *Application contact:* Dr. Ron Shiffler, Dean, 912-478-5106, Fax: 912-478-0292, E-mail: shiffler@georgiasouthern.edu.

HEC Montreal, School of Business Administration, Master of Science Programs in Administration, Program in Applied Economics, Montréal, QC H3T 2A7, Canada. Offers M Sc. All courses are given in French. Part-time programs available. *Students:* 29 full-time (8 women). 21 applicants, 52% accepted, 7 enrolled. In 2008, 6 master's awarded. *Degree requirements:* For master's, one foreign language, thesis. Application fee: $76 Canadian dollars. Electronic applications accepted. Tuition and fees charges are reported in Canadian dollars. *Expenses:* Tuition, area resident: Part-time $62.27 Canadian dollars per credit. Tuition, state resident: full-time $2241.72 Canadian dollars; part-time $179.28 Canadian dollars per credit. Tuition, nonresident: full-time $6454 Canadian dollars; part-time $419.77 Canadian dollars per credit. International tuition: $15,111.72 Canadian dollars full-time. Required fees: $1218.75 Canadian dollars; $28.25 Canadian dollars per credit. $88 Canadian dollars per term. Tuition and fees vary according to degree level and program. *Financial support:* Fellowships, research assistantships, teaching assistantships, scholarships/grants available. *Unit head:* Dr. Francois Bellavance, Director, 514-340-6485, Fax: 514-340-5690, E-mail: francois.bellavance@hec.ca. *Application contact:* Francine Blais, Administrative Director, 514-340-6112, Fax: 514-340-6411, E-mail: francine.blais@hec.ca.

The Johns Hopkins University, Zanvyl Krieger School of Arts and Sciences, Advanced Academic Programs, Program in Applied Economics, Washington, DC 20036. Offers MA. Part-time and evening/weekend programs available. *Degree requirements:* For master's, thesis (for some programs). *Entrance requirements:* For master's, minimum 3.0 GPA, coursework in microeconomics and macroeconomics. Additional exam requirements/recommendations for international students: Required—TOEFL (minimum score 250 computer-based; 100 iBT). Electronic applications accepted.

Mississippi State University, College of Business, Department of Finance and Economics, Mississippi State, MS 39762. Offers applied economics (PhD); economics (MA); finance (MSBA). Part-time programs available. Terminal master's awarded for partial completion of doctoral program. *Degree requirements:* For master's, comprehensive exam, thesis optional; for doctorate, comprehensive exam, thesis/dissertation. *Entrance requirements:* For master's and doctorate, GMAT, GRE General Test. *Faculty research:* Economics development, mergers, event studies, economic education, bank performance.

Montana State University, College of Graduate Studies, College of Agriculture, Department of Agricultural Economics and Economics, Bozeman, MT 59717. Offers applied economics

(MS). Part-time programs available. *Degree requirements:* For master's, comprehensive exam. *Entrance requirements:* For master's, GRE General Test. Additional exam requirements/recommendations for international students: Required—TOEFL (minimum score 550 paper-based; 213 computer-based). Electronic applications accepted. *Faculty research:* Agricultural production, agricultural marketing/finance, governance (private and public), natural resource management.

New York University, Graduate School of Arts and Science, Department of Economics, New York, NY 10012-1019. Offers applied economic analysis (Advanced Certificate); economics (MA, PhD); JD/MA; MD/PhD. Part-time and evening/weekend programs available. Terminal master's awarded for partial completion of doctoral program. *Degree requirements:* For master's, thesis; for doctorate, one foreign language, thesis/dissertation, 4 qualifying exams. *Entrance requirements:* For master's and doctorate, GRE General Test; for Advanced Certificate, master's degree. Additional exam requirements/recommendations for international students: Required—TOEFL. *Faculty research:* Economic theory, experimental economics, growth and development, macroeconomics and finance, international trade and international finance.

North Carolina Agricultural and Technical State University, Graduate School, School of Agriculture and Environmental Sciences, Department of Agribusiness, Applied Economics, and Agriscience Education, Greensboro, NC 27411. Offers agricultural economics (MS); agricultural education (MS). *Accreditation:* NCATE. Part-time and evening/weekend programs available. *Degree requirements:* For master's, comprehensive exam, thesis or alternative, qualifying exam. *Entrance requirements:* For master's, GRE General Test, minimum GPA of 3.0. *Faculty research:* Aid for small farmers, agricultural technology resources, labor force mobility, agrology.

Northeastern University, College of Arts and Sciences, Department of Economics, Boston, MA 02115-5096. Offers MA, PhD. Part-time and evening/weekend programs available. *Degree requirements:* For master's and doctorate, comprehensive exam. *Entrance requirements:* For master's, GRE. Additional exam requirements/recommendations for international students: Required—TOEFL. *Faculty research:* U.S. labor markets, applied economics, microeconomic theory, macroeconomic theory, econometrics.

Ohio University, Graduate College, College of Arts and Sciences, Department of Economics, Athens, OH 45701-2979. Offers applied economics (MA); financial economics (MFE). Evening/weekend programs available. *Degree requirements:* For master's, thesis or alternative. *Entrance requirements:* For master's, GRE or GMAT, minimum GPA of 3.0. Additional exam requirements/recommendations for international students: Required—TOEFL (minimum score 550 paper-based). *Faculty research:* Macroeconomics, public finance, international economics and finance, monetary theory, healthcare economics.

Old Dominion University, College of Business and Public Administration, Master's Program in Business Administration, Norfolk, VA 23529. Offers business and economic forecasting (MBA); financial analysis and valuation (MBA); information technology and enterprise integration (MBA); international business (MBA); maritime and port management (MBA); public administration (MBA). *Accreditation:* AACSB. Part-time and evening/weekend programs available. *Faculty:* 66 full-time (15 women), 6 part-time/adjunct (1 woman). *Students:* 74 full-time (26 women), 200 part-time (85 women); includes 49 minority (26 African Americans, 3 American Indian/Alaska Native, 15 Asian Americans or Pacific Islanders, 5 Hispanic Americans), 38 international. Average age 30. 169 applicants, 52% accepted, 61 enrolled. In 2008, 89 master's awarded. *Entrance requirements:* For master's, GMAT, letters of reference, resumé, essay, transcripts, coursework in calculus. Additional exam requirements/recommendations for international students: Required—TOEFL (minimum score 550 paper-based; 213 computer-based; 80 iBT). *Application deadline:* For fall admission, 6/1 priority date for domestic students, 4/15 priority date for international students; for spring admission, 11/1 priority date for domestic students, 10/1 priority date for international students. Applications are processed on a rolling basis. Application fee: $40. Electronic applications accepted. *Expenses:* Tuition, area resident: Full-time $7704; part-time $321 per credit. Tuition, state resident: full-time $7704; part-time $321 per credit. Tuition, nonresident: full-time $19,104; part-time $796 per credit. Required fees: $99 per semester. One-time fee: $40. *Financial support:* In 2008–09, 46 students received support, including 31 research assistantships with partial tuition reimbursements available (averaging $7,000 per year), 3 teaching assistantships with partial tuition reimbursements available (averaging $6,300 per year); career-related internships or fieldwork, scholarships/grants, and unspecified assistantships also available. Support available to part-time students. Financial award application deadline: 2/15; financial award applicants required to submit FAFSA. *Faculty research:* International business, buyer behavior, financial markets, strategy, operations research. *Unit head:* Dr. Bruce Rubin, Graduate Program Director, 757-683-3585, E-mail: mbainfo@odu.edu. *Application contact:* Shanna Wood, MBA Program Manager, 757-683-3585, Fax: 757-683-5750, E-mail: mbainfo@odu.edu.

Portland State University, Graduate Studies, College of Liberal Arts and Sciences, Department of Economics, Portland, OR 97207-0751. Offers applied economics (MA, MS); economics (PhD); general economics (MA, MS). Part-time programs available. *Faculty:* 17 full-time (6 women), 3 part-time/adjunct (0 women). *Students:* 12 full-time (2 women), 7 part-time (3 women); includes 2 minority (both Asian Americans or Pacific Islanders), 5 international. Average age 29. 17 applicants, 59% accepted, 8 enrolled. In 2008, 10 master's awarded. *Degree requirements:* For master's, thesis optional; for doctorate, one foreign language, thesis/dissertation. *Entrance requirements:* For master's, minimum GPA of 3.0 in upper-division course work or 2.75 overall, course work in calculus. Additional exam requirements/recommendations for international students: Required—TOEFL (minimum score 550 paper-based; 213 computer-based). *Application deadline:* For fall admission, 4/1 for domestic students, 3/1 for international students; for spring admission, 11/1 for domestic and international students. Applications are processed on a rolling basis. Application fee: $50. *Expenses:* Tuition, area resident: Full-time $8763; part-time $179 per credit hour. Tuition, state resident: full-time $8763; part-time $298 per credit hour. Tuition, nonresident: full-time $12,981; part-time $426 per credit hour. Required fees: $1242. One-time fee: $250. Tuition and fees vary according to course load and program. *Financial support:* In 2008–09, 4 research assistantships with full tuition reimbursements (averaging $6,372 per year), 1 teaching assistantship (averaging $8,820 per year) were awarded; career-related internships or fieldwork, Federal Work-Study, and unspecified assistantships also available. Support available to part-time students. Financial award application deadline: 3/1; financial award applicants required to submit FAFSA. *Faculty research:* NAFTA, economies of transition, economics of Eastern Europe, artificial intelligence, comparative economic systems. Total annual research expenditures: $64,962. *Unit head:* Dr. Randy Bluffstone, Chair, 503-725-3915, Fax: 503-725-3945. *Application contact:* Rita Spears, Office Specialist, 503-725-3941, Fax: 503-725-3945, E-mail: spearsr@pdx.edu.

Roosevelt University, Graduate Division, College of Arts and Sciences, Department of Economics, Chicago, IL 60605-1394. Offers applied economics (MA); economics (MA). Part-time and evening/weekend programs available. *Students:* 11 full-time (3 women), 13 part-time (3 women); includes 4 minority (2 African Americans, 1 American Indian/Alaska Native, 1 Asian American or Pacific Islander), 3 international. Average age 29. 48 applicants, 67% accepted, 10 enrolled. In 2008, 6 master's awarded. *Degree requirements:* For master's, thesis or alternative. *Entrance requirements:* For master's, minimum GPA of 2.7. *Application deadline:* For fall admission, 6/1 priority date for domestic students. Applications are processed on a rolling basis. Application fee: $25 ($35 for international students). *Expenses:* Tuition: Full-time $14,730; part-time $709 per credit. Required fees: $175 per semester. Tuition and fees vary according to course load and program. *Financial support:* In 2008–09, 4 students received support, including 1 teaching assistantship; career-related internships or fieldwork, Federal Work-Study, scholarships/grants, and tuition waivers (full and partial) also available. Financial award application deadline: 2/15. *Faculty research:* Labor, gender issues, international trade and development, entrepreneurship, political economy and money. Total annual research expenditures: $5,000. *Unit head:* June Lapidus, Head, 312-341-3670. *Application contact:* Joanne Canyon-Heller, Coordinator of Graduate Admission, 877-APPLY RU, Fax: 312-281-3356, E-mail: applyru@roosevelt.edu.

St. Cloud State University, School of Graduate Studies, College of Social Sciences, Department of Economics, St. Cloud, MN 56301-4498. Offers applied economics (MS); public and nonprofit institutions (MS). Part-time programs available. *Degree requirements:* For master's, thesis or alternative. *Entrance requirements:* For master's, GRE General Test, minimum GPA of 2.75. Additional exam requirements/recommendations for international students: Recommended—TOEFL (minimum score 550 paper-based; 213 computer-based), IELTS (minimum score 6.5). Electronic applications accepted.

San Jose State University, Graduate Studies and Research, College of Social Sciences, Department of Economics, San Jose, CA 95192-0001. Offers applied economics (MA); economics (MA). Part-time programs available. *Degree requirements:* For master's, comprehensive exam, thesis optional. *Entrance requirements:* For master's, GRE, minimum GPA of 3.0. Electronic applications accepted.

Southern Methodist University, Dedman College, Department of Economics, Dallas, TX 75205. Offers applied economics (MA); economics (MA, PhD); JD/MA. Part-time and evening/weekend programs available. *Faculty:* 19 full-time (5 women), 17 part-time/adjunct (5 women). *Students:* 38 full-time (18 women), 34 part-time (12 women); includes 9 minority (3 African Americans, 1 American Indian/Alaska Native, 3 Asian Americans or Pacific Islanders, 2 Hispanic Americans), 37 international. Average age 27. 85 applicants, 89% accepted, 16 enrolled. In 2008, 22 master's, 2 doctorates awarded. Terminal master's awarded for partial completion of doctoral program. *Degree requirements:* For master's, thesis, oral qualifying exam; for doctorate, thesis/dissertation, written exams. *Entrance requirements:* For master's, GRE General Test or GMAT, 12 hours course work in economics, minimum GPA of 3.0, previous course work in calculus and statistics; for doctorate, GRE General Test, minimum GPA of 3.0, 3 semesters of course work in calculus, 1 semester of course work in statistics, 1 semester of course work in linear algebra. Additional exam requirements/recommendations for international students: Required—TOEFL (minimum score 550 paper-based; 213 computer-based). *Application deadline:* For fall admission, 2/1 priority date for domestic students; for spring admission, 11/30 priority date for domestic students. Applications are processed on a rolling basis. Application fee: $75. Electronic applications accepted. *Financial support:* In 2008–09, 23 students received support, including 1 fellowship with full tuition reimbursement available (averaging $16,000 per year), 2 research assistantships with full tuition reimbursements available (averaging $16,000 per year), 20 teaching assistantships with full tuition reimbursements available (averaging $16,000 per year); tuition waivers (partial) also available. Financial award application deadline: 2/1; financial award applicants required to submit FAFSA. *Faculty research:* Economic theory, game theory, econometrics, international trade, labor. *Unit head:* Dr. Kamal Saggi, Chair, 214-768-3274, Fax: 214-768-1821, E-mail: ksaggi@mail.smu.edu. *Application contact:* Stephanie Hall, Information Contact, 214-768-2694, E-mail: eco@smu.edu.

Texas Tech University, Graduate School, College of Agricultural Sciences and Natural Resources, Department of Agricultural and Applied Economics, Lubbock, TX 79409. Offers agribusiness (MAB); agricultural and applied economics (MS, PhD); JD/MS. Part-time programs available. *Faculty:* 12 full-time (0 women). *Students:* 30 full-time (10 women), 5 part-time (2 women); includes 4 minority (2 Asian Americans or Pacific Islanders, 2 Hispanic Americans), 15 international. Average age 29. 48 applicants, 69% accepted, 15 enrolled. In 2008, 2 master's, 3 doctorates awarded. *Degree requirements:* For master's, thesis or alternative; for doctorate, thesis/dissertation. *Entrance requirements:* For master's and doctorate, GRE General Test. Additional exam requirements/recommendations for international students: Required—TOEFL (minimum score 550 paper-based; 213 computer-based). *Application deadline:* For fall admission, 3/1 priority date for international students; for spring admission, 11/1 priority date for international students. Applications are processed on a rolling basis. Application fee: $50 ($60 for international students). Electronic applications accepted. *Expenses:* Tuition, area resident: Part-time $194 per credit hour. Tuition, state resident: full-time $4648; part-time $194 per credit hour. Tuition, nonresident: full-time $11,392; part-time $475 per credit hour. Required fees: $2206; $69 per credit hour. $389 per semester. *Financial support:* In 2008–09, 26 students received support, including 22 research assistantships with partial tuition reimbursements available (averaging $12,939 per year), 2 teaching assistantships with partial tuition reimbursements available (averaging $13,770 per year); Federal Work-Study and institutionally sponsored loans also available. Support available to part-time students. Financial award application deadline: 4/15; financial award applicants required to submit FAFSA. *Faculty research:* Economics of the United States cotton and textile industries, natural resource management in semi-arid climates, commodity policy analysis, international trade in agricultural products, agribusiness analysis. Total annual research expenditures: $1 million. *Unit head:* Dr. Eduardo Segarra, Chair, 806-742-2821, Fax: 806-742-1099, E-mail: eduardo.segarra@ttu.edu. *Application contact:* Dr. Tom Knight, Graduate Adviser, 806-742-2821, Fax: 806-742-1099, E-mail: tom.knight@ttu.edu.

University of California, Santa Cruz, Division of Graduate Studies, Division of Social Sciences, Program in Applied Economics and Finance, Santa Cruz, CA 95064. Offers MS. *Degree requirements:* For master's, thesis or alternative, project. *Entrance requirements:* For master's, GRE General Test, GRE Subject Test. *Faculty research:* Economic decision-making skills for the design and operation of complex institutional systems.

University of Georgia, Graduate School, College of Agricultural and Environmental Sciences, Department of Agricultural and Applied Economics, Athens, GA 30602. Offers agricultural economics (MAE, MS, PhD); environmental economics (MS). *Degree requirements:* For master's, thesis (MS); for doctorate, thesis/dissertation. *Entrance requirements:* For master's and doctorate, GRE General Test. Electronic applications accepted.

University of Idaho, College of Graduate Studies, College of Agricultural and Life Sciences, Department of Agricultural Economics and Rural Sociology, Moscow, ID 83844-2282. Offers agricultural economics (MS); applied economics (MS), including agribusiness emphasis, agricultural economics emphasis. *Faculty:* 9 full-time, 2 part-time/adjunct. *Students:* 10 full-time, 3 part-time. Average age 29. In 2008, 6 master's awarded. *Entrance requirements:* For master's, minimum GPA of 2.8. *Application deadline:* For fall admission, 8/1 for domestic students; for spring admission, 12/15 for domestic students. Application fee: $55 ($60 for international students). *Expenses:* Tuition, nonresident: full-time $10,080; part-time $336 per credit. Required fees: $5212; $267 per credit. Tuition and fees vary according to program. *Financial support:* Research assistantships, teaching assistantships available. Financial award application deadline: 2/15. *Faculty research:* Crops: potatoes, blue grass; livestock: beef, dairy; rural and community development; natural resources and the environment; farm and ranch management. *Unit head:* Dr. Larry W Van Tassell, Department Head, 208-885-7869, Fax: 208-885-5759. *Application contact:* Dr. Larry W Van Tassell, Department Head, 208-885-7869, Fax: 208-885-5759.

University of Michigan, Horace H. Rackham School of Graduate Studies, College of Literature, Science, and the Arts, Department of Economics, Program in Applied Economics, Ann Arbor, MI 48109. Offers AM. Part-time programs available. *Entrance requirements:* For master's, GRE General Test. Additional exam requirements/recommendations for international students: Required—TOEFL (minimum score 600 paper-based; 250 computer-based). *Faculty research:* Econometric analysis transition, macro.

University of Minnesota, Twin Cities Campus, Graduate School, College of Food, Agricultural and Natural Resource Sciences, Program in Applied Economics, Minneapolis, MN 55455-0213. Offers MS, PhD. *Degree requirements:* For master's, comprehensive exam, thesis; for doctorate, comprehensive exam, thesis/dissertation. *Entrance requirements:* For master's and doctorate, GRE, minimum GPA of 3.0 preferred. Additional exam requirements/recommendations for international students: Required—TOEFL (minimum score 550 paper-based; 213 computer-based; 79 iBT). Electronic applications accepted. *Faculty research:* Consumer behavior,

Applied Economics

University of Minnesota, Twin Cities Campus (continued)
household and labor, policy analysis and health, production and marketing, resource and environmental, trade and development.

University of Nevada, Reno, Graduate School, College of Agriculture, Biotechnology and Natural Resources, Department of Resource Economics, Reno, NV 89557. Offers MS, PhD. *Faculty:* 13 full-time (4 women). *Students:* 17 full-time (10 women), 4 part-time (3 women), 10 international. Average age 33. 20 applicants, 80% accepted, 8 enrolled. In 2008, 4 master's, 2 doctorates awarded. Terminal master's awarded for partial completion of doctoral program. *Degree requirements:* For master's, thesis optional; for doctorate, thesis/dissertation. *Entrance requirements:* For master's, GRE General Test, minimum GPA of 2.75; for doctorate, GRE General Test, minimum GPA of 3.0. Additional exam requirements/recommendations for international students: Required—TOEFL (minimum score 500 paper-based; 173 computer-based; 61 iBT), IELTS (minimum score 6), TOFEL or IELTS. *Application deadline:* For fall admission, 3/1 priority date for domestic and international students; for spring admission, 11/1 priority date for domestic and international students. Applications are processed on a rolling basis. Application fee: $60 ($95 for international students). Electronic applications accepted. *Expenses:* Tuition, state resident: full-time $1710; part-time $1140 per semester. Tuition, nonresident: full-time $7115. Required fees: $158 per semester. *Financial support:* In 2008–09, 17 research assistantships with partial tuition reimbursements (averaging $20,000 per year) were awarded; Federal Work-Study, institutionally sponsored loans, scholarships/grants, health care benefits, and unspecified assistantships also available. Financial award application deadline: 3/1; financial award applicants required to submit FAFSA. *Faculty research:* Econometrics, environmental valuation, natural resource and environmental policy analysis, public lands management. Total annual research expenditures: $929,363. *Unit head:* Dr. Kim Rollins, Graduate Program Director, 775-784-1677, E-mail: krollins@cabnr.unr.edu. *Application contact:* Michele Sandberg, Application Contact, 775-784-7026, Fax: 775-784-6064, E-mail: gradschool@unr.edu.

University of New Brunswick Fredericton, School of Graduate Studies, Faculty of Arts, Department of Economics, Fredericton, NB E3B 5A3, Canada. Offers applied economics and finance (M Sc); economics (MA). Program in applied economics and finance offered at UNB Saint John Campus. Part-time programs available. *Faculty:* 110 full-time (1 woman), 3 part-time/adjunct (0 women). *Students:* 4 full-time (2 women), 4 part-time (2 women). In 2008, 5 master's awarded. *Entrance requirements:* For master's, GRE, minimum GPA of 3.0. Additional exam requirements/recommendations for international students: Required—TWE, TOEFL (minimum paper-based score of 550) or IELTS. *Application deadline:* 1/31 for domestic and international students. Applications are processed on a rolling basis. Application fee: $50 Canadian dollars. Tuition and fees charges are reported in Canadian dollars. *Expenses:* Tuition, area resident: Full-time $5562 Canadian dollars. Tuition, nonresident: full-time $9450 Canadian dollars. Required fees: $333 Canadian dollars. *Financial support:* In 2008–09, 1 research assistantship, 1 teaching assistantship were awarded; fellowships, scholarships/grants, health care benefits, and unspecified assistantships also available. Financial award application deadline: 1/31. *Faculty research:* Epidemiology and population health, micro/macro economics, economics of transportation, regional development. *Unit head:* Dr. Yuri Yevdokimov, Director of Graduate Studies, 506-447-3221, Fax: 506-453-4514, E-mail: yuri@unb.ca. *Application contact:* Lucina MacDonald, Graduate Secretary, 506-453-4828, Fax: 506-453-4514, E-mail: lmacdona@unb.ca.

The University of North Carolina at Greensboro, Graduate School, Bryan School of Business and Economics, Department of Economics, Program in Applied Economics, Greensboro, NC 27412-5001. Offers MA, MA/PhD. *Degree requirements:* For master's, comprehensive exam, thesis or alternative. *Entrance requirements:* For master's, GRE. Additional exam requirements/recommendations for international students: Required—TOEFL. Electronic applications accepted.

University of North Dakota, Graduate School, College of Business and Public Administration, Applied Economics Program, Grand Forks, ND 58202. Offers MSAE. *Degree requirements:* For master's, comprehensive exam, thesis or alternative. *Entrance requirements:* For master's, GRE General Test. Additional exam requirements/recommendations for international students: Required—TOEFL (minimum score 550 paper-based; 213 computer-based; 79 iBT), IELTS (minimum score 6.5).

University of North Texas, Robert B. Toulouse School of Graduate Studies, College of Public Affairs and Community Service, Institute of Applied Economics, Denton, TX 76203. Offers MS. Part-time programs available. *Degree requirements:* For master's, comprehensive exam, thesis or alternative. *Entrance requirements:* For master's, GRE General Test or GMAT, minimum B average in last 60 hours of course work. Additional exam requirements/recommendations for international students: Required—proof of English language proficiency required for non-native English speakers; Recommended—TOEFL (minimum score 550 paper-based; 213 computer-based). *Faculty research:* Economic/focal impact of sports and entertainment venues, economic development potential of stem cell research, state and local incentive programs, city and metropolitan area industrial targeting dispute resolution.

University of Pennsylvania, Wharton School, Program in Applied Economics, Philadelphia, PA 19104. Offers PhD.

University of Vermont, Graduate College, College of Agriculture and Life Sciences, Department of Community Development and Applied Economics, Burlington, VT 05405. Offers community development and applied economics (MS); public administration (MPA). *Students:* 23 (12 women), 1 international. 26 applicants, 65% accepted, 6 enrolled. In 2008, 6 master's awarded. *Degree requirements:* For master's, thesis. *Entrance requirements:* For master's, GRE General Test. Additional exam requirements/recommendations for international students: Required—TOEFL (minimum score 550 paper-based; 213 computer-based; 80 iBT). *Application deadline:* For fall admission, 4/1 priority date for domestic students; for spring admission, 11/15 for domestic students. Applications are processed on a rolling basis. Application fee: $40. Electronic applications accepted. *Expenses:* Tuition, state resident: part-time $488 per credit. Tuition, nonresident: part-time $1232 per credit. *Financial support:* Fellowships, research assistantships, teaching assistantships, career-related internships or fieldwork available. Financial award application deadline: 3/1. *Faculty research:* Agricultural production and marketing. *Unit head:* Dr. J. Kolodinsky, Chairperson, 802-656-2001. *Application contact:* Dr. J. Kolodinsky, Chairperson, 802-656-2001.

University of Wisconsin–Madison, Graduate School, College of Agricultural and Life Sciences, Department of Agricultural and Applied Economics, Madison, WI 53706-1380. Offers MA, MS, PhD. Part-time programs available. *Degree requirements:* For doctorate, thesis/dissertation, preliminary exams. *Entrance requirements:* For master's and doctorate, GRE General Test. Additional exam requirements/recommendations for international students: Required—TOEFL. Electronic applications accepted. *Faculty research:* Environmental and resource economics, international development, state and local economics, food systems, markets and trade.

University of Wyoming, Graduate School, College of Agriculture, Department of Agricultural and Applied Economics, Laramie, WY 82070. Offers MS. Part-time programs available. *Faculty:* 12 full-time (2 women), 2 part-time/adjunct (1 woman). *Students:* 9 full-time (4 women), 5 part-time (1 woman), 2 international. Average age 27. 9 applicants, 67% accepted, 6 enrolled. In 2008, 2 master's awarded. *Degree requirements:* For master's, thesis (for some programs). *Entrance requirements:* For master's, GRE General Test, minimum GPA of 3.0. Additional exam requirements/recommendations for international students: Required—TOEFL. *Application deadline:* For fall admission, 2/15 priority date for domestic students, 2/1 for international students; for spring admission, 10/1 priority date for domestic students. Applications are processed on a rolling basis. Application fee: $50. Electronic applications accepted. *Financial support:* In 2008–09, 9 research assistantships with tuition reimbursements (averaging $11,072 per year) were awarded; career-related internships or fieldwork, Federal Work-Study, and institutionally sponsored loans also available. Financial award application deadline: 2/1; financial award applicants required to submit FAFSA. *Faculty research:* Farm management, agricultural markets, water economics, community development, agricultural business. Total annual research expenditures: $250,000. *Unit head:* Dr. Roger H. Coupal, Interim Department Head, 307-766-2386, Fax: 307-766-5544, E-mail: coupal@uwyo.edu. *Application contact:* Michell Anderson, Graduate Admissions Coordinator, 307-766-2287, Fax: 307-766-2374, E-mail: manders2@uwyo.edu.

Utah State University, School of Graduate Studies, College of Business and College of Agriculture, Department of Economics, Program in Applied Economics, Logan, UT 84322. Offers MS. Part-time programs available. *Degree requirements:* For master's, thesis optional. *Entrance requirements:* For master's, GRE General Test, minimum GPA of 3.0.

Virginia Polytechnic Institute and State University, Graduate School, College of Agriculture and Life Sciences, Department of Agricultural and Applied Economics, Blacksburg, VA 24061. Offers agribusiness (MS); agricultural economics (MS, PhD); applied economics (MS); developmental and international economics (PhD); econometrics (PhD); macro and micro economics (PhD); markets and industrial organizations (PhD); public and regional/urban economics (PhD); resource and environmental economics (PhD). *Entrance requirements:* For master's and doctorate, GRE General Test. Additional exam requirements/recommendations for international students: Required—TOEFL (minimum score 575 paper-based; 231 computer-based). Electronic applications accepted. *Faculty research:* Rural development.

Washington State University, Graduate School, College of Agricultural, Human, and Natural Resource Sciences, School of Economic Sciences, Department of Economics, Pullman, WA 99164. Offers applied economics (MA); economics (MA, PhD); international business economics (Certificate). *Degree requirements:* For master's, comprehensive exam (for some programs), thesis (for some programs), oral exam; for doctorate, comprehensive exam, thesis/dissertation, oral exam, written exam, field exams. *Entrance requirements:* For master's, GRE General Test, minimum GPA of 3.0; for doctorate, GRE General Test or GMAT, minimum GPA of 3.0. Additional exam requirements/recommendations for international students: Required—TOEFL. *Faculty research:* Economic theory and quantitative methods, applied microeconomics.

Western Michigan University, Graduate College, College of Arts and Sciences, Department of Economics, Kalamazoo, MI 49008-5202. Offers applied economics (MA, PhD). *Degree requirements:* For master's, thesis, oral or written exams; for doctorate, thesis/dissertation, oral exam, internship. *Entrance requirements:* For doctorate, GRE General Test.

Wright State University, School of Graduate Studies, Raj Soin College of Business, Department of Economics, Program in Social and Applied Economics, Dayton, OH 45435. Offers MS.

Economic Development

Albany State University, College of Arts and Humanities, Department of History, Political Science and Public Administration, Albany, GA 31705-2717. Offers community and economic development (MPA); criminal justice (MPA); fiscal management (MPA); general management (MPA); health administration and policy (MPA); human resources management (MPA); public policy (MPA); water resource management and policy (MPA). *Accreditation:* NASPAA. Part-time programs available. *Faculty:* 5 full-time (2 women). *Students:* 10 full-time (8 women), 42 part-time (29 women); includes 50 minority (49 African Americans, 1 Asian American or Pacific Islander). Average age 35. In 2008, 12 master's awarded. *Degree requirements:* For master's, comprehensive exam, thesis. *Entrance requirements:* For master's, GRE General Test, minimum GPA of 2.5. *Application deadline:* For fall admission, 4/15 for domestic and international students; for spring admission, 11/15 for domestic and international students. Applications are processed on a rolling basis. Application fee: $20. Electronic applications accepted. *Expenses:* Tuition, area resident: Full-time $4296; part-time $154 per semester hour. Tuition, state resident: full-time $4296; part-time $154 per semester hour. Tuition, nonresident: full-time $15,338; part-time $614 per semester hour. Required fees: $306 per semester. Tuition and fees vary according to course load. *Financial support:* Tuition waivers available. Financial award application deadline: 4/1; financial award applicants required to submit FAFSA. *Faculty research:* Transportation, urban affairs, political economy. *Unit head:* Dr. Rita Henry-Brown, Chair, 229-430-4870, Fax: 229-430-7895, E-mail: rita.brown@asurams.edu. *Application contact:* Diane P. Frink, Graduate Admission Counselor, 229-430-5118, Fax: 229-430-6398, E-mail: diane.frink@asurams.edu.

Boston University, Metropolitan College (Continuing Education), Department of Administrative Sciences, Boston, MA 02215. Offers banking and financial management (MSM); business continuity in emergency management (MSM); economics development and tourism management (MSAS); electronic commerce, systems, and technology (MSAS); financial economics (MSAS); human resource management (MSM); innovation and technology (MSAS); insurance management (MSM); international market management (MSM); multinational commerce (MSAS); project management (MSM). *Accreditation:* AACSB. Part-time and evening/weekend programs available. Postbaccalaureate distance learning degree programs offered (no on-campus study). *Degree requirements:* For master's, thesis optional. *Entrance requirements:* For master's, 1 year of work experience, minimum GPA of 3.0. Additional exam requirements/recommendations for international students: Required—TOEFL (minimum score 560 paper-based; 220 computer-based; 84 iBT). Electronic applications accepted. *Faculty research:* International business, innovative process.

Cape Breton University, Shannon School of Business, Sydney, NS B1P 6L2, Canada. Offers community economic development (MBA). *Faculty:* 13 full-time (5 women), 11 part-time/adjunct (5 women). *Students:* 98 full-time (46 women), 11 part-time (4 women). Average age 38. 60 applicants, 92% accepted. In 2008, 6 master's awarded. *Degree requirements:* For master's, research project, research essay. *Entrance requirements:* For master's, interview, letters of reference. *Application deadline:* For spring admission, 5/31 for domestic students. Applications are processed on a rolling basis. Application fee: $80. *Expenses:* Contact institution. *Financial support:* In 2008–09, 6 students received support. Scholarships/grants and tuition waivers (full and partial) available. Financial award application deadline: 5/31. *Faculty research:* Community entrepreneurship, CED theory, transportation, governance, business and environmental issues in Canada. Total annual research expenditures: $20,000. *Unit head:* Ed Grimm, Dean, School of Business, 902-563-1221, Fax: 902-563-1453, E-mail: ed_grimm@cbu.ca. *Application contact:* Anne Michelle Chiasson, Program Coordinator, 902-563-1664, Fax: 902-563-1366, E-mail: anne_chiasson@cbu.ca.

Chicago State University, School of Graduate and Professional Studies, College of Arts and Sciences, Department of Geography, Sociology, Economics, and Anthropology, Chicago, IL

60628. Offers geography and economic development (MA). *Entrance requirements:* For master's, minimum GPA of 2.75.

Claremont Graduate University, Graduate Programs, School of Politics and Economics, Department of Economics, Claremont, CA 91711-6160. Offers business and financial economics (MA, PhD); economic development (Certificate); economics (PhD); industrial organization (PhD); international and development economics (PhD); international economics policy and development (MA); international money and finance (PhD); neuroeconomics (PhD); political economy and public policy (MA); public choice and public economics (PhD); MBA/PhD. Part-time programs available. *Faculty:* 7 full-time (1 woman). *Students:* 100 full-time (24 women), 6 part-time (1 woman); includes 12 minority (3 African Americans, 7 Asian Americans or Pacific Islanders, 2 Hispanic Americans), 56 international. Average age 32. In 2008, 15 master's, 15 doctorates awarded. *Entrance requirements:* For master's and doctorate, GRE General Test or GMAT. Additional exam requirements/recommendations for international students: Required—TOEFL (minimum score 550 paper-based; 213 computer-based; 80 iBT). *Application deadline:* For fall admission, 2/1 priority date for domestic students. Applications are processed on a rolling basis. Application fee: $60. Electronic applications accepted. *Expenses:* Tuition: Full-time $33,698; part-time $1465 per unit. Required fees: $310; $155 per semester. Tuition and fees vary according to program. *Financial support:* Fellowships, research assistantships, teaching assistantships, Federal Work-Study, institutionally sponsored loans, and scholarships/grants available. Support available to part-time students. Financial award application deadline: 2/15; financial award applicants required to submit FAFSA. *Faculty research:* International and financial economics, law and economics, regulation, public choice economics. *Unit head:* Arthur Denzau, Chair, 909-621-8782, Fax: 909-621-8545, E-mail: arthur.denzau@cgu.edu. *Application contact:* Laura Carillo, Recruiter and Admissions Coordinator, 909-621-8699, Fax: 909-621-7545, E-mail: laura.carillo@cga.edu.

Cleveland State University, College of Graduate Studies, Maxine Goodman Levin College of Urban Affairs, Program in Nonprofit Administration and Leadership, Cleveland, OH 44115. Offers geographic information systems (Certificate); local and urban management (Certificate); nonprofit administration and leadership (MNAL); nonprofit management (Certificate); urban economic development (Certificate). Part-time and evening/weekend programs available. *Faculty:* 26 full-time (10 women), 6 part-time/adjunct (4 women). *Students:* 5 full-time (4 women), 21 part-time (17 women); includes 4 minority (all African Americans), 1 international. Average age 35. 29 applicants, 45% accepted, 9 enrolled. *Degree requirements:* For master's, thesis or alternative, capstone course. *Entrance requirements:* For master's, GRE (minimum score: 40th percentile quantitative/verbal, 4.0 analytical writing), minimum GPA of 3.0. Additional exam requirements/recommendations for international students: Required—TOEFL (minimum score 525 paper-based; 197 computer-based; 65 iBT). *Application deadline:* For fall admission, 7/15 priority date for domestic students, 5/15 for international students; for spring admission, 11/1 for international students. Applications are processed on a rolling basis. Application fee: $30. Electronic applications accepted. *Financial support:* In 2008–09, 5 students received support, including research assistantships with full and partial tuition reimbursements available (averaging $6,960 per year); career-related internships or fieldwork, Federal Work-Study, scholarships/grants, tuition waivers (full and partial), and unspecified assistantships also available. Support available to part-time students. Financial award application deadline: 3/1; financial award applicants required to submit FAFSA. *Faculty research:* Human resource management, volunteerism, performance measurement in nonprofits, government-nonprofit partnerships. *Unit head:* Dr. Jennifer Alexander, Director, 216-687-5011, Fax: 216-687-2013, E-mail: j.k.alexander@csuohio.edu. *Application contact:* Graduate Program Coordinator, 216-523-7522, Fax: 216-687-5398, E-mail: urbanprograms@csuohio.edu.

Cleveland State University, College of Graduate Studies, Maxine Goodman Levin College of Urban Affairs, Program in Urban Planning, Design, and Development, Cleveland, OH 44115. Offers geographic information systems (Certificate); local and urban management (Certificate); urban economic development (Certificate); urban planning, design, and development (MUPDD); urban real estate development and finance (Certificate); JD/MUPDD. *Accreditation:* ACSP. Part-time and evening/weekend programs available. *Faculty:* 26 full-time (10 women), 12 part-time/adjunct (5 women). *Students:* 37 full-time (17 women), 41 part-time (21 women); includes 13 minority (9 African Americans, 1 American Indian/Alaska Native, 3 Hispanic Americans), 10 international. Average age 38. 63 applicants, 63% accepted, 21 enrolled. In 2008, 24 master's, 9 Certificates awarded. *Degree requirements:* For master's, project or thesis. *Entrance requirements:* For master's, GRE General Test (minimum score: verbal and quantitative 50th percentile, analytical writing 4.0), minimum GPA of 3.0. Additional exam requirements/recommendations for international students: Required—TOEFL (minimum score 525 paper-based; 197 computer-based; 65 iBT). *Application deadline:* For fall admission, 7/15 priority date for domestic students, 5/15 for international students; for spring admission, 11/1 for international students. Applications are processed on a rolling basis. Application fee: $30. Electronic applications accepted. *Financial support:* In 2008–09, 15 students received support, including 10 research assistantships with full and partial tuition reimbursements available (averaging $6,960 per year), 5 teaching assistantships with full and partial tuition reimbursements available (averaging $6,960 per year); career-related internships or fieldwork, Federal Work-Study, tuition waivers (full and partial), and unspecified assistantships also available. Support available to part-time students. Financial award application deadline: 3/1. *Faculty research:* Housing and neighborhood development, urban housing policy, environmental sustainability, economic development. *Unit head:* Dr. W. Dennis Keating, Director, 216-687-2298, Fax: 216-687-2013, E-mail: w.keating@csuohio.edu. *Application contact:* Graduate Program Coordinator, 216-523-7522, Fax: 216-687-5398, E-mail: urbanprograms@csuohio.edu.

Cleveland State University, College of Graduate Studies, Maxine Goodman Levin College of Urban Affairs, Program in Urban Studies, Cleveland, OH 44115. Offers geographic information systems (Certificate); local and urban management (Certificate); nonprofit management (Certificate); urban economic development (Certificate); urban real estate development and finance (Certificate); urban studies (MS); urban studies and public affairs (PhD). Part-time and evening/weekend programs available. *Faculty:* 26 full-time (10 women), 20 part-time/adjunct (11 women). *Students:* 26 full-time (12 women), 42 part-time (24 women); includes 13 minority (10 African Americans, 2 Asian Americans or Pacific Islanders, 1 Hispanic American), 21 international. Average age 37. 69 applicants, 35% accepted, 12 enrolled. In 2008, 6 master's, 7 doctorates, 6 other advanced degrees awarded. *Degree requirements:* For master's, thesis or alternative, exit project, capstone course; for doctorate, comprehensive exam, thesis/dissertation. *Entrance requirements:* For master's, GRE General Test, minimum GPA of 3.0; for doctorate, GRE General Test, minimum GPA of 3.5. Additional exam requirements/recommendations for international students: Required—TOEFL (minimum score 525 paper-based; 197 computer-based; 65 iBT). *Application deadline:* For fall admission, 7/15 priority date for domestic students, 5/15 for international students; for spring admission, 11/1 for international students. Applications are processed on a rolling basis. Application fee: $30. Electronic applications accepted. *Financial support:* In 2008–09, 15 students received support, including 11 research assistantships with full tuition reimbursements available (averaging $7,000 per year), 4 teaching assistantships with full and partial tuition reimbursements available (averaging $7,000 per year); career-related internships or fieldwork, Federal Work-Study, institutionally sponsored loans, scholarships/grants, tuition waivers (full and partial), and unspecified assistantships also available. Support available to part-time students. Financial award application deadline: 3/1; financial award applicants required to submit FAFSA. *Faculty research:* Environmental issues, economic development, urban and public policy, public management. *Unit head:* Dr. Wendy Kellogg, Director, 216-687-5265, Fax: 216-687-9342, E-mail: w.kellogg@csuohio.edu. *Application contact:* Graduate Program Coordinator, 216-523-7522, Fax: 216-687-5398, E-mail: urbanprograms@csuohio.edu.

Concordia University, School of Graduate Studies, Faculty of Arts and Science, School of Community and Public Affairs, Montréal, QC H3G 1M8, Canada. Offers community economic development (Diploma).

Cornell University, Graduate School, Graduate Fields of Agriculture and Life Sciences, Field of Community and Rural Development, Ithaca, NY 14853-0001. Offers community development process (MPS); economic development (MPS); local government organizations and operations (MPS); program development and planning (MPS). *Faculty:* 30 full-time (10 women). *Students:* 1 (woman) full-time. Average age 28. In 2008, 2 master's awarded. *Entrance requirements:* For master's, GRE General Test (recommended), 3 letters of recommendation. Additional exam requirements/recommendations for international students: Required—TOEFL (minimum score 550 paper-based; 213 computer-based; 77 iBT). *Application deadline:* For fall admission, 5/1 for domestic students. Application fee: $70. Electronic applications accepted. *Expenses:* Tuition: Full-time $29,500. Required fees: $70. Full-time tuition and fees vary according to degree level, program and student level. *Financial support:* In 2008–09, 1 fellowship with full tuition reimbursement, 1 teaching assistantship with full tuition reimbursement were awarded; research assistantships with full tuition reimbursements, institutionally sponsored loans, scholarships/grants, health care benefits, tuition waivers (full and partial), and unspecified assistantships also available. Financial award applicants required to submit FAFSA. *Faculty research:* Land use, community economic development, governance and leadership development, planning and evaluation, main street revitalization. *Unit head:* Director of Graduate Studies, 607-255-4916, Fax: 607-255-2231. *Application contact:* Graduate Field Assistant, 607-255-4916, Fax: 607-255-2331, E-mail: gradcrd@cornell.edu.

Cornell University, Graduate School, Graduate Fields of Architecture, Art and Planning, Field of City and Regional Planning, Ithaca, NY 14853-0001. Offers city and regional planning (MRP, PhD); environmental planning and design (MRP, PhD); historic preservation planning (MA); international development planning (MRP, PhD); planning theory and systems analysis (MRP, PhD); regional economics and development planning (MRP, PhD); regional science (MRP, PhD); social and health systems planning (MRP, PhD); urban and regional theory (MRP, PhD); urban planning history (MRP, PhD). *Accreditation:* ACSP (one or more programs are accredited). *Faculty:* 27 full-time (10 women). *Students:* 113 full-time (71 women); includes 13 minority (3 African Americans, 6 Asian Americans or Pacific Islanders, 4 Hispanic Americans), 26 international. Average age 30. 268 applicants, 47% accepted, 46 enrolled. In 2008, 23 master's, 5 doctorates awarded. *Degree requirements:* For master's, thesis (MA); for doctorate, comprehensive exam, thesis/dissertation. *Entrance requirements:* For master's and doctorate, GRE General Test, 2 letters of recommendation. Additional exam requirements/recommendations for international students: Required—TOEFL (minimum score 600 paper-based; 250 computer-based; 77 iBT). *Application deadline:* For fall admission, 1/10 for domestic students. Application fee: $70. Electronic applications accepted. *Expenses:* Tuition: Full-time $29,500. Required fees: $70. Full-time tuition and fees vary according to degree level, program and student level. *Financial support:* In 2008–09, 24 students received support, including 9 fellowships with full tuition reimbursements available, 5 research assistantships with full tuition reimbursements available, 10 teaching assistantships with full tuition reimbursements available; institutionally sponsored loans, scholarships/grants, health care benefits, tuition waivers (full and partial), and unspecified assistantships also available. Financial award applicants required to submit FAFSA. *Faculty research:* Land use planning, economic development, international development, historic preservation, community development. *Unit head:* Director of Graduate Studies, 607-255-6848, Fax: 607-255-1971. *Application contact:* Graduate Field Assistant, 607-255-6848, Fax: 607-255-1971, E-mail: crp_admissions@cornell.edu.

Cornell University, Graduate School, Graduate Fields of Arts and Sciences, Field of Economics, Ithaca, NY 14853-0001. Offers applied economics (PhD); basic analytical economics (PhD); econometrics and economic statistics (PhD); economic development and planning (PhD); economic theory (PhD); industrial organization and control (PhD); international economics (PhD); labor economics (PhD); monetary and macroeconomics (PhD); public finance (PhD). *Faculty:* 76 full-time (12 women). *Students:* 98 full-time (39 women); includes 6 minority (1 African American, 3 Asian Americans or Pacific Islanders, 2 Hispanic Americans), 54 international. Average age 29. 563 applicants, 14% accepted, 16 enrolled. In 2008, 16 doctorates awarded. *Degree requirements:* For doctorate, comprehensive exam, thesis/dissertation. *Entrance requirements:* For doctorate, GRE General Test, 3 letters of recommendation. Additional exam requirements/recommendations for international students: Required—TOEFL (minimum score 550 paper-based; 213 computer-based; 77 iBT). *Application deadline:* For fall admission, 1/15 priority date for domestic students. Application fee: $70. Electronic applications accepted. *Expenses:* Tuition: Full-time $29,500. Required fees: $70. Full-time tuition and fees vary according to degree level, program and student level. *Financial support:* In 2008–09, 81 students received support, including 18 fellowships with full tuition reimbursements available, 18 research assistantships with full tuition reimbursements available, 45 teaching assistantships with full tuition reimbursements available; institutionally sponsored loans, scholarships/grants, health care benefits, tuition waivers (full and partial), and unspecified assistantships also available. Financial award applicants required to submit FAFSA. *Faculty research:* Learning and games, economics of education, political economy, transfer payments, time series and nonparametrics. *Unit head:* Director of Graduate Studies, 607-255-4893, Fax: 607-255-2818. *Application contact:* Graduate Field Assistant, 607-255-4893, Fax: 607-255-2818, E-mail: econ_phd@cornell.edu.

Eastern Michigan University, Graduate School, College of Arts and Sciences, Department of Economics, Ypsilanti, MI 48197. Offers applied economics (MA); economics (MA); health economics (MA); international economics and development (MA); trade and development (MA). Part-time and evening/weekend programs available. Postbaccalaureate distance learning degree programs offered (minimal on-campus study). *Degree requirements:* For master's, thesis or alternative. *Entrance requirements:* Additional exam requirements/recommendations for international students: Required—TOEFL.

Eastern University, School of Leadership and Development, St. Davids, PA 19087-3696. Offers economic development (MBA), including international development, urban development (MA, MBA); international development (MA), including global development, urban development (MA, MBA); nonprofit management (MS); organizational leadership (MA); M Div/MBA. Part-time and evening/weekend programs available. *Degree requirements:* For master's, thesis (for some programs). *Entrance requirements:* For master's, GMAT (MBA), minimum GPA of 2.5. *Expenses:* Contact institution. *Faculty research:* Micro-level economic development, China welfare and economic development, macroethics, micro- and macro-level economic development in transitional economics, organizational effectiveness.

East Tennessee State University, School of Graduate Studies, College of Business and Technology, Department of Economics, Finance, and Urban Studies, Johnson City, TN 37614. Offers city management (MCM); community development (MPM); general administration (MPM); municipal service management (MPM); urban and regional economic development (MPM); urban and regional planning (MPM). *Degree requirements:* For master's, internship, oral defense of thesis, research report. *Entrance requirements:* For master's, GRE General Test, minimum GPA of 3.0. Additional exam requirements/recommendations for international students: Required—TOEFL (minimum score 550 paper-based; 213 computer-based).

Florida Atlantic University, College of Architecture, Urban and Public Affairs, School of Urban and Regional Planning, Boca Raton, FL 33431-0991. Offers economic development and tourism (Certificate); environmental planning (Certificate); sustainable community planning (Certificate); urban and regional planning (MURP); visual planning technology (Certificate). *Accreditation:* ACSP. Part-time and evening/weekend programs available. *Faculty:* 8 full-time (6 women), 1 (woman) part-time/adjunct. *Students:* 21 full-time (12 women), 11 part-time (5 women); includes 15 minority (5 African Americans, 10 Hispanic Americans), 1 international. Average age 33. 47 applicants, 47% accepted, 8 enrolled. In 2008, 12 master's awarded. *Entrance requirements:* For master's, GRE General Test, minimum GPA of 3.0. Additional exam requirements/recommendations for international students: Required—TOEFL. *Application deadline:* For fall admission, 7/1 priority date for domestic students, 2/15 for international students; for spring admission, 11/1 priority date for domestic students, 7/15 for international students. Applications are processed on a rolling basis. Application fee: $30. *Expenses:* Tuition, state resident: full-time $4867; part-time $270.40 per credit hour. Tuition, nonresident: full-time $16,486; part-time $915.87 per credit hour. *Financial support:* Fellowships with full tuition reimbursements, research assistantships, career-related internships or fieldwork, Federal

Economic Development

Florida Atlantic University (continued)

Work-Study, institutionally sponsored loans, and tuition waivers (partial) available. Financial award application deadline: 4/1. *Faculty research:* Growth management, urban design, computer applications/geographical information systems, environmental planning. *Unit head:* Dr. Jaap Vos, Chair, 954-762-5653, Fax: 954-762-5673, E-mail: jvos@fau.edu. *Application contact:* Dr. Jaap Vos, Chair, 954-762-5653, Fax: 954-762-5673, E-mail: jvos@fau.edu.

Fordham University, Graduate School of Arts and Sciences, Program in International Political Economy and Development, New York, NY 10458. Offers MA, Certificate. Part-time and evening/weekend programs available. *Degree requirements:* For master's, comprehensive exam. *Entrance requirements:* For master's, GRE General Test. Additional exam requirements/recommendations for international students: Required—TOEFL (minimum score 600 paper-based; 250 computer-based). Electronic applications accepted. *Faculty research:* International economics, comparative international politics, international banking and finance, international development, emerging markets and country risk analysis.

See Close-Up on page 865.

Georgetown University, Graduate School of Arts and Sciences, Department of Economics, Washington, DC 20057. Offers econometrics (PhD); economic development (PhD); economic theory (PhD); industrial organization (PhD); international macro and finance (PhD); international trade (PhD); labor economics (PhD); macroeconomics (PhD); public economics and political economics (PhD); MA/PhD; MS/MA. *Degree requirements:* For doctorate, comprehensive exam, thesis/dissertation. *Entrance requirements:* For doctorate, GRE General Test. Additional exam requirements/recommendations for international students: Required—TOEFL. *Faculty research:* International economics, economic development.

Georgia Institute of Technology, Graduate Studies and Research, College of Architecture, City and Regional Planning Program, Atlanta, GA 30332-0001. Offers city and regional planning (PhD); economic development (MCRP); environmental planning and management (MCRP); geographic information systems (MCRP); land and community development (MCRP); land use planning (MCRP); transportation (MCRP); urban design (MCRP); MCP/MSCE. *Accreditation:* ACSP. *Degree requirements:* For master's, thesis, internship. *Entrance requirements:* For master's, GRE General Test, minimum GPA of 2.7. Additional exam requirements/recommendations for international students: Required—TOEFL. Electronic applications accepted.

Georgia State University, Andrew Young School of Policy Studies, Department of Public Administration and Urban Studies, Atlanta, GA 30303-3083. Offers disaster management (Certificate); non-profit management (Certificate); planning and economic development (Certificate); public administration (MPA); public policy (PhD); urban policy studies (MS); JD/MPA. *Accreditation:* NASPAA (one or more programs are accredited). Part-time and evening/weekend programs available. Terminal master's awarded for partial completion of doctoral program. *Degree requirements:* For master's, thesis optional; for doctorate, comprehensive exam, thesis/dissertation. *Entrance requirements:* For master's and doctorate, GRE General Test. Additional exam requirements/recommendations for international students: Required—TOEFL. Electronic applications accepted. *Faculty research:* Public management, urban policy, policy analysis, public finance, public involvement.

New Mexico State University, Graduate School, College of Business, Department of Economics and International Business, Las Cruces, NM 88003-8001. Offers economic development (DED); economics (MA); experimental statistics (MS). Part-time programs available. *Faculty:* 11 full-time (0 women), 2 part-time/adjunct (1 woman). *Students:* 43 full-time (15 women), 8 part-time (3 women); includes 11 minority (1 Asian American or Pacific Islander, 10 Hispanic Americans), 27 international. Average age 30. 65 applicants, 75% accepted, 27 enrolled. In 2008, 18 master's awarded. *Degree requirements:* For master's, thesis or alternative; for doctorate, thesis/dissertation or alternative. *Entrance requirements:* For master's, minimum GPA of 3.0; for doctorate, appropriate master's degree. Additional exam requirements/recommendations for international students: Required—TOEFL. *Application deadline:* Applications are processed on a rolling basis. Application fee: $30 ($50 for international students). Electronic applications accepted. *Expenses:* Tuition, area resident: Full-time $3890; part-time $212.85 per credit. Tuition, state resident: full-time $3890; part-time $212.85 per credit. Tuition, nonresident: full-time $13,916; part-time $630.55 per credit. Required fees: $1218; $609 per semester. *Financial support:* In 2008–09, 37 students received support, including 15 research assistantships (averaging $9,955 per year), 19 teaching assistantships (averaging $8,614 per year); fellowships, career-related internships or fieldwork, Federal Work-Study, and health care benefits also available. Support available to part-time students. Financial award application deadline: 3/1. *Faculty research:* Public utilities, environment, linear models, biological sampling, public policy, economics development. *Unit head:* Dr. Anthony Popp, Graduate Adviser, 575-646-5198, Fax: 575-646-1915, E-mail: apopp@nmsu.edu. *Application contact:* Dr. Anthony Popp, Graduate Adviser, 575-646-5198, Fax: 575-646-1915, E-mail: apopp@nmsu.edu.

Southern New Hampshire University, School of Community Economic Development, Manchester, NH 03106-1045. Offers MA, MBA, MS, PhD. Part-time and evening/weekend programs available. *Degree requirements:* For master's, thesis or alternative, community project; for doctorate, comprehensive exam, thesis/dissertation, community project. *Entrance requirements:* For master's, 2 years of work experience, minimum GPA of 3.0, 2 letters of recommendation, application, fees, review; for doctorate, 2 years of work experience, minimum GPA of 3.5, 3 letters of recommendation, research samples. Additional exam requirements/recommendations for international students: Required—TOEFL (minimum score 550 paper-based; 300 computer-based; 70 iBT). Electronic applications accepted. *Expenses:* Contact institution.

University of Central Arkansas, Graduate School, College of Business Administration, Program in Community and Economic Development, Conway, AR 72035-0001. Offers MS. *Degree requirements:* For master's, comprehensive exam, thesis. *Entrance requirements:* For master's, GRE General Test, minimum GPA of 2.7. Additional exam requirements/recommendations for international students: Required—TOEFL (minimum score 550 paper-based; 213 computer-based). *Expenses:* Contact institution.

University of Houston–Victoria, School of Business Administration, Victoria, TX 77901-4450. Offers accounting (MBA); economic development and entrepreneurship (MS); finance (GMBA, MBA); general business (MBA); international business (MBA); management (GMBA, MBA); marketing (MBA). *Accreditation:* AACSB. Part-time and evening/weekend programs available. Postbaccalaureate distance learning degree programs offered (no on-campus study). *Entrance requirements:* For master's, GMAT. Additional exam requirements/recommendations for international students: Required—TOEFL (minimum score 550 paper-based; 213 computer-based). Electronic applications accepted. *Faculty research:* Economic development, marketing, finance.

University of Massachusetts Lowell, College of Arts and Sciences, Department of Regional Economic and Social Development, Lowell, MA 01854-2881. Offers MA, Graduate Certificate. Part-time programs available. *Entrance requirements:* For master's, GRE. Electronic applications accepted.

University of Miami, Graduate School, School of Business Administration, Department of Economics, Coral Gables, FL 33124. Offers economic development (MA, PhD); environmental economics (PhD); human resource economics (MA, PhD); international economics (MA, PhD); macroeconomics (PhD). Students admitted every two years in the fall semester. Terminal master's awarded for partial completion of doctoral program. *Degree requirements:* For master's, comprehensive exam; for doctorate, comprehensive exam, thesis/dissertation. *Entrance requirements:* For master's and doctorate, GRE General Test, minimum GPA of 3.0. Additional exam requirements/recommendations for international students: Required—TOEFL (minimum score 550 paper-based). *Faculty research:* International economics/trade, applied microeconomics, development.

University of Minnesota, Twin Cities Campus, Graduate School, Hubert H. Humphrey Institute of Public Affairs, Program in Public Policy, Minneapolis, MN 55455-0213. Offers advanced policy analysis methods (MPP); economic and community development (MPP); foreign policy (MPP); public and nonprofit leadership and management (MPP); science technology and environmental policy (MPP); social policy (MPP); women and public policy (MPP); JD/MPP; MPP/MS; MSW/MPP. Part-time programs available. *Degree requirements:* For master's, thesis or alternative, internship or equivalent work experience. *Entrance requirements:* For master's, GRE General Test, minimum undergraduate GPA of 3.0. Additional exam requirements/recommendations for international students: Required—TOEFL (minimum score 600 paper-based; 250 computer-based). Electronic applications accepted. *Faculty research:* Social policy, public and non-profit management and leadership, community and economic development, foreign policy and international affairs, women and public policy.

University of Minnesota, Twin Cities Campus, Graduate School, Hubert H. Humphrey Institute of Public Affairs, Program in Urban and Regional Planning, Minneapolis, MN 55455-0213. Offers environmental planning (MURP); housing and community development (MURP); land use and urban design (MURP); regional, economic and workforce development (MURP); transportation planning (MURP); JD/MURP; MURP/MLA; MURP/MS. *Accreditation:* ACSP (one or more programs are accredited). Part-time programs available. *Degree requirements:* For master's, thesis or alternative, internship or equivalent work experience. *Entrance requirements:* For master's, GRE General Test, minimum undergraduate GPA of 3.0. Additional exam requirements/recommendations for international students: Required—TOEFL (minimum score 600 paper-based; 250 computer-based). Electronic applications accepted. *Faculty research:* Policy planning, resource allocation planning, regulatory planning, program planning, project planning.

The University of North Carolina at Greensboro, Graduate School, College of Arts and Sciences, Department of Geography, Greensboro, NC 27412-5001. Offers applied geography (MA); geographic information science (Certificate); geography (PhD); urban and economic development (Certificate). *Degree requirements:* For master's, comprehensive exam, thesis or alternative. *Entrance requirements:* For master's, GRE General Test. Additional exam requirements/recommendations for international students: Required—TOEFL. Electronic applications accepted.

The University of North Carolina at Greensboro, Graduate School, College of Arts and Sciences, Department of Political Science, Greensboro, NC 27412-5001. Offers nonprofit management (Certificate); public affairs (MPA); urban and economic development (Certificate). *Accreditation:* NASPAA. *Degree requirements:* For master's, comprehensive exam. *Entrance requirements:* For master's, GRE General Test. Additional exam requirements/recommendations for international students: Required—TOEFL. Electronic applications accepted. *Faculty research:* U.S. Constitution, Canadian parliament, public management, ethical challenge of public service.

University of San Francisco, College of Arts and Sciences, Department of Economics, San Francisco, CA 94117-1080. Offers economics (MA); financial analysis (MS); international and development economics (MA); MS/MBA. Part-time and evening/weekend programs available. *Degree requirements:* For master's, comprehensive exam, thesis or alternative. *Entrance requirements:* For master's, GRE General Test (recommended), BA in economics (preferred). Additional exam requirements/recommendations for international students: Required—TOEFL. *Faculty research:* Economic development, forecasting and planning, labor markets, Pacific Rim, financial markets.

University of Southern California, Graduate School, College of Letters, Arts and Sciences, Department of Economics, Los Angeles, CA 90089. Offers economic development programming (MA); economics (MA, PhD). Part-time programs available. *Degree requirements:* For master's, thesis; for doctorate, thesis/dissertation. *Entrance requirements:* For master's and doctorate, GRE General Test. *Faculty research:* Theory, econometrics, development, institution, dynamic economics, industrial organization, international economics.

University of Southern Mississippi, Graduate School, College of Science and Technology, Department of Economic and Workforce Development, Hattiesburg, MS 39406-0001. Offers economic development (MS); human capital development (PhD); workforce training and development (MS). Part-time programs available. *Faculty:* 8 full-time (2 women). *Students:* 31 full-time (24 women), 38 part-time (21 women); includes 24 minority (all African Americans), 3 international. Average age 40. 32 applicants, 63% accepted, 17 enrolled. In 2008, 20 master's, 2 doctorates awarded. *Degree requirements:* For master's, comprehensive exam, thesis optional, internships; for doctorate, comprehensive exam, thesis/dissertation. *Entrance requirements:* For master's, GMAT, GRE General Test, minimum GPA of 2.75 in last 60 hours; for doctorate, GMAT, GRE General Test, minimum GPA of 3.5. Additional exam requirements/recommendations for international students: Required—TOEFL. *Application deadline:* For fall admission, 8/1 for domestic students, 3/1 for international students; for spring admission, 1/3 for domestic and international students. Application fee: $30. Electronic applications accepted. *Financial support:* In 2008–09, 11 students received support, including 2 research assistantships with full tuition reimbursements available (averaging $13,000 per year), 6 teaching assistantships with full tuition reimbursements available (averaging $6,500 per year); career-related internships or fieldwork and Federal Work-Study also available. Financial award application deadline: 3/1; financial award applicants required to submit FAFSA. *Faculty research:* Economic development, international studies, geography. *Unit head:* Dr. Kenneth Malone, Chair, 601-266-4736, Fax: 601-266-6071, E-mail: ken.malone@usm.edu. *Application contact:* Dr. Cyndi Gaudet, Graduate Coordinator, 601-266-6519, Fax: 601-266-6071.

University of Waterloo, Graduate Studies, Faculty of Environmental Studies, Program in Local Economic Development, Waterloo, ON N2L 3G1, Canada. Offers MAES. Part-time programs available. *Degree requirements:* For master's, internship, research paper. Electronic applications accepted.

Vanderbilt University, Graduate School, Department of Economics, Nashville, TN 37240-1001. Offers economic development (MA); economics (MA, MAT, PhD); JD/PhD. *Faculty:* 44 full-time (10 women). *Students:* 81 full-time (16 women), 2 part-time (0 women); includes 5 minority (1 African American, 3 Asian Americans or Pacific Islanders, 1 Hispanic American), 50 international. Average age 28. 380 applicants, 31% accepted, 31 enrolled. In 2008, 30 master's, 8 doctorates awarded. Terminal master's awarded for partial completion of doctoral program. *Degree requirements:* For master's, thesis or alternative; for doctorate, thesis/dissertation, final and qualifying exams. *Entrance requirements:* For master's and doctorate, GRE General Test, GRE Subject Test (recommended). Additional exam requirements/recommendations for international students: Required—TOEFL (minimum score 570 paper-based; 230 computer-based; 88 iBT). *Application deadline:* For fall admission, 1/15 for domestic and international students; for spring admission, 11/1 for domestic students. Applications are processed on a rolling basis. Application fee: $0. Electronic applications accepted. *Financial support:* Fellowships with full and partial tuition reimbursements, teaching assistantships with full and partial tuition reimbursements, career-related internships or fieldwork, Federal Work-Study, institutionally sponsored loans, scholarships/grants, and health care benefits available. Financial award application deadline: 1/15; financial award applicants required to submit CSS PROFILE or FAFSA. *Faculty research:* Economic theory, applied fields, developmental economics, environmental economics, health economics and policy. *Unit head:* Tong Li, PhD, Chair, 615-322-3426, Fax: 615-343-8495, E-mail: tong.li@vanderbilt.edu. *Application contact:* Bill Collins, PhD, Director of Graduate Studies, 615-322-3428, Fax: 615-343-8495, E-mail: william.collins@vanderbilt.edu.

Virginia Polytechnic Institute and State University, Graduate School, College of Agriculture and Life Sciences, Department of Agricultural and Applied Economics, Blacksburg, VA 24061. Offers agribusiness (MS); agricultural economics (MS, PhD); applied economics (MS); developmental and international economics (PhD); econometrics (PhD); macro and micro economics (PhD); markets and industrial organizations (PhD); public and regional/urban economics (PhD); resource and environmental economics (PhD). *Entrance requirements:* For master's and doctorate, GRE General Test. Additional exam requirements/recommendations for international students: Required—TOEFL (minimum score 575 paper-based; 231 computer-based). Electronic applications accepted. *Faculty research:* Rural development.

Virginia Polytechnic Institute and State University, Graduate School, College of Architecture and Urban Studies, School of Public and International Affairs, Blacksburg, VA 24061. Offers environmental planning and policy (MURP); government and international affairs (MPIA); housing, community and economic development (MURP); international development planning (MURP); land use and physical planning (MURP); planning, governance and globalization (PhD), including environmental planning and landscape analysis, physical planning and urban design, public and international affairs, urban and environmental design and planning; urban and regional planning (MURP). *Accreditation:* ACSP. *Entrance requirements:* Additional exam requirements/recommendations for international students: Required—TOEFL (minimum score 550 paper-based; 213 computer-based). Electronic applications accepted. *Faculty research:* Design theory, environmental planning, town planning, transportation planning.

Wayne State University, College of Liberal Arts and Sciences, Interdisciplinary Program in Economic Development, Detroit, MI 48202. Offers Certificate. *Entrance requirements:* Additional exam requirements/recommendations for international students: Required—TOEFL (minimum

score 550 paper-based; 213 computer-based); Recommended—TWE (minimum score 6). Electronic applications accepted.

West Virginia University, College of Business and Economics, Division of Economics and Finance, Morgantown, WV 26506. Offers business analysis (MA); developmental financial economics (PhD); environmental and resource economics (PhD); international economics (PhD); mathematical economics (MA); monetary economics (PhD); public finance (PhD); public policy (MA); regional and urban economics (PhD); statistics and economics (MA). Terminal master's awarded for partial completion of doctoral program. *Degree requirements:* For master's, thesis optional; for doctorate, comprehensive exam, thesis/dissertation. *Entrance requirements:* For master's and doctorate, GRE General Test, minimum GPA of 3.0; course work in intermediate microeconomics, intermediate macroeconomics, calculus, and statistics. Additional exam requirements/recommendations for international students: Required—TOEFL. Electronic applications accepted. *Faculty research:* Financial economics, regional/urban development, public economics, international trade/international finance/development economics, monetary economics.

Yale University, Graduate School of Arts and Sciences, Department of Economics, Program in International and Development Economics, New Haven, CT 06520. Offers MA. *Entrance requirements:* For master's, GRE General Test.

Economics

Albany State University, College of Arts and Humanities, Department of History, Political Science and Public Administration, Albany, GA 31705-2717. Offers community and economic development (MPA); criminal justice (MPA); fiscal management (MPA); general management (MPA); health administration and policy (MPA); human resources management (MPA); public policy (MPA); water resource management and policy (MPA). *Accreditation:* NASPAA. Part-time programs available. *Faculty:* 5 full-time (2 women). *Students:* 10 full-time (8 women), 42 part-time (29 women); includes 50 minority (49 African Americans, 1 Asian American or Pacific Islander). Average age 35. In 2008, 12 master's awarded. *Degree requirements:* For master's, comprehensive exam, thesis. *Entrance requirements:* For master's, GRE General Test, minimum GPA of 2.5. *Application deadline:* For fall admission, 4/15 for domestic and international students; for spring admission, 11/15 for domestic and international students. Applications are processed on a rolling basis. Application fee: $20. Electronic applications accepted. *Expenses:* Tuition, area resident: Full-time $4296; part-time $154 per semester hour. Tuition, state resident: full-time $4296; part-time $154 per semester hour. Tuition, nonresident: full-time $15,338; part-time $614 per semester hour. Required fees: $306 per semester. Tuition and fees vary according to course load. *Financial support:* Tuition waivers available. Financial award application deadline: 4/1; financial award applicants required to submit FAFSA. *Faculty research:* Transportation, urban affairs, political economy. *Unit head:* Dr. Rita Henry-Brown, Chair, 229-430-4870, Fax: 229-430-7895, E-mail: rita.brown@asurams.edu. *Application contact:* Diane P. Frink, Graduate Admission Counselor, 229-430-5118, Fax: 229-430-6398, E-mail: diane.frink@asurams.edu.

American University, College of Arts and Sciences, Department of Economics, Washington, DC 20016-8029. Offers applied microeconomics (Certificate); economics (MA, PhD); international economic relations (Certificate). Part-time and evening/weekend programs available. *Faculty:* 23 full-time (10 women), 1 part-time/adjunct (0 women). *Students:* 56 full-time (23 women), 71 part-time (31 women); includes 12 minority (8 African Americans, 1 Asian American or Pacific Islander, 3 Hispanic Americans), 60 international. Average age 30. 149 applicants, 62% accepted, 24 enrolled. In 2008, 23 master's, 9 doctorates awarded. Terminal master's awarded for partial completion of doctoral program. *Degree requirements:* For master's, comprehensive exam, thesis or alternative; for doctorate, comprehensive exam, thesis/dissertation, 2 research seminars, field requirement. *Entrance requirements:* For master's and doctorate, GRE; for Certificate, bachelor's degree. Additional exam requirements/recommendations for international students: Required—TOEFL. *Application deadline:* For spring admission, 10/1 for domestic students. Applications are processed on a rolling basis. Application fee: $80. *Expenses:* Tuition: Full-time $21,204; part-time $1178 per credit hour. Required fees: $380. Part-time tuition and fees vary according to course load and program. *Financial support:* Fellowships, research assistantships with full and partial tuition reimbursements, teaching assistantships with full and partial tuition reimbursements, career-related internships or fieldwork, Federal Work-Study, institutionally sponsored loans, and tuition waivers (full and partial) available. Financial award application deadline: 2/1. *Faculty research:* Political economy, development, labor, gender. *Unit head:* Robert A. Blecker, Chair, 202-885-3767, Fax: 202-885-3790, E-mail: blecker@american.edu. *Application contact:* Kathleen Clowery, Director of Graduate Admissions, 202-885 Ext. 3621, Fax: 202-885-1505, E-mail: clowery@american.edu.

The American University in Cairo, Graduate Studies and Research, School of Business, Economics and Communication, Department of Economics, Cairo, Egypt. Offers MA. Part-time programs available. *Degree requirements:* For master's, thesis or alternative. *Entrance requirements:* For master's, GMAT. Additional exam requirements/recommendations for international students: Required—English entrance exam. Electronic applications accepted. *Faculty research:* Macro-economic policies, agricultural growth and rural credit markets, alleviation of poverty in Egypt.

American University of Beirut, Graduate Programs, Faculty of Arts and Sciences, Beirut, Lebanon. Offers anthropology (MA); Arabic language and literature (MA); archaeology (MA); biology (MS); chemistry (MS); computer science (MS); economics (MA); education (MA); English language (MA); English literature (MA); environmental policy planning (MSES); financial economics (MAFE); geology (MS); history (MA); mathematics (MA, MS); Middle Eastern studies (MA); philosophy (MA); physics (MS); political studies (MA); psychology (MA); public administration (MA); sociology (MA); statistics (MA, MS). Part-time programs available. *Degree requirements:* For master's, one foreign language, comprehensive exam, thesis (for some programs). *Entrance requirements:* For master's, GRE, letter of recommendation. Additional exam requirements/recommendations for international students: Required—TOEFL (minimum score 600 paper-based; 250 computer-based; 100 iBT), IELTS (minimum score 7.5). *Faculty research:* String theory and supergravity; computer graphics; algebra and number theory; popular Arabic literature; marine and freshwater biology; integrating science, math and technology.

Andrews University, School of Graduate Studies, School of Business, Department of Accounting, Economics and Finance, Berrien Springs, MI 49104. Offers MBA, MSA. In 2008, 2 master's awarded. *Entrance requirements:* For master's, GMAT. Additional exam requirements/recommendations for international students: Required—TOEFL (minimum score 550 paper-based). Application fee: $40. *Expenses:* Tuition: Full-time $18,360; part-time $765 per credit hour. Required fees: $476; $765 per credit hour. $238 per semester. Tuition and fees vary according to degree level. *Unit head:* Dr. Leonard K. Gashugi, Chair, 769-471-3429, E-mail: gashugi@andrews.edu. *Application contact:* Carolyn Hurst, Supervisor of Graduate Admission, 800-253-2874, Fax: 269-471-6321, E-mail: graduate@andrews.edu.

Arizona State University, Graduate College, W.P. Carey School of Business, Department of Economics, Tempe, AZ 85287. Offers MS, PhD, JD/MS, MBA/MS. *Degree requirements:* For master's, thesis or alternative; for doctorate, thesis/dissertation. *Entrance requirements:* For master's and doctorate, GRE.

Assumption College, Graduate School, Department of Business Studies, Worcester, MA 01609-1296. Offers accounting (MBA); business administration (CAGS); finance/economics (MBA); general business (MBA); human resources (MBA); international business (MBA); management (MBA); marketing (MBA); nonprofit leadership (MBA). Part-time and evening/weekend programs available. *Faculty:* 6 full-time (1 woman), 14 part-time/adjunct (2 women). *Students:* 14 full-time (6 women), 144 part-time (74 women); includes 14 minority (7 African Americans, 4 Asian Americans or Pacific Islanders, 3 Hispanic Americans), 3 international. Average age 27. 85 applicants, 98% accepted. In 2008, 41 master's awarded. *Entrance requirements:* For master's and CAGS, 3 letters of recommendation, resumé, essay. Additional exam requirements/recommendations for international students: Required—TOEFL (minimum score 540 paper-based; 200 computer-based; 76 iBT), IELTS (minimum score 6). *Application deadline:* For fall admission, 6/1 priority date for domestic students, 5/1 priority date for international students; for spring admission, 11/1 priority date for domestic students, 9/1 priority date for international students. Applications are processed on a rolling basis. Application fee: $30. Electronic applications accepted. *Expenses:* Tuition: Part-time $468 per credit hour. Required fees: $20 per semester. One-time fee: $100. *Financial support:* In 2008–09, 47 students received support. Application deadline: 6/1; *Faculty research:* Workplace diversity, dynamics of team interaction, utilization of leased employees. *Unit head:* Dr. Jeffrey G. Hunter, Director, 508-767-7246, Fax: 508-767-7252, E-mail: jhunter@assumption.edu. *Application contact:* Adrian O. Dumas, Director of Graduate Enrollment Management and Services, 508-767-7365, Fax: 508-767-7030, E-mail: adumas@assumption.edu.

Auburn University, Graduate School, College of Business, Department of Economics, Auburn University, AL 36849. Offers MS. Part-time programs available. *Faculty:* 13 full-time (1 woman), 1 part-time/adjunct (0 women). *Students:* 13 full-time (3 women), 4 part-time (0 women), 1 international. Average age 26. 36 applicants, 67% accepted, 9 enrolled. In 2008, 6 master's awarded. *Degree requirements:* For master's, thesis. *Entrance requirements:* For master's, GMAT, GRE General Test. Additional exam requirements/recommendations for international students: Required—TOEFL. *Application deadline:* For fall admission, 7/7 for domestic students; for spring admission, 11/24 for domestic students. Applications are processed on a rolling basis. Application fee: $25 ($50 for international students). Electronic applications accepted. *Expenses:* Tuition, area resident: Full-time $5880; part-time $243 per credit hour. Tuition, state resident: full-time $5880; part-time $243 per credit hour. Tuition, nonresident: full-time $17,640; part-time $729 per credit hour. International tuition: $17,846 full-time. Required fees: $620. Tuition and fees vary according to program and reciprocity agreements. *Financial support:* Teaching assistantships, career-related internships or fieldwork and Federal Work-Study available. Support available to part-time students. Financial award application deadline: 3/15. *Unit head:* Dr. Steven B. Caudill, Interim Chair. *Application contact:* Dr. George Flowers, Dean of the Graduate School, 334-844-2125.

Baylor University, Graduate School, Hankamer School of Business, Department of Economics, Waco, TX 76798. Offers economics (MS Eco); international economics (MA, MS). *Students:* 15 full-time (9 women), 8 international. In 2008, 9 master's awarded. *Entrance requirements:* For master's, GMAT or GRE General Test. *Application deadline:* For fall admission, 8/1 for domestic students; for spring admission, 12/1 for domestic students. Applications are processed on a rolling basis. Application fee: $25. *Financial support:* Research assistantships, Federal Work-Study and institutionally sponsored loans available. Financial award application deadline: 4/1. *Faculty research:* Econometrics, international economics, private enterprise, comparative economic systems. *Unit head:* Dr. Steve Green, Chair, 254-710-4543, Fax: 254-710-3265, E-mail: steve_green@baylor.edu. *Application contact:* Susan Armstrong, Administrative Assistant, 254-710-6177, Fax: 254-710-1066, E-mail: susan_armstrong@baylor.edu.

Bernard M. Baruch College of the City University of New York, Zicklin School of Business, Department of Economics and Finance, Program in Economics, New York, NY 10010-5585. Offers MBA. Part-time and evening/weekend programs available. *Entrance requirements:* For master's, GMAT, 2 letters of recommendation, resumé, 2 years of work experience. Additional exam requirements/recommendations for international students: Required—TOEFL (minimum score 590 paper-based; 243 computer-based), TWE (minimum score 5).

Boston College, Graduate School of Arts and Sciences, Department of Economics, Chestnut Hill, MA 02467-3800. Offers PhD. *Degree requirements:* For doctorate, comprehensive exam, thesis/dissertation. *Entrance requirements:* For doctorate, GRE General Test, GRE Subject Test. Additional exam requirements/recommendations for international students: Required—TOEFL (minimum score 590 paper-based; 250 computer-based; 91 iBT). Electronic applications accepted. *Expenses:* Tuition: Part-time $1148 per credit. Required fees: $60. *Faculty research:* Econometrics, international economics, public sector economics, monetary economics, urban economics.

Boston University, Graduate School of Arts and Sciences, Department of Economics, Boston, MA 02215. Offers economic policy (MAEP); economics (MA, PhD); political economy (MAPE); MBA/MA. Terminal master's awarded for partial completion of doctoral program. *Degree requirements:* For master's, one foreign language, comprehensive exam; for doctorate, one foreign language, comprehensive exam, thesis/dissertation, qualifying exam. *Entrance requirements:* For master's and doctorate, GRE General Test, 3 letters of recommendation. Additional exam requirements/recommendations for international students: Required—TOEFL (minimum score 550 paper-based; 213 computer-based).

Boston University, Metropolitan College (Continuing Education), Department of Administrative Sciences, Boston, MA 02215. Offers banking and financial management (MSM); business continuity in emergency management (MSM); economics development and tourism management (MSAS); electronic commerce, systems, and technology (MSAS); financial economics (MSAS); human resource management (MSM); innovation and technology (MSAS); insurance management (MSM); international market management (MSM); multinational commerce (MSAS);

Economics

Boston University (continued)

project management (MSM). *Accreditation:* AACSB. Part-time and evening/weekend programs available. Postbaccalaureate distance learning degree programs offered (no on-campus study). *Degree requirements:* For master's, thesis optional. *Entrance requirements:* For master's, 1 year of work experience, minimum GPA of 3.0. Additional exam requirements/recommendations for international students: Required—TOEFL (minimum score 560 paper-based; 220 computer-based; 84 iBT). Electronic applications accepted. *Faculty research:* International business, innovative process.

Bowling Green State University, Graduate College, College of Business Administration, Department of Economics, Bowling Green, OH 43403. Offers MA. Part-time programs available. *Degree requirements:* For master's, thesis or alternative. *Entrance requirements:* For master's, GRE General Test. Additional exam requirements/recommendations for international students: Required—TOEFL. Electronic applications accepted. *Faculty research:* Labor economics, monetary economics, economic education, mathematical economics.

Brandeis University, International Business School, Waltham, MA 02454-9110. Offers finance (MSF); international business (MBAi); international economics and finance (MA, PhD); international finance/international economics (MBAi). Part-time and evening/weekend programs available. Terminal master's awarded for partial completion of doctoral program. *Degree requirements:* For master's, one foreign language, semester abroad; for doctorate, thesis/dissertation. *Entrance requirements:* For master's, GMAT or GRE General Test (MA), GMAT (MBAi and MSF); for doctorate, GRE General Test. Additional exam requirements/recommendations for international students: Required—TOEFL (minimum score 600 paper-based; 250 computer-based), IELTS (minimum score 7). Electronic applications accepted. *Faculty research:* International finance and business, trade policy, macroeconomics, Asian economic issues, developmental economics.

Brock University, Faculty of Graduate Studies, Faculty of Social Sciences, Program in Business Economics, St. Catharines, ON L2S 3A1, Canada. Offers MBE. *Degree requirements:* For master's, thesis or alternative. *Entrance requirements:* For master's, honours degree. Additional exam requirements/recommendations for international students: Required—TOEFL (minimum score 550 paper-based; 213 computer-based; 80 iBT), IELTS (minimum score 6.5), TWE (minimum score 4). Electronic applications accepted. *Faculty research:* Microeconomic theory, macroeconomics, econometrics, applied econometrics, economic development.

Brooklyn College of the City University of New York, Division of Graduate Studies, Department of Economics, Brooklyn, NY 11210-2889. Offers accounting (MS); economics (MA). Part-time and evening/weekend programs available. *Students:* 17 full-time (10 women), 122 part-time (65 women); includes 53 minority (40 African Americans, 10 Asian Americans or Pacific Islanders, 3 Hispanic Americans), 41 international. Average age 33. 135 applicants, 56% accepted, 53 enrolled. In 2008, 32 master's awarded. *Degree requirements:* For master's, comprehensive exam, thesis or alternative. *Entrance requirements:* For master's, GMAT (for MS), 2 letters of recommendation. Additional exam requirements/recommendations for international students: Required—TOEFL (minimum score 550 paper-based; 213 computer-based; 79 iBT). *Application deadline:* For fall admission, 3/1 priority date for domestic students, 2/1 priority date for international students; for spring admission, 3/1 priority date for domestic students, 2/1 priority date for international students. Applications are processed on a rolling basis. Application fee: $125. Electronic applications accepted. *Expenses:* Tuition, state resident: full-time $7360; part-time $310 per credit hour. Tuition, nonresident: full-time $13,800; part-time $575 per credit hour. *Financial support:* Career-related internships or fieldwork, Federal Work-Study, institutionally sponsored loans, and scholarships/grants available. Support available to part-time students. Financial award application deadline: 5/1; financial award applicants required to submit FAFSA. *Faculty research:* Econometrics, environmental economics, microeconomics, macroeconomics, taxation. *Unit head:* Dr. Robert Bell, Chairperson, 718-951-5317, E-mail: rbell brooklyn.cuny.edu. *Application contact:* Hernan Sierra, Graduate Admissions Coordinator, 718-951-4536, Fax: 718-951-4506, E-mail: grads@brooklyn.cuny.edu.

Brown University, Graduate School, Department of Economics, Providence, RI 02912. Offers PhD. Terminal master's awarded for partial completion of doctoral program. *Degree requirements:* For doctorate, thesis/dissertation. *Entrance requirements:* For doctorate, GRE General Test.

Buffalo State College, State University of New York, Graduate Studies and Research, Faculty of Natural and Social Sciences, Department of Economics and Finance, Buffalo, NY 14222-1095. Offers applied economics (MA). *Degree requirements:* For master's, project. *Entrance requirements:* Additional exam requirements/recommendations for international students: Required—TOEFL (minimum score 550 paper-based; 213 computer-based).

California Institute of Technology, Division of the Humanities and Social Sciences, Social Science Program, Pasadena, CA 91125-0001. Offers economics (PhD); political science (PhD); social science (MS). Terminal master's awarded for partial completion of doctoral program. *Degree requirements:* For doctorate, thesis/dissertation. *Entrance requirements:* For doctorate, GRE General Test. Electronic applications accepted. *Faculty research:* Individual and group decision making, design of political and economic institutions, experimental social science, public policy, quantitative history.

California State Polytechnic University, Pomona, Academic Affairs, College of Letters, Arts, and Social Sciences, Program in Economics, Pomona, CA 91768-2557. Offers MS. Part-time programs available. *Students:* 16 full-time (8 women), 42 part-time (15 women); includes 28 minority (1 African American, 15 Asian Americans or Pacific Islanders, 12 Hispanic Americans), 18 international. Average age 29. 44 applicants, 66% accepted, 14 enrolled. In 2008, 9 master's awarded. *Degree requirements:* For master's, thesis or alternative. *Entrance requirements:* For master's, GRE General Test. *Application deadline:* For fall admission, 5/1 priority date for domestic students; for winter admission, 10/15 priority date for domestic students; for spring admission, 1/20 priority date for domestic students. Applications are processed on a rolling basis. Application fee: $55. Electronic applications accepted. *Expenses:* Tuition, nonresident: full-time $7232; part-time $226 per credit. Required fees: $4272. One-time fee: $2694 part-time. Tuition and fees vary according to course load. *Financial support:* In 2008–09, 9 students received support. Federal Work-Study and institutionally sponsored loans available. Support available to part-time students. Financial award application deadline: 3/2; financial award applicants required to submit FAFSA. *Unit head:* Dr. Carsten Lange, Graduate Coordinator, 909-869-3843, E-mail: clange@csupomona.edu. *Application contact:* Scott J. Duncan, Director, Admissions, 909-869-3258, Fax: 909-869-4529, E-mail: sjduncan@csupomona.edu.

California State University, East Bay, Academic Programs and Graduate Studies, College of Business and Economics, Department of Economics, Hayward, CA 94542-3000. Offers business economics (MBA); economics (MA, MBA); economics for teachers (MBA). Part-time and evening/weekend programs available. *Degree requirements:* For master's, comprehensive exam, thesis optional, project or thesis. *Entrance requirements:* For master's, GMAT, minimum GPA of 2.75 during previous 2 years of course work. Additional exam requirements/recommendations for international students: Required—TOEFL (minimum score 550 paper-based; 213 computer-based). Electronic applications accepted.

California State University, Fullerton, Graduate Studies, Mihaylo College of Business and Economics, Department of Economics, Fullerton, CA 92834-9480. Offers business economics (MBA); economics (MA). Part-time and evening/weekend programs available. *Students:* 18 full-time (5 women), 17 part-time (5 women); includes 12 minority (4 African Americans, 6 Asian Americans or Pacific Islanders, 2 Hispanic Americans), 9 international. Average age 28. 42 applicants, 45% accepted, 9 enrolled. In 2008, 16 master's awarded. *Degree requirements:* For master's, thesis. *Entrance requirements:* For master's, GMAT, GRE General Test. Application fee: $55. Tuition and fees vary according to degree level. *Financial support:* Teaching assistantships, Federal Work-Study, institutionally sponsored loans, and scholarships/grants available. Support available to part-time students. Financial award application deadline: 3/1. *Faculty research:* Environmental and natural resource issues. *Unit head:* Dr. Morteza Rahmatian, Chair, 657-278-2228. *Application contact:* Dr. Jane Hall, Adviser, 657-278-2236.

California State University, Long Beach, Graduate Studies, College of Liberal Arts, Department of Economics, Long Beach, CA 90840. Offers economics (MA). Part-time programs available. *Faculty:* 8 full-time (3 women). *Students:* 13 full-time (6 women), 36 part-time (21 women); includes 18 minority (4 African Americans, 10 Asian Americans or Pacific Islanders, 4 Hispanic Americans), 20 international. Average age 31. 78 applicants, 71% accepted, 17 enrolled. *Degree requirements:* For master's, comprehensive exam or thesis. *Entrance requirements:* For master's, GRE General Test, GRE Subject Test, minimum GPA of 3.0. *Application deadline:* For fall admission, 4/1 for domestic students. Applications are processed on a rolling basis. Application fee: $55. Electronic applications accepted. *Expenses:* Tuition, nonresident: full-time $11,160; part-time $372 per unit. Required fees: $4100; $1261 per semester. *Financial support:* Federal Work-Study, institutionally sponsored loans, and scholarships/grants available. Financial award application deadline: 3/2. *Faculty research:* Trade and development, economic forecasting, resource economics. *Unit head:* Dr. Joseph P. Magaddino, Chair, 562-985-5061, Fax: 562-985-5804, E-mail: magaddin@csulb.edu. *Application contact:* Dr. Alejandra C Edwards, Graduate Advisor, 562-985-5969, Fax: 562-985-5804, E-mail: acoxedwa@csulb.edu.

California State University, Los Angeles, Graduate Studies, College of Business and Economics, Department of Economics and Statistics, Los Angeles, CA 90032-8530. Offers analytical quantitative economics (MA); business economics (MA, MBA, MS); economics (MA). Part-time and evening/weekend programs available. *Faculty:* 3 full-time (0 women), 2 part-time/adjunct (0 women). *Students:* 11 full-time (3 women), 15 part-time (5 women); includes 7 minority (1 African American, 1 Asian American or Pacific Islander, 5 Hispanic Americans), 8 international. Average age 28. 16 applicants, 94% accepted, 9 enrolled. In 2008, 2 master's awarded. *Degree requirements:* For master's, comprehensive exam or thesis. *Entrance requirements:* For master's, GMAT, minimum GPA of 2.5 during previous 2 years of course work. Additional exam requirements/recommendations for international students: Required—TOEFL (minimum score 550 paper-based; 213 computer-based). *Application deadline:* For fall admission, 6/15 for domestic students, 5/1 for international students; for winter admission, 11/1 for domestic students, 9/1 for international students; for spring admission, 2/1 for domestic students, 10/1 for international students. Applications are processed on a rolling basis. Application fee: $55. Electronic applications accepted. *Expenses:* Tuition, nonresident: part-time $226 per credit. Required fees: $4019. *Financial support:* Career-related internships or fieldwork and Federal Work-Study available. Support available to part-time students. Financial award application deadline: 3/1. *Unit head:* Dr. Dang Tran, Chair, 323-343-2930, Fax: 323-343-5462, E-mail: dtran@calstatela.edu. *Application contact:* Dr. Jose L. Galvan, Dean of Graduate Studies, 323-343-3820, Fax: 323-343-5653, E-mail: jgalvan@cslanet.calstatela.edu.

Carleton University, Faculty of Graduate Studies, Faculty of Public Affairs and Management, Department of Economics, Ottawa, ON K1S 5B6, Canada. Offers MA, PhD. *Degree requirements:* For master's, thesis optional; for doctorate, comprehensive exam, thesis/dissertation. *Entrance requirements:* For master's, honors degree; for doctorate, master's degree. Additional exam requirements/recommendations for international students: Required—TOEFL. *Faculty research:* Monetary economics, economic development, public economics, industrial organization, international trade.

Carleton University, Faculty of Graduate Studies, Faculty of Public Affairs and Management, Institute of Political Economy, Ottawa, ON K1S 5B6, Canada. Offers MA, PhD. *Degree requirements:* For master's, thesis optional. *Entrance requirements:* For master's, honors degree. Additional exam requirements/recommendations for international students: Required—TOEFL. *Faculty research:* Relationships between economy and politics as they affect the political, social and cultural life of societies; historical processes whereby social change is located in the interaction of the economic, political and cultural, and ideological moments of social life.

Carnegie Mellon University, Tepper School of Business, Program in Economics, Pittsburgh, PA 15213-3891. Offers PhD. *Degree requirements:* For doctorate, thesis/dissertation. *Entrance requirements:* For doctorate, GMAT, GRE General Test. *Faculty research:* Research allocation under asymmetric information, monetary theory, estimation of rational expectations models.

Case Western Reserve University, Weatherhead School of Management, Department of Economics, Cleveland, OH 44106. Offers MBA. Part-time and evening/weekend programs available. *Entrance requirements:* For master's, GMAT. *Faculty research:* Public finance and public choice, direct foreign investment, employment relationships, technical and institutional change, regional economics.

The Catholic University of America, School of Arts and Sciences, Department of Business and Economics, Washington, DC 20064. Offers international political economics (MA). Part-time and evening/weekend programs available. *Degree requirements:* For master's, comprehensive exam. *Entrance requirements:* For master's, GRE General Test, 3 letters of recommendation. Additional exam requirements/recommendations for international students: Required—TOEFL (minimum score 580 paper-based; 237 computer-based). Electronic applications accepted.

Central European University, Graduate Studies, Department of Legal Studies, Budapest, Hungary. Offers comparative constitutional law (LL M); economic and legal studies (LL M, MA); human rights (LL M, MA); international business law (LL M); legal studies (SJD). Terminal master's awarded for partial completion of doctoral program. *Degree requirements:* For master's, one foreign language, thesis; for doctorate, one foreign language, comprehensive exam, thesis/dissertation. *Entrance requirements:* For master's and doctorate, LSAT, CEU admissions exams. Additional exam requirements/recommendations for international students: Required—TOEFL (minimum score 570 paper-based; 230 computer-based). Electronic applications accepted. *Expenses:* Contact institution. *Faculty research:* Institutional, constitutional and human rights in European Union law, biomedical law and reproductive rights, data protection law, Islamic banking and finance.

Central European University, Graduate Studies, School of Social Sciences and Humanities, Budapest, Hungary. Offers economics (MA, PhD); gender studies (MA, PhD); international relations and European studies (MA, PhD); mathematics and its applications (MS, PhD); medieval studies (MA, PhD); nationalism studies (MA, PhD); philosophy (MA, PhD); political science (MA, PhD); public policy (MA, PhD); sociology and social anthropology (MA, PhD). Terminal master's awarded for partial completion of doctoral program. *Degree requirements:* For master's, one foreign language, thesis; for doctorate, one foreign language, comprehensive exam, thesis/dissertation. *Entrance requirements:* For master's, CEU subject tests, interview; for doctorate, GRE, CEU subject test, interview. Additional exam requirements/recommendations for international students: Required—TOEFL (minimum score 570 paper-based; 230 computer-based). Electronic applications accepted. *Faculty research:* Civil society, fiscal decentralization, party politics, political philosophy (especially Liberalism, theory of Democracy).

See Close-Up on page 349.

Central Michigan University, College of Graduate Studies, College of Business Administration, Department of Economics, Mount Pleasant, MI 48859. Offers MA. Part-time programs available. *Faculty:* 7 full-time (1 woman). *Students:* 20 full-time (4 women), 4 part-time (2 women); includes 1 Asian American or Pacific Islander, 11 international. Average age 26. *Degree requirements:* For master's, thesis or alternative. *Application deadline:* Applications are processed on a rolling basis. Application fee: $35 ($45 for international students). Electronic applications accepted. *Expenses:* Tuition, state resident: full-time $3717; part-time $413 per credit. Tuition, nonresident: full-time $6894; part-time $766 per credit. *Financial support:* Fellowships with tuition reimbursements, research assistantships with tuition reimbursements, teaching assistantships with tuition reimbursements, Federal Work-Study, unspecified assistantships, and out-of-state merit awards available. *Faculty research:* Economic development, industrial organization, international trade, monetary theory, public choice/labor. *Unit head:* Dr. Paul Natke, Chairperson,

989-774-3870, Fax: 989-774-2040, E-mail: natke1pa@cmich.edu. *Application contact:* Dr. Jason Taylor, Graduate Student Coordinator, 989-774-2578, Fax: 989-774-2040, E-mail: taylo2je@cmich.edu.

Chapman University, Graduate Studies, School of Law, Orange, CA 92866. Offers advocacy and dispute resolution (JD); entertainment law (JD); environmental, land use, and real estate (JD); international law (JD); law (LL M), including business law and economics, entertainment and media law, international and comparative law; prosecutorial science (LL M); tax law (JD); taxation (LL M); JD/MBA; JD/MFA. *Accreditation:* ABA. Part-time and evening/weekend programs available. *Faculty:* 50 full-time (20 women), 32 part-time/adjunct (4 women). *Students:* 514 full-time (238 women), 97 part-time (51 women); includes 123 minority (6 African Americans, 1 American Indian/Alaska Native, 82 Asian Americans or Pacific Islanders, 34 Hispanic Americans), 8 international. Average age 27. 2,521 applicants, 27% accepted, 225 enrolled. In 2008, 182 JDs, 13 master's awarded. *Entrance requirements:* LSAT, minimum undergraduate GPA of 2.75. Additional exam requirements/recommendations for international students: Required—TOEFL (minimum score 600 paper-based; 213 computer-based; 80 iBT). *Application deadline:* For fall admission, 4/1 priority date for domestic students. Applications are processed on a rolling basis. Application fee: $65. Electronic applications accepted. *Expenses:* Contact institution. *Financial support:* Fellowships, Federal Work-Study and scholarships/grants available. Financial award application deadline: 6/30; financial award applicants required to submit FAFSA. *Unit head:* Dr. John Eastman, Dean, 714-628-2500. *Application contact:* Marissa Vargas, Admissions Recruiter/Financial Aid Counselor, 877-CHAPLAW, E-mail: mvargas@chapman.edu.

City College of the City University of New York, Graduate School, College of Liberal Arts and Science, Division of Social Science, Department of Economics, New York, NY 10031-9198. Offers MA. Part-time programs available. *Degree requirements:* For master's, comprehensive exam, proficiency in a foreign language or advanced statistics. *Entrance requirements:* For master's, GRE. Additional exam requirements/recommendations for international students: Required—TOEFL (minimum score 550 paper-based; 213 computer-based). *Faculty research:* International economics, health, banking.

Claremont Graduate University, Graduate Programs, School of Politics and Economics, Department of Economics, Claremont, CA 91711-6160. Offers business and financial economics (MA, PhD); economic development (Certificate); economics (PhD); industrial organization (PhD); international and development economics (PhD); international economics policy and development (MA); international money and finance (PhD); neuroeconomics (PhD); political economy and public policy (MA); public choice and public economics (PhD); MBA/PhD. Part-time programs available. *Faculty:* 7 full-time (1 woman). *Students:* 100 full-time (24 women), 6 part-time (1 woman); includes 12 minority (3 African Americans, 7 Asian Americans or Pacific Islanders, 2 Hispanic Americans), 56 international. Average age 32. In 2008, 15 master's, 15 doctorates awarded. *Entrance requirements:* For master's and doctorate, GRE General Test or GMAT. Additional exam requirements/recommendations for international students: Required—TOEFL (minimum score 550 paper-based; 213 computer-based; 80 iBT). *Application deadline:* For fall admission, 2/1 priority date for domestic students. Applications are processed on a rolling basis. Application fee: $60. Electronic applications accepted. *Expenses:* Tuition: Full-time $33,698; part-time $1465 per unit. Required fees: $310; $155 per semester. Tuition and fees vary according to program. *Financial support:* Fellowships, research assistantships, teaching assistantships, Federal Work-Study, institutionally sponsored loans, and scholarships/grants available. Support available to part-time students. Financial award application deadline: 2/15; financial award applicants required to submit FAFSA. *Faculty research:* International and financial economics, law and economics, regulation, public choice economics. *Unit head:* Arthur Denzau, Chair, 909-621-8782, Fax: 909-621-8545, E-mail: arthur.denzau@cgu.edu. *Application contact:* Laura Carillo, Recruiter and Admissions Coordinator, 909-621-8699, Fax: 909-621-7545, E-mail: laura.carillo@cga.edu.

Claremont Graduate University, Graduate Programs, School of Politics and Economics, Department of Politics and Policy, Claremont, CA 91711-6160. Offers American politics (MA, PhD); comparative politics (PhD); international political economy (MA); international studies (MA); political philosophy (PhD); political science (PhD); politics, economics and business (MA); public policy (MA, PhD); world politics (PhD); MBA/PhD. Part-time programs available. *Faculty:* 10 full-time (4 women), 4 part-time/adjunct (0 women). *Students:* 166 full-time (60 women), 19 part-time (6 women); includes 28 minority (4 African Americans, 9 Asian Americans or Pacific Islanders, 15 Hispanic Americans), 40 international. Average age 32. In 2008, 24 master's, 17 doctorates awarded. Terminal master's awarded for partial completion of doctoral program. *Entrance requirements:* For master's and doctorate, GRE General Test. Additional exam requirements/recommendations for international students: Required—TOEFL (minimum score 550 paper-based; 213 computer-based; 80 iBT). *Application deadline:* For fall admission, 2/1 priority date for domestic students. Applications are processed on a rolling basis. Application fee: $60. Electronic applications accepted. *Expenses:* Tuition: Full-time $33,698; part-time $1465 per unit. Required fees: $310; $155 per semester. Tuition and fees vary according to program. *Financial support:* Fellowships, research assistantships, teaching assistantships, Federal Work-Study, institutionally sponsored loans, and scholarships/grants available. Support available to part-time students. Financial award application deadline: 2/15; financial award applicants required to submit FAFSA. *Faculty research:* Environmental policy, international debt, global democratization, Third World development, public sector discrimination. *Unit head:* Jean Schroedel, Chair, 909-621-8696, Fax: 909-621-8545, E-mail: jean.schroedel@cgu.edu. *Application contact:* Laura Carillo, Recruiter and Admissions Coordinator, 909-621-8699, Fax: 909-621-7545, E-mail: laura.carillo@cga.edu.

Clark Atlanta University, School of Business Administration, Department of Economics, Atlanta, GA 30314. Offers MA. Part-time programs available. *Faculty:* 1 full-time (0 women). *Students:* 1 part-time (0 women); includes African American. Average age 26. 2 applicants, 50% accepted, 0 enrolled. *Degree requirements:* For master's, one foreign language, thesis. *Entrance requirements:* For master's, GRE General Test, minimum GPA of 2.5. Additional exam requirements/recommendations for international students: Required—TOEFL (minimum score 500 paper-based; 173 computer-based). *Application deadline:* For fall admission, 4/1 for domestic and international students; for spring admission, 11/1 for domestic and international students. Applications are processed on a rolling basis. Application fee: $40 ($55 for international students). Electronic applications accepted. *Expenses:* Tuition: Full-time $12,240; part-time $680 per credit hour. Required fees: $710; $355 per semester. *Financial support:* Career-related internships or fieldwork, Federal Work-Study, scholarships/grants, and unspecified assistantships available. Support available to part-time students. Financial award application deadline: 4/30; financial award applicants required to submit FAFSA. *Faculty research:* Minority energy demand. *Unit head:* Dr. Ajamu Nyomba, Chairperson, 404-880-6286, E-mail: anyomba@cau.edu. *Application contact:* Michelle Clark-Davis, Graduate Program Admissions, 404-880-6605, E-mail: cauadmissions@cau.edu.

Clark University, Graduate School, Department of Economics, Worcester, MA 01610-1477. Offers PhD. *Faculty:* 10 full-time (4 women), 2 part-time/adjunct (0 women). *Students:* 40 full-time (16 women), 31 international. Average age 27. 30 applicants, 73% accepted, 10 enrolled. In 2008, 2 doctorates awarded. *Degree requirements:* For doctorate, thesis/dissertation. *Entrance requirements:* For doctorate, GRE General Test. Additional exam requirements/recommendations for international students: Required—TOEFL. *Application deadline:* For fall admission, 2/1 priority date for domestic students. Applications are processed on a rolling basis. Application fee: $50. *Expenses:* Tuition: Full-time $34,900; part-time $1091 per credit hour. Required fees: $30. *Financial support:* In 2008–09, fellowships with full and partial tuition reimbursements (averaging $12,000 per year), 2 research assistantships with full and partial tuition reimbursements (averaging $12,000 per year), 9 teaching assistantships with full and partial tuition reimbursements (averaging $12,000 per year) were awarded; career-related internships or fieldwork, institutionally sponsored loans, and tuition waivers (full and partial) also available. *Faculty research:* Public finance, economic development, industrial organization, international finance and trade, environmental regulation. Total annual research

expenditures: $160,000. *Unit head:* Dr. Wayne Gray, Chair, 508-793-7226. *Application contact:* Cindy Rice, Department Secretary, 508-793-7226, Fax: 508-793-8849, E-mail: economics@clarku.edu.

Clemson University, Graduate School, College of Business and Behavioral Science, Department of Economics, Clemson, SC 29634. Offers applied economics (PhD); economics (MA). *Faculty:* 19 full-time (1 woman), 4 part-time/adjunct (0 women). *Students:* 78 full-time (33 women), 13 part-time (5 women); includes 7 minority (3 African Americans, 1 Asian American or Pacific Islander, 3 Hispanic Americans), 40 international. Average age 29. 119 applicants, 54% accepted, 32 enrolled. In 2008, 7 master's, 10 doctorates awarded. *Degree requirements:* For doctorate, thesis/dissertation. *Entrance requirements:* For master's and doctorate, GRE General Test. Additional exam requirements/recommendations for international students: Required—TOEFL. *Application deadline:* For fall admission, 6/1 for domestic students, 4/15 for international students; for spring admission, 9/15 for international students. Application fee: $55. Full-time tuition and fees vary according to program. *Financial support:* In 2008–09, 5 fellowships (averaging $6,200 per year), 7 research assistantships (averaging $13,854 per year), 57 teaching assistantships (averaging $14,429 per year) were awarded. Financial award applicants required to submit FAFSA. *Faculty research:* Applied price theory, financial economics, industrial economics, labor economics, monetary economics. Total annual research expenditures: $485,950. *Unit head:* Dr. Raymond Sauer, Interim Chair, 864-656-3969, Fax: 864-656-4192, E-mail: sauerr@clemson.edu. *Application contact:* Dr. Michael T Maloney, Director of Graduate Programs, 864-656-3430, Fax: 864-656-4192, E-mail: maloney@clemson.edu.

Cleveland State University, College of Graduate Studies, College of Liberal Arts and Social Sciences, Department of Economics, Cleveland, OH 44115. Offers MA. Part-time and evening/weekend programs available. *Faculty:* 7 full-time (1 woman), 9 part-time/adjunct (1 woman). *Students:* 9 full-time (5 women), 8 part-time (0 women); includes 4 minority (2 African Americans, 2 Asian Americans or Pacific Islanders), 1 international. Average age 29. 37 applicants, 54% accepted, 7 enrolled. In 2008, 10 master's awarded. *Entrance requirements:* For master's, minimum GPA of 2.75; coursework in micro theory, macro theory, statistics, and calculus. Additional exam requirements/recommendations for international students: Required—TOEFL (minimum score 515 paper-based; 197 computer-based). *Application deadline:* For fall admission, 8/20 priority date for domestic students, 5/20 priority date for international students. Applications are processed on a rolling basis. Application fee: $30. Electronic applications accepted. *Financial support:* In 2008–09, 4 research assistantships with full tuition reimbursements (averaging $3,780 per year) were awarded; teaching assistantships with full tuition reimbursements, scholarships/grants and unspecified assistantships also available. *Faculty research:* Labor economics, health economics, energy, environment, economics of law, organization theory, industrial organization. *Unit head:* Dr. Myong-Hun Chang, Chairperson, 216-687-4523, Fax: 216-687-9206, E-mail: m.chang@csuohio.edu. *Application contact:* Glenda Carbaugh, Administrative Secretary, 216-687-4520, Fax: 216-687-9206, E-mail: g.carbaugh@csuohio.edu.

Cleveland State University, College of Graduate Studies, Maxine Goodman Levin College of Urban Affairs, Program in Nonprofit Administration and Leadership, Cleveland, OH 44115. Offers geographic information systems (Certificate); local and urban management (Certificate); nonprofit administration and leadership (MNAL); nonprofit management (Certificate); urban economic development (Certificate). Part-time and evening/weekend programs available. *Faculty:* 26 full-time (10 women), 6 part-time/adjunct (4 women). *Students:* 5 full-time (4 women), 21 part-time (17 women); includes 4 minority (all African Americans), 1 international. Average age 35. 29 applicants, 45% accepted, 9 enrolled. *Degree requirements:* For master's, thesis or alternative, capstone course. *Entrance requirements:* For master's, GRE (minimum score: 40th percentile quantitative/verbal, 4.0 analytical writing), minimum GPA of 3.0. Additional exam requirements/recommendations for international students: Required—TOEFL (minimum score 525 paper-based; 197 computer-based; 65 iBT). *Application deadline:* For fall admission, 7/15 priority date for domestic students, 5/15 for international students; for spring admission, 11/1 for international students. Applications are processed on a rolling basis. Application fee: $30. Electronic applications accepted. *Financial support:* In 2008–09, 5 students received support, including research assistantships with full and partial tuition reimbursements available (averaging $6,960 per year); career-related internships or fieldwork, Federal Work-Study, scholarships/grants, tuition waivers (full and partial), and unspecified assistantships also available. Support available to part-time students. Financial award application deadline: 3/1; financial award applicants required to submit FAFSA. *Faculty research:* Human resource management, volunteerism, performance measurement in nonprofits, government-nonprofit partnerships. *Unit head:* Dr. Jennifer Alexander, Director, 216-687-5011, Fax: 216-687-2013, E-mail: j.k.alexander@csuohio.edu. *Application contact:* Graduate Program Coordinator, 216-523-7522, Fax: 216-687-5398, E-mail: urbanprograms@csuohio.edu.

Cleveland State University, College of Graduate Studies, Maxine Goodman Levin College of Urban Affairs, Program in Urban Planning, Design, and Development, Cleveland, OH 44115. Offers geographic information systems (Certificate); local and urban management (Certificate); urban economic development (Certificate); urban planning, design, and development (MUPDD); urban real estate development and finance (Certificate); JD/MUPDD. *Accreditation:* ACSP. Part-time and evening/weekend programs available. *Faculty:* 26 full-time (10 women), 12 part-time/adjunct (5 women). *Students:* 37 full-time (17 women), 41 part-time (21 women); includes 13 minority (9 African Americans, 1 American Indian/Alaska Native, 3 Hispanic Americans), 10 international. Average age 38. 63 applicants, 63% accepted, 21 enrolled. In 2008, 24 master's, 9 Certificates awarded. *Degree requirements:* For master's, project or thesis. *Entrance requirements:* For master's, GRE General Test (minimum score: verbal and quantitative 50th percentile, analytical writing 4.0), minimum GPA of 3.0. Additional exam requirements/recommendations for international students: Required—TOEFL (minimum score 525 paper-based; 197 computer-based; 65 iBT). *Application deadline:* For fall admission, 7/15 priority date for domestic students, 5/15 for international students; for spring admission, 11/1 for international students. Applications are processed on a rolling basis. Application fee: $30. Electronic applications accepted. *Financial support:* In 2008–09, 15 students received support, including 10 research assistantships with full and partial tuition reimbursements available (averaging $6,960 per year), 5 teaching assistantships with full and partial tuition reimbursements available (averaging $6,960 per year); career-related internships or fieldwork, Federal Work-Study, tuition waivers (full and partial), and unspecified assistantships also available. Support available to part-time students. Financial award application deadline: 3/1. *Faculty research:* Housing and neighborhood development, urban housing policy, environmental sustainability, economic development. *Unit head:* Dr. W. Dennis Keating, Director, 216-687-2298, Fax: 216-687-2013, E-mail: w.keating@csuohio.edu. *Application contact:* Graduate Program Coordinator, 216-523-7522, Fax: 216-687-5398, E-mail: urbanprograms@csuohio.edu.

Cleveland State University, College of Graduate Studies, Maxine Goodman Levin College of Urban Affairs, Program in Urban Studies, Cleveland, OH 44115. Offers geographic information systems (Certificate); local and urban management (Certificate); nonprofit management (Certificate); urban economic development (Certificate); urban real estate development and finance (Certificate); urban studies (MS); urban studies and public affairs (PhD). Part-time and evening/weekend programs available. *Faculty:* 26 full-time (10 women), 20 part-time/adjunct (11 women). *Students:* 26 full-time (12 women), 42 part-time (24 women); includes 13 minority (10 African Americans, 2 Asian Americans or Pacific Islanders, 1 Hispanic American), 21 international. Average age 37. 69 applicants, 35% accepted, 12 enrolled. In 2008, 6 master's, 7 doctorates, 6 other advanced degrees awarded. *Degree requirements:* For master's, thesis or alternative, exit project, capstone course; for doctorate, comprehensive exam, thesis/dissertation. *Entrance requirements:* For master's, GRE General Test, minimum GPA of 3.0; for doctorate, GRE General Test, minimum GPA of 3.5. Additional exam requirements/recommendations for international students: Required—TOEFL (minimum score 525 paper-based; 197 computer-based; 65 iBT). *Application deadline:* For fall admission, 7/15 priority date for domestic students, 5/15 for international students; for spring admission, 11/1 for international students. Applications are processed on a rolling basis. Application fee: $30. Electronic applications accepted. *Financial support:* In 2008–09, 15 students received support,

Economics

Cleveland State University (continued)
including 11 research assistantships with full tuition reimbursements available (averaging $7,000 per year), 4 teaching assistantships with full and partial tuition reimbursements available (averaging $7,000 per year); career-related internships or fieldwork, Federal Work-Study, institutionally sponsored loans, scholarships/grants, tuition waivers (full and partial), and unspecified assistantships also available. Support available to part-time students. Financial award application deadline: 3/1; financial award applicants required to submit FAFSA. *Faculty research:* Environmental issues, economic development, urban and public policy, public management. *Unit head:* Dr. Wendy Kellogg, Director, 216-687-5265, Fax: 216-687-9342, E-mail: w.kellogg@csuohio.edu. *Application contact:* Graduate Program Coordinator, 216-523-7522, Fax: 216-687-5398, E-mail: urbanprograms@csuohio.edu.

Colorado State University, Graduate School, College of Liberal Arts, Department of Economics, Fort Collins, CO 80523-1771. Offers MA, PhD. Part-time programs available. *Faculty:* 13 full-time (5 women), 2 part-time/adjunct (1 woman). *Students:* 29 full-time (8 women), 34 part-time (11 women); includes 2 minority (both Hispanic Americans), 22 international. Average age 33. 62 applicants, 61% accepted, 13 enrolled. In 2008, 10 master's, 4 doctorates awarded. Terminal master's awarded for partial completion of doctoral program. *Degree requirements:* For master's, variable foreign language requirement, thesis or alternative; for doctorate, variable foreign language requirement, comprehensive exam, thesis/dissertation. *Entrance requirements:* For master's and doctorate, GRE General Test (combined score of 1000 on Verbal and Quantitative sections with at least 600 on Quantitative section), minimum GPA of 3.0, letters of recommendation, statement of purpose. Additional exam requirements/recommendations for international students: Required—TOEFL. *Application deadline:* For fall admission, 1/31 priority date for domestic students. Applications are processed on a rolling basis. Application fee: $50. Electronic applications accepted. *Expenses:* Tuition, area resident: Full-time $5620; part-time $312.25 per credit. Tuition, state resident: full-time $5620; part-time $312.25 per credit. Tuition, nonresident: full-time $17,253; part-time $958.50 per credit. Required fees: $1449.56; $82.35 per credit. *Financial support:* In 2008–09, 19 students received support, including 19 teaching assistantships with full tuition reimbursements available (averaging $13,428 per year); fellowships, research assistantships, career-related internships or fieldwork, Federal Work-Study, institutionally sponsored loans, scholarships/grants, traineeships, and unspecified assistantships also available. Financial award application deadline: 3/1; financial award applicants required to submit FAFSA. *Faculty research:* Regional and development economics, political economy, international trade and investment, public finance, labor markets. Total annual research expenditures: $258,976. *Unit head:* Dr. Steven J. Shulman, Chair, 970-491-6940, Fax: 970-491-2925, E-mail: steven.shulman@colostate.edu. *Application contact:* Dr. Robert W. Kling, Coordinator of Graduate Studies, 970-491-5598, Fax: 970-491-2925, E-mail: robert.king@colostate.edu.

Columbia University, Graduate School of Arts and Sciences, Division of Social Sciences, Department of Economics, New York, NY 10027. Offers M Phil, MA, PhD, JD/MA, JD/PhD. *Degree requirements:* For master's, thesis or alternative; for doctorate, thesis/dissertation. *Entrance requirements:* For master's and doctorate, GRE General Test, GRE Subject Test, previous course work in mathematics. Additional exam requirements/recommendations for international students: Required—TOEFL. *Faculty research:* International trade.

Columbia University, Graduate School of Business, Doctoral Program in Business, New York, NY 10027. Offers business (PhD), including accounting, decision, risk, and operations, finance and economics, management, marketing. *Accreditation:* AACSB. *Degree requirements:* For doctorate, comprehensive exam, thesis/dissertation, major field exam, research paper, thesis proposal. *Entrance requirements:* For doctorate, GMAT or GRE (finance), 2 letters of reference, resumé. Additional exam requirements/recommendations for international students: Required—TOEFL. Electronic applications accepted. *Expenses:* Contact institution.

Columbia University, Graduate School of Business, MBA Program, New York, NY 10027. Offers accounting (MBA); decision, risk, and operations (MBA); entrepreneurship (MBA); finance and economics (MBA); human resource management (MBA); international business (MBA); management/leadership (MBA); marketing (MBA); media (MBA); real estate (MBA); social enterprise (MBA); DDS/MBA; JD/MBA; MBA/MIA; MBA/MPH; MBA/MS; MD/MBA. *Entrance requirements:* For master's, GMAT, 2 letters of recommendation, official transcripts, essay, personal statement, completed application. Additional exam requirements/recommendations for international students: Required—TOEFL. Electronic applications accepted.

Concordia University, School of Graduate Studies, Faculty of Arts and Science, Department of Economics, Montréal, QC H3G 1M8, Canada. Offers MA, PhD, Diploma. *Degree requirements:* For master's, thesis or alternative, research paper; for doctorate, one foreign language, comprehensive exam, thesis/dissertation, research seminar. *Entrance requirements:* For master's and doctorate, honors degree in economics or equivalent. *Faculty research:* Trade and industrial adjustment, tax policy and reform, environmental policy, economics of migration, economics of telecommunications.

Cornell University, Graduate School, Graduate Fields of Architecture, Art and Planning, Field of Regional Science, Ithaca, NY 14853-0001. Offers environmental studies (MA, MS, PhD); international spatial problems (MA, MS, PhD); location theory (MA, MS, PhD); multiregional economic analysis (MA, MS, PhD); peace science (MA, MS, PhD); planning methods (MA, MS, PhD); urban and regional economics (MA, MS, PhD). *Faculty:* 17 full-time (5 women). *Students:* 22 full-time (10 women); includes 2 minority (1 African American, 1 Asian American or Pacific Islander), 19 international. Average age 33. 18 applicants, 67% accepted, 3 enrolled. In 2008, 3 master's, 2 doctorates awarded. Terminal master's awarded for partial completion of doctoral program. *Degree requirements:* For master's, thesis; for doctorate, comprehensive exam, thesis/dissertation. *Entrance requirements:* For master's and doctorate, GRE General Test, 2 letters of recommendation. Additional exam requirements/recommendations for international students: Required—TOEFL (minimum score 600 paper-based; 250 computer-based; 77 iBT). *Application deadline:* For fall admission, 1/15 priority date for domestic students. Application fee: $70. Electronic applications accepted. *Expenses:* Tuition: Full-time $29,500. Required fees: $70. Full-time tuition and fees vary according to degree level, program and student level. *Financial support:* In 2008–09, 7 students received support, including 2 research assistantships with full tuition reimbursements available, 5 teaching assistantships with full tuition reimbursements available; fellowships with full tuition reimbursements available, institutionally sponsored loans, scholarships/grants, health care benefits, tuition waivers (full and partial), and unspecified assistantships also available. Financial award applicants required to submit FAFSA. *Faculty research:* Urban and regional growth, spatial economics, formation of spatial patterns by socioeconomic systems, non-linear dynamics and complex systems, environmental-economic systems. *Unit head:* Director of Graduate Studies, 607-255-6848, Fax: 607-255-1971. *Application contact:* Graduate Field Assistant, 607-255-6848, Fax: 607-255-1971, E-mail: regsci@cornell.edu.

Cornell University, Graduate School, Graduate Fields of Arts and Sciences, Field of Economics, Ithaca, NY 14853-0001. Offers applied economics (PhD); basic analytical economics (PhD); econometrics and economic statistics (PhD); economic development and planning (PhD); economic theory (PhD); industrial organization and control (PhD); international economics (PhD); labor economics (PhD); monetary and macroeconomics (PhD); public finance (PhD). *Faculty:* 76 full-time (12 women). *Students:* 98 full-time (39 women); includes 6 minority (1 African American, 3 Asian Americans or Pacific Islanders, 2 Hispanic Americans), 54 international. Average age 29. 563 applicants, 14% accepted, 16 enrolled. In 2008, 16 doctorates awarded. *Degree requirements:* For doctorate, comprehensive exam, thesis/dissertation. *Entrance requirements:* For doctorate, GRE General Test, 3 letters of recommendation. Additional exam requirements/recommendations for international students: Required—TOEFL (minimum score 550 paper-based; 213 computer-based; 77 iBT). *Application deadline:* For fall admission, 1/15 priority date for domestic students. Application fee: $70. Electronic applications accepted. *Expenses:* Tuition: Full-time $29,500. Required fees: $70. Full-time tuition and fees vary according to degree level, program and student level. *Financial support:* In 2008–09, 81 students received support, including 18 fellowships with full tuition reimbursements available, 18 research assistantships with full tuition reimbursements available, 45 teaching assistantships with full tuition reimbursements available; institutionally sponsored loans, scholarships/grants, health care benefits, tuition waivers (full and partial), and unspecified assistantships also available. Financial award applicants required to submit FAFSA. *Faculty research:* Learning and games, economics of education, political economy, transfer payments, time series and nonparametrics. *Unit head:* Director of Graduate Studies, 607-255-4893, Fax: 607-255-2818. *Application contact:* Graduate Field Assistant, 607-255-4893, Fax: 607-255-2818, E-mail: econ_phd@cornell.edu.

Dalhousie University, Faculty of Science, Department of Economics, Halifax, NS B3H 3J5, Canada. Offers MA, MDE, PhD. *Faculty:* 14 full-time, 1 part-time/adjunct. *Students:* 29 full-time (16 women), 12 part-time (5 women). 61 applicants, 49% accepted. In 2008, 5 master's, 1 doctorate awarded. *Degree requirements:* For master's, thesis; for doctorate, thesis/dissertation. *Entrance requirements:* For master's and doctorate, GRE (recommended). Additional exam requirements/recommendations for international students: Required—TOEFL, IELTS, 1 of the following 5 approved tests: TOEFL, IELTS, CAEL, CANTEST, Michigan English Language Assessment Battery. Application fee: $70. Electronic applications accepted. *Financial support:* In 2008–09, 8 fellowships (averaging $9,500 per year), 1 research assistantship (averaging $1,830 per year), 11 teaching assistantships (averaging $3,705 per year) were awarded; career-related internships or fieldwork, scholarships/grants, and health care benefits also available. *Faculty research:* Applied econometrics, industrial organization, labor and income distribution, economic theory (micro and macro), resource economics (fishing, forestry). Total annual research expenditures: $98,500. *Unit head:* Dr. Barry Lesser, Graduate Coordinator, 902-494-1682, Fax: 902-494-6917, E-mail: barry.lesser@dal.ca. *Application contact:* Monique Comeau, Chair, 902-494-2026, Fax: 902-494-6917, E-mail: economics@dal.ca.

DePaul University, Charles H. Kellstadt Graduate School of Business and College of Liberal Arts and Sciences, Department of Economics, Chicago, IL 60604-2287. Offers applied economics (MBA); economics (MA); economics and policy analysis (MA); international business (MBA). Part-time and evening/weekend programs available. *Faculty:* 21 full-time (5 women), 8 part-time/adjunct (1 woman). *Students:* 23 applicants, 83% accepted. In 2008, 7 master's awarded. *Degree requirements:* For master's, thesis optional. *Entrance requirements:* For master's, GMAT (MBA). Additional exam requirements/recommendations for international students: Required—TOEFL, GRE. *Application deadline:* For fall admission, 7/1 for domestic students; for winter admission, 10/1 for domestic students; for spring admission, 2/1 for domestic students. Applications are processed on a rolling basis. Application fee: $40. Electronic applications accepted. *Financial support:* In 2008–09, 3 students received support, including 2 research assistantships with partial tuition reimbursements available (averaging $9,999 per year). Support available to part-time students. *Faculty research:* Forensic economics, game theory sports, economics of education, banking in Poland and Thailand. *Unit head:* Dr. Michael S. Miller, Chairperson, 312-362-8477, Fax: 312-362-5452, E-mail: mmiller@depaul.edu. *Application contact:* Kavitha Chinthada, Director of Graduate Admissions, 773-325-7885, Fax: 773-325-7311, E-mail: kchintha@depaul.edu.

Drexel University, LeBow College of Business, Program in Business Administration, Philadelphia, PA 19104-2875. Offers business administration (MBA, PhD, APC), including accounting (MBA, PhD), decision sciences (PhD), economics (MBA, PhD), finance (MBA, PhD), legal studies (MBA), management (MBA), marketing (MBA, PhD), organizational sciences (PhD), quantitative methods (MBA), strategic management (PhD). *Accreditation:* AACSB. Part-time and evening/weekend programs available. Postbaccalaureate distance learning degree programs offered (minimal on-campus study). Terminal master's awarded for partial completion of doctoral program. *Entrance requirements:* For master's, GMAT, minimum GPA of 2.75; for doctorate, GMAT. Additional exam requirements/recommendations for international students: Required—TOEFL. Electronic applications accepted. *Faculty research:* Decision support systems, individual and group behavior, operations research, techniques and strategy.

Duke University, Graduate School, Department of Economics, Durham, NC 27708. Offers AM, PhD, JD/AM. *Degree requirements:* For doctorate, thesis/dissertation. *Entrance requirements:* For master's and doctorate, GRE General Test. Additional exam requirements/recommendations for international students: Required—TOEFL (minimum score 550 paper-based; 213 computer-based; 83 iBT), IELTS (minimum score 7). Electronic applications accepted.

East Carolina University, Graduate School, Thomas Harriot College of Arts and Sciences, Department of Economics, Greenville, NC 27858-4353. Offers applied resource economics (MS). Part-time programs available. *Degree requirements:* For master's, one foreign language, comprehensive exam. *Entrance requirements:* For master's, GRE General Test. Additional exam requirements/recommendations for international students: Required—TOEFL.

Eastern Illinois University, Graduate School, College of Sciences, Department of Economics, Charleston, IL 61920-3099. Offers MA.

Eastern Michigan University, Graduate School, College of Arts and Sciences, Department of Economics, Ypsilanti, MI 48197. Offers applied economics (MA); economics (MA); health economics (MA); international economics and development (MA); trade and development (MA). Part-time and evening/weekend programs available. Postbaccalaureate distance learning degree programs offered (minimal on-campus study). *Degree requirements:* For master's, thesis or alternative. *Entrance requirements:* Additional exam requirements/recommendations for international students: Required—TOEFL.

East Tennessee State University, School of Graduate Studies, College of Business and Technology, Department of Economics, Finance, and Urban Studies, Johnson City, TN 37614. Offers city management (MCM); community development (MPM); general administration (MPM); municipal service management (MPM); urban and regional economic development (MPM); urban and regional planning (MPM). *Degree requirements:* For master's, internship, oral defense of thesis, research report. *Entrance requirements:* For master's, GRE General Test, minimum GPA of 3.0. Additional exam requirements/recommendations for international students: Required—TOEFL (minimum score 550 paper-based; 213 computer-based).

Emory University, Graduate School of Arts and Sciences, Department of Economics, Atlanta, GA 30322-1100. Offers PhD. *Degree requirements:* For doctorate, comprehensive exam, thesis/dissertation. *Entrance requirements:* For doctorate, GRE General Test. Electronic applications accepted. *Faculty research:* Applied microeconomics, econometrics, public choice, macroeconomics, law and economics.

Florida Agricultural and Mechanical University, Division of Graduate Studies, Research, and Continuing Education, College of Arts and Sciences, Division of History and Political Sciences, Program in Applied Social Science, Tallahassee, FL 32307-3200. Offers African American history (MASS); criminal justice (MASS); economics (MASS); history (MASS); political science (MASS); public administration (MASS); public management (MASS); social work (MASS); sociology (MASS). Part-time programs available. *Degree requirements:* For master's, thesis optional. *Entrance requirements:* For master's, GRE General Test, minimum GPA of 3.0. *Faculty research:* Southern history, black history, election trends, presidential history.

Florida Atlantic University, Barry Kaye College of Business, Department of Economics, Boca Raton, FL 33431-0991. Offers MS. Part-time and evening/weekend programs available. *Faculty:* 13 full-time (3 women), 6 part-time/adjunct (0 women). *Students:* 6 full-time (2 women), 14 part-time (2 women); includes 8 minority (3 African Americans, 3 Asian Americans or Pacific Islanders, 2 Hispanic Americans), 2 international. Average age 33. 29 applicants, 41% accepted, 5 enrolled. In 2008, 5 master's awarded. *Degree requirements:* For master's, thesis optional. *Entrance requirements:* For master's, GMAT, GRE General Test, minimum GPA of 3.0. Additional exam requirements/recommendations for international students: Required—TOEFL (minimum score 600 paper-based; 250 computer-based). *Application deadline:* For fall admission, 7/1 priority date for domestic students, 2/15 priority date for international students; for winter admission, 11/1 priority date for domestic students, 8/15 priority date for international students; for spring admission, 4/1 priority date for domestic students, 1/15 priority date for international students. Applications are processed on a rolling basis. Application fee: $30. *Expenses:* Tuition, state resident: full-time $4867; part-time $270.40 per credit hour. Tuition, nonresident: full-time $16,486; part-time $915.87 per credit hour. *Financial support:* Teaching assistantships with tuition reimbursements, tuition waivers (partial) and unspecified assistantships available. Financial award application deadline: 3/1. *Faculty research:* International trade and finance, decision making, monetary conditions, economic fluctuations and growth. *Unit head:* Dr. Charles Register, Chair, 561-297-4176, Fax: 561-297-2542, E-mail: register@fau.edu. *Application contact:* Dr. Eric P. Chiang, Graduate Director, 561-297-2947, Fax: 561-297-1315, E-mail: chiang@fau.edu.

Florida International University, College of Arts and Sciences, Department of Economics, Miami, FL 33199. Offers MA, PhD. Part-time and evening/weekend programs available. *Degree requirements:* For master's, thesis or alternative; for doctorate, comprehensive exam, thesis/dissertation. *Entrance requirements:* For master's, GRE, minimum GPA of 3.0, letters of recommendation; for doctorate, GRE General Test, 3 letters of recommendation, minimum GPA of 3.0. Additional exam requirements/recommendations for international students: Required—TOEFL (minimum score 550 paper-based; 213 computer-based). Electronic applications accepted. *Faculty research:* Economic development, international economics, urban/regional economics, Latin American economics.

Florida State University, Graduate Studies, College of Social Sciences, Department of Economics, Tallahassee, FL 32306. Offers MS, PhD, JD/MS. Part-time programs available. Terminal master's awarded for partial completion of doctoral program. *Degree requirements:* For master's, thesis or alternative; for doctorate, thesis/dissertation, 2 comprehensive exams, workshops. *Entrance requirements:* For master's, GRE General Test, minimum GPA of 3.0, minimum GPA of 3.4 on graduate work, minimum 1 course each in statistics and calculus; for doctorate, GRE General Test, minimum graduate GPA of 3.4, minimum 1 course in statistics, 2 in calculus, and 1 in linear algebra. Additional exam requirements/recommendations for international students: Required—TOEFL (minimum score 550 paper-based; 213 computer-based; 80 iBT). Electronic applications accepted. *Faculty research:* Lbor, industrial organization, international, experimental/behavioral.

Fordham University, Graduate School of Arts and Sciences, Department of Economics, New York, NY 10458. Offers MA, PhD. Part-time and evening/weekend programs available. Terminal master's awarded for partial completion of doctoral program. *Degree requirements:* For master's, comprehensive exam; for doctorate, comprehensive exam, thesis/dissertation. *Entrance requirements:* For master's and doctorate, GRE General Test. Additional exam requirements/recommendations for international students: Required—TOEFL (minimum score 600 paper-based; 250 computer-based). Electronic applications accepted. *Faculty research:* Developmental economics, econometrics.

Fordham University, Graduate School of Arts and Sciences, Program in International Political Economy and Development, New York, NY 10458. Offers MA, Certificate. Part-time and evening/weekend programs available. *Degree requirements:* For master's, comprehensive exam. *Entrance requirements:* For master's, GRE General Test. Additional exam requirements/recommendations for international students: Required—TOEFL (minimum score 600 paper-based; 250 computer-based). Electronic applications accepted. *Faculty research:* International economics, comparative international politics, international banking and finance, international development, emerging markets and country risk analysis.

See Close-Up on page 865.

George Mason University, College of Humanities and Social Sciences, Department of Economics, Fairfax, VA 22030. Offers economic systems design (Graduate Certificate); economics (MA, PhD). *Degree requirements:* For master's, thesis optional, 2 comprehensive exams; for doctorate, thesis/dissertation, 2 preliminary exams, field exams. *Entrance requirements:* For master's, GRE General Test, GRE Subject Test, introductory and intermediate course work in macro and microeconomics, undergraduate course work in calculus; for doctorate, GRE General Test, GRE Subject Test, course work in analytic geometry, 1 year of course work in statistics, introductory and intermediate course work in macro and microeconomics. Electronic applications accepted.

Georgetown University, Graduate School of Arts and Sciences, Department of Economics, Washington, DC 20057. Offers econometrics (PhD); economic development (PhD); economic theory (PhD); industrial organization (PhD); international macro and finance (PhD); international trade (PhD); labor economics (PhD); macroeconomics (PhD); public economics and political economics (PhD); MA/PhD; MS/MA. *Degree requirements:* For doctorate, comprehensive exam, thesis/dissertation. *Entrance requirements:* For doctorate, GRE General Test. Additional exam requirements/recommendations for international students: Required—TOEFL. *Faculty research:* International economics, economic development.

The George Washington University, Columbian College of Arts and Sciences, Department of Economics, Washington, DC 20052. Offers MA, PhD. Part-time and evening/weekend programs available. *Faculty:* 23 full-time (6 women), 21 part-time/adjunct (8 women). *Students:* 37 full-time (19 women), 59 part-time (27 women); includes 10 minority (3 African Americans, 5 Asian Americans or Pacific Islanders, 2 Hispanic Americans), 49 international. Average age 31. 322 applicants, 23% accepted, 17 enrolled. In 2008, 25 master's, 7 doctorates awarded. Terminal master's awarded for partial completion of doctoral program. *Degree requirements:* For master's, comprehensive exam, thesis or alternative; for doctorate, thesis/dissertation, general exam. *Entrance requirements:* For master's and doctorate, GRE General Test, minimum GPA of 3.0. Additional exam requirements/recommendations for international students: Required—TOEFL (minimum score 550 paper-based; 213 computer-based; 80 IBT). *Application deadline:* For fall admission, 1/15 priority date for domestic and international students; for spring admission, 9/1 for international students. Applications are processed on a rolling basis. Application fee: $60. Electronic applications accepted. *Financial support:* In 2008–09, 25 students received support; fellowships with full tuition reimbursements available, teaching assistantships with tuition reimbursements available, Federal Work-Study available. Financial award application deadline: 1/15. *Unit head:* Robert F. Phillips, Chair, 202-994-8619, E-mail: rphil@gwu.edu. *Application contact:* Information Contact, 202-994-6150, Fax: 202-994-6147, E-mail: econgrad@gwu.edu.

Georgia Institute of Technology, Graduate Studies and Research, Ivan Allen College of Policy and International Affairs, School of Economics, Atlanta, GA 30332-0001. Offers MS. *Degree requirements:* For master's, thesis. *Entrance requirements:* For master's, GRE. Additional exam requirements/recommendations for international students: Required—TOEFL. *Faculty research:* Land use patterns in developing countries, office automation and productivity, dynamic modeling of financial markets.

Georgia State University, Andrew Young School of Policy Studies, Department of Economics, Atlanta, GA 30303-3083. Offers MA, PhD. MA offered through the College of Arts and Sciences. Part-time and evening/weekend programs available. Terminal master's awarded for partial completion of doctoral program. *Degree requirements:* For master's, thesis optional; for doctorate, comprehensive exam, thesis/dissertation. *Entrance requirements:* For master's, GRE; for doctorate, GRE General Test. Additional exam requirements/recommendations for international students: Required—TOEFL. Electronic applications accepted. *Faculty research:* Tax policy, economic growth and development, environmental economics, urban and regional economics, economics of science.

Georgia State University, J. Mack Robinson College of Business, Program in General Business Administration, Atlanta, GA 30303-3083. Offers accounting/information systems (MBA); economics (MBA, MS); enterprise risk management (MBA); general business (MBA); general business administration (EMBA, PMBA); information systems consulting (MBA); information systems risk management (MBA); international business and information technology (MBA); international entrepreneurship (MBA); MBA/JD. *Accreditation:* AACSB. Part-time and evening/weekend programs available. *Entrance requirements:* For master's, GMAT. Additional exam requirements/recommendations for international students: Required—TOEFL (minimum score 610 paper-based; 255 computer-based; 101 iBT). Electronic applications accepted.

Graduate School and University Center of the City University of New York, Graduate Studies, Program in Economics, New York, NY 10016-4039. Offers PhD. *Degree requirements:* For doctorate, thesis/dissertation. *Entrance requirements:* For doctorate, GRE General Test. Additional exam requirements/recommendations for international students: Required—TOEFL. Electronic applications accepted.

Harvard University, Graduate School of Arts and Sciences, Committee on Business Economics, Cambridge, MA 02138. Offers PhD. *Degree requirements:* For doctorate, thesis/dissertation. *Entrance requirements:* For doctorate, GMAT or GRE General Test. Additional exam requirements/recommendations for international students: Required—TOEFL. *Expenses:* Tuition: Full-time $32,556. Required fees: $1426. Full-time tuition and fees vary according to program and student level.

Harvard University, Graduate School of Arts and Sciences, Department of Economics, Cambridge, MA 02138. Offers PhD. *Degree requirements:* For doctorate, thesis/dissertation, oral exam. *Entrance requirements:* For doctorate, GRE General Test, GRE Subject Test. Additional exam requirements/recommendations for international students: Required—TOEFL. *Expenses:* Tuition: Full-time $32,556. Required fees: $1426. Full-time tuition and fees vary according to program and student level. *Faculty research:* Industrial organization, macromonetary issues, international economics.

Hawai'i Pacific University, College of Business Administration, Honolulu, HI 96813. Offers accounting/CPA (MBA); e-business (MBA); economics (MBA); finance (MBA); human resource management (MBA); information systems (MBA); international business (MBA); management (MBA); marketing (MBA); organizational change (MBA); travel industry management (MBA). Part-time and evening/weekend programs available. *Faculty:* 19 full-time (6 women), 12 part-time/adjunct (2 women). *Students:* 227 full-time (117 women), 214 part-time (102 women); includes 140 minority (11 African Americans, 5 American Indian/Alaska Native, 110 Asian Americans or Pacific Islanders, 14 Hispanic Americans), 167 international. Average age 30. 275 applicants, 80% accepted, 149 enrolled. In 2008, 183 master's awarded. *Degree requirements:* For master's, thesis. *Entrance requirements:* For master's, GMAT. Additional exam requirements/recommendations for international students: Recommended—TOEFL (minimum score 550 paper-based; 213 computer-based; 80 iBT), TWE (minimum score 5). *Application deadline:* For fall admission, 2/15 priority date for domestic students; for spring admission, 10/15 priority date for domestic students. Applications are processed on a rolling basis. Application fee: $50. Electronic applications accepted. *Expenses:* Tuition: Full-time $10,800; part-time $600 per credit. *Financial support:* In 2008–09, 164 students received support; research assistantships, career-related internships or fieldwork, Federal Work-Study, scholarships/grants, and unspecified assistantships available. Support available to part-time students. Financial award application deadline: 3/1; financial award applicants required to submit FAFSA. *Faculty research:* Statistical control process as used by management, studies in comparative cross-cultural management styles, not-for-profit management. *Unit head:* Dr. Aytun Ozturk, Dean, 808-544-9301, Fax: 808-544-0283, E-mail: uozturk@hpu.edu. *Application contact:* Danny Lam, Assistant Director of Graduate Admissions, 808-544-1135, Fax: 808-544-0280, E-mail: graduate@hpu.edu.

Howard University, Graduate School, Department of Economics, Washington, DC 20059-0002. Offers MA, PhD. Part-time programs available. *Degree requirements:* For master's, comprehensive exam, thesis optional; for doctorate, one foreign language, comprehensive exam, thesis/dissertation. *Entrance requirements:* For master's, GRE General Test, minimum GPA of 3.0; for doctorate, GRE General Test, master's degree in economics or related field, minimum GPA of 3.0. Electronic applications accepted. *Faculty research:* Economic development, international trade, urban rentalization.

Hunter College of the City University of New York, Graduate School, School of Arts and Sciences, Department of Economics, New York, NY 10021-5085. Offers accounting (MS); economics (MA). Part-time and evening/weekend programs available. *Faculty:* 5 full-time (1 woman), 6 part-time/adjunct (0 women). *Students:* 13 full-time (5 women), 29 part-time (16 women); includes 22 minority (2 African Americans, 17 Asian Americans or Pacific Islanders, 3 Hispanic Americans). Average age 28. 21 applicants, 38% accepted, 5 enrolled. In 2008, 23 master's awarded. *Degree requirements:* For master's, research paper or thesis. *Entrance requirements:* For master's, GMAT or GRE General Test, minimum GPA of 3.0, 18 credits of undergraduate course work in economics (9 in mathematics), 2 letters of recommendation (1 from a member of economics department). Additional exam requirements/recommendations for international students: Required—TOEFL. *Application deadline:* For fall admission, 4/1 for domestic students, 2/1 for international students; for spring admission, 11/1 for domestic students, 9/1 for international students. Application fee: $125. *Financial support:* Fellowships, research assistantships, teaching assistantships, career-related internships or fieldwork, Federal Work-Study, institutionally sponsored loans, and tuition waivers (partial) available. Support available to part-time students. *Faculty research:* Earnings of immigrants and minority groups, taxation and the regional economy. *Unit head:* Dr. Marjorie P. Honig, Chairperson, 212-772-5400, Fax: 212-772-5398, E-mail: mhonig@hunter.cuny.edu. *Application contact:* Randall Filer, Professor of Economics, Graduate Advisor, 212-772-5399, Fax: 212-772-5398, E-mail: grad.econadvisor@hunter.cuny.edu.

Illinois State University, Graduate School, College of Arts and Sciences, Department of Economics, Normal, IL 61790-2200. Offers MA, MS. *Degree requirements:* For master's, thesis or alternative. *Entrance requirements:* For master's, GRE General Test, minimum GPA of 2.6 in last 60 hours of course work. *Faculty research:* Stevenson Center Graduate Assistantship in Community/Economic Development; the social, economic and educational correlates of rural school closure; Stevenson Center Americorps project.

Indiana University Bloomington, Kelley School of Business, Department of Business Economics and Public Policy, Bloomington, IN 47405-7000. Offers PhD. *Faculty:* 8 full-time (1 woman), 1 part-time/adjunct (0 women). *Students:* 20 applicants, 10% accepted, 2 enrolled. In 2008, 2 doctorates awarded. *Degree requirements:* For doctorate, comprehensive exam, thesis/dissertation. *Entrance requirements:* For doctorate, GRE or GMAT, bachelor's degree. Additional exam requirements/recommendations for international students: Required—TOEFL (minimum score 630 paper-based; 267 computer-based; 80 iBT). *Expenses:* Tuition, area resident: Part-time $291.97 per credit hour. Tuition, state resident: part-time $291.97 per credit hour. Tuition, nonresident: part-time $850.33 per credit hour. Required fees: $110 per semester. Tuition and fees vary according to course load and program. *Financial support:* Fellowships with full tuition reimbursements available. *Faculty research:* Industrial organization, pricing, environmental regulation and policy, information economics, economics of law and organization. *Unit head:* Dr. John W. Maxwell, Professor of Business Economics and Public Policy, 812-855-9219, Fax: 812-855-3354, E-mail: jwmax@indiana.edu. *Application contact:* Dr. Michael R. Baye, Bert Elwert Professor of Business Economics, 812-855-9219, Fax: 812-855-3354, E-mail: mbaye@indiana.edu.

Indiana University Bloomington, University Graduate School, College of Arts and Sciences, Department of Economics, Bloomington, IN 47405-7104. Offers MA, PhD. *Faculty:* 23 full-time (3 women). *Students:* 88 full-time (26 women), 7 part-time (3 women); includes 4 minority (1 African American, 1 Asian American or Pacific Islander, 2 Hispanic Americans), 69 international. Average age 29. 172 applicants, 46% accepted, 24 enrolled. In 2008, 23 master's, 15 doctorates awarded. Terminal master's awarded for partial completion of doctoral program. *Degree requirements:* For master's, thesis optional, tool skill classes; for doctorate, comprehensive exam, thesis/dissertation, field exam, 3rd year paper, tool skill classes. *Entrance requirements:* For master's, GRE General Test, minimum one year of calculus; for doctorate, GRE General Test, minimum one year of calculus, semester of linear algebra. Additional exam requirements/recommendations for international students: Required—TOEFL (minimum score 600 paper-

Economics

Indiana University Bloomington *(continued)*
based; 250 computer-based; 100 iBT). *Application deadline:* For fall admission, 1/15 priority date for domestic students, 12/1 priority date for international students. Applications are processed on a rolling basis. Application fee: $50 ($60 for international students). Electronic applications accepted. *Expenses:* Tuition, area resident: Part-time $291.97 per credit hour. Tuition, state resident: part-time $291.97 per credit hour. Tuition, nonresident: part-time $850.33 per credit hour. Required fees: $110 per semester. Tuition and fees vary according to course load and program. *Financial support:* In 2008–09, 53 students received support, including 3 fellowships with full tuition reimbursements available (averaging $16,000 per year), 1 research assistantship with full tuition reimbursement available (averaging $14,800 per year), 49 teaching assistantships with full tuition reimbursements available (averaging $14,000 per year); institutionally sponsored loans and health care benefits also available. Financial award application deadline: 1/15. *Faculty research:* Games, experiments and organization, transition economics, growth and development, macroeconomics, econometrics. *Unit head:* Prof. Gerhard Glomm, Chair, 812-855-6160, Fax: 812-855-3736, E-mail: gglomm@indiana.edu. *Application contact:* Chris Cunningham, Graduate Services Assistant, 812-855-8453, Fax: 812-855-3736, E-mail: rcunning@indiana.edu.

Indiana University–Purdue University Indianapolis, Department of Economics, Indianapolis, IN 46202-2896. Offers MA, MA/MA. *Entrance requirements:* For master's, GRE, minimum GPA of 3.0; courses in economic theory, statistics, calculus. Additional exam requirements/recommendations for international students: Required—TOEFL (minimum score 600 paper-based). *Faculty research:* Charitable giving.

Instituto Centroamericano de Administración de Empresas, Graduate Programs, La Garita, Costa Rica. Offers agribusiness (MIAM); business administration (EMBA); economics and finance (MBA); industry and technology (MBA); sustainable development (MBA). *Degree requirements:* For master's, comprehensive exam, essay. *Entrance requirements:* For master's, GMAT or GRE, fluency in Spanish, interview, letters of recommendation, minimum 1 year of work experience. Electronic applications accepted. *Faculty research:* Competitiveness, production.

Instituto Tecnológico y de Estudios Superiores de Monterrey, Campus Ciudad de México, Division of Business, Ciudad de Mexico, Mexico. Offers business administration (EMBA, MBA, PhD); economy (MBA); finance (MBA). Part-time and evening/weekend programs available. Postbaccalaureate distance learning degree programs offered (minimal on-campus study). *Entrance requirements:* For master's and doctorate, Instituto entrance exam. Additional exam requirements/recommendations for international students: Required—TOEFL.

Iowa State University of Science and Technology, Graduate College, College of Liberal Arts and Sciences, Department of Economics, Ames, IA 50011. Offers agricultural economics (MS, PhD); economics (MS, PhD); JD/MS; JD/PhD. *Faculty:* 42 full-time (6 women), 4 part-time/adjunct (3 women). *Students:* 67 full-time (26 women), 24 part-time (12 women); includes 1 minority (Asian American or Pacific Islander), 73 international. 305 applicants, 13% accepted, 12 enrolled. In 2008, 14 master's, 8 doctorates awarded. *Degree requirements:* For master's, thesis or alternative; for doctorate, thesis/dissertation. *Entrance requirements:* For master's and doctorate, GRE General Test. Additional exam requirements/recommendations for international students: Required—TOEFL (minimum score 570 paper-based; 88 iBT), IELTS (6.5) or TOEFL. *Application deadline:* For fall admission, 1/20 priority date for domestic and international students. Application fee: $30 ($70 for international students). Electronic applications accepted. *Expenses:* Tuition, area resident: Full-time $6446; part-time $359 per credit. Tuition, state resident: full-time $6446; part-time $359 per credit. Tuition, nonresident: full-time $17,330; part-time $963 per credit. Required fees: $790; $249.25 per semester. Tuition and fees vary according to course load and program. *Financial support:* In 2008–09, 54 research assistantships with full and partial tuition reimbursements (averaging $14,400 per year), 51 teaching assistantships with full and partial tuition reimbursements (averaging $15,030 per year) were awarded; fellowships, scholarships/grants, health care benefits, and unspecified assistantships also available. *Unit head:* Dr. GianCarlo Moschini, Chair, 515-294-5761, Fax: 515-294-7755, E-mail: grad@econ.iastate.edu. *Application contact:* Dr. John Schroeter, Information Contact, 515-294-2702, E-mail: grad@econ.iastate.edu.

The Johns Hopkins University, Zanvyl Krieger School of Arts and Sciences, Department of Economics, Baltimore, MD 21218-2699. Offers PhD. *Degree requirements:* For doctorate, comprehensive exam, thesis/dissertation. *Entrance requirements:* For doctorate, GRE General Test. Additional exam requirements/recommendations for international students: Required—TOEFL (minimum score 600 paper-based; 250 computer-based). Electronic applications accepted. *Faculty research:* General economic theory, econometrics and mathematical economics, trade and development, game theory, urban economics.

Kansas State University, Graduate School, College of Arts and Sciences, Department of Economics, Manhattan, KS 66506. Offers MA, PhD. Part-time programs available. *Faculty:* 12 full-time (1 woman), 3 part-time/adjunct (1 woman). *Students:* 49 full-time (16 women), 6 part-time (2 women); includes 4 minority (2 African Americans, 2 Asian Americans or Pacific Islanders), 31 international. Average age 29. 73 applicants, 36% accepted, 11 enrolled. In 2008, 6 master's, 5 doctorates awarded. Terminal master's awarded for partial completion of doctoral program. *Degree requirements:* For master's, thesis optional; for doctorate, comprehensive exam, thesis/dissertation. *Entrance requirements:* For master's, GRE (highly recommended), minimum GPA of 3.0; course work in microeconomics, macroeconomics, calculus and statistics; for doctorate, GRE (highly recommended), course work in microeconomics, macroeconomics, and calculus. Additional exam requirements/recommendations for international students: Required—TOEFL (minimum score 550 paper-based; 213 computer-based). *Application deadline:* For fall admission, 2/1 priority date for domestic and international students; for spring admission, 10/1 for domestic students, 8/1 priority date for international students. Applications are processed on a rolling basis. Application fee: $30 ($55 for international students). Electronic applications accepted. *Expenses:* Tuition, area resident: Full-time $6466; part-time $269.40 per credit hour. Tuition, state resident: full-time $6466; part-time $269.40 per credit hour. Tuition, nonresident: full-time $14,874; part-time $619.75 per credit hour. Required fees: $673; $23.40 per credit hour. Tuition and fees vary according to campus/location. *Financial support:* In 2008–09, 1 research assistantship (averaging $17,080 per year), 31 teaching assistantships with full tuition reimbursements (averaging $12,683 per year) were awarded; fellowships, career-related internships or fieldwork, institutionally sponsored loans, and scholarships/grants also available. Support available to part-time students. Financial award application deadline: 3/1; financial award applicants required to submit FAFSA. *Faculty research:* Macroeconomics; microeconomics and labor economics; development and growth; international economics; industrial organization. Total annual research expenditures: $28,846. *Unit head:* Dr. Lloyd Thomas, Head, 785-532-7357, Fax: 785-532-6919, E-mail: lbt@ksu.edu. *Application contact:* Dr. James Ragan, Director, 785-532-4582, Fax: 785-532-6919, E-mail: jfrjr@ksu.edu.

Kent State University, Graduate School of Management, Master's Program in Economics, Kent, OH 44242-0001. Offers MA. Part-time programs available. *Entrance requirements:* For master's, GMAT or GRE General Test, minimum GPA of 2.75. Additional exam requirements/recommendations for international students: Required—TOEFL (minimum score 550 paper-based; 213 computer-based). Electronic applications accepted. *Faculty research:* Macro- and microeconomic theory, labor economics, international economics, quantitative methods.

Lakehead University, Graduate Studies, Faculty of Social Sciences and Humanities, Department of Economics, Thunder Bay, ON P7B 5E1, Canada. Offers MA. Part-time and evening/weekend programs available. *Degree requirements:* For master's, thesis or comprehensive exams, research papers. *Entrance requirements:* For master's, minimum B average. Additional exam requirements/recommendations for international students: Required—TOEFL. Tuition charges are reported in Canadian dollars. *Expenses:* Tuition, area resident: Full-time $6500

Canadian dollars. International tuition: $13,700 Canadian dollars full-time. *Faculty research:* Public finance, economic history, mathematical economics, quantitative economics.

Lehigh University, College of Business and Economics, Department of Economics, Bethlehem, PA 18015-3094. Offers economics (MS, PhD); health and bio-pharmaceutical economics (MS). Part-time programs available. *Faculty:* 11 full-time (3 women), 2 part-time/adjunct (0 women). *Students:* 35 full-time (22 women), 8 part-time (2 women); includes 1 minority (Asian American or Pacific Islander), 21 international. Average age 27. 95 applicants, 66% accepted, 23 enrolled. In 2008, 11 master's, 2 doctorates awarded. Terminal master's awarded for partial completion of doctoral program. *Degree requirements:* For master's, thesis optional; for doctorate, comprehensive exam, thesis/dissertation, proposal defense. *Entrance requirements:* For master's and doctorate, GMAT or GRE General Test. Additional exam requirements/recommendations for international students: Required—TOEFL (minimum score 600 paper-based; 250 computer-based; 94 iBT). *Application deadline:* For fall admission, 7/15 for domestic students; for spring admission, 12/1 for domestic students. Applications are processed on a rolling basis. Application fee: $100. Electronic applications accepted. *Expenses:* Contact institution. *Financial support:* In 2008–09, 3 fellowships with full tuition reimbursements (averaging $13,200 per year), 9 teaching assistantships with full tuition reimbursements (averaging $13,200 per year) were awarded; research assistantships with tuition reimbursements, scholarships/grants, health care benefits, tuition waivers (full and partial), and unspecified assistantships also available. Financial award application deadline: 1/15. *Faculty research:* Public finance, investments, applied econometrics, labor economics. Total annual research expenditures: $96,352. *Unit head:* Dr. Shin-Yi Chou, Director of PhD Program, 610-758-3444, Fax: 610-758-5283, E-mail: syc2@lehigh.edu. *Application contact:* Corinn McBride, Director of Recruitment and Admissions, 610-758-3418, Fax: 610-758-5283, E-mail: com207@lehigh.edu.

Long Island University, Brooklyn Campus, Richard L. Conolly College of Liberal Arts and Sciences, Department of Economics, Brooklyn, NY 11201-8423. Offers MA. Part-time and evening/weekend programs available. *Degree requirements:* For master's, thesis or alternative. *Entrance requirements:* For master's, 2 letters of recommendation. Additional exam requirements/recommendations for international students: Required—TOEFL (minimum score 550 paper-based; 173 computer-based). Electronic applications accepted.

Louisiana State University and Agricultural and Mechanical College, Graduate School, E. J. Ourso College of Business, Department of Economics, Baton Rouge, LA 70803. Offers MS, PhD. Terminal master's awarded for partial completion of doctoral program. *Degree requirements:* For doctorate, thesis/dissertation. *Entrance requirements:* For master's and doctorate, GRE General Test, minimum GPA of 3.0. Additional exam requirements/recommendations for international students: Required—TOEFL (minimum score 550 paper-based; 213 computer-based; 79 iBT). *Faculty research:* Microeconomics, macroeconomics, econometrics, industrial organization, public finance, labor.

Louisiana Tech University, Graduate School, College of Business, Department of Finance and Economics, Ruston, LA 71272. Offers business economics (MBA, DBA); finance (MBA, DBA). Part-time programs available. *Degree requirements:* For doctorate, thesis/dissertation. *Entrance requirements:* For master's and doctorate, GMAT.

Marquette University, Graduate School of Management, Department of Economics, Milwaukee, WI 53201-1881. Offers business economics (MSAE); financial economics (MSAE); international economics (MSAE). Part-time and evening/weekend programs available. *Degree requirements:* For master's, comprehensive exam, thesis or alternative, essay. *Entrance requirements:* For master's, GMAT or GRE General Test. Additional exam requirements/recommendations for international students: Required—TOEFL. *Faculty research:* Monetary and fiscal policy in open economy, housing and regional migration, political economy of taxation and state/local government.

Massachusetts Institute of Technology, School of Humanities, Arts, and Social Sciences, Department of Economics, Cambridge, MA 02139-4307. Offers SM, PhD. Terminal master's awarded for partial completion of doctoral program. *Degree requirements:* For master's, thesis; for doctorate, comprehensive exam, thesis/dissertation. *Entrance requirements:* For doctorate, GRE General Test. Additional exam requirements/recommendations for international students: Required—TOEFL (minimum score 600 paper-based; 250 computer-based). Electronic applications accepted. *Faculty research:* Theoretical and Applied Macroeconomics; Development Economics and Economic Growth; Public Economics and Political Economy; Labor Economics and Industrial Organization; Econometrics and Economic Theory.

McGill University, Faculty of Graduate and Postdoctoral Studies, Faculty of Arts, Department of Economics, Montréal, QC H3A 2T5, Canada. Offers economics (MA, PhD); social statistics (MA).

McMaster University, School of Graduate Studies, Faculty of Social Sciences, Department of Economics, Hamilton, ON L8S 4M2, Canada. Offers MA, PhD. Part-time programs available. *Degree requirements:* For doctorate, comprehensive exam, thesis/dissertation. *Entrance requirements:* For master's, GRE (recommended), honors BA in economics; for doctorate, GRE (recommended), B+ average in a master's degree. Additional exam requirements/recommendations for international students: Required—TOEFL (minimum score 580 paper-based; 237 computer-based). *Faculty research:* Applied microeconomics, econometrics, health economics, labor economics, public finance.

Memorial University of Newfoundland, School of Graduate Studies, Department of Economics, St. John's, NL A1C 5S7, Canada. Offers MA. *Degree requirements:* For master's, thesis optional, essay course. *Entrance requirements:* For master's, honors degree (minimum 2nd class standing). *Faculty research:* Public sector economics, natural resource economics.

Miami University, Graduate School, Farmer School of Business, Department of Economics, Oxford, OH 45056. Offers MA. Part-time programs available. *Degree requirements:* For master's, thesis or alternative, final exam. *Entrance requirements:* For master's, GMAT, minimum undergraduate GPA of 3.0 during previous 2 years or 2.75 overall. Additional exam requirements/recommendations for international students: Required—TOEFL (minimum score 550 paper-based; 213 computer-based), TWE (minimum score 4).

Michigan State University, The Graduate School, College of Social Science, Department of Economics, East Lansing, MI 48824. Offers MA, PhD. *Entrance requirements:* Additional exam requirements/recommendations for international students: Required—TOEFL. Electronic applications accepted.

Middle Tennessee State University, College of Graduate Studies, College of Business, Department of Economics and Finance, Murfreesboro, TN 37132. Offers MA, PhD. Part-time and evening/weekend programs available. Postbaccalaureate distance learning degree programs offered. *Degree requirements:* For master's, thesis optional; for doctorate, comprehensive exam, thesis/dissertation. *Entrance requirements:* For master's and doctorate, GRE or MAT. Additional exam requirements/recommendations for international students: Required—TOEFL (paper-based 525; computer-based 195; iBT 71) or IELTS (6.0). Electronic applications accepted.

Mississippi State University, College of Business, Department of Finance and Economics, Mississippi State, MS 39762. Offers applied economics (PhD); economics (MA); finance (MSBA). Part-time programs available. Terminal master's awarded for partial completion of doctoral program. *Degree requirements:* For master's, comprehensive exam, thesis optional; for doctorate, comprehensive exam, thesis/dissertation. *Entrance requirements:* For master's and doctorate, GMAT, GRE General Test. *Faculty research:* Economics development, mergers, event studies, economic education, bank performance.

Montclair State University, The Office of Graduate Admissions and Support Services, School of Business, Department of Economics and Finance, Montclair, NJ 07043-1624. Offers business economics (MBA); finance (MBA). Part-time and evening/weekend programs available. *Faculty:*

16 full-time (4 women), 7 part-time/adjunct (1 woman). *Students:* 18 full-time (7 women), 75 part-time (21 women); includes 23 minority (6 African Americans, 11 Asian Americans or Pacific Islanders, 6 Hispanic Americans), 11 international. Average age 29. 48 applicants, 58% accepted, 18 enrolled. In 2008, 37 master's awarded. *Entrance requirements:* For master's, GRE General Test, 2 letters of recommendation, resumé. Additional exam requirements/recommendations for international students: Required—TOEFL (minimum score 83 computer-based). *Application deadline:* For fall admission, 6/1 for international students; for spring admission, 10/1 for international students. Applications are processed on a rolling basis. Application fee: $60. Electronic applications accepted. *Financial support:* In 2008–09, 2 research assistantships with full tuition reimbursements (averaging $7,000 per year) were awarded; Federal Work-Study, scholarships/grants, and unspecified assistantships also available. Support available to part-time students. Financial award application deadline: 3/1; financial award applicants required to submit FAFSA. *Unit head:* Dr. Richard Lord, Chair, 973-655-5255. *Application contact:* Amy Aiello, Associate Director of Admissions, 973-655-5147, Fax: 973-655-7869, E-mail: graduate.school@montclair.edu.

Morgan State University, School of Graduate Studies, College of Liberal Arts, Department of Economics, Baltimore, MD 21251. Offers MA. *Degree requirements:* For master's, comprehensive exam. *Entrance requirements:* For master's, GRE. Additional exam requirements/recommendations for international students: Required—TOEFL (minimum score 550 paper-based; 213 computer-based).

Murray State University, College of Business and Public Affairs, Program in Economics, Murray, KY 42071. Offers MS. Part-time programs available. *Entrance requirements:* For master's, GRE General Test or GMAT, economics minor or equivalent, students may be conditionally admitted and fulfill undergraduate requirements. Additional exam requirements/recommendations for international students: Required—TOEFL. *Faculty research:* Economic education, public finance, economic development, banking, telecommunications systems management.

National University, Academic Affairs, School of Business and Management, Department of Accounting and Finance, La Jolla, CA 92037-1011. Offers accountancy (MS); corporate and international finance (MS). Part-time and evening/weekend programs available. Post-baccalaureate distance learning degree programs offered (no on-campus study). *Faculty:* 9 full-time (1 woman), 104 part-time/adjunct (30 women). *Students:* 17 full-time (3 women), 57 part-time (26 women); includes 25 minority (6 African Americans, 1 American Indian/Alaska Native, 5 Asian Americans or Pacific Islanders, 13 Hispanic Americans), 16 international. Average age 33. 57 applicants, 100% accepted, 57 enrolled. In 2008, 14 master's awarded. *Degree requirements:* For master's, thesis. *Entrance requirements:* For master's, interview, minimum GPA of 2.5. Additional exam requirements/recommendations for international students: Required—TOEFL (minimum score 550 paper-based; 213 computer-based; 79 iBT), IELTS (minimum score 6). *Application deadline:* Applications are processed on a rolling basis. Application fee: $60 ($65 for international students). Electronic applications accepted. *Expenses:* Tuition: Full-time $8694; part-time $322 per credit hour. Tuition and fees vary according to course load. *Financial support:* Career-related internships or fieldwork, institutionally sponsored loans, scholarships/grants, and tuition waivers (partial) available. Support available to part-time students. Financial award application deadline: 6/30; financial award applicants required to submit FAFSA. *Unit head:* Prof. Donald A. Schwartz, Chair and Associate Professor, 858-642-8420, Fax: 858-642-8740, E-mail: dschwartz@nu.edu. *Application contact:* Dominick Giovanniello, Associate Regional Dean—San Diego, 800-NAT-UNIV, Fax: 858-541-7792, E-mail: dgiovann@nu.edu.

New Mexico State University, Graduate School, College of Agriculture, Consumer and Environmental Sciences, Department of Agricultural Economics and Agricultural Business, Las Cruces, NM 88003-8001. Offers agribusiness (M Ag, MBA); agricultural economics (MS); economics (MA). Part-time programs available. *Faculty:* 5 full-time (1 woman), 1 part-time/adjunct (0 women). *Students:* 18 full-time (8 women), 7 part-time (4 women); includes 4 minority (1 African American, 1 American Indian/Alaska Native, 1 Asian American or Pacific Islander, 1 Hispanic American), 6 international. Average age 25. 12 applicants, 75% accepted, 5 enrolled. In 2008, 9 master's awarded. *Degree requirements:* For master's, thesis (for some programs). *Entrance requirements:* For master's, previous course work in intermediate microeconomics, intermediate macroeconomics, college-level calculus, statistics. Additional exam requirements/recommendations for international students: Required—TOEFL. *Application deadline:* For fall admission, 7/1 priority date for domestic and international students; for spring admission, 11/1 priority date for domestic and international students. Applications are processed on a rolling basis. Application fee: $30 ($50 for international students). Electronic applications accepted. *Expenses:* Tuition, area resident: Full-time $3890; part-time $212.85 per credit. Tuition, state resident: full-time $3890; part-time $212.85 per credit. Tuition, nonresident: full-time $13,916; part-time $630.55 per credit. Required fees: $1218; $609 per semester. *Financial support:* In 2008–09, 5 students received support, including 9 research assistantships (averaging $16,217 per year), 5 teaching assistantships (averaging $11,060 per year); career-related internships or fieldwork and health care benefits also available. Financial award application deadline: 3/1. *Faculty research:* Natural resource policy, production economics and farm/ranch management, agribusiness and marketing, international marketing and trade, agricultural risk management. *Unit head:* Dr. Terry Crawford, Head, 575-646-3215, Fax: 575-646-3808, E-mail: crawford@nmsu.edu. *Application contact:* Dr. L. Allen Torell, Professor, 575-646-4732, Fax: 575-646-3808, E-mail: atorell@nmsu.edu.

New Mexico State University, Graduate School, College of Business, Department of Economics and International Business, Las Cruces, NM 88003-8001. Offers economic development (DED); economics (MA); experimental statistics (MS). Part-time programs available. *Faculty:* 11 full-time (0 women), 2 part-time/adjunct (1 woman). *Students:* 43 full-time (15 women), 8 part-time (3 women); includes 11 minority (1 Asian American or Pacific Islander, 10 Hispanic Americans), 27 international. Average age 30. 65 applicants, 75% accepted, 27 enrolled. In 2008, 18 master's awarded. *Degree requirements:* For master's, thesis or alternative; for doctorate, thesis/dissertation or alternative. *Entrance requirements:* For master's, minimum GPA of 3.0; for doctorate, appropriate master's degree. Additional exam requirements/recommendations for international students: Required—TOEFL. *Application deadline:* Applications are processed on a rolling basis. Application fee: $30 ($50 for international students). Electronic applications accepted. *Expenses:* Tuition, area resident: Full-time $3890; part-time $212.85 per credit. Tuition, state resident: full-time $3890; part-time $212.85 per credit. Tuition, nonresident: full-time $13,916; part-time $630.55 per credit. Required fees: $1218; $609 per semester. *Financial support:* In 2008–09, 37 students received support, including 15 research assistantships (averaging $9,955 per year), 19 teaching assistantships (averaging $8,614 per year); fellowships, career-related internships or fieldwork, Federal Work-Study, and health care benefits also available. Support available to part-time students. Financial award application deadline: 3/1. *Faculty research:* Public utilities, environment, linear models, biological sampling, public policy, economics development. *Unit head:* Dr. Anthony Popp, Graduate Adviser, 575-646-5198, Fax: 575-646-1915, E-mail: apopp@nmsu.edu. *Application contact:* Dr. Anthony Popp, Graduate Adviser, 575-646-5198, Fax: 575-646-1915, E-mail: apopp@nmsu.edu.

The New School: A University, The New School for Social Research, Department of Economics, New York, NY 10011. Offers MA, DS Sc, PhD. Part-time and evening/weekend programs available. *Faculty:* 7 full-time (1 woman), 2 part-time/adjunct (0 women). *Students:* 83 full-time (20 women), 49 part-time (14 women); includes 21 minority (8 African Americans, 9 Asian Americans or Pacific Islanders, 4 Hispanic Americans), 64 international. Average age 33. In 2008, 21 master's, 8 doctorates awarded. Terminal master's awarded for partial completion of doctoral program. *Degree requirements:* For master's, exam; for doctorate, one foreign language, thesis/dissertation, qualifying exam. *Entrance requirements:* For master's, GRE General Test; for doctorate, GRE General Test, MA. Additional exam requirements/recommendations for international students: Required—TOEFL (minimum score 600 paper-based; 250 computer-based; 100 iBT). *Application deadline:* For fall admission, 1/15 priority date for domestic students. Applications are processed on a rolling basis. Application fee: $50. *Expenses:* Tuition: Full-time $27,144; part-time $1508 per credit. Required fees: $355 per semester. *Financial support:* Fellowships, research assistantships, teaching assistantships, career-related internships or fieldwork, Federal Work-Study, scholarships/grants, and tuition waivers (full and partial) available. Financial award application deadline: 3/1; financial award applicants required to submit FAFSA. *Faculty research:* Heterodox, history of economic thought, post-Keynesian, global political economy and finance. *Unit head:* Dr. Willi Semmler, Chair, 212-229-5717 Ext. 3050, E-mail: semmlerw@newschool.edu. *Application contact:* Robert MacDonald, Director of Admissions, 800-523-5710 Ext. 3007, Fax: 212-989-7102, E-mail: macdonar@newschool.edu.

See Close-Up on page 1251.

New York University, Graduate School of Arts and Science, Department of Economics, New York, NY 10012-1019. Offers applied economic analysis (Advanced Certificate); economics (MA, PhD); JD/MA; MD/PhD. Part-time and evening/weekend programs available. Terminal master's awarded for partial completion of doctoral program. *Degree requirements:* For master's, thesis; for doctorate, one foreign language, thesis/dissertation, 4 qualifying exams. *Entrance requirements:* For master's and doctorate, GRE General Test; for Advanced Certificate, master's degree. Additional exam requirements/recommendations for international students: Required—TOEFL. *Faculty research:* Economic theory, experimental economics, growth and development, macroeconomics and finance, international trade and international finance.

New York University, Leonard N. Stern School of Business, Department of Economics, New York, NY 10012-1019. Offers MBA, PhD. *Faculty research:* Applied macroeconomics, macroeconomics and macroeconomic policy, international financial markets, international trade and business, game theory.

North Carolina State University, Graduate School, College of Management and College of Agriculture and Life Sciences, Program in Economics, Raleigh, NC 27695. Offers M Econ, MA, PhD. Part-time programs available. Terminal master's awarded for partial completion of doctoral program. *Degree requirements:* For master's, thesis (for some programs); for doctorate, thesis/dissertation. *Entrance requirements:* For master's and doctorate, GRE General Test. Additional exam requirements/recommendations for international students: Required—TOEFL. Electronic applications accepted. *Faculty research:* Endogenous growth modeling, generalized methods of moments estimation, integration and trade, agricultural policy, path dependence and network externalities.

Northeastern University, College of Arts and Sciences, Department of Economics, Boston, MA 02115-5096. Offers MA, PhD. Part-time and evening/weekend programs available. *Degree requirements:* For master's and doctorate, comprehensive exam. *Entrance requirements:* For master's, GRE. Additional exam requirements/recommendations for international students: Required—TOEFL. *Faculty research:* U.S. labor markets, applied economics, microeconomic theory, macroeconomic theory, econometrics.

Northern Illinois University, Graduate School, College of Liberal Arts and Sciences, Department of Economics, De Kalb, IL 60115-2854. Offers MA, PhD. Part-time programs available. Terminal master's awarded for partial completion of doctoral program. *Degree requirements:* For master's, comprehensive exam, thesis or alternative; for doctorate, thesis/dissertation, candidacy exam, dissertation defense, research seminar. *Entrance requirements:* For master's, GRE General Test, minimum GPA of 2.75; for doctorate, GRE General Test, minimum GPA of 2.75 (undergraduate), 3.2 (graduate). Additional exam requirements/recommendations for international students: Required—TOEFL (minimum score 550 paper-based; 213 computer-based). Electronic applications accepted. *Faculty research:* Unemployment, behavior under uncertainty, effect of debt on compensation and capital utilization, racial inequality of earnings.

Northwestern University, The Graduate School, Judd A. and Marjorie Weinberg College of Arts and Sciences, Department of Economics, Evanston, IL 60208. Offers MA, PhD, JD/PhD. Admissions and degrees offered through The Graduate School. *Degree requirements:* For doctorate, thesis/dissertation, preliminary written exam. *Entrance requirements:* For doctorate, GRE General Test. Additional exam requirements/recommendations for international students: Required—TOEFL. *Faculty research:* Organization of industry, behavior of labor markets, effects of monetary policy, theory of markets.

Northwestern University, The Graduate School, Kellogg School of Management, Program in Managerial Economics and Strategy, Evanston, IL 60208. Offers PhD. Admissions and degree offered through The Graduate School. *Degree requirements:* For doctorate, comprehensive exam, thesis/dissertation. *Entrance requirements:* For doctorate, GMAT or GRE General Test. Additional exam requirements/recommendations for international students: Required—TOEFL. Electronic applications accepted. *Faculty research:* Competitive strategy and organization, managerial economics, decision sciences, game theory, operations management.

Oakland University, Graduate Study and Lifelong Learning, School of Business Administration, Department of Economics, Rochester, MI 48309-4401. Offers Certificate.

The Ohio State University, Graduate School, College of Social and Behavioral Sciences, School of Social and Behavioral Science, Department of Economics, Columbus, OH 43210. Offers MA, PhD. *Degree requirements:* For doctorate, thesis/dissertation. *Entrance requirements:* Additional exam requirements/recommendations for international students: Required—TOEFL (minimum score 600 paper-based; 250 computer-based). Electronic applications accepted.

Ohio University, Graduate College, College of Arts and Sciences, Department of Economics, Athens, OH 45701-2979. Offers applied economics (MA); financial economics (MFE). Evening/weekend programs available. *Degree requirements:* For master's, thesis or alternative. *Entrance requirements:* For master's, GRE or GMAT, minimum GPA of 3.0. Additional exam requirements/recommendations for international students: Required—TOEFL (minimum score 550 paper-based). *Faculty research:* Macroeconomics, public finance, international economics and finance, monetary theory, healthcare economics.

Oklahoma State University, William S. Spears School of Business, Department of Economics and Legal Studies in Business, Stillwater, OK 74078. Offers MS, PhD. *Faculty:* 21 full-time (5 women), 4 part-time/adjunct (2 women). *Students:* 27 full-time (8 women), 17 part-time (5 women); includes 2 minority (1 African American, 1 American Indian/Alaska Native), 28 international. Average age 31. 53 applicants, 45% accepted, 12 enrolled. In 2008, 6 master's, 3 doctorates awarded. *Degree requirements:* For master's, thesis or alternative; for doctorate, comprehensive exam, thesis/dissertation. *Entrance requirements:* For master's and doctorate, GRE or GMAT. Additional exam requirements/recommendations for international students: Required—TOEFL. *Application deadline:* For fall admission, 3/1 priority date for international students; for spring admission, 8/1 priority date for international students. Applications are processed on a rolling basis. Application fee: $40 ($75 for international students). Electronic applications accepted. *Expenses:* Tuition, state resident: full-time $3716.40; part-time $154.85 per credit hour. Tuition, nonresident: full-time $14,448; part-time $602 per credit hour. Required fees: $1772.40; $73.85 per credit hour. One-time fee: $50. Tuition and fees vary according to course load and campus/location. *Financial support:* In 2008–09, 22 teaching assistantships (averaging $13,205 per year) were awarded; career-related internships or fieldwork, Federal Work-Study, scholarships/grants, health care benefits, tuition waivers (partial), and unspecified assistantships also available. Support available to part-time students. Financial award application deadline: 3/1; financial award applicants required to submit FAFSA. *Faculty research:* Economics and legal studies in business regional economic modeling/econometrics, urban/regional economics, monetary economics, international trade/finance/development, environmental economics. *Unit head:* Dr. Jim Fain, Head, 405-744-5195, Fax: 405-744-5180. *Application contact:* Dr. Gordon Emslie, Dean, 405-744-6368, Fax: 405-744-0355, E-mail: grad_i@okstate.edu.

Economics

Oklahoma State University, William S. Spears School of Business, Department of Finance, Stillwater, OK 74078. Offers finance (PhD); quantitative financial economics (MS). Part-time programs available. *Faculty:* 14 full-time (2 women), 6 part-time/adjunct (1 woman). *Students:* 24 full-time (7 women), 6 part-time (2 women); includes 1 minority (Asian American or Pacific Islander), 11 international. Average age 29. 77 applicants, 21% accepted, 8 enrolled. In 2008, 14 master's, 1 doctorate awarded. *Degree requirements:* For master's, thesis or alternative; for doctorate, comprehensive exam, thesis/dissertation. *Entrance requirements:* For master's and doctorate, GRE or GMAT. Additional exam requirements/recommendations for international students: Required—TOEFL. *Application deadline:* For fall admission, 3/1 priority date for international students; for spring admission, 8/1 priority date for international students. Applications are processed on a rolling basis. Application fee: $40 ($75 for international students). Electronic applications accepted. *Expenses:* Tuition, state resident: full-time $3716.40; part-time $154.85 per credit hour. Tuition, nonresident: full-time $14,448; part-time $602 per credit hour. Required fees: $1772.40; $73.85 per credit hour. One-time fee: $50. Tuition and fees vary according to course load and campus/location. *Financial support:* In 2008–09, 4 research assistantships (averaging $18,984 per year), 4 teaching assistantships (averaging $30,492 per year) were awarded; career-related internships or fieldwork, Federal Work-Study, scholarships/grants, health care benefits, tuition waivers (partial), and unspecified assistantships also available. Support available to part-time students. Financial award application deadline: 3/1; financial award applicants required to submit FAFSA. *Faculty research:* Corporate risk management, derivatives banking, investments and securities issuance, corporate governance, banking. *Unit head:* Dr. John Polonchek, Head, 405-744-5199, Fax: 405-744-5180. *Application contact:* Dr. Gordon Emslie, Dean, 405-744-6368, Fax: 405-744-0355, E-mail: grad_i@okstate.edu.

Old Dominion University, College of Business and Public Administration, Program in Economics, Norfolk, VA 23529. Offers MA. Part-time and evening/weekend programs available. *Faculty:* 11 full-time (1 woman). *Students:* 13 full-time (3 women), 12 part-time (4 women); includes 6 minority (4 African Americans, 1 Asian American or Pacific Islander, 1 Hispanic American), 6 international. Average age 30. 25 applicants, 84% accepted, 11 enrolled. In 2008, 10 master's awarded. *Degree requirements:* For master's, comprehensive exam, thesis optional, independent research. *Entrance requirements:* For master's, GMAT or GRE General Test, minimum GPA of 2.5. Additional exam requirements/recommendations for international students: Required—TOEFL (minimum score 520 paper-based; 213 computer-based; 79 iBT). *Application deadline:* For fall admission, 8/1 priority date for domestic students; for spring admission, 10/1 priority date for domestic students. Applications are processed on a rolling basis. Application fee: $40. Electronic applications accepted. *Expenses:* Tuition, area resident: Full-time $7704; part-time $321 per credit. Tuition, state resident: full-time $7704; part-time $321 per credit. Tuition, nonresident: full-time $19,104; part-time $796 per credit. Required fees: $99 per semester. One-time fee: $40. *Financial support:* In 2008–09, 4 students received support, including 4 teaching assistantships with tuition reimbursements available (averaging $12,000 per year); research assistantships with tuition reimbursements available, career-related internships or fieldwork, scholarships/grants, tuition waivers (partial), and unspecified assistantships also available. Financial award application deadline: 8/1; financial award applicants required to submit FAFSA. *Faculty research:* International economics, transportation, monetary economics, immigration, econometrics. *Unit head:* Dr. David Duden Selover, Graduate Program Director, 757-683-3541, Fax: 757-638-5639, E-mail: dselover@odu.edu. *Application contact:* Dr. Ali Ardalan, Associate Dean, 757-683-3520, Fax: 757-683-4076, E-mail: aardalan@odu.edu.

Oregon State University, Graduate School, College of Agricultural Sciences, Department of Agricultural and Resource Economics, Corvallis, OR 97331. Offers agricultural and resource economics (M Agr, MAIS, MS, PhD); economics (MS, PhD). MS and PhD in economics offered through the University Graduate Faculty of Economics. Part-time programs available. Terminal master's awarded for partial completion of doctoral program. *Degree requirements:* For master's, thesis (for some programs); for doctorate, thesis/dissertation. *Entrance requirements:* For master's and doctorate, GRE General Test, minimum GPA of 3.0 in last 90 hours. Additional exam requirements/recommendations for international students: Required—TOEFL. *Faculty research:* Marine economics, environmental economics, effects of global climate change on agriculture, efficiency of agricultural markets, analysis of aquaculture development.

Oregon State University, Graduate School, College of Forestry, Department of Forest Resources, Corvallis, OR 97331. Offers economics (MS, PhD); forest resources (MAIS, MF, MS, PhD). MS and PhD programs in economics offered through the University Graduate Faculty of Economics. *Accreditation:* SAF (one or more programs are accredited). Part-time programs available. Terminal master's awarded for partial completion of doctoral program. *Degree requirements:* For master's, thesis (for some programs); for doctorate, thesis/dissertation. *Entrance requirements:* For master's and doctorate, GRE General Test, minimum GPA of 3.0 in last 90 hours. Additional exam requirements/recommendations for international students: Required—TOEFL. *Faculty research:* Geographic information systems, long-term productivity, recreation, silviculture, biometrics, policy.

Oregon State University, Graduate School, College of Liberal Arts, Department of Economics, Corvallis, OR 97331. Offers MA, MS, PhD. Part-time programs available. Terminal master's awarded for partial completion of doctoral program. *Degree requirements:* For master's, thesis or alternative; for doctorate, thesis/dissertation. *Entrance requirements:* For master's and doctorate, GRE General Test, minimum GPA of 3.0 in last 90 hours. Additional exam requirements/recommendations for international students: Required—TOEFL. *Faculty research:* Applied microeconomics, applied econometrics.

Pace University, Lubin School of Business, Program in Business Economics, New York, NY 10038. Offers corporate economic planning (MBA); financial economics (MBA); international economics (MBA). Part-time and evening/weekend programs available. *Entrance requirements:* For master's, GMAT. Electronic applications accepted.

Penn State University Park, Graduate School, College of the Liberal Arts, Department of Economics, State College, University Park, PA 16802-1503. Offers MA, PhD.

Pepperdine University, School of Public Policy, Malibu, CA 90263. Offers American politics (MPP); economics (MPP); international relations (MPP); public policy (MPP); state and local policy (MPP). *Entrance requirements:* For master's, GRE, 2 letters of recommendation, resumé. Additional exam requirements/recommendations for international students: Required—TOEFL. Electronic applications accepted.

Peru State College, Graduate Programs, Program in Organizational Management, Peru, NE 68421. Offers MS. Program offered online only. Part-time programs available. *Degree requirements:* For master's, thesis (for some programs). *Expenses:* Contact institution. *Faculty research:* Emotional intelligence.

Portland State University, Graduate Studies, College of Liberal Arts and Sciences, Department of Economics, Portland, OR 97207-0751. Offers applied economics (MA, MS); economics (PhD); general economics (MA, MS). Part-time programs available. *Faculty:* 17 full-time (6 women), 3 part-time/adjunct (0 women). *Students:* 12 full-time (2 women), 7 part-time (3 women); includes 2 minority (both Asian Americans or Pacific Islanders), 5 international. Average age 29. 17 applicants, 59% accepted, 8 enrolled. In 2008, 10 master's awarded. *Degree requirements:* For master's, thesis optional; for doctorate, one foreign language, thesis/dissertation. *Entrance requirements:* For master's, minimum GPA of 3.0 in upper-division course work or 2.75 overall, course work in calculus. Additional exam requirements/recommendations for international students: Required—TOEFL (minimum score 550 paper-based; 213 computer-based). *Application deadline:* For fall admission, 4/1 for domestic students, 3/1 for international students; for spring admission, 11/1 for domestic and international students. Applications are processed on a rolling basis. Application fee: $50. *Expenses:* Tuition, area resident: Full-time $8763; part-time $179 per credit hour. Tuition, state resident: full-time $8763; part-time $298 per credit hour. Tuition, nonresident: full-time $12,981; part-time $426 per credit hour. Required fees: $1242. One-time fee: $250. Tuition and fees vary according to course load and program. *Financial support:* In 2008–09, 4 research assistantships with full tuition reimbursements (averaging $6,372 per year), 1 teaching assistantship (averaging $8,820 per year) were awarded; career-related internships or fieldwork, Federal Work-Study, and unspecified assistantships also available. Support available to part-time students. Financial award application deadline: 3/1; financial award applicants required to submit FAFSA. *Faculty research:* NAFTA, economies of transition, economics of Eastern Europe, artificial intelligence, comparative economic systems. Total annual research expenditures: $64,962. *Unit head:* Dr. Randy Bluffstone, Chair, 503-725-3915, Fax: 503-725-3945. *Application contact:* Rita Spears, Office Specialist, 503-725-3941, Fax: 503-725-3945, E-mail: spearsr@pdx.edu.

Portland State University, Graduate Studies, Systems Science Program, Portland, OR 97207-0751. Offers computational intelligence (Certificate); computer modeling and simulation (Certificate); systems science (MS); systems science/anthropology (PhD); systems science/business administration (PhD); systems science/civil engineering (PhD); systems science/economics (PhD); systems science/engineering management (PhD); systems science/general (PhD); systems science/mathematical sciences (PhD); systems science/mechanical engineering (PhD); systems science/psychology (PhD); systems science/sociology (PhD). *Faculty:* 3 full-time (0 women). *Students:* 12 full-time (3 women), 13 part-time (3 women); includes 2 minority (1 American Indian/Alaska Native, 1 Asian American or Pacific Islander), 5 international. Average age 38. 14 applicants, 71% accepted, 8 enrolled. In 2008, 2 master's, 4 doctorates awarded. *Degree requirements:* For doctorate, variable foreign language requirement, thesis/dissertation. *Entrance requirements:* For master's, 2 letters of recommendation; for doctorate, GMAT, GRE General Test, minimum undergraduate GPA of 3.0. Additional exam requirements/recommendations for international students: Required—TOEFL. *Application deadline:* For fall admission, 2/1 for domestic students; for spring admission, 11/1 for domestic students. Application fee: $50. *Expenses:* Tuition, area resident: Full-time $8763; part-time $179 per credit hour. Tuition, state resident: full-time $8763; part-time $298 per credit hour. Tuition, nonresident: full-time $12,981; part-time $426 per credit hour. Required fees: $1242. One-time fee: $250. Tuition and fees vary according to course load and program. *Financial support:* In 2008–09, 1 research assistantship with full tuition reimbursement (averaging $7,704 per year) was awarded; teaching assistantships with full tuition reimbursements, career-related internships or fieldwork, Federal Work-Study, scholarships/grants, and unspecified assistantships also available. Support available to part-time students. Financial award application deadline: 3/1; financial award applicants required to submit FAFSA. *Faculty research:* Systems theory and methodology, artificial intelligence neural networks, information theory, nonlinear dynamics/chaos, modeling and simulation. *Unit head:* George Lendaris, Acting Director, 503-725-4960. *Application contact:* Dawn Sharafi, Administrative Assistant, 503-725-4960, E-mail: dawn@sysc.pdx.edu.

Princeton University, Graduate School, Department of Economics, Princeton, NJ 08544-1019. Offers PhD. *Degree requirements:* For doctorate, thesis/dissertation. *Entrance requirements:* For doctorate, GRE General Test, GRE Subject Test (recommended), working knowledge of multivariate calculus and matrix algebra. Additional exam requirements/recommendations for international students: Required—TOEFL (minimum score 600 paper-based; 250 computer-based). Electronic applications accepted.

Princeton University, Graduate School, Program in Population Studies, Princeton, NJ 08544-1019. Offers demography (PhD, Certificate); economics and demography (PhD); public affairs and demography (PhD); sociology and demography (PhD). *Degree requirements:* For doctorate, thesis/dissertation. *Entrance requirements:* For doctorate, GRE General Test. Additional exam requirements/recommendations for international students: Required—TOEFL (minimum score 600 paper-based; 250 computer-based). Electronic applications accepted. *Faculty research:* Models, fertility, infant and child mortality, migration.

Providence College, Graduate Studies, School of Business, Providence, RI 02918. Offers accountancy (MBA); economics (MBA); entrepreneurship (MBA); finance (MBA); international business (MBA); management (MBA); marketing (MBA); not-for-profit (MBA); quantitative (MBA). Part-time and evening/weekend programs available. *Faculty:* 9 full-time (2 women), 9 part-time/adjunct (2 women). *Students:* 49 full-time (15 women), 46 part-time (23 women); includes 4 minority (2 African Americans, 1 Asian American or Pacific Islander, 1 Hispanic American), 2 international. Average age 27. 56 applicants, 93% accepted, 50 enrolled. In 2008, 40 master's awarded. *Degree requirements:* For master's, thesis optional. *Entrance requirements:* For master's, GMAT. Additional exam requirements/recommendations for international students: Required—TOEFL (minimum score 550 paper-based; 213 computer-based; 80 iBT). *Application deadline:* For fall admission, 8/1 priority date for domestic and international students; for spring admission, 12/1 priority date for domestic and international students. Applications are processed on a rolling basis. Application fee: $55. *Expenses:* Contact institution. *Financial support:* In 2008–09, 34 research assistantships with full tuition reimbursements (averaging $8,400 per year) were awarded; Federal Work-Study, institutionally sponsored loans, and unspecified assistantships also available. Support available to part-time students. Financial award application deadline: 8/1; financial award applicants required to submit FAFSA. *Unit head:* Dr. MaryJane Lenon, Director, MBA Program, 401-865-2566, Fax: 401-865-2978, E-mail: mjlenon@providence.edu. *Application contact:* Katherine A. Follett, Administrative Coordinator, 401-865-2333, Fax: 401-865-2978, E-mail: kfollett@providence.edu.

Purdue University, Graduate School, Krannert School of Management, Doctoral Program in Economics, West Lafayette, IN 47907.

Regent University, Graduate School, Robertson School of Government, Virginia Beach, VA 23464. Offers health care policy and administration (MA); international politics (MA); law and public policy (MA); Mid-East Politics (MA); political leadership and management (MA); political management (MA); public administration (MA); public policy (MA); terrorism and homeland defense (MA); world economies and political development (MA); JD/MA; M Div/MA; M Ed/MA; MBA/MA. Part-time and evening/weekend programs available. Postbaccalaureate distance learning degree programs offered (minimal on-campus study). *Faculty:* 6 full-time (1 woman), 11 part-time/adjunct (1 woman). *Students:* 60 full-time (33 women), 69 part-time (34 women); includes 29 minority (22 African Americans, 1 Asian American or Pacific Islander, 6 Hispanic Americans), 3 international. Average age 30. 136 applicants, 54% accepted, 54 enrolled. In 2008, 48 master's awarded. *Degree requirements:* For master's, thesis optional, internship. *Entrance requirements:* For master's, GRE General Test or LSAT, minimum undergraduate GPA of 3.0, writing sample, resumé, interview, references, transcripts. Additional exam requirements/recommendations for international students: Required—TOEFL (minimum score 577 paper-based; 233 computer-based). *Application deadline:* For fall admission, 5/1 priority date for domestic students; for spring admission, 11/1 priority date for domestic students. Applications are processed on a rolling basis. Application fee: $50. Electronic applications accepted. *Expenses:* Contact institution. *Financial support:* Career-related internships or fieldwork, scholarships/grants, tuition waivers (full and partial), and unspecified assistantships available. Support available to part-time students. Financial award application deadline: 9/1; financial award applicants required to submit FAFSA. *Faculty research:* Education reform, political character issues, social capital concerns, administrative ethics, Biblical law and public policy. *Unit head:* Dr. Charles W. Dunn, Dean, 757-352-4322, Fax: 757-352-4643, E-mail: cwdunn@regent.edu. *Application contact:* Matthew Chadwick, Director of Admissions, 800-373-5504, Fax: 757-352-4381, E-mail: admissions@regent.edu.

Rensselaer Polytechnic Institute, Graduate School, School of Humanities and Social Sciences, Department of Economics, Program in Economics, Troy, NY 12180-3590. Offers MS. Part-time programs available. *Degree requirements:* For master's, thesis. *Entrance requirements:* For master's, GRE General Test. Additional exam requirements/recommendations for international students: Required—TOEFL (minimum score 570 paper-based; 230 computer-based), TWE. Electronic applications accepted. *Faculty research:* Economic development, cost-benefit analysis, productivity and technological change, international economics.

Rensselaer Polytechnic Institute, Graduate School, School of Humanities and Social Sciences, Program in Ecological Economics, Values, and Policy, Troy, NY 12180-3590. Offers MS. Part-time programs available. *Degree requirements:* For master's, professional project. *Entrance requirements:* For master's, GRE General Test. Additional exam requirements/recommendations for international students: Required—TOEFL (minimum score 600 paper-based; 250 computer-based). Electronic applications accepted. *Faculty research:* Environmental politics and policy, environmentalism, political economy, third world politics, environmental health.

Rice University, Graduate Programs, School of Social Sciences, Department of Economics, Houston, TX 77251-1892. Offers MA, PhD. *Degree requirements:* For master's, thesis; for doctorate, thesis/dissertation. *Entrance requirements:* For master's and doctorate, GRE General Test, minimum GPA of 3.0. Additional exam requirements/recommendations for international students: Required—TOEFL (minimum score 600 paper-based; 250 computer-based; 90 iBT). Electronic applications accepted. *Faculty research:* Income distribution and small-scale industry in less developed countries, international commodity markets, microeconomic foundations, urban development, optimal taxation.

Roosevelt University, Graduate Division, College of Arts and Sciences, Department of Economics, Chicago, IL 60605-1394. Offers applied economics (MA); economics (MA). Part-time and evening/weekend programs available. *Students:* 11 full-time (3 women), 13 part-time (3 women); includes 4 minority (2 African Americans, 1 American Indian/Alaska Native, 1 Asian American or Pacific Islander), 3 international. Average age 29. 48 applicants, 67% accepted, 10 enrolled. In 2008, 6 master's awarded. *Degree requirements:* For master's, thesis or alternative. *Entrance requirements:* For master's, minimum GPA of 2.7. *Application deadline:* For fall admission, 6/1 priority date for domestic students. Applications are processed on a rolling basis. Application fee: $25 ($35 for international students). *Expenses:* Tuition: Full-time $14,730; part-time $709 per credit. Required fees: $175 per semester. Tuition and fees vary according to course load and program. *Financial support:* In 2008–09, 4 students received support, including 1 teaching assistantship; career-related internships or fieldwork, Federal Work-Study, scholarships/grants, and tuition waivers (full and partial) also available. Financial award application deadline: 2/15. *Faculty research:* Labor, gender issues, international trade and development, entrepreneurship, political economy and money. Total annual research expenditures: $5,000. *Unit head:* June Lapidus, Head, 312-341-3670. *Application contact:* Joanne Canyon-Heller, Coordinator of Graduate Admission, 877-APPLY RU, Fax: 312-281-3356, E-mail: applyru@roosevelt.edu.

Rutgers, The State University of New Jersey, Newark, Graduate School, Program in Economics, Newark, NJ 07102. Offers MA. *Entrance requirements:* For master's, GRE, minimum undergraduate B average.

Rutgers, The State University of New Jersey, Newark, Rutgers Business SchoolûNewark and New Brunswick, Department of Finance and Economics, Newark, NJ 07102. Offers MBA, MQF. *Entrance requirements:* For master's, GMAT (MBA), GRE (MQF). Additional exam requirements/recommendations for international students: Required—TOEFL.

Rutgers, The State University of New Jersey, New Brunswick, Graduate School, Program in Economics, Piscataway, NJ 08854-8097. Offers MA, PhD. Terminal master's awarded for partial completion of doctoral program. *Degree requirements:* For master's, comprehensive exam (for some programs), thesis or alternative; for doctorate, comprehensive exam, thesis/dissertation. *Entrance requirements:* For master's and doctorate, GRE General Test. Additional exam requirements/recommendations for international students: Required—TOEFL. Electronic applications accepted. *Faculty research:* Econometrics, microeconomics, macroeconomics, economichistory.

St. Cloud State University, School of Graduate Studies, College of Social Sciences, Department of Economics, St. Cloud, MN 56301-4498. Offers applied economics (MS); public and nonprofit institutions (MS). Part-time programs available. *Degree requirements:* For master's, thesis or alternative. *Entrance requirements:* For master's, GRE General Test, minimum GPA of 2.75. Additional exam requirements/recommendations for international students: Recommended—TOEFL (minimum score 550 paper-based; 213 computer-based), IELTS (minimum score 6.5). Electronic applications accepted.

San Diego State University, Graduate and Research Affairs, College of Arts and Letters, Department of Economics, San Diego, CA 92182. Offers MA. *Entrance requirements:* For master's, GRE General Test, 2 letters of recommendation. Additional exam requirements/recommendations for international students: Required—TOEFL. Electronic applications accepted. *Faculty research:* Financing public education, demand for alternative fuel vehicles, economics of the Gold Rush, interdependence of equity and economic efficiency, economics of welfare.

San Francisco State University, Division of Graduate Studies, College of Behavioral and Social Sciences, Department of Economics, San Francisco, CA 94132-1722. Offers MA.

San Jose State University, Graduate Studies and Research, College of Social Sciences, Department of Economics, San Jose, CA 95192-0001. Offers applied economics (MA); economics (MA). Part-time programs available. *Degree requirements:* For master's, comprehensive exam, thesis optional. *Entrance requirements:* For master's, GRE, minimum GPA of 3.0. Electronic applications accepted.

Simon Fraser University, Graduate Studies, Faculty of Arts and Social Sciences, Department of Economics, Burnaby, BC V5A 1S6, Canada. Offers MA, PhD. Evening/weekend programs available. *Degree requirements:* For doctorate, comprehensive exam, thesis/dissertation. *Entrance requirements:* For master's, GRE, minimum GPA of 3.0; for doctorate, GRE, minimum GPA of 3.5. Additional exam requirements/recommendations for international students: Required—TWE or IELTS. *Faculty research:* Industrial organization, public economics, econometrics, labor, macroeconomics.

South Dakota State University, Graduate School, College of Agriculture and Biological Sciences, Department of Economics, Brookings, SD 57007. Offers MS. *Faculty:* 16 full-time (2 women). *Students:* 20 full-time (3 women), 6 part-time (2 women); includes 8 minority (2 African Americans, 6 Asian Americans or Pacific Islanders). 21 applicants, 62% accepted, 13 enrolled. In 2008, 11 master's awarded. *Degree requirements:* For master's, comprehensive exam, thesis (for some programs), oral exam. *Entrance requirements:* For master's, minimum GPA of 2.75. Additional exam requirements/recommendations for international students: Required—TOEFL (minimum score 550 paper-based; 213 computer-based; 79 iBT). *Application deadline:* For fall admission, 4/15 priority date for international students; for spring admission, 8/15 priority date for international students. Applications are processed on a rolling basis. Application fee: $35. *Financial support:* In 2008–09, 5 research assistantships with partial tuition reimbursements (averaging $15,750 per year), 2 teaching assistantships with partial tuition reimbursements (averaging $15,750 per year) were awarded; scholarships/grants and unspecified assistantships also available. *Faculty research:* Sustainable agriculture, rural finance, grain and livestock marketing, agricultural policy, applied economics. *Unit head:* Dr. Richard Shane, Acting Head, 605-688-4141, Fax: 605-688-6386, E-mail: richard.shane@sdstate.edu. *Application contact:* Dr. Joseph Santos, Graduate Coordinator, 605-688-4846, Fax: 605-688-6386, E-mail: joseph.santos@sdstate.edu.

Southern Illinois University Carbondale, Graduate School, College of Liberal Arts, Department of Economics, Carbondale, IL 62901-4701. Offers MA, MS, PhD. *Degree requirements:* For master's, thesis; for doctorate, thesis/dissertation. *Entrance requirements:* For master's, GRE General Test, minimum GPA of 2.7; for doctorate, GRE General Test, minimum GPA of 3.25. Additional exam requirements/recommendations for international students: Required—TOEFL. *Faculty research:* Advanced economic theory, applied microeconomics, economic development, finance, international economics, monetary theory and policy.

See Close-Up on page 775.

Southern Illinois University Edwardsville, Graduate Studies and Research, School of Business, Department of Economics and Finance, Edwardsville, IL 62026-0001. Offers MA, MS. Part-time and evening/weekend programs available. *Faculty:* 14 full-time (4 women). *Students:* 20 full-time (8 women), 12 part-time (4 women), 18 international. Average age 26. 44 applicants, 30% accepted. In 2008, 20 master's awarded. *Degree requirements:* For master's, thesis or alternative, final exam, portfolio. *Entrance requirements:* For master's, GMAT or GRE. Additional exam requirements/recommendations for international students: Required—TOEFL (minimum score 550 paper-based; 213 computer-based; 79 iBT), IELTS (minimum score 6.5). *Application deadline:* For fall admission, 7/20 for domestic students, 6/1 for international students; for spring admission, 12/14 for domestic students, 10/1 for international students. Applications are processed on a rolling basis. Application fee: $30. Electronic applications accepted. *Expenses:* Tuition, area resident: Full-time $5838. Tuition, nonresident: full-time $14,596. Required fees: $1525. *Financial support:* In 2008–09, 2 fellowships with full tuition reimbursements (averaging $8,370 per year), 5 research assistantships with full tuition reimbursements (averaging $8,064 per year), 14 teaching assistantships with full tuition reimbursements (averaging $8,064 per year) were awarded; career-related internships or fieldwork, Federal Work-Study, institutionally sponsored loans, traineeships, and unspecified assistantships also available. Support available to part-time students. Financial award application deadline: 3/1; financial award applicants required to submit FAFSA. *Unit head:* Dr. Rik Hafer, Chair, 618-650-2542, E-mail: rhafer@siue.edu. *Application contact:* Dr. Ali Kutan, Director, 618-650-3473, E-mail: akutan@siue.edu.

Southern Methodist University, Dedman College, Department of Economics, Dallas, TX 75205. Offers applied economics (MA); economics (MA, PhD); JD/MA. Part-time and evening/weekend programs available. *Faculty:* 19 full-time (5 women), 17 part-time/adjunct (5 women). *Students:* 38 full-time (18 women), 34 part-time (12 women); includes 9 minority (3 African Americans, 1 American Indian/Alaska Native, 3 Asian Americans or Pacific Islanders, 2 Hispanic Americans), 37 international. Average age 27. 85 applicants, 89% accepted, 16 enrolled. In 2008, 22 master's, 2 doctorates awarded. Terminal master's awarded for partial completion of doctoral program. *Degree requirements:* For master's, thesis, oral qualifying exam; for doctorate, thesis/dissertation, written exams. *Entrance requirements:* For master's, GRE General Test or GMAT, 12 hours course work in economics, minimum GPA of 3.0, previous course work in calculus and statistics; for doctorate, GRE General Test, minimum GPA of 3.0, 3 semesters of course work in calculus, 1 semester of course work in statistics, 1 semester of course work in linear algebra. Additional exam requirements/recommendations for international students: Required—TOEFL (minimum score 550 paper-based; 213 computer-based). *Application deadline:* For fall admission, 2/1 priority date for domestic students; for spring admission, 11/30 priority date for domestic students. Applications are processed on a rolling basis. Application fee: $75. Electronic applications accepted. *Financial support:* In 2008–09, 23 students received support, including 1 fellowship with full tuition reimbursement available (averaging $16,000 per year), 2 research assistantships with full tuition reimbursements available (averaging $16,000 per year), 20 teaching assistantships with full tuition reimbursements available (averaging $16,000 per year); tuition waivers (partial) also available. Financial award application deadline: 2/1; financial award applicants required to submit FAFSA. *Faculty research:* Economic theory, game theory, econometrics, international trade, labor. *Unit head:* Dr. Kamal Saggi, Chair, 214-768-3274, Fax: 214-768-1821, E-mail: ksaggi@mail.smu.edu. *Application contact:* Stephanie Hall, Information Contact, 214-768-2694, E-mail: eco@smu.edu.

Stanford University, School of Humanities and Sciences, Department of Economics, Stanford, CA 94305-9991. Offers PhD. *Degree requirements:* For doctorate, thesis/dissertation, oral exam. *Entrance requirements:* For doctorate, GRE General Test. Additional exam requirements/recommendations for international students: Required—TOEFL. Electronic applications accepted.

State University of New York at Binghamton, Graduate School, School of Arts and Sciences, Department of Economics, Binghamton, NY 13902-6000. Offers economics (MA, PhD); economics and finance (MA, PhD). *Faculty:* 23 full-time (4 women), 4 part-time/adjunct (0 women). *Students:* 53 full-time (22 women), 17 part-time (7 women); includes 4 minority (1 African American, 2 Asian Americans or Pacific Islanders, 1 Hispanic American), 52 international. Average age 28. 169 applicants, 59% accepted, 15 enrolled. In 2008, 14 master's, 1 doctorate awarded. Terminal master's awarded for partial completion of doctoral program. *Degree requirements:* For doctorate, thesis/dissertation. *Entrance requirements:* For master's and doctorate, GRE General Test. Additional exam requirements/recommendations for international students: Required—TOEFL. *Application deadline:* For fall admission, 8/15 priority date for domestic students, 1/15 priority date for international students; for spring admission, 11/1 for domestic students, 10/1 priority date for international students. Applications are processed on a rolling basis. Application fee: $60. Electronic applications accepted. *Expenses:* Tuition, area resident: Full-time $6900; part-time $288 per credit. Tuition, state resident: full-time $6900; part-time $288 per credit. Tuition, nonresident: full-time $10,920; part-time $455 per credit. Required fees: $1130. Part-time tuition and fees vary according to course load, program and student level. *Financial support:* In 2008–09, 34 students received support, including 4 fellowships with full tuition reimbursements available (averaging $14,500 per year), 1 research assistantship with full tuition reimbursement available (averaging $14,500 per year), 29 teaching assistantships with full tuition reimbursements available (averaging $14,500 per year); career-related internships or fieldwork, Federal Work-Study, institutionally sponsored loans, scholarships/grants, health care benefits, and unspecified assistantships also available. Financial award application deadline: 2/15; financial award applicants required to submit FAFSA. *Unit head:* Dr. Clifford Kern, Chairperson, 607-777-2228, E-mail: ckern@binghamton.edu. *Application contact:* Victoria Williams, Recruiting and Admissions Coordinator, 607-777-2151, Fax: 607-777-2501, E-mail: vwilliam@binghamton.edu.

Stony Brook University, State University of New York, Graduate School, College of Arts and Sciences, Department of Economics, Stony Brook, NY 11794. Offers MA, PhD. *Faculty:* 12 full-time (1 woman), 5 part-time/adjunct (0 women). *Students:* 45 full-time (28 women), 41 international. Average age 28. 139 applicants, 22% accepted. In 2008, 19 master's, 9 doctorates awarded. *Degree requirements:* For doctorate, comprehensive exam, thesis/dissertation. *Entrance requirements:* For master's and doctorate, GRE General Test. Additional exam requirements/recommendations for international students: Required—TOEFL. *Application deadline:* For fall admission, 1/15 for domestic students. Application fee: $60. *Expenses:* Tuition, area resident: Full-time $7880; part-time $328 per credit hour. Tuition, state resident: full-time $7880; part-time $328 per credit hour. Tuition, nonresident: full-time $13,250; part-time $552 per credit hour. Required fees: $848. *Financial support:* In 2008–09, 1 research assistantship, 35 teaching assistantships were awarded; fellowships also available. *Faculty research:* Economic theory, game theory, econometrics, macroeconomics, applied microeconomics. Total annual research expenditures: $134,701. *Unit head:* Dr. William Dawes, Co-Chair, 631-632-7530. *Application contact:* Dr. Sandro Brusco, Director of Graduate Studies, 631-632-7548, E-mail: sbrusco@notes.cc.sunysb.edu.

Suffolk University, College of Arts and Sciences, Department of Economics, Boston, MA 02108-2770. Offers economic policy (MSEP); economics (MSE, PhD); international economics (MSIE); JD/MSIE. Part-time and evening/weekend programs available. *Degree requirements:* For doctorate, comprehensive exam, thesis/dissertation. *Entrance requirements:* For master's, GRE General Test or GMAT, statement of professional goals, official transcripts, 2 letters of recommendation, resumé; for doctorate, GRE General Test, 3 letters of recommendation. Additional exam requirements/recommendations for international students: Required—TOEFL (minimum score 550 paper-based; 213 computer-based; 80 iBT). Electronic applications accepted. *Expenses:* Contact institution. *Faculty research:* Trade demands, fair tax, smoking, multinational firms, charitable giving, fair tax.

See Close-Up on page 777.

Syracuse University, Graduate School, Maxwell School of Citizenship and Public Affairs, Program in Economics, Syracuse, NY 13244. Offers MA, PhD. *Degree requirements:* For

Economics

Syracuse University (continued)
doctorate, comprehensive exam, thesis/dissertation. *Entrance requirements:* For master's and doctorate, GRE General Test. Additional exam requirements/recommendations for international students: Required—TOEFL. Electronic applications accepted. *Faculty research:* International economics, labor economics, public finance, urban economics.

Tarleton State University, College of Graduate Studies, College of Business Administration, Department of Accounting, Finance and Economics, Stephenville, TX 76402. Offers business administration (MBA). Part-time and evening/weekend programs available. *Faculty:* 7 full-time (0 women). *Students:* 50 full-time (21 women), 213 part-time (120 women); includes 63 minority (36 African Americans, 2 American Indian/Alaska Native, 3 Asian Americans or Pacific Islanders, 22 Hispanic Americans), 3 international. Average age 32. 157 applicants, 87% accepted, 100 enrolled. In 2008, 52 master's awarded. *Degree requirements:* For master's, comprehensive exam. *Entrance requirements:* For master's, GRE or GMAT, minimum GPA of 3.0. Additional exam requirements/recommendations for international students: Required—TOEFL (minimum score 550 paper-based; 213 computer-based; 80 iBT). *Application deadline:* For fall admission, 8/5 priority date for domestic students; for spring admission, 12/1 for domestic students. Applications are processed on a rolling basis. Application fee: $30 ($130 for international students). Electronic applications accepted. *Expenses:* Tuition, area resident: Full-time $2853; part-time $158.50 per credit hour. Tuition, state resident: full-time $2853; part-time $158.50 per credit hour. Tuition, nonresident: full-time $7551; part-time $419.50 per credit hour. Required fees: $1040; $42 per credit hour. $124 per semester. Tuition and fees vary according to course load and campus/location. *Financial support:* In 2008–09, 3 research assistantships (averaging $12,000 per year) were awarded; teaching assistantships. Financial award application deadline: 5/1; financial award applicants required to submit FAFSA. *Unit head:* Dr. Sankar Sundarrajan, Department Head, 254-968-9913, Fax: 254-968-9665, E-mail: sundar@tarleton.edu. *Application contact:* Information Contact, 254-968-9104, Fax: 254-968-9670, E-mail: gradoffice@tarleton.edu.

Teachers College, Columbia University, Graduate Faculty of Education, Department of International and Transcultural Studies, Program in Economics and Education, New York, NY 10027-6696. Offers Ed M, MA, Ed D, PhD. *Faculty:* 3 full-time (0 women). *Students:* 18 full-time (11 women), 46 part-time (27 women); includes 25 minority (3 African Americans, 14 Asian Americans or Pacific Islanders, 8 Hispanic Americans), 21 international. Average age 29. 32 applicants, 69% accepted, 4 enrolled. In 2008, 7 master's, 2 doctorates awarded. *Degree requirements:* For doctorate, variable foreign language requirement, thesis/dissertation. *Entrance requirements:* For master's and doctorate, GRE. *Application deadline:* For fall admission, 5/15 for domestic students; for spring admission, 12/1 for domestic students. Application fee: $75. *Expenses:* Tuition: Full-time $26,040; part-time $1085 per credit. Required fees: $720. *Financial support:* Career-related internships or fieldwork, Federal Work-Study, institutionally sponsored loans, and tuition waivers (full and partial) available. Support available to part-time students. Financial award application deadline: 2/1. *Faculty research:* Education and economic growth, efficiency in education, training in education, labor and education policy, economic status of immigrant groups. *Unit head:* Dr. George Bond, Chair, 212-678-3947. *Application contact:* Deanna Ghozati, Assistant Director of Admission, 212-678-4018, Fax: 212-678-4171, E-mail: ghozati@tc.edu.

Temple University, Graduate School, Fox School of Business and Management, Doctoral Programs in Business, Philadelphia, PA 19122-6096. Offers accounting (PhD); economics (PhD); finance (PhD); general and strategic management (PhD); healthcare management (PhD); human resource administration (PhD); international business administration (PhD); management information systems (PhD); management science/operations research (PhD); marketing (PhD); risk, insurance, and health-care management (PhD); statistics (PhD); tourism (PhD). *Accreditation:* AACSB. *Degree requirements:* For doctorate, thesis/dissertation. *Entrance requirements:* For doctorate, GRE General Test, GMAT, minimum GPA of 3.0, master's degree. Additional exam requirements/recommendations for international students: Required—TOEFL (minimum score 575 paper-based; 230 computer-based; 88 iBT), IELTS (minimum score 7). Electronic applications accepted.

Temple University, Graduate School, Fox School of Business and Management, Master's Programs in Business, MA Programs, Philadelphia, PA 19122-6096. Offers economics (MA). *Entrance requirements:* For master's, GRE General Test, minimum undergraduate GPA of 3.0. Additional exam requirements/recommendations for international students: Required—TOEFL (minimum score 575 paper-based; 230 computer-based; 88 iBT).

Texas A&M University, College of Liberal Arts, Department of Economics, College Station, TX 77843. Offers MS, PhD. Part-time programs available. *Faculty:* 21. *Students:* 116 full-time (36 women), 12 part-time (3 women); includes 9 minority (5 Asian Americans or Pacific Islanders, 4 Hispanic Americans), 99 international. Average age 31. In 2008, 12 master's, 12 doctorates awarded. Terminal master's awarded for partial completion of doctoral program. *Degree requirements:* For master's, comprehensive exam, thesis optional; for doctorate, comprehensive exam, thesis/dissertation. *Entrance requirements:* For master's and doctorate, GRE General Test. Additional exam requirements/recommendations for international students: Required—TOEFL. *Application deadline:* For fall admission, 3/1 priority date for domestic students; for winter admission, 8/1 priority date for domestic students; for spring admission, 11/1 priority date for domestic students. Applications are processed on a rolling basis. Application fee: $50 ($75 for international students). Electronic applications accepted. *Expenses:* Tuition, area resident: Full-time $3838.50. Tuition, state resident: full-time $3838.50. Tuition, nonresident: full-time $8897. Required fees: $2359.60. *Financial support:* In 2008–09, fellowships (averaging $14,850 per year), research assistantships (averaging $12,380 per year), teaching assistantships (averaging $10,062 per year) were awarded; scholarships/grants, tuition waivers, and unspecified assistantships also available. Financial award application deadline: 2/1; financial award applicants required to submit FAFSA. *Faculty research:* Tax policy, state tax, labor, international economics, macroeconomics. *Unit head:* Dr. Larry Oliver, Head, 979-845-8541, E-mail: l-oliver@tamu.edu. *Application contact:* Christi Essix, Graduate Admissions Supervisor, 979-845-7376, Fax: 979-847-8557, E-mail: christi@econ.tamu.edu.

Texas A&M University–Commerce, Graduate School, College of Business and Technology, Department of Economics and Finance, Commerce, TX 75429-3011. Offers economics (MA, MS). Part-time programs available. *Degree requirements:* For master's, comprehensive exam, thesis (for some programs). *Entrance requirements:* For master's, GMAT or GRE General Test. Electronic applications accepted. *Faculty research:* Economic activity, forensic economics, volatility and finance, international economics.

Texas Tech University, Graduate School, College of Arts and Sciences, Department of Economics and Geography, Lubbock, TX 79409. Offers economics (MA, PhD). Part-time programs available. *Faculty:* 13 full-time (3 women), 1 part-time/adjunct (0 women). *Students:* 32 full-time (10 women), 8 part-time (3 women); includes 5 minority (2 Asian Americans or Pacific Islanders, 3 Hispanic Americans), 25 international. Average age 30. 39 applicants, 64% accepted, 12 enrolled. In 2008, 2 master's awarded. *Degree requirements:* For master's, thesis or alternative; for doctorate, thesis/dissertation. *Entrance requirements:* For master's and doctorate, GRE General Test. Additional exam requirements/recommendations for international students: Required—TOEFL (minimum score 550 paper-based; 213 computer-based). *Application deadline:* For fall admission, 3/1 priority date for international students; for spring admission, 11/1 priority date for international students. Applications are processed on a rolling basis. Application fee: $50 ($60 for international students). Electronic applications accepted. *Expenses:* Tuition, area resident: Part-time $194 per credit hour. Tuition, state resident: full-time $4648; part-time $194 per credit hour. Tuition, nonresident: full-time $11,392; part-time $475 per credit hour. Required fees: $2206; $69 per credit hour. $389 per semester. *Financial support:* In 2008–09, 13 students received support, including 29 teaching assistantships with partial tuition reimbursements available (averaging $12,188 per year); research assistantships with partial tuition reimbursements available, Federal Work-Study and institutionally sponsored loans also available. Support available to part-time students. Financial award application deadline: 4/15; financial award applicants required to submit FAFSA. *Faculty research:* Pensions and retirement, energy economics, water, monetary and international economics, labor. Total annual research expenditures: $14,368. *Unit head:* Dr. Joseph E. King, Chair, 806-742-2201, Fax: 806-742-1137, E-mail: joseph.king@ttu.edu. *Application contact:* Dr. Klaus Becker, Graduate Advisor, 806-742-2201, Fax: 806-742-1137, E-mail: klaus.becker@ttu.edu.

Trinity College, Graduate Programs, Department of Economics, Hartford, CT 06106-3100. Offers MA. Part-time and evening/weekend programs available. *Degree requirements:* For master's, thesis optional, qualifying exam. *Entrance requirements:* For master's, minimum GPA of 3.0.

Tufts University, Graduate School of Arts and Sciences, Department of Economics, Medford, MA 02155. Offers MA. *Degree requirements:* For master's, thesis optional. *Entrance requirements:* For master's, GRE General Test. Additional exam requirements/recommendations for international students: Required—TOEFL (minimum score 550 paper-based; 213 computer-based; 80 iBT). Electronic applications accepted.

Tulane University, School of Liberal Arts, Department of Economics, New Orleans, LA 70118-5669. Offers MA, PhD. *Degree requirements:* For master's, thesis or alternative; for doctorate, one foreign language, thesis/dissertation. *Entrance requirements:* For master's, GRE General Test, minimum B average in undergraduate course work; for doctorate, GRE General Test. Additional exam requirements/recommendations for international students: Required—TOEFL. Electronic applications accepted. *Faculty research:* Economic development, public finance, labor economics, international and regional economics, industrial organization.

Universidad de las Américas–Puebla, Division of Graduate Studies, School of Social Sciences, Program in Economics, Puebla, Mexico. Offers economics (MA); finance (M Adm). Part-time and evening/weekend programs available. *Degree requirements:* For master's, one foreign language, thesis. *Faculty research:* Economic models (mathematics), industrial organization, assets and values market.

Universidad Nacional Pedro Henriquez Urena, Graduate School, Santo Domingo, Dominican Republic. Offers accounting and auditing (M Acct); animal production (M Agr); business administration (MBA, PhD); Caribbean tropical architecture (M Arch); conservation of monuments and cultural goods (M Arch); economics (M Econ); education (PhD); environmental engineering (MEE); horticulture (M Agr); hospital administration (PhD); humanities (PhD); international relations (MPS); management of natural resources (MNRM); project management (M Man, MPM); public administration (MPS); sanitary engineering (ME); social science (PhD); veterinary medicine (DVM).

Université de Moncton, Faculty of Arts and Social Sciences, Department of Economics, Moncton, NB E1A 3E9, Canada. Offers MA. *Degree requirements:* For master's, one foreign language, thesis. *Entrance requirements:* For master's, minimum GPA of 3.0. *Faculty research:* Free trade, public finance, small and medium size businesses, regional development, demography and development.

Université de Montréal, Faculty of Arts and Sciences, Department of Economic Sciences, Montréal, QC H3C 3J7, Canada. Offers M Sc, PhD. *Faculty:* 35 full-time (3 women). *Students:* 74 full-time (23 women), 95 part-time (30 women). 301 applicants, 20% accepted, 35 enrolled. In 2008, 45 master's, 10 doctorates awarded. *Degree requirements:* For master's, one foreign language, thesis; for doctorate, one foreign language, thesis/dissertation, general exam. *Application deadline:* For fall admission, 2/1 priority date for domestic students; for winter admission, 11/1 priority date for domestic students; for spring admission, 2/1 priority date for domestic students. Application fee: $100. Electronic applications accepted. *Financial support:* Fellowships, research assistantships, teaching assistantships available. Financial award application deadline: 2/1. *Faculty research:* Applied and economic theory, public choice, international trade, labor economics, industrial organization. *Unit head:* Michel Poitevin, Chair, 514-343-6539, Fax: 514-343-7221, E-mail: michel.poitevin@umontreal.ca. *Application contact:* Lyne Racine, Student Files Management Technician, 514-343-7213, Fax: 514-343-7221, E-mail: lyne.racine@umontreal.ca.

Université de Sherbrooke, Faculty of Letters and Human Sciences, Department of Economics, Sherbrooke, QC J1K 2R1, Canada. Offers MA. *Degree requirements:* For master's, thesis. *Faculty research:* Economic development, public finance, macroeconomics.

Université du Québec à Montréal, Graduate Programs, Program in Economics, Montréal, QC H3C 3P8, Canada. Offers M Sc, PhD. Part-time programs available. *Degree requirements:* For master's, thesis; for doctorate, thesis/dissertation. *Entrance requirements:* For master's, appropriate bachelor's degree or equivalent, proficiency in French; for doctorate, appropriate master's degree or equivalent, proficiency in French.

Université Laval, Faculty of Social Sciences, Department of Economics, Programs in Economics, Québec, QC G1K 7P4, Canada. Offers MA, PhD. Terminal master's awarded for partial completion of doctoral program. *Degree requirements:* For master's, thesis (for some programs); for doctorate, comprehensive exam, thesis/dissertation. *Entrance requirements:* For master's and doctorate, knowledge of French. Electronic applications accepted.

University at Albany, State University of New York, College of Arts and Sciences, Department of Economics, Albany, NY 12222-0001. Offers economics (MA, PhD); regulatory economics (Certificate). Part-time programs available. Terminal master's awarded for partial completion of doctoral program. *Degree requirements:* For doctorate, one foreign language, thesis/dissertation. *Entrance requirements:* For doctorate, GRE General Test, GRE Subject Test. Additional exam requirements/recommendations for international students: Required—TOEFL (minimum score 550 paper-based; 213 computer-based). Electronic applications accepted. *Faculty research:* Expectations of inflation and interest rates, diffusion of new technology, labor markets in developing countries, government deficits and international exchange markets.

University at Buffalo, the State University of New York, Graduate School, College of Arts and Sciences, Department of Economics, Buffalo, NY 14260. Offers economics (MA, MS, PhD); financial economics (Certificate); health services (Certificate); information and Internet economics (Certificate); international economics (Certificate); law and regulation (Certificate); urban and regional economics (Certificate). Terminal master's awarded for partial completion of doctoral program. *Degree requirements:* For master's, comprehensive exam, thesis optional, theory exam; for doctorate, thesis/dissertation, field and theory exams. *Entrance requirements:* For master's and doctorate, GRE General Test. Additional exam requirements/recommendations for international students: Required—TOEFL (minimum score 550 paper-based; 213 computer-based). Electronic applications accepted. *Faculty research:* International economics, econometrics, applied economics, urban economics, economic growth and development.

The University of Akron, Graduate School, Buchtel College of Arts and Sciences, Department of Economics, Akron, OH 44325. Offers economics (MA). Part-time programs available. *Degree requirements:* For master's, thesis optional. *Entrance requirements:* For master's, minimum GPA of 2.75, letters of recommendation. Additional exam requirements/recommendations for international students: Required—TOEFL (minimum score 550 paper-based; 213 computer-based; 79 iBT). Electronic applications accepted. *Faculty research:* Regional economic performance, effects of addiction on labor market outcomes, programmatic assessment, regional trading arrangements, agriculture production in early twentieth-century South.

The University of Alabama, Graduate School, Manderson Graduate School of Business, Economics, Finance and Legal Studies Department, Tuscaloosa, AL 35487. Offers economics (MA, PhD); finance (MS, PhD). *Faculty:* 23 full-time (1 woman). *Students:* 56 full-time (15 women), 1 (woman) part-time; includes 7 minority (5 African Americans, 2 Asian Americans or Pacific Islanders), 13 international. Average age 26. 147 applicants, 35% accepted, 25 enrolled. In 2008, 12 master's, 12 doctorates awarded. Terminal master's awarded for partial completion of doctoral program. *Degree requirements:* For master's, comprehensive exam (MA), thesis

(MS); for doctorate, comprehensive exam, thesis/dissertation. *Entrance requirements:* For master's, GMAT, GRE; for doctorate, GRE or GMAT. Additional exam requirements/recommendations for international students: Required—TOEFL (minimum score 550 paper-based; 213 computer-based). *Application deadline:* For fall admission, 7/1 priority date for domestic students, 1/15 for international students; for spring admission, 11/1 priority date for domestic students, 6/1 for international students. Applications are processed on a rolling basis. Application fee: $30. Electronic applications accepted. *Expenses:* Tuition, area resident: Full-time $6400. Tuition, state resident: full-time $6400. Tuition, nonresident: full-time $18,000. *Financial support:* In 2008–09, 10 fellowships (averaging $10,000 per year), 21 research assistantships with full and partial tuition reimbursements (averaging $12,000 per year), 15 teaching assistantships with full and partial tuition reimbursements (averaging $12,000 per year) were awarded; Federal Work-Study, institutionally sponsored loans, and unspecified assistantships also available. *Faculty research:* Taxation, futures market, monetary theory and policy, income distribution. *Unit head:* Prof. Billy P. Helms, Head, 205-348-8067, E-mail: bhelms@cba.ua.edu. *Application contact:* Prof. Billy P. Helms, Head, 205-348-8067, E-mail: bhelms@cba.ua.edu.

University of Alaska Fairbanks, School of Management, Department of Economics, Fairbanks, AK 99775-6080. Offers resource and applied economics (MS). Part-time programs available. *Faculty:* 8 full-time (2 women), 3 part-time/adjunct (0 women). *Students:* 8 full-time (1 woman), 9 part-time (2 women); includes 3 minority (1 African American, 1 Asian American or Pacific Islander, 1 Hispanic American), 2 international. Average age 38. 13 applicants, 77% accepted, 9 enrolled. In 2008, 9 master's awarded. *Degree requirements:* For master's, comprehensive exam, thesis or alternative. *Entrance requirements:* Additional exam requirements/recommendations for international students: Required—TOEFL (minimum score 550 paper-based; 213 computer-based). *Application deadline:* For fall admission, 6/1 priority date for domestic students, 3/1 for international students; for spring admission, 10/15 priority date for domestic students, 9/1 for international students. Applications are processed on a rolling basis. Application fee: $60. Electronic applications accepted. *Expenses:* Tuition, area resident: Full-time $5418; part-time $301 per credit. Tuition, state resident: full-time $5418; part-time $301 per credit. Tuition, nonresident: full-time $11,070; part-time $615 per credit. Required fees: $849; $25 per credit. $78 per semester. Tuition and fees vary according to course load and reciprocity agreements. *Financial support:* In 2008–09, 6 teaching assistantships (averaging $12,910 per year) were awarded; fellowships, research assistantships, career-related internships or fieldwork, Federal Work-Study, scholarships/grants, health care benefits, and unspecified assistantships also available. Support available to part-time students. Financial award application deadline: 2/15; financial award applicants required to submit FAFSA. *Faculty research:* Statistics; resource and agriculture economics; oil, gas, and energy; sustainability; public land management. *Unit head:* Joseph Little, Program Director, 907-474-2711, Fax: 907-474-5219, E-mail: ffjml1@uaf.edu. *Application contact:* Joseph Little, Program Director, 907-474-2711, Fax: 907-474-5219, E-mail: ffjml1@uaf.edu.

University of Alberta, Faculty of Graduate Studies and Research, Department of Economics, Edmonton, AB T6G 2E1, Canada. Offers economics (MA, PhD); economics and finance (MA); environmental and natural resource economics (PhD). Part-time programs available. *Degree requirements:* For doctorate, thesis/dissertation. *Entrance requirements:* For master's and doctorate, GRE. Additional exam requirements/recommendations for international students: Required—TOEFL. *Faculty research:* Public finance, international trade, industrial organization, Pacific Rim economics, monetary economics.

The University of Arizona, Graduate College, Eller College of Management, Department of Economics, Tucson, AZ 85721. Offers MA, PhD, JD/MA, JD/PhD. Terminal master's awarded for partial completion of doctoral program. *Degree requirements:* For master's, comprehensive exam; for doctorate, thesis/dissertation. *Entrance requirements:* For master's, GRE General Test, 3 letters of recommendation, statement of purpose; for doctorate, GRE General Test, minimum GPA of 3.0, 3 letters of recommendation, statement of purpose. Additional exam requirements/recommendations for international students: Required—TOEFL (minimum score 550 paper-based). Electronic applications accepted. *Faculty research:* Applied microeconomics, experimental economics, economic history, microeconomic theory, property rights, industrial organization.

University of Arkansas, Graduate School, Sam M. Walton College of Business Administration, Department of Economics, Fayetteville, AR 72701-1201. Offers MA, PhD. *Degree requirements:* For doctorate, variable foreign language requirement, thesis/dissertation. *Entrance requirements:* For master's and doctorate, GRE General Test.

The University of British Columbia, Faculty of Arts and Faculty of Graduate Studies, Department of Economics, Vancouver, BC V6T 1Z1, Canada. Offers MA, PhD. *Degree requirements:* For master's, thesis (for some programs); for doctorate, comprehensive exam, thesis/dissertation. *Entrance requirements:* For master's and doctorate, GRE General Test. Additional exam requirements/recommendations for international students: Required—TOEFL (minimum score 550 paper-based; 213 computer-based; 80 iBT). Electronic applications accepted. *Faculty research:* Economic theory, international economics, labor economics, public finance, economic development.

University of Calgary, Faculty of Graduate Studies, Faculty of Social Sciences, Department of Economics, Calgary, AB T2N 1N4, Canada. Offers M Ec, MA, PhD. Part-time and evening/weekend programs available. *Degree requirements:* For master's, thesis (for some programs); for doctorate, thesis/dissertation, candidacy exam. *Entrance requirements:* Additional exam requirements/recommendations for international students: Required—TOEFL. *Faculty research:* Energy economics, public finance/public choice, resource economics, international trade, monetary economics.

University of California, Berkeley, Graduate Division, College of Letters and Science, Department of Economics, Berkeley, CA 94720-1500. Offers PhD, JD/MA. *Degree requirements:* For doctorate, thesis/dissertation, field exams, oral qualifying exam. *Entrance requirements:* For doctorate, GRE General Test, minimum GPA of 3.0, 3 letters of recommendation. Additional exam requirements/recommendations for international students: Required—TOEFL.

University of California, Davis, Graduate Studies, Program in Economics, Davis, CA 95616. Offers MA, PhD. Terminal master's awarded for partial completion of doctoral program. *Degree requirements:* For master's, comprehensive exam (for some programs), thesis (for some programs); for doctorate, thesis/dissertation. *Entrance requirements:* For master's, GRE General Test, minimum GPA of 3.0; for doctorate, GRE General Test, minimum GPA of 3.25. Additional exam requirements/recommendations for international students: Required—TOEFL (minimum score 550 paper-based; 213 computer-based). Electronic applications accepted. *Faculty research:* Applied microeconomics, macroeconomics, international studies, economic theory, economic history.

University of California, Irvine, Office of Graduate Studies, School of Social Sciences, Department of Economics, Irvine, CA 92697. Offers economics (MA, PhD); public choice (MA, PhD); transportation economics (MA, PhD). *Degree requirements:* For doctorate, thesis/dissertation. *Entrance requirements:* For master's and doctorate, GRE General Test, minimum GPA of 3.0. Additional exam requirements/recommendations for international students: Required—TOEFL (minimum score 550 paper-based; 213 computer-based). Electronic applications accepted. *Faculty research:* Econometrics, urban economics, applied microeconomics.

University of California, Los Angeles, Graduate Division, College of Letters and Science, Department of Economics, Los Angeles, CA 90034. Offers MA, PhD. *Students:* 105 full-time (30 women); includes 7 minority (6 Asian Americans or Pacific Islanders, 1 Hispanic American), 65 international. Average age 27. 462 applicants, 24% accepted, 23 enrolled. In 2008, 31 master's, 24 doctorates awarded. Terminal master's awarded for partial completion of doctoral program. *Degree requirements:* For master's, comprehensive exam; for doctorate, thesis/dissertation, oral and written qualifying exams. *Entrance requirements:* For master's, GRE General Test, degree objective must be Ph.D; for doctorate, GRE General Test, minimum undergraduate GPA of 3.0. *Application deadline:* For fall admission, 12/1 for domestic and international students. Application fee: $60 ($80 for international students). Electronic applications accepted. *Expenses:* Tuition, nonresident: full-time $14,694. Required fees: $9669.50. Full-time tuition and fees vary according to course load, degree level, program and student level. *Financial support:* In 2008–09, 110 fellowships with full and partial tuition reimbursements, 24 research assistantships with full and partial tuition reimbursements, 74 teaching assistantships with full and partial tuition reimbursements were awarded; Federal Work-Study, institutionally sponsored loans, scholarships/grants, health care benefits, tuition waivers (full and partial), and unspecified assistantships also available. Financial award application deadline: 3/1; financial award applicants required to submit FAFSA. *Unit head:* Dr. Gary Hansen, Chair, 310-206-1413. *Application contact:* Departmental Office, 310-206-1413, E-mail: bgarcia@econ.ucla.edu.

University of California, Riverside, Graduate Division, Department of Economics, Riverside, CA 92521-0102. Offers MA, PhD. *Faculty:* 24 full-time (6 women). *Students:* 57 full-time (24 women); includes 8 minority (1 African American, 5 Asian Americans or Pacific Islanders, 2 Hispanic Americans), 39 international. Average age 30. 145 applicants, 35% accepted, 18 enrolled. In 2008, 3 master's, 6 doctorates awarded. Terminal master's awarded for partial completion of doctoral program. *Degree requirements:* For master's, comprehensive exam; for doctorate, thesis/dissertation, qualifying exams. *Entrance requirements:* For master's and doctorate, GRE General Test, minimum GPA of 3.2. Additional exam requirements/recommendations for international students: Required—TOEFL (minimum score 550 paper-based; 213 computer-based; 80 iBT). *Application deadline:* For fall admission, 5/1 for domestic students, 2/1 for international students. Applications are processed on a rolling basis. Application fee: $60 ($75 for international students). Electronic applications accepted. *Expenses:* Tuition, nonresident: full-time $4898. Required fees: $10,362. *Financial support:* In 2008–09, fellowships with partial tuition reimbursements (averaging $12,000 per year), teaching assistantships with partial tuition reimbursements (averaging $16,500 per year) were awarded; research assistantships, career-related internships or fieldwork, institutionally sponsored loans, and tuition waivers (full and partial) also available. Financial award application deadline: 2/1; financial award applicants required to submit FAFSA. *Faculty research:* Advanced political economy; resource and environmental economics; advanced econometrics; labor economics; advanced microeconomics theory; advanced macroeconomics theory; development economics; economic history; international trade theory; money, credit and business cycles; public economics. *Unit head:* Dr. Aman Ullah, Chair, 951-827-1474, Fax: 951-827-5685, E-mail: econgrad@ucr.edu. *Application contact:* Amanda Labagnara, Graduate Program Assistant, 951-827-1474, Fax: 951-827-5685, E-mail: econgrad@ucr.edu.

Announcement: The University of California, Riverside, 60 miles east of Los Angeles, offers undergraduate and graduate degree programs in economics. The graduate program offers PhD and MA degrees in preparation for research and teaching as well as for positions in government and the private sector. Application contact: Graduate Student Affairs, phone: 951-827-1474.

University of California, San Diego, Office of Graduate Studies, Department of Economics, La Jolla, CA 92093. Offers economics (PhD); economics and international affairs (PhD). *Degree requirements:* For doctorate, thesis/dissertation. *Entrance requirements:* For doctorate, GRE General Test. Electronic applications accepted. *Faculty research:* Microfoundations of macroeconomics, econometric model specification and testing, industrial organization.

University of California, San Diego, Office of Graduate Studies, Graduate School of International Relations and Pacific Studies, La Jolla, CA 92093-0520. Offers economics and international affairs (PhD); Pacific international affairs (MPIA); political science and international affairs (PhD). *Degree requirements:* For master's, one foreign language; for doctorate, thesis/dissertation. *Entrance requirements:* For master's, GMAT or GRE General Test; for doctorate, GRE General Test. Additional exam requirements/recommendations for international students: Required—TOEFL (minimum score 550 paper-based; 213 computer-based). Electronic applications accepted. *Faculty research:* Pacific Rim as system and placement in global relations; studies in international economics, management and finance; analysis of patterns of policymaking in countries of the Pacific.

See Close-Up on page 881.

University of California, Santa Barbara, Graduate Division, College of Letters and Sciences, Division of Social Sciences, Department of Economics, Santa Barbara, CA 93106-9210. Offers business economics (MA); economics (PhD); MA/PhD. *Faculty:* 30 full-time (4 women), 14 part-time/adjunct (4 women). *Students:* 77 full-time (28 women). Average age 26. 276 applicants, 46% accepted, 34 enrolled. In 2008, 34 master's, 10 doctorates awarded. Terminal master's awarded for partial completion of doctoral program. *Degree requirements:* For master's, comprehensive exam, thesis; for doctorate, comprehensive exam, thesis/dissertation. *Entrance requirements:* For master's and doctorate, GRE General Test, 3 letters of recommendation, statement of purpose, personal achievements/contributions statement, resumé/curriculum vitae, transcripts for post-secondary institutions attended. Additional exam requirements/recommendations for international students: Required—TOEFL (minimum score 550 paper-based; 213 computer-based; 80 iBT), TOEFL or IELTS. *Application deadline:* For fall admission, 12/1 priority date for domestic and international students. Application fee: $70 ($90 for international students). Electronic applications accepted. *Expenses:* Tuition, nonresident: full-time $25,149. Required fees: $10,143. Full-time tuition and fees vary according to campus/location, reciprocity agreements and student level. *Financial support:* In 2008–09, 30 students received support, including 29 fellowships with full and partial tuition reimbursements available (averaging $11,300 per year), 7 research assistantships with full and partial tuition reimbursements available (averaging $6,500 per year), 50 teaching assistantships with partial tuition reimbursements available (averaging $9,900 per year); Federal Work-Study, institutionally sponsored loans, scholarships/grants, health care benefits, tuition waivers (full and partial), and unspecified assistantships also available. Support available to part-time students. Financial award application deadline: 12/1; financial award applicants required to submit FAFSA. *Faculty research:* Labor economics, econometrics, macroeconomic theory and policy, environmental and natural resources economics (EES), experimental and behavioral economics. *Unit head:* Prof. Perry Shapiro, Chair, Fax: 805-893-8830, E-mail: pxshap@econ.ucsb.edu. *Application contact:* Mark Patterson, Staff Graduate Advisor, 805-893-2205, Fax: 805-893-8830, E-mail: mark@econ.ucsb.edu.

University of California, Santa Barbara, Graduate Division, Donald Bren School of Environmental Science and Management, Santa Barbara, CA 93106-5131. Offers MESM, PhD. *Faculty:* 18 full-time (4 women), 24 part-time/adjunct (7 women). *Students:* 187 full-time (112 women); includes 21 minority (1 African American, 1 American Indian/Alaska Native, 11 Asian Americans or Pacific Islanders, 8 Hispanic Americans), 15 international. Average age 27. 335 applicants, 61% accepted, 89 enrolled. In 2008, 63 master's, 8 doctorates awarded. *Degree requirements:* For master's, thesis optional, group project as student thesis; for doctorate, comprehensive exam, thesis/dissertation. *Entrance requirements:* For master's and doctorate, GRE, 3 letters of recommendation, statement of purpose, personal achievements/contributions statement, resumé/curriculum vitae, transcripts for post-secondary institutions attended. Additional exam requirements/recommendations for international students: Required—TOEFL (minimum score 550 paper-based; 213 computer-based; 80 iBT), IELTS (minimum score 7), TOEFL or IELTS. *Application deadline:* For fall admission, 1/10 priority date for domestic and international students. Application fee: $70 ($90 for international students). Electronic applications accepted. *Expenses:* Tuition, nonresident: full-time $25,149. Required fees: $10,143. Full-time tuition and fees vary according to campus/location, reciprocity agreements and student level. *Financial support:* In 2008–09, 68 students received support, including 44 fellowships with full and partial tuition reimbursements available (averaging $8,400 per year), 20 research assistantships with full and partial tuition reimbursements available (averaging $6,600 per year), 28 teaching assistantships with partial tuition reimbursements available (averaging $6,900 per year); career-related internships or fieldwork, Federal Work-Study, institutionally sponsored loans, scholarships/grants, health care benefits, and unspecified

Economics

University of California, Santa Barbara (continued)
assistantships also available. Financial award application deadline: 12/15; financial award applicants required to submit FAFSA. *Faculty research:* Ecological processes, environmental politics and policy, sustainability, conservation science and planning, water resources management. *Unit head:* Dr. John Melack, Acting Dean, 805-893-3879, Fax: 805-893-6113, E-mail: melack@bren.ucsb.edu. *Application contact:* Kristen Robinson, Graduate Program Advisor, 805-893-7611, Fax: 805-893-6113, E-mail: gradasst@bren.ucsb.edu.

University of California, Santa Cruz, Division of Graduate Studies, Division of Social Sciences, Program in International Economics, Santa Cruz, CA 95064. Offers PhD. *Degree requirements:* For doctorate, thesis/dissertation, 4 field exams, econometrics project. *Entrance requirements:* For doctorate, GRE General Test. *Faculty research:* Current and emerging issues in taxation, industrial policy, environmental regulation, market structure.

University of Central Arkansas, Graduate School, College of Business Administration, Program in Community and Economic Development, Conway, AR 72035-0001. Offers MS. *Degree requirements:* For master's, comprehensive exam, thesis. *Entrance requirements:* For master's, GRE General Test, minimum GPA of 2.7. Additional exam requirements/recommendations for international students: Required—TOEFL (minimum score 550 paper-based; 213 computer-based). *Expenses:* Contact institution.

University of Central Florida, College of Business Administration, Department of Economics, Orlando, FL 32816. Offers MS, PhD. Part-time and evening/weekend programs available. *Faculty:* 21 full-time (4 women), 2 part-time/adjunct (0 women). *Students:* 15 full-time (7 women), 9 part-time (4 women); includes 3 minority (all Asian Americans or Pacific Islanders), 11 international. In 2008, 5 master's awarded. *Degree requirements:* For master's, comprehensive exam, thesis or alternative. *Entrance requirements:* For master's, GMAT, minimum GPA of 3.0 in last 60 hours. Additional exam requirements/recommendations for international students: Required—TOEFL. *Application deadline:* For fall admission, 6/15 priority date for domestic students; for spring admission, 11/1 priority date for domestic students. Application fee: $30. Electronic applications accepted. *Expenses:* Tuition, area resident: Full-time $6816; part-time $284 per credit. Tuition, state resident: full-time $6816; part-time $1076 per credit. Tuition, nonresident: full-time $25,824. Required fees: $216; $9 per credit. *Financial support:* In 2008–09, 2 fellowships with partial tuition reimbursements (averaging $17,000 per year), 8 research assistantships with partial tuition reimbursements (averaging $4,600 per year), 11 teaching assistantships with partial tuition reimbursements (averaging $5,600 per year) were awarded; career-related internships or fieldwork, Federal Work-Study, institutionally sponsored loans, tuition waivers (partial), and unspecified assistantships also available. Financial award application deadline: 3/1; financial award applicants required to submit FAFSA. *Unit head:* Dr. J. Wally Milon, Chair, 407-823-4429, E-mail: wally.milon@bus.ucf.edu. *Application contact:* Dr. J. Wally Milon, Chair, 407-823-4429, E-mail: wally.milon@bus.ucf.edu.

University of Chicago, Division of Social Sciences, Department of Economics, Chicago, IL 60637-1513. Offers PhD. *Degree requirements:* For doctorate, one foreign language, thesis/dissertation, written exams in 2 fields. *Entrance requirements:* For doctorate, GRE General Test. Additional exam requirements/recommendations for international students: Required—TOEFL, IELTS (minimum score 7). Electronic applications accepted.

University of Cincinnati, Graduate School, McMicken College of Arts and Sciences, Department of Economics, Program in Applied Economics, Cincinnati, OH 45221. Offers MA. Part-time and evening/weekend programs available. *Degree requirements:* For master's, thesis optional. *Entrance requirements:* For master's, GRE General Test or GMAT, intermediate micro, macro theory, statistics, calculus. Additional exam requirements/recommendations for international students: Required—TOEFL. Electronic applications accepted. *Faculty research:* Econometrics, labor markets, pollution markets, transportation.

University of Colorado at Boulder, Graduate School, College of Arts and Sciences, Department of Economics, Boulder, CO 80309. Offers MA, PhD. Terminal master's awarded for partial completion of doctoral program. *Degree requirements:* For master's, comprehensive exam, thesis or alternative; for doctorate, comprehensive exam, thesis/dissertation, preliminary exam. *Entrance requirements:* For master's, GRE General Test, minimum undergraduate GPA of 2.75; for doctorate, GRE General Test. Additional exam requirements/recommendations for international students: Required—TOEFL. *Faculty research:* Public economics and natural resources and environmental economics, international, econometrics, urban and regional economics, development economics, economic history.

University of Colorado Denver, College of Liberal Arts and Sciences, Department of Economics, Denver, CO 80217-3364. Offers MA. Part-time and evening/weekend programs available. *Degree requirements:* For master's, thesis or alternative. *Entrance requirements:* For master's, GRE General Test, 15 hours of course work in economics, minimum GPA of 2.5. Additional exam requirements/recommendations for international students: Required—TOEFL (minimum score 525 paper-based; 197 computer-based). Electronic applications accepted.

University of Connecticut, Graduate School, College of Liberal Arts and Sciences, Department of Economics, Field of Economics, Storrs, CT 06269. Offers MA, PhD. *Degree requirements:* For master's, comprehensive exam; for doctorate, thesis/dissertation. *Entrance requirements:* For master's and doctorate, GRE General Test, GRE Subject Test. Additional exam requirements/recommendations for international students: Required—TOEFL (minimum score 550 paper-based; 213 computer-based). Electronic applications accepted.

University of Delaware, Alfred Lerner College of Business and Economics, Department of Economics, Newark, DE 19716. Offers economics (MA, MS, PhD); economics for entrepreneurship and educators (MA); MA/MBA. Part-time programs available. *Degree requirements:* For master's, comprehensive exam, thesis (for some programs), mathematics review exam, research project; for doctorate, comprehensive exam, thesis/dissertation, field exam. *Entrance requirements:* For master's, GMAT or GRE General Test, minimum GPA of 2.5; for doctorate, GRE General Test, minimum GPA of 3.5 in graduate economics course work. Additional exam requirements/recommendations for international students: Required—TOEFL (minimum score 550 paper-based; 225 computer-based). Electronic applications accepted. *Faculty research:* Applied quantitative economics, industrial organization, resource economics, monetary economics, labor economics.

University of Denver, Division of Arts, Humanities and Social Sciences, Department of Economics, Denver, CO 80208. Offers MA. Part-time programs available. *Faculty:* 8 full-time (1 woman), 1 part-time/adjunct (0 women). *Students:* 12 full-time (5 women), 10 part-time (5 women); includes 5 minority (1 American Indian/Alaska Native, 3 Asian Americans or Pacific Islanders, 1 Hispanic American), 8 international. Average age 26. In 2008, 3 master's awarded. *Degree requirements:* For master's, thesis. *Entrance requirements:* For master's, GRE. Additional exam requirements/recommendations for international students: Required—TOEFL. *Application deadline:* Applications are processed on a rolling basis. Application fee: $50. Electronic applications accepted. *Financial support:* In 2008–09, 3 teaching assistantships with full and partial tuition reimbursements (averaging $16,000 per year) were awarded; career-related internships or fieldwork, Federal Work-Study, and scholarships/grants also available. Support available to part-time students. Financial award application deadline: 3/1; financial award applicants required to submit FAFSA. *Unit head:* Dr. Peter Ho, Chairperson, 303-871-2685. *Application contact:* Information Contact, 303-871-2685, E-mail: econ04@denver.du.edu.

University of Florida, Graduate School, Warrington College of Business Administration, Hough Graduate School of Business, Department of Economics, Gainesville, FL 32611. Offers MA, PhD. Terminal master's awarded for partial completion of doctoral program. *Degree requirements:* For master's, thesis optional; for doctorate, thesis/dissertation. *Entrance requirements:* Additional exam requirements/recommendations for international students: Required—TOEFL (minimum score 550 paper-based; 213 computer-based). Electronic applications accepted. *Faculty research:* Econometrics, international economics, industrial organization, public finance, economic theory.

University of Georgia, Graduate School, Terry College of Business, Department of Economics, Athens, GA 30602. Offers MA, PhD. *Degree requirements:* For master's, thesis; for doctorate, thesis/dissertation. *Entrance requirements:* For master's and doctorate, GRE General Test. Electronic applications accepted.

University of Guelph, Graduate Program Services, College of Management and Economics, Department of Economics, Guelph, ON N1G 2W1, Canada. Offers MA, PhD. Part-time programs available. *Degree requirements:* For master's, thesis or alternative; for doctorate, comprehensive exam, thesis/dissertation. *Entrance requirements:* For master's, minimum B+ average during previous 2 years of course work; for doctorate, minimum A- average, MA in economics. Additional exam requirements/recommendations for international students: Required—TOEFL (minimum score 550 paper-based; 213 computer-based; 89 iBT), IELTS (minimum score 6.5). Electronic applications accepted. *Faculty research:* Resource and environmental economics, econometrics, labor economics, micro and macro economics.

University of Hawaii at Manoa, Graduate Division, Colleges of Arts and Sciences, College of Social Sciences, Department of Economics, Honolulu, HI 96822. Offers MA, PhD. Part-time programs available. Terminal master's awarded for partial completion of doctoral program. *Degree requirements:* For master's, thesis optional; for doctorate, comprehensive exam, thesis/dissertation. *Entrance requirements:* For master's and doctorate, GRE General Test. Additional exam requirements/recommendations for international students: Required—TOEFL (minimum score 500 paper-based; 173 computer-based; 61 iBT), IELTS (minimum score 5). *Faculty research:* Trade, development, demography, labor, resource economics.

University of Houston, College of Liberal Arts and Social Sciences, Department of Economics, Houston, TX 77204. Offers MA, PhD. Part-time programs available. *Faculty:* 13 full-time (4 women), 3 part-time/adjunct (1 woman). *Students:* 45 full-time (24 women), 4 part-time (2 women); includes 7 minority (1 African American, 3 Asian Americans or Pacific Islanders, 3 Hispanic Americans), 31 international. Average age 28. 77 applicants, 83% accepted, 14 enrolled. In 2008, 16 master's, 8 doctorates awarded. Terminal master's awarded for partial completion of doctoral program. *Degree requirements:* For doctorate, thesis/dissertation. *Entrance requirements:* For master's, GRE General Test, minimum GPA of 3.0; for doctorate, GRE General Test, master's degree, minimum GPA of 3.0. *Expenses:* Tuition, state resident: full-time $5164; part-time $287 per credit. Tuition, nonresident: full-time $10,222; part-time $568 per credit. *Financial support:* In 2008–09, 39 teaching assistantships with full tuition reimbursements (averaging $12,600 per year) were awarded; career-related internships or fieldwork, Federal Work-Study, institutionally sponsored loans, scholarships/grants, health care benefits, and unspecified assistantships also available. Support available to part-time students. Financial award application deadline: 2/1. *Faculty research:* Econometrics, labor economics, international economics, public finance. *Unit head:* Dr. David Papell, Graduate Director, 713-743-3800, Fax: 713-743-3798, E-mail: dpapell@uh.edu. *Application contact:* Dr. David Papell, Graduate Director, 713-743-3800, Fax: 713-743-3798, E-mail: dpapell@uh.edu.

University of Illinois at Chicago, Graduate College, College of Liberal Arts and Sciences, Department of Economics, Chicago, IL 60607-7128. Offers MA, PhD, MBA/MA. Terminal master's awarded for partial completion of doctoral program. *Degree requirements:* For master's, comprehensive exam; for doctorate, thesis/dissertation. *Entrance requirements:* For master's and doctorate, GRE General Test, minimum GPA of 2.75. Additional exam requirements/recommendations for international students: Required—TOEFL. Electronic applications accepted. *Faculty research:* International, labor, and urban economics.

University of Illinois at Urbana–Champaign, Graduate College, College of Liberal Arts and Sciences, Department of Economics, Champaign, IL 61820. Offers economics (MS, PhD); policy economics (MS). *Faculty:* 25 full-time (3 women), 3 part-time/adjunct (0 women). *Students:* 163 full-time (57 women), 8 part-time (3 women); includes 5 minority (1 African American, 3 Asian Americans or Pacific Islanders, 1 Hispanic American), 142 international. 533 applicants, 15% accepted, 64 enrolled. In 2008, 65 master's, 8 doctorates awarded. Terminal master's awarded for partial completion of doctoral program. *Entrance requirements:* For master's, minimum GPA of 3.0; for doctorate, GRE General Test, minimum GPA of 3.3. Additional exam requirements/recommendations for international students: Required—TOEFL (minimum score 550 paper-based; 213 computer-based; 79 iBT). *Application deadline:* Applications are processed on a rolling basis. Application fee: $60 ($75 for international students). Electronic applications accepted. *Financial support:* In 2008–09, 23 fellowships, 16 research assistantships, 58 teaching assistantships were awarded; tuition waivers (full and partial) also available. *Unit head:* Dr. J. Fred Giertz, Interim Head, 217-333-0120, Fax: 217-244-6678, E-mail: jgiertz@illinois.edu. *Application contact:* Carol Hartman, Assistant Director for Administration, 217-333-0120, Fax: 217-244-6678, E-mail: cbhartma@illinois.edu.

See Close-Up on page 779.

The University of Iowa, Henry B. Tippie College of Business, Department of Economics, Iowa City, IA 52242-1316. Offers PhD. *Degree requirements:* For doctorate, comprehensive exam, thesis/dissertation, thesis defense. *Entrance requirements:* For doctorate, GRE General Test. Additional exam requirements/recommendations for international students: Required—TOEFL (minimum score 600 paper-based; 250 computer-based; 100 iBT); Recommended—IELTS (minimum score 7). Electronic applications accepted. *Faculty research:* Political economy, macroeconomics, econometrics, game theory, economic development.

The University of Kansas, Graduate Studies, College of Liberal Arts and Sciences, Department of Economics, Lawrence, KS 66045. Offers MA, PhD, JD/MA. Part-time programs available. *Faculty:* 18 full-time (2 women). *Students:* 78 full-time (22 women), 6 part-time (1 woman); includes 3 minority (1 American Indian/Alaska Native, 1 Asian American or Pacific Islander, 1 Hispanic American), 59 international. Average age 29. 107 applicants, 62% accepted, 29 enrolled. In 2008, 16 master's, 4 doctorates awarded. Terminal master's awarded for partial completion of doctoral program. *Degree requirements:* For master's, comprehensive exam, thesis optional; for doctorate, thesis/dissertation, qualifying exams. *Entrance requirements:* For doctorate, GRE. Additional exam requirements/recommendations for international students: Required—TOEFL, IELTS, We go by part score of either the TOEFL or IELTS. They are as follows: TOEFL-computer =20, TOEFL-paper=52, IELTS=6.0. *Application deadline:* For fall admission, 2/1 priority date for domestic and international students; for winter admission, 5/1 priority date for domestic and international students; for spring admission, 11/1 priority date for domestic and international students. Applications are processed on a rolling basis. Application fee: $45 ($50 for international students). Electronic applications accepted. *Expenses:* Tuition, area resident: Full-time $6122; part-time $255.10 per credit hour. Tuition, state resident: full-time $6122; part-time $255.10 per credit hour. Tuition, nonresident: full-time $14,629; part-time $609.55 per credit hour. Required fees: $847; $70.56 per credit hour. Tuition and fees vary according to course load and program. *Financial support:* In 2008–09, 1 fellowship with full tuition reimbursement, 5 research assistantships with full tuition reimbursements, 22 teaching assistantships with full and partial tuition reimbursements were awarded; institutionally sponsored loans, scholarships/grants, health care benefits, and unspecified assistantships also available. Financial award application deadline: 2/1. *Faculty research:* Macroeconomics, econometrics, industrial organization, microeconomics, economic development, international economics. *Unit head:* Joseph Sicilian, Chair, 785-864-3501, Fax: 785-864-5270, E-mail: jsic@ku.edu. *Application contact:* Elizabeth Asiedu, Graduate Director, 785-864-3501, Fax: 785-864-5270, E-mail: asiedu@ku.edu.

University of Kentucky, Graduate School, Gatton College of Business and Economics, Program in Economics, Lexington, KY 40506-0032. Offers MS, PhD. *Degree requirements:* For master's, comprehensive exam; for doctorate, comprehensive exam, thesis/dissertation. *Entrance requirements:* For master's, GMAT, minimum undergraduate GPA of 2.75; for doctorate, GMAT, minimum undergraduate GPA of 3.0. Additional exam requirements/recommendations for international students: Required—TOEFL (minimum score 550 paper-based; 213 computer-based). Electronic applications accepted. *Faculty research:* Public economics, international economics and economic development, labor economics, environmental economics, industrial economics.

University of Lethbridge, School of Graduate Studies, Lethbridge, AB T1K 3M4, Canada. Offers accounting (MScM); addictions counseling (M Sc); agricultural biotechnology (M Sc); agricultural studies (M Sc, MA); anthropology (MA); archaeology (MA); art (MA); biochemistry (M Sc); biological sciences (M Sc); biomolecular science (PhD); biosystems and biodiversity (PhD); Canadian studies (MA); chemistry (M Sc); computer science (M Sc); computer science and geographical information science (M Sc); counseling psychology (M Ed); dramatic arts (MA); earth, space, and physical science (PhD); economics (MA); educational leadership (M Ed); English (MA); environmental science (M Sc); evolution and behavior (PhD); exercise science (M Sc); finance (MScM); French (MA); French/German (MA); French/Spanish (MA); general education (M Ed); general management (MScM); geography (M Sc, MA); German (MA); health sciences (M Sc, MA); history (MA); human resource management and labour relations (MScM); individualized multidisciplinary (M Sc, MA); information systems (MScM); international management (MScM); kinesiology (M Sc, MA); management (M Sc, MA); marketing (MScM); mathematics (M Sc); music (MA); Native American studies (MA); neuroscience (M Sc, PhD); new media (MA); nursing (M Sc); philosophy (MA); physics (M Sc); policy and strategy (MScM); political science (MA); psychology (M Sc, MA); religious studies (MA); sociology (MA); theoretical and computational science (PhD); urban and regional studies (MA). Part-time and evening/weekend programs available. *Degree requirements:* For doctorate, comprehensive exam, thesis/dissertation. *Entrance requirements:* For master's, GMAT (M Sc in management), bachelor's degree in related field, minimum GPA of 3.0 during previous 20 graded semester courses, 2 years teaching or related experience (M Ed); for doctorate, master's degree, minimum graduate GPA of 3.5. Additional exam requirements/recommendations for international students: Required—TOEFL. *Faculty research:* Movement and brain plasticity, gibberellin physiology, photosynthesis, carbon cycling, molecular properties of main-group ring components.

University of Maine, Graduate School, College of Business, Public Policy and Health, Department of Economics, Orono, ME 04469. Offers economics (MA); financial economics (MA). Part-time programs available. *Degree requirements:* For master's, thesis optional. *Entrance requirements:* For master's, GRE General Test. Additional exam requirements/recommendations for international students: Required—TOEFL. Electronic applications accepted. *Faculty research:* Health and marine resource economics, alternative political economy.

University of Manitoba, Faculty of Graduate Studies, Faculty of Arts, Department of Economics, Winnipeg, MB R3T 2N2, Canada. Offers MA, PhD. *Degree requirements:* For master's, thesis or alternative; for doctorate, one foreign language, thesis/dissertation.

University of Maryland, Baltimore County, Graduate School, College of Arts, Humanities and Social Sciences, Department of Economics, Program in Economic Policy Analysis, Baltimore, MD 21250. Offers MA. Part-time and evening/weekend programs available. *Faculty:* 26 full-time (10 women), 2 part-time/adjunct (0 women). *Students:* 13 full-time (4 women), 9 part-time; includes 6 minority (2 African Americans, 3 Asian Americans or Pacific Islanders, 1 Hispanic American), 4 international. Average age 27. 23 applicants, 87% accepted, 8 enrolled. In 2008, 9 master's awarded. *Degree requirements:* For master's, comprehensive exam, capstone research project. *Entrance requirements:* For master's, GRE General Test, undergraduate coursework in economic theory, econometrics, calculus. Additional exam requirements/recommendations for international students: Required—TOEFL. *Application deadline:* For fall admission, 7/1 priority date for domestic students, 3/1 priority date for international students; for spring admission, 1/1 priority date for domestic students, 9/15 priority date for international students. Applications are processed on a rolling basis. Application fee: $45. Electronic applications accepted. *Financial support:* In 2008–09, 4 students received support, including 3 research assistantships with full and partial tuition reimbursements available (averaging $11,324 per year), 1 teaching assistantship with full tuition reimbursement available (averaging $11,324 per year); Federal Work-Study, health care benefits, tuition waivers (full and partial), and unspecified assistantships also available. Support available to part-time students. Financial award application deadline: 4/15; financial award applicants required to submit FAFSA. *Faculty research:* International trade policy analysis, health and hospital policy evaluation, environmental policy analysis, economics of education, economic growth and development. Total annual research expenditures: $50,000. *Unit head:* Dr. David F. Mitch, Professor of Economics and Graduate Director, Fax: 410-455-1054, E-mail: mitch@umbc.edu. *Application contact:* Dr. David F. Mitch, Professor of Economics and Graduate Director, Fax: 410-455-1054, E-mail: mitch@umbc.edu.

University of Maryland, College Park, Graduate Studies, College of Behavioral and Social Sciences, Department of Economics, College Park, MD 20742. Offers MA, PhD. Part-time and evening/weekend programs available. Terminal master's awarded for partial completion of doctoral program. *Degree requirements:* For master's, comprehensive exam, thesis optional; for doctorate, comprehensive exam, thesis/dissertation, exams. *Entrance requirements:* For master's, GRE General Test, minimum GPA of 3.0, course work in calculus and mathematics, 3 letters of recommendation; for doctorate, GRE General Test, calculus background. Additional exam requirements/recommendations for international students: Required—TOEFL. Electronic applications accepted. *Faculty research:* International economics, natural resource and environmental economics, forecasting and policy analysis, economic growth, demography of inequality.

University of Maryland, College Park, Graduate Studies, College of Behavioral and Social Sciences, Department of Government and Politics, College Park, MD 20742. Offers American politics (PhD); comparative politics (PhD); international relations (PhD); political economy (PhD); political theory (PhD). Part-time and evening/weekend programs available. *Degree requirements:* For doctorate, comprehensive exam, thesis/dissertation, written exams in 2 fields. *Entrance requirements:* For doctorate, GRE General Test, minimum GPA of 3.5, writing sample. Additional exam requirements/recommendations for international students: Required—TOEFL. Electronic applications accepted. *Faculty research:* International development/conflict, international security, post-communist society, public service, dynamics of conflict and conflict resolution.

University of Massachusetts Amherst, Graduate School, College of Social and Behavioral Sciences, Department of Economics, Amherst, MA 01003. Offers MA, PhD. Part-time programs available. Terminal master's awarded for partial completion of doctoral program. *Degree requirements:* For master's, thesis or alternative; for doctorate, comprehensive exam, thesis/dissertation. *Entrance requirements:* For master's and doctorate, GRE General Test. Additional exam requirements/recommendations for international students: Required—TOEFL (minimum score 550 paper-based; 213 computer-based; 79 iBT), IELTS (minimum score 6.5). Electronic applications accepted. *Expenses:* Tuition, area resident: Full-time $2640. Tuition, nonresident: full-time $9936. One-time fee: $332 full-time. Tuition and fees vary according to course load.

University of Massachusetts Lowell, College of Arts and Sciences, Department of Regional Economic and Social Development, Lowell, MA 01854-2881. Offers MA, Graduate Certificate. Part-time programs available. *Entrance requirements:* For master's, GRE. Electronic applications accepted.

University of Memphis, Graduate School, Fogelman College of Business and Economics, Department of Economics, Memphis, TN 38152. Offers MA, PhD. Part-time programs available. *Faculty:* 9 full-time (1 woman), 1 part-time/adjunct (0 women). *Students:* 3 full-time (0 women), 2 part-time (0 women); includes 1 minority (African American), 1 international. Average age 26. 8 applicants, 88% accepted, 0 enrolled. In 2008, 2 master's awarded. *Degree requirements:* For master's, comprehensive exam, thesis or alternative; for doctorate, comprehensive exam, thesis/dissertation. *Entrance requirements:* For master's, GMAT or GRE General Test, previous course work in statistics, intermediate micro and macro theory; for doctorate, GMAT, interview, minimum GPA of 3.4. *Application deadline:* For fall admission, 8/1 for domestic students; for spring admission, 12/1 for domestic students. Application fee: $35 ($60 for international students). *Expenses:* Tuition, area resident: Full-time $6242; part-time $330 per credit hour. Tuition, state resident: full-time $6242; part-time $330 per credit hour. Tuition, nonresident: full-time $17,828; part-time $815 per credit hour. Required fees: $1156. *Financial support:* Research assistantships with full tuition reimbursements, teaching assistantships with full tuition reimbursements, scholarships/grants available. Financial award applicants required to submit FAFSA. *Faculty research:* Tax research, medical economics, law and economics, labor economics, U.S. and Japanese economic relations. *Unit head:* Dr. William Smith, Interim Chair, 901-678-2785, E-mail: wtsmith@memphis.edu. *Application contact:* Dr. Pinaki Bose, Master's Program Coordinator, 901-678-5528, Fax: 901-678-4705, E-mail: psbose@memphis.edu.

University of Memphis, Graduate School, Fogelman College of Business and Economics, Program in Business Administration, Memphis, TN 38152. Offers accounting (MBA, PhD); economics (MBA, PhD); executive business administration (MBA); finance (PhD); finance, insurance, and real estate (MBA, MS); international business administration (IMBA); management (MBA, MS, PhD); management information systems (MBA, MS, PhD); management science (MBA); marketing (MBA, MS); marketing and supply chain management (PhD); real estate development (MS); JD/MBA. *Accreditation:* AACSB. *Faculty:* 44 full-time (7 women), 2 part-time/adjunct (0 women). *Students:* 209 full-time (90 women), 180 part-time (53 women); includes 57 minority (38 African Americans, 2 American Indian/Alaska Native, 13 Asian Americans or Pacific Islanders, 4 Hispanic Americans), 121 international. Average age 31. 235 applicants, 66% accepted, 83 enrolled. In 2008, 146 master's, 8 doctorates awarded. *Degree requirements:* For master's, comprehensive exam; for doctorate, comprehensive exam, thesis/dissertation. *Entrance requirements:* For master's, GMAT, resumé; for doctorate, GMAT, interview, minimum GPA of 3.4, resumé, letter of recommendation. Additional exam requirements/recommendations for international students: Required—TOEFL (minimum score 550 paper-based; 220 computer-based). *Application deadline:* For fall admission, 8/1 for domestic students; for spring admission, 12/1 for domestic students. Application fee: $35 ($60 for international students). *Expenses:* Tuition, area resident: Full-time $6242; part-time $330 per credit hour. Tuition, state resident: full-time $6242; part-time $330 per credit hour. Tuition, nonresident: full-time $17,828; part-time $815 per credit hour. Required fees: $1156. *Financial support:* Research assistantships with full tuition reimbursements, teaching assistantships, career-related internships or fieldwork, scholarships/grants, and unspecified assistantships available. Financial award applicants required to submit FAFSA. *Faculty research:* Competitive business strategy, finance microstructures, supply chain management innovations, health care economics, litigation risks and corporate audits. *Unit head:* Rajiv Grover, Dean, 901-678-3759, E-mail: rgrover@memphis.edu. *Application contact:* Dr. Carol V. Danehower, Associate Dean for Programs, 901-678-5402, Fax: 901-678-3579, E-mail: fcbegp@memphis.edu.

University of Miami, Graduate School, School of Business Administration, Department of Economics, Coral Gables, FL 33124. Offers economic development (MA, PhD); environmental economics (PhD); human resource economics (MA, PhD); international economics (MA, PhD); macroeconomics (PhD). Students admitted every two years in the fall semester. Terminal master's awarded for partial completion of doctoral program. *Degree requirements:* For master's, comprehensive exam; for doctorate, comprehensive exam, thesis/dissertation. *Entrance requirements:* For master's and doctorate, GRE General Test, minimum GPA of 3.0. Additional exam requirements/recommendations for international students: Required—TOEFL (minimum score 550 paper-based). *Faculty research:* International economics/trade, applied microeconomics, development.

University of Michigan, Horace H. Rackham School of Graduate Studies, College of Literature, Science, and the Arts, Department of Economics, Ann Arbor, MI 48109. Offers applied economics (AM); economics (AM, PhD); public policy and economics (PhD); social work and economics (PhD); JD/PhD; MPP/AM. Terminal master's awarded for partial completion of doctoral program. *Degree requirements:* For doctorate, oral defense of dissertation, preliminary exam. *Entrance requirements:* For master's and doctorate, GRE General Test. Additional exam requirements/recommendations for international students: Required—TOEFL (minimum score 600 paper-based; 250 computer-based). Electronic applications accepted. *Faculty research:* Economic and econometrical analysis, industrial organization, international trade, public finance, development, health, labor, population standard, macro, theory.

University of Minnesota, Twin Cities Campus, Graduate School, College of Liberal Arts, Department of Economics, Minneapolis, MN 55455-0213. Offers PhD. *Degree requirements:* For doctorate, thesis/dissertation, preliminary exams. *Entrance requirements:* For doctorate, GRE General Test. Additional exam requirements/recommendations for international students: Required—TOEFL (minimum score 600 paper-based; 250 computer-based; 100 iBT), IELTS (minimum score 7). Electronic applications accepted. *Faculty research:* Econometrics, macro- and monetary economics, mathematical economics, industrial organization, applied micro theory.

University of Mississippi, Graduate School, College of Liberal Arts, Department of Economics, Oxford, University, MS 38677. Offers MA, PhD. Electronic applications accepted.

University of Missouri–Columbia, Graduate School, College of Arts and Sciences, Department of Economics, Columbia, MO 65211. Offers MA, PhD, JD/MA. *Faculty:* 22 full-time (6 women), 4 part-time/adjunct (1 woman). *Students:* 44 full-time (18 women), 31 part-time (13 women); includes 1 minority (African American), 60 international. Average age 29. 167 applicants, 13% accepted, 15 enrolled. In 2008, 11 master's, 3 doctorates awarded. Terminal master's awarded for partial completion of doctoral program. *Degree requirements:* For doctorate, thesis/dissertation. *Entrance requirements:* For master's and doctorate, GRE General Test, minimum GPA of 3.0. Additional exam requirements/recommendations for international students: Required—TOEFL (minimum score 550 paper-based; 213 computer-based; 79 iBT). *Application deadline:* For fall admission, 1/15 priority date for domestic students; for winter admission, 11/1 priority date for domestic students; for spring admission, 3/1 priority date for domestic students. Application fee: $45 ($60 for international students). *Financial support:* Fellowships, research assistantships, teaching assistantships, institutionally sponsored loans available. *Unit head:* Dr. David Mandy, Department Chair, E-mail: mandyd@missouri.edu. *Application contact:* Lynne Riddell, 573-884-7989, E-mail: riddelll@missouri.edu.

University of Missouri–Kansas City, College of Arts and Sciences, Department of Economics, Kansas City, MO 64110-2499. Offers MA, PhD. PhD (interdisciplinary) offered through the School of Graduate Studies. Part-time and evening/weekend programs available. *Faculty:* 11 full-time (1 woman), 3 part-time/adjunct (0 women). *Students:* 9 full-time (4 women), 27 part-time (4 women); includes 6 minority (1 African American, 4 Asian Americans or Pacific Islanders, 1 Hispanic American), 9 international. Average age 30. 30 applicants, 100% accepted, 20 enrolled. In 2008, 10 master's awarded. *Degree requirements:* For doctorate, comprehensive exam, thesis/dissertation. *Entrance requirements:* For master's, GRE or minimum undergraduate GPA of 2.5; for doctorate, GRE, master's degree in economics or equivalent. Additional exam requirements/recommendations for international students: Required—TOEFL (minimum score 550 paper-based; 213 computer-based; 80 iBT). *Application deadline:* For fall admission, 2/1 priority date for domestic and international students; for spring admission, 9/1 priority date for domestic and international students. Applications are processed on a rolling basis. Application fee: $45 ($50 for international students). Electronic applications accepted. *Expenses:* Tuition, state resident: full-time $5376; part-time $298.70 per credit hour. Tuition, nonresident: full-time $13,882; part-time $771.20 per credit hour. Required fees: $640.28; $34.65 per contact hour. $30 per semester. Tuition and fees vary according to course load and program. *Financial support:* In 2008–09, 23 teaching assistantships with partial tuition reimbursements (averaging $12,406 per year) were awarded; fellowships with partial tuition reimbursements, research assistantships with partial tuition reimbursements, career-related internships or fieldwork, Federal Work-Study, institutionally sponsored loans, and tuition waivers (full and partial) also available. Support available to part-time students. Financial award application deadline: 3/1; financial award applicants required to submit FAFSA. *Faculty research:* International trade, general theory, institutions/utilities, forensic economics, human resources. Total annual research

Economics

University of Missouri–Kansas City (continued)
expenditures: $255,064. *Unit head:* James Sturgeon, Chair, 816-235-2837, Fax: 816-238-2836, E-mail: sturgeonj@umkc.edu. *Application contact:* Fred Lee, Graduate Advisor, 816-235-2543, Fax: 816-238-2836, E-mail: leefs@umkc.edu.

University of Missouri–St. Louis, College of Arts and Sciences, Department of Economics, St. Louis, MO 63121. Offers general economics (MA), including business economics; managerial economics (Certificate). Part-time and evening/weekend programs available. *Faculty:* 10 full-time (3 women). *Students:* 10 full-time (1 woman), 8 part-time (2 women), 1 international. Average age 30. In 2008, 8 master's awarded. *Entrance requirements:* For master's, GRE General Test, 2 letters of recommendation. Additional exam requirements/recommendations for international students: Required—TOEFL (minimum score 550 paper-based; 213 computer-based). *Application deadline:* For fall admission, 7/1 priority date for domestic and international students; for spring admission, 12/1 priority date for domestic and international students. Applications are processed on a rolling basis. Application fee: $35 ($40 for international students). Electronic applications accepted. *Expenses:* Tuition, area resident: Full-time $5377; part-time $298.70 per credit hour. Tuition, nonresident: full-time $13,381; part-time $472.50 per credit hour. Required fees: $4078; $52 per credit hour. *Financial support:* In 2008–09, 4 research assistantships with full and partial tuition reimbursements (averaging $5,000 per year) were awarded; teaching assistantships with full and partial tuition reimbursements. Financial award applicants required to submit FAFSA. *Faculty research:* Health economics, public policy analysis, econometrics, public choice, telecommunications and forensic economics. *Unit head:* Dr. Donald Kridel, Director of Graduate Studies, 314-516-5351, Fax: 314-516-5562, E-mail: kridel@umsl.edu. *Application contact:* 314-516-5458, Fax: 314-516-6996, E-mail: gradadm@umsl.edu.

The University of Montana, Graduate School, College of Arts and Sciences, Department of Economics, Missoula, MT 59812-0002. Offers MA. *Degree requirements:* For master's, thesis. *Entrance requirements:* For master's, GRE General Test. Additional exam requirements/recommendations for international students: Required—TOEFL (minimum score 525 paper-based; 197 computer-based). *Faculty research:* Resource economics, public policy, environmental economics, economic development, regional economics.

University of Nebraska at Omaha, Graduate Studies and Research, College of Business Administration, Department of Economics, Omaha, NE 68182. Offers MA, MS. Part-time and evening/weekend programs available. *Degree requirements:* For master's, comprehensive exam, thesis (for some programs). *Entrance requirements:* For master's, minimum GPA of 3.0. Additional exam requirements/recommendations for international students: Required—TOEFL (minimum score 530 paper-based; 197 computer-based; 71 iBT). Electronic applications accepted. *Faculty research:* Labor, economics of science, international development, monetary economics, econometrics.

University of Nebraska–Lincoln, Graduate College, College of Business Administration, Department of Economics, Lincoln, NE 68588. Offers MA, PhD, JD/MA. *Faculty:* 12 full-time (2 women), 1 part-time/adjunct. *Students:* 23 full-time (9 women), 6 part-time (3 women); includes 4 minority (1 African American, 3 Asian Americans or Pacific Islanders), 14 international. Average age 33. In 2008, 6 master's, 2 doctorates awarded. *Degree requirements:* For master's, thesis optional; for doctorate, comprehensive exam, thesis/dissertation. *Entrance requirements:* For master's and doctorate, GRE General Test. Additional exam requirements/recommendations for international students: Required—TOEFL (minimum score 550 paper-based; 213 computer-based). *Application deadline:* For fall admission, 6/30 for domestic students, 3/1 for international students; for spring admission, 10/31 for domestic students, 9/1 for international students. Applications are processed on a rolling basis. Application fee: $40. Electronic applications accepted. *Expenses:* Tuition, state resident: full-time $4275; part-time $237.50 per credit hour. Tuition, nonresident: full-time $11,525; part-time $640.25 per credit hour. Required fees: $1068; $10.35 per credit hour. $440.70 per semester. Tuition and fees vary according to course load and program. *Financial support:* Fellowships, research assistantships, teaching assistantships, Federal Work-Study and health care benefits available. Support available to part-time students. Financial award application deadline: 2/15. *Faculty research:* Applied microeconomics, economic education, international trade and finance, public finance, regional and institutional economics. *Unit head:* Dr. John E. Anderson, Chair, 402-472-2319. *Application contact:* Ginny Gross, Director of Graduate Admissions, 402-472-2878, Fax: 402-472-0589, E-mail: grad_admissions@unl.edu.

University of Nevada, Las Vegas, Graduate College, College of Business, Department of Economics, Las Vegas, NV 89154-6005. Offers MA. Part-time and evening/weekend programs available. *Faculty:* 16 full-time (1 woman), 1 part-time/adjunct (0 women). *Students:* 11 full-time (5 women), 14 part-time (2 women); includes 4 minority (2 African Americans, 2 Hispanic Americans), 5 international. Average age 28. 27 applicants, 93% accepted, 10 enrolled. In 2008, 4 master's awarded. *Degree requirements:* For master's, thesis, oral defense of thesis. *Entrance requirements:* For master's, GRE General Test or GMAT. Additional exam requirements/recommendations for international students: Required—TOEFL (minimum score 550 paper-based; 213 computer-based; 80 iBT), IELTS (minimum score 7). *Application deadline:* For fall admission, 6/15 priority date for domestic students, 5/1 for international students; for spring admission, 11/15 priority date for domestic students, 10/1 for international students. Applications are processed on a rolling basis. Application fee: $60 ($75 for international students). Electronic applications accepted. *Expenses:* Tuition, state resident: full-time $1414; part-time $198 per credit. Tuition, nonresident: full-time $12,509; part-time $415.75 per credit. International tuition: $14,249 full-time. Required fees: $4 per credit. $252 per semester. Tuition and fees vary according to course load. *Financial support:* In 2008–09, 6 students received support, including 5 research assistantships with partial tuition reimbursements available (averaging $10,333 per year), 1 teaching assistantship with partial tuition reimbursement available (averaging $10,000 per year); institutionally sponsored loans, scholarships/grants, health care benefits, and unspecified assistantships also available. Financial award application deadline: 3/1. *Unit head:* Dr. Stephen Miller, Chair/Professor, 702-895-3969, Fax: 702-895-1354, E-mail: stephen.miller@unlv.edu. *Application contact:* Graduate College Admissions Evaluator, 702-895-3320, Fax: 702-895-4180, E-mail: gradcollege@unlv.edu.

University of Nevada, Reno, Graduate School, College of Business Administration, Department of Economics, Reno, NV 89557. Offers MA, MS. *Faculty:* 13 full-time (1 woman). *Students:* 12 full-time (5 women), 13 part-time (8 women); includes 5 minority (2 Asian Americans or Pacific Islanders, 3 Hispanic Americans), 3 international. Average age 30. 21 applicants, 76% accepted, 12 enrolled. In 2008, 7 master's awarded. *Degree requirements:* For master's, thesis. *Entrance requirements:* For master's, GMAT or GRE, minimum GPA of 2.75. Additional exam requirements/recommendations for international students: Required—TOEFL (minimum score 500 paper-based; 173 computer-based; 61 iBT), IELTS (minimum score 6), TOFEL or IELTS. *Application deadline:* For fall admission, 4/15 priority date for domestic and international students; for spring admission, 10/15 priority date for domestic and international students. Applications are processed on a rolling basis. Application fee: $60 ($95 for international students). Electronic applications accepted. *Expenses:* Tuition, state resident: full-time $1710; part-time $1140 per semester. Tuition, nonresident: full-time $7115. Required fees: $158 per semester. *Financial support:* In 2008–09, 7 research assistantships with partial tuition reimbursements (averaging $14,000 per year), 1 teaching assistantship with partial tuition reimbursement (averaging $14,000 per year) were awarded; Federal Work-Study, institutionally sponsored loans, scholarships/grants, health care benefits, and unspecified assistantships also available. Financial award application deadline: 3/1; financial award applicants required to submit FAFSA. *Faculty research:* Applied microeconomics, public finance, development, labor. Total annual research expenditures: $10,894. *Unit head:* Dr. Frederico Guerro, Graduate Program Director, 775-784-6864. *Application contact:* Dr. Frederico Guerro, Graduate Program Director, 775-784-6864.

University of New Brunswick Fredericton, School of Graduate Studies, Faculty of Arts, Department of Economics, Fredericton, NB E3B 5A3, Canada. Offers applied economics and finance (M Sc); economics (MA). Program in applied economics and finance offered at UNB

Saint John Campus. Part-time programs available. *Faculty:* 110 full-time (1 woman), 3 part-time/adjunct (0 women). *Students:* 4 full-time (2 women), 4 part-time (2 women). In 2008, 5 master's awarded. *Entrance requirements:* For master's, GRE, minimum GPA of 3.0. Additional exam requirements/recommendations for international students: Required—TWE, TOEFL (minimum paper-based score of 550) or IELTS. *Application deadline:* 1/31 for domestic and international students. Applications are processed on a rolling basis. Application fee: $50 Canadian dollars. Tuition and fees charges are reported in Canadian dollars. *Expenses:* Tuition, area resident: Full-time $5562 Canadian dollars. Tuition, nonresident: full-time $9450 Canadian dollars. Required fees: $333 Canadian dollars. *Financial support:* In 2008–09, 1 research assistantship, 1 teaching assistantship were awarded; fellowships, scholarships/grants, health care benefits, and unspecified assistantships also available. Financial award application deadline: 1/31. *Faculty research:* Epidemiology and population health, micro/macro economics, economics of transportation, regional development. *Unit head:* Dr. Yuri Yevdokimov, Director of Graduate Studies, 506-447-3221, Fax: 506-453-4514, E-mail: yuri@unb.ca. *Application contact:* Lucina MacDonald, Graduate Secretary, 506-453-4828, Fax: 506-453-4514, E-mail: lmacdona@unb.ca.

University of New Brunswick Fredericton, School of Graduate Studies, Policy Studies Program, Fredericton, NB E3B 5A3, Canada. Offers people, property and alternative dispute resolution (M Phil); philosophy politics and economics (M Phil); sustainable development (M Phil). *Faculty:* 6 full-time (2 women), 13 part-time/adjunct (2 women). *Students:* 16 full-time (9 women), 4 part-time (3 women). In 2008, 3 master's awarded. *Entrance requirements:* For master's, minimum GPA of 3.5, BA. Additional exam requirements/recommendations for international students: Required—TOEFL (minimum score 600 paper-based), TWE (minimum score 5). Application fee: $50 Canadian dollars. Tuition and fees charges are reported in Canadian dollars. *Expenses:* Tuition, area resident: Full-time $5562 Canadian dollars. Tuition, nonresident: full-time $9450 Canadian dollars. Required fees: $333 Canadian dollars. *Financial support:* In 2008–09, 4 research assistantships, 1 teaching assistantship were awarded. *Unit head:* Dr. Linda Eyre, Dean of Graduate Studies, 506-447-3044, Fax: 506-453-4817, E-mail: gradidst@unb.ca. *Application contact:* Janet Amurault, Graduate Secretary, 506-458-7558, Fax: 506-453-4817, E-mail: jamiraul@unb.ca.

University of New Hampshire, Graduate School, Whittemore School of Business and Economics, Department of Economics, Durham, NH 03824. Offers MA, PhD. Part-time programs available. *Faculty:* 13 full-time (4 women). *Students:* 27 full-time (15 women), 2 part-time (1 woman), 15 international. Average age 35. 64 applicants, 70% accepted, 17 enrolled. In 2008, 15 master's, 1 doctorate awarded. Terminal master's awarded for partial completion of doctoral program. *Degree requirements:* For master's, thesis or alternative; for doctorate, one foreign language, thesis/dissertation. *Entrance requirements:* For master's and doctorate, GRE General Test. Additional exam requirements/recommendations for international students: Required—TOEFL (minimum score 550 paper-based; 213 computer-based; 80 iBT). *Application deadline:* For fall admission, 4/1 priority date for domestic students, 4/1 for international students. Applications are processed on a rolling basis. Application fee: $60. Electronic applications accepted. *Expenses:* Tuition, area resident: Full-time $9720; part-time $540 per credit hour. Tuition, nonresident: full-time $23,200; part-time $954 per credit hour. Required fees: $1446; $361.50 per term. *Financial support:* In 2008–09, 23 students received support, including 1 fellowship, 1 research assistantship, 19 teaching assistantships; career-related internships or fieldwork, Federal Work-Study, scholarships/grants, and tuition waivers (full and partial) also available. Support available to part-time students. Financial award application deadline: 2/15. *Faculty research:* Labor economics, international development, econometrics, finance, political economy. *Unit head:* Dr. Bruce Elmslie, Chair, 603-862-3357. *Application contact:* Sinthy Kounlasa, Administrative Assistant, 603-862-3457, E-mail: wsbe.grad@unh.edu.

See Close-Up on page 781.

University of New Mexico, Graduate School, College of Arts and Sciences, Department of Economics, Albuquerque, NM 87131-2039. Offers MA, PhD. Part-time programs available. Terminal master's awarded for partial completion of doctoral program. *Degree requirements:* For master's, comprehensive exam, thesis or alternative; for doctorate, comprehensive exam, thesis/dissertation. *Entrance requirements:* For master's and doctorate, GRE General Test, 3 letters of recommendation, letter of intent. Additional exam requirements/recommendations for international students: Required—TOEFL (minimum score 550 paper-based; 213 computer-based). Electronic applications accepted. *Faculty research:* Public finance, international/development economics, labor/human resource economics, econometrics, core theory, environmental/natural resource economics.

University of New Orleans, Graduate School, College of Business Administration, Department of Economics and Finance, Program in Financial Economics, New Orleans, LA 70148. Offers PhD. Terminal master's awarded for partial completion of doctoral program. *Degree requirements:* For doctorate, one foreign language, comprehensive exam, thesis/dissertation, general exams. *Entrance requirements:* For doctorate, GRE General Test, minimum GPA of 3.0. Additional exam requirements/recommendations for international students: Required—TOEFL (minimum score 550 paper-based; 213 computer-based; 79 iBT). Electronic applications accepted. *Faculty research:* Urban and regional economics, economic development, monetary theory and policy, international finance.

The University of North Carolina at Chapel Hill, Graduate School, College of Arts and Sciences, Department of Economics, Chapel Hill, NC 27599. Offers MS, PhD. Terminal master's awarded for partial completion of doctoral program. *Degree requirements:* For master's, comprehensive exam, thesis or alternative; for doctorate, comprehensive exam, thesis/dissertation. *Entrance requirements:* For master's, GRE General Test, minimum GPA of 3.0; for doctorate, GRE General Test, minimum GPA of 3.5. Additional exam requirements/recommendations for international students: Required—TOEFL (minimum score 550 paper-based; 213 computer-based). Electronic applications accepted. *Faculty research:* Health economics, micro theory/IO, labor economics, economic history, financial econometrics.

The University of North Carolina at Charlotte, Graduate School, Belk College of Business, Department of Economics, Charlotte, NC 28223-0001. Offers MS. Part-time and evening/weekend programs available. *Faculty:* 16 full-time (4 women), 3 part-time/adjunct (0 women). *Students:* 12 full-time (4 women), 25 part-time (8 women); includes 9 minority (1 African American, 2 Asian Americans or Pacific Islanders, 6 Hispanic Americans), 7 international. Average age 27. 37 applicants, 97% accepted, 20 enrolled. In 2008, 3 master's awarded. *Degree requirements:* For master's, thesis or project. *Entrance requirements:* For master's, GRE General Test, minimum undergraduate GPA of 3.0 in major, 2.8 overall. Additional exam requirements/recommendations for international students: Required—TOEFL (minimum score 557 paper-based; 220 computer-based). *Application deadline:* For fall admission, 7/15 for domestic students, 5/1 for international students; for spring admission, 11/15 for domestic students, 10/1 for international students. Applications are processed on a rolling basis. Application fee: $55. Electronic applications accepted. *Expenses:* Tuition, area resident: Full-time $2919; part-time $122 per credit hour. Tuition, state resident: full-time $2919; part-time $122 per credit hour. Tuition, nonresident: full-time $13,126; part-time $547 per credit hour. Required fees: $1779; $91 per credit hour. Tuition and fees vary according to program. *Financial support:* In 2008–09, 22 teaching assistantships (averaging $5,340 per year) were awarded; career-related internships or fieldwork, Federal Work-Study, institutionally sponsored loans, scholarships/grants, and unspecified assistantships also available. Support available to part-time students. Financial award application deadline: 4/1; financial award applicants required to submit FAFSA. *Faculty research:* Health care, taxation, energy, economic growth, monetary policy. *Unit head:* Dr. Richard A. Zuber, Chair, 704-687-2185, Fax: 704-687-6442, E-mail: razuber@emial.uncc.edu. *Application contact:* Kathy B. Giddings, Director of Graduate Admissions, 704-687-3366, Fax: 704-687-3279, E-mail: agidding@uncc.edu.

The University of North Carolina at Greensboro, Graduate School, Bryan School of Business and Economics, Department of Economics, Program in Economics, Greensboro, NC 27412-5001. Offers PhD. *Degree requirements:* For doctorate, comprehensive exam, thesis/dissertation.

Entrance requirements: Additional exam requirements/recommendations for international students: Required—TOEFL. Electronic applications accepted.

University of North Texas, Robert B. Toulouse School of Graduate Studies, College of Arts and Sciences, Department of Economics, Denton, TX 76203. Offers economic research (MS); economics (MA, MS); labor and industrial relations (MS). Part-time programs available. *Degree requirements:* For master's, comprehensive exam, thesis (for some programs). *Entrance requirements:* For master's, GMAT, GRE General Test, 3.0 GPA, 2 letters of recommendation, 500 word essay. Additional exam requirements/recommendations for international students: Required—proof of English language proficiency required for non-native English speakers; Recommended—TOEFL (minimum score 550 paper-based; 213 computer-based). *Faculty research:* Resource economics, international trade and development, immigration, telecommunications, micro enterprise development.

University of Notre Dame, Graduate School, College of Arts and Letters, Division of Social Science, Department of Economics and Econometrics, Notre Dame, IN 46556. Offers MA, PhD. *Students:* 26 full-time (5 women); includes 2 minority (1 African American, 1 Asian American or Pacific Islander), 12 international. 83 applicants, 19% accepted, 10 enrolled. In 2008, 7 master's, 2 doctorates awarded. Terminal master's awarded for partial completion of doctoral program. *Degree requirements:* For master's, comprehensive exam (for some programs), thesis optional; for doctorate, thesis/dissertation, candidacy exam. *Entrance requirements:* For doctorate, GRE General Test. Additional exam requirements/recommendations for international students: Required—TOEFL (minimum score 600 paper-based; 250 computer-based; 80 iBT). *Application deadline:* For fall admission, 1/15 priority date for domestic and international students. Application fee: $50. Electronic applications accepted. *Financial support:* Fellowships with full tuition reimbursements, teaching assistantships with full tuition reimbursements, tuition waivers (full) available. Financial award application deadline: 1/15. *Unit head:* Dr. Kali Rath, Director of Graduate Studies, 574-631-7698, E-mail: ecoe@nd.edu. *Application contact:* Dr. Barbara Turpin, Director of Graduate Admissions, 574-631-7706.

University of Oklahoma, Graduate College, College of Arts and Sciences, Department of Economics, Norman, OK 73019. Offers MA, PhD. *Faculty:* 17 full-time (6 women), 4 part-time/adjunct (2 women). *Students:* 41 full-time (11 women), 74 part-time (10 women); includes 21 minority (10 African Americans, 1 American Indian/Alaska Native, 5 Asian Americans or Pacific Islanders, 5 Hispanic Americans), 22 international. 53 applicants, 75% accepted, 26 enrolled. In 2008, 50 master's, 3 doctorates awarded. Terminal master's awarded for partial completion of doctoral program. *Degree requirements:* For doctorate, 2 foreign languages, thesis/dissertation, general exams. *Entrance requirements:* For master's, GRE General Test, minimum GPA of 3.0 in last 60 hours of course work; for doctorate, GRE General Test. Additional exam requirements/recommendations for international students: Required—TOEFL (minimum score 550 paper-based; 213 computer-based). *Application deadline:* For fall admission, 4/1 for domestic and international students; for spring admission, 9/1 for domestic and international students. Applications are processed on a rolling basis. Application fee: $40 ($90 for international students). Electronic applications accepted. *Expenses:* Tuition, state resident: full-time $3744; part-time $156 per credit hour. Tuition, nonresident: full-time $13,577; part-time $565.70 per credit hour. Required fees: $2415.40; $90.10 per credit hour. *Financial support:* In 2008–09, 9 students received support, including 25 teaching assistantships with partial tuition reimbursements available (averaging $13,116 per year); scholarships/grants, health care benefits, unspecified assistantships, and intersession and summer teaching opportunities also available. Financial award applicants required to submit FAFSA. *Faculty research:* Industrial organization, international economics; micro growth and development; public finance. Total annual research expenditures: $34,995. *Unit head:* Dr. Lex Holmes, Chair, 405-325-2861, Fax: 405-325-5842, E-mail: aholmes@ou.edu. *Application contact:* Cynthia Rogers, Graduate Liaison, 405-235-5843, Fax: 405-325-5842, E-mail: crogers@ou.edu.

University of Oregon, Graduate School, College of Arts and Sciences, Department of Economics, Eugene, OR 97403. Offers MA, MS, PhD. Terminal master's awarded for partial completion of doctoral program. *Degree requirements:* For master's, thesis or alternative; for doctorate, thesis/dissertation, qualifying exam. *Entrance requirements:* For master's and doctorate, GRE General Test, minimum GPA of 3.0. Additional exam requirements/recommendations for international students: Required—TOEFL. *Faculty research:* Labor economics, macroeconomics, international economics, industrial organization, public finance.

University of Ottawa, Faculty of Graduate and Postdoctoral Studies, Faculty of Social Sciences, Department of Economics, Ottawa, ON K1N 6N5, Canada. Offers MA, PhD. Part-time programs available. *Degree requirements:* For master's, thesis or alternative; for doctorate, comprehensive exam, thesis/dissertation. *Entrance requirements:* For master's, honors bachelor's degree or equivalent, minimum B average; for doctorate, master's degree, minimum B+ average. Electronic applications accepted. *Faculty research:* Public economics, industrial organizations, monetary economics, international economics, economic development.

University of Pennsylvania, School of Arts and Sciences, Graduate Group in Economics, Philadelphia, PA 19104. Offers AM, PhD, JD/AM, JD/PhD. *Degree requirements:* For doctorate, thesis/dissertation. *Entrance requirements:* For doctorate, GRE General Test. Additional exam requirements/recommendations for international students: Required—TOEFL. Electronic applications accepted. *Faculty research:* Economic theory, econometrics, international economics, monetary/macroeconomics, applied microeconomics, empirical microeconomics.

University of Pittsburgh, Graduate School of Public and International Affairs, Doctoral Program in Public and International Affairs, Pittsburgh, PA 15260. Offers development policy (PhD); foreign and security policy (PhD); international political economy (PhD); public administration (PhD); public policy (PhD). *Accreditation:* NASPAA. Part-time programs available. *Degree requirements:* For doctorate, comprehensive exam, thesis/dissertation. *Entrance requirements:* For doctorate, GRE, 3 letters of recommendation, resumé, minimum GPA of 3.0, writing sample. Additional exam requirements/recommendations for international students: Required—TOEFL (minimum score 600 paper-based; 250 computer-based; 100 iBT), TWE (minimum score 4); Recommended—IELTS (minimum score 7). Electronic applications accepted. *Faculty research:* International political economy, international development, public administration, public policy, foreign policy, international security policy.

See Close-Up on page 1243.

University of Pittsburgh, Graduate School of Public and International Affairs, International Affairs Division, Program in Global Political Economy, Pittsburgh, PA 15260. Offers MPIA, JD/MPIA, MBA/MPIA, MID/MPIA, MPA/MPIA, MSIS/MPIA. Part-time and evening/weekend programs available. *Degree requirements:* For master's, thesis optional, internship, capstone seminar. *Entrance requirements:* For master's, GRE General Test, 3 letters of recommendation, resumé, minimum GPA of 3.2. Additional exam requirements/recommendations for international students: Required—TOEFL (minimum score 550 paper-based; 213 computer-based; 80 iBT), TWE (minimum score 4); Recommended—IELTS (minimum score 7). Electronic applications accepted. *Faculty research:* Political economy, international security/defense/intelligence, transnational crime, international trade, international finance, terrorism.

University of Pittsburgh, School of Arts and Sciences, Department of Economics, Pittsburgh, PA 15260. Offers PhD. Part-time programs available. Terminal master's awarded for partial completion of doctoral program. *Degree requirements:* For doctorate, comprehensive exam, thesis/dissertation, PhD Comprehensive Research Paper. *Entrance requirements:* For doctorate, GRE, 3 letters of recommendation, transcripts. Additional exam requirements/recommendations for international students: Required—TOEFL (minimum score 550 paper-based; 213 computer-based; 80 iBT), IELTS (minimum score 6.5). Electronic applications accepted. *Faculty research:* Game theory, experimental economics, regional economics, labor, international trade.

University of Puerto Rico, Río Piedras, College of Social Sciences, Department of Economics, San Juan, PR 00931-3300. Offers MA. Part-time programs available. *Degree requirements:* For master's, comprehensive exam, thesis. *Entrance requirements:* For master's, GRE, PAEG, interview, minimum GPA of 3.0, letter of recommendation.

University of Regina, Faculty of Graduate Studies and Research, Johnson-Shoyama Graduate School of Public Policy, Regina, SK S4S 0A2, Canada. Offers economic analysis for public policy (Master's Certificate); non-profit management (Master's Certificate); public management (MPA, Master's Certificate); public policy (MPA, PhD, Master's Certificate). Part-time and evening/weekend programs available. *Faculty:* 6 full-time (3 women). *Students:* 53 full-time (25 women), 63 part-time (38 women). 100 applicants, 82% accepted. In 2008, 40 master's awarded. *Entrance requirements:* Additional exam requirements/recommendations for international students: Required—TOEFL (minimum score 580 paper-based; 237 computer-based; 88 iBT). *Application deadline:* Applications are processed on a rolling basis. Application fee: $85 ($100 for international students). Electronic applications accepted. *Expenses:* Contact institution. *Financial support:* In 2008–09, 8 fellowships (averaging $15,930 per year), 2 research assistantships (averaging $13,720 per year), 5 teaching assistantships (averaging $6,650 per year) were awarded. Financial award application deadline: 6/15. *Faculty research:* Public administration and policy. *Unit head:* Dr. Ken Rasmussen, Associate Dean, 306-585-5463, E-mail: ken.rasmussen@uregina.ca. *Application contact:* Devon Anderson, Information Contact, 306-585-5462, E-mail: devon.anderson@uregina.ca.

University of Rhode Island, Graduate School, College of the Environment and Life Sciences, Department of Environmental and Natural Resource Economics, Kingston, RI 02881. Offers MS, PhD. *Expenses:* Tuition, state resident: full-time $8024; part-time $446 per credit. Tuition, nonresident: full-time $21,046; part-time $1169 per credit. Required fees: $1056; $26 per credit. $30 per semester. One-time fee: $95 part-time. *Unit head:* Dr. James Anderson, Chairperson, 401-874-4568, E-mail: jla@uri.edu. *Application contact:* Dr. James Anderson, Chairperson, 401-874-4568, E-mail: jla@uri.edu.

University of Rochester, The College, Arts and Sciences, Department of Economics, Rochester, NY 14627-0250. Offers MA, PhD. *Degree requirements:* For doctorate, thesis/dissertation, qualifying exam. *Entrance requirements:* For doctorate, GRE General Test, GRE Subject Test (strongly recommended). Additional exam requirements/recommendations for international students: Required—TOEFL.

University of San Francisco, College of Arts and Sciences, Department of Economics, San Francisco, CA 94117-1080. Offers economics (MA); financial analysis (MS); international and development economics (MA); MS/MBA. Part-time and evening/weekend programs available. *Degree requirements:* For master's, comprehensive exam, thesis or alternative. *Entrance requirements:* For master's, GRE General Test (recommended), BA in economics (preferred). Additional exam requirements/recommendations for international students: Required—TOEFL. *Faculty research:* Economic development, forecasting and planning, labor markets, Pacific Rim, financial markets.

University of San Francisco, Masagung Graduate School of Management, Program in Business Administration, San Francisco, CA 94117-1080. Offers business economics (MBA); e-business (MBA); entrepreneurship (MBA); finance (MBA); international business (MBA); management (MBA); marketing (MBA); telecommunications management and policy (MBA); JD/MBA; MSN/MBA. *Accreditation:* AACSB. *Entrance requirements:* For master's, GMAT, minimum undergraduate GPA of 3.2. Additional exam requirements/recommendations for international students: Required—TOEFL. *Faculty research:* International financial markets, technology transfer licensing, international marketing, strategic planning.

University of Saskatchewan, College of Graduate Studies and Research, College of Arts and Sciences, Department of Economics, Saskatoon, SK S7N 5A2, Canada. Offers MA. *Degree requirements:* For master's, thesis (for some programs). *Entrance requirements:* Additional exam requirements/recommendations for international students: Required—TOEFL.

University of South Africa, College of Economic and Management Sciences, Pretoria, South Africa. Offers accounting (D Admin, D Com); accounting science (DA); auditing (D Admin, D Com); business administration (M Tech); business economics (D Admin); business leadership (DBL); business management (D Admin, D Com); economic management analysis (M Tech); economics (D Admin, D Com, PhD); human resource development (M Tech); industrial psychology (D Admin, D Com, PhD); logistics (D Com); marketing (M Tech); public administration (D Admin, D Com, DPA, PhD); public management (M Tech); quantitative management (D Admin, D Com); real estate (M Tech); statistics (D Admin, PhD); tourism management (D Admin, D Com); transport economics (D Admin, D Com).

University of South Carolina, The Graduate School, Moore School of Business, Economics Program, Columbia, SC 29208. Offers MA, PhD, JD/MA. *Degree requirements:* For master's, comprehensive exam (for some programs), thesis; for doctorate, comprehensive exam, thesis/dissertation, qualifying exam. *Entrance requirements:* For master's, GMAT or GRE General Test, minimum GPA of 3.0; for doctorate, GRE General Test. Additional exam requirements/recommendations for international students: Required—TOEFL (minimum score 600 paper-based; 250 computer-based; 100 iBT). Electronic applications accepted. *Faculty research:* Monetary theory, labor economics, international economics, industrial organization.

University of Southern California, Graduate School, College of Letters, Arts and Sciences, Department of Economics, Program in Economic Development Programming, Los Angeles, CA 90089. Offers MA. Part-time and evening/weekend programs available. Terminal master's awarded for partial completion of doctoral program. *Degree requirements:* For master's, thesis. *Entrance requirements:* For master's, GRE General Test.

University of Southern California, Graduate School, College of Letters, Arts and Sciences, Department of Economics, Programs in Economics, Los Angeles, CA 90089. Offers MA, PhD. *Degree requirements:* For doctorate, thesis/dissertation. *Entrance requirements:* For master's and doctorate, GRE General Test. *Faculty research:* Economics organization and law, economic development, econometrics, theory, dynamic.

University of Southern Mississippi, Graduate School, College of Science and Technology, Department of Economic and Workforce Development, Hattiesburg, MS 39406-0001. Offers economic development (MS); human capital development (PhD); workforce training and development (MS). Part-time programs available. *Faculty:* 8 full-time (2 women). *Students:* 31 full-time (24 women), 38 part-time (21 women); includes 24 minority (all African Americans), 3 international. Average age 40. 32 applicants, 63% accepted, 17 enrolled. In 2008, 20 master's, 2 doctorates awarded. *Degree requirements:* For master's, comprehensive exam, thesis optional, internships; for doctorate, comprehensive exam, thesis/dissertation. *Entrance requirements:* For master's, GMAT, GRE General Test, minimum GPA of 2.75 in last 60 hours; for doctorate, GMAT, GRE General Test, minimum GPA of 3.5. Additional exam requirements/recommendations for international students: Required—TOEFL. *Application deadline:* For fall admission, 8/1 for domestic students, 3/1 for international students; for spring admission, 1/3 for domestic and international students. Application fee: $30. Electronic applications accepted. *Financial support:* In 2008–09, 11 students received support, including 2 research assistantships with full tuition reimbursements available (averaging $13,000 per year), 6 teaching assistantships with full tuition reimbursements available (averaging $6,500 per year); career-related internships or fieldwork and Federal Work-Study also available. Financial award application deadline: 3/1; financial award applicants required to submit FAFSA. *Faculty research:* Economic development, international studies, geography. *Unit head:* Dr. Kenneth Malone, Chair, 601-266-4736, Fax: 601-266-6071, E-mail: ken.malone@usm.edu. *Application contact:* Dr. Cyndi Gaudet, Graduate Coordinator, 601-266-6519, Fax: 601-266-6071.

University of South Florida, Graduate School, College of Business Administration, Department of Economics, Tampa, FL 33620-9951. Offers MA, PhD. Part-time and evening/weekend programs available. *Faculty:* 12 full-time (1 woman), 1 part-time/adjunct (0 women). *Students:* 14 full-time (6 women), 10 part-time (3 women); includes 3 minority (2 Asian Americans or Pacific Islanders, 1 Hispanic American), 3 international. Average age 30. 30 applicants, 63%

Economics

University of South Florida (continued)
accepted, 11 enrolled. In 2008, 14 master's awarded. *Degree requirements:* For master's, comprehensive exam; for doctorate, comprehensive exam, thesis/dissertation. *Entrance requirements:* For master's, GMAT, minimum GPA of 3.0 in last 60 hours of course work. Additional exam requirements/recommendations for international students: Required—TOEFL (minimum score 550 paper-based; 213 computer-based). *Application deadline:* For fall admission, 6/1 for domestic students, 1/2 for international students; for spring admission, 10/15 for domestic students, 6/1 for international students. Applications are processed on a rolling basis. Application fee: $30. *Expenses:* Tuition, state resident: full-time $2624.40; part-time $291.60 per credit hour. Tuition, nonresident: full-time $7822; part-time $869.13 per credit hour. *Financial support:* Unspecified assistantships available. Support available to part-time students. Financial award application deadline: 2/1; financial award applicants required to submit FAFSA. Total annual research expenditures: $104,857. *Unit head:* Dr. Kwabena Gyimah-Brempong, Chairperson, 813-974-4252, Fax: 813-974-6510, E-mail: kgyimah@coba.usf.edu. *Application contact:* Michael Loewy, Program Director, 813-974-4252, Fax: 813-974-6510, E-mail: mloewy@coba.usf.edu.

The University of Tampa, John H. Sykes College of Business, Tampa, FL 33606-1490. Offers accounting (MBA, MS); economics (MBA); entrepreneurship and innovation (MBA); finance (MBA, MS); information systems management (MBA); international business (MBA); management (MBA); marketing (MBA, MS); nonprofit management (MBA). *Accreditation:* AACSB. Part-time and evening/weekend programs available. *Faculty:* 42 full-time (14 women), 13 part-time/adjunct (3 women). *Students:* 190 full-time (80 women), 343 part-time (141 women); includes 92 minority (17 African Americans, 3 American Indian/Alaska Native, 20 Asian Americans or Pacific Islanders, 52 Hispanic Americans), 89 international. Average age 31. 496 applicants, 51% accepted, 186 enrolled. In 2008, 203 master's awarded. *Degree requirements:* For master's, minimum GPA of 3.0 in required courses and overall. *Entrance requirements:* For master's, GMAT. Additional exam requirements/recommendations for international students: Required—TOEFL (minimum score 577 paper-based; 230 computer-based; 90 iBT), IELTS. *Application deadline:* For fall admission, 7/15 for domestic students, 6/1 for international students; for spring admission, 12/15 for domestic students, 11/1 for international students. Applications are processed on a rolling basis. Application fee: $40. Electronic applications accepted. *Expenses:* Tuition: Full-time $7552; part-time $472 per credit hour. Required fees: $70; $70 per year. *Financial support:* In 2008–09, 90 students received support, including 60 research assistantships with tuition reimbursements available (averaging $6,000 per year); career-related internships or fieldwork and unspecified assistantships also available. Support available to part-time students. Financial award applicants required to submit FAFSA. *Faculty research:* Information systems, leadership, corporate governance, entrepreneurship, hedonic price estimation. *Unit head:* Dr. Don Morrill, Associate Dean, Graduate and Continuing Studies, 813-253-6100, E-mail: dmorrill@ut.edu. *Application contact:* Karen Full, Director of Admissions, Graduate and Continuing Studies, 813-257-3642, E-mail: kfull@ut.edu.

The University of Tennessee, Graduate School, College of Arts and Sciences, Department of Sociology, Knoxville, TN 37996. Offers criminology (MA, PhD); energy, environment, and resource policy (MA, PhD); political economy (MA, PhD). Part-time programs available. *Degree requirements:* For master's, thesis or alternative; for doctorate, thesis/dissertation. *Entrance requirements:* For master's, GRE General Test, minimum GPA of 3.0; for doctorate, GRE General Test, minimum GPA of 3.5. Additional exam requirements/recommendations for international students: Required—TOEFL. Electronic applications accepted. *Expenses:* Tuition, area resident: Part-time $348 per credit hour. Tuition, state resident: full-time $6262. Tuition, nonresident: full-time $18,920; part-time $1052 per credit hour. Required fees: $812; $36 per credit hour. Tuition and fees vary according to program.

The University of Tennessee, Graduate School, College of Business Administration, Department of Economics, Knoxville, TN 37996. Offers MA, PhD. *Degree requirements:* For master's, thesis or alternative; for doctorate, thesis/dissertation. *Entrance requirements:* For master's and doctorate, GRE General Test or GMAT, minimum GPA of 2.7. Additional exam requirements/recommendations for international students: Required—TOEFL. Electronic applications accepted. *Expenses:* Tuition, area resident: Part-time $348 per credit hour. Tuition, state resident: full-time $6262. Tuition, nonresident: full-time $18,920; part-time $1052 per credit hour. Required fees: $812; $36 per credit hour. Tuition and fees vary according to program.

The University of Texas at Arlington, Graduate School, College of Business, Economics Department, Arlington, TX 76019. Offers MA. Part-time and evening/weekend programs available. *Faculty:* 10 full-time (3 women). *Students:* 12 full-time (5 women), 20 part-time (2 women); includes 4 minority (3 African Americans, 1 Asian American or Pacific Islander), 4 international. 31 applicants, 97% accepted, 14 enrolled. In 2008, 6 master's awarded. *Degree requirements:* For master's, thesis optional. *Entrance requirements:* For master's, GMAT or GRE General Test. Additional exam requirements/recommendations for international students: Required—TOEFL (minimum score 550 paper-based; 213 computer-based; 79 iBT). *Application deadline:* For fall admission, 6/5 for domestic students, 4/1 for international students; for spring admission, 10/15 for domestic students, 9/1 for international students. Applications are processed on a rolling basis. Application fee: $35 ($50 for international students). *Expenses:* Tuition, area resident: Full-time $6500. Tuition, state resident: full-time $6500. Tuition, nonresident: full-time $11,558. *Financial support:* In 2008–09, 1 fellowship (averaging $1,000 per year), research assistantships (averaging $6,000 per year), 14 teaching assistantships (averaging $13,000 per year) were awarded; career-related internships or fieldwork, scholarships/grants, and unspecified assistantships also available. Support available to part-time students. Financial award application deadline: 6/1; financial award applicants required to submit FAFSA. *Unit head:* Dr. Daniel Himarios, Chair, 817-272 Ext. 2881, Fax: 817-272-2073, E-mail: himarios@uta.edu. *Application contact:* Dr. Roger Wehr, Graduate Advisor, 817-272-3287, Fax: 817-272-3145, E-mail: wehr@uta.edu.

The University of Texas at Austin, Graduate School, College of Liberal Arts, Department of Economics, Austin, TX 78712-1111. Offers MA, MS Econ, PhD. Part-time programs available. *Degree requirements:* For master's, thesis; for doctorate, comprehensive exam, thesis/dissertation. *Entrance requirements:* For master's and doctorate, GRE General Test, minimum GPA of 3.5 (based on upper-division undergraduate and graduate course work). Additional exam requirements/recommendations for international students: Required—TOEFL. Electronic applications accepted. *Faculty research:* Industrial organization, game theory, monetary economics, labor economics, public economics.

The University of Texas at Dallas, School of Economic, Political and Policy Sciences, Program in Economics, Richardson, TX 75083-0688. Offers MS, PhD. Part-time and evening/weekend programs available. *Faculty:* 13 full-time (5 women). *Students:* 29 full-time (11 women), 8 part-time (1 woman); includes 8 minority (1 African American, 6 Asian Americans or Pacific Islanders, 1 Hispanic American), 16 international. Average age 33. 68 applicants, 25% accepted, 9 enrolled. In 2008, 16 master's, 1 doctorate awarded. *Degree requirements:* For master's, internship; for doctorate, thesis/dissertation. *Entrance requirements:* For master's and doctorate, GRE General Test, minimum GPA of 3.0 in upper-level course work in field. Additional exam requirements/recommendations for international students: Required—TOEFL (minimum score 550 paper-based; 213 computer-based). *Application deadline:* For fall admission, 7/15 for domestic students, 5/1 priority date for international students; for spring admission, 11/15 for domestic students, 9/1 priority date for international students. Applications are processed on a rolling basis. Application fee: $50 ($100 for international students). Electronic applications accepted. *Expenses:* Tuition, area resident: Full-time $8320. Tuition, state resident: full-time $8320. Tuition, nonresident: full-time $15,054. Part-time tuition and fees vary according to course load. *Financial support:* In 2008–09, 6 research assistantships with tuition reimbursements (averaging $13,446 per year), 16 teaching assistantships with tuition reimbursements (averaging $12,305 per year) were awarded; fellowships, career-related internships or fieldwork, Federal Work-Study, institutionally sponsored loans, scholarships/grants, and unspecified assistantships also available. Support available to part-time students. Financial award application

deadline: 4/30; financial award applicants required to submit FAFSA. *Faculty research:* Economic base of distressed counties, analysis of nonprofits and their for-profit counterparts. *Unit head:* Dr. Daniel Arce, Program Head, 972-883-6857, Fax: 972-883-2735, E-mail: darce@utdallas.edu. *Application contact:* Dr. Nathan Berg, Associate Program Head, 972-883-2088, Fax: 972-883-2735, E-mail: nberg@utdallas.edu.

See Close-Up on page 783.

The University of Texas at Dallas, School of Economic, Political and Policy Sciences, Program in Public Policy and Political Economy, Richardson, TX 75083-0688. Offers international political economy (MS); public policy (MPP); public policy and political economy (PhD). Part-time and evening/weekend programs available. *Faculty:* 14 full-time (4 women). *Students:* 33 full-time (12 women), 43 part-time (20 women); includes 26 minority (10 African Americans, 8 Asian Americans or Pacific Islanders, 8 Hispanic Americans), 19 international. Average age 40. 42 applicants, 95% accepted, 21 enrolled. In 2008, 1 master's, 6 doctorates awarded. *Degree requirements:* For doctorate, thesis/dissertation. *Entrance requirements:* For master's and doctorate, GRE General Test, minimum GPA of 3.0 in upper-level course work in field. Additional exam requirements/recommendations for international students: Required—TOEFL (minimum score 550 paper-based; 213 computer-based). *Application deadline:* For fall admission, 7/15 for domestic students, 5/1 priority date for international students; for spring admission, 11/15 for domestic students, 9/1 priority date for international students. Applications are processed on a rolling basis. Application fee: $50 ($100 for international students). Electronic applications accepted. *Expenses:* Tuition, area resident: Full-time $8320. Tuition, state resident: full-time $8320. Tuition, nonresident: full-time $15,054. Part-time tuition and fees vary according to course load. *Financial support:* In 2008–09, 2 research assistantships with tuition reimbursements (averaging $18,188 per year), 11 teaching assistantships with tuition reimbursements (averaging $12,436 per year) were awarded; fellowships, career-related internships or fieldwork, Federal Work-Study, institutionally sponsored loans, and scholarships/grants also available. Support available to part-time students. Financial award application deadline: 4/30; financial award applicants required to submit FAFSA. *Faculty research:* New leadership development, gender and leadership, globalization and leadership opportunities in democracy. *Unit head:* Dr. Sheila Amin Gutierrez de Pineres, Program Head, 972-883-6228, Fax: 972-883-2735, E-mail: pineres@utdallas.edu. *Application contact:* Dr. Marie I Chevrier, Associate Program Head, 972-883-2727, Fax: 972-883-2735, E-mail: chevrier@utdallas.edu.

See Close-Up on page 783.

The University of Texas at El Paso, Graduate School, College of Business Administration, Department of Economics and Finance, El Paso, TX 79968-0001. Offers economics (MS). Part-time and evening/weekend programs available. *Degree requirements:* For master's, thesis optional. *Entrance requirements:* For master's, GMAT, minimum GPA of 2.7. Additional exam requirements/recommendations for international students: Required—TOEFL. Electronic applications accepted.

The University of Texas at San Antonio, College of Business, Department of Economics, San Antonio, TX 78249-0617. Offers business economics (MBA); economics (MA). Part-time and evening/weekend programs available. *Degree requirements:* For master's, comprehensive exam, thesis optional. *Entrance requirements:* For master's, GMAT or GRE, minimum GPA of 3.0. Additional exam requirements/recommendations for international students: Required—TOEFL (minimum score 500 paper-based; 173 computer-based).

The University of Texas–Pan American, College of Business Administration, Program in International Business, Edinburg, TX 78541-2999. Offers computer information systems (PhD); economics (PhD); finance (PhD); management (PhD); marketing (PhD). *Degree requirements:* For doctorate, comprehensive exam, thesis/dissertation. *Entrance requirements:* For doctorate, GMAT or GRE. Additional exam requirements/recommendations for international students: Required—TOEFL, IELTS. Electronic applications accepted. *Expenses:* Contact institution.

The University of Toledo, College of Graduate Studies, College of Arts and Sciences, Department of Economics, Toledo, OH 43606-3390. Offers MA. *Degree requirements:* For master's, comprehensive exam, paper or thesis. *Entrance requirements:* For master's, GRE General Test, minimum GPA of 2.75. Electronic applications accepted. *Faculty research:* Economic development.

The University of Toledo, College of Graduate Studies, College of Business Administration, Department of Finance and Business Economics, Toledo, OH 43606-3390. Offers MBA. Evening/weekend programs available. *Degree requirements:* For master's, thesis or alternative. *Entrance requirements:* For master's, GMAT. Additional exam requirements/recommendations for international students: Required—TOEFL. *Faculty research:* Financial management, banking, international finance, investments.

The University of Toledo, College of Graduate Studies, College of Education, Department of Curriculum and Instruction, Program in Education and Economics, Toledo, OH 43606-3390. Offers MAE.

University of Toronto, School of Graduate Studies, Social Sciences Division, Department of Economics, Toronto, ON M5S 1A1, Canada. Offers MA, MFE, PhD. Part-time programs available. *Degree requirements:* For doctorate, comprehensive exam, thesis/dissertation. *Entrance requirements:* For master's, GRE (for applicants without a degree from a Canadian university), minimum B average in final year, 2 letters of reference; for doctorate, GRE (for applicants without a degree from a Canadian university), master's degree in economics, minimum B+ average, 3 letters of reference. Additional exam requirements/recommendations for international students: Required—TOEFL (minimum score 580 paper-based; 237 computer-based), TWE (minimum score 5), IELTS (minimum score: 7) or Michigan English Language Assessment Battery (minimum score: 85).

University of Utah, The Graduate School, College of Social and Behavioral Science, Department of Economics, Salt Lake City, UT 84112-1107. Offers econometrics (M Stat, MA, MS, PhD); economics (M Phil). Part-time programs available. Terminal master's awarded for partial completion of doctoral program. *Degree requirements:* For master's, thesis or alternative, exam, oral presentation, research project; for doctorate, comprehensive exam, thesis/dissertation. *Entrance requirements:* For master's, GRE General Test, undergraduate course work in economics; for doctorate, GRE General Test, GRE Subject Test, minimum GPA of 3.0, course work in calculus and statistics. Additional exam requirements/recommendations for international students: Required—TOEFL (minimum score 500 paper-based; 173 computer-based). *Faculty research:* History of economic thought, political economy, monetary economy, labor.

University of Utah, The Graduate School, Interdepartmental Program in Statistics, Salt Lake City, UT 84112-1107. Offers biostatistics (MST); business (MST); economics (MST); educational psychology (MST); mathematics (MST); sociology (MST); statistics (M Stat). Part-time programs available. *Degree requirements:* For master's, comprehensive exam, projects. *Entrance requirements:* For master's, minimum GPA of 3.0; course work in calculus, matrix theory, statistics. Additional exam requirements/recommendations for international students: Required—TOEFL (minimum score 500 paper-based; 173 computer-based). *Faculty research:* Biostatistics, management, economics, educational psychology, mathematics.

University of Victoria, Faculty of Graduate Studies, Faculty of Social Sciences, Department of Economics, Victoria, BC V8W 2Y2, Canada. Offers MA, PhD. Part-time programs available. *Degree requirements:* For master's, comprehensive exam (for some programs), thesis optional; for doctorate, comprehensive exam, thesis/dissertation, candidacy exam. *Entrance requirements:* For master's and doctorate, GRE. Additional exam requirements/recommendations for international students: Required—TOEFL (minimum score 575 paper-based; 233 computer-based), IELTS (minimum score 7). Electronic applications accepted. *Faculty research:* Industrial organization, cost/benefit, applied economics, econometrics, airline economics, health economics.

University of Virginia, College and Graduate School of Arts and Sciences, Department of Economics, Charlottesville, VA 22903. Offers MA, PhD, JD/MA. *Faculty:* 31 full-time (5 women), 2 part-time/adjunct (0 women). *Students:* 104 full-time (45 women); includes 5 Asian Americans or Pacific Islanders, 56 international. Average age 27. 349 applicants, 34% accepted, 25 enrolled. In 2008, 25 master's, 12 doctorates awarded. *Degree requirements:* For master's, comprehensive exam (for some programs), thesis (for some programs), thesis or comprehensive exam; for doctorate, comprehensive exam, thesis/dissertation. *Entrance requirements:* For master's and doctorate, GRE General Test. Additional exam requirements/recommendations for international students: Required—TOEFL (minimum score 600 paper-based; 250 computer-based; 90 iBT), IELTS (minimum score 7). *Application deadline:* For fall admission, 4/1 for domestic and international students. Applications are processed on a rolling basis. Application fee: $60. Electronic applications accepted. *Expenses:* Tuition, area resident: Full-time $10,452. Tuition, state resident: full-time $10,452. Tuition, nonresident: full-time $20,010. Required fees: $2176. Part-time tuition and fees vary according to course load and program. *Financial support:* Fellowships, research assistantships, teaching assistantships, tuition waivers (full and partial) available. Financial award application deadline: 2/1; financial award applicants required to submit FAFSA. *Faculty research:* Macroeconomics, public economics, labor, industrial organization, economic history. *Unit head:* William Johnson, Chair, 434-924-3177, Fax: 434-982-2904, E-mail: econ-dgs@virginia.edu. *Application contact:* William Johnson, Chair, 434-924-3177, Fax: 434-982-2904, E-mail: econ-dgs@virginia.edu.

University of Washington, Graduate School, College of Arts and Sciences, Department of Economics, Seattle, WA 98195. Offers PhD. Terminal master's awarded for partial completion of doctoral program. *Degree requirements:* For doctorate, comprehensive exam, thesis/dissertation. *Entrance requirements:* For doctorate, GRE General Test, minimum GPA of 3.0. Additional exam requirements/recommendations for international students: Required—TOEFL. Electronic applications accepted. *Faculty research:* Microeconomic theory; macroeconomic theory; econometrics; natural resource economics; international, development, and industrial organization.

University of Waterloo, Graduate Studies, Faculty of Arts, Department of Economics, Waterloo, ON N2L 3G1, Canada. Offers MA, PhD. Part-time programs available. *Entrance requirements:* For master's, honors degree, minimum B average. Additional exam requirements/recommendations for international students: Required—TOEFL, TWE. Electronic applications accepted. *Faculty research:* Applied microeconomics, applied macroeconomics, public finance, international trade and finance, wage inflation and consumer problems.

The University of Western Ontario, Faculty of Graduate Studies, Social Sciences Division, Department of Economics, London, ON N6A 5B8, Canada. Offers MA, PhD. *Degree requirements:* For doctorate, thesis/dissertation. *Entrance requirements:* For master's, GRE, honours BA with B+ average. Additional exam requirements/recommendations for international students: Required—TOEFL.

University of Windsor, Faculty of Graduate Studies, Faculty of Science, Department of Economics, Windsor, ON N9B 3P4, Canada. Offers MA. Part-time programs available. *Degree requirements:* For master's, thesis or alternative. *Entrance requirements:* For master's, minimum B average. Additional exam requirements/recommendations for international students: Required—TOEFL (minimum score 560 paper-based; 220 computer-based). Electronic applications accepted. *Faculty research:* International trade, economic growth, microeconomic theory.

University of Wisconsin–Madison, Graduate School, College of Letters and Science, Department of Economics, Madison, WI 53706-1380. Offers PhD. *Degree requirements:* For doctorate, thesis/dissertation. *Entrance requirements:* For doctorate, GRE General Test, 3 semesters of course work in calculus, 1 semester of course work in algebra and mathematics/statistics. Electronic applications accepted.

University of Wisconsin–Milwaukee, Graduate School, College of Letters and Sciences, Department of Economics, Milwaukee, WI 53201-0413. Offers MA, PhD. *Faculty:* 20 full-time (2 women). *Students:* 64 full-time (24 women), 20 part-time (9 women); includes 3 minority (1 African American, 1 Asian American or Pacific Islander, 1 Hispanic American), 43 international. Average age 28. 112 applicants, 69% accepted, 39 enrolled. In 2008, 32 master's, 7 doctorates awarded. *Degree requirements:* For master's, comprehensive exam; for doctorate, comprehensive exam, thesis/dissertation. *Entrance requirements:* For master's, GRE General Test; for doctorate, GRE General Test, GRE Subject Test, minimum GPA of 3.0. Additional exam requirements/recommendations for international students: Required—TOEFL (minimum score 550 paper-based; 79 iBT), IELTS (minimum score 6.5). *Application deadline:* For fall admission, 1/1 priority date for domestic students; for spring admission, 9/1 for domestic students. Applications are processed on a rolling basis. Application fee: $45 ($75 for international students). *Expenses:* Tuition, area resident: Full-time $7320; part-time $165 per credit. Tuition, state resident: full-time $7320; part-time $165 per credit. Tuition, nonresident: full-time $17,840; part-time $714 per credit. Tuition and fees vary according to campus/location, program and reciprocity agreements. *Financial support:* In 2008–09, 29 teaching assistantships were awarded; career-related internships or fieldwork and unspecified assistantships also available. Support available to part-time students. Financial award application deadline: 4/15. Total annual research expenditures: $135,210. *Unit head:* Mohsen Bahmani-Oskooee, Representative, 414-229-4334, Fax: 414-229-3860, E-mail: bahmani@uwm.edu. *Application contact:* General Information Contact, 414-229-4982, Fax: 414-229-6967, E-mail: gradschool@uwm.edu.

University of Wyoming, Graduate School, College of Business, Department of Economics and Finance, Program in Economics, Laramie, WY 82070. Offers MS, PhD. Part-time programs available. *Faculty:* 10 full-time (0 women), 3 part-time/adjunct (1 woman). *Students:* 25 full-time (9 women), 20 part-time (6 women); includes 1 minority (African American), 18 international. Average age 31. 71 applicants, 31% accepted, 10 enrolled. In 2008, 2 doctorates awarded. *Degree requirements:* For master's, thesis; for doctorate, comprehensive exam, thesis/dissertation. *Entrance requirements:* For master's, GRE General Test or GMAT, minimum GPA of 3.0; for doctorate, GRE General Test, minimum GPA of 3.0. Additional exam requirements/recommendations for international students: Required—TOEFL (minimum score 525 paper-based; 197 computer-based). *Application deadline:* For fall admission, 3/1 for domestic students; for spring admission, 10/1 for domestic students. Applications are processed on a rolling basis. Application fee: $50. *Financial support:* In 2008–09, 10 research assistantships with full tuition reimbursements (averaging $15,408 per year), 10 teaching assistantships with full tuition reimbursements (averaging $15,408 per year) were awarded. Financial award application deadline: 3/1. *Faculty research:* Resource and environmental economics, industrial organization, regulation. *Unit head:* Dr. Rob W. Godby, Chair, 307-766-3843, Fax: 307-766-5090, E-mail: rgodby@uwyo.edu. *Application contact:* Carrie Miller, Office Associate, 307-766-2175, Fax: 307-766-5090, E-mail: carriem@uwyo.edu.

University of Wyoming, Graduate School, College of Business, Department of Economics and Finance, Program in Economics and Finance, Laramie, WY 82070. Offers MS. *Degree requirements:* For master's, thesis. *Entrance requirements:* For master's, GRE, minimum GPA of 3.0. Additional exam requirements/recommendations for international students: Required—TOEFL (minimum score 540 paper-based; 207 computer-based; 76 iBT). *Faculty research:* Financial economics.

Utah State University, School of Graduate Studies, College of Business and College of Agriculture, Department of Economics, Logan, UT 84322. Offers applied economics (MS); economics (MA, MS, PhD). Terminal master's awarded for partial completion of doctoral program. *Degree requirements:* For master's, thesis (for some programs); for doctorate, comprehensive exam, thesis/dissertation. *Entrance requirements:* For master's, GRE General Test, GMAT, minimum GPA of 3.0, TOEFL for international; for doctorate, GRE General Test, minimum GPA of 3.0, TOEFL. Additional exam requirements/recommendations for international students: Required—TOEFL. Electronic applications accepted. *Faculty research:* Resource economics, economic theory, international trade, industrial organization, development.

Vanderbilt University, Graduate School, Department of Economics, Nashville, TN 37240-1001. Offers economic development (MA); economics (MA, MAT, PhD); JD/PhD. *Faculty:* 44 full-time (10 women). *Students:* 81 full-time (16 women), 2 part-time (0 women); includes 5 minority (1 African American, 3 Asian Americans or Pacific Islanders, 1 Hispanic American), 50 international. Average age 28. 380 applicants, 31% accepted, 31 enrolled. In 2008, 30 master's, 8 doctorates awarded. Terminal master's awarded for partial completion of doctoral program. *Degree requirements:* For master's, thesis or alternative; for doctorate, thesis/dissertation, final and qualifying exams. *Entrance requirements:* For master's and doctorate, GRE General Test, GRE Subject Test (recommended). Additional exam requirements/recommendations for international students: Required—TOEFL (minimum score 570 paper-based; 230 computer-based; 88 iBT). *Application deadline:* For fall admission, 1/15 for domestic and international students; for spring admission, 11/1 for domestic students. Applications are processed on a rolling basis. Application fee: $0. Electronic applications accepted. *Financial support:* Fellowships with full and partial tuition reimbursements, teaching assistantships with full and partial tuition reimbursements, career-related internships or fieldwork, Federal Work-Study, institutionally sponsored loans, scholarships/grants, and health care benefits available. Financial award application deadline: 1/15; financial award applicants required to submit CSS PROFILE or FAFSA. *Faculty research:* Economic theory, applied fields, developmental economics, environmental economics, health economics and policy. *Unit head:* Tong Li, PhD, Chair, 615-322-3426, Fax: 615-343-8495, E-mail: tong.li@vanderbilt.edu. *Application contact:* Bill Collins, PhD, Director of Graduate Studies, 615-322-3428, Fax: 615-343-8495, E-mail: william.collins@vanderbilt.edu.

Vanderbilt University, Vanderbilt University Law School, Nashville, TN 37203. Offers law (JD, LL M); law and economics (PhD); JD/M Div; JD/MA; JD/MBA; JD/MD; JD/MPP; JD/MTS; JD/PhD; LL M/MA. *Accreditation:* ABA. *Faculty:* 51 full-time (19 women), 69 part-time/adjunct (28 women). *Students:* 608 full-time (296 women); includes 100 minority (54 African Americans, 3 American Indian/Alaska Native, 19 Asian Americans or Pacific Islanders, 24 Hispanic Americans), 48 international. Average age 24. 4,336 applicants, 25% accepted, 191 enrolled. In 2008, 222 first professional degrees, 22 master's awarded. *Entrance requirements:* For JD, LSAT; for master's, foreign law degree. Additional exam requirements/recommendations for international students: Required—TOEFL. *Application deadline:* For fall admission, 9/15 for domestic and international students; for spring admission, 3/15 for domestic and international students. Applications are processed on a rolling basis. Application fee: $50. Electronic applications accepted. *Expenses:* Contact institution. *Financial support:* In 2008–09, 413 students received support. Career-related internships or fieldwork, Federal Work-Study, institutionally sponsored loans, scholarships/grants, and health care benefits available. Financial award application deadline: 2/15; financial award applicants required to submit FAFSA. *Unit head:* G. Todd Morton, Assistant Dean for Admissions, 615-322-6452, Fax: 615-322-1531. *Application contact:* Admissions Office, 615-322-6452, Fax: 615-322-1531.

Virginia Commonwealth University, Graduate School, School of Business, Program in Economics, Richmond, VA 23284-9005. Offers MA, MBA, MS. *Degree requirements:* For master's, thesis optional. *Entrance requirements:* For master's, GRE General Test.

Virginia Polytechnic Institute and State University, Graduate School, College of Agriculture and Life Sciences, Department of Agricultural and Applied Economics, Blacksburg, VA 24061. Offers agribusiness (MS); agricultural economics (MS, PhD); applied economics (MS); developmental and international economics (PhD); econometrics (PhD); macro and micro economics (PhD); markets and industrial organizations (PhD); public and regional/urban economics (PhD); resource and environmental economics (PhD). *Entrance requirements:* For master's and doctorate, GRE General Test. Additional exam requirements/recommendations for international students: Required—TOEFL (minimum score 575 paper-based; 231 computer-based). Electronic applications accepted. *Faculty research:* Rural development.

Virginia Polytechnic Institute and State University, Graduate School, College of Science, Department of Economics, Blacksburg, VA 24061. Offers MA, PhD. *Entrance requirements:* For master's and doctorate, GRE. Additional exam requirements/recommendations for international students: Required—TOEFL (minimum score 500 paper-based; 213 computer-based). Electronic applications accepted.

Virginia State University, School of Graduate Studies, Research, and Outreach, School of Liberal Arts and Education, Department of Economics, Petersburg, VA 23806-0001. Offers MA. *Degree requirements:* For master's, thesis optional. *Entrance requirements:* For master's, GRE General Test.

Walsh College of Accountancy and Business Administration, Graduate Programs, Program in Economics, Troy, MI 48007-7006. Offers MAE.

Washington State University, Graduate School, College of Agricultural, Human, and Natural Resource Sciences, School of Economic Sciences, Department of Economics, Pullman, WA 99164. Offers applied economics (MA); economics (MA, PhD); international business economics (Certificate). *Degree requirements:* For master's, comprehensive exam (for some programs), thesis (for some programs), oral exam; for doctorate, comprehensive exam, thesis/dissertation, oral exam, written exam, field exams. *Entrance requirements:* For master's, GRE General Test, minimum GPA of 3.0; for doctorate, GRE General Test or GMAT, minimum GPA of 3.0. Additional exam requirements/recommendations for international students: Required—TOEFL. *Faculty research:* Economic theory and quantitative methods, applied microeconomics.

Washington University in St. Louis, Graduate School of Arts and Sciences, Department of Economics, St. Louis, MO 63130-4899. Offers PhD. *Students:* 87 full-time (21 women); includes 2 minority (1 Asian American or Pacific Islander, 1 Hispanic American), 75 international. 368 applicants, 11% accepted, 22 enrolled. In 2008, 11 doctorates awarded. Terminal master's awarded for partial completion of doctoral program. *Degree requirements:* For doctorate, one foreign language, thesis/dissertation. *Entrance requirements:* For doctorate, GRE General Test, GRE Subject Test. *Application deadline:* For fall admission, 1/15 priority date for domestic students. Application fee: $45. Electronic applications accepted. *Financial support:* Fellowships, research assistantships, teaching assistantships, Federal Work-Study, institutionally sponsored loans, and tuition waivers (full and partial) available. Support available to part-time students. Financial award application deadline: 1/15. *Unit head:* Dr. Michele Boldrin, Chairman, 314-935-5632. *Application contact:* Assistant to the Dean, 314-935-6880, Fax: 314-935-4887.

See Display on page 772.

Wayne State University, College of Liberal Arts and Sciences, Department of Economics, Detroit, MI 48202. Offers MA, PhD, JD/MA. *Degree requirements:* For master's, thesis optional; for doctorate, thesis/dissertation. *Entrance requirements:* For master's, minimum GPA of 3.0; for doctorate, GRE, minimum GPA of 3.0. Additional exam requirements/recommendations for international students: Required—TOEFL (minimum score 550 paper-based; 213 computer-based); Recommended—TWE (minimum score 6). Electronic applications accepted. *Faculty research:* Health economics, international economics, macro economics, urban and labor economics, econometrics.

Wayne State University, College of Liberal Arts and Sciences, Interdisciplinary Program in Economic Development, Detroit, MI 48202. Offers Certificate. *Entrance requirements:* Additional exam requirements/recommendations for international students: Required—TOEFL (minimum score 550 paper-based; 213 computer-based); Recommended—TWE (minimum score 6). Electronic applications accepted.

West Chester University of Pennsylvania, Office of Graduate Studies, College of Business and Public Affairs, Department of Economics and Finance, West Chester, PA 19383. Offers business administration: economics-finance (MBA). Part-time and evening/weekend programs available. *Students:* 1 full-time (0 women), 7 part-time (2 women); includes 1 minority (Asian

Economics

Washington University in St. Louis

Fields of Concentration

Macro/Money, Growth/Development, Labor, Public Finance, Economic History, Political Economy Urban, Industrial Organization, Econometrics, Micro Theory, Game Theory

Financial assistance based on merit is available. We provide generous financial support throughout the degree program.

All of our students receive tuition support and health insurance throughout the course of their studies.

Additional funds are available on a competitive basis for summer research projects and travel support for conference presentations.

For further information

Director of Graduate Studies
Department of Economics
Washington University
One Brookings Drive
Campus Box 1208
St. Louis, MO 63130

See http://economics.wustl.edu for more information.

The Department of Economics at Washington University has a strong reputation in training high-quality Ph.D. students for academic, private- and public-sector positions.

Students work closely with faculty in economic theory, macroeconomics and monetary Theory, public finance, econometrics, economic history, development economics, and labor economics.

West Chester University of Pennsylvania (continued)

American or Pacific Islander). Average age 32. 5 applicants, 80% accepted, 2 enrolled. In 2008, 6 master's awarded. *Degree requirements:* For master's, minimum GPA of 3.0. *Entrance requirements:* For master's, GMAT, statement of professional goals, resumé, two letters of reference. Additional exam requirements/recommendations for international students: Required—TOEFL (minimum score 550 paper-based; 213 computer-based; 80 iBT). *Application deadline:* For fall admission, 4/15 for domestic students, 3/15 for international students; for spring admission, 10/15 for domestic students, 9/1 for international students. Applications are processed on a rolling basis. Application fee: $35. Electronic applications accepted. *Expenses:* Tuition, state resident: full-time $6430; part-time $357 per credit. Tuition, nonresident: full-time $10,288; part-time $572 per credit. Required fees: $652.50; $50 per credit. $67 per semester. *Financial support:* In 2008–09, research assistantships with full and partial tuition reimbursements (averaging $5,000 per year); unspecified assistantships also available. Support available to part-time students. Financial award application deadline: 2/15; financial award applicants required to submit FAFSA. *Unit head:* Dr. Paul Christ, MBA Director and Graduate Coordinator, 610-425-5000, E-mail: pchrist@wcupa.edu. *Application contact:* Office of Graduate Studies, 610-436-2943, Fax: 610-436-2763, E-mail: gradstudy@wcupa.edu.

Western Illinois University, School of Graduate Studies, College of Business and Technology, Department of Economics, Macomb, IL 61455-1390. Offers MA, Certificate. Part-time programs available. *Students:* 26 full-time (5 women), 1 part-time (0 women); includes 7 minority (5 African Americans, 1 Asian American or Pacific Islander, 1 Hispanic American), 14 international. Average age 28. 18 applicants, 83% accepted. In 2008, 13 master's awarded. *Degree requirements:* For master's, thesis or alternative. *Entrance requirements:* Additional exam requirements/recommendations for international students: Required—TOEFL (minimum score 550 paper-based; 213 computer-based; 80 iBT). *Application deadline:* Applications are processed on a rolling basis. Application fee: $30. Electronic applications accepted. *Expenses:* Tuition, state resident: full-time $5696; part-time $237.34 per credit hour. Tuition, nonresident: full-time $11,392; part-time $474.68 per credit hour. Required fees: $1453; $60.55 per credit hour. *Financial support:* In 2008–09, 14 students received support, including 12 research assistantships with full tuition reimbursements available (averaging $7,040 per year). Financial award applicants required to submit FAFSA. *Unit head:* Dr. Warren Jones, Chairperson, 309-298-1153. *Application contact:* Evelyn Hoing, Assistant Director of Graduate Studies, 309-298-1806, Fax: 309-298-2345, E-mail: grad-office@wiu.edu.

Western Michigan University, Graduate College, College of Arts and Sciences, Department of Economics, Kalamazoo, MI 49008-5202. Offers applied economics (MA, PhD). *Degree requirements:* For master's, thesis, oral or written exams; for doctorate, thesis/dissertation, oral exam, internship. *Entrance requirements:* For doctorate, GRE General Test.

West Texas A&M University, College of Business, Department of Accounting, Economics, and Finance, Program in Finance and Economics, Canyon, TX 79016-0001. Offers MS. Part-time and evening/weekend programs available. Postbaccalaureate distance learning degree programs offered (minimal on-campus study). *Degree requirements:* For master's, comprehensive exam, thesis optional. *Entrance requirements:* For master's, GMAT. Additional exam requirements/recommendations for international students: Required—TOEFL (minimum score 550 paper-based). Electronic applications accepted. *Faculty research:* International trade composition, cycle of poverty, trade effects in Asian countries, structural problems in Japanese economy, reform and the US sugar program-Nebraska.

West Virginia University, College of Business and Economics, Division of Economics and Finance, Morgantown, WV 26506. Offers business analysis (MA); developmental financial

economics (PhD); environmental and resource economics (PhD); international economics (PhD); mathematical economics (MA); monetary economics (PhD); public finance (PhD); public policy (MA); regional and urban economics (PhD); statistics and economics (MA). Terminal master's awarded for partial completion of doctoral program. *Degree requirements:* For master's, thesis optional; for doctorate, comprehensive exam, thesis/dissertation. *Entrance requirements:* For master's and doctorate, GRE General Test, minimum GPA of 3.0; course work in intermediate microeconomics, intermediate macroeconomics, calculus, and statistics. Additional exam requirements/recommendations for international students: Required—TOEFL. Electronic applications accepted. *Faculty research:* Financial economics, regional/urban development, public economics, international trade/international finance/development economics, monetary economics.

Wichita State University, Graduate School, W. Frank Barton School of Business, Department of Economics, Wichita, KS 67260. Offers business economics (MA); economic analysis (MA). Part-time and evening/weekend programs available. *Degree requirements:* For master's, thesis or written comprehensive exam. *Entrance requirements:* For master's, GRE General Test, minimum GPA of 2.75. Additional exam requirements/recommendations for international students: Required—TOEFL. Electronic applications accepted. *Faculty research:* Law economics, general aviation industry, public choice, financial and monetary economics, labor and human resources.

Wilfrid Laurier University, Faculty of Graduate Studies, School of Business and Economics, Department of Economics, Waterloo, ON N2L 3C5, Canada. Offers MA. *Entrance requirements:* For master's, honors BA or the equivalent in economics, minimum B average in undergraduate course work. Additional exam requirements/recommendations for international students: Required—TOEFL (minimum score 230 computer-based; 89 iBT). Electronic applications accepted. *Faculty research:* Economic forecasting, economic policy analysis, industry and market studies, financial economics, strategic planning, public policy and business.

Wright State University, School of Graduate Studies, Raj Soin College of Business, Department of Economics, Dayton, OH 45435. Offers business economics (MBA); social and applied economics (MS); MBA/MS. *Entrance requirements:* For master's, GRE General Test. Additional exam requirements/recommendations for international students: Required—TOEFL.

Yale University, Graduate School of Arts and Sciences, Department of Economics, New Haven, CT 06520. Offers economics (PhD); international and development economics (MA). *Degree requirements:* For doctorate, thesis/dissertation. *Entrance requirements:* For master's, GRE General Test; for doctorate, GRE General Test, GRE Subject Test. *Faculty research:* Economic history of Western Europe, environmental economics, economic growth and development.

York University, Faculty of Graduate Studies, Faculty of Arts, Program in Economics, Toronto, ON M3J 1P3, Canada. Offers MA, PhD. Part-time programs available. *Degree requirements:* For doctorate, comprehensive exam, thesis/dissertation. Electronic applications accepted.

Youngstown State University, Graduate School, College of Liberal Arts and Social Sciences, Department of Economics, Youngstown, OH 44555-0001. Offers economics (MA); financial economics (MA). Part-time programs available. *Degree requirements:* For master's, comprehensive exam, thesis optional. *Entrance requirements:* For master's, minimum GPA of 2.7, 21 hours in economics. Additional exam requirements/recommendations for international students: Required—TOEFL. *Faculty research:* Forecasting, applied econometrics, labor economics, applied macroeconomics, industrial organization.

International Economics

Claremont Graduate University, Graduate Programs, School of Politics and Economics, Department of Economics, Claremont, CA 91711-6160. Offers business and financial economics (MA, PhD); economic development (Certificate); economics (PhD); industrial organization (PhD); international and development economics (PhD); international economics policy and development (MA); international money and finance (PhD); neuroeconomics (PhD); political economy and public policy (MA); public choice and public economics (PhD); MBA/PhD. Part-time programs available. *Faculty:* 7 full-time (1 woman). *Students:* 100 full-time (24 women), 6 part-time (1 woman); includes 12 minority (3 African Americans, 7 Asian Americans or Pacific Islanders, 2 Hispanic Americans), 56 international. Average age 32. In 2008, 15 master's, 15 doctorates awarded. *Entrance requirements:* For master's and doctorate, GRE General Test or GMAT. Additional exam requirements/recommendations for international students: Required—TOEFL (minimum score 550 paper-based; 213 computer-based; 80 iBT). *Application deadline:* For fall admission, 2/1 priority date for domestic students. Applications are processed on a rolling basis. Application fee: $60. Electronic applications accepted. *Expenses:* Tuition: Full-time $33,698; part-time $1465 per unit. Required fees: $310; $155 per semester. Tuition and fees vary according to program. *Financial support:* Fellowships, research assistantships, teaching assistantships, Federal Work-Study, institutionally sponsored loans, and scholarships/grants available. Support available to part-time students. Financial award application deadline: 2/15; financial award applicants required to submit FAFSA. *Faculty research:* International and financial economics, law and economics, regulation, public choice economics. *Unit head:* Arthur Denzau, Chair, 909-621-8782, Fax: 909-621-8545, E-mail: arthur.denzau@cgu.edu. *Application contact:* Laura Carillo, Recruiter and Admissions Coordinator, 909-621-8699, Fax: 909-621-7545, E-mail: laura.carillo@cga.edu.

Eastern Michigan University, Graduate School, College of Arts and Sciences, Department of Economics, Ypsilanti, MI 48197. Offers applied economics (MA); economics (MA); health economics (MA); international economics and development (MA); trade and development (MA). Part-time and evening/weekend programs available. Postbaccalaureate distance learning degree programs offered (minimal on-campus study). *Degree requirements:* For master's, thesis or alternative. *Entrance requirements:* Additional exam requirements/recommendations for international students: Required—TOEFL.

Fordham University, Graduate School of Arts and Sciences, Program in International Political Economy and Development, New York, NY 10458. Offers MA, Certificate. Part-time and evening/weekend programs available. *Degree requirements:* For master's, comprehensive exam. *Entrance requirements:* For master's, GRE General Test. Additional exam requirements/recommendations for international students: Required—TOEFL (minimum score 600 paper-based; 250 computer-based). Electronic applications accepted. *Faculty research:* International economics, comparative international politics, international banking and finance, international development, emerging markets and country risk analysis.

See Close-Up on page 865.

Regent University, Graduate School, Robertson School of Government, Virginia Beach, VA 23464. Offers health care policy and administration (MA); international politics (MA); law and public policy (MA); Mid-East Politics (MA); political leadership and management (MA); political management (MA); public administration (MA); public policy (MA); terrorism and homeland defense (MA); world economies and political development (MA); JD/MA; M Div/MA; M Ed/MA; MBA/MA. Part-time and evening/weekend programs available. Postbaccalaureate distance learning degree programs offered (minimal on-campus study). *Faculty:* 6 full-time (1 woman), 11 part-time/adjunct (1 woman). *Students:* 60 full-time (33 women), 69 part-time (34 women); includes 29 minority (22 African Americans, 1 Asian American or Pacific Islander, 6 Hispanic Americans), 3 international. Average age 30. 136 applicants, 54% accepted, 54 enrolled. In 2008, 48 master's awarded. *Degree requirements:* For master's, thesis optional, internship. *Entrance requirements:* For master's, GRE General Test or LSAT, minimum undergraduate GPA of 3.0, writing sample, resumé, interview, references, transcripts. Additional exam requirements/recommendations for international students: Required—TOEFL (minimum score 577 paper-based; 233 computer-based). *Application deadline:* For fall admission, 5/1 priority date for domestic students; for spring admission, 11/1 priority date for domestic students. Applications are processed on a rolling basis. Application fee: $50. Electronic applications accepted. *Expenses:* Contact institution. *Financial support:* Career-related internships or fieldwork, scholarships/grants, tuition waivers (full and partial), and unspecified assistantships available. Support available to part-time students. Financial award application deadline: 9/1; financial award applicants required to submit FAFSA. *Faculty research:* Education reform, political character issues, social capital concerns, administrative ethics, Biblical law and public policy. *Unit head:* Dr. Charles W. Dunn, Dean, 757-352-4322, Fax: 757-352-4643, E-mail: cwdunn@regent.edu. *Application contact:* Matthew Chadwick, Director of Admissions, 800-373-5504, Fax: 757-352-4381, E-mail: admissions@regent.edu.

University of Miami, Graduate School, School of Business Administration, Department of Economics, Coral Gables, FL 33124. Offers economic development (MA, PhD); environmental economics (PhD); human resource economics (MA, PhD); international economics (MA, PhD); macroeconomics (PhD). Students admitted every two years in the fall semester. Terminal master's awarded for partial completion of doctoral program. *Degree requirements:* For master's, comprehensive exam; for doctorate, comprehensive exam, thesis/dissertation. *Entrance requirements:* For master's and doctorate, GRE General Test, minimum GPA of 3.0. Additional exam requirements/recommendations for international students: Required—TOEFL (minimum score 550 paper-based). *Faculty research:* International economics/trade, applied microeconomics, development.

University of San Francisco, College of Arts and Sciences, Department of Economics, San Francisco, CA 94117-1080. Offers economics (MA); financial analysis (MS); international and development economics (MA); MS/MBA. Part-time and evening/weekend programs available. *Degree requirements:* For master's, comprehensive exam, thesis or alternative. *Entrance requirements:* For master's, GRE General Test (recommended), BA in economics (preferred). Additional exam requirements/recommendations for international students: Required—TOEFL. *Faculty research:* Economic development, forecasting and planning, labor markets, Pacific Rim, financial markets.

Virginia Polytechnic Institute and State University, Graduate School, College of Agriculture and Life Sciences, Department of Agricultural and Applied Economics, Blacksburg, VA 24061. Offers agribusiness (MS); agricultural economics (MS, PhD); applied economics (MS); developmental and international economics (PhD); econometrics (PhD); macro and micro economics (PhD); markets and industrial organizations (PhD); public and regional/urban economics (PhD); resource and environmental economics (PhD). *Entrance requirements:* For master's and doctorate, GRE General Test. Additional exam requirements/recommendations for international students: Required—TOEFL (minimum score 575 paper-based; 231 computer-based). Electronic applications accepted. *Faculty research:* Rural development.

West Virginia University, College of Business and Economics, Division of Economics and Finance, Morgantown, WV 26506. Offers business analysis (MA); developmental financial economics (PhD); environmental and resource economics (PhD); international economics (PhD); mathematical economics (MA); monetary economics (PhD); public finance (PhD); public policy (MA); regional and urban economics (PhD); statistics and economics (MA). Terminal master's awarded for partial completion of doctoral program. *Degree requirements:* For master's, thesis optional; for doctorate, comprehensive exam, thesis/dissertation. *Entrance requirements:* For master's and doctorate, GRE General Test, minimum GPA of 3.0; course work in intermediate microeconomics, intermediate macroeconomics, calculus, and statistics. Additional exam requirements/recommendations for international students: Required—TOEFL. Electronic applications accepted. *Faculty research:* Financial economics, regional/urban development, public economics, international trade/international finance/development economics, monetary economics.

Yale University, Graduate School of Arts and Sciences, Department of Economics, Program in International and Development Economics, New Haven, CT 06520. Offers MA. *Entrance requirements:* For master's, GRE General Test.

Mineral Economics

Colorado School of Mines, Graduate School, Division of Economics and Business, Golden, CO 80401-1887. Offers engineering and technology management (MS); mineral economics (MS, PhD). Part-time programs available. *Faculty:* 12 full-time (4 women), 7 part-time/adjunct (1 woman). *Students:* 67 full-time (15 women), 25 part-time (4 women); includes 8 minority (1 African American, 1 Asian American or Pacific Islander, 6 Hispanic Americans), 30 international. 114 applicants, 80% accepted, 43 enrolled. In 2008, 45 master's, 3 doctorates awarded. *Degree requirements:* For master's, thesis (for some programs); for doctorate, comprehensive exam, thesis/dissertation. *Entrance requirements:* For master's and doctorate, GRE General Test. Additional exam requirements/recommendations for international students: Required—TOEFL (minimum score 550 paper-based; 213 computer-based; 80 iBT). *Application deadline:* For fall admission, 1/15 priority date for domestic and international students; for spring admission, 9/1 priority date for domestic and international students. Application fee: $50 ($70 for international students). Electronic applications accepted. *Expenses:* Tuition, state resident: full-time $9810; part-time $477 per credit hour. Tuition, nonresident: full-time $23,814; part-time $1158 per credit hour. Required fees: $1428.76; $714.38 per semester. *Financial support:* In 2008–09, 35 students received support, including 8 fellowships with full tuition reimbursements available (averaging $20,000 per year), 2 research assistantships with full tuition reimbursements available (averaging $20,000 per year), 25 teaching assistantships with full tuition reimbursements available (averaging $20,000 per year); scholarships/grants, health care benefits, and unspecified assistantships also available. Financial award application deadline: 1/15; financial award applicants required to submit FAFSA. *Faculty research:* International trade, resource and environmental economics, energy economics, operations research. Total annual research expenditures: $11,062. *Unit head:* Dr. Rod Eggert, Division Head, 303-273-3981, Fax: 303-273-3416, E-mail: reggert@mines.edu. *Application contact:* Kathleen A. Feighny, Administrative Faculty, 303-273-3979, Fax: 303-273-3416, E-mail: kfeighny@mines.edu.

Michigan Technological University, Graduate School, School of Business and Economics, Program in Applied Natural Resource Economics, Houghton, MI 49931-1295. Offers MS. Part-time programs available. *Degree requirements:* For master's, comprehensive exam, thesis (for some programs). *Entrance requirements:* For master's, GRE. Additional exam requirements/recommendations for international students: Required—TOEFL (minimum score 550 paper-based; 213 computer-based). Electronic applications accepted.

The University of Texas at Austin, Graduate School, Cockrell School of Engineering, Department of Petroleum and Geosystems Engineering, Program in Energy and Earth Resources, Austin, TX 78712-1111. Offers MA. *Degree requirements:* For master's, thesis, seminar. *Entrance requirements:* For master's, GRE General Test. Additional exam requirements/recommendations for international students: Required—TOEFL. Electronic applications accepted.

SOUTHERN ILLINOIS UNIVERSITY CARBONDALE

Department of Economics
Doctoral Program

Program of Study

The Department of Economics at Southern Illinois University Carbondale (SIUC) offers a doctoral degree that is designed to be completed in four years. In the first year, the student takes courses in macroeconomics, microeconomics, and mathematical economics and is required to pass qualifying exams in microeconomics and macroeconomics. In the second year, the student completes one field of specialization, begins econometrics, and takes the field exam (summer of second year). In the third year, the student completes the second field, finishes econometrics, and starts on a research topic for the dissertation. The fourth year is devoted to completion of the dissertation. The fields offered by the Department are international economics, economic development, and monetary theory and policy. The student may, with the permission of the Director of Graduate Studies, pursue a field in finance. All of the courses for this field are taught in the College of Business.

Research Facilities

Research facilities include Morris Library which contains more than 2.6 million volumes and subscribes to more than 12,000 current serials. Library users have access to nearly 900 electronic data files and CD-ROM products via multiple workstations throughout the library. The University maintains an extensive and up-to-date computer system with four instructional laboratories. The Department maintains its own computer lab and its own library of software most used by economists.

Financial Aid

Departmental teaching assistantships are available on a competitive basis. Half-time assistantships with stipends of $1362 per month are available for Ph.D. students. A 15-hour tuition waiver accompanies each assistantship.

Cost of Study

In-state graduate tuition is $328 per credit hour in 2009–10. Out-of-state tuition is 2.5 times the in-state tuition rate ($820 per credit hour). Graduate students with at least a 25 percent appointment as a graduate assistant receive a tuition scholarship. Fees vary from $589.03 (1 credit hour) to $1557.50 (12 credit hours). Students with a graduate assistantship receive a 50 percent reduction in the primary care medical fee. New graduate students from Arkansas, Indiana, Kentucky, Missouri, and Tennessee qualify for the alternate tuition rate, which is equivalent to the in-state graduate tuition rate.

Living and Housing Costs

For married couples, students with families, and single graduate students, the University has 690 efficiency and one-, two-, three-, and four-bedroom apartments that rent for $499 to $720 per month in 2009–10. Residence halls for single graduate students are also available, as are accessible residence hall rooms and apartments for students with disabilities.

Student Group

There were 41 students enrolled in the graduate program in economics in fall 2007. There are more than 4,300 students enrolled in graduate programs in the University, with a total student enrollment of 21,387.

Location

SIUC is 350 miles south of Chicago and 100 miles southeast of St. Louis. Nestled in rolling hills bordered by the Ohio and Mississippi Rivers and enhanced by a mild climate, the area has state parks, national forests and wildlife refuges, and large lakes for outdoor recreation. Cultural offerings include theater, opera, concerts, art exhibits, and cinema. Educational facilities for the families of students are excellent.

The University

Southern Illinois University Carbondale is a comprehensive public university with a variety of general and professional education programs. The University offers associate, bachelor's, master's, Ph.D., J.D., and M.D. degrees. The University is fully accredited by the North Central Association of Colleges and Schools. The Graduate School has an essential role in the development and coordination of graduate instruction and research programs. The Graduate Council has academic responsibility for determining graduate standards, recommending new graduate programs and research centers, and establishing policies to facilitate the research effort.

Applying

A student with a bachelor's degree must have a grade point average of 2.7 (A = 4.0) or above in the last 60 hours of undergraduate work, while those entering with a master's degree must have a grade point average of 3.25 in all graduate course work. All applicants are required to take the Graduate Record Examinations. International applicants must earn a minimum score of 550 on the Test of English as a Foreign Language (TOEFL) exam (220 on the computerized version). Additional information can be found on the Departmental Web site listed below.

Correspondence and Information

Professor Subhash C. Sharma
Director of Graduate Studies
Department of Economics
Southern Illinois University
Carbondale, Illinois 62901-4515

Mrs. Sandra McRoy, Graduate Secretary
Department of Economics
Southern Illinois University
Carbondale, Illinois 62901-4515

Phone: 618-536-7746
Fax: 618-453-2717
Web site: http://www.siu.edu/~econ/

Southern Illinois University Carbondale

THE FACULTY AND THEIR RESEARCH

Zsolt Becsi, Assistant Professor; Ph.D., Wisconsin–Madison, 1991. Public finance, macroeconomics.

Bilateral war in a multilateral world: Carrots and sticks for conflict resolution. *Can. J. Econ.* 2006. With Lahiri.

War technology, war, and welfare. *India Macroeconomics Annual 2004–2005* ed. Sugata Marjit. Calcutta: The Reserve Bank of India Endowment. With Lahiri.

Chifeng Dai, Assistant Professor; Ph.D., Florida, 2003. Industrial organization, contract theory, public economics, health economics, applied econometrics.

Delegating management to experts. *Rand J. Econ.* 2006. With Lopomo and Lewis.

Scott Gilbert, Associate Professor; Ph.D., California, San Diego, 1996. Econometrics, macroeconomics and finance.

The impact of skewness in the hedging decision. *J. Futures Markets*, 26(5):503–20, 2006. With Jones and Hatfield.

Testing for latent factors in models with autocorrelation and heteroskedasticity of unknown form. *Southern Econ. J.* 72:236–52, 2005. With Zemcik.

Richard Grabowski, Professor; Ph.D. Utah, 1977. Economic development.

Economic growth and institutional change. *Int. J. Dev. Issues* 4:39–70, 2005.

Agricultural revolution, political development, and long run growth. *Can. J. Dev. Stud.* 26:393–407, 2005.

Sajal Lahiri, Vandeveer Chair Professor; Ph.D., Indian Statistical Institute, 1976.

On the provision of official and private foreign aid. *J. Dev. Econ.* 80:179–97, 2006. With Schweinberger.

Food for education versus school quality: A comparison of policy options to reduce child labor. *Can. J. Econ.* 38:394–419, 2005. With Jafarey.

Thomas Mitchell, Associate Professor; Ph.D., Brown, 1984. Microeconomic theory, mathematical economics.

Conservation laws for microeconomists!: Comments on economic conservation laws as indices of corporate performance. *Japan World Economy*, 16:269–76, 2004.

Indeterminate output allocations. In *Economic Theory, Dynamics and Markets: Essays in Honor of Ryuzo Sato*, pp. 429–37, eds. T. Negishi, R. V. Ramachandran, and K. Mino. Boston: Kluwer Academy Publishers, 2001.

A. K. M. Morshed, Assistant Professor; Ph.D., Washington (Seattle), 2001. Macroeconomic theory, international finance.

Is there really a "border effect?" *J. Int. Money Finance*, 26(7):1229–38, 2007.

Additional sources of bias in half-life estimation. *Computational Statistics and Data Analysis*, in press. With Seong and Ahn.

Basharat A. Pitafi, Assistant Professor; Ph.D., Hawaii, 2004. Public economics, resource economics.

Prevention, eradication, and containment of invasive species: Illustrations from Hawaii. *Agr. Resource Econ. Rev.*, in press.

The economic value of watershed conservation. *Land management impacts on coastal watershed hydrology*, in press, eds. Fares and Kadi. Southampton: WIT Press.

Daniel Primont, Professor; Ph.D., California, Santa Barbara, 1970. Microeconomic theory, mathematical economics

Directional duality theory. *Econ. Theory*, 29(1):239–47, 2006. With Färe.

Luenberger productivity indicators: Aggregation across firms. *J. Prod. Anal.*, in press. With Färe.

Subhash C. Sharma, Professor; Ph.D., Kentucky, 1983. Econometrics, statistics, time-series analysis, monetary economics, development economics.

An examination of momentum strategies in commodity futures markets. *J. Futures Markets* 2007. With Shen and Szakmary.

Currency substitution in Asian countries. *J. Asian Econ.* 16:489–532, 2005. With Kandil and Chaisrisawatsuk.

Kevin Sylwester, Associate Professor; Ph.D., Wisconsin–Madison, 1997. Macroeconomics, economic growth, and development.

A note on geography, institutions, and income inequality. *Econ. Letters* 85:235–40, 2004.

Income inequality and population density 1500 AD: A connection. *J. Econ. Development* 28(2):61–82, 2003.

Alison Watts, Associate Professor; Ph.D., Duke, 1993. Microeconomics, game theory and law and economics.

Formation of buyer-seller trade networks in a quality-differentiated product market. *Can. J. Econ.* 39:971–1004, 2006. With Wang.

Uniqueness of equilibrium in cost sharing games. *J. Math. Econ.* 37:47–70, 2002.

SUFFOLK UNIVERSITY

Graduate Programs in Economics

Programs of Study

The economics department offers three graduate programs of study: the Ph.D. in economics, the Master of Science in International Economics (M.S.I.E.), the Master of Science in Economic Policy (M.S.E.P.), and the Master of Science in Economics (M.S.E.). In addition, the department offers a joint program with the Law School (J.D./M.S.I.E.).

The Ph.D. program offers both midcareer professionals and new graduates a program with an applied focus, taught by experienced faculty members, with convenient full-time and part-time program options. As part of the Department of Economics, the program is academically rigorous and theoretically sound. The unique applied focus of the Suffolk Ph.D. program enables graduates not only to seek academic appointments but also to compete for jobs in the business sector and advance in their fields. The core required courses provide a foundation in economics; the electives allow students to tailor their studies to their particular interests in theory and research.

The Master of Science in International Economics meets the needs of today's world, where business and government decisions are made in an increasingly global environment. The M.S.I.E. is a highly focused study of international economics that equips students with sophisticated quantitative skills. It prepares students for professional careers in international business, international finance, and international economic policy as analysts and consultants. M.S.I.E. students are qualified to work for multinational corporations, financial institutions, economic consulting firms, international law firms, and various international organizations.

The Master of Science in Economic Policy prepares students for careers in government, public policy research, or government relations. It provides the knowledge and skills needed for government budgeting, tax-revenue forecasting, the regulation of public utilities, and the litigation of antitrust issues. Students find the program useful preparation for managing a government agency, providing in-house or consulting advice on policy issues, representing clients in government hearings, writing reports on public policy issues, and providing expert testimony.

The Master of Science in Economics is aimed at offering increased flexibility and an expanded menu of choices to master's students. The M.S.E. is a more broad-based program than the M.S.I.E. or M.S.E.P. programs and would allow students to have more choices in course selections based on their preferences and career plans. Students completing this program may pursue a career as a generalist in both the private and public sectors rather than being limited to the particular kinds of jobs that are directly related to a narrowly defined field.

Research Facilities

Research facilities include the Mildred F. Sawyer Library and the Moakley Law Library. Students also have access, through an interlibrary program, to other major libraries in the region. As Boston residents, all students have access to the world-class Boston Public Library. Computing facilities, which provide access to current databases and software, are available for graduate students in the department. Facilities are also available at several on-campus computer labs. In addition, the Department of Economics houses the nationally recognized Beacon Hill Institute for Public Policy Research. The Beacon Hill Institute applies state-of-the-art statistical, mathematical, and econometric methods to provide economic analyses of today's leading public policy issues. Opportunities exist for graduate students to work and intern with this leading research institution.

Financial Aid

The graduate programs offer various levels of financial support. Outstanding full-time candidates may receive financial awards, including a full tuition waiver for up to three years and teaching or research assistantships. Partial financial awards are offered to qualified full-time students. Excellent candidates for part-time study may be awarded a tuition waiver. Additional opportunities exist for grants and scholarships.

Cost of Study

For the master's programs, full-time tuition is $11,650 per semester (four courses), and part-time tuition is $2913 per course. For the Ph.D. program, tuition is $3705 per course.

Living and Housing Costs

Limited on-campus housing is offered at Suffolk's Residence Hall overlooking the Boston Common. It is a short walk to the main academic and administrative buildings. Accommodations are in single, double, triple, and quad rooms or in suites. Suffolk's Off-Campus Housing Office (OCHO) helps students find housing by gathering information on apartment sublets, rentals, and sharing opportunities. The office maintains a list of students seeking roommates, posts advertisements for roommates, and works with area realtors to better serve students. A complete list of realtors is available upon request.

Student Group

The graduate students in economics include a broad range of U.S. and international students, both recent college graduates and midcareer professionals. Full-time and part-time students are welcomed, resulting in a diverse mix of backgrounds and experiences being shared in the classrooms. Classes are typically small, giving students close working relationships with each other and the faculty members. The favorable faculty-student ratio fosters an environment of personalized mentoring, helping students achieve their individual professional and academic goals.

Location

Suffolk University is located on Boston's renowned Beacon Hill, within easy reach of Boston's governmental, financial, cultural, and historic centers. A city rich in history and culture, Boston has more than fifty of the finest colleges and universities in the nation. Founded in 1630, ten years after the Pilgrims landed at Plymouth, Boston is the capital of the commonwealth of Massachusetts and is the largest city in New England. The city of Boston has a population of more than 600,000 people, including a significant number of college students, whose heritage is worldwide.

The University and The School

Founded in 1906 as Suffolk School of Law by Gleason L. Archer, Suffolk University now offers fifty-six undergraduate and graduate degree and certificate programs. Suffolk was named in *Barron's Best Buys in College Education.* Suffolk also offers programs on the campuses of Cape Cod Community College, Merrimack College, and Dean College and has branch campuses in Madrid, Spain, and Dakar, Senegal.

Applying

Information on admission procedures and requirements is available at the Web site (http://www.suffolk.edu/economics) or by contacting the Office of Graduate Admission (information below). The Ph.D. program enrolls new students only in the fall semester. Applications must be received by February 1. The master's programs enroll new full-time students only in the fall. Applications must be received by June 15 for the fall semester (March 15 for those interested in financial aid) and November 1 for the spring semester.

Correspondence and Information

Office of Graduate Admission
Suffolk University
8 Ashburton Place
Boston, Massachusetts 02108-2701
Phone: 617-573-8302
Fax: 617-523-0116
E-mail: grad.admission@suffolk.edu
Web site: http://www.suffolk.edu

Suffolk University

THE FACULTY

The Department of Economics at Suffolk University consists of a vibrant group of 12 full-time scholars. Faculty members are active in research, policy advising, writing, and consulting. Research interests of the faculty members are diverse but are in the general area of applied economics and finance, with special emphasis on the issues of economic policy and international economics.

Specific research interests of the faculty include economic development, taxation, econometric and CGE tax modeling for states of the U.S., economic reconstruction of war-torn economies, issues in education and education reform, empirical investigation of rent-to-own agreements, welfare reform, economics of regulation, empirical viability of recent developments in contract theory, competitive dynamics, spatial competition, product differentiation in U.S. motion-pictures exhibition markets, productivity growth, international debt problems and currency crisis, foreign direct investment and capital flows to emerging markets, determinants of market-assessed sovereign risk, international trade, economic justice, political economy of international economic relations, optimal investment decisions for the long term, timing issues in the high-tech IPO aftermarket, and financial valuation of knowledge assets of biotechnology firms.

David G. Tuerck, Professor and Chairman; Ph.D., Virginia. Tax policy, public choice, macroeconomic theory.
In-Mee Baek, Professor; Ph.D., Indiana. International investment, currency crisis, foreign capital flows, international debt problems.
Darlene C. Chisholm, Professor; Ph.D., Washington (Seattle). Industrial organization, applied microeconomic theory, empirical contract studies, spatial competition and product differentiation in U.S. motion-picture industry.
A. Tolga Ergun, Assistant Professor; Ph.D., Arizona. Econometrics, financial economics.
Haldun Evrenk, Assistant Professor; Ph.D., Boston University. Political economy, development economics, public finance, industrial organization.
Lou Foglia, Instructor; M.A., Northeastern. Microeconomics, macroeconomics, money, banking.
Jonathan Haughton, Associate Professor; Ph.D., Harvard. Development economics, tax policy, competitiveness, international economics.
Jongbyung Jun, Assistant Professor; Ph.D., Michigan State. Foreign exchange rate determination, applied time-series econometrics, international trade and finance.
Alison Kelly, Professor; Ph.D., Boston College. Productivity growth, issues in education, applied statistical methods.
Sunghyun Henry Kim, Associate Professor; Ph.D., Yale. Open economy macroeconomics, international finance.
Shahruz Mohtadi, Associate Professor; Ph.D., LSU. International economics, monetary economics.
Benjamin Powell, Assistant Professor; Ph.D., George Mason. Austrian economics, economic development, public choice, applied microeconomics.
Serge Shikher, Assistant Professor; Ph.D., Boston University. International trade, international finance, macroeconomics, development.

UNIVERSITY OF ILLINOIS AT URBANA–CHAMPAIGN

Department of Economics
Program in Policy Economics

Programs of Study

The Program in Policy Economics, offered by the Department of Economics, is a specially designed, intensive program of study leading to a Master of Science degree in economics from the University of Illinois. It is intended for promising young administrators in government and private institutions, in both developing countries and advanced industrial countries, who need additional training in the areas of economic analysis and quantitative techniques. It is also for young scholars interested in a terminal master's degree.

A complementary mission of the program is to help interested students acquire the necessary background to pursue a doctorate in economics. While earning the master's degree, they learn if the pursuit of a Ph.D. degree is within their reach and suits their purposes.

The program offers more than forty courses in twelve different areas of specialization. These courses are taught by a faculty of more than 30 members.

Students with an excellent background in economics and quantitative methods and a high level of proficiency in English can complete the program in one year. Students with low proficiency in English, limited training in economics, or who completed their university course work several years ago are generally required to take an additional one or two semesters to complete the master's degree. Students who wish to take advantage of the extensive course offerings at the University and study in additional areas or fields may remain up to two years to complete their program of study.

Students select one field from advanced econometrics (this field requires special prerequisites), development economics, economic policy, environment and natural resources, health economics, industrial organization, international economics, labor economics, law and economics, monetary economics, public economics, and urban and regional economics.

Program enrichment offers special training on computers; internationally known guest speakers; field trips to business, financial, and government institutions; and tutorial help for students encountering difficulty in courses.

Research Facilities

The University library has the largest collection of any public university in the world and ranks third among U.S. academic libraries.

Financial Aid

No financial aid is available for students or their spouses.

Cost of Study

Tuition and fees for the first year were $32,900 in 2008–09. Tuition and fees are subject to change for the second year. Books and supplies cost approximately $2407 per year.

Living and Housing Costs

Students can reside in University graduate student dormitories, University married student housing, or private apartments or rooms. The estimated living allowance is $1450 per month, or $17,400 per year. The current estimated cost for accompanying dependents is as follows: for one dependent, $6200 per year; for two, $9980 per year; and, for each additional dependent, $1920 per year. The current annual rate for health insurance is $3096 for a spouse and $1542 for children (subject to change).

Student Group

Program alumni come from ninety-five different countries. The 86 students who are currently enrolled are from sixteen countries: Afghanistan, Belgium, Brazil, China, Dominican Republic, Guatemala, Indonesia, Iran, Italy, Korea, Peru, Taiwan, Tanzania, Thailand, Turkey, and the United States. All students are registered full-time, and 39 percent are women.

Student Outcomes

Upon completion of the program, participants usually return to their previous positions or similar ones with enlarged opportunities. Some continue to work on their Ph.D. degrees (at the University of Illinois and elsewhere). Jobs that graduates return to include university instructor and researcher, commercial bank manager, chief executive officer, economic journalist and senior economist at a research institute, central bank economist and manager, securities analyst, chief expert at the Ministry of Trade, associate director at the Ministry of Construction, and manager at the Ministry of Finance. Over the years, some have risen in rank to hold such positions as president, governor, and deputy governor in central banks and top government cabinet positions, including Minister of Finance, Minister of Commerce and Industry, and Minister of Rural Development.

Location

Urbana-Champaign, with its mixture of rural and urban influences, education and culture, and high technology and research, offers the feeling and sophistication of a big city while retaining its Midwestern warmth.

Available athletic facilities include two golf courses, several tennis courts, jogging tracks, basketball courts, soccer fields, handball/racquetball courts, squash courts, five swimming pools, and weightlifting rooms.

The University

Since its founding in 1867, the University of Illinois at Urbana-Champaign has steadily gained in stature and is recognized as one of the leading universities in the world. The University is known primarily for its achievements in research and graduate studies.

Another prime indicator of the campus's excellence is the success of its alumni. Eleven alumni have won Nobel Prizes for the United States and another 18 have won the Pulitzer Prize.

Applying

Required materials are an application and fee, official transcript (translated if not in English) from all universities and colleges attended, three letters of recommendation, and, for students from non-English-speaking countries, scores on the Test of English as a Foreign Language (TOEFL).

Since admission is granted on a continuing basis, students should submit their completed application materials as soon as possible. Although there is no deadline date for applications, the program is usually full by April 1.

Correspondence and Information

M.S. Program
Director, Master's Program
313 David Kinley Hall
1407 West Gregory Drive
Urbana, Illinois 61801
Phone: 217-333-7651
Fax: 217-244-7368
E-mail: mspe@illinois.edu
Web site: http://www.mspe.uiuc.edu

Ph.D. Program:
Graduate Coordinator
410 David Kinley Hall
1407 West Gregory Drive
Urbana, Illinois 61801
Phone: 217-333-0120
Fax: 217-244-6678
E-mail: econ@illinois.edu
Web site: http://www.economics.uiuc.edu

University of Illinois at Urbana-Champaign

THE FACULTY AND THEIR RESEARCH

Professors
Werner Baer, Ph.D., Harvard, 1958. Development, international economics.
Anil K. Bera, Ph.D., Australian National, 1982. Econometrics.
Daniel M. Bernhardt, Ph.D., Carnegie-Mellon, 1986. Economic theory, industrial organization, banking.
In-Koo Cho, Ph.D., Princeton, 1986. Microeconomics, macroeconomics.
*Lawrence DeBrock, Ph.D., Cornell, 1979. Industrial organization, microeconomics.
Hadi S. Esfahani, Ph.D., Berkeley, 1984. Economic development, international trade.
Firouz Gahvari: Ph.D., UCLA, 1981. Public economics.
*J. Fred Giertz, Ph.D., Northwestern, 1970. Public finance and public choice.
Fred M. Gottheil, Ph.D., Duke, 1959. Comparative economic systems, Middle East economics, history of economic thought.
*Geoffrey J. D. Hewings, Ph.D., Washington, 1969. Macroeconomics, urban and regional planning.
*Charles M. Kahn, Ph.D., Harvard, 1981. Economics of information and uncertainty, game theory.
Roger W. Koenker, Ph.D., Michigan, 1974. Econometric theory and applications, industrial organization.
Stefan Krasa, Ph.D., Vienna, 1987. Microeconomics.
*Crain Olson, Ph.D., Wisconsin, 1979. Labor economics.
Salim Rashid, Ph.D., Yale, 1976. Microeconomic theory, history of economic thought, mathematical economics.
Bart Taub, Ph.D., Chicago, 1981. Macroeconomics.
*Thomas S. Ulen, Ph.D., Stanford, 1978. Law and economics.
Anne P. Villamil, Ph.D., Minnesota, 1988. Monetary economics.
Steven R. Williams, Head of Department; Ph.D., Northwestern, 1982. Microeconomic theory, mathematical economics.
Nicholas C. Yannelis, Ph.D., Rochester, 1983. Mathematical economics, game theory.

Associate Professors
George Deltas, Ph.D., Yale, 1995. Microeconomics, industrial organization.
Stephen Parente, Ph.D., Minnesota, 1990. Macroeconomics, development and growth.
*Elizabeth Powers, Ph.D., Pennsylvania, 1994. Labor economics.

Assistant Professors
Richard Akresh, Ph.D., Yale, 2004. Economic development.
Luciano de Castro, Ph.D., Institute of Pure and Applied Mathematics (Brazil), 2004. Mathematical economics, auction theory.
Todd Elder, Ph.D., Northwestern, 2001. Labor.
Seung-Hyun Hong, Ph.D. candidate, Stanford. Industrial organization.
*Darren Lubotsky, Ph.D., Berkeley, 2000. Labor economics.
Makoto Nakajima, Ph.D., Pennsylvania, 2004. Macroeconomics.
Mattias Polborn, Ph.D., Munich, 1998. Public economics.
Daniela Puzzello, Ph.D., Purdue, 2005. Economic and monetary theory.
Leonardo Rezende, Ph.D., Stanford, 2003. Industrial organization.
Juha Seppala, Ph.D., Chicago, 2000. Macroeconomics.
Rui Zhao, Ph.D., Chicago, 2000. Macroeconomics, transition.

Lecturers
Kristine Brown, Ph.D., Berkeley, 2007. Labor economics.
Jose Jazquez, Ph.D., Rensselaer, 2001. Environmental economics.
Joseph Petry, Ph.D., Illinois, 1991. Statistics.
Colleen Schultz, Ph.D., Illinois, 1998. Industrial organization, health, law and economics.
Ali Toossi, Ph.D., Illinois, 2002. Industrial organization, political economy.

Joint appointment with other departments or institutes in the University.

UNIVERSITY OF NEW HAMPSHIRE

Whittemore School of Business and Economics
Economics Programs

Programs of Study

The Whittemore School offers programs of study leading to both the M.A. and the Ph.D. degrees in economics. Applicants may enroll in the fall. The M.A. degree can be completed in one calendar year.

The principal requirements for the M.A. degree are 30 credits of graduate course work including two required courses in economic theory and one required course in econometrics, a yearlong graduate economics seminar, and a master's research paper. M.A. students may select electives from a variety of areas. The M.A. satisfies the first year of the Ph.D. program.

Currently, the Ph.D. program is based on the following key features: a series of core courses, two fields of specialization (one major and one minor), several significant research requirements, comprehensive exams in economic theory, and a field exam in the chosen major field. The core courses consist of two courses in microeconomic theory, macroeconomic theory, and econometrics and one course each in the history of thought and in economic thought and methodology. Separate comprehensive exams are given in microeconomic and macroeconomic theory. Beyond the core, students are required to have a major field of concentration that consists of four courses and a field exam, and a minor field with two courses. The department offers fields of concentration in international economics, health economics, and environmental economics. Students should refer to the Web site for information on any revisions to the curriculum.

A continuous, integrated approach to research is a highlight of the program. New students enroll in the department's weekly seminar series and are presented research by faculty members, advanced graduate students, and well-known guest speakers. Near the end of the program, Ph.D. students generally develop a research proposal for the dissertation and present it to the workshop.

In addition to the research emphasis of the Ph.D. program, the department encourages students interested in teaching to pursue the optional 12-semester-hour cognate in college teaching. The University of New Hampshire's (UNH) Preparing Future Faculty program is designed to provide graduate students with the necessary tools to become successful faculty members. Students can visit http://www.gradschool.unh.edu/pff for more information about the program.

Research Facilities

The University library houses more than 1.1 million volumes, 6,500 periodical subscriptions, and 1 million government documents that form the core of print materials. Electronic sources include EBSCOhost, which provides indexes to general, academic, and business periodicals; LexisNexis, which accesses a wide variety of full-text news and legal information; and PubMed, which contains 9 million citations of medical materials. The library provides access to a wide variety of materials, from medieval manuscripts to electronic data sets, from nineteenth-century novels to Web-based full-text documents, and from bound periodicals to electronic journals. For more information, students should visit the Web site at http://www.library.unh.edu.

Financial Aid

Applicants with strong academic records may qualify for graduate assistantships. For 20 hours of work per week, graduate assistants receive a stipend of $14,300 (proposed) for the 2009–10 academic year plus a tuition waiver; for 10 hours a week, they receive $7150 (proposed) plus a waiver of half the tuition, of which the remainder is paid at the in-state rate. Tuition scholarships are also available, as are federally funded loans for those who qualify.

Cost of Study

In 2009–10, proposed tuition for full-time students is $14,350 per year for New Hampshire residents and $25,525 per year for nonresidents. Mandatory yearly fees are expected to be $2327 plus a health insurance fee of $1490 if the student does not already have health insurance.

Living and Housing Costs

Babcock Hall, the graduate residence hall, provides single rooms at a proposed cost of $6076 for the 2009–10 academic year. Students may remain in Babcock during the summer at reduced rates. Limited on-campus housing for married students is provided at Forest Park. Proposed prices for 2009–10 for efficiency and one- or two-bedroom apartments range from $790 to $825 per month. Off-campus housing is available in a wide range of prices. For further information, applicants should visit the UNH Housing Web site at http://www.unh.edu/housing.

Student Group

The University has an enrollment of 13,544 students, 2,481 of whom are graduate students; many are from other countries. The economics graduate program typically has between 15 and 20 students enrolled.

Location

Located 65 miles north of Boston, the University of New Hampshire occupies a picturesque 200-acre campus in the attractive New England town of Durham. It is only 10 miles from the Atlantic Ocean and 60 miles from New Hampshire's scenic lakes and mountains.

The University and The School

Founded in 1886, the University of New Hampshire serves as a cultural and scientific center for the area, with the New England Center, Space Science Center, and Paul Arts Center. The Whittemore School of Business and Economics, established in 1962 and one of the University's six schools and colleges, offers undergraduate as well as graduate degrees.

Applying

An applicant for admission must submit the following materials to the Graduate School, Room 109, Thompson Hall, University of New Hampshire: the official Graduate School application forms for admission to graduate study; two official transcripts showing the grades earned in all of the applicant's previous graduate and undergraduate academic work; three letters of recommendation from persons in a position to judge the applicant's preparation for and ability to undertake graduate study (e.g., the applicant's previous instructors or coworkers); GRE scores; and, for all international applicants, TOEFL scores.

Application deadlines are July 1 for the fall session. The fall deadline for applications from international students is April 1. Applicants who wish to be considered for graduate assistantships and tuition scholarships should submit the completed application by February 1.

Correspondence and Information

Whittemore School of Business and Economics
Graduate Programs Office
116 McConnell Hall
University of New Hampshire
15 Academic Way
Durham, New Hampshire 03824-3593
Phone: 603-862-1367
Fax: 603-862-4468
E-mail: wsbe.grad@unh.edu
Web site: http://wsbe.unh.edu/grad/

University of New Hampshire

THE FACULTY AND THEIR RESEARCH

Business Administration

E. Hachemi Aliouche, Associate Professor of Hospitality Management and Senior Research Fellow, Rosenberg International Center of Franchising; Ph.D., New Hampshire. Financial aspects of franchising and financial valuation.

Carole K. Barnett, Associate Professor of Management; Ph.D., Michigan. Organizational leadership and learning, change and transformation, design and development, culture.

Clayton Barrows, Professor of Hospitality Management; Ed.D., Massachusetts. Food and beverage management, private club management.

Brian Bolton, Assistant Professor of Finance; Ph.D., Colorado. Corporate governance and initial public offering, financial markets and infrastructure, capital structure, financial econometrics, investments.

Ludwig Bstieler, Assistant Professor of Marketing; Ph.D., Innsbruck (Austria). Design and marketing of new products, market research methods.

Stephen Ciccone, Associate Professor of Finance; Ph.D., Florida State. Investments, stock return anomalies, international corporate governance, analyst forecast issues.

Eleanne Solorzano Dowd, Associate Professor of Statistics; Ph.D., South Carolina. Nonparametric statistics, multiple comparisons, statistical computing, distribution theory, Bayesian inference.

Vanessa Urch Druskat, Associate Professor of Organizational Behavior and Management; Ph.D., Boston University. Work team and team leader effectiveness, the influence of emotional competence on team effectiveness and on leader effectiveness, effective leadership in public school systems.

Joseph F. Durocher, Associate Professor of Hospitality Management; Ph.D., Cornell. Food service management, restaurant and hotel design, computers in management and training, economic forecasting for the hospitality industry.

Devkamal Dutta, Assistant Professor of Strategic Management and Entrepreneurship; Ph.D., Western Ontario. Intersection of competitive strategies and competitive dynamics, entrepreneurial cognition, opportunity recognition, knowledge exchange in multinationals.

Ahmad Etebari, Chair and Professor of Accounting and Finance; Ph.D., North Texas State. Investments, corporate finance.

Ross Gittell, Professor of Business Administration; Ph.D., Harvard. Business, government and competition, regional and urban development, business and public policy.

Raymond J. Goodman Jr., Chair and Professor of Hospitality Management; Ph.D., Cornell. Human resources management: training and performance evaluation; retirement facilities planning, design, marketing, management and operations; lodging and restaurant industry indexing and forecasting.

Roger Grinde, Associate Dean and Associate Professor of Decision Sciences; Ph.D., Penn State. Operations research, spreadsheet model auditing and control, mathematical modeling.

Charles W. Gross, Professor of Marketing; Ph.D., Colorado. International marketing, marketing planning and strategy, forecasting.

Khole Gwebu, Assistant Professor of Decision Sciences; Ph.D., Kent State. E-commerce, reverse auctions, agent-based simulations, multicultural decision making, IT outsourcing.

Bowe Hansen, Assistant Professor of Accounting; Ph.D., Emory. International accounting, accounting quality and transparency, accounting regulation.

Paul Harvey, Assistant Professor of Organizational Behavior; Ph.D., Florida State. Emotions and perceptions, ethical decision making, stress, entitlement, and abusive supervision.

Daniel E. Innis, Dean and Professor of Marketing; Ph.D., Ohio State. Marketing, consumer behavior, customer service, strategic planning, business-to-business marketing, supply chain.

Afshad J. Irani, Associate Professor of Accounting and Academic Director, M.S. in Accounting; Ph.D., Penn State. Voluntary disclosure, earnings management, insider trading, SEC and FASB regulations.

William Johnson, Assistant Professor of Finance; Ph.D., Michigan State. Initial public offerings, conflicts of interest in investment banking, product market relationships.

Fred R. Kaen, Professor of Finance and Co-Director, International Private Enterprise Center; Ph.D., Michigan. Financial management, international finance, corporate finance, corporate governance.

Peter Lane, Chair of Marketing and Associate Professor of Strategic Management and Technology; Ph.D., Connecticut. Strategy development processes, strategic alliances and joint ventures, technology and innovation management, intellectual capital management.

Jun Li, Assistant Professor of Strategic Management and Entrepreneurship; Ph.D., Texas A&M. Strategic leadership and governance in IPO-stage firms, new-venture strategy and entrepreneurship, multinational corporations in transnational economies.

Yixin Liu, Assistant Professor of Finance; Ph.D., Iowa. Corporate governance, agency issues, capital structure and debt issues, insider trading.

Michael J. Merenda, Chair of Management and Professor of Strategic Management; Ph.D., Massachusetts Amherst. Strategic planning and management, entrepreneurship, international business and SME competitiveness.

Anthony Pescosolido, Assistant Professor of Organizational Behavior and Management; Ph.D., Case Western Reserve. Team dynamics, emotion in organizations, emergent leadership, team leadership.

Catherine Plante, Associate Professor of Accounting; Ph.D., Ohio State. Financial, governmental, and nonprofit accounting.

R. Dan Reid, Associate Professor of Operations Management; Ph.D., Ohio State. Production/operations management, purchasing, business logistics, supply chain management.

Richard Saavedra, Associate Professor of Organizational Behavior; Ph.D., Michigan. Work team design and management, mood and behavior, social influence and comparison processes.

Udo Schlentrich, Associate Professor of Hospitality Management and Director, Rosenberg International Center of Franchising; Ph.D., Strathclyde. Consumer marketing, international hospitality and tourism, franchising, finance and project development, hospitality marketing, international hospitality management.

Christine Shea, Associate Dean of Graduate Programs and Research and Associate Professor of Technology and Operations Management; Ph.D., Western Ontario. Technology and operations management, managing innovation, nanotechnology.

Barry Shore, Professor of Information Systems; Ph.D., Wisconsin. Information systems, international management.

Jeffrey E. Sohl, Professor of Entrepreneurship and Decision Sciences and Director, Center for Venture Research; Ph.D., Maryland. Early-stage equity financing of high-growth ventures, trends in the angel market, time series forecasting, entrepreneurship.

A. R. Venkatachalam, Chair of Decision Sciences, Professor of Information Systems, and Director, Enterprise Integration Research Center; Ph.D., Alabama. MIS, artificial intelligence in business, global information management, electronic commerce, enterprise integration, information technology, outsourcing, emerging technologies, technology management.

Jing Wang, Assistant Professor of Decision Sciences; Ph.D., Kent State. The role of social networks in the success of open source systems, management of information systems, managing across the enterprise.

Craig Wood, Associate Professor of Operations Management; Ph.D., Ohio State. Production and operations management, operations strategy, total quality management, technology management, project management, supply chain management.

Emily Xu, Assistant Professor of Accounting; Ph.D., Massachusetts Amherst. Financial analysis, valuation models, financial reporting.

Goksel Yalcinkaya, Assistant Professor of Marketing; Ph.D., Michigan State. Marketing and diffusion of innovations, both domestically and internationally.

Honggeng Zhou, Assistant Professor of Decision Sciences; Ph.D., Ohio State. Supply chain management, information systems and technology management, production and operations management, operations strategy.

Economics

Reagan Baughman, Assistant Professor of Economics; Ph.D., Syracuse. Labor economics, public finance, health economics and policy.

Karen Smith Conway, Professor of Economics; Ph.D., North Carolina at Chapel Hill. Public economics, applied econometrics, labor supply, health economics.

Bruce T. Elmslie, Chair and Professor of Economics; Ph.D., Utah. International trade, history of economic thought, growth theory.

Richard W. England, Professor of Economics and Natural Resources; Ph.D., Michigan. Environmental policy, ecological economics, environmental management, property taxation, smart growth, land development, local economic development, state and local government finance.

Michael Goldberg, Associate Professor of Economics; Ph.D., NYU. International finance, macroeconomic theory, financial markets, expectations.

Marc W. Herold, Associate Professor of Economic Development and Women's Studies; Ph.D., Berkeley. Third World economic development, Brazil, women and development, international studies, postmodernism, economic systems, political economy, civilian causalities of war.

Andrew Houtenville, Associate Professor of Economics and Research Director of Institute on Disability; Ph.D. New Hampshire. Economics of disability, economics of education, public finance, labor economics, applied econometrics.

Ju-Chin Huang, Associate Professor of Economics and Academic Director, Economics Graduate Program; Ph.D., North Carolina State. Applied econometrics, environmental economics.

Robert D. Mohr, Assistant Professor of Economics; Ph.D., Texas at Austin. Environmental and natural resource economics, public finance.

Neil B. Niman, Associate Professor of Economics; Ph.D., Texas at Austin. Evolutionary economics, organizational economics, history of economic thought.

Zeynep Senyus, Assistant Professor of Economics; Ph.D., California, Riverside. Macroeconomics, time series analysis, monetary economics, financial economics.

Torsten Schmidt, Associate Professor of Economics; Ph.D., Florida. Industrial organization, econometrics, microeconomic theory, economics of information and uncertainty.

Evangelos O. Simos, Professor of Economics; Ph.D., Northern Illinois. Macroeconomics, international trade and finance, modeling and forecasting, econometrics, economic growth, monetary theory and policy, international affairs.

James R. Wible, Professor of Economics; Ph.D., Penn State. Macroeconomics and monetary theory, economics of science and philosophy of science, law and economics.

Le Wang, Assistant Professor of Economics; Ph.D. SMU. Applied econometrics, labor economics, development economics, health economics.

Robert Woodward, Forrest D. McKerley Professor of Health Economics; Ph.D., Washington (St. Louis). Economics, health economics, pharmaco-economics, Medicare, health-care reform, transplantation economics.

THE UNIVERSITY OF TEXAS AT DALLAS

School of Economic, Political, and Policy Sciences

Programs of Study

The School of Economic, Political, and Policy Sciences (EPPS) at the University of Texas at Dallas (UT Dallas) offers Ph.D.s in criminology, economics, geospatial information sciences, political science, public affairs, and public policy and political economy (PPPE). It also offers master's degrees in applied sociology, criminology, economics, geospatial information sciences (in conjunction with the School of Natural Sciences), international political economy, public affairs, and public policy. Students receive education through lecture, internships, and workshop courses; a basic knowledge of statistics and computer skills is considered crucial.

EPPS offers a 36-hour M.S. program in applied sociology. This includes 12 hours of core courses in applied sociology, 15 hours of core courses, and 3 hours of internship. The program is designed for students interested in areas such as nonprofit organizations and federal, state, and local government philosophy. For more information, students should contact Judy Robertson (judy@utdallas.edu) or Dr. Richard Scotch (Richard.scotch@utdallas.edu).

The 36-hour Master of Science in criminology provides students with a coherent and intellectually challenging degree that prepares them to conduct interdisciplinary research on various aspects of criminology and/or criminal justice, depending on their specific areas of specialty. Students will be well prepared for analytical and administrative posts in international and domestic research and policy institutions, criminal justice organizations, and the private sector. For more information, students should contact Remona McLain (remonamc@utdallas.edu) or Dr. James Marquart (marquart@utdallas.edu).

The 36-hour M.S. in economics is aimed at students seeking to learn advanced economic theory and apply advanced economic tools to real socioeconomic problems. For more information, students should contact Judy Du (judy.du@utdallas.edu) or Dr. Daniel Arce (darce@utdallas.edu).

In addition, EPPS offers a 30-hour M.S. in geospatial information sciences (GIS). Offered jointly by the School of Economic, Political, and Policy Sciences and the School of Natural Sciences and Mathematics, it focuses on the use of geographic information systems. For more information, students should contact Rita Medford (rmedford@utdallas.edu) or Dr. Denis Dean (Denis.Dean@utdallas.edu).

The School also offers a 36-hour Master of Science in international political economy (IPE) that consists of three components, including required course work (18 hours), prescribed electives (12 hours), and free electives (6 hours). Moreover, students must demonstrate a foreign language proficiency equivalent to two years of study in one foreign language before graduation. For more information, students should contact Judy Robertson (judy@utdallas.edu) or Dr. Jennifer Holmes (jholmes@utdallas.edu).

The Master of Public Affairs (M.P.A.) degree is a 42-hour, interdisciplinary program that includes 21 hours of core courses and 18 hours of directed electives as well as an internship or workshop. It explores the interrelationship between economic, political, and social institutions. Students may emphasize course work in management, policy analysis, or applied technology. The curriculum places strong emphasis upon the development of computer and statistical skills that are necessary for successful performance in both the public and private sectors in the twenty-first century. For more information, students should contact Del Prisock (delfina@utdallas.edu) or Dr. Doug Kiel (dkiel@utdallas.edu).

The M.S. in public policy is an interdisciplinary 36-hour graduate degree designed to develop those skill sets critical for a career in which a solid understanding of the public policy process and the analysis and evaluation of public policies are essential. Specific skills include knowledge of the policy process and related ethical concerns, rigorous research skills that provide students with an essential grounding in statistical and data analysis and research design, and effective communication skills. Students will be prepared for analytical and administrative positions and responsibilities in a wide array of professional settings in the public, non-profit, and private sectors. For more information, students should contact Judy Robertson (judy@utdallas.edu) or Dr. Marie Chevrier (chevrier@utdallas.edu).

The Ph.D. degree in criminology is an interdisciplinary, research-oriented program that provides students with a coherent and intellectually challenging research degree that prepares them for an academic appointment as a university professor or an administrative appointment with oversight of research and development within criminal justice organizations. Graduates of the program will be competent to teach and conduct interdisciplinary research at both graduate and undergraduate levels in aspects of criminology and/or criminal justice, depending on their specific areas of specialty. They also will be well prepared for analytical and administrative posts in international and domestic research and policy institutions and in the private sector. For more information, students should contact Remona McLain (remonamc@utdallas.edu) or Dr. James Marquart (marquart@utdallas.edu).

The Ph.D. program in economics prepares students for careers in academics as well as research-oriented positions in the private and public sector. It provides cutting-edge education in micro and macroeconomic theory, rigorous training in mathematical and econometric techniques, and extensive exposure to various research areas in economics. Students complete a set of core courses, pass comprehensive exams in microeconomic and macroeconomic theory as well as econometrics, are certified in two research areas in economics, and submit and defend a dissertation. For more information, students should contact Judy Du (judy.du@utdallas.edu) or Dr. Daniel Arce (darce@utdallas.edu).

The Ph.D. program in geospatial information sciences, offered with the Schools of Natural Sciences and Mathematics as well as Engineering and Computer Science, offers advanced training in geographic information sciences and related fields. Students complete core courses and pass a qualifying exam before proceeding to the dissertation. For more information, students should contact Rita Medford (rmedford@utdallas.edu) or Dr. Denis Dean (Denis.Dean@utdallas.edu).

The Ph.D. in political science provides a rigorous, student-focused disciplinary program with multidisciplinary links. Students receive state-of-the-science graduate education in political methodology and the fields of democratization, globalization and international relations, institutions and processes, and public management and decision making. Students complete a set of core courses, course work in their designated major and minor fields, and examinations in the core courses and major and minor fields; students also write and defend a dissertation. For more information, students should contact Lynne Boyer (lynne.boyer@utdallas.edu) or Dr. Robert Lowry (robert.lowry@utdallas.edu).

The Ph.D. in public affairs is an interdisciplinary program that prepares graduates to assume positions in academe, research-producing organizations, or positions of administrative authority in public organizations. The degree is nontraditional in that it requires all students to conduct applied, field-based research as the foundation for the production of their dissertations. The Ph.D. program in public affairs is a cohort program, with entering cohorts beginning each fall semester. For more information, students should contact Del Prisock (delfina@utdallas.edu) or Dr. Doug Kiel (dkiel@utdallas.edu).

The Ph.D. in public policy and political economy is centered in critical thought and interdisciplinary research that explores the interaction of institutions, markets, and public policies. Students are expected to complete a set of core courses in topics related to public policy, including rigorous training in statistics and research design; students must also complete course work in two fields and a specialization and defend a dissertation. For more information, students should contact Judy Robertson (judy@utdallas.edu) or Dr. Sheila Pineres (pineres@utdallas.edu).

Research Facilities

The University of Texas at Dallas has advanced computing facilities. The School of Economic, Political, and Policy Sciences also houses the Bruton Center for Development Studies and the Center for Educational Studies and is affiliated with the Cecil and Ida Green Center for Science and Society. Students have access to the computing facilities in the School of Economic, Political, and Policy Sciences and the University's Computing Center. The School's two computing laboratories house over 30 computers that are network linked and equipped with major social science software packages, including E-Views, R, RATS, SPSS, and STATA. A computerized geographic information system, the LexisNexis Database, and WestLaw are also available for student use. The University's Computing Center provides personal computers and UNIX workstations. Many important data and reference materials are available online from professional associations or at UT–D via the Library's and School's memberships in the Inter-University Consortium for Political and Social Research (ICPSR), the Roper Center, the University Consortium for Geographic Information Science (UCGIS), and other organizations. The library has a substantial number of social science journals.

Financial Aid

The School of Economic, Political, and Policy Sciences (EPPS) provides teaching assistantships that range from $1100 to $1400, depending on experience. Students who are awarded a full-time, 20-hour assistantship receive in-state tuition waivers. The School also offers tuition waivers that cover all tuition for up to 12 credit hours. Teaching assistantships and graduate studies scholarships are competitive, with GRE scores and grades being important criteria in the selection process.

Cost of Study

Tuition and fees can be expected to be in the range of $8000 to $10,000 per year for full-time in-state students taking 9 hours per semester, including summers. Costs might be higher for international and out-of-state students. Students are eligible for teaching assistantships and graduate-studies scholarships, as detailed above.

Living and Housing Costs

On-campus housing is available at Waterview Park Apartments, with rents varying from $800 to $1200 per month.

Student Group

There are 6,000 graduate students and more than 8,000 undergraduates studying at UT–Dallas. UT–Dallas also has a varied international student body in both graduate and undergraduate programs of study.

Location

Richardson is located just north of Dallas and south of Plano in a pleasant suburban setting. It is near the high-technology corridor that is home to Ericsson, Nortel, and numerous other telecommunications companies.

The University

UT–Dallas was created in September 1969 by Act of the Sixty-First Texas Legislature, which provided for transfer of the privately funded Southwest Center for Advanced Studies (SCAS) to the state of Texas. Undergraduate and graduate programs grew rapidly. Today, UT–Dallas has a distinguished faculty that includes numerous members of the National Academy of Sciences and National Academy of Engineering.

Applying

Application for admission to the graduate school can be made for fall, spring, or summer. GRE scores are required for degree-seeking students, although applicants may be admitted provisionally as nondegree students. A combined verbal and quantitative GRE score of at least 1100 is recommended for doctoral students, and a combined score of at least 1000 is recommended for master's degree students.

Correspondence and Information

Euel Elliott, Associate Dean for Academic Programs
School of Economic, Political, and Policy Sciences
Box 830688
The University of Texas at Dallas
Richardson, Texas 75083-0688
E-mail: eelliott@utdallas.edu
Web site: http://epps.utdallas.edu/

The University of Texas at Dallas

THE FACULTY AND THEIR RESEARCH

Bobby C. Alexander, Associate Professor of Sociology; Ph.D. (religious studies/social-scientific study of religion), Columbia, 1985. Religious studies.

Sheila Amin Gutiérrez de Piñeres, Professor of Economics; Ph.D. (economics), Duke, 1992. Latin American development, trade policy.

Donald R. Arbuckle, Clinical Research Professor; Ph.D. (American civilizations), Pennsylvania. Public management, bureaucratic behavior, policymaking.

Daniel Arce, Professor of Economics; Ph.D. (economics), Illinois at Urbana-Champaign, 1992. Economics, defense economics.

Philip K. Armour, Associate Professor of Sociology; Ph.D. (sociology), Berkeley, 1979. Sociology of religion, medical sociology.

Paul Battaglio, Assistant Professor of Public Affairs; Ph.D. (public administration), Georgia, 2005. Comparative policy and administration, public human resource management, comparative political attitudes.

Ted Benavides, Senior Lecturer; M.P.A., SMU, 1994. Public management, human resources management.

Nathan Berg, Associate Professor of Economics; Ph.D. (economics), Kansas, 2001. Finance, behavioral economics.

Kurt J. Beron, Professor of Economics and Political Economy; Ph.D. (economics), North Carolina at Chapel Hill, 1985. Education policy, tax compliance, Internet economics.

Brian J. L. Berry, Lloyd Viel Berkner Regental Professor, Professor of Political Economy, and Dean; Ph.D. (geography), Washington (Seattle), 1958. Urban economics and geography, development, cycles of growth and decline.

Denise Paquette Boots, Assistant Professor; Ph.D. (criminology), South Florida, 2006. American correction systems, family and interpersonal violence, juvenile delinquency.

Patrick T. Brandt, Assistant Professor of Political Science; Ph.D. (political science), Indiana, 2001. Presidency, congressional behavior, time series analysis, Bayesian econometrics.

Timothy Bray, Clinical Assistant Professor of Criminology and Sociology; Ph.D. (criminology), Missouri–St. Louis, 2002. Criminology.

Thomas Brunell, Professor of Political Science; Ph.D. (political science), California, Irvine, 1997. Congressional behavior, congressional elections.

Anthony Champagne, Professor of Political Science; Ph.D. (political science), Illinois, 1973. Law and public policy, judicial politics.

Marie Isabelle Chevrier, Professor of Public Policy and Political Economy; Ph.D. (public policy), Harvard, 1991. Arms control, international negotiation.

Yongwan Chun, Clinical Assistant Professor of GIS; Ph.D. (GIS), Ohio State, 2007. Spatial analysis and modeling, spatial statistics.

Harold D. Clarke, Professor of Political Science and Program Head for Political Science; Ph.D. (political science), Duke, 1971. Electoral behavior, public opinion and political support.

Rachel Croson, Professor of Economics; Ph.D. (economics), Harvard, 1994. Economics, experimental economics, behavioral economics.

Chetan Dave, Assistant Professor of Economics; Ph.D. (economics), Pittsburgh, 2004. Macroeconomics, econometrics.

Kruti R. Dholakia, Clinical Assistant Professor of Political Economy and Associate Dean for Undergraduate Programs; Ph.D. (public policy and political economy), Texas at Dallas, 2006. Methodology, global economy, development economics, health policy.

Lloyd J. Dumas, Professor of Public Policy and Political Economy; Ph.D. (economics), Columbia, 1972. International security, economic conversion, human and technical reliability.

Catherine C. Eckel, Professor of Economics; Ph.D. (economics), Virginia, 1983. Experimental economics, risk and decision making, economic education.

Euel Elliott, Professor of Public Policy and Political Economy, Senior Associate Dean, and Director of Graduate Studies; Ph.D. (political science), Duke, 1987. Public policy (general), regulatory policy, electoral behavior, nonlinear dynamics.

Simon Fass, Associate Professor of Public Policy and Political Economy; Ph.D. (urban planning), UCLA, 1978. Economic and political development.

Daniel Griffith, Ashbel Smith Professor of Geography and Geospatial Sciences; Ph.D. (geography), Toronto, 1978. Spatial statistics, quantitative urban-economic geography, applied statistics.

Jeremy Hall, Assistant Professor of Public Affairs; Ph.D. (public administration), Kentucky, 2005. Human resource management, public budgeting.

Edward J. Harpham, Professor of Political Science and Political Economy and Director of Collegium V Honors Program; Ph.D. (government), Cornell, 1980. Political theory, public policy.

Wendy L. Hassett, Clinical Associate Professor; Ph.D. (public administration and public policy), Auburn, 2003. Public management, human resource development.

Karen Hayslett-McCall, Assistant Professor of Sociology; Ph.D. (sociology), Penn State, 2002. Criminology, spatial analysis of crime, crime and neighborhoods.

Donald A. Hicks, Professor of Public Policy and Political Economy and Vice Chairman, Bruton Center for Development Studies; Ph.D. (sociology), North Carolina at Chapel Hill, 1976. Urban and regional policy, technology innovation and diffusion.

Bruce Jacobs, Professor of Sociology and Criminology; Ph.D. (sociology), USC, 1994. Street offenders, drugs and crime, qualitative methods.

Paul A. Jargowsky, Professor of Sociology and of Public Policy and Political Economy; Ph.D. (public policy), Harvard, 1991. Welfare policy.

Linda Camp Keith, Associate Professor of Political Science; Ph.D. (political science), North Texas, 1999. Public law/judicial process, human rights.

L. Douglas Kiel, Professor of Public Administration; Ph.D. (political science), Oklahoma, 1986. Public administration, organizational change, productivity improvement, nonlinear dynamics.

Tom Kovandzic, Associate Professor of Criminology; Ph.D. (criminal justice and criminology), Florida State, 1999. Firearms and violence, criminal justice policy, quantitative methods, inequality and crime, and policing, with particular interest in use of econometric methods as a tool to evaluate criminal justice policy initiatives.

Murray Leaf, Professor of Public Policy and Political Economy; Ph.D. (social anthropology), Chicago, 1966. Comparative social and economic development.

Xin Li, Assistant Professor of Economics; Ph.D. (economics), Michigan, 2006. Public economics, labor economics, experimental economics, economics of the Internet.

Robert Lowry, Professor of Political Science and of Public Policy and Political Economy and Program Head for Political Science; Ph.D. (political science), Harvard, 1993. Institutions and organizations, methodology.

James W. Marquart, Professor of Criminology and Program Head for Criminology; Ph.D. (sociology), Texas A&M, 1983. Criminology, legal reform, victimology, health issues in prison populations, community-based corrections.

Susan McElroy, Associate Professor of Economics and Political Economy; Ph.D. (economics of education), Stanford, 1996. Education policy.

Robert Morris, Assistant Professor of Criminology; Ph.D. (criminology), Sam Houston State, 2007. White-collar offending over the life course, computer crime and computer deviance, identity theft, quantitative methods.

Stuart B. Murchison, Clinical Associate Professor of Geospatial Sciences and Geography; Ph.D. (geography), Utah, 1989. Remote sensing, global positioning systems.

James C. Murdoch, Professor of Economics and Program Head for Economics; Ph.D. (economics), Wyoming, 1982. Environmental policy, public goods provision, coalition theory.

Clint W. Peinhardt, Assistant Professor of Political Science; Ph.D. (political science), Michigan, 2004. International political economy, economic development and transition, formal modeling.

Fang Qiu, Associate Professor of Geospatial Sciences and Political Economy; Ph.D. (geography), South Carolina, 2000. Geographic information sciences (GIS), remote sensing.

Todd Sandler, Professor of Economics and Political Science; Ph.D. (economics), SUNY at Binghamton, 1971. International relations, public economics, collective action, theories of terrorism.

Richard K. Scotch, Professor of Sociology and of Public Policy and Political Economy; Ph.D. (sociology), Harvard, 1982. Social policy, health policy, disabilities policy.

Barry J. Seldon, Professor of Economics; Ph.D. (economics), Duke, 1985. Microeconomics, industrial organization, advertising.

Kevin Siqueira, Associate Professor of Economics; Ph.D. (economics), Iowa State, 1998. Public economics, environmental economics, microeconomic theory, game theory.

Sheryl Skaggs, Associate Professor of Sociology; Ph.D. (sociology), North Carolina State, 2001. Work, organizations and industry, social inequality.

Marianne C. Stewart, Professor of Political Science; Ph.D. (political science), Duke, 1986. Comparative politics, Anglo-American voting behavior, political participation.

Gregory S. Thielemann, Associate Professor of Political Economy; Ph.D. (political science), Rice, 1988. Southern politics, gay and lesbian politics.

Michael Tiefelsdorf, Associate Professor of Geography and Geospatial Sciences; Ph.D. (geography), Free University of Berlin, 1988. Spatial processes, spatial statistics, quantitative geography.

Paul E. Tracy, Professor of Sociology and of Public Policy and Political Economy; Ph.D. (sociology and criminology), Pennsylvania, 1978. Criminology, juvenile delinquency.

Nicholas Valcik, Clinical Assistant Professor of Public Affairs; Ph.D. (public affairs), Texas at Dallas, 2005. Facilities management, hazardous material safety.

Lynne Vieraitis, Associate Professor of Criminology; Ph.D. (criminal justice and criminology), Florida State, 2000. Inequality and crime, gender and crime, violence against women, theoretical criminology.

Douglas Watson, Professor of Public Administration and Program Head for Public Affairs; Ph.D. (public policy and public administration), Auburn, 1992. State and local government.

John L. Worrall, Professor of Criminology; Ph.D. (political science), Washington State, 1999. Crime central policy, legal issues in policing, methodology.

Section 20
Family and Consumer Sciences

This section contains a directory of institutions offering graduate work in family and consumer sciences. Additional information about programs listed in the directory may be obtained by writing directly to the dean of a graduate school or chair of a department at the address given in the directory.

For programs offering related work, see also in this book *Economics, Psychology and Counseling,* and *Sociology, Anthropology, and Archaeology.* In another guide in this series:

Graduate Programs in Business, Education, Health, Information Studies, Law & Social Work
See *Social Work*

CONTENTS

Program Directories

Family and Consumer Sciences-General   786
Child and Family Studies   789
Child Development   796

Clothing and Textiles   798
Consumer Economics   800
Gerontology   802

Announcement

Tufts University   797

Close-Ups

See:

Adler School of Professional Psychology—
   Psychology   1051
Alliant International University–Los Angeles—Marital
   and Family Therapy   1061
Fashion Institute of Technology—Graduate Studies   117

Family and Consumer Sciences-General

Alabama Agricultural and Mechanical University, School of Graduate Studies, School of Agricultural and Environmental Sciences, Department of Family and Consumer Sciences, Huntsville, AL 35811. Offers family and consumer sciences (MS); food science (MS, PhD). Part-time and evening/weekend programs available. *Students:* 10 full-time (8 women), 21 part-time (19 women); includes 26 minority (all African Americans), 2 international. In 2008, 14 master's awarded. *Degree requirements:* For master's, comprehensive exam, thesis optional; for doctorate, one foreign language, thesis/dissertation. *Entrance requirements:* For master's, GRE General Test; for doctorate, GRE General Test, MS. Additional exam requirements/recommendations for international students: Required—TOEFL (minimum score 500 paper-based; 173 computer-based; 61 iBT). *Application deadline:* For fall admission, 5/1 for domestic students. Applications are processed on a rolling basis. Application fee: $25. Electronic applications accepted. *Expenses:* Tuition, area resident: Full-time $3924; part-time $2616 per term. Tuition, nonresident: part-time $5234 per year. International tuition: $7848 full-time. Required fees: $198; $396 per credit hour. $2841 per term. One-time fee: $8498 full-time; $5682 part-time. Full-time tuition and fees vary according to program. *Financial support:* In 2008–09, 2 research assistantships with tuition reimbursements (averaging $9,000 per year), teaching assistantships with tuition reimbursements (averaging $9,000 per year) were awarded; career-related internships or fieldwork, Federal Work-Study, and traineeships also available. Financial award application deadline: 4/1. *Faculty research:* Food biotechnology, nutrition, food microbiology, food engineering, food chemistry. *Unit head:* Dr. Cynthia Smith, Chair, 256-372-5455, Fax: 256-372-5433. *Application contact:* Dr. Caula Beyl, Dean, School of Graduate Studies, 256-372-5266, Fax: 256-372-5269, E-mail: caula.beyl@aamu.edu.

Appalachian State University, Cratis D. Williams Graduate School, Department of Family and Consumer Sciences, Boone, NC 28608. Offers child development (MA); family and consumer science (MA), including family studies, food and nutrition; family and consumer science education (MA). Part-time programs available. Postbaccalaureate distance learning degree programs offered (no on-campus study). *Faculty:* 12 full-time (11 women), 2 part-time/adjunct (1 woman). *Students:* 12 full-time (all women), 6 part-time (all women); includes 1 minority (Hispanic American), 1 international. 27 applicants, 44% accepted, 9 enrolled. In 2008, 6 master's awarded. *Degree requirements:* For master's, comprehensive exam, thesis optional. *Entrance requirements:* For master's, GRE General Test, 3 letters of recommendation. Additional exam requirements/recommendations for international students: Required—TOEFL (minimum score 550 paper-based; 230 computer-based; 79 iBT), IELTS (minimum score 6.5). *Application deadline:* For fall admission, 7/1 for domestic students, 2/1 for international students; for spring admission, 11/1 for domestic students, 7/1 for international students. Applications are processed on a rolling basis. Application fee: $50. Electronic applications accepted. *Expenses:* Tuition, area resident: Full-time $2600; part-time $700 per course. Tuition, state resident: full-time $2600; part-time $700 per course. Tuition, nonresident: full-time $5000; part-time $3300 per course. Required fees: $2150; $330 per course. Tuition and fees vary according to campus/location. *Financial support:* In 2008–09, 5 teaching assistantships (averaging $7,000 per year) were awarded; fellowships, research assistantships, career-related internships or fieldwork, scholarships/grants, and unspecified assistantships also available. Financial award application deadline: 7/1; financial award applicants required to submit FAFSA. *Faculty research:* Food antioxidants, preschool curriculum, children with special needs, family child care, FCS curriculum content. *Unit head:* Dr. Sarah Jordan, Chairperson, 828-262-2661, E-mail: jordansr@appstate.edu. *Application contact:* Dr. Sammie Garner, Graduate Director, 828-262-2698, E-mail: garnersg@appstate.edu.

Ball State University, Graduate School, College of Applied Science and Technology, Department of Family and Consumer Sciences, Muncie, IN 47306-1099. Offers MA, MS. *Entrance requirements:* For master's, resumé. *Faculty research:* Maternal and infant nutrition, nutrition education.

Bowling Green State University, Graduate College, College of Education and Human Development, School of Family and Consumer Sciences, Bowling Green, OH 43403. Offers food and nutrition (MFCS); human development and family studies (MFCS). Part-time programs available. *Degree requirements:* For master's, thesis. *Entrance requirements:* For master's, GRE General Test, minimum GPA of 3.0. Additional exam requirements/recommendations for international students: Required—TOEFL. Electronic applications accepted. *Faculty research:* Public health, wellness, social issues and policies, ethnic foods, nutrition and aging.

California State University, Fresno, Division of Graduate Studies, College of Agricultural Sciences and Technology, Department of Child, Family and Consumer Sciences, Fresno, CA 93740-8027. Offers family and consumer sciences (MS). Currently not accepting applications. Part-time and evening/weekend programs available. *Degree requirements:* For master's, thesis (for some programs). *Entrance requirements:* For master's, GRE General Test, minimum GPA of 3.0 in last 60 hours. Additional exam requirements/recommendations for international students: Required—TOEFL. Electronic applications accepted.

California State University, Long Beach, Graduate Studies, College of Health and Human Services, Department of Family and Consumer Sciences, Long Beach, CA 90840. Offers family and consumer sciences (MA); nutritional science (MS), including food science, hospitality foodservice and hotel management, nutritional sciences/dietetics and food administration. Part-time and evening/weekend programs available. *Faculty:* 9 full-time (7 women). *Students:* 7 part-time (6 women); includes 3 minority (2 Asian Americans or Pacific Islanders, 1 Hispanic American). Average age 33. 6 applicants, 17% accepted, 1 enrolled. *Degree requirements:* For master's, comprehensive exam or thesis. *Entrance requirements:* For master's, GRE (MS), minimum GPA of 3.0. *Application deadline:* For fall admission, 5/1 for domestic students. Applications are processed on a rolling basis. Application fee: $55. Electronic applications accepted. *Expenses:* Tuition, nonresident: full-time $11,160; part-time $372 per unit. Required fees: $4100; $1261 per semester. *Financial support:* Federal Work-Study, institutionally sponsored loans, and scholarships/grants available. Financial award application deadline: 3/2. *Faculty research:* School uniforms, consumer complaining behavior, nutrition and fitness education and behavior change, curriculum change, teaching experience of interns. *Unit head:* Dr. Wendy Reiboldt, Chair, 562-985-4484, Fax: 562-985-4414, E-mail: reiboldt@csulb.edu. *Application contact:* Dr. Jacqueline J Lee, Graduate Coordinator, 562-985-4545, Fax: 562-985-4414, E-mail: jjlee@csulb.edu.

California State University, Northridge, Graduate Studies, College of Health and Human Development, Department of Family and Consumer Sciences, Northridge, CA 91330. Offers MS. Part-time and evening/weekend programs available. *Faculty:* 14 full-time (10 women), 41 part-time/adjunct (31 women). *Students:* 66 full-time (63 women), 94 part-time (85 women); includes 11 African Americans, 20 Asian Americans or Pacific Islanders, 26 Hispanic Americans, 15 international. Average age 31. 129 applicants, 81% accepted, 65 enrolled. In 2008, 28 master's awarded. *Degree requirements:* For master's, thesis, project, or comprehensive exam. *Entrance requirements:* For master's, GRE General Test or minimum GPA of 3.0. Additional exam requirements/recommendations for international students: Required—TOEFL. *Application deadline:* For fall admission, 11/30 for domestic students. Application fee: $55. *Financial support:* Teaching assistantships, career-related internships or fieldwork, Federal Work-Study, and institutionally sponsored loans available. Financial award application deadline: 3/1. *Unit head:* Dr. Alyce Akers, Chair, 818-677-3051. *Application contact:* Dr. Alyce Akers, Chair, 818-677-3051.

Central Michigan University, College of Graduate Studies, College of Education and Human Services, Department of Human Environmental Studies, Mount Pleasant, MI 48859. Offers apparel product development and merchandising technology (MS); human development and family studies (MA); nutrition and dietetics (MS). Part-time and evening/weekend programs available. *Faculty:* 15 full-time (11 women), 1 part-time/adjunct (0 women). *Degree requirements:* For master's, thesis or alternative. *Application deadline:* Applications are processed on a

rolling basis. Application fee: $35 ($45 for international students). Electronic applications accepted. *Expenses:* Tuition, state resident: full-time $3717; part-time $413 per credit. Tuition, nonresident: full-time $6894; part-time $766 per credit. *Financial support:* Fellowships with tuition reimbursements, research assistantships, career-related internships or fieldwork, Federal Work-Study, unspecified assistantships, and out-of-state merit awards available. *Faculty research:* Human growth and development, family studies and human sexuality, human nutrition and dietetics, apparel and textile retailing, computer-aided design for apparel. *Unit head:* Dr. Phame Camerena, Chairperson, 989-774-3218, Fax: 989-774-2435, E-mail: camar1pm@cmich.edu. *Application contact:* Dr. Candace Maylee, Assistant Coordinator of Graduate Programs, 989-774-2613, Fax: 989-774-2435, E-mail: mayle1ce@cmich.edu.

Central Washington University, Graduate Studies, Research and Continuing Education, College of Education and Professional Studies, Department of Family and Consumer Sciences, Ellensburg, WA 98926. Offers family and consumer sciences education (MS); family studies (MS); nutrition (MS). Part-time programs available. *Degree requirements:* For master's, thesis or alternative. *Entrance requirements:* For master's, GRE General Test (nutrition), minimum GPA of 3.0. Additional exam requirements/recommendations for international students: Required—TOEFL (minimum score 550 paper-based; 213 computer-based; 79 iBT). Electronic applications accepted.

Cornell University, Graduate School, Graduate Fields of Human Ecology, Ithaca, NY 14853-0001. Offers MA, MHA, MPS, MS, PhD. *Accreditation:* CAHME (one or more programs are accredited). *Faculty:* 92 full-time (40 women). *Students:* 116 full-time (74 women); includes 21 minority (6 African Americans, 1 American Indian/Alaska Native, 10 Asian Americans or Pacific Islanders, 4 Hispanic Americans), 32 international. Average age 29. 258 applicants, 31% accepted, 36 enrolled. In 2008, 43 master's, 14 doctorates awarded. *Degree requirements:* For doctorate, comprehensive exam, thesis/dissertation. *Entrance requirements:* For master's and doctorate, GRE General Test. Additional exam requirements/recommendations for international students: Required—TOEFL. Application fee: $70. Electronic applications accepted. *Expenses:* Contact institution. *Financial support:* In 2008–09, 75 students received support, including 10 fellowships with full tuition reimbursements available, 20 research assistantships with full tuition reimbursements available, 45 teaching assistantships with full tuition reimbursements available; institutionally sponsored loans, scholarships/grants, health care benefits, tuition waivers (full and partial), and unspecified assistantships also available. Financial award applicants required to submit FAFSA. *Application contact:* Graduate School Application Requests, Caldwell Hall, 607-255-5820.

Eastern Illinois University, Graduate School, Lumpkin College of Business and Applied Sciences, School of Family and Consumer Sciences, Charleston, IL 61920-3099. Offers dietetics (MS); family and consumer sciences (MS). Part-time programs available. *Degree requirements:* For master's, comprehensive exam.

Florida State University, Graduate Studies, College of Human Sciences, Tallahassee, FL 32306. Offers MS, PhD. *Accreditation:* AAMFT/COAMFTE. Part-time programs available. *Degree requirements:* For master's, comprehensive exam (for some programs), thesis optional; for doctorate, thesis/dissertation. *Entrance requirements:* For master's and doctorate, GRE General Test, minimum GPA of 3.0. Additional exam requirements/recommendations for international students: Required—TOEFL (minimum score 80 iBT). Electronic applications accepted. *Faculty research:* Child and adolescent development, merchandising, accessible housing, culturally diverse classrooms, motor behavior.

Fontbonne University, Graduate Programs, Department of Human Environmental Sciences, St. Louis, MO 63105-3098. Offers family and consumer sciences (MA). *Faculty:* 4 full-time (all women), 5 part-time/adjunct (all women). *Students:* 2 full-time (both women), 8 part-time (7 women); includes 3 minority (all African Americans). Average age 40. In 2008, 4 master's awarded. *Degree requirements:* For master's, action paper/presentation portfolio. *Entrance requirements:* For master's, minimum GPA of 3.0. *Application deadline:* For fall admission, 8/8 priority date for domestic students; for spring admission, 1/8 priority date for domestic students. Application fee: $25. *Expenses:* Tuition: Part-time $540 per credit hour. Required fees: $270 per year. *Financial support:* Application deadline: 4/1; *Faculty research:* Early intervention, public policy: children and families, program designer. *Unit head:* Cheryl Houston, Chairperson, 314-719-8020, Fax: 314-719-8615. *Application contact:* Dr. Janine Duncan, Director, Graduate Programs, 314-719-3639, Fax: 314-719-8015.

Illinois State University, Graduate School, College of Applied Science and Technology, Department of Family and Consumer Sciences, Normal, IL 61790-2200. Offers MA, MS. *Degree requirements:* For master's, thesis or alternative. *Entrance requirements:* For master's, GRE General Test, minimum GPA of 2.8 in last 60 hours of course work. *Faculty research:* Graduate practicum assistantships, startup for Jump Start of McLean County grant, providing low-income preschool children with early literacy experiences, generations of Hope-ICI replication.

Indiana State University, School of Graduate Studies, College of Arts and Sciences, Department of Family and Consumer Sciences, Terre Haute, IN 47809-1401. Offers dietetics (MS); family and consumer sciences education (MS); inter-area option (MS). *Accreditation:* ADtA. Part-time programs available. *Degree requirements:* For master's, thesis optional. Electronic applications accepted.

Iowa State University of Science and Technology, Graduate College, College of Human Sciences, Program in Family and Consumer Sciences, Ames, IA 50011. Offers MFCS. *Students:* 4 full-time (3 women), 42 part-time (32 women); includes 3 minority (all African Americans), 1 international. 23 applicants, 83% accepted, 18 enrolled. In 2008, 6 master's awarded. *Degree requirements:* For master's, thesis or alternative. *Entrance requirements:* For master's, GRE General Test. Additional exam requirements/recommendations for international students: Required—TOEFL (minimum score 550 paper-based; 79 iBT), IELTS (6.5) or TOEFL. *Application deadline:* For fall admission, 4/15 priority date for domestic and international students; for spring admission, 10/15 priority date for domestic and international students. Application fee: $30 ($70 for international students). Electronic applications accepted. *Expenses:* Tuition, area resident: Full-time $6446; part-time $359 per credit. Tuition, state resident: full-time $6446; part-time $359 per credit. Tuition, nonresident: full-time $17,330; part-time $963 per credit. Required fees: $790; $249.25 per semester. Tuition and fees vary according to course load and program. *Financial support:* In 2008–09, 1 research assistantship with full and partial tuition reimbursement (averaging $13,392 per year) was awarded; teaching assistantships with full and partial tuition reimbursements, scholarships/grants, health care benefits, and unspecified assistantships also available. *Unit head:* Dr. Carla Peterson, Supervisory Committee Chair, 515-294-7804, E-mail: mfcsinfo@iastate.edu. *Application contact:* Dr. Carla Peterson, Supervisory Committee Chair, 515-294-7804, E-mail: mfcsinfo@iastate.edu.

Kansas State University, Graduate School, College of Human Ecology, Manhattan, KS 66506. Offers MS, PhD. Part-time programs available. Postbaccalaureate distance learning degree programs offered. *Faculty:* 48 full-time (33 women), 6 part-time/adjunct (5 women). *Students:* 159 full-time (128 women), 212 part-time (139 women); includes 39 minority (25 African Americans, 4 American Indian/Alaska Native, 5 Asian Americans or Pacific Islanders, 5 Hispanic Americans), 39 international. 257 applicants, 55% accepted, 110 enrolled. In 2008, 71 master's, 18 doctorates awarded. *Degree requirements:* For master's, residency; for doctorate, thesis/dissertation, residency. *Application deadline:* For fall admission, 2/1 priority date for domestic and international students; for spring admission, 9/1 for domestic students, 9/1 priority date for international students. Application fee: $30 ($55 for international students). Electronic applications accepted. *Expenses:* Tuition, area resident: Full-time $6466; part-time $269.40 per credit hour. Tuition, state resident: full-time $6466; part-time $269.40 per credit hour. Tuition, nonresident: full-time $14,874; part-time $619.75 per credit hour. Required fees:

$673; $23.40 per credit hour. Tuition and fees vary according to campus/location. *Financial support:* In 2008–09, 61 research assistantships (averaging $13,041 per year), 37 teaching assistantships with full and partial tuition reimbursements (averaging $12,222 per year) were awarded; career-related internships or fieldwork, Federal Work-Study, institutionally sponsored loans, scholarships/grants, and tuition waivers (full) also available. Support available to part-time students. Financial award application deadline: 3/1; financial award applicants required to submit FAFSA. *Faculty research:* Apparel and textiles, food service and hospitality management, life span human development, family life education and consultation, marriage and family therapy. Total annual research expenditures: $12.7 million. *Unit head:* Virginia Moxley, Dean, 785-532-5500, Fax: 785-532-5504, E-mail: moxley@ksu.edu. *Application contact:* Patricia Haas, Administrative Specialist, 785-532-5500, Fax: 785-532-5504, E-mail: haas@humec.ksu.edu.

Kent State University, Graduate School of Education, Health, and Human Services, School of Family and Consumer Studies, Kent, OH 44242-0001. Offers MA, MS. Part-time programs available. *Degree requirements:* For master's, thesis (for some programs). *Entrance requirements:* For master's, GRE, minimum GPA of 3.0, 3 letters of recommendation. Additional exam requirements/recommendations for international students: Required—TOEFL. Electronic applications accepted. *Faculty research:* Training human service workers, health care services for older adults, early adolescent development, caregiving arrangements with aging families, peace and war.

Lamar University, College of Graduate Studies, College of Education and Human Development, Department of Family and Consumer Sciences, Beaumont, TX 77710. Offers family and consumer science (MS); vocational home economics (Certificate). Part-time and evening/weekend programs available. *Faculty:* 4 full-time (all women). *Students:* 11 full-time (all women), 8 part-time (all women); includes 6 minority (2 African Americans, 1 American Indian/Alaska Native, 1 Asian American or Pacific Islander, 2 Hispanic Americans). Average age 28. 18 applicants, 67% accepted, 3 enrolled. In 2008, 3 master's awarded. *Degree requirements:* For master's, thesis optional. *Entrance requirements:* For master's, GRE General Test. Additional exam requirements/recommendations for international students: Required—TOEFL. *Application deadline:* For fall admission, 8/1 for domestic students; for spring admission, 12/1 for domestic students. Applications are processed on a rolling basis. Application fee: $25 ($50 for international students). *Expenses:* Tuition, state resident: full-time $5000; part-time $195 per credit. Tuition, nonresident: full-time $12,376; part-time $476 per credit. Required fees: $1570. *Financial support:* In 2008–09, 3 students received support, including 3 teaching assistantships (averaging $5,000 per year); fellowships, research assistantships, career-related internships or fieldwork, Federal Work-Study, and institutionally sponsored loans also available. Support available to part-time students. Financial award application deadline: 4/1. *Faculty research:* Maternal and infant nutrition, eating disorders, sports nutrition, human sexuality, family violence. *Unit head:* Dr. Connie Ruiz, Chair, 409-880-8663, Fax: 409-880-8666. *Application contact:* Sandy Drane, Coordinator of Graduate Admissions, 409-880-8356, Fax: 409-880-8414, E-mail: gradmissions@hal.lamar.edu.

Louisiana State University and Agricultural and Mechanical College, Graduate School, College of Agriculture, School of Human Ecology, Baton Rouge, LA 70803. Offers MS, PhD. Part-time programs available. *Degree requirements:* For master's, thesis; for doctorate, thesis/dissertation. *Entrance requirements:* For master's and doctorate, GRE General Test, minimum GPA of 3.0. Additional exam requirements/recommendations for international students: Required—TOEFL (minimum score 550 paper-based; 213 computer-based; 79 iBT). Electronic applications accepted. *Faculty research:* Nutrition for optimum health, textile and apparel production development, children's relationships with parents and caregivers, contextual influences on families.

Louisiana Tech University, Graduate School, College of Applied and Natural Sciences, School for Human Ecology, Ruston, LA 71272. Offers dietetics (MS); human ecology (MS). Part-time programs available. *Degree requirements:* For master's, thesis or alternative, Registered Dietician Exam eligibility. *Entrance requirements:* For master's, GRE General Test.

Marshall University, Academic Affairs Division, College of Education and Human Services, Division of Human Development and Allied Technology, Department of Family and Consumer Sciences, Huntington, WV 25755. Offers MA. *Degree requirements:* For master's, thesis optional, comprehensive assessment.

Missouri State University, Graduate College, College of Natural and Applied Sciences, Department of Fashion and Interior Design, Springfield, MO 65804-0094. Offers secondary education (MS Ed), including consumer sciences. Part-time programs available. *Faculty:* 2 full-time (both women), 1 (woman) part-time/adjunct. *Students:* 1 (woman) part-time. Average age 46. 1 applicant, 100% accepted, 0 enrolled. *Degree requirements:* For master's, comprehensive exam, thesis or alternative. *Entrance requirements:* For master's, GRE (MNAS), 9-12 teaching certification (MS Ed), minimum GPA of 3.0 (MNAS). Additional exam requirements/recommendations for international students: Required—TOEFL (minimum score 550 paper-based; 213 computer-based; 79 iBT). *Application deadline:* For fall admission, 7/20 priority date for domestic students, 5/1 for international students; for spring admission, 12/20 priority date for domestic students, 9/1 for international students. Applications are processed on a rolling basis. Application fee: $35 ($50 for international students). Electronic applications accepted. *Expenses:* Tuition, state resident: full-time $3852; part-time $214 per credit hour. Tuition, nonresident: full-time $7524; part-time $418 per credit hour. Required fees: $230 per semester. Tuition and fees vary according to course level and course load. *Financial support:* Career-related internships or fieldwork, Federal Work-Study, institutionally sponsored loans, scholarships/grants, and unspecified assistantships available. Financial award application deadline: 3/31; financial award applicants required to submit FAFSA. *Unit head:* Dr. Jeannie Ireland, Head, 417-836-5497, Fax: 417-836-4341, E-mail: jeannieireland@missouristate.edu. *Application contact:* Eric Eckert, Coordinator of Graduate Admissions and Recruitment, 417-836-5331, Fax: 417-836-6888, E-mail: ericeckert@missouristate.edu.

New Mexico State University, Graduate School, College of Agriculture, Consumer and Environmental Sciences, Department of Family and Consumer Sciences, Las Cruces, NM 88003-8001. Offers MS. Part-time programs available. *Faculty:* 13 full-time (11 women). *Students:* 30 full-time (28 women), 12 part-time (9 women); includes 19 minority (1 African American, 1 American Indian/Alaska Native, 17 Hispanic Americans), 5 international. Average age 30. 29 applicants, 97% accepted, 21 enrolled. In 2008, 10 master's awarded. *Degree requirements:* For master's, comprehensive exam (for some programs), thesis (for some programs), oral exam. *Entrance requirements:* For master's, GRE, 3 letters of reference, resumé. Additional exam requirements/recommendations for international students: Required—TOEFL. *Application deadline:* For fall admission, 6/30 priority date for domestic students, 3/1 priority date for international students; for spring admission, 11/30 for domestic and international students. Applications are processed on a rolling basis. Application fee: $30 ($50 for international students). Electronic applications accepted. *Expenses:* Tuition, area resident: Full-time $3890; part-time $212.85 per credit. Tuition, state resident: full-time $3890; part-time $212.85 per credit. Tuition, nonresident: full-time $13,916; part-time $630.55 per credit. Required fees: $1218; $609 per semester. *Financial support:* In 2008–09, 19 students received support, including 1 research assistantship (averaging $7,900 per year), 12 teaching assistantships (averaging $6,396 per year); career-related internships or fieldwork, Federal Work-Study, scholarships/grants, health care benefits, and unspecified assistantships also available. Support available to part-time students. Financial award application deadline: 3/1. *Faculty research:* Work, stress, and family functioning; youth at risk; food product analysis; diet and health. *Unit head:* Dr. Martha Archuleta, Head, 575-646-3936, Fax: 575-646-1889, E-mail: maarchul@nmsu.edu. *Application contact:* Dr. Wanda A Eastman, Coordinator, 575-646-1180, Fax: 575-646-1889, E-mail: wmorgan@nmsu.edu.

North Carolina Central University, Division of Academic Affairs, College of Behavioral and Social Sciences, Department of Human Sciences, Durham, NC 27707-3129. Offers family and consumer sciences (MS). Part-time and evening/weekend programs available. *Degree requirements:* For master's, one foreign language, comprehensive exam, thesis. *Entrance requirements:* For master's, GRE, minimum GPA of 3.0 in major, 2.5 overall. Additional exam requirements/recommendations for international students: Required—TOEFL.

North Dakota State University, College of Graduate and Interdisciplinary Studies, College of Human Development and Education, School of Education, Program in Family and Consumer Sciences Education, Fargo, ND 58105. Offers M Ed, MS. *Accreditation:* NCATE. Part-time programs available. *Faculty:* 1 (woman) full-time. *Students:* 1 (woman) full-time. Average age 40. 1 applicant, 100% accepted, 1 enrolled. In 2008, 2 master's awarded. *Degree requirements:* For master's, comprehensive exam, thesis or alternative. *Entrance requirements:* For master's, MAT. Additional exam requirements/recommendations for international students: Required—TOEFL. *Application deadline:* Applications are processed on a rolling basis. Application fee: $45 ($60 for international students). *Financial support:* Teaching assistantships, career-related internships or fieldwork and institutionally sponsored loans available. Financial award application deadline: 4/15. *Faculty research:* Needs of beginning teachers, learning styles and achievement, school-level variables and curriculum change. *Unit head:* Dr. William Martin, Chair, 701-231-7202, Fax: 701-231-7416, E-mail: william.martin@ndsu.edu. *Application contact:* Dr. Mari Borr, Assistant Professor, 701-231-7968, Fax: 701-231-9685, E-mail: mari.borr@ndsu.edu.

The Ohio State University, Graduate School, College of Education and Human Ecology, Program in Family and Consumer Sciences Education, Columbus, OH 43210. Offers M Ed, MS. *Accreditation:* ADtA. *Degree requirements:* For master's, thesis optional. *Entrance requirements:* Additional exam requirements/recommendations for international students: Required—TOEFL (minimum score 577 paper-based; 233 computer-based). Electronic applications accepted.

Ohio University, Graduate College, College of Health and Human Services, School of Human and Consumer Sciences, Athens, OH 45701-2979. Offers child development and family life (MS); early childhood education (MS); family studies (MS); food and nutrition (MS). Part-time programs available. *Degree requirements:* For master's, thesis. *Entrance requirements:* For master's, GRE. Additional exam requirements/recommendations for international students: Required—TOEFL. Electronic applications accepted. *Faculty research:* Diversity, developmentally appropriate activities, death and dying, gerontology, sexuality education.

Oklahoma State University, College of Human Environmental Sciences, Dean of Human Environmental Sciences—MS in Family Financial Planning Program and PhD in HES, Stillwater, OK 74078. Offers human environmental sciences (MS), including family financial planning. Part-time programs available. Postbaccalaureate distance learning degree programs offered. *Faculty:* 1 full-time (0 women). *Students:* 14 part-time (9 women); includes 2 minority (1 African American, 1 American Indian/Alaska Native). Average age 38. 51 applicants, 59% accepted, 12 enrolled. In 2008, 3 master's awarded. *Degree requirements:* For master's, thesis or alternative, creative component; for doctorate, comprehensive exam, thesis/dissertation. *Entrance requirements:* For master's and doctorate, GRE or GMAT. Additional exam requirements/recommendations for international students: Required—TOEFL. *Application deadline:* For fall admission, 3/1 priority date for international students; for spring admission, 8/1 priority date for international students. Applications are processed on a rolling basis. Application fee: $40 ($75 for international students). Electronic applications accepted. *Expenses:* Tuition, state resident: full-time $3716.40; part-time $154.85 per credit hour. Tuition, nonresident: full-time $14,448; part-time $602 per credit hour. Required fees: $1772.40; $73.85 per credit hour. One-time fee: $50. Tuition and fees vary according to course load and campus/location. *Financial support:* Career-related internships or fieldwork, Federal Work-Study, scholarships/grants, health care benefits, tuition waivers, and unspecified assistantships available. Support available to part-time students. Financial award application deadline: 3/1; financial award applicants required to submit FAFSA. *Unit head:* Dr. Stephan Wilson, Dean, 405-744-5053, Fax: 405-744-7113. *Application contact:* Dr. Shiretta Ownbey, Professor and Graduate Coordinator, 405-744-5053, Fax: 405-744-7113.

Oregon State University, Graduate School, College of Education, Program in Family and Consumer Sciences Education, Corvallis, OR 97331. Offers MAT, MS. Part-time programs available. *Degree requirements:* For master's, thesis (for some programs). *Entrance requirements:* For master's, NTE, California Basic Educational Skills Test, minimum GPA of 3.0 in last 90 hours of course work. Additional exam requirements/recommendations for international students: Required—TOEFL. *Faculty research:* Economy of time and methods.

Prairie View A&M University, College of Agriculture and Human Sciences, Prairie View, TX 77446-0519. Offers agricultural economics (MS); animal sciences (MS); interdisciplinary human sciences (MS); soil science (MS). Part-time and evening/weekend programs available. *Degree requirements:* For master's, comprehensive exam, thesis (for some programs), field placement. *Entrance requirements:* For master's, GRE General Test, minimum GPA of 2.45. Additional exam requirements/recommendations for international students: Required—TOEFL (minimum score 550 paper-based). *Faculty research:* Domestic violence prevention, water quality, food growth regulators, wetland dynamics, biochemistry, poultry disaster, obesity and nutrition, family therapy.

Purdue University, Graduate School, College of Consumer and Family Sciences, West Lafayette, IN 47907. Offers MS, PhD. Part-time programs available. *Degree requirements:* For doctorate, thesis/dissertation. *Entrance requirements:* Additional exam requirements/recommendations for international students: Required—TOEFL. Electronic applications accepted.

Queens College of the City University of New York, Division of Graduate Studies, Mathematics and Natural Sciences Division, Department of Family, Nutrition and Exercise Sciences, Flushing, NY 11367-1597. Offers home economics (MS Ed); physical education and exercise sciences (MS Ed). Part-time and evening/weekend programs available. *Degree requirements:* For master's, research project. *Entrance requirements:* For master's, minimum GPA of 3.0. Additional exam requirements/recommendations for international students: Required—TOEFL. *Faculty research:* Exercise and environmental physiology, interdisciplinary approaches to school curricula using outdoor education, program development in cardiac rehabilitation and adult fitness, nutrition education.

Sam Houston State University, College of Humanities and Social Sciences, Department of Family and Consumer Sciences, Huntsville, TX 77341. Offers dietetics (MS); family and consumer sciences (MS). Part-time and evening/weekend programs available. *Faculty:* 2 full-time (both women). *Students:* 18 full-time (all women), 3 part-time (all women); includes 5 minority (1 American Indian/Alaska Native, 2 Asian Americans or Pacific Islanders, 2 Hispanic Americans), 1 international. Average age 25. 11 applicants, 91% accepted, 10 enrolled. In 2008, 8 master's awarded. *Entrance requirements:* For master's, GRE General Test, minimum GPA of 2.5. Additional exam requirements/recommendations for international students: Required—TOEFL (minimum score 550 paper-based; 213 computer-based; 79 iBT). *Application deadline:* For fall admission, 8/1 for domestic students; for spring admission, 12/1 for domestic students. Application fee: $20. *Expenses:* Tuition, state resident: full-time $3564; part-time $198 per credit hour. Tuition, nonresident: full-time $8622; part-time $479 per credit hour. Required fees: $1290. Tuition and fees vary according to course load and campus/location. *Financial support:* Teaching assistantships available. Financial award application deadline: 5/31; financial award applicants required to submit FAFSA. *Unit head:* Dr. Janis White, Chair, 936-294-1242, Fax: 936-294-4204, E-mail: jwhite@shsu.edu. *Application contact:* Dr. Claudia Sealey-Potts, Advisor, 936-294-1250, E-mail: clapotts@shsu.edu.

San Francisco State University, Division of Graduate Studies, College of Health and Human Services, Department of Consumer and Family Studies/Dietetics, San Francisco, CA 94132-1722. Offers family and consumer sciences (MA). Part-time programs available.

South Carolina State University, School of Graduate Studies, Department of Family and Consumer Sciences, Orangeburg, SC 29117-0001. Offers individual and family development (MS); nutritional sciences (MS). Part-time and evening/weekend programs available. *Faculty:* 2 full-time (both women). *Students:* 13 full-time (all women), 15 part-time (13 women); includes

Family and Consumer Sciences-General

South Carolina State University (continued)
27 minority (all African Americans). Average age 33. 8 applicants, 88% accepted, 7 enrolled. In 2008, 12 master's awarded. *Degree requirements:* For master's, comprehensive exam, thesis optional, departmental qualifying exam. *Entrance requirements:* For master's, GRE, MAT, or NTE, minimum GPA of 2.7. *Application deadline:* For fall admission, 6/15 priority date for domestic students, 6/15 for international students; for spring admission, 11/1 for domestic and international students. Applications are processed on a rolling basis. Application fee: $25. Electronic applications accepted. *Expenses:* Tuition, state resident: full-time $7806; part-time $434 per credit hour. Tuition, nonresident: full-time $15,298; part-time $850 per credit hour. *Financial support:* In 2008–09, 3 fellowships (averaging $6,319 per year) were awarded; institutionally sponsored loans also available. Financial award application deadline: 6/1. *Faculty research:* Societal competence, relationship of parent-child interaction to adult, quality of well-being of rural elders. *Unit head:* Dr. Ethel G. Jones, Chair, 803-536-8958, Fax: 803-533-3268, E-mail: egjones@scsu.edu. *Application contact:* Annette Hazzard-Jones, Program Coordinator II, 803-536-8809, Fax: 803-536-8812, E-mail: zs_ahazzard@scsu.edu.

South Dakota State University, Graduate School, College of Family and Consumer Sciences, Department of Human Development, Consumer and Family Sciences, Brookings, SD 57007. Offers MFCS. *Faculty:* 12 full-time (11 women). *Students:* 3 full-time (2 women), 12 part-time (all women). 8 applicants, 100% accepted, 7 enrolled. In 2008, 9 master's awarded. *Entrance requirements:* For master's, resumé. Additional exam requirements/recommendations for international students: Required—TOEFL (minimum score 525 paper-based). *Application deadline:* For fall admission, 4/15 for international students; for spring admission, 8/15 for international students. Application fee: $35. *Financial support:* In 2008–09, 3 research assistantships with partial tuition reimbursements (averaging $15,750 per year), 4 teaching assistantships with partial tuition reimbursements (averaging $15,750 per year) were awarded. *Unit head:* Dr. Andrew Stremmel, Head, 605-688-6418, Fax: 605-688-4888, E-mail: andrew.stremmel@sdstate.edu. *Application contact:* The Graduate School, 605-688-4181, E-mail: sdsu_gradschool@sdstate.edu.

State University of New York College at Oneonta, Graduate Education, Division of Education, Department of Secondary Education, Oneonta, NY 13820-4015. Offers adolescence education (MS Ed); family and consumer science education (MS Ed). *Accreditation:* NCATE. Part-time and evening/weekend programs available. *Students:* 2 full-time (1 woman), 11 part-time (4 women). Average age 26. 3 applicants, 100% accepted, 3 enrolled. In 2008, 2 master's awarded. *Entrance requirements:* For master's, GRE General Test. *Application deadline:* For fall admission, 3/25 priority date for domestic students; for spring admission, 10/1 priority date for domestic students. Applications are processed on a rolling basis. Application fee: $50. *Expenses:* Tuition, area resident: Full-time $6900. Tuition, state resident: full-time $6900. Tuition, nonresident: full-time $10,920. Required fees: $916. Part-time tuition and fees vary according to program. *Unit head:* Dr. Dennis Banks, Chair, 607-436-3075, Fax: 607-436-2554, E-mail: banksdn@oneonta.edu. *Application contact:* Dean, 607-436-2523, Fax: 607-436-3084, E-mail: gradoffice@oneonta.edu.

Stephen F. Austin State University, Graduate School, College of Education, Department of Human Sciences, Nacogdoches, TX 75962. Offers MS. *Degree requirements:* For master's, comprehensive exam, thesis or alternative. *Entrance requirements:* For master's, GRE General Test. Additional exam requirements/recommendations for international students: Required—TOEFL. *Faculty research:* Consumer economics, nutrition education, clothing and textiles, family, interior design.

Tennessee State University, The School of Graduate Studies and Research, School of Agriculture and Consumer Sciences, Nashville, TN 37209-1561. Offers agricultural sciences (MS), including agribusiness, agricultural education, animal science, plant science. Part-time and evening/weekend programs available. *Faculty:* 6 full-time (0 women). *Students:* 11 full-time (9 women), 6 part-time (1 woman); includes 12 minority (9 African Americans, 3 Asian Americans or Pacific Islanders). Average age 31. 9 applicants, 56% accepted, 3 enrolled. In 2008, 10 master's awarded. *Degree requirements:* For master's, thesis. *Entrance requirements:* For master's, GRE General Test, GRE Subject Test, MAT. *Application deadline:* For fall admission, 4/1 priority date for domestic students. Application fee: $25. *Financial support:* In 2008–09, 2 research assistantships (averaging $9,511 per year), 1 teaching assistantship (averaging $9,511 per year) were awarded. *Faculty research:* Small farm economics, ornamental horticulture, beef cattle production, rural elderly. *Unit head:* Dr. Chandra Reddy, Dean, 615-963-7620, Fax: 615-963-5888. *Application contact:* Deborah Chisom, Director of Graduate Admissions, 615-963-5962, Fax: 615-963-5963, E-mail: dchiscom@tnstate.edu.

Texas A&M University–Kingsville, College of Graduate Studies, College of Agriculture and Home Economics, Department of Human Sciences, Kingsville, TX 78363. Offers MS. Part-time and evening/weekend programs available. *Degree requirements:* For master's, comprehensive exam, thesis or alternative. *Entrance requirements:* For master's, GRE General Test, minimum GPA of 3.0. Additional exam requirements/recommendations for international students: Required—TOEFL. *Faculty research:* Mexican-American families, abuse in families, nontraditional students.

Texas Southern University, Graduate School, College of Liberal Arts and Behavioral Sciences, Department of Human Services and Consumer Sciences, Houston, TX 77004-4584. Offers MS. Part-time and evening/weekend programs available. *Faculty:* 2 full-time (both women). *Students:* 7 full-time (all women), 29 part-time (26 women); includes 35 African Americans. Average age 33. 18 applicants, 100% accepted, 16 enrolled. In 2008, 4 master's awarded. *Degree requirements:* For master's, comprehensive exam, thesis (for some programs). *Entrance requirements:* For master's, GRE General Test, minimum GPA of 2.5. Additional exam requirements/recommendations for international students: Required—TOEFL. *Application deadline:* For fall admission, 7/15 priority date for domestic students. Applications are processed on a rolling basis. Application fee: $50 ($75 for international students). *Expenses:* Tuition, area resident: Full-time $1912; part-time $96 per credit hour. Tuition, state resident: full-time $1912; part-time $96 per credit hour. Tuition, nonresident: full-time $6302; part-time $343 per credit hour. Required fees: $3542. *Financial support:* Research assistantships, teaching assistantships, career-related internships or fieldwork and institutionally sponsored loans available. Financial award application deadline: 5/1. *Faculty research:* Food radiation/food for space travel, adolescent parenting, gerontology/grandparenting. *Unit head:* Dr. Shirley R. Nealy, Chair, 713-313-7638, Fax: 713-313-7228, E-mail: nealy_sr@tsu.edu. *Application contact:* Dr. Gregory Maddox, Interim Dean of the Graduate School, 713-313-7011 Ext. 4410, Fax: 713-639-1876, E-mail: maddox_gh@tsu.edu.

Texas Tech University, Graduate School, College of Human Sciences, Lubbock, TX 79409. Offers MS, PhD, JD/MS. Part-time and evening/weekend programs available. Postbaccalaureate distance learning degree programs offered (minimal on-campus study). *Faculty:* 48 full-time (32 women), 1 (woman) part-time/adjunct. *Students:* 208 full-time (126 women), 109 part-time (67 women); includes 48 minority (15 African Americans, 4 American Indian/Alaska Native, 12 Asian Americans or Pacific Islanders, 17 Hispanic Americans), 54 international. Average age 32. 301 applicants, 67% accepted, 93 enrolled. In 2008, 50 master's, 11 doctorates awarded. Terminal master's awarded for partial completion of doctoral program. *Degree requirements:* For master's, thesis (for some programs); for doctorate, thesis/dissertation. *Entrance requirements:* For master's, GRE; for doctorate, GRE General Test. Additional exam requirements/recommendations for international students: Required—TOEFL (minimum score 550 paper-based; 213 computer-based). *Application deadline:* For fall admission, 3/1 priority date for domestic students; for spring admission, 11/1 priority date for domestic students. Applications are processed on a rolling basis. Application fee: $50 ($60 for international students). Electronic applications accepted. *Expenses:* Contact institution. *Financial support:* In 2008–09, 207 students received support, including 36 research assistantships with partial tuition reimbursements available (averaging $12,954 per year), 87 teaching assistantships with partial tuition reimbursements available (averaging $12,099 per year); career-related internships or fieldwork, Federal Work-Study, institutionally sponsored loans, and scholarships/grants also available. Support available to part-time students. Financial award application deadline: 4/15; financial award applicants required to submit FAFSA. *Faculty research:* Substance abuse and recovery; the role of nutrition in the prevention of obesity; cancer and illness; the role of family factors in children's treatment response to cancer and serious illness; financial planning and credit management. Total annual research expenditures: $1.3 million. *Unit head:* Dr. Linda C. Hoover, Dean, 806-742-3031, Fax: 806-742-1849. *Application contact:* Dr. Lynn Huffman, Executive Associate Dean, 806-742-3031, Fax: 806-742-1849, E-mail: lynn.huffman@ttu.edu.

Tufts University, Graduate School of Arts and Sciences, Department of Child Development, Medford, MA 02155. Offers applied developmental psychology (PhD); child development (MA, CAGS); early childhood education (MAT). Part-time programs available. *Degree requirements:* For master's, thesis (for some programs); for doctorate, thesis/dissertation. *Entrance requirements:* For master's and doctorate, GRE General Test. Additional exam requirements/recommendations for international students: Required—TOEFL (minimum score 550 paper-based; 213 computer-based; 80 iBT). Electronic applications accepted.

The University of Akron, Graduate School, College of Fine and Applied Arts, School of Family and Consumer Sciences, Akron, OH 44325. Offers child and family development (MA), including child development, family development; child life (MA); clothing, textiles and interiors (MA); nutrition and dietetics (MS). Part-time and evening/weekend programs available. *Degree requirements:* For master's, comprehensive exam, thesis optional, oral exam. *Entrance requirements:* For master's, GRE, minimum GPA of 2.75, letters of recommendation, personal statement of goals, interview. Additional exam requirements/recommendations for international students: Required—TOEFL (minimum score 550 paper-based; 213 computer-based; 79 iBT). Electronic applications accepted. *Faculty research:* Nutritional health wellness/sports nutrition; historical/cultural aspects of clothing, textiles, interiors; FCS curriculum development; life span gender roles; families in international and historical perspectives.

The University of Alabama, Graduate School, College of Human Environmental Sciences, Tuscaloosa, AL 35487. Offers MA, MS, MSHES, PhD. Part-time and evening/weekend programs available. Postbaccalaureate distance learning degree programs offered (no on-campus study). *Faculty:* 28 full-time (21 women), 1 part-time/adjunct (0 women). *Students:* 158 full-time (102 women), 235 part-time (169 women); includes 75 minority (61 African Americans, 4 American Indian/Alaska Native, 5 Asian Americans or Pacific Islanders, 5 Hispanic Americans), 6 international. Average age 31. 271 applicants, 78% accepted, 71 enrolled. In 2008, 152 master's, 2 doctorates awarded. *Degree requirements:* For doctorate, thesis/dissertation. *Entrance requirements:* For master's, GRE General Test or MAT (minimum score: 50th percentile), minimum GPA of 3.0; for doctorate, GRE General Test or MAT, minimum GPA of 3.0. *Application deadline:* For fall admission, 7/6 for domestic students. Applications are processed on a rolling basis. Application fee: $30. Electronic applications accepted. *Expenses:* Tuition, area resident: Full-time $6400. Tuition, state resident: full-time $6400. Tuition, nonresident: full-time $18,000. *Financial support:* In 2008–09, 2 research assistantships with full tuition reimbursements (averaging $9,000 per year) were awarded; fellowships with tuition reimbursements, teaching assistantships with full tuition reimbursements, career-related internships or fieldwork, Federal Work-Study, institutionally sponsored loans, and scholarships/grants also available. *Faculty research:* Student's use of credit, determinants of income differential: comparing Asians with Blacks and Whites, expenditure patterns of Chinese, racial and ethnic differences in the likelihood of charitable contributions, health insurance coverage and precautionary behavior savings. Total annual research expenditures: $1.9 million. *Unit head:* Dr. Milla D. Boschung, Dean, 205-348-6250, Fax: 205-348-1786, E-mail: mboschun@ches.ua.edu. *Application contact:* Dr. Milla D. Boschung, Dean, 205-348-6250, Fax: 205-348-1786, E-mail: mboschun@ches.ua.edu.

University of Alberta, Faculty of Graduate Studies and Research, Department of Human Ecology, Edmonton, AB T6G 2E1, Canada. Offers family ecology and practice (M Sc, PhD); textiles and clothing (M Sc, MA, PhD). Postbaccalaureate distance learning degree programs offered (no on-campus study). *Degree requirements:* For master's, thesis (for some programs); for doctorate, comprehensive exam, thesis/dissertation. *Entrance requirements:* For master's and doctorate, minimum GPA of 7.0 on a 9.0 scale. Additional exam requirements/recommendations for international students: Required—TOEFL (minimum score 580 paper-based; 237 computer-based). *Faculty research:* Families and aging, family and child poverty, paid and unpaid work of families, textiles and clothing, parent-child relationships.

The University of Arizona, Graduate College, College of Agriculture and Life Sciences, School of Family and Consumer Sciences, Tucson, AZ 85721. Offers MS, PhD. Part-time programs available. *Entrance requirements:* For master's and doctorate, GRE General Test, minimum GPA of 3.0. Additional exam requirements/recommendations for international students: Required—TOEFL.

University of Arkansas, Graduate School, Dale Bumpers College of Agricultural, Food and Life Sciences, School of Human Environmental Sciences, Fayetteville, AR 72701-1201. Offers MS. Part-time programs available. Postbaccalaureate distance learning degree programs offered (minimal on-campus study). *Degree requirements:* For master's, comprehensive exam, thesis (for some programs).

University of Central Arkansas, Graduate School, College of Health and Behavioral Sciences, Department of Family and Consumer Sciences, Conway, AR 72035-0001. Offers MS. *Degree requirements:* For master's, comprehensive exam, thesis optional. *Entrance requirements:* For master's, GRE General Test, minimum GPA of 2.7. Additional exam requirements/recommendations for international students: Required—TOEFL (minimum score 550 paper-based; 213 computer-based). *Expenses:* Contact institution. *Faculty research:* Neurology, developmental disabilities, diet consequences.

University of Central Oklahoma, College of Graduate Studies and Research, College of Education, Department of Human Environmental Sciences, Edmond, OK 73034-5209. Offers family and child studies (MS); family and consumer science education (MS); interior design (MS); nutrition-food management (MS). Part-time programs available. *Entrance requirements:* Additional exam requirements/recommendations for international students: Required—TOEFL (minimum score 550 paper-based; 213 computer-based). Electronic applications accepted. *Faculty research:* Dietetics and food science.

University of Florida, Graduate School, College of Agricultural and Life Sciences, Department of Family, Youth, and Community Sciences, Gainesville, FL 32611. Offers MFYCS, MS.

University of Georgia, Graduate School, College of Family and Consumer Sciences, Athens, GA 30602. Offers MAT, MFCS, MS, PhD. *Degree requirements:* For doctorate, thesis/dissertation. *Entrance requirements:* For master's and doctorate, GRE General Test. Electronic applications accepted.

University of Houston, College of Technology, Department of Human Development and Consumer Science, Houston, TX 77204. Offers MS. *Faculty:* 2 full-time (1 woman), 1 part-time/adjunct (0 women). *Students:* 27 full-time (18 women), 35 part-time (22 women); includes 24 minority (17 African Americans, 5 Asian Americans or Pacific Islanders, 2 Hispanic Americans), 12 international. Average age 33. 37 applicants, 84% accepted, 27 enrolled. In 2008, 15 master's awarded. *Expenses:* Tuition, state resident: full-time $5164; part-time $287 per credit. Tuition, nonresident: full-time $10,222; part-time $568 per credit. *Financial support:* In 2008–09, 11 research assistantships (averaging $10,700 per year), 8 teaching assistantships (averaging $10,700 per year) were awarded. *Unit head:* Carole Goodson, Chairperson, 713-743-4046, Fax: 713-743-4033. *Application contact:* Holly Rosenthal, Graduate Academic Adviser, 713-743-4098, Fax: 713-743-4032, E-mail: hrosenthal@uh.edu.

University of Louisiana at Lafayette, BI Moody III College of Business Administration MBA Program, School of Human Resources, Lafayette, LA 70504. Offers MS. Part-time programs available. *Degree requirements:* For master's, thesis or alternative. *Entrance requirements:*

For master's, GRE General Test, minimum GPA of 2.75. Additional exam requirements/ recommendations for international students: Required—TOEFL (minimum score 550 paper-based; 213 computer-based). Electronic applications accepted. *Faculty research:* Nutrition education, crawfish use and nutrients.

University of Manitoba, Faculty of Graduate Studies, Faculty of Human Ecology, Winnipeg, MB R3T 2N2, Canada. Offers M Sc. *Degree requirements:* For master's, thesis.

University of Maryland, College Park, Graduate Studies, School of Public Health, Department of Family Science, College Park, MD 20742. Offers family studies (PhD); marriage and family therapy (MS). *Accreditation:* AAMFT/COAMFTE. Part-time and evening/weekend programs available. *Degree requirements:* For master's, thesis or alternative; for doctorate, comprehensive exam, thesis/dissertation, oral defense. *Entrance requirements:* For master's, GRE General Test, minimum GPA of 3.0, 3 letters of recommendation; for doctorate, GRE General Test, minimum GPA of 3.0, 3 letters of recommendation, research sample. Electronic applications accepted. *Faculty research:* Family life quality, interracial couples, child support, homeless families, family and child well-being.

University of Memphis, Graduate School, University College, Memphis, TN 38152. Offers liberal studies (MALS); merchandising and consumer science (MS), including consumer science and education; strategic leadership (MPS). Part-time and evening/weekend programs available. *Faculty:* 8 full-time (4 women). *Students:* 19 full-time (14 women), 83 part-time (59 women); includes 46 African Americans, 1 Asian American or Pacific Islander. Average age 41. 52 applicants, 85% accepted, 6 enrolled. In 2008, 43 master's awarded. *Degree requirements:* For master's, comprehensive exam, thesis (for some programs). *Entrance requirements:* For master's, MAT, GRE General Test (MS), interview (MALS). Additional exam requirements/ recommendations for international students: Required—TOEFL (minimum score 550 paper-based; 210 computer-based). *Application deadline:* For fall admission, 7/1 for domestic students, 5/1 for international students; for spring admission, 11/1 for domestic students, 9/15 for international students. Applications are processed on a rolling basis. Application fee: $35 ($60 for international students). Electronic applications accepted. *Expenses:* Tuition, area resident: Full-time $6242; part-time $330 per credit hour. Tuition, state resident: full-time $6242; part-time $330 per credit hour. Tuition, nonresident: full-time $17,828; part-time $815 per credit hour. Required fees: $1156. *Financial support:* In 2008–09, 98 students received support; research assistantships with full tuition reimbursements available, teaching assistantships, unspecified assistantships available. Financial award application deadline: 6/1; financial award applicants required to submit FAFSA. *Faculty research:* Media ethics, history of psychiatry, public relations. Total annual research expenditures: $9,333. *Unit head:* Dr. Dan Lattimore, Dean, 901-678-2991. *Application contact:* Dr. Herbert McCree, Coordinator of Graduate Studies, 901-678-4171, Fax: 901-678-3363, E-mail: hmccree@memphis.edu.

University of Mississippi, Graduate School, School of Applied Sciences, Department of Family and Consumer Sciences, Oxford, University, MS 38677. Offers MS.

University of Missouri–Columbia, Graduate School, College of Human Environmental Science, Columbia, MO 65211. Offers MA, MS, PhD. Part-time programs available. *Faculty:* 33 full-time (19 women), 1 (woman) part-time/adjunct. *Students:* 71 full-time (53 women), 61 part-time (39 women); includes 15 minority (11 African Americans, 3 Asian Americans or Pacific Islanders, 1 Hispanic American), 24 international. Average age 32. 119 applicants, 43% accepted, 29 enrolled. In 2008, 18 master's, 6 doctorates awarded. *Degree requirements:* For doctorate, thesis/dissertation. *Entrance requirements:* For master's and doctorate, GRE General Test, minimum GPA of 3.0. Additional exam requirements/recommendations for international students: Required—TOEFL. *Application deadline:* Applications are processed on a rolling basis. Application fee: $45 ($60 for international students). *Financial support:* Fellowships, research assistantships, teaching assistantships, institutionally sponsored loans available. *Unit head:* Dr. Stephen R. Jorgensen, Dean, 573-882-6227, E-mail: jorgens@missouri.edu. *Application contact:* Carla J. Beckmann, Academic Advisor, 573-882-6423, E-mail: jeromebeckmannc@missouri.edu.

University of Nebraska–Lincoln, Graduate College, College of Education and Human Sciences, Department of Child, Youth and Family Studies, Lincoln, NE 68588. Offers child development/early childhood education (MS, PhD); child, youth and family studies (MS); family and consumer sciences education (MS, PhD); family financial planning (MS); family science (MS, PhD); gerontology (PhD); human sciences (PhD), including child, youth and family studies, gerontology, medical family therapy; marriage and family therapy (MS); medical family therapy (PhD); youth development (MS). *Accreditation:* AAMFT/COAMFTE (one or more programs are accredited). Postbaccalaureate distance learning degree programs offered. *Faculty:* 16 full-time (11 women). *Students:* 23 full-time (18 women), 53 part-time (40 women); includes 8 minority (2 African Americans, 2 American Indian/Alaska Native, 2 Asian Americans or Pacific Islanders, 2 Hispanic Americans), 1 international. Average age 32. In 2008, 27 master's awarded. *Degree requirements:* For master's, thesis optional. *Entrance requirements:* For master's, GRE. Additional exam requirements/recommendations for international students: Required—TOEFL (minimum score 550 paper-based; 213 computer-based). *Application deadline:* For fall admission, 1/15 for domestic and international students; for spring admission, 10/1 for domestic and international students. Application fee: $40. Electronic applications accepted. *Expenses:* Tuition, state resident: full-time $4275; part-time $237.50 per credit hour. Tuition, nonresident: full-time $11,525; part-time $640.25 per credit hour. Required fees: $1068; $10.35 per credit hour. $440.70 per semester. Tuition and fees vary according to course load and program. *Financial support:* Fellowships, research assistantships, teaching assistantships, Federal Work-Study, health care benefits, and unspecified assistantships available. Financial award application deadline: 2/15. *Faculty research:* Marriage and family therapy, child development/early childhood education, family financial management. *Unit head:* Dr. Julie Johnson, Chair, 402-472-2957. *Application contact:* Dr. Julie Johnson, Chair, 402-472-2957.

The University of North Carolina at Greensboro, Graduate School, School of Human Environmental Sciences, Greensboro, NC 27412-5001. Offers M Ed, MS, MSW, PhD, Certificate. *Degree requirements:* For master's, thesis (for some programs); for doctorate, thesis/ dissertation. *Entrance requirements:* For master's and doctorate, GRE General Test. Additional exam requirements/recommendations for international students: Required—TOEFL. Electronic applications accepted. *Faculty research:* Impact of phosphate removal, protective clothing for pesticide workers, adolescent mothers, cancer prevention, immuno-stimulant effects.

University of Puerto Rico, Río Piedras, College of Education, Program in Family Ecology and Nutrition, San Juan, PR 00931-3300. Offers M Ed. Part-time programs available. *Degree requirements:* For master's, thesis. *Entrance requirements:* For master's, PAEG or GRE, minimum GPA of 3.0, letter of recommendation.

University of South Africa, College of Agriculture and Environmental Sciences, Pretoria, South Africa. Offers agriculture (MS); consumer science (MCS); environmental management (MA, MS, PhD); environmental science (MA, MS, PhD); geography (MA, MS, PhD); horticulture (M Tech); human ecology (MHE); life sciences (MS); nature conservation (M Tech).

The University of Tennessee, Graduate School, College of Education, Health and Human Sciences, Program in Human Ecology, Knoxville, TN 37996. Offers child and family studies (PhD); community health (PhD); nutrition science (PhD); retailing and consumer sciences (PhD); textile science (PhD). *Degree requirements:* For doctorate, thesis/dissertation. *Entrance requirements:* For doctorate, GRE General Test, minimum GPA of 2.7. Additional exam requirements/recommendations for international students: Required—TOEFL. Electronic applications accepted. *Expenses:* Tuition, area resident: Part-time $348 per credit hour. Tuition, state resident: full-time $6262. Tuition, nonresident: full-time $18,920; part-time $1052 per credit hour. Required fees: $812; $36 per credit hour. Tuition and fees vary according to program.

The University of Tennessee at Martin, Graduate Programs, College of Agriculture and Applied Sciences, Department of Family and Consumer Sciences, Martin, TN 38238-1000. Offers dietetics (MSFCS); general family and consumer sciences (MSFCS). Part-time programs available. *Faculty:* 6. *Students:* 32 (29 women). 30 applicants, 100% accepted, 16 enrolled. In 2008, 5 master's awarded. *Degree requirements:* For master's, comprehensive exam, thesis optional. *Entrance requirements:* For master's, GRE General Test, minimum GPA of 2.5. Additional exam requirements/recommendations for international students: Required—TOEFL (minimum score 525 paper-based; 197 computer-based; 71 iBT). *Application deadline:* For fall admission, 8/1 priority date for domestic students, 8/1 for international students; for spring admission, 1/1 for domestic and international students. Applications are processed on a rolling basis. Application fee: $30 ($50 for international students). Electronic applications accepted. *Expenses:* Tuition, state resident: full-time $6084; part-time $340 per semester hour. Tuition, nonresident: full-time $16,726; part-time $932 per semester hour. *Financial support:* In 2008–09, 6 students received support, including 6 research assistantships with full tuition reimbursements available (averaging $6,585 per year); scholarships/grants and unspecified assistantships also available. Financial award application deadline: 3/1. *Faculty research:* Children with developmental disabilities, regional food product development and marketing, parent education. *Unit head:* Dr. Lisa LeBleu, Coordinator, 731-881-7116, Fax: 731-881-7106, E-mail: llebleu@utm.edu. *Application contact:* Linda S. Arant, Student Services Specialist, 731-881-7012, Fax: 731-881-7499, E-mail: larant@utm.edu.

The University of Texas at Austin, Graduate School, College of Natural Sciences, School of Human Ecology, Austin, TX 78712-1111. Offers human development and family sciences (MA, PhD); nutritional sciences (MA, PhD), including nutrition (MA), nutritional sciences (PhD); textile and apparel technology (MS). *Degree requirements:* For master's, thesis; for doctorate, thesis/dissertation. *Entrance requirements:* For master's and doctorate, GRE General Test. Electronic applications accepted.

University of Wisconsin–Madison, Graduate School, School of Human Ecology, Madison, WI 53706-1380. Offers consumer behavior and family economics (MS, PhD); design studies (MFA, MS, PhD); human development and family studies (MS, PhD). *Degree requirements:* For master's, thesis (for some programs); for doctorate, comprehensive exam, thesis/ dissertation. *Entrance requirements:* For master's, GRE General Test, portfolio (design studies), 3 letters of recommendation; for doctorate, GRE General Test. Additional exam requirements/ recommendations for international students: Required—TOEFL (minimum score 580 paper-based; 237 computer-based). Electronic applications accepted.

University of Wisconsin–Stevens Point, College of Professional Studies, School of Health Promotion and Human Development, Program in Human and Community Resources, Stevens Point, WI 54481-3897. Offers MS. Part-time programs available. *Students:* 12 full-time (8 women), 7 part-time (6 women); includes 2 African Americans, 1 international. *Degree requirements:* For master's, thesis or alternative. *Entrance requirements:* For master's, minimum GPA of 2.75. *Application deadline:* For fall admission, 5/1 priority date for domestic students. Applications are processed on a rolling basis. Application fee: $45. *Expenses:* Tuition, state resident: full-time $7410. Tuition, nonresident: full-time $17,756. Full-time tuition and fees vary according to reciprocity agreements. *Financial support:* Research assistantships, teaching assistantships, Federal Work-Study available. Support available to part-time students. Financial award application deadline: 5/1; financial award applicants required to submit FAFSA. *Unit head:* Dr. Marty Loy, Head, 715-346-2830, Fax: 715-346-2720. *Application contact:* Dr. Jasia Steinmetz, Information Contact, 715-346-2830, Fax: 715-346-2720, E-mail: jsteinme@uwsp.edu.

Utah State University, School of Graduate Studies, College of Education and Human Services, Department of Family, Consumer, and Human Development, Logan, UT 84322. Offers family and human development (MFHD); family, consumer, and human development (MS, PhD), including adolescence/youth (MS), adult development/aging (MS), consumer science (MS), infancy/childhood (MS), marriage and family relations (MS), marriage and family therapy (MS). *Accreditation:* AAMFT/COAMFTE (one or more programs are accredited). Part-time and evening/ weekend programs available. Postbaccalaureate distance learning degree programs offered (minimal on-campus study). *Degree requirements:* For master's, thesis; for doctorate, comprehensive exam, thesis/dissertation, competencies. *Entrance requirements:* For master's, GRE General Test or MAT, minimum GPA of 3.0, 3 letters of recommendation; for doctorate, GRE, minimum GPA of 3.0, 3 letters of recommendation. Additional exam requirements/ recommendations for international students: Required—TOEFL. Electronic applications accepted. *Faculty research:* Marriage and family relations, adolescent problem behavior, family financial management, early literacy, mental health in the elderly, parent child attachment.

Western Michigan University, Graduate College, College of Education, Department of Family and Consumer Sciences, Program in Family and Consumer Sciences, Kalamazoo, MI 49008-5202. Offers MA. *Faculty research:* Parenting education, kinship care, entrepreneurship, textiles and dress, nutrition.

Child and Family Studies

Arizona State University, Graduate College, College of Liberal Arts and Sciences, Division of Social Sciences, School of Social and Family Dynamics, Tempe, AZ 85287. Offers family and human development (MS, PhD); infant-family practice (MAS); marriage and family therapy (MAS); sociology (MA, PhD). *Degree requirements:* For master's, thesis or alternative; for doctorate, thesis/dissertation. *Entrance requirements:* For master's and doctorate, GRE.

Assumption College, Graduate School, Counseling Psychology Program, Worcester, MA 01609-1296. Offers child and family interventions (MA); cognitive and behavioral therapies (MA); general psychology (MA). Part-time and evening/weekend programs available. *Faculty:* 4 full-time (1 woman), 6 part-time/adjunct (2 women). *Students:* 41 full-time (34 women), 30 part-time (22 women); includes 4 minority (2 African Americans, 2 Hispanic Americans), 2 international. Average age 24. 83 applicants, 81% accepted. In 2008, 28 master's, 1 other advanced degree awarded. *Degree requirements:* For master's, comprehensive exam, internship, practicum, oral exam; for CAGS, comprehensive exam, oral exam. *Entrance requirements:* For master's, 3 letters of recommendation, resumé, essay; for CAGS, 3 letters of recommendation, resumé, interview, essay. Additional exam requirements/recommendations for international students: Required—TOEFL (minimum score 540 paper-based; 200 computer-based; 76 iBT), IELTS (minimum score 6). *Application deadline:* For fall admission, 6/1 priority date for domestic students, 5/1 priority date for international students; for spring admission, 11/1 priority date for domestic students, 9/1 priority date for international students. Applications are processed on a rolling basis. Application fee: $30. Electronic applications accepted. *Expenses:* Tuition: Part-time $468 per credit hour. Required fees: $20 per semester. One-time fee: $100. *Financial support:* In 2008–09, 19 fellowships with partial tuition reimbursements

Child and Family Studies

Assumption College (continued)
(averaging $6,808 per year), 2 teaching assistantships with full tuition reimbursements (averaging $9,940 per year) were awarded. Financial award application deadline: 3/1; financial award applicants required to submit FAFSA. *Faculty research:* Mood disorders, adjustment to life-threatening illness, perception of movement, socioemotional development of young children, discovery versus disclosure. *Unit head:* Dr. Leonard A. Doerfler, Director, 508-767-7549, Fax: 508-767-7263, E-mail: doerfler@assumption.edu. *Application contact:* Adrian O. Dumas, Director of Graduate Enrollment Management and Services, 508-767-7365, Fax: 508-767-7030, E-mail: adumas@assumption.edu.

Auburn University, Graduate School, College of Human Sciences, Department of Human Development and Family Studies, Auburn University, AL 36849. Offers MS, PhD. *Accreditation:* AAMFT/COAMFTE (one or more programs are accredited). Part-time programs available. *Faculty:* 20 full-time (12 women), 1 (woman) part-time/adjunct. *Students:* 18 full-time (13 women), 34 part-time (31 women); includes 14 minority (8 African Americans, 5 Asian Americans or Pacific Islanders, 1 Hispanic American), 7 international. Average age 28. 55 applicants, 42% accepted, 9 enrolled. In 2008, 6 master's, 3 doctorates awarded. *Degree requirements:* For master's, thesis, oral exam; for doctorate, thesis/dissertation. *Entrance requirements:* For master's, GRE General Test; for doctorate, GRE General Test, master's degree. *Application deadline:* For fall admission, 7/7 for domestic students; for spring admission, 11/24 for domestic students. Applications are processed on a rolling basis. Application fee: $25 ($50 for international students). *Expenses:* Tuition, area resident: Full-time $5880; part-time $243 per credit hour. Tuition, state resident: full-time $5880; part-time $243 per credit hour. Tuition, nonresident: full-time $17,640; part-time $729 per credit hour. International tuition: $17,846 full-time. Required fees: $620. Tuition and fees vary according to program and reciprocity agreements. *Financial support:* Research assistantships, teaching assistantships, Federal Work-Study available. Support available to part-time students. Financial award application deadline: 3/15. *Faculty research:* Family influences on personality and social development, parent-child relations, infancy, day care, parent education. *Unit head:* Dr. Leanne K. Lamke, Head, 334-844-4151, E-mail: mbradbar@humsci.auburn.edu. *Application contact:* Dr. George Flowers, Interim Dean of the Graduate School, 334-844-2125.

Bank Street College of Education, Graduate School, Department of Curriculum and Instruction, Program in Infant and Parent Development, New York, NY 10025. Offers infant and family development (MS Ed); infant and family development and early intervention/early childhood special and general education (MS Ed); infant and family development and early intervention/ early childhood special education (Ed M). *Students:* 15 full-time (all women), 39 part-time (38 women); includes 8 minority (3 African Americans, 5 Hispanic Americans), 1 international. Average age 31. 27 applicants, 81% accepted, 15 enrolled. In 2008, 16 master's awarded. *Degree requirements:* For master's, thesis. *Entrance requirements:* For master's, interview. Additional exam requirements/recommendations for international students: Required—TOEFL (minimum score 600 paper-based; 250 computer-based; 100 iBT), IELTS (minimum score 7). *Application deadline:* For fall admission, 3/1 priority date for domestic students; for spring admission, 11/1 priority date for domestic students. Applications are processed on a rolling basis. Application fee: $50. *Expenses:* Tuition: Full-time $1060; part-time $1060 per credit. Required fees: $250. One-time fee: $600. *Financial support:* Career-related internships or fieldwork, Federal Work-Study, scholarships/grants, and unspecified assistantships available. Support available to part-time students. Financial award application deadline: 4/15; financial award applicants required to submit FAFSA. *Faculty research:* Early intervention, early attachment practice in infant and toddler childcare, parenting skills in adolescents. *Unit head:* Sue Cabary, Director, 212-875-4509, Fax: 212-875-4753, E-mail: scarbary@bankstreet.edu. *Application contact:* Ann Morgan, Director of Graduate Admissions, 212-875-4403, Fax: 212-875-4678, E-mail: amorgan@bankstreet.edu.

Bank Street College of Education, Graduate School, Program in Child Life, New York, NY 10025. Offers MS. *Students:* 21 full-time (all women), 8 part-time (all women); includes 4 minority (1 African American, 2 Asian Americans or Pacific Islanders, 1 Hispanic American). Average age 26. 20 applicants, 80% accepted, 10 enrolled. In 2008, 12 master's awarded. *Degree requirements:* For master's, thesis. *Entrance requirements:* For master's, interview. Additional exam requirements/recommendations for international students: Required—TOEFL (minimum score 600 paper-based; 250 computer-based), IELTS (minimum score 7). *Application deadline:* For fall admission, 3/1 priority date for domestic students; for spring admission, 11/1 priority date for domestic students. Applications are processed on a rolling basis. Application fee: $50. *Expenses:* Tuition: Full-time $1060; part-time $1060 per credit. Required fees: $250. One-time fee: $600. *Financial support:* Career-related internships or fieldwork, Federal Work-Study, scholarships/grants, and unspecified assistantships available. Support available to part-time students. Financial award application deadline: 4/15; financial award applicants required to submit FAFSA. *Faculty research:* Therapeutic play in child life setting, child advocacy, psychosocial and educational intervention with care of sick children. *Unit head:* Troy Pinkney-Ragsdale, Director, 212-875-4473, Fax: 212-875-4753, E-mail: tpinkneyragsdale@bankstreet.edu. *Application contact:* Ann Morgan, Director of Graduate Admissions, 212-875-4403, Fax: 212-875-4678, E-mail: amorgan@bankstreet.edu.

Bowling Green State University, Graduate College, College of Education and Human Development, School of Family and Consumer Sciences, Bowling Green, OH 43403. Offers food and nutrition (MFCS); human development and family studies (MFCS). Part-time programs available. *Degree requirements:* For master's, thesis. *Entrance requirements:* For master's, GRE General Test, minimum GPA of 3.0. Additional exam requirements/recommendations for international students: Required—TOEFL. Electronic applications accepted. *Faculty research:* Public health, wellness, social issues and policies, ethnic foods, nutrition and aging.

Brandeis University, The Heller School for Social Policy and Management, Program in Public Policy, Waltham, MA 02454-9110. Offers aging (MPP); behavioral health (MPP); children, youth and families (MPP); general social policy (MPP); health (MPP); poverty alleviation and development (MPP). Part-time programs available. *Entrance requirements:* Additional exam requirements/recommendations for international students: Required—TOEFL (minimum score 600 paper-based). Electronic applications accepted. *Faculty research:* Health policy, child and family policy, mental health policy, disability policy, aging policy, substance abuse, work, inequality and social change.

Brandeis University, The Heller School for Social Policy and Management, Program in Social Policy, Waltham, MA 02454-9110. Offers assets and inequalities (PhD); children, youth and families (PhD); health and behavioral health (PhD). *Degree requirements:* For doctorate, thesis/dissertation, qualifying paper, 2-year residency. *Entrance requirements:* For doctorate, GRE General Test.

Brigham Young University, Graduate Studies, College of Family, Home, and Social Sciences, Program in Marriage, Family and Human Development, Provo, UT 84602. Offers MS, PhD. *Accreditation:* AAMFT/COAMFTE. *Faculty:* 24 full-time (5 women). *Students:* 21 full-time (15 women); includes 1 minority (Asian American or Pacific Islander), 2 international. Average age 30. 27 applicants, 41% accepted, 8 enrolled. In 2008, 3 master's, 1 doctorate awarded. *Degree requirements:* For master's, thesis; for doctorate, comprehensive exam, thesis/dissertation, 2 publishable papers. *Entrance requirements:* For master's and doctorate, GRE General Test, minimum GPA of 3.0 in last 60 semester hours, letters of recommendation. Additional exam requirements/recommendations for international students: Required—TOEFL (minimum score 580 paper-based; 237 computer-based; 85 iBT), IELTS (minimum score 7). *Application deadline:* For fall admission, 1/10 for domestic and international students. Application fee: $50. Electronic applications accepted. *Expenses:* Tuition: Full-time $5160; part-time $287 per credit hour. Tuition and fees vary according to program and student's religious affiliation. *Financial support:* In 2008–09, 9 students received support, including 20 research assistantships with full and partial tuition reimbursements available (averaging $5,096 per year), 5 teaching assistantships with full and partial tuition reimbursements available (averaging $5,096 per year); scholarships/grants and unspecified assistantships also available. Financial award

application deadline: 3/27. *Faculty research:* Family studies and family process; marriage; adolescence and emerging adulthood; adult development and aging; child development. *Unit head:* Dr. Richard Miller, Director, School of Life, 801-422-2069, Fax: 801-422-0230, E-mail: rick_miller@byu.edu. *Application contact:* Graduate Secretary, 801-422-2060, E-mail: mfhdgrad@byu.edu.

Brock University, Faculty of Graduate Studies, Faculty of Social Sciences, Program in Child and Youth Studies, St. Catharines, ON L2S 3A1, Canada. Offers MA. Part-time programs available. *Degree requirements:* For master's, thesis. *Entrance requirements:* For master's, honors BA. Additional exam requirements/recommendations for international students: Required—TOEFL (minimum score 550 paper-based; 213 computer-based; 80 iBT), IELTS (minimum score 6.5), TWE (minimum score 4). Electronic applications accepted. *Faculty research:* Cognitive mechanisms, youth resilience, developmental disabilities, parent-child interactions and communication.

California State University, Los Angeles, Graduate Studies, College of Health and Human Services, Department of Child and Family Studies, Los Angeles, CA 90032-8530. Offers child development (MA). Part-time and evening/weekend programs available. *Faculty:* 3 full-time (2 women), 2 part-time/adjunct (both women). *Students:* 8 full-time (7 women), 15 part-time (all women); includes 16 minority (1 African American, 6 Asian Americans or Pacific Islanders, 9 Hispanic Americans), 1 international. Average age 29. 14 applicants, 93% accepted, 8 enrolled. In 2008, 6 master's awarded. *Degree requirements:* For master's, comprehensive exam, project or thesis. *Entrance requirements:* Additional exam requirements/recommendations for international students: Required—TOEFL (minimum score 500 paper-based; 173 computer-based). *Application deadline:* For fall admission, 6/15 for domestic students, 5/1 for international students; for winter admission, 11/1 for domestic students, 9/1 for international students; for spring admission, 2/1 for domestic students, 10/1 for international students. Applications are processed on a rolling basis. Application fee: $55. *Expenses:* Tuition, nonresident: part-time $226 per credit. Required fees: $4019. *Financial support:* Career-related internships or fieldwork and Federal Work-Study available. Support available to part-time students. Financial award application deadline: 3/1. *Faculty research:* Nutrition education, laundry product and fabric durability, computer usage in public school home economics. *Unit head:* Dr. Marlene Zepeda, Co-Chair, 323-343-4590, Fax: 323-343-5019, E-mail: mzepeda@calstatela.edu. *Application contact:* Dr. Jose L. Galvan, Dean of Graduate Studies, 323-343-3820, Fax: 323-343-5653, E-mail: jgalvan@cslanet.calstatela.edu.

Capella University, School of Human Services, Minneapolis, MN 55402. Offers addictions counseling (Certificate); counseling studies (MS, PhD); criminal justice (MS, PhD, Certificate); diversity studies (Certificate); general human services (MS, PhD); health care administration (MS, PhD, Certificate); management of nonprofit agencies (MS, PhD, Certificate); marital, couple and family counseling/therapy (MS); marriage and family services (Certificate); mental health counseling (MS); professional counseling (Certificate); social and community services (MS, PhD, Certificate). Part-time and evening/weekend programs available. Postbaccalaureate distance learning degree programs offered (minimal on-campus study). Terminal master's awarded for partial completion of doctoral program. *Degree requirements:* For master's, thesis optional, integrative project; for doctorate, comprehensive exam, thesis/dissertation. *Entrance requirements:* Additional exam requirements/recommendations for international students: Required—TOEFL (minimum score 550 paper-based; 213 computer-based), TWE (minimum score 4). Electronic applications accepted. *Faculty research:* Compulsive and addictive behaviors, substance abuse, assessment of psychopathology and neuropsychology.

Central Michigan University, College of Graduate Studies, College of Education and Human Services, Department of Human Environmental Studies, Mount Pleasant, MI 48859. Offers apparel product development and merchandising technology (MS); human development and family studies (MA); nutrition and dietetics (MS). Part-time and evening/weekend programs available. *Faculty:* 15 full-time (11 women), 1 part-time/adjunct (0 women). *Degree requirements:* For master's, thesis or alternative. *Application deadline:* Applications are processed on a rolling basis. Application fee: $35 ($45 for international students). Electronic applications accepted. *Expenses:* Tuition, state resident: full-time $3717; part-time $413 per credit. Tuition, nonresident: full-time $6894; part-time $766 per credit. *Financial support:* Fellowships with tuition reimbursements, research assistantships, career-related internships or fieldwork, Federal Work-Study, unspecified assistantships, and out-of-state merit awards available. *Faculty research:* Human growth and development, family studies and human sexuality, human nutrition and dietetics, apparel and textile retailing, computer-aided design for apparel. *Unit head:* Dr. Phame Camerena, Chairperson, 989-774-3218, Fax: 989-774-2435, E-mail: camar1pm@cmich.edu. *Application contact:* Dr. Candace Maylee, Assistant Coordinator of Graduate Programs, 989-774-2613, Fax: 989-774-2435, E-mail: mayle1ce@cmich.edu.

Central Washington University, Graduate Studies, Research and Continuing Education, College of Education and Professional Studies, Department of Family and Consumer Sciences, Ellensburg, WA 98926. Offers family and consumer sciences education (MS); family studies (MS); nutrition (MS). Part-time programs available. *Degree requirements:* For master's, thesis or alternative. *Entrance requirements:* For master's, GRE General Test (nutrition), minimum GPA of 3.0. Additional exam requirements/recommendations for international students: Required—TOEFL (minimum score 550 paper-based; 213 computer-based; 79 iBT). Electronic applications accepted.

Colorado State University, Graduate School, College of Applied Human Sciences, Department of Human Development and Family Studies, Fort Collins, CO 80523-1570. Offers MS. *Accreditation:* AAMFT/COAMFTE. Part-time programs available. *Faculty:* 14 full-time (10 women). *Students:* 24 full-time (22 women), 17 part-time (15 women); includes 2 minority (1 Asian American or Pacific Islander, 1 Hispanic American), 2 international. Average age 32. 80 applicants, 28% accepted, 12 enrolled. In 2008, 10 master's awarded. Terminal master's awarded for partial completion of doctoral program. *Degree requirements:* For master's, thesis or alternative, research project or thesis. *Entrance requirements:* For master's, GRE General Test, minimum GPA of 3.0; course work in human development, family studies, and statistics; letters of recommendation forms; additional departmental application; interview; BS/BA degree in human development and family studies or related field. Additional exam requirements/recommendations for international students: Required—TOEFL (minimum score 550 paper-based; 213 computer-based; 80 iBT). *Application deadline:* For fall admission, 1/15 for domestic and international students. Application fee: $50. Electronic applications accepted. *Expenses:* Tuition, area resident: Full-time $5620; part-time $312.25 per credit. Tuition, state resident: full-time $5620; part-time $312.25 per credit. Tuition, nonresident: full-time $17,253; part-time $958.50 per credit. Required fees: $1449.56; $82.35 per credit. *Financial support:* In 2008–09, 16 students received support, including 1 fellowship (averaging $9,792 per year), 4 research assistantships with full and partial tuition reimbursements available (averaging $10,454 per year), 11 teaching assistantships with full and partial tuition reimbursements available (averaging $7,846 per year); career-related internships or fieldwork, Federal Work-Study, institutionally sponsored loans, scholarships/grants, health care benefits, and unspecified assistantships also available. Financial award application deadline: 1/15; financial award applicants required to submit FAFSA. *Faculty research:* Promoting resiliency and optimal development; gender, culture and diversity; gerontology/aging; child and adolescent health; disabilities. Total annual research expenditures: $838,638. *Unit head:* Dr. Lise Youngblade, Department Head, 970-491-5558, Fax: 970-491-7975, E-mail: lise.youngblade@colostate.edu. *Application contact:* Dr. Karen C. Barrett, Graduate Chair, 970-491-7382, Fax: 970-491-7975, E-mail: karen.barrett@colostate.edu.

Concordia University, School of Graduate Studies, Faculty of Arts and Science, Department of Education, Program in Child Study, Montréal, QC H3G 1M8, Canada. Offers MA. *Degree requirements:* For master's, one foreign language, thesis optional. *Entrance requirements:* For master's, minimum B average in undergraduate course work. *Faculty research:* Development and family relations, children and technology, cooperative learning strategies, exceptional children, second language acquisition.

Concordia University, St. Paul, College of Education, St. Paul, MN 55104-5494. Offers curriculum and instruction (MA Ed); differentiated instruction (MA Ed); early childhood education (MA Ed); educational leadership (MA Ed); family life education (MA); special education (Certificate); sports management (MA). *Accreditation:* NCATE. Evening/weekend programs available. Postbaccalaureate distance learning degree programs offered (minimal on-campus study). *Faculty:* 16 full-time (13 women), 46 part-time/adjunct (32 women). *Students:* 651 full-time (532 women), 5 part-time (4 women); includes 60 minority (36 African Americans, 17 Asian Americans or Pacific Islanders, 7 Hispanic Americans), 1 international. Average age 35. In 2008, 95 master's, 4 other advanced degrees awarded. *Application deadline:* Applications are processed on a rolling basis. Application fee: $50. Electronic applications accepted. *Financial support:* Applicants required to submit FAFSA. *Unit head:* Prof. Lonn Maly, Dean, 651-641-8278, Fax: 651-641-8807, E-mail: maly@csp.edu. *Application contact:* Kimberly Craig, Director of Graduate and Cohort Admission, 651-603-6223, Fax: 651-603-6320, E-mail: craig@csp.edu.

Concordia University Wisconsin, Graduate Programs, Department of Education, Program in Family Studies, Mequon, WI 53097-2402. Offers MS Ed. *Degree requirements:* For master's, comprehensive exam, thesis or alternative. *Entrance requirements:* For master's, minimum GPA of 3.0. Additional exam requirements/recommendations for international students: Required—TOEFL.

Cornell University, Graduate School, Graduate Fields of Human Ecology, Field of Human Development, Ithaca, NY 14853-0001. Offers developmental psychology (PhD), including cognitive development, developmental psychopathology, ecology of human development, social and personality development; human development and family studies (PhD), including ecology of human development, family studies and the life course. *Faculty:* 30 full-time (14 women). *Students:* 27 full-time (19 women); includes 2 minority (both Asian Americans or Pacific Islanders), 11 international. Average age 29. 71 applicants, 10% accepted, 5 enrolled. In 2008, 5 doctorates awarded. *Degree requirements:* For doctorate, comprehensive exam, thesis/dissertation, pre-doctoral research project, teaching experience. *Entrance requirements:* For doctorate, GRE General Test, 2 letters of recommendation. Additional exam requirements/recommendations for international students: Required—TOEFL (minimum score 550 paper-based; 213 computer-based; 77 iBT). *Application deadline:* For fall admission, 1/15 for domestic students. Application fee: $70. Electronic applications accepted. *Expenses:* Tuition: Full-time $29,500. Required fees: $70. Full-time tuition and fees vary according to degree level, program and student level. *Financial support:* In 2008–09, 26 students received support, including 3 fellowships with full tuition reimbursements available, 3 research assistantships with full tuition reimbursements available, 20 teaching assistantships with full tuition reimbursements available; institutionally sponsored loans, scholarships/grants, health care benefits, tuition waivers (full and partial), and unspecified assistantships also available. Financial award applicants required to submit FAFSA. *Faculty research:* Cognitive development, developmental psychopathology, ecology of human development, family studies and the life course, social and personality development. *Unit head:* Director of Graduate Studies, 607-255-3181, Fax: 607-255-9856. *Application contact:* Graduate Field Assistant, 607-255-3181, Fax: 607-255-9856, E-mail: hdfs@cornell.edu.

East Carolina University, Graduate School, College of Human Ecology, Department of Child Development and Family Relations, Greenville, NC 27858-4353. Offers child development and family relations (MS); marriage and family therapy (MS). *Accreditation:* AAMFT/COAMFTE. Part-time programs available. *Degree requirements:* For master's, comprehensive exam, thesis optional. *Faculty research:* Child care quality, mental health delivery systems for children, family violence.

Eastern Michigan University, Graduate School, College of Health and Human Services, School of Social Work, Ypsilanti, MI 48197. Offers family and children's services (MSW); gerontology (Graduate Certificate); gerontology-dementia (Graduate Certificate); mental health and chemical dependency (MSW); services to the aging (MSW). *Accreditation:* CSWE. Part-time and evening/weekend programs available. Postbaccalaureate distance learning degree programs offered (minimal on-campus study). *Entrance requirements:* Additional exam requirements/recommendations for international students: Required—TOEFL.

Florida State University, Graduate Studies, College of Human Sciences, Department of Family and Child Sciences, Tallahassee, FL 32306. Offers child development (MS, PhD); family relations (MS, PhD); marriage and family therapy (PhD). *Accreditation:* AAMFT/COAMFTE. Part-time programs available. *Degree requirements:* For master's, comprehensive exam, thesis optional; for doctorate, thesis/dissertation. *Entrance requirements:* For master's and doctorate, GRE General Test, minimum GPA of 3.0. Additional exam requirements/recommendations for international students: Required—TOEFL (minimum score 80 iBT). Electronic applications accepted. *Faculty research:* Addictions, family therapy, sexuality, parent-child relations, adolescent development.

Indiana University Bloomington, School of Health, Physical Education and Recreation, Department of Applied Health Science, Bloomington, IN 47405-7000. Offers health behavior (PhD); health promotion (MS); human development/family studies (MS); nutrition science (MS); public health (MPH); safety management (MS); school and college health programs (MS). *Accreditation:* CEPH (one or more programs are accredited). *Faculty:* 24 full-time (12 women). *Students:* 93 full-time (64 women), 53 part-time (38 women); includes 48 minority (17 African Americans, 1 American Indian/Alaska Native, 27 Asian Americans or Pacific Islanders, 3 Hispanic Americans), 2 international. Average age 31. 104 applicants, 66% accepted, 47 enrolled. In 2008, 40 master's, 5 doctorates awarded. *Degree requirements:* For master's, thesis optional; for doctorate, thesis/dissertation. *Entrance requirements:* For master's, GRE (MS in nutrition science), 3 recommendations; for doctorate, GRE, 3 recommendations. Additional exam requirements/recommendations for international students: Required—TOEFL (minimum score 550 paper-based; 213 computer-based; 79 iBT). *Application deadline:* For fall admission, 4/30 priority date for domestic students, 12/1 priority date for international students; for spring admission, 11/15 priority date for domestic students, 9/1 priority date for international students. Application fee: $50 ($60 for international students). *Expenses:* Tuition, area resident: Part-time $291.97 per credit hour. Tuition, state resident: part-time $291.97 per credit hour. Tuition, nonresident: part-time $850.33 per credit hour. Required fees: $110 per semester. Tuition and fees vary according to course load and program. *Financial support:* In 2008–09, 80 students received support, including 12 fellowships (averaging $2,316 per year), 50 research assistantships with full and partial tuition reimbursements available (averaging $6,973 per year), 27 teaching assistantships with full and partial tuition reimbursements available (averaging $11,067 per year); career-related internships or fieldwork, Federal Work-Study, institutionally sponsored loans, scholarships/grants, tuition waivers (partial), and fee remissions also available. Financial award application deadline: 3/1. *Faculty research:* Cancer education, HIV/AIDS and drug education, public health, parent-child interactions, safety education. Total annual research expenditures: $2.8 million. *Unit head:* Dr. Mohammad R. Torabi, Chair, 812-855-4808, Fax: 812-855-3936, E-mail: torabi@indiana.edu. *Application contact:* Dr. Mohammad R. Torabi, Chair, 812-855-4808, Fax: 812-855-3936, E-mail: torabi@indiana.edu.

Indiana University–Purdue University Indianapolis, School of Liberal Arts, Department of Sociology, Indianapolis, IN 46202-2896. Offers family/gender studies (MA); medical sociology (MA); work/occupations (MA).

Iowa State University of Science and Technology, Graduate College, College of Human Sciences, Department of Human Development and Family Studies, Ames, IA 50011. Offers human development and family studies (MFCS, MS, PhD). *Accreditation:* AAMFT/COAMFTE. *Faculty:* 24 full-time (18 women), 7 part-time/adjunct (5 women). *Students:* 54 full-time (45 women), 16 part-time (15 women); includes 3 minority (1 Asian American or Pacific Islander, 2 Hispanic Americans), 9 international. 22 applicants, 86% accepted, 13 enrolled. In 2008, 12 master's, 6 doctorates awarded. *Degree requirements:* For master's, thesis; for doctorate, thesis/dissertation. *Entrance requirements:* For master's and doctorate, GRE General Test. Additional exam requirements/recommendations for international students: Required—TOEFL

(minimum score 550 paper-based; 79 iBT), IELTS (6.5) or TOEFL. *Application deadline:* For fall admission, 12/1 priority date for domestic and international students. Application fee: $30 ($70 for international students). Electronic applications accepted. *Expenses:* Tuition, area resident: Full-time $6446; part-time $359 per credit. Tuition, state resident: full-time $6446; part-time $359 per credit. Tuition, nonresident: full-time $17,330; part-time $963 per credit. Required fees: $790; $249.25 per semester. Tuition and fees vary according to course load and program. *Financial support:* In 2008–09, 40 research assistantships with full and partial tuition reimbursements (averaging $13,392 per year), 11 teaching assistantships with full and partial tuition reimbursements (averaging $13,392 per year) were awarded; fellowships, scholarships/grants also available. *Faculty research:* Child development, early childhood education, family resource management and housing, life span studies. *Unit head:* Dr. Dianne Draper, Interim Chair, 515-294-6316, Fax: 515-294-2502, E-mail: hdfs-grad-adm@iastate.edu. *Application contact:* Dr. Dianne Draper, Interim Chair, 515-294-6316, Fax: 515-294-2502, E-mail: hdfs-grad-adm@iastate.edu.

Kansas State University, Graduate School, College of Human Ecology, Program in Human Ecology, Manhattan, KS 66506. Offers apparel and textiles (PhD); family life education and consultation (PhD); food service, hospitality management, and administrative dietetics (PhD); institutional management (PhD); lifespan and human development (PhD); marriage and family therapy (PhD). *Faculty:* 3 full-time (all women). *Students:* 37 full-time (25 women), 24 part-time (15 women); includes 10 minority (8 African Americans, 1 American Indian/Alaska Native, 1 Asian American or Pacific Islander), 18 international. Average age 37. 25 applicants, 80% accepted, 18 enrolled. In 2008, 14 doctorates awarded. *Application deadline:* For fall admission, 2/1 priority date for domestic and international students; for spring admission, 8/1 priority date for domestic and international students. Application fee: $30 ($55 for international students). *Expenses:* Tuition, area resident: Full-time $6466; part-time $269.40 per credit hour. Tuition, state resident: full-time $6466; part-time $269.40 per credit hour. Tuition, nonresident: full-time $14,874; part-time $619.75 per credit hour. Required fees: $673; $23.40 per credit hour. Tuition and fees vary according to campus/location. *Unit head:* Elizabeth McCullough, Director, 785-532-2284, Fax: 785-532-3796, E-mail: lizm@ksu.edu. *Application contact:* Connie Fechter, Application Contact, 785-532-1473, Fax: 785-532-3796, E-mail: fechter@ksu.edu.

Kansas State University, Graduate School, College of Human Ecology, School of Family Studies and Human Services, Manhattan, KS 66506. Offers MS. *Accreditation:* AAMFT/COAMFTE; ASHA. Part-time programs available. *Faculty:* 22 full-time (15 women), 2 part-time/adjunct (both women). *Students:* 80 full-time (68 women), 164 part-time (106 women); includes 25 minority (15 African Americans, 1 American Indian/Alaska Native, 3 Asian Americans or Pacific Islanders, 6 Hispanic Americans), 4 international. Average age 32. 171 applicants, 46% accepted, 70 enrolled. In 2008, 53 master's awarded. *Degree requirements:* For master's, thesis or alternative, oral exam, residency. *Entrance requirements:* For master's, GRE, minimum GPA of 3.0 in last 2 years of undergraduate study. Additional exam requirements/recommendations for international students: Required—TOEFL (minimum score 600 paper-based; 250 computer-based). *Application deadline:* For fall admission, 2/1 priority date for domestic students, 1/15 priority date for international students; for spring admission, 10/1 priority date for domestic students, 8/1 for international students. Applications are processed on a rolling basis. Application fee: $30 ($55 for international students). *Expenses:* Tuition, area resident: Full-time $6466; part-time $269.40 per credit hour. Tuition, state resident: full-time $6466; part-time $269.40 per credit hour. Tuition, nonresident: full-time $14,874; part-time $619.75 per credit hour. Required fees: $673; $23.40 per credit hour. Tuition and fees vary according to campus/location. *Financial support:* In 2008–09, 33 research assistantships (averaging $11,781 per year), 18 teaching assistantships with full and partial tuition reimbursements (averaging $12,946 per year) were awarded; Federal Work-Study, institutionally sponsored loans, scholarships/grants, and unspecified assistantships also available. Support available to part-time students. Financial award application deadline: 3/1; financial award applicants required to submit FAFSA. *Faculty research:* Health and security of military families, personal and family risk assessment and evaluation, disorders of communication and swallowing, families and health. Total annual research expenditures: $6.3 million. *Unit head:* Dr. William Meredith, Head, 785-532-1472, Fax: 785-532-5505, E-mail: meredith@ksu.edu. *Application contact:* Connie Fechter, Application Contact, 785-532-1473, Fax: 785-532-5505, E-mail: fechter@ksu.edu.

Loma Linda University, School of Science and Technology, Department of Counseling and Family Science, Loma Linda, CA 92350. Offers MA, MS, DMFT, PhD, Certificate, MA/Certificate. *Degree requirements:* For master's, comprehensive exam, thesis optional; for doctorate, comprehensive exam, thesis/dissertation (for some programs). *Entrance requirements:* For master's, minimum 3.0 GPA; for doctorate, GRE. Additional exam requirements/recommendations for international students: Required—TOEFL (minimum score 550 paper-based; 213 computer-based), MTELP. Electronic applications accepted.

Miami University, Graduate School, School of Education and Allied Professions, Department of Family Studies and Social Work, Oxford, OH 45056. Offers child and family studies (MS). Part-time programs available. *Degree requirements:* For master's, thesis or alternative, final exam. *Entrance requirements:* For master's, MAT, minimum undergraduate GPA of 3.0 during previous 2 years or 2.75 overall.

Michigan State University, The Graduate School, College of Social Science, Department of Family and Child Ecology, East Lansing, MI 48824. Offers child development (MA); community services (MS); family and child ecology (PhD); family studies (MA); marriage and family therapy (MA); youth development (MA). *Accreditation:* AAMFT/COAMFTE (one or more programs are accredited). *Entrance requirements:* For master's, GRE General Test, minimum GPA of 3.0 in last 2 years of undergraduate course work, 3 letters of recommendation; for doctorate, GRE General Test, minimum GPA of 3.0, 3 letters of recommendation, background in behavioral sciences. Additional exam requirements/recommendations for international students: Required—TOEFL. Electronic applications accepted.

Middle Tennessee State University, College of Graduate Studies, College of Education and Behavioral Science, Department of Human Sciences, Murfreesboro, TN 37132. Offers child development and family studies (MS); nutrition and food science (MS). Part-time and evening/weekend programs available. Postbaccalaureate distance learning degree programs offered. *Degree requirements:* For master's, comprehensive exam, thesis. *Entrance requirements:* For master's, GRE or MAT. Additional exam requirements/recommendations for international students: Required—TOEFL (paper-based 525; computer-based 195; IBT 71) or IELTS (6.0). Electronic applications accepted. *Faculty research:* Courtship relationships, feminist methodology and epistemology in family studies, school uniforms, body fat in elderly, asynchronous distance education.

Missouri State University, Graduate College, College of Education, Department of Childhood Education and Family Studies, Program in Early Childhood and Family Development, Springfield, MO 65804-0094. Offers MS. Part-time programs available. Postbaccalaureate distance learning degree programs offered. *Students:* 6 full-time (all women), 8 part-time (all women). Average age 27. 4 applicants, 100% accepted, 4 enrolled. In 2008, 2 master's awarded. *Entrance requirements:* For master's, GRE, minimum GPA of 3.0. Additional exam requirements/recommendations for international students: Required—TOEFL (minimum score 550 paper-based; 213 computer-based; 79 iBT). *Application deadline:* For fall admission, 7/20 priority date for domestic students, 5/1 for international students; for spring admission, 12/20 priority date for domestic students, 9/1 for international students. Applications are processed on a rolling basis. Application fee: $35 ($50 for international students). Electronic applications accepted. *Expenses:* Tuition, state resident: full-time $3852; part-time $214 per credit hour. Tuition, nonresident: full-time $7524; part-time $418 per credit hour. Required fees: $230 per semester. Tuition and fees vary according to course level and course load. *Financial support:* In 2008–09, 2 research assistantships with full tuition reimbursements (averaging $7,340 per year) were awarded; teaching assistantships with full tuition reimbursements, Federal Work-Study, institutionally sponsored loans, scholarships/grants, and unspecified assistantships

Child and Family Studies

Missouri State University (continued)
also available. Financial award application deadline: 3/31; financial award applicants required to submit FAFSA. *Unit head:* Dr. Sue George, Program Director, 417-836-5984, Fax: 417-836-8900, E-mail: suegeorge@missouristate.edu. *Application contact:* Eric Eckert, Coordinator of Admissions and Recruitment, 417-836-5331, Fax: 417-836-6888, E-mail: ericeckert@missouristate.edu.

Mount Saint Vincent University, Graduate Programs, Department of Child and Youth Study, Halifax, NS B3M 2J6, Canada. Offers MA. Part-time and evening/weekend programs available. *Degree requirements:* For master's, thesis. *Entrance requirements:* For master's, bachelor's degree in related field, minimum B+ average, professional experience. Electronic applications accepted.

Mount Saint Vincent University, Graduate Programs, Department of Family Studies and Gerontology, Halifax, NS B3M 2J6, Canada. Offers MA. Part-time programs available. Postbaccalaureate distance learning degree programs offered (minimal on-campus study). *Degree requirements:* For master's, thesis. *Entrance requirements:* For master's, minimum GPA of 3.0; course work in statistics, research methods, family and social theories.

North Dakota State University, College of Graduate and Interdisciplinary Studies, College of Human Development and Education, Department of Child Development and Family Science, Fargo, ND 58105. Offers child development and family science (MS); couple and family therapy (MS); family financial planning (MS); gerontology (MS, PhD). *Accreditation:* AAMFT/COAMFTE. Part-time and evening/weekend programs available. Postbaccalaureate distance learning degree programs offered (no on-campus study). *Faculty:* 12 full-time (7 women). *Students:* 26 full-time (25 women), 21 part-time (18 women); includes 1 African American, 2 international. 22 applicants, 64% accepted, 12 enrolled. In 2008, 12 master's awarded. *Degree requirements:* For master's, thesis or alternative; for doctorate, thesis/dissertation. *Entrance requirements:* Additional exam requirements/recommendations for international students: Required—TOEFL (minimum score 525 paper-based; 197 computer-based; 71 iBT). *Application deadline:* For fall admission, 2/1 for domestic and international students; for spring admission, 10/1 for domestic and international students. Application fee: $45 ($60 for international students). *Financial support:* In 2008–09, 17 students received support, including research assistantships with full tuition reimbursements available (averaging $3,000 per year), 17 teaching assistantships with full tuition reimbursements available (averaging $3,000 per year); career-related internships or fieldwork, Federal Work-Study, institutionally sponsored loans, and tuition waivers (full) also available. Financial award application deadline: 4/1. *Faculty research:* Family therapy, resilience, parenting, adolescent development, mental health. Total annual research expenditures: $333,582. *Unit head:* Dr. James Deal, Head, 701-231-7568, Fax: 701-231-9645, E-mail: jim_deal@ndsu.edu. *Application contact:* Theresa Anderson, Administrative Assistant, 701-231-8628, Fax: 701-231-9645, E-mail: theresa.anderson@ndsu.edu.

Northern Illinois University, Graduate School, College of Health and Human Sciences, School of Family, Consumer and Nutrition Sciences, De Kalb, IL 60115-2854. Offers applied family and child studies (MS); nutrition and dietetics (MS). *Accreditation:* AAMFT/COAMFTE. Part-time programs available. *Degree requirements:* For master's, comprehensive exam, internship, thesis (nutrition and dietetics). *Entrance requirements:* For master's, GRE General Test, minimum GPA of 2.75. Additional exam requirements/recommendations for international students: Required—TOEFL (minimum score 550 paper-based; 213 computer-based). Electronic applications accepted. *Faculty research:* Preliminary child development, hospitality administration in Asia, sports nutrition, eating disorders.

Nova Southeastern University, Fischler School of Education and Human Services, Programs in Human Services, Fort Lauderdale, FL 33314-7796. Offers child and youth studies (Ed D); child protection (MHS); education (MS), including human services; health professions education (MS); substance abuse counseling and education (MS). Part-time and evening/weekend programs available. *Students:* 138 full-time (118 women), 11 part-time (10 women); includes 99 minority (80 African Americans, 2 Asian Americans or Pacific Islanders, 17 Hispanic Americans), 2 international. In 2008, 8 master's, 57 doctorates awarded. *Degree requirements:* For master's, thesis, practicum; for doctorate, thesis/dissertation, practicum. *Entrance requirements:* For master's, GRE or MAT, work experience in field, minimum GPA of 2.5; for doctorate, GRE or MAT, master's degree, minimum GPA of 3.0, work experience. Additional exam requirements/recommendations for international students: Recommended—TOEFL (minimum score 550 paper-based; 213 computer-based), IELTS (minimum score 6). *Application deadline:* Applications are processed on a rolling basis. Application fee: $50. Electronic applications accepted. *Expenses:* Contact institution. *Financial support:* Career-related internships or fieldwork and Federal Work-Study available. Support available to part-time students. Financial award application deadline: 4/15; financial award applicants required to submit FAFSA. *Unit head:* Dr. Elda Veloso, Associate Dean, 954-262-8538, Fax: 954-262-2917, E-mail: veloso@nova.edu. *Application contact:* Dr. Jennifer Quinones Nottingham, Dean of Student Affairs, 800-986-3223 Ext. 8500.

The Ohio State University, Graduate School, College of Education and Human Ecology, Department of Human Development and Family Science, Columbus, OH 43210. Offers M Ed, MS, PhD. *Degree requirements:* For master's, thesis optional; for doctorate, thesis/dissertation. *Entrance requirements:* For master's and doctorate, GRE General Test. Additional exam requirements/recommendations for international students: Required—TOEFL (minimum score 577 paper-based; 233 computer-based). Electronic applications accepted.

Ohio University, Graduate College, College of Health and Human Services, School of Human and Consumer Sciences, Athens, OH 45701-2979. Offers child development and family life (MS); early childhood education (MS); family studies (MS); food and nutrition (MS). Part-time programs available. *Degree requirements:* For master's, thesis. *Entrance requirements:* For master's, GRE. Additional exam requirements/recommendations for international students: Required—TOEFL. Electronic applications accepted. *Faculty research:* Diversity, developmentally appropriate activities, death and dying, gerontology, sexuality education.

Oklahoma State University, College of Human Environmental Sciences, Department of Human Development and Family Science, Stillwater, OK 74078. Offers MS, PhD. *Accreditation:* AAMFT/COAMFTE (one or more programs are accredited). Postbaccalaureate distance learning degree programs offered. *Faculty:* 30 full-time (21 women), 7 part-time/adjunct (6 women). *Students:* 21 full-time (15 women), 47 part-time (38 women); includes 7 minority (1 African American, 4 American Indian/Alaska Native, 2 Hispanic Americans), 6 international. Average age 31. 57 applicants, 37% accepted, 18 enrolled. In 2008, 16 master's awarded. *Degree requirements:* For master's, thesis (for some programs); for doctorate, comprehensive exam, thesis/dissertation. *Entrance requirements:* For master's and doctorate, GRE or GMAT. Additional exam requirements/recommendations for international students: Required—TOEFL. *Application deadline:* For fall admission, 3/1 priority date for international students; for spring admission, 8/1 priority date for international students. Applications are processed on a rolling basis. Application fee: $40 ($75 for international students). Electronic applications accepted. *Expenses:* Tuition, state resident: full-time $3716.40; part-time $154.85 per credit hour. Tuition, nonresident: full-time $14,448; part-time $602 per credit hour. Required fees: $1772.40; $73.85 per credit hour. One-time fee: $50. Tuition and fees vary according to course load and campus/location. *Financial support:* In 2008–09, 30 research assistantships (averaging $10,352 per year), 14 teaching assistantships (averaging $9,044 per year) were awarded; career-related internships or fieldwork, Federal Work-Study, scholarships/grants, health care benefits, tuition waivers (partial), and unspecified assistantships also available. Support available to part-time students. Financial award application deadline: 3/1; financial award applicants required to submit FAFSA. *Faculty research:* Family relations and child development, consequences of adolescent parenting, family stress and coping, impacts of sexual abuse on families, children's social cognition and self-competence, gerontology and health care. *Unit head:* Dr. Sue Williams, Head, 405-744-5057, Fax: 405-744-2800. *Application contact:* Dr. Gordon Emslie, Dean, 405-744-6368, Fax: 405-744-0355, E-mail: grad_i@okstate.edu.

Oregon State University, Graduate School, College of Health and Human Sciences, Department of Human Development and Family Sciences, Corvallis, OR 97331. Offers gerontology (MAIS); human development and family studies (MS, PhD). *Degree requirements:* For doctorate, thesis/dissertation. *Entrance requirements:* For master's and doctorate, GRE, minimum GPA of 3.0 in last 90 hours. Additional exam requirements/recommendations for international students: Required—TOEFL.

Oxford Graduate School, Graduate Programs, Dayton, TN 37321-6736. Offers family life education (M Litt); organizational leadership in nonprofits (M Litt); religion and society (D Phil).

Penn State University Park, Graduate School, College of Health and Human Development, Department of Human Development and Family Studies, State College, University Park, PA 16802-1503. Offers MS, PhD.

Purdue University, Graduate School, College of Consumer and Family Sciences, Department of Child Development and Family Studies, West Lafayette, IN 47907. Offers developmental studies (MS, PhD); family studies (MS, PhD); marriage and family therapy (MS, PhD). *Accreditation:* AAMFT/COAMFTE (one or more programs are accredited). Part-time programs available. Terminal master's awarded for partial completion of doctoral program. *Degree requirements:* For master's, thesis; for doctorate, thesis/dissertation. *Entrance requirements:* For master's and doctorate, GRE General Test. Additional exam requirements/recommendations for international students: Required—TWE. Electronic applications accepted. *Faculty research:* Inclusion of children with special needs, families as learning environments, relationships in child care, work-family relations, AIDS prevention.

Roberts Wesleyan College, Division of Social Work, Rochester, NY 14624-1997. Offers child and family practice (MSW); congregational and community practice (MSW); mental health practice (MSW). *Accreditation:* CSWE. *Entrance requirements:* For master's, minimum GPA of 2.75. *Faculty research:* Religion and social work, family studies, values and ethics.

Sage Graduate School, Graduate School, Department of Psychology, Program in Community Psychology, Troy, NY 12180-4115. Offers child care and children's services (MA); community counseling (MA); community health education (MA); counseling and community psychology (MA); general psychology (MA). Part-time and evening/weekend programs available. *Faculty:* 4 full-time (all women), 5 part-time/adjunct (2 women). *Students:* 24 full-time (23 women), 58 part-time (54 women); includes 12 minority (6 African Americans, 2 American Indian/Alaska Native, 4 Hispanic Americans). Average age 30. 39 applicants, 54% accepted, 11 enrolled. In 2008, 29 master's awarded. *Degree requirements:* For master's, thesis or alternative. *Entrance requirements:* For master's, minimum GPA of 2.75; official transcripts; 2 letters of reference; undergraduate courses in statistics, history, and systems of psychology; three other courses in behavioral science; personal prospectus statement; current resumée. Additional exam requirements/recommendations for international students: Required—TOEFL (minimum score 550 paper-based; 213 computer-based). *Application deadline:* Applications are processed on a rolling basis. Application fee: $40. *Expenses:* Tuition: Full-time $10,080; part-time $560 per credit hour. *Financial support:* Fellowships, research assistantships, teaching assistantships, Federal Work-Study, scholarships/grants, and unspecified assistantships available. Support available to part-time students. Financial award application deadline: 3/1; financial award applicants required to submit FAFSA. *Unit head:* Dr. Bronna Romanoff, Director, 518-244-2260, E-mail: romanb@sage.edu. *Application contact:* Wendy D. Diefendorf, Director of Graduate and Adult Admission, 518-244-2443, Fax: 518-244-6880, E-mail: diefew@sage.edu.

St. Cloud State University, School of Graduate Studies, College of Education, Department of Child and Family Studies, St. Cloud, MN 56301-4498. Offers MS. *Degree requirements:* For master's, thesis or alternative. *Entrance requirements:* For master's, GRE General Test, minimum GPA of 2.75. Additional exam requirements/recommendations for international students: Required—Michigan English Language Assessment Battery; Recommended—TOEFL (minimum score 550 paper-based; 213 computer-based), IELTS (minimum score 6.5). Electronic applications accepted.

Saint Joseph College, Graduate School, Department of Counselor Education, West Hartford, CT 06117-2700. Offers community counseling (MA), including child welfare; school counseling (MA). Part-time and evening/weekend programs available. *Students:* 28 full-time (26 women), 84 part-time (74 women). *Degree requirements:* For master's, comprehensive exam, thesis optional, capstone project. *Entrance requirements:* For master's, PRAXIS I (school counseling), 2 letters of recommendation. *Application deadline:* Applications are processed on a rolling basis. Application fee: $50. Electronic applications accepted. *Expenses:* Tuition: Part-time $560 per credit. Required fees: $30 per credit. *Financial support:* Career-related internships or fieldwork, health care benefits, and unspecified assistantships available. Support available to part-time students. Financial award applicants required to submit FAFSA. *Application contact:* Graduate Admissions Office, 860-231-5261, E-mail: graduate@sjc.edu.

San Diego State University, Graduate and Research Affairs, College of Education, Department of Child and Family Development, San Diego, CA 92182. Offers child development (MS). Part-time programs available. *Degree requirements:* For master's, thesis. *Entrance requirements:* For master's, GRE General Test, 3 letters of recommendation, interview. Additional exam requirements/recommendations for international students: Required—TOEFL. Electronic applications accepted.

San Jose State University, Graduate Studies and Research, College of Education, Department of Child and Adolescent Development, San Jose, CA 95192-0001. Offers MA. Electronic applications accepted.

South Carolina State University, School of Graduate Studies, Department of Family and Consumer Sciences, Orangeburg, SC 29117-0001. Offers individual and family development (MS); nutritional sciences (MS). Part-time and evening/weekend programs available. *Faculty:* 2 full-time (both women). *Students:* 13 full-time (all women), 15 part-time (13 women); includes 27 minority (all African Americans). Average age 33. 8 applicants, 88% accepted, 7 enrolled. In 2008, 12 master's awarded. *Degree requirements:* For master's, comprehensive exam, thesis optional, departmental qualifying exam. *Entrance requirements:* For master's, GRE, MAT, or NTE, minimum GPA of 2.7. *Application deadline:* For fall admission, 6/15 priority date for domestic students, 6/15 for international students; for spring admission, 11/1 for domestic and international students. Applications are processed on a rolling basis. Application fee: $25. Electronic applications accepted. *Expenses:* Tuition, state resident: full-time $7806; part-time $434 per credit hour. Tuition, nonresident: full-time $15,298; part-time $850 per credit hour. *Financial support:* In 2008–09, 3 fellowships (averaging $6,319 per year) were awarded; institutionally sponsored loans also available. Financial award application deadline: 6/1. *Faculty research:* Societal competence, relationship of parent-child interaction to adult, quality of well-being of rural elders. *Unit head:* Dr. Ethel G. Jones, Chair, 803-536-8958, Fax: 803-533-3268, E-mail: egjones@scsu.edu. *Application contact:* Annette Hazzard-Jones, Program Coordinator II, 803-536-8809, Fax: 803-536-8812, E-mail: zs_ahazzard@scsu.edu.

Spring Arbor University, School of Graduate and Professional Studies, Spring Arbor, MI 49283-9799. Offers counseling (MAC); family studies (MAFS); nursing (MSN); organizational management (MAOM). Part-time and evening/weekend programs available. Postbaccalaureate distance learning degree programs offered (no on-campus study). *Faculty:* 8 full-time (3 women), 99 part-time/adjunct (45 women). *Students:* 509 full-time (427 women), 306 part-time (245 women); includes 208 minority (179 African Americans, 2 American Indian/Alaska Native, 9 Asian Americans or Pacific Islanders, 18 Hispanic Americans), 3 international. Average age 39. In 2008, 249 master's awarded. *Entrance requirements:* For master's, minimum GPA of 3.0, interview, writing sample, 2 professional references. Additional exam requirements/recommendations for international students: Required—TOEFL (minimum score 550 paper-based; 220 computer-based). *Application deadline:* Applications are processed on a rolling basis. Application fee: $40. Electronic applications accepted. *Expenses:* Tuition: Full-time $5280; part-time $440 per credit hour. Required fees: $240; $150. Tuition and fees vary according to program. *Financial support:* Scholarships/grants available. Support available to part-time students. Financial award applicants required to submit FAFSA. *Unit head:* Dr. Robert Hamill, Dean of Graduate and Professional Studies, 517-750-1200 Ext. 1343, Fax: 517-750-6602, E-mail: rhamill@arbor.edu. *Application contact:* John Ball, Coordinator of Admissions, GPS Undergraduate Programs, 517-750-6459, Fax: 517-750-6602, E-mail: jball@arbor.edu.

Stanford University, School of Education, Program in Psychological Studies in Education, Stanford, CA 94305-9991. Offers child and adolescent development (PhD); counseling psychology (PhD); educational psychology (PhD). *Degree requirements:* For doctorate, thesis/dissertation. *Entrance requirements:* For doctorate, GRE General Test. Electronic applications accepted.

State University of New York at Oswego, Graduate Studies, School of Education, Department of Vocational Teacher Preparation, Oswego, NY 13126. Offers agriculture (MS Ed); business and marketing (MS Ed); family and consumer sciences (MS Ed); health careers (MS Ed); technical education (MS Ed); trade education (MS Ed). *Accreditation:* NCATE. Part-time and evening/weekend programs available. *Degree requirements:* For master's, thesis or alternative. *Entrance requirements:* Additional exam requirements/recommendations for international students: Required—TOEFL (minimum score 560 paper-based; 220 computer-based).

Syracuse University, Graduate School, College of Human Ecology, Program in Child and Family Studies, Syracuse, NY 13244. Offers MA, MS, PhD. *Accreditation:* AAMFT/COAMFTE (one or more programs are accredited). Part-time programs available. *Degree requirements:* For master's, comprehensive exam (for some programs); for doctorate, thesis/dissertation. *Entrance requirements:* For master's and doctorate, GRE General Test. Additional exam requirements/recommendations for international students: Required—TOEFL. Electronic applications accepted.

Texas State University–San Marcos, Graduate School, College of Applied Arts, Department of Family and Consumer Science, Program in Family and Child Studies, San Marcos, TX 78666. Offers MS. *Degree requirements:* For master's, thesis (for some programs). *Entrance requirements:* For master's, minimum GPA of 2.75 in last 60 hours of course work. Additional exam requirements/recommendations for international students: Required—TOEFL (minimum score 550 paper-based; 213 computer-based).

Texas Tech University, Graduate School, College of Human Sciences, Department of Human Development and Family Studies, Lubbock, TX 79409. Offers gerontology (MS); human development and family studies (MS, PhD). *Accreditation:* AAMFT/COAMFTE (one or more programs are accredited). Part-time programs available. *Faculty:* 19 full-time (15 women), 1 (woman) part-time/adjunct. *Students:* 38 full-time (30 women), 18 part-time (11 women); includes 9 minority (2 African Americans, 2 American Indian/Alaska Native, 2 Asian Americans or Pacific Islanders, 3 Hispanic Americans), 13 international. Average age 36. 32 applicants, 78% accepted, 7 enrolled. In 2008, 7 master's awarded. *Degree requirements:* For master's, thesis; for doctorate, thesis/dissertation. *Entrance requirements:* For master's and doctorate, GRE General Test. Additional exam requirements/recommendations for international students: Required—TOEFL (minimum score 550 paper-based; 213 computer-based). *Application deadline:* For fall admission, 3/1 priority date for international students; for spring admission, 11/1 priority date for international students. Applications are processed on a rolling basis. Application fee: $50 ($60 for international students). Electronic applications accepted. *Expenses:* Tuition, area resident: Part-time $194 per credit hour. Tuition, state resident: full-time $4648; part-time $194 per credit hour. Tuition, nonresident: full-time $11,392; part-time $475 per credit hour. Required fees: $2206; $69 per credit hour. $389 per semester. *Financial support:* In 2008–09, 55 students received support, including 3 research assistantships with partial tuition reimbursements available (averaging $13,107 per year), 30 teaching assistantships with partial tuition reimbursements available (averaging $13,126 per year); career-related internships or fieldwork, Federal Work-Study, institutionally sponsored loans, and scholarships/grants also available. Support available to part-time students. Financial award application deadline: 4/15; financial award applicants required to submit FAFSA. *Faculty research:* Parenting, marital and premarital relationships, adolescent risky behaviors, life span; child development. Total annual research expenditures: $352,679. *Unit head:* Anisa Zvonkovic, Chair, 806-742-3000 Ext. 279, Fax: 806-742-0285, E-mail: anisa.zvonkovic@ttu.edu. *Application contact:* Monya Castle, Graduate Secretary, 806-742-3000 Ext. 250, Fax: 806-742-0285, E-mail: monya.castle@ttu.edu.

Texas Woman's University, Graduate School, College of Professional Education, Department of Family Sciences, Denton, TX 76201. Offers child development (MS, PhD); counseling and development (MS); early childhood education (M Ed, MA, MS, Ed D); family studies (MS, PhD); family therapy (MS, PhD). *Accreditation:* ACA (one or more programs are accredited). Part-time and evening/weekend programs available. *Faculty:* 22 full-time (17 women), 11 part-time/adjunct (10 women). *Students:* 90 full-time (86 women), 317 part-time (294 women); includes 133 minority (92 African Americans, 3 American Indian/Alaska Native, 9 Asian Americans or Pacific Islanders, 29 Hispanic Americans), 18 international. Average age 37. In 2008, 91 master's, 24 doctorates awarded. *Degree requirements:* For doctorate, comprehensive exam, thesis/dissertation. *Entrance requirements:* For master's, interview, writing sample; for doctorate, interview, minimum GPA of 3.25 in last 60 hours of course work. Additional exam requirements/recommendations for international students: Required—TOEFL (minimum score 550 paper-based; 213 computer-based; 79 iBT). *Application deadline:* For fall admission, 2/15 for domestic students, 4/15 for international students; for spring admission, 9/15 for domestic students, 8/1 for international students. Applications are processed on a rolling basis. Application fee: $30 ($50 for international students). Electronic applications accepted. *Expenses:* Tuition, state resident: full-time $3564; part-time $198 per semester hour. Tuition, nonresident: full-time $8622; part-time $479 per semester hour. Required fees: $1158; $64 per semester hour. Tuition and fees vary according to course load. *Financial support:* In 2008–09, 18 research assistantships (averaging $10,746 per year), 10 teaching assistantships (averaging $10,746 per year) were awarded; career-related internships or fieldwork, Federal Work-Study, institutionally sponsored loans, scholarships/grants, traineeships, health care benefits, and unspecified assistantships also available. Support available to part-time students. Financial award application deadline: 3/1; financial award applicants required to submit FAFSA. *Faculty research:* Parenting/parent education, distance education, play therapy, family sexuality, diversity, ANTHEM healthy marriages initiative. *Unit head:* Dr. Larry LeFlore, Chair, 940-898-2685, Fax: 940-898-2676, E-mail: famsci@twu.edu. *Application contact:* Samuel Wheeler, Assistant Director of Admissions, 940-898-3188, Fax: 940-898-3081, E-mail: wheelersr@twu.edu.

Towson University, College of Graduate Studies and Research, Program in Family-Professional Collaboration, Towson, MD 21252-0001. Offers Certificate.

Tufts University, Graduate School of Arts and Sciences, Department of Child Development, Medford, MA 02155. Offers applied developmental psychology (PhD); child development (MA, CAGS); early childhood education (MAT). Part-time programs available. *Degree requirements:* For master's, thesis (for some programs); for doctorate, thesis/dissertation. *Entrance requirements:* For master's and doctorate, GRE General Test. Additional exam requirements/recommendations for international students: Required—TOEFL (minimum score 550 paper-based; 213 computer-based; 80 iBT). Electronic applications accepted.

The University of Akron, Graduate School, College of Fine and Applied Arts, School of Family and Consumer Sciences, Program in Child and Family Development, Akron, OH 44325. Offers child development (MA); family development (MA). *Degree requirements:* For master's, comprehensive exam, thesis optional, project or thesis. *Entrance requirements:* For master's, GRE, minimum GPA of 2.75, letters of recommendation, personal statement of goals; interview. Additional exam requirements/recommendations for international students: Required—TOEFL (minimum score 550 paper-based; 213 computer-based; 79 iBT). Electronic applications accepted.

The University of Akron, Graduate School, College of Fine and Applied Arts, School of Family and Consumer Sciences, Program in Child Life, Akron, OH 44325. Offers MA. *Degree requirements:* For master's, comprehensive exam, thesis optional, project or thesis. *Entrance requirements:* For master's, GRE, minimum GPA of 2.75, letters of recommendation, personal statement of goals, interview. Additional exam requirements/recommendations for international students: Required—TOEFL (minimum score 550 paper-based; 213 computer-based; 79 iBT). Electronic applications accepted.

The University of Alabama, Graduate School, College of Human Environmental Sciences, Department of Human Development and Family Studies, Tuscaloosa, AL 35487. Offers MSHES. *Faculty:* 7 full-time (5 women). *Students:* 20 full-time (all women), 10 part-time (all women); includes 5 African Americans, 1 Asian American or Pacific Islander, 1 international. Average age 26. 26 applicants, 58% accepted, 9 enrolled. In 2008, 13 master's awarded. *Degree requirements:* For master's, thesis (for some programs). *Entrance requirements:* For master's, GRE General Test or MAT, minimum GPA of 3.0. Additional exam requirements/recommendations for international students: Required—TOEFL. *Application deadline:* For fall admission, 2/1 priority date for domestic and international students. Applications are processed on a rolling basis. Application fee: $50. Electronic applications accepted. *Expenses:* Tuition, area resident: Full-time $6400. Tuition, state resident: full-time $6400. Tuition, nonresident: full-time $18,000. *Financial support:* In 2008–09, 11 students received support, including 1 fellowship with full tuition reimbursement available (averaging $15,000 per year), 6 research assistantships with full tuition reimbursements available (averaging $10,908 per year), 4 teaching assistantships (averaging $10,908 per year); career-related internships or fieldwork, Federal Work-Study, scholarships/grants, and health care benefits also available. Financial award application deadline: 3/15. *Faculty research:* Parent/child relationships, preschool curricula and quality measures for child care programs, family strengths and adolescent behaviors, depression in mothers and infants, word association and word learning in young children. *Unit head:* Dr. Carroll M. Tingle, Chair, 205-348-6158, Fax: 205-348-8153, E-mail: ctingle@ches.ua.edu. *Application contact:* Dr. Maria Hernandez-Reif, Associate Professor, 205-348-5894, E-mail: mhernandez-reif@ches.ua.edu.

The University of Arizona, Graduate College, College of Agriculture and Life Sciences, School of Family and Consumer Sciences, Division of Family Studies and Human Development, Tucson, AZ 85721. Offers family and consumer sciences education (MS); family studies and human development (PhD). Terminal master's awarded for partial completion of doctoral program. *Entrance requirements:* For master's, GRE General Test, minimum undergraduate GPA of 3.0, personal resumé, personal statement, 3 letters of recommendation. Additional exam requirements/recommendations for international students: Required—TOEFL.

University of California, Santa Barbara, Graduate Division, Gevirtz Graduate School of Education, Santa Barbara, CA 93106-9490. Offers counseling, clinical and school psychology (PhD), including clinical psychology, counseling psychology, school psychology; education (M Ed, MA, PhD), including child and adolescent development (MA, PhD), cultural perspectives and comparative education (MA, PhD), educational leadership and organizations (MA, PhD), research methodology (MA, PhD), special education disabilities and risk studies (MA), special education, disabilities and risk studies (PhD), teaching (M Ed), teaching and learning (MA, PhD); educational leadership (Ed D); school psychology (M Ed); MA/PhD. *Accreditation:* APA (one or more programs are accredited). Postbaccalaureate distance learning degree programs offered (minimal on-campus study). *Faculty:* 42 full-time (20 women), 10 part-time/adjunct (4 women). *Students:* 390 full-time (303 women); includes 149 minority (14 African Americans, 3 American Indian/Alaska Native, 57 Asian Americans or Pacific Islanders, 75 Hispanic Americans), 16 international. Average age 31. 717 applicants, 40% accepted, 170 enrolled. In 2008, 140 master's, 46 doctorates awarded. Terminal master's awarded for partial completion of doctoral program. *Degree requirements:* For master's, comprehensive exam (for some programs), thesis (for some programs); for doctorate, comprehensive exam (for some programs), thesis/dissertation, qualifying exam. *Entrance requirements:* For master's and doctorate, GRE, 3 letters of recommendation, statement of purpose, personal achievements/contributions statement, resumé/curriculum vitae, transcripts for post-secondary institutions attended. Additional exam requirements/recommendations for international students: Required—TOEFL (minimum score 550 paper-based; 213 computer-based; 80 iBT), IELTS (minimum score 7), TOEFL or IELTS. Application fee: $70 ($90 for international students). Electronic applications accepted. *Expenses:* Tuition, nonresident: full-time $25,149. Required fees: $10,143. Full-time tuition and fees vary according to campus/location, reciprocity agreements and student level. *Financial support:* In 2008–09, 253 students received support, including 206 fellowships with full and partial tuition reimbursements available (averaging $5,000 per year), 62 research assistantships with full and partial tuition reimbursements available (averaging $6,200 per year), 87 teaching assistantships with partial tuition reimbursements available (averaging $6,500 per year); career-related internships or fieldwork, Federal Work-Study, institutionally sponsored loans, scholarships/grants, traineeships, health care benefits, and unspecified assistantships also available. Financial award applicants required to submit FAFSA. *Faculty research:* Professional development, early childhood development, school violence, literacy, science/math initiative. Total annual research expenditures: $4.4 million. *Unit head:* Dr. Jane Conoley, Chair, 805-893-2185, E-mail: jane-conoley@education.ucsb.edu. *Application contact:* Kathryn Marie Tucciarone, Student Affairs Officer, 805-893-2137, E-mail: katiet@education.ucsb.edu.

University of Central Florida, College of Health and Public Affairs, School of Social Work, Orlando, FL 32816. Offers addictions (Certificate); aging studies (Certificate); children's services (Certificate); school social work (Certificate); social work (MSW); social work administration (Certificate). *Accreditation:* CSWE. Part-time and evening/weekend programs available. *Faculty:* 15 full-time (11 women), 17 part-time/adjunct (15 women). *Students:* 113 full-time (99 women), 79 part-time (64 women); includes 61 minority (35 African Americans, 1 American Indian/Alaska Native, 2 Asian Americans or Pacific Islanders, 23 Hispanic Americans), 2 international. In 2008, 80 master's, 15 other advanced degrees awarded. *Degree requirements:* For master's, thesis or alternative, field education. *Entrance requirements:* For master's, resumé. Additional exam requirements/recommendations for international students: Required—TOEFL. *Application deadline:* For fall admission, 3/1 for domestic students. Application fee: $30. Electronic applications accepted. *Expenses:* Tuition, area resident: Full-time $6816; part-time $284 per credit. Tuition, state resident: full-time $6816; part-time $1076 per credit. Tuition, nonresident: full-time $25,824. Required fees: $216; $9 per credit. *Financial support:* In 2008–09, 2 fellowships with partial tuition reimbursements (averaging $10,000 per year), 18 research assistantships with partial tuition reimbursements (averaging $6,800 per year) were awarded; teaching assistantships with partial tuition reimbursements, career-related internships or fieldwork, Federal Work-Study, institutionally sponsored loans, and unspecified assistantships also available. Financial award application deadline: 3/1; financial award applicants required to submit FAFSA. *Unit head:* Dr. John Ronnau, Director, 407-823-2114, Fax: 407-823-5697, E-mail: jronnau@mail.ucf.edu. *Application contact:* Dr. John Ronnau, Director, 407-823-2114, Fax: 407-823-5697, E-mail: jronnau@mail.ucf.edu.

University of Connecticut, Graduate School, College of Liberal Arts and Sciences, Department of Human Development and Family Studies, Field of Human Development and Family Studies, Storrs, CT 06269. Offers culture, health and human development (Graduate Certificate); human development and family studies (MA, PhD). *Accreditation:* AAMFT/COAMFTE. Terminal master's awarded for partial completion of doctoral program. *Degree requirements:* For master's, comprehensive exam; for doctorate, thesis/dissertation. *Entrance requirements:* For master's and doctorate, GRE General Test. Additional exam requirements/recommendations for international students: Required—TOEFL (minimum score 550 paper-based; 213 computer-based). Electronic applications accepted.

University of Delaware, College of Human Services, Education and Public Policy, Department of Individual and Family Studies, Newark, DE 19716. Offers human development and family studies (MS, PhD). Part-time programs available. Terminal master's awarded for partial completion of doctoral program. *Degree requirements:* For master's, thesis or alternative; for

Child and Family Studies

University of Delaware (continued)

doctorate, comprehensive exam, thesis/dissertation. *Entrance requirements:* For master's and doctorate, GRE General Test, 3 letters of recommendation. Additional exam requirements/recommendations for international students: Required—TOEFL. Electronic applications accepted. *Faculty research:* Early childhood inclusive education, relationships, family risk and resilience, disability issues, program development and evaluation.

University of Denver, College of Education, Denver, CO 80208. Offers counseling psychology (MA, PhD); curriculum and instruction (MA, PhD, Certificate), including curriculum leadership (MA, PhD); educational administration and policy studies (Certificate); educational psychology (MA, PhD, Ed S), including child and family studies (MA, PhD), quantitative research methods (MA, PhD), school psychology (PhD, Ed S); higher education and adult studies (MA, PhD); library and information science (MLIS); library and information sciences (Certificate); school administration (PhD). *Accreditation:* ALA; APA (one or more programs are accredited). Part-time and evening/weekend programs available. Postbaccalaureate distance learning degree programs offered (no on-campus study). *Faculty:* 30 full-time (20 women), 58 part-time/adjunct (40 women). *Students:* 334 full-time (259 women), 454 part-time (350 women); includes 136 minority (28 African Americans, 8 American Indian/Alaska Native, 14 Asian Americans or Pacific Islanders, 86 Hispanic Americans), 20 international. Average age 34. 851 applicants, 76% accepted, 356 enrolled. In 2008, 214 master's, 43 doctorates, 85 other advanced degrees awarded. Terminal master's awarded for partial completion of doctoral program. *Degree requirements:* For master's, comprehensive exam; for doctorate, 2 foreign languages, comprehensive exam, thesis/dissertation. *Entrance requirements:* For master's and doctorate, GRE General Test or MAT. *Application deadline:* Applications are processed on a rolling basis. Application fee: $50. Electronic applications accepted. *Financial support:* In 2008–09, 74 teaching assistantships with full and partial tuition reimbursements (averaging $6,000 per year) were awarded; career-related internships or fieldwork, Federal Work-Study, institutionally sponsored loans, and scholarships/grants also available. Support available to part-time students. Financial award application deadline: 3/1; financial award applicants required to submit FAFSA. *Faculty research:* Parkinson's disease, personnel training, development and assessments, gifted education, service learning, transportation, public schools. Total annual research expenditures: $340,000. *Unit head:* Dr. Cheryl Lovell, Associate Dean, 303-871-2479. *Application contact:* Linda McCarthy, Student Services Coordinator, 303-871-2509, E-mail: edinfo@du.edu.

University of Georgia, Graduate School, College of Education, Department of Elementary and Social Studies Education, Athens, GA 30602. Offers early childhood education (M Ed, MAT, PhD, Ed S), including child and family development (MAT); elementary education (PhD); middle school education (M Ed, PhD, Ed S); social studies education (M Ed, Ed D, PhD, Ed S). *Entrance requirements:* For master's and Ed S, GRE General Test or MAT; for doctorate, GRE General Test. Electronic applications accepted.

University of Georgia, Graduate School, College of Family and Consumer Sciences, Department of Child and Family Development, Athens, GA 30602. Offers child and family development (MS, PhD); early childhood education (MAT), including child and family development. *Accreditation:* AAMFT/COAMFTE (one or more programs are accredited). *Degree requirements:* For master's, thesis (MS); for doctorate, thesis/dissertation. *Entrance requirements:* For master's and doctorate, GRE General Test. Electronic applications accepted.

University of Guelph, Graduate Program Services, College of Social and Applied Human Sciences, Department of Family Relations and Applied Nutrition, Guelph, ON N1G 2W1, Canada. Offers applied nutrition (MAN); family relations and human development (M Sc, PhD), including applied human nutrition, couple and family therapy (M Sc), family relations and human development. *Accreditation:* AAMFT/COAMFTE (one or more programs are accredited). Part-time programs available. *Degree requirements:* For master's, thesis (for some programs); for doctorate, comprehensive exam, thesis/dissertation. *Entrance requirements:* For master's, minimum B+ average; for doctorate, master's degree in family relations and human development or related field with a minimum B+ average or master's degree in applied human nutrition. Additional exam requirements/recommendations for international students: Required—TOEFL (minimum score 600 paper-based; 250 computer-based). Electronic applications accepted. *Faculty research:* Child and adolescent development, social gerontology, family roles and relations, couple and family therapy, applied human nutrition.

University of Illinois at Springfield, Graduate Programs, College of Education and Human Services, Program in Human Services, Springfield, IL 62703-5407. Offers alcoholism and substance abuse (MA); child and family services (MA); gerontology (MA); social services administration (MA). Part-time and evening/weekend programs available. Postbaccalaureate distance learning degree programs offered (no on-campus study). *Faculty:* 4 full-time (2 women), 3 part-time/adjunct (all women). *Students:* 28 full-time (22 women), 70 part-time (56 women); includes 17 minority (16 African Americans, 1 American Indian/Alaska Native). Average age 35. 64 applicants, 42% accepted, 22 enrolled. In 2008, 24 master's awarded. *Degree requirements:* For master's, thesis optional, internship; project or thesis. *Entrance requirements:* For master's, minimum undergraduate GPA of 3.0, 2 letters of recommendation, personal statement. Additional exam requirements/recommendations for international students: Required—TOEFL (minimum score 500 paper-based; 176 computer-based; 61 iBT). Application fee: $50 ($60 for international students). Electronic applications accepted. *Expenses:* Tuition, state resident: full-time $6144; part-time $256 per credit hour. Tuition, nonresident: full-time $13,980; part-time $582.50 per credit hour. Required fees: $1800. *Financial support:* In 2008–09, research assistantships with full tuition reimbursements (averaging $8,109 per year), teaching assistantships with full tuition reimbursements (averaging $8,109 per year) were awarded; career-related internships or fieldwork, scholarships/grants, health care benefits, and unspecified assistantships also available. Support available to part-time students. Financial award application deadline: 11/15. *Unit head:* Dr. Carolyn Peck, Program Administrator, 217-206-7577, Fax: 217-206-6775, E-mail: peck.carolyn@uis.edu. *Application contact:* Dr. Lynn Pardie, Office of Graduate Studies, 800-252-8533, Fax: 217-206-7623, E-mail: pardie.lynn@uis.edu.

University of Kentucky, Graduate School, College of Agriculture, Program in Family Studies, Human Development, and Resource Management, Lexington, KY 40506-0032. Offers MSFAM, PhD. *Accreditation:* AAMFT/COAMFTE. *Degree requirements:* For master's, comprehensive exam, thesis optional. *Entrance requirements:* For master's, GRE General Test, minimum undergraduate GPA of 2.75; for doctorate, GRE General Test, minimum undergraduate GPA of 3.0. Additional exam requirements/recommendations for international students: Required—TOEFL (minimum score 550 paper-based; 213 computer-based). Electronic applications accepted. *Faculty research:* Early childhood education, family therapy, family resource management and consumer studies, human development.

University of La Verne, College of Education and Organizational Leadership, Department of Education, Programs in Child Development/Child Life, La Verne, CA 91750-4443. Offers child development (MS); child life (MS). Part-time programs available. *Faculty:* 11 full-time (8 women), 18 part-time/adjunct (14 women). *Students:* 31 full-time (30 women), 41 part-time (all women); includes 33 minority (3 African Americans, 10 Asian Americans or Pacific Islanders, 20 Hispanic Americans), 1 international. Average age 31. In 2008, 15 master's awarded. *Entrance requirements:* For master's, minimum GPA of 3.0, 3 letters of reference, writing sample. Additional exam requirements/recommendations for international students: Required—TOEFL (minimum score 550 paper-based; 213 computer-based). *Application deadline:* Applications are processed on a rolling basis. Application fee: $50. *Expenses:* Contact institution. *Financial support:* Institutionally sponsored loans, scholarships/grants, and unspecified assistantships available. Financial award application deadline: 3/2; financial award applicants required to submit FAFSA. *Unit head:* Dr. Barbara Nicoll, Chairperson, 909-593-3511 Ext. 4632, Fax: 909-392-2710, E-mail: nicollb@ulv.edu. *Application contact:* Christy Ranells, Program and Admission Specialist, 909-593-3511 Ext. 4644, Fax: 909-392-2761, E-mail: cranells@ulv.edu.

University of Manitoba, Faculty of Graduate Studies, Faculty of Human Ecology, Department of Family Social Sciences, Winnipeg, MB R3T 2N2, Canada. Offers M Sc. *Degree requirements:* For master's, thesis.

University of Maryland, College Park, Graduate Studies, School of Public Health, Department of Family Science, College Park, MD 20742. Offers family studies (PhD); marriage and family therapy (MS). *Accreditation:* AAMFT/COAMFTE. Part-time and evening/weekend programs available. *Degree requirements:* For master's, thesis or alternative; for doctorate, comprehensive exam, thesis/dissertation, oral defense. *Entrance requirements:* For master's, GRE General Test, minimum GPA of 3.0, 3 letters of recommendation; for doctorate, GRE General Test, minimum GPA of 3.0, 3 letters of recommendation, research sample. Electronic applications accepted. *Faculty research:* Family life quality, interracial couples, child support, homeless families, family and child well-being.

University of Massachusetts Amherst, Graduate School, School of Education, Program in Education, Amherst, MA 01003. Offers cultural diversity and curriculum reform (M Ed, Ed D, CAGS); early childhood education and development (M Ed, Ed D, CAGS); educational administration (M Ed, Ed D, CAGS); elementary teacher education (M Ed, Ed D, CAGS); higher education (M Ed, Ed D, CAGS); international education (M Ed, Ed D, CAGS); mathematics, science, and instructional technology (M Ed, Ed D, CAGS); physical education teacher education (M Ed, Ed D, CAGS); reading and writing (M Ed, Ed D, CAGS); research and evaluation methods (M Ed, Ed D, CAGS); school psychology and school counseling (M Ed, Ed D, CAGS); secondary teacher education (M Ed, Ed D, CAGS); social justice education (M Ed, Ed D, CAGS); special education (M Ed, Ed D, CAGS). *Accreditation:* NCATE. *Degree requirements:* For doctorate, thesis/dissertation. *Entrance requirements:* For master's and doctorate, GRE General Test. Additional exam requirements/recommendations for international students: Required—TOEFL (minimum score 530 paper-based; 197 computer-based). Electronic applications accepted. *Expenses:* Tuition, state resident: full-time $2,640; part-time $110 per credit. Tuition, nonresident: full-time $9,936; part-time $414 per credit. Required fees: $7,455. One-time fee: $332. Tuition and fees vary according to course load, campus/location, program and reciprocity agreements.

University of Minnesota, Twin Cities Campus, Graduate School, College of Education and Human Development, Department of Family Social Science, Minneapolis, MN 55455-0213. Offers marriage and family therapy (MA, PhD). *Accreditation:* AAMFT/COAMFTE (one or more programs are accredited). *Degree requirements:* For master's, thesis; for doctorate, thesis/dissertation. *Entrance requirements:* For master's and doctorate, GRE General Test, minimum undergraduate GPA of 3.0 (preferred). Additional exam requirements/recommendations for international students: Required—TOEFL. *Faculty research:* Families and diversity, families and health, families and economic well-being, individuals and relationships across the lifespan.

University of Missouri–Columbia, Graduate School, College of Human Environmental Science, Department of Human Development and Family Studies, Columbia, MO 65211. Offers MA, MS, PhD. *Faculty:* 10 full-time (6 women). *Students:* 40 full-time (29 women), 11 part-time (8 women); includes 7 minority (6 African Americans, 1 Hispanic American), 5 international. Average age 29. 38 applicants, 61% accepted, 17 enrolled. In 2008, 8 master's, 1 doctorate awarded. *Entrance requirements:* For master's, GRE General Test, minimum GPA of 3.0. Additional exam requirements/recommendations for international students: Required—TOEFL (minimum score 550 paper-based; 213 computer-based; 80 iBT). *Application deadline:* For fall admission, 2/1 priority date for domestic students; for winter admission, 11/15 priority date for domestic students. Applications are processed on a rolling basis. Application fee: $45 ($60 for international students). *Financial support:* Fellowships, research assistantships, teaching assistantships, institutionally sponsored loans available. *Unit head:* Dr. Jean Ispa, Director of Graduate Studies, E-mail: ispaj@missouri.edu. *Application contact:* Dr. Marilyn Coleman, Director of Graduate Studies, 573-882-4360, E-mail: colemanma@missouri.edu.

University of Nevada, Reno, Graduate School, College of Education, Department of Human Development and Family Studies, Reno, NV 89557. Offers MS. *Faculty:* 11 full-time (7 women). *Students:* 6 full-time (all women), 12 part-time (10 women); includes 5 minority (1 African American, 2 Asian Americans or Pacific Islanders, 2 Hispanic Americans), 1 international. Average age 33. 11 applicants, 45% accepted, 4 enrolled. In 2008, 2 master's awarded. *Degree requirements:* For master's, thesis optional. *Entrance requirements:* For master's, GRE General Test, minimum GPA of 2.75. Additional exam requirements/recommendations for international students: Required—TOEFL (minimum score 500 paper-based; 173 computer-based; 61 iBT), IELTS (minimum score 6), TOFEL or IELTS. *Application deadline:* For fall admission, 3/30 priority date for domestic and international students; for spring admission, 10/1 priority date for domestic and international students. Applications are processed on a rolling basis. Application fee: $60 ($95 for international students). Electronic applications accepted. *Expenses:* Tuition, state resident: full-time $1710; part-time $1140 per semester. Tuition, nonresident: full-time $7115. Required fees: $158 per semester. *Financial support:* In 2008–09, 1 research assistantship with partial tuition reimbursement (averaging $14,000 per year), 2 teaching assistantships with partial tuition reimbursements were awarded; Federal Work-Study, scholarships/grants, health care benefits, and unspecified assistantships also available. Financial award application deadline: 3/1; financial award applicants required to submit FAFSA. *Faculty research:* Early childhood/adolescent development, family studies. Total annual research expenditures: $21.1 million. *Unit head:* Dr. Bill Evans, Graduate Program Director, 775-784-6490, E-mail: evans@unr.nevada.edu. *Application contact:* Michele Sandberg, Application Contact, 775-784 7026, Fax: 775-784 6064, E-mail: gradschool@unr.edu.

University of New Hampshire, Graduate School, School of Health and Human Services, Department of Family Studies, Durham, NH 03824. Offers family studies (MS); marriage and family therapy (MS). *Accreditation:* AAMFT/COAMFTE. Part-time programs available. *Faculty:* 9 full-time (6 women). *Students:* 13 full-time (11 women), 9 part-time (8 women); includes 3 minority (1 African American, 2 Asian Americans or Pacific Islanders). Average age 30. 27 applicants, 56% accepted, 10 enrolled. In 2008, 7 master's awarded. *Degree requirements:* For master's, thesis or alternative. *Entrance requirements:* For master's, GRE General Test. Additional exam requirements/recommendations for international students: Required—TOEFL (minimum score 550 paper-based; 213 computer-based; 80 iBT). *Application deadline:* For fall admission, 4/1 priority date for domestic students, 4/1 for international students; for winter admission, 12/1 for domestic students. Applications are processed on a rolling basis. Application fee: $60. Electronic applications accepted. *Expenses:* Tuition, area resident: Full-time $9720; part-time $540 per credit hour. Tuition, nonresident: full-time $23,200; part-time $954 per credit hour. Required fees: $1446; $361.50 per term. *Financial support:* In 2008–09, 12 students received support, including 1 research assistantship, 5 teaching assistantships; fellowships, career-related internships or fieldwork, Federal Work-Study, scholarships/grants, and tuition waivers (full and partial) also available. Support available to part-time students. Financial award application deadline: 2/15. *Unit head:* Dr. Elizabeth Dolan, Chairperson, 603-862-2137. *Application contact:* Matty Leighton, Administrative Assistant, 603-862-5021, E-mail: family.studies@unh.edu.

University of New Mexico, Graduate School, College of Education, Department of Individual, Family and Community Education, Program in Family Studies, Albuquerque, NM 87131-2039. Offers MA, PhD. Part-time and evening/weekend programs available. *Degree requirements:* For master's, comprehensive exam, thesis (for some programs); for doctorate, comprehensive exam, thesis/dissertation. *Entrance requirements:* For master's, written paper, 3 letters of recommendation, personal statement, departmental application; for doctorate, GRE General Test, written paper, 3 letters of recommendation, personal statement, departmental application, interview. Electronic applications accepted. *Faculty research:* Home, community and school relations; multicultural issues; parent-child interactions; grandparents as primary caretakers for grandchildren; fathering, early childhood evaluation.

The University of North Carolina at Greensboro, Graduate School, School of Human Environmental Sciences, Department of Human Development and Family Studies, Greensboro, NC 27412-5001. Offers M Ed, MS, PhD. *Degree requirements:* For master's, one foreign language; for doctorate, one foreign language, thesis/dissertation. *Entrance requirements:* For master's and doctorate, GRE General Test. Additional exam requirements/recommendations for international students: Required—TOEFL. Electronic applications accepted. *Expenses:* Contact institution. *Faculty research:* Adolescent mothers, multi-handicapped, older adults.

University of North Texas, Robert B. Toulouse School of Graduate Studies, College of Education, Department of Educational Psychology, Program in Development and Family Studies, Denton, TX 76203. Offers MS. Evening/weekend programs available. *Degree requirements:* For master's, comprehensive exam, thesis optional. *Entrance requirements:* For master's, GRE General Test, letter of application, resumé, references. Additional exam requirements/recommendations for international students: Required—proof of English language proficiency required for non-native English speakers; Recommended—TOEFL (minimum score 550 paper-based; 213 computer-based). *Faculty research:* Parent-child issues, cognitive development, social development.

University of Rhode Island, Graduate School, College of Human Science and Services, Department of Human Development and Family Studies, Kingston, RI 02881. Offers college student personnel (MS); human development and family studies (MS); marriage and family therapy (MS). *Accreditation:* AAMFT/COAMFTE. Evening/weekend programs available. *Entrance requirements:* For master's, GRE or MAT. *Expenses:* Tuition, state resident: full-time $8024; part-time $446 per credit. Tuition, nonresident: full-time $21,046; part-time $1169 per credit. Required fees: $1056; $26 per credit. $30 per semester. One-time fee: $95 part-time. *Unit head:* Dr. Jerome Adams, Chair, 401-874-5962, E-mail: jadams@uri.edu. *Application contact:* Harold D. Bibb, Associate Dean of the Graduate School, 401-874-2262, Fax: 401-874-5491.

University of Southern Mississippi, Graduate School, College of Education and Psychology, Department of Child and Family Studies, Hattiesburg, MS 39406-0001. Offers child and family studies (MS); early intervention (MS); marriage and family therapy (MS). *Accreditation:* AAMFT/COAMFTE. Part-time programs available. *Faculty:* 8 full-time (4 women). *Students:* 33 full-time (32 women), 21 part-time (20 women); includes 14 minority (12 African Americans, 1 Asian American or Pacific Islander, 1 Hispanic American), 1 international. Average age 29. 55 applicants, 47% accepted, 23 enrolled. In 2008, 15 master's awarded. *Degree requirements:* For master's, comprehensive exam, thesis optional. *Entrance requirements:* For master's, GRE General Test, minimum GPA of 2.75 in last 60 hours. Additional exam requirements/recommendations for international students: Required—TOEFL. *Application deadline:* For fall admission, 3/1 priority date for domestic students, 3/1 for international students. Applications are processed on a rolling basis. Application fee: $30. Electronic applications accepted. *Financial support:* In 2008–09, 21 students received support, including 3 research assistantships with full tuition reimbursements available (averaging $7,300 per year); fellowships, career-related internships or fieldwork, Federal Work-Study, institutionally sponsored loans, scholarships/grants, and unspecified assistantships also available. Financial award application deadline: 3/15; financial award applicants required to submit FAFSA. *Faculty research:* School food service, teen pregnancy, diet and cholesterol metabolism. *Unit head:* Dr. Ann Blackwell, Chair, 601-266-5661, Fax: 601-266-4680. *Application contact:* Dr. Ann Blackwell, Chair, 601-266-5661, Fax: 601-266-4680.

The University of Tennessee, Graduate School, College of Education, Health and Human Sciences, Department of Child and Family Studies, Knoxville, TN 37996. Offers child and family studies (MS); early childhood education (MS). Part-time programs available. *Degree requirements:* For master's, thesis or alternative. *Entrance requirements:* For master's, GRE General Test, minimum GPA of 2.7. Additional exam requirements/recommendations for international students: Required—TOEFL. Electronic applications accepted. *Expenses:* Tuition, area resident: Part-time $348 per credit hour. Tuition, state resident: full-time $6262. Tuition, nonresident: full-time $18,920; part-time $1052 per credit hour. Required fees: $812; $36 per credit hour. Tuition and fees vary according to program.

The University of Tennessee, Graduate School, College of Education, Health and Human Sciences, Program in Human Ecology, Knoxville, TN 37996. Offers child and family studies (PhD); community health (PhD); nutrition science (PhD); retailing and consumer sciences (PhD); textile science (PhD). *Degree requirements:* For doctorate, thesis/dissertation. *Entrance requirements:* For doctorate, GRE General Test, minimum GPA of 2.7. Additional exam requirements/recommendations for international students: Required—TOEFL. Electronic applications accepted. *Expenses:* Tuition, area resident: Part-time $348 per credit hour. Tuition, state resident: full-time $6262. Tuition, nonresident: full-time $18,920; part-time $1052 per credit hour. Required fees: $812; $36 per credit hour. Tuition and fees vary according to program.

The University of Tennessee at Martin, Graduate Programs, College of Agriculture and Applied Sciences, Department of Family and Consumer Sciences, Martin, TN 38238-1000. Offers dietetics (MSFCS); general family and consumer sciences (MSFCS). Part-time programs available. *Faculty:* 6. *Students:* 32 (29 women). 30 applicants, 100% accepted, 16 enrolled. In 2008, 5 master's awarded. *Degree requirements:* For master's, comprehensive exam, thesis optional. *Entrance requirements:* For master's, GRE General Test, minimum GPA of 2.5. Additional exam requirements/recommendations for international students: Required—TOEFL (minimum score 525 paper-based; 197 computer-based; 71 iBT). *Application deadline:* For fall admission, 8/1 priority date for domestic students, 8/1 for international students; for spring admission, 1/1 for domestic and international students. Applications are processed on a rolling basis. Application fee: $30 ($50 for international students). Electronic applications accepted. *Expenses:* Tuition, state resident: full-time $6084; part-time $340 per semester hour. Tuition, nonresident: full-time $16,726; part-time $932 per semester hour. *Financial support:* In 2008–09, 6 students received support, including 6 research assistantships with full tuition reimbursements available (averaging $6,585 per year); scholarships/grants and unspecified assistantships also available. Financial award application deadline: 3/1. *Faculty research:* Children with developmental disabilities, regional food product development and marketing, parent education. *Unit head:* Dr. Lisa LeBleu, Coordinator, 731-881-7116, Fax: 731-881-7106, E-mail: llebleu@utm.edu. *Application contact:* Linda S. Arant, Student Services Specialist, 731-881-7012, Fax: 731-881-7499, E-mail: larant@utm.edu.

The University of Texas at Austin, Graduate School, College of Natural Sciences, School of Human Ecology, Program in Human Development and Family Sciences, Austin, TX 78712-1111. Offers MA, PhD. *Degree requirements:* For master's, thesis; for doctorate, thesis/dissertation. *Entrance requirements:* For master's and doctorate, GRE General Test. Additional exam requirements/recommendations for international students: Required—TOEFL. Electronic applications accepted. *Faculty research:* Marriage and family relationships, parenting, impact of television on children, courtship, family policy.

The University of Texas at Dallas, School of Behavioral and Brain Sciences, Program in Psychological Sciences, Richardson, TX 75083-0688. Offers early childhood disorders (MS); psychological sciences (MS, PhD). Part-time and evening/weekend programs available. *Faculty:* 31 full-time (16 women), 1 (woman) part-time/adjunct. *Students:* 47 full-time (38 women), 20 part-time (all women); includes 13 minority (3 African Americans, 5 Asian Americans or Pacific Islanders, 5 Hispanic Americans), 8 international. Average age 30. 75 applicants, 60% accepted, 32 enrolled. In 2008, 12 master's, 1 doctorate awarded. *Degree requirements:* For master's, directed project or internship; for doctorate, thesis/dissertation. *Entrance requirements:* For master's and doctorate, GRE General Test, minimum GPA of 3.0 in upper-level course work. Additional exam requirements/recommendations for international students: Required—TOEFL (minimum score 550 paper-based; 213 computer-based). *Application deadline:* For fall admission, 7/15 for domestic students, 5/1 priority date for international students; for spring admission, 11/15 for domestic students, 9/1 priority date for international students. Applications are processed on a rolling basis. Application fee: $50 ($100 for international students). Electronic applications accepted. *Expenses:* Tuition, area resident: Full-time $8320. Tuition, state resident: full-time $8320. Tuition, nonresident: full-time $15,054. Part-time tuition and fees vary according to course load. *Financial support:* In 2008–09, 14 teaching assistantships with tuition reimbursements (averaging $10,930 per year) were awarded; fellowships, research assistantships with tuition reimbursements, career-related internships or fieldwork, Federal Work-Study, scholarships/grants, and unspecified assistantships also available. Support available to part-time students. Financial award application deadline: 4/30; financial award applicants required to submit FAFSA. *Faculty research:* Social competence in normal and hyperactive youth, preschool number development, social-emotional development, family and peer relationships. *Unit head:* Dr. Melanie J. Spence, Head, PhD Programs, 972-883-2206, Fax: 972-883-2491, E-mail: mspence@utdallas.edu. *Application contact:* Dr. Robert D. Stillman, Program Head, 972-883-3106, Fax: 972-883-3022, E-mail: stillman@utdallas.edu.

University of Utah, The Graduate School, College of Social and Behavioral Science, Department of Family and Consumer Studies, Salt Lake City, UT 84112-1107. Offers MS. *Degree requirements:* For master's, thesis optional. *Entrance requirements:* For master's, GRE General Test, minimum undergraduate GPA of 3.0. Additional exam requirements/recommendations for international students: Required—TOEFL (minimum score 500 paper-based; 173 computer-based). *Faculty research:* Social, physical and economic contexts of families and communities.

University of Victoria, Faculty of Graduate Studies, Faculty of Human and Social Development, School of Child and Youth Care, Victoria, BC V8W 2Y2, Canada. Offers MA, PhD. Part-time programs available. *Degree requirements:* For master's, thesis. *Entrance requirements:* For master's, resumé, professional references, sample of academic writing. Additional exam requirements/recommendations for international students: Required—TOEFL (minimum score 575 paper-based; 233 computer-based), IELTS (minimum score 7). Electronic applications accepted.

University of Wisconsin–Madison, Graduate School, School of Human Ecology, Program in Human Development and Family Studies, Madison, WI 53706-1380. Offers MS, PhD. Part-time programs available. Terminal master's awarded for partial completion of doctoral program. *Degree requirements:* For master's, thesis; for doctorate, comprehensive exam, thesis/dissertation. *Entrance requirements:* For master's, GRE General Test, 3 letters of recommendation; for doctorate, GRE General Test, MS or MA, 3 letters of recommendation. Additional exam requirements/recommendations for international students: Required—TOEFL. Electronic applications accepted. *Faculty research:* Human development, adolescence, adulthood, prevention, intervention.

University of Wisconsin–Stout, Graduate School, College of Human Development, Program in Family Studies and Human Development, Menomonie, WI 54751. Offers MS. Part-time programs available. *Students:* 2 full-time (both women), 17 part-time (16 women); includes 1 minority (African American), 1 international. Average age 32. In 2008, 7 master's awarded. *Degree requirements:* For master's, thesis. *Entrance requirements:* For master's, minimum GPA of 2.75. Additional exam requirements/recommendations for international students: Required—TOEFL (minimum score 500 paper-based; 173 computer-based; 61 iBT). *Application deadline:* Applications are processed on a rolling basis. Application fee: $45. Electronic applications accepted. *Expenses:* Tuition, state resident: full-time $6227; part-time $345.93 per credit. Tuition, nonresident: full-time $9998; part-time $555.42 per credit. International tuition: $10,512 full-time. Tuition and fees vary according to course load, program and reciprocity agreements. *Financial support:* In 2008–09, 2 research assistantships with partial tuition reimbursements (averaging $4,343 per year) were awarded; teaching assistantships with partial tuition reimbursements, Federal Work-Study, scholarships/grants, tuition waivers (partial), and unspecified assistantships also available. Support available to part-time students. Financial award application deadline: 5/1; financial award applicants required to submit FAFSA. *Faculty research:* Diversity, work and family medical ethics, family policy, dementia and families. *Unit head:* Dr. Dale Hawley, Director, 715-232-1273, Fax: 715-232-2524, E-mail: hawleyd@uwstout.edu. *Application contact:* Anne E. Johnson, Graduate Student Evaluator (Admissions and Assistantship Coordinator), 715-232-1322, Fax: 715-232-2413, E-mail: johnsona@uwstout.edu.

Utah State University, School of Graduate Studies, College of Education and Human Services, Department of Family, Consumer, and Human Development, Logan, UT 84322. Offers family and human development (MFHD); family, consumer, and human development (MS, PhD), including adolescence/youth (MS), adult development/aging (MS), consumer science (MS), infancy/childhood (MS), marriage and family relations (MS), marriage and family therapy (MS). *Accreditation:* AAMFT/COAMFTE (one or more programs are accredited). Part-time and evening/weekend programs available. Postbaccalaureate distance learning degree programs offered (minimal on-campus study). *Degree requirements:* For master's, thesis; for doctorate, comprehensive exam, thesis/dissertation, competencies. *Entrance requirements:* For master's, GRE General Test or MAT, minimum GPA of 3.0, 3 letters of recommendation; for doctorate, GRE, minimum GPA of 3.0, 3 letters of recommendation. Additional exam requirements/recommendations for international students: Required—TOEFL. Electronic applications accepted. *Faculty research:* Marriage and family relations, adolescent problem behavior, family financial management, early literacy, mental health in the elderly, parent child attachment.

Vanderbilt University, Peabody College, Department of Psychology and Human Development, Nashville, TN 37240-1001. Offers child studies (M Ed). *Accreditation:* APA. Part-time programs available. *Faculty:* 25 full-time (12 women), 2 part-time/adjunct (1 woman). *Students:* 18 full-time (17 women), 2 part-time (both women); includes 2 minority (1 African American, 1 Asian American or Pacific Islander). Average age 25. 50 applicants, 36% accepted, 9 enrolled. In 2008, 8 master's awarded. *Degree requirements:* For master's, comprehensive exam, thesis optional. *Entrance requirements:* For master's, GRE General Test. Additional exam requirements/recommendations for international students: Required—TOEFL (minimum score 550 paper-based; 213 computer-based). *Application deadline:* For fall admission, 12/31 for domestic and international students; for spring admission, 11/1 for domestic and international students. Applications are processed on a rolling basis. Application fee: $0. Electronic applications accepted. *Financial support:* In 2008–09, 11 students received support, including 7 research assistantships with full and partial tuition reimbursements available; fellowships with full and partial tuition reimbursements available, teaching assistantships with full and partial tuition reimbursements available, Federal Work-Study, institutionally sponsored loans, scholarships/grants, and unspecified assistantships also available. Financial award application deadline: 2/1; financial award applicants required to submit FAFSA. *Faculty research:* Cognitive, language and social development; stress, coping and emotion; quantitative methods and evaluation; clinical intervention and prevention; individual differences, disabilities and developmental psychopathology. *Unit head:* Dr. David Cole, Acting Chair, 615-322-8141, Fax: 615-343-9494, E-mail: david.cole@vanderbilt.edu. *Application contact:* Sharone Hall, Educational Coordinator, 615-343-4963, Fax: 615-343-9494, E-mail: sharone.k.hall@vanderbilt.edu.

Virginia Polytechnic Institute and State University, Graduate School, College of Liberal Arts and Human Sciences, Department of Human Development, Blacksburg, VA 24061. Offers adult development and aging (MS, PhD); adult learning and human resource development (MS, PhD); child development (MS, PhD); family studies (MS, PhD); marriage and family therapy (MS, PhD). *Accreditation:* AAMFT/COAMFTE (one or more programs are accredited). *Entrance requirements:* For master's and doctorate, GRE General Test. Additional exam requirements/recommendations for international students: Required—TOEFL (minimum score 600 paper-based; 250 computer-based). Electronic applications accepted. *Faculty research:* Stress management, children's play, dual-career families, social cognition, relationships of elderly.

Walden University, Graduate Programs, School of Counseling and Social Service, Minneapolis, MN 55401. Offers human services (PhD), including clinical social work, counseling, criminal justice, family studies and intervention strategies, general program in human services, human services administration, self-designed program in human services, social policy analysis and planning; mental health counseling (MS). Part-time and evening/weekend programs available. Postbaccalaureate distance learning degree programs offered (minimal on-campus study). *Faculty:* 6 full-time, 76 part-time/adjunct. *Students:* 1,235 full-time (1,026 women), 129 part-time (111 women); includes 595 minority (505 African Americans, 21 American Indian/Alaska Native, 16 Asian Americans or Pacific Islanders, 53 Hispanic Americans), 18 international.

Child and Family Studies

Walden University (continued)
Average age 39. 724 applicants, 50% accepted, 250 enrolled. In 2008, 12 master's, 5 doctorates awarded. *Degree requirements:* For master's, thesis optional, residency; for doctorate, thesis/dissertation, residency. *Entrance requirements:* For master's, bachelor's degree or equivalent in related field, minimum GPA of 2.5, two references, goal statement, official transcripts, computer and Internet access; for doctorate, master's degree or equivalent in related field, minimum GPA of 3.0, three years related professional/academic experience, two references, goal statement, official transcripts, computer and Internet access. Additional exam requirements/recommendations for international students: Required—TOEFL (minimum score 550 paper-based; 213 computer-based), IELTS (minimum score 6.5), TOEFL, IELTS, or Michigan English Language Assessment Battery (minimum score 82). *Application deadline:* Applications are processed on a rolling basis. Application fee: $50. Electronic applications accepted. *Expenses:* Tuition: Full-time $12,877; part-time $520 per credit. Required fees: $1230. Tuition and fees vary according to course load, degree level and program. *Financial support:* Fellowships, Federal Work-Study, scholarships/grants, unspecified assistantships, and family tuition reduction; active duty/veteran tuition reduction; group tuition reduction; interest-free payment plans available. Support available to part-time students. Financial award applicants required to submit FAFSA. *Unit head:* Dr. Savitri Dixon-Saxon, Associate Dean, 800-925-3368. *Application contact:* Jennifer Hall, Director of Enrollment, 866-4-WALDEN, E-mail: info@waldenu.edu.

Wayne State University, Graduate School, Interdisciplinary Program in Infant Mental Health, Detroit, MI 48202. Offers Certificate. *Entrance requirements:* For degree, concurrent admission to a master's or doctoral program, or master's degree; letters of reference. Additional exam requirements/recommendations for international students: Required—TOEFL (minimum score 550 paper-based; 213 computer-based); Recommended—TWE (minimum score 6). Electronic applications accepted. *Faculty research:* Infant mental health treatment, early intervention, child abuse and neglect, readiness, attachment.

West Virginia University, College of Human Resources and Education, Department of Technology, Learning and Culture, Program in Child Development and Family Studies, Morgantown, WV 26506. Offers MA. Part-time programs available. *Degree requirements:* For master's, thesis. *Entrance requirements:* For master's, GRE General Test, Minimum GPA 3.0, Interview. Additional exam requirements/recommendations for international students: Required—TOEFL. Electronic applications accepted.

Wheelock College, Graduate Programs, Division of Child and Family Studies, Boston, MA 02215-4176. Offers family studies (MS); family support and parent education (MS); family, culture, and society (MS). Part-time programs available. Postbaccalaureate distance learning degree programs offered (minimal on-campus study). *Degree requirements:* For master's, comprehensive exam. Electronic applications accepted. *Faculty research:* Cross-cultural studies of parenting, effects of chronic illness on families, parenting education.

Child Development

American International College, School of Arts, Education and Science, Department of Education, Springfield, MA 01109-3189. Offers administration (M Ed, CAGS); child development (MA, Ed D), including educational psychology; elementary education (M Ed, CAGS); reading (M Ed, CAGS); secondary education (M Ed, CAGS); special education (M Ed, CAGS); teaching (MAT). Part-time and evening/weekend programs available. Terminal master's awarded for partial completion of doctoral program. *Degree requirements:* For master's, comprehensive exam (for some programs), thesis (for some programs), practicum; for doctorate, comprehensive exam (for some programs), thesis/dissertation; for CAGS, practicum. *Entrance requirements:* For master's, minimum B- average in undergraduate course work, BS or BA; for doctorate, GRE General Test, interview. Additional exam requirements/recommendations for international students: Required—TOEFL. Electronic applications accepted.

American International College, School of Arts, Education and Science, Department of Psychology, Springfield, MA 01109-3189. Offers child development (MA, Ed D), including educational psychology; clinical psychology (MA); forensic psychology (MS). Part-time and evening/weekend programs available. *Degree requirements:* For master's, comprehensive exam (for some programs), thesis (for some programs), practicum. *Entrance requirements:* For master's, minimum GPA of 3.0, BS or BA; for doctorate, GRE General Test, interview. Additional exam requirements/recommendations for international students: Required—TOEFL. Electronic applications accepted.

Appalachian State University, Cratis D. Williams Graduate School, Department of Family and Consumer Sciences, Boone, NC 28608. Offers child development (MA); family and consumer science (MA), including family studies, food and nutrition; family and consumer science education (MA). Part-time programs available. Postbaccalaureate distance learning degree programs offered (no on-campus study). *Faculty:* 12 full-time (11 women), 2 part-time/adjunct (1 woman). *Students:* 12 full-time (all women), 6 part-time (all women); includes 1 minority (Hispanic American), 1 international. 27 applicants, 44% accepted, 9 enrolled. In 2008, 6 master's awarded. *Degree requirements:* For master's, comprehensive exam, thesis optional. *Entrance requirements:* For master's, GRE General Test, 3 letters of recommendation. Additional exam requirements/recommendations for international students: Required—TOEFL (minimum score 550 paper-based; 230 computer-based; 79 iBT), IELTS (minimum score 6.5). *Application deadline:* For fall admission, 7/1 for domestic students, 2/1 for international students; for spring admission, 11/1 for domestic students, 7/1 for international students. Applications are processed on a rolling basis. Application fee: $50. Electronic applications accepted. *Expenses:* Tuition, area resident: Full-time $2600; part-time $700 per course. Tuition, state resident: full-time $2600; part-time $700 per course. Tuition, nonresident: full-time $5000; part-time $3300 per course. Required fees: $2150; $330 per course. Tuition and fees vary according to campus/location. *Financial support:* In 2008–09, 5 teaching assistantships (averaging $7,000 per year) were awarded; fellowships, research assistantships, career-related internships or fieldwork, scholarships/grants, and unspecified assistantships also available. Financial award application deadline: 7/1; financial award applicants required to submit FAFSA. *Faculty research:* Food antioxidants, preschool curriculum, children with special needs, family child care, FCS curriculum content. *Unit head:* Dr. Sarah Jordan, Chairperson, 828-262-2661, E-mail: jordansr@appstate.edu. *Application contact:* Dr. Sammie Garner, Graduate Director, 828-262-2698, E-mail: garnersg@appstate.edu.

Arcadia University, Graduate Studies, Department of Education, Glenside, PA 19038-3295. Offers art education (M Ed, MA Ed); biology education (MA Ed); chemistry education (MA Ed); child development (CAS); computer education (M Ed, CAS); computer education 7–12 (MA Ed); early childhood education (M Ed, CAS), including individualized (M Ed), master teacher (M Ed), research in child development (M Ed); educational leadership (M Ed, CAS); educational psychology (CAS); elementary education (M Ed, CAS); English education (MA Ed); environmental education (MA Ed, CAS); history education (MA Ed); language arts (M Ed, CAS); mathematics education (M Ed, MA Ed, CAS); music education (MA Ed); psychology (MA Ed); pupil personnel services (CAS); reading (M Ed, CAS); school library science (M Ed); science education (M Ed, CAS); secondary education (M Ed, CAS); special education (M Ed, Ed D, CAS); theater arts (MA Ed); written communication (MA Ed). *Accreditation:* NASAD. Part-time and evening/weekend programs available. Postbaccalaureate distance learning degree programs offered (minimal on-campus study). Electronic applications accepted.

California State University, Los Angeles, Graduate Studies, College of Health and Human Services, Department of Child and Family Studies, Los Angeles, CA 90032-8530. Offers child development (MA). Part-time and evening/weekend programs available. *Faculty:* 3 full-time (2 women), 2 part-time/adjunct (both women). *Students:* 8 full-time (7 women), 15 part-time (all women); includes 16 minority (1 African American, 6 Asian Americans or Pacific Islanders, 9 Hispanic Americans), 1 international. Average age 29. 14 applicants, 93% accepted, 8 enrolled. In 2008, 6 master's awarded. *Degree requirements:* For master's, comprehensive exam, project or thesis. *Entrance requirements:* Additional exam requirements/recommendations for international students: Required—TOEFL (minimum score 500 paper-based; 173 computer-based). *Application deadline:* For fall admission, 6/15 for domestic students, 5/1 for international students; for winter admission, 11/1 for domestic students, 9/1 for international students; for spring admission, 2/1 for domestic students, 10/1 for international students. Applications are processed on a rolling basis. Application fee: $55. *Expenses:* Tuition, nonresident: part-time $226 per credit. Required fees: $4019. *Financial support:* Career-related internships or fieldwork and Federal Work-Study available. Support available to part-time students. Financial award application deadline: 3/1. *Faculty research:* Nutrition education, laundry product and fabric durability, computer usage in public school home economics. *Unit head:* Dr. Marlene Zepeda, Co-Chair, 323-343-4590, Fax: 323-343-5019, E-mail: mzepeda@calstatela.edu. *Application contact:* Dr. Jose L. Galvan, Dean of Graduate Studies, 323-343-3820, Fax: 323-343-5653, E-mail: jgalvan@cslanet.calstatela.edu.

California State University, San Bernardino, Graduate Studies, College of Social and Behavioral Sciences, Department of Psychology, San Bernardino, CA 92407-2397. Offers child development (MA), including psychology-life span; clinical/counseling psychology (MS), including clinical psychology; general/experimental psychology (MA), including psychology; industrial/organizational psychology (MS), including organizational psychology. *Faculty:* 22 full-time (8 women), 3 part-time/adjunct (1 woman). *Students:* 98 full-time (77 women), 28 part-time (19 women); includes 44 minority (7 African Americans, 6 Asian Americans or Pacific Islanders, 31 Hispanic Americans), 4 international. Average age 29. 186 applicants, 26% accepted, 41 enrolled. In 2008, 20 master's awarded. *Degree requirements:* For master's, comprehensive exam, thesis (for some programs), advancement to candidacy. *Entrance requirements:* For master's, Graduate Writing Exam, minimum GPA of 3.0 in major. *Application deadline:* For fall admission, 8/31 priority date for domestic students. Application fee: $55. *Expenses:* Tuition, area resident: Full-time $1252; part-time $726 per quarter. Required fees: $334 per quarter. Tuition and fees vary according to degree level and student level. *Financial support:* Fellowships, research assistantships, teaching assistantships, career-related internships or fieldwork, Federal Work-Study, institutionally sponsored loans, and unspecified assistantships available. *Faculty research:* Perceptual development, human memory, psychopharmacology, psychology of women, language acquisition. *Unit head:* Dr. Joanna S. Worthley, Associate Dean, 909-537-5595, Fax: 909-537-7003, E-mail: jworthley@csusb.edu. *Application contact:* Stacy Brooks, Graduate Secretary, 909-537-5570, Fax: 909-537-7003, E-mail: sbrooks@csusb.edu.

California State University, Stanislaus, College of Human and Health Sciences, Department of Psychology, Turlock, CA 95382. Offers behavior analysis (MS); child development (Graduate Certificate); counseling (MS); psychology (MA, MS). Part-time programs available. *Degree requirements:* For master's, thesis. *Entrance requirements:* For master's, GRE General Test, minimum GPA of 3.0, 3 letters of reference, personal statement. Additional exam requirements/recommendations for international students: Required—TOEFL (minimum score 550 paper-based; 213 computer-based). Electronic applications accepted. *Faculty research:* Hedonic tone judgement, syntax and autism, early literacy assessment and native and non-native languages.

East Carolina University, Graduate School, College of Human Ecology, Department of Child Development and Family Relations, Greenville, NC 27858-4353. Offers child development and family relations (MS); marriage and family therapy (MS). *Accreditation:* AAMFT/COAMFTE. Part-time programs available. *Degree requirements:* For master's, comprehensive exam, thesis optional. *Faculty research:* Child care quality, mental health delivery systems for children, family violence.

Erikson Institute, Academic Programs, Program in Child Development, Chicago, IL 60654. Offers MS. *Degree requirements:* For master's, comprehensive exam, internship. *Entrance requirements:* For master's, 3 letters of recommendation, minimum GPA of 2.75. Additional exam requirements/recommendations for international students: Required—TOEFL.

Michigan State University, The Graduate School, College of Social Science, Department of Family and Child Ecology, East Lansing, MI 48824. Offers child development (MA); community services (MS); family and child ecology (PhD); family studies (MA); marriage and family therapy (MA); youth development (MA). *Accreditation:* AAMFT/COAMFTE (one or more programs are accredited). *Entrance requirements:* For master's, GRE General Test, minimum GPA of 3.0 in last 2 years of undergraduate course work, 3 letters of recommendation; for doctorate, GRE General Test, minimum GPA of 3.0, 3 letters of recommendation, background in behavioral sciences. Additional exam requirements/recommendations for international students: Required—TOEFL. Electronic applications accepted.

Middle Tennessee State University, College of Graduate Studies, College of Education and Behavioral Science, Department of Human Sciences, Murfreesboro, TN 37132. Offers child development and family studies (MS); nutrition and food science (MS). Part-time and evening/weekend programs available. Postbaccalaureate distance learning degree programs offered. *Degree requirements:* For master's, comprehensive exam, thesis. *Entrance requirements:* For master's, GRE or MAT. Additional exam requirements/recommendations for international students: Required—TOEFL (paper-based 525; computer-based 195; IBT 71) or IELTS (6.0). Electronic applications accepted. *Faculty research:* Courtship relationships, feminist methodology and epistemology in family studies, school uniforms, body fat in elderly, asynchronous distance education.

North Dakota State University, College of Graduate and Interdisciplinary Studies, College of Human Development and Education, Department of Child Development and Family Science, Fargo, ND 58105. Offers child development and family science (MS); couple and family therapy (MS); family financial planning (MS); gerontology (MS, PhD). *Accreditation:* AAMFT/COAMFTE. Part-time and evening/weekend programs available. Postbaccalaureate distance learning degree programs offered (no on-campus study). *Faculty:* 12 full-time (7 women). *Students:* 26 full-time (25 women), 21 part-time (18 women); includes 1 African American, 2 international. 22 applicants, 64% accepted, 12 enrolled. In 2008, 12 master's awarded. *Degree requirements:* For master's, thesis or alternative; for doctorate, thesis/dissertation. *Entrance requirements:* Additional exam requirements/recommendations for international students: Required—TOEFL (minimum score 525 paper-based; 197 computer-based; 71 iBT). *Application deadline:* For fall admission, 2/1 for domestic and international students; for spring admission, 10/1 for domestic and international students. Application fee: $45 ($60 for international students). *Financial support:* In 2008–09, 17 students received support, including research assistantships with full tuition reimbursements available (averaging $3,000 per year), 17 teaching assistantships with full tuition reimbursements available (averaging $3,000 per year); career-related internships or fieldwork, Federal Work-Study, institutionally sponsored loans, and tuition waivers (full) also available. Financial award application deadline: 4/1. *Faculty research:* Family therapy, resilience, parenting, adolescent development, mental health. Total annual research expenditures: $333,582. *Unit head:* Dr. James Deal, Head, 701-231-7568, Fax: 701-231-9645, E-mail: jim_deal@ndsu.edu. *Application contact:* Theresa Anderson, Administrative Assistant, 701-231-8628, Fax: 701-231-9645, E-mail: theresa.anderson@ndsu.edu.

Ohio University, Graduate College, College of Health and Human Services, School of Human and Consumer Sciences, Athens, OH 45701-2979. Offers child development and family life (MS); early childhood education (MS); family studies (MS); food and nutrition (MS). Part-time programs available. *Degree requirements:* For master's, thesis. *Entrance requirements:* For master's, GRE. Additional exam requirements/recommendations for international students: Required—TOEFL. Electronic applications accepted. *Faculty research:* Diversity, developmentally appropriate activities, death and dying, gerontology, sexuality education.

Purdue University, Graduate School, College of Consumer and Family Sciences, Department of Child Development and Family Studies, West Lafayette, IN 47907. Offers developmental studies (MS, PhD); family studies (MS, PhD); marriage and family therapy (MS, PhD). *Accreditation:* AAMFT/COAMFTE (one or more programs are accredited). Part-time programs available. Terminal master's awarded for partial completion of doctoral program. *Degree requirements:* For master's, thesis; for doctorate, thesis/dissertation. *Entrance requirements:* For master's and doctorate, GRE General Test. Additional exam requirements/recommendations for international students: Required—TWE. Electronic applications accepted. *Faculty research:* Inclusion of children with special needs, families as learning environments, relationships in child care, work-family relations, AIDS prevention.

Rutgers, The State University of New Jersey, Camden, Graduate School of Arts and Sciences, Program in Childhood Studies, Camden, NJ 08102-1401. Offers MA, PhD. Part-time and evening/weekend programs available. *Degree requirements:* For master's, thesis (for some programs). *Entrance requirements:* Additional exam requirements/recommendations for international students: Required—TOEFL, IELTS. *Faculty research:* Children's consumer culture, moral development, development of personality and social relations, children's literature, commodification of childhood.

San Diego State University, Graduate and Research Affairs, College of Education, Department of Child and Family Development, San Diego, CA 92182. Offers child development (MS). Part-time programs available. *Degree requirements:* For master's, thesis. *Entrance requirements:* For master's, GRE General Test, 3 letters of recommendation, interview. Additional exam requirements/recommendations for international students: Required—TOEFL. Electronic applications accepted.

Sarah Lawrence College, Graduate Studies, Program in Child Development, Bronxville, NY 10708-5999. Offers MA. Part-time programs available. *Faculty:* 7 part-time/adjunct (5 women). *Students:* 10 full-time (9 women), 3 part-time (all women); includes 4 minority (1 African American, 1 Asian American or Pacific Islander, 2 Hispanic Americans). Average age 30. 61 applicants, 23% accepted, 8 enrolled. In 2008, 6 master's awarded. *Degree requirements:* For master's, thesis, fieldwork. *Entrance requirements:* For master's, minimum B average in undergraduate coursework. *Application deadline:* For fall admission, 2/1 for domestic and international students. Applications are processed on a rolling basis. Application fee: $60. *Expenses:* Tuition: Full-time $26,544; part-time $1106 per credit. Required fees: $450. Tuition and fees vary according to program. *Financial support:* In 2008–09, 9 fellowships were awarded; career-related internships or fieldwork and scholarships/grants also available. Support available to part-time students. Financial award application deadline: 3/1; financial award applicants required to submit FAFSA. *Unit head:* Barbara Schecter, Director, 914-395-2247. *Application contact:* Susan Guma, Dean of Graduate Studies, 914-395-2373, E-mail: sguma@mail.slc.edu.

Southern New Hampshire University, School of Education, Manchester, NH 03106-1045. Offers business education (MS); child development (M Ed); computer technology education (Certificate); curriculum and instruction (M Ed); education (M Ed, CAS); elementary education (M Ed); general special education (Certificate); school business administrator (Certificate); secondary education (M Ed); training and development (Certificate). Part-time and evening/weekend programs available. Postbaccalaureate distance learning degree programs offered (no on-campus study). *Degree requirements:* For master's, comprehensive exam (for some programs), thesis or alternative. *Entrance requirements:* For master's, PRAXIS I, minimum GPA of 2.75. Additional exam requirements/recommendations for international students: Required—TOEFL (minimum score 550 paper-based; 213 computer-based). Electronic applications accepted. *Expenses:* Contact institution.

Texas Woman's University, Graduate School, College of Professional Education, Department of Family Sciences, Denton, TX 76201. Offers child development (MS, PhD); counseling and development (MS); early childhood education (M Ed, MA, MS, Ed D); family studies (MS, PhD); family therapy (MS, PhD). *Accreditation:* ACA (one or more programs are accredited). Part-time and evening/weekend programs available. *Faculty:* 22 full-time (17 women), 11 part-time/adjunct (10 women). *Students:* 90 full-time (86 women), 317 part-time (294 women); includes 133 minority (92 African Americans, 3 American Indian/Alaska Native, 9 Asian Americans or Pacific Islanders, 29 Hispanic Americans), 18 international. Average age 37. In 2008, 91 master's, 24 doctorates awarded. *Degree requirements:* For doctorate, comprehensive exam, thesis/dissertation. *Entrance requirements:* For master's, interview, writing sample; for doctorate, interview, minimum GPA of 3.25 in last 60 hours of course work. Additional exam requirements/recommendations for international students: Required—TOEFL (minimum score 550 paper-based; 213 computer-based; 79 iBT). *Application deadline:* For fall admission, 2/15 for domestic students, 4/15 for international students; for spring admission, 9/15 for domestic students, 8/1 for international students. Applications are processed on a rolling basis. Application fee: $30 ($50 for international students). Electronic applications accepted. *Expenses:* Tuition, state resident: full-time $3564; part-time $198 per semester hour. Tuition, nonresident: full-time $8622; part-time $479 per semester hour. Required fees: $1158; $64 per semester hour. Tuition and fees vary according to course load. *Financial support:* In 2008–09, 18 research assistantships (averaging $10,746 per year), 10 teaching assistantships (averaging $10,746 per year) were awarded; career-related internships or fieldwork, Federal Work-Study, institutionally sponsored loans, scholarships/grants, traineeships, health care benefits, and unspecified assistantships also available. Support available to part-time students. Financial award application deadline: 3/1; financial award applicants required to submit FAFSA. *Faculty research:* Parenting/parent education, distance education, play therapy, family sexuality, diversity, ANTHEM healthy marriages initiative. *Unit head:* Dr. Larry LeFlore, Chair, 940-898-2685, Fax: 940-898-2676, E-mail: famsci@twu.edu. *Application contact:* Samuel Wheeler, Assistant Director of Admissions, 940-898-3188, Fax: 940-898-3081, E-mail: wheelersr@twu.edu.

Tufts University, Graduate School of Arts and Sciences, Department of Child Development, Medford, MA 02155. Offers applied developmental psychology (PhD); child development (MA, CAGS); early childhood education (MAT). Part-time programs available. *Degree requirements:* For master's, thesis (for some programs); for doctorate, thesis/dissertation. *Entrance requirements:* For master's and doctorate, GRE General Test. Additional exam requirements/recommendations for international students: Required—TOEFL (minimum score 550 paper-based; 213 computer-based; 80 iBT). Electronic applications accepted.

Announcement: The Eliot-Pearson Department of Child Development is one of the country's leading departments serving children, youth, and families through its research, practice, and teaching. Noted for its interdisciplinary work and integration of research and practice, the department prepares students, through its MA, MAT, and PhD programs, to become leaders in a variety of fields, including education, developmental science, early intervention, advocacy, program evaluation, the arts and technology, and a variety of health-related fields. Please consult the department's Web site: http://ase.tufts.edu/epcd.

The University of Akron, Graduate School, College of Fine and Applied Arts, School of Family and Consumer Sciences, Program in Child and Family Development, Akron, OH 44325. Offers child development (MA); family development (MA). *Degree requirements:* For master's, comprehensive exam, thesis optional, project or thesis. *Entrance requirements:* For master's, GRE, minimum GPA of 2.75, letters of recommendation, personal statement of goals; interview. Additional exam requirements/recommendations for international students: Required—TOEFL (minimum score 550 paper-based; 213 computer-based; 79 iBT). Electronic applications accepted.

University of California, Davis, Graduate Studies, Graduate Group in Child Development, Davis, CA 95616. Offers MS. *Degree requirements:* For master's, comprehensive exam (for some programs), thesis (for some programs). *Entrance requirements:* For master's, GRE General Test, minimum GPA of 3.0. Additional exam requirements/recommendations for international students: Required—TOEFL (minimum score 550 paper-based; 213 computer-based). Electronic applications accepted. *Faculty research:* Cognitive development, socio-emotional development, early childhood.

University of La Verne, College of Education and Organizational Leadership, Department of Education, Programs in Child Development/Child Life, La Verne, CA 91750-4443. Offers child development (MS); child life (MS). Part-time programs available. *Faculty:* 11 full-time (8 women), 18 part-time/adjunct (14 women). *Students:* 31 full-time (30 women), 41 part-time (all women); includes 33 minority (3 African Americans, 10 Asian Americans or Pacific Islanders, 20 Hispanic Americans), 1 international. Average age 31. In 2008, 15 master's awarded. *Entrance requirements:* For master's, minimum GPA of 3.0, 3 letters of reference, writing sample. Additional exam requirements/recommendations for international students: Required—TOEFL (minimum score 550 paper-based; 213 computer-based). *Application deadline:* Applications are processed on a rolling basis. Application fee: $50. *Expenses:* Contact institution. *Financial support:* Institutionally sponsored loans, scholarships/grants, and unspecified assistantships available. Financial award application deadline: 3/2; financial award applicants required to submit FAFSA. *Unit head:* Dr. Barbara Nicoll, Chairperson, 909-593-3511 Ext. 4632, Fax: 909-392-2710, E-mail: nicollb@ulv.edu. *Application contact:* Christy Ranells, Program and Admission Specialist, 909-593-3511 Ext. 4644, Fax: 909-392-2761, E-mail: cranells@ulv.edu.

University of Minnesota, Twin Cities Campus, Graduate School, College of Education and Human Development, Institute of Child Development, Minneapolis, MN 55455-0213. Offers child psychology (MA, PhD); early childhood education (M Ed, MA, PhD); school psychology (MA, PhD). *Faculty research:* Developmental affective and cognitive neuroscience; developmental psychopathology; intervention and prevention science; social and emotional development; cognitive, language, and perceptual development.

University of Nebraska–Lincoln, Graduate College, College of Education and Human Sciences, Department of Child, Youth and Family Studies, Lincoln, NE 68588. Offers child development/early childhood education (MS, PhD); child, youth and family studies (MS); family and consumer sciences education (MS, PhD); family financial planning (MS); family science (MS, PhD); gerontology (PhD); human sciences (PhD), including child, youth and family studies, gerontology, medical family therapy; marriage and family therapy (MS); medical family therapy (PhD); youth development (MS). *Accreditation:* AAMFT/COAMFTE (one or more programs are accredited). Postbaccalaureate distance learning degree programs offered. *Faculty:* 16 full-time (11 women). *Students:* 23 full-time (18 women), 53 part-time (40 women); includes 8 minority (2 African Americans, 2 American Indian/Alaska Native, 2 Asian Americans or Pacific Islanders, 2 Hispanic Americans), 1 international. Average age 32. In 2008, 27 master's awarded. *Degree requirements:* For master's, thesis optional. *Entrance requirements:* For master's, GRE. Additional exam requirements/recommendations for international students: Required—TOEFL (minimum score 550 paper-based; 213 computer-based). *Application deadline:* For fall admission, 1/15 for domestic and international students; for spring admission, 10/1 for domestic and international students. Application fee: $40. Electronic applications accepted. *Expenses:* Tuition, state resident: full-time $4275; part-time $237.50 per credit hour. Tuition, nonresident: full-time $11,525; part-time $640.25 per credit hour. Required fees: $1068; $10.35 per credit hour. $440.70 per semester. Tuition and fees vary according to course load and program. *Financial support:* Fellowships, research assistantships, teaching assistantships, Federal Work-Study, health care benefits, and unspecified assistantships available. Financial award application deadline: 2/15. *Faculty research:* Marriage and family therapy, child development/early childhood education, family financial management. *Unit head:* Dr. Julie Johnson, Chair, 402-472-2957. *Application contact:* Dr. Julie Johnson, Chair, 402-472-2957.

The University of North Carolina at Charlotte, Graduate School, College of Education, Department of Special Education and Child Development, Charlotte, NC 28223-0001. Offers special education (M Ed, PhD), including academically gifted (M Ed), behavioral—emotional handicaps (M Ed), cross-categorical disabilities (M Ed), learning disabilities (M Ed), mental handicaps (M Ed), severe and profound handicaps (M Ed). Part-time programs available. *Faculty:* 29 full-time (20 women), 6 part-time/adjunct (all women). *Students:* 13 full-time (11 women), 50 part-time (47 women); includes 5 minority (1 African American, 3 American Indian/Alaska Native, 1 Hispanic American), 2 international. Average age 33. 23 applicants, 87% accepted, 19 enrolled. In 2008, 6 master's, 4 doctorates awarded. *Degree requirements:* For doctorate, comprehensive exam, thesis/dissertation, portfolio, qualifying exam. *Entrance requirements:* For master's, GRE or MAT; for doctorate, GRE or MAT, 3 letters of reference, resumé or curriculum vitae, minimum GPA of 3.5, master's degree in special education or related field, 3 years of teaching experience. Additional exam requirements/recommendations for international students: Required—TOEFL (paper-based 550; computer-based 220) or Michigan English Language Assessment Battery. *Application deadline:* For fall admission, 7/15 for domestic students, 5/1 for international students; for spring admission, 11/15 for domestic students, 10/1 for international students. Application fee: $55. *Expenses:* Tuition, area resident: Full-time $2919; part-time $122 per credit hour. Tuition, state resident: full-time $2919; part-time $122 per credit hour. Tuition, nonresident: full-time $13,126; part-time $547 per credit hour. Required fees: $1779; $91 per credit hour. Tuition and fees vary according to program. *Financial support:* In 2008–09, 1 fellowship (averaging $23,919 per year), 20 research assistantships (averaging $13,272 per year), 1 teaching assistantship (averaging $8,000 per year) were awarded. Financial award application deadline: 4/1; financial award applicants required to submit FAFSA. *Faculty research:* Transition to adulthood and self-determination, teaching reading and other academic skills to students with disabilities, alternate assessment, early intervention, preschool education. *Unit head:* David Gilmore, Unit Head, 704-687-8186, Fax: 704-687-2916. *Application contact:* Kathy B. Giddings, Director of Graduate Admissions, 704-687-3366, Fax: 704-687-3279, E-mail: agidding@uncc.edu.

The University of Tennessee at Martin, Graduate Programs, College of Agriculture and Applied Sciences, Department of Family and Consumer Sciences, Martin, TN 38238-1000. Offers dietetics (MSFCS); general family and consumer sciences (MSFCS). Part-time programs available. *Faculty:* 6. *Students:* 32 (29 women). 30 applicants, 100% accepted, 16 enrolled. In 2008, 5 master's awarded. *Degree requirements:* For master's, comprehensive exam, thesis optional. *Entrance requirements:* For master's, GRE General Test, minimum GPA of 2.5. Additional exam requirements/recommendations for international students: Required—TOEFL (minimum score 525 paper-based; 197 computer-based; 71 iBT). *Application deadline:* For fall admission, 8/1 priority date for domestic students, 8/1 for international students; for spring admission, 1/1 for domestic and international students. Applications are processed on a rolling basis. Application fee: $30 ($50 for international students). Electronic applications accepted. *Expenses:* Tuition, state resident: full-time $6084; part-time $340 per semester hour. Tuition, nonresident: full-time $16,726; part-time $932 per semester hour. *Financial support:* In 2008–09, 6 students received support, including 6 research assistantships with full tuition reimbursements available (averaging $6,585 per year); scholarships/grants and unspecified assistantships also available. Financial award application deadline: 3/1. *Faculty research:* Children with developmental disabilities, regional food product development and marketing, parent education. *Unit head:* Dr. Lisa LeBleu, Coordinator, 731-881-7116, Fax: 731-881-7106, E-mail: llebleu@

Child Development

The University of Tennessee at Martin (continued)
utm.edu. *Application contact:* Linda S. Arant, Student Services Specialist, 731-881-7012, Fax: 731-881-7499, E-mail: larant@utm.edu.

The University of Texas at Austin, Graduate School, College of Natural Sciences, School of Human Ecology, Austin, TX 78712-1111. Offers human development and family sciences (MA, PhD); nutritional sciences (MA, PhD), including nutrition (MA), nutritional sciences (PhD); textile and apparel technology (MS). *Degree requirements:* For master's, thesis; for doctorate, thesis/dissertation. *Entrance requirements:* For master's and doctorate, GRE General Test. Electronic applications accepted.

University of Wyoming, Graduate School, College of Agriculture, Department of Family and Consumer Sciences, Laramie, WY 82070. Offers early childhood development (MS); family and consumer sciences (MS); food science and human nutrition (MS). Part-time programs available. *Faculty:* 13 full-time (8 women), 13 part-time/adjunct (all women). *Students:* 2 full-time (both women), 5 part-time (all women); includes 1 minority (American Indian/Alaska Native). Average age 34. 4 applicants, 100% accepted, 4 enrolled. In 2008, 2 master's awarded. *Degree requirements:* For master's, thesis, project. *Entrance requirements:* For master's, GRE General Test or MCAT, minimum GPA of 3.0. Additional exam requirements/recommendations for international students: Required—TOEFL (minimum score 540 paper-based; 207 computer-based; 76 iBT). *Application deadline:* For fall admission, 4/1 priority date for domestic students, 3/1 priority date for international students; for spring admission, 10/1 priority date for domestic students, 9/1 priority date for international students. Applications are processed on a rolling basis. Application fee: $50. Electronic applications accepted. *Financial support:* In 2008–09, 2 research assistantships with full tuition reimbursements (averaging $11,072 per year), 2 teaching assistantships with full tuition reimbursements (averaging $11,072 per year) were awarded; career-related internships or fieldwork, Federal Work-Study, institutionally sponsored loans, scholarships/grants, and health care benefits also available. Support available to part-time students. Financial award application deadline: 5/1; financial award applicants required to submit FAFSA. *Faculty research:* Asthma, obesity and healthy weights, nutrition concerns of children with special health care needs, food product development, food safety, postpartum health, exercise nutrition. *Unit head:* Dr. Karen C. Williams, Professor and Department Head, 307-766-4145, Fax: 307-766-5686, E-mail: fam-consci@uwyo.edu. *Application contact:* Michell Anderson, Graduate Admissions Coordinator, 307-766-2287, Fax: 307-766-2374, E-mail: manders2@uwyo.edu.

Virginia Polytechnic Institute and State University, Graduate School, College of Liberal Arts and Human Sciences, Department of Human Development, Blacksburg, VA 24061. Offers adult development and aging (MS, PhD); adult learning and human resource development (MS, PhD); child development (MS, PhD); family studies (MS, PhD); marriage and family therapy (MS, PhD). *Accreditation:* AAMFT/COAMFTE (one or more programs are accredited). *Entrance requirements:* For master's and doctorate, GRE General Test. Additional exam requirements/recommendations for international students: Required—TOEFL (minimum score 600 paper-based; 250 computer-based). Electronic applications accepted. *Faculty research:* Stress management, children's play, dual-career families, social cognition, relationships of elderly.

Whittier College, Graduate Programs, Department of Education and Child Development, Whittier, CA 90608-0634. Offers educational administration (MA Ed); elementary education (MA Ed); secondary education (MA Ed). Part-time and evening/weekend programs available. *Degree requirements:* For master's, thesis. *Entrance requirements:* For master's, GRE General Test, MAT, minimum GPA of 3.5, academic writing sample.

Clothing and Textiles

Academy of Art University, Graduate Program, School of Fashion, San Francisco, CA 94105-3410. Offers fashion design (MFA); fashion merchandising (MFA); fashion textiles (MFA); knitwear (MFA). Part-time programs available. Postbaccalaureate distance learning degree programs offered (no on-campus study). *Faculty:* 16 full-time (12 women), 32 part-time/adjunct (22 women). *Students:* 353 full-time (313 women), 130 part-time (119 women); includes 95 minority (36 African Americans, 2 American Indian/Alaska Native, 39 Asian Americans or Pacific Islanders, 18 Hispanic Americans), 225 international. Average age 28. 179 applicants. In 2008, 48 master's awarded. *Degree requirements:* For master's, thesis, final review. *Entrance requirements:* For master's, minimum GPA of 3.0, portfolio. *Application deadline:* For fall admission, 9/7 for domestic and international students; for spring admission, 2/2 for domestic and international students. Applications are processed on a rolling basis. Application fee: $100 ($500 for international students). Electronic applications accepted. *Expenses:* Tuition: Full-time $18,400; part-time $770 per term. Tuition and fees vary according to program. *Financial support:* Career-related internships or fieldwork and Federal Work-Study available. Support available to part-time students. Financial award application deadline: 8/10; financial award applicants required to submit FAFSA. *Unit head:* Simon Ungless, Director, 800-544-ARTS, Fax: 415-296-2089, E-mail: info@academyart.edu. *Application contact:* Prospective Student Services, 800-544-ARTS, Fax: 415-263-4130, E-mail: info@academyart.edu.

Auburn University, Graduate School, College of Human Sciences, Department of Consumer Affairs, Auburn University, AL 36849. Offers apparel and textiles (MS). Part-time programs available. *Faculty:* 15 full-time (all women). *Students:* 5 full-time (4 women), 5 part-time (all women); includes 6 minority (2 African Americans, 1 Asian American or Pacific Islander, 3 Hispanic Americans), 4 international. Average age 29. 4 applicants, 75% accepted, 2 enrolled. In 2008, 6 master's awarded. *Degree requirements:* For master's, thesis (for some programs). *Entrance requirements:* For master's, GRE General Test. *Application deadline:* For fall admission, 7/7 for domestic students; for spring admission, 11/24 for domestic students. Applications are processed on a rolling basis. Application fee: $25 ($50 for international students). Electronic applications accepted. *Expenses:* Tuition, area resident: Full-time $5880; part-time $243 per credit hour. Tuition, state resident: full-time $5880; part-time $243 per credit hour. Tuition, nonresident: full-time $17,640; part-time $729 per credit hour. International tuition: $17,846 full-time. Required fees: $620. Tuition and fees vary according to program and reciprocity agreements. *Financial support:* Fellowships, research assistantships, teaching assistantships, career-related internships or fieldwork and Federal Work-Study available. Support available to part-time students. Financial award application deadline: 3/15. *Faculty research:* Merchandising, consumer behavior, international marketing of textiles and apparel, apparel product development. Total annual research expenditures: $875,000. *Unit head:* Dr. Carol L. Warfield, Head, 334-844-4084, E-mail: cwarfiel@humsci.auburn.edu. *Application contact:* Dr. George Flowers, Dean of the Graduate School, 334-844-2125.

Central Michigan University, College of Graduate Studies, College of Education and Human Services, Department of Human Environmental Studies, Mount Pleasant, MI 48859. Offers apparel product development and merchandising technology (MS); human development and family studies (MA); nutrition and dietetics (MS). Part-time and evening/weekend programs available. *Faculty:* 15 full-time (11 women), 1 part-time/adjunct (0 women). *Degree requirements:* For master's, thesis or alternative. *Application deadline:* Applications are processed on a rolling basis. Application fee: $35 ($45 for international students). Electronic applications accepted. *Expenses:* Tuition, state resident: full-time $3717; part-time $413 per credit. Tuition, nonresident: full-time $6894; part-time $766 per credit. *Financial support:* Fellowships with tuition reimbursements, research assistantships, career-related internships or fieldwork, Federal Work-Study, unspecified assistantships, and out-of-state merit awards available. *Faculty research:* Human growth and development, family studies and human sexuality, human nutrition and dietetics, apparel and textile retailing, computer-aided design for apparel. *Unit head:* Dr. Phame Camerena, Chairperson, 989-774-3218, Fax: 989-774-2435, E-mail: camar1pm@cmich.edu. *Application contact:* Dr. Candace Maylee, Assistant Coordinator of Graduate Programs, 989-774-2613, Fax: 989-774-2435, E-mail: mayle1ce@cmich.edu.

Cornell University, Graduate School, Graduate Fields of Human Ecology, Field of Textiles, Ithaca, NY 14853-0001. Offers apparel design (MA, MPS); fiber science (MS, PhD); polymer science (MS, PhD); textile science (MS, PhD). *Faculty:* 17 full-time (7 women). *Students:* 20 full-time (14 women); includes 2 minority (1 African American, 1 Hispanic American), 12 international. Average age 30. 33 applicants, 15% accepted, 4 enrolled. In 2008, 4 master's, 3 doctorates awarded. *Degree requirements:* For master's, thesis (MA, MS), project paper (MPS); for doctorate, comprehensive exam, thesis/dissertation. *Entrance requirements:* For master's, GRE General Test, 2 letters of recommendation, portfolio (functional apparel design); for doctorate, GRE General Test, 2 letters of recommendation. Additional exam requirements/recommendations for international students: Required—TOEFL (minimum score 600 paper-based; 250 computer-based; 77 iBT). *Application deadline:* For fall admission, 3/1 for domestic students; for spring admission, 10/1 for domestic students. Application fee: $70. Electronic applications accepted. *Expenses:* Tuition: Full-time $29,500. Required fees: $70. Full-time tuition and fees vary according to degree level, program and student level. *Financial support:* In 2008–09, 19 students received support, including 2 fellowships with full tuition reimbursements available, 12 research assistantships with full tuition reimbursements available, 5 teaching assistantships with full tuition reimbursements available; institutionally sponsored loans, scholarships/grants, health care benefits, tuition waivers (full and partial), and unspecified assistantships also available. Financial award applicants required to submit FAFSA. *Faculty research:* Apparel design, consumption, mass customization, 3-D body scanning. *Unit head:* Director of Graduate Studies, 607-255-3151, Fax: 607-255-1093. *Application contact:* Graduate Field Assistant, 607-255-3151, Fax: 607-255-1093, E-mail: textiles_grad@cornell.edu.

Eastern Michigan University, Graduate School, College of Technology, School of Technology Studies, Program in Apparel, Textile Merchandising, Ypsilanti, MI 48197. Offers MS. Part-time and evening/weekend programs available. Postbaccalaureate distance learning degree programs offered (minimal on-campus study). *Entrance requirements:* Additional exam requirements/recommendations for international students: Required—TOEFL.

Fashion Institute of Technology, School of Graduate Studies, Programs in Fashion and Textile Studies: History, Theory, and Museum Practice, New York, NY 10001-5992. Offers MA. *Accreditation:* NASAD. *Degree requirements:* For master's, one foreign language, thesis, internship. *Entrance requirements:* For master's, GRE General Test or GRE Subject Test, previous course work in art history and chemistry, 4 semesters of a foreign language. Additional exam requirements/recommendations for international students: Required—TOEFL (minimum score 550 paper-based; 213 computer-based). Electronic applications accepted.

See Close-Up on page 117.

Iowa State University of Science and Technology, Graduate College, College of Human Sciences, Department of Apparel, Education Studies, and Hospitality Management, Program in Textiles and Clothing, Ames, IA 50011. Offers MFCS, MS, PhD. *Students:* 19 full-time (17 women), 5 part-time (4 women); includes 4 minority (3 African Americans, 1 Asian American or Pacific Islander), 13 international. In 2008, 5 master's, 3 doctorates awarded. *Degree requirements:* For master's, thesis; for doctorate, thesis/dissertation. *Entrance requirements:* For master's and doctorate, GRE General Test. Additional exam requirements/recommendations for international students: Required—TOEFL (minimum score 55 paper-based; 79 iBT), IELTS (6.5) or TOEFL. *Application deadline:* For fall admission, 2/1 priority date for domestic and international students. Applications are processed on a rolling basis. Application fee: $30 ($70 for international students). Electronic applications accepted. *Expenses:* Tuition, area resident: Full-time $6446; part-time $359 per credit. Tuition, state resident: full-time $6446; part-time $359 per credit. Tuition, nonresident: full-time $17,330; part-time $963 per credit. Required fees: $790; $249.25 per semester. Tuition and fees vary according to course load and program. *Financial support:* In 2008–09, 10 research assistantships with full and partial tuition reimbursements (averaging $13,266 per year), 8 teaching assistantships with full and partial tuition reimbursements (averaging $12,420 per year) were awarded; scholarships/grants also available. *Unit head:* Dr. Ann Marie Fiore, Director of Graduate Education, 515-294-9303, E-mail: amfiore@iastate.edu. *Application contact:* Dr. Ann Marie Fiore, Director of Graduate Education, 515-294-9303, E-mail: amfiore@iastate.edu.

Kansas State University, Graduate School, College of Human Ecology, Department of Apparel, Textiles, and Interior Design, Manhattan, KS 66506. Offers apparel and textiles (MS). *Faculty:* 7 full-time (all women), 2 part-time/adjunct (both women). *Students:* 9 full-time (8 women), 12 part-time (10 women); includes 3 minority (1 African American, 1 Asian American or Pacific Islander, 1 Hispanic American), 2 international. Average age 29. 17 applicants, 65% accepted, 7 enrolled. In 2008, 2 master's awarded. *Degree requirements:* For master's, thesis optional, residency. *Entrance requirements:* For master's, GRE General Test, minimum undergraduate GPA of 3.0. Additional exam requirements/recommendations for international students: Required—TOEFL (minimum score 600 paper-based; 250 computer-based). *Application deadline:* For fall admission, 2/1 priority date for domestic and international students; for spring admission, 9/1 for domestic and international students. Applications are processed on a rolling basis. Application fee: $30 ($55 for international students). Electronic applications accepted. *Expenses:* Tuition, area resident: Full-time $6466; part-time $269.40 per credit hour. Tuition, state resident: full-time $6466; part-time $269.40 per credit hour. Tuition, nonresident: full-time $14,874; part-time $619.75 per credit hour. Required fees: $673; $23.40 per credit hour. Tuition and fees vary according to campus/location. *Financial support:* In 2008–09, 1 research assistantship (averaging $13,950 per year), 5 teaching assistantships with full tuition reimbursements (averaging $11,330 per year) were awarded; fellowships, career-related internships or fieldwork, Federal Work-Study, institutionally sponsored loans, and scholarships/grants also available. Support available to part-time students. Financial award application deadline: 3/1; financial award applicants required to submit FAFSA. *Faculty research:* Apparel marketing and consumer behavior, protective and functional clothing and textiles, social and environmental responsibility, apparel design, new product development. *Unit head:* Jana Hawley, Head, 785-532-1318, Fax: 785-532-3796, E-mail: hawleyj@ksu.edu. *Application contact:* Gina Jackson, Application Contact, 785-532-6693, Fax: 785-532-3796, E-mail: gjackson@ksu.edu.

Kansas State University, Graduate School, College of Human Ecology, Program in Human Ecology, Manhattan, KS 66506. Offers apparel and textiles (PhD); family life education and consultation (PhD); food service, hospitality management, and administrative dietetics (PhD); institutional management (PhD); lifespan and human development (PhD); marriage and family therapy (PhD). *Faculty:* 3 full-time (all women). *Students:* 37 full-time (25 women), 24 part-time (15 women); includes 10 minority (8 African Americans, 1 American Indian/Alaska Native, 1 Asian American or Pacific Islander), 18 international. Average age 37. 25 applicants, 80%

accepted, 18 enrolled. In 2008, 14 doctorates awarded. *Application deadline:* For fall admission, 2/1 priority date for domestic and international students; for spring admission, 8/1 priority date for domestic and international students. Application fee: $30 ($55 for international students). *Expenses:* Tuition, area resident: Full-time $6466; part-time $269.40 per credit hour. Tuition, state resident: full-time $6466; part-time $269.40 per credit hour. Tuition, nonresident: full-time $14,874; part-time $619.75 per credit hour. Required fees: $673; $23.40 per credit hour. Tuition and fees vary according to campus/location. *Unit head:* Elizabeth McCullough, Director, 785-532-2284, Fax: 785-532-3796, E-mail: lizm@ksu.edu. *Application contact:* Connie Fechter, Application Contact, 785-532-1473, Fax: 785-532-3796, E-mail: fechter@ksu.edu.

North Carolina State University, Graduate School, College of Textiles, Program in Textile Technology Management, Raleigh, NC 27695. Offers PhD. *Degree requirements:* For doctorate, one foreign language, thesis/dissertation, cumulative exams. *Entrance requirements:* For doctorate, GRE or GMAT. Electronic applications accepted. *Faculty research:* Niche markets, supply chain, globalization, logistics.

The Ohio State University, Graduate School, College of Education and Human Ecology, Program in Textiles and Clothing, Columbus, OH 43210. Offers MS, PhD. *Degree requirements:* For master's, thesis optional; for doctorate, thesis/dissertation. *Entrance requirements:* For master's and doctorate, GRE General Test. Additional exam requirements/recommendations for international students: Required—TOEFL (minimum score 577 paper-based; 233 computer-based). Electronic applications accepted.

Oklahoma State University, College of Human Environmental Sciences, Department of Design, Housing and Merchandising, Stillwater, OK 74078. Offers MS, PhD. Postbaccalaureate distance learning degree programs offered. *Faculty:* 19 full-time (15 women), 3 part-time/adjunct (all women). *Students:* 13 full-time (8 women), 23 part-time (21 women); includes 3 minority (1 African American, 2 Asian Americans or Pacific Islanders), 17 international. Average age 31. 15 applicants, 67% accepted, 6 enrolled. In 2008, 8 master's awarded. *Degree requirements:* For master's, thesis (for some programs); for doctorate, comprehensive exam, thesis/dissertation. *Entrance requirements:* For master's and doctorate, GRE or GMAT. Additional exam requirements/recommendations for international students: Required—TOEFL. *Application deadline:* For fall admission, 3/1 priority date for international students; for spring admission, 8/1 priority date for international students. Applications are processed on a rolling basis. Application fee: $40 ($75 for international students). Electronic applications accepted. *Expenses:* Tuition, state resident: full-time $3716.40; part-time $154.85 per credit hour. Tuition, nonresident: full-time $14,448; part-time $602 per credit hour. Required fees: $1772.40; $73.85 per credit hour. One-time fee: $50. Tuition and fees vary according to course load and campus/location. *Financial support:* In 2008–09, 18 research assistantships (averaging $10,775 per year), 8 teaching assistantships (averaging $11,595 per year) were awarded; career-related internships or fieldwork, Federal Work-Study, scholarships/grants, health care benefits, tuition waivers (partial), and unspecified assistantships also available. Support available to part-time students. Financial award application deadline: 3/1; financial award applicants required to submit FAFSA. *Faculty research:* Environmental sciences design, housing and merchandising, creativity and physical environment; product development, production and evaluation; experimental learning and critical thinking, technology strategies and assessment, customer expectation and satisfaction. *Unit head:* Dr. Randall Russ, Interim Head, 405-744-5049, Fax: 405-744-6910. *Application contact:* Dr. Gordon Emslie, Dean, 405-744-6368, Fax: 405-744-0355, E-mail: grad_i@okstate.edu.

Oregon State University, Graduate School, College of Health and Human Sciences, Department of Design and Human Environment, Corvallis, OR 97331. Offers MA, MAIS, MS, PhD. Terminal master's awarded for partial completion of doctoral program. *Degree requirements:* For master's, thesis or alternative; for doctorate, thesis/dissertation. *Entrance requirements:* For master's and doctorate, GRE General Test, minimum GPA of 3.0 in last 90 hours. Additional exam requirements/recommendations for international students: Required—TOEFL.

Philadelphia University, School of Engineering and Textiles, Program in Fashion Apparel Studies, Philadelphia, PA 19144-5497. Offers MS. Part-time programs available. *Entrance requirements:* For master's, GRE or GMAT, minimum GPA of 2.8. Additional exam requirements/recommendations for international students: Required—TOEFL (minimum score 550 paper-based; 213 computer-based; 79 iBT). Electronic applications accepted.

Purdue University, Graduate School, College of Consumer and Family Sciences, Department of Consumer Sciences and Retailing, West Lafayette, IN 47907. Offers consumer behavior (MS, PhD); family and consumer economics (MS, PhD); retail management (MS, PhD); textile science (MS, PhD). Part-time programs available. *Degree requirements:* For master's, thesis; for doctorate, thesis/dissertation. *Entrance requirements:* For master's and doctorate, GMAT or GRE General Test. Additional exam requirements/recommendations for international students: Required—TOEFL. Electronic applications accepted. *Faculty research:* Family financial resources, retail management and patronage, chemical analysis of textile dyes and finishes.

South Dakota State University, Graduate School, College of Family and Consumer Sciences, Department of Apparel Merchandising and Interior Design, Brookings, SD 57007. Offers MFCS. Part-time and evening/weekend programs available. Postbaccalaureate distance learning degree programs offered. *Faculty:* 4 full-time (all women). *Students:* 3 part-time (all women). *Entrance requirements:* Additional exam requirements/recommendations for international students: Required—TOEFL (minimum score 550 paper-based; 213 computer-based; 79 iBT). *Application deadline:* For fall admission, 4/15 for international students; for spring admission, 8/15 for international students. Application fee: $35. *Faculty research:* Rural internet shopping, professional development in apparel merchandising, gender, aesthetics. *Unit head:* Prof. Jane E. Hegland, Department Head, 605-688-5196, Fax: 605-688-5578, E-mail: jane.hegland@sdstate.edu. *Application contact:* The Graduate School, 605-688-4181, E-mail: sdsu_gradschool@sdstate.edu.

The University of Akron, Graduate School, College of Fine and Applied Arts, School of Family and Consumer Sciences, Program in Clothing, Textiles and Interiors, Akron, OH 44325. Offers MA. *Degree requirements:* For master's, comprehensive exam, thesis optional, thesis or project. *Entrance requirements:* For master's, GRE, minimum GPA of 2.75, letters of recommendation, personal statement of goals, interview. Additional exam requirements/recommendations for international students: Required—TOEFL (minimum score 550 paper-based; 213 computer-based; 79 iBT). Electronic applications accepted.

The University of Alabama, Graduate School, College of Human Environmental Sciences, Department of Clothing, Textiles, and Interior Design, Tuscaloosa, AL 35487. Offers MSHES. *Faculty:* 4 full-time (all women). In 2008, 1 master's awarded. *Degree requirements:* For master's, comprehensive exam, thesis optional. *Entrance requirements:* For master's, GRE General Test or MAT, minimum GPA of 3.0. *Application deadline:* For fall admission, 7/6 for domestic students. Applications are processed on a rolling basis. Application fee: $30. *Expenses:* Tuition, area resident: Full-time $6400. Tuition, state resident: full-time $6400. Tuition, nonresident: full-time $18,000. *Financial support:* In 2008–09, 1 research assistantship with full tuition reimbursement (averaging $8,100 per year), 2 teaching assistantships with full tuition reimbursements (averaging $8,100 per year) were awarded; fellowships, career-related internships or fieldwork, Federal Work-Study, and scholarships/grants also available. Financial award application deadline: 3/15. *Faculty research:* Archeological textiles, textile science, material culture, social psychology, international trade. *Unit head:* Dr. Carolyn Callis, Chair and Associate Professor, 205-348-6176, Fax: 205-348-0022, E-mail: ccallis@ches.ua.edu. *Application contact:* Dr. Carolyn Callis, Chair and Associate Professor, 205-348-6176, Fax: 205-348-0022, E-mail: ccallis@ches.ua.edu.

University of Alberta, Faculty of Graduate Studies and Research, Department of Human Ecology, Edmonton, AB T6G 2E1, Canada. Offers family ecology and practice (M Sc, PhD); textiles and clothing (M Sc, MA, PhD). Postbaccalaureate distance learning degree programs offered (no on-campus study). *Degree requirements:* For master's, thesis (for some programs); for doctorate, comprehensive exam, thesis/dissertation. *Entrance requirements:* For master's and doctorate, minimum GPA of 7.0 on a 9.0 scale. Additional exam requirements/recommendations for international students: Required—TOEFL (minimum score 580 paper-based; 237 computer-based). *Faculty research:* Families and aging, family and child poverty, paid and unpaid work of families, textiles and clothing, parent-child relationships.

University of California, Davis, Graduate Studies, Graduate Group in Textiles, Davis, CA 95616. Offers MS. *Degree requirements:* For master's, comprehensive exam (for some programs), thesis (for some programs). *Entrance requirements:* For master's, GRE General Test, minimum GPA of 3.0. Additional exam requirements/recommendations for international students: Required—TOEFL (minimum score 550 paper-based; 213 computer-based). Electronic applications accepted. *Faculty research:* Fiber science, social psychology, consumer psychology, chemical and physical properties of fibrous and polymeric materials.

University of Georgia, Graduate School, College of Family and Consumer Sciences, Department of Textiles, Merchandising, and Interiors, Athens, GA 30602. Offers historic costume and textiles (MS); merchandising/international trade (MS); textile analysis (PhD); textile chemical processes (PhD); textile products and standards (PhD); textile science (MS). *Degree requirements:* For master's, thesis; for doctorate, thesis/dissertation. *Entrance requirements:* For master's and doctorate, GRE General Test. Electronic applications accepted.

University of Kentucky, Graduate School, College of Design, Program in Interior Design, Merchandising, and Textiles, Lexington, KY 40506-0032. Offers MAIDM, MSIDM. *Degree requirements:* For master's, comprehensive exam, thesis optional. *Entrance requirements:* For master's, GRE General Test, minimum undergraduate GPA of 2.75. Additional exam requirements/recommendations for international students: Required—TOEFL (minimum score 550 paper-based; 213 computer-based). Electronic applications accepted. *Faculty research:* Interior design, apparel merchandising, textile evaluation, creativity in design, social-psychological aspects of dress and interiors.

University of Manitoba, Faculty of Graduate Studies, Faculty of Human Ecology, Department of Textile Sciences, Winnipeg, MB R3T 2N2, Canada. Offers M Sc. *Degree requirements:* For master's, thesis.

University of Minnesota, Twin Cities Campus, Graduate School, College of Design, Department of Design, Housing, and Apparel, Minneapolis, MN 55455-0213. Offers apparel (MA, MS, PhD); design communication (MA, MS, PhD); housing studies (MA, MS, PhD, Postbaccalaureate Certificate); interactive design (MFA); interior design (MA, MS, PhD). Part-time programs available. *Degree requirements:* For master's and Postbaccalaureate Certificate, comprehensive exam, thesis (for some programs); for doctorate, comprehensive exam, thesis/dissertation. *Entrance requirements:* For master's, GRE General Test, minimum GPA of 3.0 (preferred), portfolio, 3 letters of recommendation; for doctorate, GRE General Test, minimum GPA of 3.0 (preferred), portfolio, 3 letters of recommendation, writing sample; for Postbaccalaureate Certificate, GRE General Test, minimum GPA of 3.0 (preferred). Additional exam requirements/recommendations for international students: Required—TOEFL (minimum score 550 paper-based; 213 computer-based; 79 iBT). Electronic applications accepted. *Faculty research:* Housing policy and community development; consumer behavior; interactive design; design history; social, cultural, and behavioral issues related to designed environments.

University of Missouri–Columbia, Graduate School, College of Human Environmental Science, Department of Textile and Apparel Management, Columbia, MO 65211. Offers MA, MS. *Faculty:* 5 full-time (all women). *Students:* 9 full-time (8 women), 5 part-time (all women); includes 1 minority (African American), 3 international. Average age 31. 21 applicants, 48% accepted, 3 enrolled. In 2008, 2 master's awarded. *Entrance requirements:* For master's, GRE General Test, minimum GPA of 3.0. Additional exam requirements/recommendations for international students: Required—TOEFL (minimum score 550 paper-based; 213 computer-based; 79 iBT). *Application deadline:* For fall admission, 2/1 priority date for domestic students; for winter admission, 6/1 priority date for domestic students; for spring admission, 10/1 priority date for domestic students. Applications are processed on a rolling basis. Application fee: $45 ($60 for international students). *Financial support:* Research assistantships, teaching assistantships, institutionally sponsored loans available. *Unit head:* Dr. Pam Norum, Director of Graduate Studies, 573-882-2934, E-mail: norump@missouri.edu. *Application contact:* Dr. Pam Norum, Director of Graduate Studies, 573-882-2934, E-mail: norump@missouri.edu.

University of North Texas, Robert B. Toulouse School of Graduate Studies, School of Merchandising and Hospitality Management, Denton, TX 76203. Offers hospitality management (MS); merchandising (MS). Part-time programs available. Postbaccalaureate distance learning degree programs offered (no on-campus study). *Degree requirements:* For master's, comprehensive exam, thesis or alternative. *Entrance requirements:* For master's, GRE General Test or GMAT, minimum GPA of 2.8, course work in major area, essay, 3 references, resumé. Additional exam requirements/recommendations for international students: Required—proof of English language proficiency required for non-native English speakers; Recommended—TOEFL (minimum score 550 paper-based; 213 computer-based). *Faculty research:* Management, hospitality, merchandising, globalization, consumer behavior and experiences.

University of Rhode Island, Graduate School, College of Human Science and Services, Department of Textiles, Fashion Merchandising and Design, Kingston, RI 02881. Offers MS. *Entrance requirements:* For master's, GRE. Application fee: $35. *Expenses:* Tuition, state resident: full-time $8024; part-time $446 per credit. Tuition, nonresident: full-time $21,046; part-time $1169 per credit. Required fees: $1056; $26 per credit. $30 per semester. One-time fee: $95 part-time. *Unit head:* Dr. Linda Welters, Chair, 401-874-4525, E-mail: lwelters@uri.edu. *Application contact:* Dr. Linda Welters, Chair/Graduate Director, 401-874-4525, E-mail: lwelters@uri.edu.

The University of Tennessee, Graduate School, College of Education, Health and Human Sciences, Department of Consumer and Industry Services Management, Program in Consumer Services Management, Knoxville, TN 37996. Offers retail and consumer sciences (MS); textile science (MS). Part-time programs available. *Degree requirements:* For master's, thesis or alternative. *Entrance requirements:* For master's, GRE General Test, minimum GPA of 2.7. Additional exam requirements/recommendations for international students: Required—TOEFL. Electronic applications accepted. *Expenses:* Tuition, area resident: Part-time $348 per credit hour. Tuition, state resident: full-time $6262. Tuition, nonresident: full-time $18,920; part-time $1052 per credit hour. Required fees: $812; $36 per credit hour. Tuition and fees vary according to program.

The University of Tennessee, Graduate School, College of Education, Health and Human Sciences, Program in Human Ecology, Knoxville, TN 37996. Offers child and family studies (PhD); community health (PhD); nutrition science (PhD); retailing and consumer sciences (PhD); textile science (PhD). *Degree requirements:* For doctorate, thesis/dissertation. *Entrance requirements:* For doctorate, GRE General Test, minimum GPA of 2.7. Additional exam requirements/recommendations for international students: Required—TOEFL. Electronic applications accepted. *Expenses:* Tuition, area resident: Part-time $348 per credit hour. Tuition, state resident: full-time $6262. Tuition, nonresident: full-time $18,920; part-time $1052 per credit hour. Required fees: $812; $36 per credit hour. Tuition and fees vary according to program.

Virginia Polytechnic Institute and State University, Graduate School, College of Liberal Arts and Human Sciences, Department of Apparel, Housing, and Resource Management, Blacksburg, VA 24061. Offers apparel business and economics (MS, PhD); apparel product design and analysis (MS, PhD); apparel quality analysis (MS, PhD); consumer studies (MS, PhD); family financial management (MS, PhD); household equipment (MS, PhD); housing (MS, PhD); interior design (MS, PhD); resource management (MS, PhD). *Degree requirements:* For master's, thesis; for doctorate, thesis/dissertation. *Entrance requirements:* For master's and doctorate, GRE General Test. Additional exam requirements/recommendations for international students: Required—TOEFL (minimum score 550 paper-based; 213 computer-

Clothing and Textiles

Virginia Polytechnic Institute and State University (continued) based). Electronic applications accepted. *Faculty research:* Housing for elderly, affordable housing, household time use, phosphate laundry study, economic well-living.

Washington State University, Graduate School, College of Agricultural, Human, and Natural Resource Sciences, Department of Apparel, Merchandising, Design, and Textiles, Pullman, WA 99164. Offers apparel, merchandising, design and textiles (MA); interdisciplinary (PhD);

interior design (MA). *Degree requirements:* For master's, comprehensive exam (for some programs), thesis, oral exam; for doctorate, comprehensive exam, thesis/dissertation. *Entrance requirements:* For master's, GRE, minimum GPA of 3.0, 3 writing samples, 3 letters of recommendation, portfolio. Additional exam requirements/recommendations for international students: Required—TOEFL. Electronic applications accepted. *Faculty research:* Product development, design theory, cultural diversity, computer design accessibility.

Consumer Economics

California State University, Long Beach, Graduate Studies, College of Health and Human Services, Department of Family and Consumer Sciences, Long Beach, CA 90840. Offers family and consumer sciences (MA); nutritional science (MS), including food science, hospitality foodservice and hotel management, nutritional sciences/dietetics and food administration. Part-time and evening/weekend programs available. *Faculty:* 9 full-time (7 women). *Students:* 7 part-time (6 women); includes 3 minority (2 Asian Americans or Pacific Islanders, 1 Hispanic American). Average age 33. 6 applicants, 17% accepted, 1 enrolled. *Degree requirements:* For master's, comprehensive exam or thesis. *Entrance requirements:* For master's, GRE (MS), minimum GPA of 3.0. *Application deadline:* For fall admission, 5/1 for domestic students. Applications are processed on a rolling basis. Application fee: $55. Electronic applications accepted. *Expenses:* Tuition, nonresident: full-time $11,160; part-time $372 per unit. Required fees: $4100; $1261 per semester. *Financial support:* Federal Work-Study, institutionally sponsored loans, and scholarships/grants available. Financial award application deadline: 3/2. *Faculty research:* School uniforms, consumer complaining behavior, nutrition and fitness education and behavior change, curriculum change, teaching experience of interns. *Unit head:* Dr. Wendy Reiboldt, Chair, 562-985-4484, Fax: 562-985-4414, E-mail: reiboldt@csulb.edu. *Application contact:* Dr. Jacqueline J Lee, Graduate Coordinator, 562-985-4545, Fax: 562-985-4414, E-mail: jjlee@csulb.edu.

Colorado State University, Graduate School, College of Applied Human Sciences, Department of Design and Merchandising, Fort Collins, CA 80523-1574. Offers MS. Part-time programs available. Postbaccalaureate distance learning degree programs offered (no on-campus study). *Faculty:* 13 full-time (10 women). *Students:* 8 full-time (7 women), 15 part-time (12 women); includes 3 minority (1 African American, 1 American Indian/Alaska Native, 1 Asian American or Pacific Islander), 4 international. Average age 32. 9 applicants, 56% accepted, 4 enrolled. In 2008, 6 master's awarded. *Degree requirements:* For master's, thesis. *Entrance requirements:* For master's, GRE General Test, minimum GPA of 3.0, resumé, portfolio (if applicable to area of study), statement of purpose, letters of recommendation. Additional exam requirements/recommendations for international students: Required—TOEFL (minimum score 550 paper-based; 213 computer-based). *Application deadline:* For fall admission, 2/1 priority date for domestic students, 2/15 priority date for international students; for spring admission, 8/1 priority date for domestic students, 7/15 priority date for international students. Applications are processed on a rolling basis. Application fee: $50. Electronic applications accepted. *Expenses:* Tuition, area resident: full-time $5620; part-time $312.25 per credit. Tuition, state resident: full-time $5620; part-time $312.25 per credit. Tuition, nonresident: full-time $17,253; part-time $958.50 per credit. Required fees: $1449.56; $82.35 per credit. *Financial support:* In 2008–09, 8 students received support, including 1 research assistantship with partial tuition reimbursement available (averaging $6,165 per year), 7 teaching assistantships with partial tuition reimbursements available (averaging $6,539 per year); fellowships, career-related internships or fieldwork, Federal Work-Study, institutionally sponsored loans, scholarships/grants, traineeships, and unspecified assistantships also available. Support available to part-time students. Financial award application deadline: 1/15; financial award applicants required to submit FAFSA. *Faculty research:* Consumer and textile end use, apparel design, consumer behavior, interior design, historic costume and textiles. Total annual research expenditures: $157,951. *Unit head:* Dr. Mary A. Littrell, Head, 970-491-7890, Fax: 970-491-4855, E-mail: mary.littrell@colostate.edu. *Application contact:* Dr. Jen Ogle, Graduate Coordinator, 970-491-3794, Fax: 970-491-4855, E-mail: jennifer.ogle@colostate.edu.

Cornell University, Graduate School, Graduate Fields of Human Ecology, Field of Policy Analysis and Management, Ithaca, NY 14853-0001. Offers consumer policy (PhD); evaluation (PhD); family and social welfare policy (PhD); health administration (MHA); health management and policy (PhD). *Faculty:* 31 full-time (13 women). *Students:* 47 full-time (21 women); includes 12 minority (5 African Americans, 6 Asian Americans or Pacific Islanders, 1 Hispanic American), 5 international. Average age 29. 115 applicants, 39% accepted, 16 enrolled. In 2008, 20 master's, 6 doctorates awarded. *Degree requirements:* For master's, thesis, for doctorate, thesis/dissertation. *Entrance requirements:* For master's, GRE General Test or GMAT, 2 letters of recommendation; for doctorate, GRE General Test, 2 letters of recommendation. Additional exam requirements/recommendations for international students: Required—TOEFL (minimum score 550 paper-based; 213 computer-based; 77 iBT). *Application deadline:* For fall admission, 1/15 for domestic students. Application fee: $70. Electronic applications accepted. *Expenses:* Tuition: Full-time $29,500. Required fees: $70. Full-time tuition and fees vary according to degree level, program and student level. *Financial support:* In 2008–09, 17 students received support, including 3 fellowships with full and partial tuition reimbursements available, 5 research assistantships with full and partial tuition reimbursements available, 9 teaching assistantships with full and partial tuition reimbursements available; institutionally sponsored loans, scholarships/grants, health care benefits, tuition waivers (full and partial), and unspecified assistantships also available. Financial award applicants required to submit FAFSA. *Faculty research:* Health policy, family policy, social welfare policy, program evaluation, consumer policy. *Unit head:* Director of Graduate Studies, 607-255-7772. *Application contact:* Graduate Field Assistant, 607-255-7772, Fax: 607-255-4071, E-mail: pam_phd@cornell.edu.

Eastern Illinois University, Graduate School, Lumpkin College of Business and Applied Sciences, School of Family and Consumer Sciences, Charleston, IL 61920-3099. Offers dietetics (MS); family and consumer sciences (MS). Part-time programs available. *Degree requirements:* For master's, comprehensive exam.

Indiana State University, School of Graduate Studies, College of Arts and Sciences, Department of Family and Consumer Sciences, Terre Haute, IN 47809-1401. Offers dietetics (MS); family and consumer sciences education (MS); inter-area option (MS). *Accreditation:* ADtA. Part-time programs available. *Degree requirements:* For master's, thesis optional. Electronic applications accepted.

Iowa State University of Science and Technology, Graduate College, College of Human Sciences, Department of Apparel, Education Studies, and Hospitality Management, Program in Family and Consumer Sciences Education and Studies, Ames, IA 50011. Offers M Ed, MS, PhD. *Students:* 2 full-time (1 woman), 29 part-time (27 women); includes 3 minority (all African Americans), 3 international. In 2008, 7 master's, 10 doctorates awarded. *Degree requirements:* For master's, thesis (for some programs); for doctorate, thesis/dissertation. *Entrance requirements:* For master's and doctorate, GRE General Test. Additional exam requirements/recommendations for international students: Required—TOEFL (paper-based 550; computer-based 213; iBT 80) or IELTS (6.5). Application fee: $30 ($70 for international students). *Expenses:* Tuition, area resident: Full-time $6446; part-time $359 per credit. Tuition, state resident: full-time $6446; part-time $359 per credit. Tuition, nonresident: full-time $17,330; part-time $963 per credit. Required fees: $790; $249.25 per semester. Tuition and fees vary

according to course load and program. *Financial support:* In 2008–09, 1 research assistantship with full and partial tuition reimbursement (averaging $13,275 per year) was awarded; teaching assistantships with full and partial tuition reimbursements, scholarships/grants also available. *Unit head:* Dr. Robert Bosselman, Director of Graduate Education, 515-294-7474. *Application contact:* Dr. Robert Bosselman, Director of Graduate Education, 515-294-7474.

North Dakota State University, College of Graduate and Interdisciplinary Studies, College of Human Development and Education, Department of Child Development and Family Science, Fargo, ND 58105. Offers child development and family science (MS); couple and family therapy (MS); family financial planning (MS); gerontology (MS, PhD). *Accreditation:* AAMFT/COAMFTE. Part-time and evening/weekend programs available. Postbaccalaureate distance learning degree programs offered (no on-campus study). *Faculty:* 12 full-time (7 women). *Students:* 26 full-time (25 women), 21 part-time (18 women); includes 1 African American, 2 international. 22 applicants, 64% accepted, 12 enrolled. In 2008, 12 master's awarded. *Degree requirements:* For master's, thesis or alternative; for doctorate, thesis/dissertation. *Entrance requirements:* Additional exam requirements/recommendations for international students: Required—TOEFL (minimum score 525 paper-based; 197 computer-based; 71 iBT). *Application deadline:* For fall admission, 2/1 for domestic and international students; for spring admission, 10/1 for domestic and international students. Application fee: $45 ($60 for international students). *Financial support:* In 2008–09, 17 students received support, including research assistantships with full tuition reimbursements available (averaging $3,000 per year), 17 teaching assistantships with full tuition reimbursements available (averaging $3,000 per year); career-related internships or fieldwork, Federal Work-Study, institutionally sponsored loans, and tuition waivers (full) also available. Financial award application deadline: 4/1. *Faculty research:* Family therapy, resilience, parenting, adolescent development, mental health. Total annual research expenditures: $333,582. *Unit head:* Dr. James Deal, Head, 701-231-7568, Fax: 701-231-9645, E-mail: jim_deal@ndsu.edu. *Application contact:* Theresa Anderson, Administrative Assistant, 701-231-8628, Fax: 701-231-9645, E-mail: theresa.anderson@ndsu.edu.

The Ohio State University, Graduate School, College of Education and Human Ecology, Program in Family Resource Management, Columbus, OH 43210. Offers MS, PhD. *Degree requirements:* For master's, thesis optional; for doctorate, thesis/dissertation. *Entrance requirements:* For master's and doctorate, GRE General Test. Additional exam requirements/recommendations for international students: Required—TOEFL (minimum score 577 paper-based; 233 computer-based). Electronic applications accepted.

Oklahoma State University, College of Human Environmental Sciences, Dean of Human Environmental Sciences—MS in Family Financial Planning Program and PhD in HES, Stillwater, OK 74078. Offers human environmental sciences (MS), including family financial planning. Part-time programs available. Postbaccalaureate distance learning degree programs offered. *Faculty:* 1 full-time (0 women). *Students:* 14 part-time (9 women); includes 2 minority (1 African American, 1 American Indian/Alaska Native). Average age 38. 51 applicants, 59% accepted, 12 enrolled. In 2008, 3 master's awarded. *Degree requirements:* For master's, thesis or alternative, creative component; for doctorate, comprehensive exam, thesis/dissertation. *Entrance requirements:* For master's and doctorate, GRE or GMAT. Additional exam requirements/recommendations for international students: Required—TOEFL. *Application deadline:* For fall admission, 3/1 priority date for international students; for spring admission, 8/1 priority date for international students. Applications are processed on a rolling basis. Application fee: $40 ($75 for international students). Electronic applications accepted. *Expenses:* Tuition, state resident: full-time $3716.40; part-time $154.85 per credit hour. Tuition, nonresident: full-time $14,448; part-time $602 per credit hour. Required fees: $1772.40; $73.85 per credit hour. One-time fee: $50. Tuition and fees vary according to course load and campus/location. *Financial support:* Career-related internships or fieldwork, Federal Work-Study, scholarships/grants, health care benefits, tuition waivers, and unspecified assistantships available. Support available to part-time students. Financial award application deadline: 3/1; financial award applicants required to submit FAFSA. *Unit head:* Dr. Stephan Wilson, Dean, 405-744-5053, Fax: 405-744-7113. *Application contact:* Dr. Shiretta Ownbey, Professor and Graduate Coordinator, 405-744-5053, Fax: 405-744-7113.

Purdue University, Graduate School, College of Consumer and Family Sciences, Department of Consumer Sciences and Retailing, West Lafayette, IN 47907. Offers consumer behavior (MS, PhD); family and consumer economics (MS, PhD); retail management (MS, PhD); textile science (MS, PhD). Part-time programs available. *Degree requirements:* For master's, thesis; for doctorate, thesis/dissertation. *Entrance requirements:* For master's and doctorate, GMAT or GRE General Test. Additional exam requirements/recommendations for international students: Required—TOEFL. Electronic applications accepted. *Faculty research:* Family financial resources, retail management and patronage, chemical analysis of textile dyes and finishes.

State University of New York at Oswego, Graduate Studies, School of Education, Department of Vocational Teacher Preparation, Oswego, NY 13126. Offers agriculture (MS Ed); business and marketing (MS Ed); family and consumer sciences (MS Ed); health careers (MS Ed); technical education (MS Ed); trade education (MS Ed). *Accreditation:* NCATE. Part-time and evening/weekend programs available. *Degree requirements:* For master's, thesis or alternative. *Entrance requirements:* Additional exam requirements/recommendations for international students: Required—TOEFL (minimum score 560 paper-based; 220 computer-based).

Texas Tech University, Graduate School, College of Human Sciences, Department of Applied and Professional Studies, Division of Personal Financial Planning, Lubbock, TX 79409. Offers MS, PhD. Part-time programs available. *Students:* 54 full-time (15 women), 26 part-time (6 women); includes 14 minority (8 African Americans, 6 Hispanic Americans), 6 international. Average age 31. 76 applicants, 93% accepted, 26 enrolled. In 2008, 24 master's awarded. *Degree requirements:* For master's, thesis or alternative; for doctorate, thesis/dissertation. *Entrance requirements:* For doctorate, GRE General Test, GMAT. Additional exam requirements/recommendations for international students: Required—TOEFL (minimum score 550 paper-based; 213 computer-based). *Application deadline:* For fall admission, 3/1 priority date for international students; for spring admission, 11/1 priority date for international students. Applications are processed on a rolling basis. Application fee: $50 ($60 for international students). *Expenses:* Tuition, area resident: Part-time $194 per credit hour. Tuition, state resident: full-time $4648; part-time $194 per credit hour. Tuition, nonresident: full-time $11,392; part-time $475 per credit hour. Required fees: $2206; $69 per credit hour. $389 per semester. *Financial support:* Research assistantships, teaching assistantships, career-related internships or fieldwork, Federal Work-Study, and institutionally sponsored loans available. Support available to part-time students. Financial award application deadline: 4/15; financial award applicants required to submit FAFSA. *Faculty research:* Financial risk tolerance, determinants of success on CFP exam, financial literacy, retirement planning. *Unit head:* Dr. Vickie Hampton, Director, 806-

742-5050 Ext. 272, Fax: 806-742-5033, E-mail: vickie.hampton@ttu.edu. *Application contact:* Dr. Vickie Hampton, Director, 806-742-5050 Ext. 272, Fax: 806-742-5033, E-mail: vickie.hampton@ttu.edu.

Université Laval, Faculty of Agricultural and Food Sciences, Department of Agricultural Economics and Consumer Sciences, Program in Consumer Sciences, Québec, QC G1K 7P4, Canada. Offers Diploma. Part-time programs available. *Entrance requirements:* For degree, knowledge of French and English. Electronic applications accepted.

The University of Alabama, Graduate School, College of Human Environmental Sciences, Department of Consumer Sciences, Tuscaloosa, AL 35487. Offers MS. Part-time and evening/weekend programs available. Postbaccalaureate distance learning degree programs offered (minimal on-campus study). *Faculty:* 6 full-time (4 women). *Students:* 1 applicant, 0% accepted. In 2008, 1 master's awarded. *Degree requirements:* For master's, thesis. *Entrance requirements:* For master's, GRE or MAT. Additional exam requirements/recommendations for international students: Required—TOEFL. *Application deadline:* Applications are processed on a rolling basis. Application fee: $30. *Expenses:* Tuition, area resident: Full-time $6400. Tuition, state resident: full-time $6400. Tuition, nonresident: full-time $18,000. *Financial support:* In 2008–09, 2 students received support, including 1 research assistantship (averaging $8,100 per year), 1 teaching assistantship (averaging $8,100 per year); fellowships also available. Financial award application deadline: 3/15. *Faculty research:* Consumer economics, financial planning.

The University of Arizona, Graduate College, College of Agriculture and Life Sciences, School of Family and Consumer Sciences, Division of Family Studies and Human Development, Tucson, AZ 85721. Offers family and consumer sciences education (MS); family studies and human development (PhD). Terminal master's awarded for partial completion of doctoral program. *Entrance requirements:* For master's, GRE General Test, minimum undergraduate GPA of 3.0, personal resumé, personal statement, 3 letters of recommendation. Additional exam requirements/recommendations for international students: Required—TOEFL.

The University of Arizona, Graduate College, College of Agriculture and Life Sciences, School of Family and Consumer Sciences, Division of Retailing and Consumer Sciences, Tucson, AZ 85721. Offers MS, PhD. Part-time programs available. Terminal master's awarded for partial completion of doctoral program. *Degree requirements:* For master's, thesis; for doctorate, thesis/dissertation. *Entrance requirements:* For master's and doctorate, GRE General Test or GMAT, minimum GPA of 3.0. Additional exam requirements/recommendations for international students: Required—TOEFL. Electronic applications accepted.

University of Georgia, Graduate School, College of Family and Consumer Sciences, Department of Housing and Consumer Economics, Athens, GA 30602. Offers MS, PhD. Part-time programs available. *Degree requirements:* For master's, thesis; for doctorate, thesis/dissertation. *Entrance requirements:* For master's and doctorate, GRE General Test. Additional exam requirements/recommendations for international students: Required—TOEFL (minimum score 575 paper-based; 230 computer-based). Electronic applications accepted. *Faculty research:* Demographics, consumer decision making, home ownership counseling, financial management, economics of divorce and poverty.

University of Guelph, Graduate Program Services, College of Management and Economics, Department of Marketing and Consumer Studies, Guelph, ON N1G 2W1, Canada. Offers M Sc. *Degree requirements:* For master's, thesis. *Entrance requirements:* For master's, GMAT or GRE General Test, minimum B average during previous 2 years of course work. Additional exam requirements/recommendations for international students: Required—TOEFL (minimum score 575 paper-based; 213 computer-based). Electronic applications accepted. *Faculty research:* Marketing, quality management, consumer economics, housing and real estate management, problem gambling.

University of Idaho, College of Graduate Studies, College of Agricultural and Life Sciences, Margaret Ritchie School of Family and Consumer Sciences, Moscow, ID 83844-3183. Offers MS. *Faculty:* 8 full-time, 1 part-time/adjunct. *Students:* 10 full-time, 9 part-time. Average age 35. In 2008, 2 master's awarded. *Degree requirements:* For master's, thesis. *Entrance requirements:* For master's, minimum GPA of 2.8. *Application deadline:* For fall admission, 8/1 for domestic students; for spring admission, 12/15 for domestic students. Application fee: $55 ($60 for international students). *Expenses:* Tuition, nonresident: full-time $10,080; part-time $336 per credit. Required fees: $5212; $267 per credit. Tuition and fees vary according to program. *Financial support:* Research assistantships, teaching assistantships available. Financial award application deadline: 2/15. *Faculty research:* Food and nutrition; clothing, textiles and design; child, family and consumer studies; early childhood development. *Unit head:* Dr. Sandra Evenson, Interim Chair, 208-885-6546. *Application contact:* Dr. Sandra Evenson, Interim Chair, 208-885-6546.

University of Illinois at Urbana–Champaign, Graduate College, College of Agricultural, Consumer and Environmental Sciences, Department of Agricultural and Consumer Economics, Champaign, IL 61820. Offers MS, PhD. *Faculty:* 33 full-time (9 women), 2 part-time/adjunct (both women). *Students:* 59 full-time (28 women), 15 part-time (6 women); includes 8 minority (2 African Americans, 3 Asian Americans or Pacific Islanders, 3 Hispanic Americans), 41 international. 81 applicants, 40% accepted, 21 enrolled. In 2008, 9 master's, 12 doctorates awarded. *Entrance requirements:* For master's, GRE, minimum GPA of 3.0; for doctorate, GRE, writing sample. Additional exam requirements/recommendations for international students: Required—TOEFL (minimum score 570 paper-based; 230 computer-based; 88 iBT), IELTS (minimum score 6.5), TOEFL or IELTS. *Application deadline:* Applications are processed on a rolling basis. Application fee: $60 ($75 for international students). Electronic applications accepted. *Financial support:* In 2008–09, 17 fellowships, 41 research assistantships, 25 teaching assistantships were awarded; tuition waivers (full and partial) also available. *Unit head:* Robert J. Hauser, Head, 217-333-8859, Fax: 217-333-5538, E-mail: r-hauser@illinois.edu. *Application contact:* Linda Foste, Administrative Assistant, 217-333-1830, Fax: 217-244-7088, E-mail: l-foste@illinois.edu.

University of Missouri–Columbia, Graduate School, College of Human Environmental Science, Department of Personal Financial Planning, Columbia, MO 65211. Offers MS. *Faculty:* 4 full-time (2 women), 1 (woman) part-time/adjunct. *Students:* 9 full-time (7 women), 6 part-time (4 women); includes 2 minority (1 African American, 1 Asian American or Pacific Islander), 6 international. Average age 34. 17 applicants, 41% accepted, 3 enrolled. In 2008, 4 master's awarded. *Entrance requirements:* For master's, GRE General Test, minimum GPA of 3.0. Additional exam requirements/recommendations for international students: Required—TOEFL (minimum score 550 paper-based; 213 computer-based; 79 iBT). *Application deadline:* Applications are processed on a rolling basis. Application fee: $45 ($60 for international students). *Financial support:* Research assistantships, teaching assistantships, institutionally sponsored

loans available. *Unit head:* Dr. Robert Weagley, Department Chair, E-mail: weagleyr@missouri.edu. *Application contact:* Voronica Bonaparte, 573-882-7836, E-mail: bonapartv@missouri.edu.

University of South Carolina, The Graduate School, College of Hospitality, Retail, and Sport Management, Department of Retailing, Columbia, SC 29208. Offers MR. Part-time programs available. *Degree requirements:* For master's, comprehensive exam, Internship or Thesis. *Entrance requirements:* For master's, GMAT or GRE General Test, minimum GPA of 3.0. Additional exam requirements/recommendations for international students: Required—TOEFL (minimum score 80 iBT). Electronic applications accepted. *Faculty research:* Retail technology, retail strategy, international retailing.

The University of Tennessee, Graduate School, College of Education, Health and Human Sciences, Department of Consumer and Industry Services Management, Program in Consumer Services Management, Knoxville, TN 37996. Offers retail and consumer sciences (MS); textile science (MS). Part-time programs available. *Degree requirements:* For master's, thesis or alternative. *Entrance requirements:* For master's, GRE General Test, minimum GPA of 2.7. Additional exam requirements/recommendations for international students: Required—TOEFL. Electronic applications accepted. *Expenses:* Tuition, area resident: Part-time $348 per credit hour. Tuition, state resident: full-time $6262. Tuition, nonresident: full-time $18,920; part-time $1052 per credit hour. Required fees: $812; $36 per credit hour. Tuition and fees vary according to program.

The University of Tennessee, Graduate School, College of Education, Health and Human Sciences, Program in Human Ecology, Knoxville, TN 37996. Offers child and family studies (PhD); community health (PhD); nutrition science (PhD); retailing and consumer sciences (PhD); textile science (PhD). *Degree requirements:* For doctorate, thesis/dissertation. *Entrance requirements:* For doctorate, GRE General Test, minimum GPA of 2.7. Additional exam requirements/recommendations for international students: Required—TOEFL. Electronic applications accepted. *Expenses:* Tuition, area resident: Part-time $348 per credit hour. Tuition, state resident: full-time $6262. Tuition, nonresident: full-time $18,920; part-time $1052 per credit hour. Required fees: $812; $36 per credit hour. Tuition and fees vary according to program.

University of Utah, The Graduate School, College of Social and Behavioral Science, Department of Family and Consumer Studies, Salt Lake City, UT 84112-1107. Offers MS. *Degree requirements:* For master's, thesis optional. *Entrance requirements:* For master's, GRE General Test, minimum undergraduate GPA of 3.0. Additional exam requirements/recommendations for international students: Required—TOEFL (minimum score 500 paper-based; 173 computer-based). *Faculty research:* Social, physical and economic contexts of families and communities.

University of Wisconsin–Madison, Graduate School, School of Human Ecology, Program in Consumer Behavior and Family Economics, Madison, WI 53706-1380. Offers MS, PhD. *Degree requirements:* For master's, thesis; for doctorate, comprehensive exam, thesis/dissertation. *Entrance requirements:* For master's and doctorate, GRE General Test, 3 letters of recommendation. Additional exam requirements/recommendations for international students: Required—TOEFL (minimum score 580 paper-based; 237 computer-based). Electronic applications accepted. *Faculty research:* Economic well-being of elderly, finance, financial planning, health care policy, consumer behavior.

University of Wyoming, Graduate School, College of Agriculture, Department of Family and Consumer Sciences, Laramie, WY 82070. Offers early childhood development (MS); family and consumer sciences (MS); food science and human nutrition (MS). Part-time programs available. *Faculty:* 13 full-time (8 women), 13 part-time/adjunct (all women). *Students:* 2 full-time (both women), 5 part-time (all women); includes 1 minority (American Indian/Alaska Native). Average age 34. 4 applicants, 100% accepted, 4 enrolled. In 2008, 2 master's awarded. *Degree requirements:* For master's, thesis, project. *Entrance requirements:* For master's, GRE General Test or MCAT, minimum GPA of 3.0. Additional exam requirements/recommendations for international students: Required—TOEFL (minimum score 540 paper-based; 207 computer-based; 76 iBT). *Application deadline:* For fall admission, 4/1 priority date for domestic students, 3/1 priority date for international students; for spring admission, 10/1 priority date for domestic students, 9/1 priority date for international students. Applications are processed on a rolling basis. Application fee: $50. Electronic applications accepted. *Financial support:* In 2008–09, 2 research assistantships with full tuition reimbursements (averaging $11,072 per year), 2 teaching assistantships with full tuition reimbursements (averaging $11,072 per year) were awarded; career-related internships or fieldwork, Federal Work-Study, institutionally sponsored loans, scholarships/grants, and health care benefits also available. Support available to part-time students. Financial award application deadline: 5/1; financial award applicants required to submit FAFSA. *Faculty research:* Asthma, obesity and healthy weights, nutrition concerns of children with special health care needs, food product development, food safety, postpartum health, exercise nutrition. *Unit head:* Dr. Karen C. Williams, Professor and Department Head, 307-766-4145, Fax: 307-766-5686, E-mail: fam-consci@uwyo.edu. *Application contact:* Michell Anderson, Graduate Admissions Coordinator, 307-766-2287, Fax: 307-766-2374, E-mail: manders2@uwyo.edu.

Utah State University, School of Graduate Studies, College of Agriculture, Department of Agricultural Systems Technology and Education, Logan, UT 84322. Offers agricultural systems technology (MS), including agricultural extension education, agricultural mechanization, international agricultural extension, secondary and postsecondary agricultural education; family and consumer sciences education (MS). Part-time programs available. Postbaccalaureate distance learning degree programs offered (minimal on-campus study). *Degree requirements:* For master's, comprehensive exam (for some programs), thesis (for some programs). *Entrance requirements:* For master's, GRE General Test, MAT, BS in agricultural education, agricultural extension, or related agricultural or science discipline; minimum GPA of 3.0. Additional exam requirements/recommendations for international students: Required—TOEFL. *Faculty research:* Extension and adult education; structures and environment; low-input agriculture; farm safety, systems, and mechanizations.

Virginia Polytechnic Institute and State University, Graduate School, College of Liberal Arts and Human Sciences, Department of Apparel, Housing, and Resource Management, Blacksburg, VA 24061. Offers apparel business and economics (MS, PhD); apparel product design and analysis (MS, PhD); apparel quality analysis (MS, PhD); consumer studies (MS, PhD); family financial management (MS, PhD); household equipment (MS, PhD); housing (MS, PhD); interior design (MS, PhD); resource management (MS, PhD). *Degree requirements:* For master's, thesis; for doctorate, thesis/dissertation. *Entrance requirements:* For master's and doctorate, GRE General Test. Additional exam requirements/recommendations for international students: Required—TOEFL (minimum score 550 paper-based; 213 computer-based). Electronic applications accepted. *Faculty research:* Housing for elderly, affordable housing, household time use, phosphate laundry study, economic well-living.

Gerontology

Abilene Christian University, Graduate School, College of Arts and Sciences, Department of Sociology and Family Studies, Program in Gerontology, Abilene, TX 79699-9100. Offers MS, Certificate. *Faculty:* 3 part-time/adjunct (0 women). *Students:* 2 full-time (both women), 1 (woman) part-time; includes 2 minority (1 African American, 1 Hispanic American), 1 international. 2 applicants, 100% accepted, 1 enrolled. In 2008, 2 master's, 1 other advanced degree awarded. *Degree requirements:* For master's, comprehensive exam. *Entrance requirements:* For master's, GRE General Test or MAT. *Application deadline:* For fall admission, 4/1 priority date for domestic students; for spring admission, 11/1 for domestic students. Applications are processed on a rolling basis. Application fee: $40 ($45 for international students). Electronic applications accepted. *Expenses:* Tuition: Full-time $10,728; part-time $640 per hour. Required fees: $1090; $53.50 per hour. $10 per term. Tuition and fees vary according to campus/location. *Financial support:* In 2008–09, 3 students received support. Career-related internships or fieldwork and Federal Work-Study available. Support available to part-time students. Financial award application deadline: 4/1; financial award applicants required to submit FAFSA. *Unit head:* Dr. Charlie D. Pruett, Director of the Center for Aging, 325-674-2350, Fax: 325-674-6804, E-mail: pruettc@acu.edu. *Application contact:* William Horn, Graduate Admissions Counselor, 325-674-2656, Fax: 325-674-6717, E-mail: gradinfo@acu.edu.

Adelphi University, School of Education, Program in Physical Education and Human Performance Science, Garden City, NY 11530-0701. Offers aging (Certificate); physical/educational human performance science (MA). Part-time and evening/weekend programs available. *Students:* 39 full-time (20 women), 107 part-time (42 women); includes 12 minority (6 African Americans, 3 Asian Americans or Pacific Islanders, 3 Hispanic Americans), 4 international. Average age 28. In 2008, 64 master's awarded. *Degree requirements:* For master's, internship. *Entrance requirements:* For master's, 3 letters of recommendation, resumé. Additional exam requirements/recommendations for international students: Required—TOEFL (minimum score 550 paper-based; 213 computer-based; 80 iBT). *Application deadline:* For fall admission, 4/1 for international students; for spring admission, 11/1 for international students. Applications are processed on a rolling basis. Application fee: $50. Electronic applications accepted. *Expenses:* Tuition: Full-time $25,700; part-time $775 per credit hour. Required fees: $500. Tuition and fees vary according to course load, degree level, campus/location, program and student level. *Financial support:* Fellowships, research assistantships with full and partial tuition reimbursements, teaching assistantships, career-related internships or fieldwork, Federal Work-Study, institutionally sponsored loans, and tuition waivers (full) available. Support available to part-time students. Financial award application deadline: 2/15; financial award applicants required to submit FAFSA. *Faculty research:* Physical education for the handicapped, sport sociology, sport pedagogy. *Unit head:* Dr. Stephen J. Virgilio, Chair, 516-877-4262, E-mail: virgilio@adelphi.edu. *Application contact:* Christine Murphy, Director of Admissions, 516-877-3050, Fax: 516-877-3039, E-mail: graduateadmissions@adelphi.edu.

Adler School of Professional Psychology, Programs in Psychology, Chicago, IL 60601-7203. Offers art therapy (Certificate); clinical hypnosis (Certificate); clinical psychology (Psy D); counseling psychology (MACP); counseling psychology/art therapy (MACAT); gerontology (MAGP); marriage and family counseling (MAMFC); marriage and family therapy (Certificate); organizational psychology (MAO); substance abuse counseling (MASAC, Certificate); Psy D/Certificate; Psy D/MACAT; Psy D/MACP; Psy D/MAMFC; Psy D/MASAC. *Accreditation:* APA. Part-time and evening/weekend programs available. Postbaccalaureate distance learning degree programs offered (minimal on-campus study). *Faculty:* 36 full-time (17 women), 45 part-time/adjunct (18 women). *Students:* 514 full-time (404 women), 128 part-time (100 women); includes 147 minority (69 African Americans, 2 American Indian/Alaska Native, 30 Asian Americans or Pacific Islanders, 46 Hispanic Americans), 53 international. Average age 27. 855 applicants, 46% accepted, 195 enrolled. In 2008, 110 master's, 136 doctorates awarded. Terminal master's awarded for partial completion of doctoral program. *Degree requirements:* For master's, thesis or alternative, oral exam, practicum; for doctorate, thesis/dissertation, clinical exam, internship, oral exam, practicum, written qualifying exam. *Entrance requirements:* For master's, 12 semester hours in psychology, minimum GPA of 3.0; for doctorate, 18 semester hours in psychology, minimum GPA of 3.25; for Certificate, appropriate master's or doctoral degree. Additional exam requirements/recommendations for international students: Required—TOEFL (minimum score 550 paper-based; 213 computer-based; 79 iBT). *Application deadline:* For fall admission, 2/15 priority date for domestic students, 12/1 priority date for international students. Applications are processed on a rolling basis. Application fee: $50. Electronic applications accepted. *Expenses:* Tuition: Part-time $850 per credit. Tuition and fees vary according to degree level, campus/location and program. *Financial support:* Career-related internships or fieldwork, Federal Work-Study, scholarships/grants, and tuition waivers (full and partial) available. Support available to part-time students. Financial award application deadline: 5/15; financial award applicants required to submit FAFSA. *Unit head:* Dr. Frank Gruba-McAllister, Vice President of Academic Affairs, 312-201-5900, Fax: 312-207-5917. *Application contact:* Craig A Hines, Director of Admissions, 312-201-5900 Ext. 226, Fax: 312-201-5917, E-mail: chines@adler.edu.

See Close-Up on page 1051.

Alliant International University–Los Angeles, California School of Professional Psychology, Program in Marital and Family Therapy, Alhambra, CA 91803-1360. Offers biofeedback (MA); chemical dependency (MA); gerontology (MA); Latin American family therapy (MA). *Accreditation:* AAMFT/COAMFTE.

See Close-Up on page 1061.

Appalachian State University, Cratis D. Williams Graduate School, Department of Sociology, Boone, NC 28608. Offers gerontology (MA). Part-time programs available. *Faculty:* 10 full-time (2 women), 1 (woman) part-time/adjunct. *Students:* 9 full-time (7 women), 1 (woman) part-time; includes 1 minority (Hispanic American). 4 applicants, 100% accepted, 2 enrolled. In 2008, 15 master's awarded. *Degree requirements:* For master's, comprehensive exam, thesis optional. *Entrance requirements:* For master's, GRE General Test, 3 letters of recommendation. Additional exam requirements/recommendations for international students: Required—TOEFL (minimum score 570 paper-based; 230 computer-based), IELTS (minimum score 6.5). *Application deadline:* For fall admission, 7/1 for domestic students, 2/1 for international students; for spring admission, 11/1 for domestic students, 7/1 for international students. Applications are processed on a rolling basis. Application fee: $50. Electronic applications accepted. *Expenses:* Tuition, area resident: Full-time $2600; part-time $700 per course. Tuition, state resident: full-time $2600; part-time $700 per course. Tuition, nonresident: full-time $5000; part-time $3300 per course. Required fees: $2150; $330 per course. Tuition and fees vary according to campus/location. *Financial support:* In 2008–09, 4 research assistantships (averaging $7,000 per year) were awarded; fellowships with partial tuition reimbursements, teaching assistantships, career-related internships or fieldwork, Federal Work-Study, scholarships/grants, and unspecified assistantships also available. Financial award application deadline: 4/1; financial award applicants required to submit FAFSA. *Faculty research:* Aging, criminology, deviance. *Unit head:* Dr. Ed Folts, Chairman, 828-262-2293, E-mail: foltswe@appstate.edu. *Application contact:* Dr. Ed Rosenberg, Graduate Program Director, 828-262-2293, E-mail: rosenberge@appstate.edu.

Arizona State University at the West campus, College of Human Services, School of Aging and Lifespan Development, Phoenix, AZ 85069-7100. Offers aging and lifespan development (MS); gerontology (Certificate). Part-time and evening/weekend programs available. *Degree requirements:* For master's, applied project. *Entrance requirements:* For master's, 3 letters of recommendation, personal statement/essay; for Certificate, 2 letters of recommendation. Additional exam requirements/recommendations for international students: Required—TOEFL (minimum score 550 paper-based; 213 computer-based; 83 iBT). Electronic applications accepted.

Arkansas State University, Graduate School, College of Nursing and Health Professions, Department of Physical Therapy, Jonesboro, State University, AR 72467. Offers aging studies (Certificate); health sciences (MS); physical therapy (MPT, DPT). *Accreditation:* APTA. Part-time programs available. *Faculty:* 8 full-time (4 women), 1 (woman) part-time/adjunct. *Students:* 34 full-time (19 women), 46 part-time (29 women); includes 12 minority (all African Americans), 17 international. Average age 27. 98 applicants, 95% accepted, 38 enrolled. In 2008, 27 master's awarded. *Degree requirements:* For master's, comprehensive exam; for doctorate, comprehensive exam, thesis/dissertation. *Entrance requirements:* For master's, GRE General Test, Allied Health Profession Admissions Test, writing exam, appropriate bachelor's degree, letters of reference, resumé, official transcript, writing sample; for doctorate, GRE, Allied Health Professions Admissions Test, appropriate master's degree, letters of reference, resumé, official transcript. Additional exam requirements/recommendations for international students: Required—TOEFL (minimum score 550 paper-based; 213 computer-based; 79 iBT), IELTS (minimum score 6). *Application deadline:* Applications are processed on a rolling basis. Application fee: $50. Electronic applications accepted. *Expenses:* Contact institution. *Financial support:* In 2008–09, 12 students received support. Career-related internships or fieldwork, scholarships/grants, and unspecified assistantships available. Financial award application deadline: 7/1; financial award applicants required to submit FAFSA. *Faculty research:* Obesity, nutrition and exercise, orthotics, training and nutrition for competitive sports, youth sports. *Unit head:* Dr. Patricia King, Chair, 870-972-3591, Fax: 870-972-3652, E-mail: pking@astate.edu. *Application contact:* Dr. Andrew Sustich, Dean of the Graduate School, 870-972-3029, Fax: 870-972-3857, E-mail: sustich@astate.edu.

A.T. Still University of Health Sciences, School of Health Management, Kirksville, MO 63501. Offers geriatric healthcare (MGH); health administration (MHA); health education (MH Ed, DH Ed); public health (MPH). Part-time and evening/weekend programs available. Postbaccalaureate distance learning degree programs offered (no on-campus study). *Faculty:* 1 (woman) full-time, 52 part-time/adjunct (24 women). *Students:* 47 full-time (33 women), 477 part-time (310 women); includes 179 minority (106 African Americans, 8 American Indian/Alaska Native, 38 Asian Americans or Pacific Islanders, 27 Hispanic Americans). Average age 32. In 2008, 110 master's, 4 doctorates awarded. *Degree requirements:* For master's, thesis (for some programs), integrated terminal project; for doctorate, thesis/dissertation. *Entrance requirements:* For master's, minimum GPA of 2.5, bachelor's degree or equivalent from U.S. institution; for doctorate, minimum GPA of 2.5, master's or terminal degree, employment. Additional exam requirements/recommendations for international students: Required—TOEFL (minimum score 550 paper-based; 213 computer-based; 80 iBT). *Application deadline:* For fall admission, 8/7 for domestic students, 7/27 for international students; for winter admission, 11/30 for domestic students, 10/26 for international students; for spring admission, 2/20 for domestic students, 2/15 for international students. Applications are processed on a rolling basis. Application fee: $60. Electronic applications accepted. *Expenses:* Contact institution. *Financial support:* In 2008–09, 277 students received support; fellowships, research assistantships, teaching assistantships available. Financial award application deadline: 5/1; financial award applicants required to submit FAFSA. *Unit head:* Dr. Kimberly O'Reilly, Interim Dean, 660-626-2820, Fax: 660-626-2826, E-mail: koreilley@atsu.edu. *Application contact:* Sarah Bartlett, Director of Recruitment, 660-626-2820, Fax: 660-626-2826, E-mail: sbartlett@atsu.edu.

Ball State University, Graduate School, College of Applied Science and Technology, Fisher Institute for Wellness, Program in Applied Gerontology, Muncie, IN 47306-1099. Offers MA.

Bethel University, Graduate School, Department of Anthropology and Sociology, St. Paul, MN 55112-6999. Offers gerontology (MA). Evening/weekend programs available. *Degree requirements:* For master's, thesis. *Entrance requirements:* For master's, interview, 5 years of work experience, minimum GPA of 3.0, letters of reference. Additional exam requirements/recommendations for international students: Required—TOEFL (minimum score 550 paper-based; 213 computer-based). Electronic applications accepted.

California State University, Fullerton, Graduate Studies, College of Humanities and Social Sciences, Program in Gerontology, Fullerton, CA 92834-9480. Offers MS. *Students:* 17 full-time (all women), 25 part-time (20 women); includes 15 minority (5 Asian Americans or Pacific Islanders, 10 Hispanic Americans), 2 international. Average age 37. 21 applicants, 76% accepted, 12 enrolled. In 2008, 10 master's awarded. Tuition and fees vary according to degree level. *Financial support:* Teaching assistantships available. *Unit head:* Dr. Joseph Weber, Coordinator, 657-278-7057. *Application contact:* Admissions/Applications, 657-278-2300.

California State University, Long Beach, Graduate Studies, College of Health and Human Services, Department of Social Work, Long Beach, CA 90840. Offers children, youth and families (MSW); older adults and families (MSW). *Accreditation:* CSWE. Part-time and evening/weekend programs available. Postbaccalaureate distance learning degree programs offered (no on-campus study). *Faculty:* 20 full-time (13 women), 35 part-time/adjunct (28 women). *Students:* 257 full-time (223 women), 279 part-time (246 women); includes 383 minority (67 African Americans, 5 American Indian/Alaska Native, 62 Asian Americans or Pacific Islanders, 249 Hispanic Americans), 9 international. Average age 33. 763 applicants, 39% accepted, 229 enrolled. *Degree requirements:* For master's, thesis. *Application deadline:* For fall admission, 3/1 for domestic students. Applications are processed on a rolling basis. Application fee: $55. Electronic applications accepted. *Expenses:* Tuition, nonresident: full-time $11,160; part-time $372 per unit. Required fees: $4100; $1261 per semester. *Financial support:* Federal Work-Study, institutionally sponsored loans, and scholarships/grants available. Financial award application deadline: 3/2. *Unit head:* Dr. John Oliver, Director, 562-985-5655, Fax: 562-985-5514, E-mail: joliver@csulb.edu. *Application contact:* Dr. Christine Kleinpeter, Graduate Coordinator, 562-985-5655, Fax: 562-985-5514, E-mail: ckleinpe@csulb.edu.

California State University, Long Beach, Graduate Studies, College of Health and Human Services, Program in Gerontology, Long Beach, CA 90840. Offers MS. Part-time programs available. *Faculty:* 6 full-time (1 woman). *Students:* 15 full-time (13 women), 19 part-time (17 women); includes 16 minority (2 African Americans, 9 Asian Americans or Pacific Islanders, 5 Hispanic Americans), 3 international. Average age 32. 18 applicants, 56% accepted, 9 enrolled. *Degree requirements:* For master's, thesis optional. *Application deadline:* For fall admission, 7/1 for domestic students. Applications are processed on a rolling basis. Application fee: $55. Electronic applications accepted. *Expenses:* Tuition, nonresident: full-time $11,160; part-time $372 per unit. Required fees: $4100; $1261 per semester. *Financial support:* Federal Work-Study, institutionally sponsored loans, and scholarships/grants available. Financial award application deadline: 3/2. *Unit head:* Dr. Barbara White, Director, 562-985-1582, Fax: 562-985-4414, E-mail: bwhite@csulb.edu. *Application contact:* Dr. Barbara White, Director, 562-985-1582, Fax: 562-985-4414.

California State University, Stanislaus, College of Humanities and Social Sciences, Department of Sociology, Turlock, CA 95382. Offers gerontology (Certificate). *Entrance requirements:* For degree, minimum GPA of 2.5.

Case Western Reserve University, School of Graduate Studies, Department of Communication Sciences, Cleveland, OH 44106. Offers gerontology (Certificate); speech-language pathology (MA, PhD). *Accreditation:* ASHA (one or more programs are accredited). Terminal master's awarded for partial completion of doctoral program. *Degree requirements:* For master's, comprehensive exam, thesis optional; for doctorate, thesis/dissertation. *Entrance requirements:* For master's and doctorate, GRE General Test. Additional exam requirements/recommendations for international students: Required—TOEFL. Electronic applications accepted. *Faculty research:* Traumatic brain injury, phonological disorders, child language disorders, communication problems in the aged and Alzheimer's patients, cleft palate, voice disorders.

Chestnut Hill College, School of Graduate Studies, Program in Administration of Human Services, Philadelphia, PA 19118-2693. Offers administration of human services (MS); adult and aging services (CAS); leadership development (CAS). Part-time and evening/weekend programs available. *Faculty:* 3 full-time (all women), 7 part-time/adjunct (3 women). *Students:* 17 full-time (13 women), 35 part-time (32 women); includes 21 minority (all African Americans). 22 applicants, 50% accepted. In 2008, 14 master's awarded. *Degree requirements:* For master's, special projects or internship. *Entrance requirements:* For master's, GRE General Test or MAT, 100 volunteer hours or 1 year work-related human services experience, statement of professional goals, writing sample, transcripts, letters of recommendation; for CAS, GRE or MAT, transcripts, letters of recommendation, statement of professional goals, writing sample. Additional exam requirements/recommendations for international students: Required—TOEFL (minimum score 500 paper-based; 213 computer-based). *Application deadline:* For fall admission, 7/17 priority date for domestic students, 7/17 for international students; for spring admission, 12/15 priority date for domestic students, 12/15 for international students. Applications are processed on a rolling basis. Application fee: $50. *Expenses:* Tuition: Part-time $510 per credit hour. *Financial support:* Institutionally sponsored loans available. *Unit head:* Dr. Elaine Green, Dean of the School of Continuing and Professional Studies/Program Coordinator, 215-248-7172, Fax: 215-248-7065, E-mail: green@chc.edu. *Application contact:* Amy Boorse, Administrative Assistant, School of Graduate Studies Office, 215-248-7170, Fax: 215-248-7161, E-mail: gradadmissions@chc.edu.

Cleveland State University, College of Graduate Studies, College of Science, Department of Psychology, Cleveland, OH 44115. Offers adult development and aging (PhD); clinical psychology (MA); consumer/industrial research (MA); diversity management (MA); experimental research psychology (MA); school psychology (Psy S). *Faculty:* 20 full-time (7 women), 16 part-time/adjunct (8 women). *Students:* 66 full-time (44 women), 62 part-time (46 women); includes 25 minority (19 African Americans, 1 American Indian/Alaska Native, 2 Asian Americans or Pacific Islanders, 3 Hispanic Americans), 3 international. Average age 30. 180 applicants, 40% accepted, 55 enrolled. In 2008, 39 master's, 4 other advanced degrees awarded. *Degree requirements:* For master's, comprehensive exam (for some programs), thesis (for some programs); for doctorate, comprehensive exam, thesis/dissertation; for Psy S, internship. *Entrance requirements:* For master's and doctorate, GRE General Test. Additional exam requirements/recommendations for international students: Required—TOEFL (minimum score 525 paper-based; 197 computer-based). *Application deadline:* For fall admission, 2/1 priority date for domestic and international students. Applications are processed on a rolling basis. Application fee: $30. Electronic applications accepted. *Financial support:* In 2008–09, 45 students received support. Career-related internships or fieldwork, Federal Work-Study, tuition waivers (partial), and unspecified assistantships available. Financial award applicants required to submit FAFSA. *Faculty research:* Cognitive and social psychology, consumer psychology, clinical psychology, school psychology, aging. Total annual research expenditures: $112,607. *Unit head:* Dr. Albert F Smith, Interim Chair, 216-687-3723, Fax: 216-687-9294, E-mail: a.f.smith@csuohio.edu. *Application contact:* Karen R Colston, Administrative Coordinator, 216-687-2552, Fax: 216-687-9294, E-mail: k.colston@csuohio.edu.

The College of New Rochelle, Graduate School, Division of Human Services, Program in Gerontology, New Rochelle, NY 10805-2308. Offers MS, Certificate. Part-time and evening/weekend programs available. *Degree requirements:* For master's, fieldwork, internship. *Entrance requirements:* For master's, interview, minimum GPA of 3.0, writing sample.

Concordia University Chicago, College of Graduate and Innovative Programs, Program in Gerontology, River Forest, IL 60305-1499. Offers MA. Part-time and evening/weekend programs available. *Degree requirements:* For master's, comprehensive exam, thesis. *Entrance requirements:* For master's, minimum GPA of 2.9. Additional exam requirements/recommendations for international students: Required—TOEFL (minimum score 550 paper-based; 195 computer-based). Electronic applications accepted.

Dominican University of California, Graduate Programs, School of Arts and Sciences, Program in Nursing, San Rafael, CA 94901-2298. Offers geriatric and nurse educator (MS); integrated health practices (clinical nursing specialist) (MS). *Accreditation:* AACN. Part-time and evening/weekend programs available. *Faculty:* 3 full-time (all women), 16 part-time/adjunct (14 women). *Students:* 20 full-time (19 women), 11 part-time (9 women); includes 11 minority (5 African Americans, 1 American Indian/Alaska Native, 4 Asian Americans or Pacific Islanders, 1 Hispanic American). Average age 44. 15 applicants, 47% accepted, 7 enrolled. In 2008, 8 master's awarded. *Degree requirements:* For master's, thesis. *Entrance requirements:* For master's, minimum GPA of 3.0; clinical experience; course work in nursing research and statistics; CPR certification; professional liability and malpractice insurance; interview. Additional exam requirements/recommendations for international students: Required—TOEFL (minimum score 550 paper-based; 213 computer-based). *Application deadline:* Applications are processed on a rolling basis. Application fee: $40. Electronic applications accepted. *Expenses:* Tuition: Full-time $14,040; part-time $780 per unit. *Financial support:* In 2008–09, 20 students received support, including 10 fellowships (averaging $3,200 per year); scholarships/grants also available. Support available to part-time students. Financial award applicants required to submit FAFSA. *Unit head:* Dr. Barbara Ganley, Chair, 415-482-1829, Fax: 415-485-0120, E-mail: bganley@dominican.edu. *Application contact:* Lawrence Schwaltz, Associate Director, 415-458-3748, Fax: 415-485-3214, E-mail: larry.schwaltz@dominican.edu.

Eastern Illinois University, Graduate School, Lumpkin College of Business and Applied Sciences, Program in Gerontology, Charleston, IL 61920-3099. Offers MA.

Eastern Michigan University, Graduate School, College of Health and Human Services, School of Social Work, Ypsilanti, MI 48197. Offers family and children's services (MSW); gerontology (Graduate Certificate); gerontology-dementia (Graduate Certificate); mental health and chemical dependency (MSW); services to the aging (MSW). *Accreditation:* CSWE. Part-time and evening/weekend programs available. Postbaccalaureate distance learning degree programs offered (minimal on-campus study). *Entrance requirements:* Additional exam requirements/recommendations for international students: Required—TOEFL.

East Tennessee State University, School of Graduate Studies, College of Public and Allied Health, Department of Public Health, Johnson City, TN 37614. Offers community health (MPH); epidemiology (Certificate); gerontology (Certificate); health care management (Certificate); public health (MPH); public health administration (MPH). *Accreditation:* CEPH. Part-time programs available. *Degree requirements:* For master's, comprehensive exam, thesis optional. *Entrance requirements:* For master's, GRE General Test, 2 years of community health experience. Additional exam requirements/recommendations for international students: Required—TOEFL (minimum score 550 paper-based; 213 computer-based). *Faculty research:* Rural health issues, youth and adolescent health, health of the elderly, environmental epidemiology, spatial analysis of data.

Emory University, Nell Hodgson Woodruff School of Nursing, Atlanta, GA 30322-1100. Offers adult and elder health advanced practice nursing (MSN), including acute and critical care, adult nurse practitioner, gerontology, oncology; emergency nurse practitioner (MSN); family nurse practitioner (MSN); family nurse-midwife (MSN); leadership in healthcare (MSN); nurse midwifery (MSN); nursing administration (MSN); pediatric advanced nursing practice (MSN); public health nursing (MSN); women's health nurse practitioner (MSN); MSN/MPH. *Accreditation:* AACN; ACNM/DOA (one or more programs are accredited). Part-time programs available. *Entrance requirements:* For master's, GRE General Test or MAT, minimum GPA of 3.0, BS in nursing, RN license and additional course work, 3 letters of recommendation. Additional exam requirements/recommendations for international students: Required—TOEFL (minimum score 600 paper-based; 250 computer-based). Electronic applications accepted. *Expenses:* Contact institution. *Faculty research:* Older adult falls and injuries, minority health issues, cardiac symptoms amd quality of life, bio-ethics and decision making, menopausal issues.

Gannon University, School of Graduate Studies, College of Humanities, Education, and Social Sciences, School of Humanities, Program in Gerontology, Erie, PA 16541-0001. Offers Certificate. Part-time and evening/weekend programs available. *Entrance requirements:* For degree, interview. Additional exam requirements/recommendations for international students: Required—TOEFL (minimum score 500 paper-based; 173 computer-based). *Application deadline:* Applications are processed on a rolling basis. Application fee: $25. Electronic applications accepted. *Expenses:* Tuition: Full-time $13,050; part-time $725 per credit. Required fees: $502; $16 per credit. Tuition and fees vary according to course load, degree level, campus/location and program. *Financial support:* Career-related internships or fieldwork available. Financial award application deadline: 7/1; financial award applicants required to submit FAFSA. *Unit head:* Charles Murphy, Director, 814-871-7542, E-mail: murphy001@gannon.edu. *Application contact:* Kara Morgan, Assistant Director of Graduate Admissions, 814-871-5831, Fax: 814-871-5827, E-mail: graduate@gannon.edu.

Georgia State University, College of Arts and Sciences, Gerontology Institute, Atlanta, GA 30303-3083. Offers MA. Part-time programs available. *Degree requirements:* For master's, thesis, internship. *Entrance requirements:* For master's, GRE, 3 letters of reference. Additional exam requirements/recommendations for international students: Required—TOEFL, TWE. Electronic applications accepted. *Faculty research:* Long-term care, assisted living, ethnicity and aging dementia, memory.

Hofstra University, School of Education, Health, and Human Services, Department of Counseling, Research, Special Education and Rehabilitation, Program in Gerontology, Hempstead, NY 11549. Offers MS, Advanced Certificate. Part-time programs available. *Students:* 3 full-time (2 women), 11 part-time (9 women); includes 4 minority (3 African Americans, 1 Hispanic American), 1 international. Average age 42. 8 applicants, 100% accepted, 4 enrolled. In 2008, 8 master's, 1 other advanced degree awarded. *Degree requirements:* For master's and Advanced Certificate, thesis optional, internship. *Entrance requirements:* For master's, interview, letter of recommendation; for Advanced Certificate, letter of recommendation, interview. Additional exam requirements/recommendations for international students: Required—TOEFL (minimum score 550 paper-based; 213 computer-based; 80 iBT). *Application deadline:* Applications are processed on a rolling basis. Application fee: $60. Electronic applications accepted. *Expenses:* Tuition: Full-time $15,300; part-time $850 per credit. Required fees: $970; $165 per term. Tuition and fees vary according to program. *Financial support:* In 2008–09, 8 students received support, including 1 fellowship with full and partial tuition reimbursement available (averaging $4,000 per year); research assistantships with full and partial tuition reimbursements available, career-related internships or fieldwork, Federal Work-Study, institutionally sponsored loans, scholarships/grants, and tuition waivers (full and partial) also available. Support available to part-time students. Financial award applicants required to submit FAFSA. *Faculty research:* Elder abuse, geropsychology, environmental gerontology, later life education. *Unit head:* Dr. Jeffrey P. Rosenfeld, Director, 516-463-5752, Fax: 516-463-6184, E-mail: cprjzr@hofstra.edu. *Application contact:* Carol Drummer, Dean of Graduate Admissions, 516-463-4876, Fax: 516-463-4664, E-mail: gradstudent@hofstra.edu.

Kent State University, Graduate School of Education, Health, and Human Services, School of Family and Consumer Studies, Program in Family Studies, Kent, OH 44242-0001. Offers gerontology (MA); human development and family studies (MA).

Lakehead University, Graduate Studies, Department of History, Thunder Bay, ON P7B 5E1, Canada. Offers gerontology (MA); history (MA); women's studies (MA). Part-time programs available. *Degree requirements:* For master's, one foreign language, thesis. *Entrance requirements:* For master's, minimum B average. Additional exam requirements/recommendations for international students: Required—TOEFL. Tuition charges are reported in Canadian dollars. *Expenses:* Tuition, area resident: Full-time $6500 Canadian dollars. International tuition: $13,700 Canadian dollars full-time. *Faculty research:* Canadian history, British history, Russian/German history, women's studies.

Lakehead University, Graduate Studies, Faculty of Education, Thunder Bay, ON P7B 5E1, Canada. Offers educational studies (PhD); gerontology (M Ed); women's studies (M Ed). Part-time and evening/weekend programs available. *Degree requirements:* For master's, project or thesis. *Entrance requirements:* For master's, minimum B average. Additional exam requirements/recommendations for international students: Required—TOEFL. Tuition charges are reported in Canadian dollars. *Expenses:* Tuition, area resident: Full-time $6500 Canadian dollars. International tuition: $13,700 Canadian dollars full-time. *Faculty research:* Art education, AIDS education, language arts education, gerontology, women's studies.

Lakehead University, Graduate Studies, Faculty of Social Sciences and Humanities, Department of Sociology, Thunder Bay, ON P7B 5E1, Canada. Offers gerontology (MA); health services and policy research (MA); sociology (MA); women's studies (MA). Part-time and evening/weekend programs available. *Degree requirements:* For master's, research project or thesis. *Entrance requirements:* For master's, minimum B average. Additional exam requirements/recommendations for international students: Required—TOEFL. Tuition charges are reported in Canadian dollars. *Expenses:* Tuition, area resident: Full-time $6500 Canadian dollars. International tuition: $13,700 Canadian dollars full-time. *Faculty research:* Sociology of medicine, cultural and social change, health human resources, gerontology, women's studies.

Lakehead University, Graduate Studies, Gerontology Collaborative Program-Northern Educational Center for Aging and Health, Thunder Bay, ON P7B 5E1, Canada. Offers specialization gerontology (M Ed, M Sc, MA, MSW). Part-time programs available. *Degree requirements:* For master's, thesis (for some programs). *Entrance requirements:* Additional exam requirements/recommendations for international students: Required—TOEFL. Tuition charges are reported in Canadian dollars. *Expenses:* Tuition, area resident: Full-time $6500 Canadian dollars. International tuition: $13,700 Canadian dollars full-time. *Faculty research:* Integrated health information systems.

Lakehead University, Graduate Studies, School of Kinesiology, Thunder Bay, ON P7B 5E1, Canada. Offers kinesiology (M Sc); kinesiology and gerontology (M Sc). Part-time programs available. *Degree requirements:* For master's, thesis. *Entrance requirements:* For master's, minimum B average. Additional exam requirements/recommendations for international students: Required—TOEFL. Tuition charges are reported in Canadian dollars. *Expenses:* Tuition, area resident: Full-time $6500 Canadian dollars. International tuition: $13,700 Canadian dollars full-time. *Faculty research:* Social psychology and physical education, sport history, sports medicine, exercise physiology, gerontology.

Lakehead University, Graduate Studies, School of Social Work, Thunder Bay, ON P7B 5E1, Canada. Offers gerontology (MSW); social work (MSW); women's studies (MSW). Part-time programs available. *Degree requirements:* For master's, thesis or project. *Entrance requirements:* For master's, minimum B average. Additional exam requirements/recommendations for international students: Required—TOEFL. Tuition charges are reported in Canadian dollars. *Expenses:* Tuition, area resident: Full-time $6500 Canadian dollars. International tuition: $13,700 Canadian dollars full-time. *Faculty research:* Clinical psychology, social work and practice theory, long-term care, health care for frail elderly, women's studies.

Lindenwood University, Graduate Programs, College of Individualized Education, St. Charles, MO 63301-1695. Offers administration (MSA); business administration (MBA); communication (MS); communications (MA); criminal justice and administration (MS); gerontology (MA); health management (MS); human resource management (MS); information technology (MBA, Certificate); management (MSA); managing information technology (MS); marketing (MSA); writing (MFA). Part-time and evening/weekend programs available. *Faculty:* 14 full-time (7 women), 119 part-time/adjunct (50 women). *Students:* 750 full-time (489 women), 138 part-time (91 women); includes 196 minority (182 African Americans, 1 American Indian/Alaska Native, 5 Asian Americans or Pacific Islanders, 8 Hispanic Americans), 14 international. Average age 34. In 2008, 349 master's awarded. *Degree requirements:* For master's, thesis (for some programs), minimum GPA of 3.0, 1 colloquium per term. *Entrance requirements:* For master's, interview, minimum GPA of 3.0. Additional exam requirements/recommendations for international students: Required—TOEFL (minimum score 550 paper-based; 213 computer-based; 80 iBT). *Application deadline:* For fall admission, 9/30 priority date for domestic and international students; for winter admission, 12/30 priority date for domestic and international

Gerontology

Lindenwood University (continued)

students; for spring admission, 3/30 priority date for domestic and international students. Applications are processed on a rolling basis. Application fee: $30 ($100 for international students). *Expenses:* Tuition: Full-time $12,700; part-time $360 per credit hour. *Financial support:* Career-related internships or fieldwork, institutionally sponsored loans, tuition waivers (partial), and unspecified assistantships available. Financial award application deadline: 6/30; financial award applicants required to submit FAFSA. *Unit head:* Dan Kemper, Dean of Lindenwood College for Individual Education, 636-949-4501, Fax: 636-949-4505, E-mail: dkemper@lindenwood.edu. *Application contact:* Brett Barger, Dean of Evening Admissions and Extension Campuses, 636-949-4934, Fax: 636-949-4109, E-mail: adultadmissions@lindenwood.edu.

Long Island University, C.W. Post Campus, College of Management, Department of Health Care and Public Administration, Brookville, NY 11548-1300. Offers gerontology (Certificate); health care administration (MPA); health care administration/gerontology (MPA); nonprofit management (MPA, Certificate); public administration (MPA). *Accreditation:* NASPAA (one or more programs are accredited). Part-time and evening/weekend programs available. *Degree requirements:* For master's, thesis. *Entrance requirements:* For master's, GMAT, minimum GPA of 2.5; for Certificate, minimum GPA of 2.5. Electronic applications accepted. *Faculty research:* Critical issues in sexuality, social work in religious communities, gerontological social work.

Long Island University, Rockland Graduate Campus, Graduate School, Programs in Health and Public Administration, Orangeburg, NY 10962. Offers gerontology (Advanced Certificate); health administration (MPA); public administration (MPA). *Entrance requirements:* For master's, GRE General Test. *Expenses:* Tuition: Full-time $882; part-time $882 per credit. Required fees: $200; $100 per semester.

Marywood University, Academic Affairs, College of Health and Human Services, Department of Nursing and Public Administration, Program in Gerontology, Scranton, PA 18509-1598. Offers MS, Certificate.

Miami University, Graduate School, College of Arts and Sciences, Department of Sociology and Gerontology, Program in Gerontology, Oxford, OH 45056. Offers MGS. *Degree requirements:* For master's, final exam. *Entrance requirements:* For master's, GRE General Test, minimum undergraduate GPA of 3.0 during previous 2 years or 2.75 overall. Additional exam requirements/recommendations for international students: Required—TOEFL (minimum score 550 paper-based; 213 computer-based), TWE (minimum score 4). Electronic applications accepted.

Middle Tennessee State University, College of Graduate Studies, Program in Gerontology, Murfreesboro, TN 37132. Offers Graduate Certificate. Part-time and evening/weekend programs available. Postbaccalaureate distance learning degree programs offered. *Entrance requirements:* Additional exam requirements/recommendations for international students: Required—TOEFL (paper-based 525; computer-based 195; IBT 71) or IELTS (6.0).

Minnesota State University Mankato, College of Graduate Studies, College of Social and Behavioral Sciences, Program in Gerontology, Mankato, MN 56001. Offers MS, Certificate. *Students:* 4 full-time (2 women), 8 part-time (7 women). *Degree requirements:* For master's, comprehensive exam, thesis. *Entrance requirements:* For master's, GRE, minimum GPA of 3.0 during previous 2 years, letters of recommendation. Additional exam requirements/recommendations for international students: Required—TOEFL. *Application deadline:* For fall admission, 7/1 priority date for domestic students; for spring admission, 11/1 for domestic students. Applications are processed on a rolling basis. Application fee: $40. Electronic applications accepted. *Financial support:* Federal Work-Study and unspecified assistantships available. Support available to part-time students. Financial award application deadline: 3/15; financial award applicants required to submit FAFSA. *Unit head:* Jim Tift, Director, 507-389-5188. *Application contact:* 507-389-2321, E-mail: grad@mnsu.edu.

Morehead State University, Graduate Programs, Caudill College of Humanities, Department of Sociology, Social Work and Criminology, Morehead, KY 40351. Offers criminology (MA); general sociology (MA); gerontology (MA). Part-time and evening/weekend programs available. *Faculty:* 7 full-time (4 women), 4 part-time/adjunct (1 woman). *Students:* 9 full-time (7 women), 18 part-time (12 women); includes 1 minority (African American). Average age 30. 20 applicants, 55% accepted, 7 enrolled. In 2008, 4 master's awarded. *Degree requirements:* For master's, comprehensive exam, thesis optional. *Entrance requirements:* For master's, GRE General Test, minimum GPA of 3.0 in sociology, 2.5 overall; 18 hours of course work in sociology, writing sample. Additional exam requirements/recommendations for international students: Required—TOEFL (minimum score 500 paper-based; 173 computer-based). *Application deadline:* For fall admission, 8/1 priority date for domestic and international students; for spring admission, 12/1 priority date for domestic and international students. Applications are processed on a rolling basis. Application fee: $30 ($55 for international students). Electronic applications accepted. *Expenses:* Tuition: area resident: Full-time $6084; part-time $338 per credit hour. Tuition, state resident: full-time $6084; part-time $338 per credit hour. Tuition, nonresident: full-time $15,804; part-time $878 per credit hour. *Financial support:* In 2008–09, 5 teaching assistantships (averaging $6,000 per year) were awarded; career-related internships or fieldwork, Federal Work-Study, and unspecified assistantships also available. Financial award application deadline: 4/1; financial award applicants required to submit FAFSA. *Faculty research:* Death and dying; aging, drinking, and drugs; economic development; adult children of alcoholics. *Unit head:* Dr. Clarenda Phillips, Department Chair, 606-783-2656, Fax: 606-783-5027, E-mail: r.bylund@moreheadstate.edu. *Application contact:* Michelle Barber, Graduate Admissions Counselor, 606-783-2039, Fax: 606-783-5061, E-mail: m.barber@moreheadstate.edu.

Mount Saint Vincent University, Graduate Programs, Department of Family Studies and Gerontology, Halifax, NS B3M 2J6, Canada. Offers MA. Part-time programs available. Postbaccalaureate distance learning degree programs offered (minimal on-campus study). *Degree requirements:* For master's, thesis. *Entrance requirements:* For master's, minimum GPA of 3.0; course work in statistics, research methods, family and social theories.

National-Louis University, College of Arts and Sciences, Department of Counseling and Human Services, Chicago, IL 60603. Offers addictions counseling (Certificate); addictions treatment (Certificate); career counseling and development studies (Certificate); community counseling (MS); community wellness and prevention (Certificate); counseling (Certificate); eating disorders counseling (Certificate); employee assistance programs (MS, Certificate); gerontology administration (Certificate); gerontology counseling (MS, Certificate); human services administration (MS, Certificate); long-term care administration (Certificate); school counseling (MS). Part-time programs available. *Students:* 8 full-time (7 women), 239 part-time (199 women); includes 71 minority (49 African Americans, 5 Asian Americans or Pacific Islanders, 17 Hispanic Americans). Average age 39. In 2008, 53 master's, 6 other advanced degrees awarded. *Degree requirements:* For master's and Certificate, internship. *Entrance requirements:* For master's and Certificate, GRE, MAT, or Watson-Glaser Critical Thinking Appraisal, interview, minimum GPA of 3.0. *Application deadline:* Applications are processed on a rolling basis. *Financial support:* Federal Work-Study, institutionally sponsored loans, scholarships/grants, and tuition waivers available. Support available to part-time students. Financial award applicants required to submit FAFSA. *Faculty research:* Religion and aging, drug abuse prevention, hunger, homelessness, multicultural diversity. *Unit head:* Dr. Susan Thorne-Devin, Assistant Professor, 630-874-4560, E-mail: stdevin@nl.edu. *Application contact:* Dr. Larry Poselli, Vice President of Enrollment and Student Services, 800-443-5522 Ext. 5718, Fax: 312-261-.3550, E-mail: larry.polselli@nl.edu.

North Dakota State University, College of Graduate and Interdisciplinary Studies, College of Human Development and Education, Department of Child Development and Family Science, Fargo, ND 58105. Offers child development and family science (MS); couple and family therapy (MS); family financial planning (MS); gerontology (MS, PhD). *Accreditation:* AAMFT/COAMFTE. Part-time and evening/weekend programs available. Postbaccalaureate distance

learning degree programs offered (no on-campus study). *Faculty:* 12 full-time (7 women). *Students:* 26 full-time (25 women), 21 part-time (18 women); includes 1 African American, 2 international. 22 applicants, 64% accepted, 12 enrolled. In 2008, 12 master's awarded. *Degree requirements:* For master's, thesis or alternative; for doctorate, thesis/dissertation. *Entrance requirements:* Additional exam requirements/recommendations for international students: Required—TOEFL (minimum score 525 paper-based; 197 computer-based; 71 iBT). *Application deadline:* For fall admission, 2/1 for domestic and international students; for spring admission, 10/1 for domestic and international students. Application fee: $45 ($60 for international students). *Financial support:* In 2008–09, 17 students received support, including research assistantships with full tuition reimbursements available (averaging $3,000 per year), 17 teaching assistantships with full tuition reimbursements available (averaging $3,000 per year); career-related internships or fieldwork, Federal Work-Study, institutionally sponsored loans, and tuition waivers (full) also available. Financial award application deadline: 4/1. *Faculty research:* Family therapy, resilience, parenting, adolescent development, mental health. Total annual research expenditures: $333,582. *Unit head:* Dr. James Deal, Head, 701-231-7568, Fax: 701-231-9645, E-mail: jim_deal@ndsu.edu. *Application contact:* Theresa Anderson, Administrative Assistant, 701-231-8628, Fax: 701-231-9645, E-mail: theresa.anderson@ndsu.edu.

Northeastern Illinois University, Graduate College, College of Arts and Sciences, Department of Gerontology, Program in Gerontology, Chicago, IL 60625-4699. Offers MA. Part-time and evening/weekend programs available. *Degree requirements:* For master's, comprehensive exam, paper and project or thesis, practicum, minimum GPA of 3.0. *Entrance requirements:* For master's, 15 hours in social sciences (3 hours in gerontology), 1 course in research methods or statistics, minimum GPA of 2.75. Additional exam requirements/recommendations for international students: Required—TOEFL (minimum score 550 paper-based; 213 computer-based; 80 iBT). Electronic applications accepted. *Faculty research:* Later life development, cultural diversity, humanities and aging, elder abuse, AIDS and aging, computer training.

Notre Dame de Namur University, Division of Academic Affairs, School of Sciences, Department of Clinical Psychology and Gerontology, Belmont, CA 94002-1908. Offers clinical gerontology (Certificate); clinical psychology (MA); marital and family therapy (MAMFT). Part-time and evening/weekend programs available. *Faculty:* 2 full-time (both women), 6 part-time/adjunct (5 women). *Students:* 29 full-time (25 women), 65 part-time (56 women); includes 31 minority (5 African Americans, 11 Asian Americans or Pacific Islanders, 15 Hispanic Americans), 1 international. Average age 35. 26 applicants, 81% accepted, 16 enrolled. In 2008, 27 master's awarded. *Entrance requirements:* For master's, interview, minimum GPA of 2.5. Additional exam requirements/recommendations for international students: Required—TOEFL (minimum score 550 paper-based; 213 computer-based; 79 iBT). *Application deadline:* For fall admission, 8/1 priority date for domestic students; for spring admission, 12/1 priority date for domestic students. Applications are processed on a rolling basis. Application fee: $60. Electronic applications accepted. *Expenses:* Tuition: Part-time $699 per unit. Required fees: $3 per unit. $35 per semester. *Financial support:* Career-related internships or fieldwork available. Support available to part-time students. Financial award applicants required to submit FAFSA. *Unit head:* Dr. Nusha Askari, Chair, 650-508-3728, E-mail: naskari@ndnu.edu. *Application contact:* Candace Hallmark, Assistant Director of Graduate Admissions, 650-508-3592, Fax: 650-508-3426, E-mail: grad.admit@ndnu.edu.

Oregon Health & Science University, School of Nursing, Program in Nursing Education, Portland, OR 97239-3098. Offers MN, MS, Post Master's Certificate.

Oregon State University, Graduate School, College of Health and Human Sciences, Department of Human Development and Family Sciences, Program in Gerontology, Corvallis, OR 97331. Offers MAIS. *Degree requirements:* For master's, thesis optional. *Entrance requirements:* For master's, GRE, minimum GPA of 3.0 in last 90 hours. Additional exam requirements/recommendations for international students: Required—TOEFL. *Faculty research:* Aging/families, social/psychological aspects of aging, osteoporosis, nutrition, disease and aging.

Portland State University, Graduate Studies, College of Urban and Public Affairs, School of Community Health, Institute on Aging, Portland, OR 97207-0751. Offers Certificate. Part-time programs available. *Students:* 1 (woman) full-time, 6 part-time (3 women). Average age 41. 5 applicants, 100% accepted, 4 enrolled. *Application deadline:* For fall admission, 2/1 for domestic and international students. Application fee: $50. *Expenses:* Tuition, area resident: Full-time $8763; part-time $179 per credit hour. Tuition, state resident: full-time $8763; part-time $298 per credit hour. Tuition, nonresident: full-time $12,981; part-time $426 per credit hour. Required fees: $1242. One-time fee: $250. Tuition and fees vary according to course load and program. *Financial support:* In 2008–09, 3 research assistantships with full tuition reimbursements (averaging $9,456 per year) were awarded; teaching assistantships, career-related internships or fieldwork and Federal Work-Study also available. Support available to part-time students. Financial award application deadline: 3/1; financial award applicants required to submit FAFSA. Total annual research expenditures: $582,820. *Unit head:* Dr. Margaret Neal, Director, 503-725-3952, Fax: 503-725-5199, E-mail: nealm@pdx.edu. *Application contact:* Dr. Margaret Neal, Director, 503-725-3952, Fax: 503-725-5199, E-mail: nealm@pdx.edu.

Rochester Institute of Technology, Graduate Enrollment Services, College of Applied Science and Technology, Department of Hospitality and Service Management, Program in Senior Living Management, Rochester, NY 14623-5603. Offers AC. *Entrance requirements:* Additional exam requirements/recommendations for international students: Required—TOEFL (minimum score 550 paper-based; 213 computer-based; 79 iBT).

Sacred Heart University, Graduate Programs, College of Education and Health Professions, Program in Geriatric Health and Wellness, Fairfield, CT 06825-1000. Offers MS. Part-time and evening/weekend programs available. Postbaccalaureate distance learning degree programs offered. *Entrance requirements:* Additional exam requirements/recommendations for international students: Required—TOEFL (minimum score 550 paper-based; 213 computer-based; 75 iBT). Electronic applications accepted. *Expenses:* Contact institution.

Sage Graduate School, Graduate School, Department of Management, Program in Health Services Administration, Troy, NY 12180-4115. Offers dietetic internship (Certificate); gerontology (MS). Part-time and evening/weekend programs available. *Faculty:* 3 full-time (2 women), 7 part-time/adjunct (0 women). *Students:* 18 part-time (13 women); includes 2 minority (1 Asian American or Pacific Islander, 1 Hispanic American). Average age 34. 13 applicants, 62% accepted, 5 enrolled. In 2008, 8 master's awarded. *Entrance requirements:* For master's, minimum GPA of 2.75, completed application, current resumée, essay, official transcripts, 2 letters of recommendation. Additional exam requirements/recommendations for international students: Required—TOEFL (minimum score 550 paper-based; 213 computer-based). Application fee: $40. *Expenses:* Tuition: Full-time $10,080; part-time $560 per credit hour. *Financial support:* Fellowships, research assistantships, Federal Work-Study, scholarships/grants, and unspecified assistantships available. Support available to part-time students. Financial award application deadline: 3/1; financial award applicants required to submit FAFSA. *Unit head:* Dr. Kimberly Fredricks, Program Director, 518-292-1700, Fax: 518-292-5414, E-mail: fredek1@sage.edu. *Application contact:* Wendy D. Diefendorf, Director of Graduate and Adult Admission, 518-244-2443, Fax: 518-244-6880, E-mail: diefew@sage.edu.

St. Cloud State University, School of Graduate Studies, College of Social Sciences, Program in Gerontology, St. Cloud, MN 56301-4498. Offers MS. Part-time programs available. *Degree requirements:* For master's, thesis or alternative. *Entrance requirements:* For master's, GRE General Test, minimum GPA of 2.75. Additional exam requirements/recommendations for international students: Required—Michigan English Language Assessment Battery; Recommended—TOEFL (minimum score 550 paper-based; 213 computer-based), IELTS (minimum score 6.5). Electronic applications accepted.

Saint Joseph College, Graduate School, Institute in Gerontology, West Hartford, CT 06117-2700. Offers human development/gerontology (MA, Certificate). Part-time and evening/

weekend programs available. *Students:* 4 full-time (3 women), 15 part-time (14 women). *Application deadline:* Applications are processed on a rolling basis. Application fee: $50. Electronic applications accepted. *Expenses:* Tuition: Part-time $560 per credit. Required fees: $30 per credit. *Financial support:* Career-related internships or fieldwork, health care benefits, and unspecified assistantships available. Support available to part-time students. Financial award applicants required to submit FAFSA. *Application contact:* Graduate Admissions Office, 860-231-5261, E-mail: graduate@sjc.edu.

Saint Joseph's University, College of Arts and Sciences, Program in Gerontological Services, Philadelphia, PA 19131-1395. Offers gerontological counseling (MS); gerontological services (Post-Master's Certificate); human services administration (MS). Part-time and evening/weekend programs available. *Students:* 3 full-time (0 women), 9 part-time (4 women); includes 5 minority (all African Americans), 5 international. Average age 34. In 2008, 6 master's awarded. *Entrance requirements:* For master's, 2 letters of recommendation, application, official transcripts, personal statement. Additional exam requirements/recommendations for international students: Required—TOEFL (minimum score 550 paper-based; 213 computer-based; 79 iBT). *Application deadline:* For fall admission, 7/15 priority date for domestic students, 4/15 for international students; for winter admission, 1/15 for international students; for spring admission, 11/15 priority date for domestic students, 10/15 for international students. Applications are processed on a rolling basis. Application fee: $35. Electronic applications accepted. *Expenses:* Tuition: Part-time $745 per credit. Tuition and fees vary according to course load, degree level and program. *Financial support:* Fellowships available. Financial award applicants required to submit FAFSA. *Unit head:* Dr. Catherine Murray, Director, 610-660-1805, E-mail: cmurray@sju.edu. *Application contact:* Coralee Dixon, Assistant Director of Graduate Admissions, 610-660-1102, Fax: 610-660-1224, E-mail: coralee.dixon@sju.edu.

San Diego State University, Graduate and Research Affairs, College of Health and Human Services, Department of Gerontology, San Diego, CA 92182. Offers MS. Part-time and evening/weekend programs available. *Degree requirements:* For master's, thesis. *Entrance requirements:* For master's, GRE General Test. Additional exam requirements/recommendations for international students: Required—TOEFL. Electronic applications accepted.

San Francisco State University, Division of Graduate Studies, College of Health and Human Services, Gerontology Program, San Francisco, CA 94132-1722. Offers geriatric care management (MA); health, wellness and aging (MA); long-term care administration (MA). Part-time programs available.

San Jose State University, Graduate Studies and Research, College of Applied Sciences and Arts, Department of Health Science, San Jose, CA 95192-0001. Offers applied social gerontology (Certificate); community health education (MPH). *Accreditation:* CEPH (one or more programs are accredited). Postbaccalaureate distance learning degree programs offered. *Entrance requirements:* For master's, GRE General Test. Electronic applications accepted. *Faculty research:* Behavioral science in occupational and health care settings, epidemiology in health care settings.

Shippensburg University of Pennsylvania, School of Graduate Studies, College of Education and Human Services, Department of Social Work and Gerontology, Shippensburg, PA 17257-2299. Offers aging (Certificate); social work (MSW). Part-time and evening/weekend programs available. Postbaccalaureate distance learning degree programs offered. *Faculty:* 6 full-time (5 women), 2 part-time/adjunct (both women). *Students:* 17 full-time (15 women), 23 part-time (20 women); includes 2 minority (both African Americans). Average age 29. 5 applicants, 60% accepted, 3 enrolled. In 2008, 16 master's awarded. *Degree requirements:* For master's, thesis, practicum. *Entrance requirements:* For master's, GRE or MAT, personal statement; 3 letters of reference; resumé; minimum GPA of 2.8; coursework in human biology, economics, government/political science, psychology, sociology/anthropology and statistics. Additional exam requirements/recommendations for international students: Required—TOEFL (minimum score 560 paper-based; 220 computer-based); Recommended—IELTS (minimum score 6). *Application deadline:* For fall admission, 3/1 for international students. Applications are processed on a rolling basis. Application fee: $30. Electronic applications accepted. *Expenses:* Tuition, state resident: full-time $6430; part-time $357 per credit. Tuition, nonresident: full-time $10,288; part-time $572 per credit. Required fees: $1127; $38 per credit. One-time fee: $44 part-time. *Financial support:* In 2008–09, 3 research assistantships with full tuition reimbursements (averaging $5,000 per year) were awarded; career-related internships or fieldwork, scholarships/grants, unspecified assistantships, and resident hall directors, student payroll positions also available. Support available to part-time students. Financial award application deadline: 3/1; financial award applicants required to submit FAFSA. *Unit head:* Dr. Deborah F. Jacobs, Chairperson, 717-477-1276, Fax: 717-477-4051, E-mail: dfjaco@ship.edu. *Application contact:* Renee Payne, Associate Dean of Graduate Admissions, 717-477-1231, Fax: 717-477-4016, E-mail: rmpayn@ship.edu.

Simon Fraser University, Graduate Studies, Faculty of Arts and Social Sciences, Department of Gerontology, Burnaby, BC V5A 1S6, Canada. Offers MA, PhD. *Degree requirements:* For master's, thesis (for some programs). *Entrance requirements:* For master's, minimum GPA of 3.5. Additional exam requirements/recommendations for international students: Required—TOEFL or IELTS. *Faculty research:* Aging and the built environment, health promotion and aging.

Texas A&M University–Kingsville, College of Graduate Studies, College of Arts and Sciences, Department of Psychology and Sociology, Kingsville, TX 78363. Offers gerontology (MS); psychology (MA, MS); sociology (MA, MS). Part-time and evening/weekend programs available. *Degree requirements:* For master's, comprehensive exam, thesis or alternative. *Entrance requirements:* For master's, GRE General Test, minimum GPA of 2.5. Additional exam requirements/recommendations for international students: Required—TOEFL. *Faculty research:* Hispanic female voting behavior, attitudes toward criminal justice, immigration of aged into south Texas, folk medicine.

Texas Tech University, Graduate School, College of Human Sciences, Department of Human Development and Family Studies, Lubbock, TX 79409. Offers gerontology (MS); human development and family studies (MS, PhD). *Accreditation:* AAMFT/COAMFTE (one or more programs are accredited). Part-time programs available. *Faculty:* 19 full-time (15 women), 1 (woman) part-time/adjunct. *Students:* 38 full-time (30 women), 18 part-time (11 women); includes 9 minority (2 African Americans, 2 American Indian/Alaska Native, 2 Asian Americans or Pacific Islanders, 3 Hispanic Americans), 13 international. Average age 36. 32 applicants, 78% accepted, 7 enrolled. In 2008, 7 master's awarded. *Degree requirements:* For master's, thesis; for doctorate, thesis/dissertation. *Entrance requirements:* For master's and doctorate, GRE General Test. Additional exam requirements/recommendations for international students: Required—TOEFL (minimum score 550 paper-based; 213 computer-based). *Application deadline:* For fall admission, 3/1 priority date for international students; for spring admission, 11/1 priority date for international students. Applications are processed on a rolling basis. Application fee: $50 ($60 for international students). Electronic applications accepted. *Expenses:* Tuition, area resident: Part-time $194 per credit hour. Tuition, state resident: full-time $4648; part-time $194 per credit hour. Tuition, nonresident: full-time $11,392; part-time $475 per credit hour. Required fees: $2206; $69 per credit hour. $389 per semester. *Financial support:* In 2008–09, 55 students received support, including 3 research assistantships with partial tuition reimbursements available (averaging $13,107 per year), 30 teaching assistantships with partial tuition reimbursements available (averaging $13,126 per year); career-related internships or fieldwork, Federal Work-Study, institutionally sponsored loans, and scholarships/grants also available. Support available to part-time students. Financial award application deadline: 4/15; financial award applicants required to submit FAFSA. *Faculty research:* Parenting, marital and premarital relationships, adolescent risky behaviors, life span; child development. Total annual research expenditures: $352,679. *Unit head:* Anisa Zvonkovic, Chair, 806-742-3000 Ext. 279, Fax: 806-742-0285, E-mail: anisa.zvonkovic@ttu.edu. *Application contact:* Monya Castle, Graduate Secretary, 806-742-3000 Ext. 250, Fax: 806-742-0285, E-mail: monya.castle@ttu.edu.

Towson University, College of Graduate Studies and Research, Program in Applied Gerontology, Towson, MD 21252-0001. Offers MS, Certificate. *Entrance requirements:* For master's, minimum of 9 credits of upper-level related coursework, 2 letters of recommendation, admission essay; for Certificate, minimum of 9 credits of upper-level related coursework. Electronic applications accepted.

Université de Montréal, Faculty of Medicine, Program in Specialized Studies, Montréal, QC H3C 3J7, Canada. Offers anesthesia (DESS); diagnostic radiology (DESS); family medicine (DESS); gastroenterology (DESS); geriatry (DESS); intensive care (DESS); medical biochemistry (DESS); medical genetics (DESS); medicine (DESS); microbiology and infectious diseases (DESS); nuclear medicine (DESS); obstetrics and gynecology (DESS); ophthalmology (DESS); pediatrics (DESS); pneumology (DESS); psychiatry (DESS); radiology-oncology (DESS); rheumatology (DESS); surgery (DESS). *Faculty:* 154 full-time (40 women), 333 part-time/adjunct (100 women). *Students:* 930 full-time (580 women), 7 part-time (all women). 74 applicants, 77% accepted, 29 enrolled. In 2008, 151 DESSs awarded. *Entrance requirements:* For degree, proficiency in French. *Application deadline:* For fall admission, 2/1 priority date for domestic students; for winter admission, 11/1 priority date for domestic students; for spring admission, 2/1 priority date for domestic students. Application fee: $100. Electronic applications accepted. *Unit head:* Lorraine Locas, Assistant to the Vice Dean of Graduate Studies, 514-343-6269, Fax: 514-343-5751, E-mail: lorraine.locas@umontreal.ca. *Application contact:* Dr. Andre Ferron, Vice Dean Graduate Studies, 514-343-6111 Ext. 0933, Fax: 514-343-5751, E-mail: andre.ferron@umontreal.ca.

Université de Sherbrooke, Faculty of Letters and Human Sciences, Department of Psychology, Sherbrooke, QC J1K 2R1, Canada. Offers gerontology (MA). *Degree requirements:* For master's, thesis. *Faculty research:* Human relations.

Université Laval, Faculty of Medicine, Post-Professional Programs in Medical Studies, Québec, QC G1K 7P4, Canada. Offers anatomy–pathology (DESS); anesthesiology (DESS); cardiology (DESS); care of older people (Diploma); clinical research (DESS); community health (DESS); dermatology (DESS); diagnostic radiology (DESS); emergency medicine (Diploma); family medicine (DESS); general surgery (DESS); geriatrics (DESS); hematology (DESS); internal medicine (DESS); maternal and fetal medicine (Diploma); medical biochemistry (DESS); medical microbiology and infectious diseases (DESS); medical oncology (DESS); nephrology (DESS); neurology (DESS); neurosurgery (DESS); obstetrics and gynecology (DESS); ophthalmology (DESS); orthopedic surgery (DESS); oto-rhino-laryngology (DESS); palliative medicine (Diploma); pediatrics (DESS); plastic surgery (DESS); psychiatry (DESS); pulmonary medicine (DESS); radiology–oncology (DESS); thoracic surgery (DESS); urology (DESS). *Degree requirements:* For other advanced degree, comprehensive exam. *Entrance requirements:* For degree, knowledge of French. Electronic applications accepted.

University of Arkansas at Little Rock, Graduate School, College of Arts, Humanities, and Social Science, Program in Gerontology, Little Rock, AR 72204-1099. Offers Graduate Certificate.

University of Central Florida, College of Health and Public Affairs, School of Social Work, Orlando, FL 32816. Offers addictions (Certificate); aging studies (Certificate); children's services (Certificate); school social work (Certificate); social work (MSW); social work administration (Certificate). *Accreditation:* CSWE. Part-time and evening/weekend programs available. *Faculty:* 15 full-time (11 women), 17 part-time/adjunct (15 women). *Students:* 113 full-time (99 women), 79 part-time (64 women); includes 61 minority (35 African Americans, 1 American Indian/Alaska Native, 2 Asian Americans or Pacific Islanders, 23 Hispanic Americans), 2 international. In 2008, 80 master's, 15 other advanced degrees awarded. *Degree requirements:* For master's, thesis or alternative, field education. *Entrance requirements:* For master's, resumé. Additional exam requirements/recommendations for international students: Required—TOEFL. *Application deadline:* For fall admission, 3/1 for domestic students. Application fee: $30. Electronic applications accepted. *Expenses:* Tuition, area resident: Full-time $6816; part-time $284 per credit. Tuition, state resident: full-time $6816; part-time $1076 per credit. Tuition, nonresident: full-time $25,824. Required fees: $216; $9 per credit. *Financial support:* In 2008–09, 2 fellowships with partial tuition reimbursements (averaging $10,000 per year), 18 research assistantships with partial tuition reimbursements (averaging $6,800 per year) were awarded; teaching assistantships with partial tuition reimbursements, career-related internships or fieldwork, Federal Work-Study, institutionally sponsored loans, and unspecified assistantships also available. Financial award application deadline: 3/1; financial award applicants required to submit FAFSA. *Unit head:* Dr. John Ronnau, Director, 407-823-2114, Fax: 407-823-5697, E-mail: jronnau@mail.ucf.edu. *Application contact:* Dr. John Ronnau, Director, 407-823-2114, Fax: 407-823-5697, E-mail: jronnau@mail.ucf.edu.

University of Central Missouri, The Graduate School, College of Health and Human Services, Department of Sociology and Social Work, Warrensburg, MO 64093. Offers social gerontology (MS); sociology (MA). Part-time programs available. *Degree requirements:* For master's, comprehensive exam. *Entrance requirements:* For master's, minimum GPA of 2.5. Additional exam requirements/recommendations for international students: Required—TOEFL (minimum score 500 paper-based; 173 computer-based). *Faculty research:* Suicide, end of life decision making, aging/gerontology, race/ethic relations, religion.

University of Central Oklahoma, College of Graduate Studies and Research, College of Education, Department of Occupational and Technical Education, Program in Adult Education, Edmond, OK 73034-5209. Offers community services (M Ed); gerontology (M Ed). *Accreditation:* NCATE. Part-time programs available. *Entrance requirements:* For master's, GRE General Test. Additional exam requirements/recommendations for international students: Required—TOEFL (minimum score 550 paper-based; 213 computer-based). Electronic applications accepted.

University of Georgia, College of Public Health, Institute of Gerontology, Athens, GA 30602. Offers Certificate.

University of Illinois at Springfield, Graduate Programs, College of Education and Human Services, Program in Human Services, Springfield, IL 62703-5407. Offers alcoholism and substance abuse (MA); child and family services (MA); gerontology (MA); social services administration (MA). Part-time and evening/weekend programs available. Postbaccalaureate distance learning degree programs offered (no on-campus study). *Faculty:* 4 full-time (2 women), 3 part-time/adjunct (all women). *Students:* 28 full-time (22 women), 70 part-time (56 women); includes 17 minority (16 African Americans, 1 American Indian/Alaska Native). Average age 35. 64 applicants, 42% accepted, 22 enrolled. In 2008, 24 master's awarded. *Degree requirements:* For master's, thesis optional, internship; project or thesis. *Entrance requirements:* For master's, minimum undergraduate GPA of 3.0, 2 letters of recommendation, personal statement. Additional exam requirements/recommendations for international students: Required—TOEFL (minimum score 500 paper-based; 176 computer-based; 61 iBT). Application fee: $50 ($60 for international students). Electronic applications accepted. *Expenses:* Tuition, state resident: full-time $6144; part-time $256 per credit hour. Tuition, nonresident: full-time $13,980; part-time $582.50 per credit hour. Required fees: $1800. *Financial support:* In 2008–09, research assistantships with full tuition reimbursements (averaging $8,109 per year), teaching assistantships with full tuition reimbursements (averaging $8,109 per year) were awarded; career-related internships or fieldwork, scholarships/grants, health care benefits, and unspecified assistantships also available. Support available to part-time students. Financial award application deadline: 11/15. *Unit head:* Dr. Carolyn Peck, Program Administrator, 217-206-7577, Fax: 217-206-6775, E-mail: peck.carolyn@uis.edu. *Application contact:* Dr. Lynn Pardie, Office of Graduate Studies, 800-252-8533, Fax: 217-206-7623, E-mail: pardie.lynn@uis.edu.

University of Indianapolis, Graduate Programs, Center for Aging and Community, Indianapolis, IN 46227-3697. Offers gerontology (MS, Certificate). Part-time and evening/weekend programs available. Postbaccalaureate distance learning degree programs offered. *Faculty:* 1 (woman) full-time, 1 (woman) part-time/adjunct. *Students:* 24 part-time (21 women); includes 3 minority (2 African Americans, 1 Hispanic American), 4 international. Average age 37. *Degree*

Gerontology

University of Indianapolis (continued)
requirements: For master's, capstone course. *Entrance requirements:* For master's, 1 page essay, 3 letters of recommendation. Additional exam requirements/recommendations for international students: Required—TOEFL (minimum score 550 paper-based; 213 computer-based). *Application deadline:* Applications are processed on a rolling basis. Application fee: $50. *Financial support:* Scholarships/grants available. *Unit head:* Dr. Ellen Miller, Executive Director, 317-791-5930, Fax: 317-791-5945, E-mail: emiller@uindy.edu. *Application contact:* Tamora Wolske, Academic Program Director, 317-791-5930, Fax: 317-791-5945, E-mail: wolsketl@uindy.edu.

University of Indianapolis, Graduate Programs, School of Nursing, Indianapolis, IN 46227-3697. Offers family practice (post-RN) (MSN); gerontological nurse practitioner (MSN); nurse-midwifery (MSN); nursing (MSN); nursing administration (MSN); nursing education (MSN); MBA/MSN. *Accreditation:* AACN; ACNM. *Faculty:* 10 full-time (9 women), 7 part-time/adjunct (6 women). *Students:* 21 full-time (18 women), 108 part-time (103 women); includes 16 minority (15 African Americans, 1 Hispanic American). Average age 39. *Entrance requirements:* For master's, minimum GPA of 3.0, interview, letters of recommendation, resumé, IN nursing license, 1 year professional practice. Additional exam requirements/recommendations for international students: Required—TOEFL (minimum score 550 paper-based; 213 computer-based). *Application deadline:* For fall admission, 8/1 for domestic students; for winter admission, 12/15 for domestic students; for spring admission, 4/15 for domestic students. Applications are processed on a rolling basis. Application fee: $50. *Financial support:* Federal Work-Study available. *Unit head:* Dr. Mary McHugh, Dean, 317-788-3206, E-mail: issac@uindy.edu. *Application contact:* T.C. Crum, Information Contact, 317-788-2128, Fax: 317-788-3542, E-mail: tcrum@uindy.edu.

The University of Kansas, Graduate Studies, College of Liberal Arts and Sciences, Program in Gerontology, Lawrence, KS 66045. Offers MA, PhD, Graduate Certificate. *Faculty:* 5. *Students:* 1 (woman) full-time, all international. Average age 30. 4 applicants, 0% accepted. In 2008, 1 master's, 1 doctorate awarded. *Degree requirements:* For master's, thesis; for doctorate, comprehensive exam, thesis/dissertation, written preliminary exam. *Entrance requirements:* For master's and doctorate, GRE, 3 letters of reference. Additional exam requirements/recommendations for international students: Required—TOEFL. *Application deadline:* For fall admission, 2/1 priority date for domestic and international students. Applications are processed on a rolling basis. Application fee: $45 ($50 for international students). Electronic applications accepted. *Expenses:* Tuition, area resident: Full-time $6122; part-time $255.10 per credit hour. Tuition, state resident: full-time $6122; part-time $255.10 per credit hour. Tuition, nonresident: full-time $14,629; part-time $609.55 per credit hour. Required fees: $847; $70.56 per credit hour. Tuition and fees vary according to course load and program. *Financial support:* Fellowships with full tuition reimbursements, research assistantships with full tuition reimbursements, career-related internships or fieldwork, traineeships, and unspecified assistantships available. Financial award application deadline: 1/15. *Faculty research:* Communication and aging, work and retirement, family studies, cognitive aging, exercise and disability. *Unit head:* David J. Ekerdt, Center Director, 785-864-4130, Fax: 785-864-2666, E-mail: gerontology@ku.edu. *Application contact:* Susan Kemper, Graduate Adviser, 785-864-0748, E-mail: skemper@ku.edu.

University of Kentucky, Graduate School, College of Public Health, Program in Gerontology, Lexington, KY 40506-0032. Offers PhD. *Degree requirements:* For doctorate, comprehensive exam, thesis/dissertation. *Entrance requirements:* For doctorate, GRE General Test, minimum undergraduate GPA of 2.75, graduate work GPA of 3.0. Additional exam requirements/recommendations for international students: Required—TOEFL (minimum score 550 paper-based; 213 computer-based). Electronic applications accepted.

University of La Verne, College of Business and Public Management, Program in Gerontology, La Verne, CA 91750-4443. Offers business administration (MS); counseling (MS); gerontology (Certificate); gerontology administration (MS); health services management (MS); public administration (MS). Part-time programs available. *Faculty:* 4 part-time/adjunct (3 women). *Students:* 14 full-time (13 women), 19 part-time (18 women); includes 13 minority (9 African Americans, 4 Hispanic Americans). Average age 44. In 2008, 11 master's awarded. *Entrance requirements:* For master's, minimum GPA of 2.5. Additional exam requirements/recommendations for international students: Required—TOEFL (minimum score 550 paper-based; 213 computer-based). *Application deadline:* Applications are processed on a rolling basis. Application fee: $50. *Expenses:* Contact institution. *Financial support:* Institutionally sponsored loans available. Financial award application deadline: 3/2; financial award applicants required to submit FAFSA. *Unit head:* Joan Branin, Chairperson, 909-593-3511 Ext. 4247. *Application contact:* Barbara Cox, Program and Admissions Specialist, 909-593-3511 Ext. 4004, Fax: 909-392-2761, E-mail: bcox@ulv.edu.

University of Louisiana at Monroe, Graduate School, College of Arts and Sciences, Program in Gerontology, Monroe, LA 71209-0001. Offers MA, CGS. *Faculty:* 3 full-time (1 woman), 3 part-time/adjunct (1 woman). *Students:* 11 full-time (10 women), 16 part-time (14 women); includes 5 African Americans. Average age 30. In 2008, 7 master's awarded. *Degree requirements:* For master's, thesis (for some programs), internship. *Entrance requirements:* For master's, GRE General Test, minimum GPA of 2.75. Additional exam requirements/recommendations for international students: Required—TOEFL (minimum score 500 paper-based; 173 computer-based; 61 iBT). *Application deadline:* For fall admission, 8/22 priority date for domestic students, 7/1 for international students; for winter admission, 12/12 priority date for domestic students; for spring admission, 1/17 for domestic students, 11/1 for international students. Applications are processed on a rolling basis. Application fee: $20 ($30 for international students). Electronic applications accepted. *Expenses:* Tuition, area resident: Full-time $2403; part-time $1202 per semester. Tuition, state resident: full-time $2403; part-time $1202 per semester. Tuition, nonresident: full-time $2403; part-time $1202 per semester. International tuition: $8352 full-time. Required fees: $1239.40; $141 per credit hour. *Financial support:* In 2008–09, 4 research assistantships with full tuition reimbursements (averaging $2,500 per year) were awarded; career-related internships or fieldwork, Federal Work-Study, and unspecified assistantships also available. Financial award application deadline: 4/1; financial award applicants required to submit FAFSA. *Unit head:* Dr. James Bulot, Unit Head, 318-342-1465, Fax: 318-342-1431, E-mail: bulot@ulm.edu. *Application contact:* Paul Karlowitz, Assistant Dean, 318-342-1758, Fax: 318-342-1755, E-mail: karlowitz@ulm.edu.

University of Louisville, Graduate School, Raymond A. Kent School of Social Work, Louisville, KY 40292-0001. Offers marriage and family therapy (PMC); social work (MSSW, PhD), including alcohol and drug counseling (MSSW), gerontology (MSSW), school social work (MSSW). *Accreditation:* AAMFT/COAMFTE; CSWE (one or more programs are accredited). Part-time and evening/weekend programs available. *Faculty:* 23 full-time (15 women), 38 part-time/adjunct (21 women). *Students:* 282 full-time (229 women), 67 part-time (54 women); includes 93 minority (84 African Americans, 2 American Indian/Alaska Native, 2 Asian Americans or Pacific Islanders, 5 Hispanic Americans), 7 international. Average age 32. 314 applicants, 78% accepted, 142 enrolled. In 2008, 156 master's, 5 doctorates awarded. *Degree requirements:* For doctorate, comprehensive exam, thesis/dissertation. *Entrance requirements:* For master's, GRE or minimum GPA of 2.75; for doctorate, GRE General Test, interview, writing sample. Additional exam requirements/recommendations for international students: Required—TOEFL (minimum score 550 paper-based; 213 computer-based; 79 iBT). *Application deadline:* For fall admission, 7/31 for domestic and international students. Applications are processed on a rolling basis. Application fee: $50. Electronic applications accepted. *Financial support:* In 2008–09, 80 students received support, including 2 fellowships with full tuition reimbursements available (averaging $19,000 per year), 8 research assistantships with full tuition reimbursements available (averaging $19,000 per year); Federal Work-Study, institutionally sponsored loans, scholarships/grants, health care benefits, tuition waivers (full), and unspecified assistantships also available. Support available to part-time students. Financial award application deadline: 6/1; financial award applicants required to submit FAFSA. *Faculty research:* Child welfare, substance abuse, gerontology, family functioning, health behavior. *Unit head:* Dr. Terry Singer, Dean, 502-852-6402, Fax: 502-852-0422, E-mail: terry.singer@louisville.edu. *Application contact:* Libby Leggett, Director, Graduate Admissions, 502-852-3101, Fax: 502-852-6536, E-mail: gradadm@louisville.edu.

University of Maryland, Baltimore, Graduate School, Program in Gerontology, Baltimore, MD 21201. Offers PhD. *Degree requirements:* For doctorate, comprehensive exam, thesis/dissertation. *Entrance requirements:* For doctorate, GRE General Test. Additional exam requirements/recommendations for international students: Required—TOEFL (minimum score 550 paper-based; 213 computer-based; 80 iBT), TOEFL or IELTS; Recommended—IELTS (minimum score 7). Electronic applications accepted.

University of Maryland, Baltimore County, Graduate School, Program in Gerontology, Baltimore, MD 21201. Offers aging policy for the elderly (PhD); epidemiology of aging (PhD); social, cultural, and behavioral sciences (PhD). Part-time programs available. *Faculty:* 17 part-time/adjunct (10 women). *Students:* 19 full-time (14 women), 6 part-time (all women); includes 4 minority (all African Americans), 1 international. Average age 33. 18 applicants, 22% accepted, 4 enrolled. In 2008, 3 doctorates awarded. *Degree requirements:* For doctorate, comprehensive exam, thesis/dissertation. *Entrance requirements:* For doctorate, GRE General Test. Additional exam requirements/recommendations for international students: Required—TOEFL, TWE. *Application deadline:* For spring admission, 1/15 for domestic and international students. Application fee: $45. Electronic applications accepted. *Financial support:* In 2008–09, 12 students received support, including 3 fellowships with full tuition reimbursements available (averaging $19,000 per year), 8 research assistantships with full tuition reimbursements available (averaging $19,000 per year), 1 teaching assistantship with full tuition reimbursement available (averaging $19,000 per year); career-related internships or fieldwork, scholarships/grants, traineeships, health care benefits, tuition waivers (partial), and unspecified assistantships also available. Support available to part-time students. Financial award application deadline: 2/1; financial award applicants required to submit FAFSA. *Faculty research:* Aging and health policy, behavioral aspects of aging, caregiving, LTC, epidemiology of aging. Total annual research expenditures: $44.2 million. *Unit head:* Dr. Leslie Morgan, Co-Director at UMBC, 410-455-2074, Fax: 410-455-1154, E-mail: lmorgan@umbc.edu. *Application contact:* Justine Golden, Academic Coordinator, 410-706-4926, Fax: 410-706-4433, E-mail: jgold002@umaryland.edu.

University of Massachusetts Boston, Office of Graduate Studies, John W. McCormack Graduate School of Policy Studies, Program in Gerontology, Boston, MA 02125-3393. Offers gerontology (MS, PhD, Certificate); gerontology research (MA); management in aging services (MA). Part-time programs available. *Degree requirements:* For doctorate, comprehensive exam, thesis/dissertation. *Entrance requirements:* For doctorate, GRE General Test, minimum GPA of 3.0. *Faculty research:* Aging with a chronic disability, pension policy and social security system, elderly minorities, health services research, living arrangements.

University of Missouri–St. Louis, College of Arts and Sciences, Program in Gerontology, St. Louis, MO 63121. Offers gerontology (MS, Certificate); long term care administration (Certificate). Part-time and evening/weekend programs available. *Faculty:* 4 full-time (3 women), 5 part-time/adjunct (4 women). *Students:* 5 full-time (3 women), 9 part-time (8 women); includes 2 minority (both African Americans), 1 international. Average age 43. In 2008, 13 master's awarded. *Entrance requirements:* For master's, 3 letters of recommendation. Additional exam requirements/recommendations for international students: Required—TOEFL (minimum score 550 paper-based; 213 computer-based). *Application deadline:* For fall admission, 7/1 priority date for domestic and international students; for spring admission, 12/1 priority date for domestic and international students. Applications are processed on a rolling basis. Application fee: $35 ($40 for international students). Electronic applications accepted. *Expenses:* Tuition, area resident: Full-time $5377; part-time $298.70 per credit hour. Tuition, nonresident: full-time $13,381; part-time $472.50 per credit hour. Required fees: $4078; $52 per credit hour. *Financial support:* Research assistantships with full and partial tuition reimbursements, teaching assistantships with full and partial tuition reimbursements, career-related internships or fieldwork and Federal Work-Study available. Financial award applicants required to submit FAFSA. *Faculty research:* Health care policy, social support and stress, retirement policy health behavior, ethnic differences in aging. *Unit head:* Thomas Meuser, Director, 314-516-5421, Fax: 314-516-5210, E-mail: meusert@umsl.edu. *Application contact:* 314-516-5458, Fax: 314-516-6996, E-mail: gradadm@umsl.edu.

University of Nebraska at Omaha, Graduate Studies and Research, College of Education, Department of Counseling, Omaha, NE 68182. Offers community counseling (MA, MS); counseling gerontology (MA, MS); school counseling (MA, MS); student affairs practice in higher education (MA, MS). *Accreditation:* ACA (one or more programs are accredited); NCATE. Part-time and evening/weekend programs available. *Degree requirements:* For master's, comprehensive exam, thesis (for some programs). *Entrance requirements:* For master's, GRE General Test, MAT, department test, interview, minimum GPA of 3.0. Additional exam requirements/recommendations for international students: Required—TOEFL (minimum score 550 paper-based; 213 computer-based; 80 iBT). Electronic applications accepted.

University of Nebraska at Omaha, Graduate Studies and Research, College of Public Affairs and Community Service, Department of Gerontology, Omaha, NE 68182. Offers gerontology (Certificate); social gerontology (MA). Part-time and evening/weekend programs available. *Degree requirements:* For master's, comprehensive exam, thesis. *Entrance requirements:* For master's, GRE General Test, MAT, minimum GPA of 3.0, writing sample, letters of recommendation. Additional exam requirements/recommendations for international students: Required—TOEFL (minimum score 550 paper-based; 213 computer-based; 80 iBT). Electronic applications accepted.

University of Nebraska–Lincoln, Graduate College, College of Education and Human Sciences, Department of Child, Youth and Family Studies, Lincoln, NE 68588. Offers child development/early childhood education (MS, PhD); child, youth and family studies (MS); family and consumer sciences education (MS, PhD); family financial planning (MS); family science (MS, PhD); gerontology (PhD); human sciences (PhD), including child, youth and family studies, gerontology, medical family therapy; marriage and family therapy (MS); medical family therapy (PhD); youth development (MS). *Accreditation:* AAMFT/COAMFTE (one or more programs are accredited). Postbaccalaureate distance learning degree programs offered. *Faculty:* 16 full-time (11 women). *Students:* 23 full-time (18 women), 53 part-time (40 women); includes 8 minority (2 African Americans, 2 American Indian/Alaska Native, 2 Asian Americans or Pacific Islanders, 2 Hispanic Americans), 1 international. Average age 32. In 2008, 27 master's awarded. *Degree requirements:* For master's, thesis optional. *Entrance requirements:* For master's, GRE. Additional exam requirements/recommendations for international students: Required—TOEFL (minimum score 550 paper-based; 213 computer-based). *Application deadline:* For fall admission, 1/15 for domestic and international students; for spring admission, 10/1 for domestic and international students. Application fee: $40. Electronic applications accepted. *Expenses:* Tuition, state resident: full-time $4275; part-time $237.50 per credit hour. Tuition, nonresident: full-time $11,525; part-time $640.25 per credit hour. Required fees: $1068; $10.35 per credit hour. $440.70 per semester. Tuition and fees vary according to course load and program. *Financial support:* Fellowships, research assistantships, teaching assistantships, Federal Work-Study, health care benefits, and unspecified assistantships available. Financial award application deadline: 2/15. *Faculty research:* Marriage and family therapy, child development/early childhood education, family financial management. *Unit head:* Dr. Julie Johnson, Chair, 402-472-2957. *Application contact:* Dr. Julie Johnson, Chair, 402-472-2957.

University of New England, College of Health Professions, School of Social Work, Biddeford, ME 04005-9526. Offers addictions counseling (Certificate); gerontology (Certificate); social work (MSW). *Accreditation:* CSWE. Part-time programs available. *Degree requirements:* For master's, field internships. *Entrance requirements:* Additional exam requirements/recommendations for international students: Required—TOEFL (minimum score 550 paper-based; 213 computer-based). Electronic applications accepted. *Faculty research:* Domestic violence, solution focused practice, empowerment models, adverse childhood experiences.

The University of North Carolina at Charlotte, Graduate School, College of Arts and Sciences, Program in Gerontology, Charlotte, NC 28223-0001. Offers MA. *Students:* 1 (woman) full-time, 16 part-time (14 women); includes 4 minority (all African Americans), 3 international. Average age 27. 8 applicants, 100% accepted, 6 enrolled. In 2008, 1 master's awarded. *Degree requirements:* For master's, thesis optional. *Entrance requirements:* For master's, GRE or MAT. Additional exam requirements/recommendations for international students: Required—TOEFL (minimum score 557 paper-based; 220 computer-based). *Application deadline:* For fall admission, 7/1 for domestic students, 5/1 for international students; for spring admission, 11/1 for domestic students, 10/1 for international students. Applications are processed on a rolling basis. Application fee: $55. Electronic applications accepted. *Expenses:* Tuition, area resident: Full-time $2919; part-time $122 per credit hour. Tuition, state resident: full-time $2919; part-time $122 per credit hour. Tuition, nonresident: full-time $13,126; part-time $547 per credit hour. Required fees: $1779; $91 per credit hour. Tuition and fees vary according to program. *Financial support:* In 2008–09, 4 research assistantships (averaging $6,670 per year), 1 teaching assistantship (averaging $10,000 per year) were awarded; career-related internships or fieldwork, Federal Work-Study, institutionally sponsored loans, scholarships/grants, and unspecified assistantships also available. Support available to part-time students. Financial award application deadline: 4/1; financial award applicants required to submit FAFSA. *Faculty research:* Rural older adults, person-centered dementia care, formal and informal systems of care, health care issues: gay, lesbian, and African American aging. *Unit head:* Dr. Dena Shenk, Director, 704-687-4349, Fax: 704-687-4347, E-mail: dshenk@email.uncc.edu. *Application contact:* Kathy B. Giddings, Director of Graduate Admissions, 704-687-3366, Fax: 704-687-3279, E-mail: agidding@uncc.edu.

The University of North Carolina at Greensboro, Graduate School, Program in Gerontology, Greensboro, NC 27412-5001. Offers MS, Certificate, MS/MBA. Electronic applications accepted.

The University of North Carolina Wilmington, College of Arts and Sciences, Department of Health and Applied Human Sciences, Wilmington, NC 28403-3297. Offers applied gerontology (MS). Part-time programs available. Postbaccalaureate distance learning degree programs offered. *Faculty:* 2 full-time (both women), 3 part-time/adjunct (all women). *Students:* 4 full-time (all women), 4 part-time (all women); includes 1 minority (African American). 5 applicants, 80% accepted, 4 enrolled. In 2008, 1 master's awarded. *Degree requirements:* For master's, comprehensive exam, thesis or alternative. *Entrance requirements:* For master's, GRE, Undergraduate GPA of B or better. Additional exam requirements/recommendations for international students: Required—TOEFL (minimum score 550 paper-based; 217 computer-based; 79 iBT), IELTS (minimum score 6.5). *Application deadline:* For fall admission, 3/15 for domestic students. Application fee: $60. *Expenses:* Tuition, area resident: Full-time $4838. Tuition, state resident: full-time $4838. Tuition, nonresident: full-time $14,898. Required fees: $969.38 per semester. Tuition and fees vary according to course load, campus/location and program. *Financial support:* In 2008–09, 6 teaching assistantships with full and partial tuition reimbursements (averaging $9,500 per year) were awarded; scholarships/grants and unspecified assistantships also available. Support available to part-time students. *Unit head:* Dr. Terry Kinney, Chair, 910-962-7570, E-mail: kinneyt@uncw.edu. *Application contact:* Dr. Candy Ashton, Graduate Coordinator, 910-962-7794, Fax: 910-962-3787, E-mail: ashtonc@uncw.edu.

University of Northern Colorado, Graduate School, College of Natural and Health Sciences, School of Human Sciences, Program in Gerontology, Greeley, CO 80639. Offers MA. Part-time programs available. *Faculty:* 2 full-time (both women). *Students:* 4 full-time (all women), 3 part-time (all women), 1 international. Average age 35. 5 applicants, 100% accepted, 4 enrolled. In 2008, 5 master's awarded. *Degree requirements:* For master's, comprehensive exam. *Entrance requirements:* For master's, GRE General Test or MAT, 2 letters of recommendation. *Application deadline:* Applications are processed on a rolling basis. Application fee: $50 ($60 for international students). Electronic applications accepted. *Expenses:* Tuition, state resident: full-time $4370; part-time $242.75 per credit hour. Tuition, nonresident: full-time $12,366; part-time $687 per credit hour. Required fees: $664.20; $36.90 per credit hour. *Financial support:* Fellowships, research assistantships, teaching assistantships, unspecified assistantships available. Financial award application deadline: 3/1; financial award applicants required to submit FAFSA. *Unit head:* Dr. Susan Collins, Program Coordinator, 970-351-2403. *Application contact:* Linda Sisson, Graduate Student Admission Coordinator, 970-351-1807, Fax: 970-351-2371, E-mail: linda.sisson@unco.edu.

University of North Florida, Brooks College of Health, Department of Public Health, Jacksonville, FL 32224-2645. Offers community health (MPH); geriatric management (MSH); health administration (MHA); health behavior research and evaluation (Certificate); nutrition (MSH); rehabilitation counseling (MS). *Accreditation:* CORE. Part-time and evening/weekend programs available. *Faculty:* 23 full-time (17 women). *Students:* 92 full-time (69 women), 59 part-time (44 women); includes 39 minority (25 African Americans, 9 Asian Americans or Pacific Islanders, 5 Hispanic Americans), 15 international. Average age 30. 172 applicants, 42% accepted, 41 enrolled. In 2008, 46 master's awarded. *Degree requirements:* For master's, thesis optional. *Entrance requirements:* For master's, GRE General Test (MSH, MS, MPH), GMAT or GRE General Test (MHA), minimum GPA of 3.0 in last 60 hours. Additional exam requirements/recommendations for international students: Required—TOEFL (minimum score 500 paper-based; 173 computer-based). *Application deadline:* For fall admission, 7/1 priority date for domestic students, 5/1 for international students; for spring admission, 11/10 priority date for domestic students, 10/1 for international students. Applications are processed on a rolling basis. Application fee: $30. Electronic applications accepted. *Expenses:* Tuition, area resident: Full-time $5782.08; part-time $240.92 per credit hour. Tuition, state resident: full-time $5782.08; part-time $240.92 per credit hour. Tuition, nonresident: full-time $19,974; part-time $832.26 per credit hour. Required fees: $952.80; $39.70 per credit hour. *Financial support:* In 2008–09, 49 students received support; research assistantships, teaching assistantships, career-related internships or fieldwork, Federal Work-Study, scholarships/grants, and tuition waivers (partial) available. Support available to part-time students. Financial award application deadline: 4/1; financial award applicants required to submit FAFSA. *Faculty research:* Dietary supplements; alcohol, tobacco, and other drug use prevention; turnover among health professionals; aging; psychosocial aspects of disabilities. Total annual research expenditures: $498,043. *Unit head:* Dr. JoAnn Nolin, Chair, 904-620-2840, Fax: 904-620-2848, E-mail: jnolin@unf.edu. *Application contact:* Heather Kenney, Director of Advising, 904-620-2810, Fax: 904-620-1030, E-mail: heather.kenney@unf.edu.

University of North Texas, Robert B. Toulouse School of Graduate Studies, College of Public Affairs and Community Service, Department of Applied Gerontology, Denton, TX 76203. Offers aging (Certificate); applied gerontology (PhD); general studies in aging (MA, MS); long term care, senior housing, and aging services (MA, MS). Part-time and evening/weekend programs available. Postbaccalaureate distance learning degree programs offered (minimal on-campus study). *Degree requirements:* For master's, comprehensive exam (for some programs), thesis, internship; for doctorate, thesis/dissertation. *Entrance requirements:* For master's and doctorate, GRE General Test. Additional exam requirements/recommendations for international students: Required—proof of English language proficiency required for non-native English speakers; Recommended—TOEFL (minimum score 550 paper-based; 213 computer-based). *Faculty research:* Minority aging, housing for the elderly, aging and developmental disability, caregiving, public policy and aging.

University of Phoenix, The Artemis School, College of Health and Human Services, Phoenix, AZ 85034-7209. Offers administration of justice and security (MS); community counseling (MSC); education (MHA); family nurse practitioner (MSN); gerontology (MHA); health administration (MHA); health care education (MSN); health care management (MBA, MSN); informatics (MHA); marriage, family, and child therapy (MSC); nursing (MSN); nursing for nurse practitioners (MSN); psychology (MS); MSN/MBA; MSN/MHA. *Accreditation:* AACN. Evening/weekend programs available. Postbaccalaureate distance learning degree programs

offered. *Degree requirements:* For master's, thesis (for some programs). *Entrance requirements:* For master's, 3 years of work experience, minimum undergraduate GPA of 2.5, RN license. Additional exam requirements/recommendations for international students: Required—TOEFL (minimum score 550 paper-based; 213 computer-based; 79 iBT). Electronic applications accepted.

University of Phoenix–Birmingham Campus, College of Health and Human Services, Birmingham, AL 35244. Offers education (MHA); gerontology (MHA); health administration (MHA); health care management (MBA); informatics (MHA); nursing (MSN); nursing/health care education (MSN); MSN/MBA; MSN/MHA.

University of Phoenix–Central Valley Campus, College of Health and Human Services, Fresno, CA 93720-1562. Offers education (MHA); gerontology (MHA); health administration (MHA); health care management (MBA); nursing (MSN); MSN/MBA.

University of Phoenix–Chattanooga Campus, College of Health and Human Services, Chattanooga, TN 37421-3707. Offers education (MHA); gerontology (MHA); health administration (MHA); health care management (MBA).

University of Phoenix–Hawaii Campus, The Artemis School, College of Health and Human Services, Honolulu, HI 96813-4317. Offers administration of justice and security (MS); community counseling (MSC); education (MHA); family nurse practitioner (MSN); gerontology (MHA); health administration (MHA); health care management (MBA); marriage, family and child therapy (MSC); nursing (MSN); nursing/health care education (MSN); psychology (MS); MSN/MBA. Evening/weekend programs available. *Degree requirements:* For master's, thesis (for some programs). *Entrance requirements:* For master's, minimum undergraduate GPA of 2.5, 3 years of work experience, RN license. Additional exam requirements/recommendations for international students: Required—TOEFL (minimum score 550 paper-based; 213 computer-based; 79 iBT). Electronic applications accepted.

University of Phoenix–Phoenix Campus, The Artemis School, College of Health and Human Services, Phoenix, AZ 85040-1958. Offers community counseling (MSC); education (MHA); family nurse practitioner (MSN); gerontology (MHA); health administration (MHA); health care education (MSN); health care management (MBA); informatics (MHA); marriage, family, and child therapy (MSC); nurse practitioner (Certificate); nursing (MSN); nursing health care education (Certificate); psychology (MS); MSN/MBA; MSN/MHA. Evening/weekend programs available. *Degree requirements:* For master's, thesis (for some programs). *Entrance requirements:* For master's, 3 years of work experience in field, minimum undergraduate GPA of 2.5, RN license. Additional exam requirements/recommendations for international students: Required—TOEFL (minimum score 550 paper-based; 213 computer-based; 79 iBT). Electronic applications accepted.

University of Phoenix–Southern Colorado Campus, The Artemis School, College of Health and Human Services, Colorado Springs, CO 80919-2335. Offers administration of justice and security (MS); community counseling (MSC); education (MHA); gerontology (MHA); health administration (MHA); health care management (MBA); marriage, family and child therapy (MSC); nursing (MSN); psychology (MS); MSN/MBA. Evening/weekend programs available. *Degree requirements:* For master's, thesis (for some programs). *Entrance requirements:* For master's, minimum undergraduate GPA of 2.5, 3 years of work experience, RN license. Additional exam requirements/recommendations for international students: Required—TOEFL (minimum score 550 paper-based; 213 computer-based; 79 iBT). Electronic applications accepted.

University of Pittsburgh, Graduate School of Public Health, Department of Behavioral and Community Health Science, Pittsburgh, PA 15260. Offers behavioral and community health sciences (MPH, Dr PH); lesbian, gay, bisexual and transgender health and wellness (Certificate); minority health and health disparities (Certificate); program evaluation (Certificate); public health and aging (Certificate); public health preparedness (Certificate); MID/MPH; MPH/MPA; MPH/MSW; MPH/PhD. *Accreditation:* CAHME (one or more programs are accredited). Part-time programs available. *Degree requirements:* For master's, thesis; for doctorate, comprehensive exam, thesis/dissertation, preliminary exams. *Entrance requirements:* For master's and Certificate, GRE; for doctorate, GRE, master's degree in public health or related field. Additional exam requirements/recommendations for international students: Required—TOEFL (minimum score 550 paper-based; 213 computer-based; 80 iBT). Electronic applications accepted. *Faculty research:* Maternal and child health, program evaluation, community-based participatory research, minority health and health disparities, aging.

University of Pittsburgh, School of Social Work, Pittsburgh, PA 15260. Offers gerontology (Certificate); social work (MSW, PhD); M Div/MSW; MPA/MSW; MPH/PhD; MPIA/MSW; MSW/JD; MSW/MAJCS; MSW/MPH. *Accreditation:* CSWE (one or more programs are accredited). Part-time programs available. Postbaccalaureate distance learning degree programs offered (no on-campus study). *Degree requirements:* For master's, practicum; for doctorate, comprehensive exam, thesis/dissertation; for Certificate, thesis. *Entrance requirements:* For master's, minimum QPA of 3.0, course work in and statistics; for doctorate, GRE, MSW or related degree, course work in statistics. Additional exam requirements/recommendations for international students: Required—TOEFL (minimum score 550 paper-based; 213 computer-based). Electronic applications accepted. *Faculty research:* Mental health services research, child abuse and neglect, geriatrics, criminal justice race issues.

University of Puerto Rico, Medical Sciences Campus, Graduate School of Public Health, Program in Gerontology, San Juan, PR 00936-5067. Offers MPH, Certificate. Part-time and evening/weekend programs available. *Entrance requirements:* For master's, GRE, previous course work in social sciences, biology, psychology, and algebra.

University of Regina, Faculty of Graduate Studies and Research, Faculty of Arts, Program in Gerontology, Regina, SK S4S 0A2, Canada. Offers M Sc, MA. *Faculty:* 10 full-time (3 women). *Students:* 4 full-time (3 women), 3 part-time (all women). 5 applicants, 100% accepted. *Degree requirements:* For master's, thesis. *Entrance requirements:* Additional exam requirements/recommendations for international students: Required—TOEFL (minimum score 580 paper-based; 237 computer-based; 88 iBT). *Application deadline:* For fall admission, 3/31 for domestic students. Application fee: $85 ($100 for international students). Electronic applications accepted. *Financial support:* In 2008–09, 1 teaching assistantship (averaging $6,558 per year) was awarded; fellowships, research assistantships also available. *Unit head:* Dr. David Malloy, Program Coordinator, 306-337-3181. *Application contact:* Dr. David Malloy, Program Coordinator, 306-337-3181.

University of Rhode Island, Graduate School, College of Nursing, Kingston, RI 02881. Offers administration (MS); clinical nurse leader (MS); clinical specialist in gerontology (MS); clinical specialist in psychiatric/mental health (MS); family nurse practitioner (MS); gerontological nurse practitioner (MS); nursing (PhD); nursing education (MS). *Accreditation:* AACN; ACNM/DOA (one or more programs are accredited). *Expenses:* Tuition, state resident: full-time $8024; part-time $446 per credit. Tuition, nonresident: full-time $21,046; part-time $1169 per credit. Required fees: $1056; $26 per credit. $30 per semester. One-time fee: $95 part-time. *Unit head:* Dr. Dayle Joseph, Dean, 401-874-2766, E-mail: dayle@uri.edu. *Application contact:* Harold D. Bibb, Associate Dean of the Graduate School, 401-874-2262, Fax: 401-874-5491.

University of South Alabama, Graduate School, College of Arts and Sciences, Program in Gerontology, Mobile, AL 36688-0002. Offers Certificate. Part-time programs available. *Students:* 2 part-time (both women). 2 applicants, 50% accepted, 1 enrolled. In 2008, 1 Certificate awarded. *Entrance requirements:* For degree, GRE General Test. *Application deadline:* For fall admission, 7/15 priority date for domestic students, 6/15 priority date for international students; for spring admission, 12/1 priority date for domestic students, 11/1 priority date for international students. Applications are processed on a rolling basis. Application fee: $25 ($35 for international students). *Expenses:* Tuition, area resident: Full-time $4656. Tuition, nonresident:

Gerontology

University of South Alabama (continued)
full-time $9312. Required fees: $1102. *Financial support:* Application deadline: 4/1. *Unit head:* Dr. Roma Hanks, Chair, 251-460-6347. *Application contact:* Dr. Roma Hanks, Chair, 251-460-6347.

University of South Carolina, The Graduate School, Program in Gerontology, Columbia, SC 29208. Offers Certificate. Part-time programs available. *Degree requirements:* For Certificate, practicum. Electronic applications accepted.

University of Southern California, Graduate School, School of Gerontology, Los Angeles, CA 90089. Offers MA, MS, PhD, Certificate, DDS/MS, JD/MS, M Pl/MS, MAJCS/MS, MBA/MS, MHA/MS, MPA/MS, MSW/MS. Part-time programs available. Postbaccalaureate distance learning degree programs offered (no on-campus study). *Degree requirements:* For doctorate, thesis/dissertation. *Entrance requirements:* For master's and doctorate, GRE General Test. *Faculty research:* Cognition in aging, biodemographic of aging, health outcomes research, families and intergenerational relatives, care-giving of elderly.

University of South Florida, College of Medicine and Graduate School, Graduate Programs in Medical Sciences, Tampa, FL 33620-9951. Offers aging and neuroscience (MSMS); allergy, immunology and infectious disease (PhD); anatomy (PhD); biochemistry and molecular biology (MS, PhD), including biochemistry and molecular biology (PhD), bioinformatics and computational biology (MS); clinical and translational research (MSMS, PhD); health sciences (MSMS); medical microbiology and immunology (PhD); medical science (MSMS); molecular medicine (PhD); molecular pharmacology and physiology (PhD); neuroscience (PhD); pathology (PhD); pharmacology and therapeutics (PhD), including medical sciences; physiology and biophysics (PhD); womens health (MSMS). *Students:* 286 full-time (162 women), 62 part-time (36 women); includes 147 minority (59 African Americans, 1 American Indian/Alaska Native, 37 Asian Americans or Pacific Islanders, 50 Hispanic Americans), 28 international. 415 applicants, 69% accepted, 214 enrolled. In 2008, 65 master's, 12 doctorates awarded. Terminal master's awarded for partial completion of doctoral program. *Degree requirements:* For master's, comprehensive exam, thesis; for doctorate, comprehensive exam, thesis/dissertation. *Entrance requirements:* For doctorate, GRE General Test, minimum GPA of 3.0 in last 60 hours of coursework. Additional exam requirements/recommendations for international students: Required—TOEFL (minimum score 550 paper-based; 213 computer-based). *Application deadline:* For fall admission, 2/15 for domestic students, 1/2 for international students. Application fee: $30. *Expenses:* Contact institution. *Financial support:* Institutionally sponsored loans and scholarships/grants available. Financial award application deadline: 4/1; financial award applicants required to submit FAFSA. *Unit head:* Michael Barber, Program Director, 813-974-9702, Fax: 813-974-4317, E-mail: mbarber@health.usf.edu. *Application contact:* Franjesca Jackson, Contact Person, 813-974-2256, Fax: 813-974-4317, E-mail: fjackson@health.usf.edu.

University of South Florida, Graduate School, College of Arts and Sciences, School of Aging Studies, Tampa, FL 33620-9951. Offers aging studies (PhD); gerontology (MA). Part-time and evening/weekend programs available. *Faculty:* 12 full-time (8 women). *Students:* 26 full-time (24 women), 10 part-time (9 women); includes 7 minority (5 African Americans, 2 Hispanic Americans), 3 international. 33 applicants, 48% accepted, 10 enrolled. In 2008, 11 master's, 5 doctorates awarded. *Degree requirements:* For master's, comprehensive exam, thesis; for doctorate, comprehensive exam, thesis/dissertation. *Entrance requirements:* For master's, GRE General Test, minimum GPA of 3.0 in last 60 hours; for doctorate, GRE General Test, minimum GPA of 3.25, letter of recommendation. Additional exam requirements/recommendations for international students: Required—TOEFL (minimum score 550 paper-based; 213 computer-based). *Application deadline:* For fall admission, 2/1 priority date for domestic students, 1/2 priority date for international students. Application fee: $30. Electronic applications accepted. *Expenses:* Tuition, state resident: full-time $2624.40; part-time $291.60 per credit hour. Tuition, nonresident: full-time $7822; part-time $869.13 per credit hour. *Financial support:* Health care benefits available. Financial award application deadline: 2/3. *Faculty research:* Minorities, caregiving, guardianship, Alzheimer's disease, cognitive aging. Total annual research expenditures: $836,309. *Unit head:* Cathy L. McEvoy, Director, 813-974-1940, Fax: 813-974-9754, E-mail: cmcevoy@cas.usf.edu. *Application contact:* Amy Woodberry, Contact Person, 813-974-2419, Fax: 813-974-9754, E-mail: amwoodbu@chuma1.cas.usf.edu.

The University of Tennessee, Graduate School, College of Education, Health and Human Sciences, Program in Public Health, Knoxville, TN 37996. Offers community health education (MPH); gerontology (MPH); health planning/administration (MPH); MS/MPH. *Accreditation:* CEPH. *Degree requirements:* For master's, thesis optional. *Entrance requirements:* For master's, minimum GPA of 2.7. Additional exam requirements/recommendations for international students: Required—TOEFL. Electronic applications accepted. *Expenses:* Tuition, area resident: Part-time $348 per credit hour. Tuition, state resident: full-time $6262. Tuition, nonresident: full-time $18,920; part-time $1052 per credit hour. Required fees: $812; $36 per credit hour. Tuition and fees vary according to program.

The University of Toledo, College of Graduate Studies, College of Medicine, Biomedical Science Programs, Program in Gerontology, Toledo, OH 43606-3390. Offers contemporary gerontological practice (Certificate).

University of Utah, The Graduate School, College of Nursing, Gerontology Interdisciplinary Program, Salt Lake City, UT 84112-1107. Offers MS, Certificate. *Accreditation:* AACN. Part-time programs available. *Degree requirements:* For master's, thesis optional. *Entrance requirements:* For master's, GRE General Test, minimum undergraduate GPA of 3.0. Additional exam requirements/recommendations for international students: Required—TOEFL (minimum score 500 paper-based; 173 computer-based). *Expenses:* Contact institution. *Faculty research:* Spousal bereavement, family caregiving, healthy promotion and self-care, environmental issues, geriatric care management.

University of Wisconsin–Milwaukee, Graduate School, School of Social Welfare, Department of Social Work, Milwaukee, WI 53201-0413. Offers applied gerontology (Certificate); marriage and family therapy (Certificate); non-profit management (Certificate); social work (MSW, PhD). *Accreditation:* CSWE. Part-time programs available. *Faculty:* 19 full-time (12 women). *Students:* 173 full-time (157 women), 101 part-time (92 women); includes 55 minority (38 African Americans, 2 American Indian/Alaska Native, 7 Asian Americans or Pacific Islanders, 8 Hispanic Americans). Average age 31. 313 applicants, 57% accepted, 105 enrolled. In 2008, 133 master's awarded. *Degree requirements:* For master's, thesis or alternative. *Entrance requirements:* For doctorate, GRE, bachelor's degree. Additional exam requirements/recommendations for international students: Required—TOEFL (minimum score 550 paper-based; 79 iBT), IELTS (minimum score 6.5). *Application deadline:* For fall admission, 1/1 priority date for domestic students; for spring admission, 9/1 for domestic students. Applications are processed on a rolling basis. Application fee: $45 ($75 for international students). *Expenses:* Tuition, area resident: Full-time $7320; part-time $165 per credit. Tuition, state resident: full-time $7320; part-time $165 per credit. Tuition, nonresident: full-time $17,840; part-time $714 per credit. Tuition and fees vary according to campus/location, program and reciprocity agreements. *Financial support:* In 2008–09, 5 fellowships, 4 teaching assistantships were awarded; research assistantships, career-related internships or fieldwork and unspecified assistantships also available. Support available to part-time students. Financial award application deadline: 4/15. Total annual research expenditures: $2.9 million. *Unit head:* Deborah Padgett, Representative, 414-229-4851, Fax: 414-229-5311, E-mail: dpadgett@uwm.edu. *Application contact:* Steve McMurtry, General Information Contact, 414-229-2249, Fax: 414-229-6967, E-mail: Mcmurtry@uwm.edu.

Valparaiso University, Graduate Division, Program in Liberal Studies, Concentration in Gerontology, Valparaiso, IN 46383. Offers MALS, Post-Master's Certificate, JD/MALS. Part-time and evening/weekend programs available. *Students:* 1 full-time (0 women), 1 (woman) part-time; includes 1 minority (Hispanic American). Average age 35. In 2008, 1 master's awarded. *Entrance requirements:* For master's, minimum GPA of 3.0. Additional exam requirements/recommendations for international students: Required—TOEFL (minimum score 550 paper-based; 213 computer-based). *Application deadline:* Applications are processed on a rolling basis. Application fee: $30 ($50 for international students). Electronic applications accepted. *Financial support:* Available to part-time students. Applicants required to submit FAFSA. *Unit head:* Dr. David L. Rowland, Dean, Graduate Studies and Continuing Education, 219-464-5313, Fax: 219-464-5381, E-mail: David.Rowland@valpo.edu. *Application contact:* Jamie Haney, Coordinator of Recruitment Activities, 219-464-5313, Fax: 219-464-5381, E-mail: Jamie.Haney@valpo.edu.

Virginia Commonwealth University, Graduate School, School of Allied Health Professions, Department of Gerontology, Richmond, VA 23284-9005. Offers aging studies (CAS); gerontology (MS). *Entrance requirements:* For master's, GRE General Test or MAT. *Faculty research:* Alzheimer's disease, age-related alcoholism and suicide, pain perception, curriculum development and evaluation in gerontology/geriatrics.

Virginia Commonwealth University, Graduate School, School of Allied Health Professions, Department of Health Administration, Doctoral Program in Health Related Sciences, Richmond, VA 23284-9005. Offers clinical laboratory sciences (PhD); gerontology (PhD); health administration (PhD); nurse anesthesia (PhD); occupational therapy (PhD); physical therapy (PhD); radiation sciences (PhD); rehabilitation leadership (PhD).

Virginia Polytechnic Institute and State University, Graduate School, College of Liberal Arts and Human Sciences, Department of Human Development, Blacksburg, VA 24061. Offers adult development and aging (MS, PhD); adult learning and human resource development (MS, PhD); child development (MS, PhD); family studies (MS, PhD); marriage and family therapy (MS, PhD). *Accreditation:* AAMFT/COAMFTE (one or more programs are accredited). *Entrance requirements:* For master's and doctorate, GRE General Test. Additional exam requirements/recommendations for international students: Required—TOEFL (minimum score 600 paper-based; 250 computer-based). Electronic applications accepted. *Faculty research:* Stress management, children's play, dual-career families, social cognition, relationships of elderly.

Wayne State University, Graduate School, Interdisciplinary Program in Gerontology, Detroit, MI 48202. Offers Certificate. *Entrance requirements:* For degree, personal statement; letters of reference; interview. Additional exam requirements/recommendations for international students: Required—TOEFL (minimum score 550 paper-based; 213 computer-based); Recommended—TWE (minimum score 6). Electronic applications accepted. *Faculty research:* Aging and health, cognitive and neuroscience, aging and disability, minority aging, human factors and aging.

Webster University, College of Arts and Sciences, Department of Behavioral and Social Sciences, Program in Gerontology, St. Louis, MO 63119-3194. Offers MA.

West Chester University of Pennsylvania, Office of Graduate Studies, College of Arts and Sciences, Department of Anthropology and Sociology, West Chester, PA 19383. Offers gerontology (Certificate); long term health care (MSA). Part-time and evening/weekend programs available. *Students:* 1 (woman) part-time. Average age 43. 1 applicant, 100% accepted, 1 enrolled. In 2008, 2 Certificates awarded. *Degree requirements:* For master's, comprehensive exam. *Entrance requirements:* For master's, MAT, GRE, or GMAT, interview, statement of professional goals, resumé, two letters of reference. Additional exam requirements/recommendations for international students: Required—TOEFL (minimum score 550 paper-based; 213 computer-based; 80 iBT). *Application deadline:* For fall admission, 4/15 priority date for domestic students, 3/15 for international students; for spring admission, 10/15 for domestic students, 9/1 for international students. Applications are processed on a rolling basis. Application fee: $35. Electronic applications accepted. *Expenses:* Tuition, state resident: full-time $6430; part-time $357 per credit. Tuition, nonresident: full-time $10,288; part-time $572 per credit. Required fees: $652.50; $50 per credit. $67 per semester. *Financial support:* In 2008–09, research assistantships with full tuition reimbursements (averaging $5,000 per year); unspecified assistantships also available. Support available to part-time students. Financial award application deadline: 2/15; financial award applicants required to submit FAFSA. *Faculty research:* West African communities in the U.S., life long learning-distance education, comparative religions. *Unit head:* Dr. Douglas McConatha, Chair and Graduate Coordinator, 610-436-2556, E-mail: dmcconatha@wcupa.edu. *Application contact:* Dr. Douglas McConatha, Chair and Graduate Coordinator, 610-436-2556, E-mail: dmcconatha@wcupa.edu.

Wichita State University, Graduate School, Fairmount College of Liberal Arts and Sciences, School of Community Affairs, Wichita, KS 67260. Offers criminal justice (MA); gerontology (MA). Part-time programs available. Electronic applications accepted.

Wilmington University, Division of Nursing and Allied Health, New Castle, DE 19720-6491. Offers adult nurse practitioner (MSN); family nurse practitioner (MSN); gerontology (MSN); leadership (MSN); nursing (MSN); women's nurse practitioner (MSN). *Accreditation:* AACN. Part-time programs available. *Degree requirements:* For master's, thesis. *Entrance requirements:* For master's, BSN, RN license, interview, 3 letters of recommendation. Additional exam requirements/recommendations for international students: Required—TOEFL (minimum score 500 paper-based; 173 computer-based). Electronic applications accepted. *Faculty research:* Outcomes assessment, student writing ability.

Section 21
Geography

This section contains a directory of institutions offering graduate work in geography. Additional information about programs listed in the directory may be obtained by writing directly to the dean of a graduate school or chair of a department at the address given in the directory.

For programs offering related work, see also in this book *Area and Cultural Studies* and *Humanities.* In another guide in this series:

Graduate Programs in the Physical Sciences, Mathematics, Agricultural Sciences, the Environment & Natural Resources
See *Geosciences*

CONTENTS

Program Directories
Geographic Information Systems   .   810
Geography   813

Close-Up

See:

The University of Texas at Dallas—Economic, Political, and Policy Sciences   783

Geographic Information Systems

Acadia University, Faculty of Pure and Applied Science, Program in Applied Geomatics, Wolfville, NS B4P 2R6, Canada. Offers M Sc. Program jointly offered with Nova Scotia Community College. *Students:* 2 full-time (1 woman), 1 (woman) part-time. 4 applicants, 50% accepted, 2 enrolled. In 2008, 2 master's awarded. *Degree requirements:* For master's, thesis optional. *Entrance requirements:* Additional exam requirements/recommendations for international students: Required—TOEFL (minimum score 580 paper-based; 237 computer-based; 93 iBT), IELTS (minimum score 6.5). *Application deadline:* For fall admission, 2/1 for domestic students. Tuition and fees charges are reported in Canadian dollars. *Expenses:* Tuition, area resident: Full-time $3873.50 Canadian dollars; part-time $844 Canadian dollars per course. Tuition, state resident: full-time $4634.50 Canadian dollars; part-time $844 Canadian dollars per course. Tuition, nonresident: full-time $9103 Canadian dollars; part-time $1687 Canadian dollars per course. Required fees: $503.22 Canadian dollars; $5 Canadian dollars per course. *Financial support:* Scholarships/grants and unspecified assistantships available. *Unit head:* Dr. Ian Spooner, Coordinator, 902-585-1312, E-mail: ian.spooner@acadiau.ca. *Application contact:* Dr. Ian Spooner, Coordinator, 902-585-1312, E-mail: ian.spooner@acadiau.ca.

Appalachian State University, Cratis D. Williams Graduate School, Department of Geography and Planning, Boone, NC 28608. Offers geography (MA), including GIS, planning. Part-time programs available. Postbaccalaureate distance learning degree programs offered (no on-campus study). *Faculty:* 12 full-time (2 women), 3 part-time/adjunct (1 woman). *Students:* 23 full-time (3 women), 15 part-time (6 women). 38 applicants, 84% accepted, 25 enrolled. In 2008, 6 master's awarded. *Degree requirements:* For master's, comprehensive exam, thesis or alternative. *Entrance requirements:* For master's, GRE General Test, 3 letters of recommendation. Additional exam requirements/recommendations for international students: Required—TOEFL (minimum score 570 paper-based; 230 computer-based; 79 iBT), IELTS (minimum score 6.5). *Application deadline:* For fall admission, 7/1 for domestic students, 2/1 for international students; for spring admission, 11/1 for domestic students, 7/1 for international students. Applications are processed on a rolling basis. Application fee: $50. Electronic applications accepted. *Expenses:* Tuition, area resident: Full-time $2600; part-time $700 per course. Tuition, state resident: full-time $2600; part-time $700 per course. Tuition, nonresident: full-time $5000; part-time $3300 per course. Required fees: $2150; $330 per course. Tuition and fees vary according to campus/location. *Financial support:* In 2008–09, 10 research assistantships (averaging $7,500 per year) were awarded; fellowships, teaching assistantships, career-related internships or fieldwork, Federal Work-Study, scholarships/grants, and unspecified assistantships also available. Financial award application deadline: 4/1; financial award applicants required to submit FAFSA. *Faculty research:* Global change, climatology, production cartography, geographic information systems, North Carolina geography, Latin America. Total annual research expenditures: $250,000. *Unit head:* Dr. James Young, Chairperson, 828-262-3000, Fax: 828-262-3067. *Application contact:* Dr. Kathleen Schroeder, Graduate Program Director, 828-262-3000.

Arizona State University, Graduate College, College of Liberal Arts and Sciences, Division of Social Sciences, School of Geographical Sciences, Tempe, AZ 85287. Offers geographic education (MAS); geographic information systems (MAS); geography (MA, PhD). *Degree requirements:* For master's, thesis; for doctorate, thesis/dissertation. *Entrance requirements:* For master's and doctorate, GRE.

Boston University, Graduate School of Arts and Sciences, Department of Geography and Environment, Boston, MA 02215. Offers energy and environmental analysis (MA); environmental remote sensing and GIs (MA); geography (MA); geography and environment (PhD); international relations and environmental policy (MA). Terminal master's awarded for partial completion of doctoral program. *Degree requirements:* For master's, one foreign language, comprehensive exam, thesis; for doctorate, one foreign language, comprehensive exam, thesis/dissertation. *Entrance requirements:* For master's and doctorate, GRE General Test, GRE Subject Test, 3 letters of recommendation. Additional exam requirements/recommendations for international students: Required—TOEFL (minimum score 600 paper-based; 250 computer-based).

Clark University, Graduate School, Department of Geography, Program in Geographic Information Science, Worcester, MA 01610-1477. Offers MA. *Students:* 3 full-time (1 woman), 1 (woman) part-time, 1 international. Average age 23. 4 applicants, 100% accepted, 4 enrolled. In 2008, 1 master's awarded. *Application deadline:* For fall admission, 12/31 priority date for domestic students. Application fee: $50. *Expenses:* Tuition: Full-time $34,900; part-time $1091 per credit hour. Required fees: $30. *Unit head:* Dr. Billie Lee Turner, Director, 508-793-7336. *Application contact:* Christine Silva, Admission Coordinator, 508-793-7337, Fax: 508-793-8881, E-mail: geography@clarku.edu.

Clark University, Graduate School, Department of International Development, Community, and Environment, Program in Geographic Information Science for Development and Environment, Worcester, MA 01610-1477. Offers MA. *Students:* 14 full-time (8 women), 1 part-time (0 women); includes 2 minority (both African Americans), 8 international. Average age 27. 54 applicants, 46% accepted, 9 enrolled. In 2008, 9 master's awarded. *Degree requirements:* For master's, thesis. *Entrance requirements:* Additional exam requirements/recommendations for international students: Required—TOEFL. *Application deadline:* For fall admission, 1/15 for domestic students. Application fee: $50. *Expenses:* Tuition: Full-time $34,900; part-time $1091 per credit hour. Required fees: $30. *Financial support:* In 2008–09, research assistantships with full and partial tuition reimbursements (averaging $5,000 per year), teaching assistantships with full and partial tuition reimbursements (averaging $5,000 per year) were awarded; fellowships, tuition waivers (full and partial) also available. *Faculty research:* Dynamic modeling, image processing, land use and land cover change modeling, image classification, spatial econometrics. *Unit head:* Dr. William F. Fisher, Director, 508-421-3765, Fax: 508-793-8820, E-mail: wfisher@clarku.edu. *Application contact:* Paula Hall, IDCE Graduate Admissions, 508-793-7201, Fax: 508-793-8820, E-mail: idce@clarku.edu.

Cleveland State University, College of Graduate Studies, Maxine Goodman Levin College of Urban Affairs, Program in Environmental Studies, Cleveland, OH 44115. Offers environmental studies (MAES); geographic information systems (Certificate); urban real estate development and finance (Certificate); JD/MAES. Part-time and evening/weekend programs available. *Faculty:* 26 full-time (10 women), 3 part-time/adjunct (0 women). *Students:* 6 full-time (2 women), 16 part-time (9 women), 3 international. 16 applicants, 50% accepted, 6 enrolled. In 2008, 7 master's awarded. *Degree requirements:* For master's, thesis or alternative, exit project. *Entrance requirements:* For master's, GRE General Test (minimum score: verbal and quantitative 40th percentile, analytical writing 4.0), minimum GPA of 3.0. Additional exam requirements/recommendations for international students: Required—TOEFL (minimum score 525 paper-based; 197 computer-based; 65 iBT). *Application deadline:* For fall admission, 7/15 priority date for domestic students, 5/15 for international students; for spring admission, 11/1 for international students. Applications are processed on a rolling basis. Application fee: $30. Electronic applications accepted. *Financial support:* In 2008–09, 1 student received support, including 1 research assistantship with full and partial tuition reimbursement available (averaging $6,960 per year); career-related internships or fieldwork, Federal Work-Study, scholarships/grants, tuition waivers (full and partial), and unspecified assistantships also available. Support available to part-time students. Financial award application deadline: 3/1; financial award applicants required to submit FAFSA. *Faculty research:* Environmental policy and administration, environmental planning, geographic information systems (GIS), nonprofit management. *Unit head:* Dr. Sanda Kaufman, Director, 216-687-2367, Fax: 216-687-9342, E-mail: s.kaufman@csuohio.edu. *Application contact:* Graduate Program Coordinator, 216-523-7522, Fax: 216-687-5398, E-mail: urbanprograms@csuohio.edu.

Cleveland State University, College of Graduate Studies, Maxine Goodman Levin College of Urban Affairs, Program in Nonprofit Administration and Leadership, Cleveland, OH 44115.

Offers geographic information systems (Certificate); local and urban management (Certificate); nonprofit administration and leadership (MNAL); nonprofit management (Certificate); urban economic development (Certificate). Part-time and evening/weekend programs available. *Faculty:* 26 full-time (10 women), 6 part-time/adjunct (4 women). *Students:* 5 full-time (4 women), 21 part-time (17 women); includes 4 minority (all African Americans), 1 international. Average age 35. 29 applicants, 45% accepted, 9 enrolled. *Degree requirements:* For master's, thesis or alternative, capstone course. *Entrance requirements:* For master's, GRE (minimum score: 40th percentile quantitative/verbal, 4.0 analytical writing), minimum GPA of 3.0. Additional exam requirements/recommendations for international students: Required—TOEFL (minimum score 525 paper-based; 197 computer-based; 65 iBT). *Application deadline:* For fall admission, 7/15 priority date for domestic students, 5/15 for international students; for spring admission, 11/1 for international students. Applications are processed on a rolling basis. Application fee: $30. Electronic applications accepted. *Financial support:* In 2008–09, 5 students received support, including research assistantships with full and partial tuition reimbursements available (averaging $6,960 per year); career-related internships or fieldwork, Federal Work-Study, scholarships/grants, tuition waivers (full and partial), and unspecified assistantships also available. Support available to part-time students. Financial award application deadline: 3/1; financial award applicants required to submit FAFSA. *Faculty research:* Human resource management, volunteerism, performance measurement in nonprofits, government-nonprofit partnerships. *Unit head:* Dr. Jennifer Alexander, Director, 216-687-5011, Fax: 216-687-2013, E-mail: j.k.alexander@csuohio.edu. *Application contact:* Graduate Program Coordinator, 216-523-7522, Fax: 216-687-5398, E-mail: urbanprograms@csuohio.edu.

Cleveland State University, College of Graduate Studies, Maxine Goodman Levin College of Urban Affairs, Program in Public Administration, Cleveland, OH 44115. Offers geographic information systems (Certificate); local and urban management (Certificate); non-profit management (Certificate); public administration (MPA); urban real estate development (Certificate); JD/MPA. *Accreditation:* NASPAA. Part-time and evening/weekend programs available. *Faculty:* 26 full-time (10 women), 14 part-time/adjunct (8 women). *Students:* 14 full-time (8 women), 79 part-time (44 women); includes 7 minority (all African Americans), 1 international. Average age 36. 82 applicants, 41% accepted, 15 enrolled. In 2008, 37 master's, 8 other advanced degrees awarded. *Degree requirements:* For master's, thesis or alternative, capstone course. *Entrance requirements:* For master's, GRE General Test (minimum score: verbal and quantitative 40th percentile, analytical writing 4.0), minimum GPA of 3.0. Additional exam requirements/recommendations for international students: Required—TOEFL (minimum score 525 paper-based; 197 computer-based; 65 iBT). *Application deadline:* For fall admission, 7/15 priority date for domestic students, 5/15 for international students; for spring admission, 11/1 for international students. Applications are processed on a rolling basis. Application fee: $30. Electronic applications accepted. *Financial support:* In 2008–09, 10 students received support, including 7 research assistantships with full and partial tuition reimbursements available (averaging $6,960 per year), 3 teaching assistantships with full and partial tuition reimbursements available (averaging $6,960 per year); career-related internships or fieldwork, institutionally sponsored loans, tuition waivers (full and partial), and unspecified assistantships also available. Financial award application deadline: 3/1; financial award applicants required to submit FAFSA. *Faculty research:* Health care administration, public management, economic development, city management, nonprofit management. *Unit head:* Dr. Jessica Sowa, Director, 216-875-9972, Fax: 216-687-2013, E-mail: j.e.sowa@csuohio.edu. *Application contact:* Graduate Program Coordinator, 216-523-7522, Fax: 216-687-5398, E-mail: urbanprograms@csuohio.edu.

Cleveland State University, College of Graduate Studies, Maxine Goodman Levin College of Urban Affairs, Program in Urban Planning, Design, and Development, Cleveland, OH 44115. Offers geographic information systems (Certificate); local and urban management (Certificate); urban economic development (Certificate); urban planning, design, and development (MUPDD); urban real estate development and finance (Certificate); JD/MUPDD. *Accreditation:* ACSP. Part-time and evening/weekend programs available. *Faculty:* 26 full-time (10 women), 12 part-time/adjunct (5 women). *Students:* 37 full-time (17 women), 41 part-time (21 women); includes 13 minority (9 African Americans, 1 American Indian/Alaska Native, 3 Hispanic Americans), 10 international. Average age 38. 63 applicants, 63% accepted, 21 enrolled. In 2008, 24 master's, 9 Certificates awarded. *Degree requirements:* For master's, project or thesis. *Entrance requirements:* For master's, GRE General Test (minimum score: verbal and quantitative 50th percentile, analytical writing 4.0), minimum GPA of 3.0. Additional exam requirements/recommendations for international students: Required—TOEFL (minimum score 525 paper-based; 197 computer-based; 65 iBT). *Application deadline:* For fall admission, 7/15 priority date for domestic students, 5/15 for international students; for spring admission, 11/1 for international students. Applications are processed on a rolling basis. Application fee: $30. Electronic applications accepted. *Financial support:* In 2008–09, 15 students received support, including 10 research assistantships with full and partial tuition reimbursements available (averaging $6,960 per year), 5 teaching assistantships with full and partial tuition reimbursements available (averaging $6,960 per year); career-related internships or fieldwork, Federal Work-Study, tuition waivers (full and partial), and unspecified assistantships also available. Support available to part-time students. Financial award application deadline: 3/1. *Faculty research:* Housing and neighborhood development, urban housing policy, environmental sustainability, economic development. *Unit head:* Dr. W. Dennis Keating, Director, 216-687-2298, Fax: 216-687-2013, E-mail: w.keating@csuohio.edu. *Application contact:* Graduate Program Coordinator, 216-523-7522, Fax: 216-687-5398, E-mail: urbanprograms@csuohio.edu.

Cleveland State University, College of Graduate Studies, Maxine Goodman Levin College of Urban Affairs, Program in Urban Studies, Cleveland, OH 44115. Offers geographic information systems (Certificate); local and urban management (Certificate); nonprofit management (Certificate); urban economic development (Certificate); urban real estate development and finance (Certificate); urban studies (MS); urban studies and public affairs (PhD). Part-time and evening/weekend programs available. *Faculty:* 26 full-time (10 women), 20 part-time/adjunct (11 women). *Students:* 26 full-time (12 women), 42 part-time (24 women); includes 13 minority (10 African Americans, 2 Asian Americans or Pacific Islanders, 1 Hispanic American), 21 international. Average age 37. 69 applicants, 35% accepted, 12 enrolled. In 2008, 6 master's, 7 doctorates, 6 other advanced degrees awarded. *Degree requirements:* For master's, thesis or alternative, exit project, capstone course; for doctorate, comprehensive exam, thesis/dissertation. *Entrance requirements:* For master's, GRE General Test, minimum GPA of 3.0; for doctorate, GRE General Test, minimum GPA of 3.5. Additional exam requirements/recommendations for international students: Required—TOEFL (minimum score 525 paper-based; 197 computer-based; 65 iBT). *Application deadline:* For fall admission, 7/15 priority date for domestic students, 5/15 for international students; for spring admission, 11/1 for international students. Applications are processed on a rolling basis. Application fee: $30. Electronic applications accepted. *Financial support:* In 2008–09, 15 students received support, including 11 research assistantships with full tuition reimbursements available (averaging $7,000 per year), 4 teaching assistantships with full and partial tuition reimbursements available (averaging $7,000 per year); career-related internships or fieldwork, Federal Work-Study, institutionally sponsored loans, scholarships/grants, tuition waivers (full and partial), and unspecified assistantships also available. Support available to part-time students. Financial award application deadline: 3/1; financial award applicants required to submit FAFSA. *Faculty research:* Environmental issues, economic development, urban and public policy, public management. *Unit head:* Dr. Wendy Kellogg, Director, 216-687-5265, Fax: 216-687-9342, E-mail: w.kellogg@csuohio.edu. *Application contact:* Graduate Program Coordinator, 216-523-7522, Fax: 216-687-5398, E-mail: urbanprograms@csuohio.edu.

Eastern Michigan University, Graduate School, College of Arts and Sciences, Department of Geography and Geology, Program in Geographic Information Systems, Ypsilanti, MI 48197. Offers geographic information systems (MS); GIS educator (Graduate Certificate); GIS professional (Graduate Certificate); GIS-planning (MS).

Geographic Information Systems

Florida State University, Graduate Studies, College of Social Sciences, Department of Geography, Tallahassee, FL 32306. Offers geographic information systems (MS); geography (MA, MS, PhD). Part-time programs available. Terminal master's awarded for partial completion of doctoral program. *Degree requirements:* For master's, thesis (for some programs); for doctorate, thesis/dissertation. *Entrance requirements:* For master's and doctorate, GRE General Test, minimum GPA of 3.0. Additional exam requirements/recommendations for international students: Required—TOEFL. Electronic applications accepted. *Faculty research:* Society-nature interaction, geographic information science.

George Mason University, College of Science, Department of Earth Systems and Geoinformation Sciences, Fairfax, VA 22030. Offers MS, PhD, Certificate.

George Mason University, College of Science, Department of Geography, Fairfax, VA 22030. Offers geographic and cartographic sciences (MS). *Degree requirements:* For master's, thesis optional. *Entrance requirements:* For master's, GRE General Test, minimum GPA of 3.0 in last 60 hours; BS or BA in geography, cartography, or related field. Electronic applications accepted.

Georgia Institute of Technology, Graduate Studies and Research, College of Architecture, City and Regional Planning Program, Atlanta, GA 30332-0001. Offers city and regional planning (PhD); economic development (MCRP); environmental planning and management (MCRP); geographic information systems (MCRP); land and community development (MCRP); land use planning (MCRP); transportation (MCRP); urban design (MCRP); MCP/MSCE. *Accreditation:* ACSP. *Degree requirements:* For master's, thesis, internship. *Entrance requirements:* For master's, GRE General Test, minimum GPA of 2.7. Additional exam requirements/ recommendations for international students: Required—TOEFL. Electronic applications accepted.

Georgia State University, College of Arts and Sciences, Department of Geosciences, Program in Geographic Information Systems, Atlanta, GA 30303-3083. Offers Certificate. Part-time programs available. *Entrance requirements:* Additional exam requirements/recommendations for international students: Required—TOEFL. Electronic applications accepted. *Faculty research:* Cartography, remote sensing.

Hunter College of the City University of New York, Graduate School, School of Arts and Sciences, Department of Geography, New York, NY 10021-5085. Offers analytical geography (MA); earth system science (MA); environmental and social issues (MA); geographic information science (Certificate); geographic information systems (MA); teaching earth science (MA). Part-time and evening/weekend programs available. *Faculty:* 12 full-time (6 women), 4 part-time/adjunct (2 women). *Students:* 36 part-time (16 women); includes 3 minority (1 Asian American or Pacific Islander, 2 Hispanic Americans). Average age 33. 13 applicants, 69% accepted, 7 enrolled. In 2008, 9 master's awarded. *Degree requirements:* For master's, comprehensive exam or thesis. *Entrance requirements:* For master's, GRE General Test, minimum B average in major, minimum B- average overall, 18 credits of course work in geography, 2 letters of recommendation; for Certificate, minimum of B average in major, B- overall. Additional exam requirements/recommendations for international students: Required—TOEFL. *Application deadline:* For fall admission, 4/1 for domestic students; for spring admission, 11/1 for domestic students. Applications are processed on a rolling basis. Application fee: $125. *Financial support:* In 2008–09, 1 fellowship (averaging $3,000 per year), 2 research assistantships (averaging $10,000 per year), 10 teaching assistantships (averaging $6,000 per year) were awarded; career-related internships or fieldwork, Federal Work-Study, institutionally sponsored loans, and unspecified assistantships also available. Financial award application deadline: 3/1. *Faculty research:* Urban geography, economic geography, geographic information science, demographic methods, climate change. *Unit head:* Prof. William Solecki, Chair, 212-772-4536, Fax: 212-772-5268, E-mail: wsolecki@hunter.cuny.edu. *Application contact:* Prof. Marianna Pavlovskaya, Graduate Adviser, 212-772-5320, Fax: 212-772-5268, E-mail: mpavlov@geo.hunter.cuny.edu.

Idaho State University, Office of Graduate Studies, College of Arts and Sciences, Department of Geosciences, Pocatello, ID 83209. Offers geographic information science (MS); geology (MNS, MS); geophysics/hydrology (MS); geotechnology (Postbaccalaureate Certificate). Part-time programs available. *Faculty:* 8 full-time (1 woman). *Students:* 21 full-time (8 women), 20 part-time (7 women); includes 1 minority (Asian American or Pacific Islander), 7 international. Average age 34. In 2008, 9 master's, 2 other advanced degrees awarded. *Degree requirements:* For master's, comprehensive exam, thesis; for Postbaccalaureate Certificate, thesis optional. *Entrance requirements:* For master's and Postbaccalaureate Certificate, GRE General Test, 3 letters of recommendation. Additional exam requirements/recommendations for international students: Required—TOEFL (minimum score 550 paper-based; 213 computer-based; 80 iBT). *Application deadline:* For fall admission, 7/1 for domestic students, 6/1 for international students; for spring admission, 12/1 for domestic students, 11/1 for international students. Applications are processed on a rolling basis. Application fee: $55. Electronic applications accepted. *Expenses:* Tuition, area resident: Full-time $3114; part-time $276 per credit hour. Tuition, state resident: full-time $3114; part-time $276 per credit hour. Tuition, nonresident: full-time $12,318; part-time $404 per credit hour. Required fees: $2360. Tuition and fees vary according to course load and reciprocity agreements. *Financial support:* In 2008–09, 7 research assistantships with full and partial tuition reimbursements (averaging $6,800 per year), 8 teaching assistantships with full and partial tuition reimbursements (averaging $9,401 per year) were awarded; career-related internships or fieldwork, Federal Work-Study, institutionally sponsored loans, scholarships/grants, health care benefits, tuition waivers (full and partial), and unspecified assistantships also available. Support available to part-time students. Financial award application deadline: 1/1; financial award applicants required to submit FAFSA. *Faculty research:* Quantitative field mapping and sampling: microscopic, geochemical, and isotopic analysis of rocks, minerals and water; remote sensing, geographic information systems, and global positioning systems: environmental and watershed management; surficial and fluvial processes: landscape change; regional tectonics, structural geology; planetary geology. *Unit head:* Dr. David Rodgers, Chairman, 208-282-3365, Fax: 208-282-4414, E-mail: rodgdavi@isu.edu. *Application contact:* Ellen Combs, Graduate School Technical Records Specialist, 208-282-2150, Fax: 208-282-4847, E-mail: combelle@isu.edu.

Indiana University–Purdue University Indianapolis, School of Liberal Arts, Department of Geography, Indianapolis, IN 46202-2896. Offers geographic information systems (MS, Certificate). *Entrance requirements:* For master's, GRE, GPA of 3.0.

Montclair State University, The Office of Graduate Admissions and Support Services, College of Science and Mathematics, Department of Earth and Environmental Studies, Montclair, NJ 07043-1624. Offers earth science (Certificate); environmental management (MA, D Env M, PhD); environmental studies (MS), including environmental education, environmental health, environmental management, environmental science; geographic information science (Certificate); geoscience (MS, Certificate), including geoscience (MS), water resource management (Certificate). Part-time and evening/weekend programs available. *Faculty:* 16 full-time (2 women), 12 part-time/adjunct (4 women). *Students:* 26 full-time (11 women), 44 part-time (16 women); includes 5 minority (4 African Americans, 1 Hispanic American), 7 international. Average age 32. 21 applicants, 90% accepted, 14 enrolled. In 2008, 8 master's awarded. *Degree requirements:* For master's, comprehensive exam, thesis or alternative; for doctorate, thesis/dissertation. *Entrance requirements:* For master's, GRE General Test, 2 letters of recommendation. Additional exam requirements/recommendations for international students: Required—TOEFL (minimum score 83 computer-based). *Application deadline:* For fall admission, 6/1 for international students; for spring admission, 10/1 for international students. Applications are processed on a rolling basis. Application fee: $60. Electronic applications accepted. *Financial support:* In 2008–09, 3 research assistantships with full tuition reimbursements were awarded; Federal Work-Study, scholarships/grants, and unspecified assistantships also available. Support available to part-time students. Financial award application deadline: 3/1; financial award applicants required to submit FAFSA. *Faculty research:* Antarctica, carbon pools, contaminated sediments, wetlands. *Unit head:* Dr. Duke Ophori, Chairperson, 973-655-7558. *Application contact:* Amy Aiello, Associate Director of Admissions, 973-655-5147, Fax: 973-655-7869, E-mail: graduate.school@montclair.edu.

North Carolina State University, Graduate School, College of Natural Resources, Department of Parks, Recreation and Tourism Management, Raleigh, NC 27695. Offers natural resource management (MPRTM, MS); park and recreation management (MPRTM, MS); parks, recreation and tourism management (PhD); recreational sport management (MPRTM, MS); spatial information science (MPRTM, MS); tourism policy and development (MPRTM, MS). *Degree requirements:* For master's, thesis (for some programs); for doctorate, thesis/dissertation. *Entrance requirements:* For master's and doctorate, GRE General Test. Additional exam requirements/recommendations for international students: Required—TOEFL. Electronic applications accepted. *Faculty research:* Tourism policy and development, spatial information systems, natural resource management, recreational sports management, park and recreation management.

Northern Arizona University, Graduate College, College of Social and Behavioral Sciences, Department of Geography, Planning, and Recreation, Flagstaff, AZ 86011. Offers applied geographic information science (MS); geographic information systems (Certificate); rural geography (MA). *Degree requirements:* For master's, thesis. *Entrance requirements:* For master's, GRE General Test.

Northwest Missouri State University, Graduate School, College of Arts and Sciences, Department of Geology/Geography, Program in Geographic Information Sciences, Maryville, MO 64468-6001. Offers MS, Certificate. Part-time programs available. *Degree requirements:* For master's, comprehensive exam, thesis. *Entrance requirements:* For master's, GRE General Test, 2 letters of recommendation, writing sample, minimum undergraduate GPA of 2.5. Additional exam requirements/recommendations for international students: Required—TOEFL (minimum score 550 paper-based; 213 computer-based).

Saint Louis University, Graduate School, College of Education and Public Service and Graduate School, Department of Public Policy Studies, St. Louis, MO 63103-2097. Offers geographic information systems (Certificate); organizational development (Certificate); public administration (MAPA); public policy analysis (PhD); urban affairs (MAUA); urban planning and real estate development (MUPRED). *Accreditation:* NASPAA. Part-time programs available. *Degree requirements:* For master's, comprehensive exam (for some programs), thesis (for some programs); for doctorate, comprehensive exam, thesis/dissertation, preliminary exams. *Entrance requirements:* For master's and doctorate, GMAT, GRE General Test, or LSAT, letters of recommendation, resumé, interview, transcripts, goal statement. Additional exam requirements/ recommendations for international students: Required—TOEFL (minimum score 525 paper-based; 194 computer-based). Electronic applications accepted. *Faculty research:* Urban politics, brown fields, e-government, and administration, evaluation research, community development, electronic government and governance.

Saint Mary's University of Minnesota, Schools of Graduate and Professional Programs, Graduate School of Business and Technology, Geographic Information Science Program, Winona, MN 55987-1399. Offers MS, Certificate.

Salisbury University, Graduate Division, Master of Science in Geographic Information Systems and Public Administration Program, Salisbury, MD 21801-6837. Offers MS. Part-time programs available. Postbaccalaureate distance learning degree programs offered (minimal on-campus study). *Faculty:* 4 full-time (1 woman), 1 (woman) part-time/adjunct. *Students:* 3 full-time (0 women), 6 part-time (1 woman). Average age 32. 12 applicants, 83% accepted, 10 enrolled. *Degree requirements:* For master's, cooperative project. *Entrance requirements:* For master's, GRE (for recent graduates), GIS experience, administration experience. Additional exam requirements/recommendations for international students: Required—TOEFL (minimum score 550 paper-based; 213 computer-based). *Application deadline:* For fall admission, 2/15 for domestic students. Application fee: $45. Electronic applications accepted. *Expenses:* Tuition, area resident: Part-time $270 per credit hour. Tuition, state resident: part-time $270 per credit hour. Tuition, nonresident: part-time $566 per credit hour. Required fees: $52 per credit hour. *Faculty research:* GIS in local governments, parallel applications of GIS, GIS and vulnerability, GIS and crime analysis. *Unit head:* Dr. Michael Scott, Master's Program Director, 410-543-6456, Fax: 410-548-4506, E-mail: msscott@salisbury.edu. *Application contact:* Susan Parks, Program Management Specialist, 410-543-6460, Fax: 410-548-4506, E-mail: slparks@salisbury.edu.

San Jose State University, Graduate Studies and Research, College of Social Sciences, Department of Geography, San Jose, CA 95192-0001. Offers geographic information science (Certificate); geography (MA). *Entrance requirements:* For master's, minimum GPA of 3.0. Electronic applications accepted.

Texas State University–San Marcos, Graduate School, College of Liberal Arts, Department of Geography, Program in Environmental Geography, Geography Education, and Geography Information Science, San Marcos, TX 78666. Offers environmental geography (PhD); geography education (PhD); information science (PhD). Part-time programs available. *Degree requirements:* For doctorate, thesis/dissertation. *Entrance requirements:* For doctorate, GRE General Test, minimum GPA of 3.5, master's degree in geography, demonstrated scholarly research. Additional exam requirements/recommendations for international students: Required—TOEFL (minimum score 550 paper-based; 213 computer-based). Electronic applications accepted.

Texas State University–San Marcos, Graduate School, College of Liberal Arts, Department of Geography, Program in Geographic Information Science, San Marcos, TX 78666. Offers MAG. Part-time and evening/weekend programs available. *Degree requirements:* For master's, comprehensive exam, internship or thesis. *Entrance requirements:* For master's, GRE General Test, minimum GPA of 3.0 in last 60 hours of course work. Additional exam requirements/ recommendations for international students: Required—TOEFL (minimum score 550 paper-based; 213 computer-based). Electronic applications accepted.

Université du Québec à Montréal, Graduate Programs, Program in Geographical Information Systems, Montréal, QC H3C 3P8, Canada. Offers Diploma. Part-time programs available. *Entrance requirements:* For degree, appropriate bachelor's degree or equivalent, proficiency in French.

Université Laval, Faculty of Administrative Sciences, Programs in Business Administration, Québec, QC G1K 7P4, Canada. Offers accounting (MBA); agri-food management (MBA); electronic business (MBA, Diploma); factory management and logistics (MBA); finance (MBA); firm management (MBA); geomatic management (MBA); information technology management (MBA); international management (MBA); management (MBA); management accounting (MBA, Diploma); marketing (MBA); modeling and organizational decision (MBA); occupational health and safety management (MBA); pharmacy management (MBA); social and environmental responsibility (MBA); technological entrepreneurship (Diploma). *Accreditation:* AACSB. Part-time and evening/weekend programs available. Postbaccalaureate distance learning degree programs offered (no on-campus study). *Entrance requirements:* For master's and Diploma, knowledge of French and English. Electronic applications accepted.

University at Albany, State University of New York, College of Arts and Sciences, Department of Geography and Planning, Program in Geography, Albany, NY 12222-0001. Offers geographic information systems and spatial analysis (Certificate); geography (MA). *Degree requirements:* For master's, thesis or alternative. *Entrance requirements:* Additional exam requirements/ recommendations for international students: Required—TOEFL (minimum score 550 paper-based; 213 computer-based). Electronic applications accepted. *Faculty research:* Remote sensing, cultural/social geography, urban geography.

University at Buffalo, the State University of New York, Graduate School, College of Arts and Sciences, Department of Geography, Buffalo, NY 14260. Offers geographic information science (Certificate); geography (MA, MS, PhD); transportation and business geographics (Certificate); MA/MBA. *Degree requirements:* For master's, thesis (for some programs), project; for doctorate, thesis/dissertation; for Certificate, portfolio. *Entrance requirements:* For master's, GRE General Test, minimum GPA of 2.9; for doctorate, GRE General Test, minimum GPA of

Geographic Information Systems

University at Buffalo, the State University of New York (continued)

3.0. Additional exam requirements/recommendations for international students: Required—TOEFL (minimum score 550 paper-based; 213 computer-based; 79 iBT). Electronic applications accepted. *Faculty research:* International business and world trade, geographic information systems and cartography, transportation, urban and regional analysis, physical and environmental geography.

The University of Akron, Graduate School, Buchtel College of Arts and Sciences, Department of Geography and Planning, Program in Geographic Information Science, Akron, OH 44325. Offers MS. *Entrance requirements:* Additional exam requirements/recommendations for international students: Required—TOEFL (minimum score 550 paper-based; 213 computer-based; 79 iBT). Electronic applications accepted.

University of Central Arkansas, Graduate School, College of Liberal Arts, Department of Geography, Conway, AR 72035-0001. Offers geographic information systems (MGIS, Certificate). Part-time programs available. Postbaccalaureate distance learning degree programs offered (minimal on-campus study). *Entrance requirements:* Additional exam requirements/recommendations for international students: Required—TOEFL (minimum score 550 paper-based; 213 computer-based).

University of Colorado Denver, College of Engineering and Applied Science, Department of Civil Engineering, Denver, CO 80217-3364. Offers civil engineering (MS, PhD); geographic information systems (M Eng). Part-time and evening/weekend programs available. *Degree requirements:* For master's, comprehensive exam, thesis or alternative; for doctorate, comprehensive exam, thesis/dissertation. *Entrance requirements:* For master's and doctorate, GRE. Additional exam requirements/recommendations for international students: Required—TOEFL (minimum score 525 paper-based; 197 computer-based). Electronic applications accepted.

University of Connecticut, Graduate School, College of Liberal Arts and Sciences, Department of Geography, Field of Geography, Storrs, CT 06269. Offers geographic information systems (Certificate); geography (MS, PhD). Part-time programs available. Terminal master's awarded for partial completion of doctoral program. *Degree requirements:* For master's, comprehensive exam; for doctorate, thesis/dissertation. *Entrance requirements:* For master's and doctorate, GRE General Test. Additional exam requirements/recommendations for international students: Required—TOEFL (minimum score 550 paper-based; 213 computer-based). Electronic applications accepted.

University of Denver, University College, Denver, CO 80208. Offers applied communication (MAS, MPS, Certificate); computer information systems (MAS, Certificate); environmental policy and management (MAS, Certificate); geographic information systems (MAS, Certificate); human resource administration (MPS, Certificate); knowledge and information technologies (MAS); liberal studies (MLS, Certificate); modern languages (MLS, Certificate); organizational leadership (MPS, Certificate); security management (Certificate); technology management (MAS, Certificate), including 21st century strategic management (MAS), international markets (MAS), project management (MAS), research and development management (MAS); telecommunications (MAS, Certificate), including broadband (MAS), telecommunications management and policy (MAS), telecommunications technology (MAS), wireless networks (MAS). Part-time and evening/weekend programs available. Postbaccalaureate distance learning degree programs offered (no on-campus study). *Faculty:* 137 part-time/adjunct (55 women). *Students:* 28 full-time (15 women), 699 part-time (401 women); includes 129 minority (54 African Americans, 8 American Indian/Alaska Native, 22 Asian Americans or Pacific Islanders, 45 Hispanic Americans), 4 international. Average age 36. 845 applicants, 96% accepted, 326 enrolled. In 2008, 221 master's, 3 Certificates awarded. *Entrance requirements:* Additional exam requirements/recommendations for international students: Required—TOEFL (minimum score 550 paper-based; 213 computer-based). *Application deadline:* Applications are processed on a rolling basis. Application fee: $75. Electronic applications accepted. *Expenses:* Contact institution. *Financial support:* Applicants required to submit FAFSA. *Unit head:* Dr. James Davis, Dean, 303-871-2291, Fax: 303-871-4047, E-mail: jdavis@du.edu. *Application contact:* Information Contact, 303-871-3155.

University of Lethbridge, School of Graduate Studies, Lethbridge, AB T1K 3M4, Canada. Offers accounting (MScM); addictions counseling (M Sc); agricultural biotechnology (M Sc); agricultural studies (M Sc, MA); anthropology (MA); archaeology (MA); art (MA); biochemistry (M Sc); biological sciences (M Sc); biomolecular science (PhD); biosystems and biodiversity (PhD); Canadian studies (MA); chemistry (M Sc); computer science (M Sc); computer science and geographical information science (M Sc); counseling psychology (M Ed); dramatic arts (MA); earth, space, and physical science (PhD); economics (MA); educational leadership (M Ed); English (MA); environmental science (M Sc); evolution and behavior (PhD); exercise science (M Sc); finance (MScM); French (MA); French/German (MA); French/Spanish (MA); general education (M Ed); general management (MScM); geography (M Sc, MA); German (MA); health sciences (M Sc, MA); history (MA); human resource management and labour relations (MScM); individualized multidisciplinary (M Sc, MA); information systems (MScM); international management (MScM); kinesiology (M Sc, MA); management (M Sc, MA); marketing (MScM); mathematics (M Sc); music (MA); Native American studies (MA); neuroscience (M Sc, PhD); new media (MA); nursing (M Sc); philosophy (MA); physics (M Sc); policy and strategy (MScM); political science (MA); psychology (M Sc, MA); religious studies (MA); sociology (MA); theoretical and computational science (PhD); urban and regional studies (MA). Part-time and evening/weekend programs available. *Degree requirements:* For doctorate, comprehensive exam, thesis/dissertation. *Entrance requirements:* For master's, GMAT (M Sc in management), bachelor's degree in related field, minimum GPA of 3.0 during previous 20 graded semester courses, 2 years teaching or related experience (M Ed); for doctorate, master's degree, minimum graduate GPA of 3.5. Additional exam requirements/recommendations for international students: Required—TOEFL. *Faculty research:* Movement and brain plasticity, gibberellin physiology, photosynthesis, carbon cycling, molecular properties of main-group ring components.

University of Maryland, Baltimore County, Graduate School, College of Arts, Humanities and Social Sciences, Department of Geography and Environmental Systems, Program in Geographic Information Systems, Baltimore, MD 21250. Offers MPS, Certificate. Part-time and evening/weekend programs available. *Faculty:* 10 part-time/adjunct (3 women). *Students:* 1 (woman) full-time, 31 part-time (5 women); includes 6 minority (1 African American, 2 Asian Americans or Pacific Islanders, 3 Hispanic Americans), 4 international. Average age 31. 38 applicants, 92% accepted, 31 enrolled. *Entrance requirements:* Additional exam requirements/recommendations for international students: Required—TOEFL. *Application deadline:* For fall admission, 6/1 for domestic and international students; for spring admission, 11/1 for domestic and international students. Applications are processed on a rolling basis. Application fee: $70. Electronic applications accepted. *Faculty research:* Enterprise GIS. *Unit head:* Dr. Sandy Parker, Chair, 410-455-2002, E-mail: eparker@umbc.edu. *Application contact:* Kathryn Nee, Coordinator of Domestic Admissions, 410-455-2944, E-mail: nee@umbc.edu.

University of Minnesota, Twin Cities Campus, Graduate School, College of Liberal Arts, Department of Geography, Program in Geographic Information Science, Minneapolis, MN 55455-0213. Offers MGIS. Part-time programs available. *Degree requirements:* For master's, 3 plan B projects/papers. *Entrance requirements:* For master's, minimum GPA of 3.0; course work in college-level math, statistics, and computer programming. Additional exam requirements/recommendations for international students: Required—TOEFL (minimum score 600 paper-based; 250 computer-based; 100 iBT). *Expenses:* Contact institution. *Faculty research:* Accuracy assessment, geographic information science and society, spatial analysis and modeling, spatial databases, remote sensing.

The University of Montana, Graduate School, College of Arts and Sciences, Department of Geography, Missoula, MT 59812-0002. Offers geography (MA), including cartography and GIS, community and environmental planning. *Entrance requirements:* For master's, GRE General Test. Additional exam requirements/recommendations for international students: Required—TOEFL.

The University of North Carolina at Greensboro, Graduate School, College of Arts and Sciences, Department of Geography, Greensboro, NC 27412-5001. Offers applied geography (MA); geographic information science (Certificate); geography (PhD); urban and economic development (Certificate). *Degree requirements:* For master's, comprehensive exam, thesis or alternative. *Entrance requirements:* For master's, GRE General Test. Additional exam requirements/recommendations for international students: Required—TOEFL. Electronic applications accepted.

University of Pittsburgh, School of Arts and Sciences, Department of Geology and Planetary Science, Pittsburgh, PA 15260. Offers geographical information systems (PM Sc); geology and planetary science (MS, PhD). Part-time programs available. *Degree requirements:* For master's, thesis, oral thesis defense; for doctorate, thesis/dissertation, oral dissertation defense. *Entrance requirements:* For master's and doctorate, GRE General Test. Additional exam requirements/recommendations for international students: Required—TOEFL (minimum score 550 paper-based; 213 computer-based; 80 iBT). Electronic applications accepted. *Faculty research:* Geographical information systems, hydrology, low temperature geochemistry, volcanology, paleoclimatology.

University of Redlands, College of Arts and Sciences, Program in Geographic Information Systems, Redlands, CA 92373-0999. Offers MS. *Entrance requirements:* For master's, 2 years of professional experience using GIS or 2 university-level GIS courses plus internship, minimum undergraduate GPA of 3.0, 2 letters of recommendation. Additional exam requirements/recommendations for international students: Required—TOEFL (minimum score 550 paper-based; 210 computer-based); Recommended—IELTS (minimum score 5.5). Electronic applications accepted. *Expenses:* Contact institution.

University of Southern California, Graduate School, College of Letters, Arts and Sciences, Department of Geography, Los Angeles, CA 90089. Offers geographic information science and technology (Graduate Certificate); geography (MA, MS, PhD). Part-time and evening/weekend programs available. Postbaccalaureate distance learning degree programs offered (no on-campus study). Terminal master's awarded for partial completion of doctoral program. *Degree requirements:* For master's, thesis; for doctorate, thesis/dissertation. *Entrance requirements:* For master's and doctorate, GRE General Test. *Faculty research:* Landscape dynamics, geomorphology, geographic information science, urban geography and nature-society relations, GIS.

The University of Texas at Dallas, School of Economic, Political and Policy Sciences, Program in Geospatial Sciences, Richardson, TX 75083-0688. Offers MS, PhD. Part-time and evening/weekend programs available. *Faculty:* 6 full-time (1 woman), 3 part-time/adjunct (0 women). *Students:* 21 full-time (7 women), 36 part-time (14 women); includes 7 minority (3 African Americans, 2 Asian Americans or Pacific Islanders, 2 Hispanic Americans), 24 international. Average age 34. 44 applicants, 84% accepted, 17 enrolled. In 2008, 16 master's awarded. *Degree requirements:* For master's, internship; for doctorate, thesis/dissertation. *Entrance requirements:* For master's and doctorate, GRE General Test, minimum GPA of 3.0 in upper-level coursework in field. Additional exam requirements/recommendations for international students: Required—TOEFL (minimum score 550 paper-based; 213 computer-based). *Application deadline:* For fall admission, 7/15 for domestic students, 5/1 priority date for international students; for spring admission, 11/15 for domestic students, 9/1 priority date for international students. Applications are processed on a rolling basis. Application fee: $50 ($100 for international students). Electronic applications accepted. *Expenses:* Tuition, area resident: Full-time $8320. Tuition, state resident: full-time $8320. Tuition, nonresident: full-time $15,054. Part-time tuition and fees vary according to course load. *Financial support:* In 2008–09, 7 teaching assistantships with tuition reimbursements (averaging $11,710 per year) were awarded; fellowships, research assistantships with tuition reimbursements, career-related internships or fieldwork, Federal Work-Study, institutionally sponsored loans, scholarships/grants, and unspecified assistantships also available. Support available to part-time students. Financial award application deadline: 4/30; financial award applicants required to submit FAFSA. *Faculty research:* Neighborhood evaluation using geographical information systems. *Unit head:* Dr. Denis Dean, Program Head, 972-883-6852, Fax: 972-883-2735, E-mail: djd081000@utdallas.edu. *Application contact:* Dr. Daniel A. Griffith, Associate Program Head, 972-883-4950, Fax: 972-883-2735, E-mail: dagriffith@utdallas.edu.

See Close-Up on page 783.

The University of Toledo, College of Graduate Studies, College of Arts and Sciences, Department of Geography and Planning, Toledo, OH 43606-3390. Offers geographic information systems and applied geographics (Certificate); geography (MA); planning (MA). Part-time programs available. *Degree requirements:* For master's, thesis. *Entrance requirements:* For master's, GRE General Test. Electronic applications accepted.

University of West Georgia, Graduate School, College of Arts and Sciences, Department of Geosciences, Program in Geographic Information Systems, Carrollton, GA 30118. Offers Certificate. *Students:* 1 full-time (0 women), 2 part-time (0 women). Average age 32. Application fee: $30. *Expenses:* Tuition, state resident: full-time $2844; part-time $158 per semester hour. Tuition, nonresident: full-time $11,340; part-time $630 per semester hour. Required fees: $1120; $41.56 per semester hour. $186 per semester. Tuition and fees vary according to course load. *Unit head:* Dr. Curtis L. Hollabaugh, Chair, 678-839-6479, Fax: 678-839-5009, E-mail: chollaba@westga.edu. *Application contact:* Dr. Charles W. Clark, Interim Dean, 678-839-6508, E-mail: cclark@westga.edu.

University of Wisconsin–Madison, Graduate School, College of Letters and Science, Department of Geography, Madison, WI 53706-1380. Offers cartography and geographic information systems (MS); geographic information systems (Certificate); geography (MS, PhD). Part-time programs available. *Degree requirements:* For master's, thesis; for doctorate, thesis/dissertation; for Certificate, internship. *Entrance requirements:* For master's and doctorate, GRE General Test, minimum GPA of 3.25. Electronic applications accepted. *Faculty research:* Physical geography, urban/historical geography, people-environment, history of cartography, GIS.

University of Wisconsin–Milwaukee, Graduate School, School of Architecture and Urban Planning, Department of Urban Planning, Milwaukee, WI 53201-0413. Offers geographic information systems (Certificate); urban planning (MUP); M Arch/MUP; MPA/MUP; MUP/MS. *Accreditation:* ACSP. Part-time programs available. *Faculty:* 5 full-time (2 women). *Students:* 29 full-time (11 women), 5 part-time (3 women), 2 international. Average age 27. 59 applicants, 66% accepted, 16 enrolled. In 2008, 17 master's awarded. *Degree requirements:* For master's, comprehensive exam, thesis or alternative. *Entrance requirements:* For master's, GRE General Test. Additional exam requirements/recommendations for international students: Required—TOEFL (minimum score 550 paper-based; 213 computer-based; 79 iBT), IELTS (minimum score 6.5). *Application deadline:* For fall admission, 1/1 priority date for domestic students; for spring admission, 9/1 for domestic students. Applications are processed on a rolling basis. Application fee: $45 ($75 for international students). *Expenses:* Tuition, area resident: Full-time $7320; part-time $165 per credit. Tuition, state resident: full-time $7320; part-time $165 per credit. Tuition, nonresident: full-time $17,840; part-time $714 per credit. Tuition and fees vary according to campus/location, program and reciprocity agreements. *Financial support:* In 2008–09, 3 teaching assistantships were awarded; career-related internships or fieldwork and unspecified assistantships also available. Support available to part-time students. Financial award application deadline: 4/15. Total annual research expenditures: $157,104. *Unit head:* Joan Simuncak, Representative, 414-229-4015, Fax: 414-229-6976, E-mail: joanarch@uwm.edu. *Application contact:* General Information Contact, 414-229-4982, Fax: 414-229-6967, E-mail: gradschool@uwm.edu.

Virginia Commonwealth University, Graduate School, College of Humanities and Sciences, Wilder School of Government and Public Affairs, Department of Urban Studies and Planning, Program in Geographic Information Systems, Richmond, VA 23284-9005. Offers Certificate.

West Chester University of Pennsylvania, Office of Graduate Studies, College of Business and Public Affairs, Department of Geography and Planning, West Chester, PA 19383. Offers geographic technology (Certificate); geography (MA); regional planning (MSA). Part-time and evening/weekend programs available. *Students:* 12 full-time (1 woman), 16 part-time (4 women); includes 5 minority (4 African Americans, 1 Hispanic American). Average age 33. 15 applicants, 100% accepted, 9 enrolled. In 2008, 7 master's, 10 other advanced degrees awarded. *Degree requirements:* For master's, comprehensive exam, thesis optional. *Entrance requirements:* For master's, GRE, GMAT, or MAT, minimum GPA of 2.8, resumé, two letters of recommendation; for Certificate, minimum GPA of 2.8, resumé, three letters of recommendation. Additional exam requirements/recommendations for international students: Required—TOEFL (minimum score 550 paper-based; 213 computer-based; 80 iBT). *Application deadline:* For fall admission, 4/15 priority date for domestic students, 3/15 for international students; for spring admission, 10/15 for domestic students, 9/1 for international students. Applications are processed on a rolling basis. Application fee: $35. Electronic applications accepted. *Expenses:* Tuition, state resident: full-time $6430; part-time $357 per credit. Tuition, nonresident: full-time $10,288; part-time $572 per credit. Required fees: $652.50; $50 per credit. $67 per semester. *Financial support:* In 2008–09, 3 research assistantships with full and partial tuition reimbursements (averaging $5,000 per year) were awarded; unspecified assistantships also available. Support available to part-time students. Financial award application deadline: 2/15; financial award applicants required to submit FAFSA. *Faculty research:* Environmental education, land use/suburban planning, landscapes of Catalunya. *Unit head:* Dr. Joan Welch, Chair and Graduate Coordinator, 610-436-2940, E-mail: jwelch@wcupa.edu. *Application contact:* Rabbi Dottie Ives Dewey, MSA Graduate Coordinator, 610-436-2746, E-mail: divesdewey@wcupa.edu.

Western Illinois University, School of Graduate Studies, College of Arts and Sciences, Department of Biological Sciences, Macomb, IL 61455-1390. Offers biological sciences (MS); environmental geographic information systems (Certificate); zoo and aquarium studies (Certificate). Part-time programs available. *Students:* 58 full-time (33 women), 25 part-time (16 women); includes 5 minority (4 African Americans, 1 Hispanic American), 7 international. Average age 26. 48 applicants, 58% accepted. In 2008, 13 master's, 11 other advanced degrees awarded. *Degree requirements:* For master's, thesis or alternative. *Entrance requirements:* Additional exam requirements/recommendations for international students: Required—TOEFL (minimum score 550 paper-based; 213 computer-based; 80 iBT). *Application deadline:* Applications are processed on a rolling basis. Application fee: $30. Electronic applications accepted. *Expenses:* Tuition, state resident: full-time $5696; part-time $237.34 per credit hour. Tuition, nonresident: full-time $11,392; part-time $474.68 per credit hour. Required fees: $1453; $60.55 per credit hour. *Financial support:* In 2008–09, 25 students received support, including 11 research assistantships with full tuition reimbursements available (averaging $7,040 per year), 14 teaching assistantships with full tuition reimbursements available (averaging $8,120 per year). Financial award applicants required to submit FAFSA. *Unit head:* Dr. Richard V. Anderson, Chairperson, 309-298-2408. *Application contact:* Evelyn Hoing, Assistant Director of Graduate Studies, 309-298-1806, Fax: 309-298-2345, E-mail: grad-office@wiu.edu.

West Virginia University, Eberly College of Arts and Sciences, Department of Geology and Geography, Program in Geography, Morgantown, WV 26506. Offers energy and environmental resources (MA); geographic information systems (PhD); geography-regional development (PhD); GIS/cartographic analysis (MA); regional development (MA). Part-time programs available. *Degree requirements:* For master's, thesis, oral and written exams; for doctorate, comprehensive exam, thesis/dissertation, oral and written exams. *Entrance requirements:* For master's and doctorate, GRE General Test, minimum GPA of 3.0. Additional exam requirements/recommendations for international students: Required—TOEFL. Electronic applications accepted. *Faculty research:* Space, place and development, geographic information science, environmental geography.

Geography

Appalachian State University, Cratis D. Williams Graduate School, Department of Geography and Planning, Boone, NC 28608. Offers geography (MA), including GIS, planning. Part-time programs available. Postbaccalaureate distance learning degree programs offered (no on-campus study). *Faculty:* 12 full-time (2 women), 3 part-time/adjunct (1 woman). *Students:* 23 full-time (3 women), 15 part-time (6 women). 38 applicants, 84% accepted, 25 enrolled. In 2008, 6 master's awarded. *Degree requirements:* For master's, comprehensive exam, thesis or alternative. *Entrance requirements:* For master's, GRE General Test, 3 letters of recommendation. Additional exam requirements/recommendations for international students: Required—TOEFL (minimum score 570 paper-based; 230 computer-based; 79 iBT), IELTS (minimum score 6.5). *Application deadline:* For fall admission, 7/1 for domestic students, 2/1 for international students; for spring admission, 11/1 for domestic students, 7/1 for international students. Applications are processed on a rolling basis. Application fee: $50. Electronic applications accepted. *Expenses:* Tuition, area resident: Full-time $2600; part-time $700 per course. Tuition, state resident: full-time $2600; part-time $700 per course. Tuition, nonresident: full-time $5000; part-time $3300 per course. Required fees: $2150; $330 per course. Tuition and fees vary according to campus/location. *Financial support:* In 2008–09, 10 research assistantships (averaging $7,500 per year) were awarded; fellowships, teaching assistantships, career-related internships or fieldwork, Federal Work-Study, scholarships/grants, and unspecified assistantships also available. Financial award application deadline: 4/1; financial award applicants required to submit FAFSA. *Faculty research:* Global change, climatology, production cartography, geographic information systems, North Carolina geography, Latin America. Total annual research expenditures: $250,000. *Unit head:* Dr. James Young, Chairperson, 828-262-3000, Fax: 828-262-3067. *Application contact:* Dr. Kathleen Schroeder, Graduate Program Director, 828-262-3000.

Arizona State University, Graduate College, College of Liberal Arts and Sciences, Division of Social Sciences, School of Geographical Sciences, Tempe, AZ 85287. Offers geographic education (MAS); geographic information systems (MAS); geography (MA, PhD). *Degree requirements:* For master's, thesis; for doctorate, thesis/dissertation. *Entrance requirements:* For master's and doctorate, GRE.

Auburn University, Graduate School, College of Sciences and Mathematics, Department of Geology and Geography, Auburn University, AL 36849. Offers geography (MS); geology (MS). Part-time programs available. *Faculty:* 14 full-time (2 women), 2 part-time/adjunct (0 women). *Students:* 13 full-time (3 women), 7 part-time (3 women), 4 international. Average age 28. 17 applicants, 59% accepted, 7 enrolled. In 2008, 12 master's awarded. *Degree requirements:* For master's, computer language or geographic information systems, field camp. *Entrance requirements:* For master's, GRE General Test. *Application deadline:* For fall admission, 7/7 for domestic students; for spring admission, 11/24 for domestic students. Applications are processed on a rolling basis. Application fee: $25 ($50 for international students). Electronic applications accepted. *Expenses:* Tuition, area resident: Full-time $5880; part-time $243 per credit hour. Tuition, state resident: full-time $5880; part-time $243 per credit hour. Tuition, nonresident: full-time $17,640; part-time $729 per credit hour. International tuition: $17,846 full-time. Required fees: $620. Tuition and fees vary according to program and reciprocity agreements. *Financial support:* Research assistantships, teaching assistantships, Federal Work-Study available. Support available to part-time students. Financial award application deadline: 3/15. *Faculty research:* Empirical magma dynamics and melt migration, ore mineralogy, role of terrestrial plant biomass in deposition, metamorphic petrology and isotope geochemistry, reef development, crinoid topology. *Unit head:* Dr. Charles E. Savrda, Chair, 334-844-4282. *Application contact:* Dr. George Flowers, Dean of the Graduate School, 334-844-2125.

Boston University, Graduate School of Arts and Sciences, Department of Geography and Environment, Boston, MA 02215. Offers energy and environmental analysis (MA); environmental remote sensing and GIs (MA); geography (MA); geography and environment (PhD); international relations and environmental policy (MA). Terminal master's awarded for partial completion of doctoral program. *Degree requirements:* For master's, one foreign language, comprehensive exam, thesis; for doctorate, one foreign language, comprehensive exam, thesis/dissertation. *Entrance requirements:* For master's and doctorate, GRE General Test, GRE Subject Test, 3 letters of recommendation. Additional exam requirements/recommendations for international students: Required—TOEFL (minimum score 600 paper-based; 250 computer-based).

Brigham Young University, Graduate Studies, College of Family, Home, and Social Sciences, Department of Geography, Provo, UT 84602-1001. Offers MS. *Faculty:* 9 full-time (0 women), 1 part-time/adjunct (0 women). *Students:* 4 full-time (1 woman). Average age 26. In 2008, 4 master's awarded. *Expenses:* Tuition: Full-time $5160; part-time $287 per credit hour. Tuition and fees vary according to program and student's religious affiliation. *Financial support:* In 2008–09, 3 students received support. . *Faculty research:* Global studies, physical environment, urban planning, travel and tourism, geospatial intelligence, geographic information systems. *Unit head:* Dr. J. Matthew Shumway, Chair, 801-422-2707, Fax: 801-422-0266, E-mail: jms7@byu.edu. *Application contact:* Adviser, 801-422-4541, Fax: 801-378-5238, E-mail: gradstudies@byu.edu.

Brock University, Faculty of Graduate Studies, Faculty of Social Sciences, Program in Geography, St. Catharines, ON L2S 3A1, Canada. Offers MA. Part-time programs available. *Degree requirements:* For master's, thesis optional. *Entrance requirements:* For master's, honors degree. Additional exam requirements/recommendations for international students: Required—TOEFL (minimum score 550 paper-based; 213 computer-based; 80 iBT), IELTS (minimum score 6.5), TWE (minimum score 4).

California State University, Chico, Graduate School, College of Behavioral and Social Sciences, Department of Geography and Planning, Program in Geography, Chico, CA 95929-0425. Offers MA. Part-time programs available. *Entrance requirements:* For master's, GRE General Test, 2 letters of recommendation, statement of purpose, writing sample. Additional exam requirements/recommendations for international students: Required—TOEFL (minimum score 550 paper-based; 213 computer-based; 80 iBT), IELTS (minimum score 6.5). Electronic applications accepted.

California State University, East Bay, Academic Programs and Graduate Studies, College of Letters, Arts, and Social Sciences, Department of Geography and Environmental Studies, Hayward, CA 94542-3000. Offers geography (MA). Part-time programs available. *Degree requirements:* For master's, variable foreign language requirement, project or thesis. *Entrance requirements:* For master's, GRE, minimum GPA of 3.0 in field. Additional exam requirements/recommendations for international students: Required—TOEFL (minimum score 550 paper-based; 213 computer-based). Electronic applications accepted.

California State University, Fullerton, Graduate Studies, College of Humanities and Social Sciences, Department of Geography, Fullerton, CA 92834-9480. Offers MA. *Students:* 11 full-time (4 women), 17 part-time (8 women); includes 8 minority (6 Asian Americans or Pacific Islanders, 2 Hispanic Americans), 2 international. Average age 28. 23 applicants, 74% accepted, 14 enrolled. In 2008, 7 master's awarded. *Degree requirements:* For master's, comprehensive exam or thesis. *Entrance requirements:* For master's, minimum GPA of 3.0, 18 undergraduate credits in field. Application fee: $55. Tuition and fees vary according to degree level. *Financial support:* Teaching assistantships, career-related internships or fieldwork, Federal Work-Study, institutionally sponsored loans, and scholarships/grants available. Support available to part-time students. Financial award application deadline: 3/1. *Faculty research:* Human geography, physical geography. *Unit head:* Dr. John Carroll, Chair, 657-278-3161. *Application contact:* Admissions/Applications, 657-278-2300.

California State University, Long Beach, Graduate Studies, College of Liberal Arts, Department of Geography, Long Beach, CA 90840. Offers MA. Part-time programs available. *Faculty:* 8 full-time (4 women), 1 part-time/adjunct (0 women). *Students:* 14 full-time (6 women), 28 part-time (12 women); includes 6 minority (1 African American, 2 Asian Americans or Pacific Islanders, 3 Hispanic Americans), 3 international. Average age 33. 32 applicants, 63% accepted, 16 enrolled. *Degree requirements:* For master's, thesis. *Application deadline:* For fall admission, 4/15 for domestic students; for spring admission, 10/15 for domestic students. Applications are processed on a rolling basis. Application fee: $55. Electronic applications accepted. *Expenses:* Tuition, nonresident: full-time $11,160; part-time $372 per unit. Required fees: $4100; $1261 per semester. *Financial support:* Career-related internships or fieldwork, Federal Work-Study, institutionally sponsored loans, and scholarships/grants available. Financial award application deadline: 3/2. *Faculty research:* Demography, geographic information systems, world landforms and societies. *Unit head:* Dr. Vicent DelCasino, Chair, 562-985-4977, Fax: 562-985-8993, E-mail: vdelcasi@csulb.edu. *Application contact:* Dr. Christopher T Lee, Graduate Advisor, 562-985-2358, Fax: 562-985-8993, E-mail: clee@csulb.edu.

California State University, Los Angeles, Graduate Studies, College of Natural and Social Sciences, Department of Geography and Urban Analysis, Los Angeles, CA 90032-8530. Offers geography (MA). Part-time and evening/weekend programs available. *Faculty:* 2 full-time (1 woman), 3 part-time/adjunct (0 women). *Students:* 7 full-time (3 women), 29 part-time (12 women); includes 16 minority (5 Asian Americans or Pacific Islanders, 11 Hispanic Americans), 7 international. Average age 32. 9 applicants, 89% accepted, 5 enrolled. In 2008, 2 master's awarded. *Degree requirements:* For master's, one foreign language, comprehensive exam or thesis. *Entrance requirements:* Additional exam requirements/recommendations for international students: Required—TOEFL (minimum score 500 paper-based; 173 computer-based). *Application deadline:* For fall admission, 6/15 for domestic students, 5/1 for international students; for winter admission, 11/1 for domestic students, 9/1 for international students; for spring admission, 2/1 for domestic students, 10/1 for international students. Applications are processed on a rolling basis. Application fee: $55. Electronic applications accepted. *Expenses:* Tuition, nonresident: part-time $226 per credit. Required fees: $4019. *Financial support:* Career-related internships or fieldwork and Federal Work-Study available. Support available to part-time students. Financial award application deadline: 3/1. *Faculty research:* Technique focus–air photography, cartography, locational analysis. *Unit head:* Dr. Killian Ying, Chair, 323-343-2220, Fax: 323-343-6494, E-mail: kying@calstatela.edu. *Application contact:* Dr. Jose L. Galvan, Dean of Graduate Studies, 323-343-3820, Fax: 323-343-5653, E-mail: jgalvan@cslanet.calstatela.edu.

Geography

California State University, Northridge, Graduate Studies, College of Social and Behavioral Sciences, Department of Geography, Northridge, CA 91330. Offers MA. Part-time programs available. *Faculty:* 14 full-time (4 women), 17 part-time/adjunct (7 women). *Students:* 17 full-time (7 women), 21 part-time (12 women); includes 1 African American, 3 Asian Americans or Pacific Islanders, 6 Hispanic Americans, 1 international. Average age 36. 39 applicants, 46% accepted, 11 enrolled. In 2008, 8 master's awarded. *Degree requirements:* For master's, one foreign language, thesis. *Entrance requirements:* For master's, GRE General Test or minimum GPA of 3.0. Additional exam requirements/recommendations for international students: Required—TOEFL. *Application deadline:* For fall admission, 11/30 for domestic students. Application fee: $55. *Financial support:* Teaching assistantships available. Financial award application deadline: 3/1. *Unit head:* Darrick Danta, Chair, 818-677-3532. *Application contact:* Dr. Edward Jackiewicz, Graduate Advisor, 818-677-4565.

Carleton University, Faculty of Graduate Studies, Faculty of Arts and Social Sciences, Department of Geography and Environmental Studies, Ottawa, ON K1S 5B6, Canada. Offers geography (M Sc, MA, PhD). *Degree requirements:* For master's, thesis, seminar; for doctorate, one foreign language, thesis/dissertation, 2 comprehensive exams. *Entrance requirements:* For master's, honors degree; for doctorate, master's degree in geography. Additional exam requirements/recommendations for international students: Required—TOEFL. *Faculty research:* Human dimensions of global environmental change, winter environments, population studies, historical geography, globalization.

Central Connecticut State University, School of Graduate Studies, School of Arts and Sciences, Department of Geography, New Britain, CT 06050-4010. Offers MS. Part-time and evening/weekend programs available. *Faculty:* 10 full-time (2 women), 8 part-time/adjunct (1 woman). *Students:* 5 full-time (2 women), 11 part-time (5 women); includes 2 minority (1 Asian American or Pacific Islander, 1 Hispanic American). Average age 30. 20 applicants, 75% accepted, 8 enrolled. In 2008, 8 master's awarded. *Degree requirements:* For master's, comprehensive exam, thesis or alternative. *Entrance requirements:* For master's, minimum undergraduate GPA of 2.7. Additional exam requirements/recommendations for international students: Required—TOEFL. *Application deadline:* For fall admission, 7/1 for domestic students; for spring admission, 12/1 for domestic students. Applications are processed on a rolling basis. Application fee: $50. Electronic applications accepted. *Expenses:* Tuition, area resident: Full-time $4377; part-time $420 per credit. Tuition, state resident: full-time $6566; part-time $420 per credit. Tuition, nonresident: full-time $12,195; part-time $420 per credit. Required fees: $3462. One-time fee: $62 part-time. *Financial support:* In 2008–09, 2 students received support, including 1 research assistantship; career-related internships or fieldwork, Federal Work-Study, scholarships/grants, and unspecified assistantships also available. Support available to part-time students. Financial award application deadline: 3/1; financial award applicants required to submit FAFSA. *Faculty research:* Regional planning, environmental protection, tourism, computer mapping and geographic information systems. *Unit head:* Dr. Xiaoping Shen, Chair, 860-832-2785. *Application contact:* Dr. Xiaoping Shen, Chair, 860-832-2785.

Chicago State University, School of Graduate and Professional Studies, College of Arts and Sciences, Department of Geography, Sociology, Economics, and Anthropology, Chicago, IL 60628. Offers geography and economic development (MA). *Entrance requirements:* For master's, minimum GPA of 2.75.

Clark University, Graduate School, Department of Geography, Worcester, MA 01610-1477. Offers geographic information science (MA); geography (PhD). *Faculty:* 16 full-time (5 women), 1 part-time/adjunct (0 women). *Students:* 61 full-time (29 women), 2 part-time (0 women); includes 1 minority (Asian American or Pacific Islander), 28 international. Average age 31. 109 applicants, 27% accepted, 15 enrolled. In 2008, 4 master's, 11 doctorates awarded. *Degree requirements:* For doctorate, thesis/dissertation. *Entrance requirements:* For doctorate, GRE General Test. Additional exam requirements/recommendations for international students: Required—TOEFL. *Application deadline:* For fall admission, 12/31 priority date for domestic students. Applications are processed on a rolling basis. Application fee: $50. *Expenses:* Tuition: Full-time $34,900; part-time $1091 per credit hour. Required fees: $30. *Financial support:* In 2008–09, 5 fellowships with full tuition reimbursements (averaging $15,700 per year), 14 research assistantships with full tuition reimbursements (averaging $15,700 per year), 15 teaching assistantships with full tuition reimbursements (averaging $15,700 per year) were awarded; career-related internships or fieldwork and tuition waivers (full) also available. *Faculty research:* Global environmental change, geographic information systems, natural and technological hazards, water resources, urbanization. Total annual research expenditures: $1.8 million. *Unit head:* Dr. Billie Lee Turner, Director, 508-793-7336. *Application contact:* Christine Silva, Admission Coordinator, 508-793-7337, Fax: 508-793-8881, E-mail: geography@clarku.edu.

Concordia University, School of Graduate Studies, Faculty of Arts and Science, Department of Geography, Planning and Environment, Montréal, QC H3G 1M8, Canada. Offers environmental impact assessment (Diploma); geography, urban and environmental studies (M Sc).

Concordia University, School of Graduate Studies, Faculty of Arts and Science, Department of Political Science, Montréal, QC H3G 1M8, Canada. Offers political science (PhD); public policy and public administration (MA), including geography. *Degree requirements:* For master's, one foreign language, comprehensive exam, thesis optional, internship. *Entrance requirements:* For master's, honors degree or equivalent. Additional exam requirements/recommendations for international students: Required—TOEFL. *Faculty research:* International public policy and administration, Quebec public administration, public policy and social/political theory, geography and public policy, public administration and decision making.

East Carolina University, Graduate School, Thomas Harriot College of Arts and Sciences, Department of Geography, Greenville, NC 27858-4353. Offers MA. Part-time and evening/weekend programs available. *Degree requirements:* For master's, one foreign language, comprehensive exam, thesis optional. *Entrance requirements:* For master's, GRE General Test. Additional exam requirements/recommendations for international students: Required—TOEFL.

Eastern Michigan University, Graduate School, College of Arts and Sciences, Department of Geography and Geology, Program in Geography and Geology, Ypsilanti, MI 48197. Offers geography (MA, MS); water resources (Graduate Certificate). Part-time and evening/weekend programs available. Postbaccalaureate distance learning degree programs offered (minimal on-campus study). *Degree requirements:* For master's, thesis optional. *Entrance requirements:* Additional exam requirements/recommendations for international students: Required—TOEFL.

Florida Atlantic University, Charles E. Schmidt College of Science, Department of Geosciences, Program in Geography, Boca Raton, FL 33431-0991. Offers MA. Part-time programs available. *Students:* 8 full-time (3 women), 8 part-time (2 women); includes 3 minority (1 American Indian/Alaska Native, 2 Hispanic Americans), 1 international. Average age 35. 8 applicants, 38% accepted, 3 enrolled. In 2008, 6 master's awarded. *Degree requirements:* For master's, thesis (for some programs). *Entrance requirements:* For master's, GRE General Test, minimum GPA of 3.0. *Application deadline:* For fall admission, 3/15 priority date for domestic students, 3/15 for international students; for spring admission, 10/15 for domestic and international students. Applications are processed on a rolling basis. Application fee: $30. Electronic applications accepted. *Expenses:* Tuition, state resident: full-time $4867; part-time $270.40 per credit hour. Tuition, nonresident: full-time $16,486; part-time $915.87 per credit hour. *Financial support:* Research assistantships with partial tuition reimbursements, teaching assistantships with partial tuition reimbursements, career-related internships or fieldwork, Federal Work-Study, institutionally sponsored loans, and unspecified assistantships available. Financial award application deadline: 4/15. *Faculty research:* Remote sensing/digital images, location-allocation modeling, analysis of less-developed countries, historical settlement patterns, urban form. *Unit head:* Dr. Russell Ivy, Chair, 561-297-3295, Fax: 561-297-2745, E-mail: ivy@fau.edu. *Application contact:* Dr. David Warburton, Graduate Coordinator, 561-297-3312, Fax: 561-297-2745, E-mail: warburto@fau.edu.

Florida State University, Graduate Studies, College of Social Sciences, Department of Geography, Tallahassee, FL 32306. Offers geographic information systems (MS); geography (MA, MS, PhD). Part-time programs available. Terminal master's awarded for partial completion of doctoral program. *Degree requirements:* For master's, thesis (for some programs); for doctorate, thesis/dissertation. *Entrance requirements:* For master's and doctorate, GRE General Test, minimum GPA of 3.0. Additional exam requirements/recommendations for international students: Required—TOEFL. Electronic applications accepted. *Faculty research:* Society-nature interaction, geographic information science.

Fort Hays State University, Graduate School, College of Arts and Sciences, Department of Geosciences, Program in Geosciences, Hays, KS 67601-4099. Offers geography (MS); geology (MS). *Degree requirements:* For master's, comprehensive exam, thesis. *Entrance requirements:* For master's, GRE General Test. Additional exam requirements/recommendations for international students: Required—TOEFL (minimum score 550 paper-based; 213 computer-based). Electronic applications accepted. *Faculty research:* Cretaceous and late Cenozoic stratigraphy, sedimentation, paleontology.

George Mason University, College of Science, Department of Geography, Fairfax, VA 22030. Offers geographic and cartographic sciences (MS). *Degree requirements:* For master's, thesis optional. *Entrance requirements:* For master's, GRE General Test, minimum GPA of 3.0 in last 60 hours; BS or BA in geography, cartography, or related field. Electronic applications accepted.

The George Washington University, Columbian College of Arts and Sciences, Department of Geography, Washington, DC 20052. Offers MA. *Faculty:* 7 full-time (3 women), 13 part-time/adjunct (5 women). *Students:* 10 full-time (2 women), 8 part-time (4 women); includes 2 minority (1 African American, 1 Hispanic American), 1 international. Average age 25. 18 applicants, 89% accepted, 6 enrolled. In 2008, 6 master's awarded. *Degree requirements:* For master's, comprehensive exam, thesis or alternative. *Entrance requirements:* For master's, GRE General Test, BA in geography or related field, minimum GPA of 3.0. Additional exam requirements/recommendations for international students: Required—TOEFL (minimum score 550 paper-based; 213 computer-based; 80 iBT). *Application deadline:* For fall admission, 4/1 priority date for domestic students, 1/15 priority date for international students; for spring admission, 10/1 priority date for domestic students, 9/1 priority date for international students. Applications are processed on a rolling basis. Application fee: $60. Electronic applications accepted. *Financial support:* In 2008–09, 10 students received support; fellowships with tuition reimbursements available, teaching assistantships with tuition reimbursements available, Federal Work-Study, institutionally sponsored loans, and tuition waivers available. Financial award application deadline: 1/15. *Unit head:* Dr. Marie Price, Chair, 202-994-6187. *Application contact:* Information Contact, 202-994-6185, Fax: 202-994-2484.

Georgia State University, College of Arts and Sciences, Department of Geosciences, Program in Geography, Atlanta, GA 30303-3083. Offers MA. Part-time programs available. *Degree requirements:* For master's, one foreign language, thesis or alternative, written and oral exams. *Entrance requirements:* For master's, GRE General Test. Additional exam requirements/recommendations for international students: Required—TOEFL. Electronic applications accepted. *Faculty research:* Urban economics, biogeography, cartography, GIS, environmental.

Hunter College of the City University of New York, Graduate School, School of Arts and Sciences, Department of Geography, New York, NY 10021-5085. Offers analytical geography (MA); earth system science (MA); environmental and social issues (MA); geographic information science (Certificate); geographic information systems (MA); teaching earth science (MA). Part-time and evening/weekend programs available. *Faculty:* 12 full-time (6 women), 4 part-time/adjunct (2 women). *Students:* 36 part-time (16 women); includes 3 minority (1 Asian American or Pacific Islander, 2 Hispanic Americans). Average age 33. 13 applicants, 69% accepted, 7 enrolled. In 2008, 9 master's awarded. *Degree requirements:* For master's, comprehensive exam or thesis. *Entrance requirements:* For master's, GRE General Test, minimum B average in major, minimum B- average overall, 18 credits of course work in geography, 2 letters of recommendation; for Certificate, minimum of B average in major, B-overall. Additional exam requirements/recommendations for international students: Required—TOEFL. *Application deadline:* For fall admission, 4/1 for domestic students; for spring admission, 11/1 for domestic students. Applications are processed on a rolling basis. Application fee: $125. *Financial support:* In 2008–09, 1 fellowship (averaging $3,000 per year), 2 research assistantships (averaging $10,000 per year), 10 teaching assistantships (averaging $6,000 per year) were awarded; career-related internships or fieldwork, Federal Work-Study, institutionally sponsored loans, and unspecified assistantships also available. Financial award application deadline: 3/1. *Faculty research:* Urban geography, economic geography, geographic information science, demographic methods, climate change. *Unit head:* Prof. William Solecki, Chair, 212-772-4536, Fax: 212-772-5268, E-mail: wsolecki@hunter.cuny.edu. *Application contact:* Prof. Marianna Pavlovskaya, Graduate Adviser, 212-772-5320, Fax: 212-772-5268, E-mail: mpavlov@geo.hunter.cuny.edu.

Indiana State University, School of Graduate Studies, College of Arts and Sciences, Department of Geography, Geology and Anthropology, Terre Haute, IN 47809-1401. Offers geography (MA); geology (MS); physical geography (PhD). *Degree requirements:* For master's, thesis or alternative; for doctorate, comprehensive exam, thesis/dissertation, departmental qualifying exam. *Entrance requirements:* For doctorate, GRE General Test. Additional exam requirements/recommendations for international students: Required—TOEFL (minimum score 550 paper-based). Electronic applications accepted.

Indiana University Bloomington, University Graduate School, College of Arts and Sciences, Department of Geography, Bloomington, IN 47405-7000. Offers MA, MAT, MS, PhD, MSES/MA, MSES/MS. *Faculty:* 13 full-time (5 women), 15 part-time/adjunct (1 woman). *Students:* 24 full-time (13 women), 3 part-time (1 woman); includes 1 minority (Hispanic American), 8 international. Average age 30. 32 applicants, 34% accepted, 5 enrolled. In 2008, 5 master's, 5 doctorates awarded. *Degree requirements:* For master's, comprehensive exam, thesis; for doctorate, comprehensive exam, thesis/dissertation. *Entrance requirements:* For master's and doctorate, GRE General Test, minimum GPA of 3.0. Additional exam requirements/recommendations for international students: Required—TOEFL (minimum score 620 paper-based; 260 computer-based; 104 iBT). *Application deadline:* For fall admission, 2/15 priority date for domestic students, 12/15 priority date for international students; for spring admission, 11/15 priority date for domestic students, 11/1 priority date for international students. Application fee: $50 ($60 for international students). Electronic applications accepted. *Expenses:* Tuition, area resident: Part-time $291.97 per credit hour. Tuition, state resident: part-time $291.97 per credit hour. Tuition, nonresident: part-time $850.33 per credit hour. Required fees: $110 per semester. Tuition and fees vary according to course load and program. *Financial support:* In 2008–09, 17 students received support, including 1 fellowship with full tuition reimbursement available (averaging $21,000 per year), 4 research assistantships with full tuition reimbursements available (averaging $16,625 per year), 16 teaching assistantships with full tuition reimbursements available (averaging $12,901 per year); health care benefits also available. Financial award application deadline: 2/15; financial award applicants required to submit FAFSA. *Faculty research:* Synoptic climatology, urban and regional modeling, regional development, hydrology and statistical climatology, migration, atmospheric science, GIS human environment interaction, human geography. Total annual research expenditures: $2 million. *Unit head:* Dr. Scott Robeson, Chair and Professor, 812-855-6303, Fax: 812-855-1661, E-mail: srobeson@indiana.edu. *Application contact:* Susan White, Graduate Secretary, 812-855-6303, Fax: 812-855-1661, E-mail: suswhite@indiana.edu.

Indiana University of Pennsylvania, School of Graduate Studies and Research, College of Humanities and Social Sciences, Department of Geography and Regional Planning, Program in Geography, Indiana, PA 15705-1087. Offers MA, MS. Part-time programs available. *Faculty:* 9 full-time (1 woman). *Students:* 17 full-time (5 women), 3 part-time (1 woman), 2 international. Average age 31. 20 applicants, 35% accepted, 7 enrolled. In 2008, 7 master's awarded. *Degree requirements:* For master's, thesis optional. *Entrance requirements:* For master's, GRE, 2 letters of recommendation. Additional exam requirements/recommendations for international students: Required—TOEFL. *Application deadline:* For fall admission, 7/1 priority date for domestic students; for spring admission, 11/1 for domestic students. Applications are processed on a rolling basis. Application fee: $30. *Expenses:* Tuition, area resident: Full-time $6430; part-time $357 per credit. Tuition, nonresident: full-time $10,288; part-time $572 per credit. Required fees: $1547.50; $107 per credit. $283 per year. *Financial support:* In 2008–09, 12 research assistantships with full and partial tuition reimbursements (averaging $4,703 per year) were awarded; Federal Work-Study also available. Support available to part-time students. Financial award application deadline: 3/15; financial award applicants required to submit FAFSA. *Unit head:* Dr. Kevin Patrick, E-mail: Kevin.Patrick@iup.edu. *Application contact:* Dr. John E. Benhart, Jr., Chairperson, 724-357-2250, E-mail: jbenhart@iup.edu.

The Johns Hopkins University, G. W. C. Whiting School of Engineering, Department of Geography and Environmental Engineering, Baltimore, MD 21218-2699. Offers MA, MS, MSE, PhD. Terminal master's awarded for partial completion of doctoral program. *Degree requirements:* For master's, thesis (for some programs), 1 year full-time residency; for doctorate, comprehensive exam, thesis/dissertation, oral exam, 2 year full-time residency. *Entrance requirements:* For master's and doctorate, GRE General Test. Additional exam requirements/recommendations for international students: Required—TOEFL (minimum score 670 paper-based; 300 computer-based; 120 iBT); Recommended—IELTS. Electronic applications accepted. *Faculty research:* Environmental engineering; environmental chemistry; water resources engineering; systems analysis and economics for public decision making; geomorphology, hydrology and ecology.

Kansas State University, Graduate School, College of Arts and Sciences, Department of Geography, Manhattan, KS 66506. Offers MA, PhD. *Faculty:* 13 full-time (5 women). *Students:* 9 full-time (2 women), 7 part-time (2 women), 2 international. Average age 28. 32 applicants, 56% accepted, 10 enrolled. In 2008, 3 master's, 1 doctorate awarded. *Degree requirements:* For master's, thesis optional, oral exam; for doctorate, one foreign language, thesis/dissertation. *Entrance requirements:* For master's and doctorate, GRE General Test, minimum GPA of 3.0. *Application deadline:* For fall admission, 2/15 priority date for domestic students, 2/1 priority date for international students; for spring admission, 11/15 priority date for domestic students, 8/1 priority date for international students. Applications are processed on a rolling basis. Application fee: $30 ($55 for international students). Electronic applications accepted. *Expenses:* Tuition, area resident: Full-time $6466; part-time $269.40 per credit hour. Tuition, state resident: full-time $6466; part-time $269.40 per credit hour. Tuition, nonresident: full-time $14,874; part-time $619.75 per credit hour. Required fees: $673; $23.40 per credit hour. Tuition and fees vary according to campus/location. *Financial support:* In 2008–09, 5 research assistantships (averaging $15,342 per year), 18 teaching assistantships with full tuition reimbursements (averaging $13,166 per year) were awarded; Federal Work-Study, institutionally sponsored loans, and scholarships/grants also available. Support available to part-time students. Financial award application deadline: 3/1; financial award applicants required to submit FAFSA. *Faculty research:* Human environment interaction, health and population, culture and landscape, physical geography, geospatial analysis and applications. Total annual research expenditures: $232,379. *Unit head:* Richard Marston, Head, 785-532-5412, Fax: 785-532-7310, E-mail: rmarston@ksu.edu. *Application contact:* Kevin Blake, Director, 785-532-3406, Fax: 785-532-7310, E-mail: kblake@ksu.edu.

Kent State University, College of Arts and Sciences, Department of Geography, Kent, OH 44242-0001. Offers MA, PhD. Part-time programs available. *Degree requirements:* For master's, thesis optional; for doctorate, comprehensive exam, thesis/dissertation. *Entrance requirements:* For master's and doctorate, GRE, minimum GPA of 3.0. Additional exam requirements/recommendations for international students: Required—TOEFL. Electronic applications accepted.

Louisiana State University and Agricultural and Mechanical College, Graduate School, College of Arts and Sciences, Department of Geography and Anthropology, Baton Rouge, LA 70803. Offers anthropology (MA); geography (MA, MS, PhD). Part-time programs available. Terminal master's awarded for partial completion of doctoral program. *Degree requirements:* For master's, 2 foreign languages, thesis (for some programs); for doctorate, 2 foreign languages, thesis/dissertation. *Entrance requirements:* For master's and doctorate, GRE General Test, minimum GPA of 3.0. Additional exam requirements/recommendations for international students: Required—TOEFL (minimum score 550 paper-based; 213 computer-based; 79 iBT). Electronic applications accepted. *Faculty research:* Cultural, coastal, climate, GIS-geography, cultural, linguistics, archaeology-anthropology.

Marshall University, Academic Affairs Division, College of Liberal Arts, Department of Geography, Huntington, WV 25755. Offers MA, MS. *Degree requirements:* For master's, thesis optional.

McGill University, Faculty of Graduate and Postdoctoral Studies, Faculty of Science, Department of Geography, Montréal, QC H3A 2T5, Canada. Offers geography (M Sc, MA, PhD); neo-tropical environment (MA, PhD); social statistics (MA).

McMaster University, School of Graduate Studies, Faculty of Science, School of Geography and Earth Sciences, Hamilton, ON L8S 4M2, Canada. Offers geochemistry (PhD); geology (M Sc, PhD); human geography (MA, PhD); physical geography (M Sc, PhD). Part-time programs available. Terminal master's awarded for partial completion of doctoral program. *Degree requirements:* For master's, thesis; for doctorate, comprehensive exam, thesis/dissertation. *Entrance requirements:* For master's, minimum B+ average. Additional exam requirements/recommendations for international students: Required—TOEFL (minimum score 550 paper-based; 213 computer-based).

Memorial University of Newfoundland, School of Graduate Studies, Department of Geography, St. John's, NL A1C 5S7, Canada. Offers M Sc, MA, PhD. *Degree requirements:* For master's, thesis; for doctorate, comprehensive exam, thesis/dissertation, seminar, oral defense of thesis. *Entrance requirements:* For master's, 2nd class degree; for doctorate, master's degree. Electronic applications accepted. *Faculty research:* Cultural/historical geography, physical geography, economic geography, cartography, geographical information systems.

Miami University, Graduate School, College of Arts and Sciences, Department of Geography, Oxford, OH 45056. Offers MA. Part-time programs available. *Degree requirements:* For master's, thesis (for some programs), final exam. *Entrance requirements:* For master's, minimum undergraduate GPA of 3.0 during previous 2 years or 2.75 overall. Additional exam requirements/recommendations for international students: Required—TOEFL (minimum score 550 paper-based; 213 computer-based), TWE (minimum score 4). Electronic applications accepted.

Michigan State University, The Graduate School, College of Social Science, Department of Geography, East Lansing, MI 48824. Offers geographic information science (MS); geography (MA, PhD). *Degree requirements:* For master's, comprehensive exam, thesis (for some programs), presentation of poster/paper or oral defense of thesis; for doctorate, comprehensive exam, thesis/dissertation, presentation of poster/paper, presentation and defense of dissertation proposal, oral exam in defense of dissertation . *Entrance requirements:* Additional exam requirements/recommendations for international students: Required—TOEFL (minimum score 600 paper-based; 250 computer-based). Electronic applications accepted.

Minnesota State University Mankato, College of Graduate Studies, College of Social and Behavioral Sciences, Department of Geography, Mankato, MN 56001. Offers geography (MS); geography education (MT). Part-time programs available. *Students:* 5 full-time (2 women), 22 part-time (9 women). *Degree requirements:* For master's, one foreign language, comprehensive exam. *Entrance requirements:* For master's, GRE General Test (if GPA is below 2.8 for the last 2 years), minimum GPA of 3.0 during previous 2 years. *Application deadline:* For fall admission, 7/1 priority date for domestic students; for spring admission, 11/1 for domestic students. Applications are processed on a rolling basis. Application fee: $40. Electronic applications accepted. *Financial support:* Research assistantships, teaching assistantships with full tuition reimbursements, career-related internships or fieldwork, Federal Work-Study, institutionally sponsored loans, and unspecified assistantships available. Support available to part-time students. Financial award application deadline: 3/15; financial award applicants required to submit FAFSA. *Unit head:* Dr. Donald Friend, Chairperson, 507-389-2617. *Application contact:* 507-389-2321, E-mail: grad@mnsu.edu.

Missouri State University, Graduate College, College of Natural and Applied Sciences, Department of Geography, Geology, and Planning, Springfield, MO 65804-0094. Offers geospatial sciences (MS); natural and applied science (MNAS), including geography, geology and planning; secondary education (MS Ed), including earth science, geography. Part-time and evening/weekend programs available. *Faculty:* 19 full-time (3 women). *Students:* 24 full-time (10 women), 11 part-time (4 women), 7 international. Average age 26. 14 applicants, 100% accepted, 11 enrolled. In 2008, 5 master's awarded. *Degree requirements:* For master's, comprehensive exam, thesis (for some programs). *Entrance requirements:* For master's, GRE General Test (MS, MNAS), minimum undergraduate GPA of 3.0 (MS, MNAS), 9-12 teacher certification (MS Ed). Additional exam requirements/recommendations for international students: Required—TOEFL (minimum score 550 paper-based; 213 computer-based; 79 iBT). *Application deadline:* For fall admission, 7/20 priority date for domestic students, 5/1 for international students; for spring admission, 12/20 priority date for domestic students, 9/1 for international students. Applications are processed on a rolling basis. Application fee: $35 ($50 for international students). Electronic applications accepted. *Expenses:* Tuition, state resident: full-time $3852; part-time $214 per credit hour. Tuition, nonresident: full-time $7524; part-time $418 per credit hour. Required fees: $230 per semester. Tuition and fees vary according to course level and course load. *Financial support:* In 2008–09, 15 research assistantships with full tuition reimbursements (averaging $9,092 per year), 7 teaching assistantships with full tuition reimbursements (averaging $7,340 per year) were awarded; career-related internships or fieldwork, Federal Work-Study, institutionally sponsored loans, scholarships/grants, and unspecified assistantships also available. Financial award application deadline: 3/31; financial award applicants required to submit FAFSA. *Faculty research:* Stratigraphy and ancient meteorite impacts, environmental geochemistry of karst, hyperspectral image processing, water quality, small town planning. *Unit head:* Dr. Tom Plymate, Head, 417-836-5800, Fax: 417-836-6934, E-mail: tomplymate@missouristate.edu. *Application contact:* Eric Eckert, Coordinator of Graduate Admissions and Recruitment, 417-836-5331, Fax: 417-836-6888, E-mail: ericeckert@missouristate.edu.

New Mexico State University, Graduate School, College of Arts and Sciences, Department of Geography, Las Cruces, NM 88003-8001. Offers MAG. Part-time programs available. *Faculty:* 4 full-time (0 women). *Students:* 11 full-time (5 women), 5 part-time (2 women); includes 4 minority (1 African American, 1 American Indian/Alaska Native, 2 Hispanic Americans). Average age 33. 10 applicants, 100% accepted, 7 enrolled. In 2008, 7 master's awarded. *Degree requirements:* For master's, thesis or alternative. *Entrance requirements:* For master's, GRE General Test, previous course work in geography, map use, and physical geography. Additional exam requirements/recommendations for international students: Required—TOEFL. *Application deadline:* For fall admission, 7/1 priority date for domestic students; for spring admission, 11/1 for domestic students. Applications are processed on a rolling basis. Application fee: $30 ($50 for international students). Electronic applications accepted. *Expenses:* Tuition, area resident: Full-time $3890; part-time $212.85 per credit. Tuition, state resident: full-time $3890; part-time $212.85 per credit. Tuition, nonresident: full-time $13,916; part-time $630.55 per credit. Required fees: $1218; $609 per semester. *Financial support:* In 2008–09, 9 students received support, including 2 research assistantships (averaging $11,890 per year), 6 teaching assistantships (averaging $7,900 per year); career-related internships or fieldwork and health care benefits also available. Financial award application deadline: 3/1. *Faculty research:* Landscape ecology, land use, geomorphology, Latin America and the U.S.-Mexico border, geographic information systems. *Unit head:* Dr. John Wright, Head, 575-646-3509, Fax: 575-646-7430, E-mail: jowright@nmsu.edu. *Application contact:* Dr. Daniel Dugas, Assistant Professor, 575-646-3509, Fax: 575-646-7430, E-mail: ddugas@nmsu.edu.

Northeastern Illinois University, Graduate College, College of Arts and Sciences, Department of Geography, Environmental Studies and Economics, Program in Geography and Environmental Studies, Chicago, IL 60625-4699. Offers MA. Part-time and evening/weekend programs available. *Degree requirements:* For master's, comprehensive exam, thesis optional, minimum GPA of 3.0. *Entrance requirements:* For master's, undergraduate minor in geography or environmental studies, minimum GPA of 2.75. Additional exam requirements/recommendations for international students: Required—TOEFL (minimum score 550 paper-based; 213 computer-based; 80 iBT). Electronic applications accepted. *Faculty research:* Segregation and urbanization of minority groups in the Chicago area, scale dependence and parameterization in nonpoint source pollution modeling, ecological land classification and mapping, ecosystem restoration, soil-vegetation relationships.

Northern Arizona University, Graduate College, College of Social and Behavioral Sciences, Department of Geography, Planning, and Recreation, Flagstaff, AZ 86011. Offers applied geographic information science (MS); geographic information systems (Certificate); rural geography (MA). *Degree requirements:* For master's, thesis. *Entrance requirements:* For master's, GRE General Test.

Northern Illinois University, Graduate School, College of Liberal Arts and Sciences, Department of Geography, De Kalb, IL 60115-2854. Offers MS. Part-time programs available. *Degree requirements:* For master's, comprehensive exam, thesis optional, research seminar. *Entrance requirements:* For master's, GRE General Test, minimum GPA of 2.75. Additional exam requirements/recommendations for international students: Required—TOEFL (minimum score 550 paper-based; 213 computer-based). Electronic applications accepted. *Faculty research:* Synoptic meteorology, human impacts on soil properties, plant soil relationships, hydrological cycle, climate variability.

Northwest Missouri State University, Graduate School, College of Arts and Sciences, Department of Geology/Geography, Maryville, MO 64468-6001. Offers geographic information sciences (MS, Certificate). Part-time programs available. *Degree requirements:* For master's, comprehensive exam, thesis. *Entrance requirements:* For master's, GRE General Test, 2 letters of recommendation, writing sample, minimum undergraduate GPA of 2.5.

The Ohio State University, Graduate School, College of Social and Behavioral Sciences, School of Social and Behavioral Science, Department of Geography, Columbus, OH 43210. Offers atmospheric sciences (MS, PhD); geography (MA, PhD). *Degree requirements:* For doctorate, variable foreign language requirement, thesis/dissertation. *Entrance requirements:* Additional exam requirements/recommendations for international students: Recommended—TOEFL (minimum score 600 paper-based; 250 computer-based). Electronic applications accepted.

Ohio University, Graduate College, College of Arts and Sciences, Department of Geography, Athens, OH 45701-2979. Offers MA. Part-time programs available. *Degree requirements:* For master's, thesis. *Entrance requirements:* For master's, GRE General Test, minimum GPA of 3.0. Additional exam requirements/recommendations for international students: Required—TOEFL (minimum score 600 paper-based; 250 computer-based). Electronic applications accepted. *Faculty research:* Environmental geography, cartography and geographic information systems, cultural ecology, area studies, historical geography.

Oklahoma State University, College of Arts and Sciences, Department of Geography, Stillwater, OK 74078. Offers MS, PhD. *Faculty:* 14 full-time (3 women). *Students:* 16 full-time (4 women), 19 part-time (5 women); includes 4 minority (1 American Indian/Alaska Native, 2 Asian Americans or Pacific Islanders, 1 Hispanic American), 12 international. Average age 31. 22 applicants, 36% accepted, 6 enrolled. In 2008, 6 master's, 1 doctorate awarded. *Degree requirements:* For master's, thesis or alternative; for doctorate, comprehensive exam, thesis/dissertation. *Entrance requirements:* For master's and doctorate, GRE. Additional exam requirements/recommendations for international students: Required—TOEFL. *Application deadline:* For fall admission, 3/1 priority date for international students; for spring admission, 8/1 priority date for international students. Applications are processed on a rolling basis. Application fee: $40 ($75 for international students). Electronic applications accepted. *Expenses:* Tuition, state resident:

Geography

Oklahoma State University *(continued)*
full-time $3716.40; part-time $154.85 per credit hour. Tuition, nonresident: full-time $14,448; part-time $602 per credit hour. Required fees: $1772.40; $73.85 per credit hour. One-time fee: $50. Tuition and fees vary according to course load and campus/location. *Financial support:* In 2008–09, 9 research assistantships (averaging $14,586 per year), 17 teaching assistantships (averaging $16,002 per year) were awarded; career-related internships or fieldwork, Federal Work-Study, scholarships/grants, health care benefits, tuition waivers (partial), and unspecified assistantships also available. Support available to part-time students. Financial award application deadline: 3/1; financial award applicants required to submit FAFSA. *Faculty research:* Cultural ecology, resource management, historical/cultural geography, central Asia, geographic information systems. *Unit head:* Dr. Dale R. Lightfoot, Head, 405-744-6250, Fax: 405-744-5620. *Application contact:* Dr. Gordon Emslie, Dean, 405-744-6368, Fax: 405-744-0355, E-mail: grad_i@okstate.edu.

Oregon State University, Graduate School, College of Science, Department of Geosciences, Program in Geography, Corvallis, OR 97331. Offers MA, MAIS, MS, PhD. Part-time programs available. Terminal master's awarded for partial completion of doctoral program. *Degree requirements:* For master's, variable foreign language requirement, thesis optional; for doctorate, one foreign language, thesis/dissertation. *Entrance requirements:* For master's and doctorate, GRE General Test, GRE Subject Test, minimum GPA of 3.0 in last 90 hours. Additional exam requirements/recommendations for international students: Required—TOEFL. *Faculty research:* Resources, physical geography, cartography, remote sensing.

Penn State University Park, Graduate School, College of Earth and Mineral Sciences, Department of Geography, State College, University Park, PA 16802-1503. Offers geography (MS, PhD).

Portland State University, Graduate Studies, College of Liberal Arts and Sciences, Department of Geography, Portland, OR 97207-0751. Offers MA, MAT, MS, MST, PhD. Part-time programs available. *Faculty:* 9 full-time (2 women), 6 part-time/adjunct (1 woman). *Students:* 25 full-time (19 women), 30 part-time (9 women); includes 5 minority (1 African American, 1 American Indian/Alaska Native, 2 Asian Americans or Pacific Islanders, 1 Hispanic American), 1 international. Average age 33. 22 applicants, 82% accepted, 11 enrolled. In 2008, 9 master's awarded. *Degree requirements:* For master's, thesis (for some programs). *Entrance requirements:* For master's, GRE General Test, minimum GPA of 3.0 in upper-division course work or 2.75 overall, 3 letters of recommendation. Additional exam requirements/recommendations for international students: Required—TOEFL (minimum score 550 paper-based; 213 computer-based). *Application deadline:* For fall admission, 4/1 for domestic students, 3/1 for international students. Applications are processed on a rolling basis. Application fee: $50. *Expenses:* Tuition, area resident: Full-time $8763; part-time $179 per credit hour. Tuition, state resident: full-time $8763; part-time $298 per credit hour. Tuition, nonresident: full-time $12,981; part-time $426 per credit hour. Required fees: $1242. One-time fee: $250. Tuition and fees vary according to course load and program. *Financial support:* In 2008–09, 4 research assistantships with full tuition reimbursements (averaging $5,778 per year), 8 teaching assistantships with full tuition reimbursements (averaging $5,778 per year) were awarded; career-related internships or fieldwork, Federal Work-Study, scholarships/grants, and unspecified assistantships also available. Support available to part-time students. Financial award application deadline: 3/1; financial award applicants required to submit FAFSA. *Faculty research:* Geographic information systems, natural lands, Latin American subsistence farming, climatic change, urban perspectives. Total annual research expenditures: $188,052. *Unit head:* Dr. Thomas Harvey, Chair, 503-725-3916, Fax: 503-725-3166. *Application contact:* Angelica Nelson, Coordinator, 503-725-3916, Fax: 503-725-3166, E-mail: anelson@pdx.edu.

Queen's University at Kingston, School of Graduate Studies and Research, Faculty of Arts and Sciences, Department of Geography, Kingston, ON K7L 3N6, Canada. Offers M Sc, MA, PhD. *Degree requirements:* For master's, thesis; for doctorate, comprehensive exam, thesis/dissertation. *Entrance requirements:* Additional exam requirements/recommendations for international students: Required—TOEFL. *Faculty research:* Urban and economic geography, historical-cultural geography, earth system science.

Rutgers, The State University of New Jersey, New Brunswick, Graduate School, Program in Geography, Piscataway, NJ 08854-8097. Offers MA, MS, PhD. Terminal master's awarded for partial completion of doctoral program. *Degree requirements:* For master's, thesis or alternative; for doctorate, comprehensive exam, thesis/dissertation. *Entrance requirements:* For master's and doctorate, GRE General Test. Additional exam requirements/recommendations for international students: Required—TOEFL. *Faculty research:* Urban social theory, climate, political biology, hazards, economic development.

St. Cloud State University, School of Graduate Studies, College of Social Sciences, Department of Geography, St. Cloud, MN 56301-4498. Offers MS. *Degree requirements:* For master's, comprehensive exam (for some programs), thesis or alternative. *Entrance requirements:* For master's, GRE General Test, minimum GPA of 2.75. Additional exam requirements/recommendations for international students: Required—Michigan English Language Assessment Battery; Recommended—TOEFL (minimum score 550 paper-based; 213 computer-based), IELTS (minimum score 6.5). Electronic applications accepted.

Salem State College, School of Graduate Studies, Program in Geo-Information Science, Salem, MA 01970-5353. Offers geo-information science (MS). Part-time and evening/weekend programs available. *Students:* 10 part-time (3 women). Average age 35. In 2008, 2 master's awarded. *Degree requirements:* For master's, thesis optional. *Entrance requirements:* For master's, GRE General Test or MAT. *Application deadline:* Applications are processed on a rolling basis. Application fee: $35. *Unit head:* Keith Ratner, Coordinator, 978-542-6321, E-mail: kratner@salemstate.edu. *Application contact:* Dr. Marc Glasser, Dean of the Graduate School, 978-542-6323, Fax: 978-542-7215.

San Diego State University, Graduate and Research Affairs, College of Arts and Letters, Department of Geography, San Diego, CA 92182. Offers MA, PhD. *Degree requirements:* For master's, thesis; for doctorate, thesis/dissertation. *Entrance requirements:* For master's, GRE General Test, bachelor's degree in related field, 3 letters of recommendation. Additional exam requirements/recommendations for international students: Required—TOEFL. Electronic applications accepted. *Faculty research:* Physical geography, human geography, biogeography, environmental resources, geographic analysis.

San Francisco State University, Division of Graduate Studies, College of Behavioral and Social Sciences, Department of Geography and Human Environmental Studies, San Francisco, CA 94132-1722. Offers geography (MA), including resource management and environmental planning.

San Jose State University, Graduate Studies and Research, College of Social Sciences, Department of Geography, San Jose, CA 95192-0001. Offers geographic information science (Certificate); geography (MA). *Entrance requirements:* For master's, minimum GPA of 3.0. Electronic applications accepted.

Shippensburg University of Pennsylvania, School of Graduate Studies, College of Education and Human Services, Department of Teacher Education, Shippensburg, PA 17257-2299. Offers curriculum and instruction (M Ed), including biology, early childhood education, elementary education, English, foreign languages, geography/earth science, history, mathematics, middle school education; reading (M Ed). *Accreditation:* NCATE. Part-time and evening/weekend programs available. *Faculty:* 12 full-time (8 women), 7 part-time/adjunct (6 women). *Students:* 10 full-time (6 women), 171 part-time (154 women); includes 6 minority (2 African Americans, 2 Asian Americans or Pacific Islanders, 2 Hispanic Americans), 2 international. Average age 31. 56 applicants, 59% accepted, 24 enrolled. In 2008, 66 master's awarded. *Degree requirements:* For master's, comprehensive exam (for some programs), thesis optional, practicum or internship (for some programs). *Entrance requirements:* For master's, MAT (if GPA is

below 2.75), interview, 3 letters of recommendation, writing sample of teaching background and future goals. Additional exam requirements/recommendations for international students: Required—TOEFL (minimum score 560 paper-based; 220 computer-based); Recommended—IELTS (minimum score 6). *Application deadline:* For fall admission, 6/1 priority date for domestic students, 3/1 for international students; for spring admission, 9/1 priority date for domestic students, 7/1 for international students. Applications are processed on a rolling basis. Application fee: $30. Electronic applications accepted. *Expenses:* Tuition, state resident: full-time $6430; part-time $357 per credit. Tuition, nonresident: full-time $10,288; part-time $572 per credit. Required fees: $1127; $38 per credit. One-time fee: $44 part-time. *Financial support:* In 2008–09, 5 research assistantships with full tuition reimbursements (averaging $5,000 per year) were awarded; career-related internships or fieldwork, scholarships/grants, unspecified assistantships, and resident hall directors, student payroll positions also available. Support available to part-time students. Financial award application deadline: 3/1; financial award applicants required to submit FAFSA. *Unit head:* Dr. Christine A. Royce, Chairperson, 717-477-1688, Fax: 717-477-4046, E-mail: caroyc@ship.edu. *Application contact:* Renee Payne, Associate Dean of Graduate Admissions, 717-477-1231, Fax: 717-477-4016, E-mail: rmpayn@ship.edu.

Simon Fraser University, Graduate Studies, Faculty of Arts and Social Sciences, Department of Geography, Burnaby, BC V5A 1S6, Canada. Offers M Sc, MA, PhD. *Degree requirements:* For master's, one foreign language, thesis or alternative; for doctorate, one foreign language, thesis/dissertation, qualifying exams. *Entrance requirements:* For master's, minimum GPA of 3.0; for doctorate, minimum GPA of 3.5. Additional exam requirements/recommendations for international students: Required—TOEFL or IELTS. Electronic applications accepted. *Faculty research:* Theoretical and systematic aspects of geography, ginseng research, geographic information sciences, tourism and community planning, geomorphology.

South Dakota State University, Graduate School, College of Arts and Science, Department of Geography, Brookings, SD 57007. Offers MS. Part-time programs available. *Faculty:* 6 full-time (1 woman). *Students:* 5 full-time (1 woman), 22 part-time (7 women); includes 5 minority (1 American Indian/Alaska Native, 4 Asian Americans or Pacific Islanders). 11 applicants, 100% accepted, 11 enrolled. In 2008, 4 master's awarded. *Degree requirements:* For master's, thesis, oral exam. *Entrance requirements:* Additional exam requirements/recommendations for international students: Required—TOEFL (minimum score 525 paper-based; 197 computer-based; 71 iBT). *Application deadline:* For fall admission, 4/15 priority date for international students; for spring admission, 8/15 priority date for international students. Applications are processed on a rolling basis. Application fee: $35. *Financial support:* In 2008–09, 7 teaching assistantships with partial tuition reimbursements (averaging $15,750 per year) were awarded; career-related internships or fieldwork and unspecified assistantships also available. *Faculty research:* Contemporary agriculture and rural land use, geography of Indian casino gambling, geography of illegal drug trade, geography of crop circles. *Unit head:* Dr. Roger Sandness, Head, 605-688-4511, Fax: 605-688-4030, E-mail: roger.sandness@sdstate.edu. *Application contact:* Dr. Charles F. Gritzner, Graduate Coordinator, 605-688-4511, Fax: 605-688-4030, E-mail: charles.gritzner@sdstate.edu.

Southern Illinois University Carbondale, Graduate School, College of Liberal Arts, Department of Geography, Carbondale, IL 62901-4701. Offers MS, PhD. *Degree requirements:* For master's, thesis; for doctorate, thesis/dissertation. *Entrance requirements:* For master's, minimum GPA of 2.7; for doctorate, minimum GPA of 3.25. Additional exam requirements/recommendations for international students: Required—TOEFL. *Faculty research:* Natural resources management emphasizing water resources and environmental quality of air, water, and land systems.

Southern Illinois University Edwardsville, Graduate Studies and Research, College of Arts and Sciences, Department of Geography, Edwardsville, IL 62026-0001. Offers MS. Part-time and evening/weekend programs available. *Faculty:* 11 full-time (4 women). *Students:* 7 full-time (5 women), 23 part-time (11 women); includes 2 minority (1 American Indian/Alaska Native, 1 Asian American or Pacific Islander), 3 international. Average age 26. 23 applicants, 48% accepted. In 2008, 2 master's awarded. *Degree requirements:* For master's, thesis or alternative, final exam. *Entrance requirements:* For master's, GRE. Additional exam requirements/recommendations for international students: Required—TOEFL (minimum score 550 paper-based; 213 computer-based; 79 iBT), IELTS (minimum score 6.5). *Application deadline:* For fall admission, 7/20 for domestic students, 6/1 for international students; for spring admission, 12/14 for domestic students, 10/1 for international students. Applications are processed on a rolling basis. Application fee: $30. Electronic applications accepted. *Expenses:* Tuition, area resident: Full-time $5838. Tuition, nonresident: full-time $14,596. Required fees: $1525. *Financial support:* In 2008–09, 1 fellowship with full tuition reimbursement (averaging $8,370 per year), 8 teaching assistantships with full tuition reimbursements (averaging $8,064 per year) were awarded; research assistantships with full tuition reimbursements, career-related internships or fieldwork, Federal Work-Study, institutionally sponsored loans, and unspecified assistantships also available. Support available to part-time students. Financial award application deadline: 3/1; financial award applicants required to submit FAFSA. *Unit head:* Dr. Randall Pearson, Chair, 618-650-2090, E-mail: rapears@siue.edu. *Application contact:* Dr. Michael Starr, Director, 618-650-2492, E-mail: mstarr@siue.edu.

State University of New York at Binghamton, Graduate School, School of Arts and Sciences, Department of Geography, Binghamton, NY 13902-6000. Offers MA. *Faculty:* 7 full-time (2 women), 1 part-time/adjunct (0 women). *Students:* 22 full-time (11 women); includes 6 minority (1 African American, 1 Asian American or Pacific Islander, 4 Hispanic Americans), 4 international. Average age 26. 24 applicants, 96% accepted, 9 enrolled. In 2008, 12 master's awarded. *Degree requirements:* For master's, one foreign language, thesis (for some programs), oral and written exams. *Entrance requirements:* For master's, GRE General Test, GRE Subject Test. Additional exam requirements/recommendations for international students: Required—TOEFL. *Application deadline:* For fall admission, 4/15 priority date for domestic students, 1/15 priority date for international students; for spring admission, 11/1 for domestic students, 10/1 priority date for international students. Applications are processed on a rolling basis. Application fee: $60. Electronic applications accepted. *Expenses:* Tuition, area resident: Full-time $6900; part-time $288 per credit. Tuition, state resident: full-time $6900; part-time $288 per credit. Tuition, nonresident: full-time $10,920; part-time $455 per credit. Required fees: $1130. Part-time tuition and fees vary according to course load, program and student level. *Financial support:* In 2008–09, 14 students received support, including 3 fellowships with full tuition reimbursements available (averaging $10,000 per year), 10 teaching assistantships with full tuition reimbursements available (averaging $10,000 per year); research assistantships with full tuition reimbursements available, career-related internships or fieldwork, Federal Work-Study, institutionally sponsored loans, scholarships/grants, health care benefits, and unspecified assistantships also available. Financial award application deadline: 2/15; financial award applicants required to submit FAFSA. *Unit head:* Dr. Florence Margai, Chairperson, 607-777-6731, E-mail: margai@binghamton.edu. *Application contact:* Victoria Williams, Recruiting and Admissions Coordinator, 607-777-2151, Fax: 607-777-2501, E-mail: vwilliam@binghamton.edu.

Syracuse University, Graduate School, Maxwell School of Citizenship and Public Affairs, Program in Geography, Syracuse, NY 13244. Offers MA, PhD. Part-time and evening/weekend programs available. *Degree requirements:* For master's, thesis or alternative; for doctorate, thesis/dissertation. *Entrance requirements:* For master's and doctorate, GRE General Test. Additional exam requirements/recommendations for international students: Required—TOEFL. Electronic applications accepted.

Temple University, Graduate School, College of Liberal Arts, Department of Geography and Urban Studies, Philadelphia, PA 19122-6096. Offers geography (MA); urban studies (MA). *Degree requirements:* For master's, comprehensive exam, thesis or alternative. *Entrance requirements:* For master's, GRE General Test, minimum GPA of 3.0. Additional exam requirements/recommendations for international students: Required—TOEFL (minimum score 550 paper-based; 213 computer-based; 79 iBT). Electronic applications accepted. *Faculty* *research:* Environmental issues, urban political economy, poverty and unemployment, neighborhood development, African and Asian urbanization, housing, computer cartography.

Texas A&M University, College of Geosciences, Department of Geography, College Station, TX 77843. Offers MS, PhD. Part-time programs available. *Faculty:* 15. *Students:* 59 full-time (22 women), 22 part-time (10 women); includes 7 minority (3 African Americans, 1 American Indian/Alaska Native, 1 Asian American or Pacific Islander, 2 Hispanic Americans), 30 international. Average age 34. In 2008, 5 master's, 2 doctorates awarded. *Degree requirements:* For master's, thesis optional; for doctorate, thesis/dissertation. *Entrance requirements:* For master's and doctorate, GRE General Test. Additional exam requirements/recommendations for international students: Required—TOEFL. *Application deadline:* For fall admission, 3/1 priority date for domestic students; for spring admission, 10/1 for domestic students. Applications are processed on a rolling basis. Application fee: $50 ($75 for international students). Electronic applications accepted. *Expenses:* Tuition, area resident: Full-time $3838.50. Tuition, state resident: full-time $3838.50. Tuition, nonresident: full-time $8897. Required fees: $2359.60. *Financial support:* Fellowships, research assistantships, teaching assistantships, career-related internships or fieldwork, Federal Work-Study, and institutionally sponsored loans available. Financial award application deadline: 3/1; financial award applicants required to submit FAFSA. *Faculty research:* Geomorphology, historical geography, urban-economic geography, geographic education and technology, human-environment interaction. *Unit head:* Dr. Douglas Sherman, Head, 979-845-7188, E-mail: sherman@tamu.edu. *Application contact:* Daniel J. Sui, Graduate Advisor, 979-845-7154, Fax: 979-862-4487, E-mail: d-sui@tamu.edu.

Texas State University–San Marcos, Graduate School, College of Liberal Arts, Department of Geography, Program in Environmental Geography, Geography Education, and Geography Information Science, San Marcos, TX 78666. Offers environmental geography (PhD); geography education (PhD); information science (PhD). Part-time programs available. *Degree requirements:* For doctorate, thesis/dissertation. *Entrance requirements:* For doctorate, GRE General Test, minimum GPA of 3.5, master's degree in geography, demonstrated scholarly research. Additional exam requirements/recommendations for international students: Required—TOEFL (minimum score 550 paper-based; 213 computer-based). Electronic applications accepted.

Texas State University–San Marcos, Graduate School, College of Liberal Arts, Department of Geography, Program in Geography, San Marcos, TX 78666. Offers applied geography (MAG); geography (MS). Part-time and evening/weekend programs available. *Degree requirements:* For master's, comprehensive exam, internship or thesis. *Entrance requirements:* For master's, GRE General Test, minimum GPA of 3.0 in last 60 hours of course work. Additional exam requirements/recommendations for international students: Required—TOEFL (minimum score 550 paper-based; 213 computer-based). Electronic applications accepted. *Faculty research:* Applied cartography and geographic information systems, physical and environmental studies, land/area development and management.

Texas State University–San Marcos, Graduate School, College of Liberal Arts, Department of Geography, Program in Land/Area Studies, San Marcos, TX 78666. Offers MAG. Part-time and evening/weekend programs available. *Degree requirements:* For master's, comprehensive exam, internship or thesis. *Entrance requirements:* For master's, GRE General Test, minimum GPA of 3.0 in last 60 hours of course work. Additional exam requirements/recommendations for international students: Required—TOEFL (minimum score 550 paper-based; 213 computer-based). Electronic applications accepted.

Towson University, College of Graduate Studies and Research, Program in Geography and Environmental Planning, Towson, MD 21252-0001. Offers MA. Part-time and evening/weekend programs available. *Degree requirements:* For master's, thesis optional. *Entrance requirements:* For master's, 9 credits of course work in geography, minimum GPA of 3.0 in geography, admission essay, (2) narrative letters of recomendation, official transcripts. Additional exam requirements/recommendations for international students: Required—TOEFL. Electronic applications accepted. *Faculty research:* Geographic information systems, regional planning, hazards, development issues, urban fluvial systems.

Trent University, Graduate Studies, Program in Applications of Modeling in the Natural and Social Sciences, Peterborough, ON K9J 7B8, Canada. Offers applications of modeling in the natural and social sciences (MA); biology (M Sc, PhD); chemistry (M Sc); computer studies (M Sc); geography (M Sc, PhD); physics (M Sc). Part-time programs available. *Degree requirements:* For master's, thesis. *Entrance requirements:* For master's, honours degree. *Faculty research:* Computation of heat transfer, atmospheric physics, statistical mechanics, stress and coping, evolutionary ecology.

Trent University, Graduate Studies, Program in Environmental and Life Sciences and Program in Applications of Modeling in the Natural and Social Sciences, Department of Geography, Peterborough, ON K9J 7B8, Canada. Offers M Sc, PhD. Part-time programs available. *Degree requirements:* For master's, thesis; for doctorate, thesis/dissertation. *Entrance requirements:* For master's, honors degree; for doctorate, master's degree. *Faculty research:* Hydrometeorology, snow and ice, urban hydrology, fluvial geomorphology.

Université de Montréal, Faculty of Arts and Sciences, Department of Geography, Montréal, QC H3C 3J7, Canada. Offers environment and durable development (DESS); geography (M Sc, PhD, DESS); geomatical and spatial analysis (Certificate). *Faculty:* 27 full-time (5 women). *Students:* 37 full-time (22 women), 42 part-time (19 women). 70 applicants, 46% accepted, 25 enrolled. In 2008, 16 master's, 5 doctorates, 2 other advanced degrees awarded. *Degree requirements:* For master's, 2 foreign languages, thesis (for some programs); for doctorate, 3 foreign languages, thesis/dissertation, general exam. *Entrance requirements:* For master's, bachelor's degree in related field; for doctorate, MA in geography or related field. *Application deadline:* For fall admission, 2/1 priority date for domestic students; for winter admission, 11/1 priority date for domestic students; for spring admission, 2/1 priority date for domestic students. Applications are processed on a rolling basis. Application fee: $100. Electronic applications accepted. *Financial support:* Fellowships, research assistantships, teaching assistantships, career-related internships or fieldwork and scholarships/grants available. Support available to part-time students. *Faculty research:* Cartography, palynology, geomorphology, economic geography, regional and urban development. *Unit head:* Paul Comtois, Chairman, 514-343-8012, Fax: 514-343-8008, E-mail: paul.comtois@umontreal.ca. *Application contact:* Pierre Andr??, 514-343-8016, Fax: 514-343-8008, E-mail: pierre.andre@umonteal.ca.

Université de Sherbrooke, Faculty of Letters and Human Sciences, Department of Geography and Remote Sensing, Sherbrooke, QC J1K 2R1, Canada. Offers M Sc, PhD. *Degree requirements:* For master's, one foreign language, thesis; for doctorate, thesis/dissertation. *Faculty research:* Cartography.

Université du Québec à Montréal, Graduate Programs, Program in Geography, Montréal, QC H3C 3P8, Canada. Offers M Sc. Part-time programs available. *Degree requirements:* For master's, thesis optional. *Entrance requirements:* For master's, appropriate bachelor's degree or equivalent and proficiency in French.

Université Laval, Faculty of Forestry and Geomatics, Department of Geography, Program in Geographical Sciences, Québec, QC G1K 7P4, Canada. Offers M Sc Geogr, PhD. Terminal master's awarded for partial completion of doctoral program. *Degree requirements:* For master's, thesis; for doctorate, comprehensive exam, thesis/dissertation. *Entrance requirements:* For master's, knowledge of French; for doctorate, knowledge of French, knowledge of a second language. Electronic applications accepted.

University at Albany, State University of New York, College of Arts and Sciences, Department of Geography and Planning, Program in Geography, Albany, NY 12222-0001. Offers geographic information systems and spatial analysis (Certificate); geography (MA). *Degree requirements:* For master's, thesis or alternative. *Entrance requirements:* Additional exam requirements/recommendations for international students: Required—TOEFL (minimum score 550 paper-

based; 213 computer-based). Electronic applications accepted. *Faculty research:* Remote sensing, cultural/social geography, urban geography.

University at Buffalo, the State University of New York, Graduate School, College of Arts and Sciences, Department of Geography, Buffalo, NY 14260. Offers geographic information science (Certificate); geography (MA, MS, PhD); transportation and business geographics (Certificate); MA/MBA. *Degree requirements:* For master's, thesis (for some programs), project; for doctorate, thesis/dissertation; for Certificate, portfolio. *Entrance requirements:* For master's, GRE General Test, minimum GPA of 2.9; for doctorate, GRE General Test, minimum GPA of 3.0. Additional exam requirements/recommendations for international students: Required—TOEFL (minimum score 550 paper-based; 213 computer-based; 79 iBT). Electronic applications accepted. *Faculty research:* International business and world trade, geographic information systems and cartography, transportation, urban and regional analysis, physical and environmental geography.

The University of Akron, Graduate School, Buchtel College of Arts and Sciences, Department of Geography and Planning, Akron, OH 44325. Offers geographic information science (MS); urban planning (MA). Part-time and evening/weekend programs available. *Degree requirements:* For master's, thesis optional. *Entrance requirements:* For master's, minimum GPA of 2.75. Additional exam requirements/recommendations for international students: Required—TOEFL (minimum score 550 paper-based; 213 computer-based; 79 iBT). Electronic applications accepted. *Faculty research:* Geographic information sciences, urban and regional planning, human geography especially cultural, political, and urban, regional geography, especially Native America, Asia, and Middle East.

The University of Alabama, Graduate School, College of Arts and Sciences, Department of Geography, Tuscaloosa, AL 35487. Offers MS. Part-time and evening/weekend programs available. *Faculty:* 11 full-time (1 woman). *Students:* 19 full-time (7 women), 6 part-time (1 woman); includes 2 minority (both African Americans). Average age 26. 10 applicants, 70% accepted, 4 enrolled. In 2008, 6 master's awarded. *Degree requirements:* For master's, comprehensive exam, thesis or alternative. *Entrance requirements:* For master's, GRE, minimum GPA of 3.0. Additional exam requirements/recommendations for international students: Required—TOEFL. *Application deadline:* For fall admission, 2/1 priority date for domestic and international students; for spring admission, 10/1 priority date for domestic and international students. Applications are processed on a rolling basis. Application fee: $30. Electronic applications accepted. *Expenses:* Tuition, area resident: Full-time $6400. Tuition, state resident: full-time $6400. Tuition, nonresident: full-time $18,000. *Financial support:* In 2008–09, 16 students received support, including fellowships (averaging $12,500 per year), 3 research assistantships with full tuition reimbursements available (averaging $10,908 per year), 12 teaching assistantships with full tuition reimbursements available (averaging $10,908 per year); career-related internships or fieldwork, health care benefits, and unspecified assistantships also available. *Faculty research:* Land use, regional and urban planning, geographic information systems, forest ecology, environmental management, geomorphology, climatology, planning urban-economic geography. Total annual research expenditures: $171,391. *Unit head:* Prof. Luoheng Han, Chair, 205-348-5047, Fax: 205-348-2278, E-mail: lhan@bama.ua.edu. *Application contact:* Information Contact, 205-348-5047, Fax: 205-348-2278.

The University of Arizona, Graduate College, College of Social and Behavioral Sciences, Department of Geography and Regional Development, Tucson, AZ 85721. Offers geography (MA, PhD). Part-time programs available. Terminal master's awarded for partial completion of doctoral program. *Degree requirements:* For master's, thesis or additional course work; for doctorate, variable foreign language requirement, thesis/dissertation. *Entrance requirements:* For master's, GRE General Test, minimum GPA of 3.0, master's degree, statement of purpose, 2 letters of recommendation; for doctorate, GRE General Test, minimum GPA of 3.0, statement of purpose, 2 letters of recommendation, master's degree. Additional exam requirements/recommendations for international students: Required—TOEFL (minimum score 550 paper-based). *Faculty research:* Population, Latin America, Anglo America, the former Soviet Union, Middle East.

University of Arkansas, Graduate School, J. William Fulbright College of Arts and Sciences, Department of Geosciences, Program in Geography, Fayetteville, AR 72701-1201. Offers MA. Part-time programs available. *Degree requirements:* For master's, thesis.

The University of British Columbia, Faculty of Arts and Faculty of Graduate Studies, Department of Geography, Vancouver, BC V6T 1Z1, Canada. Offers M Sc, MA, PhD. Part-time programs available. Terminal master's awarded for partial completion of doctoral program. *Degree requirements:* For master's, thesis; for doctorate, comprehensive exam, thesis/dissertation. *Entrance requirements:* For master's and doctorate, minimum B average, 2nd class honors, upper division (class II, division I). Additional exam requirements/recommendations for international students: Required—TOEFL (minimum score 600 paper-based; 250 computer-based; 100 iBT). Electronic applications accepted. *Faculty research:* Earth system science, environmental geography, historical geography, social geography, urban geography.

University of Calgary, Faculty of Graduate Studies, Faculty of Social Sciences, Department of Geography, Calgary, AB T2N 1N4, Canada. Offers M Sc, MA, MGIS, PhD. Part-time programs available. *Degree requirements:* For master's, thesis, departmental conference; for doctorate, thesis/dissertation, candidacy exam, departmental conference. *Entrance requirements:* For master's, minimum undergraduate GPA of 3.0 during last 2 years; for doctorate, minimum GPA of 3.0 during previous 2 years, master's degree. Additional exam requirements/recommendations for international students: Required—TOEFL (minimum score 550 paper-based; 213 computer-based). Electronic applications accepted. *Faculty research:* Geographic information systems, remote sensing, geomorphology, earth system processes, urban and required environmental health research.

University of California, Berkeley, Graduate Division, College of Letters and Science, Department of Geography, Berkeley, CA 94720-1500. Offers PhD. *Degree requirements:* For doctorate, thesis/dissertation, qualifying exam. *Entrance requirements:* For doctorate, GRE General Test, minimum GPA of 3.0, 3 letters of recommendation. Electronic applications accepted.

University of California, Davis, Graduate Studies, Graduate Group in Geography, Davis, CA 95616. Offers MA, PhD. Terminal master's awarded for partial completion of doctoral program. *Degree requirements:* For master's, comprehensive exam (for some programs), thesis (for some programs); for doctorate, thesis/dissertation. *Entrance requirements:* For master's, GRE General Test, minimum GPA of 3.0; for doctorate, GRE General Test, master's degree, minimum GPA of 3.0. Additional exam requirements/recommendations for international students: Required—TOEFL (minimum score 550 paper-based; 213 computer-based). Electronic applications accepted. *Faculty research:* Cultural agrosystems, mountain society habitat and South Asia.

University of California, Los Angeles, Graduate Division, College of Letters and Science, Department of Geography, Los Angeles, CA 90095. Offers MA, PhD. *Students:* 48 full-time (23 women); includes 12 minority (1 African American, 7 Asian Americans or Pacific Islanders, 4 Hispanic Americans), 8 international. Average age 29. 68 applicants, 28% accepted, 10 enrolled. In 2008, 3 master's, 6 doctorates awarded. Terminal master's awarded for partial completion of doctoral program. *Degree requirements:* For master's, thesis; for doctorate, thesis/dissertation, oral and written qualifying exams. *Entrance requirements:* For master's, GRE General Test, minimum GPA of 3.3; for doctorate, GRE General Test, minimum undergraduate GPA of 3.3, sample of research writing or thesis. *Application deadline:* For fall admission, 12/31 for domestic and international students. Application fee: $60 ($80 for international students). Electronic applications accepted. *Expenses:* Tuition, nonresident: full-time $14,694. Required fees: $9669.50. Full-time tuition and fees vary according to course load, degree level, program and student level. *Financial support:* In 2008–09, 40 fellowships with full and partial tuition reimbursements, 11 research assistantships with full and partial tuition

Geography

University of California, Los Angeles (continued)

reimbursements, 34 teaching assistantships with full and partial tuition reimbursements were awarded; Federal Work-Study, institutionally sponsored loans, scholarships/grants, health care benefits, tuition waivers (full and partial), and unspecified assistantships also available. Financial award application deadline: 3/1; financial award applicants required to submit FAFSA. *Unit head:* Dr. David Rigby, Chair, 310-825-1071. *Application contact:* Departmental Office, 310-825-1071, E-mail: gradapps@geog.ucla.edu.

University of California, Santa Barbara, Graduate Division, College of Letters and Sciences, Division of Mathematics, Life, and Physical Sciences, Department of Geography, Geography, CA 93106-4060. Offers cognitive science (PhD); geography (MA); quantitative methods in the social sciences (PhD); transportation (PhD); MA/PhD. *Students:* 67 full-time (33 women). Average age 30. 92 applicants, 28% accepted, 15 enrolled. In 2008, 3 master's, 13 doctorates awarded. *Degree requirements:* For master's, comprehensive exam (for some programs), thesis; for doctorate, comprehensive exam, thesis/dissertation. *Entrance requirements:* For master's and doctorate, GRE General Test, 3 letters of recommendation, statement of purpose, personal achievements/contributions statement, resumé/curriculum vitae, transcripts for post-secondary institutions attended. Additional exam requirements/recommendations for international students: Required—TOEFL (paper: 550, computer: 213, IBT: 80) or IELTS (7). *Application deadline:* For fall admission, 2/1 for domestic and international students. Application fee: $70 ($90 for international students). Electronic applications accepted. *Expenses:* Tuition, nonresident: full-time $25,149. Required fees: $10,143. Full-time tuition and fees vary according to campus/location, reciprocity agreements and student level. *Financial support:* In 2008–09, 59 students received support, including 36 fellowships with full and partial tuition reimbursements available (averaging $10,700 per year), 29 research assistantships with full and partial tuition reimbursements available (averaging $8,600 per year), 31 teaching assistantships with partial tuition reimbursements available (averaging $8,000 per year); Federal Work-Study, institutionally sponsored loans, scholarships/grants, health care benefits, and unspecified assistantships also available. Financial award applicants required to submit FAFSA. *Faculty research:* Earth system science, human environment relations, modeling, measurement and computation, quantitative methods in social sciences. *Unit head:* Dr. Oliver Chadwick, Chair, 805-893-4223, E-mail: oac@geog.ucsb.edu. *Application contact:* Graduate Program Assistant, 805-893-3663, Fax: 805-893-3146, E-mail: grad_assistant@geog.ucsb.edu.

University of Central Arkansas, Graduate School, College of Liberal Arts, Department of Geography, Conway, AR 72035-0001. Offers geographic information systems (MGIS, Certificate). Part-time programs available. Postbaccalaureate distance learning degree programs offered (minimal on-campus study). *Entrance requirements:* Additional exam requirements/recommendations for international students: Required—TOEFL (minimum score 550 paper-based; 213 computer-based).

University of Cincinnati, Graduate School, McMicken College of Arts and Sciences, Department of Geography, Cincinnati, OH 45221. Offers MA, PhD. Terminal master's awarded for partial completion of doctoral program. *Degree requirements:* For master's, thesis optional; for doctorate, one foreign language, comprehensive exam, thesis/dissertation. *Entrance requirements:* For master's and doctorate, GRE General Test. Additional exam requirements/recommendations for international students: Required—TOEFL. Electronic applications accepted. *Faculty research:* Urban-economics, GIS, physical-environmental.

University of Colorado at Boulder, Graduate School, College of Arts and Sciences, Department of Geography, Boulder, CO 80309. Offers MA, PhD. Part-time programs available. Terminal master's awarded for partial completion of doctoral program. *Degree requirements:* For master's, thesis; for doctorate, one foreign language, comprehensive exam, thesis/dissertation. *Entrance requirements:* For master's, GRE General Test, minimum undergraduate GPA of 3.0; for doctorate, GRE General Test. *Faculty research:* Physical geography, human geography, environmental society relations, technical geography, GIS and cartography.

University of Colorado at Colorado Springs, Graduate School, College of Letters, Arts and Sciences, Department of Geography and Environmental Studies, Colorado Springs, CO 80933-7150. Offers MA. *Faculty:* 8 full-time (2 women), 1 part-time/adjunct (0 women). *Students:* 7 full-time (1 woman), 8 part-time (4 women); includes 2 minority (1 Asian American or Pacific Islander, 1 Hispanic American). Average age 37. 9 applicants, 100% accepted, 7 enrolled. In 2008, 7 master's awarded. *Degree requirements:* For master's, thesis optional. *Entrance requirements:* For master's, GRE. *Application deadline:* For fall admission, 4/1 for domestic students. *Faculty research:* Natural hazard mitigation and policy issues, applied geography, geographic information systems, population geography. Total annual research expenditures: $107,300. *Unit head:* Dr. Robert Larkin, Associate Professor, 719-255-4053, Fax: 719-255-4066, E-mail: rlarkin@uccs.edu. *Application contact:* Mary McGill, Program Assistant, 719-255-3016, E-mail: mmcgill@uccs.edu.

University of Connecticut, Graduate School, College of Liberal Arts and Sciences, Department of Geography, Field of Geography, Storrs, CT 06269. Offers geographic information systems (Certificate); geography (MS, PhD). Part-time programs available. Terminal master's awarded for partial completion of doctoral program. *Degree requirements:* For master's, comprehensive exam; for doctorate, thesis/dissertation. *Entrance requirements:* For master's and doctorate, GRE General Test. Additional exam requirements/recommendations for international students: Required—TOEFL (minimum score 550 paper-based; 213 computer-based). Electronic applications accepted.

University of Delaware, College of Arts and Sciences, Department of Geography, Newark, DE 19716. Offers climatology (PhD); geography (MA, MS). *Degree requirements:* For master's, thesis; for doctorate, thesis/dissertation. *Entrance requirements:* For master's and doctorate, GRE General Test. Additional exam requirements/recommendations for international students: Required—TOEFL. Electronic applications accepted. *Faculty research:* Permafrost, Glaciers, Climatology, Physical Geography, Human Geography.

University of Denver, Faculty of Natural Sciences and Mathematics, Department of Geography, Denver, CO 80208. Offers MA, MS, PhD. Part-time programs available. *Faculty:* 12 full-time (4 women). *Students:* 11 full-time (3 women), 26 part-time (9 women); includes 1 minority (Asian American or Pacific Islander), 4 international. Average age 33. In 2008, 10 master's, 1 doctorate awarded. Terminal master's awarded for partial completion of doctoral program. *Degree requirements:* For master's, thesis or alternative; for doctorate, one foreign language, thesis/dissertation. *Entrance requirements:* For master's, GRE General Test; for doctorate, GRE General Test, MA. Additional exam requirements/recommendations for international students: Required—TOEFL. *Application deadline:* Applications are processed on a rolling basis. Application fee: $50. Electronic applications accepted. *Financial support:* In 2008–09, 14 teaching assistantships with full and partial tuition reimbursements (averaging $15,500 per year) were awarded; research assistantships with full and partial tuition reimbursements, career-related internships or fieldwork, Federal Work-Study, institutionally sponsored loans, and scholarships/grants also available. Support available to part-time students. Financial award application deadline: 3/1; financial award applicants required to submit FAFSA. *Faculty research:* Transportation and land use, fluvial geography and water resources, climatology, geographic information systems, biogeography. Total annual research expenditures: $158,000. *Unit head:* Dr. Andrew Goetz, Chair, 303-871-2201. *Application contact:* Information Contact, 303-871-2201, E-mail: kescobar@du.edu.

University of Florida, Graduate School, College of Liberal Arts and Sciences, Department of Geography, Gainesville, FL 32611. Offers MA, MS, PhD. *Degree requirements:* For master's, variable foreign language requirement, thesis (for some programs); for doctorate, thesis/dissertation. *Entrance requirements:* For master's and doctorate, GRE General Test, minimum GPA of 3.0. Additional exam requirements/recommendations for international students: Required—TOEFL (minimum score 550 paper-based; 213 computer-based). Electronic applica-

tions accepted. *Faculty research:* Economic development, physical geography, hydrology, climatology, tropical agriculture.

University of Georgia, Graduate School, College of Arts and Sciences, Department of Geography, Athens, GA 30602. Offers MA, MS, PhD. *Degree requirements:* For master's, one foreign language, thesis; for doctorate, one foreign language, thesis/dissertation. *Entrance requirements:* For master's and doctorate, GRE General Test. Electronic applications accepted.

University of Guelph, Graduate Program Services, College of Social and Applied Human Sciences, Department of Geography, Guelph, ON N1G 2W1, Canada. Offers M Sc, MA, PhD. Part-time programs available. *Degree requirements:* For master's, thesis (for some programs); for doctorate, comprehensive exam, thesis/dissertation. *Entrance requirements:* For master's, minimum B average during previous 2 years of course work; for doctorate, minimum A-average. Additional exam requirements/recommendations for international students: Required—TOEFL (minimum score 550 paper-based; 213 computer-based). Electronic applications accepted. *Faculty research:* Rural resource evaluation, environmental analysis, biophysical process, rural settlement and land use, resource assessment.

University of Hawaii at Manoa, Graduate Division, Colleges of Arts and Sciences, College of Social Sciences, Department of Geography, Honolulu, HI 96822. Offers geography (MA, PhD); ocean policy (Graduate Certificate). Part-time programs available. *Degree requirements:* For master's, one foreign language, comprehensive exam, thesis; for doctorate, one foreign language, comprehensive exam, thesis/dissertation. *Entrance requirements:* For master's, GRE General Test; for doctorate, GRE General Test, sample of written work. Additional exam requirements/recommendations for international students: Required—TOEFL (minimum score 500 paper-based; 173 computer-based; 61 iBT), IELTS (minimum score 5). *Faculty research:* Physical geography, human geography, methodology.

University of Idaho, College of Graduate Studies, College of Science, Department of Geography, Moscow, ID 83844-2282. Offers Geography (MS, PhD). *Faculty:* 7 full-time, 1 part-time/adjunct. *Students:* 10 full-time, 7 part-time. Average age 34. In 2008, 4 master's, 4 doctorates awarded. *Degree requirements:* For doctorate, one foreign language, thesis/dissertation. *Entrance requirements:* For master's, minimum GPA of 2.8; for doctorate, minimum undergraduate GPA of 2.8, graduate 3.0. *Application deadline:* For fall admission, 8/1 for domestic students; for spring admission, 12/15 for domestic students. Application fee: $55 ($60 for international students). *Expenses:* Tuition, nonresident: full-time $10,080; part-time $336 per credit. Required fees: $5212; $267 per credit. Tuition and fees vary according to program. *Financial support:* Research assistantships, teaching assistantships available. Financial award application deadline: 2/15. *Faculty research:* Land cover land use changes, rural development, geographic trade models, climate change and effects on ecosystems, migration and regional development. *Unit head:* Dr. Harley E. Johansen, Head, 208-885-6216. *Application contact:* Dr. Harley E. Johansen, Head, 208-885-6216.

University of Illinois at Chicago, Graduate College, College of Liberal Arts and Sciences, Department of Anthropology, Program in Environmental and Urban Geography, Chicago, IL 60607-7128. Offers environmental studies (MA); urban geography (MA). Part-time programs available. *Degree requirements:* For master's, thesis. *Entrance requirements:* For master's, GRE General Test, minimum GPA of 2.75. Additional exam requirements/recommendations for international students: Required—TOEFL. Electronic applications accepted.

University of Illinois at Urbana–Champaign, Graduate College, College of Liberal Arts and Sciences, School of Earth, Society and Environment, Department of Geography, Champaign, IL 61820. Offers MA, MS, PhD. *Faculty:* 14 full-time (2 women). *Students:* 30 full-time (11 women), 12 part-time (4 women); includes 4 minority (2 African Americans, 2 Asian Americans or Pacific Islanders), 13 international. 47 applicants, 17% accepted, 8 enrolled. In 2008, 5 master's, 2 doctorates awarded. *Entrance requirements:* For master's, GRE, minimum GPA of 3.0; for doctorate, GRE, minimum GPA of 3.5. Additional exam requirements/recommendations for international students: Required—TOEFL. *Application deadline:* Applications are processed on a rolling basis. Application fee: $60 ($75 for international students). Electronic applications accepted. *Financial support:* In 2008–09, 13 fellowships, 9 research assistantships, 15 teaching assistantships were awarded; tuition waivers (full and partial) also available. *Unit head:* Bruce Rhoads, Head, 217-333-1322, Fax: 217-244-1785, E-mail: brhoads@illinois.edu. *Application contact:* Chris Wilcock, Admissions and Records Officer, I, 217-244-3486, Fax: 217-244-1785, E-mail: cwilcock@illinois.edu.

The University of Iowa, Graduate College, College of Liberal Arts and Sciences, Department of Geography, Iowa City, IA 52242-1316. Offers MA, PhD. *Degree requirements:* For master's, thesis optional, exam; for doctorate, comprehensive exam, thesis/dissertation. *Entrance requirements:* For master's and doctorate, GRE General Test, minimum GPA of 3.0. Additional exam requirements/recommendations for international students: Required—TOEFL (minimum score 550 paper-based; 213 computer-based; 81 iBT). Electronic applications accepted.

The University of Kansas, Graduate Studies, College of Liberal Arts and Sciences, Department of Geography, Lawrence, KS 66045-7613. Offers MA, PhD, MUP/MA. Part-time programs available. *Faculty:* 23. *Students:* 73 full-time (24 women), 10 part-time (2 women); includes 1 minority (African American), 13 international. Average age 32. 50 applicants, 62% accepted, 14 enrolled. In 2008, 9 master's, 2 doctorates awarded. *Degree requirements:* For master's, comprehensive exam, thesis, thesis defense; for doctorate, one foreign language, comprehensive exam, thesis/dissertation, dissertation defense. *Entrance requirements:* For master's and doctorate, GRE General Test, 3 letters of reference, transcripts, statement of interests. Additional exam requirements/recommendations for international students: Required—TOEFL. *Application deadline:* For fall admission, 1/15 for domestic students, 1/15 priority date for international students; for spring admission, 11/1 for domestic and international students. Applications are processed on a rolling basis. Application fee: $45 ($50 for international students). Electronic applications accepted. *Expenses:* Tuition, area resident: Full-time $6122; part-time $255.10 per credit hour. Tuition, state resident: full-time $6122; part-time $255.10 per credit hour. Tuition, nonresident: full-time $14,629; part-time $609.55 per credit hour. Required fees: $847; $70.56 per credit hour. Tuition and fees vary according to course load and program. *Financial support:* Fellowships with full tuition reimbursements, research assistantships with full tuition reimbursements, teaching assistantships with full and partial tuition reimbursements, unspecified assistantships available. Financial award application deadline: 1/15. *Faculty research:* Physical geography, techniques (cartography-GIS-remote sensing), cultural/regional geography. *Unit head:* Johannes Feddema, Chair, 785-864-5534, Fax: 785-864-5378, E-mail: t-slocum@ku.edu. *Application contact:* Stephen Egbert, Graduate Director, 785-864-4252, Fax: 785-864-5378, E-mail: s-egbert@ku.edu.

University of Kentucky, Graduate School, College of Arts and Sciences, Program in Geography, Lexington, KY 40506-0032. Offers MA, PhD. *Degree requirements:* For master's, comprehensive exam, thesis optional; for doctorate, one foreign language, comprehensive exam, thesis/dissertation. *Entrance requirements:* For master's, GRE General Test, minimum undergraduate GPA of 2.75; for doctorate, GRE General Test, minimum graduate GPA of 3.0. Additional exam requirements/recommendations for international students: Required—TOEFL (minimum score 550 paper-based; 213 computer-based). Electronic applications accepted. *Faculty research:* Cultural, industrial, medical, political, social, population, and transportation geography; geographic analysis; Third World (especially Southeast Asia theory); Eastern Europe.

University of Lethbridge, School of Graduate Studies, Lethbridge, AB T1K 3M4, Canada. Offers accounting (MScM); addictions counseling (M Sc); agricultural biotechnology (M Sc); agricultural studies (M Sc, MA); anthropology (MA); archaeology (MA); art (MA); biochemistry (M Sc); biological sciences (M Sc); biomolecular science (PhD); biosystems and biodiversity (PhD); Canadian studies (MA); chemistry (M Sc); computer science (M Sc); computer science and geographical information science (M Sc); counseling psychology (M Ed); dramatic arts (MA); earth, space, and physical science (PhD); economics (MA); educational leadership (M Ed); English (MA); environmental science (M Sc); evolution and behavior (PhD); exercise science (M Sc); finance (MScM); French (MA); French/German (MA); French/Spanish (MA); general education (M Ed); general management (MScM); geography (M Sc, MA); German (MA); health sciences (M Sc, MA); history (MA); human resource management and labour relations (MScM); individualized multidisciplinary (M Sc, MA); information systems (MScM); international management (MScM); kinesiology (M Sc, MA); management (M Sc, MA); marketing (MScM); mathematics (M Sc); music (MA); Native American studies (MA); neuroscience (M Sc, PhD); new media (MA); nursing (M Sc); philosophy (MA); physics (M Sc); policy and strategy (MScM); political science (MA); psychology (M Sc, MA); religious studies (MA); sociology (MA); theoretical and computational science (PhD); urban and regional studies (MA). Part-time and evening/weekend programs available. *Degree requirements:* For doctorate, comprehensive exam, thesis/dissertation. *Entrance requirements:* For master's, GMAT (M Sc in management), bachelor's degree in related field, minimum GPA of 3.0 during previous 20 graded semester courses, 2 years teaching or related experience (M Ed); for doctorate, master's degree, minimum graduate GPA of 3.5. Additional exam requirements/recommendations for international students: Required—TOEFL. *Faculty research:* Movement and brain plasticity, gibberellin physiology, photosynthesis, carbon cycling, molecular properties of main-group ring components.

University of Manitoba, Faculty of Graduate Studies, Clayton H. Riddell Faculty of Environment, Earth, and Resources, Department of Environment and Geography, Winnipeg, MB R3T 2N2, Canada. Offers environment (M Env); environment and geography (M Sc); geography (MA, PhD). *Degree requirements:* For master's, thesis; for doctorate, one foreign language, thesis/dissertation.

University of Maryland, Baltimore County, Graduate School, College of Arts, Humanities and Social Sciences, Department of Geography and Environmental Systems, Program in Geography and Environmental Systems, Baltimore, MD 21250. Offers MS, PhD. *Faculty:* 11 full-time (4 women), 6 part-time/adjunct (1 woman). *Students:* 11 full-time (8 women), 4 part-time (3 women); includes 1 African American, 1 Asian American or Pacific Islander, 1 international. Average age 32. 33 applicants, 52% accepted, 13 enrolled.Terminal master's awarded for partial completion of doctoral program. *Degree requirements:* For master's, thesis optional, annual faculty evaluation, research paper; for doctorate, comprehensive exam, thesis/dissertation, annual faculty evaluation, qualifying exams, proposal and dissertation defense. *Entrance requirements:* For master's and doctorate, GRE, minimum GPA of 3.0 overall, 3.3 in major. Additional exam requirements/recommendations for international students: Required—TOEFL (minimum score 550 paper-based; 213 computer-based; 80 iBT). *Application deadline:* For fall admission, 2/1 for domestic and international students. Application fee: $50. Electronic applications accepted. *Financial support:* In 2008–09, 9 students received support, including 5 fellowships with full tuition reimbursements available (averaging $30,000 per year), 4 teaching assistantships with full tuition reimbursements available (averaging $18,392 per year). Financial award application deadline: 2/1. *Faculty research:* Watershed processes, climate and weather systems; ecology and biogeography; landscape ecology and land-use change; human geography, urban sustainability and environmental health; environmental policy; geographic information science and remote sensing. *Unit head:* Dr. Christopher M. Swan, Graduate Program Director, 410-455-2002, E-mail: gpd.ges@umbc.edu. *Application contact:* Kathryn Nee, Coordinator of Domestic Admissions, 410-455-2944, E-mail: nee@umbc.edu.

University of Maryland, College Park, Graduate Studies, College of Behavioral and Social Sciences, Department of Geography, College Park, MD 20742. Offers MA, PhD, MA/MLS. Part-time and evening/weekend programs available. Terminal master's awarded for partial completion of doctoral program. *Degree requirements:* For master's, thesis, oral exam; for doctorate, comprehensive exam, thesis/dissertation. *Entrance requirements:* For master's, GRE General Test, minimum GPA of 3.0, 3 letters of recommendation; for doctorate, GRE General Test. Additional exam requirements/recommendations for international students: Required—TOEFL, TWE. Electronic applications accepted. *Faculty research:* Cartography and automated mapping, environmental systems analysis, metropolitan analysis and planning, historical and human geography, coastal geomorphology.

University of Maryland, College Park, Graduate Studies, Interdepartmental Programs, Program in Geography, Library, and Information Services, College Park, MD 20742. Offers MA/MLS. Electronic applications accepted.

University of Massachusetts Amherst, Graduate School, College of Natural Sciences and Mathematics, Department of Geosciences, Program in Geography, Amherst, MA 01003. Offers MS. Part-time programs available. *Degree requirements:* For master's, thesis optional. *Entrance requirements:* For master's, GRE General Test. Additional exam requirements/recommendations for international students: Required—TOEFL (minimum score 550 paper-based; 213 computer-based; 79 iBT), IELTS (minimum score 6.5). Electronic applications accepted. *Expenses:* Tuition, area resident: Full-time $2640. Tuition, nonresident: full-time $9936. One-time fee: $332 full-time. Tuition and fees vary according to course load.

University of Miami, Graduate School, College of Arts and Sciences, Department of Geography and Regional Studies, Coral Gables, FL 33124. Offers geography (MA). Part-time programs available. *Degree requirements:* For master's, thesis. *Entrance requirements:* For master's, GRE, 3 letters of recommendation, official transcripts. Additional exam requirements/recommendations for international students: Required—TOEFL. Electronic applications accepted. *Faculty research:* Urbanization, globalization, environmental change.

University of Minnesota, Twin Cities Campus, Graduate School, College of Liberal Arts, Department of Geography, Program in Geography, Minneapolis, MN 55455-0213. Offers MA, PhD. *Degree requirements:* For master's, comprehensive exam, thesis or 3 papers; for doctorate, comprehensive exam, thesis/dissertation. *Entrance requirements:* For master's and doctorate, GRE General Test, minimum GPA of 3.5. Additional exam requirements/recommendations for international students: Required—TOEFL (minimum score 600 paper-based; 250 computer-based; 100 iBT). Electronic applications accepted. *Faculty research:* Space, place, and the environment, biogeography/forest dynamics, international labor migration, political economy of development/globalization, historical urban geography.

University of Missouri–Columbia, Graduate School, College of Arts and Sciences, Department of Geography, Columbia, MO 65211. Offers MA. *Faculty:* 10 full-time (2 women). *Students:* 11 full-time (3 women), 6 part-time (4 women); includes 1 minority (Asian American or Pacific Islander), 3 international. Average age 30. 13 applicants, 46% accepted, 4 enrolled. In 2008, 3 master's awarded. *Entrance requirements:* For master's, GRE General Test, minimum GPA of 3.0. Additional exam requirements/recommendations for international students: Required—TOEFL (minimum score 500 paper-based; 173 computer-based; 61 iBT). *Application deadline:* For fall admission, 2/15 priority date for domestic students; for winter admission, 10/1 priority date for domestic students; for spring admission, 4/1 priority date for domestic students. Applications are processed on a rolling basis. Application fee: $45 ($60 for international students). *Financial support:* Research assistantships, teaching assistantships, institutionally sponsored loans available. *Unit head:* Dr. Joseph Hobbs, Department Chair, E-mail: hobbsj@missouri.edu. *Application contact:* Nancy Burke, 573-882-8370, E-mail: burken@missouri.edu.

The University of Montana, Graduate School, College of Arts and Sciences, Department of Geography, Missoula, MT 59812-0002. Offers geography (MA), including cartography and GIS, community and environmental planning. *Entrance requirements:* For master's, GRE General Test. Additional exam requirements/recommendations for international students: Required—TOEFL.

University of Nebraska at Omaha, Graduate Studies and Research, College of Arts and Sciences, Department of Geography and Geology, Omaha, NE 68182. Offers geographic information science (Certificate); geography (MA). Part-time programs available. *Degree requirements:* For master's, comprehensive exam, thesis (for some programs). *Entrance requirements:* For master's, GRE, minimum GPA of 3.0, 15 undergraduate geography hours, resumé. Additional exam requirements/recommendations for international students: Required—TOEFL (minimum score 550 paper-based; 213 computer-based; 80 iBT). Electronic applications accepted.

University of Nebraska–Lincoln, Graduate College, College of Arts and Sciences, Department of Anthropology and Geography, Lincoln, NE 68588. Offers anthropology (MA); geography (MA, PhD), including geography (MA), indigenous peoples (PhD); professional archaeology (MA). *Faculty:* 15 full-time (6 women). *Students:* 27 full-time (13 women), 28 part-time (14 women); includes 4 minority (2 American Indian/Alaska Native, 2 Hispanic Americans), 8 international. Average age 29. In 2008, 10 master's, 4 doctorates awarded. *Degree requirements:* For master's, thesis optional. *Entrance requirements:* For master's, GRE General Test. Additional exam requirements/recommendations for international students: Required—TOEFL. Application fee: $40. Electronic applications accepted. *Expenses:* Tuition, state resident: full-time $4275; part-time $237.50 per credit hour. Tuition, nonresident: full-time $11,525; part-time $640.25 per credit hour. Required fees: $1068; $10.35 per credit hour. $440.70 per semester. Tuition and fees vary according to course load and program. *Financial support:* Fellowships, research assistantships, teaching assistantships, health care benefits available. *Unit head:* Dr. Raymond Hames, Chair, 402-472-2411. *Application contact:* Ginny Gross, Director of Graduate Admissions, 402-472-2878, Fax: 402-472-0589, E-mail: grad_admissions@unl.edu.

University of Nevada, Reno, Graduate School, College of Science, Mackay School of Earth Sciences and Engineering, Department of Geography, Program in Geography, Reno, NV 89557. Offers MS, PhD. *Faculty:* 14 full-time (4 women). *Students:* 9 full-time (7 women), 7 part-time (1 woman). Average age 34. 22 applicants, 55% accepted, 8 enrolled. In 2008, 7 master's awarded. Terminal master's awarded for partial completion of doctoral program. *Degree requirements:* For master's, comprehensive exam, thesis; for doctorate, comprehensive exam, thesis/dissertation. *Entrance requirements:* For master's and doctorate, GRE General Test, minimum GPA of 2.75. Additional exam requirements/recommendations for international students: Required—TOEFL (minimum score 500 paper-based; 173 computer-based; 61 iBT), IELTS (minimum score 6), TOFEL or IELTS. *Application deadline:* For fall admission, 2/1 priority date for domestic and international students. Applications are processed on a rolling basis. Application fee: $60 ($95 for international students). Electronic applications accepted. *Expenses:* Tuition, state resident: full-time $1710; part-time $1140 per semester. Tuition, nonresident: full-time $7115. Required fees: $158 per semester. *Financial support:* In 2008–09, 4 research assistantships with partial tuition reimbursements (averaging $14,000 per year), 6 teaching assistantships with partial tuition reimbursements (averaging $14,000 per year) were awarded; Federal Work-Study, institutionally sponsored loans, scholarships/grants, health care benefits, and unspecified assistantships also available. Financial award application deadline: 3/1; financial award applicants required to submit FAFSA. *Faculty research:* Natural resources, education, climatology, biogeography, ethnic/cultural geography . Total annual research expenditures: $788,353. *Unit head:* Dr. Gary Hausladen, Graduate Program Director, 775-784-6995, E-mail: hausl@unr.edu. *Application contact:* Michele Sandberg, Application Contact, 775-784-7026, Fax: 775-784-6064, E-mail: gradschool@unr.edu.

University of New Mexico, Graduate School, College of Arts and Sciences, Department of Geography, Albuquerque, NM 87131-2039. Offers MS. Part-time programs available. *Degree requirements:* For master's, comprehensive exam (for some programs), thesis (for some programs). *Entrance requirements:* For master's, GRE. Additional exam requirements/recommendations for international students: Required—TOEFL. Electronic applications accepted. *Faculty research:* Geographic information science, water resources, economic development, environmental management.

University of New Orleans, Graduate School, College of Liberal Arts, Department of Geography, New Orleans, LA 70148. Offers MA. *Entrance requirements:* For master's, GRE General Test. Additional exam requirements/recommendations for international students: Required—TOEFL (minimum score 550 paper-based; 213 computer-based; 79 iBT). Electronic applications accepted.

The University of North Carolina at Chapel Hill, Graduate School, College of Arts and Sciences, Department of Geography, Chapel Hill, NC 27599. Offers MA, PhD. *Degree requirements:* For master's, one foreign language, comprehensive exam, thesis; for doctorate, 2 foreign languages, comprehensive exam, thesis/dissertation. *Entrance requirements:* For master's and doctorate, GRE General Test, minimum GPA of 3.0. *Faculty research:* Geographic information systems, climatology, hydrology, population research, Latino immigration.

The University of North Carolina at Charlotte, Graduate School, College of Arts and Sciences, Department of Geography and Earth Sciences, Charlotte, NC 28223-0001. Offers earth sciences (MS), including climatology and hydrology, environmental systems analysis, solid earth sciences; geography (MA), including community planning, location analysis, transportation studies, urban regional analysis; geography and urban and regional analysis (PhD). Part-time and evening/weekend programs available. *Faculty:* 28 full-time (8 women), 1 part-time/adjunct (0 women). *Students:* 52 full-time (20 women), 41 part-time (16 women); includes 5 minority (3 African Americans, 2 Hispanic Americans), 17 international. Average age 29. 66 applicants, 67% accepted, 28 enrolled. In 2008, 14 master's awarded. *Degree requirements:* For master's, comprehensive exam, project. *Entrance requirements:* For master's, GRE General Test or MAT, Doppelt Mathematical Reasoning Test, minimum GPA of 3.0 in undergraduate major, 2.75 overall. Additional exam requirements/recommendations for international students: Required—TOEFL (minimum score 557 paper-based; 220 computer-based). *Application deadline:* For fall admission, 7/1 for domestic students, 5/1 for international students; for spring admission, 11/1 for domestic students, 10/1 for international students. Applications are processed on a rolling basis. Application fee: $55. Electronic applications accepted. *Expenses:* Tuition, area resident: Full-time $2919; part-time $122 per credit hour. Tuition, state resident: full-time $2919; part-time $122 per credit hour. Tuition, nonresident: full-time $13,126; part-time $547 per credit hour. Required fees: $1779; $91 per credit hour. Tuition and fees vary according to program. *Financial support:* In 2008–09, 64 research assistantships (averaging $7,684 per year), 41 teaching assistantships (averaging $9,529 per year) were awarded; career-related internships or fieldwork, Federal Work-Study, institutionally sponsored loans, scholarships/grants, unspecified assistantships, and 3 administrative assistantships ($5,386) also available. Support available to part-time students. Financial award application deadline: 4/1; financial award applicants required to submit FAFSA. *Faculty research:* Location analysis, applications of GIS technology, community planning and development, regional economic modeling, retail geography. *Unit head:* Dr. Gerald L. Ingalls, Chair, 704-687-2293, Fax: 704-687-3182, E-mail: gingalls@email.uncc.edu. *Application contact:* Kathy B. Giddings, Director of Graduate Admissions, 704-687-3366, Fax: 704-687-3279, E-mail: agidding@uncc.edu.

The University of North Carolina at Greensboro, Graduate School, College of Arts and Sciences, Department of Geography, Greensboro, NC 27412-5001. Offers applied geography (MA); geographic information science (Certificate); geography (PhD); urban and economic development (Certificate). *Degree requirements:* For master's, comprehensive exam, thesis or alternative. *Entrance requirements:* For master's, GRE General Test. Additional exam requirements/recommendations for international students: Required—TOEFL. Electronic applications accepted.

University of North Dakota, Graduate School, College of Arts and Sciences, Department of Geography, Grand Forks, ND 58202. Offers MA, MS. Part-time programs available. *Degree requirements:* For master's, comprehensive exam, thesis or alternative. *Entrance requirements:* For master's, minimum GPA of 3.0. Additional exam requirements/recommendations for international students: Required—TOEFL (minimum score 550 paper-based; 213 computer-based; 79 iBT), IELTS (minimum score 6.5). Electronic applications accepted. *Faculty research:* Regional and urban development, environmental geography, geographic education, geographic techniques.

Geography

University of Northern Iowa, Graduate College, College of Social and Behavioral Sciences, Department of Geography, Cedar Falls, IA 50614. Offers MA. Part-time programs available. *Students:* 10 full-time (3 women), 5 part-time (3 women); includes 1 minority (African American), 7 international. 6 applicants, 83% accepted, 3 enrolled. In 2008, 1 master's awarded. *Degree requirements:* For master's, thesis or alternative. *Entrance requirements:* For master's, minimum GPA of 3.0; 2 letters of recommendation; brief statement about professional interests and career objectives. Additional exam requirements/recommendations for international students: Required—TOEFL (minimum score 500 paper-based; 180 computer-based; 61 iBT). *Application deadline:* For fall admission, 8/1 priority date for domestic students. Applications are processed on a rolling basis. Application fee: $30 ($50 for international students). Electronic applications accepted. *Expenses:* Tuition, state resident: full-time $6446. Tuition, nonresident: full-time $14,874. Required fees: $852. *Financial support:* Career-related internships or fieldwork, Federal Work-Study, scholarships/grants, and tuition waivers (full and partial) available. Support available to part-time students. Financial award application deadline: 2/1. *Unit head:* Dr. Patrick P. Pease, Interim Head, 319-273-2772, Fax: 319-273-7103, E-mail: patrick.pease@uni.edu. *Application contact:* Laurie S. Russell, Record Analyst, 319-273-2623, Fax: 319-273-6792, E-mail: laurie.russell@uni.edu.

University of North Texas, Robert B. Toulouse School of Graduate Studies, College of Arts and Sciences, Department of Geography, Denton, TX 76203. Offers MS. *Degree requirements:* For master's, comprehensive exam (for some programs), thesis (for some programs), 36 hours or more total. *Entrance requirements:* For master's, GRE General Test, GPA; BA/BS. Additional exam requirements/recommendations for international students: Required—proof of English language proficiency required for non-native English speakers; Recommended—TOEFL (minimum score 550 paper-based; 213 computer-based). *Faculty research:* Environmental monitoring and modeling; health and economic geography; environmental archaeology.

University of Oklahoma, Graduate College, College of Atmospheric and Geographic Sciences, Department of Geography, Norman, OK 73019. Offers MA, PhD. Part-time programs available. *Faculty:* 12 full-time (2 women), 2 part-time/adjunct (both women). *Students:* 22 full-time (9 women), 15 part-time (6 women); includes 1 minority (American Indian/Alaska Native), 13 international. 15 applicants, 67% accepted, 4 enrolled. In 2008, 11 master's, 5 doctorates awarded. Terminal master's awarded for partial completion of doctoral program. *Degree requirements:* For master's, thesis, oral and written exams; for doctorate, one foreign language, thesis/dissertation, general exams. *Entrance requirements:* For master's, GRE, minimum GPA of 3.0, writing sample, 3 letters of recommendation. Additional exam requirements/recommendations for international students: Required—TOEFL (minimum score 550 paper-based; 213 computer-based). *Application deadline:* For fall admission, 2/1 for domestic students, 4/1 for international students; for spring admission, 12/1 for domestic students, 9/1 for international students. Applications are processed on a rolling basis. Application fee: $40 ($90 for international students). Electronic applications accepted. *Expenses:* Tuition, state resident: full-time $3744; part-time $156 per credit hour. Tuition, nonresident: full-time $13,577; part-time $565.70 per credit hour. Required fees: $2415.40; $90.10 per credit hour. *Financial support:* In 2008–09, 12 students received support, including 6 fellowships with full tuition reimbursements available (averaging $5,000 per year), 1 research assistantship with partial tuition reimbursement available (averaging $17,000 per year), 12 teaching assistantships with partial tuition reimbursements available (averaging $11,966 per year); career-related internships or fieldwork, Federal Work-Study, scholarships/grants, health care benefits, and unspecified assistantships also available. Financial award application deadline: 2/1; financial award applicants required to submit FAFSA. *Faculty research:* Renewable energy, sustainability, and environmental policy; hydroclimatic variability, landscape change, and fluvial process; natural hazards and response; Latin America (environment & social movements); Indigenous peoples, colonialism, and post-colonialism . Total annual research expenditures: $507,124. *Unit head:* Fred Shelley, Chair, 405-325-5325, Fax: 405-325-6090, E-mail: fshelley@ou.edu. *Application contact:* Dr. Karl Offen, Associate Professor & Graduate Liaison, 405-325-23912, Fax: 405-325-6090, E-mail: koffen@ou.edu.

University of Oregon, Graduate School, College of Arts and Sciences, Department of Geography, Eugene, OR 97403. Offers MA, MS, PhD. *Degree requirements:* For master's, one foreign language, thesis; for doctorate, one foreign language, thesis/dissertation. *Entrance requirements:* For master's and doctorate, GRE General Test, minimum GPA of 3.0. Additional exam requirements/recommendations for international students: Required—TOEFL. *Faculty research:* Place-name research, past climates, quaternary environments, plant diffusions, population redistributions.

University of Ottawa, Faculty of Graduate and Postdoctoral Studies, Faculty of Arts, Department of Geography, Ottawa, ON K1N 6N5, Canada. Offers M Geog, M Sc, MA, PhD. *Degree requirements:* For master's, one foreign language, thesis; for doctorate, one foreign language, comprehensive exam, thesis/dissertation. *Entrance requirements:* For master's, honors degree or equivalent, minimum B average; for doctorate, master's degree, minimum B+ average. Electronic applications accepted. *Faculty research:* The physical geography of cold environment; space, place and society, environmental change.

University of Prince Edward Island, Faculty of Arts, Charlottetown, PE C1A 4P3, Canada. Offers island studies (MA). Part-time programs available. *Degree requirements:* For master's, thesis. *Entrance requirements:* Additional exam requirements/recommendations for international students: Required—TOEFL (minimum score 550 paper-based; 213 computer-based; 80 iBT), Canadian Academic English Language Assessment, Michigan English Language Assessment Battery, Canadian Test of English for Scholars and Trainees. *Faculty research:* International island studies.

University of Regina, Faculty of Graduate Studies and Research, Faculty of Arts, Department of Geography, Regina, SK S4S 0A2, Canada. Offers M Sc, MA, PhD. *Faculty:* 12 full-time (3 women), 2 part-time/adjunct (both women). *Students:* 4 full-time (3 women), 2 part-time (1 woman). 6 applicants, 50% accepted, 3 enrolled. In 2008, 3 master's awarded. *Degree requirements:* For master's, thesis. *Entrance requirements:* Additional exam requirements/recommendations for international students: Required—TOEFL (minimum score 580 paper-based; 237 computer-based; 88 iBT). *Application deadline:* Applications are processed on a rolling basis. Application fee: $85 ($100 for international students). Electronic applications accepted. *Financial support:* In 2008–09, 1 fellowship (averaging $15,000 per year), 1 research assistantship (averaging $13,500 per year) were awarded; teaching assistantships, scholarships/grants also available. Financial award application deadline: 6/15. *Faculty research:* Cultural, historical, economic, rural, and urban geography; cartography; resource management; hydrology. *Unit head:* Dr. Bernard Thraves, Graduate Program Coordinator, 306-585-4104, E-mail: bernard.thraves@uregina.ca. *Application contact:* Dr. Joe Piwowar, Graduate Program Coordinator, 306-585-5273, E-mail: joe.piwowar@uregina.ca.

University of Saskatchewan, College of Graduate Studies and Research, College of Arts and Sciences, Department of Geography, Saskatoon, SK S7N 5A2, Canada. Offers M Sc, MA, PhD. *Degree requirements:* For master's, thesis; for doctorate, thesis/dissertation. *Entrance requirements:* Additional exam requirements/recommendations for international students: Required—TOEFL.

University of South Africa, College of Agriculture and Environmental Sciences, Pretoria, South Africa. Offers agriculture (MS); consumer science (MCS); environmental management (MA, MS, PhD); environmental science (MA, MS, PhD); geography (MA, MS, PhD); horticulture (M Tech); human ecology (MHE); life sciences (MS); nature conservation (M Tech).

University of South Carolina, The Graduate School, College of Arts and Sciences, Department of Geography, Columbia, SC 29208. Offers geography (MA, MS, PhD); geography education (IMA). IMA and MAT offered in cooperation with the College of Education. Part-time programs available. *Degree requirements:* For master's, comprehensive exam, thesis (for some programs); for doctorate, comprehensive exam, thesis/dissertation. *Entrance requirements:* For master's, GRE General Test; for doctorate, GRE General Test, master's degree. Electronic applications accepted. *Faculty research:* Geographic information processing; economic, cultural, physical, and environmental geography.

University of Southern California, Graduate School, College of Letters, Arts and Sciences, Department of Geography, Los Angeles, CA 90089. Offers geographic information science and technology (Graduate Certificate); geography (MA, MS, PhD). Part-time and evening/weekend programs available. Postbaccalaureate distance learning degree programs offered (no on-campus study). Terminal master's awarded for partial completion of doctoral program. *Degree requirements:* For master's, thesis; for doctorate, thesis/dissertation. *Entrance requirements:* For master's and doctorate, GRE General Test. *Faculty research:* Landscape dynamics, geomorphology, geographic information science, urban geography and nature-society relations, GIS.

University of Southern Mississippi, Graduate School, College of Science and Technology, Department of Geography and Geology, Hattiesburg, MS 39406-0001. Offers geography (MS, PhD); geology (MS). Part-time programs available. *Faculty:* 11 full-time (2 women), 2 part-time/adjunct (0 women). *Students:* 11 full-time (5 women), 14 part-time (5 women); includes 2 minority (both African Americans). Average age 34. 12 applicants, 42% accepted, 4 enrolled. In 2008, 3 master's awarded. *Degree requirements:* For master's, comprehensive exam, thesis (for some programs), internships; for doctorate, comprehensive exam, thesis/dissertation. *Entrance requirements:* For master's, GMAT, GRE General Test, minimum GPA of 3.0. Additional exam requirements/recommendations for international students: Required—TOEFL. *Application deadline:* For fall admission, 3/15 for domestic and international students; for spring admission, 1/3 for domestic students. Applications are processed on a rolling basis. Application fee: $30. Electronic applications accepted. *Financial support:* In 2008–09, 1 research assistantship with tuition reimbursement (averaging $18,000 per year), 8 teaching assistantships with full tuition reimbursements (averaging $8,632 per year) were awarded; fellowships with full tuition reimbursements, career-related internships or fieldwork, Federal Work-Study, and institutionally sponsored loans also available. Financial award application deadline: 3/15; financial award applicants required to submit FAFSA. *Faculty research:* City and regional planning, geographic techniques, physical geography, human geography. *Unit head:* Dr. Clifton Dixon, Chair, 601-266-4729, Fax: 601-266-6219, E-mail: c.dixon@usm.edu. *Application contact:* Dr. Gail Russell, Graduate Coordinator, 601-266-6519, Fax: 601-266-6219.

University of South Florida, Graduate School, College of Arts and Sciences, Department of Geography, Tampa, FL 33620-9951. Offers MA, MURP, PhD. Part-time and evening/weekend programs available. *Faculty:* 16 full-time (6 women). *Students:* 9 full-time (4 women), 13 part-time (5 women); includes 2 minority (both Hispanic Americans), 1 international. 28 applicants, 54% accepted, 6 enrolled. In 2008, 11 master's awarded. *Degree requirements:* For master's, comprehensive exam, thesis; for doctorate, comprehensive exam, thesis/dissertation. *Entrance requirements:* For master's, GRE General Test, minimum GPA of 3.0 in last 60 hours of course work. Additional exam requirements/recommendations for international students: Required—TOEFL (minimum score 550 paper-based; 213 computer-based). *Application deadline:* For fall admission, 2/15 for domestic students, 1/2 for international students; for spring admission, 10/1 for domestic students, 6/1 for international students. Application fee: $30. *Expenses:* Tuition, state resident: full-time $2624.40; part-time $291.60 per credit hour. Tuition, nonresident: full-time $7822; part-time $869.13 per credit hour. *Financial support:* Unspecified assistantships available. Financial award application deadline: 3/1. *Faculty research:* Natural hazards, geographic information systems models, soil contamination, urban geography and social theory. Total annual research expenditures: $55,163. *Unit head:* Dr. Robert Brinkmann, Associate Professor/Chair, 813-974-4939, Fax: 813-974-4808, E-mail: rbrinkmann@cas.usf.edu. *Application contact:* Philip Van beynen, Program Director, 813-974-3026, Fax: 813-974-4808, E-mail: vanbeynen@cas.usf.edu.

The University of Tennessee, Graduate School, College of Arts and Sciences, Department of Geography, Knoxville, TN 37996. Offers MS, PhD. *Degree requirements:* For master's, thesis or alternative; for doctorate, thesis/dissertation. *Entrance requirements:* For master's and doctorate, GRE General Test, minimum GPA of 2.7. Additional exam requirements/recommendations for international students: Required—TOEFL. Electronic applications accepted. *Expenses:* Tuition, area resident: Part-time $348 per credit hour. Tuition, state resident: full-time $6262. Tuition, nonresident: full-time $18,920; part-time $1052 per credit hour. Required fees: $812; $36 per credit hour. Tuition and fees vary according to program.

The University of Texas at Austin, Graduate School, College of Liberal Arts, Department of Geography and the Environment, Austin, TX 78712-1111. Offers MA, PhD, MSCRP/PhD. *Degree requirements:* For master's, thesis or alternative; for doctorate, thesis/dissertation. *Entrance requirements:* For master's and doctorate, GRE General Test. Additional exam requirements/recommendations for international students: Required—TOEFL. Electronic applications accepted. *Faculty research:* Cultural and historical geography, environmental and physical geography, human-environment interactions, electronic technology and hypermedia, international area studies.

The University of Toledo, College of Graduate Studies, College of Arts and Sciences, Department of Geography and Planning, Toledo, OH 43606-3390. Offers geographic information systems and applied geographics (Certificate); geography (MA); planning (MA). Part-time programs available. *Degree requirements:* For master's, thesis. *Entrance requirements:* For master's, GRE General Test. Electronic applications accepted.

University of Toronto, School of Graduate Studies, Social Sciences Division, Department of Geography, Toronto, ON M5S 1A1, Canada. Offers geography (M Sc, MA, PhD); planning (M Sc Pl); urban design studies (MUD). Part-time programs available. *Degree requirements:* For master's, thesis optional; for doctorate, thesis/dissertation. *Entrance requirements:* For master's, bachelor's degree or equivalent in geography or a closely related field, minimum B+ average in each of 2 final years of degree, 3 letters of reference; for doctorate, master of geography degree, minimum A–average.

University of Utah, The Graduate School, College of Social and Behavioral Science, Department of Geography, Salt Lake City, UT 84112-1107. Offers MA, MS, PhD. Part-time programs available. *Degree requirements:* For master's, variable foreign language requirement, thesis or alternative, 6 research hours; for doctorate, comprehensive exam, thesis/dissertation, 14 research hours. *Entrance requirements:* For master's and doctorate, GRE General Test, minimum undergraduate GPA of 3.0. Additional exam requirements/recommendations for international students: Required—TOEFL (minimum score 500 paper-based; 173 computer-based; 61 iBT). Electronic applications accepted. *Faculty research:* Urban geography, earth system science, geographic information systems, remote sensing, hazards.

University of Victoria, Faculty of Graduate Studies, Faculty of Social Sciences, Department of Geography, Victoria, BC V8W 2Y2, Canada. Offers M Sc, MA, PhD. Part-time programs available. *Degree requirements:* For master's, thesis; for doctorate, comprehensive exam, thesis/dissertation, candidacy exam. *Entrance requirements:* For master's, minimum B+ average in undergraduate course work; for doctorate, master's degree. Additional exam requirements/recommendations for international students: Required—TOEFL (minimum score 575 paper-based; 233 computer-based), IELTS (minimum score 7). Electronic applications accepted. *Faculty research:* Resources and protected areas, remote sensing and forestry, geographic information systems and cartography, urban regional planning, physical climatology.

University of Washington, Graduate School, College of Arts and Sciences, Department of Geography, Seattle, WA 98195. Offers MA, PhD. *Degree requirements:* For master's, thesis; for doctorate, thesis/dissertation. *Entrance requirements:* For master's and doctorate, GRE General Test. Additional exam requirements/recommendations for international students: Required—TOEFL. Electronic applications accepted. *Faculty research:* Globalization and social theory, nature and society, regional economic development, urban patterns and processes, geographic information systems.

University of Waterloo, Graduate Studies, Faculty of Environmental Studies, Department of Geography, Waterloo, ON N2L 3G1, Canada. Offers MA, PhD. *Degree requirements:* For master's, thesis optional; for doctorate, one foreign language, comprehensive exam, thesis/dissertation. *Entrance requirements:* For master's, honors degree, minimum B average; for doctorate, master's degree, minimum A- average. Additional exam requirements/recommendations for international students: Required—TOEFL, TWE. Electronic applications accepted. *Faculty research:* Urban economic geography; physical geography; resource management; cultural, regional, historical geography; spatial data.

The University of Western Ontario, Faculty of Graduate Studies, Social Sciences Division, Department of Geography, London, ON N6A 5B8, Canada. Offers M Sc, MA, PhD. *Degree requirements:* For master's, thesis; for doctorate, thesis/dissertation. *Entrance requirements:* For master's, honors degree, minimum B average, GRE exam; for doctorate, honors degree, minimum B average. Additional exam requirements/recommendations for international students: Required—TOEFL.

University of Wisconsin–Madison, Graduate School, College of Letters and Science, Department of Geography, Madison, WI 53706-1380. Offers cartography and geographic information systems (MS); geographic information systems (Certificate); geography (MS, PhD). Part-time programs available. *Degree requirements:* For master's, thesis; for doctorate, thesis/dissertation; for Certificate, internship. *Entrance requirements:* For master's and doctorate, GRE General Test, minimum GPA of 3.25. Electronic applications accepted. *Faculty research:* Physical geography, urban/historical geography, people-environment, history of cartography, GIS.

University of Wisconsin–Milwaukee, Graduate School, College of Letters and Sciences, Department of Geography, Milwaukee, WI 53201-0413. Offers MA, MS, PhD, MLIS/MA. *Faculty:* 13 full-time (6 women). *Students:* 15 full-time (8 women), 13 part-time (6 women); includes 3 minority (2 Asian Americans or Pacific Islanders, 1 Hispanic American), 10 international. Average age 30. 28 applicants, 39% accepted, 6 enrolled. In 2008, 5 master's, 4 doctorates awarded. *Degree requirements:* For master's, comprehensive exam, thesis; for doctorate, thesis/dissertation. *Entrance requirements:* For master's and doctorate, GRE. Additional exam requirements/recommendations for international students: Required—TOEFL (minimum score 550 paper-based; 79 iBT), IELTS (minimum score 6.5). *Application deadline:* For fall admission, 1/1 priority date for domestic students; for spring admission, 9/1 for domestic students. Applications are processed on a rolling basis. Application fee: $45 ($75 for international students). *Expenses:* Tuition, area resident: Full-time $7320; part-time $165 per credit. Tuition, state resident: full-time $7320; part-time $165 per credit. Tuition, nonresident: full-time $17,840; part-time $714 per credit. Tuition and fees vary according to campus/location, program and reciprocity agreements. *Financial support:* In 2008–09, 1 research assistantship, 18 teaching assistantships were awarded; career-related internships or fieldwork and unspecified assistantships also available. Support available to part-time students. Financial award application deadline: 4/15. Total annual research expenditures: $224,300. *Unit head:* Rina Ghose, Representative, 414-229-4797, Fax: 414-229-3981, E-mail: rghose@uwm.edu. *Application contact:* General Information Contact, 414-229-4982, Fax: 414-229-6967, E-mail: gradschool@uwm.edu.

University of Wyoming, Graduate School, College of Arts and Sciences, Department of Geography, Laramie, WY 82070. Offers geography (MA, MP, MST); geography/water resources (MA); rural planning and natural resources (MP), including community and regional planning and natural resources. Postbaccalaureate distance learning degree programs offered (minimal on-campus study). *Faculty:* 5 full-time (1 woman). *Students:* 9 full-time (3 women), 10 part-time (4 women); includes 1 minority (Asian American or Pacific Islander). Average age 32. 13 applicants, 62% accepted, 8 enrolled. In 2008, 2 master's awarded. *Degree requirements:* For master's, thesis optional. *Entrance requirements:* For master's, GRE General Test, minimum GPA of 3.0. Additional exam requirements/recommendations for international students: Required—TOEFL. *Application deadline:* For fall admission, 2/15 for domestic students. Applications are processed on a rolling basis. Application fee: $50. Electronic applications accepted. *Financial support:* In 2008–09, 3 research assistantships with full and partial tuition reimbursements (averaging $11,072 per year), 6 teaching assistantships with full and partial tuition reimbursements (averaging $11,072 per year) were awarded; career-related internships or fieldwork, Federal Work-Study, scholarships/grants, health care benefits, and unspecified assistantships also available. Financial award application deadline: 3/1; financial award applicants required to submit FAFSA. *Faculty research:* Landscape ecology, landscape change, public land management, rural and small town planning, GIS. Total annual research expenditures: $112,940. *Unit head:* Dr. Gerald R. Webster, Chair, 307-766-3311, Fax: 307-766-3294, E-mail: geography-info@uwyo.edu. *Application contact:* Barbara Powell, Office Associate Senior, 307-766-3311, Fax: 307-766-3294, E-mail: geography-info@uwyo.edu.

Utah State University, School of Graduate Studies, College of Natural Resources, Department of Environment and Society, Logan, UT 84322. Offers bioregional planning (MS); geography (MA, MS); human dimensions of ecosystem science and management (MS, PhD); recreation resource management (MS, PhD). *Degree requirements:* For master's, comprehensive exam, thesis (for some programs). *Entrance requirements:* For master's and doctorate, GRE General Test, minimum GPA of 3.0. Additional exam requirements/recommendations for international students: Required—TOEFL. Electronic applications accepted. *Faculty research:* Geographic information systems/geographic and environmental education, bioregional planning, natural resource and environmental policy, outdoor recreation and tourism, natural resource and environmental management.

Virginia Polytechnic Institute and State University, Graduate School, College of Natural Resources, Department of Geography, Blacksburg, VA 24061. Offers MS, PhD. *Entrance requirements:* For master's, GRE. Additional exam requirements/recommendations for international students: Required—TOEFL (minimum score 550 paper-based; 213 computer-based). Electronic applications accepted. *Faculty research:* Third World development, geographical information systems, remote sensing, critical geopolitics, medical geography.

Wayne State University, College of Liberal Arts and Sciences, Department of Geography and Urban Planning, Detroit, MI 48202. Offers geography (MA); urban planning (MUP). Evening/weekend programs available. *Entrance requirements:* For master's, minimum 3.0 GPA; statement of interest; two letters of recommendations. Additional exam requirements/recommendations for international students: Required—TOEFL (minimum score 550 paper-based; 213 computer-based); Recommended—TWE (minimum score 6). Electronic applications accepted. *Faculty research:* Housing and community development, urban and regional economic development, urban development and land use, transportation policy and planning, environmental policy and planning.

Wayne State University, College of Liberal Arts and Sciences, Program in Geography, Detroit, MI 48202. Offers MA. *Entrance requirements:* For master's, GRE General Test. Additional exam requirements/recommendations for international students: Required—TOEFL (minimum score 550 paper-based; 213 computer-based); Recommended—TWE (minimum score 6). Electronic applications accepted.

West Chester University of Pennsylvania, Office of Graduate Studies, College of Business and Public Affairs, Department of Geography and Planning, West Chester, PA 19383. Offers geographic technology (Certificate); geography (MA); regional planning (MSA). Part-time and evening/weekend programs available. *Students:* 12 full-time (1 woman), 16 part-time (4 women); includes 5 minority (4 African Americans, 1 Hispanic American). Average age 33. 15 applicants, 100% accepted, 9 enrolled. In 2008, 7 master's, 10 other advanced degrees awarded. *Degree requirements:* For master's, comprehensive exam, thesis optional. *Entrance requirements:* For master's, GRE, GMAT, or MAT, minimum GPA of 2.8, resumé, two letters of recommendation; for Certificate, minimum GPA of 2.8, resumé, three letters of recommendation. Additional exam requirements/recommendations for international students: Required—TOEFL (minimum score 550 paper-based; 213 computer-based; 80 iBT). *Application deadline:* For fall admission, 4/15 priority date for domestic students, 3/15 for international students; for spring admission, 10/15 for domestic students, 9/1 for international students. Applications are processed on a rolling basis. Application fee: $35. Electronic applications accepted. *Expenses:* Tuition, state resident: full-time $6430; part-time $357 per credit. Tuition, nonresident: full-time $10,288; part-time $572 per credit. Required fees: $652.50; $50 per credit. $67 per semester. *Financial support:* In 2008–09, 3 research assistantships with full and partial tuition reimbursements (averaging $5,000 per year) were awarded; unspecified assistantships also available. Support available to part-time students. Financial award application deadline: 2/15; financial award applicants required to submit FAFSA. *Faculty research:* Environmental education, land use/suburban planning, landscapes of Catalunya. *Unit head:* Dr. Joan Welch, Chair and Graduate Coordinator, 610-436-2940, E-mail: jwelch@wcupa.edu. *Application contact:* Rabbi Dottie Ives Dewey, MSA Graduate Coordinator, 610-436-2746, E-mail: divesdewey@wcupa.edu.

Western Illinois University, School of Graduate Studies, College of Arts and Sciences, Department of Geography, Macomb, IL 61455-1390. Offers community development (Certificate); geography (MA). Part-time programs available. *Students:* 17 full-time (4 women), 3 part-time (0 women); includes 2 minority (both Asian Americans or Pacific Islanders), 5 international. Average age 31. 5 applicants, 80% accepted. In 2008, 1 master's, 4 other advanced degrees awarded. *Degree requirements:* For master's, thesis or alternative. *Entrance requirements:* Additional exam requirements/recommendations for international students: Required—TOEFL (minimum score 550 paper-based; 213 computer-based; 80 iBT). *Application deadline:* Applications are processed on a rolling basis. Application fee: $30. Electronic applications accepted. *Expenses:* Tuition, state resident: full-time $5696; part-time $237.34 per credit hour. Tuition, nonresident: full-time $11,392; part-time $474.68 per credit hour. Required fees: $1453; $60.55 per credit hour. *Financial support:* In 2008–09, 13 students received support, including 13 research assistantships with full tuition reimbursements available (averaging $7,040 per year). Financial award applicants required to submit FAFSA. *Unit head:* Dr. Sam Thompson, Chairperson, 309-298-1648. *Application contact:* Evelyn Hoing, Assistant Director of Graduate Studies, 309-298-1806, Fax: 309-298-2345, E-mail: grad-office@wiu.edu.

Western Kentucky University, Graduate Studies, Ogden College of Science and Engineering, Department of Geography and Geology, Bowling Green, KY 42101. Offers MAE, MS. *Degree requirements:* For master's, comprehensive exam, thesis or alternative. *Entrance requirements:* For master's, GRE General Test, minimum GPA of 2.75. Additional exam requirements/recommendations for international students: Required—TOEFL (minimum score 555 paper-based; 213 computer-based; 79 iBT). *Faculty research:* Hydroclimatology, electronic data sets, groundwater, sinkhole liquification potential, meteorological analysis.

Western Michigan University, Graduate College, College of Arts and Sciences, Department of Geography, Kalamazoo, MI 49008-5202. Offers MA. *Degree requirements:* For master's, thesis, internship.

Western Washington University, Graduate School, Huxley College of the Environment, Department of Environmental Studies, Program in Geography, Bellingham, WA 98225-5996. Offers MS. *Entrance requirements:* Additional exam requirements/recommendations for international students: Required—TOEFL (minimum score 567 paper-based; 227 computer-based). Electronic applications accepted.

West Virginia University, Eberly College of Arts and Sciences, Department of Geology and Geography, Program in Geography, Morgantown, WV 26506. Offers energy and environmental resources (MA); geographic information systems (PhD); geography-regional development (PhD); GIS/cartographic analysis (MA); regional development (MA). Part-time programs available. *Degree requirements:* For master's, thesis, oral and written exams; for doctorate, comprehensive exam, thesis/dissertation, oral and written exams. *Entrance requirements:* For master's and doctorate, GRE General Test, minimum GPA of 3.0. Additional exam requirements/recommendations for international students: Required—TOEFL. Electronic applications accepted. *Faculty research:* Space, place and development, geographic information science, environmental geography.

Wilfrid Laurier University, Faculty of Graduate Studies, Faculty of Arts, Department of Geography and Environmental Studies, Waterloo, ON N2L 3C5, Canada. Offers M Sc, MA, MES, PhD. *Degree requirements:* For master's, thesis optional; for doctorate, thesis/dissertation. *Entrance requirements:* For master's, honors BA in geography, minimum B average in undergraduate course work; honors BSc with minimum B+ or honors BES or BA in physical geography, environmental or earth sciences or the equivalent; for doctorate, MA in geography, minimum A-average. Additional exam requirements/recommendations for international students: Required—TOEFL (minimum score 230 computer-based; 89 iBT). Electronic applications accepted. *Faculty research:* Resources management, urban/economic/physical/cultural/earth surfaces/geomatics/historical/regional, spatial data handling.

York University, Faculty of Graduate Studies, Faculty of Arts and Faculty of Science and Engineering, Program in Geography, Toronto, ON M3J 1P3, Canada. Offers M Sc, MA, PhD. Part-time programs available. *Degree requirements:* For master's, thesis or alternative; for doctorate, comprehensive exam, thesis/dissertation. Electronic applications accepted.

Section 22
Military and Defense Studies

This section contains a directory of institutions offering graduate work in military and defense studies, followed by in-depth entries submitted by institutions that chose to prepare detailed program descriptions. Additional information about programs listed in the directory but not augmented by an in-depth entry may be obtained by writing directly to the dean of a graduate school or chair of a department at the address given in the directory.

For programs offering related work, see also in this book *History* and *Political Science and International Affairs*.

CONTENTS

Program Directories

Military and Defense Studies   824
National Security   825

Close-Ups
Hawai'i Pacific University   827
University of New Haven   829

See also:
The Institute of World Politics—Statecraft and World
    Politics   867
University of Pittsburgh—Public and International
    Affairs   1243

Military and Defense Studies

American Public University System, AMU/APU Graduate Programs, Charles Town, WV 25414. Offers air warfare (MA Military Studies); American Revolution (MA Military Studies); business administration (MBA); Civil War (MA Military Studies); criminal justice (MA); defense management (MA Military Studies); emergency and disaster management (MA); environmental policy and management (MS); fire science management (MA); global engagement (MA); history (MA); homeland security (MA); humanities (MA); intelligence (MA Military Studies, MA Strategic Intelligence); international peace and conflict resolution (MA); international relations and conflict resolution (MA); joint warfare (MA Military Studies); land warfare international perspective (MA Military Studies); management (MA); military history (MA); military leadership (MA Military Studies); national security studies (MA); naval warfare international (MA Military Studies); naval warfare US (MA Military Studies); political science (MA); public administration (MA); public health (MA); security management (MA); space studies (MS); special ops/LIC (MA Military Studies); sports management (MA); transportation and logistics management (MA); transportation management (MA); unconventional warfare (MA Military Studies); World War II (MA Military Studies). Programs offered via distance learning only. Part-time and evening/weekend programs available. Postbaccalaureate distance learning degree programs offered (no on-campus study). *Degree requirements:* For master's, comprehensive exam. *Entrance requirements:* For master's, bachelor's degree or equivalent, minimum GPA of 2.7 in last 60 hours of course work. Electronic applications accepted. *Faculty research:* Military history, criminal justice, management performance, national security.

Austin Peay State University, College of Graduate Studies, College of Arts and Letters, Department of History and Philosophy, Clarksville, TN 37044. Offers military history (MA). Part-time programs available. Postbaccalaureate distance learning degree programs offered (minimal on-campus study). *Faculty:* 8 full-time (0 women), 1 part-time/adjunct (0 women). *Students:* 13 full-time (4 women), 30 part-time (7 women); includes 3 minority (1 African American, 2 Asian Americans or Pacific Islanders). Average age 35. 36 applicants, 94% accepted, 17 enrolled. In 2008, 2 master's awarded. *Degree requirements:* For master's, comprehensive exam, thesis optional. *Entrance requirements:* For master's, GRE General Test, minimum undergraduate GPA of 2.75, 3 letters of recommendation, bachelor's degree. Additional exam requirements/recommendations for international students: Required—TOEFL (minimum score 500 paper-based; 173 computer-based). *Application deadline:* For fall admission, 7/27 priority date for domestic students; for spring admission, 12/17 priority date for domestic students. Applications are processed on a rolling basis. Application fee: $25. Electronic applications accepted. *Expenses:* Tuition, area resident: Full-time $5772; part-time $305 per credit hour. Tuition, state resident: full-time $5772; part-time $305 per credit hour. Tuition, nonresident: full-time $16,664; part-time $778 per credit hour. Required fees: $1224. *Financial support:* In 2008–09, 1 research assistantship with full tuition reimbursement (averaging $6,996 per year) was awarded; career-related internships or fieldwork, Federal Work-Study, institutionally sponsored loans, scholarships/grants, and unspecified assistantships also available. Support available to part-time students. Financial award application deadline: 3/1; financial award applicants required to submit FAFSA. *Unit head:* Dr. Dewey Browder, Chair, 931-221-7919, Fax: 931-221-9917, E-mail: browderd@apsu.edu. *Application contact:* Dr. Charles Pinder, Dean, College of Graduate Studies, 931-221-7414, Fax: 931-221-7641, E-mail: pinderc@apsu.edu.

The George Washington University, Elliott School of International Affairs, Program in Security Policy Studies, Washington, DC 20052. Offers MA, JD/MA. Part-time and evening/weekend programs available. *Students:* 67 full-time (25 women), 62 part-time (20 women); includes 15 minority (13 Asian Americans or Pacific Islanders, 2 Hispanic Americans), 4 international. Average age 26. 251 applicants, 49% accepted, 52 enrolled. In 2008, 45 master's awarded. *Degree requirements:* For master's, one foreign language, capstone project. *Entrance requirements:* For master's, GRE General Test, 2 semesters of introductory economics, 2 years of a modern foreign language or one semester of statistics. Additional exam requirements/recommendations for international students: Required—TOEFL. *Application deadline:* For fall admission, 2/1 for domestic students; for spring admission, 10/1 for domestic students. Application fee: $60. Electronic applications accepted. *Financial support:* In 2008–09, 22 students received support; fellowships with tuition reimbursements available, research assistantships with tuition reimbursements available, career-related internships or fieldwork, Federal Work-Study, institutionally sponsored loans, and tuition waivers (full) available. Financial award application deadline: 1/15; financial award applicants required to submit FAFSA. *Faculty research:* U.S. arms transfer policies, military balance in the Third World, U.S. foreign policy, technology and security policy. *Unit head:* Joanna Spear, Director, 202-994-1088, E-mail: jspear@gwu.edu. *Application contact:* Jeff V. Miles, Director of Graduate Admissions, 202-994-7050, Fax: 202-994-9537, E-mail: esiagrad@gwu.edu.

Hawai'i Pacific University, College of Liberal Arts, Honolulu, HI 96813. Offers diplomacy and military studies (MA); secondary education (M Ed); social work (MSW). Part-time and evening/weekend programs available. *Faculty:* 17 full-time (8 women), 8 part-time/adjunct (1 woman). *Students:* 86 full-time (52 women), 136 part-time (76 women); includes 87 minority (9 African Americans, 4 American Indian/Alaska Native, 69 Asian Americans or Pacific Islanders, 5 Hispanic Americans), 13 international. Average age 32. 152 applicants, 82% accepted, 71 enrolled. In 2008, 49 master's awarded. *Degree requirements:* For master's, thesis. *Entrance requirements:* Additional exam requirements/recommendations for international students: Recommended—TOEFL (minimum score 550 paper-based; 213 computer-based), TWE (minimum score 5). *Application deadline:* For fall admission, 2/15 priority date for domestic students; for spring admission, 10/15 priority date for domestic students. Applications are processed on a rolling basis. Application fee: $50. Electronic applications accepted. *Expenses:* Tuition: Full-time $10,800; part-time $600 per credit. *Financial support:* In 2008–09, 116 students received support. Career-related internships or fieldwork, Federal Work-Study, scholarships/grants, and unspecified assistantships available. Support available to part-time students. Financial award application deadline: 3/1; financial award applicants required to submit FAFSA. *Unit head:* Dr. William Potter, Associate Vice President and Dean, 808-544-0228, Fax: 808-544-1424, E-mail: wpotter@hpu.edu. *Application contact:* Danny Lam, Assistant Director of Graduate Admissions, 808-544-1135, Fax: 808-544-0280, E-mail: graduate@hpu.edu.

See Close-Up on page 827.

The Institute of World Politics, Graduate Programs in National Security, Intelligence, and International Affairs, Washington, DC 20036. Offers American foreign policy (Certificate); comparative political culture (Certificate); counterintelligence (Certificate); democracy building (Certificate); intelligence (Certificate); international politics (Certificate); national security affairs (Certificate); public diplomacy and political warfare (Certificate); statecraft and national security affairs (MA); statecraft and world politics (MA); strategic intelligence studies (MA). Part-time and evening/weekend programs available. *Degree requirements:* For master's, comprehensive exam, thesis optional. *Entrance requirements:* For master's, GRE General Test. Additional exam requirements/recommendations for international students: Required—TOEFL. Electronic applications accepted. *Faculty research:* Intelligence, national security, statecraft.

See Close-Up on page 867.

The Johns Hopkins University, School of Education, Division of Public Safety Leadership, Baltimore, MD 21218-2699. Offers homeland security (MS); intelligence analysis (MS); management (MS). Part-time and evening/weekend programs available. *Entrance requirements:* For master's, minimum GPA of 3.0, interview, resumé, letters of recommendation. Additional exam requirements/recommendations for international students: Required—TOEFL (minimum score 600 paper-based; 250 computer-based; 100 iBT). *Faculty research:* Ethics and integrity, counter terrorism, school safety, Homeland Security, identity theft.

Joint Military Intelligence College, School of Intelligence Studies, Washington, DC 20340-5100. Offers MSSI. Open only to federal government employees. Part-time and evening/weekend programs available. *Degree requirements:* For master's, thesis. *Entrance requirements:* For master's, MAT, authorized nomination. *Faculty research:* Law and intelligence, intelligence and higher education, low-intensity conflict, intelligence information systems.

The Judge Advocate General's School, U.S. Army, Graduate Programs, Charlottesville, VA 22903-1781. Offers military law (LL M). Only active duty military lawyers attend this school. *Accreditation:* ABA. *Degree requirements:* For master's, thesis optional. *Entrance requirements:* For master's, active duty military lawyer, international military officer, or DOD civilian attorney, JD or LL B. *Faculty research:* Criminal law, administrative and civil law, contract law, international law, legal research and writing.

Missouri State University, Graduate College, College of Humanities and Public Affairs, Department of Defense and Strategic Studies, Fairfax, VA 22031. Offers MS. Part-time programs available. *Faculty:* 1 full-time (0 women), 25 part-time/adjunct (3 women). *Students:* 34 full-time (6 women), 20 part-time (4 women); includes 5 minority (2 African Americans, 1 Asian American or Pacific Islander, 2 Hispanic Americans), 2 international. Average age 24. 34 applicants, 94% accepted, 17 enrolled. In 2008, 19 master's awarded. *Degree requirements:* For master's, comprehensive exam, thesis or alternative. *Entrance requirements:* For master's, GRE, minimum GPA of 2.75, 3 letters of recommendation. Additional exam requirements/recommendations for international students: Required—TOEFL (minimum score 550 paper-based; 213 computer-based; 79 iBT). *Application deadline:* For fall admission, 7/20 priority date for domestic students, 5/1 for international students; for spring admission, 12/20 priority date for domestic students, 9/1 for international students. Applications are processed on a rolling basis. Application fee: $35 ($50 for international students). Electronic applications accepted. *Expenses:* Tuition, state resident: full-time $3852; part-time $214 per credit hour. Tuition, nonresident: full-time $7524; part-time $418 per credit hour. Required fees: $230 per semester. Tuition and fees vary according to course level and course load. *Financial support:* Career-related internships or fieldwork, Federal Work-Study, institutionally sponsored loans, and scholarships/grants available. Financial award application deadline: 3/31; financial award applicants required to submit FAFSA. *Faculty research:* Middle East, terrorism, arms control, U.S.-Soviet military balance, Strategic Defense Initiative. *Unit head:* Dr. Keith Payne, Head, 703-218-3565, Fax: 703-218-3568, E-mail: kbpayne@missouristate.edu. *Application contact:* Dr. Keith Payne, Head, 703-218-3565, Fax: 703-218-3568, E-mail: kbpayne@missouristate.edu.

National Defense University, Industrial College of the Armed Forces, Washington, DC 20319-5066. Offers national resource strategy (MS). Open only to Department of Defense employees and specific federal agencies. *Faculty:* 102 full-time. *Students:* 320 full-time (70 women); includes 54 minority (33 African Americans, 1 American Indian/Alaska Native, 9 Asian Americans or Pacific Islanders, 11 Hispanic Americans). Average age 46. 339 applicants, 94% accepted, 320 enrolled. In 2008, 296 master's awarded. *Degree requirements:* For master's, comprehensive exam. *Entrance requirements:* Additional exam requirements/recommendations for international students: Required—TOEFL. *Application deadline:* For fall admission, 3/15 for domestic students. *Faculty research:* Industrial base and relation to national security, acquisition and relation to national security, resourcing the national security strategy. *Unit head:* Rear Adm. Garry E. Hall, Commandant, 202-685-4333. *Application contact:* Rear Adm. Garry E. Hall, Commandant, 202-685-4333.

National Defense University, Joint Advanced Warfighting School, Norfolk, AB 23511. Offers joint campaign planning and strategy (MS). Open only to Department of Defense employees and specific federal agencies. *Faculty:* 10 full-time (1 woman). *Students:* 41 full-time (3 women); includes 8 minority (4 African Americans, 2 Asian Americans or Pacific Islanders, 2 Hispanic Americans). Average age 42. 41 applicants, 100% accepted, 41 enrolled. In 2008, 41 master's awarded. *Degree requirements:* For master's, thesis. *Entrance requirements:* For master's, Phase 1 JPME. *Application deadline:* For spring admission, 4/15 for domestic and international students. Application fee: $0. *Faculty research:* Irregular warfare, national policy and strategy, international organizations and policies, modern military history and applications of lessons learned, historical military leadership relating to present-day environments. *Unit head:* Dr. Linda B. McCluney, Academic Dean, 757-443-6185, Fax: 757-443-6034, E-mail: mccluneyl@jfsc.ndu.edu. *Application contact:* Shirley A. Wallace, Chief of Plans and Policy/Registrar, 757-443-6189, Fax: 757-443-6034, E-mail: wallaces@jfsc.ndu.edu.

National Defense University, National War College, Washington, DC 20319-5066. Offers national security strategy (MS). Open only to Department of Defense employees and specific federal agencies. *Faculty:* 62 full-time (10 women). *Students:* 223 full-time (29 women); includes 28 minority (11 African Americans, 10 Asian Americans or Pacific Islanders, 7 Hispanic Americans). Average age 45. 227 applicants, 98% accepted, 223 enrolled. *Degree requirements:* For master's, comprehensive exam. *Entrance requirements:* For master's, bachelor's degree. Additional exam requirements/recommendations for international students: Required—TOEFL. *Application deadline:* For fall admission, 3/15 for domestic students. Application fee: $0. *Faculty research:* National security policy, regional security, US national security strategy, US military, strategy. *Unit head:* Brig. Gen. Robert P. Steel, Commandant, 202-685-2128, Fax: 202-685-3993. *Application contact:* Brig. Gen. Robert P. Steel, Commandant, 202-685-2128, Fax: 202-685-3993.

Naval Postgraduate School, Graduate Programs, Department of Computer Science, Program in Modeling of Virtual Environments and Simulations, Monterey, CA 93943. Offers MS, PhD. Program only open to commissioned officers of the United States and friendly nations and selected United States federal civilian employees. Part-time programs available. *Degree requirements:* For master's, thesis; for doctorate, one foreign language, thesis/dissertation.

Naval Postgraduate School, Graduate Programs, Department of Defense Analysis, Monterey, CA 93943. Offers defense analysis (MS); joint information operations (MS); special operations (MS). Program only open to commissioned officers of the United States and friendly nations and selected United States federal civilian employees. Part-time programs available. *Degree requirements:* For master's, thesis.

Naval Postgraduate School, Graduate Programs, Program in Undersea Warfare, Monterey, CA 93943. Offers applied science (MS); electrical engineering (MS); engineering acoustics (MS); operations research (MS); physical oceanography (MS). Program only open to commissioned officers of the United States and friendly nations and selected United States federal civilian employees. Part-time programs available. *Degree requirements:* For master's, thesis.

Naval Postgraduate School, Graduate Programs, School of Business and Public Policy, Monterey, CA 93943. Offers contract management (MS); defense-focused business administration (MBA); executive business administration (MBA); leadership and human resource development (MS); management (MS); program management (MS); systems engineering management (MS). Program only open to commissioned officers of the United States and friendly nations and selected United States federal civilian employees. *Accreditation:* AACSB; NASPAA. Part-time programs available. Postbaccalaureate distance learning degree programs offered (minimal on-campus study). *Degree requirements:* For master's, thesis.

Norwich University, School of Graduate Studies, Program in Military History, Northfield, VT 05663. Offers MA. Evening/weekend programs available. *Faculty:* 30 part-time/adjunct (2 women). *Students:* 207 full-time (34 women); includes 10 minority (2 African Americans, 1 American Indian/Alaska Native, 2 Asian Americans or Pacific Islanders, 5 Hispanic Americans). Average age 41. 289 applicants, 76% accepted, 211 enrolled. In 2008, 207 master's awarded. *Entrance requirements:* For master's, minimum undergraduate GPA of 2.75. Additional exam requirements/recommendations for international students: Required—TOEFL (minimum score 550 paper-based; 212 computer-based; 83 iBT). *Application deadline:* For fall admission, 8/10 for domestic and international students; for winter admission, 11/7 for domestic and international students; for spring admission, 2/6 for domestic and international students. Application fee: $50. Electronic applications accepted. *Expenses:* Tuition: Full-time $8000. Full-time tuition and fees vary according to degree level and program. *Financial support:* Scholarships/grants available. Financial award applicants required to submit FAFSA. *Unit head:* Dr. James Erhman, Program Director, 802-485-2567, Fax: 802-485-2533. *Application contact:* Lars Nielsen, Administrative Director, 802-485-2853, Fax: 802-485-2533, E-mail: lnielsen@norwich.edu.

Royal Military College of Canada, Division of Graduate Studies and Research, Continuing Studies, Department of History, Kingston, ON K7K 7B4, Canada. Offers defense management and policy (MA); history (PhD); war studies (MA). *Faculty:* 7 full-time (1 woman). *Degree requirements:* For master's, thesis. *Entrance requirements:* For master's, honours degree with second-class standing; for doctorate, master's degree. *Application deadline:* For fall admission, 5/1 priority date for domestic students; for winter admission, 9/1 priority date for domestic students. Applications are processed on a rolling basis. Application fee: $50. Electronic applications accepted. Tuition charges are reported in Canadian dollars. *Expenses:* Tuition, area resident: Full-time $4500 Canadian dollars; part-time $950 Canadian dollars per course. International tuition: $12,000 Canadian dollars full-time. Tuition and fees vary according to program. *Unit head:* Dr. Roch Legault, 613-541-6000 Ext. 6511, E-mail: legault-r@rmc.ca. *Application contact:* Suzanne Paquette, Administrative Assistant, Graduate Studies, 613-541-6000 Ext. 3728, Fax: 613-542-8612, E-mail: suzanne.paquette@rmc.ca.

School of Advanced Air and Space Studies, Program in Airpower Art and Science, Maxwell AFB, AL 36112-6424. Offers MA. Available to active duty military officers only. *Degree requirements:* For master's, comprehensive exam, thesis, minimum GPA of 3.0. *Entrance requirements:* For master's, less than 16 years total of active commissioned service; master's degree or undergraduate degree with a minimum GPA of 2.75. Additional exam requirements/recommendations for international students: Required—TOEFL. *Faculty research:* Military history, political science, international relations, social history, technology.

United States Army Command and General Staff College, Graduate Program, Fort Leavenworth, KS 66027-2301. Offers military art and science (MMAS). Only career military officers are selected to attend United States Army Command and General Staff College; Graduate Program is voluntary for first-year students, but mandatory for second-year students.

University of Calgary, Faculty of Graduate Studies, Centre for Military and Strategic Studies, Calgary, AB T2N 1N4, Canada. Offers MSS, PhD. PhD offered in special cases only. Part-time programs available. *Degree requirements:* For master's, thesis; for doctorate, comprehensive exam, thesis/dissertation. *Entrance requirements:* For master's, minimum GPA of 3.4. Additional exam requirements/recommendations for international students: Recommended—TOEFL (minimum score 550 paper-based). *Faculty research:* Military history, Israeli studies, strategic studies, int'l relations, Arctic security.

University of Detroit Mercy, College of Liberal Arts and Education, Department of Criminal Justice and Human Services, Detroit, MI 48221. Offers criminal justice (MA); intelligence analysis (MS); security administration (MS).

University of Pittsburgh, Graduate School of Public and International Affairs, International Affairs Division, Program in Security and Intelligence Studies, Pittsburgh, PA 15260. Offers MPIA, JD/MPIA, MBA/MPIA, MID/MPIA, MPA/MPIA, MSIS/MPIA. Part-time and evening/weekend programs available. *Degree requirements:* For master's, thesis optional, internship, capstone seminar. *Entrance requirements:* For master's, GRE General Test, 3 letters of recommendation, resumé, minimum GPA of 3.2. Additional exam requirements/recommendations for international students: Required—TOEFL (minimum score 550 paper-based; 213 computer-based; 80 iBT), TWE (minimum score 4.5); Recommended—IELTS (minimum score 7). Electronic applications accepted. *Faculty research:* Political economy, international security/defense/intelligence, transnational crime, international trade, international finance, terrorism.

The University of Texas at El Paso, Graduate School, Institute for Policy and Economic Development, El Paso, TX 79968-0001. Offers intelligence and national security studies (MS); leadership studies (MLS); public administration (MPA).

National Security

American Public University System, AMU/APU Graduate Programs, Charles Town, WV 25414. Offers air warfare (MA Military Studies); American Revolution (MA Military Studies); business administration (MBA); Civil War (MA Military Studies); criminal justice (MA); defense management (MA Military Studies); emergency and disaster management (MA); environmental policy and management (MS); fire science management (MA); global engagement (MA); history (MA); homeland security (MA); humanities (MA); intelligence (MA Military Studies, MA Strategic Intelligence); international peace and conflict resolution (MA); international relations and conflict resolution (MA); joint warfare (MA Military Studies); land warfare international perspective (MA Military Studies); management (MA); military history (MA); military leadership (MA Military Studies); national security studies (MA); naval warfare international (MA Military Studies); naval warfare US (MA Military Studies); political science (MA); public administration (MA); public health (MA); security management (MA); space studies (MS); special ops/LIC (MA Military Studies); sports management (MA); transportation and logistics management (MA); transportation management (MA); unconventional warfare (MA Military Studies); World War II (MA Military Studies). Programs offered via distance learning only. Part-time and evening/weekend programs available. Postbaccalaureate distance learning degree programs offered (no on-campus study). *Degree requirements:* For master's, comprehensive exam. *Entrance requirements:* For master's, bachelor's degree or equivalent, minimum GPA of 2.7 in last 60 hours of course work. Electronic applications accepted. *Faculty research:* Military history, criminal justice, management performance, national security.

California State University, San Bernardino, Graduate Studies, College of Social and Behavioral Sciences, National Security Studies Program, San Bernardino, CA 92407-2397. Offers MA. Part-time and evening/weekend programs available. *Degree requirements:* For master's, comprehensive exam. *Entrance requirements:* For master's, minimum GPA of 2.5. *Expenses:* Tuition, area resident: Full-time $1252; part-time $726 per quarter. Required fees: $334 per quarter. Tuition and fees vary according to degree level and student level. *Faculty research:* Strategy, arms control, defense policy, terrorism, U.S. foreign policy, operations analysis.

Hult International Business School, Program in International Relations—Hult London Campus, Cambridge, MA 02141. Offers conflict resolution (MA); diplomacy (MA); international public law (MA); international relations (MA); Middle East international security (MA); politics (MA); security studies (MA); terrorism (MA); U.S. foreign policy (MA). Part-time programs available. *Entrance requirements:* Additional exam requirements/recommendations for international students: Required—TOEFL (minimum score 580 paper-based; 237 computer-based), TWE (minimum score 5). Electronic applications accepted. *Faculty research:* American foreign politics, Middle East, security studies.

The Institute of World Politics, Graduate Programs in National Security, Intelligence, and International Affairs, Washington, DC 20036. Offers American foreign policy (Certificate); comparative political culture (Certificate); counterintelligence (Certificate); democracy building (Certificate); intelligence (Certificate); international politics (Certificate); national security affairs (Certificate); public diplomacy and political warfare (Certificate); statecraft and national security affairs (MA); statecraft and world politics (MA); strategic intelligence studies (MA). Part-time and evening/weekend programs available. *D*
exam, thesis optional. *Entrance requireme*
exam requirements/recommendations for int
applications accepted. *Faculty research:* Int

Kansas State University, Graduate Scho
History, Manhattan, KS 66506. Offers hist
programs available. *Faculty:* 17 full-time (6
42 full-time (11 women), 72 part-time (17 wo
Pacific Islanders), 7 international. Average a
2008, 4 master's, 2 doctorates awarded. *De*
programs); for doctorate, one foreign langua
requirements: For master's, GRE General
for doctorate, GRE General Test or MAT. Ad
international students: Required—TOEFL
deadline: For fall admission, 5/1 for dom
students; for spring admission, 11/1 for do
students. Applications are processed on a rolling basis. Application fee: $30 ($55 for international students). *Expenses:* Tuition, area resident: Full-time $6466; part-time $269.40 per credit hour. Tuition, state resident: full-time $6466; part-time $269.40 per credit hour. Tuition, nonresident: full-time $14,874; part-time $619.75 per credit hour. Required fees: $673; $23.40 per credit hour. Tuition and fees vary according to campus/location. *Financial support:* In 2008–09, 5 research assistantships (averaging $16,414 per year), 9 teaching assistantships with full tuition reimbursements (averaging $9,000 per year) were awarded; career-related internships or fieldwork, Federal Work-Study, institutionally sponsored loans, and scholarships/grants also available. Support available to part-time students. Financial award application deadline: 3/1; financial award applicants required to submit FAFSA. *Faculty research:* Environmental history, history of Christianity, American social history, history of war and society, history of international relations and diplomacy. Total annual research expenditures: $16,186. *Unit head:* Sue Zschoche, Head, 785-532-6730, Fax: 785-532-7004, E-mail: suez@ksu.edu. *Application contact:* Louise Breen, Recruiting Program Director, 785-532-0365, Fax: 785-532-7004, E-mail: breen@ksu.edu.

National Defense University, College of International Security Affairs, Washington, DC 20319-5066. Offers strategic security studies (MA), including conflict management, counterterrorism, homeland defense/ security, international security studies. Part-time and evening/weekend programs available. *Faculty:* 13 full-time (3 women), 14 part-time/adjunct (2 women). *Students:* 33 full-time (2 women), 305 part-time (75 women). Average age 30. 133 applicants, 100% accepted, 133 enrolled. In 2008, 39 master's awarded. *Degree requirements:* For master's, thesis. *Entrance requirements:* Additional exam requirements/recommendations for international students: Required—TOEFL. *Unit head:* Dr. R. Joseph DeSutter, Director, 202-685-3871. *Application contact:* Dr. R. Joseph DeSutter, Director, 202-685-3871.

National Defense University, National War College, Washington, DC 20319-5066. Offers national security strategy (MS). Open only to Department of Defense employees and specific federal agencies. *Faculty:* 62 full-time (10 women). *Students:* 223 full-time (29 women); includes 28 minority (11 African Americans, 10 Asian Americans or Pacific Islanders, 7 Hispanic Americans). Average age 45. 227 applicants, 98% accepted, 223 enrolled. *Degree requirements:* For master's, comprehensive exam. *Entrance requirements:* For master's, bachelor's degree. Additional exam requirements/recommendations for international students: Required—TOEFL. *Application deadline:* For fall admission, 3/15 for domestic students. Application fee: $0. *Faculty research:* National security policy, regional security, US national security strategy, US military, strategy. *Unit head:* Brig. Gen. Robert P. Steel, Commandant, 202-685-2128, Fax: 202-685-3993. *Application contact:* Brig. Gen. Robert P. Steel, Commandant, 202-685-2128, Fax: 202-685-3993.

Naval Postgraduate School, Graduate Programs, Department of National Security Affairs, Monterey, CA 93943. Offers intelligence (MA); international relations (MA); political science (MA); regional security education (MA); security building (MA); security studies (MA). Program only open to commissioned officers of the United States and friendly nations and selected United States federal civilian employees. Part-time programs available. *Degree requirements:* For master's, thesis.

Naval War College, Program in National Security and Strategic Studies, Newport, RI 02841-1207. Offers MA. Program open only to full-time military personnel.

Texas A&M University, George Bush School of Government and Public Service, College Station, TX 77843. Offers advanced international affairs (Certificate); homeland security (Certificate); international affairs (MPIA), including international economics and development, national security affairs; nonprofit management (Certificate); public service and administration (MPSA), including public management, public policy analysis. *Accreditation:* NASPAA. *Faculty:* 43. *Students:* 188 full-time (80 women), 101 part-time (37 women); includes 40 minority (10 African Americans, 5 Asian Americans or Pacific Islanders, 25 Hispanic Americans), 22 international. Average age 24. In 2008, 64 master's awarded. *Degree requirements:* For master's, summer internship. *Entrance requirements:* For master's, GRE (preferred) or GMAT. *Application deadline:* For fall admission, 1/24 for domestic and international students. Application fee: $50 ($75 for international students). Electronic applications accepted. *Expenses:* Tuition, area resident: Full-time $3838.50. Tuition, state resident: full-time $3838.50. Tuition, nonresident: full-time $8897. Required fees: $2359.60. *Financial support:* In 2008–09, fellowships (averaging $11,000 per year), research assistantships (averaging $11,250 per year) were awarded; career-related internships or fieldwork, Federal Work-Study, and institutionally sponsored loans also available. Financial award application deadline: 2/1; financial award applicants required to submit FAFSA. *Faculty research:* Public policy, presidential studies, public leadership, economic policy, social policy. *Unit head:* A. Benton Cocanougher, Dean, 979-862-8842, E-mail: bushschool@tamu.edu. *Application contact:* Kathryn Meyer, Recruitment/Placement Officer, 979-458-4767, Fax: 979-845-4155, E-mail: admissions@bushschool.tamu.edu.

Trinity (Washington) University, School of Professional Studies, Washington, DC 20017-1094. Offers business administration (MBA); communication (MA); international security studies (MA); organizational management (MSA), including federal program management, human resource management, nonprofit management, organizational development, public and community health. Part-time and evening/weekend programs available. *Degree requirements:* For master's, thesis (for some programs), capstone project (MSA). *Entrance requirements:* For master's, minimum GPA of 2.5. Additional exam requirements/recommendations for international students: Required—TOEFL (minimum score 550 paper-based; 213 computer-based).

University of New Haven, Graduate School, Henry C. Lee College of Criminal Justice and Forensic Sciences, National Security and Public Safety Program, West Haven, CT 06516-1916. Offers MS. *Faculty:* 3 full-time (0 women), 3 part-time/adjunct (0 women). *Students:* 24

National Security

University of New Haven (continued)

full-time (12 women), 30 part-time (11 women); includes 15 minority (6 African Americans, 2 Asian Americans or Pacific Islanders, 7 Hispanic Americans), 1 international. Average age 31. 30 applicants, 77% accepted, 17 enrolled. In 2008, 57 master's awarded. *Entrance requirements:* Additional exam requirements/recommendations for international students: Required—TOEFL (minimum score 520 paper-based; 190 computer-based; 70 iBT); Recommended—IELTS (minimum score 5.5). *Application deadline:* For fall admission, 5/31 for international students; for winter admission, 10/15 for international students; for spring admission, 1/15 for international students. Application fee: $50. *Expenses:* Tuition: Full-time $15,075; part-time $670 per credit. Required fees: $240; $45 per trimester. Tuition and fees vary according to course load and program. *Financial support:* Research assistantships with partial tuition reimbursements, teaching assistantships with partial tuition reimbursements, career-related internships or fieldwork, Federal Work-Study, scholarships/grants, tuition waivers, and unspecified assistantships available. Support available to part-time students. Financial award applicants required to submit FAFSA. *Unit head:* Dr. William L Tafoya, Dean, 203-932-7260. *Application contact:* Eloise Gormley, Director of Graduate Admissions, 203-932-7449, Fax: 203-932-7137, E-mail: gradinfo@newhaven.edu.

See Close-Up on page 829.

University of Pittsburgh, Graduate School of Public and International Affairs, Executive Programs in Public Policy and Management, Pittsburgh, PA 15260. Offers development planning (MPPM); international development (MPPM); international political economy (MPPM); international security studies (MPPM); management of non profit organizations (MPPM); metropolitan management and regional development (MPPM); policy analysis and evaluation (MPPM). Part-time programs available. *Degree requirements:* For master's, thesis optional, capstone seminar. *Entrance requirements:* For master's, 2 letters of recommendation, resumé, 5 years of supervisory or budgetary experience. Additional exam requirements/recommendations for international students: Required—TOEFL (minimum score 600 paper-based; 250 computer-based; 100 iBT), TWE (minimum score 4); Recommended—IELTS (minimum score 7). Electronic applications accepted. *Faculty research:* Executive training and technical assistance for U.S. and international clients.

See Close-Up on page 1243.

The University of Texas at El Paso, Graduate School, Institute for Policy and Economic Development, El Paso, TX 79968-0001. Offers intelligence and national security studies (MS); leadership studies (MLS); public administration (MPA).

HAWAI'I PACIFIC UNIVERSITY

Diplomacy and Military Studies Program

Program of Study	Hawai'i Pacific University's (HPU's) Master of Arts in diplomacy and military studies (M.A./DMS) is designed to provide students with an interdisciplinary view of the role of diplomacy and the military in world affairs from both historical and contemporary perspectives. The program combines courses in history, art history, literature, philosophy, anthropology, international relations, strategic studies, and political science to acquaint students with different approaches and methods in the study of diplomacy and the military.
	The M.A./DMS program is an excellent opportunity for those wishing to explore the complex relationships of politics, society, and the military. It is a useful degree for those who are either professional military officers or those who work in a variety of government positions. It is also outstanding preparation for more advanced graduate studies in history, political science, or international relations.
	Courses for the diplomacy and military studies degree fall into four major categories: core classes, electives in diplomatic and military history, supporting field electives, and capstone courses. Moreover, unlike other similar programs which have a focus on the United States and Europe, the M.A./DMS integrates a variety of courses in Asia and the Pacific as well as courses of a comparative nature.
	The core classes are drawn from the disciplines of history, interdisciplinary humanities, philosophy, and political science and provide students with the historical, ethical, and practical background necessary to fully understand the multifaceted character of the military. They are also intended to give students a sound introduction to the fundamental literature dealing with the history of foreign relations and the military.
Research Facilities	To support graduate studies, HPU's Meader and Atherton Libraries hold more than 110,000 bound volumes, 350,000 microfiche items, and periodical subscriptions to 1,500 print titles and 30,000 electronic journals. Databases of public and state university libraries, legislative information, and business-oriented statistical data are also available in the library or online. Students can access HPU's library databases, course information, their academic information, and an e-mail account through Pipeline, the university's internal Web site for students. The University's accessible on-campus computer center houses more than 100 computers with specialized software to support graduate academic programs. HPU also provides free Wi-Fi so that students can access Pipeline resources anywhere on campus using laptops. A significant number of online courses are available.
Financial Aid	The University participates in all federal financial aid programs designated for graduate students. These programs provide aid in the form of subsidized (need-based) and unsubsidized (non-need-based) Federal Stafford Student Loans. Through these loans, funds may be available to cover the student's entire cost of education. To apply for aid, students must submit the Free Application for Federal Student Aid (FAFSA) beginning January 1. Mailing of student award letters usually begins by the end of March. The University also offers several institutional scholarships and assistantships to new full-time, degree-seeking students. The Trustees' Scholar Program provides a 50 percent tuition waiver for two semesters; the Deans' Scholarship Program, a 20 percent tuition waiver for one semester; and the International Scholar Program, a 20 to 50 percent tuition waiver. Graduate assistantships, which give students a 50 percent tuition waiver for one semester, are also available. Priority consideration is given to those students who apply by the deadline.
Cost of Study	Tuition for graduate students enrolled in fall and spring semesters is determined on a per-credit basis; full-time status for a graduate student is 9 credits. Tuition for the optional winter and summer sessions is also determined on a per-credit basis. The estimated minimum funds needed for a nine-month academic year (September to May) based on 2009–10 school-year expenses is $25,739. For the 2009–10 academic year, full-time tuition is $11,880 for most graduate degree programs. Books, supplies, and transportation cost $1885, and health insurance costs $880.
Living and Housing Costs	Most graduate students live in off-campus housing. The cost of living in off-campus apartments is approximately $11,094 for a double-occupancy room.
Student Group	University enrollment currently stands at more than 8,200. HPU is one of the most culturally diverse universities in America with students from all 50 U.S. states and more than 100 countries.
Location	Hawai'i Pacific University combines the excitement of an urban, downtown campus with the serenity of a residential campus and a pristine marine institute. The main campus is ideally located in downtown Honolulu, the business and financial center of the Pacific. Eight miles away, situated on 135 acres in Kaneohe, the windward Hawai'i Loa campus is the site of environmental sciences, marine biology, nursing, oceanography, and several liberal arts programs. The third campus, The Oceanic Institute, an affiliate of HPU, is an applied aquaculture research facility located on a 56-acre site at Makapu'u Point on the windward coast of Oahu, Hawaii. Students can travel between the three sites using the convenient HPU shuttle service. There are also eight military campus programs located at Pearl Harbor, Barbers Point, Hickam Air Force Base, Schofield Barracks, Fort Shafter, Tripler Army Medical Center, Kaneohe Marine Corps Air Station, and Camp Smith.
The University	HPU is a private, nonprofit university with approximately 8,200 students. Founded in 1965, HPU prides itself on maintaining strong academic programs, small class sizes, individual attention to students, and a diverse faculty and student population. HPU is recognized as a "Best in the West" college by the *Princeton Review* and a "Best Buy" by *Barron's* business magazine. HPU offers more than fifty acclaimed undergraduate programs and twelve distinguished graduate programs. The University has a faculty of more than 500, a student-faculty ratio of 18:1, and an average class size of 20. A wide range of counseling and other student support services are available. There are more than seventy student organizations on campus, including the Graduate Student Organization.
Applying	Students must have a baccalaureate degree from an accredited college or university in the United States or an equivalent degree from another country. Applicants should complete and forward a graduate admissions application, send in the $50 nonrefundable application fee, have official transcripts sent from all colleges or universities previously attended, and forward two letters of recommendation. A personal statement about the applicant's academic and career goals is required; submitting a resume is optional. Applicants who have taken the Graduate Record Examination (GRE) should have their scores sent directly to the Graduate Admissions Office. International students should submit scores of a recognized English proficiency test such as TOEFL. Admissions decisions are made on a rolling basis, and applicants are notified between one and two weeks after all documents have been submitted. Applicants are encouraged to submit their applications online.
Correspondence and Information	Graduate Admissions Hawai'i Pacific University 1164 Bishop Street, #911 Honolulu, Hawaii 96813 Phone: 808-544-1135 866-GRAD-HPU (toll-free) Fax: 808-544-0280 E-mail: graduate@hpu.edu Web site: http://www.hpu.edu/hpumadms

Hawai'i Pacific University

THE FACULTY

Pierre Asselin, Associate Professor of History; Ph.D., Hawai'i at Manoa.
Patrick Bratton, Assistant Professor of Political Science; Ph.D., Catholic University.
Grace Cheng, Associate Professor of Political Science; Ph.D., Hawai'i.
Allison Gough, Associate Professor of History; Ph.D., Ohio State.
Russell Hart, Associate Professor of History; Ph.D., Ohio State.
Carlos Juarez, Professor of Political Science; Ph.D., UCLA.
James Primm, Associate Professor of Political Science; Ph.D., Hawai'i.
George Satterfield, Associate Professor of History; Ph.D., Illinois at Urbana-Champaign.

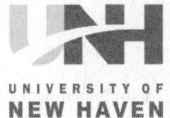

UNIVERSITY OF
NEW HAVEN

UNIVERSITY OF NEW HAVEN

Program in National Security and Public Safety

Program of Study

The National Security and Public Safety program, the result of a collaborative effort of the Criminal Justice and Political Science Departments, is administered by the dean's office of the Henry C. Lee College of Criminal Justice and Forensic Sciences, operating at the main campus in West Haven, Connecticut, as well as being hosted by Sandia National Laboratories in Albuquerque, New Mexico. Although the number of such programs has grown nationwide, UNH's program was the first of its kind, having been developed prior to 9/11.

Students gain an understanding of the fundamental principles of the legal charter, presidential executive orders, and the framework that guides the operation of national security agencies. The role and function of the U.S. agencies composing the intelligence community are analyzed, with emphasis on information protection and security. The concentration in information protection and security provides a unique approach to the issues of cyberterrorism and the protection of information management systems within national security agencies. Research issues in public safety emergency management and homeland security are emphasized. Corporate security and its new relationship to the role of homeland and national security are rich elements of research inquiry.

A total of 36 credits are required for the Master of Science degree. Students are required to complete 15 credit hours of required core courses, 9 credit hours of restricted electives, and 12 credits of electives, with advisor approval. As part of the program, students must either complete a capstone requirement of a research project or a national security internship or a do a thesis option

Research Facilities

The holdings of the Marvin K. Peterson Library include more than 249,000 volumes and 1,400 print journals and newspaper subscriptions, electronic access to more than 17,940 full-text journal and newspaper titles, U.S. government documents, and numerous corporate annual reports, pamphlet files, and microfilm as well as current and extensive back-issue files of periodicals. Faculty members and students—in their offices, residence halls, or at home—have access to a variety of online databases and library support from the Web site. UNH subscribes to many online databases, including LexisNexis, ABI/INFORM, Criminal Justice Periodicals Index, CCH Online, CountryWatch, and FORENSICnetBASE. Computers with Internet access, the Microsoft Office Suite, and SPSS are available for research purposes. Students and faculty members can plug in their laptop computers to connect to the campus network via ports available throughout the library's three floors.

The UNH Center for Computing Services provides both administrative and academic computing support. The general-access Internet labs are dedicated to providing students with access to e-mail, Web, and other standard uses. The University maintains, on behalf of its colleges or departments, numerous computer laboratories and teaching classrooms at various locations around campus. The hardware and software available in the labs are continuously upgraded as computer technology changes.

Financial Aid

Financial aid is available for graduate students through assistantships and loans. The University participates in Federal Stafford Student Loan programs. Teaching, research, and administrative assistantships are available to full-time students. Compensation includes $7.65 per hour as well as a 50 percent tuition reduction; students typically work 15–20 hours per week.

Cost of Study

Tuition for master's degree students for the 2008–09 academic year was $670 per graduate credit. The Graduate Student Council and technology fees were $20 and $25 per term, respectively. All charges and fees are subject to change.

Living and Housing Costs

There is no on-campus housing for graduate students, but the Office of Residential Life maintains a listing of apartments in the local area at a range of costs.

Student Group

Many students are from Connecticut, but each year, an increasing number come from other states and many other countries. The graduate student body of more than 1,700 ranges from recent college graduates to professionals with several years of experience in their fields. About 51 percent of the graduate students are women, about 12 percent receive some sort of financial aid, approximately 19 percent are international students, and nearly 16 percent are members of minority groups.

Student Outcomes

UNH stands apart from other institutions of higher learning because of its commitment to the concept of experiential learning—bringing practice into the classroom to educate its students and show them the world ahead. With the skills UNH teaches and the foundation it builds, graduates go on to excellent jobs in their field or to further study in business, law, and education. Graduates are employed in government service, teaching, private agencies, and business.

Location

The University of New Haven maintains a close relationship with the surrounding community. Although the campus is located in West Haven, it is less than 3 miles from downtown New Haven, and students can easily take advantage of the cultural offerings of the city. New Haven has rail, bus, and air service, and its location at the junction of two major interstate highways places the school within easy driving distance of New York, Boston, and Providence.

The University

The University of New Haven, founded in 1920, comprises five colleges—the College of Arts and Sciences, the College of Business, the Tagliatela College of Engineering, the Henry C. Lee College of Criminal Justice and Forensic Sciences, and University College. The University offers more than eighty undergraduate-degree and more than twenty-five graduate-degree programs; many are available through part-time, evening, and executive programs.

Applying

Applicants must hold a baccalaureate degree from an accredited college or university. Students must submit a formal application, the nonrefundable $50 application fee, official college transcripts from all undergraduate course work, two letters of recommendation, and a resume. In addition, a satisfactory TOEFL score (except for students whose native language is English) and certified financial support forms are required for all international students.

Correspondence and Information

James J. Cassidy, Director of the Criminal Justice Graduate Programs
Henry C. Lee College of Criminal Justice and Forensic Sciences
University of New Haven
300 Boston Post Road
West Haven, Connecticut 06516
Phone: 203-479-4510
E-mail: jcassidy@newhaven.edu
Web site: http://www.newhaven.edu/5924/

University of New Haven

THE FACULTY AND THEIR RESEARCH

Katherine Brown, Assistant Professor; Ph.D., Sam Houston State, 2008. Child victimization, child abduction murder, solvability factors affecting murder investigations.

William Carbone, Practitioner-In-Residence; M.P.A., New Haven, 1974.

James Cassidy, Associate Professor, Director of the Center for Forensic Psychology, and Coordinator of the Criminal Justice Graduate Programs; Ph.D., Hahnemann, 1993; J.D., Villanova, 1989.

Ernest Dorling, Instructor and Co-Director of International Justice and Security; M.P.A., Troy State, 1989.

Leila Dutton, Assistant Professor; Ph.D., Rhode Island, 2004.

Mario Gaboury, Professor and Chair of the Criminal Justice Department, Oskar Schindler Endowed Professor, and Director of the Crime Victims Study Center; J.D., Georgetown, 1987. Global human trafficking, victimology, victims' rights and services, juvenile justice and community policing.

Thomas Johnson, Professor Emeritus; D.Crim., Berkeley, 1970.

Robert Keppel, Associate Professor; Ph.D., Washington (Seattle), 1992. Murder and its investigation.

Michael Lawlor, Assistant Professor; J.D., George Washington, 1983.

Martin Looney, Practitioner-In-Residence; J.D., Connecticut, 1985.

Daniel Mabrey, Visiting Professor; Ph.D., Sam Houston State, 2006.

James Matschulat, Associate Professor; M.B.A., St. John's (New York), 1974. Risk management, administration of national security organizations.

Daniel Maxwell, Instructor; M.P.A., New Haven, 1994; M.S., New Haven, 1986. Law enforcement and police work, investigations and issues in the security field.

David Maxwell, Professor Emeritus; J.D., Miami, 1954.

James Monahan, Associate Professor and Co-Director of the International Justice and Security Concentration; Ph.D., Florida State, 1974. Community policing, prison reform strategies, empathy and crime.

Lynn Monahan, Professor and Coordinator of the Juvenile and Family Justice and Corrections Programs; Ph.D., Oregon, 1971.

Donna Morris, Assistant Professor and Director of the Legal Studies Program; J.D., Yale, 1979. Alternative forms of dispute resolution, restorative justice, conflict management.

Fadia Narchet, Assistant Professor and Coordinator of the Undergraduate Forensic Psychology Program; Ph.D., Florida International, 2005.

William Norton, Professor and Associate Dean; Ph.D., Florida State, 1983. Policy and program evaluation research to identify best practices in the criminal justice field.

Martin O'Connor, Associate Professor; M.Div., Yale, 2002.

Craig Parker Jr., Professor Emeritus; Ph.D., SUNY at Buffalo, 1968.

Joseph Polio, Instructor; M.S., New Haven, 2000.

Gerald Robin, Professor Emeritus; Ph.D., Pennsylvania, 1965. Legal issues, depiction of law enforcement in the media.

David Schroeder, Assistant Professor; CUNY Graduate Center, 2007. Principles of criminal investigation.

Chris Sedelmaier, Assistant Professor and Coordinator of the Crime Analysis Program; Ph.D., Rutgers, 2003.

William Tafoya, Professor, Director of the National Security Program, and Director of the Forensic Computer Investigation Program; Ph.D., Maryland, 1986. Analytical (software) tools in intelligence studies, behavioral assessment of computer criminals.

Tracy Tamborra, Assistant Professor; Ph.D., CUNY, John Jay, 2008. Domestic violence, sexual assault/abuse, and the effects of the criminal justice system on women, persons of color, persons affected by poverty, and other traditionally marginalized groups.

Max Theil, Practitioner-In-Residence; B.A., St. Mary's, 1963.

Richard H. Ward, Professor and Dean; D.Crim., Berkeley, 1971.

Section 23
Political Science and International Affairs

This section contains a directory of institutions offering graduate work in political science and international affairs, followed by in-depth entries submitted by institutions that chose to prepare detailed program descriptions. Additional information about programs listed in the directory but not augmented by an in-depth entry may be obtained by writing directly to the dean of a graduate school or chair of a department at the address given in the directory.

For programs offering related work, see also in this book *Area and Cultural Studies, History, Language and Literature,* and *Public, Regional, and Industrial Affairs.* In another guide in this series: **Graduate Programs in Business, Education, Health, Information Studies, Law & Social Work**
See *International Business*

CONTENTS

Program Directories

International Affairs	832
International Development	841
International Trade Policy	843
Political Science	844

Display

University of California, San Diego	838

Close-Ups

American University	861
Columbia University	863
Fordham University	865
The Institute of World Politics	867
Missouri State University	869
Monterey Institute of International Studies	871
The New School: A University	873
Seton Hall University	875
Southern Illinois University Carbondale	877
Tufts University	879
University of California, San Diego	881
Villanova University	883

See also:

Central European University—Social Sciences and Humanities	349
The New School: A University—Political and Social Science	1251
New York University—Public Service	1229
Tufts University—Urban and Environmental Policy and Planning	1237
University of Pittsburgh—Public and International Affairs	1243
University of Southern California—Communication, Journalism, Public Diplomacy, and Public Relations	709
The University of Texas at Dallas—Economic, Political, and Policy Sciences	783

International Affairs

Alliant International University–México City, International Studies Division, Mexico City, Mexico. Offers international relations (MA).

Alliant International University–México City, Marshall Goldsmith School of Management, Mexico City, Mexico. Offers international business administration (MIBA); international relations (MA). Part-time and evening/weekend programs available. *Entrance requirements:* For master's, GMAT, minimum GPA of 3.0. Additional exam requirements/recommendations for international students: Required—TOEFL (minimum score 550 paper-based; 213 computer-based), TWE (minimum score 5). Electronic applications accepted. *Faculty research:* Environmental impact and business in Mexico.

Alliant International University–México City, Programs in Arts and Science, Mexico City, Mexico. Offers counseling psychology (MA); international relations (MA). Part-time programs available. *Degree requirements:* For master's, thesis optional. *Entrance requirements:* For master's, GRE General Test, letters of recommendation. Additional exam requirements/recommendations for international students: Required—TOEFL. Electronic applications accepted.

Alliant International University–San Diego, Marshall Goldsmith School of Management, International Studies Division, San Diego, CA 92131-1799. Offers international relations (MA). Part-time programs available. *Degree requirements:* For master's, thesis. *Entrance requirements:* For master's, GRE, minimum GPA of 2.5, letters of recommendation. Additional exam requirements/recommendations for international students: Required—TOEFL (minimum score 550 paper-based).

American Graduate School of International Relations and Diplomacy, Program in International Relations and Diplomacy, Paris, France. Offers MA, PhD.

American Public University System, AMU/APU Graduate Programs, Charles Town, WV 25414. Offers air warfare (MA Military Studies); American Revolution (MA Military Studies); business administration (MBA); Civil War (MA Military Studies); criminal justice (MA); defense management (MA Military Studies); emergency and disaster management (MA); environmental policy and management (MS); fire science management (MA); global engagement (MA); history (MA); homeland security (MA); humanities (MA); intelligence (MA Military Studies, MA Strategic Intelligence); international peace and conflict resolution (MA); international relations and conflict resolution (MA); joint warfare (MA Military Studies); land warfare international perspective (MA Military Studies); management (MA); military history (MA); military leadership (MA Military Studies); national security studies (MA); naval warfare international (MA Military Studies); naval warfare US (MA Military Studies); political science (MA); public administration (MA); public health (MA); security management (MA); space studies (MS); special ops/LIC (MA Military Studies); sports management (MA); transportation and logistics management (MA); transportation management (MA); unconventional warfare (MA Military Studies); World War II (MA Military Studies). Programs offered via distance learning only. Part-time and evening/weekend programs available. Postbaccalaureate distance learning degree programs offered (no on-campus study). *Degree requirements:* For master's, comprehensive exam. *Entrance requirements:* For master's, bachelor's degree or equivalent, minimum GPA of 2.7 in last 60 hours of course work. Electronic applications accepted. *Faculty research:* Military history, criminal justice, management performance, national security.

American University, College of Arts and Sciences, Department of Economics, Washington, DC 20016-8029. Offers applied microeconomics (Certificate); economics (MA, PhD); international economic relations (Certificate). Part-time and evening/weekend programs available. *Faculty:* 23 full-time (10 women), 1 part-time/adjunct (0 women). *Students:* 56 full-time (23 women), 71 part-time (31 women); includes 12 minority (8 African Americans, 1 Asian American or Pacific Islander, 3 Hispanic Americans), 60 international. Average age 30. 149 applicants, 62% accepted, 24 enrolled. In 2008, 23 master's, 9 doctorates awarded. Terminal master's awarded for partial completion of doctoral program. *Degree requirements:* For master's, comprehensive exam, thesis or alternative; for doctorate, comprehensive exam, thesis/dissertation, 2 research seminars, field requirement. *Entrance requirements:* For master's and doctorate, GRE; for Certificate, bachelor's degree. Additional exam requirements/recommendations for international students: Required—TOEFL. *Application deadline:* For spring admission, 10/1 for domestic students. Applications are processed on a rolling basis. Application fee: $80. *Expenses:* Tuition: Full-time $21,204; part-time $1178 per credit hour. Required fees: $380. Part-time tuition and fees vary according to course load and program. *Financial support:* Fellowships, research assistantships with full and partial tuition reimbursements, teaching assistantships with full and partial tuition reimbursements, career-related internships or fieldwork, Federal Work-Study, institutionally sponsored loans, and tuition waivers (full and partial) available. Financial award application deadline: 2/1. *Faculty research:* Political economy, development, labor, gender. *Unit head:* Robert A. Blecker, Chair, 202-885-3767, Fax: 202-885-3790, E-mail: blecker@american.edu. *Application contact:* Kathleen Clowery, Director of Graduate Admissions, 202-885 Ext. 3621, Fax: 202-885-1505, E-mail: clowery@american.edu.

American University, School of International Service, Washington, DC 20016-8071. Offers comparative and regional studies (Certificate); cross-cultural communication (Certificate); development management (MS); ethics, peace, and global affairs (MA); European studies (Certificate); global environmental policy (MA, Certificate); international affairs (MA), including comparative and regional studies, environmental policy, international economic policy, international politics, natural resources and sustainable development, U.S. foreign policy; international communication (MA, Certificate); international development (MA, Certificate); international development management (Certificate); international economic policy (Certificate); international economic relations (Certificate); international media (MA); international peace and conflict resolution (MA, Certificate); international relations (PhD); international service (MIS); peace building (Certificate); the Americas (Certificate); United States foreign policy (Certificate); JD/MA. Part-time and evening/weekend programs available. *Faculty:* 70 full-time (28 women), 51 part-time/adjunct (20 women). *Students:* 519 full-time (317 women), 335 part-time (205 women); includes 157 minority (54 African Americans, 2 American Indian/Alaska Native, 45 Asian Americans or Pacific Islanders, 56 Hispanic Americans), 116 international. Average age 27. 1,901 applicants, 58% accepted, 277 enrolled. In 2008, 358 master's, 5 doctorates, 9 other advanced degrees awarded. Terminal master's awarded for partial completion of doctoral program. *Degree requirements:* For master's, one foreign language, comprehensive exam, thesis or alternative; for doctorate, one foreign language, comprehensive exam, thesis/dissertation, research practicum; for Certificate, minimum 15 credit hours related course work. *Entrance requirements:* For master's, GRE, 24 credits of course work in related social sciences, minimum GPA of 3.5, 2 letters of recommendation, bachelor's degree, resumé, statement of purpose; for doctorate, GRE, 2 letters of recommendation, 24 credits in related social sciences; for Certificate, bachelor's degree. Additional exam requirements/recommendations for international students: Required—TOEFL (minimum score 600 paper-based; 250 computer-based; 100 iBT). *Application deadline:* For fall admission, 1/15 priority date for domestic students; for spring admission, 10/1 priority date for domestic students. Applications are processed on a rolling basis. Application fee: $50. *Expenses:* Tuition: Full-time $21,204; part-time $1178 per credit hour. Required fees: $380. Part-time tuition and fees vary according to course load and program. *Financial support:* Career-related internships or fieldwork, Federal Work-Study, and institutionally sponsored loans available. Financial award application deadline: 1/15. *Faculty research:* International intellectual property, international environmental issues, international law and legal order, international telecommunications/technology, international sustainable development. *Unit head:* Dr. Louis W. Goodman, Dean, 202-885-1600, Fax: 202-885-2494. *Application contact:* Yasmin Quianzon, Director of Graduate Admissions and Financial Aid, 202-885-2496, Fax: 202-885-1109.

See Close-Up on page 861.

The American University of Paris, Graduate Programs, Paris, France. Offers finance (MSF); global communications (MAGC); international affairs, conflict resolution and civil society development (MA); Middle Eastern and Islamic studies (MA); public administration (MPA). *Degree requirements:* For master's, thesis. *Entrance requirements:* For master's, minimum undergraduate GPA of 3.0.

Appalachian State University, Cratis D. Williams Graduate School, Department of Government and Justice Studies, Boone, NC 28608. Offers criminal justice (MS); political science (MA), including American government, international relations; public administration (MPA), including public management, town, city and county management. Part-time programs available. Postbaccalaureate distance learning degree programs offered (no on-campus study). *Faculty:* 27 full-time (5 women), 12 part-time/adjunct (1 woman). *Students:* 70 full-time (29 women), 51 part-time (14 women); includes 9 minority (7 African Americans, 1 American Indian/Alaska Native, 1 Asian American or Pacific Islander), 4 international. 60 applicants, 92% accepted, 32 enrolled. In 2008, 58 master's awarded. *Degree requirements:* For master's, variable foreign language requirement, comprehensive exam, thesis optional. *Entrance requirements:* For master's, GRE General Test, 3 letters of recommendation. Additional exam requirements/recommendations for international students: Required—TOEFL (minimum score 570 paper-based; 230 computer-based; 79 iBT), IELTS (minimum score 6.5). *Application deadline:* For fall admission, 7/1 for domestic students, 2/1 for international students; for spring admission, 11/1 for domestic students, 7/1 for international students. Applications are processed on a rolling basis. Application fee: $50. Electronic applications accepted. *Expenses:* Tuition, area resident: Full-time $2600; part-time $700 per course. Tuition, state resident: full-time $2600; part-time $700 per course. Tuition, nonresident: full-time $5000; part-time $3300 per course. Required fees: $2150; $330 per course. Tuition and fees vary according to campus/location. *Financial support:* In 2008–09, 35 research assistantships (averaging $7,500 per year) were awarded; fellowships, teaching assistantships, career-related internships or fieldwork, Federal Work-Study, scholarships/grants, and unspecified assistantships also available. Financial award application deadline: 4/1; financial award applicants required to submit FAFSA. *Faculty research:* Campaign finance, emerging democracies, bureaucratic politics, judicial behavior, administration of justice. Total annual research expenditures: $8,500. *Unit head:* Dr. Brian Ellison, Chairperson, 828-262-3085, E-mail: ellisonba@appstate.edu. *Application contact:* Sandy Krause, Director of Admissions and Recruiting, 828-262-2130, Fax: 828-262-2709, E-mail: krausesl@appstate.edu.

Arcadia University, Graduate Studies, Program in International Relations and Diplomacy, Glenside, PA 19038-3295. Offers MA.

Baylor University, Graduate School, College of Arts and Sciences, Department of Political Science, Waco, TX 76798. Offers international studies (MA); political science (MA, PhD); public policy and administration (MPPA); JD/MPPA. *Students:* 24 full-time (7 women), 2 part-time (1 woman), 3 international. In 2008, 9 master's awarded. *Entrance requirements:* For master's, GRE General Test. *Application deadline:* Applications are processed on a rolling basis. Application fee: $25. *Financial support:* Research assistantships, career-related internships or fieldwork, Federal Work-Study, and institutionally sponsored loans available. Financial award application deadline: 3/1. *Unit head:* Dr. David Corey, Graduate Program Director, 254-710-3161, Fax: 254-710-3122, E-mail: david_d_corey@baylor.edu. *Application contact:* Jenice Langston, Administrative Assistant, 254-710-3161, Fax: 254-710-3870, E-mail: jenice_langston@baylor.edu.

Baylor University, Graduate School, Hankamer School of Business, Department of Economics, Waco, TX 76798. Offers economics (MS Eco); international economics (MA, MS). *Students:* 15 full-time (9 women), 8 international. In 2008, 9 master's awarded. *Entrance requirements:* For master's, GMAT or GRE General Test. *Application deadline:* For fall admission, 8/1 for domestic students; for spring admission, 12/1 for domestic students. Applications are processed on a rolling basis. Application fee: $25. *Financial support:* Research assistantships, Federal Work-Study and institutionally sponsored loans available. Financial award application deadline: 4/1. *Faculty research:* Econometrics, international economics, private enterprise, comparative economic systems. *Unit head:* Dr. Steve Green, Chair, 254-710-4543, Fax: 254-710-3265, E-mail: steve_green@baylor.edu. *Application contact:* Susan Armstrong, Administrative Assistant, 254-710-6177, Fax: 254-710-1066, E-mail: susan_armstrong@baylor.edu.

Boston University, Graduate School of Arts and Sciences, Department of Geography and Environment, Boston, MA 02215. Offers energy and environmental analysis (MA); environmental remote sensing and GIs (MA); geography (MA); geography and environment (PhD); international relations and environmental policy (MA). Terminal master's awarded for partial completion of doctoral program. *Degree requirements:* For master's, one foreign language, comprehensive exam, thesis; for doctorate, one foreign language, comprehensive exam, thesis/dissertation. *Entrance requirements:* For master's and doctorate, GRE General Test, GRE Subject Test, 3 letters of recommendation. Additional exam requirements/recommendations for international students: Required—TOEFL (minimum score 600 paper-based; 250 computer-based).

Boston University, Graduate School of Arts and Sciences, Department of International Relations, Boston, MA 02215. Offers African studies (Certificate); international relations (MA); international relations and environmental policy management (MA); international relations and international communication (MA); JD/MA; MBA/MA. *Degree requirements:* For master's, one foreign language, comprehensive exam, thesis. *Entrance requirements:* For master's, GRE General Test, 3 letters of recommendation; for Certificate, GRE General Test. Additional exam requirements/recommendations for international students: Required—TOEFL (minimum score 600 paper-based; 250 computer-based).

Brandeis University, International Business School, Waltham, MA 02454-9110. Offers finance (MSF); international business (MBAi); international economics and finance (MA, PhD); international finance/international economics (MBAi). Part-time and evening/weekend programs available. Terminal master's awarded for partial completion of doctoral program. *Degree requirements:* For master's, one foreign language, semester abroad; for doctorate, thesis/dissertation. *Entrance requirements:* For master's, GMAT or GRE General Test (MA), GMAT (MBAi and MSF); for doctorate, GRE General Test. Additional exam requirements/recommendations for international students: Required—TOEFL (minimum score 600 paper-based; 250 computer-based), IELTS (minimum score 7). Electronic applications accepted. *Faculty research:* International finance and business, trade policy, macroeconomics, Asian economic issues, developmental economics.

British American College London, Webster Graduate School, London, United Kingdom. Offers business (MBA); finance (MS); human resources (MA); information technology management (MA); international business (MA); international non-governmental organizations (MA); international relations (MA); management and leadership (MA); marketing (MA). Part-time programs available.

Brock University, Faculty of Graduate Studies, Faculty of Social Sciences, Program in Political Science, St. Catharines, ON L2S 3A1, Canada. Offers Canadian politics (MA); international and comparative politics (MA); political philosophy (MA); public administration (MA). Part-time programs available. *Degree requirements:* For master's, thesis optional. *Entrance requirements:* For master's, honors degree. Additional exam requirements/recommendations for international students: Required—TOEFL (minimum score 550 paper-based; 213 computer-based; 80 iBT), IELTS (minimum score 6.5), TWE (minimum score 4). Electronic applications accepted. *Faculty research:* Public administration reform, economic and social justice, politics of societies, Canadian politics, international relations.

Brooklyn College of the City University of New York, Division of Graduate Studies, Department of Political Science, Brooklyn, NY 11210-2889. Offers international affairs (MA); political science (MA, PhD); political science, urban policy and administration (MA). The department offers courses at Brooklyn College that are creditable toward the CUNY doctoral degree (with permission of the executive officer of the doctoral program). Part-time and evening/weekend programs available. *Students:* 13 full-time (6 women), 142 part-time (82 women); includes 91 minority (68 African Americans, 5 Asian Americans or Pacific Islanders, 18 Hispanic Americans), 15 international. Average age 33. 95 applicants, 83% accepted, 45 enrolled. In 2008, 43 master's awarded. *Degree requirements:* For master's, comprehensive exam (for some programs), thesis or alternative, foreign language exam (for international affairs program). *Entrance requirements:* For master's, 2 letters of recommendation, personal statement. *Expenses:* Tuition, state resident: full-time $7360; part-time $310 per credit hour. Tuition, nonresident: full-time $13,800; part-time $575 per credit hour. *Financial support:* Career-related internships or fieldwork and Federal Work-Study available. Support available to part-time students. Financial award application deadline: 5/1; financial award applicants required to submit FAFSA. *Faculty research:* Ethics and politics, politics of criminal justice, Western Europe, international law and politics, labor politics. *Unit head:* Dr. Sally Bermanzohn, Chairperson, 718-951-5306, E-mail: sallyb@brooklyn.cuny.edu. *Application contact:* Hernan Sierra, Graduate Admissions Coordinator, 718-951-4536, Fax: 718-951-4506, E-mail: grads@brooklyn.cuny.edu.

California State University, Fresno, Division of Graduate Studies, College of Social Sciences, Department of Political Science, Program in International Relations, Fresno, CA 93740-8027. Offers MA. Part-time and evening/weekend programs available. *Degree requirements:* For master's, one foreign language, thesis or alternative. *Entrance requirements:* For master's, GRE General Test, minimum GPA of 3.0. Additional exam requirements/recommendations for international students: Required—TOEFL. Electronic applications accepted.

California State University, Sacramento, Graduate Studies, College of Social Sciences and Interdisciplinary Studies, International Affairs Graduate Program, Sacramento, CA 95819-6048. Offers MA. Part-time programs available. *Degree requirements:* For master's, one foreign language, thesis or alternative, writing proficiency exam. *Entrance requirements:* For master's, GRE General Test, appropriate bachelor's degree, minimum GPA of 3.0 in last 2 years of course work. Additional exam requirements/recommendations for international students: Required—TOEFL. Electronic applications accepted.

California State University, Stanislaus, College of Humanities and Social Sciences, Department of History, Turlock, CA 95382. Offers history (MA); international relations (MA); secondary school teachers (MA). Part-time programs available. *Degree requirements:* For master's, one foreign language, comprehensive exam, thesis or alternative. *Entrance requirements:* For master's, GRE General Test, minimum undergraduate GPA of 3.0, personal statement. Additional exam requirements/recommendations for international students: Required—TOEFL (minimum score 550 paper-based; 213 computer-based). Electronic applications accepted. *Faculty research:* History of Ancient Greece, history and ecology of the central valley, acculturation and gender.

Carleton University, Faculty of Graduate Studies, Faculty of Public Affairs and Management, Norman Paterson School of International Affairs, Ottawa, ON K1S 5B6, Canada. Offers MA, PhD. Part-time programs available. *Degree requirements:* For master's, one foreign language, comprehensive exam, thesis optional. *Entrance requirements:* For master's, honors degree. Additional exam requirements/recommendations for international students: Required—TOEFL. *Faculty research:* International conflict, development, political economy, conflict analysis.

The Catholic University of America, School of Arts and Sciences, Department of Business and Economics, Washington, DC 20064. Offers international political economics (MA). Part-time and evening/weekend programs available. *Degree requirements:* For master's, comprehensive exam. *Entrance requirements:* For master's, GRE General Test, 3 letters of recommendation. Additional exam requirements/recommendations for international students: Required—TOEFL (minimum score 580 paper-based; 237 computer-based). Electronic applications accepted.

The Catholic University of America, School of Arts and Sciences, Department of Politics, Washington, DC 20064. Offers American government (MA, PhD); congressional studies (MA); international affairs (MA); international political economics (MA); political theory (MA, PhD); world politics (MA, PhD); JD/MA. Part-time programs available. *Degree requirements:* For master's, one foreign language, comprehensive exam, thesis or alternative; for doctorate, 2 foreign languages, comprehensive exam, thesis/dissertation. *Entrance requirements:* For master's and doctorate, GRE General Test, 3 letters of recommendation, minimum GPA of 3.0. Additional exam requirements/recommendations for international students: Required—TOEFL (minimum score 580 paper-based; 237 computer-based). Electronic applications accepted. *Faculty research:* Political philosophy, American political institutions and processes, political economy, national security.

Central Connecticut State University, School of Graduate Studies, School of Arts and Sciences, Program in International Area Studies, New Britain, CT 06050-4010. Offers international studies (MS). Part-time and evening/weekend programs available. *Students:* 10 full-time (4 women), 26 part-time (16 women); includes 10 minority (6 African Americans, 1 Asian American or Pacific Islander, 3 Hispanic Americans). Average age 34. 27 applicants, 70% accepted, 12 enrolled. In 2008, 10 master's awarded. *Degree requirements:* For master's, comprehensive exam, thesis or alternative. *Entrance requirements:* For master's, minimum undergraduate GPA of 2.7, essay. Additional exam requirements/recommendations for international students: Required—TOEFL. *Application deadline:* For fall admission, 7/1 for domestic students; for spring admission, 12/1 for domestic students. Applications are processed on a rolling basis. Application fee: $50. Electronic applications accepted. *Expenses:* Tuition, area resident: Full-time $4377; part-time $420 per credit. Tuition, state resident: full-time $6566; part-time $420 per credit. Tuition, nonresident: full-time $12,195; part-time $420 per credit. Required fees: $3462. One-time fee: $62 part-time. *Financial support:* In 2008–09, 3 students received support, including 2 research assistantships; career-related internships or fieldwork, Federal Work-Study, scholarships/grants, and unspecified assistantships also available. Support available to part-time students. Financial award application deadline: 3/1; financial award applicants required to submit FAFSA. *Unit head:* Dr. Evelyn Newman Phillips, Program Director, 860-832-2617. *Application contact:* Dr. Evelyn Newman Phillips, Program Director, 860-832-2617.

Central European University, Graduate Studies, School of Social Sciences and Humanities, Budapest, Hungary. Offers economics (MA, PhD); gender studies (MA, PhD); international relations and European studies (MA, PhD); mathematics and its applications (MS, PhD); medieval studies (MA, PhD); nationalism studies (MA, PhD); philosophy (MA, PhD); political science (MA, PhD); public policy (MA, PhD); sociology and social anthropology (MA, PhD). Terminal master's awarded for partial completion of doctoral program. *Degree requirements:* For master's, one foreign language, thesis; for doctorate, one foreign language, comprehensive exam, thesis/dissertation. *Entrance requirements:* For master's, CEU subject tests, interview; for doctorate, GRE, CEU subject test, interview. Additional exam requirements/recommendations for international students: Required—TOEFL (minimum score 570 paper-based; 230 computer-based). Electronic applications accepted. *Faculty research:* Civil society, fiscal decentralization, party politics, political philosophy (especially Liberalism, theory of Democracy).

See Close-Up on page 349.

Central Michigan University, Central Michigan University Off-Campus Programs, Program in Administration, Mount Pleasant, MI 48859. Offers acquisitions administration (MSA, Certificate); general administration (MSA, Certificate); health services administration (MSA, Certificate); human resources administration (MSA, Certificate); information resource management (MSA, Certificate); international administration (MSA, Certificate); leadership (MSA, Certificate); public administration (MSA, Certificate); vehicle design and manufacturing administration (MSA, Certificate). Part-time and evening/weekend programs available. Postbaccalaureate distance learning degree programs offered (no on-campus study). *Students:* Average age 38. *Entrance requirements:* For master's, minimum GPA of 2.7 in major. *Application deadline:* Applications are processed on a rolling basis. Application fee: $50. Electronic applications accepted. *Expenses:* Tuition, state resident: full-time $3717; part-time $413 per credit. Tuition, nonresident: full-time $6894; part-time $766 per credit. *Financial support:* Scholarships/grants available. Support available to part-time students. Financial award applicants required to submit FAFSA. *Unit head:* Dr. Nana Korsah, Director, MSA Programs, 989-774-6525, E-mail: korsa1na@cmich.edu. *Application contact:* 877-268-4636, E-mail: cmuoffcampus@cmich.edu.

Chapman University, Graduate Studies, Wilkinson College of Humanities and Social Sciences, International Studies Program, Orange, CA 92866. Offers MA. Part-time and evening/weekend programs available. *Entrance requirements:* For master's, GRE, 2 letters of recommendation. Additional exam requirements/recommendations for international students: Required—TOEFL (minimum score 550 paper-based; 213 computer-based; 80 iBT). Application fee: $50. *Expenses:* Tuition: Full-time $11,970; part-time $665 per credit. Required fees: $456; $456 per year. Tuition and fees vary according to course load, degree level and program. *Financial support:* Fellowships, Federal Work-Study and scholarships/grants available. Financial award applicants required to submit FAFSA. *Unit head:* Dr. James Coyle, Director, 714-744-7074, E-mail: coyle@chapman.edu. *Application contact:* Priscilla Garcia Powers, Graduate Admission Counselor, 714-997-6711, E-mail: pgarcia@chapman.edu.

City College of the City University of New York, Graduate School, College of Liberal Arts and Science, Division of Social Science, Program in International Relations, New York, NY 10031-9198. Offers MA. Part-time programs available. *Degree requirements:* For master's, one foreign language, thesis. *Entrance requirements:* For master's, GRE, 3 letters of recommendation. Additional exam requirements/recommendations for international students: Required—TOEFL (minimum score 600 paper-based; 250 computer-based). *Faculty research:* International finance, international economics, European diplomatic history, area studies, international politics and diplomacy.

Claremont Graduate University, Graduate Programs, School of Politics and Economics, Department of Politics and Policy, Claremont, CA 91711-6160. Offers American politics (MA, PhD); comparative politics (PhD); international political economy (MA); international studies (MA); political philosophy (PhD); political science (PhD); politics, economics and business (MA); public policy (MA, PhD); world politics (PhD); MBA/PhD. Part-time programs available. *Faculty:* 10 full-time (4 women), 4 part-time/adjunct (0 women). *Students:* 166 full-time (60 women), 19 part-time (6 women); includes 28 minority (4 African Americans, 9 Asian Americans or Pacific Islanders, 15 Hispanic Americans), 40 international. Average age 32. In 2008, 24 master's, 17 doctorates awarded. Terminal master's awarded for partial completion of doctoral program. *Entrance requirements:* For master's and doctorate, GRE General Test. Additional exam requirements/recommendations for international students: Required—TOEFL (minimum score 550 paper-based; 213 computer-based; 80 iBT). *Application deadline:* For fall admission, 2/1 priority date for domestic students. Applications are processed on a rolling basis. Application fee: $60. Electronic applications accepted. *Expenses:* Tuition: Full-time $33,698; part-time $1465 per unit. Required fees: $310; $155 per semester. Tuition and fees vary according to program. *Financial support:* Fellowships, research assistantships, teaching assistantships, Federal Work-Study, institutionally sponsored loans, and scholarships/grants available. Support available to part-time students. Financial award application deadline: 2/15; financial award applicants required to submit FAFSA. *Faculty research:* Environmental policy, international debt, global democratization, Third World development, public sector discrimination. *Unit head:* Jean Schroedel, Chair, 909-621-8696, Fax: 909-621-8545, E-mail: jean.schroedel@cgu.edu. *Application contact:* Laura Carillo, Recruiter and Admissions Coordinator, 909-621-8699, Fax: 909-621-7545, E-mail: laura.carillo@cga.edu.

Colorado School of Mines, Graduate School, Division of Liberal Arts and International Studies, Golden, CO 80401-1887. Offers international political economy (Graduate Certificate); liberal arts and international studies (MIPER); science and technology policy (Graduate Certificate). Part-time programs available. *Faculty:* 23 full-time (11 women), 24 part-time/adjunct (11 women). *Students:* 17 full-time (6 women), 7 part-time (0 women); includes 9 minority (2 African Americans, 1 American Indian/Alaska Native, 2 Asian Americans or Pacific Islanders, 4 Hispanic Americans), 3 international. 16 applicants, 88% accepted, 10 enrolled. In 2008, 12 master's awarded. *Degree requirements:* For master's, thesis (for some programs). *Entrance requirements:* For master's, GRE. Additional exam requirements/recommendations for international students: Required—TOEFL (minimum score 550 paper-based; 213 computer-based; 80 iBT). *Application deadline:* For fall admission, 1/15 priority date for domestic and international students; for spring admission, 9/1 priority date for domestic and international students. Application fee: $50 ($70 for international students). Electronic applications accepted. *Expenses:* Tuition, state resident: full-time $9810; part-time $477 per credit hour. Tuition, nonresident: full-time $23,814; part-time $1158 per credit hour. Required fees: $1428.76; $714.38 per semester. *Financial support:* In 2008–09, 10 students received support, including fellowships with full tuition reimbursements available (averaging $20,000 per year), 1 research assistantship with full tuition reimbursement available (averaging $20,000 per year), 9 teaching assistantships with full tuition reimbursements available (averaging $20,000 per year); scholarships/grants, health care benefits, and unspecified assistantships also available. Financial award application deadline: 1/15. Total annual research expenditures: $160,595. *Unit head:* Dr. James Jesudason, Director, 303-273-3425, Fax: 303-273-3751, E-mail: jjesudas@mines.edu. *Application contact:* Connie Warren, Program Assistant, 303-273-3590, Fax: 303-273-3751, E-mail: cwarren@mines.edu.

Columbia University, School of International and Public Affairs, Program in International Affairs, New York, NY 10027. Offers MIA, JD/MIA, MBA/MIA, MIA/MS, MPH/MIA, MSJ/MIA. *Degree requirements:* For master's, one foreign language. *Entrance requirements:* For master's, GRE General Test. Additional exam requirements/recommendations for international students: Required—TOEFL (minimum score 600 paper-based; 250 computer-based; 100 iBT). Electronic applications accepted.

See Close-Up on page 863.

Concordia University, School of Business and Professional Studies, Irvine, CA 92612-3299. Offers entrepreneurial business administration (MBA); international studies (MA). Part-time programs available. *Entrance requirements:* Additional exam requirements/recommendations for international students: Required—TOEFL (minimum score 550 paper-based; 213 computer-based).

Cornell University, Graduate School, Graduate Fields of Arts and Sciences, Field of Government, Ithaca, NY 14853-0001. Offers American politics (PhD); comparative politics (PhD); international relations (PhD); political methodology (PhD); political thought (PhD); public policy (PhD). *Faculty:* 40 full-time (14 women). *Students:* 70 full-time (37 women); includes 11 minority (2 African Americans, 1 American Indian/Alaska Native, 4 Asian Americans or Pacific Islanders, 4 Hispanic Americans), 23 international. Average age 30. 350 applicants, 9% accepted, 15 enrolled. In 2008, 13 doctorates awarded. *Degree requirements:* For doctorate, comprehensive exam, thesis/dissertation. *Entrance requirements:* For doctorate, GRE General Test, sample of written work, 3 letters of recommendation. Additional exam requirements/recommendations for international students: Required—TOEFL (minimum score 550 paper-based; 213 computer-based; 77 iBT). *Application deadline:* For fall admission, 1/15 for domestic students. Application fee: $70. Electronic applications accepted. *Expenses:* Tuition: Full-time $29,500. Required fees: $70. Full-time tuition and fees vary according to degree level, program and student level. *Financial support:* In 2008–09, 60 students received support, including 30 fellowships with full tuition reimbursements available, 2 research assistantships with full tuition reimbursements available, 28 teaching assistantships with full tuition reimbursements available; institutionally sponsored loans, scholarships/grants, health care benefits, tuition waivers (full and partial), and unspecified assistantships also available. Financial award applicants required to submit FAFSA. *Faculty research:* Political theory, American politics, comparative politics,

International Affairs

Cornell University (continued)
international relations, methodology. *Unit head:* Director of Graduate Studies, 607-255-3567, Fax: 607-255-4530. *Application contact:* Graduate Field Assistant, 607-255-3567, Fax: 607-255-4530, E-mail: cu_govt@cornell.edu.

Creighton University, Graduate School, College of Arts and Sciences, Program in International Relations, Omaha, NE 68178-0001. Offers MA. Part-time and evening/weekend programs available. *Degree requirements:* For master's, one foreign language, thesis. *Entrance requirements:* For master's, GRE General Test, 3 letters of recommendation. Additional exam requirements/recommendations for international students: Required—TOEFL (minimum score 550 paper-based; 213 computer-based; 80 iBT). Electronic applications accepted.

East Carolina University, Graduate School, Thomas Harriot College of Arts and Sciences, Program in International Studies, Greenville, NC 27858-4353. Offers MA. Part-time programs available. *Degree requirements:* For master's, comprehensive exam. *Entrance requirements:* For master's, GRE General Test. Additional exam requirements/recommendations for international students: Required—TOEFL.

Fairleigh Dickinson University, Metropolitan Campus, University College: Arts, Sciences, and Professional Studies, School of History, Political and International Studies, Program in International Studies, Teaneck, NJ 07666-1914. Offers MA. *Students:* 8 full-time (5 women), 6 part-time (5 women), 4 international. Average age 30. 18 applicants, 28% accepted, 0 enrolled. *Application deadline:* Applications are processed on a rolling basis. Application fee: $40. *Application contact:* Susan Brooman, University Director of Graduate Admissions, 201-692-2554, Fax: 201-692-2560, E-mail: globaleducation@fdu.edu.

Florida Agricultural and Mechanical University, Division of Graduate Studies, Research, and Continuing Education, College of Engineering Science, Technology, and Agriculture, Division of Agricultural Sciences, Tallahassee, FL 32307-3200. Offers agribusiness (MS); animal science (MS); engineering technology (MS); entomology (MS); food science (MS); international programs (MS); plant science (MS). *Degree requirements:* For master's, thesis. *Entrance requirements:* For master's, GRE General Test, minimum GPA of 3.0. Additional exam requirements/recommendations for international students: Required—TOEFL (minimum score 500 paper-based).

Florida International University, College of Arts and Sciences, Department of International Relations, Miami, FL 33199. Offers international relations (PhD); international studies (MA). Fall admission only for PhD. Part-time programs available. *Degree requirements:* For master's, one foreign language, thesis optional; for doctorate, one foreign language, thesis/dissertation. *Entrance requirements:* For master's and doctorate, GRE General Test, minimum GPA of 3.0, letters of recommendatikon. Additional exam requirements/recommendations for international students: Required—TOEFL (minimum score 550 paper-based; 213 computer-based). *Faculty research:* International relations theory (particularly constructivist and feminist IR theory), comparative regional studies (including Latin America and the Caribbean, Europe, East and Central Asia, Africa, and the Middle East), foreign policy and security, international law and human rights, identity and geopolitics.

Florida State University, Graduate Studies, College of Social Sciences, Program in International Affairs, Tallahassee, FL 32306. Offers MA, MS, JD/MA, JD/MS. Part-time programs available. *Degree requirements:* For master's, one foreign language, comprehensive exam, thesis optional. *Entrance requirements:* For master's, GRE General Test, minimum GPA of 3.0.

Fordham University, Graduate School of Arts and Sciences, Program in International Political Economy and Development, New York, NY 10458. Offers MA, Certificate. Part-time and evening/weekend programs available. *Degree requirements:* For master's, comprehensive exam. *Entrance requirements:* For master's, GRE General Test. Additional exam requirements/recommendations for international students: Required—TOEFL (minimum score 600 paper-based; 250 computer-based). Electronic applications accepted. *Faculty research:* International economics, comparative international politics, international banking and finance, international development, emerging markets and country risk analysis.

See Close-Up on page 865.

George Mason University, School of Public Policy, Program in International Commerce and Policy, Fairfax, VA 22030. Offers MA. Part-time programs available. *Degree requirements:* For master's, thesis or alternative. *Entrance requirements:* For master's, minimum undergraduate GPA of 3.0, 2 letters of recommendation, resumé, goals statement. Additional exam requirements/recommendations for international students: Required—TOEFL. Electronic applications accepted. *Expenses:* Contact institution.

Georgetown University, Graduate School of Arts and Sciences, BMW Center for German and European Studies, Washington, DC 20057. Offers MA, MA/JD, MA/PhD. *Degree requirements:* For master's, 2 foreign languages, comprehensive exam. *Entrance requirements:* For master's, GRE General Test. Additional exam requirements/recommendations for international students: Required—TOEFL. *Faculty research:* Trans-Atlantic relations, European Union, German and European Studies.

Georgetown University, Graduate School of Arts and Sciences, Department of Government, Washington, DC 20057. Offers American government (MA, PhD); comparative government (PhD); conflict resolution (MA); democracy and governance (MA); international law and government (MA); international relations (PhD); political theory (PhD); MA/PhD. Terminal master's awarded for partial completion of doctoral program. *Degree requirements:* For master's, one foreign language, comprehensive exam; for doctorate, one foreign language, comprehensive exam, thesis/dissertation. *Entrance requirements:* For master's, GRE General Test, minimum B average; for doctorate, GRE General Test, MA. Additional exam requirements/recommendations for international students: Required—TOEFL. *Faculty research:* Western Europe, Latin America, the Middle East, political theory, international relations and law, methodology, American politics and institutions.

Georgetown University, Graduate School of Arts and Sciences, Edmund A. Walsh School of Foreign Service, Washington, DC 20057. Offers foreign service (MS); security studies (MA); JD/MS; MA/JD; MA/PhD; MBA/MS; MS/MA. *Degree requirements:* For master's, one foreign language, comprehensive exam. *Entrance requirements:* For master's, GRE General Test, 3 semesters of undergraduate course work in economics. Additional exam requirements/recommendations for international students: Required—TOEFL. *Faculty research:* International business diplomacy, political risk analysis, foreign policy decision making, intercultural perspectives on contemporary issues.

Georgetown University, Graduate School of Arts and Sciences, School of Continuing Studies, Washington, DC 20057. Offers American studies (MALS); Catholic studies (MALS); classical civilizations (MALS); ethics and the professions (MALS); human resources management (MPS); humanities (MALS); individualized study (MALS); international affairs (MALS); Islam and Muslim-Christian relations (MALS); journalism (MPS); liberal studies (DLS); literature and society (MALS); medieval and early modern European studies (MALS); public relations (MPS); real estate (MPS); religious studies (MALS); social and public policy (MALS); sports industry management (MPS); the theory and practice of American democracy (MALS); visual culture (MALS). *Entrance requirements:* Additional exam requirements/recommendations for international students: Required—TOEFL.

Georgetown University, Law Center, Washington, DC 20001. Offers general (LL M); global health law (LL M); international and comparative law (LL M); international business and economic law (LL M); international legal studies (LL M); law (JD, SJD); securities and financial regulation (LL M); taxation (LL M); JD/LL M; JD/MA; JD/MBA; JD/MPH; JD/PhD. Accreditation: ABA. Part-time and evening/weekend programs available. *Degree requirements:* For master's, thesis; for doctorate, thesis/dissertation. *Entrance requirements:* For JD, LSAT; for master's and

doctorate, JD, LL B, or first law degree earned in country of origin. Additional exam requirements/recommendations for international students: Required—TOEFL. *Expenses:* Contact institution. *Faculty research:* Constitutional law, legal history, jurisprudence.

The George Washington University, Elliott School of International Affairs, Program in International Affairs, Washington, DC 20052. Offers MA, JD/MA, MBA/MA, MPH/MA. Part-time and evening/weekend programs available. *Faculty:* 37 full-time (6 women), 84 part-time/adjunct (22 women). *Students:* 222 full-time (130 women), 91 part-time (64 women); includes 47 minority (9 African Americans, 1 American Indian/Alaska Native, 21 Asian Americans or Pacific Islanders, 16 Hispanic Americans), 40 international. Average age 26. 702 applicants, 63% accepted, 119 enrolled. In 2008, 116 master's awarded. *Degree requirements:* For master's, one foreign language, capstone project. *Entrance requirements:* For master's, GRE General Test, 2 years of a modern foreign language, 2 semesters of introductory economics. Additional exam requirements/recommendations for international students: Required—TOEFL. *Application deadline:* For fall admission, 2/1 for domestic students; for spring admission, 10/1 for domestic students. Application fee: $60. Electronic applications accepted. *Financial support:* In 2008–09, 61 students received support; fellowships with tuition reimbursements available, research assistantships with tuition reimbursements available, career-related internships or fieldwork, Federal Work-Study, institutionally sponsored loans, and tuition waivers (full) available. Financial award application deadline: 1/15; financial award applicants required to submit FAFSA. *Faculty research:* Area studies, international economics, national security policy studies, international economic development, Sino-Soviet studies. *Unit head:* Dr. Karl F. Inderfurth, Director, 202-994-2619, E-mail: ambkfi@gwu.edu. *Application contact:* Jeff V. Miles, Director of Graduate Admissions, 202-994-7050, Fax: 202-994-9537, E-mail: esiagrad@gwu.edu.

The George Washington University, Elliott School of International Affairs, Program in International Policy and Practice, Washington, DC 20052. Offers MIPP. Part-time and evening/weekend programs available. *Students:* 20 full-time (9 women), 21 part-time (10 women); includes 4 minority (1 African American, 3 Asian Americans or Pacific Islanders), 12 international. Average age 40. 1 applicant, 0% accepted. In 2008, 26 master's awarded. *Degree requirements:* For master's, one foreign language, capstone project. *Entrance requirements:* For master's, GRE (recommended), advanced degree or 8 years experience plus BA. Additional exam requirements/recommendations for international students: Required—TOEFL. *Application deadline:* For fall admission, 2/1 for domestic students; for spring admission, 10/1 for domestic students. Application fee: $60. Electronic applications accepted. *Financial support:* In 2008–09, 13 students received support; fellowships with tuition reimbursements available, research assistantships with tuition reimbursements available, career-related internships or fieldwork, Federal Work-Study, institutionally sponsored loans, and tuition waivers available. Financial award application deadline: 1/15; financial award applicants required to submit FAFSA. *Unit head:* Dr. Chris Kojm, Director, 202-994-7969, E-mail: ckojm@gwu.edu. *Application contact:* Jeff V. Miles, Director of Graduate Admissions, 202-994-7050, Fax: 202-994-9537, E-mail: esiagrad@gwu.edu.

The George Washington University, Elliott School of International Affairs, Program in International Studies, Washington, DC 20052. Offers MIS. *Application deadline:* For fall admission, 2/1 for domestic students; for spring admission, 10/1 for domestic students. *Financial support:* Application deadline: 1/15. *Unit head:* David Alan Grier, Director, 202-994-6240, E-mail: grier@gwu.edu. *Application contact:* Jeff V. Miles, Director of Graduate Admissions, 202-994-7050, Fax: 202-994-9537, E-mail: esiagrad@gwu.edu.

Georgia Institute of Technology, Graduate Studies and Research, Ivan Allen College of Policy and International Affairs, Sam Nunn School of International Affairs, Atlanta, GA 30332-0001. Offers MS Int A, PhD. *Degree requirements:* For master's, one foreign language. *Entrance requirements:* Additional exam requirements/recommendations for international students: Required—TOEFL. Electronic applications accepted. *Faculty research:* International political economy, international security, Asian and European studies.

Harvard University, Graduate School of Arts and Sciences, Department of Government, Cambridge, MA 02138. Offers political science (PhD), including American politics, comparative politics, international relations, political thought, quantitative methods. *Degree requirements:* For doctorate, one foreign language, thesis/dissertation, general exams. *Entrance requirements:* For doctorate, GRE General Test. Additional exam requirements/recommendations for international students: Required—TOEFL. *Expenses:* Tuition: Full-time $32,556. Required fees: $1426. Full-time tuition and fees vary according to program and student level.

Harvard University, Law School, Professional Programs in Law, Cambridge, MA 02138. Offers international and comparative law (JD); law and business (JD); law and government (JD); law and social change (JD); law, science and technology (JD); JD/MALD; JD/MBA; JD/MPH; JD/MPP; JD/PhD. Accreditation: ABA. *Degree requirements:* For JD, 3rd-year paper. *Entrance requirements:* LSAT. *Expenses:* Tuition: Full-time $32,556. Required fees: $1426. Full-time tuition and fees vary according to program and student level. *Faculty research:* Constitutional law, voting rights law, cyber law.

Hult International Business School, Program in International Relations—Hult London Campus, Cambridge, MA 02141. Offers conflict resolution (MA); diplomacy (MA); international public law (MA); international relations (MA); Middle East international security (MA); politics (MA); security studies (MA); terrorism (MA); U.S. foreign policy (MA). Part-time programs available. *Entrance requirements:* Additional exam requirements/recommendations for international students: Required—TOEFL (minimum score 580 paper-based; 237 computer-based), TWE (minimum score 5). Electronic applications accepted. *Faculty research:* American foreign politics, Middle East, security studies.

Instituto Tecnológico y de Estudios Superiores de Monterrey, Campus Ciudad Obregón, Program in International Relations, Ciudad Obregón, Mexico. Offers MIR.

The Johns Hopkins University, Paul H. Nitze School of Advanced International Studies, Washington, DC 20036. Offers international development (Certificate); international public policy (MIPP); international relations (MA, PhD), including African studies (MA), American foreign policy (MA), Asian studies (MA), Canadian studies (MA), conflict management (MA), European studies (MA), global theory and history (MA), international development (MA), international law, and organizations (MA), international policy (MA), international relations (general) (MA), Latin American studies (MA), Middle East studies (MA), Russian and Eurasian studies (MA), strategic studies (MA); international studies (Certificate); JD/MA; MBA/MA; MHS/MA. Terminal master's awarded for partial completion of doctoral program. *Degree requirements:* For master's, one foreign language, 16 non-language courses (8 for MIPP), 2 core examinations, comprehensive oral exam, paper (for some programs); for doctorate, 2 foreign languages, thesis/dissertation, 3 comprehensive exams, defense. *Entrance requirements:* For master's, GMAT or GRE General Test, previous course work in economics, foreign language, undergraduate degree; for doctorate, GRE General Test, master's degree. Additional exam requirements/recommendations for international students: Required—TOEFL (minimum paper-based score of 600, computer-based 250, iBT 100) or IELTS (minimum 7.0). Electronic applications accepted. *Expenses:* Contact institution. *Faculty research:* Regional studies and functional fields of international relations, international economics, conflict management, global theory and history, international law and organizations, international policy, strategic studies.

Kansas State University, Graduate School, College of Arts and Sciences, Department of Political Science, Program in Political Science, Manhattan, KS 66506. Offers international service (MA); political science (MA). Part-time programs available. *Students:* 13 full-time (6 women), 11 part-time (6 women); includes 3 minority (all African Americans), 5 international. Average age 27. 16 applicants, 94% accepted, 8 enrolled. In 2008, 10 master's awarded. *Degree requirements:* For master's, thesis or alternative. *Entrance requirements:* For master's, GRE (recommended), minimum GPA of 3.0. Additional exam requirements/recommendations for international students: Required—TOEFL (minimum score 550 paper-based; 213 computer-based). *Application deadline:* For fall admission, 2/1 priority date for domestic and international students; for spring admission, 10/1 for domestic students, 8/1 priority date for international students. Applications are processed on a rolling basis. Application fee: $30 ($55 for international students). *Expenses:* Tuition, area resident: Full-time $6466; part-time $269.40 per credit hour. Tuition, state resident: full-time $6466; part-time $269.40 per credit hour. Tuition, nonresident: full-time $14,874; part-time $619.75 per credit hour. Required fees: $673; $23.40 per credit hour. Tuition and fees vary according to campus/location. *Financial support:* Fellowships, research assistantships, teaching assistantships, institutionally sponsored loans and scholarships/grants available. Support available to part-time students. Financial award application deadline: 3/1; financial award applicants required to submit FAFSA. *Application contact:* James Franke, Director, 785-532-0451, Fax: 785-532-2339, E-mail: jfranke@ksu.edu.

Kentucky State University, College of Professional Studies, Frankfort, KY 40601. Offers business administration (MBA), including accounting, finance, management, marketing; public administration (MPA), including human resource management, international administration and development, management information systems, nonprofit management; special education (MA). Part-time and evening/weekend programs available. Postbaccalaureate distance learning degree programs offered (minimal on-campus study). *Faculty:* 12 full-time (2 women), 1 (woman) part-time/adjunct. *Students:* 48 full-time (27 women), 75 part-time (39 women); includes 68 minority (66 African Americans, 2 Asian Americans or Pacific Islanders), 5 international. Average age 34. 90 applicants, 73% accepted, 45 enrolled. In 2008, 37 master's awarded. *Degree requirements:* For master's, comprehensive exam, thesis optional. *Entrance requirements:* For master's, GMAT. Additional exam requirements/recommendations for international students: Required—TOEFL (minimum score 525 paper-based; 173 computer-based). *Application deadline:* For fall admission, 7/1 priority date for domestic students, 4/1 priority date for international students; for spring admission, 11/15 priority date for domestic students, 8/15 priority date for international students. Applications are processed on a rolling basis. Application fee: $30 ($100 for international students). Electronic applications accepted. *Expenses:* Tuition, area resident: Full-time $5400; part-time $325 per credit hour. Tuition, state resident: full-time $5400; part-time $325 per credit hour. Tuition, nonresident: full-time $13,230; part-time $760 per credit hour. Required fees: $450. Tuition and fees vary according to course load. *Financial support:* In 2008–09, 103 students received support. Scholarships/grants, tuition waivers (partial), and unspecified assistantships available. Financial award application deadline: 4/15; financial award applicants required to submit FAFSA. *Unit head:* Dr. Gashaw Lake, Dean, E-mail: gashaw.lake@kysu.edu. *Application contact:* Cedric Cunningham, Coordinator, Office of Graduate Studies, 502-597-6536, E-mail: cedric.cunningham@kysu.edu.

Lebanese American University, School of Arts and Sciences, Beirut, Lebanon. Offers computer science (MS); international affairs (MA).

Lesley University, Graduate School of Arts and Social Sciences, Program in Intercultural Relations, Cambridge, MA 02138-2790. Offers MA, CAGS. Part-time and evening/weekend programs available. *Degree requirements:* For master's, one foreign language, internship, practicum; for CAGS, one foreign language, thesis. *Entrance requirements:* For master's, interview; for CAGS, interview, master's degree. Additional exam requirements/recommendations for international students: Required—TOEFL (minimum score 550 paper-based; 213 computer-based; 80 iBT). *Expenses:* Tuition: Full-time $13,770; part-time $765 per credit hour. Required fees: $150. Tuition and fees vary according to course load, degree level, campus/location and program. *Faculty research:* Sociolinguistics, cross-cultural feminist theory, immigration and diaspora, intercultural business training.

Long Island University, Brooklyn Campus, Richard L. Conolly College of Liberal Arts and Sciences, Program in Social Science, Brooklyn, NY 11201-8423. Offers history (MS); United Nations studies (Certificate). Part-time and evening/weekend programs available. *Entrance requirements:* For master's, 2 letters of recommendation. Additional exam requirements/recommendations for international students: Required—TOEFL (minimum score 500 paper-based; 173 computer-based). Electronic applications accepted.

Long Island University, C.W. Post Campus, College of Liberal Arts and Sciences, Department of Political Science/International Studies, Brookville, NY 11548-1300. Offers MA. Part-time and evening/weekend programs available. *Degree requirements:* For master's, comprehensive exam, thesis or alternative. *Entrance requirements:* For master's, GRE. Electronic applications accepted. *Faculty research:* International relations, Middle Eastern politics, political philosophy.

Marquette University, Graduate School, College of Arts and Sciences, Department of Political Science/International Affairs, Milwaukee, WI 53201-1881. Offers international affairs (MA), including comparative politics, international political economy, international politics; political science (MA), including American politics, comparative politics, international politics, political philosophy; JD/MA. Part-time programs available. *Degree requirements:* For master's, comprehensive exam, thesis optional. *Entrance requirements:* For master's, GRE General Test. Additional exam requirements/recommendations for international students: Required—TOEFL. *Faculty research:* Public opinion and electoral behavior, public policy analysis, Congress and the Presidency, judicial behavior, political system transitions.

McMaster University, School of Graduate Studies, Faculty of Humanities and Faculty of Social Sciences, Institute on Globalization and the Human Condition, Hamilton, ON L8S 4M2, Canada. Offers globalization studies (MA).

McMaster University, School of Graduate Studies, Faculty of Social Sciences, Department of Political Science, Hamilton, ON L8S 4M2, Canada. Offers international relations (PhD); political science (MA); public and the global economy (MA); public policy (PhD); public policy and administration (MA). Part-time programs available. *Degree requirements:* For master's, thesis or alternative. *Entrance requirements:* For master's, minimum B+ average. Additional exam requirements/recommendations for international students: Required—TOEFL (minimum score 580 paper-based; 237 computer-based). *Faculty research:* Organizational theory, internationalization of public policy, water resource policies, political interest intermediation, comparative politics.

Michigan State University, The Graduate School, College of Social Science, Interdisciplinary Studies in Social Science—Global Applications, East Lansing, MI 48824. Offers MA. *Degree requirements:* For master's, internship/practicum or field experience, policy paper or analytical report. *Entrance requirements:* Additional exam requirements/recommendations for international students: Required—TOEFL, Michigan State University ELT (85), Michigan English Language Assessment Battery (83). Electronic applications accepted.

Missouri State University, Graduate College, College of Humanities and Public Affairs, Department of Political Science, Program in International Affairs and Administration, Springfield, MO 65804-0094. Offers MIAA. Part-time programs available. *Students:* 29 full-time (8 women), 5 part-time (3 women); includes 7 minority (2 African Americans, 3 Asian Americans or Pacific Islanders, 2 Hispanic Americans), 9 international. Average age 27. 18 applicants, 94% accepted, 15 enrolled. In 2008, 14 master's awarded. *Degree requirements:* For master's, 2 foreign languages, comprehensive exam, thesis or alternative. *Entrance requirements:* For master's, GRE, minimum GPA of 3.0. Additional exam requirements/recommendations for international students: Required—TOEFL (minimum score 550 paper-based; 213 computer-based; 79 iBT). *Application deadline:* For fall admission, 7/20 priority date for domestic students, 5/1 for international students; for spring admission, 12/20 priority date for domestic students, 9/1 for international students. Applications are processed on a rolling basis. Application fee: $35 ($50 for international students). Electronic applications accepted. *Expenses:* Tuition, state resident: full-time $3852; part-time $214 per credit hour. Tuition, nonresident: full-time $7524; part-time $418 per credit hour. Required fees: $230 per semester. Tuition and fees vary according to course level and course load. *Financial support:* In 2008–09, 1 research assistantship with full tuition reimbursement (averaging $9,730 per year), 2 teaching assistantships with full tuition reimbursements (averaging $8,535 per year) were awarded; Federal Work-Study, scholarships/grants, and unspecified assistantships also available. Support available to part-time students. Financial award application deadline: 3/31; financial award applicants required to submit FAFSA. *Faculty research:* U.S.-China policy, Eastern European politics, South American political

reform, landmine use policy. *Unit head:* Dr. Beat Kernen, Graduate Director, 417-836-6957, Fax: 417-836-6655, E-mail: beatkernen@missouristate.edu. *Application contact:* Dr. Beat Kernen, Graduate Director, 417-836-6957, Fax: 417-836-6655, E-mail: beatkernen@missouristate.edu.

See Close-Up on page 869.

Monterey Institute of International Studies, Graduate School of International Policy Studies, Program in International Policy Studies, Monterey, CA 93940-2691. Offers MA. *Students:* 240 full-time (128 women), 6 part-time (4 women); includes 26 minority (5 African Americans, 1 American Indian/Alaska Native, 8 Asian Americans or Pacific Islanders, 12 Hispanic Americans), 60 international. Average age 27. In 2008, 98 master's awarded. *Degree requirements:* For master's, one foreign language. *Entrance requirements:* For master's, minimum GPA of 3.0, proficiency in a foreign language. Additional exam requirements/recommendations for international students: Required—TOEFL (minimum score 550 paper-based; 213 computer-based; 80 iBT). *Application deadline:* For fall admission, 3/15 priority date for domestic and international students; for spring admission, 10/1 priority date for domestic and international students. Applications are processed on a rolling basis. Application fee: $50. Electronic applications accepted. *Expenses:* Tuition: Full-time $29,300; part-time $1400 per credit. Required fees: $56. *Financial support:* In 2008–09, 241 students received support. Application deadline: 3/15. *Application contact:* 831-647-4123, Fax: 831-647-6405, E-mail: admit@miis.edu.

See Close-Up on page 871.

Monterey Institute of International Studies, Graduate School of International Policy Studies, Program in International Public Administration, Monterey, CA 93940-2691. Offers international management (MPA). *Students:* 67 full-time (52 women), 1 (woman) part-time; includes 15 minority (6 African Americans, 4 Asian Americans or Pacific Islanders, 5 Hispanic Americans), 17 international. Average age 26. 74 applicants, 93% accepted, 28 enrolled. In 2008, 38 master's awarded. *Degree requirements:* For master's, one foreign language. *Entrance requirements:* For master's, minimum GPA of 3.0, proficiency in a foreign language. Additional exam requirements/recommendations for international students: Required—TOEFL (minimum score 550 paper-based; 213 computer-based; 80 iBT). *Application deadline:* For fall admission, 3/15 priority date for domestic and international students; for spring admission, 10/1 priority date for domestic and international students. Applications are processed on a rolling basis. Application fee: $50. Electronic applications accepted. *Expenses:* Tuition: Full-time $29,300; part-time $1400 per credit. Required fees: $56. *Financial support:* In 2008–09, 76 students received support. Career-related internships or fieldwork, Federal Work-Study, and institutionally sponsored loans available. Support available to part-time students. Financial award application deadline: 3/15; financial award applicants required to submit FAFSA. *Application contact:* 831-647-4123, Fax: 831-647-6405, E-mail: admit@miis.edu.

See Close-Up on page 871.

Morgan State University, School of Graduate Studies, College of Liberal Arts, Department of World Languages and International Studies, Baltimore, MD 21251. Offers international studies (MA). Part-time and evening/weekend programs available. *Degree requirements:* For master's, one foreign language, comprehensive exam, thesis. *Entrance requirements:* For master's, GRE. Additional exam requirements/recommendations for international students: Required—TOEFL (minimum score 550 paper-based; 213 computer-based).

Naval Postgraduate School, Graduate Programs, Department of National Security Affairs, Monterey, CA 93943. Offers intelligence (MA); international relations (MA); political science (MA); regional security education (MA); security building (MA); security studies (MA). Program only open to commissioned officers of the United States and friendly nations and selected United States federal civilian employees. Part-time programs available. *Degree requirements:* For master's, thesis.

The New School: A University, The New School for General Studies, Program in International Affairs, New York, NY 10011. Offers global management, trade, and finance (MA, MS); international development (MA, MS); international media and communication (MA, MS); international politics and diplomacy (MA, MS); service, civic, and non-profit management (MS). Part-time programs available. *Faculty:* 10 full-time (6 women), 26 part-time/adjunct (11 women). *Students:* 198 full-time (142 women), 147 part-time (92 women); includes 77 minority (25 African Americans, 19 Asian Americans or Pacific Islanders, 33 Hispanic Americans), 63 international. Average age 30. In 2008, 86 master's awarded. *Entrance requirements:* Additional exam requirements/recommendations for international students: Required—TOEFL (minimum score 600 paper-based; 250 computer-based; 100 iBT). *Application deadline:* For fall admission, 4/15 for domestic students; for spring admission, 10/15 for domestic students. Application fee: $50. *Expenses:* Tuition: Full-time $27,144; part-time $1508 per credit. Required fees: $355 per semester. *Financial support:* Fellowships with partial tuition reimbursements, research assistantships, teaching assistantships with partial tuition reimbursements, career-related internships or fieldwork, Federal Work-Study, scholarships/grants, tuition waivers (partial), and unspecified assistantships available. Support available to part-time students. Financial award application deadline: 3/1; financial award applicants required to submit FAFSA. *Unit head:* Dr. Michael Cohen, Director, 212-206-3524, Fax: 212-645-0661, E-mail: cohenm2@newschool.edu. *Application contact:* David Norris, Director of Admissions, 212-229-5630, Fax: 212-989-3887, E-mail: nsadmissions@newschool.edu.

See Close-Up on page 873.

New York University, Graduate School of Arts and Science, Department of Politics, New York, NY 10012-1019. Offers political campaign management (MA); politics (MA, PhD); JD/MA; MBA/MA. Part-time programs available. Terminal master's awarded for partial completion of doctoral program. *Degree requirements:* For master's, one foreign language, thesis or alternative; for doctorate, 2 foreign languages, comprehensive exam, thesis/dissertation. *Entrance requirements:* For master's, GRE General Test; for doctorate, GRE General Test, master's degree in political science, minimum GPA of 2.5. Additional exam requirements/recommendations for international students: Required—TOEFL. *Faculty research:* Comparative politics, democratic theory and practice, rational choice, political economy; international relations.

New York University, Robert F. Wagner Graduate School of Public Service, Program in Public Administration, New York, NY 10012-1019. Offers public administration (PhD); public and nonprofit management and policy (MPA, Advanced Certificate), including developmental administration (Advanced Certificate), financial management and public finance, human resources management (Advanced Certificate), international administration (Advanced Certificate), management (MPA), management for public and nonprofit organizations (Advanced Certificate), public policy analysis, quantitative analysis and computer applications (Advanced Certificate), urban public policy (Advanced Certificate); JD/MPA; MBA/MPA; MPA/MA. *Accreditation:* NASPAA (one or more programs are accredited). Part-time and evening/weekend programs available. *Degree requirements:* For master's, thesis or alternative, capstone/end event; for doctorate, one foreign language, thesis/dissertation. *Entrance requirements:* For master's, minimum undergraduate GPA of 3.0; for doctorate, GMAT or GRE General Test, minimum GPA of 3.5. Additional exam requirements/recommendations for international students: Required—TOEFL (minimum score 600 paper-based; 250 computer-based; 100 iBT), TWE (minimum score 4). Electronic applications accepted. *Expenses:* Contact institution.

See Close-Up on page 1229.

New York University, School of Continuing and Professional Studies, Center for Global Affairs, New York, NY 10012-1019. Offers global studies (MS), including energy policy/environment/oil, human rights and humanitarian assistance, international law, dispute settlement, and institutions, international relations, private sector: international business, economics, and development. Part-time and evening/weekend programs available. *Entrance requirements:* For master's, GRE General Test or GMAT (for recent graduates), 2 letters of recommendation, resumé, essay. Additional exam requirements/recommendations for international students:

International Affairs

New York University (continued)
Required—TOEFL (minimum score 600 paper-based; 250 computer-based; 100 iBT), TWE. Electronic applications accepted.

North Carolina State University, Graduate School, College of Humanities and Social Sciences, School of Public and International Affairs, Program in International Studies, Raleigh, NC 27695. Offers MIS. *Degree requirements:* For master's, thesis optional. *Entrance requirements:* For master's, GRE General Test, minimum GPA of 3.0 during previous 2 years. Electronic applications accepted. *Faculty research:* Global environmental policy and climate change, drug policy and the Caribbean, U.S. national security politics, local responses to globalization, the political economy of the European Union.

Northeastern University, College of Arts and Sciences, Department of Political Science, Boston, MA 02115-5096. Offers political science (MA); public administration (MPA, Certificate), including development administration (MPA), health administration and policy (MPA), state and local government (MPA), urban studies (Certificate); public and international affairs (PhD). Part-time and evening/weekend programs available. *Degree requirements:* For master's, thesis optional; for doctorate, thesis/dissertation. *Entrance requirements:* For master's, GRE General Test. Additional exam requirements/recommendations for international students: Required—TOEFL. *Faculty research:* Presidency, public opinion, Congress, democratization, national identity.

Northwestern University, The Graduate School, Center for International and Comparative Studies, Evanston, IL 60208. Offers Certificate.

Northwestern University, Law School, Chicago, IL 60611-3069. Offers executive law (LL M); international human rights (LL M); international law (JD); law (JD, LL M); JD/LL M; JD/MBA; JD/PhD; LL M/Certificate; MSJ/MSL. *Accreditation:* ABA. *Entrance requirements:* For JD, LSAT, 1 letter of recommendation, resumé; for master's, law degree or equivalent, letter of recommendation, resumé. Additional exam requirements/recommendations for international students: Required—TOEFL. Electronic applications accepted. *Expenses:* Contact institution. *Faculty research:* Constitutional law, corporate law, international law, law and social policy, ethical studies.

Norwich University, School of Graduate Studies, Program in Diplomacy, Northfield, VT 05663. Offers international commerce (MA); international conflict management (MA); international terrorism (MA). Evening/weekend programs available. *Faculty:* 1 full-time (0 women), 15 part-time/adjunct (3 women). *Students:* 156 full-time (50 women); includes 49 minority (9 African Americans, 8 American Indian/Alaska Native, 5 Asian Americans or Pacific Islanders, 27 Hispanic Americans), 2 international. Average age 33. 353 applicants, 95% accepted, 301 enrolled. In 2008, 145 master's awarded. *Degree requirements:* For master's, comprehensive exam, thesis optional. *Entrance requirements:* For master's, minimum undergraduate GPA of 2.75. Additional exam requirements/recommendations for international students: Required—TOEFL. *Application deadline:* For fall admission, 8/10 for domestic and international students; for winter admission, 11/7 for domestic and international students; for spring admission, 2/6 for domestic and international students. Application fee: $50. Electronic applications accepted. *Expenses:* Tuition: Full-time $8000. Full-time tuition and fees vary according to degree level and program. *Financial support:* Scholarships/grants available. Financial award applicants required to submit FAFSA. *Unit head:* Dr. Hal Kearsley, Program Director, 802-485-2730, E-mail: hkearsley@norwich.edu. *Application contact:* Fianna Verret, Administrative Director, 802-485-2783, Fax: 802-485-2533, E-mail: fverret@norwich.edu.

Ohio University, Graduate College, Center for International Studies, Program in Communications and Development Studies, Athens, OH 45701-2979. Offers MA. Part-time programs available. *Degree requirements:* For master's, one foreign language, thesis optional, internship. *Entrance requirements:* For master's, minimum GPA of 3.0. Additional exam requirements/recommendations for international students: Required—TOEFL (minimum score 550 paper-based; 213 computer-based). *Faculty research:* National development processes, public relations and participatory research, audio and video production, health communication, urban development.

Old Dominion University, College of Arts and Letters, Graduate Programs in International Studies, Norfolk, VA 23529. Offers conflict and cooperation (PhD), including women's studies certificate; U.S. foreign policy (MA), including modeling and simulation certificate. Part-time programs available. *Faculty:* 14 full-time (3 women). *Students:* 40 full-time (16 women), 34 part-time (15 women); includes 6 minority (2 African Americans, 1 Asian American or Pacific Islander, 3 Hispanic Americans), 24 international. Average age 32. 99 applicants, 54% accepted, 30 enrolled. In 2008, 10 master's, 5 doctorates awarded. Terminal master's awarded for partial completion of doctoral program. *Degree requirements:* For master's, one foreign language, comprehensive exam, thesis optional; for doctorate, one foreign language, comprehensive exam, thesis/dissertation. *Entrance requirements:* For master's, GRE General Test, sample of written work, 2 letters of recommendation; for doctorate, GRE General Test, sample of written work, 3 letters of recommendation. Additional exam requirements/recommendations for international students: Required—TOEFL (minimum score 570 paper-based; 230 computer-based). *Application deadline:* For fall admission, 3/15 for domestic students, 2/15 for international students; for spring admission, 10/15 for domestic and international students. Application fee: $40. Electronic applications accepted. *Expenses:* Tuition: area resident: Full-time $7704; part-time $321 per credit. Tuition, state resident: full-time $7704; part-time $321 per credit. Tuition, nonresident: full-time $19,104; part-time $796 per credit. Required fees: $99 per semester. One-time fee: $40. *Financial support:* In 2008–09, 20 students received support, including 2 fellowships (averaging $13,000 per year), 9 research assistantships with tuition reimbursements available (averaging $11,000 per year), 9 teaching assistantships with tuition reimbursements available (averaging $11,000 per year); career-related internships or fieldwork, institutionally sponsored loans, scholarships/grants, and unspecified assistantships also available. Support available to part-time students. Financial award application deadline: 2/15; financial award applicants required to submit FAFSA. *Faculty research:* U.S. foreign policy, international security, transatlantic and transpacific relations, transnational issues, IPE and development. Total annual research expenditures: $330,391. *Unit head:* Dr. Regina Karp, Graduate Program Director, 757-683-5700, Fax: 757-683-5701, E-mail: rkarp@odu.edu. *Application contact:* Dr. Angelica Huizar, 757-683-3988, Fax: 757-683-5701, E-mail: ahuizar@odu.edu.

Pepperdine University, School of Public Policy, Malibu, CA 90263. Offers American politics (MPP); economics (MPP); international relations (MPP); public policy (MPP); state and local policy (MPP). *Entrance requirements:* For master's, GRE, 2 letters of recommendation, resumé. Additional exam requirements/recommendations for international students: Required—TOEFL. Electronic applications accepted.

Princeton University, Graduate School, Woodrow Wilson School of Public and International Affairs, Princeton, NJ 08544-1019. Offers public affairs (MPA, PhD); public policy (MPP); JD/MPA. Terminal master's awarded for partial completion of doctoral program. *Degree requirements:* For master's, internship; for doctorate, one foreign language, thesis/dissertation. *Entrance requirements:* For master's, GRE General Test, original policy memo; for doctorate, GRE General Test. Additional exam requirements/recommendations for international students: Required—TOEFL (minimum score 600 paper-based; 250 computer-based). Electronic applications accepted.

Queen's University at Kingston, School of Graduate Studies and Research, Faculty of Arts and Sciences, Department of Political Studies, Kingston, ON K7L 3N6, Canada. Offers Canadian politics (PhD); comparative politics (PhD); gender and politics (PhD); international relations (PhD); political theory (PhD). *Degree requirements:* For master's, thesis or alternative; for doctorate, one foreign language, thesis/dissertation, qualifying exams. *Entrance requirements:* Additional exam requirements/recommendations for international students: Required—TOEFL (minimum score 600 paper-based; 250 computer-based). *Faculty research:* Canadian politics, comparative politics, political thought, international politics, women and politics.

Rutgers, The State University of New Jersey, Camden, Graduate School of Arts and Sciences, Department of Public Policy and Administration, Camden, NJ 08102-1401. Offers education policy and leadership (MPA); international public service and development (MPA); public management (MPA); JD/MPA; MPA/MA. *Accreditation:* NASPAA. Part-time and evening/weekend programs available. *Degree requirements:* For master's, directed study, research workshop. *Entrance requirements:* For master's, GRE General Test, GMAT or LSAT, 3 letters of recommendation; resumé; statement of personal, professional, and academic goals. Additional exam requirements/recommendations for international students: Required—TOEFL (minimum score 550 paper-based; 213 computer-based), IELTS. Electronic applications accepted. *Faculty research:* Nonprofit management, county and municipal administration, health and human services, government communication, administrative law, educational finance.

Rutgers, The State University of New Jersey, Newark, Graduate School, Division of Global Affairs, Newark, NJ 07102. Offers MS, PhD. Part-time and evening/weekend programs available. *Degree requirements:* For master's, one foreign language, thesis optional. *Entrance requirements:* For master's and doctorate, GRE General Test, minimum B average. Electronic applications accepted. *Faculty research:* International organizations, diplomacy, world history, international political economy, global environment.

Rutgers, The State University of New Jersey, Newark, Graduate School, Program in Political Science, Newark, NJ 07102. Offers American political system (MA); international relations (MA); JD/MA. Part-time and evening/weekend programs available. *Degree requirements:* For master's, comprehensive exam, thesis optional. *Entrance requirements:* For master's, GRE, minimum undergraduate B average. Electronic applications accepted. *Faculty research:* Policymaking and policy evaluation in the United States; government and politics in Europe, Middle East, Asia, Africa, and Latin America.

Rutgers, The State University of New Jersey, New Brunswick, Graduate School, Department of Political Science, Piscataway, NJ 08854-8097. Offers American politics (PhD); comparative politics (PhD); international relations (PhD); political theory (PhD); public law (PhD); women and politics (PhD). *Degree requirements:* For doctorate, one foreign language, comprehensive exam, thesis/dissertation. *Entrance requirements:* For doctorate, GRE General Test. Additional exam requirements/recommendations for international students: Required—TOEFL.

St. John Fisher College, School of Arts and Sciences, Program in International Studies, Rochester, NY 14618-3597. Offers MS. Part-time and evening/weekend programs available. *Faculty:* 5 full-time (0 women), 2 part-time/adjunct (0 women). *Students:* 7 full-time (3 women), 28 part-time (12 women); includes 3 minority (2 African Americans, 1 Hispanic American). Average age 30. 14 applicants, 86% accepted, 11 enrolled. In 2008, 10 master's awarded. *Degree requirements:* For master's, research project. *Entrance requirements:* For master's, 2 letters of recommendation, personal statement, current resumé. Additional exam requirements/recommendations for international students: Required—TOEFL (minimum score 575 paper-based; 233 computer-based; 80 iBT). *Application deadline:* For fall admission, 7/1 for domestic students; for spring admission, 10/30 for domestic students. Applications are processed on a rolling basis. Application fee: $30. Electronic applications accepted. *Expenses:* Tuition: Part-time $655 per credit hour. Required fees: $25 per semester. *Financial support:* In 2008–09, 24 students received support. Federal Work-Study and scholarships/grants available. Financial award applicants required to submit FAFSA. *Faculty research:* International relations, international affairs, international economics, Chinese politics. *Unit head:* Dr. David Baronov, Program Director, 585-385-8220, E-mail: dbaronov@sjfc.edu. *Application contact:* Jose Perales, Director of Graduate Admissions, 585-385-8067, E-mail: jperales@sjfc.edu.

St. Mary's University, Graduate School, Department of Political Science, Interdisciplinary Program in International Relations, San Antonio, TX 78228-8507. Offers MA, JD/MA. Part-time programs available. Postbaccalaureate distance learning degree programs offered (no on-campus study). *Faculty:* 2 full-time (1 woman), 9 part-time/adjunct (2 women). *Students:* 41 full-time (27 women), 96 part-time (43 women); includes 46 minority (8 African Americans, 7 Asian Americans or Pacific Islanders, 31 Hispanic Americans), 7 international. Average age 29. 88 applicants, 76% accepted, 47 enrolled. In 2008, 56 master's awarded. *Degree requirements:* For master's, one foreign language, comprehensive exam. *Entrance requirements:* For master's, GRE General Test. Additional exam requirements/recommendations for international students: Required—TOEFL (minimum score 550 paper-based; 213 computer-based; 80 iBT). *Application deadline:* Applications are processed on a rolling basis. Application fee: $0. Electronic applications accepted. *Expenses:* Tuition: Full-time $12,006; part-time $667 per credit hour. Required fees: $440; $220 per semester. *Financial support:* In 2008–09, 17 students received support, including 15 fellowships (averaging $3,818 per year), 2 research assistantships (averaging $4,500 per year); career-related internships or fieldwork, Federal Work-Study, institutionally sponsored loans, scholarships/grants, health care benefits, tuition waivers (full), and unspecified assistantships also available. Financial award application deadline: 3/31; financial award applicants required to submit FAFSA. *Faculty research:* Eastern Europe, Soviet Union, Balkans, modern Asia, Latin America. *Unit head:* Dr. Leona Pallansch, Director, 210-436-3204, Fax: 210-431-4336, E-mail: lpallansch@stmarytx.edu. *Application contact:* Dr. Henry Flores, Dean of the Graduate School, 210-436-3101, Fax: 210-431-2220, E-mail: hflores@stmarytx.edu.

Salve Regina University, Graduate Studies, Program in International Relations, Newport, RI 02840-4192. Offers homeland security (Certificate); international relations (MA, Certificate). Part-time and evening/weekend programs available. Postbaccalaureate distance learning degree programs offered (minimal on-campus study). *Faculty:* 3 full-time (0 women), 5 part-time/adjunct (2 women). *Students:* 21 full-time (9 women), 66 part-time (24 women); includes 5 minority (1 African American, 1 Asian American or Pacific Islander, 3 Hispanic Americans), 4 international. Average age 34. 59 applicants, 59% accepted, 311 enrolled. In 2008, 38 master's awarded. *Entrance requirements:* For master's, GMAT, GRE General Test, MAT or LSAT. Additional exam requirements/recommendations for international students: Required—TOEFL (minimum score 600 paper-based; 250 computer-based; 100 iBT), TOEFL or IELTS. *Application deadline:* For fall admission, 3/15 priority date for domestic and international students; for spring admission, 9/15 priority date for domestic and international students. Applications are processed on a rolling basis. Application fee: $60. Electronic applications accepted. *Expenses:* Tuition: Part-time $395 per credit. Required fees: $40 per term. Tuition and fees vary according to degree level. *Financial support:* Career-related internships or fieldwork and Federal Work-Study available. Support available to part-time students. Financial award application deadline: 3/1; financial award applicants required to submit FAFSA. *Unit head:* Dr. Symeon Giannakos, Director, 401-341-3177, Fax: 401-341-2993, E-mail: symeon.giannakos@salve.edu. *Application contact:* Kelly Alverson, Graduate Admissions Counselor, 401-341-2153, Fax: 401-341-2973, E-mail: kelly.alverson@salve.edu.

San Francisco State University, Division of Graduate Studies, College of Behavioral and Social Sciences, Department of International Relations, San Francisco, CA 94132-1722. Offers MA.

Schiller International University, Graduate Programs, London, Program in International Relations and Diplomacy, London, United Kingdom. Offers MA. Part-time programs available. *Degree requirements:* For master's, thesis optional, GMAT before graduation. *Entrance requirements:* For master's, 1 year of undergraduate economics, 1 foreign language. Additional exam requirements/recommendations for international students: Required—TOEFL (minimum score 550 paper-based; 213 computer-based).

Schiller International University, Program in International Relations and Diplomacy, Paris, France. Offers MA. Part-time and evening/weekend programs available. *Degree requirements:* For master's, one foreign language, thesis or alternative, final comprehensive exam or thesis. *Entrance requirements:* For master's, undergraduate mathematics (strongly advised). Additional exam requirements/recommendations for international students: Required—TOEFL (minimum score 550 paper-based; 213 computer-based).

Seton Hall University, Whitehead School of Diplomacy and International Relations, South Orange, NJ 07079-2697. Offers MA, JD/MA, MBA/MA, MPA/MA. Part-time and evening/weekend programs available. *Degree requirements:* For master's, thesis (for some programs), research project, internship. *Entrance requirements:* For master's, GMAT, GRE, or LSAT, minimum GPA of 3.2. Additional exam requirements/recommendations for international students: Required—TOEFL (minimum score 600 paper-based; 250 computer-based; 100 iBT). Electronic applications accepted. *Faculty research:* International economics and development, global health, United Nations conflict negotiation and conflict management.

See Close-Up on page 875.

SIT Graduate Institute, Graduate Programs, Master's Programs in Intercultural Service, Leadership, and Management, Brattleboro, VT 05302-0676. Offers conflict transformation (MA); intercultural service, leadership, and management (MA); international education (MA); management (MS); social justice in intercultural relations (MA); sustainable development (MA). Postbaccalaureate distance learning degree programs offered (minimal on-campus study). *Degree requirements:* For master's, one foreign language, thesis. *Entrance requirements:* For master's, 3 letters of reference. Additional exam requirements/recommendations for international students: Required—TOEFL. *Faculty research:* Intercultural communication, conflict resolution, advising and training, world issues, international business.

Stanford University, School of Humanities and Sciences, Program in International Policy Studies, Stanford, CA 94305-9991. Offers MA. *Degree requirements:* For master's, thesis optional. *Entrance requirements:* For master's, GRE General Test. Additional exam requirements/recommendations for international students: Required—TOEFL. Electronic applications accepted.

Syracuse University, Graduate School, Maxwell School of Citizenship and Public Affairs and S. I. Newhouse School of Public Communications, Program in Public Diplomacy, Syracuse, NY 13244. Offers MS/MA. *Entrance requirements:* Additional exam requirements/recommendations for international students: Required—TOEFL.

Syracuse University, Graduate School, Maxwell School of Citizenship and Public Affairs, Programs in International Relations, Syracuse, NY 13244. Offers public diplomacy (MA); MS/MA. Part-time and evening/weekend programs available. *Degree requirements:* For master's, thesis or alternative. *Entrance requirements:* For master's, GRE General Test. Additional exam requirements/recommendations for international students: Required—TOEFL. Electronic applications accepted.

Syracuse University, Graduate School, S. I. Newhouse School of Public Communications and Maxwell School of Citizenship and Public Affairs, Program in Public Diplomacy, Syracuse, NY 13244. Offers MS/MA. *Entrance requirements:* Additional exam requirements/recommendations for international students: Required—TOEFL.

Texas A&M University, George Bush School of Government and Public Service, College Station, TX 77843. Offers advanced international affairs (Certificate); homeland security (Certificate); international affairs (MPIA), including international economics and development, national security affairs; nonprofit management (Certificate); public service and administration (MPSA), including public management, public policy analysis. *Accreditation:* NASPAA. *Faculty:* 43. *Students:* 188 full-time (80 women), 101 part-time (37 women); includes 40 minority (10 African Americans, 5 Asian Americans or Pacific Islanders, 25 Hispanic Americans), 22 international. Average age 24. In 2008, 64 master's awarded. *Degree requirements:* For master's, summer internship. *Entrance requirements:* For master's, GRE (preferred) or GMAT. *Application deadline:* For fall admission, 1/24 for domestic and international students. Application fee: $50 ($75 for international students). Electronic applications accepted. *Expenses:* Tuition, area resident: Full-time $3838.50. Tuition, state resident: full-time $3838.50. Tuition, nonresident: full-time $8897. Required fees: $2359.60. *Financial support:* In 2008–09, fellowships (averaging $11,000 per year), research assistantships (averaging $11,250 per year) were awarded; career-related internships or fieldwork, Federal Work-Study, and institutionally sponsored loans also available. Financial award application deadline: 2/1; financial award applicants required to submit FAFSA. *Faculty research:* Public policy, presidential studies, public leadership, economic policy, social policy. *Unit head:* A. Benton Cocanougher, Dean, 979-862-8842, E-mail: bushschool@tamu.edu. *Application contact:* Kathryn Meyer, Recruitment/Placement Officer, 979-458-4767, Fax: 979-845-4155, E-mail: admissions@bushschool.tamu.edu.

Texas State University–San Marcos, Graduate School, Program in International Studies, San Marcos, TX 78666. Offers MA. *Degree requirements:* For master's, comprehensive exam. *Entrance requirements:* For master's, minimum 3.0 GPA on last 60 hours of undergraduate work, 2 to 5 page essay, 2 letters of reference. Additional exam requirements/recommendations for international students: Required—TOEFL (minimum score 550 paper-based; 213 computer-based).

Troy University, Graduate School, College of Arts and Sciences, Program in International Relations, Troy, AL 36082. Offers MS. Part-time and evening/weekend programs available. Postbaccalaureate distance learning degree programs offered (no on-campus study). *Degree requirements:* For master's, comprehensive exam (for some programs), thesis optional. *Entrance requirements:* For master's, GRE General Test, MAT, or GMAT, minimum GPA of 2.5. Additional exam requirements/recommendations for international students: Required—TOEFL (minimum score 523 paper-based; 200 computer-based). Electronic applications accepted. *Faculty research:* Elections, religion and world politics, terrorism.

Tufts University, Fletcher School of Law and Diplomacy, Medford, MA 02155. Offers LL M, MA, MAHA, MALD, MIB, PhD, DVM/MA, JD/MALD, MALD/MA, MALD/MBA, MALD/MS, MD/MA. Postbaccalaureate distance learning degree programs offered (minimal on-campus study). *Degree requirements:* For master's, one foreign language, thesis; for doctorate, one foreign language, comprehensive exam, thesis/dissertation, dissertation defense. *Entrance requirements:* For master's and doctorate, GMAT or GRE General Test. Additional exam requirements/recommendations for international students: Required—TOEFL (minimum score 600 paper-based; 250 computer-based; 100 iBT), IELTS (minimum score 7). Electronic applications accepted. *Expenses:* Contact institution. *Faculty research:* Negotiation and conflict resolution, international organizations, international business and economic law, security studies, development economics.

See Close-Up on page 879.

United States International University, School of Arts and Sciences, Nairobi, Kenya. Offers counseling psychology (MA); international relations (MA). Part-time and evening/weekend programs available. *Degree requirements:* For master's, thesis, practicum. *Entrance requirements:* For master's, GRE General Test, 2 letters of recommendation, resumé. Additional exam requirements/recommendations for international students: Required—TOEFL (minimum score 550 paper-based; 213 computer-based). *Faculty research:* Trauma in children, African intellectualism, psychological assessment tools.

Universidad de las Americas, A.C., Program in International Organizations and Institutions, Mexico City, Mexico. Offers MA.

Universidad Nacional Pedro Henriquez Urena, Graduate School, Santo Domingo, Dominican Republic. Offers accounting and auditing (M Acct); animal production (M Agr); business administration (MBA, PhD); Caribbean tropical architecture (M Arch); conservation of monuments and cultural goods (M Arch); economics (M Econ); education (PhD); environmental engineering (MEE); horticulture (M Agr); hospital administration (PhD); humanities (PhD); international relations (MPS); management of natural resources (MNRM); project management (M Man, MPM); public administration (MPS); sanitary engineering (ME); social science (PhD); veterinary medicine (DVM).

Université Laval, Québec Institute for Advanced International Studies, Program in International Relations, Québec, QC G1K 7P4, Canada. Offers MA, PhD. *Degree requirements:* For master's, thesis (for some programs). *Entrance requirements:* For master's, English exam, French exam. Electronic applications accepted.

University of Bridgeport, International College, Bridgeport, CT 06604. Offers global development and peace (MA). Part-time and evening/weekend programs available. *Faculty:* 7 full-time (4 women), 8 part-time/adjunct (3 women). *Students:* 12 full-time (7 women), 3 part-time (2 women); includes 3 minority (all African Americans), 7 international. Average age 28. 28 applicants, 75% accepted, 11 enrolled. *Degree requirements:* For master's, thesis. *Entrance requirements:* Additional exam requirements/recommendations for international students: Recommended—TOEFL (minimum score 550 paper-based; 213 computer-based; 80 iBT), IELTS (minimum score 6.5). *Application deadline:* For fall admission, 8/1 priority date for domestic and international students; for spring admission, 12/1 priority date for domestic and international students. Application fee: $40 ($35 for international students). *Expenses:* Tuition: Full-time $19,820; part-time $595 per credit hour. Required fees: $75 per semester. *Unit head:* Dr. Thomas J Ward, Dean, 203-576-4966, Fax: 203-4967, E-mail: ward@bridgeport.edu. *Application contact:* Barbara L Maryak, Vice President of Enrollment Management, 203-576-4552, Fax: 203-576-4941, E-mail: admit@bridgeport.edu.

The University of British Columbia, Faculty of Graduate Studies, Institute of Asian Research, Vancouver, BC V6T 1Z1, Canada. Offers MAPPS. Part-time programs available. *Degree requirements:* For master's, thesis optional. *Entrance requirements:* Additional exam requirements/recommendations for international students: Required—TOEFL (minimum score 600 paper-based; 250 computer-based; 100 iBT), GRE (recommended). Electronic applications accepted. *Faculty research:* Social cohesion, globalization, social safety nets, research and development alliances, knowledge-based workshops.

University of California, Berkeley, Graduate Division, Group in International and Area Studies, Berkeley, CA 94720-1500. Offers MA, JD/MA, MBA/MA, MJ/MA.

University of California, Berkeley, Graduate Division, Haas School of Business and Group in International and Area Studies, Concurrent MBA/MIAS Program in International and Area Studies, Berkeley, CA 94720-1500. Offers MBA/MIAS. *Accreditation:* AACSB. *Entrance requirements:* Additional exam requirements/recommendations for international students: Required—TOEFL.

University of California, San Diego, Office of Graduate Studies, Department of Economics, La Jolla, CA 92093. Offers economics (PhD); economics and international affairs (PhD). *Degree requirements:* For doctorate, thesis/dissertation. *Entrance requirements:* For doctorate, GRE General Test. Electronic applications accepted. *Faculty research:* Microfoundations of macroeconomics, econometric model specification and testing, industrial organization.

University of California, San Diego, Office of Graduate Studies, Department of Political Science, La Jolla, CA 92093. Offers Latin American studies (MA); political science (PhD); political science and international affairs (PhD). *Entrance requirements:* For master's and doctorate, GRE General Test. Electronic applications accepted.

University of California, San Diego, Office of Graduate Studies, Graduate School of International Relations and Pacific Studies, La Jolla, CA 92093-0520. Offers economics and international affairs (PhD); Pacific international affairs (MPIA); political science and international affairs (PhD). *Degree requirements:* For master's, one foreign language; for doctorate, thesis/dissertation. *Entrance requirements:* For master's, GMAT or GRE General Test; for doctorate, GRE General Test. Additional exam requirements/recommendations for international students: Required—TOEFL (minimum score 550 paper-based; 213 computer-based). Electronic applications accepted. *Faculty research:* Pacific Rim as system and placement in global relations; studies in international economics, management and finance; analysis of patterns of policymaking in countries of the Pacific.

See Display on page 838. See Close-Up on page 881.

University of California, Santa Barbara, Graduate Division, College of Letters and Sciences, Division of Humanities and Fine Arts, Department of English, Santa Barbara, CA 93106-3170. Offers English (PhD); feminist studies (PhD); global studies (PhD); MA/PhD. *Faculty:* 26 full-time (13 women), 17 part-time/adjunct (12 women). *Students:* 81 full-time (43 women). Average age 30. 151 applicants, 19% accepted, 13 enrolled. In 2008, 12 doctorates awarded. Terminal master's awarded for partial completion of doctoral program. *Degree requirements:* For doctorate, one foreign language, comprehensive exam, thesis/dissertation. *Entrance requirements:* For doctorate, GRE General Test, GRE Subject Test (literature), sample of written work, 3 letters of recommendation, statement of purpose, personal achievements/contributions statement, resumé/curriculum vitae, transcripts for post-secondary institutions attended. Additional exam requirements/recommendations for international students: Required—TOEFL (paper: 550, computer: 213, IBT: 80) or IELTS (7). *Application deadline:* For fall admission, 12/15 for domestic and international students. Application fee: $70 ($90 for international students). Electronic applications accepted. *Expenses:* Tuition, nonresident: full-time $25,149. Required fees: $10,143. Full-time tuition and fees vary according to campus/location, reciprocity agreements and student level. *Financial support:* In 2008–09, 70 students received support, including 32 fellowships with full and partial tuition reimbursements available (averaging $10,800 per year), 6 research assistantships with full and partial tuition reimbursements available (averaging $4,200 per year), 54 teaching assistantships with partial tuition reimbursements available (averaging $10,800 per year); Federal Work-Study, institutionally sponsored loans, scholarships/grants, health care benefits, tuition waivers (full and partial), and unspecified assistantships also available. Financial award application deadline: 12/15; financial award applicants required to submit FAFSA. *Faculty research:* Renaissance literature, 18th century literature, American literature, race and ethnic studies, literature and theory of technology/media/information. *Unit head:* Prof. Alan Liu, Chair, 805-893-3478, Fax: 805-893-4622, E-mail: ayliu@english.ucsb.edu. *Application contact:* Chelsea Houdyshell, Staff Graduate Advisor, 805-893-2639, Fax: 805-893-4622, E-mail: chelsea@english.ucsb.edu.

University of California, Santa Barbara, Graduate Division, College of Letters and Sciences, Division of Humanities and Fine Arts, Department of History, Santa Barbara, CA 93106-9410. Offers feminist studies (PhD); global studies (PhD); public history (PhD); MA/PhD. *Faculty:* 40 full-time (17 women), 11 part-time/adjunct (6 women). *Students:* 120 full-time (62 women). Average age 34. 130 applicants, 38% accepted, 22 enrolled. In 2008, 9 doctorates awarded. Terminal master's awarded for partial completion of doctoral program. *Degree requirements:* For doctorate, comprehensive exam, thesis/dissertation, one or more languages depending on field of study. *Entrance requirements:* For doctorate, GRE, 3 letters of recommendation, statement of purpose, personal achievements/contributions statement, resumé/curriculum vitae, transcripts for post-secondary institutions attended. Additional exam requirements/recommendations for international students: Required—TOEFL (minimum score 550 paper-based; 213 computer-based; 80 iBT), IELTS (minimum score 7), TOEFL or IELTS. *Application deadline:* For fall admission, 12/5 for domestic and international students. Application fee: $70 ($90 for international students). Electronic applications accepted. *Expenses:* Tuition, nonresident: full-time $25,149. Required fees: $10,143. Full-time tuition and fees vary according to campus/location, reciprocity agreements and student level. *Financial support:* In 2008–09, 94 students received support, including 53 fellowships with full and partial tuition reimbursements available (averaging $8,600 per year), 2 research assistantships with full and partial tuition reimbursements available (averaging $7,400 per year), 70 teaching assistantships with partial tuition reimbursements available (averaging $9,400 per year); Federal Work-Study, institutionally sponsored loans, scholarships/grants, traineeships, health care benefits, tuition waivers (full and partial), and unspecified assistantships also available. Financial award application deadline: 12/5; financial award applicants required to submit FAFSA. *Faculty research:* Europe, U.S., Latin America, Africa, Middle East, East Asia. *Unit head:* Kenneth J. Moure, Chair, 805-893-2993, Fax: 805-893-8795, E-mail: moure@history.ucrb.edu. *Application contact:* Prof. Sharon Farmer, Director of Graduate Studies, 805-893-2543, Fax: 805-893-8795, E-mail: farmer@history.ucsb.edu.

International Affairs

Shaping the Pacific Century

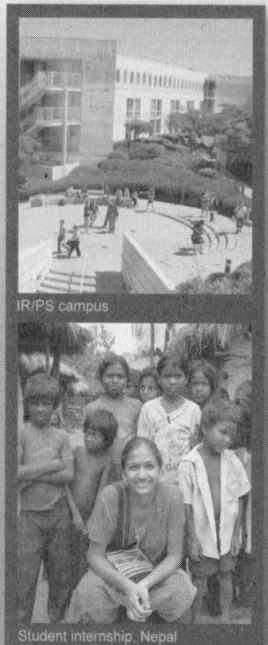

IR/PS campus

Student internship, Nepal

University of California, San Diego
School of International Relations & Pacific Studies

Uniquely located on the Pacific Ocean sharing the busiest border crossing in the world with Tijuana, Mexico, San Diego is rapidly becoming one of the most important economic centers of the Pacific region.

UC San Diego, ranked among the top public universities in the nation, receives top-ten rankings for International Relations and International Public Policy programs. At the center of UC San Diego's international studies is the School of International Relations and Pacific Studies (IR/PS).

IR/PS's faculty and innovative curriculum provide our Master's and Executive Education students with a unique blend of international relations, public policy, and management, and knowledge for leadership in the Pacific Century.

Shape Your Future
irps.ucsd.edu

University of California, Santa Barbara, Graduate Division, College of Letters and Sciences, Division of Humanities and Fine Arts, Department of Religious Studies, Santa Barbara, CA 93106-3130. Offers European Medieval studies (PhD); feminist studies (PhD); global studies (PhD); religous studies (MA, PhD); MA/PhD. *Faculty:* 18 full-time (8 women), 11 part-time/adjunct (5 women). *Students:* 86 full-time (33 women). Average age 31. 151 applicants, 31% accepted, 17 enrolled. In 2008, 7 master's, 6 doctorates awarded. Terminal master's awarded for partial completion of doctoral program. *Degree requirements:* For master's, one foreign language, comprehensive exam (for some programs), thesis (for some programs); for doctorate, one foreign language, thesis/dissertation. *Entrance requirements:* For master's, GRE General Test; for doctorate, GRE General Test, MA in related field, 3 letters of recommendation, statement of purpose, personal achievements/contributions statement, resumé/curriculum vitae, transcripts for post-secondary institutions attended. Additional exam requirements/recommendations for international students: Required—TOEFL (paper: 550, computer: 213, IBT: 80) or IELTS (7). *Application deadline:* For fall admission, 12/1 for domestic and international students. Application fee: $70 ($90 for international students). Electronic applications accepted. *Expenses:* Tuition, nonresident: full-time $25,149. Required fees: $10,143. Full-time tuition and fees vary according to campus/location, reciprocity agreements and student level. *Financial support:* In 2008–09, 67 students received support, including 29 fellowships with full and partial tuition reimbursements available (averaging $12,600 per year), 5 research assistantships with full and partial tuition reimbursements available (averaging $7,900 per year), 46 teaching assistantships with partial tuition reimbursements available (averaging $8,400 per year); career-related internships or fieldwork, Federal Work-Study, institutionally sponsored loans, scholarships/grants, traineeships, health care benefits, tuition waivers (full and partial), and unspecified assistantships also available. Financial award application deadline: 12/1; financial award applicants required to submit FAFSA. *Faculty research:* Religion and politics, religion and violence, contemporary spirituality, religious traditions, theoretical approaches to the study of religion, area studies. *Unit head:* Prof. Catherine L. Albanese, Chair, 805-893-3564, Fax: 805-893-2059, E-mail: albanese@religion.ucsb.edu. *Application contact:* Sally J. Lombrozo, Graduate Program Assistant, 805-893-2744, Fax: 805-893-2059, E-mail: lombrozo@religion.ucsb.edu.

University of California, Santa Barbara, Graduate Division, College of Letters and Sciences, Division of Social Sciences, Department of Anthropology, Santa Barbara, CA 93106-3210. Offers European archaeology (MA); global studies (PhD); North American archeology (MA); sociocultural anthropology (MA); South American archaeology (MA); MA/PhD. *Faculty:* 13 full-time (2 women), 2 part-time/adjunct (both women). *Students:* 57 full-time (36 women). Average age 31. 64 applicants, 41% accepted, 11 enrolled. In 2008, 7 master's, 3 doctorates awarded. Terminal master's awarded for partial completion of doctoral program. *Degree requirements:* For master's, comprehensive exam, thesis; for doctorate, comprehensive exam, thesis/dissertation. *Entrance requirements:* For master's and doctorate, GRE General Test, sample of written work, 3 letters of recommendation, statement of purpose, personal achievements/contributions statement, resumé/curriculum vitae, transcripts for post-secondary institutions attended. Additional exam requirements/recommendations for international students: Required—TOEFL (paper: 550, computer: 213, IBT: 80) or IELTS (7). *Application deadline:* For fall admission, 12/1 for domestic and international students. Application fee: $70 ($90 for international students). Electronic applications accepted. *Expenses:* Tuition, nonresident: full-time $25,149. Required fees: $10,143. Full-time tuition and fees vary according to campus/location, reciprocity agreements and student level. *Financial support:* In 2008–09, 51 students received support, including 47 fellowships with full and partial tuition reimbursements available (averaging $4,000 per year), 9 research assistantships with full and partial tuition reimbursements available (averaging $7,400 per year), 30 teaching assistantships with partial tuition reimbursements available (averaging $10,500 per year); career-related internships or fieldwork, Federal Work-Study, institutionally sponsored loans, scholarships/grants, traineeships, health care benefits, and unspecified assistantships also available. Financial award application deadline: 3/1; financial

award applicants required to submit FAFSA. *Faculty research:* Archaeology, bioarchaeology, biosocial anthropology, evolutionary ecology, evolutionary psychology, sociocultural anthropology. *Unit head:* Prof. Katharina Schreiber, Chair, 805-893-2519, Fax: 805-893-8707, E-mail: kschreiber@anth.ucsb.edu. *Application contact:* Robin Roe, Graduate Program Assistant, 805-893-2516, Fax: 805-893-8707, E-mail: roe@anth.ucsb.edu.

University of California, Santa Barbara, Graduate Division, College of Letters and Sciences, Division of Social Sciences, Department of Global and International Studies, Santa Barbara, CA 93106-7065. Offers MA. *Faculty:* 7 full-time (1 woman), 9 part-time/adjunct (5 women). *Students:* 22 full-time (18 women). Average age 27. 69 applicants, 45% accepted, 18 enrolled. In 2008, 15 master's awarded. *Degree requirements:* For master's, one foreign language, comprehensive exam (for some programs), thesis or alternative, internship/study abroad. *Entrance requirements:* For master's, GRE, 2 years of a 2nd language with grade B or better, 3 letters of recommendation, statement of purpose, personal achievements/contributions statement, resumé/curriculum vitae, transcripts for post-secondary institutions attended. Additional exam requirements/recommendations for international students: Required—TOEFL (paper: 550, computer: 213, IBT: 80) or IELTS. *Application deadline:* For fall admission, 12/15 for domestic and international students. Application fee: $70 ($90 for international students). Electronic applications accepted. *Expenses:* Tuition, nonresident: full-time $25,149. Required fees: $10,143. Full-time tuition and fees vary according to campus/location, reciprocity agreements and student level. *Financial support:* In 2008–09, 25 fellowships with full and partial tuition reimbursements (averaging $4,700 per year), 27 teaching assistantships with partial tuition reimbursements (averaging $5,400 per year) were awarded; career-related internships or fieldwork, Federal Work-Study, institutionally sponsored loans, scholarships/grants, health care benefits, tuition waivers (partial), unspecified assistantships, and travel support for internships also available. Financial award applicants required to submit FAFSA. *Faculty research:* Globalization, NGO/non-profit organizations, world system theory, international/global conflict resolution, international/global ethics. *Unit head:* Prof. Giles Gunn, Chair, 805-893-4299, Fax: 805-893-8003, E-mail: ggunn@global.ucsb.edu. *Application contact:* Jessea Gay Marie, Graduate Program Advisor/Internship Assistance Officer, 805-893-4668, Fax: 805-893-8003, E-mail: jmarie@global.ucsb.edu.

University of California, Santa Barbara, Graduate Division, College of Letters and Sciences, Division of Social Sciences, Department of Sociology, Santa Barbara, CA 93106-9430. Offers global studies (PhD); human development (PhD); language, interaction and social organization (PhD); technology and society (PhD); women's studies (PhD); MA/PhD. *Faculty:* 35 full-time (14 women). *Students:* 77 full-time (50 women). Average age 30. 155 applicants, 9% accepted, 8 enrolled. In 2008, 10 doctorates awarded. Terminal master's awarded for partial completion of doctoral program. *Degree requirements:* For doctorate, comprehensive exam, thesis/dissertation. *Entrance requirements:* For doctorate, GRE General Test, sample of written work, 3 letters of recommendation, statement of purpose, personal achievements/contributions statement, resumé/curriculum vitae, transcripts for post-secondary institutions attended. Additional exam requirements/recommendations for international students: Required—TOEFL (minimum score 550 paper-based; 213 computer-based; 80 iBT), TOEFL or IELTS. *Application deadline:* For fall admission, 12/10 for domestic students. Application fee: $70 ($90 for international students). Electronic applications accepted. *Expenses:* Tuition, nonresident: full-time $25,149. Required fees: $10,143. Full-time tuition and fees vary according to campus/location, reciprocity agreements and student level. *Financial support:* In 2008–09, 69 students received support, including 50 fellowships with full tuition reimbursements available (averaging $7,900 per year), 6 research assistantships with full and partial tuition reimbursements available (averaging $2,600 per year), 53 teaching assistantships with partial tuition reimbursements available (averaging $9,200 per year); career-related internships or fieldwork, Federal Work-Study, institutionally sponsored loans, scholarships/grants, health care benefits, and unspecified assistantships also available. Financial award applicants required to submit FAFSA. *Faculty* *research:* Conversation analysis, social movements, human sexuality, urban sociology, race and ethnic relations. *Unit head:* Prof. Verta Taylor, Chair, 805-893-3118, Fax: 805-893-3324, E-mail: grad-soc@soc.ucsb.edu. *Application contact:* Ra Thea, Graduate Staff Advisor, 805-893-3328, Fax: 805-893-3324, E-mail: grad-soc@soc.ucsb.edu.

University of California, Santa Cruz, Division of Graduate Studies, Division of Social Sciences, Program in International Economics, Santa Cruz, CA 95064. Offers PhD. *Degree requirements:* For doctorate, thesis/dissertation, 4 field exams, econometrics project. *Entrance requirements:* For doctorate, GRE General Test. *Faculty research:* Current and emerging issues in taxation, industrial policy, environmental regulation, market structure.

University of Central Florida, College of Sciences, Department of Political Science, Orlando, FL 32816. Offers environmental politics (MA); international studies (MA); political analysis and policy (MA). Part-time and evening/weekend programs available. *Faculty:* 24 full-time (7 women), 7 part-time/adjunct (1 woman). *Students:* 31 full-time (15 women), 37 part-time (13 women); includes 11 minority (2 Asian Americans or Pacific Islanders, 9 Hispanic Americans), 2 international. In 2008, 7 master's awarded. *Degree requirements:* For master's, comprehensive exam, thesis. *Entrance requirements:* For master's, GRE General Test, minimum GPA of 3.0 in last 60 hours. Additional exam requirements/recommendations for international students: Required—TOEFL. *Application deadline:* For fall admission, 7/15 for domestic students; for spring admission, 12/1 for domestic students. Application fee: $30. Electronic applications accepted. *Expenses:* Tuition, area resident: Full-time $6816; part-time $284 per credit. Tuition, state resident: full-time $6816; part-time $1076 per credit. Tuition, nonresident: full-time $25,824. Required fees: $216; $9 per credit. *Financial support:* In 2008–09, 2 fellowships with partial tuition reimbursements (averaging $10,000 per year), 3 research assistantships with partial tuition reimbursements (averaging $5,800 per year), 7 teaching assistantships with partial tuition reimbursements (averaging $7,600 per year) were awarded; career-related internships or fieldwork, Federal Work-Study, institutionally sponsored loans, tuition waivers (partial), and unspecified assistantships also available. Financial award application deadline: 3/1; financial award applicants required to submit FAFSA. *Faculty research:* Environment, presidential campaigning, term limits for elected officials. *Unit head:* Dr. Roger Handberg, Chair, 407-823-2608, Fax: 407-823-0051. *Application contact:* Dr. Roger Handberg, Chair, 407-823-2608, Fax: 407-823-0051.

University of Central Oklahoma, College of Graduate Studies and Research, College of Liberal Arts, Department of Political Science, Program in International Affairs, Edmond, OK 73034-5209. Offers MA. Part-time programs available. *Entrance requirements:* Additional exam requirements/recommendations for international students: Required—TOEFL (minimum score 550 paper-based; 213 computer-based). Electronic applications accepted. *Faculty research:* Korean and Japanese politics.

University of Chicago, Division of Social Sciences, Committee on International Relations, Chicago, IL 60637-1513. Offers AM, MBA/AM. Part-time programs available. *Degree requirements:* For master's, thesis. *Entrance requirements:* For master's, GRE General Test. Additional exam requirements/recommendations for international students: Required—TOEFL. Electronic applications accepted.

University of Colorado at Boulder, Graduate School, College of Arts and Sciences, Department of Political Science, Boulder, CO 80309. Offers international affairs (MA); political science (MA, PhD); public policy (MA). Terminal master's awarded for partial completion of doctoral program. *Degree requirements:* For master's, comprehensive exam, thesis; for doctorate, one foreign language, thesis/dissertation. *Entrance requirements:* For master's, GRE General Test, minimum undergraduate GPA of 3.0; for doctorate, GRE General Test, minimum GPA of 3.5 (undergraduate), 3.0 (graduate). *Faculty research:* American government and politics, comparative politics, international relations, law and politics, public policy, political philosophy, empirical theory and methodology.

University of Connecticut, Graduate School, College of Liberal Arts and Sciences, Field of International Studies, Program in International Studies, Storrs, CT 06269. Offers MA. *Degree requirements:* For master's, comprehensive exam. *Entrance requirements:* For master's, GRE General Test. Additional exam requirements/recommendations for international students: Required—TOEFL (minimum score 550 paper-based; 213 computer-based). Electronic applications accepted.

University of Delaware, College of Arts and Sciences, Department of Political Science and International Relations, Newark, DE 19716. Offers MA, PhD. Terminal master's awarded for partial completion of doctoral program. *Degree requirements:* For master's, research paper; for doctorate, one foreign language, comprehensive exam, thesis/dissertation. *Entrance requirements:* For master's and doctorate, GRE General Test, minimum GPA of 3.2 in major, 3.0 overall. Additional exam requirements/recommendations for international students: Required—TOEFL (minimum score 600 paper-based). Electronic applications accepted. *Faculty research:* Social constructivism. international migration, international security, democratization, human rights.

University of Denver, Division of Arts, Humanities and Social Sciences, School of Communication, Program in International and Intercultural Communication, Denver, CO 80208. Offers MA. *Students:* 29 full-time (25 women), 12 part-time (11 women); includes 2 minority (1 African American, 1 Hispanic American), 4 international. Average age 28. In 2008, 13 master's awarded. *Degree requirements:* For master's, one foreign language. *Entrance requirements:* For master's, GRE. Additional exam requirements/recommendations for international students: Required—TOEFL, TWE. *Application deadline:* Applications are processed on a rolling basis. Application fee: $50. Electronic applications accepted. *Financial support:* Career-related internships or fieldwork, Federal Work-Study, institutionally sponsored loans, and scholarships/grants available. Support available to part-time students. Financial award application deadline: 3/1; financial award applicants required to submit FAFSA. *Unit head:* Dr. Margaret Thompson, Chairperson, 303-871-2088. *Application contact:* Information Contact, 303-871-2088, Fax: 303-871-4949, E-mail: iic@du.edu.

University of Denver, Josef Korbel School of International Studies, Denver, CO 80208. Offers global studies (MGS); international studies (MA, PhD). Part-time programs available. *Faculty:* 27 full-time (7 women), 34 part-time/adjunct (13 women). *Students:* 344 full-time (205 women), 52 part-time (28 women); includes 35 minority (5 African Americans, 3 American Indian/Alaska Native, 7 Asian Americans or Pacific Islanders, 20 Hispanic Americans), 25 international. Average age 28. 819 applicants, 79% accepted, 213 enrolled. In 2008, 234 master's, 7 doctorates awarded. *Degree requirements:* For master's, one foreign language, thesis; for doctorate, one foreign language, thesis/dissertation. *Entrance requirements:* For master's and doctorate, GRE General Test. Additional exam requirements/recommendations for international students: Required—TOEFL. *Application deadline:* For fall admission, 1/15 priority date for domestic students, 12/1 priority date for international students; for winter admission, 10/15 priority date for domestic and international students. Applications are processed on a rolling basis. Application fee: $60. Electronic applications accepted. *Financial support:* Career-related internships or fieldwork, Federal Work-Study, institutionally sponsored loans, and scholarships/grants available. Support available to part-time students. Financial award applicants required to submit FAFSA. *Faculty research:* Human rights and international security, international politics and economics, economic-social and political development international technology analysis and management, economic-social and political development. *Unit head:* Brad Miller, Director of Graduate Admissions, 303-871-2544. *Application contact:* Office of Graduate Admissions, 303-871-2544, E-mail: korbeladm@du.edu.

University of Florida, Graduate School, College of Liberal Arts and Sciences, Department of Political Science, Program in International Relations, Gainesville, FL 32611. Offers MA, MAT. Part-time programs available. Terminal master's awarded for partial completion of doctoral program. *Degree requirements:* For master's, variable foreign language requirement, thesis or alternative. *Entrance requirements:* For master's, GRE General Test, minimum GPA of 3.0.

Additional exam requirements/recommendations for international students: Required—TOEFL (minimum score 550 paper-based; 213 computer-based). Electronic applications accepted. *Faculty research:* American and comparative foreign policy, North-South relations, international political economy.

University of Hawaii at Manoa, Graduate Division, East-West Center, Honolulu, HI 96822. Offers international cultural studies (Graduate Certificate). Part-time programs available. *Entrance requirements:* For degree, GRE General Test. Additional exam requirements/recommendations for international students: Required—TOEFL (minimum score 540 paper-based; 207 computer-based; 76 iBT), IELTS (minimum score 5).

University of Indianapolis, Graduate Programs, College of Arts and Sciences, Department of History and Political Science, Indianapolis, IN 46227-3697. Offers history (MA); international relations (MA). Part-time and evening/weekend programs available. *Faculty:* 6 full-time (2 women). *Students:* 2 full-time (1 woman), 7 part-time (4 women). Average age 30. *Degree requirements:* For master's, thesis optional. *Entrance requirements:* For master's, GRE Subject Test, minimum GPA of 3.0, 3 letters of recommendation, statement of purpose. Additional exam requirements/recommendations for international students: Required—TOEFL (minimum score 550 paper-based; 213 computer-based). *Application deadline:* Applications are processed on a rolling basis. Application fee: $30. Electronic applications accepted. *Financial support:* Federal Work-Study available. Financial award application deadline: 5/1; financial award applicants required to submit FAFSA. *Unit head:* Dr. Lawrence Sondhaus, Chairperson, 317-788-2196, Fax: 317-788-3480, E-mail: sondhaus@uindy.edu. *Application contact:* Dr. Lawrence Sondhaus, Chairperson, 317-788-2196, Fax: 317-788-3480, E-mail: sondhaus@uindy.edu.

The University of Kansas, Graduate Studies, College of Liberal Arts and Sciences, Global and International Studies, Lawrence, KS 66045. Offers MA. Part-time and evening/weekend programs available. *Faculty:* 17. *Students:* 18 full-time (4 women), 35 part-time (18 women); includes 7 minority (1 African American, 3 Asian Americans or Pacific Islanders, 3 Hispanic Americans), 4 international. Average age 33. 30 applicants, 57% accepted, 11 enrolled. In 2008, 15 master's awarded. *Degree requirements:* For master's, one foreign language, thesis optional, exam (in lieu of thesis). *Entrance requirements:* For master's, GRE, minimum GPA of 3.0, 3 letters of reference, curriculum vitae. Additional exam requirements/recommendations for international students: Required—TOEFL. *Application deadline:* For fall admission, 6/1 priority date for domestic and international students; for spring admission, 11/15 priority date for domestic and international students. Applications are processed on a rolling basis. Application fee: $45 ($55 for international students). Electronic applications accepted. *Expenses:* Tuition, area resident: Full-time $6122; part-time $255.10 per credit hour. Tuition, state resident: full-time $6122; part-time $255.10 per credit hour. Tuition, nonresident: full-time $14,629; part-time $609.55 per credit hour. Required fees: $847; $70.56 per credit hour. Tuition and fees vary according to course load and program. *Financial support:* Scholarships/grants available. *Faculty research:* Globalization, environmental sociology. *Unit head:* Dr. Eric Hanley, Program Director, 913-897-8510, Fax: 913-897-8491, E-mail: hanley@ku.edu. *Application contact:* Rebecca Cates, Program Advisor, 913-897-8510, Fax: 913-897-8491, E-mail: rjcates@ku.edu.

University of Kentucky, Graduate School, Patterson School of Diplomacy and International Commerce, Lexington, KY 40506-0027. Offers MA. *Degree requirements:* For master's, one foreign language, comprehensive exam, 30 credit hours, statistics. *Entrance requirements:* For master's, GRE General Test, minimum undergraduate GPA of 3.0. Additional exam requirements/recommendations for international students: Required—TOEFL (minimum score 550 paper-based; 213 computer-based; 79 iBT). Electronic applications accepted. *Faculty research:* International relations, foreign and defense policy, cross-cultural negotiation, international science and technology, diplomacy, international economics and development, geopolitical modeling.

University of Miami, Graduate School, College of Arts and Sciences, Department of International Studies, Coral Gables, FL 33124. Offers MA, PhD. *Degree requirements:* For master's, one foreign language, comprehensive exam; for doctorate, one foreign language, comprehensive exam, thesis/dissertation. *Entrance requirements:* For master's, GRE General Test, minimum GPA of 3.0; for doctorate, GRE General Test. Additional exam requirements/recommendations for international students: Required—TOEFL. Electronic applications accepted. *Faculty research:* Latin American studies, international economics, international security and conflict, comparative development, international health policy.

University of Miami, Graduate School, Program in International Administration, Coral Gables, FL 33124. Offers MAIA. Part-time and evening/weekend programs available. *Degree requirements:* For master's, practicum. *Entrance requirements:* For master's, GRE General Test. Additional exam requirements/recommendations for international students: Required—TOEFL (minimum score 550 paper-based; 213 computer-based), IELTS (minimum score 6.5). Electronic applications accepted.

University of Northern British Columbia, Office of Graduate Studies, Prince George, BC V2N 4Z9, Canada. Offers business administration (Diploma); community health science (M Sc); disability management (MA); education (M Ed); first nations studies (MA); gender studies (MA); history (MA); interdisciplinary studies (MA); international studies (MA); mathematical, computer and physical sciences (M Sc); natural resources and environmental studies (M Sc, MA, MNRES, PhD); political science (MA); psychology (M Sc, PhD); social work (MSW). Part-time and evening/weekend programs available. Postbaccalaureate distance learning degree programs offered (no on-campus study). *Degree requirements:* For master's, thesis; for doctorate, thesis/dissertation. *Entrance requirements:* For master's, GRE, minimum B average in undergraduate course work; for doctorate, candidacy exam, minimum A average in graduate course work.

University of Oklahoma, Graduate College, School of International and Area Studies, Norman, OK 73019-0390. Offers international studies (MA), including global affairs, global management. *Faculty:* 16 full-time (3 women), 1 part-time/adjunct (0 women). *Students:* 6 full-time (5 women), 3 part-time (1 woman); includes 1 minority (Hispanic American). 7 applicants, 57% accepted, 2 enrolled. In 2008, 2 master's awarded. *Degree requirements:* For master's, one foreign language, thesis optional. *Entrance requirements:* For master's, GMAT or GRE. Additional exam requirements/recommendations for international students: Required—TOEFL (minimum score 550 paper-based; 213 computer-based). *Application deadline:* For fall admission, 2/15 for domestic students, 4/1 for international students; for spring admission, 10/15 for domestic students, 9/1 for international students. Applications are processed on a rolling basis. Application fee: $40 ($90 for international students). Electronic applications accepted. *Expenses:* Tuition, state resident: full-time $3744; part-time $156 per credit hour. Tuition, nonresident: full-time $13,577; part-time $565.70 per credit hour. Required fees: $2415.40; $90.10 per credit hour. *Financial support:* In 2008–09, 8 students received support, including 4 research assistantships (averaging $10,564 per year), 6 teaching assistantships with partial tuition reimbursements available (averaging $13,170 per year); tuition waivers (full) and unspecified assistantships also available. Financial award applicants required to submit FAFSA. *Faculty research:* Political economy; foreign policy; linguistics; environmental affairs; international law. Total annual research expenditures: $461,607. *Unit head:* Dr. Millie C Audas, Director, 405-325-1606, Fax: 405-325-7387, E-mail: maudas@ou.edu. *Application contact:* Mitchell Smith, Associate Professor, 405-325-8893, Fax: 405-325-0718, E-mail: mps@ou.edu.

University of Oregon, Graduate School, College of Arts and Sciences, Program in International Studies, Eugene, OR 97403. Offers MA. Part-time programs available. *Degree requirements:* For master's, one foreign language, thesis, internship. *Entrance requirements:* For master's, minimum GPA of 3.0. Additional exam requirements/recommendations for international students: Required—TOEFL. *Faculty research:* International development studies; environmental studies; cross-cultural communications; planning, public policy, and management; several world regions.

International Affairs

University of Pennsylvania, School of Arts and Sciences, Graduate Group in International Studies, Philadelphia, PA 19104. Offers AM.

University of Pittsburgh, Graduate School of Public and International Affairs, Doctoral Program in Public and International Affairs, Pittsburgh, PA 15260. Offers development policy (PhD); foreign and security policy (PhD); international political economy (PhD); public administration (PhD); public policy (PhD). *Accreditation:* NASPAA. Part-time programs available. *Degree requirements:* For doctorate, comprehensive exam, thesis/dissertation. *Entrance requirements:* For doctorate, GRE, 3 letters of recommendation, resumé, minimum GPA of 3.0, writing sample. Additional exam requirements/recommendations for international students: Required—TOEFL (minimum score 600 paper-based; 250 computer-based; 100 iBT), TWE (minimum score 4); Recommended—IELTS (minimum score 7). Electronic applications accepted. *Faculty research:* International political economy, international development, public administration, public policy, foreign policy, international security policy.

See Close-Up on page 1243.

University of Pittsburgh, Graduate School of Public and International Affairs, International Affairs Division, Pittsburgh, PA 15260. Offers global political economy (MPIA); human security (MPIA); security and intelligence studies (MPIA); JD/MPIA; MBA/MPIA; MID/MPIA; MPA/MPIA; MSIS/MPIA. Part-time and evening/weekend programs available. *Degree requirements:* For master's, thesis optional, internship, capstone seminar. *Entrance requirements:* For master's, GRE General Test, 3 letters of recommendation, resumé, minimum GPA of 3.2. Additional exam requirements/recommendations for international students: Required—TOEFL (minimum score 550 paper-based; 213 computer-based), TWE (minimum score 4); Recommended—IELTS (minimum score 7). Electronic applications accepted. *Faculty research:* Political economy, international security, transnational crime, international trade, international finance, terrorism.

See Close-Up on page 1243.

University of Pittsburgh, University Center for International Studies, Pittsburgh, PA 15260. Offers African studies (Certificate); Asian studies (Certificate); European Union studies (Certificate); global studies (Certificate); Latin American studies (Certificate); Russian and East European studies (Certificate); West European studies (Certificate).

University of Rhode Island, Graduate School, College of Arts and Sciences, Department of Political Science, Kingston, RI 02881. Offers political science (MA), including American politics, comparative government, international relations, public policy; public policy and administration (MA, MPA, Certificate). In 2008, 6 master's awarded. Application fee: $35. *Expenses:* Tuition, state resident: full-time $8024; part-time $446 per credit. Tuition, nonresident: full-time $21,046; part-time $1169 per credit. Required fees: $1056; $26 per credit. $30 per semester. One-time fee: $95 part-time. *Unit head:* Dr. Gerry Tyler, Chairperson, 401-874-4053, E-mail: gtyler@uri.edu. *Application contact:* Harold D. Bibb, Associate Dean of the Graduate School, 401-874-2262, Fax: 401-874-5491.

University of San Diego, College of Arts and Sciences, Department of Political Science and International Relations, San Diego, CA 92110-2492. Offers international relations (MA); JD/MA. Part-time and evening/weekend programs available. *Faculty:* 4 full-time (3 women), 2 part-time/adjunct (0 women). *Students:* 12 full-time (6 women), 9 part-time (6 women); includes 6 minority (all Hispanic Americans), 1 international. Average age 28. 48 applicants, 50% accepted, 8 enrolled. In 2008, 19 master's awarded. *Degree requirements:* For master's, comprehensive exam. *Entrance requirements:* For master's, GRE General Test, minimum GPA of 3.1. Additional exam requirements/recommendations for international students: Required—TOEFL (minimum score 580 paper-based; 237 computer-based; 83 iBT), TWE. *Application deadline:* For fall admission, 8/31 for domestic and international students; for spring admission, 1/15 for domestic students, 11/15 for international students. Applications are processed on a rolling basis. Application fee: $45. Electronic applications accepted. *Expenses:* Tuition: Full-time $19,710; part-time $1129 per unit. Required fees: $154. Full-time tuition and fees vary according to course load and degree level. *Financial support:* In 2008–09, 17 students received support. Federal Work-Study, institutionally sponsored loans, and unspecified assistantships available. Support available to part-time students. Financial award application deadline: 3/15; financial award applicants required to submit FAFSA. *Faculty research:* Soviet politics, Latin American politics, China, Canada, international organizations. *Unit head:* Dr. Emily Edmonds-Poli, Graduate Program Director, 619-260-7802, Fax: 619-260-6840, E-mail: edmonds@sandiego.edu. *Application contact:* Dr. John Mosby, Associate Director of Graduate Admissions, 619-260-4524, Fax: 619-260-4158, E-mail: grads@sandiego.edu.

University of San Francisco, College of Arts and Sciences, Department of Economics, San Francisco, CA 94117-1080. Offers economics (MA); financial analysis (MS); international and development economics (MA); MS/MBA. Part-time and evening/weekend programs available. *Degree requirements:* For master's, comprehensive exam, thesis or alternative. *Entrance requirements:* For master's, GRE General Test (recommended), BA in economics (preferred). Additional exam requirements/recommendations for international students: Required—TOEFL. *Faculty research:* Economic development, forecasting and planning, labor markets, Pacific Rim, financial markets.

University of San Francisco, College of Arts and Sciences, International Studies Graduate Program, San Francisco, CA 94117-1080. Offers MA.

University of South Carolina, The Graduate School, College of Arts and Sciences, Department of Political Science, Program in International Studies, Columbia, SC 29208. Offers MA, PhD. Part-time programs available. Terminal master's awarded for partial completion of doctoral program. *Degree requirements:* For master's, one foreign language, thesis or alternative; for doctorate, one foreign language, comprehensive exam, thesis/dissertation. *Entrance requirements:* For master's, GRE General Test, minimum GPA of 3.3; for doctorate, GRE General Test, minimum GPA of 3.5. Additional exam requirements/recommendations for international students: Required—TOEFL. Electronic applications accepted. *Faculty research:* International relations, international organization, foreign policy, comparative politics.

University of Southern California, Graduate School, Annenberg School for Communication, School of Communication, Program in Public Diplomacy, Los Angeles, CA 90089. Offers MPD. *Degree requirements:* For master's, thesis. *Entrance requirements:* For master's, GRE, resumé, writing samples, recommendation letters. Additional exam requirements/recommendations for international students: Required—TOEFL (minimum score 280 computer-based; 114 iBT). Electronic applications accepted.

See Close-Up on page 709.

University of Southern California, Graduate School, College of Letters, Arts and Sciences, Department of Political Science, Los Angeles, CA 90089. Offers politics and international relations (MA, PhD). *Degree requirements:* For doctorate, one foreign language, thesis/dissertation. *Entrance requirements:* For doctorate, GRE General Test. *Faculty research:* Public law, urban politics, political communication, Pacific Rim studies, environmental politics.

University of Southern California, Graduate School, College of Letters, Arts and Sciences, School of International Relations, Los Angeles, CA 90089. Offers politics and international relations (PhD); public diplomacy (MPD); JD/MA; MPA/MA. Part-time programs available. Terminal master's awarded for partial completion of doctoral program. *Degree requirements:* For master's, one foreign language, thesis optional, substantive paper; for doctorate, one foreign language, thesis/dissertation, substantive paper, written/oral exams. *Entrance requirements:* For master's and doctorate, GRE General Test. *Faculty research:* International environmental agreements and regimes, Middle East regional and domestic political economies, negotiation and conflict among states on economic issues.

University of Southern Mississippi, Graduate School, College of Arts and Letters, Department of Political Science, International Development, and International Affairs, Hattiesburg, MS 39406-0001. Offers international development (PhD); political science (MA, MS). Part-time programs available. *Faculty:* 14 full-time (2 women), 1 part-time/adjunct (0 women). *Students:* 36 full-time (14 women), 44 part-time (17 women); includes 18 minority (12 African Americans, 1 American Indian/Alaska Native, 2 Asian Americans or Pacific Islanders, 3 Hispanic Americans), 6 international. Average age 41. 25 applicants, 68% accepted, 15 enrolled. In 2008, 8 master's awarded. *Degree requirements:* For master's, comprehensive exam, thesis (for some programs). *Entrance requirements:* For master's, GRE General Test, minimum GPA of 2.75 in last 2 years, 3.0 in field of study. *Application deadline:* For fall admission, 3/1 priority date for domestic students, 3/1 for international students. Applications are processed on a rolling basis. Application fee: $30. *Financial support:* In 2008–09, 4 research assistantships with full and partial tuition reimbursements (averaging $9,000 per year), 8 teaching assistantships with full tuition reimbursements (averaging $7,000 per year) were awarded; career-related internships or fieldwork, Federal Work-Study, scholarships/grants, and unspecified assistantships also available. Financial award application deadline: 3/15; financial award applicants required to submit FAFSA. *Faculty research:* American politics, international politics, political theory, comparative politics, public law. *Unit head:* Dr. Thomas Lansford, Interim Chair, 601-266-4310. *Application contact:* Dr. Robert Pauley, Graduate Coordinator, 601-266-4310, Fax: 601-266-4172.

University of South Florida, Graduate School, College of Arts and Sciences, Department of Government and International Affairs, Tampa, FL 33620-9951. Offers Latin American Caribbean and Latino Studies (MA); political science (MA); public administration (MPA). Part-time and evening/weekend programs available. *Faculty:* 18 full-time (3 women), 1 (woman) part-time/adjunct. *Students:* 33 full-time (21 women), 98 part-time (50 women); includes 39 minority (20 African Americans, 5 Asian Americans or Pacific Islanders, 14 Hispanic Americans), 6 international. 81 applicants, 62% accepted, 29 enrolled. In 2008, 27 master's awarded. *Degree requirements:* For master's, comprehensive exam, thesis; for doctorate, comprehensive exam, thesis/dissertation. *Entrance requirements:* For master's, GRE (minimum score: 470 verbal, 470 quantitative), minimum GPA of 3.0 in last 60 hours of course work. Additional exam requirements/recommendations for international students: Required—TOEFL (minimum score 550 paper-based; 213 computer-based). *Application deadline:* For fall admission, 2/15 for domestic students; for spring admission, 10/15 for domestic students. Applications are processed on a rolling basis. Application fee: $30. Electronic applications accepted. *Expenses:* Tuition, state resident: full-time $2624.40; part-time $291.60 per credit hour. Tuition, nonresident: full-time $7822; part-time $869.13 per credit hour. *Financial support:* Scholarships/grants and unspecified assistantships available. Financial award application deadline: 4/1. *Unit head:* Dr. Mohsen Milani, Chairperson, 813-974-2384, Fax: 813-974-0832, E-mail: milani@chuma1.cas.usf.edu. *Application contact:* Dr. Stephen Tauber, Graduate Coordinator, 813-974-0781, Fax: 813-974-0832, E-mail: stauber@chuma1.cas.usf.edu.

University of the Pacific, McGeorge School of Law, Sacramento, CA 95817. Offers advocacy (JD); advocacy practice and teaching (LL M); criminal justice (JD); intellectual property (JD); international legal studies (JD); international water resources law (LL M, JSD); law (JD); public law and policy (JD); public policy and law (LL M); tax (JD); transnational business practice (LL M); JD/MBA; JD/MPPA. *Accreditation:* ABA. Part-time and evening/weekend programs available. *Faculty:* 55 full-time (22 women), 73 part-time/adjunct (34 women). *Students:* 620 full-time (304 women), 396 part-time (194 women); includes 271 minority (33 African Americans, 14 American Indian/Alaska Native, 134 Asian Americans or Pacific Islanders, 90 Hispanic Americans). Average age 24. 2,627 applicants, 41% accepted. In 2008, 301 JDs, 49 master's awarded. *Degree requirements:* For master's, thesis (for some programs); for doctorate, thesis/dissertation. *Entrance requirements:* For JD, LSAT; for master's, JD; for doctorate, LL M. Additional exam requirements/recommendations for international students: Required—TOEFL (minimum score 600 paper-based; 250 computer-based; 100 iBT). *Application deadline:* For fall admission, 3/15 priority date for domestic students. Applications are processed on a rolling basis. Application fee: $50. Electronic applications accepted. *Expenses:* Contact institution. *Financial support:* In 2008–09, 925 students received support, including 9 fellowships, 76 research assistantships (averaging $1,961 per year); career-related internships or fieldwork, Federal Work-Study, institutionally sponsored loans, and scholarships/grants also available. Support available to part-time students. Financial award applicants required to submit FAFSA. *Faculty research:* International Legal Studies, Public Policy & Law, Advocacy, Intellectual Property Law, Taxation, & Criminal Law. *Unit head:* Elizabeth Rindskopf Parker, Dean, 916-739-7151, E-mail: elizabeth@uop.edu. *Application contact:* 916-739-7105, Fax: 916-739-7134, E-mail: admissionsmcgeorge@uop.edu.

University of the Pacific, School of International Studies, Program in Intercultural Relations, Stockton, CA 95211-0197. Offers MA. In 2008, 6 master's awarded. *Entrance requirements:* Additional exam requirements/recommendations for international students: Required—TOEFL (minimum score 475 paper-based; 150 computer-based). Application fee: $75. *Expenses:* Tuition: Full-time $30,380; part-time $950 per unit. Required fees: $300. *Financial support:* Application deadline: 3/1; *Unit head:* Dr. Margee Ensign, Dean, 209-946-2650, E-mail: mensign@pacific.edu. *Application contact:* Office of Graduate Admissions, 209-946-2344.

University of Utah, The Graduate School, College of Social and Behavioral Science, Department of Political Science, Program in Public Policy, Salt Lake City, UT 84112-1107. Offers international affairs and global enterprises (MS); public policy (MPP).

University of Virginia, College and Graduate School of Arts and Sciences, Department of Politics, Program in Foreign Affairs, Charlottesville, VA 22903. Offers MA, PhD. *Students:* 47 full-time (22 women), 1 part-time (0 women); includes 3 minority (all Asian Americans or Pacific Islanders), 14 international. Average age 29. 117 applicants, 30% accepted, 9 enrolled. In 2008, 7 master's, 5 doctorates awarded. *Degree requirements:* For master's, one foreign language, thesis (for some programs), 2 research/statistics courses or thesis; for doctorate, variable foreign language requirement, thesis/dissertation, 2 research/statistics courses. *Entrance requirements:* For master's and doctorate, GRE General Test, long writing sample; 2 letters of recommendation. Additional exam requirements/recommendations for international students: Required—TOEFL (minimum score 600 paper-based; 250 computer-based; 90 iBT), IELTS (minimum score 7). *Application deadline:* For fall admission, 12/4 for domestic and international students. Applications are processed on a rolling basis. Application fee: $60. Electronic applications accepted. *Expenses:* Tuition, area resident: Full-time $10,452. Tuition, state resident: full-time $10,452. Tuition, nonresident: full-time $20,010. Required fees: $2176. Part-time tuition and fees vary according to course load and program. *Financial support:* Fellowships, teaching assistantships available. Financial award application deadline: 12/4; financial award applicants required to submit FAFSA. *Unit head:* Jeffrey W. Legro, Chair, 434-924-3192, Fax: 434-924-3359. *Application contact:* Jeffrey W. Legro, Chair, 434-924-3192, Fax: 434-924-3359.

University of Washington, Graduate School, College of Arts and Sciences, Henry M. Jackson School of International Studies, Seattle, WA 98195. Offers China studies (MAIS); comparative religion (MAIS); international studies (MAIS); Japan studies (MAIS); Korea studies (MAIS); Middle Eastern studies (MAIS); Russian, East European and Central Asian studies (MAIS), including Central Asian studies, East European studies, Russian studies; South Asian studies (MAIS); JD/MAIS; MBA/MAIS; MFR/MAIS; MMA/MAIS; MPA/MAIS; MPH/MAIS. *Entrance requirements:* For master's, GRE General Test, minimum GPA of 3.0. Additional exam requirements/recommendations for international students: Required—TOEFL (minimum score 500 paper-based; 213 computer-based). Electronic applications accepted.

University of Waterloo, Graduate Studies, Faculty of Arts, Department of Political Science, Global Governance Program, Waterloo, ON N2L 3G1, Canada. Offers MA, PhD. *Entrance requirements:* For master's, BA, B+ average; for doctorate, MA. Additional exam requirements/recommendations for international students: Required—TOEFL. Electronic applications accepted. *Faculty research:* Global political economy, global environment, peace and security, global justice and human rights, multilateral institutions and diplomacy.

University of Wyoming, Graduate School, College of Arts and Sciences, Program in International Studies, Laramie, WY 82070. Offers international peace corps (MA); international studies (MA). Part-time programs available. *Faculty:* 1 (woman) full-time, 24 part-time/adjunct (7 women). *Students:* 11 full-time (6 women), 13 part-time (9 women); includes 1 minority (Asian American or Pacific Islander), 1 international. Average age 28. 25 applicants, 36% accepted, 8 enrolled. In 2008, 9 master's awarded. *Degree requirements:* For master's, one foreign language, thesis. *Entrance requirements:* For master's, GRE General Test, minimum GPA of 3.0. Additional exam requirements/recommendations for international students: Required—TOEFL (minimum score 525 paper-based; 195 computer-based). *Application deadline:* For fall admission, 2/1 for domestic and international students. Applications are processed on a rolling basis. Application fee: $50. Electronic applications accepted. *Financial support:* In 2008–09, 3 research assistantships with full and partial tuition reimbursements (averaging $11,072 per year), 3 teaching assistantships with full and partial tuition reimbursements (averaging $10,062 per year) were awarded. Financial award application deadline: 2/1. *Faculty research:* International political economy, comparative social institutions, foreign policy, economic development. *Unit head:* Dr. Jean Garrison, Director, 307-766-6119, Fax: 307-766-3812, E-mail: garrison@uwyo.edu. *Application contact:* Jennette Reisenburg, Office Associate, 307-766-3415, Fax: 307-766-3812, E-mail: jeanette@uwyo.edu.

Virginia Polytechnic Institute and State University, Graduate School, College of Architecture and Urban Studies, School of Public and International Affairs, Blacksburg, VA 24061. Offers environmental planning and policy (MURP); government and international affairs (MPIA); housing, community and economic development (MURP); international development planning (MURP); land use and physical planning (MURP); planning, governance and globalization (PhD), including environmental planning and landscape analysis, physical planning and urban design, public and international affairs, urban and environmental design and planning; urban and regional planning (MURP). *Accreditation:* ACSP. *Entrance requirements:* Additional exam requirements/recommendations for international students: Required—TOEFL (minimum score 550 paper-based; 213 computer-based). Electronic applications accepted. *Faculty research:* Design theory, environmental planning, town planning, transportation planning.

Walden University, Graduate Programs, School of Public Policy and Administration, Minneapolis, MN 55401. Offers general public policy and administration (MPA); government management (Certificate); health policy (MPA); homeland security policy (MPA); interdisciplinary policy studies (MPA); law and public policy (MPA); local government management for sustainable communities (MPA); nonprofit management (Certificate); nonprofit management and leadership (MPA, MS); policy analysis (MPA); public management and leadership (MPA); public policy and administration (PhD), including criminal justice, health services, homeland security policy and coordination, international nongovernmental organizations, knowledge management, nonprofit management and leadership, public management and leadership, public policy, public safety management; terrorism, mediation, and peace (MPA). Part-time and evening/weekend programs available. Postbaccalaureate distance learning degree programs offered (minimal on-campus study). *Faculty:* 2 full-time, 55 part-time/adjunct. *Students:* 1,285 full-time (794 women), 144 part-time (96 women); includes 657 minority (591 African Americans, 8 American Indian/Alaska Native, 17 Asian Americans or Pacific Islanders, 41 Hispanic Americans), 20 international. Average age 39. 727 applicants, 54% accepted, 284 enrolled. In 2008, 101 master's, 6 doctorates awarded. *Degree requirements:* For doctorate, thesis/dissertation, residency. *Entrance requirements:* For master's, bachelor's degree or equivalent in related field, minimum GPA of 2.5, two references, goal statement, official transcripts, access to computer and Internet; for doctorate, master's degree or equivalent in related field, minimum GPA of 3.0, three years related professional/academic experience, two references, goal statement, official transcripts, access to computer and Internet. Additional exam requirements/recommendations for international students: Required—TOEFL (minimum score 550 paper-based; 213 computer-based), IELTS (minimum score 6.5), TOEFL, IELTS, or Michigan English Language Assessment Battery (minimum score 82). *Application deadline:* Applications are processed on a rolling basis. Application fee: $50. Electronic applications accepted. *Expenses:* Tuition: Full-time $12,877; part-time $520 per credit. Required fees: $1230. Tuition and fees vary according to course load, degree level and program. *Financial support:* In 2008–09, 3 students received support; fellowships with tuition reimbursements available, Federal Work-Study, scholarships/grants, unspecified assistantships, and family tuition reduction; active duty/veteran tuition reduction; group tuition reduction; interest-free payment plans available. Support available to part-time students. Financial award applicants required to submit FAFSA. *Unit head:* Dr. Mark Gordon, Interim Associate Dean, 800-925-3368. *Application contact:* Jennifer Hall, 866-4-WALDEN, E-mail: info@waldenu.edu.

Washington State University, Graduate School, College of Liberal Arts, Edward R. Murrow College of Communication, Pullman, WA 99164. Offers health communications (MA, PhD); intercultural and international communications (MA, PhD); media and society (MA, PhD); media process and effects (MA, PhD); organizational communications (MA, PhD). *Degree requirements:* For master's, comprehensive exam (for some programs), thesis optional, oral exam; for doctorate, comprehensive exam, thesis/dissertation. *Entrance requirements:* For master's, GRE General Test, minimum GPA of 3.25, 3 letters of recommendation; for doctorate, GRE General Test, minimum undergraduate GPA of 3.25, graduate 3.5; MA in communication; 3 letters of recommendation. Additional exam requirements/recommendations for international students: Required—TOEFL (minimum score 580 paper-based; 237 computer-based). Electronic applications accepted. *Faculty research:* Advocacy communication, mediated communication in decision making, communication technology policy and effects, multicultural and international psychology and physiology of communication.

Webster University, College of Arts and Sciences, Department of History, Politics and International Relations, Program in International Relations, St. Louis, MO 63119-3194. Offers MA. Part-time and evening/weekend programs available. *Degree requirements:* For master's, thesis optional. *Faculty research:* International organizations, international political economy, politics of development, environmental law, Latin American law.

West Virginia University, Eberly College of Arts and Sciences, Department of Political Science, Morgantown, WV 26506. Offers American public policy and politics (MA); international and comparative public policy and politics (MA); political science (PhD); public policy analysis (PhD). Terminal master's awarded for partial completion of doctoral program. *Degree requirements:* For master's, thesis optional; for doctorate, comprehensive exam, thesis/dissertation. *Entrance requirements:* For master's, GRE General Test, minimum GPA of 2.75; for doctorate, GRE General Test, minimum GPA of 3.0. Additional exam requirements/recommendations for international students: Required—TOEFL. *Faculty research:* Public policy, research methods, foreign policy analysis, judicial politics, environmental and energy policy.

Wilfrid Laurier University, Faculty of Graduate Studies, Faculty of Arts and School of Business and Economics, Global Governance Program, Waterloo, ON N2L 3C5, Canada. Offers PhD. *Degree requirements:* For doctorate, thesis/dissertation. *Entrance requirements:* For doctorate, MA in political science, history, economics, international development studies, international peace studies, globalization studies, environmental studies or related field with minimum A-. Additional exam requirements/recommendations for international students: Required—TOEFL (minimum score 230 computer-based; 89 iBT). Electronic applications accepted. *Faculty research:* Global political economy, global environment, conflict and security, global justice and human rights, multilateral institutions and diplomacy.

Wilfrid Laurier University, Faculty of Graduate Studies, Faculty of Arts and School of Business and Economics, International Public Policy Program, Waterloo, ON N2L 3C5, Canada. Offers MIPP. *Entrance requirements:* For master's, honours BA with minimum B average. Additional exam requirements/recommendations for international students: Required—TOEFL (minimum score 230 computer-based; 89 iBT). Electronic applications accepted. *Faculty research:* International environmental policy, international economic relations, human security, global governance.

Yale University, Graduate School of Arts and Sciences, Department of Economics, Program in International and Development Economics, New Haven, CT 06520. Offers MA. *Entrance requirements:* For master's, GRE General Test.

Yale University, Graduate School of Arts and Sciences, Graduate Program in International Relations, New Haven, CT 06520. Offers MA, JD/MA, MBA/MA, MEM/MA, MES/MA, MF/MA, MFS/MA, MPH/MA. *Degree requirements:* For master's, one foreign language, research paper, summer project, specified grade average. *Entrance requirements:* For master's, GRE General Test, previous course work in microeconomics and macroeconomics, professional experience (preferred). Additional exam requirements/recommendations for international students: Required—TOEFL (minimum score 610 paper-based; 253 computer-based; 102 iBT). Electronic applications accepted. *Faculty research:* International security studies, international human rights, international economic development, political economy, policy studies, religion and politics.

York University, Faculty of Graduate Studies, Glendon College, Program in Public and International Affairs, Toronto, ON M3J 1P3, Canada. Offers MA.

International Development

American University, School of International Service, Washington, DC 20016-8071. Offers comparative and regional studies (Certificate); cross-cultural communication (Certificate); development management (MS); ethics, peace, and global affairs (MA); European studies (Certificate); global environmental policy (MA, Certificate); international affairs (MA), including comparative and regional studies, environmental policy, international economic policy, international politics, natural resources and sustainable development, U.S. foreign policy; international communication (MA, Certificate); international development (MA, Certificate); international development management (Certificate); international economic policy (Certificate); international economic relations (Certificate); international media (MA); international peace and conflict resolution (MA, Certificate); international relations (PhD); international service (MIS); peace building (Certificate); the Americas (Certificate); United States foreign policy (Certificate); JD/MA. Part-time and evening/weekend programs available. *Faculty:* 70 full-time (28 women), 51 part-time/adjunct (20 women). *Students:* 519 full-time (317 women), 335 part-time (205 women); includes 157 minority (54 African Americans, 2 American Indian/Alaska Native, 45 Asian Americans or Pacific Islanders, 56 Hispanic Americans), 116 international. Average age 27. 1,901 applicants, 58% accepted, 277 enrolled. In 2008, 358 master's, 5 doctorates, 9 other advanced degrees awarded. Terminal master's awarded for partial completion of doctoral program. *Degree requirements:* For master's, one foreign language, comprehensive exam, thesis or alternative; for doctorate, one foreign language, comprehensive exam, thesis/dissertation, research practicum; for Certificate, minimum 15 credit hours related course work. *Entrance requirements:* For master's, GRE, 24 credits of course work in related social sciences, minimum GPA of 3.5, 2 letters of recommendation, bachelor's degree, resumé, statement of purpose; for doctorate, GRE, 2 letters of recommendation, 24 credits in related social sciences; for Certificate, bachelor's degree. Additional exam requirements/recommendations for international students: Required—TOEFL (minimum score 600 paper-based; 250 computer-based; 100 iBT). *Application deadline:* For fall admission, 1/15 priority date for domestic students; for spring admission, 10/1 priority date for domestic students. Applications are processed on a rolling basis. Application fee: $50. *Expenses:* Tuition: Full-time $21,204; part-time $1178 per credit hour. Required fees: $380. Part-time tuition and fees vary according to course load and program. *Financial support:* Career-related internships or fieldwork, Federal Work-Study, and institutionally sponsored loans available. Financial award application deadline: 1/15. *Faculty research:* International intellectual property, international environmental issues, international law and legal order, international telecommunications/technology, international sustainable development. *Unit head:* Dr. Louis W. Goodman, Dean, 202-885-1600, Fax: 202-885-2494. *Application contact:* Yasmin Quianzon, Director of Graduate Admissions and Financial Aid, 202-885-2496, Fax: 202-885-1109.

See Close-Up on page 861.

Andrews University, School of Graduate Studies, College of Arts and Sciences, Department of Behavioral Science, Program in International Development, Berrien Springs, MI 49104. Offers MSA. Postbaccalaureate distance learning degree programs offered. *Students:* 12 full-time (8 women), 2 part-time (1 woman); includes 5 minority (3 African Americans, 2 Hispanic Americans), 7 international. Average age 33. In 2008, 6 master's awarded. *Entrance requirements:* For master's, GRE General Test. Additional exam requirements/recommendations for international students: Required—TOEFL (minimum score 550 paper-based). Application fee: $40. *Expenses:* Tuition: Full-time $18,360; part-time $765 per credit hour. Required fees: $476; $765 per credit hour. $238 per semester. Tuition and fees vary according to degree level. *Unit head:* Dr. Duane C. McBride, Director, 269-471-3152. *Application contact:* Carolyn Hurst, Supervisor of Graduate Admission, 800-253-2874, Fax: 269-471-6321, E-mail: graduate@andrews.edu.

Athabasca University, Centre for Integrated Studies, Athabasca, AB T9S 3A3, Canada. Offers adult education (MA); community studies (MA); cultural studies (MA); educational studies (MA); global change (MA); work, organization, and leadership (MA). Part-time and evening/weekend programs available. Postbaccalaureate distance learning degree programs offered (no on-campus study). *Faculty:* 8 full-time (3 women), 16 part-time/adjunct (13 women). *Students:* 651 part-time (467 women). Average age 36. 150 applicants, 87% accepted, 112 enrolled. In 2008, 39 master's awarded. *Degree requirements:* For master's, project. *Entrance requirements:* For master's, 3- or 4-year BA. Additional exam requirements/recommendations for international students: Required—TOEFL (minimum score 560 paper-based; 220 computer-based). *Application deadline:* For fall admission, 3/1 for domestic and international students; for winter admission, 10/1 for domestic and international students. Application fee: $65. Electronic applications accepted. Tuition and fees charges are reported in Canadian dollars. *Expenses:* Tuition, area resident: Full-time $13,255 Canadian dollars; part-time $1205 Canadian dollars per course. Tuition, state resident: full-time $13,255 Canadian dollars; part-time $1205 Canadian dollars per course. Tuition, nonresident: full-time $13,255 Canadian dollars; part-time $1205 Canadian dollars per course. International tuition: $15,455 Canadian dollars full-time. One-time fee: $280 Canadian dollars. *Faculty research:* Women's history, literature and culture studies, sustainable development, labor and education. *Unit head:* Dr. Michael Gismondi, Program Director, 780-675-6218, Fax: 780-675-6921, E-mail: mikeg@athabascau.ca. *Application contact:* Derek Stovin, Program Administrator, 780-675-6236, Fax: 780-675-6921, E-mail: dereks@athabascau.ca.

Brandeis University, The Heller School for Social Policy and Management, Program in Sustainable International Development, Waltham, MA 02454-9110. Offers international development (MA); sustainable development (MA). *Degree requirements:* For master's, 2nd-year fieldwork or internship. *Entrance requirements:* For master's, 3 letters of recommendation;

International Development

Brandeis University (continued)
curriculum vitae or resumé. Additional exam requirements/recommendations for international students: Required—TOEFL, IELTS. Electronic applications accepted. *Expenses:* Contact institution. *Faculty research:* Water resource management, human rights, biosphere management, rural development, public policy and governance.

Clark University, Graduate School, Department of International Development, Community, and Environment, Program in International Development and Social Change, Worcester, MA 01610-1477. Offers MA. *Students:* 31 full-time (22 women), 32 part-time (22 women); includes 4 minority (2 African Americans, 1 American Indian/Alaska Native, 1 Asian American or Pacific Islander), 24 international. Average age 29. 136 applicants, 71% accepted, 32 enrolled. In 2008, 25 master's awarded. *Degree requirements:* For master's, thesis. *Application deadline:* For fall admission, 1/15 for domestic students. Application fee: $50. *Expenses:* Tuition: Full-time $34,900; part-time $1091 per credit hour. Required fees: $30. *Financial support:* In 2008–09, research assistantships with full and partial tuition reimbursements (averaging $5,000 per year), teaching assistantships with full and partial tuition reimbursements (averaging $5,000 per year) were awarded; fellowships, tuition waivers (full and partial) also available. *Faculty research:* Participatory rural appraisal, gender issues, sustainable resource management, community building, geographic information sciences, AIDS research. *Unit head:* Dr. William F. Fisher, Director, 508-421-3765, Fax: 508-793-8820, E-mail: wfisher@clarku.edu. *Application contact:* Paula Hall, IDCE Graduate Admissions, 508-793-7201, Fax: 508-793-8820, E-mail: idce@clarku.edu.

Cornell University, Graduate School, Graduate Fields of Arts and Sciences, Field of International Development, Ithaca, NY 14853-0001. Offers development policy (MPS); international nutrition (MPS); international planning (MPS); international population (MPS); science and technology policy (MPS). *Faculty:* 46 full-time (17 women). *Students:* 14 full-time (6 women); includes 4 minority (3 African Americans, 1 Asian American or Pacific Islander), 8 international. Average age 34. 46 applicants, 39% accepted, 5 enrolled. In 2008, 6 master's awarded. *Degree requirements:* For master's, project paper. *Entrance requirements:* For master's, GRE General Test (recommended), 2 academic recommendations, 2 years of development experience. Additional exam requirements/recommendations for international students: Required—TOEFL (minimum score 77 iBT). *Application deadline:* Applications are processed on a rolling basis. Application fee: $70. Electronic applications accepted. *Expenses:* Tuition: Full-time $29,500. Required fees: $70. Full-time tuition and fees vary according to degree level, program and student level. *Financial support:* In 2008–09, 1 student received support, including 1 fellowship with full tuition reimbursement available; research assistantships with full tuition reimbursements available, teaching assistantships with full tuition reimbursements available, institutionally sponsored loans, scholarships/grants, health care benefits, tuition waivers (full and partial), and unspecified assistantships also available. Financial award applicants required to submit FAFSA. *Faculty research:* Development policy, international nutrition, international planning, science and technology policy, international population. *Unit head:* Director of Graduate Studies, 607-255-3037, Fax: 607-255-1005. *Application contact:* Graduate Field Assistant, 607-255-0831, Fax: 607-255-1005, E-mail: mpsid@cornell.edu.

Dalhousie University, Faculty of Arts and Social Science, Department of International Development Studies, Halifax, NS B3H 4R2, Canada. Offers MA. In 2008, 2 master's awarded. *Entrance requirements:* Additional exam requirements/recommendations for international students: Required—TOEFL, IELTS, 1 of five approved tests: TOEFL, IELTS, CANTEST, CAEL, Michigan English Language Assessment Battery. *Application deadline:* For fall admission, 6/1 for domestic students, 4/1 for international students; for winter admission, 10/31 for domestic students, 8/31 for international students; for spring admission, 2/28 for domestic students, 12/31 for international students. Application fee: $70. Electronic applications accepted. *Financial support:* Career-related internships or fieldwork, scholarships/grants, and health care benefits available. *Unit head:* Dr. Owen Willis, Graduate Coordinator, 902-494-3814, Fax: 902-494-2105, E-mail: idsgrad@dal.ca. *Application contact:* Marian MacKinnon, Graduate Administrator, 902-494-3814, Fax: 902-494-2105, E-mail: idsgrad@dal.ca.

Duke University, Graduate School, Terry Sanford Institute of Public Policy, Program in International Development Policy, Durham, NC 27708-0237. Offers AM, Certificate. *Degree requirements:* For master's, internship, project. *Entrance requirements:* For master's, minimum 3 years of professional experience in a development-related field. Additional exam requirements/recommendations for international students: Required—TOEFL (minimum score 550 paper-based; 213 computer-based; 83 iBT), IELTS (minimum score 7). Electronic applications accepted. *Expenses:* Contact institution.

Eastern University, School of Leadership and Development, St. Davids, PA 19087-3696. Offers economic development (MBA), including international development, urban development (MA, MBA); international development (MA), including global development, urban development (MA, MBA); nonprofit management (MS); organizational leadership (MA); M Div/MBA. Part-time and evening/weekend programs available. *Degree requirements:* For master's, thesis (for some programs). *Entrance requirements:* For master's, GMAT (MBA), minimum GPA of 2.5. *Expenses:* Contact institution. *Faculty research:* Micro-level economic development, China welfare and economic development, macroethics, micro- and macro-level economic development in transitional economics, organizational effectiveness.

Fordham University, Graduate School of Arts and Sciences, Program in International Political Economy and Development, New York, NY 10458. Offers MA, Certificate. Part-time and evening/weekend programs available. *Degree requirements:* For master's, comprehensive exam. *Entrance requirements:* For master's, GRE General Test. Additional exam requirements/recommendations for international students: Required—TOEFL (minimum score 600 paper-based; 250 computer-based). Electronic applications accepted. *Faculty research:* International economics, comparative international politics, international banking and finance, international development, emerging markets and country risk analysis.

See Close-Up on page 865.

The George Washington University, Columbian College of Arts and Sciences, Department of Anthropology, Concentration in International Development, Washington, DC 20052. Offers MA. *Unit head:* Prof. Barbara Miller, Director, 202-994-6075, E-mail: barbar@gwu.edu. *Application contact:* Information Contact, 202-994-6075, E-mail: anth@gwu.edu.

The George Washington University, Columbian College of Arts and Sciences, Trachtenberg School of Public Policy and Public Administration, Programs in Public Administration, Washington, DC 20052. Offers budget and public finance (MPA); federal policy, politics, and management (MPA); international development management (MPA); managing public organizations (MPA); managing state and local governments (MPA); nonprofit management (MPA); policy analysis and evaluation (MPA); public administration (MPA); public-private policy and management (MPA). *Accreditation:* NASPAA. Part-time programs available. *Faculty:* 16 full-time (5 women), 4 part-time/adjunct (1 woman). *Students:* 58 full-time (39 women), 55 part-time (37 women); includes 18 minority (5 African Americans, 9 Asian Americans or Pacific Islanders, 4 Hispanic Americans), 7 international. Average age 28. 206 applicants, 66% accepted, 41 enrolled. In 2008, 55 master's awarded. *Entrance requirements:* For master's, GRE General Test. Additional exam requirements/recommendations for international students: Required—TOEFL (minimum score 600 paper-based; 250 computer-based; 100 iBT). *Application deadline:* For fall admission, 4/1 priority date for domestic students, 4/1 for international students; for spring admission, 10/1 for domestic students, 9/1 for international students. Applications are processed on a rolling basis. Application fee: $60. *Financial support:* In 2008–09, 28 students received support; fellowships, teaching assistantships, career-related internships or fieldwork, Federal Work-Study, institutionally sponsored loans, and tuition waivers available. Financial award application deadline: 1/15. *Faculty research:* Regulatory reform, policy and program evaluation, ethics and public management, managing not-for-profits, policy making in the White House and Congress.

Unit head: Dr. Lori Brainard, Director, 202-994-6295, E-mail: brainard@gwu.edu. *Application contact:* David Toomer, Director of Enrollment Management, 202-994-6584, Fax: 202-994-6382.

The George Washington University, Elliott School of International Affairs, Program in International Development Studies, Washington, DC 20052. Offers MA, JD/MA, MPH/MA. *Students:* 58 full-time (44 women), 26 part-time (22 women); includes 6 minority (5 Asian Americans or Pacific Islanders, 1 Hispanic American), 7 international. Average age 27. 331 applicants, 52% accepted, 34 enrolled. In 2008, 22 master's awarded. *Degree requirements:* For master's, one foreign language, capstone project. *Entrance requirements:* For master's, GRE General Test, 2 years (or the equivalent) of a modern foreign language, introductory course in microeconomics and 1 semester of statistics. Additional exam requirements/recommendations for international students: Required—TOEFL. *Application deadline:* For fall admission, 2/1 for domestic students; for spring admission, 10/1 for domestic students. Application fee: $60. Electronic applications accepted. *Financial support:* In 2008–09, 27 students received support; fellowships with tuition reimbursements available, research assistantships with tuition reimbursements available, career-related internships or fieldwork, Federal Work-Study, institutionally sponsored loans, and tuition waivers available. Financial award application deadline: 1/15; financial award applicants required to submit FAFSA. *Faculty research:* Development, anthropology, health and development, political science, education. *Unit head:* Sean Roberts, 202-994-7739, E-mail: seanrr@gwu.edu. *Application contact:* Jeff V. Miles, Director of Graduate Admissions, 202-994-7050, Fax: 202-994-9537, E-mail: esiagrad@gwu.edu.

Harvard University, John F. Kennedy School of Government, Master in Public Administration/International Development Program, Cambridge, MA 02138. Offers MPAID. *Students:* 71 full-time (21 women); includes 8 minority (6 Asian Americans or Pacific Islanders, 2 Hispanic Americans), 48 international. Average age 27. 330 applicants, 32% accepted, 71 enrolled. *Entrance requirements:* For master's, GMAT or GRE General Test (for joint Business School applicants only), one course each in microeconomics and macroeconomics; two college-level calculus courses (one must contain multivariable calculus); bachelor's degree; 2-3 years of professional experience in development (strongly encouraged). Additional exam requirements/recommendations for international students: Required—TOEFL (minimum score 600 paper-based; 250 computer-based; 100 iBT). *Application deadline:* For fall admission, 1/4 for domestic students. Application fee: $80. Electronic applications accepted. *Expenses:* Tuition: Full-time $32,556. Required fees: $1426. Full-time tuition and fees vary according to program and student level. *Financial support:* Fellowships, research assistantships, teaching assistantships, career-related internships or fieldwork, Federal Work-Study, institutionally sponsored loans, scholarships/grants, health care benefits, and unspecified assistantships available. Financial award application deadline: 2/2; financial award applicants required to submit CSS PROFILE or FAFSA. *Unit head:* Carol Finney, Director, 617-495-7799, E-mail: carol_finney@harvard.edu. *Application contact:* 617-495-2133.

Hope International University, School of Graduate Studies, Program in Business Administration, Fullerton, CA 92831-3138. Offers business administration (MBA); educational administration (MSM); international development (MBA, MSM); management (MBA); nonprofit management (MBA). Part-time programs available. Postbaccalaureate distance learning degree programs offered (no on-campus study). *Degree requirements:* For master's, comprehensive exam (for some programs), thesis (for some programs), project. *Entrance requirements:* For master's, minimum GPA of 3.0; Bachelor's degree/official transcripts; 2 references; statement of purpose. Additional exam requirements/recommendations for international students: Required—TOEFL (minimum score 550 paper-based; 213 computer-based; 86 iBT); Recommended—IELTS (minimum score 6.5). Electronic applications accepted. *Expenses:* Contact institution.

The Johns Hopkins University, Paul H. Nitze School of Advanced International Studies, Washington, DC 20036. Offers international development (Certificate); international public policy (MIPP); international relations (MA, PhD), including African studies (MA), American foreign policy (MA), Asian studies (MA), Canadian studies (MA), conflict management (MA), European studies (MA), global theory and history (MA), international development (MA), international law, and organizations (MA), international policy (MA), international relations (general) (MA), Latin American studies (MA), Middle East studies (MA), Russian and Eurasian studies (MA), strategic studies (MA); international studies (Certificate); JD/MA; MBA/MA; MHS/MA. Terminal master's awarded for partial completion of doctoral program. *Degree requirements:* For master's, one foreign language, 16 non-language courses (8 for MIPP), 2 core examinations, comprehensive oral exam, paper (for some programs); for doctorate, 2 foreign languages, thesis/dissertation, 3 comprehensive exams, defense. *Entrance requirements:* For master's, GMAT or GRE General Test, previous course work in economics, foreign language, undergraduate degree; for doctorate, GRE General Test, master's degree. Additional exam requirements/recommendations for international students: Required—TOEFL (minimum paper-based score of 600, computer-based 250, iBT 100) or IELTS (minimum 7.0). Electronic applications accepted. *Expenses:* Contact institution. *Faculty research:* Regional studies and functional fields of international relations, international economics, conflict management, global theory and history, international law and organizations, international policy, strategic studies.

McGill University, Faculty of Graduate and Postdoctoral Studies, Desautels Faculty of Management, Montréal, QC H3A 2T5, Canada. Offers administration (PhD); entrepreneurial studies (MBA); finance (MBA); general management (Post Master's Certificate); information systems (MBA); international business (exchange program) (MBA); international Master's program in practicing management (MM); management (MBA); management for development (MBA); manufacturing management (MMM); marketing (MBA); operations management (MBA); public accountancy (Diploma); strategic management (MBA); MBA/LL B; MD/MBA.

The New School: A University, The New School for General Studies, Program in International Affairs, New York, NY 10011. Offers global management, trade, and finance (MA, MS); international development (MA, MS); international media and communication (MA, MS); international politics and diplomacy (MA, MS); service, civic, and non-profit management (MS). Part-time programs available. *Faculty:* 10 full-time (6 women), 26 part-time/adjunct (11 women). *Students:* 198 full-time (142 women), 147 part-time (92 women); includes 77 minority (25 African Americans, 19 Asian Americans or Pacific Islanders, 33 Hispanic Americans), 63 international. Average age 30. In 2008, 86 master's awarded. *Entrance requirements:* Additional exam requirements/recommendations for international students: Required—TOEFL (minimum score 600 paper-based; 250 computer-based; 100 iBT). *Application deadline:* For fall admission, 4/15 for domestic students; for spring admission, 10/15 for domestic students. Application fee: $50. *Expenses:* Tuition: Full-time $27,144; part-time $1508 per credit. Required fees: $355 per semester. *Financial support:* Fellowships with partial tuition reimbursements, research assistantships, teaching assistantships with partial tuition reimbursements, career-related internships or fieldwork, Federal Work-Study, scholarships/grants, tuition waivers (partial), and unspecified assistantships available. Support available to part-time students. Financial award application deadline: 3/1; financial award applicants required to submit FAFSA. *Unit head:* Dr. Michael Cohen, Director, 212-206-3524, Fax: 212-645-0661, E-mail: cohenm2@newschool.edu. *Application contact:* David Norris, Director of Admissions, 212-229-5630, Fax: 212-989-3887, E-mail: nsadmissions@newschool.edu.

See Close-Up on page 873.

Ohio University, Graduate College, Center for International Studies, Program in Development Studies, Athens, OH 45701-2979. Offers MA. Part-time programs available. *Degree requirements:* For master's, one foreign language, thesis optional. *Entrance requirements:* For master's, minimum GPA of 3.0. Additional exam requirements/recommendations for international students: Required—TOEFL (minimum score 550 paper-based; 213 computer-based). *Faculty research:* Problems and issues in social, economic, political, health and environmental development.

Rutgers, The State University of New Jersey, Camden, Graduate School of Arts and Sciences, Department of Public Policy and Administration, Camden, NJ 08102-1401. Offers education policy and leadership (MPA); international public service and development (MPA);

public management (MPA); JD/MPA; MPA/MA. *Accreditation:* NASPAA. Part-time and evening/weekend programs available. *Degree requirements:* For master's, directed study, research workshop. *Entrance requirements:* For master's, GRE General Test, GMAT or LSAT, 3 letters of recommendation; resumé; statement of personal, professional, and academic goals. Additional exam requirements/recommendations for international students: Required—TOEFL (minimum score 550 paper-based; 213 computer-based), IELTS. Electronic applications accepted. *Faculty research:* Nonprofit management, county and municipal administration, health and human services, government communication, administrative law, educational finance.

Saint Mary's University, Faculty of Arts, International Development Studies Program, Halifax, NS B3H 3C3, Canada. Offers MA. Part-time programs available. *Degree requirements:* For master's, thesis. *Entrance requirements:* For master's, honors degree. *Faculty research:* Dynamics of global development, gender and development, policy analysis, models and strategies for development, Latin American and Caribbean development.

Texas A&M University, George Bush School of Government and Public Service, College Station, TX 77843. Offers advanced international affairs (Certificate); homeland security (Certificate); international affairs (MPIA), including international economics and development, national security affairs; nonprofit management (Certificate); public service and administration (MPSA), including public management, public policy analysis. *Accreditation:* NASPAA. *Faculty:* 43. *Students:* 188 full-time (80 women), 101 part-time (37 women); includes 40 minority (10 African Americans, 5 Asian Americans or Pacific Islanders, 25 Hispanic Americans), 22 international. Average age 24. In 2008, 64 master's awarded. *Degree requirements:* For master's, summer internship. *Entrance requirements:* For master's, GRE (preferred) or GMAT. *Application deadline:* For fall admission, 1/24 for domestic and international students. Application fee: $50 ($75 for international students). Electronic applications accepted. *Expenses:* Tuition, area resident: Full-time $3838.50. Tuition, state resident: full-time $3838.50. Tuition, nonresident: full-time $8897. Required fees: $2359.60. *Financial support:* In 2008–09, fellowships (averaging $11,000 per year), research assistantships (averaging $11,250 per year) were awarded; career-related internships or fieldwork, Federal Work-Study, and institutionally sponsored loans also available. Financial award application deadline: 2/1; financial award applicants required to submit FAFSA. *Faculty research:* Public policy, presidential studies, public leadership, economic policy, social policy. *Unit head:* A. Benton Cocanougher, Dean, 979-862-8842, E-mail: bushschool@tamu.edu. *Application contact:* Kathryn Meyer, Recruitment/Placement Officer, 979-458-4767, Fax: 979-845-4155, E-mail: admissions@bushschool.tamu.edu.

Tufts University, Fletcher School of Law and Diplomacy, Medford, MA 02155. Offers LL M, MA, MAHA, MALD, MIB, PhD, DVM/MA, JD/MALD, MALD/MA, MALD/MBA, MALD/MS, MD/MA. Postbaccalaureate distance learning degree programs offered (minimal on-campus study). *Degree requirements:* For master's, one foreign language, thesis; for doctorate, one foreign language, comprehensive exam, thesis/dissertation, dissertation defense. *Entrance requirements:* For master's and doctorate, GMAT or GRE General Test. Additional exam requirements/recommendations for international students: Required—TOEFL (minimum score 600 paper-based; 250 computer-based; 100 iBT), IELTS (minimum score 7). Electronic applications accepted. *Expenses:* Contact institution. *Faculty research:* Negotiation and conflict resolution, international organizations, international business and economic law, security studies, development economics.

See Close-Up on page 879.

Tufts University, Graduate School of Arts and Sciences, Department of Urban and Environmental Policy and Planning, Medford, MA 02155. Offers community development (MA); environmental policy (MA); health and human welfare (MA); housing policy (MA); international environment/development policy (MA); public policy (MPP); public policy and citizen participation (MA); MA/MS; MALD/MA. *Accreditation:* ACSP (one or more programs are accredited). Part-time programs available. *Degree requirements:* For master's, thesis, internship. *Entrance requirements:* For master's, GRE General Test. Additional exam requirements/recommendations for international students: Required—TOEFL (minimum score 550 paper-based; 213 computer-based; 80 iBT). Electronic applications accepted. *Expenses:* Contact institution.

See Close-Up on page 1237.

Tulane University, School of Liberal Arts, The Payson Center for International Development and Technology Transfer, New Orleans, LA 70118-5669. Offers international development (MS, PhD). Part-time programs available. *Degree requirements:* For master's, comprehensive exam (for some programs), thesis optional; for doctorate, comprehensive exam, thesis/dissertation. *Entrance requirements:* For master's, GRE General Test, minimum B average in undergraduate course work. Additional exam requirements/recommendations for international students: Required—TOEFL. Electronic applications accepted. *Faculty research:* Third World development.

University of Florida, Graduate School, College of Liberal Arts and Sciences, Department of Political Science, Gainesville, FL 32611. Offers international development policy and administration (MA, Certificate); international relations (MA, MAT); political campaigning (MA, Certificate); political science (MA, MAT, PhD); public affairs (MA, Certificate); JD/MA. Part-time programs available. Terminal master's awarded for partial completion of doctoral program. *Degree requirements:* For master's, variable foreign language requirement, thesis or alternative; for doctorate, variable foreign language requirement, thesis/dissertation. *Entrance requirements:* For master's and doctorate, GRE General Test, minimum GPA of 3.0. Additional exam requirements/recommendations for international students: Required—TOEFL (minimum score 550 paper-based; 213 computer-based). Electronic applications accepted. *Faculty research:* U.S. political development, religion and politics, environmental politics and policy, developing societies, international relations.

University of Guelph, Graduate Program Services, Collaborative International Development Studies, Guelph, ON N1G 2W1, Canada. Offers M Eng, M Sc, MA, MBA, PhD. Part-time

programs available. *Degree requirements:* For master's, thesis (for some programs), seminar, economics course, sociology/anthropology course, geography course, political science course; for doctorate, comprehensive exam (for some programs), thesis/dissertation. *Entrance requirements:* For master's, honours degree with courses in economics, social science, and empirical methods. *Faculty research:* Transformation of developing societies, regional differences, national and international processes of development, long-term change.

University of Ottawa, Faculty of Graduate and Postdoctoral Studies, Program in Globalization and International Development, Ottawa, ON K1N 6N5, Canada. Offers MA. *Degree requirements:* For master's, thesis or alternative. *Entrance requirements:* For master's, honours bachelor's degree or equivalent, minimum B average.

University of Pittsburgh, Graduate School of Public and International Affairs, Division of International Development, Program in Human Security, Pittsburgh, PA 15260. Offers MID, MPA/MID, MID/JD, MID/MBA, MID/MPH, MID/MPIA, MID/MSIS, MID/MSW. *Degree requirements:* For master's, thesis optional, internship, capstone seminar. *Entrance requirements:* For master's, GRE General Test, 3 letters of recommendation, minimum GPA of 3.2, resumé. Additional exam requirements/recommendations for international students: Required—TOEFL (minimum score 550 paper-based; 213 computer-based; 80 iBT), TWE (minimum score 4); Recommended—IELTS (minimum score 7). Electronic applications accepted. *Faculty research:* Human rights, threats to civilian populations, human trafficking, child soldiers, post-conflict reconstruction.

University of Pittsburgh, Graduate School of Public and International Affairs, Division of International Development, Program in Nongovernmental Organizations and Civil Society, Pittsburgh, PA 15260. Offers MID, MPA/MID, MID/JD, MID/MBA, MID/MPH, MID/MPIA, MID/MSIS, MID/MSW. Part-time programs available. *Degree requirements:* For master's, thesis optional, internship, capstone seminar. *Entrance requirements:* For master's, GRE General Test, 3 letters of recommendation, resumé, minimum GPA of 3.2. Additional exam requirements/recommendations for international students: Required—TOEFL (minimum score 550 paper-based; 213 computer-based; 80 iBT), TWE (minimum score 4); Recommended—IELTS (minimum score 7). Electronic applications accepted. *Faculty research:* Project/program evaluation, population and environment, international development, development economics, civil society.

University of Pittsburgh, Graduate School of Public and International Affairs, Executive Programs in Public Policy and Management, Pittsburgh, PA 15260. Offers development planning (MPPM); international development (MPPM); international political economy (MPPM); international security studies (MPPM); management of non profit organizations (MPPM); metropolitan management and regional development (MPPM); policy analysis and evaluation (MPPM). Part-time programs available. *Degree requirements:* For master's, thesis optional, capstone seminar. *Entrance requirements:* For master's, 2 letters of recommendation, resumé, 5 years of supervisory or budgetary experience. Additional exam requirements/recommendations for international students: Required—TOEFL (minimum score 600 paper-based; 250 computer-based; 100 iBT), TWE (minimum score 4); Recommended—IELTS (minimum score 7). Electronic applications accepted. *Faculty research:* Executive training and technical assistance for U.S. and international clients.

See Close-Up on page 1243.

University of San Francisco, College of Arts and Sciences, Department of Economics, Program in International and Development Economics, San Francisco, CA 94117-1080. Offers MA.

University of Southern Mississippi, Graduate School, College of Arts and Letters, Department of Political Science, International Development, and International Affairs, Hattiesburg, MS 39406-0001. Offers international development (PhD); political science (MA, MS). Part-time programs available. *Faculty:* 14 full-time (2 women), 1 part-time/adjunct (0 women). *Students:* 36 full-time (14 women), 44 part-time (17 women); includes 18 minority (12 African Americans, 1 American Indian/Alaska Native, 2 Asian Americans or Pacific Islanders, 3 Hispanic Americans), 6 international. Average age 41. 25 applicants, 68% accepted, 15 enrolled. In 2008, 8 master's awarded. *Degree requirements:* For master's, comprehensive exam, thesis (for some programs). *Entrance requirements:* For master's, GRE General Test, minimum GPA of 2.75 in last 2 years, 3.0 in field of study. *Application deadline:* For fall admission, 3/1 priority date for domestic students, 3/1 for international students. Applications are processed on a rolling basis. Application fee: $30. *Financial support:* In 2008–09, 4 research assistantships with full and partial tuition reimbursements (averaging $9,000 per year), 8 teaching assistantships with full tuition reimbursements (averaging $7,000 per year) were awarded; career-related internships or fieldwork, Federal Work-Study, scholarships/grants, and unspecified assistantships also available. Financial award application deadline: 3/15; financial award applicants required to submit FAFSA. *Faculty research:* American politics, international politics, political theory, comparative politics, public law. *Unit head:* Dr. Thomas Lansford, Interim Chair, 601-266-4310. *Application contact:* Dr. Robert Pauley, Graduate Coordinator, 601-266-4310, Fax: 601-266-4172.

Virginia Polytechnic Institute and State University, Graduate School, College of Architecture and Urban Studies, School of Public and International Affairs, Blacksburg, VA 24061. Offers environmental planning and policy (MURP); government and international affairs (MPIA); housing, community and economic development (MURP); international development planning (MURP); land use and physical planning (MURP); planning, governance and globalization (PhD), including environmental planning and landscape analysis, physical planning and urban design, public and international affairs, urban and environmental design and planning; urban and regional planning (MURP). *Accreditation:* ACSP. *Entrance requirements:* Additional exam requirements/recommendations for international students: Required—TOEFL (minimum score 550 paper-based; 213 computer-based). Electronic applications accepted. *Faculty research:* Design theory, environmental planning, town planning, transportation planning.

International Trade Policy

The George Washington University, Elliott School of International Affairs, Program in International Trade and Investment Policy, Washington, DC 20052. Offers MA, JD/MA, MBA/MA. Part-time and evening/weekend programs available. *Students:* 28 full-time (12 women), 15 part-time (9 women); includes 7 minority (1 African American, 4 Asian Americans or Pacific Islanders, 2 Hispanic Americans), 6 international. Average age 26. 108 applicants, 56% accepted, 21 enrolled. In 2008, 23 master's awarded. *Degree requirements:* For master's, one foreign language, capstone project. *Entrance requirements:* For master's, GRE General Test, 2 years of a modern foreign language and 2 semesters of introductory economics. Additional exam requirements/recommendations for international students: Required—TOEFL. *Application deadline:* For fall admission, 2/1 for domestic students; for spring admission, 10/1 for domestic students. Application fee: $60. Electronic applications accepted. *Financial support:* In 2008–09, 11 students received support; fellowships with tuition reimbursements available, research assistantships with tuition reimbursements available, career-related internships or fieldwork, Federal Work-Study, institutionally sponsored loans, and tuition waivers available. Financial award application deadline: 1/15. *Unit head:* Steven Suranovic, Director, 202-994-7579, Fax: 202-994-5477, E-mail: smsuran@gwu.edu. *Application contact:* Jeff V. Miles, Director of Graduate Admissions, 202-994-7050, Fax: 202-994-9537, E-mail: esiagrad@gwu.edu.

Monterey Institute of International Studies, Graduate School of International Policy Studies, Program in International Trade Policy, Monterey, CA 93940-2691. Offers MA. *Students:* 26 full-time (13 women), 2 part-time (1 woman); includes 7 minority (1 African American, 1 American Indian/Alaska Native, 5 Asian Americans or Pacific Islanders), 6 international. Average age 27. In 2008, 21 master's awarded. *Degree requirements:* For master's, one foreign language. *Entrance requirements:* For master's, minimum GPA of 3.0, proficiency in a foreign language. Additional exam requirements/recommendations for international students: Required—TOEFL (minimum score 550 paper-based; 213 computer-based; 80 iBT). *Application deadline:* For fall admission, 3/15 priority date for domestic and international students; for spring admission, 10/1 priority date for domestic and international students. Applications are processed on a rolling basis. Application fee: $50. Electronic applications accepted. *Expenses:* Tuition: Full-time $29,300; part-time $1400 per credit. Required fees: $56. *Financial support:* In 2008–09, 20 students received support. Application deadline: 3/15. *Application contact:* 831-647-4123, Fax: 831-647-6405, E-mail: admit@miis.edu.

See Close-Up on page 871.

Political Science

Acadia University, Faculty of Arts, Department of Political Science, Wolfville, NS B4P 2R6, Canada. Offers MA. *Faculty:* 7 full-time (2 women), 1 part-time/adjunct (0 women). *Students:* 3 full-time (1 woman), 3 part-time (2 women). Average age 26. 13 applicants, 46% accepted, 3 enrolled. In 2008, 1 master's awarded. *Degree requirements:* For master's, thesis. *Entrance requirements:* For master's, honors degree or equivalent. Additional exam requirements/recommendations for international students: Required—TOEFL (minimum score 580 paper-based; 237 computer-based; 93 iBT), IELTS (minimum score 6.5). *Application deadline:* For fall admission, 2/1 priority date for domestic and international students. Application fee: $50. Tuition and fees charges are reported in Canadian dollars. *Expenses:* Tuition, area resident: Full-time $3873.50 Canadian dollars; part-time $844 Canadian dollars per course. Tuition, state resident: full-time $4634.50 Canadian dollars; part-time $844 Canadian dollars per course. Tuition, nonresident: full-time $9103 Canadian dollars; part-time $1687 Canadian dollars per course. Required fees: $503.22 Canadian dollars; $5 Canadian dollars per course. *Financial support:* In 2008–09, 1 student received support, including 3 teaching assistantships (averaging $9,000 per year). Financial award application deadline: 2/1. *Faculty research:* Atlantic Canada, international relations and organization, human rights, Canadian politics, political thought, technology. *Unit head:* Dr. Greg Pyrez, Head, 902-585-1293, Fax: 902-585-1070, E-mail: greg.pyrez@acadiau.ca. *Application contact:* Danielle Fraser, Administrative Secretary, 902-585-1506, Fax: 902-585-1070, E-mail: polisci@acadiau.ca.

American Public University System, AMU/APU Graduate Programs, Charles Town, WV 25414. Offers air warfare (MA Military Studies); American Revolution (MA Military Studies); business administration (MBA); Civil War (MA Military Studies); criminal justice (MA); defense management (MA Military Studies); emergency and disaster management (MA); environmental policy and management (MS); fire science management (MA); global engagement (MA); history (MA); homeland security (MA); humanities (MA); intelligence (MA Military Studies, MA Strategic Intelligence); international peace and conflict resolution (MA); international relations and conflict resolution (MA); joint warfare (MA Military Studies); land warfare international perspective (MA Military Studies); management (MA); military history (MA); military leadership (MA Military Studies); national security studies (MA); naval warfare international (MA Military Studies); naval warfare US (MA Military Studies); political science (MA); public administration (MA); public health (MA); security management (MA); space studies (MS); special ops/LIC (MA Military Studies); sports management (MA); transportation and logistics management (MA); transportation management (MA); unconventional warfare (MA Military Studies); World War II (MA Military Studies). Programs offered via distance learning only. Part-time and evening/weekend programs available. Postbaccalaureate distance learning degree programs offered (no on-campus study). *Degree requirements:* For master's, comprehensive exam. *Entrance requirements:* For master's, bachelor's degree or equivalent, minimum GPA of 2.7 in last 60 hours of course work. Electronic applications accepted. *Faculty research:* Military history, criminal justice, management performance, national security.

American University, School of Public Affairs, Department of Government, Washington, DC 20016-8130. Offers political science (MA, PhD), including American politics (MA), comparative politics (MA); women, policy and political leadership (Certificate). Part-time and evening/weekend programs available. *Faculty:* 23 full-time (13 women), 14 part-time/adjunct (2 women). *Students:* 39 full-time (17 women), 40 part-time (21 women); includes 8 minority (2 African Americans, 1 American Indian/Alaska Native, 3 Asian Americans or Pacific Islanders, 2 Hispanic Americans), 6 international. Average age 27. 156 applicants, 54% accepted, 28 enrolled. In 2008, 36 master's, 1 doctorate, 1 other advanced degree awarded. Terminal master's awarded for partial completion of doctoral program. *Degree requirements:* For master's, comprehensive exam; for doctorate, comprehensive exam, thesis/dissertation. *Entrance requirements:* For master's, GRE, statement of purpose, 2 recommendations; for doctorate, GRE, statement of purpose, 3 recommendations; for Certificate, bachelor's degree. Additional exam requirements/recommendations for international students: Required—TOEFL. *Application deadline:* For fall admission, 2/1 for domestic students; for spring admission, 11/1 for domestic students. Application fee: $55. *Expenses:* Tuition: Full-time $21,204; part-time $1178 per credit hour. Required fees: $380. Part-time tuition and fees vary according to course load and program. *Financial support:* Fellowships, research assistantships, teaching assistantships, career-related internships or fieldwork and institutionally sponsored loans available. Financial award application deadline: 2/1. *Faculty research:* Political leadership, interest groups, politics of regulation, public law, political behavior. *Unit head:* Dr. Candice Nelson, Chair, 202-885-2338, E-mail: cnelson@american.edu. *Application contact:* Dr. Candice Nelson, Chair, 202-885-2338, E-mail: cnelson@american.edu.

The American University in Cairo, Graduate Studies and Research, School of Humanities and Social Sciences, Department of Political Science, Cairo, Egypt. Offers MA. *Degree requirements:* For master's, thesis. *Entrance requirements:* Additional exam requirements/recommendations for international students: Required—English entrance exam and/or TOEFL. Electronic applications accepted. *Faculty research:* African and Middle East politics, international relations, development of human rights, international law.

The American University of Athens, The School of Graduate Studies, Athens, Greece. Offers biomedical sciences (MS); business (MBA); business communication (MA); computer sciences (MS); engineering and applied sciences (MS); politics and policy making (MA); systems engineering (MS); telecommunications (MS). *Entrance requirements:* For master's, University Degree/Resum&e, 2 recommendation letters/TOEFL score 550. Additional exam requirements/recommendations for international students: Required—TOEFL (minimum score 550 paper-based; 213 computer-based). *Faculty research:* Nanotechnology, environmental sciences, rock mechanics, human skin studies, Monte Carlo algorithms and software.

American University of Beirut, Graduate Programs, Faculty of Arts and Sciences, Beirut, Lebanon. Offers anthropology (MA); Arabic language and literature (MA); archaeology (MA); biology (MS); chemistry (MS); computer science (MS); economics (MA); education (MA); English language (MA); English literature (MA); environmental policy planning (MSES); financial economics (MAFE); geology (MS); history (MA); mathematics (MA, MS); Middle Eastern studies (MA); philosophy (MA); physics (MS); political studies (MA); psychology (MA); public administration (MA); sociology (MA); statistics (MA, MS). Part-time programs available. *Degree requirements:* For master's, one foreign language, comprehensive exam, thesis (for some programs). *Entrance requirements:* For master's, GRE, letter of recommendation. Additional exam requirements/recommendations for international students: Required—TOEFL (minimum score 600 paper-based; 250 computer-based; 100 iBT), IELTS (minimum score 7.5). *Faculty research:* String theory and supergravity; computer graphics; algebra and number theory; popular Arabic literature; marine and freshwater biology; integrating science, math and technology.

Appalachian State University, Cratis D. Williams Graduate School, Department of Government and Justice Studies, Boone, NC 28608. Offers criminal justice (MS); political science (MA), including American government, international relations; public administration (MPA), including public management, town, city and county management. Part-time programs available. Post-baccalaureate distance learning degree programs offered (no on-campus study). *Faculty:* 27 full-time (5 women), 12 part-time/adjunct (1 woman). *Students:* 70 full-time (29 women), 51 part-time (14 women); includes 9 minority (7 African Americans, 1 American Indian/Alaska Native, 1 Asian American or Pacific Islander), 4 international. 60 applicants, 92% accepted, 32 enrolled. In 2008, 58 master's awarded. *Degree requirements:* For master's, variable foreign language requirement, comprehensive exam, thesis optional. *Entrance requirements:* For master's, GRE General Test, 3 letters of recommendation. Additional exam requirements/

recommendations for international students: Required—TOEFL (minimum score 570 paper-based; 230 computer-based; 79 iBT), IELTS (minimum score 6.5). *Application deadline:* For fall admission, 7/1 for domestic students, 2/1 for international students; for spring admission, 11/1 for domestic students, 7/1 for international students. Applications are processed on a rolling basis. Application fee: $50. Electronic applications accepted. *Expenses:* Tuition, area resident: Full-time $2600; part-time $700 per course. Tuition, state resident: full-time $2600; part-time $700 per course. Tuition, nonresident: full-time $5000; part-time $3300 per course. Required fees: $2150; $330 per course. Tuition and fees vary according to campus/location. *Financial support:* In 2008–09, 35 research assistantships (averaging $7,500 per year) were awarded; fellowships, teaching assistantships, career-related internships or fieldwork, Federal Work-Study, scholarships/grants, and unspecified assistantships also available. Financial award application deadline: 4/1; financial award applicants required to submit FAFSA. *Faculty research:* Campaign finance, emerging democracies, bureaucratic politics, judicial behavior, administration of justice. Total annual research expenditures: $8,500. *Unit head:* Dr. Brian Ellison, Chairperson, 828-262-3085, E-mail: ellisonba@appstate.edu. *Application contact:* Sandy Krause, Director of Admissions and Recruiting, 828-262-2130, Fax: 828-262-2709, E-mail: krausesl@appstate.edu.

Arizona State University, Graduate College, College of Liberal Arts and Sciences, Division of Social Sciences, Department of Political Science, Tempe, AZ 85287. Offers MA, PhD. *Degree requirements:* For master's, thesis or alternative; for doctorate, thesis/dissertation. *Entrance requirements:* For master's and doctorate, GRE.

Arkansas State University, Graduate School, College of Humanities and Social Sciences, Department of Political Science, Jonesboro, State University, AR 72467. Offers political science (MA); political science education (SCCT); public administration (MPA). *Accreditation:* NASPAA (one or more programs are accredited). Part-time programs available. *Faculty:* 8 full-time (3 women), 1 (woman) part-time/adjunct. *Students:* 18 full-time (12 women), 20 part-time (10 women); includes 12 minority (all African Americans), 2 international. Average age 31. 24 applicants, 71% accepted, 7 enrolled. In 2008, 14 master's awarded. *Degree requirements:* For master's, comprehensive exam, thesis or alternative; for SCCT, comprehensive exam. *Entrance requirements:* For master's, GRE General Test or MAT, GMAT, appropriate bachelor's degree, letters of reference, official transcript, letters of recommendation, statement of purpose; for SCCT, GRE General Test or MAT, GMAT, interview, master's degree, official transcript, letters of recommendation. Additional exam requirements/recommendations for international students: Required—TOEFL (minimum score 550 paper-based; 213 computer-based; 79 iBT), IELTS (minimum score 6). *Application deadline:* For fall admission, 7/15 for domestic students, 7/1 for international students; for spring admission, 12/1 for domestic students, 11/13 for international students. Applications are processed on a rolling basis. Application fee: $30 ($40 for international students). Electronic applications accepted. *Expenses:* Tuition, state resident: full-time $3744; part-time $208 per credit hour. Tuition, nonresident: full-time $9540; part-time $530 per credit hour. International tuition: $7938 full-time. Required fees: $896; $47 per credit hour. $25 per term. One-time fee: $50. Tuition and fees vary according to course load and program. *Financial support:* In 2008–09, 12 students received support; teaching assistantships, career-related internships or fieldwork, scholarships/grants, and unspecified assistantships available. Financial award application deadline: 7/1; financial award applicants required to submit FAFSA. *Faculty research:* Peace Corps, political communication, political psychology, public opinion, elections. *Unit head:* Dr. Richard Wang, Chair, 870-972-3048, Fax: 870-972-2720, E-mail: rwang@astate.edu. *Application contact:* Dr. Andrew Sustich, Dean of the Graduate School, 870-972-3029, Fax: 870-972-3857, E-mail: sustich@astate.edu.

Ashland University, College of Arts and Sciences, Program in American History and Government, Ashland, OH 44805-3702. Offers MAHG. Part-time programs available. *Faculty:* 5 full-time (0 women), 33 part-time/adjunct (2 women). *Students:* 41 full-time (19 women), 74 part-time (34 women); includes 9 minority (3 African Americans, 1 Asian American or Pacific Islander, 5 Hispanic Americans). Average age 38. 101 applicants, 69% accepted, 56 enrolled. In 2008, 1 master's awarded. *Degree requirements:* For master's, thesis optional. *Entrance requirements:* For master's, minimum GPA of 3.0. *Application deadline:* Applications are processed on a rolling basis. Application fee: $30. Electronic applications accepted. *Expenses:* Contact institution. *Financial support:* Application deadline: 4/15. *Faculty research:* American founding, United States Civil War, Progressive Era. *Unit head:* Dr. Peter W. Schramm, Executive Director, Ashbrook Center, 419-289-5414, Fax: 419-289-5425, E-mail: pschramm@ashland.edu. *Application contact:* Christian A Pascarella, Associate Director, 419-289-5411, Fax: 419-289-5425, E-mail: cpascare@ashland.edu.

Auburn University, Graduate School, College of Liberal Arts, Department of Political Science, Auburn University, AL 36849. Offers public administration (MPA, PhD); MPA/MCP. Part-time programs available. *Faculty:* 21 full-time (5 women), 5 part-time/adjunct (1 woman). *Students:* 27 full-time (14 women), 43 part-time (22 women); includes 14 minority (12 African Americans, 1 Asian American or Pacific Islander, 1 Hispanic American), 6 international. Average age 35. 69 applicants, 54% accepted, 18 enrolled. In 2008, 20 master's, 6 doctorates awarded. *Degree requirements:* For doctorate, thesis/dissertation. *Entrance requirements:* For master's, GRE General Test, minimum GPA of 3.0 in political science, 2.5 overall; for doctorate, GRE General Test. *Application deadline:* For fall admission, 7/7 for domestic students; for spring admission, 11/24 for domestic students. Applications are processed on a rolling basis. Application fee: $25 ($50 for international students). Electronic applications accepted. *Expenses:* Tuition, area resident: Full-time $5880; part-time $243 per credit hour. Tuition, state resident: full-time $5880; part-time $243 per credit hour. Tuition, nonresident: full-time $17,640; part-time $729 per credit hour. International tuition: $17,846 full-time. Required fees: $620. Tuition and fees vary according to program and reciprocity agreements. *Financial support:* Fellowships, research assistantships, teaching assistantships, career-related internships or fieldwork and Federal Work-Study available. Support available to part-time students. Financial award application deadline: 3/15. *Faculty research:* Policy evaluation, political economy, privatization, participation, election administration. Total annual research expenditures: $200,000. *Unit head:* Dr. Gerard Gryski, Chair, 334-844-5370. *Application contact:* Dr. George Flowers, Dean of the Graduate School, 334-844-2125.

Auburn University Montgomery, School of Sciences, Department of Public Administration and Political Science, Montgomery, AL 36124-4023. Offers MPA, MPS, PhD. *Accreditation:* NASPAA (one or more programs are accredited). Part-time and evening/weekend programs available. *Faculty:* 6 full-time (1 woman), 5 part-time/adjunct (1 woman). *Students:* 19 full-time (11 women), 103 part-time (64 women); includes 48 minority (46 African Americans, 2 Asian Americans or Pacific Islanders), 4 international. Average age 30. In 2008, 25 master's awarded. *Degree requirements:* For master's, comprehensive exam; for doctorate, thesis/dissertation. *Entrance requirements:* For master's, GRE General Test or MAT; for doctorate, GRE General Test. *Application deadline:* Applications are processed on a rolling basis. Application fee: $25. Electronic applications accepted. *Expenses:* Tuition, state resident: full-time $5088; part-time $212 per credit. Tuition, nonresident: full-time $15,264; part-time $636 per credit. Required fees: $234. *Financial support:* In 2008–09, 1 research assistantship was awarded; career-related internships or fieldwork and scholarships/grants also available. Support available to part-time students. Financial award application deadline: 3/1; financial award applicants required to submit FAFSA. *Unit head:* Dr. Thomas Vocino, Head, 334-244-3696, Fax: 334-244-3826, E-mail: vocino@mail.aum.edu. *Application contact:* Dr. Glen Ray, Acting Graduate Coordinator, 334-244-3590, Fax: 334-244-3826, E-mail: gray@mail.aum.edu.

Augusta State University, Graduate Studies, College of Arts and Sciences, Department of Political Science, Augusta, GA 30904-2200. Offers MPA. Part-time and evening/weekend programs available. *Faculty:* 4 full-time (2 women), 3 part-time/adjunct (1 woman). *Students:* 8 full-time (2 women), 26 part-time (21 women); includes 7 African Americans, 5 Hispanic Americans. Average age 31. 19 applicants, 89% accepted, 14 enrolled. In 2008, 15 master's awarded. *Degree requirements:* For master's, comprehensive exam, thesis. *Entrance requirements:* For master's, GRE General Test. *Application deadline:* For fall admission, 7/16 priority date for domestic students. Applications are processed on a rolling basis. Application fee: $20. Electronic applications accepted. *Expenses:* Tuition, state resident: full-time $2520; part-time $140 per credit hour. Tuition, nonresident: full-time $10,080; part-time $560 per credit hour. Required fees: $546; $273 per semester. *Financial support:* In 2008–09, 1 student received support. Federal Work-Study and institutionally sponsored loans available. Financial award application deadline: 4/15; financial award applicants required to submit FAFSA. *Faculty research:* Political behavior, administrative law, political participation, human resources administration. *Unit head:* Dr. Sudha Ratan, Chair, 706-737-1710, E-mail: sratan@aug.edu. *Application contact:* Dr. Saundra J. Reinke, MPA Director, 706-667-4424, Fax: 706-667-4083, E-mail: sreinke@aug.edu.

Ball State University, Graduate School, College of Sciences and Humanities, Department of Political Science, Program in Political Science, Muncie, IN 47306-1099. Offers MA. *Faculty research:* Survey research, public policy.

Baylor University, Graduate School, College of Arts and Sciences, Department of Political Science, Waco, TX 76798. Offers international studies (MA); political science (MA, PhD); public policy and administration (MPPA); JD/MPPA. *Students:* 24 full-time (7 women), 2 part-time (1 woman), 3 international. In 2008, 9 master's awarded. *Entrance requirements:* For master's, GRE General Test. *Application deadline:* Applications are processed on a rolling basis. Application fee: $25. *Financial support:* Research assistantships, career-related internships or fieldwork, Federal Work-Study, and institutionally sponsored loans available. Financial award application deadline: 3/1. *Unit head:* Dr. David Corey, Graduate Program Director, 254-710-3161, Fax: 254-710-3122, E-mail: david_d_corey@baylor.edu. *Application contact:* Jenice Langston, Administrative Assistant, 254-710-3161, Fax: 254-710-3870, E-mail: jenice_langston@baylor.edu.

Baylor University, Graduate School, College of Arts and Sciences, J. M. Dawson Institute of Church-State Studies, Waco, TX 76798. Offers MA, PhD. *Students:* 34 full-time (11 women), 4 part-time (2 women); includes 6 minority (1 American Indian/Alaska Native, 2 Asian Americans or Pacific Islanders, 3 Hispanic Americans), 6 international. In 2008, 6 master's, 4 doctorates awarded. *Degree requirements:* For master's, thesis, oral exam; for doctorate, one foreign language, thesis/dissertation, preliminary exams. *Entrance requirements:* For master's, GRE General Test; for doctorate, GRE General Test, MA or equivalent. *Application deadline:* For fall admission, 3/1 for domestic students. Applications are processed on a rolling basis. Application fee: $25. *Financial support:* Fellowships, research assistantships, teaching assistantships, Federal Work-Study and institutionally sponsored loans available. Financial award application deadline: 3/1. *Faculty research:* Religion and politics, religion and public education, religious freedom and international politics, First Amendment jurisprudence. *Unit head:* Dr. Christopher Marsh, Graduate Program Director, 254-710-4412, Fax: 254-710-1571, E-mail: chris_marsh@baylor.edu. *Application contact:* Suzanne Seller, Administrative Assistant, 254-710-1510, Fax: 254-710-1571, E-mail: suzanne_sellers@baylor.edu.

Boston College, Graduate School of Arts and Sciences, Department of Political Science, Chestnut Hill, MA 02467-3800. Offers MA, PhD. Terminal master's awarded for partial completion of doctoral program. *Degree requirements:* For master's, thesis or alternative; for doctorate, one foreign language, thesis/dissertation. *Entrance requirements:* For master's and doctorate, GRE General Test. Additional exam requirements/recommendations for international students: Required—TOEFL (minimum score 590 paper-based; 250 computer-based; 91 iBT). Electronic applications accepted. *Expenses:* Tuition: Part-time $1148 per credit. Required fees: $60. *Faculty research:* Political theory, American politics, international politics.

Boston University, Graduate School of Arts and Sciences, Department of Political Science, Boston, MA 02215. Offers MA, PhD. Terminal master's awarded for partial completion of doctoral program. *Degree requirements:* For master's, one foreign language; for doctorate, 2 foreign languages, comprehensive exam, thesis/dissertation. *Entrance requirements:* For master's and doctorate, GRE General Test, 3 letters of recommendation. Additional exam requirements/recommendations for international students: Required—TOEFL (minimum score 600 paper-based; 250 computer-based).

Bowling Green State University, Graduate College, College of Arts and Sciences, Department of Political Science, Program in Political Science, Bowling Green, OH 43403. Offers MA/MA. *Entrance requirements:* Additional exam requirements/recommendations for international students: Required—TOEFL. Electronic applications accepted.

Brandeis University, Graduate School of Arts and Sciences, Department of Politics, Waltham, MA 02454-9110. Offers MA, PhD. Terminal master's awarded for partial completion of doctoral program. *Degree requirements:* For master's, thesis; for doctorate, one foreign language, comprehensive exam, thesis/dissertation. *Entrance requirements:* For master's and doctorate, GRE General Test, sample of written work, resumé, 3 letters of recommendation. Additional exam requirements/recommendations for international students: Required—TOEFL (minimum score 600 paper-based; 250 computer-based; 100 iBT), IELTS (minimum score 7). Electronic applications accepted. *Faculty research:* American institutions, international law and foreign policy, political theory, comparative politics, European politics.

Brigham Young University, Graduate Studies, College of Family, Home, and Social Sciences, Public Policy Graduate Program, Provo, UT 84602. Offers MPP, JD/MPP. *Faculty:* 3 full-time (0 women), 3 part-time/adjunct (1 woman). *Students:* 14 full-time (8 women); includes 5 minority (1 American Indian/Alaska Native, 3 Asian Americans or Pacific Islanders, 1 Hispanic American), 1 international. Average age 28. 18 applicants, 83% accepted, 10 enrolled. In 2008, 5 master's awarded. *Degree requirements:* For master's, internship. *Entrance requirements:* For master's, GRE. Additional exam requirements/recommendations for international students: Required—TOEFL (minimum score 580 paper-based; 237 computer-based; 85 iBT). *Application deadline:* For fall admission, 3/1 priority date for domestic and international students. Application fee: $50. Electronic applications accepted. *Expenses:* Tuition: Full-time $5160; part-time $287 per credit hour. Tuition and fees vary according to program and student's religious affiliation. *Financial support:* In 2008–09, 11 students received support, including 7 research assistantships with full and partial tuition reimbursements available (averaging $2,357 per year), 2 teaching assistantships with full and partial tuition reimbursements available (averaging $4,800 per year); fellowships also available. Financial award application deadline: 3/1. *Faculty research:* Welfare, environment, and health policy issues. *Unit head:* Dr. Sven E. Wilson, Graduate Program Director, 801-422-9018, Fax: 801-422-0224, E-mail: sven_wilson@byu.edu. *Application contact:* Jessica A. McArthur, Department Secretary, 801-422-7146, Fax: 801-422-0224, E-mail: publicpolicy@byu.edu.

Brock University, Faculty of Graduate Studies, Faculty of Social Sciences, Program in Political Science, St. Catharines, ON L2S 3A1, Canada. Offers Canadian politics (MA); international and comparative politics (MA); political philosophy (MA); public administration (MA). Part-time programs available. *Degree requirements:* For master's, thesis optional. *Entrance requirements:* For master's, honors degree. Additional exam requirements/recommendations for international students: Required—TOEFL (minimum score 550 paper-based; 213 computer-based; 80 iBT), IELTS (minimum score 6.5), TWE (minimum score 4). Electronic applications accepted. *Faculty research:* Public administration reform, economic and social justice, politics of societies, Canadian politics, international relations.

Brooklyn College of the City University of New York, Division of Graduate Studies, Department of Political Science, Brooklyn, NY 11210-2889. Offers international affairs (MA); political science (MA, PhD); political science, urban policy and administration (MA). The department offers courses at Brooklyn College that are creditable toward the CUNY doctoral degree (with permission of the executive officer of the doctoral program). Part-time and evening/weekend programs available. *Students:* 13 full-time (6 women), 142 part-time (82 women); includes 91 minority (68 African Americans, 5 Asian Americans or Pacific Islanders, 18 Hispanic Americans), 15 international. Average age 33. 95 applicants, 83% accepted, 45 enrolled. In 2008, 43 master's awarded. *Degree requirements:* For master's, comprehensive exam (for some programs), thesis or alternative, foreign language exam (for international affairs program). *Entrance requirements:* For master's, 2 letters of recommendation, personal statement. *Expenses:* Tuition, state resident: full-time $7360; part-time $310 per credit hour. Tuition, nonresident: full-time $13,800; part-time $575 per credit hour. *Financial support:* Career-related internships or fieldwork and Federal Work-Study available. Support available to part-time students. Financial award application deadline: 5/1; financial award applicants required to submit FAFSA. *Faculty research:* Ethics and politics, politics of criminal justice, Western Europe, international law and politics, labor politics. *Unit head:* Dr. Sally Bermanzohn, Chairperson, 718-951-5306, E-mail: sallyb@brooklyn.cuny.edu. *Application contact:* Hernan Sierra, Graduate Admissions Coordinator, 718-951-4536, Fax: 718-951-4506, E-mail: grads@brooklyn.cuny.edu.

Brown University, Graduate School, Department of Political Science, Providence, RI 02912. Offers PhD, MA/PhD. *Degree requirements:* For doctorate, thesis/dissertation. *Entrance requirements:* For doctorate, GRE General Test.

California Institute of Technology, Division of the Humanities and Social Sciences, Social Science Program, Pasadena, CA 91125-0001. Offers economics (PhD); political science (PhD); social science (MS). Terminal master's awarded for partial completion of doctoral program. *Degree requirements:* For doctorate, thesis/dissertation. *Entrance requirements:* For doctorate, GRE General Test. Electronic applications accepted. *Faculty research:* Individual and group decision making, design of political and economic institutions, experimental social science, public policy, quantitative history.

California Polytechnic State University, San Luis Obispo, College of Liberal Arts, Department of Political Science, San Luis Obispo, CA 93407. Offers MPP. Part-time programs available. *Faculty:* 3 full-time (all women). *Students:* 7 full-time (3 women), 24 part-time (13 women); includes 5 minority (1 African American, 4 Hispanic Americans). Average age 30. 46 applicants, 61% accepted, 15 enrolled. In 2008, 16 master's awarded. *Degree requirements:* For master's, thesis or alternative. *Entrance requirements:* For master's, minimum GPA of 2.75 in last 90 quarter units of course work, three letters of recommendation. Additional exam requirements/recommendations for international students: Required—TOEFL (minimum score 550 paper-based; 213 computer-based), IELTS (minimum score 6), Either TOEFL or IELTS is acceptable. *Application deadline:* For fall admission, 2/15 for domestic students, 11/30 for international students; for winter admission, 6/30 for international students. Application fee: $55. *Expenses:* Tuition, nonresident: full-time $10,170; part-time $226 per unit. Required fees: $5751; $1265 per quarter. *Financial support:* Career-related internships or fieldwork, Federal Work-Study, and scholarships/grants available. Support available to part-time students. Financial award application deadline: 3/2; financial award applicants required to submit FAFSA. *Unit head:* Dr. Elizabeth Lowham, Graduate Coordinator, 805-756-2919, Fax: 805-756-7168, E-mail: elowham@calpoly.edu. *Application contact:* Dr. Elizabeth Lowham, Graduate Coordinator, 805-756-2919, Fax: 805-756-7168, E-mail: elowham@calpoly.edu.

California State University, Chico, Graduate School, College of Behavioral and Social Sciences, Department of Political Science, Program in Political Science, Chico, CA 95929-0455. Offers MA. Part-time programs available. *Entrance requirements:* For master's, 2 letters of recommendation, statement of purpose. Additional exam requirements/recommendations for international students: Required—TOEFL (minimum score 550 paper-based; 213 computer-based; 80 iBT), IELTS (minimum score 6.5). Electronic applications accepted.

California State University, Fullerton, Graduate Studies, College of Humanities and Social Sciences, Division of Politics, Administration, and Justice, Fullerton, CA 92834-9480. Offers political science (MA); public administration (MPA). *Accreditation:* NASPAA (one or more programs are accredited). Part-time programs available. *Students:* 44 full-time (22 women), 160 part-time (84 women); includes 103 minority (6 African Americans, 1 American Indian/Alaska Native, 42 Asian Americans or Pacific Islanders, 54 Hispanic Americans), 5 international. Average age 30. 138 applicants, 55% accepted, 41 enrolled. In 2008, 45 master's awarded. *Degree requirements:* For master's, comprehensive exam, project or thesis. *Entrance requirements:* For master's, minimum GPA of 2.5 in last 60 units of course work, 12 units of course work in social sciences. Application fee: $55. Tuition and fees vary according to degree level. *Financial support:* Teaching assistantships, career-related internships or fieldwork, Federal Work-Study, institutionally sponsored loans, and scholarships/grants available. Support available to part-time students. Financial award application deadline: 3/1. *Faculty research:* Emergency management plans. *Unit head:* Dr. Phil Gianos, Chair, 657-278-3521. *Application contact:* Admissions/Applications, 657-278-2300.

California State University, Long Beach, Graduate Studies, College of Liberal Arts, Department of Political Science, Long Beach, CA 90840. Offers MA. Part-time programs available. *Faculty:* 7 full-time (3 women), 3 part-time/adjunct (1 woman). *Students:* 10 full-time (6 women), 20 part-time (8 women); includes 13 minority (2 African Americans, 2 Asian Americans or Pacific Islanders, 9 Hispanic Americans). Average age 33. 48 applicants, 40% accepted, 9 enrolled. *Degree requirements:* For master's, one foreign language, comprehensive exam or thesis. *Entrance requirements:* For master's, GRE General Test, minimum GPA of 3.0 in field. *Application deadline:* For fall admission, 4/1 for domestic students. Applications are processed on a rolling basis. Application fee: $55. Electronic applications accepted. *Expenses:* Tuition, nonresident: full-time $11,160; part-time $372 per unit. Required fees: $4100; $1261 per semester. *Financial support:* In 2008–09, 6 students received support; teaching assistantships, Federal Work-Study, institutionally sponsored loans, and scholarships/grants available. Financial award application deadline: 3/2. *Faculty research:* Social welfare policy, international political economy, Marxism, voting behavior. *Unit head:* Dr. Teresa Wright, Chair, 562-985-4704, Fax: 562-985-4979, E-mail: twright@csulb.edu. *Application contact:* Dr. Liesl Haas, Graduate Advisor, 562-985-5860, Fax: 562-985-4979, E-mail: lhaas@csulb.edu.

California State University, Los Angeles, Graduate Studies, College of Natural and Social Sciences, Department of Political Science, Los Angeles, CA 90032-8530. Offers political science (MA); public administration (MS). Part-time and evening/weekend programs available. *Faculty:* 7 full-time (2 women), 1 part-time/adjunct (0 women). *Students:* 23 full-time (15 women), 104 part-time (62 women); includes 76 minority (10 African Americans, 17 Asian Americans or Pacific Islanders, 49 Hispanic Americans), 19 international. Average age 31. In 2008, 26 master's awarded. *Degree requirements:* For master's, comprehensive exam or thesis. *Entrance requirements:* Additional exam requirements/recommendations for international students: Required—TOEFL (minimum score 500 paper-based; 173 computer-based). *Application deadline:* For fall admission, 6/15 for domestic students, 5/1 for international students; for winter admission, 11/1 for domestic students, 9/1 for international students; for spring admission, 2/1 for domestic students, 10/1 for international students. Applications are processed on a rolling basis. Application fee: $55. Electronic applications accepted. *Expenses:* Tuition, nonresident: part-time $226 per credit. Required fees: $4019. *Financial support:* Career-related internships or fieldwork and Federal Work-Study available. Support available to part-time students. Financial award application deadline: 3/1. *Faculty research:* Government; public policy and law; international, political, and economic relations; comparative politics. *Unit head:* Dr. Scott Bowman, Chair, 323-343-2230, Fax: 323-343-6452, E-mail: sbowman@calstatela.edu. *Application contact:* Dr. Jose L. Galvan, Dean of Graduate Studies, 323-343-3820, Fax: 323-343-5653, E-mail: jgalvan@cslanet.calstatela.edu.

California State University, Northridge, Graduate Studies, College of Social and Behavioral Sciences, Department of Political Science, Northridge, CA 91330. Offers MA. *Faculty:* 16 full-time (6 women), 7 part-time/adjunct (2 women). *Students:* 9 full-time (5 women), 21

Political Science

California State University, Northridge (continued)
part-time (9 women); includes 8 minority (3 Asian Americans or Pacific Islanders, 5 Hispanic Americans), 3 international. Average age 32. 413 applicants, 85% accepted, 5 enrolled. In 2008, 143 master's awarded. *Degree requirements:* For master's, comprehensive exam. *Entrance requirements:* For master's, GRE if cumulative undergraduate GPA below 3.0, 2 letters of recommendation. Additional exam requirements/recommendations for international students: Required—TOEFL. *Application deadline:* For fall admission, 11/30 for domestic students. Application fee: $55. *Financial support:* Application deadline: 3/1. *Unit head:* Dr. Matthew Cahn, Chair, 818-677-3566. *Application contact:* Dr. Matthew Cahn, Chair, 818-677-3566.

California State University, Sacramento, Graduate Studies, College of Social Sciences and Interdisciplinary Studies, Department of Government, Sacramento, CA 95819-6048. Offers MA. Part-time programs available. *Degree requirements:* For master's, thesis or alternative, writing proficiency exam. *Entrance requirements:* For master's, GRE General Test, minimum GPA of 3.0 during previous 2 years. Additional exam requirements/recommendations for international students: Required—TOEFL. Electronic applications accepted.

Carleton University, Faculty of Graduate Studies, Faculty of Public Affairs and Management, Department of Political Science, Ottawa, ON K1S 5B6, Canada. Offers MA, PhD. *Degree requirements:* For master's, one foreign language, comprehensive exam, thesis optional; for doctorate, one foreign language, comprehensive exam, thesis/dissertation. *Entrance requirements:* For master's, honors degree in political science, minimum B average; for doctorate, master's degree in political science. Additional exam requirements/recommendations for international students: Required—TOEFL. *Faculty research:* Canadian politics, comparative politics, international relations, public administration and policy analysis, political theory.

Carleton University, Faculty of Graduate Studies, Faculty of Public Affairs and Management, Institute of Political Economy, Ottawa, ON K1S 5B6, Canada. Offers MA, PhD. *Degree requirements:* For master's, thesis optional. *Entrance requirements:* For master's, honors degree. Additional exam requirements/recommendations for international students: Required—TOEFL. *Faculty research:* Relationships between economy and politics as they affect the political, social and cultural life of societies; historical processes whereby social change is located in the interaction of the economic, political and cultural, and ideological moments of social life.

Case Western Reserve University, School of Graduate Studies, Department of Political Science, Cleveland, OH 44106. Offers MA, PhD. Part-time programs available. Terminal master's awarded for partial completion of doctoral program. *Degree requirements:* For doctorate, thesis/dissertation. *Entrance requirements:* For master's, GRE General Test, 18 hours in political science; for doctorate, GRE General Test, GRE Subject Test (political science), master's degree in political science. Additional exam requirements/recommendations for international students: Required—TOEFL. Electronic applications accepted. *Faculty research:* American cultural politics and policy, Western and Eastern European governments, African politics in international affairs, American legislative and presidential politics, women and politics, Southern politics.

The Catholic University of America, School of Arts and Sciences, Department of Politics, Washington, DC 20064. Offers American government (MA, PhD); congressional studies (MA); international affairs (MA); international political economics (MA); political theory (MA, PhD); world politics (MA, PhD); JD/MA. Part-time programs available. *Degree requirements:* For master's, one foreign language, comprehensive exam, thesis or alternative; for doctorate, 2 foreign languages, comprehensive exam, thesis/dissertation. *Entrance requirements:* For master's and doctorate, GRE General Test, 3 letters of recommendation, minimum GPA of 3.0. Additional exam requirements/recommendations for international students: Required—TOEFL (minimum score 580 paper-based; 237 computer-based). Electronic applications accepted. *Faculty research:* Political philosophy, American political institutions and processes, political economy, national security.

Central European University, Graduate Studies, School of Social Sciences and Humanities, Budapest, Hungary. Offers economics (MA, PhD); gender studies (MA, PhD); international relations and European studies (MA, PhD); mathematics and its applications (MS, PhD); medieval studies (MA, PhD); nationalism studies (MA, PhD); philosophy (MA, PhD); political science (MA, PhD); public policy (MA, PhD); sociology and social anthropology (MA, PhD). Terminal master's awarded for partial completion of doctoral program. *Degree requirements:* For master's, one foreign language, thesis; for doctorate, one foreign language, comprehensive exam, thesis/dissertation. *Entrance requirements:* For master's, CEU subject tests, interview; for doctorate, GRE, CEU subject test, interview. Additional exam requirements/recommendations for international students: Required—TOEFL (minimum score 570 paper-based; 230 computer-based). Electronic applications accepted. *Faculty research:* Civil society, fiscal decentralization, party politics, political philosophy (especially Liberalism, theory of Democracy).

See Close-Up on page 349.

Central Michigan University, Central Michigan University Off-Campus Programs, Program in Public Administration, Mount Pleasant, MI 48859. Offers public management (MPA); state and local government (MPA). Part-time and evening/weekend programs available. *Entrance requirements:* For master's, minimum GPA of 2.8. Additional exam requirements/recommendations for international students: Required—TOEFL. Electronic applications accepted. *Expenses:* Tuition, state resident: full-time $3717; part-time $413 per credit. Tuition, nonresident: full-time $6894; part-time $766 per credit. *Financial support:* Scholarships/grants available. Support available to part-time students. *Unit head:* Dr. Lawrence Sych, Program Director, 989-774-3316, E-mail: sych1l@cmich.edu. *Application contact:* 877-268-4636, E-mail: cmuoffcampus@cmich.edu.

Central Michigan University, College of Graduate Studies, College of Humanities and Social and Behavioral Sciences, Department of Political Science, Program in Political Science, Mount Pleasant, MI 48859. Offers political science (MA), including American concentration, comparative/international concentration. Part-time programs available. *Students:* 9 full-time (2 women), 5 part-time (2 women); includes 2 African Americans, 2 international. Average age 25. *Degree requirements:* For master's, thesis or alternative. *Application deadline:* Applications are processed on a rolling basis. Application fee: $35 ($45 for international students). Electronic applications accepted. *Expenses:* Tuition, state resident: full-time $3717; part-time $413 per credit. Tuition, nonresident: full-time $6894; part-time $766 per credit. *Financial support:* Fellowships with tuition reimbursements, career-related internships or fieldwork, Federal Work-Study, unspecified assistantships, and out-of-state merit awards available. *Unit head:* Dr. Rick Kurtz, Chairperson, 989-774-3442, Fax: 989-774-1136, E-mail: kurtz1rs@cmich.edu. *Application contact:* Dr. Chris Owens, Graduate Advisor, 989-774-3165, Fax: 989-774-1136, E-mail: owens2ct@cmich.edu.

Central Michigan University, College of Graduate Studies, College of Humanities and Social and Behavioral Sciences, Department of Political Science, Program in Public Administration, Mount Pleasant, MI 48859. Offers professional development in public administration (Graduate Certificate); public administration (MPA), including cognate courses option; public management (MPA); state and local government (MPA). Part-time programs available. *Students:* 14 full-time (5 women), 11 part-time (6 women); includes 3 African Americans, 2 American Indian/Alaska Native, 4 international. Average age 32. *Degree requirements:* For master's, thesis or alternative. *Application deadline:* Applications are processed on a rolling basis. Application fee: $35 ($45 for international students). Electronic applications accepted. *Expenses:* Tuition, state resident: full-time $3717; part-time $413 per credit. Tuition, nonresident: full-time $6894; part-time $766 per credit. *Financial support:* Fellowships with tuition reimbursements, career-related internships or fieldwork, Federal Work-Study, unspecified assistantships, and out-of-state merit awards available. *Unit head:* Dr. Rick Kurtz, Chairperson, 989-774-3442, Fax: 989-774-1136, E-mail: kurtz1rs@cmich.edu. *Application contact:* Dr. Lawrence Sych, Program Director, 989-774-3316, Fax: 989-774-1136, E-mail: sych1l@cmich.edu.

Claremont Graduate University, Graduate Programs, School of Politics and Economics, Department of Politics and Policy, Claremont, CA 91711-6160. Offers American politics (MA, PhD); comparative politics (PhD); international political economy (MA); international studies (MA); political philosophy (PhD); political science (PhD); politics, economics and business (MA); public policy (MA, PhD); world politics (PhD); MBA/PhD. Part-time programs available. *Faculty:* 10 full-time (4 women), 4 part-time/adjunct (0 women). *Students:* 166 full-time (60 women), 19 part-time (6 women); includes 28 minority (4 African Americans, 9 Asian Americans or Pacific Islanders, 15 Hispanic Americans), 40 international. Average age 32. In 2008, 24 master's, 17 doctorates awarded. Terminal master's awarded for partial completion of doctoral program. *Entrance requirements:* For master's and doctorate, GRE General Test. Additional exam requirements/recommendations for international students: Required—TOEFL (minimum score 550 paper-based; 213 computer-based; 80 iBT). *Application deadline:* For fall admission, 2/1 priority date for domestic students. Applications are processed on a rolling basis. Application fee: $60. Electronic applications accepted. *Expenses:* Tuition: Full-time $33,698; part-time $1465 per unit. Required fees: $310; $155 per semester. Tuition and fees vary according to program. *Financial support:* Fellowships, research assistantships, teaching assistantships, Federal Work-Study, institutionally sponsored loans, and scholarships/grants available. Support available to part-time students. Financial award application deadline: 2/15; financial award applicants required to submit FAFSA. *Faculty research:* Environmental policy, international debt, global democratization, Third World development, public sector discrimination. *Unit head:* Jean Schroedel, Chair, 909-621-8696, Fax: 909-621-8545, E-mail: jean.schroedel@cgu.edu. *Application contact:* Laura Carillo, Recruiter and Admissions Coordinator, 909-621-8699, Fax: 909-621-7545, E-mail: laura.carillo@cga.edu.

Clark Atlanta University, School of Arts and Sciences, Department of Political Science, Atlanta, GA 30314. Offers MA, PhD. Part-time programs available. *Faculty:* 6 full-time (1 woman), 2 part-time/adjunct (0 women). *Students:* 6 full-time (3 women), 42 part-time (18 women); includes 44 minority (all African Americans). Average age 39. 14 applicants, 71% accepted, 4 enrolled. In 2008, 1 master's, 2 doctorates awarded. Terminal master's awarded for partial completion of doctoral program. *Degree requirements:* For master's, one foreign language, thesis; for doctorate, 2 foreign languages, thesis/dissertation. *Entrance requirements:* For master's, GRE General Test, minimum GPA of 2.5; for doctorate, GRE General Test, minimum graduate GPA of 3.0. Additional exam requirements/recommendations for international students: Required—TOEFL (minimum score 500 paper-based; 173 computer-based). *Application deadline:* For fall admission, 4/1 for domestic and international students; for spring admission, 11/1 for domestic and international students. Applications are processed on a rolling basis. Application fee: $40 ($55 for international students). *Expenses:* Tuition: Full-time $12,240; part-time $680 per credit hour. Required fees: $710; $355 per semester. *Financial support:* In 2008–09, 8 fellowships, 5 teaching assistantships were awarded; career-related internships or fieldwork, Federal Work-Study, scholarships/grants, and unspecified assistantships also available. Support available to part-time students. Financial award application deadline: 4/30; financial award applicants required to submit FAFSA. *Faculty research:* Public policy and education, rural politics, women and state economic programs, reconstruction after war in Africa, environmental policies. *Unit head:* Dr. Abi Awomolo, Chairperson, 404-880-8721, Fax: 404-880-8717, E-mail: aawomolo@cau.edu. *Application contact:* Michelle Clark-Davis, Graduate Program Admissions, 404-880-6605, E-mail: cauadmissions@cau.edu.

The College of Saint Rose, Graduate Studies, School of Arts and Humanities, Program in History/Political Science, Albany, NY 12203-1419. Offers MA. Part-time and evening/weekend programs available. *Degree requirements:* For master's, final paper/project, thesis or comprehensive exam. *Entrance requirements:* For master's, minimum undergraduate GPA of 3.0, 12 undergraduate credits in US history and/or political science. Additional exam requirements/recommendations for international students: Required—TOEFL (minimum score 550 paper-based; 213 computer-based). Electronic applications accepted.

Colorado State University, Graduate School, College of Liberal Arts, Department of Political Science, Fort Collins, CO 80523-1782. Offers MA, PhD. Part-time programs available. *Faculty:* 16 full-time (7 women), 1 (woman) part-time/adjunct. *Students:* 22 full-time (11 women), 21 part-time (7 women); includes 2 minority (1 African American, 1 Hispanic American), 1 international. Average age 31. 35 applicants, 29% accepted, 6 enrolled. In 2008, 9 master's awarded. *Degree requirements:* For master's, variable foreign language requirement, comprehensive exam (for some programs), thesis (for some programs); for doctorate, variable foreign language requirement, comprehensive exam (for some programs), thesis/dissertation (for some programs). *Entrance requirements:* For master's, GRE General Test (minimum combined score of 1050 on Verbal and Quantitative sections), minimum GPA of 3.0, BA/BS, letters of recommendation; for doctorate, GRE General Test (minimum combined score of 1200 on Verbal and Quantitative sections), minimum GPA of 3.5, 15-page writing sample, MA/MS or at least 24 credits in a master's program, letters of recommendation. Additional exam requirements/recommendations for international students: Required—TOEFL (minimum score 600 paper-based; 250 computer-based). *Application deadline:* For fall admission, 2/15 priority date for domestic and international students; for spring admission, 10/15 priority date for domestic students, 8/1 priority date for international students. Applications are processed on a rolling basis. Application fee: $50. Electronic applications accepted. *Expenses:* Tuition, area resident: Full-time $5620; part-time $312.25 per credit. Tuition, state resident: full-time $5620; part-time $312.25 per credit. Tuition, nonresident: full-time $17,253; part-time $958.50 per credit. Required fees: $1449.56; $82.35 per credit. *Financial support:* In 2008–09, 26 students received support, including 1 research assistantship (averaging $15,606 per year), 25 teaching assistantships with full tuition reimbursements available (averaging $13,554 per year); fellowships, career-related internships or fieldwork, Federal Work-Study, institutionally sponsored loans, scholarships/grants, traineeships, and unspecified assistantships also available. Financial award application deadline: 3/1; financial award applicants required to submit FAFSA. *Faculty research:* Environmental politics and policy, international relations, politics of developing nations, state and local politics and administration, political behavior. *Unit head:* Dr. Robert Duffy, Chair, 970-491-6225, Fax: 970-491-2490, E-mail: robert.duffy@colostate.edu. *Application contact:* Dr. Sandra K. Davis, Coordinator, 970-491-5281, Fax: 970-491-2490, E-mail: sandra.davis@colostate.edu.

Columbia University, Graduate School of Arts and Sciences, Division of Social Sciences, Department of Political Science, New York, NY 10027. Offers M Phil, MA, PhD, JD/MA, JD/PhD. *Degree requirements:* For master's, one foreign language; for doctorate, 2 foreign languages, thesis/dissertation. *Entrance requirements:* For master's and doctorate, GRE General Test. Additional exam requirements/recommendations for international students: Required—TOEFL. *Faculty research:* Comparative politics, American government, international relations.

Concordia University, School of Graduate Studies, Faculty of Arts and Science, Department of Political Science, Montréal, QC H3G 1M8, Canada. Offers political science (PhD); public policy and public administration (MA), including geography. *Degree requirements:* For master's, one foreign language, comprehensive exam, thesis optional, internship. *Entrance requirements:* For master's, honors degree or equivalent. Additional exam requirements/recommendations for international students: Required—TOEFL. *Faculty research:* International public policy and administration, Quebec public administration, public policy and social/political theory, geography and public policy, public administration and decision making.

Converse College, School of Education and Graduate Studies, Program in Liberal Arts, Spartanburg, SC 29302-0006. Offers English (MLA); history (MLA); political science (MLA). *Degree requirements:* For master's, capstone paper. *Entrance requirements:* For master's, minimum GPA of 3.0, 2 recommendations.

Cornell University, Graduate School, Graduate Fields of Arts and Sciences, Field of Government, Ithaca, NY 14853-0001. Offers American politics (PhD); comparative politics (PhD); international relations (PhD); political methodology (PhD); political thought (PhD); public policy (PhD). *Faculty:* 40 full-time (14 women). *Students:* 70 full-time (37 women); includes 11 minority (2 African Americans, 1 American Indian/Alaska Native, 4 Asian Americans or Pacific Islanders, 4 Hispanic Americans), 23 international. Average age 30. 350 applicants, 9% accepted, 15 enrolled. In 2008, 13 doctorates awarded. *Degree requirements:* For doctorate, comprehensive exam, thesis/dissertation. *Entrance requirements:* For doctorate, GRE General Test, sample of written work, 3 letters of recommendation. Additional exam requirements/recommendations for international students: Required—TOEFL (minimum score 550 paper-based; 213 computer-based; 77 iBT). *Application deadline:* For fall admission, 1/15 for domestic students. Application fee: $70. Electronic applications accepted. *Expenses:* Tuition: Full-time $29,500. Required fees: $70. Full-time tuition and fees vary according to degree level, program and student level. *Financial support:* In 2008–09, 60 students received support, including 30 fellowships with full tuition reimbursements available, 2 research assistantships with full tuition reimbursements available, 28 teaching assistantships with full tuition reimbursements available; institutionally sponsored loans, scholarships/grants, health care benefits, tuition waivers (full and partial), and unspecified assistantships also available. Financial award applicants required to submit FAFSA. *Faculty research:* Political theory, American politics, comparative politics, international relations, methodology. *Unit head:* Director of Graduate Studies, 607-255-3567, Fax: 607-255-4530. *Application contact:* Graduate Field Assistant, 607-255-3567, Fax: 607-255-4530, E-mail: cu_govt@cornell.edu.

Dalhousie University, Faculty of Arts and Social Science, Department of Political Science, Halifax, NS B3H 4R2, Canada. Offers MA, PhD. *Entrance requirements:* Additional exam requirements/recommendations for international students: Required—TOEFL, IELTS, 1 of 5 approved tests: TOEFL, IELTS, CANTEST, CAEL, Michigan English Language Assessment Battery. *Application deadline:* For fall admission, 6/1 for domestic students, 4/1 for international students; for winter admission, 10/31 for domestic students, 8/31 for international students; for spring admission, 2/28 for domestic students, 12/31 for international students. Application fee: $70. Electronic applications accepted. *Financial support:* Career-related internships or fieldwork, scholarships/grants, and health care benefits available. *Faculty research:* Canadian political behavior and institutions, international politics, foreign policy, African politics, liberalism and modern political theory. *Unit head:* Dr. Louise Carbert, Graduate Coordinator, 902-494-6628, Fax: 902-494-3825, E-mail: psadmin@dal.ca. *Application contact:* Karen Watts, Graduate Administrator, 902-494-2396, Fax: 902-494-3825, E-mail: psadmin@dal.ca.

Duke University, Graduate School, Department of Political Science, Durham, NC 27708. Offers AM, PhD, JD/AM, JD/PhD. Terminal master's awarded for partial completion of doctoral program. *Degree requirements:* For doctorate, 2 foreign languages, thesis/dissertation. *Entrance requirements:* For master's and doctorate, GRE General Test. Additional exam requirements/recommendations for international students: Required—TOEFL (minimum score 550 paper-based; 213 computer-based; 83 iBT), IELTS (minimum score 7). Electronic applications accepted.

East Carolina University, Graduate School, Thomas Harriot College of Arts and Sciences, Department of Political Science, Greenville, NC 27858-4353. Offers public administration (MPA). *Accreditation:* NASPAA. Part-time and evening/weekend programs available. *Degree requirements:* For master's, one foreign language, comprehensive exam. *Entrance requirements:* For master's, GRE General Test. Additional exam requirements/recommendations for international students: Required—TOEFL.

Eastern Illinois University, Graduate School, College of Sciences, Department of Political Science, Charleston, IL 61920-3099. Offers MA.

Eastern Kentucky University, The Graduate School, College of Arts and Sciences, Department of Government, Program in Political Science, Richmond, KY 40475-3102. Offers MA. *Entrance requirements:* For master's, GRE General Test, minimum GPA of 2.5.

Eastern Michigan University, Graduate School, College of Arts and Sciences, Department of Political Science, Program in Political Science, Ypsilanti, MI 48197. Offers MPA.

East Stroudsburg University of Pennsylvania, Graduate School, College of Arts and Sciences, Department of Political Science, East Stroudsburg, PA 18301-2999. Offers M Ed, MA. Part-time and evening/weekend programs available. *Faculty:* 9 full-time (4 women). *Students:* 21 full-time (11 women), 35 part-time (22 women); includes 12 minority (6 African Americans, 1 Asian American or Pacific Islander, 5 Hispanic Americans), 3 international. Average age 31. In 2008, 14 master's awarded. *Degree requirements:* For master's, variable foreign language requirement, comprehensive exam, thesis or alternative. *Entrance requirements:* Additional exam requirements/recommendations for international students: Required—TOEFL (minimum score 560 paper-based; 220 computer-based; 83 iBT), The department follows the requirements of the Graduate School for admission. *Application deadline:* For fall admission, 7/31 priority date for domestic students, 5/1 priority date for international students; for spring admission, 11/30 for domestic students, 10/1 for international students. Applications are processed on a rolling basis. Application fee: $50. *Expenses:* Tuition, state resident: full-time $6430; part-time $357 per credit. Tuition, nonresident: full-time $10,288; part-time $572 per credit. *Financial support:* In 2008–09, 13 research assistantships with full and partial tuition reimbursements (averaging $2,098 per year) were awarded; Federal Work-Study and institutionally sponsored loans also available. Financial award application deadline: 3/1; financial award applicants required to submit FAFSA. *Unit head:* Dr. Patricia Crotty, Graduate Coordinator, 570-422-3271, Fax: 570-422-3506, E-mail: pcrotty@po-box.esu.edu. *Application contact:* Kevin Quintero, Graduate Admissions Coordinator, 570-422-3890, Fax: 570-422-2711, E-mail: kquintero@po-box.esu.edu.

Emory University, Graduate School of Arts and Sciences, Department of Political Science, Atlanta, GA 30322-1100. Offers PhD. *Degree requirements:* For doctorate, comprehensive exam, thesis/dissertation. *Entrance requirements:* For doctorate, GRE General Test, minimum GPA of 3.0. Additional exam requirements/recommendations for international students: Required—TOEFL. Electronic applications accepted. *Faculty research:* Post-Soviet politics, comparative politics, international politics, judicial politics and methodology, American national political institutions.

Fairleigh Dickinson University, Metropolitan Campus, University College: Arts, Sciences, and Professional Studies, School of History, Political and International Studies, Program in Political Science, Teaneck, NJ 07666-1914. Offers MA. *Students:* 2 part-time (1 woman). Average age 24. 4 applicants, 25% accepted, 0 enrolled. In 2008, 1 master's awarded. *Application deadline:* Applications are processed on a rolling basis. Application fee: $40. *Application contact:* Susan Brooman, University Director of Graduate Admissions, 201-692-2554, Fax: 201-692-2560, E-mail: globaleducation@fdu.edu.

Fayetteville State University, Graduate School, Department of Geography, History and Political Science, Fayetteville, NC 28301-4298. Offers history (MA); political science (MA). Part-time and evening/weekend programs available. *Degree requirements:* For master's, comprehensive exam, internship. *Entrance requirements:* For master's, GRE General Test. Electronic applications accepted.

Florida Agricultural and Mechanical University, Division of Graduate Studies, Research, and Continuing Education, College of Arts and Sciences, Division of History and Political Sciences, Program in Applied Social Science, Tallahassee, FL 32307-3200. Offers African American history (MASS); criminal justice (MASS); economics (MASS); history (MASS); political science (MASS); public administration (MASS); public management (MASS); social work (MASS); sociology (MASS). Part-time programs available. *Degree requirements:* For master's, thesis optional. *Entrance requirements:* For master's, GRE General Test, minimum GPA of 3.0. *Faculty research:* Southern history, black history, election trends, presidential history.

Florida Atlantic University, Dorothy F. Schmidt College of Arts and Letters, Department of Political Science, Boca Raton, FL 33431-0991. Offers MA, MAT. Part-time programs available. *Faculty:* 15 full-time (3 women), 6 part-time/adjunct (1 woman). *Students:* 7 full-time (3 women), 16 part-time (6 women); includes 4 minority (2 African Americans, 1 Asian American or Pacific Islander, 1 Hispanic American). Average age 33. 22 applicants, 45% accepted, 6 enrolled. In 2008, 6 master's awarded. *Degree requirements:* For master's, one foreign language, thesis or alternative. *Entrance requirements:* For master's, GRE General Test, minimum GPA of 3.0 during last 60 hours of course work. *Application deadline:* For fall admission, 7/1 for domestic students, 2/15 for international students; for spring admission, 11/1 for domestic students, 7/15 for international students. Applications are processed on a rolling basis. Application fee: $30. Electronic applications accepted. *Expenses:* Tuition, state resident: full-time $4867; part-time $270.40 per credit hour. Tuition, nonresident: full-time $16,486; part-time $915.87 per credit hour. *Financial support:* Research assistantships, teaching assistantships with partial tuition reimbursements, career-related internships or fieldwork, Federal Work-Study, and institutionally sponsored loans available. Support available to part-time students. Financial award application deadline: 4/16. *Faculty research:* Public policy, comparative policy affecting women, Congress, international system, urban policy. *Unit head:* Dr. Timothy Lenz, Chair, 561-297-3212, Fax: 561-297-2997, E-mail: lenz@fau.edu. *Application contact:* Dr. Robert Rabil, Director of Graduate Studies, 561-297-3215, Fax: 561-297-2997, E-mail: rrabil@fau.edu.

Florida International University, College of Arts and Sciences, Department of Political Science, Miami, FL 33199. Offers MS, PhD. Part-time and evening/weekend programs available. *Degree requirements:* For master's, one foreign language, thesis, research project; for doctorate, one foreign language, thesis/dissertation. *Entrance requirements:* For master's, GRE General Test, minimum GPA of 3.2, 2 letters of recommendation; for doctorate, GRE General Test, minimum GPA of 3.2 (undergraduate), 3.25 (graduate), 2 letters of recommendation. Additional exam requirements/recommendations for international students: Required—TOEFL (minimum score 550 paper-based; 213 computer-based). Electronic applications accepted.

Florida State University, Graduate Studies, College of Social Sciences, Department of Political Science, Tallahassee, FL 32306. Offers MA, MS, PhD. Part-time programs available. Terminal master's awarded for partial completion of doctoral program. *Degree requirements:* For master's, thesis optional; for doctorate, comprehensive exam, thesis/dissertation. *Entrance requirements:* For master's, GRE General Test, minimum undergraduate GPA of 3.0; for doctorate, GRE General Test, minimum graduate GPA of 3.5 and/or minimum undergraduate GPA of 3.0. Additional exam requirements/recommendations for international students: Required—TOEFL (minimum score 600 paper-based). Electronic applications accepted. *Faculty research:* American government, international relations, comparative government, public policy.

Fordham University, Graduate School of Arts and Sciences, Department of Political Science, New York, NY 10458. Offers elections and campaign management (MA). Part-time and evening/weekend programs available. *Degree requirements:* For master's, comprehensive exam. *Entrance requirements:* For master's, GRE General Test. Additional exam requirements/recommendations for international students: Required—TOEFL (minimum score 600 paper-based; 250 computer-based). Electronic applications accepted. *Faculty research:* Protest in emerging democracies, impact of religion on presidential elections, increasing partisan polarization in U.S. politics, comparative urban development, democracy vs. authoritarianism in the Middle East, election and campaign management.

Fordham University, Graduate School of Arts and Sciences, Program in International Political Economy and Development, Program in Elections and Campaign Management, New York, NY 10458. Offers MA.

George Mason University, College of Humanities and Social Sciences, Department of Public and International Affairs, Fairfax, VA 22030. Offers biodefense (MS, PhD); political science (MA, PhD); public administration (MPA). *Accreditation:* NASPAA (one or more programs are accredited). *Entrance requirements:* For master's, GRE General Test, minimum GPA of 3.0 in last 60 hours of course work. Electronic applications accepted.

Georgetown University, Graduate School of Arts and Sciences, Department of Government, Program in Democracy and Governance, Washington, DC 20057. Offers MA.

Georgetown University, Graduate School of Arts and Sciences, School of Continuing Studies, Washington, DC 20057. Offers American studies (MALS); Catholic studies (MALS); classical civilizations (MALS); ethics and the professions (MALS); human resources management (MPS); humanities (MALS); individualized study (MALS); international affairs (MALS); Islam and Muslim-Christian relations (MALS); journalism (MPS); liberal studies (DLS); literature and society (MALS); medieval and early modern European studies (MALS); public relations (MPS); real estate (MPS); religious studies (MALS); social and public policy (MALS); sports industry management (MPS); the theory and practice of American democracy (MALS); visual culture (MALS). *Entrance requirements:* Additional exam requirements/recommendations for international students: Required—TOEFL.

The George Washington University, College of Professional Studies, Graduate School of Political Management, Program in Legislative Affairs, Washington, DC 20052. Offers MA. Part-time and evening/weekend programs available. *Students:* 8 full-time (5 women), 40 part-time (22 women); includes 4 minority (1 African American, 2 Asian Americans or Pacific Islanders, 1 Hispanic American). Average age 27. 44 applicants, 77% accepted, 21 enrolled. In 2008, 17 master's awarded. *Degree requirements:* For master's, comprehensive exam. *Entrance requirements:* For master's, GRE General Test, minimum GPA of 3.0. Additional exam requirements/recommendations for international students: Required—TOEFL (minimum score 550 paper-based; 213 computer-based). *Application deadline:* For fall admission, 4/1 priority date for domestic and international students; for spring admission, 10/1 priority date for domestic and international students. Applications are processed on a rolling basis. Application fee: $60. Electronic applications accepted. *Financial support:* Application deadline: 2/1. *Unit head:* Dr. Steven E. Billet, Director, 202-994-6000, E-mail: sbillet@gwu.edu. *Application contact:* Information Contact, 202-994-6000, Fax: 202-994-6006, E-mail: gspmmail@gwu.edu.

The George Washington University, Columbian College of Arts and Sciences, Department of Political Science, Washington, DC 20052. Offers MA, PhD. Part-time and evening/weekend programs available. *Faculty:* 29 full-time (9 women). *Students:* 41 full-time (13 women), 45 part-time (17 women); includes 5 minority (1 American Indian/Alaska Native, 3 Asian Americans or Pacific Islanders, 1 Hispanic American), 18 international. Average age 32. 290 applicants, 27% accepted, 17 enrolled. In 2008, 8 master's, 2 doctorates awarded. Terminal master's awarded for partial completion of doctoral program. *Degree requirements:* For master's, one foreign language, comprehensive exam, thesis or alternative; for doctorate, 2 foreign languages, thesis/dissertation, general exam. *Entrance requirements:* For master's and doctorate, GRE General Test, minimum GPA of 3.0. Additional exam requirements/recommendations for international students: Required—TOEFL (minimum score 550 paper-based; 213 computer-based; 80 iBT). *Application deadline:* For fall admission, 1/15 priority date for domestic students; for spring admission, 10/1 priority date for domestic students. Applications are processed on a rolling basis. Application fee: $60. Electronic applications accepted. *Financial support:* In 2008–09, 43 students received support; fellowships with tuition reimbursements available, teaching assistantships with tuition reimbursements available, Federal Work-Study and tuition waivers available. *Unit head:* Christopher J Deering, Chair, 202-994-6564, E-mail: rocket@gwu.edu. *Application contact:* Christopher J Deering, Chair, 202-994-6564, E-mail: rocket@gwu.edu.

The George Washington University, Elliott School of International Affairs, Program in Security Policy Studies, Washington, DC 20052. Offers MA, JD/MA. Part-time and evening/weekend programs available. *Students:* 67 full-time (25 women), 62 part-time (20 women); includes 15 minority (13 Asian Americans or Pacific Islanders, 2 Hispanic Americans), 4 international. Average age 26. 251 applicants, 49% accepted, 52 enrolled. In 2008, 45 master's awarded. *Degree requirements:* For master's, one foreign language, capstone project. *Entrance requirements:* For master's, GRE General Test, 2 semesters of introductory economics, 2 years of a modern foreign language or one semester of statistics. Additional exam requirements/recommendations for international students: Required—TOEFL. *Application deadline:* For fall admission, 2/1 for domestic students; for spring admission, 10/1 for domestic students. Application fee: $60. Electronic applications accepted. *Financial support:* In 2008–09, 22

Political Science

The George Washington University (continued)
students received support; fellowships with tuition reimbursements available, research assistantships with tuition reimbursements available, career-related internships or fieldwork, Federal Work-Study, institutionally sponsored loans, and tuition waivers (full) available. Financial award application deadline: 1/15; financial award applicants required to submit FAFSA. *Faculty research:* U.S. arms transfer policies, military balance in the Third World, U.S. foreign policy, technology and security policy. *Unit head:* Joanna Spear, Director, 202-994-1088, E-mail: jspear@gwu.edu. *Application contact:* Jeff V. Miles, Director of Graduate Admissions, 202-994-7050, Fax: 202-994-9537, E-mail: esiagrad@gwu.edu.

Georgia State University, College of Arts and Sciences, Department of Political Science, Atlanta, GA 30303-3083. Offers MA, PhD. Part-time and evening/weekend programs available. Terminal master's awarded for partial completion of doctoral program. *Degree requirements:* For master's, thesis or alternative, exam; for doctorate, one foreign language, comprehensive exam, thesis/dissertation, exam. *Entrance requirements:* For master's, GRE General Test, 2 letters of recommendation; for doctorate, GRE General Test, 3 letters of recommendation, writing sample. Additional exam requirements/recommendations for international students: Required—TOEFL. Electronic applications accepted. *Faculty research:* International politics, American politics, comparative politics, public administration, international political economy.

Governors State University, College of Arts and Sciences, Program in Political and Justice Studies, University Park, IL 60466-0975. Offers MA. Part-time and evening/weekend programs available. *Degree requirements:* For master's, thesis or alternative. *Entrance requirements:* For master's, bachelor's degree in related field.

Graduate School and University Center of the City University of New York, Graduate Studies, Program in Political Science, New York, NY 10016-4039. Offers MA, PhD. Terminal master's awarded for partial completion of doctoral program. *Degree requirements:* For master's, one foreign language, thesis; for doctorate, one foreign language, thesis/dissertation. *Entrance requirements:* For master's and doctorate, GRE General Test. Additional exam requirements/recommendations for international students: Required—TOEFL. Electronic applications accepted.

Grambling State University, School of Graduate Studies and Research, College of Arts and Sciences, Program in Public Administration, Grambling, LA 71270. Offers health service administration (MPA); human resource management (MPA); public management (MPA); state and local government (MPA). *Accreditation:* NASPAA. Part-time programs available. *Faculty:* 3 full-time (0 women), 2 part-time/adjunct (1 woman). *Students:* 18 full-time (13 women), 25 part-time (18 women); includes 37 minority (all African Americans), 5 international. Average age 29. In 2008, 22 master's awarded. *Degree requirements:* For master's, comprehensive exam (for some programs), thesis optional. *Entrance requirements:* For master's, GRE, minimum GPA of 2.75 on last degree. Additional exam requirements/recommendations for international students: Required—TOEFL (minimum score 500 paper-based; 173 computer-based; 61 iBT). *Application deadline:* For fall admission, 7/1 for domestic and international students; for spring admission, 12/1 for domestic and international students. Applications are processed on a rolling basis. Application fee: $20 ($30 for international students). Electronic applications accepted. *Expenses:* Tuition, area resident: Full-time $3637; part-time $134 per credit hour. Tuition, nonresident: full-time $7651; part-time $134 per credit hour. Required fees: $1225; $134 per credit hour. $430 per semester. *Financial support:* In 2008–09, 1 research assistantship (averaging $6,500 per year) was awarded; health care benefits, tuition waivers (full), and unspecified assistantships also available. Financial award application deadline: 5/31. *Unit head:* Dr. Rose Harris, Director, 318-274-2310, Fax: 318-274-3427, E-mail: harrisr@gram.edu. *Application contact:* Sarah Dennis, Admissions Coordinator, 318-274-2319, Fax: 318-274-3427, E-mail: denniss@alpha0.gram.edu.

Harvard University, Graduate School of Arts and Sciences, Committee on Political Economy and Government, Cambridge, MA 02138. Offers PhD. *Entrance requirements:* For doctorate, GRE General Test or GMAT. Additional exam requirements/recommendations for international students: Required—TOEFL. *Expenses:* Tuition: Full-time $32,556. Required fees: $1426. Full-time tuition and fees vary according to program and student level.

Harvard University, Graduate School of Arts and Sciences, Department of Government, Cambridge, MA 02138. Offers political science (PhD), including American politics, comparative politics, international relations, political thought, quantitative methods. *Degree requirements:* For doctorate, one foreign language, thesis/dissertation, general exams. *Entrance requirements:* For doctorate, GRE General Test. Additional exam requirements/recommendations for international students: Required—TOEFL. *Expenses:* Tuition: Full-time $32,556. Required fees: $1426. Full-time tuition and fees vary according to program and student level.

Harvard University, John F. Kennedy School of Government, Cambridge, MA 02138. Offers MPA, MPAID, MPP, MPPUP, PhD, JD/MPP, MBA/MPP, MD/MPP. *Accreditation:* NASPAA. *Faculty:* 70. *Students:* 587 full-time (239 women); includes 113 minority (27 African Americans, 8 American Indian/Alaska Native, 48 Asian Americans or Pacific Islanders, 30 Hispanic Americans), 252 international. Average age 30. 2,426 applicants, 36% accepted, 587 enrolled. *Degree requirements:* For doctorate, thesis/dissertation. *Entrance requirements:* For master's, GMAT or GRE General Test; for doctorate, GRE General Test. Additional exam requirements/recommendations for international students: Required—TOEFL (minimum score 600 paper-based; 250 computer-based; 100 iBT), TWE. Application fee: $80. Electronic applications accepted. *Expenses:* Tuition: Full-time $32,556. Required fees: $1426. Full-time tuition and fees vary according to program and student level. *Financial support:* Fellowships, research assistantships, teaching assistantships, career-related internships or fieldwork, Federal Work-Study, institutionally sponsored loans, scholarships/grants, and unspecified assistantships available. Support available to part-time students. Financial award applicants required to submit CSS PROFILE or FAFSA. *Unit head:* Dr. David Ellwood, Dean, 617-495-1122. *Application contact:* 617-495-1155, Fax: 617-496-1165, E-mail: hks_admissions@harvard.edu.

Howard University, Graduate School, Department of Political Science, Program in Political Science, Washington, DC 20059-0002. Offers MA, PhD. *Degree requirements:* For master's, comprehensive exam. *Entrance requirements:* For master's, GRE General Test, minimum GPA of 3.0; for doctorate, GRE General Test, minimum GPA of 2.8.

Hult International Business School, Program in International Relations—Hult London Campus, Cambridge, MA 02141. Offers conflict resolution (MA); diplomacy (MA); international public law (MA); international relations (MA); Middle East international security (MA); politics (MA); security studies (MA); terrorism (MA); U.S. foreign policy (MA). Part-time programs available. *Entrance requirements:* Additional exam requirements/recommendations for international students: Required—TOEFL (minimum score 580 paper-based; 237 computer-based), TWE (minimum score 5). Electronic applications accepted. *Faculty research:* American foreign politics, Middle East, security studies.

Idaho State University, Office of Graduate Studies, College of Arts and Sciences, Department of Political Science, Pocatello, ID 83209. Offers political science (MA, DA); public administration (MPA). Part-time programs available. *Faculty:* 7 full-time (1 woman). *Students:* 29 full-time (10 women), 24 part-time (11 women); includes 2 minority (both Hispanic Americans). Average age 36. In 2008, 9 master's, 1 doctorate awarded. *Degree requirements:* For master's, comprehensive exam, thesis optional, coursework in 2 subfields; for doctorate, comprehensive exam, thesis/dissertation, teaching internship. *Entrance requirements:* For master's, GRE General Test, minimum GPA of 3.0 in last 2 years of undergraduate study, 3 letters of recommendation; for doctorate, GRE General Test, major field of American politics, minimum GPA of 3.0 in last 2 years of undergraduate study, 3 letters of recommendation. Additional exam requirements/recommendations for international students: Required—TOEFL (minimum score 550 paper-based; 213 computer-based; 80 iBT). *Application deadline:* For fall admission, 7/1 for domestic students, 6/1 for international students; for spring admission, 12/1 for domestic students, 11/1 for international students. Applications are processed on a rolling basis. Application fee: $55. Electronic applications accepted. *Expenses:* Tuition, area resident: Full-time $3114; part-time $276 per credit hour. Tuition, state resident: full-time $3114; part-time $276 per credit hour. Tuition, nonresident: full-time $12,318; part-time $404 per credit hour. Required fees: $2360. Tuition and fees vary according to course load and reciprocity agreements. *Financial support:* In 2008–09, 10 teaching assistantships with full and partial tuition reimbursements (averaging $9,401 per year) were awarded; fellowships with full and partial tuition reimbursements, career-related internships or fieldwork, Federal Work-Study, institutionally sponsored loans, scholarships/grants, health care benefits, tuition waivers (full and partial), and unspecified assistantships also available. Support available to part-time students. Financial award application deadline: 1/1; financial award applicants required to submit FAFSA. *Faculty research:* International affairs, environmental policy, decision making, Constitution, executive/legislative relations. *Unit head:* Dr. Wayne Gabardi, Chairman, 208-282-4536, Fax: 208-282-4833, E-mail: gabawayn@isu.edu. *Application contact:* Ellen Combs, Graduate School Technical Records Specialist, 208-282-2150, Fax: 208-282-4847, E-mail: combelle@isu.edu.

Illinois State University, Graduate School, College of Arts and Sciences, Department of Politics and Government, Normal, IL 61790-2200. Offers MA, MS. *Degree requirements:* For master's, thesis or alternative. *Entrance requirements:* For master's, GRE General Test, minimum GPA of 3.0 in last 60 hours of course work, 15 hours of course work in political science. *Faculty research:* Political tolerance in a democracy under external threats: a survey of public opinion.

Indiana State University, School of Graduate Studies, College of Arts and Sciences, Department of Political Science, Terre Haute, IN 47809-1401. Offers political science (MA, MS); public administration (MPA). *Degree requirements:* For master's, thesis (for some programs). *Entrance requirements:* For master's, GRE or minimum undergraduate GPA of 2.75, 18 semester hours of course work in political science. Additional exam requirements/recommendations for international students: Required—TOEFL (minimum score 550 paper-based). Electronic applications accepted.

Indiana University Bloomington, University Graduate School, College of Arts and Sciences, Department of Political Science, Bloomington, IN 47405-7000. Offers MA, PhD. *Faculty:* 26 full-time (9 women). *Students:* 88 full-time (35 women); includes 10 minority (5 African Americans, 5 Asian Americans or Pacific Islanders), 20 international. Average age 30. 148 applicants, 27% accepted, 11 enrolled. In 2008, 6 master's, 5 doctorates awarded. Terminal master's awarded for partial completion of doctoral program. *Degree requirements:* For master's, thesis, 30 credit hours; for doctorate, comprehensive exam, thesis/dissertation, 90 credit hours. *Entrance requirements:* For master's, GRE, personal statement, transcripts, 3 letters of recommendation; for doctorate, GRE, sample of written work, personal statement, 3 letters of recommendation. Additional exam requirements/recommendations for international students: Required—TOEFL (minimum score 640 paper-based; 273 computer-based; 112 iBT). *Application deadline:* For fall admission, 1/15 for domestic students, 12/1 for international students. Application fee: $50 ($60 for international students). Electronic applications accepted. *Expenses:* Tuition, area resident: Part-time $291.97 per credit hour. Tuition, state resident: part-time $291.97 per credit hour. Tuition, nonresident: part-time $850.33 per credit hour. Required fees: $110 per semester. Tuition and fees vary according to course load and program. *Financial support:* In 2008–09, 56 students received support, including 3 fellowships with full tuition reimbursements available (averaging $17,551 per year), 14 research assistantships with full tuition reimbursements available (averaging $15,542 per year), 39 teaching assistantships with full tuition reimbursements available (averaging $15,542 per year); Federal Work-Study, institutionally sponsored loans, scholarships/grants, health care benefits, and unspecified assistantships also available. Financial award application deadline: 2/26. *Faculty research:* American politics, international relations, public policy, political theory, comparative politics, theory and methodology. Total annual research expenditures: $291,773. *Unit head:* Russell Hanson, Chair, 812-855-1209, Fax: 812-855-2027, E-mail: hansonr@indiana.edu. *Application contact:* Sharon LaRoche, Graduate Secretary, 812-855-1208, Fax: 812-855-2027, E-mail: laroches@indiana.edu.

Indiana University of Pennsylvania, School of Graduate Studies and Research, College of Humanities and Social Sciences, Department of Political Science, Indiana, PA 15705-1087. Offers public affairs (MA). Part-time programs available. *Faculty:* 5 full-time (3 women). *Students:* 8 full-time (1 woman), 2 part-time (1 woman), 4 international. Average age 38. 8 applicants, 50% accepted, 4 enrolled. In 2008, 5 master's awarded. *Degree requirements:* For master's, thesis optional. *Entrance requirements:* For master's, GRE, 2 letters of recommendation. Additional exam requirements/recommendations for international students: Required—TOEFL. *Application deadline:* For fall admission, 7/1 priority date for domestic students; for spring admission, 11/1 for domestic students. Applications are processed on a rolling basis. Application fee: $30. *Expenses:* Tuition, area resident: Full-time $6430; part-time $357 per credit. Tuition, nonresident: full-time $10,288; part-time $572 per credit. Required fees: $1547.50; $107 per credit. $283 per year. *Financial support:* In 2008–09, 6 research assistantships with full and partial tuition reimbursements (averaging $4,533 per year) were awarded; Federal Work-Study also available. Support available to part-time students. Financial award application deadline: 3/15; financial award applicants required to submit FAFSA. *Unit head:* Dr. Steven Jackson, Chairperson, 724-357-2776, E-mail: sjackson@iup.edu. *Application contact:* Dr. David Chambers, Graduate Coordinator, 724-357-2776, E-mail: chambers@iup.edu.

Indiana University–Purdue University Indianapolis, School of Liberal Arts, Department of Political Science, Indianapolis, IN 46202-2896. Offers MA, Certificate.

Institute for Christian Studies, Graduate Programs, Toronto, ON M5T 1R4, Canada. Offers education (M Phil F, PhD); history of philosophy (M Phil F, PhD); philosophical aesthetics (M Phil F, PhD); philosophy of religion (M Phil F, PhD); political theory (M Phil F, PhD); systematic philosophy (M Phil F, PhD); theology (M Phil F, PhD); worldview studies (MWS). Part-time programs available. Postbaccalaureate distance learning degree programs offered (minimal on-campus study). *Degree requirements:* For master's, one foreign language, thesis; for doctorate, 2 foreign languages, thesis/dissertation. *Entrance requirements:* For master's and doctorate, philosophy background. Additional exam requirements/recommendations for international students: Required—TOEFL (minimum score 600 paper-based; 250 computer-based). *Faculty research:* Human rights, anthropology of self, medieval discourse, gender and body, post-modern thought; biblical hermeneutics, creational aesthetics, ecumenism, epistemology, political theory and public policy, relational psychotherapy.

The Institute of World Politics, Graduate Programs in National Security, Intelligence, and International Affairs, Washington, DC 20036. Offers American foreign policy (Certificate); comparative political culture (Certificate); counterintelligence (Certificate); democracy building (Certificate); intelligence (Certificate); international politics (Certificate); national security affairs (Certificate); public diplomacy and political warfare (Certificate); statecraft and national security affairs (MA); statecraft and world politics (MA); strategic intelligence studies (MA). Part-time and evening/weekend programs available. *Degree requirements:* For master's, comprehensive exam, thesis optional. *Entrance requirements:* For master's, GRE General Test. Additional exam requirements/recommendations for international students: Required—TOEFL. Electronic applications accepted. *Faculty research:* Intelligence, national security, statecraft.

See Close-Up on page 867.

Iowa State University of Science and Technology, Graduate College, College of Liberal Arts and Sciences, Department of Political Science, Ames, IA 50011. Offers political science (MA); public administration (MPA); JD/MA. *Accreditation:* NASPAA. *Faculty:* 11 full-time (3 women), 5 part-time/adjunct (3 women). *Students:* 22 full-time (8 women), 35 part-time (20 women); includes 3 minority (1 African American, 2 Asian Americans or Pacific Islanders), 9 international. 58 applicants, 67% accepted, 22 enrolled. In 2008, 13 master's awarded. *Degree requirements:* For master's, thesis (for some programs). *Entrance requirements:* For master's, GRE General Test, GMAT or LSAT. Additional exam requirements/recommendations for international students: Required—TOEFL (minimum score 570 paper-based; 80 iBT), IELTS (6.5) or TOEFL. *Application deadline:* For fall admission, 1/1 priority date for domestic and international students; for spring admission, 10/1 for domestic and international students. Applications are processed on a rolling basis. Application fee: $30 ($70 for international students). Electronic applications accepted. *Expenses:* Tuition, area resident: Full-time $6446; part-time $359 per credit. Tuition, state resident: full-time $6446; part-time $359 per credit. Tuition, nonresident: full-time $17,330; part-time $963 per credit. Required fees: $790; $249.25 per semester. Tuition and fees vary according to course load and program. *Financial support:* In 2008–09, 14 research assistantships with full and partial tuition reimbursements (averaging $12,150 per year), 1 teaching assistantship with full and partial tuition reimbursement (averaging $12,600 per year) were awarded; fellowships, scholarships/grants, health care benefits, and unspecified assistantships also available. *Unit head:* Dr. James M. McCormick, Chair, 515-294-8682, Fax: 515-294-1003, E-mail: polsc@iastate.edu. *Application contact:* Dr. Mack Shelley, Director of Graduate Education, 515-294-1075, E-mail: polsci@iastate.edu.

Jackson State University, Graduate School, School of Liberal Arts, Department of Political Science, Jackson, MS 39217. Offers MA. Part-time and evening/weekend programs available. *Degree requirements:* For master's, comprehensive exam, thesis or alternative. *Entrance requirements:* For master's, GRE General Test. Additional exam requirements/recommendations for international students: Required—TOEFL.

Jacksonville State University, College of Graduate Studies and Continuing Education, College of Arts and Sciences, Department of Political Science, Jacksonville, AL 36265-1602. Offers MPA. Part-time and evening/weekend programs available. *Faculty:* 6 full-time (1 woman). *Students:* 23 full-time (16 women), 130 part-time (59 women); includes 57 minority (55 African Americans, 1 Asian American or Pacific Islander, 1 Hispanic American), 7 international. Average age 32. 93 applicants, 46% accepted, 38 enrolled. In 2008, 42 master's awarded. *Degree requirements:* For master's, comprehensive exam, thesis (for some programs). *Entrance requirements:* For master's, GRE General Test or MAT. *Application deadline:* Applications are processed on a rolling basis. Application fee: $30. Electronic applications accepted. *Expenses:* Tuition, area resident: Full-time $4560; part-time $225 per credit hour. Tuition, state resident: full-time $4560; part-time $450 per credit hour. Tuition, nonresident: full-time $9120; part-time $450 per credit hour. *Financial support:* In 2008–09, 105 students received support. Available to part-time students. Application deadline: 4/1; *Unit head:* Dr. Lawson Veasey, Head, 256-782-8130. *Application contact:* Dr. Jean Pugliese, Associate Dean, 256-782-8278, Fax: 256-782-5321, E-mail: pugliese@jsu.edu.

James Madison University, The Graduate School, College of Arts and Letters, Department of Political Science, Program in Political Science, Harrisonburg, VA 22807. Offers MA. Part-time programs available. *Students:* 16 full-time (12 women); includes 2 minority (1 Asian American or Pacific Islander, 1 Hispanic American). Average age 27. *Entrance requirements:* For master's, GRE General Test, GRE Writing Test, 2 letters of recommendation; resumé; goals, language proficiency and policy interest statements. Additional exam requirements/recommendations for international students: Required—TOEFL. *Application deadline:* For fall admission, 5/1 priority date for domestic students; for spring admission, 9/1 priority date for domestic students. Applications are processed on a rolling basis. Application fee: $55. Electronic applications accepted. *Expenses:* Tuition, area resident: Full-time $7008; part-time $292 per credit hour. Tuition, state resident: full-time $7008; part-time $292 per credit hour. Tuition, nonresident: full-time $20,352; part-time $848 per credit hour. *Financial support:* Application deadline: 3/1; *Unit head:* Dr. Jessica Adolino, Academic Unit Head, 540-568-6149, E-mail: adolinjr@jmu.edu. *Application contact:* Dr. B. Douglas Skelley, Graduate Coordinator, 540-568-6149.

The Johns Hopkins University, Zanvyl Krieger School of Arts and Sciences, Advanced Academic Programs, Program in Government, Washington, DC 20036. Offers government (MA); national securities study (Certificate); MA/MBA. Part-time and evening/weekend programs available. *Degree requirements:* For master's, thesis. *Entrance requirements:* For master's, minimum GPA of 3.0. Additional exam requirements/recommendations for international students: Required—TOEFL (minimum score 250 computer-based; 100 iBT). Electronic applications accepted.

The Johns Hopkins University, Zanvyl Krieger School of Arts and Sciences, Department of Political Science, Baltimore, MD 21218-2699. Offers MA, PhD. *Degree requirements:* For doctorate, one foreign language, thesis/dissertation. *Entrance requirements:* For doctorate, GRE General Test. Additional exam requirements/recommendations for international students: Required—TOEFL. Electronic applications accepted. *Faculty research:* American politics, comparative politics, international relations, political theory, urban politics.

Kansas State University, Graduate School, College of Arts and Sciences, Department of Political Science, Program in Political Science, Manhattan, KS 66506. Offers international service (MA); political science (MA). Part-time programs available. *Students:* 13 full-time (6 women), 11 part-time (6 women); includes 3 minority (all African Americans), 5 international. Average age 27. 16 applicants, 94% accepted, 8 enrolled. In 2008, 10 master's awarded. *Degree requirements:* For master's, thesis or alternative. *Entrance requirements:* For master's, GRE (recommended), minimum GPA of 3.0. Additional exam requirements/recommendations for international students: Required—TOEFL (minimum score 550 paper-based; 213 computer-based). *Application deadline:* For fall admission, 2/1 priority date for domestic and international students; for spring admission, 10/1 for domestic students, 8/1 priority date for international students. Applications are processed on a rolling basis. Application fee: $30 ($55 for international students). *Expenses:* Tuition, area resident: Full-time $6466; part-time $269.40 per credit hour. Tuition, state resident: full-time $6466; part-time $269.40 per credit hour. Tuition, nonresident: full-time $14,874; part-time $619.75 per credit hour. Required fees: $673; $23.40 per credit hour. Tuition and fees vary according to campus/location. *Financial support:* Fellowships, research assistantships, teaching assistantships, institutionally sponsored loans and scholarships/grants available. Support available to part-time students. Financial award application deadline: 3/1; financial award applicants required to submit FAFSA. *Application contact:* James Franke, Director, 785-532-0451, Fax: 785-532-2339, E-mail: jfranke@ksu.edu.

Kaplan University–Davenport Campus, School of Legal Studies, Davenport, IA 52807-2095. Offers health care delivery (MS); pathway to paralegal (Postbaccalaureate Certificate); state and local government (MS). Part-time and evening/weekend programs available. Postbaccalaureate distance learning degree programs offered (no on-campus study). *Entrance requirements:* For master's, GPA requirement. Additional exam requirements/recommendations for international students: Required—TOEFL (minimum score 550 paper-based; 218 computer-based; 80 iBT).

Kean University, College of Humanities and Social Sciences, Program in Political Science, Union, NJ 07083. Offers MA. Part-time and evening/weekend programs available. *Faculty:* 7 full-time (0 women). *Students:* 7 full-time (3 women), 9 part-time (3 women); includes 2 African Americans, 5 Hispanic Americans, 1 international. Average age 29. 9 applicants, 89% accepted, 7 enrolled. In 2008, 7 master's awarded. *Degree requirements:* For master's, comprehensive exam, thesis. *Entrance requirements:* For master's, GRE General Test, minimum GPA of 3.0, 3 letters of recommendation. *Application deadline:* For fall admission, 5/1 for domestic students; for spring admission, 11/1 for domestic students. Application fee: $60 ($150 for international students). Electronic applications accepted. *Expenses:* Tuition, state resident: full-time $10,128; part-time $422 per credit. Tuition, nonresident: full-time $13,728; part-time $572 per credit. Required fees: $2570; $107 per credit. Part-time tuition and fees vary according to course load, degree level and program. *Financial support:* In 2008–09, 2 research assistantships with full tuition reimbursements (averaging $3,217 per year) were awarded; unspecified assistantships also available. *Unit head:* Dr. Lawrence S. Chang, Program Coordinator, 908-737-3990, E-mail: lchang@kean.edu. *Application contact:* Steven Koch, Pre-Admissions Coordinator, 908-737-4723, Fax: 908-737-5965, E-mail: grad-adm@kean.edu.

Kent State University, College of Arts and Sciences, Department of Political Science, Kent, OH 44242-0001. Offers political science (MA); public administration (MPA); public policy (PhD). Part-time programs available. Postbaccalaureate distance learning degree programs offered. *Degree requirements:* For master's, thesis optional; for doctorate, 2 foreign languages, thesis/dissertation. *Entrance requirements:* For master's, GRE General Test, minimum GPA of 2.75; for doctorate, GRE General Test, minimum GPA of 3.0. Additional exam requirements/recommendations for international students: Required—TOEFL. Electronic applications accepted.

Lamar University, College of Graduate Studies, College of Arts and Sciences, Department of Political Science, Beaumont, TX 77710. Offers public administration (MPA). Part-time programs available. *Faculty:* 3 full-time (0 women). *Students:* 6 full-time (3 women), 4 part-time (2 women); includes 5 minority (4 African Americans, 1 Asian American or Pacific Islander). Average age 26. 18 applicants, 39% accepted, 5 enrolled. In 2008, 2 master's awarded. *Entrance requirements:* For master's, GRE General Test. Additional exam requirements/recommendations for international students: Required—TOEFL. *Application deadline:* For fall admission, 8/1 for domestic students; for spring admission, 12/1 for domestic students. Applications are processed on a rolling basis. Application fee: $25 ($50 for international students). *Expenses:* Tuition, state resident: full-time $5000; part-time $195 per credit. Tuition, nonresident: full-time $12,376; part-time $476 per credit. Required fees: $1570. *Financial support:* Fellowships, research assistantships, teaching assistantships, career-related internships or fieldwork, Federal Work-Study, and institutionally sponsored loans available. Financial award application deadline: 4/1. *Faculty research:* Political activities of administrators, administrative response to Hurricane Rita, budgeting, environmental politics, urban planning. *Unit head:* Dr. Glenn Utter, Chair, 409-880-8526, Fax: 409-880-8710. *Application contact:* Dr. Terri Davis, Director, 409-880-8533, Fax: 409-880-1710, E-mail: davistb@hal.lamar.edu.

Lehigh University, College of Arts and Sciences, Department of Political Science, Bethlehem, PA 18015. Offers politics and policy (MA). Part-time programs available. *Faculty:* 10 full-time (5 women), 1 (woman) part-time/adjunct. *Students:* 13 full-time (8 women), 4 part-time (3 women); includes 3 minority (1 African American, 1 Asian American or Pacific Islander, 1 Hispanic American), 1 international. Average age 25. 22 applicants, 59% accepted, 11 enrolled. In 2008, 13 master's awarded. *Degree requirements:* For master's, comprehensive exam (for some programs), thesis optional. *Entrance requirements:* For master's, GRE General Test. Additional exam requirements/recommendations for international students: Required—TOEFL (minimum score 560 paper-based; 223 computer-based). *Application deadline:* For fall admission, 7/15 for domestic and international students; for spring admission, 12/1 for domestic and international students. Applications are processed on a rolling basis. Application fee: $65. Electronic applications accepted. *Financial support:* In 2008–09, 2 teaching assistantships with full tuition reimbursements were awarded; fellowships, research assistantships, career-related internships or fieldwork and tuition waivers (partial) also available. Financial award application deadline: 1/15. *Faculty research:* American politics and institutions, comparative politics. *Unit head:* Dr. Richard K. Matthews, Chairman, 610-758-3340, Fax: 610-758-3348, E-mail: rm02@lehigh.edu. *Application contact:* Dr. Frank L. Davis, Director, Graduate Studies, 610-758-5987, Fax: 610-758-3348, E-mail: fld1@lehigh.edu.

Lincoln University, School of Graduate Studies and Continuing Education, College of Liberal Arts, Education and Journalism, Department of Social and Behavioral Sciences, Jefferson City, MO 65102. Offers history (MA); social science (MA), including history, political science, sociology; sociology (MA); sociology/criminal justice (MA). Part-time and evening/weekend programs available. *Faculty:* 11 full-time (4 women), 4 part-time/adjunct (2 women). *Students:* 6 full-time (3 women), 21 part-time (11 women); includes 8 minority (all African Americans), 5 international. Average age 33. 13 applicants, 100% accepted, 9 enrolled. In 2008, 14 master's awarded. *Degree requirements:* For master's, comprehensive exam, thesis optional. *Entrance requirements:* For master's, GRE General Test or MAT, 15 undergraduate hours of course work in social science including 6 hours upper-division, with 9 hours in the area of concentration. Additional exam requirements/recommendations for international students: Required—TOEFL (minimum score 500 paper-based; 173 computer-based; 61 iBT). *Application deadline:* For fall admission, 7/1 priority date for domestic and international students; for spring admission, 12/1 priority date for domestic and international students. Applications are processed on a rolling basis. Application fee: $20. *Expenses:* Tuition, area resident: Full-time $4185; part-time $232.50 per credit hour. Tuition, nonresident: full-time $7767; part-time $431.50 per credit hour. Required fees: $270; $15 per credit hour. $252.50 per semester. One-time fee: $20. Tuition and fees vary according to course load. *Financial support:* Federal Work-Study and scholarships/grants available. Financial award application deadline: 4/1; financial award applicants required to submit FAFSA. *Faculty research:* Suicide prevention. *Unit head:* Dr. Debra F. Greene, Department Head, 573-681-5145, Fax: 573-681-5150, E-mail: greened@lincolnu.edu. *Application contact:* Irasema Steck, Administrative Assistant, 573-681-5247, Fax: 573-681-5106, E-mail: gradschool@lincolnu.edu.

Long Island University, Brooklyn Campus, Richard L. Conolly College of Liberal Arts and Sciences, Department of Political Science, Brooklyn, NY 11201-8423. Offers MA. Part-time and evening/weekend programs available. *Degree requirements:* For master's, thesis or alternative. *Entrance requirements:* For master's, 2 letters of recommendation. Additional exam requirements/recommendations for international students: Required—TOEFL (minimum score 550 paper-based; 173 computer-based). Electronic applications accepted.

Long Island University, C.W. Post Campus, College of Liberal Arts and Sciences, Department of Political Science/International Studies, Brookville, NY 11548-1300. Offers MA. Part-time and evening/weekend programs available. *Degree requirements:* For master's, comprehensive exam, thesis or alternative. *Entrance requirements:* For master's, GRE. Electronic applications accepted. *Faculty research:* International relations, Middle Eastern politics, political philosophy.

Louisiana State University and Agricultural and Mechanical College, Graduate School, College of Arts and Sciences, Department of Political Science, Baton Rouge, LA 70803. Offers MA, PhD. Terminal master's awarded for partial completion of doctoral program. *Degree requirements:* For master's, thesis or alternative; for doctorate, one foreign language, thesis/dissertation. *Entrance requirements:* For master's and doctorate, GRE General Test, minimum GPA of 3.0. Additional exam requirements/recommendations for international students: Required—TOEFL (minimum score 550 paper-based; 213 computer-based; 79 iBT). Electronic applications accepted. *Faculty research:* American government and policy, political theory, international relations and comparative politics.

Loyola University Chicago, Graduate School, Department of Political Science, Chicago, IL 60611-2196. Offers political science (MA, PhD); public policy (MPP); JD/MA. Part-time and evening/weekend programs available. *Faculty:* 18 full-time (2 women), 1 (woman) part-time/adjunct. *Students:* 27 full-time (13 women), 6 part-time (1 woman); includes 1 minority (African American), 3 international. Average age 29. 88 applicants, 50% accepted, 14 enrolled. In 2008, 11 master's, 2 doctorates awarded. *Degree requirements:* For master's, thesis or alternative; for doctorate, variable foreign language requirement, comprehensive exam, thesis/dissertation. *Entrance requirements:* For master's and doctorate, GRE General Test. *Application deadline:* For fall admission, 6/1 for domestic students; for spring admission, 10/1 for domestic students. Applications are processed on a rolling basis. Application fee: $50. Electronic applications accepted. *Expenses:* Tuition: Full-time $13,500; part-time $750 per credit hour. Required fees: $60 per semester. Full-time tuition and fees vary according to program. *Financial support:* In 2008–09, 5 fellowships with full tuition reimbursements (averaging $14,000 per year), 5 research assistantships with full tuition reimbursements (averaging $14,000 per year) were awarded; Federal Work-Study, institutionally sponsored loans, scholarships/grants, tuition waivers (partial), and unspecified assistantships also available. Financial award application deadline: 2/15; financial award applicants required to submit FAFSA. *Faculty research:* American parties and elections, state and local politics, American political institutions, international political economy, modern and contemporary political thought. *Unit head:* Prof. Peter M. Sanchez, Chair, 773-508-8658, Fax: 773-508-3131, E-mail: psanche@luc.edu. *Application contact:* Prof. Peter M. Sanchez, Chair, 773-508-8658, Fax: 773-508-3131, E-mail: psanche@luc.edu.

Marquette University, Graduate School, College of Arts and Sciences, Department of Political Science/International Affairs, Milwaukee, WI 53201-1881. Offers international affairs (MA), including comparative politics, international political economy, international politics; political

Political Science

Marquette University (continued)
science (MA), including American politics, comparative politics, international politics, political philosophy; JD/MA. Part-time programs available. *Degree requirements:* For master's, comprehensive exam, thesis optional. *Entrance requirements:* For master's, GRE General Test. Additional exam requirements/recommendations for international students: Required—TOEFL. *Faculty research:* Public opinion and electoral behavior, public policy analysis, Congress and the Presidency, judicial behavior, political system transitions.

Marshall University, Academic Affairs Division, College of Liberal Arts, Department of Political Science, Huntington, WV 25755. Offers MA. *Degree requirements:* For master's, thesis optional. *Entrance requirements:* For master's, GRE General Test.

Massachusetts Institute of Technology, School of Humanities, Arts, and Social Sciences, Department of Political Science, Cambridge, MA 02139-4307. Offers SM, PhD. Terminal master's awarded for partial completion of doctoral program. *Degree requirements:* For master's, thesis; for doctorate, one foreign language, comprehensive exam, thesis/dissertation. *Entrance requirements:* For master's and doctorate, GRE General Test. Additional exam requirements/recommendations for international students: Required—TOEFL (minimum score 600 paper-based; 250 computer-based). *Faculty research:* International security; American politics; political economy; ethnic conflict and politics; democratization.

McGill University, Faculty of Graduate and Postdoctoral Studies, Faculty of Arts, Department of Political Science, Montréal, QC H3A 2T5, Canada. Offers MA, PhD.

McMaster University, School of Graduate Studies, Faculty of Social Sciences, Department of Political Science, Hamilton, ON L8S 4M2, Canada. Offers international relations (PhD); political science (MA); public and the global economy (MA); public policy (PhD); public policy and administration (MA). Part-time programs available. *Degree requirements:* For master's, thesis or alternative. *Entrance requirements:* For master's, minimum B+ average. Additional exam requirements/recommendations for international students: Required—TOEFL (minimum score 580 paper-based; 237 computer-based). *Faculty research:* Organizational theory, internationalization of public policy, water resource policies, political interest intermediation, comparative politics.

Memorial University of Newfoundland, School of Graduate Studies, Department of Political Science, St. John's, NL A1C 5S7, Canada. Offers MA. Part-time and evening/weekend programs available. *Degree requirements:* For master's, thesis optional. *Entrance requirements:* For master's, minimum 2nd class bachelor's degree. Electronic applications accepted. *Faculty research:* Comparative politics, Canadian government and politics, Newfoundland politics, and the politics of multi-level systems.

Miami University, Graduate School, College of Arts and Sciences, Department of Political Science, Oxford, OH 45056. Offers MA, MAT, PhD. *Degree requirements:* For master's, thesis (for some programs), final exam; for doctorate, comprehensive exam, thesis/dissertation, final exams. *Entrance requirements:* For master's, GRE, minimum undergraduate GPA of 3.0 during previous 2 years or 2.75 overall; for doctorate, GRE, minimum undergraduate GPA of 2.75, 3.0 graduate. Additional exam requirements/recommendations for international students: Required—TOEFL (minimum score 550 paper-based; 213 computer-based), TWE (minimum score 4). Electronic applications accepted.

Michigan State University, The Graduate School, College of Social Science, Department of Political Science, East Lansing, MI 48824. Offers political science (MA, PhD); public policy (MPP). *Degree requirements:* For master's, practicum; for doctorate, comprehensive exam, presentation of dissertation. *Entrance requirements:* Additional exam requirements/recommendations for international students: Required—TOEFL. Electronic applications accepted.

Midwestern State University, Graduate Studies, College of Humanities and Social Sciences, Department of Political Science, Wichita Falls, TX 76308. Offers MA. *Degree requirements:* For master's, one foreign language, comprehensive exam. *Entrance requirements:* For master's, GRE General Test. Additional exam requirements/recommendations for international students: Required—TOEFL (minimum score 550 paper-based; 213 computer-based). Electronic applications accepted.

Mississippi College, Graduate School, College of Arts and Sciences, School of Humanities and Social Sciences, Department of History and Political Science, Clinton, MS 39058. Offers administration of justice (MSS); history (M Ed, MA, MSS); paralegal studies (Certificate); political science (MSS); social sciences (M Ed, MSS). Part-time programs available. *Degree requirements:* For master's, one foreign language, comprehensive exam, thesis (for some programs). *Entrance requirements:* For master's, GRE or NTE, minimum GPA of 2.5. Additional exam requirements/recommendations for international students: Recommended—IELTS. Electronic applications accepted.

Mississippi State University, College of Arts and Sciences, Department of Political Science and Public Administration, Mississippi State, MS 39762. Offers political science (MA); public policy and administration (MPPA, PhD). *Accreditation:* NASPAA (one or more programs are accredited). Evening/weekend programs available. *Degree requirements:* For master's, comprehensive oral or written exam; for doctorate, thesis/dissertation, comprehensive oral and written exam. *Entrance requirements:* For master's, minimum GPA of 3.0; for doctorate, GRE General Test, minimum graduate GPA of 3.35. Additional exam requirements/recommendations for international students: Required—TOEFL. *Faculty research:* American politics, international relations, state and local government, comparative government, public administration.

Missouri State University, Graduate College, College of Humanities and Public Affairs, Department of Political Science, Springfield, MO 65804-0094. Offers international affairs and administration (MIAA); public administration (MPA). Part-time programs available. *Faculty:* 12 full-time (1 woman). *Students:* 47 full-time (16 women), 17 part-time (7 women); includes 8 minority (3 African Americans, 3 Asian Americans or Pacific Islanders, 2 Hispanic Americans), 10 international. Average age 27. 34 applicants, 91% accepted, 24 enrolled. In 2008, 25 master's awarded. *Degree requirements:* For master's, variable foreign language requirement, comprehensive exam, thesis or alternative. *Entrance requirements:* For master's, GRE, minimum GPA of 3.0. Additional exam requirements/recommendations for international students: Required—TOEFL (minimum score 550 paper-based; 213 computer-based; 79 iBT). *Application deadline:* For fall admission, 7/20 priority date for domestic students, 5/1 for international students; for spring admission, 12/20 priority date for domestic students, 9/1 for international students. Applications are processed on a rolling basis. Application fee: $35 ($50 for international students). Electronic applications accepted. *Expenses:* Tuition, state resident: full-time $3852; part-time $214 per credit hour. Tuition, nonresident: full-time $7524; part-time $418 per credit hour. Required fees: $230 per semester. Tuition and fees vary according to course level and course load. *Financial support:* In 2008–09, 1 research assistantship with full tuition reimbursement (averaging $9,730 per year), 2 teaching assistantships with full tuition reimbursements (averaging $8,535 per year) were awarded; career-related internships or fieldwork, Federal Work-Study, scholarships/grants, and unspecified assistantships also available. Support available to part-time students. Financial award application deadline: 3/31; financial award applicants required to submit FAFSA. *Unit head:* Dr. George Connor, Acting Head, 417-836-5630, Fax: 417-836-6655, E-mail: georgeconnor@missouristate.edu. *Application contact:* Dr. George Connor, Acting Head, 417-836-5630, Fax: 417-836-6655, E-mail: georgeconnor@missouristate.edu.

Naval Postgraduate School, Graduate Programs, Department of National Security Affairs, Monterey, CA 93943. Offers intelligence (MA); international relations (MA); political science (MA); regional security education (MA); security building (MA); security studies (MA). Program only open to commissioned officers of the United States and friendly nations and selected United States federal civilian employees. Part-time programs available. *Degree requirements:* For master's, thesis.

New Mexico State University, Graduate School, College of Arts and Sciences, Department of Government, Las Cruces, NM 88003-8001. Offers MA, MPA. *Accreditation:* NASPAA (one or more programs are accredited). Part-time and evening/weekend programs available. *Faculty:* 11 full-time (4 women). *Students:* 27 full-time (14 women), 16 part-time (5 women); includes 13 minority (1 American Indian/Alaska Native, 1 Asian American or Pacific Islander, 11 Hispanic Americans), 4 international. Average age 30. 36 applicants, 94% accepted, 25 enrolled. In 2008, 13 master's awarded. *Degree requirements:* For master's, comprehensive exam (for some programs), thesis optional. *Entrance requirements:* For master's, GRE (if GPA is below 3.0), writing sample, 3 letters of recommendation, resumé. Additional exam requirements/recommendations for international students: Required—TOEFL (minimum score 530 paper-based; 197 computer-based). *Application deadline:* Applications are processed on a rolling basis. Application fee: $30 ($50 for international students). Electronic applications accepted. *Expenses:* Tuition, area resident: Full-time $3890; part-time $212.85 per credit. Tuition, state resident: full-time $3890; part-time $212.85 per credit. Tuition, nonresident: full-time $13,916; part-time $630.55 per credit. Required fees: $1218; $609 per semester. *Financial support:* In 2008–09, 15 students received support, including 1 research assistantship (averaging $15,800 per year), 13 teaching assistantships with tuition reimbursements available (averaging $8,246 per year); career-related internships or fieldwork, Federal Work-Study, scholarships/grants, health care benefits, and unspecified assistantships also available. Support available to part-time students. Financial award application deadline: 3/1. *Faculty research:* U.S./Mexico border studies, public administration and policy, international relations, Latin America, American politics and theory. *Unit head:* Dr. Nancy Baker, Head, 575-646-4935, Fax: 575-646-2052, E-mail: nbaker@nmsu.edu. *Application contact:* Rona M. Lujan, Department Secretary, 575-646-4734, Fax: 575-646-2052, E-mail: rona@nmsu.edu.

The New School: A University, The New School for Social Research, Department of Political Science, New York, NY 10011. Offers MA, DS Sc, PhD. Part-time and evening/weekend programs available. *Faculty:* 13 full-time (5 women), 2 part-time/adjunct (1 woman). *Students:* 125 full-time (56 women), 30 part-time (18 women); includes 20 minority (8 African Americans, 2 Asian Americans or Pacific Islanders, 10 Hispanic Americans), 56 international. Average age 32. In 2008, 21 master's, 10 doctorates awarded. Terminal master's awarded for partial completion of doctoral program. *Degree requirements:* For master's, exam or major paper; for doctorate, one foreign language, thesis/dissertation, qualifying exam. *Entrance requirements:* For master's, GRE General Test; for doctorate, GRE General Test, MA. Additional exam requirements/recommendations for international students: Required—TOEFL (minimum score 600 paper-based; 250 computer-based; 100 iBT). *Application deadline:* For fall admission, 1/15 priority date for domestic students. Applications are processed on a rolling basis. Application fee: $50. *Expenses:* Tuition: Full-time $27,144; part-time $1508 per credit. Required fees: $355 per semester. *Financial support:* Fellowships, research assistantships, teaching assistantships, career-related internships or fieldwork, Federal Work-Study, scholarships/grants, and tuition waivers (full and partial) available. Financial award application deadline: 3/1; financial award applicants required to submit FAFSA. *Faculty research:* Democratic transitions and institution; race, class and gender; immigration and incorporation. *Unit head:* Dr. Victoria Hattam, Chair, 212-229-5747 Ext. 3082, Fax: 212-229-5315, E-mail: hattamv@newschool.edu. *Application contact:* Robert MacDonald, Director of Admissions, 800-523-5710 Ext. 3007, Fax: 212-989-7102, E-mail: macdonar@newschool.edu.

See Close-Up on page 1251.

New York University, Graduate School of Arts and Science, Department of Politics, New York, NY 10012-1019. Offers political campaign management (MA); politics (MA, PhD); JD/MA; MBA/MA. Part-time programs available. Terminal master's awarded for partial completion of doctoral program. *Degree requirements:* For master's, one foreign language, thesis or alternative; for doctorate, 2 foreign languages, comprehensive exam, thesis/dissertation. *Entrance requirements:* For master's, GRE General Test; for doctorate, GRE General Test, master's degree in political science, minimum GPA of 2.5. Additional exam requirements/recommendations for international students: Required—TOEFL. *Faculty research:* Comparative politics, democratic theory and practice, rational choice, political economy; international relations.

Northeastern Illinois University, Graduate College, College of Arts and Sciences, Department of Political Science, Program in Political Science, Chicago, IL 60625-4699. Offers MA. Part-time and evening/weekend programs available. *Degree requirements:* For master's, comprehensive exam, thesis optional, minimum GPA of 3.0. *Entrance requirements:* For master's, minimum GPA of 2.75. Additional exam requirements/recommendations for international students: Required—TOEFL (minimum score 550 paper-based; 213 computer-based; 80 iBT). Electronic applications accepted. *Faculty research:* Chinese politics, Latin American democratization, Jewish feminism, administration and delegation.

Northeastern University, College of Arts and Sciences, Department of Political Science, Boston, MA 02115-5096. Offers political science (MA); public administration (MPA, Certificate), including development administration (MPA), health administration and policy (MPA), state and local government (MPA), urban studies (Certificate); public and international affairs (PhD). Part-time and evening/weekend programs available. *Degree requirements:* For master's, thesis optional; for doctorate, thesis/dissertation. *Entrance requirements:* For master's, GRE General Test. Additional exam requirements/recommendations for international students: Required—TOEFL. *Faculty research:* Presidency, public opinion, Congress, democratization, national identity.

Northern Arizona University, Graduate College, College of Social and Behavioral Sciences, Department of Political Science, Program in Political Science, Flagstaff, AZ 86011. Offers political science (MA, PhD); public management (Certificate). *Degree requirements:* For master's, thesis optional; for doctorate, one foreign language, thesis/dissertation. *Entrance requirements:* For doctorate, GRE General Test.

Northern Illinois University, Graduate School, College of Liberal Arts and Sciences, Department of Political Science, De Kalb, IL 60115-2854. Offers political science (MA, PhD); public administration (MPA). Part-time and evening/weekend programs available. Terminal master's awarded for partial completion of doctoral program. *Degree requirements:* For master's, comprehensive exam, thesis optional; for doctorate, variable foreign language requirement, thesis/dissertation, candidacy exam, dissertation defense. *Entrance requirements:* For master's, GRE General Test, minimum GPA of 2.75, 9 hours of course work in political science; for doctorate, GRE General Test, minimum GPA of 2.75 (undergraduate), 3.2 (graduate); undergraduate major in related field. Additional exam requirements/recommendations for international students: Required—TOEFL (minimum score 550 paper-based; 213 computer-based). Electronic applications accepted. *Faculty research:* Terrorism and dynamics of trade, U.S. foreign policy, political economy of development, biopolitical theory, women and politics.

Northwestern University, The Graduate School, Judd A. and Marjorie Weinberg College of Arts and Sciences, Department of Political Science, Evanston, IL 60208. Offers MA, PhD, JD/PhD. Admissions and degrees offered through The Graduate School. Terminal master's awarded for partial completion of doctoral program. *Degree requirements:* For master's, thesis or alternative; for doctorate, thesis/dissertation, qualifying exams. *Entrance requirements:* For master's and doctorate, GRE General Test, sample of written work. Additional exam requirements/recommendations for international students: Required—TOEFL. *Faculty research:* Formal theory/formal political economy, political economy of development/state-business relations, labor market institutions and welfare policy, public opinion and political behavior, feminist political theory.

The Ohio State University, Graduate School, College of Social and Behavioral Sciences, School of Social and Behavioral Science, Department of Political Science, Columbus, OH 43210. Offers MA, PhD. *Degree requirements:* For master's, thesis optional; for doctorate, thesis/dissertation. *Entrance requirements:* For master's and doctorate, GRE General Test. Additional exam requirements/recommendations for international students: Recommended—

TOEFL (minimum score 620 paper-based; 260 computer-based). Electronic applications accepted. *Faculty research:* American, comparative, and international politics; political theory.

Ohio University, Graduate College, College of Arts and Sciences, Department of Political Science, Athens, OH 45701-2979. Offers political science (MA); public administration (MPA). Part-time programs available. *Degree requirements:* For master's, comprehensive exam, thesis or alternative. *Entrance requirements:* For master's, GRE General Test, minimum GPA of 3.0. Additional exam requirements/recommendations for international students: Required—TOEFL. Electronic applications accepted. *Faculty research:* International relations, Latin American politics, public policy, economic development, political theory.

Oklahoma State University, College of Arts and Sciences, Department of Political Science, Stillwater, OK 74078. Offers fire and emergency management administration (MS, PhD); political science (MA). *Faculty:* 20 full-time (5 women), 4 part-time/adjunct (1 woman). *Students:* 15 full-time (5 women), 29 part-time (5 women); includes 9 minority (4 African Americans, 4 American Indian/Alaska Native, 1 Asian American or Pacific Islander), 3 international. Average age 35. 41 applicants, 71% accepted, 18 enrolled. In 2008, 23 master's awarded. *Degree requirements:* For master's, comprehensive exam, thesis or creative component; for doctorate, comprehensive exam, thesis/dissertation. *Entrance requirements:* For master's, GRE; for doctorate, GRE. Additional exam requirements/recommendations for international students: Required—TOEFL. *Application deadline:* For fall admission, 3/1 priority date for international students; for spring admission, 8/1 priority date for international students. Applications are processed on a rolling basis. Application fee: $40 ($75 for international students). Electronic applications accepted. *Expenses:* Tuition, state resident: full-time $3716.40; part-time $154.85 per credit hour. Tuition, nonresident: full-time $14,448; part-time $602 per credit hour. Required fees: $1772.40; $73.85 per credit hour. One-time fee: $50. Tuition and fees vary according to course load and campus/location. *Financial support:* In 2008–09, 6 teaching assistantships (averaging $12,199 per year) were awarded; career-related internships or fieldwork, Federal Work-Study, scholarships/grants, health care benefits, tuition waivers (partial), and unspecified assistantships also available. Support available to part-time students. Financial award application deadline: 3/1; financial award applicants required to submit FAFSA. *Faculty research:* Fire and emergency management, environmental dispute resolution, voting and elections, women and politics, urban politics. *Unit head:* Dr. James Scott, Head, 405-744-5569, Fax: 405-744-6534. *Application contact:* Dr. Gordon Emslie, Dean, 405-744-6368, Fax: 405-744-0355, E-mail: grad_i@okstate.edu.

Penn State University Park, Graduate School, College of the Liberal Arts, Department of Political Science, State College, University Park, PA 16802-1503. Offers MA, PhD.

Pepperdine University, School of Public Policy, Malibu, CA 90263. Offers American politics (MPP); economics (MPP); international relations (MPP); public policy (MPP); state and local policy (MPP). *Entrance requirements:* For master's, GRE, 2 letters of recommendation, resumé. Additional exam requirements/recommendations for international students: Required—TOEFL. Electronic applications accepted.

Portland State University, Graduate Studies, College of Urban and Public Affairs, Hatfield School of Government, Division of Political Science, Portland, OR 97207-0751. Offers MA, MAT, MS, MST, PhD. Part-time programs available. *Faculty:* 12 full-time (3 women), 6 part-time/adjunct (1 woman). *Students:* 15 full-time (6 women), 13 part-time (4 women); includes 2 minority (both Asian Americans or Pacific Islanders), 4 international. Average age 28. 27 applicants, 70% accepted, 18 enrolled. In 2008, 6 master's awarded. *Degree requirements:* For master's, one foreign language, comprehensive exam, thesis; for doctorate, comprehensive exam, thesis/dissertation, residency. *Entrance requirements:* For master's, GRE General Test or MAT, minimum GPA of 3.1, 2 letters of recommendation; for doctorate, GRE General Test. Additional exam requirements/recommendations for international students: Required—TOEFL (minimum score 550 paper-based; 213 computer-based). *Application deadline:* For fall admission, 4/1 priority date for domestic students, 3/1 priority date for international students. Applications are processed on a rolling basis. Application fee: $50. *Expenses:* Tuition, area resident: Full-time $8763; part-time $179 per credit hour. Tuition, state resident: full-time $8763; part-time $298 per credit hour. Tuition, nonresident: full-time $12,981; part-time $426 per credit hour. Required fees: $1242. One-time fee: $250. Tuition and fees vary according to course load and program. *Financial support:* In 2008–09, 3 research assistantships with full tuition reimbursements (averaging $9,930 per year) were awarded; teaching assistantships, career-related internships or fieldwork, Federal Work-Study, and unspecified assistantships also available. Support available to part-time students. Financial award application deadline: 3/1; financial award applicants required to submit FAFSA. *Faculty research:* Congress, presidency, political reform, international environment, hate speech. Total annual research expenditures: $30,805. *Unit head:* Melody Rose, Chair, 503-725-3921, Fax: 503-725-8444, E-mail: rosem@pdx.edu. *Application contact:* Melody Rose, Chair, 503-725-3921, Fax: 503-725-8444, E-mail: rosem@pdx.edu.

Princeton University, Graduate School, Department of Politics, Princeton, NJ 08544-1019. Offers political philosophy (PhD); politics (PhD). *Degree requirements:* For doctorate, comprehensive exam, thesis/dissertation, teaching experience. *Entrance requirements:* For doctorate, GRE General Test, sample of written work, letters of recommendation. Additional exam requirements/recommendations for international students: Required—TOEFL (minimum score 600 paper-based; 250 computer-based). Electronic applications accepted. *Faculty research:* American politics, comparative politics, formal and quantitative methods, international relations, public law, political theory.

Purdue University, Graduate School, College of Liberal Arts, Department of Political Science, West Lafayette, IN 47907. Offers MA, PhD. Part-time and evening/weekend programs available. Terminal master's awarded for partial completion of doctoral program. *Degree requirements:* For doctorate, 2 foreign languages, thesis/dissertation. *Entrance requirements:* For master's and doctorate, GRE General Test, minimum GPA of 3.0. Additional exam requirements/recommendations for international students: Required—TOEFL. Electronic applications accepted. *Faculty research:* American politics, comparative politics, political theory, public policy/public administration, international relations.

Queen's University at Kingston, School of Graduate Studies and Research, Faculty of Arts and Sciences, Department of Political Studies, Kingston, ON K7L 3N6, Canada. Offers Canadian politics (PhD); comparative politics (PhD); gender and politics (PhD); international relations (PhD); political theory (PhD). *Degree requirements:* For master's, thesis or alternative; for doctorate, one foreign language, thesis/dissertation, qualifying exams. *Entrance requirements:* Additional exam requirements/recommendations for international students: Required—TOEFL (minimum score 600 paper-based; 250 computer-based). *Faculty research:* Canadian politics, comparative politics, political thought, international politics, women and politics.

Regent University, Graduate School, Robertson School of Government, Virginia Beach, VA 23464. Offers health care policy and administration (MA); international politics (MA); law and public policy (MA); Mid-East Politics (MA); political leadership and management (MA); political management (MA); public administration (MA); public policy (MA); terrorism and homeland defense (MA); world economies and political development (MA); JD/MA; M Div/MA; M Ed/MA; MBA/MA. Part-time and evening/weekend programs available. Postbaccalaureate distance learning degree programs offered (minimal on-campus study). *Faculty:* 6 full-time (1 woman), 11 part-time/adjunct (1 woman). *Students:* 60 full-time (33 women), 69 part-time (34 women); includes 29 minority (22 African Americans, 1 Asian American or Pacific Islander, 6 Hispanic Americans), 3 international. Average age 30. 136 applicants, 54% accepted, 54 enrolled. In 2008, 48 master's awarded. *Degree requirements:* For master's, thesis optional, internship. *Entrance requirements:* For master's, GRE General Test or LSAT, minimum undergraduate GPA of 3.0, writing sample, resumé, interview, references, transcripts. Additional exam requirements/recommendations for international students: Required—TOEFL (minimum score 577 paper-based; 233 computer-based). *Application deadline:* For fall admission, 5/1 priority date for domestic students; for spring admission, 11/1 priority date for domestic students.

Applications are processed on a rolling basis. Application fee: $50. Electronic applications accepted. *Expenses:* Contact institution. *Financial support:* Career-related internships or fieldwork, scholarships/grants, tuition waivers (full and partial), and unspecified assistantships available. Support available to part-time students. Financial award application deadline: 9/1; financial award applicants required to submit FAFSA. *Faculty research:* Education reform, political character issues, social capital concerns, administrative ethics, Biblical law and public policy. *Unit head:* Dr. Charles W. Dunn, Dean, 757-352-4322, Fax: 757-352-4643, E-mail: cwdunn@regent.edu. *Application contact:* Matthew Chadwick, Director of Admissions, 800-373-5504, Fax: 757-352-4381, E-mail: admissions@regent.edu.

Rice University, Graduate Programs, School of Social Sciences, Department of Political Science, Houston, TX 77251-1892. Offers MA, PhD. Terminal master's awarded for partial completion of doctoral program. *Degree requirements:* For master's, thesis optional; for doctorate, comprehensive exam, thesis/dissertation. *Entrance requirements:* For doctorate, GRE General Test. Additional exam requirements/recommendations for international students: Required—TOEFL (minimum score 600 paper-based; 250 computer-based; 90 iBT). Electronic applications accepted. *Faculty research:* Comparative government in Western Europe and the former Soviet Union, international relations, Congress and public policy in American government, minority politics.

Roosevelt University, Graduate Division, College of Arts and Sciences, Department of Political Science and Public Administration, Program in Political Science, Chicago, IL 60605-1394. Offers MA. Part-time and evening/weekend programs available. *Students:* 3 part-time (2 women); all minorities (all African Americans). Average age 41. In 2008, 1 master's awarded. *Degree requirements:* For master's, thesis or alternative. *Entrance requirements:* For master's, minimum GPA of 2.7. *Application deadline:* For fall admission, 6/1 priority date for domestic students. Applications are processed on a rolling basis. Application fee: $25 ($35 for international students). *Expenses:* Tuition: Full-time $14,730; part-time $709 per credit. Required fees: $175 per semester. Tuition and fees vary according to course load and program. *Financial support:* Application deadline: 2/15. *Faculty research:* Metropolitan social movements, American politics, comparative politics, political theory. *Unit head:* Jeffrey Edwards, Head, 312-341-3670. *Application contact:* Joanne Canyon-Heller, Coordinator of Graduate Admission, 877-APPLY RU, Fax: 312-281-3356, E-mail: applyru@roosevelt.edu.

Rutgers, The State University of New Jersey, Newark, Graduate School, Program in Political Science, Newark, NJ 07102. Offers American political system (MA); international relations (MA); JD/MA. Part-time and evening/weekend programs available. *Degree requirements:* For master's, comprehensive exam, thesis optional. *Entrance requirements:* For master's, GRE, minimum undergraduate B average. Electronic applications accepted. *Faculty research:* Policymaking and policy evaluation in the United States; government and politics in Europe, Middle East, Asia, Africa, and Latin America.

Rutgers, The State University of New Jersey, New Brunswick, Graduate School, Department of Political Science, Piscataway, NJ 08854-8097. Offers American politics (PhD); comparative politics (PhD); international relations (PhD); political theory (PhD); public law (PhD); women and politics (PhD). *Degree requirements:* For doctorate, one foreign language, comprehensive exam, thesis/dissertation. *Entrance requirements:* For doctorate, GRE General Test. Additional exam requirements/recommendations for international students: Required—TOEFL.

St. John's University, St. John's College of Liberal Arts and Sciences, Department of Government and Politics, Program in Government and Politics, Queens, NY 11439. Offers MA, Adv C, JD/MA. Part-time and evening/weekend programs available. *Students:* 15 full-time (9 women), 84 part-time (44 women); includes 27 minority (8 African Americans, 1 American Indian/Alaska Native, 4 Asian Americans or Pacific Islanders, 14 Hispanic Americans), 10 international. Average age 28. 132 applicants, 57% accepted, 33 enrolled. In 2008, 44 master's, 26 other advanced degrees awarded. *Degree requirements:* For master's, comprehensive exam, thesis optional. *Entrance requirements:* For master's, minimum GPA of 3.0. Additional exam requirements/recommendations for international students: Required—TOEFL (minimum score 500 paper-based; 173 computer-based; 61 iBT), IELTS (minimum score 5.5). *Application deadline:* For fall admission, 5/1 priority date for domestic and international students; for spring admission, 11/1 priority date for domestic and international students. Applications are processed on a rolling basis. Application fee: $70. Electronic applications accepted. *Expenses:* Tuition: Full-time $20,760; part-time $865 per credit. Required fees: $300; $150 per semester. Tuition and fees vary according to program. *Financial support:* Research assistantships, scholarships/grants available. Support available to part-time students. Financial award application deadline: 3/1; financial award applicants required to submit FAFSA. *Unit head:* Dr. Luba Racanska, Chair, 718-990-6329, E-mail: racanskl@stjohns.edu. *Application contact:* Kathleen Davis, Director of Graduate Admissions, 718-990-2790, Fax: 718-990-5686, E-mail: gradhelp@stjohns.edu.

St. John's University, St. John's College of Liberal Arts and Sciences, Department of Government and Politics and Division of Library and Information Science, Program in Government Information Specialist, Queens, NY 11439. Offers MA/MLS. Part-time and evening/weekend programs available. *Students:* 2 applicants, 0% accepted. *Entrance requirements:* Additional exam requirements/recommendations for international students: Required—TOEFL (minimum score 500 paper-based; 173 computer-based; 61 iBT), IELTS (minimum score 5.5). *Application deadline:* For fall admission, 5/1 priority date for domestic and international students; for spring admission, 11/1 priority date for domestic and international students. Applications are processed on a rolling basis. Application fee: $70. *Expenses:* Tuition: Full-time $20,760; part-time $865 per credit. Required fees: $300; $150 per semester. Tuition and fees vary according to program. *Financial support:* Research assistantships, career-related internships or fieldwork and scholarships/grants available. Support available to part-time students. Financial award application deadline: 3/1; financial award applicants required to submit FAFSA. *Application contact:* Kathleen Davis, Director of Graduate Admission, 718-990-2790, Fax: 718-990-5686, E-mail: gradhelp@stjohns.edu.

Saint Louis University, Graduate School, College of Arts and Sciences and Graduate School, Department of Political Science, St. Louis, MO 63103-2097. Offers MA. Part-time programs available. *Entrance requirements:* For master's, GRE or LSAT, letters of recommendation, resumé, writing sample, goal statement, transcripts. Additional exam requirements/recommendations for international students: Required—TOEFL (minimum score 525 paper-based; 194 computer-based). Electronic applications accepted. *Faculty research:* Part of Asia, Africa, Latin America, and Russia; international political economy; diplomacy and international organization; theories of democracy and justice; American political institutions.

St. Mary's University, Graduate School, Department of Political Science, San Antonio, TX 78228-8507. Offers international relations (MA); political communications and applied science (MA); political science (MA); public administration (MPA), including inter-American administration, public management; JD/MA; JD/MPA. Part-time programs available. *Faculty:* 2 full-time (1 woman), 14 part-time/adjunct (3 women). *Students:* 47 full-time (30 women), 108 part-time (51 women); includes 59 minority (9 African Americans, 7 Asian Americans or Pacific Islanders, 43 Hispanic Americans), 9 international. Average age 29. 111 applicants, 74% accepted, 56 enrolled. In 2008, 79 master's awarded. *Degree requirements:* For master's, one foreign language, comprehensive exam. *Entrance requirements:* For master's, GRE General Test. Additional exam requirements/recommendations for international students: Required—TOEFL (minimum score 550 paper-based; 213 computer-based; 80 iBT). *Application deadline:* Applications are processed on a rolling basis. Application fee: $0. Electronic applications accepted. *Expenses:* Tuition: Full-time $12,006; part-time $667 per credit hour. Required fees: $440; $220 per semester. *Financial support:* In 2008–09, 21 students received support, including 18 fellowships (averaging $3,669 per year), 3 research assistantships (averaging $4,500 per year); career-related internships or fieldwork, Federal Work-Study, institutionally sponsored loans, scholarships/grants, health care benefits, and unspecified assistantships also available. Financial award application deadline: 3/31; financial award applicants required to submit FAFSA. *Faculty research:* Voting rights, natural resources and urban policy, comparative politics and international relations. *Unit head:* Dr. Sonia Garcia, Chair, 210-436-2013, Fax:

Political Science

St. Mary's University (continued)
210-431-4336, E-mail: sgarcia@stmarytx.edu. *Application contact:* Dr. Henry Flores, Dean of the Graduate School, 210-436-3101, Fax: 210-431-2220, E-mail: hflores@stmarytx.edu.

Sam Houston State University, College of Humanities and Social Sciences, Department of Political Science, Huntsville, TX 77341. Offers political science (MA); public administration (MPA). Evening/weekend programs available. *Faculty:* 7 full-time (2 women). *Students:* 10 full-time (5 women), 17 part-time (9 women); includes 5 minority (2 African Americans, 1 Asian American or Pacific Islander, 2 Hispanic Americans). Average age 29. 13 applicants, 77% accepted, 9 enrolled. In 2008, 3 master's awarded. *Degree requirements:* For master's, thesis or alternative. *Entrance requirements:* For master's, GRE General Test. Additional exam requirements/recommendations for international students: Required—TOEFL (minimum score 550 paper-based; 213 computer-based; 79 iBT). *Application deadline:* For fall admission, 8/1 for domestic students; for spring admission, 12/1 for domestic students. Applications are processed on a rolling basis. Application fee: $20. *Expenses:* Tuition, state resident: full-time $3564; part-time $198 per credit hour. Tuition, nonresident: full-time $8622; part-time $479 per credit hour. Required fees: $1290. Tuition and fees vary according to course load and campus/location. *Financial support:* Research assistantships, teaching assistantships, career-related internships or fieldwork and institutionally sponsored loans available. Support available to part-time students. Financial award application deadline: 5/31; financial award applicants required to submit FAFSA. *Unit head:* Dr. Rhonda Callaway, Chair, 936-294-4108, Fax: 936-294-4172, E-mail: rlc005@shsu.edu. *Application contact:* Dr. Corliss Lentz, Advisor, 936-294-1459.

San Diego State University, Graduate and Research Affairs, College of Arts and Letters, Department of Political Science, San Diego, CA 92182. Offers MA. Part-time programs available. *Degree requirements:* For master's, thesis. *Entrance requirements:* For master's, GRE General Test, minimum GPA of 3.0, 2 letters of reference. Additional exam requirements/recommendations for international students: Required—TOEFL. Electronic applications accepted.

San Francisco State University, Division of Graduate Studies, College of Behavioral and Social Sciences, Department of Political Science, San Francisco, CA 94132-1722. Offers MA.

Simon Fraser University, Graduate Studies, Faculty of Arts and Social Sciences, Department of Political Science, Burnaby, BC V5A 1S6, Canada. Offers MA, PhD. *Degree requirements:* For master's, thesis (for some programs); for doctorate, one foreign language, comprehensive exam, thesis/dissertation. *Entrance requirements:* For master's, minimum GPA of 3.0; for doctorate, minimum GPA of 3.67, master's in political science. Additional exam requirements/recommendations for international students: Required—TOEFL or IELTS. *Faculty research:* Theory, comparative government, public policy and administration, federalism, international relations, Canadian politics.

Sonoma State University, School of Social Sciences, Department of Political Science, Rohnert Park, CA 94928-3609. Offers public administration (MPA). Part-time and evening/weekend programs available. *Degree requirements:* For master's, thesis or alternative. *Entrance requirements:* For master's, GRE General Test, minimum GPA of 3.0. *Faculty research:* Cross-disciplinary viewpoint in public administration, public policy implementation and evaluation with emphasis on state & local politics and non-profit organizations.

Southern Connecticut State University, School of Graduate Studies, School of Arts and Sciences, Department of Political Science, New Haven, CT 06515-1355. Offers MS. Part-time and evening/weekend programs available. *Degree requirements:* For master's, thesis or alternative. *Entrance requirements:* For master's, interview. Electronic applications accepted.

Southern Illinois University Carbondale, Graduate School, College of Liberal Arts, Department of Political Science, Program in Political Science, Carbondale, IL 62901-4701. Offers MA, PhD, JD/PhD. Part-time programs available. *Degree requirements:* For doctorate, thesis/dissertation. *Entrance requirements:* For master's, GRE General Test, minimum GPA of 2.7; for doctorate, GRE General Test, minimum GPA of 3.5. Additional exam requirements/recommendations for international students: Required—TOEFL. *Faculty research:* Public law, international relations, comparative government, American government.

See Close-Up on page 877.

Southern University and Agricultural and Mechanical College, Graduate School, Nelson Mandela School of Public Policy and Urban Affairs, Department of Political Science and Geography, Baton Rouge, LA 70813. Offers social sciences (MA). *Degree requirements:* For master's, thesis. *Entrance requirements:* For master's, GMAT or GRE General Test, minimum GPA of 3.0. Additional exam requirements/recommendations for international students: Required—TOEFL. *Faculty research:* Redistricting, comparative studies, environmental politics, political geography, mayoral elections.

Stanford University, School of Humanities and Sciences, Department of Political Science, Stanford, CA 94305-9991. Offers MA, PhD. Terminal master's awarded for partial completion of doctoral program. *Degree requirements:* For doctorate, one foreign language, thesis/dissertation, oral exam. *Entrance requirements:* For master's and doctorate, GRE General Test. Additional exam requirements/recommendations for international students: Required—TOEFL. Electronic applications accepted.

State University of New York at Binghamton, Graduate School, School of Arts and Sciences, Department of Political Science, Binghamton, NY 13902-6000. Offers political science (MA, PhD); public policy (MA, PhD). *Faculty:* 11 full-time (2 women), 1 part-time/adjunct (0 women). *Students:* 33 full-time (15 women), 12 part-time (5 women); includes 3 minority (all African Americans), 19 international. Average age 27. 67 applicants, 52% accepted, 10 enrolled. In 2008, 18 master's, 1 doctorate awarded. Terminal master's awarded for partial completion of doctoral program. *Degree requirements:* For master's, thesis or alternative, written exam; for doctorate, 2 foreign languages, thesis/dissertation, written exam. *Entrance requirements:* For master's and doctorate, GRE General Test, GRE Subject Test. Additional exam requirements/recommendations for international students: Required—TOEFL. *Application deadline:* For fall admission, 4/15 priority date for domestic students, 1/15 priority date for international students; for spring admission, 11/1 for domestic students, 10/1 priority date for international students. Applications are processed on a rolling basis. Application fee: $60. Electronic applications accepted. *Expenses:* Tuition, area resident: Full-time $6900; part-time $288 per credit. Tuition, state resident: full-time $6900; part-time $288 per credit. Tuition, nonresident: full-time $10,920; part-time $455 per credit. Required fees: $1130. Part-time tuition and fees vary according to course load, program and student level. *Financial support:* In 2008–09, 27 students received support, including 1 fellowship with full tuition reimbursement available (averaging $15,000 per year), 4 research assistantships with full tuition reimbursements available (averaging $15,000 per year), 21 teaching assistantships with full tuition reimbursements available (averaging $15,000 per year); career-related internships or fieldwork, Federal Work-Study, institutionally sponsored loans, scholarships/grants, health care benefits, tuition waivers (full), and unspecified assistantships also available. Financial award application deadline: 2/15; financial award applicants required to submit FAFSA. *Unit head:* Dr. David Clark, Chairperson, 607-777-6786, E-mail: dclark@binghamton.edu. *Application contact:* Victoria Williams, Recruiting and Admissions Coordinator, 607-777-2151, Fax: 607-777-2501, E-mail: vwilliam@binghamton.edu.

Stony Brook University, State University of New York, Graduate School, College of Arts and Sciences, Department of Political Science, Stony Brook, NY 11794. Offers political science (MA, PhD); public policy (MAPP). Evening/weekend programs available. *Faculty:* 16 full-time (3 women), 1 part-time/adjunct (0 women). *Students:* 64 full-time (19 women), 16 part-time (9 women); includes 22 minority (11 African Americans, 7 Asian Americans or Pacific Islanders, 4 Hispanic Americans), 11 international. Average age 27. 125 applicants, 52% accepted. In 2008, 36 master's, 3 doctorates awarded. *Degree requirements:* For doctorate, thesis/dissertation. *Entrance requirements:* For master's and doctorate, GRE General Test. *Application*

---

deadline: For fall admission, 1/15 for domestic students. Application fee: $60. *Expenses:* Tuition, area resident: Full-time $7880; part-time $328 per credit hour. Tuition, state resident: full-time $7880; part-time $328 per credit hour. Tuition, nonresident: full-time $13,250; part-time $552 per credit hour. Required fees: $848. *Financial support:* In 2008–09, 32 teaching assistantships were awarded; fellowships, research assistantships also available. Total annual research expenditures: $93,902. *Unit head:* Dr. Jeffrey Segal, Chair, 631-632-7640. *Application contact:* Dr. Charles Taber, Director, 631-632-7667, Fax: 631-632-4116, E-mail: charles.taber@stonybrook.edu.

Suffolk University, College of Arts and Sciences, Department of Government, Boston, MA 02108-2770. Offers international relations (MSPS); political science (MSPS); professional politics (MSPS, CAGS); MPA/MSPS. Part-time and evening/weekend programs available. *Degree requirements:* For master's, thesis optional. *Entrance requirements:* For master's, GRE General Test or MAT, statement of professional goals, official transcripts, 2 letters of recommendation, resumé. Additional exam requirements/recommendations for international students: Required—TOEFL (minimum score 550 paper-based; 213 computer-based; 80 iBT). Electronic applications accepted. *Expenses:* Contact institution. *Faculty research:* Political parties, women in politics, Canadian politics, public policy, legislative policies.

Sul Ross State University, School of Arts and Sciences, Department of Behavioral and Social Sciences, Program in Political Science, Alpine, TX 79832. Offers MA. Part-time and evening/weekend programs available. *Degree requirements:* For master's, thesis optional. *Entrance requirements:* For master's, GRE General Test, minimum undergraduate GPA of 2.5 in last 60 hours. *Faculty research:* Local government, state government, borderland studies, British studies.

Syracuse University, Graduate School, Maxwell School of Citizenship and Public Affairs, Program in Political Science, Syracuse, NY 13244. Offers MA, PhD. *Degree requirements:* For doctorate, thesis/dissertation. *Entrance requirements:* For master's and doctorate, GRE General Test. Additional exam requirements/recommendations for international students: Required—TOEFL. Electronic applications accepted.

Tarleton State University, College of Graduate Studies, College of Liberal and Fine Arts, Department of Social Sciences, Stephenville, TX 76402. Offers history (MA); political science (MA). Part-time and evening/weekend programs available. Postbaccalaureate distance learning degree programs offered (minimal on-campus study). *Faculty:* 7 full-time (2 women), 1 part-time/adjunct (0 women). *Students:* 8 full-time (3 women), 27 part-time (13 women); includes 7 minority (3 African Americans, 4 Hispanic Americans). Average age 36. 21 applicants, 67% accepted, 13 enrolled. In 2008, 11 master's awarded. *Degree requirements:* For master's, variable foreign language requirement, comprehensive exam, thesis optional. *Entrance requirements:* For master's, GRE General Test, minimum GPA of 3.0. Additional exam requirements/recommendations for international students: Required—TOEFL (minimum score 550 paper-based; 213 computer-based; 80 iBT). *Application deadline:* For fall admission, 8/5 priority date for domestic students; for spring admission, 12/1 for domestic students. Applications are processed on a rolling basis. Application fee: $30 ($130 for international students). Electronic applications accepted. *Expenses:* Tuition, area resident: Full-time $2853; part-time $158.50 per credit hour. Tuition, state resident: full-time $2853; part-time $158.50 per credit hour. Tuition, nonresident: full-time $7551; part-time $419.50 per credit hour. Required fees: $1040; $42 per credit hour. $124 per semester. Tuition and fees vary according to course load and campus/location. *Financial support:* In 2008–09, 2 research assistantships (averaging $13,200 per year) were awarded; teaching assistantships, career-related internships or fieldwork and Federal Work-Study also available. Support available to part-time students. Financial award application deadline: 5/1; financial award applicants required to submit FAFSA. *Unit head:* Dr. Malcom Cross, Department Head, 254-968-9627, Fax: 254-968-9798, E-mail: cross@tarleton.edu. *Application contact:* Information Contact, 254-968-9104, Fax: 254-968-9670, E-mail: gradoffice@tarleton.edu.

Teachers College, Columbia University, Graduate Faculty of Education, Department of Organization and Leadership, Program in Politics and Education, New York, NY 10027-6696. Offers Ed M, MA, Ed D, PhD. *Faculty:* 2 part-time/adjunct. *Students:* 22 full-time (14 women), 19 part-time (8 women); includes 13 minority (5 African Americans, 4 Asian Americans or Pacific Islanders, 4 Hispanic Americans), 6 international. Average age 30. 43 applicants, 60% accepted, 11 enrolled. In 2008, 6 master's, 2 doctorates awarded. *Degree requirements:* For doctorate, thesis/dissertation. *Application deadline:* For fall admission, 5/15 for domestic students. Application fee: $75. *Expenses:* Tuition: Full-time $26,040; part-time $1085 per credit. Required fees: $720. *Financial support:* Career-related internships or fieldwork, Federal Work-Study, institutionally sponsored loans, and tuition waivers (full and partial) available. Support available to part-time students. Financial award application deadline: 2/1. *Faculty research:* Urban and social programs in education. *Unit head:* Warner Burke, Chair, 212-678-3258. *Application contact:* Debbie Lesperance, Assistant Director of Admission, 212-678-3710, Fax: 212-678-4171.

Temple University, Graduate School, College of Liberal Arts, Department of Political Science, Philadelphia, PA 19122-6096. Offers MA, PhD. Part-time programs available. Terminal master's awarded for partial completion of doctoral program. *Degree requirements:* For master's, comprehensive exam; for doctorate, thesis/dissertation, preliminary and oral exams. *Entrance requirements:* For master's and doctorate, GRE General Test, minimum GPA of 3.0. Additional exam requirements/recommendations for international students: Required—TOEFL (minimum score 550 paper-based; 213 computer-based; 79 iBT). Electronic applications accepted. *Faculty research:* American politics, international politics, comparative politics, political theory, urban politics, public policy.

Texas A&M International University, Office of Graduate Studies and Research, College of Arts and Sciences, Department of Social Sciences, Laredo, TX 78041-1900. Offers history (MA); political science (MA); public administration (MPA). *Degree requirements:* For master's, thesis (for some programs). *Entrance requirements:* For master's, GRE General Test. Additional exam requirements/recommendations for international students: Required—TOEFL (minimum score 550 paper-based; 213 computer-based).

Texas A&M University, College of Liberal Arts, Department of Political Science, College Station, TX 77843. Offers MA, PhD. *Faculty:* 23. *Students:* 45 full-time (22 women), 14 part-time (4 women); includes 12 minority (5 African Americans, 2 Asian Americans or Pacific Islanders, 5 Hispanic Americans), 10 international. Average age 30. In 2008, 3 master's, 6 doctorates awarded. *Degree requirements:* For master's, thesis optional; for doctorate, comprehensive exam, thesis/dissertation. *Entrance requirements:* For master's and doctorate, GRE General Test, minimum GPA of 3.4. Additional exam requirements/recommendations for international students: Required—TOEFL. *Application deadline:* For fall admission, 12/20 for domestic and international students. Application fee: $50 ($75 for international students). Electronic applications accepted. *Expenses:* Tuition, area resident: Full-time $3838.50. Tuition, state resident: full-time $3838.50. Tuition, nonresident: full-time $8897. Required fees: $2359.60. *Financial support:* In 2008–09, fellowships (averaging $3,000 per year), research assistantships (averaging $15,600 per year) were awarded; institutionally sponsored loans and assistant lecturer positions also available. Financial award application deadline: 12/20; financial award applicants required to submit FAFSA. *Faculty research:* American politics, international relations, comparative politics, political theory, public policy. *Unit head:* Dr. James Rogers, Head, 979-845-2905, E-mail: rogers@tamu.edu. *Application contact:* Dr. Cary J. Nederman, Graduate Advisor, 979-845-4845, Fax: 979-845-4845, E-mail: nederman@polisci.tamu.edu.

Texas A&M University–Kingsville, College of Graduate Studies, College of Arts and Sciences, Program in History and Political Science, Kingsville, TX 78363. Offers MA, MS. Part-time and evening/weekend programs available. *Degree requirements:* For master's, comprehensive exam, thesis or alternative. *Entrance requirements:* For master's, GRE General Test. Additional exam requirements/recommendations for international students: Required—TOEFL.

Texas State University–San Marcos, Graduate School, College of Liberal Arts, Department of Political Science, Program in Political Science, San Marcos, TX 78666. Offers MA. Part-time and evening/weekend programs available. *Degree requirements:* For master's, comprehensive exam, thesis (for some programs). *Entrance requirements:* For master's, minimum GPA of 2.9 in last 60 hours of course work. Additional exam requirements/recommendations for international students: Required—TOEFL (minimum score 550 paper-based; 213 computer-based). Electronic applications accepted. *Faculty research:* Religion in American public life, international humanitarian and refugee policy, judicial biography and history, citizenship and ethics, business and government policy making.

Texas State University–San Marcos, Graduate School, Interdisciplinary Studies in Political Science, San Marcos, TX 78666. Offers MAIS. *Degree requirements:* For master's, comprehensive exam.

Texas Tech University, Graduate School, College of Arts and Sciences, Department of Political Science, Lubbock, TX 79409. Offers political science (MA, PhD); public administration (MPA); JD/MPA. *Accreditation:* NASPAA (one or more programs are accredited). Part-time programs available. *Faculty:* 12 full-time (2 women). *Students:* 54 full-time (23 women), 18 part-time (6 women); includes 15 minority (1 African American, 1 American Indian/Alaska Native, 4 Asian Americans or Pacific Islanders, 9 Hispanic Americans), 7 international. Average age 28. 53 applicants, 57% accepted, 11 enrolled. In 2008, 11 master's, 3 doctorates awarded. *Degree requirements:* For master's, thesis or alternative; for doctorate, thesis/dissertation. *Entrance requirements:* For master's and doctorate, GRE General Test. Additional exam requirements/recommendations for international students: Required—TOEFL (minimum score 550 paper-based; 213 computer-based). *Application deadline:* For fall admission, 3/1 priority date for international students; for spring admission, 11/1 priority date for international students. Applications are processed on a rolling basis. Application fee: $50 ($60 for international students). Electronic applications accepted. *Expenses:* Tuition, area resident: Part-time $194 per credit hour. Tuition, state resident: full-time $4648; part-time $194 per credit hour. Tuition, nonresident: full-time $11,392; part-time $475 per credit hour. Required fees: $2206; $69 per credit hour. $389 per semester. *Financial support:* In 2008–09, 53 students received support, including 24 teaching assistantships with partial tuition reimbursements available (averaging $12,958 per year); research assistantships with partial tuition reimbursements available, Federal Work-Study and institutionally sponsored loans also available. Support available to part-time students. Financial award application deadline: 4/15; financial award applicants required to submit FAFSA. *Faculty research:* State politics, American institutions and behavior, Asian politics, international and comparative political relations and economics, public administration and organizations. Total annual research expenditures: $119,879. *Unit head:* Dr. Philip H. Marshall, Chair, 806-742-3121, Fax: 806-742-0850, E-mail: philip.marshall@ttu.edu. *Application contact:* Donna Barnes, Administrative Assistant, 806-742-3121, Fax: 806-742-0850, E-mail: donna.barnes@ttu.edu.

Texas Woman's University, Graduate School, College of Arts and Sciences, Department of History and Government, Denton, TX 76201. Offers government (MA); history (MA). Part-time and evening/weekend programs available. *Faculty:* 9 full-time (4 women), 5 part-time/adjunct (2 women). *Students:* 5 full-time (3 women), 29 part-time (26 women); includes 6 minority (2 African Americans, 1 Asian American or Pacific Islander, 3 Hispanic Americans), 2 international. Average age 36. In 2008, 12 master's awarded. *Degree requirements:* For master's, thesis. *Entrance requirements:* For master's, GRE (waived if completed a graduate degree), minimum GPA of 3.3, writing sample/portfolio. Additional exam requirements/recommendations for international students: Required—TOEFL (minimum score 550 paper-based; 213 computer-based; 79 iBT). *Application deadline:* For fall admission, 4/1 for international students; for spring admission, 8/1 for international students. Applications are processed on a rolling basis. Application fee: $30 ($50 for international students). Electronic applications accepted. *Expenses:* Tuition, state resident: full-time $3564; part-time $198 per semester hour. Tuition, nonresident: full-time $8622; part-time $479 per semester hour. Required fees: $1158; $64 per semester hour. Tuition and fees vary according to course load. *Financial support:* In 2008–09, 21 research assistantships (averaging $9,684 per year), 2 teaching assistantships (averaging $9,684 per year) were awarded; career-related internships or fieldwork, Federal Work-Study, institutionally sponsored loans, scholarships/grants, traineeships, health care benefits, and unspecified assistantships also available. Support available to part-time students. Financial award application deadline: 3/1; financial award applicants required to submit FAFSA. *Faculty research:* Recent American history, civil liberties, military history, legal studies, women and politics. *Unit head:* Dr. Mark Kessler, Chair, 940-898-2133, Fax: 940-898-2130, E-mail: HistoryGov@twu.edu. *Application contact:* Samuel Wheeler, Assistant Director of Admissions, 940-898-3188, Fax: 940-898-3081, E-mail: wheelersr@twu.edu.

Tulane University, School of Liberal Arts, Department of Political Science, New Orleans, LA 70118-5669. Offers MA, PhD, MA/JD. *Degree requirements:* For master's, one foreign language, thesis optional, seminar; for doctorate, 2 foreign languages, thesis/dissertation. *Entrance requirements:* For master's, GRE General Test, minimum B average in undergraduate course work; for doctorate, GRE General Test. Additional exam requirements/recommendations for international students: Required—TOEFL. Electronic applications accepted.

Université de Montréal, Faculty of Arts and Sciences, Department of Political Science, Montréal, QC H3C 3J7, Canada. Offers M Sc, PhD. *Faculty:* 27 full-time (6 women), 5 part-time/adjunct (1 woman). *Students:* 70 full-time (30 women), 117 part-time (54 women). 173 applicants, 25% accepted, 34 enrolled. In 2008, 45 master's, 6 doctorates awarded. *Degree requirements:* For master's, thesis; for doctorate, thesis/dissertation, general exam. *Entrance requirements:* For master's, minimum GPA of 2.8; for doctorate, master's degree, minimum GPA of 3.0. *Application deadline:* For fall admission, 2/1 priority date for domestic students; for winter admission, 11/1 priority date for domestic students; for spring admission, 2/1 priority date for domestic students. Application fee: $100. Electronic applications accepted. *Financial support:* Fellowships, research assistantships, teaching assistantships, career-related internships or fieldwork available. *Unit head:* Denis Moni??re, Chairman, 514-343-6588, Fax: 514-343-2360, E-mail: denis.moniere@umontreal.ca. *Application contact:* Alain No??l, Graduate Chairman, 514-343-2079, Fax: 514-343-2360, E-mail: alain.noel@umontreal.ca.

Université du Québec à Montréal, Graduate Programs, Program in Political Science, Montréal, QC H3C 3P8, Canada. Offers MA, PhD. Part-time programs available. *Degree requirements:* For master's, thesis; for doctorate, thesis/dissertation. *Entrance requirements:* For master's, appropriate bachelor's degree or equivalent, proficiency in French; for doctorate, appropriate master's degree or equivalent, proficiency in French.

Université Laval, Faculty of Social Sciences, Department of Political Science, Program in Policy Analysis, Québec, QC G1K 7P4, Canada. Offers MA. *Degree requirements:* For master's, thesis (for some programs). *Entrance requirements:* For master's, knowledge of French, comprehension of written English. Electronic applications accepted.

Université Laval, Faculty of Social Sciences, Department of Political Science, Programs in Political Science, Québec, QC G1K 7P4, Canada. Offers MA, PhD. Terminal master's awarded for partial completion of doctoral program. *Degree requirements:* For master's, thesis (for some programs); for doctorate, comprehensive exam, thesis/dissertation. *Entrance requirements:* For master's, knowledge of French; for doctorate, knowledge of French, comprehension of written English. Electronic applications accepted.

University at Albany, State University of New York, Nelson A. Rockefeller College of Public Affairs and Policy, Department of Political Science, Albany, NY 12222-0001. Offers MA, PhD. *Degree requirements:* For doctorate, one foreign language, thesis/dissertation. *Entrance requirements:* For doctorate, GRE General Test. Additional exam requirements/recommendations for international students: Required—TOEFL (minimum score 550 paper-based; 213 computer-based). Electronic applications accepted.

University at Buffalo, the State University of New York, Graduate School, College of Arts and Sciences, Department of Political Science, Buffalo, NY 14260. Offers MA, PhD. Terminal master's awarded for partial completion of doctoral program. *Degree requirements:* For master's, thesis or alternative, paper, project; for doctorate, comprehensive exam, thesis/dissertation. *Entrance requirements:* For master's, GRE General Test, minimum GPA of 3.0; for doctorate, GRE General Test, minimum GPA of 3.3. Additional exam requirements/recommendations for international students: Required—TOEFL (minimum score 550 paper-based; 213 computer-based; 79 iBT). Electronic applications accepted. *Faculty research:* American politics, public law, comparative politics, international politics.

The University of Akron, Graduate School, Buchtel College of Arts and Sciences, Department of Political Science, Akron, OH 44325. Offers applied politics (MA); political science (MA); JD/MAP. Part-time programs available. *Degree requirements:* For master's, comprehensive exam, essay, seminars (political science); portfolio (applied politics). *Entrance requirements:* For master's, minimum GPA of 2.75, letters of recommendation. Additional exam requirements/recommendations for international students: Required—TOEFL (minimum score 550 paper-based; 213 computer-based; 79 iBT). Electronic applications accepted. *Faculty research:* Public opinion and public policy, applied/electrical politics, international/comparative politics, the politics of criminal justice, conflict management.

The University of Alabama, Graduate School, College of Arts and Sciences, Department of Political Science, Tuscaloosa, AL 35487. Offers political science (MA, PhD); public administration (MPA). Part-time programs available. *Faculty:* 16 full-time (4 women). *Students:* 39 full-time (17 women), 18 part-time (8 women); includes 7 minority (4 African Americans, 1 Asian American or Pacific Islander, 2 Hispanic Americans), 8 international. Average age 29. 47 applicants, 64% accepted, 12 enrolled. In 2008, 7 master's, 1 doctorate awarded. Terminal master's awarded for partial completion of doctoral program. *Degree requirements:* For master's, thesis optional; for doctorate, comprehensive exam, thesis/dissertation. *Entrance requirements:* For master's and doctorate, GRE (minimum score: 1000), minimum undergraduate GPA of 3.0. Additional exam requirements/recommendations for international students: Required—TOEFL. *Application deadline:* For fall admission, 6/30 for domestic and international students; for spring admission, 10/15 for domestic and international students. Applications are processed on a rolling basis. Application fee: $30. *Expenses:* Tuition, area resident: Full-time $6400. Tuition, state resident: full-time $6400. Tuition, nonresident: full-time $18,000. *Financial support:* In 2008–09, 15 students received support, including teaching assistantships with full tuition reimbursements available (averaging $10,908 per year); career-related internships or fieldwork and Federal Work-Study also available. Financial award application deadline: 2/15. *Faculty research:* American politics, comparative politics, international relations, public administration, political theory. Total annual research expenditures: $15,183. *Unit head:* Dr. David U. Lanoue, Chair and Professor, 205-348-5981, Fax: 205-348-5298, E-mail: dlanoue@bama.ua.edu. *Application contact:* Dr. Terry Royed, Graduate Advisor, 205-348-3801, Fax: 205-348-5248, E-mail: troyed@tenhoor.as.ua.edu.

University of Alberta, Faculty of Graduate Studies and Research, Department of Political Science, Edmonton, AB T6G 2E1, Canada. Offers MA, PhD. Part-time programs available. *Degree requirements:* For master's, thesis (for some programs); for doctorate, one foreign language, thesis/dissertation. *Entrance requirements:* Additional exam requirements/recommendations for international students: Required—TOEFL. *Faculty research:* Canadian politics, international relations, globalization, classical and contemporary political theory, gender and politics.

The University of Arizona, Graduate College, College of Social and Behavioral Sciences, Department of Political Science, Tucson, AZ 85721. Offers MA, PhD. Terminal master's awarded for partial completion of doctoral program. *Degree requirements:* For master's, thesis or alternative; for doctorate, variable foreign language requirement, comprehensive exam, thesis/dissertation. *Entrance requirements:* For master's and doctorate, GRE General Test, GRE Subject Test, minimum GPA of 3.2, 3 letters of recommendation, statement of purpose, writing sample. Additional exam requirements/recommendations for international students: Required—TOEFL (minimum score 550 paper-based). Electronic applications accepted. *Faculty research:* Voting behavior, political participation, Soviet domestic and Sino-Soviet relations, presidential leadership and congressional behavior.

University of Arkansas, Graduate School, J. William Fulbright College of Arts and Sciences, Department of Political Science, Program in Political Science, Fayetteville, AR 72701-1201. Offers MA. *Degree requirements:* For master's, thesis or alternative. *Entrance requirements:* For master's, GRE General Test.

The University of British Columbia, Faculty of Arts and Faculty of Graduate Studies, Department of Political Science, Vancouver, BC V6T 1Z1, Canada. Offers MA, PhD. Part-time programs available. *Degree requirements:* For master's, thesis; for doctorate, comprehensive exam, thesis/dissertation. *Entrance requirements:* For master's, BA in political science; for doctorate, GRE, BA and MA in political science. Additional exam requirements/recommendations for international students: Required—TOEFL (minimum score 580 paper-based; 237 computer-based), TWE (minimum score 5). Electronic applications accepted. *Faculty research:* Canadian politics, international relations, political theory, comparative politics, public policy.

University of Calgary, Faculty of Graduate Studies, Faculty of Social Sciences, Department of Political Science, Calgary, AB T2N 1N4, Canada. Offers MA, PhD. *Degree requirements:* For master's, thesis; for doctorate, one foreign language, comprehensive exam, thesis/dissertation, prospectus, oral and written candidacy exams. *Entrance requirements:* For master's, minimum GPA of 3.4; for doctorate, minimum GPA of 3.7. Additional exam requirements/recommendations for international students: Required—TOEFL (minimum score 620 paper-based; 260 computer-based). Electronic applications accepted. *Faculty research:* Canadian politics, international relations, comparative politics, theory, public policy.

University of California, Berkeley, Graduate Division, College of Letters and Science, Department of Political Science, Berkeley, CA 94720-1500. Offers PhD. *Degree requirements:* For doctorate, thesis/dissertation, oral qualifying exams. *Entrance requirements:* For doctorate, GRE General Test, minimum GPA of 3.0, 3 letters of recommendation. Electronic applications accepted.

University of California, Davis, Graduate Studies, Program in Political Science, Davis, CA 95616. Offers MA, PhD. Terminal master's awarded for partial completion of doctoral program. *Degree requirements:* For master's, thesis; for doctorate, thesis/dissertation. *Entrance requirements:* For master's and doctorate, GRE General Test, minimum GPA of 3.0, writing sample. Additional exam requirements/recommendations for international students: Required—TOEFL (minimum score 550 paper-based; 213 computer-based). Electronic applications accepted. *Faculty research:* American government and politics, political theory, comparative politics, international relations, public law.

University of California, Irvine, Office of Graduate Studies, School of Social Sciences, Department of Political Science, Irvine, CA 92697. Offers political psychology (PhD); political sciences (PhD); public choice (PhD). *Degree requirements:* For doctorate, thesis/dissertation. *Entrance requirements:* For doctorate, GRE General Test, minimum GPA of 3.0. Additional exam requirements/recommendations for international students: Required—TOEFL (minimum score 550 paper-based; 213 computer-based). Electronic applications accepted. *Faculty research:* Political behavior, political economy, international relations.

University of California, Los Angeles, Graduate Division, College of Letters and Science, Department of Political Science, Los Angeles, CA 90095. Offers MA, PhD. *Students:* 143 full-time (63 women); includes 33 minority (7 African Americans, 10 Asian Americans or Pacific Islanders, 16 Hispanic Americans), 23 international. Average age 29. 314 applicants, 29% accepted, 28 enrolled. In 2008, 3 master's, 14 doctorates awarded. *Degree requirements:* For master's, comprehensive exam; for doctorate, one foreign language, thesis/dissertation, oral and written qualifying exams. *Entrance requirements:* For master's, GRE General Test, minimum

Political Science

University of California, Los Angeles (continued)
GPA of 3.0, sample of written work, degree objective of Ph.D; for doctorate, GRE General Test, minimum undergraduate GPA of 3.0, sample of written work. *Application deadline:* For fall admission, 12/15 for domestic and international students. Application fee: $60 ($80 for international students). Electronic applications accepted. *Expenses:* Tuition, nonresident: full-time $14,694. Required fees: $9669.50. Full-time tuition and fees vary according to course load, degree level, program and student level. *Financial support:* In 2008–09, 125 fellowships with full tuition reimbursements, 34 research assistantships with full tuition reimbursements, 82 teaching assistantships with full tuition reimbursements were awarded; Federal Work-Study, institutionally sponsored loans, scholarships/grants, health care benefits, tuition waivers (full and partial), and unspecified assistantships also available. Financial award application deadline: 3/1; financial award applicants required to submit FAFSA. *Unit head:* Dr. Edmond Keller, Chair, 310-825-2566. *Application contact:* Joseph Brown, Graduate Advisor, 310-825-3372, Fax: 310-825-0778, E-mail: joseph@polisci.ucla.edu.

University of California, Riverside, Graduate Division, Department of Political Science, Riverside, CA 92521-0102. Offers MA, PhD. Part-time programs available. Terminal master's awarded for partial completion of doctoral program. *Degree requirements:* For master's, comprehensive exams or thesis; for doctorate, thesis/dissertation, qualifying exams. *Entrance requirements:* For master's and doctorate, GRE General Test, minimum GPA of 3.2. Additional exam requirements/recommendations for international students: Required—TOEFL (minimum score 550 paper-based; 213 computer-based; 80 iBT). Electronic applications accepted. *Expenses:* Tuition, nonresident: full-time $4898. Required fees: $10,362. *Faculty research:* American politics, mass political behavior, comparative politics, international relations, political theory.

University of California, San Diego, Office of Graduate Studies, Department of Political Science, La Jolla, CA 92093. Offers Latin American studies (MA); political science (PhD); political science and international affairs (PhD). *Entrance requirements:* For master's and doctorate, GRE General Test. Electronic applications accepted.

University of California, San Diego, Office of Graduate Studies, Graduate School of International Relations and Pacific Studies, La Jolla, CA 92093-0520. Offers economics and international affairs (PhD); Pacific international affairs (MPIA); political science and international affairs (PhD). *Degree requirements:* For master's, one foreign language; for doctorate, thesis/dissertation. *Entrance requirements:* For master's, GMAT or GRE General Test; for doctorate, GRE General Test. Additional exam requirements/recommendations for international students: Required—TOEFL (minimum score 550 paper-based; 213 computer-based). Electronic applications accepted. *Faculty research:* Pacific Rim as system and placement in global relations; studies in international economics, management and finance; analysis of patterns of policymaking in countries of the Pacific.

See Close-Up on page 881.

University of California, Santa Barbara, Graduate Division, College of Letters and Sciences, Division of Social Sciences, Department of Political Science, Santa Barbara, CA 93106-9420. Offers political science (MA); women's studies (PhD); MA/PhD. Part-time programs available. *Faculty:* 22 full-time (10 women), 5 part-time/adjunct (2 women). *Students:* 51 full-time (22 women). Average age 30. 94 applicants, 32% accepted, 7 enrolled. In 2008, 9 master's, 4 doctorates awarded. Terminal master's awarded for partial completion of doctoral program. *Degree requirements:* For master's, comprehensive exam (for some programs), thesis optional; for doctorate, one foreign language, comprehensive exam, thesis/dissertation. *Entrance requirements:* For master's, GRE General Test, bachelor's degree with minimum GPA of 3.0, 3 letters of recommendation, statement of purpose, personal achievements/contributions statement, resumé/curriculum vitae, transcripts for post-secondary institutions attended; for doctorate, GRE General Test, master's degree with minimum GPA of 3.0, 3 letters of recommendation, statement of purpose, personal achievements/contributions statement, resumé/curriculum vitae, transcripts for post-secondary institutions attended. Additional exam requirements/recommendations for international students: Required—TOEFL (minimum score 600 paper-based; 250 computer-based; 100 iBT), TOEFL or IELTS. *Application deadline:* For fall admission, 1/1 priority date for domestic and international students. Application fee: $70 ($90 for international students). Electronic applications accepted. *Expenses:* Tuition, nonresident: full-time $25,149. Required fees: $10,143. Full-time tuition and fees vary according to campus/location, reciprocity agreements and student level. *Financial support:* In 2008–09, 43 students received support, including 25 fellowships with full tuition reimbursements available (averaging $8,200 per year), 42 teaching assistantships with partial tuition reimbursements available (averaging $8,900 per year); Federal Work-Study, institutionally sponsored loans, scholarships/grants, and health care benefits also available. Financial award applicants required to submit FAFSA. *Faculty research:* American politics, comparative politics, international relations, political theory, methodology. *Unit head:* Dr. John Woolley, Chair, 805-893-3432, Fax: 805-893-3309, E-mail: woolley@polsci.ucsb.edu. *Application contact:* Linda James, Staff Graduate Advisor, 805-893-3626, Fax: 805-893-3309, E-mail: james@polsci.ucsb.edu.

University of California, Santa Cruz, Division of Graduate Studies, Division of Social Sciences, Politics Department, Santa Cruz, CA 95064. Offers PhD. *Entrance requirements:* Additional exam requirements/recommendations for international students: Required—TOEFL. Electronic applications accepted.

University of Central Florida, College of Sciences, Department of Political Science, Orlando, FL 32816. Offers environmental politics (MA); international studies (MA); political analysis and policy (MA). Part-time and evening/weekend programs available. *Faculty:* 24 full-time (7 women), 7 part-time/adjunct (1 woman). *Students:* 31 full-time (15 women), 37 part-time (13 women); includes 11 minority (2 Asian Americans or Pacific Islanders, 9 Hispanic Americans), 2 international. In 2008, 7 master's awarded. *Degree requirements:* For master's, comprehensive exam, thesis. *Entrance requirements:* For master's, GRE General Test, minimum GPA of 3.0 in last 60 hours. Additional exam requirements/recommendations for international students: Required—TOEFL. *Application deadline:* For fall admission, 7/15 for domestic students; for spring admission, 12/1 for domestic students. Application fee: $30. Electronic applications accepted. *Expenses:* Tuition, area resident: Full-time $6816; part-time $284 per credit. Tuition, state resident: full-time $6816; part-time $1076 per credit. Tuition, nonresident: full-time $25,824. Required fees: $216; $9 per credit. *Financial support:* In 2008–09, 2 fellowships with partial tuition reimbursements (averaging $10,000 per year), 3 research assistantships with partial tuition reimbursements (averaging $5,800 per year), 7 teaching assistantships with partial tuition reimbursements (averaging $7,600 per year) were awarded; career-related internships or fieldwork, Federal Work-Study, institutionally sponsored loans, tuition waivers (partial), and unspecified assistantships also available. Financial award application deadline: 3/1; financial award applicants required to submit FAFSA. *Faculty research:* Environment, presidential campaigning, term limits for elected officials. *Unit head:* Dr. Roger Handberg, Chair, 407-823-2608, Fax: 407-823-0051. *Application contact:* Dr. Roger Handberg, Chair, 407-823-2608, Fax: 407-823-0051.

University of Central Oklahoma, College of Graduate Studies and Research, College of Liberal Arts, Department of Political Science, Program in Political Science, Edmond, OK 73034-5209. Offers MA. Part-time programs available. *Entrance requirements:* Additional exam requirements/recommendations for international students: Required—TOEFL (minimum score 550 paper-based; 213 computer-based). Electronic applications accepted. *Faculty research:* U. S. Congress.

University of Chicago, Division of Social Sciences, Department of Political Science, Chicago, IL 60637-1513. Offers PhD. *Degree requirements:* For doctorate, one foreign language, thesis/dissertation, exam, qualifying paper. *Entrance requirements:* For doctorate, GRE General Test. Additional exam requirements/recommendations for international students: Required—TOEFL, IELTS (minimum score 7). Electronic applications accepted. *Faculty research:* Political philosophy, international political economy, strategic studies, public policy and race relations, comparative politics (China, Middle East, Soviet Union, Africa, India, Japan).

University of Cincinnati, Graduate School, McMicken College of Arts and Sciences, Department of Political Science, Cincinnati, OH 45221. Offers MA, PhD. Terminal master's awarded for partial completion of doctoral program. *Degree requirements:* For master's, thesis (for some programs); for doctorate, thesis/dissertation. *Entrance requirements:* For master's and doctorate, GRE General Test, GRE Subject Test. Additional exam requirements/recommendations for international students: Required—TOEFL. Electronic applications accepted. *Faculty research:* International security, methodology, American politics, comparative politics.

University of Colorado at Boulder, Graduate School, College of Arts and Sciences, Department of Political Science, Boulder, CO 80309. Offers international affairs (MA); political science (MA, PhD); public policy (MA). Terminal master's awarded for partial completion of doctoral program. *Degree requirements:* For master's, comprehensive exam, thesis; for doctorate, one foreign language, thesis/dissertation. *Entrance requirements:* For master's, GRE General Test, minimum undergraduate GPA of 3.0; for doctorate, GRE General Test, minimum GPA of 3.5 (undergraduate), 3.0 (graduate). *Faculty research:* American government and politics, comparative politics, international relations, law and politics, public policy, political philosophy, empirical theory and methodology.

University of Colorado Denver, College of Liberal Arts and Sciences, Department of Political Science, Denver, CO 80217-3364. Offers MA. Part-time and evening/weekend programs available. *Degree requirements:* For master's, thesis or alternative. *Entrance requirements:* For master's, GRE, 18 hours of course work in political science. Additional exam requirements/recommendations for international students: Required—TOEFL (minimum score 525 paper-based; 197 computer-based). Electronic applications accepted. *Faculty research:* Palestinian peace process, post-Soviet governmental corruption, gender/racial/ethnic politics in the U.S.A., U.S. immigration.

University of Connecticut, Graduate School, College of Liberal Arts and Sciences, Department of Political Science, Field of Political Science, Storrs, CT 06269. Offers MA, PhD. Terminal master's awarded for partial completion of doctoral program. *Degree requirements:* For master's, comprehensive exam; for doctorate, 2 foreign languages, thesis/dissertation. *Entrance requirements:* For master's and doctorate, GRE General Test. Additional exam requirements/recommendations for international students: Required—TOEFL (minimum score 550 paper-based; 213 computer-based). Electronic applications accepted.

University of Dallas, Braniff Graduate School of Liberal Arts, Institute of Philosophic Studies, Doctoral Program in Politics, Irving, TX 75062-4736. Offers PhD. *Degree requirements:* For doctorate, 2 foreign languages, comprehensive exam, thesis/dissertation. *Entrance requirements:* For doctorate, GRE General Test. Additional exam requirements/recommendations for international students: Required—TOEFL. *Faculty research:* Classical, medieval, and modern political philosophy; American political thought and institutions; politics and literature.

University of Dallas, Braniff Graduate School of Liberal Arts, Master's Program in Politics, Irving, TX 75062-4736. Offers M Pol, MA. Part-time programs available. *Degree requirements:* For master's, one foreign language, comprehensive exam, thesis. *Entrance requirements:* For master's, GRE General Test. Additional exam requirements/recommendations for international students: Required—TOEFL. *Faculty research:* Classical, medieval, and modern political philosophy; American political thought and institutions; politics and literature.

University of Delaware, College of Arts and Sciences, Department of Political Science and International Relations, Newark, DE 19716. Offers MA, PhD. Terminal master's awarded for partial completion of doctoral program. *Degree requirements:* For master's, research paper; for doctorate, one foreign language, comprehensive exam, thesis/dissertation. *Entrance requirements:* For master's and doctorate, GRE General Test, minimum GPA of 3.2 in major, 3.0 overall. Additional exam requirements/recommendations for international students: Required—TOEFL (minimum score 600 paper-based). Electronic applications accepted. *Faculty research:* Social constructivism. international migration, international security, democratization, human rights.

University of Florida, Graduate School, College of Liberal Arts and Sciences, Department of Political Science, Gainesville, FL 32611. Offers international development policy and administration (MA, Certificate); international relations (MA, MAT); political campaigning (MA, Certificate); political science (MA, MAT, PhD); public affairs (MA, Certificate); JD/MA. Part-time programs available. Terminal master's awarded for partial completion of doctoral program. *Degree requirements:* For master's, variable foreign language requirement, thesis or alternative; for doctorate, variable foreign language requirement, thesis/dissertation. *Entrance requirements:* For master's and doctorate, GRE General Test, minimum GPA of 3.0. Additional exam requirements/recommendations for international students: Required—TOEFL (minimum score 550 paper-based; 213 computer-based). Electronic applications accepted. *Faculty research:* U.S. political development, religion and politics, environmental politics and policy, developing societies, international relations.

University of Georgia, School of Public and International Affairs, Program in Political Science, Athens, GA 30602. Offers MA, PhD. *Degree requirements:* For master's, one foreign language, thesis; for doctorate, one foreign language, thesis/dissertation. *Entrance requirements:* For master's and doctorate, GRE General Test. Electronic applications accepted.

University of Guelph, Graduate Program Services, College of Social and Applied Human Sciences, Department of Political Science, Guelph, ON N1G 2W1, Canada. Offers comparative politics (MA); international development (MA); political science (MA); public policy and public administration (MA); the Americas (Canada emphasis) (MA). MA in public policy and public administration offered in collaboration with Department of Political Science of McMaster University. *Degree requirements:* For master's, thesis or paper. *Entrance requirements:* For master's, minimum B average during previous 2 years of course work, 4 year Honours Degree in Political Science. Additional exam requirements/recommendations for international students: Required—TOEFL. Electronic applications accepted. *Faculty research:* Political ethics, constitutional power.

University of Hawaii at Manoa, Graduate Division, Colleges of Arts and Sciences, College of Social Sciences, Department of Political Science, Honolulu, HI 96822. Offers MA, PhD. Part-time programs available. Terminal master's awarded for partial completion of doctoral program. *Degree requirements:* For master's, thesis optional; for doctorate, comprehensive exam, thesis/dissertation. *Entrance requirements:* Additional exam requirements/recommendations for international students: Required—TOEFL (minimum score 540 paper-based; 207 computer-based; 76 iBT), IELTS (minimum score 5). *Faculty research:* Asia/Pacific, political economy, human rights, futures, postmodernism.

University of Houston, College of Liberal Arts and Social Sciences, Department of Political Science, Houston, TX 77204. Offers MA, PhD. Part-time and evening/weekend programs available. *Faculty:* 18 full-time (3 women), 2 part-time/adjunct (0 women). *Students:* 35 full-time (19 women), 43 part-time (22 women); includes 18 minority (8 African Americans, 1 American Indian/Alaska Native, 4 Asian Americans or Pacific Islanders, 5 Hispanic Americans), 12 international. Average age 32. 71 applicants, 38% accepted, 17 enrolled. In 2008, 8 master's, 2 doctorates awarded. *Degree requirements:* For doctorate, thesis/dissertation. *Entrance requirements:* For master's and doctorate, GRE General Test, minimum GPA of 3.0. *Application deadline:* For fall admission, 4/1 for domestic students; for spring admission, 10/1 for domestic students. Applications are processed on a rolling basis. Application fee: $0. *Expenses:* Tuition, state resident: full-time $5164; part-time $287 per credit. Tuition, nonresident: full-time $10,222; part-time $568 per credit. *Financial support:* In 2008–09, 2 fellowships with full tuition reimbursements (averaging $10,000 per year), 28 teaching assistantships with full tuition reimbursements (averaging $13,000 per year) were awarded; career-related internships or fieldwork, Federal Work-Study, institutionally sponsored loans, scholarships/grants, health care benefits, and unspecified assistantships also available. Support available to part-time students. Financial award application deadline: 2/1. *Faculty research:* American politics, political theory, judicial process, public policy, comparative politics. *Unit head:* Dr. Harrell Rodgers, Chairperson, 713-743-3890, Fax: 713-743-3927, E-mail: hrodgers@uh.edu. *Application contact:* Director of Graduate Studies, 713-743-3890, E-mail: polsgrad@bayou.uh.edu.

University of Idaho, College of Graduate Studies, College of Letters, Arts and Social Sciences, Department of Political Science and Public Affairs Research, Program in Political Science, Moscow, ID 83844-2282. Offers MA, PhD. *Students:* 8 full-time, 3 part-time. Average age 35. In 2008, 1 master's, 1 doctorate awarded. *Degree requirements:* For doctorate, thesis/dissertation. *Entrance requirements:* For master's, minimum GPA of 2.8; for doctorate, minimum undergraduate GPA of 2.8, 3.0 graduate. *Application deadline:* For fall admission, 8/1 for domestic students; for spring admission, 12/15 for domestic students. Application fee: $55 ($60 for international students). *Expenses:* Tuition, nonresident: full-time $10,080; part-time $336 per credit. Required fees: $5212; $267 per credit. Tuition and fees vary according to program. *Financial support:* Application deadline: 2/15. *Unit head:* Dr. Donald W. Crowley, Chair, 208-885-6328. *Application contact:* Dr. Donald W. Crowley, Chair, 208-885-6328.

University of Illinois at Chicago, Graduate College, College of Liberal Arts and Sciences, Department of Political Science, Chicago, IL 60607-7128. Offers MA, PhD. Part-time programs available. Terminal master's awarded for partial completion of doctoral program. *Degree requirements:* For master's, thesis or comprehensive exam. *Entrance requirements:* For master's, GRE General Test, minimum GPA of 3.0. Additional exam requirements/recommendations for international students: Required—TOEFL. Electronic applications accepted. *Faculty research:* Policy analysis/national urban politics and policy, electoral behavior.

University of Illinois at Springfield, Graduate Programs, College of Public Affairs and Administration, Program in Political Studies, Springfield, IL 62703-5407. Offers MA. Part-time and evening/weekend programs available. *Faculty:* 10 full-time (2 women), 3 part-time/adjunct (0 women). *Students:* 23 full-time (4 women), 36 part-time (16 women); includes 13 minority (9 African Americans, 2 Asian Americans or Pacific Islanders, 2 Hispanic Americans). Average age 31. 29 applicants, 72% accepted, 14 enrolled. In 2008, 30 master's awarded. *Degree requirements:* For master's, comprehensive exam, participant/observer case study, or thesis. *Entrance requirements:* Additional exam requirements/recommendations for international students: Required—TOEFL (minimum score 500 paper-based; 176 computer-based; 61 iBT). *Application deadline:* Applications are processed on a rolling basis. Application fee: $50 ($60 for international students). Electronic applications accepted. *Expenses:* Tuition, state resident: full-time $6144; part-time $256 per credit hour. Tuition, nonresident: full-time $13,980; part-time $582.50 per credit hour. Required fees: $1800. *Financial support:* In 2008–09, research assistantships with full tuition reimbursements (averaging $8,109 per year), teaching assistantships with full tuition reimbursements (averaging $8,109 per year) were awarded; career-related internships or fieldwork, Federal Work-Study, scholarships/grants, health care benefits, and unspecified assistantships also available. Support available to part-time students. Financial award application deadline: 11/15; financial award applicants required to submit FAFSA. *Unit head:* Dr. Pinky Sue Wassenberg, Interim Program Administrator, 217-206-6523, Fax: 217-206-7807, E-mail: wassenberg.pinky@uis.edu. *Application contact:* Dr. Lynn Pardie, Office of Graduate Studies, 800-252-8533, Fax: 217-206-7623, E-mail: pardie.lynn@uis.edu.

University of Illinois at Urbana–Champaign, Graduate College, College of Liberal Arts and Sciences, Department of Political Science, Champaign, IL 61820. Offers MA, PhD, PhD/JD. *Faculty:* 30 full-time (11 women), 5 part-time/adjunct (1 woman). *Students:* 75 full-time (30 women), 1 (woman) part-time; includes 9 minority (3 African Americans, 6 Asian Americans or Pacific Islanders), 13 international. 127 applicants, 15% accepted, 18 enrolled. In 2008, 14 master's, 7 doctorates awarded. *Entrance requirements:* For master's, GRE General Test, minimum GPA of 3.0; for doctorate, GRE General Test, writing sample, minimum GPA of 3.0. Additional exam requirements/recommendations for international students: Required—TOEFL (minimum score 79 iBT). *Application deadline:* Applications are processed on a rolling basis. Application fee: $60 ($75 for international students). Electronic applications accepted. *Financial support:* In 2008–09, 55 fellowships, 26 research assistantships, 45 teaching assistantships were awarded; tuition waivers (full and partial) also available. *Unit head:* William Bernhard, Head, 217-333-3880, Fax: 217-244-5712, E-mail: bernhard@illinois.edu. *Application contact:* Brenda R. Stamm, Secretary, 217-333-2602, Fax: 217-244-5712, E-mail: stamm@illinois.edu.

The University of Iowa, Graduate College, College of Liberal Arts and Sciences, Department of Political Science, Iowa City, IA 52242-1316. Offers MA, PhD. *Degree requirements:* For master's, thesis optional, exam; for doctorate, comprehensive exam, thesis/dissertation. *Entrance requirements:* For master's and doctorate, GRE General Test, minimum GPA of 3.0. Additional exam requirements/recommendations for international students: Required—TOEFL (minimum score 600 paper-based; 250 computer-based; 100 iBT). Electronic applications accepted.

The University of Kansas, Graduate Studies, College of Liberal Arts and Sciences, Department of Political Science, Lawrence, KS 66045. Offers MA, PhD. Part-time programs available. *Faculty:* 25 full-time. *Students:* 46 full-time (20 women), 4 part-time (1 woman); includes 2 minority (1 African American, 1 Asian American or Pacific Islander), 11 international. Average age 30. 78 applicants, 50% accepted, 18 enrolled. In 2008, 8 master's, 2 doctorates awarded. Terminal master's awarded for partial completion of doctoral program. *Degree requirements:* For master's, comprehensive exam, thesis or alternative; for doctorate, comprehensive exam, thesis/dissertation, research skills. *Entrance requirements:* For master's and doctorate, GRE General Test, 3 letters of recommendation, transcripts, personal statement, curriculum vitae. Additional exam requirements/recommendations for international students: Required—TOEFL. *Application deadline:* For fall admission, 1/9 priority date for domestic and international students. Application fee: $45 ($50 for international students). Electronic applications accepted. *Expenses:* Tuition, area resident: Full-time $6122; part-time $255.10 per credit hour. Tuition, state resident: full-time $6122; part-time $255.10 per credit hour. Tuition, nonresident: full-time $14,629; part-time $609.55 per credit hour. Required fees: $847; $70.56 per credit hour. Tuition and fees vary according to course load and program. *Financial support:* Fellowships with full tuition reimbursements, research assistantships, teaching assistantships with full tuition reimbursements, scholarships/grants, health care benefits, and unspecified assistantships available. Financial award application deadline: 1/9. *Faculty research:* Public policy, political economy and development, political institutions and organized interests, international conflict and cooperation. *Unit head:* Elaine Sharp, Chair, 785-864-3523, Fax: 785-864-5700, E-mail: esharp@ku.edu. *Application contact:* Prof. Paul E Johnson, Graduate Director, 785-864-3523, Fax: 785-864-5700, E-mail: pauljohn@ku.edu.

University of Kentucky, Graduate School, College of Arts and Sciences, Program in Political Science, Lexington, KY 40506-0032. Offers MA, PhD. *Degree requirements:* For master's, comprehensive exam, thesis optional; for doctorate, comprehensive exam, thesis/dissertation. *Entrance requirements:* For master's, GRE General Test, minimum undergraduate GPA of 2.75; for doctorate, GRE General Test, minimum graduate GPA of 3.0. Additional exam requirements/recommendations for international students: Required—TOEFL (minimum score 550 paper-based; 213 computer-based). Electronic applications accepted. *Faculty research:* International political economy, critical policy studies, regional conflict and integration, race and American politics, media studies.

University of Lethbridge, School of Graduate Studies, Lethbridge, AB T1K 3M4, Canada. Offers accounting (MScM); addictions counseling (M Sc); agricultural biotechnology (M Sc); agricultural studies (M Sc, MA); anthropology (MA); archaeology (MA); art (MA); biochemistry (M Sc); biological sciences (M Sc); biomolecular science (PhD); biosystems and biodiversity (PhD); Canadian studies (MA); chemistry (M Sc); computer science (M Sc); computer science and geographical information science (M Sc); counseling psychology (M Ed); dramatic arts (MA); earth, space, and physical science (PhD); economics (MA); educational leadership (M Ed); English (MA); environmental science (M Sc); evolution and behavior (PhD); exercise science (M Sc); finance (MScM); French (MA); French/German (MA); French/Spanish (MA); general education (M Ed); general management (MScM); geography (M Sc, MA); German (MA); health sciences (M Sc, MA); history (MA); human resource management and labour relations (MScM); individualized multidisciplinary (M Sc, MA); information systems (MScM); international management (MScM); kinesiology (M Sc, MA); management (M Sc, MA); marketing (MScM); mathematics (M Sc); music (MA); Native American studies (MA); neuroscience (M Sc, PhD); new media (MA); nursing (M Sc); philosophy (MA); physics (M Sc); policy and strategy (MScM); political science (MA); psychology (M Sc, MA); religious studies (MA); sociology (MA); theoretical and computational science (PhD); urban and regional studies (MA). Part-time and evening/weekend programs available. *Degree requirements:* For doctorate, comprehensive exam, thesis/dissertation. *Entrance requirements:* For master's, GMAT (M Sc in management), bachelor's degree in related field, minimum GPA of 3.0 during previous 20 graded semester courses, 2 years teaching or related experience (M Ed); for doctorate, master's degree, minimum graduate GPA of 3.5. Additional exam requirements/recommendations for international students: Required—TOEFL. *Faculty research:* Movement and brain plasticity, gibberellin physiology, photosynthesis, carbon cycling, molecular properties of main-group ring components.

University of Louisville, Graduate School, College of Arts and Sciences, Department of Political Science, Louisville, KY 40292-0001. Offers MA. Part-time and evening/weekend programs available. *Faculty:* 13 full-time (5 women), 3 part-time/adjunct. *Students:* 12 full-time (5 women), 12 part-time (5 women); includes 2 African Americans, 1 Hispanic American. Average age 30. 20 applicants, 70% accepted, 11 enrolled. In 2008, 8 master's awarded. *Degree requirements:* For master's, thesis (for some programs), thesis or directed research paper. *Entrance requirements:* For master's, GRE General Test, letters of recommendation (2 academic); personal statement; transcripts. Additional exam requirements/recommendations for international students: Required—TOEFL. *Application deadline:* For fall admission, 8/1 for domestic and international students; for winter admission, 8/1 for domestic students; for spring admission, 12/1 for domestic and international students. Applications are processed on a rolling basis. Application fee: $30 ($40 for international students). *Financial support:* In 2008–09, 2 research assistantships with full tuition reimbursements (averaging $12,000 per year) were awarded. Financial award application deadline: 6/1. *Faculty research:* International law; politics of East Asia; comparative political systems; environmental policy; international relations. Total annual research expenditures: $45,000. *Unit head:* Dr. Ronald K. Vogel, Chair, 502-852-3312, Fax: 502-852-7923, E-mail: ron.vogel@louisvile.edu. *Application contact:* Libby Leggett, Director, Graduate Admissions, 502-852-3101, Fax: 502-852-6536, E-mail: gradadm@louisville.edu.

University of Manitoba, Faculty of Graduate Studies, Faculty of Arts, Department of Political Studies, Winnipeg, MB R3T 2N2, Canada. Offers political studies (MA); public administration (MPA). *Degree requirements:* For master's, one foreign language, thesis or alternative.

University of Maryland, College Park, Graduate Studies, College of Behavioral and Social Sciences, Department of Government and Politics, College Park, MD 20742. Offers American politics (PhD); comparative politics (PhD); international relations (PhD); political economy (PhD); political theory (PhD). Part-time and evening/weekend programs available. *Degree requirements:* For doctorate, comprehensive exam, thesis/dissertation, written exams in 2 fields. *Entrance requirements:* For doctorate, GRE General Test, minimum GPA of 3.5, writing sample. Additional exam requirements/recommendations for international students: Required—TOEFL. Electronic applications accepted. *Faculty research:* International development/conflict, international security, post-communist society, public service, dynamics of conflict and conflict resolution.

University of Massachusetts Amherst, Graduate School, College of Social and Behavioral Sciences, Department of Political Science, Amherst, MA 01003. Offers MA, PhD. Part-time programs available. Terminal master's awarded for partial completion of doctoral program. *Degree requirements:* For master's, one foreign language, thesis or alternative; for doctorate, one foreign language, comprehensive exam, thesis/dissertation. *Entrance requirements:* For master's and doctorate, GRE General Test, writing sample, 3 letters of recommendation. Additional exam requirements/recommendations for international students: Required—TOEFL (minimum score 550 paper-based; 213 computer-based; 79 iBT), IELTS (minimum score 6.5). Electronic applications accepted. *Expenses:* Tuition, area resident: Full-time $2640. Tuition, nonresident: full-time $9936. One-time fee: $332 full-time. Tuition and fees vary according to course load.

University of Massachusetts Boston, Office of Graduate Studies, Division of Continuing Education and John W. McCormack Graduate School of Policy Studies, Program in Women in Politics and Government, Boston, MA 02125-3393. Offers Certificate. Part-time and evening/weekend programs available. *Degree requirements:* For Certificate, practicum, final project. *Entrance requirements:* For degree, interview, minimum GPA of 2.75.

University of Massachusetts Boston, Office of Graduate Studies, John W. McCormack Graduate School of Policy Studies, Boston, MA 02125-3393. Offers gerontology (MA, MS, PhD, Certificate), including gerontology (MS, PhD, Certificate), gerontology research (MA), management in aging services (MA); public affairs (MS); public policy (PhD); women in politics and government (Certificate). Certificate program in women in politics and government offered jointly with Division of Continuing Education. Part-time and evening/weekend programs available. *Degree requirements:* For doctorate, thesis/dissertation; for Certificate, practicum, final project. *Entrance requirements:* For doctorate, GRE General Test; for Certificate, interview, minimum GPA of 2.5.

University of Memphis, Graduate School, College of Arts and Sciences, Department of Political Science, Memphis, TN 38152. Offers MA. *Faculty:* 6 full-time (2 women). *Students:* 12 full-time (8 women), 7 part-time (3 women); includes 1 minority (African American). Average age 28. 9 applicants, 100% accepted, 3 enrolled. In 2008, 3 master's awarded. *Degree requirements:* For master's, comprehensive exam, thesis or alternative, internship. *Entrance requirements:* For master's, GRE General Test or GMAT, minimum GPA of 3.0. *Application deadline:* For fall admission, 8/1 for domestic students; for spring admission, 12/1 for domestic students. Applications are processed on a rolling basis. Application fee: $35 ($60 for international students). *Expenses:* Tuition, area resident: Full-time $6242; part-time $330 per credit hour. Tuition, state resident: full-time $6242; part-time $330 per credit hour. Tuition, nonresident: full-time $17,828; part-time $815 per credit hour. Required fees: $1156. *Financial support:* Research assistantships with full tuition reimbursements available. Financial award applicants required to submit FAFSA. *Faculty research:* Political philosophy, comparative judicial studies, conflict studies, legislative studies, foreign policy. *Unit head:* Dr. Robert Blanton, Interim Chair, 901-678-2395, Fax: 901-678-2983, E-mail: rblanton@memphis.edu. *Application contact:* Dr. David Richards, Graduate Studies Coordinator, 901-678-3348, Fax: 901-678-2983, E-mail: drich1@memphis.edu.

University of Miami, Graduate School, College of Arts and Sciences, Department of Political Science, Coral Gables, FL 33124. Offers MPA, MPA/MPH. Part-time and evening/weekend programs available. *Degree requirements:* For master's, thesis optional. *Entrance requirements:* For master's, GRE General Test. Additional exam requirements/recommendations for international students: Required—TOEFL.

University of Michigan, Horace H. Rackham School of Graduate Studies, College of Literature, Science, and the Arts, Department of Political Science, Ann Arbor, MI 48109. Offers political science (AM, PhD); social work and political science (PhD); JD/AM. Terminal master's awarded for partial completion of doctoral program. *Degree requirements:* For master's, thesis; for doctorate, comprehensive exam, thesis/dissertation, oral defense of dissertation, preliminary exam. *Entrance requirements:* For master's and doctorate, GRE General Test. Additional exam requirements/recommendations for international students: Required—TOEFL. Electronic applications accepted. *Faculty research:* Political theory, American politics, world politics, comparative politics.

University of Minnesota, Twin Cities Campus, Graduate School, College of Liberal Arts, Department of Political Science, Minneapolis, MN 55455-0213. Offers PhD. Part-time programs available. *Degree requirements:* For doctorate, thesis/dissertation, 1 foreign language or

Political Science

University of Minnesota, Twin Cities Campus (continued)
statistics. *Entrance requirements:* For doctorate, GRE. Additional exam requirements/recommendations for international students: Required—TOEFL; Recommended—IELTS. Electronic applications accepted. *Faculty research:* Political psychology, political economy, social policy, legislative studies, history of political thought.

University of Mississippi, Graduate School, College of Liberal Arts, Department of Political Science, Oxford, University, MS 38677. Offers MA, PhD. *Degree requirements:* For doctorate, thesis/dissertation. *Entrance requirements:* For master's, GRE General Test, minimum GPA of 3.0; for doctorate, GRE General Test. Additional exam requirements/recommendations for international students: Required—TOEFL. Electronic applications accepted.

University of Missouri–Columbia, Graduate School, College of Arts and Sciences, Department of Political Science, Columbia, MO 65211. Offers MA, PhD. *Faculty:* 18 full-time (4 women), 2 part-time/adjunct (0 women). *Students:* 55 full-time (20 women), 13 part-time (5 women); includes 2 minority (1 Asian American or Pacific Islander, 1 Hispanic American), 24 international. Average age 28. 50 applicants, 50% accepted, 21 enrolled. In 2008, 3 master's, 5 doctorates awarded. Terminal master's awarded for partial completion of doctoral program. *Degree requirements:* For doctorate, one foreign language, thesis/dissertation. *Entrance requirements:* For master's and doctorate, GRE General Test, minimum GPA of 3.0. Additional exam requirements/recommendations for international students: Required—TOEFL (minimum score 570 paper-based; 240 computer-based; 88 iBT). *Application deadline:* For fall admission, 2/15 priority date for domestic students. Applications are processed on a rolling basis. Application fee: $45 ($60 for international students). *Financial support:* Fellowships, research assistantships, teaching assistantships, institutionally sponsored loans available. *Unit head:* Dr. John Petrocik, Department Chair, E-mail: petrocikj@missouri.edu. *Application contact:* Dana Davis, Administrative Assistant, 573-882-2062, E-mail: davisdana@missouri.edu.

University of Missouri–Kansas City, College of Arts and Sciences, Department of Political Science, Kansas City, MO 64110-2499. Offers MA, PhD. PhD (interdisciplinary) offered through the School of Graduate Studies. Part-time and evening/weekend programs available. *Faculty:* 7 full-time (2 women), 6 part-time/adjunct (1 woman). *Students:* 9 part-time (3 women); includes 2 minority (1 African American, 1 Hispanic American). Average age 42. 4 applicants, 100% accepted, 1 enrolled. In 2008, 2 master's awarded. Terminal master's awarded for partial completion of doctoral program. *Degree requirements:* For master's, thesis optional; for doctorate, thesis/dissertation. *Entrance requirements:* For master's, GRE, minimum GPA of 3.0, course work in political science, 2 letters of recommendation; for doctorate, GRE, minimum GPA of 3.0, MA in political science or related area, writing sample. Additional exam requirements/recommendations for international students: Required—TOEFL (minimum score 550 paper-based; 213 computer-based; 80 iBT). *Application deadline:* For fall admission, 4/1 priority date for domestic and international students; for spring admission, 11/1 priority date for domestic and international students. Applications are processed on a rolling basis. Application fee: $45 ($50 for international students). Electronic applications accepted. *Expenses:* Tuition, state resident: full-time $5376; part-time $298.70 per credit hour. Tuition, nonresident: full-time $13,882; part-time $771.20 per credit hour. Required fees: $640.28; $34.65 per contact hour. $30 per semester. Tuition and fees vary according to course load and program. *Financial support:* In 2008–09, 2 research assistantships (averaging $14,250 per year), 1 teaching assistantship with partial tuition reimbursement (averaging $11,400 per year) were awarded; career-related internships or fieldwork and institutionally sponsored loans also available. Financial award application deadline: 3/1; financial award applicants required to submit FAFSA. *Faculty research:* Sex and gender, Chinese politics, voting behavior, politics of presidency and social security, public law. *Unit head:* Dr. Harris Mirkin, Chair, 816-235-2792, Fax: 816-235-5594, E-mail: mirkinh@umkc.edu. *Application contact:* Dr. Harris Mirkin, Chair, 816-235-2792, Fax: 816-235-5594, E-mail: mirkinh@umkc.edu.

University of Missouri–St. Louis, College of Arts and Sciences, Department of Political Science, St. Louis, MO 63121. Offers American politics (MA); comparative politics (MA); international politics (MA); political process and behavior (MA); political science (PhD); public administration and public policy (MA); urban and regional politics (MA). Part-time and evening/weekend programs available. *Faculty:* 19 full-time (7 women). *Students:* 19 full-time (8 women), 23 part-time (14 women); includes 9 minority (6 African Americans, 1 American Indian/Alaska Native, 2 Asian Americans or Pacific Islanders), 4 international. Average age 36. In 2008, 6 master's, 2 doctorates awarded. Terminal master's awarded for partial completion of doctoral program. *Degree requirements:* For master's, thesis optional; for doctorate, thesis/dissertation. *Entrance requirements:* For master's, GRE General Test, 2 letters of recommendation; for doctorate, GRE General Test, 3 letters of recommendation. Additional exam requirements/recommendations for international students: Required—TOEFL (minimum score 550 paper-based; 213 computer-based). *Application deadline:* For fall admission, 2/15 priority date for domestic and international students; for spring admission, 10/15 priority date for domestic and international students. Applications are processed on a rolling basis. Application fee: $35 ($40 for international students). Electronic applications accepted. *Expenses:* Tuition, area resident: Full-time $5377; part-time $298.70 per credit hour. Tuition, nonresident: full-time $13,381; part-time $472.50 per credit hour. Required fees: $4078; $52 per credit hour. *Financial support:* In 2008–09, 10 research assistantships with full and partial tuition reimbursements (averaging $10,800 per year), 6 teaching assistantships with full and partial tuition reimbursements (averaging $10,800 per year) were awarded; fellowships, career-related internships or fieldwork also available. Support available to part-time students. Financial award application deadline: 3/15; financial award applicants required to submit FAFSA. *Faculty research:* Public policy, urban politics and administration, American government. *Unit head:* Dr. Barbara Graham, Director of Graduate Studies, 314-516-5522, Fax: 314-516-5268, E-mail: umslpolisci@umsl.edu. *Application contact:* 314-516-5458, Fax: 314-516-6996, E-mail: gradadm@umsl.edu.

The University of Montana, Graduate School, College of Arts and Sciences, Department of Political Science, Program in Political Science, Missoula, MT 59812-0002. Offers MA. *Degree requirements:* For master's, thesis. *Entrance requirements:* For master's, GRE General Test.

University of Nebraska at Omaha, Graduate Studies and Research, College of Arts and Sciences, Department of Political Science, Omaha, NE 68182. Offers MS. Part-time and evening/weekend programs available. *Degree requirements:* For master's, comprehensive exam, thesis (for some programs). *Entrance requirements:* For master's, 15 undergraduate political science hours, minimum undergraduate GPA of 3.0, 2 letters of recommendation. Additional exam requirements/recommendations for international students: Required—TOEFL (minimum score 500 paper-based; 173 computer-based; 61 iBT). Electronic applications accepted.

University of Nevada, Las Vegas, Graduate College, College of Liberal Arts, Department of Political Science, Las Vegas, NV 89154-5029. Offers ethics and policy studies (MA); political science (PhD). Part-time programs available. *Faculty:* 13 full-time (3 women). *Students:* 13 full-time (6 women), 10 part-time (3 women); includes 8 minority (1 African American, 1 American Indian/Alaska Native, 3 Asian Americans or Pacific Islanders, 3 Hispanic Americans). Average age 30. 19 applicants, 79% accepted, 12 enrolled. In 2008, 3 master's awarded. *Degree requirements:* For master's, comprehensive exam (for some programs), thesis (for some programs); for doctorate, comprehensive exam, thesis/dissertation, oral examination. *Entrance requirements:* For master's and doctorate, GRE General Test. Additional exam requirements/recommendations for international students: Required—TOEFL (minimum score 550 paper-based; 213 computer-based; 80 iBT), IELTS (minimum score 7). *Application deadline:* For fall admission, 2/1 priority date for domestic and international students; for spring admission, 10/1 priority date for domestic and international students. Applications are processed on a rolling basis. Application fee: $60 ($75 for international students). Electronic applications accepted. *Expenses:* Tuition, state resident: full-time $1414; part-time $198 per credit. Tuition, nonresident: full-time $12,509; part-time $415.75 per credit. International tuition: $14,249 full-time. Required fees: $4 per credit. $252 per semester. Tuition and fees vary according to course load. *Financial support:* In 2008–09, 10 students received support, including 5 research assistantships with partial tuition reimbursements available (averaging $10,000 per year), 5 teaching assistantships with partial tuition reimbursements available (averaging $11,000 per year); institutionally sponsored loans, scholarships/grants, health care benefits, and unspecified assistantships also available. Financial award application deadline: 3/1. *Faculty research:* Religion and politics, internal security and environmental cooperation, US elections and campaigns, party systems and democratization, judicial behavior. *Unit head:* Dr. Mehran Tamadonfar, Chair/Associate Professor, 702-895-5258, Fax: 702-895-1065, E-mail: mehran.tamadorfar@unlv.edu. *Application contact:* Graduate College Admissions Evaluator, 702-895-3320, Fax: 702-895-4180, E-mail: gradcollege@unlv.edu.

University of Nevada, Reno, Graduate School, College of Liberal Arts, Department of Political Science, Program in Political Science, Reno, NV 89557. Offers MA, PhD. *Faculty:* 16 full-time (6 women). *Students:* 9 full-time (3 women), 28 part-time (14 women); includes 6 minority (1 African American, 1 American Indian/Alaska Native, 4 Hispanic Americans), 2 international. Average age 40. 10 applicants, 90% accepted, 4 enrolled. In 2008, 6 master's, 1 doctorate awarded. Terminal master's awarded for partial completion of doctoral program. *Degree requirements:* For master's, comprehensive exam, oral exam/thesis or professional paper; for doctorate, thesis/dissertation, 2 field exams, oral exam. *Entrance requirements:* For master's, GRE General Test, GMAT, LSAT, minimum GPA of 2.75; for doctorate, GRE General Test, GMAT, LSAT, minimum GPA of 3.0. Additional exam requirements/recommendations for international students: Required—TOEFL (minimum score 500 paper-based; 173 computer-based; 61 iBT), IELTS (minimum score 6), TOFEL or IELTS. *Application deadline:* For fall admission, 3/31 priority date for domestic and international students. Applications are processed on a rolling basis. Application fee: $60 ($95 for international students). Electronic applications accepted. *Expenses:* Tuition, state resident: full-time $1710; part-time $1140 per semester. Tuition, nonresident: full-time $7115. Required fees: $158 per semester. *Financial support:* In 2008–09, 2 research assistantships with partial tuition reimbursements (averaging $14,000 per year), 6 teaching assistantships with partial tuition reimbursements (averaging $14,000 per year) were awarded; Federal Work-Study, institutionally sponsored loans, scholarships/grants, health care benefits, and unspecified assistantships also available. Financial award application deadline: 3/1; financial award applicants required to submit FAFSA. *Faculty research:* Analysis of political processes, institutions, and policies. Total annual research expenditures: $90,725. *Unit head:* Dr. Christopher Simon, Graduate Program Director, 775-682-7769, Fax: 775-784-1473, E-mail: casimon@unr.nevada.edu. *Application contact:* Michele Sandberg, Application Contact, 775-784-7026, Fax: 775-784-6064, E-mail: gradschool@unr.edu.

University of New Brunswick Fredericton, School of Graduate Studies, Faculty of Arts, Department of Political Science, Fredericton, NB E3B 5A3, Canada. Offers MA. Part-time programs available. *Faculty:* 6 full-time (2 women), 1 part-time/adjunct (0 women). *Students:* 10 full-time (2 women), 1 (woman) part-time. In 2008, 8 master's awarded. *Degree requirements:* For master's, thesis. *Entrance requirements:* For master's, minimum GPA of 3.0. Additional exam requirements/recommendations for international students: Required—TOEFL, TWE. *Application deadline:* For fall admission, 3/1 priority date for domestic students. Applications are processed on a rolling basis. Application fee: $50 Canadian dollars. Tuition and fees charges are reported in Canadian dollars. *Expenses:* Tuition, area resident: Full-time $5562 Canadian dollars. Tuition, nonresident: full-time $9450 Canadian dollars. Required fees: $333 Canadian dollars. *Financial support:* In 2008–09, 3 research assistantships, 2 teaching assistantships were awarded; fellowships also available. *Faculty research:* Canadian politics, political theory, public policy, gender and politics, international studies. *Unit head:* Dr. Joanne Wright, Director of Graduate Studies, 506-458-7422, Fax: 506-453-4755, E-mail: jwright@unb.ca. *Application contact:* Deborah Sloan, Graduate Secretary, 506-453-4826, Fax: 506-453-4755, E-mail: dsloan@unb.ca.

University of New Hampshire, Graduate School, College of Liberal Arts, Department of Political Science, Program in Political Science, Durham, NH 03824. Offers MA. Part-time programs available. *Faculty:* 15 full-time. *Students:* 5 full-time (1 woman), 14 part-time (6 women); includes 4 minority (1 African American, 1 American Indian/Alaska Native, 1 Asian American or Pacific Islander, 1 Hispanic American). Average age 28. 8 applicants, 88% accepted, 3 enrolled. In 2008, 8 master's awarded. *Degree requirements:* For master's, thesis. *Entrance requirements:* For master's, GRE General Test. Additional exam requirements/recommendations for international students: Required—TOEFL (minimum score 550 paper-based; 213 computer-based; 80 iBT). *Application deadline:* For fall admission, 4/1 priority date for domestic students, 4/1 for international students; for winter admission, 12/1 for domestic students. Applications are processed on a rolling basis. Application fee: $60. Electronic applications accepted. *Expenses:* Tuition, area resident: Full-time $9720; part-time $540 per credit hour. Tuition, nonresident: full-time $23,200; part-time $954 per credit hour. Required fees: $1446; $361.50 per term. *Financial support:* In 2008–09, 6 students received support, including 3 teaching assistantships; fellowships, research assistantships, career-related internships or fieldwork, Federal Work-Study, scholarships/grants, and tuition waivers (full and partial) also available. Support available to part-time students. Financial award application deadline: 2/15. *Unit head:* Dr. Warren Brown, Chairperson, 603-862-3225. *Application contact:* Tama Andrews, Administrative Assistant, 603-862-1750, E-mail: mpa.ma.political.science.grad@unh.edu.

University of New Mexico, Graduate School, College of Arts and Sciences, Department of Political Science, Albuquerque, NM 87131-2039. Offers MA, PhD. Part-time programs available. Terminal master's awarded for partial completion of doctoral program. *Degree requirements:* For master's, comprehensive exam, thesis optional, minimum cumulative GPA of 3.2; for doctorate, comprehensive exam, thesis/dissertation, field research paper, minimum cumulative GPA of 3.5. *Entrance requirements:* For master's and doctorate, GRE, 3 letters of recommendation, writing sample, letter of intent. Additional exam requirements/recommendations for international students: Required—TOEFL. Electronic applications accepted. *Faculty research:* Latin American politics, American politics, comparative politics, public policy, international relations, methodology.

University of New Orleans, Graduate School, College of Liberal Arts, Department of Political Science, New Orleans, LA 70148. Offers political science (MA, PhD); public administration (MPA). Evening/weekend programs available. *Degree requirements:* For master's, one foreign language, thesis or alternative; for doctorate, one foreign language, thesis/dissertation. *Entrance requirements:* For master's, GRE General Test; for doctorate, GRE General Test, GRE Subject Test. Additional exam requirements/recommendations for international students: Required—TOEFL (minimum score 550 paper-based; 213 computer-based; 79 iBT). Electronic applications accepted. *Faculty research:* Judicial politics, public policy, voting rights, Southern politics, presidential-congressional relations.

The University of North Carolina at Chapel Hill, Graduate School, College of Arts and Sciences, Department of Political Science, Program in Political Science, Chapel Hill, NC 27599. Offers MA, PhD. *Degree requirements:* For master's, comprehensive exam, thesis; for doctorate, one foreign language, comprehensive exam, thesis/dissertation. *Entrance requirements:* For master's and doctorate, GRE General Test, GRE Subject Test, minimum GPA of 3.0.

The University of North Carolina at Greensboro, Graduate School, College of Arts and Sciences, Department of Political Science, Greensboro, NC 27412-5001. Offers nonprofit management (Certificate); public affairs (MPA); urban and economic development (Certificate). *Accreditation:* NASPAA. *Degree requirements:* For master's, comprehensive exam. *Entrance requirements:* For master's, GRE General Test. Additional exam requirements/recommendations for international students: Required—TOEFL. Electronic applications accepted. *Faculty research:* U.S. Constitution, Canadian parliament, public management, ethical challenge of public service.

University of Northern British Columbia, Office of Graduate Studies, Prince George, BC V2N 4Z9, Canada. Offers business administration (Diploma); community health science (M Sc); disability management (MA); education (M Ed); first nations studies (MA); gender studies (MA); history (MA); interdisciplinary studies (MA); international studies (MA); mathematical, computer and physical sciences (M Sc); natural resources and environmental studies (M Sc, MA, MNRES, PhD); political science (MA); psychology (M Sc, PhD); social work (MSW).

Part-time and evening/weekend programs available. Postbaccalaureate distance learning degree programs offered (no on-campus study). *Degree requirements:* For master's, thesis; for doctorate, thesis/dissertation. *Entrance requirements:* For master's, GRE, minimum B average in undergraduate course work; for doctorate, candidacy exam, minimum A average in graduate course work.

University of Northern Iowa, Graduate College, College of Social and Behavioral Sciences, Department of Political Science, Cedar Falls, IA 50614. Offers MA. *Students:* 1 part-time (0 women). *Entrance requirements:* For master's, minimum GPA of 3.0. Additional exam requirements/recommendations for international students: Required—TOEFL (minimum score 500 paper-based; 180 computer-based; 61 iBT). *Expenses:* Tuition, state resident: full-time $6446. Tuition, nonresident: full-time $14,874. Required fees: $852. *Unit head:* Dr. Philip Mauceri, Head, 319-273-2528, Fax: 319-273-7103, E-mail: philip.mauceri@uni.edu. *Application contact:* Laurie S. Russell, Record Analyst, 319-273-2623, Fax: 319-273-6792, E-mail: laurie.russell@uni.edu.

University of North Texas, Robert B. Toulouse School of Graduate Studies, College of Arts and Sciences, Department of Political Science, Denton, TX 76203. Offers MA, MS, PhD. Evening/weekend programs available. *Degree requirements:* For master's, comprehensive exam, thesis (for some programs); for doctorate, 2 foreign languages, comprehensive exam, thesis/dissertation. *Entrance requirements:* For master's, GRE General Test, minimum GPA of 3.0, 3 letters of recommendation, statement of interest; for doctorate, GRE General Test, 3 letters of recommendation, statement of interest. Additional exam requirements/recommendations for international students: Required—proof of English language proficiency; Recommended—TOEFL (minimum score 550 paper-based; 213 computer-based). *Faculty research:* Political parties, international conflict, judicial politics, comparative politics.

University of Notre Dame, Graduate School, College of Arts and Letters, Division of Social Science, Department of Political Science, Notre Dame, IN 46556. Offers PhD. *Faculty:* 42 full-time (8 women), 5 part-time/adjunct (1 woman). *Students:* 82 full-time (34 women); includes 13 minority (2 African Americans, 1 American Indian/Alaska Native, 1 Asian American or Pacific Islander, 9 Hispanic Americans), 28 international. 173 applicants, 14% accepted, 11 enrolled. In 2008, 9 doctorates awarded. *Degree requirements:* For doctorate, one foreign language, comprehensive exam, thesis/dissertation, candidacy exam. *Entrance requirements:* For doctorate, GRE General Test. Additional exam requirements/recommendations for international students: Required—TOEFL (minimum score 600 paper-based; 250 computer-based; 80 iBT). *Application deadline:* For fall admission, 1/10 priority date for domestic and international students. Application fee: $50. Electronic applications accepted. *Financial support:* Fellowships with full tuition reimbursements, research assistantships with full tuition reimbursements, teaching assistantships with full tuition reimbursements, career-related internships or fieldwork and tuition waivers (full) available. Financial award application deadline: 2/1. *Faculty research:* American government, comparative politics, international relations, political theory. *Unit head:* Dr. Christina Wolbrecht, Director of Graduate Studies, 574-631-9017, E-mail: govtgrad@nd.edu. *Application contact:* Dr. Barbara Turpin, Director of Graduate Admissions, 574-631-7706, Fax: 574-631-4183.

University of Oklahoma, Graduate College, College of Arts and Sciences, Department of Political Science, Program in Political Science, Norman, OK 73019-0390. Offers MA, PhD. *Students:* 38 full-time (14 women), 23 part-time (11 women); includes 6 minority (3 African Americans, 1 American Indian/Alaska Native, 2 Asian Americans or Pacific Islanders), 11 international. 25 applicants, 84% accepted, 7 enrolled. In 2008, 8 master's, 2 doctorates awarded. Terminal master's awarded for partial completion of doctoral program. *Degree requirements:* For master's, thesis or alternative; for doctorate, thesis/dissertation, language or quantitative techniques. *Entrance requirements:* For master's and doctorate, GRE General Test, 3 letters of recommendation. Additional exam requirements/recommendations for international students: Required—TOEFL (minimum score 600 paper-based; 250 computer-based). *Application deadline:* For fall admission, 2/1 for domestic and international students; for spring admission, 10/15 for domestic students, 9/1 for international students. Applications are processed on a rolling basis. Application fee: $40 ($90 for international students). Electronic applications accepted. *Expenses:* Tuition, state resident: full-time $3744; part-time $156 per credit hour. Tuition, nonresident: full-time $13,577; part-time $565.70 per credit hour. Required fees: $2415.40; $90.10 per credit hour. *Financial support:* In 2008–09, 23 students received support. Tuition waivers (partial) and unspecified assistantships available. *Faculty research:* American politics; institutions, processes and political behavior; Democratization; international security; terrorism; knowledge utilization in the policy process; comparative administration systems. *Application contact:* Mitchell P. Smith, Graduate Programs Director, 405-325-8893, Fax: 405-325-0718, E-mail: mps@ou.edu.

University of Oregon, Graduate School, College of Arts and Sciences, Department of Political Science, Eugene, OR 97403. Offers MA, MS, PhD. Terminal master's awarded for partial completion of doctoral program. *Degree requirements:* For master's, thesis or alternative; for doctorate, thesis/dissertation. *Entrance requirements:* For master's and doctorate, GRE General Test, minimum GPA of 3.0. Additional exam requirements/recommendations for international students: Required—TOEFL. *Faculty research:* Public policy, public choice, comparative politics, political economy, international relations.

University of Ottawa, Faculty of Graduate and Postdoctoral Studies, Faculty of Social Sciences, Department of Political Studies, Ottawa, ON K1N 6N5, Canada. Offers MA, PhD. *Degree requirements:* For master's, thesis or alternative, fluency in English and French; for doctorate, comprehensive exam, thesis/dissertation. *Entrance requirements:* For master's, honors bachelor's degree or equivalent, minimum B average; for doctorate, master's degree, minimum B+ average. Electronic applications accepted. *Faculty research:* Political thought and analysis of ideologies, Canadian and Québécois policies, international and comparative policies.

University of Pennsylvania, School of Arts and Sciences, Graduate Group in Political Science, Philadelphia, PA 19104. Offers AM, PhD, MGA/AM. Terminal master's awarded for partial completion of doctoral program. *Degree requirements:* For doctorate, one foreign language, thesis/dissertation. *Entrance requirements:* For master's and doctorate, GRE General Test. Additional exam requirements/recommendations for international students: Required—TOEFL. Electronic applications accepted.

University of Pittsburgh, Graduate School of Public and International Affairs, Executive Programs in Public Policy and Management, Pittsburgh, PA 15260. Offers development planning (MPPM); international development (MPPM); international political economy (MPPM); international security studies (MPPM); management of non profit organizations (MPPM); metropolitan management and regional development (MPPM); policy analysis and evaluation (MPPM). Part-time programs available. *Degree requirements:* For master's, thesis optional, capstone seminar. *Entrance requirements:* For master's, 2 letters of recommendation, resumé, 5 years of supervisory or budgetary experience. Additional exam requirements/recommendations for international students: Required—TOEFL (minimum score 600 paper-based; 250 computer-based; 100 iBT), TWE (minimum score 4); Recommended—IELTS (minimum score 7). Electronic applications accepted. *Faculty research:* Executive training and technical assistance for U.S. and international clients.

See Close-Up on page 1243.

University of Pittsburgh, Graduate School of Public and International Affairs, International Affairs Division, Program in Global Political Economy, Pittsburgh, PA 15260. Offers MPIA, JD/MPIA, MBA/MPIA, MID/MPIA, MPA/MPIA, MSIS/MPIA. Part-time and evening/weekend programs available. *Degree requirements:* For master's, thesis optional, internship, capstone seminar. *Entrance requirements:* For master's, GRE General Test, 3 letters of recommendation, resumé, minimum GPA of 3.2. Additional exam requirements/recommendations for international students: Required—TOEFL (minimum score 550 paper-based; 213 computer-

based; 80 iBT), TWE (minimum score 4); Recommended—IELTS (minimum score 7). Electronic applications accepted. *Faculty research:* Political economy, international security/defense/intelligence, transnational crime, international trade, international finance, terrorism.

University of Pittsburgh, School of Arts and Sciences, Department of Political Science, Pittsburgh, PA 15260. Offers MA, PhD. Part-time programs available. Terminal master's awarded for partial completion of doctoral program. *Degree requirements:* For master's, comprehensive exam; for doctorate, comprehensive exam, thesis/dissertation. *Entrance requirements:* For master's and doctorate, GRE General Test, minimum QPA of 3.0. Additional exam requirements/recommendations for international students: Required—TOEFL. Electronic applications accepted.

University of Regina, Faculty of Graduate Studies and Research, Faculty of Arts, Department of Philosophy, Regina, SK S4S 0A2, Canada. Offers philosophy (MA); social and political thought (MA). *Faculty:* 9 full-time (3 women). *Students:* 3 full-time (2 women). 2 applicants, 100% accepted. *Degree requirements:* For master's, thesis. *Entrance requirements:* Additional exam requirements/recommendations for international students: Required—TOEFL (minimum score 580 paper-based; 237 computer-based; 88 iBT). *Application deadline:* Applications are processed on a rolling basis. Application fee: $85 ($100 for international students). Electronic applications accepted. *Financial support:* Fellowships, research assistantships, teaching assistantships, scholarships/grants available. Financial award application deadline: 6/15. *Faculty research:* History of philosophy, ethics, aesthetics, metaphysics, epistemology. *Unit head:* Dr. Eldon Soifer, Head, 306-585-4301, Fax: 306-585-4827, E-mail: eldon.soifer@uregina.ca. *Application contact:* Dr. Eldon Soifer, Head, 306-585-4301, Fax: 306-585-4827, E-mail: eldon.soifer@uregina.ca.

University of Regina, Faculty of Graduate Studies and Research, Faculty of Arts, Department of Political Science, Regina, SK S4S 0A2, Canada. Offers MA. Part-time programs available. *Faculty:* 10 full-time (3 women), 1 (woman) part-time/adjunct. *Students:* 11 full-time (6 women), 11 part-time (6 women). 10 applicants, 60% accepted, 4 enrolled. In 2008, 3 master's awarded. *Degree requirements:* For master's, thesis. *Entrance requirements:* Additional exam requirements/recommendations for international students: Required—TOEFL (minimum score 580 paper-based; 237 computer-based; 88 iBT). *Application deadline:* For fall admission, 3/15 for domestic students. Applications are processed on a rolling basis. Application fee: $85 ($100 for international students). Electronic applications accepted. *Financial support:* In 2008–09, 2 fellowships (averaging $15,000 per year), 2 research assistantships (averaging $13,500 per year), 1 teaching assistantship (averaging $6,558 per year) were awarded; scholarships/grants also available. Financial award application deadline: 6/15. *Faculty research:* Canadian politics, comparative politics, international politics. *Unit head:* Dr. Jeremy Rayner, Head, 306-585-5679, Fax: 306-585-4815, E-mail: jeremy.rayner@uregina.ca. *Application contact:* Dr. Yuchao Zhu, Graduate Coordinator, 306-585-4060, E-mail: yuchao.zhu@uregina.ca.

University of Regina, Faculty of Graduate Studies and Research, Faculty of Arts, Program in Social and Political Thought, Regina, SK S4S 0A2, Canada. Offers MA. *Faculty:* 9 full-time (3 women). *Students:* 5 full-time (1 woman), 4 part-time (0 women). 3 applicants, 100% accepted. In 2008, 1 master's awarded. *Degree requirements:* For master's, thesis. *Entrance requirements:* Additional exam requirements/recommendations for international students: Required—TOEFL (minimum score 580 paper-based; 237 computer-based; 88 iBT). *Application deadline:* For fall admission, 3/15 for domestic students. Application fee: $85 ($100 for international students). Electronic applications accepted. *Financial support:* In 2008–09, 1 fellowship (averaging $15,000 per year), 1 research assistantship (averaging $13,500 per year), 1 teaching assistantship (averaging $6,558 per year) were awarded. *Unit head:* Dr. Shadia Drury, Program Coordinator, 306-585-4073, E-mail: shadia.drury@uregina.ca. *Application contact:* Dr. Shadia Drury, Program Coordinator, 306-585-4073, E-mail: shadia.drury@uregina.ca.

University of Rhode Island, Graduate School, College of Arts and Sciences, Department of Political Science, Kingston, RI 02881. Offers political science (MA), including American politics, comparative government, international relations, public policy; public policy and administration (MA, MPA, Certificate). In 2008, 6 master's awarded. Application fee: $35. *Expenses:* Tuition, state resident: full-time $8024; part-time $446 per credit. Tuition, nonresident: full-time $21,046; part-time $1169 per credit. Required fees: $1056; $26 per credit. $30 per semester. One-time fee: $95 part-time. *Unit head:* Dr. Gerry Tyler, Chairperson, 401-874-4053, E-mail: gtyler@uri.edu. *Application contact:* Harold D. Bibb, Associate Dean of the Graduate School, 401-874-2262, Fax: 401-874-5491.

University of Rochester, The College, Arts and Sciences, Department of Political Science, Rochester, NY 14627-0250. Offers MA, PhD, MPH/MS, MS/PhD. Terminal master's awarded for partial completion of doctoral program. *Degree requirements:* For doctorate, thesis/dissertation, qualifying exam. *Entrance requirements:* For master's and doctorate, GRE General Test. Additional exam requirements/recommendations for international students: Required—TOEFL.

University of Saskatchewan, College of Graduate Studies and Research, College of Arts and Sciences, Department of Political Studies, Saskatoon, SK S7N 5A2, Canada. Offers MA. *Degree requirements:* For master's, thesis. *Entrance requirements:* Additional exam requirements/recommendations for international students: Required—TOEFL.

University of South Africa, College of Human Sciences, Pretoria, South Africa. Offers adult education (M Ed); African languages (MA, PhD); African politics (MA, PhD); Afrikaans (MA, PhD); ancient history (MA, PhD); ancient Near Eastern studies (MA, PhD); anthropology (MA, PhD); applied linguistics (MA); Arabic (MA, PhD); archaeology (MA); art history (MA); Biblical archaeology (MA); Biblical studies (M Th, D Th, PhD); Christian spirituality (M Th, D Th); church history (M Th, D Th); classical studies (MA, PhD); clinical psychology (MA); communication (MA, PhD); comparative education (M Ed, Ed D); consulting psychology (D Admin, D Com, PhD); curriculum studies (M Ed, Ed D); development studies (M Admin, MA, D Admin, PhD); didactics (M Ed, Ed D); education (M Tech); education management (M Ed, Ed D); educational psychology (M Ed); English (MA); environmental education (M Ed); French (MA, PhD); German (MA, PhD); Greek (MA); guidance and counseling (M Ed); health studies (MA, PhD), including health sciences education (MA), health services management (MA), medical and surgical nursing science (critical care general) (MA), midwifery and neonatal nursing science (MA), trauma and emergency care (MA); history (MA, PhD); history of education (Ed D); inclusive education (M Ed, Ed D); information and communications technology policy and regulation (MA); information science (MA, MIS, PhD); international politics (MA, PhD); Islamic studies (MA, PhD); Italian (MA, PhD); Judaica (MA, PhD); linguistics (MA, PhD); mathematical education (M Ed); mathematics education (MA); missiology (M Th, D Th); modern Hebrew (MA, PhD); musicology (MA, MMus, D Mus, PhD); natural science education (M Ed); New Testament (M Th, D Th); Old Testament (D Th); pastoral therapy (M Th, D Th); philosophy (MA); philosophy of education (M Ed, Ed D); politics (MA, PhD); Portuguese (MA, PhD); practical theology (M Th, D Th); psychology (MA, MS, PhD); psychology of education (M Ed, Ed D); public health (MA); religious studies (MA, D Th, PhD); Romance languages (MA); Russian (MA, PhD); Semitic languages (MA, PhD); social behavior studies in HIV/AIDS (MA); social science (mental health) (MA); social science in development studies (MA); social science in psychology (MA); social science in social work (MA); social science in sociology (MA); social work (MSW, DSW, PhD); socio-education (M Ed, Ed D); sociolinguistics (MA); sociology (MA, PhD); Spanish (MA, PhD); systematic theology (M Th, D Th); TESOL (teaching English to speakers of other languages) (MA); theological ethics (M Th, D Th); theory of literature (MA, PhD); urban ministries (D Th); urban ministry (M Th).

University of South Carolina, The Graduate School, College of Arts and Sciences, Department of Political Science, Program in Political Science, Columbia, SC 29208. Offers MA, PhD. Part-time programs available. Terminal master's awarded for partial completion of doctoral program. *Degree requirements:* For master's, one foreign language, thesis; for doctorate, one foreign language, comprehensive exam, thesis/dissertation. *Entrance requirements:* For master's and doctorate, GRE General Test, minimum GPA of 3.5. Additional exam requirements/recommendations for international students: Required—TOEFL. Electronic applications accepted.

Political Science

University of South Carolina (continued)
Faculty research: American government and politics, comparative politics, political theory, international politics, public administration and policy.

The University of South Dakota, Graduate School, College of Arts and Sciences, Department of Political Science, Vermillion, SD 57069-2390. Offers American political institutions (PhD); political science (MA); public administration (MPA, PhD); public policy (PhD); JD/MA; JD/MPA. *Accreditation:* NASPAA (one or more programs are accredited). Part-time programs available. Postbaccalaureate distance learning degree programs offered. *Degree requirements:* For master's, comprehensive exam, thesis (for some programs). *Entrance requirements:* For master's, GRE or LSAT (MPA), GRE General Test (MA), minimum GPA of 2.7. Additional exam requirements/recommendations for international students: Required—TOEFL (minimum score 550 paper-based; 213 computer-based; 79 iBT). Electronic applications accepted.

University of Southern California, Graduate School, Annenberg School for Communication, School of Communication, Program in Public Diplomacy, Los Angeles, CA 90089. Offers MPD. *Degree requirements:* For master's, thesis. *Entrance requirements:* For master's, GRE, resumé, writing samples, recommendation letters. Additional exam requirements/recommendations for international students: Required—TOEFL (minimum score 280 computer-based; 114 iBT). Electronic applications accepted.

See Close-Up on page 709.

University of Southern California, Graduate School, College of Letters, Arts and Sciences, Department of Political Science, Los Angeles, CA 90089. Offers politics and international relations (MA, PhD). *Degree requirements:* For doctorate, one foreign language, thesis/dissertation. *Entrance requirements:* For doctorate, GRE General Test. *Faculty research:* Public law, urban politics, political communication, Pacific Rim studies, environmental politics.

University of Southern Mississippi, Graduate School, College of Arts and Letters, Department of Political Science, International Development, and International Affairs, Hattiesburg, MS 39406-0001. Offers international development (PhD); political science (MA, MS). Part-time programs available. *Faculty:* 14 full-time (2 women), 1 part-time/adjunct (0 women). *Students:* 36 full-time (14 women), 44 part-time (17 women); includes 18 minority (12 African Americans, 1 American Indian/Alaska Native, 2 Asian Americans or Pacific Islanders, 3 Hispanic Americans), 6 international. Average age 41. 25 applicants, 68% accepted, 15 enrolled. In 2008, 8 master's awarded. *Degree requirements:* For master's, comprehensive exam, thesis (for some programs). *Entrance requirements:* For master's, GRE General Test, minimum GPA of 2.75 in last 2 years, 3.0 in field of study. *Application deadline:* For fall admission, 3/1 priority date for domestic students, 3/1 for international students. Applications are processed on a rolling basis. Application fee: $30. *Financial support:* In 2008–09, 4 research assistantships with full and partial tuition reimbursements (averaging $9,000 per year), 8 teaching assistantships with full tuition reimbursements (averaging $7,000 per year) were awarded; career-related internships or fieldwork, Federal Work-Study, scholarships/grants, and unspecified assistantships also available. Financial award application deadline: 3/15; financial award applicants required to submit FAFSA. *Faculty research:* American politics, international politics, political theory, comparative politics, public law. *Unit head:* Dr. Thomas Lansford, Interim Chair, 601-266-4310. *Application contact:* Dr. Robert Pauley, Graduate Coordinator, 601-266-4310, Fax: 601-266-4172.

University of South Florida, Graduate School, College of Arts and Sciences, Department of Government and International Affairs, Tampa, FL 33620-9951. Offers Latin American Caribbean and Latino Studies (MA); political science (MA); public administration (MPA). Part-time and evening/weekend programs available. *Faculty:* 18 full-time (3 women), 1 (woman) part-time/adjunct. *Students:* 33 full-time (21 women), 98 part-time (50 women); includes 39 minority (20 African Americans, 5 Asian Americans or Pacific Islanders, 14 Hispanic Americans), 6 international. 81 applicants, 62% accepted, 29 enrolled. In 2008, 27 master's awarded. *Degree requirements:* For master's, comprehensive exam, thesis; for doctorate, comprehensive exam, thesis/dissertation. *Entrance requirements:* For master's, GRE (minimum score: 470 verbal, 470 quantitative), minimum GPA of 3.0 in last 60 hours of course work. Additional exam requirements/recommendations for international students: Required—TOEFL (minimum score 550 paper-based; 213 computer-based). *Application deadline:* For fall admission, 2/15 for domestic students; for spring admission, 10/15 for domestic students. Applications are processed on a rolling basis. Application fee: $30. Electronic applications accepted. *Expenses:* Tuition, state resident: full-time $2624.40; part-time $291.60 per credit hour. Tuition, nonresident: full-time $7822; part-time $869.13 per credit hour. *Financial support:* Scholarships/grants and unspecified assistantships available. Financial award application deadline: 4/1. *Unit head:* Dr. Mohsen Milani, Chairperson, 813-974-2384, Fax: 813-974-0832, E-mail: milani@chuma1.cas.usf.edu. *Application contact:* Dr. Stephen Tauber, Graduate Coordinator, 813-974-0781, Fax: 813-974-0832, E-mail: stauber@chuma1.cas.usf.edu.

The University of Tennessee, Graduate School, College of Arts and Sciences, Department of Political Science, Program in Political Science, Knoxville, TN 37996. Offers MA, PhD. Part-time programs available. *Degree requirements:* For master's, thesis or alternative; for doctorate, one foreign language, thesis/dissertation. *Entrance requirements:* For master's and doctorate, GRE General Test, minimum GPA of 2.7. Additional exam requirements/recommendations for international students: Required—TOEFL. Electronic applications accepted. *Expenses:* Tuition, area resident: Part-time $348 per credit hour. Tuition, state resident: full-time $6262. Tuition, nonresident: full-time $18,920; part-time $1052 per credit hour. Required fees: $812; $36 per credit hour. Tuition and fees vary according to program.

The University of Tennessee, Graduate School, College of Arts and Sciences, Department of Sociology, Knoxville, TN 37996. Offers criminology (MA, PhD); energy, environment, and resource policy (MA, PhD); political economy (MA, PhD). Part-time programs available. *Degree requirements:* For master's, thesis or alternative; for doctorate, thesis/dissertation. *Entrance requirements:* For master's, GRE General Test, minimum GPA of 3.0; for doctorate, GRE General Test, minimum GPA of 3.5. Additional exam requirements/recommendations for international students: Required—TOEFL. Electronic applications accepted. *Expenses:* Tuition, area resident: Part-time $348 per credit hour. Tuition, state resident: full-time $6262. Tuition, nonresident: full-time $18,920; part-time $1052 per credit hour. Required fees: $812; $36 per credit hour. Tuition and fees vary according to program.

The University of Texas at Arlington, Graduate School, College of Liberal Arts, Department of Political Science, Arlington, TX 76019. Offers MA. Part-time and evening/weekend programs available. *Faculty:* 4 full-time (1 woman), 1 part-time/adjunct (0 women). *Students:* 9 full-time (5 women), 21 part-time (10 women); includes 6 minority (3 African Americans, 3 Hispanic Americans), 3 international. 30 applicants, 73% accepted, 12 enrolled. In 2008, 15 master's awarded. *Degree requirements:* For master's, comprehensive exam, thesis optional. *Entrance requirements:* For master's, GRE, minimum GPA of 3.0 in last 60 hours of course work. Additional exam requirements/recommendations for international students: Required—TOEFL (minimum score 550 paper-based; 213 computer-based). *Application deadline:* For fall admission, 6/16 for domestic students. Applications are processed on a rolling basis. Application fee: $35 ($50 for international students). *Expenses:* Tuition, area resident: Full-time $6500. Tuition, state resident: full-time $6500. Tuition, nonresident: full-time $11,558. *Financial support:* In 2008–09, 2 students received support, including 2 teaching assistantships (averaging $5,000 per year); career-related internships or fieldwork, institutionally sponsored loans, and scholarships/grants also available. Support available to part-time students. Financial award application deadline: 6/1; financial award applicants required to submit FAFSA. *Unit head:* Dr. Rebecca Deen, Chair, 817-272-2991, Fax: 817-272-2525, E-mail: deen@uta.edu. *Application contact:* Dr. Brent Boyea, Graduate Advisor, 817-272-2991, E-mail: boyea@uta.edu.

The University of Texas at Austin, Graduate School, College of Liberal Arts, Department of Government, Austin, TX 78712-1111. Offers PhD. *Degree requirements:* For doctorate, comprehensive exam, thesis/dissertation. *Entrance requirements:* For doctorate, GRE General Test. Electronic applications accepted.

The University of Texas at Brownsville, Graduate Studies, College of Liberal Arts, Department of Government, Brownsville, TX 78520-4991. Offers MAIS. Part-time and evening/weekend programs available. *Degree requirements:* For master's, comprehensive exam, thesis optional. *Entrance requirements:* For master's, GRE General Test. Additional exam requirements/recommendations for international students: Required—TOEFL.

The University of Texas at Dallas, School of Economic, Political and Policy Sciences, Program in Political Science, Richardson, TX 75083-0688. Offers legislative studies (MA); political science (PhD). Part-time and evening/weekend programs available. *Faculty:* 12 full-time (4 women). *Students:* 30 full-time (8 women), 10 part-time (6 women); includes 10 minority (2 African Americans, 2 American Indian/Alaska Native, 3 Asian Americans or Pacific Islanders, 3 Hispanic Americans), 7 international. Average age 38. 20 applicants, 75% accepted, 8 enrolled. In 2008, 1 doctorate awarded. *Degree requirements:* For doctorate, thesis/dissertation. *Entrance requirements:* For master's and doctorate, GRE General Test, minimum GPA of 3.0 in upper-level course work in field. Additional exam requirements/recommendations for international students: Required—TOEFL (minimum score 550 paper-based; 213 computer-based). *Application deadline:* For fall admission, 7/15 for domestic students, 5/1 priority date for international students; for spring admission, 11/15 for domestic students, 9/1 priority date for international students. Applications are processed on a rolling basis. Application fee: $50 ($100 for international students). Electronic applications accepted. *Expenses:* Tuition, area resident: Full-time $8320. Tuition, state resident: full-time $8320. Tuition, nonresident: full-time $15,054. Part-time tuition and fees vary according to course load. *Financial support:* In 2008–09, 5 research assistantships with tuition reimbursements (averaging $15,329 per year), 16 teaching assistantships with tuition reimbursements (averaging $12,300 per year) were awarded; fellowships, career-related internships or fieldwork, Federal Work-Study, institutionally sponsored loans, and scholarships/grants also available. Support available to part-time students. Financial award application deadline: 4/30; financial award applicants required to submit FAFSA. *Unit head:* Dr. Robert C. Lowry, Program Head, 972-883-6720, Fax: 972-883-2735, E-mail: robert.lowry@utdallas.edu. *Application contact:* Dr. Thomas L. Brunell, Associate Program Head, 972-883-4963, Fax: 972-883-2735, E-mail: tbrunell@utdallas.edu.

The University of Texas at Dallas, School of Economic, Political and Policy Sciences, Program in Public Policy and Political Economy, Richardson, TX 75083-0688. Offers international political economy (MS); public policy (MPP); public policy and political economy (PhD). Part-time and evening/weekend programs available. *Faculty:* 14 full-time (4 women). *Students:* 33 full-time (12 women), 43 part-time (20 women); includes 26 minority (10 African Americans, 8 Asian Americans or Pacific Islanders, 8 Hispanic Americans), 19 international. Average age 40. 42 applicants, 95% accepted, 21 enrolled. In 2008, 1 master's, 6 doctorates awarded. *Degree requirements:* For doctorate, thesis/dissertation. *Entrance requirements:* For master's and doctorate, GRE General Test, minimum GPA of 3.0 in upper-level course work in field. Additional exam requirements/recommendations for international students: Required—TOEFL (minimum score 550 paper-based; 213 computer-based). *Application deadline:* For fall admission, 7/15 for domestic students, 5/1 priority date for international students; for spring admission, 11/15 for domestic students, 9/1 priority date for international students. Applications are processed on a rolling basis. Application fee: $50 ($100 for international students). Electronic applications accepted. *Expenses:* Tuition, area resident: Full-time $8320. Tuition, state resident: full-time $8320. Tuition, nonresident: full-time $15,054. Part-time tuition and fees vary according to course load. *Financial support:* In 2008–09, 2 research assistantships with tuition reimbursements (averaging $18,188 per year), 11 teaching assistantships with tuition reimbursements (averaging $12,436 per year) were awarded; fellowships, career-related internships or fieldwork, Federal Work-Study, institutionally sponsored loans, and scholarships/grants also available. Support available to part-time students. Financial award application deadline: 4/30; financial award applicants required to submit FAFSA. *Faculty research:* New leadership development, gender and leadership, globalization and leadership opportunities in democracy. *Unit head:* Dr. Sheila Amin Gutierrez de Pineres, Program Head, 972-883-6228, Fax: 972-883-2735, E-mail: pineres@utdallas.edu. *Application contact:* Dr. Marie I Chevrier, Associate Program Head, 972-883-2727, Fax: 972-883-2735, E-mail: chevrier@utdallas.edu.

See Close-Up on page 783.

The University of Texas at El Paso, Graduate School, College of Liberal Arts, Department of Political Science, El Paso, TX 79968-0001. Offers MA. Part-time and evening/weekend programs available. *Degree requirements:* For master's, thesis (for some programs). *Entrance requirements:* For master's, GMAT, GRE General Test, minimum GPA of 3.0. Electronic applications accepted.

The University of Texas at San Antonio, College of Liberal and Fine Arts, Department of Political Science and Geography, San Antonio, TX 78249-0617. Offers political science (MA). Part-time and evening/weekend programs available. *Degree requirements:* For master's, thesis optional. *Entrance requirements:* For master's, GRE General Test. Additional exam requirements/recommendations for international students: Required—TOEFL (minimum score 500 paper-based; 173 computer-based). Electronic applications accepted.

The University of Texas at Tyler, College of Arts and Sciences, Department of Political Science, Tyler, TX 75799-0001. Offers MA. Part-time and evening/weekend programs available. *Degree requirements:* For master's, comprehensive exam, thesis optional, 36 hours of course work, minimum GPA of 3.0. *Entrance requirements:* Additional exam requirements/recommendations for international students: Required—TOEFL (minimum score 79 computer-based). *Faculty research:* American politics, comparative politics, international relations, political theory and philosophy.

The University of Texas of the Permian Basin, Office of Graduate Studies, College of Arts and Sciences, Department of Social Sciences, Odessa, TX 79762-0001. Offers criminal justice administration (MS); political science (MPA). Part-time and evening/weekend programs available. *Degree requirements:* For master's, comprehensive exam (for some programs), thesis (for some programs). *Entrance requirements:* For master's, GRE General Test. Additional exam requirements/recommendations for international students: Required—TOEFL (minimum score 550 paper-based; 213 computer-based).

The University of Toledo, College of Graduate Studies, College of Arts and Sciences, Department of Political Science and Public Administration, Program in Political Science, Toledo, OH 43606-3390. Offers MA. *Degree requirements:* For master's, thesis. *Entrance requirements:* For master's, GRE General Test, GRE Subject Test, minimum GPA of 2.7. Electronic applications accepted. *Faculty research:* Economic policy, development, Third World, Eastern Europe, Africa.

University of Toronto, School of Graduate Studies, Social Sciences Division, Department of Political Science, Toronto, ON M5S 1A1, Canada. Offers MA, PhD. Part-time programs available. *Degree requirements:* For master's, thesis optional; for doctorate, one foreign language, thesis/dissertation, reading competency in a language other than English. *Entrance requirements:* For master's, 3 letters of recommendation, writing sample; for doctorate, 4 letters of recommendation, writing sample.

University of Utah, The Graduate School, College of Humanities, Program in Middle East Studies, Salt Lake City, UT 84112-1107. Offers anthropology (MA); Arabic (MA, PhD); Arabic and linguistics (MA, PhD); Hebrew (MA); history (MA, PhD); Persian (MA, PhD); political science (MA, PhD); Turkish (MA). Terminal master's awarded for partial completion of doctoral program. *Degree requirements:* For master's, 2 foreign languages, comprehensive exam, thesis optional; for doctorate, 3 foreign languages, comprehensive exam, thesis/dissertation. *Entrance requirements:* For master's, GRE General Test, minimum GPA of 3.2; for doctorate, GRE General Test, MA in Middle East studies or equivalent, minimum GPA of 3.2. Additional exam requirements/recommendations for international students: Required—TOEFL (minimum score 580 paper-based; 237 computer-based; 92 iBT). *Faculty research:* Arabic literature and linguistics, Islamic studies, Middle East history, political science, Judaic studies.

University of Utah, The Graduate School, College of Social and Behavioral Science, Department of Political Science, Program in Political Science, Salt Lake City, UT 84112-1107. Offers MA, MS, PhD. Part-time programs available. *Degree requirements:* For master's, one foreign language, thesis or research paper; for doctorate, variable foreign language requirement, thesis/dissertation. *Entrance requirements:* For master's, GRE General Test, minimum GPA of 3.2; for doctorate, GRE General Test. Additional exam requirements/recommendations for international students: Required—TOEFL (minimum score 500 paper-based; 173 computer-based). *Faculty research:* Middle East politics, environmental politics, democratic theory, political participation, Latin-American politics.

University of Victoria, Faculty of Graduate Studies, Faculty of Social Sciences, Department of Political Science, Victoria, BC V8W 2Y2, Canada. Offers MA, PhD. Part-time programs available. *Degree requirements:* For master's, thesis; for doctorate, thesis/dissertation, candidacy exam. *Entrance requirements:* For master's, minimum B+ average in last 2 years of undergraduate course work. Additional exam requirements/recommendations for international students: Required—TOEFL (minimum score 600 paper-based; 250 computer-based). Electronic applications accepted. *Faculty research:* Political theory, political parties, international political economy, comparative public policy, British Columbian politics.

University of Virginia, College and Graduate School of Arts and Sciences, Department of Politics, Program in Government, Charlottesville, VA 22903. Offers MA, PhD, JD/MA, MBA/MA. *Students:* 34 full-time (11 women); includes 1 minority (African American), 11 international. Average age 29. 61 applicants, 31% accepted, 3 enrolled. In 2008, 3 master's, 7 doctorates awarded. *Degree requirements:* For master's, 2 research/statistics courses or thesis; for doctorate, variable foreign language requirement, thesis/dissertation, 2 research/statistics courses. *Entrance requirements:* For master's and doctorate, GRE General Test, long writing sample; 2 letters of recommendation. Additional exam requirements/recommendations for international students: Required—TOEFL (minimum score 600 paper-based; 250 computer-based; 90 iBT), IELTS (minimum score 7). *Application deadline:* For fall admission, 12/4 for domestic and international students. Applications are processed on a rolling basis. Application fee: $60. Electronic applications accepted. *Expenses:* Tuition, area resident: Full-time $10,452. Tuition, state resident: full-time $10,452. Tuition, nonresident: full-time $20,010. Required fees: $2176. Part-time tuition and fees vary according to course load and program. *Financial support:* Fellowships, teaching assistantships available. Financial award application deadline: 12/4; financial award applicants required to submit FAFSA. *Unit head:* Jeffrey W. Legro, Chair, 434-924-3192, Fax: 434-924-3159. *Application contact:* Jeffrey W. Legro, Chair, 434-924-3192, Fax: 434-924-3159.

University of Washington, Graduate School, College of Arts and Sciences, Department of Political Science, Seattle, WA 98195. Offers MA, PhD. *Degree requirements:* For doctorate, thesis/dissertation. *Entrance requirements:* For master's and doctorate, GRE General Test, minimum GPA of 3.0. Additional exam requirements/recommendations for international students: Required—TOEFL. Electronic applications accepted. *Faculty research:* American politics, comparative politics, international relations, political theory, political economy.

University of Waterloo, Graduate Studies, Faculty of Arts, Department of Political Science, Global Governance Program, Waterloo, ON N2L 3G1, Canada. Offers MA, PhD. *Entrance requirements:* For master's, BA, B+ average; for doctorate, MA. Additional exam requirements/recommendations for international students: Required—TOEFL. Electronic applications accepted. *Faculty research:* Global political economy, global environment, peace and security, global justice and human rights, multilateral institutions and diplomacy.

The University of Western Ontario, Faculty of Graduate Studies, Social Sciences Division, Department of Political Science, London, ON N6A 5B8, Canada. Offers MA, MPA, PhD. Part-time programs available. *Degree requirements:* For master's, thesis; for doctorate, comprehensive exam, thesis/dissertation. *Entrance requirements:* For master's, minimum B average, honors BA in political science or equivalent, sample of written work; for doctorate, MA in political science or equivalent. *Faculty research:* Political theory, Canadian politics, local government, comparative politics, international relations.

University of West Florida, College of Arts and Sciences: Arts, Department of Government, Pensacola, FL 32514-5750. Offers political science (MA), including public administration, security and diplomacy. Part-time and evening/weekend programs available. *Faculty:* 3 full-time (1 woman), 2 part-time/adjunct (1 woman). *Students:* 4 full-time (0 women), 18 part-time (8 women); includes 4 minority (1 African American, 3 Hispanic Americans). Average age 32. 18 applicants, 56% accepted, 6 enrolled. In 2008, 8 master's awarded. *Degree requirements:* For master's, thesis or alternative. *Entrance requirements:* For master's, GRE General Test, minimum GPA of 3.0. Additional exam requirements/recommendations for international students: Required—TOEFL (minimum score 550 paper-based; 213 computer-based). *Application deadline:* For fall admission, 6/1 for domestic students, 5/15 for international students; for spring admission, 11/1 for domestic students, 10/1 for international students. Applications are processed on a rolling basis. Application fee: $30. *Expenses:* Tuition, state resident: full-time $6095; part-time $253.97 per credit hour. Tuition, nonresident: full-time $21,919; part-time $913.31 per credit hour. *Financial support:* Fellowships, research assistantships with partial tuition reimbursements, career-related internships or fieldwork, Federal Work-Study, institutionally sponsored loans, and tuition waivers (full and partial) available. Support available to part-time students. Financial award application deadline: 4/15; financial award applicants required to submit FAFSA. *Faculty research:* Political campaigns, elections, law enforcement, growth management. *Unit head:* Dr. Alfred Cuzan, Chairperson, 850-474-2337, E-mail: govt@uwf.edu. *Application contact:* Terry McCray, Assistant Director of Graduate Admissions, 850-473-7718, Fax: 850-473-7714, E-mail: gradadmissions@uwf.edu.

University of Windsor, Faculty of Graduate Studies, Faculty of Arts and Social Sciences, Department of Political Science, Windsor, ON N9B 3P4, Canada. Offers MA. Part-time programs available. *Entrance requirements:* For master's, minimum B+ average. Additional exam requirements/recommendations for international students: Required—TOEFL (minimum score 600 paper-based; 250 computer-based). Electronic applications accepted. *Faculty research:* Canadian politics and government, local government, comparative political Canadian public administration, public policy.

University of Wisconsin–Madison, Graduate School, College of Letters and Science, Department of Political Science, Madison, WI 53706-1380. Offers PhD. *Degree requirements:* For doctorate, thesis/dissertation. *Entrance requirements:* For doctorate, GRE General Test. Electronic applications accepted. *Faculty research:* Comparative politics, American politics, international relations, political theory, political methodology.

University of Wisconsin–Milwaukee, Graduate School, College of Letters and Sciences, Department of Political Science, Milwaukee, WI 53201-0413. Offers MA, PhD. *Faculty:* 19 full-time (5 women). *Students:* 32 full-time (13 women), 18 part-time (8 women); includes 5 minority (1 African American, 1 Asian American or Pacific Islander, 3 Hispanic Americans), 7 international. Average age 29. 57 applicants, 49% accepted, 15 enrolled. In 2008, 9 master's, 3 doctorates awarded. *Degree requirements:* For master's, thesis or alternative; for doctorate, one foreign language, thesis/dissertation. *Entrance requirements:* For master's and doctorate, GRE General Test, minimum GPA of 3.0. Additional exam requirements/recommendations for international students: Required—TOEFL (minimum score 550 paper-based; 79 iBT), IELTS (minimum score 6.5). *Application deadline:* For fall admission, 1/1 priority date for domestic students; for spring admission, 9/1 for domestic students. Applications are processed on a rolling basis. Application fee: $45 ($75 for international students). *Expenses:* Tuition, area resident: Full-time $7320; part-time $165 per credit. Tuition, state resident: full-time $7320; part-time $165 per credit. Tuition, nonresident: full-time $17,840; part-time $714 per credit. Tuition and fees vary according to campus/location, program and reciprocity agreements.

Financial support: In 2008–09, 21 teaching assistantships were awarded; career-related internships or fieldwork and unspecified assistantships also available. Support available to part-time students. Financial award application deadline: 4/15. Total annual research expenditures: $3,503. *Unit head:* John Bohte, Representative, 414-229-4328, Fax: 414-229-5021, E-mail: jbohte@uwm.edu. *Application contact:* General Information Contact, 414-229-4982, Fax: 414-229-6967, E-mail: gradschool@uwm.edu.

University of Wyoming, Graduate School, College of Arts and Sciences, Department of Political Science, Program in Political Science, Laramie, WY 82070. Offers MA. Part-time programs available. *Faculty:* 10 full-time (3 women), 2 part-time/adjunct (1 woman). *Students:* 7 full-time (4 women), 4 part-time (0 women); includes 1 minority (American Indian/Alaska Native), 6 international. Average age 28. 6 applicants, 83% accepted, 2 enrolled. In 2008, 2 master's awarded. *Degree requirements:* For master's, thesis or alternative. *Entrance requirements:* For master's, GRE General Test, bachelor's degree in political science, minimum GPA of 3.0. Additional exam requirements/recommendations for international students: Required—TOEFL (minimum score 525 paper-based; 195 computer-based). *Application deadline:* For fall admission, 6/1 priority date for domestic students. Applications are processed on a rolling basis. Application fee: $50. Electronic applications accepted. *Financial support:* In 2008–09, 6 students received support, including 5 research assistantships with full tuition reimbursements available (averaging $11,072 per year), 1 teaching assistantship with full tuition reimbursement available (averaging $11,072 per year); career-related internships or fieldwork and unspecified assistantships also available. Financial award application deadline: 3/15. *Faculty research:* American government, public law, judicial politics, political theory, international relations. *Unit head:* Dr. Jim King, Department Head, Professor, 307-766-6484, Fax: 307-766—771, E-mail: jking@uwyo.edu. *Application contact:* Jamie L. LeJambre, Graduate Coordinator, 307-766-6484, Fax: 307-766-6771, E-mail: lejambre@uwyo.edu.

Utah State University, School of Graduate Studies, College of Humanities, Arts and Social Sciences, Department of Political Science, Logan, UT 84322. Offers MA, MS. Part-time programs available. *Degree requirements:* For master's, one foreign language, thesis. *Entrance requirements:* For master's, GRE General Test, minimum GPA of 3.0. Additional exam requirements/recommendations for international students: Required—TOEFL. *Faculty research:* Political parties; social choice; international political economics; foreign policy; politics, markets, and public policy.

Vanderbilt University, Graduate School, Department of Political Science, Nashville, TN 37240-1001. Offers MA, MAT, PhD. *Faculty:* 25 full-time (9 women). *Students:* 34 full-time (19 women), 1 part-time (0 women); includes 5 minority (2 African Americans, 3 Hispanic Americans), 12 international. Average age 30. 129 applicants, 10% accepted, 7 enrolled. In 2008, 5 master's, 2 doctorates awarded. Terminal master's awarded for partial completion of doctoral program. *Degree requirements:* For master's, thesis; for doctorate, thesis/dissertation, final and qualifying exams. *Entrance requirements:* For master's and doctorate, GRE General Test, writing sample. Additional exam requirements/recommendations for international students: Required—TOEFL (minimum score 570 paper-based; 230 computer-based; 88 iBT). *Application deadline:* For fall admission, 1/15 for domestic and international students. Application fee: $0. Electronic applications accepted. *Financial support:* Fellowships with full tuition reimbursements, research assistantships with full tuition reimbursements, teaching assistantships with full tuition reimbursements, Federal Work-Study, institutionally sponsored loans, scholarships/grants, and health care benefits available. Financial award application deadline: 1/15; financial award applicants required to submit CSS PROFILE or FAFSA. *Faculty research:* American politics, comparative politics, international politics, political theory, political culture and life. *Unit head:* John Geer, Chair, 615-322-6222, Fax: 615-343-6003, E-mail: john.g.geer@vanderbilt.edu. *Application contact:* Jonathan Hiskey, Director of Graduate Studies, 615-322-6236, Fax: 615-343-6003, E-mail: j.hiskey@vanderbilt.edu.

Villanova University, Graduate School of Liberal Arts and Sciences, Department of Political Science, Program in Political Science, Villanova, PA 19085-1699. Offers MA. *Students:* 22 full-time (11 women), 21 part-time (6 women); includes 3 minority (2 Asian Americans or Pacific Islanders, 1 Hispanic American), 2 international. Average age 27. 45 applicants, 93% accepted, 17 enrolled. In 2008, 20 master's awarded. *Degree requirements:* For master's, thesis or alternative. *Entrance requirements:* For master's, GRE, minimum GPA of 3.0. *Application deadline:* For fall admission, 8/1 for domestic and international students; for spring admission, 12/1 for domestic and international students. Applications are processed on a rolling basis. Application fee: $50. Electronic applications accepted. *Financial support:* Scholarships/grants and unspecified assistantships available. Financial award application deadline: 3/15; financial award applicants required to submit FAFSA. *Unit head:* Dr. Markus Kreuzer, Director, 610-519-4710. *Application contact:* Matthew Kerbel, Information Contact, 610-519-4553, Fax: 610-519-7487, E-mail: matthew.kerbel@villanova.edu.

See Close-Up on page 883.

Virginia Commonwealth University, Graduate School, College of Humanities and Sciences, Wilder School of Government and Public Affairs, Richmond, VA 23284-9005. Offers MA, MPA, MS, MURP, PhD, CASR, CCJA, CPM, CURP, Certificate, Graduate Certificate, JD/MURP, MSW/Certificate.

Virginia Polytechnic Institute and State University, Graduate School, College of Liberal Arts and Human Sciences, Department of Political Science, Blacksburg, VA 24061. Offers MA. *Entrance requirements:* For master's, GRE General Test. Additional exam requirements/recommendations for international students: Required—TOEFL (minimum score 600 paper-based; 250 computer-based). Electronic applications accepted. *Faculty research:* Comparative politics, international relations, American government and politics, research methods.

Washington State University, Graduate School, College of Liberal Arts, Department of Political Science, Program in Political Science, Pullman, WA 99164. Offers MA, PhD. Terminal master's awarded for partial completion of doctoral program. *Degree requirements:* For master's, comprehensive exam (for some programs), thesis, oral exam; for doctorate, comprehensive exam, thesis/dissertation, oral exam, written exam. *Entrance requirements:* For master's, GRE General Test, minimum GPA of 3.0; for doctorate, GRE General Test, minimum GPA of 3.5. Additional exam requirements/recommendations for international students: Required—TOEFL. Electronic applications accepted. *Faculty research:* Political psychology and image theory, grass roots environmental policy, federal juvenile policy.

Washington University in St. Louis, Graduate School of Arts and Sciences, Department of Political Science, St. Louis, MO 63130-4899. Offers political economy and public policy (MA); political science (PhD). *Students:* 41 full-time (14 women); includes 1 minority (Hispanic American), 17 international. 120 applicants, 11% accepted, 7 enrolled. In 2008, 7 master's, 3 doctorates awarded. Terminal master's awarded for partial completion of doctoral program. *Degree requirements:* For master's, thesis or alternative; for doctorate, thesis/dissertation. *Entrance requirements:* For master's and doctorate, GRE General Test. *Application deadline:* For fall admission, 1/15 priority date for domestic students. Application fee: $45. Electronic applications accepted. *Financial support:* Fellowships, research assistantships, teaching assistantships, career-related internships or fieldwork, Federal Work-Study, institutionally sponsored loans, and tuition waivers (full and partial) available. Support available to part-time students. Financial award application deadline: 1/15. *Unit head:* Dr. Andrew Martin, Chairperson, 314-935-5822. *Application contact:* Assistant to the Dean, 314-935-6880, Fax: 314-935-4887.

Wayne State University, College of Liberal Arts and Sciences, Department of Political Science, Program in Political Science, Detroit, MI 48202. Offers MA, PhD, JD/MA. *Degree requirements:* For doctorate, thesis/dissertation. *Entrance requirements:* For master's, GRE General Test, minimum GPA of 3.0; for doctorate, GRE General Test, minimum GPA of 3.0, 3 letters of recommendation. Additional exam requirements/recommendations for international students: Required—TOEFL (minimum score 550 paper-based; 213 computer-based); Recommended—TWE (minimum score 6). Electronic applications accepted. *Faculty research:* Political theory and

Political Science

Wayne State University (continued)

thought, international relations, American politics, comparative politics, public policy, public administration, urban politics.

West Chester University of Pennsylvania, Office of Graduate Studies, College of Business and Public Affairs, Department of Political Science, West Chester, PA 19383. Offers administration (Certificate); human resource management (MSA, Certificate); individualized (MSA); non profit administration (Certificate); nonprofit administration (MSA); public administration (MSA); training and development (MSA). Part-time and evening/weekend programs available. *Students:* 4 full-time (all women), 31 part-time (24 women); includes 8 minority (7 African Americans, 1 Hispanic American). Average age 33. 32 applicants, 97% accepted, 26 enrolled. In 2008, 17 master's, 2 Certificates awarded. *Degree requirements:* For master's, comprehensive exam (for some programs). *Entrance requirements:* For master's and Certificate, GMAT, GRE General Test, or MAT, statement of professional goals, resumé, two letters of reference. Additional exam requirements/recommendations for international students: Required—TOEFL (minimum score 550 paper-based; 213 computer-based; 80 iBT). *Application deadline:* For fall admission, 4/15 priority date for domestic students, 3/15 for international students; for spring admission, 10/15 for domestic students, 9/1 for international students. Applications are processed on a rolling basis. Application fee: $35. Electronic applications accepted. *Expenses:* Tuition, state resident: full-time $6430; part-time $357 per credit. Tuition, nonresident: full-time $10,288; part-time $572 per credit. Required fees: $652.50; $50 per credit. $67 per semester. *Financial support:* In 2008–09, 4 research assistantships with full and partial tuition reimbursements (averaging $5,000 per year) were awarded; unspecified assistantships also available. Support available to part-time students. Financial award application deadline: 2/15; financial award applicants required to submit FAFSA. *Unit head:* Dr. Christopher Fiorentino, Dean, College of Business and Public Affairs, 610-436-2930, E-mail: cfiorentino@wcupa.edu. *Application contact:* Dr. Lorraine Bernotsky, Graduate Coordinator, 610-738-0576, E-mail: lbernotsky@wcupa.edu.

Western Illinois University, School of Graduate Studies, College of Arts and Sciences, Department of Political Science, Macomb, IL 61455-1390. Offers political science (MA); public and non-profit management (Certificate). Part-time programs available. *Students:* 15 full-time (4 women), 3 part-time (1 woman); includes 3 minority (all African Americans), 3 international. Average age 27. 21 applicants, 62% accepted. In 2008, 7 master's, 2 other advanced degrees awarded. *Degree requirements:* For master's, comprehensive exam, thesis or alternative. *Entrance requirements:* Additional exam requirements/recommendations for international students: Required—TOEFL (minimum score 550 paper-based; 213 computer-based; 80 iBT). *Application deadline:* Applications are processed on a rolling basis. Electronic applications accepted. *Expenses:* Tuition, state resident: full-time $5696; part-time $237.34 per credit hour. Tuition, nonresident: full-time $11,392; part-time $474.68 per credit hour. Required fees: $1453; $60.55 per credit hour. *Financial support:* In 2008–09, 9 students received support, including 9 research assistantships with full tuition reimbursements available (averaging $7,040 per year). Financial award applicants required to submit FAFSA. *Unit head:* Dr. Richard Hardy, Chairperson, 309-298-1055. *Application contact:* Evelyn Hoing, Assistant Director of Graduate Studies, 309-298-1806, Fax: 309-298-2345, E-mail: grad-office@wiu.edu.

Western Kentucky University, Graduate Studies, Potter College of Arts and Letters, Department of Political Science, Bowling Green, KY 42101. Offers MPA. Part-time and evening/weekend programs available. *Degree requirements:* For master's, comprehensive exam, final exam. *Entrance requirements:* For master's, GRE General Test, minimum GPA of 2.75. Additional exam requirements/recommendations for international students: Required—TOEFL (minimum score 555 paper-based; 213 computer-based; 79 iBT). *Faculty research:* Role of non-profits, comparative policy analysis, social welfare policy, rural administration, ethics and bureaucracy.

Western Michigan University, Graduate College, College of Arts and Sciences, Department of Political Science, Program in Political Science, Kalamazoo, MI 49008-5202. Offers MA, PhD. *Degree requirements:* For master's, thesis optional, oral exams; for doctorate, thesis/dissertation, oral exam. *Entrance requirements:* For doctorate, GRE General Test.

Western Washington University, Graduate School, College of Humanities and Social Sciences, Department of Political Science, Bellingham, WA 98225-5996. Offers MA. Part-time programs available. *Degree requirements:* For master's, comprehensive exam, thesis (for some programs). *Entrance requirements:* For master's, GRE General Test, minimum GPA of 3.0 in last 60 semester hours or last 90 quarter hours. Additional exam requirements/recommendations for international students: Required—TOEFL (minimum score 567 paper-based; 227 computer-based). Electronic applications accepted. *Faculty research:* Elections, environment, identity, international relations.

West Texas A&M University, College of Education and Social Sciences, Department of History and Political Science, Program in Political Science, Canyon, TX 79016-0001. Offers MA. Part-time and evening/weekend programs available. *Degree requirements:* For master's, comprehensive exam, thesis optional. *Entrance requirements:* For master's, GRE General Test. Additional exam requirements/recommendations for international students: Required—TOEFL (minimum score 550 paper-based). Electronic applications accepted. *Faculty research:* American government, public administration, state and local government, international politics.

West Virginia University, Eberly College of Arts and Sciences, Department of Political Science, Morgantown, WV 26506. Offers American public policy and politics (MA); international and comparative public policy and politics (MA); political science (PhD); public policy analysis (PhD). Terminal master's awarded for partial completion of doctoral program. *Degree requirements:* For master's, thesis optional; for doctorate, comprehensive exam, thesis/dissertation. *Entrance requirements:* For master's, GRE General Test, minimum GPA of 2.75; for doctorate, GRE General Test, minimum GPA of 3.0. Additional exam requirements/recommendations for international students: Required—TOEFL. *Faculty research:* Public policy, research methods, foreign policy analysis, judicial politics, environmental and energy policy.

Wichita State University, Graduate School, Fairmount College of Liberal Arts and Sciences, Department of Political Science, Wichita, KS 67260. Offers MA. Part-time and evening/weekend programs available. *Degree requirements:* For master's, comprehensive exam, thesis optional, internship. *Entrance requirements:* For master's, GRE, minimum GPA of 3.0. Additional exam requirements/recommendations for international students: Required—TOEFL. Electronic applications accepted. *Faculty research:* Foreign intelligence, political participation of U.S. parties, Southern civil rights policy.

Wilfrid Laurier University, Faculty of Graduate Studies, Faculty of Arts, Department of Political Science, Waterloo, ON N2L 3C5, Canada. Offers MA. *Degree requirements:* For master's, thesis optional. *Entrance requirements:* For master's, honors bachelor's degree or the equivalent in political science, minimum B average in undergraduate course work. Additional exam requirements/recommendations for international students: Required—TOEFL (minimum score 230 computer-based; 89 iBT). Electronic applications accepted. *Faculty research:* Political behavior/political psychology, Canadian political studies, comparative, politics/relations, public opinion and electoral studies, international.

Yale University, Graduate School of Arts and Sciences, Department of Political Science, New Haven, CT 06520. Offers PhD. *Degree requirements:* For doctorate, one foreign language, thesis/dissertation. *Entrance requirements:* For doctorate, GRE General Test. *Faculty research:* U.N. and international security.

York University, Faculty of Graduate Studies, Faculty of Arts, Program in Political Science, Toronto, ON M3J 1P3, Canada. Offers MA, PhD. Part-time programs available. *Degree requirements:* For master's, thesis or alternative; for doctorate, one foreign language, comprehensive exam, thesis/dissertation. Electronic applications accepted.

York University, Faculty of Graduate Studies, Faculty of Arts, Program in Social and Political Thought, Toronto, ON M3J 1P3, Canada. Offers MA, PhD. Part-time programs available. *Degree requirements:* For master's, one foreign language, thesis or alternative, oral exams; for doctorate, one foreign language, comprehensive exam, thesis/dissertation. Electronic applications accepted.

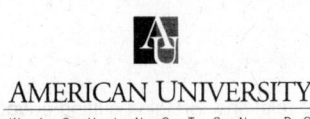

AMERICAN UNIVERSITY
WASHINGTON, DC

School of International Service

Programs of Study

A founding member of the Association of Professional Schools of International Affairs, American University's (AU) School of International Service (SIS) is the largest and most-applied-to school of international affairs in the United States. SIS offers the following two-year standard master's programs: comparative and regional studies, global environmental politics, international communication, international development, international economic relations, international politics, international peace and conflict resolution, and U.S. foreign policy.

SIS also offers a one-year executive master's program (Master of International Service) for midcareer professionals with five to seven years of work experience, preferably in international affairs, and a Ph.D. program in international relations. In addition, the School has dual-degree programs with Ritsumeikan University in Japan, Korea University and Sookmyung Women's University in Korea, and the University of Peace in Costa Rica. Joint-degree programs in international media, ethics, peace, and global affairs and dual J.D./M.A., M.A./M.B.A., M.A./M.A.T., and M.A./M.T.S. programs are also available on the American University campus.

Within the graduate curriculum, students can tailor their programs to reflect their special interest and career paths and are also encouraged to integrate professional experience, including internships. General M.A. degree requirements include 39–42 credit hours of approved graduate course work, a comprehensive examination, demonstration of research and writing skills through completion of a master's thesis, substantial research paper requirement or research practicum, and proficiency in a modern foreign language. General Ph.D. degree requirements include 72 credit hours of approved graduate course work consisting of 60 hours of course credits and 12 credit hours of independent dissertation supervision.

Teaching styles at SIS are highly collegial. The curriculum is distinguished by linking theory and practice and addressing emerging issues both conceptually and empirically. SIS students have the opportunity to participate in cutting-edge faculty-led research projects and are constantly challenged to care about the moral, philosophical, and practical implications of an increasingly interdependent world.

The University's nationally recognized Career Center and SIS partner with domestic and international employers to offer substantive internship experiences for which students may earn academic credit. SIS students have interned and worked at such organizations as the International Monetary Fund, Amnesty International, Global Fund for Women, U.N. Higher Commissioner for Refugees, the U.S. Department of State, the World Bank, Search for Common Ground, foreign embassies, and many others.

Research Facilities

The School of International Service offers research opportunities through a number of research programs and centers, such as the Center for Asian Studies, the Center for Global Peace, Intercultural Management Institute, Center for Human Rights, Peacebuilding and Development Institute, and Public International Law and Policy Program.

During the summer, SIS also offers specialized study tours to sites including South Africa, Malaysia, Egypt, Italy, India, China, and the United Arab Emirates, where students are encouraged to pursue self-designed research in conjunction with a faculty adviser.

The American University's Bender Library and Learning Resources Center house more than 780,000 titles, as well as journals, film/video/multimedia recordings, and microforms. The library also contains special collections in music, mathematics, Japanese materials, and broadcast journalism. The library provides online access to 2,000 other member libraries. The University is also ranked by Intel as one of the top ten "most unwired college campuses" and was selected as T-Mobile's first HotSpot WiFi Internet campus.

Financial Aid

SIS offers merit-based awards to a limited number of eligible domestic and international graduate students upon notification of admission. Only full-time students are eligible to receive merit-based assistance. These awards are normally awarded for two years, provided that the recipient follows American University academic regulations and remains in good academic standing. The award amounts and types vary but can include partial- to full-tuition remission and/or a monthly stipend and/or a research assistantship with a faculty member. All admitted Ph.D. students are fully funded for their course work during their study at SIS. Students should note that all required application materials need to be received by the posted deadline in order to be considered for merit-based aid.

Cost of Study

Tuition for the 2009–10 academic year is $22,266, based on two semesters of full-time enrollment, 9 credits/semester, at the rate of $1237 per credit. Fees are $1930, which includes an SIS fee of $750 per semester for full-time students (registering for 9 credits or above) or $500 per semester for part-time students (registering for 6 to 8 credits), plus $300 for other estimated University fees. Students should anticipate an increase of 5 to 8 percent for each succeeding academic year.

Living and Housing Costs

Washington, D.C., is a diverse and eclectic city with many options for graduate students looking for housing. The best place to start searching is the American University Housing and Dining Web site (http://www.american.edu/ocl/housing/), where information about housing in Washington, D.C., and current postings for a variety of accommodations are listed. Some students choose to live on their own, renting a studio or one-bedroom apartment in the AU neighborhood or in one of the many centers around the city; others opt for group housing, sharing costs with several people in a house or apartment. Washington, D.C., has plenty of options from which to choose. There are many resources for finding housing in the city, including the American University Housing and Dining Programs (http://www.american.edu/ocl/housing/), Apartment Search (http://www.apartmentsearch.com), craigslist–Washington D.C. (http://www.washingtondc.craigslist.org), Off Campus Network (http://www.offcampusnetwork.com/index.asp), Washington City Paper classifieds (http://www.washingtoncitypaper.com/class/classifieds.html), Washington Post classifieds (http://www.washingtonpost.com), Washington D.C. ForRent (http://www.washingtondc.forrent.com), Washington D.C. Convention and Visitors Bureau (http://www.2chambers.com/tourist5.htm), and Washington Metropolitan Transit Authority (http://www.wmata.com).

Student Group

With a graduate student body of more than 800, SIS is the largest and most-applied-to school of international affairs in the U.S. A very diverse student body is composed of about 20 percent international students from more than 130 countries, and an additional 25 percent are members of domestic minority groups.

Location

American University is located in northwest Washington, D.C., home to some 192 foreign embassies, chanceries, and the headquarters of many international organizations. In addition, the Smithsonian Institution, National Institutes of Health, John F. Kennedy Center for the Performing Arts, National Archives, Brookings Institute, World Bank, and Library of Congress are all just a short distance from the campus. There are also a host of research and internship sites related to each field, including the Office of European Union Commission, Organization of American States, TransAfrica Forum, and Asia Society.

The University and The School

American University was chartered by an Act of the United States Congress in 1893. The first graduate students were admitted in 1914, and President Woodrow Wilson officially dedicated the University on May 27, 1914. Today, as a premiere global university, American University has more than 11,000 students enrolled and attracts students from all fifty states, the District of Columbia, Puerto Rico and the territories, and nearly 150 other countries.

During the Cold War, U.S. President Dwight Eisenhower was aware that the world needed to prepare for a time when the U.S.-Soviet rivalry no longer dominated foreign policy. He encouraged thirteen university presidents, including AU's Hurst Anderson, to incorporate human-focused international affairs into higher education. Anderson and the Methodist Bishop of Washington shared a similar vision: a school predicated on service to the global community. Eisenhower embraced the idea and spoke at the School's groundbreaking ceremony in 1957. The School of International Service opened in 1958 to an inaugural class of 80 students from thirty-six countries.

Applying

To be considered for admission to the master's programs, all applicants must possess a bachelor's degree or its equivalent from an accredited institution and submit the application form; a resume; a statement of purpose; two letters of recommendation (three for the Ph.D. program); official transcripts; official test scores, such as GRE scores and/or TOEFL/IELTS scores (if applicable, for international students); and a $50 application fee. GRE scores are required for all Ph.D. applicants. The minimum TOEFL requirement for international students is 100 on the iBT, 250 on the CBT, or 600 on the PBT. The minimum IELTS requirement is 7.0. International students who do not hold a higher education degree from an English-speaking university are not required to take the GRE but do need to take the TOEFL/IELTS. The M.A. application deadline for spring semester is October 1 for domestic students and September 15 for international students; the M.A. application deadline for fall semester is January 15 for all applicants. The Ph.D. application deadline is January 1. All application materials must reach the Graduate Admissions Office by the deadline if students wish to be considered for merit-based financial aid.

Correspondence and Information

Office of Graduate Admissions
School of International Service
American University
4400 Massachusetts Avenue, NW
Washington, D.C. 20016-8071
Phone: 202-885-1646
Fax: 202-885-1109
E-mail: sisgrad@american.edu
Web site: http://www.american.edu/sis

American University

THE FACULTY AND THEIR RESEARCH

The diversity of SIS faculty members exemplifies the multidisciplinary and cross-cultural aspects of international relations. Bringing cutting-edge research into their classrooms, the faculty members use a variety of interactive approaches, such as simulations and case studies, in their teaching. The School regularly appoints adjunct and visiting professors and benefits from their expertise in the field of international relations.

Comparative and Regional Studies: Michelle Egan, Director
Global Environmental Politics: Paul Wapner, Director
International Communication: Nanette Levinson, Director
International Development: David Hirschmann, Director
International Economic Relations: Tamar Gutner, Interim Director
International Peace and Conflict Resolution: Ronald Fisher, Director
International Politics: Tamar Gutner, Director
U.S. Foreign Policy: Shoon Murray, Director

COLUMBIA UNIVERSITY

COLUMBIA | SIPA
School of International and Public Affairs
www.sipa.columbia.edu

School of International and Public Affairs
Master of International Affairs
and Master of Public Administration

Programs of Study	The School of International and Public Affairs (SIPA) offers two full-time graduate policy degree programs: the Master of International Affairs (M.I.A.) and the Master of Public Administration (M.P.A.). The M.P.A. program also includes a unique specialization in Development Practice (M.P.A. D.P.) These programs and their student bodies share a great deal in common. Employers demand the reliable skill set of a common core curriculum and an area of solid specialization of both sets of graduates. The School offers the same concentration choices to students in both the M.I.A. and M.P.A. programs, reflecting the fact that most policy questions can no longer be neatly categorized as domestic or international issues. As a result, the content and the structure of SIPA's M.I.A. and M.P.A. programs have slowly converged. Prospective students still notice differences in the programs that reflect their histories and student bodies: There is more international content in the M.I.A. core; the M.P.A. core has more national and local policy content. Students in both programs choose SIPA for its balance of theory and practice, and find their classmates' perspectives are as varied as their diverse backgrounds. Nonetheless, most students would say that an M.I.A. student tends toward a more global and theoretical approach to policy questions, while an M.P.A. student is more likely to focus on questions of policy processes and implementation at a local level. The M.P.A. D.P. student has a desire to understand and manage approaches to sustainable development challenges. The rigorous cross-disciplinary M.P.A. D.P. program emphasizes the development of critical knowledge, skills, and attributes of an effective professional in developing societies.
	The School of International and Public Affairs also participates in combined programs with the Graduate School of Business; the School of Law; the School of Public Health; the Graduate School of Journalism; the Graduate School of Architecture, Planning, and Preservation; the Graduate School of Arts and Sciences; the School of Social Work; Institut d'Études Politiques (Paris); the London School of Economics; Hertie School of Governance (Berlin); and the National University of Singapore.
Research Facilities	The International Affairs Building contains Lehman Library, which holds 265,000 volumes, including virtually all significant American and international publications in foreign relations, foreign policy, and the areas covered by the Regional Institutes. The Lehman Library is part of the University library system, with holdings in excess of 6 million volumes.
	Associated with the School are the University's eight regional institutes, the Institute of War and Peace Studies, the Center for the Study of Human Rights, the United Nations Study Program, and the Columbia Earth Institute. Scholars from all parts of the world are invited to study and participate in the institutes' activities and, while in residence, to teach courses.
Financial Aid	The School offers a number of fellowships. In 2008–09 approximately 11 percent of first-year students received fellowship funding, while over 68 percent of second-year students received funding. The average first-year fellowship award was $14,222, and the average second-year fellowship amount was $17,771. Students are also encouraged to apply for outside fellowships. Long-term loans are available to help pay for tuition, fees, and living expenses. For additional information about financial aid, interested students should visit http://sipa.columbia.edu/resources_services/financial_aid/index.html.
Cost of Study	Tuition and fees for the 2008–09 academic year were $37,884. Additional expenses for the academic year, including housing in New York City, food, and books, are estimated to be approximately $22,356.
Living and Housing Costs	The University provides housing for a limited number of single and married graduate students at varying costs. Inquiries about accommodations should be directed to the Office of University Apartment Housing. International House, a privately owned student residence near the campus, also has accommodations for graduate students. Inquiries should be addressed to the Committee on Admissions, International House, 500 Riverside Drive, New York, New York 10027. The Off-Campus Housing Registry in the Office of University Apartment Housing maintains a listing of privately owned apartments and rooms for rent.
Student Group	The School's student body, with approximately 1,200 students across seven degree programs, consists of men and women from the United States and many other countries. In 2008–09 students at SIPA came from more than ninety different countries. Approximately 45 percent of the students are international scholars, and about 60 percent are women.
Location	New York City is truly an exciting city in which to live and study. Its educational and cultural opportunities are unparalleled in their scope and diversity, as are its professional options.
The University and The School	Established as King's College in 1754, Columbia was given a state charter and a new name after the Revolutionary War. Today, the University community of over 26,000 students and faculty members has at its disposal extensive library collections and a computer center for academic research projects. The University is one of the world's leading centers for studies in international affairs.
	The School of International and Public Affairs is a graduate professional school established in 1946 for the purpose of training students for careers in such fields as international business and banking, government service, international organizations, and journalism. The School has an active placement program that is constantly seeking the best opportunities for its graduates. Apart from its own resources, the School draws upon the faculties of the Graduate School of Arts and Sciences, the School of Law, the Graduate School of Business, Teachers College, the Graduate School of Journalism, and the School of Public Health.
Applying	A bachelor's degree or the equivalent is required. M.I.A. candidates must be proficient in a second language to graduate. It is thus recommended that M.I.A. candidates possess at least an elementary understanding of a second language at the time of admission. GRE General Test scores are required and GMAT scores can be submitted with approval of the Office of Admissions. Six credits in the principles of macroeconomics and microeconomics are strongly recommended. A high level math class is also highly recommended. The application deadline for fall admission is January 5. Students are encouraged to apply early. The School prefers to accept students for September (fall) matriculation; however, applications for admission to the spring semester (starting in January) are also accepted. The January application deadline is October 1. Fellowships are not awarded to January entrants. All qualified applicants receive consideration for admission without regard to race, creed, color, sex, or national origin.
Correspondence and Information	Office of Admissions and Financial Aid 420 West 118th Street, Room 408 Mail Code 3325 School of International and Public Affairs Columbia University New York, New York 10027 Phone: 212-854-6216 Fax: 212-854-3010 E-mail: sipa_admission@columbia.edu Web site: http://sipa.columbia.edu/admissions

Columbia University

FACULTY HEADS AND SPECIALIZATIONS

ADMINISTRATION
John H. Coatsworth, Ph.D., Dean.
Patrick Bohan, M.A., Associate Dean.
Robert Garris, Ph.D., Associate Dean.
Cassandra Simmons, Ph.D., Associate Dean.
Meg Heenehan, M.Ed., Director, Office of Career Services.
Matt Clemons, M.B.A., Director, Office of Admissions and Financial Aid.

CONCENTRATIONS/SPECIALIZATIONS
Students choose a policy concentration and pair this with a specialization. Specializations are either functional or regional in nature.

Concentrations
Economic and Political Development, Energy and Environment, Human Rights, International Finance and Economic Policy, International Security Policy, and Urban and Social Policy.

Functional Specializations
Advanced Policy and Economic Analysis, Applied Science, Communications and Media, International Organizations, and Management.

Regional Specializations
Africa, East Asia, Europe, Latin America, Middle East, Russia, Eurasia and Eastern Europe, Southern Asia, and the United States.

—————

Applicants should note that M.P.A. D.P. students do not choose from the above list of concentrations and specializations. The M.PA. D.P. program is designed to train aspiring practitioners to understand and manage approaches to sustainable development challenge and integrates insights from a range of disciplines, including the natural and health sciences.

FORDHAM UNIVERSITY

Graduate Program in International Political Economy and Development

Programs of Study	The Graduate Program in International Political Economy and Development (IPED) is internationally known for its academic excellence. This excellence is achieved through a unique and innovative interdisciplinary approach to analyzing contemporary global economic relations as well as international development issues. The program is a twelve-course curriculum designed primarily for future and present professionals involved with international economic issues as financial analysts, economists, policy analysts, and program administrators. The IPED curriculum begins by providing a rigorous graduate-level foundation in economic, political, and quantitative analysis. Building on this solid foundation, the curriculum then offers an advanced interdisciplinary study of global economic relations and international development issues. Students can complete their professional training in the IPED Master of Arts (M.A.) curriculum with specializations in international banking and finance, international development studies, international economics, or international policy analysis. As a capstone experience, students must pass a comprehensive examination. A full-time student can complete the program in three semesters. Part-time students can complete the program in two years, including two summers.

The M.A. program also provides important practical training. Students must complete an approved internship with an international organization in the business, government, or nonprofit sector if they do not already possess relevant professional experience. The IPED program sponsors a number of internships, both in the United States and abroad, as well as an emerging markets travel program. On a competitive basis, the Graduate Program also offers several international travel scholarships, overseas language immersion study awards, and internship fellowships.

As part of their twelve M.A. courses, IPED students may also fulfill the requirements for two Advanced Certificates: one in Emerging Markets and Country Risk Analysis and the other in Financial Econometrics and Data Analysis. These certificates are also open to qualified visiting students from other universities as well as currently employed professionals. IPED students who wish to strengthen their financial analysis skills may take an additional five courses in the Business School and earn an Advanced Certificate in International Business and Finance.

Two dual-degree programs are offered: IPED students may pursue a second M.A. in economics and Fordham Law students may pursue the IPED M.A.

Research Facilities
Fordham University supports academic and scientific research with exceptional resources that include sophisticated computer facilities and state-of-the-art laboratories. The combined libraries of the University contain more than 1.8 million bound volumes and more than 15,500 periodicals and serials. The 240,000-square-foot William D. Walsh Family Library, one of the most technologically advanced academic libraries in the world, is an open-stack library that seats 1,600 readers. The Law School library and the Gerald Quinn Library Lincoln Center may also be used by Fordham students. In addition to the University libraries, graduate students may use the New York Public Library system, and they also have access to the libraries of the City University of New York, Columbia University, the New School, and New York University.

Financial Aid
Each year, the Graduate Program in International Political Economy and Development offers a number of fellowships. In addition to regular fellowships, there are specialized fellowships that enable the recruitment of an extremely talented and diverse student body. For example, Ricci Fellowships ensure that individuals who are actively involved in international affairs, usually from the UN diplomatic community, are enrolled; Global Markets Assistantships attract highly qualified individuals interested in the analysis of international commercial and financial markets; Public Service Assistantships are available for U.S. citizens with international experience who wish to pursue a career with the U.S. federal government; and Arrupe Fellowships attract very promising students who want to pursue a career with a nonprofit international relief and development organization. The program also participates in the U.S. Peace Corps Fellows/U.S.A. Program. Once enrolled in the IPED program, students become eligible for additional scholarships that help them prepare for the job market by gaining overseas experience (International Peace and Development Scholarships, Emerging Markets Travel Program), enhancing their language proficiency (Language Immersion Study Awards), or interning with a specially selected organization (Intern Fellowships). Educational Loans are also available for most students.

Cost of Study
Tuition for the 2009–10 academic year is $1190 per credit. Annual general fees are $268.

Living and Housing Costs
Rental costs for single students living in University apartments range from $8650 to $9860 per year. Shared rental units range from $700 to $1000 per month in the immediate off-campus neighborhood. An up-to-date rental database is maintained by the Office of the Associate Dean.

Student Group
The IPED program has an entering class of approximately 25 students each year from diverse backgrounds who share a common enthusiasm for international and development issues. About 40 percent of the students come from Africa, Asia, Eastern Europe, and Latin America.

Student Outcomes
Approximately half of the program's alumni are employed in the business sector, usually as analysts in the financial services industry with firms such as JP Morgan Chase and Ernst & Young. About a quarter work in the public sector as economists, analysts, or managers at agencies ranging from the U.S. International Trade Administration to the United Nations Children's Fund (UNICEF). About 15 percent work in the nonprofit sector, usually as project managers with organizations such as Catholic Relief Services and Freedom House. On average over the last five years, more than 20 percent of the program's graduates have won distinguished awards, ranging from Fulbrights and Soros Foundation Scholarships to U.S. Presidential Management Fellowships.

Location
The program's New York City location is ideal for anyone who wishes to be at the center of the world economy. New York City exposes students to the best the world has to offer in art, culture, and business and has the highly diversified atmosphere of a truly international city. Professors draw upon the resources of the city to enrich their courses.

The University
Fordham is a university in the Jesuit tradition. Founded in 1841, it is governed as an institution under a charter granted by the State of New York. The IPED program is offered through the Graduate School of Arts and Sciences. Founded in 1916, it carries on Fordham's oldest academic tradition, the education of talented men and women in the liberal arts and sciences, at the postgraduate level.

Applying
Admission to the program is very selective. Students are chosen from among the top 50 percent of applicants to U.S. graduate programs. Fellowship recipients are selected from among the top 15 percent of applicants to U.S. graduate schools. All applicants must have the equivalent of a U.S. bachelor's degree with a B or better average and must submit a statement of purpose, the general aptitude scores of the GRE, transcripts of all previous undergraduate and graduate course work, and three letters of recommendation. International applicants must also submit TOEFL scores. Applicants who do not wish to be considered for University financial aid may substitute LSAT scores or GMAT scores in place of the GRE. These individuals are still eligible for financial aid in the form of loans. There are additional admission materials required for some of the fellowship programs. Admission is for fall entrance only. To guarantee full consideration, the Graduate Admissions Office must receive students' complete applications by January 4 if aid is also applied for and by April 1 for applications without aid as well as those for Ricci Fellowships.

Correspondence and Information
International Political Economy and Development Program
Fordham University
Bronx, New York 10458

Phone: 718-817-4064
E-mail: iped@fordham.edu
Web site: http://www.fordham.edu/iped

Fordham University

THE FACULTY AND THEIR RESEARCH

All of the faculty members in the program are full-time, and all have doctorates from prominent universities. The faculty members are not only distinguished by their research and consultancy work, but also by their personal interest in mentoring and teaching the students. To complement the faculty, up to 2 visiting lecturers who are practitioners in their fields also teach each year.

Economists

Robert Brent, Professor; Ph.D., Manchester (U.K.). Project evaluation, taxation and development, tax reform, health evaluations and developing countries.

Michael Buckley, Senior Lecturer of Economics and Finance, Ph.D., Wayne State (Michigan). Global financial markets, financial analysis, financial consulting.

Mary Burke, Senior Lecturer of Economics; Ph.D., Fordham. Banking, management consulting.

Mary Beth Combs, Associate Professor; Ph.D., Iowa. Economic rights of women, economic history.

Ralf Hepp, Assistant Professor; Ph.D., California, Santa Cruz. International finance, open macroeconomics.

Baybars Karacaovali, Assistant Professor; Ph.D., Maryland, College Park. International trade, international political economy.

Subha Mani, Assistant Professor, Ph.D., USC. Microeconomics of development, microfinance, health, education, demography, applied econometrics.

Darryl L. McLeod, Associate Professor; Ph.D., Berkeley. Consultant to the World Bank, Inter-American Development Bank, the Organization of American States, and Lehman Brothers Emerging Markets Group. Development economics, stabilization and developing countries, poverty and income distribution in Latin America and Asia.

Sophie Mitra, Assistant Professor; Ph.D., Paris. Sustainable development, agricultural economics, and labor.

Erick Rengifo, Assistant Professor, Ph.D., Louvain (Belgium). Financial economics, financial econometrics, risk management.

Dominick Salvatore, Distinguished Professor; Ph.D., CUNY Graduate Center. Consultant to UN. Fulbright Awardee (Europe). Commercial policies and trade protectionism, international trade and economic development, international and European monetary systems.

Henry M. Schwalbenberg, Associate Professor and Director of the Graduate Program in International Political Economy and Development; Ph.D., Columbia. Political economy of trade and development, Southeast Asia and the Pacific economies, North-South capital flows.

Troy Tassier, Assistant Professor; Ph.D., Iowa. Microeconomics, public policy, economics of networks, complex systems, epidemics and development.

Booi Themeli, Senior Lecturer of Economics and Director of the Africa Rising Project; M.Comm., Rhodes (South Africa); Ph.D., Fordham. Rockefeller Fellow, Fulbright Fellow, Mandela Fellow. Privatization and development, the economies of Sub-Saharan Africa.

Political Scientists

Bruce E. Andrews, Associate Professor; Ph.D., Harvard. Political economy of the world system, interpretation of foreign policy, theories of international politics.

Susan A. Berger, Associate Professor; Ph.D., Columbia. Political economy of development, comparative politics, political economy of Latin America and the Caribbean.

Jonathan Crystal, Associate Professor; Ph.D., Harvard. Political economy of direct foreign investment.

John P. Entelis, Professor; Ph.D., NYU. Comparative politics, political risk analysis, political economy of the Middle East and North Africa.

Melissa Labonte, Assistant Professor, Ph.D., Brown. Comparative politics, post-conflict peace building, human rights, West Africa.

Joachim Rennstich, Assistant Professor, Ph.D., Indiana Bloomington. International politics, technology and political change.

Sociologists and Anthropologists

O. Hugo Benavides, Assistant Professor of Anthropology; Ph.D., CUNY Graduate Center. Ethnographic research in Ecuador.

Evelyn L. Bush, Assistant Professor; Ph.D., Cornell. Social movements and transnational politics, sociology of religion, human rights.

Donald F. Heisel, Research Director, Center for Migration Studies; Ph.D., Wisconsin. International migration, population, and social-economic development.

Historians

Michael Latham, Associate Professor; Ph.D., UCLA. Diplomatic history, the Kennedy administration and the Alliance for Progress.

Hector Lindo-Fuentes, Professor; Ph.D., Chicago. Economic history, nineteenth- and twentieth-century Latin America.

Visiting Lecturers

Arancha Garcia de Soto, Helen Hamlyn Senior Fellow, Institute of International Humanitarian Affairs, Ph.D., Salamanca (Spain). Complex emergencies and humanitarian assistance.

William Seltzer, Senior Research Scholar and Chair of the American Statistical Association's Committee on Professional Ethics; B.A., Chicago. Consultant, UN International Criminal Tribunal for Rwanda (1996); Director of the UN Statistics Division (1986–94); Chief of Demographic and Social Statistics, UN Statistics Division (1974–86). Demographic measurement, statistical organization and policy, the interface between human rights and population data systems, the promotion of ethical standards in demographic and statistical work.

THE INSTITUTE OF WORLD POLITICS

A Graduate School of National Security and International Affairs
Master of Arts in Statecraft and International Affairs,
Master of Arts in Statecraft and National Security Affairs,
and Master of Arts in Strategic Intelligence Studies

Program of Study

The Institute of World Politics (IWP) is an accredited graduate school of national security, intelligence, and international affairs dedicated to developing leaders with a sound understanding of international realities and the ethical conduct of statecraft, based on knowledge and appreciation of the principles of the American political economy and the Western moral tradition. The Institute's curriculum includes the study of all the elements of statecraft, including the arts of war, peacemaking, and diplomacy; public diplomacy and cultural diplomacy; psychological strategy and political action; economic strategy; intelligence and counterintelligence; the exercise of intangible instruments of power such as moral leadership, will-power, courage, rhetoric, etc.; and the integration of these elements into overall national strategy.

The Institute emphasizes the development of a capacity to think strategically so as to detect and understand strategic threats and opportunities; prevent, manage, resolve, and prevail in international conflicts; match the ends and means of policy; and do all of these in ways that minimize the necessity to use force.

Because true statesmanship requires that power not be misused, IWP's educational philosophy posits that the responsible conduct of statecraft must be guided by ethics and personal and civic virtue. Hence it incorporates character development and the study of applied ethics—another aspect that contributes to its uniqueness.

IWP currently offers three Master of Arts degree programs: Statecraft and National Security Affairs, Statecraft and International Affairs, and Strategic Intelligence Studies. Statecraft and International Affairs includes a foreign language requirement. All degrees contain the same foundational core curriculum in history, international politics, comparative ideologies, the Western moral tradition and the application of ethics to the use of power, American founding principles, and an overview of all the elements of statecraft. The Statecraft and National Security Affairs program offers specializations in intelligence, national security affairs, and public diplomacy and political warfare. The Statecraft and International Affairs program offers specializations in comparative political culture, international politics, American foreign policy, and democracy building. The Strategic Intelligence Studies program is designed for recent graduates who seek careers in the intelligence field as well as professionals whose agencies or clientele are charged with the acquisition and interpretation of intelligence. Each degree consists of eight core courses (4 credits each) and four elective courses in one of the specializations. All students also take or test out of two shorter courses (2-credits) on strategic geography and economics. Students may study full-time or part-time. Most classes are offered in the evenings for the convenience of those students who are midcareer professionals.

For their foreign language requirement, students in the Statecraft and International Affairs program must demonstrate proficiency in a strategic foreign language. IWP provides a list of these languages.

IWP also offers eight graduate-level certificate programs: American foreign policy, comparative political culture, democracy building, intelligence, counterintelligence, international politics, national security affairs, and public diplomacy and political warfare. The certificate programs are designed for students who wish to pursue graduate studies but do not need or seek a degree and/or those students who already have an advanced degree yet require additional graduate credentials. These programs are also intended to encourage students' continued professional growth and to serve as valuable indicators of achievement and knowledge for current or prospective employers and professional colleagues and peers.

Research Facilities

The IWP library contains more than 30,000 volumes, including the private library of William J. Casey, a former Director of Central Intelligence. In addition, the library maintains an extensive collection of foreign affairs periodicals and reference works, many of which are unique and available only through IWP. The IWP library also has specialized collections in U.S. foreign policy, Soviet/Russian affairs, Middle Eastern history, and intelligence/counterintelligence. High-speed Internet access is available to students through the library, as are extensive electronic databases.

Financial Aid

IWP offers merit-based scholarships to attract and retain high-achieving, academically talented graduate students. A more modest, need-based grant program is also available. IWP is eligible for Title IV federal funds, which enable students to use federal student loans to fund their IWP education. Students at the Institute are also eligible for Veterans' Affairs benefits. Prospective students should visit the IWP Web site for complete details.

Cost of Study

Tuition for the 2009–10 academic year is $1000 per credit hour; each 4-credit course is $4000 ($2000 for each 2-credit course). An application fee of $75 (nonrefundable and nontransferable) and a $300 per course deposit (applied toward tuition) are required to seek and hold an accepted student's place in the entering class. In addition, there is a mandatory Student Services fee of $150 per semester ($75 in the summer session). Classes are held throughout the year, with sessions beginning in spring, summer, and fall. Classes are small, conducted in seminar settings, and most are held during evening and weekend hours for the convenience of the students and their employers.

Living and Housing Costs

The Institute does not provide student housing. However, housing is available at several locations near the Institute. Students are responsible for making their own housing arrangements. Neighborhoods in northwest Washington, D.C., and many areas of Maryland and Virginia are proximate and accessible via public transportation. Students should consider personal safety and transportation availability as well as price when searching for housing. For a list of off-campus housing search engines and apartment locator services, students should visit the Institute's Web site.

Student Group

IWP's average class size per course is 10. In addition to recent college graduates, midcareer professionals from a wide range of U.S. and foreign government agencies and private organizations enroll at the Institute to advance their careers. The result is an ever-expanding network of IWP students and alumni from—and graduates earning key positions throughout—the organizations that develop and implement policy for the United States and countries around the world.

Student Outcomes

Successful recipients of IWP's master's degrees are prepared for a wide range of careers, including defense, intelligence, foreign policy making and implementation, policy research, journalism, and a variety of private-sector professions. These advanced degrees complement many undergraduate pursuits, thereby enhancing a bachelor's degree in political science, history, international relations, economics, or business.

Location

The Institute of World Politics is located in the historical Marlatt Mansion and Bently Hall on 16th Street, NW, in downtown Washington, D.C. The school's location, just eight blocks from the White House, offers students access to the seat of federal government and to the heart of U.S. foreign policy and governmental decision-making processes. Experts at the Institute, whether they are faculty members, guest lecturers, or speakers at extracurricular functions are drawn from the highest ranks of the U.S. government, foreign embassies, and domestic and international organizations specializing in national security affairs.

Applying

Admission to the master's degree programs is competitive. The Institute of World Politics seeks a culturally diverse student body to enhance the international classroom experience. Half the student body consists of recent college graduates who have an interest in international affairs, foreign policy, intelligence, or national security. Other students include personnel from the U.S. government, international diplomats, and working professionals with interests in international affairs and national security.

An earned bachelor's degree from a regionally accredited or similarly recognized college or university is required. Applicants without significant undergraduate course work or job experience in IWP's subject fields may be required to complete related prerequisite course work. Application requirements include a current resume, official (sealed) transcripts from all institutions attended, Graduate Record Examinations (GRE) General Test scores (or the LSAT), three letters of recommendation, a short description of educational and professional goals, and an essay. Prospective students may apply online or request further information through the Institute's address, phone number, or Web site.

Correspondence and Information

Colin Parks
Director of Student Recruitment
The Institute of World Politics
1521 16th Street, NW
Washington, D.C. 20036-1464
Phone: 202-462-2101
        888-KNOW-IWP (toll-free)
E-mail: parks@iwp.edu
Web site: http://www.iwp.edu

The Institute of World Politics

THE FACULTY

Norman A. Bailey, Adjunct Professor; Ph.D., Columbia, 1962. Mission Manager for Cuba and Venezuela, Office of the Director of National Intelligence; former Senior Director of International Economic Affairs, National Security Council.

Raymond J. Batvinis, Adjunct Professor; Ph.D., Catholic University, 2002. Consultant/investigator for RJB Associates; former supervisory special agent, FBI.

David Burgess, Adjunct Professor; J.D., Georgetown, 1978. Senior official, U.S. Peace Corps and former State Department official.

Marek Jan Chodakiewicz, Professor of History and Academic Dean; Ph.D., Columbia, 2002.

Kenneth deGraffenreid, Professor of Intelligence Studies; M.A., Catholic University, 1977. Former Deputy National Counterintelligence Executive and former Senior Director of Intelligence Programs, National Security Council.

Lee Edwards, Adjunct Professor; Ph.D., Catholic University, 1986. Distinguished Scholar, The Heritage Foundation.

Roger W. Fontaine, Adjunct Professor; Ph.D., Johns Hopkins (SAIS), 1970. Former Director of Latin American Affairs, National Security Council.

Paul A. Goble, Adjunct Professor; M.A., Chicago, 1973. Formerly with the International Broadcasting Bureau, CIA, and Department of State.

Christopher C. Harmon, Adjunct Professor; Ph.D., Claremont, 1984. Author, *Terrorism Today;* Professor, Marine Corps University.

Walter Jajko, Defense Advanced Research Projects Agency Professor of Defense Studies; M.A., Columbia, 1964. Former Assistant to the Secretary of Defense for Intelligence Oversight; Brigadier General, USAF (retired).

Brian Kelley, Adjunct Professor; M.A., Florida State, 1974. Retired senior CIA official.

David M. L. Klocek, Professor of Political Science, Vice Dean of Academic Affairs, Faculty Chairman, and Director of Admissions; Ph.D., Georgetown, 2000. Former analyst, CIA.

Mark P. Lagon, Adjunct Professor; Ph.D., Georgetown, 1991. Deputy Assistant Secretary of State; formerly with the Senate Foreign Relations Committee.

John Lenczowski, Professor, Founder, and President of The Institute of World Politics; Ph.D., Johns Hopkins (SAIS), 1980. Former Director of European and Soviet Affairs, National Security Council; formerly with the Department of State.

Thomas P. Melady, Senior Diplomat in Residence; Ph.D., Catholic University, 1954. Former U.S. Ambassador to the Vatican, Uganda, and Burundi.

Ross H. Munro, Adjunct Professor; B.A., British Columbia, 1965. Director of Asian Studies, Center for Security Studies.

Joshua Muravchik, Adjunct Professor; Ph.D., Georgetown, 1984. Resident Scholar, American Enterprise Institute.

Alberto M. Piedra, Donald E. Bently Professor of Political Economy; Ph.D., Madrid, 1957; Ph.D., Georgetown, 1962. Former U.S. Ambassador to Guatemala.

Juliana Geran Pilon, Adjunct Research Professor and Earhart Fellow; Ph.D., Chicago, 1974.

S. Eugene Poteat, Adjunct Professor; M.A., Institute of World Politics, 2001. President, Association for Intelligence Officers; former CIA official.

Herbert Romerstein, Adjunct Professor. Author, researcher, and former Director, Office to Counter Soviet Disinformation and Active Measures, U.S. Information Agency.

Charles R. Smith, Adjunct Professor; Ph.D., Catholic University, 1982.

Henry D. Sokolski, Adjunct Professor; M.A., Chicago, 1980. Former Deputy for Nonproliferation, Department of Defense.

Robert W. Stephan, Adjunct Professor; Ph.D., George Washington, 1997. Senior CIA official.

Douglas E. Streusand, Adjunct Professor; Ph.D., Chicago, 1987. Associate Professor, Marine Corps Command and Staff College.

David Thomas, Adjunct Professor; D.Phil., Oxford, 1980. Department of Defense.

John J. Tierney Jr., Walter Kohler Professor of International Relations; Ph.D., Pennsylvania, 1969.

J. Michael Waller, Walter and Leonore Annenberg Professor of International Communication; Ph.D., Boston University, 1993.

John J. Yurechko, Adjunct Professor; Ph.D., Berkeley, 1980. Director of Analysis and Collection, Office of the National Counterintelligence Executive; formerly with Defense Intelligence Agency.

MISSOURI STATE UNIVERSITY

Department of Political Science
Master of Global Studies

Program of Study

The Department of Political Science offers a Master of Global Studies (M.G.S.) degree to meet the growing societal and occupational needs in a highly competitive and yet increasingly interdependent world. The main mission of the M.G.S. program is to produce well-rounded and educated persons who understand and appreciate the diversity and complexity of international affairs and the role of global citizenship and who can bring imaginative and creative problem-solving skills to problems faced by the global community.

The M.G.S. is designed to equip students with skills in areas such as quantitative analysis, policy analysis, administration/management, foreign languages, communication, and problem solving that allow them to pursue careers in both public and private-sector agencies in an international environment. The M.G.S. also prepares students to continue their education at the doctoral level in international relations, political science, or other related fields.

Students enrolled in the M.G.S. program must complete a series of core courses that have been crafted to provide them with a firm foundation in international affairs and administration. These courses include seminars in international relations theory, international organizations and administration, international political economy, comparative politics, foreign policy decision making, and comparative public administration. In addition to the core curriculum, each student selects a cognate field and specializes in it. These fields include international relations and comparative politics, international economics and business, public administration, and national security. The student completes a total of 15 to 18 hours in his or her cognate field. Students also must either complete an independent research project supervised by a faculty member or opt for the 6-hour thesis option, whereby the student writes a full-fledged thesis. Finally, students must complete the equivalent of two years of training in a modern foreign language. Those students who earn a grade point average of less than 3.75 in the program must pass a comprehensive exam composed of both written and oral assessments. This exam is designed to measure the extent to which these students have absorbed the core body of knowledge included in the curriculum.

Students are encouraged to enroll in an internship. In the past, students have secured positions in internships in locations ranging from the local area to Japan. Students may receive 3 hours of credit for the internship, and it may be counted in the cognate field portion of the program requirements. Graduate students enrolled in the M.G.S. program also participate in numerous international conferences and a wide variety of other academic-related events. Such activities play a critical role in helping students learn about the global community (and help make them more competitive job candidates after graduation).

The M.G.S. program also encourages students to participate in study-abroad trips. Past study tours have included China and various European countries, including Russia. In addition, the M.G.S. program has established an exchange program with the Graduate Institute of Political Science at National Sun Yat-sen University (NSYSU) in Kaohsiung, Taiwan. NSYSU has been named by the Ministry of Education as one of Taiwan's seven major research-intensive universities. With a population of over 2 million, Kaohsiung is the second-largest city in Taiwan. NSYSU's Political Science Program only has exchange programs with a small number of other universities—including the two best universities in China (Peking University and Fudan University). M.G.S. students may spend the equivalent of a semester studying international relations and/or Chinese at NSYSU (all graduate classes are taught in English) and receive credit for those classes. In addition to the exchange program with NSYSU, there are other exchange program opportunities.

Research Facilities

Missouri State University libraries have comprehensive electronic resources, including an online catalog, electronic indexes and full-text resources, and Internet accessibility. The University is a member of the Center for Research Libraries and is both a U.S. and United Nations document depository.

Financial Aid

Graduate assistantships are awarded on a competitive basis in the Department and elsewhere on campus. The Department typically awards up to five graduate assistantships per year to students in the M.G.S. program. All students applying for a graduate assistantship must have their GRE scores (verbal and quantitative) on file at the time of application. Each award is granted for an academic year. A stipend and a waiver of tuition accompany the assistantship. Student research grants of up to $2000 are available to students who wish to conduct research in East Asia.

Cost of Study

Missouri residents pay $3852 for 9 hours plus approximately $1500 in fees; nonresidents pay $7524 for 9 hours plus approximately $1500 in fees.

Living and Housing Costs

Graduate student housing with meal plans costs between $7810 and $9820 per person; without a meal plan, it costs between $6090 and $8100. A twelve-month family meal plan can be purchased for $1177 per semester. Two-bedroom apartments in the community rent for approximately $540 a month.

Student Group

The total enrollment at Missouri State University is approximately 20,000 students, of whom 16 percent are graduate students. Students come from across the United States and from more than sixty countries. There are 40 students enrolled in the M.G.S. program. Students in the program come from the surrounding area, the state of Missouri, across the U.S., and from many other nations.

Student Outcomes

The M.G.S. program enjoys a record of nearly 100 percent in placing its graduates in Ph.D. programs in America and abroad. Graduates have been admitted to the American University, Cambridge University, University of New Mexico, Catholic University, University of Southern California, University of Missouri, University of Northern Illinois, University of North Texas, University of South Carolina and University of Essex. It is noteworthy that many of these students have received prestigious and highly competitive scholarships and/or graduate assistantships.

A vast majority of graduates who have opted for a career have managed to secure employment in prestigious organizations. These include the National Defense University, Television Tokyo, the Landmine Survivors Network, and the United Nations in New York City or the UN branch offices in various countries overseas. Some international students who have earned the M.G.S. degree have found employment with their respective home governments or with international businesses.

Location

Missouri State University is located in Springfield, the third-largest city in Missouri, with a metropolitan service region of 400,000. Located in the heart of the Ozarks recreational area, the University is within easy driving distance of numerous lakes, streams, and parks. The community of Springfield is supported by an industrial/manufacturing base and an expanding service industry in tourism, with people drawn by the natural beauty and recreation of the Ozarks and the musical attractions in nearby Branson. Springfield has an extensive health and medical economy serving southwest Missouri, northwest Arkansas, southeast Kansas, and northeast Oklahoma.

The University

Missouri State University, founded in 1905, is a multicampus metropolitan university system with a statewide mission in public affairs. The University offers more than 150 undergraduate majors and forty-three graduate programs, many of which are the strongest of their kind in the state. The students experience college life at its best, with NCAA Division I athletics and more than 250 student organizations.

Applying

Individuals interested in applying to the M.G.S. program may obtain an application from the Graduate College, Carrington Hall, Room 306, Missouri State University, 901 South National, Springfield, Missouri 65897 (417-836-5335). Downloadable forms and an online application are provided at the Graduate College Web site at http://graduate.missouristate.edu/admissions.htm/. International students must also follow all directions as outlined on the Graduate College Web site at http://graduate.missouristate.edu/international.htm/.

Correspondence and Information

Dr. Beat Kernen
M.G.S. Program Director
Missouri State University
Springfield, Missouri 65897

Phone: 417-836-5733
E-mail: beatkernen@missouristate.edu
Web site: http://polsci.missouristate.edu/mgs/

Missouri State University

THE FACULTY AND THEIR RESEARCH

M.G.S. faculty members are student oriented. They are also among the most productive and visible faculty at MSU. M.G.S. faculty members have published a string of policy-relevant publications (books and articles) focusing on international affairs. As a consequence, M.G.S. faculty have been asked to provide testimony before the U.S. Congress and served as consultants to various agencies and departments within the executive branch of the national government. Moreover, they are regularly invited to appear on local television and radio programs and have made appearances on national or international television broadcasts including *Dateline, CNN World News, Nightline, The Oprah Winfrey Show,* and the Voice of America's *Issues & Opinions* (a television program broadcast into China) and China Central Television (CCTV). With respect to the print media, faculty members have contributed opinion pieces to many of the world's major newspapers, including the *China Daily, Wall Street Journal, Los Angeles Times, Chicago Tribune, Denver Post, Taipei Times, Rocky Mountain News,* and *Kansas City Star.* Not surprisingly, the M.G.S. program has hosted a number of important international conferences. Students are strongly encouraged to participate in these events.

Dennis Hickey, Professor; Ph.D., Texas. Dr. Hickey's research and teaching interests include international relations, Asian politics, national security, and American foreign policy. During the spring semester of 2008, Dr. Hickey was a Fulbright Exchange Scholar at the China Foreign Affairs University in Beijing, China. His most recent book, *Foreign Policy Making in Taiwan: From Principle to Pragmatism,* was published by Routledge in 2007. (dennishickey@missouristate.edu)
Beat R. Kernen, Professor and Director of the M.G.S. Program; Ph.D., Kansas. Dr. Kernen's teaching and research interests include international relations, post-Soviet politics, and the politics of the European Union. His most recent research focuses on Russia's geo-strategic interests in other former Soviet republics, especially in the Caucasus. He has published articles in *The Soviet and Post-Soviet Review, Crossroads, Political Chronicle, Yearbook of East European Economies,* and *East European Quarterly.* (beatkernen@missouristate.edu)
Gabriel Ondetti, Assistant Professor; Ph.D., North Carolina at Chapel Hill. Dr. Ondetti's teaching and research interests include Latin American politics and international political economy. His current research focuses on the impact of democracy on redistributive policies in Latin America. In spring 2008 he published *Land, Protest, and Politics: The Landless Movement and the Struggle for Agrarian Reform in Brazil* (Penn State Press). (gabrielondetti@missouristate.edu)
Kenneth R. Rutherford, Associate Professor; M.B.A., Colorado; M.A.L.S., Ph.D., Georgetown. Dr. Rutherford's research and teaching interests include international law, international organization, and international security. He is cofounder of Survivor Corps, formerly the Landmine Survivors Network. His most recent book is *Humanitarianism Under Fire: The United States and United Nations Intervention in Somalia* (Kumarian Press) published in July 2008. (kenrutherford@missouristate.edu)

Monterey Institute
of International Studies
An affiliate of Middlebury College

MONTEREY INSTITUTE OF INTERNATIONAL STUDIES
Graduate School of International Policy and Management

Programs of Study

The Graduate School of International Policy and Management (GSIPM) offers three two-year professional master's degree programs: the Master of Arts in international policy studies (MAIPS), the Master of Public Administration (M.P.A.) in international management, and the Master of Arts in international environmental policy (MAIEP).

The MAIPS program combines language and policy studies to train students for careers in the public, nonprofit, or private sectors in cross-cultural settings. The curriculum combines courses in policy analysis, economics, quantitative analysis, international relations, comparative politics, area studies, and language, with an in-depth focus on specific policy problems or sectors.

Within the MAIPS program, GSIPM offers three specialized tracks: international development, international security, and international trade. Many students will focus these tracks on more specific areas, such as international negotiation/conflict resolution, international norms/humans rights/justice, Asian studies, terrorism studies, or international organizations/nonprofit management.

The M.P.A. program focuses on the knowledge, professional skills, and leadership abilities needed to effectively help local, national, and global organizations build or improve community developments. The curriculum includes courses in public and nonprofit management, organizational theory, data analysis, budgeting, accounting, and program evaluation.

The MAIEP program responds to the growing need for policymakers to address environmental problems with international dimensions, such as biodiversity protection, climate-change policy, sustainable development, renewable energy, water and air quality, coastal watersheds, and marine policy. Courses include the scientific foundations of environmental policy, international environmental law and policy, environmental economics, and conflict management

In addition to the degree programs, GSIPM offers stand-alone certificate programs structured around defined clusters of courses that examine specific policy areas: Nonproliferation Studies, Conflict Resolution, International Environmental Policy, and International Trade Policy.

Research Facilities

Internships and research opportunities are available through the Institute's James Martin Center for Nonproliferation Studies; the Center for East Asian Studies; the Monterey Center for Humanitarian Assistance, Development, and Security; and the Monterey Terrorism Research and Education Program.

The William Tell Coleman Library includes 95,000 volumes, more than 500 print periodicals, over 50 online databases, more than 400 academic journals, about thirty-five newspapers, and approximately 15,000 electronic books. One third of the collection is in languages other than English. Innovative and challenging curricula at the Institute require appropriate facilities and cutting-edge technology. Classrooms vary in size from large halls where plenary sessions with simultaneous interpretation can be held to smaller classrooms and labs befitting seminar-style classes for 5 to 15 students.

The Max Kade Language and Technology Center is a fully equipped language-learning center. It provides multimedia classrooms and conference rooms with state-of-the-art technology, including a multimedia resource center and the campus Teaching and Learning Collaborative.

In addition to numerous computer labs, the campus is fully wireless. Every student is encouraged to have a personal laptop computer adapted for wireless connectivity.

Financial Aid

Candidates with a minimum grade point average of 3.3 on a 4.0 scale (or equivalent) are considered for merit scholarships ranging from $4000 to $15,000 per year. Veterans of military service or orphans/dependants of veterans may be eligible for veteran's benefits. The Monterey Institute Grant is awarded to students demonstrating exceptional financial need who do not qualify for merit scholarships. Other scholarships may be awarded by outside foundations.

Under the Federal Stafford Loan program, students may borrow up to $8500 in subsidized loans or $20,500 in unsubsidized loans, less any subsidized amount. Graduate PLUS Loans cover the cost of college minus other financial aid resources. The Federal Work-Study Program allows students to work up to $4000 per academic year, working a maximum of 20 hours per week.

Cost of Study

Tuition and fees for 2009–10 are $31,056.

Living and Housing Costs

The estimated variable expenses for books, supplies, housing, food, local transportation, personal expenses, and health insurance is $17,592.

Student Group

Institute enrollment is approximately 800. About one third of the students are from outside the United States, representing more than sixty countries. More than 90 percent of students from the U.S. have worked or studied abroad. More than fifty languages are spoken by students on campus. Language classes are regularly offered in English, Spanish, Arabic, French, Russian, Japanese, Chinese (Mandarin), and German. Other languages are offered by request.

Student Outcomes

The School's graduates are prepared for careers in policy research, project coordination, and management. They apply those skills in a wide range of settings and organizations, such as international development (UNDP, World Bank), environmental protection (UNEP, World Wildlife Fund), intergovernmental organizations (World Trade Organization, United Nations), national governments (Japan, China, Kazakhstan, Russia, India), the U.S. government (Departments of State, Energy, and Commerce; USAID; DIA; CIA), and international NGOs (Save the Children, Mercy Corps).

Location

The Monterey Institute is situated in one of the most spectacular natural environments in the world. The Monterey Peninsula is 130 miles south of San Francisco on California's central coast, surrounded by ocean and mountains. Silicon Valley is only a short drive away. With a population of 100,000, the area combines a variety of rich cultural resources and agricultural activities.

The Institute

Established in 1955 with summer classes in language and culture, the Monterey Institute of Foreign Studies was the first institute dedicated to the then-revolutionary concept that a living language should be taught as such: French in French, German in German, etc. Year-round degree programs began in 1961. By 1979, the Institute had grown to international distinction and was renamed the Monterey Institute of International Studies.

The Monterey Institute is an affiliate of Middlebury College. Founded in 1800, Middlebury is one of the country's top liberal arts colleges. It offers students a broad curriculum embracing the arts, humanities, literature, foreign languages, social sciences, and natural sciences. The affiliation further enriches the curriculum, creates a bicoastal presence, and offers valuable connections to build greater global connection.

Applying

The Monterey Institute of International Studies has a rolling application process and allows students to begin in both fall and spring semesters. The priority deadlines for applicants who wish to be considered for merit-based scholarships are October 1 for the spring semester, and December 1, February 1, or March 15 for the fall semester.

Prospective students are required to have a U.S. bachelor's degree or the equivalent from an accredited college/university and a minimum GPA of 3.0 on a 4.0 scale. Applicants with a GPA below 3.0 should submit a GRE score; otherwise, a GRE score is optional. In order to complete the application process, prospective students are required to submit the following: a completed application form, a personal statement (600 words), a resume/CV, official transcripts from all colleges attended, two letters of recommendation, and a nonrefundable $50 application fee.

Nonnative English speakers must also provide a TOEFL or IELTS score. The minimum TOEFL requirements are as follows: paper-based test, 550; test of written English, 4.0; Computer-based test: 213, test of written English: 4.0; Internet-based test: 80, test of written English: 213, no other subscores below 19. The IELTS minimum is 6.5 overall with no subscore below 6.0 on the Academic module. International students should apply three months before enrollment to allow enough time for the visa process.

Correspondence and Information

Admissions Office
Monterey Institute of International Studies
460 Pierce Street
Monterey, California 93940
Phone: 831-647-4123
      800-824-7235 (toll-free within the United States)
Fax: 831-647-6405
E-mail: admit@miis.edu
Web site: http://www.miis.edu

Monterey Institute of International Studies

THE FULL-TIME FACULTY AND THEIR RESEARCH

Tsuneo Akaha, Professor and Director, Center for East Asian Studies; Ph.D. (political science), USC. Dr. Akaha teaches courses on security in Northeast Asia and public policy in Japan, especially foreign and environmental.

William Arrocha, Assistant Professor; Ph.D. (international relations), Queen's at Kingston. Dr. Arrocha teaches courses on international political economy, trade policy with special reference to NAFTA, and politics of Mexico.

Mahabat Baimyrzaeva; Ph.D. (public administration), USC. Professor Baimyrzaeva teaches courses in public administration, management, policy, and international development.

Jeffrey M. Bale, Assistant Professor and Director, Monterey Terrorism Research and Education Program (MonTREP); Ph.D. (European history), Berkeley. Dr. Bale teaches courses in terrorism and security issues.

Jan Knippers Black, Professor; Ph.D. (international studies), American. Dr. Black teaches courses on Latin American politics and development (media, foreign policy, women, and human rights).

Fernando DePaolis, Assistant Professor; Ph.D. (regional analysis), UCLA. Dr. DePaolis teaches courses on regional analysis, data analysis, and the labor and income effects of trade policies.

Stephen Garrett, Professor; Ph.D. (international affairs), Virginia. Dr. Garrett spent academic year 1978–79 in Bangkok, Thailand, as a senior lecturer on a Fulbright Fellowship and was appointed to the Gordon Paul Smith Chair of International Policy Studies in 1988–89. Dr. Garrett teaches courses on ethics and force in international relations, comparative approaches to transitional justice, and humanitarian intervention.

Gordon Hahn, Professor; Ph.D. (political science), Boston University. Dr. Hahn is the author of *Russia's Islamic Threat* (Yale University Press, 2007), and numerous scholarly and analytical articles on politics, Islam, and jihadism in Russia. Dr. Hahn teaches courses within the terrorism program.

Pushpa Iyer, Assistant Professor; Ph.D. (conflict analysis and resolution), George Mason. Dr. Iyer teaches courses in conflict resolution, identity conflicts, civil wars, peace processes and non-state armed actors.

Nuket Kardam, Associate Professor; Ph.D. (political science), Michigan State. Dr. Kardam teaches courses on international organizations, organization behavior, and women and civil society in Islamic countries, especially Turkey.

Sharad Joshi, Associate Professor; Ph.D., Pittsburgh. Dr. Sharad Joshi is a researcher in the Monterey Terrorism Research and Education Program (MonTREP). Dr. Joshi teaches courses on terrorism and international security.

Jeffrey Langholz, Professor; Ph.D. (natural resource policy and management), Cornell. Dr. Langholz teaches courses on natural resource policy and management, international environmental policy, and sustainable development.

Edward J. Laurance, Professor; Ph.D. (international relations), Pennsylvania. Dr. Laurance has served as a consultant to the UN Department of Disarmament Affairs since 1992. He also cofounded the International Action Network on Small Arms, the largest transnational small arms NGO. Dr. Laurance teaches courses on international organizations, multilateral problem solving, and small arms control.

Beryl Levinger, Distinguished Professor of Nonprofit Management; Ph.D. (educational planning), Alabama. Dr. Levinger teaches courses on nonprofit organization and management, and human capacity building.

Wei Liang, Professor; Ph.D. USC. Dr. Liang teaches courses in international trade negotiation, international relations, international political economy, and Asian studies.

Robert McCleery, Professor; Ph.D. (economics), Stanford. Dr. McCleery teaches courses on international economics, quantitative analysis for trade policy, and economic development, especially East Asia and Mexico.

Philip Murphy, Associate Professor; Ph.D. (political science), Pittsburgh. Dr. Murphy teaches course work in quantitative methods and public policy analysis.

William Potter, Professor and Director, Center for Russian and Eurasian Studies and the James Martin Center for Nonproliferation Studies; Ph.D. (political science), Michigan. Dr. Potter teaches courses on disarmament and nonproliferation of weapons of mass destruction.

Moyara de Moraes Ruehsen, Associate Professor; Ph.D. (international economics and Middle Eastern studies), Johns Hopkins. Dr. Ruehsen teaches courses on international economics, illegal markets, and data analysis.

Jason Scorse, Assistant Professor; Ph.D. (environmental economics and policy), Berkeley. Dr. Scorse teaches courses on environmental and resource economics, sustainable development, international trade, and international economics.

Sheikh Shahnawaz, Assistant Professor; Ph.D. (economics), USC. Dr. Shahnawaz teaches courses on trade services, international economics, and the political economy of the Middle East.

Fred Wehling, Assistant Professor; Ph.D. (political science), UCLA. Dr. Wehling teaches courses on international security, fissile material control, terrorism with nuclear/chemical/biological/radiological weapons, and nuclear nonproliferation

Jim Williams, Associate Professor; Ph.D., M.S. (energy and resources) Berkeley. Prior to coming to the Monterey Institute, Dr. Williams worked at Energy and Environmental Economics (E3) where he was lead analyst on the E3 team modeling implementation of California's Global Warming Solutions Act (AB32) for California state agencies. Dr. Williams teaches courses on energy and climate change policy.

Jing-dong Yuan, Associate Professor; Ph.D. (political science), Queen's at Kingston. Dr. Yuan teaches courses on Chinese security and foreign policy, Chinese politics, arms control, East Asia security, Sino-Indian relations, and Sino-U.S. relations.

Lyuba Zarsky, Associate Professor; Ph.D. (economics), Massachusetts Amherst. Dr. Zarsky teaches courses in trade, sustainable development, globalization, environmental governance, development economics, and macroeconomics of sustainable development.

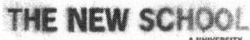

THE NEW SCHOOL: A UNIVERSITY

International Affairs

Programs of Study	The graduate program in international affairs offers two degree options: a 42-credit Master of Arts in international affairs designed for students who wish to enter the field, and a 30-credit Master of Science in international affairs for those with prior professional experience in the field. Both programs of study combine a set of core courses with a wide range of electives and opportunities for hands-on experience. Students may pursue the M.A. or M.S. degree on a full-time or part-time basis; courses are offered both days and evenings.
	The New School's International Affairs programs emphasize practice and real-world problem solving. They combine analysis of the changing global economy and culture with an examination of the economic and social problems facing developing countries. Upon graduation, students are in a position to begin or advance careers in public service, nongovernmental organizations, academia, media, the private sector, and more.
	The curriculum is supplemented by internships, fieldwork, conferences, weekly seminars on international affairs, and other special workshops and talks. The program also offers opportunities for fieldwork overseas during the summer, in such locations as Barcelona, Bombay, Buenos Aires, Cameroon, Geneva, Ghana, Hong Kong, Johannesburg, and Kenya. Students also have access to The New School's extensive academic resources, including the graduate program in media studies, Milano The New School for Management and Urban Policy, and the World Policy and India China institutes.
	The program's full-time and part-time M.A. and M.S. students come from a wide range of backgrounds; they include former UN staff members, Peace Corps volunteers, NGO workers, journalists, filmmakers, lawyers, and stockbrokers. Some seek new careers, whereas others are looking for ways to address the limitations of their current ones. Above all, students enroll in the program because they want to expand and build upon their unique experiences in the service of a better world.
Research Facilities	The New School is a member of the Research Library Association of South Manhattan, one of the largest interuniversity library consortia in the country. Members of the consortium include The New School's Raymond Fogelman Library, which houses 173,000 volumes in the social sciences and philosophy; New York University's Elmer Holmes Bobst Library; and the Cooper Union Library. Total holdings of these libraries exceed 4.1 million volumes and 25,000 journals. Beyond the consortium are the rich resources of New York City, including 250 METRO-member libraries and the public library systems of the five New York boroughs. Extensive computer facilities are available.
Financial Aid	Scholarships and awards are available to all matriculated students, whether full-time or part-time. The University considers both merit and need in granting available funds. The University Scholars fund provides additional financial support for students from underrepresented groups. An extended payment plan allows students to pay tuition in installments throughout the academic year.
Cost of Study	Tuition for the 2009–10 academic year is $1175 per credit. A $100 University services fee, a $15 divisional fee, and a $5 student senate fee are charged each term. Prospective students should visit http://www.newschool.edu/tuition for more information.
Living and Housing Costs	The University Housing Office maintains a comprehensive resource center with apartment listings. University-operated apartments and residence halls are also an option for graduate students. The cost of housing, food, transportation, and living expenses averages $17,000 per year. For more information, students should visit: http://www.newschool.edu/studentservices.
Student Group	More than 300 students from 62 countries work directly with international practitioners and scholars and focus on today's top global issues, including global economics, poverty and development, cities and urbanization, international institutions, NGOs, human rights, conflict and security, and media and culture.
Location	New York City offers numerous opportunities for students of international affairs. The U.N. General Assembly is located there, as are many major NGOs and multinational corporations. New York is an international center for media business and production and is the financial center of the world.
The University and The School	Located in the heart of New York's Greenwich Village, The New School is a center of academic excellence where intellectual and artistic freedoms thrive. The 9,000 matriculated students and more than 6,000 continuing education students who attend the university's eight schools enjoy a disciplined education supported by small class sizes, superior resources, and renowned working faculty members who practice what they teach. When The New School was founded in 1919, its mission was to create a place where global peace and justice were more than theoretical goals. Today, The New School continues to pursue that mission and strives to foster worthy and just citizens of the world. For more information about the University, students should visit http://www.newschool.edu.
	The eight schools that make up The New School are The New School for General Studies, The New School for Social Research, Milano The New School for Management and Urban Policy, Parsons The New School for Design, Eugene Lang College The New School for Liberal Arts, Mannes College The New School for Music, The New School for Drama, and The New School for Jazz and Contemporary Music.
Applying	Applications are welcome from students in all academic disciplines. Students must submit official transcripts, letters of recommendation, a statement of purpose, an academic writing sample, a one-page resume, and a $40 application fee. A personal interview is conducted after the application has been reviewed. Standardized test scores are not required. Application deadlines are February 15 for fall and October 15 for spring admission. Early application is strongly encouraged.
Correspondence and Information	International Affairs Program Office of Admissions The New School 66 West 12th Street, Room 401 New York, New York 10011 Phone: 212-229-5630 E-mail: nsadmissions@newschool.edu Web site: http://www.ia.newschool.edu

The New School: A University

THE FACULTY

Michael A. Cohen, Program Director; Ph.D., Chicago.
Jonathan Bach, Associate Director; Ph.D., Syracuse.

Core Faculty

Stephen J. Collier, Ph.D., Berkeley.
David Gold, Ph.D., City University of New York.
Ashok Gurung, M.I.A., Columbia.
Nina Khrushcheva, Ph.D., Princeton.
Lily Ling, Ph.D., MIT.

For a complete listing of courses and faculty members, including visiting and part-time faculty members, students should visit the Web site at http://www.ia.newschool.edu.

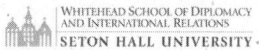
WHITEHEAD SCHOOL OF DIPLOMACY
AND INTERNATIONAL RELATIONS
SETON HALL UNIVERSITY

SETON HALL UNIVERSITY

The Whitehead School of Diplomacy and International Relations

Programs of Study

The John C. Whitehead School of Diplomacy and International Relations educates students from around the world to bring diplomatic skills and a solid understanding of international affairs to careers in public service, business, law, and the nonprofit sector. The only school of its kind in the United States to share a unique link with the United Nations Association of the USA, the Whitehead School of Diplomacy exposes students to the policymakers and practitioners addressing today's worldwide concerns. Innovative graduate and undergraduate degree programs, taught by a distinguished faculty of scholars and professionals, prepare students to be effective and ethical leaders in their professional careers. The Whitehead School of Diplomacy is an affiliate member of the Association of Professional Schools of International Affairs (APSIA).

The graduate curriculum combines interdisciplinary global studies with research methodology and policy analysis, culminating in a professional internship and significant research project. The School's Director of Internships and Career Development works closely with students to tailor their internships to their specific career goals. To attain the M.A. degree, students complete a total of 45 credit hours, satisfying core curriculum requirements, and two specializations. Students select from an array of functional and regional specializations structuring their academic studies according to their particular interests, career goals, and backgrounds. Functional specializations include foreign policy analysis, global health and human security, global negotiation and conflict management, international economics and development, international law and human rights, international organizations, and international security. Regional specializations in Africa, Asia, Europe, Latin America and the Caribbean, and the Middle East are also available.

Joint graduate degree programs combine an M.A. in diplomacy and international relations with a J.D., an M.B.A., an M.P.A. (with a focus on government or nonprofit management), an M.A. in Asian studies, or an M.A. in strategic communications.

At the Whitehead School, graduate students of diverse cultural, educational, and professional backgrounds form an international academic community. The graduate program fosters leadership and civic responsibility and sharpens analytical and practical skills. Small classes create a supportive environment that encourages mentoring relationships. An active graduate student association takes on a variety of projects and activities. Graduate assistantships, scholarships, and positions on the student-edited *Whitehead Journal of Diplomacy and International Relations* are awarded on a competitive basis.

Research Facilities

Walsh Library is a state-of-the-art facility built in 1994. In addition to housing print materials, library services include expert research support, bibliographic searching with online text retrieval (also available remotely), extensive CD-ROM databases, and interlibrary borrowing. As a U.N. depository, optical disk technology makes available up-to-date documentation from the U.N. The library's computer labs and study carrels are all Internet-linked and offer wireless Internet.

Financial Aid

In addition to federal loan and work-study programs, the Whitehead School of Diplomacy may award graduate assistantships and scholarships to full-time students who exhibit high academic and professional potential. The School's Office of Internships and Career Development guides students' career development activities.

Cost of Study

In 2009–10, tuition is $901 per credit. Full-time students pay $305 per semester in University and technology fees; part-time students pay $185.

Living and Housing Costs

On-campus housing is not available for graduate students. Housing and living costs in South Orange and surrounding towns are comparable to most suburban cities, with studio and one-bedroom apartments renting for $750 to $1000 per month. The member organization of graduate students, the Graduate Diplomacy Council, supports an online housing database on the University's online posting board. This forum helps students to find roommates and discuss various apartment buildings and neighborhoods in the area.

Student Group

Approximately 250 full-time graduate students are enrolled in the program. Students come from throughout the United States and nearly forty countries. Their diverse backgrounds are a tremendous asset, offering students a truly international experience. The student body includes recent college graduates as well as midcareer professionals from various disciplines. The School's graduate student association organizes academic, professional, and social events and serves as a support network for mentoring new students.

Location

Nestled on 58 acres in the suburban town of South Orange, New Jersey, Seton Hall is just 14 miles from New York City.

The University and The School

For 150 years, Seton Hall University has been a catalyst for leadership, developing the whole student—mind, heart, and spirit. Seton Hall combines the resources of a large university with the personal attention of a small liberal arts college. Composed of 5,200 undergraduate students and 4,800 graduate students, Seton Hall is a Catholic university that embraces students of all races and religions, challenging each to better the world through integrity, compassion, and a commitment to serving others.

Through a unique alliance with the United Nations Association of the USA, the Whitehead School of Diplomacy and International Relations provides students with a link to the United Nations system, the diplomatic community, nongovernmental organizations, and global business. A continuous exchange of people and ideas between the School and the U.N. brings students in direct contact with policymakers and practitioners and exposes them to ongoing opportunities to foster professional growth and development. The curriculum is enhanced by the perspectives and insights of practitioners from all sectors of the international community who participate in panel discussions, video conferences, and as adjunct professors and guest lecturers.

Beyond the classroom, the Whitehead School actively promotes dialogue on critical global issues. A prestigious World Leaders Forum has brought to the campus thought-provoking lectures and discussions with former Prime Minister of Great Britain and Northern Ireland Tony Blair, former Polish President Lech Walesa, former Soviet President Mikhail Gorbachev, United Nations Secretary-General Kofi Annan, Iranian President Mohammad Khatami, former Prime Minister of Israel Shimon Peres, and many others.

Applying

The Whitehead School of Diplomacy and International Relations selects students from around the world who have completed undergraduate degrees in a variety of disciplines, and whose academic record, international experience, or professional achievements and personal goals show promise of leadership. English proficiency is a requirement, and students whose education was not in English are required to submit TOEFL scores. Applications are evaluated on a rolling basis, and students may begin the program in September, January, or May. Students applying to the dual-degree programs should submit separate applications to each school.

Correspondence and Information

Catherine Ruby, Ph.D., Director
Office of Graduate Admissions
The Whitehead School of Diplomacy and International Relations
Seton Hall University
400 South Orange Avenue
South Orange, New Jersey 07079

Phone: 973-275-2515
Fax: 973-275-2519
E-mail: diplomat@shu.edu
Web site: http://diplomacy.shu.edu

Seton Hall University

THE FACULTY

Administrative Organization
Ambassador John K. Menzies, Ph.D., Dean.
Courtney Smith, Ph.D., Associate Dean of Academic Affairs.
Ursula Sanjamino, Ph.D., Associate Dean of Graduate Studies.
Elizabeth Bakes, M.A., Assistant Dean of External Affairs.
Catherine Ruby, Ph.D., Director of Graduate Admissions.

Faculty
Margarita Balmaceda, Associate Professor; Ph.D., Princeton. Central and Eastern Europe, security and energy policy.
Assefaw Bariagaber, Professor; Ph.D., Southern Illinois. Ethno-political analysis, refugee policy, Africa.
Martin Edwards, Assistant Professor; Ph.D., Rutgers. International organizations and international political economy.
Omer Gokcekus, Professor; Ph.D., Duke. Interest groups and trade policy, organizational architecture and corruption.
Benjamin Goldfrank, Assistant Professor; Ph.D., Berkeley. Comparative analysis of Latin American politics, sub-national governments, participatory budgeting, political parties.
Yinan He, Assistant Professor; Ph.D., M.I.T. Security studies.
Yanzhong Huang, Associate Professor; Ph.D., Chicago. Global health studies, U.S.-China relations, Chinese politics.
Fredline M'Cormack-Hale; Ph.D., Florida. African Studies, non-governmental organizations, democratization.
Philip Moremen, Associate Professor; J.D., UCLA; Ph.D., Tufts (Fletcher). International law, environmental policy.
Ann Marie Murphy, Assistant Professor; Ph.D., Columbia. Comparative foreign policy.
Jesse Russell, Assistant Professor; Ph.D., California, Santa Barbara. International relations theory, research methods.
Courtney Smith, Associate Professor; Ph.D., Ohio State. United Nations studies.
Yui Suzuki, Assistant Professor; Ph.D., Michigan. International macro/finance, economic development and transition, macroeconomics and international trade.
Zheng Wang, Assistant Professor; Ph.D., George Mason. Negotiation and conflict management.
Elizabeth Wilson; J.D., Harvard; Ph.D., Pennsylvania. International law, human rights.

Distinguished Adjunct Faculty Members
Ambassador Marc Grossman, former U.S. Under Secretary of State for Political Affairs.
Ambassador Ahmad Kamal, M.A., former Permanent Representative of Pakistan to the United Nations.
Ambassador Laszlo Molnar, Ph.D., former Permanent Representative of Hungary to the United Nations.
Ambassador Slavi Pachovski, J.D., Ph.D., former Permanent Representative of Bulgaria to the United Nations.

SOUTHERN ILLINOIS UNIVERSITY CARBONDALE

Department of Political Science
Ph.D. Program

Program of Study

The Doctor of Philosophy (Ph.D.) in political science at Southern Illinois University Carbondale (SIUC) provides advanced specialized training for careers in teaching and research in colleges, universities, and the public sector. The minimum requirements to graduate are 33 semester credit hours in three different fields, 9 credit hours in research methodology, and a dissertation, for a total of 66 credit hours. Credits earned at the master's level may apply toward this total. The fields of study are American politics and government, comparative politics, international relations, political theory, public administration and policy, public law, and methodology. The normal time commitment for completion of the Ph.D. is three to four years beyond the M.A.

The program strives to accommodate divergent career goals. Students may also choose between a quantitative or qualitative emphasis in methodology, depending on their research objectives.

The Department of Political Science is dedicated to providing a stimulating and challenging environment for its students and to advancing knowledge in the political and social sciences. A highly favorable faculty-student ratio guarantees small class size, individualized instruction, and opportunities for research collaboration. The Department also cooperates with the Law School in offering a concurrent Ph.D./J.D. program to serve the needs of both the political science and legal education communities.

Research Facilities

SIUC's Morris Library is a member of the Association of Research Libraries, the Center of Research Libraries in Chicago, the Online Computer Library Center (OCLC), and ILLINET Online (IO), the statewide automated catalog and interlibrary loan system, with records of more than 600 libraries. The library's own collection holds 2.8 million volumes, 4.5 million microforms, and more than 12,200 current serial subscriptions. It is a regional depository for U.S. government publications. SIUC offers abundant and accessible computing facilities, and it is among the 180 universities working in partnership with industry and government to develop Internet2. Students also have access to important data archives, including full membership with the Interuniversity Consortium for Political and Social Research and the Roper Public Opinion Archive.

Financial Aid

Graduate students with a graduate assistant appointment of at least 25 percent receive a tuition waiver and stipend sufficient to cover all expenses of the student's education; any admitted student is eligible to apply. Students with outstanding qualifications may be nominated for fellowships awarded by the Graduate School. SIUC provides a large number of on-campus work opportunities, while federally subsidized loans are available through the Office of Financial Aid.

Cost of Study

In-state graduate tuition is $328 per credit hour in 2009–10. Out-of-state tuition is 2.5 times the in-state tuition rate ($820 per credit hour). Graduate students with at least a 25 percent appointment as a graduate assistant receive a tuition scholarship. Fees vary from $589.03 (1 credit hour) to $1557.50 (12 credit hours). Students with a graduate assistantship receive a 50 percent reduction in the primary care medical fee. New graduate students from Arkansas, Indiana, Kentucky, Missouri, and Tennessee qualify for the alternate tuition rate, which is equivalent to the in-state graduate tuition rate.

Living and Housing Costs

For married couples, students with families, and single graduate students, the University has 690 efficiency and one-, two-, three-, and four-bedroom apartments that rent for $499 to $720 per month in 2009–10. Residence halls for single graduate students are also available, as are accessible residence hall rooms and apartments for students with disabilities.

Student Group

The Ph.D. program enrolls about two dozen students annually. Including students in M.A. and M.P.A. programs, total graduate student enrollment in the Department is about 100. In 2006, forty percent of Ph.D. students are women and twenty-five percent are international. About half of all Ph.D. students work as graduate assistants in the Department, while the remainder are supported by fellowships or hold jobs on campus.

Student Outcomes

The large majority of Ph.D. graduates look forward to careers in teaching and research in colleges and universities, although a few find employment as researchers in the private and public sectors. Recent graduates hold positions at the University of Illinois, National Defense University, Clarion University, Austin Peay University, Seton Hall University, Loras College (Dubuque), Georgia Southern University, University of Missouri–Rolla, and Hankuk University (Korea). Graduates are also employed in various governmental agencies at the national, state, and local levels and in the private sector.

Location

Carbondale is approximately 100 miles southeast of St. Louis, Missouri, and on the edge of the 263,000-acre Shawnee National Forest. Two state parks and four recreational lakes are located within 10 miles of campus, which is noted for its landscaping and wooded areas. Surrounded by forest, farmland, and Illinois's nascent wine industry, the city of Carbondale has been cited as one of the fifty most desirable places to live in the United States.

The University and The Department

Founded in 1869, Southern Illinois University Carbondale enrolls 21,000 students, of whom 4,000 are graduate and professional students. SIUC has fifty-eight master's and twenty-seven doctoral degree programs, placing it in the Carnegie Foundation's premier category, Doctoral/Research University–Extensive.

The Political Science Graduate Student Association and the Public Administration Student Organization (PASO) host visiting speakers, brown-bag seminars, and social events throughout the year. The Mileur Endowment enables the Department to bring noted scholars and public figures to campus for varying periods of time. The Public Policy Institute, founded by the late Senator Paul Simon, provides additional opportunities for students to participate in discussions of major issues facing government leaders and society at large.

Applying

Applications may be obtained by writing to the Director of Graduate Studies or downloading forms from the Department's Web site. Applications must include the standard forms, transcripts from all colleges and universities previously attended, three letters of reference, a statement of purpose, and GRE scores. An appropriate M.A. degree is normally a prerequisite, but suitably qualified students lacking the M.A. may apply for direct entry to the doctoral program. Deadlines for applications that include a request for financial assistance are January 15 for doctoral fellowships and February 15 for graduate assistantships. Applications for admission without assistance should be received no later than three months (domestic students) or six months (international students) before the start of the semester. Admission to spring semester (starting in January) is possible.

Correspondence and Information

Director of Graduate Studies
Department of Political Science
Southern Illinois University Carbondale
Carbondale, Illinois 62901-4501

Phone: 618-536-2371
E-mail: polsdept@siu.edu
Web site: http://www.siu.edu/~polysci

Southern Illinois University Carbondale

THE FACULTY AND THEIR RESEARCH

Stephen Bloom, Assistant Professor; Ph.D., UCLA, 2004. Comparative politics, international relations, nationalism, ethnic politics, political economy, Ukraine and Latvia.

Randolph Burnside, Assistant Professor; Ph.D., New Orleans, 2005. American political institutions, public opinion, urban and minority politics.

Robert Clinton, Professor and Chair; Ph.D., Texas, 1984. Public law and political theory, challenge of long-held assumptions about the power of the Supreme Court.

Scott A. Comparato, Associate Professor; Ph.D., Washington (St. Louis), 2000. Public law, judicial politics and interest-group strategies in argumentation before the courts.

J. Tobin Grant, Associate Professor and Director of Graduate Studies; Ph.D., Ohio State, 2001. American politics, religion in politics, and political methodology.

Phillip Habel, Assistant Professor; Ph.D., Illinois at Urbana-Champaign, 2006. American politics, media and politics, political methodology.

Laura Hatcher, Assistant Professor; Ph.D., Massachusetts, 2002. Public law, law and society, the legal profession, conservative legal movements, regulation and administrative law, qualitative research methods.

John A. Hamman, Associate Professor; Ph.D., Illinois, 1988. The American presidency, executive leadership, public management.

Roudy W. Hildreth, Assistant Professor; Ph.D., Minnesota, 2005. Democratic theory, American political thought, political theory of John Dewey, youth civic engagement.

Scott D. McClurg, Associate Professor; Ph.D., Washington (St. Louis), 2000. American politics, political participation, public opinion, electoral behavior, political geography, spatial statistics, campaign dynamics.

Ken Mulligan, Assistant Professor; Ph.D., Ohio State, 2004. American politics, mass political behavior, political psychology, voting behavior, religion and politics.

Stephen Shulman, Associate Professor; Ph.D., Michigan, 1996; postdoctoral study at Yale. National identity and the role of culture in international politics, with special reference to Ukraine and Russia.

Keith Snavely, Professor and Director of the M.P.A. Program; Ph.D., California, Davis, 1984. Domestic and international nonprofit organizations, local economic development.

Frederick Solt, Assistant Professor; Ph.D., North Carolina, 2003. Comparative politics, democratization, institutions, Latin America.

THE FLETCHER SCHOOL
TUFTS UNIVERSITY

TUFTS UNIVERSITY
The Fletcher School

Programs of Study

The Fletcher School provides students with the theoretical knowledge and practical skills needed to be leaders in the global community. A Fletcher education is designed to be as flexible as it is rigorous. A variety of degree programs allows students to tailor their Fletcher education to meet a specific international interest or career goal. All students are required to pass written and oral comprehension exams in a language other than their native tongue. The master's degrees require the completion of a substantial thesis. Ph.D. candidates must write and defend a dissertation. In addition, each degree program has specific graduation requirements.

The School offers several degree programs. The Master of Arts in Law and Diplomacy (M.A.L.D.) is a two-year, highly flexible, interdisciplinary, professional degree in international affairs.

The Master of International Business (M.I.B.) is a two-year hybrid international business/international affairs professional degree.

The Master of Arts (M.A.) is a one-year degree program designed for midcareer or senior-level professionals with eight or more years of professional experience.

The Master of Laws (LL.M.) is a one-year program in international law for professionals practicing law or for those eligible to practice law.

The Global Master of Arts Program (GMAP) is a twelve-month program for midcareer or senior-level professionals with eight or more years of professional experience. Courses are conducted through a combination of Internet-mediated instruction and three 2-week residencies.

The Doctor of Philosophy (Ph.D.) is an advanced interdisciplinary study of international affairs.

Upon graduation, students pursue careers in government, business, journalism, international agencies, teaching, and research in international affairs.

The School takes a multidisciplinary approach to the study of international issues, offering courses in three divisions: international law and organizations; diplomacy, history, and politics; and economics and international business. Students choose from an array of fields of study in which they concentrate their studies. The program is conducted on a semester basis.

Through cooperative arrangements, Fletcher students may take approved courses in the graduate departments and professional schools of Tufts University and Harvard University. Formal exchange programs exist with prominent institutions throughout the world. In addition, the Fletcher School offers several formal joint programs with other institutions: a four-year joint program leading to the M.A.L.D. from Fletcher and the J.D. from the law schools at Harvard or Berkeley (Boalt Hall); a three-year joint program leading to the M.A.L.D. from Fletcher and the M.B.A. from the Amos Tuck School of Business Administration at Dartmouth, from Instituto de Empresa, Madrid, or from HEC M.B.A. Program, HEC School of Management; and joint programs of international affairs studies leading to the M.A.L.D. from Fletcher and the M.A.I.S. from the Diplomatische Akademie, Vienna, or the MIA from University of St. Gallen, Switzerland. Fletcher also offers joint degrees with several programs at Tufts University, including the Department of Urban and Environmental Policy, the Cummings School of Veterinary Medicine, the Gerald J. and Dorothy R. Friedman School of Nutrition Science and Policy, the Faculty of Arts and Sciences, the College of Engineering, and the School of Medicine. Students who wish to enroll in a joint-degree program must be admitted independently to both the Fletcher School and the other institution. Ad hoc joint-degree programs also may be arranged with other law, business, or professional schools.

Research Facilities

The research facilities available to Fletcher students are unparalleled. The Edwin Ginn Library of the Fletcher School is one of the largest specialized international affairs teaching libraries in the world. In addition, Fletcher students have full access to the libraries of Tufts and Harvard Universities and the major public and private libraries participating in the Boston Library Consortium. Extensive microcomputer facilities are also available at the School.

Financial Aid

Fellowship grants are available up to the cost of tuition. Loan programs and work-study funds are also available, as are teaching assistantships at Tufts University and research assistantships at Fletcher.

Cost of Study

Tuition varies by the program, depending on special program features. In 2009–10, tuition for the M.A.L.D., M.A., and Ph.D. programs at the Fletcher School was $35,200. LL.M. tuition was $40,200, and M.I.B. tuition was $41,200. Reduced fees are charged to doctoral candidates once they have completed course work.

Living and Housing Costs

Single first-year students are encouraged to live in the Fletcher residence hall. For 2009–10, room rates were $4750; a typical meal plan was $3575. Off-campus room and board expenses ranged from $12,000 to $14,500 on average.

Student Group

Students are drawn to the Fletcher School from all parts of the United States and throughout the world. Diversity is a hallmark of the school. In most years, 46 percent of Fletcher's students come from abroad, while 25 percent of the U.S. citizens attending are members of minority groups. The very first class in 1933 included women and international and minority students; the School remains firmly committed to enrolling a multinational and multiethnic student body. In addition to recent college graduates, the student body includes midcareer executives and government officials from the United States and abroad. Total enrollment is approximately 400 students; 190 master's degree candidates are admitted annually.

Location

The Fletcher School is located on the Tufts campus in Medford, Massachusetts. The metropolitan area of Cambridge and Boston, with its famous academic institutions, is 10 minutes away, providing students with easy access to many intellectual, cultural, and social opportunities. At the same time, the small-campus environment of the School fosters the contemplative pursuit of academic interests and contributes to a supportive and cohesive student community.

The School

Established by Tufts with the assistance of Harvard University in 1933, the Fletcher School was the first graduate and professional school in the United States devoted to the study of international relations. The curriculum is designed to combine practice and theory. Fletcher students live, study, and attend classes within the School's own complex of four contiguous buildings and share social, cultural, and intellectual interests to a degree unusual in graduate school. Since its founding, Fletcher has graduated more than 7,000 students, and its alumni are engaged in careers in public service; in business, banking, and other private pursuits; and in education and research in international affairs. Fletcher alumni, students, administrators, and faculty and staff members share a sense of pride in the School, motivation for high endeavor, and desire to be of service. All members of the faculty are in residence at the School; most have had practical experience in international public, not-for-profit, or private organizations. They regularly contribute to the policy and scholarly debates of the day in print and broadcast media, in refereed journals, and in books on topics in international affairs.

Applying

The School selects students whose academic background, interest in international affairs, related experience and achievements, and personal qualities support expectation of distinguished graduate study and professional careers. The School welcomes applications from college graduates in all areas of concentration—the social sciences, the humanities, the physical sciences, engineering, and business. Applicants who are graduates of colleges and universities where the language of instruction is English are required to take the GRE General Test or the GMAT. International applicants whose native language is not English are required to take the TOEFL or the IELTS and are encouraged to take the GRE General Test or the GMAT. Application materials, including requests for financial assistance, should be filed no later than January 15 for admission for the following September. Notification of admission for fall is mailed by April 1. In addition, Fletcher offers limited admission to the spring semester class; the deadline for applying is October 15.

Correspondence and Information

Director of Admissions and Financial Aid
The Fletcher School
Tufts University
Medford, Massachusetts 02155

Phone: 617-627-3040
Fax: 617-627-3712
E-mail: fletcheradmissions@tufts.edu
Web site: http://fletcher.tufts.edu

Tufts University

THE RESIDENT FACULTY

The faculty members listed here teach the majority of courses offered each year at the Fletcher School. They also serve as students' primary advisers and directors of thesis and dissertation writing. Additional courses may be offered to enhance the curriculum by professors from other units of Tufts University, experts in the field, and international affairs practitioners.

Stephen W. Bosworth, Dean; LL.D. (hon.), B.A., Dartmouth.
Jenny C. Aker, Assistant Professor of Development Economics; Ph.D., Berkeley.
Eileen Babbitt, Professor of International Conflict Management Practice; Ph.D., MIT.
Steven A. Block, Associate Professor of International Economics; Ph.D., Harvard.
Jonathan Brookfield, Associate Professor of Strategic Management and International Business; Ph.D., Pennsylvania.
Katrina Burgess, Associate Professor of International Political Economy; Ph.D., Princeton.
Daniel Drezner, Associate Director of International Politics; Ph.D., Stanford.
Leila Fawaz, Issam M. Fares Professor of Lebanese and Eastern Mediterranean Studies; Ph.D., Harvard.
Kelly Sims Gallagher, Associate Professor of Energy and Environmental Policy; Ph.D., Tufts.
Carolyn Gideon, Assistant Professor of International Communications and Technology Policy; Ph.D., Harvard.
Michael J. Glennon, Professor of International Law; J.D., Minnesota.
John Hammock, Associate Professor of Public Policy; Ph.D., Tufts.
Hurst Hannum, Professor of International Law; J.D., Berkeley.
Alan K. Henrikson, Associate Professor of Diplomatic History; Ph.D., Harvard.
Andrew C. Hess, Professor of Diplomacy; Ph.D., Harvard.
Laurent L. Jacque, Walter B. Wriston Professor of International Business; Ph.D., Pennsylvania.
Ayesha Jalal, Professor of History; Ph.D., Cambridge.
Ian Johnstone, Associate Professor of International Law; LL.M., Columbia.
Michael W. Klein, Professor of International Economics; Ph.D., Columbia.
Carsten Kowalczyk, Associate Professor of International Economics; Ph.D., Rochester.
William C. Martel, Associate Professor of International Security Studies; Ph.D., Massachusetts Amherst.
William R. Moomaw, Professor of International Environmental Policy; Ph.D., MIT.
Vali Nasr, Professor of International Politics; Ph.D., MIT.
John C. Perry, Henry Willard Denison Professor of Japanese Diplomacy; Ph.D., Harvard.
Robert L. Pfaltzgraff Jr., Shelby Cullom Davis Professor of International Security Studies; Ph.D., Pennsylvania.
Jeswald W. Salacuse, Henry J. Braker Professor of Commercial Law; J.D., Harvard.
Richard H. Shultz, Professor of International Politics; Ph.D., Miami (Ohio).
Bernard Simonin, Associate Professor of Marketing and International Business; Ph.D., Michigan.
Joel P. Trachtman, Professor of International Law; J.D., Harvard.
Peter Uvin, Henry J. Leir Associate Professor of International Humanitarian Studies; Ph.D., Geneva.
Alan Wachman, Assistant Professor of International Politics; Ph.D., Harvard.

The Fletcher School.

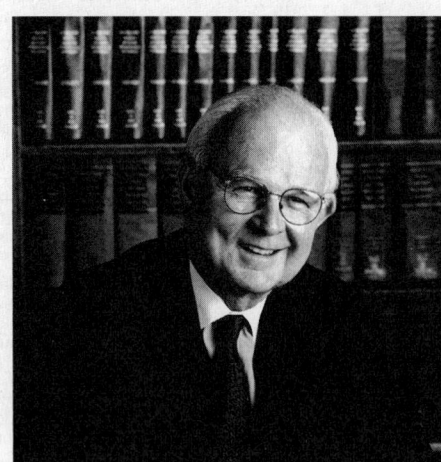

Stephen W. Bosworth, Dean of the Fletcher School.

UNIVERSITY OF CALIFORNIA, SAN DIEGO

School of International Relations and Pacific Studies (IR/PS)

University of California, San Diego
School of International Relations
and Pacific Studies

Programs of Study

The School of International Relations and Pacific Studies (IR/PS) is the University of California San Diego's only professional school of international relations as well as the only such program in the U.S. focused on the Pacific region—Asia and the Americas. Only 20 years old, it was recently ranked in the top ten for foreign affairs by *Foreign Policy*. IR/PS has become recognized internationally for its superb faculty and outstanding students. The school's innovative curriculum integrates the strengths of the traditional professional school programs of business management, international affairs, and public policy. Courses offered at IR/PS are designed to foster interdisciplinary understanding with special attention to the Pacific region.

IR/PS offers four different degree programs: the two-year professional Master of Pacific International Affairs (M.P.I.A.), the one-year executive Master of Advanced Studies-International Affairs (MAS-IA), the Bachelor of Arts/Master of International Affairs (B.A./M.I.A.), and a joint Ph.D. degree in political science and international affairs in collaboration with the University of California San Diego (UCSD) political science department.

The M.P.I.A. is a two year program that provides professional training for internationally minded individuals pursuing careers in the private, public, and nonprofit sectors. Students are able to choose career tracks in the fields of international management, international politics, international economics, public policy, nonprofit management and international development, and international environmental policy. In addition to choosing a career concentration, students acquire expertise in the language and society of one of the following regions: China, Japan, Korea, Southeast Asia, or Latin America. Finally, students choose from a variety of elective courses in order to suit their personal and professional needs.

The MAS-IA is a one-year, full-time program designed for mid-career executives and professionals who seek specialized and advanced training in the field of international affairs. It is designed to complement their professional experience by offering advanced education and training to prepare them to assume leadership positions in their fields. In addition to taking two classes specially designed for the MAS-IA, students also take classes from one of three career tracks: international security, international political economy, or international public policy. Students also take classes about their chosen regional focus of China, Japan, Korea, Latin America, or Southeast Asia.

The B.A./M.I.A. is a combined five-year degree program offered in conjunction with the international studies program at UCSD. It is open only to UCSD undergraduates in select majors within the International Studies Program. The program retains and builds upon the interdisciplinary core of the existing International Studies B.A. degree by incorporating graduate level courses during the student's fourth year, and then adds the professional training of IR/PS in the fifth year.

The joint Ph.D. program offers interdisciplinary academic education to a very small number of elite students pursuing international careers requiring advanced research capabilities in economics and political science within the international arena. Students are able to work with faculty at both IR/PS and the political science department while pursuing their research interests in political science and international affairs.

In addition to these degree granting programs, IR/PS also sponsors a certificate program, the Global Leadership Institute (GLI), which is designed for working professionals seeking to expand their international knowledge and experience within their field, as well as enhance their professional development in public and private finance, international economics, public policy and program evaluation, management, marketing, accounting, nonprofit management, quantitative methods, econometrics, long-range strategic planning, and international affairs. GLI fellows take regularly scheduled IR/PS classes, along with classes designed specifically for fellows.

Research Facilities

IR/PS houses the first academic library in the United States to focus exclusively on contemporary political, economic, and business affairs in the countries of the Pacific Basin. The library's current collection consists of more than 60,000 bound volumes and some 2,000 periodical subscriptions in Japanese, Chinese, Spanish, Portuguese, Korean, English, and other languages as well as company annual reports, computerized data files, maps, and other special materials. The language laboratory currently has facilities for instruction in Mandarin Chinese, Japanese, Korean, Portuguese, Vietnamese, Bahasa Indonesian, and Spanish. Computers equipped with Chinese and Japanese software and several Japanese word processors are also available. Supporting resources include the Center for Iberian and Latin American Studies, the Center for U.S.-Mexican Studies, the Institute of the Americas, the Program in Chinese Studies, the Program in Japanese Studies, the Melanesian Studies Resource Center, the Institute for Global Conflict and Cooperation, and the numerous University departments of science and engineering. The University of California, San Diego (UCSD), library contains more than 2 million volumes. An additional 7.6 million titles are available through the MELVYL online catalog, which provides easy access to the other University of California campus libraries.

Financial Aid

Financial assistance is available in the form of merit-based awards, campus employment, and need-based financial aid. Many students receive partial- or full-tuition scholarships or fellowship awards each year. More than $1 million is awarded to the incoming class. International and U.S. applicants are eligible.

Cost of Study

The 2009–10 M.P.I.A. and Ph.D. resident fees are approximately $16,000 and the out-of-state tuition and fees are approximately $30,000. The MAS-IA fees are approximately $30,000.

Living and Housing Costs

The University provides housing for both single and married graduate students. It is somewhat limited, but ample housing is available in the region surrounding the campus, particularly in an area called University Town Center. About 25 percent of master's students live in University apartments or affiliated housing.

Student Group

Approximately 250 graduate students from the United States and overseas are enrolled in the School. About 51 percent are women, 40 percent are international, and 19 percent are members of minority groups. The students represent a variety of universities and backgrounds.

Student Outcomes

IR/PS has firmly established itself as a leader in training professionals to compete in the global arena. M.P.I.A. program graduates have gone on to rewarding positions in the private, public, and nonprofit sectors in Japan, Korea, Hong Kong, Taiwan, and other parts of Asia as well as in the United States, Mexico, South America, and Europe. They have skills in finance, marketing, management, foreign languages and culture, and trade and public policy. Program graduates are employed in government, international trade, nonprofit organizations, media/telecommunications, manufacturing/high technology, financial services, and consulting. Major public sector organizations that have employed IR/PS graduates include the U.S. Departments of State and the Treasury, the CIA, the GAO, the National Park Service, the Environmental Protection Agency, and the World Bank. Major non-profit sector organizations include the Latino Economic Development Corporation, Project Concern International, the Asia Foundation, and the Peterson Institute. Major private sector employers include American Airlines, KPMG, Sony, Morgan Stanley, Nomura, Hewlett Packard, Deloitte Consulting, and the Nielsen Company.

Location

UCSD is located minutes from downtown San Diego, which offers a rich variety of social and cultural opportunities, coupled with widespread recreational activities. With a strong concentration of academic institutions, San Diego has become an important center for advanced research. The city hosts a large number of rapidly growing international trade and service firms and has more Ph.D.'s, more personal computers, and more miles of fiber-optic cable per capita than any other American city.

San Diego borders Tijuana, one of Mexico's most dynamic cities. The San Diego/Tijuana area is one of the most important economic centers on the Pacific Rim. San Diego is in a prime location for international businesses involved in the Maquiladora industry, and more than 2,000 companies have U.S.-Mexico production-sharing operations. In recognition of the increasing influence of international business on the economy, the San Diego World Trade Center serves the business community to promote increased trade in the Pacific Rim.

The University and The School

The University of California San Diego, part of the ten-campus University of California System, is recognized as one of the top teaching and research institutions in the United States. The University has a total enrollment of approximately 30,000 students. Its graduate and professional students are drawn from the upper ranks of the nation's finest colleges and universities and from institutions of comparable standing throughout the world. IR/PS is the University of California's only professional school of international affairs and the only one in the United States focused exclusively on the Pacific Rim.

Applying

The Admissions Committee looks for students who have strong academic records, previous professional employment, a history of meaningful international experience, and demonstrated leadership ability. Students interested in pursuing a degree program at IR/PS must have earned a B.A. or its equivalent at an institution of comparable standing to that of the University of California System. An applicant must submit a completed application, three letters of recommendation, transcripts, and scores on the GRE General Test. (MAS-IA applicants are not required to submit GRE scores and waivers of the GRE requirement are offered to M.P.I.A. applicants on a case-by-case basis. In addition, scores from the GMAT may be substituted for the GRE for M.P.I.A. applicants.) A minimum score of 575 on the paper-based version of the TOEFL or 7.0 on the IELTS is required of international applicants whose native language is not English and whose undergraduate education was conducted in a language other than English. The Priority deadline for M.P.I.A. applications for admission is December 1, and the standard deadline is January 15; late applications are considered on a rolling admissions basis. The priority deadline for MAS-IA applications for admission is October 30, and the standard deadline is January 15; late applications are accepted until April 2. The deadline for Ph.D. applications is January 12. Students are admitted without regard to race, creed, color, sex, or national origin. The application process is online.

Correspondence and Information

Admissions Office
School of International Relations and Pacific Studies
University of California, San Diego
9500 Gilman Drive, 0520
La Jolla, California 92093-0520

Phone: 858-534-5914
Fax: 858-534-1135
E-mail: irps-apply@ucsd.edu
Web site: http://irps.ucsd.edu

University of California, San Diego

THE FACULTY

Peter F. Cowhey, Dean; Ph.D., Berkeley.
Roger E. Bohn, Ph.D., MIT.
Marsha A. Chandler, Ph.D., North Carolina at Chapel Hill.
Alberto Díaz-Cayeros, Ph.D., Duke.
Richard E. Feinberg, Ph.D., Stanford
Peter A. Gourevitch, Ph.D., Harvard.
Emily Hafner-Burton, Ph.D., Wisconsin–Madison
Stephan M. Haggard, Ph.D., Berkeley.
Gordon H. Hanson, Ph.D., MIT.
Takeo Hoshi, Ph.D., MIT.
Miles E. Kahler, Ph.D., Harvard.
Alex Kane, Ph.D., NYU.
Ellis S. Krauss, Ph.D., Stanford.
Bruce N. Lehmann, Ph.D., Chicago.
Edmund J. Malesky, Ph.D., Duke.
Craig T. McIntosh, Ph.D., Berkeley.
Barry J. Naughton, Ph.D., Yale.
Krislert Samphantharak, Ph.D., Chicago.
Ulrike Scheade, Ph.D., Marburg (Germany).
Susan L. Shirk, Ph.D., MIT.
Matthew F. Shugart, Ph.D., California, Irvine.
Y.-H. Tohsaku, Ph.D., California, San Diego.
David Victor, Ph.D., M.I.T.
Barbara F. Walter, Ph.D., Chicago.
Christopher M. Woodruff, Ph.D., Texas at Austin.

Junjie Zhang, Ph.D., Duke.
Josh Graff Zivin, Ph.D., Berkeley.

Language Instructors

Sandra Pedregal, M.A., California, San Diego.
Yvonee Swun, M.B.A., National.
Eiko Uchida, Ph.D., Carnegie Mellon.

Adjunct Faculty

George Belch, Ph.D., UCLA.
Samuel A. Bozzette, Ph.D., RAND.
Lewis M. Branscomb, Ph.D., Harvard.
Richard T. Carson, Ph.D., Ph.D., Berkeley.
Mary Delmage, M.B.A., UCLA.
Robert Hooper, Ph.D., California, Davis.
Christina Klien, , Ph.D., California, Irvine.
David R. Mares, Ph.D., Harvard.
Richard Sinkin, Ph.D., Michigan.
Peter H. Smith, Ph.D., Columbia.
Dale E. Squires, Ph.D., Cornell.
Christena L. Turner, Ph.D., Stanford.

Emeritus Faculty

Lawrence Krause, Ph.D., Harvard.

The Robinson Building Complex, home to the School of International Relations and Pacific Studies.

Students at the School of International Relations and Pacific Studies.

VILLANOVA UNIVERSITY

Graduate Studies
Liberal Arts and Sciences
Department of Political Science

Program of Study	The Department of Political Science at Villanova University offers two graduate programs: the Master of Arts (M.A.) in political science and the Master of Public Administration (M.P.A.).

The M.A. program features courses on American government, comparative government, international relations, and political theory. A degree requires ten courses and a capstone oral exam that involves the defense of the student's portfolio or eight courses and a 6-credit thesis. All students pursuing the M.A. must complete PSC 7000 and one course from each of the three concentrations: American government, international relations, and political philosophy.

The M.P.A. is a 36- to 39-credit program, designed to prepare students for management careers in the public and nonprofit sectors. Required courses provide students with knowledge of public administration theory and history, statistical analysis and research methods, organization theory and design, and how to manage financial and human resources in order to be successful in their careers. Elective courses include 3-credit and 1-credit courses. The M.P.A. program is fully accredited by the National Association of Schools of Public Affairs and Administration (NASPAA).

Both graduate programs also offer graduate certificates (five courses or 15 credits are required) for students not seeking a master's degree or for those looking for a specialization within their degree. Both graduate degree programs admit part-time students. Class size ranges from 4 to 20 students, with the average around 12. Courses meet for 2 hours once per week in the evening. |
Research Facilities	The Falvey Memorial Library provides resources and facilities for study and research by students and faculty members, with a book capacity of more than half a million volumes. The Office of University Information Technologies (UNIT) provides data and voice communication, computing services, and access to remote computing and information services over the Internet. Student computer laboratories throughout campus are open 24 hours a day.
Financial Aid	Financial support (tuition remission and/or stipends) is available through the political science department in the form of graduate assistantships and tuition scholarships. Loan programs and need-based financial aid are available through the Office of Financial Assistance, Kennedy Hall, Villanova University, Villanova, Pennsylvania 19085; telephone: 610-519-4010.
Cost of Study	Graduate tuition is $630 per credit hour in 2009–10. In addition, there is a University fee of $60 each semester.
Living and Housing Costs	Various affordable housing possibilities are available near the Villanova University campus or are easily accessible by public transportation. Housing costs vary in accordance with the option chosen. Room and board for a single graduate student may average about $8000 for a twelve-month period. Villanova University does not provide on-campus housing for graduate students.
Student Group	Students in the M.A. and M.P.A. programs combine a variety of academic backgrounds, professional interests, and personal aims. The M.A. program enrolls 40 to 50 students per year, and the M.P.A. program enrolls 50 to 60 students per year. The ratio of men to women is 1:1. About 20 percent of the students in both programs are international. The majority of students in both programs are part-time.
Student Outcomes	Recent graduates of both programs have been admitted to doctoral programs at schools such as Cornell, Penn, Emory, Johns Hopkins, Duke, Maryland, Michigan, NYU, and Penn State. Others attend law schools, such as Georgetown, George Washington, Seton Hall, and Villanova. Graduates also pursue public service careers in the national, state, and local governments and with nonprofit organizations.
Location	Villanova University provides a tranquil setting for study and reflection. Situated on the historic Main Line, a western suburb of Philadelphia, Villanova is located on Lancaster Avenue (Route 30), 2 minutes from the Blue Route (Route 476) and 5 minutes from the Pennsylvania Turnpike, Schuylkill Expressway, and Route 202. Philadelphia's revitalized Center City is 25 minutes away by train, and historic Valley Forge and the Brandywine Valley are easily accessible by car. Villanova is within easy driving distance of several other premier institutions of higher learning, including Bryn Mawr, Haverford, and Swarthmore Colleges; Temple University; and the University of Pennsylvania. With ample parking and mass transit stops right on University grounds, the campus allows for easy travel by car, bus, or train.
The University	Villanova University is an institute rich in history and tradition. For more than 150 years, Villanova has been directed by one of the oldest teaching orders of the Catholic Church, the Order of St. Augustine. From modest beginnings on a country estate of a Revolutionary War officer, the University has seen significant growth in its student population as well as its position as a leading coeducational institute of higher learning.
Applying	Applications for admission and financial aid are available from the Office of Graduate Studies. Applications should be sent to the Office of Graduate Studies, College of Liberal Arts and Sciences, Villanova University, 800 Lancaster Avenue, Villanova, Pennsylvania 19085. Completed applications include an application for admission, nonrefundable application fee of $50, official postsecondary academic transcripts, and GRE scores (General Test only). In addition, applicants should send three letters of recommendation and a two-page narrative explaining anticipated career objectives and reasons for seeking admission to the Director of Graduate Studies at the address listed below. No interviews are necessary. Applicants from non-English-speaking countries must submit TOEFL scores. Applications are considered on a rolling basis. Financial aid decisions are made by April 15. Only applicants seeking full-time admission are considered for financial aid.
Correspondence and Information	Director of Graduate Studies (specify M.A. or M.P.A. or both)
Department of Political Science
Villanova University
Villanova, Pennsylvania 19085
Phone: 610-519-4710
Fax: 610-519-7487
Web site: http://www.villanova.edu/artsci/psc/graduate

Villanova University

THE FACULTY AND THEIR RESEARCH

David Barrett, Ph.D., Notre Dame. National security policy, intelligence policy, foreign policy formation.

Lara Brown, Ph.D., UCLA. Presidents, elections, political parties, congress.

Kail C. Ellis, O.S.A., Dean, College of Arts and Sciences; Ph.D., Catholic University. Comparative politics of Arab states.

Lowell S. Gustafson, Associate Dean; Ph.D., Virginia. Latin American politics, international political economy, theories of international relations.

John R. Johannes, Vice President for Academic Affairs; Ph.D., Harvard. American government, congress.

Christine Kelleher Palus, Ph.D., North Carolina at Chapel Hill. American politics, state and local government, urban politics, research methods.

Matthew R. Kerbel, Ph.D., Michigan. Political communications, the presidency.

Marcus L. Kreuzer, Ph.D., Columbia. Parties, comparative political economy, democratization, European politics.

Robert W. Langran, Ph.D., Bryn Mawr. Constitutional development, constitutional law, civil rights and civil liberties, congress, government and business, women and politics.

Robert A. Maranto, Ph.D., Minnesota. Public policy, public administration, American government.

Colleen A. Sheehan, Ph.D., Claremont. American political theory.

Thomas W. Smith, Associate Dean, Ph.D., Notre Dame. Ancient political theory, religion and politics.

Joseph E. Thompson, Ph.D., Catholic University. International relations, American foreign policy, comparative politics, Ireland.

A. Maria Toyoda, Chair, Ph.D., Georgetown. East Asia, comparative politics.

Catherine E. Warrick, Ph.D., Georgetown. Comparative politics, Middle East, South Asia, gender and Islamic politics.

Craig Wheeland, Associate Vice President for Academic Affairs; Ph.D., Penn State. Public administration, urban politics, intergovernmental management.

Catherine Wilson, Ph.D., Pennsylvania. Public administration, nonprofit management, immigration, religion and politics.

Section 24
Psychology and Counseling

This section contains a directory of institutions offering graduate work in psychology and counseling, followed by in-depth entries submitted by institutions that chose to prepare detailed program descriptions. Additional information about programs listed in the directory but not augmented by an in-depth entry may be obtained by writing directly to the dean of a graduate school or chair of a department at the address given in the directory.

For programs offering related work, see also in this book *Criminology and Forensics, Family and Consumer Sciences,* and *Sociology, Anthropology, and Archaeology.* In the other guides in this series:

Graduate Programs in the Biological Sciences

See *Biological and Biomedical Sciences; Genetics, Developmental Biology, and Reproductive Biology; Neuroscience and Neurobiology;* and *Pharmacology and Toxicology*

Graduate Programs in Business, Education, Health, Information Studies, Law & Social Work

See *Education, Nursing (Psychiatric Nursing), Pharmacy and Pharmaceutical Sciences, Public Health,* and *Social Work*

CONTENTS

Program Directories

Psychology—General	887
Addictions/Substance Abuse Counseling	922
Clinical Psychology	925
Cognitive Sciences	944
Counseling Psychology	948
Developmental Psychology	970
Experimental Psychology	974
Forensic Psychology	980
Genetic Counseling	982
Health Psychology	982
Human Development	985
Industrial and Organizational Psychology	992
Marriage and Family Therapy	1001
Psychoanalysis and Psychotherapy	1011
Rehabilitation Counseling	1012
School Psychology	1017
Social Psychology	1034
Sport Psychology	1044
Thanatology	1046
Transpersonal and Humanistic Psychology	1046

Announcements

Midwestern University, Downers Grove Campus	933
Northwestern University	902
Roger Williams University	981

Cross-Discipline Announcement

Northwestern University	1047

Close-Ups

Adelphi University	1049
Adler School of Professional Psychology	1051
Alfred University	1053
Alliant International University–Fresno	
Clinical Psychology-Ph.D.	1057
Clinical Psychology-Psy.D.	1059
Forensic Psychology	1055
Alliant International University–Irvine	
Forensic Psychology	1055
Marital and Family Therapy	1061
Alliant International University–Los Angeles	
Clinical Psychology-Ph.D.	1057
Clinical Psychology-Psy.D.	1059
Forensic Psychology	1055
Marital and Family Therapy	1061
Alliant International University–Sacramento	
Clinical Psychology-Psy.D.	1059
Marital and Family Therapy	1061
Alliant International University–San Diego	
Clinical Psychology-Ph.D.	1057
Clinical Psychology-Psy.D.	1059
Marital and Family Therapy	1061
Alliant International University–San Francisco	
Clinical Psychology-Ph.D.	1057
Clinical Psychology-Psy.D.	1059
Antioch University New England	1063
Argosy University, Atlanta	1065
Argosy University, Chicago	1067
Argosy University, Dallas	1069
Argosy University, Denver	1071
Argosy University, Hawai'i	1073
Argosy University, Inland Empire	1075
Argosy University, Los Angeles	1077
Argosy University, Nashville	1079
Argosy University, Orange County	1081
Argosy University, Phoenix	1083
Argosy University, Salt Lake City	1085
Argosy University, San Diego	1087
Argosy University, San Francisco Bay Area	1089
Argosy University, Sarasota	1091
Argosy University, Schaumburg	1093
Argosy University, Seattle	1095
Argosy University, Tampa	1097
Argosy University, Twin Cities	1099
Argosy University, Washington DC	1101
Barry University	1103
California Institute of Integral Studies	1105
Fairleigh Dickinson University, College at Florham	1107
Fairleigh Dickinson University, Metropolitan Campus	1107
Felician College	1109
Fielding Graduate University	1111
Florida Institute of Technology	1113
George Fox University	1115
Lesley University	1117
Loyola University Maryland	1119
Naropa University	1121
Palo Alto University	
Clinical Psychology	1123
Doctor of Psychology	1125
Philadelphia College of Osteopathic Medicine	1127
Roger Williams University	1129
Rutgers, The State University of New Jersey, Newark	1131
Seton Hall University	1133
Southern Illinois University Carbondale	
Psychology	1135
Rehabilitation	1137
South University (Columbia Campus)	1139

South University (Montgomery Campus)   1141
South University (Savannah Campus)   1143
South University (West Palm Beach Campus)   1145
Southwestern College   1147
University of New Haven   1149
Villanova University   1151
Widener University   1153

See also:
California Institute of Integral Studies—Humanities   347
The New School: A University—Political and Social
   Science   1251
Northwestern University—Human Development and
   Social Policy   1231

Psychology—General

Abilene Christian University, Graduate School, College of Arts and Sciences, Department of Psychology, Program in Psychology, Abilene, TX 79699-9100. Offers MS. *Students:* 2 full-time (both women), 3 part-time (2 women); includes 1 minority (African American), 1 international. In 2008, 3 master's awarded. *Degree requirements:* For master's, comprehensive exam, thesis optional. *Entrance requirements:* For master's, GRE General Test. *Application deadline:* For fall admission, 4/1 priority date for domestic students; for spring admission, 11/1 for domestic students. Applications are processed on a rolling basis. Application fee: $40 ($45 for international students). Electronic applications accepted. *Expenses:* Tuition: Full-time $10,728; part-time $640 per hour. Required fees: $1090; $53.50 per hour. $10 per term. Tuition and fees vary according to campus/location. *Financial support:* In 2008–09, 1 student received support. Federal Work-Study available. Support available to part-time students. Financial award application deadline: 4/1; financial award applicants required to submit FAFSA. *Unit head:* Dr. Robert McKelvain, Graduate Advisor, 325-674-2472, Fax: 325-674-6968, E-mail: beckr@acu.edu. *Application contact:* William Horn, Graduate Admissions Counselor, 325-674-2656, Fax: 325-674-6717, E-mail: gradinfo@acu.edu.

Acadia University, Faculty of Pure and Applied Science, Department of Psychology, Wolfville, NS B4P 2R6, Canada. Offers clinical psychology (M Sc). *Faculty:* 12 full-time (6 women), 11 part-time/adjunct (5 women). *Students:* 9 full-time (8 women). Average age 26. 45 applicants, 18% accepted, 4 enrolled. In 2008, 5 master's awarded. *Degree requirements:* For master's, thesis. *Entrance requirements:* For master's, GRE General Test, GRE Subject Test, honors degree or equivalent. Additional exam requirements/recommendations for international students: Required—TOEFL (minimum score 580 paper-based; 237 computer-based; 93 iBT), IELTS (minimum score 6.5). *Application deadline:* For fall admission, 2/1 priority date for domestic students. Applications are processed on a rolling basis. Application fee: $50. Electronic applications accepted. Tuition and fees charges are reported in Canadian dollars. *Expenses:* Tuition, area resident: Full-time $3873.50 Canadian dollars; part-time $844 Canadian dollars per course. Tuition, state resident: full-time $4634.50 Canadian dollars; part-time $844 Canadian dollars per course. Tuition, nonresident: full-time $9103 Canadian dollars; part-time $1687 Canadian dollars per course. Required fees: $503.22 Canadian dollars; $5 Canadian dollars per course. *Financial support:* In 2008–09, 5 students received support, including 5 teaching assistantships; career-related internships or fieldwork, scholarships/grants, and unspecified assistantships also available. Financial award application deadline: 2/1. *Faculty research:* Social psychology, job stress, psychotherapy, cognition perception, development. *Unit head:* Dr. Douglas K. Symons, Head, 902-585-1301, Fax: 902-585-1078, E-mail: doug.symons@acadiau.ca. *Application contact:* Dr. Peter Horvath, Information Contact, 902-585-1200, Fax: 902-585-1078, E-mail: peter.horvath@acadiau.ca.

Adelphi University, Derner Institute of Advanced Psychological Studies, Garden City, NY 11530-0701. Offers clinical psychology (PhD); general psychology (MA); mental health counseling (MA); school psychology (MA). *Accreditation:* APA (one or more programs are accredited). Part-time programs available. *Faculty:* 23 full-time (11 women), 78 part-time/adjunct (51 women). *Students:* 187 full-time (151 women), 128 part-time (101 women); includes 43 minority (21 African Americans, 10 Asian Americans or Pacific Islanders, 12 Hispanic Americans), 17 international. Average age 29. 590 applicants, 44% accepted, 95 enrolled. In 2008, 81 master's, 21 doctorates awarded. *Degree requirements:* For master's, comprehensive exam; for doctorate, thesis/dissertation, research (second year), 1 year internship. *Entrance requirements:* For master's, 3 letters of recommendation, minimum GPA of 3.0; for doctorate, GRE General Test, GRE Subject Test, interview; resumé; undergraduate course work in psychology, experimental psychology, statistics, developmental psychology, and abnormal psychology. Additional exam requirements/recommendations for international students: Required—TOEFL (minimum score 550 paper-based; 213 computer-based; 80 iBT). *Application deadline:* For fall admission, 4/1 priority date for domestic students, 5/1 priority date for international students; for spring admission, 11/1 priority date for international students. Application fee: $50. Electronic applications accepted. *Expenses:* Contact institution. *Financial support:* In 2008–09, 77 research assistantships with full and partial tuition reimbursements (averaging $5,527 per year) were awarded; teaching assistantships, career-related internships or fieldwork, Federal Work-Study, institutionally sponsored loans, and unspecified assistantships also available. Financial award application deadline: 2/15; financial award applicants required to submit FAFSA. *Faculty research:* Psychoanalytic processes, trauma and resilience, personality disorders, program evaluation, psychotherapy process. *Unit head:* Dr. Jeau Lau Chin, Dean, 516-877-4800, E-mail: Chin@adelphi.edu. *Application contact:* Christine Murphy, Director of Admissions, 516-877-3050, Fax: 516-877-3039, E-mail: graduateadmissions@adelphi.edu.

See Close-Up on page 1049.

Adler School of Professional Psychology, Programs in Psychology, Chicago, IL 60601-7203. Offers art therapy (Certificate); clinical hypnosis (Certificate); clinical psychology (Psy D); counseling psychology (MACP); counseling psychology/art therapy (MACAT); gerontology (MAGP); marriage and family counseling (MAMFC); marriage and family therapy (Certificate); organizational psychology (MAO); substance abuse counseling (MASAC, Certificate); Psy D/Certificate; Psy D/MACAT; Psy D/MACP; Psy D/MAMFC; Psy D/MASAC. *Accreditation:* APA. Part-time and evening/weekend programs available. Postbaccalaureate distance learning degree programs offered (minimal on-campus study). *Faculty:* 36 full-time (17 women), 45 part-time/adjunct (18 women). *Students:* 514 full-time (404 women), 128 part-time (100 women); includes 147 minority (69 African Americans, 2 American Indian/Alaska Native, 30 Asian Americans or Pacific Islanders, 46 Hispanic Americans), 53 international. Average age 27. 855 applicants, 46% accepted, 195 enrolled. In 2008, 110 master's, 136 doctorates awarded. Terminal master's awarded for partial completion of doctoral program. *Degree requirements:* For master's, thesis or alternative, oral exam, practicum; for doctorate, thesis/dissertation, clinical exam, internship, oral exam, practicum, written qualifying exam. *Entrance requirements:* For master's, 12 semester hours in psychology, minimum GPA of 3.0; for doctorate, 18 semester hours in psychology, minimum GPA of 3.25; for Certificate, appropriate master's or doctoral degree. Additional exam requirements/recommendations for international students: Required—TOEFL (minimum score 550 paper-based; 213 computer-based; 79 iBT). *Application deadline:* For fall admission, 2/15 priority date for domestic students, 12/1 priority date for international students. Applications are processed on a rolling basis. Application fee: $50. Electronic applications accepted. *Expenses:* Tuition: Part-time $850 per credit. Tuition and fees vary according to degree level, campus/location and program. *Financial support:* Career-related internships or fieldwork, Federal Work-Study, scholarships/grants, and tuition waivers (full and partial) available. Support available to part-time students. Financial award application deadline: 5/15; financial award applicants required to submit FAFSA. *Unit head:* Dr. Frank Gruba-McAllister, Vice President of Academic Affairs, 312-201-5900, Fax: 312-207-5917. *Application contact:* Craig A Hines, Director of Admissions, 312-201-5900 Ext. 226, Fax: 312-201-5917, E-mail: chines@adler.edu.

See Close-Up on page 1051.

Alabama Agricultural and Mechanical University, School of Graduate Studies, School of Education, Department of Counseling and Special Education, Huntsville, AL 35811. Offers communicative disorders (M Ed, MS); psychology and counseling (MS, Ed S), including clinical psychology (MS), counseling and guidance, counseling psychology (MS), personnel management (MS), psychometry (MS), school psychology (MS); special education (M Ed, MS). *Accreditation:* CORE; NCATE. Part-time and evening/weekend programs available. *Students:* 13 full-time (9 women), 57 part-time (46 women); includes 52 minority (51 African Americans, 1 Hispanic American), 2 international. In 2008, 24 master's awarded. *Degree requirements:* For master's, comprehensive exam. *Entrance requirements:* For master's, GRE General Test. Additional exam requirements/recommendations for international students: Required—TOEFL (minimum score 500 paper-based; 173 computer-based; 61 iBT). *Application deadline:* For fall admission, 5/1 for domestic students. Application fee: $15 ($20 for international students). *Expenses:* Tuition, area resident: Full-time $3924; part-time $2616 per term. Tuition, nonresident: part-time $5234 per year. International tuition: $7848 full-time. Required fees: $198; $396 per credit hour. $2841 per term. One-time fee: $8498 full-time; $5682 part-time. Full-time tuition and fees vary according to program. *Financial support:* Career-related internships or fieldwork available. Support available to part-time students. Financial award application deadline: 4/1. *Faculty research:* Increasing numbers of minorities in special education and speech-language pathology. *Unit head:* Dr. Shirley King, Chair, 256-372-5520, Fax: 256-372-5526. *Application contact:* Dr. Caula Beyl, Dean, School of Graduate Studies, 256-372-5266, Fax: 256-372-5269, E-mail: caula.beyl@aamu.edu.

Alliant International University–Fresno, California School of Professional Psychology, Fresno, CA 93727. Offers PhD, Psy D. *Accreditation:* APA. *Degree requirements:* For doctorate, thesis/dissertation. *Entrance requirements:* For doctorate, interview, 3.0 GPA, letters of recommendation, essay. *Faculty research:* Child and family, body image, psychoanalysis, neuropsychology, teaching of psychology.

See Close-Up on page 1057.

Alliant International University–Los Angeles, California School of Professional Psychology, Alhambra, CA 91803-1360. Offers MA, PhD, Psy D. *Accreditation:* APA. *Degree requirements:* For doctorate, comprehensive exam, thesis/dissertation. *Entrance requirements:* For doctorate, interview, minimum GPA of 3.0 in psychology and overall, letters of recommendation, essay. Additional exam requirements/recommendations for international students: Required—TOEFL (minimum score 600 paper-based; 250 computer-based), TWE (minimum score 5). Electronic applications accepted. *Faculty research:* Family therapy, pregnancy-related issues, multicultural psychology, post-traumatic stress.

See Close-Up on page 1057.

Alliant International University–Sacramento, California School of Professional Psychology, Sacramento, CA 95825. Offers MA, Psy D. Electronic applications accepted.

See Close-Ups on pages 1059 and 1061.

Alliant International University–San Diego, California School of Professional Psychology, San Diego, CA 92131-1799. Offers MA, PhD, Psy D. *Accreditation:* APA. Part-time programs available. *Degree requirements:* For doctorate, thesis/dissertation. *Entrance requirements:* For doctorate, interview, minimum GPA of 3.0 in both psychology and overall. *Faculty research:* Native American studies, cross-cultural family therapy, families.

Alliant International University–San Francisco, California School of Professional Psychology, San Francisco, CA 94133-1221. Offers Post-Doctoral MS, PhD, Psy D, Certificate. *Accreditation:* APA (one or more programs are accredited). *Degree requirements:* For doctorate, comprehensive exam, thesis/dissertation. *Entrance requirements:* For master's and doctorate, interview, minimum GPA of 3.0. Additional exam requirements/recommendations for international students: Required—TOEFL (minimum score 600 paper-based; 250 computer-based), TWE (minimum score 5). Electronic applications accepted. *Faculty research:* Multicultural issues, lesbian/gay/bisexual/transgender issues, health psychology, family systems, substance abuse.

See Close-Ups on pages 1057 and 1059.

American International College, School of Arts, Education and Science, Department of Psychology, Springfield, MA 01109-3189. Offers child development (MA, Ed D), including educational psychology; clinical psychology (MA); forensic psychology (MS). Part-time and evening/weekend programs available. *Degree requirements:* For master's, comprehensive exam (for some programs), thesis (for some programs), practicum. *Entrance requirements:* For master's, minimum GPA of 3.0, BS or BA; for doctorate, GRE General Test, interview. Additional exam requirements/recommendations for international students: Required—TOEFL. Electronic applications accepted.

American University, College of Arts and Sciences, Department of Psychology, Program in Behavior, Cognition, and Neuroscience, Washington, DC 22016-8062. Offers psychology (PhD), including behavior, cognition and neuroscience. *Students:* 11 full-time (5 women), 10 part-time (9 women); includes 4 minority (1 African American, 2 Asian Americans or Pacific Islanders, 1 Hispanic American), 3 international. Average age 27. 34 applicants, 21% accepted, 6 enrolled. In 2008, 3 doctorates awarded. *Degree requirements:* For doctorate, comprehensive exam, thesis/dissertation, 2 lab rotations, 2 tools of research. *Entrance requirements:* For doctorate, GRE General Test, GRE Subject Test, 3 recommendations. Additional exam requirements/recommendations for international students: Required—TOEFL. *Application deadline:* For fall admission, 1/1 for domestic students. Application fee: $80. *Expenses:* Tuition: Full-time $21,204; part-time $1178 per credit hour. Required fees: $380. Part-time tuition and fees vary according to course load and program. *Financial support:* Fellowships, research assistantships, teaching assistantships, career-related internships or fieldwork, Federal Work-Study, institutionally sponsored loans, and tuition waivers (full and partial) available. Support available to part-time students. Financial award application deadline: 2/1. *Faculty research:* Psychophysics, drug discrimination learning, choice behavior, conditioning and learning, olfaction and taste. *Application contact:* Sara Holland, Senior Administrative Assistant, 202-885-1717, Fax: 202-885-1023.

American University, College of Arts and Sciences, Department of Psychology, Program in Clinical Psychology, Washington, DC 22016-8062. Offers psychology (PhD), including clinical psychology. *Accreditation:* APA. *Students:* 20 full-time (15 women), 18 part-time (16 women); includes 8 minority (2 African Americans, 1 Asian American or Pacific Islander, 5 Hispanic Americans). Average age 28. 213 applicants, 5% accepted, 7 enrolled. In 2008, 4 doctorates awarded. *Degree requirements:* For doctorate, comprehensive exam, thesis/dissertation, internship. *Entrance requirements:* For doctorate, GRE General Test, GRE Subject Test, recommendations. Additional exam requirements/recommendations for international students: Required—TOEFL. *Application deadline:* For fall admission, 1/1 for domestic students. Application fee: $80. *Expenses:* Tuition: Full-time $21,204; part-time $1178 per credit hour. Required fees: $380. Part-time tuition and fees vary according to course load and program. *Financial support:* Fellowships, research assistantships, teaching assistantships, career-related internships or fieldwork, Federal Work-Study, institutionally sponsored loans, tuition waivers (full and partial), and unspecified assistantships available. Support available to part-time students. Financial award application deadline: 2/1. *Faculty research:* Depression, eating disorders, anxiety disorders, addictions, behavior therapy. *Application contact:* Sara Holland, Senior Administrative Assistant, 202-885-1717, Fax: 202-885-1023.

American University of Beirut, Graduate Programs, Faculty of Arts and Sciences, Beirut, Lebanon. Offers anthropology (MA); Arabic language and literature (MA); archaeology (MA); biology (MS); chemistry (MS); computer science (MS); economics (MA); education (MA); English language (MA); English literature (MA); environmental policy planning (MSES); financial economics (MAFE); geology (MS); history (MA); mathematics (MA, MS); Middle Eastern studies (MA); philosophy (MA); physics (MS); political studies (MA); psychology (MA); public administration (MA); sociology (MA); statistics (MA, MS). Part-time programs available. *Degree requirements:* For master's, one foreign language, comprehensive exam, thesis (for some programs). *Entrance requirements:* For master's, GRE, letter of recommendation. Additional exam requirements/recommendations for international students: Required—TOEFL (minimum score 600 paper-based; 250 computer-based; 100 iBT), IELTS (minimum score 7.5). *Faculty research:* String theory and supergravity; computer graphics; algebra and number theory; popular Arabic literature; marine and freshwater biology; integrating science, math and technology.

Andrews University, School of Graduate Studies, School of Education, Department of Educational and Counseling Psychology, Berrien Springs, MI 49104. Offers community

Psychology—General

Andrews University (continued)

counseling (MA); counseling psychology (PhD); educational and developmental psychology (MA, Ed D, PhD), including educational and developmental psychology (MA), educational psychology (Ed D, PhD); school counseling (MA); school psychology (Ed S). *Accreditation:* ACA (one or more programs are accredited). Part-time programs available. *Students:* 42 full-time (29 women), 51 part-time (38 women); includes 34 minority (19 African Americans, 2 Asian Americans or Pacific Islanders, 13 Hispanic Americans), 11 international. Average age 33. In 2008, 17 master's, 1 doctorate, 4 other advanced degrees awarded. Terminal master's awarded for partial completion of doctoral program. *Degree requirements:* For master's, thesis optional; for doctorate, thesis/dissertation. *Entrance requirements:* For master's, GRE Subject Test, minimum GPA of 2.6; for doctorate, GRE General Test, MA, minimum GPA of 3.5, sample of research. Additional exam requirements/recommendations for international students: Required—TOEFL (minimum score 550 paper-based). *Application deadline:* Applications are processed on a rolling basis. Application fee: $40. *Expenses:* Tuition: Full-time $18,360; part-time $765 per credit hour. Required fees: $476; $765 per credit hour. $238 per semester. Tuition and fees vary according to degree level. *Faculty research:* Testing methods, temperament, African-American studies, counseling process, multicultural issues. *Unit head:* Dr. Rudi Bailey, Chair, 269-471-3473. *Application contact:* Carolyn Hurst, Supervisor of Graduate Admission, 800-253-2874, Fax: 269-471-6321, E-mail: graduate@andrews.edu.

Angelo State University, College of Graduate Studies, College of Liberal and Fine Arts, Department of Psychology and Sociology, San Angelo, TX 76909. Offers psychology (MS), including counseling psychology, general psychology, industrial and organizational psychology. Part-time and evening/weekend programs available. *Faculty:* 8 full-time (2 women). *Students:* 28 full-time (18 women), 9 part-time (8 women); includes 7 minority (1 American Indian/Alaska Native, 6 Hispanic Americans), 1 international. Average age 25. 20 applicants, 70% accepted, 11 enrolled. In 2008, 23 master's awarded. *Degree requirements:* For master's, comprehensive exam, thesis optional. *Entrance requirements:* For master's, GRE General Test. Additional exam requirements/recommendations for international students: Required—TOEFL or IELTS. *Application deadline:* For fall admission, 7/15 priority date for domestic students, 6/10 for international students; for spring admission, 12/1 priority date for domestic students, 11/1 for international students. Applications are processed on a rolling basis. Application fee: $40 ($50 for international students). Electronic applications accepted. *Financial support:* In 2008–09, 44 students received support, including 3 teaching assistantships (averaging $10,251 per year); career-related internships or fieldwork, Federal Work-Study, scholarships/grants, and unspecified assistantships also available. Support available to part-time students. Financial award application deadline: 3/1; financial award applicants required to submit FAFSA. *Faculty research:* Toddlers use of actors' intentions to learn verbs. Total annual research expenditures: $116,915. *Unit head:* Dr. William B. Davidson, Department Head, 325-942-2068 Ext. 248, E-mail: bill.davidson@angelo.edu. *Application contact:* Theresa Fortin, Graduate Admissions Assistant, 325-942-2169, Fax: 325-942-2194, E-mail: theresa.fortin@angelo.edu.

Antioch University Los Angeles, Graduate Programs, Program in Psychology, Culver City, CA 90230. Offers clinical psychology (MA); psychology (MA). Part-time programs available. *Degree requirements:* For master's, thesis (for some programs), internship. *Entrance requirements:* For master's, interview. Additional exam requirements/recommendations for international students: Required—TOEFL. *Faculty research:* Creativity and humor, ethnic humor, adult development, Jungian theory, psychoanalytic theory.

Antioch University McGregor, Graduate Programs, Individualized Liberal and Professional Studies Program, Yellow Springs, OH 45387-1609. Offers liberal and professional studies (MA), including counseling, creative writing, education, film studies, liberal studies, management, modern literature, psychology, theatre, visual arts. Part-time and evening/weekend programs available. Postbaccalaureate distance learning degree programs offered (minimal on-campus study). *Degree requirements:* For master's, thesis or alternative. *Entrance requirements:* For master's, resumé, 2 letters of reference. Electronic applications accepted. *Expenses:* Contact institution.

Antioch University New England, Graduate School, Department of Applied Psychology, Keene, NH 03431-3552. Offers autism spectrum disorders (Certificate); clinical mental health counseling (MA); dance/movement therapy and counseling (M Ed, MA); marriage and family therapy (MA, PhD). *Degree requirements:* For master's, internship, practicum. *Entrance requirements:* For master's, previous course work and work experience in psychology. Additional exam requirements/recommendations for international students: Required—TOEFL (minimum score 600 paper-based; 250 computer-based). Electronic applications accepted. *Expenses:* Contact institution. *Faculty research:* Diversity, descendents of survivors of the Holocaust and American slavery.

See Close-Up on page 1063.

Antioch University Santa Barbara, Program in Psychology, Santa Barbara, CA 93101-1581. Offers MA. Part-time and evening/weekend programs available. *Faculty:* 1 (woman) full-time, 22 part-time/adjunct (12 women). *Students:* 103 full-time (89 women), 23 part-time (21 women); includes 36 minority (3 African Americans, 1 American Indian/Alaska Native, 5 Asian Americans or Pacific Islanders, 27 Hispanic Americans), 4 international. In 2008, 69 master's awarded. *Degree requirements:* For master's, internship. *Entrance requirements:* Additional exam requirements/recommendations for international students: Required—TOEFL (minimum score 550 paper-based; 213 computer-based). *Application deadline:* Applications are processed on a rolling basis. Application fee: $60. Electronic applications accepted. *Expenses:* Tuition: Full-time $17,025; part-time $570 per unit. Required fees: $26. Tuition and fees vary according to course load, degree level and program. *Unit head:* Catherine Radecki-Bush, PhD, Chair, 805-962-8179 Ext. 229, Fax: 805-962-4786, E-mail: cradecki-bush@antioch.edu. *Application contact:* Steve Weir, Director of Marketing and Enrollment Management, 805-962-8179 Ext. 152, Fax: 805-962-4786, E-mail: sweir@antioch.edu.

Antioch University Seattle, Graduate Programs, Program in Psychology, Seattle, WA 98121-1814. Offers MA, Psy D. Part-time and evening/weekend programs available. *Degree requirements:* For master's, internship. Electronic applications accepted. *Faculty research:* Trauma and post-traumatic stress disorders, workplace harassment and violence, multicultural issues and diversity.

Appalachian State University, Cratis D. Williams Graduate School, Department of Psychology, Boone, NC 28608. Offers clinical health psychology (MA); general experimental psychology (MA); industrial and organizational psychology (MA). Part-time programs available. *Faculty:* 31 full-time (11 women). *Students:* 59 full-time (45 women), 15 part-time (12 women); includes 3 minority (2 African Americans, 1 Asian American or Pacific Islander), 4 international. 185 applicants, 30% accepted, 18 enrolled. In 2008, 23 master's, 3 other advanced degrees awarded. *Degree requirements:* For master's and MA/SSP, comprehensive exam, thesis optional, GRE Subject Test exit exam. *Entrance requirements:* For master's and MA/SSP, GRE General Test, 3 letters of recommendation. Additional exam requirements/recommendations for international students: Required—TOEFL (minimum score 550 paper-based; 230 computer-based; 79 iBT), IELTS (minimum score 6.5), TOEFL or IELTS. *Application deadline:* For fall admission, 3/1 for domestic students, 2/1 for international students. Applications are processed on a rolling basis. Application fee: $50. Electronic applications accepted. *Expenses:* Tuition, area resident: Full-time $2600; part-time $700 per course. Tuition, state resident: full-time $2600; part-time $700 per course. Tuition, nonresident: full-time $5000; part-time $3300 per course. Required fees: $2150; $330 per course. Tuition and fees vary according to campus/location. *Financial support:* In 2008–09, 34 research assistantships (averaging $3,500 per year), 25 teaching assistantships (averaging $3,500 per year) were awarded; fellowships, career-related internships or fieldwork, Federal Work-Study, scholarships/grants, and unspecified assistantships also available. Financial award application deadline: 4/1; financial award applicants required to submit FAFSA. *Faculty research:* Eating disorders, school-based consultations, organizational behavior management, brain mechanisms of sound localization, parenting styles.

Total annual research expenditures: $83,000. *Unit head:* Dr. James Denniston, Chair, 828-262-2272, Fax: 828-262-2272, E-mail: dennistonjc@appstate.edu. *Application contact:* Dr. Denise Martz, Graduate Coordinator, 828-262-2715, E-mail: martzdm@appstate.edu.

Arcadia University, Graduate Studies, Department of Education, Glenside, PA 19038-3295. Offers art education (M Ed, MA Ed); biology education (MA Ed); chemistry education (MA Ed); child development (CAS); computer education (M Ed, CAS); computer education 7–12 (MA Ed); early childhood education (M Ed, CAS), including individualized (M Ed), master teacher (M Ed), research in child development (M Ed); educational leadership (M Ed, CAS); educational psychology (CAS); elementary education (M Ed, CAS); English education (MA Ed); environmental education (MA Ed, CAS); history education (MA Ed); language arts (M Ed, CAS); mathematics education (M Ed, MA Ed, CAS); music education (MA Ed); psychology (MA Ed); pupil personnel services (CAS); reading (M Ed, CAS); school library science (M Ed); science education (M Ed, CAS); secondary education (M Ed, CAS); special education (M Ed, Ed D, CAS); theater arts (MA Ed); written communication (MA Ed). *Accreditation:* NASAD. Part-time and evening/weekend programs available. Postbaccalaureate distance learning degree programs offered (minimal on-campus study). Electronic applications accepted.

Arcadia University, Graduate Studies, Department of Psychology, Glenside, PA 19038-3295. Offers community counseling (MACP); school counseling (MACP). Part-time programs available. *Degree requirements:* For master's, practicum. *Entrance requirements:* For master's, GRE General Test or MAT.

Argosy University, Atlanta, College of Psychology and Behavioral Sciences, Atlanta, GA 30328. Offers clinical psychology (MA, Psy D, Postdoctoral Respecialization Certificate), including child and family psychology (Psy D), general adult clinical (Psy D), health psychology (Psy D), neuropsychology/geropsychology (Psy D); community counseling (MA), including marriage and family therapy; counselor education and supervision (Ed D); marriage and family therapy (Certificate). *Accreditation:* APA.

See Close-Up on page 1065.

Argosy University, Chicago, College of Psychology and Behavioral Sciences, Chicago, IL 60654. Offers clinical psychology (MA, Psy D), including child and adolescent psychology (Psy D), client-centered and experiential psychotherapies (Psy D), diversity and multicultural psychology (Psy D), family psychology (Psy D), forensic psychology (Psy D), health psychology (Psy D), psychoanalytic psychology (Psy D), psychology and spirituality (Psy D); community counseling (MA); counseling psychology (Ed D), including counselor education and supervision; counselor education and supervision (Ed D); organizational leadership (Ed D). *Accreditation:* APA (one or more programs are accredited). Postbaccalaureate distance learning degree programs offered (minimal on-campus study).

See Close-Up on page 1067.

Argosy University, Dallas, College of Psychology and Behavioral Sciences, Dallas, TX 75231. Offers MA, Psy D.

See Close-Up on page 1069.

Argosy University, Denver, College of Psychology and Behavioral Sciences, Denver, CO 80203. Offers clinical psychology (MA, Psy D); community counseling (MA); counseling psychology (Ed D), including counselor education and supervision; counselor education and supervision (Ed D); forensic psychology (MA); marriage and family therapy (MA); organizational leadership (Ed D).

See Close-Up on page 1071.

Argosy University, Hawai'i, College of Psychology and Behavioral Sciences, Honolulu, HI 96813. Offers MA, MS, Ed D, Psy D, Certificate, Postdoctoral Respecialization Certificate. *Accreditation:* APA.

See Close-Up on page 1073.

Argosy University, Inland Empire, College of Psychology and Behavioral Sciences, San Bernardino, CA 92408. Offers clinical psychology/marriage and family therapy (MA); counseling psychology (MA, Ed D); counseling psychology/marriage and family therapy (MA); forensic psychology (MA).

See Close-Up on page 1075.

Argosy University, Los Angeles, College of Psychology and Behavioral Sciences, Santa Monica, CA 90405. Offers clinical psychology/marriage and family therapy (MA); counseling psychology (Ed D); counseling psychology/marriage and family therapy (MA); organizational leadership (Ed D).

See Close-Up on page 1077.

Argosy University, Nashville, College of Psychology and Behavioral Sciences, Nashville, TN 37214. Offers counselor education and supervision (Ed D); mental health counseling (MA).

See Close-Up on page 1079.

Argosy University, Orange County, College of Psychology and Behavioral Sciences, Santa Ana, CA 92704. Offers MA, Ed D, Psy D, Postdoctoral Respecialization Certificate. *Accreditation:* APA. Part-time and evening/weekend programs available. *Degree requirements:* For master's, comprehensive exam; for doctorate, comprehensive exam, thesis/dissertation. *Entrance requirements:* For master's and doctorate, 3 letters of recommendation, interview, resumé. Additional exam requirements/recommendations for international students: Required—TOEFL. Electronic applications accepted. *Faculty research:* The psychological aspects of infertility medicine, depression, psychoanalytic therapy, experiential approaches to teaching.

See Close-Up on page 1081.

Argosy University, Phoenix, College of Psychology and Behavioral Sciences, Phoenix, AZ 85021. Offers MA, Psy D.

See Close-Up on page 1083.

Argosy University, Salt Lake City, College of Psychology and Behavioral Sciences, Draper, UT 84020. Offers counseling psychology (Ed D); marriage and family therapy (MA).

See Close-Up on page 1085.

Argosy University, San Diego, College of Psychology and Behavioral Sciences, San Diego, CA 92108. Offers clinical psychology/marriage and family therapy (MA); counseling psychology (MA, Ed D); counseling psychology/marriage and family therapy (MA).

See Close-Up on page 1087.

Argosy University, San Francisco Bay Area, College of Psychology and Behavioral Sciences, Alameda, CA 94501. Offers clinical psychology (MA, Psy D); counseling psychology (MA, Ed D); forensic psychology (MA); organizational leadership (Ed D). *Accreditation:* APA (one or more programs are accredited).

See Close-Up on page 1089.

Argosy University, Sarasota, College of Psychology and Behavioral Sciences, Sarasota, FL 34235. Offers community counseling (MA); counseling psychology (Ed D); counselor education and supervision (Ed D); forensic psychology (MA); marriage and family therapy (MA); mental health counseling (MA); organizational leadership (Ed D); pastoral community counseling (Ed D); school counseling (MA, Ed S); school psychology (MA).

See Close-Up on page 1091.

Argosy University, Schaumburg, College of Psychology and Behavioral Sciences, Schaumburg, IL 60173-5403. Offers clinical health psychology (Post-Graduate Certificate); clinical psychology (MA, Psy D), including child and family psychology (Psy D), clinical health psychology (Psy D), diversity and multicultural psychology (Psy D), forensic psychology (Psy D); community counseling (MA); counseling psychology (Ed D), including counselor education and supervision; counselor education and supervision (Ed D); forensic psychology (Post-Graduate Certificate); organizational leadership (Ed D). *Accreditation:* ACA; APA.

See Close-Up on page 1093.

Argosy University, Seattle, College of Psychology and Behavioral Sciences, Seattle, WA 98121. Offers MA, Ed D, Psy D, Postdoctoral Respecialization Certificate.

See Close-Up on page 1095.

Argosy University, Tampa, College of Psychology and Behavioral Sciences, Tampa, FL 33614. Offers clinical psychology (MA, Psy D), including clinical psychology; counselor education and supervision (Ed D); marriage and family therapy (MA); mental health counseling (MA); organizational leadership (Ed D); school counseling (MA).

See Close-Up on page 1097.

Argosy University, Twin Cities, College of Psychology and Behavioral Sciences, Eagan, MN 55121. Offers clinical psychology (MA, Psy D), including child and family psychology (Psy D), forensic psychology (Psy D), health psychology (Psy D), marriage/couples and family therapy (Psy D), neuropsychology (Psy D); forensic counseling (Post-Graduate Certificate); forensic psychology (MA); marriage and family therapy (MA, DMFT), including forensic counseling (MA); organizational leadership (Ed D). *Accreditation:* APA.

See Close-Up on page 1099.

Argosy University, Washington DC, College of Psychology and Behavioral Sciences, Arlington, VA 22209. Offers clinical psychology (MA, Psy D), including child and family psychology (Psy D), diversity and multicultural psychology (Psy D), forensic psychology (Psy D), health and neuropsychology (Psy D); community counseling (MA); counseling psychology (Ed D), including counselor education and supervision; counselor education and supervision (Ed D); forensic psychology (MA); organizational leadership (Ed D). *Accreditation:* APA.

See Close-Up on page 1101.

Arizona State University, Graduate College, College of Liberal Arts and Sciences, Division of Natural Sciences, Department of Psychology, Tempe, AZ 85287. Offers behavioral neuroscience (PhD); clinical psychology (PhD); cognition, action and perception (PhD); developmental psychology (PhD); quantitative psychology (PhD); social psychology (PhD). *Accreditation:* APA. *Degree requirements:* For doctorate, thesis/dissertation. *Entrance requirements:* For doctorate, GRE General Test, GRE Subject Test.

Arizona State University at the Polytechnic Campus, School of Applied Arts and Sciences, Applied Psychology Program, Mesa, AZ 85212. Offers MS. *Degree requirements:* For master's, thesis or applied project with oral defense. *Entrance requirements:* For master's, GRE, 3 letters of recommendation, minimum GPA of 3.0. Additional exam requirements/recommendations for international students: Required—TOEFL (minimum score 550 paper-based; 213 computer-based; 83 iBT); Recommended—TWE. Electronic applications accepted.

Assumption College, Graduate School, Counseling Psychology Program, Worcester, MA 01609-1296. Offers child and family interventions (MA); cognitive and behavioral therapies (MA); general psychology (MA). Part-time and evening/weekend programs available. *Faculty:* 4 full-time (1 woman), 6 part-time/adjunct (2 women). *Students:* 41 full-time (34 women), 30 part-time (22 women); includes 4 minority (2 African Americans, 2 Hispanic Americans), 2 international. Average age 24. 83 applicants, 81% accepted. In 2008, 28 master's, 1 other advanced degree awarded. *Degree requirements:* For master's, comprehensive exam, internship, practicum, oral exam; for CAGS, comprehensive exam, oral exam. *Entrance requirements:* For master's, 3 letters of recommendation, resumé, essay; for CAGS, 3 letters of recommendation, resumé, interview, essay. Additional exam requirements/recommendations for international students: Required—TOEFL (minimum score 540 paper-based; 200 computer-based; 76 iBT), IELTS (minimum score 6). *Application deadline:* For fall admission, 6/1 priority date for domestic students, 5/1 priority date for international students; for spring admission, 11/1 priority date for domestic students, 9/1 priority date for international students. Applications are processed on a rolling basis. Application fee: $30. Electronic applications accepted. *Expenses:* Tuition: Part-time $468 per credit hour. Required fees: $20 per semester. One-time fee: $100. *Financial support:* In 2008–09, 19 fellowships with partial tuition reimbursements (averaging $6,808 per year), 2 teaching assistantships with full tuition reimbursements (averaging $9,940 per year) were awarded. Financial award application deadline: 3/1; financial award applicants required to submit FAFSA. *Faculty research:* Mood disorders, adjustment to life-threatening illness, perception of movement, socioemotional development of young children, discovery versus disclosure. *Unit head:* Dr. Leonard A. Doerfler, Director, 508-767-7549, Fax: 508-767-7263, E-mail: doerfler@assumption.edu. *Application contact:* Adrian O. Dumas, Director of Graduate Enrollment Management and Services, 508-767-7365, Fax: 508-767-7030, E-mail: adumas@assumption.edu.

Athabasca University, Graduate Centre for Applied Psychology, Athabasca, AB T9S 3A3, Canada. Offers art therapy (MC); career counseling (MC); counseling (Advanced Certificate); counseling psychology (MC); school counseling (MC). *Faculty:* 3 full-time (2 women), 2 part-time/adjunct (0 women). Tuition and fees charges are reported in Canadian dollars. *Expenses:* Tuition, area resident: Full-time $13,255 Canadian dollars; part-time $1205 Canadian dollars per course. Tuition, state resident: full-time $13,255 Canadian dollars; part-time $1205 Canadian dollars per course. Tuition, nonresident: full-time $13,255 Canadian dollars; part-time $1205 Canadian dollars per course. International tuition: $15,455 Canadian dollars full-time. One-time fee: $280 Canadian dollars. *Unit head:* Dr. Sandra Collins, Program Director, 888-611-7121, E-mail: sandrac@athabascau.ca. *Application contact:* Information Contact, 800-788-9041, Fax: 780-675-6437, E-mail: inquire@athabascau.ca.

Auburn University, Graduate School, College of Liberal Arts, Department of Psychology, Auburn University, AL 36849. Offers applied behavior analysis in developmental disabilities (MS); clinical psychology (PhD); experimental psychology (PhD); industrial/organizational psychology (PhD). *Accreditation:* APA (one or more programs are accredited). Part-time programs available. *Faculty:* 24 full-time (6 women), 2 part-time/adjunct (both women). *Students:* 37 full-time (25 women), 67 part-time (33 women); includes 13 minority (7 African Americans, 2 Asian Americans or Pacific Islanders, 4 Hispanic Americans). Average age 27. 248 applicants, 13% accepted, 30 enrolled. In 2008, 27 master's, 11 doctorates awarded. *Degree requirements:* For doctorate, thesis/dissertation. *Entrance requirements:* For master's, GRE General Test, GRE Subject Test, minimum GPA of 3.25 in psychology, 3.0 overall; for doctorate, GRE General Test, GRE Subject Test. *Application deadline:* For fall admission, 7/7 for domestic students; for spring admission, 11/24 for domestic students. Applications are processed on a rolling basis. Application fee: $25 ($50 for international students). Electronic applications accepted. *Expenses:* Tuition, area resident: Full-time $5880; part-time $243 per credit hour. Tuition, state resident: full-time $5880; part-time $243 per credit hour. Tuition, nonresident: full-time $17,640; part-time $729 per credit hour. International tuition: $17,846 full-time. Required fees: $620. Tuition and fees vary according to program and reciprocity agreements. *Financial support:* Research assistantships, teaching assistantships, Federal Work-Study available. Support available to part-time students. Financial award application deadline: 3/15. *Faculty research:* Clinical psychology, learning, industrial psychology, organizational psychology. Total annual research expenditures: $200,000. *Unit head:* Dr. Barry Burkhart, Chair, 334-844-4412. *Application contact:* Dr. George Flowers, Dean of the Graduate School, 334-844-2125.

Auburn University Montgomery, School of Sciences, Department of Psychology, Montgomery, AL 36124-4023. Offers MSPG. Part-time and evening/weekend programs available. *Faculty:* 7 full-time (2 women), 1 part-time/adjunct (0 women). *Students:* 12 full-time (7 women), 11 part-time (all women); includes 8 minority (all African Americans), 1 international. Average age 26. In 2008, 7 master's awarded. *Degree requirements:* For master's, comprehensive exam, thesis optional. *Entrance requirements:* For master's, GRE General Test or MAT. *Application deadline:* Applications are processed on a rolling basis. Application fee: $25. Electronic applications accepted. *Expenses:* Tuition, state resident: full-time $5088; part-time $212 per credit. Tuition, nonresident: full-time $15,264; part-time $636 per credit. Required fees: $234. *Financial support:* In 2008–09, 7 teaching assistantships were awarded; career-related internships or fieldwork and scholarships/grants also available. Support available to part-time students. Financial award application deadline: 3/1; financial award applicants required to submit FAFSA. *Faculty research:* Community service, diagnosis, behavior modification. *Unit head:* Dr. Peter Zachar, Chair, 334-244-3311, Fax: 334-244-3826, E-mail: pzachar@mail.aum.edu. *Application contact:* Dr. Steve LoBello, Graduate Coordinator, 334-244-3309, Fax: 334-244-3826, E-mail: slobello@mail.aum.edu.

Augusta State University, Graduate Studies, College of Arts and Sciences, Department of Psychology, Augusta, GA 30904-2200. Offers MS. Part-time programs available. *Faculty:* 7 full-time (4 women). *Students:* 28 full-time (26 women), 6 part-time (4 women); includes 7 African Americans, 2 Asian Americans or Pacific Islanders. Average age 27. 43 applicants, 42% accepted, 15 enrolled. In 2008, 8 master's awarded. *Degree requirements:* For master's, thesis optional, written/oral exam. *Entrance requirements:* For master's, GRE General Test, minimum GPA of 2.5, bachelor's degree in psychology or equivalent course work. *Application deadline:* For fall admission, 8/1 priority date for domestic students. Applications are processed on a rolling basis. Application fee: $20. *Expenses:* Tuition, state resident: full-time $2520; part-time $140 per credit hour. Tuition, nonresident: full-time $10,080; part-time $560 per credit hour. Required fees: $546; $273 per semester. *Financial support:* Research assistantships with partial tuition reimbursements, career-related internships or fieldwork, Federal Work-Study, and institutionally sponsored loans available. Financial award application deadline: 4/15; financial award applicants required to submit FAFSA. *Faculty research:* Developmental, cognitive, gender and aging issues, consumer behavior, conditioned taste aversions, circadian rhythms, use of slang and offensive language. *Unit head:* Dr. Deborah S. Richardson, Chair, 706-737-1694. *Application contact:* Connie Bradley, Degree Program Specialist, 706-737-1694, Fax: 706-737-1773, E-mail: cbradley@aug.edu.

Austin Peay State University, College of Graduate Studies, College of Professional Programs and Social Sciences, Department of Psychology, Clarksville, TN 37044. Offers counseling (MS); psychology (MA). Part-time programs available. Postbaccalaureate distance learning degree programs offered (no on-campus study). *Faculty:* 12 full-time (5 women), 3 part-time/adjunct (2 women). *Students:* 48 full-time (36 women), 28 part-time (23 women); includes 10 minority (6 African Americans, 3 Asian Americans or Pacific Islanders, 1 Hispanic American), 1 international. Average age 29. 34 applicants, 100% accepted, 28 enrolled. In 2008, 14 master's awarded. *Degree requirements:* For master's, comprehensive exam, thesis (for some programs). *Entrance requirements:* For master's, GRE General Test, minimum undergraduate GPA of 2.5, 3 letters of recommendation, bachelor's degree. Additional exam requirements/recommendations for international students: Required—TOEFL (minimum score 500 paper-based; 173 computer-based). *Application deadline:* For fall admission, 3/27 priority date for domestic students; for spring admission, 11/1 priority date for domestic students. Applications are processed on a rolling basis. Application fee: $25. Electronic applications accepted. *Expenses:* Tuition, area resident: Full-time $5772; part-time $305 per credit hour. Tuition, state resident: full-time $5772; part-time $305 per credit hour. Tuition, nonresident: full-time $16,664; part-time $778 per credit hour. Required fees: $1224. *Financial support:* In 2008–09, 12 research assistantships with full tuition reimbursements (averaging $6,996 per year) were awarded; career-related internships or fieldwork, Federal Work-Study, institutionally sponsored loans, scholarships/grants, and unspecified assistantships also available. Support available to part-time students. Financial award application deadline: 3/1; financial award applicants required to submit FAFSA. *Unit head:* Dr. Samuel Fung, Chair, 931-221-7233, Fax: 931-221-6267, E-mail: fungs@apsu.edu. *Application contact:* Dr. Charles Pinder, Dean, College of Graduate Studies, 931-221-7414, Fax: 931-221-7641, E-mail: pinderc@apsu.edu.

Avila University, Department of Psychology, Kansas City, MO 64145-1698. Offers counseling psychology (MS); general psychology (MS). Part-time and evening/weekend programs available. *Faculty:* 7 full-time (5 women), 12 part-time/adjunct (9 women). *Students:* 116 full-time (93 women), 29 part-time (25 women); includes 31 minority (27 African Americans, 2 Asian Americans or Pacific Islanders, 2 Hispanic Americans), 6 international. Average age 32. 72 applicants, 72% accepted, 41 enrolled. In 2008, 31 master's awarded. *Entrance requirements:* For master's, minimum GPA of 3.0 in last 60 hours, 2 letters of recommendation, transcripts, application with letter of intent. Additional exam requirements/recommendations for international students: Required—TOEFL. *Application deadline:* Applications are processed on a rolling basis. Application fee: $0. *Expenses:* Tuition: Full-time $7776; part-time $432 per credit hour. Required fees: $414; $24 per credit hour. Tuition and fees vary according to program. *Financial support:* In 2008–09, 108 students received support. Career-related internships or fieldwork and scholarships/grants available. Support available to part-time students. Financial award applicants required to submit FAFSA. *Faculty research:* Preparation for working in mental health services. *Unit head:* Dr. Regina Staves, Director of Graduate Psychology, 816-501-3665, Fax: 816-501-2455, E-mail: gradpsych@avila.edu. *Application contact:* Ann Grubbs, Administrative Assistant, 816-501-3698, E-mail: gradpsych@avila.edu.

Azusa Pacific University, School of Behavioral and Applied Sciences, Department of Graduate Psychology, Azusa, CA 91702-7000. Offers clinical psychology (MA, Psy D), including family therapy (MA). *Accreditation:* APA (one or more programs are accredited). Part-time and evening/weekend programs available. *Degree requirements:* For master's, comprehensive exam, 250 hours of clinical experience, individual and group therapy. *Entrance requirements:* For master's, interview, minimum GPA of 3.0, Minnesota Multiphasic Personality Inventory. Additional exam requirements/recommendations for international students: Required—TOEFL (minimum score 600 paper-based).

Ball State University, Graduate School, College of Sciences and Humanities, Department of Psychological Science, Muncie, IN 47306-1099. Offers clinical psychology (MA); cognitive and social processes (MA).

Barry University, School of Arts and Sciences, Department of Psychology, Miami Shores, FL 33161-6695. Offers clinical psychology (MS); school psychology (MS, SSP). Part-time and evening/weekend programs available. *Degree requirements:* For master's, thesis, practicum. *Entrance requirements:* For master's, GRE General Test, minimum GPA of 3.0, course work in psychology. Electronic applications accepted. *Faculty research:* Closed head injury, memory and aging, infant/mother interaction, evolutionary aspects of behavior, gender roles.

See Close-Up on page 1103.

Bayamón Central University, Graduate Programs, Program in Psychology, Bayamón, PR 00960-1725. Offers MA. Part-time and evening/weekend programs available. *Degree requirements:* For master's, comprehensive exam. *Entrance requirements:* For master's, EXADEP, bachelor's degree in psychology or related field.

Baylor University, Graduate School, College of Arts and Sciences, Department of Psychology and Neuroscience, Waco, TX 76798. Offers clinical psychology (MSCP, Psy D); neuroscience (MA, PhD). *Accreditation:* APA (one or more programs are accredited). *Students:* 42 full-time (30 women), 3 part-time (all women); includes 8 minority (5 Asian Americans or Pacific Islanders, 3 Hispanic Americans), 1 international. In 2008, 5 master's, 2 doctorates awarded. *Degree requirements:* For doctorate, comprehensive exam. *Entrance requirements:* For master's, GRE General Test; for doctorate, GRE General Test, GRE Subject Test (Psy D). *Application deadline:* Applications are processed on a rolling basis. Application fee: $25. *Financial support:* Research assistantships, teaching assistantships, career-related internships or fieldwork, Federal Work-Study, institutionally sponsored loans, tuition waivers (partial), and practicum stipends

Psychology—General

Baylor University *(continued)*
available. Financial award applicants required to submit FAFSA. *Application contact:* Barbara Prisco, Graduate Coordinator, 254-757-0535, Fax: 254-710-3870, E-mail: barbara_prisco@baylor.edu.

Biola University, Rosemead School of Psychology, La Mirada, CA 90639-0001. Offers MA, PhD, Psy D. *Accreditation:* APA. Terminal master's awarded for partial completion of doctoral program. *Degree requirements:* For master's, thesis, internship; for doctorate, comprehensive exam, thesis/dissertation, internship. *Entrance requirements:* For master's and doctorate, GRE General Test, GRE Subject Test, Minnesota Multiphasic Personality Inventory, interview, 30 undergraduate credits in psychology. Additional exam requirements/recommendations for international students: Required—TOEFL (minimum score 250 computer-based). *Expenses:* Contact institution. *Faculty research:* Integration of psychology and theology, practice of psychotherapy, therapy process and outcomes.

Boston College, Graduate School of Arts and Sciences, Department of Psychology, Chestnut Hill, MA 02467-3800. Offers MA, PhD. *Degree requirements:* For doctorate, thesis/dissertation, fieldwork. *Entrance requirements:* For master's, GRE General Test; for doctorate, GRE General Test, GRE Subject Test. Additional exam requirements/recommendations for international students: Required—TOEFL (minimum score 590 paper-based; 250 computer-based; 91 iBT). Electronic applications accepted. *Expenses:* Tuition: Part-time $1148 per credit. Required fees: $60. *Faculty research:* Social, cognitive, and biological processes.

Boston Graduate School of Psychoanalysis, Master's Program—New York, New York, NY 10011. Offers MA. Part-time programs available. *Entrance requirements:* For master's, interview, writing sample.

Boston University, Graduate School of Arts and Sciences, Department of Psychology, Boston, MA 02215. Offers MA, PhD. *Accreditation:* APA (one or more programs are accredited). Terminal master's awarded for partial completion of doctoral program. *Degree requirements:* For master's, one foreign language, comprehensive exam; for doctorate, one foreign language, comprehensive exam, thesis/dissertation. *Entrance requirements:* For master's and doctorate, GRE General Test. Additional exam requirements/recommendations for international students: Required—TOEFL.

Boston University, School of Medicine, Division of Graduate Medical Sciences, Program in Mental Health and Behavioral Medicine, Boston, MA 02215. Offers MA. *Entrance requirements:* For master's, GRE General Test. Additional exam requirements/recommendations for international students: Required—TOEFL. *Faculty research:* HIV/AIDS, trauma, behavioral medicine (obesity, breast cancer), neurosciences, autism, serious mental illness, sports psychology.

Bowling Green State University, Graduate College, College of Arts and Sciences, Department of Psychology, Bowling Green, OH 43403. Offers clinical psychology (MA, PhD); developmental psychology (MA, PhD); experimental psychology (MA, PhD); industrial/organizational psychology (MA, PhD); quantitative psychology (MA, PhD). *Accreditation:* APA (one or more programs are accredited). *Degree requirements:* For doctorate, thesis/dissertation. *Entrance requirements:* For doctorate, GRE General Test, GRE Subject Test. Additional exam requirements/recommendations for international students: Required—TOEFL. Electronic applications accepted. *Faculty research:* Personnel psychology, developmental-mathematical models, behavioral medication, brain process, child/adolescent social cognition.

Brandeis University, Graduate School of Arts and Sciences, Department of Psychology, Program in General Psychology, Waltham, MA 02454-9110. Offers MA. Part-time programs available. *Degree requirements:* For master's, thesis. *Entrance requirements:* For master's, GRE General Test, 3 letters of recommendation. Additional exam requirements/recommendations for international students: Required—TOEFL (minimum score 600 paper-based; 250 computer-based). Electronic applications accepted. *Faculty research:* Developmental, cognition, social aging, perception.

Brenau University, Graduate Programs, School of Health and Science, Gainesville, GA 30501. Offers family nurse practitioner (MSN); nurse educator (MSN); nursing management (MSN); occupational therapy (MS); psychology (MS). *Accreditation:* AOTA; NLN. Part-time and evening/weekend programs available. *Faculty:* 22 full-time (17 women), 8 part-time/adjunct (7 women). *Students:* 69 full-time (67 women), 59 part-time (54 women); includes 36 minority (28 African Americans, 2 American Indian/Alaska Native, 3 Asian Americans or Pacific Islanders, 3 Hispanic Americans), 2 international. Average age 33. 75 applicants, 55% accepted, 28 enrolled. In 2008, 40 master's awarded. *Degree requirements:* For master's, comprehensive exam (for some programs), thesis (for some programs), clinical practicum hours. *Entrance requirements:* For master's, GRE General Test or MAT, interview, writing sample, references (for some programs). Additional exam requirements/recommendations for international students: Required—TOEFL (minimum score 500 paper-based). *Application deadline:* Applications are processed on a rolling basis. Application fee: $35. Electronic applications accepted. *Expenses:* Contact institution. *Financial support:* In 2008–09, 32 students received support. Scholarships/grants and traineeships available. Support available to part-time students. Financial award application deadline: 7/15; financial award applicants required to submit FAFSA. *Unit head:* Dr. Gale Starich, Dean, 777-718-5305, Fax: 770-297-5929, E-mail: gstarich@brenau.edu. *Application contact:* Michelle Leavell, Admissions Coordinator, 770-538-4390, Fax: 770-538-4701, E-mail: mleavell@brenau.edu.

Bridgewater State College, School of Graduate Studies, School of Arts and Sciences, Department of Psychology, Bridgewater, MA 02325-0001. Offers MA. Part-time and evening/weekend programs available. *Entrance requirements:* For master's, GRE General Test.

Brigham Young University, Graduate Studies, College of Family, Home, and Social Sciences, Department of Psychology, Provo, UT 84602-1001. Offers clinical psychology (PhD); general psychology (MS); psychology (PhD), including applied social psychology, behavioral neurobiology, theoretical/philosophical psychology. *Accreditation:* APA (one or more programs are accredited). *Faculty:* 30 full-time (7 women), 10 part-time/adjunct (4 women). *Students:* 94 full-time (31 women); includes 13 minority (3 African Americans, 6 Asian Americans or Pacific Islanders, 4 Hispanic Americans), 9 international. Average age 24. 73 applicants, 32% accepted, 23 enrolled. In 2008, 9 master's, 14 doctorates awarded. *Degree requirements:* For master's, thesis; for doctorate, thesis/dissertation, publishable paper. *Entrance requirements:* For master's and doctorate, GRE General Test, minimum GPA of 3.0 in last 60 hours of upper division course work. Additional exam requirements/recommendations for international students: Required—TOEFL. *Application deadline:* For fall admission, 1/3 for domestic students. Application fee: $50. Electronic applications accepted. *Expenses:* Tuition: Full-time $5160; part-time $287 per credit hour. Tuition and fees vary according to program and student's religious affiliation. *Financial support:* In 2008–09, 85 students received support, including 13 research assistantships with partial tuition reimbursements available (averaging $3,000 per year), 26 teaching assistantships with partial tuition reimbursements available (averaging $3,000 per year); fellowships, career-related internships or fieldwork, scholarships/grants, tuition waivers (partial), and unspecified assistantships also available. Financial award application deadline: 5/31. *Faculty research:* Psychotherapy process, Alzheimer's disease/dementia, psychology and law, health, psychology, developmental. Total annual research expenditures: $533,878. *Unit head:* Dr. Ramona Hopkins, Chair, 801-422-1170, Fax: 801-422-0602, E-mail: ramona_hopkins@byu.edu. *Application contact:* Karen A. Christensen, Coordinator of Student Programs, 801-422-4560, Fax: 801-422-0602, E-mail: karen_christensen@byu.edu.

Brock University, Faculty of Graduate Studies, Faculty of Social Sciences, Program in Psychology, St. Catharines, ON L2S 3A1, Canada. Offers behavioral neuroscience (MA, PhD); life span development (MA, PhD); social personality (MA, PhD). Part-time programs available. *Degree requirements:* For master's, thesis; for doctorate, thesis/dissertation. *Entrance requirements:* For master's, GRE, honors degree; for doctorate, GRE, master's degree. Additional exam requirements/recommendations for international students: Required—TOEFL (minimum

score 550 paper-based; 213 computer-based; 80 iBT), IELTS (minimum score 6.5), TWE (minimum score 4). Electronic applications accepted. *Faculty research:* Social personality, behavioral neuroscience, life-span development.

Brooklyn College of the City University of New York, Division of Graduate Studies, Department of Psychology, Brooklyn, NY 11210-2889. Offers experimental psychology (MA); industrial and organizational psychology (MA), including industrial and organizational psychology-human relations, psychology-organizational psychology and behavior; mental health counseling (MA); psychology (PhD). The City University doctoral program in experimental psychology is based at Brooklyn College; candidates who complete the MA may apply for admission to the doctoral program. MA programs in industrial and organizational psychology and mental health counseling are fall admissions only. Part-time programs available. *Students:* 79 full-time (68 women), 121 part-time (93 women); includes 77 minority (48 African Americans, 1 American Indian/Alaska Native, 10 Asian Americans or Pacific Islanders, 18 Hispanic Americans), 18 international. Average age 31. 254 applicants, 59% accepted, 101 enrolled. In 2008, 48 master's awarded. *Degree requirements:* For master's, comprehensive exam, thesis (for some programs). *Entrance requirements:* For master's, minimum GPA of 3.0, 2 letters of recommendation, essay; for doctorate, GRE. Additional exam requirements/recommendations for international students: Required—TOEFL. *Application deadline:* For fall admission, 3/1 for domestic students, 2/1 for international students; for spring admission, 11/1 for domestic students, 10/1 for international students. Applications are processed on a rolling basis. Application fee: $125. Electronic applications accepted. *Expenses:* Tuition, state resident: full-time $7360; part-time $310 per credit hour. Tuition, nonresident: full-time $13,800; part-time $575 per credit hour. *Financial support:* Career-related internships or fieldwork, Federal Work-Study, institutionally sponsored loans, scholarships/grants, and tuition waivers (partial) available. Support available to part-time students. Financial award application deadline: 5/1; financial award applicants required to submit FAFSA. *Unit head:* Dr. Glen Hass, Chairperson, 718-951-5601, Fax: 718-951-4814, E-mail: ghass@brooklyn.cuny.edu. *Application contact:* Hernan Sierra, Graduate Admissions Coordinator, 718-951-4536, Fax: 718-951-4506, E-mail: grads@brooklyn.cuny.edu.

Brown University, Graduate School, Department of Psychology, Providence, RI 02912. Offers behavioral neuroscience (PhD); cognitive processes (PhD); sensation and perception (PhD); social/developmental (PhD); MS/PhD. *Degree requirements:* For doctorate, thesis/dissertation. *Entrance requirements:* For doctorate, GRE General Test, GRE Subject Test.

Bryn Mawr College, Graduate School of Arts and Sciences, Department of Psychology, Bryn Mawr, PA 19010-2899. Offers clinical developmental psychology (PhD). Part-time programs available. *Degree requirements:* For doctorate, one foreign language, comprehensive exam, thesis/dissertation. *Entrance requirements:* For doctorate, GRE General Test. Additional exam requirements/recommendations for international students: Required—TOEFL (minimum score 600 paper-based; 250 computer-based).

Bucknell University, Graduate Studies, College of Arts and Sciences, Department of Psychology, Lewisburg, PA 17837. Offers MA, MS. Part-time programs available. *Degree requirements:* For master's, thesis. *Entrance requirements:* For master's, GRE General Test, GRE Subject Test, minimum GPA of 2.8. Additional exam requirements/recommendations for international students: Required—TOEFL.

Caldwell College, Graduate Studies, Program in Applied Behavior Analysis, Caldwell, NJ 07006-6195. Offers MA. *Entrance requirements:* For master's, GRE, minimum GPA of 3.0, writing sample. Additional exam requirements/recommendations for international students: Required—TOEFL (minimum score 580 paper-based; 237 computer-based).

California Coast University, Program in Psychology, Santa Ana, CA 92701. Offers MS. Part-time programs available. Postbaccalaureate distance learning degree programs offered (no on-campus study).

California Institute of Integral Studies, Graduate Programs, School of Consciousness and Transformation, San Francisco, CA 94103. Offers cultural anthropology and social transformation (MA); East-West psychology (MA, PhD); integrative health studies (MA); philosophy and religion (MA, PhD), including Asian and comparative studies, philosophy, cosmology, and consciousness, women's spirituality, women's spirituality flex format; social and cultural anthropology (PhD); transformative leadership (MA); transformative studies (PhD). Part-time and evening/weekend programs available. Postbaccalaureate distance learning degree programs offered (minimal on-campus study). *Faculty:* 29 full-time, 32 part-time/adjunct. *Students:* 334 full-time (218 women), 126 part-time (77 women); includes 102 minority (39 African Americans, 4 American Indian/Alaska Native, 35 Asian Americans or Pacific Islanders, 24 Hispanic Americans), 1 international. Average age 37. 223 applicants, 78% accepted, 110 enrolled. In 2008, 93 master's, 30 doctorates awarded. Terminal master's awarded for partial completion of doctoral program. *Degree requirements:* For master's, comprehensive exam (for some programs), thesis optional; for doctorate, comprehensive exam, thesis/dissertation. *Entrance requirements:* For master's, minimum GPA of 3.0, letters of recommendation, writing sample; for doctorate, master's degree, minimum GPA of 3.0, letters of recommendation, writing sample. Additional exam requirements/recommendations for international students: Required—TOEFL. *Application deadline:* For fall admission, 2/1 priority date for domestic and international students; for spring admission, 10/15 priority date for domestic and international students. Applications are processed on a rolling basis. Application fee: $65. Electronic applications accepted. *Expenses:* Tuition: Part-time $815 per contact hour. Required fees: $270; $135 per semester. Tuition and fees vary according to degree level. *Financial support:* In 2008–09, 271 students received support; research assistantships, teaching assistantships, career-related internships or fieldwork, Federal Work-Study, institutionally sponsored loans, scholarships/grants, and tuition waivers (partial) available. Support available to part-time students. Financial award application deadline: 3/15; financial award applicants required to submit FAFSA. *Faculty research:* Altered states of consciousness, dreams, cosmology, postcolonial studies, integrative health studies. *Application contact:* Allyson Werner, Senior Admissions Counselor, 415-575-6155, Fax: 415-575-1268.

See Close-Up on page 347.

California Institute of Integral Studies, Graduate Programs, School of Professional Psychology, San Francisco, CA 94103. Offers clinical psychology (Psy D); community mental health (MA); drama therapy (MA); expressive arts therapy (MA); integral counseling psychology (MA); integral counseling, psychology-weekend (MA); somatic psychology (MA). *Accreditation:* APA. Part-time programs available. *Faculty:* 28 full-time, 59 part-time/adjunct. *Students:* 553 full-time (408 women), 88 part-time (69 women); includes 132 minority (25 African Americans, 3 American Indian/Alaska Native, 57 Asian Americans or Pacific Islanders, 47 Hispanic Americans). Average age 37. 506 applicants, 61% accepted, 181 enrolled. In 2008, 109 master's, 20 doctorates awarded. *Degree requirements:* For master's, comprehensive exam; for doctorate, comprehensive exam, thesis/dissertation. *Entrance requirements:* For master's, minimum GPA of 3.0, letters of recommendation, writing sample; for doctorate, GRE, MA in psychology or social work with appropriate practical experience for advanced standing, or BA with a minimum GPA of 3.1; letters of recommendation; writing sample. Additional exam requirements/recommendations for international students: Required—TOEFL. *Application deadline:* For fall admission, 2/1 priority date for domestic and international students; for spring admission, 10/15 priority date for domestic and international students. Applications are processed on a rolling basis. Application fee: $65. Electronic applications accepted. *Expenses:* Tuition: Part-time $815 per contact hour. Required fees: $270; $135 per semester. Tuition and fees vary according to degree level. *Financial support:* In 2008–09, 496 students received support; research assistantships with tuition reimbursements available, teaching assistantships with tuition reimbursements available, career-related internships or fieldwork, Federal Work-Study, institutionally sponsored loans, scholarships/grants, and tuition waivers (partial) available. Support available to part-time students. Financial award application deadline: 3/15; financial award applicants required to submit FAFSA. *Faculty research:* Somatic psychology, comparative psychology, art therapy, transpersonal psychology, eco-psychology. *Application contact:* David Townes, Senior Admissions Counselor, 415-575-6152, Fax: 415-575-1268, E-mail: dtownes@ciis.edu.

See Close-Up on page 1105.

California Lutheran University, Graduate Studies, Department of Psychology, Thousand Oaks, CA 91360-2787. Offers clinical psychology (MS); marital and family therapy (MS). Part-time programs available. *Faculty:* 3 full-time (2 women), 12 part-time/adjunct (10 women). *Students:* 129 full-time (110 women), 4 part-time (3 women); includes 31 minority (2 African Americans, 1 American Indian/Alaska Native, 6 Asian Americans or Pacific Islanders, 22 Hispanic Americans), 6 international. Average age 30. 118 applicants, 70% accepted. In 2008, 49 master's awarded. *Degree requirements:* For master's, thesis or comprehensive exams. *Entrance requirements:* For master's, GRE General Test, interview, minimum GPA of 3.0. *Application deadline:* For fall admission, 2/15 priority date for domestic students. Applications are processed on a rolling basis. Application fee: $50. *Financial support:* In 2008–09, 60 students received support. *Unit head:* Dr. Mindy Puopolo, Director, 805-493-3528. *Application contact:* 805-493-3127, Fax: 805-493-3542, E-mail: clugrad@clunet.edu.

California Polytechnic State University, San Luis Obispo, College of Liberal Arts, Department of Psychology and Child Development, San Luis Obispo, CA 93407. Offers psychology (MS). Part-time programs available. *Faculty:* 3 full-time (2 women), 1 (woman) part-time/adjunct. *Students:* 25 full-time (24 women), 12 part-time (11 women); includes 4 minority (1 African American, 1 Asian American or Pacific Islander, 2 Hispanic Americans). Average age 30. 65 applicants, 29% accepted, 17 enrolled. In 2008, 15 master's awarded. *Degree requirements:* For master's, comprehensive exam, thesis (for some programs). *Entrance requirements:* For master's, GRE General Test, minimum GPA of 3.0 in last 90 quarter units of course work, 4 letters of recommendation, interview. Additional exam requirements/recommendations for international students: Required—TOEFL (minimum score 550 paper-based; 213 computer-based), IELTS (minimum score 6), Either TOEFL or IELTS is acceptable. *Application deadline:* For fall admission, 12/1 for domestic students, 11/30 for international students. Application fee: $55. Electronic applications accepted. *Expenses:* Tuition, nonresident: full-time $10,170; part-time $226 per unit. Required fees: $5751; $1265 per quarter. *Financial support:* Career-related internships or fieldwork, Federal Work-Study, and institutionally sponsored loans available. Support available to part-time students. Financial award application deadline: 3/2; financial award applicants required to submit FAFSA. *Faculty research:* Eating disorders, mood disorders, neuropsychology, forensic psychology, group therapy. *Unit head:* Dr. Kelly Moreno, Graduate Coordinator, 805-756-2805, Fax: 805-756-1134, E-mail: kmoreno@calpoly.edu. *Application contact:* Margaret Booker, Administrative Analyst, 805-756-2456, Fax: 805-756-1134, E-mail: mbooker@calpoly.edu.

California State Polytechnic University, Pomona, Academic Affairs, College of Letters, Arts, and Social Sciences, Program in Psychology, Pomona, CA 91768-2557. Offers MS. Part-time programs available. *Students:* 22 full-time (all women), 5 part-time (all women); includes 11 minority (1 African American, 1 American Indian/Alaska Native, 3 Asian Americans or Pacific Islanders, 6 Hispanic Americans), 1 international. Average age 28. 75 applicants, 16% accepted, 12 enrolled. In 2008, 11 master's awarded. *Degree requirements:* For master's, thesis or alternative. *Application deadline:* For fall admission, 4/15 for domestic students. Applications are processed on a rolling basis. Application fee: $55. Electronic applications accepted. *Expenses:* Tuition, nonresident: full-time $7232; part-time $226 per credit. Required fees: $4272. One-time fee: $2694 part-time. Tuition and fees vary according to course load. *Financial support:* Application deadline: 3/2. *Unit head:* Dr. Jeffery Mio, Director of Graduate Studies, 909-869-3899, E-mail: jsmio@csupomona.edu. *Application contact:* Scott J. Duncan, Director, Admissions, 909-869-3258, Fax: 909-869-4529, E-mail: sjduncan@csupomona.edu.

California State University, Bakersfield, Division of Graduate Studies, School of Humanities and Social Sciences, Program in Psychology, Bakersfield, CA 93311-1022. Offers MA. Part-time programs available. *Degree requirements:* For master's, comprehensive exam, thesis. *Entrance requirements:* For master's, GRE General Test, 3 letters of recommendation.

California State University, Chico, Graduate School, College of Behavioral and Social Sciences, Department of Psychology, Program in Psychological Science, Chico, CA 95929-0722. Offers MA. *Degree requirements:* For master's, thesis or alternative. *Entrance requirements:* For master's, GRE General Test or MAT, 3 letters of recommendation on departmental form, statement of purpose. Additional exam requirements/recommendations for international students: Required—TOEFL (minimum score 550 paper-based; 213 computer-based; 80 iBT), IELTS (minimum score 6.5).

California State University, Dominguez Hills, College of Natural and Behavioral Sciences, Program in Psychology, Carson, CA 90747-0001. Offers clinical psychology (MA). Part-time and evening/weekend programs available. *Faculty:* 7 full-time (5 women). *Students:* 19 full-time (17 women), 16 part-time (12 women); includes 20 minority (6 African Americans, 14 Hispanic Americans). Average age 32. 45 applicants, 64% accepted, 17 enrolled. In 2008, 9 master's awarded. Terminal master's awarded for partial completion of doctoral program. *Degree requirements:* For master's, comprehensive exam, thesis optional. *Entrance requirements:* For master's, GRE General Test or MAT, interview, minimum GPA of 3.0, prerequisite psychology courses. Additional exam requirements/recommendations for international students: Required—TOEFL (minimum score 550 paper-based). *Application deadline:* For fall admission, 3/1 for domestic and international students. Application fee: $55. Electronic applications accepted. *Expenses:* Tuition, nonresident: part-time $339 per unit. Required fees: $1300 per semester. *Faculty research:* Culture and health, neuropsychology and HIV, psychohistory of the Holocaust, community and adolescents, malingering. *Unit head:* Dr. Ramona Davis, Chair, 310-243-3474, E-mail: rdavis@csudh.edu. *Application contact:* Dr. Karen I. Mason, Coordinator, 310-243-3642, Fax: 310-516-3642, E-mail: kmason@csudh.edu.

California State University, Fresno, Division of Graduate Studies, College of Science and Mathematics, Department of Psychology, Fresno, CA 93740-8027. Offers MA, MS. *Degree requirements:* For master's, thesis. *Entrance requirements:* For master's, GRE General Test, GRE Subject Test, minimum GPA of 3.0. Additional exam requirements/recommendations for international students: Required—TOEFL. Electronic applications accepted. *Faculty research:* Oncology prediction, parenting stress, wellness, aging and memory, retrieval inhibition, anger, minority mental health.

California State University, Fullerton, Graduate Studies, College of Humanities and Social Sciences, Department of Psychology, Fullerton, CA 92834-9480. Offers clinical/community psychology (MS); psychology (MA). Part-time programs available. *Students:* 60 full-time (45 women), 14 part-time (8 women); includes 26 minority (4 African Americans, 15 Asian Americans or Pacific Islanders, 7 Hispanic Americans), 7 international. Average age 27. 141 applicants, 29% accepted, 33 enrolled. In 2008, 18 master's awarded. *Degree requirements:* For master's, thesis. *Entrance requirements:* For master's, GRE General Test, GRE Subject Test, undergraduate major in psychology or related field. *Application deadline:* For fall admission, 3/15 for domestic students. Application fee: $55. Tuition and fees vary according to degree level. *Financial support:* Teaching assistantships, career-related internships or fieldwork, Federal Work-Study, institutionally sponsored loans, and scholarships/grants available. Support available to part-time students. Financial award application deadline: 3/1. *Unit head:* Dr. Daniel Kee, Chair, 657-278-3514. *Application contact:* Admissions/Applications, 657-278-2300.

California State University, Long Beach, Graduate Studies, College of Liberal Arts, Department of Psychology, Long Beach, CA 90840. Offers human factors (MS); psychology (MA). Part-time and evening/weekend programs available. *Faculty:* 15 full-time (3 women), 4 part-time/adjunct (3 women). *Students:* 39 full-time (27 women), 18 part-time (10 women); includes 24 minority (5 African Americans, 10 Asian Americans or Pacific Islanders, 9 Hispanic Americans), 3 international. Average age 30. 161 applicants, 25% accepted, 34 enrolled. *Degree requirements:* For master's, comprehensive exam, thesis. *Entrance requirements:* For master's, GRE General Test, GRE Subject Test. *Application deadline:* For fall admission, 3/1 for domestic students. Applications are processed on a rolling basis. Application fee: $55. Electronic applications accepted. *Expenses:* Tuition, nonresident: full-time $11,160; part-time $372 per unit. Required fees: $4100; $1261 per semester. *Financial support:* Federal Work-Study, institutionally sponsored loans, and scholarships/grants available. Financial award application deadline: 3/2. *Faculty research:* Physiological psychology, social and personality psychology, community-clinical psychology, industrial-organizational psychology, developmental psychology. *Unit head:* Dr. Kenneth F Green, Chair, 562-985-5001, Fax: 562-985-8004, E-mail: kgreen@csulb.edu. *Application contact:* Diane Roe, Graduate Adviser, 562-985-5000, Fax: 562-985-8004, E-mail: droe@csulb.edu.

California State University, Los Angeles, Graduate Studies, College of Natural and Social Sciences, Department of Psychology, Los Angeles, CA 90032-8530. Offers MA, MS. Part-time and evening/weekend programs available. *Faculty:* 8 full-time (5 women), 3 part-time/adjunct (1 woman). *Students:* 61 full-time (51 women), 53 part-time (40 women); includes 62 minority (11 African Americans, 11 Asian Americans or Pacific Islanders, 40 Hispanic Americans), 8 international. Average age 29. 128 applicants, 98% accepted, 45 enrolled. In 2008, 17 master's awarded. *Degree requirements:* For master's, comprehensive exam or thesis. *Entrance requirements:* Additional exam requirements/recommendations for international students: Required—TOEFL (minimum score 500 paper-based; 173 computer-based). *Application deadline:* For fall admission, 6/15 for domestic students, 5/1 for international students; for winter admission, 11/1 for domestic students, 9/1 for international students; for spring admission, 2/1 for domestic students, 10/1 for international students. Applications are processed on a rolling basis. Application fee: $55. Electronic applications accepted. *Expenses:* Tuition, nonresident: part-time $226 per credit. Required fees: $4019. *Financial support:* Career-related internships or fieldwork and Federal Work-Study available. Support available to part-time students. Financial award application deadline: 3/1. *Faculty research:* Binaural resolution of the size of an acoustic array, response and generalization of matching to sample in children. *Unit head:* Dr. Fary Cachelin, Chair, 323-343-2250, Fax: 323-343-2281, E-mail: fcachel@calstatela.edu. *Application contact:* Dr. Jose L. Galvan, Dean of Graduate Studies, 323-343-3820, Fax: 323-343-5653, E-mail: jgalvan@cslanet.calstatela.edu.

California State University, Northridge, Graduate Studies, College of Social and Behavioral Sciences, Department of Psychology, Northridge, CA 91330. Offers clinical psychology (MA); general-experimental psychology (MA); human factors and applied experimental psychology (MA). *Faculty:* 31 full-time (18 women), 24 part-time/adjunct (8 women). *Students:* 64 full-time (38 women), 15 part-time (10 women); includes 27 minority (2 African Americans, 6 Asian Americans or Pacific Islanders, 19 Hispanic Americans), 3 international. Average age 27. 136 applicants, 32% accepted, 35 enrolled. In 2008, 29 master's awarded. *Degree requirements:* For master's, thesis. *Entrance requirements:* For master's, GRE General Test, GRE Subject Test, minimum GPA of 3.0, letters of recommendation. Additional exam requirements/recommendations for international students: Required—TOEFL. *Application deadline:* For fall admission, 11/30 for domestic students. Application fee: $55. *Financial support:* Application deadline: 3/1. *Unit head:* Dr. Carrie Saetermoe, Chair, 818-677-3506. *Application contact:* Dr. Carrie Saetermoe, Chair, 818-677-3506.

California State University, Sacramento, Graduate Studies, College of Social Sciences and Interdisciplinary Studies, Department of Psychology, Sacramento, CA 95819-6048. Offers counseling psychology (MA). Part-time programs available. *Degree requirements:* For master's, thesis, writing proficiency exam. *Entrance requirements:* For master's, GRE Subject Test, minimum GPA of 3.0 during previous 2 years. Additional exam requirements/recommendations for international students: Required—TOEFL. Electronic applications accepted.

California State University, San Bernardino, Graduate Studies, College of Social and Behavioral Sciences, Department of Psychology, San Bernardino, CA 92407-2397. Offers child development (MA), including psychology-life span; clinical/counseling psychology (MS), including clinical psychology; general/experimental psychology (MA), including psychology; industrial/organizational psychology (MS), including organizational psychology. *Faculty:* 22 full-time (8 women), 3 part-time/adjunct (1 woman). *Students:* 98 full-time (77 women), 28 part-time (19 women); includes 44 minority (7 African Americans, 6 Asian Americans or Pacific Islanders, 31 Hispanic Americans), 4 international. Average age 29. 186 applicants, 26% accepted, 41 enrolled. In 2008, 20 master's awarded. *Degree requirements:* For master's, comprehensive exam, thesis (for some programs), advancement to candidacy. *Entrance requirements:* For master's, Graduate Writing Exam, minimum GPA of 3.0 in major. *Application deadline:* For fall admission, 8/31 priority date for domestic students. Application fee: $55. *Expenses:* Tuition, area resident: Full-time $1252; part-time $726 per quarter. Required fees: $334 per quarter. Tuition and fees vary according to degree level and student level. *Financial support:* Fellowships, research assistantships, teaching assistantships, career-related internships or fieldwork, Federal Work-Study, institutionally sponsored loans, and unspecified assistantships available. *Faculty research:* Perceptual development, human memory, psychopharmacology, psychology of women, language acquisition. *Unit head:* Dr. Joanna S. Worthley, Associate Dean, 909-537-5595, Fax: 909-537-7003, E-mail: jworthley@csusb.edu. *Application contact:* Stacy Brooks, Graduate Secretary, 909-537-5570, Fax: 909-537-7003, E-mail: sbrooks@csusb.edu.

California State University, San Marcos, College of Arts and Sciences, Program in Psychology, San Marcos, CA 92096-0001. Offers MA. *Degree requirements:* For master's, thesis. *Entrance requirements:* For master's, GRE General Test, GRE Subject Test (recommended), 3 letters of recommendation. Additional exam requirements/recommendations for international students: Required—TOEFL (minimum score 550 paper-based). *Faculty research:* Psychopharmacology, recovery from major surgery, computer literacy in children, neuropsychology of hemispheric differences, conservation psychology.

California State University, Stanislaus, College of Human and Health Sciences, Department of Psychology, Turlock, CA 95382. Offers behavior analysis (MS); child development (Graduate Certificate); counseling (MS); psychology (MA, MS). Part-time programs available. *Degree requirements:* For master's, thesis. *Entrance requirements:* For master's, GRE General Test, minimum GPA of 3.0, 3 letters of reference, personal statement. Additional exam requirements/recommendations for international students: Required—TOEFL (minimum score 550 paper-based; 213 computer-based). Electronic applications accepted. *Faculty research:* Hedonic tone judgement, syntax and autism, early literacy assessment and native and non-native languages.

Cambridge College, School of Psychology and Counseling, Cambridge, MA 02138-5304. Offers addiction counseling (M Ed); counseling psychology (M Ed); counseling psychology: forensic counseling (M Ed); marriage and family therapy (M Ed); mental health and addiction counseling (M Ed); mental health counseling (M Ed); mental health counseling for school guidance counselors (Certificate); mental health, addiction and school adjustment counseling (M Ed); psychological studies (M Ed); school adjustment counseling (M Ed); school guidance counseling (M Ed). Part-time and evening/weekend programs available. *Faculty:* 5 full-time (2 women), 183 part-time/adjunct (85 women). *Students:* 476 full-time (384 women), 313 part-time (245 women); includes 396 minority (300 African Americans, 2 American Indian/Alaska Native, 13 Asian Americans or Pacific Islanders, 81 Hispanic Americans), 13 international. Average age 37. 307 applicants, 81% accepted, 192 enrolled. In 2008, 226 master's, 9 CAGSs awarded. *Degree requirements:* For master's, thesis, practicum/internship; for other advanced degree, thesis, practicum/Internship. *Entrance requirements:* For master's, evidence of a bachelor's degree from an accredited institution; essay; 2 references; health insurance; for other advanced degree, evidence of a master's degree from an accredited institution; essay; 2 references; health insurance. Additional exam requirements/recommendations for international students: Required—TOEFL (minimum score 550 paper-based; 213 computer-based; 79 iBT). *Application deadline:* Applications are processed on a rolling basis. Application fee: $30. Electronic applications accepted. *Expenses:* Tuition: Full-time $6960; part-time $435 per credit. One-time fee: $140 full-time. Tuition and fees vary according to degree level, campus/

Psychology—General

Cambridge College *(continued)*
location and program. *Financial support:* In 2008–09, 857 students received support. Career-related internships or fieldwork, Federal Work-Study, and scholarships/grants available. Financial award applicants required to submit FAFSA. *Unit head:* Dr. Niti Seth, EdD, Dean, 617-873-0208, Fax: 617-349-3545, E-mail: nseth@cambridgecollege.edu. *Application contact:* Kathryn Lenehan, Admission Counselor, 800-877-0280, E-mail: kathryn.lenehan@cambridgecollege.edu.

Cameron University, Office of Graduate Studies, Program in Behavioral Sciences, Lawton, OK 73505-6377. Offers MS. Part-time and evening/weekend programs available. *Degree requirements:* For master's, comprehensive exam, thesis optional. *Entrance requirements:* Additional exam requirements/recommendations for international students: Required—TOEFL (minimum score 550 paper-based; 213 computer-based). Electronic applications accepted. *Faculty research:* Student burnout, attention deficit hyperactivity disorder, group decision making, counseling outcomes, smoking cessation.

Capella University, Harold Abel School of Psychology, Minneapolis, MN 55402. Offers clinical psychology (MS); counseling psychology (MS); educational psychology (MS, PhD); general psychology (MS, PhD); industrial/organizational psychology (MS, PhD); school psychology (MS, Certificate); sport psychology (MS). Part-time and evening/weekend programs available. Postbaccalaureate distance learning degree programs offered (minimal on-campus study). Terminal master's awarded for partial completion of doctoral program. *Degree requirements:* For master's, thesis optional, project; for doctorate, thesis/dissertation. *Entrance requirements:* For degree, master's degree in school psychology. Additional exam requirements/recommendations for international students: Required—TOEFL (minimum score 550 paper-based; 213 computer-based), TWE (minimum score 4). Electronic applications accepted. *Faculty research:* Correctional mental health delivery, community mental health, attachment and caregiving in adult and family relationships, influence of encouragement on motivation, and moral dilemmas in business.

Cardinal Stritch University, College of Arts and Sciences, Department of Psychology, Milwaukee, WI 53217-3985. Offers clinical psychology (MA). Part-time and evening/weekend programs available. *Degree requirements:* For master's, thesis, portfolio, clinical practicum. *Entrance requirements:* For master's, GRE General Test, GRE Subject Test (psychology), interview, minimum GPA of 3.0, 3 letters of recommendation.

Carleton University, Faculty of Graduate Studies, Faculty of Arts and Social Sciences, Department of Psychology, Ottawa, ON K1S 5B6, Canada. Offers neuroscience (M Sc); psychology (MA, PhD). Part-time programs available. *Degree requirements:* For master's, thesis; for doctorate, comprehensive exam, thesis/dissertation. *Entrance requirements:* For master's, honors degree; for doctorate, GRE, master's degree. Additional exam requirements/recommendations for international students: Required—TOEFL. *Faculty research:* Behavioral neuroscience, social and personality psychology, cognitive/perception, developmental psychology, computer user research and evaluation, forensic psychology, health psychology.

Carlos Albizu University, Graduate Programs, San Juan, PR 00901. Offers clinical psychology (MS, PhD, Psy D); general psychology (PhD); industrial/organizational psychology (MS, PhD); speech and language pathology (MS). *Accreditation:* APA (one or more programs are accredited). Part-time and evening/weekend programs available. *Faculty:* 22 full-time (11 women), 52 part-time/adjunct (38 women). *Students:* 566 full-time (470 women), 149 part-time (122 women); all minorities (all Hispanic Americans). Average age 28. 238 applicants, 79% accepted, 170 enrolled. In 2008, 100 master's, 84 doctorates awarded. Terminal master's awarded for partial completion of doctoral program. *Degree requirements:* For master's, one foreign language, comprehensive exam, thesis; for doctorate, one foreign language, comprehensive exam, thesis/dissertation, written qualifying exams. *Entrance requirements:* For master's, GRE General Test or EXADEP, interview; minimum GPA of 3.0 (industrial/organizational psychology), 3.25 (speech and language pathology); for doctorate, GRE General Test or EXADEP, interview; minimum GPA of 3.0 (industrial/organizational psychology), 3.25 (PhD and Psy D in clinical psychology). *Application deadline:* For fall admission, 2/15 for domestic students, 7/19 for international students; for winter admission, 11/15 for international students; for spring admission, 11/15 for domestic students, 4/21 for international students. Application fee: $75. *Expenses:* Tuition: Full-time $6912; part-time $288 per credit. Required fees: $512 per semester. Tuition and fees vary according to degree level. *Financial support:* In 2008–09, 564 students received support, including 272 fellowships (averaging $1,786 per year); career-related internships or fieldwork, Federal Work-Study, institutionally sponsored loans, scholarships/grants, traineeships, and tuition waivers (partial) also available. Support available to part-time students. Financial award application deadline: 4/21; financial award applicants required to submit FAFSA. *Faculty research:* Psychotherapeutic techniques for Hispanics, psychology of the aged, school dropouts, stress, violence. *Unit head:* Dr. Jose J Cabiya, Chancellor, 787-725-6500 Ext. 1435, Fax: 787-721-7187, E-mail: jcabiya@sju.albizu.edu. *Application contact:* Carlos Rodriguez, Director of Admission's Office, 787-725-6500 Ext. 1521, Fax: 787-721-7187, E-mail: jveray@albizu.edu.

Carlos Albizu University, Miami Campus, Graduate Programs, Miami, FL 33172-2209. Offers clinical psychology (Psy D); entrepreneurship (MBA); exceptional student education (MS); industrial/organizational psychology (MS); marriage and family therapy (MS); mental health counseling (MS); nonprofit management (MBA); organizational management (MBA); psychology (MS); school counseling (MS); teaching English as a second language (MS). *Accreditation:* APA. Part-time and evening/weekend programs available. *Faculty:* 19 full-time (12 women), 70 part-time/adjunct (35 women). *Students:* 498 full-time (409 women), 199 part-time (153 women); includes 515 minority (56 African Americans, 1 American Indian/Alaska Native, 7 Asian Americans or Pacific Islanders, 451 Hispanic Americans). Average age 33. 179 applicants, 67% accepted, 113 enrolled. In 2008, 185 master's, 21 doctorates awarded. Terminal master's awarded for partial completion of doctoral program. *Degree requirements:* For master's, one foreign language, comprehensive exam, integrative project (MBA), research project (MSESE and MSTESOL); for doctorate, one foreign language, comprehensive exam, internship, doctoral project. *Entrance requirements:* For master's, 3 letters of recommendation, interview, minimum GPA of 3.0, resumé, statement of purpose, official transcripts; for doctorate, 3 letters of recommendation, minimum GPA of 3.0, resumé, interview. *Application deadline:* For fall admission, 8/1 priority date for domestic students; for spring admission, 11/30 priority date for domestic students. Applications are processed on a rolling basis. Application fee: $50. Electronic applications accepted. *Expenses:* Tuition: Full-time $9090; part-time $505 per credit. Required fees: $298 per term. Tuition and fees vary according to course load, degree level and program. *Financial support:* In 2008–09, 111 students received support. Federal Work-Study, scholarships/grants, and tuition discounts available. Financial award application deadline: 6/1; financial award applicants required to submit FAFSA. *Faculty research:* Psychotherapy, forensic psychology, neuropsychology, marketing strategy, entrepreneurship, special education. *Unit head:* Dr. Carmen S. Roca, PhD, Chancellor, 305-593-1223 Ext. 120, Fax: 305-629-8052, E-mail: croca@albizu.edu. *Application contact:* Barbara De la Cruz, Admission Officer, 305-593-1223 Ext. 218, Fax: 305-593-1854, E-mail: bdelacruz@albizu.edu.

Carnegie Mellon University, College of Humanities and Social Sciences, Department of Psychology, Pittsburgh, PA 15213-3891. Offers cognitive neuroscience (PhD); cognitive psychology (PhD); developmental psychology (PhD); social/personality/health psychology (PhD). *Degree requirements:* For doctorate, comprehensive exam, thesis/dissertation. *Entrance requirements:* For doctorate, GRE General Test. Additional exam requirements/recommendations for international students: Required—TOEFL. *Faculty research:* Artificial intelligence, stress and the immune system, children's learning strategies, neural basis of cognition.

Case Western Reserve University, School of Graduate Studies, Department of Psychology, Cleveland, OH 44106. Offers clinical psychology (PhD); experimental psychology (PhD). *Accreditation:* APA. *Degree requirements:* For doctorate, thesis/dissertation, internship. *Entrance requirements:* For doctorate, GRE General Test, GRE Subject Test. Additional exam requirements/recommendations for international students: Required—TOEFL. Electronic applica-

tions accepted. *Faculty research:* Adolescent suicide, cognitive processing, repressive responses, visual perception, impact of HIV infection, neuropsychology.

Castleton State College, Division of Graduate Studies, Department of Psychology, Castleton, VT 05735. Offers forensic psychology (MA). *Degree requirements:* For master's, thesis. *Entrance requirements:* For master's, GRE General Test, minimum undergraduate GPA of 3.5, previous course work in research methodology and statistics. Additional exam requirements/recommendations for international students: Required—TOEFL. *Faculty research:* Psychology and law, juvenile delinquency, criminal psychology, correctional psychology, police psychology.

The Catholic University of America, School of Arts and Sciences, Department of Psychology, Washington, DC 20064. Offers applied experimental psychology (MA, PhD); clinical psychology (PhD); general psychology (MA, PhD); human development (PhD); human factors (MA); JD/MA. *Accreditation:* APA (one or more programs are accredited). Part-time programs available. Terminal master's awarded for partial completion of doctoral program. *Degree requirements:* For master's, comprehensive exam; for doctorate, comprehensive exam, thesis/dissertation. *Entrance requirements:* For master's, GRE General Test, 3 letters of recommendation; for doctorate, GRE General Test, GRE Subject Test, 3 letters of recommendation. Additional exam requirements/recommendations for international students: Required—TOEFL (minimum score 580 paper-based; 237 computer-based). Electronic applications accepted. *Faculty research:* Social development, family interaction, human perception and cognition, applied cognitive science, individual and group psychotherapy.

Central Connecticut State University, School of Graduate Studies, School of Arts and Sciences, Department of Psychology, New Britain, CT 06050-4010. Offers community psychology (MA); general psychology (MA); health psychology (MA). Part-time and evening/weekend programs available. *Faculty:* 21 full-time (12 women), 20 part-time/adjunct (6 women). *Students:* 17 full-time (14 women), 22 part-time (14 women); includes 8 minority (3 African Americans, 1 Asian American or Pacific Islander, 4 Hispanic Americans), 3 international. Average age 27. 35 applicants, 54% accepted, 10 enrolled. In 2008, 1 master's awarded. *Degree requirements:* For master's, comprehensive exam, thesis or alternative. *Entrance requirements:* For master's, minimum undergraduate GPA of 2.7, essay. Additional exam requirements/recommendations for international students: Required—TOEFL. *Application deadline:* For fall admission, 4/25 for domestic students; for spring admission, 12/1 for domestic students. Applications are processed on a rolling basis. Application fee: $50. Electronic applications accepted. *Expenses:* Tuition, area resident: Full-time $4377; part-time $420 per credit. Tuition, state resident: full-time $6566; part-time $420 per credit. Tuition, nonresident: full-time $12,195; part-time $420 per credit. Required fees: $3462. One-time fee: $62 part-time. *Financial support:* In 2008–09, 9 students received support, including 6 research assistantships; career-related internships or fieldwork, Federal Work-Study, scholarships/grants, and unspecified assistantships also available. Support available to part-time students. Financial award application deadline: 3/1; financial award applicants required to submit FAFSA. *Faculty research:* Clinical psychology, general psychology, child development, cognitive development, drugs/behavior. *Unit head:* Dr. Bradley M. Waite, Chair, 860-832-3100. *Application contact:* Dr. Bradley M. Waite, Chair, 860-832-3100.

Central Michigan University, College of Graduate Studies, College of Humanities and Social and Behavioral Sciences, Department of Psychology, Mount Pleasant, MI 48859. Offers clinical psychology (MA, PhD); experimental psychology (MS, PhD), including applied experimental psychology (PhD), experimental psychology (MS); industrial and organizational psychology (MA, PhD); neuroscience (MS, PhD); school psychology (PhD, S Psy S), including psychological services (S Psy S), school psychology (PhD). *Accreditation:* APA (one or more programs are accredited). *Faculty:* 25 full-time (8 women), 1 (woman) part-time/adjunct. *Students:* 80 full-time (53 women), 63 part-time (35 women); includes 2 African Americans, 2 American Indian/Alaska Native, 1 Asian American or Pacific Islander, 14 international. Average age 27. In 2008, 5 other advanced degrees awarded. Terminal master's awarded for partial completion of doctoral program. *Degree requirements:* For master's, thesis or alternative; for doctorate, thesis/dissertation; for S Psy S, thesis. *Entrance requirements:* For doctorate, GRE. Application fee: $35 ($45 for international students). Electronic applications accepted. *Expenses:* Tuition, state resident: full-time $3717; part-time $413 per credit. Tuition, nonresident: full-time $6894; part-time $766 per credit. *Financial support:* Fellowships with tuition reimbursements, research assistantships with tuition reimbursements, teaching assistantships with tuition reimbursements, career-related internships or fieldwork, Federal Work-Study, unspecified assistantships, and out-of-state merit awards available. *Faculty research:* Experimental psychology; clinical psychology; industrial/organizational psychology; school psychology; neuroscience. *Unit head:* Dr. Hajime Otani, Chairperson, 989-774-6494, Fax: 989-774-2553, E-mail: otani1h@cmich.edu. *Application contact:* Judith L. Prince, Director of Graduate Student Services, 989-774-1059, Fax: 989-774-1857, E-mail: judith.l.prince@cmich.edu.

Central Washington University, Graduate Studies, Research and Continuing Education, College of the Sciences, Department of Psychology, Ellensburg, WA 98926. Offers experimental psychology (MS); mental health counseling (MS); school counseling (M Ed); school psychology (M Ed). Evening/weekend programs available. *Degree requirements:* For master's, thesis. *Entrance requirements:* For master's, GRE General Test, minimum GPA of 3.0. Additional exam requirements/recommendations for international students: Required—TOEFL (minimum score 550 paper-based; 213 computer-based; 79 iBT).

Chestnut Hill College, School of Graduate Studies, Division of Psychology, Philadelphia, PA 19118-2693. Offers clinical and counseling psychology (MA, MS, CAS); clinical psychology (Psy D). Part-time and evening/weekend programs available. *Faculty:* 11 full-time (5 women), 33 part-time/adjunct (14 women). *Students:* 149 full-time (126 women), 205 part-time (162 women); includes 54 minority (42 African Americans, 6 Asian Americans or Pacific Islanders, 6 Hispanic Americans), 1 international. 308 applicants, 40% accepted. In 2008, 55 master's, 18 doctorates awarded. *Degree requirements:* For master's, thesis optional, practica; for doctorate, comprehensive exam, thesis/dissertation, internship, practica, clinical competency exam. *Entrance requirements:* For master's, GRE General Test, statement of professional goals, writing sample, official transcripts, letters of recommendation; for doctorate, GRE General Test, master's degree in clinical counseling or closely related field, transcripts, letters of recommendation, statement of professional goals, writing sample; for CAS, GRE General Test, official transcripts, letters of recommendation, statement of professional goals, writing sample. Additional exam requirements/recommendations for international students: Required—TOEFL (minimum score 500 paper-based; 213 computer-based). *Application deadline:* For fall admission, 7/17 priority date for domestic students, 7/17 for international students; for spring admission, 12/15 priority date for domestic students, 12/15 for international students. Applications are processed on a rolling basis. *Expenses:* Tuition: Part-time $510 per credit hour. *Faculty research:* Adolescent development, trauma and sexual abuse, cultural diversity, family psychology and family therapy, psychodynamic therapy. *Unit head:* Dr. Joseph Micucci, Division Chair, 215-248-7162, Fax: 215-248-7155. *Application contact:* Amy Boorse, Administrative Assistant, School of Graduate Studies Office, 215-248-7170, Fax: 215-248-7161, E-mail: gradadmissions@chc.edu.

The Chicago School of Professional Psychology, Graduate School, Program in Clinical Psychology, Chicago, IL 60610. Offers applied behavior analysis (MA, Psy D, Certificate); clinical counseling (MA); clinical psychology (Psy D); general psychology (Certificate); Latino mental health (Certificate). *Degree requirements:* For master's, thesis (for some programs); for doctorate, comprehensive exam, thesis/dissertation. *Entrance requirements:* For master's, minimum undergraduate GPA of 3.0; 1 course in psychology and 1 course in either statistics or research methods; for doctorate, GRE, 18 hours of psychology credit (including courses in statistics, normal psychology and human development); minimum GPA of 3.2. Additional exam requirements/recommendations for international students: Required—TOEFL (minimum score 550 paper-based; 213 computer-based; 79 iBT). Electronic applications accepted.

The Citadel, The Military College of South Carolina, Citadel Graduate College, Department of Psychology, Charleston, SC 29409. Offers psychology (MA), including clinical counseling.

Part-time and evening/weekend programs available. *Faculty:* 8 full-time (2 women), 3 part-time/adjunct (1 woman). *Students:* 20 full-time (15 women), 41 part-time (35 women); includes 5 minority (2 African Americans, 1 American Indian/Alaska Native, 1 Asian American or Pacific Islander, 1 Hispanic American), 1 international. Average age 28. In 2008, 10 master's awarded. *Degree requirements:* For master's, comprehensive exam, thesis optional. *Entrance requirements:* For master's, GRE (minimum 1000) or MAT (minimum 410), minimum undergraduate GPA of 3.0; 2 letters of reference. Additional exam requirements/recommendations for international students: Required—TOEFL (minimum score 550 paper-based; 213 computer-based). *Application deadline:* For fall admission, 3/15 for domestic students. Application fee: $30. Electronic applications accepted. *Expenses:* Tuition, state resident: full-time $5850; part-time $325 per credit hour. Tuition, nonresident: full-time $9612; part-time $534 per credit hour. Required fees: $15 per semester. *Financial support:* Research assistantships, career-related internships or fieldwork, health care benefits, and unspecified assistantships available. Support available to part-time students. Financial award application deadline: 7/1; financial award applicants required to submit FAFSA. *Faculty research:* Ostracism and social exclusion; bullying; social concerns of special-needs children; childhood obesity; phantom limb pain; validation of psychological tests; perfectionism; school-based interventions with at-risk children. *Unit head:* Dr. Steve A. Nida, Department Head, 843-953-5322, Fax: 843-953-6797, E-mail: steve.nida@citadel.edu. *Application contact:* Dr. William G. Johnson, Program Director, 843-953-6827, Fax: 843-953-6769, E-mail: will.johnson@citadel.edu.

City College of the City University of New York, Graduate School, College of Liberal Arts and Science, Division of Social Science, Department of Psychology, New York, NY 10031-9198. Offers clinical psychology (PhD); experimental cognition (PhD); general psychology (MA); mental health counseling (MA). *Accreditation:* APA (one or more programs are accredited). Part-time programs available. *Degree requirements:* For master's, one foreign language, comprehensive exam, thesis. *Entrance requirements:* For master's, GRE. Additional exam requirements/recommendations for international students: Required—TOEFL (minimum score 550 paper-based; 213 computer-based). *Faculty research:* Social/personality psychology, physiological psychology, cognition and development.

Claremont Graduate University, Graduate Programs, School of Behavioral and Organizational Sciences, Department of Psychology, Claremont, CA 91711-6160. Offers advanced study in evaluation (Certificate); cognitive psychology (MA, PhD); developmental psychology (MA, PhD); evaluation and applied research methods (MA, PhD); health behavior research and evaluation (MA, PhD); human resource development and evaluation (MA); industrial/organizational psychology (MA, PhD); organizational behavior (MA, PhD); organizational psychology (MA, PhD); social psychology (MA, PhD); MBA/PhD. Part-time programs available. *Faculty:* 17 full-time (7 women), 1 part-time/adjunct (0 women). *Students:* 218 full-time (158 women), 24 part-time (18 women); includes 51 minority (15 African Americans, 1 American Indian/Alaska Native, 22 Asian Americans or Pacific Islanders, 13 Hispanic Americans), 11 international. Average age 30. In 2008, 38 master's, 12 doctorates, 2 other advanced degrees awarded. Terminal master's awarded for partial completion of doctoral program. *Entrance requirements:* For master's and doctorate, GRE General Test. Additional exam requirements/recommendations for international students: Required—TOEFL (minimum score 550 paper-based; 213 computer-based; 80 iBT). *Application deadline:* For fall admission, 1/15 priority date for domestic students. Applications are processed on a rolling basis. Application fee: $60. Electronic applications accepted. *Expenses:* Tuition: Full-time $33,698; part-time $1465 per unit. Required fees: $310; $155 per semester. Tuition and fees vary according to program. *Financial support:* Fellowships, research assistantships, teaching assistantships, Federal Work-Study, institutionally sponsored loans, scholarships/grants, and tuition waivers (full and partial) available. Support available to part-time students. Financial award application deadline: 2/15; financial award applicants required to submit FAFSA. *Faculty research:* Social intervention, diversity in organizations, eyewitness memory, aging and cognition, drug policy. *Unit head:* Stewart Donaldson, Dean, 909-607-9001, Fax: 909-621-8905, E-mail: stewart.donaldson@cgu.edu. *Application contact:* Paul Thomas, Director, External Affairs, 909-607-9016, Fax: 909-621-8905, E-mail: paul.thomas@cgu.edu.

Clark University, Graduate School, Department of Psychology, Worcester, MA 01610-1477. Offers clinical psychology (PhD); developmental psychology (PhD); social-personality psychology (PhD). *Accreditation:* APA. *Faculty:* 15 full-time (7 women), 6 part-time/adjunct (4 women). *Students:* 41 full-time (35 women), 1 (woman) part-time; includes 6 minority (1 African American, 1 Asian American or Pacific Islander, 4 Hispanic Americans), 8 international. Average age 30. 165 applicants, 13% accepted, 11 enrolled. In 2008, 6 doctorates awarded. *Degree requirements:* For doctorate, thesis/dissertation. *Entrance requirements:* For doctorate, GRE General Test. Additional exam requirements/recommendations for international students: Required—TOEFL. *Application deadline:* For fall admission, 12/28 priority date for domestic students. Applications are processed on a rolling basis. Application fee: $50. *Expenses:* Tuition: Full-time $34,900; part-time $1091 per credit hour. Required fees: $30. *Financial support:* In 2008–09, 2 fellowships with full tuition reimbursements (averaging $15,700 per year), 11 research assistantships with full tuition reimbursements (averaging $15,700 per year), 15 teaching assistantships with full tuition reimbursements (averaging $15,700 per year) were awarded; career-related internships or fieldwork and tuition waivers (full and partial) also available. *Faculty research:* Development of psychological processes in sociocultural context, conceptualizing and reasoning, symbolization, psychotherapy, metaphor, emotions and personalities. Total annual research expenditures: $1.2 million. *Unit head:* Dr. Wendy Grolnick, Chair, 508-793-7273. *Application contact:* Peggy Moskowitz, Graduate School Secretary, 508-793-7274, Fax: 508-793-7265, E-mail: psychology@clarku.edu.

Clemson University, Graduate School, College of Business and Behavioral Science, Department of Psychology, Program in Applied Psychology, Clemson, SC 29634. Offers MS. *Students:* 1 (woman) full-time, 1 (woman) part-time. Average age 30. 43 applicants, 7% accepted, 2 enrolled. In 2008, 10 master's awarded. *Degree requirements:* For master's, thesis, internship. *Entrance requirements:* For master's, GRE General Test, 18 hours of course work in psychology. Additional exam requirements/recommendations for international students: Required—TOEFL. *Application deadline:* For fall admission, 3/15 for domestic students, 4/15 for international students; for spring admission, 9/15 for international students. Application fee: $55. Full-time tuition and fees vary according to program. *Financial support:* In 2008–09, 3 research assistantships were awarded; teaching assistantships, career-related internships or fieldwork and unspecified assistantships also available. Financial award application deadline: 3/15; financial award applicants required to submit FAFSA. *Faculty research:* Personnel selection and validation; performance evaluation; training, motivation and decision making; human factors; TOEFL. *Unit head:* Dr. Chris Pagano, Coordinator, 864-656-4984, Fax: 864-656-0358, E-mail: cpagano@clemson.edu. *Application contact:* Interim Associate Dean.

Clemson University, Graduate School, College of Business and Behavioral Science, Department of Psychology, Program in Human Factors Psychology, Clemson, SC 29634. Offers PhD. *Students:* 14 full-time (7 women), 1 (woman) part-time. Average age 27. 33 applicants, 24% accepted, 5 enrolled. In 2008, 1 doctorate awarded. Application fee: $55. Full-time tuition and fees vary according to program. *Unit head:* Dr. Chris Pagano, Coordinator, 864-656-4984, Fax: 864-656-0358, E-mail: cpagano@clemson.edu. *Application contact:* Dr. Chris Pagano, Coordinator, 864-656-4984, Fax: 864-656-0358, E-mail: cpagano@clemson.edu.

Cleveland State University, College of Graduate Studies, College of Science, Department of Psychology, Cleveland, OH 44115. Offers adult development and aging (PhD); clinical psychology (MA); consumer/industrial research (MA); diversity management (MA); experimental research psychology (MA); school psychology (Psy S). *Faculty:* 20 full-time (7 women), 16 part-time/adjunct (8 women). *Students:* 66 full-time (44 women), 62 part-time (46 women); includes 25 minority (19 African Americans, 1 American Indian/Alaska Native, 2 Asian Americans or Pacific Islanders, 3 Hispanic Americans), 3 international. Average age 30. 180 applicants, 40% accepted, 55 enrolled. In 2008, 39 master's, 4 other advanced degrees awarded. *Degree requirements:* For master's, comprehensive exam (for some programs), thesis (for some programs); for doctorate, comprehensive exam, thesis/dissertation; for Psy S, internship.

Entrance requirements: For master's and doctorate, GRE General Test. Additional exam requirements/recommendations for international students: Required—TOEFL (minimum score 525 paper-based; 197 computer-based). *Application deadline:* For fall admission, 2/1 priority date for domestic and international students. Applications are processed on a rolling basis. Application fee: $30. Electronic applications accepted. *Financial support:* In 2008–09, 45 students received support. Career-related internships or fieldwork, Federal Work-Study, tuition waivers (partial), and unspecified assistantships available. Financial award applicants required to submit FAFSA. *Faculty research:* Cognitive and social psychology, consumer psychology, clinical psychology, school psychology, aging. Total annual research expenditures: $112,607. *Unit head:* Dr. Albert F Smith, Interim Chair, 216-687-3723, Fax: 216-687-9294, E-mail: a.f.smith@csuohio.edu. *Application contact:* Karen R Colston, Administrative Coordinator, 216-687-2552, Fax: 216-687-9294, E-mail: k.colston@csuohio.edu.

The College at Brockport, State University of New York, School of Letters and Sciences, Department of Psychology, Brockport, NY 14420-2997. Offers MA. *Degree requirements:* For master's, thesis optional. *Entrance requirements:* For master's, GRE General Test, letters of recommendation, interview, minimum GPA of 3.0. Additional exam requirements/recommendations for international students: Required—TOEFL (minimum score 550 paper-based; 213 computer-based; 79 iBT). *Faculty research:* Positive psychology, decision-making and applied behavior analysis, family processes and close relationships, cognition and neuropsychology, social/personality and industrial/organizational psychology.

College of Saint Elizabeth, Department of Psychology, Morristown, NJ 07960-6989. Offers counseling psychology (MA); forensic psychology (MA); student affairs in higher education (Certificate). Part-time and evening/weekend programs available. *Faculty:* 4 full-time (2 women), 10 part-time/adjunct (5 women). *Students:* 11 full-time (10 women), 84 part-time (77 women); includes 23 minority (10 African Americans, 3 Asian Americans or Pacific Islanders, 10 Hispanic Americans), 2 international. Average age 34. 104 applicants, 58% accepted, 47 enrolled. In 2008, 11 master's, 1 other advanced degree awarded. *Degree requirements:* For master's, thesis or alternative, portfolio. *Entrance requirements:* For master's, minimum GPA of 3.0, BA in psychology (preferred), 12 credits of course work in psychology. *Application deadline:* For fall admission, 4/14 priority date for domestic students; for spring admission, 11/15 for domestic students. Applications are processed on a rolling basis. Application fee: $35. Electronic applications accepted. *Expenses:* Tuition: Part-time $759 per credit. Required fees: $380 per semester. *Financial support:* Career-related internships or fieldwork, tuition waivers (partial), and unspecified assistantships available. Support available to part-time students. Financial award application deadline: 3/15; financial award applicants required to submit FAFSA. *Faculty research:* Family systems, dissociative identity disorder, multicultural counseling, outcomes assessment. *Unit head:* Dr. Valerie Scott, Director of the Graduate Program in Counseling Psychology, 973-290-4102, Fax: 973-290-4676, E-mail: vscott@cse.edu. *Application contact:* Donna Tatarka, Dean of Admission, 973-290-4705, Fax: 973-290-4710, E-mail: dtatarka@cse.edu.

College of St. Joseph, Graduate Programs, Division of Psychology and Human Services, Rutland, VT 05701-3899. Offers alcohol and substance abuse counseling (MS); clinical mental health counseling (MS); clinical psychology (MS); community counseling (MS); school guidance counseling (MS). Part-time and evening/weekend programs available. *Degree requirements:* For master's, comprehensive exam, thesis. *Entrance requirements:* For master's, 2 letters of reference, interview. Electronic applications accepted.

The College of William and Mary, Faculty of Arts and Sciences, Department of Psychology, Williamsburg, VA 23187-8795. Offers clinical psychology (Psy D); general experimental psychology (MA). Psy D is offered through the Virginia Consortium for Professional Psychology. *Degree requirements:* For master's, comprehensive exam, thesis, oral exams. *Entrance requirements:* For master's, GRE, passed course work in statistics and experimental psychology. Additional exam requirements/recommendations for international students: Required—TOEFL. Electronic applications accepted. *Expenses:* Tuition, state resident: full-time $6400; part-time $300 per credit hour. Tuition, nonresident: full-time $19,720; part-time $800 per credit hour. International tuition: $19,720 full-time. Required fees: $3860. *Faculty research:* Personality, developmental, cognition, applied decision theory, social psychology.

Colorado State University, Graduate School, College of Natural Sciences, Department of Psychology, Fort Collins, CO 80523-1876. Offers MS, PhD. *Accreditation:* APA. Post-baccalaureate distance learning degree programs offered (no on-campus study). *Faculty:* 26 full-time (13 women), 2 part-time/adjunct (0 women). *Students:* 67 full-time (49 women), 47 part-time (34 women); includes 24 minority (1 African American, 7 American Indian/Alaska Native, 6 Asian Americans or Pacific Islanders, 10 Hispanic Americans), 4 international. Average age 28. 436 applicants, 5% accepted, 22 enrolled. In 2008, 21 master's, 12 doctorates awarded. Terminal master's awarded for partial completion of doctoral program. *Degree requirements:* For master's, comprehensive exam (for some programs), thesis (for some programs); for doctorate, comprehensive exam, thesis/dissertation. *Entrance requirements:* For master's and doctorate, GRE General Test, GRE Subject Test, minimum GPA of 3.0; transcripts; 3 letters of recommendation; resumé or curriculum vitae; statement of interest; sample of scientific writing (for some areas of study). Additional exam requirements/recommendations for international students: Required—TOEFL (minimum score 550 paper-based; 213 computer-based; 80 iBT). *Application deadline:* For fall admission, 9/15 priority date for domestic and international students; for spring admission, 1/15 priority date for domestic and international students. Applications are processed on a rolling basis. Application fee: $50. Electronic applications accepted. *Expenses:* Tuition, area resident: full-time $5620; part-time $312.25 per credit. Tuition, state resident: full-time $5620; part-time $312.25 per credit. Tuition, nonresident: full-time $17,253; part-time $958.50 per credit. Required fees: $1449.56; $82.35 per credit. *Financial support:* In 2008–09, 65 students received support, including 2 fellowships (averaging $30,300 per year), 10 research assistantships with full tuition reimbursements available (averaging $8,998 per year), 53 teaching assistantships with full tuition reimbursements available (averaging $11,448 per year); health care benefits also available. Financial award application deadline: 1/15; financial award applicants required to submit FAFSA. *Faculty research:* Environmental psychology, cognitive learning, health psychology, counseling and clinical issues, industrial and organizational psychology. Total annual research expenditures: $3.9 million. *Unit head:* Dr. Ernest L. Chavez, Chair and Professor, 970-491-6364, Fax: 970-491-1032, E-mail: ernest.chavez@colostate.edu. *Application contact:* Joanne Moran, Program Assistant I, 970-491-7298, Fax: 970-491-1032, E-mail: joanne.moran@colostate.edu.

Columbia University, Graduate School of Arts and Sciences, Division of Natural Sciences, Department of Psychology, New York, NY 10027. Offers experimental psychology (M Phil, MA, PhD); psychobiology (M Phil, MA, PhD); social psychology (M Phil, MA, PhD); JD/MA; JD/PhD; MD/PhD. *Degree requirements:* For master's, thesis; for doctorate, thesis/dissertation. *Entrance requirements:* For master's and doctorate, GRE General Test. Additional exam requirements/recommendations for international students: Required—TOEFL.

Concordia University, School of Graduate Studies, Faculty of Arts and Science, Department of Psychology, Program in Psychology (General), Montréal, QC H3G 1M8, Canada. Offers MA, PhD. *Degree requirements:* For master's, comprehensive exam, thesis; for doctorate, comprehensive exam, thesis/dissertation. *Entrance requirements:* For master's, GRE General Test, GRE Subject Test, honors degree in psychology or equivalent; for doctorate, master's degree in psychology. *Faculty research:* Appetitive motivation and drug dependence, human information processing, psychology of physical activity.

Concordia University Chicago, College of Graduate and Innovative Programs, Program in Psychology, River Forest, IL 60305-1499. Offers MA. Part-time and evening/weekend programs available. *Degree requirements:* For master's, comprehensive exam, thesis optional. *Entrance requirements:* For master's, minimum GPA of 2.9. Additional exam requirements/recommendations for international students: Required—TOEFL (minimum score 550 paper-based; 195 computer-based). Electronic applications accepted. *Faculty research:* Lutheran high school counseling research.

Psychology—General

Concordia University Wisconsin, Graduate Programs, Department of Psychology, Mequon, WI 53097-2402. Offers professional counseling (MPC).

Connecticut College, Graduate School, Department of Psychology, New London, CT 06320-4196. Offers MA. Part-time programs available. *Students:* 1 (woman) full-time, 6 part-time (5 women), 1 international. Average age 25. 7 applicants, 57% accepted, 2 enrolled. In 2008, 10 master's awarded. *Degree requirements:* For master's, comprehensive exam (for some programs), thesis. *Entrance requirements:* For master's, GRE General Test. Additional exam requirements/recommendations for international students: Required—TOEFL (minimum score 600 paper-based). *Application deadline:* For fall admission, 2/15 for domestic and international students. Application fee: $60. *Expenses:* Tuition: Full-time $11,900; part-time $1700 per course. *Financial support:* In 2008–09, 2 students received support. 5 course remissions for 1 student; 3 course remissions for 1 student available. Financial award application deadline: 2/15; financial award applicants required to submit CSS PROFILE or FAFSA. *Faculty research:* Behavioral medicine, personality-social psychology, clinical, neuroscience/psychobiology. *Unit head:* Dr. Ann Sloan Devlin, Chair, 860-439-2333, Fax: 860-439-5300, E-mail: ann.devlin@conncoll.edu. *Application contact:* Nancy M. MacLeod, Academic Department Assistant, 860-439-2330, Fax: 860-439-5300, E-mail: nancy.macleod@conncoll.edu.

Cornell University, Graduate School, Graduate Fields of Arts and Sciences, Field of Psychology, Ithaca, NY 14853-0001. Offers biopsychology (PhD); human experimental psychology (PhD); personality and social psychology (PhD). *Faculty:* 42 full-time (15 women). *Students:* 35 full-time (19 women); includes 5 minority (1 African American, 2 Asian Americans or Pacific Islanders, 2 Hispanic Americans), 11 international. Average age 30. 179 applicants, 7% accepted, 7 enrolled. In 2008, 5 doctorates awarded. *Degree requirements:* For doctorate, comprehensive exam, thesis/dissertation, 2 semesters of teaching experience. *Entrance requirements:* For doctorate, GRE General Test, 3 letters of recommendation. Additional exam requirements/recommendations for international students: Required—TOEFL (minimum score 550 paper-based; 213 computer-based; 77 iBT). *Application deadline:* For fall admission, 12/15 for domestic students. Application fee: $70. Electronic applications accepted. *Expenses:* Tuition: Full-time $29,500. Required fees: $70. Full-time tuition and fees vary according to degree level, program and student level. *Financial support:* In 2008–09, 36 students received support, including 10 fellowships with full tuition reimbursements available, 2 research assistantships with full tuition reimbursements available, 24 teaching assistantships with full tuition reimbursements available; institutionally sponsored loans, scholarships/grants, health care benefits, tuition waivers (full and partial), and unspecified assistantships also available. Financial award applicants required to submit FAFSA. *Faculty research:* Sensory and perceptual systems, social cognition, cognitive development, quantitative and computational modeling, behavioral neuroscience. *Unit head:* Director of Graduate Studies, 607-255-6364, Fax: 607-255-8433. *Application contact:* Graduate Field Assistant, 607-255-3834, Fax: 607-255-8433, E-mail: psychapp@cornell.edu.

Dalhousie University, Faculty of Science, Department of Psychology, Halifax, NS B3H 4J1, Canada. Offers clinical psychology (PhD); psychology (M Sc, PhD); psychology/neuroscience (M Sc, PhD). *Accreditation:* APA (one or more programs are accredited). *Faculty:* 30 full-time (8 women), 34 part-time/adjunct (14 women). *Students:* 56 full-time (35 women); includes 2 minority (both Asian Americans or Pacific Islanders). 200 applicants, 8% accepted. In 2008, 8 master's, 7 doctorates awarded. *Degree requirements:* For master's, thesis; for doctorate, thesis/dissertation. *Entrance requirements:* For doctorate, GRE General Test. Additional exam requirements/recommendations for international students: Required—TOEFL, IELTS, 1 of the following 5 approved tests: IELTS, TOEFL, CAEL, CANTEST, Michigan English Language Assessment Battery. Application fee: $70. Electronic applications accepted. *Financial support:* In 2008–09, 19 fellowships, 26 teaching assistantships (averaging $1,853 per year) were awarded; career-related internships or fieldwork, scholarships/grants, and health care benefits also available. Financial award application deadline: 2/1. *Faculty research:* Physiological psychology, psychology of learning, learning and behavior, forensic clinical health psychology, development perception and cognition. Total annual research expenditures: $1.9 million. *Unit head:* Dr. Tracy Taylor-Helmick, Graduate Coordinator, 902-494-3001, Fax: 902-494-6585, E-mail: tracy.taylor.helmick@dal.ca. *Application contact:* Mary Macconnachie, Graduate Secretary, 902-494-3839, Fax: 902-494-6585, E-mail: mary.macconnachie@dal.ca.

Dartmouth College, Arts and Sciences Graduate Programs, Department of Psychological and Brain Sciences, Hanover, NH 03755. Offers cognitive neuroscience (PhD); psychology (PhD). *Degree requirements:* For doctorate, thesis/dissertation. *Entrance requirements:* For doctorate, GRE General Test, GRE Subject Test. Additional exam requirements/recommendations for international students: Required—TOEFL. *Faculty research:* Behavioral neuroscience, cognitive neuroscience, cognitive science, social/personality psychology.

DePaul University, College of Liberal Arts and Sciences, Department of Psychology, Chicago, IL 60604-2287. Offers clinical psychology (MA, PhD), including child clinical psychology, community clinical psychology; experimental psychology (MA, PhD); general psychology (MS); industrial/organizational psychology (MA, PhD); MA/PhD. *Accreditation:* APA (one or more programs are accredited). *Faculty:* 31 full-time (19 women), 6 part-time/adjunct (4 women). *Students:* 33 full-time (17 women), 23 part-time (20 women); includes 9 minority (4 African Americans, 1 American Indian/Alaska Native, 1 Asian American or Pacific Islander, 3 Hispanic Americans), 2 international. Average age 28. 332 applicants, 14% accepted, 23 enrolled. In 2008, 14 master's, 17 doctorates awarded. *Degree requirements:* For master's, thesis, oral exam; for doctorate, comprehensive exam, thesis/dissertation, oral and written exams. *Entrance requirements:* For master's and doctorate, GRE General Test, GRE Subject Test, 32 quarter hours of course work in psychology, 3 letters of recommendation. Additional exam requirements/recommendations for international students: Required—TOEFL. Application fee: $40. Electronic applications accepted. *Financial support:* In 2008–09, 48 students received support, including 35 research assistantships with full tuition reimbursements available (averaging $11,800 per year), 13 teaching assistantships with full tuition reimbursements available (averaging $11,800 per year); career-related internships or fieldwork, scholarships/grants, traineeships, tuition waivers (full and partial), and unspecified assistantships also available. Financial award application deadline: 1/10. *Faculty research:* Adolescent stress and depression, minority adolescents sexuality, public policy, community influences in child adjustment. *Unit head:* Dr. Christopher B Keys, Chairman, 773-325-7887, Fax: 773-325-7888. *Application contact:* Alison Pereida Knapp, Graduate Admissions Assistant, 773-325-7887, Fax: 773-325-7888.

Drexel University, College of Arts and Sciences, Department of Psychology, Philadelphia, PA 19104-2875. Offers clinical psychology (PhD), including clinical psychology, forensic psychology, health psychology, neuropsychology; law-psychology (PhD); psychology (MS); JD/PhD. *Accreditation:* APA (one or more programs are accredited). *Degree requirements:* For doctorate, thesis/dissertation, internship. *Entrance requirements:* For doctorate, GRE General Test. Additional exam requirements/recommendations for international students: Required—TOEFL. Electronic applications accepted. *Expenses:* Contact institution. *Faculty research:* Neurosciences, rehabilitation psychology, cognitive science, neurological assessment.

Duke University, Graduate School, Department of Psychology, Durham, NC 27708-0586. Offers biological psychology (PhD); clinical psychology (PhD); cognitive psychology (PhD); developmental psychology (PhD); experimental psychology (PhD); health psychology (PhD); human social development (PhD); JD/MA. *Accreditation:* APA (one or more programs are accredited). *Degree requirements:* For doctorate, thesis/dissertation. *Entrance requirements:* For doctorate, GRE General Test. Additional exam requirements/recommendations for international students: Required—TOEFL (minimum score 550 paper-based; 213 computer-based; 83 iBT), IELTS (minimum score 7). Electronic applications accepted.

Duquesne University, Graduate School of Liberal Arts, Department of Psychology, Pittsburgh, PA 15282-0001. Offers clinical psychology (PhD). *Accreditation:* APA. *Faculty:* 14 full-time (5 women). *Students:* 55 full-time (28 women); includes 2 minority (1 African American, 1 Hispanic American), 9 international. Average age 25. 79 applicants, 9% accepted, 7 enrolled. In 2008, 9 doctorates awarded. *Degree requirements:* For doctorate, comprehensive exam, thesis/dissertation. *Entrance requirements:* For doctorate, GRE General Test, MA in psychology. Additional exam requirements/recommendations for international students: Required—TOEFL. *Application deadline:* For fall admission, 12/15 for domestic and international students. Application fee: $50. Electronic applications accepted. *Expenses:* Tuition: Part-time $819 per credit. Required fees: $78 per credit. Tuition and fees vary according to course load. *Financial support:* In 2008–09, 1 research assistantship with full tuition reimbursement (averaging $13,000 per year), 14 teaching assistantships with full tuition reimbursements (averaging $13,000 per year) were awarded; fellowships with full tuition reimbursements, career-related internships or fieldwork, scholarships/grants, tuition waivers (partial), and unspecified assistantships also available. Financial award application deadline: 5/1. *Faculty research:* Emotion, language motivation, imagination, development. *Unit head:* Dr. Daniel Burston, Chair, 412-396-5067. *Application contact:* Linda L. Rendulic, Assistant to the Dean, 412-396-6400, Fax: 412-396-5265, E-mail: rendulic@duq.edu.

East Carolina University, Graduate School, Thomas Harriot College of Arts and Sciences, Department of Psychology, Program in General Psychology, Greenville, NC 27858-4353. Offers MA. *Degree requirements:* For master's, one foreign language, comprehensive exam, thesis. *Entrance requirements:* For master's, GRE General Test, GRE Subject Test. Additional exam requirements/recommendations for international students: Required—TOEFL.

East Central University, School of Graduate Studies, Department of Psychology, Ada, OK 74820-6899. Offers MSPS. Part-time and evening/weekend programs available. *Entrance requirements:* For master's, GRE General Test, MAT. Electronic applications accepted.

Eastern Illinois University, Graduate School, College of Sciences, Department of Psychology, Charleston, IL 61920-3099. Offers clinical psychology (MA); school psychology (SSP). *Degree requirements:* For master's, comprehensive exam; for SSP, thesis. *Entrance requirements:* For master's and SSP, GRE General Test.

Eastern Kentucky University, The Graduate School, College of Arts and Sciences, Department of Psychology, Richmond, KY 40475-3102. Offers clinical psychology (MS); industrial/organizational psychology (MS); school psychology (Psy S). Part-time programs available. *Entrance requirements:* For master's and Psy S, GRE General Test, minimum GPA of 2.5. *Faculty research:* Autism, social psychology, parenting, assessment of depression/anxiety, reading.

Eastern Michigan University, Graduate School, College of Arts and Sciences, Department of Psychology, Ypsilanti, MI 48197. Offers clinical behavioral psychology (MS); clinical psychology (MS, PhD); psychology (MS). *Accreditation:* APA.

Eastern Washington University, Graduate Studies, College of Education and Human Development, Department of Counseling, Educational, and Developmental Psychology, Cheney, WA 99004-2431. Offers mental health counseling (MS), including applied psychology, mental health counseling; school counseling (MS), including applied psychology, school counseling; school psychology (MS); special education (M Ed). *Accreditation:* ACA (one or more programs are accredited); NCATE (one or more programs are accredited). *Degree requirements:* For master's, comprehensive exam, thesis or alternative. *Entrance requirements:* For master's, GRE General Test, minimum GPA of 3.0. *Faculty research:* 21.

Eastern Washington University, Graduate Studies, College of Social and Behavioral Sciences, Department of Psychology, Cheney, WA 99004-2431. Offers clinical psychology (MS); experimental psychology (MS); psychology (MS); school psychology (MS). *Degree requirements:* For master's, comprehensive exam, thesis or alternative. *Entrance requirements:* For master's, GRE General Test, minimum GPA of 3.0.

East Tennessee State University, School of Graduate Studies, College of Arts and Sciences, Department of Psychology, Johnson City, TN 37614. Offers clinical psychology (MA); general psychology (MA). *Degree requirements:* For master's, thesis, oral exams. *Entrance requirements:* For master's, GRE General Test, GRE Subject Test, minimum GPA of 3.0. Additional exam requirements/recommendations for international students: Required—TOEFL (minimum score 550 paper-based; 213 computer-based). *Faculty research:* Language acquisition, recovery of brain function after injury or damage, violence in domestic relationships and road rage, reasons for living, unhealthy tanning behaviors.

Edinboro University of Pennsylvania, Graduate Studies and Research, School of Liberal Arts, Department of Psychology, Edinboro, PA 16444. Offers clinical psychology (MA). Part-time and evening/weekend programs available. *Faculty:* 3 full-time (1 woman). *Students:* 24 full-time (20 women), 9 part-time (8 women); includes 1 minority (Asian American or Pacific Islander), 3 international. Average age 29. In 2008, 12 master's awarded. *Degree requirements:* For master's, comprehensive exam, thesis or alternative, project. *Entrance requirements:* For master's, GRE or MAT, minimum QPA of 2.5. *Application deadline:* For fall admission, 3/15 priority date for domestic students. Applications are processed on a rolling basis. Application fee: $30. Electronic applications accepted. *Expenses:* Tuition, state resident: full-time $6430; part-time $357 per credit. Tuition, nonresident: full-time $8038; part-time $572 per credit. International tuition: $15,171.58 full-time. Required fees: $2113; $60 per credit. Tuition and fees vary according to course load. *Financial support:* In 2008–09, 10 research assistantships with full and partial tuition reimbursements (averaging $3,850 per year) were awarded; career-related internships or fieldwork, Federal Work-Study, scholarships/grants, and unspecified assistantships also available. Support available to part-time students. Financial award application deadline: 2/15; financial award applicants required to submit FAFSA. *Unit head:* Dr. Cynthia Legin-Bucell, Chairperson, 814-732-2774, E-mail: leginbucell@edinboro.edu. *Application contact:* Dr. Cynthia Legin-Bucell, Chairperson, 814-732-2774, E-mail: leginbucell@edinboro.edu.

Emory University, Graduate School of Arts and Sciences, Department of Psychology, Atlanta, GA 30322-1100. Offers clinical psychology (PhD); cognition and development (PhD); neuroscience and animal behavior (PhD). *Accreditation:* APA. *Degree requirements:* For doctorate, comprehensive exam, thesis/dissertation. *Entrance requirements:* For doctorate, GRE General Test, minimum GPA of 3.25. Additional exam requirements/recommendations for international students: Required—TOEFL. Electronic applications accepted. *Faculty research:* Neuroscience and animal behavior; adult and child psychopathology, cognition development assessment.

Emporia State University, School of Graduate Studies, The Teachers College, Department of Psychology, Art Therapy, Rehabilitation and Mental Health Counseling, Program in Psychology, Emporia, KS 66801-5087. Offers general psychology (MS); industrial/organizational psychology (MS). Part-time programs available. *Students:* 15 full-time (10 women), 11 part-time (7 women); includes 3 minority (2 African Americans, 1 Hispanic American), 4 international. 9 applicants, 44% accepted, 4 enrolled. In 2008, 7 master's awarded. *Degree requirements:* For master's, comprehensive exam or thesis, internship. *Entrance requirements:* For master's, GRE General Test or MAT, graduate essay exam, appropriate bachelor's degree, letters of recommendation. Additional exam requirements/recommendations for international students: Required—TOEFL. *Application deadline:* For fall admission, 6/1 priority date for domestic students; for spring admission, 10/1 for domestic students. Applications are processed on a rolling basis. Application fee: $30 ($75 for international students). Electronic applications accepted. *Expenses:* Tuition, area resident: Full-time $3976; part-time $166 per credit hour. Tuition, state resident: full-time $3976; part-time $166 per credit hour. Tuition, nonresident: full-time $12,028; part-time $501 per credit hour. Required fees: $51 per credit hour. Tuition and fees vary according to campus/location. *Financial support:* Career-related internships or fieldwork, Federal Work-Study, institutionally sponsored loans, health care benefits, and unspecified assistantships available. Financial award application deadline: 3/15; financial award applicants required to submit FAFSA. *Faculty research:* Driving under the influence (DUI) personality, lifestyles and imposter phenomenon. *Unit head:* Dr. Kenneth A. Weaver, Chair, 620-341-5317, E-mail: kweaver@emporia.edu. *Application contact:* Mary Sewell, Admissions Coordinator, 800-950-GRAD, Fax: 620-341-5909, E-mail: msewell@emporia.edu.

Evangel University, Department of Psychology, Springfield, MO 65802-2191. Offers clinical psychology (MS); counseling psychology (MS). Part-time and evening/weekend programs available. *Degree requirements:* For master's, comprehensive exam, thesis (for some programs). *Entrance requirements:* For master's, GRE General Test or MAT, minimum undergraduate GPA of 3.0, undergraduate major or minor in psychology, teaching certificate (school counseling). Additional exam requirements/recommendations for international students: Required—TOEFL (minimum score 550 paper-based; 213 computer-based).

Fairfield University, Graduate School of Education and Allied Professions, Department of Psychological and Educational Consultation, Fairfield, CT 06824-5195. Offers applied psychology (MA), including foundations of advanced psychology, human services, industrial/organizational/personnel; media/educational technology (MA); school media specialist (MA); school psychology (MA, CAS); special education (MA, CAS). Part-time and evening/weekend programs available. *Faculty:* 6 full-time (2 women), 7 part-time/adjunct (4 women). *Students:* 49 full-time (42 women), 111 part-time (97 women); includes 19 minority (2 African Americans, 1 American Indian/Alaska Native, 2 Asian Americans or Pacific Islanders, 14 Hispanic Americans), 2 international. 96 applicants, 58% accepted, 30 enrolled. In 2008, 44 master's, 14 other advanced degrees awarded. *Degree requirements:* For master's, comprehensive exam, thesis optional, educational technology course (for some programs). *Entrance requirements:* For master's, PRAXIS I (PPST), minimum QPA of 3.0, 2 recommendations, resumé, essay. Additional exam requirements/recommendations for international students: Required—TOEFL (minimum score 550 paper-based; 213 computer-based; 80 iBT). Application fee: $60. Electronic applications accepted. *Expenses:* Tuition: Full-time $9450; part-time $525 per credit hour. Required fees: $25 per semester. Tuition and fees vary according to course load and program. *Financial support:* Unspecified assistantships and Federal Grant (Project SETTEL) funds tuition for future special education, bilingual, and/or TESOL educators available. Financial award applicants required to submit FAFSA. *Faculty research:* Child neuropsychology, disabilities, effect of pre-treatment orientation on treatment, autism, technology in business and classroom, collaboration with schools, communities and industry. *Unit head:* Dr. Daniel Geller, Chair, 203-254-4000 Ext. 2324, Fax: 203-254-4047, E-mail: dgeller@fairfield.edu. *Application contact:* Marianne Gumpper, Director of Graduate and Continuing Studies Admissions, 203-254-4184, Fax: 203-254-4073, E-mail: gradadmis@fairfield.edu.

Fairleigh Dickinson University, College at Florham, Maxwell Becton College of Arts and Sciences, Department of Psychology, Madison, NJ 07940-1099. Offers counseling (MA); industrial/organizational psychology (MA); organizational behavior (MA, Certificate), including organizational behavior (MA), organizational leadership (Certificate); MA/MBA. *Students:* 63 full-time (42 women), 78 part-time (44 women), 5 international. Average age 30. 133 applicants, 60% accepted, 40 enrolled. In 2008, 55 master's awarded. *Application deadline:* Applications are processed on a rolling basis. Application fee: $40. *Unit head:* Dr. Diane Wentworth, Chairperson, 973-443-8548. *Application contact:* Susan Brooman, University Director, Graduate Admissions, 973-443-8905, Fax: 973-443-8088, E-mail: grad@fdu.edu.

See Close-Up on page 1107.

Fairleigh Dickinson University, Metropolitan Campus, University College: Arts, Sciences, and Professional Studies, School of Psychology, Teaneck, NJ 07666-1914. Offers clinical psychology (MA, PhD); clinical psychopharmacology (MA); forensic psychology (MA); general-theoretical psychology (MA, Certificate); school psychology (MA, Psy D). *Accreditation:* APA (one or more programs are accredited). *Students:* 198 full-time (145 women), 50 part-time (31 women), 7 international. Average age 32. 174 applicants, 79% accepted, 79 enrolled. In 2008, 27 master's, 11 doctorates awarded. *Application deadline:* Applications are processed on a rolling basis. Application fee: $40. *Application contact:* Susan Brooman, University Director of Graduate Admissions, 201-692-2554, Fax: 201-692-2560, E-mail: globaleducation@fdu.edu.

Fayetteville State University, Graduate School, Program in Psychology, Fayetteville, NC 28301-4298. Offers MA. Part-time and evening/weekend programs available. *Degree requirements:* For master's, comprehensive exam, internship. Electronic applications accepted. *Faculty research:* Coping strategies, reasons for living, hypnosis, cultural differences in expression of emotions, ethics, morals, stress, adult development.

Fielding Graduate University, Graduate Programs, School of Psychology, Santa Barbara, CA 93105-3538. Offers clinical psychology (PhD); clinical psychology respecialization (Post-Doctoral Certificate); media psychology (PhD); media psychology and social change (MA); neuropsychology (Post-Doctoral Certificate). *Accreditation:* APA. Postbaccalaureate distance learning degree programs offered (minimal on-campus study). *Faculty:* 35 full-time (17 women), 2 part-time/adjunct (0 women). *Students:* 522 full-time (382 women), 76 part-time (47 women); includes 121 minority (38 African Americans, 6 American Indian/Alaska Native, 28 Asian Americans or Pacific Islanders, 49 Hispanic Americans), 12 international. Average age 44. 284 applicants, 38% accepted, 76 enrolled. In 2008, 38 doctorates, 29 other advanced degrees awarded. Terminal master's awarded for partial completion of doctoral program. *Degree requirements:* For master's, capstone project; for doctorate, comprehensive exam, thesis/dissertation. *Entrance requirements:* For doctorate, writing sample, minimum GPA of 3.0, 3 letters of recommendation, resumé. *Application deadline:* For fall admission, 2/23 for domestic and international students; for spring admission, 8/25 for domestic and international students. Application fee: $75. Electronic applications accepted. *Expenses:* Contact institution. *Financial support:* In 2008–09, 440 students received support, including 3 research assistantships (averaging $2,565 per year); scholarships/grants and health care benefits also available. Support available to part-time students. Financial award application deadline: 5/15; financial award applicants required to submit FAFSA. *Unit head:* Dr. Raymond Trybus, Dean, 805-898-2909, E-mail: rtrybus@fielding.edu. *Application contact:* Kathryn Romero, Admission Counselor, 800-340-1099, Fax: 805-687-9793, E-mail: kromero@fielding.edu.

See Close-Up on page 1111.

Fisk University, Graduate Programs, Department of Psychology, Nashville, TN 37208-3051. Offers clinical psychology (MA); psychology (MA). *Degree requirements:* For master's, thesis. *Entrance requirements:* For master's, GRE General Test, GRE Subject Test, minimum GPA of 3.0. *Faculty research:* Ethnic and gender identity, development, female adolescent development, juvenile delinquency prevention.

Florida Agricultural and Mechanical University, Division of Graduate Studies, Research, and Continuing Education, College of Arts and Sciences, Department of Psychology, Tallahassee, FL 32307-3200. Offers community psychology (MS); school psychology (MS). *Degree requirements:* For master's, thesis. *Entrance requirements:* For master's, GRE General Test, minimum GPA of 3.0. Additional exam requirements/recommendations for international students: Required—TOEFL.

Florida Atlantic University, Charles E. Schmidt College of Science, Department of Psychology, Boca Raton, FL 33431-0991. Offers MA, PhD. *Faculty:* 26 full-time (8 women), 6 part-time/adjunct (2 women). *Students:* 58 full-time (39 women), 13 part-time (9 women); includes 13 minority (3 African Americans, 1 American Indian/Alaska Native, 4 Asian Americans or Pacific Islanders, 5 Hispanic Americans), 5 international. Average age 39. 115 applicants, 29% accepted, 10 enrolled. In 2008, 12 master's, 8 doctorates awarded. Terminal master's awarded for partial completion of doctoral program. *Degree requirements:* For master's, one foreign language, thesis or alternative; for doctorate, one foreign language, comprehensive exam, thesis/dissertation. *Entrance requirements:* For master's and doctorate, GRE General Test, minimum GPA of 3.0 during previous 2 years. *Application deadline:* For fall admission, 5/1 for domestic students, 5/15 for international students. Application fee: $30. Electronic applications accepted. *Expenses:* Tuition, state resident: full-time $4867; part-time $270.40 per credit hour. Tuition, nonresident: full-time $16,486; part-time $915.87 per credit hour. *Financial support:* Research assistantships with partial tuition reimbursements, teaching assistantships with partial tuition reimbursements, Federal Work-Study, institutionally sponsored loans, scholarships/grants, and unspecified assistantships available. Financial award application deadline: 3/1; financial award applicants required to submit FAFSA. *Faculty research:* Cognition, psychobiology,

developmental psychology, social psychology, neuroscience. *Unit head:* Dr. David L. Wolgin, Chair, 561-297-3366, Fax: 561-297-2160, E-mail: wolgindl@fau.edu. *Application contact:* Dr. David F. Bjorklund, Graduate Program Coordinator, 561-297-3368, Fax: 561-297-2160, E-mail: dbjorklu@fau.edu.

Florida Institute of Technology, Graduate Programs, College of Psychology and Liberal Arts, School of Psychology, Melbourne, FL 32901-6975. Offers applied behavior analysis (MS); clinical psychology (Psy D); industrial/organizational psychology (MS, PhD). *Accreditation:* APA (one or more programs are accredited). Part-time programs available. *Degree requirements:* For master's, comprehensive exam (for some programs), thesis (for some programs); for doctorate, comprehensive exam, thesis/dissertation (for some programs), internship. *Entrance requirements:* For master's, GRE General Test, 3 letters of recommendation, minimum GPA of 3.0, resumé, statement of objectives; for doctorate, GRE General Test, GRE Subject Test, 3 letters of recommendation, minimum GPA of 3.2, resumé, statement of objectives. Additional exam requirements/recommendations for international students: Required—TOEFL (minimum score 550 paper-based; 213 computer-based). Electronic applications accepted. *Expenses:* Tuition: Part-time $980 per credit hour. *Faculty research:* Addictions, neuropsychology, child abuse, assessment, psychological trauma.

See Close-Up on page 1113.

Florida International University, College of Arts and Sciences, Department of Psychology, Miami, FL 33199. Offers developmental psychology (PhD); general psychology (MS); psychology (MS). Part-time programs available. Terminal master's awarded for partial completion of doctoral program. *Degree requirements:* For master's, thesis; for doctorate, comprehensive exam, thesis/dissertation. *Entrance requirements:* For master's, GRE General Test, minimum GPA of 3.0, resumé, writing samples; for doctorate, GRE General Test, 3 letters of recommendation, resumé, writing samples, minimum GPA of 3.0. Additional exam requirements/recommendations for international students: Required—TOEFL (minimum score 550 paper-based; 213 computer-based). Electronic applications accepted. *Faculty research:* Community psychology.

Florida State University, Graduate Studies, College of Arts and Sciences, Department of Psychology, Tallahassee, FL 32306. Offers applied behavior analysis (MS); clinical psychology (PhD); cognitive psychology (PhD); developmental psychology (PhD); neuroscience (PhD); social psychology (PhD). *Accreditation:* APA (one or more programs are accredited). Terminal master's awarded for partial completion of doctoral program. *Degree requirements:* For master's, comprehensive exam; for doctorate, thesis/dissertation, preliminary exam. *Entrance requirements:* For master's and doctorate, GRE General Test, minimum GPA of 3.0. Additional exam requirements/recommendations for international students: Required—TOEFL (minimum score 550 paper-based; 213 computer-based; 80 iBT). Electronic applications accepted.

Fordham University, Graduate School of Arts and Sciences, Department of Psychology, New York, NY 10458. Offers applied developmental psychology (PhD); clinical psychology (PhD); psychometrics (PhD). Terminal master's awarded for partial completion of doctoral program. *Degree requirements:* For doctorate, comprehensive exam, thesis/dissertation. *Entrance requirements:* For doctorate, GRE General Test, GRE Subject Test. Additional exam requirements/recommendations for international students: Required—TOEFL (minimum score 600 paper-based; 250 computer-based). Electronic applications accepted.

Fort Hays State University, Graduate School, College of Arts and Sciences, Department of Psychology, Hays, KS 67601-4099. Offers psychology (MS); school psychology (Ed S). *Degree requirements:* For master's and Ed S, comprehensive exam, thesis. *Entrance requirements:* For master's, GRE General Test. Additional exam requirements/recommendations for international students: Required—TOEFL (minimum score 550 paper-based; 213 computer-based). Electronic applications accepted. *Faculty research:* Memory, learning, motivation, clinical and experimental psychology, history and systems of psychological stressors in rural environments.

Framingham State College, Division of Graduate and Continuing Education, Program in Counseling Psychology, Framingham, MA 01701-9101. Offers MA. Part-time and evening/weekend programs available.

Francis Marion University, Graduate Programs, Department of Psychology, Florence, SC 29501-0547. Offers applied clinical psychology (MS); applied community psychology (MS); school psychology (MS). Part-time and evening/weekend programs available. *Faculty:* 10 full-time (4 women), 6 part-time/adjunct (4 women). *Students:* 15 full-time (all women), 28 part-time (25 women); includes 5 minority (all African Americans), 1 international. Average age 38. 39 applicants, 100% accepted, 12 enrolled. In 2008, 15 master's awarded. *Degree requirements:* For master's, internship. *Entrance requirements:* For master's, GRE General Test. *Application deadline:* For fall admission, 4/15 for domestic students; for spring admission, 10/15 for domestic students. Applications are processed on a rolling basis. Application fee: $30. *Expenses:* Tuition, state resident: full-time $7547; part-time $377.35 per credit hour. Tuition, nonresident: full-time $15,094; part-time $754.70 per credit hour. Required fees: $22 per credit hour. $30 per semester. *Financial support:* In 2008–09, 1 research assistantship (averaging $7,000 per year), 3 teaching assistantships (averaging $8,000 per year) were awarded; career-related internships or fieldwork and unspecified assistantships also available. Support available to part-time students. Financial award application deadline: 3/1; financial award applicants required to submit FAFSA. *Faculty research:* Critical thinking, spatial localization, cognition and aging, family psychology. *Unit head:* Dr. John R. Hester, Chair, 843-661-1635, Fax: 843-661-1628. *Application contact:* Jennifer Taylor, Administrative Assistant, 843-661-1378, Fax: 843-661-1628.

Frostburg State University, Graduate School, College of Liberal Arts and Sciences, Department of Psychology, Frostburg, MD 21532-1099. Offers counseling psychology (MS). Part-time and evening/weekend programs available. *Degree requirements:* For master's, internship. *Entrance requirements:* For master's, GRE General Test or MAT, interview, minimum GPA of 3.0, resumé. Electronic applications accepted.

Fuller Theological Seminary, Graduate School of Psychology, Pasadena, CA 91182. Offers MA, MS, PhD, Psy D, Certificate. *Accreditation:* APA (one or more programs are accredited). Terminal master's awarded for partial completion of doctoral program. *Degree requirements:* For master's, practicum; for doctorate, thesis/dissertation, internships. *Entrance requirements:* For master's, GRE General Test; for doctorate, GRE General Test, GRE Subject Test, interview. Additional exam requirements/recommendations for international students: Required—TOEFL. *Faculty research:* Psychology of religion, depression, shame, psychoneuroimmunology, marital intimacy, sex roles, psychoanalytic theory, men's issues, family relations.

Gallaudet University, The Graduate School, College of Arts and Sciences, Department of Psychology, Washington, DC 20002-3625. Offers clinical psychology (PhD); school psychology (MA, Psy S), including developmental psychology (MA), school psychology (Psy S). *Accreditation:* APA (one or more programs are accredited). *Degree requirements:* For master's, thesis optional; for doctorate, thesis/dissertation. *Entrance requirements:* For master's, GRE General Test or MAT; for doctorate, GRE General Test or MAT, interview. Electronic applications accepted.

Gardner-Webb University, Graduate School, School of Psychology, Boiling Springs, NC 28017. Offers mental health counseling (MA); school counseling (MA). Part-time and evening/weekend programs available. *Degree requirements:* For master's, comprehensive exam. *Entrance requirements:* For master's, GRE General Test, MAT, minimum GPA of 2.7. Electronic applications accepted.

Geneva College, Program in Counseling, Beaver Falls, PA 15010-3599. Offers marriage and family (MA); mental health (MA); school counseling (MA). *Accreditation:* ACA. Part-time and evening/weekend programs available. *Degree requirements:* For master's, internship. *Entrance*

Psychology—General

Geneva College (continued)
requirements: For master's, GRE General Test or MAT, minimum GPA of 3.0, letters of recommendation, faith statement, 12 credits in undergraduate psychology. Additional exam requirements/recommendations for international students: Required—TOEFL. Electronic applications accepted.

George Fox University, Graduate Department of Clinical Psychology, Newberg, OR 97132-2697. Offers MA, Psy D. *Accreditation:* APA. *Faculty:* 8 full-time (3 women), 8 part-time/adjunct (3 women). *Students:* 105 full-time (69 women), 4 part-time (all women); includes 11 minority (2 African Americans, 3 American Indian/Alaska Native, 2 Asian Americans or Pacific Islanders, 4 Hispanic Americans). Average age 29. 76 applicants, 45% accepted, 24 enrolled. In 2008, 21 master's, 21 doctorates awarded. *Degree requirements:* For master's, comprehensive exam, 60 semester hours of required and elective courses; for doctorate, thesis/dissertation, internship plus 125 semester hours of required and elective courses. *Entrance requirements:* For master's and doctorate, GRE General Test, minimum undergraduate GPA of 3.0 during previous 2 years. Additional exam requirements/recommendations for international students: Required—TOEFL (minimum score 550 paper-based; 213 computer-based; 80 iBT). *Application deadline:* For fall admission, 1/15 priority date for domestic and international students. Applications are processed on a rolling basis. Application fee: $40. Electronic applications accepted. *Expenses:* Contact institution. *Financial support:* In 2008–09, 15 students received support, including 8 research assistantships (averaging $2,000 per year), 6 teaching assistantships (averaging $3,000 per year); scholarships/grants also available. Financial award application deadline: 5/15; financial award applicants required to submit FAFSA. *Faculty research:* Psychological assessment; impact of psychological services on medical outcome; spirituality and wellness; effectiveness of clinical training and supervision; shame. Total annual research expenditures: $22,000. *Unit head:* Dr. Wayne Adams, Professor and Chairperson, Graduate Department of Clinical Psychology, 800-765-4369 Ext. 2372, E-mail: wadams@georgefox.edu. *Application contact:* Adina McConaughey, Admission Counselor, 800-631-0921 Ext. 2263, Fax: 503-554-2263, E-mail: amcconaughey@georgefox.edu.

See Close-Up on page 1115.

George Mason University, College of Humanities and Social Sciences, Department of Psychology, Fairfax, VA 22030. Offers applied developmental psychology (MA, PhD); biopsychology (MA, PhD); clinical psychology (MA, PhD); human factors engineering psychology (MA, PhD); industrial/organizational psychology (MA, PhD); psychology (MA, PhD); school psychology (MA). *Accreditation:* APA. Terminal master's awarded for partial completion of doctoral program. *Degree requirements:* For master's, thesis (for applied developmental psychology and biopsychology); for doctorate, comprehensive exam, thesis/dissertation or alternative. *Entrance requirements:* For master's, GRE General Test, minimum GPA of 3.0 in last 60 hours of course work, undergraduate course work in psychology; for doctorate, GRE General Test, minimum undergraduate GPA of 3.0, 3.3 in major. Additional exam requirements/recommendations for international students: Required—TOEFL (minimum score 575 paper-based; 230 computer-based; 88 iBT), IELTS (minimum score 6). Electronic applications accepted.

Georgetown University, Graduate School of Arts and Sciences, Department of Psychology, Washington, DC 20057. Offers PhD, JD/MPP. *Degree requirements:* For doctorate, thesis/dissertation. *Entrance requirements:* For doctorate, GRE General Test, GRE Subject Test. Additional exam requirements/recommendations for international students: Required—TOEFL.

The George Washington University, Columbian College of Arts and Sciences, Department of Psychology, Washington, DC 20052. Offers applied social psychology (PhD); clinical psychology (PhD); cognitive neuroscience (PhD). *Accreditation:* APA. Part-time and evening/weekend programs available. *Faculty:* 27 full-time (14 women), 19 part-time/adjunct (12 women). *Students:* 119 full-time (99 women), 83 part-time (64 women); includes 56 minority (14 African Americans, 2 American Indian/Alaska Native, 24 Asian Americans or Pacific Islanders, 16 Hispanic Americans), 6 international. Average age 29. 873 applicants, 5% accepted, 47 enrolled. In 2008, 41 doctorates awarded. *Degree requirements:* For doctorate, thesis/dissertation or alternative, general exam. *Entrance requirements:* For doctorate, GRE General Test, minimum GPA of 3.0. Additional exam requirements/recommendations for international students: Required—TOEFL (minimum score 550 paper-based; 213 computer-based; 80 iBT). *Application deadline:* For fall admission, 1/15 for domestic and international students. Application fee: $60. *Financial support:* In 2008–09, 62 students received support; fellowships with tuition reimbursements available, teaching assistantships with tuition reimbursements available, career-related internships or fieldwork, Federal Work-Study, and tuition waivers available. *Unit head:* Dr. Paul Poppen, Chair, 202-994-6324, E-mail: pjp@gwu.edu. *Application contact:* Information Contact, 202-994-6320, Fax: 202-994-1602, E-mail: psydept@gwu.edu.

The George Washington University, Columbian College of Arts and Sciences, Program in Professional Psychology, Washington, DC 20052. Offers Psy D. *Accreditation:* APA. *Faculty:* 2 full-time (0 women), 1 (woman) part-time/adjunct. *Students:* 90 full-time (69 women), 72 part-time (55 women); includes 24 minority (10 African Americans, 2 American Indian/Alaska Native, 6 Asian Americans or Pacific Islanders, 6 Hispanic Americans), 9 international. Average age 30. 359 applicants, 10% accepted, 36 enrolled. In 2008, 37 doctorates awarded. *Entrance requirements:* For doctorate, GRE General Test, interview, minimum GPA of 3.0. Additional exam requirements/recommendations for international students: Required—TOEFL (minimum score 550 paper-based; 213 computer-based; 80 iBT). *Application deadline:* For fall admission, 12/1 priority date for domestic students. Applications are processed on a rolling basis. Application fee: $60. Electronic applications accepted. *Financial support:* Fellowships with partial tuition reimbursements available. *Unit head:* Dr. Dorothy Holmes, Director, 202-496-6282, Fax: 202-496-6263, E-mail: crescent@gwu.edu. *Application contact:* Dr. Dorothy Holmes, Director, 202-496-6282, Fax: 202-496-6263, E-mail: crescent@gwu.edu.

Georgia Institute of Technology, Graduate Studies and Research, College of Sciences, School of Psychology, Atlanta, GA 30332-0001. Offers human computer interaction (MSHCI); psychology (MS, MS Psy, PhD), including engineering psychology (PhD), experimental psychology (PhD), industrial/organizational psychology (PhD). Terminal master's awarded for partial completion of doctoral program. *Degree requirements:* For master's, thesis; for doctorate, thesis/dissertation. *Entrance requirements:* For master's and doctorate, GRE General Test, GRE Subject Test, minimum GPA of 3.0. Additional exam requirements/recommendations for international students: Required—TOEFL. Electronic applications accepted. *Faculty research:* Experimental, industrial-organizational, and engineering psychology; cognitive aging and processes; leadership; human factors.

Georgia Southern University, Jack N. Averitt College of Graduate Studies, College of Liberal Arts and Social Sciences, Department of Psychology, Statesboro, GA 30460. Offers MS, Psy D. *Students:* 25 full-time (14 women); includes 2 minority (both African Americans). Average age 25. 39 applicants, 74% accepted, 15 enrolled. In 2008, 14 master's awarded. *Degree requirements:* For master's, thesis (for some programs), terminal exam; for doctorate, practical internship. *Entrance requirements:* For master's, GRE General Test, minimum GPA of 3.0, introductory courses in psychology and statistics, letter of recommendation; for doctorate, minimum undergraduate GPA of 3.25; 3 letters of reference; statement of purpose. Additional exam requirements/recommendations for international students: Required—TOEFL (minimum score 550 paper-based; 213 computer-based; 80 iBT). *Application deadline:* For fall admission, 3/1 priority date for domestic students, 3/1 for international students. Applications are processed on a rolling basis. Application fee: $50. Electronic applications accepted. *Expenses:* Tuition, area resident: Full-time $3840; part-time $160 per semester hour. Tuition, state resident: full-time $3840; part-time $160 per semester hour. Tuition, nonresident: full-time $15,336; part-time $639 per semester hour. Required fees: $1152. *Financial support:* In 2008–09, 25 students received support, including research assistantships with partial tuition reimbursements available (averaging $6,850 per year), teaching assistantships with partial tuition reimbursements available (averaging $6,850 per year); career-related internships or fieldwork, Federal Work-Study, scholarships/grants, tuition waivers (partial), and unspecified assistantships also available. Support available to part-time students. Financial award application deadline: 4/15; financial award applicants required to submit FAFSA. *Faculty research:* Scholarship related to the teaching of psychology, psychology of religion, animal models of stress, reading and discourse processing, health and psychological response to illness. Total annual research expenditures: $50,396. *Unit head:* Dr. John Murray, Chair, 912-478-5539, Fax: 912-478-0751, E-mail: jmurray@kmccurdy@georgiasouthern.edu. *Application contact:* 912-478-5384, Fax: 912-478-0740, E-mail: gradadmissions@georgiasouthern.edu.

Georgia State University, College of Arts and Sciences, Department of Psychology, Atlanta, GA 30303-3083. Offers MA, PhD. *Accreditation:* APA (one or more programs are accredited). *Degree requirements:* For master's, thesis; for doctorate, comprehensive exam, thesis/dissertation. *Entrance requirements:* For doctorate, GRE General Test, departmental supplemental form. Additional exam requirements/recommendations for international students: Required—TOEFL. Electronic applications accepted. *Faculty research:* Social psychology, developmental and comparative psychology, neuropsychology, clinical psychology, neuropsychology.

Golden Gate University, Ageno School of Business, San Francisco, CA 94105-2968. Offers accounting (MBA); business administration (EMBA, MBA, DBA); finance (MBA, MS, Certificate); financial planning (MS, Certificate); human resource management (MBA, MS); human resources management (Certificate); information technology (MBA); information technology management (MS, Certificate); integrated marketing and communications (MS, Certificate); international business (MBA); management (MBA); marketing (MBA, MS, Certificate); operations management (Certificate); psychology (MA, Certificate); public relations (MS, Certificate); JD/MBA. Part-time and evening/weekend programs available. *Degree requirements:* For doctorate, thesis/dissertation. *Entrance requirements:* For master's, GMAT (MBA), minimum GPA of 2.5 (MS). Additional exam requirements/recommendations for international students: Required—TOEFL.

Governors State University, College of Education, Program in Psychology, University Park, IL 60466-0975. Offers MA. Part-time and evening/weekend programs available. *Degree requirements:* For master's, thesis or alternative, practicum. *Entrance requirements:* For master's, GRE or MAT.

Graduate School and University Center of the City University of New York, Graduate Studies, Program in Psychology, New York, NY 10016-4039. Offers basic applied neurocognition (PhD); biopsychology (PhD); clinical psychology (PhD); developmental psychology (PhD); environmental psychology (PhD); experimental psychology (PhD); industrial psychology (PhD); learning processes (PhD); neuropsychology (PhD); psychology (PhD); social personality (PhD). *Degree requirements:* For doctorate, one foreign language, thesis/dissertation. *Entrance requirements:* For doctorate, GRE General Test. Additional exam requirements/recommendations for international students: Required—TOEFL. Electronic applications accepted.

Hardin-Simmons University, Graduate School, Cynthia Ann Parker College of Liberal Arts, Department of Psychology, Abilene, TX 79698-0001. Offers family psychology (MA). Part-time programs available. *Faculty:* 5 full-time (1 woman). *Students:* 14 full-time (7 women), 8 part-time (6 women); includes 5 minority (2 African Americans, 3 Hispanic Americans). Average age 26. 12 applicants, 58% accepted, 7 enrolled. In 2008, 8 master's awarded. *Degree requirements:* For master's, comprehensive exam, clinical experience, project. *Entrance requirements:* For master's, 21 semester hours of course work in psychology (18 in upper division classes); minimum undergraduate GPA of 3.0 in major, 2.7 overall; writing sample; letters of recommendation. Additional exam requirements/recommendations for international students: Required—TOEFL (minimum score 550 paper-based; 213 computer-based; 75 iBT). *Application deadline:* For fall admission, 8/15 priority date for domestic students, 4/1 for international students; for spring admission, 1/5 priority date for domestic students, 9/1 for international students. Applications are processed on a rolling basis. Application fee: $50. *Expenses:* Tuition: Full-time $10,620; part-time $590 per credit hour. Required fees: $590; $110 per semester. Tuition and fees vary according to course load and degree level. *Financial support:* In 2008–09, 22 students received support, including 13 fellowships (averaging $1,154 per year); career-related internships or fieldwork and scholarships/grants also available. Support available to part-time students. Financial award application deadline: 6/30; financial award applicants required to submit FAFSA. *Faculty research:* Spirituality in marriage, intimacy and sexuality in marriage, sex education in the church, role of faith in marital satisfaction, family stress management. *Unit head:* Dr. Doug Thomas, Head, 325-670-1534, Fax: 325-670-1458, E-mail: dthomas@hsutx.edu. *Application contact:* Dr. Gary Stanlake, Dean of Graduate Studies, 325-670-1298, Fax: 325-670-1564, E-mail: gradoff@hsutx.edu.

Harvard University, Graduate School of Arts and Sciences, Department of Psychology, Cambridge, MA 02138. Offers psychology (PhD), including behavior and decision analysis, cognition, developmental psychology, experimental psychology, personality, psychobiology, psychopathology; social psychology (PhD). *Degree requirements:* For doctorate, thesis/dissertation, general exams. *Entrance requirements:* For doctorate, GRE General Test. Additional exam requirements/recommendations for international students: Required—TOEFL. *Expenses:* Tuition: Full-time $32,556. Required fees: $1426. Full-time tuition and fees vary according to program and student level.

Hodges University, Graduate Programs, Naples, FL 34119. Offers business administration (MBA); computer information technology (MS); criminal justice (MCJ); education (MPS); information systems management (MIS); interdisciplinary (MPS); law (MPS); management (MSM); professional studies (MPS); psychology (MPS); public administration (MPA). Part-time and evening/weekend programs available. Postbaccalaureate distance learning degree programs offered (no on-campus study). *Faculty:* 13 full-time (4 women), 3 part-time/adjunct (2 women). *Students:* 21 full-time (13 women), 210 part-time (138 women); includes 68 minority (33 African Americans, 2 Asian Americans or Pacific Islanders, 33 Hispanic Americans). Average age 36. In 2008, 82 master's awarded. *Degree requirements:* For master's, comprehensive exam (for some programs). *Entrance requirements:* For master's, in-house entrance exam. *Application deadline:* Applications are processed on a rolling basis. Application fee: $50. Electronic applications accepted. *Expenses:* Tuition: Full-time $16,200; part-time $600 per credit hour. Required fees: $570. *Financial support:* In 2008–09, 200 students received support. Federal Work-Study and scholarships/grants available. Financial award application deadline: 7/9; financial award applicants required to submit FAFSA. *Unit head:* Terry McMahan, President, 239-513-1122, Fax: 239-598-6253, E-mail: tmcmahan@hodges.edu. *Application contact:* Rita Lampus, Vice President of Student Enrollment Management, 239-513-1122, Fax: 239-598-6253, E-mail: rlampus@hodges.edu.

Hofstra University, College of Liberal Arts and Sciences, Department of Psychology, Hempstead, NY 11549. Offers applied organizational psychology (PhD); clinical psychology (MA, PhD); industrial/organizational psychology (MA); school-community psychology (MS, Psy D, CAS). Part-time and evening/weekend programs available. *Faculty:* 29 full-time (9 women), 13 part-time/adjunct (4 women). *Students:* 196 full-time (131 women), 35 part-time (20 women); includes 34 minority (12 African Americans, 15 Asian Americans or Pacific Islanders, 7 Hispanic Americans), 2 international. Average age 27. 345 applicants, 33% accepted, 56 enrolled. In 2008, 54 master's, 26 doctorates, 8 other advanced degrees awarded. Terminal master's awarded for partial completion of doctoral program. *Degree requirements:* For master's, comprehensive exam, thesis optional, internship; for doctorate, comprehensive exam, thesis/dissertation, oral defense, internship. *Entrance requirements:* For master's, GRE, interview, essay; for doctorate, GRE General Test, GRE Subject Test (psychology), letters of recommendation, interview, essay. Additional exam requirements/recommendations for international students: Required—TOEFL (minimum score 550 paper-based; 213 computer-based; 80 iBT). *Application deadline:* For fall admission, 1/15 priority date for domestic and international students. Application fee: $60. Electronic applications accepted. *Expenses:* Tuition: Full-time $15,300; part-time $850 per credit. Required fees: $970; $165 per term. Tuition and fees vary according to program. *Financial support:* In 2008–09, 155 students received support, including 80 fellowships with full and partial tuition reimbursements available (averaging $7,968 per year), 9 research assistantships with full and partial tuition reimbursements available (averaging $8,820 per year); career-related internships or fieldwork, Federal Work-Study, institutionally sponsored loans, scholarships/grants, tuition waivers (full and partial), and unspecified assistantships also available. Support available to part-time students. Financial award applicants required to submit FAFSA. *Faculty research:* Virtual reality treatment of phobias and trauma, school psychology, occupational health, performance management, treatment of anger. Total annual research expenditures: $130,000. *Unit head:* Dr. Charles Levinthal, Chairperson, 516-463-5627, Fax: 516-463-6052, E-mail: psycfl@hofstra.edu. *Application contact:* Carol Drummer, Dean of Graduate Admissions, 516-463-4876, Fax: 516-463-4664, E-mail: gradstudent@hofstra.edu.

Hood College, Graduate School, Programs in Human Sciences, Frederick, MD 21701-8575. Offers human sciences (MA), including psychology; thanatology (MA, Certificate). Part-time and evening/weekend programs available. *Faculty:* 5 full-time (2 women), 7 part-time/adjunct (4 women). *Students:* 19 full-time (all women), 89 part-time (77 women); includes 19 minority (15 African Americans, 1 American Indian/Alaska Native, 3 Asian Americans or Pacific Islanders), 2 international. Average age 35. 34 applicants, 85% accepted, 20 enrolled. In 2008, 30 master's, 16 other advanced degrees awarded. *Degree requirements:* For master's, comprehensive exam, capstone/research project. *Entrance requirements:* For master's, minimum GPA of 2.75. Additional exam requirements/recommendations for international students: Required—TOEFL (minimum score 575 paper-based; 231 computer-based; 89 iBT). *Application deadline:* For fall admission, 7/15 for domestic and international students; for spring admission, 12/15 for domestic and international students. Applications are processed on a rolling basis. Application fee: $35. Electronic applications accepted. *Expenses:* Tuition: Full-time $6480. Required fees: $100; $50 per semester. *Financial support:* Applicants required to submit FAFSA. *Faculty research:* Mind-body medicine and multicultural healing, the New Orleans jazz funeral, death practices in African-American culture, bereavement theories and gender differences, Piaget's theory of cognitive development as a formal mathematical model. *Unit head:* Dr. Dana G. Cable, Director, 301-696-3758, Fax: 301-696-3597, E-mail: cable@hood.edu. *Application contact:* Dr. Allen P. Flora, Dean of Graduate School, 301-696-3811, Fax: 301-696-3597, E-mail: gofurther@hood.edu.

Houston Baptist University, College of Education and Behavioral Sciences, Program in Psychology, Houston, TX 77074-3298. Offers MAP. Part-time and evening/weekend programs available. *Degree requirements:* For master's, comprehensive exam. *Entrance requirements:* For master's, GRE General Test, minimum GPA of 3.0. Additional exam requirements/recommendations for international students: Required—TOEFL (minimum score 550 paper-based; 213 computer-based).

Howard University, Graduate School, Department of Psychology, Washington, DC 20059-0002. Offers clinical psychology (PhD); developmental psychology (PhD); experimental psychology (PhD); neuropsychology (PhD); personality psychology (PhD); psychology (MS); social psychology (PhD). *Accreditation:* APA (one or more programs are accredited). Part-time programs available. *Degree requirements:* For master's, thesis; for doctorate, comprehensive exam, thesis/dissertation, qualifying exam. *Entrance requirements:* For master's, GRE General Test, minimum GPA of 2.5, bachelor's degree in psychology or related field; for doctorate, GRE General Test, minimum GPA of 3.0. *Faculty research:* Personality and psychophysiology, educational and social development of African-American children, child and adult psychopathology.

Humboldt State University, Graduate Studies, College of Natural Resources and Sciences, Department of Psychology, Arcata, CA 95521-8299. Offers psychology (MA), including academic research, counseling, school psychology. *Students:* 64 full-time (52 women), 6 part-time (3 women); includes 13 minority (1 African American, 3 American Indian/Alaska Native, 2 Asian Americans or Pacific Islanders, 7 Hispanic Americans), 1 international. Average age 29. 71 applicants, 45% accepted, 26 enrolled. In 2008, 12 master's awarded. *Degree requirements:* For master's, thesis. *Entrance requirements:* For master's, appropriate bachelor's degree, minimum GPA of 2.5. Additional exam requirements/recommendations for international students: Required—TOEFL (minimum score 500 paper-based; 173 computer-based). *Application deadline:* For fall admission, 2/15 for domestic and international students. Applications are processed on a rolling basis. Application fee: $55. *Expenses:* Tuition, state resident: full-time $5236. Tuition, nonresident: full-time $11,338. *Financial support:* Career-related internships or fieldwork available. Financial award application deadline: 3/1; financial award applicants required to submit FAFSA. *Faculty research:* School psychology, counseling, eating disorders, mood induction, depression. *Unit head:* Dr. Brent Duncan, Chair, 707-826-3755, Fax: 707-826-4993, E-mail: bbd1@humboldt.edu. *Application contact:* Dr. Brent Duncan, Administrative Support Coordinator, 707-826-3755, Fax: 707-826-4993, E-mail: bbd1@humboldt.edu.

Hunter College of the City University of New York, Graduate School, School of Arts and Sciences, Department of Psychology, New York, NY 10021-5085. Offers applied and evaluative psychology (MA); biopsychology and comparative psychology (MA); social, cognitive, and developmental psychology (MA). Part-time and evening/weekend programs available. *Faculty:* 15 full-time (7 women), 2 part-time/adjunct (0 women). *Students:* 9 full-time (8 women), 55 part-time (43 women); includes 9 minority (2 African Americans, 1 Asian American or Pacific Islander, 6 Hispanic Americans). Average age 29. 107 applicants, 42% accepted, 17 enrolled. In 2008, 29 master's awarded. *Degree requirements:* For master's, comprehensive exam, thesis. *Entrance requirements:* For master's, GRE General Test, minimum 12 credits of course work in psychology, including statistics and experimental psychology; 2 letters of recommendation. Additional exam requirements/recommendations for international students: Required—TOEFL. *Application deadline:* For fall admission, 4/1 for domestic students, 2/1 for international students; for spring admission, 11/1 for domestic students, 9/1 for international students. Applications are processed on a rolling basis. Application fee: $125. *Financial support:* Federal Work-Study, scholarships/grants, and tuition waivers (partial) available. Support available to part-time students. *Faculty research:* Personality, cognitive and linguistic development, hormonal and neural control of behavior, gender and culture, social cognition of health and attitudes. *Unit head:* Dr. Jeffrey Parsons, Chairperson, 212-772-5550, Fax: 212-772-5620, E-mail: jeffrey.parsons@hunter.cuny.edu. *Application contact:* Martin Braun, MA Program Director (Acting), 212-772-4482, Fax: 212-650-3336, E-mail: cbraun@hunter.cuny.edu.

Idaho State University, Office of Graduate Studies, College of Arts and Sciences, Department of Psychology, Pocatello, ID 83209. Offers clinical psychology (PhD); psychology (MS). *Accreditation:* APA (one or more programs are accredited). Part-time programs available. *Faculty:* 10 full-time (6 women). *Students:* 24 full-time (16 women), 13 part-time (12 women); includes 3 minority (1 Asian American or Pacific Islander, 2 Hispanic Americans). Average age 30. In 2008, 4 master's, 7 doctorates awarded. *Degree requirements:* For master's, comprehensive exam, thesis, active participation in the research process; for doctorate, comprehensive exam, thesis/dissertation, 1 year full-time clinical internship. *Entrance requirements:* For master's, GRE General Test, GRE Subject Test, BS in psychology, minimum GPA of 3.0 in last 2 years of undergraduate courses; for doctorate, GRE General Test, GRE Subject Test, MS in psychology, recommendation from Clinical Admissions Committee. Additional exam requirements/recommendations for international students: Required—TOEFL (minimum score 550 paper-based; 213 computer-based; 80 iBT). *Application deadline:* For fall admission, 7/1 for domestic students, 6/1 for international students; for spring admission, 12/1 for domestic students, 11/1 for international students. Applications are processed on a rolling basis. Application fee: $55. Electronic applications accepted. *Expenses:* Tuition, area resident: Full-time $3114; part-time $276 per credit hour. Tuition, state resident: full-time $3114; part-time $276 per credit hour. Tuition, nonresident: full-time $12,318; part-time $404 per credit hour. Required fees: $2360. Tuition and fees vary according to course load and reciprocity agreements. *Financial support:* In 2008–09, 15 teaching assistantships with full and partial tuition reimbursements (averaging $9,401 per year) were awarded; research assistantships with full and partial tuition reimbursements, career-related internships or fieldwork, Federal Work-Study, institutionally sponsored loans, scholarships/grants, traineeships, health care benefits, tuition waivers (full and partial), and unspecified assistantships also available. Support available to part-time students. Financial award application deadline: 1/1; financial award applicants required to submit FAFSA. *Faculty research:* Substance abuse, sexual decision making, trauma, behavioral pharmacology, developmental psychopathology, working memory and strategies, goal setting, person perception, developmental psychobiology, parent-child interactions. *Unit head:* Dr. Kandi Turley-Ames, Chairman, 208-282-2462, Fax: 208-282-4832, E-mail: turlkand@isu.edu. *Application contact:* Ellen Combs, Graduate School Technical Records Specialist, 208-282-2150, Fax: 208-282-4847, E-mail: combelle@isu.edu.

Illinois Institute of Technology, Graduate College, Institute of Psychology, Chicago, IL 60616-3793. Offers clinical psychology (PhD); industrial/organizational psychology (PhD); personnel/human resource development (MS); psychology (MS); rehabilitation counseling (MS); rehabilitation counselor education (PhD). *Accreditation:* APA (one or more programs are accredited); CORE. Evening/weekend programs available. *Faculty:* 19 full-time (8 women), 5 part-time/adjunct (all women). *Students:* 98 full-time (78 women), 94 part-time (69 women); includes 36 minority (10 African Americans, 16 Asian Americans or Pacific Islanders, 10 Hispanic Americans), 24 international. Average age 29. 301 applicants, 40% accepted, 54 enrolled. In 2008, 37 master's, 13 doctorates awarded. Terminal master's awarded for partial completion of doctoral program. *Degree requirements:* For master's, comprehensive exam, thesis (for some programs); for doctorate, comprehensive exam, thesis/dissertation, qualifying exams. *Entrance requirements:* For master's, GRE General Test, minimum GPA of 3.0; for doctorate, GRE General Test, minimum GPA of 3.2. Additional exam requirements/recommendations for international students: Required—TOEFL (minimum score 550 paper-based; 213 computer-based; 80 iBT). *Application deadline:* For fall admission, 1/15 for domestic and international students. Application fee: $40. Electronic applications accepted. *Financial support:* In 2008–09, 39 fellowships with partial tuition reimbursements (averaging $2,798 per year), 1 research assistantship with partial tuition reimbursement, 24 teaching assistantships with partial tuition reimbursements (averaging $4,405 per year) were awarded; career-related internships or fieldwork, Federal Work-Study, institutionally sponsored loans, scholarships/grants, traineeships, health care benefits, tuition waivers (partial), and unspecified assistantships also available. Support available to part-time students. Financial award applicants required to submit FAFSA. *Faculty research:* Stigma and mental illness, depression, couples communication, leadership, psychometric theory. Total annual research expenditures: $426,090. *Unit head:* Dr. M. Ellen Mitchell, Dean, 312-567-3362, Fax: 312-567-3493, E-mail: mitchelle@itt.edu. *Application contact:* Application Contact, 312-567-3500, Fax: 312-567-3493, E-mail: psychology@iit.edu.

Illinois State University, Graduate School, College of Arts and Sciences, Department of Psychology, Normal, IL 61790-2200. Offers psychology (MA, MS), including clinical psychology, counseling psychology, developmental psychology, educational psychology, experimental psychology, measurement-evaluation, organizational-industrial psychology; school psychology (PhD, SSP). *Accreditation:* APA. *Degree requirements:* For master's, thesis or alternative; for doctorate, variable foreign language requirement, thesis/dissertation, 2 terms of residency, internship, practicum. *Entrance requirements:* For master's, GRE General Test, GRE Subject Test, minimum GPA of 3.0 in last 60 hours of course work; for doctorate, GRE General Test. *Faculty research:* Comprehensive evaluation system for the central region professional development grant, Illinois school psychology internship consortium, for children's sake.

Immaculata University, College of Graduate Studies, Department of Psychology, Immaculata, PA 19345. Offers clinical psychology (Psy D); counseling psychology (MA, Certificate), including school guidance counselor (Certificate), school psychologist (Certificate). *Accreditation:* APA. Part-time and evening/weekend programs available. *Degree requirements:* For master's, comprehensive exam, thesis optional; for doctorate, comprehensive exam, thesis/dissertation. *Entrance requirements:* For master's, GRE General Test or MAT, minimum GPA of 3.0; for doctorate, GRE General Test, minimum GPA of 3.5. Additional exam requirements/recommendations for international students: Required—TOEFL, IELTS. *Faculty research:* Supervision ethics, psychology of teaching, gender.

Indiana State University, School of Graduate Studies, College of Arts and Sciences, Department of Psychology, Terre Haute, IN 47809-1401. Offers clinical psychology (Psy D); general psychology (MA, MS). *Accreditation:* APA (one or more programs are accredited). Terminal master's awarded for partial completion of doctoral program. *Degree requirements:* For master's, thesis (for some programs); for doctorate, comprehensive exam, thesis/dissertation, internship, professional research project. *Entrance requirements:* For master's, GRE General Test, 12 semester hours of course work in psychology, minimum GPA of 2.75; for doctorate, GRE General Test, minimum GPA of 3.0. Additional exam requirements/recommendations for international students: Required—TOEFL (minimum score 550 paper-based). Electronic applications accepted.

Indiana University Bloomington, University Graduate School, College of Arts and Sciences, Department of Criminal Justice, Bloomington, IN 47405. Offers criminal justice (MA, PhD); criminology (MA, PhD); cross-cultural perspectives of crime and justice (MA, PhD); law and society (MA, PhD); psychology and the law (MA). Part-time programs available. *Faculty:* 15 full-time (5 women). *Students:* 41 full-time (23 women), 1 (woman) part-time; includes 5 minority (2 African Americans, 2 American Indian/Alaska Native, 1 Hispanic American), 5 international. Average age 31. 22 applicants, 64% accepted, 6 enrolled. In 2008, 4 master's awarded. Terminal master's awarded for partial completion of doctoral program. *Degree requirements:* For master's, thesis optional; for doctorate, thesis/dissertation, foreign language or research practicum. *Entrance requirements:* For master's and doctorate, GRE General Test. Additional exam requirements/recommendations for international students: Required—TOEFL (minimum score 600 paper-based; 250 computer-based; 100 iBT). *Application deadline:* For fall admission, 1/15 for domestic students, 12/1 for international students. Application fee: $55 ($65 for international students). Electronic applications accepted. *Expenses:* Contact institution. *Financial support:* In 2008–09, 1 fellowship with full tuition reimbursement (averaging $25,000 per year), 2 research assistantships with full tuition reimbursements (averaging $11,721 per year), 24 teaching assistantships with full tuition reimbursements (averaging $11,721 per year) were awarded; Federal Work-Study, health care benefits, tuition waivers (full), and unspecified assistantships also available. Financial award application deadline: 1/15. *Faculty research:* Violence, crime, juveniles, psychology and law, cross-cultural studies. *Unit head:* Roger J.R. Levesque, JD, PhD, Chair, 812-856-1210, E-mail: rlevesqu@indiana.edu. *Application contact:* Ruth Cord, Graduate Secretary, 812-856-4675, Fax: 812-855-5522, E-mail: rkapusti@indiana.edu.

Indiana University Bloomington, University Graduate School, College of Arts and Sciences, Department of Psychological and Brain Sciences, Bloomington, IN 47405-7000. Offers biology and behavior (PhD); clinical science (PhD); cognitive psychology (PhD); developmental psychology (PhD); psychological and brain sciences (MA); social psychology (PhD). *Accreditation:* APA (one or more programs are accredited). *Faculty:* 53 full-time (16 women). *Students:* 95 full-time (52 women), 1 part-time (0 women); includes 11 minority (3 African Americans, 3 Asian Americans or Pacific Islanders, 5 Hispanic Americans), 18 international. Average age 28. 210 applicants, 15% accepted, 17 enrolled. In 2008, 1 master's, 10 doctorates awarded. *Degree requirements:* For doctorate, comprehensive exam, thesis/dissertation, 1st and 2nd year projects, 1 year as associate instructor, qualifying exam, student teaching. *Entrance requirements:* For doctorate, GRE. Additional exam requirements/recommendations for international students: Required—TOEFL (minimum score 550 paper-based; 213 computer-based). *Application deadline:* For fall admission, 12/15 for domestic students, 12/1 for international students. Application fee: $50 ($60 for international students). Electronic applications accepted. *Expenses:* Tuition, area resident: Part-time $291.97 per credit hour. Tuition, state resident: part-time $291.97 per credit hour. Tuition, nonresident: part-time $850.33 per credit hour. Required fees: $110 per semester. Tuition and fees vary according to course load and program. *Financial support:* Fellowships with full tuition reimbursements, research assistantships with full tuition reimbursements, teaching assistantships with full tuition reimbursements, scholarships/grants, health care benefits, and unspecified assistantships available. *Unit head:* Dr. Linda B. Smith, Chair, 812-855-3991, Fax: 812-855-4691, E-mail: smith4@indiana.edu. *Application contact:* Patricia G. Crouch, Academic Services Coordinator, 812-855-4528, Fax: 812-855-4691, E-mail: pcrouch@indiana.edu.

Psychology—General

Indiana University of Pennsylvania, School of Graduate Studies and Research, College of Natural Sciences and Mathematics, Department of Psychology, Indiana, PA 15705-1087. Offers clinical psychology (Psy D); psychology (MA). *Accreditation:* APA (one or more programs are accredited). Part-time programs available. *Faculty:* 15 full-time (8 women). *Students:* 43 full-time (37 women), 18 part-time (15 women); includes 3 minority (1 African American, 1 Asian American or Pacific Islander, 1 Hispanic American). Average age 27. 94 applicants, 12% accepted, 11 enrolled. In 2008, 8 master's, 15 doctorates awarded. Terminal master's awarded for partial completion of doctoral program. *Degree requirements:* For doctorate, comprehensive exam, thesis/dissertation, internship, practicum. *Entrance requirements:* For master's, GRE General Test; for doctorate, GRE General Test, minimum GPA of 3.0, interview, letters of recommendation. Additional exam requirements/recommendations for international students: Required—TOEFL. *Application deadline:* For fall admission, 1/10 for domestic students. Applications are processed on a rolling basis. Application fee: $30. *Expenses:* Tuition, area resident: Full-time $6430; part-time $357 per credit. Tuition, nonresident: full-time $10,288; part-time $572 per credit. Required fees: $1547.50; $107 per credit. $283 per year. *Financial support:* In 2008–09, 5 fellowships (averaging $2,200 per year), 41 research assistantships with full and partial tuition reimbursements (averaging $3,822 per year), 2 teaching assistantships (averaging $20,909 per year) were awarded; Federal Work-Study and scholarships/grants also available. Financial award application deadline: 3/15; financial award applicants required to submit FAFSA. *Unit head:* Dr. Mary Lou Zanich, Chairperson, 724-357-2426, E-mail: mtzanich@iup.edu. *Application contact:* Dr. Donald Robertson, Graduate Coordinator, 724-357-4522, E-mail: durobert@iup.edu.

Indiana University–Purdue University Indianapolis, School of Science, Department of Psychology, Indianapolis, IN 46202-3275. Offers clinical rehabilitation psychology (MS); industrial/organizational psychology (MS); psychobiology of addictions (MS, PhD). *Accreditation:* APA (one or more programs are accredited). Terminal master's awarded for partial completion of doctoral program. *Degree requirements:* For master's, thesis; for doctorate, thesis/dissertation. *Entrance requirements:* For master's, GRE General Test, minimum undergraduate GPA of 3.0; for doctorate, GRE General Test, GRE Subject Test (clinical rehabilitation psychology), minimum undergraduate GPA of 3.2. *Faculty research:* Psychiatric rehabilitation, chronic stress, neurological research, language and cognitive development in infants. alcoholism and psychopathology.

Indiana University South Bend, College of Liberal Arts and Sciences, South Bend, IN 46634-7111. Offers applied mathematics and computer science (MS); applied psychology (MA); English (MA); liberal studies (MLS). Part-time and evening/weekend programs available. *Degree requirements:* For master's, thesis (for some programs). *Entrance requirements:* For master's, minimum GPA of 3.0. Additional exam requirements/recommendations for international students: Required—TOEFL. *Faculty research:* Artificial intelligence, bioinformatics, English language and literature, creative writing, computer networks.

Institute of Transpersonal Psychology, Global Programs, Palo Alto, CA 94303. Offers psychology (PhD); transpersonal psychology (MTP); transpersonal studies (Certificate). Postbaccalaureate distance learning degree programs offered (minimal on-campus study). *Faculty:* 8 full-time (4 women), 27 part-time/adjunct (20 women). *Students:* 184 full-time (153 women), 25 part-time (21 women); includes 32 minority (11 African Americans, 2 American Indian/Alaska Native, 5 Asian Americans or Pacific Islanders, 14 Hispanic Americans), 15 international. Average age 43. 142 applicants, 83% accepted, 90 enrolled. In 2008, 19 master's, 8 doctorates awarded. Terminal master's awarded for partial completion of doctoral program. *Degree requirements:* For master's, thesis (for some programs); for doctorate, thesis/dissertation. *Entrance requirements:* For master's and doctorate, bachelor's degree. Additional exam requirements/recommendations for international students: Required—TOEFL. *Application deadline:* Applications are processed on a rolling basis. Application fee: $55. *Expenses:* Contact institution. *Financial support:* In 2008–09, 68 students received support. Federal Work-Study and scholarships/grants available. Support available to part-time students. Financial award application deadline: 6/30; financial award applicants required to submit FAFSA. *Unit head:* Dr. Paul Roy, Academic Vice President, 650-493-4430 Ext. 243, Fax: 650-493-6835, E-mail: proy@itp.edu. *Application contact:* Dawn Campagnola, Admissions Assistant, 650-493-4430 Ext. 240, Fax: 650-493-6835, E-mail: info@itp.edu.

Institute of Transpersonal Psychology, Residential Programs, Palo Alto, CA 94303. Offers clinical psychology (PhD); counseling psychology (MA); transpersonal psychology (MA, PhD); women's spirituality (PhD). Part-time and evening/weekend programs available. *Faculty:* 17 full-time (9 women), 31 part-time/adjunct (18 women). *Students:* 268 full-time (189 women), 40 part-time (31 women); includes 53 minority (9 African Americans, 3 American Indian/Alaska Native, 21 Asian Americans or Pacific Islanders, 20 Hispanic Americans), 14 international. Average age 38. 168 applicants, 52% accepted, 56 enrolled. In 2008, 47 master's, 16 doctorates awarded. Terminal master's awarded for partial completion of doctoral program. *Degree requirements:* For doctorate, thesis/dissertation. *Entrance requirements:* For master's and doctorate, bachelor's degree. *Application deadline:* For fall admission, 2/15 priority date for domestic students. Applications are processed on a rolling basis. Application fee: $55. *Expenses:* Tuition: Full-time $24,543; part-time $577 per unit. Tuition and fees vary according to degree level. *Financial support:* In 2008–09, 178 students received support; teaching assistantships, career-related internships or fieldwork, Federal Work-Study, and scholarships/grants available. Support available to part-time students. Financial award application deadline: 7/1; financial award applicants required to submit FAFSA. *Unit head:* Dr. Paul Roy, Academic Vice President, 650-493-4430 Ext. 243, Fax: 650-493-6835, E-mail: proy@itp.edu. *Application contact:* 650-493-4430 Ext. 16, Fax: 650-493-6835, E-mail: itpinfo@itp.edu.

Instituto Tecnologico de Santo Domingo, Graduate School, Santo Domingo, Dominican Republic. Offers applied linguistics (MA); corporate finance (M Mgmt); education (M Ed); engineering (M Eng), including data telecommunications, industrial engineering, sanitary and environmental engineering, structural engineering; environmental science (M En S), including environmental education, environmental management, marine and coastal ecosystems, natural resources management; human resources administration (M Mgmt); management (M Mgmt); psychology (MA); social science (M Ed). *Entrance requirements:* For master's, birth certificate, minimum GPA of 2.0.

Inter American University of Puerto Rico, Metropolitan Campus, Graduate Programs, Program in Psychology, San Juan, PR 00919-1293. Offers industrial/organizational psychology (MA, PhD); labor relations (MA); psychology (MA, PhD); school psychology (MA, PhD). *Degree requirements:* For master's, comprehensive exam. *Entrance requirements:* For master's, GRE or EXADEP, interview. Electronic applications accepted.

Inter American University of Puerto Rico, San Germán Campus, Graduate Studies Center, Program in Psychology, San Germán, PR 00683-5008. Offers counseling psychology (MA, PhD); school psychology (MA, PhD). Part-time and evening/weekend programs available. *Degree requirements:* For master's, comprehensive exam, thesis; for doctorate, comprehensive exam, thesis/dissertation. *Entrance requirements:* For master's, GRE General Test or EXADEP, minimum GPA of 3.0; for doctorate, GRE, EXADEP or MAT, minimum GPA of 3.0.

Iona College, School of Arts and Science, Department of Psychology, New Rochelle, NY 10801-1890. Offers experimental psychology (MA); industrial-organizational psychology (MA); mental health counseling (MA); psychology (MA); school psychology (MA). Part-time and evening/weekend programs available. *Faculty:* 11 full-time (5 women), 6 part-time/adjunct (3 women). *Students:* 71 full-time (54 women), 42 part-time (35 women); includes 26 minority (9 African Americans, 5 Asian Americans or Pacific Islanders, 12 Hispanic Americans), 1 international. Average age 25. 120 applicants, 73% accepted, 39 enrolled. In 2008, 19 master's awarded. *Degree requirements:* For master's, thesis. *Entrance requirements:* For master's, GRE or minimum GPA of 3.0. Additional exam requirements/recommendations for international students: Required—TOEFL (minimum score 550 paper-based; 213 computer-based). *Application deadline:* Applications are processed on a rolling basis. Application fee: $50. Electronic applications accepted. *Expenses:* Tuition: Part-time $755 per credit. Required fees: $175 per term. *Financial support:* Career-related internships or fieldwork, tuition waivers (partial), and unspecified assistantships available. Support available to part-time students. Financial award application deadline: 4/15; financial award applicants required to submit FAFSA. *Unit head:* Dr. Pauline Jirik-Babb, Chair, 914-633-2191, E-mail: pjirikbabb@iona.edu. *Application contact:* Veronica Jarek-Prinz, Director of Graduate Admissions, 914-633-2420, Fax: 914-633-2277, E-mail: vjarekprinz@iona.edu.

Iowa State University of Science and Technology, Graduate College, College of Liberal Arts and Sciences, Department of Psychology, Ames, IA 50011. Offers cognitive psychology (PhD); counseling psychology (PhD); social psychology (PhD). *Accreditation:* APA. *Faculty:* 25 full-time (8 women), 8 part-time/adjunct (4 women). *Students:* 63 full-time (43 women); includes 10 minority (3 African Americans, 7 Asian Americans or Pacific Islanders), 4 international. Average age 26. 117 applicants, 14% accepted, 11 enrolled. In 2008, 8 doctorates awarded. *Degree requirements:* For doctorate, comprehensive exam, thesis/dissertation. *Entrance requirements:* For doctorate, GRE General Test, GRE Subject Test (psychology). Additional exam requirements/recommendations for international students: Required—TOEFL (minimum score 560 paper-based; 220 computer-based). *Application deadline:* For fall admission, 1/5 priority date for domestic and international students. Application fee: $30 ($70 for international students). Electronic applications accepted. *Expenses:* Tuition, area resident: Full-time $6446; part-time $359 per credit. Tuition, state resident: full-time $6446; part-time $359 per credit. Tuition, nonresident: full-time $17,330; part-time $963 per credit. Required fees: $790; $249.25 per semester. Tuition and fees vary according to course load and program. *Financial support:* In 2008–09, 45 students received support, including 2 fellowships with full tuition reimbursements available (averaging $14,055 per year), 13 research assistantships with full tuition reimbursements available (averaging $12,200 per year), 30 teaching assistantships with full tuition reimbursements available (averaging $12,200 per year); scholarships/grants, health care benefits, and unspecified assistantships also available. *Faculty research:* Counseling psychology, cognitive psychology, social psychology, health psychology, psychology and public policy. Total annual research expenditures: $2 million. *Unit head:* Dr. Stephanie Madon, Director of Graduate Education, 515-294-1742, Fax: 515-294-6424, E-mail: madon@iastate.edu. *Application contact:* Ann K Schmidt, Graduate Admissions Secretary, 515-294-1743, Fax: 515-294-6424, E-mail: psychadm@iastate.edu.

Jackson State University, Graduate School, School of Liberal Arts, Department of Psychology, Jackson, MS 39217. Offers clinical psychology (PhD). *Accreditation:* APA. *Degree requirements:* For doctorate, comprehensive exam, thesis/dissertation. *Entrance requirements:* For doctorate, MAT, GRE.

Jacksonville State University, College of Graduate Studies and Continuing Education, College of Arts and Sciences, Department of Psychology, Jacksonville, AL 36265-1602. Offers MS. Part-time and evening/weekend programs available. *Faculty:* 5 full-time (2 women). *Students:* 32 full-time (23 women), 17 part-time (12 women); includes 15 minority (13 African Americans, 1 American Indian/Alaska Native, 1 Hispanic American), 3 international. Average age 29. 31 applicants, 48% accepted, 15 enrolled. In 2008, 8 master's awarded. *Degree requirements:* For master's, comprehensive exam, thesis (for some programs). *Entrance requirements:* For master's, GRE General Test or MAT. *Application deadline:* Applications are processed on a rolling basis. Application fee: $30. Electronic applications accepted. *Expenses:* Tuition, area resident: Full-time $4560; part-time $225 per credit hour. Tuition, state resident: full-time $4560; part-time $450 per credit hour. Tuition, nonresident: full-time $9120; part-time $450 per credit hour. *Financial support:* In 2008–09, 43 students received support. Available to part-time students. Application deadline: 4/1; *Unit head:* Dr. Steven Dworkin, Interim Department Head, 256-782-5804. *Application contact:* Dr. Jean Pugliese, Associate Dean, 256-782-8278, Fax: 256-782-5321, E-mail: pugliese@jsu.edu.

James Madison University, The Graduate School, College of Integrated Science and Technology, Department of Graduate Psychology, Harrisonburg, VA 22807. Offers assessment and measurement (PhD); college student personnel administration (M Ed); combined-integrated clinical and school psychology (PhD, Psy D); community counseling psychology (M Ed, MA, Ed S); psychological sciences (MA); school counseling (Ed S); school psychology (M Ed, MA, Ed S), including school counseling (M Ed, Ed S), school psychology (MA, Ed S). *Accreditation:* ACA (one or more programs are accredited); APA (one or more programs are accredited). Part-time and evening/weekend programs available. *Faculty:* 25 full-time (13 women), 17 part-time/adjunct (10 women). *Students:* 121 full-time (90 women), 53 part-time (44 women); includes 22 minority (17 African Americans, 4 Asian Americans or Pacific Islanders, 1 Hispanic American), 4 international. Average age 27. In 2008, 43 master's, 10 doctorates, 25 other advanced degrees awarded. *Degree requirements:* For doctorate, thesis/dissertation; for Ed S, thesis. *Entrance requirements:* For master's, GRE General Test, GRE Subject Test; for doctorate, GRE General Test. Additional exam requirements/recommendations for international students: Required—TOEFL. *Application deadline:* For fall admission, 2/1 priority date for domestic students; for spring admission, 9/1 for domestic students. Applications are processed on a rolling basis. Application fee: $55. Electronic applications accepted. *Expenses:* Tuition, area resident: Full-time $7008; part-time $292 per credit hour. Tuition, state resident: full-time $7008; part-time $292 per credit hour. Tuition, nonresident: full-time $20,352; part-time $848 per credit hour. *Financial support:* In 2008–09, 91 students received support, including 2 teaching assistantships with full tuition reimbursements available (averaging $8,664 per year); research assistantships, career-related internships or fieldwork, Federal Work-Study, and 21 doctoral ($14,500), 62 graduate assistantships ($7,382) also available. Financial award application deadline: 3/1; financial award applicants required to submit FAFSA. *Unit head:* Sheena J. Rogers, Academic Unit Head, 540-568-6439, Fax: 540-568-3322, E-mail: rogerssj@cisat.jmu.edu. *Application contact:* Sheena J. Rogers, Academic Unit Head, 540-568-6439, Fax: 540-568-3322, E-mail: rogerssj@cisat.jmu.edu.

John F. Kennedy University, Graduate School of Holistic Studies, Department of Integral Studies, Program in Integral Psychology, Pleasant Hill, CA 94523-4817. Offers dream studies (Certificate); integral psychology (MA); life coaching (Certificate). Part-time and evening/weekend programs available.

John F. Kennedy University, Graduate School of Professional Psychology, Pleasant Hill, CA 94523-4817. Offers MA, Psy D, Certificate. *Accreditation:* APA. Part-time and evening/weekend programs available. *Degree requirements:* For master's, thesis or alternative. *Entrance requirements:* For master's, interview. Additional exam requirements/recommendations for international students: Required—TOEFL.

The Johns Hopkins University, Zanvyl Krieger School of Arts and Sciences, Department of Psychological and Brain Sciences, Baltimore, MD 21218-2699. Offers PhD. *Degree requirements:* For doctorate, thesis/dissertation, research project, teaching experience. *Entrance requirements:* For doctorate, GRE General Test, GRE Subject Test. Additional exam requirements/recommendations for international students: Required—TOEFL. Electronic applications accepted. *Faculty research:* Biopsychology, cognitive psychology, cognitive neuroscience, developmental psychology, neurobiology.

Kansas State University, Graduate School, College of Arts and Sciences, Department of Psychology, Manhattan, KS 66506. Offers MS, PhD. Part-time programs available. *Faculty:* 13 full-time (3 women), 1 part-time/adjunct (0 women). *Students:* 36 full-time (23 women), 47 part-time (34 women); includes 12 minority (4 African Americans, 1 American Indian/Alaska Native, 1 Asian American or Pacific Islander, 6 Hispanic Americans), 5 international. Average age 29. 97 applicants, 25% accepted, 12 enrolled. In 2008, 24 master's, 8 doctorates awarded. *Degree requirements:* For master's, thesis or alternative; for doctorate, thesis/dissertation, preliminary exam. *Entrance requirements:* For master's, GRE General Test, minimum undergraduate GPA of 3.0; for doctorate, GRE General Test, minimum GPA of 3.0. Additional exam requirements/recommendations for international students: Required—TOEFL (minimum score 600 paper-based; 250 computer-based). *Application deadline:* For fall admission, 2/1 priority date for domestic and international students; for spring admission, 10/1 for domestic students, 8/1 priority date for international students. Applications are processed on a rolling basis. Application fee: $30 ($55 for international students). Electronic applications accepted. *Expenses:* Tuition, area resident: Full-time $6466; part-time $269.40 per credit hour. Tuition, state resident: full-time $6466; part-time $269.40 per credit hour. Tuition, nonresident: full-time $14,874; part-time $619.75 per credit hour. Required fees: $673; $23.40 per credit hour. Tuition and fees vary according to campus/location. *Financial support:* In 2008–09, 2 research assistantships (averaging $15,950 per year), 17 teaching assistantships with full tuition reimbursements (averaging $10,845 per year) were awarded; fellowships, career-related internships or fieldwork, institutionally sponsored loans, and scholarships/grants also available. Support available to part-time students. Financial award application deadline: 3/1; financial award applicants required to submit FAFSA. *Faculty research:* Personal and occupational health, neurological bases of drug use and abuse, measurement and reduction of prejudice, judgment and decision making, and visual perception. Total annual research expenditures: $218,217. *Unit head:* Jerry Frieman, Head, 785-532-0607, Fax: 785-532-5401, E-mail: frieman@ksu.edu. *Application contact:* Clive Fullagar, Director, 785-532-0608, Fax: 785-532-5401, E-mail: fullagar@ksu.edu.

Kean University, College of Humanities and Social Sciences, Program in Psychology, Union, NJ 07083. Offers human behavior and organizational psychology (MA); psychological services (MA). Part-time and evening/weekend programs available. *Faculty:* 18 full-time (13 women). *Students:* 13 full-time (10 women), 25 part-time (23 women); includes 7 African Americans, 1 Asian American or Pacific Islander, 3 Hispanic Americans, 1 international. Average age 28. 23 applicants, 65% accepted, 5 enrolled. In 2008, 23 master's awarded. *Degree requirements:* For master's, comprehensive exam, thesis, research. *Entrance requirements:* For master's, GRE General Test, 2 letters of recommendation, interview, prerequisite coursework in behavioral sciences, 12 credits in psychology. *Application deadline:* For fall admission, 5/1 for domestic students; for spring admission, 11/1 for domestic students. Application fee: $60 ($150 for international students). Electronic applications accepted. *Expenses:* Tuition, state resident: full-time $10,128; part-time $422 per credit. Tuition, nonresident: full-time $13,728; part-time $572 per credit. Required fees: $2570; $107 per credit. Part-time tuition and fees vary according to course load, degree level and program. *Financial support:* In 2008–09, 4 research assistantships with full tuition reimbursements (averaging $3,217 per year) were awarded; unspecified assistantships also available. *Unit head:* Dr. Joanne Walsh, Program Coordinator, 908-737-5870, E-mail: jwalsh@kean.edu. *Application contact:* Steven Koch, Pre-Admissions Coordinator, 908-737-4723, Fax: 908-737-5965, E-mail: grad-adm@kean.edu.

Kent State University, College of Arts and Sciences, Department of Psychology, Kent, OH 44242-0001. Offers clinical psychology (MA, PhD); experimental psychology (MA, PhD). *Accreditation:* APA (one or more programs are accredited). *Degree requirements:* For master's, thesis; for doctorate, thesis/dissertation. *Entrance requirements:* For master's, GRE, minimum GPA of 3.0, minimum 18 semester hours in psychology with one course in statistics and one experimental course with a lab component; for doctorate, GRE, minimum GPA of 3.0. Additional exam requirements/recommendations for international students: Required—TOEFL (minimum score 525 paper-based), Michigan English Language Assessment Battery (minimum score: 77).

Lakehead University, Graduate Studies, Department of Psychology, Thunder Bay, ON P7B 5E1, Canada. Offers clinical psychology (PhD); experimental psychology (MA). Part-time and evening/weekend programs available. *Degree requirements:* For master's, thesis optional; for doctorate, thesis/dissertation, 2 comprehensive exams, internship. *Entrance requirements:* For master's, GRE, honors degree in psychology, advanced course work in statistics, minimum B average; for doctorate, GRE, minimum B average. Additional exam requirements/recommendations for international students: Required—TOEFL. Tuition charges are reported in Canadian dollars. *Expenses:* Tuition, area resident: Full-time $6500 Canadian dollars. International tuition: $13,700 Canadian dollars full-time. *Faculty research:* Chaos theory, health psychology, counseling psychology, gerontology, women's studies.

Lamar University, College of Graduate Studies, College of Arts and Sciences, Department of Psychology, Beaumont, TX 77710. Offers community/clinical psychology (MS); industrial/organizational psychology (MS). Part-time programs available. *Faculty:* 7 full-time (4 women). *Students:* 21 full-time (10 women), 5 part-time (3 women); includes 4 minority (1 African American, 3 Hispanic Americans), 2 international. Average age 25. 32 applicants, 41% accepted, 10 enrolled. In 2008, 6 master's awarded. *Degree requirements:* For master's, thesis, practicum. *Entrance requirements:* For master's, GRE General Test, minimum GPA of 2.75 in last 60 hours of undergraduate course work. Additional exam requirements/recommendations for international students: Required—TOEFL. *Application deadline:* For fall admission, 8/1 for domestic students; for spring admission, 12/1 for domestic students. Application fee: $25 ($50 for international students). *Expenses:* Tuition, state resident: full-time $5000; part-time $195 per credit. Tuition, nonresident: full-time $12,376; part-time $476 per credit. Required fees: $1570. *Financial support:* In 2008–09, 12 students received support, including 3 teaching assistantships (averaging $4,500 per year); fellowships, research assistantships, career-related internships or fieldwork, Federal Work-Study, scholarships/grants, and tuition waivers (partial) also available. Support available to part-time students. Financial award application deadline: 4/1. *Faculty research:* Groupthink, health psychology, school psychology, behavioral neuroscience. *Unit head:* Dr. Oney D. Fitzpatrick, Chair, 409-880-8285, Fax: 409-880-1779, E-mail: fitzpatrod@hal.lamar.edu. *Application contact:* Dr. James W. Westgate, Assistant Dean, 409-880-7978, E-mail: westgate@hal.lamar.edu.

La Salle University, School of Arts and Sciences, Program in Psychology, Philadelphia, PA 19141-1199. Offers clinical psychology (Psy D); family psychology (Psy D); rehabilitation psychology (Psy D). Part-time and evening/weekend programs available. *Entrance requirements:* For doctorate, GRE, minimum GPA of 3.0. *Expenses:* Contact institution. *Faculty research:* Cognitive therapy, attribution theory, treatment of addiction.

Laurentian University, School of Graduate Studies and Research, Programme in Psychology, Sudbury, ON P3E 2C6, Canada. Offers applied psychology (MA); experimental psychology (MA).

Leadership Institute of Seattle, School of Applied Behavioral Science, Kenmore, WA 98028-4966. Offers consulting and coaching in organizations (MA); systems counseling (MA). *Degree requirements:* For master's, thesis (for some programs), oral exams. *Entrance requirements:* For master's, bachelor's degree from an accredited university or college.

Lehigh University, College of Arts and Sciences, Department of Psychology, Bethlehem, PA 18015-3094. Offers human cognition and development (MS, PhD). *Faculty:* 12 full-time (7 women). *Students:* 14 full-time (11 women), 4 international. Average age 26. 68 applicants, 4% accepted, 1 enrolled. In 2008, 5 master's, 1 doctorate awarded. *Degree requirements:* For master's, thesis; for doctorate, comprehensive exam, thesis/dissertation. *Entrance requirements:* For doctorate, GRE General Test. Additional exam requirements/recommendations for international students: Required—TOEFL. *Application deadline:* For fall admission, 1/15 for domestic and international students. Application fee: $65. Electronic applications accepted. *Expenses:* Contact institution. *Financial support:* In 2008–09, 11 students received support, including 1 fellowship with full tuition reimbursement available (averaging $20,000 per year), 2 research assistantships with full tuition reimbursements available (averaging $16,900 per year), 11 teaching assistantships with full tuition reimbursements available (averaging $16,900 per year); scholarships/grants, tuition waivers (full and partial), and unspecified assistantships also available. Financial award application deadline: 1/15. *Faculty research:* Social-cognitive developmental psychology, cognition and language, social cognition and personality. Total annual research expenditures: $206,022. *Unit head:* Diane Hyland, Chairperson, 610-758-3631, Fax: 610-758-6277, E-mail: dthl@lehigh.edu. *Application contact:* Dr. Michael Gill, Program Director, 610-758-3630, Fax: 610-758-6277, E-mail: inpsy@lehigh.edu.

Lesley University, Graduate School of Arts and Social Sciences, Cambridge, MA 02138-2790. Offers clinical mental health counseling (MA), including expressive therapies counseling, holistic counseling, school and community counseling; counseling psychology (MA, CAGS), including professional counseling (MA), school counseling (MA); creative arts in learning (CAGS); creative writing (MFA); ecological teaching and learning (MS); environmental education (MS); expressive therapies (MA, PhD, CAGS), including art (MA), dance (MA), expressive therapies, music (MA); independent studies (CAGS); independent study (MA); intercultural relations (MA, CAGS); interdisciplinary studies (MA), including individualized studies, integrative holistic health, women's studies; urban environmental leadership (MA); visual arts (MFA). Part-time and evening/weekend programs available. Postbaccalaureate distance learning degree programs offered (minimal on-campus study). *Degree requirements:* For master's, internship, practicum, thesis (expressive therapies); for doctorate, thesis/dissertation, arts apprenticeship, field placement; for CAGS, thesis, internship (counseling psychology, expressive therapies). *Entrance requirements:* For master's, MAT (counseling psychology), interview, writing samples, art portfolio; for doctorate, GRE or MAT; for CAGS, interview, master's degree. Additional exam requirements/recommendations for international students: Required—TOEFL (minimum score 550 paper-based; 213 computer-based; 80 iBT). Electronic applications accepted. *Expenses:* Tuition: Full-time $13,770; part-time $765 per credit hour. Required fees: $150. Tuition and fees vary according to course load, degree level, campus/location and program. *Faculty research:* Psychotherapy and culture; psychotherapy and psychological trauma; women's issues in art, teaching and psychotherapy; community based art, psycho-spiritual inquiry.

Lewis & Clark College, Graduate School of Education and Counseling, Department of Counseling Psychology, Portland, OR 97219-7899. Offers addictions treatment (MA); counseling psychology (MA, MS); marriage, couple and family therapy (MA); psychological and cultural studies (MA); school psychology (MS, Ed S). Part-time and evening/weekend programs available. *Degree requirements:* For master's, thesis proposal (MS). *Entrance requirements:* For master's, GRE General Test, minimum undergraduate GPA of 2.75. Additional exam requirements/recommendations for international students: Required—TOEFL (minimum score 575 paper-based; 233 computer-based). Electronic applications accepted. *Faculty research:* Treatment of depression, substance abuse, child-family problems, health psychology, marital relations.

Lipscomb University, Program in Counseling, Nashville, TN 37204-3951. Offers counseling psychology (Certificate); professional counseling (MS); psychology (MS). Part-time and evening/weekend programs available. Postbaccalaureate distance learning degree programs offered (minimal on-campus study). *Entrance requirements:* For master's, GRE, resumé, 3 reference letters, minimum GPA of 3.0. Electronic applications accepted. *Faculty research:* Cognitive psychology, neuroscience, health psychology, grief issues.

Loma Linda University, School of Science and Technology, Department of Psychology, Loma Linda, CA 92350. Offers PhD, Psy D. *Accreditation:* APA. *Degree requirements:* For doctorate, comprehensive exam, thesis/dissertation. *Entrance requirements:* For doctorate, GRE General Test. Additional exam requirements/recommendations for international students: Required—TOEFL (minimum score 550 paper-based; 213 computer-based), MTELP. Electronic applications accepted.

Long Island University, Brooklyn Campus, Richard L. Conolly College of Liberal Arts and Sciences, Department of Psychology, Brooklyn, NY 11201-8423. Offers clinical psychology (PhD); psychology (MA). *Accreditation:* APA (one or more programs are accredited). Part-time and evening/weekend programs available. Terminal master's awarded for partial completion of doctoral program. *Degree requirements:* For master's, thesis or alternative; for doctorate, thesis/dissertation. *Entrance requirements:* For master's, GRE Subject Test, GRE General Test, 2 letters of recommendation; for doctorate, GRE Subject Test, GRE General Test. Additional exam requirements/recommendations for international students: Required—TOEFL (minimum score 500 paper-based; 173 computer-based). Electronic applications accepted.

Long Island University, C.W. Post Campus, College of Liberal Arts and Sciences, Department of Psychology, Brookville, NY 11548-1300. Offers clinical psychology (Psy D); psychology (MA). *Accreditation:* APA. Part-time programs available. *Degree requirements:* For master's, thesis; for doctorate, thesis/dissertation, internship. *Entrance requirements:* For master's, GRE General Test, GRE Subject Test, minimum GPA of 3.0 in psychology, 2.8 overall; for doctorate, GRE General Test, GRE Subject Test, bachelor's degree in psychology, minimum GPA of 3.25. Electronic applications accepted. *Faculty research:* Visual perception, animal learning, attachment, neuropsychology, developmental disabilities, severe mental illness.

Loras College, Graduate Division, Program in Applied Psychology, Dubuque, IA 52004-0178. Offers MA. Part-time and evening/weekend programs available. *Degree requirements:* For master's, comprehensive exam, thesis (for some programs). *Entrance requirements:* For master's, Ohio State University Psychological Test or GRE General Test, minimum undergraduate GPA of 2.75.

Louisiana State University and Agricultural and Mechanical College, Graduate School, College of Arts and Sciences, Department of Psychology, Baton Rouge, LA 70803. Offers biological psychology (MA, PhD); clinical psychology (MA, PhD); cognitive psychology (MA, PhD); developmental psychology (MA, PhD); industrial/organizational psychology (MA, PhD); school psychology (MA, PhD). *Accreditation:* APA (one or more programs are accredited). Terminal master's awarded for partial completion of doctoral program. *Degree requirements:* For master's, thesis; for doctorate, thesis/dissertation, 1 year internship. *Entrance requirements:* For master's and doctorate, GRE General Test, minimum GPA of 3.0. Additional exam requirements/recommendations for international students: Required—TOEFL (minimum score 550 paper-based; 213 computer-based; 79 iBT). Electronic applications accepted. *Faculty research:* Clinical psychology, autism, anxiety, addition, neuro-psychology, school psychology, cognitive psychology, experimental psychology.

Louisiana Tech University, Graduate School, College of Education, Department of Behavioral Sciences and Psychology, Ruston, LA 71272. Offers counseling (MA); counseling psychology (PhD); industrial/organizational psychology (MA); special education (MA). *Accreditation:* APA (one or more programs are accredited). Part-time programs available. *Degree requirements:* For master's, thesis or alternative; for doctorate, thesis/dissertation. *Entrance requirements:* For master's and doctorate, GRE General Test.

Loyola University Chicago, Graduate School, Department of Psychology, Chicago, IL 60611-2196. Offers applied social psychology (MA, PhD); clinical psychology (MA, PhD); developmental psychology (MA, PhD); human perception (MS). *Accreditation:* APA (one or more programs are accredited). *Faculty:* 27 full-time (12 women), 1 part-time/adjunct (0 women). *Students:* 81 full-time (65 women), 7 part-time (all women); includes 13 minority (5 African Americans, 1 American Indian/Alaska Native, 3 Asian Americans or Pacific Islanders, 4 Hispanic Americans), 5 international. Average age 28. 380 applicants, 6% accepted, 15 enrolled. In 2008, 16 master's, 10 doctorates awarded. Terminal master's awarded for partial completion of doctoral program. *Degree requirements:* For master's, comprehensive exam, thesis; for doctorate, comprehensive exam, thesis/dissertation. *Entrance requirements:* For master's and doctorate, GRE General Test, GRE Subject Test. Application fee: $50. Electronic applications accepted. *Expenses:* Tuition: Full-time $13,500; part-time $750 per credit hour. Required fees: $60 per semester. Full-time tuition and fees vary according to program. *Financial support:* In 2008–09, 7 fellowships with full tuition reimbursements (averaging $12,000 per year), 24 research assistantships with full tuition reimbursements (averaging $12,000 per year), 10 teaching assistantships with full tuition reimbursements (averaging $12,000 per year) were awarded; career-related internships or fieldwork, Federal Work-Study, scholarships/grants, and traineeships also available. Financial award applicants required to submit FAFSA. *Faculty research:* Cognitive development, hearing and vision, attitude and prejudice, child and family, AIDS and health promotion. Total annual research expenditures: $2.5 million. *Unit head:* Dr. R. Scott Tindale, Chair, 773-508-3014, E-mail: rtindal@luc.edu. *Application contact:* Ron Martin, Assistant Director of Enrollment Management, 312-915-8950, Fax: 312-915-8905, E-mail: gradapp@luc.edu.

Loyola University Maryland, Graduate Programs, College of Arts and Sciences, Department of Psychology, Baltimore, MD 21210-2699. Offers clinical psychology (MS, Psy D, CAS);

Psychology—General

Loyola University Maryland (continued)

counseling psychology (MS, CAS). *Accreditation:* APA. Part-time and evening/weekend programs available. *Faculty:* 47 full-time (25 women), 29 part-time/adjunct (16 women). *Students:* 140 full-time (117 women), 94 part-time (80 women); includes 36 minority (20 African Americans, 1 American Indian/Alaska Native, 9 Asian Americans or Pacific Islanders, 6 Hispanic Americans). Average age 29. In 2008, 60 master's, 11 doctorates, 1 other advanced degree awarded. *Entrance requirements:* For master's, doctorate, and CAS, GRE General Test, GRE Subject Test (recommended). Additional exam requirements/recommendations for international students: Required—TOEFL (minimum score 550 paper-based; 213 computer-based). *Application deadline:* Applications are processed on a rolling basis. Application fee: $50. *Financial support:* Research assistantships available. Financial award applicants required to submit FAFSA. *Unit head:* Dr. Amanda Thomas, Associate Dean, 410-617-5590. *Application contact:* Maureen Faux, Interim Director, Graduate Admissions, 410-617-5020, Fax: 410-617-2002, E-mail: graduate@loyola.edu.

See Close-Up on page 1119.

Lynn University, College of Arts and Sciences, Boca Raton, FL 33431-5598. Offers applied psychology (MS); criminal justice administration (MS); emergency planning and administration (MS, Certificate). Part-time and evening/weekend programs available. Postbaccalaureate distance learning degree programs offered. *Entrance requirements:* For master's, GRE, resumé, 2 letters of recommendation, minimum undergraduate GPA of 3.0. Additional exam requirements/recommendations for international students: Required—TOEFL (minimum score 550 paper-based; 213 computer-based). *Faculty research:* Terrorism, criminological theory, corrections, emergency planning.

Madonna University, Department of Psychology, Livonia, MI 48150-1173. Offers clinical psychology (MSCP). Part-time and evening/weekend programs available. *Degree requirements:* For master's, thesis or alternative. *Entrance requirements:* Additional exam requirements/recommendations for international students: Required—TOEFL. Electronic applications accepted.

Marietta College, Program in Psychology, Marietta, OH 45750-4000. Offers MAP. *Faculty:* 3 full-time (1 woman). *Students:* 10 full-time (8 women), 9 part-time (7 women). Average age 22. *Unit head:* Dr. Mark E. Sibicky, Chair, 740-376-4762, E-mail: sibickym@marietta.edu. *Application contact:* Cathy J. Brown, Director of Graduate and Continuing Studies, 740-376-4740, Fax: 740-376-4423, E-mail: ce@marietta.edu.

Marist College, Graduate Programs, School of Social and Behavioral Sciences, Poughkeepsie, NY 12601-1387. Offers counseling psychology (MA); education (M Ed); education psychology (MA); school psychology (MA, Adv C). Part-time and evening/weekend programs available. *Degree requirements:* For master's, thesis optional. *Entrance requirements:* For master's, GRE General Test, letters of recommendation, minimum undergraduate GPA of 3.0, interview, essay, official transcript. Additional exam requirements/recommendations for international students: Required—TOEFL (minimum score 550 paper-based; 213 computer-based; 80 iBT); Recommended—IELTS (minimum score 6.5). Electronic applications accepted. *Faculty research:* AIDS prevention, educational intervention, humanistic counseling research, aging and development, neuroimaging.

Marquette University, Graduate School, College of Arts and Sciences, Department of Psychology, Milwaukee, WI 53201-1881. Offers clinical psychology (MS); psychology (PhD). *Accreditation:* APA. Part-time programs available. *Degree requirements:* For master's, comprehensive exam, thesis or alternative; for doctorate, thesis/dissertation, internship, qualifying exam. *Entrance requirements:* For master's, GRE General Test, GRE Subject Test, MAT; for doctorate, GRE General Test, GRE Subject Test, sample of scholarly writing. Additional exam requirements/recommendations for international students: Required—TOEFL. *Faculty research:* Mental imagery, moral development, organizational behavior, depression, psychotherapy outcomes.

Marshall University, Academic Affairs Division, College of Liberal Arts, Department of Psychology, Huntington, WV 25755. Offers clinical psychology (MA); general psychology (MA); industrial and organizational psychology (MA); psychology (Psy D). *Accreditation:* APA. *Degree requirements:* For master's, thesis optional. *Entrance requirements:* For master's, GRE General Test or MAT.

Martin University, Division of Psychology, Indianapolis, IN 46218-3867. Offers community psychology (MS). Part-time and evening/weekend programs available. *Degree requirements:* For master's, thesis. *Entrance requirements:* For master's, GRE General Test, GRE Subject Test.

Marywood University, Academic Affairs, College of Education and Human Development, Department of Psychology and Counseling, Program in Psychology, Scranton, PA 18509-1598. Offers child/clinical school psychology (MA); clinical services (MA); general theoretical psychology (MA). Part-time and evening/weekend programs available. *Degree requirements:* For master's, comprehensive exam, thesis or alternative, internship/practicum. *Entrance requirements:* For master's, GRE or MAT. Additional exam requirements/recommendations for international students: Required—TOEFL (minimum score 550 paper-based; 213 computer-based). Electronic applications accepted. *Faculty research:* Personality disorders, counselor training, preschool development, self-esteem measurement, family dynamics.

Massachusetts School of Professional Psychology, Graduate Programs, Boston, MA 02132. Offers clinical psychology (Psy D); clinical psychopharmacology (Post-Doctoral MS); counseling psychology (MA); executive coaching (Graduate Certificate); forensic psychology (MA); organizational psychology (MA); respecialization in clinical psychology (Certificate); MA/CAGS. *Accreditation:* APA. *Degree requirements:* For master's, comprehensive exam; for doctorate, thesis/dissertation. *Entrance requirements:* For doctorate, GRE General Test. Additional exam requirements/recommendations for international students: Required—TOEFL (minimum score 550 paper-based; 213 computer-based). Electronic applications accepted.

McGill University, Faculty of Graduate and Postdoctoral Studies, Faculty of Medicine, Department of Psychiatry, Montréal, QC H3A 2T5, Canada. Offers M Sc.

McGill University, Faculty of Graduate and Postdoctoral Studies, Faculty of Science, Department of Psychology, Montréal, QC H3A 2T5, Canada. Offers clinical psychology (PhD); experimental psychology (M Sc, MA, PhD). *Accreditation:* APA (one or more programs are accredited).

McMaster University, School of Graduate Studies, Faculty of Science, Department of Psychology, Hamilton, ON L8S 4M2, Canada. Offers M Sc, PhD. *Degree requirements:* For doctorate, comprehensive exam, thesis/dissertation. *Entrance requirements:* For doctorate, GRE General Test, honors degree, minimum B+ average. Additional exam requirements/recommendations for international students: Required—TOEFL (minimum score 550 paper-based; 213 computer-based).

McNeese State University, Doré School of Graduate Studies, Burton College of Education, Department of Psychology, Lake Charles, LA 70609. Offers addiction treatment (MA); applied behavior analysis (MA); counseling psychology (MA); general/experimental psychology (MA). Evening/weekend programs available. *Faculty:* 6 full-time (3 women), 1 (woman) part-time/adjunct. *Students:* 40 full-time (27 women), 23 part-time (17 women); includes 8 minority (7 African Americans, 1 Asian American or Pacific Islander), 4 international. In 2008, 12 master's awarded. *Entrance requirements:* For master's, GRE. *Application deadline:* For fall admission, 5/15 priority date for domestic and international students; for spring admission, 10/15 priority date for domestic and international students. Applications are processed on a rolling basis. Application fee: $20 ($30 for international students). *Expenses:* Tuition, area resident: Full-time $2386. Tuition, state resident: full-time $2386. Required fees: $885. Tuition and fees vary according to course load. *Financial support:* Application deadline: 5/1. *Unit head:* Dr. Dena L. Matzenbacher, Head, 337-475-5457, Fax: 337-562-4115, E-mail: dena@mcneese.edu. *Application contact:* Dr. George F. Mead, Interim Dean of Dore' School of Graduate Studies, 337-475-5396, Fax: 337-475-5397, E-mail: admissions@mcneese.edu.

Medaille College, Programs in Psychology, Buffalo, NY 14214-2695. Offers mental health counseling (MA); psychology (MA). Part-time and evening/weekend programs available. *Faculty:* 6 full-time (3 women), 10 part-time/adjunct (8 women). *Students:* 148 full-time (118 women); includes 30 minority (29 African Americans, 1 Hispanic American). Average age 34. 85 applicants, 94% accepted, 75 enrolled. In 2008, 37 master's awarded. *Degree requirements:* For master's, comprehensive exam (for some programs), thesis (for some programs). *Entrance requirements:* For master's, GRE General Test (psychology), minimum GPA of 2.75 (psychology). Additional exam requirements/recommendations for international students: Required—TOEFL (minimum score 550 paper-based; 213 computer-based). *Application deadline:* Applications are processed on a rolling basis. Application fee: $35. Electronic applications accepted. *Expenses:* Tuition: Full-time $15,480; part-time $645 per credit hour. *Financial support:* In 2008–09, 90 students received support. Federal Work-Study available. Financial award applicants required to submit FAFSA. *Faculty research:* Schizophrenia, Parkinson's Disease, eyewitness testimony, methodology. *Unit head:* Dr. Judith Horowitz, Dean of Adult and Graduate Studies, 716-880-2229, Fax: 716-884-0291, E-mail: jhorowitz@medaille.edu. *Application contact:* Jacqueline Matheny, Executive Director of Marketing and Enrollment, 716-932-2541, Fax: 716-632-1811, E-mail: jmatheny@medaille.edu.

Memorial University of Newfoundland, School of Graduate Studies, Department of Psychology, St. John's, NL A1C 5S7, Canada. Offers applied social psychology (MASP); experimental psychology (M Sc, PhD). Part-time programs available. *Degree requirements:* For master's, workterms (MASP), thesis (M Sc); for doctorate, comprehensive exam, thesis/dissertation, oral thesis defense. *Entrance requirements:* For master's, GRE, honors bachelor's degree of high second class standing or equivalent; for doctorate, GRE, master's or honors degree. Electronic applications accepted. *Faculty research:* Behavioral neuroscience, cognition, theory and research on abnormal behavior.

Mercy College, School of Social and Behavioral Sciences, Program in Psychology, Dobbs Ferry, NY 10522-1189. Offers psychology (MS); school psychology (MS). Part-time and evening/weekend programs available. Postbaccalaureate distance learning degree programs offered (minimal on-campus study). *Students:* 11 full-time (9 women), 15 part-time (10 women); includes 13 minority (7 African Americans, 1 American Indian/Alaska Native, 5 Hispanic Americans), 1 international. Average age 33. 34 applicants, 47% accepted, 10 enrolled. In 2008, 5 master's awarded. *Degree requirements:* For master's, completion of written comprehensive exam or six-credit thesis. *Entrance requirements:* For master's, BA in psychology, sociology, behavioral science or education; interview; letters of recommendation; minimum GPA of 3.0; resumé; 3- to 5-page essay stating reason for pursuing master's degree in psychology. Additional exam requirements/recommendations for international students: Required—TOEFL (minimum score 600 paper-based; 250 computer-based; 100 iBT). *Application deadline:* For fall admission, 8/1 for international students. Applications are processed on a rolling basis. Application fee: $40. Electronic applications accepted. *Expenses:* Tuition: Full-time $12,330; part-time $685 per credit. Required fees: $240; $120 per semester. Tuition and fees vary according to program. *Financial support:* In 2008–09, 6 students received support. Career-related internships or fieldwork, Federal Work-Study, scholarships/grants, and unspecified assistantships available. Support available to part-time students. Financial award applicants required to submit FAFSA. *Unit head:* Dr. Barbara Melamed, Program Director, 914-674-7345, E-mail: bmelamed@mercy.edu. *Application contact:* Dr. Barbara Melamed, Program Director, 914-674-7345, E-mail: bmelamed@mercy.edu.

Metropolitan State University, College of Professional Studies, St. Paul, MN 55106-5000. Offers psychology (MA). Part-time and evening/weekend programs available. *Degree requirements:* For master's, thesis. *Entrance requirements:* For master's, transcripts, resumée, letters of reference, BA, 3.0 GPA. Additional exam requirements/recommendations for international students: Required—TOEFL (minimum score 550 paper-based; 213 computer-based).

Miami University, Graduate School, College of Arts and Sciences, Department of Psychology, Oxford, OH 45056. Offers clinical psychology (PhD); experimental psychology (PhD); social psychology (PhD). *Accreditation:* APA. *Degree requirements:* For doctorate, comprehensive exam, thesis/dissertation, final exams. *Entrance requirements:* For doctorate, GRE General Test, GRE Subject Test, minimum GPA of 2.75 (undergraduate), 3.0 (graduate). Additional exam requirements/recommendations for international students: Required—TOEFL (minimum score 550 paper-based; 213 computer-based), TWE (minimum score 4). Electronic applications accepted.

Michigan School of Professional Psychology, Programs in Humanistic and Clinical Psychology, Farmington Hills, MI 48334. Offers humanistic and clinical psychology (MA, Psy D). *Degree requirements:* For master's, thesis, practicum; for doctorate, thesis/dissertation, internship, practicum. *Entrance requirements:* For master's, 1 year of work experience, interview, minimum GPA of 3.0, curriculum vitae, personal essay, Bachelor's completion; for doctorate, 3 years of work experience, 2 interviews, minimum graduate GPA of 3.0, scholarly writing sample, curriculum vitae, personal essay, MA degree completion. Additional exam requirements/recommendations for international students: Required—TOEFL. Electronic applications accepted. *Faculty research:* Qualitative research, existential-phenomenological psychology, applications to clinical practice.

Michigan State University, The Graduate School, College of Social Science, Department of Psychology, East Lansing, MI 48824. Offers MA, PhD. *Accreditation:* APA (one or more programs are accredited). *Entrance requirements:* Additional exam requirements/recommendations for international students: Required—TOEFL (minimum score 550 paper-based; 213 computer-based), Michigan State University ELT (85), Michigan ELAB (83). Electronic applications accepted.

Middle Tennessee State University, College of Graduate Studies, College of Education and Behavioral Science, Department of Psychology, Program in Psychology, Murfreesboro, TN 37132. Offers MA. Part-time and evening/weekend programs available. Postbaccalaureate distance learning degree programs offered. *Degree requirements:* For master's, one foreign language, comprehensive exam, thesis. *Entrance requirements:* For master's, GRE. Additional exam requirements/recommendations for international students: Required—TOEFL (paper-based 525; computer-based 195; IBT 71) or IELTS (6.0). Electronic applications accepted.

Midwestern State University, Graduate Studies, College of Humanities and Social Sciences, Department of Psychology, Wichita Falls, TX 76308. Offers MA. Part-time and evening/weekend programs available. *Degree requirements:* For master's, one foreign language, comprehensive exam, thesis optional. *Entrance requirements:* For master's, GRE General Test, 3 recommendation forms. Additional exam requirements/recommendations for international students: Required—TOEFL (minimum score 550 paper-based; 213 computer-based). Electronic applications accepted. *Faculty research:* Personality disorders, child sexual abuse and sexual coercion, educational psychology.

Millersville University of Pennsylvania, Graduate School, School of Education, Department of Psychology, Millersville, PA 17551-0302. Offers psychology (MS), including clinical psychology, school psychology; school counseling (M Ed). Part-time programs available. *Faculty:* 20 full-time (14 women), 6 part-time/adjunct (3 women). *Students:* 65 full-time (55 women), 78 part-time (65 women); includes 9 minority (5 African Americans, 1 Asian American or Pacific Islander, 3 Hispanic Americans), 1 international. Average age 29. 89 applicants, 40% accepted, 20 enrolled. In 2008, 41 master's awarded. *Degree requirements:* For master's, comprehensive exam, thesis optional. *Entrance requirements:* For master's, GRE, in-person interview. Additional exam requirements/recommendations for international students: Required—TOEFL (minimum score 500 paper-based; 183 computer-based; 65 iBT), TOEFL may be replaced by IELTS with score of 6 or higher. *Application deadline:* For fall admission, 2/1 for domestic and international students; for winter admission, 10/1 for domestic and international students; for spring admission, 10/1 for domestic and international students. Application fee: $40. Electronic applications accepted. *Expenses:* Tuition, state resident: full-time $6430; part-time $357 per credit. Tuition, nonresident: full-time $10,288; part-time $572 per credit. Required fees: $1937; $73.50 per credit. One-time fee: $88 part-time. Tuition and fees vary according to course load. *Financial support:* In 2008–09, 44 students received support, including 44 research assistantships with full and partial tuition reimbursements available (averaging $4,700 per year); institutionally sponsored loans and unspecified assistantships also available. Support available to part-time students. Financial award application deadline: 3/15; financial award applicants required to submit FAFSA. *Unit head:* Dr. Helena Tuleya-Payne, Chair, 717-872-3925, Fax: 717-871-2480, E-mail: helena.tuleya-payne@millersville.edu. *Application contact:* Dr. Victor S. DeSantis, Dean of Graduate and Professional Studies, 717-872-3099, Fax: 717-872-3453, E-mail: victor.desantis@millersville.edu.

Minnesota State University Mankato, College of Graduate Studies, College of Social and Behavioral Sciences, Department of Psychology, Mankato, MN 56001. Offers clinical psychology (MA); industrial/organizational psychology (MA); psychology (MT); school psychology (Psy D). Part-time programs available. *Students:* 38 full-time (23 women), 5 part-time (1 woman). *Degree requirements:* For master's, one foreign language, comprehensive exam, thesis (for some programs). *Entrance requirements:* For master's, GRE General Test, GRE Subject Test (clinical psychology), minimum GPA of 3.0 during previous 2 years, 3 letters of reference. Additional exam requirements/recommendations for international students: Required—TOEFL. *Application deadline:* For fall admission, 1/1 priority date for domestic students. Applications are processed on a rolling basis. Application fee: $40. Electronic applications accepted. *Financial support:* Research assistantships, teaching assistantships with full tuition reimbursements, career-related internships or fieldwork, Federal Work-Study, institutionally sponsored loans, and unspecified assistantships available. Support available to part-time students. Financial award application deadline: 3/15; financial award applicants required to submit FAFSA. *Faculty research:* Professional competency in hospitals, mood disturbance, 360-degree feedback, employee selection, planning fallacy. *Unit head:* Dr. Barry Ries, Chairperson, 507-389-2724. *Application contact:* 507-389-2321, E-mail: grad@mnsu.edu.

Mississippi State University, College of Arts and Sciences, Department of Psychology, Mississippi State, MS 39762. Offers clinical psychology (MS); cognitive science (PhD); experimental psychology (MS). Terminal master's awarded for partial completion of doctoral program. *Degree requirements:* For master's, comprehensive exam, thesis; for doctorate, thesis/dissertation, qualifying exam, comprehensive written and oral exam. *Entrance requirements:* For master's, GRE General Test, minimum GPA of 2.75; for doctorate, GRE General Test, proficiency in at least 1 computer language. Additional exam requirements/recommendations for international students: Required—TOEFL. *Faculty research:* Personality type, alcoholism, blindness and low vision, mental retardation, language comprehension.

Missouri State University, Graduate College, College of Health and Human Services, Department of Psychology, Springfield, MO 65804-0094. Offers psychology (MS), including clinical, experimental, industrial/organizational. *Faculty:* 26 full-time (10 women), 1 part-time/adjunct (0 women). *Students:* 44 full-time (30 women), 3 part-time (all women); includes 1 minority (Hispanic American). Average age 24. 71 applicants, 45% accepted, 20 enrolled. In 2008, 17 master's awarded. *Degree requirements:* For master's, comprehensive exam, thesis. *Entrance requirements:* For master's, GRE General Test, GRE Subject Test, minimum GPA of 3.25 in major, 3.0 overall; 20 hours of course work in psychology (experimental and statistics). Additional exam requirements/recommendations for international students: Required—TOEFL (minimum score 550 paper-based; 213 computer-based; 79 iBT). *Application deadline:* For fall admission, 3/1 priority date for domestic and international students. Application fee: $35 ($50 for international students). Electronic applications accepted. *Expenses:* Tuition, state resident: full-time $3852; part-time $214 per credit hour. Tuition, nonresident: full-time $7524; part-time $418 per credit hour. Required fees: $230 per semester. Tuition and fees vary according to course level and course load. *Financial support:* In 2008–09, 10 research assistantships with full tuition reimbursements (averaging $7,340 per year), 3 teaching assistantships with full tuition reimbursements (averaging $9,730 per year) were awarded; career-related internships or fieldwork, Federal Work-Study, institutionally sponsored loans, scholarships/grants, and unspecified assistantships also available. Financial award application deadline: 3/31; financial award applicants required to submit FAFSA. *Faculty research:* Work-family conflict, child forensic psychology, sports psychology, body image assessment, visual learning. *Unit head:* Dr. Robert G. Jones, Head, 417-836-5797, Fax: 417-836-830, E-mail: psychology@missouristate.edu. *Application contact:* Eric Eckert, Coordinator of Admissions and Recruitment, 417-836-5331, Fax: 417-836-6888, E-mail: ericeckert@missouristate.edu.

Monmouth University, Graduate School, Department of Psychology, West Long Branch, NJ 07764-1898. Offers professional counseling (PMC); psychological counseling (MA). Part-time and evening/weekend programs available. *Faculty:* 7 full-time (3 women), 3 part-time/adjunct (all women). *Students:* 84 full-time (72 women), 121 part-time (100 women); includes 29 minority (13 African Americans, 2 American Indian/Alaska Native, 4 Asian Americans or Pacific Islanders, 10 Hispanic Americans), 3 international. Average age 31. 122 applicants, 99% accepted, 53 enrolled. In 2008, 69 master's awarded. *Degree requirements:* For master's, thesis optional, fieldwork. *Entrance requirements:* For master's, GRE General Test, minimum GPA of 3.0 in major, 24 credits in psychology. Additional exam requirements/recommendations for international students: Required—TOEFL (minimum score 550 paper-based; 213 computer-based; 79 iBT), IELTS (minimum score 5), Michigan English Language Assessment Battery (minimum score: 77), Cambridge A, B, C. *Application deadline:* For fall admission, 7/15 priority date for domestic students, 6/1 for international students; for spring admission, 11/15 priority date for domestic students, 11/1 for international students. Applications are processed on a rolling basis. Application fee: $50. Electronic applications accepted. *Expenses:* Tuition: Full-time $13,914; part-time $773 per credit. Required fees: $628; $157 per semester. *Financial support:* In 2008–09, 91 students received support, including 91 fellowships (averaging $2,044 per year), 8 research assistantships (averaging $8,667 per year); career-related internships or fieldwork, scholarships/grants, tuition waivers (partial), and unspecified assistantships also available. Support available to part-time students. Financial award application deadline: 3/1; financial award applicants required to submit FAFSA. *Faculty research:* Violent crime, single parenting, the African-American male, counseling older women, successful behavior for under-achieving youth. *Unit head:* Dr. Frances K. Trotman, Director, 732-571-7593, Fax: 732-263-5159, E-mail: ftrotman@monmouth.edu. *Application contact:* Kevin Roane, Director, Office of Graduate Admission, 732-571-3452, Fax: 732-263-5123, E-mail: gradadm@monmouth.edu.

Montana State University, College of Graduate Studies, College of Letters and Science, Department of Psychology, Bozeman, MT 59717. Offers MS. Part-time programs available. *Degree requirements:* For master's, comprehensive exam, thesis (for some programs). *Entrance requirements:* For master's, GRE General Test. Additional exam requirements/recommendations for international students: Required—TOEFL (minimum score 550 paper-based; 213 computer-based). Electronic applications accepted. *Faculty research:* Cognitive psychology, social psychology, biopsychology, health psychology.

Montana State University–Billings, College of Arts and Sciences, Department of Psychology, Billings, MT 59101-0298. Offers MS. Part-time programs available. *Degree requirements:* For master's, thesis optional. *Entrance requirements:* For master's, GRE General Test, 3 letters of recommendation, resumé.

Montclair State University, The Office of Graduate Admissions and Support Services, College of Humanities and Social Sciences, Department of Psychology, Montclair, NJ 07043-1624. Offers educational psychology (MA), including child/adolescent clinical psychology, clinical psychology for Spanish/English bilinguals; psychology (MA, Certificate), including industrial and organizational psychology (MA); school psychologist (Certificate). Part-time and evening/weekend programs available. *Faculty:* 28 full-time (13 women), 32 part-time/adjunct (16 women). *Students:* 28 full-time (20 women), 31 part-time (26 women); includes 14 minority (4 African Americans, 6 Asian Americans or Pacific Islanders, 4 Hispanic Americans), 2 international. Average age 27. 62 applicants, 56% accepted, 23 enrolled. In 2008, 26 master's awarded. *Degree requirements:* For master's, comprehensive exam, thesis or alternative. *Entrance requirements:* For master's, GRE General Test, GRE Subject Test, previous course work in psychology, interview, 2 letters of recommendation. Additional exam requirements/recommendations for international students: Required—TOEFL (minimum score 83 computer-based). *Application deadline:* For fall admission, 2/1 for domestic and international students; for spring admission, 10/1 for domestic and international students. Applications are processed on a rolling basis. Application fee: $60. Electronic applications accepted. *Financial support:* In 2008–09, 10 research assistantships with full tuition reimbursements (averaging $7,000 per year) were awarded; Federal Work-Study, scholarships/grants, and unspecified assistantships also available. Support available to part-time students. Financial award application deadline: 3/1; financial award applicants required to submit FAFSA. *Faculty research:* Engaged learning, academic and civic development. Total annual research expenditures: $10,000. *Unit head:* Dr. Peter Vietze, Chairperson, 973-655-5201. *Application contact:* Amy Aiello, Associate Director of Admissions, 973-655-5147, Fax: 973-655-7869, E-mail: graduate.school@montclair.edu.

Morehead State University, Graduate Programs, College of Science and Technology, Department of Psychology, Morehead, KY 40351. Offers clinical psychology (MS); counseling psychology (MS); experimental/general psychology (MS). Part-time programs available. *Faculty:* 8 full-time (3 women). *Students:* 22 full-time (18 women), 3 part-time (1 woman). Average age 26. 30 applicants, 53% accepted, 9 enrolled. In 2008, 10 master's awarded. *Degree requirements:* For master's, comprehensive exam, thesis optional. *Entrance requirements:* For master's, GRE General Test, 18 undergraduate hours in psychology, minimum GPA of 3.0. Additional exam requirements/recommendations for international students: Required—TOEFL (minimum score 500 paper-based; 173 computer-based). *Application deadline:* For fall admission, 8/1 priority date for domestic and international students; for spring admission, 12/1 for domestic students, 12/1 priority date for international students. Applications are processed on a rolling basis. Application fee: $30 ($55 for international students). Electronic applications accepted. *Expenses:* Tuition, area resident: Full-time $6084; part-time $338 per credit hour. Tuition, state resident: full-time $6084; part-time $338 per credit hour. Tuition, nonresident: full-time $15,804; part-time $878 per credit hour. *Financial support:* In 2008–09, 19 research assistantships (averaging $6,000 per year) were awarded; career-related internships or fieldwork, Federal Work-Study, and institutionally sponsored loans also available. Financial award application deadline: 4/1; financial award applicants required to submit FAFSA. *Faculty research:* Mood induction effects, serotonin receptor activity, stress, perceptual processes. *Unit head:* Dr. Laurie Couch, Interim Department Chair. *Application contact:* Michelle Barber, Graduate Admissions Counselor, 606-783-2039, Fax: 606-783-5061, E-mail: m.barber@moreheadstate.edu.

Morgan State University, School of Graduate Studies, College of Liberal Arts, Department of Psychology, Baltimore, MD 21251. Offers psychometrics (MS, PhD). *Entrance requirements:* For master's and doctorate, GRE.

Mount Aloysius College, Program in Psychology, Cresson, PA 16630-1999. Offers MS. *Entrance requirements:* For master's, GRE General Test.

Mount Holyoke College, Department of Psychology and Education, South Hadley, MA 01075. Offers MA.

Murray State University, College of Humanities and Fine Arts, Program in Psychology, Murray, KY 42071. Offers clinical psychology (MA, MS); psychology (MA, MS). Part-time programs available. *Degree requirements:* For master's, one foreign language, comprehensive exam (for some programs), thesis. *Entrance requirements:* For master's, GRE General Test. Additional exam requirements/recommendations for international students: Required—TOEFL.

National-Louis University, College of Arts and Sciences, Program in Psychology, Chicago, IL 60603. Offers cultural psychology (MA); health psychology (MA); human development (MA); organizational psychology (MA); psychology (Certificate). Part-time and evening/weekend programs available. *Students:* 4 full-time (all women), 214 part-time (30 women); includes 145 minority (121 African Americans, 3 American Indian/Alaska Native, 3 Asian Americans or Pacific Islanders, 18 Hispanic Americans), 2 international. Average age 38. In 2008, 30 master's awarded. *Degree requirements:* For master's, thesis, internship (health psychology). *Entrance requirements:* For master's, GRE, MAT, or Watson-Glaser Critical Thinking Appraisal, interview, minimum GPA of 3.0; for Certificate, GRE, MAT, or Watson-Glaser Critical Thinking Appraisal, interview, minimum GPA of 3.0, undergraduate course work in psychology. *Application deadline:* Applications are processed on a rolling basis. *Financial support:* Federal Work-Study, institutionally sponsored loans, scholarships/grants, and tuition waivers available. Support available to part-time students. Financial award applicants required to submit FAFSA. *Faculty research:* Human development, personality theory, abnormal psychology. *Unit head:* Dr. Edward Risinger, Professor, 224-233-2533, Fax: 224-233-2533, E-mail: erisinger@nl.edu. *Application contact:* David McCulloch, Vice President for University Services, 800-443-5522 Ext. 5151, Fax: 847-465-0593, E-mail: dmcc@wheeling1.nl.edu.

National University, Academic Affairs, College of Letters and Sciences, Department of Psychology, La Jolla, CA 92037-1011. Offers counseling psychology (MA); human behavior (MA). Part-time and evening/weekend programs available. Postbaccalaureate distance learning degree programs offered (no on-campus study). *Faculty:* 16 full-time (8 women), 166 part-time/adjunct (101 women). *Students:* 396 full-time (312 women), 375 part-time (293 women); includes 281 minority (114 African Americans, 8 American Indian/Alaska Native, 34 Asian Americans or Pacific Islanders, 125 Hispanic Americans), 6 international. Average age 36. 510 applicants, 100% accepted, 510 enrolled. In 2008, 226 master's awarded. *Degree requirements:* For master's, thesis (for some programs). *Entrance requirements:* For master's, interview, minimum GPA of 2.5. Additional exam requirements/recommendations for international students: Required—TOEFL (minimum score 550 paper-based; 213 computer-based; 79 iBT), IELTS (minimum score 6). *Application deadline:* Applications are processed on a rolling basis. Application fee: $60 ($65 for international students). Electronic applications accepted. *Expenses:* Tuition: Full-time $8694; part-time $322 per credit hour. Tuition and fees vary according to course load. *Financial support:* Career-related internships or fieldwork, institutionally sponsored loans, scholarships/grants, and tuition waivers (partial) available. Support available to part-time students. Financial award application deadline: 6/30; financial award applicants required to submit FAFSA. *Unit head:* Dr. Maureen O'Hara, Chair and Professor, 858-642-8464, Fax: 858-642-8715, E-mail: mohara@nu.edu. *Application contact:* Dominick Giovanniello, Associate Regional Dean—San Diego, 800-NAT-UNIV, Fax: 858-541-7792, E-mail: dgiovann@nu.edu.

New Jersey City University, Graduate Studies and Continuing Education, College of Arts and Sciences, Department of Psychology, Jersey City, NJ 07305-1597. Offers counseling (MA); educational psychology (MA, PD), including educational psychology (MA), school psychology (PD). *Degree requirements:* For PD, summer internship or externship. *Entrance requirements:* For master's, GRE General Test or MAT; for PD, GRE General Test. Additional exam requirements/recommendations for international students: Required—TOEFL.

New Mexico Highlands University, Graduate Studies, College of Arts and Sciences, Department of Behavioral Sciences, Las Vegas, NM 87701. Offers psychology (MS), including clinical psychology, general psychology. Part-time programs available. *Faculty:* 12 full-time (7 women). *Students:* 18 full-time (13 women), 6 part-time (3 women); includes 9 minority (all Hispanic Americans), 1 international. Average age 28. 13 applicants, 85% accepted, 7 enrolled. In 2008, 3 master's awarded. *Degree requirements:* For master's, comprehensive exam, thesis or alternative. *Entrance requirements:* For master's, minimum undergraduate GPA of 3.0. Additional exam requirements/recommendations for international students: Required—TOEFL (minimum score 540 paper-based; 207 computer-based). *Application deadline:* For fall admission, 8/1 priority date for domestic students. Applications are processed on a rolling basis. Application fee: $15. *Expenses:* Tuition, state resident: full-time $2880; part-time $120 per credit hour. Tuition, nonresident: full-time $4234; part-time $176 per credit hour. Inter-

Psychology—General

New Mexico Highlands University (continued)
national tuition: $5645 full-time. One-time fee: $20. *Financial support:* In 2008–09, 17 students received support, including 14 teaching assistantships (averaging $5,250 per year); career-related internships or fieldwork, Federal Work-Study, institutionally sponsored loans, scholarships/grants, tuition waivers (full and partial), and unspecified assistantships also available. Support available to part-time students. Financial award application deadline: 3/1; financial award applicants required to submit FAFSA. *Faculty research:* Southwest Native American resettlement development, community-level interventions, neurochemistry of personality, comparative criminal justice, social theory and activism. *Unit head:* Dr. Ian Williamson, Chair, 505-454-3342, E-mail: iwilliamson@nmhu.edu. *Application contact:* Diane Trujillo, Administrative Assistant for Graduate Studies, 505-454-3266, Fax: 505-426-2117, E-mail: dtrujillo@nmhu.edu.

New Mexico State University, Graduate School, College of Arts and Sciences, Department of Psychology, Las Cruces, NM 88003-8001. Offers MA, PhD. Part-time programs available. *Faculty:* 7 full-time (1 woman). *Students:* 44 full-time (28 women), 11 part-time (3 women); includes 8 minority (all Hispanic Americans), 5 international. Average age 30. 42 applicants, 95% accepted, 11 enrolled. In 2008, 5 master's, 2 doctorates awarded. *Degree requirements:* For master's, thesis; for doctorate, comprehensive exam, thesis/dissertation. *Entrance requirements:* For master's, GRE General Test, letters of recommendation, curriculum vitae; for doctorate, GRE General Test, letters of recommendation, master's thesis or proposal, curriculum vitae. *Application deadline:* For fall admission, 2/1 priority date for domestic students, 2/1 for international students. Applications are processed on a rolling basis. Application fee: $30 ($50 for international students). Electronic applications accepted. *Expenses:* Tuition, area resident: Full-time $3890; part-time $212.85 per credit. Tuition, state resident: full-time $3890; part-time $212.85 per credit. Tuition, nonresident: full-time $13,916; part-time $630.55 per credit. Required fees: $1218; $609 per semester. *Financial support:* In 2008–09, 45 students received support, including 7 research assistantships with partial tuition reimbursements available (averaging $10,421 per year), 33 teaching assistantships with partial tuition reimbursements available (averaging $10,482 per year); fellowships, career-related internships or fieldwork, Federal Work-Study, and health care benefits also available. Support available to part-time students. Financial award application deadline: 2/15. *Faculty research:* Engineering, cognitive, and social psychology; human/computer interaction; cognitive science. *Unit head:* Dr. James E. McDonald, Head, 575-646-5130, Fax: 575-646-6212, E-mail: jemcdon@nmsu.edu. *Application contact:* Dr. Laura J Madson, Associate Professor/Chair of Graduate Committee, 575-646-6207, Fax: 575-646-6212, E-mail: lmadson@nmsu.edu.

The New School: A University, The New School for Social Research, Department of Psychology, New York, NY 10011. Offers clinical psychology (PhD); general psychology (MA, PhD). *Accreditation:* APA (one or more programs are accredited). Part-time and evening/weekend programs available. *Faculty:* 17 full-time (8 women), 6 part-time/adjunct (1 woman). *Students:* 152 full-time (118 women), 90 part-time (72 women); includes 46 minority (11 African Americans, 2 American Indian/Alaska Native, 10 Asian Americans or Pacific Islanders, 23 Hispanic Americans), 28 international. Average age 29. In 2008, 54 master's, 5 doctorates awarded. Terminal master's awarded for partial completion of doctoral program. *Degree requirements:* For doctorate, one foreign language, thesis/dissertation, qualifying exam. *Entrance requirements:* For master's, GRE General Test; for doctorate, GRE General Test, MA. Additional exam requirements/recommendations for international students: Required—TOEFL (minimum score 600 paper-based; 250 computer-based; 100 iBT). *Application deadline:* For fall admission, 1/15 priority date for domestic students. Applications are processed on a rolling basis. Application fee: $50. *Expenses:* Tuition: Full-time $27,144; part-time $1508 per credit. Required fees: $355 per semester. *Financial support:* Fellowships, research assistantships, teaching assistantships, career-related internships or fieldwork, Federal Work-Study, scholarships/grants, and tuition waivers (full and partial) available. Financial award application deadline: 3/1; financial award applicants required to submit FAFSA. *Faculty research:* Consciousness, memory, language, perceptions, psychopathology. *Unit head:* Dr. Joan Miller, Chair, 212-229-5727 Ext. 3106. *Application contact:* Robert MacDonald, Director of Admissions, 800-523-5710 Ext. 3007, Fax: 212-989-7102, E-mail: macdonar@newschool.edu.

See Close-Up on page 1251.

New York University, Graduate School of Arts and Science, Department of Psychology, New York, NY 10012-1019. Offers cognition and perception (PhD); community psychology (PhD); general psychology (MA); industrial/organizational psychology (MA); psychotherapy and psychoanalysis (Advanced Certificate); social/personality psychology (PhD). Part-time programs available. Terminal master's awarded for partial completion of doctoral program. *Degree requirements:* For master's, comprehensive exam, thesis or alternative; for doctorate, thesis/dissertation. *Entrance requirements:* For master's, GRE General Test, minimum GPA of 3.0; for doctorate, GRE General Test, GRE Subject Test; for Advanced Certificate, doctoral degree, minimum GPA of 3.0. Additional exam requirements/recommendations for international students: Required—TOEFL. *Faculty research:* Vision, memory, social cognition, social and cognitive development, relationships.

New York University, Steinhardt School of Culture, Education and Human Development, Department of Applied Psychology, New York, NY 10012-1019. Offers counselor education (MA, PhD, Advanced Certificate), including counseling and guidance (MA, Advanced Certificate), counseling for mental health and wellness (MA), counseling psychology (PhD); educational and developmental psychology (MA, PhD), including educational psychology (MA), psychological development (PhD), school psychology (PhD). *Accreditation:* APA (one or more programs are accredited). Part-time and evening/weekend programs available. Terminal master's awarded for partial completion of doctoral program. *Degree requirements:* For master's, thesis (for some programs); for doctorate, thesis/dissertation. *Entrance requirements:* For doctorate, GRE General Test, interview. Additional exam requirements/recommendations for international students: Required—TOEFL. *Faculty research:* Urban children; adolescents and families; culture, race and ethnicity; risk-taking behaviors and health; early childhood.

Norfolk State University, School of Graduate Studies, School of Liberal Arts, Department of Psychology, Norfolk, VA 23504. Offers community/clinical psychology (MA); psychology (Psy D). Psy D offered through the Virginia Consortium for Professional Psychology; for information call 757-431-4950. Part-time programs available. *Degree requirements:* For master's, comprehensive exam, thesis or alternative; for doctorate, comprehensive exam, thesis/dissertation. *Entrance requirements:* For master's, minimum GPA of 2.7.

North Carolina Central University, Division of Academic Affairs, College of Behavioral and Social Sciences, Department of Psychology, Durham, NC 27707-3129. Offers MA. Part-time and evening/weekend programs available. *Degree requirements:* For master's, one foreign language, comprehensive exam, thesis. *Entrance requirements:* For master's, GRE, minimum GPA of 3.0 in major, 2.5 overall. Additional exam requirements/recommendations for international students: Required—TOEFL. *Faculty research:* Aggression, hypertension, faces, anger, teaching.

North Carolina State University, Graduate School, College of Humanities and Social Sciences, Department of Psychology, Raleigh, NC 27695. Offers developmental psychology (PhD); ergonomics and experimental psychology (PhD); industrial/organizational psychology (PhD); psychology in the public interest (PhD); school psychology (PhD). *Accreditation:* APA. *Degree requirements:* For doctorate, comprehensive exam, thesis/dissertation. *Entrance requirements:* For doctorate, GRE General Test, GRE Subject Test (industrial/organizational psychology), MAT (recommended), minimum GPA of 3.0 in major. Electronic applications accepted. *Faculty research:* Cognitive and social development (human factors, families, the workplace, community issues and health, aging).

Northcentral University, Graduate Studies, Prescott Valley, AZ 86314. Offers business (MBA, DBA, PhD, CAGS); education (M Ed, Ed D, PhD, CAGS); psychology (MA, PhD, CAGS).

North Dakota State University, College of Graduate and Interdisciplinary Studies, College of Science and Mathematics, Department of Psychology, Fargo, ND 58105. Offers clinical psychology (MS); cognitive and visual neuroscience (PhD); health and social psychology (PhD); psychology (MS). *Faculty:* 18 full-time (4 women), 2 part-time/adjunct (1 woman). *Students:* 36 full-time (27 women); includes 4 minority (1 African American, 2 Asian Americans or Pacific Islanders, 1 Hispanic American), 1 international. Average age 24. 48 applicants, 33% accepted, 10 enrolled. In 2008, 3 master's, 1 doctorate awarded. *Degree requirements:* For master's, thesis; for doctorate, thesis/dissertation. *Entrance requirements:* For master's and doctorate, GRE General Test, GRE Subject Test. Additional exam requirements/recommendations for international students: Required—TOEFL (minimum score 525 paper-based; 197 computer-based; 71 iBT). *Application deadline:* For fall admission, 3/1 for domestic and international students. Application fee: $45 ($60 for international students). Electronic applications accepted. *Financial support:* In 2008–09, 36 students received support, including 2 fellowships with full tuition reimbursements available (averaging $16,000 per year), 23 research assistantships with full tuition reimbursements available (averaging $16,000 per year), 11 teaching assistantships with full tuition reimbursements available (averaging $6,000 per year); career-related internships or fieldwork, Federal Work-Study, institutionally sponsored loans, tuition waivers (full and partial), and unspecified assistantships also available. Support available to part-time students. Financial award application deadline: 3/1. *Faculty research:* Cognition science, neuropsychology, group behavior, applied behavior analysis, behavior therapy. Total annual research expenditures: $2 million. *Unit head:* Dr. Paul D. Rokke, Chair, 701-231-8622, Fax: 701-231-8426, E-mail: paul.rokke@ndsu.edu. *Application contact:* Dr. Paul D. Rokke, Chair, 701-231-8622, Fax: 701-231-8426, E-mail: paul.rokke@ndsu.edu.

Northeastern State University, Graduate College, College of Education, Department of Psychology and Counseling, Tahlequah, OK 74464-2399. Offers counseling psychology (MS); school counseling (M Ed). Part-time and evening/weekend programs available. *Students:* 107 full-time (83 women), 52 part-time (42 women); includes 39 minority (10 African Americans, 22 American Indian/Alaska Native, 1 Asian American or Pacific Islander, 6 Hispanic Americans), 2 international. In 2008, 40 master's awarded. *Degree requirements:* For master's, thesis (for some programs), written and oral examinations. *Entrance requirements:* For master's, GRE, minimum GPA of 2.5. *Application deadline:* Applications are processed on a rolling basis. Application fee: $0. *Financial support:* Teaching assistantships, career-related internships or fieldwork and Federal Work-Study available. Financial award application deadline: 3/1. *Unit head:* Dr. Kathryn Sanders, Chair, 918-456-5511 Ext. 3016, Fax: 918-458-2397, E-mail: sanderka@nsuok.edu. *Application contact:* Margie Railey, Administrative Assistant, 918-456-5511 Ext. 2093, Fax: 918-458-2061, E-mail: railey@nsouk.edu.

Northeastern University, Bouvé College of Health Sciences Graduate School, Department of Counseling and Applied Educational Psychology, Boston, MA 02115-5096. Offers applied behavior analysis (MS); applied educational psychology (MS), including school counseling, school psychology; college student development and counseling (MS); counseling psychology (MS, PhD, CAGS); school psychology (PhD, CAGS); special needs and intensive special needs (MS Ed). *Accreditation:* APA (one or more programs are accredited). Part-time and evening/weekend programs available. *Degree requirements:* For doctorate, comprehensive exam, thesis/dissertation, qualifying exams; for CAGS, comprehensive exam. *Entrance requirements:* For master's and CAGS, GRE General Test or MAT; for doctorate, GRE General Test. Additional exam requirements/recommendations for international students: Required—TOEFL. *Faculty research:* Early intervention, career development and choice, crisis intervention, family systems, bilingual education in special education.

Northern Arizona University, Graduate College, College of Social and Behavioral Sciences, Department of Psychology, Flagstaff, AZ 86011. Offers applied health psychology (MA); clinical psychology (MA); general psychology (MA); teaching of psychology (MA). Part-time programs available. *Degree requirements:* For master's, thesis, oral defense. *Entrance requirements:* For master's, GRE General Test.

Northern Illinois University, Graduate School, College of Liberal Arts and Sciences, Department of Psychology, De Kalb, IL 60115-2854. Offers MA, PhD. *Accreditation:* APA (one or more programs are accredited). *Degree requirements:* For master's, comprehensive exam, thesis optional; for doctorate, thesis/dissertation, candidacy exam, dissertation defense. *Entrance requirements:* For master's, GRE General Test, minimum GPA of 3.0 for last 2 years of undergraduate work; for doctorate, GRE General Test, minimum undergraduate GPA of 2.75, graduate GPA of 3.2; master's degree with research thesis. Additional exam requirements/recommendations for international students: Required—TOEFL (minimum score 550 paper-based; 213 computer-based). Electronic applications accepted. *Faculty research:* Neglect syndrome, ADHD, workplace discrimination, adolescent suicide, social dilemmas.

Northern Michigan University, College of Graduate Studies, College of Arts and Sciences, Department of Psychology, Marquette, MI 49855-5301. Offers MS. Part-time and evening/weekend programs available. *Degree requirements:* For master's, thesis (for some programs). *Entrance requirements:* For master's, GRE, minimum GPA of 3.0.

Northwestern State University of Louisiana, Graduate Studies and Research, Department of Psychology, Natchitoches, LA 71497. Offers clinical psychology (MS). *Faculty:* 6 full-time (4 women), 1 (woman) part-time/adjunct. *Students:* 22 full-time (17 women), 8 part-time (6 women); includes 11 minority (9 African Americans, 2 Hispanic Americans). Average age 27. 20 applicants, 95% accepted, 18 enrolled. In 2008, 6 master's awarded. *Degree requirements:* For master's, comprehensive exam, thesis or alternative. *Entrance requirements:* For master's, GRE General Test, GRE Subject Test, minimum undergraduate GPA of 2.5. *Application deadline:* For fall admission, 8/1 priority date for domestic students; for spring admission, 1/10 for domestic students. Applications are processed on a rolling basis. Application fee: $20 ($30 for international students). *Financial support:* Application deadline: 7/15. *Unit head:* Dr. Cynthia Lindsey, Head, 318-357-6594, Fax: 318-357-6802, E-mail: lindseyc@nsula.edu. *Application contact:* Dr. Steven G. Horton, Associate Provost/Dean, Graduate Studies, Research, and Information Systems, 318-357-5851, Fax: 318-357-5019, E-mail: grad_school@nsula.edu.

Northwestern University, The Graduate School, Judd A. and Marjorie Weinberg College of Arts and Sciences, Department of Psychology, Evanston, IL 60208. Offers brain, behavior and cognition (PhD); clinical psychology (PhD); cognitive psychology (PhD); personality (PhD); social psychology (PhD); JD/PhD. Admissions and degrees offered through The Graduate School. *Accreditation:* APA (one or more programs are accredited). Part-time programs available. *Degree requirements:* For doctorate, thesis/dissertation. *Entrance requirements:* For doctorate, GRE General Test, GRE Subject Test. Additional exam requirements/recommendations for international students: Required—TOEFL. Electronic applications accepted. *Faculty research:* Memory and higher order cognition, anxiety and depression, effectiveness of psychotherapy, social cognition, molecular basis of memory.

Announcement: The Department of Psychology offers PhD programs in brain, behavior, and cognition (BBC); cognitive psychology; social psychology; personality; and clinical psychology. There is a special emphasis on genuine interdisciplinary cooperation. Study and research programs are tailored to the individual. For more information, prospective students should contact the Graduate Admissions Coordinator.

Northwest Missouri State University, Graduate School, College of Education and Human Services, Department of Psychology and Sociology, Maryville, MO 64468-6001. Offers guidance and counseling (MS Ed). Part-time programs available. *Degree requirements:* For master's, comprehensive exam, thesis. *Entrance requirements:* For master's, GRE General Test, minimum undergraduate GPA of 2.5, 3.0 in major; writing sample. Additional exam requirements/recommendations for international students: Required—TOEFL (minimum score 550 paper-based; 213 computer-based). Electronic applications accepted.

Northwest University, College of Social and Behavioral Sciences, Kirkland, WA 98033. Offers counseling psychology (MA); international care and community development (MA).

Evening/weekend programs available. *Faculty:* 1 full-time (0 women), 7 part-time/adjunct (4 women). *Students:* 82 full-time (70 women), 6 part-time (5 women); includes 9 minority (5 African Americans, 2 Asian Americans or Pacific Islanders, 2 Hispanic Americans), 2 international. 108 applicants, 69% accepted, 54 enrolled. In 2008, 28 master's awarded. *Entrance requirements:* For master's, essay, 3 character references. Additional exam requirements/recommendations for international students: Required—TOEFL (minimum score 580 paper-based; 237 computer-based). *Application deadline:* For fall admission, 12/1 priority date for domestic and international students; for spring admission, 4/1 priority date for domestic and international students. Applications are processed on a rolling basis. Application fee: $75. *Expenses:* Contact institution. *Financial support:* In 2008–09, 2 students received support. Career-related internships or fieldwork, health care benefits, and interational student scholarships available. Financial award application deadline: 6/30. *Unit head:* Dr. William Herkelrath, Dean, 425-889-5328, Fax: 425-739-4602, E-mail: william.herkelrath@northwestu.edu. *Application contact:* Sara Bickerstaff, Student Services Coordinator, 425-889-5249, Fax: 425-739-4602, E-mail: sara.bickerstaff@northwestu.edu.

Notre Dame de Namur University, Division of Academic Affairs, School of Sciences, Department of Clinical Psychology and Gerontology, Belmont, CA 94002-1908. Offers clinical gerontology (Certificate); clinical psychology (MA); marital and family therapy (MAMFT). Part-time and evening/weekend programs available. *Faculty:* 2 full-time (both women), 6 part-time/adjunct (5 women). *Students:* 29 full-time (25 women), 65 part-time (56 women); includes 31 minority (5 African Americans, 11 Asian Americans or Pacific Islanders, 15 Hispanic Americans), 1 international. Average age 35. 26 applicants, 81% accepted, 16 enrolled. In 2008, 27 master's awarded. *Entrance requirements:* For master's, interview, minimum GPA of 2.5. Additional exam requirements/recommendations for international students: Required—TOEFL (minimum score 550 paper-based; 213 computer-based; 79 iBT). *Application deadline:* For fall admission, 8/1 priority date for domestic students; for spring admission, 12/1 priority date for domestic students. Applications are processed on a rolling basis. Application fee: $60. Electronic applications accepted. *Expenses:* Tuition: Part-time $699 per unit. Required fees: $3 per unit. $35 per semester. *Financial support:* Career-related internships or fieldwork available. Support available to part-time students. Financial award applicants required to submit FAFSA. *Unit head:* Dr. Nusha Askari, Chair, 650-508-3728, E-mail: naskari@ndnu.edu. *Application contact:* Candace Hallmark, Assistant Director of Graduate Admissions, 650-508-3592, Fax: 650-508-3426, E-mail: grad.admit@ndnu.edu.

Nova Southeastern University, Center for Psychological Studies, Fort Lauderdale, FL 33314-7796. Offers MS, PhD, Psy D, Psy S, SPS. *Accreditation:* APA (one or more programs are accredited). Postbaccalaureate distance learning degree programs offered. *Faculty:* 34 full-time (11 women), 68 part-time/adjunct (32 women). *Students:* 827 full-time (706 women), 662 part-time (591 women); includes 631 minority (283 African Americans, 5 American Indian/Alaska Native, 31 Asian Americans or Pacific Islanders, 312 Hispanic Americans), 27 international. 1,433 applicants, 49% accepted, 520 enrolled. In 2008, 340 master's, 77 doctorates, 20 other advanced degrees awarded. Terminal master's awarded for partial completion of doctoral program. *Degree requirements:* For master's, comprehensive exam, 3 practica; for doctorate, thesis/dissertation, clinical internship, competency exam; for other advanced degree, comprehensive exam, internship. *Entrance requirements:* For doctorate, GRE General Test, GRE Subject Test (recommended), minimum undergraduate GPA of 3.0; for other advanced degree, GRE General Test. Additional exam requirements/recommendations for international students: Required—TOEFL (minimum score 550 paper-based; 213 computer-based). *Application deadline:* Applications are processed on a rolling basis. Application fee: $50. Electronic applications accepted. *Expenses:* Contact institution. *Financial support:* In 2008–09, 5 research assistantships, 34 teaching assistantships (averaging $1,000 per year) were awarded; career-related internships or fieldwork, Federal Work-Study, institutionally sponsored loans, scholarships/grants, and unspecified assistantships also available. Support available to part-time students. Financial award application deadline: 4/1. *Faculty research:* Clinical and child clinical psychology, geriatrics, interpersonal violence. *Unit head:* Karen Grosby, Dean, 954-262-5701, Fax: 954-262-3859, E-mail: grosby@nova.edu. *Application contact:* Carlos Perez, Enrollment Management, 954-262-5790, Fax: 954-262-3893, E-mail: cpsinfo@cps.nova.edu.

The Ohio State University, Graduate School, College of Social and Behavioral Sciences, School of Social and Behavioral Science, Department of Psychology, Columbus, OH 43210. Offers behavioral neuroscience (PhD); clinical psychology (PhD); cognitive psychology (PhD); developmental psychology (PhD); mental retardation and developmental disabilities (PhD); psychology (MA); quantitative psychology (PhD); social psychology (PhD). *Accreditation:* APA (one or more programs are accredited). *Degree requirements:* For doctorate, thesis/dissertation. *Entrance requirements:* For master's and doctorate, GRE General Test. Additional exam requirements/recommendations for international students: Required—TOEFL (minimum score 600 paper-based; 250 computer-based). Electronic applications accepted.

Ohio University, Graduate College, College of Arts and Sciences, Department of Psychology, Athens, OH 45701-2979. Offers clinical psychology (PhD); experimental psychology (PhD); organizational psychology (PhD). *Accreditation:* APA. *Degree requirements:* For doctorate, one foreign language, comprehensive exam, thesis/dissertation. *Entrance requirements:* For doctorate, GRE General Test, GRE Subject Test. Additional exam requirements/recommendations for international students: Required—TOEFL. *Faculty research:* Health, cognitive, child clinical, and social psychology.

Oklahoma State University, College of Arts and Sciences, Department of Psychology, Stillwater, OK 74078. Offers clinical psychology (PhD); general psychology (MS); lifespan development psychology (PhD). *Accreditation:* APA (one or more programs are accredited). *Faculty:* 26 full-time (12 women), 1 part-time/adjunct (0 women). *Students:* 38 full-time (22 women), 16 part-time (12 women); includes 10 minority (2 African Americans, 3 American Indian/Alaska Native, 2 Asian Americans or Pacific Islanders, 3 Hispanic Americans), 2 international. Average age 28. 145 applicants, 8% accepted, 10 enrolled. In 2008, 10 master's, 4 doctorates awarded. *Degree requirements:* For master's, thesis or alternative; for doctorate, comprehensive exam, thesis/dissertation. *Entrance requirements:* For master's and doctorate, GRE General Test. Additional exam requirements/recommendations for international students: Required—TOEFL. *Application deadline:* For fall admission, 3/1 priority date for international students; for spring admission, 8/1 priority date for international students. Applications are processed on a rolling basis. Application fee: $40 ($75 for international students). Electronic applications accepted. *Expenses:* Tuition, state resident: full-time $3716.40; part-time $154.85 per credit hour. Tuition, nonresident: full-time $14,448; part-time $602 per credit hour. Required fees: $1772.40; $73.85 per credit hour. One-time fee: $50. Tuition and fees vary according to course load and campus/location. *Financial support:* In 2008–09, 15 research assistantships (averaging $14,338 per year), 32 teaching assistantships (averaging $13,493 per year) were awarded; career-related internships or fieldwork, Federal Work-Study, scholarships/grants, health care benefits, tuition waivers (partial), and unspecified assistantships also available. Support available to part-time students. Financial award application deadline: 3/1; financial award applicants required to submit FAFSA. *Unit head:* Dr. Maureen A. Sullivan, Head, 405-744-6028, Fax: 405-744-8067. *Application contact:* Dr. Gordon Emslie, Dean, 405-744-6368, Fax: 405-744-0355, E-mail: grad_i@okstate.edu.

Old Dominion University, College of Sciences, Doctoral Program in Psychology, Norfolk, VA 23529. Offers applied experimental psychology (PhD); human factors psychology (PhD); industrial/organizational psychology (PhD). *Faculty:* 17 full-time (7 women), 1 part-time/adjunct (0 women). *Students:* 16 full-time (7 women), 20 part-time (15 women); includes 1 minority (Hispanic American). Average age 29. 65 applicants, 18% accepted, 10 enrolled. In 2008, 6 doctorates awarded. *Degree requirements:* For doctorate, thesis/dissertation, qualifying exam. *Entrance requirements:* For doctorate, GRE General Test, GRE Subject Test, 3 recommendation letters. Additional exam requirements/recommendations for international students: Required—TOEFL (minimum score 550 paper-based). *Application deadline:* For winter admission, 1/5 for domestic and international students. Application fee: $40. *Expenses:* Tuition, area resident: Full-time $7704; part-time $321 per credit. Tuition, state resident: full-time $7704; part-time $321 per credit. Tuition, nonresident: full-time $19,104; part-time $796 per credit. Required fees: $99 per semester. One-time fee: $40. *Financial support:* In 2008–09, 13 students received support, including 2 fellowships with full tuition reimbursements available (averaging $18,000 per year), research assistantships with full tuition reimbursements available (averaging $12,000 per year), 11 teaching assistantships with full tuition reimbursements available (averaging $12,000 per year). Financial award application deadline: 1/15. *Faculty research:* Human-computer interaction, simulation, neuroergonomics, attention and workload. Total annual research expenditures: $399,161. *Unit head:* Dr. Barbara Winstead, Graduate Program Director, 757-683-4239, Fax: 757-683-5087, E-mail: psychgpd@odu.edu. *Application contact:* Dr. Barbara Winstead, Graduate Program Director, 757-683-4239, Fax: 757-683-5087, E-mail: psychgpd@odu.edu.

Old Dominion University, College of Sciences, Program in Psychology, Norfolk, VA 23529. Offers MS. Part-time programs available. *Faculty:* 17 full-time (7 women), 1 part-time/adjunct (0 women). *Students:* 13 full-time (11 women), 6 part-time (3 women); includes 3 minority (2 African Americans, 1 Hispanic American). Average age 25. 28 applicants, 61% accepted, 9 enrolled. In 2008, 6 master's awarded. *Degree requirements:* For master's, comprehensive exam, thesis optional. *Entrance requirements:* For master's, GRE General Test, minimum GPA of 3.0 in major, previous course work in psychology. Additional exam requirements/recommendations for international students: Required—TOEFL. *Application deadline:* For fall admission, 5/15 for domestic and international students. Applications are processed on a rolling basis. Application fee: $40. Electronic applications accepted. *Expenses:* Tuition, area resident: Full-time $7704; part-time $321 per credit. Tuition, state resident: full-time $7704; part-time $321 per credit. Tuition, nonresident: full-time $19,104; part-time $796 per credit. Required fees: $99 per semester. One-time fee: $40. *Financial support:* In 2008–09, 7 students received support, including research assistantships with partial tuition reimbursements available (averaging $9,000 per year), 7 teaching assistantships with partial tuition reimbursements available (averaging $9,000 per year); career-related internships or fieldwork, scholarships/grants, and tuition waivers (partial) also available. Financial award application deadline: 2/15; financial award applicants required to submit FAFSA. *Faculty research:* Social psychology, developmental psychology, physiopsychology, community psychology, industrial/organizational psychology. *Unit head:* Dr. Louis H. Janda, Graduate Program Director, 757-683-4211, Fax: 757-683-5087, E-mail: ljanda@odu.edu. *Application contact:* Dr. Louis H. Janda, Graduate Program Director, 757-683-4211, Fax: 757-683-5087, E-mail: ljanda@odu.edu.

Our Lady of the Lake University of San Antonio, School of Professional Studies, Program in Psychology, San Antonio, TX 78207-4689. Offers counseling psychology (MS, Psy D); marriage and family therapy (MS); school psychology (MS). *Accreditation:* APA (one or more programs are accredited). Part-time and evening/weekend programs available. *Students:* 99 full-time (83 women), 97 part-time (86 women); includes 117 minority (25 African Americans, 1 American Indian/Alaska Native, 3 Asian Americans or Pacific Islanders, 88 Hispanic Americans), 2 international. Average age 30. In 2008, 42 master's, 3 doctorates awarded. *Degree requirements:* For master's, comprehensive exam, thesis optional, practicum; for doctorate, thesis/dissertation, internship, qualifying exam. *Entrance requirements:* For master's and doctorate, GRE General Test or MAT, interview. Additional exam requirements/recommendations for international students: Required—TOEFL. *Application deadline:* For fall admission, 3/1 priority date for domestic and international students. Applications are processed on a rolling basis. Application fee: $25 ($50 for international students). Electronic applications accepted. *Expenses:* Tuition: Full-time $11,970; part-time $665 per credit hour. Required fees: $500; $250 per term. *Financial support:* Research assistantships, teaching assistantships, career-related internships or fieldwork available. Support available to part-time students. Financial award application deadline: 4/15. *Faculty research:* Marriage and family therapy, supervision, cross-cultural counseling, violence. *Unit head:* Dr. Kathryn Anderson, Chair, 210-434-6711, E-mail: andek@lake.ollusa.edu. *Application contact:* 210-434-6711 Ext. 2314, Fax: 210-431-4036, E-mail: gradadm@lake.ollusa.edu.

Pace University, Dyson College of Arts and Sciences, Department of Psychology, New York, NY 10038. Offers bilingual school psychology (MS Ed); counseling-substance abuse (MS); psychology (MA); school psychology (MS Ed); school-clinical child psychology (Psy D). *Accreditation:* APA (one or more programs are accredited). Part-time and evening/weekend programs available. Terminal master's awarded for partial completion of doctoral program. *Degree requirements:* For master's, comprehensive exam, qualifying exams, internship; for doctorate, comprehensive exam, qualifying exams, externship, internship, project. *Entrance requirements:* For master's, interview; for doctorate, GRE General Test, GRE Subject Test, interview. Electronic applications accepted.

Pacifica Graduate Institute, Graduate Programs, Carpinteria, CA 93013. Offers clinical psychology (PhD); counseling psychology (MA); depth psychology (MA, PhD); mythological studies (MA, PhD). Terminal master's awarded for partial completion of doctoral program. *Degree requirements:* For master's, thesis (for some programs), practicum; for doctorate, comprehensive exam, thesis/dissertation, internship. *Entrance requirements:* For master's, resumé, 3 letters of recommendation, writing sample, interview; for doctorate, resumé, 4 letters of recommendation, writing sample, interview. Additional exam requirements/recommendations for international students: Required—TOEFL. *Faculty research:* Imaginal and archetypal theory; post-Colonial psychoanalytic and Jungian theory; myth literature as it applies to the theory and practice of psychology.

Pacific University, School of Professional Psychology, Forest Grove, OR 97116-1797. Offers clinical psychology (MS, Psy D); counseling psychology (MA). *Accreditation:* APA (one or more programs are accredited). Part-time programs available. *Degree requirements:* For master's, comprehensive exam (for some programs), thesis (for some programs); for doctorate, comprehensive exam, thesis/dissertation. *Entrance requirements:* For master's, course work in introductory psychology, statistics, and abnormal psychology; minimum GPA of 3.0; for doctorate, GRE General Test, minimum GPA of 3.0, undergraduate course work in psychology, minimum GPA of 3.1 in last 2 years. Additional exam requirements/recommendations for international students: Required—TOEFL (minimum score 600 paper-based; 105 computer-based). Electronic applications accepted. *Expenses:* Contact institution. *Faculty research:* Neuropsychological assessment, assessment and treatment of anxiety, forensic psychology, cross-cultural psychology, child and adolescent psychopathology.

Palo Alto University, Distance Learning Program in Psychology, Palo Alto, CA 94303-4232. Offers MS. Postbaccalaureate distance learning degree programs offered (no on-campus study). *Entrance requirements:* For master's, GRE General Test. Additional exam requirements/recommendations for international students: Required—TOEFL (minimum score 550 paper-based; 220 computer-based). Electronic applications accepted.

Palo Alto University, Program in Clinical Psychology, Palo Alto, CA 94303-4232. Offers PhD, JD/PhD, MBA/PhD. *Accreditation:* APA. *Degree requirements:* For doctorate, comprehensive exam, thesis/dissertation, 2000 hour clinical internship, oral clinical competency exam. *Entrance requirements:* For doctorate, GRE General Test, BA or MA in psychology or related area, minimum undergraduate GPA of 3.0, 3.3 graduate. Additional exam requirements/recommendations for international students: Required—TOEFL. Electronic applications accepted. *Faculty research:* Child/family studies, health psychology, neuropsychology, personality development, assessment.

See Close-Up on page 1123.

Penn State Harrisburg, Graduate School, School of Behavioral Sciences and Education, Middletown, PA 17057-4898. Offers adult education (D Ed); applied behavior analysis (MA); applied clinical psychology (MA); applied psychological research (MA); community psychology and social change (MA); health education (M Ed); teaching and curriculum (M Ed); training and development (M Ed). Part-time and evening/weekend programs available.

Psychology—General

Penn State University Park, Graduate School, College of the Liberal Arts, Department of Psychology, State College, University Park, PA 16802-1503. Offers clinical psychology (MS, PhD); cognitive psychology (MS, PhD); developmental psychology (MS, PhD); industrial/organizational psychology (MS, PhD); psychobiology (MS, PhD); social psychology (MS, PhD). *Accreditation:* APA (one or more programs are accredited).

Pepperdine University, Graduate School of Education and Psychology, Division of Psychology, Malibu, CA 90263. Offers clinical psychology (MA). *Entrance requirements:* For master's, GRE General Test or MAT, 2 professional recommendations. Additional exam requirements/recommendations for international students: Required—TOEFL (minimum score 550 paper-based; 220 computer-based).

Pepperdine University, Graduate School of Education and Psychology, Division of Psychology, Los Angeles, CA 90045. Offers clinical psychology (MA, Psy D), including clinical psychology, clinical psychology (daytime) (MA), clinical psychology (evening) (MA); psychology (MA). Part-time and evening/weekend programs available. *Faculty:* 32 full-time (11 women), 76 part-time/adjunct (42 women). *Students:* 762 full-time (661 women), 98 part-time (82 women); includes 252 minority (76 African Americans, 7 American Indian/Alaska Native, 65 Asian Americans or Pacific Islanders, 104 Hispanic Americans), 38 international. In 2008, 313 master's, 22 doctorates awarded. *Entrance requirements:* For master's and doctorate, GRE General Test. Additional exam requirements/recommendations for international students: Required—TOEFL. *Application deadline:* For fall admission, 2/1 for domestic students. Applications are processed on a rolling basis. Application fee: $55. *Expenses:* Contact institution. *Financial support:* Research assistantships, teaching assistantships, career-related internships or fieldwork and scholarships/grants available. Support available to part-time students. Financial award application deadline: 7/1; financial award applicants required to submit FAFSA. *Unit head:* Dr. Robert deMayo, Associate Dean, 310-568-5747, E-mail: robert.demayo@pepperdine.edu. *Application contact:* Brenden Wysocki, Admissions Manager, 310-568-5786.

Philadelphia College of Osteopathic Medicine, Graduate and Professional Programs, Department of Psychology, Philadelphia, PA 19131-1694. Offers clinical psychology (Psy D); counseling and clinical health psychology (MS); organizational leadership and development (MS); psychology (Certificate); school psychology (MS, Psy D, Ed S). *Accreditation:* APA. *Degree requirements:* For master's, thesis; for doctorate, comprehensive exam, thesis/dissertation, final project, fieldwork. *Entrance requirements:* For master's, GRE or MAT, minimum GPA of 3.0; course work in biology, chemistry, English, physics; for other advanced degree, PRAXIS. *Faculty research:* Depression in primary care, integrated primary care, geriatric mental health.

See Close-Up on page 1127.

Pittsburg State University, Graduate School, College of Education, Department of Psychology and Counseling, Program in Psychology, Pittsburg, KS 66762. Offers MS. *Degree requirements:* For master's, thesis or alternative. *Entrance requirements:* For master's, GRE General Test, minimum GPA of 2.8.

Polytechnic Institute of NYU, Department of Humanities and Social Sciences, Major in Environment-Behavior Studies, Brooklyn, NY 11201-2990. Offers MS. Part-time and evening/weekend programs available. *Degree requirements:* For master's, comprehensive exam (for some programs), thesis (for some programs). *Entrance requirements:* Additional exam requirements/recommendations for international students: Required—TOEFL (minimum score 550 paper-based; 213 computer-based); Recommended—IELTS (minimum score 6.5). Electronic applications accepted.

Pontifical Catholic University of Puerto Rico, Institute of Graduate Studies in Behavioral Science and Community Affairs, Ponce, PR 00717-0777. Offers clinical psychology (MA, MS, PhD); clinical social work (MSW); criminology (MA); industrial psychology (MS, PhD); psychology (PhD); public administration (MA); vocational rehabilitation counseling (MSS). Part-time and evening/weekend programs available. *Degree requirements:* For master's, thesis; for doctorate, comprehensive exam, thesis/dissertation. *Entrance requirements:* For master's, EXADEP, GRE, 3 letters of recommendation, interview, minimum GPA of 2.75.

Portland State University, Graduate Studies, College of Liberal Arts and Sciences, Department of Psychology, Portland, OR 97207-0751. Offers MA, MS, PhD. *Faculty:* 18 full-time (8 women), 22 part-time/adjunct (8 women). *Students:* 50 full-time (37 women), 13 part-time (10 women); includes 11 minority (1 African American, 1 American Indian/Alaska Native, 1 Asian American or Pacific Islander, 8 Hispanic Americans), 6 international. Average age 32. 84 applicants, 24% accepted, 15 enrolled. In 2008, 11 master's awarded. *Degree requirements:* For master's, variable foreign language requirement, thesis; for doctorate, variable foreign language requirement, comprehensive exam, thesis/dissertation. *Entrance requirements:* For master's, GRE General Test, minimum GPA of 3.0 in upper-division course work or 2.75 overall, 3 letters of recommendation. Additional exam requirements/recommendations for international students: Required—TOEFL (minimum score 550 paper-based; 213 computer-based). *Application deadline:* For fall admission, 12/15 for domestic and international students. Application fee: $50. *Expenses:* Tuition, area resident: Full-time $8763; part-time $179 per credit hour. Tuition, state resident: full-time $8763; part-time $298 per credit hour. Tuition, nonresident: full-time $12,981; part-time $426 per credit hour. Required fees: $1242. One-time fee: $250. Tuition and fees vary according to course load and program. *Financial support:* In 2008–09, 1 research assistantship with full tuition reimbursement (averaging $10,657 per year), 37 teaching assistantships with full tuition reimbursements (averaging $10,094 per year) were awarded; career-related internships or fieldwork, Federal Work-Study, scholarships/grants, tuition waivers (partial), and unspecified assistantships also available. Support available to part-time students. Financial award application deadline: 3/1; financial award applicants required to submit FAFSA. *Faculty research:* Organizational psychology, work and the family, quantitative psychology, decision making, psychosocial factors affecting health. Total annual research expenditures: $633,568. *Unit head:* Sherwin Davidson, Chair, 503-725-3923, Fax: 503-725-3904, E-mail: davidsons@pdx.edu. *Application contact:* Sherwin Davidson, Chair, 503-725-3923, Fax: 503-725-3904, E-mail: davidsons@pdx.edu.

Portland State University, Graduate Studies, Systems Science Program, Portland, OR 97207-0751. Offers computational intelligence (Certificate); computer modeling and simulation (Certificate); systems science (MS); systems science/anthropology (PhD); systems science/business administration (PhD); systems science/civil engineering (PhD); systems science/economics (PhD); systems science/engineering management (PhD); systems science/general (PhD); systems science/mathematical sciences (PhD); systems science/mechanical engineering (PhD); systems science/psychology (PhD); systems science/sociology (PhD). *Faculty:* 3 full-time (0 women). *Students:* 12 full-time (3 women), 13 part-time (3 women); includes 2 minority (1 American Indian/Alaska Native, 1 Asian American or Pacific Islander), 5 international. Average age 38. 14 applicants, 71% accepted, 8 enrolled. In 2008, 2 master's, 4 doctorates awarded. *Degree requirements:* For doctorate, variable foreign language requirement, thesis/dissertation. *Entrance requirements:* For master's, 2 letters of recommendation; for doctorate, GMAT, GRE General Test, minimum undergraduate GPA of 3.0. Additional exam requirements/recommendations for international students: Required—TOEFL. *Application deadline:* For fall admission, 2/1 for domestic students; for spring admission, 11/1 for domestic students. Application fee: $50. *Expenses:* Tuition, area resident: Full-time $8763; part-time $179 per credit hour. Tuition, state resident: full-time $8763; part-time $298 per credit hour. Tuition, nonresident: full-time $12,981; part-time $426 per credit hour. Required fees: $1242. One-time fee: $250. Tuition and fees vary according to course load and program. *Financial support:* In 2008–09, 1 research assistantship with full tuition reimbursement (averaging $7,704 per year) was awarded; teaching assistantships with full tuition reimbursements, career-related internships or fieldwork, Federal Work-Study, scholarships/grants, and unspecified assistantships also available. Support available to part-time students. Financial award application deadline: 3/1; financial award applicants required to submit FAFSA. *Faculty research:* Systems theory and methodology, artificial intelligence neural networks, information theory, nonlinear dynamics/chaos, modeling and simulation. *Unit head:* George Lendaris, Acting Director, 503-725-4960. *Application contact:* Dawn Sharafi, Administrative Assistant, 503-725-4960, E-mail: dawn@sysc.pdx.edu.

Princeton University, Graduate School, Department of Psychology, Princeton, NJ 08544-1019. Offers neuroscience (PhD); psychology (PhD). *Degree requirements:* For doctorate, thesis/dissertation. *Entrance requirements:* For doctorate, GRE General Test, GRE Subject Test. Additional exam requirements/recommendations for international students: Required—TOEFL (minimum score 550 paper-based). Electronic applications accepted.

Purdue University, Graduate School, College of Liberal Arts, Department of Psychological Sciences, West Lafayette, IN 47907. Offers PhD. *Accreditation:* APA. *Entrance requirements:* For doctorate, GRE General Test. Additional exam requirements/recommendations for international students: Required—TOEFL. Electronic applications accepted. *Faculty research:* Career development of women in science, development of friendships during childhood and adolescence, social competence, human information processing.

Queens College of the City University of New York, Division of Graduate Studies, Mathematics and Natural Sciences Division, Department of Psychology, Flushing, NY 11367-1597. Offers clinical behavioral applications in mental health settings (MA); psychology (MA). Part-time programs available. *Degree requirements:* For master's, comprehensive exam, thesis or alternative. *Entrance requirements:* For master's, GRE, minimum GPA of 3.0. Additional exam requirements/recommendations for international students: Required—TOEFL.

Queen's University at Kingston, School of Graduate Studies and Research, Faculty of Arts and Sciences, Department of Psychology, Kingston, ON K7L 3N6, Canada. Offers brain behavior and cognitive science (MA, PhD); clinical psychology (MA, PhD); developmental psychology (MA, PhD); social personality psychology (MA, PhD). *Accreditation:* APA (one or more programs are accredited). *Degree requirements:* For master's, thesis; for doctorate, comprehensive exam, thesis/dissertation. *Entrance requirements:* For master's and doctorate, GRE General Test. Additional exam requirements/recommendations for international students: Required—TOEFL. *Faculty research:* Human development, social, personality, behavioral neuroscience, forensic.

Radford University, College of Graduate and Professional Studies, College of Humanities and Behavioral Sciences, Program in Psychology, Radford, VA 24142. Offers clinical psychology (MA, MS); counseling psychology (Psy D); experimental psychology (MA); general psychology (MS); industrial/organizational psychology (MA, MS); school psychology (Ed S). Part-time programs available. *Faculty:* 23 full-time (9 women), 1 part-time/adjunct (0 women). *Students:* 46 full-time (28 women), 5 part-time (4 women); includes 4 minority (3 African Americans, 1 Asian American or Pacific Islander), 2 international. Average age 26. 114 applicants, 42% accepted, 20 enrolled. In 2008, 36 master's awarded. *Degree requirements:* For master's, comprehensive exam, thesis (for some programs). *Entrance requirements:* For master's, GRE, minimum GPA of 3.0; 3 letters of reference; essay. Additional exam requirements/recommendations for international students: Required—TOEFL (minimum score 550 paper-based; 213 computer-based; 79 iBT). *Application deadline:* For fall admission, 3/1 priority date for domestic students, 12/1 for international students; for spring admission, 10/1 for domestic students, 7/1 for international students. Applications are processed on a rolling basis. Application fee: $40. Electronic applications accepted. *Expenses:* Tuition, area resident: Full-time $4845; part-time $202 per credit. Tuition, state resident: full-time $4845; part-time $202 per credit. Tuition, nonresident: full-time $11,483; part-time $478 per credit. Required fees: $2349; $98 per credit. *Financial support:* In 2008–09, 47 students received support, including 33 research assistantships with partial tuition reimbursements available (averaging $8,000 per year), 12 teaching assistantships with partial tuition reimbursements available (averaging $8,700 per year); career-related internships or fieldwork, institutionally sponsored loans, scholarships/grants, and unspecified assistantships also available. Financial award application deadline: 3/1; financial award applicants required to submit FAFSA. *Unit head:* Dr. Hilary M. Lips, Chair, 540-831-5387, Fax: 540-831-6113, E-mail: hlips@radford.edu. *Application contact:* Graduate Admissions Office, 540-831-5431, Fax: 540-831-6061, E-mail: gradcollege@radford.edu.

Regis University, College for Professional Studies, MA Program, Denver, CO 80221-1099. Offers criminology (MA); fine arts administration (Certificate); language and communication (MA); mediation (Certificate); psychology (MA); self-designed major (MA); social justice, peace, and reconciliation (Certificate); social science (MA); technical communication (Certificate). Program also offered in Henderson and Las Vegas (Summerlin), NV. Part-time and evening/weekend programs available. Postbaccalaureate distance learning degree programs offered (minimal on-campus study). *Degree requirements:* For master's, thesis, research project. *Entrance requirements:* For master's, resumé, recommendations, essays. Additional exam requirements/recommendations for international students: Required—TOEFL (minimum score 213 computer-based), TWE (minimum score 5). Electronic applications accepted. *Expenses:* Contact institution. *Faculty research:* Independent/nonresidential graduate study: new methods and models, adult learning and the capstone experience, Goal Setting, behavior of Adult students, Innovative Studies for Community Colleges.

Rhode Island College, School of Graduate Studies, Faculty of Arts and Sciences, Department of Psychology, Providence, RI 02908-1991. Offers MA. Part-time and evening/weekend programs available. *Faculty:* 12 full-time (6 women). *Students:* 4 full-time (all women), 10 part-time (9 women); includes 2 minority (1 African American, 1 Hispanic American). Average age 32. In 2008, 1 master's awarded. *Degree requirements:* For master's, comprehensive exam. *Entrance requirements:* For master's, GRE or MAT, 3 letters of recommendation. Additional exam requirements/recommendations for international students: Recommended—TOEFL (minimum score 550 paper-based; 213 computer-based; 79 iBT). *Application deadline:* For fall admission, 4/1 for domestic students; for spring admission, 11/1 for domestic students. Applications are processed on a rolling basis. Application fee: $50. *Expenses:* Tuition, area resident: Full-time $6816; part-time $284 per credit hour. Tuition, state resident: full-time $6816; part-time $284 per credit hour. Tuition, nonresident: full-time $13,920; part-time $580 per credit hour. Required fees: $454; $16 per credit. $68 per term. *Financial support:* In 2008–09, 1 teaching assistantship with full tuition reimbursement (averaging $5,200 per year) was awarded; Federal Work-Study, scholarships/grants, health care benefits, and unspecified assistantships also available. Support available to part-time students. Financial award application deadline: 5/15; financial award applicants required to submit FAFSA. *Unit head:* Dr. Thomas Malloy, Chair, 401-456-8015. *Application contact:* Graduate Studies, 401-456-8700.

Rice University, Graduate Programs, School of Social Sciences, Department of Psychology, Houston, TX 77251-1892. Offers cognitive sciences (MA, PhD); industrial-organizational/social psychology (MA, PhD); psychology (MA, PhD). Terminal master's awarded for partial completion of doctoral program. *Degree requirements:* For master's, thesis; for doctorate, thesis/dissertation. *Entrance requirements:* For doctorate, GRE General Test, minimum GPA of 3.0. Additional exam requirements/recommendations for international students: Required—TOEFL. Electronic applications accepted. *Faculty research:* Learning and memory, information processing, decision theory.

Richmont Graduate University, Graduate Programs, Atlanta, GA 30327. Offers Christian psychological studies (MS); marriage and family therapy (MA); professional counseling (MA).

Rochester Institute of Technology, Graduate Enrollment Services, College of Liberal Arts, Department of Psychology, Rochester, NY 14623-5603. Offers MS. *Entrance requirements:* Additional exam requirements/recommendations for international students: Required—TOEFL.

Roosevelt University, Graduate Division, College of Arts and Sciences, Department of Psychology, Program in Psychology, Chicago, IL 60605-1394. Offers Psy D. *Students:* 76 full-time (57 women), 46 part-time (33 women); includes 15 minority (10 African Americans, 2 Asian Americans or Pacific Islanders, 3 Hispanic Americans), 1 international. Average age 30. 530 applicants, 19% accepted, 27 enrolled. In 2008, 5 doctorates awarded. Application fee: $25 ($35 for international students). *Expenses:* Tuition: Full-time $14,730; part-time $709 per credit. Required fees: $175 per semester. Tuition and fees vary according to course load and program. *Unit head:* Steven Kvaal, Director, 312-341-6374. *Application contact:* Joanne Canyon-Heller, Coordinator of Graduate Admission, 877-APPLY RU, Fax: 312-281-3356, E-mail: applyru@roosevelt.edu.

Rosalind Franklin University of Medicine and Science, College of Health Professions, Department of Psychology, North Chicago, IL 60064-3095. Offers clinical counseling (MS); psychology (MS, PhD). Terminal master's awarded for partial completion of doctoral program. *Degree requirements:* For master's, capstone experience. *Entrance requirements:* For master's, GRE (optional), minimum 3.0 GPA, bachelor's degree (preferably in related subject); for doctorate, GRE, minimum 3.0 GPA, bachelors or master's degree. Additional exam requirements/recommendations for international students: Required—TOEFL. *Faculty research:* Anxiety, pain, psychopathy, epilepsy, neuropsychology.

Rowan University, Graduate School, College of Liberal Arts and Sciences, Department of Psychology, Glassboro, NJ 08028-1701. Offers mental health counseling (MA). Part-time and evening/weekend programs available. *Students:* 15 full-time (12 women), 21 part-time (19 women); includes 4 minority (1 African American, 3 Asian Americans or Pacific Islanders). Average age 27. 43 applicants, 40% accepted, 13 enrolled. In 2008, 8 master's awarded. *Degree requirements:* For master's, thesis. *Entrance requirements:* For master's, GRE. Additional exam requirements/recommendations for international students: Required—TOEFL. *Application deadline:* Applications are processed on a rolling basis. Electronic applications accepted. *Expenses:* Tuition, area resident: Full-time $10,624; part-time $590 per credit. Tuition, state resident: full-time $10,624; part-time $590 per credit. Tuition, nonresident: full-time $10,624; part-time $590 per credit. Required fees: $2258; $124.90 per credit. *Financial support:* Career-related internships or fieldwork, scholarships/grants, health care benefits, and unspecified assistantships available. *Unit head:* Dr. Mira Lalovic-Hand, Interim Associate Provost/Director of Graduate School, 856-256-5120, E-mail: Lalovic-hand@rowan.edu. *Application contact:* Karen Haynes, Graduate Coordinator, 856-256-4052, Fax: 856-256-4436, E-mail: Haynes@rowan.edu.

Rowan University, Graduate School, College of Liberal Arts and Sciences, Program in Mental Health Counseling and Applied Psychology, Glassboro, NJ 08028-1701. Offers MA. Part-time and evening/weekend programs available. *Students:* 6 full-time (4 women), 18 part-time (16 women); includes 3 minority (1 African American, 2 Asian Americans or Pacific Islanders). Average age 28. 28 applicants, 7% accepted, 1 enrolled. In 2008, 7 master's awarded. *Degree requirements:* For master's, thesis. *Entrance requirements:* For master's, GRE. Additional exam requirements/recommendations for international students: Required—TOEFL. *Application deadline:* Applications are processed on a rolling basis. Application fee: $50. Electronic applications accepted. *Expenses:* Tuition, area resident: Full-time $10,624; part-time $590 per credit. Tuition, state resident: full-time $10,624; part-time $590 per credit. Tuition, nonresident: full-time $10,624; part-time $590 per credit. Required fees: $2258; $124.90 per credit. *Financial support:* Career-related internships or fieldwork, scholarships/grants, health care benefits, and unspecified assistantships available. *Unit head:* Dr. Mira Lalovic-Hand, Interim Associate Provost/Director of Graduate School, 856-256-5120, E-mail: Lalovic-hand@rowan.edu. *Application contact:* Karen Haynes, Graduate Coordinator, 856-256-4052, Fax: 856-256-4436, E-mail: Haynes@rowan.edu.

Rutgers, The State University of New Jersey, Camden, Graduate School of Arts and Sciences, Program in Psychology, Camden, NJ 08102-1401. Offers MA. Part-time and evening/weekend programs available. *Degree requirements:* For master's, thesis. *Entrance requirements:* For master's, GRE, 3 letters of recommendation; statement of goals; prerequisite coursework in introductory psychology, statistics and experimental psychology. Additional exam requirements/recommendations for international students: Required—TOEFL, IELTS. Electronic applications accepted. *Faculty research:* Cognitive psychology, sexuality, health psychology, personality psychology, clinical psychology.

Rutgers, The State University of New Jersey, Newark, Graduate School, Program in Psychology, Newark, NJ 07102. Offers cognitive neuroscience (PhD); cognitive science (PhD); perception (PhD); psychobiology (PhD); social cognition (PhD). *Degree requirements:* For doctorate, comprehensive exam, thesis/dissertation. *Entrance requirements:* For doctorate, GRE General Test, GRE Subject Test, minimum undergraduate B average. Electronic applications accepted. *Faculty research:* Visual perception (luminance, motion), neuroendocrine mechanisms in behavior (reproduction, pain), attachment theory, connectionist modeling of cognition.

See Close-Up on page 1131.

Rutgers, The State University of New Jersey, New Brunswick, Graduate School of Applied and Professional Psychology, Piscataway, NJ 08854-8097. Offers Psy M, Psy D. *Accreditation:* APA (one or more programs are accredited). *Degree requirements:* For doctorate, comprehensive exam, thesis/dissertation, 1 year internship. *Entrance requirements:* For doctorate, GRE General Test, GRE Subject Test, bachelor's degree in psychology or equivalent. Additional exam requirements/recommendations for international students: Required—TOEFL. Electronic applications accepted. *Expenses:* Contact institution. *Faculty research:* Organizational psychology, behavior modification, long- and short-term dynamic therapy, school psychology, addictive behaviors.

Rutgers, The State University of New Jersey, New Brunswick, Graduate School, Program in Psychology, Piscataway, NJ 08854-8097. Offers behavioral neuroscience (PhD); clinical psychology (PhD); cognitive psychology (PhD); interdisciplinary health psychology (PhD); social psychology (PhD). *Accreditation:* APA. *Degree requirements:* For doctorate, comprehensive exam, thesis/dissertation. *Entrance requirements:* For doctorate, GRE General Test, 3 letters of recommendation. Additional exam requirements/recommendations for international students: Required—TOEFL (minimum score 577 paper-based; 233 computer-based). Electronic applications accepted. *Faculty research:* Learning and memory, behavioral ecology, hormones and behavior, psychopharmacology, anxiety disorders.

Sage Graduate School, Graduate School, Department of Psychology, Troy, NY 12180-4115. Offers community psychology (MA), including child care and children's services, community counseling, community health education, counseling and community psychology, general psychology; forensic psychology (Certificate). Part-time and evening/weekend programs available. *Faculty:* 4 full-time (all women), 5 part-time/adjunct (2 women). *Students:* 24 full-time (23 women), 58 part-time (54 women); includes 12 minority (6 African Americans, 2 American Indian/Alaska Native, 4 Hispanic Americans). Average age 30. 39 applicants, 54% accepted, 11 enrolled. In 2008, 29 master's, 3 other advanced degrees awarded. *Degree requirements:* For master's, thesis or alternative. *Entrance requirements:* For master's, GRE General Test. Additional exam requirements/recommendations for international students: Required—TOEFL (minimum score 550 paper-based; 213 computer-based). *Application deadline:* Applications are processed on a rolling basis. Application fee: $40. *Expenses:* Tuition: Full-time $10,080; part-time $560 per credit hour. *Financial support:* Fellowships, research assistantships, Federal Work-Study, scholarships/grants, and unspecified assistantships available. Support available to part-time students. Financial award application deadline: 3/1; financial award applicants required to submit FAFSA. *Faculty research:* Effectiveness of arts integration programs in elementary/secondary schools, literacy-based substance abuse program, outcome evaluation of program to increase college entry among urban youth. Total annual research expenditures: $10,000. *Unit head:* Dr. Jean Poppei, Chair, 518-244-2076, Fax: 518-244-4545, E-mail: poppei@sage.edu. *Application contact:* Wendy D. Diefendorf, Director of Graduate and Adult Admission, 518-244-2443, Fax: 518-244-6880, E-mail: diefew@sage.edu.

St. Cloud State University, School of Graduate Studies, College of Education, Department of Counselor Education and Educational Psychology, St. Cloud, MN 56301-4498. Offers college counseling and student development (MS); rehabilitation counseling (MS); school counseling (MS). *Degree requirements:* For master's, thesis or alternative. *Entrance requirements:* For master's, GRE General Test, minimum GPA of 2.75. Additional exam requirements/recommendations for international students: Required—Michigan English Language Assessment Battery; Recommended—TOEFL (minimum score 550 paper-based; 213 computer-based), IELTS (minimum score 6.5). Electronic applications accepted.

St. Cloud State University, School of Graduate Studies, College of Education, Department of Educational Leadership and Community Psychology, Program in Applied Behavior Analysis, St. Cloud, MN 56301-4498. Offers MS. Part-time programs available. Postbaccalaureate distance learning degree programs offered (no on-campus study). *Degree requirements:* For master's, comprehensive exam (for some programs), thesis or alternative. *Entrance requirements:* For master's, GRE General Test, minimum GPA of 2.75. Additional exam requirements/recommendations for international students: Required—Michigan English Language Assessment Battery; Recommended—TOEFL (minimum score 550 paper-based; 213 computer-based), IELTS (minimum score 6.5).

St. John's University, St. John's College of Liberal Arts and Sciences, Department of Psychology, Queens, NY 11439. Offers clinical psychology (PhD), including clinical psychology-child, clinical psychology-general; general experimental psychology (MA); school psychology (MS, Psy D). *Accreditation:* APA (one or more programs are accredited). Part-time and evening/weekend programs available. *Students:* 174 full-time (151 women), 86 part-time (73 women); includes 46 minority (11 African Americans, 17 Asian Americans or Pacific Islanders, 18 Hispanic Americans), 8 international. Average age 27. 438 applicants, 24% accepted, 59 enrolled. In 2008, 39 master's, 26 doctorates awarded. *Degree requirements:* For master's, comprehensive exam, thesis optional; for doctorate, comprehensive exam, thesis/dissertation, internship. *Entrance requirements:* For master's, GRE, minimum GPA of 3.0, 2 writing samples; for doctorate, GRE General Test, GRE Subject Test, interview. Additional exam requirements/recommendations for international students: Required—TOEFL (minimum score 500 paper-based; 173 computer-based; 61 iBT), IELTS (minimum score 5.5). *Application deadline:* For fall admission, 2/1 for domestic students, 5/1 priority date for international students; for spring admission, 11/1 priority date for international students. Applications are processed on a rolling basis. Application fee: $70. Electronic applications accepted. *Expenses:* Contact institution. *Financial support:* Fellowships, research assistantships, career-related internships or fieldwork, scholarships/grants, and unspecified assistantships available. Support available to part-time students. Financial award application deadline: 3/1; financial award applicants required to submit FAFSA. *Faculty research:* Clinical psychology, school psychology, developmental psychology, health psychology and psychotherapies. *Unit head:* Dr. Raymond DiGiuseppe, Chair, 718-990-1955, E-mail: digiuser@stjohns.edu. *Application contact:* Kathleen Davis, Director of Graduate Admissions, 718-990-2790, Fax: 718-990-5686, E-mail: gradhelp@stjohns.edu.

Saint Joseph's University, College of Arts and Sciences, Department of Criminal Justice, Philadelphia, PA 19131-1395. Offers administration/police executive (MS); behavior analysis (MS, Post-Master's Certificate); criminal justice (MS, Post-Master's Certificate); criminology (MS); federal law (MS); intelligence and crime (MS); probation, parole, and corrections (MS). Part-time and evening/weekend programs available. Postbaccalaureate distance learning degree programs offered. *Students:* 2 full-time (1 woman), 178 part-time (107 women); includes 56 minority (49 African Americans, 1 Asian American or Pacific Islander, 6 Hispanic Americans), 2 international. Average age 33. In 2008, 118 master's awarded. *Degree requirements:* For master's, thesis. *Entrance requirements:* For master's, GRE General Test or minimum GPA of 3.0, 2 letters of recommendation, personal statement, application, official transcripts. Additional exam requirements/recommendations for international students: Required—TOEFL (minimum score 550 paper-based; 213 computer-based; 79 iBT). *Application deadline:* For fall admission, 7/15 priority date for domestic students, 4/15 for international students; for winter admission, 1/15 for international students; for spring admission, 11/15 priority date for domestic students, 10/15 for international students. Applications are processed on a rolling basis. Application fee: $35. Electronic applications accepted. *Expenses:* Tuition: Part-time $745 per credit. Tuition and fees vary according to course load, degree level and program. *Financial support:* Career-related internships or fieldwork and unspecified assistantships available. Financial award applicants required to submit FAFSA. *Unit head:* Patricia Griffin, Director, 610-660-1294, E-mail: pgriffin@sju.edu. *Application contact:* Coralee Dixon, Assistant Director of Graduate Admissions, 610-660-1102, Fax: 610-660-1224, E-mail: coralee.dixon@sju.edu.

Saint Joseph's University, College of Arts and Sciences, Department of Psychology, Philadelphia, PA 19131-1395. Offers MS. Evening/weekend programs available. *Students:* 17 full-time (13 women); includes 2 minority (1 African American, 1 Hispanic American), 1 international. Average age 24. In 2008, 8 master's awarded. *Entrance requirements:* For master's, GRE General Test, 2 letters of recommendation, application, official transcripts, personal statement, psychology insert. Additional exam requirements/recommendations for international students: Required—TOEFL (minimum score 550 paper-based; 213 computer-based; 79 iBT). *Application deadline:* For fall admission, 3/1 priority date for domestic and international students; for winter admission, 1/15 for international students; for spring admission, 11/15 priority date for domestic students, 10/15 priority date for international students. Applications are processed on a rolling basis. Application fee: $35. Electronic applications accepted. *Expenses:* Tuition: Part-time $745 per credit. Tuition and fees vary according to course load, degree level and program. *Financial support:* In 2008–09, 7,200 teaching assistantships with full tuition reimbursements were awarded; unspecified assistantships also available. Financial award applicants required to submit FAFSA. *Unit head:* Dr. Jodi Mindell, Director, 610-660-1806, E-mail: jmindell@sju.edu. *Application contact:* Coralee Dixon, Assistant Director of Graduate Admissions, 610-660-1102, Fax: 610-660-1224, E-mail: coralee.dixon@sju.edu.

Saint Louis University, Graduate School, College of Arts and Sciences and Graduate School, Department of Psychology, St. Louis, MO 63103-2097. Offers clinical psychology (MS-R, PhD); experimental psychology (MS-R, PhD); industrial-organizational psychology (PhD); psychology (PhD). *Accreditation:* APA (one or more programs are accredited). Part-time programs available. *Degree requirements:* For master's, comprehensive exam, thesis; for doctorate, thesis/dissertation, clinical internship (for clinical psychology PhD). *Entrance requirements:* For master's and doctorate, GRE General Test, interview, letters of recommendation, resumé, transcripts, goal statement. Additional exam requirements/recommendations for international students: Required—TOEFL (minimum score 550 paper-based; 213 computer-based). Electronic applications accepted. *Faculty research:* Violence and trauma; neural basis of learning and memory function; eating disorders; body image and health behavior; prejudice, stereotyping, and victimization; memory, cognitive aging and language processing.

Saint Mary's University, Faculty of Science, Department of Psychology, Halifax, NS B3H 3C3, Canada. Offers applied psychology (M Sc, PhD), including industrial/organizational psychology. Part-time programs available. *Degree requirements:* For master's, thesis, internship. *Entrance requirements:* For master's, GRE General Test, honors degree, minimum QPA of 3.25. *Faculty research:* Assessment, health psychology, social psychology, cognition.

St. Mary's University, Graduate School, Department of Psychology, San Antonio, TX 78228-8507. Offers clinical psychology (MA, MS); industrial/organizational psychology (MA, MS). Part-time programs available. *Faculty:* 6 full-time (3 women), 5 part-time/adjunct (2 women). *Students:* 24 full-time (20 women), 17 part-time (8 women); includes 12 minority (1 African American, 1 American Indian/Alaska Native, 1 Asian American or Pacific Islander, 9 Hispanic Americans), 2 international. Average age 25. 40 applicants, 73% accepted, 22 enrolled. In 2008, 17 master's awarded. *Degree requirements:* For master's, comprehensive exam. *Entrance requirements:* For master's, GRE General Test, letters of recommendation, work experience. Additional exam requirements/recommendations for international students: Required—TOEFL (minimum score 550 paper-based; 213 computer-based; 80 iBT). *Application deadline:* Applications are processed on a rolling basis. Application fee: $0. Electronic applications accepted. *Expenses:* Tuition: Full-time $12,006; part-time $667 per credit hour. Required fees: $440; $220 per semester. *Financial support:* In 2008–09, 6 students received support, including 4 fellowships (averaging $3,125 per year), 2 research assistantships (averaging $4,500 per year); career-related internships or fieldwork, Federal Work-Study, institutionally sponsored

Psychology—General

St. Mary's University (continued)

loans, scholarships/grants, and health care benefits also available. Financial award application deadline: 3/31; financial award applicants required to submit FAFSA. *Unit head:* Dr. Patricia Owen, Director, 210-436-3314, Fax: 210-431-4301, E-mail: psycpat@stmarytx.edu. *Application contact:* Dr. Henry Flores, Dean of the Graduate School, 210-436-3101, Fax: 210-431-2220, E-mail: hflores@stmarytx.edu.

Saint Xavier University, Graduate Studies, School of Arts and Sciences, Department of Psychology, Chicago, IL 60655-3105. Offers adult counseling (Certificate); child/adolescent counseling (Certificate); core counseling (Certificate); counseling psychology (MA). Part-time and evening/weekend programs available. *Entrance requirements:* For master's, GRE General Test, minimum GPA of 3.0, interview.

Salem State College, School of Graduate Studies, Program in Counseling and Psychological Services, Salem, MA 01970-5353. Offers MS. Part-time and evening/weekend programs available. *Students:* 36 full-time (29 women), 40 part-time (36 women); includes 3 minority (1 Asian American or Pacific Islander, 2 Hispanic Americans), 4 international. Average age 31. In 2008, 11 master's awarded. *Entrance requirements:* For master's, GRE General Test or MAT. *Application deadline:* Applications are processed on a rolling basis. Application fee: $35. *Unit head:* Dr. Patrice Miller, Coordinator, 978-542-6075, Fax: 978-542-6596, E-mail: pmiller@salemstate.edu. *Application contact:* Dr. Marc Glasser, Dean of the Graduate School, 978-542-6323, Fax: 978-542-7215.

Sam Houston State University, College of Humanities and Social Sciences, Department of Psychology and Philosophy, Huntsville, TX 77341. Offers clinical psychology (PhD); psychology (MA). *Accreditation:* APA. Part-time programs available. *Faculty:* 14 full-time (5 women), 1 part-time/adjunct (0 women). *Students:* 69 full-time (55 women), 33 part-time (28 women); includes 20 minority (6 African Americans, 6 Asian Americans or Pacific Islanders, 8 Hispanic Americans), 3 international. Average age 26. 139 applicants, 26% accepted, 31 enrolled. In 2008, 13 master's, 4 doctorates awarded. *Degree requirements:* For master's, thesis. *Entrance requirements:* For master's, GRE General Test or MAT, minimum GPA of 3.0. Additional exam requirements/recommendations for international students: Required—TOEFL (minimum score 550 paper-based; 213 computer-based; 79 iBT). *Application deadline:* For fall admission, 8/1 for domestic students; for spring admission, 12/1 for domestic students. Applications are processed on a rolling basis. Application fee: $20. *Expenses:* Tuition, state resident: full-time $3564; part-time $198 per credit hour. Tuition, nonresident: full-time $8622; part-time $479 per credit hour. Required fees: $1290. Tuition and fees vary according to course load and campus/location. *Financial support:* Research assistantships, teaching assistantships, career-related internships or fieldwork and institutionally sponsored loans available. Support available to part-time students. Financial award application deadline: 5/31; financial award applicants required to submit FAFSA. *Unit head:* Dr. Christopher Wilson, Chair, 936-294-3052, Fax: 936-294-3798, E-mail: psy_dcw@shsu.edu. *Application contact:* Dr. Rowland Miller, Graduate Coordinator, 936-294-1176, Fax: 936-294-3798, E-mail: psy_rsm@shsu.edu.

San Diego State University, Graduate and Research Affairs, College of Sciences, Department of Psychology, San Diego, CA 92182. Offers clinical psychology (MS, PhD); industrial and organizational psychology (MS); program evaluation (MS); psychology (MA). *Accreditation:* APA (one or more programs are accredited). Terminal master's awarded for partial completion of doctoral program. *Degree requirements:* For master's, thesis, oral exam; for doctorate, thesis/dissertation. *Entrance requirements:* For master's, GRE General Test, GRE Subject Test, 3 letters of recommendation; for doctorate, GRE General Test, GRE Subject Test, minimum GPA of 3.0, 3 letters of recommendation. Additional exam requirements/recommendations for international students: Required—TOEFL. Electronic applications accepted.

San Francisco State University, Division of Graduate Studies, College of Behavioral and Social Sciences, Department of Psychology, San Francisco, CA 94132-1722. Offers MA, MS.

San Jose State University, Graduate Studies and Research, College of Social Sciences, Department of Psychology, San Jose, CA 95192-0001. Offers clinical psychology (MS); experimental psychology (MA); industrial/organizational psychology (MS); psychology (MA). *Degree requirements:* For master's, comprehensive exam, thesis (for some programs). *Entrance requirements:* For master's, GRE General Test, minimum GPA of 3.0. Electronic applications accepted. *Faculty research:* Drug and alcohol abuse, neurohormonal mechanisms in motion sickness, behavior modification, sleep research, genetics.

Saybrook Graduate School and Research Center, Programs in Psychology, Human Science and Organizational Systems, San Francisco, CA 94111-1920. Offers clinical psychology (PhD); creativity studies (MA); human science (MA, PhD), including consciousness and spirituality, individualized (PhD), integrative health studies, organizational systems, social transformation; marriage and family therapy (MA); organizational systems (MA, PhD), including individualized (PhD), organizational systems; psychology (MA, PhD), including consciousness and spirituality, humanistic and transpersonal psychology, individualized (PhD), integrative health studies, licensure track (MA), organizational systems, social transformation. Postbaccalaureate distance learning degree programs offered (minimal on-campus study). Terminal master's awarded for partial completion of doctoral program. *Degree requirements:* For master's, thesis or alternative; for doctorate, thesis/dissertation. Electronic applications accepted. *Faculty research:* Humanistic theory, health studies, organizational systems, consciousness and spirituality, social transformation.

The School of Professional Psychology at Forest Institute, Graduate Programs, Springfield, MO 65807. Offers clinical psychology (Psy D); counseling psychology (MA); marriage and family therapy (MA, PGC). *Accreditation:* AAMFT/COAMFTE; APA (one or more programs are accredited). *Faculty:* 18 full-time (9 women), 28 part-time/adjunct (15 women). *Students:* 208 full-time (141 women), 34 part-time (27 women). 153 applicants, 42% accepted, 40 enrolled. In 2008, 36 master's, 36 doctorates awarded. Terminal master's awarded for partial completion of doctoral program. *Median time to degree:* Of those who began their doctoral program in fall 2000, 100% received their degree in 8 years or less. *Degree requirements:* For master's, thesis, practice; for doctorate, comprehensive exam, thesis/dissertation, internship, practice. *Entrance requirements:* For master's, GRE General Test, interview, minimum GPA of 3.0, 12 hours in psychology; for doctorate, GRE General Test, interview, minimum GPA of 3.0, 18 hours in psychology. Additional exam requirements/recommendations for international students: Required—TOEFL (minimum score 550 paper-based; 213 computer-based). *Application deadline:* For fall admission, 1/15 priority date for domestic and international students; for spring admission, 8/1 priority date for domestic and international students. Applications are processed on a rolling basis. Application fee: $50. Electronic applications accepted. *Expenses:* Tuition: Full-time $22,500. *Financial support:* In 2008–09, 91 students received support. Career-related internships or fieldwork, Federal Work-Study, and scholarships/grants available. Support available to part-time students. Financial award applicants required to submit FAFSA. *Faculty research:* Forensics/corrections, marriage and family therapy, child and adolescent, integrated health care, neuropsychology. *Unit head:* Dr. Mark E. Skrade, President, 417-823-3477, Fax: 417-823-3442, E-mail: mskrade@forest.edu. *Application contact:* Dawn Medley, Director of Enrollment Management, 417-823-3477, Fax: 417-823-3442, E-mail: dmedley@forest.edu.

Seattle University, College of Arts and Sciences, Department of Psychology, Seattle, WA 98122-1090. Offers existential and phenomenological therapeutic psychology (MA Psych). *Degree requirements:* For master's, thesis. *Entrance requirements:* For master's, interview, minimum GPA of 3.0, previous undergraduate course work in psychology. *Faculty research:* Healing, transformations in relationships, therapy, dialogical research.

Seton Hall University, College of Arts and Sciences, Department of Psychology, South Orange, NJ 07079-2697. Offers experimental psychology (MS), including behavioral neuroscience. Part-time and evening/weekend programs available. *Entrance requirements:* Additional exam requirements/recommendations for international students: Required—TOEFL. Electronic applica-

tions accepted. *Faculty research:* Behavioral neuroscience, cognitive psychology, social psychology, perception/motor skills, memory, depression, anxiety.

See Close-Up on page 1133.

Seton Hall University, College of Education and Human Services, Department of Professional Psychology and Family Therapy, South Orange, NJ 07079-2697. Offers counseling psychology (MA, PhD); marriage and family therapy (MS, PhD, Ed S); psychological studies (MA); school psychology (Ed S). *Accreditation:* APA. Part-time and evening/weekend programs available. Postbaccalaureate distance learning degree programs offered (minimal on-campus study). Terminal master's awarded for partial completion of doctoral program. *Degree requirements:* For master's, comprehensive exam, case study; for doctorate, comprehensive exam, thesis/dissertation, internship; for Ed S, comprehensive exam, internship. *Entrance requirements:* For master's, GRE or MAT; for doctorate, GRE, interview; for Ed S, GRE or MAT, interview. *Faculty research:* Counseling process, ethics, family systems, child pathology.

Shippensburg University of Pennsylvania, School of Graduate Studies, College of Arts and Sciences, Department of Psychology, Shippensburg, PA 17257-2299. Offers MS. Part-time and evening/weekend programs available. *Faculty:* 10 full-time (3 women). *Students:* 18 full-time (13 women), 14 part-time (8 women); includes 1 minority (Asian American or Pacific Islander). Average age 27. 35 applicants, 51% accepted, 9 enrolled. In 2008, 10 master's awarded. *Degree requirements:* For master's, thesis optional. *Entrance requirements:* For master's, GRE Subject Test (psychology), minimum GPA of 2.75, 1 course in statistics, 6 undergraduate credit hours in psychology, supplemental application with goals statement. Additional exam requirements/recommendations for international students: Required—TOEFL (minimum score 560 paper-based; 220 computer-based); Recommended—IELTS (minimum score 6). *Application deadline:* For fall admission, 4/1 priority date for domestic students, 3/1 for international students; for spring admission, 11/1 priority date for domestic students, 7/1 for international students. Applications are processed on a rolling basis. Application fee: $30. Electronic applications accepted. *Expenses:* Tuition, state resident: full-time $6430; part-time $357 per credit. Tuition, nonresident: full-time $10,288; part-time $572 per credit. Required fees: $1127; $38 per credit. One-time fee: $44 part-time. *Financial support:* In 2008–09, 10 research assistantships with full tuition reimbursements (averaging $5,000 per year) were awarded; career-related internships or fieldwork, scholarships/grants, unspecified assistantships, and resident hall directors, student payroll positions also available. Support available to part-time students. Financial award application deadline: 3/1; financial award applicants required to submit FAFSA. *Unit head:* Dr. Suzanne Morin, Chairperson, 717-477-1657, Fax: 717-477-4057, E-mail: smmori@ship.edu. *Application contact:* Renee Payne, Associate Dean of Graduate Admissions, 717-477-1231, Fax: 717-477-4016, E-mail: rmpayn@ship.edu.

Simon Fraser University, Graduate Studies, Faculty of Arts and Social Sciences, Department of Psychology, Burnaby, BC V5A 1S6, Canada. Offers MA, PhD. *Accreditation:* APA (one or more programs are accredited). *Degree requirements:* For master's, thesis; for doctorate, thesis/dissertation. *Entrance requirements:* For master's and doctorate, GRE, minimum GPA of 3.5. Additional exam requirements/recommendations for international students: Required—TOEFL or IELTS. *Expenses:* Contact institution. *Faculty research:* Social cognition/biological neuropsychology, theory and methods.

Southeastern Baptist Theological Seminary, Graduate and Professional Programs, Wake Forest, NC 27588-1889. Offers advanced biblical studies (M Div); Christian education (M Div, MACE); Christian ethics (PhD); Christian ministry (M Div); Christian planting (M Div); church music (MACM); counseling (MACO); evangelism (PhD); language (M Div); ministry (D Min); New Testament (PhD); Old Testament (PhD); philosophy (PhD); theology (Th M, PhD); women's studies (M Div). *Accreditation:* ACIPE; ATS (one or more programs are accredited). *Degree requirements:* For master's, thesis (for some programs), oral exam; for doctorate, thesis/dissertation, fieldwork; for M Div, supervised ministry. *Entrance requirements:* For master's, Cooperative English Test, minimum GPA of 2.0, M Div or equivalent (Th M); for doctorate, GRE General Test or MAT, Cooperative English Test, M Div or equivalent, 3 years of professional experience.

Southeastern Louisiana University, College of Arts, Humanities and Social Sciences, Department of Psychology, Hammond, LA 70402. Offers MA. Part-time programs available. *Faculty:* 5 full-time (1 woman). *Students:* 10 full-time (6 women), 14 part-time (10 women), 2 international. Average age 25. 11 applicants, 91% accepted, 5 enrolled. In 2008, 4 master's awarded. *Degree requirements:* For master's, comprehensive exam, thesis. *Entrance requirements:* For master's, GRE General Test, minimum GPA of 3.0, 18 undergraduate hours in psychology/educational psychology, 3 letters of reference. Additional exam requirements/recommendations for international students: Required—TOEFL (minimum score 500 paper-based; 173 computer-based; 61 iBT). *Application deadline:* For fall admission, 7/15 priority date for domestic students, 6/1 priority date for international students; for spring admission, 12/1 priority date for domestic students, 10/1 priority date for international students. Applications are processed on a rolling basis. Application fee: $20 ($30 for international students). Electronic applications accepted. *Expenses:* Tuition, area resident: Full-time $2376. Tuition, state resident: full-time $2376. Tuition, nonresident: full-time $6876. Required fees: $1105. *Financial support:* In 2008–09, 10 students received support, including 10 research assistantships with full tuition reimbursements available (averaging $10,100 per year); career-related internships or fieldwork, Federal Work-Study, institutionally sponsored loans, unspecified assistantships, and administrative assistantship also available. Support available to part-time students. Financial award application deadline: 5/1; financial award applicants required to submit FAFSA. *Faculty research:* Social cognition, police lineup identification, body image, cross-cultural parenting strategy, organizational performance. *Unit head:* Dr. Matt Rossano, Department Head, 985-549-2154, Fax: 985-549-6892, E-mail: mrossano@selu.edu. *Application contact:* Sandra Meyers, Graduate Admissions Analyst, 985-549-2066, Fax: 985-549-5632, E-mail: admissions@selu.edu.

Southern Adventist University, School of Education and Psychology, Collegedale, TN 37315-0370. Offers curriculum and instruction (MS Ed); educational administration and supervision (MS Ed); inclusive education (MS Ed); literacy education (MS Ed); outdoor teacher education (MS Ed); professional counseling (MS); school counseling (MS). *Accreditation:* NCATE. Part-time and evening/weekend programs available. *Degree requirements:* For master's, comprehensive exam (for some programs), thesis optional, position paper (MS), portfolio (MS Ed in outdoor teacher education). *Entrance requirements:* For master's, GRE General Test, interview (MS); 9 semester hours of upper division course work in psychology or related field, including 1 course in psychology research or statistics; 9 semester hours of education (MS Ed). Additional exam requirements/recommendations for international students: Required—TOEFL (minimum score 600 paper-based; 250 computer-based; 100 iBT). Electronic applications accepted.

Southern California Seminary, Graduate and Professional Programs, El Cajon, CA 92019. Offers biblical studies (MA); counseling psychology (MACP); psychology (Psy D); religious studies (MRS); theology (M Div). Part-time and evening/weekend programs available. Postbaccalaureate distance learning degree programs offered (minimal on-campus study). *Degree requirements:* For master's, thesis (for some programs); for doctorate, thesis/dissertation; for M Div, 2 foreign languages. *Entrance requirements:* For doctorate, master's degree in psychology. Additional exam requirements/recommendations for international students: Required—TOEFL (minimum score 550 paper-based). Electronic applications accepted.

Southern Connecticut State University, School of Graduate Studies, School of Arts and Sciences, Department of Psychology, New Haven, CT 06515-1355. Offers MA. Part-time and evening/weekend programs available. *Degree requirements:* For master's, thesis or alternative. *Entrance requirements:* For master's, interview, previous course work in psychology. Electronic applications accepted.

Southern Illinois University Carbondale, Graduate School, College of Education, Department of Behavior Analysis and Therapy, Carbondale, IL 62901-4701. Offers MS.

Southern Illinois University Carbondale, Graduate School, College of Liberal Arts, Department of Psychology, Carbondale, IL 62901-4701. Offers clinical psychology (MA, MS, PhD); counseling psychology (MA, MS, PhD); experimental psychology (MA, MS, PhD). *Accreditation:* APA (one or more programs are accredited). *Degree requirements:* For master's, thesis; for doctorate, thesis/dissertation. *Entrance requirements:* For master's, GRE General Test, GRE Subject Test, minimum GPA of 2.7; for doctorate, GRE General Test, GRE Subject Test, minimum GPA of 3.25. Additional exam requirements/recommendations for international students: Required—TOEFL. *Faculty research:* Developmental neuropsychology; smoking, affect, and cognition; personality measurement; vocational psychology; program evaluation.

See Close-Up on page 1135.

Southern Illinois University Edwardsville, Graduate Studies and Research, School of Education, Department of Psychology, Edwardsville, IL 62026-0001. Offers clinical child and school psychology (MS); clinical-adult psychology (MA); industrial-organizational psychology (MA); school psychology (SD). Part-time programs available. *Faculty:* 20 full-time (9 women). *Students:* 41 full-time (35 women), 40 part-time (33 women); includes 4 minority (3 African Americans, 1 Asian American or Pacific Islander), 2 international. Average age 26. 157 applicants, 18% accepted. In 2008, 29 master's, 12 other advanced degrees awarded. *Degree requirements:* For master's, thesis (for some programs), research paper; for SD, thesis. *Entrance requirements:* For master's, GRE. Additional exam requirements/recommendations for international students: Required—TOEFL (minimum score 550 paper-based; 213 computer-based; 79 iBT), IELTS (minimum score 6.5). *Application deadline:* For fall admission, 2/1 for domestic and international students. Application fee: $30. Electronic applications accepted. *Expenses:* Tuition, area resident: Full-time $5838. Tuition, nonresident: full-time $14,596. Required fees: $1525. *Financial support:* In 2008–09, 1 fellowship with full tuition reimbursement (averaging $8,370 per year), 2 research assistantships (averaging $8,064 per year), 44 teaching assistantships with full tuition reimbursements (averaging $8,064 per year) were awarded; career-related internships or fieldwork, Federal Work-Study, institutionally sponsored loans, traineeships, and unspecified assistantships also available. Support available to part-time students. Financial award application deadline: 3/1; financial award applicants required to submit FAFSA. *Unit head:* Dr. Lynn Bartels, Co-Chair, 618-650-2202, E-mail: lbartel@siue.edu. *Application contact:* Dr. Lynn Bartels, Co-Chair, 618-650-2202, E-mail: lbartel@siue.edu.

Southern Methodist University, Dedman College, Department of Psychology, Dallas, TX 75275. Offers clinical psychology (PhD). Part-time programs available. *Faculty:* 18 full-time (7 women), 4 part-time/adjunct (all women). *Students:* 21 full-time (18 women); includes 3 minority (1 American Indian/Alaska Native, 2 Hispanic Americans). Average age 29. 164 applicants, 10% accepted, 8 enrolled. *Degree requirements:* For doctorate, comprehensive exam, thesis/dissertation, oral exam, practicum, research presentation and publication. *Entrance requirements:* For doctorate, GRE General Test, minimum GPA of 3.0. Additional exam requirements/recommendations for international students: Required—TOEFL (minimum score 550 paper-based). *Application deadline:* For fall admission, 2/1 priority date for domestic and international students. Application fee: $60. Electronic applications accepted. *Financial support:* In 2008–09, 9 students received support, including 8 research assistantships with tuition reimbursements available (averaging $14,000 per year); teaching assistantships, career-related internships or fieldwork, Federal Work-Study, and institutionally sponsored loans also available. Support available to part-time students. Financial award application deadline: 1/1; financial award applicants required to submit FAFSA. *Faculty research:* Experimental, social, developmental, and cognitive psychology; anger/violence; mood disorders; depression and anxiety; family assessment and development; chronic pain and mental health. *Unit head:* Dr. Ernest Jouriles, Chair, 214-768-2360, Fax: 214-768-3910, E-mail: ejourile@mail.smu.edu. *Application contact:* Dr. Robert B. Hampson, Director, 214-768-2734, Fax: 214-768-3910, E-mail: rhampson@smu.edu.

Southern Nazarene University, Graduate College, School of Psychology, Bethany, OK 73008. Offers counseling psychology (MSCP); marriage and family therapy (MA). *Degree requirements:* For master's, thesis optional. *Entrance requirements:* For master's, English proficiency exam, minimum GPA of 3.0 in last 60 hours/major, 2.7 overall.

Southern New Hampshire University, School of Liberal Arts, Manchester, NH 03106-1045. Offers clinical services for adults psychiatric disabilities (Certificate); clinical services for children and adolescents with psychiatric disabilities (Certificate); clinical services for persons with co-occurring substance abuse and psychiatric disabilities (Certificate); community mental health (MS); fiction writing (MFA); non-fiction writing (MFA); teaching English as a foreign language (MS). Part-time and evening/weekend programs available. *Degree requirements:* For master's, one foreign language, thesis. *Entrance requirements:* For master's, minimum GPA of 2.75: MS-TEFL, 3.0: MFA. Additional exam requirements/recommendations for international students: Required—TOEFL (minimum score 550 paper-based; 213 computer-based; 79 iBT), IELTS (minimum score 6.5), TWE (minimum score 5). Electronic applications accepted. *Expenses:* Contact institution. *Faculty research:* Action research, state of the art practice in behavioral health services, wraparound approaches to working with youth, learning styles.

Southern Oregon University, Graduate Studies, School of Social Sciences, Department of Psychology, Ashland, OR 97520. Offers applied psychology (MAP); human service-organizational training and development (MA, MS); social science (MA, MS), including professional counseling, psychology. Part-time programs available. *Degree requirements:* For master's, thesis, portfolio and oral defense. *Entrance requirements:* For master's, GRE General Test, minimum GPA of 3.0. Electronic applications accepted.

Southern University and Agricultural and Mechanical College, Graduate School, College of Sciences, Department of Psychology, Baton Rouge, LA 70813. Offers rehabilitation counseling (MS). *Degree requirements:* For master's, comprehensive exam, thesis optional. *Entrance requirements:* For master's, GMAT or GRE General Test. Additional exam requirements/recommendations for international students: Required—TOEFL (minimum score 525 paper-based; 193 computer-based). *Faculty research:* Cultural diversity, professional preparation and participation of minorities, needs and satisfaction of students with disabilities, prediction model for rehabilitation outcome, diabetes.

Southwestern College, Program in Psychodrama and Action Methods, Santa Fe, NM 87502-4788. Offers Certificate. *Entrance requirements:* For degree, 3 letters of reference, interview application.

Spalding University, Graduate Studies, College of Social Sciences and Humanities, School of Professional Psychology, Louisville, KY 40203-2188. Offers clinical psychology (MA, Psy D). *Accreditation:* APA (one or more programs are accredited). Part-time programs available. Terminal master's awarded for partial completion of doctoral program. *Degree requirements:* For master's, comprehensive exam; for doctorate, thesis/dissertation. *Entrance requirements:* For master's, GRE General Test, 18 hours of undergraduate course work in psychology, interview; for doctorate, GRE General Test, interview, 18 hours of coursework in psychology. Additional exam requirements/recommendations for international students: Required—TOEFL (minimum score 535 paper-based; 203 computer-based). *Expenses:* Tuition: Full-time $11,340; part-time $630 per credit hour. Tuition and fees vary according to program. *Faculty research:* Substance abuse, prayer research, end-of-life issues, complementary and alternative medicine, research methodology and statistical inference.

Stanford University, School of Humanities and Sciences, Department of Psychology, Stanford, CA 94305-9991. Offers PhD. *Degree requirements:* For doctorate, thesis/dissertation, oral exam. *Entrance requirements:* For doctorate, GRE General Test, GRE Subject Test. Additional exam requirements/recommendations for international students: Required—TOEFL. Electronic applications accepted.

State University of New York at Binghamton, Graduate School, School of Arts and Sciences, Department of Psychology, Binghamton, NY 13902-6000. Offers behavioral neuroscience (MA, PhD); clinical psychology (MA, PhD); cognitive and behavioral science (MA, PhD). *Accreditation:* APA (one or more programs are accredited). *Faculty:* 27 full-time (11 women), 7 part-time/adjunct (2 women). *Students:* 71 full-time (49 women), 21 part-time (16 women); includes 12 minority (4 African Americans, 1 Asian American or Pacific Islander, 7 Hispanic Americans), 6 international. Average age 27. 271 applicants, 10% accepted, 17 enrolled. In 2008, 10 doctorates awarded. Terminal master's awarded for partial completion of doctoral program. *Degree requirements:* For master's, thesis; for doctorate, thesis/dissertation, departmental qualifying exam. *Entrance requirements:* For master's and doctorate, GRE General Test, GRE Subject Test. Additional exam requirements/recommendations for international students: Required—TOEFL. *Application deadline:* For fall admission, 4/15 priority date for domestic students, 1/15 priority date for international students; for spring admission, 11/1 for domestic students, 10/1 priority date for international students. Applications are processed on a rolling basis. Application fee: $60. Electronic applications accepted. *Expenses:* Tuition, area resident: Full-time $6900; part-time $288 per credit. Tuition, state resident: full-time $6900; part-time $288 per credit. Tuition, nonresident: full-time $10,920; part-time $455 per credit. Required fees: $1130. Part-time tuition and fees vary according to course load, program and student level. *Financial support:* In 2008–09, 72 students received support, including 9 fellowships with full tuition reimbursements available (averaging $17,500 per year), 19 research assistantships with full tuition reimbursements available (averaging $17,500 per year), 40 teaching assistantships with full tuition reimbursements available (averaging $17,500 per year); career-related internships or fieldwork, Federal Work-Study, institutionally sponsored loans, scholarships/grants, health care benefits, and unspecified assistantships also available. Financial award application deadline: 2/15; financial award applicants required to submit FAFSA. *Unit head:* Dr. Peter Gerhardstein, Chair, 607-777-4387, E-mail: gerhard@binghamton.edu. *Application contact:* Victoria Williams, Recruiting and Admissions Coordinator, 607-777-2151, Fax: 607-777-2501, E-mail: vwilliam@binghamton.edu.

State University of New York at New Paltz, Graduate School, School of Liberal Arts and Sciences, Department of Psychology, New Paltz, NY 12561. Offers mental health counseling (MS); psychology (MA); school counseling (MS). Part-time and evening/weekend programs available. *Faculty:* 13 full-time (8 women), 1 (woman) part-time/adjunct. *Students:* 23 full-time (18 women), 14 part-time (12 women); includes 3 minority (1 Asian American or Pacific Islander, 2 Hispanic Americans). Average age 27. 71 applicants, 54% accepted, 17 enrolled. In 2008, 12 master's awarded. *Degree requirements:* For master's, comprehensive exam, thesis. *Entrance requirements:* For master's, GRE General Test, minimum GPA of 3.0. Additional exam requirements/recommendations for international students: Required—TOEFL (minimum score 550 paper-based; 213 computer-based; 80 iBT). *Application deadline:* For fall admission, 3/15 priority date for domestic students, 3/15 for international students; for spring admission, 11/15 for domestic and international students. Application fee: $50. Electronic applications accepted. *Financial support:* In 2008–09, 5 students received support, including 5 teaching assistantships with partial tuition reimbursements available (averaging $5,000 per year); career-related internships or fieldwork, Federal Work-Study, institutionally sponsored loans, traineeships, and unspecified assistantships also available. Financial award application deadline: 8/1; financial award applicants required to submit FAFSA. *Faculty research:* Disaster mental health, women's objectification, mate selection, cultural psychology, achievement motivation. *Unit head:* Dr. Douglas Maynard, Chair, 845-257-3426, E-mail: maynardd@newpaltz.edu. *Application contact:* Dr. Jonathan Raskin, Coordinator, 845-257-3471, E-mail: raskinj@newpaltz.edu.

State University of New York at Plattsburgh, Faculty of Arts and Science, Department of Psychology, Plattsburgh, NY 12901-2681. Offers school psychology (MA, CAS). Part-time programs available. *Faculty:* 2 full-time (1 woman), 3 part-time/adjunct (2 women). *Students:* 18 full-time (14 women), 7 part-time (5 women); includes 3 minority (1 Asian American or Pacific Islander, 2 Hispanic Americans), 1 international. Average age 26. 22 applicants, 77% accepted, 9 enrolled. In 2008, 8 master's, 8 other advanced degrees awarded. *Degree requirements:* For master's, thesis, internship. *Entrance requirements:* For master's, GRE General Test, minimum GPA of 3.0. Additional exam requirements/recommendations for international students: Required—TOEFL (minimum score 550 paper-based; 213 computer-based; 79 iBT). *Application deadline:* For fall admission, 2/15 priority date for domestic students. Applications are processed on a rolling basis. Application fee: $75. *Expenses:* Tuition, area resident: Full-time $7880; part-time $328 per credit hour. Tuition, state resident: full-time $7880; part-time $328 per credit hour. Tuition, nonresident: full-time $13,250; part-time $552 per credit hour. Required fees: $1060. *Financial support:* Federal Work-Study available. Support available to part-time students. Financial award application deadline: 4/15; financial award applicants required to submit FAFSA. *Faculty research:* Alzheimer's disease, adolescent behavior, intellectual assessment, learning disabilities, reading skill acquisition. *Unit head:* Dr. Wendy Braje, Chair, 518-564-3383, E-mail: brajewl@plattsburgh.edu. *Application contact:* Marguerite Adelman, Assistant Director, Graduate Admissions, 518-564-4723, Fax: 518-564-4722, E-mail: adelmaml@plattsburgh.edu.

Stephen F. Austin State University, Graduate School, College of Liberal Arts, Department of Psychology, Nacogdoches, TX 75962. Offers MA. *Degree requirements:* For master's, comprehensive exam, thesis. *Entrance requirements:* For master's, GRE General Test. Additional exam requirements/recommendations for international students: Required—TOEFL.

Stony Brook University, State University of New York, Graduate School, College of Arts and Sciences, Department of Psychology, Stony Brook, NY 11794. Offers biopsychology (PhD); clinical psychology (PhD); cognitive/experimental psychology (PhD); social and health psychology (PhD). *Accreditation:* APA. *Faculty:* 31 full-time (13 women), 1 (woman) part-time/adjunct. *Students:* 96 full-time (70 women); includes 17 minority (2 African Americans, 8 Asian Americans or Pacific Islanders, 7 Hispanic Americans), 11 international. Average age 27. 477 applicants, 6% accepted. In 2008, 23 doctorates awarded. *Degree requirements:* For doctorate, thesis/dissertation. *Entrance requirements:* For doctorate, GRE General Test, GRE Subject Test. Additional exam requirements/recommendations for international students: Required—TOEFL. *Application deadline:* For fall admission, 1/15 for domestic students. Application fee: $60. *Expenses:* Tuition, area resident: Full-time $7880; part-time $328 per credit hour. Tuition, state resident: full-time $7880; part-time $328 per credit hour. Tuition, nonresident: full-time $13,250; part-time $552 per credit hour. Required fees: $848. *Financial support:* In 2008–09, 20 research assistantships, 53 teaching assistantships were awarded; fellowships, career-related internships or fieldwork also available. *Faculty research:* Behavior therapy, memory and cognition, child and family studies, quantitative methods, health psychology. Total annual research expenditures: $4.3 million. *Unit head:* Dr. Nancy Squires, Chair, 631-632-7855, Fax: 631-632-7876, E-mail: nancy.squires@stonybrook.edu. *Application contact:* Graduate Director, 631-632-7855, Fax: 631-632-7876.

Suffolk University, College of Arts and Sciences, Department of Psychology, Boston, MA 02108-2770. Offers clinical psychology (PhD). *Accreditation:* APA. *Degree requirements:* For doctorate, thesis/dissertation, practicum. *Entrance requirements:* For doctorate, GRE General Test or MAT, statement of professional goals, official transcripts, 2 letters of recommendation, resumé. Additional exam requirements/recommendations for international students: Required—TOEFL (minimum score 550 paper-based; 213 computer-based; 80 iBT). Electronic applications accepted. *Expenses:* Contact institution. *Faculty research:* Olfaction decision-making in substance-dependent individuals, ego development, experiential avoidance in generalized anxiety disorder.

Sul Ross State University, School of Arts and Sciences, Department of Behavioral and Social Sciences, Program in Psychology, Alpine, TX 79832. Offers MA. *Entrance requirements:* For master's, GRE General Test, minimum GPA of 2.5 in last 60 hours of undergraduate work.

Temple University, Graduate School, College of Liberal Arts, Department of Psychology, Philadelphia, PA 19122-6096. Offers clinical psychology (PhD); cognitive psychology (PhD); developmental psychology (PhD); social psychology (PhD). *Accreditation:* APA. *Degree requirements:* For doctorate, thesis/dissertation. *Entrance requirements:* For doctorate, GRE General Test, minimum GPA of 3.0. Additional exam requirements/recommendations for inter-

Psychology—General

Temple University (continued)

national students: Required—TOEFL (minimum score 550 paper-based; 213 computer-based; 79 iBT). Electronic applications accepted.

Tennessee State University, The School of Graduate Studies and Research, College of Education, Department of Psychology, Nashville, TN 37209-1561. Offers counseling and guidance (MS), including counseling, elementary school counseling, organizational counseling, secondary school counseling; counseling psychology (PhD); psychology (MS, PhD); school psychology (MS, PhD). *Accreditation:* APA. *Faculty:* 15 full-time (9 women), 1 (woman) part-time/adjunct. *Students:* 83 full-time (63 women), 94 part-time (79 women); includes 17 African Americans, 1 American Indian/Alaska Native, 1 Asian American or Pacific Islander. Average age 33. 205 applicants, 45% accepted, 44 enrolled. In 2008, 14 master's, 7 doctorates awarded. *Degree requirements:* For doctorate, thesis/dissertation (for some programs). *Entrance requirements:* For master's, GRE General Test or MAT; for doctorate, GRE General Test or MAT, minimum GPA of 3.25, work experience. *Application deadline:* For fall admission, 3/1 priority date for international students. Applications are processed on a rolling basis. Application fee: $25. Electronic applications accepted. *Unit head:* Dr. Linda Guthrie, Head, 615-963-2920, Fax: 615-963-5140, E-mail: lguthrie@tnstate.edu. *Application contact:* Dr. Linda Guthrie, Head, 615-963-2920, Fax: 615-963-5140, E-mail: lguthrie@tnstate.edu.

Texas A&M International University, Office of Graduate Studies and Research, College of Arts and Sciences, Department of Behavioral, Applied Sciences, and Criminal Justice, Laredo, TX 78041-1900. Offers counseling psychology (MACP); criminal justice (MS); psychology (MS); sociology (MA). *Degree requirements:* For master's, thesis (for some programs). *Entrance requirements:* For master's, GRE General Test. Additional exam requirements/recommendations for international students: Required—TOEFL (minimum score 550 paper-based; 213 computer-based).

Texas A&M University, College of Liberal Arts, Department of Psychology, College Station, TX 77843. Offers behavioral and cellular neuroscience (MS, PhD); clinical psychology (MS, PhD); cognitive psychology (MS, PhD); developmental psychology (MS, PhD); industrial/organizational psychology (MS, PhD); social psychology (MS, PhD). *Accreditation:* APA (one or more programs are accredited). *Faculty:* 35. *Students:* 74 full-time (47 women), 11 part-time (9 women); includes 30 minority (7 African Americans, 5 Asian Americans or Pacific Islanders, 18 Hispanic Americans), 4 international. In 2008, 11 master's, 12 doctorates awarded. *Degree requirements:* For master's, thesis; for doctorate, comprehensive exam (for some programs), thesis/dissertation. *Entrance requirements:* For master's and doctorate, GRE General Test. Additional exam requirements/recommendations for international students: Required—TOEFL. *Application deadline:* For fall admission, 1/5 for domestic and international students. Application fee: $50 ($75 for international students). Electronic applications accepted. *Expenses:* Tuition, area resident: Full-time $3838.50. Tuition, state resident: full-time $3838.50. Tuition, nonresident: full-time $8897. Required fees: $2359.60. *Financial support:* Fellowships with partial tuition reimbursements, research assistantships with partial tuition reimbursements, teaching assistantships with partial tuition reimbursements, career-related internships or fieldwork, institutionally sponsored loans, health care benefits, and unspecified assistantships available. Financial award application deadline: 1/5; financial award applicants required to submit FAFSA. *Unit head:* Dr. Les Morey, Head, 979-845-2581, Fax: 979-845-4727, E-mail: lmorey@psych.tamu.edu. *Application contact:* Sharon Starr, Graduate Admissions Supervisor, 979-458-1710, Fax: 979-845-4727, E-mail: gradadv@psyc.tamu.edu.

Texas A&M University–Commerce, Graduate School, College of Education and Human Services, Department of Psychology and Special Education, Commerce, TX 75429-3011. Offers cognition and instruction (PhD); psychology (MA, MS); special education (M Ed, MA, MS). Part-time programs available. Terminal master's awarded for partial completion of doctoral program. *Degree requirements:* For master's, comprehensive exam, thesis (for some programs); for doctorate, thesis/dissertation, departmental qualifying exam. *Entrance requirements:* For master's, GRE General Test; for doctorate, GRE General Test, 3 letters of recommendation. Electronic applications accepted. *Faculty research:* Human learning, study skills, multicultural bilingual, diversity and special education, educationally handicapped.

Texas A&M University–Corpus Christi, Graduate Studies and Research, College of Liberal Arts, Program in Psychology, Corpus Christi, TX 78412-5503. Offers MA. Part-time and evening/weekend programs available. *Degree requirements:* For master's, comprehensive exam, thesis (for some programs). *Entrance requirements:* For master's, GRE General Test. Additional exam requirements/recommendations for international students: Required—TOEFL. Electronic applications accepted.

Texas A&M University–Kingsville, College of Graduate Studies, College of Arts and Sciences, Department of Psychology and Sociology, Kingsville, TX 78363. Offers gerontology (MS); psychology (MA, MS); sociology (MA, MS). Part-time and evening/weekend programs available. *Degree requirements:* For master's, comprehensive exam, thesis or alternative. *Entrance requirements:* For master's, GRE General Test, minimum GPA of 2.5. Additional exam requirements/recommendations for international students: Required—TOEFL. *Faculty research:* Hispanic female voting behavior, attitudes toward criminal justice, immigration of aged into south Texas, folk medicine.

Texas A&M University–Texarkana, Graduate Studies and Research, College of Health and Behavioral Sciences, Texarkana, TX 75505-5518. Offers counseling psychology (MS). Part-time and evening/weekend programs available. *Degree requirements:* For master's, comprehensive exam (for some programs), thesis or alternative. *Entrance requirements:* For master's, minimum GPA of 3.0 in last 60 hours of bachelor's degree. Additional exam requirements/recommendations for international students: Required—TOEFL. Electronic applications accepted.

Texas Christian University, College of Science and Engineering, Department of Psychology, Fort Worth, TX 76129-0002. Offers MA, MS, PhD. Part-time and evening/weekend programs available. *Degree requirements:* For master's, thesis, foreign language (MA); for doctorate, thesis/dissertation. *Entrance requirements:* For master's and doctorate, GRE General Test. Additional exam requirements/recommendations for international students: Required—TOEFL. *Application deadline:* For fall admission, 3/1 for domestic students; for spring admission, 12/1 for domestic students. Applications are processed on a rolling basis. Application fee: $0. *Expenses:* Tuition: Full-time $17,640. *Financial support:* Fellowships, teaching assistantships, unspecified assistantships available. Financial award application deadline: 3/1. *Unit head:* Dr. Timothy Barth, Chairperson, 817-257-7410, E-mail: t.barth@tcu.edu. *Application contact:* Dr. Timothy Barth, Chairperson, 817-257-7410, E-mail: t.barth@tcu.edu.

Texas Southern University, Graduate School, College of Liberal Arts and Behavioral Sciences, Department of Psychology, Houston, TX 77004-4584. Offers MA. *Faculty:* 6 full-time (3 women). *Students:* 32 full-time (30 women), 42 part-time (33 women); includes 68 African Americans, 1 Asian American or Pacific Islander, 3 Hispanic Americans. Average age 32. 13 applicants, 100% accepted, 10 enrolled. In 2008, 15 master's awarded. Application fee: $50. *Expenses:* Tuition, area resident: Full-time $1912; part-time $96 per credit hour. Tuition, state resident: full-time $1912; part-time $96 per credit hour. Tuition, nonresident: full-time $6302; part-time $343 per credit hour. Required fees: $3542. *Financial support:* Research assistantships, teaching assistantships available. *Unit head:* Dr. Leon H Belcher, Chair, 713-313-7062, E-mail: belcher_lh@tsu.edu. *Application contact:* Dr. Gregory Maddox, Interim Dean of the Graduate School, 713-313-7011 Ext. 4410, Fax: 713-639-1876, E-mail: maddox_gh@tsu.edu.

Texas State University–San Marcos, Graduate School, College of Liberal Arts, Department of Psychology, San Marcos, TX 78666. Offers health psychology (MA). *Degree requirements:* For master's, thesis, 450 hours of practicum courses. *Entrance requirements:* For master's, GRE General Test, minimum GPA of 3.0 in last 60 hours and in psychology, 3 letters of rec, 3.0 GPA in psy core courses, statement of purpose. Additional exam requirements/recommendations for international students: Required—TOEFL (minimum score 550 paper-based; 213 computer-based). Electronic applications accepted.

Texas State University–San Marcos, Graduate School, Interdisciplinary Studies Program in Educational Administration and Psychological Services, San Marcos, TX 78666. Offers MAIS. *Degree requirements:* For master's, comprehensive exam.

Texas State University–San Marcos, Graduate School, Interdisciplinary Studies Program in Psychology, San Marcos, TX 78666. Offers MAIS. *Degree requirements:* For master's, comprehensive exam.

Texas Tech University, Graduate School, College of Arts and Sciences, Department of Psychology, Lubbock, TX 79409. Offers clinical psychology (PhD); counseling psychology (MA, PhD); experimental psychology (MA, PhD); psychology (MA, PhD). *Accreditation:* APA (one or more programs are accredited). Part-time programs available. *Faculty:* 25 full-time (11 women). *Students:* 87 full-time (58 women), 20 part-time (13 women); includes 16 minority (5 African Americans, 1 American Indian/Alaska Native, 2 Asian Americans or Pacific Islanders, 8 Hispanic Americans), 6 international. Average age 28. 290 applicants, 13% accepted, 17 enrolled. In 2008, 13 master's, 6 doctorates awarded. *Degree requirements:* For doctorate, thesis/dissertation. *Entrance requirements:* For master's and doctorate, GRE General Test, GRE Subject Test. Additional exam requirements/recommendations for international students: Required—TOEFL (minimum score 550 paper-based; 213 computer-based). *Application deadline:* For fall admission, 3/1 priority date for international students; for spring admission, 11/1 priority date for international students. Applications are processed on a rolling basis. Application fee: $50 ($60 for international students). Electronic applications accepted. *Expenses:* Tuition, area resident: Part-time $194 per credit hour. Tuition, state resident: full-time $4648; part-time $194 per credit hour. Tuition, nonresident: full-time $11,392; part-time $475 per credit hour. Required fees: $2206; $69 per credit hour. $389 per semester. *Financial support:* In 2008–09, 91 students received support, including 4 research assistantships with partial tuition reimbursements available (averaging $12,762 per year), 69 teaching assistantships with partial tuition reimbursements available (averaging $11,835 per year); career-related internships or fieldwork, Federal Work-Study, and institutionally sponsored loans also available. Support available to part-time students. Financial award application deadline: 4/15; financial award applicants required to submit FAFSA. *Faculty research:* Failure/success in relationships, peer rejection in school, stress and coping, group processes, clinical and health psychology. Total annual research expenditures: $564,495. *Unit head:* Dr. Susan S. Hendrick, Chair, 806-742-3711 Ext. 224, Fax: 806-742-0818, E-mail: s.hendrick@ttu.edu. *Application contact:* Dr. Lee M. Cohen, Director of Clinical Program, 806-742-3711 Ext. 254, Fax: 806-742-0818, E-mail: lee.cohen@ttu.edu.

Texas Woman's University, Graduate School, College of Arts and Sciences, Department of Psychology and Philosophy, Denton, TX 76201. Offers counseling psychology (MA, PhD); school psychology (PhD, SSP). *Accreditation:* APA (one or more programs are accredited). *Faculty:* 14 full-time (9 women), 3 part-time/adjunct (1 woman). *Students:* 61 full-time (50 women), 60 part-time (55 women); includes 27 minority (9 African Americans, 8 Asian Americans or Pacific Islanders, 10 Hispanic Americans), 3 international. Average age 29. In 2008, 24 master's, 5 doctorates awarded. Terminal master's awarded for partial completion of doctoral program. *Degree requirements:* For master's, thesis; for doctorate, comprehensive exam, thesis/dissertation, internship, residency. *Entrance requirements:* For master's, BA/BS or 18 hours in psychology, minimum GPA of 3.5 in undergraduate psychology classes, essay, 3 letters of reference; for doctorate, 3 letters of reference; minimum overall and psychology undergraduate GPA of 3.5; BS/BA in psychology or 18 hours of required psychology classes. Additional exam requirements/recommendations for international students: Required—TOEFL (minimum score 550 paper-based; 213 computer-based; 79 iBT). *Application deadline:* For fall admission, 12/15 for domestic and international students. Applications are processed on a rolling basis. Application fee: $30 ($50 for international students). Electronic applications accepted. *Expenses:* Tuition, state resident: full-time $3564; part-time $198 per semester hour. Tuition, nonresident: full-time $8622; part-time $479 per semester hour. Required fees: $1158; $64 per semester hour. Tuition and fees vary according to course load. *Financial support:* In 2008–09, 14 research assistantships (averaging $10,746 per year), 8 teaching assistantships (averaging $10,746 per year) were awarded; career-related internships or fieldwork, Federal Work-Study, institutionally sponsored loans, scholarships/grants, traineeships, health care benefits, and unspecified assistantships also available. Support available to part-time students. Financial award application deadline: 3/1; financial award applicants required to submit FAFSA. *Faculty research:* Women's anger, pre-school assessments, body image dysfunction, traumatic stress, classical ethics, mental health and behavioral needs of adolescents in alternative education. *Unit head:* Dr. Dan Miller, Chair, 940-898-2303, Fax: 940-898-2301, E-mail: dmiller@twu.edu. *Application contact:* Samuel Wheeler, Assistant Director of Admissions, 940-898-3188, Fax: 940-898-3081, E-mail: wheelersr@twu.edu.

Trevecca Nazarene University, Graduate Division, Graduate Psychology Programs, Nashville, TN 37210-2877. Offers clinical counseling (Ed D); counseling (MA); counseling psychology (MA); marriage and family therapy (MMFT). Part-time and evening/weekend programs available. *Faculty:* 4 full-time (1 woman), 15 part-time/adjunct (7 women). *Students:* 191 full-time (151 women), 36 part-time (24 women); includes 41 minority (37 African Americans, 1 Asian American or Pacific Islander, 3 Hispanic Americans), 1 international. Average age 33. In 2008, 56 master's awarded. *Degree requirements:* For master's, comprehensive exam; for doctorate, comprehensive exam, thesis/dissertation. *Entrance requirements:* For master's, GRE General Test or MAT, minimum GPA of 2.7, 2 reference assessment forms; for doctorate, GRE, minimum GPA of 3.25, 3 recommendation forms, 400-word letter of intent, interview. Additional exam requirements/recommendations for international students: Required—TOEFL. *Application deadline:* Applications are processed on a rolling basis. *Expenses:* Contact institution. *Financial support:* Applicants required to submit FAFSA. *Unit head:* Dr. Peter Wilson, Director, 615-248-1384, Fax: 615-248-1662, E-mail: pwilson@trevecca.edu. *Application contact:* Heather Ambrefe, Department Secretary, 615-248-1384, Fax: 615-248-1662, E-mail: admissions_psy@trevecca.edu.

Tufts University, Graduate School of Arts and Sciences, Department of Psychology, Medford, MA 02155. Offers MS, PhD. Terminal master's awarded for partial completion of doctoral program. *Degree requirements:* For master's, thesis; for doctorate, one foreign language, thesis/dissertation. *Entrance requirements:* For master's and doctorate, GRE General Test, GRE Subject Test. Additional exam requirements/recommendations for international students: Required—TOEFL (minimum score 550 paper-based; 213 computer-based; 80 iBT). Electronic applications accepted.

Tulane University, School of Science and Engineering, Department of Psychology, New Orleans, LA 70118-5669. Offers MS, PhD. *Accreditation:* APA (one or more programs are accredited). Terminal master's awarded for partial completion of doctoral program. *Degree requirements:* For master's, variable foreign language requirement, thesis; for doctorate, thesis/dissertation. *Entrance requirements:* For master's, GRE General Test, minimum B average in undergraduate course work; for doctorate, GRE General Test. Additional exam requirements/recommendations for international students: Required—TOEFL. Electronic applications accepted. *Faculty research:* Hormones and behavior, aggression, personnel selection, cognitive development, stereotyping, diabetes.

Uniformed Services University of the Health Sciences, School of Medicine, Graduate Programs in the Biomedical Sciences and Public Health, Department of Medical and Clinical Psychology, Bethesda, MD 20814-4799. Offers clinical psychology (PhD); medical psychology (PhD). Clinical psychology available to active duty military only. *Accreditation:* APA. Terminal master's awarded for partial completion of doctoral program. *Degree requirements:* For doctorate, comprehensive exam, thesis/dissertation, qualifying exam. *Entrance requirements:* For doctorate, GRE General Test, minimum GPA of 3.0, U.S. citizenship. Additional exam requirements/recommendations for international students: Required—TOEFL. Electronic applications accepted. *Faculty research:* Addictive and appetitive behavior, psychopharmacology, stress and eating, obesity, health.

Union College, Graduate Programs, Department of Psychology, Barbourville, KY 40906-1499. Offers clinical psychology (MA); counseling psychology (MA); school psychology (MA).

Union Institute & University, Online MA Programs, Cincinnati, OH 45206-1925. Offers health and wellness (MA); history and culture (MA); leadership (MA); literature and writing (MA); psychology (MA). Part-time programs available. Postbaccalaureate distance learning degree programs offered (no on-campus study). *Degree requirements:* For master's, thesis. *Expenses:* Contact institution.

Union Institute & University, Program in Psychology and Counseling, Cincinnati, OH 45206-1925. Offers MA.

Universidad de las Americas, A.C., Program in Psychology, Mexico City, Mexico. Offers family therapy (MA).

Universidad de las Américas–Puebla, Division of Graduate Studies, School of Social Sciences, Program in Psychology, Puebla, Mexico. Offers MA. Part-time and evening/weekend programs available. *Degree requirements:* For master's, one foreign language, thesis. *Entrance requirements:* For master's, minimum B+ average. *Faculty research:* Testing, social hemispheric specialization, clinical psychology.

Université de Montréal, Faculty of Arts and Sciences, Department of Psychology, Montréal, QC H3C 3J7, Canada. Offers M Sc, PhD. *Faculty:* 80 full-time (32 women), 7 part-time/adjunct (3 women). *Students:* 180 full-time (142 women), 149 part-time (111 women). 332 applicants, 25% accepted, 77 enrolled. In 2008, 40 master's, 41 doctorates awarded. Terminal master's awarded for partial completion of doctoral program. *Degree requirements:* For master's, one foreign language, thesis; for doctorate, one foreign language, thesis/dissertation, general exam. *Application deadline:* For fall admission, 2/1 for domestic students. Application fee: $100. Electronic applications accepted. *Faculty research:* Vision, marital counseling, memory. *Unit head:* Serge larochelle, Director, 514-343-6503, Fax: 514-343-2285, E-mail: serge.larochelle@umontreal.ca. *Application contact:* Th??r??se Lauz??, Graduate Studies Chairman, 514-343-4607, Fax: 514-343-2285, E-mail: therese.lauze@umontreal.ca.

Université de Sherbrooke, Faculty of Letters and Human Sciences, Department of Psychology, Sherbrooke, QC J1K 2R1, Canada. Offers gerontology (MA). *Degree requirements:* For master's, thesis. *Faculty research:* Human relations.

Université du Québec à Montréal, Graduate Programs, Program in Psychology, Montréal, QC H3C 3P8, Canada. Offers D Ps, PhD. Part-time programs available. *Degree requirements:* For doctorate, thesis/dissertation. *Entrance requirements:* For doctorate, appropriate master's degree or equivalent, proficiency in French.

Université du Québec à Trois-Rivières, Graduate Programs, Program in Psychology, Trois-Rivières, QC G9A 5H7, Canada. Offers PhD, Certificate. Part-time programs available. *Degree requirements:* For doctorate, thesis/dissertation. *Entrance requirements:* For doctorate, appropriate master's degree, proficiency in French. *Faculty research:* Child and family development, gerontology, mental health.

Université Laval, Faculty of Social Sciences, School of Psychology, Programs in Psychology, Québec, QC G1K 7P4, Canada. Offers clinical psychology (PhD); community psychology (PhD); psychology (PhD, Psy D). *Degree requirements:* For doctorate, comprehensive exam, thesis/dissertation. *Entrance requirements:* For doctorate, comprehension of written English, knowledge of French, interview. Electronic applications accepted.

University at Albany, State University of New York, College of Arts and Sciences, Department of Psychology, Albany, NY 12222-0001. Offers autism (Certificate); biopsychology (PhD); clinical psychology (PhD); general/experimental psychology (PhD); industrial/organizational psychology (PhD); psychology (MA); social/personality psychology (PhD). *Accreditation:* APA (one or more programs are accredited). *Degree requirements:* For doctorate, thesis/dissertation. *Entrance requirements:* For doctorate, GRE General Test, GRE Subject Test. Additional exam requirements/recommendations for international students: Required—TOEFL (minimum score 550 paper-based; 213 computer-based). Electronic applications accepted.

University at Buffalo, the State University of New York, Graduate School, College of Arts and Sciences, Department of Psychology, Buffalo, NY 14260. Offers behavioral neuroscience (PhD); clinical psychology (PhD); cognitive psychology (PhD); general psychology (MA); social-personality psychology (PhD). *Accreditation:* APA (one or more programs are accredited). Terminal master's awarded for partial completion of doctoral program. *Degree requirements:* For master's, project; for doctorate, thesis/dissertation. *Entrance requirements:* For master's and doctorate, GRE General Test. Additional exam requirements/recommendations for international students: Required—TOEFL (minimum score 550 paper-based; 213 computer-based; 79 iBT). Electronic applications accepted. *Faculty research:* Neural, endocrine, and molecular bases of behavior; adult mood and anxiety disorders; relationship dysfunction; attention deficit/hyperactivity disorder; psycho-linguistics.

The University of Akron, Graduate School, Buchtel College of Arts and Sciences, Department of Psychology, Akron, OH 44325. Offers applied cognitive aging (MA, PhD); counseling psychology (MA, PhD); industrial/gerontological psychology (PhD); industrial/organizational psychology (MA, PhD); psychology (MA). *Accreditation:* APA (one or more programs are accredited). Terminal master's awarded for partial completion of doctoral program. *Degree requirements:* For master's, thesis optional, thesis or specialty exam; for doctorate, one foreign language, comprehensive exam, thesis/dissertation. *Entrance requirements:* For master's, GRE General Test, GRE Subject Test, minimum GPA of 2.75, letters of recommendation, minimum GPA of 3.0 in psychology courses; for doctorate, GRE General Test, GRE Subject Test, minimum graduate GPA of 3.25, letters of recommendation, personal statement. Additional exam requirements/recommendations for international students: Required—TOEFL (minimum score 550 paper-based; 213 computer-based; 79 iBT). Electronic applications accepted. *Faculty research:* Social cognitive determinants of behaviour, the application of psychological principles to the workplace and career planning/development, the psychological processes of aging.

The University of Alabama, Graduate School, College of Arts and Sciences, Department of Psychology, Tuscaloosa, AL 35487. Offers clinical psychology (PhD); experimental psychology (PhD). *Accreditation:* APA. *Faculty:* 20 full-time (8 women), 3 part-time/adjunct (2 women). *Students:* 78 full-time (60 women), 16 part-time (12 women); includes 16 minority (9 African Americans, 3 Asian Americans or Pacific Islanders, 4 Hispanic Americans), 2 international. Average age 27. 252 applicants, 11% accepted, 19 enrolled. In 2008, 13 doctorates awarded. *Degree requirements:* For doctorate, thesis/dissertation. *Entrance requirements:* For doctorate, GRE. Additional exam requirements/recommendations for international students: Required—TOEFL (minimum score 550 paper-based). *Application deadline:* For fall admission, 12/1 for domestic and international students. Application fee: $30. Electronic applications accepted. *Expenses:* Tuition, area resident: Full-time $6400. Tuition, state resident: full-time $6400. Tuition, nonresident: full-time $18,000. *Financial support:* In 2008–09, 73 students received support, including 12 fellowships with full tuition reimbursements available (averaging $15,000 per year), 34 research assistantships with full and partial tuition reimbursements available (averaging $11,142 per year), 26 teaching assistantships with tuition reimbursements available (averaging $11,142 per year); career-related internships or fieldwork, institutionally sponsored loans, scholarships/grants, health care benefits, and unspecified assistantships also available. Financial award application deadline: 12/1. *Faculty research:* Cognitive development/disability, child clinical, psychology and law, health/aging, social psychology. Total annual research expenditures: $2.3 million. *Unit head:* Dr. Kenneth Lichstein, Chair, 205-348-4962, Fax: 205-348-8648, E-mail: lichstein@ua.edu. *Application contact:* Mary Beth Hubbard, Information Contact, 205-348-1919, Fax: 205-348-8648, E-mail: mbhubbard@as.ua.edu.

The University of Alabama at Birmingham, School of Social and Behavioral Sciences, Department of Psychology, Birmingham, AL 35294. Offers MA, PhD. *Accreditation:* APA (one or more programs are accredited). Electronic applications accepted. *Faculty research:* Biological basis of behavior structure, function of the nervous system.

The University of Alabama in Huntsville, School of Graduate Studies, College of Liberal Arts, Department of Psychology, Huntsville, AL 35899. Offers MA. Part-time and evening/weekend programs available. *Faculty:* 4 full-time (2 women). *Students:* 5 full-time (all women), 8 part-time (6 women), 1 international. Average age 26. 13 applicants, 46% accepted, 5 enrolled. In 2008, 5 master's awarded. *Degree requirements:* For master's, comprehensive exam, thesis or alternative, oral and written exams. *Entrance requirements:* For master's, GRE General Test, 15 hours of course work in psychology, minimum GPA of 3.25, sample of written work. Additional exam requirements/recommendations for international students: Required—TOEFL (minimum score 500 paper-based; 173 computer-based; 62 iBT). *Application deadline:* For fall admission, 7/15 for domestic students, 4/1 for international students; for spring admission, 11/30 for domestic students, 9/1 for international students. Applications are processed on a rolling basis. Application fee: $40 ($50 for international students). Electronic applications accepted. *Expenses:* Tuition, area resident: Full-time $5214; part-time $323 per credit hour. Tuition, state resident: full-time $5214; part-time $323 per credit hour. Tuition, nonresident: full-time $11,444; part-time $705 per credit hour. Required fees: $540; $120 per semester. Tuition and fees vary according to course load. *Financial support:* In 2008–09, 5 students received support, including 2 teaching assistantships with full tuition reimbursements available (averaging $8,460 per year); career-related internships or fieldwork, Federal Work-Study, institutionally sponsored loans, scholarships/grants, health care benefits, and unspecified assistantships also available. Support available to part-time students. Financial award application deadline: 4/1; financial award applicants required to submit FAFSA. *Faculty research:* Personal and social cognition, development and aging, human factors, perception, biological psychology: hormones and behavior. Total annual research expenditures: $22,140. *Unit head:* Dr. Sandra L. Carpenter, Chair, 256-824-6191, Fax: 256-824-2387, E-mail: carpens@email.uah.edu. *Application contact:* Kathy Biggs, Graduate Studies Admissions Manager, 256-824-6199, Fax: 256-824-6405, E-mail: deangrad@uah.edu.

University of Alaska Anchorage, College of Arts and Sciences, Department of Psychology, Anchorage, AK 99508-8060. Offers clinical psychology (MS); clinical-community psychology with rural-indigenous emphasis (PhD). Part-time programs available. *Degree requirements:* For master's, thesis. *Entrance requirements:* For master's, GRE General Test, GRE Subject Test, interview, references; for doctorate, interview, bachelor's or master's degree in psychology. Additional exam requirements/recommendations for international students: Required—TOEFL (minimum score 550 paper-based; 213 computer-based). *Faculty research:* Substance abuse, childhood autism, biofeedback, psychological assessment, mental health in Native Alaskans.

University of Alaska Fairbanks, College of Liberal Arts, Department of Psychology, Fairbanks, AK 99775-6480. Offers clinical-community psychology (PhD), including rural cross-cultural emphasis. *Faculty:* 5 full-time (1 woman), 4 part-time/adjunct (0 women). *Students:* 2 full-time (0 women), 20 part-time (16 women); includes 8 minority (1 African American, 5 American Indian/Alaska Native, 2 Hispanic Americans), 1 international. Average age 38. 21 applicants, 48% accepted, 9 enrolled. In 2008, 1 doctorate awarded. *Degree requirements:* For doctorate, comprehensive exam, thesis/dissertation, oral exam, oral defense. *Entrance requirements:* For doctorate, disclosure statement. Additional exam requirements/recommendations for international students: Required—TOEFL (minimum score 550 paper-based; 213 computer-based; 80 iBT). *Application deadline:* For fall admission, 12/15 for domestic and international students. Application fee: $60. *Expenses:* Tuition, area resident: Full-time $5418; part-time $301 per credit. Tuition, state resident: full-time $5418; part-time $301 per credit. Tuition, nonresident: full-time $11,070; part-time $615 per credit. Required fees: $849; $25 per credit. $78 per semester. Tuition and fees vary according to course load and reciprocity agreements. *Financial support:* In 2008–09, 2 fellowships (averaging $15,270 per year), 7 research assistantships (averaging $16,089 per year), 8 teaching assistantships (averaging $15,611 per year) were awarded; career-related internships or fieldwork, Federal Work-Study, scholarships/grants, health care benefits, and unspecified assistantships also available. Support available to part-time students. Financial award application deadline: 7/1; financial award applicants required to submit FAFSA. *Faculty research:* Clinical and community psychology, rural, indigenous, and cultural psychology. *Unit head:* Dr. Dani Sheppard, Department Chair, 907-474-7007, Fax: 907-474-5781, E-mail: fypsych@uaf.edu. *Application contact:* Dr. Dani Sheppard, Department Chair, 907-474-7007, Fax: 907-474-5781, E-mail: fypsych@uaf.edu.

University of Alberta, Faculty of Graduate Studies and Research, Department of Psychology, Edmonton, AB T6G 2E1, Canada. Offers M Sc, MA, PhD. Terminal master's awarded for partial completion of doctoral program. *Degree requirements:* For master's, thesis (for some programs); for doctorate, thesis/dissertation. *Entrance requirements:* For master's and doctorate, GRE. Additional exam requirements/recommendations for international students: Required—TOEFL (minimum score 550 paper-based; 213 computer-based). Electronic applications accepted. *Faculty research:* Animal behavior processes; cognitive, social and perceptual processes; development and aging; neuroscience.

The University of Arizona, Graduate College, College of Social and Behavioral Sciences, Department of Psychology, Tucson, AZ 85721. Offers PhD, JD/PhD. *Accreditation:* APA (one or more programs are accredited). *Degree requirements:* For doctorate, comprehensive exam, thesis/dissertation. *Entrance requirements:* For doctorate, GRE General Test, GRE Subject Test, 3 letters of recommendation, statement of purpose. Additional exam requirements/recommendations for international students: Required—TOEFL (minimum score 550 paper-based; 80 iBT). Electronic applications accepted. *Faculty research:* Cognitive neuroscience, aging, law and psychology, psycholinguistics, family psychology.

University of Arkansas, Graduate School, J. William Fulbright College of Arts and Sciences, Department of Psychology, Fayetteville, AR 72701-1201. Offers MA, PhD. *Accreditation:* APA (one or more programs are accredited). *Degree requirements:* For master's, thesis; for doctorate, variable foreign language requirement, thesis/dissertation. *Entrance requirements:* For doctorate, GRE General Test, GRE Subject Test.

University of Arkansas at Little Rock, Graduate School, College of Arts, Humanities, and Social Science, Department of Psychology, Little Rock, AR 72204-1099. Offers applied psychology (MAP). Part-time and evening/weekend programs available. *Entrance requirements:* For master's, GRE General Test, minimum GPA of 2.7. *Faculty research:* Psychological methods and theories in business industry, government, and organizations; personnel program evaluation; training; affirmative action; organizational analysis and development.

University of Baltimore, Graduate School, The Yale Gordon College of Liberal Arts, Program in Applied Psychology, Baltimore, MD 21201-5779. Offers applied psychology (MS), including counseling, industrial and organizational psychology, psychological applications. Part-time and evening/weekend programs available. *Faculty:* 7 full-time (5 women), 7 part-time/adjunct (2 women). *Students:* 59 full-time (41 women), 40 part-time (31 women); includes 28 minority (21 African Americans, 6 Asian Americans or Pacific Islanders, 1 Hispanic American), 4 international. Average age 27. 163 applicants, 34% accepted, 46 enrolled. In 2008, 31 master's awarded. *Degree requirements:* For master's, thesis optional. *Entrance requirements:* For master's, GRE, minimum GPA of 3.0. Additional exam requirements/recommendations for international students: Required—TOEFL (minimum score 550 paper-based; 213 computer-based). *Application deadline:* For fall admission, 8/1 for domestic students, 6/1 for international students; for spring admission, 12/1 for domestic students, 11/1 for international students. Applications are processed on a rolling basis. Application fee: $30. Electronic applications accepted. *Expenses:* Contact institution. *Financial support:* In 2008–09, 5 research assistantships with full and partial tuition reimbursements were awarded; fellowships, career-related internships or fieldwork and Federal Work-Study also available. Support available to part-time students. Financial award application deadline: 4/1; financial award applicants required to submit FAFSA. *Faculty research:* Participatory decision making, counter productive workplace behavior, organizational consulting, substance abuse treatment, cognitive functioning in head injured. Total annual research expenditures: $93,146. *Unit head:* Dr. Thomas Mitchell, Director, 410-837-

Psychology—General

University of Baltimore (continued)
5348, Fax: 410-837-4793, E-mail: tmitchell@ubalt.edu. *Application contact:* Kevin Nies, Assistant Director, Office of Graduate Admission, 410-837-6565, E-mail: knies@ubalt.edu.

The University of British Columbia, Faculty of Arts and Faculty of Graduate Studies, Department of Psychology, Vancouver, BC V6T 1Z1, Canada. Offers behavioral neuroscience (MA, PhD); clinical psychology (MA, PhD); cognitive science (MA, PhD); developmental psychology (MA, PhD); forensic psychology (PhD); health psychology (MA, PhD); quantitative methods (MA, PhD); social/personality psychology (MA, PhD). *Accreditation:* APA (one or more programs are accredited). Terminal master's awarded for partial completion of doctoral program. *Degree requirements:* For master's, thesis; for doctorate, comprehensive exam, thesis/dissertation. *Entrance requirements:* For master's and doctorate, GRE General Test, GRE Subject Test. Additional exam requirements/recommendations for international students: Required—TOEFL (minimum score 550 paper-based; 230 computer-based; 80 iBT). Electronic applications accepted. *Faculty research:* Clinical, developmental, social/personality, cognition, behavioral neuroscience.

University of Calgary, Faculty of Graduate Studies, Faculty of Social Sciences, Department of Psychology, Calgary, AB T2N 1N4, Canada. Offers clinical psychology (M Sc, PhD); psychology (M Sc, PhD). *Degree requirements:* For master's, thesis; for doctorate, thesis/dissertation. *Entrance requirements:* For master's, GRE General Test, bachelor's degree in psychology, minimum GPA of 3.4. Additional exam requirements/recommendations for international students: Required—TOEFL (minimum score 550 paper-based; 213 computer-based). Electronic applications accepted. *Faculty research:* Cognition and cognitive development, social psychology, theoretical psychology, perception, aging.

University of California, Berkeley, Graduate Division, College of Letters and Science, Department of Psychology, Berkeley, CA 94720-1500. Offers PhD. *Accreditation:* APA. *Degree requirements:* For doctorate, thesis/dissertation, qualifying exam. *Entrance requirements:* For doctorate, GRE General Test, GRE Subject Test, minimum GPA of 3.0, 3 letters of recommendation. Electronic applications accepted.

University of California, Davis, Graduate Studies, Program in Psychology, Davis, CA 95616. Offers PhD. *Degree requirements:* For doctorate, thesis/dissertation. *Entrance requirements:* For doctorate, GRE General Test, GRE Subject Test, minimum GPA of 3.0. Additional exam requirements/recommendations for international students: Required—TOEFL (minimum score 550 paper-based; 213 computer-based). Electronic applications accepted. *Faculty research:* Social personality, perception, cognition, psychobiology.

University of California, Irvine, Office of Graduate Studies, School of Social Ecology, Department of Psychology and Social Behavior, Irvine, CA 92697. Offers PhD. *Degree requirements:* For doctorate, thesis/dissertation, research project. *Entrance requirements:* For doctorate, GRE General Test, minimum GPA of 3.0. Additional exam requirements/recommendations for international students: Required—TOEFL (minimum score 550 paper-based; 213 computer-based). Electronic applications accepted. *Faculty research:* Psychosocial development in children, adolescents, and adults; gerontology; childhood behavior disorders; and developmental psychopathology; sex differences; attitude change; social psychology.

University of California, Irvine, Office of Graduate Studies, School of Social Sciences, Department of Cognitive Science, Irvine, CA 92697. Offers psychology (PhD). *Degree requirements:* For doctorate, thesis/dissertation. *Entrance requirements:* For doctorate, GRE General Test, minimum GPA of 3.0. Additional exam requirements/recommendations for international students: Required—TOEFL (minimum score 550 paper-based; 213 computer-based). Electronic applications accepted. *Faculty research:* Mathematical psychology, visual and auditory perception, cognitive development, problem solving, experimental psychology.

University of California, Los Angeles, Graduate Division, College of Letters and Science, Department of Psychology, Los Angeles, CA 90034. Offers MA, PhD. *Accreditation:* APA (one or more programs are accredited). *Students:* 187 full-time (124 women); includes 44 minority (7 African Americans, 22 Asian Americans or Pacific Islanders, 15 Hispanic Americans), 10 international. Average age 26. 620 applicants, 12% accepted, 41 enrolled. In 2008, 32 master's, 33 doctorates awarded. Terminal master's awarded for partial completion of doctoral program. *Degree requirements:* For master's, comprehensive exam; for doctorate, thesis/dissertation, oral and written qualifying exams, teaching experience. *Entrance requirements:* For master's, GRE General Test, GRE Subject Test, minimum GPA of 3.0, degree objective of Ph.D; for doctorate, GRE General Test, GRE Subject Test, MAT, minimum undergraduate GPA of 3.0. Additional exam requirements/recommendations for international students: Required—TOEFL. Application fee: $60 ($80 for international students). Electronic applications accepted. *Expenses:* Tuition, nonresident: full-time $14,694. Required fees: $9669.50. Full-time tuition and fees vary according to course load, degree level, program and student level. *Financial support:* In 2008–09, 146 fellowships with full and partial tuition reimbursements, 60 research assistantships with full and partial tuition reimbursements, 109 teaching assistantships with full and partial tuition reimbursements were awarded; Federal Work-Study, institutionally sponsored loans, scholarships/grants, health care benefits, tuition waivers (full and partial), and unspecified assistantships also available. Financial award application deadline: 3/1; financial award applicants required to submit FAFSA. *Unit head:* Robert Bjork, Chair, 310-825-7028. *Application contact:* Departmental Office, 310-825-2617, E-mail: gradadm@psych.ucla.edu.

University of California, Riverside, Graduate Division, Department of Psychology, Riverside, CA 92521-0102. Offers MA, PhD. *Accreditation:* APA. *Degree requirements:* For doctorate, comprehensive exam, thesis/dissertation, 3 quarters of teaching experience, qualifying exams. *Entrance requirements:* For doctorate, GRE General Test, minimum GPA of 3.2. Additional exam requirements/recommendations for international students: Required—TOEFL (minimum score 550 paper-based; 213 computer-based; 80 iBT). Electronic applications accepted. *Expenses:* Tuition, nonresident: full-time $4898. Required fees: $10,362. *Faculty research:* Neuroscience, personality and social psychology, developmental psychology, cognition, health psychology, quantitative psychology.

University of California, San Diego, Office of Graduate Studies, Department of Psychology, La Jolla, CA 92093. Offers PhD. *Degree requirements:* For doctorate, thesis/dissertation. *Entrance requirements:* For doctorate, GRE General Test. Electronic applications accepted.

University of California, San Diego, Office of Graduate Studies, Interdisciplinary Program in Cognitive Science, La Jolla, CA 92093. Offers cognitive science/anthropology (PhD); cognitive science/communication (PhD); cognitive science/computer science and engineering (PhD); cognitive science/linguistics (PhD); cognitive science/neuroscience (PhD); cognitive science/philosophy (PhD); cognitive science/psychology (PhD); cognitive science/sociology (PhD). Admissions offered through affiliated departments. *Degree requirements:* For doctorate, thesis/dissertation. *Entrance requirements:* For doctorate, GRE General Test, acceptance into one of the 8 participating departments. *Faculty research:* Language and cognition, philosophy of mind, visual perception, biological anthropology, sociolinguistics.

University of California, Santa Barbara, Graduate Division, College of Letters and Sciences, Division of Mathematics, Life, and Physical Sciences, Department of Psychology, Santa Barbara, CA 93106-9660. Offers MA, PhD. *Faculty:* 30 full-time (10 women), 1 (woman) part-time/adjunct. *Students:* 75 full-time (43 women). Average age 27. 229 applicants, 10% accepted, 9 enrolled. In 2008, 4 master's, 7 doctorates awarded. Terminal master's awarded for partial completion of doctoral program. *Degree requirements:* For master's, thesis; for doctorate, comprehensive exam, thesis/dissertation, teaching assistant training, progress report, papers, mini-convention presentation, 1 quarter of student teaching or teaching assistant class with section lab. *Entrance requirements:* For doctorate, GRE General Test, 3 letters of recommendation, statement of purpose, personal achievements/contributions statement, resumé/curriculum vitae, transcripts for post-secondary institutions attended. Additional exam requirements/recommendations for international students: Required—TOEFL (paper: 550,

computer: 213, IBT: 80) or IELTS (7). *Application deadline:* For fall admission, 12/1 for domestic and international students. Application fee: $70 ($90 for international students). Electronic applications accepted. *Expenses:* Tuition, nonresident: full-time $25,149. Required fees: $10,143. Full-time tuition and fees vary according to campus/location, reciprocity agreements and student level. *Financial support:* In 2008–09, 74 students received support, including 60 fellowships with full and partial tuition reimbursements available (averaging $4,800 per year), 29 research assistantships with full and partial tuition reimbursements available (averaging $8,200 per year), 45 teaching assistantships with partial tuition reimbursements available (averaging $8,000 per year); Federal Work-Study, institutionally sponsored loans, scholarships/grants, health care benefits, and unspecified assistantships also available. Financial award application deadline: 12/15; financial award applicants required to submit FAFSA. *Faculty research:* Social psychology; developmental and evolutionary psychology; neuroscience and behavior; cognition, perception and cognitive neuroscience. Total annual research expenditures: $6 million. *Unit head:* Dr. F. Gregory Ashby, Chair, 805-893-2130, Fax: 805-893-4303, E-mail: ashby@psych.ucsb.edu. *Application contact:* Sondra Gordon, Staff Graduate Advisor, 805-893-2793, Fax: 805-893-4303, E-mail: gordon@psych.ucsb.edu.

University of California, Santa Cruz, Division of Graduate Studies, Division of Social Sciences, Program in Psychology, Santa Cruz, CA 95064. Offers PhD. *Degree requirements:* For doctorate, thesis/dissertation, qualifying exam. *Entrance requirements:* For doctorate, GRE General Test. *Faculty research:* Cognitive psychology, human information processing, sensation perceptions, psychobiology.

University of Central Arkansas, Graduate School, College of Health and Behavioral Sciences, Department of Counseling and Psychology, Conway, AR 72035-0001. Offers community service counseling (MS); counseling psychology (MS); school psychology (MS, PhD). *Accreditation:* APA. Terminal master's awarded for partial completion of doctoral program. *Degree requirements:* For master's, comprehensive exam, thesis optional, internship; for doctorate, comprehensive exam, thesis/dissertation, internship. *Entrance requirements:* For master's, GRE General Test, minimum GPA of 2.75; for doctorate, GRE General Test, minimum GPA of 3.25. Additional exam requirements/recommendations for international students: Required—TOEFL (minimum score 550 paper-based; 213 computer-based).

University of Central Florida, College of Sciences, Department of Psychology, Orlando, FL 32816. Offers applied experimental and human factors psychology (MA, PhD); clinical psychology (MA, MS, PhD); industrial/organizational psychology (MS, PhD). *Accreditation:* APA. Part-time and evening/weekend programs available. *Faculty:* 43 full-time (17 women), 13 part-time/adjunct (5 women). *Students:* 148 full-time (97 women), 24 part-time (15 women); includes 31 minority (9 African Americans, 6 Asian Americans or Pacific Islanders, 16 Hispanic Americans), 8 international. In 2008, 35 master's, 18 doctorates awarded. *Degree requirements:* For doctorate, thesis/dissertation, candidacy exam. *Entrance requirements:* For master's, GRE General Test, minimum GPA of 3.0 in last 60 hours. Additional exam requirements/recommendations for international students: Required—TOEFL. *Application deadline:* For fall admission, 2/15 for domestic students. Application fee: $30. Electronic applications accepted. *Expenses:* Tuition, area resident: Full-time $6816; part-time $284 per credit. Tuition, state resident: full-time $6816; part-time $1076 per credit. Tuition, nonresident: full-time $25,824. Required fees: $216; $9 per credit. *Financial support:* In 2008–09, 20 fellowships with partial tuition reimbursements (averaging $9,900 per year), 43 research assistantships with partial tuition reimbursements (averaging $11,600 per year), 56 teaching assistantships with partial tuition reimbursements (averaging $7,200 per year) were awarded; career-related internships or fieldwork, Federal Work-Study, institutionally sponsored loans, tuition waivers (partial), and unspecified assistantships also available. Financial award application deadline: 3/1; financial award applicants required to submit FAFSA. *Faculty research:* Professional ethical decision making, electronic selection systems, psychometrics. *Unit head:* Dr. Robert Dipboye, Chair, 407-823-2216, E-mail: rdipboye@mail.ucf.edu. *Application contact:* Dr. Robert Dipboye, Chair, 407-823-2216, E-mail: rdipboye@mail.ucf.edu.

University of Central Missouri, The Graduate School, College of Health and Human Services, Department of Psychology, Warrensburg, MO 64093. Offers MS. Part-time programs available. *Degree requirements:* For master's, comprehensive exam, thesis optional. *Entrance requirements:* For master's, GRE General Test, GRE Subject Test, minimum GPA of 2.75, Missouri teaching certificate, course work in psychology, 3 letters of recommendation. Additional exam requirements/recommendations for international students: Required—TOEFL (minimum score 500 paper-based; 173 computer-based).

University of Central Oklahoma, College of Graduate Studies and Research, College of Education, Department of Psychology, Program in General Psychology, Edmond, OK 73034-5209. Offers MA. *Degree requirements:* For master's, thesis. *Entrance requirements:* For master's, GRE General Test. Additional exam requirements/recommendations for international students: Required—TOEFL (minimum score 550 paper-based; 213 computer-based). Electronic applications accepted.

University of Chicago, Division of Social Sciences, Department of Psychology, Chicago, IL 60637-1513. Offers PhD. *Degree requirements:* For doctorate, one foreign language, thesis/dissertation, exams. *Entrance requirements:* For doctorate, GRE General Test, GRE Subject Test. Additional exam requirements/recommendations for international students: Required—TOEFL, IELTS (minimum score 7). Electronic applications accepted.

University of Cincinnati, Graduate School, McMicken College of Arts and Sciences, Department of Psychology, Cincinnati, OH 45221. Offers clinical psychology (PhD); experimental psychology (PhD). *Accreditation:* APA. *Degree requirements:* For doctorate, comprehensive exam, thesis/dissertation. *Entrance requirements:* For doctorate, GRE General Test. Additional exam requirements/recommendations for international students: Required—TOEFL. *Faculty research:* Neuropsychology, human factors, health.

University of Colorado at Boulder, Graduate School, College of Arts and Sciences, Department of Psychology, Boulder, CO 80309. Offers MA, PhD. *Accreditation:* APA (one or more programs are accredited). *Degree requirements:* For master's, comprehensive exam; for doctorate, thesis/dissertation. *Entrance requirements:* For master's, GRE General Test, minimum undergraduate GPA of 2.75; for doctorate, GRE General Test. *Faculty research:* Clinical psychology, behavioral genetics, behavioral neuroscience, cognitive psychology, social psychology.

University of Colorado at Colorado Springs, Graduate School, College of Letters, Arts and Sciences, Department of Psychology, Colorado Springs, CO 80933-7150. Offers MA, PhD. *Accreditation:* APA. Part-time programs available. *Faculty:* 14 full-time (5 women), 3 part-time/adjunct (1 woman). *Students:* 34 full-time (26 women), 6 part-time (4 women); includes 6 minority (1 African American, 2 Asian Americans or Pacific Islanders, 3 Hispanic Americans). Average age 28. 21 applicants, 95% accepted, 18 enrolled. In 2008, 10 master's awarded. *Degree requirements:* For master's, thesis; for doctorate, comprehensive exam, thesis/dissertation. *Entrance requirements:* For master's, GRE, BA in psychology or equivalent background; minimum GPA of 3.0. *Application deadline:* For fall admission, 1/1 for domestic students. Applications are processed on a rolling basis. *Financial support:* Research assistantships, teaching assistantships, career-related internships or fieldwork and Federal Work-Study available. Support available to part-time students. Financial award applicants required to submit FAFSA. *Faculty research:* Aging, social psychology, learning and memory, personality disorders, psychology and law. Total annual research expenditures: $429,985. *Unit head:* Dr. Kelli Klebe, Chair, 719-255-4181, Fax: 719-255-4166, E-mail: kklebe@uccs.edu. *Application contact:* Dr. Hasker Davis, Graduate Student Advisor, 719-255-4148, Fax: 719-255-4166, E-mail: hdavis@uccs.edu.

University of Colorado Denver, College of Liberal Arts and Sciences, Department of Psychology, Denver, CO 80217-3364. Offers PhD. Part-time and evening/weekend programs available. *Entrance requirements:* Additional exam requirements/recommendations for international students: Required—TOEFL (minimum score 525 paper-based; 197 computer-based). Electronic applications accepted. *Faculty research:* Organizational behavior, body image perception, professional ethics, infant perception and cognition, charismatic leadership.

University of Connecticut, Graduate School, College of Liberal Arts and Sciences, Department of Psychology, Field of Psychology, Storrs, CT 06269. Offers behavioral neuroscience (PhD); biopsychology (PhD); clinical psychology (MA, PhD); cognition and instruction (PhD); developmental psychology (MA, PhD); ecological psychology (PhD); experimental psychology (PhD); general psychology (MA, PhD); health psychology (Graduate Certificate); industrial/organizational psychology (PhD); language and cognition (PhD); neuroscience (PhD); occupational health psychology (Graduate Certificate); social psychology (MA, PhD). *Accreditation:* APA (one or more programs are accredited). Terminal master's awarded for partial completion of doctoral program. *Degree requirements:* For master's, comprehensive exam; for doctorate, thesis/dissertation. *Entrance requirements:* For master's and doctorate, GRE General Test, GRE Subject Test. Additional exam requirements/recommendations for international students: Required—TOEFL (minimum score 550 paper-based; 213 computer-based). Electronic applications accepted.

University of Dallas, Braniff Graduate School of Liberal Arts, Program in Psychology, Irving, TX 75062-4736. Offers M Psych, MA. Part-time programs available. *Degree requirements:* For master's, one foreign language, comprehensive exam (for some programs), thesis (for some programs). *Entrance requirements:* Additional exam requirements/recommendations for international students: Required—TOEFL.

University of Dayton, Graduate School, College of Arts and Sciences, Department of Psychology, Dayton, OH 45469-1300. Offers clinical psychology (MA); general psychology (MA). *Faculty:* 18 full-time (5 women), 2 part-time/adjunct (1 woman). *Students:* 35 full-time (27 women), 3 part-time (2 women); includes 7 minority (3 African Americans, 1 Asian American or Pacific Islander, 3 Hispanic Americans), 1 international. Average age 25. 123 applicants, 24% accepted, 16 enrolled. In 2008, 8 master's awarded. *Degree requirements:* For master's, thesis. *Entrance requirements:* For master's, GRE General Test, GRE Subject Test (recommended). Additional exam requirements/recommendations for international students: Required—TOEFL (minimum score 550 paper-based; 213 computer-based; 80 iBT). *Application deadline:* For fall admission, 3/1 priority date for domestic students, 2/1 priority date for international students. Application fee: $0 ($50 for international students). Electronic applications accepted. *Expenses:* Tuition: Full-time $6950; part-time $1737.50 per semester. Required fees: $25 per semester. Tuition and fees vary according to course level, course load, degree level and program. *Financial support:* In 2008–09, 27 students received support, including 9 research assistantships with full tuition reimbursements available (averaging $9,980 per year); institutionally sponsored loans, traineeships, and tuition waivers (partial) also available. Financial award application deadline: 3/1; financial award applicants required to submit FAFSA. *Faculty research:* Cognitive processes, television and children, interpersonal process, modes and mechanisms of therapy. *Unit head:* Dr. David W. Biers, Chair, 937-229-2713, Fax: 937-229-3900, E-mail: biers@udayton.edu. *Application contact:* Angela Jones-Glukhov, Associate Director of Graduate Admissions, 937-229-4305, Fax: 937-229-4729, E-mail: jonesgas@notes.udayton.edu.

University of Delaware, College of Arts and Sciences, Department of Psychology, Newark, DE 19716. Offers behavioral neuroscience (PhD); clinical psychology (PhD); cognitive psychology (PhD); social psychology (PhD). *Accreditation:* APA. *Degree requirements:* For doctorate, thesis/dissertation. *Entrance requirements:* For doctorate, GRE General Test. Additional exam requirements/recommendations for international students: Required—TOEFL (minimum score 600 paper-based; 250 computer-based). Electronic applications accepted. *Faculty research:* Emotion development, neural and cognitive aspects of memory, neural control of feeding, intergroup relations, social cognition and communication.

University of Denver, Division of Arts, Humanities and Social Sciences, Department of Psychology, Denver, CO 80208. Offers MA, PhD. *Accreditation:* APA (one or more programs are accredited). *Faculty:* 23 full-time (11 women), 3 part-time/adjunct (2 women). *Students:* 30 full-time (25 women), 3 part-time (2 women); includes 5 minority (3 Asian Americans or Pacific Islanders, 2 Hispanic Americans), 2 international. Average age 27. In 2008, 6 master's, 8 doctorates awarded. *Degree requirements:* For doctorate, thesis/dissertation. *Entrance requirements:* For master's and doctorate, GRE General Test. Additional exam requirements/recommendations for international students: Required—TOEFL. *Application deadline:* Applications are processed on a rolling basis. Application fee: $50. Electronic applications accepted. *Financial support:* In 2008–09, 13 research assistantships with full and partial tuition reimbursements (averaging $15,000 per year), 23 teaching assistantships with full and partial tuition reimbursements (averaging $14,400 per year) were awarded; career-related internships or fieldwork, Federal Work-Study, institutionally sponsored loans, and scholarships/grants also available. Support available to part-time students. Financial award application deadline: 1/1; financial award applicants required to submit FAFSA. *Faculty research:* Developmental neuropsychology, self-esteem and peer relationships, child abuse and neglect, marital and family interactions, adolescent peer and romantic relationships. Total annual research expenditures: $3.9 million. *Unit head:* Dr. Ralph J. Roberts, Chairperson, 303-871-3803. *Application contact:* Paula Houghtaling, Information Contact, 303-871-3803, E-mail: info@psy.du.edu.

University of Denver, Graduate School of Professional Psychology, Denver, CO 80208. Offers clinical psychology (Psy D); psychology (MA). *Accreditation:* APA. *Faculty:* 12 full-time (6 women), 31 part-time/adjunct (16 women). *Students:* 198 full-time (162 women), 25 part-time (15 women); includes 26 minority (6 African Americans, 3 American Indian/Alaska Native, 9 Asian Americans or Pacific Islanders, 8 Hispanic Americans), 8 international. Average age 26. 525 applicants, 36% accepted, 92 enrolled. In 2008, 75 master's, 31 doctorates awarded. *Degree requirements:* For doctorate, paper, internship. *Entrance requirements:* For master's and doctorate, GRE General Test. Additional exam requirements/recommendations for international students: Required—TOEFL. *Application deadline:* For fall admission, 1/5 for domestic students. Application fee: $50. Electronic applications accepted. *Financial support:* In 2008–09, 30 teaching assistantships with full and partial tuition reimbursements (averaging $3,500 per year) were awarded; career-related internships or fieldwork, Federal Work-Study, institutionally sponsored loans, scholarships/grants, and clinical assistantships also available. Support available to part-time students. Financial award application deadline: 3/1; financial award applicants required to submit FAFSA. *Unit head:* Dr. Peter Buirski, Dean, 303-871-2382. *Application contact:* Admissions, 303-871-3873, Fax: 303-871-4220, E-mail: gsppinfo@du.edu.

University of Detroit Mercy, College of Liberal Arts and Education, Department of Psychology, Detroit, MI 48221. Offers clinical psychology (MA, PhD); industrial/organizational psychology (MA); school psychology (Spec). *Accreditation:* APA. Evening/weekend programs available. *Degree requirements:* For doctorate, departmental qualifying exam. *Faculty research:* Gerontology.

University of Florida, Graduate School, College of Liberal Arts and Sciences, Department of Psychology, Gainesville, FL 32611. Offers behavior analysis (PhD); behavioral neuroscience (MS, PhD); cognitive and sensory processes (PhD); counseling psychology (PhD); developmental psychology (PhD); social psychology (MS, PhD); JD/PhD. *Degree requirements:* For master's, thesis or alternative; for doctorate, thesis/dissertation. *Entrance requirements:* For master's and doctorate, GRE General Test, minimum GPA of 3.0. Additional exam requirements/recommendations for international students: Required—TOEFL (minimum score 550 paper-based; 213 computer-based). Electronic applications accepted. *Faculty research:* Experimental analysis of behavior, psychobiology, cognition and sensory processes, counseling psychology, social psychology, developmental psychology.

University of Georgia, Graduate School, College of Arts and Sciences, Department of Psychology, Athens, GA 30602. Offers MS, PhD. *Accreditation:* APA (one or more programs are accredited). *Degree requirements:* For master's, thesis; for doctorate, one foreign language, thesis/dissertation. *Entrance requirements:* For master's and doctorate, GRE General Test. Additional exam requirements/recommendations for international students: Required—TOEFL. Electronic applications accepted.

University of Guelph, Graduate Program Services, College of Social and Applied Human Sciences, Department of Psychology, Guelph, ON N1G 2W1, Canada. Offers applied social psychology (MA, PhD); clinical psychology applied development emphasis (PhD); clinical psychology applied developmental emphasis (MA); industrial/organizational psychology (MA, PhD); neuroscience and applied cognitive science (MA, PhD). *Degree requirements:* For master's, thesis; for doctorate, comprehensive exam, thesis/dissertation. *Entrance requirements:* For master's, GRE General Test, GRE Subject Test, minimum B+ average during previous 2 years of course work; for doctorate, GRE General Test, GRE Subject Test, minimum A- average. Additional exam requirements/recommendations for international students: Required—TOEFL (minimum score 89 iBT). Electronic applications accepted. *Faculty research:* Organizational psychology, reading comprehension and mathematical ability, drug addiction and relapse, gender issues and culture, memory, clinical psychology.

University of Hartford, College of Arts and Sciences, Department of Psychology, West Hartford, CT 06117-1599. Offers clinical practices (MA, Psy D), including clinical practices (Psy D), psychology (MA); general experimental psychology (MA); organizational behavior (MS); school psychology (MS). *Accreditation:* APA. Part-time programs available. *Degree requirements:* For master's, comprehensive exam, thesis (for some programs). *Entrance requirements:* For master's, GRE General Test, GRE Subject Test, minimum GPA of 3.0; for doctorate, GRE General Test, GRE Subject Test. Additional exam requirements/recommendations for international students: Required—TOEFL (minimum score 550 paper-based; 213 computer-based). Electronic applications accepted. *Expenses:* Contact institution.

University of Hawaii at Manoa, Graduate Division, Colleges of Arts and Sciences, College of Social Sciences, Department of Psychology, Honolulu, HI 96822. Offers clinical psychology (PhD); community and cultural psychology (PhD); community and culture (MA); psychology (MA, PhD, Graduate Certificate). *Accreditation:* APA (one or more programs are accredited). Part-time programs available. Terminal master's awarded for partial completion of doctoral program. *Degree requirements:* For master's, comprehensive exam, thesis; for doctorate, comprehensive exam, thesis/dissertation. *Entrance requirements:* For master's and doctorate, GRE General Test, GRE Subject Test. Additional exam requirements/recommendations for international students: Required—TOEFL (minimum score 600 paper-based; 250 computer-based; 100 iBT), IELTS (minimum score 7). *Faculty research:* Cross-cultural psychology, health psychology, marine mammals, child/adult psychopathology.

University of Houston, College of Liberal Arts and Social Sciences, Department of Psychology, Houston, TX 77204. Offers clinical psychology (PhD); industrial/organizational psychology (PhD); psychology (MA); social psychology (PhD). *Accreditation:* APA (one or more programs are accredited). *Faculty:* 26 full-time (11 women), 8 part-time/adjunct (3 women). *Students:* 99 full-time (75 women), 15 part-time (11 women); includes 20 minority (5 African Americans, 3 Asian Americans or Pacific Islanders, 12 Hispanic Americans), 10 international. Average age 27. 386 applicants, 7% accepted, 23 enrolled. In 2008, 19 master's, 17 doctorates awarded. *Degree requirements:* For doctorate, thesis/dissertation. *Entrance requirements:* For doctorate, GRE General Test, minimum GPA of 3.0. *Application deadline:* For fall admission, 1/1 for domestic students. Application fee: $40 ($75 for international students). *Expenses:* Tuition, state resident: full-time $5164; part-time $287 per credit. Tuition, nonresident: full-time $10,222; part-time $568 per credit. *Financial support:* In 2008–09, 15 fellowships with full tuition reimbursements (averaging $11,500 per year), 14 research assistantships with full tuition reimbursements (averaging $12,050 per year), 76 teaching assistantships with full tuition reimbursements (averaging $12,050 per year) were awarded; career-related internships or fieldwork, Federal Work-Study, institutionally sponsored loans, scholarships/grants, health care benefits, and unspecified assistantships also available. Support available to part-time students. Financial award application deadline: 2/1; financial award applicants required to submit FAFSA. *Faculty research:* Health psychology, depression, child/family process, organizational effectiveness, close relationships. *Unit head:* Dr. David Francis, Chairperson, 713-743-7036, Fax: 713-743-8588, E-mail: dfrancis@uh.edu. *Application contact:* Sherry A. Berun, Coordinator, Academic Affairs, 713-743-8508, Fax: 713-743-8588, E-mail: sherryr@uh.edu.

University of Houston–Clear Lake, School of Human Sciences and Humanities, Programs in Human Sciences, Houston, TX 77058-1098. Offers behavioral sciences (MA), including criminology, cross cultural studies, general psychology, sociology; clinical psychology (MA); criminology (MA); cross cultural studies (MA); family therapy (MA); fitness and human performance (MA); school psychology (MA). *Accreditation:* AAMFT/COAMFTE. Part-time and evening/weekend programs available. Postbaccalaureate distance learning degree programs offered (minimal on-campus study). *Degree requirements:* For master's, thesis or alternative. *Entrance requirements:* For master's, GRE General Test. Additional exam requirements/recommendations for international students: Required—TOEFL (minimum score 550 paper-based; 213 computer-based). Electronic applications accepted. *Faculty research:* Smoking cessation, adolescent sexuality, white collar crime, serial murder, human factors/human computer interaction.

University of Houston–Victoria, School of Arts and Sciences, Program in Psychology, Victoria, TX 77901-4450. Offers counseling psychology (MA); school psychology (MA). Part-time and evening/weekend programs available. Postbaccalaureate distance learning degree programs offered. *Degree requirements:* For master's, project or thesis. *Entrance requirements:* For master's, GRE General Test. Additional exam requirements/recommendations for international students: Required—TOEFL (minimum score 550 paper-based; 213 computer-based). Electronic applications accepted.

University of Idaho, College of Graduate Studies, College of Letters, Arts and Social Sciences, Department of Psychology and Communication Studies, Moscow, ID 83844-2282. Offers psychology (MS). *Faculty:* 8 full-time, 6 part-time/adjunct. *Students:* 9 full-time, 18 part-time. Average age 31. In 2008, 9 master's awarded. *Entrance requirements:* For master's, GRE, minimum GPA of 2.8. *Application deadline:* For fall admission, 8/1 for domestic students; for spring admission, 12/15 for domestic students. Application fee: $55 ($60 for international students). *Expenses:* Tuition, nonresident: full-time $10,080; part-time $336 per credit. Required fees: $5212; $267 per credit. Tuition and fees vary according to program. *Financial support:* Fellowships, research assistantships, teaching assistantships available. Financial award application deadline: 2/15. *Faculty research:* Clinical, experimental, and cognitive psychology. *Unit head:* Dr. Richard D. Locke, Chair, 208-885-6324. *Application contact:* Dr. Richard D. Locke, Chair, 208-885-6324.

University of Illinois at Chicago, Graduate College, College of Liberal Arts and Sciences, Department of Psychology, Chicago, IL 60607-7128. Offers PhD. *Accreditation:* APA. *Degree requirements:* For doctorate, thesis/dissertation, departmental qualifying exam. *Entrance requirements:* For doctorate, GRE General Test, minimum GPA of 2.75. Additional exam requirements/recommendations for international students: Required—TOEFL. Electronic applications accepted.

University of Illinois at Urbana–Champaign, Graduate College, College of Liberal Arts and Sciences, Department of Psychology, Champaign, IL 61820. Offers MA, MS, PhD. *Accreditation:* APA (one or more programs are accredited). *Faculty:* 53 full-time (18 women), 2 part-time/adjunct (1 woman). *Students:* 174 full-time (113 women); includes 25 minority (7 African Americans, 2 American Indian/Alaska Native, 13 Asian Americans or Pacific Islanders, 3 Hispanic Americans), 53 international. 479 applicants, 11% accepted, 23 enrolled. In 2008, 25 master's, 24 doctorates awarded. *Entrance requirements:* For master's and doctorate, GRE General Test, minimum GPA of 3.0. Additional exam requirements/recommendations for international students: Required—TOEFL (minimum score 79 iBT), IELTS (minimum score 6.5), TOEFL or IELTS. *Application deadline:* Applications are processed on a rolling basis. Application fee: $60 ($75 for international students). Electronic applications accepted. *Financial support:* In 2008–09, 26 fellowships with full tuition reimbursements, 101 research assistantships with

Psychology—General

University of Illinois at Urbana–Champaign (continued)
full tuition reimbursements, 92 teaching assistantships with full tuition reimbursements were awarded; tuition waivers (full) also available. *Unit head:* Dr. David Irwin, Head, 217-333-0632, Fax: 217-244-5876, E-mail: irwin@illinois.edu. *Application contact:* Cheryl Berger, Assistant Head for Graduate Affairs, 217-333-0631, Fax: 217-244-5876, E-mail: gradstdy@cyrus.psych.uiuc.edu.

University of Indianapolis, Graduate Programs, School of Psychological Sciences, Indianapolis, IN 46227-3697. Offers clinical psychology (Psy D); clinical psychology/mental health counseling (MA). *Accreditation:* APA. *Faculty:* 10 full-time (4 women), 4 part-time/adjunct (1 woman). *Students:* 112 full-time (101 women), 55 part-time (43 women); includes 6 minority (5 African Americans, 1 Asian American or Pacific Islander), 8 international. Average age 27. *Degree requirements:* For master's, practicum; for doctorate, comprehensive exam, thesis/dissertation, 1200 hours of clinical practicum, 2000 hour internship. *Entrance requirements:* For master's, GRE, 3 letters of recommendation; for doctorate, GRE, minimum GPA of 3.0, 18 hours of course work in psychology, 3 letters of recommendation. Additional exam requirements/recommendations for international students: Required—TOEFL (minimum score 550 paper-based; 213 computer-based). *Application deadline:* For fall admission, 2/25 for domestic students. Application fee: $50. *Financial support:* Federal Work-Study available. *Unit head:* Dr. E. John McIlvried, Dean, 317-788-3247, Fax: 317-788-3480, E-mail: jmcilvried@uindy.edu. *Application contact:* Dr. E. John McIlvried, Associate Provost for Graduate Programs and International Programs, 317-788-3274, E-mail: jmcilvried@uindy.edu.

The University of Iowa, Graduate College, College of Education, Department of Psychological and Quantitative Foundations, Iowa City, IA 52242-1316. Offers counseling psychology (PhD); educational measurement and statistics (MA, PhD); educational psychology (MA, PhD); school psychology (PhD, Ed S); JD/PhD. *Accreditation:* APA. *Degree requirements:* For master's, thesis optional, exam; for doctorate, comprehensive exam, thesis/dissertation; for Ed S, exam. *Entrance requirements:* For master's, doctorate, and Ed S, GRE General Test, minimum GPA of 3.0. Additional exam requirements/recommendations for international students: Required—TOEFL (minimum score 550 paper-based; 213 computer-based; 81 iBT). Electronic applications accepted.

The University of Iowa, Graduate College, College of Liberal Arts and Sciences, Department of Psychology, Iowa City, IA 52242-1316. Offers neural and behavioral sciences (PhD); psychology (MA, PhD). *Degree requirements:* For master's, thesis optional, exam; for doctorate, comprehensive exam, thesis/dissertation. *Entrance requirements:* For master's and doctorate, GRE General Test, minimum GPA of 3.0. Additional exam requirements/recommendations for international students: Required—TOEFL (minimum score 550 paper-based; 213 computer-based; 81 iBT). Electronic applications accepted.

The University of Kansas, Graduate Studies, College of Liberal Arts and Sciences, Department of Applied Behavioral Science, Lawrence, KS 66045. Offers applied behavioral science (MA); behavioral psychology (PhD). *Faculty:* 18. *Students:* 55 full-time (38 women), 4 part-time (all women); includes 5 minority (1 African American, 2 Asian Americans or Pacific Islanders, 2 Hispanic Americans), 3 international. Average age 32. 65 applicants, 18% accepted, 11 enrolled. In 2008, 6 master's, 5 doctorates awarded. Terminal master's awarded for partial completion of doctoral program. *Degree requirements:* For master's, thesis; for doctorate, thesis/dissertation, comprehensive oral and written exams, journal reviews. *Entrance requirements:* For master's and doctorate, curriculum vitae, 3 letters of recommendation. Additional exam requirements/recommendations for international students: Required—TOEFL, TWE. *Application deadline:* For fall admission, 1/12 priority date for domestic and international students. Application fee: $45 ($50 for international students). Electronic applications accepted. *Expenses:* Tuition, area resident: Full-time $6122; part-time $255.10 per credit hour. Tuition, state resident: full-time $6122; part-time $255.10 per credit hour. Tuition, nonresident: full-time $14,629; part-time $609.55 per credit hour. Required fees: $847; $70.56 per credit hour. Tuition and fees vary according to course load and program. *Financial support:* Fellowships, research assistantships with full and partial tuition reimbursements, teaching assistantships with full and partial tuition reimbursements, career-related internships or fieldwork, traineeships, tuition waivers (full), and unspecified assistantships available. Financial award application deadline: 2/1. *Faculty research:* Early childhood, developmental disabilities, community health and development, adults with disabilities, applied behavior analysis. *Unit head:* Dr. Edward K. Morris, Chair, 785-864-4840, Fax: 785-864-5202, E-mail: ekm@ku.edu. *Application contact:* Dr. Gregory J. Madden, Graduate Director, 785-864-4840, Fax: 785-864-5202, E-mail: gmadden@ku.edu.

The University of Kansas, Graduate Studies, College of Liberal Arts and Sciences, Department of Psychology, Lawrence, KS 66045. Offers clinical child psychology (MA, PhD); cognitive (PhD); developmental (PhD); psychology (MA, PhD); quantitative (PhD). *Accreditation:* APA (one or more programs are accredited). *Faculty:* 38. *Students:* 90 full-time (65 women), 6 part-time (5 women); includes 15 minority (5 African Americans, 1 American Indian/Alaska Native, 7 Asian Americans or Pacific Islanders, 2 Hispanic Americans), 6 international. Average age 27. 195 applicants, 14% accepted, 10 enrolled. In 2008, 15 master's, 16 doctorates awarded. *Degree requirements:* For master's, thesis; for doctorate, comprehensive exam, thesis/dissertation. *Entrance requirements:* For doctorate, GRE General Test, minimum GPA of 3.0. Additional exam requirements/recommendations for international students: Required—TOEFL. *Application deadline:* For fall admission, 1/15 for domestic and international students. Application fee: $45 ($55 for international students). Electronic applications accepted. *Expenses:* Tuition, area resident: Full-time $6122; part-time $255.10 per credit hour. Tuition, state resident: full-time $6122; part-time $255.10 per credit hour. Tuition, nonresident: full-time $14,629; part-time $609.55 per credit hour. Required fees: $847; $70.56 per credit hour. Tuition and fees vary according to course load and program. *Financial support:* Fellowships with full tuition reimbursements, research assistantships with partial tuition reimbursements, teaching assistantships with full and partial tuition reimbursements, career-related internships or fieldwork and unspecified assistantships available. Financial award application deadline: 1/4; financial award applicants required to submit FAFSA. *Faculty research:* Cognitive psychology, methodology and statistics, developmental clinical/health psychology. *Unit head:* Greg Simpson, Chair, 785-864-9821, Fax: 785-864-5696, E-mail: gsimpson@ku.edu. *Application contact:* Cathy L. O'Keefe, Graduate Admissions Officer, 785-864-4195, Fax: 785-864-5696, E-mail: psycgrad@ku.edu.

University of Kentucky, Graduate School, College of Arts and Sciences, Program in Psychology, Lexington, KY 40506-0032. Offers clinical psychology (MA); experimental psychology (MA). *Accreditation:* APA (one or more programs are accredited). *Degree requirements:* For master's, comprehensive exam, thesis; for doctorate, comprehensive exam, thesis/dissertation. *Entrance requirements:* For master's, GRE General Test, minimum undergraduate GPA of 2.75; for doctorate, GRE General Test, minimum graduate GPA of 3.0. Additional exam requirements/recommendations for international students: Required—TOEFL (minimum score 550 paper-based; 213 computer-based). Electronic applications accepted. *Faculty research:* Psychopharmacology and teratology, behavioral neuroscience, social psychology, cognitive psychology, development and developmental psychobiology.

University of La Verne, College of Arts and Sciences, Department of Psychology, La Verne, CA 91750-4443. Offers clinical-community psychology (Psy D); counseling (MS), including general counseling, higher education counseling, marriage and family therapy. *Accreditation:* APA (one or more programs are accredited). Part-time programs available. *Faculty:* 11 full-time (5 women), 16 part-time/adjunct (9 women). *Students:* 89 full-time (76 women), 106 part-time (94 women); includes 114 minority (23 African Americans, 12 Asian Americans or Pacific Islanders, 79 Hispanic Americans). Average age 30. In 2008, 24 master's, 20 doctorates awarded. *Degree requirements:* For master's, thesis, competency exam, personal psychotherapy; for doctorate, thesis/dissertation, clinical internship, competency exams, practicum, personal psychotherapy. *Entrance requirements:* For master's, minimum undergraduate GPA of 3.0, 3 letters of recommendation, interview; for doctorate, minimum GPA of 3.25 undergraduate, 3.65

graduate; 3 recommendations; interview; curriculum vitae. Additional exam requirements/recommendations for international students: Required—TOEFL (minimum score 600 paper-based; 250 computer-based). *Application deadline:* Applications are processed on a rolling basis. *Expenses:* Contact institution. *Financial support:* Career-related internships or fieldwork, institutionally sponsored loans, and scholarships/grants available. Financial award application deadline: 3/2; financial award applicants required to submit FAFSA. *Faculty research:* Developmental therapy and counseling. *Unit head:* Dr. Glenn Gamst, Department Chair, 909-593-3511, E-mail: gamstg@ulv.edu. *Application contact:* Connie Hamlow, Admissions Information Specialist, 909-593-3511 Ext. 4244, Fax: 909-392-2761, E-mail: gradadmission@ulv.edu.

University of Lethbridge, School of Graduate Studies, Lethbridge, AB T1K 3M4, Canada. Offers accounting (MScM); addictions counseling (M Sc); agricultural biotechnology (M Sc); agricultural studies (M Sc, MA); anthropology (MA); archaeology (MA); art (MA); biochemistry (M Sc); biological sciences (M Sc); biomolecular science (PhD); biosystems and biodiversity (PhD); Canadian studies (MA); chemistry (M Sc); computer science (M Sc); computer science and geographical information science (M Sc); counseling psychology (M Ed); dramatic arts (MA); earth, space, and physical science (PhD); economics (MA); educational leadership (M Ed); English (MA); environmental science (M Sc); evolution and behavior (PhD); exercise science (M Sc); finance (MScM); French (MA); French/German (MA); French/Spanish (MA); general education (M Ed); general management (MScM); geography (M Sc, MA); German (MA); health sciences (M Sc, MA); history (MA); human resource management and labour relations (MScM); individualized multidisciplinary (M Sc, MA); information systems (MScM); international management (MScM); kinesiology (M Sc, MA); management (M Sc, MA); marketing (MScM); mathematics (M Sc); music (MA); Native American studies (MA); neuroscience (M Sc, PhD); new media (MA); nursing (M Sc); philosophy (MA); physics (M Sc); policy and strategy (MScM); political science (MA); psychology (M Sc, MA); religious studies (MA); sociology (MA); theoretical and computational science (PhD); urban and regional studies (MA). Part-time and evening/weekend programs available. *Degree requirements:* For doctorate, comprehensive exam, thesis/dissertation. *Entrance requirements:* For master's, GMAT (M Sc in management), bachelor's degree in related field, minimum GPA of 3.0 during previous 20 graded semester courses, 2 years teaching or related experience (M Ed); for doctorate, master's degree, minimum graduate GPA of 3.5. Additional exam requirements/recommendations for international students: Required—TOEFL. *Faculty research:* Movement and brain plasticity, gibberellin physiology, photosynthesis, carbon cycling, molecular properties of main-group ring components.

University of Louisiana at Lafayette, BI Moody III College of Business Administration MBA Program, College of Liberal Arts, Department of Psychology, Program in Psychology, Lafayette, LA 70504. Offers MS. *Degree requirements:* For master's, comprehensive exam, thesis (for some programs). *Entrance requirements:* For master's, GRE General Test. Additional exam requirements/recommendations for international students: Required—TOEFL (minimum score 550 paper-based; 213 computer-based).

University of Louisiana at Monroe, Graduate School, College of Education and Human Development, Department of Psychology, Monroe, LA 71209-0001. Offers general psychology (MS); school psychology (MS, SSP). Part-time and evening/weekend programs available. *Faculty:* 6 full-time (3 women), 2 part-time/adjunct (1 woman). *Students:* 18 full-time (10 women), 8 part-time (5 women); includes 8 minority (all African Americans). Average age 28. In 2008, 7 master's, 7 other advanced degrees awarded. *Degree requirements:* For master's, thesis; for SSP, comprehensive exam, thesis, minimum GPA of 3.0, field and practicum experiences (400 hours), internship (1250 hours). *Entrance requirements:* For master's, minimum GPA of 2.75 or GRE General Test; for SSP, GRE General Test, minimum GPA of 3.25. Additional exam requirements/recommendations for international students: Required—TOEFL (minimum score 500 paper-based; 173 computer-based; 61 iBT). *Application deadline:* For fall admission, 8/22 priority date for domestic students, 7/1 for international students; for winter admission, 12/12 priority date for domestic students; for spring admission, 1/17 for domestic students, 11/1 for international students. Applications are processed on a rolling basis. Application fee: $20 ($30 for international students). Electronic applications accepted. *Expenses:* Tuition, area resident: Full-time $2403; part-time $1202 per semester. Tuition, state resident: full-time $2403; part-time $1202 per semester. Tuition, nonresident: full-time $2403; part-time $1202 per semester. International tuition: $8352 full-time. Required fees: $1239.40; $141 per credit hour. *Financial support:* In 2008–09, 11 research assistantships with full tuition reimbursements (averaging $2,500 per year) were awarded; career-related internships or fieldwork, Federal Work-Study, and unspecified assistantships also available. Financial award application deadline: 4/1; financial award applicants required to submit FAFSA. *Faculty research:* Identity development comparison, alcohol and drug problems. *Unit head:* Dr. David Williamson, Head, 318-342-1331, Fax: 318-342-1352, E-mail: williamson@ulm.edu. *Application contact:* Dr. David Williamson, Head, 318-342-1331, Fax: 318-342-1352, E-mail: williamson@ulm.edu.

University of Louisville, Graduate School, College of Arts and Sciences, Department of Psychological and Brain Sciences, Louisville, KY 40292-0001. Offers clinical psychology (MA, PhD); experimental psychology (PhD); psychology (MA). *Accreditation:* APA (one or more programs are accredited). *Students:* 68 full-time (47 women), 2 part-time (1 woman); includes 2 African Americans, 2 Asian Americans or Pacific Islanders, 1 Hispanic American, 7 international. Average age 30. In 2008, 20 master's, 13 doctorates awarded. *Degree requirements:* For doctorate, thesis/dissertation, internship. *Entrance requirements:* For master's and doctorate, GRE General Test. *Application deadline:* Applications are processed on a rolling basis. Application fee: $50. *Financial support:* In 2008–09, 29 teaching assistantships with tuition reimbursements (averaging $20,500 per year) were awarded; career-related internships or fieldwork also available. *Unit head:* Dr. Barbara Burns, Chair, 502-852-5947, Fax: 502-852-8904, E-mail: bburns@louisville.edu. *Application contact:* Libby Leggett, Director, Graduate Admissions, 502-852-3101, Fax: 502-852-6536, E-mail: gradadm@louisville.edu.

University of Maine, Graduate School, College of Liberal Arts and Sciences, Department of Psychology, Orono, ME 04469. Offers clinical psychology (PhD); developmental psychology (MA); experimental psychology (MA, PhD); social psychology (MA). *Accreditation:* APA (one or more programs are accredited). *Degree requirements:* For master's, thesis; for doctorate, thesis/dissertation. *Entrance requirements:* For master's and doctorate, GRE General Test, GRE Subject Test. Additional exam requirements/recommendations for international students: Required—TOEFL. Electronic applications accepted. *Faculty research:* Social development, hypertension and aging, attitude change, self-confidence in achievement situations, health psychology.

University of Manitoba, Faculty of Graduate Studies, Faculty of Arts, Department of Psychology, Winnipeg, MB R3T 2N2, Canada. Offers clinical psychology (PhD); psychology (MA, PhD); school psychology (MA). *Accreditation:* APA (one or more programs are accredited). *Degree requirements:* For master's, thesis; for doctorate, one foreign language, thesis/dissertation. *Entrance requirements:* For master's and doctorate, GRE General Test.

University of Mary Hardin-Baylor, College of Sciences and Humanities, Department of Psychology, Belton, TX 76513. Offers community counseling (MA); marriage and family Christian counseling (MA); psychology and counseling (MA); school counseling and psychology (MA). Part-time and evening/weekend programs available. *Degree requirements:* For master's, comprehensive exam. *Entrance requirements:* For master's, GRE General Test, minimum GPA of 3.0 in last 60 hours or 2.75 overall. Electronic applications accepted.

University of Maryland, Baltimore County, Graduate School, College of Arts, Humanities and Social Sciences, Department of Psychology, Baltimore, MD 21250. Offers applied developmental psychology (PhD); human services psychology (MA, PhD), including applied behavioral analysis (MA), human services psychology/clinical (PhD); industrial and organizational psychology (MPS); psychology (MPS). *Accreditation:* APA (one or more programs are accredited). *Faculty:* 23 full-time (9 women), 11 part-time/adjunct (4 women). *Students:* 117 full-time (97 women), 14 part-time (11 women); includes 24 minority (9 African Americans, 8 Asian Americans or Pacific Islanders, 7 Hispanic Americans), 9 international. Average age 30.

182 applicants, 23% accepted, 32 enrolled. In 2008, 20 master's, 13 doctorates awarded. Terminal master's awarded for partial completion of doctoral program. *Degree requirements:* For master's, thesis or alternative; for doctorate, comprehensive exam, thesis/dissertation. *Entrance requirements:* For master's, GRE General Test; for doctorate, GRE General Test, GRE Subject Test. Additional exam requirements/recommendations for international students: Required—TOEFL. *Application deadline:* For fall admission, 12/1 for domestic and international students. Application fee: $50. Electronic applications accepted. *Financial support:* In 2008–09, 1 fellowship with full and partial tuition reimbursement (averaging $22,000 per year), 29 research assistantships with full and partial tuition reimbursements (averaging $14,857 per year), 34 teaching assistantships with full and partial tuition reimbursements (averaging $14,857 per year) were awarded; career-related internships or fieldwork, Federal Work-Study, health care benefits, and tuition waivers (full and partial) also available. Financial award application deadline: 3/1; financial award applicants required to submit FAFSA. *Faculty research:* Prevention and treatment of behavior problems, early intervention, cultural contexts, applications to education, behavioral medicine. Total annual research expenditures: $2.3 million. *Unit head:* Dr. Linda Baker, Chair, 410-455-2415, Fax: 410-455-1055, E-mail: baker@umbc.edu. *Application contact:* Cara Lane, Program Management Specialist, 410-455-2567, Fax: 410-455-1055, E-mail: psycdept@umbc.edu.

University of Maryland, College Park, Graduate Studies, College of Behavioral and Social Sciences, Department of Psychology, College Park, MD 20742. Offers clinical psychology (PhD); developmental psychology (PhD); experimental psychology (PhD); industrial psychology (MA, MS, PhD); social psychology (PhD). *Accreditation:* APA (one or more programs are accredited). *Degree requirements:* For master's, thesis; for doctorate, variable foreign language requirement, comprehensive exam, thesis/dissertation. *Entrance requirements:* For master's and doctorate, GRE General Test, GRE Subject Test, minimum GPA of 3.5, research and/or work experience, 3 letters of recommendation. Electronic applications accepted. *Faculty research:* Social stereotyping and prejudice, anxiety disorders, auditory neuroethology, counseling and social psychology.

University of Massachusetts Amherst, Graduate School, College of Social and Behavioral Sciences, Department of Psychology, Amherst, MA 01003. Offers clinical psychology (MS, PhD); cognitive psychology (MS, PhD); developmental science (MS, PhD); psychology of peace and violence (MS, PhD); social psychology (MS, PhD). *Accreditation:* APA (one or more programs are accredited). Terminal master's awarded for partial completion of doctoral program. *Degree requirements:* For master's, thesis; for doctorate, comprehensive exam, thesis/dissertation. *Entrance requirements:* For master's and doctorate, GRE General Test, 3 letters of recommendation. Additional exam requirements/recommendations for international students: Required—TOEFL (minimum score 550 paper-based; 213 computer-based; 79 iBT), IELTS (minimum score 6.5). Electronic applications accepted. *Expenses:* Tuition, area resident: Full-time $2640. Tuition, nonresident: full-time $9936. One-time fee: $332 full-time. Tuition and fees vary according to course load.

University of Massachusetts Dartmouth, Graduate School, College of Arts and Sciences, Department of Psychology, North Dartmouth, MA 02747-2300. Offers behavior analyst (PMC); clinical psychology (MA); general psychology (MA). Part-time programs available. *Faculty:* 17 full-time (8 women), 8 part-time/adjunct (5 women). *Students:* 17 full-time (11 women), 26 part-time (23 women); includes 6 minority (4 African Americans, 2 Asian Americans or Pacific Islanders). Average age 29. 52 applicants, 46% accepted, 16 enrolled. In 2008, 18 master's awarded. *Degree requirements:* For master's, thesis (for some programs). *Entrance requirements:* For master's, GRE General Test, minimum GPA of 2.75, 3 letters of recommendation. Additional exam requirements/recommendations for international students: Required—TOEFL (minimum score 500 paper-based). *Application deadline:* For fall admission, 3/31 for domestic students, 1/31 for international students. Application fee: $40 ($60 for international students). Electronic applications accepted. *Expenses:* Tuition, state resident: full-time $2071; part-time $86.29 per credit. Tuition, nonresident: full-time $8099; part-time $337.46 per credit. Required fees: $7946. Tuition and fees vary according to class time, course load and reciprocity agreements. *Financial support:* In 2008–09, 9 teaching assistantships with full tuition reimbursements (averaging $3,500 per year) were awarded; career-related internships or fieldwork, Federal Work-Study, and unspecified assistantships also available. Support available to part-time students. Financial award application deadline: 3/1; financial award applicants required to submit FAFSA. *Faculty research:* Emotion, nonverbal communication, behavioral medicine, children's theatre and self-confidence, psychosocial stress. Total annual research expenditures: $14,000. *Unit head:* Dr. Paul Donnelly, Director, Clinical Psychology, 508-999-8334, E-mail: pdonnelly@umassd.edu. *Application contact:* Elan Turcotte-Shamski, Graduate Admissions Officer, 508-999-8604, Fax: 508-999-8183, E-mail: graduate@umassd.edu.

University of Massachusetts Lowell, College of Arts and Sciences, Department of Psychology, Lowell, MA 01854-2881. Offers community social psychology (MA). Part-time programs available. *Degree requirements:* For master's, thesis optional. *Entrance requirements:* For master's, GRE General Test or MAT. Electronic applications accepted. *Faculty research:* Domestic violence, youth sports, teen pregnancy, substance abuse, family and work roles.

University of Memphis, Graduate School, College of Arts and Sciences, Department of Psychology, Memphis, TN 38152. Offers clinical psychology (PhD); experimental psychology (PhD); general psychology (MS); school psychology (MA, PhD). Part-time programs available. *Faculty:* 29 full-time (9 women), 1 part-time/adjunct (0 women). *Students:* 119 full-time (80 women), 21 part-time (13 women); includes 23 minority (16 African Americans, 1 American Indian/Alaska Native, 2 Asian Americans or Pacific Islanders, 4 Hispanic Americans), 9 international. Average age 27. 197 applicants, 23% accepted, 31 enrolled. In 2008, 28 master's, 11 doctorates awarded. Terminal master's awarded for partial completion of doctoral program. *Degree requirements:* For master's, comprehensive exam, thesis (for some programs), oral exam (MS); for doctorate, thesis/dissertation, internship. *Entrance requirements:* For master's, GRE General Test, 18 undergraduate hours in psychology, minimum GPA of 2.5; for doctorate, GRE General Test, GRE Subject Test. *Application deadline:* For fall admission, 2/1 for domestic students. Applications are processed on a rolling basis. Application fee: $35 ($60 for international students). *Expenses:* Tuition, area resident: Full-time $6242; part-time $330 per credit hour. Tuition, state resident: full-time $6242; part-time $330 per credit hour. Tuition, nonresident: full-time $17,828; part-time $815 per credit hour. Required fees: $1156. *Financial support:* Fellowships with full tuition reimbursements, research assistantships with full tuition reimbursements, teaching assistantships with full tuition reimbursements, tuition waivers (partial) and unspecified assistantships available. Financial award applicants required to submit FAFSA. *Faculty research:* Psychotherapy and psychopathology, behavioral medicine and community psychology, child and family studies, cognitive and social processes, neuropsychology and behavioral neuroscience. *Unit head:* Dr. William Zachry, Chair, 901-678-2145, Fax: 901-678-2579, E-mail: wzachry@memphis.edu. *Application contact:* Dr. Robert Cohen, Graduate Studies Coordinator, 901-678-2146.

University of Miami, Graduate School, College of Arts and Sciences, Department of Psychology, Coral Gables, FL 33124. Offers adult clinical (PhD); behavioral neuroscience (PhD); child clinical (PhD); developmental psychology (PhD); health clinical (PhD); psychology (MS). *Accreditation:* APA (one or more programs are accredited). *Degree requirements:* For doctorate, comprehensive exam, thesis/dissertation. *Entrance requirements:* For doctorate, GRE General Test, minimum GPA of 3.5. Additional exam requirements/recommendations for international students: Required—TOEFL. Electronic applications accepted. *Faculty research:* Behavioral factors in cardiovascular disease and cancer adult psychopathology, developmental disabilities, social and emotional development, mechanisms of coping.

University of Michigan, Horace H. Rackham School of Graduate Studies, College of Literature, Science, and the Arts, Department of Psychology, Ann Arbor, MI 48109. Offers biopsychology (PhD); clinical psychology (PhD); cognition and perception (PhD); developmental psychology (PhD); personality and social contexts (PhD); social psychology (PhD). *Accreditation:* APA. *Degree requirements:* For doctorate, comprehensive exam, thesis/dissertation, oral defense of dissertation, preliminary exam. *Entrance requirements:* For doctorate, GRE General Test (optional), GRE Subject Test (optional). Additional exam requirements/recommendations for international students: Required—TOEFL. Electronic applications accepted.

University of Michigan, Horace H. Rackham School of Graduate Studies, College of Literature, Science, and the Arts, Department of Women's Studies, Ann Arbor, MI 48109. Offers English and women's studies (PhD); history and women's studies (PhD); lesbian, gay, bisexual, transgender, queer (LGBTQ) studies (Certificate); psychology and women's studies (PhD); sociology and women's studies (PhD); women's studies (Certificate). *Degree requirements:* For doctorate, variable foreign language requirement, thesis/dissertation. *Entrance requirements:* For doctorate, GRE General Test, previous undergraduate course work in women's studies. Electronic applications accepted. *Faculty research:* Gender issues; LGBTQ studies; sexuality; women and science; global feminism.

University of Michigan, Horace H. Rackham School of Graduate Studies, Combined Program in Education and Psychology, Ann Arbor, MI 48109. Offers PhD. *Degree requirements:* For doctorate, thesis/dissertation, oral defense of dissertation, preliminary exam, independent research project. *Entrance requirements:* For doctorate, GRE General Test. Additional exam requirements/recommendations for international students: Required—TOEFL (minimum score 600 paper-based; 250 computer-based; 100 iBT). Electronic applications accepted. *Faculty research:* Classroom research, instructional psychology.

University of Minnesota, Twin Cities Campus, Graduate School, College of Liberal Arts, Department of Psychology, Minneapolis, MN 55455-0213. Offers biological psychopathology (PhD); clinical psychology (PhD); cognitive and biological psychology (PhD); counseling psychology (PhD); industrial/organizational psychology (PhD); personality, individual differences, and behavior genetics (PhD); quantitative/psychometric methods (PhD); school psychology (PhD); social psychology (PhD). *Accreditation:* APA. *Degree requirements:* For doctorate, comprehensive exam, thesis/dissertation. *Entrance requirements:* For doctorate, GRE General Test, GRE Subject Test (recommended), 12 credits of upper-level psychology courses, including a course in statistics or psychological measurement. Additional exam requirements/recommendations for international students: Required—TOEFL (minimum score 550 paper-based; 213 computer-based; 79 iBT).

University of Mississippi, Graduate School, College of Liberal Arts, Department of Psychology, Oxford, University, MS 38677. Offers clinical psychology (PhD); experimental psychology (PhD); psychology (MA). *Accreditation:* APA (one or more programs are accredited). *Degree requirements:* For master's, thesis; for doctorate, thesis/dissertation. *Entrance requirements:* For master's, GRE General Test, minimum GPA of 3.0; for doctorate, GRE General Test. Additional exam requirements/recommendations for international students: Required—TOEFL. Electronic applications accepted.

University of Missouri–Columbia, Graduate School, College of Arts and Sciences, Department of Psychological Sciences, Columbia, MO 65211. Offers MA, MS, PhD. *Accreditation:* APA (one or more programs are accredited). *Faculty:* 40 full-time (15 women), 2 part-time/adjunct (0 women). *Students:* 69 full-time (43 women), 19 part-time (15 women); includes 11 minority (2 African Americans, 3 Asian Americans or Pacific Islanders, 6 Hispanic Americans), 15 international. Average age 27. 239 applicants, 12% accepted, 18 enrolled. In 2008, 9 master's, 11 doctorates awarded. Terminal master's awarded for partial completion of doctoral program. *Degree requirements:* For doctorate, thesis/dissertation. *Entrance requirements:* For master's and doctorate, GRE General Test, minimum GPA of 3.0. Additional exam requirements/recommendations for international students: Required—TOEFL (minimum score 500 paper-based; 173 computer-based; 61 iBT). *Application deadline:* For fall admission, 2/1 priority date for domestic students. Applications are processed on a rolling basis. Application fee: $45 ($60 for international students). *Financial support:* Fellowships, research assistantships, teaching assistantships, career-related internships or fieldwork and institutionally sponsored loans available. *Unit head:* Dr. Ann Bettencourt, Department Chair, E-mail: bettencourta@missouri.edu. *Application contact:* Linda Jacobs, Office Support Staff IV, 573-882-0838, E-mail: jacobsl@missouri.edu.

University of Missouri–Kansas City, College of Arts and Sciences, Department of Psychology, Kansas City, MO 64110-2499. Offers psychology (MA, PhD), including clinical psychology (PhD), community psychology (PhD). *Accreditation:* APA. *Faculty:* 15 full-time (12 women), 1 part-time/adjunct (0 women). *Students:* 18 full-time (15 women), 6 part-time (5 women); includes 3 minority (2 African Americans, 1 Hispanic American). Average age 31. 90 applicants, 6% accepted, 5 enrolled. In 2008, 3 master's, 2 doctorates awarded. Terminal master's awarded for partial completion of doctoral program. *Degree requirements:* For master's, thesis; for doctorate, comprehensive exam, thesis/dissertation, residency. *Entrance requirements:* For master's, GRE, minimum GPA of 3.5, letter of recommendation; for doctorate, GRE, minimum GPA of 3.25. Additional exam requirements/recommendations for international students: Required—TOEFL (minimum score 550 paper-based; 213 computer-based; 80 iBT). *Application deadline:* For fall admission, 1/15 for domestic and international students. Applications are processed on a rolling basis. Application fee: $45 ($50 for international students). Electronic applications accepted. *Expenses:* Tuition, state resident: full-time $5376; part-time $298.70 per credit hour. Tuition, nonresident: full-time $13,882; part-time $771.20 per credit hour. Required fees: $640.28; $34.65 per contact hour. $30 per semester. Tuition and fees vary according to course load and program. *Financial support:* In 2008–09, 14 research assistantships (averaging $12,402 per year), 3 teaching assistantships (averaging $10,000 per year) were awarded; career-related internships or fieldwork, Federal Work-Study, and institutionally sponsored loans also available. Support available to part-time students. Financial award application deadline: 3/1; financial award applicants required to submit FAFSA. *Faculty research:* HIV/AIDS research group, psycho-oncology, sensory and cognitive neuroscience, cognitive psychophysiology, obesity and related metabolic disorders. Total annual research expenditures: $750,913. *Unit head:* Dr. Diane Filion, Chairperson, 816-235-1061, E-mail: filiond@umkc.edu. *Application contact:* 816-235-1111.

University of Missouri–St. Louis, College of Arts and Sciences, Department of Psychology, St. Louis, MO 63121. Offers behavioral neuroscience (PhD); clinical psychology respecialization (Certificate); community psychology (PhD); general psychology (MA); industrial/organizational psychology (PhD). *Accreditation:* APA (one or more programs are accredited). Evening/weekend programs available. *Faculty:* 21 full-time (10 women). *Students:* 56 full-time (46 women), 15 part-time (11 women); includes 4 minority (1 American Indian/Alaska Native, 2 Asian Americans or Pacific Islanders, 1 Hispanic American), 1 international. Average age 28. In 2008, 16 master's, 8 doctorates awarded. Terminal master's awarded for partial completion of doctoral program. *Degree requirements:* For doctorate, thesis/dissertation. *Entrance requirements:* For master's and doctorate, GRE General Test, GRE Subject Test, 3 letters of recommendation. Additional exam requirements/recommendations for international students: Required—TOEFL (minimum score 550 paper-based; 213 computer-based). *Application deadline:* For fall admission, 2/1 priority date for domestic and international students. Applications are processed on a rolling basis. Application fee: $35 ($40 for international students). Electronic applications accepted. *Expenses:* Tuition, area resident: Full-time $5377; part-time $298.70 per credit hour. Tuition, nonresident: full-time $13,381; part-time $472.50 per credit hour. Required fees: $4078; $52 per credit hour. *Financial support:* In 2008–09, 3 research assistantships with full and partial tuition reimbursements (averaging $9,225 per year), 15 teaching assistantships with full and partial tuition reimbursements (averaging $9,000 per year) were awarded; fellowships with full tuition reimbursements also available. Financial award applicants required to submit FAFSA. *Faculty research:* Bereavement and loss, neuroscience, post-traumatic stress disorder, conflict and negotiation, social psychology. *Unit head:* Dr. George Taylor, Chair, 314-516-5391, Fax: 314-516-5392, E-mail: umslpsychology@msx.umsl.edu. *Application contact:* 314-516-5458, Fax: 314-516-6996, E-mail: gradadm@umsl.edu.

The University of Montana, Graduate School, College of Arts and Sciences, Department of Psychology, Missoula, MT 59812-0002. Offers clinical psychology (PhD); experimental

Psychology—General

The University of Montana (continued)
psychology (PhD), including animal behavior psychology, developmental psychology; school psychology (MA, PhD, Ed S). *Accreditation:* APA (one or more programs are accredited). Terminal master's awarded for partial completion of doctoral program. *Degree requirements:* For master's, thesis; for doctorate, thesis/dissertation. *Entrance requirements:* For master's, doctorate, and Ed S, GRE General Test. Additional exam requirements/recommendations for international students: Required—TOEFL.

University of Nebraska at Omaha, Graduate Studies and Research, College of Arts and Sciences, Department of Psychology, Omaha, NE 68182. Offers developmental psychology (PhD); industrial/organizational psychology (MS, PhD); psychobiology (PhD); psychology (MA); school psychology (MS, Ed S). Part-time programs available. *Degree requirements:* For master's, comprehensive exam, thesis (for some programs). *Entrance requirements:* For master's, GRE General Test, GRE Subject Test, previous course work in psychology, including statistics and a laboratory course; minimum GPA of 3.0, 3 letters of recommendation; for doctorate, GRE General Test. Additional exam requirements/recommendations for international students: Required—TOEFL (minimum score 500 paper-based; 173 computer-based; 61 iBT). Electronic applications accepted.

University of Nebraska–Lincoln, Graduate College, College of Arts and Sciences, Department of Psychology, Lincoln, NE 68588. Offers biopsychology (PhD); clinical psychology (PhD); cognitive psychology (PhD); developmental psychology (PhD); psychology (MA); social/personality psychology (PhD); JD/MA; JD/PhD. *Accreditation:* APA (one or more programs are accredited). *Faculty:* 24 full-time (8 women). *Students:* 84 full-time (66 women), 29 part-time (15 women); includes 15 minority (1 African American, 1 American Indian/Alaska Native, 4 Asian Americans or Pacific Islanders, 9 Hispanic Americans), 9 international. Average age 32. In 2008, 16 master's, 18 doctorates awarded. *Degree requirements:* For master's, thesis optional; for doctorate, comprehensive exam, thesis/dissertation. *Entrance requirements:* For master's and doctorate, GRE General Test. Additional exam requirements/recommendations for international students: Required—TOEFL (minimum score 550 paper-based; 213 computer-based). *Application deadline:* For fall admission, 1/3 for domestic and international students. Application fee: $40. Electronic applications accepted. *Expenses:* Tuition, state resident: full-time $4275; part-time $237.50 per credit hour. Tuition, nonresident: full-time $11,525; part-time $640.25 per credit hour. Required fees: $1068; $10.35 per credit hour. $440.70 per semester. Tuition and fees vary according to course load and program. *Financial support:* Fellowships, research assistantships, teaching assistantships, Federal Work-Study, health care benefits, and unspecified assistantships available. Support available to part-time students. Financial award application deadline: 1/3. *Faculty research:* Law and psychology, rural mental health, chronic mental illness, neuropsychology, child clinical psychology. *Unit head:* Dr. David Hansen, Chair, 402-472-3721, Fax: 402-472-4637. *Application contact:* Ginny Gross, Director of Graduate Admissions, 402-472-2878, Fax: 402-472-0589, E-mail: grad_admissions@unl.edu.

University of Nevada, Las Vegas, Graduate College, College of Liberal Arts, Department of Psychology, Las Vegas, NV 89154-5030. Offers psychology (PhD). *Accreditation:* APA. Part-time programs available. *Faculty:* 22 full-time (9 women), 4 part-time/adjunct (2 women). *Students:* 60 full-time (44 women), 18 part-time (12 women); includes 11 minority (4 African Americans, 4 Asian Americans or Pacific Islanders, 3 Hispanic Americans), 3 international. Average age 31. 112 applicants, 16% accepted, 15 enrolled. In 2008, 13 doctorates awarded. *Degree requirements:* For doctorate, comprehensive exam, thesis/dissertation, oral defense of dissertation. *Entrance requirements:* For doctorate, GRE General and Subject Tests. Additional exam requirements/recommendations for international students: Required—TOEFL (minimum score 550 paper-based; 213 computer-based; 80 iBT), IELTS (minimum score 7). *Application deadline:* For fall admission, 12/15 priority date for domestic students, 5/1 for international students. Applications are processed on a rolling basis. Application fee: $60 ($75 for international students). Electronic applications accepted. *Expenses:* Tuition, state resident: full-time $1414; part-time $198 per credit. Tuition, nonresident: full-time $12,509; part-time $415.75 per credit. International tuition: $14,249 full-time. Required fees: $4 per credit. $252 per semester. Tuition and fees vary according to course load. *Financial support:* In 2008–09, 52 students received support, including 1 fellowship (averaging $14,000 per year), 4 research assistantships with partial tuition reimbursements available (averaging $10,666 per year), 47 teaching assistantships with partial tuition reimbursements available (averaging $12,275 per year); institutionally sponsored loans, scholarships/grants, health care benefits, and unspecified assistantships also available. Financial award application deadline: 3/1. *Faculty research:* Childhood anxiety disorders, text comprehension, infant face recognition, auditory perception in schizophrenia, treatment of substance abuse. *Unit head:* Dr. Mark Ashcraft, Chair/Professor, 702-895-3305, Fax: 702-895-0195, E-mail: mark.ashcraft@unlv.edu. *Application contact:* Graduate College Admissions Evaluator, 702-895-3320, Fax: 702-895-4180, E-mail: gradcollege@unlv.edu.

University of Nevada, Reno, Graduate School, College of Liberal Arts, Department of Psychology, Reno, NV 89557. Offers behavior analysis (MA, PhD); clinical psychology (MA, PhD); cognitive brain science (MA, PhD). *Accreditation:* APA (one or more programs are accredited). *Faculty:* 24 full-time (11 women). *Students:* 76 full-time (50 women), 40 part-time (26 women); includes 7 minority (1 African American, 4 Asian Americans or Pacific Islanders, 2 Hispanic Americans), 11 international. Average age 30. 202 applicants, 18% accepted, 23 enrolled. In 2008, 40 master's, 20 doctorates awarded. Terminal master's awarded for partial completion of doctoral program. *Degree requirements:* For master's, thesis optional; for doctorate, thesis/dissertation. *Entrance requirements:* For master's, GRE General Test, GRE Subject Test, minimum GPA of 2.75; for doctorate, GRE General Test, GRE Subject Test, minimum GPA of 3.0. Additional exam requirements/recommendations for international students: Required—TOEFL (minimum score 500 paper-based; 173 computer-based; 61 iBT), IELTS (minimum score 6), TOFEL or IELTS. *Application deadline:* For fall admission, 1/1 priority date for domestic and international students. Applications are processed on a rolling basis. Application fee: $60 ($95 for international students). Electronic applications accepted. *Expenses:* Tuition, state resident: full-time $1710; part-time $1140 per semester. Tuition, nonresident: full-time $7115. Required fees: $158 per semester. *Financial support:* In 2008–09, 40 research assistantships with partial tuition reimbursements (averaging $14,000 per year), 27 teaching assistantships with partial tuition reimbursements (averaging $14,000 per year) were awarded; Federal Work-Study, institutionally sponsored loans, scholarships/grants, health care benefits, and unspecified assistantships also available. Financial award application deadline: 3/1; financial award applicants required to submit FAFSA. *Faculty research:* Cognitive psychology, social psychological theory, animal and human intelligence, psychotherapy outcome, perception. Total annual research expenditures: $1.5 million. *Unit head:* Dr. Victoria Follette, Chair, 775-784-6828, E-mail: vmf@unr.edu. *Application contact:* Michele Sandberg, Application Contact, 775-784-7026, Fax: 775-784-6064, E-mail: gradschool@unr.edu.

University of New Brunswick Fredericton, School of Graduate Studies, Faculty of Arts, Department of Psychology, Fredericton, NB E3B 5A3, Canada. Offers MA, PhD. *Accreditation:* APA. Part-time programs available. *Faculty:* 14 full-time (9 women). *Students:* 41 full-time (35 women), 1 (woman) part-time. In 2008, 7 doctorates awarded. *Degree requirements:* For doctorate, variable foreign language requirement, comprehensive exam, thesis/dissertation. *Entrance requirements:* For master's and doctorate, GRE, minimum GPA of 3.7. Additional exam requirements/recommendations for international students: Required—TOEFL, TWE. *Application deadline:* For fall admission, 1/15 priority date for domestic and international students. Applications are processed on a rolling basis. Application fee: $50 Canadian dollars. Tuition and fees charges are reported in Canadian dollars. *Expenses:* Tuition, area resident: Full-time $5562 Canadian dollars. Tuition, nonresident: full-time $9450 Canadian dollars. Required fees: $333 Canadian dollars. *Financial support:* In 2008–09, 11 research assistantships were awarded; fellowships, teaching assistantships also available. Financial award application deadline: 1/15. *Faculty research:* Depression, adolescence, human sexuality, family violence, autism. *Unit head:* Dr. Heather Sears, Director of Graduate Studies, 506-458-7122, Fax: 506-447-3063, E-mail: hsears@unb.ca. *Application contact:* Theresa Mills, Graduate Secretary, 506-453-4707, Fax: 506-447-3063, E-mail: tmills@unb.ca.

University of New Brunswick Saint John, Department of Psychology, Fredericton, NB, NB E2L 4L5, Canada. Offers applied and experimental psychology (PhD); clinical psychology (PhD); experimental psychology (MA). *Faculty:* 9 full-time (4 women). *Students:* 4 full-time (all women). In 2008, 1 master's awarded. *Degree requirements:* For master's, thesis; for doctorate, comprehensive exam, thesis/dissertation. *Entrance requirements:* For master's, GRE General Test. Additional exam requirements/recommendations for international students: Required—TOEFL (minimum score 550 paper-based). *Application deadline:* For fall admission, 2/1 for domestic students. Application fee: $50. Electronic applications accepted. *Expenses:* Tuition, area resident: Full-time $5562. International tuition: $9450 full-time. Required fees: $333. *Financial support:* In 2008–09, 1 fellowship, 7 research assistantships, 2 teaching assistantships were awarded; unspecified assistantships also available. Support available to part-time students. Financial award application deadline: 2/1. *Faculty research:* Psychopharmacology and addictions, forensic psychology and criminal justice, interpersonal relations, perception and graphical perception, lie detection. *Unit head:* Dr. Lily Both, Director of Graduate Studies, 506-648-5769, Fax: 506-648-5780, E-mail: lboth@unbsj.ca. *Application contact:* Frances Stevens, Secretary, 506-648-5640, Fax: 506-648-5780, E-mail: fstevens@unb.ca.

University of New Hampshire, Graduate School, College of Liberal Arts, Department of Psychology, Durham, NH 03824. Offers PhD. *Faculty:* 23 full-time (7 women). *Students:* 28 full-time (17 women), 3 part-time (2 women), 2 international. Average age 27. 87 applicants, 9% accepted, 6 enrolled. In 2008, 3 doctorates awarded. *Degree requirements:* For doctorate, thesis/dissertation. *Entrance requirements:* For doctorate, GRE General Test, GRE Subject Test. Additional exam requirements/recommendations for international students: Required—TOEFL (minimum score 550 paper-based; 213 computer-based; 80 iBT). *Application deadline:* For fall admission, 2/15 priority date for domestic students, 2/15 for international students. Applications are processed on a rolling basis. Application fee: $60. Electronic applications accepted. *Expenses:* Tuition, area resident: Full-time $9720; part-time $540 per credit hour. Tuition, nonresident: full-time $23,200; part-time $954 per credit hour. Required fees: $1446; $361.50 per term. *Financial support:* In 2008–09, 30 students received support, including 3 fellowships, 27 teaching assistantships; research assistantships, career-related internships or fieldwork, Federal Work-Study, scholarships/grants, and tuition waivers (full and partial) also available. Support available to part-time students. Financial award application deadline: 2/15. *Faculty research:* History of psychology; cognition and perception; learning, developmental, physiological, and social psychology. *Unit head:* Dr. Robert Mair, Chairperson, 603-862-3198. *Application contact:* Janice Chadwich, Administrative Assistant, 603-862-3167, E-mail: psychology.ph.d@unh.edu.

University of New Mexico, Graduate School, College of Arts and Sciences, Department of Psychology, Albuquerque, NM 87131-2039. Offers clinical psychology (MS, PhD); psychology (PhD). *Accreditation:* APA (one or more programs are accredited). *Degree requirements:* For master's, thesis; for doctorate, comprehensive exam, thesis/dissertation, pre-doctoral internship. *Entrance requirements:* For doctorate, GRE General Test, GRE Subject Test (psychology), minimum GPA of 3.0. Additional exam requirements/recommendations for international students: Required—TOEFL. Electronic applications accepted. *Faculty research:* Addictions, learning cognition and memory, neuropsychology, quantitative behavioral neuroscience, evolutionary development psychology, physiological psychology, cognitive neuroscience.

University of New Orleans, Graduate School, College of Sciences, Department of Psychology, New Orleans, LA 70148. Offers MS, PhD. *Degree requirements:* For doctorate, thesis/dissertation. *Entrance requirements:* For doctorate, GRE General Test, minimum GPA of 3.0, 21 hours of course work in psychology. Additional exam requirements/recommendations for international students: Required—TOEFL (minimum score 550 paper-based; 213 computer-based; 79 iBT). Electronic applications accepted. *Faculty research:* Biofeedback, visual and auditory perception, psychopharmacology, neuropeptides.

The University of North Carolina at Chapel Hill, Graduate School, College of Arts and Sciences, Department of Psychology, Chapel Hill, NC 27599. Offers biological psychology (PhD); clinical psychology (PhD); cognitive psychology (PhD); developmental psychology (PhD); quantitative psychology (PhD); social psychology (PhD). *Accreditation:* APA. *Degree requirements:* For doctorate, comprehensive exam, thesis/dissertation. *Entrance requirements:* For doctorate, GRE General Test, minimum GPA of 3.0. Electronic applications accepted. *Faculty research:* Expressed emotion, cognitive development, social cognitive neuroscience, human memory personality.

The University of North Carolina at Charlotte, Graduate School, College of Arts and Sciences, Department of Psychology, Charlotte, NC 28223-0001. Offers community/clinical psychology (MA); health psychology (PhD); industrial/organizational psychology (MA); organizational science (PhD). Part-time programs available. *Faculty:* 35 full-time (14 women), 3 part-time/adjunct (1 woman). *Students:* 61 full-time (47 women), 18 part-time (17 women); includes 16 minority (7 African Americans, 9 Hispanic Americans), 2 international. Average age 27. 306 applicants, 10% accepted, 25 enrolled. In 2008, 21 master's awarded. *Degree requirements:* For master's, thesis. *Entrance requirements:* For master's, GRE General Test, GRE Subject Test, minimum GPA of 3.0 in undergraduate major, 2.8 overall. Additional exam requirements/recommendations for international students: Required—TOEFL (minimum score 557 paper-based; 220 computer-based). *Application deadline:* Applications are processed on a rolling basis. Application fee: $55. Electronic applications accepted. *Expenses:* Tuition, area resident: Full-time $2919; part-time $122 per credit hour. Tuition, state resident: full-time $2919; part-time $122 per credit hour. Tuition, nonresident: full-time $13,126; part-time $547 per credit hour. Required fees: $1779; $91 per credit hour. Tuition and fees vary according to program. *Financial support:* In 2008–09, 3 fellowships (averaging $17,667 per year), 40 research assistantships (averaging $10,209 per year), 20 teaching assistantships (averaging $10,181 per year) were awarded; career-related internships or fieldwork, Federal Work-Study, institutionally sponsored loans, scholarships/grants, unspecified assistantships, and 6 administrative assistantships ($6,173 average) also available. Support available to part-time students. Financial award application deadline: 4/1; financial award applicants required to submit FAFSA. *Faculty research:* Health psychology, industrial-organizational psychology, cognitive science. *Unit head:* Dr. Brian L. Cutler, Chair, 704-687-4731, Fax: 704-687-3096, E-mail: blcutler@email.uncc.edu. *Application contact:* Kathy B. Giddings, Director of Graduate Admissions, 704-687-3366, Fax: 704-687-3279, E-mail: agidding@uncc.edu.

The University of North Carolina at Greensboro, Graduate School, College of Arts and Sciences, Department of Psychology, Greensboro, NC 27412-5001. Offers clinical psychology (MA, PhD); cognitive psychology (MA, PhD); developmental psychology (MA, PhD); social psychology (MA, PhD). *Accreditation:* APA (one or more programs are accredited). Terminal master's awarded for partial completion of doctoral program. *Degree requirements:* For master's, comprehensive exam, thesis; for doctorate, one foreign language, thesis/dissertation, preliminary exam. *Entrance requirements:* For master's and doctorate, GRE General Test. Additional exam requirements/recommendations for international students: Required—TOEFL. Electronic applications accepted. *Faculty research:* Sensory and perceptual determinants; evoked potential: disorders, deafness, and development.

The University of North Carolina Wilmington, College of Arts and Sciences, Department of Psychology, Wilmington, NC 28403-3297. Offers MA. Part-time programs available. *Students:* 26 full-time (17 women), 43 part-time (26 women); includes 6 minority (1 African American, 3 Asian Americans or Pacific Islanders, 2 Hispanic Americans), 4 international. Average age 27. 121 applicants, 21% accepted, 23 enrolled. In 2008, 17 master's awarded. *Degree requirements:* For master's, comprehensive exam, thesis. *Entrance requirements:* For master's, GRE General Test, GRE Subject Test, minimum B average in undergraduate major. Additional exam requirements/recommendations for international students: Required—TOEFL (minimum score 550 paper-based; 217 computer-based; 79 iBT), IELTS (minimum score 6.5). *Application deadline:* For fall admission, 1/15 for domestic students. Applications are processed on a rolling basis. Application fee: $60. *Expenses:* Tuition, area resident: Full-time $4838. Tuition, state resident: full-time $4838. Tuition, nonresident: full-time $14,898. Required fees: $969.38 per semester. Tuition and fees vary according to course load, campus/location and program. *Financial support:* In 2008–09, 16 teaching assistantships with partial tuition reimbursements (averaging $10,000 per year) were awarded; career-related internships or fieldwork and Federal Work-Study also available. Financial award application deadline: 3/15. *Unit head:* Dr. Mark Galizio, Chairman, 910-962-3813, Fax: 910-962-7010, E-mail: galizio@uncw.edu. *Application contact:* Dr. Richard Ogle, Graduate Coordinator, E-mail: ogler@uncw.edu.

University of North Dakota, Graduate School, College of Arts and Sciences, Department of Psychology, Grand Forks, ND 58202. Offers clinical psychology (PhD); counseling psychology (PhD); experimental psychology (PhD); forensic psychology (MA, MS); psychology (MA). *Accreditation:* APA (one or more programs are accredited). *Degree requirements:* For master's, thesis, final exam; for doctorate, comprehensive exam, thesis/dissertation, internship, final exam. *Entrance requirements:* For master's, GRE General Test, GRE Subject Test, minimum GPA of 3.0; for doctorate, GRE General Test, GRE Subject Test, minimum GPA of 3.5. Additional exam requirements/recommendations for international students: Required—TOEFL (minimum score 550 paper-based; 213 computer-based; 79 iBT), IELTS (minimum score 6.5). Electronic applications accepted. *Faculty research:* Developmental psychology, clinical social psychology, educational psychology, personality disorders.

University of Northern British Columbia, Office of Graduate Studies, Prince George, BC V2N 4Z9, Canada. Offers business administration (Diploma); community health science (M Sc); disability management (MA); education (M Ed); first nations studies (MA); gender studies (MA); history (MA); interdisciplinary studies (MA); international studies (MA); mathematical, computer and physical sciences (M Sc); natural resources and environmental studies (M Sc, MA, MNRES, PhD); political science (MA); psychology (M Sc, PhD); social work (MSW). Part-time and evening/weekend programs available. Postbaccalaureate distance learning degree programs offered (no on-campus study). *Degree requirements:* For master's, thesis; for doctorate, thesis/dissertation. *Entrance requirements:* For master's, GRE, minimum B average in undergraduate course work; for doctorate, candidacy exam, minimum A average in graduate course work.

University of Northern Colorado, Graduate School, College of Education and Behavioral Sciences, School of Psychological Sciences, Greeley, CO 80639. Offers MA, PhD. Part-time programs available. *Faculty:* 15 full-time (6 women). *Students:* 21 full-time (12 women), 14 part-time (11 women); includes 4 minority (2 Asian Americans or Pacific Islanders, 2 Hispanic Americans), 6 international. Average age 34. 12 applicants, 100% accepted, 6 enrolled. In 2008, 3 master's, 3 doctorates awarded. *Degree requirements:* For master's, comprehensive exam, thesis or alternative; for doctorate, comprehensive exam, thesis/dissertation. *Entrance requirements:* For master's and doctorate, GRE General Test, letters of recommendation. *Application deadline:* Applications are processed on a rolling basis. Application fee: $50 ($60 for international students). Electronic applications accepted. *Expenses:* Tuition, state resident: full-time $4370; part-time $242.75 per credit hour. Tuition, nonresident: full-time $12,366; part-time $687 per credit hour. Required fees: $664.20; $36.90 per credit hour. *Financial support:* In 2008–09, 5 research assistantships (averaging $3,418 per year), 8 teaching assistantships (averaging $4,898 per year) were awarded; fellowships, unspecified assistantships also available. Financial award application deadline: 3/1; financial award applicants required to submit FAFSA. *Unit head:* Dr. Mark Alcorn, Director, 970-351-2957, Fax: 970-351-1103. *Application contact:* Linda Sisson, Graduate Student Admission Coordinator, 970-351-1807, Fax: 970-351-2371, E-mail: linda.sisson@unco.edu.

University of Northern Iowa, Graduate College, College of Social and Behavioral Sciences, Department of Psychology, Cedar Falls, IA 50614. Offers MA. Part-time programs available. *Students:* 36 full-time (26 women), 4 part-time (2 women); includes 5 minority (2 African Americans, 3 Asian Americans or Pacific Islanders), 2 international. 94 applicants, 34% accepted, 17 enrolled. In 2008, 14 master's awarded. *Degree requirements:* For master's, comprehensive exam, thesis. *Entrance requirements:* For master's, GRE, minimum GPA of 3.0, 3 letters of recommendation. Additional exam requirements/recommendations for international students: Required—TOEFL (minimum score 500 paper-based; 180 computer-based; 61 iBT). *Application deadline:* For fall admission, 4/30 for domestic students. Applications are processed on a rolling basis. Application fee: $30 ($50 for international students). Electronic applications accepted. *Expenses:* Tuition, state resident: full-time $6446. Tuition, nonresident: full-time $14,874. Required fees: $852. *Financial support:* Career-related internships or fieldwork, Federal Work-Study, and tuition waivers (full and partial) available. Support available to part-time students. Financial award application deadline: 2/1. *Unit head:* Dr. Carolyn Hildebramdt, Acting Head, 319-273-2303, Fax: 319-273-6188. *Application contact:* Laurie S. Russell, Record Analyst, 319-273-2623, Fax: 319-273-6792, E-mail: laurie.russell@uni.edu.

University of North Florida, College of Arts and Sciences, Department of Psychology, Jacksonville, FL 32224-2645. Offers counseling psychology (MAC); general psychology (MA). Part-time and evening/weekend programs available. *Faculty:* 18 full-time (7 women). *Students:* 50 full-time (37 women), 8 part-time (7 women); includes 11 minority (6 African Americans, 5 Hispanic Americans). Average age 26. 128 applicants, 41% accepted, 36 enrolled. In 2008, 20 master's awarded. *Degree requirements:* For master's, comprehensive exam, thesis optional, practicum. *Entrance requirements:* For master's, GRE General Test, 2 letters of recommendation, minimum GPA of 3.0 in last 60 hours of course work. Additional exam requirements/recommendations for international students: Required—TOEFL (minimum score 500 paper-based; 173 computer-based). *Application deadline:* For fall admission, 3/1 priority date for domestic students, 3/1 for international students. Applications are processed on a rolling basis. Application fee: $30. Electronic applications accepted. *Expenses:* Tuition, area resident: Full-time $5782.08; part-time $240.92 per credit hour. Tuition, state resident: full-time $5782.08; part-time $240.92 per credit hour. Tuition, nonresident: full-time $19,974; part-time $832.26 per credit hour. Required fees: $952.80; $39.70 per credit hour. *Financial support:* In 2008–09, 27 students received support, including 4 teaching assistantships (averaging $2,250 per year); Federal Work-Study and tuition waivers (partial) also available. Support available to part-time students. Financial award application deadline: 4/1; financial award applicants required to submit FAFSA. *Faculty research:* Sensory perception, social cognition, sexual behavior, evolutionary psychology, psychology and law. Total annual research expenditures: $80,377. *Unit head:* Dr. Michael Toglia, PhD, Chair, 904-620-1624, E-mail: m.toglia@unf.edu. *Application contact:* Dr. Randy Russac, Graduate Coordinator for General Psychology, 904-620-2807, Fax: 904-620-3814, E-mail: rrussac@unf.edu.

University of North Texas, Robert B. Toulouse School of Graduate Studies, College of Arts and Sciences, Department of Psychology, Denton, TX 76203. Offers clinical psychology (PhD); counseling psychology (MA, MS, PhD); experimental psychology (MA, MS, PhD); health psychology and behavioral medicine (PhD). *Accreditation:* APA (one or more programs are accredited). Terminal master's awarded for partial completion of doctoral program. *Degree requirements:* For master's, comprehensive exam, thesis or alternative; for doctorate, one foreign language, comprehensive exam, thesis/dissertation. *Entrance requirements:* For master's and doctorate, GRE General Test, interview. Additional exam requirements/recommendations for international students: Required—proof of English language proficiency required for non-native English speakers; Recommended—TOEFL (minimum score 550 paper-based; 213 computer-based). *Faculty research:* Very broad range of topics and approaches.

University of North Texas, Robert B. Toulouse School of Graduate Studies, College of Public Affairs and Community Service, Department of Behavior Analysis, Denton, TX 76203. Offers MS. *Accreditation:* APA. *Degree requirements:* For master's, thesis. *Entrance requirements:* For master's, GRE General Test. Additional exam requirements/recommendations for international students: Required—proof of English language proficiency required for non-native English speakers; Recommended—TOEFL (minimum score 550 paper-based; 213 computer-based). *Faculty research:* Human operant research, applied behavior analysis, animal training autism.

University of Notre Dame, Graduate School, College of Arts and Letters, Division of Social Science, Department of Psychology, Notre Dame, IN 46556. Offers cognitive psychology (PhD); counseling psychology (PhD); developmental psychology (PhD); quantitative psychology (PhD). *Accreditation:* APA. *Faculty:* 28 full-time (11 women), 5 part-time/adjunct (4 women). *Students:* 70 full-time (49 women); includes 11 minority (3 African Americans, 3 Asian Americans or Pacific Islanders, 5 Hispanic Americans), 13 international. 146 applicants, 18% accepted, 18 enrolled. In 2008, 8 doctorates awarded. *Degree requirements:* For doctorate, comprehensive exam, thesis/dissertation, candidacy exam. *Entrance requirements:* For doctorate, GRE General Test, GRE Subject Test (strongly recommended). Additional exam requirements/recommendations for international students: Required—TOEFL (minimum score 600 paper-based; 250 computer-based; 80 iBT). *Application deadline:* For fall admission, 1/2 for domestic and international students. Application fee: $50. Electronic applications accepted. *Financial support:* Fellowships with full tuition reimbursements, research assistantships with full tuition reimbursements, teaching assistantships with full tuition reimbursements, career-related internships or fieldwork and tuition waivers (full) available. Financial award application deadline: 1/2. *Faculty research:* Cognitive and socio-emotional development, statistical methods and quantitative models applicable to psychology, interpersonal relations, life span development and developmental delay, childhood depression, structural equation and dynamical systems. *Unit head:* Dr. Dan Lapsley, Director of Graduate Studies, 574-631-8789. *Application contact:* Dr. Barbara Turpin, Director of Graduate Admissions, 574-631-7706, Fax: 574-631-4183.

University of Oklahoma, Graduate College, College of Arts and Sciences, Department of Psychology, Norman, OK 73019. Offers organizational dynamics (MS); psychology (MS, PhD). Part-time programs available. *Faculty:* 22 full-time (10 women), 1 part-time/adjunct (0 women). *Students:* 63 full-time (31 women), 31 part-time (19 women); includes 15 minority (4 African Americans, 4 American Indian/Alaska Native, 1 Asian American or Pacific Islander, 6 Hispanic Americans), 3 international. 92 applicants, 23% accepted, 20 enrolled. In 2008, 23 master's, 7 doctorates awarded. Terminal master's awarded for partial completion of doctoral program. *Degree requirements:* For master's, thesis or alternative; for doctorate, thesis/dissertation, general exam. *Entrance requirements:* For master's, GRE General Test, GRE Subject Test, minimum GPA of 3.0, 3 letters of recommendation; for doctorate, GRE General Test, GRE Subject Test, 3 letters of recommendation. Additional exam requirements/recommendations for international students: Required—TOEFL (minimum score 550 paper-based; 213 computer-based). *Application deadline:* For fall admission, 4/1 priority date for domestic students, 4/1 for international students; for spring admission, 11/1 for domestic students, 9/1 for international students. Applications are processed on a rolling basis. Application fee: $40 ($90 for international students). Electronic applications accepted. *Expenses:* Tuition, state resident: full-time $3744; part-time $156 per credit hour. Tuition, nonresident: full-time $13,577; part-time $565.70 per credit hour. Required fees: $2415.40; $90.10 per credit hour. *Financial support:* In 2008–09, 48 students received support, including 16 fellowships with full tuition reimbursements available (averaging $5,563 per year), 8 research assistantships with partial tuition reimbursements available (averaging $12,381 per year), 37 teaching assistantships with partial tuition reimbursements available (averaging $13,916 per year); career-related internships or fieldwork, scholarships/grants, health care benefits, and unspecified assistantships also available. Financial award application deadline: 3/1; financial award applicants required to submit FAFSA. *Faculty research:* Leadership process, cognition, social, personality, attention human judgement and decision-making; human performance; creativity of leadership; comparative psychology; methodology and statistics. Total annual research expenditures: $1.6 million. *Unit head:* Dr. Jorge Mendoza, Chair, 405-325-4511, Fax: 405-325-4737, E-mail: jmendoza@ou.edu. *Application contact:* Kathryn Paine, Administrative Assistant, 405-325-4512, Fax: 405-325-4737, E-mail: psychology@ou.edu.

University of Oregon, Graduate School, College of Arts and Sciences, Department of Psychology, Eugene, OR 97403. Offers clinical psychology (PhD); cognitive psychology (MA, MS, PhD); developmental psychology (MA, MS, PhD); physiological psychology (MA, MS, PhD); psychology (MA, MS, PhD); social/personality psychology (MA, MS, PhD). *Accreditation:* APA (one or more programs are accredited). Terminal master's awarded for partial completion of doctoral program. *Degree requirements:* For doctorate, thesis/dissertation. *Entrance requirements:* For master's, GRE General Test, minimum GPA of 3.0; for doctorate, GRE General Test. Additional exam requirements/recommendations for international students: Required—TOEFL.

University of Ottawa, Faculty of Graduate and Postdoctoral Studies, Faculty of Social Sciences, School of Psychology, Ottawa, ON K1N 6N5, Canada. Offers PhD. *Accreditation:* APA. *Degree requirements:* For doctorate, thesis/dissertation. *Entrance requirements:* For doctorate, minimum B+ average. Electronic applications accepted. *Faculty research:* Behavioral neuroscience, social psychology, developmental psychology, cognition.

University of Pennsylvania, School of Arts and Sciences, Graduate Group in Psychology, Philadelphia, PA 19104. Offers PhD. *Accreditation:* APA. *Degree requirements:* For doctorate, thesis/dissertation. *Entrance requirements:* For doctorate, GRE General Test, GRE Subject Test. Additional exam requirements/recommendations for international students: Required—TOEFL. Electronic applications accepted. *Faculty research:* Cognitive psychology, sensation and perception, biological psychology, clinical psychology, social psychology.

University of Phoenix, The Artemis School, College of Health and Human Services, Phoenix, AZ 85034-7209. Offers administration of justice and security (MS); community counseling (MSC); education (MHA); family nurse practitioner (MSN); gerontology (MHA); health administration (MHA); health care education (MSN); health care management (MBA, MSN); informatics (MHA); marriage, family, and child therapy (MSC); nursing (MSN); nursing for nurse practitioners (MSN); psychology (MS); MSN/MBA; MSN/MHA. *Accreditation:* AACN. Evening/weekend programs available. Postbaccalaureate distance learning degree programs offered. *Degree requirements:* For master's, thesis (for some programs). *Entrance requirements:* For master's, 3 years of work experience, minimum undergraduate GPA of 2.5, RN license. Additional exam requirements/recommendations for international students: Required—TOEFL (minimum score 550 paper-based; 213 computer-based; 79 iBT). Electronic applications accepted.

University of Phoenix–Austin Campus, College of Social and Behavioral Science, Austin, TX 78759. Offers administration of justice and security (MS); psychology (MS). Postbaccalaureate distance learning degree programs offered.

University of Phoenix–Birmingham Campus, College of Social and Behavioral Science, Birmingham, AL 35244. Offers administration of justice and security (MS); psychology (MS).

University of Phoenix–Chattanooga Campus, College of Social and Behavioral Science, Chattanooga, TN 37421-3707. Offers administration of justice and security (MS); psychology (MSP). Postbaccalaureate distance learning degree programs offered.

University of Phoenix–Cheyenne Campus, College of Social and Behavioral Science, Cheyenne, WY 82009. Offers administration of justice and security (MS); psychology (MS). Postbaccalaureate distance learning degree programs offered.

University of Phoenix–Cincinnati Campus, The Artemis School, College of Health and Human Services, West Chester, OH 45069-4875. Offers administration of justice and security (MS); health care management (MBA); nursing (MSN); psychology (MS). Evening/weekend programs available. Postbaccalaureate distance learning degree programs offered. *Degree requirements:* For master's, thesis (for some programs). *Entrance requirements:* For master's, minimum undergraduate GPA of 2.5, 3 years of work experience. Additional exam requirements/recommendations for international students: Required—TOEFL (minimum score 550 paper-based; 79 iBT). Electronic applications accepted.

University of Phoenix–Cleveland Campus, The Artemis School, College of Health and Human Services, Independence, OH 44131-2194. Offers administration of justice and security (MS); health care management (MBA); nursing (MSN); psychology (MS). Evening/weekend

Psychology—General

University of Phoenix–Cleveland Campus (continued)
programs available. Postbaccalaureate distance learning degree programs offered. *Degree requirements:* For master's, thesis (for some programs). *Entrance requirements:* For master's, minimum undergraduate GPA of 2.5, 3 years of work experience. Additional exam requirements/ recommendations for international students: Required—TOEFL (minimum score 550 paper-based; 213 computer-based; 79 iBT). Electronic applications accepted.

University of Phoenix–Columbus Ohio Campus, The Artemis School, College of Health and Human Services, Columbus, OH 43240-4032. Offers administration of justice and security (MS); health care management (MBA); nursing (MSN); psychology (MS). Evening/weekend programs available. Postbaccalaureate distance learning degree programs offered. *Degree requirements:* For master's, thesis (for some programs). *Entrance requirements:* For master's, minimum undergraduate GPA of 2.5, 3 years work experience. Additional exam requirements/ recommendations for international students: Required—TOEFL (minimum score 550 paper-based; 213 computer-based; 79 iBT). Electronic applications accepted.

University of Phoenix–Dallas Campus, The Artemis School, College of Health and Human Services, Dallas, TX 75251-2009. Offers administration of justice and security (MS); health administration (MHA); health care management (MBA); psychology (MS). Postbaccalaureate distance learning degree programs offered. *Degree requirements:* For master's, thesis (for some programs). *Entrance requirements:* For master's, minimum undergraduate GPA of 2.5, 3 years of work experience. Additional exam requirements/recommendations for international students: Required—TOEFL (minimum score 550 paper-based; 213 computer-based; 79 iBT). Electronic applications accepted.

University of Phoenix–Denver Campus, The Artemis School, College of Health and Human Services, Lone Tree, CO 80124-5453. Offers administration of justice and security (MS); community counseling (MSC); health administration (MHA); health care management (MBA); marriage, family and child therapy (MSC); nursing (MSN); psychology (MS); MSN/MBA; MSN/MHA. Evening/weekend programs available. Postbaccalaureate distance learning degree programs offered. *Degree requirements:* For master's, thesis (for some programs). *Entrance requirements:* For master's, minimum undergraduate GPA of 2.5, 3 years work experience, RN license. Additional exam requirements/recommendations for international students: Required—TOEFL (minimum score 550 paper-based; 213 computer-based; 79 iBT). Electronic applications accepted.

University of Phoenix–Harrisburg Campus, College of Social and Behavioral Science, Harrisburg, PA 17112. Offers administration of justice and security (MS); psychology (MS). Postbaccalaureate distance learning degree programs offered.

University of Phoenix–Hawaii Campus, The Artemis School, College of Health and Human Services, Honolulu, HI 96813-4317. Offers administration of justice and security (MS); community counseling (MSC); education (MHA); family nurse practitioner (MSN); gerontology (MHA); health administration (MHA); health care management (MBA); marriage, family and child therapy (MSC); nursing (MSN); nursing/health care education (MSN); psychology (MS); MSN/MBA. Evening/weekend programs available. *Degree requirements:* For master's, thesis (for some programs). *Entrance requirements:* For master's, minimum undergraduate GPA of 2.5, 3 years of work experience, RN license. Additional exam requirements/recommendations for international students: Required—TOEFL (minimum score 550 paper-based; 213 computer-based; 79 iBT). Electronic applications accepted.

University of Phoenix–Houston Campus, The Artemis School, College of Health and Human Services, Houston, TX 77079-2004. Offers administration of justice and security (MS); health administration (MHA); health care management (MBA); psychology (MS). Postbaccalaureate distance learning degree programs offered. *Degree requirements:* For master's, thesis (for some programs). *Entrance requirements:* For master's, minimum undergraduate GPA of 2.5, 3 years of work experience. Additional exam requirements/recommendations for international students: Required—TOEFL (minimum score 550 paper-based; 213 computer-based; 79 iBT). Electronic applications accepted.

University of Phoenix–Idaho Campus, The Artemis School, College of Health and Human Services, Meridian, ID 83642-3014. Offers administration of justice and security (MS); health administration (MHA); health care management (MBA); nursing (MSN); nursing/health care education (MSN); psychology (MS); MSN/MBA. Evening/weekend programs available. Postbaccalaureate distance learning degree programs offered. *Degree requirements:* For master's, thesis (for some programs). *Entrance requirements:* For master's, minimum undergraduate GPA of 2.5, 3 years of work experience. Additional exam requirements/recommendations for international students: Required—TOEFL (minimum score 550 paper-based; 213 computer-based). Electronic applications accepted.

University of Phoenix–Indianapolis Campus, The Artemis School, College of Health and Human Services, Indianapolis, IN 46250-932. Offers administration of justice and security (MS); health administration (MHA); health care management (MBA); nursing (MSN); nursing/ health care education (MSN); psychology (MS); MSN/MBA; MSN/MHA. Evening/weekend programs available. Postbaccalaureate distance learning degree programs offered. *Degree requirements:* For master's, thesis. *Entrance requirements:* For master's, 3 years work experience, minimum undergraduate GPA of 2.5. Additional exam requirements/ recommendations for international students: Required—TOEFL (minimum score 500 paper-based; 213 computer-based). Electronic applications accepted.

University of Phoenix–Jersey City Campus, College of Social and Behavioral Science, Jersey City, NJ 07310. Offers administration of justice and security (MS); psychology (MS). Postbaccalaureate distance learning degree programs offered.

University of Phoenix–Las Vegas Campus, The Artemis School, College of Health and Human Services, Las Vegas, NV 89128. Offers administration of justice and security (MS); health administration (MHA); health care management (MBA); marriage, family, and child therapy (MSC); mental health counseling (MSC); nursing (MSN); nursing/health care education (MSN); psychology (MS); MSN/MBA; MSN/MHA. Postbaccalaureate distance learning degree programs offered. *Entrance requirements:* For master's, minimum undergraduate GPA of 2.5, 3 years of work experience. Additional exam requirements/recommendations for international students: Required—TOEFL (minimum score 550 paper-based; 213 computer-based; 79 iBT). Electronic applications accepted.

University of Phoenix–Louisiana Campus, The Artemis School, College of Health and Human Services, Metairie, LA 70001-2082. Offers administration of justice and security (MS); health administration (MHA); health care management (MBA); nursing (MSN); psychology (MS); MSN/MBA. Evening/weekend programs available. Postbaccalaureate distance learning degree programs offered (no on-campus study). *Degree requirements:* For master's, thesis (for some programs). *Entrance requirements:* For master's, minimum undergraduate GPA of 2.5, 3 years work experience, RN license. Additional exam requirements/recommendations for international students: Required—TOEFL (minimum score 550 paper-based; 213 computer-based; 79 iBT). Electronic applications accepted.

University of Phoenix–Maryland Campus, The Artemis School, College of Health and Human Services, Columbia, MD 21045-5424. Offers administration of justice and security (MS); health administration (MHA); health care education (MSN); health care management (MBA); nursing (MSN); psychology (MS); MSN/MBA; MSN/MHA. Evening/weekend programs available. *Degree requirements:* For master's, thesis (for some programs). *Entrance requirements:* For master's, minimum undergraduate GPA of 2.5, 3 years work experience. Additional exam requirements/recommendations for international students: Required—TOEFL (minimum score 550 paper-based; 213 computer-based; 79 iBT). Electronic applications accepted.

University of Phoenix–New Mexico Campus, The Artemis School, College of Health and Human Services, Albuquerque, NM 87109-4645. Offers administration of justice and security (MS); health administration (MHA); health care education (MSN); health care management (MBA); marriage and family therapy (MSC); nursing (MSN); psychology (MS); MSN/MBA. Evening/weekend programs available. *Degree requirements:* For master's, thesis (for some programs). *Entrance requirements:* For master's, minimum undergraduate GPA of 2.5, 3 years of work experience, RN license. Additional exam requirements/recommendations for international students: Required—TOEFL (minimum score 550 paper-based; 213 computer-based; 79 iBT). Electronic applications accepted.

University of Phoenix–Northern Nevada Campus, College of Social and Behavioral Science, Reno, NV 89511. Offers administration of justice and security (MS); marriage, family and child therapy (MSC); psychology (MS); school counseling (MSC).

University of Phoenix–Oklahoma City Campus, College of Health and Human Services, Oklahoma City, OK 73116-8244. Offers administration of justice and security (MS); health care management (MBA); nursing (MSN); psychology (MS).

University of Phoenix–Oregon Campus, The Artemis School, College of Health and Human Services, Tigard, OR 97223. Offers administration of justice and security (MS); health administration (MHA); health care management (MBA); nursing (MSN); psychology (MS); MSN/MBA. Evening/weekend programs available. *Degree requirements:* For master's, thesis (for some programs). *Entrance requirements:* For master's, minimum undergraduate GPA of 2.5, 3 years of work experience, current RN license (nursing). Additional exam requirements/ recommendations for international students: Required—TOEFL (minimum score 550 paper-based; 213 computer-based; 79 iBT). Electronic applications accepted.

University of Phoenix–Philadelphia Campus, The Artemis School, College of Health and Human Services, Wayne, PA 19087-2121. Offers administration of justice and security (MS); health administration (MHA); health care education (MSN); health care management (MBA); nursing (MSN); psychology (MS); MSN/MBA. Evening/weekend programs available. *Degree requirements:* For master's, thesis (for some programs). *Entrance requirements:* For master's, minimum undergraduate GPA of 2.5, 3 years work experience. Additional exam requirements/ recommendations for international students: Required—TOEFL (minimum score 550 paper-based; 213 computer-based; 79 iBT). Electronic applications accepted.

University of Phoenix–Phoenix Campus, The Artemis School, College of Health and Human Services, Phoenix, AZ 85040-1958. Offers community counseling (MSC); education (MHA); family nurse practitioner (MSN); gerontology (MHA); health administration (MHA); health care education (MSN); health care management (MBA); informatics (MHA); marriage, family, and child therapy (MSC); nurse practitioner (Certificate); nursing (MSN); nursing health care education (Certificate); psychology (MS); MSN/MBA; MSN/MHA. Evening/weekend programs available. *Degree requirements:* For master's, thesis (for some programs). *Entrance requirements:* For master's, 3 years of work experience in field, minimum undergraduate GPA of 2.5, RN license. Additional exam requirements/recommendations for international students: Required—TOEFL (minimum score 550 paper-based; 213 computer-based; 79 iBT). Electronic applications accepted.

University of Phoenix–Pittsburgh Campus, The Artemis School, College of Health and Human Services, Pittsburgh, PA 15276. Offers administration of justice and security (MS); health administration (MHA); health care education (MSN); health care management (MBA); nursing (MSN); psychology (MS); MSN/MBA; MSN/MHA. Evening/weekend programs available. *Degree requirements:* For master's, thesis (for some programs). *Entrance requirements:* For master's, minimum undergraduate GPA of 2.5, 3 years work experience, current RN license (nursing). Additional exam requirements/recommendations for international students: Required—TOEFL (minimum score 550 paper-based; 213 computer-based; 79 iBT). Electronic applications accepted.

University of Phoenix–Richmond Campus, The Artemis School, College of Health and Human Services, Richmond, VA 23230. Offers administration of justice and security (MS); health administration (MHA); health care education (MSN); health care management (MBA); nursing (MSN); psychology (MS); MSN/MBA; MSN/MHA. Evening/weekend programs available. *Degree requirements:* For master's, thesis (for some programs). *Entrance requirements:* For master's, minimum undergraduate GPA of 2.5, 3 years work experience, current RN license for nursing programs. Additional exam requirements/recommendations for international students: Required—TOEFL (minimum score 500 paper-based; 213 computer-based; 79 iBT). Electronic applications accepted.

University of Phoenix–Sacramento Valley Campus, The Artemis School, College of Health and Human Services, Sacramento, CA 95833-3632. Offers administration of justice and security (MS); community counseling (MSC); family nurse practitioner (MSN); health administration (MHA); health care education (MSN); health care management (MBA); marriage, family and child counseling (MSC); nursing (MSN); psychology (MS); MSN/MBA. Evening/ weekend programs available. *Degree requirements:* For master's, thesis (for some programs). *Entrance requirements:* For master's, RN license, minimum undergraduate GPA of 2.5, 3 years work experience. Additional exam requirements/recommendations for international students: Required—TOEFL (minimum score 550 paper-based; 213 computer-based; 79 iBT). Electronic applications accepted.

University of Phoenix–San Antonio Campus, College of Social and Behavioral Science, San Antonio, TX 78230. Offers administration of justice and security (MS); psychology (MS).

University of Phoenix–Southern Arizona Campus, The Artemis School, College of Health and Human Services, Tucson, AZ 85711. Offers administration of justice and security (MS); family nurse practitioner (MSN, Certificate); health administration (MHA); health care management (MBA); marriage, family and child therapy (MSC); nursing (MSN); psychology (MS). Evening/weekend programs available. *Degree requirements:* For master's, thesis (for some programs). *Entrance requirements:* For master's, minimum undergraduate GPA of 2.5, 3 years of work experience, RN license. Additional exam requirements/recommendations for international students: Required—TOEFL (minimum score 550 paper-based; 213 computer-based; 79 iBT). Electronic applications accepted.

University of Phoenix–Southern California Campus, The Artemis School, College of Health and Human Services, Costa Mesa, CA 92626. Offers administration of justice and security (MS); family nurse practitioner (MSN, Certificate); health administration (MHA); health care education (MSN); health care management (MBA); marriage, family and child therapy (MSC); nursing (MSN); psychology (MS); MSN/MBA; MSN/MHA. Evening/weekend programs available. *Degree requirements:* For master's, thesis (for some programs). *Entrance requirements:* For master's, minimum undergraduate GPA of 2.5, 3 years work experience, RN license. Additional exam requirements/recommendations for international students: Required—TOEFL (minimum score 550 paper-based; 213 computer-based; 79 iBT). Electronic applications accepted.

University of Phoenix–Southern Colorado Campus, The Artemis School, College of Health and Human Services, Colorado Springs, CO 80919-2335. Offers administration of justice and security (MS); community counseling (MSC); education (MHA); gerontology (MHA); health administration (MHA); health care management (MBA); marriage, family and child therapy (MSC); nursing (MSN); psychology (MS); MSN/MBA. Evening/weekend programs available. *Degree requirements:* For master's, thesis (for some programs). *Entrance requirements:* For master's, minimum undergraduate GPA of 2.5, 3 years of work experience, RN license. Additional exam requirements/recommendations for international students: Required—TOEFL (minimum score 550 paper-based; 213 computer-based; 79 iBT). Electronic applications accepted.

Psychology—General

University of Phoenix–Tulsa Campus, College of Health and Human Services, Tulsa, OK 74146-3801. Offers administration of justice and security (MS); health care management (MBA); nursing (MSN); psychology (MS).

University of Pittsburgh, School of Arts and Sciences, Department of Psychology, Pittsburgh, PA 15260. Offers MS, PhD. *Accreditation:* APA (one or more programs are accredited). Terminal master's awarded for partial completion of doctoral program. *Degree requirements:* For master's, comprehensive exam, thesis; for doctorate, comprehensive exam, thesis/dissertation. *Entrance requirements:* For doctorate, GRE General Test, minimum GPA of 3.0. Additional exam requirements/recommendations for international students: Required—TOEFL (minimum score 550 paper-based; 213 computer-based), TOEFL (paper-based 550, computer-based 213) or IELTS (score 7). Electronic applications accepted. *Faculty research:* Behavioral medicine and psychoneuroimmunology; learning, reasoning and memory; psychopathology and behavioral problems; social cognition; social influence and group processes; social and cognitive development.

University of Puerto Rico, Río Piedras, College of Social Sciences, Department of Psychology, San Juan, PR 00931-3300. Offers clinical psychology (MA); industrial organizational psychology (MA); investigative academic psychology (MA); psychology (PhD). Part-time programs available. *Degree requirements:* For master's, comprehensive exam, thesis; for doctorate, comprehensive exam, thesis/dissertation, internship. *Entrance requirements:* For master's, GRE or PAEG, interview, minimum GPA of 3.0; for doctorate, GRE or PAEG, interview, master's degree, minimum GPA of 3.0. *Faculty research:* Intervention on Depressed Latino Youth, biosychosocial training.

University of Regina, Faculty of Graduate Studies and Research, Faculty of Arts, Department of Psychology, Regina, SK S4S 0A2, Canada. Offers clinical psychology (MA, PhD); experimental and applied psychology (MA, PhD). *Faculty:* 18 full-time (10 women). *Students:* 54 full-time (44 women), 3 part-time (all women). 57 applicants, 28% accepted. In 2008, 6 master's, 3 doctorates awarded. *Degree requirements:* For master's, thesis; for doctorate, comprehensive exam, thesis/dissertation. *Entrance requirements:* For master's, GRE General Test, GRE Subject Test; for doctorate, GRE General Test, GRE Subject Test (optional for students who hold a master's degree from a Canadian university). Additional exam requirements/recommendations for international students: Required—TOEFL (minimum score 580 paper-based; 237 computer-based; 88 iBT). *Application deadline:* For fall admission, 2/15 for domestic students. Application fee: $85 ($100 for international students). Electronic applications accepted. *Financial support:* In 2008–09, 17 fellowships (averaging $16,764 per year), 4 research assistantships (averaging $13,875 per year), 11 teaching assistantships (averaging $6,675 per year) were awarded; career-related internships or fieldwork and scholarships/grants also available. Financial award application deadline: 6/15. *Faculty research:* Clinical, experimental and applied psychology. *Unit head:* Dr. William E. Smythe, Head, 306-585-4157, Fax: 306-585-5429, E-mail: william.smythe@uregina.ca. *Application contact:* Dr. Dongyan Blachford, Associate Dean, 306-585-5186, Fax: 306-337-2444, E-mail: dongyan.blachford@uregina.ca.

University of Rhode Island, Graduate School, College of Arts and Sciences, Department of Psychology, Program in Behavioral Science, Kingston, RI 02881. Offers PhD. *Expenses:* Tuition, state resident: full-time $8024; part-time $446 per credit. Tuition, nonresident: full-time $21,046; part-time $1169 per credit. Required fees: $1056; $26 per credit. $30 per semester. One-time fee: $95 part-time. *Unit head:* Kathryn Quina, Director, 401-874-2777, E-mail: kquina@uri.edu. *Application contact:* Harold D. Bibb, Associate Dean of the Graduate School, 401-874-2262, Fax: 401-874-5491.

University of Rochester, The College, Arts and Sciences, Department of Clinical and Social Sciences in Psychology, Rochester, NY 14627-0250. Offers clinical psychology (PhD); developmental psychology (PhD); psychology (MA); social-personality psychology (PhD). *Accreditation:* APA (one or more programs are accredited). Terminal master's awarded for partial completion of doctoral program. *Degree requirements:* For doctorate, thesis/dissertation, qualifying exam. *Entrance requirements:* For doctorate, GRE General Test. Additional exam requirements/recommendations for international students: Required—TOEFL.

University of Saint Francis, Graduate School, Department of Psychology and Counseling, Fort Wayne, IN 46808-3994. Offers general psychology (MS); mental health counseling (MS); pastoral counseling (MS); school counseling (MS Ed). Part-time and evening/weekend programs available. *Entrance requirements:* For master's, interview, minimum undergraduate GPA of 3.0.

University of Saint Mary, Graduate Programs, Program in Psychology, Leavenworth, KS 66048-5082. Offers MA. Part-time and evening/weekend programs available. *Degree requirements:* For master's, thesis. *Entrance requirements:* For master's, minimum undergraduate GPA of 2.75.

University of St. Thomas, Graduate Studies, Graduate School of Professional Psychology, St. Paul, MN 55105-1096. Offers counseling psychology (MA, Psy D); family psychology (Certificate). *Accreditation:* APA. Part-time and evening/weekend programs available. *Degree requirements:* For master's, comprehensive exam, practicum; for doctorate, comprehensive exam, thesis/dissertation, qualifying exam, practicum, internship. *Entrance requirements:* For master's, MAT or GRE, minimum GPA of 2.75, letters of recommendation; for doctorate, GRE, minimum GPA of 3.2, letters of recommendation. Additional exam requirements/recommendations for international students: Required—TOEFL. *Expenses:* Contact institution. *Faculty research:* Elderly, eating disorders, anxiety.

University of Saskatchewan, College of Graduate Studies and Research, College of Arts and Sciences, Department of Psychology, Saskatoon, SK S7N 5A2, Canada. Offers MA, PhD. *Accreditation:* APA (one or more programs are accredited). *Degree requirements:* For master's, thesis; for doctorate, thesis/dissertation. *Entrance requirements:* Additional exam requirements/recommendations for international students: Required—TOEFL.

University of South Africa, College of Human Sciences, Pretoria, South Africa. Offers adult education (M Ed); African languages (MA, PhD); African politics (MA, PhD); Afrikaans (MA, PhD); ancient history (MA, PhD); ancient Near Eastern studies (MA, PhD); anthropology (MA, PhD); applied linguistics (MA); Arabic (MA, PhD); archaeology (MA); art history (MA); Biblical archaeology (MA); Biblical studies (M Th, D Th, PhD); Christian spirituality (M Th, D Th); church history (M Th, D Th); classical studies (MA, PhD); clinical psychology (MA); communication (MA, PhD); comparative education (M Ed, Ed D); consulting psychology (D Admin, D Com, PhD); curriculum studies (M Ed, Ed D); development studies (M Admin, MA, D Admin, PhD); didactics (M Ed, Ed D); education (M Tech); education management (M Ed, Ed D); educational psychology (M Ed); English (MA); environmental education (M Ed); French (MA, PhD); German (MA, PhD); Greek (MA); guidance and counseling (M Ed); health studies (MA, PhD), including health sciences education (MA), health services management (MA), medical and surgical nursing science (critical care general) (MA), midwifery and neonatal nursing science (MA), trauma and emergency care (MA); history (MA, PhD); history of education (Ed D); inclusive education (M Ed, Ed D); information and communications technology policy and regulation (MA); information science (MA, MIS, PhD); international politics (MA, PhD); Islamic studies (MA, PhD); Italian (MA, PhD); Judaica (MA, PhD); linguistics (MA, PhD); mathematical education (M Ed); mathematics education (MA); missiology (M Th, D Th); modern Hebrew (MA, PhD); musicology (MA, MMus, D Mus, PhD); natural science education (M Ed); New Testament (M Th, D Th); Old Testament (D Th); pastoral therapy (M Th, D Th); philosophy (MA); philosophy of education (M Ed, Ed D); politics (MA, PhD); Portuguese (MA, PhD); practical theology (M Th, D Th); psychology (MA, MS, PhD); psychology of education (M Ed, Ed D); public health (MA); religious studies (MA, D Th, PhD); Romance languages (MA); Russian (MA, PhD); Semitic languages (MA, PhD); social behavior studies in HIV/AIDS (MA); social science (mental health) (MA); social science in development studies (MA); social science in psychology (MA); social science in social work (MA); social science in sociology (MA); social work (MSW, DSW, PhD); socio-education (M Ed, Ed D); sociolinguistics (MA); sociology (MA, PhD); Spanish (MA, PhD); systematic theology (M Th, D Th); TESOL (teaching English to speakers of other languages) (MA); theological ethics (M Th, D Th); theory of literature (MA, PhD); urban ministries (D Th); urban ministry (M Th).

University of South Alabama, Graduate School, College of Arts and Sciences, Department of Psychology, Mobile, AL 36688-0002. Offers MS. Part-time and evening/weekend programs available. *Faculty:* 12 full-time (4 women), 1 (woman) part-time/adjunct. *Students:* 20 full-time (16 women), 5 part-time (2 women); includes 3 minority (1 African American, 2 Asian Americans or Pacific Islanders). 39 applicants, 31% accepted, 10 enrolled. In 2008, 13 master's awarded. *Degree requirements:* For master's, comprehensive exam, thesis optional. *Entrance requirements:* For master's, GRE General Test, GRE Subject Test (recommended), minimum GPA of 3.0, major in psychology or equivalent. *Application deadline:* For fall admission, 3/1 priority date for domestic students, 3/1 for international students. Applications are processed on a rolling basis. Application fee: $35. *Expenses:* Tuition, area resident: Full-time $4656. Tuition, nonresident: full-time $9312. Required fees: $1102. *Financial support:* Fellowships, research assistantships available. Support available to part-time students. Financial award application deadline: 4/1. *Faculty research:* Language acquisition and development. *Unit head:* Dr. Larry Christensen, Chair, 251-460-6371. *Application contact:* Dr. Elise E Labbe'- ColdSmith, Graduate Coordinator.

University of South Carolina, The Graduate School, College of Arts and Sciences, Department of Psychology, Columbia, SC 29208. Offers clinical/community psychology (MA, PhD), including clinical/community psychology (PhD), general psychology (MA); experimental psychology (MA, PhD); school psychology (PhD). *Accreditation:* APA (one or more programs are accredited). Terminal master's awarded for partial completion of doctoral program. *Degree requirements:* For master's, thesis; for doctorate, comprehensive exam, thesis/dissertation. *Entrance requirements:* For master's and doctorate, GRE General Test. Additional exam requirements/recommendations for international students: Required—TOEFL. Electronic applications accepted. *Faculty research:* Developmental cognitive neuroscience, alcohol and drug addictions, reading and language processing, child and family, prevention.

The University of South Dakota, Graduate School, College of Arts and Sciences, Department of Psychology, Vermillion, SD 57069-2390. Offers clinical psychology (MA, PhD); human factors (MA, PhD). *Accreditation:* APA (one or more programs are accredited). *Degree requirements:* For master's, comprehensive exam, thesis; for doctorate, comprehensive exam, thesis/dissertation. *Entrance requirements:* For master's, GRE, minimum GPA of 2.7; for doctorate, GRE General Test, GRE Subject Test, minimum GPA of 2.7. Additional exam requirements/recommendations for international students: Required—TOEFL (minimum score 550 paper-based; 213 computer-based; 79 iBT). Electronic applications accepted. *Faculty research:* Human-computer interactions, perceptual-cognitive processing, medical psychology, depression, moral psychology.

University of Southern California, Graduate School, College of Letters, Arts and Sciences, Department of Psychology, Los Angeles, CA 90089. *Accreditation:* APA. *Faculty research:* Affective neuroscience, vision, aggression and violence, language and reading development, substance abuse.

University of Southern Mississippi, Graduate School, College of Education and Psychology, Department of Psychology, Hattiesburg, MS 39406-0001. Offers clinical psychology (MA, PhD); counseling psychology (PhD); experimental psychology (MA, PhD); psychology (MS); school psychology (MA, PhD). *Accreditation:* ACA; APA (one or more programs are accredited). *Faculty:* 28 full-time (11 women). *Students:* 104 full-time (83 women), 34 part-time (24 women); includes 13 minority (7 African Americans, 2 Asian Americans or Pacific Islanders, 4 Hispanic Americans), 7 international. Average age 28. 189 applicants, 21% accepted, 31 enrolled. In 2008, 24 master's, 13 doctorates awarded. Terminal master's awarded for partial completion of doctoral program. *Degree requirements:* For master's, comprehensive exam, thesis; for doctorate, comprehensive exam, thesis/dissertation. *Entrance requirements:* For master's, GRE General Test, minimum GPA of 3.0; for doctorate, GRE General Test, interview, minimum GPA of 3.0. Additional exam requirements/recommendations for international students: Required—TOEFL. *Application deadline:* For fall admission, 3/1 priority date for domestic students, 3/1 for international students. Applications are processed on a rolling basis. Application fee: $30. *Financial support:* In 2008–09, 48 research assistantships with full tuition reimbursements (averaging $8,802 per year), 48 teaching assistantships with full tuition reimbursements (averaging $6,500 per year) were awarded; career-related internships or fieldwork, Federal Work-Study, and institutionally sponsored loans also available. Financial award application deadline: 3/15; financial award applicants required to submit FAFSA. *Faculty research:* Dolphin cognition, sleep, neuropsychology, health-related behaviors, psychopathology. Total annual research expenditures: $101,200. *Unit head:* Dr. Joseph Olmi, Chair, 601-266-4177, Fax: 601-266-5580. *Application contact:* Dr. Heather Sterling-Turner, Graduate Coordinator, 601-266-4177, Fax: 601-266-5580.

University of South Florida, Graduate School, College of Arts and Sciences, Department of Psychology, Tampa, FL 33620-9951. Offers clinical psychology (MA, PhD); cognitive and neural sciences (MA, PhD); industrial-organizational psychology (MA, PhD). *Accreditation:* APA (one or more programs are accredited). *Faculty:* 30 full-time (10 women). *Students:* 93 full-time (53 women), 22 part-time (15 women); includes 12 minority (2 African Americans, 4 Asian Americans or Pacific Islanders, 6 Hispanic Americans), 16 international. 421 applicants, 3% accepted, 11 enrolled. In 2008, 21 master's, 12 doctorates awarded. *Degree requirements:* For master's, comprehensive exam, thesis; for doctorate, comprehensive exam, thesis/dissertation. *Entrance requirements:* For master's and doctorate, GRE General Test, minimum GPA of 3.0 in last 60 hours of course work. Additional exam requirements/recommendations for international students: Required—TOEFL (minimum score 550 paper-based; 213 computer-based). *Application deadline:* For fall admission, 11/15 for domestic students, 12/15 for international students. Application fee: $30. Electronic applications accepted. *Expenses:* Contact institution. *Financial support:* Fellowships with full and partial tuition reimbursements, research assistantships with partial tuition reimbursements, teaching assistantships with partial tuition reimbursements, career-related internships or fieldwork, scholarships/grants, tuition waivers (partial), and unspecified assistantships available. Financial award applicants required to submit FAFSA. *Faculty research:* Human memory; job analysis; stress, drug and alcohol abuse; neuroscience. Total annual research expenditures: $2.9 million. *Unit head:* Emanual Donchin, Program Director, 813-974-0466, Fax: 813-974-4617, E-mail: dochin@shell.cas.usf.edu. *Application contact:* William Sacco, Program Director, 813-974-0375, Fax: 813-974-4617, E-mail: sacco@cas.usf.edu.

The University of Tennessee, Graduate School, College of Arts and Sciences, Department of Psychology, Knoxville, TN 37996. Offers clinical psychology (PhD); experimental psychology (MA, PhD); psychology (MA). *Accreditation:* APA (one or more programs are accredited). Terminal master's awarded for partial completion of doctoral program. *Degree requirements:* For master's, thesis; for doctorate, thesis/dissertation. *Entrance requirements:* For master's and doctorate, GRE General Test, GRE Subject Test, minimum GPA of 2.7. Additional exam requirements/recommendations for international students: Required—TOEFL. Electronic applications accepted. *Expenses:* Tuition, area resident: Part-time $348 per credit hour. Tuition, state resident: full-time $6262. Tuition, nonresident: full-time $18,920; part-time $1052 per credit hour. Required fees: $812; $36 per credit hour. Tuition and fees vary according to program.

The University of Tennessee at Chattanooga, Graduate School, College of Arts and Sciences, Department of Psychology, Chattanooga, TN 37403. Offers industrial/organizational psychology (MS); research psychology (MS). Part-time and evening/weekend programs available. *Faculty:* 8 full-time (1 woman), 1 (woman) part-time/adjunct. *Students:* 43 full-time (26 women), 9 part-time (6 women); includes 9 minority (4 African Americans, 3 Asian Americans or Pacific Islanders, 2 Hispanic Americans), 2 international. Average age 28. 70 applicants, 71% accepted, 19 enrolled. In 2008, 17 master's awarded. *Degree requirements:* For master's, comprehensive exam (for some programs), thesis optional, practicum (industrial/organizational psychology). *Entrance requirements:* For master's, GRE General Test, minimum GPA of 2.5 on all undergraduate coursework or 3.0 in senior year. Additional exam requirements/

Psychology—General

The University of Tennessee at Chattanooga (continued)
recommendations for international students: Required—TOEFL (minimum score 550 paper-based; 213 computer-based; 79 iBT); Recommended—IELTS (minimum score 6). *Application deadline:* For fall admission, 8/1 priority date for domestic students, 6/1 for international students; for spring admission, 12/1 priority date for domestic students, 10/1 for international students. Applications are processed on a rolling basis. Application fee: $30 ($35 for international students). *Expenses:* Tuition, area resident: Full-time $6150; part-time $281 per credit hour. Tuition, nonresident: full-time $16,710; part-time $867 per credit hour. Required fees: $1100; $128 per credit hour. $550 per semester. *Financial support:* In 2008–09, 12 fellowships with full and partial tuition reimbursements (averaging $3,438 per year) were awarded; career-related internships or fieldwork, Federal Work-Study, institutionally sponsored loans, scholarships/grants, tuition waivers (partial), and unspecified assistantships also available. Support available to part-time students. Financial award application deadline: 4/1; financial award applicants required to submit FAFSA. *Faculty research:* Decision processes, philosophical psychology, memory, social cognition, employee selection. Total annual research expenditures: $47,807. *Unit head:* Dr. Paul J. Watson, Department Head, 423-425-4262, Fax: 423-425-4284, E-mail: paul-watson@utc.edu. *Application contact:* Dr. Stephanie Bellar, Dean of Graduate Studies, 423-425-4666, Fax: 423-425-5223, E-mail: stephanie-bellar@utc.edu.

The University of Texas at Arlington, Graduate School, College of Science, Department of Psychology, Arlington, TX 76019. Offers experimental psychology (PhD); health psychology (PhD); industrial organizational psychology (MS); psychology (MS). Part-time programs available. *Faculty:* 16 full-time (5 women), 1 part-time/adjunct (0 women). *Students:* 53 full-time (38 women), 12 part-time (9 women); includes 11 minority (6 African Americans, 1 Asian American or Pacific Islander, 4 Hispanic Americans), 9 international. 81 applicants, 35% accepted, 15 enrolled. In 2008, 16 master's, 4 doctorates awarded. Terminal master's awarded for partial completion of doctoral program. *Degree requirements:* For master's, comprehensive exam or thesis; for doctorate, thesis/dissertation (for some programs). *Entrance requirements:* For master's and doctorate, GRE General Test, minimum GPA of 3.0 in last 60 hours of course work. Additional exam requirements/recommendations for international students: Required—TOEFL (minimum score 550 paper-based; 213 computer-based). *Application deadline:* For fall admission, 6/16 for domestic students. Applications are processed on a rolling basis. Application fee: $35 ($50 for international students). *Expenses:* Tuition, area resident: Full-time $6500. Tuition, state resident: full-time $6500. Tuition, nonresident: full-time $11,558. *Financial support:* In 2008–09, 4 fellowships (averaging $1,000 per year), 2 research assistantships with tuition reimbursements (averaging $15,000 per year), 28 teaching assistantships with tuition reimbursements (averaging $15,000 per year) were awarded; career-related internships or fieldwork, Federal Work-Study, institutionally sponsored loans, scholarships/grants, traineeships, tuition waivers (partial), and unspecified assistantships also available. Financial award application deadline: 6/1; financial award applicants required to submit FAFSA. *Unit head:* Dr. Robert Gatchel, Chair, 817-272-2281, Fax: 817-272-2364, E-mail: gatchel@uta.edu. *Application contact:* Dr. Jared Kenworthy, Graduate Advisor, 817-272-2281, Fax: 817-272-2364, E-mail: kenworthy@uta.edu.

The University of Texas at Austin, Graduate School, College of Liberal Arts, Department of Psychology, Austin, TX 78712-1111. Offers PhD. *Accreditation:* APA. *Degree requirements:* For doctorate, thesis/dissertation. *Entrance requirements:* For doctorate, GRE General Test. Electronic applications accepted. *Faculty research:* Behavioral neuroscience, sensory neuroscience, evolutionary psychology, cognitive processes in psychopathology, cognitive processes and their development.

The University of Texas at Brownsville, Graduate Studies, College of Liberal Arts, Department of Behavioral Sciences, Brownsville, TX 78520-4991. Offers MAIS. Part-time and evening/weekend programs available. *Degree requirements:* For master's, thesis or comprehensive exam. *Entrance requirements:* For master's, GRE General Test. Additional exam requirements/recommendations for international students: Required—TOEFL. *Faculty research:* Memory, socio-political structure of South America, cartography of Mexico and Central America, family economic structure of Spain.

The University of Texas at Dallas, School of Behavioral and Brain Sciences, Program in Psychological Sciences, Richardson, TX 75083-0688. Offers early childhood disorders (MS); psychological sciences (MS, PhD). Part-time and evening/weekend programs available. *Faculty:* 31 full-time (16 women), 1 (woman) part-time/adjunct. *Students:* 47 full-time (38 women), 20 part-time (all women); includes 13 minority (3 African Americans, 5 Asian Americans or Pacific Islanders, 5 Hispanic Americans), 8 international. Average age 30. 75 applicants, 60% accepted, 32 enrolled. In 2008, 12 master's, 1 doctorate awarded. *Degree requirements:* For master's, directed project or internship; for doctorate, thesis/dissertation. *Entrance requirements:* For master's and doctorate, GRE General Test, minimum GPA of 3.0 in upper-level course work. Additional exam requirements/recommendations for international students: Required—TOEFL (minimum score 550 paper-based; 213 computer-based). *Application deadline:* For fall admission, 7/15 for domestic students, 5/1 priority date for international students; for spring admission, 11/15 for domestic students, 9/1 priority date for international students. Applications are processed on a rolling basis. Application fee: $50 ($100 for international students). Electronic applications accepted. *Expenses:* Tuition, area resident: Full-time $8320. Tuition, state resident: full-time $8320. Tuition, nonresident: full-time $15,054. Part-time tuition and fees vary according to course load. *Financial support:* In 2008–09, 14 teaching assistantships with tuition reimbursements (averaging $10,930 per year) were awarded; fellowships, research assistantships with tuition reimbursements, career-related internships or fieldwork, Federal Work-Study, scholarships/grants, and unspecified assistantships also available. Support available to part-time students. Financial award application deadline: 4/30; financial award applicants required to submit FAFSA. *Faculty research:* Social competence in normal and hyperactive youth, preschool number development, social-emotional development, family and peer relationships. *Unit head:* Dr. Melanie J. Spence, Head, PhD Programs, 972-883-2206, Fax: 972-883-2491, E-mail: mspence@utdallas.edu. *Application contact:* Dr. Robert D. Stillman, Program Head, 972-883-3106, Fax: 972-883-3022, E-mail: stillman@utdallas.edu.

The University of Texas at El Paso, Graduate School, College of Liberal Arts, Department of Psychology, El Paso, TX 79968-0001. Offers clinical psychology (MA); experimental psychology (MA); psychology (PhD). Part-time and evening/weekend programs available. *Degree requirements:* For master's, thesis; for doctorate, thesis/dissertation. *Entrance requirements:* For master's and doctorate, GRE General Test. Additional exam requirements/recommendations for international students: Required—TOEFL. Electronic applications accepted.

The University of Texas at San Antonio, College of Liberal and Fine Arts, Department of Psychology, San Antonio, TX 78249-0617. Offers MS. Part-time and evening/weekend programs available. *Degree requirements:* For master's, comprehensive exam, thesis. *Entrance requirements:* For master's, GRE General Test, minimum GPA of 3.0 in last 60 hours and in all psychology courses. Additional exam requirements/recommendations for international students: Required—TOEFL (minimum score 500 paper-based; 173 computer-based). Electronic applications accepted.

The University of Texas at Tyler, College of Education and Psychology, Department of Psychology, Tyler, TX 75799-0001. Offers clinical psychology (MS), including neuropsychology, school psychology; counseling psychology (MA), including general, marriage and family; interdisciplinary studies (MSIS); school counseling (MA). Part-time and evening/weekend programs available. *Degree requirements:* For master's, comprehensive exam, thesis optional. *Entrance requirements:* For master's, GRE General Test, minimum GPA of 3.0. Additional exam requirements/recommendations for international students: Required—TOEFL (minimum score 79 computer-based). Electronic applications accepted. *Faculty research:* Neuropsychology, child abuse, psychometric properties of psychological instruments, maternal behavior, clinical practice issues, victimization of women, post-traumatic stress disorder.

The University of Texas of the Permian Basin, Office of Graduate Studies, College of Arts and Sciences, Deparment of Psychology, Odessa, TX 79762-0001. Offers applied research psychology (MA); clinical psychology (MA). Part-time and evening/weekend programs available. *Degree requirements:* For master's, comprehensive exam, thesis, practicum. *Entrance requirements:* For master's, GRE General Test, 3 letters of recommendation. Additional exam requirements/recommendations for international students: Required—TOEFL (minimum score 550 paper-based; 213 computer-based).

The University of Texas–Pan American, College of Social and Behavioral Sciences, Department of Psychology and Anthropology, Edinburg, TX 78541-2999. Offers psychology (MA), including clinical psychology, experimental psychology. Part-time and evening/weekend programs available. *Degree requirements:* For master's, comprehensive exam, thesis optional, internship. *Entrance requirements:* For master's, GRE, letters of recommendation. Additional exam requirements/recommendations for international students: Required—TOEFL. Electronic applications accepted. *Faculty research:* Biofeedback, acculturation, health, stress/trauma, neuropsychological assessment, false memories, children's theory of mind.

University of the Pacific, College of the Pacific, Department of Psychology, Stockton, CA 95211-0197. Offers MA. *Faculty:* 7 full-time (4 women). *Students:* 14 part-time (9 women); includes 5 minority (1 American Indian/Alaska Native, 1 Asian American or Pacific Islander, 3 Hispanic Americans), 1 international. Average age 26. 21 applicants, 57% accepted, 7 enrolled. In 2008, 7 master's awarded. *Degree requirements:* For master's, thesis. *Entrance requirements:* For master's, GRE General Test. Additional exam requirements/recommendations for international students: Required—TOEFL (minimum score 475 paper-based; 150 computer-based). *Application deadline:* For fall admission, 3/1 priority date for domestic students. Applications are processed on a rolling basis. Application fee: $75. *Expenses:* Tuition: Full-time $30,380; part-time $950 per unit. Required fees: $300. *Financial support:* In 2008–09, 7 teaching assistantships were awarded; institutionally sponsored loans also available. Support available to part-time students. Financial award application deadline: 3/1; financial award applicants required to submit FAFSA. *Unit head:* Dr. Roseann Hannon, Chairperson, 209-946-2133, E-mail: rhannon@pacific.edu. *Application contact:* Information Contact, 209-946-2261.

The University of Toledo, College of Graduate Studies, College of Arts and Sciences, Department of Psychology, Toledo, OH 43606-3390. Offers behavioral (PhD), including cognitive, psychobiology and learning, social; clinical psychology (PhD); experimental psychology (MA). *Accreditation:* APA. *Degree requirements:* For master's, thesis; for doctorate, one foreign language, thesis/dissertation. *Entrance requirements:* For master's and doctorate, GRE General Test, GRE Subject Test. *Faculty research:* Neural taste response.

University of Toronto, School of Graduate Studies, Life Sciences Division, Department of Psychology, Toronto, ON M5S 1A1, Canada. Offers MA, PhD. *Accreditation:* APA (one or more programs are accredited). *Degree requirements:* For master's, thesis; for doctorate, thesis/dissertation, oral exam. *Entrance requirements:* For master's, minimum A– average in last two years, 6 full courses in psychology, laboratory experience; for doctorate, minimum A– average, research experience.

University of Tulsa, Graduate School, College of Arts and Sciences, Department of Psychology, Tulsa, OK 74104-3189. Offers clinical psychology (MA, PhD); industrial/organizational psychology (MA, PhD); JD/MA. *Accreditation:* APA (one or more programs are accredited). Part-time programs available. *Faculty:* 13 full-time (5 women), 1 (woman) part-time/adjunct. *Students:* 41 full-time (33 women), 31 part-time (24 women); includes 7 minority (4 African Americans, 1 American Indian/Alaska Native, 2 Hispanic Americans), 2 international. Average age 28. 132 applicants, 39% accepted, 19 enrolled. In 2008, 12 master's, 9 doctorates awarded. Terminal master's awarded for partial completion of doctoral program. *Degree requirements:* For doctorate, comprehensive exam, thesis/dissertation. *Entrance requirements:* For master's and doctorate, GRE General Test. Additional exam requirements/recommendations for international students: Required—TOEFL (minimum score 575 paper-based; 231 computer-based; 91 iBT), IELTS (minimum score 6.5). *Application deadline:* Applications are processed on a rolling basis. Application fee: $40. Electronic applications accepted. *Expenses:* Tuition: Full-time $15,408; part-time $899 per credit hour. Required fees: $3.33 per credit hour. One-time fee: $200 full-time. Tuition and fees vary according to course load and program. *Financial support:* In 2008–09, 56 students received support, including 13 fellowships with full and partial tuition reimbursements available (averaging $4,535 per year), 17 research assistantships with full and partial tuition reimbursements available (averaging $11,228 per year), 26 teaching assistantships with full and partial tuition reimbursements available (averaging $9,995 per year); career-related internships or fieldwork, Federal Work-Study, scholarships/grants, tuition waivers (full and partial), and unspecified assistantships also available. Support available to part-time students. Financial award application deadline: 2/1; financial award applicants required to submit FAFSA. *Faculty research:* Personality and social psychology, cognitive psychology, neuropsychology, training assessment, trauma studies, personnel testing and selection, training, performance appraisal, organizational development, job attitudes and motivation, and leadership. Total annual research expenditures: $1.1 million. *Unit head:* Dr. Judy Berry, Chairperson, 918-631-2834, Fax: 918-631-2833, E-mail: judy-berry@utulsa.edu. *Application contact:* Graduate School, 918-631-2336, Fax: 918-631-2156, E-mail: grad@utulsa.edu.

University of Utah, The Graduate School, College of Social and Behavioral Science, Department of Psychology, Salt Lake City, UT 84112-1107. Offers clinical psychology (PhD); psychology (PhD). *Accreditation:* APA. *Degree requirements:* For doctorate, thesis/dissertation. *Entrance requirements:* For doctorate, GRE General Test. Additional exam requirements/recommendations for international students: Required—TOEFL (minimum score 500 paper-based; 173 computer-based). *Faculty research:* Cognitive neuroscience, health, social cognition, psychopathology, cognitive and social development.

University of Vermont, Graduate College, College of Arts and Sciences, Department of Psychology, Burlington, VT 05405. Offers clinical psychology (PhD); psychology (PhD). *Accreditation:* APA. *Students:* 50 (40 women); includes 5 minority (1 African American, 4 Hispanic Americans), 2 international. 186 applicants, 15% accepted, 10 enrolled. In 2008, 8 doctorates awarded. *Degree requirements:* For doctorate, thesis/dissertation. *Entrance requirements:* For doctorate, GRE General Test. Additional exam requirements/recommendations for international students: Required—TOEFL (minimum score 550 paper-based; 213 computer-based; 80 iBT). *Application deadline:* For fall admission, 12/1 for domestic students. Application fee: $40. Electronic applications accepted. *Expenses:* Tuition, state resident: part-time $488 per credit. Tuition, nonresident: part-time $1232 per credit. *Financial support:* Fellowships, research assistantships, teaching assistantships available. Financial award application deadline: 2/1. *Unit head:* Dr. William Falls, Chairperson, 802-656-2670. *Application contact:* Dr. Rex Forehand, Coordinator, 802-656-2670.

University of Victoria, Faculty of Graduate Studies, Faculty of Social Sciences, Department of Psychology, Victoria, BC V8W 2Y2, Canada. Offers clinical psychology (PhD); clinical psychology (neuropsychology) (M Sc); cognition and brain science (M Sc, PhD); experimental neuropsychology (M Sc, PhD); individualized study (M Sc, PhD); life span development psychology (PhD); life span developmental psychology (M Sc); social psychology (M Sc, PhD). *Accreditation:* APA (one or more programs are accredited). *Degree requirements:* For master's, thesis; for doctorate, thesis/dissertation, candidacy exam. *Entrance requirements:* For master's and doctorate, GRE General Test. Additional exam requirements/recommendations for international students: Required—TOEFL (minimum score 600 paper-based; 250 computer-based). Electronic applications accepted. *Faculty research:* Life span development psychology and aging, behavioral neuroscience, cognitive psychology, behavioral psychology, environmental psychology.

University of Virginia, College and Graduate School of Arts and Sciences, Department of Psychology, Program in Psychology, Charlottesville, VA 22903. Offers MA, PhD. *Accreditation:* APA. *Students:* 79 full-time (53 women), 1 (woman) part-time; includes 6 minority (3 African Americans, 3 Asian Americans or Pacific Islanders), 10 international. Average age 27. 491

applicants, 5% accepted, 11 enrolled. In 2008, 21 master's, 15 doctorates awarded. *Degree requirements:* For master's, thesis; for doctorate, comprehensive exam, thesis/dissertation. *Entrance requirements:* For master's and doctorate, GRE General Test, GRE Subject Test. *Application deadline:* Applications are processed on a rolling basis. Application fee: $60. Electronic applications accepted. *Expenses:* Tuition, area resident: Full-time $10,452. Tuition, state resident: full-time $10,452. Tuition, nonresident: full-time $20,010. Required fees: $2176. Part-time tuition and fees vary according to course load and program. *Financial support:* Applicants required to submit FAFSA. *Unit head:* David Hill, Chair, 434-982-4750, Fax: 434-982-4766, E-mail: dh2t@virginia.edu. *Application contact:* David Hill, Chair, 434-982-4750, Fax: 434-982-4766, E-mail: dh2t@virginia.edu.

University of Washington, Graduate School, College of Arts and Sciences, Department of Psychology, Seattle, WA 98195. Offers animal behavior (PhD); child psychology (PhD); clinical psychology (PhD); cognition and perception (PhD); developmental psychology (PhD); quantitative psychology (PhD); social psychology and personality (PhD). *Accreditation:* APA. *Degree requirements:* For doctorate, thesis/dissertation. *Entrance requirements:* For doctorate, GRE General Test, minimum GPA of 3.0. Electronic applications accepted. *Faculty research:* Addictive behaviors, artificial intelligence, child psychopathology, mechanisms and development of vision, physiology of ingestive behaviors.

University of Waterloo, Graduate Studies, Faculty of Arts, Department of Psychology, Waterloo, ON N2L 3G1, Canada. Offers MA, MA Sc, PhD. *Accreditation:* APA (one or more programs are accredited). Terminal master's awarded for partial completion of doctoral program. *Degree requirements:* For master's, thesis (for some programs); for doctorate, thesis/dissertation. *Entrance requirements:* For master's, GRE, honors degree in psychology, minimum B average; for doctorate, GRE, master's degree in psychology, minimum B average. Additional exam requirements/recommendations for international students: Required—TOEFL, TWE. Electronic applications accepted. *Faculty research:* Memory and attention, attitudes and behavior in the workplace, object recognition, judgment and decision making, communication and knowledge in toddlers.

The University of Western Ontario, Faculty of Graduate Studies, Biosciences Division, Department of Psychology, London, ON N6A 5B8, Canada. Offers MA, PhD. *Degree requirements:* For master's, thesis; for doctorate, thesis/dissertation. *Entrance requirements:* For master's, minimum B average during last 2 years; for doctorate, MA in psychology. Additional exam requirements/recommendations for international students: Required—TOEFL. *Faculty research:* Clinical, applied and social/personality psychology; psychobiology; cognitive processes.

University of West Florida, College of Arts and Sciences: Arts, Department of Psychology, Pensacola, FL 32514-5750. Offers counseling (MA); counseling-licensed mental health counselor (MA); general (MA); industrial-organizational (MA). Part-time programs available. *Faculty:* 11 full-time (3 women). *Students:* 61 full-time (46 women), 42 part-time (34 women); includes 22 minority (13 African Americans, 2 Asian Americans or Pacific Islanders, 7 Hispanic Americans), 2 international. Average age 26. 119 applicants, 65% accepted, 38 enrolled. In 2008, 16 master's awarded. *Degree requirements:* For master's, thesis (for some programs). *Entrance requirements:* For master's, GRE General Test, GRE Subject Test, minimum GPA of 3.0. Additional exam requirements/recommendations for international students: Required—TOEFL (minimum score 550 paper-based; 213 computer-based). *Application deadline:* For fall admission, 6/1 for domestic students, 5/15 for international students; for spring admission, 11/1 for domestic students, 10/1 for international students. Applications are processed on a rolling basis. Application fee: $30. *Expenses:* Tuition, state resident: full-time $6095; part-time $253.97 per credit hour. Tuition, nonresident: full-time $21,919; part-time $913.31 per credit hour. *Financial support:* In 2008–09, 3 research assistantships with partial tuition reimbursements (averaging $3,760 per year), 2 teaching assistantships with partial tuition reimbursements (averaging $3,760 per year) were awarded; career-related internships or fieldwork and Federal Work-Study also available. Financial award application deadline: 4/15; financial award applicants required to submit FAFSA. *Faculty research:* Prose recall, brain imaging, peak performance, biofeedback and pain control, comparable worth. Total annual research expenditures: $15,000. *Unit head:* Dr. Laura Koppes, Chairperson, 850-474-3493. *Application contact:* Terry McCray, Assistant Director of Graduate Admissions, 850-473-7718, Fax: 850-473-7714, E-mail: gradadmissions@uwf.edu.

University of West Georgia, Graduate School, College of Arts and Sciences, Department of Psychology, Carrollton, GA 30118. Offers individual, organizational, and community transformation: consciousness and society (Psy D); psychology (MA). Part-time programs available. *Faculty:* 14 full-time (2 women). *Students:* 33 full-time (20 women), 18 part-time (12 women); includes 5 minority (2 African Americans, 3 Hispanic Americans). Average age 31. 38 applicants, 53% accepted, 5 enrolled. In 2008, 25 master's awarded. Terminal master's awarded for partial completion of doctoral program. *Degree requirements:* For master's, one foreign language, comprehensive exam, thesis optional; for doctorate, comprehensive exam, thesis/dissertation. *Entrance requirements:* For master's, GRE General Test, interview, minimum GPA of 2.5, written statement; for doctorate, GRE or MAT, interview, written statement. *Application deadline:* For fall admission, 7/18 priority date for domestic students; for spring admission, 11/27 for domestic students. Application fee: $30. Electronic applications accepted. *Expenses:* Tuition, state resident: full-time $2844; part-time $158 per semester hour. Tuition, nonresident: full-time $11,340; part-time $630 per semester hour. Required fees: $1120; $41.56 per semester hour. $186 per semester. Tuition and fees vary according to course load. *Financial support:* In 2008–09, 12 students received support, including 12 research assistantships with full tuition reimbursements available (averaging $3,000 per year); career-related internships or fieldwork, tuition waivers (full), and unspecified assistantships also available. Support available to part-time students. Financial award applicants required to submit FAFSA. *Faculty research:* Creativity, inspiration and consciousness; symbolism and metaphor in psychotherapy; spirituality of children; feminism and culture; mind/body connection. Total annual research expenditures: $30,000. *Unit head:* Dr. Donadrian Lawrence Rice, Chair, 678-839-6510, Fax: 678-839-0611, E-mail: drice@westga.edu. *Application contact:* Dr. Charles W. Clark, Dean, 678-839-6508, E-mail: cclark@westga.edu.

University of Windsor, Faculty of Graduate Studies, Faculty of Arts and Social Sciences, Department of Psychology, Windsor, ON N9B 3P4, Canada. Offers adult clinical (MA, PhD); applied social psychology (MA, PhD); child clinical (MA, PhD); clinical neuropsychology (MA, PhD). *Accreditation:* APA (one or more programs are accredited). *Degree requirements:* For master's, thesis; for doctorate, comprehensive exam, thesis/dissertation. *Entrance requirements:* For master's, GRE General Test, GRE Subject Test in psychology, minimum B average; for doctorate, GRE General Test, GRE Subject Test in psychology, master's degree. Additional exam requirements/recommendations for international students: Required—TOEFL (minimum score 600 paper-based; 250 computer-based). Electronic applications accepted. *Faculty research:* Gambling, suicidology, emotional competence, psychotherapy and trauma.

University of Wisconsin–Eau Claire, College of Arts and Sciences, Department of Psychology, Eau Claire, WI 54702-4004. Offers school psychology (MSE, Ed S). Part-time programs available. *Faculty:* 12 full-time (6 women). *Students:* 16 full-time (11 women), 7 part-time (all women), 1 international. Average age 24. 49 applicants, 33% accepted, 16 enrolled. In 2008, 16 master's awarded. *Degree requirements:* For master's, comprehensive exam, thesis, NASP Professional Exam, written exam, externship. *Entrance requirements:* For master's, GRE, minimum undergraduate GPA of 3.07. Additional exam requirements/recommendations for international students: Required—TOEFL (minimum score 550 paper-based; 213 computer-based; 79 iBT). *Application deadline:* For fall admission, 3/1 priority date for domestic students, 6/1 priority date for international students; for spring admission, 11/1 priority date for international students. Applications are processed on a rolling basis. Application fee: $56. Electronic applications accepted. *Expenses:* Tuition, state resident: full-time $6426; part-time $400.60 per credit. Tuition, nonresident: full-time $17,560; part-time $975.32 per credit. One-time fee: $56 full-time. *Financial support:* In 2008–09, 16 students received support, including 8 fellowships (averaging $3,000 per year); Federal Work-Study and unspecified assistantships also available. Financial award application deadline: 3/1; financial award applicants required to submit FAFSA. *Unit head:* Dr. Lori Bica, Chair, 715-836-5733, Fax: 715-836-2214, E-mail: bicala@uwec.edu. *Application contact:* Kristina Anderson, Director of Admissions, 715-836-5415, Fax: 715-836-2409, E-mail: admissions@uwec.edu.

University of Wisconsin–La Crosse, Office of University Graduate Studies, College of Liberal Studies, Department of Psychology, La Crosse, WI 54601-3742. Offers school psychology (MS Ed, Ed S); student affairs administration (MS Ed). *Faculty:* 19 full-time (12 women). *Students:* 47 full-time (33 women), 63 part-time (55 women); includes 5 minority (1 African American, 1 Asian American or Pacific Islander, 3 Hispanic Americans), 1 international. Average age 26. 63 applicants, 100% accepted, 42 enrolled. In 2008, 29 master's awarded. *Degree requirements:* For master's, thesis, seminar, or comprehensive exams. *Entrance requirements:* For master's, GRE General Test, minimum GPA of 2.85, interview, writing sample, resumé. Additional exam requirements/recommendations for international students: Required—TOEFL (minimum score 550 paper-based; 213 computer-based). *Application deadline:* For fall admission, 2/15 for domestic students. Application fee: $45. *Expenses:* Tuition, state resident: full-time $6485; part-time $360 per credit hour. Tuition, nonresident: full-time $16,830; part-time $935 per credit hour. Required fees: $846. Tuition and fees vary according to program and reciprocity agreements. *Financial support:* In 2008–09, 31 research assistantships with partial tuition reimbursements (averaging $7,309 per year) were awarded; career-related internships or fieldwork, Federal Work-Study, institutionally sponsored loans, scholarships/grants, health care benefits, and unspecified assistantships also available. Support available to part-time students. *Unit head:* Dr. Emily Johnson, Chair, 608-785-6888, Fax: 608-785-8443, E-mail: johnson.emil@uwlax.edu. *Application contact:* Kathryn Kiefer, Associate Director of Admissions, 608-785-8939, E-mail: admissions@uwlax.edu.

University of Wisconsin–Madison, Graduate School, College of Letters and Science, Department of Psychology, Madison, WI 53706-1380. Offers biology of brain and behavior (PhD); clinical psychology (PhD); cognitive neurosciences (PhD); developmental psychology (PhD); perception (PhD); psychology (PhD); social and personality psychology (PhD). *Accreditation:* APA. *Degree requirements:* For doctorate, comprehensive exam, thesis/dissertation. *Entrance requirements:* For doctorate, GRE General Test, minimum undergraduate GPA of 3.0. Additional exam requirements/recommendations for international students: Required—TOEFL. Electronic applications accepted.

University of Wisconsin–Milwaukee, Graduate School, College of Letters and Sciences, Department of Psychology, Milwaukee, WI 53201-0413. Offers clinical psychology (MS, PhD); psychology (MS, PhD). *Accreditation:* APA (one or more programs are accredited). *Faculty:* 22 full-time (6 women). *Students:* 54 full-time (32 women), 17 part-time (11 women); includes 12 minority (3 African Americans, 2 Asian Americans or Pacific Islanders, 7 Hispanic Americans), 4 international. Average age 29. 188 applicants, 10% accepted, 14 enrolled. In 2008, 4 master's, 10 doctorates awarded. *Degree requirements:* For master's, thesis; for doctorate, variable foreign language requirement, thesis/dissertation. *Entrance requirements:* For master's and doctorate, GRE General Test, GRE Subject Test. Additional exam requirements/recommendations for international students: Required—TOEFL (minimum score 550 paper-based; 79 iBT), IELTS (minimum score 6.5). *Application deadline:* For fall admission, 1/1 priority date for domestic students; for spring admission, 9/1 for domestic students. Applications are processed on a rolling basis. Application fee: $45 ($75 for international students). *Expenses:* Tuition, area resident: Full-time $7320; part-time $165 per credit. Tuition, state resident: full-time $7320; part-time $165 per credit. Tuition, nonresident: full-time $17,840; part-time $714 per credit. Tuition and fees vary according to campus/location, program and reciprocity agreements. *Financial support:* In 2008–09, 7 research assistantships, 48 teaching assistantships were awarded; career-related internships or fieldwork and unspecified assistantships also available. Support available to part-time students. Financial award application deadline: 4/15. Total annual research expenditures: $1.3 million. *Unit head:* Hobart Davies, Representative, 414-229-6594, Fax: 414-229-5219, E-mail: hobart@uwm.edu. *Application contact:* Susan Lima, General Information Contact, 414-229-4359, Fax: 414-229-6967, E-mail: suelima@uwm.edu.

University of Wisconsin–Oshkosh, The Office of Graduate Studies, College of Letters and Science, Department of Psychology, Oshkosh, WI 54901. Offers experimental psychology (MS); industrial/organizational psychology (MS). *Degree requirements:* For master's, thesis. *Entrance requirements:* For master's, GRE, 10 semester hours of undergraduate course work in psychology. Additional exam requirements/recommendations for international students: Required—TOEFL (minimum score 550 paper-based; 213 computer-based; 79 iBT). Electronic applications accepted. *Faculty research:* Performance evaluation, training, biological bases of behavior, tactile perception, aging.

University of Wisconsin–Stout, Graduate School, College of Human Development, Program in Applied Psychology, Menomonie, WI 54751. Offers MS. Part-time programs available. *Students:* 26 full-time (17 women), 3 part-time (2 women); includes 5 minority (2 African Americans, 1 Asian American or Pacific Islander, 2 Hispanic Americans), 3 international. Average age 24. 24 applicants, 79% accepted, 12 enrolled. In 2008, 10 master's awarded. *Degree requirements:* For master's, thesis. *Entrance requirements:* For master's, GRE General Test, GRE Subject Test, minimum GPA of 3.0, 15 semester credits of undergraduate course work in psychology, 8 semester credits in research methods and statistics. Additional exam requirements/recommendations for international students: Required—TOEFL (minimum score 500 paper-based; 173 computer-based; 61 iBT). *Application deadline:* For fall admission, 2/1 priority date for domestic and international students; for spring admission, 10/1 priority date for domestic and international students. Application fee: $45. Electronic applications accepted. *Expenses:* Tuition, state resident: full-time $6227; part-time $345.93 per credit. Tuition, nonresident: full-time $9998; part-time $555.42 per credit. International tuition: $10,512 full-time. Tuition and fees vary according to course load, program and reciprocity agreements. *Financial support:* In 2008–09, 12 research assistantships with partial tuition reimbursements (averaging $4,165 per year), 11 teaching assistantships with tuition reimbursements (averaging $2,798 per year) were awarded; Federal Work-Study, scholarships/grants, tuition waivers (partial), and unspecified assistantships also available. Support available to part-time students. Financial award application deadline: 5/1; financial award applicants required to submit FAFSA. *Faculty research:* Health complementary therapies, motivation, group dynamics, social reasoning, stress. *Unit head:* Dr. Kristina Gorbatenko-Roth, Director, 715-232-2451, Fax: 715-232-5303, E-mail: gorbatenkok@uwstout.edu. *Application contact:* Anne E. Johnson, Graduate Student Evaluator (Admissions and Assistantship Coordinator), 715-232-1322, Fax: 715-232-2413, E-mail: johnsona@uwstout.edu.

University of Wisconsin–Whitewater, School of Graduate Studies, College of Letters and Sciences, Department of Psychology, Whitewater, WI 53190-1790. Offers school psychology (MS Ed, Ed S). Part-time and evening/weekend programs available. Postbaccalaureate distance learning degree programs offered (no on-campus study). *Degree requirements:* For master's, comprehensive exam or thesis. *Entrance requirements:* For master's, MAT or GRE, interview, minimum GPA of 3.0, 3 letters of recommendation. Additional exam requirements/recommendations for international students: Required—TOEFL (minimum score 550 paper-based; 213 computer-based). Electronic applications accepted. *Faculty research:* School violence/youth violence; anger/aggression interventions; women's mental health; pedagogy of empathy, social psychology, and personality.

University of Wyoming, Graduate School, College of Arts and Sciences, Department of Psychology, Laramie, WY 82070. Offers MA, MS, PhD. *Accreditation:* APA (one or more programs are accredited). *Faculty:* 15 full-time (6 women), 2 part-time/adjunct (1 woman). *Students:* 29 full-time (19 women), 10 part-time (7 women); includes 4 minority (1 American Indian/Alaska Native, 2 Asian Americans or Pacific Islanders, 1 Hispanic American), 2 international. Average age 27. 81 applicants, 9% accepted, 5 enrolled. In 2008, 4 master's, 5 doctorates awarded. Terminal master's awarded for partial completion of doctoral program.

Psychology—General

University of Wyoming (continued)
Degree requirements: For master's, thesis; for doctorate, comprehensive exam, thesis/dissertation. *Entrance requirements:* For master's and doctorate, GRE General Test, GRE Subject Test, minimum GPA of 3.0. Additional exam requirements/recommendations for international students: Required—TOEFL. *Application deadline:* For fall admission, 1/15 for domestic and international students. Application fee: $50. *Financial support:* In 2008–09, 17 research assistantships with full tuition reimbursements (averaging $10,100 per year), 12 teaching assistantships with full tuition reimbursements (averaging $10,100 per year) were awarded; career-related internships or fieldwork, Federal Work-Study, and institutionally sponsored loans also available. Financial award application deadline: 3/1. *Faculty research:* Child development, health psychology, psychology and law, social psychology, mood/anxiety disorders. Total annual research expenditures: $1.1 million. *Unit head:* Dr. Carolyn M. Pepper, Associate Professor and Chair, 307-766-2951, Fax: 307-766-2926, E-mail: cpepper@uwyo.edy. *Application contact:* Dr. Carolyn M. Pepper, Associate Professor and Chair, 307-766-2951, Fax: 307-766-2926, E-mail: cpepper@uwyo.edu.

Utah State University, School of Graduate Studies, College of Education and Human Services, Department of Psychology, Logan, UT 84322. Offers clinical/counseling/school psychology (PhD); research and evaluation methodology (PhD); school counseling (MS); school psychology (MS). *Accreditation:* APA (one or more programs are accredited). Part-time and evening/weekend programs available. Postbaccalaureate distance learning degree programs offered (no on-campus study). Terminal master's awarded for partial completion of doctoral program. *Degree requirements:* For master's, thesis (for some programs); for doctorate, thesis/dissertation. *Entrance requirements:* For master's, GRE General Test (school psychology), MAT (school counseling), minimum GPA of 3.5; for doctorate, GRE General Test, minimum GPA of 3.5. Additional exam requirements/recommendations for international students: Required—TOEFL. *Faculty research:* Hearing loss detection in infancy, ADHD, eating disorders, domestic violence, neuropsychology, bilingual/Spanish speaking students/parents.

Valdosta State University, Graduate School, College of Education, Department of Psychology and Counseling, Valdosta, GA 31698. Offers clinical/counseling psychology (MS); industrial/organizational psychology (MS); school counseling (M Ed, Ed S); school psychology (Ed S). Part-time and evening/weekend programs available. *Faculty:* 16 full-time (2 women). *Students:* 65 full-time (54 women), 40 part-time (36 women); includes 32 minority (27 African Americans, 5 Hispanic Americans). Average age 27. 105 applicants, 60% accepted, 29 enrolled. In 2008, 25 master's awarded. *Degree requirements:* For master's, thesis or alternative, comprehensive written and/or oral exams; for Ed S, thesis. *Entrance requirements:* For master's and Ed S, GRE General Test or MAT. Additional exam requirements/recommendations for international students: Required—TOEFL (minimum score 523 paper-based; 193 computer-based). *Application deadline:* For fall admission, 7/1 for domestic and international students; for spring admission, 11/15 for domestic and international students. Applications are processed on a rolling basis. Application fee: $40. Electronic applications accepted. *Financial support:* In 2008–09, 2 students received support, including 2 research assistantships with full tuition reimbursements available (averaging $2,452 per year); institutionally sponsored loans and unspecified assistantships also available. Support available to part-time students. Financial award application deadline: 7/1; financial award applicants required to submit FAFSA. *Faculty research:* Using Bender-Gestalt to predict graphomotor dimensions of the draw-a-person test, neurobehavioral hemispheric dominance. *Unit head:* Dr. Robert Bauer, Chair, 229-333-5930, Fax: 229-259-5576, E-mail: bbauer@valdosta.edu. *Application contact:* Rebecca Waters, Coordinator of Graduate Admissions, 229-333-5694, Fax: 229-245-3853, E-mail: rlwaters@valdosta.edu.

Valparaiso University, Graduate Division, Department of Psychology, Valparaiso, IN 46383. Offers business management (for counseling students) (Certificate); clinical mental health counseling (MA); community counseling (MA); JD/MA. Part-time and evening/weekend programs available. *Faculty:* 7 part-time/adjunct (3 women). *Students:* 33 full-time (24 women), 16 part-time (9 women); includes 6 minority (2 African Americans, 1 Asian American or Pacific Islander, 3 Hispanic Americans), 2 international. Average age 28. In 2008, 16 master's awarded. *Degree requirements:* For master's, thesis or alternative, internship. *Entrance requirements:* For master's, minimum GPA of 3.0; 15 credits in the social/behavioral sciences (psychology, sociology, human development, etc.) with a minimum GPA of 3.0 or better; a course in introductory psychology; a recent statistics course with a B or better . Additional exam requirements/recommendations for international students: Required—TOEFL (minimum score 550 paper-based; 213 computer-based). *Application deadline:* For fall admission, 3/1 priority date for domestic students. Applications are processed on a rolling basis. Application fee: $30 ($50 for international students). Electronic applications accepted. *Financial support:* Career-related internships or fieldwork, traineeships, and unspecified assistantships available. Support available to part-time students. Financial award applicants required to submit FAFSA. *Faculty research:* Environmental psychology, human sexuality, racial identity development models, social psychology. *Unit head:* Dr. James Nelson, Director of Graduate Porgrams, 219-464-5443, Fax: 219-464-6878, E-mail: Jim.Nelson@valpo.edu. *Application contact:* Jamie Haney, Coordinator of Recruitment Activities, 219-464-5313, Fax: 219-464-5381, E-mail: Jamie.Haney@valpo.edu.

Vanderbilt University, Graduate School, Program in Psychological Sciences, Nashville, TN 37240-1001. Offers MA, PhD. *Accreditation:* APA (one or more programs are accredited). *Faculty:* 90 full-time (35 women). *Students:* 92 full-time (67 women); includes 13 minority (6 African Americans, 3 Asian Americans or Pacific Islanders, 4 Hispanic Americans), 19 international. Average age 28. 394 applicants, 8% accepted, 15 enrolled. In 2008, 4 master's, 10 doctorates awarded. *Degree requirements:* For doctorate, comprehensive exam, thesis/dissertation, final and qualifying exams. *Entrance requirements:* For doctorate, GRE General Test, GRE Subject Test. Additional exam requirements/recommendations for international students: Required—TOEFL (minimum score 570 paper-based; 230 computer-based; 88 iBT). *Application deadline:* For fall admission, 12/15 for domestic and international students. Application fee: $0. Electronic applications accepted. *Financial support:* Fellowships with full and partial tuition reimbursements, research assistantships with full and partial tuition reimbursements, teaching assistantships with full and partial tuition reimbursements, career-related internships or fieldwork, Federal Work-Study, institutionally sponsored loans, scholarships/grants, traineeships, and health care benefits available. Financial award application deadline: 1/15; financial award applicants required to submit CSS PROFILE or FAFSA. *Faculty research:* Clinical, cognitive, developmental, and social psychology; neuroscience; vision; behavior. *Unit head:* Andrew J. Tomarken, Co-Chair, 615-322-2874, Fax: 615-343-8449, E-mail: andrew.j.tomarken@vanderbilt.edu. *Application contact:* Thomas J. Palmeri, Co-Director of Graduate Studies, 615-322-2874, Fax: 615-343-8449, E-mail: thomas.j.palmeri@vanderbilt.edu.

Vanderbilt University, Peabody College, Department of Psychology and Human Development, Nashville, TN 37240-1001. Offers child studies (M Ed). *Accreditation:* APA. Part-time programs available. *Faculty:* 25 full-time (12 women), 2 part-time/adjunct (1 woman). *Students:* 18 full-time (17 women), 2 part-time (both women); includes 2 minority (1 African American, 1 Asian American or Pacific Islander). Average age 25. 50 applicants, 36% accepted, 9 enrolled. In 2008, 8 master's awarded. *Degree requirements:* For master's, comprehensive exam, thesis optional. *Entrance requirements:* For master's, GRE General Test. Additional exam requirements/recommendations for international students: Required—TOEFL (minimum score 550 paper-based; 213 computer-based). *Application deadline:* For fall admission, 12/31 for domestic and international students; for spring admission, 11/1 for domestic and international students. Applications are processed on a rolling basis. Application fee: $0. Electronic applications accepted. *Financial support:* In 2008–09, 11 students received support, including 7 research assistantships with full and partial tuition reimbursements available; fellowships with full and partial tuition reimbursements available, teaching assistantships with full and partial tuition reimbursements available, Federal Work-Study, institutionally sponsored loans, scholarships/grants, and unspecified assistantships also available. Financial award application deadline: 2/1; financial award applicants required to submit FAFSA. *Faculty research:* Cognitive, language and social development; stress, coping and emotion; quantitative methods and evaluation; clinical intervention and prevention; individual differences, disabilities and developmental psychopathology. *Unit head:* Dr. David Cole, Acting Chair, 615-322-8141, Fax: 615-343-9494, E-mail: david.cole@vanderbilt.edu. *Application contact:* Sharone Hall, Educational Coordinator, 615-343-4963, Fax: 615-343-9494, E-mail: sharone.k.hall@vanderbilt.edu.

Villanova University, Graduate School of Liberal Arts and Sciences, Department of Psychology, Villanova, PA 19085-1699. Offers MS. Part-time and evening/weekend programs available. *Faculty:* 8 full-time (3 women), 2 part-time/adjunct (1 woman). *Students:* 42 full-time (28 women), 3 part-time (2 women); includes 1 minority (African American). Average age 24. 88 applicants, 48% accepted, 21 enrolled. In 2008, 14 master's awarded. *Degree requirements:* For master's, thesis. *Entrance requirements:* For master's, GRE General Test, minimum GPA of 3.0. *Application deadline:* For fall admission, 8/1 for domestic and international students; for spring admission, 12/1 for domestic and international students. Applications are processed on a rolling basis. Application fee: $50. Electronic applications accepted. *Financial support:* Research assistantships, Federal Work-Study and scholarships/grants available. Financial award applicants required to submit FAFSA. *Unit head:* Dr. Thomas Toppino, Chair, 610-519-4720. *Application contact:* Dr. Gerald Long, Dean, Graduate School of Liberal Arts and Sciences, 610-519-7093, Fax: 610-519-7096.

See Close-Up on page 1151.

Virginia Commonwealth University, Graduate School, College of Humanities and Sciences, Department of Psychology, Program in General Psychology, Richmond, VA 23284-9005. Offers PhD. *Degree requirements:* For doctorate, thesis/dissertation. *Entrance requirements:* For doctorate, GRE General Test.

Virginia Polytechnic Institute and State University, Graduate School, College of Science, Department of Psychology, Blacksburg, VA 24061. Offers bio-behavioral sciences (PhD); clinical psychology (PhD); developmental psychology (PhD); industrial/organizational psychology (PhD); psychology (MS). *Accreditation:* APA (one or more programs are accredited). *Entrance requirements:* For master's and doctorate, GRE General Test. Additional exam requirements/recommendations for international students: Required—TOEFL (minimum score 550 paper-based; 213 computer-based). Electronic applications accepted. *Faculty research:* Infant development from electrophysical point of view, work motivation and personnel selection, EEG, ERP and hypnosis with reference to chronic pain, intimate violence.

Virginia State University, School of Graduate Studies, Research, and Outreach, School of Engineering, Science and Technology, Department of Psychology, Petersburg, VA 23806-0001. Offers behavioral and community health sciences (PhD); clinical health psychology (PhD); clinical psychology (MS); general psychology (MS). *Degree requirements:* For master's, one foreign language, thesis. *Entrance requirements:* For master's, GRE General Test.

Wake Forest University, Graduate School of Arts and Sciences, Department of Psychology, Winston-Salem, NC 27109. Offers MA. *Degree requirements:* For master's, one foreign language, comprehensive exam, thesis. *Entrance requirements:* For master's, GRE General Test. Additional exam requirements/recommendations for international students: Required—TOEFL (minimum score 213 computer-based; 79 iBT). Electronic applications accepted. *Faculty research:* Developmental, social, personality, experimental, and physiological psychology.

Walden University, Graduate Programs, School of Psychology, Minneapolis, MN 55401. Offers clinical assessment (Post-Doctoral Certificate); clinical child psychology (Post-Doctoral Certificate); clinical psychology (Post-Doctoral Certificate); counseling psychology (Post-Doctoral Certificate); forensic psychology (MS), including forensic psychology in the community, general forensic psychology, mental health applications, program planning and evaluation in forensic settings, psychology and legal systems; general psychology (Post-Doctoral Certificate); health psychology (Post-Doctoral Certificate); organizational psychology (Post-Doctoral Certificate); organizational psychology and development (Certificate); psychology (MS, PhD), including clinical psychology, counseling psychology, crisis management and response (MS), general psychology, health psychology, leadership development and coaching (MS), media psychology (MS), organizational psychology, organizational psychology and development (MS), organizational psychology and nonprofit management (MS), program evaluation and research (MS), psychology of culture (MS), psychology, public administration, and social change (MS), school psychology, social psychology (MS), terrorism and security (MS); school psychology (Post-Doctoral Certificate); teaching online (Post-Master's Certificate). Part-time and evening/weekend programs available. Postbaccalaureate distance learning degree programs offered (minimal on-campus study). *Faculty:* 16 full-time, 190 part-time/adjunct. *Students:* 3,198 full-time (2,489 women), 810 part-time (664 women); includes 1,319 minority (1,013 African Americans, 51 American Indian/Alaska Native, 68 Asian Americans or Pacific Islanders, 187 Hispanic Americans), 72 international. Average age 40. 1,468 applicants, 60% accepted, 612 enrolled. In 2008, 203 master's, 37 doctorates awarded. Terminal master's awarded for partial completion of doctoral program. *Degree requirements:* For master's, thesis optional; for doctorate, thesis/dissertation, residency. *Entrance requirements:* For master's, bachelor's degree or equivalent in related field, minimum GPA of 2.5, two references, goal statement, official transcripts, access to computer and Internet; for doctorate, master's degree or equivalent in related field, minimum GPA of 3.0, three years related professional/academic experience, two references, goal statement, official transcripts, access to computer and Internet. Additional exam requirements/recommendations for international students: Required—TOEFL (minimum score 550 paper-based; 213 computer-based), IELTS (minimum score 6.5), TOEFL, IELTS, or Michigan English Language Assessment Battery (minimum score 82). *Application deadline:* Applications are processed on a rolling basis. Application fee: $50. Electronic applications accepted. *Expenses:* Tuition: Full-time $12,877; part-time $520 per credit. Required fees: $1230. Tuition and fees vary according to course load, degree level and program. *Financial support:* In 2008–09, 1 fellowship was awarded; Federal Work-Study, scholarships/grants, unspecified assistantships, and family tuition reduction; active duty/veteran tuition reduction; group tuition reduction; interest-free payment plans also available. Support available to part-time students. Financial award applicants required to submit FAFSA. *Unit head:* Dr. Nina Nabors, Associate Dean, 800-925-3368. *Application contact:* Jennifer Hall, 866-4-WALDEN, E-mail: info@waldenu.edu.

Washburn University, College of Arts and Sciences, Department of Psychology, Topeka, KS 66621. Offers clinical psychology (MA). Part-time programs available. *Degree requirements:* For master's, thesis. *Entrance requirements:* For master's, GRE General Test, 15 hours of course work in psychology. Electronic applications accepted. *Faculty research:* Animal behavior, correctional psychology, children's social development, metacognition and metamemory, psychology of exercise, Gibsonian Ecological Psychology, treatment of anxiety disorders.

Washington College, Graduate Programs, Department of Psychology, Chestertown, MD 21620-1197. Offers MA. Part-time and evening/weekend programs available. *Entrance requirements:* For master's, GRE General Test.

Washington State University, Graduate School, College of Liberal Arts, Department of Psychology, Pullman, WA 99164. Offers clinical psychology (PhD); experimental psychology (PhD); psychology (MS). *Accreditation:* APA (one or more programs are accredited). *Degree requirements:* For master's, comprehensive exam (for some programs), thesis (for some programs), oral exam; for doctorate, comprehensive exam, thesis/dissertation, oral exam, written exam. *Entrance requirements:* For master's, GRE General Test, minimum GPA of 3.0, research or clinical experience, 3 letters of recommendation; for doctorate, GRE General Test, minimum GPA of 3.0, 1 course in statistics and research methodology, research or clinical experience, 3 letters of recommendation. *Faculty research:* Childhood conduct disorders, etiology of depression, treatment of reading disorders, applied behavior analysis, selective attention.

Washington University in St. Louis, Graduate School of Arts and Sciences, Department of Philosophy, Program in Philosophy/Neuroscience/Psychology, St. Louis, MO 63130-4899.

Offers PhD. *Students:* 14 full-time (3 women); includes 1 Hispanic American, 5 international. 35 applicants, 9% accepted, 2 enrolled. *Degree requirements:* For doctorate, thesis/dissertation. *Entrance requirements:* For doctorate, GRE General Test, sample of written work. *Application deadline:* For fall admission, 1/15 priority date for domestic students. Applications are processed on a rolling basis. Application fee: $45. Electronic applications accepted. *Financial support:* Fellowships, Federal Work-Study and tuition waivers (full and partial) available. Financial award application deadline: 1/15. *Unit head:* Dr. Jose Bermudez, Head, 314-935-4297. *Application contact:* Assistant to the Dean, 314-935-6880, Fax: 314-935-4887.

Washington University in St. Louis, Graduate School of Arts and Sciences, Department of Psychology, St. Louis, MO 63130-4899. Offers clinical psychology (PhD); general experimental psychology (PhD); social psychology (PhD). *Accreditation:* APA. *Students:* 102 full-time (63 women); includes 23 minority (6 African Americans, 13 Asian Americans or Pacific Islanders, 4 Hispanic Americans), 12 international. 291 applicants, 11% accepted, 18 enrolled. In 2008, 11 doctorates awarded. Terminal master's awarded for partial completion of doctoral program. *Degree requirements:* For doctorate, thesis/dissertation. *Entrance requirements:* For doctorate, GRE General Test. *Application deadline:* For fall admission, 12/15 priority date for domestic students. Application fee: $45. Electronic applications accepted. *Financial support:* Fellowships, research assistantships, teaching assistantships, career-related internships or fieldwork, Federal Work-Study, institutionally sponsored loans, and tuition waivers (full and partial) available. Support available to part-time students. Financial award application deadline: 1/15. *Unit head:* Dr. Randy Larsen, Chairperson, 314-935-6520. *Application contact:* Assistant to the Dean, 314-935-6880, Fax: 314-935-4887.

Wayne State University, College of Liberal Arts and Sciences, Department of Psychology, Detroit, MI 48202. Offers human development (MA); psychology (MA, MS, PhD), including behavioral and cognitive neuroscience (PhD), clinical psychology (PhD), cognitive and social psychology (PhD), industrial/organizational psychology (PhD), psychology (MA, MS). *Accreditation:* APA (one or more programs are accredited). *Degree requirements:* For doctorate, thesis/dissertation. *Entrance requirements:* For doctorate, GRE General Test, GRE Subject Test, personal statement; letters of recommendation. Additional exam requirements/recommendations for international students: Required—TOEFL (minimum score 550 paper-based; 213 computer-based); Recommended—TWE (minimum score 6). Electronic applications accepted. *Faculty research:* Clinical neuropsychology; high risk factors in development; human aging and neuroscience; industrial/organizational psychology; health psychology.

Wesleyan University, Graduate Programs, Department of Psychology, Middletown, CT 06459-0260. Offers MA. *Degree requirements:* For master's, thesis. *Entrance requirements:* For master's, GRE General Test, GRE Subject Test, MAT. Additional exam requirements/recommendations for international students: Required—TOEFL. Electronic applications accepted. *Faculty research:* Human perception and cognition; cognitive, social, and moral development; history of psychology; biopsychology; psycholinguistics.

West Chester University of Pennsylvania, Office of Graduate Studies, College of Arts and Sciences, Department of Psychology, West Chester, PA 19383. Offers clinical mental health (Certificate); clinical psychology (MA); general psychology (MA); industrial psychology (MA). Part-time and evening/weekend programs available. *Students:* 63 full-time (47 women), 28 part-time (20 women); includes 5 minority (4 African Americans, 1 Hispanic American), 1 international. Average age 30. 179 applicants, 79% accepted, 43 enrolled. In 2008, 32 master's awarded. *Degree requirements:* For master's, comprehensive exam, thesis (for some programs). *Entrance requirements:* For master's, GRE General Test or MAT, minimum GPA of 3.0, psychology 3.25; three letters of reference. Additional exam requirements/recommendations for international students: Required—TOEFL (minimum score 550 paper-based; 213 computer-based; 80 iBT). *Application deadline:* For fall admission, 4/15 priority date for domestic students, 3/15 for international students; for spring admission, 10/15 for domestic students, 9/1 for international students. Applications are processed on a rolling basis. Application fee: $35. Electronic applications accepted. *Expenses:* Tuition, state resident: full-time $6430; part-time $357 per credit. Tuition, nonresident: full-time $10,288; part-time $572 per credit. Required fees: $652.50; $50 per credit. $67 per semester. *Financial support:* In 2008–09, 9 research assistantships with full and partial tuition reimbursements (averaging $5,000 per year) were awarded; unspecified assistantships also available. Support available to part-time students. Financial award application deadline: 2/15; financial award applicants required to submit FAFSA. *Faculty research:* Animal learning and cognition. *Unit head:* Dr. Sandra Kerr, Chair, 610-436-2949, E-mail: skerr@wcupa.edu. *Application contact:* Dr. Stefani Yorges, Graduate Coordinator, 610-436-3154, E-mail: syorges@wcupa.edu.

Western Carolina University, Graduate School, College of Education and Allied Professions, Department of Psychology, Cullowhee, NC 28723. Offers general psychology (MA); school psychology (MA). Part-time programs available. *Degree requirements:* For master's, comprehensive exam, thesis. *Entrance requirements:* For master's, GRE General Test, appropriate undergraduate, interview, 3 letters of recommendation, personal statement. Additional exam requirements/recommendations for international students: Required—TOEFL (minimum score 550 paper-based; 270 computer-based; 79 iBT). *Faculty research:* Five-factor model of personality, evolutionary psychology, stress and worry, body image and physical attractiveness, moral decision-making, memory, learning styles.

Western Illinois University, School of Graduate Studies, College of Arts and Sciences, Department of Psychology, Macomb, IL 61455-1390. Offers clinical/community mental health (MS); general psychology (MS); psychology (MS, SSP); school psychology (SSP). Part-time programs available. *Students:* 42 full-time (21 women), 14 part-time (11 women); includes 1 minority (Asian American or Pacific Islander), 2 international. Average age 25. 66 applicants, 53% accepted. In 2008, 13 master's, 10 other advanced degrees awarded. *Degree requirements:* For master's, comprehensive exam (for some programs), thesis or alternative. *Entrance requirements:* For master's and SSP, GRE General Test. Additional exam requirements/recommendations for international students: Required—TOEFL (minimum score 550 paper-based; 213 computer-based; 80 iBT). *Application deadline:* Applications are processed on a rolling basis. Application fee: $30. Electronic applications accepted. *Expenses:* Tuition, state resident: full-time $5696; part-time $237.34 per credit hour. Tuition, nonresident: full-time $11,392; part-time $474.68 per credit hour. Required fees: $1453; $60.55 per credit hour. *Financial support:* In 2008–09, 36 students received support, including 36 research assistantships with full tuition reimbursements available (averaging $7,040 per year). Financial award applicants required to submit FAFSA. *Unit head:* Dr. Steven Dworkin, Chairperson, 309-298-1593. *Application contact:* Evelyn Hoing, Assistant Director of Graduate Studies, 309-298-1806, Fax: 309-298-2345, E-mail: grad-office@wiu.edu.

Western Kentucky University, Graduate Studies, College of Education and Behavioral Sciences, Department of Psychology, Bowling Green, KY 42101. Offers psychology (MA); school psychology (Ed S). *Degree requirements:* For master's, comprehensive exam, thesis (for some programs); for Ed S, thesis, oral exam. *Entrance requirements:* For master's, GRE General Test; for Ed S, GRE General Test, minimum GPA of 3.5. Additional exam requirements/recommendations for international students: Required—TOEFL (minimum score 555 paper-based; 213 computer-based; 79 iBT). *Faculty research:* Neural regeneration, enhancing mobility in the elderly, improvement in visual processing in older adults, lifespan development.

Western Michigan University, Graduate College, College of Arts and Sciences, Department of Psychology, Kalamazoo, MI 49008-5202. Offers behavior analysis (MA, PhD); clinical psychology (MA, PhD); experimental psychology (MA); industrial/organizational psychology (MA). *Accreditation:* APA (one or more programs are accredited). *Degree requirements:* For master's, variable foreign language requirement, thesis, oral exams; for doctorate, 2 foreign languages, comprehensive exam, thesis/dissertation, oral exams. *Entrance requirements:* For master's and doctorate, GRE General Test.

Western New England College, School of Arts and Sciences, Program in Behavior Analysis, Springfield, MA 01119. Offers PhD. *Entrance requirements:* For doctorate, GRE, master's degree in behavior analysis with minimum GPA of 3.6.

Western Washington University, Graduate School, College of Humanities and Social Sciences, Department of Psychology, Bellingham, WA 98225-5996. Offers experimental psychology (MS); mental health counseling (MS); school counseling (M Ed). *Accreditation:* ACA (one or more programs are accredited). *Degree requirements:* For master's, comprehensive exam, thesis (for some programs). *Entrance requirements:* For master's, GRE General Test, minimum GPA of 3.0 in last 60 semester hours or last 90 quarter hours. Additional exam requirements/recommendations for international students: Required—TOEFL (minimum score 567 paper-based; 227 computer-based). *Faculty research:* Social, cognitive, behavioral neuroscience, counseling/clinical, developmental.

Westfield State College, Division of Graduate and Continuing Education, Department of Psychology, Westfield, MA 01086. Offers applied behavior analysis (MA); mental health counseling (MA); school guidance (MA). Part-time and evening/weekend programs available. *Faculty:* 9 part-time/adjunct (6 women). *Students:* 13 full-time (12 women), 17 part-time (13 women). Average age 37. In 2008, 13 master's awarded. *Degree requirements:* For master's, comprehensive exam. *Entrance requirements:* For master's, GRE General Test, MAT, minimum undergraduate GPA of 2.7. *Application deadline:* Applications are processed on a rolling basis. Application fee: $30. *Financial support:* In 2008–09, 5 research assistantships (averaging $1,600 per year) were awarded; teaching assistantships, career-related internships or fieldwork, Federal Work-Study, and tuition waivers (full and partial) also available. Support available to part-time students. Financial award application deadline: 4/1; financial award applicants required to submit CSS PROFILE. *Unit head:* Dr. Ricki Kantrowitz, Director, 413-572-5378. *Application contact:* Michelle Janke, Admissions Coordinator, 413-572-8022, Fax: 413-572-5227, E-mail: mjanke@wsc.ma.edu.

West Texas A&M University, College of Education and Social Sciences, Department of Behavioral Sciences, Canyon, TX 79016-0001. Offers psychology (MA). Part-time and evening/weekend programs available. *Degree requirements:* For master's, comprehensive exam, thesis optional. *Entrance requirements:* For master's, GRE General Test, 3 letters of recommendation; interview; minimum GPA of 3.25 in psychology, 3.0 overall. Additional exam requirements/recommendations for international students: Required—TOEFL (minimum score 550 paper-based). Electronic applications accepted. *Faculty research:* Application of sociological principles to historical and contemporary analyses of social systems.

West Virginia University, Eberly College of Arts and Sciences, Department of Psychology, Morgantown, WV 26506. Offers behavior analysis (PhD); clinical psychology (MA, PhD); development psychology (PhD); psychology (MS). *Accreditation:* APA (one or more programs are accredited). Part-time programs available. Terminal master's awarded for partial completion of doctoral program. *Degree requirements:* For master's, thesis optional; for doctorate, comprehensive exam, thesis/dissertation. *Entrance requirements:* For master's and doctorate, GRE General Test, minimum GPA of 3.0. Additional exam requirements/recommendations for international students: Required—TOEFL. *Faculty research:* Adult and child clinical psychology, behavioral assessment and therapy, child and adolescent behavior, life span development, experimental and applied behavior analysis.

Wheaton College, Graduate School, Department of Psychology, Wheaton, IL 60187-5593. Offers clinical psychology (MA, Psy D); counseling ministries (MA). *Accreditation:* APA (one or more programs are accredited). Terminal master's awarded for partial completion of doctoral program. *Degree requirements:* For master's, thesis or alternative; for doctorate, thesis/dissertation, internship. *Entrance requirements:* For master's, GRE General Test, 18 hours of course work in psychology; for doctorate, GRE General Test.

Wichita State University, Graduate School, Fairmount College of Liberal Arts and Sciences, Department of Psychology, Wichita, KS 67260. Offers community/clinical psychology (PhD); human factors (PhD); psychology (MA). *Accreditation:* APA. Part-time programs available. *Degree requirements:* For doctorate, thesis/dissertation. *Entrance requirements:* For doctorate, GRE. Additional exam requirements/recommendations for international students: Required—TOEFL. Electronic applications accepted. *Faculty research:* Behavioral evolution, women and alcohol, behavioral medicine, delinquency prevention.

Widener University, School of Human Service Professions, Institute for Graduate Clinical Psychology, Law-Psychology Program, Chester, PA 19013-5792. Offers JD/Psy D. *Faculty:* 15 full-time (6 women), 18 part-time/adjunct (10 women). *Students:* 13 full-time (9 women); includes 2 minority (1 American Indian/Alaska Native, 1 Asian American or Pacific Islander). Average age 23. 21 applicants, 19% accepted. *Application deadline:* For fall admission, 2/1 for domestic students. Applications are processed on a rolling basis. Application fee: $60. Electronic applications accepted. *Financial support:* In 2008–09, 12 students received support; research assistantships, career-related internships or fieldwork, Federal Work-Study, institutionally sponsored loans, and scholarships/grants available. Financial award application deadline: 5/31. *Unit head:* Dr. Amiram Elwork, Director, 610-499-1206, Fax: 610-499-4625, E-mail: amiram.elwork@widener.edu. *Application contact:* Maureen A. Brennan, Admissions Coordinator, 610-499-1206, Fax: 610-499-4625, E-mail: maureen.a.brennan@widener.edu.

See Close-Up on page 1153.

Wilfrid Laurier University, Faculty of Graduate Studies, Faculty of Science, Department of Psychology, Waterloo, ON N2L 3C5, Canada. Offers brain and cognition (M Sc, PhD); community psychology (MA, PhD); social and developmental psychology (MA, PhD). *Degree requirements:* For master's, thesis; for doctorate, thesis/dissertation. *Entrance requirements:* For master's, honors BA or the equivalent in psychology, minimum B average in undergraduate course work, GRE (General Test); for doctorate, master's degree, minimum A- average, GRE (General Test). Additional exam requirements/recommendations for international students: Required—TOEFL (minimum score 230 computer-based; 89 iBT). Electronic applications accepted. *Faculty research:* Brain and cognition, community psychology, social and developmental psychology.

William Carey University, School of Psychology and Counseling, Hattiesburg, MS 39401-5499. Offers counseling psychology (MS). Part-time programs available. *Entrance requirements:* For master's, GRE, PRAXIS, MAT, minimum GPA of 2.5. Additional exam requirements/recommendations for international students: Required—TOEFL (minimum score 550 paper-based; 213 computer-based). *Expenses:* Contact institution. *Faculty research:* Addiction prevention, psychometric measurement, crisis counseling, gerontology.

Winthrop University, College of Arts and Sciences, Department of Psychology, Rock Hill, SC 29733. Offers MS, SSP. *Degree requirements:* For master's and SSP, comprehensive exam. *Entrance requirements:* For master's, GRE General Test, interview, minimum GPA of 3.0, 3 letters of recommendation, 15 hours of psychology courses in specified subject areas. Electronic applications accepted.

Wisconsin School of Professional Psychology, Program in Clinical Psychology, Milwaukee, WI 53225-4960. Offers MA, Psy D. *Accreditation:* APA. Part-time and evening/weekend programs available. Terminal master's awarded for partial completion of doctoral program. *Degree requirements:* For master's, candidacy exam, 500 hours of supervised clinical practica; for doctorate, thesis/dissertation, 1 year clinical intern and practicum experience (2000 hrs), candidacy and clinical exams. *Entrance requirements:* For master's, GRE General Test, GRE Subject Test, bachelor's degree in psychology, writing sample; for doctorate, GRE General Test, GRE Subject Test, master's degree in clinical psychology or equivalent, writing sample. *Faculty research:* Violence prevention, psychology of women, forensic psychology, custody evaluation, aging, harm reduction in AODA.

Wright Institute, Program in Clinical Psychology, Berkeley, CA 94704-1796. Offers Psy D. *Accreditation:* APA. *Degree requirements:* For doctorate, thesis/dissertation. *Entrance requirements:* Additional exam requirements/recommendations for international students: Required—TOEFL (minimum score 600 paper-based). Electronic applications accepted.

Psychology—General

Wright State University, School of Graduate Studies, College of Liberal Arts, Program in Applied Behavioral Science, Dayton, OH 45435. Offers criminal justice and social problems (MA); international and comparative politics (MA). *Degree requirements:* For master's, thesis optional. *Entrance requirements:* Additional exam requirements/recommendations for international students: Required—TOEFL. *Faculty research:* Training and development, criminal justice and social problems, community systems, human factors, industrial/organizational psychology.

Wright State University, School of Graduate Studies, College of Science and Mathematics, Department of Psychology, Dayton, OH 45435. Offers human factors and industrial/organizational psychology (MS, PhD). *Degree requirements:* For master's, thesis; for doctorate, thesis/dissertation. *Entrance requirements:* For master's, GRE General Test. Additional exam requirements/recommendations for international students: Required—TOEFL.

Wright State University, School of Professional Psychology, Dayton, OH 45435. Offers clinical psychology (Psy D). *Accreditation:* APA. *Degree requirements:* For doctorate, thesis/dissertation. *Entrance requirements:* For doctorate, GRE General Test, GRE Subject Test. Additional exam requirements/recommendations for international students: Required—TOEFL. *Expenses:* Contact institution.

Xavier University, College of Social Sciences, Health and Education, Department of Psychology, Cincinnati, OH 45207. Offers clinical psychology (Psy D); psychology (MA), including general experimental, industrial-organizational. *Accreditation:* APA (one or more programs are accredited). *Faculty:* 16 full-time (8 women), 5 part-time/adjunct (3 women). *Students:* 83 full-time (61 women), 30 part-time (22 women); includes 8 minority (4 African Americans, 4 Asian Americans or Pacific Islanders), 2 international. Average age 27. 242 applicants, 31% accepted, 25 enrolled. In 2008, 27 master's, 12 doctorates awarded. *Degree requirements:* For master's, comprehensive exam, thesis, internship; for doctorate, comprehensive exam, thesis/dissertation, internship. *Entrance requirements:* For master's and doctorate, GRE.

Additional exam requirements/recommendations for international students: Required—TOEFL. *Application deadline:* For fall admission, 1/15 for domestic and international students. Application fee: $35. Electronic applications accepted. *Expenses:* Contact institution. *Financial support:* In 2008–09, 57 students received support, including 39 research assistantships with partial tuition reimbursements available, 18 teaching assistantships with partial tuition reimbursements available. Financial award application deadline: 3/1; financial award applicants required to submit FAFSA. *Unit head:* Dr. Christine M. Dacey, Chair, 513-745-3533, Fax: 513-745-3327, E-mail: dacey@xavier.edu. *Application contact:* Margaret Maybury, Assistant Director, Enrollment and Student Services, 513-745-1053, Fax: 513-745-3347, E-mail: maybury@xavier.edu.

Yale University, Graduate School of Arts and Sciences, Department of Psychology, New Haven, CT 06520. Offers behavioral neuroscience (PhD); clinical psychology (PhD); cognitive psychology (PhD); developmental psychology (PhD); social/personality psychology (PhD). *Accreditation:* APA. *Degree requirements:* For doctorate, thesis/dissertation. *Entrance requirements:* For doctorate, GRE General Test.

Yeshiva University, Ferkauf Graduate School of Psychology, New York, NY 10033-3201. Offers MA, PhD, Psy D. *Accreditation:* APA (one or more programs are accredited). Part-time programs available. *Degree requirements:* For doctorate, comprehensive exam, thesis/dissertation. *Entrance requirements:* For master's and doctorate, GRE General Test.

York University, Faculty of Graduate Studies, Faculty of Health, Program in Psychology, Toronto, ON M3J 1P3, Canada. Offers MA, PhD. *Accreditation:* APA (one or more programs are accredited). Part-time programs available. *Degree requirements:* For master's, thesis, practicum; for doctorate, thesis/dissertation, practicum. *Entrance requirements:* For master's, GRE. Electronic applications accepted.

Youngstown State University, Graduate School, College of Liberal Arts and Social Sciences, Department of Psychology, Youngstown, OH 44555-0001. Offers applied behavior analysis (MS).

Addictions/Substance Abuse Counseling

Adler School of Professional Psychology, Programs in Psychology, Chicago, IL 60601-7203. Offers art therapy (Certificate); clinical hypnosis (Certificate); clinical psychology (Psy D); counseling psychology (MACP); counseling psychology/art therapy (MACAT); gerontology (MAGP); marriage and family counseling (MAMFC); marriage and family therapy (Certificate); organizational psychology (MAO); substance abuse counseling (MASAC, Certificate); Psy D/Certificate; Psy D/MACAT; Psy D/MACP; Psy D/MAMFC; Psy D/MASAC. *Accreditation:* APA. Part-time and evening/weekend programs available. Postbaccalaureate distance learning degree programs offered (minimal on-campus study). *Faculty:* 36 full-time (17 women), 45 part-time/adjunct (18 women). *Students:* 514 full-time (404 women), 128 part-time (100 women); includes 147 minority (69 African Americans, 2 American Indian/Alaska Native, 30 Asian Americans or Pacific Islanders, 46 Hispanic Americans), 53 international. Average age 27. 855 applicants, 46% accepted, 195 enrolled. In 2008, 110 master's, 136 doctorates awarded. Terminal master's awarded for partial completion of doctoral program. *Degree requirements:* For master's, thesis or alternative, oral exam, practicum; for doctorate, thesis/dissertation, clinical exam, internship, oral exam, practicum, written qualifying exam. *Entrance requirements:* For master's, 12 semester hours in psychology, minimum GPA of 3.0; for doctorate, 18 semester hours in psychology, minimum GPA of 3.25; for Certificate, appropriate master's or doctoral degree. Additional exam requirements/recommendations for international students: Required—TOEFL (minimum score 550 paper-based; 213 computer-based; 79 iBT). *Application deadline:* For fall admission, 2/15 priority date for domestic students, 12/1 priority date for international students. Applications are processed on a rolling basis. Application fee: $50. Electronic applications accepted. *Expenses:* Tuition: Part-time $850 per credit. Tuition and fees vary according to degree level, campus/location and program. *Financial support:* Career-related internships or fieldwork, Federal Work-Study, scholarships/grants, and tuition waivers (full and partial) available. Support available to part-time students. Financial award application deadline: 5/15; financial award applicants required to submit FAFSA. *Unit head:* Dr. Frank Gruba-McAllister, Vice President of Academic Affairs, 312-201-5900, Fax: 312-207-5917. *Application contact:* Craig A Hines, Director of Admissions, 312-201-5900 Ext. 226, Fax: 312-201-5917, E-mail: chines@adler.edu.

See Close-Up on page 1051.

Alliant International University–Los Angeles, California School of Professional Psychology, Program in Marital and Family Therapy, Alhambra, CA 91803-1360. Offers biofeedback (MA); chemical dependency (MA); gerontology (MA); Latin American family therapy (MA). *Accreditation:* AAMFT/COAMFTE.

See Close-Up on page 1061.

Argosy University, Hawai'i, College of Psychology and Behavioral Sciences, Program in Substance Abuse Counseling, Honolulu, HI 96813. Offers Certificate.

See Close-Up on page 1073.

Cambridge College, School of Psychology and Counseling, Cambridge, MA 02138-5304. Offers addiction counseling (M Ed); counseling psychology (M Ed); counseling psychology: forensic counseling (M Ed); marriage and family therapy (M Ed); mental health and addiction counseling (M Ed); mental health counseling (M Ed); mental health counseling for school guidance counselors (Certificate); mental health, addiction and school adjustment counseling (M Ed); psychological studies (M Ed); school adjustment counseling (M Ed); school guidance counseling (M Ed). Part-time and evening/weekend programs available. *Faculty:* 5 full-time (2 women), 183 part-time/adjunct (85 women). *Students:* 476 full-time (384 women), 313 part-time (245 women); includes 396 minority (300 African Americans, 2 American Indian/Alaska Native, 13 Asian Americans or Pacific Islanders, 81 Hispanic Americans), 13 international. Average age 37. 307 applicants, 81% accepted, 192 enrolled. In 2008, 226 master's, 9 CAGSs awarded. *Degree requirements:* For master's, thesis, practicum/internship; for other advanced degree, thesis, practicum/internship. *Entrance requirements:* For master's, evidence of a bachelor's degree from an accredited institution; essay; 2 references; health insurance; for other advanced degree, evidence of a master's degree from an accredited institution; essay; 2 references; health insurance. Additional exam requirements/recommendations for international students: Required—TOEFL (minimum score 550 paper-based; 213 computer-based; 79 iBT). *Application deadline:* Applications are processed on a rolling basis. Application fee: $30. Electronic applications accepted. *Expenses:* Tuition: Full-time $6960; part-time $435 per credit. One-time fee: $140 full-time. Tuition and fees vary according to degree level, campus/location and program. *Financial support:* In 2008–09, 857 students received support. Career-related internships or fieldwork, Federal Work-Study, and scholarships/grants available. Financial award applicants required to submit FAFSA. *Unit head:* Dr. Niti Seth, EdD, Dean, 617-873-0208, Fax: 617-349-3545, E-mail: nseth@cambridgecollege.edu. *Application contact:* Kathryn Lenehan, Admission Counselor, 800-877-0280, E-mail: kathryn.lenehan@cambridgecollege.edu.

Capella University, School of Human Services, Minneapolis, MN 55402. Offers addictions counseling (Certificate); counseling studies (MS, PhD); criminal justice (MS, PhD, Certificate); diversity studies (Certificate); general human services (MS, PhD); health care administration (MS, PhD, Certificate); management of nonprofit agencies (MS, PhD, Certificate); marital, couple and family counseling/therapy (MS); marriage and family services (Certificate); mental

health counseling (MS); professional counseling (Certificate); social and community services (MS, PhD, Certificate). Part-time and evening/weekend programs available. Postbaccalaureate distance learning degree programs offered (minimal on-campus study). Terminal master's awarded for partial completion of doctoral program. *Degree requirements:* For master's, thesis optional, integrative project; for doctorate, comprehensive exam, thesis/dissertation. *Entrance requirements:* Additional exam requirements/recommendations for international students: Required—TOEFL (minimum score 550 paper-based; 213 computer-based), TWE (minimum score 4). Electronic applications accepted. *Faculty research:* Compulsive and addictive behaviors, substance abuse, assessment of psychopathology and neuropsychology.

Cleveland State University, College of Graduate Studies, College of Education and Human Services, Department of Counseling, Administration, Supervision and Adult Learning (CASAL), Cleveland, OH 44115. Offers accelerated degree in adult learning and development (M Ed); adult learning and development (M Ed); chemical dependency counseling (Certificate); community agency counseling (M Ed); counseling and pupil personnel administration (Ed S); early childhood mental health counseling (Certificate); educational administration and supervision (M Ed); school administration (Ed S); school counseling (M Ed). *Accreditation:* ACA (one or more programs are accredited). Part-time and evening/weekend programs available. *Faculty:* 16 full-time (10 women), 8 part-time/adjunct (4 women). *Students:* 62 full-time (54 women), 351 part-time (274 women); includes 146 minority (127 African Americans, 3 Asian Americans or Pacific Islanders, 16 Hispanic Americans), 2 international. Average age 35. 235 applicants, 56% accepted, 104 enrolled. In 2008, 138 master's, 10 Certificates awarded. *Degree requirements:* For master's, comprehensive exam (for some programs), thesis optional; for other advanced degree, comprehensive exam, thesis optional, internship. *Entrance requirements:* For master's, GRE General Test or MAT, letter of recommendation, minimum GPA of 2.75. Additional exam requirements/recommendations for international students: Required—TOEFL (minimum score 525 paper-based; 197 computer-based), IELTS (minimum score 6). *Application deadline:* For fall admission, 6/21 for domestic students, 5/15 for international students; for spring admission, 8/31 for domestic students, 11/1 for international students. Application fee: $30. Electronic applications accepted. *Financial support:* In 2008–09, 8 students received support, including research assistantships with full and partial tuition reimbursements available (averaging $3,287 per year), teaching assistantships with full and partial tuition reimbursements available (averaging $3,480 per year); career-related internships or fieldwork, scholarships/grants, tuition waivers (full), and unspecified assistantships also available. Support available to part-time students. *Faculty research:* Education law, career development, women in school administration, psychopharmacology, counseling and spirituality. Total annual research expenditures: $478,265. *Unit head:* Dr. Ann L Bauer, Chairperson, 216-687-4582, Fax: 216-687-5378, E-mail: a.l.bauer@csuohio.edu. *Application contact:* Deborah L Brown, Interim Assistant Director, Graduate Admissions, 216-523-7572, Fax: 216-687-5400, E-mail: d.l.brown@csuohio.edu.

The College of New Jersey, Graduate Division, School of Education, Department of Counselor Education, Program in Community Counseling: Substance Abuse and Addiction Specialization, Ewing, NJ 08628. Offers MA, Certificate. *Degree requirements:* For master's, comprehensive exam. *Entrance requirements:* For master's, GRE, minimum GPA of 3.0 in field or 2.75 overall; for Certificate, M Ed. Additional exam requirements/recommendations for international students: Required—TOEFL. Electronic applications accepted.

College of St. Joseph, Graduate Programs, Division of Psychology and Human Services, Program in Alcohol and Substance Abuse Counseling, Rutland, VT 05701-3899. Offers MS. Part-time programs available. *Entrance requirements:* For master's, 2 letters of reference, interview. Electronic applications accepted.

The College of William and Mary, School of Education, Program in Counselor Education, Williamsburg, VA 23187-8795. Offers community and addictions counseling (M Ed); community counseling (M Ed); counselor education (PhD); family counseling (M Ed); school counseling (M Ed). *Accreditation:* ACA; NCATE. Part-time and evening/weekend programs available. *Degree requirements:* For doctorate, comprehensive exam, thesis/dissertation. *Entrance requirements:* For master's, GRE, minimum GPA of 2.5; for doctorate, GRE, minimum GPA of 3.5. Additional exam requirements/recommendations for international students: Required—TOEFL. Electronic applications accepted. *Expenses:* Tuition, state resident: full-time $6400; part-time $300 per credit hour. Tuition, nonresident: full-time $19,720; part-time $800 per credit hour. International tuition: $19,720 full-time. Required fees: $3860. *Faculty research:* Sexuality, multicultural education, substance abuse, transpersonal psychology.

Coppin State University, Division of Graduate Studies, Division of Arts and Sciences, Department of Applied Psychology and Rehabilitation Counseling, Program in Alcohol and Substance Abuse Counseling, Baltimore, MD 21216-3698. Offers MS. Part-time programs available. *Degree requirements:* For master's, comprehensive exam (for some programs), thesis optional, internship, clinical requirement. *Entrance requirements:* For master's, GRE General Test, interview, minimum GPA of 3.0.

East Carolina University, Graduate School, School of Allied Health Sciences, Program in Rehabilitation Studies, Greenville, NC 27858-4353. Offers rehabilitation counseling (MS);

substance abuse and clinical counseling (MS); vocational evaluation (MS). *Accreditation:* CORE. Part-time and evening/weekend programs available. *Degree requirements:* For master's, comprehensive exam, thesis or alternative, internship. *Entrance requirements:* For master's, GRE General Test or MAT. Additional exam requirements/recommendations for international students: Required—TOEFL.

Eastern Michigan University, Graduate School, College of Health and Human Services, School of Social Work, Ypsilanti, MI 48197. Offers family and children's services (MSW); gerontology (Graduate Certificate); gerontology-dementia (Graduate Certificate); mental health and chemical dependency (MSW); services to the aging (MSW). *Accreditation:* CSWE. Part-time and evening/weekend programs available. Postbaccalaureate distance learning degree programs offered (minimal on-campus study). *Entrance requirements:* Additional exam requirements/ recommendations for international students: Required—TOEFL.

Governors State University, College of Health Professions, Program in Addictions Studies, University Park, IL 60466-0975. Offers MHS. Part-time and evening/weekend programs available. *Degree requirements:* For master's, comprehensive exam, thesis or alternative, internship. *Entrance requirements:* For master's, minimum undergraduate GPA of 2.5; 9 hours of course work in behavioral sciences; 6 hours of course work in biological sciences or chemistry, statistics or research methods.

Grand Canyon University, College of Nursing and Health Sciences, Phoenix, AZ 85017-1097. Offers addiction counseling (MS); nursing (MS), including adult clinical nurse specialist, family nurse practitioner, nursing education, nursing leadership in health care system; professional counseling (MS). Part-time and evening/weekend programs available. Postbaccalaureate distance learning degree programs offered (no on-campus study). *Faculty:* 21 full-time (16 women), 224 part-time/adjunct (164 women). *Students:* 87 full-time (72 women), 783 part-time (665 women); includes 123 minority (71 African Americans, 6 American Indian/Alaska Native, 13 Asian Americans or Pacific Islanders, 33 Hispanic Americans), 5 international. Average age 44. In 2008, 151 master's awarded. *Entrance requirements:* Additional exam requirements/ recommendations for international students: Required—TOEFL (minimum score 575 paper-based; 233 computer-based; 90 iBT), IELTS (minimum score 7). *Application deadline:* For fall admission, 8/21 for domestic students, 7/2 for international students; for spring admission, 12/24 for domestic students, 11/1 for international students. Application fee: $100. *Financial support:* Federal Work-Study available. Support available to part-time students. Financial award applicants required to submit FAFSA. *Unit head:* Dr. Fran Roberts, Vice President, 602-639-6163, E-mail: froberts@gcu.edu. *Application contact:* Andrea Wolochuk, Information Contact, 602-639-6429, E-mail: awolochuk@gcu.edu.

Hazelden Graduate School of Addiction Studies, Graduate Programs, Center City, MN 55012. Offers addiction counseling (MA, Certificate). Part-time programs available. *Entrance requirements:* Additional exam requirements/recommendations for international students: Required—TOEFL.

Indiana University–Purdue University Indianapolis, School of Science, Department of Psychology, Psychobiology of Addictions Program, Indianapolis, IN 46202-2896. Offers MS, PhD. *Entrance requirements:* For master's, GRE General Test, minimum undergraduate GPA of 3.2. *Faculty research:* Behavioral genetics, behavior pharmacology, animal models, developmental psychology, neurobehavioral toxicology, neuropsychology of learning and memory, animal models of fetal alcohol syndrome.

Indiana Wesleyan University, College of Graduate Studies, Graduate Studies in Counseling, Marion, IN 46953. Offers addictions counseling (MS); community counseling (MS); marriage and family counseling (MS); school counseling (MS). *Accreditation:* ACA. Part-time programs available. *Faculty:* 7 full-time (4 women), 6 part-time/adjunct (3 women). *Students:* 60 full-time (46 women), 47 part-time (38 women); includes 4 minority (all African Americans). Average age 36. In 2008, 26 master's awarded. *Degree requirements:* For master's, thesis or alternative. *Entrance requirements:* For master's, GRE General Test. Additional exam requirements/ recommendations for international students: Required—TOEFL. *Application deadline:* For fall admission, 6/14 priority date for domestic students. Application fee: $25. Electronic applications accepted. *Expenses:* Contact institution. *Financial support:* In 2008–09, 1 research assistantship with partial tuition reimbursement, 1 teaching assistantship with partial tuition reimbursement were awarded. Support available to part-time students. Financial award application deadline: 3/1; financial award applicants required to submit FAFSA. *Faculty research:* Community counseling, multicultural counseling, addictions. *Unit head:* Dr. Mark Gerig, Director of Graduate Counseling Studies, 765-677-2995, Fax: 765-677-1456, E-mail: mark.gerig@indwes.edu. *Application contact:* Tom Leas, Director of Adult Enrollment Services, 800-895-0036, Fax: 765-677-2404, E-mail: graduate@indwes.edu.

The Johns Hopkins University, Bloomberg School of Public Health, Department of Mental Health, Baltimore, MD 21218-2699. Offers children's mental health services (PhD); drug dependence epidemiology (PhD); mental health (MHS); psychiatric epidemiology (PhD). *Degree requirements:* For master's, thesis (for some programs); for doctorate, thesis/dissertation, 1 year full-time residency, oral and written exams. *Entrance requirements:* For master's, GRE General Test, MCAT, 3 letters of recommendation, curriculum vitae; for doctorate, GRE General Test, MCAT or GMAT, 3 letters of recommendation, curriculum vitae. Additional exam requirements/recommendations for international students: Required—TOEFL (minimum score 550 paper-based; 250 computer-based). Electronic applications accepted. *Faculty research:* Etiology, development and prevention of aggressive and antisocial behavior; epidemiology of mental disorders; genetic epidemiology of mental disorders.

The Johns Hopkins University, School of Education, Department of Counseling and Human Services, Baltimore, MD 21218-2699. Offers addictions counseling (Certificate); clinical community counseling (Certificate); clinical supervision (Certificate); contemporary trauma (Certificate); counseling (MS, CAGS); counseling at-risk youth (Certificate); organizational counseling (Certificate); play therapy (Certificate); spiritual and existential counseling and therapy (Certificate). Part-time and evening/weekend programs available. *Entrance requirements:* For master's, minimum GPA of 3.0, interview, resumé, letters of recommendation; for other advanced degree, master's or doctoral degree, interview, resumé, minimum GPA of 3.0, letters of recommendation. Additional exam requirements/recommendations for international students: Required—TOEFL (minimum score 600 paper-based; 250 computer-based; 100 iBT).

Kean University, College of Education, Program in Counselor Education, Union, NJ 07083. Offers alcohol and drug abuse counseling (MA); business and industry counseling (MA); community/agency counseling (MA); school counseling (MA). *Accreditation:* ACA; NCATE. Part-time programs available. *Faculty:* 6 full-time (3 women). *Students:* 48 full-time (41 women), 188 part-time (165 women); includes 41 African Americans, 1 Asian American or Pacific Islander, 22 Hispanic Americans. Average age 31. 120 applicants, 77% accepted, 58 enrolled. In 2008, 38 master's awarded. *Degree requirements:* For master's, comprehensive exam, thesis, practicum, internship. *Entrance requirements:* For master's, GRE General Test or MAT, minimum GPA of 3.0, 2 letters of recommendation, interview, initial teacher certification (school counseling). *Application deadline:* For fall admission, 5/1 for domestic students; for spring admission, 11/1 for domestic students. Application fee: $60 ($150 for international students). Electronic applications accepted. *Expenses:* Tuition, state resident: full-time $10,128; part-time $422 per credit. Tuition, nonresident: full-time $13,728; part-time $572 per credit. Required fees: $2570; $107 per credit. Part-time tuition and fees vary according to course load, degree level and program. *Financial support:* In 2008–09, 6 research assistantships with full tuition reimbursements (averaging $3,217 per year) were awarded; unspecified assistantships also available. *Unit head:* Dr. J. Barry Mascari, Coordinator, 908-737-3850, E-mail: jmascari@kean.edu. *Application contact:* Steven Koch, Pre-Admissions Coordinator, 908-737-4723, Fax: 908-737-5965, E-mail: grad-adm@kean.edu.

Lewis & Clark College, Graduate School of Education and Counseling, Department of Counseling Psychology, Program in Addictions Treatment, Portland, OR 97219-7899. Offers MA. Part-time and evening/weekend programs available. *Entrance requirements:* For master's, GRE General Test, minimum undergraduate GPA of 2.75. Additional exam requirements/ recommendations for international students: Required—TOEFL (minimum score 575 paper-based; 233 computer-based). Electronic applications accepted.

Maryville University of Saint Louis, School of Health Professions, Program in Rehabilitation Counseling, St. Louis, MO 63141-7299. Offers marriage and family therapy (MARC); music therapy (MARC); substance abuse (MARC). *Accreditation:* CORE. Part-time and evening/ weekend programs available. *Students:* 45. In 2008, 17 master's awarded. *Degree requirements:* For master's, internship, seminar. *Entrance requirements:* For master's, minimum cumulative GPA of 3.0, 2 letters of recommendation, interview. Additional exam requirements/ recommendations for international students: Required—TOEFL (minimum score 550 paper-based). *Application deadline:* For fall admission, 1/15 for domestic students; for spring admission, 10/1 for domestic students. Application fee: $40. Electronic applications accepted. *Expenses:* Tuition: Full-time $19,650; part-time $605 per credit hour. Required fees: $100 per semester. Part-time tuition and fees vary according to degree level and program. *Financial support:* Career-related internships or fieldwork, Federal Work-Study, and campus employment available. Financial award application deadline: 7/31. *Unit head:* Barbara Parker, Director, 314-529-9437, E-mail: bparker@maryville.edu. *Application contact:* Barbara Parker, Director, 314-529-9437, E-mail: bparker@maryville.edu.

Marywood University, Academic Affairs, College of Education and Human Development, Department of Psychology and Counseling, Program in Mental Health Counseling, Scranton, PA 18509-1598. Offers addiction (MA); general (MA); pastoral (MA). *Accreditation:* ACA.

McNeese State University, Doré School of Graduate Studies, Burton College of Education, Department of Psychology, Lake Charles, LA 70609. Offers addiction treatment (MA); applied behavior analysis (MA); counseling psychology (MA); general/experimental psychology (MA). Evening/weekend programs available. *Faculty:* 6 full-time (3 women), 1 (woman) part-time/ adjunct. *Students:* 40 full-time (27 women), 23 part-time (17 women); includes 8 minority (7 African Americans, 1 Asian American or Pacific Islander), 4 international. In 2008, 12 master's awarded. *Entrance requirements:* For master's, GRE. *Application deadline:* For fall admission, 5/15 priority date for domestic and international students; for spring admission, 10/15 priority date for domestic and international students. Applications are processed on a rolling basis. Application fee: $20 ($30 for international students). *Expenses:* Tuition, area resident: Full-time $2386. Tuition, state resident: full-time $2386. Required fees: $885. Tuition and fees vary according to course load. *Financial support:* Application deadline: 5/1. *Unit head:* Dr. Dena L. Matzenbacher, Head, 337-475-5457, Fax: 337-562-4115, E-mail: dena@mcneese.edu. *Application contact:* Dr. George F. Mead, Interim Dean of Dore' School of Graduate Studies, 337-475-5396, Fax: 337-475-5397, E-mail: admissions@mcneese.edu.

Mercy College, School of Social and Behavioral Sciences, Program in Counseling, Dobbs Ferry, NY 10522-1189. Offers alcohol and substance abuse counseling (Certificate); counseling (MS); retirement counseling (Certificate). Part-time and evening/weekend programs available. Postbaccalaureate distance learning degree programs offered (no on-campus study). *Students:* 121 full-time (106 women), 200 part-time (170 women); includes 113 minority (98 African Americans, 1 American Indian/Alaska Native, 4 Asian Americans or Pacific Islanders, 10 Hispanic Americans), 1 international. Average age 35. 169 applicants, 47% accepted, 52 enrolled. In 2008, 66 master's awarded. *Degree requirements:* For master's, comprehensive exam. *Entrance requirements:* For master's, interview, two professional letters of recommendation, minimum undergraduate GPA of 3.0, resumé. Additional exam requirements/ recommendations for international students: Required—TOEFL (minimum score 600 paper-based; 250 computer-based; 100 iBT). *Application deadline:* For fall admission, 8/1 for international students. Applications are processed on a rolling basis. Application fee: $40. Electronic applications accepted. *Expenses:* Tuition: Full-time $12,330; part-time $685 per credit. Required fees: $240; $120 per semester. Tuition and fees vary according to program. *Financial support:* In 2008–09, 92 students received support. Career-related internships or fieldwork, Federal Work-Study, scholarships/grants, and unspecified assistantships available. Support available to part-time students. Financial award applicants required to submit FAFSA. *Faculty research:* Ethics, drug abuse problems, human development, domestic violence. *Unit head:* Dr. Fernando Cabrera, Assistant Professor, Psychology and Behavioral Science, 914-674-7334, E-mail: fcabrera@mercy.edu. *Application contact:* Dr. Fernando Cabrera, Assistant Professor, Psychology and Behavioral Science, 914-674-7334, E-mail: fcabrera@mercy.edu.

Monmouth University, Graduate School, The Marjorie K. Unterberg School of Nursing and Health Studies, West Long Branch, NJ 07764-1898. Offers advanced practice nursing (Post-Master's Certificate); nursing (MSN); school nursing (Certificate); substance awareness coordinator (Certificate). *Accreditation:* AACN. Part-time and evening/weekend programs available. *Faculty:* 11 full-time (all women), 2 part-time/adjunct (both women). *Students:* 8 full-time (all women), 211 part-time (206 women); includes 47 minority (10 African Americans, 1 American Indian/Alaska Native, 29 Asian Americans or Pacific Islanders, 7 Hispanic Americans), 1 international. Average age 44. 113 applicants, 100% accepted, 62 enrolled. In 2008, 36 master's awarded. *Degree requirements:* For master's, 39-45 credits, practicum (for some tracks). *Entrance requirements:* For master's, GRE General Test, RN license, 1 year of work experience, minimum undergraduate GPA of 2.75. Additional exam requirements/ recommendations for international students: Required—TOEFL (minimum score 550 paper-based; 213 computer-based; 79 iBT), IELTS (minimum score 5), Michigan English Language Assessment Battery (minimum score: 77), Cambridge A, B, C. *Application deadline:* For fall admission, 7/15 priority date for domestic students, 6/1 for international students; for spring admission, 11/15 priority date for domestic students, 11/1 for international students. Applications are processed on a rolling basis. Application fee: $50. Electronic applications accepted. *Expenses:* Tuition: Full-time $13,914; part-time $773 per credit. Required fees: $628; $157 per semester. *Financial support:* In 2008–09, 113 students received support, including 113 fellowships (averaging $1,340 per year), 3 research assistantships (averaging $5,136 per year); career-related internships or fieldwork, scholarships/grants, tuition waivers (partial), and unspecified assistantships also available. Support available to part-time students. Financial award application deadline: 3/1; financial award applicants required to submit FAFSA. *Faculty research:* Relationship of undergraduate GPA and GRE to succeed in a graduate nursing program. *Unit head:* Dr. Janet Mahoney, Director, 732-571-3443, Fax: 732-263-5131, E-mail: jmahoney@monmouth.edu. *Application contact:* Kevin Roane, Director, Office of Graduate Admission, 732-571-3452, Fax: 732-263-5123, E-mail: gradadm@monmouth.edu.

Montclair State University, The Office of Graduate Admissions and Support Services, College of Education and Human Services, Department of Counseling, Human Development, and Educational Leadership, Montclair, NJ 07043-1624. Offers administration and supervision (MA), including administration and supervision, educator/trainer; advanced counseling (Certificate); counseling and guidance (MA), including addictions counseling, community counseling, student affairs; counselor education (PhD); principal (Certificate); school administrator (Certificate); school business administrator (Certificate); school counselor (Certificate); substance awareness coordinator (Certificate). *Accreditation:* NCATE. Part-time and evening/weekend programs available. *Faculty:* 18 full-time (12 women), 16 part-time/adjunct (10 women). *Students:* 134 full-time (109 women), 422 part-time (299 women); includes 86 minority (48 African Americans, 8 Asian Americans or Pacific Islanders, 30 Hispanic Americans), 4 international. Average age 31. 164 applicants, 55% accepted, 74 enrolled. In 2008, 115 master's awarded. *Degree requirements:* For master's, comprehensive exam, thesis or alternative; for doctorate, comprehensive exam, thesis/dissertation. *Entrance requirements:* For master's, GRE General Test, interview, 2 letters of recommendation. Additional exam requirements/recommendations for international students: Required—TOEFL (minimum score 83 computer-based). *Application deadline:* For fall admission, 6/1 for international students; for spring admission, 10/1 for international students. Applications are processed on a rolling basis. Application fee: $60. Electronic applications accepted. *Financial support:* In 2008–09, 15 research assistantships with full tuition reimbursements (averaging $7,000 per year) were awarded; Federal Work-Study, scholarships/grants, and unspecified assistantships also available. Support available to

Addictions/Substance Abuse Counseling

Montclair State University (continued)
part-time students. Financial award application deadline: 3/1; financial award applicants required to submit FAFSA. *Faculty research:* K-12 education, data collection. *Unit head:* Dr. Catherine Roland, Chairperson, 973-655-7216, E-mail: rolandc@mail.montclair.edu. *Application contact:* Amy Aiello, Associate Director of Admissions, 973-655-5147, Fax: 973-655-7869, E-mail: graduate.school@montclair.edu.

National-Louis University, College of Arts and Sciences, Department of Counseling and Human Services, Chicago, IL 60603. Offers addictions counseling (Certificate); addictions treatment (Certificate); career counseling and development studies (Certificate); community counseling (MS); community wellness and prevention (Certificate); counseling (Certificate); eating disorders counseling (Certificate); employee assistance programs (MS, Certificate); gerontology administration (Certificate); gerontology counseling (MS, Certificate); human services administration (MS, Certificate); long-term care administration (Certificate); school counseling (MS). Part-time programs available. *Students:* 8 full-time (7 women), 239 part-time (199 women); includes 71 minority (49 African Americans, 5 Asian Americans or Pacific Islanders, 17 Hispanic Americans). Average age 39. In 2008, 53 master's, 6 other advanced degrees awarded. *Degree requirements:* For master's and Certificate, internship. *Entrance requirements:* For master's and Certificate, GRE, MAT, or Watson-Glaser Critical Thinking Appraisal, interview, minimum GPA of 3.0. *Application deadline:* Applications are processed on a rolling basis. *Financial support:* Federal Work-Study, institutionally sponsored loans, scholarships/grants, and tuition waivers available. Support available to part-time students. Financial award applicants required to submit FAFSA. *Faculty research:* Religion and aging, drug abuse prevention, hunger, homelessness, multicultural diversity. *Unit head:* Dr. Susan Thorne-Devin, Assistant Professor, 630-874-4560, E-mail: stdevin@nl.edu. *Application contact:* Dr. Larry Poselli, Vice President of Enrollment and Student Services, 800-443-5522 Ext. 5718, Fax: 312-261-.3550, E-mail: larry.polselli@nl.edu.

Pace University, Dyson College of Arts and Sciences, Department of Psychology, Program in Counseling-Substance Abuse, New York, NY 10038. Offers MS. Offered at Pleasantville, NY location only. Part-time and evening/weekend programs available. *Degree requirements:* For master's, comprehensive exam, qualifying exams, internship. *Entrance requirements:* For master's, GRE, interview. Electronic applications accepted.

Palm Beach Atlantic University, School of Education and Behavioral Studies, West Palm Beach, FL 33416-4708. Offers counseling psychology (MSCP), including addictions/mental health, marriage and family therapy, mental health counseling, school guidance counseling; elementary education (M Ed). Part-time and evening/weekend programs available. *Entrance requirements:* For master's, GRE General Test, minimum GPA of 3.0 in last 60 hours of course work. Additional exam requirements/recommendations for international students: Required—TOEFL (minimum score 550 paper-based; 213 computer-based). Electronic applications accepted.

St. Mary's University, Graduate School, Department of Counseling and Human Services, San Antonio, TX 78228-8507. Offers community counseling (MA); counseling (Sp C); counseling education and supervision (PhD); marriage and family relations (Certificate); marriage and family therapy (MA, PhD); mental health (MA); mental health and substance abuse counseling (Certificate); substance abuse (MA). *Accreditation:* AAMFT/COAMFTE (one or more programs are accredited); ACA (one or more programs are accredited). Postbaccalaureate distance learning degree programs offered (minimal on-campus study). *Faculty:* 7 full-time (3 women). *Students:* 97 full-time (76 women), 73 part-time (60 women); includes 63 minority (13 African Americans, 5 Asian Americans or Pacific Islanders, 45 Hispanic Americans), 7 international. Average age 35. 91 applicants, 78% accepted, 57 enrolled. In 2008, 31 master's, 14 doctorates awarded. *Degree requirements:* For master's, comprehensive exam, internship; for doctorate, comprehensive exam, thesis/dissertation, internship. *Entrance requirements:* For master's, GRE General Test, MAT; for doctorate, GRE General Test, recommendation from employers, admissions committee and department faculty. Additional exam requirements/recommendations for international students: Required—TOEFL (minimum score 550 paper-based; 213 computer-based; 80 iBT). *Application deadline:* Applications are processed on a rolling basis. Application fee: $0. Electronic applications accepted. *Expenses:* Contact institution. *Financial support:* In 2008–09, 42 students received support, including 34 fellowships (averaging $4,709 per year), 8 research assistantships (averaging $9,313 per year); career-related internships or fieldwork, Federal Work-Study, institutionally sponsored loans, scholarships/grants, and health care benefits also available. Financial award application deadline: 3/31; financial award applicants required to submit FAFSA. *Unit head:* Dr. Dana Comstock, Chair, 210-436-3226, Fax: 210-431-6886, E-mail: dcomstock@stmarytx.edu. *Application contact:* Dr. Henry Flores, Dean of the Graduate School, 210-436-3101, Fax: 210-431-2220, E-mail: hflores@stmarytx.edu.

Shippensburg University of Pennsylvania, School of Graduate Studies, College of Education and Human Services, Department of Counseling, Shippensburg, PA 17257-2299. Offers Adlerian studies (Certificate); advanced study in counseling (Certificate); alcohol and drug counseling (Certificate); counseling (M Ed, MS), including college counseling (MS), community counseling (MS), elementary school counseling, mental health counseling (MS), secondary school counseling (MS), student personnel services (MS); couple and family counseling (Certificate). *Accreditation:* ACA (one or more programs are accredited); NCATE. Part-time and evening/weekend programs available. *Faculty:* 8 full-time (3 women), 3 part-time/adjunct (2 women). *Students:* 71 full-time (60 women), 109 part-time (91 women); includes 22 minority (16 African Americans, 4 Asian Americans or Pacific Islanders, 2 Hispanic Americans), 2 international. Average age 29. 128 applicants, 39% accepted, 32 enrolled. In 2008, 48 master's awarded. *Degree requirements:* For master's, fieldwork, research project, internship, candidacy. *Entrance requirements:* For master's, GRE or MAT (for community, mental health, student personnel, and college counseling applicants if GPA is less than 2.75), minimum GPA of 2.75 (3.0 for M Ed), interview, resumé, 3 letters of recommendation, supplemental data forms, one year of relevant work experience, on-campus interview. Additional exam requirements/recommendations for international students: Required—TOEFL (minimum score 560 paper-based; 220 computer-based); Recommended—IELTS (minimum score 6). *Application deadline:* For fall admission, 3/1 for international students; for spring admission, 7/1 for international students. Applications are processed on a rolling basis. Application fee: $30. Electronic applications accepted. *Expenses:* Tuition, state resident: full-time $6430; part-time $357 per credit. Tuition, nonresident: full-time $10,288; part-time $572 per credit. Required fees: $1127; $38 per credit. One-time fee: $44 part-time. *Financial support:* In 2008–09, 44 research assistantships with full tuition reimbursements (averaging $5,000 per year) were awarded; career-related internships or fieldwork, scholarships/grants, unspecified assistantships, and resident hall directors, student payroll positions also available. Support available to part-time students. Financial award application deadline: 3/1; financial award applicants required to submit FAFSA. *Unit head:* Dr. Jan Arminio, Chairperson, 717-477-1668, Fax: 717-477-4016, E-mail: jlarmi@ship.edu. *Application contact:* Renee Payne, Associate Dean of Graduate Admissions, 717-477-1231, Fax: 717-477-4016, E-mail: rmpayn@ship.edu.

Southern New Hampshire University, School of Liberal Arts, Manchester, NH 03106-1045. Offers clinical services for adults psychiatric disabilities (Certificate); clinical services for children and adolescents with psychiatric disabilities (Certificate); clinical services for persons with co-occurring substance abuse and psychiatric disabilities (Certificate); community mental health (MS); fiction writing (MFA); non-fiction writing (MFA); teaching English as a foreign language (MS). Part-time and evening/weekend programs available. *Degree requirements:* For master's, one foreign language, thesis. *Entrance requirements:* For master's, minimum GPA of 2.75: MS-TEFL, 3.0: MFA. Additional exam requirements/recommendations for international students: Required—TOEFL (minimum score 550 paper-based; 213 computer-based; 79 iBT), IELTS (minimum score 6.5), TWE (minimum score 5). Electronic applications accepted. *Expenses:* Contact institution. *Faculty research:* Action research, state of the art practice in behavioral health services, wraparound approaches to working with youth, learning styles.

Springfield College, Graduate Programs, Programs in Rehabilitation Counseling and Services, Springfield, MA 01109-3797. Offers alcohol rehabilitation/substance abuse counseling (M Ed, MS); deaf counseling (M Ed, MS); developmental disabilities (M Ed, MS); general counseling and casework (M Ed, MS); psychiatric rehabilitation/mental health counseling (M Ed, MS); special services (M Ed, MS). *Accreditation:* CORE (one or more programs are accredited). Part-time programs available. *Faculty:* 8 full-time (2 women), 6 part-time/adjunct (4 women). *Students:* 26 full-time, 7 part-time. Average age 30. 20 applicants, 90% accepted, 11 enrolled. In 2008, 18 master's awarded. *Degree requirements:* For master's, comprehensive exam. *Entrance requirements:* Additional exam requirements/recommendations for international students: Required—TOEFL (minimum score 550 paper-based; 213 computer-based). *Application deadline:* For fall admission, 1/15 for domestic and international students; for winter admission, 11/1 for international students; for spring admission, 11/1 for domestic and international students. Applications are processed on a rolling basis. Application fee: $50. Electronic applications accepted. *Expenses:* Tuition: Full-time $9132; part-time $761 per semester hour. Required fees: $150. Tuition and fees vary according to course load. *Financial support:* Fellowships with partial tuition reimbursements, teaching assistantships with partial tuition reimbursements, career-related internships or fieldwork, Federal Work-Study, institutionally sponsored loans, and unspecified assistantships available. Financial award application deadline: 3/1; financial award applicants required to submit FAFSA. *Unit head:* Dr. Robert Hewes, Director, 413-748-3318, E-mail: rhewes@spfldcol.edu. *Application contact:* Donald James Shaw, Director of Graduate Admissions, 413-748-3479, Fax: 413-748-3694, E-mail: donald_shaw_jr@spfldcol.edu.

Stony Brook University, State University of New York, Stony Brook University Medical Center, School of Medicine, Program in Public Health, Stony Brook, NY 11794. Offers community health (MPH); evaluation sciences (MPH); family violence (MPH); health economics (MPH); population health (MPH); substance abuse (MPH). *Students:* 16 full-time (8 women), 29 part-time (24 women); includes 14 minority (6 African Americans, 6 Asian Americans or Pacific Islanders, 2 Hispanic Americans), 5 international. Average age 39. 77 applicants, 64% accepted. In 2008, 10 master's awarded. *Entrance requirements:* For master's, GRE, 3 references. Additional exam requirements/recommendations for international students: Required—TOEFL. *Application deadline:* For fall admission, 1/15 for domestic and international students. Application fee: $60. Electronic applications accepted. *Expenses:* Tuition, area resident: Full-time $7880; part-time $328 per credit hour. Tuition, state resident: full-time $7880; part-time $328 per credit hour. Tuition, nonresident: full-time $13,250; part-time $552 per credit hour. Required fees: $848. *Faculty research:* Population health, health service research, health economics. *Unit head:* Dr. Raymond L. Goldsteen, Director, 631-444-2074, Fax: 631-444-3480, E-mail: raymond.goldsteen@stonybrook.edu. *Application contact:* Dr. Raymond L. Goldsteen, Director, 631-444-2074, Fax: 631-444-3480, E-mail: raymond.goldsteen@stonybrook.edu.

Universidad Central del Caribe, Program in Substance Abuse Counseling, Bayamón, PR 00960-6032. Offers MHS.

University of Arkansas at Pine Bluff, School of Arts and Sciences, Pine Bluff, AR 71601-2799. Offers MS.

University of Central Florida, College of Health and Public Affairs, School of Social Work, Orlando, FL 32816. Offers addictions (Certificate); aging studies (Certificate); children's services (Certificate); school social work (Certificate); social work (MSW); social work administration (Certificate). *Accreditation:* CSWE. Part-time and evening/weekend programs available. *Faculty:* 15 full-time (11 women), 17 part-time/adjunct (15 women). *Students:* 113 full-time (99 women), 79 part-time (64 women); includes 61 minority (35 African Americans, 1 American Indian/Alaska Native, 2 Asian Americans or Pacific Islanders, 23 Hispanic Americans), 2 international. In 2008, 80 master's, 15 other advanced degrees awarded. *Degree requirements:* For master's, thesis or alternative, field education. *Entrance requirements:* For master's, resumé. Additional exam requirements/recommendations for international students: Required—TOEFL. *Application deadline:* For fall admission, 3/1 for domestic students. Application fee: $30. Electronic applications accepted. *Expenses:* Tuition, area resident: Full-time $6816; part-time $284 per credit. Tuition, state resident: full-time $6816; part-time $1076 per credit. Tuition, nonresident: full-time $25,824. Required fees: $216; $9 per credit. *Financial support:* In 2008–09, 2 fellowships with partial tuition reimbursements (averaging $10,000 per year), 18 research assistantships with partial tuition reimbursements (averaging $6,800 per year) were awarded; teaching assistantships with partial tuition reimbursements, career-related internships or fieldwork, Federal Work-Study, institutionally sponsored loans, and unspecified assistantships also available. Financial award application deadline: 3/1; financial award applicants required to submit FAFSA. *Unit head:* Dr. John Ronnau, Director, 407-823-2114, Fax: 407-823-5697, E-mail: jronnau@mail.ucf.edu. *Application contact:* Dr. John Ronnau, Director, 407-823-2114, Fax: 407-823-5697, E-mail: jronnau@mail.ucf.edu.

University of Central Oklahoma, College of Graduate Studies and Research, College of Liberal Arts, Department of Sociology, Criminal Justice and Substance Abuse Studies, Edmond, OK 73034-5209. Offers criminal justice management and administration (MA). Part-time programs available. *Entrance requirements:* Additional exam requirements/recommendations for international students: Required—TOEFL (minimum score 550 paper-based; 213 computer-based). Electronic applications accepted. *Faculty research:* Gender issues, violent offenders.

University of Detroit Mercy, College of Liberal Arts and Education, Department of Counseling and Addiction Studies, Program in Addiction Studies, Detroit, MI 48221. Offers Certificate. Part-time programs available.

University of Detroit Mercy, College of Liberal Arts and Education, Department of Counseling and Addiction Studies, Program in Counseling, Detroit, MI 48221. Offers addiction counseling (MA); community counseling (MA); school counseling (MA). *Accreditation:* ACA. Part-time and evening/weekend programs available. *Degree requirements:* For master's, thesis or alternative. *Entrance requirements:* For master's, minimum GPA of 2.75.

University of Great Falls, Graduate Studies, Program in Addictions Counseling, Great Falls, MT 59405. Offers Certificate. Part-time and evening/weekend programs available. *Degree requirements:* For Certificate, thesis optional. *Entrance requirements:* For degree, GRE General Test or MAT, 3 letters of recommendation. Additional exam requirements/recommendations for international students: Required—TOEFL (minimum score 500 paper-based; 205 computer-based). Electronic applications accepted.

University of Illinois at Springfield, Graduate Programs, College of Education and Human Services, Program in Human Services, Springfield, IL 62703-5407. Offers alcoholism and substance abuse (MA); child and family services (MA); gerontology (MA); social services administration (MA). Part-time and evening/weekend programs available. Postbaccalaureate distance learning degree programs offered (no on-campus study). *Faculty:* 4 full-time (2 women), 3 part-time/adjunct (all women). *Students:* 28 full-time (22 women), 70 part-time (56 women); includes 17 minority (16 African Americans, 1 American Indian/Alaska Native). Average age 35. 64 applicants, 42% accepted, 22 enrolled. In 2008, 24 master's awarded. *Degree requirements:* For master's, thesis optional, internship; project or thesis. *Entrance requirements:* For master's, minimum undergraduate GPA of 3.0, 2 letters of recommendation, personal statement. Additional exam requirements/recommendations for international students: Required—TOEFL (minimum score 500 paper-based; 176 computer-based; 61 iBT). Application fee: $50 ($60 for international students). Electronic applications accepted. *Expenses:* Tuition, state resident: full-time $6144; part-time $256 per credit hour. Tuition, nonresident: full-time $13,980; part-time $582.50 per credit hour. Required fees: $1800. *Financial support:* In 2008–09, research assistantships with full tuition reimbursements (averaging $8,109 per year), teaching assistantships with full tuition reimbursements (averaging $8,109 per year) were awarded; career-related internships or fieldwork, scholarships/grants, health care benefits, and unspecified assistantships also available. Support available to part-time students. Financial award application deadline: 11/15. *Unit head:* Dr. Carolyn Peck, Program Administrator, 217-206-7577, Fax:

217-206-6775, E-mail: peck.carolyn@uis.edu. *Application contact:* Dr. Lynn Pardie, Office of Graduate Studies, 800-252-8533, Fax: 217-206-7623, E-mail: pardie.lynn@uis.edu.

University of Lethbridge, School of Graduate Studies, Lethbridge, AB T1K 3M4, Canada. Offers accounting (MScM); addictions counseling (M Sc); agricultural biotechnology (M Sc); agricultural studies (M Sc, MA); anthropology (MA); archaeology (MA); art (MA); biochemistry (M Sc); biological sciences (M Sc); biomolecular science (PhD); biosystems and biodiversity (PhD); Canadian studies (MA); chemistry (M Sc); computer science (M Sc); computer science and geographical information science (M Sc); counseling psychology (M Ed); dramatic arts (MA); earth, space, and physical science (PhD); economics (MA); educational leadership (M Ed); English (MA); environmental science (M Sc); evolution and behavior (PhD); exercise science (M Sc); finance (MScM); French (MA); French/German (MA); French/Spanish (MA); general education (M Ed); general management (MScM); geography (M Sc, MA); German (MA); health sciences (M Sc, MA); history (MA); human resource management and labour relations (MScM); individualized multidisciplinary (M Sc, MA); information systems (MScM); international management (MScM); kinesiology (M Sc, MA); management (M Sc, MA); marketing (MScM); mathematics (M Sc); music (MA); Native American studies (MA); neuroscience (M Sc, PhD); new media (MA); nursing (M Sc); philosophy (MA); physics (M Sc); policy and strategy (MScM); political science (MA); psychology (M Sc, MA); religious studies (MA); sociology (MA); theoretical and computational science (PhD); urban and regional studies (MA). Part-time and evening/weekend programs available. *Degree requirements:* For doctorate, comprehensive exam, thesis/dissertation. *Entrance requirements:* For master's, GMAT (M Sc in management), bachelor's degree in related field, minimum GPA of 3.0 during previous 20 graded semester courses, 2 years teaching or related experience (M Ed); for doctorate, master's degree, minimum graduate GPA of 3.5. Additional exam requirements/recommendations for international students: Required—TOEFL. *Faculty research:* Movement and brain plasticity, gibberellin physiology, photosynthesis, carbon cycling, molecular properties of main-group ring components.

University of Louisiana at Monroe, Graduate School, College of Education and Human Development, Department of Educational Leadership and Counseling, Program in Substance Abuse Counseling, Monroe, LA 71209-0001. Offers MA. Part-time and evening/weekend programs available. *Faculty:* 1 full-time (0 women). *Students:* 9 full-time (5 women), 2 part-time (1 woman); includes 2 minority (both African Americans). Average age 37. In 2008, 4 master's awarded. *Degree requirements:* For master's, thesis optional, 600 hours clinical internship. *Entrance requirements:* For master's, GRE General Test, minimum GPA of 2.8 in last 60 hours. Additional exam requirements/recommendations for international students: Required—TOEFL (minimum score 500 paper-based; 173 computer-based; 61 iBT). *Application deadline:* For fall admission, 8/22 priority date for domestic students, 7/1 for international students; for winter admission, 12/12 for domestic students; for spring admission, 1/17 for domestic students, 11/1 for international students. Applications are processed on a rolling basis. Application fee: $20 ($30 for international students). Electronic applications accepted. *Expenses:* Tuition, area resident: Full-time $2403; part-time $1202 per semester. Tuition, state resident: full-time $2403; part-time $1202 per semester. Tuition, nonresident: full-time $2403; part-time $1202 per semester. International tuition: $8352 full-time. Required fees: $1239.40; $141 per credit hour. *Financial support:* Research assistantships with full tuition reimbursements, teaching assistantships with full tuition reimbursements, career-related internships or fieldwork, Federal Work-Study, and unspecified assistantships available. Financial award application deadline: 4/1; financial award applicants required to submit FAFSA. *Faculty research:* Addictionology. *Unit head:* Dr. Mitchell Young, Coordinator, 318-342-1255, Fax: 318-342-3131, E-mail: myoung@ulm.edu. *Application contact:* Dr. Mitchell Young, Coordinator, 318-342-1255, Fax: 318-342-3131, E-mail: myoung@ulm.edu.

University of Louisville, Graduate School, Raymond A. Kent School of Social Work, Louisville, KY 40292-0001. Offers marriage and family therapy (PMC); social work (MSSW, PhD), including alcohol and drug counseling (MSSW), gerontology (MSSW), school social work (MSSW). *Accreditation:* AAMFT/COAMFTE; CSWE (one or more programs are accredited). Part-time and evening/weekend programs available. *Faculty:* 23 full-time (15 women), 38 part-time/adjunct (21 women). *Students:* 282 full-time (229 women), 67 part-time (54 women); includes 93 minority (84 African Americans, 2 American Indian/Alaska Native, 2 Asian Americans or Pacific Islanders, 5 Hispanic Americans), 7 international. Average age 32. 314 applicants, 78% accepted, 142 enrolled. In 2008, 156 master's, 5 doctorates awarded. *Degree requirements:* For doctorate, comprehensive exam, thesis/dissertation. *Entrance requirements:* For master's,

GRE or minimum GPA of 2.75; for doctorate, GRE General Test, interview, writing sample. Additional exam requirements/recommendations for international students: Required—TOEFL (minimum score 550 paper-based; 213 computer-based; 79 iBT). *Application deadline:* For fall admission, 7/31 for domestic and international students. Applications are processed on a rolling basis. Application fee: $50. Electronic applications accepted. *Financial support:* In 2008–09, 80 students received support, including 2 fellowships with full tuition reimbursements available (averaging $19,000 per year), 8 research assistantships with full tuition reimbursements available (averaging $19,000 per year); Federal Work-Study, institutionally sponsored loans, scholarships/grants, health care benefits, tuition waivers (full), and unspecified assistantships also available. Support available to part-time students. Financial award application deadline: 6/1; financial award applicants required to submit FAFSA. *Faculty research:* Child welfare, substance abuse, gerontology, family functioning, health behavior. *Unit head:* Dr. Terry Singer, Dean, 502-852-6402, Fax: 502-852-0422, E-mail: terry.singer@louisville.edu. *Application contact:* Libby Leggett, Director, Graduate Admissions, 502-852-3101, Fax: 502-852-6536, E-mail: gradadm@louisville.edu.

University of Mary, Divison of Social and Behavioral Sciences, Bismarck, ND 58504-9652. Offers addiction counseling (MSC); community counseling (MSC); school counseling (MSC).

University of Nevada, Las Vegas, Graduate College, College of Education, Department of Counselor Education, Las Vegas, NV 89154-3066. Offers addiction studies (Advanced Certificate); community mental health (MS); rehabilitation counseling (Advanced Certificate); school counseling (M Ed). *Faculty:* 7 full-time (2 women), 10 part-time/adjunct (7 women). *Students:* 47 full-time (39 women), 37 part-time (31 women); includes 13 minority (1 African American, 4 Asian Americans or Pacific Islanders, 8 Hispanic Americans). Average age 35. 31 applicants, 81% accepted, 15 enrolled. In 2008, 20 master's awarded. *Degree requirements:* For master's, comprehensive exam (for some programs), thesis (for some programs); for Advanced Certificate, thesis (for some programs). *Entrance requirements:* Additional exam requirements/recommendations for international students: Required—TOEFL (minimum score 550 paper-based; 213 computer-based; 80 iBT), IELTS (minimum score 7). *Application deadline:* For fall admission, 2/1 priority date for domestic and international students. Applications are processed on a rolling basis. Application fee: $60 ($75 for international students). Electronic applications accepted. *Expenses:* Tuition, state resident: full-time $1414; part-time $198 per credit. Tuition, nonresident: full-time $12,509; part-time $415.75 per credit. International tuition: $14,249 full-time. Required fees: $4 per credit; $252 per semester. Tuition and fees vary according to course load. *Financial support:* In 2008–09, 11 students received support, including 7 research assistantships with partial tuition reimbursements available (averaging $10,000 per year), 4 teaching assistantships with partial tuition reimbursements available (averaging $10,000 per year); institutionally sponsored loans, scholarships/grants, health care benefits, and unspecified assistantships also available. Financial award application deadline: 3/1. *Faculty research:* Social justice and multicultural competencies for counselors, therapeutic storytelling and bibliotherapy, school counselor education pedagogy, counseling program evaluation, addictions prevention and related trauma. *Unit head:* Dr. Dale Pehrsson, Chair/Associate Professor, 702-895-5994, Fax: 702-895-5550, E-mail: dale.pehrsson@unlv.edu. *Application contact:* Graduate College Admissions Evaluator, 702-895-3320, Fax: 702-895-4180, E-mail: gradcollege@unlv.edu.

University of New England, College of Health Professions, School of Social Work, Biddeford, ME 04005-9526. Offers addictions counseling (Certificate); gerontology (Certificate); social work (MSW). *Accreditation:* CSWE. Part-time programs available. *Degree requirements:* For master's, field internships. *Entrance requirements:* Additional exam requirements/recommendations for international students: Required—TOEFL (minimum score 550 paper-based; 213 computer-based). Electronic applications accepted. *Faculty research:* Domestic violence, solution focused practice, empowerment models, adverse childhood experiences.

Wayne State University, Graduate School, Interdisciplinary Program in Alcohol and Drug Abuse Studies, Detroit, MI 48202. Offers Certificate. *Entrance requirements:* For degree, graduate degree or enrolled in graduate program; letter of reference. Additional exam requirements/recommendations for international students: Required—TOEFL (minimum score 550 paper-based; 213 computer-based); Recommended—TWE (minimum score 6). Electronic applications accepted. *Faculty research:* Epidemiology and etiology of substance use, substance abuse prevention and treatment; treatment for substance abuse and co-occurring disorders; faculty and professional development in substance abuse.

Clinical Psychology

Abilene Christian University, Graduate School, College of Arts and Sciences, Department of Psychology, Program in Clinical Psychology, Abilene, TX 79699-9100. Offers MS. Part-time programs available. *Students:* 17 full-time (11 women), 1 (woman) part-time; includes 1 minority (African American), 1 international. 11 applicants, 73% accepted, 6 enrolled. In 2008, 4 master's awarded. *Degree requirements:* For master's, comprehensive exam, thesis. *Entrance requirements:* For master's, GRE General Test. *Application deadline:* For fall admission, 4/1 priority date for domestic students; for spring admission, 11/1 for domestic students. Applications are processed on a rolling basis. Application fee: $40 ($45 for international students). Electronic applications accepted. *Expenses:* Tuition: Full-time $10,728; part-time $640 per hour. Required fees: $1090; $53.50 per hour. $10 per term. Tuition and fees vary according to campus/location. *Financial support:* In 2008–09, 18 students received support. Career-related internships or fieldwork and Federal Work-Study available. Support available to part-time students. Financial award application deadline: 4/1; financial award applicants required to submit FAFSA. *Unit head:* Dr. Robert McKelvain, Graduate Advisor, 325-674-2472, Fax: 325-674-6968, E-mail: beckr@acu.edu. *Application contact:* William Horn, Graduate Admissions Counselor, 325-674-2656, Fax: 325-674-6717, E-mail: gradinfo@acu.edu.

Acadia University, Faculty of Pure and Applied Science, Department of Psychology, Wolfville, NS B4P 2R6, Canada. Offers clinical psychology (M Sc). *Faculty:* 12 full-time (6 women), 11 part-time/adjunct (5 women). *Students:* 9 full-time (8 women). Average age 26. 45 applicants, 18% accepted, 4 enrolled. In 2008, 5 master's awarded. *Degree requirements:* For master's, thesis. *Entrance requirements:* For master's, GRE General Test, GRE Subject Test, honors degree or equivalent. Additional exam requirements/recommendations for international students: Required—TOEFL (minimum score 580 paper-based; 237 computer-based; 93 iBT), IELTS (minimum score 6.5). *Application deadline:* For fall admission, 2/1 priority date for domestic students. Applications are processed on a rolling basis. Application fee: $50. Electronic applications accepted. Tuition and fees charges are reported in Canadian dollars. *Expenses:* Tuition, area resident: Full-time $3873.50 Canadian dollars; part-time $844 Canadian dollars per course. Tuition, state resident: full-time $4634.50 Canadian dollars; part-time $844 Canadian dollars per course. Tuition, nonresident: full-time $9103 Canadian dollars; part-time $1687 Canadian dollars per course. Required fees: $503.22 Canadian dollars; $5 Canadian dollars per course. *Financial support:* In 2008–09, 5 students received support, including 5 teaching assistantships; career-related internships or fieldwork, scholarships/grants, and unspecified assistantships also available. Financial award application deadline: 2/1. *Faculty research:* Social psychology, job stress, psychotherapy, cognition perception, development. *Unit head:* Dr. Douglas K. Symons, Head, 902-585-1301, Fax: 902-585-1078, E-mail: doug.symons@acadiau.ca. *Application contact:* Dr. Peter Horvath, Information Contact, 902-585-1200, Fax: 902-585-1078, E-mail: peter.horvath@acadiau.ca.

Adelphi University, Derner Institute of Advanced Psychological Studies, Program in Clinical Psychology, Garden City, NY 11530-0701. Offers PhD. *Students:* 77 full-time (59 women), 44 part-time (32 women); includes 15 minority (5 African Americans, 8 Asian Americans or Pacific Islanders, 2 Hispanic Americans), 12 international. Average age 32. In 2008, 21 doctorates awarded. *Degree requirements:* For doctorate, thesis/dissertation, research (second year), 1 year internship. *Entrance requirements:* For doctorate, GRE General Test, GRE Subject Test, interview; resumé, undergraduate courses in psychology, experimental psychology, statistics, developmental psychology, and abnormal psychology. Additional exam requirements/recommendations for international students: Required—TOEFL (minimum score 550 paper-based; 213 computer-based; 80 iBT). *Application deadline:* For fall admission, 1/15 priority date for domestic and international students. Application fee: $50. Electronic applications accepted. *Expenses:* Tuition: Full-time $25,700; part-time $775 per credit hour. Required fees: $500. Tuition and fees vary according to course load, degree level, campus/location, program and student level. *Financial support:* Research assistantships with full and partial tuition reimbursements, teaching assistantships, career-related internships or fieldwork, Federal Work-Study, institutionally sponsored loans, and unspecified assistantships available. Financial award application deadline: 2/15; financial award applicants required to submit FAFSA. *Unit head:* Dr. Christopher J Muran, Associate Dean, 516-877-4803, E-mail: jcmuran@adelphi.edu. *Application contact:* Christine Murphy, Director of Admissions, 516-877-3050, Fax: 516-877-3039, E-mail: graduateadmissions@adelphi.edu.

Adler School of Professional Psychology, Programs in Psychology, Chicago, IL 60601-7203. Offers art therapy (Certificate); clinical hypnosis (Certificate); clinical psychology (Psy D); counseling psychology (MACP); counseling psychology/art therapy (MACAT); gerontology (MAGP); marriage and family counseling (MAMFC); marriage and family therapy (Certificate); organizational psychology (MAO); substance abuse counseling (MASAC, Certificate); Psy D/Certificate; Psy D/MACAT; Psy D/MACP; Psy D/MAMFC; Psy D/MASAC. *Accreditation:* APA. Part-time and evening/weekend programs available. Postbaccalaureate distance learning degree programs offered (minimal on-campus study). *Faculty:* 36 full-time (17 women), 45 part-time/adjunct (18 women). *Students:* 514 full-time (404 women), 128 part-time (100 women); includes 147 minority (69 African Americans, 2 American Indian/Alaska Native, 30 Asian Americans or Pacific Islanders, 46 Hispanic Americans), 53 international. Average age 27. 855 applicants, 46% accepted, 195 enrolled. In 2008, 110 master's, 136 doctorates awarded. Terminal master's awarded for partial completion of doctoral program. *Degree requirements:* For master's, thesis or alternative, oral exam, practicum; for doctorate, thesis/dissertation, clinical exam, internship, oral exam, practicum, written qualifying exam. *Entrance requirements:* For master's, 12 semester hours in psychology, minimum GPA of 3.0; for doctorate, 18 semester hours in psychology, minimum GPA of 3.25; for Certificate, appropriate master's or doctoral degree. Additional exam requirements/recommendations for international students: Required—TOEFL (minimum score

Clinical Psychology

Adler School of Professional Psychology (continued)
550 paper-based; 213 computer-based; 79 iBT). *Application deadline:* For fall admission, 2/15 priority date for domestic students, 12/1 priority date for international students. Applications are processed on a rolling basis. Application fee: $50. Electronic applications accepted. *Expenses:* Tuition: Part-time $850 per credit. Tuition and fees vary according to degree level, campus/location and program. *Financial support:* Career-related internships or fieldwork, Federal Work-Study, scholarships/grants, and tuition waivers (full and partial) available. Support available to part-time students. Financial award application deadline: 5/15; financial award applicants required to submit FAFSA. *Unit head:* Dr. Frank Gruba-McAllister, Vice President of Academic Affairs, 312-201-5900, Fax: 312-207-5917. *Application contact:* Craig A Hines, Director of Admissions, 312-201-5900 Ext. 226, Fax: 312-201-5917, E-mail: chines@adler.edu.

See Close-Up on page 1051.

Alabama Agricultural and Mechanical University, School of Graduate Studies, School of Education, Department of Counseling and Special Education, Huntsville, AL 35811. Offers communicative disorders (M Ed, MS); psychology and counseling (MS, Ed S), including clinical psychology (MS), counseling and guidance, counseling psychology (MS), personnel management (MS), psychometry (MS), school psychology (MS); special education (M Ed, MS). *Accreditation:* CORE; NCATE. Part-time and evening/weekend programs available. *Students:* 13 full-time (9 women), 57 part-time (46 women); includes 52 minority (51 African Americans, 1 Hispanic American), 2 international. In 2008, 24 master's awarded. *Degree requirements:* For master's, comprehensive exam. *Entrance requirements:* For master's, GRE General Test. Additional exam requirements/recommendations for international students: Required—TOEFL (minimum score 500 paper-based; 173 computer-based; 61 iBT). *Application deadline:* For fall admission, 5/1 for domestic students. Application fee: $15 ($20 for international students). *Expenses:* Tuition, area resident: Full-time $3924; part-time $2616 per term. Tuition, nonresident: part-time $5234 per year. International tuition: $7848 full-time. Required fees: $198; $396 per credit hour. $2841 per term. One-time fee: $8498 full-time; $5682 part-time. Full-time tuition and fees vary according to program. *Financial support:* Career-related internships or fieldwork available. Support available to part-time students. Financial award application deadline: 4/1. *Faculty research:* Increasing numbers of minorities in special education and speech-language pathology. *Unit head:* Dr. Shirley King, Chair, 256-372-5520, Fax: 256-372-5526. *Application contact:* Dr. Caula Beyl, Dean, School of Graduate Studies, 256-372-5266, Fax: 256-372-5269, E-mail: caula.beyl@aamu.edu.

Alliant International University–Fresno, California School of Professional Psychology, PhD Program in Clinical Psychology, Fresno, CA 93727. Offers PhD. *Degree requirements:* For doctorate, thesis/dissertation. *Entrance requirements:* For doctorate, interview, minimum GPA of 3.0 in both psychology and overall, letters of recommendation, essay. Additional exam requirements/recommendations for international students: Required—TOEFL (minimum score 600 paper-based; 250 computer-based), TWE (minimum score 5). *Faculty research:* Teaching, ecosystemic child psychology, health psychology, clinical forensic psychology.

See Close-Up on page 1057.

Alliant International University–Fresno, California School of Professional Psychology, Psy D Program in Clinical Psychology, Fresno, CA 93727. Offers Psy D. *Accreditation:* APA. *Degree requirements:* For doctorate, comprehensive exam, thesis/dissertation. *Entrance requirements:* For doctorate, interview, minimum GPA of 3.0 in both psychology and overall, letters of recommendation, essay. Additional exam requirements/recommendations for international students: Required—TOEFL (minimum score 600 paper-based; 250 computer-based), TWE (minimum score 5). Electronic applications accepted. *Faculty research:* Ecosystemic child clinical health psychology, eating disorders.

See Close-Up on page 1059.

Alliant International University–Los Angeles, California School of Professional Psychology, PhD Program in Clinical Psychology, Alhambra, CA 91803-1360. Offers PhD. *Accreditation:* APA. *Degree requirements:* For doctorate, comprehensive exam, thesis/dissertation. *Entrance requirements:* For doctorate, interview, minimum GPA of 3.0 in both psychology and overall. Additional exam requirements/recommendations for international students: Required—TOEFL (minimum score 600 paper-based; 250 computer-based), TWE (minimum score 5). Electronic applications accepted. *Faculty research:* Multicultural and community clinical psychology, health psychology, individual and family psychology.

See Close-Up on page 1057.

Alliant International University–Los Angeles, California School of Professional Psychology, Psy D Program in Clinical Psychology, Alhambra, CA 91803-1360. Offers Psy D. *Accreditation:* APA. *Degree requirements:* For doctorate, thesis/dissertation. *Entrance requirements:* For doctorate, interview, minimum GPA of 3.0 in both psychology and overall. Additional exam requirements/recommendations for international students: Required—TOEFL (minimum score 600 paper-based; 250 computer-based), TWE. Electronic applications accepted. *Faculty research:* Child and family psychology, multicultural and community psychology, acculturation, lesbian and gay issues, women's health.

See Close-Up on page 1059.

Alliant International University–Sacramento, California School of Professional Psychology, Program in Clinical Psychology, Sacramento, CA 95825. Offers Psy D. *Entrance requirements:* For doctorate, minimum GPA of 3.0, letters of recommendation, interview. Electronic applications accepted. *Faculty research:* Health psychology, infant-preschool mental health, community mental, health trauma, aging.

See Close-Up on page 1059.

Alliant International University–San Diego, California School of Professional Psychology, PhD Program in Clinical Psychology, San Diego, CA 92131-1799. Offers PhD. *Accreditation:* APA. *Degree requirements:* For doctorate, thesis/dissertation. *Entrance requirements:* For doctorate, interview, minimum GPA of 3.0 in both psychology and overall. Additional exam requirements/recommendations for international students: Required—TOEFL (minimum score 600 paper-based; 250 computer-based), TWE (minimum score 5). Electronic applications accepted. *Faculty research:* Family conflict in adolescence, anxiety disorders, PTSD, childhood psychopathology, regressed memory.

See Close-Up on page 1057.

Alliant International University–San Diego, California School of Professional Psychology, Psy D Program in Clinical Psychology, San Diego, CA 92131-1799. Offers Psy D. *Accreditation:* APA. *Degree requirements:* For doctorate, thesis/dissertation. *Entrance requirements:* For doctorate, interview, minimum GPA of 3.0 in both psychology and overall. Additional exam requirements/recommendations for international students: Required—TOEFL (minimum score 600 paper-based; 250 computer-based), TWE (minimum score 5). Electronic applications accepted. *Faculty research:* Forensic psychology, health psychology, integrative psychology, family and child psychology.

See Close-Up on page 1059.

Alliant International University–San Diego, Marshall Goldsmith School of Management, Organizational Psychology Division, San Diego, CA 92131-1799. Offers clinical/industrial organizational psychology (PhD); consulting psychology (PhD); industrial/organizational psychology (MA, MS, PhD); organizational behavior (MA). Part-time and evening/weekend programs available. Terminal master's awarded for partial completion of doctoral program. *Degree requirements:* For doctorate, thesis/dissertation. *Entrance requirements:* For master's and doctorate, interview, minimum GPA of 3.0 in both psychology and overall. Additional exam requirements/recommendations for international students: Required—TOEFL (minimum score 600 paper-based; 250 computer-based), TWE (minimum score 5). Electronic applications accepted. *Faculty research:* Cultural diversity in the workplace, work motivation, personnel, performance management.

Alliant International University–San Francisco, California School of Professional Psychology, PhD Program in Clinical Psychology, San Francisco, CA 94133-1221. Offers PhD. *Degree requirements:* For doctorate, thesis/dissertation. *Entrance requirements:* For doctorate, interview, minimum GPA of 3.0 in both psychology and overall. Additional exam requirements/recommendations for international students: Required—TOEFL (minimum score 600 paper-based; 250 computer-based), TWE (minimum score 5). Electronic applications accepted. *Faculty research:* Social model of disability, feminist models of clinical training, post-traumatic stress disorder, HIV, psychology of women.

See Close-Up on page 1057.

Alliant International University–San Francisco, California School of Professional Psychology, Psy D Program in Clinical Psychology, San Francisco, CA 94133-1221. Offers Psy D, Certificate. *Accreditation:* APA (one or more programs are accredited). *Degree requirements:* For doctorate, thesis/dissertation. *Entrance requirements:* For doctorate, interview, minimum GPA of 3.0 in both psychology and overall. Additional exam requirements/recommendations for international students: Required—TOEFL (minimum score 600 paper-based; 250 computer-based), TWE (minimum score 5). Electronic applications accepted. *Faculty research:* Health psychology, family and child psychology, psychodynamic psychology, multicultural and community psychology, gender issues.

See Close-Up on page 1059.

American International College, School of Arts, Education and Science, Department of Psychology, Program in Clinical Psychology, Springfield, MA 01109-3189. Offers MA. *Degree requirements:* For master's, practicum. *Entrance requirements:* For master's, minimum B average in undergraduate course work, BS or BA. Additional exam requirements/recommendations for international students: Required—TOEFL. Electronic applications accepted.

American University, College of Arts and Sciences, Department of Psychology, Program in Clinical Psychology, Washington, DC 22016-8062. Offers psychology (PhD), including clinical psychology. *Accreditation:* APA. *Students:* 20 full-time (15 women), 18 part-time (16 women); includes 8 minority (2 African Americans, 1 Asian American or Pacific Islander, 5 Hispanic Americans). Average age 28. 213 applicants, 5% accepted, 7 enrolled. In 2008, 4 doctorates awarded. *Degree requirements:* For doctorate, comprehensive exam, thesis/dissertation, internship. *Entrance requirements:* For doctorate, GRE General Test, GRE Subject Test, recommendations. Additional exam requirements/recommendations for international students: Required—TOEFL. *Application deadline:* For fall admission, 1/1 for domestic students. Application fee: $80. *Expenses:* Tuition: Full-time $21,204; part-time $1178 per credit hour. Required fees: $380. Part-time tuition and fees vary according to course load and program. *Financial support:* Fellowships, research assistantships, teaching assistantships, career-related internships or fieldwork, Federal Work-Study, institutionally sponsored loans, tuition waivers (full and partial), and unspecified assistantships available. Support available to part-time students. Financial award application deadline: 2/1. *Faculty research:* Depression, eating disorders, anxiety disorders, addictions, behavior therapy. *Application contact:* Sara Holland, Senior Administrative Assistant, 202-885-1717, Fax: 202-885-1023.

Antioch University Los Angeles, Graduate Programs, Program in Psychology, Culver City, CA 90230. Offers clinical psychology (MA); psychology (MA). Part-time programs available. *Degree requirements:* For master's, thesis (for some programs), internship. *Entrance requirements:* For master's, interview. Additional exam requirements/recommendations for international students: Required—TOEFL. *Faculty research:* Creativity and humor, ethnic humor, adult development, Jungian theory, psychoanalytic theory.

Antioch University New England, Graduate School, Department of Applied Psychology, Program in Clinical Mental Health Counseling, Keene, NH 03431-3552. Offers MA. *Degree requirements:* For master's, internship, practicum. *Entrance requirements:* For master's, previous course work and work experience in psychology. Additional exam requirements/recommendations for international students: Required—TOEFL (minimum score 600 paper-based; 250 computer-based). Electronic applications accepted. *Expenses:* Contact institution. *Faculty research:* Multicultural issues in field supervision.

Antioch University New England, Graduate School, Department of Clinical Psychology, Keene, NH 03431-3552. Offers Psy D. *Accreditation:* APA. *Degree requirements:* For doctorate, thesis/dissertation, internship, practicum. *Entrance requirements:* For doctorate, GRE General Test, GRE Subject Test, previous course work in psychology. Additional exam requirements/recommendations for international students: Required—TOEFL (minimum score 600 paper-based; 250 computer-based). *Expenses:* Contact institution. *Faculty research:* Psychotherapy outcome and process in private practice, neuropsychiatric evaluations, effects of trauma on adults, supervision, clinical training evaluation.

Antioch University Santa Barbara, Program in Clinical Psychology, Santa Barbara, CA 93101-1581. Offers Psy D. *Faculty:* 6 full-time (4 women), 7 part-time/adjunct (3 women). *Students:* 50 full-time (37 women), 5 part-time (3 women); includes 17 minority (3 African Americans, 2 Asian Americans or Pacific Islanders, 12 Hispanic Americans), 1 international. *Entrance requirements:* Additional exam requirements/recommendations for international students: Required—TOEFL (minimum score 550 paper-based; 213 computer-based). *Application deadline:* Applications are processed on a rolling basis. Application fee: $60. Electronic applications accepted. *Expenses:* Tuition: Full-time $17,025; part-time $570 per unit. Required fees: $26. Tuition and fees vary according to course load, degree level and program. *Unit head:* Michele Harway, PhD, Director, 805-962-8179 Ext. 320, Fax: 805-962-4786, E-mail: mharway@antioch.edu. *Application contact:* Steve Weir, Director of Marketing and Enrollment Management, 805-962-8179 Ext. 152, Fax: 805-962-4786, E-mail: sweir@antioch.edu.

Appalachian State University, Cratis D. Williams Graduate School, Department of Psychology, Boone, NC 28608. Offers clinical health psychology (MA); general experimental psychology (MA); industrial and organizational psychology (MA). Part-time programs available. *Faculty:* 31 full-time (11 women). *Students:* 59 full-time (45 women), 15 part-time (12 women); includes 3 minority (2 African Americans, 1 Asian American or Pacific Islander), 4 international. 185 applicants, 30% accepted, 18 enrolled. In 2008, 23 master's, 3 other advanced degrees awarded. *Degree requirements:* For master's and MA/SSP, comprehensive exam, thesis optional, GRE Subject Test exit exam. *Entrance requirements:* For master's and MA/SSP, GRE General Test, 3 letters of recommendation. Additional exam requirements/recommendations for international students: Required—TOEFL (minimum score 550 paper-based; 230 computer-based; 79 iBT), IELTS (minimum score 6.5), TOEFL or IELTS. *Application deadline:* For fall admission, 3/1 for domestic students, 2/1 for international students. Applications are processed on a rolling basis. Application fee: $50. Electronic applications accepted. *Expenses:* Tuition, area resident: Full-time $2600; part-time $700 per course. Tuition, state resident: full-time $2600; part-time $700 per course. Tuition, nonresident: full-time $5000; part-time $3300 per course. Required fees: $2150; $330 per course. Tuition and fees vary according to campus/location. *Financial support:* In 2008–09, 34 research assistantships (averaging $3,500 per year), 25 teaching assistantships (averaging $3,500 per year) were awarded; fellowships, career-related internships or fieldwork, Federal Work-Study, scholarships/grants, and unspecified assistantships also available. Financial award application deadline: 4/1; financial award applicants required to submit FAFSA. *Faculty research:* Eating disorders, school-based consultations, organizational behavior management, brain mechanisms of sound localization, parenting styles. Total annual research expenditures: $83,000. *Unit head:* Dr. James Denniston, Chair, 828-262-2272, Fax: 828-262-2272, E-mail: dennistonjc@appstate.edu. *Application contact:* Dr. Denise Martz, Graduate Coordinator, 828-262-2715, E-mail: martzdm@appstate.edu.

Argosy University, Atlanta, College of Psychology and Behavioral Sciences, Atlanta, GA 30328. Offers clinical psychology (MA, Psy D, Postdoctoral Respecialization Certificate), including child and family psychology (Psy D), general adult clinical (Psy D), health psychology (Psy D), neuropsychology/geropsychology (Psy D); community counseling (MA), including marriage and family therapy; counselor education and supervision (Ed D); marriage and family therapy (Certificate). *Accreditation:* APA.

See Close-Up on page 1065.

Argosy University, Chicago, College of Psychology and Behavioral Sciences, Doctoral Program in Clinical Psychology, Chicago, IL 60654. Offers child and adolescent psychology (Psy D); client-centered and experiential psychotherapies (Psy D); diversity and multicultural psychology (Psy D); family psychology (Psy D); forensic psychology (Psy D); health psychology (Psy D); psychoanalytic psychology (Psy D); psychology and spirituality (Psy D). *Accreditation:* APA.

See Close-Up on page 1067.

Argosy University, Chicago, College of Psychology and Behavioral Sciences, Master's Program in Clinical Psychology, Chicago, IL 60654. Offers MA.

See Close-Up on page 1067.

Argosy University, Dallas, College of Psychology and Behavioral Sciences, Program in Clinical Psychology, Dallas, TX 75231. Offers MA, Psy D.

See Close-Up on page 1069.

Argosy University, Denver, College of Psychology and Behavioral Sciences, Denver, CO 80203. Offers clinical psychology (MA, Psy D); community counseling (MA); counseling psychology (Ed D), including counselor education and supervision; counselor education and supervision (Ed D); forensic psychology (MA); marriage and family therapy (MA); organizational leadership (Ed D).

See Close-Up on page 1071.

Argosy University, Hawai'i, College of Psychology and Behavioral Sciences, Program in Clinical Psychology, Honolulu, HI 96813. Offers clinical psychology (MA, Psy D, Postdoctoral Respecialization Certificate), including child and family clinical practice (Psy D), diversity in clinical practice (Psy D). *Accreditation:* APA.

See Close-Up on page 1073.

Argosy University, Inland Empire, College of Psychology and Behavioral Sciences, San Bernardino, CA 92408. Offers clinical psychology/marriage and family therapy (MA); counseling psychology (MA, Ed D); counseling psychology/marriage and family therapy (MA); forensic psychology (MA).

See Close-Up on page 1075.

Argosy University, Los Angeles, College of Psychology and Behavioral Sciences, Santa Monica, CA 90405. Offers clinical psychology/marriage and family therapy (MA); counseling psychology (Ed D); counseling psychology/marriage and family therapy (MA); organizational leadership (Ed D).

See Close-Up on page 1077.

Argosy University, Orange County, College of Psychology and Behavioral Sciences, Program in Clinical Psychology, Santa Ana, CA 92704. Offers child and adolescent psychology (Psy D); forensic psychology (Psy D); marriage and family therapy (MA).

See Close-Up on page 1081.

Argosy University, Phoenix, College of Psychology and Behavioral Sciences, Program in Clinical Psychology, Phoenix, AZ 85021. Offers clinical psychology (MA); sports-exercise psychology (Psy D). *Accreditation:* APA (one or more programs are accredited).

See Close-Up on page 1083.

Argosy University, San Diego, College of Psychology and Behavioral Sciences, San Diego, CA 92108. Offers clinical psychology/marriage and family therapy (MA); counseling psychology (MA, Ed D); counseling psychology/marriage and family therapy (MA).

See Close-Up on page 1087.

Argosy University, San Francisco Bay Area, College of Psychology and Behavioral Sciences, Alameda, CA 94501. Offers clinical psychology (MA, Psy D); counseling psychology (MA, Ed D); forensic psychology (MA); organizational leadership (Ed D). *Accreditation:* APA (one or more programs are accredited).

See Close-Up on page 1089.

Argosy University, Schaumburg, College of Psychology and Behavioral Sciences, Schaumburg, IL 60173-5403. Offers clinical health psychology (Post-Graduate Certificate); clinical psychology (MA, Psy D), including child and family psychology (Psy D), clinical health psychology (Psy D), diversity and multicultural psychology (Psy D), forensic psychology (Psy D); community counseling (MA); counseling psychology (Ed D), including counselor education and supervision; counselor education and supervision (Ed D); forensic psychology (Post-Graduate Certificate); organizational leadership (Ed D). *Accreditation:* ACA; APA.

See Close-Up on page 1093.

Argosy University, Seattle, College of Psychology and Behavioral Sciences, Program in Clinical Psychology, Seattle, WA 98121. Offers MA, Psy D, Postdoctoral Respecialization Certificate.

See Close-Up on page 1095.

Argosy University, Tampa, College of Psychology and Behavioral Sciences, Program in Clinical Psychology, Tampa, FL 33614. Offers clinical psychology (MA, Psy D), including child and adolescent psychology (Psy D), geropsychology (Psy D), marriage/couples and family therapy (Psy D), neuropsychology (Psy D). *Accreditation:* APA.

See Close-Up on page 1097.

Argosy University, Twin Cities, College of Psychology and Behavioral Sciences, Eagan, MN 55121. Offers clinical psychology (MA, Psy D), including child and family psychology (Psy D), forensic psychology (Psy D), health psychology (Psy D), marriage/couples and family therapy (Psy D), neuropsychology (Psy D); forensic counseling (Post-Graduate Certificate); forensic psychology (MA); marriage and family therapy (MA, DMFT), including forensic counseling (MA); organizational leadership (Ed D). *Accreditation:* APA.

See Close-Up on page 1099.

Argosy University, Washington DC, College of Psychology and Behavioral Sciences, Arlington, VA 22209. Offers clinical psychology (MA, Psy D), including child and family psychology (Psy D), diversity and multicultural psychology (Psy D), forensic psychology (Psy D), health and neuropsychology (Psy D); community counseling (MA); counseling psychology (Ed D), including counselor education and supervision; counselor education and supervision (Ed D); forensic psychology (MA); organizational leadership (Ed D). *Accreditation:* APA.

See Close-Up on page 1101.

Arizona State University, Graduate College, College of Liberal Arts and Sciences, Division of Natural Sciences, Department of Psychology, Tempe, AZ 85287. Offers behavioral neuroscience (PhD); clinical psychology (PhD); cognition, action and perception (PhD); developmental psychology (PhD); quantitative psychology (PhD); social psychology (PhD). *Accreditation:* APA. *Degree requirements:* For doctorate, thesis/dissertation. *Entrance requirements:* For doctorate, GRE General Test, GRE Subject Test.

Azusa Pacific University, School of Behavioral and Applied Sciences, Department of Graduate Psychology, Azusa, CA 91702-7000. Offers clinical psychology (MA, Psy D), including family therapy (MA). *Accreditation:* APA (one or more programs are accredited). Part-time and evening/weekend programs available. *Degree requirements:* For master's, comprehensive exam, 250 hours of clinical experience, individual and group therapy. *Entrance requirements:* For master's, interview, minimum GPA of 3.0, Minnesota Multiphasic Personality Inventory. Additional exam requirements/recommendations for international students: Required—TOEFL (minimum score 600 paper-based).

Ball State University, Graduate School, College of Sciences and Humanities, Department of Psychological Science, Program in Clinical Psychology, Muncie, IN 47306-1099. Offers MA. *Entrance requirements:* For master's, GRE General Test, interview.

Barry University, School of Arts and Sciences, Department of Psychology, Miami Shores, FL 33161-6695. Offers clinical psychology (MS); school psychology (MS, SSP). Part-time and evening/weekend programs available. *Degree requirements:* For master's, thesis, practicum. *Entrance requirements:* For master's, GRE General Test, minimum GPA of 3.0, course work in psychology. Electronic applications accepted. *Faculty research:* Closed head injury, memory and aging, infant/mother interaction, evolutionary aspects of behavior, gender roles.

See Close-Up on page 1103.

Baylor University, Graduate School, College of Arts and Sciences, Department of Psychology and Neuroscience, Program in Clinical Psychology, Waco, TX 76798. Offers MSCP, Psy D. *Accreditation:* APA. *Students:* 26 full-time (19 women), 3 part-time (all women); includes 7 minority (5 Asian Americans or Pacific Islanders, 2 Hispanic Americans). In 2008, 3 master's awarded. *Degree requirements:* For doctorate, comprehensive exam. *Entrance requirements:* For master's, GRE General Test; for doctorate, GRE General Test, interview. *Application deadline:* For fall admission, 2/1 for domestic students. Applications are processed on a rolling basis. Application fee: $25. *Financial support:* Research assistantships, teaching assistantships, career-related internships or fieldwork, institutionally sponsored loans, tuition waivers (partial), and practicum stipends available. Financial award applicants required to submit FAFSA. *Faculty research:* Professional training in clinical psychology, human systems and dynamics, social skills validation, child therapy and assessment. *Unit head:* Dr. Gary Elkins, Graduate Program Director, 254-710-2961, Fax: 254-710-3033, E-mail: gary_elkins@baylor.edu. *Application contact:* Barbara Prisco, Graduate Coordinator, 254-757-0535, Fax: 254-710-3033, E-mail: barbara_prisco@baylor.edu.

Benedictine University, Graduate Programs, Program in Clinical Psychology, Lisle, IL 60532-0900. Offers MS. Part-time programs available. *Degree requirements:* For master's, comprehensive exam, internship. *Entrance requirements:* For master's, MAT. Additional exam requirements/recommendations for international students: Required—TOEFL (minimum score 550 paper-based; 213 computer-based). Electronic applications accepted.

Bethany University, Program in Clinical Psychology, Scotts Valley, CA 95066-2820. Offers MS. Part-time and evening/weekend programs available.

Bowling Green State University, Graduate College, College of Arts and Sciences, Department of Psychology, Bowling Green, OH 43403. Offers clinical psychology (MA, PhD); developmental psychology (MA, PhD); experimental psychology (MA, PhD); industrial/organizational psychology (MA, PhD); quantitative psychology (MA, PhD). *Accreditation:* APA (one or more programs are accredited). *Degree requirements:* For doctorate, thesis/dissertation. *Entrance requirements:* For doctorate, GRE General Test, GRE Subject Test. Additional exam requirements/recommendations for international students: Required—TOEFL. Electronic applications accepted. *Faculty research:* Personnel psychology, developmental-mathematical models, behavioral medication, brain process, child/adolescent social cognition.

Brigham Young University, Graduate Studies, College of Family, Home, and Social Sciences, Department of Psychology, Provo, UT 84602-1001. Offers clinical psychology (PhD); general psychology (MS); psychology (PhD), including applied social psychology, behavioral neurobiology, theoretical/philosophical psychology. *Accreditation:* APA (one or more programs are accredited). *Faculty:* 30 full-time (7 women), 10 part-time/adjunct (4 women). *Students:* 94 full-time (31 women); includes 13 minority (3 African Americans, 6 Asian Americans or Pacific Islanders, 4 Hispanic Americans), 9 international. Average age 24. 73 applicants, 32% accepted, 23 enrolled. In 2008, 9 master's, 14 doctorates awarded. *Degree requirements:* For master's, thesis; for doctorate, thesis/dissertation, publishable paper. *Entrance requirements:* For master's and doctorate, GRE General Test, minimum GPA of 3.0 in last 60 hours of upper division course work. Additional exam requirements/recommendations for international students: Required—TOEFL. *Application deadline:* For fall admission, 1/3 for domestic students. Application fee: $50. Electronic applications accepted. *Expenses:* Tuition: Full-time $5160; part-time $287 per credit hour. Tuition and fees vary according to program and student's religious affiliation. *Financial support:* In 2008–09, 85 students received support, including 13 research assistantships with partial tuition reimbursements available (averaging $3,000 per year), 26 teaching assistantships with partial tuition reimbursements available (averaging $3,000 per year); fellowships, career-related internships or fieldwork, scholarships/grants, tuition waivers (partial), and unspecified assistantships also available. Financial award application deadline: 5/31. *Faculty research:* Psychotherapy process, Alzheimer's disease/dementia, psychology and law, health, psychology, developmental. Total annual research expenditures: $533,878. *Unit head:* Dr. Ramona Hopkins, Chair, 801-422-1170, Fax: 801-422-0602, E-mail: ramona_hopkins@byu.edu. *Application contact:* Karen A. Christensen, Coordinator of Student Programs, 801-422-4560, Fax: 801-422-0602, E-mail: karen_christensen@byu.edu.

Bryn Mawr College, Graduate School of Arts and Sciences, Department of Psychology, Bryn Mawr, PA 19010-2899. Offers clinical developmental psychology (PhD). Part-time programs available. *Degree requirements:* For doctorate, one foreign language, comprehensive exam, thesis/dissertation. *Entrance requirements:* For doctorate, GRE General Test. Additional exam requirements/recommendations for international students: Required—TOEFL (minimum score 600 paper-based; 250 computer-based).

California Institute of Integral Studies, Graduate Programs, School of Professional Psychology, San Francisco, CA 94103. Offers clinical psychology (Psy D); community mental health (MA); drama therapy (MA); expressive arts therapy (MA); integral counseling psychology (MA); integral counseling, psychology-weekend (MA); somatic psychology (MA). *Accreditation:* APA. Part-time programs available. *Faculty:* 28 full-time, 59 part-time/adjunct. *Students:* 553 full-time (408 women), 88 part-time (69 women); includes 132 minority (25 African Americans, 3 American Indian/Alaska Native, 57 Asian Americans or Pacific Islanders, 47 Hispanic Americans). Average age 37. 506 applicants, 61% accepted, 181 enrolled. In 2008, 109 master's, 20 doctorates awarded. *Degree requirements:* For master's, comprehensive exam; for doctorate, comprehensive exam, thesis/dissertation. *Entrance requirements:* For master's, minimum GPA of 3.0, letters of recommendation, writing sample; for doctorate, GRE, MA in psychology or social work with appropriate practical experience for advanced standing, or BA with a minimum GPA of 3.1; letters of recommendation; writing sample. Additional exam requirements/recommendations for international students: Required—TOEFL. *Application deadline:* For fall admission, 2/1 priority date for domestic and international students; for spring admission, 10/15 priority date for domestic and international students. Applications are processed on a rolling basis. Application fee: $65. Electronic applications accepted. *Expenses:* Tuition: Part-time $815 per contact hour. Required fees: $270; $135 per semester. Tuition and fees vary according to degree level. *Financial support:* In 2008–09, 496 students received support; research assistantships with tuition reimbursements available, teaching assistantships with tuition reimbursements available, career-related internships or fieldwork, Federal Work-Study,

Clinical Psychology

California Institute of Integral Studies (continued)
institutionally sponsored loans, scholarships/grants, and tuition waivers (partial) available. Support available to part-time students. Financial award application deadline: 3/15; financial award applicants required to submit FAFSA. *Faculty research:* Somatic psychology, comparative psychology, art therapy, transpersonal psychology, eco-psychology. *Application contact:* David Townes, Senior Admissions Counselor, 415-575-6152, Fax: 415-575-1268, E-mail: dtownes@ciis.edu.

See Close-Up on page 1105.

California Lutheran University, Graduate Studies, Department of Psychology, Thousand Oaks, CA 91360-2787. Offers clinical psychology (MS); marital and family therapy (MS). Part-time programs available. *Faculty:* 3 full-time (2 women), 12 part-time/adjunct (10 women). *Students:* 129 full-time (110 women), 4 part-time (3 women); includes 31 minority (2 African Americans, 1 American Indian/Alaska Native, 6 Asian Americans or Pacific Islanders, 22 Hispanic Americans), 6 international. Average age 30. 118 applicants, 70% accepted. In 2008, 49 master's awarded. *Degree requirements:* For master's, thesis or comprehensive exams. *Entrance requirements:* For master's, GRE General Test, interview, minimum GPA of 3.0. *Application deadline:* For fall admission, 2/15 priority date for domestic students. Applications are processed on a rolling basis. Application fee: $50. *Financial support:* In 2008–09, 60 students received support. *Unit head:* Dr. Mindy Puopolo, Director, 805-493-3528. *Application contact:* 805-493-3127, Fax: 805-493-3542, E-mail: clugrad@clunet.edu.

California State University, Dominguez Hills, College of Natural and Behavioral Sciences, Program in Psychology, Carson, CA 90747-0001. Offers clinical psychology (MA). Part-time and evening/weekend programs available. *Faculty:* 7 full-time (5 women). *Students:* 19 full-time (17 women), 16 part-time (12 women); includes 20 minority (6 African Americans, 14 Hispanic Americans). Average age 32. 45 applicants, 64% accepted, 17 enrolled. In 2008, 9 master's awarded. Terminal master's awarded for partial completion of doctoral program. *Degree requirements:* For master's, comprehensive exam, thesis optional. *Entrance requirements:* For master's, GRE General Test or MAT, interview, minimum GPA of 3.0, prerequisite psychology courses. Additional exam requirements/recommendations for international students: Required—TOEFL (minimum score 550 paper-based). *Application deadline:* For fall admission, 3/1 for domestic and international students. Application fee: $55. Electronic applications accepted. *Expenses:* Tuition, nonresident: part-time $339 per unit. Required fees: $1300 per semester. *Faculty research:* Culture and health, neuropsychology and HIV, psychohistory of the Holocaust, community and adolescents, malingering. *Unit head:* Dr. Ramona Davis, Chair, 310-243-3474, E-mail: rdavis@csudh.edu. *Application contact:* Dr. Karen I. Mason, Coordinator, 310-243-3642, Fax: 310-516-3642, E-mail: kmason@csudh.edu.

California State University, Fullerton, Graduate Studies, College of Humanities and Social Sciences, Department of Psychology, Fullerton, CA 92834-9480. Offers clinical/community psychology (MS); psychology (MA). Part-time programs available. *Students:* 60 full-time (45 women), 14 part-time (8 women); includes 26 minority (4 African Americans, 15 Asian Americans or Pacific Islanders, 7 Hispanic Americans), 7 international. Average age 27. 141 applicants, 29% accepted, 33 enrolled. In 2008, 18 master's awarded. *Degree requirements:* For master's, thesis. *Entrance requirements:* For master's, GRE General Test, GRE Subject Test, undergraduate major in psychology or related field. *Application deadline:* For fall admission, 3/15 for domestic students. Application fee: $55. Tuition and fees vary according to degree level. *Financial support:* Teaching assistantships, career-related internships or fieldwork, Federal Work-Study, institutionally sponsored loans, and scholarships/grants available. Support available to part-time students. Financial award application deadline: 3/1. *Unit head:* Dr. Daniel Kee, Chair, 657-278-3514. *Application contact:* Admissions/Applications, 657-278-2300.

California State University, Northridge, Graduate Studies, College of Social and Behavioral Sciences, Department of Psychology, Northridge, CA 91330. Offers clinical psychology (MA); general-experimental psychology (MA); human factors and applied experimental psychology (MA). *Faculty:* 31 full-time (18 women), 24 part-time/adjunct (8 women). *Students:* 64 full-time (38 women), 15 part-time (10 women); includes 27 minority (2 African Americans, 6 Asian Americans or Pacific Islanders, 19 Hispanic Americans), 3 international. Average age 27. 136 applicants, 32% accepted, 35 enrolled. In 2008, 29 master's awarded. *Degree requirements:* For master's, thesis. *Entrance requirements:* For master's, GRE General Test, GRE Subject Test, minimum GPA of 3.0, letters of recommendation. Additional exam requirements/recommendations for international students: Required—TOEFL. *Application deadline:* For fall admission, 11/30 for domestic students. Application fee: $55. *Financial support:* Application deadline: 3/1. *Unit head:* Dr. Carrie Saetermoe, Chair, 818-677-3506. *Application contact:* Dr. Carrie Saetermoe, Chair, 818-677-3506.

California State University, San Bernardino, Graduate Studies, College of Social and Behavioral Sciences, Department of Psychology, Program in Clinical/Counseling Psychology, San Bernardino, CA 92407-2397. Offers clinical psychology (MS). *Students:* 28 full-time (25 women), 1 (woman) part-time; includes 13 minority (3 African Americans, 2 Asian Americans or Pacific Islanders, 8 Hispanic Americans), 1 international. Average age 30. 64 applicants, 16% accepted, 9 enrolled. In 2008, 5 master's awarded. *Degree requirements:* For master's, comprehensive exam (for some programs), thesis optional, comprehensive exam or thesis. *Entrance requirements:* For master's, minimum GPA of 3.0 in major. *Application deadline:* For fall admission, 8/31 priority date for domestic students. Application fee: $55. *Expenses:* Tuition, area resident: Full-time $1252; part-time $726 per quarter. Required fees: $334 per quarter. Tuition and fees vary according to degree level and student level. *Financial support:* Fellowships, research assistantships, teaching assistantships, career-related internships or fieldwork, Federal Work-Study, and unspecified assistantships available. Financial award application deadline: 3/1. *Faculty research:* Psychology of women, fathering, depression, families, cross-cultural counseling. *Unit head:* Dr. Robert Cramer, Chair, 909-537-5576, Fax: 909-537-7003, E-mail: rcramer@csusb.edu. *Application contact:* Stacy Brooks, Graduate Secretary, 909-880-5570, Fax: 909-880-7003, E-mail: sbrooks@csusb.edu.

Capella University, Harold Abel School of Psychology, Minneapolis, MN 55402. Offers clinical psychology (MS); counseling psychology (MS); educational psychology (MS, PhD); general psychology (MS, PhD); industrial/organizational psychology (MS, PhD); school psychology (MS, Certificate); sport psychology (MS). Part-time and evening/weekend programs available. Postbaccalaureate distance learning degree programs offered (minimal on-campus study). Terminal master's awarded for partial completion of doctoral program. *Degree requirements:* For master's, thesis optional, project; for doctorate, thesis/dissertation. *Entrance requirements:* For degree, master's degree in school psychology. Additional exam requirements/recommendations for international students: Required—TOEFL (minimum score 550 paper-based; 213 computer-based), TWE (minimum score 4). Electronic applications accepted. *Faculty research:* Correctional mental health delivery, community mental health, attachment and caregiving in adult and family relationships, influence of encouragement on motivation, and moral dilemmas in business.

Cardinal Stritch University, College of Arts and Sciences, Department of Psychology, Milwaukee, WI 53217-3985. Offers clinical psychology (MA). Part-time and evening/weekend programs available. *Degree requirements:* For master's, thesis, portfolio, clinical practicum. *Entrance requirements:* For master's, GRE General Test, GRE Subject Test (psychology), interview, minimum GPA of 3.0, 3 letters of recommendation.

Carlos Albizu University, Graduate Programs, San Juan, PR 00901. Offers clinical psychology (MS, PhD, Psy D); general psychology (PhD); industrial/organizational psychology (MS, PhD); speech and language pathology (MS). *Accreditation:* APA (one or more programs are accredited). Part-time and evening/weekend programs available. *Faculty:* 22 full-time (11 women), 52 part-time/adjunct (38 women). *Students:* 566 full-time (470 women), 149 part-time (122 women); all minorities (all Hispanic Americans). Average age 28. 238 applicants, 79% accepted, 170 enrolled. In 2008, 100 master's, 84 doctorates awarded. Terminal master's awarded for partial completion of doctoral program. *Degree requirements:* For master's, one foreign language,

comprehensive exam, thesis; for doctorate, one foreign language, comprehensive exam, thesis/dissertation, written qualifying exams. *Entrance requirements:* For master's, GRE General Test or EXADEP, interview; minimum GPA of 3.0 (industrial/organizational psychology), 3.25 (speech and language pathology); for doctorate, GRE General Test or EXADEP, interview; minimum GPA of 3.0 (industrial/organizational psychology), 3.25 (PhD and Psy D in clinical psychology). *Application deadline:* For fall admission, 2/15 for domestic students, 7/19 for international students; for winter admission, 11/15 for international students; for spring admission, 11/15 for domestic students, 4/21 for international students. Application fee: $75. *Expenses:* Tuition: Full-time $6912; part-time $288 per credit. Required fees: $512 per semester. Tuition and fees vary according to degree level. *Financial support:* In 2008–09, 564 students received support, including 272 fellowships (averaging $1,786 per year); career-related internships or fieldwork, Federal Work-Study, institutionally sponsored loans, scholarships/grants, traineeships, and tuition waivers (partial) also available. Support available to part-time students. Financial award application deadline: 4/21; financial award applicants required to submit FAFSA. *Faculty research:* Psychotherapeutic techniques for Hispanics, psychology of the aged, school dropouts, stress, violence. *Unit head:* Dr. Jose J Cabiya, Chancellor, 787-725-6500 Ext. 1435, Fax: 787-721-7187, E-mail: jcabiya@sju.albizu.edu. *Application contact:* Carlos Rodriguez, Director of Admission's Office, 787-725-6500 Ext. 1521, Fax: 787-721-7187, E-mail: jveray@albizu.edu.

Carlos Albizu University, Miami Campus, Graduate Programs, Miami, FL 33172-2209. Offers clinical psychology (Psy D); entrepreneurship (MBA); exceptional student education (MS); industrial/organizational psychology (MS); marriage and family therapy (MS); mental health counseling (MS); nonprofit management (MBA); organizational management (MBA); psychology (MS); school counseling (MS); teaching English as a second language (MS). *Accreditation:* APA. Part-time and evening/weekend programs available. *Faculty:* 19 full-time (12 women), 70 part-time/adjunct (35 women). *Students:* 498 full-time (409 women), 199 part-time (153 women); includes 515 minority (56 African Americans, 1 American Indian/Alaska Native, 7 Asian Americans or Pacific Islanders, 451 Hispanic Americans). Average age 33. 179 applicants, 67% accepted, 113 enrolled. In 2008, 185 master's, 21 doctorates awarded. Terminal master's awarded for partial completion of doctoral program. *Degree requirements:* For master's, one foreign language, comprehensive exam, integrative project (MBA), research project (MSESE and MSTESOL); for doctorate, one foreign language, comprehensive exam, internship, doctoral project. *Entrance requirements:* For master's, 3 letters of recommendation, interview, minimum GPA of 3.0, resumé, statement of purpose, official transcripts; for doctorate, 3 letters of recommendation, minimum GPA of 3.0, resumé, interview. *Application deadline:* For fall admission, 8/1 priority date for domestic students; for spring admission, 11/30 priority date for domestic students. Applications are processed on a rolling basis. Application fee: $50. Electronic applications accepted. *Expenses:* Tuition: Full-time $9090; part-time $505 per credit. Required fees: $298 per term. Tuition and fees vary according to course load, degree level and program. *Financial support:* In 2008–09, 111 students received support. Federal Work-Study, scholarships/grants, and tuition discounts available. Financial award application deadline: 6/1; financial award applicants required to submit FAFSA. *Faculty research:* Psychotherapy, forensic psychology, neuropsychology, marketing strategy, entrepreneurship, special education. *Unit head:* Dr. Carmen S. Roca, PhD, Chancellor, 305-593-1223 Ext. 120, Fax: 305-629-8052, E-mail: croca@albizu.edu. *Application contact:* Barbara De la Cruz, Admission Officer, 305-593-1223 Ext. 218, Fax: 305-593-1854, E-mail: bdelacruz@albizu.edu.

Case Western Reserve University, School of Graduate Studies, Department of Psychology, Program in Clinical Psychology, Cleveland, OH 44106. Offers PhD. *Accreditation:* APA. *Degree requirements:* For doctorate, thesis/dissertation, internship. *Entrance requirements:* For doctorate, GRE General Test, GRE Subject Test. Additional exam requirements/recommendations for international students: Required—TOEFL. Electronic applications accepted. *Faculty research:* Pediatric psychology, family functioning, depression, geriatric psychopathology, creativity and play.

The Catholic University of America, School of Arts and Sciences, Department of Psychology, Washington, DC 20064. Offers applied experimental psychology (MA, PhD); clinical psychology (PhD); general psychology (MA, PhD); human development (PhD); human factors (MA); JD/MA. *Accreditation:* APA (one or more programs are accredited). Part-time programs available. Terminal master's awarded for partial completion of doctoral program. *Degree requirements:* For master's, comprehensive exam; for doctorate, comprehensive exam, thesis/dissertation. *Entrance requirements:* For master's, GRE General Test, 3 letters of recommendation; for doctorate, GRE General Test, GRE Subject Test, 3 letters of recommendation. Additional exam requirements/recommendations for international students: Required—TOEFL (minimum score 580 paper-based; 237 computer-based). Electronic applications accepted. *Faculty research:* Social development, family interaction, human perception and cognition, applied cognitive science, individual and group psychotherapy.

Central Michigan University, College of Graduate Studies, College of Humanities and Social and Behavioral Sciences, Department of Psychology, Program in Clinical Psychology, Mount Pleasant, MI 48859. Offers MA, PhD. *Accreditation:* APA. *Faculty:* 8 full-time (3 women). *Students:* 7 full-time (2 women), 23 part-time (18 women), 4 international. Average age 26. Terminal master's awarded for partial completion of doctoral program. *Degree requirements:* For master's, thesis, completion of first two years of the PhD program in clinical psychology; for doctorate, thesis/dissertation. *Entrance requirements:* For master's and doctorate, GRE. *Application deadline:* For fall admission, 1/15 for domestic and international students. Application fee: $35 ($45 for international students). Electronic applications accepted. *Expenses:* Tuition, state resident: full-time $3717; part-time $413 per credit. Tuition, nonresident: full-time $6894; part-time $766 per credit. *Financial support:* In 2008–09, 3 fellowships with tuition reimbursements were awarded; research assistantships with tuition reimbursements, career-related internships or fieldwork, Federal Work-Study, unspecified assistantships, and out-of-state merit awards also available. *Faculty research:* Applied youth development; emotional processes, personality disorders, and assessment; influence of affective variables on cognitive performance; post-traumatic stress disorder and panic disorder; validation of clinical inferences from psychological tests. *Unit head:* Dr. Reid Skeel, Director, 989-774-6463, Fax: 989-774-2553, E-mail: skeel1rl@cmich.edu. *Application contact:* Judith L. Prince, Director of Graduate Student Services, 989-774-1059, Fax: 989-774-1857, E-mail: judith.l.prince@cmich.edu.

Chestnut Hill College, School of Graduate Studies, Division of Psychology, Program in Clinical and Counseling Psychology, Philadelphia, PA 19118-2693. Offers MA, MS, CAS. Part-time and evening/weekend programs available. *Faculty:* 11 full-time (5 women), 33 part-time/adjunct (14 women). *Students:* 144 full-time (133 women), 103 part-time (72 women); includes 47 minority (37 African Americans, 5 Asian Americans or Pacific Islanders, 5 Hispanic Americans). 147 applicants, 52% accepted. In 2008, 55 master's awarded. *Degree requirements:* For master's, thesis optional, practica. *Entrance requirements:* For master's, GRE, statement of professional goals, writing sample, transcripts, letters of recommendation; for CAS, GRE, master's degree in counseling or related discipline, transcripts, letters of recommendation, statement of professional goals, writing sample. Additional exam requirements/recommendations for international students: Required—TOEFL (minimum score 550 paper-based; 213 computer-based). *Application deadline:* For fall admission, 7/17 priority date for domestic students, 7/17 for international students; for spring admission, 12/15 priority date for domestic students, 12/15 for international students. Applications are processed on a rolling basis. Application fee: $50. *Expenses:* Tuition: Part-time $510 per credit hour. *Faculty research:* Play therapy, eating disorders, addictions, group psychology and group therapy, health psychology. *Application contact:* Amy Boorse, Administrative Assistant, School of Graduate Studies Office, 215-248-7170, Fax: 215-248-7161, E-mail: gradadmissions@chc.edu.

Chestnut Hill College, School of Graduate Studies, Division of Psychology, Program in Clinical Psychology, Philadelphia, PA 19118-2693. Offers Psy D. *Accreditation:* APA. Part-time and evening/weekend programs available. *Faculty:* 11 full-time (5 women), 33 part-time/adjunct (14 women). *Students:* 66 full-time (54 women), 41 part-time (29 women); includes 7 minority (5 African Americans, 1 Asian American or Pacific Islander, 1 Hispanic American), 1 international. 161 applicants, 29% accepted. In 2008, 18 doctorates awarded. *Degree requirements:* For doctorate, comprehensive exam, thesis/dissertation, internships, practica. *Entrance requirements:* For doctorate, GRE, transcripts, letters of recommendation, statement of professional goals, writing sample, master's degree in clinical/counseling psychology or closely related field. Additional exam requirements/recommendations for international students: Required—TOEFL (minimum score 500 paper-based; 213 computer-based). *Application deadline:* For fall admission, 7/17 priority date for domestic students, 7/17 for international students; for spring admission, 12/15 priority date for domestic students, 12/15 for international students. Applications are processed on a rolling basis. Application fee: $75. *Expenses:* Tuition: Part-time $510 per credit hour. *Faculty research:* Psychological testing and assessment, GLBT issues, autism and developmental disorders, stepfamilies, gender issues. *Application contact:* Mary Steinmetz, Director of Psy D Admissions, 215-248-7077, Fax: 215-753-3619, E-mail: profpsyc@chc.edu.

The Chicago School of Professional Psychology, Graduate School, Program in Clinical Psychology, Chicago, IL 60610. Offers applied behavior analysis (MA, Psy D, Certificate); clinical counseling (MA); clinical psychology (Psy D); general psychology (Certificate); Latino mental health (Certificate). *Degree requirements:* For master's, thesis (for some programs); for doctorate, comprehensive exam, thesis/dissertation. *Entrance requirements:* For master's, minimum undergraduate GPA of 3.0; 1 course in psychology and 1 course in either statistics or research methods; for doctorate, GRE, 18 hours of psychology credit (including courses in statistics, normal psychology and human development); minimum GPA of 3.2. Additional exam requirements/recommendations for international students: Required—TOEFL (minimum score 550 paper-based; 213 computer-based; 79 iBT). Electronic applications accepted.

The Chicago School of Professional Psychology, Graduate School, Program in Psychodynamic Psychology, Chicago, IL 60610. Offers Psy D.

City College of the City University of New York, Graduate School, College of Liberal Arts and Science, Division of Social Science, Department of Psychology, New York, NY 10031-9198. Offers clinical psychology (PhD); experimental cognition (PhD); general psychology (MA); mental health counseling (MA). *Accreditation:* APA (one or more programs are accredited). Part-time programs available. *Degree requirements:* For master's, one foreign language, comprehensive exam, thesis. *Entrance requirements:* For master's, GRE. Additional exam requirements/recommendations for international students: Required—TOEFL (minimum score 550 paper-based; 213 computer-based). *Faculty research:* Social/personality psychology, physiological psychology, cognition and development.

Clark University, Graduate School, Department of Psychology, Program in Clinical Psychology, Worcester, MA 01610-1477. Offers PhD. *Accreditation:* APA. *Degree requirements:* For doctorate, thesis/dissertation. *Entrance requirements:* For doctorate, GRE General Test. Additional exam requirements/recommendations for international students: Required—TOEFL. *Application deadline:* For fall admission, 12/28 priority date for domestic students. Applications are processed on a rolling basis. Application fee: $50. *Expenses:* Tuition: Full-time $34,900; part-time $1091 per credit hour. Required fees: $30. *Financial support:* In 2008–09, fellowships with full tuition reimbursements (averaging $15,700 per year), research assistantships with full tuition reimbursements (averaging $15,700 per year), teaching assistantships with full tuition reimbursements (averaging $15,700 per year) were awarded; tuition waivers (full) also available. *Unit head:* Dr. James Cordova, Chair, 508-793-7268. *Application contact:* Peggy Moskowitz, Graduate School Secretary, 508-793-7274, Fax: 508-793-7265, E-mail: psychology@clarku.edu.

Cleveland State University, College of Graduate Studies, College of Science, Department of Psychology, Cleveland, OH 44115. Offers adult development and aging (PhD); clinical psychology (MA); consumer/industrial research (MA); diversity management (MA); experimental research psychology (MA); school psychology (Psy S). *Faculty:* 20 full-time (7 women), 16 part-time/adjunct (8 women). *Students:* 66 full-time (44 women), 62 part-time (46 women); includes 25 minority (19 African Americans, 1 American Indian/Alaska Native, 2 Asian Americans or Pacific Islanders, 3 Hispanic Americans), 3 international. Average age 30. 180 applicants, 40% accepted, 55 enrolled. In 2008, 39 master's, 4 other advanced degrees awarded. *Degree requirements:* For master's, comprehensive exam (for some programs), thesis (for some programs); for doctorate, comprehensive exam, thesis/dissertation; for Psy S, internship. *Entrance requirements:* For master's and doctorate, GRE General Test. Additional exam requirements/recommendations for international students: Required—TOEFL (minimum score 525 paper-based; 197 computer-based). *Application deadline:* For fall admission, 2/1 priority date for domestic and international students. Applications are processed on a rolling basis. Application fee: $30. Electronic applications accepted. *Financial support:* In 2008–09, 45 students received support. Career-related internships or fieldwork, Federal Work-Study, tuition waivers (partial), and unspecified assistantships available. Financial award applicants required to submit FAFSA. *Faculty research:* Cognitive and social psychology, consumer psychology, clinical psychology, school psychology, aging. Total annual research expenditures: $112,607. *Unit head:* Dr. Albert F Smith, Interim Chair, 216-687-3723, Fax: 216-687-9294, E-mail: a.f.smith@csuohio.edu. *Application contact:* Karen R Colston, Administrative Coordinator, 216-687-2552, Fax: 216-687-9294, E-mail: k.colston@csuohio.edu.

College of St. Joseph, Graduate Programs, Division of Psychology and Human Services, Program in Clinical Mental Health Counseling, Rutland, VT 05701-3899. Offers MS. Part-time programs available. *Degree requirements:* For master's, comprehensive exam. *Entrance requirements:* For master's, 2 letters of reference, interview. Electronic applications accepted.

College of St. Joseph, Graduate Programs, Division of Psychology and Human Services, Program in Clinical Psychology, Rutland, VT 05701-3899. Offers MS. Part-time and evening/weekend programs available. *Degree requirements:* For master's, comprehensive exam, thesis optional. *Entrance requirements:* For master's, 2 letters of reference, interview. Electronic applications accepted.

Concordia University, School of Graduate Studies, Faculty of Arts and Science, Department of Psychology, Program in Psychology (Clinical), Montréal, QC H3G 1M8, Canada. Offers MA, PhD, Certificate. *Accreditation:* APA (one or more programs are accredited). *Degree requirements:* For master's, comprehensive exam, thesis; for doctorate, comprehensive exam, thesis/dissertation. *Entrance requirements:* For master's, GRE General Test, GRE Subject Test, honors degree in psychology or equivalent; for doctorate, master's degree in psychology. *Faculty research:* Developmental-clinical psychology, sensory deficits, sexual dysfunction.

Dalhousie University, Faculty of Science, Department of Psychology, Halifax, NS B3H 4J1, Canada. Offers clinical psychology (PhD); psychology (M Sc, PhD); psychology/neuroscience (M Sc, PhD). *Accreditation:* APA (one or more programs are accredited). *Faculty:* 30 full-time (8 women), 34 part-time/adjunct (14 women). *Students:* 56 full-time (35 women); includes 2 minority (both Asian Americans or Pacific Islanders). 200 applicants, 8% accepted. In 2008, 8 master's, 7 doctorates awarded. *Degree requirements:* For master's, thesis; for doctorate, thesis/dissertation. *Entrance requirements:* For doctorate, GRE General Test. Additional exam requirements/recommendations for international students: Required—TOEFL, IELTS, 1 of the following 5 approved tests: IELTS, TOEFL, CAEL, CANTEST, Michigan English Language Assessment Battery. Application fee: $70. Electronic applications accepted. *Financial support:* In 2008–09, 19 fellowships, 26 teaching assistantships (averaging $1,853 per year) were awarded; career-related internships or fieldwork, scholarships/grants, and health care benefits also available. Financial award application deadline: 2/1. *Faculty research:* Physiological psychology, psychology of learning, learning and behavior, forensic clinical health psychology, development perception and cognition. Total annual research expenditures: $1.9 million. *Unit head:* Dr. Tracy Taylor-Helmick, Graduate Coordinator, 902-494-3001, Fax: 902-494-6585, E-mail: tracy.taylor.helmick@dal.ca. *Application contact:* Mary Macconnachie, Graduate Secretary, 902-494-3839, Fax: 902-494-6585, E-mail: mary.macconnachie@dal.ca.

DePaul University, College of Liberal Arts and Sciences, Department of Psychology, Chicago, IL 60604-2287. Offers clinical psychology (MA, PhD), including child clinical psychology, community clinical psychology; experimental psychology (MA, PhD); general psychology (MS); industrial/organizational psychology (MA, PhD); MA/PhD. *Accreditation:* APA (one or more programs are accredited). *Faculty:* 31 full-time (19 women), 6 part-time/adjunct (4 women). *Students:* 33 full-time (17 women), 23 part-time (20 women); includes 9 minority (4 African Americans, 1 American Indian/Alaska Native, 1 Asian American or Pacific Islander, 3 Hispanic Americans), 2 international. Average age 28. 332 applicants, 14% accepted, 23 enrolled. In 2008, 14 master's, 17 doctorates awarded. *Degree requirements:* For master's, thesis, oral exam; for doctorate, comprehensive exam, thesis/dissertation, oral and written exams. *Entrance requirements:* For master's and doctorate, GRE General Test, GRE Subject Test, 32 quarter hours of course work in psychology, 3 letters of recommendation. Additional exam requirements/recommendations for international students: Required—TOEFL. Application fee: $40. Electronic applications accepted. *Financial support:* In 2008–09, 48 students received support, including 35 research assistantships with full tuition reimbursements available (averaging $11,800 per year), 13 teaching assistantships with full tuition reimbursements available (averaging $11,800 per year); career-related internships or fieldwork, scholarships/grants, traineeships, tuition waivers (full and partial), and unspecified assistantships also available. Financial award application deadline: 1/10. *Faculty research:* Adolescent stress and depression, minority adolescents sexuality, public policy, community influences in child adjustment. *Unit head:* Dr. Christopher B Keys, Chairman, 773-325-7887, Fax: 773-325-7888. *Application contact:* Alison Pereida Knapp, Graduate Admissions Assistant, 773-325-7887, Fax: 773-325-7888.

Drexel University, College of Arts and Sciences, Department of Psychology, Clinical Psychology Program, Philadelphia, PA 19104-2875. Offers clinical psychology (PhD); forensic psychology (PhD); health psychology (PhD); neuropsychology (PhD). *Accreditation:* APA. Terminal master's awarded for partial completion of doctoral program. *Degree requirements:* For doctorate, thesis/dissertation, qualifying exam. *Entrance requirements:* For doctorate, GRE General Test, GRE Subject Test, minimum GPA of 3.0. Electronic applications accepted. *Expenses:* Contact institution. *Faculty research:* Cognitive behavioral therapy, stress and coping, eating disorders, substance abuse, developmental disabilities.

Drexel University, College of Arts and Sciences, Department of Psychology, Program in Law-Psychology, Philadelphia, PA 19104-2875. Offers JD/PhD. Electronic applications accepted. *Expenses:* Contact institution. *Faculty research:* Mental health law issues, professional ethics, social science applications to law.

Duke University, Graduate School, Department of Psychology, Durham, NC 27708-0586. Offers biological psychology (PhD); clinical psychology (PhD); cognitive psychology (PhD); developmental psychology (PhD); experimental psychology (PhD); health psychology (PhD); human social development (PhD); JD/MA. *Accreditation:* APA (one or more programs are accredited). *Degree requirements:* For doctorate, thesis/dissertation. *Entrance requirements:* For doctorate, GRE General Test. Additional exam requirements/recommendations for international students: Required—TOEFL (minimum score 550 paper-based; 213 computer-based; 83 iBT), IELTS (minimum score 7). Electronic applications accepted.

Duquesne University, Graduate School of Liberal Arts, Department of Psychology, Pittsburgh, PA 15282-0001. Offers clinical psychology (PhD). *Accreditation:* APA. *Faculty:* 14 full-time (5 women). *Students:* 55 full-time (28 women); includes 2 minority (1 African American, 1 Hispanic American), 9 international. Average age 25. 79 applicants, 9% accepted, 7 enrolled. In 2008, 9 doctorates awarded. *Degree requirements:* For doctorate, comprehensive exam, thesis/dissertation. *Entrance requirements:* For doctorate, GRE General Test, MA in psychology. Additional exam requirements/recommendations for international students: Required—TOEFL. *Application deadline:* For fall admission, 12/15 for domestic and international students. Application fee: $50. Electronic applications accepted. *Expenses:* Tuition: Part-time $819 per credit. Required fees: $78 per credit. Tuition and fees vary according to course load. *Financial support:* In 2008–09, 1 research assistantship with full tuition reimbursement (averaging $13,000 per year), 14 teaching assistantships with full tuition reimbursements (averaging $13,000 per year) were awarded; fellowships with full tuition reimbursements, career-related internships or fieldwork, scholarships/grants, tuition waivers (partial), and unspecified assistantships also available. Financial award application deadline: 5/1. *Faculty research:* Emotion, language motivation, imagination, development. *Unit head:* Dr. Daniel Burston, Chair, 412-396-5067. *Application contact:* Linda L. Rendulic, Assistant to the Dean, 412-396-6400, Fax: 412-396-5265, E-mail: rendulic@duq.edu.

East Carolina University, Graduate School, Thomas Harriot College of Arts and Sciences, Department of Psychology, Program in Clinical Psychology, Greenville, NC 27858-4353. Offers MA. *Degree requirements:* For master's, one foreign language, comprehensive exam, thesis. *Entrance requirements:* For master's, GRE General Test, GRE Subject Test. Additional exam requirements/recommendations for international students: Required—TOEFL.

Eastern Illinois University, Graduate School, College of Sciences, Charleston, IL 61920-3099. Offers biological sciences (MS); chemistry (MS); communication disorders and sciences (MS); economics (MA); mathematics and computer science (MA), including mathematics, mathematics education; natural sciences (MS); political science (MA); psychology (MA, SSP), including clinical psychology (MA), school psychology (SSP). Part-time programs available. *Degree requirements:* For SSP, thesis. *Entrance requirements:* For degree, GRE General Test.

Eastern Illinois University, Graduate School, College of Sciences, Department of Psychology, Program in Clinical Psychology, Charleston, IL 61920-3099. Offers MA. *Degree requirements:* For master's, comprehensive exam. *Entrance requirements:* For master's, GRE General Test.

Eastern Kentucky University, The Graduate School, College of Arts and Sciences, Department of Psychology, Richmond, KY 40475-3102. Offers clinical psychology (MS); industrial/organizational psychology (MS); school psychology (Psy S). Part-time programs available. *Entrance requirements:* For master's and Psy S, GRE General Test, minimum GPA of 2.5. *Faculty research:* Autism, social psychology, parenting, assessment of depression/anxiety, reading.

Eastern Michigan University, Graduate School, College of Arts and Sciences, Department of Psychology, Ypsilanti, MI 48197. Offers clinical behavioral psychology (MS); clinical psychology (MS, PhD); psychology (MS). *Accreditation:* APA.

Eastern Virginia Medical School, The Virginia Consortium Program in Clinical Psychology, Norfolk, VA 23501-1980. Offers Psy D. *Accreditation:* APA. *Faculty:* 33. *Students:* 53. 249 applicants, 6% accepted, 10 enrolled. In 2008, 4 doctorates awarded. *Entrance requirements:* For doctorate, GRE, BS in behavioral sciences or equivalent. Additional exam requirements/recommendations for international students: Required—TOEFL. *Application deadline:* For fall admission, 1/15 for domestic students. Application fee: $40. *Expenses:* Contact institution. *Unit head:* Dr. Michael L. Stutts, Director, 757-446-8400, Fax: 757-446-8401, E-mail: stuttsml@evms.edu. *Application contact:* Eileen O'Neill, Administrative Coordinator, 757-368-1820, Fax: 757-446-8401, E-mail: exoneill@odu.edu.

Eastern Washington University, Graduate Studies, College of Social and Behavioral Sciences, Department of Psychology, Cheney, WA 99004-2431. Offers clinical psychology (MS); experimental psychology (MS); psychology (MS); school psychology (MS). *Degree requirements:* For master's, comprehensive exam, thesis or alternative. *Entrance requirements:* For master's, GRE General Test, minimum GPA of 3.0.

East Tennessee State University, School of Graduate Studies, College of Arts and Sciences, Department of Psychology, Johnson City, TN 37614. Offers clinical psychology (MA); general psychology (MA). *Degree requirements:* For master's, thesis, oral exams. *Entrance requirements:* For master's, GRE General Test, GRE Subject Test, minimum GPA of 3.0. Additional exam requirements/recommendations for international students: Required—TOEFL (minimum score 550 paper-based; 213 computer-based). *Faculty research:* Language acquisition, recovery of brain function after injury or damage, violence in domestic relationships and road rage, reasons for living, unhealthy tanning behaviors.

Clinical Psychology

Edinboro University of Pennsylvania, Graduate Studies and Research, School of Liberal Arts, Department of Psychology, Edinboro, PA 16444. Offers clinical psychology (MA). Part-time and evening/weekend programs available. *Faculty:* 3 full-time (1 woman). *Students:* 24 full-time (20 women), 9 part-time (8 women); includes 1 minority (Asian American or Pacific Islander), 3 international. Average age 29. In 2008, 12 master's awarded. *Degree requirements:* For master's, comprehensive exam, thesis or alternative, project. *Entrance requirements:* For master's, GRE or MAT, minimum QPA of 2.5. *Application deadline:* For fall admission, 3/15 priority date for domestic students. Applications are processed on a rolling basis. Application fee: $30. Electronic applications accepted. *Expenses:* Tuition, state resident: full-time $6430; part-time $357 per credit. Tuition, nonresident: full-time $8038; part-time $572 per credit. International tuition: $15,171.58 full-time. Required fees: $2113; $60 per credit. Tuition and fees vary according to course load. *Financial support:* In 2008–09, 10 research assistantships with full and partial tuition reimbursements (averaging $3,850 per year) were awarded; career-related internships or fieldwork, Federal Work-Study, scholarships/grants, and unspecified assistantships also available. Support available to part-time students. Financial award application deadline: 2/15; financial award applicants required to submit FAFSA. *Unit head:* Dr. Cynthia Legin-Bucell, Chairperson, 814-732-2774, E-mail: leginbucell@edinboro.edu. *Application contact:* Dr. Cynthia Legin-Bucell, Chairperson, 814-732-2774, E-mail: leginbucell@edinboro.edu.

Emory University, Graduate School of Arts and Sciences, Department of Psychology, Atlanta, GA 30322-1100. Offers clinical psychology (PhD); cognition and development (PhD); neuroscience and animal behavior (PhD). *Accreditation:* APA. *Degree requirements:* For doctorate, comprehensive exam, thesis/dissertation. *Entrance requirements:* For doctorate, GRE General Test, minimum GPA of 3.25. Additional exam requirements/recommendations for international students: Required—TOEFL. Electronic applications accepted. *Faculty research:* Neuroscience and animal behavior; adult and child psychopathology, cognition development assessment.

Emporia State University, School of Graduate Studies, The Teachers College, Department of Psychology, Art Therapy, Rehabilitation and Mental Health Counseling, Program in Clinical Psychology, Emporia, KS 66801-5087. Offers MS. Part-time programs available. *Students:* 17 full-time (12 women), 4 part-time (2 women); includes 2 minority (1 African American, 1 Asian American or Pacific Islander), 2 international. 14 applicants, 50% accepted, 7 enrolled. In 2008, 8 master's awarded. *Degree requirements:* For master's, comprehensive exam, clinical internship. *Entrance requirements:* For master's, GRE or MAT, 24 hours of course work in undergraduate psychology, 3 letters of recommendation. Additional exam requirements/recommendations for international students: Required—TOEFL (minimum score 450 paper-based; 133 computer-based). *Application deadline:* For fall admission, 8/15 for domestic students. Applications are processed on a rolling basis. Application fee: $30 ($75 for international students). Electronic applications accepted. *Expenses:* Tuition, area resident: Full-time $3976; part-time $166 per credit hour. Tuition, state resident: full-time $3976; part-time $166 per credit hour. Tuition, nonresident: full-time $12,028; part-time $501 per credit hour. Required fees: $51 per credit hour. Tuition and fees vary according to campus/location. *Financial support:* Career-related internships or fieldwork, Federal Work-Study, institutionally sponsored loans, health care benefits, and unspecified assistantships available. Support available to part-time students. Financial award application deadline: 3/15; financial award applicants required to submit FAFSA. *Unit head:* Dr. Kenneth A. Weaver, Chair, 620-341-5317, E-mail: kweaver@emporia.edu. *Application contact:* Mary Sewell, Admissions Coordinator, 800-950-GRAD, Fax: 620-341-5909, E-mail: msewell@emporia.edu.

Evangel University, Department of Psychology, Springfield, MO 65802-2191. Offers clinical psychology (MS); counseling psychology (MS). Part-time and evening/weekend programs available. *Degree requirements:* For master's, comprehensive exam, thesis (for some programs). *Entrance requirements:* For master's, GRE General Test or MAT, minimum undergraduate GPA of 3.0, undergraduate major or minor in psychology, teaching certificate (school counseling). Additional exam requirements/recommendations for international students: Required—TOEFL (minimum score 550 paper-based; 213 computer-based).

Fairleigh Dickinson University, Metropolitan Campus, University College: Arts, Sciences, and Professional Studies, School of Psychology, Program in Clinical Psychology, Teaneck, NJ 07666-1914. Offers MA, PhD. *Accreditation:* APA. *Students:* 81 full-time (57 women), 1 (woman) part-time, 2 international. Average age 31. 19 applicants, 89% accepted, 17 enrolled. In 2008, 8 doctorates awarded. *Application deadline:* Applications are processed on a rolling basis. Application fee: $40. *Application contact:* Susan Brooman, University Director of Graduate Admissions, 201-692-2554, Fax: 201-692-2560, E-mail: globaleducation@fdu.edu.

See Close-Up on page 1107.

Fairleigh Dickinson University, Metropolitan Campus, University College: Arts, Sciences, and Professional Studies, School of Psychology, Program in Clinical Psychopharmacology, Teaneck, NJ 07666-1914. Offers MA. *Students:* 34 part-time (20 women), 1 international. Average age 45. 25 applicants, 100% accepted, 15 enrolled. In 2008, 8 master's awarded. *Application contact:* Susan Brooman, University Director of Graduate Admissions, 201-692-2554, Fax: 201-692-2560, E-mail: globaleducation@fdu.edu.

Fielding Graduate University, Graduate Programs, School of Psychology, Santa Barbara, CA 93105-3538. Offers clinical psychology (PhD); clinical psychology respecialization (Post-Doctoral Certificate); media psychology (PhD); media psychology and social change (MA); neuropsychology (Post-Doctoral Certificate). *Accreditation:* APA. Postbaccalaureate distance learning degree programs offered (minimal on-campus study). *Faculty:* 35 full-time (17 women), 2 part-time/adjunct (0 women). *Students:* 522 full-time (382 women), 76 part-time (47 women); includes 121 minority (38 African Americans, 6 American Indian/Alaska Native, 28 Asian Americans or Pacific Islanders, 49 Hispanic Americans), 12 international. Average age 44. 284 applicants, 38% accepted, 76 enrolled. In 2008, 38 doctorates, 29 other advanced degrees awarded. Terminal master's awarded for partial completion of doctoral program. *Degree requirements:* For master's, capstone project; for doctorate, comprehensive exam, thesis/ dissertation. *Entrance requirements:* For doctorate, writing sample, minimum GPA of 3.0, 3 letters of recommendation, resumé. *Application deadline:* For fall admission, 2/23 for domestic and international students; for spring admission, 8/25 for domestic and international students. Application fee: $75. Electronic applications accepted. *Expenses:* Contact institution. *Financial support:* In 2008–09, 440 students received support, including 3 research assistantships (averaging $2,565 per year); scholarships/grants and health care benefits also available. Support available to part-time students. Financial award application deadline: 5/15; financial award applicants required to submit FAFSA. *Unit head:* Dr. Raymond Trybus, Dean, 805-898-2909, E-mail: rtrybus@fielding.edu. *Application contact:* Kathryn Romero, Admission Counselor, 800-340-1099, Fax: 805-687-9793, E-mail: kromero@fielding.edu.

See Close-Up on page 1111.

Fisk University, Graduate Programs, Department of Psychology, Nashville, TN 37208-3051. Offers clinical psychology (MA); psychology (MA). *Degree requirements:* For master's, thesis. *Entrance requirements:* For master's, GRE General Test, GRE Subject Test, minimum GPA of 3.0. *Faculty research:* Ethnic and gender identity, development, female adolescent development, juvenile delinquency prevention.

Florida Institute of Technology, Graduate Programs, College of Psychology and Liberal Arts, School of Psychology, Melbourne, FL 32901-6975. Offers applied behavior analysis (MS); clinical psychology (Psy D); industrial/organizational psychology (MS, PhD). *Accreditation:* APA (one or more programs are accredited). Part-time programs available. *Degree requirements:* For master's, comprehensive exam (for some programs), thesis (for some programs); for doctorate, comprehensive exam, thesis/dissertation (for some programs), internship. *Entrance requirements:* For master's, GRE General Test, 3 letters of recommendation, minimum GPA of 3.0, resumé, statement of objectives; for doctorate, GRE General Test, GRE Subject Test, 3 letters of recommendation, minimum GPA of 3.2, resumé, statement of objectives. Additional exam requirements/recommendations for international students: Required—TOEFL (minimum score 550 paper-based; 213 computer-based). Electronic applications accepted. *Expenses:* Tuition: Part-time $980 per credit hour. *Faculty research:* Addictions, neuropsychology, child abuse, assessment, psychological trauma.

See Close-Up on page 1113.

Florida State University, Graduate Studies, College of Arts and Sciences, Department of Psychology, Program in Clinical Psychology, Tallahassee, FL 32306. Offers PhD. *Accreditation:* APA. *Degree requirements:* For doctorate, thesis/dissertation, preliminary exam, independent project. *Entrance requirements:* For doctorate, GRE General Test, minimum GPA of 3.2, research experience, letters of recommendation. Additional exam requirements/recommendations for international students: Required—TOEFL (minimum score 550 paper-based; 213 computer-based; 80 iBT). Electronic applications accepted. *Faculty research:* Antisocial behavior, depression, addictive behavior, developmental psychopathology, anxiety.

Fordham University, Graduate School of Arts and Sciences, Department of Psychology, Program in Clinical Psychology, New York, NY 10458. Offers PhD. Terminal master's awarded for partial completion of doctoral program. *Degree requirements:* For doctorate, comprehensive exam, thesis/dissertation, clinical internship. *Entrance requirements:* For doctorate, GRE General Test, GRE Subject Test. Additional exam requirements/recommendations for international students: Required—TOEFL (minimum score 600 paper-based; 250 computer-based). Electronic applications accepted.

Francis Marion University, Graduate Programs, Department of Psychology, Florence, SC 29501-0547. Offers applied clinical psychology (MS); applied community psychology (MS); school psychology (MS). Part-time and evening/weekend programs available. *Faculty:* 10 full-time (4 women), 6 part-time/adjunct (4 women). *Students:* 15 full-time (all women), 28 part-time (25 women); includes 5 minority (all African Americans), 1 international. Average age 38. 39 applicants, 100% accepted, 12 enrolled. In 2008, 15 master's awarded. *Degree requirements:* For master's, internship. *Entrance requirements:* For master's, GRE General Test. *Application deadline:* For fall admission, 4/15 for domestic students; for spring admission, 10/15 for domestic students. Applications are processed on a rolling basis. Application fee: $30. *Expenses:* Tuition, state resident: full-time $7547; part-time $377.35 per credit hour. Tuition, nonresident: full-time $15,094; part-time $754.70 per credit hour. Required fees: $22 per credit hour. $30 per semester. *Financial support:* In 2008–09, 1 research assistantship (averaging $7,000 per year), 3 teaching assistantships (averaging $8,000 per year) were awarded; career-related internships or fieldwork and unspecified assistantships also available. Support available to part-time students. Financial award application deadline: 3/1; financial award applicants required to submit FAFSA. *Faculty research:* Critical thinking, spatial localization, cognition and aging, family psychology. *Unit head:* Dr. John R. Hester, Chair, 843-661-1635, Fax: 843-661-1628. *Application contact:* Jennifer Taylor, Administrative Assistant, 843-661-1378, Fax: 843-661-1628.

Fuller Theological Seminary, Graduate School of Psychology, Department of Clinical Psychology, Pasadena, CA 91182. Offers PhD, Psy D. *Accreditation:* APA (one or more programs are accredited). *Degree requirements:* For doctorate, thesis/dissertation, internships. *Entrance requirements:* For doctorate, GRE General Test, GRE Subject Test, interview. Additional exam requirements/recommendations for international students: Required—TOEFL. *Expenses:* Contact institution. *Faculty research:* Psychoneuroimmunology, psychology of religion, coping, shame, depression.

Gallaudet University, The Graduate School, College of Arts and Sciences, Department of Psychology, Program in Clinical Psychology, Washington, DC 20002-3625. Offers PhD. MA in psychology given as part of PhD program. *Accreditation:* APA. *Degree requirements:* For doctorate, thesis/dissertation. *Entrance requirements:* For doctorate, GRE General Test or MAT, interview. Electronic applications accepted.

George Fox University, Graduate Department of Clinical Psychology, Newberg, OR 97132-2697. Offers MA, Psy D. *Accreditation:* APA. *Faculty:* 8 full-time (3 women), 8 part-time/adjunct (3 women). *Students:* 105 full-time (69 women), 4 part-time (all women); includes 11 minority (2 African Americans, 3 American Indian/Alaska Native, 2 Asian Americans or Pacific Islanders, 4 Hispanic Americans). Average age 29. 76 applicants, 45% accepted, 24 enrolled. In 2008, 21 master's, 21 doctorates awarded. *Degree requirements:* For master's, comprehensive exam, 60 semester hours of required and elective courses; for doctorate, thesis/dissertation, internship plus 125 semester hours of required and elective courses. *Entrance requirements:* For master's and doctorate, GRE General Test, minimum undergraduate GPA of 3.0 during previous 2 years. Additional exam requirements/recommendations for international students: Required—TOEFL (minimum score 550 paper-based; 213 computer-based; 80 iBT). *Application deadline:* For fall admission, 1/15 priority date for domestic and international students. Applications are processed on a rolling basis. Application fee: $40. Electronic applications accepted. *Expenses:* Contact institution. *Financial support:* In 2008–09, 15 students received support, including 8 research assistantships (averaging $2,000 per year), 6 teaching assistantships (averaging $3,000 per year); scholarships/grants also available. Financial award application deadline: 5/15; financial award applicants required to submit FAFSA. *Faculty research:* Psychological assessment; impact of psychological services on medical outcome; spirituality and wellness; effectiveness of clinical training and supervision; shame. Total annual research expenditures: $22,000. *Unit head:* Dr. Wayne Adams, Professor and Chairperson, Graduate Department of Clinical Psychology, 800-765-4369 Ext. 2372, E-mail: wadams@georgefox.edu. *Application contact:* Adina McConaughey, Admission Counselor, 800-631-0921 Ext. 2263, Fax: 503-554-2263, E-mail: amcconaughey@georgefox.edu.

See Close-Up on page 1115.

George Mason University, College of Humanities and Social Sciences, Department of Psychology, Fairfax, VA 22030. Offers applied developmental psychology (MA, PhD); bio-psychology (MA, PhD); clinical psychology (MA, PhD); human factors engineering psychology (MA, PhD); industrial/organizational psychology (MA, PhD); psychology (MA, PhD); school psychology (MA). *Accreditation:* APA. Terminal master's awarded for partial completion of doctoral program. *Degree requirements:* For master's, thesis (for applied developmental psychology and biopsychology); for doctorate, comprehensive exam, thesis/dissertation or alternative. *Entrance requirements:* For master's, GRE General Test, minimum GPA of 3.0 in last 60 hours of course work, undergraduate course work in psychology; for doctorate, GRE General Test, minimum undergraduate GPA of 3.0, 3.3 in major. Additional exam requirements/recommendations for international students: Required—TOEFL (minimum score 575 paper-based; 230 computer-based; 88 iBT), IELTS (minimum score 6). Electronic applications accepted.

The George Washington University, Columbian College of Arts and Sciences, Department of Psychology, Washington, DC 20052. Offers applied social psychology (PhD); clinical psychology (PhD); cognitive neuroscience (PhD). *Accreditation:* APA. Part-time and evening/weekend programs available. *Faculty:* 27 full-time (14 women), 19 part-time/adjunct (12 women). *Students:* 119 full-time (99 women), 83 part-time (64 women); includes 56 minority (14 African Americans, 2 American Indian/Alaska Native, 24 Asian Americans or Pacific Islanders, 16 Hispanic Americans), 6 international. Average age 29. 873 applicants, 5% accepted, 47 enrolled. In 2008, 41 doctorates awarded. *Degree requirements:* For doctorate, thesis/dissertation or alternative, general exam. *Entrance requirements:* For doctorate, GRE General Test, minimum GPA of 3.0. Additional exam requirements/recommendations for international students: Required—TOEFL (minimum score 550 paper-based; 213 computer-based; 80 iBT). *Application deadline:* For fall admission, 1/15 for domestic and international students. Application fee: $60. *Financial support:* In 2008–09, 62 students received support; fellowships with tuition reimbursements available, teaching assistantships with tuition reimbursements available, career-related internships or fieldwork, Federal Work-Study, and tuition waivers available. *Unit head:* Dr. Paul Poppen, Chair, 202-994-6324, E-mail: pjp@gwu.edu. *Application contact:* Information Contact, 202-994-6320, Fax: 202-994-1602, E-mail: psydept@gwu.edu.

Graduate School and University Center of the City University of New York, Graduate Studies, Program in Psychology, New York, NY 10016-4039. Offers basic applied neurocognition (PhD); biopsychology (PhD); clinical psychology (PhD); developmental psychology (PhD); environmental psychology (PhD); experimental psychology (PhD); industrial psychology (PhD); learning processes (PhD); neuropsychology (PhD); psychology (PhD); social personality (PhD). *Degree requirements:* For doctorate, one foreign language, thesis/dissertation. *Entrance requirements:* For doctorate, GRE General Test. Additional exam requirements/recommendations for international students: Required—TOEFL. Electronic applications accepted.

Hofstra University, College of Liberal Arts and Sciences, Department of Psychology, Program in Clinical Psychology, Hempstead, NY 11549. Offers MA, PhD. *Accreditation:* APA (one or more programs are accredited); NCATE (one or more programs are accredited). *Students:* 91 full-time (62 women); includes 10 minority (2 African Americans, 4 Asian Americans or Pacific Islanders, 4 Hispanic Americans), 2 international. Average age 27. 159 applicants, 14% accepted, 14 enrolled. In 2008, 16 master's, 13 doctorates awarded. Terminal master's awarded for partial completion of doctoral program. *Degree requirements:* For doctorate, comprehensive exam, thesis/dissertation, oral defense, full time internship. *Entrance requirements:* For doctorate, GRE General Test, GRE Subject Test (psychology), 3 letters of recommendation, interview, essay, curriculum vitae. Additional exam requirements/recommendations for international students: Required—TOEFL (minimum score 550 paper-based; 213 computer-based; 80 iBT). *Application deadline:* For fall admission, 1/15 for domestic and international students. Application fee: $60. Electronic applications accepted. *Expenses:* Tuition: Full-time $15,300; part-time $850 per credit. Required fees: $970; $165 per term. Tuition and fees vary according to program. *Financial support:* In 2008–09, 67 students received support, including 15 fellowships with full and partial tuition reimbursements available (averaging $21,740 per year), 5 research assistantships with full and partial tuition reimbursements available (averaging $4,500 per year); career-related internships or fieldwork, Federal Work-Study, institutionally sponsored loans, scholarships/grants, tuition waivers (full and partial), and unspecified assistantships also available. Support available to part-time students. Financial award applicants required to submit FAFSA. *Faculty research:* Self-help approach to cigarette cessation, treatment of anger, cognitions of cocaine-addicted schizophrenics, use of mindfulness in treatment of chronic medical conditions, virtual reality treatment phobia and trauma, parent/child interventions, meditation, CBT for anxiety and depression. *Unit head:* Dr. Mitchell L. Schare, Program Director, 516-463-5009, Fax: 516-463-6052, E-mail: psymls@hofstra.edu. *Application contact:* Carol Drummer, Dean of Graduate Admissions, 516-463-4876, Fax: 516-463-4664, E-mail: gradstudent@hofstra.edu.

Howard University, Graduate School, Department of Psychology, Washington, DC 20059-0002. Offers clinical psychology (PhD); developmental psychology (PhD); experimental psychology (PhD); neuropsychology (PhD); personality psychology (PhD); psychology (MS); social psychology (PhD). *Accreditation:* APA (one or more programs are accredited). Part-time programs available. *Degree requirements:* For master's, thesis; for doctorate, comprehensive exam, thesis/dissertation, qualifying exam. *Entrance requirements:* For master's, GRE General Test, minimum GPA of 2.5, bachelor's degree in psychology or related field; for doctorate, GRE General Test, minimum GPA of 3.0. *Faculty research:* Personality and psychophysiology, educational and social development of African-American children, child and adult psychopathology.

Idaho State University, Office of Graduate Studies, College of Arts and Sciences, Department of Psychology, Department of Clinical Psychology, Pocatello, ID 83209. Offers PhD. *Students:* 22 full-time (15 women), 11 part-time (10 women); includes 2 minority (1 Asian American or Pacific Islander, 1 Hispanic American). Average age 30. In 2008, 7 doctorates awarded. *Degree requirements:* For doctorate, comprehensive exam, thesis/dissertation, 1 year full-time clinical internship. *Entrance requirements:* For doctorate, GRE General Test, GRE Subject Test, MS in psychology. Additional exam requirements/recommendations for international students: Required—TOEFL (minimum score 550 paper-based; 213 computer-based; 80 iBT). *Application deadline:* For fall admission, 7/1 for domestic students, 6/1 for international students; for spring admission, 12/1 for domestic students, 11/1 for international students. Applications are processed on a rolling basis. Application fee: $55. Electronic applications accepted. *Expenses:* Tuition, area resident: Full-time $3114; part-time $276 per credit hour. Tuition, state resident: full-time $3114; part-time $276 per credit hour. Tuition, nonresident: full-time $12,318; part-time $404 per credit hour. Required fees: $2360. Tuition and fees vary according to course load and reciprocity agreements. *Financial support:* Career-related internships or fieldwork, Federal Work-Study, institutionally sponsored loans, scholarships/grants, traineeships, health care benefits, tuition waivers (full and partial), and unspecified assistantships available. Support available to part-time students. Financial award application deadline: 1/1; financial award applicants required to submit FAFSA. *Faculty research:* Pre-adolescent behavior, substance abuse training, trauma related problems. *Unit head:* Dr. Kandi Turley-Ames, Chairman, 208-282-2462, Fax: 208-282-4832, E-mail: turlkand@isu.edu. *Application contact:* Ellen Combs, Graduate School Technical Records Specialist, 208-282-2150, Fax: 208-282-4847, E-mail: combelle@isu.edu.

Illinois Institute of Technology, Graduate College, Institute of Psychology, Chicago, IL 60616-3793. Offers clinical psychology (PhD); industrial/organizational psychology (PhD); personnel/human resource development (MS); psychology (MS); rehabilitation counseling (MS); rehabilitation counselor education (PhD). *Accreditation:* APA (one or more programs are accredited); CORE. Evening/weekend programs available. *Faculty:* 19 full-time (8 women), 5 part-time/adjunct (all women). *Students:* 98 full-time (78 women), 94 part-time (69 women); includes 36 minority (10 African Americans, 16 Asian Americans or Pacific Islanders, 10 Hispanic Americans), 24 international. Average age 29. 301 applicants, 40% accepted, 54 enrolled. In 2008, 37 master's, 13 doctorates awarded. Terminal master's awarded for partial completion of doctoral program. *Degree requirements:* For master's, comprehensive exam, thesis (for some programs); for doctorate, comprehensive exam, thesis/dissertation, qualifying exams. *Entrance requirements:* For master's, GRE General Test, minimum GPA of 3.0; for doctorate, GRE General Test, minimum GPA of 3.2. Additional exam requirements/recommendations for international students: Required—TOEFL (minimum score 550 paper-based; 213 computer-based; 80 iBT). *Application deadline:* For fall admission, 1/15 for domestic and international students. Application fee: $40. Electronic applications accepted. *Financial support:* In 2008–09, 39 fellowships with partial tuition reimbursements (averaging $2,798 per year), 1 research assistantship with partial tuition reimbursement, 24 teaching assistantships with partial tuition reimbursements (averaging $4,405 per year) were awarded; career-related internships or fieldwork, Federal Work-Study, institutionally sponsored loans, scholarships/grants, traineeships, health care benefits, tuition waivers (partial), and unspecified assistantships also available. Support available to part-time students. Financial award applicants required to submit FAFSA. *Faculty research:* Stigma and mental illness, depression, couples communication, leadership, psychometric theory. Total annual research expenditures: $426,090. *Unit head:* Dr. M. Ellen Mitchell, Dean, 312-567-3362, Fax: 312-567-3493, E-mail: mitchelle@itt.edu. *Application contact:* Application Contact, 312-567-3500, Fax: 312-567-3493, E-mail: psychology@iit.edu.

Illinois State University, Graduate School, College of Arts and Sciences, Department of Psychology, Normal, IL 61790-2200. Offers psychology (MA, MS), including clinical psychology, counseling psychology, developmental psychology, educational psychology, experimental psychology, measurement-evaluation, organizational-industrial psychology; school psychology (PhD, SSP). *Accreditation:* APA. *Degree requirements:* For master's, thesis or alternative; for doctorate, variable foreign language requirement, thesis/dissertation, 2 terms of residency, internship, practicum. *Entrance requirements:* For master's, GRE General Test, GRE Subject Test, minimum GPA of 3.0 in last 60 hours of course work; for doctorate, GRE General Test. *Faculty research:* Comprehensive evaluation system for the central region professional development grant, Illinois school psychology internship consortium, for children's sake.

Immaculata University, College of Graduate Studies, Department of Psychology, Immaculata, PA 19345. Offers clinical psychology (Psy D); counseling psychology (MA, Certificate), including school guidance counselor (Certificate), school psychologist (Certificate). *Accreditation:* APA. Part-time and evening/weekend programs available. *Degree requirements:* For master's, comprehensive exam, thesis optional; for doctorate, comprehensive exam, thesis/dissertation. *Entrance requirements:* For master's, GRE General Test or MAT, minimum GPA of 3.0; for doctorate, GRE General Test, minimum GPA of 3.5. Additional exam requirements/recommendations for international students: Required—TOEFL, IELTS. *Faculty research:* Supervision ethics, psychology of teaching, gender.

Indiana State University, School of Graduate Studies, College of Arts and Sciences, Department of Psychology, Terre Haute, IN 47809-1401. Offers clinical psychology (Psy D); general psychology (MA, MS). *Accreditation:* APA (one or more programs are accredited). Terminal master's awarded for partial completion of doctoral program. *Degree requirements:* For master's, thesis (for some programs); for doctorate, comprehensive exam, thesis/dissertation, internship, professional research project. *Entrance requirements:* For master's, GRE General Test, 12 semester hours of course work in psychology, minimum GPA of 2.75; for doctorate, GRE General Test, minimum GPA of 3.0. Additional exam requirements/recommendations for international students: Required—TOEFL (minimum score 550 paper-based). Electronic applications accepted.

Indiana University of Pennsylvania, School of Graduate Studies and Research, College of Natural Sciences and Mathematics, Department of Psychology, Program in Clinical Psychology, Indiana, PA 15705-1087. Offers Psy D. *Accreditation:* APA. Part-time programs available. *Faculty:* 15 full-time (8 women). *Students:* 43 full-time (37 women), 18 part-time (15 women); includes 3 minority (1 African American, 1 Asian American or Pacific Islander, 1 Hispanic American). Average age 27. 94 applicants, 12% accepted, 11 enrolled. In 2008, 15 doctorates awarded. *Degree requirements:* For doctorate, comprehensive exam, thesis/dissertation, internship, practicum. *Entrance requirements:* For doctorate, GRE General Test, minimum GPA of 3.0, 3 letters of recommendation, interview. Additional exam requirements/recommendations for international students: Required—TOEFL. *Application deadline:* For fall admission, 1/10 for domestic students. Application fee: $30. *Expenses:* Tuition, area resident: Full-time $6430; part-time $357 per credit. Tuition, nonresident: full-time $10,288; part-time $572 per credit. Required fees: $1547.50; $107 per credit. $283 per year. *Financial support:* In 2008–09, 5 fellowships (averaging $2,200 per year), 41 research assistantships with full and partial tuition reimbursements (averaging $3,822 per year), 2 teaching assistantships (averaging $20,909 per year) were awarded; Federal Work-Study and scholarships/grants also available. Financial award application deadline: 3/15; financial award applicants required to submit FAFSA. *Unit head:* Dr. Beverly Goodwin, Graduate Coordinator, 724-357-4522, E-mail: Beverly.Goodwin@iup.edu. *Application contact:* Dr. Donald Robertson, Graduate Coordinator, 724-357-4522, E-mail: durobert@iup.edu.

Indiana University–Purdue University Indianapolis, School of Science, Department of Psychology, Indianapolis, IN 46202-3275. Offers clinical rehabilitation psychology (MS); industrial/organizational psychology (MS); psychobiology of addictions (MS, PhD). *Accreditation:* APA (one or more programs are accredited). Terminal master's awarded for partial completion of doctoral program. *Degree requirements:* For master's, thesis; for doctorate, thesis/dissertation. *Entrance requirements:* For master's, GRE General Test, minimum undergraduate GPA of 3.0; for doctorate, GRE General Test, GRE Subject Test (clinical rehabilitation psychology), minimum undergraduate GPA of 3.2. *Faculty research:* Psychiatric rehabilitation, chronic stress, neurological research, language and cognitive development in infants. alcoholism and psychopathology.

Institute of Transpersonal Psychology, Residential Programs, Palo Alto, CA 94303. Offers clinical psychology (PhD); counseling psychology (MA); transpersonal psychology (MA, PhD); women's spirituality (PhD). Part-time and evening/weekend programs available. *Faculty:* 17 full-time (9 women), 31 part-time/adjunct (18 women). *Students:* 268 full-time (189 women), 40 part-time (31 women); includes 53 minority (9 African Americans, 3 American Indian/Alaska Native, 21 Asian Americans or Pacific Islanders, 20 Hispanic Americans), 14 international. Average age 38. 168 applicants, 52% accepted, 56 enrolled. In 2008, 47 master's, 16 doctorates awarded. Terminal master's awarded for partial completion of doctoral program. *Degree requirements:* For doctorate, thesis/dissertation. *Entrance requirements:* For master's and doctorate, bachelor's degree. *Application deadline:* For fall admission, 2/15 priority date for domestic students. Applications are processed on a rolling basis. Application fee: $55. *Expenses:* Tuition: Full-time $24,543; part-time $577 per unit. Tuition and fees vary according to degree level. *Financial support:* In 2008–09, 178 students received support; teaching assistantships, career-related internships or fieldwork, Federal Work-Study, and scholarships/grants available. Support available to part-time students. Financial award application deadline: 7/1; financial award applicants required to submit FAFSA. *Unit head:* Dr. Paul Roy, Academic Vice President, 650-493-4430 Ext. 243, Fax: 650-493-6835, E-mail: proy@itp.edu. *Application contact:* 650-493-4430 Ext. 16, Fax: 650-493-6835, E-mail: itpinfo@itp.edu.

Jackson State University, Graduate School, School of Liberal Arts, Department of Psychology, Jackson, MS 39217. Offers clinical psychology (PhD). *Accreditation:* APA. *Degree requirements:* For doctorate, comprehensive exam, thesis/dissertation. *Entrance requirements:* For doctorate, MAT, GRE.

James Madison University, The Graduate School, College of Integrated Science and Technology, Department of Graduate Psychology, Program in Combined-Integrated Clinical and School Psychology, Harrisonburg, VA 22807. Offers PhD, Psy D. Part-time and evening/weekend programs available. *Students:* 19 full-time (16 women); includes 2 minority (1 African American, 1 Asian American or Pacific Islander), 2 international. Average age 27. In 2008, 9 doctorates awarded. *Degree requirements:* For doctorate, thesis/dissertation, 12-month internship. *Entrance requirements:* For doctorate, GRE General Test, GRE Subject Test (advanced psychology), 3 letters of recommendation. Additional exam requirements/recommendations for international students: Required—TOEFL. *Application deadline:* For fall admission, 2/1 for domestic students. Applications are processed on a rolling basis. Application fee: $55. Electronic applications accepted. *Expenses:* Tuition, area resident: Full-time $7008; part-time $292 per credit hour. Tuition, state resident: full-time $7008; part-time $292 per credit hour. Tuition, nonresident: full-time $20,352; part-time $848 per credit hour. *Financial support:* In 2008–09, 12 students received support. 14 doctoral assistantships ($14,500) available. Financial award application deadline: 3/1; financial award applicants required to submit FAFSA. *Unit head:* Dr. Gregg R. Henriques, Program Director, 540-568-7857. *Application contact:* Dr. Gregg R. Henriques, Program Director, 540-568-7857.

The Johns Hopkins University, Bloomberg School of Public Health, Department of Mental Health, Baltimore, MD 21218-2699. Offers children's mental health services (PhD); drug dependence epidemiology (PhD); mental health (MHS); psychiatric epidemiology (PhD). *Degree requirements:* For master's, thesis (for some programs); for doctorate, thesis/dissertation, 1 year full-time residency, oral and written exams. *Entrance requirements:* For master's, GRE General Test, MCAT, 3 letters of recommendation, curriculum vitae; for doctorate, GRE General Test, MCAT or GMAT, 3 letters of recommendation, curriculum vitae. Additional exam requirements/recommendations for international students: Required—TOEFL (minimum score 550 paper-based; 250 computer-based). Electronic applications accepted. *Faculty research:* Etiology, development and prevention of aggressive and antisocial behavior; epidemiology of mental disorders; genetic epidemiology of mental disorders.

Kean University, Nathan Weiss Graduate College, Program in School and Clinical Psychology, Union, NJ 07083. Offers Psy D. Evening/weekend programs available. *Faculty:* 18 full-time (13 women). *Degree requirements:* For doctorate, comprehensive exam, thesis/dissertation, externship. *Entrance requirements:* For doctorate, GRE General Test (minimum score: verbal 500, quantitative 500, writing 4.0), GRE Subject Test in Psychology within the last 5 years (minimum score: 550), minimum undergraduate GPA of 3.3, graduate 3.5; personal statement of goals and objectives, three letters of recommendation (at least one from a professor), personal interview, prerequisite coursework in theories of personality, abnormal psychology, tests and measurements, statistics, and experimental psychology. *Application deadline:* For fall admission, 1/30 for domestic students. Application fee: $60 ($150 for international students).

Clinical Psychology

Kean University (continued)

Electronic applications accepted. *Expenses:* Contact institution. *Financial support:* In 2008–09, research assistantships (averaging $3,217 per year); unspecified assistantships also available. *Unit head:* Dr. Dennis Finger, Program Coordinator, 908-737-5870, E-mail: dfinger@kean.edu. *Application contact:* Steven Koch, Pre-Admissions Coordinator, 908-737-4723, Fax: 908-737-5965, E-mail: grad-adm@kean.edu.

Kent State University, College of Arts and Sciences, Department of Psychology, Kent, OH 44242-0001. Offers clinical psychology (MA, PhD); experimental psychology (MA, PhD). *Accreditation:* APA (one or more programs are accredited). *Degree requirements:* For master's, thesis; for doctorate, thesis/dissertation. *Entrance requirements:* For master's, GRE, minimum GPA of 3.0, minimum 18 semester hours in psychology with one course in statistics and one experimental course with a lab component; for doctorate, GRE, minimum GPA of 3.0. Additional exam requirements/recommendations for international students: Required—TOEFL (minimum score 525 paper-based), Michigan English Language Assessment Battery (minimum score: 77).

Lakehead University, Graduate Studies, Department of Psychology, Thunder Bay, ON P7B 5E1, Canada. Offers clinical psychology (PhD); experimental psychology (MA). Part-time and evening/weekend programs available. *Degree requirements:* For master's, thesis optional; for doctorate, thesis/dissertation, 2 comprehensive exams, internship. *Entrance requirements:* For master's, GRE, honors degree in psychology, advanced course work in statistics, minimum B average; for doctorate, GRE, minimum B average. Additional exam requirements/recommendations for international students: Required—TOEFL. Tuition charges are reported in Canadian dollars. *Expenses:* Tuition, area resident: Full-time $6500 Canadian dollars. International tuition: $13,700 Canadian dollars full-time. *Faculty research:* Chaos theory, health psychology, counseling psychology, gerontology, women's studies.

Lamar University, College of Graduate Studies, College of Arts and Sciences, Department of Psychology, Beaumont, TX 77710. Offers community/clinical psychology (MS); industrial/organizational psychology (MS). Part-time programs available. *Faculty:* 7 full-time (4 women). *Students:* 21 full-time (10 women), 5 part-time (3 women); includes 4 minority (1 African American, 3 Hispanic Americans), 2 international. Average age 25. 32 applicants, 41% accepted, 10 enrolled. In 2008, 6 master's awarded. *Degree requirements:* For master's, thesis, practicum. *Entrance requirements:* For master's, GRE General Test, minimum GPA of 2.75 in last 60 hours of undergraduate course work. Additional exam requirements/recommendations for international students: Required—TOEFL. *Application deadline:* For fall admission, 8/1 for domestic students; for spring admission, 12/1 for domestic students. Application fee: $25 ($50 for international students). *Expenses:* Tuition, state resident: full-time $5000; part-time $195 per credit. Tuition, nonresident: full-time $12,376; part-time $476 per credit. Required fees: $1570. *Financial support:* In 2008–09, 12 students received support, including 3 teaching assistantships (averaging $4,500 per year); fellowships, research assistantships, career-related internships or fieldwork, Federal Work-Study, scholarships/grants, and tuition waivers (partial) also available. Support available to part-time students. Financial award application deadline: 4/1. *Faculty research:* Groupthink, health psychology, school psychology, behavioral neuroscience. *Unit head:* Dr. Oney D. Fitzpatrick, Chair, 409-880-8285, Fax: 409-880-1779, E-mail: fitzpatrod@hal.lamar.edu. *Application contact:* Dr. James W. Westgate, Assistant Dean, 409-880-7978, E-mail: westgate@hal.lamar.edu.

La Salle University, School of Arts and Sciences, Program in Clinical-Counseling Psychology, Philadelphia, PA 19141-1199. Offers MA. *Accreditation:* APA. Part-time and evening/weekend programs available. *Degree requirements:* For master's, comprehensive exam. *Entrance requirements:* For master's, GRE or MAT, 15 undergraduate credits in psychology. *Expenses:* Contact institution. *Faculty research:* Cognitive therapy, attribution theory, work habits, single parent families, treatment of addictions.

La Salle University, School of Arts and Sciences, Program in Psychology, Philadelphia, PA 19141-1199. Offers clinical psychology (Psy D); family psychology (Psy D); rehabilitation psychology (Psy D). Part-time and evening/weekend programs available. *Entrance requirements:* For doctorate, GRE, minimum GPA of 3.0. *Expenses:* Contact institution. *Faculty research:* Cognitive therapy, attribution theory, treatment of addiction.

Lesley University, Graduate School of Arts and Social Sciences, Cambridge, MA 02138-2790. Offers clinical mental health counseling (MA), including expressive therapies counseling, holistic counseling, school and community counseling; counseling psychology (MA, CAGS), including professional counseling (MA), school counseling (MA); creative arts in learning (CAGS); creative writing (MFA); ecological teaching and learning (MS); environmental education (MS); expressive therapies (MA, PhD, CAGS), including art (MA), dance (MA), expressive therapies, music (MA); independent studies (CAGS); independent study (MA); intercultural relations (MA, CAGS); interdisciplinary studies (MA), including individualized studies, integrative holistic health, women's studies; urban environmental leadership (MA); visual arts (MFA). Part-time and evening/weekend programs available. Postbaccalaureate distance learning degree programs offered (minimal on-campus study). *Degree requirements:* For master's, internship, practicum, thesis (expressive therapies); for doctorate, thesis/dissertation, arts apprenticeship, field placement; for CAGS, thesis, internship (counseling psychology, expressive therapies). *Entrance requirements:* For master's, MAT (counseling psychology), interview, writing samples, art portfolio; for doctorate, GRE or MAT; for CAGS, interview, master's degree. Additional exam requirements/recommendations for international students: Required—TOEFL (minimum score 550 paper-based; 213 computer-based; 80 iBT). Electronic applications accepted. *Expenses:* Tuition: Full-time $13,770; part-time $765 per credit hour. Required fees: $150. Tuition and fees vary according to course load, degree level, campus/location and program. *Faculty research:* Psychotherapy and culture; psychotherapy and psychological trauma; women's issues in art, teaching and psychotherapy; community based art, psycho-spiritual inquiry.

Long Island University, Brooklyn Campus, Richard L. Conolly College of Liberal Arts and Sciences, Department of Psychology, Program in Clinical Psychology, Brooklyn, NY 11201-8423. Offers PhD. *Accreditation:* APA. *Degree requirements:* For doctorate, thesis/dissertation. *Entrance requirements:* For doctorate, GRE Subject Test, GRE General Test. Additional exam requirements/recommendations for international students: Required—TOEFL (minimum score 500 paper-based; 173 computer-based). Electronic applications accepted. *Faculty research:* Ethnicity and human development.

Long Island University, C.W. Post Campus, College of Liberal Arts and Sciences, Department of Psychology, Program in Clinical Psychology, Brookville, NY 11548-1300. Offers Psy D. *Accreditation:* APA. *Degree requirements:* For doctorate, thesis/dissertation, internship. *Entrance requirements:* For doctorate, GRE General Test, GRE Subject Test, GRE analytical writing, bachelor's degree in psychology, minimum GPA of 3.25, 18 credit hours of undergraduate psychology, 3 letters of recommendation. *Expenses:* Contact institution. *Faculty research:* Family violence, schizophrenia, developmental disabilities, psychotherapy, terror and trauma.

Louisiana State University and Agricultural and Mechanical College, Graduate School, College of Arts and Sciences, Department of Psychology, Baton Rouge, LA 70803. Offers biological psychology (MA, PhD); clinical psychology (MA, PhD); cognitive psychology (MA, PhD); developmental psychology (MA, PhD); industrial/organizational psychology (MA, PhD); school psychology (MA, PhD). *Accreditation:* APA (one or more programs are accredited). Terminal master's awarded for partial completion of doctoral program. *Degree requirements:* For master's, thesis; for doctorate, thesis/dissertation, 1 year internship. *Entrance requirements:* For master's and doctorate, GRE General Test, minimum GPA of 3.0. Additional exam requirements/recommendations for international students: Required—TOEFL (minimum score 550 paper-based; 213 computer-based; 79 iBT). Electronic applications accepted. *Faculty research:* Clinical psychology, autism, anxiety, addition, neuro-psychology, school psychology, cognitive psychology, experimental psychology.

Loyola University Chicago, Graduate School, Department of Psychology, Program in Clinical Psychology, Chicago, IL 60611-2196. Offers MA, PhD. *Accreditation:* APA. *Faculty:* 10 full-time (5 women). *Students:* 35 full-time (29 women); includes 4 minority (3 African Americans, 1 Hispanic American), 1 international. Average age 27. 309 applicants, 2% accepted, 6 enrolled. In 2008, 7 master's, 4 doctorates awarded. Terminal master's awarded for partial completion of doctoral program. *Degree requirements:* For master's, thesis; for doctorate, comprehensive exam, thesis/dissertation. *Entrance requirements:* For doctorate, GRE General Test, GRE Subject Test, letters of recommendation. *Application deadline:* For fall admission, 12/1 for domestic students. Application fee: $50. Electronic applications accepted. *Expenses:* Tuition: Full-time $13,500; part-time $750 per credit hour. Required fees: $60 per semester. Full-time tuition and fees vary according to program. *Financial support:* In 2008–09, 2 fellowships with full tuition reimbursements (averaging $15,000 per year), 17 research assistantships with full tuition reimbursements (averaging $15,000 per year), 7 teaching assistantships with full tuition reimbursements (averaging $15,000 per year) were awarded; career-related internships or fieldwork, Federal Work-Study, scholarships/grants, traineeships, and unspecified assistantships also available. Financial award application deadline: 12/1; financial award applicants required to submit FAFSA. *Faculty research:* Child and family, AIDS, ethics and professional practice, psychotherapy, stress and coping, positive youth development, pediatric psychology, adolescence, inner city youth. *Unit head:* Dr. Grayson Holmbeck, Director, 773-508-2967, Fax: 773-508-8713, E-mail: gholmbe@luc.edu. *Application contact:* Jacquie Hamilton, Senior Secretary, 773-508-2974, Fax: 773-508-8713, E-mail: jhamilt@luc.edu.

Loyola University Maryland, Graduate Programs, College of Arts and Sciences, Department of Psychology, Program in Clinical Psychology, Baltimore, MD 21210-2699. Offers MS, Psy D, CAS. *Accreditation:* APA. Part-time and evening/weekend programs available. *Faculty:* 47 full-time (25 women), 29 part-time/adjunct (16 women). *Students:* 110 full-time (93 women), 54 part-time (48 women); includes 21 minority (9 African Americans, 1 American Indian/Alaska Native, 8 Asian Americans or Pacific Islanders, 3 Hispanic Americans). Average age 26. In 2008, 36 master's, 11 doctorates, 1 other advanced degree awarded. *Entrance requirements:* For master's, doctorate, and CAS, GRE General Test, GRE Subject Test (recommended). Additional exam requirements/recommendations for international students: Required—TOEFL (minimum score 550 paper-based; 213 computer-based). *Application deadline:* Applications are processed on a rolling basis. Application fee: $50. *Financial support:* Applicants required to submit FAFSA. *Unit head:* Mary Jo Coiro, Assistant Director, Clinical, 410-614-2175, E-mail: tpmartino@loyola.edu. *Application contact:* Maureen Faux, interim Director, Graduate Admissions, 410-617-5020, Fax: 410-617-2002, E-mail: graduate@loyola.edu.

Madonna University, Department of Psychology, Livonia, MI 48150-1173. Offers clinical psychology (MSCP). Part-time and evening/weekend programs available. *Degree requirements:* For master's, thesis or alternative. *Entrance requirements:* Additional exam requirements/recommendations for international students: Required—TOEFL. Electronic applications accepted.

Marquette University, Graduate School, College of Arts and Sciences, Department of Psychology, Milwaukee, WI 53201-1881. Offers clinical psychology (MS); psychology (PhD). *Accreditation:* APA. Part-time programs available. *Degree requirements:* For master's, comprehensive exam, thesis or alternative; for doctorate, thesis/dissertation, internship, qualifying exam. *Entrance requirements:* For master's, GRE General Test, GRE Subject Test, MAT; for doctorate, GRE General Test, GRE Subject Test, sample of scholarly writing. Additional exam requirements/recommendations for international students: Required—TOEFL. *Faculty research:* Mental imagery, moral development, organizational behavior, depression, psychotherapy outcomes.

Marshall University, Academic Affairs Division, College of Liberal Arts, Department of Psychology, Huntington, WV 25755. Offers clinical psychology (MA); general psychology (MA); industrial and organizational psychology (MA); psychology (Psy D). *Accreditation:* APA. *Degree requirements:* For master's, thesis optional. *Entrance requirements:* For master's, GRE General Test or MAT.

Marywood University, Academic Affairs, College of Education and Human Development, Department of Psychology and Counseling, Program in Clinical Psychology, Scranton, PA 18509-1598. Offers Psy D. *Accreditation:* APA. *Entrance requirements:* For doctorate, GRE, official transcripts, 3 letters of recomendation, personal statement, minimum overall GPA of 3.3.

Marywood University, Academic Affairs, College of Education and Human Development, Department of Psychology and Counseling, Program in Psychology, Scranton, PA 18509-1598. Offers child/clinical school psychology (MA); clinical services (MA); general theoretical psychology (MA). Part-time and evening/weekend programs available. *Degree requirements:* For master's, comprehensive exam, thesis or alternative, internship/practicum. *Entrance requirements:* For master's, GRE or MAT. Additional exam requirements/recommendations for international students: Required—TOEFL (minimum score 550 paper-based; 213 computer-based). Electronic applications accepted. *Faculty research:* Personality disorders, counselor training, preschool development, self-esteem measurement, family dynamics.

Massachusetts School of Professional Psychology, Graduate Programs, Boston, MA 02132. Offers clinical psychology (Psy D); clinical psychopharmacology (Post-Doctoral MS); counseling psychology (MA); executive coaching (Graduate Certificate); forensic psychology (MA); organizational psychology (MA); respecialization in clinical psychology (Certificate); MA/CAGS. *Accreditation:* APA. *Degree requirements:* For master's, comprehensive exam; for doctorate, thesis/dissertation. *Entrance requirements:* For doctorate, GRE General Test. Additional exam requirements/recommendations for international students: Required—TOEFL (minimum score 550 paper-based; 213 computer-based). Electronic applications accepted.

McGill University, Faculty of Graduate and Postdoctoral Studies, Faculty of Science, Department of Psychology, Montréal, QC H3A 2T5, Canada. Offers clinical psychology (PhD); experimental psychology (M Sc, MA, PhD). *Accreditation:* APA (one or more programs are accredited).

Miami University, Graduate School, College of Arts and Sciences, Department of Psychology, Oxford, OH 45056. Offers clinical psychology (PhD); experimental psychology (PhD); social psychology (PhD). *Accreditation:* APA. *Degree requirements:* For doctorate, comprehensive exam, thesis/dissertation, final exams. *Entrance requirements:* For doctorate, GRE General Test, GRE Subject Test, minimum GPA of 2.75 (undergraduate), 3.0 (graduate). Additional exam requirements/recommendations for international students: Required—TOEFL (minimum score 550 paper-based; 213 computer-based), TWE (minimum score 4). Electronic applications accepted.

Michigan School of Professional Psychology, Programs in Humanistic and Clinical Psychology, Farmington Hills, MI 48334. Offers humanistic and clinical psychology (MA, Psy D). *Degree requirements:* For master's, thesis, practicum; for doctorate, thesis/dissertation, internship, practicum. *Entrance requirements:* For master's, 1 year of work experience, interview, minimum GPA of 3.0, curriculum vitae, personal essay, Bachelor's completion; for doctorate, 3 years of work experience, 2 interviews, minimum graduate GPA of 3.0, scholarly writing sample, curriculum vitae, personal essay, MA degree completion. Additional exam requirements/recommendations for international students: Required—TOEFL. Electronic applications accepted. *Faculty research:* Qualitative research, existential-phenomenological psychology, applications to clinical practice.

Midwestern University, Downers Grove Campus, College of Health Sciences, Illinois Campus, Program in Clinical Psychology, Downers Grove, IL 60515-1235. Offers MA, Psy D. *Faculty:* 1 part-time/adjunct (0 women). *Students:* 86 full-time (71 women), 3 part-time (all women); includes 11 minority (6 African Americans, 2 Asian Americans or Pacific Islanders, 3 Hispanic Americans), 2 international. Average age 27. 77 applicants, 61% accepted, 26 enrolled. In 2008, 16 master's awarded. *Degree requirements:* For doctorate, thesis/dissertation, qualifying examination. *Entrance requirements:* For master's and doctorate, GRE, minimum overall GPA of 2.75, 3 letters of recommendation. Additional exam requirements/recommendations for international students: Required—TOEFL. *Application deadline:* Applications are processed on a rolling basis. Application fee: $50. *Unit head:* Dr. Frank J. Prerost, Director, 630-515-7405, Fax: 630-971-6402, E-mail: fprero@midwestern.edu. *Application contact:* Michael Laken, Director of Admissions, 630-515-6171, Fax: 630-971-6086, E-mail: admissil@midwestern.edu.

Announcement: Midwestern University is committed to educating the health-care team of the new century. The University administers the Chicago College of Osteopathic Medicine, the Chicago College of Pharmacy, the College of Health Sciences, the Arizona College of Osteopathic Medicine, and the College of Pharmacy-Glendale. The University operates campuses in Downers Grove, Illinois, and in Glendale, Arizona. The Clinical Psychology Program offers an MA/Doctor of Psychology (PsyD) degree on the Downers Grove campus. The four-year curriculum incorporates didactic courses, practical experiences, internships, and a clinical dissertation. The Master of Arts degree is awarded after the successful completion of the first two years of the program, and the Doctor of Psychology degree is awarded after two additional years of study. Contact the Office of Admissions, Midwestern University (Downers Grove campus); 800-458-6253; e-mail: admissil@midwestern.edu; Web site: http://www.midwestern.edu.

Midwestern University, Glendale Campus, College of Health Sciences, Arizona Campus, Program in Clinical Psychology, Glendale, AZ 85308. Offers Psy D.

Millersville University of Pennsylvania, Graduate School, School of Education, Department of Psychology, Program in Psychology, Millersville, PA 17551-0302. Offers clinical psychology (MS); school psychology (MS). Part-time programs available. *Faculty:* 20 full-time (14 women), 6 part-time/adjunct (3 women). *Students:* 49 full-time (41 women), 45 part-time (38 women); includes 6 minority (5 African Americans, 1 Hispanic American), 1 international. Average age 29. 74 applicants, 45% accepted, 17 enrolled. In 2008, 28 master's awarded. *Degree requirements:* For master's, comprehensive exam, thesis optional. *Entrance requirements:* For master's, GRE, in-person interview. Additional exam requirements/recommendations for international students: Required—TOEFL (minimum score 500 paper-based; 183 computer-based; 65 iBT), TOEFL may be replaced by IELTS with score of 6 or higher. *Application deadline:* For fall admission, 2/1 for domestic and international students; for winter admission, 10/1 for domestic and international students; for spring admission, 10/1 for domestic and international students. Application fee: $40. Electronic applications accepted. *Expenses:* Tuition, state resident: full-time $6430; part-time $357 per credit. Tuition, nonresident: full-time $10,288; part-time $572 per credit. Required fees: $1937; $73.50 per credit. One-time fee: $88 part-time. Tuition and fees vary according to course load. *Financial support:* In 2008–09, 31 students received support, including 31 research assistantships with full and partial tuition reimbursements available (averaging $4,718 per year); institutionally sponsored loans and unspecified assistantships also available. Support available to part-time students. Financial award application deadline: 3/15; financial award applicants required to submit FAFSA. *Faculty research:* Childhood disorders, family stress, anxiety and worry treatments, solution-focused counseling, creativity, personality correlates. *Unit head:* Dr. Claudia Haferkamp, Coordinator of Clinical Psychology Program, 717-872-3826, Fax: 717-871-2480, E-mail: claudia.haferkamp@millersville.edu. *Application contact:* Dr. Victor S. DeSantis, Dean of Graduate and Professional Studies, 717-872-3099, Fax: 717-872-3453, E-mail: victor.desantis@millersville.edu.

Minnesota State University Mankato, College of Graduate Studies, College of Social and Behavioral Sciences, Department of Psychology, Mankato, MN 56001. Offers clinical psychology (MA); industrial/organizational psychology (MA); psychology (MT); school psychology (Psy D). Part-time programs available. *Students:* 38 full-time (23 women), 5 part-time (1 woman). *Degree requirements:* For master's, one foreign language, comprehensive exam, thesis (for some programs). *Entrance requirements:* For master's, GRE General Test, GRE Subject Test (clinical psychology), minimum GPA of 3.0 during previous 2 years, 3 letters of reference. Additional exam requirements/recommendations for international students: Required—TOEFL. *Application deadline:* For fall admission, 1/1 priority date for domestic students. Applications are processed on a rolling basis. Application fee: $40. Electronic applications accepted. *Financial support:* Research assistantships, teaching assistantships with full tuition reimbursements, career-related internships or fieldwork, Federal Work-Study, institutionally sponsored loans, and unspecified assistantships available. Support available to part-time students. Financial award application deadline: 3/15; financial award applicants required to submit FAFSA. *Faculty research:* Professional competency in hospitals, mood disturbance, 360-degree feedback, employee selection, planning fallacy. *Unit head:* Dr. Barry Ries, Chairperson, 507-389-2724. *Application contact:* 507-389-2321, E-mail: grad@mnsu.edu.

Mississippi State University, College of Arts and Sciences, Department of Psychology, Mississippi State, MS 39762. Offers clinical psychology (MS); cognitive science (PhD); experimental psychology (MS). Terminal master's awarded for partial completion of doctoral program. *Degree requirements:* For master's, comprehensive exam, thesis; for doctorate, thesis/dissertation, qualifying exam, comprehensive written and oral exam. *Entrance requirements:* For master's, GRE General Test, minimum GPA of 2.75; for doctorate, GRE General Test, proficiency in at least 1 computer language. Additional exam requirements/recommendations for international students: Required—TOEFL. *Faculty research:* Personality type, alcoholism, blindness and low vision, mental retardation, language comprehension.

Missouri State University, Graduate College, College of Health and Human Services, Department of Psychology, Springfield, MO 65804-0094. Offers psychology (MS), including clinical, experimental, industrial/organizational. *Faculty:* 26 full-time (10 women), 1 part-time/adjunct (0 women). *Students:* 44 full-time (30 women), 3 part-time (all women); includes 1 minority (Hispanic American). Average age 24. 71 applicants, 45% accepted, 20 enrolled. In 2008, 17 master's awarded. *Degree requirements:* For master's, comprehensive exam, thesis. *Entrance requirements:* For master's, GRE General Test, GRE Subject Test, minimum GPA of 3.25 in major, 3.0 overall; 20 hours of course work in psychology (experimental and statistics). Additional exam requirements/recommendations for international students: Required—TOEFL (minimum score 550 paper-based; 213 computer-based; 79 iBT). *Application deadline:* For fall admission, 3/1 priority date for domestic and international students. Application fee: $35 ($50 for international students). Electronic applications accepted. *Expenses:* Tuition, state resident: full-time $3852; part-time $214 per credit hour. Tuition, nonresident: full-time $7524; part-time $418 per credit hour. Required fees: $230 per semester. Tuition and fees vary according to course level and course load. *Financial support:* In 2008–09, 10 research assistantships with full tuition reimbursements (averaging $7,340 per year), 3 teaching assistantships with full tuition reimbursements (averaging $9,730 per year) were awarded; career-related internships or fieldwork, Federal Work-Study, institutionally sponsored loans, scholarships/grants, and unspecified assistantships also available. Financial award application deadline: 3/31; financial award applicants required to submit FAFSA. *Faculty research:* Work-family conflict, child forensic psychology, sports psychology, body image assessment, visual learning. *Unit head:* Dr. Robert G. Jones, Head, 417-836-5797, Fax: 417-836-830, E-mail: psychology@missouristate.edu. *Application contact:* Eric Eckert, Coordinator of Admissions and Recruitment, 417-836-5331, Fax: 417-836-6888, E-mail: ericeckert@missouristate.edu.

Montclair State University, The Office of Graduate Admissions and Support Services, College of Humanities and Social Sciences, Department of Psychology, Montclair, NJ 07043-1624. Offers educational psychology (MA), including child/adolescent clinical psychology, clinical psychology for Spanish/English bilinguals; psychology (MA, Certificate), including industrial and organizational psychology (MA); school psychologist (Certificate). Part-time and evening/weekend programs available. *Faculty:* 28 full-time (13 women), 32 part-time/adjunct (16 women). *Students:* 28 full-time (20 women), 31 part-time (26 women); includes 14 minority (4 African Americans, 6 Asian Americans or Pacific Islanders, 4 Hispanic Americans), 2 international. Average age 27. 62 applicants, 56% accepted, 23 enrolled. In 2008, 26 master's awarded. *Degree requirements:* For master's, comprehensive exam, thesis or alternative. *Entrance requirements:* For master's, GRE General Test, GRE Subject Test, previous course work in psychology, interview, 2 letters of recommendation. Additional exam requirements/recommendations for international students: Required—TOEFL (minimum score 83 computer-based). *Application deadline:* For fall admission, 2/1 for domestic and international students; for spring admission, 10/1 for domestic and international students. Applications are processed on a rolling basis. Application fee: $60. Electronic applications accepted. *Financial support:* In 2008–09, 10 research assistantships with full tuition reimbursements (averaging $7,000 per year) were awarded; Federal Work-Study, scholarships/grants, and unspecified assistantships also available. Support available to part-time students. Financial award application deadline: 3/1; financial award applicants required to submit FAFSA. *Faculty research:* Engaged learning, academic and civic development. Total annual research expenditures: $10,000. *Unit head:* Dr. Peter Vietze, Chairperson, 973-655-5201. *Application contact:* Amy Aiello, Associate Director of Admissions, 973-655-5147, Fax: 973-655-7869, E-mail: graduate.school@montclair.edu.

Morehead State University, Graduate Programs, College of Science and Technology, Department of Psychology, Morehead, KY 40351. Offers clinical psychology (MS); counseling psychology (MS); experimental/general psychology (MS). Part-time programs available. *Faculty:* 8 full-time (3 women). *Students:* 22 full-time (18 women), 3 part-time (1 woman). Average age 26. 30 applicants, 53% accepted, 9 enrolled. In 2008, 10 master's awarded. *Degree requirements:* For master's, comprehensive exam, thesis optional. *Entrance requirements:* For master's, GRE General Test, 18 undergraduate hours in psychology, minimum GPA of 3.0. Additional exam requirements/recommendations for international students: Required—TOEFL (minimum score 500 paper-based; 173 computer-based). *Application deadline:* For fall admission, 8/1 priority date for domestic and international students; for spring admission, 12/1 for domestic students, 12/1 priority date for international students. Applications are processed on a rolling basis. Application fee: $30 ($55 for international students). Electronic applications accepted. *Expenses:* Tuition, area resident: Full-time $6084; part-time $338 per credit hour. Tuition, state resident: full-time $6084; part-time $338 per credit hour. Tuition, nonresident: full-time $15,804; part-time $878 per credit hour. *Financial support:* In 2008–09, 19 research assistantships (averaging $6,000 per year) were awarded; career-related internships or fieldwork, Federal Work-Study, and institutionally sponsored loans also available. Financial award application deadline: 4/1; financial award applicants required to submit FAFSA. *Faculty research:* Mood induction effects, serotonin receptor activity, stress, perceptual processes. *Unit head:* Dr. Laurie Couch, Interim Department Chair. *Application contact:* Michelle Barber, Graduate Admissions Counselor, 606-783-2039, Fax: 606-783-5061, E-mail: m.barber@moreheadstate.edu.

Murray State University, College of Humanities and Fine Arts, Program in Psychology, Murray, KY 42071. Offers clinical psychology (MA, MS); psychology (MA, MS). Part-time programs available. *Degree requirements:* For master's, one foreign language, comprehensive exam (for some programs), thesis. *Entrance requirements:* For master's, GRE General Test. Additional exam requirements/recommendations for international students: Required—TOEFL.

Naropa University, Graduate Programs, Program in Transpersonal Psychology, Boulder, CO 80302-6697. Offers ecopsychology (MA); transpersonal psychology (MA). Part-time and evening/weekend programs available. Postbaccalaureate distance learning degree programs offered (minimal on-campus study). *Faculty:* 4 full-time (2 women), 13 part-time/adjunct (7 women). *Students:* 40 part-time (34 women); includes 2 minority (1 Asian American or Pacific Islander, 1 Hispanic American), 4 international. Average age 42. 38 applicants, 58% accepted, 18 enrolled. In 2008, 10 master's awarded. *Degree requirements:* For master's, thesis, service learning. *Entrance requirements:* For master's, interview (by phone or in-person), technology form, resumé, letter of interest, 3 letters of recommendation. Additional exam requirements/recommendations for international students: Required—TOEFL (minimum score 600 paper-based; 250 computer-based). *Application deadline:* For fall admission, 1/15 for domestic and international students. Applications are processed on a rolling basis. Application fee: $60. Electronic applications accepted. *Expenses:* Tuition: Full-time $14,767; part-time $726 per credit hour. Required fees: $45 per term. *Financial support:* In 2008–09, 2 students received support. Career-related internships or fieldwork, Federal Work-Study, scholarships/grants, health care benefits, and tuition waivers (partial) available. Support available to part-time students. Financial award application deadline: 3/1; financial award applicants required to submit FAFSA. *Unit head:* Dr. John Davis, Director, 303-245-4654, Fax: 303-546-4044, E-mail: jdavis@naropa.edu. *Application contact:* Kate Levene, Admissions Counselor, 303-245-4657, Fax: 303-546-3583, E-mail: klevene@naropa.edu.

See Close-Up on page 1121.

New Mexico Highlands University, Graduate Studies, College of Arts and Sciences, Department of Behavioral Sciences, Las Vegas, NM 87701. Offers psychology (MS), including clinical psychology, general psychology. Part-time programs available. *Faculty:* 12 full-time (7 women). *Students:* 18 full-time (13 women), 6 part-time (3 women); includes 9 minority (all Hispanic Americans), 1 international. Average age 28. 13 applicants, 85% accepted, 7 enrolled. In 2008, 3 master's awarded. *Degree requirements:* For master's, comprehensive exam, thesis or alternative. *Entrance requirements:* For master's, minimum undergraduate GPA of 3.0. Additional exam requirements/recommendations for international students: Required—TOEFL (minimum score 540 paper-based; 207 computer-based). *Application deadline:* For fall admission, 8/1 priority date for domestic students. Applications are processed on a rolling basis. Application fee: $15. *Expenses:* Tuition, state resident: full-time $2880; part-time $120 per credit hour. Tuition, nonresident: full-time $4234; part-time $176 per credit hour. International tuition: $5645 full-time. One-time fee: $20. *Financial support:* In 2008–09, 17 students received support, including 14 teaching assistantships (averaging $5,250 per year); career-related internships or fieldwork, Federal Work-Study, institutionally sponsored loans, scholarships/grants, tuition waivers (full and partial), and unspecified assistantships also available. Support available to part-time students. Financial award application deadline: 3/1; financial award applicants required to submit FAFSA. *Faculty research:* Southwest Native American resettlement development, community-level interventions, neurochemistry of personality, comparative criminal justice, social theory and activism. *Unit head:* Dr. Ian Williamson, Chair, 505-454-3342, E-mail: iwilliamson@nmhu.edu. *Application contact:* Diane Trujillo, Administrative Assistant for Graduate Studies, 505-454-3266, Fax: 505-426-2117, E-mail: dtrujillo@nmhu.edu.

The New School: A University, The New School for Social Research, Department of Psychology, New York, NY 10011. Offers clinical psychology (PhD); general psychology (MA, PhD). *Accreditation:* APA (one or more programs are accredited). Part-time and evening/weekend programs available. *Faculty:* 17 full-time (8 women), 6 part-time/adjunct (1 woman). *Students:* 152 full-time (118 women), 90 part-time (72 women); includes 46 minority (11 African Americans, 2 American Indian/Alaska Native, 10 Asian Americans or Pacific Islanders, 23 Hispanic Americans), 28 international. Average age 29. In 2008, 54 master's, 5 doctorates awarded. Terminal master's awarded for partial completion of doctoral program. *Degree requirements:* For doctorate, one foreign language, thesis/dissertation, qualifying exam. *Entrance requirements:* For master's, GRE General Test; for doctorate, GRE General Test, MA. Additional exam requirements/recommendations for international students: Required—TOEFL (minimum score 600 paper-based; 250 computer-based; 100 iBT). *Application deadline:* For fall admission, 1/15 priority date for domestic students. Applications are processed on a rolling basis. Application fee: $50. *Expenses:* Tuition: Full-time $27,144; part-time $1508 per credit. Required fees: $355 per semester. *Financial support:* Fellowships, research assistantships, teaching assistantships, career-related internships or fieldwork, Federal Work-Study, scholarships/grants, and tuition waivers (full and partial) available. Financial award application deadline: 3/1; financial award applicants required to submit FAFSA. *Faculty research:* Consciousness, memory, language, perceptions, psychopathology. *Unit head:* Dr. Joan Miller, Chair, 212-229-5727 Ext. 3106. *Application contact:* Robert MacDonald, Director of Admissions, 800-523-5710 Ext. 3007, Fax: 212-989-7102, E-mail: macdonar@newschool.edu.

See Close-Up on page 1251.

Norfolk State University, School of Graduate Studies, School of Liberal Arts, Department of Psychology, Program in Community/Clinical Psychology, Norfolk, VA 23504. Offers MA. *Degree requirements:* For master's, comprehensive exam, thesis or alternative. *Entrance requirements:* For master's, minimum GPA of 2.7.

Clinical Psychology

North Dakota State University, College of Graduate and Interdisciplinary Studies, College of Science and Mathematics, Department of Psychology, Fargo, ND 58105. Offers clinical psychology (MS); cognitive and visual neuroscience (PhD); health and social psychology (PhD); psychology (MS). *Faculty:* 18 full-time (4 women), 2 part-time/adjunct (1 woman). *Students:* 36 full-time (27 women); includes 4 minority (1 African American, 2 Asian Americans or Pacific Islanders, 1 Hispanic American), 1 international. Average age 24. 48 applicants, 33% accepted, 10 enrolled. In 2008, 3 master's, 1 doctorate awarded. *Degree requirements:* For master's, thesis; for doctorate, thesis/dissertation. *Entrance requirements:* For master's and doctorate, GRE General Test, GRE Subject Test. Additional exam requirements/recommendations for international students: Required—TOEFL (minimum score 525 paper-based; 197 computer-based; 71 iBT). *Application deadline:* For fall admission, 3/1 for domestic and international students. Application fee: $45 ($60 for international students). Electronic applications accepted. *Financial support:* In 2008–09, 36 students received support, including 2 fellowships with full tuition reimbursements available (averaging $16,000 per year), 23 research assistantships with full tuition reimbursements available (averaging $16,000 per year), 11 teaching assistantships with full tuition reimbursements available (averaging $6,000 per year); career-related internships or fieldwork, Federal Work-Study, institutionally sponsored loans, tuition waivers (full and partial), and unspecified assistantships also available. Support available to part-time students. Financial award application deadline: 3/1. *Faculty research:* Cognition science, neuropsychology, group behavior, applied behavior analysis, behavior therapy. Total annual research expenditures: $2 million. *Unit head:* Dr. Paul D. Rokke, Chair, 701-231-8622, Fax: 701-231-8426, E-mail: paul.rokke@ndsu.edu. *Application contact:* Dr. Paul D. Rokke, Chair, 701-231-8622, Fax: 701-231-8426, E-mail: paul.rokke@ndsu.edu.

Northern Arizona University, Graduate College, College of Social and Behavioral Sciences, Department of Psychology, Flagstaff, AZ 86011. Offers applied health psychology (MA); clinical psychology (MA); general psychology (MA); teaching of psychology (MA). Part-time programs available. *Degree requirements:* For master's, thesis, oral defense. *Entrance requirements:* For master's, GRE General Test.

Northwestern State University of Louisiana, Graduate Studies and Research, Department of Psychology, Natchitoches, LA 71497. Offers clinical psychology (MS). *Faculty:* 6 full-time (4 women), 1 (woman) part-time/adjunct. *Students:* 22 full-time (17 women), 8 part-time (6 women); includes 11 minority (9 African Americans, 2 Hispanic Americans). Average age 27. 20 applicants, 95% accepted, 18 enrolled. In 2008, 6 master's awarded. *Degree requirements:* For master's, comprehensive exam, thesis or alternative. *Entrance requirements:* For master's, GRE General Test, GRE Subject Test, minimum undergraduate GPA of 2.5. *Application deadline:* For fall admission, 8/1 priority date for domestic students; for spring admission, 1/10 for domestic students. Applications are processed on a rolling basis. Application fee: $20 ($30 for international students). *Financial support:* Application deadline: 7/15. *Unit head:* Dr. Cynthia Lindsey, Head, 318-357-6594, Fax: 318-357-6802, E-mail: lindseyc@nsula.edu. *Application contact:* Dr. Steven G. Horton, Associate Provost/Dean, Graduate Studies, Research, and Information Systems, 318-357-5851, Fax: 318-357-5019, E-mail: grad_school@nsula.edu.

Northwestern University, The Graduate School, Judd A. and Marjorie Weinberg College of Arts and Sciences, Department of Psychology, Evanston, IL 60208. Offers brain, behavior and cognition (PhD); clinical psychology (PhD); cognitive psychology (PhD); personality (PhD); social psychology (PhD); JD/PhD. Admissions and degrees offered through The Graduate School. *Accreditation:* APA (one or more programs are accredited). Part-time programs available. *Degree requirements:* For doctorate, thesis/dissertation. *Entrance requirements:* For doctorate, GRE General Test, GRE Subject Test. Additional exam requirements/recommendations for international students: Required—TOEFL. Electronic applications accepted. *Faculty research:* Memory and higher order cognition, anxiety and depression, effectiveness of psychotherapy, social cognition, molecular basis of memory.

Northwestern University, The Graduate School and Northwestern University Feinberg School of Medicine, Program in Clinical Psychology, Evanston, IL 60208. Offers clinical psychology (PhD), including clinical neuropsychology, general clinical. PhD admissions and degree offered through The Graduate School. *Accreditation:* APA. *Degree requirements:* For doctorate, thesis/dissertation, clinical internship. *Entrance requirements:* For doctorate, GRE General Test, GRE Subject Test, minimum GPA of 3.2, course work in psychology. Additional exam requirements/recommendations for international students: Required—TOEFL. *Faculty research:* Cancer and cardiovascular risk reduction, evaluation of mental health services and policy, neuropsychological assessment, outcome of psychotherapy, cognitive therapy, pediatric and clinical child psychology.

Notre Dame de Namur University, Division of Academic Affairs, School of Sciences, Department of Clinical Psychology and Gerontology, Program in Clinical Psychology, Belmont, CA 94002-1908. Offers MA. Part-time programs available. *Students:* 25 full-time (21 women), 45 part-time (38 women); includes 24 minority (3 African Americans, 9 Asian Americans or Pacific Islanders, 12 Hispanic Americans), 2 international. Average age 34. In 2008, 24 master's awarded. *Entrance requirements:* Additional exam requirements/recommendations for international students: Required—TOEFL (minimum score 550 paper-based; 213 computer-based; 79 iBT). Application fee: $60. *Expenses:* Tuition: Part-time $699 per unit. Required fees: $3 per unit. $35 per semester. *Financial support:* Available to part-time students. Applicants required to submit FAFSA. *Unit head:* Dr. Nusha Askari, 650-5083728, E-mail: naskari@ndnu.edu. *Application contact:* Candace Hallmark, Assistant Director of Graduate Admissions, 650-508-3592, Fax: 650-508-3426, E-mail: grad.admit@ndnu.edu.

Nova Southeastern University, Center for Psychological Studies, Program in Clinical Psychology, Fort Lauderdale, FL 33314-7796. Offers PhD, Psy D, SPS. *Accreditation:* APA. *Faculty:* 31 full-time (9 women), 12 part-time/adjunct (6 women). *Students:* 502 full-time (407 women); includes 138 minority (30 African Americans, 2 American Indian/Alaska Native, 15 Asian Americans or Pacific Islanders, 91 Hispanic Americans), 6 international. 474 applicants, 30% accepted, 95 enrolled. In 2008, 87 doctorates awarded. *Degree requirements:* For doctorate, thesis/dissertation, clinical internship, competency exam; for SPS, comprehensive exam, internship. *Entrance requirements:* For doctorate, GRE General Test, GRE Subject Test (recommended), 18 credits of course work in psychology including 1 hour of experimental psychology and 3 hours of statistics, minimum undergraduate GPA of 3.0; for SPS, GRE General Test. Additional exam requirements/recommendations for international students: Required—TOEFL (minimum score 550 paper-based; 213 computer-based). *Application deadline:* For fall admission, 1/8 for domestic students. Application fee: $50. Electronic applications accepted. *Expenses:* Contact institution. *Financial support:* In 2008–09, 5 research assistantships, 33 teaching assistantships (averaging $1,000 per year) were awarded; career-related internships or fieldwork, Federal Work-Study, scholarships/grants, and unspecified assistantships also available. Financial award application deadline: 4/1. *Faculty research:* Eating disorders, neuropsychology, family violence, sports psychology, child-pediatric psychology. *Unit head:* Karen Grosby, Dean, 954-262-5701, Fax: 954-262-3859, E-mail: grosby@nova.edu. *Application contact:* Carlos Perez, Enrollment Management, 954-262-5790, Fax: 954-262-3893, E-mail: cpsinfo@cps.nova.edu.

The Ohio State University, Graduate School, College of Social and Behavioral Sciences, School of Social and Behavioral Science, Department of Psychology, Columbus, OH 43210. Offers behavioral neuroscience (PhD); clinical psychology (PhD); cognitive psychology (PhD); developmental psychology (PhD); mental retardation and developmental disabilities (PhD); psychology (MA); quantitative psychology (PhD); social psychology (PhD). *Accreditation:* APA (one or more programs are accredited). *Degree requirements:* For doctorate, thesis/dissertation. *Entrance requirements:* For master's and doctorate, GRE General Test. Additional exam requirements/recommendations for international students: Required—TOEFL (minimum score 600 paper-based; 250 computer-based). Electronic applications accepted.

Ohio University, Graduate College, College of Arts and Sciences, Department of Psychology, Program in Clinical Psychology, Athens, OH 45701-2979. Offers PhD. *Accreditation:* APA. *Degree requirements:* For doctorate, one foreign language, comprehensive exam, thesis/dissertation. *Entrance requirements:* For doctorate, GRE General Test, GRE Subject Test, minimum graduate GPA of 3.4. Additional exam requirements/recommendations for international students: Required—TOEFL. *Faculty research:* Health psychology, child clinical psychology, psychotherapy outcome.

Oklahoma State University, College of Arts and Sciences, Department of Psychology, Stillwater, OK 74078. Offers clinical psychology (PhD); general psychology (MS); lifespan development psychology (PhD). *Accreditation:* APA (one or more programs are accredited). *Faculty:* 26 full-time (12 women), 1 part-time/adjunct (0 women). *Students:* 38 full-time (22 women), 16 part-time (12 women); includes 10 minority (2 African Americans, 3 American Indian/Alaska Native, 2 Asian Americans or Pacific Islanders, 3 Hispanic Americans), 2 international. Average age 28. 145 applicants, 8% accepted, 10 enrolled. In 2008, 10 master's, 4 doctorates awarded. *Degree requirements:* For master's, thesis or alternative; for doctorate, comprehensive exam, thesis/dissertation. *Entrance requirements:* For master's and doctorate, GRE General Test. Additional exam requirements/recommendations for international students: Required—TOEFL. *Application deadline:* For fall admission, 3/1 priority date for international students; for spring admission, 8/1 priority date for international students. Applications are processed on a rolling basis. Application fee: $40 ($75 for international students). Electronic applications accepted. *Expenses:* Tuition, state resident: full-time $3716.40; part-time $154.85 per credit hour. Tuition, nonresident: full-time $14,448; part-time $602 per credit hour. Required fees: $1772.40; $73.85 per credit hour. One-time fee: $50. Tuition and fees vary according to course load and campus/location. *Financial support:* In 2008–09, 15 research assistantships (averaging $14,338 per year), 32 teaching assistantships (averaging $13,493 per year) were awarded; career-related internships or fieldwork, Federal Work-Study, scholarships/grants, health care benefits, tuition waivers (partial), and unspecified assistantships also available. Support available to part-time students. Financial award application deadline: 3/1; financial award applicants required to submit FAFSA. *Unit head:* Dr. Maureen A. Sullivan, Head, 405-744-6028, Fax: 405-744-8067. *Application contact:* Dr. Gordon Emslie, Dean, 405-744-6368, Fax: 405-744-0355, E-mail: grad_i@okstate.edu.

Old Dominion University, College of Sciences, Virginia Consortium Program in Clinical Psychology, Norfolk, VA 23529. Offers Psy D. *Accreditation:* APA. *Faculty:* 10 full-time (5 women). *Students:* 20 full-time (16 women), 32 part-time (25 women); includes 16 minority (6 African Americans, 7 Asian Americans or Pacific Islanders, 3 Hispanic Americans). Average age 28. 207 applicants, 8% accepted, 10 enrolled. In 2008, 3 doctorates awarded. *Degree requirements:* For doctorate, comprehensive exam, thesis/dissertation, internship. *Entrance requirements:* For doctorate, GRE General Test. Additional exam requirements/recommendations for international students: Required—TOEFL. *Application deadline:* For fall admission, 1/2 for domestic and international students. Application fee: $40. *Expenses:* Contact institution. *Financial support:* In 2008–09, 29 students received support, including 26 research assistantships with partial tuition reimbursements available (averaging $7,550 per year), 3 teaching assistantships with partial tuition reimbursements available (averaging $8,000 per year); career-related internships or fieldwork, scholarships/grants, and unspecified assistantships also available. Financial award application deadline: 1/2; financial award applicants required to submit FAFSA. *Faculty research:* Body image, depression, coping with stress, minority and women's issues, family therapy, neuropsychology. *Unit head:* Dr. Robin J. Lewis, Graduate Program Director, 757-683-4210, Fax: 757-368-1823, E-mail: psydgpd@odu.edu. *Application contact:* Eileen O'Neill, Coordinator, 757-368-1820, Fax: 757-368-1823, E-mail: exoneill@odu.edu.

Pace University, Dyson College of Arts and Sciences, Department of Psychology, Program in School-Clinical Child Psychology, New York, NY 10038. Offers Psy D. *Accreditation:* APA. Terminal master's awarded for partial completion of doctoral program. *Degree requirements:* For doctorate, comprehensive exam, qualifying exams, externship, internship, project. *Entrance requirements:* For doctorate, GRE General Test, GRE Subject Test, interview. Electronic applications accepted.

Pacifica Graduate Institute, Graduate Programs, Carpinteria, CA 93013. Offers clinical psychology (PhD); counseling psychology (MA); depth psychology (MA, PhD); mythological studies (MA, PhD). Terminal master's awarded for partial completion of doctoral program. *Degree requirements:* For master's, thesis (for some programs), practicum; for doctorate, comprehensive exam, thesis/dissertation, internship. *Entrance requirements:* For master's, resumé, 3 letters of recommendation, writing sample, interview; for doctorate, resumé, 4 letters of recommendation, writing sample, interview. Additional exam requirements/recommendations for international students: Required—TOEFL. *Faculty research:* Imaginal and archetypal theory; post-Colonial psychoanalytic and Jungian theory; myth literature as it applies to the theory and practice of psychology.

Palo Alto University, PGSP-Stanford Psy D Consortium Program, Palo Alto, CA 94303-4232. Offers Psy D. *Degree requirements:* For doctorate, thesis/dissertation. *Entrance requirements:* For doctorate, GRE, BA or MA in psychology or related area, minimum undergraduate GPA of 3.0, minimum graduate GPA of 3.3. Additional exam requirements/recommendations for international students: Required—TOEFL. Electronic applications accepted. *Faculty research:* Biopsychosocial research, neurobiology, psychopharmacology.

See Close-Up on page 1125.

Palo Alto University, Program in Clinical Psychology, Palo Alto, CA 94303-4232. Offers PhD, JD/PhD, MBA/PhD. *Accreditation:* APA. *Degree requirements:* For doctorate, comprehensive exam, thesis/dissertation, 2000 hour clinical internship, oral clinical competency exam. *Entrance requirements:* For doctorate, GRE General Test, BA or MA in psychology or related area, minimum undergraduate GPA of 3.0, 3.3 graduate. Additional exam requirements/recommendations for international students: Required—TOEFL. Electronic applications accepted. *Faculty research:* Child/family studies, health psychology, neuropsychology, personality development, assessment.

See Close-Up on page 1123.

Penn State Harrisburg, Graduate School, School of Behavioral Sciences and Education, Middletown, PA 17057-4898. Offers adult education (D Ed); applied behavior analysis (MA); applied clinical psychology (MA); applied psychological research (MA); community psychology and social change (MA); health education (M Ed); teaching and curriculum (M Ed); training and development (M Ed). Part-time and evening/weekend programs available.

Penn State University Park, Graduate School, College of the Liberal Arts, Department of Psychology, State College, University Park, PA 16802-1503. Offers clinical psychology (MS, PhD); cognitive psychology (MS, PhD); developmental psychology (MS, PhD); industrial/organizational psychology (MS, PhD); psychobiology (MS, PhD); social psychology (MS, PhD). *Accreditation:* APA (one or more programs are accredited).

Pepperdine University, Graduate School of Education and Psychology, Division of Psychology, Malibu, CA 90263. Offers clinical psychology (MA). *Entrance requirements:* For master's, GRE General Test or MAT, 2 professional recommendations. Additional exam requirements/recommendations for international students: Required—TOEFL (minimum score 550 paper-based; 220 computer-based).

Pepperdine University, Graduate School of Education and Psychology, Division of Psychology, Program in Clinical Psychology, Los Angeles, CA 90045. Offers clinical psychology (Psy D); clinical psychology (daytime) (MA), including marriage and family therapy; clinical psychology (evening) (MA), including marriage and family therapy. *Accreditation:* APA. Part-time and evening/weekend programs available. *Students:* 590 full-time (523 women), 71 part-time (59 women); includes 191 minority (58 African Americans, 7 American Indian/Alaska Native, 51 Asian Americans or Pacific Islanders, 75 Hispanic Americans), 22 international. 541 applicants, 64% accepted, 203 enrolled. In 2008, 195 master's awarded. *Entrance requirements:* For master's, GRE General Test, bachelor's degree in psychology or related field. Additional exam requirements/recommendations for international students: Required—TOEFL. *Application* *deadline:* For fall admission, 11/17 priority date for domestic students. Applications are processed on a rolling basis. Application fee: $55. *Financial support:* Research assistantships, teaching assistantships available. Financial award application deadline: 7/1; financial award applicants required to submit FAFSA. *Unit head:* Dr. Cary Mitchell, Director, 310-568-8553, E-mail: cary.mitchell@pepperdine.edu. *Application contact:* Lindsy Blanco, Recruitment and Admissions Manager, 310-506-5605.

Philadelphia College of Osteopathic Medicine, Graduate and Professional Programs, Department of Psychology, Philadelphia, PA 19131-1694. Offers clinical psychology (Psy D); counseling and clinical health psychology (MS); organizational leadership and development (MS); psychology (Certificate); school psychology (MS, Psy D, Ed S). *Accreditation:* APA. *Degree requirements:* For master's, thesis; for doctorate, comprehensive exam, thesis/dissertation, final project, fieldwork. *Entrance requirements:* For master's, GRE or MAT, minimum GPA of 3.0; course work in biology, chemistry, English, physics; for other advanced degree, PRAXIS. *Faculty research:* Depression in primary care, integrated primary care, geriatric mental health.

See Close-Up on page 1127.

Phillips Graduate Institute, Program in Clinical Family Psychology and Organizational Consulting, Encino, CA 91316-1509. Offers clinical psychology (Psy D); organizational consulting (Psy D). Evening/weekend programs available. *Degree requirements:* For doctorate, thesis/dissertation. *Entrance requirements:* For doctorate, minimum GPA of 3.0, interview.

Ponce School of Medicine, Program in Clinical Psychology, Ponce, PR 00732-7004. Offers Psy D. *Accreditation:* APA. *Faculty:* 26 full-time (9 women), 5 part-time/adjunct (2 women). *Students:* 186 full-time (157 women); all minorities (all Hispanic Americans). Average age 28. 92 applicants, 34% accepted, 31 enrolled. In 2008, 37 doctorates awarded. *Degree requirements:* For doctorate, one foreign language, comprehensive exam, thesis/dissertation, internship. *Entrance requirements:* For doctorate, GRE General Test or EXADEP, proficiency in Spanish and English, 2 letters of recommendation, minimum undergraduate GPA of 2.7. *Application deadline:* For fall admission, 4/15 for domestic and international students. Application fee: $100. *Financial support:* In 2008–09, 153 students received support; fellowships, scholarships/grants available. Financial award application deadline: 4/30; financial award applicants required to submit FAFSA. *Unit head:* Dr. Jose Pons, Head, 787-840-2575, E-mail: jpons@psm.edu. *Application contact:* Maria Colon, Admissions Officer, 787-840-2575 Ext. 2143, E-mail: mcolon@psm.edu.

Pontifical Catholic University of Puerto Rico, Institute of Graduate Studies in Behavioral Science and Community Affairs, Program in Clinical Psychology (Doctorate), Ponce, PR 00717-0777. Offers PhD. Part-time and evening/weekend programs available. *Degree requirements:* For doctorate, comprehensive exam, thesis/dissertation. *Entrance requirements:* For doctorate, EXADEP, minimum GPA of 2.75.

Pontifical Catholic University of Puerto Rico, Institute of Graduate Studies in Behavioral Science and Community Affairs, Program in Clinical Psychology (Master's), Ponce, PR 00717-0777. Offers MA, MS. Part-time and evening/weekend programs available. *Degree requirements:* For master's, thesis. *Entrance requirements:* For master's, EXADEP, 3 letters of recommendation, interview, minimum GPA of 2.75.

Prairie View A&M University, College of Juvenile Justice and Psychology, Prairie View, TX 77446-0519. Offers clinical adolescent psychology (PhD); juvenile forensic psychology (MSJFP); juvenile justice (MSJJ, PhD). Part-time and evening/weekend programs available. *Degree requirements:* For master's, comprehensive exam (for some programs), thesis (for some programs); for doctorate, comprehensive exam, thesis/dissertation. *Entrance requirements:* For master's, GRE, minimum GPA of 2.75; for doctorate, GRE, previous course work in clinical adolescent psychology, minimum GPA of 3.5. Additional exam requirements/recommendations for international students: Required—TOEFL. *Faculty research:* Juvenile justice, juvenile forensic psychology, teen court, graduate education, capital punishment.

Queens College of the City University of New York, Division of Graduate Studies, Mathematics and Natural Sciences Division, Department of Psychology, Flushing, NY 11367-1597. Offers clinical behavioral applications in mental health settings (MA); psychology (MA). Part-time programs available. *Degree requirements:* For master's, comprehensive exam, thesis or alternative. *Entrance requirements:* For master's, GRE, minimum GPA of 3.0. Additional exam requirements/recommendations for international students: Required—TOEFL.

Queen's University at Kingston, School of Graduate Studies and Research, Faculty of Arts and Sciences, Department of Psychology, Kingston, ON K7L 3N6, Canada. Offers brain behavior and cognitive science (MA, PhD); clinical psychology (MA, PhD); developmental psychology (MA, PhD); social personality psychology (MA, PhD). *Accreditation:* APA (one or more programs are accredited). *Degree requirements:* For master's, thesis; for doctorate, comprehensive exam, thesis/dissertation. *Entrance requirements:* For master's and doctorate, GRE General Test. Additional exam requirements/recommendations for international students: Required—TOEFL. *Faculty research:* Human development, social, personality, behavioral neuroscience, forensic.

Radford University, College of Graduate and Professional Studies, College of Humanities and Behavioral Sciences, Program in Psychology, Radford, VA 24142. Offers clinical psychology (MA, MS); counseling psychology (Psy D); experimental psychology (MA); general psychology (MS); industrial/organizational psychology (MA, MS); school psychology (Ed S). Part-time programs available. *Faculty:* 23 full-time (9 women), 1 part-time/adjunct (0 women). *Students:* 46 full-time (28 women), 5 part-time (4 women); includes 4 minority (3 African Americans, 1 Asian American or Pacific Islander), 2 international. Average age 26. 114 applicants, 42% accepted, 20 enrolled. In 2008, 36 master's awarded. *Degree requirements:* For master's, comprehensive exam, thesis (for some programs). *Entrance requirements:* For master's, GRE, minimum GPA of 3.0; 3 letters of reference; essay. Additional exam requirements/recommendations for international students: Required—TOEFL (minimum score 550 paper-based; 213 computer-based; 79 iBT). *Application deadline:* For fall admission, 3/1 priority date for domestic students, 12/1 for international students; for spring admission, 10/1 for domestic students, 7/1 for international students. Applications are processed on a rolling basis. Application fee: $40. Electronic applications accepted. *Expenses:* Tuition, area resident: Full-time $4845; part-time $202 per credit. Tuition, state resident: full-time $4845; part-time $202 per credit. Tuition, nonresident: full-time $11,483; part-time $478 per credit. Required fees: $2349; $98 per credit. *Financial support:* In 2008–09, 47 students received support, including 33 research assistantships with partial tuition reimbursements available (averaging $8,000 per year), 12 teaching assistantships with partial tuition reimbursements available (averaging $8,700 per year); career-related internships or fieldwork, institutionally sponsored loans, scholarships/grants, and unspecified assistantships also available. Financial award application deadline: 3/1; financial award applicants required to submit FAFSA. *Unit head:* Dr. Hilary M. Lips, Chair, 540-831-5387, Fax: 540-831-6113, E-mail: hlips@radford.edu. *Application contact:* Graduate Admissions Office, 540-831-5431, Fax: 540-831-6061, E-mail: gradcollege@radford.edu.

Regent University, Graduate School, School of Psychology and Counseling, Virginia Beach, VA 23464-9800. Offers clinical psychology (MA, Psy D); counseling (MA), including community counseling, human services counseling, school counseling; counseling studies (CAGS); counselor education and supervision (PhD); M Div/MA; M Ed/MA; MBA/MA. PhD program offered online only. *Accreditation:* ACA; APA (one or more programs are accredited). Part-time and evening/weekend programs available. Postbaccalaureate distance learning degree programs offered (minimal on-campus study). *Faculty:* 25 full-time (12 women), 19 part-time/adjunct (9 women). *Students:* 176 full-time (142 women), 192 part-time (144 women); includes 100 minority (78 African Americans, 2 American Indian/Alaska Native, 10 Asian Americans or Pacific Islanders, 10 Hispanic Americans), 13 international. Average age 32. 317 applicants, 47% accepted, 112 enrolled. In 2008, 129 master's, 22 doctorates awarded. *Degree requirements:* For master's, thesis or alternative, internship, practicum, written competency exam; for doctorate, thesis/dissertation or alternative. *Entrance requirements:* For master's, GRE General Test including writing exam, minimum undergraduate GPA of 2.75, 3 recommendations, resumé, transcripts, writing sample; for doctorate, GRE General Test including writing exam, GRE Subject Test, minimum undergraduate GPA of 3.0, 3.5 (PhD), 10-15 minute VHS tape demonstrating counseling skills, writing sample, 3 recommendations, resumé, transcripts. Additional exam requirements/recommendations for international students: Required—TOEFL (minimum score 577 paper-based; 233 computer-based). *Application deadline:* For fall admission, 4/1 priority date for domestic students; for spring admission, 11/1 priority date for domestic students. Applications are processed on a rolling basis. Application fee: $50. Electronic applications accepted. *Expenses:* Contact institution. *Financial support:* Research assistantships with full and partial tuition reimbursements, teaching assistantships with full and partial tuition reimbursements, career-related internships or fieldwork, scholarships/grants, and tuition waivers (full and partial) available. Support available to part-time students. Financial award application deadline: 9/1; financial award applicants required to submit FAFSA. *Faculty research:* Marriage enrichment, AIDS counseling, troubled youth, faith and learning, trauma. *Unit head:* Dr. Rosemarie Hughes, Dean, 757-352-4269, Fax: 757-352-4282, E-mail: rosehug@regent.edu. *Application contact:* Matthew Chadwick, Director of Admissions, 800-373-5504, Fax: 757-352-4381, E-mail: admissions@regent.edu.

Roosevelt University, Graduate Division, College of Arts and Sciences, Department of Psychology, Program in Clinical Professional Psychology, Chicago, IL 60605-1394. Offers MA, Psy D. *Accreditation:* APA. *Students:* 115 full-time (96 women), 111 part-time (95 women); includes 70 minority (38 African Americans, 12 Asian Americans or Pacific Islanders, 20 Hispanic Americans), 6 international. Average age 30. 274 applicants, 45% accepted, 52 enrolled. In 2008, 44 master's, 4 doctorates awarded. *Expenses:* Tuition: Full-time $14,730; part-time $709 per credit. Required fees: $175 per semester. Tuition and fees vary according to course load and program. *Unit head:* Judith Dygdon, Director, 312-341-6362. *Application contact:* Joanne Canyon-Heller, Coordinator of Graduate Admission, 877-APPLY RU, Fax: 312-281-3356, E-mail: applyru@roosevelt.edu.

Rosalind Franklin University of Medicine and Science, School of Graduate and Postdoctoral Studies, Department of Clinical Psychology, North Chicago, IL 60064-3095. Offers MS, PhD. *Accreditation:* APA. Terminal master's awarded for partial completion of doctoral program. *Degree requirements:* For master's, thesis; for doctorate, comprehensive exam, thesis/dissertation, 1 year full-time clinical internship. *Entrance requirements:* For master's, GRE General Test; for doctorate, GRE General Test, GRE Subject Test. Additional exam requirements/recommendations for international students: Required—TOEFL, TWE. *Expenses:* Contact institution. *Faculty research:* Hormonal influences on human sexually dimorphic behavior, nutrition and mood, aging, anxiety disorders.

Rutgers, The State University of New Jersey, New Brunswick, Graduate School of Applied and Professional Psychology, Department of Clinical Psychology, Piscataway, NJ 08854-8097. Offers Psy M, Psy D. *Accreditation:* APA (one or more programs are accredited). *Degree requirements:* For doctorate, comprehensive exam, thesis/dissertation, 1 year internship. *Entrance requirements:* For doctorate, GRE General Test, GRE Subject Test, bachelor's degree in psychology or equivalent. Additional exam requirements/recommendations for international students: Required—TOEFL. Electronic applications accepted. *Expenses:* Contact institution. *Faculty research:* Long- and short-term dynamic therapy, community psychology, cognitive-behavioral therapy: anxiety and depressive disorders, addictive behaviors: eating disorders and alcoholism.

Rutgers, The State University of New Jersey, New Brunswick, Graduate School, Program in Psychology, Piscataway, NJ 08854-8097. Offers behavioral neuroscience (PhD); clinical psychology (PhD); cognitive psychology (PhD); interdisciplinary health psychology (PhD); social psychology (PhD). *Accreditation:* APA. *Degree requirements:* For doctorate, comprehensive exam, thesis/dissertation. *Entrance requirements:* For doctorate, GRE General Test, 3 letters of recommendation. Additional exam requirements/recommendations for international students: Required—TOEFL (minimum score 577 paper-based; 233 computer-based). Electronic applications accepted. *Faculty research:* Learning and memory, behavioral ecology, hormones and behavior, psychopharmacology, anxiety disorders.

St. John's University, St. John's College of Liberal Arts and Sciences, Department of Psychology, Program in Clinical Psychology, Queens, NY 11439. Offers clinical psychology-child (PhD); clinical psychology-general (PhD). *Accreditation:* APA. *Students:* 35 full-time (24 women), 32 part-time (28 women); includes 17 minority (5 African Americans, 8 Asian Americans or Pacific Islanders, 4 Hispanic Americans), 4 international. Average age 28. 244 applicants, 9% accepted, 12 enrolled. In 2008, 10 doctorates awarded. *Degree requirements:* For doctorate, comprehensive exam, thesis/dissertation, internship, externship. *Entrance requirements:* For doctorate, GRE General Test, GRE Subject Test, 24 credits of undergraduate course work in psychology, 2 writing samples. Additional exam requirements/recommendations for international students: Required—TOEFL (minimum score 500 paper-based; 173 computer-based; 61 iBT), IELTS (minimum score 5.5). *Application deadline:* For fall admission, 2/1 for domestic students, 5/1 priority date for international students; for spring admission, 11/1 priority date for international students. Applications are processed on a rolling basis. Application fee: $70. Electronic applications accepted. *Expenses:* Contact institution. *Financial support:* Fellowships, research assistantships, career-related internships or fieldwork and scholarships/grants available. Support available to part-time students. Financial award application deadline: 3/1; financial award applicants required to submit FAFSA. *Faculty research:* Cognitive-behavioral therapy, sucking cessation pedagogical research and implicit attitudes. *Unit head:* Dr. Jeffrey S. Nevid, Director, 718-990-1548, E-mail: nevidj@stjohns.edu. *Application contact:* Kathleen Davis, Director of Graduate Admission, 718-990-2790, Fax: 718-990-5686, E-mail: gradhelp@stjohns.edu.

Saint Louis University, Graduate School, College of Arts and Sciences and Graduate School, Department of Psychology, St. Louis, MO 63103-2097. Offers clinical psychology (MS-R, PhD); experimental psychology (MS-R, PhD); industrial-organizational psychology (PhD); psychology (PhD). *Accreditation:* APA (one or more programs are accredited). Part-time programs available. *Degree requirements:* For master's, comprehensive exam, thesis; for doctorate, thesis/dissertation, clinical internship (for clinical psychology PhD). *Entrance requirements:* For master's and doctorate, GRE General Test, interview, letters of recommendation, resumé, transcripts, goal statement. Additional exam requirements/recommendations for international students: Required—TOEFL (minimum score 550 paper-based; 213 computer-based). Electronic applications accepted. *Faculty research:* Violence and trauma; neural basis of learning and memory function; eating disorders; body image and health behavior; prejudice, stereotyping, and victimization; memory, cognitive aging and language processing.

St. Mary's University, Graduate School, Department of Psychology, Program in Clinical Psychology, San Antonio, TX 78228-8507. Offers MA, MS. Part-time programs available. *Faculty:* 4 full-time (2 women), 2 part-time/adjunct (1 woman). *Students:* 15 full-time (14 women), 6 part-time (3 women); includes 7 minority (1 African American, 1 American Indian/Alaska Native, 5 Hispanic Americans), 2 international. Average age 25. 24 applicants, 54% accepted, 11 enrolled. In 2008, 6 master's awarded. *Degree requirements:* For master's, comprehensive exam, practica. *Entrance requirements:* For master's, GRE General Test. Additional exam requirements/recommendations for international students: Required—TOEFL (minimum score 550 paper-based; 213 computer-based; 80 iBT). *Application deadline:* Applications are processed on a rolling basis. Application fee: $0. Electronic applications accepted. *Expenses:* Tuition: Full-time $12,006; part-time $667 per credit hour. Required fees: $440; $220 per semester. *Financial support:* In 2008–09, 4 students received support, including 3 fellowships (averaging $3,167 per year), 1 research assistantship (averaging $4,500 per year); career-related internships or fieldwork, Federal Work-Study, institutionally sponsored loans, scholarships/grants, health care benefits, and unspecified assistantships also available. Financial award application deadline: 3/31; financial award applicants required to submit FAFSA. *Unit head:* Dr. Patricia Owen, Interim Director, 210-436-3314, Fax: 210-431-4301, E-mail: powen@

Clinical Psychology

St. Mary's University (continued)

stmarytx.edu. *Application contact:* Dr. Henry Flores, Dean of the Graduate School, 210-436-3101, Fax: 210-431-2220, E-mail: hflores@stmarytx.edu.

Saint Michael's College, Graduate Programs, Program in Clinical Psychology, Colchester, VT 05439. Offers MA. Part-time and evening/weekend programs available. *Degree requirements:* For master's, thesis or alternative, internship, practicum, research seminar. *Entrance requirements:* For master's, GRE General Test, GRE Subject Test, undergraduate major in psychology or related area, minimum 12 credits in psychology, minimum GPA of 3.0. Electronic applications accepted. *Faculty research:* Psychodynamic psychotherapy, family therapy, philosophical foundations of clinical psychology.

Sam Houston State University, College of Humanities and Social Sciences, Department of Psychology and Philosophy, Huntsville, TX 77341. Offers clinical psychology (PhD); psychology (MA). *Accreditation:* APA. Part-time programs available. *Faculty:* 14 full-time (5 women), 1 part-time/adjunct (0 women). *Students:* 69 full-time (55 women), 33 part-time (28 women); includes 20 minority (6 African Americans, 6 Asian Americans or Pacific Islanders, 8 Hispanic Americans), 3 international. Average age 26. 139 applicants, 26% accepted, 31 enrolled. In 2008, 13 master's, 4 doctorates awarded. *Degree requirements:* For master's, thesis. *Entrance requirements:* For master's, GRE General Test or MAT, minimum GPA of 3.0. Additional exam requirements/recommendations for international students: Required—TOEFL (minimum score 550 paper-based; 213 computer-based; 79 iBT). *Application deadline:* For fall admission, 8/1 for domestic students; for spring admission, 12/1 for domestic students. Applications are processed on a rolling basis. Application fee: $20. *Expenses:* Tuition, state resident: full-time $3564; part-time $198 per credit hour. Tuition, nonresident: full-time $8622; part-time $479 per credit hour. Required fees: $1290. Tuition and fees vary according to course load and campus/location. *Financial support:* Research assistantships, teaching assistantships, career-related internships or fieldwork and institutionally sponsored loans available. Support available to part-time students. Financial award application deadline: 5/31; financial award applicants required to submit FAFSA. *Unit head:* Dr. Christopher Wilson, Chair, 936-294-3052, Fax: 936-294-3798, E-mail: psy_dcw@shsu.edu. *Application contact:* Dr. Rowland Miller, Graduate Coordinator, 936-294-1176, Fax: 936-294-3798, E-mail: psy_rsm@shsu.edu.

San Diego State University, Graduate and Research Affairs, College of Sciences, Department of Psychology, San Diego, CA 92182. Offers clinical psychology (MS, PhD); industrial and organizational psychology (MS); program evaluation (MS); psychology (MA). *Accreditation:* APA (one or more programs are accredited). Terminal master's awarded for partial completion of doctoral program. *Degree requirements:* For master's, thesis, oral exam; for doctorate, thesis/dissertation. *Entrance requirements:* For master's, GRE General Test, GRE Subject Test, 3 letters of recommendation; for doctorate, GRE General Test, GRE Subject Test, minimum GPA of 3.0, 3 letters of recommendation. Additional exam requirements/recommendations for international students: Required—TOEFL. Electronic applications accepted.

San Jose State University, Graduate Studies and Research, College of Social Sciences, Department of Psychology, San Jose, CA 95192-0001. Offers clinical psychology (MS); experimental psychology (MA); industrial/organizational psychology (MS); psychology (MA). *Degree requirements:* For master's, comprehensive exam, thesis (for some programs). *Entrance requirements:* For master's, GRE General Test, minimum GPA of 3.0. Electronic applications accepted. *Faculty research:* Drug and alcohol abuse, neurohormonal mechanisms in motion sickness, behavior modification, sleep research, genetics.

Saybrook Graduate School and Research Center, Programs in Psychology, Human Science and Organizational Systems, San Francisco, CA 94111-1920. Offers clinical psychology (PhD); creativity studies (MA); human science (MA, PhD), including consciousness and spirituality, individualized (PhD), integrative health studies, organizational systems, social transformation; marriage and family therapy (MA); organizational systems (MA, PhD), including individualized (PhD), organizational systems; psychology (MA, PhD), including consciousness and spirituality, humanistic and transpersonal psychology, individualized (PhD), integrative health studies, licensure track (MA), organizational systems, social transformation. Postbaccalaureate distance learning degree programs offered (minimal on-campus study). Terminal master's awarded for partial completion of doctoral program. *Degree requirements:* For master's, thesis or alternative; for doctorate, thesis/dissertation. Electronic applications accepted. *Faculty research:* Humanistic theory, health studies, organizational systems, consciousness and spirituality, social transformation.

The School of Professional Psychology at Forest Institute, Graduate Programs, Springfield, MO 65807. Offers clinical psychology (Psy D); counseling psychology (MA); marriage and family therapy (MA, PGC). *Accreditation:* AAMFT/COAMFTE; APA (one or more programs are accredited). *Faculty:* 18 full-time (9 women), 28 part-time/adjunct (15 women). *Students:* 208 full-time (141 women), 34 part-time (27 women). 153 applicants, 42% accepted, 40 enrolled. In 2008, 36 master's, 36 doctorates awarded. Terminal master's awarded for partial completion of doctoral program. *Median time to degree:* Of those who began their doctoral program in fall 2000, 100% received their degree in 8 years or less. *Degree requirements:* For master's, thesis, practice; for doctorate, comprehensive exam, thesis/dissertation, internship, practice. *Entrance requirements:* For master's, GRE General Test, interview, minimum GPA of 3.0, 12 hours in psychology; for doctorate, GRE General Test, interview, minimum GPA of 3.0, 18 hours in psychology. Additional exam requirements/recommendations for international students: Required—TOEFL (minimum score 550 paper-based; 213 computer-based). *Application deadline:* For fall admission, 1/15 priority date for domestic and international students; for spring admission, 8/1 priority date for domestic and international students. Applications are processed on a rolling basis. Application fee: $50. Electronic applications accepted. *Expenses:* Tuition: Full-time $22,500. *Financial support:* In 2008–09, 91 students received support. Career-related internships or fieldwork, Federal Work-Study, and scholarships/grants available. Support available to part-time students. Financial award applicants required to submit FAFSA. *Faculty research:* Forensics/corrections, marriage and family therapy, child and adolescent, integrated health care, neuropsychology. *Unit head:* Dr. Mark E. Skrade, President, 417-823-3477, Fax: 417-823-3442, E-mail: mskrade@forest.edu. *Application contact:* Dawn Medley, Director of Enrollment Management, 417-823-3477, Fax: 417-823-3442, E-mail: dmedley@forest.edu.

Seattle Pacific University, PhD in Clinical Psychology Program, Seattle, WA 98119-1997. Offers PhD. *Accreditation:* APA. *Faculty:* 9 full-time (5 women), 3 part-time/adjunct (0 women). *Students:* 49 full-time (36 women), 29 part-time (27 women); includes 11 minority (1 African American, 1 American Indian/Alaska Native, 5 Asian Americans or Pacific Islanders, 4 Hispanic Americans). Average age 29. 107 applicants, 10% accepted, 11 enrolled. In 2008, 16 doctorates awarded. *Degree requirements:* For doctorate, thesis/dissertation, clinical internship, practicum. *Entrance requirements:* For doctorate, GRE General Test or MAT. *Application deadline:* For fall admission, 2/1 for domestic students. Electronic applications accepted. *Expenses:* Contact institution. *Financial support:* In 2008–09, 63 students received support; fellowships, scholarships/grants available. Financial award applicants required to submit FAFSA. *Faculty research:* Social network support, attachment, integration of faith and family psychology, developmental psychology. *Unit head:* Dr. Jay Skidmore, Chair, 706-281-2916. *Application contact:* Grad Center The, 206-281-2091.

Southern Illinois University Carbondale, Graduate School, College of Liberal Arts, Department of Psychology, Carbondale, IL 62901-4701. Offers clinical psychology (MA, MS, PhD); counseling psychology (MA, MS, PhD); experimental psychology (MA, MS, PhD). *Accreditation:* APA (one or more programs are accredited). *Degree requirements:* For master's, thesis; for doctorate, thesis/dissertation. *Entrance requirements:* For master's, GRE General Test, GRE Subject Test, minimum GPA of 2.7; for doctorate, GRE General Test, GRE Subject Test, minimum GPA of 3.25. Additional exam requirements/recommendations for international students: Required—TOEFL. *Faculty research:* Developmental neuropsychology; smoking, affect, and cognition; personality measurement; vocational psychology; program evaluation.

See Close-Up on page 1135.

Southern Illinois University Edwardsville, Graduate Studies and Research, School of Education, Department of Psychology, Program in Clinical-Adult Psychology, Edwardsville, IL 62026-0001. Offers MA. Part-time programs available. *Students:* 14 full-time (9 women), 11 part-time (8 women); includes 2 minority (1 African American, 1 Asian American or Pacific Islander). Average age 26. 44 applicants, 25% accepted. In 2008, 11 master's awarded. *Degree requirements:* For master's, thesis. *Entrance requirements:* For master's, GRE. Additional exam requirements/recommendations for international students: Required—TOEFL (minimum score 550 paper-based; 213 computer-based; 79 iBT), IELTS (minimum score 6.5). *Application deadline:* For fall admission, 2/1 for domestic and international students. Application fee: $30. Electronic applications accepted. *Expenses:* Tuition, area resident: Full-time $5838. Tuition, nonresident: full-time $14,596. Required fees: $1525. *Financial support:* Application deadline: 3/1; *Unit head:* Dr. Lynn Bartels, Director, 618-650-2202, E-mail: lbartel@siue.edu. *Application contact:* Dr. Lynn Bartels, Director, 618-650-2202, E-mail: lbartel@siue.edu.

Southern Illinois University Edwardsville, Graduate Studies and Research, School of Education, Department of Psychology, Program in Clinical Child and School Psychology, Edwardsville, IL 62026-0001. Offers MS. Part-time programs available. *Students:* 11 full-time (all women), 9 part-time (all women), 2 international. Average age 26. 63 applicants, 14% accepted. In 2008, 11 master's awarded. *Degree requirements:* For master's, thesis (for some programs), research project. *Entrance requirements:* For master's, GRE. Additional exam requirements/recommendations for international students: Required—TOEFL (minimum score 550 paper-based; 213 computer-based; 79 iBT), IELTS (minimum score 6.5). *Application deadline:* For fall admission, 2/1 for domestic and international students. Application fee: $30. Electronic applications accepted. *Expenses:* Tuition, area resident: Full-time $5838. Tuition, nonresident: full-time $14,596. Required fees: $1525. *Financial support:* Application deadline: 3/1; *Unit head:* Dr. Lynn Bartels, Director, 618-650-2202, E-mail: lbartel@siue.edu. *Application contact:* Dr. Lynn Bartels, Director, 618-650-2202, E-mail: lbartel@siue.edu.

Southern Methodist University, Dedman College, Department of Psychology, Program in Clinical Psychology, Dallas, TX 75275. Offers PhD. *Faculty:* 11 full-time (5 women), 3 part-time/adjunct (2 women). *Students:* 16 full-time (14 women); includes 4 minority (1 American Indian/Alaska Native, 1 Asian American or Pacific Islander, 2 Hispanic Americans). Average age 32. 84 applicants, 8% accepted, 4 enrolled. In 2008, 1 doctorate awarded. *Degree requirements:* For doctorate, comprehensive exam, thesis/dissertation, research presentation and publication. *Entrance requirements:* For doctorate, GRE General Test, minimum GPA of 3.0, 3 letters of recommendation. Additional exam requirements/recommendations for international students: Required—TOEFL (minimum score 550 paper-based). *Application deadline:* For fall admission, 1/1 priority date for domestic and international students. Application fee: $60. Electronic applications accepted. *Financial support:* In 2008–09, 9 students received support, including 8 research assistantships with full tuition reimbursements available (averaging $14,000 per year); career-related internships or fieldwork also available. Financial award application deadline: 1/1; financial award applicants required to submit FAFSA. *Faculty research:* Family violence, family assessment, anxiety disorders, personality disorders. Total annual research expenditures: $500,000. *Unit head:* Dr. Robert B. Hampson, Director, 214-768-2734, Fax: 214-768-3910, E-mail: rhampson@smu.edu. *Application contact:* Ann Conner, Assistant to Director of Graduate Studies, 214-768-4924, Fax: 214-768-3910, E-mail: aconner@smu.edu.

Southern New Hampshire University, School of Liberal Arts, Manchester, NH 03106-1045. Offers clinical services for adults psychiatric disabilities (Certificate); clinical services for children and adolescents with psychiatric disabilities (Certificate); clinical services for persons with co-occurring substance abuse and psychiatric disabilities (Certificate); community mental health (MS); fiction writing (MFA); non-fiction writing (MFA); teaching English as a foreign language (MS). Part-time and evening/weekend programs available. *Degree requirements:* For master's, one foreign language, thesis. *Entrance requirements:* For master's, minimum GPA of 2.75: MS-TEFL, 3.0: MFA. Additional exam requirements/recommendations for international students: Required—TOEFL (minimum score 550 paper-based; 213 computer-based; 79 iBT), IELTS (minimum score 6.5), TWE (minimum score 5). Electronic applications accepted. *Expenses:* Contact institution. *Faculty research:* Action research, state of the art practice in behavioral health services, wraparound approaches to working with youth, learning styles.

Spalding University, Graduate Studies, College of Social Sciences and Humanities, School of Professional Psychology, Louisville, KY 40203-2188. Offers clinical psychology (MA, Psy D). *Accreditation:* APA (one or more programs are accredited). Part-time programs available. Terminal master's awarded for partial completion of doctoral program. *Degree requirements:* For master's, comprehensive exam; for doctorate, thesis/dissertation. *Entrance requirements:* For master's, GRE General Test, 18 hours of undergraduate course work in psychology, interview; for doctorate, GRE General Test, interview, 18 hours of coursework in psychology. Additional exam requirements/recommendations for international students: Required—TOEFL (minimum score 535 paper-based; 203 computer-based). *Expenses:* Tuition: Full-time $11,340; part-time $630 per credit hour. Tuition and fees vary according to program. *Faculty research:* Substance abuse, prayer research, end-of-life issues, complementary and alternative medicine, research methodology and statistical inference.

State University of New York at Binghamton, Graduate School, School of Arts and Sciences, Department of Psychology, Specialization in Clinical Psychology, Binghamton, NY 13902-6000. Offers MA, PhD. *Accreditation:* APA (one or more programs are accredited). *Students:* 29 full-time (23 women), 15 part-time (12 women); includes 7 minority (3 African Americans, 4 Hispanic Americans), 2 international. Average age 28. 212 applicants, 4% accepted, 6 enrolled. In 2008, 3 doctorates awarded. *Degree requirements:* For master's, thesis; for doctorate, thesis/dissertation, departmental qualifying exam. *Entrance requirements:* For master's and doctorate, GRE General Test, GRE Subject Test. Additional exam requirements/recommendations for international students: Required—TOEFL. *Application deadline:* For fall admission, 4/15 priority date for domestic students, 1/15 priority date for international students; for spring admission, 11/1 for domestic students, 10/1 priority date for international students. Applications are processed on a rolling basis. Application fee: $60. Electronic applications accepted. *Expenses:* Tuition, area resident: Full-time $6900; part-time $288 per credit. Tuition, state resident: full-time $6900; part-time $288 per credit. Tuition, nonresident: full-time $10,920; part-time $455 per credit. Required fees: $1130. Part-time tuition and fees vary according to course load, program and student level. *Financial support:* Fellowships, research assistantships, teaching assistantships, career-related internships or fieldwork, Federal Work-Study, institutionally sponsored loans, scholarships/grants, traineeships, health care benefits, and unspecified assistantships available. Financial award application deadline: 2/15; financial award applicants required to submit FAFSA. *Unit head:* Dr. Steven Lisman, Graduate Coordinator, 607-777-4929, E-mail: slisman@binghamton.edu. *Application contact:* Victoria Williams, Recruiting and Admissions Coordinator, 607-777-2151, Fax: 607-777-2501, E-mail: vwilliam@binghamton.edu.

Stony Brook University, State University of New York, Graduate School, College of Arts and Sciences, Department of Psychology, Program in Clinical Psychology, Stony Brook, NY 11794. Offers PhD. *Accreditation:* APA. *Students:* 38 full-time (35 women); includes 5 minority (2 Asian Americans or Pacific Islanders, 3 Hispanic Americans). Average age 27. 322 applicants, 3% accepted. In 2008, 7 doctorates awarded. *Degree requirements:* For doctorate, thesis/dissertation. *Entrance requirements:* For doctorate, GRE General Test, GRE Subject Test. Additional exam requirements/recommendations for international students: Required—TOEFL. *Application deadline:* For fall admission, 1/15 for domestic students. Application fee: $60. *Expenses:* Tuition, area resident: Full-time $7880; part-time $328 per credit hour. Tuition, state resident: full-time $7880; part-time $328 per credit hour. Tuition, nonresident: full-time $13,250; part-time $552 per credit hour. Required fees: $848. *Unit head:* Dr. Daniel O'Leary, Head, 631-632-7850, E-mail: k.d.oleary@stonybrook.edu. *Application contact:* Graduate Director, 631-632-7792, Fax: 631-632-7876.

Suffolk University, College of Arts and Sciences, Department of Psychology, Boston, MA 02108-2770. Offers clinical psychology (PhD). *Accreditation:* APA. *Degree requirements:* For doctorate, thesis/dissertation, practicum. *Entrance requirements:* For doctorate, GRE General Test or MAT, statement of professional goals, official transcripts, 2 letters of recommendation, resumé. Additional exam requirements/recommendations for international students: Required—TOEFL (minimum score 550 paper-based; 213 computer-based; 80 iBT). Electronic applications accepted. *Expenses:* Contact institution. *Faculty research:* Olfaction decision-making in substance-dependent individuals, ego development, experiential avoidance in generalized anxiety disorder.

Syracuse University, Graduate School, College of Arts and Sciences, Program in Clinical Psychology, Syracuse, NY 13244. Offers PhD. *Accreditation:* APA. *Degree requirements:* For doctorate, thesis/dissertation. *Entrance requirements:* For doctorate, GRE General Test, GRE Subject Test. Additional exam requirements/recommendations for international students: Required—TOEFL. Electronic applications accepted.

Teachers College, Columbia University, Graduate Faculty of Education, Department of Counseling and Clinical Psychology, Program in Clinical Psychology, New York, NY 10027-6696. Offers PhD. *Accreditation:* APA. *Faculty:* 4 full-time (2 women), 8 part-time/adjunct. *Students:* 25 full-time (18 women), 22 part-time (17 women); includes 11 minority (2 African Americans, 8 Asian Americans or Pacific Islanders, 1 Hispanic American), 2 international. Average age 31. 415 applicants, 79% accepted, 115 enrolled. In 2008, 11 doctorates awarded. *Application deadline:* For fall admission, 12/15 for domestic students. Application fee: $75. *Expenses:* Tuition: Full-time $26,040; part-time $1085 per credit. Required fees: $720. *Financial support:* Career-related internships or fieldwork, Federal Work-Study, institutionally sponsored loans, and tuition waivers (partial) available. Support available to part-time students. Financial award application deadline: 2/1. *Faculty research:* Psychotherapy education, trauma, stress, psychopathology, life span and aging issues. *Unit head:* Maria Miville, Head, 212-678-3257. *Application contact:* Melba Remice, Assistant Director of Admission, 212-678-4035, Fax: 212-678-4171, E-mail: ms2545@columbia.edu.

Temple University, Graduate School, College of Liberal Arts, Department of Psychology, Program in Clinical Psychology, Philadelphia, PA 19122-6096. Offers PhD. *Accreditation:* APA. *Degree requirements:* For doctorate, thesis/dissertation. *Entrance requirements:* For doctorate, GRE General Test, minimum GPA of 3.0. Additional exam requirements/recommendations for international students: Required—TOEFL (minimum score 550 paper-based; 213 computer-based; 79 iBT). Electronic applications accepted. *Faculty research:* Depression, addictive disorders, parenting and families, social phobia, child and adolescent treatment research.

Texas A&M University, College of Liberal Arts, Department of Psychology, College Station, TX 77843. Offers behavioral and cellular neuroscience (MS, PhD); clinical psychology (MS, PhD); cognitive psychology (MS, PhD); developmental psychology (MS, PhD); industrial/organizational psychology (MS, PhD); social psychology (MS, PhD). *Accreditation:* APA (one or more programs are accredited). *Faculty:* 35. *Students:* 74 full-time (47 women), 11 part-time (9 women); includes 30 minority (7 African Americans, 5 Asian Americans or Pacific Islanders, 18 Hispanic Americans), 4 international. In 2008, 11 master's, 12 doctorates awarded. *Degree requirements:* For master's, thesis; for doctorate, comprehensive exam (for some programs), thesis/dissertation. *Entrance requirements:* For master's and doctorate, GRE General Test. Additional exam requirements/recommendations for international students: Required—TOEFL. *Application deadline:* For fall admission, 1/5 for domestic and international students. Application fee: $50 ($75 for international students). Electronic applications accepted. *Expenses:* Tuition, area resident: Full-time $3838.50. Tuition, state resident: full-time $3838.50. Tuition, nonresident: full-time $8897. Required fees: $2359.60. *Financial support:* Fellowships with partial tuition reimbursements, research assistantships with partial tuition reimbursements, teaching assistantships with partial tuition reimbursements, career-related internships or fieldwork, institutionally sponsored loans, health care benefits, and unspecified assistantships available. Financial award application deadline: 1/5; financial award applicants required to submit FAFSA. *Unit head:* Dr. Les Morey, Head, 979-845-2581, Fax: 979-845-4727, E-mail: lmorey@psych.tamu.edu. *Application contact:* Sharon Starr, Graduate Admissions Supervisor, 979-458-1710, Fax: 979-845-4727, E-mail: gradadv@psyc.tamu.edu.

Texas Tech University, Graduate School, College of Arts and Sciences, Department of Psychology, Lubbock, TX 79409. Offers clinical psychology (PhD); counseling psychology (MA, PhD); experimental psychology (MA, PhD); psychology (MA, PhD). *Accreditation:* APA (one or more programs are accredited). Part-time programs available. *Faculty:* 25 full-time (11 women). *Students:* 87 full-time (58 women), 20 part-time (13 women); includes 16 minority (5 African Americans, 1 American Indian/Alaska Native, 2 Asian Americans or Pacific Islanders, 8 Hispanic Americans), 6 international. Average age 28. 290 applicants, 13% accepted, 17 enrolled. In 2008, 13 master's, 6 doctorates awarded. *Degree requirements:* For doctorate, thesis/dissertation. *Entrance requirements:* For master's and doctorate, GRE General Test, GRE Subject Test. Additional exam requirements/recommendations for international students: Required—TOEFL (minimum score 550 paper-based; 213 computer-based). *Application deadline:* For fall admission, 3/1 priority date for international students; for spring admission, 11/1 priority date for international students. Applications are processed on a rolling basis. Application fee: $50 ($60 for international students). Electronic applications accepted. *Expenses:* Tuition, area resident: Part-time $194 per credit hour. Tuition, state resident: full-time $4648; part-time $194 per credit hour. Tuition, nonresident: full-time $11,392; part-time $475 per credit hour. Required fees: $2206; $69 per credit hour. $389 per semester. *Financial support:* In 2008–09, 91 students received support, including 4 research assistantships with partial tuition reimbursements available (averaging $12,762 per year), 69 teaching assistantships with partial tuition reimbursements available (averaging $11,835 per year); career-related internships or fieldwork, Federal Work-Study, and institutionally sponsored loans also available. Support available to part-time students. Financial award application deadline: 4/15; financial award applicants required to submit FAFSA. *Faculty research:* Failure/success in relationships, peer rejection in school, stress and coping, group processes, clinical and health psychology. Total annual research expenditures: $564,495. *Unit head:* Dr. Susan S. Hendrick, Chair, 806-742-3711 Ext. 224, Fax: 806-742-0818, E-mail: s.hendrick@ttu.edu. *Application contact:* Dr. Lee M. Cohen, Director of Clinical Program, 806-742-3711 Ext. 254, Fax: 806-742-0818, E-mail: lee.cohen@ttu.edu.

Towson University, College of Graduate Studies and Research, Program in Clinical Psychology, Towson, MD 21252-0001. Offers MA. Part-time and evening/weekend programs available. *Degree requirements:* For master's, thesis (for some programs), exams. *Entrance requirements:* For master's, GRE, minimum GPA of 3.0, 15 credits in related course work. Additional exam requirements/recommendations for international students: Required—TOEFL. Electronic applications accepted. *Faculty research:* Cognitive behavior, issues affecting the aging, relaxation hypnosis and imagery, medicalization of male sexuality.

Troy University, Graduate School, College of Education, Program in Counseling and Psychology, Troy, AL 36082. Offers clinical mental health (MS); community counseling (MS); school psychology (MS); student affairs counseling (MS). *Accreditation:* ACA; CORE; NCATE. Part-time and evening/weekend programs available. *Degree requirements:* For master's, comprehensive exam, thesis. *Entrance requirements:* For master's, MAT, minimum GPA of 2.5. Additional exam requirements/recommendations for international students: Required—TOEFL (minimum score 523 paper-based; 200 computer-based). Electronic applications accepted.

Uniformed Services University of the Health Sciences, School of Medicine, Graduate Programs in the Biomedical Sciences and Public Health, Department of Medical and Clinical Psychology, Bethesda, MD 20814-4799. Offers clinical psychology (PhD); medical psychology (PhD). Clinical psychology available to active duty military only. *Accreditation:* APA. Terminal master's awarded for partial completion of doctoral program. *Degree requirements:* For doctorate, comprehensive exam, thesis/dissertation, qualifying exam. *Entrance requirements:* For doctorate, GRE General Test, minimum GPA of 3.0, U.S. citizenship. Additional exam requirements/recommendations for international students: Required—TOEFL. Electronic applications accepted. *Faculty research:* Addictive and appetitive behavior, psychopharmacology, stress and eating, obesity, health.

Union College, Graduate Programs, Department of Psychology, Barbourville, KY 40906-1499. Offers clinical psychology (MA); counseling psychology (MA); school psychology (MA).

Union Institute & University, Program in Clinical Psychology, Cincinnati, OH 45206-1925. Offers Psy D. *Degree requirements:* For doctorate, thesis/dissertation, internship, residency, practicum. *Entrance requirements:* For doctorate, master's degree, letters of recommendation, interview.

Universidad de Iberoamerica, Graduate School, San Jose, Costa Rica. Offers clinical psychology (M Psych); educational psychology (M Psych); forensic psychology (M Psych); hospital management (MHA); intensive care nursing (MN); medicine (MD). *Entrance requirements:* For master's, 2 letters of recommendation, interview.

Université Laval, Faculty of Social Sciences, School of Psychology, Programs in Psychology, Québec, QC G1K 7P4, Canada. Offers clinical psychology (PhD); community psychology (PhD); psychology (PhD, Psy D). *Degree requirements:* For doctorate, comprehensive exam, thesis/dissertation. *Entrance requirements:* For doctorate, comprehension of written English, knowledge of French, interview. Electronic applications accepted.

University at Albany, State University of New York, College of Arts and Sciences, Department of Psychology, Albany, NY 12222-0001. Offers autism (Certificate); biopsychology (PhD); clinical psychology (PhD); general/experimental psychology (PhD); industrial/organizational psychology (PhD); psychology (MA); social/personality psychology (PhD). *Accreditation:* APA (one or more programs are accredited). *Degree requirements:* For doctorate, thesis/dissertation. *Entrance requirements:* For doctorate, GRE General Test, GRE Subject Test. Additional exam requirements/recommendations for international students: Required—TOEFL (minimum score 550 paper-based; 213 computer-based). Electronic applications accepted.

University at Buffalo, the State University of New York, Graduate School, College of Arts and Sciences, Department of Psychology, Buffalo, NY 14260. Offers behavioral neuroscience (PhD); clinical psychology (PhD); cognitive psychology (PhD); general psychology (MA); social-personality psychology (PhD). *Accreditation:* APA (one or more programs are accredited). Terminal master's awarded for partial completion of doctoral program. *Degree requirements:* For master's, project; for doctorate, thesis/dissertation. *Entrance requirements:* For master's and doctorate, GRE General Test. Additional exam requirements/recommendations for international students: Required—TOEFL (minimum score 550 paper-based; 213 computer-based; 79 iBT). Electronic applications accepted. *Faculty research:* Neural, endocrine, and molecular bases of behavior; adult mood and anxiety disorders; relationship dysfunction; attention deficit/hyperactivity disorder; psycho-linguistics.

The University of Alabama, Graduate School, College of Arts and Sciences, Department of Psychology, Tuscaloosa, AL 35487. Offers clinical psychology (PhD); experimental psychology (PhD). *Accreditation:* APA. *Faculty:* 20 full-time (8 women), 3 part-time/adjunct (2 women). *Students:* 78 full-time (60 women), 16 part-time (12 women); includes 16 minority (9 African Americans, 3 Asian Americans or Pacific Islanders, 4 Hispanic Americans), 2 international. Average age 27. 252 applicants, 11% accepted, 19 enrolled. In 2008, 13 doctorates awarded. *Degree requirements:* For doctorate, thesis/dissertation. *Entrance requirements:* For doctorate, GRE. Additional exam requirements/recommendations for international students: Required—TOEFL (minimum score 550 paper-based). *Application deadline:* For fall admission, 12/1 for domestic and international students. Application fee: $30. Electronic applications accepted. *Expenses:* Tuition, area resident: Full-time $6400. Tuition, state resident: full-time $6400. Tuition, nonresident: full-time $18,000. *Financial support:* In 2008–09, 73 students received support, including 12 fellowships with full tuition reimbursements available (averaging $15,000 per year), 34 research assistantships with full and partial tuition reimbursements available (averaging $11,142 per year), 26 teaching assistantships with tuition reimbursements available (averaging $11,142 per year); career-related internships or fieldwork, institutionally sponsored loans, scholarships/grants, health care benefits, and unspecified assistantships also available. Financial award application deadline: 12/1. *Faculty research:* Cognitive development/disability, child clinical, psychology and law, health/aging, social psychology. Total annual research expenditures: $2.3 million. *Unit head:* Dr. Kenneth Lichstein, Chair, 205-348-4962, Fax: 205-348-8648, E-mail: lichstein@ua.edu. *Application contact:* Mary Beth Hubbard, Information Contact, 205-348-1919, Fax: 205-348-8648, E-mail: mbhubbard@as.ua.edu.

University of Alaska Anchorage, College of Arts and Sciences, Department of Psychology, Anchorage, AK 99508-8060. Offers clinical psychology (MS); clinical-community psychology with rural-indigenous emphasis (PhD). Part-time programs available. *Degree requirements:* For master's, thesis. *Entrance requirements:* For master's, GRE General Test, GRE Subject Test, interview, references; for doctorate, interview, bachelor's or master's degree in psychology. Additional exam requirements/recommendations for international students: Required—TOEFL (minimum score 550 paper-based; 213 computer-based). *Faculty research:* Substance abuse, childhood autism, biofeedback, psychological assessment, mental health in Native Alaskans.

University of Alaska Fairbanks, College of Liberal Arts, Department of Psychology, Fairbanks, AK 99775-6480. Offers clinical-community psychology (PhD), including rural cross-cultural emphasis. *Faculty:* 5 full-time (1 woman), 4 part-time/adjunct (0 women). *Students:* 2 full-time (0 women), 20 part-time (16 women); includes 8 minority (1 African American, 5 American Indian/Alaska Native, 2 Hispanic Americans), 1 international. Average age 38. 21 applicants, 48% accepted, 9 enrolled. In 2008, 1 doctorate awarded. *Degree requirements:* For doctorate, comprehensive exam, thesis/dissertation, oral exam, oral defense. *Entrance requirements:* For doctorate, disclosure statement. Additional exam requirements/recommendations for international students: Required—TOEFL (minimum score 550 paper-based; 213 computer-based; 80 iBT). *Application deadline:* For fall admission, 12/15 for domestic and international students. Application fee: $60. *Expenses:* Tuition, area resident: Full-time $5418; part-time $301 per credit. Tuition, state resident: full-time $5418; part-time $301 per credit. Tuition, nonresident: full-time $11,070; part-time $615 per credit. Required fees: $849; $25 per credit. $78 per semester. Tuition and fees vary according to course load and reciprocity agreements. *Financial support:* In 2008–09, 2 fellowships (averaging $15,270 per year), 7 research assistantships (averaging $16,089 per year), 8 teaching assistantships (averaging $15,611 per year) were awarded; career-related internships or fieldwork, Federal Work-Study, scholarships/grants, health care benefits, and unspecified assistantships also available. Support available to part-time students. Financial award application deadline: 7/1; financial award applicants required to submit FAFSA. *Faculty research:* Clinical and community psychology, rural, indigenous, and cultural psychology. *Unit head:* Dr. Dani Sheppard, Department Chair, 907-474-7007, Fax: 907-474-5781, E-mail: fypsych@uaf.edu. *Application contact:* Dr. Dani Sheppard, Department Chair, 907-474-7007, Fax: 907-474-5781, E-mail: fypsych@uaf.edu.

The University of British Columbia, Faculty of Arts and Faculty of Graduate Studies, Department of Psychology, Vancouver, BC V6T 1Z1, Canada. Offers behavioral neuroscience (MA, PhD); clinical psychology (MA, PhD); cognitive science (MA, PhD); developmental psychology (MA, PhD); forensic psychology (PhD); health psychology (MA, PhD); quantitative methods (MA, PhD); social/personality psychology (MA, PhD). *Accreditation:* APA (one or more programs are accredited). Terminal master's awarded for partial completion of doctoral program. *Degree requirements:* For master's, thesis; for doctorate, comprehensive exam, thesis/dissertation. *Entrance requirements:* For master's and doctorate, GRE General Test, GRE Subject Test. Additional exam requirements/recommendations for international students: Required—TOEFL (minimum score 550 paper-based; 230 computer-based; 80 iBT). Electronic applications accepted. *Faculty research:* Clinical, developmental, social/personality, cognition, behavioral neuroscience.

University of Calgary, Faculty of Graduate Studies, Faculty of Social Sciences, Department of Psychology, Program in Clinical Psychology, Calgary, AB T2N 1N4, Canada. Offers M Sc,

Clinical Psychology

University of Calgary (continued)

PhD. *Degree requirements:* For master's, thesis, practical training; for doctorate, thesis/dissertation, practical training. *Entrance requirements:* For master's, GRE General Test, bachelor's degree in psychology or equivalent, minimum GPA of 3.6; for doctorate, GRE General Test, bachelor's degree in psychology, master's degree. Additional exam requirements/recommendations for international students: Required—TOEFL (minimum score 600 paper-based; 250 computer-based). Electronic applications accepted. *Faculty research:* Depression, schizophrenia, aging, neuropsychology, cognitive and linguistic development in infancy.

University of California, San Diego, Office of Graduate Studies, Group in Clinical Psychology, La Jolla, CA 92093. Offers PhD. Electronic applications accepted.

University of California, Santa Barbara, Graduate Division, Gevirtz Graduate School of Education, Santa Barbara, CA 93106-9490. Offers counseling, clinical and school psychology (PhD), including clinical psychology, counseling psychology, school psychology; education (M Ed, MA, PhD), including child and adolescent development (MA, PhD), cultural perspectives and comparative education (MA, PhD), educational leadership and organizations (MA, PhD), research methodology (MA, PhD), special education disabilities and risk studies (MA), special education, disabilities and risk studies (PhD), teaching (M Ed), teaching and learning (MA, PhD); educational leadership (Ed D); school psychology (M Ed); MA/PhD. *Accreditation:* APA (one or more programs are accredited). Postbaccalaureate distance learning degree programs offered (minimal on-campus study). *Faculty:* 42 full-time (20 women), 10 part-time/adjunct (4 women). *Students:* 390 full-time (303 women); includes 149 minority (14 African Americans, 3 American Indian/Alaska Native, 57 Asian Americans or Pacific Islanders, 75 Hispanic Americans), 16 international. Average age 31. 717 applicants, 40% accepted, 170 enrolled. In 2008, 140 master's, 46 doctorates awarded. Terminal master's awarded for partial completion of doctoral program. *Degree requirements:* For master's, comprehensive exam (for some programs), thesis (for some programs); for doctorate, comprehensive exam (for some programs), thesis/dissertation, qualifying exam. *Entrance requirements:* For master's and doctorate, GRE, 3 letters of recommendation, statement of purpose, personal achievements/contributions statement, resumé/curriculum vitae, transcripts for post-secondary institutions attended. Additional exam requirements/recommendations for international students: Required—TOEFL (minimum score 550 paper-based; 213 computer-based; 80 iBT), IELTS (minimum score 7), TOEFL or IELTS. Application fee: $70 ($90 for international students). Electronic applications accepted. *Expenses:* Tuition, nonresident: full-time $25,149. Required fees: $10,143. Full-time tuition and fees vary according to campus/location, reciprocity agreements and student level. *Financial support:* In 2008–09, 253 students received support, including 206 fellowships with full and partial tuition reimbursements available (averaging $5,000 per year), 62 research assistantships with full and partial tuition reimbursements available (averaging $6,200 per year), 87 teaching assistantships with partial tuition reimbursements available (averaging $6,500 per year); career-related internships or fieldwork, Federal Work-Study, institutionally sponsored loans, scholarships/grants, traineeships, health care benefits, and unspecified assistantships also available. Financial award applicants required to submit FAFSA. *Faculty research:* Professional development, early childhood development, school violence, literacy, science/math initiative. Total annual research expenditures: $4.4 million. *Unit head:* Dr. Jane Conoley, Chair, 805-893-2185, E-mail: jane-conoley@education.ucsb.edu. *Application contact:* Kathryn Marie Tucciarone, Student Affairs Officer, 805-893-2137, E-mail: katiet@education.ucsb.edu.

University of Central Florida, College of Sciences, Department of Psychology, Program in Clinical Psychology, Orlando, FL 32816. Offers MA, MS, PhD. *Accreditation:* APA. Part-time and evening/weekend programs available. *Students:* 55 full-time (44 women), 5 part-time (3 women); includes 7 minority (1 African American, 2 Asian Americans or Pacific Islanders, 4 Hispanic Americans), 3 international. In 2008, 15 master's, 1 doctorate awarded. *Degree requirements:* For master's, thesis or alternative, clinical internship; for doctorate, thesis/dissertation, candidacy exam, internship. *Entrance requirements:* For master's and doctorate, GRE General Test, minimum GPA of 3.0 in last 60 hours, resumé. Additional exam requirements/recommendations for international students: Required—TOEFL. *Application deadline:* For fall admission, 2/15 for domestic students. Application fee: $30. Electronic applications accepted. *Expenses:* Tuition, area resident: Full-time $6816; part-time $284 per credit. Tuition, state resident: full-time $6816; part-time $1076 per credit. Tuition, nonresident: full-time $25,824. Required fees: $216; $9 per credit. *Financial support:* In 2008–09, 12 fellowships with partial tuition reimbursements (averaging $10,400 per year), 7 research assistantships with partial tuition reimbursements (averaging $5,000 per year), 23 teaching assistantships with partial tuition reimbursements (averaging $6,800 per year) were awarded; career-related internships or fieldwork, Federal Work-Study, institutionally sponsored loans, tuition waivers (partial), and unspecified assistantships also available. Financial award application deadline: 3/1; financial award applicants required to submit FAFSA. *Faculty research:* Professional ethical decision making, computer experience and anxiety, effects of expert testimony on decision making in a rape trial, religiosity, relationship beliefs and marital adjustment. *Unit head:* Dr. Deborah Beidel, Director, 407-254-3908, E-mail: dbeidel@mail.ucf.edu. *Application contact:* Dr. Deborah Beidel, Director, 407-254-3908, E-mail: dbeidel@mail.ucf.edu.

University of Cincinnati, Graduate School, McMicken College of Arts and Sciences, Department of Psychology, Cincinnati, OH 45221. Offers clinical psychology (PhD); experimental psychology (PhD). *Accreditation:* APA. *Degree requirements:* For doctorate, comprehensive exam, thesis/dissertation. *Entrance requirements:* For doctorate, GRE General Test. Additional exam requirements/recommendations for international students: Required—TOEFL. *Faculty research:* Neuropsychology, human factors, health.

University of Colorado Denver, College of Liberal Arts and Sciences, Program in Clinical Health Psychology, Denver, CO 80217-3364. Offers PhD.

University of Connecticut, Graduate School, College of Liberal Arts and Sciences, Department of Psychology, Field of Psychology, Storrs, CT 06269. Offers behavioral neuroscience (PhD); biopsychology (PhD); clinical psychology (MA, PhD); cognition and instruction (PhD); developmental psychology (MA, PhD); ecological psychology (PhD); experimental psychology (PhD); general psychology (MA, PhD); health psychology (Graduate Certificate); industrial/organizational psychology (PhD); language and cognition (PhD); neuroscience (PhD); occupational health psychology (Graduate Certificate); social psychology (MA, PhD). *Accreditation:* APA (one or more programs are accredited). Terminal master's awarded for partial completion of doctoral program. *Degree requirements:* For master's, comprehensive exam; for doctorate, thesis/dissertation. *Entrance requirements:* For master's and doctorate, GRE General Test, GRE Subject Test. Additional exam requirements/recommendations for international students: Required—TOEFL (minimum score 550 paper-based; 213 computer-based). Electronic applications accepted.

University of Dayton, Graduate School, College of Arts and Sciences, Department of Psychology, Program in Clinical Psychology, Dayton, OH 45469-1300. Offers MA. Part-time programs available. *Faculty:* 8 full-time (3 women), 2 part-time/adjunct (1 woman). *Students:* 26 full-time (23 women), 1 (woman) part-time; includes 6 minority (3 African Americans, 1 Asian American or Pacific Islander, 2 Hispanic Americans). Average age 24. 98 applicants, 20% accepted, 13 enrolled. In 2008, 5 master's awarded. *Degree requirements:* For master's, thesis. *Entrance requirements:* For master's, GRE General Test, GRE Subject Test (recommended), minimum undergraduate GPA of 3.0, 3.3 during final 2 years of course work. Additional exam requirements/recommendations for international students: Required—TOEFL (minimum score 550 paper-based; 213 computer-based; 80 iBT). *Application deadline:* For fall admission, 3/1 priority date for domestic and international students; for winter admission, 7/1 priority date for international students; for spring admission, 1/1 priority date for international students. Application fee: $0 ($50 for international students). Electronic applications accepted. *Expenses:* Tuition: Full-time $6950; part-time $1737.50 per semester. Required fees: $25 per semester. Tuition and fees vary according to course level, course load, degree level and program. *Financial support:* In 2008–09, 18 students received support, including 3 research assistantships with full tuition reimbursements available (averaging $10,096 per year); institutionally sponsored loans, traineeships, and tuition waivers (partial) also available. Financial award application deadline: 3/1. *Faculty research:* Family issues, modes and mechanisms of therapy, gender issues, personality disorders, stress and coping. *Unit head:* Dr. Roger N. Reeb, Director, 937-229-2395, Fax: 937-229-3900, E-mail: roger.reeb@notes.udayton.edu. *Application contact:* Angela Jones-Glukhov, Associate Director of Graduate Admissions, 937-229-4305, Fax: 937-229-4729, E-mail: jonesgas@notes.udayton.edu.

University of Delaware, College of Arts and Sciences, Department of Psychology, Newark, DE 19716. Offers behavioral neuroscience (PhD); clinical psychology (PhD); cognitive psychology (PhD); social psychology (PhD). *Accreditation:* APA. *Degree requirements:* For doctorate, thesis/dissertation. *Entrance requirements:* For doctorate, GRE General Test. Additional exam requirements/recommendations for international students: Required—TOEFL (minimum score 600 paper-based; 250 computer-based). Electronic applications accepted. *Faculty research:* Emotion development, neural and cognitive aspects of memory, neural control of feeding, intergroup relations, social cognition and communication.

University of Denver, Graduate School of Professional Psychology, Denver, CO 80208. Offers clinical psychology (Psy D); psychology (MA). *Accreditation:* APA. *Faculty:* 12 full-time (6 women), 31 part-time/adjunct (16 women). *Students:* 198 full-time (162 women), 25 part-time (15 women); includes 26 minority (6 African Americans, 3 American Indian/Alaska Native, 9 Asian Americans or Pacific Islanders, 8 Hispanic Americans), 8 international. Average age 26. 525 applicants, 36% accepted, 92 enrolled. In 2008, 75 master's, 31 doctorates awarded. *Degree requirements:* For doctorate, paper, internship. *Entrance requirements:* For master's and doctorate, GRE General Test. Additional exam requirements/recommendations for international students: Required—TOEFL. *Application deadline:* For fall admission, 1/5 for domestic students. Application fee: $50. Electronic applications accepted. *Financial support:* In 2008–09, 30 teaching assistantships with full and partial tuition reimbursements (averaging $3,500 per year) were awarded; career-related internships or fieldwork, Federal Work-Study, institutionally sponsored loans, scholarships/grants, and clinical assistantships also available. Support available to part-time students. Financial award application deadline: 3/1; financial award applicants required to submit FAFSA. *Unit head:* Dr. Peter Buirski, Dean, 303-871-2382. *Application contact:* Admissions, 303-871-3873, Fax: 303-871-4220, E-mail: gsppinfo@du.edu.

University of Detroit Mercy, College of Liberal Arts and Education, Department of Psychology, Program in Clinical Psychology, Detroit, MI 48221. Offers MA, PhD. *Accreditation:* APA. *Degree requirements:* For doctorate, departmental qualifying exam.

University of Florida, Graduate School, College of Public Health and Health Professions, Department of Clinical and Health Psychology, Gainesville, FL 32611. Offers PhD. *Accreditation:* APA. *Degree requirements:* For doctorate, thesis/dissertation. *Entrance requirements:* For doctorate, GRE General Test, minimum GPA of 3.0. Additional exam requirements/recommendations for international students: Required—TOEFL (minimum score 550 paper-based; 213 computer-based). Electronic applications accepted. *Faculty research:* Child psychology, pediatric psychology, health/medical psychology, neuropsychology.

University of Guelph, Graduate Program Services, College of Social and Applied Human Sciences, Department of Psychology, Guelph, ON N1G 2W1, Canada. Offers applied social psychology (MA, PhD); clinical psychology applied development emphasis (PhD); clinical psychology applied developmental emphasis (MA); industrial/organizational psychology (MA, PhD); neuroscience and applied cognitive science (MA, PhD). *Degree requirements:* For master's, thesis; for doctorate, comprehensive exam, thesis/dissertation. *Entrance requirements:* For master's, GRE General Test, GRE Subject Test, minimum B+ average during previous 2 years of course work; for doctorate, GRE General Test, GRE Subject Test, minimum A-average. Additional exam requirements/recommendations for international students: Required—TOEFL (minimum score 89 iBT). Electronic applications accepted. *Faculty research:* Organizational psychology, reading comprehension and mathematical ability, drug addiction and relapse, gender issues and culture, memory, clinical psychology.

University of Hartford, College of Arts and Sciences, Department of Psychology, Program in Clinical Practices, West Hartford, CT 06117-1599. Offers clinical practices (Psy D); psychology (MA). *Accreditation:* APA. *Degree requirements:* For master's, comprehensive exam, thesis optional. *Entrance requirements:* For master's, GRE General Test, GRE Subject Test, minimum GPA of 3.0, 3 letters of recommendation. Additional exam requirements/recommendations for international students: Required—TOEFL (minimum score 550 paper-based; 213 computer-based). Electronic applications accepted. *Faculty research:* Attachment issues, child abuse prevention, master's psychologist issues, neuropsychology.

University of Hawaii at Manoa, Graduate Division, Colleges of Arts and Sciences, College of Social Sciences, Department of Psychology, Honolulu, HI 96822. Offers clinical psychology (PhD); community and cultural psychology (PhD); community and culture (MA); psychology (MA, PhD, Graduate Certificate). *Accreditation:* APA (one or more programs are accredited). Part-time programs available. Terminal master's awarded for partial completion of doctoral program. *Degree requirements:* For master's, comprehensive exam, thesis; for doctorate, comprehensive exam, thesis/dissertation. *Entrance requirements:* For master's and doctorate, GRE General Test, GRE Subject Test. Additional exam requirements/recommendations for international students: Required—TOEFL (minimum score 600 paper-based; 250 computer-based; 100 iBT), IELTS (minimum score 7). *Faculty research:* Cross-cultural psychology, health psychology, marine mammals, child/adult psychopathology.

University of Houston, College of Liberal Arts and Social Sciences, Department of Psychology, Houston, TX 77204. Offers clinical psychology (PhD); industrial/organizational psychology (PhD); psychology (MA); social psychology (PhD). *Accreditation:* APA (one or more programs are accredited). *Faculty:* 26 full-time (11 women), 8 part-time/adjunct (3 women). *Students:* 99 full-time (75 women), 15 part-time (11 women); includes 20 minority (5 African Americans, 3 Asian Americans or Pacific Islanders, 12 Hispanic Americans), 10 international. Average age 27. 386 applicants, 7% accepted, 23 enrolled. In 2008, 19 master's, 17 doctorates awarded. *Degree requirements:* For doctorate, thesis/dissertation. *Entrance requirements:* For doctorate, GRE General Test, minimum GPA of 3.0. *Application deadline:* For fall admission, 1/1 for domestic students. Application fee: $40 ($75 for international students). *Expenses:* Tuition, state resident: full-time $5164; part-time $287 per credit. Tuition, nonresident: full-time $10,222; part-time $568 per credit. *Financial support:* In 2008–09, 15 fellowships with full tuition reimbursements (averaging $11,500 per year), 14 research assistantships with full tuition reimbursements (averaging $12,050 per year), 76 teaching assistantships with full tuition reimbursements (averaging $12,050 per year) were awarded; career-related internships or fieldwork, Federal Work-Study, institutionally sponsored loans, scholarships/grants, health care benefits, and unspecified assistantships also available. Support available to part-time students. Financial award application deadline: 2/1; financial award applicants required to submit FAFSA. *Faculty research:* Health psychology, depression, child/family process, organizational effectiveness, close relationships. *Unit head:* Dr. David Francis, Chairperson, 713-743-7036, Fax: 713-743-8588, E-mail: dfrancis@uh.edu. *Application contact:* Sherry A. Berun, Coordinator, Academic Affairs, 713-743-8508, Fax: 713-743-8588, E-mail: sherryr@uh.edu.

University of Houston–Clear Lake, School of Human Sciences and Humanities, Programs in Human Sciences, Houston, TX 77058-1098. Offers behavioral sciences (MA), including criminology, cross cultural studies, general psychology, sociology; clinical psychology (MA); criminology (MA); cross cultural studies (MA); family therapy (MA); fitness and human performance (MA); school psychology (MA). *Accreditation:* AAMFT/COAMFTE. Part-time and evening/weekend programs available. Postbaccalaureate distance learning degree programs offered (minimal on-campus study). *Degree requirements:* For master's, thesis or alternative. *Entrance requirements:* For master's, GRE General Test. Additional exam requirements/recommendations for international students: Required—TOEFL (minimum score 550 paper-based; 213 computer-based). Electronic applications accepted. *Faculty research:* Smoking cessation, adolescent sexuality, white collar crime, serial murder, human factors/human computer interaction.

University of Indianapolis, Graduate Programs, School of Psychological Sciences, Indianapolis, IN 46227-3697. Offers clinical psychology (Psy D); clinical psychology/mental health counseling (MA). *Accreditation:* APA. *Faculty:* 10 full-time (4 women), 4 part-time/adjunct (1 woman). *Students:* 112 full-time (101 women), 55 part-time (43 women); includes 6 minority (5 African Americans, 1 Asian American or Pacific Islander), 8 international. Average age 27. *Degree requirements:* For master's, practicum; for doctorate, comprehensive exam, thesis/dissertation, 1200 hours of clinical practicum, 2000 hour internship. *Entrance requirements:* For master's, GRE, 3 letters of recommendation; for doctorate, GRE, minimum GPA of 3.0, 18 hours of course work in psychology, 3 letters of recommendation. Additional exam requirements/recommendations for international students: Required—TOEFL (minimum score 550 paper-based; 213 computer-based). *Application deadline:* For fall admission, 2/25 for domestic students. Application fee: $50. *Financial support:* Federal Work-Study available. *Unit head:* Dr. E. John McIlvried, Dean, 317-788-3247, Fax: 317-788-3480, E-mail: jmcilvried@uindy.edu. *Application contact:* Dr. E. John McIlvried, Associate Provost for Graduate Programs and International Programs, 317-788-3274, E-mail: jmcilvried@uindy.edu.

The University of Kansas, Graduate Studies, College of Liberal Arts and Sciences, Department of Psychology and Department of Psychology, Program in Clinical Child Psychology, Lawrence, KS 66045. Offers MA, PhD. *Accreditation:* APA. *Faculty:* 16. *Students:* 18 full-time (11 women), 6 part-time (3 women); includes 6 minority (2 African Americans, 3 Asian Americans or Pacific Islanders, 1 Hispanic American). Average age 28. 115 applicants, 5% accepted, 5 enrolled. In 2008, 4 master's, 3 doctorates awarded. *Degree requirements:* For master's, thesis; for doctorate, comprehensive exam, thesis/dissertation, clinical internship. *Entrance requirements:* For master's, GRE General Test, GRE Subject Test; for doctorate, GRE General Test, GRE Subject Test, minimum GPA of 3.5. Additional exam requirements/recommendations for international students: Required—TOEFL. *Application deadline:* For fall admission, 12/1 for domestic and international students. Application fee: $45 ($55 for international students). Electronic applications accepted. *Expenses:* Tuition, area resident: Full-time $6122; part-time $255.10 per credit hour. Tuition, state resident: full-time $6122; part-time $255.10 per credit hour. Tuition, nonresident: full-time $14,629; part-time $609.55 per credit hour. Required fees: $847; $70.56 per credit hour. Tuition and fees vary according to course load and program. *Financial support:* Fellowships with tuition reimbursements, research assistantships with tuition reimbursements, teaching assistantships with tuition reimbursements, career-related internships or fieldwork, scholarships/grants, traineeships, health care benefits, and unspecified assistantships available. Financial award application deadline: 12/1. *Faculty research:* Pediatric psychology; serious emotional disorders; responses to disasters and terrorism; anxiety, stress, and coping; psychotherapy with children. *Unit head:* Michael Roberts, Director, 785-864-4226, Fax: 785-864-5024, E-mail: mroberts@ku.edu. *Application contact:* Graduate Admissions, 785-864-4226, Fax: 785-864-5024, E-mail: ccpp@ku.edu.

University of Kentucky, Graduate School, College of Arts and Sciences, Program in Psychology, Lexington, KY 40506-0032. Offers clinical psychology (MA); experimental psychology (MA). *Accreditation:* APA (one or more programs are accredited). *Degree requirements:* For master's, comprehensive exam, thesis; for doctorate, comprehensive exam, thesis/dissertation. *Entrance requirements:* For master's, GRE General Test, minimum undergraduate GPA of 2.75; for doctorate, GRE General Test, minimum graduate GPA of 3.0. Additional exam requirements/recommendations for international students: Required—TOEFL (minimum score 550 paper-based; 213 computer-based). Electronic applications accepted. *Faculty research:* Psychopharmacology and teratology, behavioral neuroscience, social psychology, cognitive psychology, development and developmental psychobiology.

University of La Verne, College of Arts and Sciences, Department of Psychology, Program in Clinical-Community Psychology, La Verne, CA 91750-4443. Offers Psy D. Part-time programs available. *Faculty:* 9 full-time (3 women), 6 part-time/adjunct (1 woman). *Students:* 53 full-time (43 women), 33 part-time (29 women); includes 38 minority (9 African Americans, 6 Asian Americans or Pacific Islanders, 23 Hispanic Americans). Average age 29. In 2008, 20 doctorates awarded. *Degree requirements:* For doctorate, thesis/dissertation, clinical internship, competency exams, practicum, personal psychotherapy. *Entrance requirements:* For doctorate, minimum GPA of 3.25 undergraduate, 3.65 graduate; 3 recommendations; interview; curriculum vitae. Additional exam requirements/recommendations for international students: Required—TOEFL (minimum score 600 paper-based; 250 computer-based). *Application deadline:* For fall admission, 1/15 for domestic and international students. Application fee: $75. *Expenses:* Contact institution. *Financial support:* Career-related internships or fieldwork, institutionally sponsored loans, scholarships/grants, and unspecified assistantships available. Financial award application deadline: 3/2; financial award applicants required to submit FAFSA. *Unit head:* Dr. Raymond Scott, Chairperson, 909-593-3511 Ext. 4181, E-mail: rscott@ulv.edu. *Application contact:* Connie Hamlow, Admissions Information Specialist, 909-593-3511 Ext. 4244, Fax: 909-392-2761, E-mail: gradadmission@ulv.edu.

University of Louisville, Graduate School, College of Arts and Sciences, Department of Psychological and Brain Sciences, Program in Clinical Psychology, Louisville, KY 40292. Offers MA, PhD. *Accreditation:* APA. *Faculty:* 14 full-time (8 women). *Students:* 36 full-time (27 women), 1 (woman) part-time; includes 2 African Americans, 1 Asian American or Pacific Islander, 1 international. Average age 30. 115 applicants, 10% accepted, 5 enrolled. In 2008, 6 master's, 8 doctorates awarded. *Degree requirements:* For doctorate, thesis/dissertation, core curriculum; preliminary exam; research. *Entrance requirements:* For doctorate, GRE General Test. Additional exam requirements/recommendations for international students: Required—TOEFL. *Application deadline:* For fall admission, 12/1 for international students. Application fee: $50. Electronic applications accepted. *Financial support:* In 2008–09, 6 fellowships with full tuition reimbursements (averaging $22,000 per year), 4 research assistantships with full tuition reimbursements (averaging $22,000 per year), 17 teaching assistantships with full tuition reimbursements (averaging $22,000 per year) were awarded; career-related internships or fieldwork also available. *Faculty research:* Health psychology, geropsychology, psychopathology. *Unit head:* Dr. Janet Woodruff-Borden, Director of Clinical Training, 502-852-6070, Fax: 502-852-8904, E-mail: j.woodruff-borden@louisville.edu. *Application contact:* Libby Leggett, Director, Graduate Admissions, 502-852-3101, Fax: 502-852-6536, E-mail: gradadm@louisville.edu.

University of Maine, Graduate School, College of Liberal Arts and Sciences, Department of Psychology, Orono, ME 04469. Offers clinical psychology (PhD); developmental psychology (MA); experimental psychology (MA, PhD); social psychology (MA). *Accreditation:* APA (one or more programs are accredited). *Degree requirements:* For master's, thesis; for doctorate, thesis/dissertation. *Entrance requirements:* For master's and doctorate, GRE General Test, GRE Subject Test. Additional exam requirements/recommendations for international students: Required—TOEFL. Electronic applications accepted. *Faculty research:* Social development, hypertension and aging, attitude change, self-confidence in achievement situations, health psychology.

University of Manitoba, Faculty of Graduate Studies, Faculty of Arts, Department of Psychology, Winnipeg, MB R3T 2N2, Canada. Offers clinical psychology (PhD); psychology (MA, PhD); school psychology (MA). *Accreditation:* APA (one or more programs are accredited). *Degree requirements:* For master's, thesis; for doctorate, one foreign language, thesis/dissertation. *Entrance requirements:* For master's and doctorate, GRE General Test.

University of Maryland, College Park, Graduate Studies, College of Behavioral and Social Sciences, Department of Psychology, College Park, MD 20742. Offers clinical psychology (PhD); developmental psychology (PhD); experimental psychology (PhD); industrial psychology (MA, MS, PhD); social psychology (PhD). *Accreditation:* APA (one or more programs are accredited). *Degree requirements:* For master's, thesis; for doctorate, variable foreign language requirement, comprehensive exam, thesis/dissertation. *Entrance requirements:* For master's

and doctorate, GRE General Test, GRE Subject Test, minimum GPA of 3.5, research and/or work experience, 3 letters of recommendation. Electronic applications accepted. *Faculty research:* Social stereotyping and prejudice, anxiety disorders, auditory neuroethology, counseling and social psychology.

University of Massachusetts Amherst, Graduate School, College of Social and Behavioral Sciences, Department of Psychology, Amherst, MA 01003. Offers clinical psychology (MS, PhD); cognitive psychology (MS, PhD); developmental science (MS, PhD); psychology of peace and violence (MS, PhD); social psychology (MS, PhD). *Accreditation:* APA (one or more programs are accredited). Terminal master's awarded for partial completion of doctoral program. *Degree requirements:* For master's, thesis; for doctorate, comprehensive exam, thesis/dissertation. *Entrance requirements:* For master's and doctorate, GRE General Test, 3 letters of recommendation. Additional exam requirements/recommendations for international students: Required—TOEFL (minimum score 550 paper-based; 213 computer-based; 79 iBT), IELTS (minimum score 6.5). Electronic applications accepted. *Expenses:* Tuition, area resident: Full-time $2640. Tuition, nonresident: full-time $9936. One-time fee: $332 full-time. Tuition and fees vary according to course load.

University of Massachusetts Boston, Office of Graduate Studies, College of Liberal Arts, Program in Clinical Psychology, Boston, MA 02125-3393. Offers PhD. *Accreditation:* APA. Part-time and evening/weekend programs available. *Degree requirements:* For doctorate, comprehensive exam, thesis/dissertation, oral exams, practicum. *Entrance requirements:* For doctorate, GRE General Test, GRE Subject Test, minimum GPA of 2.75. *Faculty research:* Community psychology, psychology, racism and mental health, gender and culture, posttraumatic stress disorder.

University of Massachusetts Dartmouth, Graduate School, College of Arts and Sciences, Department of Psychology, North Dartmouth, MA 02747-2300. Offers behavior analyst (PMC); clinical psychology (MA); general psychology (MA). Part-time programs available. *Faculty:* 17 full-time (8 women), 8 part-time/adjunct (5 women). *Students:* 17 full-time (11 women), 26 part-time (23 women); includes 6 minority (4 African Americans, 2 Asian Americans or Pacific Islanders). Average age 29. 52 applicants, 46% accepted, 16 enrolled. In 2008, 18 master's awarded. *Degree requirements:* For master's, thesis (for some programs). *Entrance requirements:* For master's, GRE General Test, minimum GPA of 2.75, 3 letters of recommendation. Additional exam requirements/recommendations for international students: Required—TOEFL (minimum score 500 paper-based). *Application deadline:* For fall admission, 3/31 for domestic students, 1/31 for international students. Application fee: $40 ($60 for international students). Electronic applications accepted. *Expenses:* Tuition, state resident: full-time $2071; part-time $86.29 per credit. Tuition, nonresident: full-time $8099; part-time $337.46 per credit. Required fees: $7946. Tuition and fees vary according to class time, course load and reciprocity agreements. *Financial support:* In 2008–09, 9 teaching assistantships with full tuition reimbursements (averaging $3,500 per year) were awarded; career-related internships or fieldwork, Federal Work-Study, and unspecified assistantships also available. Support available to part-time students. Financial award application deadline: 3/1; financial award applicants required to submit FAFSA. *Faculty research:* Emotion, nonverbal communication, behavioral medicine, children's theatre and self-confidence, psychosocial stress. Total annual research expenditures: $14,000. *Unit head:* Dr. Paul Donnelly, Director, Clinical Psychology, 508-999-8334, E-mail: pdonnelly@umassd.edu. *Application contact:* Elan Turcotte-Shamski, Graduate Admissions Officer, 508-999-8604, Fax: 508-999-8183, E-mail: graduate@umassd.edu.

University of Memphis, Graduate School, College of Arts and Sciences, Department of Psychology, Memphis, TN 38152. Offers clinical psychology (PhD); experimental psychology (PhD); general psychology (MS); school psychology (MA, PhD). Part-time programs available. *Faculty:* 29 full-time (9 women), 1 part-time/adjunct (0 women). *Students:* 119 full-time (80 women), 21 part-time (13 women); includes 23 minority (16 African Americans, 1 American Indian/Alaska Native, 2 Asian Americans or Pacific Islanders, 4 Hispanic Americans), 9 international. Average age 27. 197 applicants, 23% accepted, 31 enrolled. In 2008, 28 master's, 11 doctorates awarded. Terminal master's awarded for partial completion of doctoral program. *Degree requirements:* For master's, comprehensive exam, thesis (for some programs), oral exam (MS); for doctorate, thesis/dissertation, internship. *Entrance requirements:* For master's, GRE General Test, 18 undergraduate hours in psychology, minimum GPA of 2.5; for doctorate, GRE General Test, GRE Subject Test. *Application deadline:* For fall admission, 2/1 for domestic students. Applications are processed on a rolling basis. Application fee: $35 ($60 for international students). *Expenses:* Tuition, area resident: Full-time $6242; part-time $330 per credit hour. Tuition, state resident: full-time $6242; part-time $330 per credit hour. Tuition, nonresident: full-time $17,828; part-time $815 per credit hour. Required fees: $1156. *Financial support:* Fellowships with full tuition reimbursements, research assistantships with full tuition reimbursements, teaching assistantships with full tuition reimbursements, tuition waivers (partial) and unspecified assistantships available. Financial award applicants required to submit FAFSA. *Faculty research:* Psychotherapy and psychopathology, behavioral medicine and community psychology, child and family studies, cognitive and social processes, neuropsychology and behavioral neuroscience. *Unit head:* Dr. William Zachry, Chair, 901-678-2145, Fax: 901-678-2579, E-mail: wzachry@memphis.edu. *Application contact:* Dr. Robert Cohen, Graduate Studies Coordinator, 901-678-2146.

University of Miami, Graduate School, College of Arts and Sciences, Department of Psychology, Coral Gables, FL 33124. Offers adult clinical (PhD); behavioral neuroscience (PhD); child clinical (PhD); developmental psychology (PhD); health clinical (PhD); psychology (MS). *Accreditation:* APA (one or more programs are accredited). *Degree requirements:* For doctorate, comprehensive exam, thesis/dissertation. *Entrance requirements:* For doctorate, GRE General Test, minimum GPA of 3.5. Additional exam requirements/recommendations for international students: Required—TOEFL. Electronic applications accepted. *Faculty research:* Behavioral factors in cardiovascular disease and cancer adult psychopathology, developmental disabilities, social and emotional development, mechanisms of coping.

University of Michigan, Horace H. Rackham School of Graduate Studies, College of Literature, Science, and the Arts, Department of Psychology, Ann Arbor, MI 48109. Offers biopsychology (PhD); clinical psychology (PhD); cognition and perception (PhD); developmental psychology (PhD); personality and social contexts (PhD); social psychology (PhD). *Accreditation:* APA. *Degree requirements:* For doctorate, comprehensive exam, thesis/dissertation, oral defense of dissertation, preliminary exam. *Entrance requirements:* For doctorate, GRE General Test (optional), GRE Subject Test (optional). Additional exam requirements/recommendations for international students: Required—TOEFL. Electronic applications accepted.

University of Michigan–Dearborn, College of Arts, Sciences, and Letters, Master of Science in Psychology Health/Clinical Program, Dearborn, MI 48128. Offers clinical health psychology (MS); health psychology (MS). Part-time programs available. *Faculty:* 8 full-time (4 women), 1 part-time/adjunct (0 women). *Students:* 20 full-time (17 women), 13 part-time (10 women); includes 7 minority (1 African American, 4 Asian Americans or Pacific Islanders, 2 Hispanic Americans). Average age 36. 52 applicants, 23% accepted, 10 enrolled. In 2008, 6 master's awarded. *Degree requirements:* For master's, thesis or alternative, oral defense of thesis. *Entrance requirements:* For master's, GRE, 3 letters of recommendation, statement of purpose, official transcripts from all universities attended. Additional exam requirements/recommendations for international students: Required—TOEFL (minimum score 560 paper-based; 220 computer-based). *Application deadline:* For fall admission, 3/15 for domestic and international students. Application fee: $60 ($75 for international students). *Financial support:* In 2008–09, 4 students received support. Scholarships/grants available. *Faculty research:* Cardiovascular reactivity, coping, addiction, psychoneuroimmunology. *Unit head:* Dr. Pam McAuslan, Program Director, 313-593-5376, E-mail: pmcausla@umd.umich.edu. *Application contact:* Carol Ligienza, Graduate Program Coordinator, CASL Graduate Programs, 313-593-1183, Fax: 313-583-6498, E-mail: caslgrad@umd.umich.edu.

Clinical Psychology

University of Minnesota, Twin Cities Campus, Graduate School, College of Liberal Arts, Department of Psychology, Program in Clinical Psychology, Minneapolis, MN 55455-0213. Offers PhD. *Accreditation:* APA. *Degree requirements:* For doctorate, comprehensive exam, thesis/dissertation, internship. *Entrance requirements:* For doctorate, GRE General Test, minimum GPA of 3.5; 12 credits of upper-level psychology courses, including statistics or psychological measurement; previous course work in abnormal psychology. Additional exam requirements/recommendations for international students: Required—TOEFL (minimum score 550 paper-based; 213 computer-based; 79 iBT).

University of Mississippi, Graduate School, College of Liberal Arts, Department of Psychology, Oxford, University, MS 38677. Offers clinical psychology (PhD); experimental psychology (PhD); psychology (MA). *Accreditation:* APA (one or more programs are accredited). *Degree requirements:* For master's, thesis; for doctorate, thesis/dissertation. *Entrance requirements:* For master's, GRE General Test, minimum GPA of 3.0; for doctorate, GRE General Test. Additional exam requirements/recommendations for international students: Required—TOEFL. Electronic applications accepted.

University of Missouri–Kansas City, College of Arts and Sciences, Department of Psychology, Kansas City, MO 64110-2499. Offers psychology (MA, PhD), including clinical psychology (PhD), community psychology (PhD). *Accreditation:* APA. *Faculty:* 15 full-time (12 women), 1 part-time/adjunct (0 women). *Students:* 18 full-time (15 women), 6 part-time (5 women); includes 3 minority (2 African Americans, 1 Hispanic American). Average age 31. 90 applicants, 6% accepted, 5 enrolled. In 2008, 3 master's, 2 doctorates awarded. Terminal master's awarded for partial completion of doctoral program. *Degree requirements:* For master's, thesis; for doctorate, comprehensive exam, thesis/dissertation, residency. *Entrance requirements:* For master's, GRE, minimum GPA of 3.5, letter of recommendation; for doctorate, GRE, minimum GPA of 3.25. Additional exam requirements/recommendations for international students: Required—TOEFL (minimum score 550 paper-based; 213 computer-based; 80 iBT). *Application deadline:* For fall admission, 1/15 for domestic and international students. Applications are processed on a rolling basis. Application fee: $45 ($50 for international students). Electronic applications accepted. *Expenses:* Tuition, state resident: full-time $5376; part-time $298.70 per credit hour. Tuition, nonresident: full-time $13,882; part-time $771.20 per credit hour. Required fees: $640.28; $34.65 per contact hour. $30 per semester. Tuition and fees vary according to course load and program. *Financial support:* In 2008–09, 14 research assistantships (averaging $12,402 per year), 3 teaching assistantships (averaging $10,000 per year) were awarded; career-related internships or fieldwork, Federal Work-Study, and institutionally sponsored loans also available. Support available to part-time students. Financial award application deadline: 3/1; financial award applicants required to submit FAFSA. *Faculty research:* HIV/AIDS research group, psycho-oncology, sensory and cognitive neuroscience, cognitive psychophysiology, obesity and related metabolic disorders. Total annual research expenditures: $750,913. *Unit head:* Dr. Diane Filion, Chairperson, 816-235-1061, E-mail: filiond@umkc.edu. *Application contact:* 816-235-1111.

University of Missouri–St. Louis, College of Arts and Sciences, Department of Psychology, St. Louis, MO 63121. Offers behavioral neuroscience (PhD); clinical psychology respecialization (Certificate); community psychology (PhD); general psychology (MA); industrial/organizational psychology (PhD). *Accreditation:* APA (one or more programs are accredited). Evening/weekend programs available. *Faculty:* 21 full-time (10 women). *Students:* 56 full-time (46 women), 15 part-time (11 women); includes 4 minority (1 American Indian/Alaska Native, 2 Asian Americans or Pacific Islanders, 1 Hispanic American), 1 international. Average age 28. In 2008, 16 master's, 8 doctorates awarded. Terminal master's awarded for partial completion of doctoral program. *Degree requirements:* For doctorate, thesis/dissertation. *Entrance requirements:* For master's and doctorate, GRE General Test, GRE Subject Test, 3 letters of recommendation. Additional exam requirements/recommendations for international students: Required—TOEFL (minimum score 550 paper-based; 213 computer-based). *Application deadline:* For fall admission, 2/1 priority date for domestic and international students. Applications are processed on a rolling basis. Application fee: $35 ($40 for international students). Electronic applications accepted. *Expenses:* Tuition, area resident: Full-time $5377; part-time $298.70 per credit hour. Tuition, nonresident: full-time $13,381; part-time $472.50 per credit hour. Required fees: $4078; $52 per credit hour. *Financial support:* In 2008–09, 3 research assistantships with full and partial tuition reimbursements (averaging $9,225 per year), 15 teaching assistantships with full and partial tuition reimbursements (averaging $9,000 per year) were awarded; fellowships with full tuition reimbursements also available. Financial award applicants required to submit FAFSA. *Faculty research:* Bereavement and loss, neuroscience, post-traumatic stress disorder, conflict and negotiation, social psychology. *Unit head:* Dr. George Taylor, Chair, 314-516-5391, Fax: 314-516-5392, E-mail: umslpsychology@msx.umsl.edu. *Application contact:* 314-516-5458, Fax: 314-516-6996, E-mail: gradadm@umsl.edu.

The University of Montana, Graduate School, College of Arts and Sciences, Department of Psychology, Missoula, MT 59812-0002. Offers clinical psychology (PhD); experimental psychology (PhD), including animal behavior psychology, developmental psychology; school psychology (MA, PhD, Ed S). *Accreditation:* APA (one or more programs are accredited). Terminal master's awarded for partial completion of doctoral program. *Degree requirements:* For master's, thesis; for doctorate, thesis/dissertation. *Entrance requirements:* For master's, doctorate, and Ed S, GRE General Test. Additional exam requirements/recommendations for international students: Required—TOEFL.

University of Nebraska–Lincoln, Graduate College, College of Arts and Sciences, Department of Psychology, Lincoln, NE 68588. Offers biopsychology (PhD); clinical psychology (PhD); cognitive psychology (PhD); developmental psychology (PhD); psychology (MA); social/personality psychology (PhD); JD/MA; JD/PhD. *Accreditation:* APA (one or more programs are accredited). *Faculty:* 24 full-time (8 women). *Students:* 84 full-time (66 women), 29 part-time (15 women); includes 15 minority (1 African American, 1 American Indian/Alaska Native, 4 Asian Americans or Pacific Islanders, 9 Hispanic Americans), 9 international. Average age 32. In 2008, 16 master's, 18 doctorates awarded. *Degree requirements:* For master's, thesis optional; for doctorate, comprehensive exam, thesis/dissertation. *Entrance requirements:* For master's and doctorate, GRE General Test. Additional exam requirements/recommendations for international students: Required—TOEFL (minimum score 550 paper-based; 213 computer-based). *Application deadline:* For fall admission, 1/3 for domestic and international students. Application fee: $40. Electronic applications accepted. *Expenses:* Tuition, state resident: full-time $4275; part-time $237.50 per credit hour. Tuition, nonresident: full-time $11,525; part-time $640.25 per credit hour. Required fees: $1068; $10.35 per credit hour. $440.70 per semester. Tuition and fees vary according to course load and program. *Financial support:* Fellowships, research assistantships, teaching assistantships, Federal Work-Study, health care benefits, and unspecified assistantships available. Support available to part-time students. Financial award application deadline: 1/3. *Faculty research:* Law and psychology, rural mental health, chronic mental illness, neuropsychology, child clinical psychology. *Unit head:* Dr. David Hansen, Chair, 402-472-3721, Fax: 402-472-4637. *Application contact:* Ginny Gross, Director of Graduate Admissions, 402-472-2878, Fax: 402-472-0589, E-mail: grad_admissions@unl.edu.

University of Nevada, Reno, Graduate School, College of Liberal Arts, Department of Psychology, Program in Clinical Psychology, Reno, NV 89557. Offers MA, PhD. *Faculty:* 9 full-time (4 women). *Students:* 33 full-time (24 women), 19 part-time (13 women); includes 5 minority (1 African American, 3 Asian Americans or Pacific Islanders, 1 Hispanic American), 6 international. Average age 30. 105 applicants, 8% accepted, 5 enrolled. In 2008, 40 master's, 10 doctorates awarded. Terminal master's awarded for partial completion of doctoral program. *Degree requirements:* For master's, thesis optional; for doctorate, comprehensive exam, thesis/dissertation. *Entrance requirements:* For master's, GRE Subject Test (psychology), minimum GPA of 2.75; for doctorate, GRE Subject Test (psychology), minimum GPA of 3.0. Additional exam requirements/recommendations for international students: Required—TOEFL (minimum score 500 paper-based; 173 computer-based; 61 iBT), IELTS (minimum score 6), TOFEL or IELTS. *Application deadline:* For fall admission, 1/1 priority date for domestic and international students. Application fee: $60 ($95 for international students). Electronic applications accepted. *Expenses:* Tuition, state resident: full-time $1710; part-time $1140 per semester. Tuition, nonresident: full-time $7115. Required fees: $158 per semester. *Financial support:* In 2008–09, 26 research assistantships with partial tuition reimbursements (averaging $14,000 per year), 12 teaching assistantships with partial tuition reimbursements (averaging $14,000 per year) were awarded; Federal Work-Study, institutionally sponsored loans, scholarships/grants, health care benefits, and unspecified assistantships also available. Financial award application deadline: 3/1; financial award applicants required to submit FAFSA. *Faculty research:* Health behavior, domestic violence, verbal relations, anxiety. Total annual research expenditures: $404,823. *Unit head:* Dr. William Follette, Program Director, 775-784-6828, E-mail: follette@unr.edu. *Application contact:* Michele Sandberg, Application Contact, 775-784-7026, Fax: 775-784-6064, E-mail: gradschool@unr.edu.

University of New Brunswick Saint John, Department of Psychology, Fredericton, NB, NB E2L 4L5, Canada. Offers applied and experimental psychology (PhD); clinical psychology (PhD); experimental psychology (MA). *Faculty:* 9 full-time (4 women). *Students:* 4 full-time (all women). In 2008, 1 master's awarded. *Degree requirements:* For master's, thesis; for doctorate, comprehensive exam, thesis/dissertation. *Entrance requirements:* For master's, GRE General Test. Additional exam requirements/recommendations for international students: Required—TOEFL (minimum score 550 paper-based). *Application deadline:* For fall admission, 2/1 for domestic students. Application fee: $50. Electronic applications accepted. *Expenses:* Tuition, area resident: Full-time $5562. International tuition: $9450 full-time. Required fees: $333. *Financial support:* In 2008–09, 1 fellowship, 7 research assistantships, 2 teaching assistantships were awarded; unspecified assistantships also available. Support available to part-time students. Financial award application deadline: 2/1. *Faculty research:* Psychopharmacology and addictions, forensic psychology and criminal justice, interpersonal relations, perception and graphical perception, lie detection. *Unit head:* Dr. Lily Both, Director of Graduate Studies, 506-648-5769, Fax: 506-648-5780, E-mail: lboth@unbsj.ca. *Application contact:* Frances Stevens, Secretary, 506-648-5640, Fax: 506-648-5780, E-mail: fstevens@unb.ca.

University of New Mexico, Graduate School, College of Arts and Sciences, Department of Psychology, Program in Clinical Psychology, Albuquerque, NM 87131-2039. Offers MS, PhD. *Accreditation:* APA (one or more programs are accredited). *Degree requirements:* For master's, thesis; for doctorate, comprehensive exam, thesis/dissertation, pre-doctoral internship. *Entrance requirements:* For doctorate, GRE General Test, GRE Subject Test (psychology), minimum GPA of 3.0. Additional exam requirements/recommendations for international students: Required—TOEFL. Electronic applications accepted.

The University of North Carolina at Chapel Hill, Graduate School, College of Arts and Sciences, Department of Psychology, Chapel Hill, NC 27599. Offers biological psychology (PhD); clinical psychology (PhD); cognitive psychology (PhD); developmental psychology (PhD); quantitative psychology (PhD); social psychology (PhD). *Accreditation:* APA. *Degree requirements:* For doctorate, comprehensive exam, thesis/dissertation. *Entrance requirements:* For doctorate, GRE General Test, minimum GPA of 3.0. Electronic applications accepted. *Faculty research:* Expressed emotion, cognitive development, social cognitive neuroscience, human memory personality.

The University of North Carolina at Charlotte, Graduate School, College of Arts and Sciences, Department of Psychology, Program in Community/Clinical Psychology, Charlotte, NC 28223-0001. Offers MA. *Students:* 9 full-time (8 women), 11 part-time (10 women); includes 6 minority (4 African Americans, 2 Hispanic Americans). Average age 26. 129 applicants, 3% accepted, 4 enrolled. In 2008, 8 master's awarded. *Degree requirements:* For master's, comprehensive exam, thesis. *Entrance requirements:* For master's, GRE General Test, GRE Subject Test, minimum GPA of 3.0 in undergraduate major, 2.8 overall. Additional exam requirements/recommendations for international students: Required—TOEFL (minimum score 557 paper-based; 220 computer-based). *Application deadline:* For fall admission, 3/1 for domestic and international students. Application fee: $55. Electronic applications accepted. *Expenses:* Tuition, area resident: Full-time $2919; part-time $122 per credit hour. Tuition, state resident: full-time $2919; part-time $122 per credit hour. Tuition, nonresident: full-time $13,126; part-time $547 per credit hour. Required fees: $1779; $91 per credit hour. Tuition and fees vary according to program. *Financial support:* In 2008–09, 1 research assistantship (averaging $2,250 per year), 3 teaching assistantships (averaging $9,000 per year) were awarded; career-related internships or fieldwork, Federal Work-Study, institutionally sponsored loans, scholarships/grants, unspecified assistantships, and 2 administrative assistantships ($8,100 average) also available. Support available to part-time students. Financial award application deadline: 4/1; financial award applicants required to submit FAFSA. *Unit head:* Dr. Richard G. Tedeschi, Coordinator, 704-687-4754, Fax: 704-687-3096, E-mail: rtedesch@email.uncc.edu. *Application contact:* Kathy B. Giddings, Director of Graduate Admissions, 704-687-3366, Fax: 704-687-3279, E-mail: agidding@uncc.edu.

The University of North Carolina at Greensboro, Graduate School, College of Arts and Sciences, Department of Psychology, Greensboro, NC 27412-5001. Offers clinical psychology (MA, PhD); cognitive psychology (MA, PhD); developmental psychology (MA, PhD); social psychology (MA, PhD). *Accreditation:* APA (one or more programs are accredited). Terminal master's awarded for partial completion of doctoral program. *Degree requirements:* For master's, comprehensive exam, thesis; for doctorate, one foreign language, thesis/dissertation, preliminary exam. *Entrance requirements:* For master's and doctorate, GRE General Test. Additional exam requirements/recommendations for international students: Required—TOEFL. Electronic applications accepted. *Faculty research:* Sensory and perceptual determinants; evoked potential: disorders, deafness, and development.

University of North Dakota, Graduate School, College of Arts and Sciences, Department of Psychology, Grand Forks, ND 58202. Offers clinical psychology (PhD); counseling psychology (PhD); experimental psychology (PhD); forensic psychology (MA, MS); psychology (MA). *Accreditation:* APA (one or more programs are accredited). *Degree requirements:* For master's, thesis, final exam; for doctorate, comprehensive exam, thesis/dissertation, internship, final exam. *Entrance requirements:* For master's, GRE General Test, GRE Subject Test, minimum GPA of 3.0; for doctorate, GRE General Test, GRE Subject Test, minimum GPA of 3.5. Additional exam requirements/recommendations for international students: Required—TOEFL (minimum score 550 paper-based; 213 computer-based; 79 iBT), IELTS (minimum score 6.5). Electronic applications accepted. *Faculty research:* Developmental psychology, clinical social psychology, educational psychology, personality disorders.

University of North Texas, Robert B. Toulouse School of Graduate Studies, College of Arts and Sciences, Department of Psychology, Denton, TX 76203. Offers clinical psychology (PhD); counseling psychology (MA, MS, PhD); experimental psychology (MA, MS, PhD); health psychology and behavioral medicine (PhD). *Accreditation:* APA (one or more programs are accredited). Terminal master's awarded for partial completion of doctoral program. *Degree requirements:* For master's, comprehensive exam, thesis or alternative; for doctorate, one foreign language, comprehensive exam, thesis/dissertation. *Entrance requirements:* For master's and doctorate, GRE General Test, interview. Additional exam requirements/recommendations for international students: Required—proof of English language proficiency required for non-native English speakers; Recommended—TOEFL (minimum score 550 paper-based; 213 computer-based). *Faculty research:* Very broad range of topics and approaches.

University of Oregon, Graduate School, College of Arts and Sciences, Department of Psychology, Program in Clinical Psychology, Eugene, OR 97403. Offers PhD. *Accreditation:* APA. *Degree requirements:* For doctorate, thesis/dissertation. *Entrance requirements:* For doctorate, GRE General Test. Additional exam requirements/recommendations for international students: Required—TOEFL.

University of Pennsylvania, Graduate School of Education, Division of Applied Psychology and Human Development, Program in School, Community, and Clinical Child Psychology, Philadelphia, PA 19104. Offers PhD. *Degree requirements:* For doctorate, thesis/dissertation, exams. *Entrance requirements:* For doctorate, GRE General Test, GRE Subject Test. Electronic applications accepted. *Expenses:* Contact institution. *Faculty research:* Therapeutic interventions at a preschool level, childhood stress, college psychology, school and community psychology.

University of Puerto Rico, Río Piedras, College of Social Sciences, Department of Psychology, San Juan, PR 00931-3300. Offers clinical psychology (MA); industrial organizational psychology (MA); investigative academic psychology (MA); psychology (PhD). Part-time programs available. *Degree requirements:* For master's, comprehensive exam, thesis; for doctorate, comprehensive exam, thesis/dissertation, internship. *Entrance requirements:* For master's, GRE or PAEG, interview, minimum GPA of 3.0; for doctorate, GRE or PAEG, interview, master's degree, minimum GPA of 3.0. *Faculty research:* Intervention on Depressed Latino Youth, biosychosocial training.

University of Regina, Faculty of Graduate Studies and Research, Faculty of Arts, Department of Psychology, Regina, SK S4S 0A2, Canada. Offers clinical psychology (MA, PhD); experimental and applied psychology (MA, PhD). *Faculty:* 18 full-time (10 women). *Students:* 54 full-time (44 women), 3 part-time (all women). 57 applicants, 28% accepted. In 2008, 6 master's, 3 doctorates awarded. *Degree requirements:* For master's, thesis; for doctorate, comprehensive exam, thesis/dissertation. *Entrance requirements:* For master's, GRE General Test, GRE Subject Test; for doctorate, GRE General Test, GRE Subject Test (optional for students who hold a master's degree from a Canadian university). Additional exam requirements/recommendations for international students: Required—TOEFL (minimum score 580 paper-based; 237 computer-based; 88 iBT). *Application deadline:* For fall admission, 2/15 for domestic students. Application fee: $85 ($100 for international students). Electronic applications accepted. *Financial support:* In 2008–09, 17 fellowships (averaging $16,764 per year), 4 research assistantships (averaging $13,875 per year), 11 teaching assistantships (averaging $6,675 per year) were awarded; career-related internships or fieldwork and scholarships/grants also available. Financial award application deadline: 6/15. *Faculty research:* Clinical, experimental and applied psychology. *Unit head:* Dr. William E. Smythe, Head, 306-585-4157, Fax: 306-585-5429, E-mail: william.smythe@uregina.ca. *Application contact:* Dr. Dongyan Blachford, Associate Dean, 306-585-5186, Fax: 306-337-2444, E-mail: dongyan.blachford@uregina.ca.

University of Rhode Island, Graduate School, College of Arts and Sciences, Department of Psychology, Program in Clinical Psychology, Kingston, RI 02881. Offers MA, PhD. *Accreditation:* APA. Application fee: $35. *Expenses:* Tuition, state resident: full-time $8024; part-time $446 per credit. Tuition, nonresident: full-time $21,046; part-time $1169 per credit. Required fees: $1056; $26 per credit. $30 per semester. One-time fee: $95 part-time. *Unit head:* Dr. Allan Berman, Director, 401-874-4257, E-mail: alberman@uri.edu. *Application contact:* Harold D. Bibb, Associate Dean of the Graduate School, 401-874-2262, Fax: 401-874-5491.

University of Rochester, The College, Arts and Sciences, Department of Clinical and Social Sciences in Psychology, Rochester, NY 14627-0250. Offers clinical psychology (PhD); developmental psychology (PhD); psychology (MA); social-personality psychology (PhD). *Accreditation:* APA (one or more programs are accredited). Terminal master's awarded for partial completion of doctoral program. *Degree requirements:* For doctorate, thesis/dissertation, qualifying exam. *Entrance requirements:* For doctorate, GRE General Test. Additional exam requirements/recommendations for international students: Required—TOEFL.

University of South Africa, College of Human Sciences, Pretoria, South Africa. Offers adult education (M Ed); African languages (MA, PhD); African politics (MA, PhD); Afrikaans (MA, PhD); ancient history (MA, PhD); ancient Near Eastern studies (MA, PhD); anthropology (MA, PhD); applied linguistics (MA); Arabic (MA, PhD); archaeology (MA); art history (MA); Biblical archaeology (MA); Biblical studies (M Th, D Th, PhD); Christian spirituality (M Th, D Th); church history (M Th, D Th); classical studies (MA, PhD); clinical psychology (MA); communication (MA, PhD); comparative education (M Ed, Ed D); consulting psychology (D Admin, D Com, PhD); curriculum studies (M Ed, Ed D); development studies (M Admin, MA, D Admin, PhD); didactics (M Ed, Ed D); education (M Tech); education management (M Ed, Ed D); educational psychology (M Ed); English (MA); environmental education (M Ed); French (MA, PhD); German (MA, PhD); Greek (MA); guidance and counseling (M Ed); health studies (MA, PhD), including health sciences education (MA), health services management (MA), medical and surgical nursing science (critical care general) (MA), midwifery and neonatal nursing science (MA), trauma and emergency care (MA); history (MA, PhD); history of education (Ed D); inclusive education (M Ed, Ed D); information and communications technology policy and regulation (MA); information science (MA, MIS, PhD); international politics (MA, PhD); Islamic studies (MA, PhD); Italian (MA, PhD); Judaica (MA, PhD); linguistics (MA, PhD); mathematical education (M Ed); mathematics education (MA); missiology (M Th, D Th); modern Hebrew (MA, PhD); musicology (MA, MMus, D Mus, PhD); natural science education (M Ed); New Testament (M Th, D Th); Old Testament (D Th); pastoral therapy (M Th, D Th); philosophy (MA); philosophy of education (M Ed, Ed D); politics (MA, PhD); Portuguese (MA, PhD); practical theology (M Th, D Th); psychology (MA, MS, PhD); psychology of education (M Ed, Ed D); public health (MA); religious studies (MA, D Th, PhD); Romance languages (MA); Russian (MA, PhD); Semitic languages (MA, PhD); social behavior studies in HIV/AIDS (MA); social science (mental health) (MA); social science in development studies (MA); social science in psychology (MA); social science in social work (MA); social science in sociology (MA); social work (MSW, DSW, PhD); socio-education (M Ed, Ed D); sociolinguistics (MA); sociology (MA, PhD); Spanish (MA, PhD); systematic theology (M Th, D Th); TESOL (teaching English to speakers of other languages) (MA); theological ethics (M Th, D Th); theory of literature (MA, PhD); urban ministries (D Th); urban ministry (M Th).

University of South Carolina, The Graduate School, College of Arts and Sciences, Department of Psychology, Program in Clinical/Community Psychology, Columbia, SC 29208. Offers clinical/community psychology (PhD); general psychology (MA). *Accreditation:* APA. *Degree requirements:* For master's, comprehensive exam, thesis; for doctorate, comprehensive exam, thesis/dissertation. *Entrance requirements:* For doctorate, GRE General Test, minimum GPA of 3.2. Additional exam requirements/recommendations for international students: Required—TOEFL. Electronic applications accepted. *Faculty research:* Developmental psychopathology, health disparities, community-level interventions for psychological well being.

University of South Carolina Aiken, Program in Applied Clinical Psychology, Aiken, SC 29801-6309. Offers MS. Part-time and evening/weekend programs available. *Degree requirements:* For master's, thesis. *Entrance requirements:* For master's, GRE General Test, GRE Subject Test (psychology). Electronic applications accepted.

The University of South Dakota, Graduate School, College of Arts and Sciences, Department of Psychology, Vermillion, SD 57069-2390. Offers clinical psychology (MA, PhD); human factors (MA, PhD). *Accreditation:* APA (one or more programs are accredited). *Degree requirements:* For master's, comprehensive exam, thesis; for doctorate, comprehensive exam, thesis/dissertation. *Entrance requirements:* For master's, GRE, minimum GPA of 2.7; for doctorate, GRE General Test, GRE Subject Test, minimum GPA of 2.7. Additional exam requirements/recommendations for international students: Required—TOEFL (minimum score 550 paper-based; 213 computer-based; 79 iBT). Electronic applications accepted. *Faculty research:* Human-computer interactions, perceptual-cognitive processing, medical psychology, depression, moral psychology.

University of Southern Mississippi, Graduate School, College of Education and Psychology, Department of Psychology, Hattiesburg, MS 39406-0001. Offers clinical psychology (MA, PhD); counseling psychology (PhD); experimental psychology (MA, PhD); psychology (MS); school psychology (MA, PhD). *Accreditation:* ACA; APA (one or more programs are accredited). *Faculty:* 28 full-time (11 women). *Students:* 104 full-time (83 women), 34 part-time (24 women); includes 13 minority (7 African Americans, 2 Asian Americans or Pacific Islanders, 4 Hispanic Americans), 7 international. Average age 28. 189 applicants, 21% accepted, 31 enrolled. In 2008, 24 master's, 13 doctorates awarded. Terminal master's awarded for partial completion of doctoral program. *Degree requirements:* For master's, comprehensive exam, thesis; for doctorate, comprehensive exam, thesis/dissertation. *Entrance requirements:* For master's, GRE General Test, minimum GPA of 3.0; for doctorate, GRE General Test, interview, minimum GPA of 3.0. Additional exam requirements/recommendations for international students: Required—TOEFL. *Application deadline:* For fall admission, 3/1 priority date for domestic students, 3/1 for international students. Applications are processed on a rolling basis. Application fee: $30. *Financial support:* In 2008–09, 48 research assistantships with full tuition reimbursements (averaging $8,802 per year), 48 teaching assistantships with full tuition reimbursements (averaging $6,500 per year) were awarded; career-related internships or fieldwork, Federal Work-Study, and institutionally sponsored loans also available. Financial award application deadline: 3/15; financial award applicants required to submit FAFSA. *Faculty research:* Dolphin cognition, sleep, neuropsychology, health-related behaviors, psychopathology. Total annual research expenditures: $101,200. *Unit head:* Dr. Joesph Olmi, Chair, 601-266-4177, Fax: 601-266-5580. *Application contact:* Dr. Heather Sterling-Turner, Graduate Coordinator, 601-266-4177, Fax: 601-266-5580.

University of South Florida, Graduate School, College of Arts and Sciences, Department of Psychology, Tampa, FL 33620-9951. Offers clinical psychology (MA, PhD); cognitive and neural sciences (MA, PhD); industrial-organizational psychology (MA, PhD). *Accreditation:* APA (one or more programs are accredited). *Faculty:* 30 full-time (10 women). *Students:* 93 full-time (53 women), 22 part-time (15 women); includes 12 minority (2 African Americans, 4 Asian Americans or Pacific Islanders, 6 Hispanic Americans), 16 international. 421 applicants, 3% accepted, 11 enrolled. In 2008, 21 master's, 12 doctorates awarded. *Degree requirements:* For master's, comprehensive exam, thesis; for doctorate, comprehensive exam, thesis/dissertation. *Entrance requirements:* For master's and doctorate, GRE General Test, minimum GPA of 3.0 in last 60 hours of course work. Additional exam requirements/recommendations for international students: Required—TOEFL (minimum score 550 paper-based; 213 computer-based). *Application deadline:* For fall admission, 11/15 for domestic students, 12/15 for international students. Application fee: $30. Electronic applications accepted. *Expenses:* Contact institution. *Financial support:* Fellowships with full and partial tuition reimbursements, research assistantships with partial tuition reimbursements, teaching assistantships with partial tuition reimbursements, career-related internships or fieldwork, scholarships/grants, tuition waivers (partial), and unspecified assistantships available. Financial award applicants required to submit FAFSA. *Faculty research:* Human memory; job analysis; stress, drug and alcohol abuse; neuroscience. Total annual research expenditures: $2.9 million. *Unit head:* Emanual Donchin, Program Director, 813-974-0466, Fax: 813-974-4617, E-mail: dochin@shell.cas.usf.edu. *Application contact:* William Sacco, Program Director, 813-974-0375, Fax: 813-974-4617, E-mail: sacco@cas.usf.edu.

The University of Tennessee, Graduate School, College of Arts and Sciences, Department of Psychology, Knoxville, TN 37996. Offers clinical psychology (PhD); experimental psychology (MA, PhD); psychology (MA). *Accreditation:* APA (one or more programs are accredited). Terminal master's awarded for partial completion of doctoral program. *Degree requirements:* For master's, thesis; for doctorate, thesis/dissertation. *Entrance requirements:* For master's and doctorate, GRE General Test, GRE Subject Test, minimum GPA of 2.7. Additional exam requirements/recommendations for international students: Required—TOEFL. Electronic applications accepted. *Expenses:* Tuition, area resident: Part-time $348 per credit hour. Tuition, state resident: full-time $6262. Tuition, nonresident: full-time $18,920; part-time $1052 per credit hour. Required fees: $812; $36 per credit hour. Tuition and fees vary according to program.

The University of Texas at El Paso, Graduate School, College of Liberal Arts, Department of Psychology, El Paso, TX 79968-0001. Offers clinical psychology (MA); experimental psychology (MA); psychology (PhD). Part-time and evening/weekend programs available. *Degree requirements:* For master's, thesis; for doctorate, thesis/dissertation. *Entrance requirements:* For master's and doctorate, GRE General Test. Additional exam requirements/recommendations for international students: Required—TOEFL. Electronic applications accepted.

The University of Texas at Tyler, College of Education and Psychology, Department of Psychology, Tyler, TX 75799-0001. Offers clinical psychology (MS), including neuropsychology, school psychology; counseling psychology (MA), including general, marriage and family; interdisciplinary studies (MSIS); school counseling (MA). Part-time and evening/weekend programs available. *Degree requirements:* For master's, comprehensive exam, thesis optional. *Entrance requirements:* For master's, GRE General Test, minimum GPA of 3.0. Additional exam requirements/recommendations for international students: Required—TOEFL (minimum score 79 computer-based). Electronic applications accepted. *Faculty research:* Neuropsychology, child abuse, psychometric properties of psychological instruments, maternal behavior, clinical practice issues, victimization of women, post-traumatic stress disorder.

The University of Texas of the Permian Basin, Office of Graduate Studies, College of Arts and Sciences, Deparment of Psychology, Odessa, TX 79762-0001. Offers applied research psychology (MA); clinical psychology (MA). Part-time and evening/weekend programs available. *Degree requirements:* For master's, comprehensive exam, thesis, practicum. *Entrance requirements:* For master's, GRE General Test, 3 letters of recommendation. Additional exam requirements/recommendations for international students: Required—TOEFL (minimum score 550 paper-based; 213 computer-based).

The University of Texas–Pan American, College of Social and Behavioral Sciences, Department of Psychology and Anthropology, Edinburg, TX 78541-2999. Offers psychology (MA), including clinical psychology, experimental psychology. Part-time and evening/weekend programs available. *Degree requirements:* For master's, comprehensive exam, thesis optional, internship. *Entrance requirements:* For master's, GRE, letters of recommendation. Additional exam requirements/recommendations for international students: Required—TOEFL. Electronic applications accepted. *Faculty research:* Biofeedback, acculturation, health, stress/trauma, neuropsychological assessment, false memories, children's theory of mind.

The University of Texas Southwestern Medical Center at Dallas, Southwestern Graduate School of Biomedical Sciences, Division of Clinical Science, Clinical Psychology Program, Dallas, TX 75390. Offers PhD. *Accreditation:* APA. *Faculty:* 41 full-time (20 women), 30 part-time/adjunct (11 women). *Students:* 45 full-time (31 women); includes 9 minority (1 African American, 4 Asian Americans or Pacific Islanders, 4 Hispanic Americans), 1 international. Average age 26. 139 applicants, 7% accepted, 10 enrolled. In 2008, 9 doctorates awarded. *Degree requirements:* For doctorate, thesis/dissertation, clinical and qualifying exams. *Entrance requirements:* For doctorate, GRE General Test, minimum undergraduate GPA of 3.0. *Application deadline:* For fall admission, 1/1 for domestic students. Application fee: $0. Electronic applications accepted. *Expenses:* Tuition, state resident: full-time $3600. Tuition, nonresident: full-time $10,344. Required fees: $763. *Financial support:* Research assistantships, career-related internships or fieldwork and institutionally sponsored loans available. Financial award application deadline: 3/1; financial award applicants required to submit FAFSA. *Faculty research:* Health psychology, depression, cross-cultural research, neuropsychology, sequelae children's illness. *Unit head:* Dr. C. Munro Cullum, Chair, 214-648-4640, Fax: 214-648-5250, E-mail: munro.cullum@utsouthwestern.edu. *Application contact:* Kimberly Jones, Education Coordinator, 214-648-5267, Fax: 214-648-5297, E-mail: kelsey.stutzman@utsouthwestern.edu.

University of the District of Columbia, College of Arts and Sciences, Department of Psychology and Counseling, Program in Clinical Psychology, Washington, DC 20008-1175. Offers MS.

The University of Toledo, College of Graduate Studies, College of Arts and Sciences, Department of Psychology, Toledo, OH 43606-3390. Offers behavioral (PhD), including cognitive, psychobiology and learning, social; clinical psychology (PhD); experimental psychology (MA). *Accreditation:* APA. *Degree requirements:* For master's, thesis; for doctorate, one foreign language, thesis/dissertation. *Entrance requirements:* For master's and doctorate, GRE General Test, GRE Subject Test. *Faculty research:* Neural taste response.

Clinical Psychology

University of Tulsa, Graduate School, College of Arts and Sciences, Department of Psychology, Program in Clinical Psychology, Tulsa, OK 74104-3189. Offers MA, PhD, JD/MA. *Accreditation:* APA (one or more programs are accredited). Part-time programs available. *Faculty:* 9 full-time (3 women), 1 (woman) part-time/adjunct. *Students:* 26 full-time (22 women), 25 part-time (22 women); includes 5 minority (2 African Americans, 1 American Indian/Alaska Native, 2 Hispanic Americans), 1 international. Average age 29. 63 applicants, 35% accepted, 8 enrolled. In 2008, 5 master's, 7 doctorates awarded. Terminal master's awarded for partial completion of doctoral program. *Degree requirements:* For master's, thesis (for some programs), 6 credit hours of practicum training; for doctorate, comprehensive exam, thesis/dissertation, 1 year pre-doctoral internship. *Entrance requirements:* For master's and doctorate, GRE General Test, interview. Additional exam requirements/recommendations for international students: Required—TOEFL (minimum score 575 paper-based; 231 computer-based; 91 iBT), IELTS (minimum score 6.5). *Application deadline:* For fall admission, 12/1 for domestic and international students. Application fee: $40. Electronic applications accepted. *Expenses:* Tuition: Full-time $15,408; part-time $899 per credit hour. Required fees: $3.33 per credit hour. One-time fee: $200 full-time. Tuition and fees vary according to course load and program. *Financial support:* In 2008–09, 34 students received support, including 13 fellowships with full and partial tuition reimbursements available (averaging $4,535 per year), 17 research assistantships with full and partial tuition reimbursements available (averaging $11,228 per year), 11 teaching assistantships with full and partial tuition reimbursements available (averaging $8,749 per year); career-related internships or fieldwork, Federal Work-Study, tuition waivers (full and partial), and unspecified assistantships also available. Support available to part-time students. Financial award application deadline: 2/1; financial award applicants required to submit FAFSA. *Faculty research:* Traumatic stress studies, randomized control trials of exposure treatments, pain modulation, neuropsychological assessment of health/mental health, psychological assessment, psychometrics, ethics, longitudinal assessment of child development, trauma and journalism, and MMPI studies. Total annual research expenditures: $815,707. *Unit head:* Dr. Elana Newman, Director, 918-631-3151, Fax: 918-631-2836, E-mail: elana-newman@utulsa.edu. *Application contact:* Information Contact, E-mail: grad@utulsa.edu.

University of Utah, The Graduate School, College of Social and Behavioral Science, Department of Psychology, Salt Lake City, UT 84112-1107. Offers clinical psychology (PhD); psychology (PhD). *Accreditation:* APA. *Degree requirements:* For doctorate, thesis/dissertation. *Entrance requirements:* For doctorate, GRE General Test. Additional exam requirements/recommendations for international students: Required—TOEFL (minimum score 500 paper-based; 173 computer-based). *Faculty research:* Cognitive neuroscience, health, social cognition, psychopathology, cognitive and social development.

University of Vermont, Graduate College, College of Arts and Sciences, Department of Psychology, Burlington, VT 05405. Offers clinical psychology (PhD); psychology (PhD). *Accreditation:* APA. *Students:* 50 (40 women); includes 5 minority (1 African American, 4 Hispanic Americans), 2 international. 186 applicants, 15% accepted, 10 enrolled. In 2008, 8 doctorates awarded. *Degree requirements:* For doctorate, thesis/dissertation. *Entrance requirements:* For doctorate, GRE General Test. Additional exam requirements/recommendations for international students: Required—TOEFL (minimum score 550 paper-based; 213 computer-based; 80 iBT). *Application deadline:* For fall admission, 12/1 for domestic students. Application fee: $40. Electronic applications accepted. *Expenses:* Tuition, state resident: part-time $488 per credit. Tuition, nonresident: part-time $1232 per credit. *Financial support:* Fellowships, research assistantships, teaching assistantships available. Financial award application deadline: 2/1. *Unit head:* Dr. William Falls, Chairperson, 802-656-2670. *Application contact:* Dr. Rex Forehand, Coordinator, 802-656-2670.

University of Victoria, Faculty of Graduate Studies, Faculty of Social Sciences, Department of Psychology, Victoria, BC V8W 2Y2, Canada. Offers clinical psychology (PhD); clinical psychology (neuropsychology) (M Sc); cognition and brain science (M Sc, PhD); experimental neuropsychology (M Sc, PhD); individualized study (M Sc, PhD); life span development psychology (PhD); life span developmental psychology (M Sc); social psychology (M Sc, PhD). *Accreditation:* APA (one or more programs are accredited). *Degree requirements:* For master's, thesis; for doctorate, thesis/dissertation, candidacy exam. *Entrance requirements:* For master's and doctorate, GRE General Test. Additional exam requirements/recommendations for international students: Required—TOEFL (minimum score 600 paper-based; 250 computer-based). Electronic applications accepted. *Faculty research:* Life span development psychology and aging, behavioral neuroscience, cognitive psychology, behavioral psychology, environmental psychology.

University of Virginia, Curry School of Education, Department of Human Services, Charlottesville, VA 22903. Offers clinical and school psychology (PhD); communication disorders (M Ed); counselor education (M Ed, Ed D, Ed S); health and physical education (M Ed, Ed D), including kinesiology. *Accreditation:* APA (one or more programs are accredited). *Faculty:* 26 full-time (14 women), 2 part-time/adjunct (1 woman). *Students:* 103 full-time (97 women), 8 part-time (all women); includes 10 minority (2 African Americans, 4 Asian Americans or Pacific Islanders, 4 Hispanic Americans). Average age 25. 180 applicants, 50% accepted, 38 enrolled. In 2008, 41 master's awarded. *Entrance requirements:* For master's, doctorate, and Ed S, GRE General Test, 2 letters of recommendation. Additional exam requirements/recommendations for international students: Required—TOEFL (minimum score 600 paper-based; 250 computer-based; 90 iBT), IELTS (minimum score 7). *Application deadline:* Applications are processed on a rolling basis. Application fee: $60. Electronic applications accepted. *Expenses:* Tuition, area resident: Full-time $10,452. Tuition, state resident: full-time $10,452. Tuition, nonresident: full-time $20,010. Required fees: $2176. Part-time tuition and fees vary according to course load and program. *Financial support:* Fellowships with tuition reimbursements, research assistantships with tuition reimbursements, teaching assistantships with tuition reimbursements available. Financial award applicants required to submit FAFSA. *Unit head:* Chris Ingersoll, Chair. *Application contact:* Lynn Renfroe, Information Contact, 434-924-6254, E-mail: ldr9t@virginia.edu.

University of Washington, Graduate School, College of Arts and Sciences, Department of Psychology, Seattle, WA 98195. Offers animal behavior (PhD); child psychology (PhD); clinical psychology (PhD); cognition and perception (PhD); developmental psychology (PhD); quantitative psychology (PhD); social psychology and personality (PhD). *Accreditation:* APA. *Degree requirements:* For doctorate, thesis/dissertation. *Entrance requirements:* For doctorate, GRE General Test, minimum GPA of 3.0. Electronic applications accepted. *Faculty research:* Addictive behaviors, artificial intelligence, child psychopathology, mechanisms and development of vision, physiology of ingestive behaviors.

University of Windsor, Faculty of Graduate Studies, Faculty of Arts and Social Sciences, Department of Psychology, Windsor, ON N9B 3P4, Canada. Offers adult clinical (MA, PhD); applied social psychology (MA, PhD); child clinical (MA, PhD); clinical neuropsychology (MA, PhD). *Accreditation:* APA (one or more programs are accredited). *Degree requirements:* For master's, thesis; for doctorate, comprehensive exam, thesis/dissertation. *Entrance requirements:* For master's, GRE General Test, GRE Subject Test in psychology, minimum B average; for doctorate, GRE General Test, GRE Subject Test in psychology, master's degree. Additional exam requirements/recommendations for international students: Required—TOEFL (minimum score 600 paper-based; 250 computer-based). Electronic applications accepted. *Faculty research:* Gambling, suicidology, emotional competence, psychotherapy and trauma.

University of Wisconsin–Madison, Graduate School, College of Letters and Science, Department of Psychology, Program in Clinical Psychology, Madison, WI 53706-1380. Offers PhD. *Accreditation:* APA. *Degree requirements:* For doctorate, comprehensive exam, thesis/dissertation. *Entrance requirements:* For doctorate, GRE General Test, minimum undergraduate GPA of 3.0. Additional exam requirements/recommendations for international students: Required—TOEFL. Electronic applications accepted.

University of Wisconsin–Milwaukee, Graduate School, College of Letters and Sciences, Department of Psychology, Milwaukee, WI 53201-0413. Offers clinical psychology (MS, PhD); psychology (MS, PhD). *Accreditation:* APA (one or more programs are accredited). *Faculty:* 22 full-time (6 women). *Students:* 54 full-time (32 women), 17 part-time (11 women); includes 12 minority (3 African Americans, 2 Asian Americans or Pacific Islanders, 7 Hispanic Americans), 4 international. Average age 29. 188 applicants, 10% accepted, 14 enrolled. In 2008, 4 master's, 10 doctorates awarded. *Degree requirements:* For master's, thesis; for doctorate, variable foreign language requirement, thesis/dissertation. *Entrance requirements:* For master's and doctorate, GRE General Test, GRE Subject Test. Additional exam requirements/recommendations for international students: Required—TOEFL (minimum score 550 paper-based; 79 iBT), IELTS (minimum score 6.5). *Application deadline:* For fall admission, 1/1 priority date for domestic students; for spring admission, 9/1 for domestic students. Applications are processed on a rolling basis. Application fee: $45 ($75 for international students). *Expenses:* Tuition, area resident: Full-time $7320; part-time $165 per credit. Tuition, state resident: full-time $7320; part-time $165 per credit. Tuition, nonresident: full-time $17,840; part-time $714 per credit. Tuition and fees vary according to campus/location, program and reciprocity agreements. *Financial support:* In 2008–09, 7 research assistantships, 48 teaching assistantships were awarded; career-related internships or fieldwork and unspecified assistantships also available. Support available to part-time students. Financial award application deadline: 4/15. Total annual research expenditures: $1.3 million. *Unit head:* Hobart Davies, Representative, 414-229-6594, Fax: 414-229-5219, E-mail: hobart@uwm.edu. *Application contact:* Susan Lima, General Information Contact, 414-229-4359, Fax: 414-229-6967, E-mail: suelima@uwm.edu.

Utah State University, School of Graduate Studies, College of Education and Human Services, Department of Psychology, Logan, UT 84322. Offers clinical/counseling/school psychology (PhD); research and evaluation methodology (PhD); school counseling (MS); school psychology (MS). *Accreditation:* APA (one or more programs are accredited). Part-time and evening/weekend programs available. Postbaccalaureate distance learning degree programs offered (no on-campus study). Terminal master's awarded for partial completion of doctoral program. *Degree requirements:* For master's, thesis (for some programs); for doctorate, thesis/dissertation. *Entrance requirements:* For master's, GRE General Test (school psychology), MAT (school counseling), minimum GPA of 3.5; for doctorate, GRE General Test, minimum GPA of 3.5. Additional exam requirements/recommendations for international students: Required—TOEFL. *Faculty research:* Hearing loss detection in infancy, ADHD, eating disorders, domestic violence, neuropsychology, bilingual/Spanish speaking students/parents.

Valdosta State University, Graduate School, College of Education, Department of Psychology and Counseling, Valdosta, GA 31698. Offers clinical/counseling psychology (MS); industrial/organizational psychology (MS); school counseling (M Ed, Ed S); school psychology (Ed S). Part-time and evening/weekend programs available. *Faculty:* 16 full-time (2 women). *Students:* 65 full-time (54 women), 40 part-time (36 women); includes 32 minority (27 African Americans, 5 Hispanic Americans). Average age 27. 105 applicants, 60% accepted, 29 enrolled. In 2008, 25 master's awarded. *Degree requirements:* For master's, thesis or alternative, comprehensive written and/or oral exams; for Ed S, thesis. *Entrance requirements:* For master's and Ed S, GRE General Test or MAT. Additional exam requirements/recommendations for international students: Required—TOEFL (minimum score 523 paper-based; 193 computer-based). *Application deadline:* For fall admission, 7/1 for domestic and international students; for spring admission, 11/15 for domestic and international students. Applications are processed on a rolling basis. Application fee: $40. Electronic applications accepted. *Financial support:* In 2008–09, 2 students received support, including 2 research assistantships with full tuition reimbursements available (averaging $2,452 per year); institutionally sponsored loans and unspecified assistantships also available. Support available to part-time students. Financial award application deadline: 7/1; financial award applicants required to submit FAFSA. *Faculty research:* Using Bender-Gestalt to predict graphomotor dimensions of the draw-a-person test, neurobehavioral hemispheric dominance. *Unit head:* Dr. Robert Bauer, Chair, 229-333-5930, Fax: 229-259-5576, E-mail: bbauer@valdosta.edu. *Application contact:* Rebecca Waters, Coordinator of Graduate Admissions, 229-333-5694, Fax: 229-245-3853, E-mail: rlwaters@valdosta.edu.

Valparaiso University, Graduate Division, Department of Psychology, Valparaiso, IN 46383. Offers business management (for counseling students) (Certificate); clinical mental health counseling (MA); community counseling (MA); JD/MA. Part-time and evening/weekend programs available. *Faculty:* 7 part-time/adjunct (3 women). *Students:* 33 full-time (24 women), 16 part-time (9 women); includes 6 minority (2 African Americans, 1 Asian American or Pacific Islander, 3 Hispanic Americans), 2 international. Average age 28. In 2008, 16 master's awarded. *Degree requirements:* For master's, thesis or alternative, internship. *Entrance requirements:* For master's, minimum GPA of 3.0; 15 credits in the social/behavioral sciences (psychology, sociology, human development, etc.) with a minimum GPA of 3.0 or better; a course in introductory psychology; a recent statistics course with a B or better . Additional exam requirements/recommendations for international students: Required—TOEFL (minimum score 550 paper-based; 213 computer-based). *Application deadline:* For fall admission, 3/1 priority date for domestic students. Applications are processed on a rolling basis. Application fee: $30 ($50 for international students). Electronic applications accepted. *Financial support:* Career-related internships or fieldwork, traineeships, and unspecified assistantships available. Support available to part-time students. Financial award applicants required to submit FAFSA. *Faculty research:* Environmental psychology, human sexuality, racial identity development models, social psychology. *Unit head:* Dr. James Nelson, Director of Graduate Porgrams, 219-464-5443, Fax: 219-464-6878, E-mail: Jim.Nelson@valpo.edu. *Application contact:* Jamie Haney, Coordinator of Recruitment Activities, 219-464-5313, Fax: 219-464-5381, E-mail: Jamie.Haney@valpo.edu.

Vanguard University of Southern California, Graduate Program in Clinical Psychology, Costa Mesa, CA 92626-9601. Offers clinical psychology (MS). Part-time and evening/weekend programs available. *Faculty:* 3 full-time (all women), 5 part-time/adjunct (2 women). *Students:* 41 full-time (34 women), 27 part-time (24 women); includes 19 minority (1 African American, 2 American Indian/Alaska Native, 3 Asian Americans or Pacific Islanders, 13 Hispanic Americans). Average age 30. 93 applicants, 49% accepted, 26 enrolled. *Degree requirements:* For master's, thesis or alternative. *Entrance requirements:* For master's, minimum GPA of 3.0. Additional exam requirements/recommendations for international students: Required—TOEFL (minimum score 550 paper-based; 213 computer-based; 79 iBT). *Application deadline:* For fall admission, 4/1 priority date for domestic and international students; for winter admission, 11/1 for domestic and international students. Applications are processed on a rolling basis. Application fee: $45. Electronic applications accepted. *Expenses:* Contact institution. *Financial support:* In 2008–09, 62 students received support. Scholarships/grants and unspecified assistantships available. Financial award application deadline: 3/2; financial award applicants required to submit FAFSA. *Faculty research:* Children, play therapy, death and dying, trauma, marital and family counseling. *Unit head:* Dr. Jerre White, Director, 714-556-3610 Ext. 3550, Fax: 714-662-5226, E-mail: jwhite@vanguard.edu. *Application contact:* Asha Harrington, Graduate Psychology Coordinator, 714-556-3610 Ext. 3550, Fax: 714-662-5226, E-mail: gradpsych@vanguard.edu.

Virginia Commonwealth University, Graduate School, College of Humanities and Sciences, Department of Psychology, Program in Clinical Psychology, Richmond, VA 23284-9005. Offers PhD. *Accreditation:* APA. *Degree requirements:* For doctorate, thesis/dissertation. *Entrance requirements:* For doctorate, GRE General Test.

Virginia Polytechnic Institute and State University, Graduate School, College of Science, Department of Psychology, Blacksburg, VA 24061. Offers bio-behavioral sciences (PhD); clinical psychology (PhD); developmental psychology (PhD); industrial/organizational psychology (PhD); psychology (MS). *Accreditation:* APA (one or more programs are accredited). *Entrance requirements:* For master's and doctorate, GRE General Test. Additional exam requirements/recommendations for international students: Required—TOEFL (minimum score 550 paper-based; 213 computer-based). Electronic applications accepted. *Faculty research:* Infant development from electrophysical point of view, work motivation and personnel selection, EEG, ERP and hypnosis with reference to chronic pain, intimate violence.

Virginia State University, School of Graduate Studies, Research, and Outreach, School of Engineering, Science and Technology, Department of Psychology, Petersburg, VA 23806-0001. Offers behavioral and community health sciences (PhD); clinical health psychology (PhD); clinical psychology (MS); general psychology (MS). *Degree requirements:* For master's, one foreign language, thesis. *Entrance requirements:* For master's, GRE General Test.

Walden University, Graduate Programs, School of Psychology, Minneapolis, MN 55401. Offers clinical assessment (Post-Doctoral Certificate); clinical child psychology (Post-Doctoral Certificate); clinical psychology (Post-Doctoral Certificate); counseling psychology (Post-Doctoral Certificate); forensic psychology (MS), including forensic psychology in the community, general forensic psychology, mental health applications, program planning and evaluation in forensic settings, psychology and legal systems; general psychology (Post-Doctoral Certificate); health psychology (Post-Doctoral Certificate); organizational psychology (Post-Doctoral Certificate); organizational psychology and development (Certificate); psychology (MS, PhD), including clinical psychology, counseling psychology, crisis management and response (MS), general psychology, health psychology, leadership development and coaching (MS), media psychology (MS), organizational psychology, organizational psychology and development (MS), organizational psychology and nonprofit management (MS), program evaluation and research (MS), psychology of culture (MS), psychology, public administration, and social change (MS), school psychology, social psychology (MS), terrorism and security (MS); school psychology (Post-Doctoral Certificate); teaching online (Post-Master's Certificate). Part-time and evening/weekend programs available. Postbaccalaureate distance learning degree programs offered (minimal on-campus study). *Faculty:* 16 full-time, 190 part-time/adjunct. *Students:* 3,198 full-time (2,489 women), 810 part-time (664 women); includes 1,319 minority (1,013 African Americans, 51 American Indian/Alaska Native, 68 Asian Americans or Pacific Islanders, 187 Hispanic Americans), 72 international. Average age 40. 1,468 applicants, 60% accepted, 612 enrolled. In 2008, 203 master's, 37 doctorates awarded. Terminal master's awarded for partial completion of doctoral program. *Degree requirements:* For master's, thesis optional; for doctorate, thesis/dissertation, residency. *Entrance requirements:* For master's, bachelor's degree or equivalent in related field, minimum GPA of 2.5, two references, goal statement, official transcripts, access to computer and Internet; for doctorate, master's degree or equivalent in related field, minimum GPA of 3.0, three years related professional/academic experience, two references, goal statement, official transcripts, access to computer and Internet. Additional exam requirements/recommendations for international students: Required—TOEFL (minimum score 550 paper-based; 213 computer-based), IELTS (minimum score 6.5), TOEFL, IELTS, or Michigan English Language Assessment Battery (minimum score 82). *Application deadline:* Applications are processed on a rolling basis. Application fee: $50. Electronic applications accepted. *Expenses:* Tuition: Full-time $12,877; part-time $520 per credit. Required fees: $1230. Tuition and fees vary according to course load, degree level and program. *Financial support:* In 2008–09, 1 fellowship was awarded; Federal Work-Study, scholarships/grants, unspecified assistantships, and family tuition reduction; active duty/veteran tuition reduction; group tuition reduction; interest-free payment plans also available. Support available to part-time students. Financial award applicants required to submit FAFSA. *Unit head:* Dr. Nina Nabors, Associate Dean, 800-925-3368. *Application contact:* Jennifer Hall, 866-4-WALDEN, E-mail: info@waldenu.edu.

Washburn University, College of Arts and Sciences, Department of Psychology, Topeka, KS 66621. Offers clinical psychology (MA). Part-time programs available. *Degree requirements:* For master's, thesis. *Entrance requirements:* For master's, GRE General Test, 15 hours of course work in psychology. Electronic applications accepted. *Faculty research:* Animal behavior, correctional psychology, children's social development, metacognition and metamemory, psychology of exercise, Gibsonian Ecological Psychology, treatment of anxiety disorders.

Washington State University, Graduate School, College of Liberal Arts, Department of Psychology, Pullman, WA 99164. Offers clinical psychology (PhD); experimental psychology (PhD); psychology (MS). *Accreditation:* APA (one or more programs are accredited). *Degree requirements:* For master's, comprehensive exam (for some programs), thesis (for some programs), oral exam; for doctorate, comprehensive exam, thesis/dissertation, oral exam, written exam. *Entrance requirements:* For master's, GRE General Test, minimum GPA of 3.0, research or clinical experience, 3 letters of recommendation; for doctorate, GRE General Test, minimum GPA of 3.0, 1 course in statistics and research methodology, research or clinical experience, 3 letters of recommendation. *Faculty research:* Childhood conduct disorders, etiology of depression, treatment of reading disorders, applied behavior analysis, selective attention.

Washington University in St. Louis, Graduate School of Arts and Sciences, Department of Psychology, St. Louis, MO 63130-4899. Offers clinical psychology (PhD); general experimental psychology (PhD); social psychology (PhD). *Accreditation:* APA. *Students:* 102 full-time (63 women); includes 23 minority (6 African Americans, 13 Asian Americans or Pacific Islanders, 4 Hispanic Americans), 12 international. 291 applicants, 11% accepted, 18 enrolled. In 2008, 11 doctorates awarded. Terminal master's awarded for partial completion of doctoral program. *Degree requirements:* For doctorate, thesis/dissertation. *Entrance requirements:* For doctorate, GRE General Test. *Application deadline:* For fall admission, 12/15 priority date for domestic students. Application fee: $45. Electronic applications accepted. *Financial support:* Fellowships, research assistantships, teaching assistantships, career-related internships or fieldwork, Federal Work-Study, institutionally sponsored loans, and tuition waivers (full and partial) available. Support available to part-time students. Financial award application deadline: 1/15. *Unit head:* Dr. Randy Larsen, Chairperson, 314-935-6520. *Application contact:* Assistant to the Dean, 314-935-6880, Fax: 314-935-4887.

Wayne State University, College of Education, Division of Theoretical and Behavioral Foundations, Detroit, MI 48202. Offers counseling (M Ed, MA, Ed D, PhD, Ed S); education evaluation and research (M Ed, Ed D, PhD); educational psychology (M Ed, Ed D, PhD, Ed S); educational sociology (M Ed, Ed D, PhD, Ed S); history and philosophy of education (M Ed, Ed D, PhD); rehabilitation counseling and community inclusion (MA, Ed S); school and community psychology (MA, Ed S); school clinical psychology (Ed S). *Accreditation:* ACA (one or more programs are accredited); CORE (one or more programs are accredited). Evening/weekend programs available. *Degree requirements:* For doctorate, thesis/dissertation. *Entrance requirements:* For master's, GRE; for doctorate, GRE, interview, minimum GPA of 3.0, curriculum vitae, references. Additional exam requirements/recommendations for international students: Required—TOEFL (minimum score 550 paper-based; 213 computer-based), TWE (minimum score 6). Electronic applications accepted. *Faculty research:* Adolescents at risk, supervision of counseling.

Wayne State University, College of Liberal Arts and Sciences, Department of Psychology, Program in Psychology, Detroit, MI 48202. Offers behavioral and cognitive neuroscience (PhD); clinical psychology (PhD); cognitive and social psychology (PhD); industrial/organizational psychology (PhD); psychology (MA, MS). *Accreditation:* APA (one or more programs are accredited). *Degree requirements:* For doctorate, thesis/dissertation. *Entrance requirements:* For doctorate, GRE General Test, GRE Subject Test. Additional exam requirements/recommendations for international students: Required—TOEFL (minimum score 550 paper-based; 213 computer-based); Recommended—TWE (minimum score 6). Electronic applications accepted.

West Chester University of Pennsylvania, Office of Graduate Studies, College of Arts and Sciences, Department of Psychology, West Chester, PA 19383. Offers clinical mental health (Certificate); clinical psychology (MA); general psychology (MA); industrial psychology (MA). Part-time and evening/weekend programs available. *Students:* 63 full-time (47 women), 28 part-time (20 women); includes 5 minority (4 African Americans, 1 Hispanic American), 1 international. Average age 30. 179 applicants, 79% accepted, 43 enrolled. In 2008, 32 master's awarded. *Degree requirements:* For master's, comprehensive exam, thesis (for some programs). *Entrance requirements:* For master's, GRE General Test or MAT, minimum GPA of 3.0, psychology 3.25; three letters of reference. Additional exam requirements/recommendations for international students: Required—TOEFL (minimum score 550 paper-based; 213 computer-

based; 80 iBT). *Application deadline:* For fall admission, 4/15 priority date for domestic students, 3/15 for international students; for spring admission, 10/15 for domestic students, 9/1 for international students. Applications are processed on a rolling basis. Application fee: $35. Electronic applications accepted. *Expenses:* Tuition, state resident: full-time $6430; part-time $357 per credit. Tuition, nonresident: full-time $10,288; part-time $572 per credit. Required fees: $652.50; $50 per credit. $67 per semester. *Financial support:* In 2008–09, 9 research assistantships with full and partial tuition reimbursements (averaging $5,000 per year) were awarded; unspecified assistantships also available. Support available to part-time students. Financial award application deadline: 2/15; financial award applicants required to submit FAFSA. *Faculty research:* Animal learning and cognition. *Unit head:* Dr. Sandra Kerr, Chair, 610-436-2949, E-mail: skerr@wcupa.edu. *Application contact:* Dr. Stefani Yorges, Graduate Coordinator, 610-436-3154, E-mail: syorges@wcupa.edu.

Western Illinois University, School of Graduate Studies, College of Arts and Sciences, Department of Psychology, Macomb, IL 61455-1390. Offers clinical/community mental health (MS); general psychology (MS); psychology (MS, SSP); school psychology (SSP). Part-time programs available. *Students:* 42 full-time (21 women), 14 part-time (11 women); includes 1 minority (Asian American or Pacific Islander), 2 international. Average age 25. 66 applicants, 53% accepted. In 2008, 13 master's, 10 other advanced degrees awarded. *Degree requirements:* For master's, comprehensive exam (for some programs), thesis or alternative. *Entrance requirements:* For master's and SSP, GRE General Test. Additional exam requirements/recommendations for international students: Required—TOEFL (minimum score 550 paper-based; 213 computer-based; 80 iBT). *Application deadline:* Applications are processed on a rolling basis. Application fee: $30. Electronic applications accepted. *Expenses:* Tuition, state resident: full-time $5696; part-time $237.34 per credit hour. Tuition, nonresident: full-time $11,392; part-time $474.68 per credit hour. Required fees: $1453; $60.55 per credit hour. *Financial support:* In 2008–09, 36 students received support, including 36 research assistantships with full tuition reimbursements available (averaging $7,040 per year). Financial award applicants required to submit FAFSA. *Unit head:* Dr. Steven Dworkin, Chairperson, 309-298-1593. *Application contact:* Evelyn Hoing, Assistant Director of Graduate Studies, 309-298-1806, Fax: 309-298-2345, E-mail: grad-office@wiu.edu.

Western Michigan University, Graduate College, College of Arts and Sciences, Department of Psychology, Kalamazoo, MI 49008-5202. Offers behavior analysis (MA, PhD); clinical psychology (MA, PhD); experimental psychology (MA); industrial/organizational psychology (MA). *Accreditation:* APA (one or more programs are accredited). *Degree requirements:* For master's, variable foreign language requirement, thesis, oral exams; for doctorate, 2 foreign languages, comprehensive exam, thesis/dissertation, oral exams. *Entrance requirements:* For master's and doctorate, GRE General Test.

West Virginia University, Eberly College of Arts and Sciences, Department of Psychology, Morgantown, WV 26506. Offers behavior analysis (PhD); clinical psychology (MA, PhD); development psychology (PhD); psychology (MS). *Accreditation:* APA (one or more programs are accredited). Part-time programs available. Terminal master's awarded for partial completion of doctoral program. *Degree requirements:* For master's, thesis optional; for doctorate, comprehensive exam, thesis/dissertation. *Entrance requirements:* For master's and doctorate, GRE General Test, minimum GPA of 3.0. Additional exam requirements/recommendations for international students: Required—TOEFL. *Faculty research:* Adult and child clinical psychology, behavioral assessment and therapy, child and adolescent behavior, life span development, experimental and applied behavior analysis.

Wheaton College, Graduate School, Department of Psychology, Wheaton, IL 60187-5593. Offers clinical psychology (MA, Psy D); counseling ministries (MA). *Accreditation:* APA (one or more programs are accredited). Terminal master's awarded for partial completion of doctoral program. *Degree requirements:* For master's, thesis or alternative; for doctorate, thesis/dissertation, internship. *Entrance requirements:* For master's, GRE General Test, 18 hours of course work in psychology; for doctorate, GRE General Test.

Wichita State University, Graduate School, Fairmount College of Liberal Arts and Sciences, Department of Psychology, Wichita, KS 67260. Offers community/clinical psychology (PhD); human factors (PhD); psychology (MA). *Accreditation:* APA. Part-time programs available. *Degree requirements:* For doctorate, thesis/dissertation. *Entrance requirements:* For doctorate, GRE. Additional exam requirements/recommendations for international students: Required—TOEFL. Electronic applications accepted. *Faculty research:* Behavioral evolution, women and alcohol, behavioral medicine, delinquency prevention.

Widener University, School of Human Service Professions, Institute for Graduate Clinical Psychology, Program in Clinical Psychology, Chester, PA 19013-5792. Offers Psy D, Psy D/M Ed, Psy D/MA, Psy D/MBA, Psy D/MHA, Psy D/MPA, Psy D/MSHR. *Accreditation:* APA. *Students:* Average age 24. In 2008, 26 doctorates awarded. *Degree requirements:* For doctorate, thesis/dissertation, final oral and written qualifying exams. *Entrance requirements:* For doctorate, GRE General Test or MAT. *Application deadline:* For fall admission, 12/31 for domestic students. Application fee: $75. Electronic applications accepted. *Expenses:* Contact institution. *Financial support:* Career-related internships or fieldwork, Federal Work-Study, institutionally sponsored loans, scholarships/grants, and stipends available. Financial award application deadline: 4/15. *Faculty research:* Cognitive and personality diagnostic testing, depression, child and adolescent competencies, learning disabilities, family therapy. *Unit head:* Dr. Virginia Brabender, Associate Dean/Director, 610-499-1208, Fax: 610-499-4625, E-mail: graduate.psychology@widener.edu. *Application contact:* Ellen Madison, Admissions Coordinator, 611-499-1206, Fax: 610-499-4625, E-mail: ellen.t.madison@widener.edu.

See Close-Up on page 1153.

Widener University, School of Human Service Professions, Institute for Graduate Clinical Psychology, Program in Clinical Psychology and Health and Medical Services Administration, Chester, PA 19013-5792. Offers Psy D/MBA, Psy D/MHA. *Accreditation:* APA (one or more programs are accredited); CAHME. *Faculty:* 15 full-time (6 women), 18 part-time/adjunct (10 women). *Students:* 6 full-time (4 women), 1 part-time (0 women); includes 1 minority (African American). Average age 28. *Application deadline:* For fall admission, 12/31 for domestic students. Application fee: $75. Electronic applications accepted. *Financial support:* Career-related internships or fieldwork, Federal Work-Study, and institutionally sponsored loans available. Financial award application deadline: 5/31. *Faculty research:* Psychosocial competence, family systems, medical care systems and financing. *Unit head:* Dr. Hal Shorey, Director, 610-499-4598, Fax: 610-499-4625. *Application contact:* Admissions Coordinator

See Close-Up on page 1153.

William Paterson University of New Jersey, College of the Humanities and Social Sciences, Program in Clinical and Counseling Psychology, Wayne, NJ 07470-8420. Offers MA. *Entrance requirements:* For master's, GRE General Test. Electronic applications accepted.

Wisconsin School of Professional Psychology, Program in Clinical Psychology, Milwaukee, WI 53225-4960. Offers MA, Psy D. *Accreditation:* APA. Part-time and evening/weekend programs available. Terminal master's awarded for partial completion of doctoral program. *Degree requirements:* For master's, candidacy exam, 500 hours of supervised clinical practica; for doctorate, thesis/dissertation, 1 year clinical intern and practicum experience (2000 hrs), candidacy and clinical exams. *Entrance requirements:* For master's, GRE General Test, GRE Subject Test, bachelor's degree in psychology, writing sample; for doctorate, GRE General Test, GRE Subject Test, master's degree in clinical psychology or equivalent, writing sample. *Faculty research:* Violence prevention, psychology of women, forensic psychology, custody evaluation, aging, harm reduction in AODA.

Wright Institute, Program in Clinical Psychology, Berkeley, CA 94704-1796. Offers Psy D. *Accreditation:* APA. *Degree requirements:* For doctorate, thesis/dissertation. *Entrance*

Clinical Psychology

Wright Institute (continued)
requirements: Additional exam requirements/recommendations for international students: Required—TOEFL (minimum score 600 paper-based). Electronic applications accepted.

Wright State University, School of Professional Psychology, Dayton, OH 45435. Offers clinical psychology (Psy D). *Accreditation:* APA. *Degree requirements:* For doctorate, thesis/dissertation. *Entrance requirements:* For doctorate, GRE General Test, GRE Subject Test. Additional exam requirements/recommendations for international students: Required—TOEFL. *Expenses:* Contact institution.

Xavier University, College of Social Sciences, Health and Education, Department of Psychology, Cincinnati, OH 45207. Offers clinical psychology (Psy D); psychology (MA), including general experimental, industrial-organizational. *Accreditation:* APA (one or more programs are accredited). *Faculty:* 16 full-time (8 women), 5 part-time/adjunct (3 women). *Students:* 83 full-time (61 women), 30 part-time (22 women); includes 8 minority (4 African Americans, 4 Asian Americans or Pacific Islanders), 2 international. Average age 27. 242 applicants, 31% accepted, 25 enrolled. In 2008, 27 master's, 12 doctorates awarded. *Degree requirements:* For master's, comprehensive exam, thesis, internship; for doctorate, comprehensive exam, thesis/dissertation, internship. *Entrance requirements:* For master's and doctorate, GRE. Additional exam requirements/recommendations for international students: Required—TOEFL. *Application deadline:* For fall admission, 1/15 for domestic and international students. Application fee: $35. Electronic applications accepted. *Expenses:* Contact institution. *Financial support:* In 2008–09, 57 students received support, including 39 research assistantships with partial tuition reimbursements available, 18 teaching assistantships with partial tuition reimbursements available. Financial award application deadline: 3/1; financial award applicants required to submit FAFSA. *Unit head:* Dr. Christine M. Dacey, Chair, 513-745-3533, Fax: 513-745-3327, E-mail: dacey@xavier.edu. *Application contact:* Margaret Maybury, Assistant Director, Enrollment and Student Services, 513-745-1053, Fax: 513-745-3347, E-mail: maybury@xavier.edu.

Yale University, Graduate School of Arts and Sciences, Department of Psychology, New Haven, CT 06520. Offers behavioral neuroscience (PhD); clinical psychology (PhD); cognitive psychology (PhD); developmental psychology (PhD); social/personality psychology (PhD). *Accreditation:* APA. *Degree requirements:* For doctorate, thesis/dissertation. *Entrance requirements:* For doctorate, GRE General Test.

Yeshiva University, Ferkauf Graduate School of Psychology, Program in Clinical Psychology, New York, NY 10033-3201. Offers Psy D. *Accreditation:* APA. Part-time programs available. *Degree requirements:* For doctorate, comprehensive exam, thesis/dissertation. *Entrance requirements:* For doctorate, GRE General Test. *Faculty research:* Psychotherapy, family therapy, psychoanalysis, cognitive behavior therapy.

Yeshiva University, Ferkauf Graduate School of Psychology, Program in School/Clinical-Child Psychology, New York, NY 10033-3201. Offers Psy D. *Accreditation:* APA. Part-time programs available. *Degree requirements:* For doctorate, comprehensive exam, thesis/dissertation. *Entrance requirements:* For doctorate, GRE General Test. *Faculty research:* Testing, early childhood intervention, child and adolescent psychotherapy, clinical child psychology.

Cognitive Sciences

Arizona State University, Graduate College, College of Liberal Arts and Sciences, Division of Natural Sciences, Department of Psychology, Tempe, AZ 85287. Offers behavioral neuroscience (PhD); clinical psychology (PhD); cognition, action and perception (PhD); developmental psychology (PhD); quantitative psychology (PhD); social psychology (PhD). *Accreditation:* APA. *Degree requirements:* For doctorate, thesis/dissertation. *Entrance requirements:* For doctorate, GRE General Test, GRE Subject Test.

Ball State University, Graduate School, College of Sciences and Humanities, Department of Psychological Science, Program in Cognitive and Social Processes, Muncie, IN 47306-1099. Offers MA.

Boston University, Graduate School of Arts and Sciences, Department of Cognitive and Neural Systems, Boston, MA 02215. Offers MA, PhD. Terminal master's awarded for partial completion of doctoral program. *Degree requirements:* For master's, one foreign language, comprehensive exam; for doctorate, one foreign language, comprehensive exam, thesis/dissertation. *Entrance requirements:* For master's and doctorate, GRE General Test, GRE Subject Test (recommended), 3 letters of recommendation. Additional exam requirements/recommendations for international students: Required—TOEFL (minimum score 550 paper-based; 213 computer-based).

Brandeis University, Graduate School of Arts and Sciences, Department of Psychology, Waltham, MA 02454-9110. Offers cognitive neuroscience (PhD); general psychology (MA); social/developmental psychology (PhD). MA program offered to students enrolled in PhD program only. *Degree requirements:* For doctorate, comprehensive exam, thesis/dissertation. *Entrance requirements:* For doctorate, GRE General Test, GRE Subject Test (recommended), 3 letters of recommendation. Additional exam requirements/recommendations for international students: Required—TOEFL (minimum score 600 paper-based; 250 computer-based). Electronic applications accepted. *Faculty research:* Development, cognition, social aging, perception.

Brown University, Graduate School, Department of Cognitive and Linguistic Sciences, Providence, RI 02912. Offers cognitive science (Sc M, PhD); linguistics (AM, PhD). *Degree requirements:* For master's, one foreign language, thesis or alternative; for doctorate, 2 foreign languages, thesis/dissertation.

Brown University, Graduate School, Department of Psychology, Providence, RI 02912. Offers behavioral neuroscience (PhD); cognitive processes (PhD); sensation and perception (PhD); social/developmental (PhD); MS/PhD. *Degree requirements:* For doctorate, thesis/dissertation. *Entrance requirements:* For doctorate, GRE General Test, GRE Subject Test.

Carleton University, Faculty of Graduate Studies, Faculty of Arts and Social Sciences, Program in Cognitive Science, Ottawa, ON K1S 5B6, Canada. Offers PhD. *Degree requirements:* For doctorate, thesis/dissertation. *Entrance requirements:* For doctorate, master's degree. *Faculty research:* Language, attention, artificial intelligence, symbol recognition, consciousness.

Carnegie Mellon University, College of Humanities and Social Sciences, Department of Psychology, Area of Cognitive Neuroscience, Pittsburgh, PA 15213-3891. Offers PhD. *Degree requirements:* For doctorate, comprehensive exam, thesis/dissertation. *Entrance requirements:* For doctorate, GRE General Test. Additional exam requirements/recommendations for international students: Required—TOEFL.

Carnegie Mellon University, College of Humanities and Social Sciences, Department of Psychology, Area of Cognitive Psychology, Pittsburgh, PA 15213-3891. Offers PhD. *Degree requirements:* For doctorate, comprehensive exam, thesis/dissertation. *Entrance requirements:* For doctorate, GRE General Test. Additional exam requirements/recommendations for international students: Required—TOEFL.

Case Western Reserve University, School of Graduate Studies, Department of Cognitive Science, Cleveland, OH 44106. Offers cognitive linguistics (MA). Part-time programs available. *Degree requirements:* For master's, thesis. *Entrance requirements:* For master's, GRE, writing sample, recommendations. Additional exam requirements/recommendations for international students: Required—TOEFL. Electronic applications accepted. *Faculty research:* Application of metaphor and conceptual integration theories to a wide range of non-linguistic phenomena.

Claremont Graduate University, Graduate Programs, School of Behavioral and Organizational Sciences, Department of Psychology, Claremont, CA 91711-6160. Offers advanced study in evaluation (Certificate); cognitive psychology (MA, PhD); developmental psychology (MA, PhD); evaluation and applied research methods (MA, PhD); health behavior research and evaluation (MA, PhD); human resource development and evaluation (MA); industrial/organizational psychology (MA, PhD); organizational behavior (MA, PhD); organizational psychology (MA, PhD); social psychology (MA, PhD); MBA/PhD. Part-time programs available. *Faculty:* 17 full-time (7 women), 1 part-time/adjunct (0 women). *Students:* 218 full-time (158 women), 24 part-time (18 women); includes 51 minority (15 African Americans, 1 American Indian/Alaska Native, 22 Asian Americans or Pacific Islanders, 13 Hispanic Americans), 11 international. Average age 30. In 2008, 38 master's, 12 doctorates, 2 other advanced degrees awarded. Terminal master's awarded for partial completion of doctoral program. *Entrance requirements:* For master's and doctorate, GRE General Test. Additional exam requirements/recommendations for international students: Required—TOEFL (minimum score 550 paper-based; 213 computer-based; 80 iBT). *Application deadline:* For fall admission, 1/15 priority date for domestic students. Applications are processed on a rolling basis. Application fee: $60. Electronic applications accepted. *Expenses:* Tuition: Full-time $33,698; part-time $1465 per unit. Required fees: $310; $155 per semester. Tuition and fees vary according to program. *Financial support:* Fellowships, research assistantships, teaching assistantships, Federal Work-Study, institutionally sponsored loans, scholarships/grants, and tuition waivers (full and partial) available. Support available to part-time students. Financial award application deadline: 2/15; financial award applicants required to submit FAFSA. *Faculty research:* Social intervention, diversity in organizations, eyewitness memory, aging and cognition, drug policy. *Unit head:* Stewart Donaldson, Dean, 909-607-9001, Fax: 909-621-8905, E-mail: stewart.donaldson@cgu.edu. *Application contact:* Paul Thomas, Director, External Affairs, 909-607-9016, Fax: 909-621-8905, E-mail: paul.thomas@cgu.edu.

Cornell University, Graduate School, Graduate Fields of Arts and Sciences, Field of Information Science, Ithaca, NY 14853-0001. Offers cognition (PhD); human computer interaction (PhD); information systems (PhD); social aspects of information (PhD). *Faculty:* 32 full-time (10 women). *Students:* 13 full-time (4 women), 7 international. Average age 34. 58 applicants, 5% accepted, 2 enrolled. *Degree requirements:* For doctorate, comprehensive exam, thesis/dissertation. *Entrance requirements:* For doctorate, GRE General Test, 3 letters of recommendation. Additional exam requirements/recommendations for international students: Required—TOEFL (minimum score 550 paper-based; 213 computer-based; 77 iBT). *Application deadline:* For fall admission, 1/1 for domestic students. Application fee: $70. Electronic applications accepted. *Expenses:* Tuition: Full-time $29,500. Required fees: $70. Full-time tuition and fees vary according to degree level, program and student level. *Financial support:* In 2008–09, 10 students received support, including 2 fellowships with full tuition reimbursements available, 4 research assistantships with full tuition reimbursements available, 4 teaching assistantships with full tuition reimbursements available; institutionally sponsored loans, scholarships/grants, tuition waivers (full and partial), and unspecified assistantships also available. Financial award applicants required to submit FAFSA. *Faculty research:* Digital libraries, game theory, data mining, human-computer interaction, computational linguistics. *Unit head:* Director of Graduate Studies, 607-255-5925. *Application contact:* Graduate Field Assistant, 607-255-5925, E-mail: info@infosci.cornell.edu.

Dartmouth College, Arts and Sciences Graduate Programs, Department of Psychological and Brain Sciences, Program in Cognitive Neuroscience, Hanover, NH 03755. Offers PhD.

Duke University, Graduate School, Department of Psychology, Durham, NC 27708-0586. Offers biological psychology (PhD); clinical psychology (PhD); cognitive psychology (PhD); developmental psychology (PhD); experimental psychology (PhD); health psychology (PhD); human social development (PhD); JD/MA. *Accreditation:* APA (one or more programs are accredited). *Degree requirements:* For doctorate, thesis/dissertation. *Entrance requirements:* For doctorate, GRE General Test. Additional exam requirements/recommendations for international students: Required—TOEFL (minimum score 550 paper-based; 213 computer-based; 83 iBT), IELTS (minimum score 7). Electronic applications accepted.

Emory University, Graduate School of Arts and Sciences, Department of Psychology, Atlanta, GA 30322-1100. Offers clinical psychology (PhD); cognition and development (PhD); neuroscience and animal behavior (PhD). *Accreditation:* APA. *Degree requirements:* For doctorate, comprehensive exam, thesis/dissertation. *Entrance requirements:* For doctorate, GRE General Test, minimum GPA of 3.25. Additional exam requirements/recommendations for international students: Required—TOEFL. Electronic applications accepted. *Faculty research:* Neuroscience and animal behavior; adult and child psychopathology, cognition development assessment.

Florida State University, Graduate Studies, College of Arts and Sciences, Department of Psychology, Program in Cognitive Psychology, Tallahassee, FL 32306. Offers PhD. *Degree requirements:* For doctorate, thesis/dissertation, preliminary exam. *Entrance requirements:* For doctorate, GRE General Test, minimum GPA of 3.0, research experience, letters of recommendation. Additional exam requirements/recommendations for international students: Required—TOEFL (minimum score 550 paper-based; 213 computer-based; 80 iBT). Electronic applications accepted. *Faculty research:* Memory, learning and reading disabilities, expert performance, aging.

The George Washington University, Columbian College of Arts and Sciences, Department of Psychology, Washington, DC 20052. Offers applied social psychology (PhD); clinical psychology (PhD); cognitive neuroscience (PhD). *Accreditation:* APA. Part-time and evening/weekend programs available. *Faculty:* 27 full-time (14 women), 19 part-time/adjunct (12 women). *Students:* 119 full-time (99 women), 83 part-time (64 women); includes 56 minority (14 African Americans, 2 American Indian/Alaska Native, 24 Asian Americans or Pacific Islanders, 16 Hispanic Americans), 6 international. Average age 29. 873 applicants, 5% accepted, 47 enrolled. In 2008, 41 doctorates awarded. *Degree requirements:* For doctorate, thesis/dissertation or alternative, general exam. *Entrance requirements:* For doctorate, GRE General Test, minimum GPA of 3.0. Additional exam requirements/recommendations for international students: Required—TOEFL (minimum score 550 paper-based; 213 computer-based; 80 iBT). *Application deadline:* For fall admission, 1/15 for domestic and international students. Application fee: $60. *Financial support:* In 2008–09, 62 students received support; fellowships with tuition reimbursements available, teaching assistantships with tuition reimbursements available, career-related internships or fieldwork, Federal Work-Study, and tuition waivers available. *Unit head:* Dr. Paul Poppen, Chair, 202-994-6324, E-mail: pjp@gwu.edu. *Application contact:* Information Contact, 202-994-6320, Fax: 202-994-1602, E-mail: psydept@gwu.edu.

Graduate School and University Center of the City University of New York, Graduate Studies, Program in Psychology, New York, NY 10016-4039. Offers basic applied neurocognition

(PhD); biopsychology (PhD); clinical psychology (PhD); developmental psychology (PhD); environmental psychology (PhD); experimental psychology (PhD); industrial psychology (PhD); learning processes (PhD); neuropsychology (PhD); psychology (PhD); social personality (PhD). *Degree requirements:* For doctorate, one foreign language, thesis/dissertation. *Entrance requirements:* For doctorate, GRE General Test. Additional exam requirements/recommendations for international students: Required—TOEFL. Electronic applications accepted.

Harvard University, Graduate School of Arts and Sciences, Department of Psychology, Cambridge, MA 02138. Offers psychology (PhD), including behavior and decision analysis, cognition, developmental psychology, experimental psychology, personality, psychobiology, psychopathology; social psychology (PhD). *Degree requirements:* For doctorate, thesis/dissertation, general exams. *Entrance requirements:* For doctorate, GRE General Test. Additional exam requirements/recommendations for international students: Required—TOEFL. *Expenses:* Tuition: Full-time $32,556. Required fees: $1426. Full-time tuition and fees vary according to program and student level.

Harvard University, Graduate School of Education, Master's Programs in Education, Cambridge, MA 02138. Offers arts in education (Ed M); education policy and management (Ed M); higher education (Ed M); human development and psychology (Ed M); international education policy (Ed M); language and literacy (Ed M); learning and teaching (Ed M); mid-career mathematics and science (teaching certificate) (Ed M); mind brain and education (Ed M); risk and prevention (Ed M); school leadership (Ed M); special studies (Ed M); teaching and curriculum (teaching certificate) (Ed M); technology innovation and education (Ed M). Part-time programs available. *Faculty:* 61 full-time (29 women), 40 part-time/adjunct (24 women). *Students:* 504 full-time (403 women), 66 part-time (53 women); includes 129 minority (40 African Americans, 1 American Indian/Alaska Native, 59 Asian Americans or Pacific Islanders, 29 Hispanic Americans), 84 international. Average age 28. 1,255 applicants, 59% accepted, 533 enrolled. In 2008, 610 master's awarded. *Entrance requirements:* For master's, GRE General Test, 3 letters of recommendation, official transcripts, statement of purpose. Additional exam requirements/recommendations for international students: Required—TOEFL (minimum score 600 paper-based; 250 computer-based; 100 iBT), TWE (minimum score 5). *Application deadline:* For fall admission, 1/5 for domestic and international students. Application fee: $85. Electronic applications accepted. *Expenses:* Contact institution. *Financial support:* In 2008–09, 336 students received support, including 30 fellowships with full and partial tuition reimbursements available (averaging $15,975 per year); career-related internships or fieldwork, Federal Work-Study, institutionally sponsored loans, scholarships/grants, health care benefits, tuition waivers (full and partial), and unspecified assistantships also available. Support available to part-time students. Financial award application deadline: 2/1; financial award applicants required to submit FAFSA. *Faculty research:* Learning and development; educational leadership and organizations; educational policy analysis. Total annual research expenditures: $14.7 million. *Unit head:* Jennifer L. Petrallia, Assistant Dean for Master's Studies, 617-495-8445. *Application contact:* Information Contact, 617-495-3414, Fax: 617-496-3577, E-mail: gseadmissions@harvard.edu.

Hunter College of the City University of New York, Graduate School, School of Arts and Sciences, Department of Psychology, New York, NY 10021-5085. Offers applied and evaluative psychology (MA); biopsychology and comparative psychology (MA); social, cognitive, and developmental psychology (MA). Part-time and evening/weekend programs available. *Faculty:* 15 full-time (7 women), 2 part-time/adjunct (0 women). *Students:* 9 full-time (8 women), 55 part-time (43 women); includes 9 minority (2 African Americans, 1 Asian American or Pacific Islander, 6 Hispanic Americans). Average age 29. 107 applicants, 42% accepted, 17 enrolled. In 2008, 29 master's awarded. *Degree requirements:* For master's, comprehensive exam, thesis. *Entrance requirements:* For master's, GRE General Test, minimum 12 credits of course work in psychology, including statistics and experimental psychology; 2 letters of recommendation. Additional exam requirements/recommendations for international students: Required—TOEFL. *Application deadline:* For fall admission, 4/1 for domestic students, 2/1 for international students; for spring admission, 11/1 for domestic students, 9/1 for international students. Applications are processed on a rolling basis. Application fee: $125. *Financial support:* Federal Work-Study, scholarships/grants, and tuition waivers (partial) available. Support available to part-time students. *Faculty research:* Personality, cognitive and linguistic development, hormonal and neural control of behavior, gender and culture, social cognition of health and attitudes. *Unit head:* Dr. Jeffrey Parsons, Chairperson, 212-772-5550, Fax: 212-772-5620, E-mail: jeffrey.parsons@hunter.cuny.edu. *Application contact:* Martin Braun, MA Program Director (Acting), 212-772-4482, Fax: 212-650-3336, E-mail: cbraun@hunter.cuny.edu.

Indiana University Bloomington, University Graduate School, College of Arts and Sciences, Cognitive Science Program, Bloomington, IN 47406-7512. Offers PhD. *Faculty:* 76 full-time (17 women). *Students:* 12 full-time (3 women); includes 1 minority (Hispanic American), 5 international. Average age 31. 49 applicants, 10% accepted, 2 enrolled. In 2008, 6 doctorates awarded. *Degree requirements:* For doctorate, comprehensive exam, thesis/dissertation. *Entrance requirements:* For doctorate, GRE, 3 letters of reference, statement of purpose, transcripts, departmental questions form. Additional exam requirements/recommendations for international students: Required—TOEFL (minimum score 600 paper-based; 94 iBT). *Application deadline:* For fall admission, 1/15 for domestic students, 12/1 for international students. Application fee: $50 ($60 for international students). Electronic applications accepted. *Expenses:* Tuition, area resident: Part-time $291.97 per credit hour. Tuition, state resident: part-time $291.97 per credit hour. Tuition, nonresident: part-time $850.33 per credit hour. Required fees: $110 per semester. Tuition and fees vary according to course load and program. *Financial support:* In 2008–09, 13 students received support, including 2 fellowships (averaging $20,000 per year), 3 research assistantships (averaging $17,850 per year), 5 teaching assistantships (averaging $17,850 per year). *Faculty research:* Learning concepts, neural network models, language, animal cognition, dynamic and robotics systems approaches to behavior and cognition. *Unit head:* Robert Goldstone, Director, 812-856-3889, E-mail: rgoldsto@indiana.edu. *Application contact:* Susan Towle, Information Contact, 812-855-0031, E-mail: stowle@indiana.edu.

Indiana University Bloomington, University Graduate School, College of Arts and Sciences, Department of Psychological and Brain Sciences, Bloomington, IN 47405-7000. Offers biology and behavior (PhD); clinical science (PhD); cognitive psychology (PhD); developmental psychology (PhD); psychological and brain sciences (MA); social psychology (PhD). *Accreditation:* APA (one or more programs are accredited). *Faculty:* 53 full-time (16 women). *Students:* 95 full-time (52 women), 1 part-time (0 women); includes 11 minority (3 African Americans, 3 Asian Americans or Pacific Islanders, 5 Hispanic Americans), 18 international. Average age 28. 210 applicants, 15% accepted, 17 enrolled. In 2008, 1 master's, 10 doctorates awarded. *Degree requirements:* For doctorate, comprehensive exam, thesis/dissertation, 1st and 2nd year projects, 1 year as associate instructor, qualifying exam, student teaching. *Entrance requirements:* For doctorate, GRE. Additional exam requirements/recommendations for international students: Required—TOEFL (minimum score 550 paper-based; 213 computer-based). *Application deadline:* For fall admission, 12/15 for domestic students, 12/1 for international students. Application fee: $50 ($60 for international students). Electronic applications accepted. *Expenses:* Tuition, area resident: Part-time $291.97 per credit hour. Tuition, state resident: part-time $291.97 per credit hour. Tuition, nonresident: part-time $850.33 per credit hour. Required fees: $110 per semester. Tuition and fees vary according to course load and program. *Financial support:* Fellowships with full tuition reimbursements, research assistantships with full tuition reimbursements, teaching assistantships with full tuition reimbursements, scholarships/grants, health care benefits, and unspecified assistantships also available. *Unit head:* Dr. Linda B. Smith, Chair, 812-855-3991, Fax: 812-855-4691, E-mail: smith4@indiana.edu. *Application contact:* Patricia G. Crouch, Academic Services Coordinator, 812-855-4528, Fax: 812-855-4691, E-mail: pcrouch@indiana.edu.

Iowa State University of Science and Technology, Graduate College, College of Liberal Arts and Sciences, Department of Psychology, Ames, IA 50011. Offers cognitive psychology (PhD); counseling psychology (PhD); social psychology (PhD). *Accreditation:* APA. *Faculty:* 25 full-time (8 women), 8 part-time/adjunct (4 women). *Students:* 63 full-time (43 women); includes 10 minority (3 African Americans, 7 Asian Americans or Pacific Islanders), 4 international. Average age 26. 117 applicants, 14% accepted, 11 enrolled. In 2008, 8 doctorates awarded. *Degree requirements:* For doctorate, comprehensive exam, thesis/dissertation. *Entrance requirements:* For doctorate, GRE General Test, GRE Subject Test (psychology). Additional exam requirements/recommendations for international students: Required—TOEFL (minimum score 560 paper-based; 220 computer-based). *Application deadline:* For fall admission, 1/5 priority date for domestic and international students. Application fee: $30 ($70 for international students). Electronic applications accepted. *Expenses:* Tuition, area resident: Full-time $6446; part-time $359 per credit. Tuition, state resident: full-time $6446; part-time $359 per credit. Tuition, nonresident: full-time $17,330; part-time $963 per credit. Required fees: $790; $249.25 per semester. Tuition and fees vary according to course load and program. *Financial support:* In 2008–09, 45 students received support, including 2 fellowships with full tuition reimbursements available (averaging $14,055 per year), 13 research assistantships with full tuition reimbursements available (averaging $12,200 per year), 30 teaching assistantships with full tuition reimbursements available (averaging $12,200 per year); scholarships/grants, health care benefits, and unspecified assistantships also available. *Faculty research:* Counseling psychology, cognitive psychology, social psychology, health psychology, psychology and public policy. Total annual research expenditures: $2 million. *Unit head:* Dr. Stephanie Madon, Director of Graduate Education, 515-294-1742, Fax: 515-294-6424, E-mail: madon@iastate.edu. *Application contact:* Ann K Schmidt, Graduate Admissions Secretary, 515-294-1743, Fax: 515-294-6424, E-mail: psychadm@iastate.edu.

The Johns Hopkins University, Zanvyl Krieger School of Arts and Sciences, Department of Cognitive Science, Baltimore, MD 21218-2699. Offers PhD. *Degree requirements:* For doctorate, one foreign language, thesis/dissertation, 2 research papers. *Entrance requirements:* For doctorate, GRE General Test, letters of recommendation, sample of work. Additional exam requirements/recommendations for international students: Required—TOEFL (minimum score 600 paper-based; 250 computer-based). Electronic applications accepted. *Faculty research:* Acquisition and development, cognitive neuropsychology and neuroscience, computational studies, psycholinguistics and cognitive psychology, theoretical linguistics.

Louisiana State University and Agricultural and Mechanical College, Graduate School, College of Arts and Sciences, Department of Psychology, Baton Rouge, LA 70803. Offers biological psychology (MA, PhD); clinical psychology (MA, PhD); cognitive psychology (MA, PhD); developmental psychology (MA, PhD); industrial/organizational psychology (MA, PhD); school psychology (MA, PhD). *Accreditation:* APA (one or more programs are accredited). Terminal master's awarded for partial completion of doctoral program. *Degree requirements:* For master's, thesis; for doctorate, thesis/dissertation, 1 year internship. *Entrance requirements:* For master's and doctorate, GRE General Test, minimum GPA of 3.0. Additional exam requirements/recommendations for international students: Required—TOEFL (minimum score 550 paper-based; 213 computer-based; 79 iBT). Electronic applications accepted. *Faculty research:* Clinical psychology, autism, anxiety, addition, neuro-psychology, school psychology, cognitive psychology, experimental psychology.

Loyola University Chicago, Graduate School, Department of Psychology, Program in Human Perception, Chicago, IL 60611-2196. Offers MS. *Students:* 1 (woman) part-time. Average age 38. In 2008, 1 master's awarded. *Entrance requirements:* For master's, two letters of recommendation, 3.5 GPA. Application fee: $50. *Expenses:* Tuition: Full-time $13,500; part-time $750 per credit hour. Required fees: $60 per semester. Full-time tuition and fees vary according to program. *Faculty research:* Auditory information processing, visual information processing, attention, sensory memory, decision theory. *Unit head:* Dr. Raymond Dye, Program Director, 773-508-3018, Fax: 773-508-8713, E-mail: rdye@luc.edu. *Application contact:* Ron Martin, Assistant Director of Enrollment Management, 312-915-8950, Fax: 312-915-8905, E-mail: gradapp@luc.edu.

Massachusetts Institute of Technology, School of Science, Department of Brain and Cognitive Sciences, Cambridge, MA 02139-4307. Offers cognitive science (PhD); neuroscience (PhD). *Degree requirements:* For doctorate, comprehensive exam, thesis/dissertation. *Entrance requirements:* For doctorate, GRE General Test. Additional exam requirements/recommendations for international students: Required—TOEFL (minimum score 577 paper-based; 233 computer-based). Electronic applications accepted. *Faculty research:* Vision, learning and memory, motor control, plasticity.

Mississippi State University, College of Arts and Sciences, Department of Psychology, Mississippi State, MS 39762. Offers clinical psychology (MS); cognitive science (PhD); experimental psychology (MS). Terminal master's awarded for partial completion of doctoral program. *Degree requirements:* For master's, comprehensive exam, thesis; for doctorate, thesis/dissertation, qualifying exam, comprehensive written and oral exam. *Entrance requirements:* For master's, GRE General Test, minimum GPA of 2.75; for doctorate, GRE General Test, proficiency in at least 1 computer language. Additional exam requirements/recommendations for international students: Required—TOEFL. *Faculty research:* Personality type, alcoholism, blindness and low vision, mental retardation, language comprehension.

New York University, Graduate School of Arts and Science, Department of Psychology, New York, NY 10012-1019. Offers cognition and perception (PhD); community psychology (PhD); general psychology (MA); industrial/organizational psychology (MA); psychotherapy and psychoanalysis (Advanced Certificate); social/personality psychology (PhD). Part-time programs available. Terminal master's awarded for partial completion of doctoral program. *Degree requirements:* For master's, comprehensive exam, thesis or alternative; for doctorate, thesis/dissertation. *Entrance requirements:* For master's, GRE General Test, minimum GPA of 3.0; for doctorate, GRE General Test, GRE Subject Test; for Advanced Certificate, doctoral degree, minimum GPA of 3.0. Additional exam requirements/recommendations for international students: Required—TOEFL. *Faculty research:* Vision, memory, social cognition, social and cognitive development, relationships.

North Dakota State University, College of Graduate and Interdisciplinary Studies, College of Science and Mathematics, Department of Psychology, Fargo, ND 58105. Offers clinical psychology (MS); cognitive and visual neuroscience (PhD); health and social psychology (PhD); psychology (MS). *Faculty:* 18 full-time (4 women), 2 part-time/adjunct (1 woman). *Students:* 36 full-time (27 women); includes 4 minority (1 African American, 2 Asian Americans or Pacific Islanders, 1 Hispanic American), 1 international. Average age 24. 48 applicants, 33% accepted, 10 enrolled. In 2008, 3 master's, 1 doctorate awarded. *Degree requirements:* For master's, thesis; for doctorate, thesis/dissertation. *Entrance requirements:* For master's and doctorate, GRE General Test, GRE Subject Test. Additional exam requirements/recommendations for international students: Required—TOEFL (minimum score 525 paper-based; 197 computer-based; 71 iBT). *Application deadline:* For fall admission, 3/1 for domestic and international students. Application fee: $45 ($60 for international students). Electronic applications accepted. *Financial support:* In 2008–09, 36 students received support, including 2 fellowships with full tuition reimbursements available (averaging $16,000 per year), 23 research assistantships with full tuition reimbursements available (averaging $16,000 per year), 11 teaching assistantships with full tuition reimbursements available (averaging $6,000 per year); career-related internships or fieldwork, Federal Work-Study, institutionally sponsored loans, tuition waivers (full and partial), and unspecified assistantships also available. Support available to part-time students. Financial award application deadline: 3/1. *Faculty research:* Cognition science, neuropsychology, group behavior, applied behavior analysis, behavior therapy. Total annual research expenditures: $2 million. *Unit head:* Dr. Paul D. Rokke, Chair, 701-231-8622, Fax: 701-231-8426, E-mail: paul.rokke@ndsu.edu. *Application contact:* Dr. Paul D. Rokke, Chair, 701-231-8622, Fax: 701-231-8426, E-mail: paul.rokke@ndsu.edu.

Northwestern University, The Graduate School, Judd A. and Marjorie Weinberg College of Arts and Sciences, Department of Psychology, Evanston, IL 60208. Offers brain, behavior and cognition (PhD); clinical psychology (PhD); cognitive psychology (PhD); personality (PhD); social psychology (PhD); JD/PhD. Admissions and degrees offered through The Graduate School. *Accreditation:* APA (one or more programs are accredited). Part-time programs available.

Cognitive Sciences

Northwestern University (continued)
Degree requirements: For doctorate, thesis/dissertation. *Entrance requirements:* For doctorate, GRE General Test, GRE Subject Test. Additional exam requirements/recommendations for international students: Required—TOEFL. Electronic applications accepted. *Faculty research:* Memory and higher order cognition, anxiety and depression, effectiveness of psychotherapy, social cognition, molecular basis of memory.

The Ohio State University, Graduate School, College of Social and Behavioral Sciences, School of Social and Behavioral Science, Department of Psychology, Columbus, OH 43210. Offers behavioral neuroscience (PhD); clinical psychology (PhD); cognitive psychology (PhD); developmental psychology (PhD); mental retardation and developmental disabilities (PhD); psychology (MA); quantitative psychology (PhD); social psychology (PhD). *Accreditation:* APA (one or more programs are accredited). *Degree requirements:* For doctorate, thesis/dissertation. *Entrance requirements:* For master's and doctorate, GRE General Test. Additional exam requirements/recommendations for international students: Required—TOEFL (minimum score 600 paper-based; 250 computer-based). Electronic applications accepted.

Penn State University Park, Graduate School, College of the Liberal Arts, Department of Psychology, State College, University Park, PA 16802-1503. Offers clinical psychology (MS, PhD); cognitive psychology (MS, PhD); developmental psychology (MS, PhD); industrial/organizational psychology (MS, PhD); psychobiology (MS, PhD); social psychology (MS, PhD). *Accreditation:* APA (one or more programs are accredited).

Queen's University at Kingston, School of Graduate Studies and Research, Faculty of Arts and Sciences, Department of Psychology, Kingston, ON K7L 3N6, Canada. Offers brain behavior and cognitive science (MA, PhD); clinical psychology (MA, PhD); developmental psychology (MA, PhD); social personality psychology (MA, PhD). *Accreditation:* APA (one or more programs are accredited). *Degree requirements:* For master's, thesis; for doctorate, comprehensive exam, thesis/dissertation. *Entrance requirements:* For master's and doctorate, GRE General Test. Additional exam requirements/recommendations for international students: Required—TOEFL. *Faculty research:* Human development, social, personality, behavioral neuroscience, forensic.

Rensselaer Polytechnic Institute, Graduate School, School of Humanities and Social Sciences, Department of Cognitive Science, Troy, NY 12180-3590. Offers PhD. *Degree requirements:* For doctorate, thesis/dissertation. *Entrance requirements:* For doctorate, GRE General Test. Additional exam requirements/recommendations for international students: Required—TOEFL (minimum score 600 paper-based; 250 computer-based), IELTS (minimum score 7.5). Electronic applications accepted. *Faculty research:* Perception and action, logic, artificial intelligence, cognitive engineering, computational cognitive modeling.

Rice University, Graduate Programs, School of Social Sciences, Department of Psychology, Houston, TX 77251-1892. Offers cognitive sciences (MA, PhD); industrial-organizational/social psychology (MA, PhD); psychology (MA, PhD). Terminal master's awarded for partial completion of doctoral program. *Degree requirements:* For master's, thesis; for doctorate, thesis/dissertation. *Entrance requirements:* For doctorate, GRE General Test, minimum GPA of 3.0. Additional exam requirements/recommendations for international students: Required—TOEFL. Electronic applications accepted. *Faculty research:* Learning and memory, information processing, decision theory.

Rutgers, The State University of New Jersey, Newark, Graduate School, Program in Psychology, Newark, NJ 07102. Offers cognitive neuroscience (PhD); cognitive science (PhD); perception (PhD); psychobiology (PhD); social cognition (PhD). *Degree requirements:* For doctorate, comprehensive exam, thesis/dissertation. *Entrance requirements:* For doctorate, GRE General Test, GRE Subject Test, minimum undergraduate B average. Electronic applications accepted. *Faculty research:* Visual perception (luminance, motion), neuroendocrine mechanisms in behavior (reproduction, pain), attachment theory, connectionist modeling of cognition.

See Close-Up on page 1131.

Rutgers, The State University of New Jersey, New Brunswick, Graduate School, Program in Psychology, Piscataway, NJ 08854-8097. Offers behavioral neuroscience (PhD); clinical psychology (PhD); cognitive psychology (PhD); interdisciplinary health psychology (PhD); social psychology (PhD). *Accreditation:* APA. *Degree requirements:* For doctorate, comprehensive exam, thesis/dissertation. *Entrance requirements:* For doctorate, GRE General Test, 3 letters of recommendation. Additional exam requirements/recommendations for international students: Required—TOEFL (minimum score 577 paper-based; 233 computer-based). Electronic applications accepted. *Faculty research:* Learning and memory, behavioral ecology, hormones and behavior, psychopharmacology, anxiety disorders.

State University of New York at Binghamton, Graduate School, School of Arts and Sciences, Department of Psychology, Specialization in Cognitive and Behavioral Science, Binghamton, NY 13902-6000. Offers MA, PhD. *Students:* 18 full-time (8 women), 1 (woman) part-time; includes 2 minority (1 Asian American or Pacific Islander, 1 Hispanic American), 3 international. Average age 27. 26 applicants, 31% accepted, 5 enrolled. In 2008, 2 doctorates awarded. *Degree requirements:* For master's, thesis; for doctorate, thesis/dissertation, departmental qualifying exam. *Entrance requirements:* For master's and doctorate, GRE General Test, GRE Subject Test. Additional exam requirements/recommendations for international students: Required—TOEFL. *Application deadline:* For fall admission, 4/15 priority date for domestic students, 1/15 priority date for international students; for spring admission, 11/1 for domestic students, 10/1 priority date for international students. Applications are processed on a rolling basis. Application fee: $60. Electronic applications accepted. *Expenses:* Tuition, area resident: Full-time $6900; part-time $288 per credit. Tuition, state resident: full-time $6900; part-time $288 per credit. Tuition, nonresident: full-time $10,920; part-time $455 per credit. Required fees: $1130. Part-time tuition and fees vary according to course load, program and student level. *Financial support:* Fellowships, research assistantships, teaching assistantships, career-related internships or fieldwork, Federal Work-Study, institutionally sponsored loans, scholarships/grants, traineeships, health care benefits, and unspecified assistantships available. Financial award application deadline: 2/15; financial award applicants required to submit FAFSA. *Unit head:* Dr. Cynthia Connine, Graduate Coordinator, 607-777-2286, E-mail: connine@binghamton.edu. *Application contact:* Victoria Williams, Recruiting and Admissions Coordinator, 607-777-2151, Fax: 607-777-2501, E-mail: vwilliam@binghamton.edu.

Temple University, Graduate School, College of Liberal Arts, Department of Psychology, Program in Cognitive Psychology, Philadelphia, PA 19122-6096. Offers PhD. *Degree requirements:* For doctorate, thesis/dissertation. *Entrance requirements:* For doctorate, GRE General Test, minimum GPA of 3.0. Additional exam requirements/recommendations for international students: Required—TOEFL (minimum score 550 paper-based; 213 computer-based; 79 iBT). Electronic applications accepted. *Faculty research:* Language development, creativity, childhood memory, visual perception, aging.

Texas A&M University, College of Liberal Arts, Department of Psychology, College Station, TX 77843. Offers behavioral and cellular neuroscience (MS, PhD); clinical psychology (MS, PhD); cognitive psychology (MS, PhD); developmental psychology (MS, PhD); industrial/organizational psychology (MS, PhD); social psychology (MS, PhD). *Accreditation:* APA (one or more programs are accredited). *Faculty:* 35. *Students:* 74 full-time (47 women), 11 part-time (9 women); includes 30 minority (7 African Americans, 5 Asian Americans or Pacific Islanders, 18 Hispanic Americans), 4 international. In 2008, 11 master's, 12 doctorates awarded. *Degree requirements:* For master's, thesis; for doctorate, comprehensive exam (for some programs), thesis/dissertation. *Entrance requirements:* For master's and doctorate, GRE General Test. Additional exam requirements/recommendations for international students: Required—TOEFL. *Application deadline:* For fall admission, 1/5 for domestic and international students. Application fee: $50 ($75 for international students). Electronic applications accepted. *Expenses:* Tuition, area resident: Full-time $3838.50. Tuition, state resident: full-time $3838.50. Tuition, nonresident: full-time $8897. Required fees: $2359.60. *Financial support:* Fellowships with partial tuition reimbursements, research assistantships with partial tuition reimbursements, teaching assistantships with partial tuition reimbursements, career-related internships or fieldwork, institutionally sponsored loans, health care benefits, and unspecified assistantships available. Financial award application deadline: 1/5; financial award applicants required to submit FAFSA. *Unit head:* Dr. Les Morey, Head, 979-845-2581, Fax: 979-845-4727, E-mail: lmorey@psych.tamu.edu. *Application contact:* Sharon Starr, Graduate Admissions Supervisor, 979-458-1710, Fax: 979-845-4727, E-mail: gradadv@psyc.tamu.edu.

Texas A&M University–Commerce, Graduate School, College of Education and Human Services, Department of Psychology and Special Education, Commerce, TX 75429-3011. Offers cognition and instruction (PhD); psychology (MA, MS); special education (M Ed, MA, MS). Part-time programs available. Terminal master's awarded for partial completion of doctoral program. *Degree requirements:* For master's, comprehensive exam, thesis (for some programs); for doctorate, thesis/dissertation, departmental qualifying exam. *Entrance requirements:* For master's, GRE General Test; for doctorate, GRE General Test, 3 letters of recommendation. Electronic applications accepted. *Faculty research:* Human learning, study skills, multicultural bilingual, diversity and special education, educationally handicapped.

University at Buffalo, the State University of New York, Graduate School, College of Arts and Sciences, Department of Psychology, Buffalo, NY 14260. Offers behavioral neuroscience (PhD); clinical psychology (PhD); cognitive psychology (PhD); general psychology (MA); social-personality psychology (PhD). *Accreditation:* APA (one or more programs are accredited). Terminal master's awarded for partial completion of doctoral program. *Degree requirements:* For master's, project; for doctorate, thesis/dissertation. *Entrance requirements:* For master's and doctorate, GRE General Test. Additional exam requirements/recommendations for international students: Required—TOEFL (minimum score 550 paper-based; 213 computer-based; 79 iBT). Electronic applications accepted. *Faculty research:* Neural, endocrine, and molecular bases of behavior; adult mood and anxiety disorders; relationship dysfunction; attention deficit/hyperactivity disorder; psycho-linguistics.

The University of Akron, Graduate School, Buchtel College of Arts and Sciences, Department of Psychology, Program in Applied Cognitive Aging, Akron, OH 44325. Offers MA, PhD. *Degree requirements:* For master's, thesis optional, thesis or specialty exam; for doctorate, one foreign language, comprehensive exam, thesis/dissertation. *Entrance requirements:* For master's, GRE General Test, GRE Subject Test, minimum GPA of 2.75, letters of recommendation; for doctorate, GRE General Test, GRE Subject Test, minimum graduate GPA of 3.25, letters of recommendation, personal statement. Additional exam requirements/recommendations for international students: Required—TOEFL (minimum score 550 paper-based; 213 computer-based; 79 iBT). Electronic applications accepted. *Faculty research:* Changes in memory and cognition with age, automaticity and effects of training, models of visual word recognition, and experimental neuropsychology.

The University of British Columbia, Faculty of Arts and Faculty of Graduate Studies, Department of Psychology, Vancouver, BC V6T 1Z1, Canada. Offers behavioral neuroscience (MA, PhD); clinical psychology (MA, PhD); cognitive science (MA, PhD); developmental psychology (MA, PhD); forensic psychology (PhD); health psychology (MA, PhD); quantitative methods (MA, PhD); social/personality psychology (MA, PhD). *Accreditation:* APA (one or more programs are accredited). Terminal master's awarded for partial completion of doctoral program. *Degree requirements:* For master's, thesis; for doctorate, comprehensive exam, thesis/dissertation. *Entrance requirements:* For master's and doctorate, GRE General Test, GRE Subject Test. Additional exam requirements/recommendations for international students: Required—TOEFL (minimum score 550 paper-based; 230 computer-based; 80 iBT). Electronic applications accepted. *Faculty research:* Clinical, developmental, social/personality, cognition, behavioral neuroscience.

University of California, San Diego, Office of Graduate Studies, Department of Cognitive Science, La Jolla, CA 92093. Offers PhD. *Degree requirements:* For doctorate, one foreign language, thesis/dissertation. *Entrance requirements:* For doctorate, GRE General Test. Additional exam requirements/recommendations for international students: Required—TOEFL (minimum score 550 paper-based; 213 computer-based). Electronic applications accepted. *Faculty research:* Neural networks, neurobiology of cognition, cognitive modeling, distributed cognition, psycholinguistics.

University of California, San Diego, Office of Graduate Studies, Interdisciplinary Program in Cognitive Science, La Jolla, CA 92093. Offers cognitive science/anthropology (PhD); cognitive science/communication (PhD); cognitive science/computer science and engineering (PhD); cognitive science/linguistics (PhD); cognitive science/neuroscience (PhD); cognitive science/philosophy (PhD); cognitive science/psychology (PhD); cognitive science/sociology (PhD). Admissions offered through affiliated departments. *Degree requirements:* For doctorate, thesis/dissertation. *Entrance requirements:* For doctorate, GRE General Test, acceptance into one of the 8 participating departments. *Faculty research:* Language and cognition, philosophy of mind, visual perception, biological anthropology, sociolinguistics.

University of California, Santa Barbara, Graduate Division, College of Letters and Sciences, Division of Humanities and Fine Arts, Department of Linguistics, Santa Barbara, CA 93106-3100. Offers applied linguistics (PhD); cognitive science (PhD); human development (PhD); language, interaction, and social organizations (PhD); MA/PhD. *Faculty:* 23 full-time (12 women). *Students:* 25 full-time (14 women). Average age 32. 63 applicants, 17% accepted, 5 enrolled. In 2008, 5 doctorates awarded. *Degree requirements:* For doctorate, one foreign language, comprehensive exam, thesis/dissertation, 48 units of coursework, minimum GPA of 3.7. *Entrance requirements:* For doctorate, GRE, 3 letters of recommendation, statement of purpose, personal achievements/contributions statement, resumé/curriculum vitae, transcripts for post-secondary institutions attended. Additional exam requirements/recommendations for international students: Required—TOEFL (minimum score 550 paper-based; 213 computer-based; 80 iBT), IELTS (minimum score 7), TOEFL or IELTS. *Application deadline:* For fall admission, 12/1 priority date for domestic and international students. Application fee: $70 ($90 for international students). Electronic applications accepted. *Expenses:* Tuition, nonresident: full-time $25,149. Required fees: $10,143. Full-time tuition and fees vary according to campus/location, reciprocity agreements and student level. *Financial support:* In 2008–09, 24 students received support, including 19 fellowships with full and partial tuition reimbursements available (averaging $12,400 per year), 1 research assistantship with full and partial tuition reimbursement available (averaging $3,000 per year), 13 teaching assistantships with partial tuition reimbursements available (averaging $5,600 per year); Federal Work-Study, institutionally sponsored loans, scholarships/grants, health care benefits, and unspecified assistantships also available. Financial award application deadline: 12/1; financial award applicants required to submit FAFSA. *Faculty research:* Language, race and subcultural identities among California teenagers; language acquisition, psycholinguisticss; language documentation, fieldwork; syntax of nominalization in 5 Tibeto-Burman languages; perceptual correlates of syllable weight. *Unit head:* Prof. Patricia M. Clancy, Chair, 805-893-8658, Fax: 805-893-7769, E-mail: pclancy@linguistics.ucsb.edu. *Application contact:* Mary Rae Staton, Graduate Program Assistant, 805-893-3776, Fax: 805-893-7769, E-mail: staton@linguistics.ucsb.edu.

University of California, Santa Barbara, Graduate Division, College of Letters and Sciences, Division of Mathematics, Life, and Physical Sciences, Department of Geography, Geography, CA 93106-4060. Offers cognitive science (PhD); geography (MA); quantitative methods in the social sciences (PhD); transportation (PhD); MA/PhD. *Students:* 67 full-time (33 women). Average age 30. 92 applicants, 28% accepted, 15 enrolled. In 2008, 3 master's, 13 doctorates awarded. *Degree requirements:* For master's, comprehensive exam (for some programs), thesis; for doctorate, comprehensive exam, thesis/dissertation. *Entrance requirements:* For master's and doctorate, GRE General Test, 3 letters of recommendation, statement of purpose, personal achievements/contributions statement, resumé/curriculum vitae, transcripts for post-secondary institutions attended. Additional exam requirements/recommendations for international students: Required—TOEFL (paper: 550, computer: 213, IBT: 80) or IELTS (7). *Application deadline:* For fall admission, 2/1 for domestic and international students. Application fee: $70 ($90 for international students). Electronic applications accepted. *Expenses:* Tuition, nonresident: full-time $25,149. Required fees: $10,143. Full-time tuition and fees vary according to campus/location, reciprocity agreements and student level. *Financial support:* In 2008–09, 59 students received support, including 36 fellowships with full and partial tuition reimbursements available (averaging $10,700 per year), 29 research assistantships with full and partial tuition reimbursements available (averaging $8,600 per year), 31 teaching assistantships with partial tuition reimbursements available (averaging $8,000 per year); Federal Work-Study, institutionally sponsored loans, scholarships/grants, health care benefits, and unspecified assistantships also available. Financial award applicants required to submit FAFSA. *Faculty research:* Earth system science, human environment relations, modeling, measurement and computation, quantitative methods in social sciences. *Unit head:* Dr. Oliver Chadwick, Chair, 805-893-4223, E-mail: oac@geog.ucsb.edu. *Application contact:* Graduate Program Assistant, 805-893-3663, Fax: 805-893-3146, E-mail: grad_assistant@geog.ucsb.edu.

University of Connecticut, Graduate School, College of Liberal Arts and Sciences, Department of Psychology, Field of Psychology, Storrs, CT 06269. Offers behavioral neuroscience (PhD); biopsychology (PhD); clinical psychology (MA, PhD); cognition and instruction (PhD); developmental psychology (MA, PhD); ecological psychology (PhD); experimental psychology (PhD); general psychology (MA, PhD); health psychology (Graduate Certificate); industrial/organizational psychology (PhD); language and cognition (PhD); neuroscience (PhD); occupational health psychology (Graduate Certificate); social psychology (MA, PhD). *Accreditation:* APA (one or more programs are accredited). Terminal master's awarded for partial completion of doctoral program. *Degree requirements:* For master's, comprehensive exam; for doctorate, thesis/dissertation. *Entrance requirements:* For master's and doctorate, GRE General Test, GRE Subject Test. Additional exam requirements/recommendations for international students: Required—TOEFL (minimum score 550 paper-based; 213 computer-based). Electronic applications accepted.

University of Connecticut, Graduate School, Neag School of Education, Department of Educational Psychology, Storrs, CT 06269. Offers educational psychology (MA, PhD, Post-Master's Certificate), including cognition and instruction, counseling psychology, gifted and talented education, learning technology, measurement, evaluation, and assessment, school psychology, special education. *Degree requirements:* For master's, comprehensive exam; for doctorate, thesis/dissertation. *Entrance requirements:* For doctorate, GRE General Test. Additional exam requirements/recommendations for international students: Required—TOEFL (minimum score 550 paper-based; 213 computer-based). Electronic applications accepted.

University of Connecticut, Graduate School, Neag School of Education, Department of Educational Psychology, Field of Educational Psychology, Program in Cognition and Instruction, Storrs, CT 06269. Offers MA, PhD, Post-Master's Certificate. *Degree requirements:* For master's, comprehensive exam; for doctorate, thesis/dissertation. *Entrance requirements:* For doctorate, GRE General Test. Additional exam requirements/recommendations for international students: Required—TOEFL (minimum score 550 paper-based; 213 computer-based). Electronic applications accepted.

University of Delaware, College of Arts and Sciences, Department of Psychology, Newark, DE 19716. Offers behavioral neuroscience (PhD); clinical psychology (PhD); cognitive psychology (PhD); social psychology (PhD). *Accreditation:* APA. *Degree requirements:* For doctorate, thesis/dissertation. *Entrance requirements:* For doctorate, GRE General Test. Additional exam requirements/recommendations for international students: Required—TOEFL (minimum score 600 paper-based; 250 computer-based). Electronic applications accepted. *Faculty research:* Emotion development, neural and cognitive aspects of memory, neural control of feeding, intergroup relations, social cognition and communication.

University of Florida, Graduate School, College of Liberal Arts and Sciences, Department of Psychology, Gainesville, FL 32611. Offers behavior analysis (PhD); behavioral neuroscience (MS, PhD); cognitive and sensory processes (PhD); counseling psychology (PhD); developmental psychology (PhD); social psychology (MS, PhD); JD/PhD. *Degree requirements:* For master's, thesis or alternative; for doctorate, thesis/dissertation. *Entrance requirements:* For master's and doctorate, GRE General Test, minimum GPA of 3.0. Additional exam requirements/recommendations for international students: Required—TOEFL (minimum score 550 paper-based; 213 computer-based). Electronic applications accepted. *Faculty research:* Experimental analysis of behavior, psychobiology, cognition and sensory processes, counseling psychology, social psychology, developmental psychology.

University of Guelph, Graduate Program Services, College of Social and Applied Human Sciences, Department of Psychology, Guelph, ON N1G 2W1, Canada. Offers applied social psychology (MA, PhD); clinical psychology applied development emphasis (PhD); clinical psychology applied developmental emphasis (MA); industrial/organizational psychology (MA, PhD); neuroscience and applied cognitive science (MA, PhD). *Degree requirements:* For master's, thesis; for doctorate, comprehensive exam, thesis/dissertation. *Entrance requirements:* For master's, GRE General Test, GRE Subject Test, minimum B+ average during previous 2 years of course work; for doctorate, GRE General Test, GRE Subject Test, minimum A-average. Additional exam requirements/recommendations for international students: Required—TOEFL (minimum score 89 iBT). Electronic applications accepted. *Faculty research:* Organizational psychology, reading comprehension and mathematical ability, drug addiction and relapse, gender issues and culture, memory, clinical psychology.

The University of Kansas, Graduate Studies, College of Liberal Arts and Sciences, Department of Psychology, Lawrence, KS 66045. Offers clinical child psychology (MA, PhD); cognitive (PhD); developmental (PhD); psychology (MA, PhD); quantitative (PhD). *Accreditation:* APA (one or more programs are accredited). *Faculty:* 38. *Students:* 90 full-time (65 women), 6 part-time (5 women); includes 15 minority (5 African Americans, 1 American Indian/Alaska Native, 7 Asian Americans or Pacific Islanders, 2 Hispanic Americans), 6 international. Average age 27. 195 applicants, 14% accepted, 10 enrolled. In 2008, 15 master's, 16 doctorates awarded. *Degree requirements:* For master's, thesis; for doctorate, comprehensive exam, thesis/dissertation. *Entrance requirements:* For doctorate, GRE General Test, minimum GPA of 3.0. Additional exam requirements/recommendations for international students: Required—TOEFL. *Application deadline:* For fall admission, 1/15 for domestic and international students. Application fee: $45 ($55 for international students). Electronic applications accepted. *Expenses:* Tuition, area resident: Full-time $6122; part-time $255.10 per credit hour. Tuition, state resident: full-time $6122; part-time $255.10 per credit hour. Tuition, nonresident: full-time $14,629; part-time $609.55 per credit hour. Required fees: $847; $70.56 per credit hour. Tuition and fees vary according to course load and program. *Financial support:* Fellowships with full tuition reimbursements, research assistantships with partial tuition reimbursements, teaching assistantships with full and partial tuition reimbursements, career-related internships or fieldwork and unspecified assistantships available. Financial award application deadline: 1/4; financial award applicants required to submit FAFSA. *Faculty research:* Cognitive psychology, methodology and statistics, developmental clinical/health psychology. *Unit head:* Greg Simpson, Chair, 785-864-9821, Fax: 785-864-5696, E-mail: gsimpson@ku.edu. *Application contact:* Cathy L. O'Keefe, Graduate Admissions Officer, 785-864-4195, Fax: 785-864-5696, E-mail: psycgrad@ku.edu.

University of Louisiana at Lafayette, BI Moody III College of Business Administration MBA Program, College of Sciences, Institute of Cognitive Science, Lafayette, LA 70504. Offers PhD. *Degree requirements:* For doctorate, comprehensive exam, thesis/dissertation. *Entrance requirements:* For doctorate, GRE General Test, minimum GPA of 3.25. Additional exam requirements/recommendations for international students: Required—TOEFL (minimum score 550 paper-based; 213 computer-based). Electronic applications accepted. *Faculty research:* Computational models of cognition, comparative cognition, cognitive development, computational cognitive neuroscience, memory.

University of Maryland, Baltimore County, Graduate School, College of Natural and Mathematical Sciences, Department of Biological Sciences and Department of Psychology, Program in Neurosciences and Cognitive Sciences, Baltimore, MD 21250. Offers PhD. *Faculty:* 18 full-time (8 women). *Students:* 5 full-time (4 women); includes 3 minority (2 Asian Americans or Pacific Islanders, 1 Hispanic American). 13 applicants, 23% accepted, 0 enrolled. In 2008, 1 doctorate awarded. *Degree requirements:* For doctorate, comprehensive exam (for some programs), thesis/dissertation. *Entrance requirements:* For doctorate, GRE General Test, minimum GPA of 3.0. Additional exam requirements/recommendations for international students: Required—TOEFL. *Application deadline:* For fall admission, 1/15 for domestic students, 12/15 for international students. Applications are processed on a rolling basis. Application fee: $50. Electronic applications accepted. *Financial support:* In 2008–09, 5 students received support, including 3 research assistantships with full tuition reimbursements available (averaging $22,300 per year), 2 teaching assistantships with full tuition reimbursements available (averaging $21,300 per year). *Unit head:* Dr. Phyllis Robinson, Director, 410-455-3669, Fax: 410-455-3875, E-mail: biograd@umbc.edu. *Application contact:* Dr. Phyllis Robinson, Director, 410-455-3669, Fax: 410-455-3875, E-mail: biograd@umbc.edu.

University of Maryland, College Park, Graduate Studies, Interdepartmental Programs, Program in Neurosciences and Cognitive Sciences, College Park, MD 20742. Offers PhD. *Degree requirements:* For doctorate, comprehensive exam, thesis/dissertation. *Entrance requirements:* For doctorate, GRE General Test, 3 letters of recommendation. Additional exam requirements/recommendations for international students: Required—TOEFL. Electronic applications accepted. *Faculty research:* Molecular neurobiology, cognition, neural and behavioral systems language, memory, human development.

University of Massachusetts Amherst, Graduate School, College of Social and Behavioral Sciences, Department of Psychology, Amherst, MA 01003. Offers clinical psychology (MS, PhD); cognitive psychology (MS, PhD); developmental science (MS, PhD); psychology of peace and violence (MS, PhD); social psychology (MS, PhD). *Accreditation:* APA (one or more programs are accredited). Terminal master's awarded for partial completion of doctoral program. *Degree requirements:* For master's, thesis; for doctorate, comprehensive exam, thesis/dissertation. *Entrance requirements:* For master's and doctorate, GRE General Test, 3 letters of recommendation. Additional exam requirements/recommendations for international students: Required—TOEFL (minimum score 550 paper-based; 213 computer-based; 79 iBT), IELTS (minimum score 6.5). Electronic applications accepted. *Expenses:* Tuition, area resident: Full-time $2640. Tuition, nonresident: full-time $9936. One-time fee: $332 full-time. Tuition and fees vary according to course load.

University of Minnesota, Twin Cities Campus, Graduate School, College of Liberal Arts, Department of Psychology, Program in Cognitive and Biological Psychology, Minneapolis, MN 55455-0213. Offers PhD. *Degree requirements:* For doctorate, comprehensive exam, thesis/dissertation. *Entrance requirements:* For doctorate, GRE General Test, GRE Subject Test (recommended), 12 credits of upper-level psychology courses, including a course in statistics or psychological measurement. Additional exam requirements/recommendations for international students: Required—TOEFL (minimum score 550 paper-based; 213 computer-based; 79 iBT).

University of Nebraska–Lincoln, Graduate College, College of Arts and Sciences, Department of Psychology, Lincoln, NE 68588. Offers biopsychology (PhD); clinical psychology (PhD); cognitive psychology (PhD); developmental psychology (PhD); psychology (MA); social/personality psychology (PhD); JD/MA; JD/PhD. *Accreditation:* APA (one or more programs are accredited). *Faculty:* 24 full-time (8 women). *Students:* 84 full-time (66 women), 29 part-time (15 women); includes 15 minority (1 African American, 1 American Indian/Alaska Native, 4 Asian Americans or Pacific Islanders, 9 Hispanic Americans), 9 international. Average age 32. In 2008, 16 master's, 18 doctorates awarded. *Degree requirements:* For master's, thesis optional; for doctorate, comprehensive exam, thesis/dissertation. *Entrance requirements:* For master's and doctorate, GRE General Test. Additional exam requirements/recommendations for international students: Required—TOEFL (minimum score 550 paper-based; 213 computer-based). *Application deadline:* For fall admission, 1/3 for domestic and international students. Application fee: $40. Electronic applications accepted. *Expenses:* Tuition, state resident: full-time $4275; part-time $237.50 per credit hour. Tuition, nonresident: full-time $11,525; part-time $640.25 per credit hour. Required fees: $1068; $10.35 per credit hour. $440.70 per semester. Tuition and fees vary according to course load and program. *Financial support:* Fellowships, research assistantships, teaching assistantships, Federal Work-Study, health care benefits, and unspecified assistantships available. Support available to part-time students. Financial award application deadline: 1/3. *Faculty research:* Law and psychology, rural mental health, chronic mental illness, neuropsychology, child clinical psychology. *Unit head:* Dr. David Hansen, Chair, 402-472-3721, Fax: 402-472-4637. *Application contact:* Ginny Gross, Director of Graduate Admissions, 402-472-2878, Fax: 402-472-0589, E-mail: grad_admissions@unl.edu.

University of Nebraska–Lincoln, Graduate College, College of Education and Human Sciences, Department of Educational Psychology, Lincoln, NE 68588. Offers cognition, learning and development (MA); counseling psychology (MA); educational psychology (MA, Ed S); psychological studies in education (PhD), including cognition, learning and development, counseling psychology, quantitative, qualitative, and psychometric methods, school psychology; quantitative, qualitative, and psychometric methods (MA); school psychology (MA, Ed S). *Accreditation:* APA (one or more programs are accredited); NCATE. *Faculty:* 19 full-time (6 women). *Students:* 16 full-time (14 women), 26 part-time (18 women); includes 2 minority (1 African American, 1 Hispanic American), 2 international. Average age 30. In 2008, 22 master's, 3 other advanced degrees awarded. *Degree requirements:* For master's, thesis optional. *Entrance requirements:* For master's, GRE General Test. Additional exam requirements/recommendations for international students: Required—TOEFL (minimum score 500 paper-based; 173 computer-based). *Application deadline:* For fall admission, 12/15 for domestic and international students; for spring admission, 10/1 for domestic students. Application fee: $40. Electronic applications accepted. *Expenses:* Tuition, state resident: full-time $4275; part-time $237.50 per credit hour. Tuition, nonresident: full-time $11,525; part-time $640.25 per credit hour. Required fees: $1068; $10.35 per credit hour. $440.70 per semester. Tuition and fees vary according to course load and program. *Financial support:* Fellowships, research assistantships, teaching assistantships, Federal Work-Study, health care benefits, and unspecified assistantships available. Support available to part-time students. Financial award application deadline: 1/15. *Faculty research:* Measurement and assessment, metacognition, academic skills, child development, multicultural education and counseling. *Unit head:* Dr. Ralph De Ayala, Chair, 402-472-2210, E-mail: tcgrad2@unl.edu. *Application contact:* Dr. Ralph De Ayala, Chair, 402-472-2210, E-mail: tcgrad2@unl.edu.

University of Nevada, Reno, Graduate School, College of Liberal Arts, Department of Psychology, Program in Cognitive Brain Science, Reno, NV 89557. Offers MA, PhD. *Faculty:* 5 full-time. *Students:* 14 full-time (8 women), 6 part-time (5 women); includes 1 Asian American or Pacific Islander, 1 international. Average age 29. 3 applicants, 100% accepted, 2 enrolled. In 2008, 1 master's, 5 doctorates awarded. Terminal master's awarded for partial completion of doctoral program. *Degree requirements:* For master's, thesis optional; for doctorate, comprehensive exam, thesis/dissertation. *Entrance requirements:* For master's, GRE General Test, minimum GPA of 2.75; for doctorate, GRE General Test, minimum GPA of 3.0. Additional exam requirements/recommendations for international students: Required—TOEFL (minimum score 500 paper-based; 173 computer-based; 61 iBT), IELTS (minimum score 6), TOFEL or IELTS. *Application deadline:* For fall admission, 1/1 priority date for domestic and international students. Application fee: $60 ($95 for international students). Electronic applications accepted. *Expenses:* Tuition, state resident: full-time $1710; part-time $1140 per semester. Tuition, nonresident: full-time $7115. Required fees: $158 per semester. *Financial support:* In 2008–09, 5 research assistantships with partial tuition reimbursements (averaging $14,000 per year), 9 teaching assistantships with partial tuition reimbursements (averaging $14,000 per year) were awarded; Federal Work-Study, institutionally sponsored loans, scholarships/grants, health

Cognitive Sciences

University of Nevada, Reno (continued)
care benefits, and unspecified assistantships also available. Financial award application deadline: 3/1; financial award applicants required to submit FAFSA. *Faculty research:* Comparative psychology, cognition, perception. Total annual research expenditures: $286,168. *Unit head:* Dr. Michael Crognale, Graduate Program Director, 775-784-6828, E-mail: mikro@unr.edu. *Application contact:* Michele Sandberg, Application Contact, 775-784-7026, Fax: 775-784-6064, E-mail: gradschool@unr.edu.

The University of North Carolina at Chapel Hill, Graduate School, College of Arts and Sciences, Department of Psychology, Chapel Hill, NC 27599. Offers biological psychology (PhD); clinical psychology (PhD); cognitive psychology (PhD); developmental psychology (PhD); quantitative psychology (PhD); social psychology (PhD). *Accreditation:* APA. *Degree requirements:* For doctorate, comprehensive exam, thesis/dissertation. *Entrance requirements:* For doctorate, GRE General Test, minimum GPA of 3.0. Electronic applications accepted. *Faculty research:* Expressed emotion, cognitive development, social cognitive neuroscience, human memory personality.

The University of North Carolina at Greensboro, Graduate School, College of Arts and Sciences, Department of Psychology, Greensboro, NC 27412-5001. Offers clinical psychology (MA, PhD); cognitive psychology (MA, PhD); developmental psychology (MA, PhD); social psychology (MA, PhD). *Accreditation:* APA (one or more programs are accredited). Terminal master's awarded for partial completion of doctoral program. *Degree requirements:* For master's, comprehensive exam, thesis; for doctorate, one foreign language, thesis/dissertation, preliminary exam. *Entrance requirements:* For master's and doctorate, GRE General Test. Additional exam requirements/recommendations for international students: Required—TOEFL. Electronic applications accepted. *Faculty research:* Sensory and perceptual determinants; evoked potential: disorders, deafness, and development.

University of Notre Dame, Graduate School, College of Arts and Letters, Division of Social Science, Department of Psychology, Notre Dame, IN 46556. Offers cognitive psychology (PhD); counseling psychology (PhD); developmental psychology (PhD); quantitative psychology (PhD). *Accreditation:* APA. *Faculty:* 28 full-time (11 women), 5 part-time/adjunct (4 women). *Students:* 70 full-time (49 women); includes 11 minority (3 African Americans, 3 Asian Americans or Pacific Islanders, 5 Hispanic Americans), 13 international. 146 applicants, 18% accepted, 18 enrolled. In 2008, 8 doctorates awarded. *Degree requirements:* For doctorate, comprehensive exam, thesis/dissertation, candidacy exam. *Entrance requirements:* For doctorate, GRE General Test, GRE Subject Test (strongly recommended). Additional exam requirements/recommendations for international students: Required—TOEFL (minimum score 600 paper-based; 250 computer-based; 80 iBT). *Application deadline:* For fall admission, 1/2 for domestic and international students. Application fee: $50. Electronic applications accepted. *Financial support:* Fellowships with full tuition reimbursements, research assistantships with full tuition reimbursements, teaching assistantships with full tuition reimbursements, career-related internships or fieldwork and tuition waivers (full) available. Financial award application deadline: 1/2. *Faculty research:* Cognitive and socio-emotional development, statistical methods and quantitative models applicable to psychology, interpersonal relations, life span development and developmental delay, childhood depression, structural equation and dynamical systems. *Unit head:* Dr. Dan Lapsley, Director of Graduate Studies, 574-631-8789. *Application contact:* Dr. Barbara Turpin, Director of Graduate Admissions, 574-631-7706, Fax: 574-631-4183.

University of Oregon, Graduate School, College of Arts and Sciences, Department of Psychology, Eugene, OR 97403. Offers clinical psychology (PhD); cognitive psychology (MA, MS, PhD); developmental psychology (MA, MS, PhD); physiological psychology (MA, MS, PhD); psychology (MA, MS, PhD); social/personality psychology (MA, MS, PhD). *Accreditation:* APA (one or more programs are accredited). Terminal master's awarded for partial completion of doctoral program. *Degree requirements:* For doctorate, thesis/dissertation. *Entrance requirements:* For master's, GRE General Test, minimum GPA of 3.0; for doctorate, GRE General Test. Additional exam requirements/recommendations for international students: Required—TOEFL.

University of Pittsburgh, School of Education, Department of Instruction and Learning, Program in Cognitive Studies, Pittsburgh, PA 15260. Offers PhD. *Degree requirements:* For doctorate, thesis/dissertation. *Entrance requirements:* For doctorate, GRE General Test. Additional exam requirements/recommendations for international students: Required—TOEFL. Electronic applications accepted.

University of Rochester, The College, Arts and Sciences, Department of Brain and Cognitive Sciences, Rochester, NY 14627-0250. Offers MS, PhD. Terminal master's awarded for partial completion of doctoral program. *Degree requirements:* For doctorate, thesis/dissertation, qualifying exam. *Entrance requirements:* For master's and doctorate, GRE General Test. Additional exam requirements/recommendations for international students: Required—TOEFL. Electronic applications accepted.

University of South Florida, Graduate School, College of Arts and Sciences, Department of Psychology, Tampa, FL 33620-9951. Offers clinical psychology (MA, PhD); cognitive and neural sciences (MA, PhD); industrial-organizational psychology (MA, PhD). *Accreditation:* APA (one or more programs are accredited). *Faculty:* 30 full-time (10 women). *Students:* 93 full-time (53 women), 22 part-time (15 women); includes 12 minority (2 African Americans, 4 Asian Americans or Pacific Islanders, 6 Hispanic Americans), 16 international. 421 applicants, 3% accepted, 11 enrolled. In 2008, 21 master's, 12 doctorates awarded. *Degree requirements:* For master's, comprehensive exam, thesis; for doctorate, comprehensive exam, thesis/dissertation. *Entrance requirements:* For master's and doctorate, GRE General Test, minimum GPA of 3.0 in last 60 hours of course work. Additional exam requirements/recommendations for international students: Required—TOEFL (minimum score 550 paper-based; 213 computer-based). *Application deadline:* For fall admission, 11/15 for domestic students, 12/15 for international students. Application fee: $30. Electronic applications accepted. *Expenses:* Contact institution. *Financial support:* Fellowships with full and partial tuition reimbursements, research assistantships with partial tuition reimbursements, teaching assistantships with partial tuition reimbursements, career-related internships or fieldwork, scholarships/grants, tuition waivers (partial), and unspecified assistantships available. Financial award applicants required to submit FAFSA. *Faculty research:* Human memory; job analysis; stress, drug and alcohol abuse; neuroscience. Total annual research expenditures: $2.9 million. *Unit head:* Emanual Donchin, Program Director, 813-974-0466, Fax: 813-974-4617, E-mail: dochin@shell.cas.

usf.edu. *Application contact:* William Sacco, Program Director, 813-974-0375, Fax: 813-974-4617, E-mail: sacco@cas.usf.edu.

The University of Texas at Austin, Graduate School, College of Education, Department of Educational Psychology, Austin, TX 78712-1111. Offers academic educational psychology (M Ed, MA); counseling psychology (PhD); counselor education (M Ed); human development and culture (PhD); learning, cognition and instruction (PhD); quantitative methods (PhD); school psychology (PhD). *Accreditation:* APA (one or more programs are accredited). *Degree requirements:* For master's, thesis optional; for doctorate, thesis/dissertation. *Entrance requirements:* For master's and doctorate, GRE General Test, 3 letters of recommendation. Additional exam requirements/recommendations for international students: Required—TOEFL.

The University of Texas at Dallas, School of Behavioral and Brain Sciences, Program in Cognition and Neuroscience, Richardson, TX 75083-0688. Offers applied cognition and neuroscience (MS); cognition and neuroscience (PhD). Part-time and evening/weekend programs available. *Faculty:* 21 full-time (7 women). *Students:* 77 full-time (38 women), 28 part-time (12 women); includes 23 minority (4 African Americans, 12 Asian Americans or Pacific Islanders, 7 Hispanic Americans), 21 international. Average age 32. 70 applicants, 73% accepted, 34 enrolled. In 2008, 31 master's, 9 doctorates awarded. *Degree requirements:* For master's, internship; for doctorate, thesis/dissertation. *Entrance requirements:* For master's and doctorate, GRE General Test, minimum GPA of 3.0 in upper-level coursework in field. Additional exam requirements/recommendations for international students: Required—TOEFL (minimum score 550 paper-based; 213 computer-based). *Application deadline:* For fall admission, 7/15 for domestic students, 5/1 priority date for international students; for spring admission, 11/15 for domestic students, 9/1 priority date for international students. Applications are processed on a rolling basis. Application fee: $50 ($100 for international students). Electronic applications accepted. *Expenses:* Tuition, area resident: Full-time $8320. Tuition, state resident: full-time $8320. Tuition, nonresident: full-time $15,054. Part-time tuition and fees vary according to course load. *Financial support:* In 2008–09, 10 research assistantships with tuition reimbursements (averaging $14,238 per year), 28 teaching assistantships with tuition reimbursements (averaging $10,519 per year) were awarded; fellowships, career-related internships or fieldwork, Federal Work-Study, institutionally sponsored loans, scholarships/grants, and unspecified assistantships also available. Support available to part-time students. Financial award application deadline: 4/30; financial award applicants required to submit FAFSA. *Faculty research:* Combination of biological, behavioral, and computational approaches for evaluating biological and artificial information processing systems. *Unit head:* Dr. James C. Bartlett, Head, PhD Program, 972-883-2079, Fax: 972-883-2491, E-mail: jbartlet@utdallas.edu. *Application contact:* Dr. Robert D. Stillman, Head, 972-883-3106, Fax: 972-883-3022, E-mail: stillman@utdallas.edu.

The University of Toledo, College of Graduate Studies, College of Arts and Sciences, Department of Psychology, Toledo, OH 43606-3390. Offers behavioral (PhD), including cognitive, psychobiology and learning, social; clinical psychology (PhD); experimental psychology (MA). *Accreditation:* APA. *Degree requirements:* For master's, thesis; for doctorate, one foreign language, thesis/dissertation. *Entrance requirements:* For master's and doctorate, GRE General Test, GRE Subject Test. *Faculty research:* Neural taste response.

University of Washington, Graduate School, College of Arts and Sciences, Department of Psychology, Seattle, WA 98195. Offers animal behavior (PhD); child psychology (PhD); clinical psychology (PhD); cognition and perception (PhD); developmental psychology (PhD); quantitative psychology (PhD); social psychology and personality (PhD). *Accreditation:* APA. *Degree requirements:* For doctorate, thesis/dissertation. *Entrance requirements:* For doctorate, GRE General Test, minimum GPA of 3.0. Electronic applications accepted. *Faculty research:* Addictive behaviors, artificial intelligence, child psychopathology, mechanisms and development of vision, physiology of ingestive behaviors.

University of Wisconsin–Madison, Graduate School, College of Letters and Science, Department of Psychology, Program in Cognitive Neurosciences, Madison, WI 53706-1380. Offers PhD. *Degree requirements:* For doctorate, comprehensive exam, thesis/dissertation. *Entrance requirements:* For doctorate, GRE General Test, minimum undergraduate GPA of 3.0. Additional exam requirements/recommendations for international students: Required—TOEFL. Electronic applications accepted.

University of Wisconsin–Madison, Graduate School, College of Letters and Science, Department of Psychology, Program in Perception, Madison, WI 53706-1380. Offers PhD. *Degree requirements:* For doctorate, comprehensive exam, thesis/dissertation. *Entrance requirements:* For doctorate, GRE General Test, minimum GPA of 3.0. Electronic applications accepted.

Wayne State University, College of Liberal Arts and Sciences, Department of Psychology, Program in Psychology, Detroit, MI 48202. Offers behavioral and cognitive neuroscience (PhD); clinical psychology (PhD); cognitive and social psychology (PhD); industrial/organizational psychology (PhD); psychology (MA, MS). *Accreditation:* APA (one or more programs are accredited). *Degree requirements:* For doctorate, thesis/dissertation. *Entrance requirements:* For doctorate, GRE General Test, GRE Subject Test. Additional exam requirements/recommendations for international students: Required—TOEFL (minimum score 550 paper-based; 213 computer-based); Recommended—TWE (minimum score 6). Electronic applications accepted.

Wilfrid Laurier University, Faculty of Graduate Studies, Faculty of Science, Department of Psychology, Waterloo, ON N2L 3C5, Canada. Offers brain and cognition (M Sc, PhD); community psychology (MA, PhD); social and developmental psychology (MA, PhD). *Degree requirements:* For master's, thesis; for doctorate, thesis/dissertation. *Entrance requirements:* For master's, honors BA or the equivalent in psychology, minimum B average in undergraduate course work, GRE (General Test); for doctorate, master's degree, minimum A- average, GRE (General Test). Additional exam requirements/recommendations for international students: Required—TOEFL (minimum score 230 computer-based; 89 iBT). Electronic applications accepted. *Faculty research:* Brain and cognition, community psychology, social and developmental psychology.

Yale University, Graduate School of Arts and Sciences, Department of Psychology, New Haven, CT 06520. Offers behavioral neuroscience (PhD); clinical psychology (PhD); cognitive psychology (PhD); developmental psychology (PhD); social/personality psychology (PhD). *Accreditation:* APA. *Degree requirements:* For doctorate, thesis/dissertation. *Entrance requirements:* For doctorate, GRE General Test.

Counseling Psychology

Abilene Christian University, Graduate School, College of Arts and Sciences, Department of Psychology, Program in Counseling Psychology, Abilene, TX 79699-9100. Offers MS. *Students:* 10 full-time (7 women), 2 part-time (1 woman); includes 1 minority (African American), 1 international. 13 applicants, 62% accepted, 5 enrolled. In 2008, 4 master's awarded. *Degree requirements:* For master's, comprehensive exam, thesis optional. *Entrance requirements:* For master's, GRE General Test. *Application deadline:* For fall admission, 4/1 priority date for domestic students; for spring admission, 11/1 for domestic students. Applications are processed on a rolling basis. Application fee: $40 ($45 for international students). Electronic applications accepted. *Expenses:* Tuition: Full-time $10,728; part-time $640 per hour. Required fees:

$1090; $53.50 per hour. $10 per term. Tuition and fees vary according to campus/location. *Financial support:* In 2008–09, 12 students received support. Applicants required to submit FAFSA. *Unit head:* Dr. Robert McKelvain, Graduate Advisor, 325-674-2472, Fax: 325-674-6968, E-mail: beckr@acu.edu. *Application contact:* William Horn, Graduate Admissions Counselor, 325-674-2656, Fax: 325-674-6717, E-mail: gradinfo@acu.edu.

Adelphi University, Derner Institute of Advanced Psychological Studies, Program in Mental Health Counseling, Garden City, NY 11530-0701. Offers MA. *Students:* 30 full-time (22 women), 8 part-time (all women); includes 1 minority (African American), 3 international. Average age 27. In 2008, 13 master's awarded. *Degree requirements:* For master's, comprehensive exam.

Entrance requirements: For master's, GRE General Test, GRE Subject Test, minimum cumulative GPA of 3.1; interview; course work in developmental psychology, research methods, and psycho-pathology; 2 letters of recommendation. Additional exam requirements/recommendations for international students: Required—TOEFL (minimum score 550 paper-based; 213 computer-based; 80 iBT). *Application deadline:* For fall admission, 4/1 priority date for domestic students, 5/1 priority date for international students. Application fee: $50. Electronic applications accepted. *Expenses:* Tuition: Full-time $25,700; part-time $775 per credit hour. Required fees: $500. Tuition and fees vary according to course load, degree level, campus/location, program and student level. *Financial support:* Research assistantships with full and partial tuition reimbursements, career-related internships or fieldwork, Federal Work-Study, institutionally sponsored loans, and unspecified assistantships available. *Unit head:* Dr. Butaney Bhupin, Interim Assistant Dean, 516-877-4829, E-mail: butaney@adelphi.edu. *Application contact:* Christine Murphy, Director of Admissions, 516-877-3050, Fax: 516-877-3039, E-mail: graduateadmissions@adelphi.edu.

Adler Graduate School, Program in Adlerian Studies, Richfield, MN 55423. Offers art therapy specialization (MA); clinical counseling track (MA); coaching and consulting in organizations (Certificate); management consulting and organizational leadership (MA); marriage and family track (MA); non-clinical Adlerian studies track (MA); personal and professional life coaching (Certificate); school counseling (MA). Part-time and evening/weekend programs available. *Degree requirements:* For master's, thesis or alternative, 500-700 hour internship, depending on license choice. *Entrance requirements:* For master's, minimum undergraduate GPA of 3.0, 12 credits of course work in psychology or related field.

Adler School of Professional Psychology, Programs in Psychology, Chicago, IL 60601-7203. Offers art therapy (Certificate); clinical hypnosis (Certificate); clinical psychology (Psy D); counseling psychology (MACP); counseling psychology/art therapy (MACAT); gerontology (MAGP); marriage and family counseling (MAMFC); marriage and family therapy (Certificate); organizational psychology (MAO); substance abuse counseling (MASAC, Certificate); Psy D/Certificate; Psy D/MACAT; Psy D/MACP; Psy D/MAMFC; Psy D/MASAC. *Accreditation:* APA. Part-time and evening/weekend programs available. Postbaccalaureate distance learning degree programs offered (minimal on-campus study). *Faculty:* 36 full-time (17 women), 45 part-time/adjunct (18 women). *Students:* 514 full-time (404 women), 128 part-time (100 women); includes 147 minority (69 African Americans, 2 American Indian/Alaska Native, 30 Asian Americans or Pacific Islanders, 46 Hispanic Americans), 53 international. Average age 27. 855 applicants, 46% accepted, 195 enrolled. In 2008, 110 master's, 136 doctorates awarded. Terminal master's awarded for partial completion of doctoral program. *Degree requirements:* For master's, thesis or alternative, oral exam, practicum; for doctorate, thesis/dissertation, clinical exam, internship, oral exam, practicum, written qualifying exam. *Entrance requirements:* For master's, 12 semester hours in psychology, minimum GPA of 3.0; for doctorate, 18 semester hours in psychology, minimum GPA of 3.25; for Certificate, appropriate master's or doctoral degree. Additional exam requirements/recommendations for international students: Required—TOEFL (minimum score 550 paper-based; 213 computer-based; 79 iBT). *Application deadline:* For fall admission, 2/15 priority date for domestic students, 12/1 priority date for international students. Applications are processed on a rolling basis. Application fee: $50. Electronic applications accepted. *Expenses:* Tuition: Part-time $850 per credit. Tuition and fees vary according to degree level, campus/location and program. *Financial support:* Career-related internships or fieldwork, Federal Work-Study, scholarships/grants, and tuition waivers (full and partial) available. Support available to part-time students. Financial award application deadline: 5/15; financial award applicants required to submit FAFSA. *Unit head:* Dr. Frank Gruba-McAllister, Vice President of Academic Affairs, 312-201-5900, Fax: 312-207-5917. *Application contact:* Craig A Hines, Director of Admissions, 312-201-5900 Ext. 226, Fax: 312-201-5917, E-mail: chines@adler.edu.

See Close-Up on page 1051.

Alabama Agricultural and Mechanical University, School of Graduate Studies, School of Education, Department of Counseling and Special Education, Huntsville, AL 35811. Offers communicative disorders (M Ed, MS); psychology and counseling (MS, Ed S), including clinical psychology (MS), counseling and guidance, counseling psychology (MS), personnel management (MS), psychometry (MS), school psychology (MS); special education (M Ed, MS). *Accreditation:* CORE; NCATE. Part-time and evening/weekend programs available. *Students:* 13 full-time (9 women), 57 part-time (46 women); includes 52 minority (51 African Americans, 1 Hispanic American), 2 international. In 2008, 24 master's awarded. *Degree requirements:* For master's, comprehensive exam. *Entrance requirements:* For master's, GRE General Test. Additional exam requirements/recommendations for international students: Required—TOEFL (minimum score 500 paper-based; 173 computer-based; 61 iBT). *Application deadline:* For fall admission, 5/1 for domestic students. Application fee: $15 ($20 for international students). *Expenses:* Tuition, area resident: Full-time $3924; part-time $2616 per term. Tuition, nonresident: part-time $5234 per year. International tuition: $7848 full-time. Required fees: $198; $396 per credit hour. $2841 per term. One-time fee: $8498 full-time; $5682 part-time. Full-time tuition and fees vary according to program. *Financial support:* Career-related internships or fieldwork available. Support available to part-time students. Financial award application deadline: 4/1. *Faculty research:* Increasing numbers of minorities in special education and speech-language pathology. *Unit head:* Dr. Shirley King, Chair, 256-372-5520, Fax: 256-372-5526. *Application contact:* Dr. Caula Beyl, Dean, School of Graduate Studies, 256-372-5266, Fax: 256-372-5269, E-mail: caula.beyl@aamu.edu.

Alaska Pacific University, Graduate Programs, Department of Counseling, Psychological Studies, and Human Services, Program in Counseling Psychology, Anchorage, AK 99508-4672. Offers MSCP.

Alliant International University–México City, Programs in Arts and Science, Mexico City, Mexico. Offers counseling psychology (MA); international relations (MA). Part-time programs available. *Degree requirements:* For master's, thesis optional. *Entrance requirements:* For master's, GRE General Test, letters of recommendation. Additional exam requirements/recommendations for international students: Required—TOEFL. Electronic applications accepted.

Amberton University, Graduate School, Program in Counseling, Garland, TX 75041-5595. Offers MA. *Entrance requirements:* For master's, minimum GPA of 3.0.

Amridge University, Graduate and Professional Programs, Montgomery, AL 36117. Offers behavioral leadership and management (MA); biblical studies (MA, PhD); family therapy (D Min); leadership and management (MS); marriage and family therapy (M Div, MA, PhD), including marriage and family therapy (PhD), professional counseling (PhD); ministerial leadership (M Div, MS); pastoral counseling (M Div, MS); practical theology (MA); professional counseling (M Div, MA); theology (M Div, D Min). *Accreditation:* ATS. Part-time and evening/weekend programs available. Postbaccalaureate distance learning degree programs offered (no on-campus study). *Faculty:* 44 full-time (9 women), 18 part-time/adjunct (7 women). *Students:* 131 full-time (61 women), 218 part-time (119 women); includes 174 minority (164 African Americans, 1 American Indian/Alaska Native, 1 Asian American or Pacific Islander, 8 Hispanic Americans). Average age 35. *Degree requirements:* For master's, one foreign language, comprehensive exam (for some programs), thesis (for some programs); for doctorate, comprehensive exam (for some programs), thesis/dissertation; for M Div, comprehensive exam (for some programs). *Entrance requirements:* For M Div, master's, and doctorate, GRE General Test or MAT. Additional exam requirements/recommendations for international students: Required—TOEFL. *Application deadline:* For fall admission, 9/1 priority date for domestic students; for spring admission, 1/1 priority date for domestic students. Applications are processed on a rolling basis. Application fee: $75. Electronic applications accepted. *Expenses:* Tuition: Full-time $9630; part-time $535 per semester hour. Required fees: $600 per term. Tuition and fees vary according to course load and degree level. *Financial support:* Federal Work-Study and scholarships/grants available. Support available to part-time students. Financial award applicants required to submit FAFSA. *Faculty research:* Homiletics, hermeneutics, ancient Near Eastern history. *Unit head:* Rick Johnson, Director of Enrollment Management, 800-351-4040 Ext. 7513, Fax: 334-387-3878, E-mail: rickjohnson@amridgeuniversity.edu. *Application contact:* Ora Davis, Admissions Officer, 334-387-3877 Ext. 7524, Fax: 334-387-3878, E-mail: oradavis@amridgeuniversity.edu.

Andrews University, School of Graduate Studies, School of Education, Department of Educational and Counseling Psychology, Program in Counseling Psychology, Berrien Springs, MI 49104. Offers PhD. *Students:* 4 full-time (2 women), 13 part-time (7 women); includes 1 minority (African American). Average age 39. In 2008, 1 doctorate awarded. *Degree requirements:* For doctorate, thesis/dissertation. *Entrance requirements:* Additional exam requirements/recommendations for international students: Required—TOEFL (minimum score 550 paper-based). Application fee: $40. *Expenses:* Tuition: Full-time $18,360; part-time $765 per credit hour. Required fees: $476; $765 per credit hour. $238 per semester. Tuition and fees vary according to degree level. *Unit head:* Dr. Carole Woolford, Coordinator, 269-471-6074. *Application contact:* Carolyn Hurst, Supervisor of Graduate Admission, 800-253-2874, Fax: 269-471-6321, E-mail: graduate@andrews.edu.

Angelo State University, College of Graduate Studies, College of Liberal and Fine Arts, Department of Psychology and Sociology, San Angelo, TX 76909. Offers psychology (MS), including counseling psychology, general psychology, industrial and organizational psychology. Part-time and evening/weekend programs available. *Faculty:* 8 full-time (2 women). *Students:* 28 full-time (18 women), 9 part-time (8 women); includes 7 minority (1 American Indian/Alaska Native, 6 Hispanic Americans), 1 international. Average age 25. 20 applicants, 70% accepted, 11 enrolled. In 2008, 23 master's awarded. *Degree requirements:* For master's, comprehensive exam, thesis optional. *Entrance requirements:* For master's, GRE General Test. Additional exam requirements/recommendations for international students: Required—TOEFL or IELTS. *Application deadline:* For fall admission, 7/15 priority date for domestic students, 6/10 for international students; for spring admission, 12/1 priority date for domestic students, 11/1 for international students. Applications are processed on a rolling basis. Application fee: $40 ($50 for international students). Electronic applications accepted. *Financial support:* In 2008–09, 44 students received support, including 3 teaching assistantships (averaging $10,251 per year); career-related internships or fieldwork, Federal Work-Study, scholarships/grants, and unspecified assistantships also available. Support available to part-time students. Financial award application deadline: 3/1; financial award applicants required to submit FAFSA. *Faculty research:* Toddlers use of actors' intentions to learn verbs. Total annual research expenditures: $116,915. *Unit head:* Dr. William B. Davidson, Department Head, 325-942-2068 Ext. 248, E-mail: bill.davidson@angelo.edu. *Application contact:* Theresa Fortin, Graduate Admissions Assistant, 325-942-2169, Fax: 325-942-2194, E-mail: theresa.fortin@angelo.edu.

Anna Maria College, Graduate Division, Program in Counseling Psychology, Paxton, MA 01612. Offers counseling psychology (MA). Part-time and evening/weekend programs available. *Faculty:* 1 full-time (0 women), 7 part-time/adjunct (5 women). *Students:* 12 full-time (9 women), 26 part-time (22 women); includes 3 minority (2 African Americans, 1 Asian American or Pacific Islander). Average age 34. In 2008, 16 master's awarded. *Degree requirements:* For master's, comprehensive exam, practicum. *Entrance requirements:* Additional exam requirements/recommendations for international students: Required—TOEFL (minimum score 500 paper-based). *Application deadline:* For fall admission, 3/1 priority date for domestic and international students; for spring admission, 11/1 priority date for domestic and international students. Applications are processed on a rolling basis. Application fee: $40. Electronic applications accepted. *Expenses:* Tuition: Part-time $1400 per course. *Financial support:* Applicants required to submit FAFSA. *Unit head:* Richard L. Connors, Director, 508-849-3413, Fax: 508-849-3339, E-mail: rconnors@annamaria.edu. *Application contact:* Dennis Braun, Director, Graduate Studies and Continuing Education, 508-849-3293, Fax: 508-819-3362, E-mail: dbraun@annamaria.edu.

Antioch University McGregor, Graduate Programs, Individualized Liberal and Professional Studies Program, Yellow Springs, OH 45387-1609. Offers liberal and professional studies (MA), including counseling, creative writing, education, film studies, liberal studies, management, modern literature, psychology, theatre, visual arts. Part-time and evening/weekend programs available. Postbaccalaureate distance learning degree programs offered (minimal on-campus study). *Degree requirements:* For master's, thesis or alternative. *Entrance requirements:* For master's, resumé, 2 letters of reference. Electronic applications accepted. *Expenses:* Contact institution.

Antioch University New England, Graduate School, Department of Applied Psychology, Program in Clinical Mental Health Counseling, Keene, NH 03431-3552. Offers MA. *Degree requirements:* For master's, internship, practicum. *Entrance requirements:* For master's, previous course work and work experience in psychology. Additional exam requirements/recommendations for international students: Required—TOEFL (minimum score 600 paper-based; 250 computer-based). Electronic applications accepted. *Expenses:* Contact institution. *Faculty research:* Multicultural issues in field supervision.

Argosy University, Chicago, College of Psychology and Behavioral Sciences, Doctoral Program in Clinical Psychology, Chicago, IL 60654. Offers child and adolescent psychology (Psy D); client-centered and experiential psychotherapies (Psy D); diversity and multicultural psychology (Psy D); family psychology (Psy D); forensic psychology (Psy D); health psychology (Psy D); psychoanalytic psychology (Psy D); psychology and spirituality (Psy D). *Accreditation:* APA.

See Close-Up on page 1067.

Argosy University, Chicago, College of Psychology and Behavioral Sciences, Program in Counseling Psychology, Chicago, IL 60654. Offers counselor education and supervision (Ed D). Postbaccalaureate distance learning degree programs offered (minimal on-campus study).

See Close-Up on page 1067.

Argosy University, Denver, College of Psychology and Behavioral Sciences, Denver, CO 80203. Offers clinical psychology (MA, Psy D); community counseling (MA); counseling psychology (Ed D), including counselor education and supervision; counselor education and supervision (Ed D); forensic psychology (MA); marriage and family therapy (MA); organizational leadership (Ed D).

See Close-Up on page 1071.

Argosy University, Hawai'i, College of Psychology and Behavioral Sciences, Program in Counseling Psychology, Honolulu, HI 96813. Offers Ed D.

See Close-Up on page 1073.

Argosy University, Inland Empire, College of Psychology and Behavioral Sciences, San Bernardino, CA 92408. Offers clinical psychology/marriage and family therapy (MA); counseling psychology (MA, Ed D); counseling psychology/marriage and family therapy (MA); forensic psychology (MA).

See Close-Up on page 1075.

Argosy University, Los Angeles, College of Psychology and Behavioral Sciences, Santa Monica, CA 90405. Offers clinical psychology/marriage and family therapy (MA); counseling psychology (Ed D); counseling psychology/marriage and family therapy (MA); organizational leadership (Ed D).

See Close-Up on page 1077.

Argosy University, Nashville, College of Psychology and Behavioral Sciences, Nashville, TN 37214. Offers counselor education and supervision (Ed D); mental health counseling (MA).

See Close-Up on page 1079.

Counseling Psychology

Argosy University, Orange County, College of Psychology and Behavioral Sciences, Program in Counseling Psychology, Santa Ana, CA 92704. Offers counseling psychology (Ed D); marriage and family therapy (MA).

See Close-Up on page 1081.

Argosy University, Phoenix, College of Psychology and Behavioral Sciences, Program in Mental Health Counseling, Phoenix, AZ 85021. Offers MA.

See Close-Up on page 1083.

Argosy University, Salt Lake City, College of Psychology and Behavioral Sciences, Draper, UT 84020. Offers counseling psychology (Ed D); marriage and family therapy (MA).

See Close-Up on page 1085.

Argosy University, San Diego, College of Psychology and Behavioral Sciences, San Diego, CA 92108. Offers clinical psychology/marriage and family therapy (MA); counseling psychology (MA, Ed D); counseling psychology/marriage and family therapy (MA).

See Close-Up on page 1087.

Argosy University, San Francisco Bay Area, College of Psychology and Behavioral Sciences, Program in Counseling Psychology, Alameda, CA 94501. Offers MA, Ed D.

See Close-Up on page 1089.

Argosy University, Sarasota, College of Psychology and Behavioral Sciences, Sarasota, FL 34235. Offers community counseling (MA); counseling psychology (Ed D); counselor education and supervision (Ed D); forensic psychology (MA); marriage and family therapy (MA); mental health counseling (MA); organizational leadership (Ed D); pastoral community counseling (Ed D); school counseling (MA, Ed S); school psychology (MA).

See Close-Up on page 1091.

Argosy University, Schaumburg, College of Psychology and Behavioral Sciences, Schaumburg, IL 60173-5403. Offers clinical health psychology (Post-Graduate Certificate); clinical psychology (MA, Psy D), including child and family psychology (Psy D), clinical health psychology (Psy D), diversity and multicultural psychology (Psy D), forensic psychology (Psy D); community counseling (MA); counseling psychology (Ed D), including counselor education and supervision; counselor education and supervision (Ed D); forensic psychology (Post-Graduate Certificate); organizational leadership (Ed D). *Accreditation:* ACA; APA.

See Close-Up on page 1093.

Argosy University, Seattle, College of Psychology and Behavioral Sciences, Program in Counseling Psychology, Seattle, WA 98121. Offers MA, Ed D.

See Close-Up on page 1095.

Argosy University, Tampa, College of Psychology and Behavioral Sciences, Tampa, FL 33614. Offers clinical psychology (MA, Psy D), including clinical psychology; counselor education and supervision (Ed D); marriage and family therapy (MA); mental health counseling (MA); organizational leadership (Ed D); school counseling (MA).

See Close-Up on page 1097.

Argosy University, Washington DC, College of Psychology and Behavioral Sciences, Arlington, VA 22209. Offers clinical psychology (MA, Psy D), including child and family psychology (Psy D), diversity and multicultural psychology (Psy D), forensic psychology (Psy D), health and neuropsychology (Psy D); community counseling (MA); counseling psychology (Ed D), including counselor education and supervision; counselor education and supervision (Ed D); forensic psychology (MA); organizational leadership (Ed D). *Accreditation:* APA.

See Close-Up on page 1101.

Arizona State University, Graduate College, Mary Lou Fulton College of Education, Division of Psychology in Education, Program in Counseling Psychology, Tempe, AZ 85287. Offers PhD. *Accreditation:* APA. *Degree requirements:* For doctorate, thesis/dissertation. *Entrance requirements:* For doctorate, GRE General Test or MAT.

Assumption College, Graduate School, Counseling Psychology Program, Worcester, MA 01609-1296. Offers child and family interventions (MA); cognitive and behavioral therapies (MA); general psychology (MA). Part-time and evening/weekend programs available. *Faculty:* 4 full-time (1 woman), 6 part-time/adjunct (2 women). *Students:* 41 full-time (34 women), 30 part-time (22 women); includes 4 minority (2 African Americans, 2 Hispanic Americans), 2 international. Average age 24. 83 applicants, 81% accepted. In 2008, 28 master's, 1 other advanced degree awarded. *Degree requirements:* For master's, comprehensive exam, internship, practicum, oral exam; for CAGS, comprehensive exam, oral exam. *Entrance requirements:* For master's, 3 letters of recommendation, resumé, essay; for CAGS, 3 letters of recommendation, resumé, interview, essay. Additional exam requirements/recommendations for international students: Required—TOEFL (minimum score 540 paper-based; 200 computer-based; 76 iBT), IELTS (minimum score 6). *Application deadline:* For fall admission, 6/1 priority date for domestic students, 5/1 priority date for international students; for spring admission, 11/1 priority date for domestic students, 9/1 priority date for international students. Applications are processed on a rolling basis. Application fee: $30. Electronic applications accepted. *Expenses:* Tuition: Part-time $468 per credit hour. Required fees: $20 per semester. One-time fee: $100. *Financial support:* In 2008–09, 19 fellowships with partial tuition reimbursements (averaging $6,808 per year), 2 teaching assistantships with full tuition reimbursements (averaging $9,940 per year) were awarded. Financial award application deadline: 3/1; financial award applicants required to submit FAFSA. *Faculty research:* Mood disorders, adjustment to life-threatening illness, perception of movement, socioemotional development of young children, discovery versus disclosure. *Unit head:* Dr. Leonard A. Doerfler, Director, 508-767-7549, Fax: 508-767-7263, E-mail: doerfler@assumption.edu. *Application contact:* Adrian O. Dumas, Director of Graduate Enrollment Management and Services, 508-767-7365, Fax: 508-767-7030, E-mail: adumas@assumption.edu.

Athabasca University, Graduate Centre for Applied Psychology, Athabasca, AB T9S 3A3, Canada. Offers art therapy (MC); career counseling (MC); counseling (Advanced Certificate); counseling psychology (MC); school counseling (MC). *Faculty:* 3 full-time (2 women), 2 part-time/adjunct (0 women). Tuition and fees charges are reported in Canadian dollars. *Expenses:* Tuition, area resident: Full-time $13,255 Canadian dollars; part-time $1205 Canadian dollars per course. Tuition, state resident: full-time $13,255 Canadian dollars; part-time $1205 Canadian dollars per course. Tuition, nonresident: full-time $13,255 Canadian dollars; part-time $1205 Canadian dollars per course. International tuition: $15,455 Canadian dollars full-time. One-time fee: $280 Canadian dollars. *Unit head:* Dr. Sandra Collins, Program Director, 888-611-7121, E-mail: sandrac@athabascau.ca. *Application contact:* Information Contact, 800-788-9041, Fax: 780-675-6437, E-mail: inquire@athabascau.ca.

Auburn University, Graduate School, College of Education, Department of Counseling and Counseling Psychology, Auburn University, AL 36849. Offers community agency counseling (M Ed, MS, Ed D, PhD, Ed S); counseling psychology (PhD); counselor education (Ed D, PhD); school counseling (M Ed, MS, Ed D, PhD, Ed S); school psychometry (M Ed, MS, Ed D, PhD, Ed S). *Accreditation:* ACA (one or more programs are accredited); APA (one or more programs are accredited); NCATE. Part-time programs available. *Faculty:* 10 full-time (6 women). *Students:* 51 full-time (35 women), 41 part-time (33 women); includes 27 minority (26 African Americans, 1 Hispanic American), 5 international. Average age 31. 140 applicants, 42% accepted, 30 enrolled. In 2008, 20 master's, 9 doctorates, 4 other advanced degrees awarded. *Degree requirements:* For master's, thesis (for some programs); for doctorate, thesis/dissertation; for Ed S, thesis or alternative. *Entrance requirements:* For master's and Ed S, GRE General Test; for doctorate, GRE General Test, GRE Subject Test. *Application deadline:* For fall admission, 5/15 for domestic students. Application fee: $25 ($50 for international students). Electronic applications accepted. *Expenses:* Tuition, area resident: Full-time $5880; part-time $243 per credit hour. Tuition, state resident: full-time $5880; part-time $243 per credit hour. Tuition, nonresident: full-time $17,640; part-time $729 per credit hour. International tuition: $17,846 full-time. Required fees: $620. Tuition and fees vary according to program and reciprocity agreements. *Financial support:* Research assistantships, Federal Work-Study and traineeships available. Support available to part-time students. Financial award application deadline: 3/15. *Faculty research:* At-risk students, substance abuse, gender roles, AIDS, professional ethics. *Unit head:* Dr. Holly Stadler, Head, 334-844-5160. *Application contact:* Dr. Joe Pittman, Interim Dean of the Graduate School, 334-844-4700.

Avila University, Department of Psychology, Kansas City, MO 64145-1698. Offers counseling psychology (MS); general psychology (MS). Part-time and evening/weekend programs available. *Faculty:* 7 full-time (5 women), 12 part-time/adjunct (9 women). *Students:* 116 full-time (93 women), 29 part-time (25 women); includes 31 minority (27 African Americans, 2 Asian Americans or Pacific Islanders, 2 Hispanic Americans), 6 international. Average age 32. 72 applicants, 72% accepted, 41 enrolled. In 2008, 31 master's awarded. *Entrance requirements:* For master's, minimum GPA of 3.0 in last 60 hours, 2 letters of recommendation, transcripts, application with letter of intent. Additional exam requirements/recommendations for international students: Required—TOEFL. *Application deadline:* Applications are processed on a rolling basis. Application fee: $0. *Expenses:* Tuition: Full-time $7776; part-time $432 per credit hour. Required fees: $414; $24 per credit hour. Tuition and fees vary according to program. *Financial support:* In 2008–09, 108 students received support. Career-related internships or fieldwork and scholarships/grants available. Support available to part-time students. Financial award applicants required to submit FAFSA. *Faculty research:* Preparation for working in mental health services. *Unit head:* Dr. Regina Staves, Director of Graduate Psychology, 816-501-3665, Fax: 816-501-2455, E-mail: gradpsych@avila.edu. *Application contact:* Ann Grubbs, Administrative Assistant, 816-501-3698, E-mail: gradpsych@avila.edu.

Ball State University, Graduate School, Teachers College, Department of Counseling Psychology and Guidance Services, Program in Counseling Psychology, Muncie, IN 47306-1099. Offers MA, PhD. *Accreditation:* ACA. *Degree requirements:* For doctorate, thesis/dissertation. *Entrance requirements:* For doctorate, GRE General Test, interview, minimum graduate GPA of 3.2, resumé.

Bemidji State University, School of Graduate Studies, College of Social and Natural Sciences, Field of Counseling Psychology, Bemidji, MN 56601-2699. Offers psychology (MS). Part-time programs available. *Entrance requirements:* For master's, GRE General Test, letters of recommendation, letter of intent, curriculum vitae/resumé. Additional exam requirements/recommendations for international students: Required—TOEFL. Electronic applications accepted. *Faculty research:* Exercise and working memory; age and stability of self-esteem in rural women; traumatic stress; Post-Traumatic Stress Disorder treatment for vets; learning outcomes assessment.

Bethel University, Graduate School, Department of Psychology, St. Paul, MN 55112-6999. Offers child and adolescent mental health (Certificate); counseling psychology (MA). Evening/weekend programs available. *Degree requirements:* For master's, comprehensive exam, thesis, practicum. *Entrance requirements:* For master's, MAT, interview, minimum GPA of 3.0, course work in psychology and statistics, letters of reference. Additional exam requirements/recommendations for international students: Required—TOEFL (minimum score 550 paper-based; 213 computer-based). Electronic applications accepted.

Boston College, Lynch Graduate School of Education, Department of Counseling Psychology, Developmental, and Educational Psychology, Program in Counseling Psychology, Chestnut Hill, MA 02467-3800. Offers MA, PhD, MA/MA. *Accreditation:* APA (one or more programs are accredited). Terminal master's awarded for partial completion of doctoral program. *Degree requirements:* For master's, comprehensive exam; for doctorate, comprehensive exam, thesis/dissertation. *Entrance requirements:* For master's and doctorate, GRE General Test. Additional exam requirements/recommendations for international students: Required—TOEFL (minimum score 550 paper-based; 213 computer-based; 81 iBT). Electronic applications accepted. *Expenses:* Tuition: Part-time $1148 per credit. Required fees: $60. *Faculty research:* Reducing non-academic barriers to learning; race, gender, culture and social class issues in mental health; domestic violence; career development; community intervention and prevention.

Boston Graduate School of Psychoanalysis, Program in Psychoanalytic Counseling, Brookline, MA 02446-4602. Offers MA. *Degree requirements:* For master's, 100-hour practicum, 600-hour internship. *Entrance requirements:* For master's, interview, writing sample. Electronic applications accepted. *Faculty research:* Emotional learning in the classroom, addictions, the effect of extra-analytic contact with analysis, the geriatric setting, siblings.

Boston University, School of Education, Department of Literacy and Language, Counseling and Development, Program in Counseling Psychology, Boston, MA 02215. Offers Ed D. *Degree requirements:* For doctorate, comprehensive exam, thesis/dissertation. *Entrance requirements:* For doctorate, GRE General Test or MAT. Additional exam requirements/recommendations for international students: Required—TOEFL. Electronic applications accepted. *Faculty research:* Cross-cultural counseling, parenting, women's development, mental health.

Boston University, School of Medicine, Division of Graduate Medical Sciences, Program in Mental Health and Behavioral Medicine, Boston, MA 02215. Offers MA. *Entrance requirements:* For master's, GRE General Test. Additional exam requirements/recommendations for international students: Required—TOEFL. *Faculty research:* HIV/AIDS, trauma, behavioral medicine (obesity, breast cancer), neurosciences, autism, serious mental illness, sports psychology.

Bowie State University, Graduate Programs, Program in Counseling Psychology, Bowie, MD 20715-9465. Offers MA. Part-time and evening/weekend programs available. *Degree requirements:* For master's, comprehensive exam, thesis optional, research paper, practicum. *Entrance requirements:* For master's, self statement, 2.5 minimum GPA, 3 recommendations. Electronic applications accepted.

Bowie State University, Graduate Programs, Program in Mental Health Counseling, Bowie, MD 20715-9465. Offers MA. Part-time and evening/weekend programs available. *Degree requirements:* For master's, comprehensive exam. *Entrance requirements:* For master's, 3 letters of recommendation, 3.0 GPA, personal statement, 12 undergraduate credit hours in couseling or psycology. Electronic applications accepted.

Bowling Green State University, Graduate College, College of Education and Human Development, School of Education and Intervention Services, Intervention Services Division, Program in Counseling, Bowling Green, OH 43403. Offers mental health counseling (MA); school counseling (M Ed). *Accreditation:* NCATE. Part-time programs available. *Degree requirements:* For master's, thesis or alternative. *Entrance requirements:* For master's, GRE General Test. Additional exam requirements/recommendations for international students: Required—TOEFL. Electronic applications accepted. *Faculty research:* Perfectionism, multicultural counseling, suicide, ethics and legal issues related to counseling, play therapy.

Brigham Young University, Graduate Studies, David O. McKay School of Education, Department of Counseling Psychology and Special Education, Provo, UT 84602-1001. Offers school psychology (PhD); school psychology (Ed S); special education (MS). *Accreditation:* NCATE. Part-time programs available. *Faculty:* 12 full-time (7 women), 11 part-time/adjunct (4 women). *Students:* 64 full-time (44 women), 14 part-time (13 women); includes 13 minority (1 African American, 2 American Indian/Alaska Native, 8 Asian Americans or Pacific Islanders, 2 Hispanic Americans), 5 international. Average age 31. 67 applicants, 49% accepted, 17 enrolled. In 2008, 2 master's, 10 doctorates, 12 other advanced degrees awarded. *Degree requirements:* For master's, comprehensive exam, thesis; for doctorate, comprehensive exam, thesis/dissertation. *Entrance requirements:* For master's and doctorate, GRE General Test, minimum GPA of 3.0 in last 60 hours of undergraduate coursework. Additional exam requirements/recommendations for international students: Required—TOEFL (minimum score 580 paper-based; 237 computer-based), IELTS (minimum score 7). *Application deadline:* For fall admission, 1/15 for domestic and international students. Application fee: $50. Electronic applications accepted. *Expenses:* Tuition: Full-time $5160; part-time $287 per credit hour. Tuition and fees vary according to program and student's religious affiliation. *Financial support:* In 2008–09, 45 students received support, including 30 research assistantships with partial tuition reimbursements available (averaging $5,400 per year), 3 teaching assistantships with partial tuition reimbursements available (averaging $6,120 per year); career-related internships or fieldwork, institutionally sponsored loans, and tuition waivers (partial) also available. Financial award application deadline: 4/30. *Faculty research:* Gender issues in education, psychotherapy progress and outcome, and behavior disorders and ABA. Total annual research expenditures: $195,507. *Unit head:* Dr. Mary Anne Prater, Chair, 801-422-3857, Fax: 801-422-0198, E-mail: prater@byu.edu. *Application contact:* Diane E. Hancock, Department Secretary, 801-422-3859, Fax: 801-422-0198, E-mail: diane_hancock@byu.edu.

Brooklyn College of the City University of New York, Division of Graduate Studies, Department of Health and Nutrition Science, Brooklyn, NY 11210-2889. Offers community health (MA, MPH, MS), including community health education (MA), computer science and health science (MS), health care management (MPH), health care policy and administration (MPH), thanatology (MA); grief counseling (CAS); nutrition (MS); public health (MPH). Part-time and evening/weekend programs available. *Students:* 8 full-time (7 women), 170 part-time (142 women); includes 76 minority (53 African Americans, 14 Asian Americans or Pacific Islanders, 9 Hispanic Americans), 19 international. Average age 34. 118 applicants, 71% accepted, 50 enrolled. In 2008, 41 master's, 1 other advanced degree awarded. *Degree requirements:* For master's, thesis or alternative. *Entrance requirements:* For master's, GRE, 18 credits, essay, 2 letters of recommendation. Additional exam requirements/recommendations for international students: Required—TOEFL. *Application deadline:* For fall admission, 3/1 priority date for domestic students, 2/1 priority date for international students; for spring admission, 11/1 priority date for domestic students, 10/1 priority date for international students. Applications are processed on a rolling basis. Application fee: $125. Electronic applications accepted. *Expenses:* Tuition, state resident: full-time $7360; part-time $310 per credit hour. Tuition, nonresident: full-time $13,800; part-time $575 per credit hour. *Financial support:* Career-related internships or fieldwork, Federal Work-Study, institutionally sponsored loans, and scholarships/grants available. Support available to part-time students. Financial award application deadline: 5/1; financial award applicants required to submit FAFSA. *Faculty research:* Medical ethics, relocation stress, risk reduction, disease prevention, history of public health, computer applications. *Unit head:* Dr. Janet Kolmer Grommet, Chairperson, 718-951-5026, Fax: 718-951-4670, E-mail: jgrommet@brooklyn.cuny.edu. *Application contact:* Hernan Sierra, Graduate Admissions Coordinator, 718-951-4536, Fax: 718-951-4506, E-mail: grads@brooklyn.cuny.edu.

Brooklyn College of the City University of New York, Division of Graduate Studies, Department of Psychology, Brooklyn, NY 11210-2889. Offers experimental psychology (MA); industrial and organizational psychology (MA), including industrial and organizational psychology-human relations, psychology-organizational psychology and behavior; mental health counseling (MA); psychology (PhD). The City University doctoral program in experimental psychology is based at Brooklyn College; candidates who complete the MA may apply for admission to the doctoral program. MA programs in industrial and organizational psychology and mental health counseling are fall admissions only. Part-time programs available. *Students:* 79 full-time (68 women), 121 part-time (93 women); includes 77 minority (48 African Americans, 1 American Indian/Alaska Native, 10 Asian Americans or Pacific Islanders, 18 Hispanic Americans), 18 international. Average age 31. 254 applicants, 59% accepted, 101 enrolled. In 2008, 48 master's awarded. *Degree requirements:* For master's, comprehensive exam, thesis (for some programs). *Entrance requirements:* For master's, minimum GPA of 3.0, 2 letters of recommendation, essay; for doctorate, GRE. Additional exam requirements/recommendations for international students: Required—TOEFL. *Application deadline:* For fall admission, 3/1 for domestic students, 2/1 for international students; for spring admission, 11/1 for domestic students, 10/1 for international students. Applications are processed on a rolling basis. Application fee: $125. Electronic applications accepted. *Expenses:* Tuition, state resident: full-time $7360; part-time $310 per credit hour. Tuition, nonresident: full-time $13,800; part-time $575 per credit hour. *Financial support:* Career-related internships or fieldwork, Federal Work-Study, institutionally sponsored loans, scholarships/grants, and tuition waivers (partial) available. Support available to part-time students. Financial award application deadline: 5/1; financial award applicants required to submit FAFSA. *Unit head:* Dr. Glen Hass, Chairperson, 718-951-5601, Fax: 718-951-4814, E-mail: ghass@brooklyn.cuny.edu. *Application contact:* Hernan Sierra, Graduate Admissions Coordinator, 718-951-4536, Fax: 718-951-4506, E-mail: grads@brooklyn.cuny.edu.

Caldwell College, Graduate Studies, Program in Counseling Psychology, Caldwell, NJ 07006-6195. Offers art therapy (MA); counseling psychology (MA); school counseling (MA). Part-time and evening/weekend programs available. *Degree requirements:* For master's, comprehensive exam, practicum. *Entrance requirements:* For master's, GRE General Test, minimum GPA of 3.0. Additional exam requirements/recommendations for international students: Required—TOEFL (minimum score 580 paper-based; 237 computer-based). Electronic applications accepted.

California Baptist University, Program in Counseling Psychology, Riverside, CA 92504-3206. Offers professional counseling (MS); professional ministry (MS). Part-time programs available. *Faculty:* 4 full-time (2 women), 4 part-time/adjunct (2 women). *Students:* 79 full-time (61 women), 54 part-time (42 women); includes 58 minority (14 African Americans, 1 American Indian/Alaska Native, 9 Asian Americans or Pacific Islanders, 34 Hispanic Americans), 3 international. 116 applicants, 54% accepted, 48 enrolled. In 2008, 45 master's awarded. *Degree requirements:* For master's, comprehensive exam, 24 hours (individual) or 50 hours (group) psychotherapy. *Entrance requirements:* For master's, Minnesota Multiphasic Personality Inventory, Myers-Briggs Type Inventory, course work in developmental psychology, theories of personality, and statistics; minimum undergraduate GPA of 2.75. Additional exam requirements/recommendations for international students: Required—TOEFL (minimum score 575 paper-based; 230 computer-based; 89 iBT). *Application deadline:* For fall admission, 9/1 for domestic students, 7/1 priority date for international students; for spring admission, 1/3 for domestic students, 10/15 priority date for international students. Applications are processed on a rolling basis. Application fee: $45. Electronic applications accepted. *Expenses:* Contact institution. *Financial support:* Career-related internships or fieldwork, Federal Work-Study, and scholarships/grants available. Support available to part-time students. Financial award applicants required to submit FAFSA. *Unit head:* Dr. Gary Collins, Director and Associate Dean, School of Business, 951-343-4304, Fax: 951-343-4569, E-mail: gcollins@calbaptist.edu. *Application contact:* Gail Ronveaux, Dean of Graduate Enrollment, 951-343-5045, Fax: 951-343-5095, E-mail: graduateadmissions@calbaptist.edu.

California Institute of Integral Studies, Graduate Programs, School of Professional Psychology, San Francisco, CA 94103. Offers clinical psychology (Psy D); community mental health (MA); drama therapy (MA); expressive arts therapy (MA); integral counseling psychology (MA); integral counseling, psychology-weekend (MA); somatic psychology (MA). *Accreditation:* APA. Part-time programs available. *Faculty:* 28 full-time, 59 part-time/adjunct. *Students:* 553 full-time (408 women), 88 part-time (69 women); includes 132 minority (25 African Americans, 3 American Indian/Alaska Native, 57 Asian Americans or Pacific Islanders, 47 Hispanic Americans). Average age 37. 506 applicants, 61% accepted, 181 enrolled. In 2008, 109 master's, 20 doctorates awarded. *Degree requirements:* For master's, comprehensive exam; for doctorate, comprehensive exam, thesis/dissertation. *Entrance requirements:* For master's, minimum GPA of 3.0, letters of recommendation, writing sample; for doctorate, GRE, MA in psychology or social work with appropriate practical experience for advanced standing, or BA with a minimum GPA of 3.1; letters of recommendation; writing sample. Additional exam requirements/recommendations for international students: Required—TOEFL. *Application deadline:* For fall admission, 2/1 priority date for domestic and international students; for spring admission, 10/15 priority date for domestic and international students. Applications are processed

on a rolling basis. Application fee: $65. Electronic applications accepted. *Expenses:* Tuition: Part-time $815 per contact hour. Required fees: $270; $135 per semester. Tuition and fees vary according to degree level. *Financial support:* In 2008–09, 496 students received support; research assistantships with tuition reimbursements available, teaching assistantships with tuition reimbursements available, career-related internships or fieldwork, Federal Work-Study, institutionally sponsored loans, scholarships/grants, and tuition waivers (partial) available. Support available to part-time students. Financial award application deadline: 3/15; financial award applicants required to submit FAFSA. *Faculty research:* Somatic psychology, comparative psychology, art therapy, transpersonal psychology, eco-psychology. *Application contact:* David Townes, Senior Admissions Counselor, 415-575-6152, Fax: 415-575-1268, E-mail: dtownes@ciis.edu.

See Close-Up on page 1105.

California State University, Bakersfield, Division of Graduate Studies, School of Humanities and Social Sciences, Program in Counseling Psychology, Bakersfield, CA 93311-1022. Offers MS.

California State University, Sacramento, Graduate Studies, College of Social Sciences and Interdisciplinary Studies, Department of Psychology, Sacramento, CA 95819-6048. Offers counseling psychology (MA). Part-time programs available. *Degree requirements:* For master's, thesis, writing proficiency exam. *Entrance requirements:* For master's, GRE Subject Test, minimum GPA of 3.0 during previous 2 years. Additional exam requirements/recommendations for international students: Required—TOEFL. Electronic applications accepted.

California State University, San Bernardino, Graduate Studies, College of Social and Behavioral Sciences, Department of Psychology, Program in Clinical/Counseling Psychology, San Bernardino, CA 92407-2397. Offers clinical psychology (MS). *Students:* 28 full-time (25 women), 1 (woman) part-time; includes 13 minority (3 African Americans, 2 Asian Americans or Pacific Islanders, 8 Hispanic Americans), 1 international. Average age 30. 64 applicants, 16% accepted, 9 enrolled. In 2008, 5 master's awarded. *Degree requirements:* For master's, comprehensive exam (for some programs), thesis optional, comprehensive exam or thesis. *Entrance requirements:* For master's, minimum GPA of 3.0 in major. *Application deadline:* For fall admission, 8/31 priority date for domestic students. Application fee: $55. *Expenses:* Tuition, area resident: Full-time $1252; part-time $726 per quarter. Required fees: $334 per quarter. Tuition and fees vary according to degree level and student level. *Financial support:* Fellowships, research assistantships, teaching assistantships, career-related internships or fieldwork, Federal Work-Study, and unspecified assistantships available. Financial award application deadline: 3/1. *Faculty research:* Psychology of women, fathering, depression, families, cross-cultural counseling. *Unit head:* Dr. Robert Cramer, Chair, 909-537-5576, Fax: 909-537-7003, E-mail: rcramer@csusb.edu. *Application contact:* Stacy Brooks, Graduate Secretary, 909-880-5570, Fax: 909-880-7003, E-mail: sbrooks@csusb.edu.

Cambridge College, School of Psychology and Counseling, Cambridge, MA 02138-5304. Offers addiction counseling (M Ed); counseling psychology (M Ed); counseling psychology: forensic counseling (M Ed); marriage and family therapy (M Ed); mental health and addiction counseling (M Ed); mental health counseling (M Ed); mental health counseling for school guidance counselors (Certificate); mental health, addiction and school adjustment counseling (M Ed); psychological studies (M Ed); school adjustment counseling (M Ed); school guidance counseling (M Ed). Part-time and evening/weekend programs available. *Faculty:* 5 full-time (2 women), 183 part-time/adjunct (85 women). *Students:* 476 full-time (384 women), 313 part-time (245 women); includes 396 minority (300 African Americans, 2 American Indian/Alaska Native, 13 Asian Americans or Pacific Islanders, 81 Hispanic Americans), 13 international. Average age 37. 307 applicants, 81% accepted, 192 enrolled. In 2008, 226 master's, 9 CAGSs awarded. *Degree requirements:* For master's, thesis, practicum/internship; for other advanced degree, thesis, practicum/Internship. *Entrance requirements:* For master's, evidence of a bachelor's degree from an accredited institution; essay; 2 references; health insurance; for other advanced degree, evidence of a master's degree from an accredited institution; essay; 2 references; health insurance. Additional exam requirements/recommendations for international students: Required—TOEFL (minimum score 550 paper-based; 213 computer-based; 79 iBT). *Application deadline:* Applications are processed on a rolling basis. Application fee: $30. Electronic applications accepted. *Expenses:* Tuition: Full-time $6960; part-time $435 per credit. One-time fee: $140 full-time. Tuition and fees vary according to degree level, campus/location and program. *Financial support:* In 2008–09, 857 students received support. Career-related internships or fieldwork, Federal Work-Study, and scholarships/grants available. Financial award applicants required to submit FAFSA. *Unit head:* Dr. Niti Seth, EdD, Dean, 617-873-0208, Fax: 617-349-3545, E-mail: nseth@cambridgecollege.edu. *Application contact:* Kathryn Lenehan, Admission Counselor, 800-877-0280, E-mail: kathryn.lenehan@cambridgecollege.edu.

Capella University, Harold Abel School of Psychology, Minneapolis, MN 55402. Offers clinical psychology (MS); counseling psychology (MS); educational psychology (MS, PhD); general psychology (MS, PhD); industrial/organizational psychology (MS, PhD); school psychology (MS, Certificate); sport psychology (MS). Part-time and evening/weekend programs available. Postbaccalaureate distance learning degree programs offered (minimal on-campus study). Terminal master's awarded for partial completion of doctoral program. *Degree requirements:* For master's, thesis optional, project; for doctorate, thesis/dissertation. *Entrance requirements:* For degree, master's degree in school psychology. Additional exam requirements/recommendations for international students: Required—TOEFL (minimum score 550 paper-based; 213 computer-based), TWE (minimum score 4). Electronic applications accepted. *Faculty research:* Correctional mental health delivery, community mental health, attachment and caregiving in adult and family relationships, influence of encouragement on motivation, and moral dilemmas in business.

Capella University, School of Human Services, Minneapolis, MN 55402. Offers addictions counseling (Certificate); counseling studies (MS, PhD); criminal justice (MS, PhD, Certificate); diversity studies (Certificate); general human services (MS, PhD); health care administration (MS, PhD, Certificate); management of nonprofit agencies (MS, PhD, Certificate); marital, couple and family counseling/therapy (MS); marriage and family services (Certificate); mental health counseling (MS); professional counseling (Certificate); social and community services (MS, PhD, Certificate). Part-time and evening/weekend programs available. Postbaccalaureate distance learning degree programs offered (minimal on-campus study). Terminal master's awarded for partial completion of doctoral program. *Degree requirements:* For master's, thesis optional, integrative project; for doctorate, comprehensive exam, thesis/dissertation. *Entrance requirements:* Additional exam requirements/recommendations for international students: Required—TOEFL (minimum score 550 paper-based; 213 computer-based), TWE (minimum score 4). Electronic applications accepted. *Faculty research:* Compulsive and addictive behaviors, substance abuse, assessment of psychopathology and neuropsychology.

Carlos Albizu University, Miami Campus, Graduate Programs, Miami, FL 33172-2209. Offers clinical psychology (Psy D); entrepreneurship (MBA); exceptional student education (MS); industrial/organizational psychology (MS); marriage and family therapy (MS); mental health counseling (MS); nonprofit management (MBA); organizational management (MBA); psychology (MS); school counseling (MS); teaching English as a second language (MS). *Accreditation:* APA. Part-time and evening/weekend programs available. *Faculty:* 19 full-time (12 women), 70 part-time/adjunct (35 women). *Students:* 498 full-time (409 women), 199 part-time (153 women); includes 515 minority (56 African Americans, 1 American Indian/Alaska Native, 7 Asian Americans or Pacific Islanders, 451 Hispanic Americans). Average age 33. 179 applicants, 67% accepted, 113 enrolled. In 2008, 185 master's, 21 doctorates awarded. Terminal master's awarded for partial completion of doctoral program. *Degree requirements:* For master's, one foreign language, comprehensive exam, integrative project (MBA), research project (MSESE and MSTESOL); for doctorate, one foreign language, comprehensive exam, internship, doctoral project. *Entrance requirements:* For master's, 3 letters of recommendation, interview, minimum GPA of 3.0, resumé, statement of purpose, official transcripts; for doctorate, 3 letters of recommendation, minimum GPA of 3.0, resumé, interview. *Application deadline:*

Counseling Psychology

Carlos Albizu University, Miami Campus (continued)
For fall admission, 8/1 priority date for domestic students; for spring admission, 11/30 priority date for domestic students. Applications are processed on a rolling basis. Application fee: $50. Electronic applications accepted. *Expenses:* Tuition: Full-time $9090; part-time $505 per credit. Required fees: $298 per term. Tuition and fees vary according to course load, degree level and program. *Financial support:* In 2008–09, 111 students received support. Federal Work-Study, scholarships/grants, and tuition discounts available. Financial award application deadline: 6/1; financial award applicants required to submit FAFSA. *Faculty research:* Psychotherapy, forensic psychology, neuropsychology, marketing strategy, entrepreneurship, special education. *Unit head:* Dr. Carmen S. Roca, PhD, Chancellor, 305-593-1223 Ext. 120, Fax: 305-629-8052, E-mail: croca@albizu.edu. *Application contact:* Barbara De la Cruz, Admission Officer, 305-593-1223 Ext. 218, Fax: 305-593-1854, E-mail: bdelacruz@albizu.edu.

Carlow University, School for Social Change, Pittsburgh, PA 15213-3165. Offers professional counseling (MS); professional counseling: school counseling (MS); professional leadership: management for nonprofit organizations (MS); professional leadership: organizational influence and policy (MS); professional leadership: training and development (MS). Part-time and evening/weekend programs available. *Faculty:* 5 full-time (3 women), 10 part-time/adjunct (5 women). *Students:* 98 full-time (92 women), 85 part-time (79 women); includes 38 minority (36 African Americans, 2 Asian Americans or Pacific Islanders). Average age 31. 146 applicants, 47% accepted, 63 enrolled. In 2008, 64 master's awarded. *Entrance requirements:* Additional exam requirements/recommendations for international students: Required—TOEFL (minimum score 550 paper-based; 213 computer-based). *Application deadline:* For fall admission, 6/15 priority date for domestic and international students; for spring admission, 11/15 priority date for domestic and international students. Applications are processed on a rolling basis. Application fee: $20. Electronic applications accepted. *Expenses:* Tuition: Part-time $700 per credit. *Financial support:* Federal Work-Study available. Financial award application deadline: 4/1; financial award applicants required to submit FAFSA. *Faculty research:* Gender and leadership, cross cultural communications and leadership, organizational culture. *Unit head:* Robert A Reed, PsyD, Chair, Department of Psychology and Counseling, 412-575-6349, E-mail: reedra@carlow.edu. *Application contact:* Jo Danhires, Administrative Assistant, Admissions, 412-578-6059, Fax: 412-578-6321, E-mail: gradstudies@carlow.edu.

Centenary College, Program in Counseling Psychology, Hackettstown, NJ 07840-2100. Offers counseling (MA); counseling psychology (MA). Part-time and evening/weekend programs available. Postbaccalaureate distance learning degree programs offered (minimal on-campus study). *Degree requirements:* For master's, thesis, fieldwork.

Central Michigan University, Central Michigan University Off-Campus Programs, Program in Counseling, Mount Pleasant, MI 48859. Offers professional counseling (MA); school counseling (MA). Part-time and evening/weekend programs available. *Entrance requirements:* For master's, MAT, minimum GPA of 2.7. Additional exam requirements/recommendations for international students: Required—TOEFL. Electronic applications accepted. *Expenses:* Tuition, state resident: full-time $3717; part-time $413 per credit. Tuition, nonresident: full-time $6894; part-time $766 per credit. *Financial support:* Scholarships/grants available. Support available to part-time students. *Unit head:* Dr. Suzanne Shellady, Chair, 989-774-3507, E-mail: shell1sm@cmich.edu. *Application contact:* 877-268-4636, E-mail: cmuoffcampus@cmich.edu.

Central Michigan University, College of Graduate Studies, College of Humanities and Social and Behavioral Sciences, Department of Psychology, Program in School Psychology, Mount Pleasant, MI 48859. Offers psychological services (S Psy S); school psychology (PhD). *Accreditation:* APA; NCATE. *Students:* 20 full-time (17 women), 20 part-time (18 women); includes 1 African American, 1 international. Average age 28. In 2008, 5 other advanced degrees awarded. *Degree requirements:* For doctorate, thesis/dissertation; for S Psy S, thesis. *Entrance requirements:* For doctorate, GRE. *Application deadline:* For fall admission, 1/15 for domestic and international students. Application fee: $35 ($45 for international students). Electronic applications accepted. *Expenses:* Tuition, state resident: full-time $3717; part-time $413 per credit. Tuition, nonresident: full-time $6894; part-time $766 per credit. *Financial support:* Fellowships with tuition reimbursements, research assistantships with tuition reimbursements, teaching assistantships with tuition reimbursements, career-related internships or fieldwork, Federal Work-Study, unspecified assistantships, and out-of-state merit awards available. *Faculty research:* Psychology and education foundations, psychology and education assessment, intervention strategies. *Unit head:* Dr. Hajime Otani, Chairperson, 989-774-6494, Fax: 989-774-2553, E-mail: otani1h@cmich.edu. *Application contact:* Judith L. Prince, Director of Graduate Student Services, 989-774-1059, Fax: 989-774-1857, E-mail: judith.l.prince@cmich.edu.

Central Washington University, Graduate Studies, Research and Continuing Education, College of the Sciences, Department of Psychology, Program in Mental Health Counseling, Ellensburg, WA 98926. Offers MS. *Accreditation:* ACA. *Degree requirements:* For master's, thesis, internship. *Entrance requirements:* For master's, GRE General Test, minimum GPA of 3.0. Additional exam requirements/recommendations for international students: Required—TOEFL (minimum score 550 paper-based; 213 computer-based; 79 iBT).

Chaminade University of Honolulu, Graduate Services, Program in Counseling Psychology, Honolulu, HI 96816-1578. Offers MSCP. Part-time and evening/weekend programs available. *Degree requirements:* For master's, comprehensive exam. *Entrance requirements:* For master's, minimum undergraduate GPA of 3.0, 3 letters of recommendation. Additional exam requirements/recommendations for international students: Required—TOEFL (minimum score 550 paper-based). *Faculty research:* Taoist/Buddhist psychology, psychology of T'ai Chi Ch'uan, sleep disorders, drug/alcohol prevention with adolescent girls, anger/aggression with kids.

Chatham University, Program in Counseling Psychology, Pittsburgh, PA 15232-2826. Offers child, adolescent and family (MSCP); counseling psychology (Psy D); health and holistic (MSCP); infant mental health (MSCP); organization and supervision (MSCP); sport and exercise (MSCP). Part-time and evening/weekend programs available. *Students:* 121 full-time (104 women), 72 part-time (63 women). Average age 30. 117 applicants, 79% accepted, 60 enrolled. In 2008, 63 master's awarded. *Degree requirements:* For master's, thesis optional, supervised internship, advanced research project (optional); for doctorate, thesis/dissertation, internship. *Entrance requirements:* For master's, minimum GPA of 3.0; 2 letters of recommendation; resumé; prerequisite coursework in statistics, biology, and psychology; for doctorate, GRE. Additional exam requirements/recommendations for international students: Required—TOEFL (minimum score 600 paper-based; 250 computer-based; 100 iBT), IELTS (minimum score 6.5), TWE. *Application deadline:* For fall admission, 5/1 priority date for domestic and international students; for spring admission, 10/15 for domestic students, 10/15 priority date for international students. Applications are processed on a rolling basis. Application fee: $45. Electronic applications accepted. *Expenses:* Tuition: Part-time $686 per credit. Tuition and fees vary according to program. *Financial support:* Career-related internships or fieldwork available. Financial award applicants required to submit FAFSA. *Faculty research:* Trauma and recovery, hypnosis, psychospiritual dimensions of healing, psychotherapy of schizophrenia. *Unit head:* Dr. Mary Beth Mannarino, Director, 412-365-1196, Fax: 412-365-1505, E-mail: mmannarino@chatham.edu. *Application contact:* Dory Perry, Associate Director of Graduate Admissions, 412-365-2758, Fax: 412-365-1609, E-mail: gradadmissions@chatham.edu.

Chestnut Hill College, School of Graduate Studies, Division of Psychology, Program in Clinical and Counseling Psychology, Philadelphia, PA 19118-2693. Offers MA, MS, CAS. Part-time and evening/weekend programs available. *Faculty:* 11 full-time (5 women), 33 part-time/adjunct (14 women). *Students:* 144 full-time (133 women), 103 part-time (72 women); includes 47 minority (37 African Americans, 5 Asian Americans or Pacific Islanders, 5 Hispanic Americans). 147 applicants, 52% accepted. In 2008, 55 master's awarded. *Degree requirements:* For master's, thesis optional, practica. *Entrance requirements:* For master's, GRE, statement of professional goals, writing sample, transcripts, letters of recommendation; for CAS, GRE, master's degree in counseling or related discipline, transcripts, letters of recommendation, statement of professional goals, writing sample. Additional exam requirements/recommendations for international students: Required—TOEFL (minimum score 550 paper-based; 213 computer-based). *Application deadline:* For fall admission, 7/17 priority date for domestic students, 7/17 for international students; for spring admission, 12/15 priority date for domestic students, 12/15 for international students. Applications are processed on a rolling basis. Application fee: $50. *Expenses:* Tuition: Part-time $510 per credit hour. *Faculty research:* Play therapy, eating disorders, addictions, group psychology and group therapy, health psychology. *Application contact:* Amy Boorse, Administrative Assistant, School of Graduate Studies Office, 215-248-7170, Fax: 215-248-7161, E-mail: gradadmissions@chc.edu.

The Chicago School of Professional Psychology, Graduate School, Program in Clinical Psychology, Chicago, IL 60610. Offers applied behavior analysis (MA, Psy D, Certificate); clinical counseling (MA); clinical psychology (Psy D); general psychology (Certificate); Latino mental health (Certificate). *Degree requirements:* For master's, thesis (for some programs); for doctorate, comprehensive exam, thesis/dissertation. *Entrance requirements:* For master's, minimum undergraduate GPA of 3.0; 1 course in psychology and 1 course in either statistics or research methods; for doctorate, GRE, 18 hours of psychology credit (including courses in statistics, normal psychology and human development); minimum GPA of 3.2. Additional exam requirements/recommendations for international students: Required—TOEFL (minimum score 550 paper-based; 213 computer-based; 79 iBT). Electronic applications accepted.

City College of the City University of New York, Graduate School, College of Liberal Arts and Science, Program in Mental Health Counseling, New York, NY 10031-9198. Offers MA.

City University of Seattle, Graduate Division, Division of Arts and Sciences, Bellevue, WA 98005. Offers counseling psychology (MA). Part-time and evening/weekend programs available. Postbaccalaureate distance learning degree programs offered (no on-campus study). Electronic applications accepted. *Expenses:* Contact institution.

Cleveland State University, College of Graduate Studies, College of Education and Human Services, Department of Counseling, Administration, Supervision and Adult Learning (CASAL), Cleveland, OH 44115. Offers accelerated degree in adult learning and development (M Ed); adult learning and development (M Ed); chemical dependency counseling (Certificate); community agency counseling (M Ed); counseling and pupil personnel administration (Ed S); early childhood mental health counseling (Certificate); educational administration and supervision (M Ed); school administration (Ed S); school counseling (M Ed). *Accreditation:* ACA (one or more programs are accredited). Part-time and evening/weekend programs available. *Faculty:* 16 full-time (10 women), 8 part-time/adjunct (4 women). *Students:* 62 full-time (54 women), 351 part-time (274 women); includes 146 minority (127 African Americans, 3 Asian Americans or Pacific Islanders, 16 Hispanic Americans), 2 international. Average age 35. 235 applicants, 56% accepted, 104 enrolled. In 2008, 138 master's, 10 Certificates awarded. *Degree requirements:* For master's, comprehensive exam (for some programs), thesis optional; for other advanced degree, comprehensive exam, thesis optional, internship. *Entrance requirements:* For master's, GRE General Test or MAT, letter of recommendation, minimum GPA of 2.75. Additional exam requirements/recommendations for international students: Required—TOEFL (minimum score 525 paper-based; 197 computer-based), IELTS (minimum score 6). *Application deadline:* For fall admission, 6/21 for domestic students, 5/15 for international students; for spring admission, 8/31 for domestic students, 11/1 for international students. Application fee: $30. Electronic applications accepted. *Financial support:* In 2008–09, 8 students received support, including research assistantships with full and partial tuition reimbursements available (averaging $3,287 per year), teaching assistantships with full and partial tuition reimbursements available (averaging $3,480 per year); career-related internships or fieldwork, scholarships/grants, tuition waivers (full), and unspecified assistantships also available. Support available to part-time students. *Faculty research:* Education law, career development, women in school administration, psychopharmacology, counseling and spirituality. Total annual research expenditures: $478,265. *Unit head:* Dr. Ann L Bauer, Chairperson, 216-687-4582, Fax: 216-687-5378, E-mail: a.l.bauer@csuohio.edu. *Application contact:* Deborah L Brown, Interim Assistant Director, Graduate Admissions, 216-523-7572, Fax: 216-687-5400, E-mail: d.l.brown@csuohio.edu.

Cleveland State University, College of Graduate Studies, College of Education and Human Services, Program in Urban Education, Cleveland, OH 44115. Offers counseling (PhD); counseling psychology (PhD); leadership and lifelong learning (PhD); learning and development (PhD); policy studies (PhD); school administration (PhD). Part-time programs available. *Faculty:* 16 full-time (8 women), 15 part-time/adjunct (12 women). *Students:* 37 full-time (31 women), 76 part-time (48 women); includes 15 minority (all African Americans), 1 international. Average age 42. 53 applicants, 36% accepted, 13 enrolled. In 2008, 17 doctorates awarded. *Degree requirements:* For doctorate, one foreign language, comprehensive exam, thesis/dissertation. *Entrance requirements:* For doctorate, GRE General Test, minimum graduate GPA of 3.25. Additional exam requirements/recommendations for international students: Required—TOEFL (minimum score 525 paper-based; 197 computer-based), IELTS (minimum score 6). *Application deadline:* For fall admission, 2/5 for domestic students. Application fee: $30. *Financial support:* In 2008–09, 7 students received support, including 4 research assistantships with full and partial tuition reimbursements available (averaging $7,800 per year), 3 teaching assistantships with full and partial tuition reimbursements available (averaging $7,800 per year); tuition waivers (full) and unspecified assistantships also available. Financial award applicants required to submit FAFSA. *Faculty research:* Equity issues (race, ethnicity, and gender), education development consequences for special needs of urban populations, urban education programming, counseling the violent or aggressive adolescent. Total annual research expenditures: $5,662. *Unit head:* Dr. Joshua Bagakas, Director, 216-687-4591, Fax: 216-875-9697, E-mail: j.bagakas@csuohio.edu. *Application contact:* Wanda Butler, Administrative Assistant, 216-687-4697, Fax: 216-875-9697, E-mail: w.pruett-butler@csuohio.edu.

The College at Brockport, State University of New York, School of Professions, Department of Counselor Education, Brockport, NY 14420-2997. Offers college counseling (MS Ed); mental health counseling (MS); school counseling (MS Ed, CAS). *Accreditation:* ACA (one or more programs are accredited). Part-time programs available. *Degree requirements:* For master's, internship, project. *Entrance requirements:* For master's, interview, letters of recommendation; for CAS, master's degree, New York state school counselor certificate. Additional exam requirements/recommendations for international students: Required—TOEFL (minimum score 550 paper-based; 213 computer-based; 79 iBT). *Faculty research:* Gender and diversity issues, counseling outcomes, qualitative research, school counseling, mental health counseling and obesity.

The College of New Rochelle, Graduate School, Division of Human Services, Program in Guidance and Counseling, New Rochelle, NY 10805-2308. Offers MS. Part-time programs available. *Degree requirements:* For master's, internship. *Entrance requirements:* For master's, interview, minimum GPA of 3.0.

The College of New Rochelle, Graduate School, Division of Human Services, Program in Mental Health Counseling, New Rochelle, NY 10805-2308. Offers Certificate. *Degree requirements:* For Certificate, internship.

College of Saint Elizabeth, Department of Psychology, Morristown, NJ 07960-6989. Offers counseling psychology (MA); forensic psychology (MA); student affairs in higher education (Certificate). Part-time and evening/weekend programs available. *Faculty:* 4 full-time (2 women), 10 part-time/adjunct (5 women). *Students:* 11 full-time (10 women), 84 part-time (77 women); includes 23 minority (10 African Americans, 3 Asian Americans or Pacific Islanders, 10 Hispanic Americans), 2 international. Average age 34. 104 applicants, 58% accepted, 47 enrolled. In 2008, 11 master's, 1 other advanced degree awarded. *Degree requirements:* For master's, thesis or alternative, portfolio. *Entrance requirements:* For master's, minimum GPA of 3.0, BA in psychology (preferred), 12 credits of course work in psychology. *Application deadline:* For fall admission, 4/14 priority date for domestic students; for spring admission, 11/15 for domestic students. Applications are processed on a rolling basis. Application fee: $35. Electronic applications accepted. *Expenses:* Tuition: Part-time $759 per credit. Required fees: $380 per semester. *Financial support:* Career-related internships or fieldwork, tuition waivers (partial), and unspecified assistantships available. Support available to part-time students. Financial award application deadline: 3/15; financial award applicants required to submit FAFSA. *Faculty research:* Family systems, dissociative identity disorder, multicultural counseling, outcomes assessment. *Unit head:* Dr. Valerie Scott, Director of the Graduate Program in Counseling Psychology, 973-290-4102, Fax: 973-290-4676, E-mail: vscott@cse.edu. *Application contact:* Donna Tatarka, Dean of Admission, 973-290-4705, Fax: 973-290-4710, E-mail: dtatarka@cse.edu.

College of St. Joseph, Graduate Programs, Division of Psychology and Human Services, Program in Clinical Mental Health Counseling, Rutland, VT 05701-3899. Offers MS. Part-time programs available. *Degree requirements:* For master's, comprehensive exam. *Entrance requirements:* For master's, 2 letters of reference, interview. Electronic applications accepted.

College of Staten Island of the City University of New York, Graduate Programs, Program in Mental Health Counseling, Staten Island, NY 10314-6600. Offers MA. *Entrance requirements:* For master's, BA/BS degree with five undergraduate courses in psychology, minimum GPA of 3.0, two letters of recommendation, personal statement. Additional exam requirements/recommendations for international students: Required—TOEFL (minimum score 600 paper-based; 250 computer-based; 100 iBT). *Application deadline:* For fall admission, 6/30 priority date for domestic and international students. Applications are processed on a rolling basis. Application fee: $125. Electronic applications accepted. *Expenses:* Tuition, area resident: Full-time $6400; part-time $270 per credit. Tuition, nonresident: full-time $12,000; part-time $500 per credit. Required fees: $378; $113 per semester. *Financial support:* Federal Work-Study available. Support available to part-time students. *Unit head:* Dr. Judith Kuppersmith, PhD, Acting Program Coordinator, 718-982-3795, E-mail: kuppersmith@mail.csi.cuny.edu. *Application contact:* Sasha Spence, Assistant Director of Graduate Recruitment and Admissions, 718-982-2699, Fax: 718-982-2500, E-mail: spence@mail.csi.cuny.edu.

Colorado Christian University, Program in Counseling, Lakewood, CO 80226. Offers MA. Part-time and evening/weekend programs available. *Degree requirements:* For master's, thesis optional. *Entrance requirements:* For master's, GRE General Test, 3 letters of recommendation. Additional exam requirements/recommendations for international students: Required—TOEFL. Electronic applications accepted. *Expenses:* Contact institution.

Columbus State University, Graduate Studies, College of Education, Department of Counseling, Foundations, and Leadership, Columbus, GA 31907-5645. Offers community counseling (MS); educational leadership (M Ed, Ed S); school counseling (M Ed). *Accreditation:* ACA; NCATE. Part-time and evening/weekend programs available. Postbaccalaureate distance learning degree programs offered (minimal on-campus study). *Faculty:* 11 full-time (3 women), 7 part-time/adjunct (4 women). *Students:* 81 full-time (63 women), 72 part-time (55 women); includes 58 minority (53 African Americans, 2 Asian Americans or Pacific Islanders, 3 Hispanic Americans), 1 international. Average age 36. 127 applicants, 40% accepted, 46 enrolled. In 2008, 42 master's, 138 other advanced degrees awarded. *Degree requirements:* For master's, thesis, exit exam; for Ed S, thesis or alternative. *Entrance requirements:* For master's, GRE General Test, minimum GPA of 2.75; for Ed S, GRE General Test. Additional exam requirements/recommendations for international students: Required—TOEFL (minimum score 550 paper-based; 213 computer-based). *Application deadline:* For fall admission, 5/1 priority date for domestic students, 5/1 for international students; for spring admission, 11/1 for domestic and international students. Applications are processed on a rolling basis. Application fee: $25. Electronic applications accepted. *Expenses:* Tuition, area resident: Full-time $3410; part-time $143 per credit hour. Tuition, state resident: full-time $3411; part-time $143 per credit hour. Tuition, nonresident: full-time $13,634; part-time $569 per credit hour. Required fees: $1348. *Financial support:* In 2008–09, 64 students received support, including 7 research assistantships with partial tuition reimbursements available (averaging $3,000 per year); career-related internships or fieldwork, Federal Work-Study, institutionally sponsored loans, scholarships/grants, tuition waivers (partial), and unspecified assistantships also available. Support available to part-time students. Financial award application deadline: 5/1; financial award applicants required to submit FAFSA. *Unit head:* Dr. Paul Tom Hackett, Chair, 706-568-5061, Fax: 706-569-3134, E-mail: hackett_paul@colstate.edu. *Application contact:* Katie Thornton, Graduate Admissions Specialist, 706-568-2035, Fax: 706-568-2462, E-mail: thornton_katie@colstate.edu.

Concordia University Chicago, College of Graduate and Innovative Programs, Program in Community Counseling, River Forest, IL 60305-1499. Offers MA. *Accreditation:* ACA. *Degree requirements:* For master's, final project. *Entrance requirements:* For master's, minimum GPA of 2.9. Additional exam requirements/recommendations for international students: Required—TOEFL (minimum score 550 paper-based; 195 computer-based). Electronic applications accepted.

Concordia University Wisconsin, Graduate Programs, Department of Psychology, Program in Professional Counseling, Mequon, WI 53097-2402. Offers MPC. Postbaccalaureate distance learning degree programs offered (minimal on-campus study). *Degree requirements:* For master's, comprehensive exam, thesis or alternative. *Entrance requirements:* For master's, minimum GPA of 3.0. Additional exam requirements/recommendations for international students: Required—TOEFL.

Dallas Baptist University, College of Humanities and Social Sciences, Counseling Program (Main Campus), Dallas, TX 75211-9299. Offers MA. Part-time and evening/weekend programs available. *Faculty:* 68 full-time (30 women), 113 part-time/adjunct (47 women). *Students:* 7 full-time, 147 part-time. 44 applicants, 61% accepted, 27 enrolled. In 2008, 44 master's awarded. *Entrance requirements:* For master's, GRE General Test, minimum GPA of 3.0. Additional exam requirements/recommendations for international students: Required—TOEFL. *Application deadline:* Applications are processed on a rolling basis. Application fee: $25. Electronic applications accepted. *Expenses:* Tuition: Part-time $558 per credit hour. *Financial support:* Federal Work-Study, institutionally sponsored loans, scholarships/grants, and tuition waivers (full and partial) available. Support available to part-time students. Financial award applicants required to submit FAFSA. *Faculty research:* Therapy effectiveness. *Unit head:* Dr. Mary Becerril, Director, 214-333-5273, Fax: 214-333-5323, E-mail: graduate@dbu.edu. *Application contact:* Kit P. Montgomery, Director of Graduate Programs, 214-333-5242, Fax: 214-333-5579, E-mail: graduate@dbu.edu.

Dallas Baptist University, College of Humanities and Social Sciences, Counseling Program (North Campus), Dallas, TX 75211-9299. Offers). Part-time and evening/weekend programs available. *Faculty:* 68 full-time (30 women), 113 part-time/adjunct (47 women). *Students:* 53 part-time (44 women). 13 applicants, 77% accepted.Application fee: $25. *Expenses:* Tuition: Part-time $558 per credit hour. *Financial support:* Applicants required to submit FAFSA. *Unit head:* Dr. Joe Cook, Director, 214-333-5787, Fax: 214-333-5579. *Application contact:* Kit P. Montgomery, Director of Graduate Programs, 214-333-5242, Fax: 214-333-5579, E-mail: graduate@dbu.edu.

Dominican University of California, Graduate Programs, School of Arts and Sciences, Program in Counseling Psychology, San Rafael, CA 94901-2298. Offers MFT, MS. Part-time programs available. *Faculty:* 4 full-time (3 women), 11 part-time/adjunct (10 women). *Students:* 50 full-time (44 women), 49 part-time (44 women); includes 15 minority (5 African Americans, 1 Asian American or Pacific Islander, 9 Hispanic Americans). Average age 40. 13 applicants, 77% accepted, 7 enrolled. In 2008, 21 master's awarded. *Degree requirements:* For master's, comprehensive exam (for some programs), thesis (for some programs). *Entrance requirements:* For master's, minimum GPA of 3.0 for last 60 units. Additional exam requirements/recommendations for international students: Required—TOEFL (minimum score 550 paper-based; 213 computer-based). *Application deadline:* For fall admission, 6/15 priority date for domestic and international students; for spring admission, 11/15 priority date for domestic and international students. Applications are processed on a rolling basis. Application fee: $40. Electronic applications accepted. *Expenses:* Contact institution. *Financial support:* In 2008–09, 28 students received support, including fellowships (averaging $2,554 per year); career-related internships or fieldwork, scholarships/grants, traineeships, health care benefits, tuition waivers (partial), and tuition discounts also available. Support available to part-time students. Financial award application deadline: 7/1; financial award applicants required to submit FAFSA. *Unit head:* Dr. Charles R. Billings, Chair of the Graduate Department of Counseling Psychology, 415-485-3263. *Application contact:* Larry Schwartz, Associate Director of Graduate Admissions, 415-458-3748, E-mail: lawrence.schwartz@dominican.edu.

Eastern Nazarene College, Adult and Graduate Studies, Program in Family Counseling, Quincy, MA 02170-2999. Offers marriage and family therapy (MS). Part-time and evening/weekend programs available. *Entrance requirements:* For master's, 3 letters of recommendation, resumé. Additional exam requirements/recommendations for international students: Required—TOEFL (minimum score 550 paper-based).

Eastern University, Department of Counseling Psychology, St. Davids, PA 19087-3696. Offers community/clinical counseling (MA); school counseling (MA, Certificate); school psychology (MS, Certificate). *Degree requirements:* For master's, internship. *Entrance requirements:* For master's, minimum GPA of 2.5. Additional exam requirements/recommendations for international students: Required—TOEFL.

Eastern Washington University, Graduate Studies, College of Education and Human Development, Department of Counseling, Educational, and Developmental Psychology, Program in Mental Health Counseling, Cheney, WA 99004-2431. Offers applied psychology (MS); mental health counseling (MS).

Eastern Washington University, Graduate Studies, College of Education and Human Development, Department of Counseling, Educational, and Developmental Psychology, Program in School Counseling, Cheney, WA 99004-2431. Offers applied psychology (MS); school counseling (MS). *Accreditation:* ACA; NCATE. *Degree requirements:* For master's, comprehensive exam, thesis or alternative. *Entrance requirements:* For master's, GRE General Test, minimum GPA of 3.0.

Emporia State University, School of Graduate Studies, The Teachers College, Department of Psychology, Art Therapy, Rehabilitation and Mental Health Counseling, Program in Mental Health Counseling, Emporia, KS 66801-5087. Offers MS. *Accreditation:* ACA. Part-time programs available. *Students:* 20 full-time (17 women), 7 part-time (6 women); includes 2 minority (both African Americans), 4 international. 7 applicants, 57% accepted, 4 enrolled. In 2008, 4 master's awarded. *Degree requirements:* For master's, comprehensive exam, internship. *Entrance requirements:* For master's, GRE or MAT. Additional exam requirements/recommendations for international students: Required—TOEFL (minimum score 450 paper-based; 133 computer-based). *Application deadline:* For fall admission, 8/15 for domestic students. Applications are processed on a rolling basis. Application fee: $30 ($75 for international students). Electronic applications accepted. *Expenses:* Tuition, area resident: Full-time $3976; part-time $166 per credit hour. Tuition, state resident: full-time $3976; part-time $166 per credit hour. Tuition, nonresident: full-time $12,028; part-time $501 per credit hour. Required fees: $51 per credit hour. Tuition and fees vary according to campus/location. *Financial support:* Federal Work-Study, institutionally sponsored loans, health care benefits, and unspecified assistantships available. Financial award application deadline: 3/15; financial award applicants required to submit FAFSA. *Unit head:* Dr. Kenneth A. Weaver, Chair, 620-341-5317, E-mail: kweaver@emporia.edu. *Application contact:* Mary Sewell, Admissions Coordinator, 800-950-GRAD, Fax: 620-341-5909, E-mail: msewell@emporia.edu.

Evangel University, Department of Psychology, Springfield, MO 65802-2191. Offers clinical psychology (MS); counseling psychology (MS). Part-time and evening/weekend programs available. *Degree requirements:* For master's, comprehensive exam, thesis (for some programs). *Entrance requirements:* For master's, GRE General Test or MAT, minimum undergraduate GPA of 3.0, undergraduate major or minor in psychology, teaching certificate (school counseling). Additional exam requirements/recommendations for international students: Required—TOEFL (minimum score 550 paper-based; 213 computer-based).

Fairleigh Dickinson University, College at Florham, Maxwell Becton College of Arts and Sciences, Department of Psychology, Program in Counseling, Madison, NJ 07940-1099. Offers MA. *Students:* 51 full-time (34 women), 56 part-time (36 women), 3 international. Average age 30. 91 applicants, 58% accepted, 28 enrolled. In 2008, 33 master's awarded. *Unit head:* Dr. Diane Wentworth, Chairperson, 973-443-8548. *Application contact:* Susan Brooman, University Director, Graduate Admissions, 973-443-8905, Fax: 973-443-8088, E-mail: grad@fdu.edu.

Felician College, Program in Counseling Psychology, Lodi, NJ 07644-2117. Offers MS.

See Close-Up on page 1109.

Fitchburg State College, Division of Graduate and Continuing Education, Programs in Counseling, Fitchburg, MA 01420-2697. Offers elementary school guidance counseling (MS); marriage and family therapy (MS); mental health counseling (MS); secondary school guidance counseling (MS). *Accreditation:* NCATE. Part-time and evening/weekend programs available. *Students:* 18 full-time (16 women), 69 part-time (61 women); includes 6 minority (1 African American, 1 American Indian/Alaska Native, 4 Hispanic Americans), 2 international. Average age 31. 14 applicants, 100% accepted, 12 enrolled. In 2008, 23 master's awarded. *Entrance requirements:* For master's, GRE General Test or MAT, letters of recommendation, resumé; for Certificate, master's degree. Additional exam requirements/recommendations for international students: Required—TOEFL (minimum score 550 paper-based; 213 computer-based; 79 iBT). *Application deadline:* Applications are processed on a rolling basis. Application fee: $25 ($50 for international students). *Expenses:* Tuition, state resident: full-time $3600; part-time $150 per credit. Tuition, nonresident: full-time $3600; part-time $150 per credit. Required fees: $109 per credit. *Financial support:* In 2008–09, research assistantships with partial tuition reimbursements (averaging $5,500 per year); Federal Work-Study, scholarships/grants, and unspecified assistantships also available. Support available to part-time students. Financial award application deadline: 3/1; financial award applicants required to submit FAFSA. *Unit head:* Dr. John Hancock, Chair, 978-665-3604, Fax: 978-665-3658, E-mail: gce@fsc.edu. *Application contact:* Director of Admissions, 978-665-3144, Fax: 978-665-4540, E-mail: admissions@fsc.edu.

Florida Atlantic University, College of Education, Department of Counselor Education, Boca Raton, FL 33431-0991. Offers counselor education (M Ed, PhD, Ed S); marriage and family therapy (Ed S); mental health counseling (M Ed, Ed S); rehabilitation counseling (M Ed); school counseling (M Ed, Ed S). *Accreditation:* ACA; NCATE. Part-time and evening/weekend programs available. *Faculty:* 7 full-time (2 women), 6 part-time/adjunct (5 women). *Students:* 59 full-time (50 women), 97 part-time (84 women); includes 53 minority (18 African Americans, 3 Asian Americans or Pacific Islanders, 32 Hispanic Americans), 2 international. Average age 35. 135 applicants, 42% accepted, 39 enrolled. In 2008, 46 master's awarded. *Degree requirements:* For Ed S, departmental qualifying exam. *Entrance requirements:* For master's, GRE General Test, minimum GPA of 3.0 during previous 2 years; for Ed S, GRE General Test, minimum graduate GPA of 3.25. Additional exam requirements/recommendations for international students: Required—TOEFL. *Application deadline:* For fall admission, 3/1 for domestic students, 2/1 for international students; for spring admission, 9/15 for domestic students, 7/1 for international students. Applications are processed on a rolling basis. Application fee: $30. *Expenses:* Tuition, state resident: full-time $4867; part-time $270.40 per credit hour. Tuition, nonresident: full-time $16,486; part-time $915.87 per credit hour. *Financial support:* Research assistantships with partial tuition reimbursements, teaching assistantships, career-related internships or fieldwork, scholarships/grants, and unspecified assistantships available. *Faculty research:* Brief therapy, psychological type, marriage and family counseling, international programs, integrated services. *Unit head:* Dr. Irene Johnson, Chair, 561-297-2136, Fax: 561-297-2309. *Application contact:* Susan Foley, Senior Secretary, 561-297-3602, Fax: 561-297-2309, E-mail: cnslred@fau.edu.

Counseling Psychology

Florida International University, College of Education, Department of Educational and Psychological Studies, Program in Counselor Education, Miami, FL 33199. Offers mental health counseling (MS); rehabilitation counseling (MS); school counseling (MS). *Accreditation:* ACA; NCATE. Part-time and evening/weekend programs available. *Entrance requirements:* For master's, General Knowledge test, College Level Academic Skills Test, GRE or PRAXIS (school counseling track), minimum GPA of 3.0, interview. Additional exam requirements/recommendations for international students: Required—TOEFL (minimum score 550 paper-based; 213 computer-based; 80 iBT), IELTS (minimum score 6.3). Electronic applications accepted.

Florida State University, Graduate Studies, College of Education, Department of Educational Psychology and Learning Systems, Program in Psychological Services, Tallahassee, FL 32306. Offers MS, PhD, Ed S. *Accreditation:* ACA (one or more programs are accredited). *Degree requirements:* For master's and Ed S, comprehensive exam, thesis optional. *Entrance requirements:* For master's and Ed S, GRE General Test, minimum GPA of 3.0.

Fordham University, Graduate School of Education, Division of Psychological and Educational Services, New York, NY 10023. Offers counseling and personnel services (MSE, Adv C); counseling psychology (PhD); educational psychology (MSE, PhD); school psychology (PhD); urban and urban bilingual school psychology (Adv C). *Accreditation:* APA (one or more programs are accredited); NCATE. *Degree requirements:* For doctorate, thesis/dissertation. *Entrance requirements:* For doctorate, GRE General Test.

Fort Valley State University, College of Graduate Studies and Extended Education, Department of Counseling Psychology, Program in Mental Health Counseling, Fort Valley, GA 31030-4313. Offers MS. Part-time programs available. *Degree requirements:* For master's, comprehensive exam (for some programs), thesis optional. *Entrance requirements:* For master's, GRE General Test or MAT.

Franciscan University of Steubenville, Graduate Programs, Department of Counseling, Steubenville, OH 43952-1763. Offers MA. Part-time programs available. *Degree requirements:* For master's, case presentation, integrative paper. *Entrance requirements:* For master's, GRE General Test or MAT, minimum undergraduate GPA of 3.0.

Frostburg State University, Graduate School, College of Liberal Arts and Sciences, Department of Psychology, Program in Counseling Psychology, Frostburg, MD 21532-1099. Offers MS. Part-time and evening/weekend programs available. *Degree requirements:* For master's, internship. *Entrance requirements:* For master's, GRE General Test or MAT, interview, minimum GPA of 3.0, resumé. Electronic applications accepted.

Gallaudet University, The Graduate School, Department of Counseling, Washington, DC 20002-3625. Offers mental health counseling (MA); school counseling (MA). *Accreditation:* ACA; NCATE. *Degree requirements:* For master's, thesis optional. *Entrance requirements:* For master's, GRE General Test or MAT. Electronic applications accepted.

Gannon University, School of Graduate Studies, College of Humanities, Education, and Social Sciences, School of Humanities, Program in Counseling Psychology, Erie, PA 16541-0001. Offers PhD. Part-time and evening/weekend programs available. *Students:* 2 full-time (1 woman), 17 part-time (13 women); includes 1 minority (Asian American or Pacific Islander), 1 international. Average age 41. 3 applicants, 67% accepted, 0 enrolled. In 2008, 5 doctorates awarded. *Degree requirements:* For doctorate, thesis/dissertation, internship. *Entrance requirements:* For doctorate, GRE General Test, master's degree, minimum QPA of 3.5. Additional exam requirements/recommendations for international students: Required—TOEFL (minimum score 500 paper-based; 173 computer-based). *Application deadline:* Applications are processed on a rolling basis. Application fee: $50. Electronic applications accepted. *Expenses:* Contact institution. *Financial support:* Career-related internships or fieldwork, Federal Work-Study, scholarships/grants, and unspecified assistantships available. Financial award application deadline: 7/1; financial award applicants required to submit FAFSA. *Unit head:* Dr. Linda Fleming, Director, 814-871-7262, Fax: 814-871-5511, E-mail: fleming006@gannon.edu. *Application contact:* Kara Morgan, Assistant Director of Graduate Admissions, 814-871-5831, Fax: 814-871-5827, E-mail: graduate@gannon.edu.

Gardner-Webb University, Graduate School, School of Psychology, Program in Mental Health Counseling, Boiling Springs, NC 28017. Offers MA. *Accreditation:* ACA. Part-time and evening/weekend programs available. *Degree requirements:* For master's, comprehensive exam. *Entrance requirements:* For master's, GRE General Test, MAT, minimum GPA of 2.7. Electronic applications accepted.

Geneva College, Program in Counseling, Beaver Falls, PA 15010-3599. Offers marriage and family (MA); mental health (MA); school counseling (MA). *Accreditation:* ACA. Part-time and evening/weekend programs available. *Degree requirements:* For master's, internship. *Entrance requirements:* For master's, GRE General Test or MAT, minimum GPA of 3.0, letters of recommendation, faith statement, 12 credits in undergraduate psychology. Additional exam requirements/recommendations for international students: Required—TOEFL. Electronic applications accepted.

George Fox University, School of Education, Graduate Department of Counseling, Newberg, OR 97132-2697. Offers counseling (MA); marriage and family therapy (MA, Certificate); mental health trauma (Certificate); school counseling (MA, Certificate); school psychology (Certificate, Ed S). Part-time programs available. *Faculty:* 10 full-time (3 women), 7 part-time/adjunct (5 women). *Students:* 80 full-time (66 women), 147 part-time (117 women); includes 20 minority (6 African Americans, 3 American Indian/Alaska Native, 4 Asian Americans or Pacific Islanders, 7 Hispanic Americans). Average age 35. 89 applicants, 75% accepted, 53 enrolled. In 2008, 61 master's awarded. *Entrance requirements:* For master's, MAT or GRE. Additional exam requirements/recommendations for international students: Required—TOEFL (minimum score 550 paper-based; 213 computer-based; 80 iBT). *Application deadline:* For fall admission, 5/30 for domestic students; for winter admission, 11/1 for domestic students; for spring admission, 2/28 for domestic students. Applications are processed on a rolling basis. Application fee: $40. Electronic applications accepted. *Expenses:* Contact institution. *Financial support:* Career-related internships or fieldwork available. *Unit head:* Dr. Richard Shaw, Associate Professor of Marriage and Family Therapy/Chair, 503-554-6142, E-mail: rshaw@georgefox.edu. *Application contact:* Carol Namburi, Admissions Counselor, 800-631-0921, Fax: 503-554-6111, E-mail: counseling@georgefox.edu.

Georgian Court University, School of Sciences and Mathematics, Lakewood, NJ 08701-2697. Offers biology (MS); counseling psychology (MA); holistic health (Certificate); holistic health studies (MA); mathematics (MA); professional counselor (Certificate); school psychology (Certificate). Part-time and evening/weekend programs available. *Faculty:* 16 full-time (10 women), 6 part-time/adjunct (4 women). *Students:* 52 full-time (48 women), 102 part-time (82 women); includes 18 minority (8 African Americans, 3 Asian Americans or Pacific Islanders, 7 Hispanic Americans), 2 international. Average age 34. 119 applicants, 66% accepted, 58 enrolled. In 2008, 27 master's, 2 other advanced degrees awarded. *Degree requirements:* For master's, comprehensive exam (for some programs), thesis (for some programs). *Entrance requirements:* For master's, GRE General Test, GRE Subject Test in biology (MS), 3 letters of recommendation. Additional exam requirements/recommendations for international students: Required—TOEFL (minimum score 550 paper-based; 213 computer-based). *Application deadline:* For fall admission, 8/1 priority date for domestic students, 4/1 for international students; for spring admission, 1/1 priority date for domestic students, 7/1 for international students. Applications are processed on a rolling basis. Application fee: $40. Electronic applications accepted. *Expenses:* Tuition: Full-time $12,276; part-time $682 per credit. Required fees: $400 per year. Tuition and fees vary according to campus/location. *Financial support:* Scholarships/grants, health care benefits, and unspecified assistantships available. Financial award application deadline: 4/15; financial award applicants required to submit FAFSA. *Unit head:* Dr. Linda James, Dean, 732-987-2617, Fax: 732-987-2007. *Application contact:* Eugene Soltys, Director of Graduate Admissions, 732-987-2770, Fax: 732-987-2084, E-mail: graduateadmissions@georgian.edu.

Georgia State University, College of Education, Department of Counseling and Psychological Services, Program in Professional Counseling, Atlanta, GA 30303-3083. Offers counseling psychology (PhD); counselor education and practice (PhD); professional counseling (MS, Ed S). *Accreditation:* ACA (one or more programs are accredited); APA (one or more programs are accredited). *Degree requirements:* For master's, comprehensive exam; for doctorate, comprehensive exam, thesis/dissertation. *Entrance requirements:* For master's, GRE General Test, minimum GPA of 2.5; for doctorate, GRE General Test, minimum GPA of 3.3; for Ed S, GRE General Test, minimum graduate GPA of 3.25. *Faculty research:* Dropout prevention, school reform, school violence, lifestyle correlates, stress management.

Goddard College, Graduate Programs, Master of Arts in Psychology and Counseling Program, Plainfield, VT 05667-9432. Offers organizational development (MA); psychology and counseling (MA); sexual orientation (MA). Part-time programs available. Postbaccalaureate distance learning degree programs offered (minimal on-campus study). *Faculty:* 5 part-time/adjunct (4 women). *Students:* 58 full-time, 1 part-time. Average age 41. 26 applicants, 65% accepted, 15 enrolled. *Degree requirements:* For master's, thesis. *Entrance requirements:* For master's, recent undergraduate degree in psychology or closely related field (preparatory semester at Goddard can substitute), transcripts, three letters of recommendation, interview. *Application deadline:* Applications are processed on a rolling basis. Application fee: $40. Electronic applications accepted. *Expenses:* Tuition: Full-time $14,446. Full-time tuition and fees vary according to campus/location and program. Part-time tuition and fees vary according to course load and program. *Financial support:* In 2008–09, 45 students received support. Applicants required to submit FAFSA. *Unit head:* Dr. Steve James, Director, 802-454-8311, Fax: 802-454-7835, E-mail: steven.james@goddard.edu. *Application contact:* David DeLucca, Senior Admissions Counselor, 800-906-8312 Ext. 248, Fax: 802-454-1029, E-mail: david.delucca@goddard.edu.

Gonzaga University, School of Education, Program in Counseling Psychology, Spokane, WA 99258. Offers MAC, MAP. *Accreditation:* ACA. *Degree requirements:* For master's, comprehensive exam. *Entrance requirements:* For master's, GRE General Test or MAT, minimum B average in undergraduate course work. Additional exam requirements/recommendations for international students: Required—TOEFL.

Governors State University, College of Education, Program in Counseling, University Park, IL 60466-0975. Offers MA. *Accreditation:* ACA. Part-time and evening/weekend programs available. *Degree requirements:* For master's, practicum. *Entrance requirements:* For master's, minimum GPA of 2.5 in last 60 hours of course work or minimum GPA of 2.25 and GRE General Test.

Grace College, Graduate School in Counseling and Interpersonal Relations, Program in Counseling, Winona Lake, IN 46590-1294. Offers counseling (MA); interpersonal relations (MA). *Accreditation:* ACA. Part-time and evening/weekend programs available. *Degree requirements:* For master's, comprehensive exam, portfolio. *Entrance requirements:* For master's, GRE (counseling). Additional exam requirements/recommendations for international students: Required—TOEFL. Electronic applications accepted.

Grace University, College of Graduate Studies, Counseling Program, Omaha, NE 68108. Offers MA. *Entrance requirements:* For master's, minimum undergraduate GPA of 3.0.

Harding University, College of Bible and Religion, Program in Marriage and Family Therapy, Searcy, AR 72149-0001. Offers marriage and family therapy (MS); mental health counseling (MS). Part-time programs available. *Faculty:* 4 full-time (0 women), 4 part-time/adjunct (2 women). *Students:* 24 full-time (10 women), 1 (woman) part-time; includes 1 minority (African American). Average age 27. 20 applicants, 85% accepted, 15 enrolled. In 2008, 12 master's awarded. *Degree requirements:* For master's, comprehensive exam, 15-month practicum. *Entrance requirements:* For master's, GRE General Test, minimum undergraduate GPA of 2.75, graduate 3.0. *Application deadline:* For fall admission, 4/1 priority date for domestic students. Applications are processed on a rolling basis. Application fee: $25. *Expenses:* Tuition: Full-time $9360; part-time $520 per credit hour. Required fees: $21 per credit hour. Tuition and fees vary according to course load and program. *Financial support:* In 2008–09, 8 students received support. Career-related internships or fieldwork, Federal Work-Study, and scholarships/grants available. *Faculty research:* Forgiveness, substance abuse, PTSD. *Unit head:* Dr. Lewis L. Moore, Chairman, 501-279-4347, Fax: 501-279-4417, E-mail: lmoore@harding.edu. *Application contact:* Ruth Ann Dawson, Office Manager, 501-279-4347, Fax: 501-279-4417, E-mail: radawson@harding.edu.

Heidelberg University, Program in Counseling, Tiffin, OH 44883-2462. Offers MA. Part-time and evening/weekend programs available. *Degree requirements:* For master's, thesis or alternative, counseling practicum, internship. *Entrance requirements:* For master's, GRE General Test, 12 hours course work in behavioral sciences, minimum GPA of 2.9, 3 letters of reference. Additional exam requirements/recommendations for international students: Required—TOEFL.

Hofstra University, School of Education, Health, and Human Services, Department of Counseling, Research, Special Education and Rehabilitation, Program in Rehabilitation Counseling, Hempstead, NY 11549. Offers rehabilitation administration (PD); rehabilitation counseling (MS Ed); rehabilitation counseling in mental health (MS Ed). *Accreditation:* CORE. Part-time and evening/weekend programs available. *Students:* 16 full-time (12 women), 9 part-time (7 women); includes 10 minority (7 African Americans, 3 Hispanic Americans), 1 international. Average age 36. 12 applicants, 92% accepted, 6 enrolled. In 2008, 6 master's awarded. *Degree requirements:* For master's, comprehensive exam, 600-hour internship, 100-hour practicum; for PD, internship in rehabilitation administration. *Entrance requirements:* For master's, 4 letters of recommendation, interview, essay, professional experience; for PD, 3 letters of recommendation, master's degree in related field, professional experience. Additional exam requirements/recommendations for international students: Required—TOEFL (minimum score 550 paper-based; 213 computer-based; 80 iBT). *Application deadline:* Applications are processed on a rolling basis. Application fee: $60. Electronic applications accepted. *Expenses:* Tuition: Full-time $15,300; part-time $850 per credit. Required fees: $970; $165 per term. Tuition and fees vary according to program. *Financial support:* In 2008–09, 24 students received support, including 2 fellowships with full and partial tuition reimbursements available (averaging $2,525 per year); research assistantships with full and partial tuition reimbursements available, career-related internships or fieldwork, Federal Work-Study, institutionally sponsored loans, scholarships/grants, traineeships, tuition waivers (full and partial), and unspecified assistantships also available. Support available to part-time students. Financial award applicants required to submit FAFSA. *Faculty research:* Workplace socialization and individuals with disabilities; collaboration among rehabilitation agencies and consumer outcomes; job retention among rehabilitation counseling professionals; transition services for youth with disabilities. Total annual research expenditures: $210,000. *Unit head:* Dr. Jamie Mitus, Director, 516-463-7453, Fax: 516-463-6184, E-mail: cprjsm@hofstra.edu. *Application contact:* Carol Drummer, Dean of Graduate Admissions, 516-463-4876, Fax: 516-463-4664, E-mail: gradstudent@hofstra.edu.

Holy Family University, Graduate School, School of Arts and Sciences, Philadelphia, PA 19114-2094. Offers counseling psychology (MS); criminal justice (MA). Part-time and evening/weekend programs available. *Faculty:* 1 full-time (0 women), 4 part-time/adjunct (2 women). *Students:* 34 full-time (26 women), 122 part-time (98 women); includes 26 minority (13 African Americans, 3 Asian Americans or Pacific Islanders, 10 Hispanic Americans), 1 international. Average age 30. 72 applicants, 61% accepted, 35 enrolled. In 2008, 4 master's awarded. *Degree requirements:* For master's, comprehensive exam, thesis optional. *Entrance requirements:* For master's, MAT, interview, minimum GPA of 3.0. *Application deadline:* For fall admission, 7/1 priority date for domestic students; for winter admission, 11/1 for domestic students. Applications are processed on a rolling basis. Application fee: $25. *Expenses:* Tuition: Part-time $555 per credit. Required fees: $85 per semester. One-time fee: $25 part-time. *Financial* *support:* Research assistantships with full and partial tuition reimbursements, Federal Work-Study available. Support available to part-time students. Financial award application deadline: 2/15; financial award applicants required to submit FAFSA. *Unit head:* Dr. Regina Hobaugh, Dean of the School of Arts and Sciences, 267-341-3278, Fax: 215-827-0492, E-mail: hobaugh@holyfamily.edu. *Application contact:* Gidget Marie Montelibano, Graduate Admissions Counselor, 267-341-3558, Fax: 215-637-1478, E-mail: gmontelibano@holyfamily.edu.

Holy Names University, Graduate Division, Department of Counseling Psychology, Oakland, CA 94619-1699. Offers counseling psychology (MA); forensic psychology (MA, Certificate); pastoral counseling (MA, Certificate). Part-time and evening/weekend programs available. *Faculty:* 1 (woman) full-time, 9 part-time/adjunct (5 women). *Students:* 38 full-time (33 women), 13 part-time (12 women); includes 33 minority (25 African Americans, 2 Asian Americans or Pacific Islanders, 6 Hispanic Americans), 1 international. Average age 35. 22 applicants, 68% accepted, 11 enrolled. In 2008, 13 master's awarded. *Degree requirements:* For master's, comprehensive paper, seminars. *Entrance requirements:* For master's, minimum undergraduate GPA of 2.6 overall, 3.0 in major. Additional exam requirements/recommendations for international students: Required—TOEFL (minimum score 550 paper-based; 213 computer-based; 80 iBT). *Application deadline:* For fall admission, 8/1 priority date for domestic students, 8/1 for international students; for spring admission, 12/1 priority date for domestic students, 12/1 for international students. Applications are processed on a rolling basis. Application fee: $65. *Expenses:* Tuition: Full-time $6255; part-time $695 per unit. Required fees: $340. Tuition and fees vary according to course load, program, reciprocity agreements and student's religious affiliation. *Financial support:* In 2008–09, 38 students received support. Available to part-time students. Application deadline: 3/2; *Faculty research:* Cognitive psychology, anger management, grief and grief counseling, post-modernism and psychotherapy, spirituality and psychology. *Unit head:* Dr. Helen Shoemaker, Program Director, 510-436-1543, E-mail: shoemaker@hnu.edu. *Application contact:* 800-430-1321, Fax: 510-436-1325, E-mail: AdultEd@hnu.edu.

Houston Baptist University, College of Education and Behavioral Sciences, Program in Christian Counseling, Houston, TX 77074-3298. Offers MACC. *Degree requirements:* For master's, comprehensive exam. *Entrance requirements:* For master's, GRE General Test, minimum GPA of 3.0. Additional exam requirements/recommendations for international students: Required—TOEFL (minimum score 550 paper-based; 213 computer-based).

Howard University, School of Education, Department of Human Development and Psychoeducational Studies, Program in Counseling Psychology, Washington, DC 20059-0002. Offers M Ed, MA, PhD, CAGS. *Accreditation:* APA. Part-time programs available. Terminal master's awarded for partial completion of doctoral program. *Degree requirements:* For master's, comprehensive exam, thesis (for some programs), expository writing exam; for doctorate, one foreign language, comprehensive exam, thesis/dissertation, expository writing exam, internship. *Entrance requirements:* For master's, GRE General Test (MA), minimum GPA of 2.7; for doctorate, GRE General Test, minimum GPA of 3.4; for CAGS, GRE General Test, minimum graduate GPA of 3.0. *Faculty research:* Cultural issues in counseling and psychotherapy, counseling theory construction, self–actualization black psychology.

Humboldt State University, Graduate Studies, College of Natural Resources and Sciences, Department of Psychology, Arcata, CA 95521-8299. Offers psychology (MA), including academic research, counseling, school psychology. *Students:* 64 full-time (52 women), 6 part-time (3 women); includes 13 minority (1 African American, 3 American Indian/Alaska Native, 2 Asian Americans or Pacific Islanders, 7 Hispanic Americans), 1 international. Average age 29. 71 applicants, 45% accepted, 26 enrolled. In 2008, 12 master's awarded. *Degree requirements:* For master's, thesis. *Entrance requirements:* For master's, appropriate bachelor's degree, minimum GPA of 2.5. Additional exam requirements/recommendations for international students: Required—TOEFL (minimum score 500 paper-based; 173 computer-based). *Application deadline:* For fall admission, 2/15 for domestic and international students. Applications are processed on a rolling basis. Application fee: $55. *Expenses:* Tuition, state resident: full-time $5236. Tuition, nonresident: full-time $11,338. *Financial support:* Career-related internships or fieldwork available. Financial award application deadline: 3/1; financial award applicants required to submit FAFSA. *Faculty research:* School psychology, counseling, eating disorders, mood induction, depression. *Unit head:* Dr. Brent Duncan, Chair, 707-826-3755, Fax: 707-826-4993, E-mail: bbd1@humboldt.edu. *Application contact:* Dr. Brent Duncan, Administrative Support Coordinator, 707-826-3755, Fax: 707-826-4993, E-mail: bbd1@humboldt.edu.

Husson University, School of Graduate and Professional Studies, Program in Counseling Psychology, Bangor, ME 04401-2999. Offers MS.

Idaho State University, Office of Graduate Studies, Kasiska College of Health Professions, Department of Counseling, Pocatello, ID 83209. Offers counseling (M Coun, Ed S), including marriage and family counseling (M Coun), mental health counseling (M Coun), school counseling (M Coun), student affairs and college counseling (M Coun); counselor education and counseling (PhD). *Accreditation:* ACA (one or more programs are accredited). Part-time programs available. *Faculty:* 7 full-time (4 women). *Students:* 72 full-time (50 women), 26 part-time (18 women); includes 7 minority (2 African Americans, 1 American Indian/Alaska Native, 1 Asian American or Pacific Islander, 3 Hispanic Americans), 1 international. Average age 34. In 2008, 28 master's, 7 doctorates, 1 other advanced degree awarded. *Degree requirements:* For master's, comprehensive exam, thesis; for doctorate, comprehensive exam, thesis/dissertation, internship; for Ed S, comprehensive exam, thesis, case studies, oral exam. *Entrance requirements:* For master's, GRE General Test, MAT, minimum GPA of 3.0; for doctorate, GRE General Test, MAT, minimum graduate GPA of 3.0, resumé, interview, counseling license; for Ed S, GRE General Test, minimum graduate GPA of 3.0, master's degree in counseling, 3 letters of recommendation, 2 years work experience. Additional exam requirements/recommendations for international students: Required—TOEFL (minimum score 600 paper-based; 213 computer-based; 80 iBT). *Application deadline:* For fall admission, 7/1 for domestic students, 6/1 for international students; for spring admission, 12/1 for domestic students, 11/1 for international students. Applications are processed on a rolling basis. Application fee: $55. Electronic applications accepted. *Expenses:* Tuition, area resident: Full-time $3114; part-time $276 per credit hour. Tuition, state resident: full-time $3114; part-time $276 per credit hour. Tuition, nonresident: full-time $12,318; part-time $404 per credit hour. Required fees: $2360. Tuition and fees vary according to course load and reciprocity agreements. *Financial support:* In 2008–09, 13 teaching assistantships with full and partial tuition reimbursements (averaging $9,401 per year) were awarded; career-related internships or fieldwork, Federal Work-Study, institutionally sponsored loans, scholarships/grants, traineeships, health care benefits, tuition waivers (full and partial), and unspecified assistantships also available. Support available to part-time students. Financial award application deadline: 1/1; financial award applicants required to submit FAFSA. *Faculty research:* Group counseling, multicultural counseling, family counseling, child therapy, supervision. *Unit head:* Dr. Stephen Feit, Chair, 208-282-3663, Fax: 208-282-2583, E-mail: feitstep@isu.edu. *Application contact:* Ellen Combs, Graduate School Technical Records Specialist, 208-282-2150, Fax: 208-282-4847, E-mail: combelle@isu.edu.

Illinois State University, Graduate School, College of Arts and Sciences, Department of Psychology, Normal, IL 61790-2200. Offers psychology (MA, MS), including clinical psychology, counseling psychology, developmental psychology, educational psychology, experimental psychology, measurement-evaluation, organizational-industrial psychology; school psychology (PhD, SSP). *Accreditation:* APA. *Degree requirements:* For master's, thesis or alternative; for doctorate, variable foreign language requirement, thesis/dissertation, 2 terms of residency, internship, practicum. *Entrance requirements:* For master's, GRE General Test, GRE Subject Test, minimum GPA of 3.0 in last 60 hours of course work; for doctorate, GRE General Test. *Faculty research:* Comprehensive evaluation system for the central region professional development grant, Illinois school psychology internship consortium, for children's sake.

Immaculata University, College of Graduate Studies, Department of Psychology, Immaculata, PA 19345. Offers clinical psychology (Psy D); counseling psychology (MA, Certificate), including school guidance counselor (Certificate), school psychologist (Certificate). *Accreditation:* APA. Part-time and evening/weekend programs available. *Degree requirements:* For master's, comprehensive exam, thesis optional; for doctorate, comprehensive exam, thesis/dissertation. *Entrance requirements:* For master's, GRE General Test or MAT, minimum GPA of 3.0; for doctorate, GRE General Test, minimum GPA of 3.5. Additional exam requirements/recommendations for international students: Required—TOEFL, IELTS. *Faculty research:* Supervision ethics, psychology of teaching, gender.

Indiana State University, School of Graduate Studies, College of Education, Department of Communication Disorders, Counseling and School and Educational Psychology, Terre Haute, IN 47809-1401. Offers counseling psychology (MS, PhD); counselor education (PhD); mental health counseling (MS); school counseling (M Ed); school psychology (PhD, Ed S); MA/MS. *Accreditation:* ACA; NCATE. Part-time and evening/weekend programs available. *Degree requirements:* For master's, thesis optional; for doctorate, thesis/dissertation, research tools proficiency tests. *Entrance requirements:* For master's, GRE General Test or MAT, minimum undergraduate GPA of 2.75; for doctorate, GRE General Test, master's degree, minimum undergraduate GPA of 3.5. Electronic applications accepted. *Faculty research:* Vocational development supervision.

Indiana University Bloomington, School of Education, Department of Counseling and Educational Psychology, Bloomington, IN 47405-1006. Offers counseling (MS, PhD, Ed S); counseling psychology (PhD); counselor education (MS, Ed S); educational psychology (MS, PhD); inquiry methodology (PhD); learning and developmental sciences (MS, PhD); school psychology (PhD, Ed S). *Accreditation:* ACA (one or more programs are accredited); APA (one or more programs are accredited); NCATE. *Faculty:* 32 full-time (13 women), 20 part-time/adjunct (10 women). *Students:* 225 full-time (174 women), 51 part-time (39 women); includes 40 minority (17 African Americans, 1 American Indian/Alaska Native, 10 Asian Americans or Pacific Islanders, 12 Hispanic Americans), 46 international. Average age 29. 350 applicants, 46% accepted, 80 enrolled. In 2008, 41 master's, 45 doctorates, 24 other advanced degrees awarded. Terminal master's awarded for partial completion of doctoral program. *Degree requirements:* For master's, thesis optional; for doctorate, thesis/dissertation; for Ed S, comprehensive exam or project. *Entrance requirements:* For master's, doctorate, and Ed S, GRE General Test. Additional exam requirements/recommendations for international students: Required—TOEFL. *Application deadline:* Applications are processed on a rolling basis. Application fee: $50 ($60 for international students). Electronic applications accepted. *Expenses:* Tuition, area resident: Part-time $291.97 per credit hour. Tuition, state resident: part-time $291.97 per credit hour. Tuition, nonresident: part-time $850.33 per credit hour. Required fees: $110 per semester. Tuition and fees vary according to course load and program. *Financial support:* In 2008–09, 58 students received support, including 7 fellowships with partial tuition reimbursements available (averaging $15,000 per year), 15 research assistantships with partial tuition reimbursements available (averaging $12,000 per year), 36 teaching assistantships with partial tuition reimbursements available (averaging $14,280 per year); career-related internships or fieldwork, Federal Work-Study, institutionally sponsored loans, scholarships/grants, and unspecified assistantships also available. Support available to part-time students. Financial award application deadline: 1/1; financial award applicants required to submit FAFSA. *Faculty research:* Counseling psychology, inquiry methodology, school psychology, learning sciences, human development, educational psychology. *Unit head:* Dr. Joyce Alexander, Chairperson, 812-856-8300, Fax: 812-856-8333, E-mail: cep@indiana.edu. *Application contact:* Jessica Durnal, Student Services Specialist, 812-856-8300, Fax: 812-856-8333, E-mail: cep@indiana.edu.

Indiana Wesleyan University, College of Graduate Studies, Graduate Studies in Counseling, Marion, IN 46953. Offers addictions counseling (MS); community counseling (MS); marriage and family counseling (MS); school counseling (MS). *Accreditation:* ACA. Part-time programs available. *Faculty:* 7 full-time (4 women), 6 part-time/adjunct (3 women). *Students:* 60 full-time (46 women), 47 part-time (38 women); includes 4 minority (all African Americans). Average age 36. In 2008, 26 master's awarded. *Degree requirements:* For master's, thesis or alternative. *Entrance requirements:* For master's, GRE General Test. Additional exam requirements/recommendations for international students: Required—TOEFL. *Application deadline:* For fall admission, 6/14 priority date for domestic students. Application fee: $25. Electronic applications accepted. *Expenses:* Contact institution. *Financial support:* In 2008–09, 1 research assistantship with partial tuition reimbursement, 1 teaching assistantship with partial tuition reimbursement were awarded. Support available to part-time students. Financial award application deadline: 3/1; financial award applicants required to submit FAFSA. *Faculty research:* Community counseling, multicultural counseling, addictions. *Unit head:* Dr. Mark Gerig, Director of Graduate Counseling Studies, 765-677-2995, Fax: 765-677-1456, E-mail: mark.gerig@indwes.edu. *Application contact:* Tom Leas, Director of Adult Enrollment Services, 800-895-0036, Fax: 765-677-2404, E-mail: graduate@indwes.edu.

Institute of Transpersonal Psychology, Residential Programs, Palo Alto, CA 94303. Offers clinical psychology (PhD); counseling psychology (MA); transpersonal psychology (MA, PhD); women's spirituality (PhD). Part-time and evening/weekend programs available. *Faculty:* 17 full-time (9 women), 31 part-time/adjunct (18 women). *Students:* 268 full-time (189 women), 40 part-time (31 women); includes 53 minority (9 African Americans, 3 American Indian/Alaska Native, 21 Asian Americans or Pacific Islanders, 20 Hispanic Americans), 14 international. Average age 38. 168 applicants, 52% accepted, 56 enrolled. In 2008, 47 master's, 16 doctorates awarded. Terminal master's awarded for partial completion of doctoral program. *Degree requirements:* For doctorate, thesis/dissertation. *Entrance requirements:* For master's and doctorate, bachelor's degree. *Application deadline:* For fall admission, 2/15 priority date for domestic students. Applications are processed on a rolling basis. Application fee: $55. *Expenses:* Tuition: Full-time $24,543; part-time $577 per unit. Tuition and fees vary according to degree level. *Financial support:* In 2008–09, 178 students received support; teaching assistantships, career-related internships or fieldwork, Federal Work-Study, and scholarships/grants available. Support available to part-time students. Financial award application deadline: 7/1; financial award applicants required to submit FAFSA. *Unit head:* Dr. Paul Roy, Academic Vice President, 650-493-4430 Ext. 243, Fax: 650-493-6835, E-mail: proy@itp.edu. *Application contact:* 650-493-4430 Ext. 16, Fax: 650-493-6835, E-mail: itpinfo@itp.edu.

Inter American University of Puerto Rico, Aguadilla Campus, Graduate School, Aguadilla, PR 00605. Offers counseling psychology with an emphasis in family (MS); criminal justice (MA); educative management and leadership (MA); elementary education (MA); industrial mangement (MBA); marketing (MBA). Part-time and evening/weekend programs available. *Degree requirements:* For master's, comprehensive exam. *Entrance requirements:* For master's, EXADEP, 2 letters of recommendation, minimum GPA of 2.5. Electronic applications accepted.

Inter American University of Puerto Rico, San Germán Campus, Graduate Studies Center, Program in Psychology, San Germán, PR 00683-5008. Offers counseling psychology (MA, PhD); school psychology (MA, PhD). Part-time and evening/weekend programs available. *Degree requirements:* For master's, comprehensive exam, thesis; for doctorate, comprehensive exam, thesis/dissertation. *Entrance requirements:* For master's, GRE General Test or EXADEP, minimum GPA of 3.0; for doctorate, GRE, EXADEP or MAT, minimum GPA of 3.0.

Iona College, School of Arts and Science, Department of Psychology, New Rochelle, NY 10801-1890. Offers experimental psychology (MA); industrial-organizational psychology (MA); mental health counseling (MA); psychology (MA); school psychology (MA). Part-time and evening/weekend programs available. *Faculty:* 11 full-time (5 women), 6 part-time/adjunct (3 women). *Students:* 71 full-time (54 women), 42 part-time (35 women); includes 26 minority (9 African Americans, 5 Asian Americans or Pacific Islanders, 12 Hispanic Americans), 1 international. Average age 25. 120 applicants, 73% accepted, 39 enrolled. In 2008, 19 master's awarded. *Degree requirements:* For master's, thesis. *Entrance requirements:* For master's, GRE or minimum GPA of 3.0. Additional exam requirements/recommendations for international students: Required—TOEFL (minimum score 550 paper-based; 213 computer-based). *Application deadline:* Applications are processed on a rolling basis. Application fee: $50. Electronic applications accepted. *Expenses:* Tuition: Part-time $755 per credit. Required fees: $175 per term. *Financial support:* Career-related internships or fieldwork, tuition waivers

Counseling Psychology

Iona College (continued)

(partial), and unspecified assistantships available. Support available to part-time students. Financial award application deadline: 4/15; financial award applicants required to submit FAFSA. *Unit head:* Dr. Pauline Jirik-Babb, Chair, 914-633-2191, E-mail: pjirikbabb@iona.edu. *Application contact:* Veronica Jarek-Prinz, Director of Graduate Admissions, 914-633-2420, Fax: 914-633-2277, E-mail: vjarekprinz@iona.edu.

Iowa State University of Science and Technology, Graduate College, College of Liberal Arts and Sciences, Department of Psychology, Ames, IA 50011. Offers cognitive psychology (PhD); counseling psychology (PhD); social psychology (PhD). *Accreditation:* APA. *Faculty:* 25 full-time (8 women), 8 part-time/adjunct (4 women). *Students:* 63 full-time (43 women); includes 10 minority (3 African Americans, 7 Asian Americans or Pacific Islanders), 4 international. Average age 26. 117 applicants, 14% accepted, 11 enrolled. In 2008, 8 doctorates awarded. *Degree requirements:* For doctorate, comprehensive exam, thesis/dissertation. *Entrance requirements:* For doctorate, GRE General Test, GRE Subject Test (psychology). Additional exam requirements/recommendations for international students: Required—TOEFL (minimum score 560 paper-based; 220 computer-based). *Application deadline:* For fall admission, 1/5 priority date for domestic and international students. Application fee: $30 ($70 for international students). Electronic applications accepted. *Expenses:* Tuition, area resident: Full-time $6446; part-time $359 per credit. Tuition, state resident: full-time $6446; part-time $359 per credit. Tuition, nonresident: full-time $17,330; part-time $963 per credit. Required fees: $790; $249.25 per semester. Tuition and fees vary according to course load and program. *Financial support:* In 2008–09, 45 students received support, including 2 fellowships with full tuition reimbursements available (averaging $14,055 per year), 13 research assistantships with full tuition reimbursements available (averaging $12,200 per year), 30 teaching assistantships with full tuition reimbursements available (averaging $12,200 per year); scholarships/grants, health care benefits, and unspecified assistantships also available. *Faculty research:* Counseling psychology, cognitive psychology, social psychology, health psychology, psychology and public policy. Total annual research expenditures: $2 million. *Unit head:* Dr. Stephanie Madon, Director of Graduate Education, 515-294-1742, Fax: 515-294-6424, E-mail: madon@iastate.edu. *Application contact:* Ann K Schmidt, Graduate Admissions Secretary, 515-294-1743, Fax: 515-294-6424, E-mail: psychadm@iastate.edu.

James Madison University, The Graduate School, College of Integrated Science and Technology, Department of Graduate Psychology, Program in Community Counseling Psychology, Harrisonburg, VA 22807. Offers M Ed, MA, Ed S. *Accreditation:* ACA (one or more programs are accredited); APA (one or more programs are accredited). Part-time and evening/weekend programs available. *Students:* 58 full-time (43 women), 34 part-time (28 women); includes 12 minority (11 African Americans, 1 Asian American or Pacific Islander), 1 international. Average age 27. In 2008, 26 master's, 16 other advanced degrees awarded. *Degree requirements:* For Ed S, comprehensive exam, thesis, internship. *Entrance requirements:* For master's, GRE General Test, 3 reference forms, interview, criminal history check. Additional exam requirements/recommendations for international students: Required—TOEFL. *Application deadline:* For fall admission, 2/1 priority date for domestic students. Applications are processed on a rolling basis. Application fee: $55. Electronic applications accepted. *Expenses:* Tuition, area resident: Full-time $7008; part-time $292 per credit hour. Tuition, state resident: full-time $7008; part-time $292 per credit hour. Tuition, nonresident: full-time $20,352; part-time $848 per credit hour. *Financial support:* In 2008–09, 44 students received support; teaching assistantships with full tuition reimbursements available, career-related internships or fieldwork, Federal Work-Study, and 45 graduate assistantships ($7,382) available. Financial award application deadline: 3/1; financial award applicants required to submit FAFSA. *Unit head:* Dr. Lennis G. Echerling, Program Director, 540-568-6552. *Application contact:* Dr. Lennis G. Echerling, Program Director, 540-568-6552.

John Carroll University, Graduate School, Program in Community Counseling, University Heights, OH 44118-4581. Offers clinical counseling (Certificate); community counseling (MA). *Accreditation:* ACA. Part-time and evening/weekend programs available. *Degree requirements:* For master's, comprehensive exam, internship, practicum. *Entrance requirements:* For master's, MAT or GRE, minimum GPA of 2.75, statement of volunteer experience, interview, 12-18 hours social science course work, survey. Additional exam requirements/recommendations for international students: Required—TOEFL. Electronic applications accepted. *Faculty research:* Child and adolescent development, HIV, hypnosis, wellness, women's issues.

John F. Kennedy University, Graduate School of Holistic Studies, Department of Counseling Psychology, Program in Counseling Psychology, Pleasant Hill, CA 94523-4817. Offers holistic studies (MA); somatic psychology (MA); transpersonal psychology (MA). Part-time and evening/weekend programs available. *Degree requirements:* For master's, thesis or alternative. *Entrance requirements:* For master's, interview. Additional exam requirements/recommendations for international students: Required—TOEFL.

John F. Kennedy University, Graduate School of Professional Psychology, Program in Counseling Psychology, Pleasant Hill, CA 94523-4817. Offers MA. *Accreditation:* APA. Part-time and evening/weekend programs available. *Degree requirements:* For master's, thesis or alternative. *Entrance requirements:* For master's, interview. Additional exam requirements/recommendations for international students: Required—TOEFL.

Kean University, College of Humanities and Social Sciences, Program in Psychology, Union, NJ 07083. Offers human behavior and organizational psychology (MA); psychological services (MA). Part-time and evening/weekend programs available. *Faculty:* 18 full-time (13 women). *Students:* 13 full-time (10 women), 25 part-time (23 women); includes 7 African Americans, 1 Asian American or Pacific Islander, 3 Hispanic Americans, 1 international. Average age 28. 23 applicants, 65% accepted, 5 enrolled. In 2008, 23 master's awarded. *Degree requirements:* For master's, comprehensive exam, thesis, research. *Entrance requirements:* For master's, GRE General Test, 2 letters of recommendation, interview, prerequisite coursework in behavioral sciences, 12 credits in psychology. *Application deadline:* For fall admission, 5/1 for domestic students; for spring admission, 11/1 for domestic students. Application fee: $60 ($150 for international students). Electronic applications accepted. *Expenses:* Tuition, state resident: full-time $10,128; part-time $422 per credit. Tuition, nonresident: full-time $13,728; part-time $572 per credit. Required fees: $2570; $107 per credit. Part-time tuition and fees vary according to course load, degree level and program. *Financial support:* In 2008–09, 4 research assistantships with full tuition reimbursements (averaging $3,217 per year) were awarded; unspecified assistantships also available. *Unit head:* Dr. Joanne Walsh, Program Coordinator, 908-737-5870, E-mail: jwalsh@kean.edu. *Application contact:* Steven Koch, Pre-Admissions Coordinator, 908-737-4723, Fax: 908-737-5965, E-mail: grad-adm@kean.edu.

Kent State University, Graduate School of Education, Health, and Human Services, Department of Adult, Counseling, Health and Vocational Education, Program in Community Counseling, Kent, OH 44242-0001. Offers M Ed, MA. *Accreditation:* ACA; NCATE. *Degree requirements:* For master's, thesis (for some programs). *Entrance requirements:* Additional exam requirements/recommendations for international students: Required—TOEFL. Electronic applications accepted. *Faculty research:* Group work, personality assessment, family/child therapy, substance abuse counseling, clinical supervision.

Kutztown University of Pennsylvania, College of Graduate Studies and Extended Learning, Program in Counseling Psychology, Kutztown, PA 19530-0730. Offers agency counseling (MA); marital and family therapy (MA). Part-time and evening/weekend programs available. *Faculty:* 5 full-time (2 women). *Students:* 32 full-time (27 women), 20 part-time (19 women); includes 1 minority (Hispanic American). Average age 28. 38 applicants, 55% accepted, 11 enrolled. In 2008, 12 master's awarded. *Degree requirements:* For master's, comprehensive exam, thesis optional. *Entrance requirements:* For master's, GRE General Test, interview. Additional exam requirements/recommendations for international students: Required—TOEFL. *Application deadline:* For fall admission, 2/1 for domestic and international students; for spring admission, 8/1 for domestic and international students. Application fee: $35. Electronic applications accepted. *Expenses:* Tuition, area resident: Full-time $6430; part-time $357 per credit. Tuition, state resident: full-time $6430; part-time $357 per credit. Tuition, nonresident: full-time $10,288; part-time $572 per credit. Required fees: $1360; $72 per credit. $67 per semester. *Financial support:* Career-related internships or fieldwork, Federal Work-Study, scholarships/grants, and unspecified assistantships available. Financial award application deadline: 3/1; financial award applicants required to submit FAFSA. *Faculty research:* Addicted families. *Unit head:* Dr. Deborah Barlieb, Chairperson, 610-683-4204, Fax: 610-683-1585, E-mail: barlieb@kutztown.edu. *Application contact:* Dr. Linda Matthews, Interim Dean of Graduate Studies, 610-683-4201, Fax: 610-683-1393, E-mail: graduate@kutztown.edu.

La Salle University, School of Arts and Sciences, Program in Clinical-Counseling Psychology, Philadelphia, PA 19141-1199. Offers MA. *Accreditation:* APA. Part-time and evening/weekend programs available. *Degree requirements:* For master's, comprehensive exam. *Entrance requirements:* For master's, GRE or MAT, 15 undergraduate credits in psychology. *Expenses:* Contact institution. *Faculty research:* Cognitive therapy, attribution theory, work habits, single parent families, treatment of addictions.

Leadership Institute of Seattle, School of Applied Behavioral Science, Systems Counseling Track, Kenmore, WA 98028-4966. Offers MA. *Degree requirements:* For master's, thesis (for some programs), oral exams. *Entrance requirements:* For master's, bachelor's degree from an accredited university or college. *Faculty research:* Family systems theory, marriage and family therapy, systems consultation, family and culture of origin, personal authority.

Lee University, College of Arts and Sciences, Cleveland, TN 37320-3450. Offers mental health counseling (MS); school counseling (MS). Part-time programs available. *Faculty:* 11 full-time (5 women), 3 part-time/adjunct (1 woman). *Students:* 40 full-time (33 women), 22 part-time (18 women); includes 4 minority (2 Asian Americans or Pacific Islanders, 2 Hispanic Americans), 1 international. Average age 28. 36 applicants, 67% accepted, 17 enrolled. In 2008, 33 master's awarded. *Degree requirements:* For master's, variable foreign language requirement, comprehensive exam, thesis, internship. *Entrance requirements:* For master's, GRE General Test or MAT, minimum undergraduate GPA of 3.0, 3 letters of recommendation, interview. *Application deadline:* For fall admission, 4/1 priority date for domestic and international students; for spring admission, 10/1 priority date for domestic and international students. Applications are processed on a rolling basis. Application fee: $25. *Expenses:* Tuition: Full-time $10,824; part-time $451 per credit. Required fees: $270; $200 per semester. Tuition and fees vary according to course load and program. *Financial support:* Teaching assistantships, career-related internships or fieldwork, Federal Work-Study, institutionally sponsored loans, scholarships/grants, and unspecified assistantships available. Financial award application deadline: 3/1; financial award applicants required to submit FAFSA. *Unit head:* Dr. Doyle Goff, Director, 423-614-8126, Fax: 423-614-8129, E-mail: drgoff@leeuniversity.edu. *Application contact:* Vicki Glasscock, Graduate Admissions Director, 423-614-8059, E-mail: vglasscock@leeuniversity.edu.

Lehigh University, College of Education, Program in Counseling Psychology, Bethlehem, PA 18015-3094. Offers counseling and human services (M Ed); counseling psychology (PhD); elementary and secondary school counseling (M Ed); international counseling (M Ed, Certificate); secondary school counseling (M Ed). *Accreditation:* APA (one or more programs are accredited). Part-time and evening/weekend programs available. Postbaccalaureate distance learning degree programs offered (minimal on-campus study). *Faculty:* 5 full-time (3 women), 10 part-time/adjunct (5 women). *Students:* 46 full-time (35 women), 35 part-time (32 women); includes 13 minority (8 African Americans, 1 American Indian/Alaska Native, 2 Asian Americans or Pacific Islanders, 2 Hispanic Americans), 8 international. Average age 29. 163 applicants, 21% accepted, 17 enrolled. In 2008, 41 master's, 3 doctorates awarded. *Degree requirements:* For doctorate, comprehensive exam, thesis/dissertation. *Entrance requirements:* For master's, minimum GPA of 3.0, 2 letters of recommendation, essay, transcript; for doctorate, GRE General Test (Verbal and Quantitative), 2 letters of recommendation, supplemental application, transcript, essay. Additional exam requirements/recommendations for international students: Required—TOEFL (minimum score 600 paper-based; 250 computer-based; 93 iBT). *Application deadline:* For fall admission, 11/15 for domestic and international students; for winter admission, 2/1 for domestic and international students. Application fee: $65. Electronic applications accepted. *Financial support:* In 2008–09, 11 students received support, including 2 research assistantships with full and partial tuition reimbursements available (averaging $13,000 per year); fellowships with full and partial tuition reimbursements available, career-related internships or fieldwork, Federal Work-Study, institutionally sponsored loans, scholarships/grants, and tuition waivers (full and partial) also available. Financial award application deadline: 1/31; financial award applicants required to submit FAFSA. *Faculty research:* Supervision, violence prevention, multicultural training and counseling, career development and health interventions. *Unit head:* Dr. Nicholas Ladany, Coordinator, 610-758-3250, Fax: 610-758-3227, E-mail: nil3@lehigh.edu. *Application contact:* Donna M. Johnson, Coordinator, 610-758 Ext. 3231, Fax: 610-758-6223, E-mail: dmj4@lehigh.edu.

Lesley University, Graduate School of Arts and Social Sciences, Program in Counseling Psychology, Cambridge, MA 02138-2790. Offers professional counseling (MA); school counseling (MA). Part-time and evening/weekend programs available. Postbaccalaureate distance learning degree programs offered (no on-campus study). Terminal master's awarded for partial completion of doctoral program. *Degree requirements:* For master's, internship, practicum. *Entrance requirements:* For master's, MAT. Additional exam requirements/recommendations for international students: Required—TOEFL (minimum score 550 paper-based; 213 computer-based; 80 iBT). *Expenses:* Tuition: Full-time $13,770; part-time $765 per credit hour. Required fees: $150. Tuition and fees vary according to course load, degree level, campus/location and program.

See Close-Up on page 1117.

Lewis & Clark College, Graduate School of Education and Counseling, Department of Counseling Psychology, Portland, OR 97219-7899. Offers addictions treatment (MA); counseling psychology (MA, MS); marriage, couple and family therapy (MA); psychological and cultural studies (MA); school psychology (MS, Ed S). Part-time and evening/weekend programs available. *Degree requirements:* For master's, thesis proposal (MS). *Entrance requirements:* For master's, GRE General Test, minimum undergraduate GPA of 2.75. Additional exam requirements/recommendations for international students: Required—TOEFL (minimum score 575 paper-based; 233 computer-based). Electronic applications accepted. *Faculty research:* Treatment of depression, substance abuse, child-family problems, health psychology, marital relations.

Lewis University, College of Arts and Sciences, Program in Counseling Psychology, Romeoville, IL 60446. Offers child and adolescent counseling (MA); mental health counseling (MA). Part-time and evening/weekend programs available. *Faculty:* 6 full-time (2 women). *Students:* 29 full-time (27 women), 53 part-time (49 women); includes 18 minority (12 African Americans, 6 Hispanic Americans). Average age 30. In 2008, 22 master's awarded. *Degree requirements:* For master's, thesis optional. *Entrance requirements:* For master's, 15 hours of psychology, including statistics or research; 2 letters of recommendation; writing assessment; minimum GPA of 3.0 in last 60 hours, interview. Additional exam requirements/recommendations for international students: Required—TOEFL (minimum score 550 paper-based; 213 computer-based). *Application deadline:* For fall admission, 5/1 priority date for international students; for spring admission, 11/15 priority date for international students. Applications are processed on a rolling basis. Application fee: $40. Electronic applications accepted. *Financial support:* Federal Work-Study, scholarships/grants, tuition waivers, and unspecified assistantships available. Financial award application deadline: 5/1; financial award applicants required to submit FAFSA. *Faculty research:* Cognitive development, attitude formation, juvenile delinquency, gender issues, work-family conflict. *Unit head:* Dr. Katherine Helm, Director, 815-838-0500 Ext. 5604, Fax: 815-836-5032, E-mail: helmka@lewisu.edu. *Application contact:* Nancy Hanley, Information Contact, 815-838-0500 Ext. 5604, E-mail: hanleyna@lewisu.edu.

Liberty University, College of Arts and Sciences, Lynchburg, VA 24502. Offers counseling (MA); nursing (MSN); pastoral care and counseling (PhD); professional counseling (PhD). *Accreditation:* AACN. Part-time programs available. Postbaccalaureate distance learning degree programs offered (minimal on-campus study). *Degree requirements:* For master's, comprehensive exam (for some programs); for doctorate, comprehensive exam, thesis/dissertation. *Entrance requirements:* For master's, GRE General Test (MSN), minimum undergraduate GPA of 3.0; for doctorate, GRE General Test, minimum master's GPA of 3.25. Additional exam requirements/recommendations for international students: Required—TOEFL (minimum score 600 paper-based; 250 computer-based). Electronic applications accepted. *Expenses:* Tuition: Full-time $7286; part-time $1779 per semester. Required fees: $150 per semester. *Faculty research:* God concept and adult attachment, building marital strength, image of God and gender, breastfeeding behavior among adolescent mothers, osteoporosis.

Lindenwood University, Graduate Programs, School of Education, St. Charles, MO 63301-1695. Offers education (MA); educational administration (MA, Ed D, Ed S); instructional leadership (Ed D, Ed S); library media (MA); professional and school counseling (MA); professional counseling (MA); school counseling (MA); teaching (MA). Part-time and evening/weekend programs available. *Faculty:* 33 full-time (13 women), 176 part-time/adjunct (83 women). *Students:* 460 full-time (352 women), 1,975 part-time (1,518 women); includes 620 minority (585 African Americans, 8 American Indian/Alaska Native, 16 Asian Americans or Pacific Islanders, 11 Hispanic Americans), 9 international. Average age 37. In 2008, 883 master's, 11 doctorates, 51 other advanced degrees awarded. *Degree requirements:* For master's, thesis (for some programs), minimum GPA of 3.0; for doctorate, thesis/dissertation, minimum GPA of 3.0; for Ed S, comprehensive exam, specialist project, minimum GPA of 3.0. *Entrance requirements:* For master's, interview, minimum GPA of 3.0, writing sample, letter of recommendation; for doctorate, GRE, minimum GPA of 3.4 in graduate studies, resumé, interview, writing sample, 4 letters of recommendation; for Ed S, master's degree in education, relevant work experience. Additional exam requirements/recommendations for international students: Required—TOEFL (minimum score 550 paper-based; 213 computer-based; 80 iBT). *Application deadline:* For fall admission, 8/30 priority date for domestic and international students; for spring admission, 12/30 priority date for domestic and international students. Applications are processed on a rolling basis. Application fee: $30 ($100 for international students). Electronic applications accepted. *Expenses:* Tuition: Full-time $12,700; part-time $360 per credit hour. *Financial support:* Career-related internships or fieldwork, institutionally sponsored loans, tuition waivers (partial), and unspecified assistantships available. Financial award applicants required to submit FAFSA. *Unit head:* Dr. Cynthia Bice, Dean of Education, 636-949-4618, Fax: 636-949-4197, E-mail: cbice@lindenwood.edu. *Application contact:* Brett Barger, Dean of Evening Admissions and Extension Campuses, 636-949-4934, Fax: 636-949-4109, E-mail: adultadmissions@lindenwood.edu.

Lindsey Wilson College, School of Professional Counseling, Columbia, KY 42728-1298. Offers counseling and human development (M Ed). *Accreditation:* ACA. Part-time and evening/weekend programs available.

Lipscomb University, Program in Counseling, Nashville, TN 37204-3951. Offers counseling psychology (Certificate); professional counseling (MS); psychology (MS). Part-time and evening/weekend programs available. Postbaccalaureate distance learning degree programs offered (minimal on-campus study). *Entrance requirements:* For master's, GRE, resumé, 3 reference letters, minimum GPA of 3.0. Electronic applications accepted. *Faculty research:* Cognitive psychology, neuroscience, health psychology, grief issues.

Long Island University, Brentwood Campus, School of Education, Brentwood, NY 11717. Offers childhood education (MS); early childhood education (MS); literacy (MS); mental health counseling (MS); school counseling (MS); special education (MS). Part-time and evening/weekend programs available.

Long Island University, Rockland Graduate Campus, Graduate School, Program in Counseling and Development, Orangeburg, NY 10962. Offers mental health counseling (MS); school counselor (MS). *Expenses:* Tuition: Full-time $882; part-time $882 per credit. Required fees: $200; $100 per semester.

Long Island University, Westchester Graduate Campus, Program in Mental Health Counseling, Purchase, NY 10577. Offers MS.

Louisiana State University in Shreveport, College of Education and Human Development, Program in Counseling Psychology, Shreveport, LA 71115-2399. Offers MS. *Degree requirements:* For master's, comprehensive exam, 30 credit-hour curriculum and internship (600 clock hours). *Entrance requirements:* For master's, GRE, references, undergrad prerequisites. Additional exam requirements/recommendations for international students: Required—TOEFL (minimum score 500 paper-based; 173 computer-based; 61 iBT).

Louisiana Tech University, Graduate School, College of Education, Department of Behavioral Sciences and Psychology, Ruston, LA 71272. Offers counseling (MA); counseling psychology (PhD); industrial/organizational psychology (MA); special education (MA). *Accreditation:* APA (one or more programs are accredited). Part-time programs available. *Degree requirements:* For master's, thesis or alternative; for doctorate, thesis/dissertation. *Entrance requirements:* For master's and doctorate, GRE General Test.

Loyola University Chicago, School of Education, Program in Counseling Psychology, Chicago, IL 60611-2196. Offers PhD. Offered through the Graduate School. *Accreditation:* APA. *Faculty:* 5 full-time (3 women), 4 part-time/adjunct (2 women). *Students:* 29. Average age 26. 28 applicants, 32% accepted, 4 enrolled. In 2008, 5 doctorates awarded. *Degree requirements:* For doctorate, comprehensive exam, thesis/dissertation. *Entrance requirements:* For doctorate, GRE General Test, GRE Subject Test, interview; minimum graduate GPA of 3.5, undergraduate 3.0; letters of recommendation. Additional exam requirements/recommendations for international students: Required—TOEFL (minimum score 550 paper-based; 213 computer-based; 79 iBT). *Application deadline:* For fall admission, 12/1 for domestic and international students. Application fee: $50. Electronic applications accepted. *Expenses:* Tuition: Full-time $13,500; part-time $750 per credit hour. Required fees: $60 per semester. Full-time tuition and fees vary according to program. *Financial support:* In 2008–09, 2 fellowships with full tuition reimbursements (averaging $14,000 per year), 10 research assistantships with full tuition reimbursements (averaging $12,500 per year) were awarded; teaching assistantships with full tuition reimbursements, career-related internships or fieldwork, Federal Work-Study, traineeships, and unspecified assistantships also available. Financial award application deadline: 2/15; financial award applicants required to submit FAFSA. *Faculty research:* Career choice and development, multicultural counseling, psychological measurement, prevention and intervention, family therapy. *Unit head:* Dr. Steve Brown, Director, 312-915-6311, E-mail: sbrown@luc.edu. *Application contact:* Marie Rosin-Dittmar, Information Contact, 312-915-6800, E-mail: schleduc@luc.edu.

Loyola University Maryland, Graduate Programs, College of Arts and Sciences, Department of Psychology, Program in Counseling Psychology, Baltimore, MD 21210-2699. Offers MS, CAS. Part-time and evening/weekend programs available. *Faculty:* 47 full-time (25 women), 29 part-time/adjunct (16 women). *Students:* 28 full-time (22 women), 28 part-time (21 women); includes 10 minority (7 African Americans, 1 Asian American or Pacific Islander, 2 Hispanic Americans). Average age 28. In 2008, 24 master's awarded. *Entrance requirements:* For master's and CAS, GRE General Test, GRE Subject Test (recommended). Additional exam requirements/recommendations for international students: Required—TOEFL (minimum score 550 paper-based; 213 computer-based). *Application deadline:* Applications are processed on a rolling basis. Application fee: $50. *Financial support:* Applicants required to submit FAFSA. *Unit head:* Dr. Amanda Thomas, Associate Dean, 410-614-5590, E-mail: tpmartino@loyola.edu. *Application contact:* Maureen Faux, Interim Director, Graduate Admissions, 410-617-5020, Fax: 410-617-2002, E-mail: graduate@loyola.edu.

Marist College, Graduate Programs, School of Social and Behavioral Sciences, Poughkeepsie, NY 12601-1387. Offers counseling psychology (MA); education (M Ed); education psychology (MA); school psychology (MA, Adv C). Part-time and evening/weekend programs available. *Degree requirements:* For master's, thesis optional. *Entrance requirements:* For master's, GRE General Test, letters of recommendation, minimum undergraduate GPA of 3.0, interview, essay, official transcript. Additional exam requirements/recommendations for international students: Required—TOEFL (minimum score 550 paper-based; 213 computer-based; 80 iBT); Recommended—IELTS (minimum score 6.5). Electronic applications accepted. *Faculty research:* AIDS prevention, educational intervention, humanistic counseling research, aging and development, neuroimaging.

Mars Hill Graduate School, Graduate Programs, Seattle, WA 98121. Offers Christian studies (MA); counseling psychology (MA); divinity (MS). Part-time programs available. *Entrance requirements:* For master's, MAT.

Marylhurst University, Department of Art Therapy Counseling, Marylhurst, OR 97036-0261. Offers art therapy (PGC); art therapy counseling (MA); counseling (PGC). Part-time programs available. *Faculty:* 3 full-time (all women), 4 part-time/adjunct (all women). *Students:* 48 full-time (46 women), 5 part-time (all women); includes 2 minority (1 African American, 1 Asian American or Pacific Islander). Average age 32. 26 applicants, 96% accepted, 21 enrolled. In 2008, 19 master's awarded. *Degree requirements:* For master's, comprehensive exam, practicums. *Entrance requirements:* For master's, MAT, minimum GPA of 3.0, course work in psychology and art, slide portfolio, letters of reference, resumé, autobiography, personal statement, portfolio. Additional exam requirements/recommendations for international students: Required—TOEFL (minimum score 550 paper-based; 213 computer-based; 80 iBT). *Application deadline:* For fall admission, 1/31 priority date for domestic and international students. Applications are processed on a rolling basis. Application fee: $40 ($50 for international students). *Expenses:* Contact institution. *Financial support:* Federal Work-Study and scholarships/grants available. Support available to part-time students. Financial award applicants required to submit FAFSA. *Faculty research:* Scientific approaches to art therapy research, child and adolescent psychotherapy, multicultural counseling. *Unit head:* Christine Turner, Chair, 503-636-8141, Fax: 503-636-9526, E-mail: cturner@marylhurst.edu. *Application contact:* Kathleen Schneff, Admissions Specialist, 800-634-9982 Ext. 3322, Fax: 503-635-6585, E-mail: admissions@marylhurst.edu.

Marymount University, School of Education and Human Services, Program in Community Counseling, Arlington, VA 22207-4299. Offers MA, Certificate. *Accreditation:* ACA (one or more programs are accredited). Part-time and evening/weekend programs available. *Students:* 43 full-time (38 women), 46 part-time (42 women); includes 13 minority (8 African Americans, 2 Asian Americans or Pacific Islanders, 3 Hispanic Americans), 2 international. Average age 31. 58 applicants, 91% accepted, 33 enrolled. In 2008, 30 master's awarded. *Entrance requirements:* For master's, GRE, 2 letters of recommendation, interview, resumé, personal statement; for Certificate, master's degree in counseling. Additional exam requirements/recommendations for international students: Required—TOEFL (minimum score 600 paper-based; 250 computer-based; 100 iBT). *Application deadline:* For fall admission, 7/1 for international students; for spring admission, 10/15 for international students. Application fee: $40. Electronic applications accepted. *Expenses:* Tuition: Full-time $12,420; part-time $690 per credit hour. Required fees: $126; $7 per credit hour. Tuition and fees vary according to degree level. *Financial support:* In 2008–09, 56 students received support; research assistantships with full tuition reimbursements available, career-related internships or fieldwork, Federal Work-Study, scholarships/grants, and unspecified assistantships available. Support available to part-time students. Financial award applicants required to submit FAFSA. *Unit head:* Dr. Charles Harris, Chair, 703-284-1664, Fax: 703-284-5708, E-mail: charles.harris@marymount.edu. *Application contact:* Francesca Reed, Director, Graduate Admissions, 703-284-5901, Fax: 703-527-3815, E-mail: grad.admissions@marymount.edu.

Marywood University, Academic Affairs, College of Education and Human Development, Department of Psychology and Counseling, Program in Mental Health Counseling, Scranton, PA 18509-1598. Offers addiction (MA); general (MA); pastoral (MA). *Accreditation:* ACA.

Massachusetts School of Professional Psychology, Graduate Programs, Boston, MA 02132. Offers clinical psychology (Psy D); clinical psychopharmacology (Post-Doctoral MS); counseling psychology (MA); executive coaching (Graduate Certificate); forensic psychology (MA); organizational psychology (MA); respecialization in clinical psychology (Certificate); MA/CAGS. *Accreditation:* APA. *Degree requirements:* For master's, comprehensive exam; for doctorate, thesis/dissertation. *Entrance requirements:* For doctorate, GRE General Test. Additional exam requirements/recommendations for international students: Required—TOEFL (minimum score 550 paper-based; 213 computer-based). Electronic applications accepted.

McGill University, Faculty of Graduate and Postdoctoral Studies, Faculty of Education, Department of Educational and Counseling Psychology, Montréal, QC H3A 2T5, Canada. Offers counseling psychology (MA, PhD); educational psychology (M Ed, MA, PhD); school/applied child psychology and applied developmental psychology (M Ed, MA, PhD, Diploma), including school psychology. *Accreditation:* APA.

McKendree University, Graduate Programs, Program in Professional Counseling, Lebanon, IL 62254-1299. Offers MA. *Degree requirements:* For master's, comprehensive exam, internship. *Entrance requirements:* For master's, minimum GPA of 3.0, 3 letters of recommendation, personal statement.

McNeese State University, Doré School of Graduate Studies, Burton College of Education, Department of Psychology, Lake Charles, LA 70609. Offers addiction treatment (MA); applied behavior analysis (MA); counseling psychology (MA); general/experimental psychology (MA). Evening/weekend programs available. *Faculty:* 6 full-time (3 women), 1 (woman) part-time/adjunct. *Students:* 40 full-time (27 women), 23 part-time (17 women); includes 8 minority (7 African Americans, 1 Asian American or Pacific Islander), 4 international. In 2008, 12 master's awarded. *Entrance requirements:* For master's, GRE. *Application deadline:* For fall admission, 5/15 priority date for domestic and international students; for spring admission, 10/15 priority date for domestic and international students. Applications are processed on a rolling basis. Application fee: $20 ($30 for international students). *Expenses:* Tuition, area resident: Full-time $2386. Tuition, state resident: full-time $2386. Required fees: $885. Tuition and fees vary according to course load. *Financial support:* Application deadline: 5/1. *Unit head:* Dr. Dena L. Matzenbacher, Head, 337-475-5457, Fax: 337-562-4115, E-mail: dena@mcneese.edu. *Application contact:* Dr. George F. Mead, Interim Dean of Dore' School of Graduate Studies, 337-475-5396, Fax: 337-475-5397, E-mail: admissions@mcneese.edu.

Medaille College, Programs in Psychology, Buffalo, NY 14214-2695. Offers mental health counseling (MA); psychology (MA). Part-time and evening/weekend programs available. *Faculty:* 6 full-time (3 women), 10 part-time/adjunct (8 women). *Students:* 148 full-time (118 women); includes 30 minority (29 African Americans, 1 Hispanic American). Average age 34. 85 applicants, 94% accepted, 75 enrolled. In 2008, 37 master's awarded. *Degree requirements:* For master's, comprehensive exam (for some programs), thesis (for some programs). *Entrance requirements:* For master's, GRE General Test (psychology), minimum GPA of 2.75 (psychology). Additional exam requirements/recommendations for international students: Required—TOEFL (minimum score 550 paper-based; 213 computer-based). *Application deadline:* Applications are processed on a rolling basis. Application fee: $35. Electronic applications accepted. *Expenses:* Tuition: Full-time $15,480; part-time $645 per credit hour. *Financial support:* In 2008–09, 90 students received support. Federal Work-Study available. Financial award applicants required to submit FAFSA. *Faculty research:* Schizophrenia, Parkinson's Disease, eyewitness testimony, methodology. *Unit head:* Dr. Judith Horowitz, Dean of Adult and Graduate Studies, 716-880-2229, Fax: 716-884-0291, E-mail: jhorowitz@medaille.edu. *Application contact:* Jacqueline Matheny, Executive Director of Marketing and Enrollment, 716-932-2541, Fax: 716-632-1811, E-mail: jmatheny@medaille.edu.

Counseling Psychology

Mercy College, School of Social and Behavioral Sciences, Program in Counseling, Dobbs Ferry, NY 10522-1189. Offers alcohol and substance abuse counseling (Certificate); counseling (MS); retirement counseling (Certificate). Part-time and evening/weekend programs available. Postbaccalaureate distance learning degree programs offered (no on-campus study). *Students:* 121 full-time (106 women), 200 part-time (170 women); includes 113 minority (98 African Americans, 1 American Indian/Alaska Native, 4 Asian Americans or Pacific Islanders, 10 Hispanic Americans), 1 international. Average age 35. 169 applicants, 47% accepted, 52 enrolled. In 2008, 66 master's awarded. *Degree requirements:* For master's, comprehensive exam. *Entrance requirements:* For master's, interview, two professional letters of recommendation, minimum undergraduate GPA of 3.0, resumé. Additional exam requirements/recommendations for international students: Required—TOEFL (minimum score 600 paper-based; 250 computer-based; 100 iBT). *Application deadline:* For fall admission, 8/1 for international students. Applications are processed on a rolling basis. Application fee: $40. Electronic applications accepted. *Expenses:* Tuition: Full-time $12,330; part-time $685 per credit. Required fees: $240; $120 per semester. Tuition and fees vary according to program. *Financial support:* In 2008–09, 92 students received support. Career-related internships or fieldwork, Federal Work-Study, scholarships/grants, and unspecified assistantships available. Support available to part-time students. Financial award applicants required to submit FAFSA. *Faculty research:* Ethics, drug abuse problems, human development, domestic violence. *Unit head:* Dr. Fernando Cabrera, Assistant Professor, Psychology and Behavioral Science, 914-674-7334, E-mail: fcabrera@mercy.edu. *Application contact:* Dr. Fernando Cabrera, Assistant Professor, Psychology and Behavioral Science, 914-674-7334, E-mail: fcabrera@mercy.edu.

Mercy College, School of Social and Behavioral Sciences, Program in Mental Health Counseling, Dobbs Ferry, NY 10522-1189. Offers MS. Part-time and evening/weekend programs available. *Students:* 27 full-time (23 women), 37 part-time (32 women); includes 17 African Americans, 2 Asian Americans or Pacific Islanders, 15 Hispanic Americans, 1 international. Average age 39. 45 applicants, 87% accepted, 33 enrolled. In 2008, 7 master's awarded. *Entrance requirements:* For master's, resumé, interview, two professional letters of recommendation, 2- to 3-page essay on reason(s) for pursuing counseling degree. Additional exam requirements/recommendations for international students: Required—TOEFL (minimum score 600 paper-based; 250 computer-based; 100 iBT). *Application deadline:* For fall admission, 8/1 for international students. Application fee: $40. *Expenses:* Tuition: Full-time $12,330; part-time $685 per credit. Required fees: $240; $120 per semester. Tuition and fees vary according to program. *Financial support:* In 2008–09, 24 students received support. Career-related internships or fieldwork, Federal Work-Study, scholarships/grants, and unspecified assistantships available. Support available to part-time students. Financial award applicants required to submit FAFSA. *Unit head:* Dr. Diana Trevouledes, Program Director, 914-674-7401, E-mail: dtrevouledes@mercy.edu. *Application contact:* Dr. Diana Trevouledes, Program Director, 914-674-7401, E-mail: dtrevouledes@mercy.edu.

Michigan Theological Seminary, Graduate Programs, Plymouth, MI 48170. Offers Bible (Graduate Certificate); Christian education (MA); counseling psychology (MA); divinity (M Div); theological studies (MA). *Accreditation:* ATS. Part-time and evening/weekend programs available. *Degree requirements:* For master's, one foreign language, thesis; for M Div, 2 foreign languages. *Faculty research:* Judaism, cults, world religions.

MidAmerica Nazarene University, Graduate Studies in Counseling, Olathe, KS 66062-1899. Offers counseling (MAC); play therapy (PMC). Evening/weekend programs available. *Faculty:* 6 full-time (2 women), 7 part-time/adjunct (4 women). *Students:* 62 full-time (44 women), 28 part-time (all women); includes 9 minority (5 African Americans, 2 American Indian/Alaska Native, 2 Hispanic Americans). Average age 35. 42 applicants, 64% accepted. In 2008, 22 master's awarded. *Entrance requirements:* For master's, Minnesota Multiphasic Personality Inventory, minimum GPA of 3.0. *Application deadline:* For fall admission, 6/15 for domestic students. Application fee: $75. *Expenses:* Contact institution. *Unit head:* Dr. Todd Frye, Director, 913-971-3449, Fax: 913-971-3402, E-mail: tmfrye@mnu.edu. *Application contact:* Aileen Douglas, Secretary, 913-791-3449, Fax: 913-791-3402, E-mail: adouglas@mnu.edu.

Mississippi College, Graduate School, School of Education, Department of Psychology and Counseling, Clinton, MS 39058. Offers counseling (Ed S); marriage and family counseling (MS); mental health counseling (MS); school counseling (M Ed). Part-time programs available. *Degree requirements:* For master's and Ed S, comprehensive exam, thesis optional. *Entrance requirements:* For master's, GRE or NTE. Additional exam requirements/recommendations for international students: Recommended—IELTS. Electronic applications accepted.

Monmouth University, Graduate School, Department of Psychology, West Long Branch, NJ 07764-1898. Offers professional counseling (PMC); psychological counseling (MA). Part-time and evening/weekend programs available. *Faculty:* 7 full-time (3 women), 3 part-time/adjunct (all women). *Students:* 84 full-time (72 women), 121 part-time (100 women); includes 29 minority (13 African Americans, 2 American Indian/Alaska Native, 4 Asian Americans or Pacific Islanders, 10 Hispanic Americans), 3 international. Average age 31. 122 applicants, 99% accepted, 53 enrolled. In 2008, 69 master's awarded. *Degree requirements:* For master's, thesis optional, fieldwork. *Entrance requirements:* For master's, GRE General Test, minimum GPA of 3.0 in major, 24 credits in psychology. Additional exam requirements/recommendations for international students: Required—TOEFL (minimum score 550 paper-based; 213 computer-based; 79 iBT), IELTS (minimum score 5), Michigan English Language Assessment Battery (minimum score: 77), Cambridge A, B, C. *Application deadline:* For fall admission, 7/15 priority date for domestic students, 6/1 for international students; for spring admission, 11/15 priority date for domestic students, 11/1 for international students. Applications are processed on a rolling basis. Application fee: $50. Electronic applications accepted. *Expenses:* Tuition: Full-time $13,914; part-time $773 per credit. Required fees: $628; $157 per semester. *Financial support:* In 2008–09, 91 students received support, including 91 fellowships (averaging $2,044 per year), 8 research assistantships (averaging $8,667 per year); career-related internships or fieldwork, scholarships/grants, tuition waivers (partial), and unspecified assistantships also available. Support available to part-time students. Financial award application deadline: 3/1; financial award applicants required to submit FAFSA. *Faculty research:* Violent crime, single parenting, the African-American male, counseling older women, successful behavior for under-achieving youth. *Unit head:* Dr. Frances K. Trotman, Director, 732-571-7593, Fax: 732-263-5159, E-mail: ftrotman@monmouth.edu. *Application contact:* Kevin Roane, Director, Office of Graduate Admission, 732-571-3452, Fax: 732-263-5123, E-mail: gradadm@monmouth.edu.

Montclair State University, The Office of Graduate Admissions and Support Services, College of Education and Human Services, Department of Counseling, Human Development, and Educational Leadership, Montclair, NJ 07043-1624. Offers administration and supervision (MA), including administration and supervision, educator/trainer; advanced counseling (Certificate); counseling and guidance (MA), including addictions counseling, community counseling, student affairs; counselor education (PhD); principal (Certificate); school administrator (Certificate); school business administrator (Certificate); school counselor (Certificate); substance awareness coordinator (Certificate). *Accreditation:* NCATE. Part-time and evening/weekend programs available. *Faculty:* 18 full-time (12 women), 16 part-time/adjunct (10 women). *Students:* 134 full-time (109 women), 422 part-time (299 women); includes 86 minority (48 African Americans, 8 Asian Americans or Pacific Islanders, 30 Hispanic Americans), 4 international. Average age 31. 164 applicants, 55% accepted, 74 enrolled. In 2008, 115 master's awarded. *Degree requirements:* For master's, comprehensive exam, thesis or alternative; for doctorate, comprehensive exam, thesis/dissertation. *Entrance requirements:* For master's, GRE General Test, interview, 2 letters of recommendation. Additional exam requirements/recommendations for international students: Required—TOEFL (minimum score 83 computer-based). *Application deadline:* For fall admission, 6/1 for international students; for spring admission, 10/1 for international students. Applications are processed on a rolling basis. Application fee: $60. Electronic applications accepted. *Financial support:* In 2008–09, 15 research assistantships with full tuition reimbursements (averaging $7,000 per year) were awarded; Federal Work-Study, scholarships/grants, and unspecified assistantships also available. Support available to part-time students. Financial award application deadline: 3/1; financial award applicants required to submit FAFSA. *Faculty research:* K-12 education, data collection. *Unit head:* Dr. Catherine Roland, Chairperson, 973-655-7216, E-mail: rolandc@mail.montclair.edu. *Application contact:* Amy Aiello, Associate Director of Admissions, 973-655-5147, Fax: 973-655-7869, E-mail: graduate.school@montclair.edu.

Morehead State University, Graduate Programs, College of Science and Technology, Department of Psychology, Morehead, KY 40351. Offers clinical psychology (MS); counseling psychology (MS); experimental/general psychology (MS). Part-time programs available. *Faculty:* 8 full-time (3 women). *Students:* 22 full-time (18 women), 3 part-time (1 woman). Average age 26. 30 applicants, 53% accepted, 9 enrolled. In 2008, 10 master's awarded. *Degree requirements:* For master's, comprehensive exam, thesis optional. *Entrance requirements:* For master's, GRE General Test, 18 undergraduate hours in psychology, minimum GPA of 3.0. Additional exam requirements/recommendations for international students: Required—TOEFL (minimum score 500 paper-based; 173 computer-based). *Application deadline:* For fall admission, 8/1 priority date for domestic and international students; for spring admission, 12/1 for domestic students, 12/1 priority date for international students. Applications are processed on a rolling basis. Application fee: $30 ($55 for international students). Electronic applications accepted. *Expenses:* Tuition, area resident: Full-time $6084; part-time $338 per credit hour. Tuition, state resident: full-time $6084; part-time $338 per credit hour. Tuition, nonresident: full-time $15,804; part-time $878 per credit hour. *Financial support:* In 2008–09, 19 research assistantships (averaging $6,000 per year) were awarded; career-related internships or fieldwork, Federal Work-Study, and institutionally sponsored loans also available. Financial award application deadline: 4/1; financial award applicants required to submit FAFSA. *Faculty research:* Mood induction effects, serotonin receptor activity, stress, perceptual processes. *Unit head:* Dr. Laurie Couch, Interim Department Chair. *Application contact:* Michelle Barber, Graduate Admissions Counselor, 606-783-2039, Fax: 606-783-5061, E-mail: m.barber@moreheadstate.edu.

Mount St. Mary's College, Graduate Division, Program in Counseling Psychology, Los Angeles, CA 90049-1599. Offers MS. Part-time and evening/weekend programs available. *Degree requirements:* For master's, research project. *Entrance requirements:* For master's, MAT, minimum GPA of 2.75.

Naropa University, Graduate Programs, Program in Transpersonal Counseling Psychology, Boulder, CO 80302-6697. Offers art therapy (MA); counseling psychology (MA); wilderness therapy (MA). *Faculty:* 8 full-time (5 women), 43 part-time/adjunct (31 women). *Students:* 134 full-time (103 women), 66 part-time (52 women); includes 22 minority (2 African Americans, 6 American Indian/Alaska Native, 4 Asian Americans or Pacific Islanders, 10 Hispanic Americans), 16 international. Average age 31. 213 applicants, 57% accepted, 80 enrolled. In 2008, 60 master's awarded. *Degree requirements:* For master's, internships. *Entrance requirements:* For master's, in-person interview, course work in psychology, 3 letters of recommendation, resumé, letter of interest, supplemental application. Additional exam requirements/recommendations for international students: Required—TOEFL (minimum score 600 paper-based; 250 computer-based). *Application deadline:* For fall admission, 1/15 priority date for domestic and international students. Applications are processed on a rolling basis. Application fee: $60. Electronic applications accepted. *Expenses:* Tuition: Full-time $14,767; part-time $726 per credit hour. Required fees: $45 per term. *Financial support:* In 2008–09, 98 students received support, including 21 research assistantships with partial tuition reimbursements available (averaging $3,000 per year), 6 teaching assistantships with partial tuition reimbursements available (averaging $3,000 per year); career-related internships or fieldwork, Federal Work-Study, scholarships/grants, health care benefits, tuition waivers (partial), and unspecified assistantships also available. Support available to part-time students. Financial award application deadline: 3/1; financial award applicants required to submit FAFSA. *Unit head:* Carla Clements, Chair, 303-546-3577. *Application contact:* Alice Di Tullio, Admissions Counselor, 303-546-3598, Fax: 303-546-3583, E-mail: aliced@naropa.edu.

See Close-Up on page 1121.

National University, Academic Affairs, College of Letters and Sciences, Department of Psychology, La Jolla, CA 92037-1011. Offers counseling psychology (MA); human behavior (MA). Part-time and evening/weekend programs available. Postbaccalaureate distance learning degree programs offered (no on-campus study). *Faculty:* 16 full-time (8 women), 166 part-time/adjunct (101 women). *Students:* 396 full-time (312 women), 375 part-time (293 women); includes 281 minority (114 African Americans, 8 American Indian/Alaska Native, 34 Asian Americans or Pacific Islanders, 125 Hispanic Americans), 6 international. Average age 36. 510 applicants, 100% accepted, 510 enrolled. In 2008, 226 master's awarded. *Degree requirements:* For master's, thesis (for some programs). *Entrance requirements:* For master's, interview, minimum GPA of 2.5. Additional exam requirements/recommendations for international students: Required—TOEFL (minimum score 550 paper-based; 213 computer-based; 79 iBT), IELTS (minimum score 6). *Application deadline:* Applications are processed on a rolling basis. Application fee: $60 ($65 for international students). Electronic applications accepted. *Expenses:* Tuition: Full-time $8694; part-time $322 per credit hour. Tuition and fees vary according to course load. *Financial support:* Career-related internships or fieldwork, institutionally sponsored loans, scholarships/grants, and tuition waivers (partial) available. Support available to part-time students. Financial award application deadline: 6/30; financial award applicants required to submit FAFSA. *Unit head:* Dr. Maureen O'Hara, Chair and Professor, 858-642-8464, Fax: 858-642-8715, E-mail: mohara@nu.edu. *Application contact:* Dominick Giovanniello, Associate Regional Dean—San Diego, 800-NAT-UNIV, Fax: 858-541-7792, E-mail: dgiovann@nu.edu.

New England College, Program in Community Mental Health Counseling, Henniker, NH 03242-3293. Offers human services (MS); mental health counseling (MS). Part-time and evening/weekend programs available. *Degree requirements:* For master's, internship.

New Jersey City University, Graduate Studies and Continuing Education, College of Arts and Sciences, Department of Psychology, Program in Counseling, Jersey City, NJ 07305-1597. Offers MA.

New Mexico State University, Graduate School, College of Education, Department of Counseling and Educational Psychology, Las Cruces, NM 88003-8001. Offers counseling and guidance (MA); counseling psychology (PhD); school psychology (Ed S). *Accreditation:* ACA; APA (one or more programs are accredited); NCATE. Part-time programs available. *Faculty:* 11 full-time (8 women), 4 part-time/adjunct (2 women). *Students:* 62 full-time (46 women), 415 part-time (306 women); includes 48 minority (3 African Americans, 2 American Indian/Alaska Native, 1 Asian American or Pacific Islander, 42 Hispanic Americans), 2 international. Average age 32. 92 applicants, 93% accepted, 28 enrolled. In 2008, 10 master's, 5 doctorates, 12 other advanced degrees awarded. *Degree requirements:* For master's, comprehensive exam, thesis optional, internship; for doctorate, comprehensive exam, thesis/dissertation, internship; for Ed S, thesis or alternative, internship. *Entrance requirements:* For master's, doctorate, and Ed S, GRE General Test, minimum GPA of 3.0. *Application deadline:* For fall admission, 12/15 for domestic students; for spring admission, 4/1 priority date for domestic students. Application fee: $30 ($50 for international students). Electronic applications accepted. *Expenses:* Tuition, area resident: Full-time $3890; part-time $212.85 per credit. Tuition, state resident: full-time $3890; part-time $212.85 per credit. Tuition, nonresident: full-time $13,916; part-time $630.55 per credit. Required fees: $1218; $609 per semester. *Financial support:* In 2008–09, 68 students received support, including 3 research assistantships with partial tuition reimbursements available (averaging $12,150 per year), 32 teaching assistantships with partial tuition reimbursements available (averaging $7,990 per year); fellowships with partial tuition reimbursements available, career-related internships or fieldwork, Federal Work-Study, institutionally sponsored loans, scholarships/grants, traineeships, health care benefits, and unspecified assistantships also available. Support available to part-time students. Financial award application deadline: 4/1. *Faculty research:* Multicultural counseling, integrative health psychology group, career development school counseling. *Unit head:* Dr. Michael Waldo, Head, 575-646-2121, Fax: 575-646-8035, E-mail: miwaldo@nmsu.edu. *Application contact:* Elena Luna, Coordinator, 575-646-3498, Fax: 575-646-7721, E-mail: rosluna@nmsu.edu.

New York Institute of Technology, Graduate Division, School of Education, Program in Mental Health Counseling and School Counseling, Old Westbury, NY 11568-8000. Offers MS. *Students:* 3 full-time (all women), 15 part-time (11 women); includes 3 minority (2 African Americans, 1 Hispanic American). Average age 34. 71 applicants, 69% accepted. In 2008, 24 master's awarded. *Degree requirements:* For master's, thesis, internship. *Entrance requirements:* For master's, minimum GPA of 3.0, interview, 3 letters of reference. Additional exam requirements/recommendations for international students: Required—TOEFL. *Application deadline:* For fall admission, 7/1 priority date for domestic students; for spring admission, 12/1 priority date for domestic students. Application fee: $50. *Expenses:* Tuition: Part-time $783 per credit. *Financial support:* Research assistantships with partial tuition reimbursements, career-related internships or fieldwork, institutionally sponsored loans, and unspecified assistantships available. Support available to part-time students. Financial award applicants required to submit FAFSA. *Unit head:* Dr. Carol Dahir, Coordinator, 516-686-7616, Fax: 516-686-7655, E-mail: cdahir@nyit.edu. *Application contact:* Jacquelyn Nealon, Dean of Admissions and Financial Aid, 516-686-7925, Fax: 516-686-7613, E-mail: jnealon@nyit.edu.

New York University, Steinhardt School of Culture, Education and Human Development, Department of Applied Psychology, Program in Counselor Education, New York, NY 10012-1019. Offers counseling and guidance (MA, Advanced Certificate), including bilingual school counseling (MA), school counseling (MA); counseling for mental health and wellness (MA); counseling psychology (PhD). *Accreditation:* APA (one or more programs are accredited). Part-time and evening/weekend programs available. Terminal master's awarded for partial completion of doctoral program. *Degree requirements:* For master's, thesis (for some programs); for doctorate, thesis/dissertation. *Entrance requirements:* For doctorate, GRE General Test, interview. Additional exam requirements/recommendations for international students: Required—TOEFL. *Faculty research:* Cross-cultural counseling; group dynamics; culture, race and ethnicity; religiosity and psychological development; well-being and mental health.

Nicholls State University, Graduate Studies, College of Education, Department of Psychology and Counselor Education, Thibodaux, LA 70310. Offers psychological counseling (MA); school psychology (SSP). *Accreditation:* NCATE. Part-time and evening/weekend programs available. *Degree requirements:* For master's, comprehensive exam; for SSP, comprehensive exam, internship. *Entrance requirements:* For master's, GRE General Test. Electronic applications accepted.

Northeastern State University, Graduate College, College of Education, Department of Psychology and Counseling, Program in Counseling Psychology, Tahlequah, OK 74464-2399. Offers MS. Part-time and evening/weekend programs available. *Students:* 63 full-time (46 women), 41 part-time (33 women); includes 24 minority (5 African Americans, 14 American Indian/Alaska Native, 5 Hispanic Americans), 2 international. In 2008, 22 master's awarded. *Degree requirements:* For master's, thesis, internship, practicum. *Entrance requirements:* For master's, GRE, minimum GPA of 2.5. Additional exam requirements/recommendations for international students: Required—TOEFL (minimum score 213 computer-based). *Application deadline:* For fall admission, 3/1 priority date for domestic students; for spring admission, 10/1 for domestic students. Applications are processed on a rolling basis. Application fee: $0 ($25 for international students). Electronic applications accepted. *Financial support:* Teaching assistantships, career-related internships or fieldwork and Federal Work-Study available. Financial award application deadline: 3/1. *Application contact:* Margie Railey, Administrative Assistant, 918-456-5511 Ext. 2093, Fax: 918-458-2061, E-mail: railey@nsouk.edu.

Northeastern University, Bouvé College of Health Sciences Graduate School, Department of Counseling and Applied Educational Psychology, Program in Counseling Psychology, Boston, MA 02115-5096. Offers MS, PhD, CAGS. *Accreditation:* APA (one or more programs are accredited). Part-time programs available. *Degree requirements:* For doctorate, comprehensive exam, thesis/dissertation, qualifying exams; for CAGS, comprehensive exam. *Entrance requirements:* For master's and CAGS, GRE General Test or MAT; for doctorate, GRE General Test. Additional exam requirements/recommendations for international students: Required—TOEFL. *Faculty research:* Crisis intervention, family systems.

Northern Arizona University, Graduate College, College of Education, Program in Educational Psychology, Flagstaff, AZ 86011. Offers counseling psychology (PhD); learning and instruction (PhD); school psychology (PhD). *Degree requirements:* For doctorate, comprehensive exam, thesis/dissertation, internship. *Entrance requirements:* For doctorate, GRE General Test.

Northwestern Oklahoma State University, School of Professional Studies, Program in Counseling Psychology, Alva, OK 73717-2799. Offers MCP. Part-time programs available. *Faculty:* 5 full-time (1 woman). *Students:* 31 full-time (21 women), 31 part-time (28 women); includes 7 minority (1 African American, 2 American Indian/Alaska Native, 4 Hispanic Americans). Average age 31. 43 applicants, 100% accepted. In 2008, 22 master's awarded. *Degree requirements:* For master's, comprehensive exam. *Entrance requirements:* For master's, GRE General Test or MAT, minimum GPA of 2.75. *Application deadline:* Applications are processed on a rolling basis. Application fee: $15. *Expenses:* Required fees: $152 per hour. *Financial support:* Fellowships, Federal Work-Study available. Support available to part-time students. Financial award application deadline: 5/1; financial award applicants required to submit FAFSA. *Unit head:* Dr. Nancy Knous, Coordinator, 580-327-8443. *Application contact:* Debbie Skinner, Coordinator of Graduate Studies, 580-327-8410, E-mail: dgskinner@nwosu.edu.

Northwestern University, The Graduate School, Interdepartmental Degree Programs, Program in Counseling Psychology, Evanston, IL 60208. Offers MA. Admissions and degrees offered through The Graduate School. Part-time programs available. *Degree requirements:* For master's, comprehensive exam. *Entrance requirements:* For master's, GRE General Test. Electronic applications accepted. *Faculty research:* Family psychology, adult development and pathology, minority counseling, groups and systems, clinical training, stress and coping, health psychology.

Northwest University, College of Social and Behavioral Sciences, Kirkland, WA 98033. Offers counseling psychology (MA); international care and community development (MA). Evening/weekend programs available. *Faculty:* 1 full-time (0 women), 7 part-time/adjunct (4 women). *Students:* 82 full-time (70 women), 6 part-time (5 women); includes 9 minority (5 African Americans, 2 Asian Americans or Pacific Islanders, 2 Hispanic Americans), 2 international. 108 applicants, 69% accepted, 54 enrolled. In 2008, 28 master's awarded. *Entrance requirements:* For master's, essay, 3 character references. Additional exam requirements/recommendations for international students: Required—TOEFL (minimum score 580 paper-based; 237 computer-based). *Application deadline:* For fall admission, 12/1 priority date for domestic and international students; for spring admission, 4/1 priority date for domestic and international students. Applications are processed on a rolling basis. Application fee: $75. *Expenses:* Contact institution. *Financial support:* In 2008–09, 2 students received support. Career-related internships or fieldwork, health care benefits, and interational student scholarships available. Financial award application deadline: 6/30. *Unit head:* Dr. William Herkelrath, Dean, 425-889-5328, Fax: 425-739-4602, E-mail: william.herkelrath@northwestu.edu. *Application contact:* Sara Bickerstaff, Student Services Coordinator, 425-889-5249, Fax: 425-739-4602, E-mail: sara.bickerstaff@northwestu.edu.

Nova Southeastern University, Center for Psychological Studies, Master's Programs in Counseling, Mental Health, School Guidance, and Clinical Pharmacology, Fort Lauderdale, FL 33314-7796. Offers clinical pharmacology (MS); mental health counseling (MS); school guidance and counseling (MS). Part-time and evening/weekend programs available. *Faculty:* 7 full-time (2 women), 27 part-time/adjunct (8 women). *Students:* 263 full-time (245 women), 581 part-time (515 women); includes 430 minority (219 African Americans, 3 American Indian/Alaska Native, 11 Asian Americans or Pacific Islanders, 197 Hispanic Americans), 19 international. 562 applicants, 65% accepted, 262 enrolled. In 2008, 226 master's awarded. *Degree requirements:* For master's, comprehensive exam, 3 practica. *Entrance requirements:* Additional exam requirements/recommendations for international students: Required—TOEFL (minimum score 550 paper-based; 213 computer-based). *Application deadline:* For fall admission, 7/29 for domestic students; for winter admission, 11/29 for domestic students; for spring admission,

3/29 for domestic students. Applications are processed on a rolling basis. Application fee: $50. Electronic applications accepted. *Financial support:* Career-related internships or fieldwork, Federal Work-Study, and institutionally sponsored loans available. Financial award application deadline: 4/1. *Faculty research:* Clinical and child clinical psychology, geriatrics, interpersonal violence. *Unit head:* Karen S. Grosby, Dean, 954-262-5701, Fax: 954-262-3859. *Application contact:* Carlos Perez, Enrollment Management, 954-262-5790, Fax: 954-262-3893, E-mail: cpsinfo@cps.nova.edu.

Oakland University, Graduate Study and Lifelong Learning, School of Education and Human Services, Department of Counseling, Rochester, MI 48309-4401. Offers MA, PhD, Certificate. *Accreditation:* ACA (one or more programs are accredited). Part-time and evening/weekend programs available. *Degree requirements:* For doctorate, thesis/dissertation. *Entrance requirements:* Additional exam requirements/recommendations for international students: Required—TOEFL (minimum score 550 paper-based; 213 computer-based). Electronic applications accepted.

Ottawa University, Graduate Studies-Arizona, Program in Professional Counseling, Ottawa, KS 66067-3399. Offers Christian counseling (MA); expressive arts therapy (MA); marriage and family therapy (MA); treatment of trauma, abuse and deprivation (MA). Programs offered in Mesa, Phoenix, Tempe and West Valley, AZ. Part-time and evening/weekend programs available. Postbaccalaureate distance learning degree programs offered. *Degree requirements:* For master's, comprehensive exam, thesis or alternative, field experience, practicum. *Entrance requirements:* For master's, minimum undergraduate GPA of 3.0; course work in theories of personality, abnormal psychology, and human growth and development. Additional exam requirements/recommendations for international students: Required—TOEFL (minimum score 550 paper-based; 213 computer-based).

Our Lady of the Lake University of San Antonio, School of Professional Studies, Program in Psychology, San Antonio, TX 78207-4689. Offers counseling psychology (MS, Psy D); marriage and family therapy (MS); school psychology (MS). *Accreditation:* APA (one or more programs are accredited). Part-time and evening/weekend programs available. *Students:* 99 full-time (83 women), 97 part-time (86 women); includes 117 minority (25 African Americans, 1 American Indian/Alaska Native, 3 Asian Americans or Pacific Islanders, 88 Hispanic Americans), 2 international. Average age 30. In 2008, 42 master's, 3 doctorates awarded. *Degree requirements:* For master's, comprehensive exam, thesis optional, practicum; for doctorate, thesis/dissertation, internship, qualifying exam. *Entrance requirements:* For master's and doctorate, GRE General Test or MAT, interview. Additional exam requirements/recommendations for international students: Required—TOEFL. *Application deadline:* For fall admission, 3/1 priority date for domestic and international students. Applications are processed on a rolling basis. Application fee: $25 ($50 for international students). Electronic applications accepted. *Expenses:* Tuition: Full-time $11,970; part-time $665 per credit hour. Required fees: $500; $250 per term. *Financial support:* Research assistantships, teaching assistantships, career-related internships or fieldwork available. Support available to part-time students. Financial award application deadline: 4/15. *Faculty research:* Marriage and family therapy, supervision, cross-cultural counseling, violence. *Unit head:* Dr. Kathryn Anderson, Chair, 210-434-6711, E-mail: andek@lake.ollusa.edu. *Application contact:* 210-434-6711 Ext. 2314, Fax: 210-431-4036, E-mail: gradadm@lake.ollusa.edu.

Pacifica Graduate Institute, Graduate Programs, Carpinteria, CA 93013. Offers clinical psychology (PhD); counseling psychology (MA); depth psychology (MA, PhD); mythological studies (MA, PhD). Terminal master's awarded for partial completion of doctoral program. *Degree requirements:* For master's, thesis (for some programs), practicum; for doctorate, comprehensive exam, thesis/dissertation, internship. *Entrance requirements:* For master's, resumé, 3 letters of recommendation, writing sample, interview; for doctorate, resumé, 4 letters of recommendation, writing sample, interview. Additional exam requirements/recommendations for international students: Required—TOEFL. *Faculty research:* Imaginal and archetypal theory; post-Colonial psychoanalytic and Jungian theory; myth literature as it applies to the theory and practice of psychology.

Palm Beach Atlantic University, School of Education and Behavioral Studies, West Palm Beach, FL 33416-4708. Offers counseling psychology (MSCP), including addictions/mental health, marriage and family therapy, mental health counseling, school guidance counseling; elementary education (M Ed). Part-time and evening/weekend programs available. *Entrance requirements:* For master's, GRE General Test, minimum GPA of 3.0 in last 60 hours of course work. Additional exam requirements/recommendations for international students: Required—TOEFL (minimum score 550 paper-based; 213 computer-based). Electronic applications accepted.

Penn State University Park, Graduate School, College of Education, Department of Counselor Education, Counseling Psychology and Rehabilitation Services, State College, University Park, PA 16802-1503. Offers counseling psychology (PhD); counselor education (M Ed, MS), including elementary counseling; counselor education, counseling psychology and rehabilitation services (D Ed). *Accreditation:* ACA (one or more programs are accredited); APA (one or more programs are accredited); NCATE.

Philadelphia College of Osteopathic Medicine, Graduate and Professional Programs, Department of Psychology, Philadelphia, PA 19131-1694. Offers clinical psychology (Psy D); counseling and clinical health psychology (MS); organizational leadership and development (MS); psychology (Certificate); school psychology (MS, Psy D, Ed S). *Accreditation:* APA. *Degree requirements:* For master's, thesis; for doctorate, comprehensive exam, thesis/dissertation, final project, fieldwork. *Entrance requirements:* For master's, GRE or MAT, minimum GPA of 3.0; course work in biology, chemistry, English, physics; for other advanced degree, PRAXIS. *Faculty research:* Depression in primary care, integrated primary care, geriatric mental health.

See Close-Up on page 1127.

Prescott College, Graduate Programs, Program in Counseling and Psychology, Prescott, AZ 86301. Offers adventure-based psychotherapy (MA); counseling psychology (MA); ecopsychology (MA); ecotherapy (MA); equine-assisted mental health (MA); expressive arts therapy (MA); somatic psychology (MA); student-directed independent study (MA). Part-time programs available. Postbaccalaureate distance learning degree programs offered (minimal on-campus study). *Faculty:* 43 part-time/adjunct (29 women). *Students:* 74 full-time (66 women), 19 part-time (18 women); includes 9 minority (4 African Americans, 1 American Indian/Alaska Native, 4 Hispanic Americans), 9 international. Average age 37. 54 applicants, 70% accepted, 27 enrolled. In 2008, 29 master's awarded. *Degree requirements:* For master's, thesis, fieldwork or internship, practicum. *Entrance requirements:* For master's, 2 letters of recommendation, resumé, official academic transcripts, personal statement, application form, proposed study plan. Additional exam requirements/recommendations for international students: Required—TOEFL (minimum score 500 paper-based; 173 computer-based). *Application deadline:* For fall admission, 3/15 priority date for domestic and international students; for spring admission, 9/15 priority date for domestic and international students. Applications are processed on a rolling basis. Application fee: $40. Electronic applications accepted. *Expenses:* Tuition: Full-time $13,608; part-time $567 per credit. Required fees: $50 per term. One-time fee: $182. Tuition and fees vary according to degree level. *Financial support:* Career-related internships or fieldwork, Federal Work-Study, and scholarships/grants available. Financial award applicants required to submit FAFSA. *Unit head:* Camille Smith, Chair, Fax: 928-776-5151, E-mail: csmith@prescott.edu. *Application contact:* Kerstin Alicki, Admissions Counselor, 877-350-2102, Fax: 928-776-5242, E-mail: admissions@prescott.edu.

Providence College and Theological Seminary, Theological Seminary, Otterburne, MB R0A 1G0, Canada. Offers children's ministry (Certificate); Christian studies (MA, Certificate); counseling (MA); cross-cultural discipleship (Certificate); divinity (M Div); educational studies (MA), including counseling psychology, educational ministries, student development, teaching

Counseling Psychology

Providence College and Theological Seminary (continued)

English to speakers of other languages, training teachers of English to speakers of other languages; global studies (MA); lay counseling (Diploma); ministry (D Min); teaching English to speakers of other languages (Certificate); theological studies (MA); training teacher of English to speakers of other languages (Certificate); youth ministry (Certificate). *Accreditation:* ATS. Part-time programs available. *Degree requirements:* For master's, variable foreign language requirement, thesis (for some programs); for doctorate, thesis/dissertation; for M Div, 2 foreign languages, comprehensive exam, thesis/dissertation (for some programs). *Entrance requirements:* Additional exam requirements/recommendations for international students: Recommended—TOEFL (minimum score 550 paper-based; 213 computer-based). *Faculty research:* Studies in Isaiah, theology of sin.

Purdue University Calumet, Graduate School, School of Education, Program in Counseling, Hammond, IN 46323-2094. Offers human services (MS Ed); mental health counseling (MS Ed); school counseling (MS Ed). *Entrance requirements:* Additional exam requirements/recommendations for international students: Required—TOEFL.

Radford University, College of Graduate and Professional Studies, College of Education and Human Development, Department of Counselor Education, Radford, VA 24142. Offers community counseling (MS); school counseling (MS); student administration counseling (MS); student affairs counseling (MS). *Accreditation:* ACA; NCATE. Part-time and evening/weekend programs available. *Faculty:* 9 full-time (5 women), 1 (woman) part-time/adjunct. *Students:* 52 full-time (43 women), 75 part-time (63 women); includes 9 minority (6 African Americans, 1 Asian American or Pacific Islander, 2 Hispanic Americans). Average age 31. 91 applicants, 82% accepted, 52 enrolled. In 2008, 60 master's awarded. *Degree requirements:* For master's, comprehensive exam, thesis optional. *Entrance requirements:* For master's, GRE or MAT. Additional exam requirements/recommendations for international students: Required—TOEFL (minimum score 550 paper-based; 213 computer-based; 79 iBT). *Application deadline:* For fall admission, 3/1 priority date for domestic students, 12/1 for international students; for spring admission, 10/1 for domestic students, 7/1 for international students. Applications are processed on a rolling basis. Application fee: $40. Electronic applications accepted. *Expenses:* Tuition, area resident: Full-time $4845; part-time $202 per credit. Tuition, state resident: full-time $4845; part-time $202 per credit. Tuition, nonresident: full-time $11,483; part-time $478 per credit. Required fees: $2349; $98 per credit. *Financial support:* In 2008–09, 86 students received support, including 27 research assistantships with partial tuition reimbursements available (averaging $8,000 per year), 4 teaching assistantships with partial tuition reimbursements available (averaging $8,700 per year); career-related internships or fieldwork, Federal Work-Study, institutionally sponsored loans, scholarships/grants, and unspecified assistantships also available. Financial award application deadline: 3/1; financial award applicants required to submit FAFSA. *Unit head:* Dr. Alan Forrest, Chair, 540-831-5487, Fax: 540-831-6755, E-mail: aforrest@radford.edu. *Application contact:* Graduate Admissions, 540-831-5431, Fax: 540-831-6061, E-mail: gradcollege@radford.edu.

Radford University, College of Graduate and Professional Studies, College of Humanities and Behavioral Sciences, Program in Counseling Psychology, Radford, VA 24142. Offers Psy D. *Faculty:* 6 full-time (4 women). *Students:* 5 full-time (3 women). Average age 28. 15 applicants, 47% accepted, 5 enrolled. *Degree requirements:* For doctorate, thesis/dissertation. *Entrance requirements:* For doctorate, GRE General Test, master's degree; minimum GPA of 3.25; letter of interest; curriculum vitae; writing sample; 3 letters of recommendation. Additional exam requirements/recommendations for international students: Required—TOEFL (minimum score 550 paper-based; 213 computer-based; 79 iBT). *Application deadline:* For fall admission, 1/15 priority date for domestic students, 1/15 for international students; for spring admission, 10/1 for domestic students. Applications are processed on a rolling basis. Application fee: $40. Electronic applications accepted. *Expenses:* Tuition, area resident: Full-time $4845; part-time $202 per credit. Tuition, state resident: full-time $4845; part-time $202 per credit. Tuition, nonresident: full-time $11,483; part-time $478 per credit. Required fees: $2349; $98 per credit. *Financial support:* In 2008–09, 5 students received support. Career-related internships or fieldwork, Federal Work-Study, institutionally sponsored loans, and scholarships/grants available. Financial award application deadline: 3/1; financial award applicants required to submit FAFSA. *Unit head:* Dr. James L Werth, Program Director, 540-831-6817, Fax: 540-831-6113, E-mail: jwerth@radford.edu. *Application contact:* Graduate Admissions, 540-831-5431, Fax: 540-831-6061, E-mail: gradcollege@radford.edu.

Radford University, College of Graduate and Professional Studies, College of Humanities and Behavioral Sciences, Program in Psychology, Radford, VA 24142. Offers clinical psychology (MA, MS); counseling psychology (Psy D); experimental psychology (MA); general psychology (MS); industrial/organizational psychology (MA, MS); school psychology (Ed S). Part-time programs available. *Faculty:* 23 full-time (9 women), 1 part-time/adjunct (0 women). *Students:* 46 full-time (28 women), 5 part-time (4 women); includes 4 minority (3 African Americans, 1 Asian American or Pacific Islander), 2 international. Average age 26. 114 applicants, 42% accepted, 20 enrolled. In 2008, 36 master's awarded. *Degree requirements:* For master's, comprehensive exam, thesis (for some programs). *Entrance requirements:* For master's, GRE, minimum GPA of 3.0; 3 letters of reference; essay. Additional exam requirements/recommendations for international students: Required—TOEFL (minimum score 550 paper-based; 213 computer-based; 79 iBT). *Application deadline:* For fall admission, 3/1 priority date for domestic students, 12/1 for international students; for spring admission, 10/1 for domestic students, 7/1 for international students. Applications are processed on a rolling basis. Application fee: $40. Electronic applications accepted. *Expenses:* Tuition, area resident: Full-time $4845; part-time $202 per credit. Tuition, state resident: full-time $4845; part-time $202 per credit. Tuition, nonresident: full-time $11,483; part-time $478 per credit. Required fees: $2349; $98 per credit. *Financial support:* In 2008–09, 47 students received support, including 33 research assistantships with partial tuition reimbursements available (averaging $8,000 per year), 12 teaching assistantships with partial tuition reimbursements available (averaging $8,700 per year); career-related internships or fieldwork, institutionally sponsored loans, scholarships/grants, and unspecified assistantships also available. Financial award application deadline: 3/1; financial award applicants required to submit FAFSA. *Unit head:* Dr. Hilary M. Lips, Chair, 540-831-5387, Fax: 540-831-6113, E-mail: hlips@radford.edu. *Application contact:* Graduate Admissions Office, 540-831-5431, Fax: 540-831-6061, E-mail: gradcollege@radford.edu.

Regent University, Graduate School, School of Psychology and Counseling, Virginia Beach, VA 23464-9800. Offers clinical psychology (MA, Psy D); counseling (MA), including community counseling, human services counseling, school counseling; counseling studies (CAGS); counselor education and supervision (PhD); M Div/MA; M Ed/MA; MBA/MA. PhD program offered online only. *Accreditation:* ACA; APA (one or more programs are accredited). Part-time and evening/weekend programs available. Postbaccalaureate distance learning degree programs offered (minimal on-campus study). *Faculty:* 25 full-time (12 women), 19 part-time/adjunct (9 women). *Students:* 176 full-time (142 women), 192 part-time (144 women); includes 100 minority (78 African Americans, 2 American Indian/Alaska Native, 10 Asian Americans or Pacific Islanders, 10 Hispanic Americans), 13 international. Average age 32. 317 applicants, 47% accepted, 112 enrolled. In 2008, 129 master's, 22 doctorates awarded. *Degree requirements:* For master's, thesis or alternative, internship, practicum, written competency exam; for doctorate, thesis/dissertation or alternative. *Entrance requirements:* For master's, GRE General Test including writing exam, minimum undergraduate GPA of 2.75, 3 recommendations, resumé, transcripts, writing sample; for doctorate, GRE General Test including writing exam, GRE Subject Test, minimum undergraduate GPA of 3.0, 3.5 (PhD), 10-15 minute VHS tape demonstrating counseling skills, writing sample, 3 recommendations, resumé, transcripts. Additional exam requirements/recommendations for international students: Required—TOEFL (minimum score 577 paper-based; 233 computer-based). *Application deadline:* For fall admission, 4/1 priority date for domestic students; for spring admission, 11/1 priority date for domestic students. Applications are processed on a rolling basis. Application fee: $50. Electronic applications accepted. *Expenses:* Contact institution. *Financial support:* Research assistantships with full and partial tuition reimbursements, teaching assistantships with full and partial tuition reimbursements, career-related internships or fieldwork, scholarships/grants, and tuition waivers (full and partial) available. Support available to part-time students. Financial award application deadline: 9/1; financial award applicants required to submit FAFSA. *Faculty research:* Marriage enrichment, AIDS counseling, troubled youth, faith and learning, trauma. *Unit head:* Dr. Rosemarie Hughes, Dean, 757-352-4269, Fax: 757-352-4282, E-mail: rosehug@regent.edu. *Application contact:* Matthew Chadwick, Director of Admissions, 800-373-5504, Fax: 757-352-4381, E-mail: admissions@regent.edu.

Regis University, College for Professional Studies, Graduate Counseling Program, Denver, CO 80221-1099. Offers community counseling (MAC); counseling children and adolescents (Post-Graduate Certificate); marriage and family therapy (Post-Graduate Certificate). Program offered in Henderson and Las Vegas (Summerlin), NV. *Accreditation:* ACA. Part-time and evening/weekend programs available. *Degree requirements:* For master's, internships, practicum. *Entrance requirements:* For master's, 2 admissions essays, interview, 2 recommendations, resumé, criminal background check. Additional exam requirements/recommendations for international students: Required—TOEFL (minimum score 213 computer-based), TWE (minimum score 5). *Expenses:* Contact institution. *Faculty research:* Group Development, Counselor Education, Counsel and Therapy, Influence of Technology on Psychology, Dream finding groups, Adult Development, Depression.

Richmont Graduate University, Graduate Programs, Atlanta, GA 30327. Offers Christian psychological studies (MS); marriage and family therapy (MA); professional counseling (MA).

Rivier College, School of Graduate Studies, Department of Education, Nashua, NH 03060. Offers curriculum and instruction (M Ed); early childhood education (M Ed); educational administration (M Ed); educational studies (M Ed); elementary education (M Ed); elementary education and general special education (M Ed); emotional and behavioral disorders (M Ed); general social education (M Ed); leadership and learning (CAGS); learning disabilities (M Ed); learning disabilities and reading (M Ed); mental health counseling (MA); reading (M Ed); school counseling (M Ed). Part-time and evening/weekend programs available. *Degree requirements:* For master's, comprehensive exam (for some programs), internships. *Entrance requirements:* For master's, GRE General Test or MAT.

Rosemont College, Graduate School, Program in Counseling Psychology, Rosemont, PA 19010-1699. Offers human services (MA); school counseling (MA). Part-time and evening/weekend programs available. *Degree requirements:* For master's, thesis or alternative, practicum. *Entrance requirements:* For master's, 3.0 baccalaureate GPA, statement of purpose, 3 letters of recommendation. Additional exam requirements/recommendations for international students: Required—TOEFL. Electronic applications accepted. *Expenses:* Contact institution. *Faculty research:* Addictions counseling.

Rowan University, Graduate School, College of Liberal Arts and Sciences, Department of Psychology, Program in Mental Health Counseling, Glassboro, NJ 08028-1701. Offers MA. Part-time and evening/weekend programs available. *Students:* 9 full-time (8 women), 3 part-time (all women); includes 1 minority (Asian American or Pacific Islander). Average age 23. 15 applicants, 100% accepted, 12 enrolled. *Degree requirements:* For master's, thesis. *Entrance requirements:* For master's, GRE. Additional exam requirements/recommendations for international students: Required—TOEFL. *Application deadline:* For spring admission, 2/15 for domestic students. Electronic applications accepted. *Expenses:* Tuition, area resident: Full-time $10,624; part-time $590 per credit. Tuition, state resident: full-time $10,624; part-time $590 per credit. Tuition, nonresident: full-time $10,624; part-time $590 per credit. Required fees: $2258; $124.90 per credit. *Financial support:* Career-related internships or fieldwork, scholarships/grants, health care benefits, and unspecified assistantships available. *Unit head:* Dr. Mira Lalovic-Hand, Interim Associate Provost/Director of Graduate School, 856-256-5120, E-mail: Lalovic-hand@rowan.edu. *Application contact:* Karen Haynes, Graduate Coordinator, 856-256-4052, Fax: 856-256-4436, E-mail: Haynes@rowan.edu.

Rowan University, Graduate School, College of Liberal Arts and Sciences, Program in Mental Health Counseling and Applied Psychology, Glassboro, NJ 08028-1701. Offers MA. Part-time and evening/weekend programs available. *Students:* 6 full-time (4 women), 18 part-time (16 women); includes 3 minority (1 African American, 2 Asian Americans or Pacific Islanders). Average age 28. 28 applicants, 7% accepted, 1 enrolled. In 2008, 7 master's awarded. *Degree requirements:* For master's, thesis. *Entrance requirements:* For master's, GRE. Additional exam requirements/recommendations for international students: Required—TOEFL. *Application deadline:* Applications are processed on a rolling basis. Application fee: $50. Electronic applications accepted. *Expenses:* Tuition, area resident: Full-time $10,624; part-time $590 per credit. Tuition, state resident: full-time $10,624; part-time $590 per credit. Tuition, nonresident: full-time $10,624; part-time $590 per credit. Required fees: $2258; $124.90 per credit. *Financial support:* Career-related internships or fieldwork, scholarships/grants, health care benefits, and unspecified assistantships available. *Unit head:* Dr. Mira Lalovic-Hand, Interim Provost/Director of Graduate School, 856-256-5120, E-mail: Lalovic-hand@rowan.edu. *Application contact:* Karen Haynes, Graduate Coordinator, 856-256-4052, Fax: 856-256-4436, E-mail: Haynes@rowan.edu.

Rutgers, The State University of New Jersey, New Brunswick, Graduate School of Education, Department of Educational Psychology, Program in Counseling Psychology, Piscataway, NJ 08854-8097. Offers Ed M. Part-time and evening/weekend programs available. *Entrance requirements:* For master's, GRE General Test, 3 letters of recommendation. Additional exam requirements/recommendations for international students: Required—TOEFL (minimum score 550 paper-based; 233 computer-based; 83 iBT). Electronic applications accepted. *Faculty research:* Children and family in a cross-cultural context, attachment theory, multicultural counseling, therapy relationship.

St. Bonaventure University, School of Graduate Studies, School of Education, Program in Counselor Education, St. Bonaventure, NY 14778-2284. Offers community mental health counselor (Adv C); counseling education-school (MS Ed); school counselor (Adv C). *Degree requirements:* For master's, comprehensive exam, thesis optional. *Entrance requirements:* For master's, GRE, interview, writing sample. *Faculty research:* Parent education, learning disabilities, stress management.

St. Edward's University, New College, Program in Counseling, Austin, TX 78704. Offers MA. Part-time and evening/weekend programs available. *Students:* 81 full-time (67 women), 151 part-time (117 women); includes 49 minority (14 African Americans, 2 American Indian/Alaska Native, 5 Asian Americans or Pacific Islanders, 28 Hispanic Americans), 1 international. Average age 35. 87 applicants, 72% accepted, 54 enrolled. In 2008, 55 master's awarded. *Degree requirements:* For master's, minimum 24 resident hours. *Entrance requirements:* For master's, GRE General Test, minimum GPA of 3.0 in last 60 hours or 2.75 overall. Additional exam requirements/recommendations for international students: Required—TOEFL (minimum score 550 paper-based; 213 computer-based; 79 iBT). *Application deadline:* For fall admission, 8/1 for domestic students, 7/1 for international students; for spring admission, 12/1 for domestic students, 11/1 for international students. Applications are processed on a rolling basis. Application fee: $45 ($50 for international students). Electronic applications accepted. *Expenses:* Tuition: Full-time $13,752; part-time $764 per credit hour. Required fees: $50 per semester. Full-time tuition and fees vary according to course load and program. *Financial support:* In 2008–09, 4 students received support. Scholarships/grants available. *Unit head:* Dr. Elizabeth Katz, Director, 512-464-8833, Fax: 512-448-8492, E-mail: elizk@stedwards.edu. *Application contact:* Anna Alkin, Graduate Admissions Coordinator, 512-448-8745, Fax: 512-428-1032, E-mail: annaa@stedwards.edu.

St. Edward's University, School of Management and Business, Program in Human Services, Austin, TX 78704. Offers administration (Certificate); conflict resolution (Certificate); family mediation (Certificate); human services (MA), including administration, conflict resolution, human resource management, organization development and training, social and psychological services; mediation (Certificate); organization development and training (Certificate). Part-time and evening/weekend programs available. *Students:* 2 full-time (both women), 53 part-time (42 women); includes 23 minority (5 African Americans, 2 Asian Americans or Pacific Islanders, 16 Hispanic Americans). Average age 33. 21 applicants, 90% accepted, 16 enrolled. In 2008, 22 master's awarded. *Degree requirements:* For master's, minimum 24 resident hours. *Entrance requirements:* For master's, GRE General Test, GMAT, minimum GPA of 2.75 in last 60 hours of course work. Additional exam requirements/recommendations for international students: Required—TOEFL (minimum score 550 paper-based; 213 computer-based; 79 iBT). *Application deadline:* For fall admission, 8/1 for domestic students, 7/1 for international students; for spring admission, 12/1 for domestic students, 11/1 for international students. Applications are processed on a rolling basis. Application fee: $45 ($50 for international students). Electronic applications accepted. *Expenses:* Tuition: Full-time $13,752; part-time $764 per credit hour. Required fees: $50 per semester. Full-time tuition and fees vary according to course load and program. *Financial support:* In 2008–09, 2 students received support. Scholarships/grants available. *Faculty research:* Leadership development, organizational management, public policy. *Unit head:* Dr. Constance D Porter, Director, 512-416-5827, Fax: 512-448-8492, E-mail: constanp@stedwards.edu. *Application contact:* Kay L. Arnold, Graduate Admissions Coordinator, 512-233-1636, Fax: 512-428-1032, E-mail: kayla@stedwards.edu.

St. John Fisher College, Wegmans School of Nursing, Program in Mental Health Counseling, Rochester, NY 14618-3597. Offers MS. *Accreditation:* ACA. Part-time programs available. *Faculty:* 4 full-time (3 women), 2 part-time/adjunct (0 women). *Students:* 31 full-time (29 women), 24 part-time (19 women); includes 7 minority (5 African Americans, 2 Hispanic Americans). Average age 32. 58 applicants, 64% accepted, 25 enrolled. In 2008, 16 master's awarded. *Degree requirements:* For master's, practicum experience, internship. *Entrance requirements:* For master's, GRE (if GPA below 3.0), 2 letters of recommendation, personal statement, current resumé, undergraduate course work in abnormal psychology, interview. Additional exam requirements/recommendations for international students: Required—TOEFL (minimum score 575 paper-based; 233 computer-based; 80 iBT). *Application deadline:* For fall admission, 3/1 for domestic students. Applications are processed on a rolling basis. Application fee: $30. Electronic applications accepted. *Expenses:* Tuition: Part-time $655 per credit hour. Required fees: $25 per semester. *Financial support:* In 2008–09, 47 students received support. Federal Work-Study and scholarships/grants available. Financial award applicants required to submit FAFSA. *Faculty research:* Social class issues, clinical supervision, counselor education, play therapy. *Unit head:* Dr. Signe M. Kastberg, Director, 585-385-7222, E-mail: skastberg@sjfc.edu. *Application contact:* Jose Perales, Director of Graduate Admissions, 585-385-8067, E-mail: jperales@sjfc.edu.

Saint Joseph College, Graduate School, Department of Counselor Education, West Hartford, CT 06117-2700. Offers community counseling (MA), including child welfare; school counseling (MA). Part-time and evening/weekend programs available. *Students:* 28 full-time (26 women), 84 part-time (74 women). *Degree requirements:* For master's, comprehensive exam, thesis optional, capstone project. *Entrance requirements:* For master's, PRAXIS I (school counseling), 2 letters of recommendation. *Application deadline:* Applications are processed on a rolling basis. Application fee: $50. Electronic applications accepted. *Expenses:* Tuition: Part-time $560 per credit. Required fees: $30 per credit. *Financial support:* Career-related internships or fieldwork, health care benefits, and unspecified assistantships available. Support available to part-time students. Financial award applicants required to submit FAFSA. *Application contact:* Graduate Admissions Office, 860-231-5261, E-mail: graduate@sjc.edu.

Saint Martin's University, Graduate Programs, Program in Counseling Psychology, Lacey, WA 98503-1297. Offers MAC. Part-time and evening/weekend programs available. *Degree requirements:* For master's, clinical experience, interview. *Entrance requirements:* For master's, BA in psychology or related field, clinical experience. Additional exam requirements/recommendations for international students: Required—TOEFL. *Faculty research:* Alcohol studies, clinical effectiveness, social justice, parent adolescent interaction.

St. Mary's University, Graduate School, Department of Counseling and Human Services, Program in Mental Health, San Antonio, TX 78228-8507. Offers MA. Part-time programs available. *Faculty:* 4 full-time (2 women). *Students:* 7 full-time (6 women), 6 part-time (all women); includes 5 minority (all Hispanic Americans), 1 international. Average age 28. 8 applicants, 88% accepted, 5 enrolled. In 2008, 1 master's awarded. *Degree requirements:* For master's, comprehensive exam, internship. *Entrance requirements:* For master's, GRE, MAT. Additional exam requirements/recommendations for international students: Required—TOEFL (minimum score 550 paper-based; 213 computer-based; 80 iBT). *Application deadline:* Applications are processed on a rolling basis. Application fee: $0. Electronic applications accepted. *Expenses:* Tuition: Full-time $12,006; part-time $667 per credit hour. Required fees: $440; $220 per semester. *Financial support:* In 2008–09, 3 students received support, including 3 fellowships (averaging $2,833 per year). Financial award application deadline: 3/31; financial award applicants required to submit FAFSA. *Unit head:* Dr. Ray Wooten, Director, 210-436-3226, Fax: 210-431-6886, E-mail: hrwooten@stmarytx.edu. *Application contact:* Dr. Henry Flores, Dean of the Graduate School, 210-436-3101, Fax: 210-431-2220, E-mail: hflores@stmarytx.edu.

Saint Mary's University of Minnesota, Schools of Graduate and Professional Programs, Graduate School of Health and Human Services, Counseling and Psychological Services Program, Winona, MN 55987-1399. Offers MA.

Saint Paul University, Faculty of Human Sciences, Program in Counseling and Spirituality, Ottawa, ON K1S 1C4, Canada. Offers individual or marital/couple counseling (MA); spiritual care (MA). Part-time programs available. *Degree requirements:* For master's, research project or thesis. *Entrance requirements:* For master's, honors BA in human sciences, minimum B average, 12 theology credits.

St. Thomas University, Biscayne College, Department of Social Sciences and Counseling, Program in Mental Health Counseling, Miami Gardens, FL 33054-6459. Offers MS. Part-time and evening/weekend programs available. *Degree requirements:* For master's, comprehensive exam. *Entrance requirements:* For master's, interview, minimum GPA of 3.0 or GRE. Additional exam requirements/recommendations for international students: Required—TOEFL (minimum score 550 paper-based; 213 computer-based; 79 iBT). Electronic applications accepted.

Saint Xavier University, Graduate Studies, School of Arts and Sciences, Department of Psychology, Chicago, IL 60655-3105. Offers adult counseling (Certificate); child/adolescent counseling (Certificate); core counseling (Certificate); counseling psychology (MA). Part-time and evening/weekend programs available. *Entrance requirements:* For master's, GRE General Test, minimum GPA of 3.0, interview.

Salem State College, School of Graduate Studies, Program in Counseling and Psychological Services, Salem, MA 01970-5353. Offers MS. Part-time and evening/weekend programs available. *Students:* 36 full-time (29 women), 40 part-time (36 women); includes 3 minority (1 Asian American or Pacific Islander, 2 Hispanic Americans), 4 international. Average age 31. In 2008, 11 master's awarded. *Entrance requirements:* For master's, GRE General Test or MAT. *Application deadline:* Applications are processed on a rolling basis. Application fee: $35. *Unit head:* Dr. Patrice Miller, Coordinator, 978-542-6075, Fax: 978-542-6596, E-mail: pmiller@salemstate.edu. *Application contact:* Dr. Marc Glasser, Dean of the Graduate School, 978-542-6323, Fax: 978-542-7215.

Salve Regina University, Graduate Studies, Holistic Graduate Programs, Newport, RI 02840-4192. Offers expressive and creative arts (CAGS); holistic counseling (MA); holistic leadership (MA, CAGS); mental health (CAGS). Part-time and evening/weekend programs available. *Faculty:* 4 full-time (2 women), 9 part-time/adjunct (6 women). *Students:* 18 full-time (16 women), 90 part-time (81 women); includes 1 minority (American Indian/Alaska Native). Average age 42. 40 applicants, 83% accepted, 30 enrolled. In 2008, 18 master's, 15 other advanced degrees awarded. *Degree requirements:* For master's, internship, project. *Entrance requirements:* For master's, GMAT, GRE General Test, or MAT. Additional exam requirements/recommendations for international students: Required—TOEFL (minimum score 600 paper-based; 250 computer-based; 100 iBT), TOEFL or IELTS. *Application deadline:* For fall admission, 3/15 priority date for domestic and international students; for spring admission, 9/15 priority date for domestic and international students. Applications are processed on a rolling basis. Application fee: $60. Electronic applications accepted. *Expenses:* Tuition: Part-time $395 per credit. Required fees: $40 per term. Tuition and fees vary according to degree level. *Financial support:* Career-related internships or fieldwork and Federal Work-Study available. Support available to part-time students. Financial award application deadline: 3/1; financial award applicants required to submit FAFSA. *Unit head:* Dr. Peter F. Mullen, Director, 401-341-3278, Fax: 401-341-2977, E-mail: mullenp@salve.edu. *Application contact:* Kelly Alverson, Graduate Admissions Counselor, 401-341-2153, Fax: 401-341-2973, E-mail: kelly.alverson@salve.edu.

Salve Regina University, Graduate Studies, Program in Rehabilitation Counseling, Newport, RI 02840-4192. Offers mental health counseling (CAGS); rehabilitation counseling (MA). Part-time and evening/weekend programs available. *Faculty:* 1 (woman) full-time, 4 part-time/adjunct (all women). *Students:* 13 full-time (10 women), 25 part-time (18 women); includes 1 minority (Hispanic American). Average age 35. 18 applicants, 89% accepted, 13 enrolled. In 2008, 16 master's awarded. *Entrance requirements:* For master's, GMAT, GRE General Test or MAT. Additional exam requirements/recommendations for international students: Required—TOEFL (minimum score 600 paper-based; 250 computer-based; 100 iBT), TOEFL or IELTS. *Application deadline:* For fall admission, 3/15 priority date for domestic and international students; for spring admission, 9/15 priority date for domestic and international students. Applications are processed on a rolling basis. Application fee: $60. Electronic applications accepted. *Expenses:* Tuition: Part-time $395 per credit. Required fees: $40 per term. Tuition and fees vary according to degree level. *Financial support:* Career-related internships or fieldwork and Federal Work-Study available. Support available to part-time students. Financial award application deadline: 3/1; financial award applicants required to submit FAFSA. *Unit head:* Dr. Dimity Peter, Director, 401-341-3189, Fax: 401-341-2993, E-mail: dimity.peter@salve.edu. *Application contact:* Kelly Alverson, Graduate Admissions Counselor, 401-341-2153, Fax: 401-341-2973, E-mail: kelly.alverson@salve.edu.

San Francisco State University, Division of Graduate Studies, College of Health and Human Services, Department of Counseling, San Francisco, CA 94132-1722. Offers counseling (MS); marriage, family, and child counseling (MSC); rehabilitation counseling (MS). *Accreditation:* ACA (one or more programs are accredited). Part-time programs available.

Santa Clara University, School of Education, Counseling Psychology, and Pastoral Ministries, Department of Counseling Psychology, Program in Counseling Psychology, Santa Clara, CA 95053. Offers MA. Part-time and evening/weekend programs available. *Students:* 89 full-time (82 women), 113 part-time (90 women); includes 55 minority (1 African American, 21 Asian Americans or Pacific Islanders, 33 Hispanic Americans), 6 international. Average age 32. 88 applicants, 72% accepted, 40 enrolled. In 2008, 59 master's awarded. *Degree requirements:* For master's, comprehensive exam, thesis optional. *Entrance requirements:* For master's, GRE or MAT, minimum GPA of 3.0, 1 year of related experience. Additional exam requirements/recommendations for international students: Required—TOEFL. *Application deadline:* Applications are processed on a rolling basis. *Expenses:* Contact institution. *Financial support:* Fellowships, teaching assistantships, career-related internships or fieldwork, Federal Work-Study, institutionally sponsored loans, and scholarships/grants available. Support available to part-time students. Financial award application deadline: 3/1; financial award applicants required to submit FAFSA.

The School of Professional Psychology at Forest Institute, Graduate Programs, Springfield, MO 65807. Offers clinical psychology (Psy D); counseling psychology (MA); marriage and family therapy (MA, PGC). *Accreditation:* AAMFT/COAMFTE; APA (one or more programs are accredited). *Faculty:* 18 full-time (9 women), 28 part-time/adjunct (15 women). *Students:* 208 full-time (141 women), 34 part-time (27 women). 153 applicants, 42% accepted, 40 enrolled. In 2008, 36 master's, 36 doctorates awarded. Terminal master's awarded for partial completion of doctoral program. *Median time to degree:* Of those who began their doctoral program in fall 2000, 100% received their degree in 8 years or less. *Degree requirements:* For master's, thesis, practice; for doctorate, comprehensive exam, thesis/dissertation, internship, practice. *Entrance requirements:* For master's, GRE General Test, interview, minimum GPA of 3.0, 12 hours in psychology; for doctorate, GRE General Test, interview, minimum GPA of 3.0, 18 hours in psychology. Additional exam requirements/recommendations for international students: Required—TOEFL (minimum score 550 paper-based; 213 computer-based). *Application deadline:* For fall admission, 1/15 priority date for domestic and international students; for spring admission, 8/1 priority date for domestic and international students. Applications are processed on a rolling basis. Application fee: $50. Electronic applications accepted. *Expenses:* Tuition: Full-time $22,500. *Financial support:* In 2008–09, 91 students received support. Career-related internships or fieldwork, Federal Work-Study, and scholarships/grants available. Support available to part-time students. Financial award applicants required to submit FAFSA. *Faculty research:* Forensics/corrections, marriage and family therapy, child and adolescent, integrated health care, neuropsychology. *Unit head:* Dr. Mark E. Skrade, President, 417-823-3477, Fax: 417-823-3442, E-mail: mskrade@forest.edu. *Application contact:* Dawn Medley, Director of Enrollment Management, 417-823-3477, Fax: 417-823-3442, E-mail: dmedley@forest.edu.

Seton Hall University, College of Education and Human Services, Department of Professional Psychology and Family Therapy, Program in Counseling Psychology, South Orange, NJ 07079-2697. Offers MA, PhD. *Accreditation:* APA. *Degree requirements:* For doctorate, comprehensive exam, thesis/dissertation, internship. *Entrance requirements:* For doctorate, GRE, interview. *Faculty research:* Vocational indecision, coping skills, cognitive behavioral interventions, vocational development.

Shippensburg University of Pennsylvania, School of Graduate Studies, College of Education and Human Services, Department of Counseling, Shippensburg, PA 17257-2299. Offers Adlerian studies (Certificate); advanced study in counseling (Certificate); alcohol and drug counseling (Certificate); counseling (M Ed, MS), including college counseling (MS), community counseling (MS), elementary school counseling, mental health counseling (MS), secondary school counseling (MS), student personnel services (MS); couple and family counseling (Certificate). *Accreditation:* ACA (one or more programs are accredited); NCATE. Part-time and evening/weekend programs available. *Faculty:* 8 full-time (3 women), 3 part-time/adjunct (2 women). *Students:* 71 full-time (60 women), 109 part-time (91 women); includes 22 minority (16 African Americans, 4 Asian Americans or Pacific Islanders, 2 Hispanic Americans), 2 international. Average age 29. 128 applicants, 39% accepted, 32 enrolled. In 2008, 48 master's awarded. *Degree requirements:* For master's, fieldwork, research project, internship, candidacy. *Entrance requirements:* For master's, GRE or MAT (for community, mental health, student personnel, and college counseling applicants if GPA is less than 2.75), minimum GPA of 2.75 (3.0 for M Ed), interview, resumé, 3 letters of recommendation, supplemental data forms, one year of relevant work experience, on-campus interview. Additional exam requirements/recommendations for international students: Required—TOEFL (minimum score 560 paper-based; 220 computer-based); Recommended—IELTS (minimum score 6). *Application deadline:* For fall admission, 3/1 for international students; for spring admission, 7/1 for international students. Applications are processed on a rolling basis. Application fee: $30. Electronic applications accepted. *Expenses:* Tuition, state resident: full-time $6430; part-time $357 per credit. Tuition, nonresident: full-time $10,288; part-time $572 per credit. Required fees: $1127; $38 per credit. One-time fee: $44 part-time. *Financial support:* In 2008–09, 44 research assistantships with full tuition reimbursements (averaging $5,000 per year) were awarded; career-related internships or fieldwork, scholarships/grants, unspecified assistantships, and resident hall directors, student payroll positions also available. Support available to part-time students. Financial award application deadline: 3/1; financial award applicants required to submit FAFSA. *Unit head:* Dr. Jan Arminio, Chairperson, 717-477-1668, Fax: 717-477-4016, E-mail: jlarmi@ship.edu. *Application contact:* Renee Payne, Associate Dean of Graduate Admissions, 717-477-1231, Fax: 717-477-4016, E-mail: rmpayn@ship.edu.

Counseling Psychology

Sonoma State University, School of Social Sciences, Department of Counseling, Rohnert Park, CA 94928-3609. Offers counseling (MA); marriage, family, and child counseling (MA); pupil personnel services (MA). *Accreditation:* ACA. Part-time programs available. *Degree requirements:* For master's, internship. *Entrance requirements:* For master's, minimum GPA of 3.0. *Faculty research:* Self-esteem, relationship of emotion and health, at-risk youth, feminist issues, supervision strategies.

Southeast Missouri State University, School of Graduate Studies, Department of Educational Leadership and Counseling, Counseling Program, Cape Girardeau, MO 63701-4799. Offers counseling education (Ed S); mental health counseling (MA); school counseling (MA), including elementary counseling, secondary counseling. *Accreditation:* ACA; NCATE. Part-time and evening/weekend programs available. *Faculty:* 5 full-time (3 women). *Students:* 17 full-time (15 women), 50 part-time (44 women); includes 3 minority (2 African Americans, 1 Asian American or Pacific Islander). Average age 33. 19 applicants, 89% accepted. In 2008, 23 master's, 5 other advanced degrees awarded. *Degree requirements:* For master's, comprehensive exam, thesis optional, portfolio, oral exam; for Ed S, oral exam. *Entrance requirements:* For master's, GRE General Test, MAT, minimum undergraduate GPA of 3.0; for Ed S, GRE General Test or MAT, minimum graduate GPA of 3.5. Additional exam requirements/recommendations for international students: Required—TOEFL (minimum score 550 paper-based; 213 computer-based); Recommended—IELTS (minimum score 6). *Application deadline:* For fall admission, 8/1 for domestic students, 7/1 for international students; for spring admission, 11/21 for domestic students, 11/1 for international students. Applications are processed on a rolling basis. Application fee: $25 ($100 for international students). Electronic applications accepted. *Expenses:* Tuition, area resident: Part-time $213.30 per credit hour. Tuition, state resident: part-time $213.30 per credit hour. Tuition, nonresident: part-time $393.30 per credit hour. Required fees: $23.70 per credit hour. *Financial support:* In 2008–09, 11 students received support, including 11 research assistantships with full tuition reimbursements available (averaging $7,600 per year); unspecified assistantships also available. Financial award applicants required to submit FAFSA. *Faculty research:* Counselor development, cognitive development of counselors, counselor supervision, issues in school counseling, issues in mental health counseling. *Unit head:* Dr. Margaret Noe, Dean, College of Education, 573-651-2408, E-mail: mnoe@semo.edu. *Application contact:* Marsha L. Arant, Senior Administrative Assistant, School of Graduate Studies, 573-651-2192, Fax: 573-651-2001, E-mail: marant@semo.edu.

Southern Adventist University, School of Education and Psychology, Collegedale, TN 37315-0370. Offers curriculum and instruction (MS Ed); educational administration and supervision (MS Ed); inclusive education (MS Ed); literacy education (MS Ed); outdoor teacher education (MS Ed); professional counseling (MS); school counseling (MS). *Accreditation:* NCATE. Part-time and evening/weekend programs available. *Degree requirements:* For master's, comprehensive exam (for some programs), thesis optional, position paper (MS), portfolio (MS Ed in outdoor teacher education). *Entrance requirements:* For master's, GRE General Test, interview (MS); 9 semester hours of upper division course work in psychology or related field, including 1 course in psychology research or statistics; 9 semester hours of education (MS Ed). Additional exam requirements/recommendations for international students: Required—TOEFL (minimum score 600 paper-based; 250 computer-based; 100 iBT). Electronic applications accepted.

Southern Arkansas University–Magnolia, Graduate Programs, Magnolia, AR 71753. Offers agriculture (MS); business administration (MBA); computer and information sciences (MS); counseling (MS); education (M Ed), including counseling and development, educational administration and supervision, elementary education, secondary education; kinesiology (MS); library media and information specialist (M Ed); public administration (EMPA); school counseling (M Ed); teaching (MAT). *Accreditation:* NCATE. Part-time and evening/weekend programs available. *Faculty:* 35 full-time (19 women), 15 part-time/adjunct (8 women). *Students:* 104 full-time (73 women), 343 part-time (252 women); includes 113 minority (108 African Americans, 3 American Indian/Alaska Native, 2 Asian Americans or Pacific Islanders), 12 international. Average age 34. In 2008, 77 master's awarded. *Degree requirements:* For master's, comprehensive exam, thesis optional. *Entrance requirements:* For master's, GRE, MAT or GMAT, minimum GPA of 2.75. *Application deadline:* For fall admission, 8/15 for domestic students; for winter admission, 1/8 for domestic students; for spring admission, 1/8 for domestic students. Applications are processed on a rolling basis. Application fee: $0. *Expenses:* Tuition, area resident: Full-time $3564; part-time $198 per credit hour. Tuition, state resident: full-time $3564; part-time $198 per credit hour. Tuition, nonresident: full-time $5238; part-time $291 per credit hour. Required fees: $512. *Financial support:* Career-related internships or fieldwork, Federal Work-Study, scholarships/grants, tuition waivers (full), and unspecified assistantships available. Financial award applicants required to submit FAFSA. *Faculty research:* Alternative certification for teachers, supervision of instruction, instructional leadership, counseling. *Unit head:* Dr. Kim Bloss, Dean, Graduate Studies, 870-235-4150, Fax: 870-235-5227, E-mail: kkbloss@saumag.edu. *Application contact:* Dr. Kim Bloss, Dean, Graduate Studies, 870-235-4150, Fax: 870-235-5227, E-mail: kkbloss@saumag.edu.

Southern California Seminary, Graduate and Professional Programs, El Cajon, CA 92019. Offers biblical studies (MA); counseling psychology (MACP); psychology (Psy D); religious studies (MRS); theology (M Div). Part-time and evening/weekend programs available. Post-baccalaureate distance learning degree programs offered (minimal on-campus study). *Degree requirements:* For master's, thesis (for some programs); for doctorate, thesis/dissertation; for M Div, 2 foreign languages. *Entrance requirements:* For doctorate, master's degree in psychology. Additional exam requirements/recommendations for international students: Required—TOEFL (minimum score 550 paper-based). Electronic applications accepted.

Southern Illinois University Carbondale, Graduate School, College of Liberal Arts, Department of Psychology, Carbondale, IL 62901-4701. Offers clinical psychology (MA, MS, PhD); counseling psychology (MA, MS, PhD); experimental psychology (MA, MS, PhD). *Accreditation:* APA (one or more programs are accredited). *Degree requirements:* For master's, thesis; for doctorate, thesis/dissertation. *Entrance requirements:* For master's, GRE General Test, GRE Subject Test, minimum GPA of 2.7; for doctorate, GRE General Test, GRE Subject Test, minimum GPA of 3.25. Additional exam requirements/recommendations for international students: Required—TOEFL. *Faculty research:* Developmental neuropsychology; smoking, affect, and cognition; personality measurement; vocational psychology; program evaluation.

See Close-Up on page 1135.

Southern Nazarene University, Graduate College, School of Psychology, Bethany, OK 73008. Offers counseling psychology (MSCP); marriage and family therapy (MA). *Degree requirements:* For master's, thesis optional. *Entrance requirements:* For master's, English proficiency exam, minimum GPA of 3.0 in last 60 hours/major, 2.7 overall.

South University, Graduate Programs, College of Arts and Sciences, Program in Professional Counseling, Savannah, GA 31406. Offers MA.

See Close-Up on page 1143.

South University, Program in Professional Counseling, Montgomery, AL 36116-1120. Offers MA.

See Close-Up on page 1141.

South University, Program in Professional Counseling, Columbia, SC 29203. Offers MA.

See Close-Up on page 1139.

South University, Program in Professional Counseling, West Palm Beach, FL 33409. Offers MA.

See Close-Up on page 1145.

Southwestern Assemblies of God University, Thomas F. Harrison School of Graduate Studies, Program in Counseling Psychology, Waxahachie, TX 75165-5735. Offers counseling psychology (clinical) (MCP); human services counseling (MS). Part-time programs available. *Degree requirements:* For master's, comprehensive written and oral exams. *Entrance requirements:* For master's, GRE General Test, minimum GPA of 2.5. Electronic applications accepted.

Southwestern College, Program in Art Therapy/Counseling, Santa Fe, NM 87502-4788. Offers MA. Part-time and evening/weekend programs available. *Degree requirements:* For master's, internship. *Entrance requirements:* For master's, resumé, slide portfolio, interview, 3 letters of reference, personal statement of 3 pages.

Southwestern College, Program in Counseling, Santa Fe, NM 87502-4788. Offers MA. Part-time and evening/weekend programs available. *Degree requirements:* For master's, internship. *Entrance requirements:* For master's, resumé, 3 letters of reference, interview, personal statement of 3 pages.

See Close-Up on page 1147.

Southwestern College, Program in Grief, Loss and Trauma Counseling, Santa Fe, NM 87502-4788. Offers MA, Certificate. Part-time and evening/weekend programs available. Post-baccalaureate distance learning degree programs offered (minimal on-campus study). *Entrance requirements:* For master's, personal statement of 3 pages, interview, references, resumé; for Certificate, 3 letters of reference, interview.

Spring Arbor University, School of Graduate and Professional Studies, Spring Arbor, MI 49283-9799. Offers counseling (MAC); family studies (MAFS); nursing (MSN); organizational management (MAOM). Part-time and evening/weekend programs available. Postbaccalaureate distance learning degree programs offered (no on-campus study). *Faculty:* 8 full-time (3 women), 99 part-time/adjunct (45 women). *Students:* 509 full-time (427 women), 306 part-time (245 women); includes 208 minority (179 African Americans, 2 American Indian/Alaska Native, 9 Asian Americans or Pacific Islanders, 18 Hispanic Americans), 3 international. Average age 39. In 2008, 249 master's awarded. *Entrance requirements:* For master's, minimum GPA of 3.0, interview, writing sample, 2 professional references. Additional exam requirements/recommendations for international students: Required—TOEFL (minimum score 550 paper-based; 220 computer-based). *Application deadline:* Applications are processed on a rolling basis. Application fee: $40. Electronic applications accepted. *Expenses:* Tuition: Full-time $5280; part-time $440 per credit hour. Required fees: $240; $150. Tuition and fees vary according to program. *Financial support:* Scholarships/grants available. Support available to part-time students. Financial award applicants required to submit FAFSA. *Unit head:* Dr. Robert Hamill, Dean of Graduate and Professional Studies, 517-750-1200 Ext. 1343, Fax: 517-750-6602, E-mail: rhamill@arbor.edu. *Application contact:* John Ball, Coordinator of Admissions, GPS Undergraduate Programs, 517-750-6459, Fax: 517-750-6602, E-mail: jball@arbor.edu.

Springfield College, Graduate Programs, Program in Human Services, Springfield, MA 01109-3797. Offers human services (MS), including community counseling psychology, mental health counseling, organizational management and leadership. Part-time programs available. *Faculty:* 4 full-time (3 women). *Students:* 2 full-time, 2 part-time. Average age 30. 4 applicants, 75% accepted, 1 enrolled. In 2008, 3 master's awarded. *Degree requirements:* For master's, comprehensive exam, thesis (for some programs), research project. *Entrance requirements:* For master's, GRE. Additional exam requirements/recommendations for international students: Required—TOEFL (minimum score 550 paper-based; 213 computer-based). *Application deadline:* For fall admission, 1/15 for domestic and international students; for winter admission, 11/1 for domestic and international students; for spring admission, 11/1 for domestic and international students. Applications are processed on a rolling basis. Application fee: $50. Electronic applications accepted. *Expenses:* Contact institution. *Financial support:* Fellowships with partial tuition reimbursements, teaching assistantships with partial tuition reimbursements, career-related internships or fieldwork, Federal Work-Study, institutionally sponsored loans, and unspecified assistantships available. Financial award application deadline: 3/1; financial award applicants required to submit FAFSA. *Unit head:* Dr. Stephen Coulon, Director, 413-748-3029, E-mail: scoulon@spfldcol.edu. *Application contact:* Donald James Shaw, Director of Graduate Admissions, 413-748-3479, Fax: 413-748-3694, E-mail: donald_shaw_jr@spfldcol.edu.

Springfield College, Graduate Programs, Programs in Psychology and Counseling, Springfield, MA 01109-3797. Offers athletic counseling (M Ed, MS, CAGS); industrial/organizational psychology (M Ed, MS, CAGS); marriage and family therapy (M Ed, MS, CAGS); mental health counseling (M Ed, MS, CAGS); school guidance and counseling (M Ed, MS, CAGS); student personnel in higher education (M Ed, MS, CAGS). Part-time programs available. *Faculty:* 13 full-time (6 women), 12 part-time/adjunct (3 women). *Students:* 151 full-time, 52 part-time. Average age 30. 198 applicants, 73% accepted, 74 enrolled. In 2008, 84 master's, 4 other advanced degrees awarded. *Degree requirements:* For master's, research project, portfolio. *Entrance requirements:* Additional exam requirements/recommendations for international students: Required—TOEFL (minimum score 550 paper-based; 213 computer-based). *Application deadline:* For fall admission, 1/15 priority date for domestic students, 1/15 for international students; for winter admission, 11/1 for domestic and international students; for spring admission, 11/1 for domestic and international students. Applications are processed on a rolling basis. Application fee: $50. Electronic applications accepted. *Expenses:* Tuition: Full-time $9132; part-time $761 per semester hour. Required fees: $150. Tuition and fees vary according to course load. *Financial support:* Fellowships with partial tuition reimbursements, teaching assistantships with partial tuition reimbursements, career-related internships or fieldwork, Federal Work-Study, institutionally sponsored loans, and unspecified assistantships available. Financial award application deadline: 3/1; financial award applicants required to submit FAFSA. *Unit head:* Dr. Glenn Lowery, Director, 413-748-3301, Fax: 413-748-3854, E-mail: glowery@spfldcol.edu. *Application contact:* Donald James Shaw, Director of Graduate Admissions, 413-748-3479, Fax: 413-748-3694, E-mail: donald_shaw_jr@spfldcol.edu.

Stanford University, School of Education, Program in Psychological Studies in Education, Stanford, CA 94305-9991. Offers child and adolescent development (PhD); counseling psychology (PhD); educational psychology (PhD). *Degree requirements:* For doctorate, thesis/dissertation. *Entrance requirements:* For doctorate, GRE General Test. Electronic applications accepted.

State University of New York at New Paltz, Graduate School, School of Liberal Arts and Sciences, Department of Psychology, New Paltz, NY 12561. Offers mental health counseling (MS); psychology (MA); school counseling (MS). Part-time and evening/weekend programs available. *Faculty:* 13 full-time (8 women), 1 (woman) part-time/adjunct. *Students:* 23 full-time (18 women), 14 part-time (12 women); includes 3 minority (1 Asian American or Pacific Islander, 2 Hispanic Americans). Average age 27. 71 applicants, 54% accepted, 17 enrolled. In 2008, 12 master's awarded. *Degree requirements:* For master's, comprehensive exam, thesis. *Entrance requirements:* For master's, GRE General Test, minimum GPA of 3.0. Additional exam requirements/recommendations for international students: Required—TOEFL (minimum score 550 paper-based; 213 computer-based; 80 iBT). *Application deadline:* For fall admission, 3/15 priority date for domestic students, 3/15 for international students; for spring admission, 11/15 for domestic and international students. Application fee: $50. Electronic applications accepted. *Financial support:* In 2008–09, 5 students received support, including 5 teaching assistantships with partial tuition reimbursements available (averaging $5,000 per year); career-related internships or fieldwork, Federal Work-Study, institutionally sponsored loans, traineeships, and unspecified assistantships also available. Financial award application deadline: 8/1; financial award applicants required to submit FAFSA. *Faculty research:* Disaster mental health, women's objectification, mate selection, cultural psychology, achievement motivation. *Unit head:* Dr. Douglas Maynard, Chair, 845-257-3426, E-mail: maynardd@newpaltz.edu. *Application contact:* Dr. Jonathan Raskin, Coordinator, 845-257-3471, E-mail: raskinj@newpaltz.edu.

State University of New York at Oswego, Graduate Studies, School of Education, Department of Counseling and Psychological Services, Program in Counseling Services, Oswego, NY 13126. Offers MS, CAS, MS/CAS. *Degree requirements:* For master's, comprehensive exam, fieldwork; for CAS, thesis, fieldwork. *Entrance requirements:* For master's, GRE General Test, interview, minimum GPA of 3.0; for CAS, GRE General Test, GRE Subject Test, 18 hours of course work in behavioral science or education, interview, minimum GPA of 3.0. Additional exam requirements/recommendations for international students: Required—TOEFL (minimum score 560 paper-based; 220 computer-based). *Faculty research:* Psychological applications in education and human services, evaluation of standard tests for admissions criteria.

State University of New York at Oswego, Graduate Studies, School of Education, Department of Counseling and Psychological Services, Program in Human Services/Counseling, Oswego, NY 13126. Offers MS. Part-time programs available. *Degree requirements:* For master's, comprehensive exam. *Entrance requirements:* For master's, GRE General Test, interview, minimum GPA of 3.0. Additional exam requirements/recommendations for international students: Required—TOEFL (minimum score 560 paper-based; 220 computer-based).

Stephens College, Division of Graduate and Continuing Studies, Programs in Counseling, Columbia, MO 65215-0002. Offers counseling (M Ed), including marriage and family therapy, professional counseling, school counseling. Part-time and evening/weekend programs available. *Faculty:* 3 full-time (all women), 8 part-time/adjunct (3 women). *Students:* 104 full-time (93 women), 20 part-time (18 women); includes 11 minority (7 African Americans, 1 American Indian/Alaska Native, 1 Asian American or Pacific Islander, 2 Hispanic Americans). Average age 38. 32 applicants, 88% accepted, 28 enrolled. In 2008, 26 master's awarded. *Degree requirements:* For master's, thesis. *Entrance requirements:* For master's, minimum GPA of 3.0 in last 60 hours. Additional exam requirements/recommendations for international students: Required—TOEFL (minimum score 213 computer-based). *Application deadline:* For fall admission, 7/25 priority date for domestic and international students; for winter admission, 12/1 priority date for domestic and international students; for spring admission, 4/25 priority date for domestic and international students. Applications are processed on a rolling basis. Application fee: $40. Electronic applications accepted. *Expenses:* Tuition: Part-time $335 per credit hour. Required fees: $15 per credit hour. *Financial support:* In 2008–09, 12 students received support. Scholarships/grants and unspecified assistantships available. Financial award application deadline: 12/5; financial award applicants required to submit FAFSA. *Unit head:* Dr. Linda Taylor Thompson, Program Chair, 800-388-7579. *Application contact:* Meredith Julian, Assistant Director of Marketing and Recruitment, 800-388-7579, E-mail: online@stephens.edu.

Suffolk University, College of Arts and Sciences, Department of Education and Human Services, Program in Mental Health Counseling, Boston, MA 02108-2770. Offers MS, CAGS, MPA/MSMHC. Part-time programs available. *Entrance requirements:* For master's, GRE General Test or MAT, statement of professional goals, official transcripts, 2 letters of recommendation, resumé. *Expenses:* Tuition: Full-time $31,550; part-time $1052 per credit. Required fees: $10 per year. Tuition and fees vary according to program.

Tarleton State University, College of Graduate Studies, College of Education, Department of Psychology and Counseling, Stephenville, TX 76402. Offers counseling and psychology (M Ed), including counseling, counseling psychology, educational psychology; educational administration (M Ed); secondary education (Certificate); special education (Certificate). Part-time and evening/weekend programs available. Postbaccalaureate distance learning degree programs offered (minimal on-campus study). *Faculty:* 17 full-time (8 women), 11 part-time/adjunct (5 women). *Students:* 70 full-time (59 women), 271 part-time (244 women); includes 100 minority (59 African Americans, 4 American Indian/Alaska Native, 5 Asian Americans or Pacific Islanders, 32 Hispanic Americans). Average age 35. 104 applicants, 76% accepted, 60 enrolled. In 2008, 75 master's awarded. *Degree requirements:* For master's, comprehensive exam, thesis optional. *Entrance requirements:* For master's, GRE General Test, minimum GPA of 3.0. Additional exam requirements/recommendations for international students: Required—TOEFL (minimum score 550 paper-based; 213 computer-based; 80 iBT). *Application deadline:* For fall admission, 8/5 priority date for domestic students; for spring admission, 12/1 for domestic students. Applications are processed on a rolling basis. Application fee: $30 ($130 for international students). Electronic applications accepted. *Expenses:* Tuition, area resident: Full-time $2853; part-time $158.50 per credit hour. Tuition, state resident: full-time $2853; part-time $158.50 per credit hour. Tuition, nonresident: full-time $7551; part-time $419.50 per credit hour. Required fees: $1040; $42 per credit hour. $124 per semester. Tuition and fees vary according to course load and campus/location. *Financial support:* In 2008–09, 3 research assistantships (averaging $13,778 per year) were awarded; teaching assistantships, career-related internships or fieldwork, Federal Work-Study, institutionally sponsored loans, and tuition waivers (partial) also available. Support available to part-time students. Financial award application deadline: 5/1; financial award applicants required to submit FAFSA. *Unit head:* Dr. David Weissenburger, Department Head and Professor, 254-968-9090, Fax: 254-968-1991, E-mail: weissenburge@tarleton.edu. *Application contact:* Information Contact, 254-968-9104, Fax: 254-968-9670, E-mail: gradoffice@tarleton.edu.

Teachers College, Columbia University, Graduate Faculty of Education, Department of Counseling and Clinical Psychology, Program in Counseling Psychology, New York, NY 10027-6696. Offers Ed M, Ed D, PhD. *Accreditation:* APA (one or more programs are accredited). Part-time programs available. *Faculty:* 7 full-time (4 women). *Students:* 177 full-time (156 women), 103 part-time (93 women); includes 95 minority (41 African Americans, 27 Asian Americans or Pacific Islanders, 27 Hispanic Americans), 31 international. Average age 27. 458 applicants, 49% accepted, 107 enrolled. In 2008, 131 master's, 6 doctorates awarded. *Degree requirements:* For doctorate, thesis/dissertation. *Entrance requirements:* For doctorate, GRE General Test. *Application deadline:* For fall admission, 5/15 for domestic students. Application fee: $75. *Expenses:* Tuition: Full-time $26,040; part-time $1085 per credit. Required fees: $720. *Financial support:* Fellowships, research assistantships, teaching assistantships, career-related internships or fieldwork, Federal Work-Study, institutionally sponsored loans, and tuition waivers (full and partial) available. Support available to part-time students. Financial award application deadline: 2/1. *Faculty research:* Career development, mentoring racial identity, adult development, gender issues. *Unit head:* Maria Miville, Head, 212-678-3257. *Application contact:* Melba Remice, Assistant Director of Admission, 212-678-4035, Fax: 212-678-4171, E-mail: ms2545@columbia.edu.

Temple University, Graduate School, College of Education, Department of Psychological Studies in Education, Counseling Psychology Program, Philadelphia, PA 19122-6096. Offers Ed M, PhD. *Accreditation:* APA (one or more programs are accredited). Part-time programs available. Terminal master's awarded for partial completion of doctoral program. *Degree requirements:* For master's, thesis or alternative; for doctorate, thesis/dissertation. *Entrance requirements:* For master's, GRE General Test or MAT, minimum GPA of 2.8; for doctorate, GRE General Test, GRE Subject Test in psychology. *Faculty research:* Multi-cultural and diversity training, health psychology/supervision/addictions.

Tennessee State University, The School of Graduate Studies and Research, College of Education, Department of Psychology, Nashville, TN 37209-1561. Offers counseling and guidance (MS), including counseling, elementary school counseling, organizational counseling, secondary school counseling; counseling psychology (PhD); psychology (MS, PhD); school psychology (MS, PhD). *Accreditation:* APA. *Faculty:* 15 full-time (9 women), 1 (woman) part-time/adjunct. *Students:* 83 full-time (63 women), 94 part-time (79 women); includes 17 African Americans, 1 American Indian/Alaska Native, 1 Asian American or Pacific Islander. Average age 33. 205 applicants, 45% accepted, 44 enrolled. In 2008, 14 master's, 7 doctorates awarded. *Degree requirements:* For doctorate, thesis/dissertation (for some programs). *Entrance requirements:* For master's, GRE General Test or MAT; for doctorate, GRE General Test or MAT, minimum GPA of 3.25, work experience. *Application deadline:* For fall admission, 3/1 priority date for international students. Applications are processed on a rolling basis. Application fee: $25. Electronic applications accepted. *Unit head:* Dr. Linda Guthrie, Head, 615-963-2920, Fax: 615-963-5140, E-mail: lguthrie@tnstate.edu. *Application contact:* Dr. Linda Guthrie, Head, 615-963-2920, Fax: 615-963-5140, E-mail: lguthrie@tnstate.edu.

Texas A&M International University, Office of Graduate Studies and Research, College of Arts and Sciences, Department of Behavioral, Applied Sciences, and Criminal Justice, Laredo, TX 78041-1900. Offers counseling psychology (MACP); criminal justice (MS); psychology (MS); sociology (MA). *Degree requirements:* For master's, thesis (for some programs). *Entrance requirements:* For master's, GRE General Test. Additional exam requirements/recommendations for international students: Required—TOEFL (minimum score 550 paper-based; 213 computer-based).

Texas A&M University, College of Education and Human Development, Department of Educational Psychology, College Station, TX 77843. Offers counseling psychology (PhD); educational psychology (PhD); educational technology (M Ed); gifted and talented education (M Ed, MS); Hispanic bilingual education (M Ed, PhD); human learning and development (MS); intelligence, creativity, and giftedness (PhD); learning, development, and instruction (PhD); research, measurement and statistics (MS); research, measurement, and statistics (PhD); school counseling (M Ed); school psychology (PhD); special education (M Ed, PhD). *Accreditation:* APA (one or more programs are accredited); NCATE. Part-time and evening/weekend programs available. Postbaccalaureate distance learning degree programs offered (no on-campus study). *Faculty:* 46. *Students:* 161 full-time (129 women), 148 part-time (126 women); includes 86 minority (26 African Americans, 1 American Indian/Alaska Native, 11 Asian Americans or Pacific Islanders, 48 Hispanic Americans), 38 international. In 2008, 47 master's, 20 doctorates awarded. *Degree requirements:* For master's, thesis optional; for doctorate, thesis/dissertation. *Entrance requirements:* For master's and doctorate, GRE General Test. Additional exam requirements/recommendations for international students: Required—TOEFL. Application fee: $50 ($75 for international students). Electronic applications accepted. *Expenses:* Tuition, area resident: Full-time $3838.50. Tuition, state resident: full-time $3838.50. Tuition, nonresident: full-time $8897. Required fees: $2359.60. *Financial support:* In 2008–09, fellowships (averaging $12,000 per year), research assistantships (averaging $9,000 per year), teaching assistantships (averaging $9,000 per year) were awarded; career-related internships or fieldwork, institutionally sponsored loans, scholarships/grants, and unspecified assistantships also available. Financial award applicants required to submit FAFSA. *Unit head:* Dr. Victor Willson, Head, 979-845-1800, E-mail: v-willson@tamu.edu. *Application contact:* Carol A. Wagner, Director of Advising, 979-845-1833, Fax: 979-862-1256, E-mail: c-wagner@tamu.edu.

Texas A&M University–Commerce, Graduate School, College of Education and Human Services, Department of Counseling, Commerce, TX 75429-3011. Offers M Ed, MS, PhD. *Accreditation:* ACA (one or more programs are accredited). Part-time programs available. Terminal master's awarded for partial completion of doctoral program. *Degree requirements:* For master's, comprehensive exam, thesis (for some programs); for doctorate, thesis/dissertation, departmental qualifying exam. *Entrance requirements:* For master's and doctorate, GRE General Test. *Faculty research:* Emergency responders, efficacy and effect of web-based instruction, family violence, play therapy.

Texas A&M University–Texarkana, Graduate Studies and Research, College of Health and Behavioral Sciences, Texarkana, TX 75505-5518. Offers counseling psychology (MS). Part-time and evening/weekend programs available. *Degree requirements:* For master's, comprehensive exam (for some programs), thesis or alternative. *Entrance requirements:* For master's, minimum GPA of 3.0 in last 60 hours of bachelor's degree. Additional exam requirements/recommendations for international students: Required—TOEFL. Electronic applications accepted.

Texas Tech University, Graduate School, College of Arts and Sciences, Department of Psychology, Lubbock, TX 79409. Offers clinical psychology (PhD); counseling psychology (MA, PhD); experimental psychology (MA, PhD); psychology (MA, PhD). *Accreditation:* APA (one or more programs are accredited). Part-time programs available. *Faculty:* 25 full-time (11 women). *Students:* 87 full-time (58 women), 20 part-time (13 women); includes 16 minority (5 African Americans, 1 American Indian/Alaska Native, 2 Asian Americans or Pacific Islanders, 8 Hispanic Americans), 6 international. Average age 28. 290 applicants, 13% accepted, 17 enrolled. In 2008, 13 master's, 6 doctorates awarded. *Degree requirements:* For doctorate, thesis/dissertation. *Entrance requirements:* For master's and doctorate, GRE General Test, GRE Subject Test. Additional exam requirements/recommendations for international students: Required—TOEFL (minimum score 550 paper-based; 213 computer-based). *Application deadline:* For fall admission, 3/1 priority date for international students; for spring admission, 11/1 priority date for international students. Applications are processed on a rolling basis. Application fee: $50 ($60 for international students). Electronic applications accepted. *Expenses:* Tuition, area resident: Part-time $194 per credit hour. Tuition, state resident: full-time $4648; part-time $194 per credit hour. Tuition, nonresident: full-time $11,392; part-time $475 per credit hour. Required fees: $2206; $69 per credit hour. $389 per semester. *Financial support:* In 2008–09, 91 students received support, including 4 research assistantships with partial tuition reimbursements available (averaging $12,762 per year), 69 teaching assistantships with partial tuition reimbursements available (averaging $11,835 per year); career-related internships or fieldwork, Federal Work-Study, and institutionally sponsored loans also available. Support available to part-time students. Financial award application deadline: 4/15; financial award applicants required to submit FAFSA. *Faculty research:* Failure/success in relationships, peer rejection in school, stress and coping, group processes, clinical and health psychology. Total annual research expenditures: $564,495. *Unit head:* Dr. Susan S. Hendrick, Chair, 806-742-3711 Ext. 224, Fax: 806-742-0818, E-mail: s.hendrick@ttu.edu. *Application contact:* Dr. Lee M. Cohen, Director of Clinical Program, 806-742-3711 Ext. 254, Fax: 806-742-0818, E-mail: lee.cohen@ttu.edu.

Texas Wesleyan University, Graduate Programs, Programs in Education, Fort Worth, TX 76105-1536. Offers education (M Ed); mental health/school counseling (MSP); professional counseling (MA). Part-time and evening/weekend programs available. Postbaccalaureate distance learning degree programs offered (no on-campus study). *Faculty:* 37 full-time (11 women), 40 part-time/adjunct (13 women). *Students:* 86 full-time (70 women), 164 part-time (143 women); includes 85 minority (44 African Americans, 3 Asian Americans or Pacific Islanders, 38 Hispanic Americans). Average age 35. 309 applicants, 54% accepted, 91 enrolled. In 2008, 90 master's awarded. *Entrance requirements:* For master's, GRE General Test, minimum GPA of 3.0 in final 60 hours of undergraduate course work, interview, essay. *Application deadline:* For fall admission, 6/15 priority date for domestic students; for spring admission, 10/15 priority date for domestic students. Applications are processed on a rolling basis. Application fee: $40 ($50 for international students). Tuition and fees vary according to degree level. *Financial support:* Career-related internships or fieldwork, Federal Work-Study, scholarships/grants, and tuition waivers (full and partial) available. Support available to part-time students. Financial award application deadline: 3/15; financial award applicants required to submit FAFSA. *Faculty research:* Teacher effectiveness, bilingual education, analytic teaching. *Unit head:* Dr. Carlos Martinez, Dean, School of Education, 817-531-4940, Fax: 817-531-4943. *Application contact:* DeTrae Warren, Graduate Admission Recruiter, 817-531-4931, Fax: 817-531-4935, E-mail: dwarren@txwes.edu.

Texas Woman's University, Graduate School, College of Arts and Sciences, Department of Psychology and Philosophy, Denton, TX 76201. Offers counseling psychology (MA, PhD); school psychology (PhD, SSP). *Accreditation:* APA (one or more programs are accredited). *Faculty:* 14 full-time (9 women), 3 part-time/adjunct (1 woman). *Students:* 61 full-time (50 women), 60 part-time (55 women); includes 27 minority (9 African Americans, 8 Asian Americans or Pacific Islanders, 10 Hispanic Americans), 3 international. Average age 29. In 2008, 24 master's, 5 doctorates awarded. Terminal master's awarded for partial completion of doctoral program. *Degree requirements:* For master's, thesis; for doctorate, comprehensive exam, thesis/dissertation, internship, residency. *Entrance requirements:* For master's, BA/BS or 18 hours in psychology, minimum GPA of 3.5 in undergraduate psychology classes, essay, 3 letters of reference; for doctorate, 3 letters of reference; minimum overall and psychology

Counseling Psychology

Texas Woman's University (continued)

undergraduate GPA of 3.5; BS/BA in psychology or 18 hours of required psychology classes. Additional exam requirements/recommendations for international students: Required—TOEFL (minimum score 550 paper-based; 213 computer-based; 79 iBT). *Application deadline:* For fall admission, 12/15 for domestic and international students. Applications are processed on a rolling basis. Application fee: $30 ($50 for international students). Electronic applications accepted. *Expenses:* Tuition, state resident: full-time $3564; part-time $198 per semester hour. Tuition, nonresident: full-time $8622; part-time $479 per semester hour. Required fees: $1158; $64 per semester hour. Tuition and fees vary according to course load. *Financial support:* In 2008–09, 14 research assistantships (averaging $10,746 per year), 8 teaching assistantships (averaging $10,746 per year) were awarded; career-related internships or fieldwork, Federal Work-Study, institutionally sponsored loans, scholarships/grants, traineeships, health care benefits, and unspecified assistantships also available. Support available to part-time students. Financial award application deadline: 3/1; financial award applicants required to submit FAFSA. *Faculty research:* Women's anger, pre-school assessments, body image dysfunction, traumatic stress, classical ethics, mental health and behavioral needs of adolescents in alternative education. *Unit head:* Dr. Dan Miller, Chair, 940-898-2303, Fax: 940-898-2301, E-mail: dmiller@twu.edu. *Application contact:* Samuel Wheeler, Assistant Director of Admissions, 940-898-3188, Fax: 940-898-3081, E-mail: wheelersr@twu.edu.

Towson University, College of Graduate Studies and Research, Program in Counseling Psychology, Towson, MD 21252-0001. Offers CAS. Part-time and evening/weekend programs available.

Trevecca Nazarene University, Graduate Division, Graduate Psychology Programs, Major in Counseling Psychology, Nashville, TN 37210-2877. Offers MA. Part-time and evening/weekend programs available. *Students:* 36 full-time (25 women), 5 part-time (3 women); includes 14 minority (12 African Americans, 1 Asian American or Pacific Islander, 1 Hispanic American). In 2008, 4 master's awarded. *Degree requirements:* For master's, comprehensive exam, thesis, practicum. *Entrance requirements:* For master's, GRE General Test or MAT, minimum GPA of 2.7, 2 reference assessment forms. Additional exam requirements/recommendations for international students: Required—TOEFL (minimum score 500 paper-based; 173 computer-based). *Application deadline:* Applications are processed on a rolling basis. Application fee: $25. *Expenses:* Contact institution. *Financial support:* Applicants required to submit FAFSA. *Unit head:* Dr. Peter Wilson, Director of Graduate Psychology Program, 615-248-1384, Fax: 615-248-1662, E-mail: admissions_psy@trevecca.edu. *Application contact:* Heather Ambrefe, Department Secretary, 615-248-1384, Fax: 615-248-1662, E-mail: admissions_psy@trevecca.edu.

Trinity International University, Trinity Evangelical Divinity School, Deerfield, IL 60015-1284. Offers Biblical and Near Eastern archaeology and languages (MA); Christian studies (MA, Certificate); Christian thought (MA); church history (MA, Th M); congregational ministry: pastor-teacher (M Div); congregational ministry: team ministry (M Div); counseling ministries (MA); counseling psychology (MA); cross-cultural ministry (M Div); educational studies (PhD); evangelism (MA); history of Christianity in America (MA); intercultural studies (MA, PhD); leadership and ministry management (D Min); military chaplaincy -(D Min); ministry (MA); mission and evangelism (Th M); missions and evangelism (D Min); New Testament (MA, Th M); Old Testament (Th M); Old Testament and Semitic languages (MA); pastoral care (M Div); pastoral care and counseling (D Min); pastoral counseling and psychology (Th M); pastoral theology (Th M); philosophy of religion (MA); preaching (D Min); religion (MA); research ministry (M Div); systematic theology (Th M); theological studies (PhD); urban ministry (MA). *Accreditation:* ATS (one or more programs are accredited). Part-time programs available. Postbaccalaureate distance learning degree programs offered (minimal on-campus study). *Degree requirements:* For master's, comprehensive exam, thesis, fieldwork; for doctorate, comprehensive exam (for some programs), thesis/dissertation; for M Div, 2 foreign languages, fieldwork; for Certificate, comprehensive exam, integrative papers. *Entrance requirements:* For M Div, GRE, MAT; for master's, GRE, MAT, minimum cumulative undergraduate GPA of 3.0; for doctorate, GRE, minimum cumulative graduate GPA of 3.2; for Certificate, GRE, MAT, minimum undergraduate GPA of 2.5. Additional exam requirements/recommendations for international students: Required—TOEFL (minimum score 580 paper-based; 237 computer-based), TWE (minimum score 4). Electronic applications accepted.

Trinity International University, Trinity Graduate School, Deerfield, IL 60015-1284. Offers bioethics (MA); communication and culture (MA); counseling psychology (MA); instructional leadership (M Ed); teaching (MA). Part-time and evening/weekend programs available. Postbaccalaureate distance learning degree programs offered (minimal on-campus study). *Degree requirements:* For master's, comprehensive exam. *Entrance requirements:* For master's, GRE General Test or MAT, minimum undergraduate GPA of 3.0. Additional exam requirements/recommendations for international students: Required—TOEFL (minimum score 580 paper-based; 237 computer-based), TWE (minimum score 4). Electronic applications accepted.

Trinity International University, South Florida Campus, Graduate School, Miami, FL 33132-1996. Offers MA.

Trinity Western University, Faculty of Graduate Studies, Program in Counseling Psychology, Langley, BC V2Y 1Y1, Canada. Offers MA. *Accreditation:* ACA. Part-time programs available. *Degree requirements:* For master's, comprehensive exam, thesis. *Entrance requirements:* For master's, GRE if out of school for 5 years prior to applying, BA in honors psychology; 3.0 GPA for 3rd and 4th year of BA. Additional exam requirements/recommendations for international students: Required—TOEFL (minimum score 600 paper-based; 250 computer-based). *Faculty research:* Meaning, group counseling, trauma, counseling supervision.

Union College, Graduate Programs, Department of Psychology, Barbourville, KY 40906-1499. Offers clinical psychology (MA); counseling psychology (MA); school psychology (MA).

Union Institute & University, Program in Psychology and Counseling, Cincinnati, OH 45206-1925. Offers MA.

United States International University, School of Arts and Sciences, Nairobi, Kenya. Offers counseling psychology (MA); international relations (MA). Part-time and evening/weekend programs available. *Degree requirements:* For master's, thesis, practicum. *Entrance requirements:* For master's, GRE General Test, 2 letters of recommendation, resumé. Additional exam requirements/recommendations for international students: Required—TOEFL (minimum score 550 paper-based; 213 computer-based). *Faculty research:* Trauma in children, African intellectualism, psychological assessment tools.

Universidad del Turabo, Graduate Programs, School of Social Sciences and Humanities, Programs in Psychology, Program in Counseling Psychology, Gurabo, PR 00778-3030. Offers MSS.

University at Albany, State University of New York, School of Education, Department of Educational and Counseling Psychology, Albany, NY 12222-0001. Offers counseling psychology (MS, PhD, CAS); educational psychology (Ed D); educational psychology and statistics (MS); measurements and evaluation (Ed D); rehabilitation counseling (MS), including counseling psychology; school counselor (CAS); school psychology (Psy D, CAS); special education (MS); statistics and research design (Ed D). *Accreditation:* APA (one or more programs are accredited). Evening/weekend programs available. *Degree requirements:* For doctorate, thesis/dissertation. *Entrance requirements:* For doctorate, GRE General Test. Additional exam requirements/recommendations for international students: Required—TOEFL (minimum score 550 paper-based; 213 computer-based). Electronic applications accepted.

University at Buffalo, the State University of New York, Graduate School, Graduate School of Education, Department of Counseling, School, and Educational Psychology, Buffalo, NY 14260. Offers counseling/school psychology (PhD); counselor education (PhD); educational psychology (MA, PhD); mental health counseling (MS); rehabilitation counseling (MS); school counseling (Ed M, Certificate); school psychology (MA). *Accreditation:* CORE (one or more programs are accredited). *Degree requirements:* For master's, comprehensive exam (for some programs), thesis (for some programs); for doctorate, comprehensive exam, thesis/dissertation. *Entrance requirements:* For master's and doctorate, GRE General Test, interview, letters of reference. Additional exam requirements/recommendations for international students: Required—TOEFL. Electronic applications accepted. *Faculty research:* Multicultural counseling, class size effects, quality of life, eating disorders, outcome assessment.

The University of Akron, Graduate School, Buchtel College of Arts and Sciences, Department of Psychology, Program in Counseling Psychology, Akron, OH 44325. Offers MA, PhD. *Accreditation:* APA (one or more programs are accredited). *Degree requirements:* For master's, thesis optional, thesis or specialty exam; for doctorate, comprehensive exam, thesis/dissertation. *Entrance requirements:* For master's, GRE General Test, GRE Subject Test, minimum GPA of 2.75, letters of recommendation; for doctorate, GRE General Test, GRE Subject Test, minimum GPA of 3.25, letters of recommendation, personal statement. Additional exam requirements/recommendations for international students: Required—TOEFL (minimum score 550 paper-based; 213 computer-based; 79 iBT). Electronic applications accepted. *Faculty research:* Counseling process and outcome, suicide, diversity issues and counseling psychology (e.g., gender, race, ethnicity, sexual orientation) vocational psychology, assessment.

The University of Akron, Graduate School, College of Education, Department of Counseling, Program in Counseling Psychology, Akron, OH 44325. Offers PhD. *Accreditation:* APA. *Degree requirements:* For doctorate, one foreign language, comprehensive exam, thesis/dissertation, written and oral exams. *Entrance requirements:* For doctorate, GRE, interview, minimum GPA of 3.25, letters of recommendation, supplemental forms, department doctoral application. Additional exam requirements/recommendations for international students: Required—TOEFL (minimum score 550 paper-based; 213 computer-based). Electronic applications accepted.

University of Alberta, Faculty of Graduate Studies and Research, Department of Educational Psychology, Edmonton, AB T6G 2E1, Canada. Offers counseling psychology (M Ed, PhD); educational psychology (M Ed, PhD); instructional technology (M Ed); school counseling (M Ed); school psychology (M Ed, PhD); special education (M Ed, PhD); special education-deafness studies (M Ed); teaching English as a second language (M Ed). Part-time programs available. *Degree requirements:* For master's, thesis optional; for doctorate, comprehensive exam, thesis/dissertation. *Entrance requirements:* For master's and doctorate, minimum GPA of 3.0. Additional exam requirements/recommendations for international students: Required—TOEFL. *Faculty research:* Human learning, development and assessment.

University of Baltimore, Graduate School, The Yale Gordon College of Liberal Arts, Program in Applied Psychology, Baltimore, MD 21201-5779. Offers applied psychology (MS), including counseling, industrial and organizational psychology, psychological applications. Part-time and evening/weekend programs available. *Faculty:* 7 full-time (5 women), 7 part-time/adjunct (2 women). *Students:* 59 full-time (41 women), 40 part-time (31 women); includes 28 minority (21 African Americans, 6 Asian Americans or Pacific Islanders, 1 Hispanic American), 4 international. Average age 27. 163 applicants, 34% accepted, 46 enrolled. In 2008, 31 master's awarded. *Degree requirements:* For master's, thesis optional. *Entrance requirements:* For master's, GRE, minimum GPA of 3.0. Additional exam requirements/recommendations for international students: Required—TOEFL (minimum score 550 paper-based; 213 computer-based). *Application deadline:* For fall admission, 8/1 for domestic students, 6/1 for international students; for spring admission, 12/1 for domestic students, 11/1 for international students. Applications are processed on a rolling basis. Application fee: $30. Electronic applications accepted. *Expenses:* Contact institution. *Financial support:* In 2008–09, 5 research assistantships with full and partial tuition reimbursements were awarded; fellowships, career-related internships or fieldwork and Federal Work-Study also available. Support available to part-time students. Financial award application deadline: 4/1; financial award applicants required to submit FAFSA. *Faculty research:* Participatory decision making, counter productive workplace behavior, organizational consulting, substance abuse treatment, cognitive functioning in head injured. Total annual research expenditures: $93,146. *Unit head:* Dr. Thomas Mitchell, Director, 410-837-5348, Fax: 410-837-4793, E-mail: tmitchell@ubalt.edu. *Application contact:* Kevin Nies, Assistant Director, Office of Graduate Admission, 410-837-6565, E-mail: knies@ubalt.edu.

The University of British Columbia, Faculty of Graduate Studies, Faculty of Education, Department of Educational and Counseling Psychology, and Special Education, Vancouver, BC V6T 1Z1, Canada. Offers counseling psychology (M Ed, MA, PhD); development, learning and culture (PhD); guidance studies (Diploma); human development, learning and culture (M Ed, MA); measurement and evaluation and research methodology (M Ed); measurement, evaluation and research methodology (MA); measurement, evaluation, and research methodology (PhD); school psychology (M Ed, MA, PhD); special education (M Ed, MA, PhD, Diploma). Part-time programs available. *Degree requirements:* For master's, thesis (for some programs); for doctorate, comprehensive exam, thesis/dissertation. *Entrance requirements:* For master's, GRE General Test (counseling psychology MA); for doctorate, GRE General Test. Additional exam requirements/recommendations for international students: Required—TOEFL. Electronic applications accepted. *Faculty research:* Women, family, social problems, career transition, stress and coping problems.

University of Calgary, Faculty of Graduate Studies, Faculty of Education, Division of Applied Psychology, Calgary, AB T2N 1N4, Canada. Offers counseling psychology (M Ed, M Sc, PhD); human development and learning (M Ed, M Sc, PhD); school psychology (M Ed, M Sc, PhD); special education (M Ed, M Sc, PhD). Part-time programs available. *Degree requirements:* For master's, thesis (for some programs), final oral exam; for doctorate, thesis/dissertation, candidacy exam, final oral exam. *Entrance requirements:* For master's, minimum GPA of 3.0, 3 letters of reference; for doctorate, minimum GPA of 3.5, 3 letters of reference. *Faculty research:* Counselor education, family life studies, learning and cognition.

University of California, Santa Barbara, Graduate Division, Gevirtz Graduate School of Education, Santa Barbara, CA 93106-9490. Offers counseling, clinical and school psychology (PhD), including clinical psychology, counseling psychology, school psychology; education (M Ed, MA, PhD), including child and adolescent development (MA, PhD), cultural perspectives and comparative education (MA, PhD), educational leadership and organizations (MA, PhD), research methodology (MA, PhD), special education disabilities and risk studies (MA), special education, disabilities and risk studies (PhD), teaching (M Ed), teaching and learning (MA, PhD); educational leadership (Ed D); school psychology (M Ed); MA/PhD. *Accreditation:* APA (one or more programs are accredited). Postbaccalaureate distance learning degree programs offered (minimal on-campus study). *Faculty:* 42 full-time (20 women), 10 part-time/adjunct (4 women). *Students:* 390 full-time (303 women); includes 149 minority (14 African Americans, 3 American Indian/Alaska Native, 57 Asian Americans or Pacific Islanders, 75 Hispanic Americans), 16 international. Average age 31. 717 applicants, 40% accepted, 170 enrolled. In 2008, 140 master's, 46 doctorates awarded. Terminal master's awarded for partial completion of doctoral program. *Degree requirements:* For master's, comprehensive exam (for some programs), thesis (for some programs); for doctorate, comprehensive exam (for some programs), thesis/dissertation, qualifying exam. *Entrance requirements:* For master's and doctorate, GRE, 3 letters of recommendation, statement of purpose, personal achievements/contributions statement, resumé/curriculum vitae, transcripts for post-secondary institutions attended. Additional exam requirements/recommendations for international students: Required—TOEFL (minimum score 550 paper-based; 213 computer-based; 80 iBT), IELTS (minimum score 7), TOEFL or IELTS. Application fee: $70 ($90 for international students). Electronic applications accepted. *Expenses:* Tuition, nonresident: full-time $25,149. Required fees: $10,143. Full-time tuition and fees vary according to campus/location, reciprocity agreements and student level. *Financial support:* In 2008–09, 253 students received support, including 206 fellowships with full and partial tuition reimbursements available (averaging $5,000 per year), 62 research assistantships with full and partial tuition reimbursements available (averaging $6,200 per year), 87 teaching assistantships with partial tuition reimbursements available (averaging $6,500 per year); career-related internships or fieldwork, Federal Work-Study, institutionally sponsored loans, scholarships/grants, traineeships, health care benefits, and unspecified assistantships also available. Financial award applicants required to submit FAFSA. *Faculty research:* Professional development, early childhood development, school violence, literacy, science/math initiative. Total annual research expenditures: $4.4 million. *Unit head:* Dr. Jane Conoley, Chair, 805-893-2185, E-mail: jane-conoley@education.ucsb.edu. *Application contact:* Kathryn Marie Tucciarone, Student Affairs Officer, 805-893-2137, E-mail: katiet@education.ucsb.edu.

University of Central Arkansas, Graduate School, College of Health and Behavioral Sciences, Department of Counseling and Psychology, Program in Counseling Psychology, Conway, AR 72035-0001. Offers MS. *Degree requirements:* For master's, comprehensive exam, thesis optional. *Entrance requirements:* For master's, GRE General Test, minimum GPA of 2.7. Additional exam requirements/recommendations for international students: Required—TOEFL (minimum score 550 paper-based; 213 computer-based).

University of Central Oklahoma, College of Graduate Studies and Research, College of Education, Department of Psychology, Program in Counseling Psychology, Edmond, OK 73034-5209. Offers MS. *Entrance requirements:* For master's, GRE General Test. Additional exam requirements/recommendations for international students: Required—TOEFL (minimum score 550 paper-based; 213 computer-based). Electronic applications accepted.

University of Colorado Denver, School of Education and Human Development, Program in Counseling Psychology and Counselor Education, Denver, CO 80217-3364. Offers MA. *Accreditation:* ACA; NCATE. Part-time and evening/weekend programs available. *Degree requirements:* For master's, comprehensive exam, thesis optional. *Entrance requirements:* For master's, GRE or MAT, minimum GPA of 2.75, 4 letters of recommendation, interview, resumé. Additional exam requirements/recommendations for international students: Required—TOEFL (minimum score 525 paper-based; 197 computer-based). Electronic applications accepted. *Faculty research:* Spiritual issues in counseling, multicultural and diversity issues in counseling, adolescent suicide, career development.

University of Connecticut, Graduate School, Neag School of Education, Department of Educational Psychology, Storrs, CT 06269. Offers educational psychology (MA, PhD, Post-Master's Certificate), including cognition and instruction, counseling psychology, gifted and talented education, learning technology, measurement, evaluation, and assessment, school psychology, special education. *Degree requirements:* For master's, comprehensive exam; for doctorate, thesis/dissertation. *Entrance requirements:* For doctorate, GRE General Test. Additional exam requirements/recommendations for international students: Required—TOEFL (minimum score 550 paper-based; 213 computer-based). Electronic applications accepted.

University of Connecticut, Graduate School, Neag School of Education, Department of Educational Psychology, Field of Educational Psychology, Program in Counseling Psychology, Storrs, CT 06269. Offers counseling psychology (PhD); school counseling (MA, Post-Master's Certificate). *Accreditation:* ACA. Terminal master's awarded for partial completion of doctoral program. *Degree requirements:* For master's, comprehensive exam, thesis or alternative; for doctorate, thesis/dissertation. *Entrance requirements:* For doctorate, GRE General Test. Additional exam requirements/recommendations for international students: Required—TOEFL (minimum score 550 paper-based; 213 computer-based). Electronic applications accepted.

University of Denver, College of Education, Denver, CO 80208. Offers counseling psychology (MA, PhD); curriculum and instruction (MA, PhD, Certificate), including curriculum leadership (MA, PhD); educational administration and policy studies (Certificate); educational psychology (MA, PhD, Ed S), including child and family studies (MA, PhD), quantitative research methods (MA, PhD), school psychology (PhD, Ed S); higher education and adult studies (MA, PhD); library and information science (MLIS); library and information sciences (Certificate); school administration (PhD). *Accreditation:* ALA; APA (one or more programs are accredited). Part-time and evening/weekend programs available. Postbaccalaureate distance learning degree programs offered (no on-campus study). *Faculty:* 30 full-time (20 women), 58 part-time/adjunct (40 women). *Students:* 334 full-time (259 women), 454 part-time (350 women); includes 136 minority (28 African Americans, 8 American Indian/Alaska Native, 14 Asian Americans or Pacific Islanders, 86 Hispanic Americans), 20 international. Average age 34. 851 applicants, 76% accepted, 356 enrolled. In 2008, 214 master's, 43 doctorates, 85 other advanced degrees awarded. Terminal master's awarded for partial completion of doctoral program. *Degree requirements:* For master's, comprehensive exam; for doctorate, 2 foreign languages, comprehensive exam, thesis/dissertation. *Entrance requirements:* For master's and doctorate, GRE General Test or MAT. *Application deadline:* Applications are processed on a rolling basis. Application fee: $50. Electronic applications accepted. *Financial support:* In 2008–09, 74 teaching assistantships with full and partial tuition reimbursements (averaging $6,000 per year) were awarded; career-related internships or fieldwork, Federal Work-Study, institutionally sponsored loans, and scholarships/grants also available. Support available to part-time students. Financial award application deadline: 3/1; financial award applicants required to submit FAFSA. *Faculty research:* Parkinson's disease, personnel training, development and assessments, gifted education, service learning, transportation, public schools. Total annual research expenditures: $340,000. *Unit head:* Dr. Cheryl Lovell, Associate Dean, 303-871-2479. *Application contact:* Linda McCarthy, Student Services Coordinator, 303-871-2509, E-mail: edinfo@du.edu.

University of Florida, Graduate School, College of Liberal Arts and Sciences, Department of Psychology, Gainesville, FL 32611. Offers behavior analysis (PhD); behavioral neuroscience (MS, PhD); cognitive and sensory processes (PhD); counseling psychology (PhD); developmental psychology (PhD); social psychology (MS, PhD); JD/PhD. *Degree requirements:* For master's, thesis or alternative; for doctorate, thesis/dissertation. *Entrance requirements:* For master's and doctorate, GRE General Test, minimum GPA of 3.0. Additional exam requirements/recommendations for international students: Required—TOEFL (minimum score 550 paper-based; 213 computer-based). Electronic applications accepted. *Faculty research:* Experimental analysis of behavior, psychobiology, cognition and sensory processes, counseling psychology, social psychology, developmental psychology.

University of Great Falls, Graduate Studies, Program in Counseling, Great Falls, MT 59405. Offers counseling psychology (MSC). Part-time and evening/weekend programs available. *Degree requirements:* For master's, thesis optional, internship. *Entrance requirements:* For master's, GRE General Test, 3 letters of recommendation. Additional exam requirements/recommendations for international students: Required—TOEFL (minimum score 500 paper-based; 205 computer-based). Electronic applications accepted. *Faculty research:* Self concept and adolescent offenders, juvenile delinquency, community mental health counseling.

University of Houston, College of Education, Department of Educational Psychology, Houston, TX 77204. Offers counseling psychology (M Ed, PhD); educational psychology (M Ed); educational psychology and individual differences (PhD); special education (M Ed, Ed D). *Accreditation:* NCATE. Part-time and evening/weekend programs available. *Faculty:* 18 full-time (8 women), 13 part-time/adjunct (8 women). *Students:* 96 full-time (79 women), 118 part-time (103 women); includes 73 minority (24 African Americans, 23 Asian Americans or Pacific Islanders, 26 Hispanic Americans), 8 international. Average age 31. 164 applicants, 49% accepted, 40 enrolled. In 2008, 43 master's, 17 doctorates awarded. *Degree requirements:* For master's, comprehensive exam or thesis; for doctorate, comprehensive exam, thesis/dissertation. *Entrance requirements:* For master's, GRE General Test or MAT, interview (counseling psychology); for doctorate, GRE General Test, interview. *Application deadline:* For fall admission, 2/1 for domestic students. Application fee: $35 ($75 for international students). *Expenses:* Tuition, state resident: full-time $5164; part-time $287 per credit. Tuition, nonresident: full-time $10,222; part-time $568 per credit. *Financial support:* In 2008–09, 3 fellowships with full tuition reimbursements (averaging $9,700 per year), 2 research assistantships with full tuition reimbursements (averaging $10,425 per year), 46 teaching assistantships with full tuition reimbursements (averaging $10,425 per year) were awarded; career-related internships or fieldwork, Federal Work-Study, institutionally sponsored loans, scholarships/grants, health care benefits, and unspecified assistantships also available. Support available to part-time students. Financial award application deadline: 2/1. *Faculty research:* Cross-cultural assessment and counseling, cognitive and psychosocial development, learning and emotional disturbances. *Unit head:* Dr. Doris Prater, Interim Chairperson, 713-743-9827, Fax: 713-743-4996, E-mail: dlprater@uh.edu. *Application contact:* Graduate Adviser, 713-743-5019, Fax: 713-743-4996, E-mail: epsy@uh.edu.

University of Houston–Victoria, School of Arts and Sciences, Program in Psychology, Victoria, TX 77901-4450. Offers counseling psychology (MA); school psychology (MA). Part-time and evening/weekend programs available. Postbaccalaureate distance learning degree programs offered. *Degree requirements:* For master's, project or thesis. *Entrance requirements:* For master's, GRE General Test. Additional exam requirements/recommendations for international students: Required—TOEFL (minimum score 550 paper-based; 213 computer-based). Electronic applications accepted.

University of Indianapolis, Graduate Programs, School of Psychological Sciences, Indianapolis, IN 46227-3697. Offers clinical psychology (Psy D); clinical psychology/mental health counseling (MA). *Accreditation:* APA. *Faculty:* 10 full-time (4 women), 4 part-time/adjunct (1 woman). *Students:* 112 full-time (101 women), 55 part-time (43 women); includes 6 minority (5 African Americans, 1 Asian American or Pacific Islander), 8 international. Average age 27. *Degree requirements:* For master's, practicum; for doctorate, comprehensive exam, thesis/dissertation, 1200 hours of clinical practicum, 2000 hour internship. *Entrance requirements:* For master's, GRE, 3 letters of recommendation; for doctorate, GRE, minimum GPA of 3.0, 18 hours of course work in psychology, 3 letters of recommendation. Additional exam requirements/recommendations for international students: Required—TOEFL (minimum score 550 paper-based; 213 computer-based). *Application deadline:* For fall admission, 2/25 for domestic students. Application fee: $50. *Financial support:* Federal Work-Study available. *Unit head:* Dr. E. John McIlvried, Dean, 317-788-3247, Fax: 317-788-3480, E-mail: jmcilvried@uindy.edu. *Application contact:* Dr. E. John McIlvried, Associate Provost for Graduate Programs and International Programs, 317-788-3274, E-mail: jmcilvried@uindy.edu.

The University of Iowa, Graduate College, College of Education, Department of Psychological and Quantitative Foundations, Iowa City, IA 52242-1316. Offers counseling psychology (PhD); educational measurement and statistics (MA, PhD); educational psychology (MA, PhD); school psychology (PhD, Ed S); JD/PhD. *Accreditation:* APA. *Degree requirements:* For master's, thesis optional, exam; for doctorate, comprehensive exam, thesis/dissertation; for Ed S, exam. *Entrance requirements:* For master's, doctorate, and Ed S, GRE General Test, minimum GPA of 3.0. Additional exam requirements/recommendations for international students: Required—TOEFL (minimum score 550 paper-based; 213 computer-based; 81 iBT). Electronic applications accepted.

The University of Kansas, Graduate Studies, School of Education, Department of Psychology and Research in Education, Program in Counseling Psychology, Lawrence, KS 66045. Offers MS, PhD. *Accreditation:* APA (one or more programs are accredited). Part-time programs available. *Faculty:* 6. *Students:* 76 full-time (57 women), 11 part-time (8 women); includes 14 minority (5 African Americans, 2 American Indian/Alaska Native, 2 Asian Americans or Pacific Islanders, 5 Hispanic Americans), 2 international. Average age 29. 120 applicants, 28% accepted, 31 enrolled. In 2008, 28 master's, 8 doctorates awarded. Terminal master's awarded for partial completion of doctoral program. *Degree requirements:* For master's, thesis or alternative; for doctorate, comprehensive exam, thesis/dissertation. *Entrance requirements:* For master's and doctorate, GRE General Test, minimum GPA of 3.0. Additional exam requirements/recommendations for international students: Required—TOEFL. *Application deadline:* For fall admission, 12/15 for domestic and international students. Application fee: $45 ($50 for international students). Electronic applications accepted. *Expenses:* Tuition, area resident: Full-time $6122; part-time $255.10 per credit hour. Tuition, state resident: full-time $6122; part-time $255.10 per credit hour. Tuition, nonresident: full-time $14,629; part-time $609.55 per credit hour. Required fees: $847; $70.56 per credit hour. Tuition and fees vary according to course load and program. *Financial support:* Fellowships, research assistantships with full and partial tuition reimbursements, teaching assistantships with full and partial tuition reimbursements, career-related internships or fieldwork, scholarships/grants, and unspecified assistantships available. Financial award application deadline: 1/15. *Faculty research:* Career development, assessment and intervention, multi-cultural counseling, counselor training, positive psychology. *Unit head:* Tom Krieshok, Professor and Director of Training, 785-864-3931, Fax: 785-864-3820. *Application contact:* Admissions Coordinator, 785-864-3931, Fax: 785-864-3820, E-mail: preadmit@ku.edu.

University of Kentucky, Graduate School, College of Education, Program in Educational and Counseling Psychology, Lexington, KY 40506-0032. Offers counseling psychology (MS Ed, PhD, Ed S); educational and counseling psychology (MS Ed); educational psychology (Ed D, PhD, Ed S); school psychometrist and school psychology (MA Ed). *Accreditation:* APA (one or more programs are accredited); NCATE. *Degree requirements:* For master's, comprehensive exam, thesis optional; for doctorate, comprehensive exam, thesis/dissertation; for Ed S, comprehensive exam. *Entrance requirements:* For master's, GRE General Test, minimum undergraduate GPA of 2.75; for doctorate, GRE General Test, minimum graduate GPA of 3.0; for Ed S, GRE General Test. Additional exam requirements/recommendations for international students: Required—TOEFL (minimum score 550 paper-based; 213 computer-based). Electronic applications accepted.

University of La Verne, College of Arts and Sciences, Department of Psychology, Programs in Counseling, La Verne, CA 91750-4443. Offers general counseling (MS); higher education counseling (MS); marriage and family therapy (MS). Part-time programs available. *Faculty:* 2 full-time (both women), 10 part-time/adjunct (8 women). *Students:* 36 full-time (33 women), 73 part-time (65 women); includes 76 minority (14 African Americans, 6 Asian Americans or Pacific Islanders, 56 Hispanic Americans). Average age 30. In 2008, 24 master's awarded. *Degree requirements:* For master's, thesis, competency exam, personal psychotherapy. *Entrance requirements:* For master's, minimum undergraduate GPA of 3.0, 3 recommendations, interview. Additional exam requirements/recommendations for international students: Required—TOEFL (minimum score 600 paper-based; 250 computer-based). *Application deadline:* Applications are processed on a rolling basis. Application fee: $50. *Expenses:* Contact institution. *Financial support:* Career-related internships or fieldwork, institutionally sponsored loans, and scholarships/grants available. Financial award application deadline: 3/2; financial award applicants required to submit FAFSA. *Application contact:* Connie Hamlow, Admissions Information Specialist, 909-593-3511 Ext. 4244, Fax: 909-392-2761, E-mail: gradadmission@ulv.edu.

University of Lethbridge, School of Graduate Studies, Lethbridge, AB T1K 3M4, Canada. Offers accounting (MScM); addictions counseling (M Sc); agricultural biotechnology (M Sc); agricultural studies (M Sc, MA); anthropology (MA); archaeology (MA); art (MA); biochemistry (M Sc); biological sciences (M Sc); biomolecular science (PhD); biosystems and biodiversity (PhD); Canadian studies (MA); chemistry (M Sc); computer science (M Sc); computer science and geographical information science (M Sc); counseling psychology (M Ed); dramatic arts (MA); earth, space, and physical science (PhD); economics (MA); educational leadership (M Ed); English (MA); environmental science (M Sc); evolution and behavior (PhD); exercise science (M Sc); finance (MScM); French (MA); French/German (MA); French/Spanish (MA); general education (M Ed); general management (MScM); geography (M Sc, MA); German (MA); health sciences (M Sc, MA); history (MA); human resource management and labour relations (MScM); individualized multidisciplinary (M Sc, MA); information systems (MScM); international management (MScM); kinesiology (M Sc, MA); management (M Sc, MA); marketing (MScM); mathematics (M Sc); music (MA); Native American studies (MA); neuroscience (M Sc, PhD); new media (MA); nursing (M Sc); philosophy (MA); physics (M Sc); policy and strategy (MScM); political science (MA); psychology (M Sc, MA); religious studies (MA); sociology (MA); theoretical and computational science (PhD); urban and regional studies (MA). Part-time and evening/weekend programs available. *Degree requirements:* For doctorate, comprehensive

Counseling Psychology

University of Lethbridge (continued)
exam, thesis/dissertation. *Entrance requirements:* For master's, GMAT (M Sc in management), bachelor's degree in related field, minimum GPA of 3.0 during previous 20 graded semester courses, 2 years teaching or related experience (M Ed); for doctorate, master's degree, minimum graduate GPA of 3.5. Additional exam requirements/recommendations for international students: Required—TOEFL. *Faculty research:* Movement and brain plasticity, gibberellin physiology, photosynthesis, carbon cycling, molecular properties of main-group ring components.

University of Mary Hardin-Baylor, College of Sciences and Humanities, Department of Psychology, Belton, TX 76513. Offers community counseling (MA); marriage and family Christian counseling (MA); psychology and counseling (MA); school counseling and psychology (MA). Part-time and evening/weekend programs available. *Degree requirements:* For master's, comprehensive exam. *Entrance requirements:* For master's, GRE General Test, minimum GPA of 3.0 in last 60 hours or 2.75 overall. Electronic applications accepted.

University of Maryland, College Park, Graduate Studies, College of Education, Department of Counseling and Personnel Services, College Park, MD 20742. Offers college student personnel (M Ed, MA); college student personnel administration (PhD); community counseling (CAGS); community/career counseling (M Ed, MA); counseling and personnel services (M Ed, MA, PhD); counseling psychology (PhD); counselor education (PhD); rehabilitation counseling (M Ed, MA, AGSC); school counseling (M Ed, MA); school psychology (M Ed, MA, PhD). *Accreditation:* ACA (one or more programs are accredited); APA (one or more programs are accredited); CORE (one or more programs are accredited); NCATE. Part-time and evening/weekend programs available. Postbaccalaureate distance learning degree programs offered (no on-campus study). *Degree requirements:* For master's, thesis (for some programs); for doctorate, thesis/dissertation. *Entrance requirements:* For master's, GRE General Test or MAT, minimum GPA of 3.0, 3 letters of recommendation; for doctorate, GRE General Test or MAT, minimum GPA of 3.5, 3 letters of recommendation. Additional exam requirements/recommendations for international students: Required—TOEFL. Electronic applications accepted. *Faculty research:* Educational psychology, counseling, health.

University of Massachusetts Boston, Office of Graduate Studies, Graduate College of Education, Counseling and School Psychology Department, Boston, MA 02125-3393. Offers family therapy (M Ed, CAGS); forensic counseling (M Ed, CAGS); mental health counseling (M Ed, CAGS); rehabilitation counseling (M Ed, CAGS); school guidance counseling (M Ed, CAGS); school psychology (M Ed, CAGS). *Degree requirements:* For master's and CAGS, comprehensive exam. *Entrance requirements:* For master's, GRE General Test or MAT; for CAGS, minimum GPA of 2.75.

University of Medicine and Dentistry of New Jersey, School of Health Related Professions, Department of Psychiatric Rehabilitation and Counseling Professions, Scotch Plains, NJ 07076. Offers professional counseling (Certificate); psychiatric rehabilitation (MS, PhD); rehabilitation counseling (MS), including psychiatric rehabilitation, vocational rehabilitation. *Accreditation:* CORE. *Degree requirements:* For master's, internship, practicum. *Entrance requirements:* For master's, minimum 2 years of psychiatric rehabilitation or related professional experience or GRE General Test, interview; for doctorate, GRE General Test. Additional exam requirements/recommendations for international students: Required—TOEFL. Electronic applications accepted.

University of Memphis, Graduate School, College of Education, Department of Counseling, Educational Psychology and Research, Memphis, TN 38152. Offers counseling (MS, Ed D), including community counseling (MS), rehabilitation counseling (MS), school counseling (MS); counseling psychology (PhD); educational psychology and research (MS, PhD), including educational psychology, educational research. *Accreditation:* ACA (one or more programs are accredited); APA (one or more programs are accredited); CORE (one or more programs are accredited); NCATE. *Faculty:* 32 full-time (14 women), 6 part-time/adjunct (4 women). *Students:* 87 full-time (68 women), 114 part-time (93 women); includes 63 minority (58 African Americans, 3 American Indian/Alaska Native, 1 Asian American or Pacific Islander, 1 Hispanic American), 10 international. Average age 32. 114 applicants, 54% accepted, 30 enrolled. In 2008, 50 master's, 22 doctorates awarded. *Degree requirements:* For master's, comprehensive exam, thesis or alternative; for doctorate, comprehensive exam, thesis/dissertation. *Entrance requirements:* For master's, GRE General Test or MAT, minimum GPA of 2.5; for doctorate, GRE General Test. *Application deadline:* For fall admission, 10/1 for domestic students; for spring admission, 4/1 for domestic students. Application fee: $35 ($60 for international students). *Expenses:* Tuition, area resident: Full-time $6242; part-time $330 per credit hour. Tuition, state resident: full-time $6242; part-time $330 per credit hour. Tuition, nonresident: full-time $17,828; part-time $815 per credit hour. Required fees: $1156. *Financial support:* Fellowships with full tuition reimbursements, research assistantships with full tuition reimbursements, teaching assistantships with full tuition reimbursements, career-related internships or fieldwork available. Financial award applicants required to submit FAFSA. *Faculty research:* Anger management, aging and disability, supervision, multicultural counseling. *Unit head:* Dr. Douglas C. Strohmer, Chair, 901-678-2841, Fax: 901-678-5114. *Application contact:* Dr. Ernest A. Rakow, Associate Dean of Administration and Graduate Programs, 901-678-2399, Fax: 901-678-4778.

University of Miami, Graduate School, School of Education, Department of Educational and Psychological Studies, Program in Counseling Psychology, Coral Gables, FL 33124. Offers PhD. *Accreditation:* APA. *Degree requirements:* For doctorate, comprehensive exam, thesis/dissertation. *Entrance requirements:* For doctorate, GRE General Test. Additional exam requirements/recommendations for international students: Required—TOEFL (minimum score 550 paper-based; 212 computer-based). Electronic applications accepted. *Faculty research:* Cocaine recidivism, family systems, behavior and health, nontraditional families, stress and coping.

University of Minnesota, Twin Cities Campus, Graduate School, College of Liberal Arts, Department of Psychology, Program in Counseling Psychology, Minneapolis, MN 55455-0213. Offers PhD. *Accreditation:* APA. *Degree requirements:* For doctorate, comprehensive exam, thesis/dissertation, internship. *Entrance requirements:* For doctorate, GRE General Test, GRE Subject Test (recommended), 12 credits of upper-level psychology courses, including a course in statistics or psychological measurement. Additional exam requirements/recommendations for international students: Required—TOEFL (minimum score 550 paper-based; 213 computer-based; 79 iBT).

University of Missouri–Columbia, Graduate School, College of Education, Department of Educational, School, and Counseling Psychology, Columbia, MO 65211. Offers counseling psychology (M Ed, MA, PhD, Ed S); educational psychology (M Ed, MA, PhD, Ed S); learning and instruction (M Ed); school psychology (M Ed, MA, PhD, Ed S). *Accreditation:* APA (one or more programs are accredited); CORE. Part-time programs available. *Faculty:* 25 full-time (13 women), 4 part-time/adjunct (2 women). *Students:* 121 full-time (89 women), 98 part-time (77 women); includes 33 minority (16 African Americans, 3 American Indian/Alaska Native, 6 Asian Americans or Pacific Islanders, 8 Hispanic Americans), 26 international. Average age 30. 215 applicants, 27% accepted, 53 enrolled. In 2008, 51 master's, 11 doctorates, 5 other advanced degrees awarded. *Degree requirements:* For doctorate, thesis/dissertation. *Entrance requirements:* For master's, doctorate, and Ed S, GRE General Test, minimum GPA of 3.0. Additional exam requirements/recommendations for international students: Required—TOEFL (minimum score 580 paper-based; 237 computer-based; 92 iBT). *Application deadline:* For fall admission, 1/8 priority date for domestic students. Applications are processed on a rolling basis. Application fee: $45 ($60 for international students). *Financial support:* Fellowships, research assistantships, teaching assistantships, institutionally sponsored loans available. *Unit head:* Dr. Deborah Carr, Department Chair, E-mail: carrd@missouri.edu. *Application contact:* Latoya Owens, 573-882-7732, E-mail: owensla@missouri.edu.

University of Missouri–Kansas City, School of Education, Kansas City, MO 64110-2499. Offers administration (Ed D); counseling and guidance (MA, Ed S); counseling psychology (PhD); curriculum and instruction (MA, Ed S); education (PhD); educational administration (Ed S); reading education (MA, Ed S); special education (MA). PhD with concentration in "education" is an interdisciplinary degree offered by the School of Graduate Studies. *Accreditation:* NCATE. Part-time and evening/weekend programs available. *Faculty:* 60 full-time (47 women), 62 part-time/adjunct (48 women). *Students:* 178 full-time (136 women), 428 part-time (302 women); includes 145 minority (110 African Americans, 4 American Indian/Alaska Native, 11 Asian Americans or Pacific Islanders, 20 Hispanic Americans), 16 international. Average age 33. 204 applicants, 76% accepted, 137 enrolled. In 2008, 147 master's, 10 doctorates, 38 other advanced degrees awarded. *Degree requirements:* For doctorate, thesis/dissertation, internship, practicum. *Entrance requirements:* For master's, GRE, minimum GPA of 2.75, 2 letters of reference, written statement of purpose; for doctorate, GRE, minimum GPA of 3.0; for Ed S, minimum GPA of 3.0. Additional exam requirements/recommendations for international students: Required—TOEFL (minimum score 550 paper-based; 213 computer-based; 80 iBT). *Application deadline:* For fall admission, 4/1 priority date for domestic and international students; for spring admission, 11/1 priority date for domestic and international students. Applications are processed on a rolling basis. Application fee: $45 ($50 for international students). *Expenses:* Tuition, state resident: full-time $5376; part-time $298.70 per credit hour. Tuition, nonresident: full-time $13,882; part-time $771.20 per credit hour. Required fees: $640.28; $34.65 per contact hour. $30 per semester. Tuition and fees vary according to course load and program. *Financial support:* In 2008–09, 16 research assistantships with partial tuition reimbursements (averaging $11,325 per year) were awarded; fellowships with full tuition reimbursements, teaching assistantships, career-related internships or fieldwork, Federal Work-Study, institutionally sponsored loans, and tuition waivers (full and partial) also available. Support available to part-time students. Financial award application deadline: 3/1; financial award applicants required to submit FAFSA. *Faculty research:* Urban education, inquiry-based field study, theories of counseling and psychotherapy, school literacy, educational technology. Total annual research expenditures: $3.6 million. *Unit head:* Dr. Linda Edwards, Dean, 816-235-2236, Fax: 816-235-5270, E-mail: education@umkc.edu. *Application contact:* Student Services Office, 816-235-2234, Fax: 816-235-6544, E-mail: education@umkc.edu.

The University of Montana, Graduate School, School of Education, Department of Educational Leadership and Counseling, Program in Counselor Education, Missoula, MT 59812-0002. Offers counselor education (Ed S); counselor education and supervision (Ed D); mental health counseling (MA); school counseling (MA). *Accreditation:* ACA; NCATE. *Degree requirements:* For doctorate, thesis/dissertation. *Entrance requirements:* For master's, doctorate, and Ed S, GRE General Test. Additional exam requirements/recommendations for international students: Required—TOEFL.

University of Nebraska–Lincoln, Graduate College, College of Education and Human Sciences, Department of Educational Psychology, Lincoln, NE 68588. Offers cognition, learning and development (MA); counseling psychology (MA); educational psychology (MA, Ed S); psychological studies in education (PhD), including cognition, learning and development, counseling psychology, quantitative, qualitative, and psychometric methods, school psychology; quantitative, qualitative, and psychometric methods (MA); school psychology (MA, Ed S). *Accreditation:* APA (one or more programs are accredited); NCATE. *Faculty:* 19 full-time (6 women). *Students:* 16 full-time (14 women), 26 part-time (18 women); includes 2 minority (1 African American, 1 Hispanic American), 2 international. Average age 30. In 2008, 22 master's, 3 other advanced degrees awarded. *Degree requirements:* For master's, thesis optional. *Entrance requirements:* For master's, GRE General Test. Additional exam requirements/recommendations for international students: Required—TOEFL (minimum score 500 paper-based; 173 computer-based). *Application deadline:* For fall admission, 12/15 for domestic and international students; for spring admission, 10/1 for domestic students. Application fee: $40. Electronic applications accepted. *Expenses:* Tuition, state resident: full-time $4275; part-time $237.50 per credit hour. Tuition, nonresident: full-time $11,525; part-time $640.25 per credit hour. Required fees: $1068; $10.35 per credit hour. $440.70 per semester. Tuition and fees vary according to course load and program. *Financial support:* Fellowships, research assistantships, teaching assistantships, Federal Work-Study, health care benefits, and unspecified assistantships available. Support available to part-time students. Financial award application deadline: 1/15. *Faculty research:* Measurement and assessment, metacognition, academic skills, child development, multicultural education and counseling. *Unit head:* Dr. Ralph De Ayala, Chair, 402-472-2210, E-mail: tcgrad2@unl.edu. *Application contact:* Dr. Ralph De Ayala, Chair, 402-472-2210, E-mail: tcgrad2@unl.edu.

The University of North Carolina at Greensboro, Graduate School, School of Education, Department of Counseling and Educational Development, Greensboro, NC 27412-5001. Offers advanced school counseling (PMC); counseling and counselor education (PhD); counseling and educational development (MS); couple and family counseling (PMC); school counseling (PMC); MS/Ed S. *Accreditation:* ACA (one or more programs are accredited); NCATE. *Degree requirements:* For master's, comprehensive exam, practicum, internship; for doctorate, comprehensive exam, thesis/dissertation. *Entrance requirements:* For master's, doctorate, and PMC, GRE General Test. Additional exam requirements/recommendations for international students: Required—TOEFL. Electronic applications accepted. *Faculty research:* Gerontology, invitational theory, career development, marriage and family therapy, drug and alcohol abuse prevention.

University of North Dakota, Graduate School, College of Education and Human Development, Department of Counseling, Grand Forks, ND 58202. Offers MA. *Degree requirements:* For master's, comprehensive exam, thesis or alternative. *Entrance requirements:* For master's, GRE General Test or MAT, minimum GPA of 3.0. Additional exam requirements/recommendations for international students: Required—TOEFL (minimum score 550 paper-based; 213 computer-based; 79 iBT), IELTS (minimum score 6.5). Electronic applications accepted. *Faculty research:* Group dynamics, addictive behavior, item response theory, geopsychology, women's health.

University of Northern Colorado, Graduate School, College of Education and Behavioral Sciences, School of Applied Psychology and Counselor Education, Program in Counseling Psychology, Greeley, CO 80639. Offers Psy D. *Accreditation:* ACA; APA; NCATE. Part-time and evening/weekend programs available. *Faculty:* 5 full-time (3 women). *Students:* 19 full-time (15 women), 15 part-time (12 women); includes 2 minority (1 Asian American or Pacific Islander, 1 Hispanic American). Average age 35. 64 applicants, 16% accepted, 8 enrolled. In 2008, 6 doctorates awarded. *Degree requirements:* For doctorate, comprehensive exam, thesis/dissertation. *Entrance requirements:* For doctorate, GRE General Test, 3 letters of reference. *Application deadline:* Applications are processed on a rolling basis. Application fee: $50 ($60 for international students). *Expenses:* Tuition, state resident: full-time $4370; part-time $242.75 per credit hour. Tuition, nonresident: full-time $12,366; part-time $687 per credit hour. Required fees: $664.20; $36.90 per credit hour. *Financial support:* Fellowships, research assistantships, teaching assistantships, unspecified assistantships available. Financial award application deadline: 3/1; financial award applicants required to submit FAFSA. *Unit head:* Dr. Brian Johnson, Program Coordinator, 970-351-2731. *Application contact:* Linda Sisson, Graduate Student Admission Coordinator, 970-351-1807, Fax: 970-351-2371, E-mail: linda.sisson@unco.edu.

University of North Florida, College of Arts and Sciences, Department of Psychology, Jacksonville, FL 32224-2645. Offers counseling psychology (MAC); general psychology (MA). Part-time and evening/weekend programs available. *Faculty:* 18 full-time (7 women). *Students:* 50 full-time (37 women), 8 part-time (7 women); includes 11 minority (6 African Americans, 5 Hispanic Americans). Average age 26. 128 applicants, 41% accepted, 36 enrolled. In 2008, 20 master's awarded. *Degree requirements:* For master's, comprehensive exam, thesis optional, practicum. *Entrance requirements:* For master's, GRE General Test, 2 letters of recommendation, minimum GPA of 3.0 in last 60 hours of course work. Additional exam requirements/recommendations for international students: Required—TOEFL (minimum score 500 paper-based; 173 computer-based). *Application deadline:* For fall admission, 3/1 priority date for domestic students, 3/1 for international students. Applications are processed on a rolling basis. Application fee: $30. Electronic applications accepted. *Expenses:* Tuition, area resident: Full-time $5782.08; part-time $240.92 per credit hour. Tuition, state resident: full-time $5782.08; part-time

$240.92 per credit hour. Tuition, nonresident: full-time $19,974; part-time $832.26 per credit hour. Required fees: $952.80; $39.70 per credit hour. *Financial support:* In 2008–09, 27 students received support, including 4 teaching assistantships (averaging $2,250 per year); Federal Work-Study and tuition waivers (partial) also available. Support available to part-time students. Financial award application deadline: 4/1; financial award applicants required to submit FAFSA. *Faculty research:* Sensory perception, social cognition, sexual behavior, evolutionary psychology, psychology and law. Total annual research expenditures: $80,377. *Unit head:* Dr. Michael Toglia, PhD, Chair, 904-620-1624, E-mail: m.toglia@unf.edu. *Application contact:* Dr. Randy Russac, Graduate Coordinator for General Psychology, 904-620-2807, Fax: 904-620-3814, E-mail: rrussac@unf.edu.

University of North Florida, College of Education and Human Services, Department of Counseling and Educational Leadership, Program in Counselor Education, Jacksonville, FL 32224-2645. Offers mental health counseling (M Ed); school counseling (M Ed). *Accreditation:* ACA; NCATE. Part-time and evening/weekend programs available. *Faculty:* 17 full-time (9 women). *Students:* 42 full-time (36 women), 53 part-time (49 women); includes 20 minority (13 African Americans, 2 Asian Americans or Pacific Islanders, 5 Hispanic Americans). Average age 30. 46 applicants, 33% accepted, 14 enrolled. In 2008, 24 master's awarded. *Entrance requirements:* For master's, GRE General Test, minimum GPA of 3.0 in last 60 hours, 3 letters of recommendation, interview, writing sample. Additional exam requirements/recommendations for international students: Required—TOEFL (minimum score 500 paper-based; 173 computer-based). *Application deadline:* For fall admission, 5/1 for domestic students, 4/23 for international students; for spring admission, 9/26 for domestic students. Application fee: $30. Electronic applications accepted. *Expenses:* Tuition, area resident: Full-time $5782.08; part-time $240.92 per credit hour. Tuition, state resident: full-time $5782.08; part-time $240.92 per credit hour. Tuition, nonresident: full-time $19,974; part-time $832.26 per credit hour. Required fees: $952.80; $39.70 per credit hour. *Financial support:* In 2008–09, 43 students received support; teaching assistantships, career-related internships or fieldwork, Federal Work-Study, and tuition waivers (partial) available. Support available to part-time students. Financial award application deadline: 4/1; financial award applicants required to submit FAFSA. *Faculty research:* Legal and ethical issues in working with minors in schools; gay, lesbian, bisexual, and transgender issues; collaboration between school counselors and classroom teachers; therapist distress and self care; school counselors as advocates for academic achievement. Total annual research expenditures: $242,391. *Unit head:* Dr. John Venn, PhD, Chair, 904-620-2990, Fax: 904-620-2982, E-mail: cstone@unf.edu. *Application contact:* Kiersten Jarvis, Graduate Admissions Coordinator, 904-620-1360, Fax: 904-620-1362, E-mail: kiersten.jarvis@unf.edu.

University of North Texas, Robert B. Toulouse School of Graduate Studies, College of Arts and Sciences, Department of Psychology, Denton, TX 76203. Offers clinical psychology (PhD); counseling psychology (MA, MS, PhD); experimental psychology (MA, MS, PhD); health psychology and behavioral medicine (PhD). *Accreditation:* APA (one or more programs are accredited). Terminal master's awarded for partial completion of doctoral program. *Degree requirements:* For master's, comprehensive exam, thesis or alternative; for doctorate, one foreign language, comprehensive exam, thesis/dissertation. *Entrance requirements:* For master's and doctorate, GRE General Test, interview. Additional exam requirements/recommendations for international students: Required—proof of English language proficiency required for non-native English speakers; Recommended—TOEFL (minimum score 550 paper-based; 213 computer-based). *Faculty research:* Very broad range of topics and approaches.

University of Notre Dame, Graduate School, College of Arts and Letters, Division of Social Science, Department of Psychology, Notre Dame, IN 46556. Offers cognitive psychology (PhD); counseling psychology (PhD); developmental psychology (PhD); quantitative psychology (PhD). *Accreditation:* APA. *Faculty:* 28 full-time (11 women), 5 part-time/adjunct (4 women). *Students:* 70 full-time (49 women); includes 11 minority (3 African Americans, 3 Asian Americans or Pacific Islanders, 5 Hispanic Americans), 13 international. 146 applicants, 18% accepted, 18 enrolled. In 2008, 8 doctorates awarded. *Degree requirements:* For doctorate, comprehensive exam, thesis/dissertation, candidacy exam. *Entrance requirements:* For doctorate, GRE General Test, GRE Subject Test (strongly recommended). Additional exam requirements/recommendations for international students: Required—TOEFL (minimum score 600 paper-based; 250 computer-based; 80 iBT). *Application deadline:* For fall admission, 1/2 for domestic and international students. Application fee: $50. Electronic applications accepted. *Financial support:* Fellowships with full tuition reimbursements, research assistantships with full tuition reimbursements, teaching assistantships with full tuition reimbursements, career-related internships or fieldwork and tuition waivers (full) available. Financial award application deadline: 1/2. *Faculty research:* Cognitive and socio-emotional development, statistical methods and quantitative models applicable to psychology, interpersonal relations, life span development and developmental delay, childhood depression, structural equation and dynamical systems. *Unit head:* Dr. Dan Lapsley, Director of Graduate Studies, 574-631-8789. *Application contact:* Dr. Barbara Turpin, Director of Graduate Admissions, 574-631-7706, Fax: 574-631-4183.

University of Oklahoma, Graduate College, College of Education, Department of Educational Psychology, Program in Counseling Psychology, Norman, OK 73019. Offers PhD. *Accreditation:* APA. *Students:* 26 full-time (17 women), 19 part-time (13 women); includes 12 minority (2 African Americans, 5 American Indian/Alaska Native, 1 Asian American or Pacific Islander, 4 Hispanic Americans), 2 international. 40 applicants, 5% accepted, 2 enrolled. In 2008, 5 doctorates awarded. *Degree requirements:* For doctorate, thesis/dissertation, general exam. *Entrance requirements:* For doctorate, GRE General Test, master's degree, 3 letters of recommendation, interview, curriculum vitae. Additional exam requirements/recommendations for international students: Required—TOEFL (minimum score 550 paper-based; 213 computer-based). *Application deadline:* For fall admission, 1/10 for domestic and international students; for spring admission, 11/1 for domestic students, 9/1 for international students. Applications are processed on a rolling basis. Application fee: $40 ($90 for international students). Electronic applications accepted. *Expenses:* Tuition, state resident: full-time $3744; part-time $156 per credit hour. Tuition, nonresident: full-time $13,577; part-time $565.70 per credit hour. Required fees: $2415.40; $90.10 per credit hour. *Financial support:* In 2008–09, 22 students received support. Career-related internships or fieldwork, institutionally sponsored loans, scholarships/grants, health care benefits, and unspecified assistantships available. Financial award application deadline: 3/1; financial award applicants required to submit FAFSA. *Faculty research:* Counseling assessment; process and outcome; diversity issues; health psychology; marriage and family; education, training and supervision. *Unit head:* Dr. Terri K Debacker, Chair, 405-325-1068, Fax: 405-325-6655, E-mail: debacker@ou.edu. *Application contact:* Rindi Ledo, Graduate Programs Officer, 405-325-4525, Fax: 405-325-6655, E-mail: gpoedpsych@ou.edu.

University of Pennsylvania, Graduate School of Education, Division of Applied Psychology and Human Development, Program in Psychological Services, Philadelphia, PA 19104. Offers counseling psychology (MS Ed). *Degree requirements:* For master's, exam. *Entrance requirements:* For master's, GRE General Test. Electronic applications accepted. *Expenses:* Contact institution. *Faculty research:* Counseling in school, college, or agency.

University of Phoenix–Las Vegas Campus, The Artemis School, College of Health and Human Services, Las Vegas, NV 89128. Offers administration of justice and security (MS); health administration (MHA); health care management (MBA); marriage, family, and child therapy (MSC); mental health counseling (MSC); nursing (MSN); nursing/health care education (MSN); psychology (MS); MSN/MBA; MSN/MHA. Postbaccalaureate distance learning degree programs offered. *Entrance requirements:* For master's, minimum undergraduate GPA of 2.5, 3 years of work experience. Additional exam requirements/recommendations for international students: Required—TOEFL (minimum score 550 paper-based; 213 computer-based; 79 iBT). Electronic applications accepted.

University of Phoenix–Puerto Rico Campus, The Artemis School, College of Health and Human Services, Guaynabo, PR 00968. Offers marriage and family counseling (MSC); mental health counseling (MSC). Evening/weekend programs available. *Degree requirements:* For master's, thesis (for some programs). *Entrance requirements:* For master's, Counselor

Preparation Comprehensive Examination, minimum undergraduate GPA of 2.5, 3 years work experience. Additional exam requirements/recommendations for international students: Required—TOEFL (minimum score 550 paper-based; 213 computer-based; 79 iBT). Electronic applications accepted.

University of Phoenix–Sacramento Valley Campus, The Artemis School, College of Health and Human Services, Sacramento, CA 95833-3632. Offers administration of justice and security (MS); community counseling (MSC); family nurse practitioner (MSN); health administration (MHA); health care education (MSN); health care management (MBA); marriage, family and child counseling (MSC); nursing (MSN); psychology (MS); MSN/MBA. Evening/weekend programs available. *Degree requirements:* For master's, thesis (for some programs). *Entrance requirements:* For master's, RN license, minimum undergraduate GPA of 2.5, 3 years work experience. Additional exam requirements/recommendations for international students: Required—TOEFL (minimum score 550 paper-based; 213 computer-based; 79 iBT). Electronic applications accepted.

University of Phoenix–Utah Campus, The Artemis School, College of Health and Human Services, Salt Lake City, UT 84123-4617. Offers health care management (MBA); healthcare education (MSN); mental health counseling (MSC); nursing (MSN); MSN/MBA. Evening/weekend programs available. *Degree requirements:* For master's, thesis (for some programs). *Entrance requirements:* For master's, minimum undergraduate GPA of 2.5, 3 years work experience, RN license. Additional exam requirements/recommendations for international students: Required—TOEFL (minimum score 550 paper-based; 213 computer-based; 79 iBT). Electronic applications accepted.

University of Puget Sound, Graduate Studies, School of Education, Program in Counseling, Tacoma, WA 98416. Offers mental health counseling (M Ed); pastoral counseling (M Ed); school counseling (M Ed). *Accreditation:* NCATE. Part-time and evening/weekend programs available. *Faculty:* 2 full-time (both women), 1 (woman) part-time/adjunct. *Students:* 1 (woman) full-time, 23 part-time (17 women); includes 1 minority (Hispanic American). Average age 30. 27 applicants, 59% accepted, 11 enrolled. In 2008, 8 master's awarded. *Entrance requirements:* For master's, GRE General Test, minimum GPA of 3.0. Additional exam requirements/recommendations for international students: Required—TOEFL (minimum score 550 paper-based; 213 computer-based; 80 iBT). *Application deadline:* For fall admission, 3/1 priority date for domestic and international students. Applications are processed on a rolling basis. Application fee: $75. Electronic applications accepted. *Expenses:* Contact institution. *Financial support:* In 2008–09, 1 student received support, including 1 teaching assistantship with tuition reimbursement available (averaging $14,204 per year); career-related internships or fieldwork and tuition waivers (full) also available. Financial award application deadline: 3/31; financial award applicants required to submit FAFSA. *Faculty research:* Cross-role professional preparation, suicide prevention. *Unit head:* Dr. John Woodward, Dean, 253-879-3375, E-mail: woodward@pugetsound.edu. *Application contact:* Dr. George H. Mills, Vice President for Enrollment, 253-879-3211, Fax: 253-879-3993, E-mail: admission@pugetsound.edu.

University of Rhode Island, Graduate School, College of Human Science and Services, Department of Human Development and Family Studies, Kingston, RI 02881. Offers college student personnel (MS); human development and family studies (MS); marriage and family therapy (MS). *Accreditation:* AAMFT/COAMFTE. Evening/weekend programs available. *Entrance requirements:* For master's, GRE or MAT. *Expenses:* Tuition, state resident: full-time $8024; part-time $446 per credit. Tuition, nonresident: full-time $21,046; part-time $1169 per credit. Required fees: $1056; $26 per credit. $30 per semester. One-time fee: $95 part-time. *Unit head:* Dr. Jerome Adams, Chair, 401-874-5962, E-mail: jadams@uri.edu. *Application contact:* Harold D. Bibb, Associate Dean of the Graduate School, 401-874-2262, Fax: 401-874-5491.

University of Saint Francis, Graduate School, Department of Psychology and Counseling, Fort Wayne, IN 46808-3994. Offers general psychology (MS); mental health counseling (MS); pastoral counseling (MS); school counseling (MS Ed). Part-time and evening/weekend programs available. *Entrance requirements:* For master's, interview, minimum undergraduate GPA of 3.0.

University of St. Thomas, Graduate Studies, Graduate School of Professional Psychology, St. Paul, MN 55105-1096. Offers counseling psychology (MA, Psy D); family psychology (Certificate). *Accreditation:* APA. Part-time and evening/weekend programs available. *Degree requirements:* For master's, comprehensive exam, practicum; for doctorate, comprehensive exam, thesis/dissertation, qualifying exam, practicum, internship. *Entrance requirements:* For master's, MAT or GRE, minimum GPA of 2.75, letters of recommendation; for doctorate, GRE, minimum GPA of 3.2, letters of recommendation. Additional exam requirements/recommendations for international students: Required—TOEFL. *Expenses:* Contact institution. *Faculty research:* Elderly, eating disorders, anxiety.

University of San Diego, School of Leadership and Education Sciences, Program in Counseling, San Diego, CA 92110-2492. Offers clinical mental health counseling (MA); school counseling (MA). Part-time and evening/weekend programs available. *Faculty:* 5 full-time (3 women), 7 part-time/adjunct (5 women). *Students:* 70 full-time (59 women), 31 part-time (30 women); includes 2 African Americans, 11 Asian Americans or Pacific Islanders, 24 Hispanic Americans, 1 international. Average age 27. 116 applicants, 70% accepted, 51 enrolled. In 2008, 40 master's awarded. *Degree requirements:* For master's, comprehensive exam. *Entrance requirements:* For master's, minimum GPA of 3.0, interview with faculty member. Additional exam requirements/recommendations for international students: Required—TOEFL (minimum score 580 paper-based; 237 computer-based; 83 iBT), TWE. *Application deadline:* For fall admission, 3/1 priority date for domestic students. Application fee: $45. Electronic applications accepted. *Expenses:* Tuition: Full-time $19,710; part-time $1129 per unit. Required fees: $154. Full-time tuition and fees vary according to course load and degree level. *Financial support:* In 2008–09, 82 students received support. Career-related internships or fieldwork, Federal Work-Study, institutionally sponsored loans, unspecified assistantships, and stipends available. Support available to part-time students. Financial award application deadline: 4/1; financial award applicants required to submit FAFSA. *Unit head:* Dr. Lonnie Rowell, Graduate Program Co-Director, 619-260-4212, Fax: 619-260-8095. *Application contact:* Dr. John Mosby, Associate Director of Graduate Admissions, 619-260-4524, Fax: 619-260-4158, E-mail: grads@sandiego.edu.

University of San Francisco, School of Education, Department of Counseling Psychology, San Francisco, CA 94117-1080. Offers counseling (MA), including educational counseling, life transitions counseling, marital and family therapy; counseling psychology (Ed D). *Degree requirements:* For doctorate, thesis/dissertation. *Entrance requirements:* For doctorate, GRE General Test.

The University of Scranton, College of Graduate and Continuing Education, Department of Counseling and Human Services, Scranton, PA 18510. Offers community counseling (MS); professional counseling (CAGS); rehabilitation counseling (MS); school counseling (MS). *Accreditation:* ACA (one or more programs are accredited). Part-time and evening/weekend programs available. *Faculty:* 9 full-time (7 women), 10 part-time/adjunct (5 women). *Students:* 137 full-time (102 women), 19 part-time (14 women); includes 9 minority (5 African Americans, 2 Asian Americans or Pacific Islanders, 2 Hispanic Americans), 2 international. Average age 29. 105 applicants, 70% accepted. In 2008, 84 master's awarded. *Degree requirements:* For master's, comprehensive exam, capstone experience. *Entrance requirements:* For master's, minimum GPA of 2.75. Additional exam requirements/recommendations for international students: Required—TOEFL (minimum score 500 paper-based; 173 computer-based), IELTS (minimum score 5.5). *Application deadline:* For fall admission, 3/1 for domestic students. Application fee: $50. *Financial support:* In 2008–09, 15 students received support, including 15 teaching assistantships with full and partial tuition reimbursements available (averaging $4,400 per year); fellowships, career-related internships or fieldwork, Federal Work-Study, and unspecified assistantships also available. Support available to part-time students. Financial award application deadline: 3/1. *Unit head:* Dr. Oliver J. Morgan, Chair, 570-941-6171, Fax: 570-941-4201,

Counseling Psychology

The University of Scranton (continued)
E-mail: morgan1@scranton.edu. *Application contact:* Joseph M Robach, Director of Admissions, 570-941-4385, Fax: 570-941-5928, E-mail: robachj2@scranton.edu.

University of South Africa, College of Human Sciences, Pretoria, South Africa. Offers adult education (M Ed); African languages (MA, PhD); African politics (MA, PhD); Afrikaans (MA, PhD); ancient history (MA, PhD); ancient Near Eastern studies (MA, PhD); anthropology (MA, PhD); applied linguistics (MA); Arabic (MA, PhD); archaeology (MA); art history (MA); Biblical archaeology (MA); Biblical studies (M Th, D Th, PhD); Christian spirituality (M Th, D Th); church history (M Th, D Th); classical studies (MA, PhD); clinical psychology (MA); communication (MA, PhD); comparative education (M Ed, Ed D); consulting psychology (D Admin, D Com, PhD); curriculum studies (M Ed, Ed D); development studies (M Admin, MA, D Admin, PhD); didactics (M Ed, Ed D); education (M Tech); education management (M Ed, Ed D); educational psychology (M Ed); English (MA); environmental education (M Ed); French (MA, PhD); German (MA, PhD); Greek (MA); guidance and counseling (M Ed); health studies (MA, PhD), including health sciences education (MA), health services management (MA), medical and surgical nursing science (critical care general) (MA), midwifery and neonatal nursing science (MA), trauma and emergency care (MA); history (MA, PhD); history of education (Ed D); inclusive education (M Ed, Ed D); information and communications technology policy and regulation (MA); information science (MA, MIS, PhD); international politics (MA, PhD); Islamic studies (MA, PhD); Italian (MA, PhD); Judaica (MA, PhD); linguistics (MA, PhD); mathematical education (M Ed); mathematics education (MA); missiology (M Th, D Th); modern Hebrew (MA, PhD); musicology (MA, MMus, D Mus, PhD); natural science education (M Ed); New Testament (M Th, D Th); Old Testament (D Th); pastoral therapy (M Th, D Th); philosophy (MA); philosophy of education (M Ed, Ed D); politics (MA, PhD); Portuguese (MA, PhD); practical theology (M Th, D Th); psychology (MA, MS, PhD); psychology of education (M Ed, Ed D); public health (MA); religious studies (MA, D Th, PhD); Romance languages (MA); Russian (MA, PhD); Semitic languages (MA, PhD); social behavior studies in HIV/AIDS (MA); social science (mental health) (MA); social science in development studies (MA); social science in psychology (MA); social science in social work (MA); social science in sociology (MA); social work (MSW, DSW, PhD); socio-education (M Ed, Ed D); sociolinguistics (MA); sociology (MA, PhD); Spanish (MA, PhD); systematic theology (M Th, D Th); TESOL (teaching English to speakers of other languages) (MA); theological ethics (M Th, D Th); theory of literature (MA, PhD); urban ministries (D Th); urban ministry (M Th).

University of Southern California, Graduate School, School of Education, Master's Programs in Education, Los Angeles, CA 90089. Offers counseling psychology (ME); curriculum and teaching (MS); instructional technology (MS); marriage, family and child counseling (MMFT); postsecondary administration and student affairs [PASA] (ME); school counseling (ME); teaching and teaching credential program (MAT); teaching English as a foreign language (ME); teaching English to speakers of other languages (MS). Part-time and evening/weekend programs available. *Entrance requirements:* For master's, GRE.

University of Southern Mississippi, Graduate School, College of Education and Psychology, Department of Psychology, Hattiesburg, MS 39406-0001. Offers clinical psychology (MA, PhD); counseling psychology (PhD); experimental psychology (MA, PhD); psychology (MS); school psychology (MA, PhD). *Accreditation:* ACA; APA (one or more programs are accredited). *Faculty:* 28 full-time (11 women). *Students:* 104 full-time (83 women), 34 part-time (24 women); includes 13 minority (7 African Americans, 2 Asian Americans or Pacific Islanders, 4 Hispanic Americans), 7 international. Average age 28. 189 applicants, 21% accepted, 31 enrolled. In 2008, 24 master's, 13 doctorates awarded. Terminal master's awarded for partial completion of doctoral program. *Degree requirements:* For master's, comprehensive exam, thesis; for doctorate, comprehensive exam, thesis/dissertation. *Entrance requirements:* For master's, GRE General Test, minimum GPA of 3.0; for doctorate, GRE General Test, interview, minimum GPA of 3.0. Additional exam requirements/recommendations for international students: Required—TOEFL. *Application deadline:* For fall admission, 3/1 priority date for domestic students, 3/1 for international students. Applications are processed on a rolling basis. Application fee: $30. *Financial support:* In 2008–09, 48 research assistantships with full tuition reimbursements (averaging $8,802 per year), 48 teaching assistantships with full tuition reimbursements (averaging $6,500 per year) were awarded; career-related internships or fieldwork, Federal Work-Study, and institutionally sponsored loans also available. Financial award application deadline: 3/15; financial award applicants required to submit FAFSA. *Faculty research:* Dolphin cognition, sleep, neuropsychology, health-related behaviors, psychopathology. Total annual research expenditures: $101,200. *Unit head:* Dr. Joesph Olmi, Chair, 601-266-4177, Fax: 601-266-5580. *Application contact:* Dr. Heather Sterling-Turner, Graduate Coordinator, 601-266-4177, Fax: 601-266-5580.

The University of Tennessee, Graduate School, College of Education, Health and Human Sciences, Department of Educational Psychology and Counseling, Knoxville, TN 37996. Offers adult education (MS); applied educational psychology (MS); collaborative learning (Ed D); college student personnel (MS); mental health counseling (MS); rehabilitation counseling (MS); school counseling (MS). *Accreditation:* ACA (one or more programs are accredited); CORE (one or more programs are accredited); NCATE. Part-time and evening/weekend programs available. *Degree requirements:* For master's, thesis optional. *Entrance requirements:* For master's, GRE General Test, minimum GPA of 2.7. Additional exam requirements/recommendations for international students: Required—TOEFL. Electronic applications accepted. *Expenses:* Tuition, area resident: Part-time $348 per credit hour. Tuition, state resident: full-time $6262. Tuition, nonresident: full-time $18,920; part-time $1052 per credit hour. Required fees: $812; $36 per credit hour. Tuition and fees vary according to program.

The University of Texas at Austin, Graduate School, College of Education, Department of Educational Psychology, Austin, TX 78712-1111. Offers academic educational psychology (M Ed, MA); counseling psychology (PhD); counselor education (M Ed); human development and culture (PhD); learning, cognition and instruction (PhD); quantitative methods (PhD); school psychology (PhD). *Accreditation:* APA (one or more programs are accredited). *Degree requirements:* For master's, thesis optional; for doctorate, thesis/dissertation. *Entrance requirements:* For master's and doctorate, GRE General Test, 3 letters of recommendation. Additional exam requirements/recommendations for international students: Required—TOEFL.

The University of Texas at Tyler, College of Education and Psychology, Department of Psychology, Tyler, TX 75799-0001. Offers clinical psychology (MS), including neuropsychology, school psychology; counseling psychology (MA), including general, marriage and family; interdisciplinary studies (MSIS); school counseling (MA). Part-time and evening/weekend programs available. *Degree requirements:* For master's, comprehensive exam, thesis optional. *Entrance requirements:* For master's, GRE General Test, minimum GPA of 3.0. Additional exam requirements/recommendations for international students: Required—TOEFL (minimum score 79 computer-based). Electronic applications accepted. *Faculty research:* Neuropsychology, child abuse, psychometric properties of psychological instruments, maternal behavior, clinical practice issues, victimization of women, post-traumatic stress disorder.

University of the District of Columbia, College of Arts and Sciences, Department of Psychology and Counseling, Program in Counseling, Washington, DC 20008-1175. Offers MS.

University of Utah, The Graduate School, College of Education, Department of Educational Psychology, Salt Lake City, UT 84112-1107. Offers counseling psychology (PhD); educational psychology (MA); professional counseling (MS); professional psychology (M Ed); school counseling (M Ed, MS); school psychology (MS, PhD); statistics (M Stat). *Accreditation:* APA (one or more programs are accredited). Evening/weekend programs available. *Degree requirements:* For master's, variable foreign language requirement, comprehensive exam, thesis (for some programs); for doctorate, variable foreign language requirement, thesis/dissertation, oral exam. *Entrance requirements:* For master's and doctorate, GRE General Test, minimum GPA of 3.0. Additional exam requirements/recommendations for international students: Required—TOEFL (minimum score 500 paper-based; 173 computer-based). *Faculty research:* Autism, computer technology and instruction, cognitive behavior, aging, group counseling.

University of Vermont, Graduate College, College of Education and Social Services, Department of Integrated Professional Studies, Counseling Program, Burlington, VT 05405. Offers MS. *Accreditation:* ACA; NCATE. *Faculty:* 3 full-time (2 women), 6 part-time/adjunct (2 women). *Students:* 39 (32 women); includes 4 minority (2 American Indian/Alaska Native, 2 Hispanic Americans). 58 applicants, 53% accepted, 14 enrolled. In 2008, 21 master's awarded. *Entrance requirements:* For master's, GRE General Test, resumé. Additional exam requirements/recommendations for international students: Required—TOEFL (minimum score 550 paper-based; 213 computer-based; 80 iBT). *Application deadline:* For fall admission, 2/1 priority date for domestic students. Applications are processed on a rolling basis. Application fee: $40. Electronic applications accepted. *Expenses:* Tuition, state resident: part-time $488 per credit. Tuition, nonresident: part-time $1232 per credit. *Financial support:* Fellowships, research assistantships, teaching assistantships available. Financial award application deadline: 2/1. *Faculty research:* Women and tenure, counseling children and adolescents. *Unit head:* Anne Geroski, Coordinator, 802-656-3888, Fax: 802-656-3173. *Application contact:* Anne Geroski, Coordinator, 802-656-3888, Fax: 802-656-3173.

University of Victoria, Faculty of Graduate Studies, Faculty of Education, Department of Educational Psychology and Leadership Studies, Victoria, BC V8W 2Y2, Canada. Offers aboriginal communities counseling (M Ed); counseling (M Ed, MA); educational psychology (M Ed, MA, PhD), including counseling psychology (M Ed, MA), leadership studies (PhD), learning and development (MA, PhD), measurement and evaluation, special education (M Ed, MA); leadership studies (M Ed, MA). Part-time programs available. *Degree requirements:* For master's, thesis (for some programs), comprehensive exam (M Ed); for doctorate, comprehensive exam, thesis/dissertation, candidacy exam. *Entrance requirements:* For master's, 2 years of work experience in a relevant field, minimum B average; for doctorate, GRE, 2 years of work experience in a relevant field, minimum B average. Additional exam requirements/recommendations for international students: Required—TOEFL (minimum score 575 paper-based; 233 computer-based), IELTS (minimum score 7). *Faculty research:* Learning and development (child, adolescent and adult), special education and exceptional children.

The University of Western Ontario, Faculty of Graduate Studies, Social Sciences Division, Faculty of Education, Program in Counseling Psychology, London, ON N6A 5B8, Canada. Offers M Ed. Part-time programs available. *Entrance requirements:* For master's, minimum B average, 3 yr experience in helping profession. *Faculty research:* Women's issues in counseling, causes for sexual harassment in the workplace, counselor memory and confidence in clinical judgements.

University of West Florida, College of Arts and Sciences: Arts, Department of Psychology, Pensacola, FL 32514-5750. Offers counseling (MA); counseling-licensed mental health counselor (MA); general (MA); industrial-organizational (MA). Part-time programs available. *Faculty:* 11 full-time (3 women). *Students:* 61 full-time (46 women), 42 part-time (34 women); includes 22 minority (13 African Americans, 2 Asian Americans or Pacific Islanders, 7 Hispanic Americans), 2 international. Average age 26. 119 applicants, 65% accepted, 38 enrolled. In 2008, 16 master's awarded. *Degree requirements:* For master's, thesis (for some programs). *Entrance requirements:* For master's, GRE General Test, GRE Subject Test, minimum GPA of 3.0. Additional exam requirements/recommendations for international students: Required—TOEFL (minimum score 550 paper-based; 213 computer-based). *Application deadline:* For fall admission, 6/1 for domestic students, 5/15 for international students; for spring admission, 11/1 for domestic students, 10/1 for international students. Applications are processed on a rolling basis. Application fee: $30. *Expenses:* Tuition, state resident: full-time $6095; part-time $253.97 per credit hour. Tuition, nonresident: full-time $21,919; part-time $913.31 per credit hour. *Financial support:* In 2008–09, 3 research assistantships with partial tuition reimbursements (averaging $3,760 per year), 2 teaching assistantships with partial tuition reimbursements (averaging $3,760 per year) were awarded; career-related internships or fieldwork and Federal Work-Study also available. Financial award application deadline: 4/15; financial award applicants required to submit FAFSA. *Faculty research:* Prose recall, brain imaging, peak performance, biofeedback and pain control, comparable worth. Total annual research expenditures: $15,000. *Unit head:* Dr. Laura Koppes, Chairperson, 850-474-3493. *Application contact:* Terry McCray, Assistant Director of Graduate Admissions, 850-473-7718, Fax: 850-473-7714, E-mail: gradadmissions@uwf.edu.

University of Wisconsin–Madison, Graduate School, School of Education, Department of Counseling Psychology, Program in Counseling Psychology, Madison, WI 53706-1380. Offers PhD. *Accreditation:* APA. *Degree requirements:* For doctorate, thesis/dissertation.

University of Wisconsin–Milwaukee, Graduate School, School of Education, Department of Educational Psychology, Milwaukee, WI 53201-0413. Offers counseling (school, community) (MS); counseling psychology (PhD); learning and development (MS); research methodology (MS, PhD); school psychology (PhD). *Accreditation:* APA. Part-time programs available. *Faculty:* 21 full-time (13 women). *Students:* 146 full-time (116 women), 60 part-time (49 women); includes 40 minority (15 African Americans, 1 American Indian/Alaska Native, 12 Asian Americans or Pacific Islanders, 12 Hispanic Americans), 6 international. Average age 30. 252 applicants, 46% accepted, 54 enrolled. In 2008, 84 master's, 1 doctorate awarded. *Degree requirements:* For master's, comprehensive exam, thesis; for doctorate, thesis/dissertation. *Entrance requirements:* For master's, minimum GPA of 3.0; for doctorate, GRE General Test, minimum GPA of 3.0. Additional exam requirements/recommendations for international students: Required—TOEFL (minimum score 550 paper-based; 79 iBT), IELTS (minimum score 6.5). *Application deadline:* For fall admission, 1/1 priority date for domestic students; for spring admission, 9/1 for domestic students. Applications are processed on a rolling basis. Application fee: $45 ($75 for international students). *Expenses:* Tuition, area resident: Full-time $7320; part-time $165 per credit. Tuition, state resident: full-time $7320; part-time $165 per credit. Tuition, nonresident: full-time $17,840; part-time $714 per credit. Tuition and fees vary according to campus/location, program and reciprocity agreements. *Financial support:* In 2008–09, 11 teaching assistantships were awarded; career-related internships or fieldwork and unspecified assistantships also available. Support available to part-time students. Financial award application deadline: 4/15. Total annual research expenditures: $673,016. *Unit head:* Anthony Hains, Chair, 414-229-5715, Fax: 414-229-4939, E-mail: aahains@uwm.edu. *Application contact:* General Information Contact, 414-229-4982, Fax: 414-229-6967, E-mail: gradschool@uwm.edu.

University of Wisconsin–Stout, Graduate School, College of Human Development, Program in Mental Health Counseling, Menomonie, WI 54751. Offers MS. Part-time programs available. *Students:* 35 full-time (33 women), 13 part-time (12 women), 1 international. Average age 30. 48 applicants, 27% accepted, 10 enrolled. In 2008, 20 master's awarded. *Degree requirements:* For master's, thesis optional, comprehensive exam or thesis. *Entrance requirements:* For master's, minimum GPA of 2.75. Additional exam requirements/recommendations for international students: Required—TOEFL (minimum score 500 paper-based; 173 computer-based; 61 iBT). *Application deadline:* For fall admission, 2/1 priority date for domestic and international students; for spring admission, 10/1 priority date for domestic and international students. Application fee: $45. Electronic applications accepted. *Expenses:* Tuition, state resident: full-time $6227; part-time $345.93 per credit. Tuition, nonresident: full-time $9998; part-time $555.42 per credit. International tuition: $10,512 full-time. Tuition and fees vary according to course load, program and reciprocity agreements. *Financial support:* In 2008–09, 5 research assistantships with partial tuition reimbursements (averaging $6,631 per year), 2 teaching assistantships with partial tuition reimbursements (averaging $4,429 per year) were awarded; Federal Work-Study, scholarships/grants, tuition waivers (partial), and unspecified assistantships also available. Support available to part-time students. Financial award application deadline: 5/1; financial award applicants required to submit FAFSA. *Faculty research:* Body image, gender issues, eating disorders, cognitive behavioral therapy. *Unit head:* Dr. John Klem, Director, 715-232-3094, Fax: 715-232-2356, E-mail: klemj@uwstout.edu. *Application* *contact:* Anne E. Johnson, Graduate Student Evaluator (Admissions and Assistantship Coordinator), 715-232-1322, Fax: 715-232-2413, E-mail: johnsona@uwstout.edu.

University of Wisconsin–Stout, Graduate School, School of Education, Program in School Counseling, Menomonie, WI 54751. Offers MS. Part-time programs available. *Students:* 48 full-time (42 women), 16 part-time (13 women); includes 7 minority (3 Asian Americans or Pacific Islanders, 4 Hispanic Americans). Average age 24. 27 applicants, 81% accepted, 19 enrolled. In 2008, 35 master's awarded. *Degree requirements:* For master's, thesis. *Entrance requirements:* For master's, minimum GPA of 2.75. Additional exam requirements/ recommendations for international students: Required—TOEFL (minimum score 500 paper-based; 173 computer-based; 61 iBT). *Application deadline:* For fall admission, 2/1 priority date for domestic and international students; for spring admission, 10/1 priority date for domestic and international students. Application fee: $45. Electronic applications accepted. *Expenses:* Tuition, state resident: full-time $6227; part-time $345.93 per credit. Tuition, nonresident: full-time $9998; part-time $555.42 per credit. International tuition: $10,512 full-time. Tuition and fees vary according to course load, program and reciprocity agreements. *Financial support:* In 2008–09, 3 research assistantships with partial tuition reimbursements (averaging $6,833 per year), 2 teaching assistantships with partial tuition reimbursements (averaging $4,839 per year) were awarded; Federal Work-Study, scholarships/grants, tuition waivers (partial), and unspecified assistantships also available. Support available to part-time students. Financial award application deadline: 5/1; financial award applicants required to submit FAFSA. *Faculty research:* Adventure-based learning, body image, domestic violence, resilience, school climate. *Unit head:* Dr. Denise Brouillard, Director, 715-232-2599, Fax: 715-232-1244, E-mail: brouillardd@uwstout.edu. *Application contact:* Anne E. Johnson, Graduate Student Evaluator (Admissions and Assistantship Coordinator), 715-232-1322, Fax: 715-232-2413, E-mail: johnsona@uwstout.edu.

Utah State University, School of Graduate Studies, College of Education and Human Services, Department of Psychology, Logan, UT 84322. Offers clinical/counseling/school psychology (PhD); research and evaluation methodology (PhD); school counseling (MS); school psychology (MS). *Accreditation:* APA (one or more programs are accredited). Part-time and evening/ weekend programs available. Postbaccalaureate distance learning degree programs offered (no on-campus study). Terminal master's awarded for partial completion of doctoral program. *Degree requirements:* For master's, thesis (for some programs); for doctorate, thesis/ dissertation. *Entrance requirements:* For master's, GRE General Test (school psychology), MAT (school counseling), minimum GPA of 3.5; for doctorate, GRE General Test, minimum GPA of 3.5. Additional exam requirements/recommendations for international students: Required—TOEFL. *Faculty research:* Hearing loss detection in infancy, ADHD, eating disorders, domestic violence, neuropsychology, bilingual/Spanish speaking students/parents.

Valdosta State University, Graduate School, College of Education, Department of Psychology and Counseling, Valdosta, GA 31698. Offers clinical/counseling psychology (MS); industrial/ organizational psychology (MS); school counseling (M Ed, Ed S); school psychology (Ed S). Part-time and evening/weekend programs available. *Faculty:* 16 full-time (2 women). *Students:* 65 full-time (54 women), 40 part-time (36 women); includes 32 minority (27 African Americans, 5 Hispanic Americans). Average age 27. 105 applicants, 60% accepted, 29 enrolled. In 2008, 25 master's awarded. *Degree requirements:* For master's, thesis or alternative, comprehensive written and/or oral exams; for Ed S, thesis. *Entrance requirements:* For master's and Ed S, GRE General Test or MAT. Additional exam requirements/recommendations for international students: Required—TOEFL (minimum score 523 paper-based; 193 computer-based). *Application deadline:* For fall admission, 7/1 for domestic and international students; for spring admission, 11/15 for domestic and international students. Applications are processed on a rolling basis. Application fee: $40. Electronic applications accepted. *Financial support:* In 2008–09, 2 students received support, including 2 research assistantships with full tuition reimbursements available (averaging $2,452 per year); institutionally sponsored loans and unspecified assistantships also available. Support available to part-time students. Financial award application deadline: 7/1; financial award applicants required to submit FAFSA. *Faculty research:* Using Bender-Gestalt to predict graphomotor dimensions of the draw-a-person test, neurobehavioral hemispheric dominance. *Unit head:* Dr. Robert Bauer, Chair, 229-333-5930, Fax: 229-259-5576, E-mail: bbauer@valdosta.edu. *Application contact:* Rebecca Waters, Coordinator of Graduate Admissions, 229-333-5694, Fax: 229-245-3853, E-mail: rlwaters@valdosta.edu.

Valparaiso University, Graduate Division, Department of Psychology, Valparaiso, IN 46383. Offers business management (for counseling students) (Certificate); clinical mental health counseling (MA); community counseling (MA); JD/MA. Part-time and evening/weekend programs available. *Faculty:* 7 part-time/adjunct (3 women). *Students:* 33 full-time (24 women), 16 part-time (9 women); includes 6 minority (2 African Americans, 1 Asian American or Pacific Islander, 3 Hispanic Americans), 2 international. Average age 28. In 2008, 16 master's awarded. *Degree requirements:* For master's, thesis or alternative, internship. *Entrance requirements:* For master's, minimum GPA of 3.0; 15 credits in the social/behavioral sciences (psychology, sociology, human development, etc.) with a minimum GPA of 3.0 or better; a course in introductory psychology; a recent statistics course with a B or better . Additional exam requirements/recommendations for international students: Required—TOEFL (minimum score 550 paper-based; 213 computer-based). *Application deadline:* For fall admission, 3/1 priority date for domestic students. Applications are processed on a rolling basis. Application fee: $30 ($50 for international students). Electronic applications accepted. *Financial support:* Career-related internships or fieldwork, traineeships, and unspecified assistantships available. Support available to part-time students. Financial award applicants required to submit FAFSA. *Faculty research:* Environmental psychology, human sexuality, racial identity development models, social psychology. *Unit head:* Dr. James Nelson, Director of Graduate Porgrams, 219-464-5443, Fax: 219-464-6878, E-mail: Jim.Nelson@valpo.edu. *Application contact:* Jamie Haney, Coordinator of Recruitment Activities, 219-464-5313, Fax: 219-464-5381, E-mail: Jamie.Haney@valpo.edu.

Virginia Commonwealth University, Graduate School, College of Humanities and Sciences, Department of Psychology, Program in Counseling Psychology, Richmond, VA 23284-9005. Offers PhD. *Accreditation:* APA. *Degree requirements:* For doctorate, thesis/dissertation. *Entrance requirements:* For doctorate, GRE General Test, GRE Subject Test. *Faculty research:* Life span development counseling, couple/family therapy, health psychology, psychotherapy.

Virginia Commonwealth University, Graduate School, School of Allied Health Professions, Program in Patient Counseling, Richmond, VA 23284-9005. Offers MS, CPC. *Entrance requirements:* For master's, GRE General Test.

Walden University, Graduate Programs, School of Counseling and Social Service, Minneapolis, MN 55401. Offers human services (PhD), including clinical social work, counseling, criminal justice, family studies and intervention strategies, general program in human services, human services administration, self-designed program in human services, social policy analysis and planning; mental health counseling (MS). Part-time and evening/weekend programs available. Postbaccalaureate distance learning degree programs offered (minimal on-campus study). *Faculty:* 6 full-time, 76 part-time/adjunct. *Students:* 1,235 full-time (1,026 women), 129 part-time (111 women); includes 595 minority (505 African Americans, 21 American Indian/ Alaska Native, 16 Asian Americans or Pacific Islanders, 53 Hispanic Americans), 18 international. Average age 39. 724 applicants, 50% accepted, 250 enrolled. In 2008, 12 master's, 5 doctorates awarded. *Degree requirements:* For master's, thesis optional, residency; for doctorate, thesis/ dissertation, residency. *Entrance requirements:* For master's, bachelor's degree or equivalent in related field, minimum GPA of 2.5, two references, goal statement, official transcripts, computer and Internet access; for doctorate, master's degree or equivalent in related field, minimum GPA of 3.0, three years related professional/academic experience, two references, goal statement, official transcripts, computer and Internet access. Additional exam requirements/ recommendations for international students: Required—TOEFL (minimum score 550 paper-based; 213 computer-based), IELTS (minimum score 6.5), TOEFL, IELTS, or Michigan English Language Assessment Battery (minimum score 82). *Application deadline:* Applications are processed on a rolling basis. Application fee: $50. Electronic applications accepted. *Expenses:* Tuition: Full-time $12,877; part-time $520 per credit. Required fees: $1230. Tuition and fees vary according to course load, degree level and program. *Financial support:* Fellowships, Federal Work-Study, scholarships/grants, unspecified assistantships, and family tuition reduction; active duty/veteran tuition reduction; group tuition reduction; interest-free payment plans available. Support available to part-time students. Financial award applicants required to submit FAFSA. *Unit head:* Dr. Savitri Dixon-Saxon, Associate Dean, 800-925-3368. *Application contact:* Jennifer Hall, Director of Enrollment, 866-4-WALDEN, E-mail: info@waldenu.edu.

Walden University, Graduate Programs, School of Psychology, Minneapolis, MN 55401. Offers clinical assessment (Post-Doctoral Certificate); clinical child psychology (Post-Doctoral Certificate); clinical psychology (Post-Doctoral Certificate); counseling psychology (Post-Doctoral Certificate); forensic psychology (MS), including forensic psychology in the community, general forensic psychology, mental health applications, program planning and evaluation in forensic settings, psychology and legal systems; general psychology (Post-Doctoral Certificate); health psychology (Post-Doctoral Certificate); organizational psychology (Post-Doctoral Certificate); organizational psychology and development (Certificate); psychology (MS, PhD), including clinical psychology, counseling psychology, crisis management and response (MS), general psychology, health psychology, leadership development and coaching (MS), media psychology (MS), organizational psychology, organizational psychology and development (MS), organizational psychology and nonprofit management (MS), program evaluation and research (MS), psychology of culture (MS), psychology, public administration, and social change (MS), school psychology, social psychology (MS), terrorism and security (MS); school psychology (Post-Doctoral Certificate); teaching online (Post-Master's Certificate). Part-time and evening/weekend programs available. Postbaccalaureate distance learning degree programs offered (minimal on-campus study). *Faculty:* 16 full-time, 190 part-time/adjunct. *Students:* 3,198 full-time (2,489 women), 810 part-time (664 women); includes 1,319 minority (1,013 African Americans, 51 American Indian/Alaska Native, 68 Asian Americans or Pacific Islanders, 187 Hispanic Americans), 72 international. Average age 40. 1,468 applicants, 60% accepted, 612 enrolled. In 2008, 203 master's, 37 doctorates awarded. Terminal master's awarded for partial completion of doctoral program. *Degree requirements:* For master's, thesis optional; for doctorate, thesis/dissertation, residency. *Entrance requirements:* For master's, bachelor's degree or equivalent in related field, minimum GPA of 2.5, two references, goal statement, official transcripts, access to computer and Internet; for doctorate, master's degree or equivalent in related field, minimum GPA of 3.0, three years related professional/academic experience, two references, goal statement, official transcripts, access to computer and Internet. Additional exam requirements/recommendations for international students: Required—TOEFL (minimum score 550 paper-based; 213 computer-based), IELTS (minimum score 6.5), TOEFL, IELTS, or Michigan English Language Assessment Battery (minimum score 82). *Application deadline:* Applications are processed on a rolling basis. Application fee: $50. Electronic applications accepted. *Expenses:* Tuition: Full-time $12,877; part-time $520 per credit. Required fees: $1230. Tuition and fees vary according to course load, degree level and program. *Financial support:* In 2008–09, 1 fellowship was awarded; Federal Work-Study, scholarships/ grants, unspecified assistantships, and family tuition reduction; active duty/veteran tuition reduction; group tuition reduction; interest-free payment plans also available. Support available to part-time students. Financial award applicants required to submit FAFSA. *Unit head:* Dr. Nina Nabors, Associate Dean, 800-925-3368. *Application contact:* Jennifer Hall, 866-4-WALDEN, E-mail: info@waldenu.edu.

Walla Walla University, Graduate School, School of Education and Psychology, Specialization in Counseling Psychology, College Place, WA 99324-1198. Offers MA. Part-time programs available. *Faculty:* 4 full-time (1 woman). *Students:* 15 full-time (8 women), 2 part-time (both women). Average age 29. *Degree requirements:* For master's, thesis (for some programs). *Entrance requirements:* For master's, GRE General Test, minimum GPA of 2.75, course work in education and psychology. Additional exam requirements/recommendations for international students: Required—TOEFL (minimum score 550 paper-based; 213 computer-based; 79 iBT). *Application deadline:* For fall admission, 4/1 priority date for domestic students. Applications are processed on a rolling basis. Application fee: $50. Electronic applications accepted. *Expenses:* Tuition: Full-time $25,584; part-time $492 per credit. Tuition and fees vary according to course load. *Financial support:* Teaching assistantships with partial tuition reimbursements available. Financial award application deadline: 4/1; financial award applicants required to submit FAFSA. *Faculty research:* Instructional psychology, moral development. *Unit head:* Dr. Lee Stough, Program Director, 509-527-2943, Fax: 509-527-2248, E-mail: lee.stough@wallawalla.edu. *Application contact:* Dr. Joe G. Galusha, Dean of Graduate Studies, 509-527-2421, Fax: 509-527-2237, E-mail: joe.galusha@wallawalla.edu.

Walsh University, Graduate Studies, Program in Counseling and Human Development, North Canton, OH 44720-3396. Offers mental health counseling (MA); school counseling (MA). *Accreditation:* ACA. Part-time and evening/weekend programs available. *Faculty:* 5 full-time (all women), 6 part-time/adjunct (4 women). *Students:* 30 full-time (26 women), 58 part-time (49 women); includes 3 minority (1 African American, 1 American Indian/Alaska Native, 1 Hispanic American), 2 international. Average age 30. 41 applicants, 56% accepted, 20 enrolled. In 2008, 26 master's awarded. *Degree requirements:* For master's, comprehensive exam, internship, practicum. *Entrance requirements:* For master's, GRE General Test, MAT, interview, minimum GPA of 3.0, writing sample. Additional exam requirements/recommendations for international students: Required—TOEFL (minimum score 500 paper-based; 173 computer-based). *Application deadline:* For fall admission, 7/15 priority date for domestic students. Applications are processed on a rolling basis. Application fee: $25. Electronic applications accepted. *Expenses:* Tuition: Full-time $9450; part-time $525 per credit. Part-time tuition and fees vary according to course load and program. *Financial support:* In 2008–09, 47 students received support, including 8 research assistantships with tuition reimbursements available (averaging $8,325 per year); tuition waivers (partial) and tuition discounts also available. Financial award application deadline: 12/31. *Faculty research:* Mind-body connections in trauma and trauma counseling, grief/loss issues regarding counselor training, supervision, family counseling and counselor education, refugee mental health, grief counseling and grief counseling training. *Unit head:* Dr. Linda Barclay, Program Director, 330-490-7264, Fax: 330-490-7165, E-mail: lbarclay@walsh.edu. *Application contact:* Angela Piverotto, Director of Graduate and Transfer Admissions, 330-490-7174, Fax: 330-490-7165, E-mail: apiverotto@walsh.edu.

Washington State University, Graduate School, College of Education, Department of Educational Leadership and Counseling Psychology, Program in Counseling Psychology, Pullman, WA 99164. Offers counseling psychology (Ed M, MA, PhD); school psychologist (Certificate). *Accreditation:* APA (one or more programs are accredited). Terminal master's awarded for partial completion of doctoral program. *Degree requirements:* For master's, comprehensive exam (for some programs), thesis (for some programs), oral or written exam; for doctorate, comprehensive exam, thesis/dissertation, oral and written exam. *Entrance requirements:* For master's and doctorate, GRE General Test, minimum GPA of 3.0, 3 letters of recommendation. Additional exam requirements/recommendations for international students: Required—TOEFL (minimum score 550 paper-based; 213 computer-based). Electronic applications accepted. *Faculty research:* Hypnosis supervision, multicultural counseling, American Indian mental health, eating disorders.

Wayland Baptist University, Graduate Programs, Program in Counseling, Plainview, TX 79072-6998. Offers counseling (MA); government administration (MPA); homeland security (MPA); justice administration (MPA). Part-time and evening/weekend programs available. Postbaccalaureate distance learning degree programs offered. *Faculty:* 8 full-time (2 women). *Students:* 2 full-time (both women), 105 part-time (81 women); includes 27 minority (3 African Americans, 2 American Indian/Alaska Native, 2 Asian Americans or Pacific Islanders, 20 Hispanic Americans). Average age 34. 39 applicants, 95% accepted, 19 enrolled. In 2008, 34 master's awarded. *Degree requirements:* For master's, comprehensive exam. *Entrance requirements:* For master's, GRE, MAT. Application fee: $50. *Expenses:* Tuition: Full-time

Counseling Psychology

Wayland Baptist University (continued)
$310; part-time $310 per credit hour. Required fees: $782; $9 per credit hour. $60 per semester. *Financial support:* Federal Work-Study, institutionally sponsored loans, and scholarships/grants available. Support available to part-time students. Financial award application deadline: 5/1; financial award applicants required to submit FAFSA. *Unit head:* Dr. Estelle Owens, Chairman, 806-291-1171, Fax: 806-291-1972, E-mail: owensest@wbu.edu. *Application contact:* Amanda Stanton, Graduate Studies, 806-291-3414, Fax: 806-291-1950, E-mail: stanton@wbu.edu.

Waynesburg University, Graduate and Professional Studies, Waynesburg, PA 15370-1222. Offers business (MBA); counseling psychology (MA); education (MAT); nursing (MSN); nursing practice (DNP); special education (M Ed); technology (M Ed); MSN/MBA. *Accreditation:* AACN. Part-time and evening/weekend programs available. Electronic applications accepted.

Webster University, College of Arts and Sciences, Department of Behavioral and Social Sciences, Program in Counseling, St. Louis, MO 63119-3194. Offers MA.

Western Michigan University, Graduate College, College of Education, Department of Counselor Education and Counseling Psychology, Kalamazoo, MI 49008-5202. Offers counselin psychology (MA); counseling psychology (PhD); counselor education (MA, PhD); human resources development (MA); marriage and family therapy (MA). *Accreditation:* ACA (one or more programs are accredited); APA (one or more programs are accredited); CORE; NCATE. *Degree requirements:* For doctorate, thesis/dissertation, oral exams. *Entrance requirements:* For doctorate, GRE General Test.

Western Washington University, Graduate School, College of Humanities and Social Sciences, Department of Psychology, Program in Mental Health Counseling, Bellingham, WA 98225-5996. Offers MS. *Accreditation:* ACA. *Degree requirements:* For master's, thesis optional. *Entrance requirements:* For master's, GRE General Test, minimum GPA of 3.0 in last 60 semester hours or last 90 quarter hours. Additional exam requirements/recommendations for international students: Required—TOEFL (minimum score 567 paper-based; 227 computer-based). Electronic applications accepted.

Westfield State College, Division of Graduate and Continuing Education, Department of Psychology, Westfield, MA 01086. Offers applied behavior analysis (MA); mental health counseling (MA); school guidance (MA). Part-time and evening/weekend programs available. *Faculty:* 9 part-time/adjunct (6 women). *Students:* 13 full-time (12 women), 17 part-time (13 women). Average age 37. In 2008, 13 master's awarded. *Degree requirements:* For master's, comprehensive exam. *Entrance requirements:* For master's, GRE General Test, MAT, minimum undergraduate GPA of 2.7. *Application deadline:* Applications are processed on a rolling basis. Application fee: $30. *Financial support:* In 2008–09, 5 research assistantships (averaging $1,600 per year) were awarded; teaching assistantships, career-related internships or fieldwork, Federal Work-Study, and tuition waivers (full and partial) also available. Support available to part-time students. Financial award application deadline: 4/1; financial award applicants required to submit CSS PROFILE. *Unit head:* Dr. Ricki Kantrowitz, Director, 413-572-5378. *Application contact:* Michelle Janke, Admissions Coordinator, 413-572-8022, Fax: 413-572-5227, E-mail: mjanke@wsc.ma.edu.

Westminster College, Program in Counseling Psychology, Salt Lake City, UT 84105-3697. Offers MSPC. Part-time and evening/weekend programs available. *Faculty:* 5 full-time (all women), 4 part-time/adjunct (3 women). *Students:* 23 full-time (18 women); includes 4 minority (1 American Indian/Alaska Native, 1 Asian American or Pacific Islander, 2 Hispanic Americans). Average age 30. 35 applicants, 66% accepted, 11 enrolled. *Degree requirements:* For master's, comprehensive exam, thesis, internship. *Entrance requirements:* For master's, GRE, 3 professional recommendations, personal statement, official transcripts, background check, baccalaureate information. Additional exam requirements/recommendations for international students: Required—TOEFL (minimum score 600 paper-based). *Application deadline:* For fall admission, 2/6 priority date for domestic and international students. Applications are processed on a rolling basis. Application fee: $40. Electronic applications accepted. *Expenses:* Contact institution. *Financial support:* In 2008–09, 18 students received support. Career-related internships or fieldwork available. Support available to part-time students. Financial award applicants required to submit FAFSA. *Faculty research:* Trauma, substance abuse treatment, object relations, refugee populations, attachment theory. *Unit head:* Janine Wanlass, Director, 801-832-2428, E-mail: jwanlass@westminstercollege.edu. *Application contact:* Joel Bauman, Vice President of Enrollment Services, 801-832-2200, Fax: 801-832-3101, E-mail: admission@westminstercollege.edu.

West Virginia University, College of Human Resources and Education, Department of Counseling, Rehabilitation Counseling, and Counseling Psychology, Program in Counseling Psychology, Morgantown, WV 26506. Offers PhD. *Accreditation:* ACA; APA. *Degree requirements:* For doctorate, comprehensive exam, thesis/dissertation, APA-approved 1 year internship. *Entrance requirements:* For doctorate, GRE General Test, interview. Additional exam requirements/recommendations for international students: Required—TOEFL (minimum score 550 paper-based; 213 computer-based; 65 iBT). Electronic applications accepted.

William Carey University, School of Psychology and Counseling, Hattiesburg, MS 39401-5499. Offers counseling psychology (MS). Part-time programs available. *Entrance requirements:* For master's, GRE, PRAXIS, MAT, minimum GPA of 2.5. Additional exam requirements/recommendations for international students: Required—TOEFL (minimum score 550 paper-based; 213 computer-based). *Expenses:* Contact institution. *Faculty research:* Addiction prevention, psychometric measurement, crisis counseling, gerontology.

William Paterson University of New Jersey, College of the Humanities and Social Sciences, Program in Clinical and Counseling Psychology, Wayne, NJ 07470-8420. Offers MA. *Entrance requirements:* For master's, GRE General Test. Electronic applications accepted.

Wright Institute, Program in Counseling Psychology, Berkeley, CA 94704-1796. Offers MA.

Yeshiva University, Ferkauf Graduate School of Psychology, Program in Mental Health Counseling Psychology, New York, NY 10033-3201. Offers MA. Part-time programs available. *Entrance requirements:* For master's, GRE General Test. *Faculty research:* Substance abuse treatment, group therapy.

Youngstown State University, Graduate School, Beeghly College of Education, Department of Counseling, Youngstown, OH 44555-0001. Offers community counseling (MS Ed); school counseling (MS Ed). *Accreditation:* ACA; NCATE. Part-time and evening/weekend programs available. *Degree requirements:* For master's, comprehensive exam. *Entrance requirements:* For master's, MAT, interview, minimum GPA of 2.7. Additional exam requirements/recommendations for international students: Required—TOEFL. *Faculty research:* Suicide, euthanasia, ethical issues, marriage and family.

Developmental Psychology

Andrews University, School of Graduate Studies, School of Education, Department of Educational and Counseling Psychology, Program in Educational and Developmental Psychology, Berrien Springs, MI 49104. Offers educational and developmental psychology (MA); educational psychology (Ed D, PhD). *Students:* 5 full-time (1 woman), 17 part-time (16 women); includes 9 minority (6 African Americans, 1 Asian American or Pacific Islander, 2 Hispanic Americans), 4 international. Average age 35. In 2008, 6 master's awarded. *Degree requirements:* For master's, thesis optional. *Entrance requirements:* For master's, GRE. Additional exam requirements/recommendations for international students: Required—TOEFL (minimum score 550 paper-based). *Application deadline:* Applications are processed on a rolling basis. Application fee: $40. *Expenses:* Tuition: Full-time $18,360; part-time $765 per credit hour. Required fees: $476; $765 per credit hour. $238 per semester. Tuition and fees vary according to degree level. *Unit head:* Dr. Jimmy Kijai, Coordinator, 269-471-6240. *Application contact:* Carolyn Hurst, Supervisor of Graduate Admission, 800-253-2874, Fax: 269-471-6321, E-mail: graduate@andrews.edu.

Arizona State University, Graduate College, College of Liberal Arts and Sciences, Division of Natural Sciences, Department of Psychology, Tempe, AZ 85287. Offers behavioral neuroscience (PhD); clinical psychology (PhD); cognition, action and perception (PhD); developmental psychology (PhD); quantitative psychology (PhD); social psychology (PhD). *Accreditation:* APA. *Degree requirements:* For doctorate, thesis/dissertation. *Entrance requirements:* For doctorate, GRE General Test, GRE Subject Test.

Boston College, Lynch Graduate School of Education, Department of Counseling Psychology, Developmental, and Educational Psychology, Program in Developmental and Educational Psychology, Chestnut Hill, MA 02467-3800. Offers MA, PhD. Part-time and evening/weekend programs available. Terminal master's awarded for partial completion of doctoral program. *Degree requirements:* For master's, comprehensive exam; for doctorate, comprehensive exam, thesis/dissertation. *Entrance requirements:* For master's and doctorate, GRE General Test. Additional exam requirements/recommendations for international students: Required—TOEFL (minimum score 550 paper-based; 213 computer-based; 81 iBT). Electronic applications accepted. *Expenses:* Tuition: Part-time $1148 per credit. Required fees: $60. *Faculty research:* Cognitive learning and culture, effects of social policy reform on children and families, psychosocial trauma, human rights and international justice; positive youth development; children and adolescents living in poverty.

Bowling Green State University, Graduate College, College of Arts and Sciences, Department of Psychology, Bowling Green, OH 43403. Offers clinical psychology (MA, PhD); developmental psychology (MA, PhD); experimental psychology (MA, PhD); industrial/organizational psychology (MA, PhD); quantitative psychology (MA, PhD). *Accreditation:* APA (one or more programs are accredited). *Degree requirements:* For doctorate, thesis/dissertation. *Entrance requirements:* For doctorate, GRE General Test, GRE Subject Test. Additional exam requirements/recommendations for international students: Required—TOEFL. Electronic applications accepted. *Faculty research:* Personnel psychology, developmental-mathematical models, behavioral medication, brain process, child/adolescent social cognition.

Brandeis University, Graduate School of Arts and Sciences, Department of Psychology, Waltham, MA 02454-9110. Offers cognitive neuroscience (PhD); general psychology (MA); social/developmental psychology (PhD). MA program offered to students enrolled in PhD program only. *Degree requirements:* For doctorate, comprehensive exam, thesis/dissertation. *Entrance requirements:* For doctorate, GRE General Test, GRE Subject Test (recommended), 3 letters of recommendation. Additional exam requirements/recommendations for international students: Required—TOEFL (minimum score 600 paper-based; 250 computer-based). Electronic applications accepted. *Faculty research:* Development, cognition, social aging, perception.

Brown University, Graduate School, Department of Psychology, Providence, RI 02912. Offers behavioral neuroscience (PhD); cognitive processes (PhD); sensation and perception (PhD); social/developmental (PhD); MS/PhD. *Degree requirements:* For doctorate, thesis/dissertation. *Entrance requirements:* For doctorate, GRE General Test, GRE Subject Test.

Bryn Mawr College, Graduate School of Arts and Sciences, Department of Psychology, Bryn Mawr, PA 19010-2899. Offers clinical developmental psychology (PhD). Part-time programs available. *Degree requirements:* For doctorate, one foreign language, comprehensive exam, thesis/dissertation. *Entrance requirements:* For doctorate, GRE General Test. Additional exam requirements/recommendations for international students: Required—TOEFL (minimum score 600 paper-based; 250 computer-based).

Carnegie Mellon University, College of Humanities and Social Sciences, Department of Psychology, Area of Developmental Psychology, Pittsburgh, PA 15213-3891. Offers PhD. *Degree requirements:* For doctorate, comprehensive exam, thesis/dissertation. *Entrance requirements:* For doctorate, GRE General Test. Additional exam requirements/recommendations for international students: Required—TOEFL. *Faculty research:* Cognitive development, language acquisition.

Chatham University, Program in Counseling Psychology, Pittsburgh, PA 15232-2826. Offers child, adolescent and family (MSCP); counseling psychology (Psy D); health and holistic (MSCP); infant mental health (MSCP); organization and supervision (MSCP); sport and exercise (MSCP). Part-time and evening/weekend programs available. *Students:* 121 full-time (104 women), 72 part-time (63 women). Average age 30. 117 applicants, 79% accepted, 60 enrolled. In 2008, 63 master's awarded. *Degree requirements:* For master's, thesis optional, supervised internship, advanced research project (optional); for doctorate, thesis/dissertation, internship. *Entrance requirements:* For master's, minimum GPA of 3.0; 2 letters of recommendation; resumé; prerequisite coursework in statistics, biology, and psychology; for doctorate, GRE. Additional exam requirements/recommendations for international students: Required—TOEFL (minimum score 600 paper-based; 250 computer-based; 100 iBT), IELTS (minimum score 6.5), TWE. *Application deadline:* For fall admission, 5/1 priority date for domestic and international students; for spring admission, 10/15 for domestic students, 10/15 priority date for international students. Applications are processed on a rolling basis. Application fee: $45. Electronic applications accepted. *Expenses:* Tuition: Part-time $686 per credit. Tuition and fees vary according to program. *Financial support:* Career-related internships or fieldwork available. Financial award applicants required to submit FAFSA. *Faculty research:* Trauma and recovery, hypnosis, psychospiritual dimensions of healing, psychotherapy of schizophrenia. *Unit head:* Dr. Mary Beth Mannarino, Director, 412-365-1196, Fax: 412-365-1505, E-mail: mmannarino@chatham.edu. *Application contact:* Dory Perry, Associate Director of Graduate Admissions, 412-365-2758, Fax: 412-365-1609, E-mail: gradadmissions@chatham.edu.

Claremont Graduate University, Graduate Programs, School of Behavioral and Organizational Sciences, Department of Psychology, Claremont, CA 91711-6160. Offers advanced study in evaluation (Certificate); cognitive psychology (MA, PhD); developmental psychology (MA, PhD); evaluation and applied research methods (MA, PhD); health behavior research and evaluation (MA, PhD); human resource development and evaluation (MA); industrial/organizational psychology (MA, PhD); organizational behavior (MA, PhD); organizational psychology (MA, PhD); social psychology (MA, PhD); MBA/PhD. Part-time programs available. *Faculty:* 17 full-time (7 women), 1 part-time/adjunct (0 women). *Students:* 218 full-time (158 women), 24 part-time (18 women); includes 51 minority (15 African Americans, 1 American Indian/Alaska Native, 22 Asian Americans or Pacific Islanders, 13 Hispanic Americans), 11 international. Average age 30. In 2008, 38 master's, 12 doctorates, 2 other advanced degrees awarded. Terminal master's awarded for partial completion of doctoral program. *Entrance* *requirements:* For master's and doctorate, GRE General Test. Additional exam requirements/recommendations for international students: Required—TOEFL (minimum score 550 paper-based; 213 computer-based; 80 iBT). *Application deadline:* For fall admission, 1/15 priority date for domestic students. Applications are processed on a rolling basis. Application fee: $60. Electronic applications accepted. *Expenses:* Tuition: Full-time $33,698; part-time $1465 per unit. Required fees: $310; $155 per semester. Tuition and fees vary according to program. *Financial support:* Fellowships, research assistantships, teaching assistantships, Federal Work-Study, institutionally sponsored loans, scholarships/grants, and tuition waivers (full and partial) available. Support available to part-time students. Financial award application deadline: 2/15; financial award applicants required to submit FAFSA. *Faculty research:* Social intervention, diversity in organizations, eyewitness memory, aging and cognition, drug policy. *Unit head:* Stewart Donaldson, Dean, 909-607-9001, Fax: 909-621-8905, E-mail: stewart.donaldson@cgu.edu. *Application contact:* Paul Thomas, Director, External Affairs, 909-607-9016, Fax: 909-621-8905, E-mail: paul.thomas@cgu.edu.

Clark University, Graduate School, Department of Psychology, Program in Developmental Psychology, Worcester, MA 01610-1477. Offers PhD. *Degree requirements:* For doctorate, thesis/dissertation. *Entrance requirements:* For doctorate, GRE General Test. Additional exam requirements/recommendations for international students: Required—TOEFL. *Application deadline:* For fall admission, 12/28 priority date for domestic students. Applications are processed on a rolling basis. Application fee: $50. *Expenses:* Tuition: Full-time $34,900; part-time $1091 per credit hour. Required fees: $30. *Financial support:* In 2008–09, fellowships with full tuition reimbursements (averaging $15,700 per year), research assistantships with full tuition reimbursements (averaging $15,700 per year), teaching assistantships with full tuition reimbursements (averaging $15,700 per year) were awarded; tuition waivers (full) also available. *Unit head:* Dr. Michael Bambert, Chair, 508-793-7274. *Application contact:* Peggy Moskowitz, Graduate School Secretary, 508-793-7274, Fax: 508-793-7265, E-mail: psychology@clarku.edu.

Cornell University, Graduate School, Graduate Fields of Human Ecology, Field of Human Development, Ithaca, NY 14853-0001. Offers developmental psychology (PhD), including cognitive development, developmental psychopathology, ecology of human development, social and personality development; human development and family studies (PhD), including ecology of human development, family studies and the life course. *Faculty:* 30 full-time (14 women). *Students:* 27 full-time (19 women); includes 2 minority (both Asian Americans or Pacific Islanders), 11 international. Average age 29. 71 applicants, 10% accepted, 5 enrolled. In 2008, 5 doctorates awarded. *Degree requirements:* For doctorate, comprehensive exam, thesis/dissertation, pre-doctoral research project, teaching experience. *Entrance requirements:* For doctorate, GRE General Test, 2 letters of recommendation. Additional exam requirements/recommendations for international students: Required—TOEFL (minimum score 550 paper-based; 213 computer-based; 77 iBT). *Application deadline:* For fall admission, 1/15 for domestic students. Application fee: $70. Electronic applications accepted. *Expenses:* Tuition: Full-time $29,500. Required fees: $70. Full-time tuition and fees vary according to degree level, program and student level. *Financial support:* In 2008–09, 26 students received support, including 3 fellowships with full tuition reimbursements available, 3 research assistantships with full tuition reimbursements available, 20 teaching assistantships with full tuition reimbursements available; institutionally sponsored loans, scholarships/grants, health care benefits, tuition waivers (full and partial), and unspecified assistantships also available. Financial award applicants required to submit FAFSA. *Faculty research:* Cognitive development, developmental psychopathology, ecology of human development, family studies and the life course, social and personality development. *Unit head:* Director of Graduate Studies, 607-255-3181, Fax: 607-255-9856. *Application contact:* Graduate Field Assistant, 607-255-3181, Fax: 607-255-9856, E-mail: hdfs@cornell.edu.

Duke University, Graduate School, Department of Psychology, Durham, NC 27708-0586. Offers biological psychology (PhD); clinical psychology (PhD); cognitive psychology (PhD); developmental psychology (PhD); experimental psychology (PhD); health psychology (PhD); human social development (PhD); JD/MA. *Accreditation:* APA (one or more programs are accredited). *Degree requirements:* For doctorate, thesis/dissertation. *Entrance requirements:* For doctorate, GRE General Test. Additional exam requirements/recommendations for international students: Required—TOEFL (minimum score 550 paper-based; 213 computer-based; 83 iBT), IELTS (minimum score 7). Electronic applications accepted.

Emory University, Graduate School of Arts and Sciences, Department of Psychology, Atlanta, GA 30322-1100. Offers clinical psychology (PhD); cognition and development (PhD); neuroscience and animal behavior (PhD). *Accreditation:* APA. *Degree requirements:* For doctorate, comprehensive exam, thesis/dissertation. *Entrance requirements:* For doctorate, GRE General Test, minimum GPA of 3.25. Additional exam requirements/recommendations for international students: Required—TOEFL. Electronic applications accepted. *Faculty research:* Neuroscience and animal behavior; adult and child psychopathology, cognition development assessment.

Erikson Institute, Academic Programs, Chicago, IL 60654. Offers administration (Certificate); bilingual/ESL (Certificate); child development (MS); early childhood education (MS); infant mental health (Certificate); infant studies (Certificate); MS/MSW. Part-time and evening/weekend programs available. *Degree requirements:* For master's, comprehensive exam, internship; for Certificate, internship. *Entrance requirements:* For master's and Certificate, minimum GPA of 2.75. Additional exam requirements/recommendations for international students: Required—TOEFL. *Faculty research:* Assessment strategies from early childhood through elementary years; language, literacy, and the arts in children's development; inclusive special education; parent-child relationships; cognitive development.

Florida International University, College of Arts and Sciences, Department of Psychology, Miami, FL 33199. Offers developmental psychology (PhD); general psychology (MS); psychology (MS). Part-time programs available. Terminal master's awarded for partial completion of doctoral program. *Degree requirements:* For master's, thesis; for doctorate, comprehensive exam, thesis/dissertation. *Entrance requirements:* For master's, GRE General Test, minimum GPA of 3.0, resumé, writing samples; for doctorate, GRE General Test, 3 letters of recommendation, resumé, writing samples, minimum GPA of 3.0. Additional exam requirements/recommendations for international students: Required—TOEFL (minimum score 550 paper-based; 213 computer-based). Electronic applications accepted. *Faculty research:* Community psychology.

Florida State University, Graduate Studies, College of Arts and Sciences, Department of Psychology, Program in Developmental Psychology, Tallahassee, FL 32306. Offers PhD. *Degree requirements:* For doctorate, thesis/dissertation, preliminary exam. *Entrance requirements:* For doctorate, GRE, minimum GPA of 3.0, research experience, letters of recommendation. Additional exam requirements/recommendations for international students: Required—TOEFL (minimum score 550 paper-based; 213 computer-based; 80 iBT). Electronic applications accepted. *Faculty research:* Learning disabilities, phonological processing, psychology of reading, emergent literacy, aging.

Fordham University, Graduate School of Arts and Sciences, Department of Psychology, Program in Applied Developmental Psychology, New York, NY 10458. Offers PhD. *Degree requirements:* For doctorate, comprehensive exam, thesis/dissertation. *Entrance requirements:* For doctorate, GRE General Test, GRE Subject Test. Additional exam requirements/recommendations for international students: Required—TOEFL (minimum score 600 paper-based; 250 computer-based). Electronic applications accepted. *Faculty research:* Development of citizenship, impact of participation in community service, impact of poverty on children, development of moral reasoning and behavior.

Gallaudet University, The Graduate School, College of Arts and Sciences, Department of Psychology, Program in School Psychology, Washington, DC 20002-3625. Offers developmental psychology (MA); school psychology (Psy S). *Accreditation:* NCATE. *Degree requirements:* For master's, thesis optional. *Entrance requirements:* For master's, GRE General Test or MAT. Electronic applications accepted.

George Mason University, College of Humanities and Social Sciences, Department of Psychology, Fairfax, VA 22030. Offers applied developmental psychology (MA, PhD); biopsychology (MA, PhD); clinical psychology (MA, PhD); human factors engineering psychology (MA, PhD); industrial/organizational psychology (MA, PhD); psychology (MA, PhD); school psychology (MA). *Accreditation:* APA. Terminal master's awarded for partial completion of doctoral program. *Degree requirements:* For master's, thesis (for applied developmental psychology and biopsychology); for doctorate, comprehensive exam, thesis/dissertation or alternative. *Entrance requirements:* For master's, GRE General Test, minimum GPA of 3.0 in last 60 hours of course work, undergraduate course work in psychology; for doctorate, GRE General Test, minimum undergraduate GPA of 3.0, 3.3 in major. Additional exam requirements/recommendations for international students: Required—TOEFL (minimum score 575 paper-based; 230 computer-based; 88 iBT), IELTS (minimum score 6). Electronic applications accepted.

Graduate School and University Center of the City University of New York, Graduate Studies, Program in Psychology, New York, NY 10016-4039. Offers basic applied neurocognition (PhD); biopsychology (PhD); clinical psychology (PhD); developmental psychology (PhD); environmental psychology (PhD); experimental psychology (PhD); industrial psychology (PhD); learning processes (PhD); neuropsychology (PhD); psychology (PhD); social personality (PhD). *Degree requirements:* For doctorate, one foreign language, thesis/dissertation. *Entrance requirements:* For doctorate, GRE General Test. Additional exam requirements/recommendations for international students: Required—TOEFL. Electronic applications accepted.

Harvard University, Graduate School of Arts and Sciences, Department of Psychology, Cambridge, MA 02138. Offers psychology (PhD), including behavior and decision analysis, cognition, developmental psychology, experimental psychology, personality, psychobiology, psychopathology; social psychology (PhD). *Degree requirements:* For doctorate, thesis/dissertation, general exams. *Entrance requirements:* For doctorate, GRE General Test. Additional exam requirements/recommendations for international students: Required—TOEFL. *Expenses:* Tuition: Full-time $32,556. Required fees: $1426. Full-time tuition and fees vary according to program and student level.

Howard University, Graduate School, Department of Psychology, Washington, DC 20059-0002. Offers clinical psychology (PhD); developmental psychology (PhD); experimental psychology (PhD); neuropsychology (PhD); personality psychology (PhD); psychology (MS); social psychology (PhD). *Accreditation:* APA (one or more programs are accredited). Part-time programs available. *Degree requirements:* For master's, thesis; for doctorate, comprehensive exam, thesis/dissertation, qualifying exam. *Entrance requirements:* For master's, GRE General Test, minimum GPA of 2.5, bachelor's degree in psychology or related field; for doctorate, GRE General Test, minimum GPA of 3.0. *Faculty research:* Personality and psychophysiology, educational and social development of African-American children, child and adult psychopathology.

Illinois State University, Graduate School, College of Arts and Sciences, Department of Psychology, Normal, IL 61790-2200. Offers psychology (MA, MS), including clinical psychology, counseling psychology, developmental psychology, educational psychology, experimental psychology, measurement-evaluation, organizational-industrial psychology; school psychology (PhD, SSP). *Accreditation:* APA. *Degree requirements:* For master's, thesis or alternative; for doctorate, variable foreign language requirement, thesis/dissertation, 2 terms of residency, internship, practicum. *Entrance requirements:* For master's, GRE General Test, GRE Subject Test, minimum GPA of 3.0 in last 60 hours of course work; for doctorate, GRE General Test. *Faculty research:* Comprehensive evaluation system for the central region professional development grant, Illinois school psychology internship consortium, for children's sake.

Indiana University Bloomington, University Graduate School, College of Arts and Sciences, Department of Psychological and Brain Sciences, Bloomington, IN 47405-7000. Offers biology and behavior (PhD); clinical science (PhD); cognitive psychology (PhD); developmental psychology (PhD); psychological and brain sciences (MA); social psychology (PhD). *Accreditation:* APA (one or more programs are accredited). *Faculty:* 53 full-time (16 women). *Students:* 95 full-time (52 women), 1 part-time (0 women); includes 11 minority (3 African Americans, 3 Asian Americans or Pacific Islanders, 5 Hispanic Americans), 18 international. Average age 28. 210 applicants, 15% accepted, 17 enrolled. In 2008, 1 master's, 10 doctorates awarded. *Degree requirements:* For doctorate, comprehensive exam, thesis/dissertation, 1st and 2nd year projects, 1 year as associate instructor, qualifying exam, student teaching. *Entrance requirements:* For doctorate, GRE. Additional exam requirements/recommendations for international students: Required—TOEFL (minimum score 550 paper-based; 213 computer-based). *Application deadline:* For fall admission, 12/15 for domestic students, 12/1 for international students. Application fee: $50 ($60 for international students). Electronic applications accepted. *Expenses:* Tuition, area resident: Part-time $291.97 per credit hour. Tuition, state resident: part-time $291.97 per credit hour. Tuition, nonresident: part-time $850.33 per credit hour. Required fees: $110 per semester. Tuition and fees vary according to course load and program. *Financial support:* Fellowships with full tuition reimbursements, research assistantships with full tuition reimbursements, teaching assistantships with full tuition reimbursements, scholarships/grants, health care benefits, and unspecified assistantships available. *Unit head:* Dr. Linda B. Smith, Chair, 812-855-3991, Fax: 812-855-4691, E-mail: smith4@indiana.edu. *Application contact:* Patricia G. Crouch, Academic Services Coordinator, 812-855-4528, Fax: 812-855-4691, E-mail: pcrouch@indiana.edu.

Louisiana State University and Agricultural and Mechanical College, Graduate School, College of Arts and Sciences, Department of Psychology, Baton Rouge, LA 70803. Offers biological psychology (MA, PhD); clinical psychology (MA, PhD); cognitive psychology (MA, PhD); developmental psychology (MA, PhD); industrial/organizational psychology (MA, PhD); school psychology (MA, PhD). *Accreditation:* APA (one or more programs are accredited). Terminal master's awarded for partial completion of doctoral program. *Degree requirements:* For master's, thesis; for doctorate, thesis/dissertation, 1 year internship. *Entrance requirements:* For master's and doctorate, GRE General Test, minimum GPA of 3.0. Additional exam requirements/recommendations for international students: Required—TOEFL (minimum score 550 paper-based; 213 computer-based; 79 iBT). Electronic applications accepted. *Faculty research:* Clinical psychology, autism, anxiety, addition, neuro-psychology, school psychology, cognitive psychology, experimental psychology.

Loyola University Chicago, Graduate School, Department of Psychology, Program in Developmental Psychology, Chicago, IL 60611-2196. Offers MA, PhD. *Faculty:* 6 full-time (4 women), 1 (woman) part-time/adjunct. *Students:* 12 full-time (11 women); includes 4 minority (1 African American, 1 American Indian/Alaska Native, 2 Hispanic Americans). Average age 27. 22 applicants, 14% accepted, 2 enrolled. In 2008, 2 doctorates awarded. *Degree requirements:* For doctorate, comprehensive exam, thesis/dissertation, internship or student teaching. *Entrance requirements:* For doctorate, GRE General Test, GRE Subject Test. Additional exam requirements/recommendations for international students: Required—TOEFL (minimum score 500 paper-based). *Application deadline:* For fall admission, 1/15 for domestic students. Application fee: $50. Electronic applications accepted. *Expenses:* Tuition: Full-time $13,500; part-time $750 per credit hour. Required fees: $60 per semester. Full-time tuition and fees vary according to program. *Financial support:* In 2008–09, 5 students received support, including fellowships with full tuition reimbursements available (averaging $14,000 per year), research assistantships with full tuition reimbursements available (averaging $14,000 per year), teaching assistantships with full tuition reimbursements available (averaging $14,000 per year); career-related internships or fieldwork, scholarships/grants, and unspecified assistantships also available. Financial award application deadline: 2/1; financial award applicants required to submit FAFSA. *Faculty research:* Cognitive development, parenting, bilingualism, memory development, emotion development, aggression and violence, racism stereotyping. Total annual research expenditures: $10,000. *Unit head:* Dr. Denise Davidson, Director, 773-508-3008, Fax: 773-508-2813, E-mail: ddavids@luc.edu. *Application contact:* Ron Martin, Assistant Director of Enrollment Management, 312-915-8950, Fax: 312-915-8905, E-mail: gradapp@luc.edu.

Developmental Psychology

McGill University, Faculty of Graduate and Postdoctoral Studies, Faculty of Education, Department of Educational and Counseling Psychology, Montréal, QC H3A 2T5, Canada. Offers counseling psychology (MA, PhD); educational psychology (M Ed, MA, PhD); school/applied child psychology and applied developmental psychology (M Ed, MA, PhD, Diploma), including school psychology. *Accreditation:* APA.

New York University, Steinhardt School of Culture, Education and Human Development, Department of Applied Psychology, Program in Educational and Developmental Psychology, New York, NY 10012-1019. Offers educational psychology (MA), including general educational psychology, psychological measurement and evaluation, psychology of parenthood; psychological development (PhD); school psychology (PhD). *Accreditation:* APA (one or more programs are accredited). Part-time and evening/weekend programs available. Terminal master's awarded for partial completion of doctoral program. *Degree requirements:* For master's, thesis (for some programs); for doctorate, thesis/dissertation. *Entrance requirements:* For doctorate, GRE General Test, interview. Additional exam requirements/recommendations for international students: Required—TOEFL. *Faculty research:* High risk children and youth; child and adolescent developments; families and schooling; infant cognition; exploration, language, and symbolic play in toddlerhood.

North Carolina State University, Graduate School, College of Humanities and Social Sciences, Department of Psychology, Raleigh, NC 27695. Offers developmental psychology (PhD); ergonomics and experimental psychology (PhD); industrial/organizational psychology (PhD); psychology in the public interest (PhD); school psychology (PhD). *Accreditation:* APA. *Degree requirements:* For doctorate, comprehensive exam, thesis/dissertation. *Entrance requirements:* For doctorate, GRE General Test, GRE Subject Test (industrial/organizational psychology), MAT (recommended), minimum GPA of 3.0 in major. Electronic applications accepted. *Faculty research:* Cognitive and social development (human factors, families, the workplace, community issues and health, aging).

The Ohio State University, Graduate School, College of Social and Behavioral Sciences, School of Social and Behavioral Science, Department of Psychology, Columbus, OH 43210. Offers behavioral neuroscience (PhD); clinical psychology (PhD); cognitive psychology (PhD); developmental psychology (PhD); mental retardation and developmental disabilities (PhD); psychology (MA); quantitative psychology (PhD); social psychology (PhD). *Accreditation:* APA (one or more programs are accredited). *Degree requirements:* For doctorate, thesis/dissertation. *Entrance requirements:* For master's and doctorate, GRE General Test. Additional exam requirements/recommendations for international students: Required—TOEFL (minimum score 600 paper-based; 250 computer-based). Electronic applications accepted.

Penn State University Park, Graduate School, College of the Liberal Arts, Department of Psychology, State College, University Park, PA 16802-1503. Offers clinical psychology (MS, PhD); cognitive psychology (MS, PhD); developmental psychology (MS, PhD); industrial/organizational psychology (MS, PhD); psychobiology (MS, PhD); social psychology (MS, PhD). *Accreditation:* APA (one or more programs are accredited).

Queen's University at Kingston, School of Graduate Studies and Research, Faculty of Arts and Sciences, Department of Psychology, Kingston, ON K7L 3N6, Canada. Offers brain behavior and cognitive science (MA, PhD); clinical psychology (MA, PhD); developmental psychology (MA, PhD); social personality psychology (MA, PhD). *Accreditation:* APA (one or more programs are accredited). *Degree requirements:* For master's, thesis; for doctorate, comprehensive exam, thesis/dissertation. *Entrance requirements:* For master's and doctorate, GRE General Test. Additional exam requirements/recommendations for international students: Required—TOEFL. *Faculty research:* Human development, social, personality, behavioral neuroscience, forensic.

Stanford University, School of Education, Program in Psychological Studies in Education, Stanford, CA 94305-9991. Offers child and adolescent development (PhD); counseling psychology (PhD); educational psychology (PhD). *Degree requirements:* For doctorate, thesis/dissertation. *Entrance requirements:* For doctorate, GRE General Test. Electronic applications accepted.

Teachers College, Columbia University, Graduate Faculty of Education, Department of Human Development, Program in Developmental Psychology, New York, NY 10027-6696. Offers MA, Ed D, PhD. *Faculty:* 6 full-time (5 women). *Students:* 37 full-time (30 women), 53 part-time (41 women); includes 20 minority (3 African Americans, 9 Asian Americans or Pacific Islanders, 8 Hispanic Americans), 19 international. Average age 28. 91 applicants, 82% accepted, 34 enrolled. In 2008, 23 master's, 1 doctorate awarded. *Degree requirements:* For doctorate, thesis/dissertation, integrative project. *Entrance requirements:* For doctorate, GRE General Test. *Application deadline:* For fall admission, 5/15 for domestic students. Application fee: $75. *Expenses:* Tuition: Full-time $26,040; part-time $1085 per credit. Required fees: $720. *Financial support:* Research assistantships, teaching assistantships, career-related internships or fieldwork, Federal Work-Study, institutionally sponsored loans, and tuition waivers (full and partial) available. Support available to part-time students. Financial award application deadline: 2/1. *Faculty research:* Language development in infants, psychology of mathematics education, intellectual development, testing and assessment, cognitive development. *Unit head:* Office of Admissions, 212-678-3710, Fax: 212-678-4171. *Application contact:* Melba Remice, Assistant Director of Admission, 212-678-4035, Fax: 212-678-4171, E-mail: ms2545@columbia.edu.

Temple University, Graduate School, College of Liberal Arts, Department of Psychology, Program in Developmental Psychology, Philadelphia, PA 19122-6096. Offers PhD. *Degree requirements:* For doctorate, thesis/dissertation. *Entrance requirements:* For doctorate, GRE General Test, minimum GPA of 3.0. Additional exam requirements/recommendations for international students: Required—TOEFL (minimum score 550 paper-based; 213 computer-based; 79 iBT). Electronic applications accepted. *Faculty research:* Social development, cognitive development, emotional development, research methodology.

Texas A&M University, College of Liberal Arts, Department of Psychology, College Station, TX 77843. Offers behavioral and cellular neuroscience (MS, PhD); clinical psychology (MS, PhD); cognitive psychology (MS, PhD); developmental psychology (MS, PhD); industrial/organizational psychology (MS, PhD); social psychology (MS, PhD). *Accreditation:* APA (one or more programs are accredited). *Faculty:* 35. *Students:* 74 full-time (47 women), 11 part-time (9 women); includes 30 minority (7 African Americans, 5 Asian Americans or Pacific Islanders, 18 Hispanic Americans), 4 international. In 2008, 11 master's, 12 doctorates awarded. *Degree requirements:* For master's, thesis; for doctorate, comprehensive exam (for some programs), thesis/dissertation. *Entrance requirements:* For master's and doctorate, GRE General Test. Additional exam requirements/recommendations for international students: Required—TOEFL. *Application deadline:* For fall admission, 1/5 for domestic and international students. Application fee: $50 ($75 for international students). Electronic applications accepted. *Expenses:* Tuition, area resident: Full-time $3838.50. Tuition, state resident: full-time $3838.50. Tuition, nonresident: full-time $8897. Required fees: $2359.60. *Financial support:* Fellowships with partial tuition reimbursements, research assistantships with partial tuition reimbursements, teaching assistantships with partial tuition reimbursements, career-related internships or fieldwork, institutionally sponsored loans, health care benefits, and unspecified assistantships available. Financial award application deadline: 1/5; financial award applicants required to submit FAFSA. *Unit head:* Dr. Les Morey, Head, 979-845-2581, Fax: 979-845-4727, E-mail: lmorey@psych.tamu.edu. *Application contact:* Sharon Starr, Graduate Admissions Supervisor, 979-458-1710, Fax: 979-845-4727, E-mail: gradadv@psyc.tamu.edu.

Tufts University, Graduate School of Arts and Sciences, Department of Child Development, Medford, MA 02155. Offers applied developmental psychology (PhD); child development (MA, CAGS); early childhood education (MAT). Part-time programs available. *Degree requirements:* For master's, thesis (for some programs); for doctorate, thesis/dissertation. *Entrance requirements:* For master's and doctorate, GRE General Test. Additional exam requirements/

recommendations for international students: Required—TOEFL (minimum score 550 paper-based; 213 computer-based; 80 iBT). Electronic applications accepted.

Université de Montréal, Faculty of Arts and Sciences, School of Psychoeducation, Montréal, QC H3C 3J7, Canada. Offers M Sc, PhD, Certificate. Part-time programs available. *Faculty:* 16 full-time (5 women), 4 part-time/adjunct (2 women). *Students:* 69 full-time (60 women), 51 part-time (47 women). 139 applicants, 36% accepted, 47 enrolled. In 2008, 23 master's awarded. *Degree requirements:* For master's, one foreign language, thesis. *Application deadline:* For fall admission, 2/1 priority date for domestic students; for winter admission, 11/1 priority date for domestic students; for spring admission, 2/1 priority date for domestic students. Application fee: $100. Electronic applications accepted. *Financial support:* Fellowships, research assistantships, teaching assistantships, career-related internships or fieldwork and institutionally sponsored loans available. Support available to part-time students. *Faculty research:* Child maladjustment, family, prevention, treatment, antisocial behavior. *Unit head:* Sophie Parent, Chairperson and Responsible for Graduate studies (PhD), 514-343-7421, Fax: 514-343-6951, E-mail: sophie.parent@umontreal.ca. *Application contact:* Lyse Turgeon, Graduate Chairperson (MSc), 514-343-6111 Ext. 2559, Fax: 514-343-6951, E-mail: lyse.turgeon@umontreal.ca.

The University of British Columbia, Faculty of Arts and Faculty of Graduate Studies, Department of Psychology, Vancouver, BC V6T 1Z1, Canada. Offers behavioral neuroscience (MA, PhD); clinical psychology (MA, PhD); cognitive science (MA, PhD); developmental psychology (MA, PhD); forensic psychology (PhD); health psychology (MA, PhD); quantitative methods (MA, PhD); social/personality psychology (MA, PhD). *Accreditation:* APA (one or more programs are accredited). Terminal master's awarded for partial completion of doctoral program. *Degree requirements:* For master's, thesis; for doctorate, comprehensive exam, thesis/dissertation. *Entrance requirements:* For master's and doctorate, GRE General Test, GRE Subject Test. Additional exam requirements/recommendations for international students: Required—TOEFL (minimum score 550 paper-based; 230 computer-based; 80 iBT). Electronic applications accepted. *Faculty research:* Clinical, developmental, social/personality, cognition, behavioral neuroscience.

University of California, Santa Barbara, Graduate Division, Gevirtz Graduate School of Education, Santa Barbara, CA 93106-9490. Offers counseling, clinical and school psychology (PhD), including clinical psychology, counseling psychology, school psychology; education (M Ed, MA, PhD), including child and adolescent development (MA, PhD); cultural perspectives and comparative education (MA, PhD), educational leadership and organizations (MA, PhD), research methodology (MA, PhD), special education disabilities and risk studies (MA), special education, disabilities and risk studies (PhD), teaching (M Ed), teaching and learning (MA, PhD); educational leadership (Ed D); school psychology (M Ed); MA/PhD. *Accreditation:* APA (one or more programs are accredited). Postbaccalaureate distance learning degree programs offered (minimal on-campus study). *Faculty:* 42 full-time (20 women), 10 part-time/adjunct (4 women). *Students:* 390 full-time (303 women); includes 149 minority (14 African Americans, 3 American Indian/Alaska Native, 57 Asian Americans or Pacific Islanders, 75 Hispanic Americans), 16 international. Average age 31. 717 applicants, 40% accepted, 170 enrolled. In 2008, 140 master's, 46 doctorates awarded. Terminal master's awarded for partial completion of doctoral program. *Degree requirements:* For master's, comprehensive exam (for some programs), thesis (for some programs); for doctorate, comprehensive exam (for some programs), thesis/dissertation, qualifying exam. *Entrance requirements:* For master's and doctorate, GRE, 3 letters of recommendation, statement of purpose, personal achievements/contributions statement, resumé/curriculum vitae, transcripts for post-secondary institutions attended. Additional exam requirements/recommendations for international students: Required—TOEFL (minimum score 550 paper-based; 213 computer-based; 80 iBT), IELTS (minimum score 7), TOEFL or IELTS. Application fee: $70 ($90 for international students). Electronic applications accepted. *Expenses:* Tuition, nonresident: full-time $25,149. Required fees: $10,143. Full-time tuition and fees vary according to campus/location, reciprocity agreements and student level. *Financial support:* In 2008–09, 253 students received support, including 206 fellowships with full and partial tuition reimbursements available (averaging $5,000 per year), 62 research assistantships with full and partial tuition reimbursements available (averaging $6,200 per year), 87 teaching assistantships with partial tuition reimbursements available (averaging $6,500 per year); career-related internships or fieldwork, Federal Work-Study, institutionally sponsored loans, scholarships/grants, traineeships, health care benefits, and unspecified assistantships also available. Financial award applicants required to submit FAFSA. *Faculty research:* Professional development, early childhood development, school violence, literacy, science/math initiative. Total annual research expenditures: $4.4 million. *Unit head:* Dr. Jane Conoley, Chair, 805-893-2185, E-mail: jane-conoley@education.ucsb.edu. *Application contact:* Kathryn Marie Tucciarone, Student Affairs Officer, 805-893-2137, E-mail: katiet@education.ucsb.edu.

University of Connecticut, Graduate School, College of Liberal Arts and Sciences, Department of Psychology, Field of Psychology, Storrs, CT 06269. Offers behavioral neuroscience (PhD); biopsychology (PhD); clinical psychology (MA, PhD); cognition and instruction (PhD); developmental psychology (MA, PhD); ecological psychology (PhD); experimental psychology (PhD); general psychology (MA, PhD); health psychology (Graduate Certificate); industrial/organizational psychology (PhD); language and cognition (PhD); neuroscience (PhD); occupational health psychology (Graduate Certificate); social psychology (MA, PhD). *Accreditation:* APA (one or more programs are accredited). Terminal master's awarded for partial completion of doctoral program. *Degree requirements:* For master's, comprehensive exam; for doctorate, thesis/dissertation. *Entrance requirements:* For master's and doctorate, GRE General Test, GRE Subject Test. Additional exam requirements/recommendations for international students: Required—TOEFL (minimum score 550 paper-based; 213 computer-based). Electronic applications accepted.

University of Florida, Graduate School, College of Liberal Arts and Sciences, Department of Psychology, Gainesville, FL 32611. Offers behavior analysis (PhD); behavioral neuroscience (MS, PhD); cognitive and sensory processes (PhD); counseling psychology (PhD); developmental psychology (PhD); social psychology (MS, PhD); JD/PhD. *Degree requirements:* For master's, thesis or alternative; for doctorate, thesis/dissertation. *Entrance requirements:* For master's and doctorate, GRE General Test, minimum GPA of 3.0. Additional exam requirements/recommendations for international students: Required—TOEFL (minimum score 550 paper-based; 213 computer-based). Electronic applications accepted. *Faculty research:* Experimental analysis of behavior, psychobiology, cognition and sensory processes, counseling psychology, social psychology, developmental psychology.

The University of Kansas, Graduate Studies, College of Liberal Arts and Sciences, Department of Psychology, Lawrence, KS 66045. Offers clinical child psychology (MA, PhD); cognitive (PhD); developmental (PhD); psychology (MA, PhD); quantitative (PhD). *Accreditation:* APA (one or more programs are accredited). *Faculty:* 38. *Students:* 90 full-time (65 women), 6 part-time (5 women); includes 15 minority (5 African Americans, 1 American Indian/Alaska Native, 7 Asian Americans or Pacific Islanders, 2 Hispanic Americans), 6 international. Average age 27. 195 applicants, 14% accepted, 10 enrolled. In 2008, 15 master's, 16 doctorates awarded. *Degree requirements:* For master's, thesis; for doctorate, comprehensive exam, thesis/dissertation. *Entrance requirements:* For doctorate, GRE General Test, minimum GPA of 3.0. Additional exam requirements/recommendations for international students: Required—TOEFL. *Application deadline:* For fall admission, 1/15 for domestic and international students. Application fee: $45 ($55 for international students). Electronic applications accepted. *Expenses:* Tuition, area resident: Full-time $6122; part-time $255.10 per credit hour. Tuition, state resident: full-time $6122; part-time $255.10 per credit hour. Tuition, nonresident: full-time $14,629; part-time $609.55 per credit hour. Required fees: $847; $70.56 per credit hour. Tuition and fees vary according to course load and program. *Financial support:* Fellowships with full tuition reimbursements, research assistantships with partial tuition reimbursements, teaching assistantships with full and partial tuition reimbursements, career-related internships or fieldwork and unspecified assistantships available. Financial award application deadline: 1/4; financial award applicants required to submit FAFSA. *Faculty research:* Cognitive psychology, methodology and statistics, developmental clinical/health psychology. *Unit head:* Greg Simpson, Chair, 785-864-9821, Fax: 785-864-5696, E-mail: gsimpson@ku.edu. *Application contact:* Cathy L. O'Keefe, Graduate Admissions Officer, 785-864-4195, Fax: 785-864-5696, E-mail: psycgrad@ku.edu.

The University of Kansas, Graduate Studies, College of Liberal Arts and Sciences, Program in Child Language, Lawrence, KS 66045. Offers MA, PhD. *Faculty:* 22. *Students:* 8 full-time (5 women), 1 international. Average age 28. 5 applicants, 60% accepted, 2 enrolled. *Degree requirements:* For master's, thesis; for doctorate, comprehensive exam, thesis/dissertation, written preliminary exam. *Entrance requirements:* For master's and doctorate, GRE, minimum GPA of 3.5, 3 letters of reference. Additional exam requirements/recommendations for international students: Required—TOEFL. *Application deadline:* For fall admission, 2/1 priority date for domestic and international students; for spring admission, 11/1 for domestic and international students. Applications are processed on a rolling basis. Application fee: $45 ($50 for international students). Electronic applications accepted. *Expenses:* Tuition, area resident: Full-time $6122; part-time $255.10 per credit hour. Tuition, state resident: full-time $6122; part-time $255.10 per credit hour. Tuition, nonresident: full-time $14,629; part-time $609.55 per credit hour. Required fees: $847; $70.56 per credit hour. Tuition and fees vary according to course load and program. *Financial support:* Fellowships with full tuition reimbursements, research assistantships with full tuition reimbursements, career-related internships or fieldwork, traineeships, and unspecified assistantships available. Financial award application deadline: 2/1. *Faculty research:* Etiology of language impairments, word recognition processes, cultural context and linguistic patterns, language acquisition. *Unit head:* Mabel Rice, Director, 785-864-4570, E-mail: mabel@ku.edu. *Application contact:* Susan Kemper, Graduate Adviser, 785-864-0748, E-mail: skemper@ku.edu.

University of Maine, Graduate School, College of Liberal Arts and Sciences, Department of Psychology, Orono, ME 04469. Offers clinical psychology (PhD); developmental psychology (MA); experimental psychology (MA, PhD); social psychology (MA). *Accreditation:* APA (one or more programs are accredited). *Degree requirements:* For master's, thesis; for doctorate, thesis/dissertation. *Entrance requirements:* For master's and doctorate, GRE General Test, GRE Subject Test. Additional exam requirements/recommendations for international students: Required—TOEFL. Electronic applications accepted. *Faculty research:* Social development, hypertension and aging, attitude change, self-confidence in achievement situations, health psychology.

University of Maryland, Baltimore County, Graduate School, College of Arts, Humanities and Social Sciences, Department of Psychology, Program in Applied Developmental Psychology, Baltimore, MD 21250. Offers PhD. *Faculty:* 6 full-time (4 women), 11 part-time/adjunct (4 women). *Students:* 29 full-time (26 women), 6 part-time (5 women); includes 5 minority (2 African Americans, 2 Asian Americans or Pacific Islanders, 1 Hispanic American), 5 international. Average age 32. 18 applicants, 39% accepted, 6 enrolled. In 2008, 3 doctorates awarded. *Degree requirements:* For doctorate, comprehensive exam, thesis/dissertation. *Entrance requirements:* For doctorate, GRE General Test, GRE Subject Test, minimum GPA of 3.0. Additional exam requirements/recommendations for international students: Required—TOEFL. *Application deadline:* For fall admission, 1/9 for domestic and international students. Application fee: $50. Electronic applications accepted. *Financial support:* In 2008–09, 4 research assistantships with full and partial tuition reimbursements (averaging $14,857 per year), 12 teaching assistantships with full and partial tuition reimbursements (averaging $14,566 per year) were awarded; fellowships with partial tuition reimbursements, career-related internships or fieldwork, Federal Work-Study, health care benefits, and unspecified assistantships also available. Financial award application deadline: 3/1; financial award applicants required to submit FAFSA. *Faculty research:* Early intervention and development, schooling and development, cultural aspects of development, development in high risk children, social-emotional development. Total annual research expenditures: $2.3 million. *Unit head:* Dr. Susan Sonnenschein, Director, 410-455-2361, Fax: 410-455-1055, E-mail: sonnenschein@umbc.edu. *Application contact:* Cara Lane, Program Management Specialist, 410-455-2567, Fax: 410-455-1055, E-mail: psycdept@umbc.edu.

University of Maryland, College Park, Graduate Studies, College of Behavioral and Social Sciences, Department of Psychology, College Park, MD 20742. Offers clinical psychology (PhD); developmental psychology (PhD); experimental psychology (PhD); industrial psychology (MA, MS, PhD); social psychology (PhD). *Accreditation:* APA (one or more programs are accredited). *Degree requirements:* For master's, thesis; for doctorate, variable foreign language requirement, comprehensive exam, thesis/dissertation. *Entrance requirements:* For master's and doctorate, GRE General Test, GRE Subject Test, minimum GPA of 3.5, research and/or work experience, 3 letters of recommendation. Electronic applications accepted. *Faculty research:* Social stereotyping and prejudice, anxiety disorders, auditory neuroethology, counseling and social psychology.

University of Massachusetts Amherst, Graduate School, College of Social and Behavioral Sciences, Department of Psychology, Amherst, MA 01003. Offers clinical psychology (MS, PhD); cognitive psychology (MS, PhD); developmental science (MS, PhD); psychology of peace and violence (MS, PhD); social psychology (MS, PhD). *Accreditation:* APA (one or more programs are accredited). Terminal master's awarded for partial completion of doctoral program. *Degree requirements:* For master's, thesis; for doctorate, comprehensive exam, thesis/dissertation. *Entrance requirements:* For master's and doctorate, GRE General Test, 3 letters of recommendation. Additional exam requirements/recommendations for international students: Required—TOEFL (minimum score 550 paper-based; 213 computer-based; 79 iBT), IELTS (minimum score 6.5). Electronic applications accepted. *Expenses:* Tuition, area resident: Full-time $2640. Tuition, nonresident: full-time $9936. One-time fee: $332 full-time. Tuition and fees vary according to course load.

University of Miami, Graduate School, College of Arts and Sciences, Department of Psychology, Coral Gables, FL 33124. Offers adult clinical (PhD); behavioral neuroscience (PhD); child clinical (PhD); developmental psychology (PhD); health clinical (PhD); psychology (MS). *Accreditation:* APA (one or more programs are accredited). *Degree requirements:* For doctorate, comprehensive exam, thesis/dissertation. *Entrance requirements:* For doctorate, GRE General Test, minimum GPA of 3.5. Additional exam requirements/recommendations for international students: Required—TOEFL. Electronic applications accepted. *Faculty research:* Behavioral factors in cardiovascular disease and cancer adult psychopathology, developmental disabilities, social and emotional development, mechanisms of coping.

University of Michigan, Horace H. Rackham School of Graduate Studies, College of Literature, Science, and the Arts, Department of Psychology, Ann Arbor, MI 48109. Offers biopsychology (PhD); clinical psychology (PhD); cognition and perception (PhD); developmental psychology (PhD); personality and social contexts (PhD); social psychology (PhD). *Accreditation:* APA. *Degree requirements:* For doctorate, comprehensive exam, thesis/dissertation, oral defense of dissertation, preliminary exam. *Entrance requirements:* For doctorate, GRE General Test (optional), GRE Subject Test (optional). Additional exam requirements/recommendations for international students: Required—TOEFL. Electronic applications accepted.

The University of Montana, Graduate School, College of Arts and Sciences, Department of Psychology, Missoula, MT 59812-0002. Offers clinical psychology (PhD); experimental psychology (PhD), including animal behavior psychology, developmental psychology; school psychology (MA, PhD, Ed S). *Accreditation:* APA (one or more programs are accredited). Terminal master's awarded for partial completion of doctoral program. *Degree requirements:* For master's, thesis; for doctorate, thesis/dissertation. *Entrance requirements:* For master's, doctorate, and Ed S, GRE General Test. Additional exam requirements/recommendations for international students: Required—TOEFL.

University of Nebraska at Omaha, Graduate Studies and Research, College of Arts and Sciences, Department of Psychology, Omaha, NE 68182. Offers developmental psychology (PhD); industrial/organizational psychology (MS, PhD); psychobiology (PhD); psychology (MA); school psychology (MS, Ed S). Part-time programs available. *Degree requirements:* For master's, comprehensive exam, thesis (for some programs). *Entrance requirements:* For master's, GRE General Test, GRE Subject Test, previous course work in psychology, including statistics and a laboratory course; minimum GPA of 3.0, 3 letters of recommendation; for doctorate, GRE General Test. Additional exam requirements/recommendations for international students: Required—TOEFL (minimum score 500 paper-based; 173 computer-based; 61 iBT). Electronic applications accepted.

University of Nebraska–Lincoln, Graduate College, College of Arts and Sciences, Department of Psychology, Lincoln, NE 68588. Offers biopsychology (PhD); clinical psychology (PhD); cognitive psychology (PhD); developmental psychology (PhD); psychology (MA); social/personality psychology (PhD); JD/MA; JD/PhD. *Accreditation:* APA (one or more programs are accredited). *Faculty:* 24 full-time (8 women). *Students:* 84 full-time (66 women), 29 part-time (15 women); includes 15 minority (1 African American, 1 American Indian/Alaska Native, 4 Asian Americans or Pacific Islanders, 9 Hispanic Americans), 9 international. Average age 32. In 2008, 16 master's, 18 doctorates awarded. *Degree requirements:* For master's, thesis optional; for doctorate, comprehensive exam, thesis/dissertation. *Entrance requirements:* For master's and doctorate, GRE General Test. Additional exam requirements/recommendations for international students: Required—TOEFL (minimum score 550 paper-based; 213 computer-based). *Application deadline:* For fall admission, 1/3 for domestic and international students. Application fee: $40. Electronic applications accepted. *Expenses:* Tuition, state resident: full-time $4275; part-time $237.50 per credit hour. Tuition, nonresident: full-time $11,525; part-time $640.25 per credit hour. Required fees: $1068; $10.35 per credit hour. $440.70 per semester. Tuition and fees vary according to course load and program. *Financial support:* Fellowships, research assistantships, teaching assistantships, Federal Work-Study, health care benefits, and unspecified assistantships available. Support available to part-time students. Financial award application deadline: 1/3. *Faculty research:* Law and psychology, rural mental health, chronic mental illness, neuropsychology, child clinical psychology. *Unit head:* Dr. David Hansen, Chair, 402-472-3721, Fax: 402-472-4637. *Application contact:* Ginny Gross, Director of Graduate Admissions, 402-472-2878, Fax: 402-472-0589, E-mail: grad_admissions@unl.edu.

University of Nebraska–Lincoln, Graduate College, College of Education and Human Sciences, Department of Educational Psychology, Lincoln, NE 68588. Offers cognition, learning and development (MA); counseling psychology (MA); educational psychology (MA, Ed S); psychological studies in education (PhD), including cognition, learning and development, counseling psychology, quantitative, qualitative, and psychometric methods, school psychology; quantitative, qualitative, and psychometric methods (MA); school psychology (MA, Ed S). *Accreditation:* APA (one or more programs are accredited); NCATE. *Faculty:* 19 full-time (6 women). *Students:* 16 full-time (14 women), 26 part-time (18 women); includes 2 minority (1 African American, 1 Hispanic American), 2 international. Average age 30. In 2008, 22 master's, 3 other advanced degrees awarded. *Degree requirements:* For master's, thesis optional. *Entrance requirements:* For master's, GRE General Test. Additional exam requirements/recommendations for international students: Required—TOEFL (minimum score 500 paper-based; 173 computer-based). *Application deadline:* For fall admission, 12/15 for domestic and international students; for spring admission, 10/1 for domestic students. Application fee: $40. Electronic applications accepted. *Expenses:* Tuition, state resident: full-time $4275; part-time $237.50 per credit hour. Tuition, nonresident: full-time $11,525; part-time $640.25 per credit hour. Required fees: $1068; $10.35 per credit hour. $440.70 per semester. Tuition and fees vary according to course load and program. *Financial support:* Fellowships, research assistantships, teaching assistantships, Federal Work-Study, health care benefits, and unspecified assistantships available. Support available to part-time students. Financial award application deadline: 1/15. *Faculty research:* Measurement and assessment, metacognition, academic skills, child development, multicultural education and counseling. *Unit head:* Dr. Ralph De Ayala, Chair, 402-472-2210, E-mail: tcgrad2@unl.edu. *Application contact:* Dr. Ralph De Ayala, Chair, 402-472-2210, E-mail: tcgrad2@unl.edu.

The University of North Carolina at Chapel Hill, Graduate School, College of Arts and Sciences, Department of Psychology, Chapel Hill, NC 27599. Offers biological psychology (PhD); clinical psychology (PhD); cognitive psychology (PhD); developmental psychology (PhD); quantitative psychology (PhD); social psychology (PhD). *Accreditation:* APA. *Degree requirements:* For doctorate, comprehensive exam, thesis/dissertation. *Entrance requirements:* For doctorate, GRE General Test, minimum GPA of 3.0. Electronic applications accepted. *Faculty research:* Expressed emotion, cognitive development, social cognitive neuroscience, human memory personality.

The University of North Carolina at Greensboro, Graduate School, College of Arts and Sciences, Department of Psychology, Greensboro, NC 27412-5001. Offers clinical psychology (MA, PhD); cognitive psychology (MA, PhD); developmental psychology (MA, PhD); social psychology (MA, PhD). *Accreditation:* APA (one or more programs are accredited). Terminal master's awarded for partial completion of doctoral program. *Degree requirements:* For master's, comprehensive exam, thesis; for doctorate, one foreign language, thesis/dissertation, preliminary exam. *Entrance requirements:* For master's and doctorate, GRE General Test. Additional exam requirements/recommendations for international students: Required—TOEFL. Electronic applications accepted. *Faculty research:* Sensory and perceptual determinants; evoked potential: disorders, deafness, and development.

University of Notre Dame, Graduate School, College of Arts and Letters, Division of Social Science, Department of Psychology, Notre Dame, IN 46556. Offers cognitive psychology (PhD); counseling psychology (PhD); developmental psychology (PhD); quantitative psychology (PhD). *Accreditation:* APA. *Faculty:* 28 full-time (11 women), 5 part-time/adjunct (4 women). *Students:* 70 full-time (49 women); includes 11 minority (3 African Americans, 3 Asian Americans or Pacific Islanders, 5 Hispanic Americans), 13 international. 146 applicants, 18% accepted, 18 enrolled. In 2008, 8 doctorates awarded. *Degree requirements:* For doctorate, comprehensive exam, thesis/dissertation, candidacy exam. *Entrance requirements:* For doctorate, GRE General Test, GRE Subject Test (strongly recommended). Additional exam requirements/recommendations for international students: Required—TOEFL (minimum score 600 paper-based; 250 computer-based; 80 iBT). *Application deadline:* For fall admission, 1/2 for domestic and international students. Application fee: $50. Electronic applications accepted. *Financial support:* Fellowships with full tuition reimbursements, research assistantships with full tuition reimbursements, teaching assistantships with full tuition reimbursements, career-related internships or fieldwork and tuition waivers (full) available. Financial award application deadline: 1/2. *Faculty research:* Cognitive and socio-emotional development, statistical methods and quantitative models applicable to psychology, interpersonal relations, life span development and developmental delay, childhood depression, structural equation and dynamical systems. *Unit head:* Dr. Dan Lapsley, Director of Graduate Studies, 574-631-8789. *Application contact:* Dr. Barbara Turpin, Director of Graduate Admissions, 574-631-7706, Fax: 574-631-4183.

University of Oregon, Graduate School, College of Arts and Sciences, Department of Psychology, Eugene, OR 97403. Offers clinical psychology (PhD); cognitive psychology (MA, MS, PhD); developmental psychology (MA, MS, PhD); physiological psychology (MA, MS, PhD); psychology (MA, MS, PhD); social/personality psychology (MA, MS, PhD). *Accreditation:* APA (one or more programs are accredited). Terminal master's awarded for partial completion of doctoral program. *Degree requirements:* For doctorate, thesis/dissertation. *Entrance requirements:* For master's, GRE General Test, minimum GPA of 3.0; for doctorate, GRE General Test. Additional exam requirements/recommendations for international students: Required—TOEFL.

University of Pittsburgh, School of Education, Department of Psychology in Education, Program in Applied Developmental Psychology, Pittsburgh, PA 15260. Offers MS, PhD. Part-time and evening/weekend programs available. *Degree requirements:* For master's, thesis. *Entrance requirements:* For doctorate, GRE. Additional exam requirements/recommendations for international students: Required—TOEFL. Electronic applications accepted.

Developmental Psychology

University of Rochester, The College, Arts and Sciences, Department of Clinical and Social Sciences in Psychology, Rochester, NY 14627-0250. Offers clinical psychology (PhD); developmental psychology (PhD); psychology (MA); social-personality psychology (PhD). *Accreditation:* APA (one or more programs are accredited). Terminal master's awarded for partial completion of doctoral program. *Degree requirements:* For doctorate, thesis/dissertation, qualifying exam. *Entrance requirements:* For doctorate, GRE General Test. Additional exam requirements/recommendations for international students: Required—TOEFL.

University of Victoria, Faculty of Graduate Studies, Faculty of Social Sciences, Department of Psychology, Victoria, BC V8W 2Y2, Canada. Offers clinical psychology (PhD); clinical psychology (neuropsychology) (M Sc); cognition and brain science (M Sc, PhD); experimental neuropsychology (M Sc, PhD); individualized study (M Sc, PhD); life span development psychology (PhD); life span developmental psychology (M Sc); social psychology (M Sc, PhD). *Accreditation:* APA (one or more programs are accredited). *Degree requirements:* For master's, thesis; for doctorate, thesis/dissertation, candidacy exam. *Entrance requirements:* For master's and doctorate, GRE General Test. Additional exam requirements/recommendations for international students: Required—TOEFL (minimum score 600 paper-based; 250 computer-based). Electronic applications accepted. *Faculty research:* Life span development psychology and aging, behavioral neuroscience, cognitive psychology, behavioral psychology, environmental psychology.

University of Washington, Graduate School, College of Arts and Sciences, Department of Psychology, Seattle, WA 98195. Offers animal behavior (PhD); child psychology (PhD); clinical psychology (PhD); cognition and perception (PhD); developmental psychology (PhD); quantitative psychology (PhD); social psychology and personality (PhD). *Accreditation:* APA. *Degree requirements:* For doctorate, thesis/dissertation. *Entrance requirements:* For doctorate, GRE General Test, minimum GPA of 3.0. Electronic applications accepted. *Faculty research:* Addictive behaviors, artificial intelligence, child psychopathology, mechanisms and development of vision, physiology of ingestive behaviors.

University of Wisconsin–Madison, Graduate School, College of Letters and Science, Department of Psychology, Program in Developmental Psychology, Madison, WI 53706-1380. Offers PhD. *Degree requirements:* For doctorate, comprehensive exam, thesis/dissertation. *Entrance requirements:* For doctorate, GRE General Test, minimum undergraduate GPA of 3.0. Additional exam requirements/recommendations for international students: Required—TOEFL. Electronic applications accepted.

University of Wisconsin–Milwaukee, Graduate School, School of Education, Department of Educational Psychology, Milwaukee, WI 53201-0413. Offers counseling (school, community) (MS); counseling psychology (PhD); learning and development (MS); research methodology (MS, PhD); school psychology (PhD). *Accreditation:* APA. Part-time programs available. *Faculty:* 21 full-time (13 women). *Students:* 146 full-time (116 women), 60 part-time (49 women); includes 40 minority (15 African Americans, 1 American Indian/Alaska Native, 12 Asian Americans or Pacific Islanders, 12 Hispanic Americans), 6 international. Average age 30. 252 applicants, 46% accepted, 54 enrolled. In 2008, 84 master's, 1 doctorate awarded. *Degree requirements:* For master's, comprehensive exam, thesis; for doctorate, thesis/dissertation. *Entrance requirements:* For master's, minimum GPA of 3.0; for doctorate, GRE General Test, minimum GPA of 3.0. Additional exam requirements/recommendations for international students: Required—TOEFL (minimum score 550 paper-based; 79 iBT), IELTS (minimum score 6.5). *Application deadline:* For fall admission, 1/1 priority date for domestic students; for spring admission, 9/1 for domestic students. Applications are processed on a rolling basis. Application fee: $45 ($75 for international students). *Expenses:* Tuition, area resident: Full-time $7320; part-time $165 per credit. Tuition, state resident: full-time $7320; part-time $165 per credit. Tuition, nonresident: full-time $17,840; part-time $714 per credit. Tuition and fees vary according to campus/location, program and reciprocity agreements. *Financial support:* In 2008–09, 11 teaching assistantships were awarded; career-related internships or fieldwork and unspecified assistantships also available. Support available to part-time students. Financial award application deadline: 4/15. Total annual research expenditures: $673,016. *Unit head:* Anthony Hains, Chair, 414-229-5715, Fax: 414-229-4939, E-mail: aahains@uwm.edu. *Application contact:* General Information Contact, 414-229-4982, Fax: 414-229-6967, E-mail: gradschool@uwm.edu.

Virginia Polytechnic Institute and State University, Graduate School, College of Science, Department of Psychology, Blacksburg, VA 24061. Offers bio-behavioral sciences (PhD); clinical psychology (PhD); developmental psychology (PhD); industrial/organizational psychology (PhD); psychology (MS). *Accreditation:* APA (one or more programs are accredited). *Entrance requirements:* For master's and doctorate, GRE General Test. Additional exam requirements/recommendations for international students: Required—TOEFL (minimum score 550 paper-based; 213 computer-based). Electronic applications accepted. *Faculty research:* Infant development from electrophysical point of view, work motivation and personnel selection, EEG, ERP and hypnosis with reference to chronic pain, intimate violence.

Walden University, Graduate Programs, School of Psychology, Minneapolis, MN 55401. Offers clinical assessment (Post-Doctoral Certificate); clinical child psychology (Post-Doctoral Certificate); clinical psychology (Post-Doctoral Certificate); counseling psychology (Post-Doctoral Certificate); forensic psychology (MS), including forensic psychology in the community, general forensic psychology, mental health applications, program planning and evaluation in forensic settings, psychology and legal systems; general psychology (Post-Doctoral Certificate); health psychology (Post-Doctoral Certificate); organizational psychology (Post-Doctoral Certificate); organizational psychology and development (Certificate); psychology (MS, PhD), including clinical psychology, counseling psychology, crisis management and response (MS), general psychology, health psychology, leadership development and coaching (MS), media psychology (MS), organizational psychology, organizational psychology and development (MS), organizational psychology and nonprofit management (MS), program evaluation and research (MS), psychology of culture (MS), psychology, public administration, and social change (MS), school psychology, social psychology (MS), terrorism and security (MS); school psychology (Post-Doctoral Certificate); teaching online (Post-Master's Certificate). Part-time and evening/weekend programs available. Postbaccalaureate distance learning degree programs offered (minimal on-campus study). *Faculty:* 16 full-time, 190 part-time/adjunct. *Students:* 3,198 full-time (2,489 women), 810 part-time (664 women); includes 1,319 minority (1,013 African Americans, 51 American Indian/Alaska Native, 68 Asian Americans or Pacific Islanders, 187 Hispanic Americans), 72 international. Average age 40. 1,468 applicants, 60% accepted, 612 enrolled. In 2008, 203 master's, 37 doctorates awarded. Terminal master's awarded for partial completion of doctoral program. *Degree requirements:* For master's, thesis optional; for doctorate, thesis/dissertation, residency. *Entrance requirements:* For master's, bachelor's degree or equivalent in related field, minimum GPA of 2.5, two references, goal statement, official transcripts, access to computer and Internet; for doctorate, master's degree or equivalent in related field, minimum GPA of 3.0, three years related professional/academic experience, two references, goal statement, official transcripts, access to computer and Internet. Additional exam requirements/recommendations for international students: Required—TOEFL (minimum score 550 paper-based; 213 computer-based), IELTS (minimum score 6.5), TOEFL, IELTS, or Michigan English Language Assessment Battery (minimum score 82). *Application deadline:* Applications are processed on a rolling basis. Application fee: $50. Electronic applications accepted. *Expenses:* Tuition: Full-time $12,877; part-time $520 per credit. Required fees: $1230. Tuition and fees vary according to course load, degree level and program. *Financial support:* In 2008–09, 1 fellowship was awarded; Federal Work-Study, scholarships/grants, unspecified assistantships, and family tuition reduction; active duty/veteran tuition reduction; group tuition reduction; interest-free payment plans also available. Support available to part-time students. Financial award applicants required to submit FAFSA. *Unit head:* Dr. Nina Nabors, Associate Dean, 800-925-3368. *Application contact:* Jennifer Hall, 866-4-WALDEN, E-mail: info@waldenu.edu.

Wayne State University, College of Liberal Arts and Sciences, Department of Psychology, Program in Psychology, Detroit, MI 48202. Offers behavioral and cognitive neuroscience (PhD); clinical psychology (PhD); cognitive and social psychology (PhD); industrial/organizational psychology (PhD); psychology (MA, MS). *Accreditation:* APA (one or more programs are accredited). *Degree requirements:* For doctorate, thesis/dissertation. *Entrance requirements:* For doctorate, GRE General Test, GRE Subject Test. Additional exam requirements/recommendations for international students: Required—TOEFL (minimum score 550 paper-based; 213 computer-based); Recommended—TWE (minimum score 6). Electronic applications accepted.

West Virginia University, Eberly College of Arts and Sciences, Department of Psychology, Morgantown, WV 26506. Offers behavior analysis (PhD); clinical psychology (MA, PhD); development psychology (PhD); psychology (MS). *Accreditation:* APA (one or more programs are accredited). Part-time programs available. Terminal master's awarded for partial completion of doctoral program. *Degree requirements:* For master's, thesis optional; for doctorate, comprehensive exam, thesis/dissertation. *Entrance requirements:* For master's and doctorate, GRE General Test, minimum GPA of 3.0. Additional exam requirements/recommendations for international students: Required—TOEFL. *Faculty research:* Adult and child clinical psychology, behavioral assessment and therapy, child and adolescent behavior, life span development, experimental and applied behavior analysis.

Wilfrid Laurier University, Faculty of Graduate Studies, Faculty of Science, Department of Psychology, Waterloo, ON N2L 3C5, Canada. Offers brain and cognition (M Sc, PhD); community psychology (MA, PhD); social and developmental psychology (MA, PhD). *Degree requirements:* For master's, thesis; for doctorate, thesis/dissertation. *Entrance requirements:* For master's, honors BA or the equivalent in psychology, minimum B average in undergraduate course work, GRE (General Test); for doctorate, master's degree, minimum A- average, GRE (General Test). Additional exam requirements/recommendations for international students: Required—TOEFL (minimum score 230 computer-based; 89 iBT). Electronic applications accepted. *Faculty research:* Brain and cognition, community psychology, social and developmental psychology.

Yale University, Graduate School of Arts and Sciences, Department of Psychology, New Haven, CT 06520. Offers behavioral neuroscience (PhD); clinical psychology (PhD); cognitive psychology (PhD); developmental psychology (PhD); social/personality psychology (PhD). *Accreditation:* APA. *Degree requirements:* For doctorate, thesis/dissertation. *Entrance requirements:* For doctorate, GRE General Test.

Experimental Psychology

American University, College of Arts and Sciences, Department of Psychology, Program in Psychology, Washington, DC 22016-8062. Offers experimental/biological psychology (MA); general psychology (MA); personality/social psychology (MA). Part-time programs available. *Students:* 39 full-time (33 women), 21 part-time (16 women); includes 12 minority (4 African Americans, 5 Asian Americans or Pacific Islanders, 3 Hispanic Americans), 1 international. Average age 26. 169 applicants, 33% accepted, 25 enrolled. In 2008, 21 master's awarded. *Degree requirements:* For master's, comprehensive exam, thesis or alternative. *Entrance requirements:* For master's, GRE General Test, GRE Subject Test. Additional exam requirements/recommendations for international students: Required—TOEFL. *Application deadline:* For fall admission, 3/1 for domestic students. Applications are processed on a rolling basis. Application fee: $80. *Expenses:* Tuition: Full-time $21,204; part-time $1178 per credit hour. Required fees: $380. Part-time tuition and fees vary according to course load and program. *Financial support:* Research assistantships, teaching assistantships available. Financial award application deadline: 2/1. *Faculty research:* Behavior therapy, cognitive behavior modification, pro-social behavior, conditioning and learning, olfaction. *Application contact:* Sara Holland, Senior Administrative Assistant, 202-885-1717, Fax: 202-885-1023.

Appalachian State University, Cratis D. Williams Graduate School, Department of Psychology, Boone, NC 28608. Offers clinical health psychology (MA); general experimental psychology (MA); industrial and organizational psychology (MA). Part-time programs available. *Faculty:* 31 full-time (11 women). *Students:* 59 full-time (45 women), 15 part-time (12 women); includes 3 minority (2 African Americans, 1 Asian American or Pacific Islander), 4 international. 185 applicants, 30% accepted, 18 enrolled. In 2008, 23 master's, 3 other advanced degrees awarded. *Degree requirements:* For master's and MA/SSP, comprehensive exam, thesis optional, GRE Subject Test exit exam. *Entrance requirements:* For master's and MA/SSP, GRE General Test, 3 letters of recommendation. Additional exam requirements/recommendations for international students: Required—TOEFL (minimum score 550 paper-based; 230 computer-based; 79 iBT), IELTS (minimum score 6.5), TOEFL or IELTS. *Application deadline:* For fall admission, 3/1 for domestic students, 2/1 for international students. Applications are processed on a rolling basis. Application fee: $50. Electronic applications accepted. *Expenses:* Tuition, area resident: Full-time $2600; part-time $700 per course. Tuition, state resident: full-time $2600; part-time $700 per course. Tuition, nonresident: full-time $5000; part-time $3300 per course. Required fees: $2150; $330 per course. Tuition and fees vary according to campus/location. *Financial support:* In 2008–09, 34 research assistantships (averaging $3,500 per year), 25 teaching assistantships (averaging $3,500 per year) were awarded; fellowships, career-related internships or fieldwork, Federal Work-Study, scholarships/grants, and unspecified assistantships also available. Financial award application deadline: 4/1; financial award applicants required to submit FAFSA. *Faculty research:* Eating disorders, school-based consultations, organizational behavior management, brain mechanisms of sound localization, parenting styles. Total annual research expenditures: $83,000. *Unit head:* Dr. James Denniston, Chair, 828-262-2272, Fax: 828-262-2272, E-mail: dennistonjc@appstate.edu. *Application contact:* Dr. Denise Martz, Graduate Coordinator, 828-262-2715, E-mail: martzdm@appstate.edu.

Auburn University, Graduate School, College of Liberal Arts, Department of Psychology, Auburn University, AL 36849. Offers applied behavior analysis in developmental disabilities (MS); clinical psychology (PhD); experimental psychology (PhD); industrial/organizational psychology (PhD). *Accreditation:* APA (one or more programs are accredited). Part-time programs available. *Faculty:* 24 full-time (6 women), 2 part-time/adjunct (both women). *Students:* 37 full-time (25 women), 57 part-time (33 women); includes 13 minority (7 African Americans, 2 Asian Americans or Pacific Islanders, 4 Hispanic Americans). Average age 27. 248 applicants, 13% accepted, 30 enrolled. In 2008, 27 master's, 11 doctorates awarded. *Degree requirements:* For doctorate, thesis/dissertation. *Entrance requirements:* For master's, GRE General Test, GRE Subject Test, minimum GPA of 3.25 in psychology, 3.0 overall; for doctorate, GRE General Test, GRE Subject Test. *Application deadline:* For fall admission, 7/7 for domestic students; for spring admission, 11/24 for domestic students. Applications are processed on a rolling basis. Application fee: $25 ($50 for international students). Electronic applications accepted. *Expenses:* Tuition, area resident: Full-time $5880; part-time $243 per credit hour. Tuition, state resident: full-time $5880; part-time $243 per credit hour. Tuition, nonresident: full-time $17,640; part-time $729 per credit hour. International tuition: $17,846 full-time. Required fees: $620. Tuition and fees vary according to program and reciprocity agreements. *Financial support:* Research assistantships, teaching assistantships, Federal Work-Study available. Support available to part-time students. Financial award application deadline: 3/15. *Faculty research:* Clinical psychology, learning, industrial psychology, organizational psychology. Total annual research expenditures: $200,000. *Unit head:* Dr. Barry Burkhart, Chair, 334-844-4412. *Application contact:* Dr. George Flowers, Dean of the Graduate School, 334-844-2125.

Bowling Green State University, Graduate College, College of Arts and Sciences, Department of Psychology, Bowling Green, OH 43403. Offers clinical psychology (MA, PhD); developmental psychology (MA, PhD); experimental psychology (MA, PhD); industrial/organizational psychology (MA, PhD); quantitative psychology (MA, PhD). *Accreditation:* APA (one or more programs are accredited). *Degree requirements:* For doctorate, thesis/dissertation. *Entrance requirements:* For doctorate, GRE General Test, GRE Subject Test. Additional exam requirements/recommendations for international students: Required—TOEFL. Electronic applications accepted. *Faculty research:* Personnel psychology, developmental-mathematical models, behavioral medication, brain process, child/adolescent social cognition.

Brooklyn College of the City University of New York, Division of Graduate Studies, Department of Psychology, Brooklyn, NY 11210-2889. Offers experimental psychology (MA); industrial and organizational psychology (MA), including industrial and organizational psychology-human relations, psychology-organizational psychology and behavior; mental health counseling (MA); psychology (PhD). The City University doctoral program in experimental psychology is based at Brooklyn College; candidates who complete the MA may apply for admission to the doctoral program. MA programs in industrial and organizational psychology and mental health counseling are fall admissions only. Part-time programs available. *Students:* 79 full-time (68 women), 121 part-time (93 women); includes 77 minority (48 African Americans, 1 American Indian/Alaska Native, 10 Asian Americans or Pacific Islanders, 18 Hispanic Americans), 18 international. Average age 31. 254 applicants, 59% accepted, 101 enrolled. In 2008, 48 master's awarded. *Degree requirements:* For master's, comprehensive exam, thesis (for some programs). *Entrance requirements:* For master's, minimum GPA of 3.0, 2 letters of recommendation, essay; for doctorate, GRE. Additional exam requirements/recommendations for international students: Required—TOEFL. *Application deadline:* For fall admission, 3/1 for domestic students, 2/1 for international students; for spring admission, 11/1 for domestic students, 10/1 for international students. Applications are processed on a rolling basis. Application fee: $125. Electronic applications accepted. *Expenses:* Tuition, state resident: full-time $7360; part-time $310 per credit hour. Tuition, nonresident: full-time $13,800; part-time $575 per credit hour. *Financial support:* Career-related internships or fieldwork, Federal Work-Study, institutionally sponsored loans, scholarships/grants, and tuition waivers (partial) available. Support available to part-time students. Financial award application deadline: 5/1; financial award applicants required to submit FAFSA. *Unit head:* Dr. Glen Hass, Chairperson, 718-951-5601, Fax: 718-951-4814, E-mail: ghass@brooklyn.cuny.edu. *Application contact:* Hernan Sierra, Graduate Admissions Coordinator, 718-951-4536, Fax: 718-951-4506, E-mail: grads@brooklyn.cuny.edu.

California State University, Northridge, Graduate Studies, College of Social and Behavioral Sciences, Department of Psychology, Northridge, CA 91330. Offers clinical psychology (MA); general-experimental psychology (MA); human factors and applied experimental psychology (MA). *Faculty:* 31 full-time (18 women), 24 part-time/adjunct (8 women). *Students:* 64 full-time (38 women), 15 part-time (10 women); includes 27 minority (2 African Americans, 6 Asian Americans or Pacific Islanders, 19 Hispanic Americans), 3 international. Average age 27. 136 applicants, 32% accepted, 35 enrolled. In 2008, 29 master's awarded. *Degree requirements:* For master's, thesis. *Entrance requirements:* For master's, GRE General Test, GRE Subject Test, minimum GPA of 3.0, letters of recommendation. Additional exam requirements/recommendations for international students: Required—TOEFL. *Application deadline:* For fall admission, 11/30 for domestic students. Application fee: $55. *Financial support:* Application deadline: 3/1. *Unit head:* Dr. Carrie Saetermoe, Chair, 818-677-3506. *Application contact:* Dr. Carrie Saetermoe, Chair, 818-677-3506.

California State University, San Bernardino, Graduate Studies, College of Social and Behavioral Sciences, Department of Psychology, Program in General/Experimental Psychology, San Bernardino, CA 92407-2397. Offers psychology (MA). *Students:* 32 full-time (26 women), 14 part-time (9 women); includes 13 minority (1 African American, 1 Asian American or Pacific Islander, 11 Hispanic Americans). Average age 28. 53 applicants, 36% accepted, 16 enrolled. In 2008, 4 master's awarded. *Degree requirements:* For master's, thesis. *Entrance requirements:* For master's, minimum GPA of 3.0 in major. *Application deadline:* For fall admission, 4/1 for domestic students; for spring admission, 3/1 for domestic students. Application fee: $55. *Expenses:* Tuition, area resident: Full-time $1252; part-time $726 per quarter. Required fees: $334 per quarter. Tuition and fees vary according to degree level and student level. *Financial support:* Unspecified assistantships available. *Unit head:* Dr. Robert Ricco, Director, 909-537-5485, Fax: 909-537-7003, E-mail: rricco@csusb.edu. *Application contact:* Stacy Brooks, Graduate Secretary, 909-537-5570, Fax: 909-537-7003, E-mail: sbrooks@csusb.edu.

Case Western Reserve University, School of Graduate Studies, Department of Psychology, Program in Experimental Psychology, Cleveland, OH 44106. Offers PhD. *Degree requirements:* For doctorate, thesis/dissertation, internship. *Entrance requirements:* For doctorate, GRE General Test, GRE Subject Test. Additional exam requirements/recommendations for international students: Required—TOEFL. Electronic applications accepted. *Faculty research:* Memory and intelligence, brain function in rats.

The Catholic University of America, School of Arts and Sciences, Department of Psychology, Washington, DC 20064. Offers applied experimental psychology (MA, PhD); clinical psychology (PhD); general psychology (MA, PhD); human development (PhD); human factors (MA); JD/MA. *Accreditation:* APA (one or more programs are accredited). Part-time programs available. Terminal master's awarded for partial completion of doctoral program. *Degree requirements:* For master's, comprehensive exam; for doctorate, comprehensive exam, thesis/dissertation. *Entrance requirements:* For master's, GRE General Test, 3 letters of recommendation; for doctorate, GRE General Test, GRE Subject Test, 3 letters of recommendation. Additional exam requirements/recommendations for international students: Required—TOEFL (minimum score 580 paper-based; 237 computer-based). Electronic applications accepted. *Faculty research:* Social development, family interaction, human perception and cognition, applied cognitive science, individual and group psychotherapy.

Central Michigan University, College of Graduate Studies, College of Humanities and Social and Behavioral Sciences, Department of Psychology, Program in Experimental Psychology, Mount Pleasant, MI 48859. Offers applied experimental psychology (PhD); experimental psychology (MS). Part-time programs available. *Students:* 13 full-time (7 women), 18 part-time (5 women); includes 1 African American, 1 Asian American or Pacific Islander, 3 international. Average age 27. *Degree requirements:* For master's, thesis or alternative; for doctorate, thesis/dissertation. *Application deadline:* For fall admission, 2/1 for domestic and international students. Application fee: $35 ($45 for international students). Electronic applications accepted. *Expenses:* Tuition, state resident: full-time $3717; part-time $413 per credit. Tuition, nonresident: full-time $6894; part-time $766 per credit. *Financial support:* In 2008–09, 3 fellowships with tuition reimbursements were awarded; research assistantships with tuition reimbursements, career-related internships or fieldwork, Federal Work-Study, unspecified assistantships, and out-of-state merit awards also available. *Faculty research:* Behavioral neuroscience; human development; perception and cognition; social/personal problem solving; psychophysiology. *Unit head:* Dr. Hajime Otani, Chairperson, 989-774-6494, Fax: 989-774-2553, E-mail: otani1h@cmich.edu. *Application contact:* Judith L. Prince, Director of Graduate Student Services, 989-774-1059, Fax: 989-774-1857, E-mail: judith.l.prince@cmich.edu.

Central Washington University, Graduate Studies, Research and Continuing Education, College of the Sciences, Department of Psychology, Program in Experimental Psychology,

Ellensburg, WA 98926. Offers MS. *Degree requirements:* For master's, thesis. *Entrance requirements:* For master's, GRE General Test, minimum GPA of 3.0. Additional exam requirements/recommendations for international students: Required—TOEFL (minimum score 550 paper-based; 213 computer-based; 79 iBT).

City College of the City University of New York, Graduate School, College of Liberal Arts and Science, Division of Social Science, Department of Psychology, New York, NY 10031-9198. Offers clinical psychology (PhD); experimental cognition (PhD); general psychology (MA); mental health counseling (MA). *Accreditation:* APA (one or more programs are accredited). Part-time programs available. *Degree requirements:* For master's, one foreign language, comprehensive exam, thesis. *Entrance requirements:* For master's, GRE. Additional exam requirements/recommendations for international students: Required—TOEFL (minimum score 550 paper-based; 213 computer-based). *Faculty research:* Social/personality psychology, physiological psychology, cognition and development.

Cleveland State University, College of Graduate Studies, College of Science, Department of Psychology, Cleveland, OH 44115. Offers adult development and aging (PhD); clinical psychology (MA); consumer/industrial research (MA); diversity management (MA); experimental research psychology (MA); school psychology (Psy S). *Faculty:* 20 full-time (7 women), 16 part-time/adjunct (8 women). *Students:* 66 full-time (44 women), 62 part-time (46 women); includes 25 minority (19 African Americans, 1 American Indian/Alaska Native, 2 Asian Americans or Pacific Islanders, 3 Hispanic Americans), 3 international. Average age 30. 180 applicants, 40% accepted, 55 enrolled. In 2008, 39 master's, 4 other advanced degrees awarded. *Degree requirements:* For master's, comprehensive exam (for some programs), thesis (for some programs); for doctorate, comprehensive exam, thesis/dissertation; for Psy S, internship. *Entrance requirements:* For master's and doctorate, GRE General Test. Additional exam requirements/recommendations for international students: Required—TOEFL (minimum score 525 paper-based; 197 computer-based). *Application deadline:* For fall admission, 2/1 priority date for domestic and international students. Applications are processed on a rolling basis. Application fee: $30. Electronic applications accepted. *Financial support:* In 2008–09, 45 students received support. Career-related internships or fieldwork, Federal Work-Study, tuition waivers (partial), and unspecified assistantships available. Financial award applicants required to submit FAFSA. *Faculty research:* Cognitive and social psychology, consumer psychology, clinical psychology, school psychology, aging. Total annual research expenditures: $112,607. *Unit head:* Dr. Albert F Smith, Interim Chair, 216-687-3723, Fax: 216-687-9294, E-mail: a.f.smith@csuohio.edu. *Application contact:* Karen R Colston, Administrative Coordinator, 216-687-2552, Fax: 216-687-9294, E-mail: k.colston@csuohio.edu.

Columbia University, Graduate School of Arts and Sciences, Division of Natural Sciences, Department of Psychology, New York, NY 10027. Offers experimental psychology (M Phil, MA, PhD); psychobiology (M Phil, MA, PhD); social psychology (M Phil, MA, PhD); JD/MA; JD/PhD; MD/PhD. *Degree requirements:* For master's, thesis; for doctorate, thesis/dissertation. *Entrance requirements:* For master's and doctorate, GRE General Test. Additional exam requirements/recommendations for international students: Required—TOEFL.

Cornell University, Graduate School, Graduate Fields of Arts and Sciences, Field of Psychology, Ithaca, NY 14853-0001. Offers biopsychology (PhD); human experimental psychology (PhD); personality and social psychology (PhD). *Faculty:* 42 full-time (15 women). *Students:* 35 full-time (19 women); includes 5 minority (1 African American, 2 Asian Americans or Pacific Islanders, 2 Hispanic Americans), 11 international. Average age 30. 179 applicants, 7% accepted, 7 enrolled. In 2008, 5 doctorates awarded. *Degree requirements:* For doctorate, comprehensive exam, thesis/dissertation, 2 semesters of teaching experience. *Entrance requirements:* For doctorate, GRE General Test, 3 letters of recommendation. Additional exam requirements/recommendations for international students: Required—TOEFL (minimum score 550 paper-based; 213 computer-based; 77 iBT). *Application deadline:* For fall admission, 12/15 for domestic students. Application fee: $70. Electronic applications accepted. *Expenses:* Tuition: Full-time $29,500. Required fees: $70. Full-time tuition and fees vary according to degree level, program and student level. *Financial support:* In 2008–09, 36 students received support, including 10 fellowships with full tuition reimbursements available, 2 research assistantships with full tuition reimbursements available, 24 teaching assistantships with full tuition reimbursements available; institutionally sponsored loans, scholarships/grants, health care benefits, tuition waivers (full and partial), and unspecified assistantships also available. Financial award applicants required to submit FAFSA. *Faculty research:* Sensory and perceptual systems, social cognition, cognitive development, quantitative and computational modeling, behavioral neuroscience. *Unit head:* Director of Graduate Studies, 607-255-6364, Fax: 607-255-8433. *Application contact:* Graduate Field Assistant, 607-255-3834, Fax: 607-255-8433, E-mail: psychapp@cornell.edu.

Dallas Baptist University, Gary Cook School of Leadership, Program in Christian Education, Dallas, TX 75211-9299. Offers adult ministry (MA); business ministry (MA); childhood ministry (MA); collegiate ministry (MA); communication ministry (MA); counseling ministry (MA); education ministry (MA); general ministry (MA); missions ministry (MA); student ministry (MA); worship ministry (MA). Part-time and evening/weekend programs available. *Faculty:* 68 full-time (30 women), 113 part-time/adjunct (47 women). *Students:* 13 full-time, 55 part-time. 45 applicants. In 2008, 22 master's awarded. *Entrance requirements:* For master's, minimum GPA of 3.0. Additional exam requirements/recommendations for international students: Required—TOEFL. *Application deadline:* Applications are processed on a rolling basis. Application fee: $25. Electronic applications accepted. *Expenses:* Tuition: Part-time $558 per credit hour. *Financial support:* Federal Work-Study, institutionally sponsored loans, scholarships/grants, and tuition waivers (full and partial) available. Support available to part-time students. Financial award applicants required to submit FAFSA. *Unit head:* Dr. Judy Morris, Director, 214-333-5246, Fax: 214-333-5115, E-mail: graduate@dbu.edu. *Application contact:* Kit P. Montgomery, Director of Graduate Programs, 214-333-5242, Fax: 214-333-5579, E-mail: graduate@dbu.edu.

DePaul University, College of Liberal Arts and Sciences, Department of Psychology, Chicago, IL 60604-2287. Offers clinical psychology (MA, PhD), including child clinical psychology, community clinical psychology; experimental psychology (MA, PhD); general psychology (MS); industrial/organizational psychology (MA, PhD); MA/PhD. *Accreditation:* APA (one or more programs are accredited). *Faculty:* 31 full-time (19 women), 6 part-time/adjunct (4 women). *Students:* 33 full-time (17 women), 23 part-time (20 women); includes 9 minority (4 African Americans, 1 American Indian/Alaska Native, 1 Asian American or Pacific Islander, 3 Hispanic Americans), 2 international. Average age 28. 332 applicants, 14% accepted, 23 enrolled. In 2008, 14 master's, 17 doctorates awarded. *Degree requirements:* For master's, thesis, oral exam; for doctorate, comprehensive exam, thesis/dissertation, oral and written exams. *Entrance requirements:* For master's and doctorate, GRE General Test, GRE Subject Test, 32 quarter hours of course work in psychology, 3 letters of recommendation. Additional exam requirements/recommendations for international students: Required—TOEFL. Application fee: $40. Electronic applications accepted. *Financial support:* In 2008–09, 48 students received support, including 35 research assistantships with full tuition reimbursements available (averaging $11,800 per year), 13 teaching assistantships with full tuition reimbursements available (averaging $11,800 per year); career-related internships or fieldwork, scholarships/grants, traineeships, tuition waivers (full and partial), and unspecified assistantships also available. Financial award application deadline: 1/10. *Faculty research:* Adolescent stress and depression, minority adolescents sexuality, public policy, community influences in child adjustment. *Unit head:* Dr. Christopher B Keys, Chairman, 773-325-7887, Fax: 773-325-7888. *Application contact:* Alison Pereida Knapp, Graduate Admissions Assistant, 773-325-7887, Fax: 773-325-7888.

Duke University, Graduate School, Department of Psychology, Durham, NC 27708-0586. Offers biological psychology (PhD); clinical psychology (PhD); cognitive psychology (PhD); developmental psychology (PhD); experimental psychology (PhD); health psychology (PhD); human social development (PhD); JD/MA. *Accreditation:* APA (one or more programs are accredited). *Degree requirements:* For doctorate, thesis/dissertation. *Entrance requirements:* For doctorate, GRE General Test. Additional exam requirements/recommendations for inter-

Experimental Psychology

Duke University (continued)
national students: Required—TOEFL (minimum score 550 paper-based; 213 computer-based; 83 iBT), IELTS (minimum score 7). Electronic applications accepted.

Eastern Washington University, Graduate Studies, College of Social and Behavioral Sciences, Department of Psychology, Cheney, WA 99004-2431. Offers clinical psychology (MS); experimental psychology (MS); psychology (MS); school psychology (MS). *Degree requirements:* For master's, comprehensive exam, thesis or alternative. *Entrance requirements:* For master's, GRE General Test, minimum GPA of 3.0.

Fairleigh Dickinson University, Metropolitan Campus, University College: Arts, Sciences, and Professional Studies, School of Psychology, Program in General-Theoretical Psychology, Teaneck, NJ 07666-1914. Offers MA, Certificate. *Students:* 18 full-time (14 women), 13 part-time (9 women), 4 international. Average age 29. 30 applicants, 93% accepted, 14 enrolled. In 2008, 10 master's awarded. *Application deadline:* Applications are processed on a rolling basis. Application fee: $40. *Application contact:* Susan Brooman, University Director of Graduate Admissions, 201-692-2554, Fax: 201-692-2560, E-mail: globaleducation@fdu.edu.

Georgia Institute of Technology, Graduate Studies and Research, College of Sciences, School of Psychology, Atlanta, GA 30332-0001. Offers human computer interaction (MSHCI); psychology (MS, MS Psy, PhD), including engineering psychology (PhD), experimental psychology (PhD), industrial/organizational psychology (PhD). Terminal master's awarded for partial completion of doctoral program. *Degree requirements:* For master's, thesis; for doctorate, thesis/dissertation. *Entrance requirements:* For master's and doctorate, GRE General Test, GRE Subject Test, minimum GPA of 3.0. Additional exam requirements/recommendations for international students: Required—TOEFL. Electronic applications accepted. *Faculty research:* Experimental, industrial-organizational, and engineering psychology; cognitive aging and processes; leadership; human factors.

Graduate School and University Center of the City University of New York, Graduate Studies, Program in Psychology, New York, NY 10016-4039. Offers basic applied neurocognition (PhD); biopsychology (PhD); clinical psychology (PhD); developmental psychology (PhD); environmental psychology (PhD); experimental psychology (PhD); industrial psychology (PhD); learning processes (PhD); neuropsychology (PhD); psychology (PhD); social personality (PhD). *Degree requirements:* For doctorate, one foreign language, thesis/dissertation. *Entrance requirements:* For doctorate, GRE General Test. Additional exam requirements/recommendations for international students: Required—TOEFL. Electronic applications accepted.

Harvard University, Graduate School of Arts and Sciences, Department of Psychology, Cambridge, MA 02138. Offers psychology (PhD), including behavior and decision analysis, cognition, developmental psychology, experimental psychology, personality, psychobiology, psychopathology; social psychology (PhD). *Degree requirements:* For doctorate, thesis/dissertation, general exams. *Entrance requirements:* For doctorate, GRE General Test. Additional exam requirements/recommendations for international students: Required—TOEFL. *Expenses:* Tuition: Full-time $32,556. Required fees: $1426. Full-time tuition and fees vary according to program and student level.

Howard University, Graduate School, Department of Psychology, Washington, DC 20059-0002. Offers clinical psychology (PhD); developmental psychology (PhD); experimental psychology (PhD); neuropsychology (PhD); personality psychology (PhD); psychology (MS); social psychology (PhD). *Accreditation:* APA (one or more programs are accredited). Part-time programs available. *Degree requirements:* For master's, thesis; for doctorate, comprehensive exam, thesis/dissertation, qualifying exam. *Entrance requirements:* For master's, GRE General Test, minimum GPA of 2.5, bachelor's degree in psychology or related field; for doctorate, GRE General Test, minimum GPA of 3.0. *Faculty research:* Personality and psychophysiology, educational and social development of African-American children, child and adult psychopathology.

Illinois State University, Graduate School, College of Arts and Sciences, Department of Psychology, Normal, IL 61790-2200. Offers psychology (MA, MS), including clinical psychology, counseling psychology, developmental psychology, educational psychology, experimental psychology, measurement-evaluation, organizational-industrial psychology; school psychology (PhD, SSP). *Accreditation:* APA. *Degree requirements:* For master's, thesis or alternative; for doctorate, variable foreign language requirement, thesis/dissertation, 2 terms of residency, internship, practicum. *Entrance requirements:* For master's, GRE General Test, GRE Subject Test, minimum GPA of 3.0 in last 60 hours of course work; for doctorate, GRE General Test. *Faculty research:* Comprehensive evaluation system for the central region professional development grant, Illinois school psychology internship consortium, for children's sake.

Iona College, School of Arts and Science, Department of Psychology, New Rochelle, NY 10801-1890. Offers experimental psychology (MA); industrial-organizational psychology (MA); mental health counseling (MA); psychology (MA); school psychology (MA). Part-time and evening/weekend programs available. *Faculty:* 11 full-time (5 women), 6 part-time/adjunct (3 women). *Students:* 71 full-time (54 women), 42 part-time (35 women); includes 26 minority (9 African Americans, 5 Asian Americans or Pacific Islanders, 12 Hispanic Americans), 1 international. Average age 25. 120 applicants, 73% accepted, 39 enrolled. In 2008, 19 master's awarded. *Degree requirements:* For master's, thesis. *Entrance requirements:* For master's, GRE or minimum GPA of 3.0. Additional exam requirements/recommendations for international students: Required—TOEFL (minimum score 550 paper-based; 213 computer-based). *Application deadline:* Applications are processed on a rolling basis. Application fee: $50. Electronic applications accepted. *Expenses:* Tuition: Part-time $755 per credit. Required fees: $175 per term. *Financial support:* Career-related internships or fieldwork, tuition waivers (partial), and unspecified assistantships available. Support available to part-time students. Financial award application deadline: 4/15; financial award applicants required to submit FAFSA. *Unit head:* Dr. Pauline Jirik-Babb, Chair, 914-633-2191, E-mail: pjirikbabb@iona.edu. *Application contact:* Veronica Jarek-Prinz, Director of Graduate Admissions, 914-633-2420, Fax: 914-633-2277, E-mail: vjarekprinz@iona.edu.

Kent State University, College of Arts and Sciences, Department of Psychology, Kent, OH 44242-0001. Offers clinical psychology (MA, PhD); experimental psychology (MA, PhD). *Accreditation:* APA (one or more programs are accredited). *Degree requirements:* For master's, thesis; for doctorate, thesis/dissertation. *Entrance requirements:* For master's, GRE, minimum GPA of 3.0, minimum 18 semester hours in psychology with one course in statistics and one experimental course with a lab component; for doctorate, GRE, minimum GPA of 3.0. Additional exam requirements/recommendations for international students: Required—TOEFL (minimum score 525 paper-based), Michigan English Language Assessment Battery (minimum score: 77).

Lakehead University, Graduate Studies, Department of Psychology, Thunder Bay, ON P7B 5E1, Canada. Offers clinical psychology (PhD); experimental psychology (MA). Part-time and evening/weekend programs available. *Degree requirements:* For master's, thesis optional; for doctorate, thesis/dissertation, 2 comprehensive exams, internship. *Entrance requirements:* For master's, GRE, honors degree in psychology, advanced course work in statistics, minimum B average; for doctorate, GRE, minimum B average. Additional exam requirements/recommendations for international students: Required—TOEFL. Tuition charges are reported in Canadian dollars. *Expenses:* Tuition, area resident: Full-time $6500 Canadian dollars. International tuition: $13,700 Canadian dollars full-time. *Faculty research:* Chaos theory, health psychology, counseling psychology, gerontology, women's studies.

Laurentian University, School of Graduate Studies and Research, Programme in Psychology, Sudbury, ON P3E 2C6, Canada. Offers applied psychology (MA); experimental psychology (MA).

McGill University, Faculty of Graduate and Postdoctoral Studies, Faculty of Science, Department of Psychology, Montréal, QC H3A 2T5, Canada. Offers clinical psychology (PhD); experimental psychology (M Sc, MA, PhD). *Accreditation:* APA (one or more programs are accredited).

McNeese State University, Doré School of Graduate Studies, Burton College of Education, Department of Psychology, Lake Charles, LA 70609. Offers addiction treatment (MA); applied behavior analysis (MA); counseling psychology (MA); general/experimental psychology (MA). Evening/weekend programs available. *Faculty:* 6 full-time (3 women), 1 (woman) part-time/adjunct. *Students:* 40 full-time (27 women), 23 part-time (17 women); includes 8 minority (7 African Americans, 1 Asian American or Pacific Islander), 4 international. In 2008, 12 master's awarded. *Entrance requirements:* For master's, GRE. *Application deadline:* For fall admission, 5/15 priority date for domestic and international students; for spring admission, 10/15 priority date for domestic and international students. Applications are processed on a rolling basis. Application fee: $20 ($30 for international students). *Expenses:* Tuition, area resident: Full-time $2386. Tuition, state resident: full-time $2386. Required fees: $885. Tuition and fees vary according to course load. *Financial support:* Application deadline: 5/1. *Unit head:* Dr. Dena L. Matzenbacher, Head, 337-475-5457, Fax: 337-562-4115, E-mail: dena@mcneese.edu. *Application contact:* Dr. George F. Mead, Interim Dean of Dore' School of Graduate Studies, 337-475-5396, Fax: 337-475-5397, E-mail: admissions@mcneese.edu.

Memorial University of Newfoundland, School of Graduate Studies, Department of Psychology, St. John's, NL A1C 5S7, Canada. Offers applied social psychology (MASP); experimental psychology (M Sc, PhD). Part-time programs available. *Degree requirements:* For master's, workterms (MASP), thesis (M Sc); for doctorate, comprehensive exam, thesis/dissertation, oral thesis defense. *Entrance requirements:* For master's, GRE, honors bachelor's degree of high second class standing or equivalent; for doctorate, GRE, master's or honors degree. Electronic applications accepted. *Faculty research:* Behavioral neuroscience, cognition, theory and research on abnormal behavior.

Miami University, Graduate School, College of Arts and Sciences, Department of Psychology, Oxford, OH 45056. Offers clinical psychology (PhD); experimental psychology (PhD); social psychology (PhD). *Accreditation:* APA. *Degree requirements:* For doctorate, comprehensive exam, thesis/dissertation, final exams. *Entrance requirements:* For doctorate, GRE General Test, GRE Subject Test, minimum GPA of 2.75 (undergraduate), 3.0 (graduate). Additional exam requirements/recommendations for international students: Required—TOEFL (minimum score 550 paper-based; 213 computer-based), TWE (minimum score 4). Electronic applications accepted.

Mississippi State University, College of Arts and Sciences, Department of Psychology, Mississippi State, MS 39762. Offers clinical psychology (MS); cognitive science (PhD); experimental psychology (MS). Terminal master's awarded for partial completion of doctoral program. *Degree requirements:* For master's, comprehensive exam, thesis; for doctorate, thesis/dissertation, qualifying exam, comprehensive written and oral exam. *Entrance requirements:* For master's, GRE General Test, minimum GPA of 2.75; for doctorate, GRE General Test, proficiency in at least 1 computer language. Additional exam requirements/recommendations for international students: Required—TOEFL. *Faculty research:* Personality type, alcoholism, blindness and low vision, mental retardation, language comprehension.

Missouri State University, Graduate College, College of Health and Human Services, Department of Psychology, Springfield, MO 65804-0094. Offers psychology (MS), including clinical, experimental, industrial/organizational. *Faculty:* 26 full-time (10 women), 1 part-time/adjunct (0 women). *Students:* 44 full-time (30 women), 3 part-time (all women); includes 1 minority (Hispanic American). Average age 24. 71 applicants, 45% accepted, 20 enrolled. In 2008, 17 master's awarded. *Degree requirements:* For master's, comprehensive exam, thesis. *Entrance requirements:* For master's, GRE General Test, GRE Subject Test, minimum GPA of 3.25 in major, 3.0 overall; 20 hours of course work in psychology (experimental and statistics). Additional exam requirements/recommendations for international students: Required—TOEFL (minimum score 550 paper-based; 213 computer-based; 79 iBT). *Application deadline:* For fall admission, 3/1 priority date for domestic and international students. Application fee: $35 ($50 for international students). Electronic applications accepted. *Expenses:* Tuition, state resident: full-time $3852; part-time $214 per credit hour. Tuition, nonresident: full-time $7524; part-time $418 per credit hour. Required fees: $230 per semester. Tuition and fees vary according to course level and course load. *Financial support:* In 2008–09, 10 research assistantships with full tuition reimbursements (averaging $7,340 per year), 3 teaching assistantships with full tuition reimbursements (averaging $9,730 per year) were awarded; career-related internships or fieldwork, Federal Work-Study, institutionally sponsored loans, scholarships/grants, and unspecified assistantships also available. Financial award application deadline: 3/31; financial award applicants required to submit FAFSA. *Faculty research:* Work-family conflict, child forensic psychology, sports psychology, body image assessment, visual learning. *Unit head:* Dr. Robert G. Jones, Head, 417-836-5797, Fax: 417-836-830, E-mail: psychology@missouristate.edu. *Application contact:* Eric Eckert, Coordinator of Admissions and Recruitment, 417-836-5331, Fax: 417-836-6888, E-mail: ericeckert@missouristate.edu.

Morehead State University, Graduate Programs, College of Science and Technology, Department of Psychology, Morehead, KY 40351. Offers clinical psychology (MS); counseling psychology (MS); experimental/general psychology (MS). Part-time programs available. *Faculty:* 8 full-time (3 women). *Students:* 22 full-time (18 women), 3 part-time (1 woman). Average age 26. 30 applicants, 53% accepted, 9 enrolled. In 2008, 10 master's awarded. *Degree requirements:* For master's, comprehensive exam, thesis optional. *Entrance requirements:* For master's, GRE General Test, 18 undergraduate hours in psychology, minimum GPA of 3.0. Additional exam requirements/recommendations for international students: Required—TOEFL (minimum score 500 paper-based; 173 computer-based). *Application deadline:* For fall admission, 8/1 priority date for domestic and international students; for spring admission, 12/1 for domestic students, 12/1 priority date for international students. Applications are processed on a rolling basis. Application fee: $30 ($55 for international students). Electronic applications accepted. *Expenses:* Tuition, area resident: Full-time $6084; part-time $338 per credit hour. Tuition, state resident: full-time $6084; part-time $338 per credit hour. Tuition, nonresident: full-time $15,804; part-time $878 per credit hour. *Financial support:* In 2008–09, 19 research assistantships (averaging $6,000 per year) were awarded; career-related internships or fieldwork, Federal Work-Study, and institutionally sponsored loans also available. Financial award application deadline: 4/1; financial award applicants required to submit FAFSA. *Faculty research:* Mood induction effects, serotonin receptor activity, stress, perceptual processes. *Unit head:* Dr. Laurie Couch, Interim Department Chair. *Application contact:* Michelle Barber, Graduate Admissions Counselor, 606-783-2039, Fax: 606-783-5061, E-mail: m.barber@moreheadstate.edu.

North Carolina State University, Graduate School, College of Humanities and Social Sciences, Department of Psychology, Raleigh, NC 27695. Offers developmental psychology (PhD); ergonomics and experimental psychology (PhD); industrial/organizational psychology (PhD); psychology in the public interest (PhD); school psychology (PhD). *Accreditation:* APA. *Degree requirements:* For doctorate, comprehensive exam, thesis/dissertation. *Entrance requirements:* For doctorate, GRE General Test, GRE Subject Test (industrial/organizational psychology), MAT (recommended), minimum GPA of 3.0 in major. Electronic applications accepted. *Faculty research:* Cognitive and social development (human factors, families, the workplace, community issues and health, aging).

Northeastern University, College of Arts and Sciences, Department of Psychology, Boston, MA 02115-5096. Offers experimental psychology (MA, PhD). *Degree requirements:* For doctorate, thesis/dissertation. *Entrance requirements:* For doctorate, GRE General Test. Additional exam requirements/recommendations for international students: Required—TOEFL. *Faculty research:* Behavioral, neuroscience language and cognition, perception, personality and social.

Ohio University, Graduate College, College of Arts and Sciences, Department of Psychology, Program in Experimental Psychology, Athens, OH 45701-2979. Offers PhD. *Degree requirements:* For doctorate, one foreign language, comprehensive exam, thesis/dissertation. *Entrance requirements:* For doctorate, GRE General Test, GRE Subject Test, minimum graduate GPA of 3.4. Additional exam requirements/recommendations for international students: Required—TOEFL. *Faculty research:* Cognitive psychology, quantitative psychology, social psychology, judgment and decision making, health psychology.

Old Dominion University, College of Sciences, Doctoral Program in Psychology, Norfolk, VA 23529. Offers applied experimental psychology (PhD); human factors psychology (PhD); industrial/organizational psychology (PhD). *Faculty:* 17 full-time (7 women), 1 part-time/adjunct (0 women). *Students:* 16 full-time (7 women), 20 part-time (15 women); includes 1 minority (Hispanic American). Average age 29. 65 applicants, 18% accepted, 10 enrolled. In 2008, 6 doctorates awarded. *Degree requirements:* For doctorate, thesis/dissertation, qualifying exam. *Entrance requirements:* For doctorate, GRE General Test, GRE Subject Test, 3 recommendation letters. Additional exam requirements/recommendations for international students: Required—TOEFL (minimum score 550 paper-based). *Application deadline:* For winter admission, 1/5 for domestic and international students. Application fee: $40. *Expenses:* Tuition, area resident: Full-time $7704; part-time $321 per credit. Tuition, state resident: full-time $7704; part-time $321 per credit. Tuition, nonresident: full-time $19,104; part-time $796 per credit. Required fees: $99 per semester. One-time fee: $40. *Financial support:* In 2008–09, 13 students received support, including 2 fellowships with full tuition reimbursements available (averaging $18,000 per year), research assistantships with full tuition reimbursements available (averaging $12,000 per year), 11 teaching assistantships with full tuition reimbursements available (averaging $12,000 per year). Financial award application deadline: 1/15. *Faculty research:* Human-computer interaction, simulation, neuroergonomics, attention and workload. Total annual research expenditures: $399,161. *Unit head:* Dr. Barbara Winstead, Graduate Program Director, 757-683-4239, Fax: 757-683-5087, E-mail: psychgpd@odu.edu. *Application contact:* Dr. Barbara Winstead, Graduate Program Director, 757-683-4239, Fax: 757-683-5087, E-mail: psychgpd@odu.edu.

Radford University, College of Graduate and Professional Studies, College of Humanities and Behavioral Sciences, Program in Psychology, Radford, VA 24142. Offers clinical psychology (MA, MS); counseling psychology (Psy D); experimental psychology (MA); general psychology (MS); industrial/organizational psychology (MA, MS); school psychology (Ed S). Part-time programs available. *Faculty:* 23 full-time (9 women), 1 part-time/adjunct (0 women). *Students:* 46 full-time (28 women), 5 part-time (4 women); includes 4 minority (3 African Americans, 1 Asian American or Pacific Islander), 2 international. Average age 26. 114 applicants, 42% accepted, 20 enrolled. In 2008, 36 master's awarded. *Degree requirements:* For master's, comprehensive exam, thesis (for some programs). *Entrance requirements:* For master's, GRE, minimum GPA of 3.0; 3 letters of reference; essay. Additional exam requirements/recommendations for international students: Required—TOEFL (minimum score 550 paper-based; 213 computer-based; 79 iBT). *Application deadline:* For fall admission, 3/1 priority date for domestic students, 12/1 for international students; for spring admission, 10/1 for domestic students, 7/1 for international students. Applications are processed on a rolling basis. Application fee: $40. Electronic applications accepted. *Expenses:* Tuition, area resident: Full-time $4845; part-time $202 per credit. Tuition, state resident: full-time $4845; part-time $202 per credit. Tuition, nonresident: full-time $11,483; part-time $478 per credit. Required fees: $2349; $98 per credit. *Financial support:* In 2008–09, 47 students received support, including 33 research assistantships with partial tuition reimbursements available (averaging $8,000 per year), 12 teaching assistantships with partial tuition reimbursements available (averaging $8,700 per year); career-related internships or fieldwork, institutionally sponsored loans, scholarships/grants, and unspecified assistantships also available. Financial award application deadline: 3/1; financial award applicants required to submit FAFSA. *Unit head:* Dr. Hilary M. Lips, Chair, 540-831-5387, Fax: 540-831-6113, E-mail: hlips@radford.edu. *Application contact:* Graduate Admissions Office, 540-831-5431, Fax: 540-831-6061, E-mail: gradcollege@radford.edu.

St. John's University, St. John's College of Liberal Arts and Sciences, Department of Psychology, Program in General Experimental Psychology, Queens, NY 11439. Offers MA. Part-time and evening/weekend programs available. *Students:* 8 full-time (7 women), 7 part-time (6 women); includes 4 minority (1 Asian American or Pacific Islander, 3 Hispanic Americans), 2 international. Average age 25. 22 applicants, 68% accepted, 6 enrolled. In 2008, 4 master's awarded. *Degree requirements:* For master's, comprehensive exam, thesis optional. *Entrance requirements:* For master's, minimum GPA of 3.0, 2 writing samples. Additional exam requirements/recommendations for international students: Required—TOEFL (minimum score 500 paper-based; 173 computer-based; 61 iBT), IELTS (minimum score 5.5). *Application deadline:* For fall admission, 5/1 priority date for domestic and international students; for spring admission, 11/1 priority date for domestic and international students. Applications are processed on a rolling basis. Application fee: $70. Electronic applications accepted. *Expenses:* Tuition: Full-time $20,760; part-time $865 per credit. Required fees: $300; $150 per semester. Tuition and fees vary according to program. *Financial support:* Research assistantships, career-related internships or fieldwork, scholarships/grants, and unspecified assistantships available. Support available to part-time students. Financial award application deadline: 3/1; financial award applicants required to submit FAFSA. *Faculty research:* Learning and memory neuropsychology, perception, social psychology, developmental psychology. *Unit head:* Dr. Leonard Brosgole, Coordinator, 718-990-1552, E-mail: brosgoll@stjohns.edu. *Application contact:* Kathleen Davis, Director of Graduate Admission, 718-990-2790, Fax: 718-990-5686, E-mail: gradhelp@stjohns.edu.

Saint Louis University, Graduate School, College of Arts and Sciences and Graduate School, Department of Psychology, St. Louis, MO 63103-2097. Offers clinical psychology (MS-R, PhD); experimental psychology (MS-R, PhD); industrial-organizational psychology (PhD); psychology (PhD). *Accreditation:* APA (one or more programs are accredited). Part-time programs available. *Degree requirements:* For master's, comprehensive exam, thesis; for doctorate, thesis/dissertation, clinical internship (for clinical psychology PhD). *Entrance requirements:* For master's and doctorate, GRE General Test, interview, letters of recommendation, resumé, transcripts, goal statement. Additional exam requirements/recommendations for international students: Required—TOEFL (minimum score 550 paper-based; 213 computer-based). Electronic applications accepted. *Faculty research:* Violence and trauma; neural basis of learning and memory function; eating disorders; body image and health behavior; prejudice, stereotyping, and victimization; memory, cognitive aging and language processing.

San Jose State University, Graduate Studies and Research, College of Social Sciences, Department of Psychology, San Jose, CA 95192-0001. Offers clinical psychology (MS); experimental psychology (MA); industrial/organizational psychology (MS); psychology (MA). *Degree requirements:* For master's, comprehensive exam, thesis (for some programs). *Entrance requirements:* For master's, GRE General Test, minimum GPA of 3.0. Electronic applications accepted. *Faculty research:* Drug and alcohol abuse, neurohormonal mechanisms in motion sickness, behavior modification, sleep research, genetics.

Seton Hall University, College of Arts and Sciences, Department of Psychology, South Orange, NJ 07079-2697. Offers experimental psychology (MS), including behavioral neuroscience. Part-time and evening/weekend programs available. *Entrance requirements:* Additional exam requirements/recommendations for international students: Required—TOEFL. Electronic applications accepted. *Faculty research:* Behavioral neuroscience, cognitive psychology, social psychology, perception/motor skills, memory, depression, anxiety.

See Close-Up on page 1133.

Southern Illinois University Carbondale, Graduate School, College of Liberal Arts, Department of Psychology, Carbondale, IL 62901-4701. Offers clinical psychology (MA, MS, PhD); counseling psychology (MA, MS, PhD); experimental psychology (MA, MS, PhD). *Accreditation:* APA (one or more programs are accredited). *Degree requirements:* For master's, thesis; for doctorate, thesis/dissertation. *Entrance requirements:* For master's, GRE General Test, GRE Subject Test, minimum GPA of 2.7; for doctorate, GRE General Test, GRE Subject Test, minimum GPA of 3.25. Additional exam requirements/recommendations for international students: Required—TOEFL. *Faculty research:* Developmental neuropsychology; smoking, affect, and cognition; personality measurement; vocational psychology; program evaluation.

See Close-Up on page 1135.

Stony Brook University, State University of New York, Graduate School, College of Arts and Sciences, Department of Psychology, Program in Cognitive/Experimental Psychology, Stony Brook, NY 11794. Offers PhD. *Students:* 16 full-time (7 women); includes 1 minority (Hispanic American), 2 international. Average age 28. 36 applicants, 28% accepted. In 2008, 4 doctorates awarded. *Degree requirements:* For doctorate, thesis/dissertation. *Entrance requirements:* For doctorate, GRE General Test, GRE Subject Test. Additional exam requirements/recommendations for international students: Required—TOEFL. *Application deadline:* For fall admission, 1/15 for domestic students. Application fee: $60. *Expenses:* Tuition, area resident: Full-time $7880; part-time $328 per credit hour. Tuition, state resident: full-time $7880; part-time $328 per credit hour. Tuition, nonresident: full-time $13,250; part-time $552 per credit hour. Required fees: $848. *Unit head:* Dr. Nancy Franklin, Head, 631-632-7840, E-mail: nancy.franklin@stonybrook.edu. *Application contact:* Graduate Director, 631-632-7792, Fax: 631-632-7876.

Syracuse University, Graduate School, College of Arts and Sciences, Program in Experimental Psychology, Syracuse, NY 13244. Offers PhD. Part-time programs available. *Degree requirements:* For doctorate, thesis/dissertation. *Entrance requirements:* For doctorate, GRE General Test. Additional exam requirements/recommendations for international students: Required—TOEFL.

Texas Tech University, Graduate School, College of Arts and Sciences, Department of Psychology, Lubbock, TX 79409. Offers clinical psychology (PhD); counseling psychology (MA, PhD); experimental psychology (MA, PhD); psychology (MA, PhD). *Accreditation:* APA (one or more programs are accredited). Part-time programs available. *Faculty:* 25 full-time (11 women). *Students:* 87 full-time (58 women), 20 part-time (13 women); includes 16 minority (5 African Americans, 1 American Indian/Alaska Native, 2 Asian Americans or Pacific Islanders, 8 Hispanic Americans), 6 international. Average age 28. 290 applicants, 13% accepted, 17 enrolled. In 2008, 13 master's, 6 doctorates awarded. *Degree requirements:* For doctorate, thesis/dissertation. *Entrance requirements:* For master's and doctorate, GRE General Test, GRE Subject Test. Additional exam requirements/recommendations for international students: Required—TOEFL (minimum score 550 paper-based; 213 computer-based). *Application deadline:* For fall admission, 3/1 priority date for international students; for spring admission, 11/1 priority date for international students. Applications are processed on a rolling basis. Application fee: $50 ($60 for international students). Electronic applications accepted. *Expenses:* Tuition, area resident: Part-time $194 per credit hour. Tuition, state resident: full-time $4648; part-time $194 per credit hour. Tuition, nonresident: full-time $11,392; part-time $475 per credit hour. Required fees: $2206; $69 per credit hour. $389 per semester. *Financial support:* In 2008–09, 91 students received support, including 4 research assistantships with partial tuition reimbursements available (averaging $12,762 per year), 69 teaching assistantships with partial tuition reimbursements available (averaging $11,835 per year); career-related internships or fieldwork, Federal Work-Study, and institutionally sponsored loans also available. Support available to part-time students. Financial award application deadline: 4/15; financial award applicants required to submit FAFSA. *Faculty research:* Failure/success in relationships, peer rejection in school, stress and coping, group processes, clinical and health psychology. Total annual research expenditures: $564,495. *Unit head:* Dr. Susan S. Hendrick, Chair, 806-742-3711 Ext. 224, Fax: 806-742-0818, E-mail: s.hendrick@ttu.edu. *Application contact:* Dr. Lee M. Cohen, Director of Clinical Program, 806-742-3711 Ext. 254, Fax: 806-742-0818, E-mail: lee.cohen@ttu.edu.

University at Albany, State University of New York, College of Arts and Sciences, Department of Psychology, Albany, NY 12222-0001. Offers autism (Certificate); biopsychology (PhD); clinical psychology (PhD); general/experimental psychology (PhD); industrial/organizational psychology (PhD); psychology (MA); social/personality psychology (PhD). *Accreditation:* APA (one or more programs are accredited). *Degree requirements:* For doctorate, thesis/dissertation. *Entrance requirements:* For doctorate, GRE General Test, GRE Subject Test. Additional exam requirements/recommendations for international students: Required—TOEFL (minimum score 550 paper-based; 213 computer-based). Electronic applications accepted.

The University of Alabama, Graduate School, College of Arts and Sciences, Department of Psychology, Tuscaloosa, AL 35487. Offers clinical psychology (PhD); experimental psychology (PhD). *Accreditation:* APA. *Faculty:* 20 full-time (8 women), 3 part-time/adjunct (2 women). *Students:* 78 full-time (60 women), 16 part-time (12 women); includes 16 minority (9 African Americans, 3 Asian Americans or Pacific Islanders, 4 Hispanic Americans), 2 international. Average age 27. 252 applicants, 11% accepted, 19 enrolled. In 2008, 13 doctorates awarded. *Degree requirements:* For doctorate, thesis/dissertation. *Entrance requirements:* For doctorate, GRE. Additional exam requirements/recommendations for international students: Required—TOEFL (minimum score 550 paper-based). *Application deadline:* For fall admission, 12/1 for domestic and international students. Application fee: $30. Electronic applications accepted. *Expenses:* Tuition, area resident: Full-time $6400. Tuition, state resident: full-time $6400. Tuition, nonresident: full-time $18,000. *Financial support:* In 2008–09, 73 students received support, including 12 fellowships with full tuition reimbursements available (averaging $15,000 per year), 34 research assistantships with full and partial tuition reimbursements available (averaging $11,142 per year), 26 teaching assistantships with tuition reimbursements available (averaging $11,142 per year); career-related internships or fieldwork, institutionally sponsored loans, scholarships/grants, health care benefits, and unspecified assistantships also available. Financial award application deadline: 12/1. *Faculty research:* Cognitive development/disability, child clinical, psychology and law, health/aging, social psychology. Total annual research expenditures: $2.3 million. *Unit head:* Dr. Kenneth Lichstein, Chair, 205-348-4962, Fax: 205-348-8648, E-mail: lichstein@ua.edu. *Application contact:* Mary Beth Hubbard, Information Contact, 205-348-1919, Fax: 205-348-8648, E-mail: mbhubbard@as.ua.edu.

University of Central Florida, College of Sciences, Department of Psychology, Program in Applied Experimental and Human Factors Psychology, Orlando, FL 32816. Offers MA, PhD. *Accreditation:* APA. *Students:* 36 full-time (18 women), 8 part-time (6 women); includes 3 minority (1 Asian American or Pacific Islander, 2 Hispanic Americans), 2 international. In 2008, 1 master's, 11 doctorates awarded. *Degree requirements:* For doctorate, thesis/dissertation, departmental candidacy exam. *Entrance requirements:* For doctorate, GRE General Test, minimum GPA of 3.2 in last 60 hours or master's qualifying exam. Additional exam requirements/recommendations for international students: Required—TOEFL. *Application deadline:* For fall admission, 2/1 for domestic students. Application fee: $30. Electronic applications accepted. *Expenses:* Tuition, area resident: Full-time $6816; part-time $284 per credit. Tuition, state resident: full-time $6816; part-time $1076 per credit. Tuition, nonresident: full-time $25,824. Required fees: $216; $9 per credit. *Financial support:* In 2008–09, 1 fellowship with partial tuition reimbursement (averaging $10,000 per year), 17 research assistantships with partial tuition reimbursements (averaging $16,000 per year), 17 teaching assistantships with partial tuition reimbursements (averaging $7,600 per year) were awarded; career-related internships or fieldwork, Federal Work-Study, institutionally sponsored loans, tuition waivers (partial), and unspecified assistantships also available. Financial award application deadline: 3/1; financial award applicants required to submit FAFSA. *Faculty research:* Visual performance, team training, controls/displays, synthetic speech, alarms/warning. *Unit head:* Dr. Edward Rinalducci, Coordinator, 407-823-5860, Fax: 407-823-5862, E-mail: erinaldu@mail.ucf.edu. *Application contact:* Dr. Edward Rinalducci, Coordinator, 407-823-5860, Fax: 407-823-5862, E-mail: erinaldu@mail.ucf.edu.

University of Cincinnati, Graduate School, McMicken College of Arts and Sciences, Department of Psychology, Cincinnati, OH 45221. Offers clinical psychology (PhD); experimental psychology (PhD). *Accreditation:* APA. *Degree requirements:* For doctorate, comprehensive exam, thesis/

Experimental Psychology

University of Cincinnati (continued)

dissertation. *Entrance requirements:* For doctorate, GRE General Test. Additional exam requirements/recommendations for international students: Required—TOEFL. *Faculty research:* Neuropsychology, human factors, health.

University of Connecticut, Graduate School, College of Liberal Arts and Sciences, Department of Psychology, Field of Psychology, Storrs, CT 06269. Offers behavioral neuroscience (PhD); biopsychology (PhD); clinical psychology (MA, PhD); cognition and instruction (PhD); developmental psychology (MA, PhD); ecological psychology (PhD); experimental psychology (PhD); general psychology (MA, PhD); health psychology (Graduate Certificate); industrial/organizational psychology (PhD); language and cognition (PhD); neuroscience (PhD); occupational health psychology (Graduate Certificate); social psychology (MA, PhD). *Accreditation:* APA (one or more programs are accredited). Terminal master's awarded for partial completion of doctoral program. *Degree requirements:* For master's, comprehensive exam; for doctorate, thesis/dissertation. *Entrance requirements:* For master's and doctorate, GRE General Test, GRE Subject Test. Additional exam requirements/recommendations for international students: Required—TOEFL (minimum score 550 paper-based; 213 computer-based). Electronic applications accepted.

University of Hartford, College of Arts and Sciences, Department of Psychology, Program in General Experimental Psychology, West Hartford, CT 06117-1599. Offers MA. Part-time programs available. *Degree requirements:* For master's, comprehensive exam, thesis or alternative. *Entrance requirements:* For master's, GRE General Test, GRE Subject Test, minimum GPA of 3.0, 3 letters of recommendation. Additional exam requirements/recommendations for international students: Required—TOEFL (minimum score 550 paper-based; 213 computer-based). Electronic applications accepted. *Faculty research:* Decision making, social judgment and stereotyping, stress and health.

University of Kentucky, Graduate School, College of Arts and Sciences, Program in Psychology, Lexington, KY 40506-0032. Offers clinical psychology (MA); experimental psychology (MA). *Accreditation:* APA (one or more programs are accredited). *Degree requirements:* For master's, comprehensive exam, thesis; for doctorate, comprehensive exam, thesis/dissertation. *Entrance requirements:* For master's, GRE General Test, minimum undergraduate GPA of 2.75; for doctorate, GRE General Test, minimum graduate GPA of 3.0. Additional exam requirements/recommendations for international students: Required—TOEFL (minimum score 550 paper-based; 213 computer-based). Electronic applications accepted. *Faculty research:* Psychopharmacology and teratology, behavioral neuroscience, social psychology, cognitive psychology, development and developmental psychobiology.

University of Louisiana at Monroe, Graduate School, College of Education and Human Development, Department of Psychology, Program in General Psychology, Monroe, LA 71209-0001. Offers MS. Part-time and evening/weekend programs available. *Faculty:* 4 full-time (1 woman). *Students:* 13 full-time (7 women), 4 part-time (2 women); includes 4 minority (all African Americans). Average age 28. In 2008, 7 master's awarded. *Degree requirements:* For master's, comprehensive exam, thesis. *Entrance requirements:* For master's, minimum GPA of 2.5 or GRE General Test. Additional exam requirements/recommendations for international students: Required—TOEFL (minimum score 500 paper-based; 173 computer-based; 61 iBT). *Application deadline:* For fall admission, 8/22 priority date for domestic students, 7/1 for international students; for winter admission, 12/12 priority date for domestic students; for spring admission, 1/7 for domestic students, 11/1 for international students. Applications are processed on a rolling basis. Application fee: $20 ($30 for international students). Electronic applications accepted. *Expenses:* Tuition, area resident: Full-time $2403; part-time $1202 per semester. Tuition, state resident: full-time $2403; part-time $1202 per semester. Tuition, nonresident: full-time $2403; part-time $1202 per semester. International tuition: $8352 full-time. Required fees: $1239.40; $141 per credit hour. *Financial support:* In 2008–09, 11 research assistantships (averaging $2,500 per year) were awarded; career-related internships or fieldwork, Federal Work-Study, and unspecified assistantships also available. Financial award application deadline: 4/1; financial award applicants required to submit FAFSA. *Unit head:* Dr. Joe McGahan, Coordinator, 818-342-1338, Fax: 318-342-1352, E-mail: mcgahan@ulm.edu. *Application contact:* Dr. Joe McGahan, Coordinator, 818-342-1338, Fax: 318-342-1352, E-mail: mcgahan@ulm.edu.

University of Louisville, Graduate School, College of Arts and Sciences, Department of Psychological and Brain Sciences, Program in Experimental Psychology, Louisville, KY 40292. Offers PhD. *Faculty:* 12 full-time (3 women), 2 part-time/adjunct (1 woman). *Students:* 32 full-time (20 women); includes 1 Asian American or Pacific Islander, 1 Hispanic American, 6 international. Average age 30. 23 applicants, 39% accepted, 5 enrolled. In 2008, 5 doctorates awarded. *Degree requirements:* For doctorate, thesis/dissertation, core curriculum; preliminary exam; research. *Entrance requirements:* For doctorate, GRE General Test. Additional exam requirements/recommendations for international students: Required—TOEFL. *Application deadline:* For fall admission, 12/1 for domestic and international students. Application fee: $50. Electronic applications accepted. *Financial support:* In 2008–09, 4 fellowships with full tuition reimbursements (averaging $22,000 per year), 11 research assistantships with full tuition reimbursements (averaging $22,000 per year), 9 teaching assistantships with full tuition reimbursements (averaging $22,000 per year) were awarded. *Faculty research:* Cognitive science, developmental science, neuroscience and neuropsychology, vision and hearing. *Unit head:* Dr. Heywood M. Petry, Head, 502-852-6031, Fax: 502-852-8904, E-mail: woody.petry@louisville.edu. *Application contact:* Libby Leggett, Director, Graduate Admissions, 502-852-3101, Fax: 502-852-6536, E-mail: gradadm@louisville.edu.

University of Maine, Graduate School, College of Liberal Arts and Sciences, Department of Psychology, Orono, ME 04469. Offers clinical psychology (PhD); developmental psychology (MA); experimental psychology (MA, PhD); social psychology (MA). *Accreditation:* APA (one or more programs are accredited). *Degree requirements:* For master's, thesis; for doctorate, thesis/dissertation. *Entrance requirements:* For master's and doctorate, GRE General Test, GRE Subject Test. Additional exam requirements/recommendations for international students: Required—TOEFL. Electronic applications accepted. *Faculty research:* Social development, hypertension and aging, attitude change, self-confidence in achievement situations, health psychology.

University of Maryland, College Park, Graduate Studies, College of Behavioral and Social Sciences, Department of Psychology, College Park, MD 20742. Offers clinical psychology (PhD); developmental psychology (PhD); experimental psychology (PhD); industrial psychology (MA, MS, PhD); social psychology (PhD). *Accreditation:* APA (one or more programs are accredited). *Degree requirements:* For master's, thesis; for doctorate, variable foreign language requirement, comprehensive exam, thesis/dissertation. *Entrance requirements:* For master's and doctorate, GRE General Test, GRE Subject Test, minimum GPA of 3.5, research and/or work experience, 3 letters of recommendation. Electronic applications accepted. *Faculty research:* Social stereotyping and prejudice, anxiety disorders, auditory neuroethology, counseling and social psychology.

University of Memphis, Graduate School, College of Arts and Sciences, Department of Psychology, Memphis, TN 38152. Offers clinical psychology (PhD); experimental psychology (PhD); general psychology (MS); school psychology (MA, PhD). Part-time programs available. *Faculty:* 29 full-time (9 women), 1 part-time/adjunct (0 women). *Students:* 119 full-time (80 women), 21 part-time (13 women); includes 23 minority (16 African Americans, 1 American Indian/Alaska Native, 2 Asian Americans or Pacific Islanders, 4 Hispanic Americans), 9 international. Average age 27. 197 applicants, 23% accepted, 31 enrolled. In 2008, 28 master's, 11 doctorates awarded. Terminal master's awarded for partial completion of doctoral program. *Degree requirements:* For master's, comprehensive exam, thesis (for some programs), oral exam (MS); for doctorate, thesis/dissertation, internship. *Entrance requirements:* For master's, GRE General Test, 18 undergraduate hours in psychology, minimum GPA of 2.5; for doctorate, GRE General Test, GRE Subject Test. *Application deadline:* For fall admission, 2/1 for domestic students. Applications are processed on a rolling basis. Application fee: $35 ($60 for international students). *Expenses:* Tuition, area resident: Full-time $6242; part-time $330 per credit hour. Tuition, state resident: full-time $6242; part-time $330 per credit hour. Tuition, nonresident: full-time $17,828; part-time $815 per credit hour. Required fees: $1156. *Financial support:* Fellowships with full tuition reimbursements, research assistantships with full tuition reimbursements, teaching assistantships with full tuition reimbursements, tuition waivers (partial) and unspecified assistantships available. Financial award applicants required to submit FAFSA. *Faculty research:* Psychotherapy and psychopathology, behavioral medicine and community psychology, child and family studies, cognitive and social processes, neuropsychology and behavioral neuroscience. *Unit head:* Dr. William Zachry, Chair, 901-678-2145, Fax: 901-678-2579, E-mail: wzachry@memphis.edu. *Application contact:* Dr. Robert Cohen, Graduate Studies Coordinator, 901-678-2146.

University of Michigan, Horace H. Rackham School of Graduate Studies, College of Literature, Science, and the Arts, Department of Psychology, Ann Arbor, MI 48109. Offers biopsychology (PhD); clinical psychology (PhD); cognition and perception (PhD); developmental psychology (PhD); personality and social contexts (PhD); social psychology (PhD). *Accreditation:* APA. *Degree requirements:* For doctorate, comprehensive exam, thesis/dissertation, oral defense of dissertation, preliminary exam. *Entrance requirements:* For doctorate, GRE General Test (optional), GRE Subject Test (optional). Additional exam requirements/recommendations for international students: Required—TOEFL. Electronic applications accepted.

University of Mississippi, Graduate School, College of Liberal Arts, Department of Psychology, Oxford, University, MS 38677. Offers clinical psychology (PhD); experimental psychology (PhD); psychology (MA). *Accreditation:* APA (one or more programs are accredited). *Degree requirements:* For master's, thesis; for doctorate, thesis/dissertation. *Entrance requirements:* For master's, GRE General Test, minimum GPA of 3.0; for doctorate, GRE General Test. Additional exam requirements/recommendations for international students: Required—TOEFL. Electronic applications accepted.

The University of Montana, Graduate School, College of Arts and Sciences, Department of Psychology, Missoula, MT 59812-0002. Offers clinical psychology (PhD); experimental psychology (PhD), including animal behavior psychology, developmental psychology; school psychology (MA, PhD, Ed S). *Accreditation:* APA (one or more programs are accredited). Terminal master's awarded for partial completion of doctoral program. *Degree requirements:* For master's, thesis; for doctorate, thesis/dissertation. *Entrance requirements:* For master's, doctorate, and Ed S, GRE General Test. Additional exam requirements/recommendations for international students: Required—TOEFL.

University of New Brunswick Saint John, Department of Psychology, Fredericton, NB, NB E2L 4L5, Canada. Offers applied and experimental psychology (PhD); clinical psychology (PhD); experimental psychology (MA). *Faculty:* 9 full-time (4 women). *Students:* 4 full-time (all women). In 2008, 1 master's awarded. *Degree requirements:* For master's, thesis; for doctorate, comprehensive exam, thesis/dissertation. *Entrance requirements:* For master's, GRE General Test. Additional exam requirements/recommendations for international students: Required—TOEFL (minimum score 550 paper-based). *Application deadline:* For fall admission, 2/1 for domestic students. Application fee: $50. Electronic applications accepted. *Expenses:* Tuition, area resident: Full-time $5562. International tuition: $9450 full-time. Required fees: $333. *Financial support:* In 2008–09, 1 fellowship, 7 research assistantships, 2 teaching assistantships were awarded; unspecified assistantships also available. Support available to part-time students. Financial award application deadline: 2/1. *Faculty research:* Psychopharmacology and addictions, forensic psychology and criminal justice, interpersonal relations, perception and graphical perception, lie detection. *Unit head:* Dr. Lily Both, Director of Graduate Studies, 506-648-5769, Fax: 506-648-5780, E-mail: lboth@unbsj.ca. *Application contact:* Frances Stevens, Secretary, 506-648-5640, Fax: 506-648-5780, E-mail: fstevens@unb.ca.

The University of North Carolina at Chapel Hill, Graduate School, College of Arts and Sciences, Department of Psychology, Chapel Hill, NC 27599. Offers biological psychology (PhD); clinical psychology (PhD); cognitive psychology (PhD); developmental psychology (PhD); quantitative psychology (PhD); social psychology (PhD). *Accreditation:* APA. *Degree requirements:* For doctorate, comprehensive exam, thesis/dissertation. *Entrance requirements:* For doctorate, GRE General Test, minimum GPA of 3.0. Electronic applications accepted. *Faculty research:* Expressed emotion, cognitive development, social cognitive neuroscience, human memory personality.

University of North Dakota, Graduate School, College of Arts and Sciences, Department of Psychology, Grand Forks, ND 58202. Offers clinical psychology (PhD); counseling psychology (PhD); experimental psychology (PhD); forensic psychology (MA, MS); psychology (MA). *Accreditation:* APA (one or more programs are accredited). *Degree requirements:* For master's, thesis, final exam; for doctorate, comprehensive exam, thesis/dissertation, internship, final exam. *Entrance requirements:* For master's, GRE General Test, GRE Subject Test, minimum GPA of 3.0; for doctorate, GRE General Test, GRE Subject Test, minimum GPA of 3.5. Additional exam requirements/recommendations for international students: Required—TOEFL (minimum score 550 paper-based; 213 computer-based; 79 iBT), IELTS (minimum score 6.5). Electronic applications accepted. *Faculty research:* Developmental psychology, clinical social psychology, educational psychology, personality disorders.

University of North Texas, Robert B. Toulouse School of Graduate Studies, College of Arts and Sciences, Department of Psychology, Denton, TX 76203. Offers clinical psychology (PhD); counseling psychology (MA, MS, PhD); experimental psychology (MA, MS, PhD); health psychology and behavioral medicine (PhD). *Accreditation:* APA (one or more programs are accredited). Terminal master's awarded for partial completion of doctoral program. *Degree requirements:* For master's, comprehensive exam, thesis or alternative; for doctorate, one foreign language, comprehensive exam, thesis/dissertation. *Entrance requirements:* For master's and doctorate, GRE General Test, interview. Additional exam requirements/recommendations for international students: Required—proof of English language proficiency required for non-native English speakers; Recommended—TOEFL (minimum score 550 paper-based; 213 computer-based). *Faculty research:* Very broad range of topics and approaches.

University of Regina, Faculty of Graduate Studies and Research, Faculty of Arts, Department of Psychology, Regina, SK S4S 0A2, Canada. Offers clinical psychology (MA, PhD); experimental and applied psychology (MA, PhD). *Faculty:* 18 full-time (10 women). *Students:* 54 full-time (44 women), 3 part-time (all women). 57 applicants, 28% accepted. In 2008, 6 master's, 3 doctorates awarded. *Degree requirements:* For master's, thesis; for doctorate, comprehensive exam, thesis/dissertation. *Entrance requirements:* For master's, GRE General Test, GRE Subject Test; for doctorate, GRE General Test, GRE Subject Test (optional for students who hold a master's degree from a Canadian university). Additional exam requirements/recommendations for international students: Required—TOEFL (minimum score 580 paper-based; 237 computer-based; 88 iBT). *Application deadline:* For fall admission, 2/15 for domestic students. Application fee: $85 ($100 for international students). Electronic applications accepted. *Financial support:* In 2008–09, 17 fellowships (averaging $16,764 per year), 4 research assistantships (averaging $13,875 per year), 11 teaching assistantships (averaging $6,675 per year) were awarded; career-related internships or fieldwork and scholarships/grants also available. Financial award application deadline: 6/15. *Faculty research:* Clinical, experimental and applied psychology. *Unit head:* Dr. William E. Smythe, Head, 306-585-4157, Fax: 306-585-5429, E-mail: william.smythe@uregina.ca. *Application contact:* Dr. Dongyan Blachford, Associate Dean, 306-585-5186, Fax: 306-337-2444, E-mail: dongyan.blachford@uregina.ca.

University of South Carolina, The Graduate School, College of Arts and Sciences, Department of Psychology, Program in Experimental Psychology, Columbia, SC 29208. Offers MA, PhD. Terminal master's awarded for partial completion of doctoral program. *Degree requirements:* For master's, comprehensive exam, thesis; for doctorate, comprehensive exam, thesis/dissertation. *Entrance requirements:* For master's and doctorate, GRE General Test. Additional exam requirements/recommendations for international students: Required—TOEFL. Electronic applications accepted. *Faculty research:* Cognition, development, neuroscience.

University of Southern Mississippi, Graduate School, College of Education and Psychology, Department of Psychology, Hattiesburg, MS 39406-0001. Offers clinical psychology (MA, PhD); counseling psychology (PhD); experimental psychology (MA, PhD); psychology (MS); school psychology (MA, PhD). *Accreditation:* ACA; APA (one or more programs are accredited). *Faculty:* 28 full-time (11 women). *Students:* 104 full-time (83 women), 34 part-time (24 women); includes 13 minority (7 African Americans, 2 Asian Americans or Pacific Islanders, 4 Hispanic Americans), 7 international. Average age 28. 189 applicants, 21% accepted, 31 enrolled. In 2008, 24 master's, 13 doctorates awarded. Terminal master's awarded for partial completion of doctoral program. *Degree requirements:* For master's, comprehensive exam, thesis; for doctorate, comprehensive exam, thesis/dissertation. *Entrance requirements:* For master's, GRE General Test, minimum GPA of 3.0; for doctorate, GRE General Test, interview, minimum GPA of 3.0. Additional exam requirements/recommendations for international students: Required—TOEFL. *Application deadline:* For fall admission, 3/1 priority date for domestic students, 3/1 for international students. Applications are processed on a rolling basis. Application fee: $30. *Financial support:* In 2008–09, 48 research assistantships with full tuition reimbursements (averaging $8,802 per year), 48 teaching assistantships with full tuition reimbursements (averaging $6,500 per year) were awarded; career-related internships or fieldwork, Federal Work-Study, and institutionally sponsored loans also available. Financial award application deadline: 3/15; financial award applicants required to submit FAFSA. *Faculty research:* Dolphin cognition, sleep, neuropsychology, health-related behaviors, psychopathology. Total annual research expenditures: $101,200. *Unit head:* Dr. Joesph Olmi, Chair, 601-266-4177, Fax: 601-266-5580. *Application contact:* Dr. Heather Sterling-Turner, Graduate Coordinator, 601-266-4177, Fax: 601-266-5580.

The University of Tennessee, Graduate School, College of Arts and Sciences, Department of Psychology, Knoxville, TN 37996. Offers clinical psychology (PhD); experimental psychology (MA, PhD); psychology (MA). *Accreditation:* APA (one or more programs are accredited). Terminal master's awarded for partial completion of doctoral program. *Degree requirements:* For master's, thesis; for doctorate, thesis/dissertation. *Entrance requirements:* For master's and doctorate, GRE General Test, GRE Subject Test, minimum GPA of 2.7. Additional exam requirements/recommendations for international students: Required—TOEFL. Electronic applications accepted. *Expenses:* Tuition, area resident: Part-time $348 per credit hour. Tuition, state resident: full-time $6262. Tuition, nonresident: full-time $18,920; part-time $1052 per credit hour. Required fees: $812; $36 per credit hour. Tuition and fees vary according to program.

The University of Tennessee at Chattanooga, Graduate School, College of Arts and Sciences, Department of Psychology, Program in Research Psychology, Chattanooga, TN 37403. Offers MS. Part-time and evening/weekend programs available. *Faculty:* 5 full-time (1 woman). *Students:* 9 full-time (7 women), 5 part-time (3 women); includes 2 minority (1 Asian American or Pacific Islander, 1 Hispanic American). Average age 31. 14 applicants, 64% accepted, 6 enrolled. In 2008, 5 master's awarded. *Degree requirements:* For master's, thesis. *Entrance requirements:* For master's, GRE General Test. Additional exam requirements/recommendations for international students: Required—TOEFL (minimum score 550 paper-based; 213 computer-based; 79 iBT); Recommended—IELTS (minimum score 6). *Application deadline:* For fall admission, 8/1 priority date for domestic students, 6/1 for international students; for spring admission, 12/1 priority date for domestic students, 10/1 for international students. Applications are processed on a rolling basis. Application fee: $30 ($35 for international students). *Expenses:* Tuition, area resident: Full-time $6150; part-time $281 per credit hour. Tuition, nonresident: full-time $16,710; part-time $867 per credit hour. Required fees: $1100; $128 per credit hour. $550 per semester. *Financial support:* In 2008–09, 4 fellowships with full and partial tuition reimbursements (averaging $4,125 per year) were awarded; career-related internships or fieldwork, Federal Work-Study, institutionally sponsored loans, scholarships/grants, tuition waivers (partial), and unspecified assistantships also available. Support available to part-time students. Financial award application deadline: 4/1; financial award applicants required to submit FAFSA. *Faculty research:* Cognition, psychology of religion, self-esteem, abnormal psychology, child development. Total annual research expenditures: $47,807. *Unit head:* Dr. David Ross, Coordinator, 423-425-4262, Fax: 423-425-4284, E-mail: david-ross@utc.edu. *Application contact:* Dr. Stephanie Bellar, Dean of Graduate Studies, 423-425-4666, Fax: 423-425-5223, E-mail: stephanie-bellar@utc.edu.

The University of Texas at Arlington, Graduate School, College of Science, Department of Psychology, Arlington, TX 76019. Offers experimental psychology (PhD); health psychology (PhD); industrial organizational psychology (MS); psychology (MS). Part-time programs available. *Faculty:* 16 full-time (5 women), 1 part-time/adjunct (0 women). *Students:* 53 full-time (38 women), 12 part-time (9 women); includes 11 minority (6 African Americans, 1 Asian American or Pacific Islander, 4 Hispanic Americans), 9 international. 81 applicants, 35% accepted, 15 enrolled. In 2008, 16 master's, 4 doctorates awarded. Terminal master's awarded for partial completion of doctoral program. *Degree requirements:* For master's, comprehensive exam or thesis; for doctorate, thesis/dissertation (for some programs). *Entrance requirements:* For master's and doctorate, GRE General Test, minimum GPA of 3.0 in last 60 hours of course work. Additional exam requirements/recommendations for international students: Required—TOEFL (minimum score 550 paper-based; 213 computer-based). *Application deadline:* For fall admission, 6/16 for domestic students. Applications are processed on a rolling basis. Application fee: $35 ($50 for international students). *Expenses:* Tuition, area resident: Full-time $6500. Tuition, state resident: full-time $6500. Tuition, nonresident: full-time $11,558. *Financial support:* In 2008–09, 4 fellowships (averaging $1,000 per year), 2 research assistantships with tuition reimbursements (averaging $15,000 per year), 28 teaching assistantships with tuition reimbursements (averaging $15,000 per year) were awarded; career-related internships or fieldwork, Federal Work-Study, institutionally sponsored loans, scholarships/grants, traineeships, tuition waivers (partial), and unspecified assistantships also available. Financial award application deadline: 6/1; financial award applicants required to submit FAFSA. *Unit head:* Dr. Robert Gatchel, Chair, 817-272-2281, Fax: 817-272-2364, E-mail: gatchel@uta.edu. *Application contact:* Dr. Jared Kenworthy, Graduate Advisor, 817-272-2281, Fax: 817-272-2364, E-mail: kenworthy@uta.edu.

The University of Texas at El Paso, Graduate School, College of Liberal Arts, Department of Psychology, El Paso, TX 79968-0001. Offers clinical psychology (MA); experimental psychology (MA); psychology (PhD). Part-time and evening/weekend programs available. *Degree requirements:* For master's, thesis; for doctorate, thesis/dissertation. *Entrance requirements:* For master's and doctorate, GRE General Test. Additional exam requirements/recommendations for international students: Required—TOEFL. Electronic applications accepted.

The University of Texas of the Permian Basin, Office of Graduate Studies, College of Arts and Sciences, Deparment of Psychology, Odessa, TX 79762-0001. Offers applied research psychology (MA); clinical psychology (MA). Part-time and evening/weekend programs available. *Degree requirements:* For master's, comprehensive exam, thesis, practicum. *Entrance requirements:* For master's, GRE General Test, 3 letters of recommendation. Additional exam requirements/recommendations for international students: Required—TOEFL (minimum score 550 paper-based; 213 computer-based).

The University of Texas–Pan American, College of Social and Behavioral Sciences, Department of Psychology and Anthropology, Edinburg, TX 78541-2999. Offers psychology (MA), including clinical psychology, experimental psychology. Part-time and evening/weekend programs available. *Degree requirements:* For master's, comprehensive exam, thesis optional, internship. *Entrahce requirements:* For master's, GRE, letters of recommendation. Additional exam requirements/recommendations for international students: Required—TOEFL. Electronic applications accepted. *Faculty research:* Biofeedback, acculturation, health, stress/trauma, neuropsychological assessment, false memories, children's theory of mind.

The University of Toledo, College of Graduate Studies, College of Arts and Sciences, Department of Psychology, Toledo, OH 43606-3390. Offers behavioral (PhD), including cognitive, psychobiology and learning, social; clinical psychology (PhD); experimental psychology (MA). *Accreditation:* APA. *Degree requirements:* For master's, thesis; for doctorate, one foreign language, thesis/dissertation. *Entrance requirements:* For master's and doctorate, GRE General Test, GRE Subject Test. *Faculty research:* Neural taste response.

University of Victoria, Faculty of Graduate Studies, Faculty of Social Sciences, Department of Psychology, Victoria, BC V8W 2Y2, Canada. Offers clinical psychology (PhD); clinical psychology (neuropsychology) (M Sc); cognition and brain science (M Sc, PhD); experimental neuropsychology (M Sc, PhD); individualized study (M Sc, PhD); life span development psychology (PhD); life span developmental psychology (M Sc); social psychology (M Sc, PhD). *Accreditation:* APA (one or more programs are accredited). *Degree requirements:* For master's, thesis; for doctorate, thesis/dissertation, candidacy exam. *Entrance requirements:* For master's and doctorate, GRE General Test. Additional exam requirements/recommendations for international students: Required—TOEFL (minimum score 600 paper-based; 250 computer-based). Electronic applications accepted. *Faculty research:* Life span development psychology and aging, behavioral neuroscience, cognitive psychology, behavioral psychology, environmental psychology.

University of Wisconsin–Oshkosh, The Office of Graduate Studies, College of Letters and Science, Department of Psychology, Oshkosh, WI 54901. Offers experimental psychology (MS); industrial/organizational psychology (MS). *Degree requirements:* For master's, thesis. *Entrance requirements:* For master's, GRE, 10 semester hours of undergraduate course work in psychology. Additional exam requirements/recommendations for international students: Required—TOEFL (minimum score 550 paper-based; 213 computer-based; 79 iBT). Electronic applications accepted. *Faculty research:* Performance evaluation, training, biological bases of behavior, tactile perception, aging.

Washington State University, Graduate School, College of Liberal Arts, Department of Psychology, Pullman, WA 99164. Offers clinical psychology (PhD); experimental psychology (PhD); psychology (MS). *Accreditation:* APA (one or more programs are accredited). *Degree requirements:* For master's, comprehensive exam (for some programs), thesis (for some programs), oral exam; for doctorate, comprehensive exam, thesis/dissertation, oral exam, written exam. *Entrance requirements:* For master's, GRE General Test, minimum GPA of 3.0, research or clinical experience, 3 letters of recommendation; for doctorate, GRE General Test, minimum GPA of 3.0, 1 course in statistics and research methodology, research or clinical experience, 3 letters of recommendation. *Faculty research:* Childhood conduct disorders, etiology of depression, treatment of reading disorders, applied behavior analysis, selective attention.

Washington University in St. Louis, Graduate School of Arts and Sciences, Department of Psychology, St. Louis, MO 63130-4899. Offers clinical psychology (PhD); general experimental psychology (PhD); social psychology (PhD). *Accreditation:* APA. *Students:* 102 full-time (63 women); includes 23 minority (6 African Americans, 13 Asian Americans or Pacific Islanders, 4 Hispanic Americans), 12 international. 291 applicants, 11% accepted, 18 enrolled. In 2008, 11 doctorates awarded. Terminal master's awarded for partial completion of doctoral program. *Degree requirements:* For doctorate, thesis/dissertation. *Entrance requirements:* For doctorate, GRE General Test. *Application deadline:* For fall admission, 12/15 priority date for domestic students. Application fee: $45. Electronic applications accepted. *Financial support:* Fellowships, research assistantships, teaching assistantships, career-related internships or fieldwork, Federal Work-Study, institutionally sponsored loans, and tuition waivers (full and partial) available. Support available to part-time students. Financial award application deadline: 1/15. *Unit head:* Dr. Randy Larsen, Chairperson, 314-935-6520. *Application contact:* Assistant to the Dean, 314-935-6880, Fax: 314-935-4887.

Western Michigan University, Graduate College, College of Arts and Sciences, Department of Psychology, Kalamazoo, MI 49008-5202. Offers behavior analysis (MA, PhD); clinical psychology (MA, PhD); experimental psychology (MA); industrial/organizational psychology (MA). *Accreditation:* APA (one or more programs are accredited). *Degree requirements:* For master's, variable foreign language requirement, thesis, oral exams; for doctorate, 2 foreign languages, comprehensive exam, thesis/dissertation, oral exams. *Entrance requirements:* For master's and doctorate, GRE General Test.

Western Washington University, Graduate School, College of Humanities and Social Sciences, Department of Psychology, Program in Experimental Psychology, Bellingham, WA 98225-5996. Offers MS. *Degree requirements:* For master's, thesis. *Entrance requirements:* For master's, GRE General Test, minimum GPA of 3.0 in last 60 semester hours or last 90 quarter hours. Additional exam requirements/recommendations for international students: Required—TOEFL (minimum score 567 paper-based; 227 computer-based). Electronic applications accepted.

Xavier University, College of Social Sciences, Health and Education, Department of Psychology, Cincinnati, OH 45207. Offers clinical psychology (Psy D); psychology (MA), including general experimental, industrial-organizational. *Accreditation:* APA (one or more programs are accredited). *Faculty:* 16 full-time (8 women), 5 part-time/adjunct (3 women). *Students:* 83 full-time (61 women), 30 part-time (22 women); includes 8 minority (4 African Americans, 4 Asian Americans or Pacific Islanders), 2 international. Average age 27. 242 applicants, 31% accepted, 25 enrolled. In 2008, 27 master's, 12 doctorates awarded. *Degree requirements:* For master's, comprehensive exam, thesis, internship; for doctorate, comprehensive exam, thesis/dissertation, internship. *Entrance requirements:* For master's and doctorate, GRE. Additional exam requirements/recommendations for international students: Required—TOEFL. *Application deadline:* For fall admission, 1/15 for domestic and international students. Application fee: $35. Electronic applications accepted. *Expenses:* Contact institution. *Financial support:* In 2008–09, 57 students received support, including 39 research assistantships with partial tuition reimbursements available, 18 teaching assistantships with partial tuition reimbursements available. Financial award application deadline: 3/1; financial award applicants required to submit FAFSA. *Unit head:* Dr. Christine M. Dacey, Chair, 513-745-3533, Fax: 513-745-3327, E-mail: dacey@xavier.edu. *Application contact:* Margaret Maybury, Assistant Director, Enrollment and Student Services, 513-745-1053, Fax: 513-745-3347, E-mail: maybury@xavier.edu.

Forensic Psychology

Alliant International University–Fresno, Center for Forensic Studies, Fresno, CA 93727. Offers forensic psychology (PhD, Psy D). *Degree requirements:* For doctorate, thesis/dissertation. *Entrance requirements:* For doctorate, interview; master's degree in psychology, forensic psychology, criminology, criminal justice, social work or law; minimum GPA of 3.0 in psychology and overall. Additional exam requirements/recommendations for international students: Required—TOEFL (minimum score 600 paper-based; 250 computer-based), TWE (minimum score 5). Electronic applications accepted. *Faculty research:* Domestic violence, serial killers, court evaluations, drug and alcohol abuse.

See Close-Up on page 1055.

Alliant International University–Irvine, Center for Forensic Studies, Irvine, CA 92612. Offers Psy D.

See Close-Up on page 1055.

Alliant International University–Los Angeles, Center for Forensic Studies, Alhambra, CA 91803-1360. Offers forensic psychology (Psy D). *Degree requirements:* For doctorate, thesis/dissertation. *Entrance requirements:* For doctorate, interview; master's degree in psychology, forensic psychology, criminology, criminal justice, social work or law; minimum GPA of 3.0 in psychology and overall. Additional exam requirements/recommendations for international students: Required—TOEFL (minimum score 600 paper-based; 250 computer-based), TWE (minimum score 5). *Faculty research:* Court testimony.

See Close-Up on page 1055.

American International College, School of Arts, Education and Science, Department of Psychology, Program in Forensic Psychology, Springfield, MA 01109-3189. Offers MS. Part-time and evening/weekend programs available. *Degree requirements:* For master's, comprehensive exam (for some programs), thesis optional. *Entrance requirements:* For master's, minimum B-average in undergraduate course work, BS or BA. Additional exam requirements/recommendations for international students: Required—TOEFL. Electronic applications accepted.

Argosy University, Chicago, College of Psychology and Behavioral Sciences, Doctoral Program in Clinical Psychology, Chicago, IL 60654. Offers child and adolescent psychology (Psy D); client-centered and experiential psychotherapies (Psy D); diversity and multicultural psychology (Psy D); family psychology (Psy D); forensic psychology (Psy D); health psychology (Psy D); psychoanalytic psychology (Psy D); psychology and spirituality (Psy D). *Accreditation:* APA.

See Close-Up on page 1067.

Argosy University, Denver, College of Psychology and Behavioral Sciences, Denver, CO 80203. Offers clinical psychology (MA, Psy D); community counseling (MA); counseling psychology (Ed D), including counselor education and supervision; counselor education and supervision (Ed D); forensic psychology (MA); marriage and family therapy (MA); organizational leadership (Ed D).

See Close-Up on page 1071.

Argosy University, Inland Empire, College of Psychology and Behavioral Sciences, San Bernardino, CA 92408. Offers clinical psychology/marriage and family therapy (MA); counseling psychology (MA, Ed D); counseling psychology/marriage and family therapy (MA); forensic psychology (MA).

See Close-Up on page 1075.

Argosy University, Orange County, College of Psychology and Behavioral Sciences, Program in Forensic Psychology, Santa Ana, CA 92704. Offers MA.

See Close-Up on page 1081.

Argosy University, Phoenix, College of Psychology and Behavioral Sciences, Program in Forensic Psychology, Phoenix, AZ 85021. Offers MA.

See Close-Up on page 1083.

Argosy University, San Francisco Bay Area, College of Psychology and Behavioral Sciences, Program in Forensic Psychology, Alameda, CA 94501. Offers MA.

See Close-Up on page 1089.

Argosy University, Sarasota, College of Psychology and Behavioral Sciences, Sarasota, FL 34235. Offers community counseling (MA); counseling psychology (Ed D); counselor education and supervision (Ed D); forensic psychology (MA); marriage and family therapy (MA); mental health counseling (MA); organizational leadership (Ed D); pastoral community counseling (Ed D); school counseling (MA, Ed S); school psychology (MA).

See Close-Up on page 1091.

Argosy University, Schaumburg, College of Psychology and Behavioral Sciences, Schaumburg, IL 60173-5403. Offers clinical health psychology (Post-Graduate Certificate); clinical psychology (MA, Psy D), including child and family psychology (Psy D), clinical health psychology (Psy D), diversity and multicultural psychology (Psy D), forensic psychology (Psy D); community counseling (MA); counseling psychology (Ed D), including counselor education and supervision; counselor education and supervision (Ed D); forensic psychology (Post-Graduate Certificate); organizational leadership (Ed D). *Accreditation:* ACA; APA.

See Close-Up on page 1093.

Argosy University, Twin Cities, College of Psychology and Behavioral Sciences, Eagan, MN 55121. Offers clinical psychology (MA, Psy D), including child and family psychology (Psy D), forensic psychology (Psy D), health psychology (Psy D), marriage/couples and family therapy (Psy D), neuropsychology (Psy D); forensic counseling (Post-Graduate Certificate); forensic psychology (MA); marriage and family therapy (MA, DMFT), including forensic counseling (MA); organizational leadership (Ed D). *Accreditation:* APA.

See Close-Up on page 1099.

Argosy University, Washington DC, College of Psychology and Behavioral Sciences, Arlington, VA 22209. Offers clinical psychology (MA, Psy D), including child and family psychology (Psy D), diversity and multicultural psychology (Psy D), forensic psychology (Psy D), health and neuropsychology (Psy D); community counseling (MA); counseling psychology (Ed D), including counselor education and supervision; counselor education and supervision (Ed D); forensic psychology (MA); organizational leadership (Ed D). *Accreditation:* APA.

See Close-Up on page 1101.

California Baptist University, Program in Forensic Psychology, Riverside, CA 92504-3206. Offers MA. Part-time programs available. *Faculty:* 2 full-time (both women), 1 part-time/adjunct (0 women). *Students:* 15 full-time (12 women), 4 part-time (3 women); includes 9 minority (2 African Americans, 1 American Indian/Alaska Native, 2 Asian Americans or Pacific Islanders, 4 Hispanic Americans). 19 applicants, 63% accepted, 11 enrolled. *Entrance requirements:* Additional exam requirements/recommendations for international students: Required—TOEFL (minimum score 575 paper-based; 230 computer-based; 89 iBT). *Application deadline:* For fall admission, 8/1 priority date for domestic students, 7/1 for international students; for spring admission, 12/1 priority date for domestic students, 10/15 for international students. Applications are processed on a rolling basis. Application fee: $45. Electronic applications accepted. *Expenses:* Tuition: Full-time $8172; part-time $454 per credit hour. Required fees: $510. *Financial support:* Federal Work-Study and scholarships/grants available. Support available to part-time students. Financial award applicants required to submit FAFSA. *Unit head:* Dr. Anne-Marie Larsen, Director, 951-343-4761. *Application contact:* Gail Ronveaux, Dean of Graduate Enrollment, 951-343-5045, Fax: 951-343-5095, E-mail: graduateadmissions@calbaptist.edu.

Cambridge College, School of Psychology and Counseling, Cambridge, MA 02138-5304. Offers addiction counseling (M Ed); counseling psychology (M Ed); counseling psychology: forensic counseling (M Ed); marriage and family therapy (M Ed); mental health and addiction counseling (M Ed); mental health counseling (M Ed); mental health counseling for school guidance counselors (Certificate); mental health, addiction and school adjustment counseling (M Ed); psychological studies (M Ed); school adjustment counseling (M Ed); school guidance counseling (M Ed). Part-time and evening/weekend programs available. *Faculty:* 5 full-time (2 women), 183 part-time/adjunct (85 women). *Students:* 476 full-time (384 women), 313 part-time (245 women); includes 396 minority (300 African Americans, 2 American Indian/Alaska Native, 13 Asian Americans or Pacific Islanders, 81 Hispanic Americans), 13 international. Average age 37. 307 applicants, 81% accepted, 192 enrolled. In 2008, 226 master's, 9 CAGSs awarded. *Degree requirements:* For master's, thesis, practicum/internship; for other advanced degree, thesis, practicum/Internship. *Entrance requirements:* For master's, evidence of a bachelor's degree from an accredited institution; essay; 2 references; health insurance; for other advanced degree, evidence of a master's degree from an accredited institution; essay; 2 references; health insurance. Additional exam requirements/recommendations for international students: Required—TOEFL (minimum score 550 paper-based; 213 computer-based; 79 iBT). *Application deadline:* Applications are processed on a rolling basis. Application fee: $30. Electronic applications accepted. *Expenses:* Tuition: Full-time $6960; part-time $435 per credit. One-time fee: $140 full-time. Tuition and fees vary according to degree level, campus/location and program. *Financial support:* In 2008–09, 857 students received support. Career-related internships or fieldwork, Federal Work-Study, and scholarships/grants available. Financial award applicants required to submit FAFSA. *Unit head:* Dr. Niti Seth, EdD, Dean, 617-873-0208, Fax: 617-349-3545, E-mail: nseth@cambridgecollege.edu. *Application contact:* Kathryn Lenehan, Admission Counselor, 800-877-0280, E-mail: kathryn.lenehan@cambridgecollege.edu.

Castleton State College, Division of Graduate Studies, Department of Psychology, Castleton, VT 05735. Offers forensic psychology (MA). *Degree requirements:* For master's, thesis. *Entrance requirements:* For master's, GRE General Test, minimum undergraduate GPA of 3.5, previous course work in research methodology and statistics. Additional exam requirements/recommendations for international students: Required—TOEFL. *Faculty research:* Psychology and law, juvenile delinquency, criminal psychology, correctional psychology, police psychology.

The Chicago School of Professional Psychology, Graduate School, Program in Forensic Psychology, Chicago, IL 60610. Offers MA. *Degree requirements:* For master's, thesis optional. *Entrance requirements:* For master's, GRE (highly recommended), 1 course in research methods, statistics, 1 course in psychology. Additional exam requirements/recommendations for international students: Required—TOEFL (minimum score 550 paper-based; 213 computer-based; 79 iBT).

College of Saint Elizabeth, Department of Psychology, Morristown, NJ 07960-6989. Offers counseling psychology (MA); forensic psychology (MA); student affairs in higher education (Certificate). Part-time and evening/weekend programs available. *Faculty:* 4 full-time (2 women), 10 part-time/adjunct (5 women). *Students:* 11 full-time (10 women), 84 part-time (77 women); includes 23 minority (10 African Americans, 3 Asian Americans or Pacific Islanders, 10 Hispanic Americans), 2 international. Average age 34. 104 applicants, 58% accepted, 47 enrolled. In 2008, 11 master's, 1 other advanced degree awarded. *Degree requirements:* For master's, thesis or alternative, portfolio. *Entrance requirements:* For master's, minimum GPA of 3.0, BA in psychology (preferred), 12 credits of course work in psychology. *Application deadline:* For fall admission, 4/14 priority date for domestic students; for spring admission, 11/15 for domestic students. Applications are processed on a rolling basis. Application fee: $35. Electronic applications accepted. *Expenses:* Tuition: Part-time $759 per credit. Required fees: $380 per semester. *Financial support:* Career-related internships or fieldwork, tuition waivers (partial), and unspecified assistantships available. Support available to part-time students. Financial award application deadline: 3/15; financial award applicants required to submit FAFSA. *Faculty research:* Family systems, dissociative identity disorder, multicultural counseling, outcomes assessment. *Unit head:* Dr. Valerie Scott, Director of the Graduate Program in Counseling Psychology, 973-290-4102, Fax: 973-290-4676, E-mail: vscott@cse.edu. *Application contact:* Donna Tatarka, Dean of Admission, 973-290-4705, Fax: 973-290-4710, E-mail: dtatarka@cse.edu.

Drexel University, College of Arts and Sciences, Department of Psychology, Clinical Psychology Program, Philadelphia, PA 19104-2875. Offers clinical psychology (PhD); forensic psychology (PhD); health psychology (PhD); neuropsychology (PhD). *Accreditation:* APA. Terminal master's awarded for partial completion of doctoral program. *Degree requirements:* For doctorate, thesis/dissertation, qualifying exam. *Entrance requirements:* For doctorate, GRE General Test, GRE Subject Test, minimum GPA of 3.0. Electronic applications accepted. *Expenses:* Contact institution. *Faculty research:* Cognitive behavioral therapy, stress and coping, eating disorders, substance abuse, developmental disabilities.

Fairleigh Dickinson University, Metropolitan Campus, University College: Arts, Sciences, and Professional Studies, School of Psychology, Program in Forensic Psychology, Teaneck, NJ 07666-1914. Offers MA. *Students:* 9 full-time (all women), 1 (woman) part-time. Average age 23. 31 applicants, 71% accepted, 9 enrolled. *Application contact:* Susan Brooman, University Director of Graduate Admissions, 201-692-2554, Fax: 201-692-2560, E-mail: globaleducation@fdu.edu.

Holy Names University, Graduate Division, Department of Counseling Psychology, Oakland, CA 94619-1699. Offers counseling psychology (MA); forensic psychology (MA, Certificate); pastoral counseling (MA, Certificate). Part-time and evening/weekend programs available. *Faculty:* 1 (woman) full-time, 9 part-time/adjunct (5 women). *Students:* 38 full-time (33 women), 13 part-time (12 women); includes 33 minority (25 African Americans, 2 Asian Americans or Pacific Islanders, 6 Hispanic Americans), 1 international. Average age 35. 22 applicants, 68% accepted, 11 enrolled. In 2008, 13 master's awarded. *Degree requirements:* For master's, comprehensive paper, seminars. *Entrance requirements:* For master's, minimum undergraduate GPA of 2.6 overall, 3.0 in major. Additional exam requirements/recommendations for international students: Required—TOEFL (minimum score 550 paper-based; 213 computer-based; 80 iBT). *Application deadline:* For fall admission, 8/1 priority date for domestic students, 8/1 for international students; for spring admission, 12/1 priority date for domestic students, 12/1 for international students. Applications are processed on a rolling basis. Application fee: $65. *Expenses:* Tuition: Full-time $6255; part-time $695 per unit. Required fees: $340. Tuition and fees vary according to course load, program, reciprocity agreements and student's religious affiliation. *Financial support:* In 2008–09, 38 students received support. Available to part-time students. Application deadline: 3/2; *Faculty research:* Cognitive psychology, anger management, grief and grief counseling, post-modernism and psychotherapy, spirituality and psychology. *Unit head:* Dr. Helen Shoemaker, Program Director, 510-436-1543, E-mail: shoemaker@hnu.edu. *Application contact:* 800-430-1321, Fax: 510-436-1325, E-mail: AdultEd@hnu.edu.

John Jay College of Criminal Justice of the City University of New York, Graduate Studies, Program in Forensic Psychology, New York, NY 10019-1093. Offers MA, PhD. Part-time and evening/weekend programs available. *Degree requirements:* For master's, thesis or alternative, externship. *Entrance requirements:* For master's, GRE General Test, minimum B average in major. Additional exam requirements/recommendations for international students: Required—TOEFL (minimum score 500 paper-based; 173 computer-based).

John Jay College of Criminal Justice of the City University of New York, Graduate Studies, Programs in Criminal Justice, New York, NY 10019-1093. Offers criminal justice (MA, PhD); criminology and deviance (PhD); forensic psychology (PhD); forensic science (PhD);

law and philosophy (PhD); organizational behavior (PhD); public policy (PhD). Part-time and evening/weekend programs available. Terminal master's awarded for partial completion of doctoral program. *Degree requirements:* For master's, thesis or alternative; for doctorate, one foreign language, thesis/dissertation. *Entrance requirements:* For master's, GRE General Test, minimum B average; for doctorate, GRE General Test. Additional exam requirements/recommendations for international students: Required—TOEFL (minimum score 500 paper-based; 173 computer-based).

Marymount University, School of Education and Human Services, Program in Community Counseling and Forensic Psychology, Arlington, VA 22207-4299. Offers MA/MA. Part-time and evening/weekend programs available. *Students:* 7 full-time (all women), 4 part-time (all women); includes 3 minority (all African Americans). Average age 27. *Entrance requirements:* Additional exam requirements/recommendations for international students: Required—TOEFL (minimum score 600 paper-based; 250 computer-based; 100 iBT). Application fee: $40. *Expenses:* Tuition: Full-time $12,420; part-time $690 per credit hour. Required fees: $126; $7 per credit hour. Tuition and fees vary according to degree level. *Financial support:* In 2008–09, 10 students received support; research assistantships with full tuition reimbursements available, career-related internships or fieldwork, Federal Work-Study, scholarships/grants, and unspecified assistantships available. Support available to part-time students. Financial award applicants required to submit FAFSA. *Unit head:* Dr. Wayne Lesko, Dean, 703-284-1620, Fax: 703-284-1631, E-mail: wayne.lesko@marymount.edu. *Application contact:* Francesca Reed, Director, Graduate Admissions, 703-284-5901, Fax: 703-527-3815, E-mail: grad.admissions@marymount.edu.

Marymount University, School of Education and Human Services, Program in Forensic Psychology, Arlington, VA 22207-4299. Offers MA. Part-time and evening/weekend programs available. *Faculty:* 4 full-time (3 women), 7 part-time/adjunct (5 women). *Students:* 121 full-time (102 women), 43 part-time (38 women); includes 24 minority (13 African Americans, 1 American Indian/Alaska Native, 6 Asian Americans or Pacific Islanders, 4 Hispanic Americans), 2 international. Average age 25. 159 applicants, 90% accepted, 81 enrolled. In 2008, 74 master's awarded. *Degree requirements:* For master's, thesis or alternative. *Entrance requirements:* For master's, GRE, 2 letters of recommendation, resumé, personal statement. Additional exam requirements/recommendations for international students: Required—TOEFL (minimum score 600 paper-based; 250 computer-based; 100 iBT). *Application deadline:* For fall admission, 2/16 for domestic and international students. Application fee: $40. Electronic applications accepted. *Expenses:* Tuition: Full-time $12,420; part-time $690 per credit hour. Required fees: $126; $7 per credit hour. Tuition and fees vary according to degree level. *Financial support:* In 2008–09, 120 students received support; research assistantships with full tuition reimbursements available, career-related internships or fieldwork, Federal Work-Study, scholarships/grants, and unspecified assistantships available. Support available to part-time students. Financial award applicants required to submit FAFSA. *Unit head:* Dr. Jason Doll, Chair, 703-526-6821, Fax: 703-284-5708, E-mail: jason.doll@marymount.edu. *Application contact:* Francesca Reed, Director, Graduate Admissions, 703-284-5901, Fax: 703-527-3815, E-mail: grad.admissions@marymount.edu.

Massachusetts School of Professional Psychology, Graduate Programs, Boston, MA 02132. Offers clinical psychology (Psy D); clinical psychopharmacology (Post-Doctoral MS); counseling psychology (MA); executive coaching (Graduate Certificate); forensic psychology (MA); organizational psychology (MA); respecialization in clinical psychology (Certificate); MA/CAGS. *Accreditation:* APA. *Degree requirements:* For master's, comprehensive exam; for doctorate, thesis/dissertation. *Entrance requirements:* For doctorate, GRE General Test. Additional exam requirements/recommendations for international students: Required—TOEFL (minimum score 550 paper-based; 213 computer-based). Electronic applications accepted.

Oklahoma State University Center for Health Sciences, Graduate Program in Forensic Sciences, Tulsa, OK 74107-1898. Offers forensic DNA/molecular biology (MS); forensic examination of questioned documents (MFSA, Certificate); forensic pathology (MS); forensic psychology (MS); forensic sciences (MFSA); forensic toxicology (MS). Part-time and evening/weekend programs available. Postbaccalaureate distance learning degree programs offered (no on-campus study). *Degree requirements:* For master's, comprehensive exam (for some programs), thesis (for some programs). *Entrance requirements:* For master's, MAT (MFSA) or GRE General Test, professional experience (MFSA). Additional exam requirements/recommendations for international students: Required—TOEFL (minimum score 600 paper-based; 250 computer-based), TWE (minimum score 5). *Faculty research:* DNA typing, DNA polymorphism, identification through DNA, disease transmission, forensic dentistry, neurotoxicity of HIV, forensic toxicology method development, toxin detection and characterization.

Prairie View A&M University, College of Juvenile Justice and Psychology, Prairie View, TX 77446-0519. Offers clinical adolescent psychology (PhD); juvenile forensic psychology (MSJFP); juvenile justice (MSJJ, PhD). Part-time and evening/weekend programs available. *Degree requirements:* For master's, comprehensive exam (for some programs), thesis (for some programs); for doctorate, comprehensive exam, thesis/dissertation. *Entrance requirements:* For master's, GRE, minimum GPA of 2.75; for doctorate, GRE, previous course work in clinical adolescent psychology, minimum GPA of 3.5. Additional exam requirements/recommendations for international students: Required—TOEFL. *Faculty research:* Juvenile justice, juvenile forensic psychology, teen court, graduate education, capital punishment.

Roger Williams University, Feinstein College of Arts and Sciences, Program in Forensic Psychology, Bristol, RI 02809. Offers MA. Part-time programs available. *Faculty:* 8 full-time (3 women). *Students:* 30 full-time (26 women), 2 part-time (1 woman); includes 1 minority (Hispanic American). Average age 25. 49 applicants, 73% accepted, 17 enrolled. In 2008, 13 master's awarded. *Degree requirements:* For master's, thesis optional. *Entrance requirements:* For master's, GRE, 3 Letters Recommendation, Personal Statement, Transcript. Additional exam requirements/recommendations for international students: Recommended—IELTS. *Application deadline:* For fall admission, 3/15 for domestic and international students. Applications are processed on a rolling basis. Application fee: $50. Electronic applications accepted. *Expenses:* Contact institution. *Financial support:* In 2008–09, 27 students received support. Application deadline: 6/15; *Unit head:* Dr. Donald Whitworth, Professor of Psychology, 401-254-3509, E-mail: dwhitworth@rwu.edu. *Application contact:* Lori Vales, Graduate Admission Coordinator, 401-254-6200, Fax: 401-254-3557, E-mail: gradadmit@rwu.edu.

Announcement: Roger Williams University is one of only a handful of academic institutions to offer a graduate degree focused specifically on forensic psychology. Faculty members provide expert training on topics ranging from sex offender risk assessment and adolescent homicide to prosecutorial misconduct and eyewitness testimony. For more information, visit www.rwu.edu/admission/graduate/.

See Close-Up on page 1129.

Sage Graduate School, Graduate School, Department of Psychology, Program in Forensic Psychology, Troy, NY 12180-4115. Offers Certificate. Part-time and evening/weekend programs available. *Faculty:* 4 full-time (all women), 5 part-time/adjunct (2 women). *Students:* 3 full-time (all women), 6 part-time (all women). Average age 29. In 2008, 3 Certificates awarded. *Entrance requirements:* Additional exam requirements/recommendations for international students: Required—TOEFL (minimum score 550 paper-based; 213 computer-based).

Application deadline: Applications are processed on a rolling basis. Application fee: $40. *Expenses:* Tuition: Full-time $10,080; part-time $560 per credit hour. *Financial support:* Fellowships, research assistantships, Federal Work-Study, scholarships/grants, and unspecified assistantships available. Support available to part-time students. Financial award application deadline: 3/1; financial award applicants required to submit FAFSA. *Unit head:* Dr. Bronna Romanoff, Director, 518-244-2260, E-mail: romanb@sage.edu. *Application contact:* Wendy D. Diefendorf, Director of Graduate and Adult Admission, 518-244-2443, Fax: 518-244-6880, E-mail: diefew@sage.edu.

Sage Graduate School, Graduate School, Department of Sociology and Criminal Justice, Program in Forensic Mental Health, Troy, NY 12180-4115. Offers MS, Certificate. Part-time and evening/weekend programs available. *Faculty:* 2 part-time/adjunct (both women). *Students:* 3 full-time (all women), 14 part-time (13 women); includes 2 minority (both African Americans). Average age 28. 32 applicants, 69% accepted, 12 enrolled. *Entrance requirements:* Additional exam requirements/recommendations for international students: Required—TOEFL (minimum score 550 paper-based; 213 computer-based). *Application deadline:* Applications are processed on a rolling basis. Application fee: $40. *Expenses:* Tuition: Full-time $10,080; part-time $560 per credit hour. *Financial support:* Fellowships, research assistantships, Federal Work-Study, scholarships/grants, and unspecified assistantships available. Support available to part-time students. *Unit head:* Dr. Maureen McLeod, Chair, 518-244-2245, E-mail: mcleom@sage.edu. *Application contact:* Wendy D. Diefendorf, Director of Graduate and Adult Admission, 518-244-2443, Fax: 518-244-6880, E-mail: diefew@sage.edu.

Tiffin University, Program in Criminal Justice, Tiffin, OH 44883-2161. Offers crime analysis (MSCJ); criminal behavior (MSCJ); forensic psychology (MSCJ); homeland security administration (MSCJ); justice administration (MSCJ). Part-time and evening/weekend programs available. Postbaccalaureate distance learning degree programs offered (no on-campus study). *Degree requirements:* For master's, thesis optional. *Entrance requirements:* For master's, minimum undergraduate GPA of 2.5, work experience. Additional exam requirements/recommendations for international students: Required—TOEFL (minimum score 550 paper-based; 213 computer-based). Electronic applications accepted. *Faculty research:* Terrorism, intelligence, homeland security, guns and crime.

Universidad de Iberoamerica, Graduate School, San Jose, Costa Rica. Offers clinical psychology (M Psych); educational psychology (M Psych); forensic psychology (M Psych); hospital management (MHA); intensive care nursing (MN); medicine (MD). *Entrance requirements:* For master's, 2 letters of recommendation, interview.

The University of British Columbia, Faculty of Arts and Faculty of Graduate Studies, Department of Psychology, Vancouver, BC V6T 1Z1, Canada. Offers behavioral neuroscience (MA, PhD); clinical psychology (MA, PhD); cognitive science (MA, PhD); developmental psychology (MA, PhD); forensic psychology (PhD); health psychology (MA, PhD); quantitative methods (MA, PhD); social/personality psychology (MA, PhD). *Accreditation:* APA (one or more programs are accredited). Terminal master's awarded for partial completion of doctoral program. *Degree requirements:* For master's, thesis; for doctorate, comprehensive exam, thesis/dissertation. *Entrance requirements:* For master's and doctorate, GRE General Test, GRE Subject Test. Additional exam requirements/recommendations for international students: Required—TOEFL (minimum score 550 paper-based; 230 computer-based; 80 iBT). Electronic applications accepted. *Faculty research:* Clinical, developmental, social/personality, cognition, behavioral neuroscience.

University of Massachusetts Boston, Office of Graduate Studies, Graduate College of Education, Counseling and School Psychology Department, Program in Mental Health Counseling, Boston, MA 02125-3393. Offers forensic counseling (M Ed, CAGS).

University of North Dakota, Graduate School, College of Arts and Sciences, Department of Psychology, Grand Forks, ND 58202. Offers clinical psychology (PhD); counseling psychology (PhD); experimental psychology (PhD); forensic psychology (MA, MS); psychology (MA). *Accreditation:* APA (one or more programs are accredited). *Degree requirements:* For master's, thesis, final exam; for doctorate, comprehensive exam, thesis/dissertation, internship, final exam. *Entrance requirements:* For master's, GRE General Test, GRE Subject Test, minimum GPA of 3.0; for doctorate, GRE General Test, GRE Subject Test, minimum GPA of 3.5. Additional exam requirements/recommendations for international students: Required—TOEFL (minimum score 550 paper-based; 213 computer-based; 79 iBT), IELTS (minimum score 6.5). Electronic applications accepted. *Faculty research:* Developmental psychology, clinical social psychology, educational psychology, personality disorders.

Walden University, Graduate Programs, School of Psychology, Minneapolis, MN 55401. Offers clinical assessment (Post-Doctoral Certificate); clinical child psychology (Post-Doctoral Certificate); clinical psychology (Post-Doctoral Certificate); counseling psychology (Post-Doctoral Certificate); forensic psychology (MS), including forensic psychology in the community, general forensic psychology, mental health applications, program planning and evaluation in forensic settings, psychology and legal systems; general psychology (Post-Doctoral Certificate); health psychology (Post-Doctoral Certificate); organizational psychology (Post-Doctoral Certificate); organizational psychology and development (Certificate); psychology (MS, PhD), including clinical psychology, counseling psychology, crisis management and response (MS), general psychology, health psychology, leadership development and coaching (MS), media psychology (MS), organizational psychology, organizational psychology and development (MS), organizational psychology and nonprofit management (MS), program evaluation and research (MS), psychology of culture (MS), psychology, public administration, and social change (MS), school psychology, social psychology (MS), terrorism and security (MS); school psychology (Post-Doctoral Certificate); teaching online (Post-Master's Certificate). Part-time and evening/weekend programs available. Postbaccalaureate distance learning degree programs offered (minimal on-campus study). *Faculty:* 16 full-time, 190 part-time/adjunct. *Students:* 3,198 full-time (2,489 women), 810 part-time (664 women); includes 1,319 minority (1,013 African Americans, 51 American Indian/Alaska Native, 68 Asian Americans or Pacific Islanders, 187 Hispanic Americans), 72 international. Average age 40. 1,468 applicants, 60% accepted, 612 enrolled. In 2008, 203 master's, 37 doctorates awarded. Terminal master's awarded for partial completion of doctoral program. *Degree requirements:* For master's, thesis optional; for doctorate, thesis/dissertation, residency. *Entrance requirements:* For master's, bachelor's degree or equivalent in related field, minimum GPA of 2.5, two references, goal statement, official transcripts, access to computer and Internet; for doctorate, master's degree or equivalent in related field, minimum GPA of 3.0, three years related professional/academic experience, two references, goal statement, official transcripts, access to computer and Internet. Additional exam requirements/recommendations for international students: Required—TOEFL (minimum score 550 paper-based; 213 computer-based), IELTS (minimum score 6.5), TOEFL, IELTS, or Michigan English Language Assessment Battery (minimum score 82). *Application deadline:* Applications are processed on a rolling basis. Application fee: $50. Electronic applications accepted. *Expenses:* Tuition: Full-time $12,877; part-time $520 per credit. Required fees: $1230. Tuition and fees vary according to course load, degree level and program. *Financial support:* In 2008–09, 1 fellowship was awarded; Federal Work-Study, scholarships/grants, unspecified assistantships, and family tuition reduction; active duty/veteran tuition reduction; group tuition reduction; interest-free payment plans also available. Support available to part-time students. Financial award applicants required to submit FAFSA. *Unit head:* Dr. Nina Nabors, Associate Dean, 800-925-3368. *Application contact:* Jennifer Hall, 866-4-WALDEN, E-mail: info@waldenu.edu.

Genetic Counseling

Arcadia University, Graduate Studies, Program in Genetic Counseling, Glenside, PA 19038-3295. Offers MSGC. *Degree requirements:* For master's, thesis. *Entrance requirements:* For master's, GRE. Additional exam requirements/recommendations for international students: Required—TOEFL. *Expenses:* Contact institution.

Brandeis University, Graduate School of Arts and Sciences, Program in Genetic Counseling, Waltham, MA 02454-9110. Offers MS. *Degree requirements:* For master's, thesis. *Entrance requirements:* For master's, GRE General Test, resumé, 3 letters of recommendation, statement of purpose. Additional exam requirements/recommendations for international students: Required—TOEFL (minimum score 600 paper-based; 250 computer-based; 100 iBT), IELTS (minimum score 7). Electronic applications accepted. *Expenses:* Contact institution.

California State University, Stanislaus, College of Natural Sciences, Department of Biological Sciences, Turlock, CA 95382. Offers ecology and sustainability (MS); genetic counseling (MS); marine sciences (MS). Part-time programs available. *Degree requirements:* For master's, thesis. *Entrance requirements:* For master's, GRE General Test, GRE Subject Test, minimum GPA of 3.0, 3 letters of reference, personal statement. Additional exam requirements/recommendations for international students: Required—TOEFL (minimum score 550 paper-based; 213 computer-based). Electronic applications accepted. *Faculty research:* Long-term smoking and pregnancy rate, vertebrate paleobiology, terrestrial animals, benthic invertebrates of central California coastline.

Case Western Reserve University, School of Medicine and School of Graduate Studies, Graduate Programs in Medicine, Department of Genetics, Program in Genetic Counseling, Cleveland, OH 44106. Offers MS. *Degree requirements:* For master's, thesis. *Entrance requirements:* For master's, GRE General Test. Additional exam requirements/recommendations for international students: Required—TOEFL. *Faculty research:* Genetic testing, ethical issues in genetics, cancer genetics, reproductive genetics, prenatal diagnosis.

The Johns Hopkins University, Bloomberg School of Public Health, Department of Health, Behavior and Society, Baltimore, MD 21218-2699. Offers behavioral sciences and health education (MHS); genetic counseling (Sc M); social and behavioral sciences (PhD, Sc D). *Degree requirements:* For master's, comprehensive exam (for some programs), thesis (for some programs); for doctorate, comprehensive exam, thesis/dissertation. *Entrance requirements:* For master's and doctorate, GRE, transcripts, curriculum vitae, statement, 3 recommendation letters. Additional exam requirements/recommendations for international students: Required—TOEFL (minimum score 250 computer-based; 100 iBT). Electronic applications accepted. *Faculty research:* Structural and community-level inventions to improve health communication and health education behavioral and social aspects of genetic counseling.

McGill University, Faculty of Graduate and Postdoctoral Studies, Faculty of Medicine, Department of Human Genetics, Montréal, QC H3A 2T5, Canada. Offers genetic counseling (M Sc); human genetics (M Sc, PhD).

Mount Sinai School of Medicine of New York University, Graduate School of Biological Sciences, New York, NY 10029-6504. Offers bioethics (MS); biological sciences (PhD); clinical research (MS); community medicine (MPH); genetic counseling (MS); neurosciences (PhD); MD/PhD. *Faculty:* 126 full-time (40 women). *Students:* 498 full-time (259 women); includes 123 minority (27 African Americans, 3 American Indian/Alaska Native, 76 Asian Americans or Pacific Islanders, 17 Hispanic Americans), 95 international. 859 applicants, 30% accepted, 102 enrolled. In 2008, 60 master's, 27 doctorates awarded. Terminal master's awarded for partial completion of doctoral program. *Degree requirements:* For master's, thesis; for doctorate, comprehensive exam, thesis/dissertation. *Entrance requirements:* For master's, GRE General Test; for doctorate, GRE General Test, GRE Subject Test, 3 years of college pre-med course work. Additional exam requirements/recommendations for international students: Required—TOEFL. *Application deadline:* For fall admission, 12/15 for domestic and international students. Applications are processed on a rolling basis. Application fee: $75. Electronic applications accepted. *Expenses:* Tuition: Full-time $23,175. Required fees: $100. Full-time tuition and fees vary according to course load, degree level, program and student level. *Financial support:* In 2008–09, fellowships with full tuition reimbursements (averaging $28,000 per year), research assistantships with full tuition reimbursements (averaging $28,000 per year) were awarded; Federal Work-Study, institutionally sponsored loans, scholarships/grants, health care benefits, and unspecified assistantships also available. Financial award application deadline: 4/30; financial award applicants required to submit FAFSA. *Faculty research:* Cancer, genetics and genomics, immunology, neuroscience, developmental and stem cell biology, translational research. Total annual research expenditures: $191.5 million. *Unit head:* Dr. John Morrison, Dean, 212-241-6546, Fax: 212-241-0651, E-mail: john.morrison@mssm.edu. *Application contact:* Lily Recanati, Manager, 212-241-2793, Fax: 212-241-0651, E-mail: lily.recantati@mssm.edu.

Northwestern University, The Graduate School, Program in Genetic Counseling, Evanston, IL 60208. Offers MS. *Degree requirements:* For master's, thesis. *Entrance requirements:* For master's, GRE General Test, interview. Additional exam requirements/recommendations for international students: Required—TOEFL. *Faculty research:* Preimplantation genetic diagnosis, gene expression in preimplantation embryos, fetal cells in maternal blood: first trimester prenatal screening for Down's Syndrome, genetic counseling efficacy and counseling issues in prenatal diagnosis.

Sarah Lawrence College, Graduate Studies, Program in Genetic Counseling, Bronxville, NY 10708-5999. Offers human genetics (MS). Part-time programs available. *Faculty:* 21 part-time/adjunct (16 women). *Students:* 37 full-time (34 women), 1 part-time (0 women); includes 4 minority (2 Asian Americans or Pacific Islanders, 2 Hispanic Americans), 18 international. 93 applicants, 61% accepted, 19 enrolled. In 2008, 21 master's awarded. *Degree requirements:* For master's, thesis, fieldwork. *Entrance requirements:* For master's, previous course work in biology, chemistry, developmental biology, genetics, probability and statistics. *Application deadline:* For fall admission, 1/15 for domestic students. Application fee: $60. *Expenses:* Contact institution. *Financial support:* In 2008–09, 26 students received support, including 26 fellowships; career-related internships or fieldwork, Federal Work-Study, scholarships/grants, and unspecified assistantships also available. Support available to part-time students. Financial award application deadline: 3/1; financial award applicants required to submit CSS PROFILE or FAFSA. *Unit head:* Caroline Lieber, Director, 914-395-2371. *Application contact:* Susan Guma, Dean of Graduate Studies, 914-395-2373, E-mail: sguma@mail.slc.edu.

University of Arkansas for Medical Sciences, Graduate School, Program in Genetic Counseling, Little Rock, AR 72205-7199. Offers MS.

The University of British Columbia, Faculty of Medicine, Department of Medical Genetics, Program in Genetic Counselling, Vancouver, BC V6T 1Z1, Canada. Offers M Sc.

University of California, Irvine, School of Medicine, Department of Pediatrics, Program in Genetic Counseling, Irvine, CA 92697. Offers MS. *Degree requirements:* For master's, thesis. *Entrance requirements:* For master's, GRE General Test, minimum GPA of 3.0. Additional exam requirements/recommendations for international students: Required—TOEFL (minimum score 550 paper-based; 213 computer-based). Electronic applications accepted. *Faculty research:* Gene mapping and linkage analysis, delineation of new malformation and chromosomal syndromes, ethical and counseling issues in genetics.

University of Cincinnati, Graduate School, College of Allied Health Sciences, Program in Genetic Counseling, Cincinnati, OH 45221. Offers medical genetics (MS). Part-time programs available. *Degree requirements:* For master's, thesis. *Entrance requirements:* For master's, GRE General Test. Additional exam requirements/recommendations for international students: Required—TOEFL. Electronic applications accepted. *Faculty research:* Lysosomal disease, Tourette's syndrome, epidemiology of Down syndrome, genetic counseling, genetic disease treatment.

University of Colorado Denver, Graduate School, Program in Genetic Counseling, Denver, CO 80217-3364. Offers MS. *Degree requirements:* For master's, comprehensive exam, thesis optional. *Entrance requirements:* For master's, GRE General Test, minimum GPA of 3.0, 4 letters of recommendation. Additional exam requirements/recommendations for international students: Required—TOEFL (minimum score 550 paper-based; 213 computer-based). *Expenses:* Contact institution.

University of Minnesota, Twin Cities Campus, Graduate School, Program in Molecular, Cellular, Developmental Biology and Genetics, Minneapolis, MN 55455-0213. Offers genetic counseling (MS); molecular, cellular, developmental biology and genetics (PhD). Part-time programs available. Terminal master's awarded for partial completion of doctoral program. *Degree requirements:* For master's, thesis optional; for doctorate, thesis/dissertation. *Entrance requirements:* For master's and doctorate, GRE General Test. Additional exam requirements/recommendations for international students: Required—TOEFL (minimum score 625 paper-based; 263 computer-based; 80 iBT). Electronic applications accepted. *Faculty research:* Membrane receptors and membrane transport, cell interactions, cytoskeleton and cell mobility, regulation of gene expression, plant cell and molecular biology.

The University of North Carolina at Greensboro, Graduate School, Program in Genetic Counseling, Greensboro, NC 27412-5001. Offers MS. Electronic applications accepted.

University of Oklahoma Health Sciences Center, College of Medicine and Graduate College, Department of Genetic Counseling, Oklahoma City, OK 73190. Offers MS. *Entrance requirements:* For master's, GRE General Test, 3 letters of recommendation.

University of Pittsburgh, Graduate School of Public Health, Department of Human Genetics, Program in Genetic Counseling, Pittsburgh, PA 15260. Offers MS. *Degree requirements:* For master's, comprehensive exam, thesis, clinical internship. *Entrance requirements:* For master's, GRE General Test, previous course work in biochemistry, calculus, and genetics. Additional exam requirements/recommendations for international students: Required—TOEFL (minimum score 550 paper-based; 213 computer-based; 80 iBT). Electronic applications accepted. *Faculty research:* Statistical genetics, molecular genetics, cytogenetics, gene therapy.

University of South Carolina, School of Medicine and The Graduate School, Graduate Programs in Medicine, Program in Genetic Counseling, Columbia, SC 29208. Offers MS. *Degree requirements:* For master's, comprehensive exam, internship, practicum. *Entrance requirements:* For master's, GRE General Test. Electronic applications accepted. *Expenses:* Contact institution. *Faculty research:* Genetic counseling, international, transition, prenatal diagnosis.

The University of Texas Health Science Center at Houston, Graduate School of Biomedical Sciences, Program in Genetic Counseling, Houston, TX 77225-0036. Offers MS. *Degree requirements:* For master's, thesis. *Entrance requirements:* For master's, GRE General Test. Additional exam requirements/recommendations for international students: Required—TOEFL, TWE. Electronic applications accepted. *Faculty research:* Genetics, molecular genetics, ctyogenetics, psychosocial issues associated with genetics counseling, research aspects of the practice of medical genetics.

University of Toronto, School of Graduate Studies, Life Sciences Division, Department of Molecular and Medical Genetics, Toronto, ON M5S 1A1, Canada. Offers genetic counseling (M Sc); molecular and medical genetics (M Sc, PhD). *Degree requirements:* For master's, thesis; for doctorate, thesis/dissertation. *Entrance requirements:* For master's, B Sc or equivalent, minimum B+ average; for doctorate, M Sc or equivalent, minimum B+ average. Additional exam requirements/recommendations for international students: Required—TOEFL, IELTS (minimum score: 7), Michigan English Language Assessment Battery (minimum score: 85) or COPE (minimum score: 4). *Faculty research:* Structural biology, developmental genetics, molecular medicine, genetic counseling.

University of Wisconsin–Madison, Graduate School, College of Agricultural and Life Sciences and Graduate Programs in Medicine, Department of Genetics, Program in Genetic Counseling, Madison, WI 53706-1380. Offers MS.

Health Psychology

American University of Beirut, Graduate Programs, Faculty of Health Sciences, Beirut, Lebanon. Offers environmental sciences (MSES), including environmental health; epidemiology (MS); epidemiology and biostatistics (MPH); health behavior and education (MPH); population health (MS); public health (MPH). Part-time programs available. *Degree requirements:* For master's, one foreign language, comprehensive exam, thesis (for some programs). *Entrance requirements:* For master's, 2 letters of recommendation, personal statement, transcripts. Additional exam requirements/recommendations for international students: Required—TOEFL (minimum score 573 paper-based; 230 computer-based; 98 iBT), IELTS (minimum score 7.5). Electronic applications accepted. *Faculty research:* Urban health, childbirth, tobacco control, HIV/AIDS surveillance, health finance and policies.

Appalachian State University, Cratis D. Williams Graduate School, Department of Psychology, Boone, NC 28608. Offers clinical health psychology (MA); general experimental psychology (MA); industrial and organizational psychology (MA). Part-time programs available. *Faculty:* 31 full-time (11 women). *Students:* 59 full-time (45 women), 15 part-time (12 women); includes 3 minority (2 African Americans, 1 Asian American or Pacific Islander), 4 international. 185 applicants, 30% accepted, 18 enrolled. In 2008, 23 master's, 3 other advanced degrees awarded. *Degree requirements:* For master's and MA/SSP, comprehensive exam, thesis optional, GRE Subject Test exit exam. *Entrance requirements:* For master's and MA/SSP, GRE General Test, 3 letters of recommendation. Additional exam requirements/recommendations for international students: Required—TOEFL (minimum score 550 paper-based; 230 computer-based; 79 iBT), IELTS (minimum score 6.5), TOEFL or IELTS. *Application deadline:* For fall admission, 3/1 for domestic students, 2/1 for international students. Applications are processed on a rolling basis. Application fee: $50. Electronic applications accepted. *Expenses:* Tuition, area resident: Full-time $2600; part-time $700 per course. Tuition, state resident: full-time $2600; part-time $700 per course. Tuition, nonresident: full-time $5000; part-time $3300 per course. Required fees: $2150; $330 per course. Tuition and fees vary according to campus/location. *Financial support:* In 2008–09, 34 research assistantships (averaging $3,500 per year), 25 teaching assistantships (averaging $3,500 per year) were awarded; fellowships, career-related internships or fieldwork, Federal Work-Study, scholarships/grants, and unspecified assistantships also available. Financial award application deadline: 4/1; financial award applicants required to submit FAFSA. *Faculty research:* Eating disorders, school-based consultations, organizational behavior management, brain mechanisms of sound localization, parenting styles. Total annual research expenditures: $83,000. *Unit head:* Dr. James Denniston, Chair, 828-262-2272, Fax: 828-262-2272, E-mail: dennistonjc@appstate.edu. *Application contact:* Dr. Denise Martz, Graduate Coordinator, 828-262-2715, E-mail: martzdm@appstate.edu.

Argosy University, Atlanta, College of Psychology and Behavioral Sciences, Atlanta, GA 30328. Offers clinical psychology (MA, Psy D, Postdoctoral Respecialization Certificate), including child and family psychology (Psy D), general adult clinical (Psy D), health psychology (Psy D), neuropsychology/geropsychology (Psy D); community counseling (MA), including marriage and family therapy; counselor education and supervision (Ed D); marriage and family therapy (Certificate). *Accreditation:* APA.

See Close-Up on page 1065.

Argosy University, Chicago, College of Psychology and Behavioral Sciences, Doctoral Program in Clinical Psychology, Chicago, IL 60654. Offers child and adolescent psychology (Psy D); client-centered and experiential psychotherapies (Psy D); diversity and multicultural psychology (Psy D); family psychology (Psy D); forensic psychology (Psy D); health psychology (Psy D); psychoanalytic psychology (Psy D); psychology and spirituality (Psy D). *Accreditation:* APA.

See Close-Up on page 1067.

Argosy University, Schaumburg, College of Psychology and Behavioral Sciences, Schaumburg, IL 60173-5403. Offers clinical health psychology (Post-Graduate Certificate); clinical psychology (MA, Psy D), including child and family psychology (Psy D), clinical health psychology (Psy D), diversity and multicultural psychology (Psy D), forensic psychology (Psy D); community counseling (MA); counseling psychology (Ed D), including counselor education and supervision; counselor education and supervision (Ed D); forensic psychology (Post-Graduate Certificate); organizational leadership (Ed D). *Accreditation:* ACA; APA.

See Close-Up on page 1093.

Argosy University, Twin Cities, College of Psychology and Behavioral Sciences, Eagan, MN 55121. Offers clinical psychology (MA, Psy D), including child and family psychology (Psy D), forensic psychology (Psy D), health psychology (Psy D), marriage/couples and family therapy (Psy D), neuropsychology (Psy D); forensic counseling (Post-Graduate Certificate); forensic psychology (MA); marriage and family therapy (MA, DMFT), including forensic counseling (MA); organizational leadership (Ed D). *Accreditation:* APA.

See Close-Up on page 1099.

Argosy University, Washington DC, College of Psychology and Behavioral Sciences, Arlington, VA 22209. Offers clinical psychology (MA, Psy D), including child and family psychology (Psy D), diversity and multicultural psychology (Psy D), forensic psychology (Psy D), health and neuropsychology (Psy D); community counseling (MA); counseling psychology (Ed D), including counselor education and supervision; counselor education and supervision (Ed D); forensic psychology (MA); organizational leadership (Ed D). *Accreditation:* APA.

See Close-Up on page 1101.

Bastyr University, Graduate and Professional Programs, School of Nutrition and Exercise Science, Kenmore, WA 98028-4966. Offers nutrition (MS); nutrition and clinical health psychology (MS). Part-time programs available. *Degree requirements:* For master's, thesis optional. *Entrance requirements:* For master's, BS with 1 year of course work in chemistry, biochemistry, physiology and nutrition. Additional exam requirements/recommendations for international students: Required—TOEFL (minimum score 550 paper-based; 213 computer-based; 79 iBT).

California Institute of Integral Studies, Graduate Programs, School of Consciousness and Transformation, San Francisco, CA 94103. Offers cultural anthropology and social transformation (MA); East-West psychology (MA, PhD); integrative health studies (MA); philosophy and religion (MA, PhD), including Asian and comparative studies, philosophy, cosmology, and consciousness, women's spirituality, women's spirituality flex format; social and cultural anthropology (PhD); transformative leadership (MA); transformative studies (PhD). Part-time and evening/weekend programs available. Postbaccalaureate distance learning degree programs offered (minimal on-campus study). *Faculty:* 29 full-time, 32 part-time/adjunct. *Students:* 334 full-time (218 women), 126 part-time (77 women); includes 102 minority (39 African Americans, 4 American Indian/Alaska Native, 35 Asian Americans or Pacific Islanders, 24 Hispanic Americans), 1 international. Average age 37. 223 applicants, 78% accepted, 110 enrolled. In 2008, 93 master's, 30 doctorates awarded. Terminal master's awarded for partial completion of doctoral program. *Degree requirements:* For master's, comprehensive exam (for some programs), thesis optional; for doctorate, comprehensive exam, thesis/dissertation. *Entrance requirements:* For master's, minimum GPA of 3.0, letters of recommendation, writing sample; for doctorate, master's degree, minimum GPA of 3.0, letters of recommendation, writing sample. Additional exam requirements/recommendations for international students: Required—TOEFL. *Application deadline:* For fall admission, 2/1 priority date for domestic and international students; for spring admission, 10/15 priority date for domestic and international students. Applications are processed on a rolling basis. Application fee: $65. Electronic applications accepted. *Expenses:* Tuition: Part-time $815 per contact hour. Required fees: $270; $135 per semester. Tuition and fees vary according to degree level. *Financial support:* In 2008–09, 271 students received support; research assistantships, teaching assistantships, career-related internships or fieldwork, Federal Work-Study, institutionally sponsored loans, scholarships/grants, and tuition waivers (partial) available. Support available to part-time students. Financial award application deadline: 3/15; financial award applicants required to submit FAFSA. *Faculty research:* Altered states of consciousness, dreams, cosmology, postcolonial studies, integrative health studies. *Application contact:* Allyson Werner, Senior Admissions Counselor, 415-575-6155, Fax: 415-575-1268.

See Close-Up on page 347.

California Institute of Integral Studies, Graduate Programs, School of Professional Psychology, San Francisco, CA 94103. Offers clinical psychology (Psy D); community mental health (MA); drama therapy (MA); expressive arts therapy (MA); integral counseling psychology (MA); integral counseling, psychology-weekend (MA); somatic psychology (MA). *Accreditation:* APA. Part-time programs available. *Faculty:* 28 full-time, 59 part-time/adjunct. *Students:* 553 full-time (408 women), 88 part-time (69 women); includes 132 minority (25 African Americans, 3 American Indian/Alaska Native, 57 Asian Americans or Pacific Islanders, 47 Hispanic Americans). Average age 37. 506 applicants, 61% accepted, 181 enrolled. In 2008, 109 master's, 20 doctorates awarded. *Degree requirements:* For master's, comprehensive exam; for doctorate, comprehensive exam, thesis/dissertation. *Entrance requirements:* For master's, minimum GPA of 3.0, letters of recommendation, writing sample; for doctorate, GRE, MA in psychology or social work with appropriate practical experience for advanced standing, or BA with a minimum GPA of 3.1; letters of recommendation; writing sample. Additional exam requirements/recommendations for international students: Required—TOEFL. *Application deadline:* For fall admission, 2/1 priority date for domestic and international students; for spring admission, 10/15 priority date for domestic and international students. Applications are processed on a rolling basis. Application fee: $65. Electronic applications accepted. *Expenses:* Tuition: Part-time $815 per contact hour. Required fees: $270; $135 per semester. Tuition and fees vary according to degree level. *Financial support:* In 2008–09, 496 students received support; research assistantships with tuition reimbursements available, teaching assistantships with tuition reimbursements available, career-related internships or fieldwork, Federal Work-Study, institutionally sponsored loans, scholarships/grants, and tuition waivers (partial) available. Support available to part-time students. Financial award application deadline: 3/15; financial award applicants required to submit FAFSA. *Faculty research:* Somatic psychology, comparative psychology, art therapy, transpersonal psychology, eco-psychology. *Application contact:* David Townes, Senior Admissions Counselor, 415-575-6152, Fax: 415-575-1268, E-mail: dtownes@ciis.edu.

See Close-Up on page 1105.

Central Connecticut State University, School of Graduate Studies, School of Arts and Sciences, Department of Psychology, New Britain, CT 06050-4010. Offers community psychology (MA); general psychology (MA); health psychology (MA). Part-time and evening/weekend programs available. *Faculty:* 21 full-time (12 women), 20 part-time/adjunct (6 women). *Students:* 17 full-time (14 women), 22 part-time (14 women); includes 8 minority (3 African Americans, 1 Asian American or Pacific Islander, 4 Hispanic Americans), 3 international. Average age 27. 35 applicants, 54% accepted, 10 enrolled. In 2008, 1 master's awarded. *Degree requirements:* For master's, comprehensive exam, thesis or alternative. *Entrance requirements:* For master's, minimum undergraduate GPA of 2.7, essay. Additional exam requirements/recommendations for international students: Required—TOEFL. *Application deadline:* For fall admission, 4/25 for domestic students; for spring admission, 12/1 for domestic students. Applications are processed on a rolling basis. Application fee: $50. Electronic applications accepted. *Expenses:* Tuition, area resident: Full-time $4377; part-time $420 per credit. Tuition, state resident: full-time $6566; part-time $420 per credit. Tuition, nonresident: full-time $12,195; part-time $420 per credit. Required fees: $3462. One-time fee: $62 part-time. *Financial support:* In 2008–09, 9 students received support, including 6 research assistantships; career-related internships or fieldwork, Federal Work-Study, scholarships/grants, and unspecified assistantships also available. Support available to part-time students. Financial award application deadline: 3/1; financial award applicants required to submit FAFSA. *Faculty research:* Clinical psychology, general psychology, child development, cognitive development, drugs/behavior. *Unit head:* Dr. Bradley M. Waite, Chair, 860-832-3100. *Application contact:* Dr. Bradley M. Waite, Chair, 860-832-3100.

Chatham University, Program in Counseling Psychology, Pittsburgh, PA 15232-2826. Offers child, adolescent and family (MSCP); counseling psychology (Psy D); health and holistic (MSCP); infant mental health (MSCP); organization and supervision (MSCP); sport and exercise (MSCP). Part-time and evening/weekend programs available. *Students:* 121 full-time (104 women), 72 part-time (63 women). Average age 30. 117 applicants, 79% accepted, 60 enrolled. In 2008, 63 master's awarded. *Degree requirements:* For master's, thesis optional, supervised internship, advanced research project (optional); for doctorate, thesis/dissertation, internship. *Entrance requirements:* For master's, minimum GPA of 3.0; 2 letters of recommendation; resumé; prerequisite coursework in statistics, biology, and psychology; for doctorate, GRE. Additional exam requirements/recommendations for international students: Required—TOEFL (minimum score 600 paper-based; 250 computer-based; 100 iBT), IELTS (minimum score 6.5), TWE. *Application deadline:* For fall admission, 5/1 priority date for domestic and international students; for spring admission, 10/15 for domestic students, 10/15 priority date for international students. Applications are processed on a rolling basis. Application fee: $45. Electronic applications accepted. *Expenses:* Tuition: Part-time $686 per credit. Tuition and fees vary according to program. *Financial support:* Career-related internships or fieldwork available. Financial award applicants required to submit FAFSA. *Faculty research:* Trauma and recovery, hypnosis, psychospiritual dimensions of healing, psychotherapy of schizophrenia. *Unit head:* Dr. Mary Beth Mannarino, Director, 412-365-1196, Fax: 412-365-1505, E-mail: mmannarino@chatham.edu. *Application contact:* Dory Perry, Associate Director of Graduate Admissions, 412-365-2758, Fax: 412-365-1609, E-mail: gradadmissions@chatham.edu.

Claremont Graduate University, Graduate Programs, School of Behavioral and Organizational Sciences, Department of Psychology, Claremont, CA 91711-6160. Offers advanced study in evaluation (Certificate); cognitive psychology (MA, PhD); developmental psychology (MA, PhD); evaluation and applied research methods (MA, PhD); health behavior research and evaluation (MA, PhD); human resource development and evaluation (MA); industrial/organizational psychology (MA, PhD); organizational behavior (MA, PhD); organizational psychology (MA, PhD); social psychology (MA, PhD); MBA/PhD. Part-time programs available. *Faculty:* 17 full-time (7 women), 1 part-time/adjunct (0 women). *Students:* 218 full-time (158 women), 24 part-time (18 women); includes 51 minority (15 African Americans, 1 American Indian/Alaska Native, 22 Asian Americans or Pacific Islanders, 13 Hispanic Americans), 11 international. Average age 30. In 2008, 38 master's, 12 doctorates, 2 other advanced degrees awarded. Terminal master's awarded for partial completion of doctoral program. *Entrance requirements:* For master's and doctorate, GRE General Test. Additional exam requirements/recommendations for international students: Required—TOEFL (minimum score 550 paper-based; 213 computer-based; 80 iBT). *Application deadline:* For fall admission, 1/15 priority date for domestic students. Applications are processed on a rolling basis. Application fee: $60. Electronic applications accepted. *Expenses:* Tuition: Full-time $33,698; part-time $1465 per unit. Required fees: $310; $155 per semester. Tuition and fees vary according to program. *Financial support:* Fellowships, research assistantships, teaching assistantships, Federal Work-Study, institutionally sponsored loans, scholarships/grants, and tuition waivers (full and partial) available. Support available to part-time students. Financial award application deadline: 2/15; financial award applicants required to submit FAFSA. *Faculty research:* Social intervention, diversity in organizations, eyewitness memory, aging and cognition, drug policy. *Unit head:* Stewart Donaldson, Dean, 909-607-9001, Fax: 909-621-8905, E-mail: stewart.donaldson@cgu.edu. *Application contact:* Paul Thomas, Director, External Affairs, 909-607-9016, Fax: 909-621-8905, E-mail: paul.thomas@cgu.edu.

Drexel University, College of Arts and Sciences, Department of Psychology, Clinical Psychology Program, Philadelphia, PA 19104-2875. Offers clinical psychology (PhD); forensic psychology (PhD); health psychology (PhD); neuropsychology (PhD). *Accreditation:* APA. Terminal master's awarded for partial completion of doctoral program. *Degree requirements:* For doctorate, thesis/dissertation, qualifying exam. *Entrance requirements:* For doctorate, GRE General Test, GRE Subject Test, minimum GPA of 3.0. Electronic applications accepted. *Expenses:* Contact institution. *Faculty research:* Cognitive behavioral therapy, stress and coping, eating disorders, substance abuse, developmental disabilities.

Drexel University, College of Arts and Sciences, Department of Psychology, Program in Law-Psychology, Philadelphia, PA 19104-2875. Offers JD/PhD. Electronic applications accepted. *Expenses:* Contact institution. *Faculty research:* Mental health law issues, professional ethics, social science applications to law.

Duke University, Graduate School, Department of Psychology, Durham, NC 27708-0586. Offers biological psychology (PhD); clinical psychology (PhD); cognitive psychology (PhD); developmental psychology (PhD); experimental psychology (PhD); health psychology (PhD); human social development (PhD); JD/MA. *Accreditation:* APA (one or more programs are accredited). *Degree requirements:* For doctorate, thesis/dissertation. *Entrance requirements:* For doctorate, GRE General Test. Additional exam requirements/recommendations for international students: Required—TOEFL (minimum score 550 paper-based; 213 computer-based; 83 iBT), IELTS (minimum score 7). Electronic applications accepted.

East Carolina University, Graduate School, Thomas Harriot College of Arts and Sciences, Department of Psychology, Program in Health Psychology, Greenville, NC 27858-4353. Offers PhD. *Entrance requirements:* For doctorate, GRE.

The George Washington University, School of Public Health and Health Services, Doctoral Program in Public Health, Washington, DC 20052. Offers environmental and occupational health (Dr PH); global health (Dr PH); health behavior (Dr PH); health policy (Dr PH). *Accreditation:* CEPH. *Students:* 5 full-time (3 women), 24 part-time (21 women); includes 12 minority (9 African Americans, 1 American Indian/Alaska Native, 1 Asian American or Pacific Islander, 1 Hispanic American), 2 international. Average age 31. 70 applicants, 27% accepted,

Health Psychology

The George Washington University (continued)
13 enrolled. *Application deadline:* For fall admission, 2/15 priority date for domestic students, 2/15 for international students. Applications are processed on a rolling basis. Application fee: $55. *Financial support:* Application deadline: 2/15. *Faculty research:* Community organization, tele-medicine, long-term care, financing for vulnerable populations, quantitative analysis in public health policy. *Unit head:* Dr. Marina S. Moses, Director, 202-994-1734, E-mail: eohmsm@gwumc.edu. *Application contact:* Jane Smith, Director of Recruitment, 202-994-0248, Fax: 202-994-3773, E-mail: sphhsinfo@gwumc.edu.

John F. Kennedy University, Graduate School of Holistic Studies, Department of Counseling Psychology, Program in Counseling Psychology, Pleasant Hill, CA 94523-4817. Offers holistic studies (MA); somatic psychology (MA); transpersonal psychology (MA). Part-time and evening/weekend programs available. *Degree requirements:* For master's, thesis or alternative. *Entrance requirements:* For master's, interview. Additional exam requirements/recommendations for international students: Required—TOEFL.

Lesley University, Graduate School of Arts and Social Sciences, Self-Designed Master's Program in Interdisciplinary Studies, Cambridge, MA 02138-2790. Offers individualized studies (MA); integrative holistic health (MA); women's studies (MA). Part-time and evening/weekend programs available. Postbaccalaureate distance learning degree programs offered (no on-campus study). *Entrance requirements:* For master's, 3 letters of recommendation. Additional exam requirements/recommendations for international students: Required—TOEFL (minimum score 550 paper-based; 213 computer-based; 80 iBT). *Expenses:* Tuition: Full-time $13,770; part-time $765 per credit hour. Required fees: $150. Tuition and fees vary according to course load, degree level, campus/location and program.

National-Louis University, College of Arts and Sciences, Program in Psychology, Chicago, IL 60603. Offers cultural psychology (MA); health psychology (MA); human development (MA); organizational psychology (MA); psychology (Certificate). Part-time and evening/weekend programs available. *Students:* 4 full-time (all women), 214 part-time (30 women); includes 145 minority (121 African Americans, 3 American Indian/Alaska Native, 3 Asian Americans or Pacific Islanders, 18 Hispanic Americans), 2 international. Average age 38. In 2008, 30 master's awarded. *Degree requirements:* For master's, thesis, internship (health psychology). *Entrance requirements:* For master's, GRE, MAT, or Watson-Glaser Critical Thinking Appraisal, interview, minimum GPA of 3.0; for Certificate, GRE, MAT, or Watson-Glaser Critical Thinking Appraisal, interview, minimum GPA of 3.0, undergraduate course work in psychology. *Application deadline:* Applications are processed on a rolling basis. *Financial support:* Federal Work-Study, institutionally sponsored loans, scholarships/grants, and tuition waivers available. Support available to part-time students. Financial award applicants required to submit FAFSA. *Faculty research:* Human development, personality theory, abnormal psychology. *Unit head:* Dr. Edward Risinger, Professor, 224-233-2533, Fax: 224-233-2533, E-mail: erisinger@nl.edu. *Application contact:* David McCulloch, Vice President for University Services, 800-443-5522 Ext. 5151, Fax: 847-465-0593, E-mail: dmcc@wheeling1.nl.edu.

North Dakota State University, College of Graduate and Interdisciplinary Studies, College of Science and Mathematics, Department of Psychology, Fargo, ND 58105. Offers clinical psychology (MS); cognitive and visual neuroscience (PhD); health and social psychology (PhD); psychology (MS). *Faculty:* 18 full-time (4 women), 2 part-time/adjunct (1 woman). *Students:* 36 full-time (27 women); includes 4 minority (1 African American, 2 Asian Americans or Pacific Islanders, 1 Hispanic American), 1 international. Average age 24. 48 applicants, 33% accepted, 10 enrolled. In 2008, 3 master's, 1 doctorate awarded. *Degree requirements:* For master's, thesis; for doctorate, thesis/dissertation. *Entrance requirements:* For master's and doctorate, GRE General Test, GRE Subject Test. Additional exam requirements/recommendations for international students: Required—TOEFL (minimum score 525 paper-based; 197 computer-based; 71 iBT). *Application deadline:* For fall admission, 3/1 for domestic and international students. Application fee: $45 ($60 for international students). Electronic applications accepted. *Financial support:* In 2008–09, 36 students received support, including 2 fellowships with full tuition reimbursements available (averaging $16,000 per year), 23 research assistantships with full tuition reimbursements available (averaging $16,000 per year), 11 teaching assistantships with full tuition reimbursements available (averaging $6,000 per year); career-related internships or fieldwork, Federal Work-Study, institutionally sponsored loans, tuition waivers (full and partial), and unspecified assistantships also available. Support available to part-time students. Financial award application deadline: 3/1. *Faculty research:* Cognition science, neuropsychology, group behavior, applied behavior analysis, behavior therapy. Total annual research expenditures: $2 million. *Unit head:* Dr. Paul D. Rokke, Chair, 701-231-8622, Fax: 701-231-8426, E-mail: paul.rokke@ndsu.edu. *Application contact:* Dr. Paul D. Rokke, Chair, 701-231-8622, Fax: 701-231-8426, E-mail: paul.rokke@ndsu.edu.

Northern Arizona University, Graduate College, College of Social and Behavioral Sciences, Department of Psychology, Flagstaff, AZ 86011. Offers applied health psychology (MA); clinical psychology (MA); general psychology (MA); teaching of psychology (MA). Part-time programs available. *Degree requirements:* For master's, thesis, oral defense. *Entrance requirements:* For master's, GRE General Test.

Northern Kentucky University, Office of Graduate Programs, College of Arts and Sciences, Program in Industrial-Organizational Psychology, Highland Heights, KY 41099. Offers industrial psychology (Certificate); industrial-organizational psychology (MS); occupational health psychology (Certificate); organizational psychology (Certificate). Part-time and evening/weekend programs available. *Students:* 8 full-time (6 women), 34 part-time (25 women); includes 4 minority (all African Americans), 2 international. Average age 29. 37 applicants, 57% accepted, 15 enrolled. In 2008, 23 master's awarded. *Degree requirements:* For master's, thesis optional, capstone. *Entrance requirements:* For master's, GRE (450 verbal, 450 quantitative, and 3.5 writing), minimum GPA of 3.0, at least 9 semester hours of undergraduate psychology, 1 course in statistics. Additional exam requirements/recommendations for international students: Required—TOEFL (minimum score 550 paper-based; 213 computer-based; 79 iBT), Michigan Test may be substituted only if taken at NKU (minimu score of 80); Recommended—IELTS (minimum score 6.5). *Application deadline:* For fall admission, 6/1 priority date for domestic students, 6/1 for international students; for spring admission, 11/1 priority date for domestic students, 10/1 for international students. Applications are processed on a rolling basis. Application fee: $40. Electronic applications accepted. *Expenses:* Tuition, area resident: Full-time $6642. Tuition, state resident: full-time $6642. Tuition, nonresident: full-time $11,682. *Financial support:* Unspecified assistantships available. Financial award applicants required to submit FAFSA. *Faculty research:* Workplace bullying, gender bias in hiring and performance appraisal, personality in training outcomes, social dilemmas. *Unit head:* Dr. Jeffrey Smith, Director, 859-572-5317, Fax: 859-572-6085, E-mail: smithj@nku.edu. *Application contact:* Dr. Peg Griffin, Director of Graduate Programs, 859-572-6934, Fax: 859-572-6670, E-mail: griffinp@nku.edu.

Philadelphia College of Osteopathic Medicine, Graduate and Professional Programs, Department of Psychology, Philadelphia, PA 19131-1694. Offers clinical psychology (Psy D); counseling and clinical health psychology (MS); organizational leadership and development (MS); psychology (Certificate); school psychology (MS, Psy D, Ed S). *Accreditation:* APA. *Degree requirements:* For master's, thesis; for doctorate, comprehensive exam, thesis/dissertation, final project, fieldwork. *Entrance requirements:* For master's, GRE or MAT, minimum GPA of 3.0; course work in biology, chemistry, English, physics; for other advanced degree, PRAXIS. *Faculty research:* Depression in primary care, integrated primary care, geriatric mental health.

See Close-Up on page 1127.

Prescott College, Graduate Programs, Program in Counseling and Psychology, Prescott, AZ 86301. Offers adventure-based psychotherapy (MA); counseling psychology (MA); ecopsychology (MA); ecotherapy (MA); equine-assisted mental health (MA); expressive arts therapy (MA); somatic psychology (MA); student-directed independent study (MA). Part-time programs

available. Postbaccalaureate distance learning degree programs offered (minimal on-campus study). *Faculty:* 43 part-time/adjunct (29 women). *Students:* 74 full-time (66 women), 19 part-time (18 women); includes 9 minority (4 African Americans, 1 American Indian/Alaska Native, 4 Hispanic Americans), 9 international. Average age 37. 54 applicants, 70% accepted, 27 enrolled. In 2008, 29 master's awarded. *Degree requirements:* For master's, thesis, fieldwork or internship, practicum. *Entrance requirements:* For master's, 2 letters of recommendation, resumé, official academic transcripts, personal statement, application form, proposed study plan. Additional exam requirements/recommendations for international students: Required—TOEFL (minimum score 500 paper-based; 173 computer-based). *Application deadline:* For fall admission, 3/15 priority date for domestic and international students; for spring admission, 9/15 priority date for domestic and international students. Applications are processed on a rolling basis. Application fee: $40. Electronic applications accepted. *Expenses:* Tuition: Full-time $13,608; part-time $567 per credit. Required fees: $50 per term. One-time fee: $182. Tuition and fees vary according to degree level. *Financial support:* Career-related internships or fieldwork, Federal Work-Study, and scholarships/grants available. Financial award applicants required to submit FAFSA. *Unit head:* Camille Smith, Chair, Fax: 928-776-5151, E-mail: csmith@prescott.edu. *Application contact:* Kerstin Alicki, Admissions Counselor, 877-350-2102, Fax: 928-776-5242, E-mail: admissions@prescott.edu.

Rutgers, The State University of New Jersey, New Brunswick, Graduate School, Program in Psychology, Piscataway, NJ 08854-8097. Offers behavioral neuroscience (PhD); clinical psychology (PhD); cognitive psychology (PhD); interdisciplinary health psychology (PhD); social psychology (PhD). *Accreditation:* APA. *Degree requirements:* For doctorate, comprehensive exam, thesis/dissertation. *Entrance requirements:* For doctorate, GRE General Test, 3 letters of recommendation. Additional exam requirements/recommendations for international students: Required—TOEFL (minimum score 577 paper-based; 233 computer-based). Electronic applications accepted. *Faculty research:* Learning and memory, behavioral ecology, hormones and behavior, psychopharmacology, anxiety disorders.

San Diego State University, Graduate and Research Affairs, College of Health and Human Services, Graduate School of Public Health, San Diego, CA 92182. Offers environmental health (MPH); epidemiology (MPH, PhD), including biostatistics (MPH); global emergency preparedness and response (MS); global health (PhD); health behavior (PhD); health promotion (MPH); health services administration (MPH); toxicology (MS); MPH/MA; MSW/MPH. *Accreditation:* ABET (one or more programs are accredited); CAHME (one or more programs are accredited); CEPH (one or more programs are accredited). Part-time programs available. *Degree requirements:* For master's, comprehensive exam (for some programs), thesis (for some programs); for doctorate, thesis/dissertation. *Entrance requirements:* For master's, GMAT (health services administration MPH), GRE General Test; for doctorate, GRE General Test. Additional exam requirements/recommendations for international students: Required—TOEFL. *Faculty research:* Evaluation of tobacco, AIDS prevalence and prevention, mammography, infant death project, Alzheimer's in elderly Chinese.

Saybrook Graduate School and Research Center, Programs in Psychology, Human Science and Organizational Systems, San Francisco, CA 94111-1920. Offers clinical psychology (PhD); creativity studies (MA); human science (MA, PhD), including consciousness and spirituality, individualized (PhD), integrative health studies, organizational systems, social transformation; marriage and family therapy (MA); organizational systems (MA, PhD), including individualized (PhD), organizational systems; psychology (MA, PhD), including consciousness and spirituality, humanistic and transpersonal psychology, individualized (PhD), integrative health studies, licensure track (MA), organizational systems, social transformation. Postbaccalaureate distance learning degree programs offered (minimal on-campus study). Terminal master's awarded for partial completion of doctoral program. *Degree requirements:* For master's, thesis or alternative; for doctorate, thesis/dissertation. Electronic applications accepted. *Faculty research:* Humanistic theory, health studies, organizational systems, consciousness and spirituality, social transformation.

Southwestern College, Program in Integral Somatic Psychology, Santa Fe, NM 87502-4788. Offers Certificate. *Entrance requirements:* For degree, applic, & certificate refeence program interview.

Stony Brook University, State University of New York, Graduate School, College of Arts and Sciences, Department of Psychology, Program in Social and Health Psychology, Stony Brook, NY 11794. Offers PhD. *Students:* 23 full-time (18 women); includes 6 minority (3 Asian Americans or Pacific Islanders, 3 Hispanic Americans), 3 international. Average age 28. 95 applicants, 12% accepted. In 2008, 9 doctorates awarded. *Degree requirements:* For doctorate, thesis/dissertation. *Entrance requirements:* For doctorate, GRE General Test, GRE Subject Test. Additional exam requirements/recommendations for international students: Required—TOEFL. *Application deadline:* For fall admission, 1/15 for domestic students. Application fee: $60. *Expenses:* Tuition, area resident: Full-time $7880; part-time $328 per credit hour. Tuition, state resident: full-time $7880; part-time $328 per credit hour. Tuition, nonresident: full-time $13,250; part-time $552 per credit hour. Required fees: $848. *Unit head:* Dr. Marci Lobel, Head, 631-632-7651, E-mail: marci.lobel@stonybrook.edu. *Application contact:* Dr. Marci Lobel, Head, 631-632-7651, E-mail: marci.lobel@stonybrook.edu.

Texas State University–San Marcos, Graduate School, College of Liberal Arts, Department of Psychology, San Marcos, TX 78666. Offers health psychology (MA). *Degree requirements:* For master's, thesis, 450 hours of practicum courses. *Entrance requirements:* For master's, GRE General Test, minimum GPA of 3.0 in last 60 hours and in psychology, 3 letters of rec, 3.0 GPA in psy core courses, statement of purpose. Additional exam requirements/recommendations for international students: Required—TOEFL (minimum score 550 paper-based; 213 computer-based). Electronic applications accepted.

The University of British Columbia, Faculty of Arts and Faculty of Graduate Studies, Department of Psychology, Vancouver, BC V6T 1Z1, Canada. Offers behavioral neuroscience (MA, PhD); clinical psychology (MA, PhD); cognitive science (MA, PhD); developmental psychology (MA, PhD); forensic psychology (PhD); health psychology (MA, PhD); quantitative methods (MA, PhD); social/personality psychology (MA, PhD). *Accreditation:* APA (one or more programs are accredited). Terminal master's awarded for partial completion of doctoral program. *Degree requirements:* For master's, thesis; for doctorate, comprehensive exam, thesis/dissertation. *Entrance requirements:* For master's and doctorate, GRE General Test, GRE Subject Test. Additional exam requirements/recommendations for international students: Required—TOEFL (minimum score 550 paper-based; 230 computer-based; 80 iBT). Electronic applications accepted. *Faculty research:* Clinical, developmental, social/personality, cognition, behavioral neuroscience.

University of Colorado Denver, College of Liberal Arts and Sciences, Program in Clinical Health Psychology, Denver, CO 80217-3364. Offers PhD.

University of Connecticut, Graduate School, College of Liberal Arts and Sciences, Department of Psychology, Field of Psychology, Storrs, CT 06269. Offers behavioral neuroscience (PhD); biopsychology (PhD); clinical psychology (MA, PhD); cognition and instruction (PhD); developmental psychology (MA, PhD); ecological psychology (PhD); experimental psychology (PhD); general psychology (MA, PhD); health psychology (Graduate Certificate); industrial/organizational psychology (PhD); language and cognition (PhD); neuroscience (PhD); occupational health psychology (Graduate Certificate); social psychology (MA, PhD). *Accreditation:* APA (one or more programs are accredited). Terminal master's awarded for partial completion of doctoral program. *Degree requirements:* For master's, comprehensive exam; for doctorate, thesis/dissertation. *Entrance requirements:* For master's and doctorate, GRE General Test, GRE Subject Test. Additional exam requirements/recommendations for international students: Required—TOEFL (minimum score 550 paper-based; 213 computer-based). Electronic applications accepted.

University of Florida, Graduate School, College of Public Health and Health Professions, Department of Clinical and Health Psychology, Gainesville, FL 32611. Offers PhD. *Accreditation:*

APA. *Degree requirements:* For doctorate, thesis/dissertation. *Entrance requirements:* For doctorate, GRE General Test, minimum GPA of 3.0. Additional exam requirements/recommendations for international students: Required—TOEFL (minimum score 550 paper-based; 213 computer-based). Electronic applications accepted. *Faculty research:* Child psychology, pediatric psychology, health/medical psychology, neuropsychology.

University of Michigan–Dearborn, College of Arts, Sciences, and Letters, Master of Science in Psychology Health/Clinical Program, Dearborn, MI 48128. Offers clinical health psychology (MS); health psychology (MS). Part-time programs available. *Faculty:* 8 full-time (4 women), 1 part-time/adjunct (0 women). *Students:* 20 full-time (17 women), 13 part-time (10 women); includes 7 minority (1 African American, 4 Asian Americans or Pacific Islanders, 2 Hispanic Americans). Average age 36. 52 applicants, 23% accepted, 10 enrolled. In 2008, 6 master's awarded. *Degree requirements:* For master's, thesis or alternative, oral defense of thesis. *Entrance requirements:* For master's, GRE, 3 letters of recommendation, statement of purpose, official transcripts from all universities attended. Additional exam requirements/recommendations for international students: Required—TOEFL (minimum score 560 paper-based; 220 computer-based). *Application deadline:* For fall admission, 3/15 for domestic and international students. Application fee: $60 ($75 for international students). *Financial support:* In 2008–09, 4 students received support. Scholarships/grants available. *Faculty research:* Cardiovascular reactivity, coping, addiction, psychoneuroimmunology. *Unit head:* Dr. Pam McAuslan, Program Director, 313-593-5376, E-mail: pmcausla@umd.umich.edu. *Application contact:* Carol Ligienza, Graduate Program Coordinator, CASL Graduate Programs, 313-593-1183, Fax: 313-583-6498, E-mail: caslgrad@umd.umich.edu.

The University of North Carolina at Charlotte, Graduate School, College of Arts and Sciences, Department of Psychology, Program in Health Psychology, Charlotte, NC 28223-0001. Offers PhD. *Students:* 25 full-time (20 women), 4 part-time (all women); includes 3 African Americans, 3 Hispanic Americans. Average age 30. 42 applicants, 24% accepted, 8 enrolled. *Entrance requirements:* For doctorate, GRE, minimum GPA of 3.0 in undergraduate major. Additional exam requirements/recommendations for international students: Required—TOEFL (minimum score 557 paper-based; 220 computer-based). *Application deadline:* For fall admission, 12/1 for domestic and international students. Application fee: $55. *Expenses:* Tuition, area resident: Full-time $2919; part-time $122 per credit hour. Tuition, state resident: full-time $2919; part-time $122 per credit hour. Tuition, nonresident: full-time $13,126; part-time $547 per credit hour. Required fees: $1779; $91 per credit hour. Tuition and fees vary according to program. *Financial support:* In 2008–09, 1 fellowship (averaging $18,000 per year), 16 research assistantships (averaging $7,567 per year), 13 teaching assistantships (averaging $10,087 per year) were awarded; career-related internships or fieldwork, Federal Work-Study, institutionally sponsored loans, scholarships/grants, unspecified assistantships, and 4 administrative assistantships ($5,210 average) also available. Support available to part-time students. Financial award application deadline: 4/1; financial award applicants required to submit FAFSA. *Unit head:* Dr. Art W. Blume, IV, Director, 704-687-4789, Fax: 704-687-3096, E-mail: awblume@email.uncc.edu. *Application contact:* Kathy B. Giddings, Director of Graduate Admissions, 704-687-3366, Fax: 704-687-3279, E-mail: agidding@uncc.edu.

University of North Texas, Robert B. Toulouse School of Graduate Studies, College of Arts and Sciences, Department of Psychology, Denton, TX 76203. Offers clinical psychology (PhD); counseling psychology (MA, MS, PhD); experimental psychology (MA, MS, PhD); health psychology and behavioral medicine (PhD). *Accreditation:* APA (one or more programs are accredited). Terminal master's awarded for partial completion of doctoral program. *Degree requirements:* For master's, comprehensive exam, thesis or alternative; for doctorate, one foreign language, comprehensive exam, thesis/dissertation. *Entrance requirements:* For master's and doctorate, GRE General Test, interview. Additional exam requirements/recommendations for international students: Required—proof of English language proficiency required for non-native English speakers; Recommended—TOEFL (minimum score 550 paper-based; 213 computer-based). *Faculty research:* Very broad range of topics and approaches.

The University of Texas at Arlington, Graduate School, College of Science, Department of Psychology, Arlington, TX 76019. Offers experimental psychology (PhD); health psychology (PhD); industrial organizational psychology (MS); psychology (MS). Part-time programs available. *Faculty:* 16 full-time (5 women), 1 part-time/adjunct (0 women). *Students:* 53 full-time (38 women), 12 part-time (9 women); includes 11 minority (6 African Americans, 1 Asian American or Pacific Islander, 4 Hispanic Americans), 9 international. 81 applicants, 35% accepted, 15 enrolled. In 2008, 16 master's, 4 doctorates awarded. Terminal master's awarded for partial completion of doctoral program. *Degree requirements:* For master's, comprehensive exam or thesis; for doctorate, thesis/dissertation (for some programs). *Entrance requirements:* For master's and doctorate, GRE General Test, minimum GPA of 3.0 in last 60 hours of course work. Additional exam requirements/recommendations for international students: Required—TOEFL (minimum score 550 paper-based; 213 computer-based). *Application deadline:* For fall admission, 6/16 for domestic students. Applications are processed on a rolling basis. Application fee: $35 ($50 for international students). *Expenses:* Tuition, area resident: Full-time $6500. Tuition, state resident: full-time $6500. Tuition, nonresident: full-time $11,558. *Financial support:* In 2008–09, 4 fellowships (averaging $1,000 per year), 2 research assistantships with tuition reimbursements (averaging $15,000 per year), 28 teaching assistantships with tuition reimbursements (averaging $15,000 per year) were awarded; career-related internships or fieldwork, Federal Work-Study, institutionally sponsored loans, scholarships/grants, traineeships, tuition waivers (partial), and unspecified assistantships also available. Financial award application deadline: 6/1; financial award applicants required to submit FAFSA. *Unit head:* Dr. Robert Gatchel, Chair, 817-272-2281, Fax: 817-272-2364, E-mail: gatchel@uta.edu. *Application contact:* Dr. Jared Kenworthy, Graduate Advisor, 817-272-2281, Fax: 817-272-2364, E-mail: kenworthy@uta.edu.

University of the Sciences in Philadelphia, College of Graduate Studies, Program in Health Psychology, Philadelphia, PA 19104-4495. Offers MS. *Faculty:* 3 full-time (1 woman), 2 part-time/adjunct (both women). *Students:* 10 full-time (9 women), 7 part-time (5 women); includes 3 minority (2 African Americans, 1 Hispanic American). Average age 27. 24 applicants, 75% accepted, 2 enrolled. In 2008, 2 master's awarded. *Entrance requirements:* For master's, bachelor's degree in related field, minimum GPA of 3.0 in major. Additional exam requirements/recommendations for international students: Required—TOEFL, TWE. *Application deadline:* For fall admission, 5/1 for international students; for winter admission, 10/1 for international students; for spring admission, 3/1 for international students. Applications are processed on a rolling basis. Application fee: $50. *Expenses:* Contact institution. *Financial support:* In 2008–09, 9 students received support, including 1 research assistantship; tuition waivers (partial) also available. Financial award application deadline: 5/1. *Faculty research:* Stress and immune system, women's health and breast cancer, memory, health care policy. *Unit head:* Dr. Philip Gehrman, Acting Program Director, 215-596-8517, E-mail: pgehrma@usp.edu. *Application contact:* Joyce D'Angelo, Administrative Assistant, 215-596-8937, E-mail: j.dangel@usp.edu.

Virginia State University, School of Graduate Studies, Research, and Outreach, School of Engineering, Science and Technology, Department of Psychology, Petersburg, VA 23806-0001. Offers behavioral and community health sciences (PhD); clinical health psychology (PhD); clinical psychology (MS); general psychology (MS). *Degree requirements:* For master's, one foreign language, thesis. *Entrance requirements:* For master's, GRE General Test.

Walden University, Graduate Programs, School of Psychology, Minneapolis, MN 55401. Offers clinical assessment (Post-Doctoral Certificate); clinical child psychology (Post-Doctoral Certificate); clinical psychology (Post-Doctoral Certificate); counseling psychology (Post-Doctoral Certificate); forensic psychology (MS), including forensic psychology in the community, general forensic psychology, mental health applications, program planning and evaluation in forensic settings, psychology and legal systems; general psychology (Post-Doctoral Certificate); health psychology (Post-Doctoral Certificate); organizational psychology (Post-Doctoral Certificate); organizational psychology and development (Certificate); psychology (MS, PhD), including clinical psychology, counseling psychology, crisis management and response (MS), general psychology, health psychology, leadership development and coaching (MS), media psychology (MS), organizational psychology, organizational psychology and development (MS), organizational psychology and nonprofit management (MS), program evaluation and research (MS), psychology of culture (MS), psychology, public administration, and social change (MS), school psychology, social psychology (MS), terrorism and security (MS); school psychology (Post-Doctoral Certificate); teaching online (Post-Master's Certificate). Part-time and evening/weekend programs available. Postbaccalaureate distance learning degree programs offered (minimal on-campus study). *Faculty:* 16 full-time, 190 part-time/adjunct. *Students:* 3,198 full-time (2,489 women), 810 part-time (664 women); includes 1,319 minority (1,013 African Americans, 51 American Indian/Alaska Native, 68 Asian Americans or Pacific Islanders, 187 Hispanic Americans), 72 international. Average age 40. 1,468 applicants, 60% accepted, 612 enrolled. In 2008, 203 master's, 37 doctorates awarded. Terminal master's awarded for partial completion of doctoral program. *Degree requirements:* For master's, thesis optional; for doctorate, thesis/dissertation, residency. *Entrance requirements:* For master's, bachelor's degree or equivalent in related field, minimum GPA of 2.5, two references, goal statement, official transcripts, access to computer and Internet; for doctorate, master's degree or equivalent in related field, minimum GPA of 3.0, three years related professional/academic experience, two references, goal statement, official transcripts, access to computer and Internet. Additional exam requirements/recommendations for international students: Required—TOEFL (minimum score 550 paper-based; 213 computer-based), IELTS (minimum score 6.5), TOEFL, IELTS, or Michigan English Language Assessment Battery (minimum score 82). *Application deadline:* Applications are processed on a rolling basis. Application fee: $50. Electronic applications accepted. *Expenses:* Tuition: Full-time $12,877; part-time $520 per credit. Required fees: $1230. Tuition and fees vary according to course load, degree level and program. *Financial support:* In 2008–09, 1 fellowship was awarded; Federal Work-Study, scholarships/grants, unspecified assistantships, and family tuition reduction; active duty/veteran tuition reduction; group tuition reduction; interest-free payment plans also available. Support available to part-time students. Financial award applicants required to submit FAFSA. *Unit head:* Dr. Nina Nabors, Associate Dean, 800-925-3368. *Application contact:* Jennifer Hall, 866-4-WALDEN, E-mail: info@waldenu.edu.

West Chester University of Pennsylvania, Office of Graduate Studies, College of Health Sciences, Department of Health, West Chester, PA 19383. Offers emergency preparedness (Certificate); health care administration (Certificate); integrative health (Certificate); public health (MPH); school health (M Ed). *Accreditation:* CEPH. Part-time and evening/weekend programs available. *Students:* 49 full-time (28 women), 90 part-time (60 women); includes 29 minority (24 African Americans, 4 Asian Americans or Pacific Islanders, 1 Hispanic American), 28 international. Average age 32. 133 applicants, 83% accepted, 39 enrolled. In 2008, 29 master's, 12 other advanced degrees awarded. *Degree requirements:* For master's, thesis (for some programs), minimum GPA of 3.0. *Entrance requirements:* For master's, one-page statement of career objectives, two letters of reference. Additional exam requirements/recommendations for international students: Required—TOEFL (minimum score 550 paper-based; 213 computer-based; 80 iBT). *Application deadline:* For fall admission, 4/15 priority date for domestic students, 3/15 for international students; for spring admission, 10/15 for domestic students, 9/1 for international students. Applications are processed on a rolling basis. Application fee: $35. Electronic applications accepted. *Expenses:* Tuition, state resident: full-time $6430; part-time $357 per credit. Tuition, nonresident: full-time $10,288; part-time $572 per credit. Required fees: $652.50; $50 per credit. $67 per semester. *Financial support:* In 2008–09, 15 research assistantships with full and partial tuition reimbursements (averaging $5,000 per year) were awarded; unspecified assistantships also available. Support available to part-time students. Financial award application deadline: 2/15; financial award applicants required to submit FAFSA. *Faculty research:* HIV/AIDS education, teacher preparation, water quality. *Unit head:* Dr. Roger Mustalish, Chair, 610-436-2931, E-mail: rmustalish@wcupa.edu. *Application contact:* Dr. Bethann Cinelli, Graduate Coordinator, 610-436-2267, E-mail: bcinelli@wcupa.edu.

Yeshiva University, Ferkauf Graduate School of Psychology, Program in Clinical Health Psychology, New York, NY 10033-3201. Offers PhD. *Accreditation:* APA. Part-time programs available. *Degree requirements:* For doctorate, comprehensive exam, thesis/dissertation. *Entrance requirements:* For doctorate, GRE General Test. *Faculty research:* Dieting, substance abuse, adolescent depression and suicide, cancer research, MS research.

Human Development

Argosy University, Chicago, College of Psychology and Behavioral Sciences, Doctoral Program in Clinical Psychology, Chicago, IL 60654. Offers child and adolescent psychology (Psy D); client-centered and experiential psychotherapies (Psy D); diversity and multicultural psychology (Psy D); family psychology (Psy D); forensic psychology (Psy D); health psychology (Psy D); psychoanalytic psychology (Psy D); psychology and spirituality (Psy D). *Accreditation:* APA.

See Close-Up on page 1067.

Arizona State University, Graduate College, College of Liberal Arts and Sciences, Division of Social Sciences, School of Social and Family Dynamics, Tempe, AZ 85287. Offers family and human development (MS, PhD); infant-family practice (MAS); marriage and family therapy (MAS); sociology (MA, PhD). *Degree requirements:* For master's, thesis or alternative; for doctorate, thesis/dissertation. *Entrance requirements:* For master's and doctorate, GRE.

Auburn University, Graduate School, College of Human Sciences, Department of Human Development and Family Studies, Auburn University, AL 36849. Offers MS, PhD. *Accreditation:* AAMFT/COAMFTE (one or more programs are accredited). Part-time programs available. *Faculty:* 20 full-time (12 women), 1 (woman) part-time/adjunct. *Students:* 18 full-time (13 women), 34 part-time (31 women); includes 14 minority (8 African Americans, 5 Asian Americans or Pacific Islanders, 1 Hispanic American), 7 international. Average age 28. 55 applicants, 42% accepted, 9 enrolled. In 2008, 6 master's, 3 doctorates awarded. *Degree requirements:* For master's, thesis, oral exam; for doctorate, thesis/dissertation. *Entrance requirements:* For master's, GRE General Test; for doctorate, GRE General Test, master's degree. *Application deadline:* For fall admission, 7/7 for domestic students; for spring admission, 11/24 for domestic students. Applications are processed on a rolling basis. Application fee: $25 ($50 for international students). *Expenses:* Tuition, area resident: Full-time $5880; part-time $243 per credit hour. Tuition, state resident: full-time $5880; part-time $243 per credit hour. Tuition, nonresident: full-time $17,640; part-time $729 per credit hour. International tuition: $17,846 full-time. Required

Human Development

Auburn University (continued)
fees: $620. Tuition and fees vary according to program and reciprocity agreements. *Financial support:* Research assistantships, teaching assistantships, Federal Work-Study available. Support available to part-time students. Financial award application deadline: 3/15. *Faculty research:* Family influences on personality and social development, parent-child relations, infancy, day care, parent education. *Unit head:* Dr. Leanne K. Lamke, Head, 334-844-4151, E-mail: mbradbar@humsci.auburn.edu. *Application contact:* Dr. George Flowers, Interim Dean of the Graduate School, 334-844-2125.

Boston University, School of Education, Department of Literacy and Language, Counseling and Development, Program in Developmental Studies, Boston, MA 02215. Offers Ed M, Ed D, CAGS. *Degree requirements:* For doctorate, comprehensive exam, thesis/dissertation; for CAGS, comprehensive exam. *Entrance requirements:* For master's, doctorate, and CAGS, GRE General Test or MAT. Additional exam requirements/recommendations for international students: Required—TOEFL. Electronic applications accepted. *Faculty research:* Moral development, social and cognitive development, language and literacy development, cross-cultural development.

Bowling Green State University, Graduate College, College of Education and Human Development, School of Family and Consumer Sciences, Bowling Green, OH 43403. Offers food and nutrition (MFCS); human development and family studies (MFCS). Part-time programs available. *Degree requirements:* For master's, thesis. *Entrance requirements:* For master's, GRE General Test, minimum GPA of 3.0. Additional exam requirements/recommendations for international students: Required—TOEFL. Electronic applications accepted. *Faculty research:* Public health, wellness, social issues and policies, ethnic foods, nutrition and aging.

Bradley University, Graduate School, College of Education and Health Sciences, Department of Educational Leadership and Human Development, Peoria, IL 61625-0002. Offers human development counseling (MA), including community and agency counseling, school counseling; leadership in educational administration (MA); leadership in human service administration (MA). *Accreditation:* ACA; NCATE. Part-time and evening/weekend programs available. *Degree requirements:* For master's, comprehensive exam, thesis optional. *Entrance requirements:* For master's, GRE General Test or MAT, interview, 3 letters of recommendation. Additional exam requirements/recommendations for international students: Required—TOEFL (minimum score 550 paper-based; 213 computer-based; 79 iBT).

Brigham Young University, Graduate Studies, College of Family, Home, and Social Sciences, Program in Marriage, Family and Human Development, Provo, UT 84602. Offers MS, PhD. *Accreditation:* AAMFT/COAMFTE. *Faculty:* 24 full-time (5 women). *Students:* 21 full-time (15 women); includes 1 minority (Asian American or Pacific Islander), 2 international. Average age 30. 27 applicants, 41% accepted, 8 enrolled. In 2008, 3 master's, 1 doctorate awarded. *Degree requirements:* For master's, thesis; for doctorate, comprehensive exam, thesis/dissertation, 2 publishable papers. *Entrance requirements:* For master's and doctorate, GRE General Test, minimum GPA of 3.0 in last 60 semester hours, letters of recommendation. Additional exam requirements/recommendations for international students: Required—TOEFL (minimum score 580 paper-based; 237 computer-based; 85 iBT), IELTS (minimum score 7). *Application deadline:* For fall admission, 1/10 for domestic and international students. Application fee: $50. Electronic applications accepted. *Expenses:* Tuition: Full-time $5160; part-time $287 per credit hour. Tuition and fees vary according to program and student's religious affiliation. *Financial support:* In 2008–09, 9 students received support, including 20 research assistantships with full and partial tuition reimbursements available (averaging $5,096 per year), 5 teaching assistantships with full and partial tuition reimbursements available (averaging $5,096 per year); scholarships/grants and unspecified assistantships also available. Financial award application deadline: 3/27. *Faculty research:* Family studies and family process; marriage; adolescence and emerging adulthood; adult development and aging; child development. *Unit head:* Dr. Richard Miller, Director, School of Life, 801-422-2069, Fax: 801-422-0230, E-mail: rick_miller@byu.edu. *Application contact:* Graduate Secretary, 801-422-2060, E-mail: mfhdgrad@byu.edu.

Brock University, Faculty of Graduate Studies, Faculty of Social Sciences, Program in Psychology, St. Catharines, ON L2S 3A1, Canada. Offers behavioral neuroscience (MA, PhD); life span development (MA, PhD); social personality (MA, PhD). Part-time programs available. *Degree requirements:* For master's, thesis; for doctorate, thesis/dissertation. *Entrance requirements:* For master's, GRE, honors degree; for doctorate, GRE, master's degree. Additional exam requirements/recommendations for international students: Required—TOEFL (minimum score 550 paper-based; 213 computer-based; 80 iBT), IELTS (minimum score 6.5), TWE (minimum score 4). Electronic applications accepted. *Faculty research:* Social personality, behavioral neuroscience, life-span development.

California State University, San Bernardino, Graduate Studies, College of Social and Behavioral Sciences, Department of Psychology, Program in Child Development, San Bernardino, CA 92407-2397. Offers psychology-life span (MA). *Students:* 17 full-time (16 women), 9 part-time (8 women); includes 8 minority (2 African Americans, 6 Hispanic Americans). Average age 30. 25 applicants, 44% accepted, 10 enrolled. In 2008, 3 master's awarded. *Degree requirements:* For master's, comprehensive exam. *Entrance requirements:* For master's, minimum GPA of 3.0 in major. *Application deadline:* For fall admission, 8/31 priority date for domestic students. Application fee: $55. *Expenses:* Tuition, area resident: Full-time $1252; part-time $726 per quarter. Required fees: $334 per quarter. Tuition and fees vary according to degree level and student level. *Unit head:* Dr. Cherie Ward, Director, 909-537-7304, E-mail: sward@csusb.edu. *Application contact:* Stacy Brooks, Graduate Secretary, 909-537-5570, Fax: 909-537-7003, E-mail: sbrooks@csusb.edu.

Central Michigan University, College of Graduate Studies, College of Education and Human Services, Department of Human Environmental Studies, Mount Pleasant, MI 48859. Offers apparel product development and merchandising technology (MS); human development and family studies (MA); nutrition and dietetics (MS). Part-time and evening/weekend programs available. *Faculty:* 15 full-time (11 women), 1 part-time/adjunct (0 women). *Degree requirements:* For master's, thesis or alternative. *Application deadline:* Applications are processed on a rolling basis. Application fee: $35 ($45 for international students). Electronic applications accepted. *Expenses:* Tuition, state resident: full-time $3717; part-time $413 per credit. Tuition, nonresident: full-time $6894; part-time $766 per credit. *Financial support:* Fellowships with tuition reimbursements, research assistantships, career-related internships or fieldwork, Federal Work-Study, unspecified assistantships, and out-of-state merit awards available. *Faculty research:* Human growth and development, family studies and human sexuality, human nutrition and dietetics, apparel and textile retailing, computer-aided design for apparel. *Unit head:* Dr. Phame Camerena, Chairperson, 989-774-3218, Fax: 989-774-2435, E-mail: camar1pm@cmich.edu. *Application contact:* Dr. Candace Maylee, Assistant Coordinator of Graduate Programs, 989-774-2613, Fax: 989-774-2435, E-mail: mayle1ce@cmich.edu.

Claremont Graduate University, Graduate Programs, School of Educational Studies, Claremont, CA 91711-6160. Offers Africana education (Certificate); education and policy (MA, PhD); higher education/student affairs (MA, PhD); human development (MA, PhD); public school administration (MA, PhD); quantitative evaluation (MA, PhD); special education (MA, PhD); teacher education (MA); teaching and learning (MA, PhD); urban leadership (PhD); MBA/PhD. Part-time programs available. *Faculty:* 19 full-time (13 women), 1 part-time/adjunct (0 women). *Students:* 267 full-time (190 women), 202 part-time (146 women); includes 204 minority (55 African Americans, 1 American Indian/Alaska Native, 43 Asian Americans or Pacific Islanders, 105 Hispanic Americans), 7 international. Average age 37. In 2008, 81 master's, 34 doctorates, 1 other advanced degree awarded. Terminal master's awarded for partial completion of doctoral program. *Entrance requirements:* For master's and doctorate, GRE General Test. Additional exam requirements/recommendations for international students: Required—TOEFL (minimum score 550 paper-based; 213 computer-based; 80 iBT). *Application deadline:* For fall admission, 2/1 priority date for domestic students. Applications are processed

on a rolling basis. Application fee: $60. Electronic applications accepted. *Expenses:* Tuition: Full-time $33,698; part-time $1465 per unit. Required fees: $310; $155 per semester. Tuition and fees vary according to program. *Financial support:* Fellowships, research assistantships, Federal Work-Study, institutionally sponsored loans, and scholarships/grants available. Support available to part-time students. Financial award application deadline: 2/15; financial award applicants required to submit FAFSA. *Faculty research:* Education administration, K-12 and higher education, multicultural education, education policy, diversity in higher education, faculty issues. *Unit head:* Margaret Grogan, Dean, 909-621-8075, Fax: 909-621-8734, E-mail: margaret.grogan@cgu.edu. *Application contact:* Nicole Kouyoumdjian, Director of External Affairs, 909-607-8493, Fax: 909-621-8734, E-mail: nicole.kouyoumdjian@cgu.edu.

Clemson University, Graduate School, College of Health, Education, and Human Development, Program in Youth Development, Clemson, SC 29634. Offers MS. *Faculty:* 3 full-time (2 women). *Students:* 1 full-time (0 women), 35 part-time (21 women); includes 14 minority (13 African Americans, 1 Hispanic American). Average age 31. 9 applicants, 78% accepted, 6 enrolled. In 2008, 9 master's awarded. Full-time tuition and fees vary according to program. Total annual research expenditures: $15,870. *Unit head:* Dr. William Quinn, Coordinator, 864-656-1501, Fax: 864-656-5488, E-mail: wquinn@clemson.edu. *Application contact:* Dr. William Quinn, Coordinator, 864-656-1501, Fax: 864-656-5488, E-mail: wquinn@clemson.edu.

Colorado State University, Graduate School, College of Applied Human Sciences, Department of Human Development and Family Studies, Fort Collins, CO 80523-1570. Offers MS. *Accreditation:* AAMFT/COAMFTE. Part-time programs available. *Faculty:* 14 full-time (10 women). *Students:* 24 full-time (22 women), 17 part-time (15 women); includes 2 minority (1 Asian American or Pacific Islander, 1 Hispanic American), 2 international. Average age 32. 80 applicants, 28% accepted, 12 enrolled. In 2008, 10 master's awarded. Terminal master's awarded for partial completion of doctoral program. *Degree requirements:* For master's, thesis or alternative, research project or thesis. *Entrance requirements:* For master's, GRE General Test, minimum GPA of 3.0; course work in human development, family studies, and statistics; letters of recommendation forms; additional departmental application; interview; BS/BA degree in human development and family studies or related field. Additional exam requirements/recommendations for international students: Required—TOEFL (minimum score 550 paper-based; 213 computer-based; 80 iBT). *Application deadline:* For fall admission, 1/15 for domestic and international students. Application fee: $50. Electronic applications accepted. *Expenses:* Tuition, area resident: Full-time $5620; part-time $312.25 per credit. Tuition, state resident: full-time $5620; part-time $312.25 per credit. Tuition, nonresident: full-time $17,253; part-time $958.50 per credit. Required fees: $1449.56; $82.35 per credit. *Financial support:* In 2008–09, 16 students received support, including 1 fellowship (averaging $9,792 per year), 4 research assistantships with full and partial tuition reimbursements available (averaging $10,454 per year), 11 teaching assistantships with full and partial tuition reimbursements available (averaging $7,846 per year); career-related internships or fieldwork, Federal Work-Study, institutionally sponsored loans, scholarships/grants, health care benefits, and unspecified assistantships also available. Financial award application deadline: 1/15; financial award applicants required to submit FAFSA. *Faculty research:* Promoting resiliency and optimal development; gender, culture and diversity; gerontology/aging; child and adolescent health; disabilities. Total annual research expenditures: $838,638. *Unit head:* Dr. Lise Youngblade, Department Head, 970-491-5558, Fax: 970-491-7975, E-mail: lise.youngblade@colostate.edu. *Application contact:* Dr. Karen C. Barrett, Graduate Chair, 970-491-7382, Fax: 970-491-7975, E-mail: karen.barrett@colostate.edu.

Cornell University, Graduate School, Graduate Fields of Human Ecology, Field of Human Development, Ithaca, NY 14853-0001. Offers developmental psychology (PhD), including cognitive development, developmental psychopathology, ecology of human development, social and personality development; human development and family studies (PhD), including ecology of human development, family studies and the life course. *Faculty:* 30 full-time (14 women). *Students:* 27 full-time (19 women); includes 2 minority (both Asian Americans or Pacific Islanders), 11 international. Average age 29. 71 applicants, 10% accepted, 5 enrolled. In 2008, 5 doctorates awarded. *Degree requirements:* For doctorate, comprehensive exam, thesis/dissertation, pre-doctoral research project, teaching experience. *Entrance requirements:* For doctorate, GRE General Test, 2 letters of recommendation. Additional exam requirements/recommendations for international students: Required—TOEFL (minimum score 550 paper-based; 213 computer-based; 77 iBT). *Application deadline:* For fall admission, 1/15 for domestic students. Application fee: $70. Electronic applications accepted. *Expenses:* Tuition: Full-time $29,500. Required fees: $70. Full-time tuition and fees vary according to degree level, program and student level. *Financial support:* In 2008–09, 26 students received support, including 3 fellowships with full tuition reimbursements available, 3 research assistantships with full tuition reimbursements available, 20 teaching assistantships with full tuition reimbursements available; institutionally sponsored loans, scholarships/grants, health care benefits, tuition waivers (full and partial), and unspecified assistantships also available. Financial award applicants required to submit FAFSA. *Faculty research:* Cognitive development, developmental psychopathology, ecology of human development, family studies and the life course, social and personality development. *Unit head:* Director of Graduate Studies, 607-255-3181, Fax: 607-255-9856. *Application contact:* Graduate Field Assistant, 607-255-3181, Fax: 607-255-9856, E-mail: hdfs@cornell.edu.

DePaul University, School of Education, Chicago, IL 60106. Offers bilingual and bicultural education (M Ed, MA); curriculum studies (M Ed, MA); education (Ed D), including curriculum studies, educational leadership; educational leadership (M Ed, MA), including administration and supervision, Catholic school leadership, physical education; human development and learning (MA); human services and counseling (M Ed, MA), including agencies, family concerns, and higher education, elementary schools, human services management, secondary schools; reading and learning disabilities (M Ed, MA); social culture studies in education and development (M Ed, MA), including curriculum studies/development; teaching and learning (early childhood, elementary and secondary) (M Ed), including elementary education (M Ed, MA), secondary education (M Ed, MA); teaching and learning (early childhood, elementary, and secondary) (MA), including elementary education (M Ed, MA), secondary education (M Ed, MA). *Accreditation:* NCATE. Part-time and evening/weekend programs available. *Faculty:* 61 full-time (40 women), 66 part-time/adjunct (41 women). *Students:* 863 full-time (694 women), 447 part-time (332 women); includes 262 minority (131 African Americans, 2 American Indian/Alaska Native, 53 Asian Americans or Pacific Islanders, 76 Hispanic Americans), 16 international. Average age 30. 635 applicants, 74% accepted, 318 enrolled. In 2008, 604 master's, 5 doctorates awarded. *Degree requirements:* For doctorate, thesis/dissertation. *Entrance requirements:* For master's, interview, minimum GPA of 2.75, 2 letters of recommendation; for doctorate, interview, master's degree, writing sample, 3 letters of recommendation. Additional exam requirements/recommendations for international students: Required—TOEFL (minimum score 550 paper-based; 213 computer-based; 80 iBT). *Application deadline:* Applications are processed on a rolling basis. Application fee: $40. Electronic applications accepted. *Financial support:* In 2008–09, 14 research assistantships with tuition reimbursements (averaging $5,800 per year) were awarded; career-related internships or fieldwork also available. *Faculty research:* Reflective teaching, children at risk, loss, ethnicity, urban education. Total annual research expenditures: $1.6 million. *Unit head:* Dr. Marie Donovan, Dean, 773-325-7581, Fax: 773-325-7713, E-mail: mdonovan@depaul.edu. *Application contact:* Brandon Washington, Data Project Manager, 773-325-1152, Fax: 773-325-2270, E-mail: bwashin3@depaul.edu.

Dowling College, Graduate Programs in Education, Oakdale, NY 11769-1999. Offers educational administration (Ed D, PD), including computers in education (PD), educational administration (Ed D); school administration and supervision (PD), school district administration (PD); human development and learning (MS Ed); literacy (MS Ed); literacy/special education (MS Ed); secondary education (MS Ed); special education (MS Ed). *Accreditation:* NCATE. Part-time and evening/weekend programs available. Postbaccalaureate distance learning degree programs offered. *Degree requirements:* For master's and PD, comprehensive exam; for doctorate, thesis/dissertation. *Entrance requirements:* For master's, minimum GPA of 3.0; for doctorate, GRE, master's degree; for PD, teaching certificate. Additional exam requirements/

recommendations for international students: Required—TOEFL (minimum score 550 paper-based). Electronic applications accepted. *Faculty research:* Natural readers, Korean styles and learning strategies, mothers of children with disabilities, computers in instruction, cultural background and organizational roadblocks to problem solving.

Duke University, Graduate School, Department of Psychology, Durham, NC 27708-0586. Offers biological psychology (PhD); clinical psychology (PhD); cognitive psychology (PhD); developmental psychology (PhD); experimental psychology (PhD); health psychology (PhD); human social development (PhD); JD/MA. *Accreditation:* APA (one or more programs are accredited). *Degree requirements:* For doctorate, thesis/dissertation. *Entrance requirements:* For doctorate, GRE General Test. Additional exam requirements/recommendations for international students: Required—TOEFL (minimum score 550 paper-based; 213 computer-based; 83 iBT), IELTS (minimum score 7). Electronic applications accepted.

East Tennessee State University, School of Graduate Studies, College of Education, Department of Human Development and Learning, Johnson City, TN 37614. Offers advanced practitioner (M Ed); community agency counseling (M Ed, MA); comprehensive concentration (M Ed); counseling (M Ed, MA); early childhood education (M Ed, MA); early childhood general (M Ed); early childhood special education (M Ed); early childhood teaching (M Ed); elementary and secondary (school counseling) (M Ed, MA); marriage and family therapy (M Ed, MA); modified concentration (M Ed). *Accreditation:* ACA; NCATE. Part-time programs available. *Degree requirements:* For master's, comprehensive exam, thesis (for some programs). *Entrance requirements:* For master's, GRE General Test, minimum GPA of 3.0. Additional exam requirements/recommendations for international students: Required—TOEFL (minimum score 550 paper-based; 213 computer-based). *Faculty research:* Drug and alcohol abuse, marriage and family counseling, severe mental retardation, parenting of children with disabilities.

Erikson Institute, Academic Programs, Chicago, IL 60654. Offers administration (Certificate); bilingual/ESL (Certificate); child development (MS); early childhood education (MS); infant mental health (Certificate); infant studies (Certificate); MS/MSW. Part-time and evening/weekend programs available. *Degree requirements:* For master's, comprehensive exam, internship; for Certificate, internship. *Entrance requirements:* For master's and Certificate, minimum GPA of 2.75. Additional exam requirements/recommendations for international students: Required—TOEFL. *Faculty research:* Assessment strategies from early childhood through elementary years; language, literacy, and the arts in children's development; inclusive special education; parent-child relationships; cognitive development.

Fielding Graduate University, Graduate Programs, School of Human and Organization Development, Santa Barbara, CA 93105-3538. Offers evidence-based coaching (Certificate); human and organizational systems (PhD); human development (PhD); integral studies (Certificate); organization management and development (MA). Postbaccalaureate distance learning degree programs offered (minimal on-campus study). *Faculty:* 28 full-time (13 women), 10 part-time/adjunct (3 women). *Students:* 498 full-time (353 women), 181 part-time (123 women); includes 126 minority (66 African Americans, 6 American Indian/Alaska Native, 27 Asian Americans or Pacific Islanders, 27 Hispanic Americans), 56 international. Average age 47. 178 applicants, 91% accepted, 120 enrolled. In 2008, 34 master's, 38 doctorates, 60 other advanced degrees awarded. Terminal master's awarded for partial completion of doctoral program. *Degree requirements:* For master's, thesis or alternative; for doctorate, comprehensive exam, thesis/dissertation. *Entrance requirements:* For master's, minimum GPA of 2.5, letter of recommendation; for doctorate, 2 letters of recommendation, writing sample, resumé, self-assessment statement. *Application deadline:* For fall admission, 3/1 for domestic and international students; for spring admission, 9/1 for domestic and international students. Application fee: $75. Electronic applications accepted. *Expenses:* Contact institution. *Financial support:* In 2008–09, 392 students received support, including 2 research assistantships (averaging $5,448 per year); scholarships/grants and health care benefits also available. Support available to part-time students. Financial award application deadline: 5/15; financial award applicants required to submit FAFSA. *Unit head:* Dr. Charles McClintock, Dean, 805-898-2930, Fax: 805-687-4590, E-mail: cmcclintock@fielding.edu. *Application contact:* Carmen Kuchera, Admission Counselor, 800-340-1099, Fax: 805-687-9793, E-mail: ckuchera@fielding.edu.

The George Washington University, Graduate School of Education and Human Development, Individualized Master's Program, Washington, DC 20052. Offers MA Ed. *Students:* 5 full-time (2 women), 7 part-time (all women); includes 2 minority (both Hispanic Americans). Average age 30. 8 applicants, 88% accepted, 4 enrolled. In 2008, 11 master's awarded. *Degree requirements:* For master's, comprehensive exam. *Entrance requirements:* For master's, GRE General Test or MAT, minimum GPA of 2.75. *Application deadline:* For fall admission, 3/1 priority date for domestic students; for spring admission, 10/1 for domestic students. Applications are processed on a rolling basis. Application fee: $60. *Financial support:* Application deadline: 1/15; *Application contact:* Sarah Lang, Director of Graduate Admissions, 202-994-1447, Fax: 202-994-7207, E-mail: slang@gwu.edu.

Harvard University, Graduate School of Education, Doctoral Program in Education, Cambridge, MA 02138. Offers culture, communities and education (Ed D); education policy, leadership and instructional practice (Ed D); higher education (Ed D); human development and education (Ed D); quantitative policy analysis in education (Ed D); urban superintendency (Ed D). Part-time programs available. *Faculty:* 61 full-time (29 women), 40 part-time/adjunct (24 women). *Students:* 298 full-time (209 women), 31 part-time (18 women); includes 96 minority (36 African Americans, 3 American Indian/Alaska Native, 35 Asian Americans or Pacific Islanders, 22 Hispanic Americans), 39 international. Average age 34. 503 applicants, 12% accepted, 44 enrolled. In 2008, 40 doctorates awarded. Terminal master's awarded for partial completion of doctoral program. *Degree requirements:* For doctorate, thesis/dissertation. *Entrance requirements:* For doctorate, GRE General Test, 3 letters of recommendation, official transcripts, statement of purpose. Additional exam requirements/recommendations for international students: Required—TOEFL (minimum score 600 paper-based; 250 computer-based; 100 iBT), TWE (minimum score 5). *Application deadline:* For fall admission, 12/15 for domestic and international students. Application fee: $85. Electronic applications accepted. *Expenses:* Contact institution. *Financial support:* In 2008–09, 244 students received support, including 119 fellowships with full and partial tuition reimbursements available (averaging $12,934 per year), 73 research assistantships (averaging $9,295 per year), 145 teaching assistantships (averaging $9,237 per year); career-related internships or fieldwork, Federal Work-Study, institutionally sponsored loans, scholarships/grants, health care benefits, tuition waivers (full and partial), and unspecified assistantships also available. Support available to part-time students. Financial award application deadline: 2/1; financial award applicants required to submit FAFSA. *Faculty research:* Learning and development; educational leadership and organizations; education policy analysis. Total annual research expenditures: $14.7 million. *Unit head:* Dr. Shu-Ling Chen, Assistant Dean for Doctoral Studies, 617-496-4406. *Application contact:* Information Contact, 617-495-3414, Fax: 617-496-3577, E-mail: gseadmissions@harvard.edu.

Harvard University, Graduate School of Education, Master's Programs in Education, Cambridge, MA 02138. Offers arts in education (Ed M); education policy and management (Ed M); higher education (Ed M); human development and psychology (Ed M); international education policy (Ed M); language and literacy (Ed M); learning and teaching (Ed M); mid-career mathematics and science (teaching certificate) (Ed M); mind brain and education (Ed M); risk and prevention (Ed M); school leadership (Ed M); special studies (Ed M); teaching and curriculum (teaching certificate) (Ed M); technology innovation and education (Ed M). Part-time programs available. *Faculty:* 61 full-time (29 women), 40 part-time/adjunct (24 women). *Students:* 504 full-time (403 women), 66 part-time (53 women); includes 129 minority (40 African Americans, 1 American Indian/Alaska Native, 59 Asian Americans or Pacific Islanders, 29 Hispanic Americans), 84 international. Average age 28. 1,255 applicants, 59% accepted, 533 enrolled. In 2008, 610 master's awarded. *Entrance requirements:* For master's, GRE General Test, 3 letters of recommendation, official transcripts, statement of purpose. Additional exam requirements/recommendations for international students: Required—TOEFL (minimum score 600 paper-based; 250 computer-based; 100 iBT), TWE (minimum score 5). *Application deadline:* For fall admission, 1/5 for domestic and international students. Application fee: $85. Electronic applications accepted. *Expenses:* Contact institution. *Financial support:* In 2008–09, 336 students received support, including 30 fellowships with full and partial tuition reimbursements available (averaging $15,975 per year); career-related internships or fieldwork, Federal Work-Study, institutionally sponsored loans, scholarships/grants, health care benefits, tuition waivers (full and partial), and unspecified assistantships also available. Support available to part-time students. Financial award application deadline: 2/1; financial award applicants required to submit FAFSA. *Faculty research:* Learning and development; educational leadership and organizations; educational policy analysis. Total annual research expenditures: $14.7 million. *Unit head:* Jennifer L. Petrallia, Assistant Dean for Master's Studies, 617-495-8445. *Application contact:* Information Contact, 617-495-3414, Fax: 617-496-3577, E-mail: gseadmissions@harvard.edu.

Hofstra University, School of Education, Health, and Human Services, Department of Curriculum and Teaching, Hempstead, NY 11549. Offers business education (MS Ed); early childhood education (MA, MS Ed), including early childhood and childhood education (MS Ed), early childhood education (MA, MS Ed, Ed D); educational technology (CAS); elementary education (MA, MS Ed); elementary education-math/science/technology (MA); English education (MA, MS Ed); fine arts education (MA, MS Ed); foreign language education (MA, MS Ed), including foreign language education; learning and teaching (Ed D), including applied linguistics, art education, arts and humanities, early childhood education (MA, MS Ed, Ed D), English education, human development, learning and teaching, math education, math, science, and technology, multicultural education, physical education, science education (MA, MS Ed, Ed D), social studies education, special education; mathematics education (MA, MS Ed); middle level education (Advanced Certificate), including middle school extension (grades 5-6), middle school extension (grades 7-9); music education (MA, MS Ed), including music education, wind conducting (MA); science education (MA, MS Ed), including science education (MA, MS Ed, Ed D); secondary education (Advanced Certificate); social studies education (MA, MS Ed); TESL/bilingual education (MA, MS Ed, CAS), including bilingual education (MA), bilingual extension education (CAS), TESOL (MS Ed, CAS). *Accreditation:* NCATE. Part-time and evening/weekend programs available. Postbaccalaureate distance learning degree programs offered. *Faculty:* 26 full-time (18 women), 28 part-time/adjunct (16 women). *Students:* 250 full-time (187 women), 258 part-time (208 women); includes 80 minority (26 African Americans, 12 Asian Americans or Pacific Islanders, 42 Hispanic Americans). Average age 28. 376 applicants, 83% accepted, 171 enrolled. In 2008, 273 master's, 17 other advanced degrees awarded. Terminal master's awarded for partial completion of doctoral program. *Degree requirements:* For master's, one foreign language, comprehensive exam (for some programs), thesis (for some programs), electronic portfolio, student teaching, fieldwork, curriculum project, exit project; for doctorate, comprehensive exam, thesis/dissertation; for other advanced degree, one foreign language, comprehensive exam, electronic portfolio. *Entrance requirements:* For master's, letters of recommendation, interview, teaching certificate (MA), essay, portfolio; for doctorate, GRE, 3 letters of recommendation, essay, interview, 2 years full-time teaching; for other advanced degree, letters of recommendation, interview, teaching certificate, essay, portfolio. Additional exam requirements/recommendations for international students: Required—TOEFL (minimum score 550 paper-based; 213 computer-based; 80 iBT). *Application deadline:* Applications are processed on a rolling basis. Application fee: $60. Electronic applications accepted. *Expenses:* Tuition: Full-time $15,300; part-time $850 per credit. Required fees: $970; $165 per term. Tuition and fees vary according to program. *Financial support:* In 2008–09, 298 students received support, including 55 fellowships with full and partial tuition reimbursements available (averaging $3,410 per year), 7 research assistantships with full and partial tuition reimbursements available (averaging $13,199 per year); career-related internships or fieldwork, Federal Work-Study, institutionally sponsored loans, scholarships/grants, health care benefits, tuition waivers (full and partial), unspecified assistantships, and tuition vouchers for cooperating teachers also available. Support available to part-time students. Financial award applicants required to submit FAFSA. *Faculty research:* Problem-based learning. Total annual research expenditures: $6,000. *Unit head:* Dr. Judith Kaufman, Chairperson, 516-463-6566, Fax: 516-463-6196, E-mail: catjsk@hofstra.edu. *Application contact:* Carol Drummer, Dean of Graduate Admissions, 516-463-4876, Fax: 516-463-4664, E-mail: gradstudent@hofstra.edu.

Hood College, Graduate School, Programs in Human Sciences, Frederick, MD 21701-8575. Offers human sciences (MA), including psychology; thanatology (MA, Certificate). Part-time and evening/weekend programs available. *Faculty:* 5 full-time (2 women), 7 part-time/adjunct (4 women). *Students:* 19 full-time (all women), 89 part-time (77 women); includes 19 minority (15 African Americans, 1 American Indian/Alaska Native, 3 Asian Americans or Pacific Islanders), 2 international. Average age 35. 34 applicants, 85% accepted, 20 enrolled. In 2008, 30 master's, 16 other advanced degrees awarded. *Degree requirements:* For master's, comprehensive exam, capstone/research project. *Entrance requirements:* For master's, minimum GPA of 2.75. Additional exam requirements/recommendations for international students: Required—TOEFL (minimum score 575 paper-based; 231 computer-based; 89 iBT). *Application deadline:* For fall admission, 7/15 for domestic and international students; for spring admission, 12/15 for domestic and international students. Applications are processed on a rolling basis. Application fee: $35. Electronic applications accepted. *Expenses:* Tuition: Full-time $6480. Required fees: $100; $50 per semester. *Financial support:* Applicants required to submit FAFSA. *Faculty research:* Mind-body medicine and multicultural healing, the New Orleans jazz funeral, death practices in African-American culture, bereavement theories and gender differences, Piaget's theory of cognitive development as a formal mathematical model. *Unit head:* Dr. Dana G. Cable, Director, 301-696-3758, Fax: 301-696-3597, E-mail: cable@hood.edu. *Application contact:* Dr. Allen P. Flora, Dean of Graduate School, 301-696-3811, Fax: 301-696-3597, E-mail: gofurther@hood.edu.

Howard University, School of Education, Department of Human Development and Psychoeducational Studies, Program in Human Development, Washington, DC 20059-0002. Offers MS. Offered through the Graduate School of Arts and Sciences. Part-time programs available. *Degree requirements:* For master's, comprehensive exam, thesis, expository writing exam. *Entrance requirements:* For master's, GRE General Test, minimum GPA of 2.7. *Faculty research:* Overweight and obesity in black youth, diabetes, sickle-cell anemia.

Indiana University Bloomington, School of Health, Physical Education and Recreation, Department of Applied Health Science, Bloomington, IN 47405-7000. Offers health behavior (PhD); health promotion (MS); human development/family studies (MS); nutrition science (MS); public health (MPH); safety management (MS); school and college health programs (MS). *Accreditation:* CEPH (one or more programs are accredited). *Faculty:* 24 full-time (12 women). *Students:* 93 full-time (64 women), 53 part-time (38 women); includes 48 minority (17 African Americans, 1 American Indian/Alaska Native, 27 Asian Americans or Pacific Islanders, 3 Hispanic Americans), 2 international. Average age 31. 104 applicants, 66% accepted, 47 enrolled. In 2008, 40 master's, 5 doctorates awarded. *Degree requirements:* For master's, thesis optional; for doctorate, thesis/dissertation. *Entrance requirements:* For master's, GRE (MS in nutrition science), 3 recommendations; for doctorate, GRE, 3 recommendations. Additional exam requirements/recommendations for international students: Required—TOEFL (minimum score 550 paper-based; 213 computer-based; 79 iBT). *Application deadline:* For fall admission, 4/30 priority date for domestic students, 12/1 priority date for international students; for spring admission, 11/15 priority date for domestic students, 9/1 priority date for international students. Application fee: $50 ($60 for international students). *Expenses:* Tuition, area resident: Part-time $291.97 per credit hour. Tuition, state resident: part-time $291.97 per credit hour. Tuition, nonresident: part-time $850.33 per credit hour. Required fees: $110 per semester. Tuition and fees vary according to course load and program. *Financial support:* In 2008–09, 80 students received support, including 12 fellowships (averaging $2,316 per year), 50 research assistantships with full and partial tuition reimbursements available (averaging $6,973 per year), 27 teaching assistantships with full and partial tuition reimbursements available (averaging $11,067 per year); career-related internships or fieldwork, Federal Work-Study, institutionally sponsored loans, scholarships/grants, tuition waivers (partial), and fee remissions also available. Financial

Human Development

Indiana University Bloomington (continued)
award application deadline: 3/1. *Faculty research:* Cancer education, HIV/AIDS and drug education, public health, parent-child interactions, safety education. Total annual research expenditures: $2.8 million. *Unit head:* Dr. Mohammad R. Torabi, Chair, 812-855-4808, Fax: 812-855-3936, E-mail: torabi@indiana.edu. *Application contact:* Dr. Mohammad R. Torabi, Chair, 812-855-4808, Fax: 812-855-3936, E-mail: torabi@indiana.edu.

Iowa State University of Science and Technology, Graduate College, College of Human Sciences, Department of Human Development and Family Studies, Ames, IA 50011. Offers human development and family studies (MFCS, MS, PhD). *Accreditation:* AAMFT/COAMFTE. *Faculty:* 24 full-time (18 women), 7 part-time/adjunct (5 women). *Students:* 54 full-time (45 women), 16 part-time (15 women); includes 3 minority (1 Asian American or Pacific Islander, 2 Hispanic Americans), 9 international. 22 applicants, 86% accepted, 13 enrolled. In 2008, 12 master's, 6 doctorates awarded. *Degree requirements:* For master's, thesis; for doctorate, thesis/dissertation. *Entrance requirements:* For master's and doctorate, GRE General Test. Additional exam requirements/recommendations for international students: Required—TOEFL (minimum score 550 paper-based; 79 iBT), IELTS (6.5) or TOEFL. *Application deadline:* For fall admission, 12/1 priority date for domestic and international students. Application fee: $30 ($70 for international students). Electronic applications accepted. *Expenses:* Tuition, area resident: Full-time $6446; part-time $359 per credit. Tuition, state resident: full-time $6446; part-time $359 per credit. Tuition, nonresident: full-time $17,330; part-time $963 per credit. Required fees: $790; $249.25 per semester. Tuition and fees vary according to course load and program. *Financial support:* In 2008–09, 40 research assistantships with full and partial tuition reimbursements (averaging $13,392 per year), 11 teaching assistantships with full and partial tuition reimbursements (averaging $13,392 per year) were awarded; fellowships, scholarships/grants also available. *Faculty research:* Child development, early childhood education, family resource management and housing, life span studies. *Unit head:* Dr. Dianne Draper, Interim Chair, 515-294-6316, Fax: 515-294-2502, E-mail: hdfs-grad-adm@iastate.edu. *Application contact:* Dr. Dianne Draper, Interim Chair, 515-294-6316, Fax: 515-294-2502, E-mail: hdfs-grad-adm@iastate.edu.

Kansas State University, Graduate School, College of Human Ecology, Program in Human Ecology, Manhattan, KS 66506. Offers apparel and textiles (PhD); family life education and consultation (PhD); food service, hospitality management, and administrative dietetics (PhD); institutional management (PhD); lifespan and human development (PhD); marriage and family therapy (PhD). *Faculty:* 3 full-time (all women). *Students:* 37 full-time (25 women), 24 part-time (15 women); includes 10 minority (8 African Americans, 1 American Indian/Alaska Native, 1 Asian American or Pacific Islander), 18 international. Average age 37. 25 applicants, 80% accepted, 18 enrolled. In 2008, 14 doctorates awarded. *Application deadline:* For fall admission, 2/1 priority date for domestic and international students; for spring admission, 8/1 priority date for domestic and international students. Application fee: $30 ($55 for international students). *Expenses:* Tuition, area resident: Full-time $6466; part-time $269.40 per credit hour. Tuition, state resident: full-time $6466; part-time $269.40 per credit hour. Tuition, nonresident: full-time $14,874; part-time $619.75 per credit hour. Required fees: $673; $23.40 per credit hour. Tuition and fees vary according to campus/location. *Unit head:* Elizabeth McCullough, Director, 785-532-2284, Fax: 785-532-3796, E-mail: lizm@ksu.edu. *Application contact:* Connie Fechter, Application Contact, 785-532-1473, Fax: 785-532-3796, E-mail: fechter@ksu.edu.

Kent State University, Graduate School of Education, Health, and Human Services, Department of Adult, Counseling, Health and Vocational Education, Program in Counseling and Human Development Services, Kent, OH 44242-0001. Offers PhD. *Accreditation:* ACA; NCATE. *Degree requirements:* For doctorate, comprehensive exam, thesis/dissertation. *Entrance requirements:* For doctorate, GRE General Test. Additional exam requirements/recommendations for international students: Required—TOEFL. Electronic applications accepted. *Faculty research:* Family/child therapy, clinical supervision, group work, experiential training methods.

Kent State University, Graduate School of Education, Health, and Human Services, School of Family and Consumer Studies, Program in Family Studies, Kent, OH 44242-0001. Offers gerontology (MA); human development and family studies (MA).

Laurentian University, School of Graduate Studies and Research, Programme in Human Development, Sudbury, ON P3E 2C6, Canada. Offers M Sc, MA. Interdisciplinary program consisting of the Departments of Psychology, Sociology, and Human Movement. Part-time programs available. *Degree requirements:* For master's, thesis or alternative. *Entrance requirements:* For master's, honors degree with second class or better. *Faculty research:* Aging and well-being, physical, social and cognitive development of children, social cognition and social relationships including peers and family, education and schooling.

Lehigh University, College of Arts and Sciences, Department of Psychology, Bethlehem, PA 18015-3094. Offers human cognition and development (MS, PhD). *Faculty:* 12 full-time (7 women). *Students:* 14 full-time (11 women), 4 international. Average age 26. 68 applicants, 4% accepted, 1 enrolled. In 2008, 5 master's, 1 doctorate awarded. *Degree requirements:* For master's, thesis; for doctorate, comprehensive exam, thesis/dissertation. *Entrance requirements:* For doctorate, GRE General Test. Additional exam requirements/recommendations for international students: Required—TOEFL. *Application deadline:* For fall admission, 1/15 for domestic and international students. Application fee: $65. Electronic applications accepted. *Expenses:* Contact institution. *Financial support:* In 2008–09, 11 students received support, including 1 fellowship with full tuition reimbursement available (averaging $20,000 per year), 2 research assistantships with full tuition reimbursements available (averaging $16,900 per year), 11 teaching assistantships with full tuition reimbursements available (averaging $16,900 per year); scholarships/grants, tuition waivers (full and partial), and unspecified assistantships also available. Financial award application deadline: 1/15. *Faculty research:* Social-cognitive developmental psychology, cognition and language, social cognition and personality. Total annual research expenditures: $206,022. *Unit head:* Diane Hyland, Chairperson, 610-758-3631, Fax: 610-758-6277, E-mail: dthl@lehigh.edu. *Application contact:* Dr. Michael Gill, Program Director, 610-758-3630, Fax: 610-758-6277, E-mail: inpsy@lehigh.edu.

Lindsey Wilson College, School of Professional Counseling, Columbia, KY 42728-1298. Offers counseling and human development (M Ed). *Accreditation:* ACA. Part-time and evening/weekend programs available.

Marywood University, Academic Affairs, College of Education and Human Development, Department of Human Development, Doctoral Program in Human Development, Scranton, PA 18509-1598. Offers PhD.

Montana State University, College of Graduate Studies, College of Education, Health, and Human Development, Department of Health and Human Development, Bozeman, MT 59717. Offers MS. *Accreditation:* ACA. Part-time programs available. Postbaccalaureate distance learning degree programs offered. *Degree requirements:* For master's, comprehensive exam. *Entrance requirements:* For master's, GRE General Test. Additional exam requirements/recommendations for international students: Required—TOEFL (minimum score 550 paper-based; 213 computer-based). Electronic applications accepted. *Faculty research:* Gait analysis, cancer prevention, obesity prevention, energy expenditure, decision making.

National-Louis University, College of Arts and Sciences, Program in Psychology, Chicago, IL 60603. Offers cultural psychology (MA); health psychology (MA); human development (MA); organizational psychology (MA); psychology (Certificate). Part-time and evening/weekend programs available. *Students:* 4 full-time (all women), 214 part-time (30 women); includes 145 minority (121 African Americans, 3 American Indian/Alaska Native, 3 Asian Americans or Pacific Islanders, 18 Hispanic Americans), 2 international. Average age 38. In 2008, 30 master's awarded. *Degree requirements:* For master's, thesis, internship (health psychology). *Entrance requirements:* For master's, GRE, MAT, or Watson-Glaser Critical Thinking Appraisal, interview, minimum GPA of 3.0; for Certificate, GRE, MAT, or Watson-Glaser Critical Thinking Appraisal, interview, minimum GPA of 3.0, undergraduate course work in psychology. *Application deadline:* Applications are processed on a rolling basis. *Financial support:* Federal Work-Study, institutionally sponsored loans, scholarships/grants, and tuition waivers available. Support available to part-time students. Financial award applicants required to submit FAFSA. *Faculty research:* Human development, personality theory, abnormal psychology. *Unit head:* Dr. Edward Risinger, Professor, 224-233-2533, Fax: 224-233-2533, E-mail: erisinger@nl.edu. *Application contact:* David McCulloch, Vice President for University Services, 800-443-5522 Ext. 5151, Fax: 847-465-0593, E-mail: dmcc@wheeling1.nl.edu.

National-Louis University, National College of Education, Doctoral Programs in Education, Program in Human Learning and Development, Chicago, IL 60603. Offers Ed D. Part-time and evening/weekend programs available. *Students:* 1 (woman) full-time, 13 part-time (9 women); includes 3 minority (1 Asian American or Pacific Islander, 2 Hispanic Americans). Average age 40. *Degree requirements:* For doctorate, comprehensive exam, thesis/dissertation, internship. *Entrance requirements:* For doctorate, GRE General Test, minimum GPA of 3.25, interview, resumé, writing sample. *Application deadline:* For fall admission, 5/1 for domestic students; for spring admission, 1/15 for domestic students. *Financial support:* Fellowships, research assistantships, teaching assistantships, career-related internships or fieldwork, Federal Work-Study, institutionally sponsored loans, and scholarships/grants available. Support available to part-time students. Financial award application deadline: 4/15; financial award applicants required to submit FAFSA. *Application contact:* Dr. Larry Poselli, Vice President of Enrollment and Student Services, 800-443-5522 Ext. 5718, Fax: 312-261-.3550, E-mail: larry.polselli@nl.edu.

National-Louis University, National College of Education, Program in Educational Psychology/Human Learning and Development, Chicago, IL 60603. Offers educational psychology (CAS, Ed S); educational psychology/human learning and development (M Ed, MS Ed). Part-time and evening/weekend programs available. *Students:* 12 full-time (all women), 12 part-time (all women); includes 3 minority (1 African American, 2 Hispanic Americans). Average age 31. In 2008, 10 master's awarded. *Degree requirements:* For master's, thesis (for some programs). *Entrance requirements:* For master's, MAT or GRE, minimum GPA of 3.0, teaching certificate; for other advanced degree, master's degree, teaching certificate. *Application deadline:* Applications are processed on a rolling basis. Electronic applications accepted. *Financial support:* Fellowships, career-related internships or fieldwork, Federal Work-Study, institutionally sponsored loans, and scholarships/grants available. Support available to part-time students. Financial award applicants required to submit FAFSA.

New York Institute of Technology, Graduate Division, School of Health Professions, Behavioral, and Life Sciences, Program in Human Relations, Old Westbury, NY 11568-8000. Offers MPS. Part-time and evening/weekend programs available. Postbaccalaureate distance learning degree programs offered. *Students:* 1 (woman) full-time, 10 part-time (8 women); includes 3 minority (1 African American, 2 Asian Americans or Pacific Islanders), 2 international. Average age 38. In 2008, 5 master's awarded. *Degree requirements:* For master's, thesis or alternative. *Entrance requirements:* For master's, minimum QPA of 2.85. Additional exam requirements/recommendations for international students: Required—TOEFL (minimum score 550 paper-based; 213 computer-based). *Application deadline:* For fall admission, 7/1 priority date for domestic students; for spring admission, 12/1 priority date for domestic students. Applications are processed on a rolling basis. Application fee: $50. Electronic applications accepted. *Expenses:* Tuition: Part-time $783 per credit. *Financial support:* Fellowships, research assistantships with partial tuition reimbursements, institutionally sponsored loans, tuition waivers (full and partial), and unspecified assistantships available. Support available to part-time students. Financial award applicants required to submit FAFSA. *Faculty research:* Distance learning delivery systems. *Unit head:* Dr. Maria LaPadula, Chair, 516-686-3869, Fax: 516-686-3850, E-mail: mlapadul@nyit.edu. *Application contact:* Dr. Jacquelyn Nealon, Vice President for Enrollment Services, 516-686-7925, Fax: 516-686-7597, E-mail: jnealon@nyit.edu.

New York University, Steinhardt School of Culture, Education and Human Development, New York, NY 10012-1019. Offers MA, MFA, MM, MPH, MS, DA, DPS, DPT, Ed D, PhD, Advanced Certificate. *Accreditation:* Teacher Education Accreditation Council. Part-time and evening/weekend programs available. *Degree requirements:* For doctorate, comprehensive exam (for some programs), thesis/dissertation. *Entrance requirements:* For doctorate, GRE General Test, interview. Additional exam requirements/recommendations for international students: Required—TOEFL. *Expenses:* Contact institution. *Faculty research:* Equity, urban adolescents, arts in education, globalization, community and public health.

North Dakota State University, College of Graduate and Interdisciplinary Studies, College of Human Development and Education, Program in Human Development, Fargo, ND 58105. Offers PhD. *Students:* 22 full-time (14 women), 16 part-time (12 women); includes 8 minority (1 African American, 5 American Indian/Alaska Native, 1 Asian American or Pacific Islander, 1 Hispanic American), 1 international. In 2008, 9 doctorates awarded. *Degree requirements:* For doctorate, comprehensive exam, thesis/dissertation. *Entrance requirements:* Additional exam requirements/recommendations for international students: Required—TOEFL (minimum score 525 paper-based; 197 computer-based; 71 iBT). *Application deadline:* For fall admission, 2/1 priority date for domestic and international students. Applications are processed on a rolling basis. Application fee: $45 ($60 for international students). *Financial support:* In 2008–09, 12 students received support; research assistantships with full tuition reimbursements available, teaching assistantships with full tuition reimbursements available, scholarships/grants, tuition waivers (partial), and unspecified assistantships available. *Faculty research:* Gerontology, wellness, counselor education. Total annual research expenditures: $1.3 million. *Unit head:* Dr. Greg Sanders, Coordinator, 701-231-8211, E-mail: greg.sanders@ndsu.edu. *Application contact:* Dr. Greg Sanders, Coordinator, 701-231-8211, E-mail: greg.sanders@ndsu.edu.

Northwestern University, The Graduate School, School of Education and Social Policy, Program in Human Development and Social Policy, Evanston, IL 60208. Offers PhD. Admissions and degrees offered through The Graduate School. *Degree requirements:* For doctorate, comprehensive exam, thesis/dissertation. *Entrance requirements:* For doctorate, GRE General Test, writing sample. Additional exam requirements/recommendations for international students: Required—TOEFL (minimum score 600 paper-based; 250 computer-based; 100 iBT). Electronic applications accepted. *Faculty research:* Social context of development; social policy issues affecting children, adolescents, adults, and families.

See Close-Up on page 1231.

The Ohio State University, Graduate School, College of Education and Human Ecology, Department of Human Development and Family Science, Columbus, OH 43210. Offers M Ed, MS, PhD. *Degree requirements:* For master's, thesis optional; for doctorate, thesis/dissertation. *Entrance requirements:* For master's and doctorate, GRE General Test. Additional exam requirements/recommendations for international students: Required—TOEFL (minimum score 577 paper-based; 233 computer-based). Electronic applications accepted.

Oklahoma State University, College of Arts and Sciences, Department of Psychology, Stillwater, OK 74078. Offers clinical psychology (PhD); general psychology (MS); lifespan development psychology (PhD). *Accreditation:* APA (one or more programs are accredited). *Faculty:* 26 full-time (12 women), 1 part-time/adjunct (0 women). *Students:* 38 full-time (22 women), 16 part-time (12 women); includes 10 minority (2 African Americans, 3 American Indian/Alaska Native, 2 Asian Americans or Pacific Islanders, 3 Hispanic Americans), 2 international. Average age 28. 145 applicants, 8% accepted, 10 enrolled. In 2008, 10 master's, 4 doctorates awarded. *Degree requirements:* For master's, thesis or alternative; for doctorate, comprehensive exam, thesis/dissertation. *Entrance requirements:* For master's and doctorate, GRE General Test. Additional exam requirements/recommendations for international students: Required—TOEFL. *Application deadline:* For fall admission, 3/1 priority date for international students; for spring admission, 8/1 priority date for international students. Applications are processed on a rolling basis. Application fee: $40 ($75 for international students). Electronic applications accepted. *Expenses:* Tuition, state resident: full-time $3716.40; part-time $154.85 per credit hour. Tuition, nonresident: full-time $14,448; part-time $602 per credit hour. Required fees: $1772.40; $73.85 per credit hour. One-time fee: $50. Tuition and fees vary according to course load and campus/location. *Financial support:* In 2008–09, 15 research assistantships (averaging $14,338 per year), 32 teaching assistantships (averaging $13,493 per year) were awarded; career-related internships or fieldwork, Federal Work-Study, scholarships/grants, health care benefits, tuition waivers (partial), and unspecified assistantships also available. Support available to part-time students. Financial award application deadline: 3/1; financial award applicants required to submit FAFSA. *Unit head:* Dr. Maureen A. Sullivan, Head, 405-744-6028, Fax: 405-744-8067. *Application contact:* Dr. Gordon Emslie, Dean, 405-744-6368, Fax: 405-744-0355, E-mail: grad_i@okstate.edu.

Oregon State University, Graduate School, College of Health and Human Sciences, Department of Human Development and Family Sciences, Corvallis, OR 97331. Offers gerontology (MAIS); human development and family studies (MS, PhD). *Degree requirements:* For doctorate, thesis/dissertation. *Entrance requirements:* For master's and doctorate, GRE, minimum GPA of 3.0 in last 90 hours. Additional exam requirements/recommendations for international students: Required—TOEFL.

Our Lady of the Lake University of San Antonio, School of Professional Studies, Program in Human Sciences, San Antonio, TX 78207-4689. Offers MA. Part-time and evening/weekend programs available. *Students:* 4 full-time (all women), 29 part-time (25 women); includes 27 minority (7 African Americans, 1 Asian American or Pacific Islander, 19 Hispanic Americans). Average age 40. In 2008, 9 master's awarded. *Entrance requirements:* For master's, GRE General Test or MAT, interview. Additional exam requirements/recommendations for international students: Required—TOEFL. *Application deadline:* Applications are processed on a rolling basis. Application fee: $25 ($50 for international students). Electronic applications accepted. *Expenses:* Tuition: Full-time $11,970; part-time $665 per credit hour. Required fees: $500; $250 per term. *Financial support:* Application deadline: 4/15. *Unit head:* Dr. Steve Blanchard, Chair, 210-434-6711 Ext. 2273, E-mail: blank@lake.ollusa.com. *Application contact:* 210-434-6711 Ext. 2314, Fax: 210-431-4036, E-mail: gradadm@lake.ollusa.edu.

Pacific Oaks College, Graduate School, Program in Human Development, Pasadena, CA 91103. Offers MA. Part-time and evening/weekend programs available. Postbaccalaureate distance learning degree programs offered (minimal on-campus study). *Degree requirements:* For master's, thesis. *Entrance requirements:* Additional exam requirements/recommendations for international students: Required—TOEFL (minimum score 550 paper-based; 213 computer-based). *Faculty research:* Bicultural development, teaching adults, art education, literacy development, adolescent development.

Penn State University Park, Graduate School, College of Health and Human Development, Department of Human Development and Family Studies, State College, University Park, PA 16802-1503. Offers MS, PhD.

Purdue University, Graduate School, College of Consumer and Family Sciences, Department of Child Development and Family Studies, West Lafayette, IN 47907. Offers developmental studies (MS, PhD); family studies (MS, PhD); marriage and family therapy (MS, PhD). *Accreditation:* AAMFT/COAMFTE (one or more programs are accredited). Part-time programs available. Terminal master's awarded for partial completion of doctoral program. *Degree requirements:* For master's, thesis; for doctorate, thesis/dissertation. *Entrance requirements:* For master's and doctorate, GRE General Test. Additional exam requirements/recommendations for international students: Required—TWE. Electronic applications accepted. *Faculty research:* Inclusion of children with special needs, families as learning environments, relationships in child care, work-family relations, AIDS prevention.

Saint Joseph College, Graduate School, Institute in Gerontology, West Hartford, CT 06117-2700. Offers human development/gerontology (MA, Certificate). Part-time and evening/weekend programs available. *Students:* 4 full-time (3 women), 15 part-time (14 women). *Application deadline:* Applications are processed on a rolling basis. Application fee: $50. Electronic applications accepted. *Expenses:* Tuition: Part-time $560 per credit. Required fees: $30 per credit. *Financial support:* Career-related internships or fieldwork, health care benefits, and unspecified assistantships available. Support available to part-time students. Financial award applicants required to submit FAFSA. *Application contact:* Graduate Admissions Office, 860-231-5261, E-mail: graduate@sjc.edu.

St. Lawrence University, Department of Education, Program in Counseling and Human Development, Canton, NY 13617-1455. Offers mental health counseling (MS); school counseling (M Ed, CAS). Part-time and evening/weekend programs available. *Entrance requirements:* For master's, GRE General Test. *Faculty research:* Defense mechanisms and mediation.

Saint Louis University, Graduate School, College of Education and Public Service and Graduate School, Department of Counseling and Family Therapy, St. Louis, MO 63103-2097. Offers counseling and family therapy (PhD); human development counseling (MA); marriage and family therapy (Certificate); school counseling (MA, MA-R). *Accreditation:* NCATE. Part-time programs available. *Degree requirements:* For master's, comprehensive exam, thesis (for some programs); for doctorate, comprehensive exam, thesis/dissertation, preliminary oral and written exams. *Entrance requirements:* For master's and doctorate, GRE General Test, letters of recommendation, resumé, transcripts, goal statement. Additional exam requirements/recommendations for international students: Required—TOEFL (minimum score 550 paper-based; 213 computer-based). Electronic applications accepted. *Faculty research:* Medical family therapy/collaborative health care multicultural counseling, mental health needs of diverse, minority, or Immigrant/refugee populations, divorce, aging families.

Saint Mary's University of Minnesota, Schools of Graduate and Professional Programs, Graduate School of Business and Technology, Human Development Program, Winona, MN 55987-1399. Offers MA.

South Dakota State University, Graduate School, College of Family and Consumer Sciences, Department of Human Development, Consumer and Family Sciences, Brookings, SD 57007. Offers MFCS. *Faculty:* 12 full-time (11 women). *Students:* 3 full-time (2 women), 12 part-time (all women). 8 applicants, 100% accepted, 7 enrolled. In 2008, 9 master's awarded. *Entrance requirements:* For master's, resumé. Additional exam requirements/recommendations for international students: Required—TOEFL (minimum score 525 paper-based). *Application deadline:* For fall admission, 4/15 for international students; for spring admission, 8/15 for international students. Application fee: $35. *Financial support:* In 2008–09, 3 research assistantships with partial tuition reimbursements (averaging $15,750 per year), 4 teaching assistantships with partial tuition reimbursements (averaging $15,750 per year) were awarded. *Unit head:* Dr. Andrew Stremmel, Head, 605-688-6418, Fax: 605-688-4888, E-mail: andrew.stremmel@sdstate.edu. *Application contact:* The Graduate School, 605-688-4181, E-mail: sdsu_gradschool@sdstate.edu.

Southern Illinois University Carbondale, Graduate School, College of Education, Department of Educational Psychology and Special Education, Program in Educational Psychology, Carbondale, IL 62901-4701. Offers counselor education (MS Ed, PhD); educational psychology (PhD); human learning and development (MS Ed); measurement and statistics (PhD). *Accreditation:* NCATE. *Degree requirements:* For master's, thesis; for doctorate, thesis/dissertation. *Entrance requirements:* For master's, GRE General Test, minimum GPA of 2.7; for doctorate, minimum GPA of 3.25. Additional exam requirements/recommendations for international students: Required—TOEFL. *Faculty research:* Career development, problem solving, learning and instruction, cognitive development, family assessment.

Texas A&M University, College of Education and Human Development, Department of Educational Psychology, College Station, TX 77843. Offers counseling psychology (PhD); educational psychology (PhD); educational technology (M Ed); gifted and talented education (M Ed, MS); Hispanic bilingual education (M Ed, PhD); human learning and development (MS); intelligence, creativity, and giftedness (PhD); learning, development, and instruction (PhD); research, measurement and statistics (MS); research, measurement, and statistics (PhD); school counseling (M Ed); school psychology (PhD); special education (M Ed, PhD). *Accreditation:* APA (one or more programs are accredited); NCATE. Part-time and evening/weekend programs available. Postbaccalaureate distance learning degree programs offered (no on-campus study). *Faculty:* 46. *Students:* 161 full-time (129 women), 148 part-time (126 women); includes 86 minority (26 African Americans, 1 American Indian/Alaska Native, 11 Asian Americans or Pacific Islanders, 48 Hispanic Americans), 38 international. In 2008, 47 master's, 20 doctorates awarded. *Degree requirements:* For master's, thesis optional; for doctorate, thesis/dissertation. *Entrance requirements:* For master's and doctorate, GRE General Test. Additional exam requirements/recommendations for international students: Required—TOEFL. Application fee: $50 ($75 for international students). Electronic applications accepted. *Expenses:* Tuition, area resident: Full-time $3838.50. Tuition, state resident: full-time $3838.50. Tuition, nonresident: full-time $8897. Required fees: $2359.60. *Financial support:* In 2008–09, fellowships (averaging $12,000 per year), research assistantships (averaging $9,000 per year), teaching assistantships (averaging $9,000 per year) were awarded; career-related internships or fieldwork, institutionally sponsored loans, scholarships/grants, and unspecified assistantships also available. Financial award applicants required to submit FAFSA. *Unit head:* Dr. Victor Willson, Head, 979-845-1800, E-mail: v-willson@tamu.edu. *Application contact:* Carol A. Wagner, Director of Advising, 979-845-1833, Fax: 979-862-1256, E-mail: c-wagner@tamu.edu.

Texas Tech University, Graduate School, College of Human Sciences, Department of Human Development and Family Studies, Lubbock, TX 79409. Offers gerontology (MS); human development and family studies (MS, PhD). *Accreditation:* AAMFT/COAMFTE (one or more programs are accredited). Part-time programs available. *Faculty:* 19 full-time (15 women), 1 (woman) part-time/adjunct. *Students:* 38 full-time (30 women), 18 part-time (11 women); includes 9 minority (2 African Americans, 2 American Indian/Alaska Native, 2 Asian Americans or Pacific Islanders, 3 Hispanic Americans), 13 international. Average age 36. 32 applicants, 78% accepted, 7 enrolled. In 2008, 7 master's awarded. *Degree requirements:* For master's, thesis; for doctorate, thesis/dissertation. *Entrance requirements:* For master's and doctorate, GRE General Test. Additional exam requirements/recommendations for international students: Required—TOEFL (minimum score 550 paper-based; 213 computer-based). *Application deadline:* For fall admission, 3/1 priority date for international students; for spring admission, 11/1 priority date for international students. Applications are processed on a rolling basis. Application fee: $50 ($60 for international students). Electronic applications accepted. *Expenses:* Tuition, area resident: Part-time $194 per credit hour. Tuition, state resident: full-time $4648; part-time $194 per credit hour. Tuition, nonresident: full-time $11,392; part-time $475 per credit hour. Required fees: $2206; $69 per credit hour. $389 per semester. *Financial support:* In 2008–09, 55 students received support, including 3 research assistantships with partial tuition reimbursements available (averaging $13,107 per year), 30 teaching assistantships with partial tuition reimbursements available (averaging $13,126 per year); career-related internships or fieldwork, Federal Work-Study, institutionally sponsored loans, and scholarships/grants also available. Support available to part-time students. Financial award application deadline: 4/15; financial award applicants required to submit FAFSA. *Faculty research:* Parenting, marital and premarital relationships, adolescent risky behaviors, life span; child development. Total annual research expenditures: $352,679. *Unit head:* Anisa Zvonkovic, Chair, 806-742-3000 Ext. 279, Fax: 806-742-0285, E-mail: anisa.zvonkovic@ttu.edu. *Application contact:* Monya Castle, Graduate Secretary, 806-742-3000 Ext. 250, Fax: 806-742-0285, E-mail: monya.castle@ttu.edu.

The University of Alabama, Graduate School, College of Human Environmental Sciences, Department of Human Development and Family Studies, Tuscaloosa, AL 35487. Offers MSHES. *Faculty:* 7 full-time (5 women). *Students:* 20 full-time (all women), 10 part-time (all women); includes 5 African Americans, 1 Asian American or Pacific Islander, 1 international. Average age 26. 26 applicants, 58% accepted, 9 enrolled. In 2008, 13 master's awarded. *Degree requirements:* For master's, thesis (for some programs). *Entrance requirements:* For master's, GRE General Test or MAT, minimum GPA of 3.0. Additional exam requirements/recommendations for international students: Required—TOEFL. *Application deadline:* For fall admission, 2/1 priority date for domestic and international students. Applications are processed on a rolling basis. Application fee: $50. Electronic applications accepted. *Expenses:* Tuition, area resident: Full-time $6400. Tuition, state resident: full-time $6400. Tuition, nonresident: full-time $18,000. *Financial support:* In 2008–09, 11 students received support, including 1 fellowship with full tuition reimbursement available (averaging $15,000 per year), 6 research assistantships with full tuition reimbursements available (averaging $10,908 per year), 4 teaching assistantships (averaging $10,908 per year); career-related internships or fieldwork, Federal Work-Study, scholarships/grants, and health care benefits also available. Financial award application deadline: 3/15. *Faculty research:* Parent/child relationships, preschool curricula and quality measures for child care programs, family strengths and adolescent behaviors, depression in mothers and infants, word association and word learning in young children. *Unit head:* Dr. Carroll M. Tingle, Chair, 205-348-6158, Fax: 205-348-8153, E-mail: ctingle@ches.ua.edu. *Application contact:* Dr. Maria Hernandez-Reif, Associate Professor, 205-348-5894, E-mail: mhernandez-reif@ches.ua.edu.

The University of Arizona, Graduate College, College of Agriculture and Life Sciences, School of Family and Consumer Sciences, Division of Family Studies and Human Development, Tucson, AZ 85721. Offers family and consumer sciences education (MS); family studies and human development (PhD). Terminal master's awarded for partial completion of doctoral program. *Entrance requirements:* For master's, GRE General Test, minimum undergraduate GPA of 3.0, personal resumé, personal statement, 3 letters of recommendation. Additional exam requirements/recommendations for international students: Required—TOEFL.

The University of British Columbia, Faculty of Graduate Studies, Faculty of Education, Department of Educational and Counseling Psychology, and Special Education, Vancouver, BC V6T 1Z1, Canada. Offers counseling psychology (M Ed, MA, PhD); development, learning and culture (PhD); guidance studies (Diploma); human development, learning and culture (M Ed, MA); measurement and evaluation and research methodology (M Ed); measurement, evaluation and research methodology (MA); measurement, evaluation, and research methodology (PhD); school psychology (M Ed, MA, PhD); special education (M Ed, MA, PhD, Diploma). Part-time programs available. *Degree requirements:* For master's, thesis (for some programs); for doctorate, comprehensive exam, thesis/dissertation. *Entrance requirements:* For master's, GRE General Test (counseling psychology MA); for doctorate, GRE General Test. Additional exam requirements/recommendations for international students: Required—TOEFL. Electronic applications accepted. *Faculty research:* Women, family, social problems, career transition, stress and coping problems.

University of Calgary, Faculty of Graduate Studies, Faculty of Education, Division of Applied Psychology, Calgary, AB T2N 1N4, Canada. Offers counseling psychology (M Ed, M Sc, PhD); human development and learning (M Ed, M Sc, PhD); school psychology (M Ed, M Sc, PhD); special education (M Ed, M Sc, PhD). Part-time programs available. *Degree requirements:* For master's, thesis (for some programs), final oral exam; for doctorate, thesis/dissertation, candidacy exam, final oral exam. *Entrance requirements:* For master's, minimum GPA of 3.0, 3 letters of reference; for doctorate, minimum GPA of 3.5, 3 letters of reference. *Faculty research:* Counselor education, family life studies, learning and cognition.

University of California, Berkeley, Graduate Division, School of Education, Division of Cognition and Development, Program in Human Development and Education, Berkeley, CA 94720-1500. Offers MA, PhD, PhD/MA. Electronic applications accepted.

University of California, Davis, Graduate Studies, Graduate Group in Human Development, Davis, CA 95616. Offers PhD. *Degree requirements:* For doctorate, thesis/dissertation. *Entrance requirements:* For doctorate, GRE General Test, GRE Subject Test, minimum GPA of 3.0. Additional exam requirements/recommendations for international students: Required—TOEFL (minimum score 550 paper-based; 213 computer-based). Electronic applications accepted. *Faculty research:* Life span socioemotional and cognitive development, individual differences,

Human Development

University of California, Davis (continued)
relationship between biological and behavioral development, cross-cultural and cross-generational development.

University of California, Santa Barbara, Graduate Division, College of Letters and Sciences, Division of Humanities and Fine Arts, Department of Linguistics, Santa Barbara, CA 93106-3100. Offers applied linguistics (PhD); cognitive science (PhD); human development (PhD); language, interaction, and social organizations (PhD); MA/PhD. *Faculty:* 23 full-time (12 women). *Students:* 25 full-time (14 women). Average age 32. 63 applicants, 17% accepted, 5 enrolled. In 2008, 5 doctorates awarded. *Degree requirements:* For doctorate, one foreign language, comprehensive exam, thesis/dissertation, 48 units of coursework, minimum GPA of 3.7. *Entrance requirements:* For doctorate, GRE, 3 letters of recommendation, statement of purpose, personal achievements/contributions statement, resumé/curriculum vitae, transcripts for post-secondary institutions attended. Additional exam requirements/recommendations for international students: Required—TOEFL (minimum score 550 paper-based; 213 computer-based; 80 iBT), IELTS (minimum score 7), TOEFL or IELTS. *Application deadline:* For fall admission, 12/1 priority date for domestic and international students. Application fee: $70 ($90 for international students). Electronic applications accepted. *Expenses:* Tuition, nonresident: full-time $25,149. Required fees: $10,143. Full-time tuition and fees vary according to campus/location, reciprocity agreements and student level. *Financial support:* In 2008–09, 24 students received support, including 19 fellowships with full and partial tuition reimbursements available (averaging $12,400 per year), 1 research assistantship with full and partial tuition reimbursement available (averaging $3,000 per year), 13 teaching assistantships with partial tuition reimbursements available (averaging $5,600 per year); Federal Work-Study, institutionally sponsored loans, scholarships/grants, health care benefits, and unspecified assistantships also available. Financial award application deadline: 12/1; financial award applicants required to submit FAFSA. *Faculty research:* Language, race and subcultural identities among California teenagers; language acquisition, psycholinguisticss; language documentation, fieldwork; syntax of nominalization in 5 Tibeto-Burman languages; perceptual correlates of syllable weight. *Unit head:* Prof. Patricia M. Clancy, Chair, 805-893-8658, Fax: 805-893-7769, E-mail: pclancy@linguistics.ucsb.edu. *Application contact:* Mary Rae Staton, Graduate Program Assistant, 805-893-3776, Fax: 805-893-7769, E-mail: staton@linguistics.ucsb.edu.

University of California, Santa Barbara, Graduate Division, College of Letters and Sciences, Division of Social Sciences, Department of Communication, Santa Barbara, CA 93106-4020. Offers human development (PhD); MA/PhD. *Faculty:* 20 full-time (8 women), 1 part-time/adjunct (0 women). *Students:* 38 full-time (26 women). Average age 28. 155 applicants, 12% accepted, 10 enrolled. In 2008, 2 doctorates awarded. *Degree requirements:* For doctorate, comprehensive exam, thesis/dissertation. *Entrance requirements:* For doctorate, GRE General Test, 3 letters of recommendation, statement of purpose, personal achievements/contributions statement, resumé/curriculum vitae, transcripts for post-secondary institutions attended. Additional exam requirements/recommendations for international students: Required—TOEFL (minimum score 600 paper-based; 213 computer-based; 80 iBT), TOEFL or IELTS. *Application deadline:* For fall admission, 1/1 for domestic and international students. Application fee: $70 ($90 for international students). Electronic applications accepted. *Expenses:* Tuition, nonresident: full-time $25,149. Required fees: $10,143. Full-time tuition and fees vary according to campus/location, reciprocity agreements and student level. *Financial support:* In 2008–09, 38 students received support, including 38 fellowships with full and partial tuition reimbursements available (averaging $5,500 per year), 5 research assistantships with full and partial tuition reimbursements available (averaging $7,800 per year), 34 teaching assistantships with partial tuition reimbursements available (averaging $11,000 per year); Federal Work-Study, institutionally sponsored loans, scholarships/grants, health care benefits, tuition waivers (full and partial), and unspecified assistantships also available. Financial award application deadline: 1/1; financial award applicants required to submit FAFSA. *Faculty research:* Interpersonal communication, organizational communication, media communication, political communication, intrapersonal communication. Total annual research expenditures: $100,000. *Unit head:* Prof. Michael Stohl, Chair, 805-893-7935, Fax: 805-893-7102, E-mail: mstohl@comm.ucsb.edu. *Application contact:* Nancy Siris-Rawls, Graduate Program Assistant, 805-893-3046, Fax: 805-893-7102, E-mail: nsiris@comm.ucsb.edu.

University of California, Santa Barbara, Graduate Division, College of Letters and Sciences, Division of Social Sciences, Department of Sociology, Santa Barbara, CA 93106-9430. Offers global studies (PhD); human development (PhD); language, interaction and social organization (PhD); technology and society (PhD); women's studies (PhD); MA/PhD. *Faculty:* 35 full-time (14 women). *Students:* 77 full-time (50 women). Average age 30. 155 applicants, 9% accepted, 8 enrolled. In 2008, 10 doctorates awarded. Terminal master's awarded for partial completion of doctoral program. *Degree requirements:* For doctorate, comprehensive exam, thesis/dissertation. *Entrance requirements:* For doctorate, GRE General Test, sample of written work, 3 letters of recommendation, statement of purpose, personal achievements/contributions statement, resumé/curriculum vitae, transcripts for post-secondary institutions attended. Additional exam requirements/recommendations for international students: Required—TOEFL (minimum score 550 paper-based; 213 computer-based; 80 iBT), TOEFL or IELTS. *Application deadline:* For fall admission, 12/10 for domestic students. Application fee: $70 ($90 for international students). Electronic applications accepted. *Expenses:* Tuition, nonresident: full-time $25,149. Required fees: $10,143. Full-time tuition and fees vary according to campus/location, reciprocity agreements and student level. *Financial support:* In 2008–09, 69 students received support, including 50 fellowships with full tuition reimbursements available (averaging $7,900 per year), 6 research assistantships with full and partial tuition reimbursements available (averaging $2,600 per year), 53 teaching assistantships with partial tuition reimbursements available (averaging $9,200 per year); career-related internships or fieldwork, Federal Work-Study, institutionally sponsored loans, scholarships/grants, health care benefits, and unspecified assistantships also available. Financial award applicants required to submit FAFSA. *Faculty research:* Conversation analysis, social movements, human sexuality, urban sociology, race and ethnic relations. *Unit head:* Prof. Verta Taylor, Chair, 805-893-3118, Fax: 805-893-3324, E-mail: grad-soc@soc.ucsb.edu. *Application contact:* Ra Thea, Graduate Staff Advisor, 805-893-3328, Fax: 805-893-3324, E-mail: grad-soc@soc.ucsb.edu.

University of Central Oklahoma, College of Graduate Studies and Research, College of Education, Department of Human Environmental Sciences, Edmond, OK 73034-5209. Offers family and child studies (MS); family and consumer science education (MS); interior design (MS); nutrition-food management (MS). Part-time programs available. *Entrance requirements:* Additional exam requirements/recommendations for international students: Required—TOEFL (minimum score 550 paper-based; 213 computer-based). Electronic applications accepted. *Faculty research:* Dietetics and food science.

University of Chicago, Division of Social Sciences, Department of Comparative Human Development, Chicago, IL 60637-1513. Offers PhD. *Degree requirements:* For doctorate, one foreign language, thesis/dissertation, pre-doctoral written exams. *Entrance requirements:* For doctorate, GRE General Test, GRE Subject Test. Additional exam requirements/recommendations for international students: Required—TOEFL, IELTS (minimum score 7). Electronic applications accepted.

University of Connecticut, Graduate School, College of Liberal Arts and Sciences, Department of Human Development and Family Studies, Field of Human Development and Family Studies, Storrs, CT 06269. Offers culture, health and human development (Graduate Certificate); human development and family studies (MA, PhD). *Accreditation:* AAMFT/COAMFTE. Terminal master's awarded for partial completion of doctoral program. *Degree requirements:* For master's, comprehensive exam; for doctorate, thesis/dissertation. *Entrance requirements:* For master's and doctorate, GRE General Test. Additional exam requirements/recommendations for international students: Required—TOEFL (minimum score 550 paper-based; 213 computer-based). Electronic applications accepted.

University of Dayton, Graduate School, School of Education and Allied Professions, Department of Counselor Education and Human Services, Dayton, OH 45469-1300. Offers college student personnel (MS Ed); community counseling (MS Ed); higher education administration (MS Ed); human services (MS Ed); school counseling (MS Ed); school psychology (MS Ed, Ed S); teacher as child/youth development specialist (MS Ed). *Accreditation:* NCATE. Part-time and evening/weekend programs available. *Faculty:* 11 full-time (8 women), 33 part-time/adjunct (22 women). *Students:* 266 full-time (222 women), 236 part-time (200 women); includes 70 minority (58 African Americans, 2 Asian Americans or Pacific Islanders, 10 Hispanic Americans), 2 international. Average age 32. 359 applicants, 47% accepted, 114 enrolled. In 2008, 175 master's, 7 Ed Ss awarded. *Degree requirements:* For master's, comprehensive exam (for some programs), thesis (for some programs), exit exam. *Entrance requirements:* For master's, MAT or GRE (if GPA is below 2.75), interview, writing sample. Additional exam requirements/recommendations for international students: Required—TOEFL (minimum score 550 paper-based; 213 computer-based; 80 iBT). *Application deadline:* For fall admission, 4/10 for domestic students, 3/1 priority date for international students; for winter admission, 9/10 for domestic students, 7/1 priority date for international students; for spring admission, 1/10 for domestic students, 1/1 priority date for international students. Applications are processed on a rolling basis. Application fee: $0 ($50 for international students). Electronic applications accepted. *Expenses:* Tuition: Full-time $6950; part-time $1737.50 per semester. Required fees: $25 per semester. Tuition and fees vary according to course level, course load, degree level and program. *Financial support:* In 2008–09, 7 research assistantships with full tuition reimbursements (averaging $8,000 per year), 1 teaching assistantship with full tuition reimbursement (averaging $8,000 per year) were awarded; career-related internships or fieldwork, institutionally sponsored loans, health care benefits, and unspecified assistantships also available. Financial award applicants required to submit FAFSA. *Faculty research:* Anger as part of the grief process, inclusion of children with severe disabilities, comparisons of school counselors in Bosnia and the U.S., graduate and professional student socialization, use of cohort groups in doctoral programs, bullying in schools, impact of space on learning, sophomore experience. *Unit head:* Dr. Alan Demmitt, Chairperson, 937-229-3644, Fax: 937-229-1055. *Application contact:* Angela Jones-Glukhov, Associate Director of Graduate Admissions, 937-229-4305, Fax: 937-229-4729, E-mail: jonesgas@notes.udayton.edu.

University of Delaware, College of Human Services, Education and Public Policy, Department of Individual and Family Studies, Newark, DE 19716. Offers human development and family studies (MS, PhD). Part-time programs available. Terminal master's awarded for partial completion of doctoral program. *Degree requirements:* For master's, thesis or alternative; for doctorate, comprehensive exam, thesis/dissertation. *Entrance requirements:* For master's and doctorate, GRE General Test, 3 letters of recommendation. Additional exam requirements/recommendations for international students: Required—TOEFL. Electronic applications accepted. *Faculty research:* Early childhood inclusive education, relationships, family risk and resilience, disability issues, program development and evaluation.

University of Guelph, Graduate Program Services, College of Social and Applied Human Sciences, Department of Family Relations and Applied Nutrition, Guelph, ON N1G 2W1, Canada. Offers applied nutrition (MAN); family relations and human development (M Sc, PhD), including applied human nutrition, couple and family therapy (M Sc), family relations and human development. *Accreditation:* AAMFT/COAMFTE (one or more programs are accredited). Part-time programs available. *Degree requirements:* For master's, thesis (for some programs); for doctorate, comprehensive exam, thesis/dissertation. *Entrance requirements:* For master's, minimum B+ average; for doctorate, master's degree in family relations and human development or related field with a minimum B+ average or master's degree in applied human nutrition. Additional exam requirements/recommendations for international students: Required—TOEFL (minimum score 600 paper-based; 250 computer-based). Electronic applications accepted. *Faculty research:* Child and adolescent development, social gerontology, family roles and relations, couple and family therapy, applied human nutrition.

University of Houston, College of Technology, Department of Human Development and Consumer Science, Houston, TX 77204. Offers MS. *Faculty:* 2 full-time (1 woman), 1 part-time/adjunct (0 women). *Students:* 27 full-time (18 women), 35 part-time (22 women); includes 24 minority (17 African Americans, 5 Asian Americans or Pacific Islanders, 2 Hispanic Americans), 12 international. Average age 33. 37 applicants, 84% accepted, 27 enrolled. In 2008, 15 master's awarded. *Expenses:* Tuition, state resident: full-time $5164; part-time $287 per credit. Tuition, nonresident: full-time $10,222; part-time $568 per credit. *Financial support:* In 2008–09, 11 research assistantships (averaging $10,700 per year), 8 teaching assistantships (averaging $10,700 per year) were awarded. *Unit head:* Carole Goodson, Chairperson, 713-743-4046, Fax: 713-743-4033. *Application contact:* Holly Rosenthal, Graduate Academic Adviser, 713-743-4098, Fax: 713-743-4032, E-mail: hrosenthal@uh.edu.

University of Illinois at Chicago, Graduate College, College of Applied Health Sciences, Department of Disability and Human Development, Chicago, IL 60607-7128. Offers disability and human development (MS); disability studies (PhD). *Accreditation:* AOTA. Part-time programs available. *Degree requirements:* For master's, thesis optional; for doctorate, thesis/dissertation. *Entrance requirements:* For master's and doctorate, GRE General Test. Additional exam requirements/recommendations for international students: Required—TOEFL. Electronic applications accepted. *Faculty research:* Emerging trends in disability, demography and financial structure of disability services, aging and disability, empowerment of people with disabilities, health promotion in disabilities.

University of Illinois at Springfield, Graduate Programs, College of Education and Human Services, Program in Human Development Counseling, Springfield, IL 62703-5407. Offers MA. *Accreditation:* ACA. Part-time and evening/weekend programs available. *Faculty:* 4 full-time (2 women), 3 part-time/adjunct (2 women). *Students:* 23 full-time (21 women), 38 part-time (33 women); includes 4 minority (3 African Americans, 1 Asian American or Pacific Islander). Average age 33. 41 applicants, 68% accepted, 11 enrolled. In 2008, 28 master's awarded. *Degree requirements:* For master's, project, thesis, or comprehensive exam. *Entrance requirements:* For master's, minimum undergraduate GPA of 3.0 in the last 60 hours of coursework, personal references, written essay, interview. Additional exam requirements/recommendations for international students: Required—TOEFL (minimum score 500 paper-based; 176 computer-based; 61 iBT). Application fee: $50 ($60 for international students). Electronic applications accepted. *Expenses:* Tuition, state resident: full-time $6144; part-time $256 per credit hour. Tuition, nonresident: full-time $13,980; part-time $582.50 per credit hour. Required fees: $1800. *Financial support:* In 2008–09, research assistantships with full tuition reimbursements (averaging $8,109 per year), teaching assistantships with full tuition reimbursements (averaging $8,109 per year) were awarded; career-related internships or fieldwork, Federal Work-Study, scholarships/grants, health care benefits, and unspecified assistantships also available. Support available to part-time students. Financial award application deadline: 11/15; financial award applicants required to submit FAFSA. *Unit head:* Dr. William Abler, Program Administrator, 217-206-7567, Fax: 217-206-6775, E-mail: abler.william@uis.edu. *Application contact:* Dr. Lynn Pardie, Office of Graduate Studies, 800-252-8533, Fax: 217-206-7623, E-mail: pardie.lynn@uis.edu.

University of Illinois at Urbana–Champaign, Graduate College, College of Agricultural, Consumer and Environmental Sciences, Department of Human and Community Development, Champaign, IL 61820. Offers agricultural education (MS); human and community development (MS, PhD); MS/MSW. *Faculty:* 16 full-time (11 women), 1 part-time/adjunct (0 women). *Students:* 28 full-time (24 women), 5 part-time (1 woman); includes 5 minority (4 African Americans, 1 Asian American or Pacific Islander), 6 international. 43 applicants, 30% accepted, 9 enrolled. In 2008, 14 master's, 1 doctorate awarded. *Entrance requirements:* For master's and doctorate, GRE, minimum GPA of 3.0. Additional exam requirements/recommendations for international students: Required—TOEFL (minimum score 550 paper-based; 213 computer-based; 79 iBT). *Application deadline:* Applications are processed on a rolling basis. Application fee: $60 ($75 for international students). Electronic applications accepted. *Financial support:* In 2008–09, 16 fellowships, 17 research assistantships, 14 teaching assistantships were awarded; tuition waivers (full and partial) also available. *Unit head:* Robert Hughes, Head, 217-333-3790, Fax: 217-244-7877, E-mail: hughesro@illinois.edu. *Application contact:* Leann Topol, Clerk, 217-333-3869, Fax: 217-244-7877, E-mail: ltopol@illinois.edu.

University of Maine, Graduate School, College of Education and Human Development, Department of Human Development and Family Relations, Orono, ME 04469. Offers human development (MS). Part-time programs available. *Degree requirements:* For master's, thesis. *Entrance requirements:* For master's, GRE General Test. Additional exam requirements/recommendations for international students: Required—TOEFL. Electronic applications accepted. *Faculty research:* Methods to assess nutrient intake and risk, carnitine-supplemented diets for protein-calorie malnutrition, nutrition education, grandfathers' perceptions of relations to grandchildren, social participation of spouses in distressed and nondistressed marriages.

University of Maryland, College Park, Graduate Studies, College of Arts and Humanities, School of Languages, Literature, and Cultures, Program in Second Language Acquisition and Application, College Park, MD 20742. Offers French (MA); German (MA); Japanese (MA); Russian (MA); second language instruction (PhD); second language learning (PhD); second language measurement and assessment (PhD); second language use (PhD); Spanish (MA). *Entrance requirements:* For master's, BA or BS in related field, demonstrated language competency, 3 letters of reference. Electronic applications accepted. *Faculty research:* Second language acquisition, pedagogical perspectives, technological applications, language use in professional contexts.

University of Maryland, College Park, Graduate Studies, College of Education, Department of Human Development, College Park, MD 20742. Offers early childhood/elementary education (M Ed, MA, Ed D, PhD); human development (M Ed, MA, Ed D, PhD). *Accreditation:* NCATE. Part-time and evening/weekend programs available. Postbaccalaureate distance learning degree programs offered. *Degree requirements:* For master's, comprehensive exam, thesis optional; for doctorate, comprehensive exam, thesis/dissertation, essay, exam, research paper. *Entrance requirements:* For master's, GRE General Test, minimum GPA of 3.0, 3 letters of recommendation; for doctorate, GRE General Test or MAT, minimum undergraduate GPA of 3.0, graduate 3.5; 3 letters of recommendation. Additional exam requirements/recommendations for international students: Required—TOEFL. Electronic applications accepted. *Faculty research:* Developmental science, educational psychology, cognitive development, language development.

University of Missouri–Columbia, Graduate School, College of Human Environmental Science, Department of Human Development and Family Studies, Columbia, MO 65211. Offers MA, MS, PhD. *Faculty:* 10 full-time (6 women). *Students:* 40 full-time (29 women), 11 part-time (8 women); includes 7 minority (6 African Americans, 1 Hispanic American), 5 international. Average age 29. 38 applicants, 61% accepted, 17 enrolled. In 2008, 8 master's, 1 doctorate awarded. *Entrance requirements:* For master's, GRE General Test, minimum GPA of 3.0. Additional exam requirements/recommendations for international students: Required—TOEFL (minimum score 550 paper-based; 213 computer-based; 80 iBT). *Application deadline:* For fall admission, 2/1 priority date for domestic students; for winter admission, 11/15 priority date for domestic students. Applications are processed on a rolling basis. Application fee: $45 ($60 for international students). *Financial support:* Fellowships, research assistantships, teaching assistantships, institutionally sponsored loans available. *Unit head:* Dr. Jean Ispa, Director of Graduate Studies, E-mail: ispaj@missouri.edu. *Application contact:* Dr. Marilyn Coleman, Director of Graduate Studies, 573-882-4360, E-mail: colemanma@missouri.edu.

University of Nebraska–Lincoln, Graduate College, College of Education and Human Sciences, Department of Child, Youth and Family Studies, Lincoln, NE 68588. Offers child development/early childhood education (MS, PhD); child, youth and family studies (MS); family and consumer sciences education (MS, PhD); family financial planning (MS); family science (MS, PhD); gerontology (PhD); human sciences (PhD), including child, youth and family studies, gerontology, medical family therapy; marriage and family therapy (MS); medical family therapy (PhD); youth development (MS). *Accreditation:* AAMFT/COAMFTE (one or more programs are accredited). Postbaccalaureate distance learning degree programs offered. *Faculty:* 16 full-time (11 women). *Students:* 23 full-time (18 women), 53 part-time (40 women); includes 8 minority (2 African Americans, 2 American Indian/Alaska Native, 2 Asian Americans or Pacific Islanders, 2 Hispanic Americans), 1 international. Average age 32. In 2008, 27 master's awarded. *Degree requirements:* For master's, thesis optional. *Entrance requirements:* For master's, GRE. Additional exam requirements/recommendations for international students: Required—TOEFL (minimum score 550 paper-based; 213 computer-based). *Application deadline:* For fall admission, 1/15 for domestic and international students; for spring admission, 10/1 for domestic and international students. Application fee: $40. Electronic applications accepted. *Expenses:* Tuition, state resident: full-time $4275; part-time $237.50 per credit hour. Tuition, nonresident: full-time $11,525; part-time $640.25 per credit hour. Required fees: $1068; $10.35 per credit hour. $440.70 per semester. Tuition and fees vary according to course load and program. *Financial support:* Fellowships, research assistantships, teaching assistantships, Federal Work-Study, health care benefits, and unspecified assistantships available. Financial award application deadline: 2/15. *Faculty research:* Marriage and family therapy, child development/early childhood education, family financial management. *Unit head:* Dr. Julie Johnson, Chair, 402-472-2957. *Application contact:* Dr. Julie Johnson, Chair, 402-472-2957.

University of Nebraska–Lincoln, Graduate College, College of Education and Human Sciences, Department of Special Education and Communication Disorders, Lincoln, NE 68588. Offers audiology research (PhD); clinical audiology (Au D); educational studies (PhD); human sciences (PhD), including communication disorders; special education (M Ed, MA, Ed S), including special education (M Ed, MA), special education and communication disorders (Ed S); speech-language pathology and audiology (MS, Au D), including audiology and hearing science (Au D), speech-language pathology (Au D), speech-language pathology and audiology (MS). *Accreditation:* ASHA (one or more programs are accredited); NCATE. *Faculty:* 19 full-time (7 women). *Students:* 76 full-time (71 women), 71 part-time (69 women); includes 3 minority (1 African American, 1 Asian American or Pacific Islander, 1 Hispanic American), 2 international. Average age 28. In 2008, 69 master's awarded. *Degree requirements:* For master's, thesis optional. *Entrance requirements:* For master's, GRE General Test. Additional exam requirements/recommendations for international students: Required—TOEFL. *Application deadline:* For fall admission, 2/15 for domestic students; for spring admission, 10/15 for domestic students. Application fee: $40. Electronic applications accepted. *Expenses:* Tuition, state resident: full-time $4275; part-time $237.50 per credit hour. Tuition, nonresident: full-time $11,525; part-time $640.25 per credit hour. Required fees: $1068; $10.35 per credit hour. $440.70 per semester. Tuition and fees vary according to course load and program. *Financial support:* Fellowships, research assistantships, teaching assistantships, Federal Work-Study, health care benefits, and unspecified assistantships available. Support available to part-time students. Financial award application deadline: 2/15. *Faculty research:* Curriculum-based assessment, paraprofessional and parent training, behavior management for special needs individuals, augmentative communication, speech/language disorders. *Unit head:* Dr. John E. Bernthal, Chair, 402-472-5496, Fax: 402-472-7697, E-mail: tcgrad2@unl.edu. *Application contact:* Dr. John E. Bernthal, Chair, 402-472-5496, Fax: 402-472-7697, E-mail: tcgrad2@unl.edu.

University of Nebraska–Lincoln, Graduate College, College of Education and Human Sciences, Department of Textiles, Clothing and Design, Lincoln, NE 68588. Offers human sciences (PhD), including textiles, clothing and design (MS, PhD); merchandising (MS); textile history/quilt studies (MA); textile science (MS); textile-apparel (MA); textiles, clothing and design (MA, MS), including textiles, clothing and design (MS, PhD). Part-time programs available. Postbaccalaureate distance learning degree programs offered (minimal on-campus study). *Faculty:* 10 full-time (8 women). *Students:* 14 full-time (12 women), 3 part-time (all women), 5 international. Average age 29. In 2008, 9 master's awarded. *Degree requirements:* For master's, thesis optional. *Entrance requirements:* For master's, GRE General Test. Additional exam requirements/recommendations for international students: Required—TOEFL (minimum score 550 paper-based; 213 computer-based). *Application deadline:* For fall admission, 3/1 for international students. Applications are processed on a rolling basis. Application fee: $40. Electronic applications accepted. *Expenses:* Tuition, state resident: full-time $4275; part-time $237.50 per credit hour. Tuition, nonresident: full-time $11,525; part-time $640.25 per credit hour. Required fees: $1068; $10.35 per credit hour. $440.70 per semester. Tuition and fees vary according to course load and program. *Financial support:* Fellowships, research assistantships, teaching assistantships, Federal Work-Study, health care benefits, and unspecified assistantships available. Financial award application deadline: 2/15. *Faculty research:* Merchandising, textile science, fiber arts, textile history, quilt studies. *Unit head:* Dr. Carol Thayer, Acting Chair, 402-472-2911. *Application contact:* Dr. Carol Thayer, Acting Chair, 402-472-2911.

University of Nevada, Reno, Graduate School, College of Education, Department of Human Development and Family Studies, Reno, NV 89557. Offers MS. *Faculty:* 11 full-time (7 women). *Students:* 6 full-time (all women), 12 part-time (10 women); includes 5 minority (1 African American, 2 Asian Americans or Pacific Islanders, 2 Hispanic Americans), 1 international. Average age 33. 11 applicants, 45% accepted, 4 enrolled. In 2008, 2 master's awarded. *Degree requirements:* For master's, thesis optional. *Entrance requirements:* For master's, GRE General Test, minimum GPA of 2.75. Additional exam requirements/recommendations for international students: Required—TOEFL (minimum score 500 paper-based; 173 computer-based; 61 iBT), IELTS (minimum score 6), TOFEL or IELTS. *Application deadline:* For fall admission, 3/30 priority date for domestic and international students; for spring admission, 10/1 priority date for domestic and international students. Applications are processed on a rolling basis. Application fee: $60 ($95 for international students). Electronic applications accepted. *Expenses:* Tuition, state resident: full-time $1710; part-time $1140 per semester. Tuition, nonresident: full-time $7115. Required fees: $158 per semester. *Financial support:* In 2008–09, 1 research assistantship with partial tuition reimbursement (averaging $14,000 per year), 2 teaching assistantships with partial tuition reimbursements were awarded; Federal Work-Study, scholarships/grants, health care benefits, and unspecified assistantships also available. Financial award application deadline: 3/1; financial award applicants required to submit FAFSA. *Faculty research:* Early childhood/adolescent development, family studies. Total annual research expenditures: $21.1 million. *Unit head:* Dr. Bill Evans, Graduate Program Director, 775-784-6490, E-mail: evans@unr.nevada.edu. *Application contact:* Michele Sandberg, Application Contact, 775-784 7026, Fax: 775-784 6064, E-mail: gradschool@unr.edu.

The University of North Carolina at Greensboro, Graduate School, School of Human Environmental Sciences, Department of Human Development and Family Studies, Greensboro, NC 27412-5001. Offers M Ed, MS, PhD. *Degree requirements:* For master's, one foreign language; for doctorate, one foreign language, thesis/dissertation. *Entrance requirements:* For master's and doctorate, GRE General Test. Additional exam requirements/recommendations for international students: Required—TOEFL. Electronic applications accepted. *Expenses:* Contact institution. *Faculty research:* Adolescent mothers, multi-handicapped, older adults.

University of North Texas, Robert B. Toulouse School of Graduate Studies, College of Education, Department of Educational Psychology, Program in Development and Family Studies, Denton, TX 76203. Offers MS. Evening/weekend programs available. *Degree requirements:* For master's, comprehensive exam, thesis optional. *Entrance requirements:* For master's, GRE General Test, letter of application, resumé, references. Additional exam requirements/recommendations for international students: Required—proof of English language proficiency required for non-native English speakers; Recommended—TOEFL (minimum score 550 paper-based; 213 computer-based). *Faculty research:* Parent-child issues, cognitive development, social development.

University of Pennsylvania, Graduate School of Education, Division of Applied Psychology and Human Development, Interdisciplinary Studies in Human Development, Philadelphia, PA 19104. Offers MS Ed, PhD. Part-time programs available. Terminal master's awarded for partial completion of doctoral program. *Degree requirements:* For master's, exam; for doctorate, thesis/dissertation, exam. *Entrance requirements:* For master's, GRE General Test; for doctorate, GRE General Test, GRE Subject Test. Electronic applications accepted. *Expenses:* Contact institution. *Faculty research:* Child development, risk and resilience among vulnerable youth in high-risk environments.

University of St. Thomas, Graduate Studies, School of Education, Program in Organization Learning and Development, St. Paul, MN 55105-1096. Offers MA, Ed D, Certificate. Part-time and evening/weekend programs available. Postbaccalaureate distance learning degree programs offered (minimal on-campus study). *Degree requirements:* For doctorate, comprehensive exam, thesis/dissertation. *Entrance requirements:* For master's, minimum GPA of 2.75, 3 letters of reference; for doctorate, MAT, minimum GPA of 3.5, interview; for Certificate, minimum graduate GPA of 3.25. Additional exam requirements/recommendations for international students: Required—TOEFL (minimum score 550 paper-based; 213 computer-based). *Expenses:* Contact institution. *Faculty research:* Workplace conflict, physician leaders, entrepreneurship education, mentoring.

University of South Africa, College of Human Sciences, Pretoria, South Africa. Offers adult education (M Ed); African languages (MA, PhD); African politics (MA, PhD); Afrikaans (MA, PhD); ancient history (MA, PhD); ancient Near Eastern studies (MA, PhD); anthropology (MA, PhD); applied linguistics (MA); Arabic (MA, PhD); archaeology (MA); art history (MA); Biblical archaeology (MA); Biblical studies (M Th, D Th, PhD); Christian spirituality (M Th, D Th); church history (M Th, D Th); classical studies (MA, PhD); clinical psychology (MA); communication (MA, PhD); comparative education (M Ed, Ed D); consulting psychology (D Admin, D Com, PhD); curriculum studies (M Ed, Ed D); development studies (M Admin, MA, D Admin, PhD); didactics (M Ed, Ed D); education (M Tech); education management (M Ed, Ed D); educational psychology (M Ed); English (MA); environmental education (M Ed); French (MA, PhD); German (MA, PhD); Greek (MA); guidance and counseling (M Ed); health studies (MA, PhD), including health sciences education (MA), health services management (MA), medical and surgical nursing science (critical care general) (MA), midwifery and neonatal nursing science (MA), trauma and emergency care (MA); history (MA, PhD); history of education (Ed D); inclusive education (M Ed, Ed D); information and communications technology policy and regulation (MA); information science (MA, MIS, PhD); international politics (MA, PhD); Islamic studies (MA, PhD); Italian (MA, PhD); Judaica (MA, PhD); linguistics (MA, PhD); mathematical education (M Ed); mathematics education (MA); missiology (M Th, D Th); modern Hebrew (MA, PhD); musicology (MA, MMus, D Mus, PhD); natural science education (M Ed); New Testament (M Th, D Th); Old Testament (D Th); pastoral therapy (M Th, D Th); philosophy (MA); philosophy of education (M Ed, Ed D); politics (MA, PhD); Portuguese (MA, PhD); practical theology (M Th, D Th); psychology (MA, MS, PhD); psychology of education (M Ed, Ed D); public health (MA); religious studies (MA, D Th, PhD); Romance languages (MA); Russian (MA, PhD); Semitic languages (MA, PhD); social behavior studies in HIV/AIDS (MA); social science (mental health) (MA); social science in development studies (MA); social science in psychology (MA); social science in social work (MA); social science in sociology (MA); social work (MSW, DSW, PhD); socio-education (M Ed, Ed D); sociolinguistics (MA); sociology (MA, PhD); Spanish (MA, PhD); systematic theology (M Th, D Th); TESOL (teaching English to speakers of other languages) (MA); theological ethics (M Th, D Th); theory of literature (MA, PhD); urban ministries (D Th); urban ministry (M Th).

The University of Texas at Austin, Graduate School, College of Education, Department of Educational Psychology, Austin, TX 78712-1111. Offers academic educational psychology (M Ed, MA); counseling psychology (PhD); counselor education (M Ed); human development and culture (PhD); learning, cognition and instruction (PhD); quantitative methods (PhD); school psychology (PhD). *Accreditation:* APA (one or more programs are accredited). *Degree requirements:* For master's, thesis optional; for doctorate, thesis/dissertation. *Entrance requirements:* For master's and doctorate, GRE General Test, 3 letters of recommendation. Additional exam requirements/recommendations for international students: Required—TOEFL.

University of Victoria, Faculty of Graduate Studies, Faculty of Education, Department of Educational Psychology and Leadership Studies, Victoria, BC V8W 2Y2, Canada. Offers

Human Development

University of Victoria (continued)
aboriginal communities counseling (M Ed); counseling (M Ed, MA); educational psychology (M Ed, MA, PhD), including counseling psychology (M Ed, MA), leadership studies (PhD), learning and development (MA, PhD), measurement and evaluation, special education (M Ed, MA); leadership studies (M Ed, MA). Part-time programs available. *Degree requirements:* For master's, thesis (for some programs), comprehensive exam (M Ed); for doctorate, comprehensive exam, thesis/dissertation, candidacy exam. *Entrance requirements:* For master's, 2 years of work experience in a relevant field, minimum B average; for doctorate, GRE, 2 years of work experience in a relevant field, minimum B average. Additional exam requirements/recommendations for international students: Required—TOEFL (minimum score 575 paper-based; 233 computer-based), IELTS (minimum score 7). *Faculty research:* Learning and development (child, adolescent and adult), special education and exceptional children.

University of Victoria, Faculty of Graduate Studies, Faculty of Human and Social Development, Studies in Policy and Practice Program, Victoria, BC V8W 2Y2, Canada. Offers MA. Part-time programs available. *Degree requirements:* For master's, thesis. *Entrance requirements:* For master's, resumé. Additional exam requirements/recommendations for international students: Required—TOEFL (minimum score 575 paper-based; 233 computer-based), IELTS (minimum score 7). Electronic applications accepted. *Faculty research:* Women's issues, public policy formation and implementation, health promotion and education, children, youth and families.

University of Washington, Graduate School, College of Education, Program in Educational Psychology, Seattle, WA 98195. Offers educational psychology (PhD); human development and cognition (M Ed); learning sciences (M Ed, PhD); measurement, statistics and research design (M Ed); school psychology (M Ed). *Accreditation:* APA. *Degree requirements:* For master's, thesis optional; for doctorate, thesis/dissertation. *Entrance requirements:* For master's and doctorate, GRE General Test, minimum GPA of 3.0. Additional exam requirements/recommendations for international students: Required—TOEFL.

University of Wisconsin–Madison, Graduate School, School of Human Ecology, Program in Human Development and Family Studies, Madison, WI 53706-1380. Offers MS, PhD. Part-time programs available. Terminal master's awarded for partial completion of doctoral program. *Degree requirements:* For master's, thesis; for doctorate, comprehensive exam, thesis/dissertation. *Entrance requirements:* For master's, GRE General Test, 3 letters of recommendation; for doctorate, GRE General Test, MS or MA, 3 letters of recommendation. Additional exam requirements/recommendations for international students: Required—TOEFL. Electronic applications accepted. *Faculty research:* Human development, adolescence, adulthood, prevention, intervention.

University of Wisconsin–Stevens Point, College of Professional Studies, School of Health Promotion and Human Development, Stevens Point, WI 54481-3897. Offers human and community resources (MS); nutritional sciences (MS). Part-time programs available. *Students:* 2 part-time (both women). *Degree requirements:* For master's, thesis or alternative. *Entrance requirements:* For master's, minimum GPA of 2.75. *Application deadline:* For fall admission, 5/1 priority date for domestic students. Applications are processed on a rolling basis. Application fee: $45. *Expenses:* Tuition, state resident: full-time $7410. Tuition, nonresident: full-time $17,756. Full-time tuition and fees vary according to reciprocity agreements. *Financial support:* Research assistantships, teaching assistantships, career-related internships or fieldwork, Federal Work-Study, and unspecified assistantships available. Support available to part-time students. Financial award application deadline: 5/1; financial award applicants required to submit FAFSA. *Unit head:* Dr. Marty Loy, Head, 715-346-2830, Fax: 715-346-2720. *Application contact:* Dr. Jasia Steinmetz, Information Contact, 715-346-2830, Fax: 715-346-2720, E-mail: jsteinme@uwsp.edu.

University of Wisconsin–Stout, Graduate School, College of Human Development, Program in Family Studies and Human Development, Menomonie, WI 54751. Offers MS. Part-time programs available. *Students:* 2 full-time (both women), 17 part-time (16 women); includes 1 minority (African American), 1 international. Average age 32. In 2008, 7 master's awarded. *Degree requirements:* For master's, thesis. *Entrance requirements:* For master's, minimum GPA of 2.75. Additional exam requirements/recommendations for international students: Required—TOEFL (minimum score 500 paper-based; 173 computer-based; 61 iBT). *Application deadline:* Applications are processed on a rolling basis. Application fee: $45. Electronic applications accepted. *Expenses:* Tuition, state resident: full-time $6227; part-time $345.93 per credit. Tuition, nonresident: full-time $9998; part-time $555.42 per credit. International tuition: $10,512 full-time. Tuition and fees vary according to course load, program and reciprocity agreements. *Financial support:* In 2008–09, 2 research assistantships with partial tuition reimbursements (averaging $4,343 per year) were awarded; teaching assistantships with partial tuition reimbursements, Federal Work-Study, scholarships/grants, tuition waivers (partial), and unspecified assistantships also available. Support available to part-time students. Financial award application deadline: 5/1; financial award applicants required to submit FAFSA. *Faculty research:* Diversity, work and family medical ethics, family policy, dementia and families. *Unit head:* Dr. Dale Hawley, Director, 715-232-1273, Fax: 715-232-2524, E-mail: hawleyd@uwstout.edu. *Application contact:* Anne E. Johnson, Graduate Student Evaluator (Admissions and Assistantship Coordinator), 715-232-1322, Fax: 715-232-2413, E-mail: johnsona@uwstout.edu.

Utah State University, School of Graduate Studies, College of Education and Human Services, Department of Family, Consumer, and Human Development, Logan, UT 84322. Offers family and human development (MFHD); family, consumer, and human development (MS, PhD), including adolescence/youth (MS), adult development/aging (MS), consumer science (MS), infancy/childhood (MS), marriage and family relations (MS), marriage and family therapy (MS). *Accreditation:* AAMFT/COAMFTE (one or more programs are accredited). Part-time and evening/weekend programs available. Postbaccalaureate distance learning degree programs offered (minimal on-campus study). *Degree requirements:* For master's, thesis; for doctorate, comprehensive exam, thesis/dissertation, competencies. *Entrance requirements:* For master's, GRE General Test or MAT, minimum GPA of 3.0, 3 letters of recommendation; for doctorate, GRE, minimum GPA of 3.0, 3 letters of recommendation. Additional exam requirements/recommendations for international students: Required—TOEFL. Electronic applications accepted. *Faculty research:* Marriage and family relations, adolescent problem behavior, family financial management, early literacy, mental health in the elderly, parent child attachment.

Vanderbilt University, Peabody College, Department of Human and Organizational Development, Nashville, TN 37240-1001. Offers community development and action (M Ed); human development counseling (M Ed). *Accreditation:* ACA; NCATE. Part-time programs available. *Faculty:* 28 full-time (14 women), 26 part-time/adjunct (20 women). *Students:* 65 full-time (63 women), 10 part-time (7 women); includes 14 minority (7 African Americans, 1 Asian American or Pacific Islander, 6 Hispanic Americans), 1 international. Average age 27. 125 applicants, 54% accepted, 38 enrolled. In 2008, 22 master's awarded. *Degree requirements:* For master's, comprehensive exam, thesis optional. *Entrance requirements:* For master's, GRE General Test, MAT. Additional exam requirements/recommendations for international students: Required—TOEFL (minimum score 550 paper-based; 213 computer-based). *Application deadline:* For fall admission, 12/31 priority date for domestic and international students; for spring admission, 11/1 priority date for domestic and international students. Applications are processed on a rolling basis. Application fee: $0. Electronic applications accepted. *Financial support:* In 2008–09, 75 students received support, including 21 research assistantships with full and partial tuition reimbursements available, 13 teaching assistantships with full and partial tuition reimbursements available; fellowships with full and partial tuition reimbursements available, Federal Work-Study, institutionally sponsored loans, scholarships/grants, tuition waivers (partial), and unspecified assistantships also available. Support available to part-time students. Financial award application deadline: 2/1; financial award applicants required to submit FAFSA. *Faculty research:* Community psychology, community development and urban policy, counseling and mental health services, organizational development and institutional change; youth physical and behavioral health in schools and communities. *Unit head:* Dr. Joseph Cunningham, Chair, 615-322-6881, Fax: 615-322-1141, E-mail: joe.cunningham@vanderbilt.edu. *Application contact:* Sherrie Lane, Office Assistant, 615-322-8484, Fax: 615-322-1141, E-mail: sherrie.a.lane@vanderbilt.edu.

Virginia Polytechnic Institute and State University, Graduate School, College of Liberal Arts and Human Sciences, Department of Human Development, Blacksburg, VA 24061. Offers adult development and aging (MS, PhD); adult learning and human resource development (MS, PhD); child development (MS, PhD); family studies (MS, PhD); marriage and family therapy (MS, PhD). *Accreditation:* AAMFT/COAMFTE (one or more programs are accredited). *Entrance requirements:* For master's and doctorate, GRE General Test. Additional exam requirements/recommendations for international students: Required—TOEFL (minimum score 600 paper-based; 250 computer-based). Electronic applications accepted. *Faculty research:* Stress management, children's play, dual-career families, social cognition, relationships of elderly.

Washington State University, Graduate School, College of Agricultural, Human, and Natural Resource Sciences, Department of Human Development, Pullman, WA 99164. Offers MA. Part-time programs available. *Degree requirements:* For master's, comprehensive exam (for some programs), thesis (for some programs), oral exam. *Entrance requirements:* For master's, GRE General Test, minimum GPA of 3.0, 3 letters of recommendation. Additional exam requirements/recommendations for international students: Required—TOEFL. Electronic applications accepted. *Faculty research:* Family processes, social development of children, quality child care, community collaborations, parent-child relationships.

Wayne State University, College of Liberal Arts and Sciences, Department of Psychology, Program in Human Development, Detroit, MI 48202. Offers MA. *Entrance requirements:* For master's, GRE General Test. Additional exam requirements/recommendations for international students: Required—TOEFL (minimum score 550 paper-based; 213 computer-based); Recommended—TWE (minimum score 6). Electronic applications accepted. *Faculty research:* Emotional expression, peer influence in adolescence, preschool concept formation and memory, mother-infant interaction.

West Virginia University, Davis College of Agriculture, Forestry and Consumer Sciences, Division of Resource Management and Sustainable Development, Morgantown, WV 26506. Offers agricultural and extension education (MS, PhD), including agricultural and extension education, teaching vocational-agriculture (MS); agricultural and resource economics (MS); human and community development (PhD); natural resource economics (PhD); resource management (PhD); resource management and sustainable development (PhD). Part-time programs available. *Degree requirements:* For master's, thesis; for doctorate, comprehensive exam, thesis/dissertation. *Entrance requirements:* For master's, GRE General Test. Additional exam requirements/recommendations for international students: Required—TOEFL. *Faculty research:* Environmental economics, energy economics, agriculture.

Wheelock College, Graduate Programs, Division of Arts and Sciences, Boston, MA 02215-4176. Offers human development (MS). *Entrance requirements:* Additional exam requirements/recommendations for international students: Required—TOEFL. Electronic applications accepted.

Industrial and Organizational Psychology

Adler Graduate School, Program in Adlerian Studies, Richfield, MN 55423. Offers art therapy specialization (MA); clinical counseling track (MA); coaching and consulting in organizations (Certificate); management consulting and organizational leadership (MA); marriage and family track (MA); non-clinical Adlerian studies track (MA); personal and professional life coaching (Certificate); school counseling (MA). Part-time and evening/weekend programs available. *Degree requirements:* For master's, thesis or alternative, 500-700 hour internship, depending on license choice. *Entrance requirements:* For master's, minimum undergraduate GPA of 3.0, 12 credits of course work in psychology or related field.

Adler School of Professional Psychology, Programs in Psychology, Chicago, IL 60601-7203. Offers art therapy (Certificate); clinical hypnosis (Certificate); clinical psychology (Psy D); counseling psychology (MACP); counseling psychology/art therapy (MACAT); gerontology (MAGP); marriage and family counseling (MAMFC); marriage and family therapy (Certificate); organizational psychology (MAO); substance abuse counseling (MASAC, Certificate); Psy D/Certificate; Psy D/MACAT; Psy D/MACP; Psy D/MAMFC; Psy D/MASAC. *Accreditation:* APA. Part-time and evening/weekend programs available. Postbaccalaureate distance learning degree programs offered (minimal on-campus study). *Faculty:* 36 full-time (17 women), 45 part-time/adjunct (18 women). *Students:* 514 full-time (404 women), 128 part-time (100 women); includes 147 minority (69 African Americans, 2 American Indian/Alaska Native, 30 Asian Americans or Pacific Islanders, 46 Hispanic Americans), 53 international. Average age 27. 855 applicants, 46% accepted, 195 enrolled. In 2008, 110 master's, 136 doctorates awarded. Terminal master's awarded for partial completion of doctoral program. *Degree requirements:* For master's, thesis or alternative, oral exam, practicum; for doctorate, thesis/dissertation, clinical exam, internship, oral exam, practicum, written qualifying exam. *Entrance requirements:* For master's, 12 semester hours in psychology, minimum GPA of 3.0; for doctorate, 18 semester hours in psychology, minimum GPA of 3.25; for Certificate, appropriate master's or doctoral degree. Additional exam requirements/recommendations for international students: Required—TOEFL (minimum score 550 paper-based; 213 computer-based; 79 iBT). *Application deadline:* For fall admission, 2/15 priority date for domestic students, 12/1 priority date for international students. Applications are processed on a rolling basis. Application fee: $50. Electronic applications accepted. *Expenses:* Tuition: Part-time $850 per credit. Tuition and fees vary according to degree level, campus/location and program. *Financial support:* Career-related internships or fieldwork, Federal Work-Study, scholarships/grants, and tuition waivers (full and partial) available. Support available to part-time students. Financial award application deadline: 5/15; financial award applicants required to submit FAFSA. *Unit head:* Dr. Frank Gruba-McAllister, Vice President of Academic Affairs, 312-201-5900, Fax: 312-207-5917. *Application contact:* Craig A Hines, Director of Admissions, 312-201-5900 Ext. 226, Fax: 312-201-5917, E-mail: chines@adler.edu.

See Close-Up on page 1051.

Alliant International University–Fresno, Marshall Goldsmith School of Management, Organizational Psychology Division, Fresno, CA 93727. Offers organizational behavior (MA); organizational development (Psy D); MA/PhD; Psy D/MA. Part-time and evening/weekend programs available. *Degree requirements:* For doctorate, thesis/dissertation. *Entrance requirements:* For doctorate, interview, minimum GPA of 3.0. Additional exam requirements/recommendations for international students: Required—TOEFL (minimum score 600 paper-based; 250 computer-based), TWE (minimum score 5). Electronic applications accepted. *Faculty research:* Leadership, ethics and management; career development, human resources management.

Alliant International University–Los Angeles, Marshall Goldsmith School of Management, Organizational Psychology Division, Alhambra, CA 91803-1360. Offers industrial/organizational psychology (MA, PhD). Part-time programs available. Terminal master's awarded for partial completion of doctoral program. *Degree requirements:* For doctorate, thesis/dissertation. *Entrance requirements:* For master's and doctorate, interview, minimum GPA of 3.0 in both psychology and overall. Additional exam requirements/recommendations for international students: Required—TOEFL (minimum score 600 paper-based; 250 computer-based), TWE (minimum score 5). Electronic applications accepted. *Faculty research:* Organizational transitions, productivity, work force demographics, management technology, comparative and international research.

Alliant International University–Sacramento, Marshall Goldsmith School of Management, Program in Organizational Development, Sacramento, CA 95825. Offers Psy D. *Entrance requirements:* For doctorate, minimum GPA of 3.0, interview, letters of recommendation.

Alliant International University–San Diego, Marshall Goldsmith School of Management, Organizational Psychology Division, San Diego, CA 92131-1799. Offers clinical/industrial organizational psychology (PhD); consulting psychology (PhD); industrial/organizational psychology (MA, MS, PhD); organizational behavior (MA). Part-time and evening/weekend programs available. Terminal master's awarded for partial completion of doctoral program. *Degree requirements:* For doctorate, thesis/dissertation. *Entrance requirements:* For master's and doctorate, interview, minimum GPA of 3.0 in both psychology and overall. Additional exam requirements/recommendations for international students: Required—TOEFL (minimum score 600 paper-based; 250 computer-based), TWE (minimum score 5). Electronic applications accepted. *Faculty research:* Cultural diversity in the workplace, work motivation, personnel, performance management.

Alliant International University–San Francisco, Marshall Goldsmith School of Management, Organizational Psychology Division, San Francisco, CA 94133-1221. Offers organization development (MA); organizational psychology (MA, PhD). Part-time and evening/weekend programs available. Terminal master's awarded for partial completion of doctoral program. *Degree requirements:* For doctorate, thesis/dissertation. *Entrance requirements:* For master's and doctorate, interview, minimum GPA of 3.0. Additional exam requirements/recommendations for international students: Required—TOEFL (minimum score 650 paper-based; 250 computer-based), TWE (minimum score 5). Electronic applications accepted. *Faculty research:* Leadership, ethics and management, career development, organizational behavior, strategic change.

American InterContinental University Online, Program in Business Administration, Hoffman Estates, IL 60192. Offers accounting and finance (MBA); finance (MBA); healthcare management (MBA); human resource management (MBA); international business (MBA); management (MBA); marketing (MBA); operations management (MBA); organizational psychology and development (MBA); project management (MBA). Evening/weekend programs available. Postbaccalaureate distance learning degree programs offered (no on-campus study). *Entrance requirements:* Additional exam requirements/recommendations for international students: Required—TOEFL (minimum score 550 paper-based; 213 computer-based). Electronic applications accepted.

Angelo State University, College of Graduate Studies, College of Liberal and Fine Arts, Department of Psychology and Sociology, San Angelo, TX 76909. Offers psychology (MS), including counseling psychology, general psychology, industrial and organizational psychology. Part-time and evening/weekend programs available. *Faculty:* 8 full-time (2 women). *Students:* 28 full-time (18 women), 9 part-time (8 women); includes 7 minority (1 American Indian/Alaska Native, 6 Hispanic Americans), 1 international. Average age 25. 20 applicants, 70% accepted, 11 enrolled. In 2008, 23 master's awarded. *Degree requirements:* For master's, comprehensive exam, thesis optional. *Entrance requirements:* For master's, GRE General Test. Additional exam requirements/recommendations for international students: Required—TOEFL or IELTS. *Application deadline:* For fall admission, 7/15 priority date for domestic students, 6/10 for international students; for spring admission, 12/1 priority date for domestic students, 11/1 for international students. Applications are processed on a rolling basis. Application fee: $40 ($50 for international students). Electronic applications accepted. *Financial support:* In 2008–09, 44 students received support, including 3 teaching assistantships (averaging $10,251 per year); career-related internships or fieldwork, Federal Work-Study, scholarships/grants, and unspecified assistantships also available. Support available to part-time students. Financial award application deadline: 3/1; financial award applicants required to submit FAFSA. *Faculty research:* Toddlers use of actors' intentions to learn verbs. Total annual research expenditures: $116,915. *Unit head:* Dr. William B. Davidson, Department Head, 325-942-2068 Ext. 248, E-mail: bill.davidson@angelo.edu. *Application contact:* Theresa Fortin, Graduate Admissions Assistant, 325-942-2169, Fax: 325-942-2194, E-mail: theresa.fortin@angelo.edu.

Antioch University Seattle, Graduate Programs, Center for Creative Change, Seattle, WA 98121-1814. Offers environment and community (MA); management (MS); organizational psychology (MA); strategic communications (MA); whole system design (MA). Evening/weekend programs available. Electronic applications accepted. *Expenses:* Contact institution.

Appalachian State University, Cratis D. Williams Graduate School, Department of Psychology, Boone, NC 28608. Offers clinical health psychology (MA); general experimental psychology (MA); industrial and organizational psychology (MA). Part-time programs available. *Faculty:* 31 full-time (11 women). *Students:* 59 full-time (45 women), 15 part-time (12 women); includes 3 minority (2 African Americans, 1 Asian American or Pacific Islander), 4 international. 185 applicants, 30% accepted, 18 enrolled. In 2008, 23 master's, 3 other advanced degrees awarded. *Degree requirements:* For master's and MA/SSP, comprehensive exam, thesis optional, GRE Subject Test exit exam. *Entrance requirements:* For master's and MA/SSP, GRE General Test, 3 letters of recommendation. Additional exam requirements/recommendations for international students: Required—TOEFL (minimum score 550 paper-based; 230 computer-based; 79 iBT), IELTS (minimum score 6.5), TOEFL or IELTS. *Application deadline:* For fall admission, 3/1 for domestic students, 2/1 for international students. Applications are processed on a rolling basis. Application fee: $50. Electronic applications accepted. *Expenses:* Tuition, area resident: Full-time $2600; part-time $700 per course. Tuition, state resident: full-time $2600; part-time $700 per course. Tuition, nonresident: full-time $5000; part-time $3300 per course. Required fees: $2150; $330 per course. Tuition and fees vary according to campus/location. *Financial support:* In 2008–09, 34 research assistantships (averaging $3,500 per year), 25 teaching assistantships (averaging $3,500 per year) were awarded; fellowships, career-related internships or fieldwork, Federal Work-Study, scholarships/grants, and unspecified assistantships also available. Financial award application deadline: 4/1; financial award applicants required to submit FAFSA. *Faculty research:* Eating disorders, school-based consultations, organizational behavior management, brain mechanisms of sound localization, parenting styles. Total annual research expenditures: $83,000. *Unit head:* Dr. James Denniston, Chair, 828-262-2272, Fax: 828-262-2272, E-mail: dennistonjc@appstate.edu. *Application contact:* Dr. Denise Martz, Graduate Coordinator, 828-262-2715, E-mail: martzdm@appstate.edu.

Auburn University, Graduate School, College of Liberal Arts, Department of Psychology, Auburn University, AL 36849. Offers applied behavior analysis in developmental disabilities (MS); clinical psychology (PhD); experimental psychology (PhD); industrial/organizational psychology (PhD). *Accreditation:* APA (one or more programs are accredited). Part-time programs available. *Faculty:* 24 full-time (6 women), 2 part-time/adjunct (both women). *Students:* 37 full-time (25 women), 57 part-time (33 women); includes 13 minority (7 African Americans, 2 Asian Americans or Pacific Islanders, 4 Hispanic Americans). Average age 27. 248 applicants, 13% accepted, 30 enrolled. In 2008, 27 master's, 11 doctorates awarded. *Degree requirements:* For doctorate, thesis/dissertation. *Entrance requirements:* For master's, GRE General Test, GRE Subject Test, minimum GPA of 3.25 in psychology, 3.0 overall; for doctorate, GRE General Test, GRE Subject Test. *Application deadline:* For fall admission, 7/7 for domestic students; for spring admission, 11/24 for domestic students. Applications are processed on a rolling basis. Application fee: $25 ($50 for international students). Electronic applications accepted. *Expenses:* Tuition, area resident: Full-time $5880; part-time $243 per credit hour. Tuition, state resident: full-time $5880; part-time $243 per credit hour. Tuition, nonresident: full-time $17,640; part-time $729 per credit hour. International tuition: $17,846 full-time. Required fees: $620. Tuition and fees vary according to program and reciprocity agreements. *Financial support:* Research assistantships, teaching assistantships, Federal Work-Study available. Support available to part-time students. Financial award application deadline: 3/15. *Faculty research:* Clinical psychology, learning, industrial psychology, organizational psychology. Total annual research expenditures: $200,000. *Unit head:* Dr. Barry Burkhart, Chair, 334-844-4412. *Application contact:* Dr. George Flowers, Dean of the Graduate School, 334-844-2125.

Bernard M. Baruch College of the City University of New York, Weissman School of Arts and Sciences, Program in Industrial Organizational Psychology, New York, NY 10010-5585. Offers MS.

Bernard M. Baruch College of the City University of New York, Zicklin School of Business, Program in Industrial and Organizational Psychology, New York, NY 10010-5585. Offers MBA, MS, PhD, Certificate. Part-time and evening/weekend programs available. *Degree requirements:* For master's, thesis or alternative; for doctorate, comprehensive exam, thesis/dissertation. *Entrance requirements:* For master's, GMAT or GRE General Test, 2 letters of recommendation, resumé, 2 years of work experience; for doctorate, GMAT or GRE General Test. Additional exam requirements/recommendations for international students: Required—TOEFL (minimum score 590 paper-based; 243 computer-based), TWE. *Faculty research:* Job attitudes, power and leadership in organizations, measurement issues in organizational behavior, work motivation, fair employment practices.

Bowling Green State University, Graduate College, College of Arts and Sciences, Department of Psychology, Bowling Green, OH 43403. Offers clinical psychology (MA, PhD); developmental psychology (MA, PhD); experimental psychology (MA, PhD); industrial/organizational psychology (MA, PhD); quantitative psychology (MA, PhD). *Accreditation:* APA (one or more programs are accredited). *Degree requirements:* For doctorate, thesis/dissertation. *Entrance requirements:* For doctorate, GRE General Test, GRE Subject Test. Additional exam requirements/recommendations for international students: Required—TOEFL. Electronic applications accepted. *Faculty research:* Personnel psychology, developmental-mathematical models, behavioral medication, brain process, child/adolescent social cognition.

Brooklyn College of the City University of New York, Division of Graduate Studies, Department of Psychology, Program in Industrial and Organizational Psychology, Brooklyn, NY 11210-2889. Offers MA. *Students:* 5 full-time (all women), 93 part-time (74 women); includes 49 minority (33 African Americans, 1 American Indian/Alaska Native, 8 Asian Americans or Pacific Islanders, 7 Hispanic Americans), 9 international. Average age 32. 96 applicants, 77% accepted, 51 enrolled. In 2008, 30 master's awarded. *Degree requirements:* For master's, comprehensive exam, thesis. *Entrance requirements:* For master's, 2 letters of recommendation. Additional exam requirements/recommendations for international students: Required—TOEFL (minimum score 520 paper-based; 190 computer-based; 69 iBT). *Application deadline:* For fall admission, 3/1 priority date for domestic students. *Expenses:* Tuition, state resident: full-time $7360; part-time $310 per credit hour. Tuition, nonresident: full-time $13,800; part-time $575 per credit hour. *Unit head:* Benzion Chanowitz, Graduate Advisor, 718-951-5601, E-mail: bchanowitz@brooklyn.cuny.edu. *Application contact:* Hernan Sierra, Graduate Admissions Coordinator, 718-951-4536, Fax: 718-951-4506, E-mail: grads@brooklyn.cuny.edu.

California State University, San Bernardino, Graduate Studies, College of Social and Behavioral Sciences, Department of Psychology, Program in Industrial/Organizational Psychology, San Bernardino, CA 92407-2397. Offers organizational psychology (MS). *Students:* 21 full-time (10 women), 4 part-time (1 woman); includes 10 minority (1 African American, 3 Asian Americans or Pacific Islanders, 6 Hispanic Americans), 3 international. Average age 27. 44 applicants, 20% accepted, 6 enrolled. In 2008, 8 master's awarded. *Degree requirements:* For master's, thesis. *Entrance requirements:* For master's, minimum GPA of 3.0 in major. *Application deadline:* For fall admission, 8/31 priority date for domestic students. Application fee: $55. *Expenses:* Tuition, area resident: Full-time $1252; part-time $726 per quarter. Required fees: $334 per quarter. Tuition and fees vary according to degree level and student level. *Unit head:* Dr. Robert Cramer, Head, 909-537-5576, Fax: 909-537-7003, E-mail: rcramer@csusb.edu. *Application contact:* Stacy Brooks, Graduate Secretary, 909-537-5570, Fax: 909-537-7003, E-mail: sbrooks@csusb.edu.

Capella University, Harold Abel School of Psychology, Minneapolis, MN 55402. Offers clinical psychology (MS); counseling psychology (MS); educational psychology (MS, PhD); general psychology (MS, PhD); industrial/organizational psychology (MS, PhD); school psychology (MS, Certificate); sport psychology (MS). Part-time and evening/weekend programs available. Postbaccalaureate distance learning degree programs offered (minimal on-campus study). Terminal master's awarded for partial completion of doctoral program. *Degree requirements:* For master's, thesis optional, project; for doctorate, thesis/dissertation. *Entrance requirements:* For degree, master's degree in school psychology. Additional exam requirements/recommendations for international students: Required—TOEFL (minimum score 550 paper-based; 213 computer-based), TWE (minimum score 4). Electronic applications accepted. *Faculty research:* Correctional mental health delivery, community mental health, attachment and caregiving in adult and family relationships, influence of encouragement on motivation, and moral dilemmas in business.

Carlos Albizu University, Graduate Programs, San Juan, PR 00901. Offers clinical psychology (MS, PhD, Psy D); general psychology (PhD); industrial/organizational psychology (MS, PhD); speech and language pathology (MS). *Accreditation:* APA (one or more programs are accredited). Part-time and evening/weekend programs available. *Faculty:* 22 full-time (11 women), 52 part-time/adjunct (38 women). *Students:* 566 full-time (470 women), 149 part-time (122 women); all minorities (all Hispanic Americans). Average age 28. 238 applicants, 79% accepted, 170 enrolled. In 2008, 100 master's, 84 doctorates awarded. Terminal master's awarded for partial completion of doctoral program. *Degree requirements:* For master's, one foreign language, comprehensive exam, thesis; for doctorate, one foreign language, comprehensive exam, thesis/dissertation, written qualifying exams. *Entrance requirements:* For master's, GRE General Test or EXADEP, interview; minimum GPA of 3.0 (industrial/organizational psychology), 3.25 (speech and language pathology); for doctorate, GRE General Test or EXADEP, interview; minimum GPA of 3.0 (industrial/organizational psychology), 3.25 (PhD and Psy D in clinical psychology). *Application deadline:* For fall admission, 2/15 for domestic students, 7/19 for international students; for winter admission, 11/15 for international students; for spring admission, 11/15 for domestic students, 4/21 for international students. Application fee: $75. *Expenses:* Tuition: Full-time $6912; part-time $288 per credit. Required fees: $512 per semester. Tuition and fees vary according to degree level. *Financial support:* In 2008–09, 564 students received support, including 272 fellowships (averaging $1,786 per year); career-related internships or fieldwork, Federal Work-Study, institutionally sponsored loans, scholarships/grants, traineeships, and tuition waivers (partial) also available. Support available to part-time students. Financial award application deadline: 4/21; financial award applicants required to submit FAFSA. *Faculty research:* Psychotherapeutic techniques for Hispanics, psychology of the aged, school dropouts, stress, violence. *Unit head:* Dr. Jose J Cabiya, Chancellor, 787-725-6500 Ext. 1435, Fax: 787-721-7187, E-mail: jcabiya@sju.albizu.edu. *Application contact:* Carlos Rodriguez, Director of Admission's Office, 787-725-6500 Ext. 1521, Fax: 787-721-7187, E-mail: jveray@albizu.edu.

Carlos Albizu University, Miami Campus, Graduate Programs, Miami, FL 33172-2209. Offers clinical psychology (Psy D); entrepreneurship (MBA); exceptional student education (MS); industrial/organizational psychology (MS); marriage and family therapy (MS); mental health counseling (MS); nonprofit management (MBA); organizational management (MBA); psychology (MS); school counseling (MS); teaching English as a second language (MS). *Accreditation:* APA. Part-time and evening/weekend programs available. *Faculty:* 19 full-time

Industrial and Organizational Psychology

Carlos Albizu University, Miami Campus *(continued)*
(12 women), 70 part-time/adjunct (35 women). *Students:* 498 full-time (409 women), 199 part-time (153 women); includes 515 minority (56 African Americans, 1 American Indian/Alaska Native, 7 Asian Americans or Pacific Islanders, 451 Hispanic Americans). Average age 33. 179 applicants, 67% accepted, 113 enrolled. In 2008, 185 master's, 21 doctorates awarded. Terminal master's awarded for partial completion of doctoral program. *Degree requirements:* For master's, one foreign language, comprehensive exam, integrative project (MBA), research project (MSESE and MSTESOL); for doctorate, one foreign language, comprehensive exam, internship, doctoral project. *Entrance requirements:* For master's, 3 letters of recommendation, interview, minimum GPA of 3.0, resumé, statement of purpose, official transcripts; for doctorate, 3 letters of recommendation, minimum GPA of 3.0, resumé, interview. *Application deadline:* For fall admission, 8/1 priority date for domestic students; for spring admission, 11/30 priority date for domestic students. Applications are processed on a rolling basis. Application fee: $50. Electronic applications accepted. *Expenses:* Tuition: Full-time $9090; part-time $505 per credit. Required fees: $298 per term. Tuition and fees vary according to course load, degree level and program. *Financial support:* In 2008–09, 111 students received support. Federal Work-Study, scholarships/grants, and tuition discounts available. Financial award application deadline: 6/1; financial award applicants required to submit FAFSA. *Faculty research:* Psychotherapy, forensic psychology, neuropsychology, marketing strategy, entrepreneurship, special education. *Unit head:* Dr. Carmen S. Roca, PhD, Chancellor, 305-593-1223 Ext. 120, Fax: 305-629-8052, E-mail: croca@albizu.edu. *Application contact:* Barbara De la Cruz, Admission Officer, 305-593-1223 Ext. 218, Fax: 305-593-1854, E-mail: bdelacruz@albizu.edu.

Central Michigan University, College of Graduate Studies, College of Humanities and Social and Behavioral Sciences, Department of Psychology, Program in Industrial and Organizational Psychology, Mount Pleasant, MI 48859. Offers MA, PhD. *Faculty:* 10 full-time (1 woman). *Students:* 24 full-time (11 women), 18 part-time (10 women); includes 2 American Indian/Alaska Native, 6 international. Average age 26. *Degree requirements:* For master's, thesis; for doctorate, comprehensive exam, thesis/dissertation. *Entrance requirements:* For master's and doctorate, GRE. *Application deadline:* For fall admission, 1/1 for domestic and international students. Application fee: $35 ($45 for international students). Electronic applications accepted. *Expenses:* Tuition, state resident: full-time $3717; part-time $413 per credit. Tuition, nonresident: full-time $6894; part-time $766 per credit. *Financial support:* Fellowships with tuition reimbursements, research assistantships with tuition reimbursements, career-related internships or fieldwork, Federal Work-Study, unspecified assistantships, and out-of-state merit awards available. *Faculty research:* Job stress, retirement, leadership, and careers; personality in the workplace, personnel selection, and structural equation modeling in I/O psychology; personnel psychology, evolutionary psychology, and influences on HRM utilization; occupational health psychology and job stress; work attitudes, psychological ownership in work, and performance appraisal. *Unit head:* Dr. Hajime Otani, Chairperson, 989-774-6461, Fax: 989-774-2553, E-mail: otani1h@cmich.edu. *Application contact:* Judith L. Prince, Director of Graduate Student Services, 989-774-1059, Fax: 989-774-1857, E-mail: judith.l.prince@cmich.edu.

Chatham University, Program in Counseling Psychology, Pittsburgh, PA 15232-2826. Offers child, adolescent and family (MSCP); counseling psychology (Psy D); health and holistic (MSCP); infant mental health (MSCP); organization and supervision (MSCP); sport and exercise (MSCP). Part-time and evening/weekend programs available. *Students:* 121 full-time (104 women), 72 part-time (63 women). Average age 30. 117 applicants, 79% accepted, 60 enrolled. In 2008, 63 master's awarded. *Degree requirements:* For master's, thesis optional, supervised internship, advanced research project (optional); for doctorate, thesis/dissertation, internship. *Entrance requirements:* For master's, minimum GPA of 3.0; 2 letters of recommendation; resumé; prerequisite coursework in statistics, biology, and psychology; for doctorate, GRE. Additional exam requirements/recommendations for international students: Required—TOEFL (minimum score 600 paper-based; 250 computer-based; 100 iBT), IELTS (minimum score 6.5), TWE. *Application deadline:* For fall admission, 5/1 priority date for domestic and international students; for spring admission, 10/15 for domestic students, 10/15 priority date for international students. Applications are processed on a rolling basis. Application fee: $45. Electronic applications accepted. *Expenses:* Tuition: Part-time $686 per credit. Tuition and fees vary according to program. *Financial support:* Career-related internships or fieldwork available. Financial award applicants required to submit FAFSA. *Faculty research:* Trauma and recovery, hypnosis, psychospiritual dimensions of healing, psychotherapy of schizophrenia. *Unit head:* Dr. Mary Beth Mannarino, Director, 412-365-1196, Fax: 412-365-1505, E-mail: mmannarino@chatham.edu. *Application contact:* Dory Perry, Associate Director of Graduate Admissions, 412-365-2758, Fax: 412-365-1609, E-mail: gradadmissions@chatham.edu.

The Chicago School of Professional Psychology, Graduate School, Program in Industrial and Organizational Psychology, Chicago, IL 60610. Offers business psychology (Psy D); industrial and organizational psychology (MA). Part-time and evening/weekend programs available. *Degree requirements:* For master's, internship; for doctorate, thesis/dissertation, internship. *Entrance requirements:* For master's, 1 course in psychology and statistics and research methods; for doctorate, GRE, writing test, 12 hours of psychology credit including a course in statistics and research methods. Additional exam requirements/recommendations for international students: Required—TOEFL (minimum score 550 paper-based; 213 computer-based; 79 iBT). Electronic applications accepted.

Claremont Graduate University, Graduate Programs, School of Behavioral and Organizational Sciences, Department of Psychology, Claremont, CA 91711-6160. Offers advanced study in evaluation (Certificate); cognitive psychology (MA, PhD); developmental psychology (MA, PhD); evaluation and applied research methods (MA, PhD); health behavior research and evaluation (MA, PhD); human resource development and evaluation (MA); industrial/organizational psychology (MA, PhD); organizational behavior (MA, PhD); organizational psychology (MA, PhD); social psychology (MA, PhD); MBA/PhD. Part-time programs available. *Faculty:* 17 full-time (7 women), 1 part-time/adjunct (0 women). *Students:* 218 full-time (158 women), 24 part-time (18 women); includes 51 minority (15 African Americans, 1 American Indian/Alaska Native, 22 Asian Americans or Pacific Islanders, 13 Hispanic Americans), 11 international. Average age 30. In 2008, 38 master's, 12 doctorates, 2 other advanced degrees awarded. Terminal master's awarded for partial completion of doctoral program. *Entrance requirements:* For master's and doctorate, GRE General Test. Additional exam requirements/recommendations for international students: Required—TOEFL (minimum score 550 paper-based; 213 computer-based; 80 iBT). *Application deadline:* For fall admission, 1/15 priority date for domestic students. Applications are processed on a rolling basis. Application fee: $60. Electronic applications accepted. *Expenses:* Tuition: Full-time $33,698; part-time $1465 per unit. Required fees: $310; $155 per semester. Tuition and fees vary according to program. *Financial support:* Fellowships, research assistantships, teaching assistantships, Federal Work-Study, institutionally sponsored loans, scholarships/grants, and tuition waivers (full and partial) available. Support available to part-time students. Financial award application deadline: 2/15; financial award applicants required to submit FAFSA. *Faculty research:* Social intervention, diversity in organizations, eyewitness memory, aging and cognition, drug policy. *Unit head:* Stewart Donaldson, Dean, 909-607-9001, Fax: 909-621-8905, E-mail: stewart.donaldson@cgu.edu. *Application contact:* Paul Thomas, Director, External Affairs, 909-607-9016, Fax: 909-621-8905, E-mail: paul.thomas@cgu.edu.

Clemson University, Graduate School, College of Business and Behavioral Science, Department of Psychology, Program in Industrial/Organizational Psychology, Clemson, SC 29634. Offers PhD. *Students:* 21 full-time (15 women), 5 part-time (2 women); includes 2 minority (1 African American, 1 Hispanic American), 1 international. Average age 28. 103 applicants, 10% accepted, 8 enrolled. In 2008, 5 doctorates awarded. *Degree requirements:* For doctorate, thesis/dissertation. *Entrance requirements:* For doctorate, GRE General Test. Additional exam requirements/recommendations for international students: Required—TOEFL. *Application deadline:* For fall admission, 3/15 for domestic students. Application fee: $55. Full-time tuition and fees vary according to program. *Financial support:* Research assistantships available. Financial award application deadline: 3/15; financial award applicants required

to submit FAFSA. *Unit head:* Dr. Chris Pagano, Coordinator, 864-656-4984, Fax: 864-656-0358, E-mail: cpagano@clemson.edu. *Application contact:* Dr. Chris Pagano, Coordinator, 864-656-4984, Fax: 864-656-0358, E-mail: cpagano@clemson.edu.

Cleveland State University, College of Graduate Studies, College of Science, Department of Psychology, Cleveland, OH 44115. Offers adult development and aging (PhD); clinical psychology (MA); consumer/industrial research (MA); diversity management (MA); experimental research psychology (MA); school psychology (Psy S). *Faculty:* 20 full-time (7 women), 16 part-time/adjunct (8 women). *Students:* 66 full-time (44 women), 62 part-time (46 women); includes 25 minority (19 African Americans, 1 American Indian/Alaska Native, 2 Asian Americans or Pacific Islanders, 3 Hispanic Americans), 3 international. Average age 30. 180 applicants, 40% accepted, 55 enrolled. In 2008, 39 master's, 4 other advanced degrees awarded. *Degree requirements:* For master's, comprehensive exam (for some programs), thesis (for some programs); for doctorate, comprehensive exam, thesis/dissertation; for Psy S, internship. *Entrance requirements:* For master's and doctorate, GRE General Test. Additional exam requirements/recommendations for international students: Required—TOEFL (minimum score 525 paper-based; 197 computer-based). *Application deadline:* For fall admission, 2/1 priority date for domestic and international students. Applications are processed on a rolling basis. Application fee: $30. Electronic applications accepted. *Financial support:* In 2008–09, 45 students received support. Career-related internships or fieldwork, Federal Work-Study, tuition waivers (partial), and unspecified assistantships available. Financial award applicants required to submit FAFSA. *Faculty research:* Cognitive and social psychology, consumer psychology, clinical psychology, school psychology, aging. Total annual research expenditures: $112,607. *Unit head:* Dr. Albert F Smith, Interim Chair, 216-687-3723, Fax: 216-687-9294, E-mail: a.f.smith@csuohio.edu. *Application contact:* Karen R Colston, Administrative Coordinator, 216-687-2552, Fax: 216-687-9294, E-mail: k.colston@csuohio.edu.

DePaul University, College of Liberal Arts and Sciences, Department of Psychology, Chicago, IL 60604-2287. Offers clinical psychology (MA, PhD), including child clinical psychology, community clinical psychology; experimental psychology (MA, PhD); general psychology (MS); industrial/organizational psychology (MA, PhD); MA/PhD. *Accreditation:* APA (one or more programs are accredited). *Faculty:* 31 full-time (19 women), 6 part-time/adjunct (4 women). *Students:* 33 full-time (17 women), 23 part-time (20 women); includes 9 minority (4 African Americans, 1 American Indian/Alaska Native, 1 Asian American or Pacific Islander, 3 Hispanic Americans), 2 international. Average age 28. 332 applicants, 14% accepted, 23 enrolled. In 2008, 14 master's, 17 doctorates awarded. *Degree requirements:* For master's, thesis, oral exam; for doctorate, comprehensive exam, thesis/dissertation, oral and written exams. *Entrance requirements:* For master's and doctorate, GRE General Test, GRE Subject Test, 32 quarter hours of course work in psychology, 3 letters of recommendation. Additional exam requirements/recommendations for international students: Required—TOEFL. Application fee: $40. Electronic applications accepted. *Financial support:* In 2008–09, 48 students received support, including 35 research assistantships with full tuition reimbursements available (averaging $11,800 per year), 13 teaching assistantships with full tuition reimbursements available (averaging $11,800 per year); career-related internships or fieldwork, scholarships/grants, traineeships, tuition waivers (full and partial), and unspecified assistantships also available. Financial award application deadline: 1/10. *Faculty research:* Adolescent stress and depression, minority adolescents sexuality, public policy, community influences in child adjustment. *Unit head:* Dr. Christopher B Keys, Chairman, 773-325-7887, Fax: 773-325-7888. *Application contact:* Alison Pereida Knapp, Graduate Admissions Assistant, 773-325-7887, Fax: 773-325-7888.

Eastern Kentucky University, The Graduate School, College of Arts and Sciences, Department of Psychology, Richmond, KY 40475-3102. Offers clinical psychology (MS); industrial/organizational psychology (MS); school psychology (Psy S). Part-time programs available. *Entrance requirements:* For master's and Psy S, GRE General Test, minimum GPA of 2.5. *Faculty research:* Autism, social psychology, parenting, assessment of depression/anxiety, reading.

Elmhurst College, Graduate Programs, Program in Industrial/Organizational Psychology, Elmhurst, IL 60126-3296. Offers MA. Part-time and evening/weekend programs available. *Faculty:* 1 full-time (0 women), 3 part-time/adjunct (1 woman). *Students:* 28 part-time (20 women); includes 2 minority (1 African American, 1 Hispanic American). Average age 23. 50 applicants, 46% accepted, 17 enrolled. In 2008, 6 master's awarded. *Degree requirements:* For master's, thesis optional. *Entrance requirements:* For master's, GRE General Test, 3 recommendations. Additional exam requirements/recommendations for international students: Required—TOEFL (minimum score 550 paper-based; 213 computer-based). *Application deadline:* Applications are processed on a rolling basis. Application fee: $25. Electronic applications accepted. *Expenses:* Tuition: Part-time $675 per semester hour. Tuition and fees vary according to program. *Financial support:* In 2008–09, 10 students received support. Federal Work-Study and scholarships/grants available. Support available to part-time students. Financial award application deadline: 6/1; financial award applicants required to submit FAFSA. *Unit head:* Dr. John E. Bohnert, Dean of Graduate Studies, 630-617-3069, Fax: 630-617-5501, E-mail: gradadm@elmhurst.edu. *Application contact:* Elizabeth D. Kuebler, Director of Adult and Graduate Admission, 630-617-3069, Fax: 630-617-5501, E-mail: betsyk@elmhurst.edu.

Emporia State University, School of Graduate Studies, The Teachers College, Department of Psychology, Art Therapy, Rehabilitation and Mental Health Counseling, Program in Psychology, Emporia, KS 66801-5087. Offers general psychology (MS); industrial/organizational psychology (MS). Part-time programs available. *Students:* 15 full-time (10 women), 11 part-time (7 women); includes 3 minority (2 African Americans, 1 Hispanic American), 4 international. 9 applicants, 44% accepted, 4 enrolled. In 2008, 7 master's awarded. *Degree requirements:* For master's, comprehensive exam or thesis, internship. *Entrance requirements:* For master's, GRE General Test or MAT, graduate essay exam, appropriate bachelor's degree, letters of recommendation. Additional exam requirements/recommendations for international students: Required—TOEFL. *Application deadline:* For fall admission, 6/1 priority date for domestic students; for spring admission, 10/1 for domestic students. Applications are processed on a rolling basis. Application fee: $30 ($75 for international students). Electronic applications accepted. *Expenses:* Tuition, area resident: Full-time $3976; part-time $166 per credit hour. Tuition, state resident: full-time $3976; part-time $166 per credit hour. Tuition, nonresident: full-time $12,028; part-time $501 per credit hour. Required fees: $51 per credit hour. Tuition and fees vary according to campus/location. *Financial support:* Career-related internships or fieldwork, Federal Work-Study, institutionally sponsored loans, health care benefits, and unspecified assistantships available. Financial award application deadline: 3/15; financial award applicants required to submit FAFSA. *Faculty research:* Driving under the influence (DUI) personality, lifestyles and imposter phenomenon. *Unit head:* Dr. Kenneth A. Weaver, Chair, 620-341-5317, E-mail: kweaver@emporia.edu. *Application contact:* Mary Sewell, Admissions Coordinator, 800-950-GRAD, Fax: 620-341-5909, E-mail: msewell@emporia.edu.

Fairfield University, Graduate School of Education and Allied Professions, Department of Psychological and Educational Consultation, Fairfield, CT 06824-5195. Offers applied psychology (MA), including foundations of advanced psychology, human services, industrial/organizational/personnel; media/educational technology (MA); school media specialist (MA); school psychology (MA, CAS); special education (MA, CAS). Part-time and evening/weekend programs available. *Faculty:* 6 full-time (2 women), 7 part-time/adjunct (4 women). *Students:* 49 full-time (42 women), 111 part-time (97 women); includes 19 minority (2 African Americans, 1 American Indian/Alaska Native, 2 Asian Americans or Pacific Islanders, 14 Hispanic Americans), 2 international. 96 applicants, 58% accepted, 30 enrolled. In 2008, 44 master's, 14 other advanced degrees awarded. *Degree requirements:* For master's, comprehensive exam, thesis optional, educational technology course (for some programs). *Entrance requirements:* For master's, PRAXIS I (PPST), minimum QPA of 3.0, 2 recommendations, resumé, essay. Additional exam requirements/recommendations for international students: Required—TOEFL (minimum score 550 paper-based; 213 computer-based; 80 iBT). *Application fee:* $60. Electronic applications accepted. *Expenses:* Tuition: Full-time $9450; part-time $525 per credit hour. Required fees: $25 per semester. Tuition and fees vary according to course load and program.

Financial support: Unspecified assistantships and Federal Grant (Project SETTEL) funds tuition for future special education, bilingual, and/or TESOL educators available. Financial award applicants required to submit FAFSA. *Faculty research:* Child neuropsychology, disabilities, effect of pre-treatment orientation on treatment, autism, technology in business and classroom, collaboration with schools, communities and industry. *Unit head:* Dr. Daniel Geller, Chair, 203-254-4000 Ext. 2324, Fax: 203-254-4047, E-mail: dgeller@fairfield.edu. *Application contact:* Marianne Gumpper, Director of Graduate and Continuing Studies Admissions, 203-254-4184, Fax: 203-254-4073, E-mail: gradadmis@fairfield.edu.

Fairleigh Dickinson University, College at Florham, Maxwell Becton College of Arts and Sciences, Department of Psychology, Program in Industrial/Organizational Psychology, Madison, NJ 07940-1099. Offers MA, MA/MBA. *Students:* 11 full-time (8 women), 4 part-time (3 women), 2 international. Average age 25. 32 applicants, 59% accepted, 6 enrolled. In 2008, 10 master's awarded. *Entrance requirements:* For master's, GRE General Test. *Application deadline:* Applications are processed on a rolling basis. Application fee: $40. *Application contact:* Susan Brooman, University Director, Graduate Admissions, 973-443-8905, Fax: 973-443-8088, E-mail: grad@fdu.edu.

Florida Institute of Technology, Graduate Programs, College of Psychology and Liberal Arts, School of Psychology, Melbourne, FL 32901-6975. Offers applied behavior analysis (MS); clinical psychology (Psy D); industrial/organizational psychology (MS, PhD). *Accreditation:* APA (one or more programs are accredited). Part-time programs available. *Degree requirements:* For master's, comprehensive exam (for some programs), thesis (for some programs); for doctorate, comprehensive exam, thesis/dissertation (for some programs), internship. *Entrance requirements:* For master's, GRE General Test, 3 letters of recommendation, minimum GPA of 3.0, resumé, statement of objectives; for doctorate, GRE General Test, GRE Subject Test, 3 letters of recommendation, minimum GPA of 3.2, resumé, statement of objectives. Additional exam requirements/recommendations for international students: Required—TOEFL (minimum score 550 paper-based; 213 computer-based). Electronic applications accepted. *Expenses:* Tuition: Part-time $980 per credit hour. *Faculty research:* Addictions, neuropsychology, child abuse, assessment, psychological trauma.

See Close-Up on page 1113.

George Mason University, College of Humanities and Social Sciences, Department of Psychology, Fairfax, VA 22030. Offers applied developmental psychology (MA, PhD); biopsychology (MA, PhD); clinical psychology (MA, PhD); human factors engineering psychology (MA, PhD); industrial/organizational psychology (MA, PhD); psychology (MA, PhD); school psychology (MA). *Accreditation:* APA. Terminal master's awarded for partial completion of doctoral program. *Degree requirements:* For master's, thesis (for applied developmental psychology and biopsychology); for doctorate, comprehensive exam, thesis/dissertation or alternative. *Entrance requirements:* For master's, GRE General Test, minimum GPA of 3.0 in last 60 hours of course work, undergraduate course work in psychology; for doctorate, GRE General Test, minimum undergraduate GPA of 3.0, 3.3 in major. Additional exam requirements/recommendations for international students: Required—TOEFL (minimum score 575 paper-based; 230 computer-based; 88 iBT), IELTS (minimum score 6). Electronic applications accepted.

The George Washington University, Columbian College of Arts and Sciences, Department of Organizational Sciences and Communication, Washington, DC 20052. Offers human resources management (MA); industrial/organizational psychology (PhD); organizational management (MA). Part-time and evening/weekend programs available. *Faculty:* 9 full-time (5 women), 10 part-time/adjunct (7 women). *Students:* 19 full-time (13 women), 41 part-time (35 women); includes 14 minority (7 African Americans, 1 American Indian/Alaska Native, 3 Asian Americans or Pacific Islanders, 3 Hispanic Americans), 3 international. Average age 29. 52 applicants, 73% accepted, 23 enrolled. In 2008, 63 master's awarded. *Degree requirements:* For master's, comprehensive exam. *Entrance requirements:* For master's, GRE General Test, minimum GPA of 3.0. Additional exam requirements/recommendations for international students: Required—TOEFL (minimum score 500 paper-based; 213 computer-based; 80 iBT). *Application deadline:* For fall admission, 1/15 priority date for domestic and international students; for spring admission, 10/1 priority date for domestic students, 9/1 priority date for international students. Applications are processed on a rolling basis. Application fee: $60. Electronic applications accepted. *Financial support:* Federal Work-Study and institutionally sponsored loans available. *Unit head:* Dr. David Costanza, Acting Director, 202-994-1875, Fax: 202-994-1881, E-mail: dconstanz@gwu.edu. *Application contact:* Information Contact, 202-994-1880, Fax: 202-994-1881.

Georgia Institute of Technology, Graduate Studies and Research, College of Sciences, School of Psychology, Atlanta, GA 30332-0001. Offers human computer interaction (MSHCI); psychology (MS, MS Psy, PhD), including engineering psychology (PhD), experimental psychology (PhD), industrial/organizational psychology (PhD). Terminal master's awarded for partial completion of doctoral program. *Degree requirements:* For master's, thesis; for doctorate, thesis/dissertation. *Entrance requirements:* For master's and doctorate, GRE General Test, GRE Subject Test, minimum GPA of 3.0. Additional exam requirements/recommendations for international students: Required—TOEFL. Electronic applications accepted. *Faculty research:* Experimental, industrial-organizational, and engineering psychology; cognitive aging and processes; leadership; human factors.

Goddard College, Graduate Programs, Master of Arts in Psychology and Counseling Program, Plainfield, VT 05667-9432. Offers organizational development (MA); psychology and counseling (MA); sexual orientation (MA). Part-time programs available. Postbaccalaureate distance learning degree programs offered (minimal on-campus study). *Faculty:* 5 part-time/adjunct (4 women). *Students:* 58 full-time, 1 part-time. Average age 41. 26 applicants, 65% accepted, 15 enrolled. *Degree requirements:* For master's, thesis. *Entrance requirements:* For master's, recent undergraduate degree in psychology or closely related field (preparatory semester at Goddard can substitute), transcripts, three letters of recommendation, interview. *Application deadline:* Applications are processed on a rolling basis. Application fee: $40. Electronic applications accepted. *Expenses:* Tuition: Full-time $14,446. Full-time tuition and fees vary according to campus/location and program. Part-time tuition and fees vary according to course load and program. *Financial support:* In 2008–09, 45 students received support. Applicants required to submit FAFSA. *Unit head:* Dr. Steve James, Director, 802-454-8311, Fax: 802-454-7835, E-mail: steven.james@goddard.edu. *Application contact:* David DeLucca, Senior Admissions Counselor, 800-906-8312 Ext. 248, Fax: 802-454-1029, E-mail: david.delucca@goddard.edu.

Graduate School and University Center of the City University of New York, Graduate Studies, Program in Psychology, New York, NY 10016-4039. Offers basic applied neurocognition (PhD); biopsychology (PhD); clinical psychology (PhD); developmental psychology (PhD); environmental psychology (PhD); experimental psychology (PhD); industrial psychology (PhD); learning processes (PhD); neuropsychology (PhD); psychology (PhD); social personality (PhD). *Degree requirements:* For doctorate, one foreign language, thesis/dissertation. *Entrance requirements:* For doctorate, GRE General Test. Additional exam requirements/recommendations for international students: Required—TOEFL. Electronic applications accepted.

Hofstra University, College of Liberal Arts and Sciences, Department of Psychology, Program in Applied Organizational Psychology, Hempstead, NY 11549. Offers PhD. *Students:* 11 full-time (4 women), 22 part-time (12 women); includes 7 minority (2 African Americans, 5 Asian Americans or Pacific Islanders). Average age 34. 19 applicants, 58% accepted, 7 enrolled. In 2008, 2 doctorates awarded. *Degree requirements:* For doctorate, comprehensive exam, thesis/dissertation. *Entrance requirements:* For doctorate, GRE, 2 letters of recommendation, essay, interview. Additional exam requirements/recommendations for international students: Required—TOEFL (minimum score 550 paper-based; 213 computer-based; 80 iBT). *Application deadline:* For fall admission, 4/1 for domestic and international students. Application fee: $60. Electronic applications accepted. *Expenses:* Tuition: Full-time $15,300; part-time $850 per credit. Required fees: $970; $165 per term. Tuition and fees vary according to program. *Financial support:* In 2008–09, 22 students received support, including 22 fellowships with full and partial tuition reimbursements available (averaging $6,769 per year); research assistantships with full and partial tuition reimbursements available, career-related internships or fieldwork, Federal Work-Study, institutionally sponsored loans, scholarships/grants, tuition waivers (full and partial), and unspecified assistantships also available. Support available to part-time students. Financial award applicants required to submit FAFSA. *Faculty research:* Customer satisfaction, personal selection, faking and personality, performance management, organizational health. Total annual research expenditures: $130,000. *Unit head:* Dr. William Metlay, Program Director, 516-463-6344, Fax: 516-463-4664, E-mail: psywzm@hofstra.edu. *Application contact:* Carol Drummer, Dean of Graduate Admissions, 516-463-4876, Fax: 516-463-4664, E-mail: gradstudent@hofstra.edu.

Hofstra University, College of Liberal Arts and Sciences, Department of Psychology, Program in Industrial/Organizational Psychology, Hempstead, NY 11549. Offers MA. Part-time and evening/weekend programs available. *Students:* 43 full-time (24 women), 9 part-time (5 women); includes 11 minority (7 African Americans, 3 Asian Americans or Pacific Islanders, 1 Hispanic American). Average age 24. 72 applicants, 72% accepted, 24 enrolled. In 2008, 27 master's awarded. *Degree requirements:* For master's, comprehensive exam, thesis optional, internship. *Entrance requirements:* For master's, GRE General Test, minimum GPA of 3.0, essay, interview. Additional exam requirements/recommendations for international students: Required—TOEFL (minimum score 550 paper-based; 213 computer-based; 80 iBT). *Application deadline:* Applications are processed on a rolling basis. Application fee: $60. Electronic applications accepted. *Expenses:* Tuition: Full-time $15,300; part-time $850 per credit. Required fees: $970; $165 per term. Tuition and fees vary according to program. *Financial support:* In 2008–09, 13 students received support, including 8 fellowships with full and partial tuition reimbursements available (averaging $7,611 per year), 4 research assistantships with full and partial tuition reimbursements available (averaging $14,220 per year); career-related internships or fieldwork, Federal Work-Study, institutionally sponsored loans, scholarships/grants, tuition waivers (full and partial), and unspecified assistantships also available. Support available to part-time students. Financial award applicants required to submit FAFSA. *Faculty research:* Selection interviews, personality testing, occupational health, multi-source feedback, customer service. *Unit head:* Dr. Comila Shahani-Denning, Director, 516-463-6343, Fax: 516-463-6354, E-mail: psyc2s@hofstra.edu. *Application contact:* Carol Drummer, Dean of Graduate Admissions, 516-463-4876, Fax: 516-463-4664, E-mail: gradstudent@hofstra.edu.

Illinois Institute of Technology, Graduate College, Institute of Psychology, Chicago, IL 60616-3793. Offers clinical psychology (PhD); industrial/organizational psychology (PhD); personnel/human resource development (MS); psychology (MS); rehabilitation counseling (MS); rehabilitation counselor education (PhD). *Accreditation:* APA (one or more programs are accredited); CORE. Evening/weekend programs available. *Faculty:* 19 full-time (8 women), 5 part-time/adjunct (all women). *Students:* 98 full-time (78 women), 94 part-time (69 women); includes 36 minority (10 African Americans, 16 Asian Americans or Pacific Islanders, 10 Hispanic Americans), 24 international. Average age 29. 301 applicants, 40% accepted, 54 enrolled. In 2008, 37 master's, 13 doctorates awarded. Terminal master's awarded for partial completion of doctoral program. *Degree requirements:* For master's, comprehensive exam, thesis (for some programs); for doctorate, comprehensive exam, thesis/dissertation, qualifying exams. *Entrance requirements:* For master's, GRE General Test, minimum GPA of 3.0; for doctorate, GRE General Test, minimum GPA of 3.2. Additional exam requirements/recommendations for international students: Required—TOEFL (minimum score 550 paper-based; 213 computer-based; 80 iBT). *Application deadline:* For fall admission, 1/15 for domestic and international students. Application fee: $40. Electronic applications accepted. *Financial support:* In 2008–09, 39 fellowships with partial tuition reimbursements (averaging $2,798 per year), 1 research assistantship with partial tuition reimbursement, 24 teaching assistantships with partial tuition reimbursements (averaging $4,405 per year) were awarded; career-related internships or fieldwork, Federal Work-Study, institutionally sponsored loans, scholarships/grants, traineeships, health care benefits, tuition waivers (partial), and unspecified assistantships also available. Support available to part-time students. Financial award applicants required to submit FAFSA. *Faculty research:* Stigma and mental illness, depression, couples communication, leadership, psychometric theory. Total annual research expenditures: $426,090. *Unit head:* Dr. M. Ellen Mitchell, Dean, 312-567-3362, Fax: 312-567-3493, E-mail: mitchelle@iit.edu. *Application contact:* Application Contact, 312-567-3500, Fax: 312-567-3493, E-mail: psychology@iit.edu.

Illinois State University, Graduate School, College of Arts and Sciences, Department of Psychology, Normal, IL 61790-2200. Offers psychology (MA, MS), including clinical psychology, counseling psychology, developmental psychology, educational psychology, experimental psychology, measurement-evaluation, organizational-industrial psychology; school psychology (PhD, SSP). *Accreditation:* APA. *Degree requirements:* For master's, thesis or alternative; for doctorate, variable foreign language requirement, thesis/dissertation, 2 terms of residency, internship, practicum. *Entrance requirements:* For master's, GRE General Test, GRE Subject Test, minimum GPA of 3.0 in last 60 hours of course work; for doctorate, GRE General Test. *Faculty research:* Comprehensive evaluation system for the central region professional development grant, Illinois school psychology internship consortium, for children's sake.

Indiana University–Purdue University Indianapolis, School of Science, Department of Psychology, Program in Industrial/Organizational Psychology, Indianapolis, IN 46202-2896. Offers MS. *Entrance requirements:* For master's, GRE General Test (minimum combined verbal and quantitative score: 1100, including quantitative score of 550), minimum undergraduate GPA of 3.0 on a 4.0 scale. *Faculty research:* Stereotyping and prejudice biases, performance feedback, personnel psychology, organizational decision making, counterproductive behaviors.

Inter American University of Puerto Rico, Metropolitan Campus, Graduate Programs, Program in Psychology, San Juan, PR 00919-1293. Offers industrial/organizational psychology (MA, PhD); labor relations (MA); psychology (MA, PhD); school psychology (MA, PhD). *Degree requirements:* For master's, comprehensive exam. *Entrance requirements:* For master's, GRE or EXADEP, interview. Electronic applications accepted.

Iona College, School of Arts and Science, Department of Psychology, New Rochelle, NY 10801-1890. Offers experimental psychology (MA); industrial-organizational psychology (MA); mental health counseling (MA); psychology (MA); school psychology (MA). Part-time and evening/weekend programs available. *Faculty:* 11 full-time (5 women), 6 part-time/adjunct (3 women). *Students:* 71 full-time (54 women), 42 part-time (35 women); includes 26 minority (9 African Americans, 5 Asian Americans or Pacific Islanders, 12 Hispanic Americans), 1 international. Average age 25. 120 applicants, 73% accepted, 39 enrolled. In 2008, 19 master's awarded. *Degree requirements:* For master's, thesis. *Entrance requirements:* For master's, GRE or minimum GPA of 3.0. Additional exam requirements/recommendations for international students: Required—TOEFL (minimum score 550 paper-based; 213 computer-based). *Application deadline:* Applications are processed on a rolling basis. Application fee: $50. Electronic applications accepted. *Expenses:* Tuition: Part-time $755 per credit. Required fees: $175 per term. *Financial support:* Career-related internships or fieldwork, tuition waivers (partial), and unspecified assistantships available. Support available to part-time students. Financial award application deadline: 4/15; financial award applicants required to submit FAFSA. *Unit head:* Dr. Pauline Jirik-Babb, Chair, 914-633-2191, E-mail: pjirikbabb@iona.edu. *Application contact:* Veronica Jarek-Prinz, Director of Graduate Admissions, 914-633-2420, Fax: 914-633-2277, E-mail: vjarekprinz@iona.edu.

John F. Kennedy University, Graduate School of Professional Psychology, Program in Organizational Psychology, Pleasant Hill, CA 94523-4817. Offers MA, Certificate. *Accreditation:* APA. Part-time and evening/weekend programs available. *Degree requirements:* For master's, thesis or alternative. *Entrance requirements:* For master's, interview. Additional exam requirements/recommendations for international students: Required—TOEFL.

Kean University, College of Humanities and Social Sciences, Program in Psychology, Union, NJ 07083. Offers human behavior and organizational psychology (MA); psychological services (MA). Part-time and evening/weekend programs available. *Faculty:* 18 full-time (13 women).

Industrial and Organizational Psychology

Kean University (continued)
Students: 13 full-time (10 women), 25 part-time (23 women); includes 7 African Americans, 1 Asian American or Pacific Islander, 3 Hispanic Americans, 1 international. Average age 28. 23 applicants, 65% accepted, 5 enrolled. In 2008, 23 master's awarded. *Degree requirements:* For master's, comprehensive exam, thesis, research. *Entrance requirements:* For master's, GRE General Test, 2 letters of recommendation, interview, prerequisite coursework in behavioral sciences, 12 credits in psychology. *Application deadline:* For fall admission, 5/1 for domestic students; for spring admission, 11/1 for domestic students. Application fee: $60 ($150 for international students). Electronic applications accepted. *Expenses:* Tuition, state resident: full-time $10,128; part-time $422 per credit. Tuition, nonresident: full-time $13,728; part-time $572 per credit. Required fees: $2570; $107 per credit. Part-time tuition and fees vary according to course load, degree level and program. *Financial support:* In 2008–09, 4 research assistantships with full tuition reimbursements (averaging $3,217 per year) were awarded; unspecified assistantships also available. *Unit head:* Dr. Joanne Walsh, Program Coordinator, 908-737-5870, E-mail: jwalsh@kean.edu. *Application contact:* Steven Koch, Pre-Admissions Coordinator, 908-737-4723, Fax: 908-737-5965, E-mail: grad-adm@kean.edu.

Lamar University, College of Graduate Studies, College of Arts and Sciences, Department of Psychology, Beaumont, TX 77710. Offers community/clinical psychology (MS); industrial/organizational psychology (MS). Part-time programs available. *Faculty:* 7 full-time (4 women). *Students:* 21 full-time (10 women), 5 part-time (3 women); includes 4 minority (1 African American, 3 Hispanic Americans), 2 international. Average age 25. 32 applicants, 41% accepted, 10 enrolled. In 2008, 6 master's awarded. *Degree requirements:* For master's, thesis, practicum. *Entrance requirements:* For master's, GRE General Test, minimum GPA of 2.75 in last 60 hours of undergraduate course work. Additional exam requirements/recommendations for international students: Required—TOEFL. *Application deadline:* For fall admission, 8/1 for domestic students; for spring admission, 12/1 for domestic students. Application fee: $25 ($50 for international students). *Expenses:* Tuition, state resident: full-time $5000; part-time $195 per credit. Tuition, nonresident: full-time $12,376; part-time $476 per credit. Required fees: $1570. *Financial support:* In 2008–09, 12 students received support, including 3 teaching assistantships (averaging $4,500 per year); fellowships, research assistantships, career-related internships or fieldwork, Federal Work-Study, scholarships/grants, and tuition waivers (partial) also available. Support available to part-time students. Financial award application deadline: 4/1. *Faculty research:* Groupthink, health psychology, school psychology, behavioral neuroscience. *Unit head:* Dr. Oney D. Fitzpatrick, Chair, 409-880-8285, Fax: 409-880-1779, E-mail: fitzpatrod@hal.lamar.edu. *Application contact:* Dr. James W. Westgate, Assistant Dean, 409-880-7978, E-mail: westgate@hal.lamar.edu.

Louisiana State University and Agricultural and Mechanical College, Graduate School, College of Arts and Sciences, Department of Psychology, Baton Rouge, LA 70803. Offers biological psychology (MA, PhD); clinical psychology (MA, PhD); cognitive psychology (MA, PhD); developmental psychology (MA, PhD); industrial/organizational psychology (MA, PhD); school psychology (MA, PhD). *Accreditation:* APA (one or more programs are accredited). Terminal master's awarded for partial completion of doctoral program. *Degree requirements:* For master's, thesis; for doctorate, thesis/dissertation, 1 year internship. *Entrance requirements:* For master's and doctorate, GRE General Test, minimum GPA of 3.0. Additional exam requirements/recommendations for international students: Required—TOEFL (minimum score 550 paper-based; 213 computer-based; 79 iBT). Electronic applications accepted. *Faculty research:* Clinical psychology, autism, anxiety, addition, neuro-psychology, school psychology, cognitive psychology, experimental psychology.

Louisiana Tech University, Graduate School, College of Education, Department of Behavioral Sciences and Psychology, Ruston, LA 71272. Offers counseling (MA); counseling psychology (PhD); industrial/organizational psychology (MA); special education (MA). *Accreditation:* APA (one or more programs are accredited). Part-time programs available. *Degree requirements:* For master's, thesis or alternative; for doctorate, thesis/dissertation. *Entrance requirements:* For master's and doctorate, GRE General Test.

Marshall University, Academic Affairs Division, College of Liberal Arts, Department of Psychology, Huntington, WV 25755. Offers clinical psychology (MA); general psychology (MA); industrial and organizational psychology (MA); psychology (Psy D). *Accreditation:* APA. *Degree requirements:* For master's, thesis optional. *Entrance requirements:* For master's, GRE General Test or MAT.

Massachusetts School of Professional Psychology, Graduate Programs, Boston, MA 02132. Offers clinical psychology (Psy D); clinical psychopharmacology (Post-Doctoral MS); counseling psychology (MA); executive coaching (Graduate Certificate); forensic psychology (MA); organizational psychology (MA); respecialization in clinical psychology (Certificate); MA/CAGS. *Accreditation:* APA. *Degree requirements:* For master's, comprehensive exam; for doctorate, thesis/dissertation. *Entrance requirements:* For doctorate, GRE General Test. Additional exam requirements/recommendations for international students: Required—TOEFL (minimum score 550 paper-based; 213 computer-based). Electronic applications accepted.

Middle Tennessee State University, College of Graduate Studies, College of Education and Behavioral Science, Department of Psychology, Murfreesboro, TN 37132. Offers industrial/organizational psychology (MA); professional counseling (M Ed, Ed S), including curriculum and instruction (Ed S), school counseling (M Ed); psychology (MA); school psychology (Ed S). Part-time and evening/weekend programs available. Postbaccalaureate distance learning degree programs offered. *Entrance requirements:* Additional exam requirements/recommendations for international students: Required—TOEFL (paper-based 525; computer-based 195; IBT 71) or IELTS (6.0). Electronic applications accepted. *Faculty research:* Industrial/organizational, social/personality/sports, counseling/clinical/school, cognitive/language/learning/perception, developmental/aging.

Minnesota State University Mankato, College of Graduate Studies, College of Social and Behavioral Sciences, Department of Psychology, Mankato, MN 56001. Offers clinical psychology (MA); industrial/organizational psychology (MA); psychology (MT); school psychology (Psy D). Part-time programs available. *Students:* 38 full-time (23 women), 5 part-time (1 woman). *Degree requirements:* For master's, one foreign language, comprehensive exam, thesis (for some programs). *Entrance requirements:* For master's, GRE General Test, GRE Subject Test (clinical psychology), minimum GPA of 3.0 during previous 2 years, 3 letters of reference. Additional exam requirements/recommendations for international students: Required—TOEFL. *Application deadline:* For fall admission, 1/1 priority date for domestic students. Applications are processed on a rolling basis. Application fee: $40. Electronic applications accepted. *Financial support:* Research assistantships, teaching assistantships with full tuition reimbursements, career-related internships or fieldwork, Federal Work-Study, institutionally sponsored loans, and unspecified assistantships available. Support available to part-time students. Financial award application deadline: 3/15; financial award applicants required to submit FAFSA. *Faculty research:* Professional competency in hospitals, mood disturbance, 360-degree feedback, employee selection, planning fallacy. *Unit head:* Dr. Barry Ries, Chairperson, 507-389-2724. *Application contact:* 507-389-2321, E-mail: grad@mnsu.edu.

Missouri State University, Graduate College, College of Health and Human Services, Department of Psychology, Springfield, MO 65804-0094. Offers psychology (MS), including clinical, experimental, industrial/organizational. *Faculty:* 26 full-time (10 women), 1 part-time/adjunct (0 women). *Students:* 44 full-time (30 women), 3 part-time (all women); includes 1 minority (Hispanic American). Average age 24. 71 applicants, 45% accepted, 20 enrolled. In 2008, 17 master's awarded. *Degree requirements:* For master's, comprehensive exam, thesis. *Entrance requirements:* For master's, GRE General Test, GRE Subject Test, minimum GPA of 3.25 in major, 3.0 overall; 20 hours of course work in psychology (experimental and statistics). Additional exam requirements/recommendations for international students: Required—TOEFL (minimum score 550 paper-based; 213 computer-based; 79 iBT). *Application deadline:* For fall admission, 3/1 priority date for domestic and international students. Application fee: $35 ($50 for international students). Electronic applications accepted. *Expenses:* Tuition, state resident: full-time $3852; part-time $214 per credit hour. Tuition, nonresident: full-time $7524; part-time $418 per credit hour. Required fees: $230 per semester. Tuition and fees vary according to course level and course load. *Financial support:* In 2008–09, 10 research assistantships with full tuition reimbursements (averaging $7,340 per year), 3 teaching assistantships with full tuition reimbursements (averaging $9,730 per year) were awarded; career-related internships or fieldwork, Federal Work-Study, institutionally sponsored loans, scholarships/grants, and unspecified assistantships also available. Financial award application deadline: 3/31; financial award applicants required to submit FAFSA. *Faculty research:* Work-family conflict, child forensic psychology, sports psychology, body image assessment, visual learning. *Unit head:* Dr. Robert G. Jones, Head, 417-836-5797, Fax: 417-836-830, E-mail: psychology@missouristate.edu. *Application contact:* Eric Eckert, Coordinator of Admissions and Recruitment, 417-836-5331, Fax: 417-836-6888, E-mail: ericeckert@missouristate.edu.

Montclair State University, The Office of Graduate Admissions and Support Services, College of Humanities and Social Sciences, Department of Psychology, Montclair, NJ 07043-1624. Offers educational psychology (MA), including child/adolescent clinical psychology, clinical psychology for Spanish/English bilinguals; psychology (MA, Certificate), including industrial and organizational psychology (MA); school psychologist (Certificate). Part-time and evening/weekend programs available. *Faculty:* 28 full-time (13 women), 32 part-time/adjunct (16 women). *Students:* 28 full-time (20 women), 31 part-time (26 women); includes 14 minority (4 African Americans, 6 Asian Americans or Pacific Islanders, 4 Hispanic Americans), 2 international. Average age 27. 62 applicants, 56% accepted, 23 enrolled. In 2008, 26 master's awarded. *Degree requirements:* For master's, comprehensive exam, thesis or alternative. *Entrance requirements:* For master's, GRE General Test, GRE Subject Test, previous course work in psychology, interview, 2 letters of recommendation. Additional exam requirements/recommendations for international students: Required—TOEFL (minimum score 83 computer-based). *Application deadline:* For fall admission, 2/1 for domestic and international students; for spring admission, 10/1 for domestic and international students. Applications are processed on a rolling basis. Application fee: $60. Electronic applications accepted. *Financial support:* In 2008–09, 10 research assistantships with full tuition reimbursements (averaging $7,000 per year) were awarded; Federal Work-Study, scholarships/grants, and unspecified assistantships also available. Support available to part-time students. Financial award application deadline: 3/1; financial award applicants required to submit FAFSA. *Faculty research:* Engaged learning, academic and civic development. Total annual research expenditures: $10,000. *Unit head:* Dr. Peter Vietze, Chairperson, 973-655-5201. *Application contact:* Amy Aiello, Associate Director of Admissions, 973-655-5147, Fax: 973-655-7869, E-mail: graduate.school@montclair.edu.

National-Louis University, College of Arts and Sciences, Program in Psychology, Chicago, IL 60603. Offers cultural psychology (MA); health psychology (MA); human development (MA); organizational psychology (MA); psychology (Certificate). Part-time and evening/weekend programs available. *Students:* 4 full-time (all women), 214 part-time (30 women); includes 145 minority (121 African Americans, 3 American Indian/Alaska Native, 3 Asian Americans or Pacific Islanders, 18 Hispanic Americans), 2 international. Average age 38. In 2008, 30 master's awarded. *Degree requirements:* For master's, thesis, internship (health psychology). *Entrance requirements:* For master's, GRE, MAT, or Watson-Glaser Critical Thinking Appraisal, interview, minimum GPA of 3.0; for Certificate, GRE, MAT, or Watson-Glaser Critical Thinking Appraisal, interview, minimum GPA of 3.0, undergraduate course work in psychology. *Application deadline:* Applications are processed on a rolling basis. *Financial support:* Federal Work-Study, institutionally sponsored loans, scholarships/grants, and tuition waivers available. Support available to part-time students. Financial award applicants required to submit FAFSA. *Faculty research:* Human development, personality theory, abnormal psychology. *Unit head:* Dr. Edward Risinger, Professor, 224-233-2533, Fax: 224-233-2533, E-mail: erisinger@nl.edu. *Application contact:* David McCulloch, Vice President for University Services, 800-443-5522 Ext. 5151, Fax: 847-465-0593, E-mail: dmcc@wheeling1.nl.edu.

New York University, Graduate School of Arts and Science, Department of Psychology, New York, NY 10012-1019. Offers cognition and perception (PhD); community psychology (PhD); general psychology (MA); industrial/organizational psychology (MA); psychotherapy and psychoanalysis (Advanced Certificate); social/personality psychology (PhD). Part-time programs available. Terminal master's awarded for partial completion of doctoral program. *Degree requirements:* For master's, comprehensive exam, thesis or alternative; for doctorate, thesis/dissertation. *Entrance requirements:* For master's, GRE General Test, minimum GPA of 3.0; for doctorate, GRE General Test, GRE Subject Test; for Advanced Certificate, doctoral degree, minimum GPA of 3.0. Additional exam requirements/recommendations for international students: Required—TOEFL. *Faculty research:* Vision, memory, social cognition, social and cognitive development, relationships.

North Carolina State University, Graduate School, College of Humanities and Social Sciences, Department of Psychology, Raleigh, NC 27695. Offers developmental psychology (PhD); ergonomics and experimental psychology (PhD); industrial/organizational psychology (PhD); psychology in the public interest (PhD); school psychology (PhD). *Accreditation:* APA. *Degree requirements:* For doctorate, comprehensive exam, thesis/dissertation. *Entrance requirements:* For doctorate, GRE General Test, GRE Subject Test (industrial/organizational psychology), MAT (recommended), minimum GPA of 3.0 in major. Electronic applications accepted. *Faculty research:* Cognitive and social development (human factors, families, the workplace, community issues and health, aging).

Northern Kentucky University, Office of Graduate Programs, College of Arts and Sciences, Program in Industrial-Organizational Psychology, Highland Heights, KY 41099. Offers industrial psychology (Certificate); industrial-organizational psychology (MS); occupational health psychology (Certificate); organizational psychology (Certificate). Part-time and evening/weekend programs available. *Students:* 8 full-time (6 women), 34 part-time (25 women); includes 4 minority (all African Americans), 2 international. Average age 29. 37 applicants, 57% accepted, 15 enrolled. In 2008, 23 master's awarded. *Degree requirements:* For master's, thesis optional, capstone. *Entrance requirements:* For master's, GRE (450 verbal, 450 quantitative, and 3.5 writing), minimum GPA of 3.0, at least 9 semester hours of undergraduate psychology, 1 course in statistics. Additional exam requirements/recommendations for international students: Required—TOEFL (minimum score 550 paper-based; 213 computer-based; 79 iBT), Michigan Test may be substituted only if taken at NKU (minimu score of 80); Recommended—IELTS (minimum score 6.5). *Application deadline:* For fall admission, 6/1 priority date for domestic students, 6/1 for international students; for spring admission, 11/1 priority date for domestic students, 10/1 for international students. Applications are processed on a rolling basis. Application fee: $40. Electronic applications accepted. *Expenses:* Tuition, area resident: Full-time $6642. Tuition, state resident: full-time $6642. Tuition, nonresident: full-time $11,682. *Financial support:* Unspecified assistantships available. Financial award applicants required to submit FAFSA. *Faculty research:* Workplace bullying, gender bias in hiring and performance appraisal, personality in training outcomes, social dilemmas. *Unit head:* Dr. Jeffrey Smith, Director, 859-572-5317, Fax: 859-572-6085, E-mail: smithj@nku.edu. *Application contact:* Dr. Peg Griffin, Director of Graduate Programs, 859-572-6934, Fax: 859-572-6670, E-mail: griffinp@nku.edu.

Ohio University, Graduate College, College of Arts and Sciences, Department of Psychology, Program in Organizational Psychology, Athens, OH 45701-2979. Offers PhD. *Degree requirements:* For doctorate, one foreign language, comprehensive exam, thesis/dissertation. *Entrance requirements:* For doctorate, GRE General Test, GRE Subject Test. Additional exam requirements/recommendations for international students: Required—TOEFL. *Faculty research:* Performance appraisal, job satisfaction, organizational entry, sexual harassment.

Old Dominion University, College of Sciences, Doctoral Program in Psychology, Norfolk, VA 23529. Offers applied experimental psychology (PhD); human factors psychology (PhD); industrial/organizational psychology (PhD). *Faculty:* 17 full-time (7 women), 1 part-time/adjunct (0 women). *Students:* 16 full-time (7 women), 20 part-time (15 women); includes 1 minority

(Hispanic American). Average age 29. 65 applicants, 18% accepted, 10 enrolled. In 2008, 6 doctorates awarded. *Degree requirements:* For doctorate, thesis/dissertation, qualifying exam. *Entrance requirements:* For doctorate, GRE General Test, GRE Subject Test, 3 recommendation letters. Additional exam requirements/recommendations for international students: Required—TOEFL (minimum score 550 paper-based). *Application deadline:* For winter admission, 1/5 for domestic and international students. Application fee: $40. *Expenses:* Tuition, area resident: Full-time $7704; part-time $321 per credit. Tuition, state resident: full-time $7704; part-time $321 per credit. Tuition, nonresident: full-time $19,104; part-time $796 per credit. Required fees: $99 per semester. One-time fee: $40. *Financial support:* In 2008–09, 13 students received support, including 2 fellowships with full tuition reimbursements available (averaging $18,000 per year), research assistantships with full tuition reimbursements available (averaging $12,000 per year), 11 teaching assistantships with full tuition reimbursements available (averaging $12,000 per year). Financial award application deadline: 1/15. *Faculty research:* Human-computer interaction, simulation, neuroergonomics, attention and workload. Total annual research expenditures: $399,161. *Unit head:* Dr. Barbara Winstead, Graduate Program Director, 757-683-4239, Fax: 757-683-5087, E-mail: psychgpd@odu.edu. *Application contact:* Dr. Barbara Winstead, Graduate Program Director, 757-683-4239, Fax: 757-683-5087, E-mail: psychgpd@odu.edu.

Penn State University Park, Graduate School, College of the Liberal Arts, Department of Psychology, State College, University Park, PA 16802-1503. Offers clinical psychology (MS, PhD); cognitive psychology (MS, PhD); developmental psychology (MS, PhD); industrial/organizational psychology (MS, PhD); psychobiology (MS, PhD); social psychology (MS, PhD). *Accreditation:* APA (one or more programs are accredited).

Philadelphia College of Osteopathic Medicine, Graduate and Professional Programs, Department of Psychology, Philadelphia, PA 19131-1694. Offers clinical psychology (Psy D); counseling and clinical health psychology (MS); organizational leadership and development (MS); psychology (Certificate); school psychology (MS, Psy D, Ed S). *Accreditation:* APA. *Degree requirements:* For master's, thesis; for doctorate, comprehensive exam, thesis/dissertation, final project, fieldwork. *Entrance requirements:* For master's, GRE or MAT, minimum GPA of 3.0; course work in biology, chemistry, English, physics; for other advanced degree, PRAXIS. *Faculty research:* Depression in primary care, integrated primary care, geriatric mental health.

See Close-Up on page 1127.

Pontifical Catholic University of Puerto Rico, Institute of Graduate Studies in Behavioral Science and Community Affairs, Program in Industrial Psychology (Doctorate), Ponce, PR 00717-0777. Offers PhD. Part-time and evening/weekend programs available. *Entrance requirements:* For doctorate, EXADEP, minimum GPA of 2.75.

Pontifical Catholic University of Puerto Rico, Institute of Graduate Studies in Behavioral Science and Community Affairs, Program in Industrial Psychology (Master's), Ponce, PR 00717-0777. Offers MS. Part-time and evening/weekend programs available. *Degree requirements:* For master's, thesis. *Entrance requirements:* For master's, EXADEP, 3 letters of recommendation, interview, minimum GPA of 2.75.

Radford University, College of Graduate and Professional Studies, College of Humanities and Behavioral Sciences, Program in Psychology, Radford, VA 24142. Offers clinical psychology (MA, MS); counseling psychology (Psy D); experimental psychology (MA); general psychology (MS); industrial/organizational psychology (MA, MS); school psychology (Ed S). Part-time programs available. *Faculty:* 23 full-time (9 women), 1 part-time/adjunct (0 women). *Students:* 46 full-time (28 women), 5 part-time (4 women); includes 4 minority (3 African Americans, 1 Asian American or Pacific Islander), 2 international. Average age 26. 114 applicants, 42% accepted, 20 enrolled. In 2008, 36 master's awarded. *Degree requirements:* For master's, comprehensive exam, thesis (for some programs). *Entrance requirements:* For master's, GRE, minimum GPA of 3.0; 3 letters of reference; essay. Additional exam requirements/recommendations for international students: Required—TOEFL (minimum score 550 paper-based; 213 computer-based; 79 iBT). *Application deadline:* For fall admission, 3/1 priority date for domestic students, 12/1 for international students; for spring admission, 10/1 for domestic students, 7/1 for international students. Applications are processed on a rolling basis. Application fee: $40. Electronic applications accepted. *Expenses:* Tuition, area resident: Full-time $4845; part-time $202 per credit. Tuition, state resident: full-time $4845; part-time $202 per credit. Tuition, nonresident: full-time $11,483; part-time $478 per credit. Required fees: $2349; $98 per credit. *Financial support:* In 2008–09, 47 students received support, including 33 research assistantships with partial tuition reimbursements available (averaging $8,000 per year), 12 teaching assistantships with partial tuition reimbursements available (averaging $8,700 per year); career-related internships or fieldwork, institutionally sponsored loans, scholarships/grants, and unspecified assistantships also available. Financial award application deadline: 3/1; financial award applicants required to submit FAFSA. *Unit head:* Dr. Hilary M. Lips, Chair, 540-831-5387, Fax: 540-831-6113, E-mail: hlips@radford.edu. *Application contact:* Graduate Admissions Office, 540-831-5431, Fax: 540-831-6061, E-mail: gradcollege@radford.edu.

Rice University, Graduate Programs, School of Social Sciences, Department of Psychology, Houston, TX 77251-1892. Offers cognitive sciences (MA, PhD); industrial-organizational/social psychology (MA, PhD); psychology (MA, PhD). Terminal master's awarded for partial completion of doctoral program. *Degree requirements:* For master's, thesis; for doctorate, thesis/dissertation. *Entrance requirements:* For doctorate, GRE General Test, minimum GPA of 3.0. Additional exam requirements/recommendations for international students: Required—TOEFL. Electronic applications accepted. *Faculty research:* Learning and memory, information processing, decision theory.

Roosevelt University, Graduate Division, College of Arts and Sciences, Department of Psychology, Program in Industrial/Organizational Psychology, Chicago, IL 60605-1394. Offers MA. *Students:* 41 full-time (27 women), 57 part-time (38 women); includes 24 minority (12 African Americans, 9 Asian Americans or Pacific Islanders, 3 Hispanic Americans), 4 international. Average age 29. 132 applicants, 52% accepted, 20 enrolled. In 2008, 33 master's awarded. *Expenses:* Tuition: Full-time $14,730; part-time $709 per credit. Required fees: $175 per semester. Tuition and fees vary according to course load and program. *Unit head:* Michael Helford, Director, 847-619-8543. *Application contact:* Joanne Canyon-Heller, Coordinator of Graduate Admission, 877-APPLY RU, Fax: 312-281-3356, E-mail: applyru@roosevelt.edu.

Rutgers, The State University of New Jersey, New Brunswick, Graduate School of Applied and Professional Psychology, Program in Organizational Psychology, Piscataway, NJ 08854-8097. Offers Psy M, Psy D. *Degree requirements:* For doctorate, comprehensive exam, thesis/dissertation, 1 year internship. *Entrance requirements:* For doctorate, GRE General Test, GRE Subject Test (psychology), BA in psychology or equivalent. Additional exam requirements/recommendations for international students: Required—TOEFL. Electronic applications accepted. *Expenses:* Contact institution. *Faculty research:* Organizational assessment, managerial and organizational practice, consultation, organizational development, decision making.

St. Cloud State University, School of Graduate Studies, College of Social Sciences, Program in Industrial-Organizational Psychology, St. Cloud, MN 56301-4498. Offers MS. *Degree requirements:* For master's, thesis or alternative. *Entrance requirements:* For master's, GRE General Test, minimum GPA of 2.75. Additional exam requirements/recommendations for international students: Required—Michigan English Language Assessment Battery; Recommended—TOEFL (minimum score 550 paper-based; 213 computer-based), IELTS (minimum score 6.5). Electronic applications accepted.

Saint Joseph's University, College of Arts and Sciences, Programs in Training and Organizational Development, Philadelphia, PA 19131-1395. Offers adult learning and training (MS, Certificate); organization dynamics and leadership (MS, Certificate); organizational psychology and development (MS, Certificate). Part-time and evening/weekend programs available. *Students:* 1 full-time (0 women), 64 part-time (47 women); includes 20 minority (18 African Americans, 1 Asian American or Pacific Islander, 1 Hispanic American), 4 international. Average age 37. In 2008, 18 master's awarded. *Entrance requirements:* For master's, GRE (if GPA is below 2.7), application, official transcripts, minimum GPA of 2.7, personal statement, 2 letters of recommendation, current resumé. Additional exam requirements/recommendations for international students: Required—TOEFL (minimum score 550 paper-based; 213 computer-based; 79 iBT). *Application deadline:* For fall admission, 7/15 priority date for domestic students, 4/15 for international students; for winter admission, 1/15 for international students; for spring admission, 11/15 priority date for domestic students, 10/15 for international students. Applications are processed on a rolling basis. Application fee: $35. Electronic applications accepted. *Expenses:* Tuition: Part-time $745 per credit. Tuition and fees vary according to course load, degree level and program. *Financial support:* Applicants required to submit FAFSA. *Unit head:* Dr. Thomas N. Tavantzis, Director, 610-660-1575, E-mail: ttavantz@sju.edu. *Application contact:* Coralee Dixon, Assistant Director of Graduate Admissions, 610-660-1102, Fax: 610-660-1224, E-mail: coralee.dixon@sju.edu.

Saint Louis University, Graduate School, College of Arts and Sciences and Graduate School, Department of Psychology, St. Louis, MO 63103-2097. Offers clinical psychology (MS-R, PhD); experimental psychology (MS-R, PhD); industrial-organizational psychology (PhD); psychology (PhD). *Accreditation:* APA (one or more programs are accredited). Part-time programs available. *Degree requirements:* For master's, comprehensive exam, thesis; for doctorate, thesis/dissertation, clinical internship (for clinical psychology PhD). *Entrance requirements:* For master's and doctorate, GRE General Test, interview, letters of recommendation, resumé, transcripts, goal statement. Additional exam requirements/recommendations for international students: Required—TOEFL (minimum score 550 paper-based; 213 computer-based). Electronic applications accepted. *Faculty research:* Violence and trauma; neural basis of learning and memory function; eating disorders; body image and health behavior; prejudice, stereotyping, and victimization; memory, cognitive aging and language processing.

Saint Mary's University, Faculty of Science, Department of Psychology, Halifax, NS B3H 3C3, Canada. Offers applied psychology (M Sc, PhD), including industrial/organizational psychology. Part-time programs available. *Degree requirements:* For master's, thesis, internship. *Entrance requirements:* For master's, GRE General Test, honors degree, minimum QPA of 3.25. *Faculty research:* Assessment, health psychology, social psychology, cognition.

St. Mary's University, Graduate School, Department of Psychology, Program in Industrial/Organizational Psychology, San Antonio, TX 78228-8507. Offers MA, MS. Part-time programs available. *Faculty:* 2 full-time (1 woman), 3 part-time/adjunct (1 woman). *Students:* 9 full-time (6 women), 11 part-time (5 women); includes 5 minority (1 Asian American or Pacific Islander, 4 Hispanic Americans). Average age 25. 16 applicants, 100% accepted, 11 enrolled. In 2008, 17 master's awarded. *Degree requirements:* For master's, comprehensive exam, thesis optional. *Entrance requirements:* For master's, GRE General Test. Additional exam requirements/recommendations for international students: Required—TOEFL (minimum score 550 paper-based; 213 computer-based; 80 iBT). *Application deadline:* Applications are processed on a rolling basis. Application fee: $0. Electronic applications accepted. *Expenses:* Tuition: Full-time $12,006; part-time $667 per credit hour. Required fees: $440; $220 per semester. *Financial support:* In 2008–09, 2 students received support, including 1 fellowship (averaging $3,000 per year), 1 research assistantship (averaging $4,500 per year); career-related internships or fieldwork, Federal Work-Study, institutionally sponsored loans, scholarships/grants, health care benefits, and unspecified assistantships also available. Financial award application deadline: 3/31; financial award applicants required to submit FAFSA. *Unit head:* Dr. Gregory Pool, Director, 210-436-3314, Fax: 210-431-4301, E-mail: gpool@stmarytx.edu. *Application contact:* Dr. Henry Flores, Dean of the Graduate School, 210-436-3101, Fax: 210-431-2220, E-mail: hflores@stmarytx.edu.

San Diego State University, Graduate and Research Affairs, College of Sciences, Department of Psychology, San Diego, CA 92182. Offers clinical psychology (MS, PhD); industrial and organizational psychology (MS); program evaluation (MS); psychology (MA). *Accreditation:* APA (one or more programs are accredited). Terminal master's awarded for partial completion of doctoral program. *Degree requirements:* For master's, thesis, oral exam; for doctorate, thesis/dissertation. *Entrance requirements:* For master's, GRE General Test, GRE Subject Test, 3 letters of recommendation; for doctorate, GRE General Test, GRE Subject Test, minimum GPA of 3.0, 3 letters of recommendation. Additional exam requirements/recommendations for international students: Required—TOEFL. Electronic applications accepted.

San Jose State University, Graduate Studies and Research, College of Social Sciences, Department of Psychology, San Jose, CA 95192-0001. Offers clinical psychology (MS); experimental psychology (MA); industrial/organizational psychology (MS); psychology (MA). *Degree requirements:* For master's, comprehensive exam, thesis (for some programs). *Entrance requirements:* For master's, GRE General Test, minimum GPA of 3.0. Electronic applications accepted. *Faculty research:* Drug and alcohol abuse, neurohormonal mechanisms in motion sickness, behavior modification, sleep research, genetics.

Seattle Pacific University, Industrial Organizational Psychology Program, Seattle, WA 98119-1997. Offers MA, PhD. *Faculty:* 6 full-time (all women), 1 (woman) part-time/adjunct. *Students:* 28 full-time (21 women), 20 part-time (14 women); includes 7 minority (2 African Americans, 4 Asian Americans or Pacific Islanders, 1 Hispanic American), 2 international. Average age 28. 74 applicants, 35% accepted, 24 enrolled. In 2008, 27 master's awarded. *Degree requirements:* For master's, research project; for doctorate, thesis/dissertation, field placement. Application fee: $50. Electronic applications accepted. *Expenses:* Tuition: Full-time $659; part-time $659 per credit hour. One-time fee: $50. Tuition and fees vary according to program. *Unit head:* Dr. Robert B McKenna, Chair, 206-281-2629, E-mail: rmckenna@spu.edu. *Application contact:* Grad Center The, 206-281-2091.

Southern Illinois University Edwardsville, Graduate Studies and Research, School of Education, Department of Psychology, Program in Industrial-Organizational Psychology, Edwardsville, IL 62026-0001. Offers MA. Part-time programs available. *Students:* 16 full-time (15 women), 12 part-time (8 women); includes 2 minority (both African Americans). Average age 26. 40 applicants. In 2008, 7 master's awarded. *Degree requirements:* For master's, thesis. *Entrance requirements:* For master's, GRE. Additional exam requirements/recommendations for international students: Required—TOEFL (minimum score 550 paper-based; 213 computer-based; 79 iBT), IELTS (minimum score 6.5). *Application deadline:* For fall admission, 2/1 for domestic and international students. Application fee: $30. Electronic applications accepted. *Expenses:* Tuition, area resident: Full-time $5838. Tuition, nonresident: full-time $14,596. Required fees: $1525. *Financial support:* Application deadline: 3/1; *Unit head:* Dr. Lynn Bartels, Director, 618-650-2202, E-mail: lbartel@siue.edu. *Application contact:* Dr. Lynn Bartels, Director, 618-650-2202, E-mail: lbartel@siue.edu.

Springfield College, Graduate Programs, Programs in Psychology and Counseling, Springfield, MA 01109-3797. Offers athletic counseling (M Ed, MS, CAGS); industrial/organizational psychology (M Ed, MS, CAGS); marriage and family therapy (M Ed, MS, CAGS); mental health counseling (M Ed, MS, CAGS); school guidance and counseling (M Ed, MS, CAGS); student personnel in higher education (M Ed, MS, CAGS). Part-time programs available. *Faculty:* 13 full-time (6 women), 12 part-time/adjunct (3 women). *Students:* 151 full-time, 52 part-time. Average age 30. 198 applicants, 73% accepted, 74 enrolled. In 2008, 84 master's, 4 other advanced degrees awarded. *Degree requirements:* For master's, research project, portfolio. *Entrance requirements:* Additional exam requirements/recommendations for international students: Required—TOEFL (minimum score 550 paper-based; 213 computer-based). *Application deadline:* For fall admission, 1/15 priority date for domestic students, 1/15 for international students; for winter admission, 11/1 for domestic and international students; for spring admission, 11/1 for domestic and international students. Applications are processed on a rolling basis. Application fee: $50. Electronic applications accepted. *Expenses:* Tuition: Full-time $9132; part-time $761 per semester hour. Required fees: $150. Tuition and fees vary according to course load. *Financial support:* Fellowships with partial tuition reimbursements, teaching assistantships with partial tuition reimbursements, career-related internships or

Industrial and Organizational Psychology

Springfield College (continued)
fieldwork, Federal Work-Study, institutionally sponsored loans, and unspecified assistantships available. Financial award application deadline: 3/1; financial award applicants required to submit FAFSA. *Unit head:* Dr. Glenn Lowery, Director, 413-748-3301, Fax: 413-748-3854, E-mail: glowery@spfldcol.edu. *Application contact:* Donald James Shaw, Director of Graduate Admissions, 413-748-3479, Fax: 413-748-3694, E-mail: donald_shaw_jr@spfldcol.edu.

Teachers College, Columbia University, Graduate Faculty of Education, Department of Organization and Leadership, Program in Social and Organizational Psychology, New York, NY 10027-6696. Offers organizational psychology (MA, Ed D, PhD); social psychology (Ed D, PhD). *Faculty:* 8 full-time (5 women), 5 part-time/adjunct. *Students:* 112 full-time (88 women), 154 part-time (94 women); includes 58 minority (13 African Americans, 27 Asian Americans or Pacific Islanders, 18 Hispanic Americans), 23 international. Average age 32. 258 applicants, 49% accepted, 58 enrolled. In 2008, 84 master's, 4 doctorates awarded. Terminal master's awarded for partial completion of doctoral program. *Degree requirements:* For master's, comprehensive exam; for doctorate, thesis/dissertation. *Entrance requirements:* For master's, minimum GPA of 3.0; for doctorate, GRE General Test. *Application deadline:* For fall admission, 5/15 for domestic students; for spring admission, 12/1 for domestic students. Application fee: $75. *Expenses:* Tuition: Full-time $26,040; part-time $1085 per credit. Required fees: $720. *Financial support:* Fellowships, research assistantships, career-related internships or fieldwork, Federal Work-Study, institutionally sponsored loans, and tuition waivers (full and partial) available. Support available to part-time students. Financial award application deadline: 2/1. *Faculty research:* Conflict resolution, human resource and organization development, management competence, organizational culture, leadership. *Unit head:* Warner Burke, Chair, 212-678-3258. *Application contact:* Debbie Lesperance, Assistant Director of Admission, 212-678-3710, Fax: 212-678-4171.

Temple University, Graduate School, College of Education, Department of Psychological Studies in Education, Program in Adult and Organizational Development, Philadelphia, PA 19122-6096. Offers Ed M. Part-time and evening/weekend programs available. *Degree requirements:* For master's, thesis or alternative. *Entrance requirements:* For master's, GRE General Test or MAT, minimum GPA of 3.0. Additional exam requirements/recommendations for international students: Required—TOEFL (minimum score 550 paper-based; 213 computer-based; 79 iBT). Electronic applications accepted.

Texas A&M University, College of Liberal Arts, Department of Psychology, College Station, TX 77843. Offers behavioral and cellular neuroscience (MS, PhD); clinical psychology (MS, PhD); cognitive psychology (MS, PhD); developmental psychology (MS, PhD); industrial/organizational psychology (MS, PhD); social psychology (MS, PhD). *Accreditation:* APA (one or more programs are accredited). *Faculty:* 35. *Students:* 74 full-time (47 women), 11 part-time (9 women); includes 30 minority (7 African Americans, 5 Asian Americans or Pacific Islanders, 18 Hispanic Americans), 4 international. In 2008, 11 master's, 12 doctorates awarded. *Degree requirements:* For master's, thesis; for doctorate, comprehensive exam (for some programs), thesis/dissertation. *Entrance requirements:* For master's and doctorate, GRE General Test. Additional exam requirements/recommendations for international students: Required—TOEFL. *Application deadline:* For fall admission, 1/5 for domestic and international students. Application fee: $50 ($75 for international students). Electronic applications accepted. *Expenses:* Tuition, area resident: Full-time $3838.50. Tuition, state resident: full-time $3838.50. Tuition, nonresident: full-time $8897. Required fees: $2359.60. *Financial support:* Fellowships with partial tuition reimbursements, research assistantships with partial tuition reimbursements, teaching assistantships with partial tuition reimbursements, career-related internships or fieldwork, institutionally sponsored loans, health care benefits, and unspecified assistantships available. Financial award application deadline: 1/5; financial award applicants required to submit FAFSA. *Unit head:* Dr. Les Morey, Head, 979-845-2581, Fax: 979-845-4727, E-mail: lmorey@psych.tamu.edu. *Application contact:* Sharon Starr, Graduate Admissions Supervisor, 979-458-1710, Fax: 979-845-4727, E-mail: gradadv@psyc.tamu.edu.

University at Albany, State University of New York, College of Arts and Sciences, Department of Psychology, Albany, NY 12222-0001. Offers autism (Certificate); biopsychology (PhD); clinical psychology (PhD); general/experimental psychology (PhD); industrial/organizational psychology (PhD); psychology (MA); social/personality psychology (PhD). *Accreditation:* APA (one or more programs are accredited). *Degree requirements:* For doctorate, thesis/dissertation. *Entrance requirements:* For doctorate, GRE General Test, GRE Subject Test. Additional exam requirements/recommendations for international students: Required—TOEFL (minimum score 550 paper-based; 213 computer-based). Electronic applications accepted.

The University of Akron, Graduate School, Buchtel College of Arts and Sciences, Department of Psychology, Program in Industrial/Organizational Psychology, Akron, OH 44325. Offers MA, PhD. Terminal master's awarded for partial completion of doctoral program. *Degree requirements:* For master's, thesis optional, thesis or specialty exam; for doctorate, one foreign language, comprehensive exam, thesis/dissertation. *Entrance requirements:* For master's, GRE General Test, GRE Subject Test, minimum GPA of 2.75, letters of recommendation; for doctorate, GRE General Test, GRE Subject Test, minimum graduate GPA of 3.25, letters of recommendation, personal statement. Additional exam requirements/recommendations for international students: Required—TOEFL (minimum score 550 paper-based; 213 computer-based; 79 iBT). Electronic applications accepted. *Faculty research:* Personnel selection, performance management, leadership, self-regulation, affect.

University of Baltimore, Graduate School, The Yale Gordon College of Liberal Arts, Program in Applied Psychology, Baltimore, MD 21201-5779. Offers applied psychology (MS), including counseling, industrial and organizational psychology, psychological applications. Part-time and evening/weekend programs available. *Faculty:* 7 full-time (5 women), 7 part-time/adjunct (2 women). *Students:* 59 full-time (41 women), 40 part-time (31 women); includes 28 minority (21 African Americans, 6 Asian Americans or Pacific Islanders, 1 Hispanic American), 4 international. Average age 27. 163 applicants, 34% accepted, 46 enrolled. In 2008, 31 master's awarded. *Degree requirements:* For master's, thesis optional. *Entrance requirements:* For master's, GRE, minimum GPA of 3.0. Additional exam requirements/recommendations for international students: Required—TOEFL (minimum score 550 paper-based; 213 computer-based). *Application deadline:* For fall admission, 8/1 for domestic students, 6/1 for international students; for spring admission, 12/1 for domestic students, 11/1 for international students. Applications are processed on a rolling basis. Application fee: $30. Electronic applications accepted. *Expenses:* Contact institution. *Financial support:* In 2008–09, 5 research assistantships with full and partial tuition reimbursements were awarded; fellowships, career-related internships or fieldwork and Federal Work-Study also available. Support available to part-time students. Financial award application deadline: 4/1; financial award applicants required to submit FAFSA. *Faculty research:* Participatory decision making, counter productive workplace behavior, organizational consulting, substance abuse treatment, cognitive functioning in head injured. Total annual research expenditures: $93,146. *Unit head:* Dr. Thomas Mitchell, Director, 410-837-5348, Fax: 410-837-4793, E-mail: tmitchell@ubalt.edu. *Application contact:* Kevin Nies, Assistant Director, Office of Graduate Admission, 410-837-6565, E-mail: knies@ubalt.edu.

University of Central Florida, College of Sciences, Department of Psychology, Program in Industrial/Organizational Psychology, Orlando, FL 32816. Offers MS, PhD. *Accreditation:* APA. Part-time and evening/weekend programs available. *Students:* 57 full-time (35 women), 11 part-time (6 women); includes 21 minority (8 African Americans, 3 Asian Americans or Pacific Islanders, 10 Hispanic Americans), 3 international. Average age 28. In 2008, 19 master's, 6 doctorates awarded. *Degree requirements:* For master's, comprehensive exam, thesis, practicum. *Entrance requirements:* For master's, GRE General Test, minimum GPA of 3.0 in last 60 hours, resumé. Additional exam requirements/recommendations for international students: Required—TOEFL. *Application deadline:* For fall admission, 2/1 for domestic students. Application fee: $30. Electronic applications accepted. *Expenses:* Tuition, area resident: Full-time $6816; part-time $284 per credit. Tuition, state resident: full-time $6816; part-time $1076 per credit. Tuition, nonresident: full-time $25,824. Required fees: $216; $9 per credit. *Financial support:* In 2008–09, 7 fellowships with partial tuition reimbursements (averaging $9,000 per year), 19 research assistantships with partial tuition reimbursements (averaging $10,000 per year), 16 teaching assistantships with partial tuition reimbursements (averaging $7,400 per year) were awarded; career-related internships or fieldwork, Federal Work-Study, institutionally sponsored loans, tuition waivers (partial), and unspecified assistantships also available. Financial award application deadline: 3/1; financial award applicants required to submit FAFSA. *Faculty research:* Sports psychology, electronic selection systems, team training, stress effects, psychometrics. *Unit head:* Dr. Barbara Fritzsche, Director, 407-823-3919, E-mail: bfritzsc@mail.ucf.edu. *Application contact:* Dr. Barbara Fritzsche, Director, 407-823-3919, E-mail: bfritzsc@mail.ucf.edu.

University of Connecticut, Graduate School, College of Liberal Arts and Sciences, Department of Psychology, Field of Psychology, Storrs, CT 06269. Offers behavioral neuroscience (PhD); biopsychology (PhD); clinical psychology (MA, PhD); cognition and instruction (PhD); developmental psychology (MA, PhD); ecological psychology (PhD); experimental psychology (PhD); general psychology (MA, PhD); health psychology (Graduate Certificate); industrial/organizational psychology (PhD); language and cognition (PhD); neuroscience (PhD); occupational health psychology (Graduate Certificate); social psychology (MA, PhD). *Accreditation:* APA (one or more programs are accredited). Terminal master's awarded for partial completion of doctoral program. *Degree requirements:* For master's, comprehensive exam; for doctorate, thesis/dissertation. *Entrance requirements:* For master's and doctorate, GRE General Test, GRE Subject Test. Additional exam requirements/recommendations for international students: Required—TOEFL (minimum score 550 paper-based; 213 computer-based). Electronic applications accepted.

University of Detroit Mercy, College of Liberal Arts and Education, Department of Psychology, Program in Industrial/Organizational Psychology, Detroit, MI 48221. Offers MA. *Entrance requirements:* For master's, GRE General Test, minimum GPA of 3.0.

University of Guelph, Graduate Program Services, College of Social and Applied Human Sciences, Department of Psychology, Guelph, ON N1G 2W1, Canada. Offers applied social psychology (MA, PhD); clinical psychology applied development emphasis (PhD); clinical psychology applied developmental emphasis (MA); industrial/organizational psychology (MA, PhD); neuroscience and applied cognitive science (MA, PhD). *Degree requirements:* For master's, thesis; for doctorate, comprehensive exam, thesis/dissertation. *Entrance requirements:* For master's, GRE General Test, GRE Subject Test, minimum B+ average during previous 2 years of course work; for doctorate, GRE General Test, GRE Subject Test, minimum A-average. Additional exam requirements/recommendations for international students: Required—TOEFL (minimum score 89 iBT). Electronic applications accepted. *Faculty research:* Organizational psychology, reading comprehension and mathematical ability, drug addiction and relapse, gender issues and culture, memory, clinical psychology.

University of Houston, College of Liberal Arts and Social Sciences, Department of Psychology, Houston, TX 77204. Offers clinical psychology (PhD); industrial/organizational psychology (PhD); psychology (MA); social psychology (PhD). *Accreditation:* APA (one or more programs are accredited). *Faculty:* 26 full-time (11 women), 8 part-time/adjunct (3 women). *Students:* 99 full-time (75 women), 15 part-time (11 women); includes 20 minority (5 African Americans, 3 Asian Americans or Pacific Islanders, 12 Hispanic Americans), 10 international. Average age 27. 386 applicants, 7% accepted, 23 enrolled. In 2008, 19 master's, 17 doctorates awarded. *Degree requirements:* For doctorate, thesis/dissertation. *Entrance requirements:* For doctorate, GRE General Test, minimum GPA of 3.0. *Application deadline:* For fall admission, 1/1 for domestic students. Application fee: $40 ($75 for international students). *Expenses:* Tuition, state resident: full-time $5164; part-time $287 per credit. Tuition, nonresident: full-time $10,222; part-time $568 per credit. *Financial support:* In 2008–09, 15 fellowships with full tuition reimbursements (averaging $11,500 per year), 14 research assistantships with full tuition reimbursements (averaging $12,050 per year), 76 teaching assistantships with full tuition reimbursements (averaging $12,050 per year) were awarded; career-related internships or fieldwork, Federal Work-Study, institutionally sponsored loans, scholarships/grants, health care benefits, and unspecified assistantships also available. Support available to part-time students. Financial award application deadline: 2/1; financial award applicants required to submit FAFSA. *Faculty research:* Health psychology, depression, child/family process, organizational effectiveness, close relationships. *Unit head:* Dr. David Francis, Chairperson, 713-743-7036, Fax: 713-743-8588, E-mail: dfrancis@uh.edu. *Application contact:* Sherry A. Berun, Coordinator, Academic Affairs, 713-743-8508, Fax: 713-743-8588, E-mail: sherryr@uh.edu.

University of Maryland, Baltimore County, Graduate School, College of Arts, Humanities and Social Sciences, Department of Psychology, Baltimore, MD 21250. Offers applied developmental psychology (PhD); human services psychology (MA, PhD), including applied behavioral analysis (MA), human services psychology/clinical (PhD); industrial and organizational psychology (MPS); psychology (MPS). *Accreditation:* APA (one or more programs are accredited). *Faculty:* 23 full-time (9 women), 11 part-time/adjunct (4 women). *Students:* 117 full-time (97 women), 14 part-time (11 women); includes 24 minority (9 African Americans, 8 Asian Americans or Pacific Islanders, 7 Hispanic Americans), 9 international. Average age 30. 182 applicants, 23% accepted, 32 enrolled. In 2008, 20 master's, 13 doctorates awarded. Terminal master's awarded for partial completion of doctoral program. *Degree requirements:* For master's, thesis or alternative; for doctorate, comprehensive exam, thesis/dissertation. *Entrance requirements:* For master's, GRE General Test; for doctorate, GRE General Test, GRE Subject Test. Additional exam requirements/recommendations for international students: Required—TOEFL. *Application deadline:* For fall admission, 12/1 for domestic and international students. Application fee: $50. Electronic applications accepted. *Financial support:* In 2008–09, 1 fellowship with full and partial tuition reimbursement (averaging $22,000 per year), 29 research assistantships with full and partial tuition reimbursements (averaging $14,857 per year), 34 teaching assistantships with full and partial tuition reimbursements (averaging $14,857 per year) were awarded; career-related internships or fieldwork, Federal Work-Study, health care benefits, and tuition waivers (full and partial) also available. Financial award application deadline: 3/1; financial award applicants required to submit FAFSA. *Faculty research:* Prevention and treatment of behavior problems, early intervention, cultural contexts, applications to education, behavioral medicine. Total annual research expenditures: $2.3 million. *Unit head:* Dr. Linda Baker, Chair, 410-455-2415, Fax: 410-455-1055, E-mail: baker@umbc.edu. *Application contact:* Cara Lane, Program Management Specialist, 410-455-2567, Fax: 410-455-1055, E-mail: psycdept@umbc.edu.

University of Maryland, College Park, Graduate Studies, College of Behavioral and Social Sciences, Department of Psychology, College Park, MD 20742. Offers clinical psychology (PhD); developmental psychology (PhD); experimental psychology (PhD); industrial psychology (MA, MS, PhD); social psychology (PhD). *Accreditation:* APA (one or more programs are accredited). *Degree requirements:* For master's, thesis; for doctorate, variable foreign language requirement, comprehensive exam, thesis/dissertation. *Entrance requirements:* For master's and doctorate, GRE General Test, GRE Subject Test, minimum GPA of 3.5, research and/or work experience, 3 letters of recommendation. Electronic applications accepted. *Faculty research:* Social stereotyping and prejudice, anxiety disorders, auditory neuroethology, counseling and social psychology.

University of Minnesota, Twin Cities Campus, Graduate School, College of Liberal Arts, Department of Psychology, Program in Industrial/Organizational Psychology, Minneapolis, MN 55455-0213. Offers PhD. *Degree requirements:* For doctorate, comprehensive exam, thesis/dissertation. *Entrance requirements:* For doctorate, GRE General Test, GRE Subject Test (recommended), 12 credits of upper-level psychology courses, including a course in statistics or psychological measurement. Additional exam requirements/recommendations for international students: Required—TOEFL (minimum score 550 paper-based; 213 computer-based; 79 iBT).

University of Missouri–St. Louis, College of Arts and Sciences, Department of Psychology, St. Louis, MO 63121. Offers behavioral neuroscience (PhD); clinical psychology respecialization

(Certificate); community psychology (PhD); general psychology (MA); industrial/organizational psychology (PhD). *Accreditation:* APA (one or more programs are accredited). Evening/weekend programs available. *Faculty:* 21 full-time (10 women). *Students:* 56 full-time (46 women), 15 part-time (11 women); includes 4 minority (1 American Indian/Alaska Native, 2 Asian Americans or Pacific Islanders, 1 Hispanic American), 1 international. Average age 28. In 2008, 16 master's, 8 doctorates awarded. Terminal master's awarded for partial completion of doctoral program. *Degree requirements:* For doctorate, thesis/dissertation. *Entrance requirements:* For master's and doctorate, GRE General Test, GRE Subject Test, 3 letters of recommendation. Additional exam requirements/recommendations for international students: Required—TOEFL (minimum score 550 paper-based; 213 computer-based). *Application deadline:* For fall admission, 2/1 priority date for domestic and international students. Applications are processed on a rolling basis. Application fee: $35 ($40 for international students). Electronic applications accepted. *Expenses:* Tuition, area resident: Full-time $5377; part-time $298.70 per credit hour. Tuition, nonresident: full-time $13,381; part-time $472.50 per credit hour. Required fees: $4078; $52 per credit hour. *Financial support:* In 2008–09, 3 research assistantships with full and partial tuition reimbursements (averaging $9,225 per year), 15 teaching assistantships with full and partial tuition reimbursements (averaging $9,000 per year) were awarded; fellowships with full tuition reimbursements also available. Financial award applicants required to submit FAFSA. *Faculty research:* Bereavement and loss, neuroscience, post-traumatic stress disorder, conflict and negotiation, social psychology. *Unit head:* Dr. George Taylor, Chair, 314-516-5391, Fax: 314-516-5392, E-mail: umslpsychology@msx.umsl.edu. *Application contact:* 314-516-5458, Fax: 314-516-6996, E-mail: gradadm@umsl.edu.

University of Nebraska at Omaha, Graduate Studies and Research, College of Arts and Sciences, Department of Psychology, Omaha, NE 68182. Offers developmental psychology (PhD); industrial/organizational psychology (MS, PhD); psychobiology (PhD); psychology (MA); school psychology (MS, Ed S). Part-time programs available. *Degree requirements:* For master's, comprehensive exam, thesis (for some programs). *Entrance requirements:* For master's, GRE General Test, GRE Subject Test, previous course work in psychology, including statistics and a laboratory course; minimum GPA of 3.0, 3 letters of recommendation; for doctorate, GRE General Test. Additional exam requirements/recommendations for international students: Required—TOEFL (minimum score 500 paper-based; 173 computer-based; 61 iBT). Electronic applications accepted.

University of New Haven, Graduate School, College of Arts and Sciences, Program in Industrial and Organizational Psychology, West Haven, CT 06516-1916. Offers MA, Certificate. Part-time and evening/weekend programs available. *Faculty:* 6 full-time (4 women), 8 part-time/adjunct (4 women). *Students:* 99 full-time (69 women), 36 part-time (25 women); includes 24 minority (10 African Americans, 2 American Indian/Alaska Native, 3 Asian Americans or Pacific Islanders, 9 Hispanic Americans), 16 international. Average age 27. 127 applicants, 80% accepted, 59 enrolled. In 2008, 54 master's awarded. *Degree requirements:* For master's, thesis or alternative. *Entrance requirements:* Additional exam requirements/recommendations for international students: Required—TOEFL (minimum score 520 paper-based; 190 computer-based; 70 iBT); Recommended—IELTS (minimum score 5.5). *Application deadline:* For fall admission, 5/31 for international students; for winter admission, 10/15 for international students; for spring admission, 1/15 for international students. Applications are processed on a rolling basis. Application fee: $50. *Expenses:* Contact institution. *Financial support:* Research assistantships with partial tuition reimbursements, teaching assistantships with partial tuition reimbursements, career-related internships or fieldwork, Federal Work-Study, scholarships/grants, tuition waivers, and unspecified assistantships available. Support available to part-time students. Financial award applicants required to submit FAFSA. *Unit head:* Dr. Stuart D Sidle, Coordinator, 203-932-7341. *Application contact:* Eloise Gormley, Information Contact, 203-932-7449.

See Close-Up on page 1149.

The University of North Carolina at Charlotte, Graduate School, College of Arts and Sciences, Department of Psychology, Program in Industrial/Organizational Psychology, Charlotte, NC 28223-0001. Offers MA. *Students:* 12 full-time (10 women), 3 part-time (all women); includes 3 Hispanic Americans. Average age 24. 80 applicants, 13% accepted, 6 enrolled. In 2008, 13 master's awarded. *Degree requirements:* For master's, comprehensive exam, thesis. *Entrance requirements:* For master's, GRE General Test, GRE Subject Test, minimum undergraduate GPA of 3.0 in major, 2.8 overall. Additional exam requirements/recommendations for international students: Required—TOEFL (minimum score 557 paper-based; 220 computer-based). *Application deadline:* For fall admission, 2/1 for domestic and international students. Application fee: $55. Electronic applications accepted. *Expenses:* Tuition, area resident: Full-time $2919; part-time $122 per credit hour. Tuition, state resident: full-time $2919; part-time $122 per credit hour. Tuition, nonresident: full-time $13,126; part-time $547 per credit hour. Required fees: $1779; $91 per credit hour. Tuition and fees vary according to program. *Financial support:* In 2008–09, 1 fellowship (averaging $10,000 per year), 4 research assistantships (averaging $11,950 per year), 2 teaching assistantships (averaging $9,000 per year) were awarded; career-related internships or fieldwork, Federal Work-Study, institutionally sponsored loans, scholarships/grants, and unspecified assistantships also available. Support available to part-time students. Financial award application deadline: 4/1; financial award applicants required to submit FAFSA. *Unit head:* Dr. Steven G. Rogelberg, Coordinator, 704-687-4731, Fax: 704-687-3096, E-mail: sgrogelb@uncc.edu. *Application contact:* Kathy B. Giddings, Director of Graduate Admissions, 704-687-3366, Fax: 704-687-3279, E-mail: agidding@uncc.edu.

The University of North Carolina at Charlotte, Graduate School, College of Arts and Sciences, Department of Psychology, Program in Organizational Science, Charlotte, NC 28223-0001. Offers PhD. *Students:* 15 full-time (9 women); includes 1 Hispanic American, 2 international. Average age 25. 55 applicants, 13% accepted, 7 enrolled. *Expenses:* Tuition, area resident: Full-time $2919; part-time $122 per credit hour. Tuition, state resident: full-time $2919; part-time $122 per credit hour. Tuition, nonresident: full-time $13,126; part-time $547 per credit hour. Required fees: $1779; $91 per credit hour. Tuition and fees vary according to program. *Financial support:* In 2008–09, 2 fellowships (averaging $21,500 per year), 19 research assistantships (averaging $12,487 per year), 1 teaching assistantship (averaging $18,500 per year) were awarded; 1 administrative assistantship ($4,000) also available. *Unit head:* Dr. Steven G. Rogelberg, Coordinator, 704-687-4731, Fax: 704-687-3096, E-mail: sgrogelb@uncc.edu. *Application contact:* Dr. Steven G. Rogelberg, Coordinator, 704-687-4731, Fax: 704-687-3096, E-mail: sgrogelb@uncc.edu.

University of Puerto Rico, Río Piedras, College of Social Sciences, Department of Psychology, San Juan, PR 00931-3300. Offers clinical psychology (MA); industrial organizational psychology (MA); investigative academic psychology (MA); psychology (PhD). Part-time programs available. *Degree requirements:* For master's, comprehensive exam, thesis; for doctorate, comprehensive exam, thesis/dissertation, internship. *Entrance requirements:* For master's, GRE or PAEG, interview, minimum GPA of 3.0; for doctorate, GRE or PAEG, interview, master's degree, minimum GPA of 3.0. *Faculty research:* Intervention on Depressed Latino Youth, biosychosocial training.

University of South Africa, College of Economic and Management Sciences, Pretoria, South Africa. Offers accounting (D Admin, D Com); accounting science (DA); auditing (D Admin, D Com); business administration (M Tech); business economics (D Admin); business leadership (DBL); business management (D Admin, D Com); economic management analysis (M Tech); economics (D Admin, D Com, PhD); human resource development (M Tech); industrial psychology (D Admin, D Com, PhD); logistics (D Com); marketing (M Tech); public administration (D Admin, D Com, DPA, PhD); public management (M Tech); quantitative management (D Admin, D Com); real estate (M Tech); statistics (D Admin, PhD); tourism management (D Admin, D Com); transport economics (D Admin, D Com).

University of South Africa, College of Human Sciences, Pretoria, South Africa. Offers adult education (M Ed); African languages (MA, PhD); African politics (MA, PhD); Afrikaans (MA, PhD); ancient history (MA, PhD); ancient Near Eastern studies (MA, PhD); anthropology (MA, PhD); applied linguistics (MA); Arabic (MA, PhD); archaeology (MA); art history (MA); Biblical archaeology (MA); Biblical studies (M Th, D Th, PhD); Christian spirituality (M Th, D Th); church history (M Th, D Th); classical studies (MA, PhD); clinical psychology (MA); communication (MA, PhD); comparative education (M Ed, Ed D); consulting psychology (D Admin, D Com, PhD); curriculum studies (M Ed, Ed D); development studies (M Admin, MA, D Admin, PhD); didactics (M Ed, Ed D); education (M Tech); education management (M Ed, Ed D); educational psychology (M Ed); English (MA); environmental education (M Ed); French (MA, PhD); German (MA, PhD); Greek (MA); guidance and counseling (M Ed); health studies (MA, PhD), including health sciences education (MA), health services management (MA), medical and surgical nursing science (critical care general) (MA), midwifery and neonatal nursing science (MA), trauma and emergency care (MA); history (MA, PhD); history of education (Ed D); inclusive education (M Ed, Ed D); information and communications technology policy and regulation (MA); information science (MA, MIS, PhD); international politics (MA, PhD); Islamic studies (MA, PhD); Italian (MA, PhD); Judaica (MA, PhD); linguistics (MA, PhD); mathematical education (M Ed); mathematics education (MA); missiology (M Th, D Th); modern Hebrew (MA, PhD); musicology (MA, MMus, D Mus, PhD); natural science education (M Ed); New Testament (M Th, D Th); Old Testament (D Th); pastoral therapy (M Th, D Th); philosophy (MA); philosophy of education (M Ed, Ed D); politics (MA, PhD); Portuguese (MA, PhD); practical theology (M Th, D Th); psychology (MA, MS, PhD); psychology of education (M Ed, Ed D); public health (MA); religious studies (MA, D Th, PhD); Romance languages (MA); Russian (MA, PhD); Semitic languages (MA, PhD); social behavior studies in HIV/AIDS (MA); social science (mental health) (MA); social science in development studies (MA); social science in psychology (MA); social science in social work (MA); social science in sociology (MA); social work (MSW, DSW, PhD); socio-education (M Ed, Ed D); sociolinguistics (MA); sociology (MA, PhD); Spanish (MA, PhD); systematic theology (M Th, D Th); TESOL (teaching English to speakers of other languages) (MA); theological ethics (M Th, D Th); theory of literature (MA, PhD); urban ministries (D Th); urban ministry (M Th).

University of South Florida, Graduate School, College of Arts and Sciences, Department of Psychology, Tampa, FL 33620-9951. Offers clinical psychology (MA, PhD); cognitive and neural sciences (MA, PhD); industrial-organizational psychology (MA, PhD). *Accreditation:* APA (one or more programs are accredited). *Faculty:* 30 full-time (10 women). *Students:* 93 full-time (53 women), 22 part-time (15 women); includes 12 minority (2 African Americans, 4 Asian Americans or Pacific Islanders, 6 Hispanic Americans), 16 international. 421 applicants, 3% accepted, 11 enrolled. In 2008, 21 master's, 12 doctorates awarded. *Degree requirements:* For master's, comprehensive exam, thesis; for doctorate, comprehensive exam, thesis/dissertation. *Entrance requirements:* For master's and doctorate, GRE General Test, minimum GPA of 3.0 in last 60 hours of course work. Additional exam requirements/recommendations for international students: Required—TOEFL (minimum score 550 paper-based; 213 computer-based). *Application deadline:* For fall admission, 11/15 for domestic students, 12/15 for international students. Application fee: $30. Electronic applications accepted. *Expenses:* Contact institution. *Financial support:* Fellowships with full and partial tuition reimbursements, research assistantships with partial tuition reimbursements, teaching assistantships with partial tuition reimbursements, career-related internships or fieldwork, scholarships/grants, tuition waivers (partial), and unspecified assistantships available. Financial award applicants required to submit FAFSA. *Faculty research:* Human memory; job analysis; stress, drug and alcohol abuse; neuroscience. Total annual research expenditures: $2.9 million. *Unit head:* Emanual Donchin, Program Director, 813-974-0466, Fax: 813-974-4617, E-mail: dochin@shell.cas.usf.edu. *Application contact:* William Sacco, Program Director, 813-974-0375, Fax: 813-974-4617, E-mail: sacco@cas.usf.edu.

The University of Tennessee, Graduate School, College of Business Administration, Program in Industrial and Organizational Psychology, Knoxville, TN 37996. Offers PhD. *Degree requirements:* For doctorate, thesis/dissertation. *Entrance requirements:* For doctorate, GRE General Test, minimum GPA of 2.7. Additional exam requirements/recommendations for international students: Required—TOEFL. Electronic applications accepted. *Expenses:* Tuition, area resident: Part-time $348 per credit hour. Tuition, state resident: full-time $6262. Tuition, nonresident: full-time $18,920; part-time $1052 per credit hour. Required fees: $812; $36 per credit hour. Tuition and fees vary according to program.

The University of Tennessee at Chattanooga, Graduate School, College of Arts and Sciences, Department of Psychology, Program in Industrial/Organizational Psychology, Chattanooga, TN 37403. Offers MS. Part-time and evening/weekend programs available. *Faculty:* 4 full-time (0 women), 1 (woman) part-time/adjunct. *Students:* 34 full-time (19 women), 4 part-time (3 women); includes 7 minority (4 African Americans, 2 Asian Americans or Pacific Islanders, 1 Hispanic American), 2 international. Average age 25. 56 applicants, 73% accepted, 13 enrolled. In 2008, 12 master's awarded. *Degree requirements:* For master's, comprehensive exam (for some programs), thesis optional, practicum. *Entrance requirements:* For master's, GRE General Test. Additional exam requirements/recommendations for international students: Required—TOEFL (minimum score 550 paper-based; 213 computer-based; 79 iBT); Recommended—IELTS (minimum score 6). *Application deadline:* For fall admission, 8/1 priority date for domestic students, 6/1 for international students; for spring admission, 12/1 priority date for domestic students, 10/1 for international students. Applications are processed on a rolling basis. Application fee: $30 ($35 for international students). *Expenses:* Tuition, area resident: Full-time $6150; part-time $281 per credit hour. Tuition, nonresident: full-time $16,710; part-time $867 per credit hour. Required fees: $1100; $128 per credit hour. $550 per semester. *Financial support:* In 2008–09, 8 fellowships with full and partial tuition reimbursements (averaging $3,094 per year) were awarded; career-related internships or fieldwork, Federal Work-Study, institutionally sponsored loans, scholarships/grants, tuition waivers (partial), and unspecified assistantships also available. Support available to part-time students. Financial award application deadline: 4/1; financial award applicants required to submit FAFSA. *Faculty research:* Employee selection, group dynamics, compensation and benefits, statistical models, organizational methods. Total annual research expenditures: $47,807. *Unit head:* Dr. Michael D. Biderman, Coordinator, 423-425-4268, Fax: 423-425-4284, E-mail: michael-biderman@utc.edu. *Application contact:* Dr. Stephanie Bellar, Dean of Graduate Studies, 423-425-4666, Fax: 423-425-5223, E-mail: stephanie-bellar@utc.edu.

The University of Texas at Arlington, Graduate School, College of Science, Department of Psychology, Arlington, TX 76019. Offers experimental psychology (PhD); health psychology (PhD); industrial organizational psychology (MS); psychology (MS). Part-time programs available. *Faculty:* 16 full-time (5 women), 1 part-time/adjunct (0 women). *Students:* 53 full-time (38 women), 12 part-time (9 women); includes 11 minority (6 African Americans, 1 Asian American or Pacific Islander, 4 Hispanic Americans), 9 international. 81 applicants, 35% accepted, 15 enrolled. In 2008, 16 master's, 4 doctorates awarded. Terminal master's awarded for partial completion of doctoral program. *Degree requirements:* For master's, comprehensive exam or thesis; for doctorate, thesis/dissertation (for some programs). *Entrance requirements:* For master's and doctorate, GRE General Test, minimum GPA of 3.0 in last 60 hours of course work. Additional exam requirements/recommendations for international students: Required—TOEFL (minimum score 550 paper-based; 213 computer-based). *Application deadline:* For fall admission, 6/16 for domestic students. Applications are processed on a rolling basis. Application fee: $35 ($50 for international students). *Expenses:* Tuition, area resident: Full-time $6500. Tuition, state resident: full-time $6500. Tuition, nonresident: full-time $11,558. *Financial support:* In 2008–09, 4 fellowships (averaging $1,000 per year), 2 research assistantships with tuition reimbursements (averaging $15,000 per year), 28 teaching assistantships with tuition reimbursements (averaging $15,000 per year) were awarded; career-related internships or fieldwork, Federal Work-Study, institutionally sponsored loans, scholarships/grants, traineeships, tuition waivers (partial), and unspecified assistantships also available. Financial award application deadline: 6/1; financial award applicants required to submit FAFSA. *Unit head:* Dr. Robert Gatchel, Chair, 817-272-2281, Fax: 817-272-2364, E-mail: gatchel@uta.edu. *Application contact:* Dr. Jared Kenworthy, Graduate Advisor, 817-272-2281, Fax: 817-272-2364, E-mail: kenworthy@uta.edu.

University of Tulsa, Graduate School, College of Arts and Sciences, Department of Psychology, Program in Industrial/Organizational Psychology, Tulsa, OK 74104-3189. Offers MA, PhD,

Industrial and Organizational Psychology

University of Tulsa *(continued)*
JD/MA. Part-time programs available. *Faculty:* 4 full-time (2 women). *Students:* 15 full-time (11 women), 6 part-time (2 women); includes 2 minority (both African Americans), 1 international. Average age 27. 69 applicants, 42% accepted, 11 enrolled. In 2008, 7 master's, 2 doctorates awarded. Terminal master's awarded for partial completion of doctoral program. *Degree requirements:* For master's, comprehensive exam, thesis (for some programs), 200 hour internship; for doctorate, comprehensive exam, thesis/dissertation. *Entrance requirements:* For master's and doctorate, GRE General Test. Additional exam requirements/recommendations for international students: Required—TOEFL (minimum score 575 paper-based; 231 computer-based; 91 iBT), IELTS (minimum score 6.5). *Application deadline:* For fall admission, 1/15 for domestic and international students. Application fee: $40. Electronic applications accepted. *Expenses:* Tuition: Full-time $15,408; part-time $899 per credit hour. Required fees: $3.33 per credit hour. One-time fee: $200 full-time. Tuition and fees vary according to course load and program. *Financial support:* In 2008–09, 15 students received support, including 15 teaching assistantships with full and partial tuition reimbursements available (averaging $11,242 per year); fellowships with full and partial tuition reimbursements available, research assistantships with full and partial tuition reimbursements available, career-related internships or fieldwork, Federal Work-Study, scholarships/grants, tuition waivers (full and partial), and unspecified assistantships also available. Support available to part-time students. Financial award application deadline: 2/1; financial award applicants required to submit FAFSA. *Faculty research:* Personnel testing and selection, training, performance appraisal, organizational development, job attitudes and motivation, and leadership. Total annual research expenditures: $286,747. *Unit head:* Dr. John McNulty, Director, 918-631-2835, Fax: 918-631-2833, E-mail: john-mcnulty@utulsa.edu. *Application contact:* Information Contact, E-mail: grad@utulsa.edu.

University of West Florida, College of Arts and Sciences: Arts, Department of Psychology, Pensacola, FL 32514-5750. Offers counseling (MA); counseling-licensed mental health counselor (MA); general (MA); industrial-organizational (MA). Part-time programs available. *Faculty:* 11 full-time (3 women). *Students:* 61 full-time (46 women), 42 part-time (34 women); includes 22 minority (13 African Americans, 2 Asian Americans or Pacific Islanders, 7 Hispanic Americans), 2 international. Average age 26. 119 applicants, 65% accepted, 38 enrolled. In 2008, 16 master's awarded. *Degree requirements:* For master's, thesis (for some programs). *Entrance requirements:* For master's, GRE General Test, GRE Subject Test, minimum GPA of 3.0. Additional exam requirements/recommendations for international students: Required—TOEFL (minimum score 550 paper-based; 213 computer-based). *Application deadline:* For fall admission, 6/1 for domestic students, 5/15 for international students; for spring admission, 11/1 for domestic students, 10/1 for international students. Applications are processed on a rolling basis. Application fee: $30. *Expenses:* Tuition, state resident: full-time $6095; part-time $253.97 per credit hour. Tuition, nonresident: full-time $21,919; part-time $913.31 per credit hour. *Financial support:* In 2008–09, 3 research assistantships with partial tuition reimbursements (averaging $3,760 per year), 2 teaching assistantships with partial tuition reimbursements (averaging $3,760 per year) were awarded; career-related internships or fieldwork and Federal Work-Study also available. Financial award application deadline: 4/15; financial award applicants required to submit FAFSA. *Faculty research:* Prose recall, brain imaging, peak performance, biofeedback and pain control, comparable worth. Total annual research expenditures: $15,000. *Unit head:* Dr. Laura Koppes, Chairperson, 850-474-3493. *Application contact:* Terry McCray, Assistant Director of Graduate Admissions, 850-473-7718, Fax: 850-473-7714, E-mail: gradadmissions@uwf.edu.

University of Wisconsin–Oshkosh, The Office of Graduate Studies, College of Letters and Science, Department of Psychology, Oshkosh, WI 54901. Offers experimental psychology (MS); industrial/organizational psychology (MS). *Degree requirements:* For master's, thesis. *Entrance requirements:* For master's, GRE, 10 semester hours of undergraduate course work in psychology. Additional exam requirements/recommendations for international students: Required—TOEFL (minimum score 550 paper-based; 213 computer-based; 79 iBT). Electronic applications accepted. *Faculty research:* Performance evaluation, training, biological bases of behavior, tactile perception, aging.

Valdosta State University, Graduate School, College of Education, Department of Psychology and Counseling, Valdosta, GA 31698. Offers clinical/counseling psychology (MS); industrial/organizational psychology (MS); school counseling (M Ed, Ed S); school psychology (Ed S). Part-time and evening/weekend programs available. *Faculty:* 16 full-time (2 women). *Students:* 65 full-time (54 women), 40 part-time (36 women); includes 32 minority (27 African Americans, 5 Hispanic Americans). Average age 27. 105 applicants, 60% accepted, 29 enrolled. In 2008, 25 master's awarded. *Degree requirements:* For master's, thesis or alternative, comprehensive written and/or oral exams; for Ed S, thesis. *Entrance requirements:* For master's and Ed S, GRE General Test or MAT. Additional exam requirements/recommendations for international students: Required—TOEFL (minimum score 523 paper-based; 193 computer-based). *Application deadline:* For fall admission, 7/1 for domestic and international students; for spring admission, 11/15 for domestic and international students. Applications are processed on a rolling basis. Application fee: $40. Electronic applications accepted. *Financial support:* In 2008–09, 2 students received support, including 2 research assistantships with full tuition reimbursements available (averaging $2,452 per year); institutionally sponsored loans and unspecified assistantships also available. Support available to part-time students. Financial award application deadline: 7/1; financial award applicants required to submit FAFSA. *Faculty research:* Using Bender-Gestalt to predict graphomotor dimensions of the draw-a-person test, neurobehavioral hemispheric dominance. *Unit head:* Dr. Robert Bauer, Chair, 229-333-5930, Fax: 229-259-5576, E-mail: bbauer@valdosta.edu. *Application contact:* Rebecca Waters, Coordinator of Graduate Admissions, 229-333-5694, Fax: 229-245-3853, E-mail: rlwaters@valdosta.edu.

Virginia Polytechnic Institute and State University, Graduate School, College of Science, Department of Psychology, Blacksburg, VA 24061. Offers bio-behavioral sciences (PhD); clinical psychology (PhD); developmental psychology (PhD); industrial/organizational psychology (PhD); psychology (MS). *Accreditation:* APA (one or more programs are accredited). *Entrance requirements:* For master's and doctorate, GRE General Test. Additional exam requirements/recommendations for international students: Required—TOEFL (minimum score 550 paper-based; 213 computer-based). Electronic applications accepted. *Faculty research:* Infant development from electrophysical point of view, work motivation and personnel selection, EEG, ERP and hypnosis with reference to chronic pain, intimate violence.

Walden University, Graduate Programs, School of Psychology, Minneapolis, MN 55401. Offers clinical assessment (Post-Doctoral Certificate); clinical child psychology (Post-Doctoral Certificate); clinical psychology (Post-Doctoral Certificate); counseling psychology (Post-Doctoral Certificate); forensic psychology (MS), including forensic psychology in the community, general forensic psychology, mental health applications, program planning and evaluation in forensic settings, psychology and legal systems; general psychology (Post-Doctoral Certificate); health psychology (Post-Doctoral Certificate); organizational psychology (Post-Doctoral Certificate); organizational psychology and development (Certificate); psychology (MS, PhD), including clinical psychology, counseling psychology, crisis management and response (MS), general psychology, health psychology, leadership development and coaching (MS), media psychology (MS), organizational psychology, organizational psychology and development (MS), organizational psychology and nonprofit management (MS), program evaluation and research (MS), psychology of culture (MS), psychology, public administration, and social change (MS), school psychology, social psychology (MS), terrorism and security (MS); school psychology (Post-Doctoral Certificate); teaching online (Post-Master's Certificate). Part-time and evening/weekend programs available. Postbaccalaureate distance learning degree programs offered (minimal on-campus study). *Faculty:* 16 full-time, 190 part-time/adjunct. *Students:* 3,198 full-time (2,489 women), 810 part-time (664 women); includes 1,319 minority (1,013 African Americans, 51 American Indian/Alaska Native, 68 Asian Americans or Pacific Islanders, 187 Hispanic Americans), 72 international. Average age 40. 1,468 applicants, 60% accepted, 612 enrolled. In 2008, 203 master's, 37 doctorates awarded. Terminal master's awarded for partial completion of doctoral program. *Degree requirements:* For master's, thesis optional; for doctorate, thesis/dissertation, residency. *Entrance requirements:* For master's, bachelor's degree or equivalent in related field, minimum GPA of 2.5, two references, goal statement, official transcripts, access to computer and Internet; for doctorate, master's degree or equivalent in related field, minimum GPA of 3.0, three years related professional/academic experience, two references, goal statement, official transcripts, access to computer and Internet. Additional exam requirements/recommendations for international students: Required—TOEFL (minimum score 550 paper-based; 213 computer-based), IELTS (minimum score 6.5), TOEFL, IELTS, or Michigan English Language Assessment Battery (minimum score 82). *Application deadline:* Applications are processed on a rolling basis. Application fee: $50. Electronic applications accepted. *Expenses:* Tuition: Full-time $12,877; part-time $520 per credit. Required fees: $1230. Tuition and fees vary according to course load, degree level and program. *Financial support:* In 2008–09, 1 fellowship was awarded; Federal Work-Study, scholarships/grants, unspecified assistantships, and family tuition reduction; active duty/veteran tuition reduction; group tuition reduction; interest-free payment plans also available. Support available to part-time students. Financial award applicants required to submit FAFSA. *Unit head:* Dr. Nina Nabors, Associate Dean, 800-925-3368. *Application contact:* Jennifer Hall, 866-4-WALDEN, E-mail: info@waldenu.edu.

Wayne State University, College of Liberal Arts and Sciences, Department of Psychology, Program in Psychology, Detroit, MI 48202. Offers behavioral and cognitive neuroscience (PhD); clinical psychology (PhD); cognitive and social psychology (PhD); industrial/organizational psychology (PhD); psychology (MA, MS). *Accreditation:* APA (one or more programs are accredited). *Degree requirements:* For doctorate, thesis/dissertation. *Entrance requirements:* For doctorate, GRE General Test, GRE Subject Test. Additional exam requirements/recommendations for international students: Required—TOEFL (minimum score 550 paper-based; 213 computer-based); Recommended—TWE (minimum score 6). Electronic applications accepted.

West Chester University of Pennsylvania, Office of Graduate Studies, College of Arts and Sciences, Department of Psychology, West Chester, PA 19383. Offers clinical mental health (Certificate); clinical psychology (MA); general psychology (MA); industrial psychology (MA). Part-time and evening/weekend programs available. *Students:* 63 full-time (47 women), 28 part-time (20 women); includes 5 minority (4 African Americans, 1 Hispanic American), 1 international. Average age 30. 179 applicants, 79% accepted, 43 enrolled. In 2008, 32 master's awarded. *Degree requirements:* For master's, comprehensive exam, thesis (for some programs). *Entrance requirements:* For master's, GRE General Test or MAT, minimum GPA of 3.0, psychology 3.25; three letters of reference. Additional exam requirements/recommendations for international students: Required—TOEFL (minimum score 550 paper-based; 213 computer-based; 80 iBT). *Application deadline:* For fall admission, 4/15 priority date for domestic students, 3/15 for international students; for spring admission, 10/15 for domestic students, 9/1 for international students. Applications are processed on a rolling basis. Application fee: $35. Electronic applications accepted. *Expenses:* Tuition, state resident: full-time $6430; part-time $357 per credit. Tuition, nonresident: full-time $10,288; part-time $572 per credit. Required fees: $652.50; $50 per credit. $67 per semester. *Financial support:* In 2008–09, 9 research assistantships with full and partial tuition reimbursements (averaging $5,000 per year) were awarded; unspecified assistantships also available. Support available to part-time students. Financial award application deadline: 2/15; financial award applicants required to submit FAFSA. *Faculty research:* Animal learning and cognition. *Unit head:* Dr. Sandra Kerr, Chair, 610-436-2949, E-mail: skerr@wcupa.edu. *Application contact:* Dr. Stefani Yorges, Graduate Coordinator, 610-436-3154, E-mail: syorges@wcupa.edu.

Western Michigan University, Graduate College, College of Arts and Sciences, Department of Psychology, Kalamazoo, MI 49008-5202. Offers behavior analysis (MA, PhD); clinical psychology (MA, PhD); experimental psychology (MA); industrial/organizational psychology (MA). *Accreditation:* APA (one or more programs are accredited). *Degree requirements:* For master's, variable foreign language requirement, thesis, oral exams; for doctorate, 2 foreign languages, comprehensive exam, thesis/dissertation, oral exams. *Entrance requirements:* For master's and doctorate, GRE General Test.

Wright State University, School of Graduate Studies, College of Science and Mathematics, Department of Psychology, Program in Human Factors and Industrial/Organizational Psychology, Dayton, OH 45435. Offers MS, PhD. *Degree requirements:* For master's, thesis; for doctorate, thesis/dissertation.

Xavier University, College of Social Sciences, Health and Education, Department of Psychology, Cincinnati, OH 45207. Offers clinical psychology (Psy D); psychology (MA), including general experimental, industrial-organizational. *Accreditation:* APA (one or more programs are accredited). *Faculty:* 16 full-time (8 women), 5 part-time/adjunct (3 women). *Students:* 83 full-time (61 women), 30 part-time (22 women); includes 8 minority (4 African Americans, 4 Asian Americans or Pacific Islanders), 2 international. Average age 27. 242 applicants, 31% accepted, 25 enrolled. In 2008, 27 master's, 12 doctorates awarded. *Degree requirements:* For master's, comprehensive exam, thesis, internship; for doctorate, comprehensive exam, thesis/dissertation, internship. *Entrance requirements:* For master's and doctorate, GRE. Additional exam requirements/recommendations for international students: Required—TOEFL. *Application deadline:* For fall admission, 1/15 for domestic and international students. Application fee: $35. Electronic applications accepted. *Expenses:* Contact institution. *Financial support:* In 2008–09, 57 students received support, including 39 research assistantships with partial tuition reimbursements available, 18 teaching assistantships with partial tuition reimbursements available. Financial award application deadline: 3/1; financial award applicants required to submit FAFSA. *Unit head:* Dr. Christine M. Dacey, Chair, 513-745-3533, Fax: 513-745-3327, E-mail: dacey@xavier.edu. *Application contact:* Margaret Maybury, Assistant Director, Enrollment and Student Services, 513-745-1053, Fax: 513-745-3347, E-mail: maybury@xavier.edu.

Marriage and Family Therapy

Abilene Christian University, Graduate School, College of Biblical Studies, Program in Marriage and Family Therapy, Abilene, TX 79699-9100. Offers MMFT. *Accreditation:* AAMFT/COAMFTE. *Faculty:* 2 full-time (both women), 5 part-time/adjunct (2 women). *Students:* 33 full-time (17 women); includes 4 minority (2 African Americans, 1 Asian American or Pacific Islander, 1 Hispanic American), 1 international. 33 applicants, 67% accepted, 17 enrolled. In 2008, 19 master's awarded. *Degree requirements:* For master's, comprehensive exam. *Entrance requirements:* For master's, GRE General Test, interview. *Application deadline:* For fall admission, 4/1 priority date for domestic students; for spring admission, 11/1 for domestic students. Applications are processed on a rolling basis. Application fee: $40 ($45 for international students). Electronic applications accepted. *Expenses:* Tuition: Full-time $10,728; part-time $640 per hour. Required fees: $1090; $53.50 per hour. $10 per term. Tuition and fees vary according to campus/location. *Financial support:* In 2008–09, 33 students received support; teaching assistantships, career-related internships or fieldwork available. Support available to part-time students. Financial award application deadline: 4/1; financial award applicants required to submit FAFSA. *Faculty research:* Overeating variables, family systems, intervention strategies. *Unit head:* Dr. Jackie Halstead, Chairperson, 325-674-3778, Fax: 325-674-3749, E-mail: halsteadj@acu.edu. *Application contact:* William Horn, Graduate Admissions Counselor, 325-674-2656, Fax: 325-674-6717, E-mail: gradinfo@acu.edu.

Adler Graduate School, Program in Adlerian Studies, Richfield, MN 55423. Offers art therapy specialization (MA); clinical counseling track (MA); coaching and consulting in organizations (Certificate); management consulting and organizational leadership (MA); marriage and family track (MA); non-clinical Adlerian studies track (MA); personal and professional life coaching (Certificate); school counseling (MA). Part-time and evening/weekend programs available. *Degree requirements:* For master's, thesis or alternative, 500-700 hour internship, depending on license choice. *Entrance requirements:* For master's, minimum undergraduate GPA of 3.0, 12 credits of course work in psychology or related field.

Adler School of Professional Psychology, Programs in Psychology, Chicago, IL 60601-7203. Offers art therapy (Certificate); clinical hypnosis (Certificate); clinical psychology (Psy D); counseling psychology (MACP); counseling psychology/art therapy (MACAT); gerontology (MAGP); marriage and family counseling (MAMFC); marriage and family therapy (Certificate); organizational psychology (MAO); substance abuse counseling (MASAC, Certificate); Psy D/Certificate; Psy D/MACAT; Psy D/MACP; Psy D/MAMFC; Psy D/MASAC. *Accreditation:* APA. Part-time and evening/weekend programs available. Postbaccalaureate distance learning degree programs offered (minimal on-campus study). *Faculty:* 36 full-time (17 women), 45 part-time/adjunct (18 women). *Students:* 514 full-time (404 women), 128 part-time (100 women); includes 147 minority (69 African Americans, 2 American Indian/Alaska Native, 30 Asian Americans or Pacific Islanders, 46 Hispanic Americans), 53 international. Average age 27. 855 applicants, 46% accepted, 195 enrolled. In 2008, 110 master's, 136 doctorates awarded. Terminal master's awarded for partial completion of doctoral program. *Degree requirements:* For master's, thesis or alternative, oral exam, practicum; for doctorate, thesis/dissertation, clinical exam, internship, oral exam, practicum, written qualifying exam. *Entrance requirements:* For master's, 12 semester hours in psychology, minimum GPA of 3.0; for doctorate, 18 semester hours in psychology, minimum GPA of 3.25; for Certificate, appropriate master's or doctoral degree. Additional exam requirements/recommendations for international students: Required—TOEFL (minimum score 550 paper-based; 213 computer-based; 79 iBT). *Application deadline:* For fall admission, 2/15 priority date for domestic students, 12/1 priority date for international students. Applications are processed on a rolling basis. Application fee: $50. Electronic applications accepted. *Expenses:* Tuition: Part-time $850 per credit. Tuition and fees vary according to degree level, campus/location and program. *Financial support:* Career-related internships or fieldwork, Federal Work-Study, scholarships/grants, and tuition waivers (full and partial) available. Support available to part-time students. Financial award application deadline: 5/15; financial award applicants required to submit FAFSA. *Unit head:* Dr. Frank Gruba-McAllister, Vice President of Academic Affairs, 312-201-5900, Fax: 312-207-5917. *Application contact:* Craig A Hines, Director of Admissions, 312-201-5900 Ext. 226, Fax: 312-201-5917, E-mail: chines@adler.edu.

See Close-Up on page 1051.

Alliant International University–Irvine, California School of Professional Psychology, Program in Marital and Family Therapy, Irvine, CA 92612. Offers MA, Psy D. *Accreditation:* AAMFT/COAMFTE. Part-time programs available. *Degree requirements:* For doctorate, thesis/dissertation. *Entrance requirements:* For master's, minimum GPA of 3.0, letters of recommendation, interview; for doctorate, letters of recommendation, minimum GPA of 3.0, interview. Additional exam requirements/recommendations for international students: Required—TOEFL (minimum score 600 paper-based; 250 computer-based), TWE (minimum score 5). Electronic applications accepted. *Faculty research:* Chemical dependency, observational research.

See Close-Up on page 1061.

Alliant International University–Los Angeles, California School of Professional Psychology, Program in Marital and Family Therapy, Alhambra, CA 91803-1360. Offers biofeedback (MA); chemical dependency (MA); gerontology (MA); Latin American family therapy (MA). *Accreditation:* AAMFT/COAMFTE.

See Close-Up on page 1061.

Alliant International University–Sacramento, California School of Professional Psychology, Program in Marital and Family Therapy, Sacramento, CA 95825. Offers MA. *Accreditation:* AAMFT/COAMFTE. *Entrance requirements:* For master's, minimum GPA of 3.0, letters of recommendation, interview. Additional exam requirements/recommendations for international students: Required—TOEFL (minimum score 600 paper-based; 250 computer-based), TWE (minimum score 5). Electronic applications accepted. *Faculty research:* Couples therapy, marital myths, cross-cultural issues.

See Close-Up on page 1061.

Alliant International University–San Diego, California School of Professional Psychology, Program in Marital and Family Therapy, San Diego, CA 92131-1799. Offers MA, Psy D. *Accreditation:* AAMFT/COAMFTE. Part-time programs available. *Degree requirements:* For doctorate, thesis/dissertation. *Entrance requirements:* For master's and doctorate, minimum GPA of 3.0, letters of recommendation, interview. Additional exam requirements/recommendations for international students: Required—TOEFL (minimum score 600 paper-based; 250 computer-based), TWE (minimum score 5). Electronic applications accepted. *Faculty research:* Chemical dependency, women's issues, emotionally focused therapy, couple relationships, work/family/parenting.

See Close-Up on page 1061.

Amridge University, Graduate and Professional Programs, Montgomery, AL 36117. Offers behavioral leadership and management (MA); biblical studies (MA, PhD); family therapy (D Min); leadership and management (MS); marriage and family therapy (M Div, MA, PhD), including marriage and family therapy (PhD), professional counseling (PhD); ministerial leadership (M Div, MS); pastoral counseling (M Div, MS); practical theology (MA); professional counseling (M Div, MA); theology (M Div, D Min). *Accreditation:* ATS. Part-time and evening/weekend programs available. Postbaccalaureate distance learning degree programs offered (no on-campus study). *Faculty:* 44 full-time (9 women), 18 part-time/adjunct (7 women). *Students:* 131 full-time (61 women), 218 part-time (119 women); includes 174 minority (164 African Americans, 1 American Indian/Alaska Native, 1 Asian American or Pacific Islander, 8 Hispanic Americans). Average age 35. *Degree requirements:* For master's, one foreign language, comprehensive exam (for some programs), thesis (for some programs); for doctorate, comprehensive exam (for some programs), thesis/dissertation; for M Div, comprehensive exam (for some programs). *Entrance requirements:* For M Div, master's, and doctorate, GRE General Test or MAT. Additional exam requirements/recommendations for international students: Required—TOEFL. *Application deadline:* For fall admission, 9/1 priority date for domestic students; for spring admission, 1/1 priority date for domestic students. Applications are processed on a rolling basis. Application fee: $75. Electronic applications accepted. *Expenses:* Tuition: Full-time $9630; part-time $535 per semester hour. Required fees: $600 per term. Tuition and fees vary according to course load and degree level. *Financial support:* Federal Work-Study and scholarships/grants available. Support available to part-time students. Financial award applicants required to submit FAFSA. *Faculty research:* Homiletics, hermeneutics, ancient Near Eastern history. *Unit head:* Rick Johnson, Director of Enrollment Management, 800-351-4040 Ext. 7513, Fax: 334-387-3878, E-mail: rickjohnson@amridgeuniversity.edu. *Application contact:* Ora Davis, Admissions Officer, 334-387-3877 Ext. 7524, Fax: 334-387-3878, E-mail: oradavis@amridgeuniversity.edu.

Antioch University New England, Graduate School, Department of Applied Psychology, Program in Marriage and Family Therapy, Keene, NH 03431-3552. Offers MA, PhD. *Accreditation:* AAMFT/COAMFTE. *Degree requirements:* For master's, internship, practicum. *Entrance requirements:* For master's, previous course work and work experience in psychology; resumé; essay; official transcripts; 3 letters of recommendation. Additional exam requirements/recommendations for international students: Required—TOEFL (minimum score 600 paper-based; 250 computer-based). Electronic applications accepted. *Expenses:* Contact institution. *Faculty research:* Use of reflective team model in case teaching and in organizational consulting, executive mentoring and coaching.

See Close-Up on page 1063.

Appalachian State University, Cratis D. Williams Graduate School, Department of Human Development and Psychological Counseling, Boone, NC 28608. Offers community counseling (MA); marriage and family therapy (MA); school counseling (MA); student development (MA). *Accreditation:* AAMFT/COAMFTE; ACA; NCATE. Part-time programs available. *Faculty:* 15 full-time (5 women), 21 part-time/adjunct (14 women). *Students:* 124 full-time (97 women), 50 part-time (39 women); includes 14 minority (12 African Americans, 1 Asian American or Pacific Islander, 1 Hispanic American). 169 applicants, 57% accepted, 66 enrolled. In 2008, 60 master's awarded. *Degree requirements:* For master's, comprehensive exam (for some programs), thesis optional, internships. *Entrance requirements:* For master's, GRE General Test, 3 letters of recommendation. Additional exam requirements/recommendations for international students: Required—TOEFL (minimum score 570 paper-based; 230 computer-based; 79 iBT), IELTS (minimum score 6.5). *Application deadline:* For fall admission, 2/1 priority date for domestic students, 2/1 for international students; for spring admission, 2/1 for international students. Applications are processed on a rolling basis. Application fee: $50. Electronic applications accepted. *Expenses:* Tuition, area resident: Full-time $2600; part-time $700 per course. Tuition, state resident: full-time $2600; part-time $700 per course. Tuition, nonresident: full-time $5000; part-time $3300 per course. Required fees: $2150; $330 per course. Tuition and fees vary according to campus/location. *Financial support:* In 2008–09, 20 research assistantships (averaging $7,000 per year), 7 teaching assistantships (averaging $7,000 per year) were awarded; fellowships, career-related internships or fieldwork, Federal Work-Study, scholarships/grants, and unspecified assistantships also available. Financial award application deadline: 4/1; financial award applicants required to submit FAFSA. *Faculty research:* Multicultural counseling, addictions counseling, play therapy, expressive arts, child and adolescent therapy, sexual abuse counseling. *Unit head:* Dr. Lee Baruth, Chairman, 828-262-2055, E-mail: baruthlg@appstate.edu. *Application contact:* Sandy Krause, Director of Admissions and Recruiting, 828-262-2130, Fax: 828-262-2709, E-mail: krausesl@appstate.edu.

Argosy University, Atlanta, College of Psychology and Behavioral Sciences, Atlanta, GA 30328. Offers clinical psychology (MA, Psy D, Postdoctoral Respecialization Certificate), including child and family psychology (Psy D), general adult clinical (Psy D), health psychology (Psy D), neuropsychology/geropsychology (Psy D); community counseling (MA), including marriage and family therapy; counselor education and supervision (Ed D); marriage and family therapy (Certificate). *Accreditation:* APA.

See Close-Up on page 1065.

Argosy University, Chicago, College of Psychology and Behavioral Sciences, Doctoral Program in Clinical Psychology, Chicago, IL 60654. Offers child and adolescent psychology (Psy D); client-centered and experiential psychotherapies (Psy D); diversity and multicultural psychology (Psy D); family psychology (Psy D); forensic psychology (Psy D); health psychology (Psy D); psychoanalytic psychology (Psy D); psychology and spirituality (Psy D). *Accreditation:* APA.

See Close-Up on page 1067.

Argosy University, Denver, College of Psychology and Behavioral Sciences, Denver, CO 80203. Offers clinical psychology (MA, Psy D); community counseling (MA); counseling psychology (Ed D), including counselor education and supervision; counselor education and supervision (Ed D); forensic psychology (MA); marriage and family therapy (MA); organizational leadership (Ed D).

See Close-Up on page 1071.

Argosy University, Hawai'i, College of Psychology and Behavioral Sciences, Program in Marriage and Family Therapy, Honolulu, HI 96813. Offers MA.

See Close-Up on page 1073.

Argosy University, Inland Empire, College of Psychology and Behavioral Sciences, San Bernardino, CA 92408. Offers clinical psychology/marriage and family therapy (MA); counseling psychology (MA, Ed D); counseling psychology/marriage and family therapy (MA); forensic psychology (MA).

See Close-Up on page 1075.

Argosy University, Los Angeles, College of Psychology and Behavioral Sciences, Santa Monica, CA 90405. Offers clinical psychology/marriage and family therapy (MA); counseling psychology (Ed D); counseling psychology/marriage and family therapy (MA); organizational leadership (Ed D).

See Close-Up on page 1077.

Argosy University, Orange County, College of Psychology and Behavioral Sciences, Program in Clinical Psychology, Santa Ana, CA 92704. Offers child and adolescent psychology (Psy D); forensic psychology (Psy D); marriage and family therapy (MA).

See Close-Up on page 1081.

Argosy University, Orange County, College of Psychology and Behavioral Sciences, Program in Counseling Psychology, Santa Ana, CA 92704. Offers counseling psychology (Ed D); marriage and family therapy (MA).

See Close-Up on page 1081.

Argosy University, Salt Lake City, College of Psychology and Behavioral Sciences, Draper, UT 84020. Offers counseling psychology (Ed D); marriage and family therapy (MA).

See Close-Up on page 1085.

Argosy University, San Diego, College of Psychology and Behavioral Sciences, San Diego, CA 92108. Offers clinical psychology/marriage and family therapy (MA); counseling psychology (MA, Ed D); counseling psychology/marriage and family therapy (MA).

See Close-Up on page 1087.

Marriage and Family Therapy

Argosy University, Sarasota, College of Psychology and Behavioral Sciences, Sarasota, FL 34235. Offers community counseling (MA); counseling psychology (Ed D); counselor education and supervision (Ed D); forensic psychology (MA); marriage and family therapy (MA); mental health counseling (MA); organizational leadership (Ed D); pastoral community counseling (Ed D); school counseling (MA, Ed S); school psychology (MA).

See Close-Up on page 1091.

Argosy University, Schaumburg, College of Psychology and Behavioral Sciences, Schaumburg, IL 60173-5403. Offers clinical health psychology (Post-Graduate Certificate); clinical psychology (MA, Psy D), including child and family psychology (Psy D), clinical health psychology (Psy D), diversity and multicultural psychology (Psy D), forensic psychology (Psy D); community counseling (MA); counseling psychology (Ed D), including counselor education and supervision; counselor education and supervision (Ed D); forensic psychology (Post-Graduate Certificate); organizational leadership (Ed D). *Accreditation:* ACA; APA.

See Close-Up on page 1093.

Argosy University, Tampa, College of Psychology and Behavioral Sciences, Program in Clinical Psychology, Tampa, FL 33614. Offers clinical psychology (MA, Psy D), including child and adolescent psychology (Psy D), geropsychology (Psy D), marriage/couples and family therapy (Psy D), neuropsychology (Psy D). *Accreditation:* APA.

See Close-Up on page 1097.

Argosy University, Twin Cities, College of Psychology and Behavioral Sciences, Eagan, MN 55121. Offers clinical psychology (MA, Psy D), including child and family psychology (Psy D), forensic psychology (Psy D), health psychology (Psy D), marriage/couples and family therapy (Psy D), neuropsychology (Psy D); forensic counseling (Post-Graduate Certificate); forensic psychology (MA); marriage and family therapy (MA, DMFT), including forensic counseling (MA); organizational leadership (Ed D). *Accreditation:* APA.

See Close-Up on page 1099.

Argosy University, Washington DC, College of Psychology and Behavioral Sciences, Arlington, VA 22209. Offers clinical psychology (MA, Psy D), including child and family psychology (Psy D), diversity and multicultural psychology (Psy D), forensic psychology (Psy D), health and neuropsychology (Psy D); community counseling (MA); counseling psychology (Ed D), including counselor education and supervision; counselor education and supervision (Ed D); forensic psychology (MA); organizational leadership (Ed D). *Accreditation:* APA.

See Close-Up on page 1101.

Arizona State University, Graduate College, College of Liberal Arts and Sciences, Division of Social Sciences, School of Social and Family Dynamics, Tempe, AZ 85287. Offers family and human development (MS, PhD); infant-family practice (MAS); marriage and family therapy (MAS); sociology (MA, PhD). *Degree requirements:* For master's, thesis or alternative; for doctorate, thesis/dissertation. *Entrance requirements:* For master's and doctorate, GRE.

Azusa Pacific University, School of Behavioral and Applied Sciences, Department of Graduate Psychology, Azusa, CA 91702-7000. Offers clinical psychology (MA, Psy D), including family therapy (MA). *Accreditation:* APA (one or more programs are accredited). Part-time and evening/weekend programs available. *Degree requirements:* For master's, comprehensive exam, 250 hours of clinical experience, individual and group therapy. *Entrance requirements:* For master's, interview, minimum GPA of 3.0, Minnesota Multiphasic Personality Inventory. Additional exam requirements/recommendations for international students: Required—TOEFL (minimum score 600 paper-based).

Barry University, School of Education, Program in Marital, Couple and Family Counseling/Therapy, Miami Shores, FL 33161-6695. Offers MS, Ed S. Part-time and evening/weekend programs available. *Degree requirements:* For master's, comprehensive exam, scholarly paper; for Ed S, comprehensive exam. *Entrance requirements:* For master's, GRE General Test or MAT, minimum GPA of 3.0; for Ed S, GRE General Test, minimum GPA of 3.0. Electronic applications accepted.

Bethel Seminary, Graduate and Professional Programs, St. Paul, MN 55112-6998. Offers applied ministry (MA); biblical studies (MATS, Certificate); children's and family ministry (MACFM); Christian education (MACE); Christian thought (M Div, MACT); church leadership (D Min); community ministry leadership (MA, Certificate); congregation and family care (D Min); global and contextual studies (MA, MATS); historical studies (MATS); lay ministry (Certificate); marriage and family studies (M Div); marriage and family therapy (MAMFT, Certificate); pastoral ministries (M Div); spiritual formation (Certificate); theological studies (MATS, Certificate); transformational leadership (MATL); youth ministries (MACE). *Accreditation:* ACIPE; ATS (one or more programs are accredited). Part-time and evening/weekend programs available. Post-baccalaureate distance learning degree programs offered (minimal on-campus study). *Faculty:* 26 full-time (2 women), 93 part-time/adjunct (29 women). *Students:* 397 full-time (124 women), 707 part-time (299 women); includes 218 minority (123 African Americans, 1 American Indian/Alaska Native, 67 Asian Americans or Pacific Islanders, 27 Hispanic Americans), 14 international. Average age 36. 470 applicants, 90% accepted, 270 enrolled. In 2008, 63 first professional degrees, 101 master's, 10 doctorates awarded. *Degree requirements:* For master's, variable foreign language requirement, thesis (for some programs); for doctorate, thesis/dissertation; for M Div, one foreign language. *Entrance requirements:* For M Div, letters of reference; for master's, letters of reference, transcripts, personal statement; for doctorate, M Div, letters of reference, essays, organizational support. Additional exam requirements/recommendations for international students: Required—TOEFL (minimum score 550 paper-based; 213 computer-based). *Application deadline:* For fall admission, 8/1 priority date for domestic students, 3/1 for international students; for winter admission, 12/1 priority date for domestic students; for spring admission, 3/1 priority date for domestic students. Applications are processed on a rolling basis. Application fee: $20. Electronic applications accepted. *Financial support:* In 2008–09, 688 students received support, including 20 teaching assistantships; career-related internships or fieldwork, Federal Work-Study, scholarships/grants, and tuition waivers (full) also available. Financial award application deadline: 7/15; financial award applicants required to submit FAFSA. *Faculty research:* Nature of theology, ethics, biblical commentaries, nature of God, science and theology. *Unit head:* Dr. Leland Eliason, Executive Vice President and Provost, 651-638-6182. *Application contact:* Joseph V. Dworak, Director of Admissions, 651-638-6288, Fax: 651-638-6002, E-mail: j-dworak@bethel.edu.

Briercrest Seminary, Graduate Programs, Program in Christian Ministries, Caronport, SK S0H 0S0, Canada. Offers leadership (MA); marriage and family counseling (MA); missions (MA); pastoral counseling (MA); worship (MA); youth and family ministry (MA). Part-time programs available. *Degree requirements:* For master's, comprehensive exam, thesis optional. *Entrance requirements:* Additional exam requirements/recommendations for international students: Required—TOEFL (minimum score 550 paper-based; 213 computer-based).

Brigham Young University, Graduate Studies, College of Family, Home, and Social Sciences, Program of Marriage and Family Therapy, Provo, UT 84602. Offers MS, PhD. *Faculty:* 8 full-time (1 woman), 4 part-time/adjunct (2 women). *Students:* 41 full-time (19 women); includes 7 minority (1 African American, 1 American Indian/Alaska Native, 1 Asian American or Pacific Islander, 4 Hispanic Americans), 1 international. Average age 29. 65 applicants, 18% accepted, 11 enrolled. In 2008, 8 master's awarded. *Degree requirements:* For master's, comprehensive exam, thesis; for doctorate, comprehensive exam, thesis/dissertation. *Entrance requirements:* For master's and doctorate, GRE General Test, GRE Writing Test, minimum GPA of 3.0 in last 60 hours of course work. Additional exam requirements/recommendations for international students: Required—TOEFL. *Application deadline:* For fall admission, 12/15 for domestic and international students. Application fee: $50. Electronic applications accepted. *Expenses:* Tuition: Full-time $5160; part-time $287 per credit hour. Tuition and fees vary according to program and student's religious affiliation. *Financial support:* In 2008–09, 38 students received support, including 26 research assistantships with full and partial tuition reimbursements available (averaging $12,900 per year); fellowships, teaching assistantships, career-related internships or fieldwork, scholarships/grants, and tuition waivers (partial) also available. Financial award application deadline: 1/10. *Faculty research:* Therapy process and outcome, preparation for marriage, family relationships across the life cycle, marriage and family therapy, healthcare costs. Total annual research expenditures: $37,018. *Unit head:* Dr. Leslie L. Feinauer, Program Director, 801-422-7750, Fax: 801-422-0163, E-mail: leslie_feinauer@byu.edu. *Application contact:* Linda Kader, Program Secretary, 801-422-5680, Fax: 801-422-0163, E-mail: linda_kader@byu.edu.

California Lutheran University, Graduate Studies, Department of Psychology, Thousand Oaks, CA 91360-2787. Offers clinical psychology (MS); marital and family therapy (MS). Part-time programs available. *Faculty:* 3 full-time (2 women), 12 part-time/adjunct (10 women). *Students:* 129 full-time (110 women), 4 part-time (3 women); includes 31 minority (2 African Americans, 1 American Indian/Alaska Native, 6 Asian Americans or Pacific Islanders, 22 Hispanic Americans), 6 international. Average age 30. 118 applicants, 70% accepted. In 2008, 49 master's awarded. *Degree requirements:* For master's, thesis or comprehensive exams. *Entrance requirements:* For master's, GRE General Test, interview, minimum GPA of 3.0. *Application deadline:* For fall admission, 2/15 priority date for domestic students. Applications are processed on a rolling basis. Application fee: $50. *Financial support:* In 2008–09, 60 students received support. *Unit head:* Dr. Mindy Puopolo, Director, 805-493-3528. *Application contact:* 805-493-3127, Fax: 805-493-3542, E-mail: clugrad@clunet.edu.

California State University, Chico, Graduate School, College of Behavioral and Social Sciences, Department of Psychology, Program in Marriage and Family Therapy, Chico, CA 95929-0722. Offers MS. *Degree requirements:* For master's, thesis or alternative. *Entrance requirements:* For master's, GRE General Test or MAT, 3 letters of recommendation on departmental form, statement of purpose. Additional exam requirements/recommendations for international students: Required—TOEFL (minimum score 550 paper-based; 213 computer-based; 80 iBT), IELTS (minimum score 6.5).

California State University, Dominguez Hills, College of Professional Studies, School of Health and Human Services, Program in Marital and Family Therapy, Carson, CA 90747-0001. Offers MS. Part-time and evening/weekend programs available. *Faculty:* 2 full-time (both women), 3 part-time/adjunct (2 women). *Students:* 78 full-time (62 women), 27 part-time (22 women); includes 66 minority (37 African Americans, 2 Asian Americans or Pacific Islanders, 27 Hispanic Americans), 1 international. Average age 37. 60 applicants, 95% accepted, 38 enrolled. In 2008, 22 master's awarded. *Degree requirements:* For master's, comprehensive exam. *Entrance requirements:* For master's, minimum GPA of 3.0. *Application deadline:* For fall admission, 8/1 for domestic students; for spring admission, 12/15 for domestic students. Applications are processed on a rolling basis. Application fee: $55. Electronic applications accepted. *Expenses:* Tuition, nonresident: part-time $339 per unit. Required fees: $1300 per semester. *Faculty research:* Sociology of the family, clinical psychology theory, employee assistance programs, race and sport, secondary trauma. *Unit head:* Dr. Michele Linden, Coordinator, 310-243-2693, E-mail: mlinden@csudh.edu. *Application contact:* Dr. Gayle Ball-Parker, Director of Admissions, 310-243-3645, E-mail: gball@csudh.edu.

California State University, Fresno, Division of Graduate Studies, School of Education and Human Development, Department of Counseling and Special Education, Program in Marriage and Family Therapy, Fresno, CA 93740-8027. Offers MS. *Accreditation:* ACA. Part-time and evening/weekend programs available. *Degree requirements:* For master's, thesis or alternative. *Entrance requirements:* For master's, GRE General Test, MAT, minimum GPA of 3.0. Additional exam requirements/recommendations for international students: Required—TOEFL. Electronic applications accepted. *Faculty research:* Child abuse prevention, early childhood education.

California State University, Long Beach, Graduate Studies, College of Education, Department of Advanced Studies in Education and Counseling, Master of Science in Counseling Program, Long Beach, CA 90840. Offers marriage and family therapy (MS); school counseling (MS). *Accreditation:* NCATE. *Students:* Average age 32. *Degree requirements:* For master's, comprehensive exam or thesis. *Application deadline:* For fall admission, 3/1 for domestic students. Applications are processed on a rolling basis. Application fee: $55. Electronic applications accepted. *Expenses:* Tuition, nonresident: full-time $11,160; part-time $372 per unit. Required fees: $4100; $1261 per semester. *Financial support:* Federal Work-Study, institutionally sponsored loans, and scholarships/grants available. Financial award application deadline: 3/2. *Unit head:* Dr. Jennifer Coots, Chair, 562-985-4517, Fax: 562-985-4534, E-mail: jcoots@csulb.edu. *Application contact:* Dr. Bita Ghafoori, Assistant Chair, 562-985-7864, Fax: 562-985-4534, E-mail: bghafoor@csulb.edu.

California State University, Northridge, Graduate Studies, College of Education, Department of Educational Psychology and Counseling, Northridge, CA 91330. Offers counseling (MS), including career counseling, college counseling and student services, marriage and family therapy, school counseling, school psychology; educational psychology (MA Ed), including development, learning, and instruction, early childhood education. *Accreditation:* ACA (one or more programs are accredited); NCATE. Part-time and evening/weekend programs available. *Faculty:* 18 full-time (11 women), 40 part-time/adjunct (19 women). *Students:* 334 full-time (297 women), 140 part-time (122 women); includes 24 African Americans, 38 Asian Americans or Pacific Islanders, 156 Hispanic Americans, 14 international. Average age 31. 450 applicants, 36% accepted, 140 enrolled. In 2008, 124 master's awarded. *Entrance requirements:* For master's, GRE General Test or minimum GPA of 3.0. Additional exam requirements/recommendations for international students: Required—TOEFL. *Application deadline:* For fall admission, 11/30 for domestic students. Application fee: $55. *Financial support:* Scholarships/grants available. Support available to part-time students. Financial award application deadline: 3/1. *Unit head:* Dr. Shari Tarver-Behring, Chair, 818-677-2599. *Application contact:* Dr. Shari Tarver-Behring, Chair, 818-677-2599.

Cambridge College, School of Psychology and Counseling, Cambridge, MA 02138-5304. Offers addiction counseling (M Ed); counseling psychology (M Ed); counseling psychology: forensic counseling (M Ed); marriage and family therapy (M Ed); mental health and addiction counseling (M Ed); mental health counseling (M Ed); mental health counseling for school guidance counselors (Certificate); mental health, addiction and school adjustment counseling (M Ed); psychological studies (M Ed); school adjustment counseling (M Ed); school guidance counseling (M Ed). Part-time and evening/weekend programs available. *Faculty:* 5 full-time (2 women), 183 part-time/adjunct (85 women). *Students:* 476 full-time (384 women), 313 part-time (245 women); includes 396 minority (300 African Americans, 2 American Indian/Alaska Native, 13 Asian Americans or Pacific Islanders, 81 Hispanic Americans), 13 international. Average age 37. 307 applicants, 81% accepted, 192 enrolled. In 2008, 226 master's, 9 CAGSs awarded. *Degree requirements:* For master's, thesis, practicum/internship; for other advanced degree, thesis, practicum/Internship. *Entrance requirements:* For master's, evidence of a bachelor's degree from an accredited institution; essay; 2 references; health insurance; for other advanced degree, evidence of a master's degree from an accredited institution; essay; 2 references; health insurance. Additional exam requirements/recommendations for international students: Required—TOEFL (minimum score 550 paper-based; 213 computer-based; 79 iBT). *Application deadline:* Applications are processed on a rolling basis. Application fee: $30. Electronic applications accepted. *Expenses:* Tuition: Full-time $6960; part-time $435 per credit. One-time fee: $140 full-time. Tuition and fees vary according to degree level, campus/location and program. *Financial support:* In 2008–09, 857 students received support. Career-related internships or fieldwork, Federal Work-Study, and scholarships/grants available. Financial award applicants required to submit FAFSA. *Unit head:* Dr. Niti Seth, EdD, Dean, 617-873-0208, Fax: 617-349-3545, E-mail: nseth@cambridgecollege.edu. *Application contact:* Kathryn Lenehan, Admission Counselor, 800-877-0280, E-mail: kathryn.lenehan@cambridgecollege.edu.

Capella University, School of Human Services, Minneapolis, MN 55402. Offers addictions counseling (Certificate); counseling studies (MS, PhD); criminal justice (MS, PhD, Certificate); diversity studies (Certificate); general human services (MS, PhD); health care administration

(MS, PhD, Certificate); management of nonprofit agencies (MS, PhD, Certificate); marital, couple and family counseling/therapy (MS); marriage and family services (Certificate); mental health counseling (MS); professional counseling (Certificate); social and community services (MS, PhD, Certificate). Part-time and evening/weekend programs available. Postbaccalaureate distance learning degree programs offered (minimal on-campus study). Terminal master's awarded for partial completion of doctoral program. *Degree requirements:* For master's, thesis optional, integrative project; for doctorate, comprehensive exam, thesis/dissertation. *Entrance requirements:* Additional exam requirements/recommendations for international students: Required—TOEFL (minimum score 550 paper-based; 213 computer-based), TWE (minimum score 4). Electronic applications accepted. *Faculty research:* Compulsive and addictive behaviors, substance abuse, assessment of psychopathology and neuropsychology.

Carlos Albizu University, Miami Campus, Graduate Programs, Miami, FL 33172-2209. Offers clinical psychology (Psy D); entrepreneurship (MBA); exceptional student education (MS); industrial/organizational psychology (MS); marriage and family therapy (MS); mental health counseling (MS); nonprofit management (MBA); organizational management (MBA); psychology (MS); school counseling (MS); teaching English as a second language (MS). *Accreditation:* APA. Part-time and evening/weekend programs available. *Faculty:* 19 full-time (12 women), 70 part-time/adjunct (35 women). *Students:* 498 full-time (409 women), 199 part-time (153 women); includes 515 minority (56 African Americans, 1 American Indian/Alaska Native, 7 Asian Americans or Pacific Islanders, 451 Hispanic Americans). Average age 33. 179 applicants, 67% accepted, 113 enrolled. In 2008, 185 master's, 21 doctorates awarded. Terminal master's awarded for partial completion of doctoral program. *Degree requirements:* For master's, one foreign language, comprehensive exam, integrative project (MBA), research project (MSESE and MSTESOL); for doctorate, one foreign language, comprehensive exam, internship, doctoral project. *Entrance requirements:* For master's, 3 letters of recommendation, interview, minimum GPA of 3.0, resumé, statement of purpose, official transcripts; for doctorate, 3 letters of recommendation, minimum GPA of 3.0, resumé, interview. *Application deadline:* For fall admission, 8/1 priority date for domestic students; for spring admission, 11/30 priority date for domestic students. Applications are processed on a rolling basis. Application fee: $50. Electronic applications accepted. *Expenses:* Tuition: Full-time $9090; part-time $505 per credit. Required fees: $298 per term. Tuition and fees vary according to course load, degree level and program. *Financial support:* In 2008–09, 111 students received support. Federal Work-Study, scholarships/grants, and tuition discounts available. Financial award application deadline: 6/1; financial award applicants required to submit FAFSA. *Faculty research:* Psychotherapy, forensic psychology, neuropsychology, marketing strategy, entrepreneurship, special education. *Unit head:* Dr. Carmen S. Roca, PhD, Chancellor, 305-593-1223 Ext. 120, Fax: 305-629-8052, E-mail: croca@albizu.edu. *Application contact:* Barbara De la Cruz, Admission Officer, 305-593-1223 Ext. 218, Fax: 305-593-1854, E-mail: bdelacruz@albizu.edu.

Central Connecticut State University, School of Graduate Studies, School of Education and Professional Studies, Department of Counseling and Family Therapy, New Britain, CT 06050-4010. Offers marriage and family therapy (MS); professional counseling (MS, Certificate); school counseling (MS); student development in higher education (MS). *Accreditation:* AAMFT/COAMFTE. Part-time and evening/weekend programs available. *Faculty:* 7 full-time (4 women), 12 part-time/adjunct (9 women). *Students:* 109 full-time (93 women), 187 part-time (151 women); includes 47 minority (24 African Americans, 2 American Indian/Alaska Native, 2 Asian Americans or Pacific Islanders, 19 Hispanic Americans), 3 international. Average age 35. 245 applicants, 47% accepted, 92 enrolled. In 2008, 67 master's, 1 other advanced degree awarded. *Degree requirements:* For master's, comprehensive exam, thesis or alternative. *Entrance requirements:* For master's, minimum undergraduate GPA of 2.7, essay. Additional exam requirements/recommendations for international students: Required—TOEFL. *Application deadline:* For fall admission, 5/1 for domestic students. Applications are processed on a rolling basis. Application fee: $50. Electronic applications accepted. *Expenses:* Tuition, area resident: Full-time $4377; part-time $420 per credit. Tuition, state resident: full-time $6566; part-time $420 per credit. Tuition, nonresident: full-time $12,195; part-time $420 per credit. Required fees: $3462. One-time fee: $62 part-time. *Financial support:* In 2008–09, 36 students received support, including 22 research assistantships; career-related internships or fieldwork, Federal Work-Study, scholarships/grants, and unspecified assistantships also available. Support available to part-time students. Financial award application deadline: 3/1; financial award applicants required to submit FAFSA. *Faculty research:* Elementary/secondary school counseling, marriage/family therapy, rehabilitation counseling, counseling in higher educational settings. *Unit head:* Dr. Connie Tait, Chair, 860-832-2154. *Application contact:* Dr. Connie Tait, Chair, 860-832-2154.

Chapman University, Graduate Studies, Schmid College of Science, Department of Psychology, Orange, CA 92866. Offers marriage and family therapy (MA). Part-time and evening/weekend programs available. *Faculty:* 13 full-time (5 women), 3 part-time/adjunct (2 women). *Students:* 31 full-time (28 women), 27 part-time (22 women); includes 15 minority (2 African Americans, 7 Asian Americans or Pacific Islanders, 6 Hispanic Americans), 5 international. Average age 29. 70 applicants, 43% accepted, 16 enrolled. In 2008, 20 master's awarded. *Degree requirements:* For master's, comprehensive exam, thesis optional. *Entrance requirements:* For master's, GRE, minimum undergraduate GPA of 2.5. Additional exam requirements/recommendations for international students: Required—TOEFL (minimum score 550 paper-based; 213 computer-based; 80 iBT). *Application deadline:* For fall admission, 3/1 for domestic students; for spring admission, 11/1 for domestic students. Application fee: $50. Electronic applications accepted. *Expenses:* Contact institution. *Financial support:* Fellowships, Federal Work-Study and scholarships/grants available. Financial award application deadline: 6/30; financial award applicants required to submit FAFSA. *Unit head:* Dr. Georg Eifert, Chair, 714-997-6776, E-mail: eifert@chapman.edu. *Application contact:* Susan Read-Weil, Coordinator, 714-744-7837, E-mail: sreadwei@chapman.edu.

Chatham University, Program in Counseling Psychology, Pittsburgh, PA 15232-2826. Offers child, adolescent and family (MSCP); counseling psychology (Psy D); health and holistic (MSCP); infant mental health (MSCP); organization and supervision (MSCP); sport and exercise (MSCP). Part-time and evening/weekend programs available. *Students:* 121 full-time (104 women), 72 part-time (63 women). Average age 30. 117 applicants, 79% accepted, 60 enrolled. In 2008, 63 master's awarded. *Degree requirements:* For master's, thesis optional, supervised internship, advanced research project (optional); for doctorate, thesis/dissertation, internship. *Entrance requirements:* For master's, minimum GPA of 3.0; 2 letters of recommendation; resumé; prerequisite coursework in statistics, biology, and psychology; for doctorate, GRE. Additional exam requirements/recommendations for international students: Required—TOEFL (minimum score 600 paper-based; 250 computer-based; 100 iBT), IELTS (minimum score 6.5), TWE. *Application deadline:* For fall admission, 5/1 priority date for domestic and international students; for spring admission, 10/15 for domestic students, 10/15 priority date for international students. Applications are processed on a rolling basis. Application fee: $45. Electronic applications accepted. *Expenses:* Tuition: Part-time $686 per credit. Tuition and fees vary according to program. *Financial support:* Career-related internships or fieldwork available. Financial award applicants required to submit FAFSA. *Faculty research:* Trauma and recovery, hypnosis, psychospiritual dimensions of healing, psychotherapy of schizophrenia. *Unit head:* Dr. Mary Beth Mannarino, Director, 412-365-1196, Fax: 412-365-1505, E-mail: mmannarino@chatham.edu. *Application contact:* Dory Perry, Associate Director of Graduate Admissions, 412-365-2758, Fax: 412-365-1609, E-mail: gradadmissions@chatham.edu.

The Chicago School of Professional Psychology, Graduate School, Program in Marital and Family Therapy, Chicago, IL 60610. Offers MA, Psy D. Part-time programs available.

Christian Theological Seminary, Graduate and Professional Programs, Indianapolis, IN 46208-3301. Offers marriage and family (MA); pastoral care and counseling (D Min); practical theology (D Min); psychotherapy and faith (MA); sacred theology (STM); specialized ministries (MA); theological studies (MTS); theology (M Div). *Accreditation:* AAMFT/COAMFTE (one or more programs are accredited); ACIPE; ATS. Part-time programs available. Terminal master's awarded for partial completion of doctoral program. *Degree requirements:* For master's,

comprehensive exam (for some programs), thesis (for some programs); for doctorate, comprehensive exam, thesis/dissertation; for M Div, comprehensive exam, thesis/dissertation (for some programs), missionary and cross-cultural experience. *Entrance requirements:* For master's, GRE General Test, MAT; for doctorate, M Div or BD. Electronic applications accepted. *Faculty research:* Faith formation, peer learning post graduation.

The College of New Jersey, Graduate Division, School of Education, Department of Counselor Education, Program in Marriage and Family Therapy, Ewing, NJ 08628. Offers Ed S. Part-time and evening/weekend programs available. *Entrance requirements:* For degree, GRE, minimum GPA of 3.0 in field or 2.75 overall. Additional exam requirements/recommendations for international students: Required—TOEFL. Electronic applications accepted.

The College of William and Mary, School of Education, Program in Counselor Education, Williamsburg, VA 23187-8795. Offers community and addictions counseling (M Ed); community counseling (M Ed); counselor education (PhD); family counseling (M Ed); school counseling (M Ed). *Accreditation:* ACA; NCATE. Part-time and evening/weekend programs available. *Degree requirements:* For doctorate, comprehensive exam, thesis/dissertation. *Entrance requirements:* For master's, GRE, minimum GPA of 2.5; for doctorate, GRE, minimum GPA of 3.5. Additional exam requirements/recommendations for international students: Required—TOEFL. Electronic applications accepted. *Expenses:* Tuition, state resident: full-time $6400; part-time $300 per credit hour. Tuition, nonresident: full-time $19,720; part-time $800 per credit hour. International tuition: $19,720 full-time. Required fees: $3860. *Faculty research:* Sexuality, multicultural education, substance abuse, transpersonal psychology.

Converse College, School of Education and Graduate Studies, Education Specialist Program, Spartanburg, SC 29302-0006. Offers administration and supervision (Ed S); curriculum and instruction (Ed S); marriage and family therapy (Ed S). *Accreditation:* AAMFT/COAMFTE. Part-time programs available. *Entrance requirements:* For degree, GRE or MAT (marriage and family therapy), minimum GPA of 3.0. Electronic applications accepted.

Denver Seminary, Graduate and Professional Programs, Littleton, CO 80120. Offers apologetics (Certificate); biblical studies (MA); Christian formation and soul care (MA, Certificate); Christian studies (MA, Certificate); church and parachurch leadership (D Min); counseling licensure (MA); counseling ministry (MA); intercultural ministry (Certificate); leadership (MA, Certificate); marriage and family counseling (D Min); pastoral ministry (D Min); philosophy of religion (MA); spiritual guidance (Certificate); theology (M Div, Certificate); worship (Certificate); youth and family ministry (MA). *Accreditation:* ACA; ACIPE; ATS (one or more programs are accredited). Part-time and evening/weekend programs available. Postbaccalaureate distance learning degree programs offered. *Degree requirements:* For master's, 2 foreign languages, thesis (for some programs); for doctorate, 2 foreign languages, thesis/dissertation; for M Div, 2 foreign languages. *Entrance requirements:* For M Div, minimum undergraduate GPA of 2.5; for master's, minimum undergraduate GPA of 3.0; for doctorate, M Div, 3 years of ministry experience. Additional exam requirements/recommendations for international students: Required—TOEFL (minimum score 575 paper-based; 233 computer-based; 90 iBT). Electronic applications accepted.

Dominican University of California, Graduate Programs, School of Arts and Sciences, Program in Counseling Psychology, San Rafael, CA 94901-2298. Offers MFT, MS. Part-time programs available. *Faculty:* 4 full-time (3 women), 11 part-time/adjunct (10 women). *Students:* 50 full-time (44 women), 49 part-time (44 women); includes 15 minority (5 African Americans, 1 Asian American or Pacific Islander, 9 Hispanic Americans). Average age 40. 13 applicants, 77% accepted, 7 enrolled. In 2008, 21 master's awarded. *Degree requirements:* For master's, comprehensive exam (for some programs), thesis (for some programs). *Entrance requirements:* For master's, minimum GPA of 3.0 for last 60 units. Additional exam requirements/recommendations for international students: Required—TOEFL (minimum score 550 paper-based; 213 computer-based). *Application deadline:* For fall admission, 6/15 priority date for domestic and international students; for spring admission, 11/15 priority date for domestic and international students. Applications are processed on a rolling basis. Application fee: $40. Electronic applications accepted. *Expenses:* Contact institution. *Financial support:* In 2008–09, 28 students received support, including fellowships (averaging $2,554 per year); career-related internships or fieldwork, scholarships/grants, traineeships, health care benefits, tuition waivers (partial), and tuition discounts also available. Support available to part-time students. Financial award application deadline: 7/1; financial award applicants required to submit FAFSA. *Unit head:* Dr. Charles R. Billings, Chair of the Graduate Department of Counseling Psychology, 415-485-3263. *Application contact:* Larry Schwartz, Associate Director of Graduate Admissions, 415-458-3748, E-mail: lawrence.schwartz@dominican.edu.

Drexel University, College of Nursing and Health Professions, Program in Couples and Family Therapy, Philadelphia, PA 19104-2875. Offers couples and family therapy (PhD); family therapy (MFT). *Accreditation:* AAMFT/COAMFTE (one or more programs are accredited). Part-time programs available. Terminal master's awarded for partial completion of doctoral program. *Degree requirements:* For master's, comprehensive exam, thesis; for doctorate, thesis/dissertation, qualifying exam. *Entrance requirements:* For master's, GRE General Test or MAT, minimum GPA of 2.75; for doctorate, GRE General Test, minimum GPA of 3.0. Electronic applications accepted. *Faculty research:* Family assessment, gender issues, chronic illness, early intervention.

East Carolina University, Graduate School, College of Human Ecology, Department of Child Development and Family Relations, Greenville, NC 27858-4353. Offers child development and family relations (MS); marriage and family therapy (MS). *Accreditation:* AAMFT/COAMFTE. Part-time programs available. *Degree requirements:* For master's, comprehensive exam, thesis optional. *Faculty research:* Child care quality, mental health delivery systems for children, family violence.

Eastern Nazarene College, Adult and Graduate Studies, Program in Family Counseling, Quincy, MA 02170-2999. Offers marriage and family therapy (MS). Part-time and evening/weekend programs available. *Entrance requirements:* For master's, 3 letters of recommendation, resumé. Additional exam requirements/recommendations for international students: Required—TOEFL (minimum score 550 paper-based).

Eastern University, Palmer Theological Seminary, Program in Ministry, St. Davids, PA 19087-3696. Offers marriage and family (D Min). *Accreditation:* ACIPE. Part-time programs available. *Degree requirements:* For doctorate, thesis/dissertation. *Entrance requirements:* For doctorate, 3 years of experience, involvement in ministry, church endorsement. *Expenses:* Contact institution.

East Tennessee State University, School of Graduate Studies, College of Education, Department of Human Development and Learning, Johnson City, TN 37614. Offers advanced practitioner (M Ed); community agency counseling (M Ed, MA); comprehensive concentration (M Ed); counseling (M Ed, MA); early childhood education (M Ed, MA); early childhood general (M Ed); early childhood special education (M Ed); early childhood teaching (M Ed); elementary and secondary (school counseling) (M Ed, MA); marriage and family therapy (M Ed, MA); modified concentration (M Ed). *Accreditation:* ACA; NCATE. Part-time programs available. *Degree requirements:* For master's, comprehensive exam, thesis (for some programs). *Entrance requirements:* For master's, GRE General Test, minimum GPA of 3.0. Additional exam requirements/recommendations for international students: Required—TOEFL (minimum score 550 paper-based; 213 computer-based). *Faculty research:* Drug and alcohol abuse, marriage and family counseling, severe mental retardation, parenting of children with disabilities.

Edgewood College, Program in Marriage and Family Therapy, Madison, WI 53711-1997. Offers MS. Part-time and evening/weekend programs available. *Students:* 13 full-time (10 women), 17 part-time (14 women); includes 3 minority (2 African Americans, 1 Hispanic American). Average age 32. In 2008, 15 master's awarded. *Degree requirements:* For master's, research project. *Entrance requirements:* For master's, minimum GPA of 2.75, 2 letters of reference, personal statement, interviews. Additional exam requirements/recommendations for international students: Required—TOEFL (minimum score 213 computer-based). *Application*

Marriage and Family Therapy

Edgewood College (continued)

deadline: For fall admission, 3/1 for domestic students. Application fee: $25. Electronic applications accepted. *Expenses:* Tuition: Part-time $655 per credit. *Unit head:* Dr. Peter Fabian, Director, 608-663-2233, Fax: 608-663-3291, E-mail: fabian@edgewood.edu. *Application contact:* Paula O'Malley, Director of Graduate and Professional Studies, 608-663-2217, Fax: 608-663-3496, E-mail: gps@edgewood.edu.

Evangelical Theological Seminary, Graduate and Professional Programs, Myerstown, PA 17067-1212. Offers divinity (M Div); marriage and family therapy (MA); ministry (Certificate); religion (MA). *Accreditation:* ATS (one or more programs are accredited). Part-time programs available. Postbaccalaureate distance learning degree programs offered (minimal on-campus study). *Degree requirements:* For master's, 2 foreign languages; for M Div, 2 foreign languages, ministry internship. *Entrance requirements:* For M Div and master's, minimum GPA of 2.5. Additional exam requirements/recommendations for international students: Required—TOEFL (minimum score 550 paper-based; 213 computer-based). *Faculty research:* Literary form and structure within the Hebrew and Greek scriptures, Wesley studies, esoteric biblical languages, the Mosaic law and the Christian, ethics.

Fairfield University, Graduate School of Education and Allied Professions, Department of Marriage and Family Therapy, Fairfield, CT 06824-5195. Offers MA. *Accreditation:* AAMFT/COAMFTE. Part-time and evening/weekend programs available. *Faculty:* 3 full-time (all women), 5 part-time/adjunct (3 women). *Students:* 21 full-time (20 women), 45 part-time (39 women); includes 1 African American, 3 Hispanic Americans. Average age 39. 35 applicants, 54% accepted, 9 enrolled. In 2008, 17 master's awarded. *Degree requirements:* For master's, comprehensive exam. *Entrance requirements:* For master's, minimum QPA of 3.0, 2 recommendations, resumé, essay. Additional exam requirements/recommendations for international students: Required—TOEFL (minimum score 550 paper-based; 213 computer-based; 80 iBT). *Application deadline:* For fall admission, 4/15 for domestic and international students; for spring admission, 10/1 for domestic and international students. Application fee: $60. Electronic applications accepted. *Expenses:* Tuition: Full-time $9450; part-time $525 per credit hour. Required fees: $25 per semester. Tuition and fees vary according to course load and program. *Financial support:* Unspecified assistantships available. Financial award applicants required to submit FAFSA. *Faculty research:* Diversity and multiculturalism, accreditation, professional ethics, program development and alumni engagement, international family therapy. *Unit head:* Dr. Rona Preli, Chair, 203-254-4000 Ext. 2475, Fax: 203-254-4047, E-mail: rpreli@fairfield.edu. *Application contact:* Marianne Gumpper, Director of Graduate and Continuing Studies Admissions, 203-254-4184, Fax: 203-254-4073, E-mail: gradadmis@fairfield.edu.

Fitchburg State College, Division of Graduate and Continuing Education, Programs in Counseling, Fitchburg, MA 01420-2697. Offers elementary school guidance counseling (MS); marriage and family therapy (Certificate); mental health counseling (MS); secondary school guidance counseling (MS). *Accreditation:* NCATE. Part-time and evening/weekend programs available. *Students:* 18 full-time (16 women), 69 part-time (61 women); includes 6 minority (1 African American, 1 American Indian/Alaska Native, 4 Hispanic Americans), 2 international. Average age 31. 14 applicants, 100% accepted, 12 enrolled. In 2008, 23 master's awarded. *Entrance requirements:* For master's, GRE General Test or MAT, letters of recommendation, resumé; for Certificate, master's degree. Additional exam requirements/recommendations for international students: Required—TOEFL (minimum score 550 paper-based; 213 computer-based; 79 iBT). *Application deadline:* Applications are processed on a rolling basis. Application fee: $25 ($50 for international students). *Expenses:* Tuition, state resident: full-time $3600; part-time $150 per credit. Tuition, nonresident: full-time $3600; part-time $150 per credit. Required fees: $109 per credit. *Financial support:* In 2008–09, research assistantships with partial tuition reimbursements (averaging $5,500 per year); Federal Work-Study, scholarships/grants, and unspecified assistantships also available. Support available to part-time students. Financial award application deadline: 3/1; financial award applicants required to submit FAFSA. *Unit head:* Dr. John Hancock, Chair, 978-665-3604, Fax: 978-665-3658, E-mail: gce@fsc.edu. *Application contact:* Director of Admissions, 978-665-3144, Fax: 978-665-4540, E-mail: admissions@fsc.edu.

Florida Atlantic University, College of Education, Department of Counselor Education, Boca Raton, FL 33431-0991. Offers counselor education (M Ed, PhD, Ed S); marriage and family therapy (Ed S); mental health counseling (M Ed, Ed S); rehabilitation counseling (M Ed); school counseling (M Ed, Ed S). *Accreditation:* ACA; NCATE. Part-time and evening/weekend programs available. *Faculty:* 7 full-time (2 women), 6 part-time/adjunct (5 women). *Students:* 59 full-time (50 women), 97 part-time (84 women); includes 53 minority (18 African Americans, 3 Asian Americans or Pacific Islanders, 32 Hispanic Americans), 2 international. Average age 35. 135 applicants, 42% accepted, 39 enrolled. In 2008, 46 master's awarded. *Degree requirements:* For Ed S, departmental qualifying exam. *Entrance requirements:* For master's, GRE General Test, minimum GPA of 3.0 during previous 2 years; for Ed S, GRE General Test, minimum graduate GPA of 3.25. Additional exam requirements/recommendations for international students: Required—TOEFL. *Application deadline:* For fall admission, 3/1 for domestic students, 2/1 for international students; for spring admission, 9/15 for domestic students, 7/1 for international students. Applications are processed on a rolling basis. Application fee: $30. *Expenses:* Tuition, state resident: full-time $4867; part-time $270.40 per credit hour. Tuition, nonresident: full-time $16,486; part-time $915.87 per credit hour. *Financial support:* Research assistantships with partial tuition reimbursements, teaching assistantships, career-related internships or fieldwork, scholarships/grants, and unspecified assistantships available. *Faculty research:* Brief therapy, psychological type, marriage and family counseling, international programs, integrated services. *Unit head:* Dr. Irene Johnson, Chair, 561-297-2136, Fax: 561-297-2309. *Application contact:* Susan Foley, Senior Secretary, 561-297-3602, Fax: 561-297-2309, E-mail: cnslred@fau.edu.

Florida State University, Graduate Studies, College of Human Sciences, Department of Family and Child Sciences, Tallahassee, FL 32306. Offers child development (MS, PhD); family relations (MS, PhD); marriage and family therapy (PhD). *Accreditation:* AAMFT/COAMFTE. Part-time programs available. *Degree requirements:* For master's, comprehensive exam, thesis optional; for doctorate, thesis/dissertation. *Entrance requirements:* For master's and doctorate, GRE General Test, minimum GPA of 3.0. Additional exam requirements/recommendations for international students: Required—TOEFL (minimum score 80 iBT). Electronic applications accepted. *Faculty research:* Addictions, family therapy, sexuality, parent-child relations, adolescent development.

Friends University, Graduate School, Division of Science, Arts, and Education, Program in Family Therapy, Wichita, KS 67213. Offers MSFT. *Accreditation:* AAMFT/COAMFTE. Evening/weekend programs available. *Entrance requirements:* Additional exam requirements/recommendations for international students: Required—TOEFL (minimum score 560 paper-based; 220 computer-based). Electronic applications accepted.

Fuller Theological Seminary, Graduate School of Psychology, Department of Marriage and Family Therapy, Pasadena, CA 91182. Offers family studies (MA); marital and family therapy (MS); marriage and family enrichment (Certificate). *Degree requirements:* For master's, practicum. *Entrance requirements:* For master's, GRE General Test. Additional exam requirements/recommendations for international students: Required—TOEFL. *Expenses:* Contact institution. *Faculty research:* Marital intimacy, sex-roles, psychoanalytical theory, men's issues.

Geneva College, Program in Counseling, Beaver Falls, PA 15010-3599. Offers marriage and family (MA); mental health (MA); school counseling (MA). *Accreditation:* ACA. Part-time and evening/weekend programs available. *Degree requirements:* For master's, internship. *Entrance requirements:* For master's, GRE General Test or MAT, minimum GPA of 3.0, letters of recommendation, faith statement, 12 credits in undergraduate psychology. Additional exam requirements/recommendations for international students: Required—TOEFL. Electronic applications accepted.

George Fox University, School of Education, Graduate Department of Counseling, Newberg, OR 97132-2697. Offers counseling (MA); marriage and family therapy (MA, Certificate); mental health trauma (Certificate); school counseling (MA, Certificate); school psychology (Certificate, Ed S). Part-time programs available. *Faculty:* 10 full-time (3 women), 7 part-time/adjunct (5 women). *Students:* 80 full-time (66 women), 147 part-time (117 women); includes 20 minority (6 African Americans, 3 American Indian/Alaska Native, 4 Asian Americans or Pacific Islanders, 7 Hispanic Americans). Average age 35. 89 applicants, 75% accepted, 53 enrolled. In 2008, 61 master's awarded. *Entrance requirements:* For master's, MAT or GRE. Additional exam requirements/recommendations for international students: Required—TOEFL (minimum score 550 paper-based; 213 computer-based; 80 iBT). *Application deadline:* For fall admission, 5/30 for domestic students; for winter admission, 11/1 for domestic students; for spring admission, 2/28 for domestic students. Applications are processed on a rolling basis. Application fee: $40. Electronic applications accepted. *Expenses:* Contact institution. *Financial support:* Career-related internships or fieldwork available. *Unit head:* Dr. Richard Shaw, Associate Professor of Marriage and Family Therapy/Chair, 503-554-6142, E-mail: rshaw@georgefox.edu. *Application contact:* Carol Namburi, Admissions Counselor, 800-631-0921, Fax: 503-554-6111, E-mail: counseling@georgefox.edu.

Harding University, College of Bible and Religion, Program in Marriage and Family Therapy, Searcy, AR 72149-0001. Offers marriage and family therapy (MS); mental health counseling (MS). Part-time programs available. *Faculty:* 4 full-time (0 women), 4 part-time/adjunct (2 women). *Students:* 24 full-time (10 women), 1 (woman) part-time; includes 1 minority (African American). Average age 27. 20 applicants, 85% accepted, 15 enrolled. In 2008, 12 master's awarded. *Degree requirements:* For master's, comprehensive exam, 15-month practicum. *Entrance requirements:* For master's, GRE General Test, minimum undergraduate GPA of 2.75, graduate 3.0. *Application deadline:* For fall admission, 4/1 priority date for domestic students. Applications are processed on a rolling basis. Application fee: $25. *Expenses:* Tuition: Full-time $9360; part-time $520 per credit hour. Required fees: $21 per credit hour. Tuition and fees vary according to course load and program. *Financial support:* In 2008–09, 8 students received support. Career-related internships or fieldwork, Federal Work-Study, and scholarships/grants available. *Faculty research:* Forgiveness, substance abuse, PTSD. *Unit head:* Dr. Lewis L. Moore, Chairman, 501-279-4347, Fax: 501-279-4417, E-mail: lmoore@harding.edu. *Application contact:* Ruth Ann Dawson, Office Manager, 501-279-4347, Fax: 501-279-4417, E-mail: radawson@harding.edu.

Hardin-Simmons University, Graduate School, Cynthia Ann Parker College of Liberal Arts, Department of Psychology, Program in Family Psychology, Abilene, TX 79698-0001. Offers MA. Part-time programs available. *Faculty:* 5 full-time (1 woman). *Students:* 14 full-time (7 women), 8 part-time (6 women); includes 5 minority (2 African Americans, 3 Hispanic Americans). Average age 26. 12 applicants, 58% accepted, 7 enrolled. In 2008, 8 master's awarded. *Degree requirements:* For master's, comprehensive exam, clinical experience, project. *Entrance requirements:* For master's, minimum undergraduate GPA of 3.0 in major, 2.7 overall; 21 semester hours of course work in psychology, 18 of those in upper division classes; writing sample; letters of recommendation. Additional exam requirements/recommendations for international students: Required—TOEFL (minimum score 550 paper-based; 213 computer-based; 75 iBT). *Application deadline:* For fall admission, 8/15 priority date for domestic students, 4/1 for international students; for spring admission, 1/5 priority date for domestic students, 9/1 for international students. Applications are processed on a rolling basis. Application fee: $50. *Expenses:* Tuition: Full-time $10,620; part-time $590 per credit hour. Required fees: $590; $110 per semester. Tuition and fees vary according to course load and degree level. *Financial support:* In 2008–09, 22 students received support, including 13 fellowships (averaging $1,154 per year); career-related internships or fieldwork and scholarships/grants also available. Support available to part-time students. Financial award application deadline: 6/30; financial award applicants required to submit FAFSA. *Faculty research:* Family stress management, spirituality in marriage, intimacy and sexuality in marriage, sex education in the church, role of faith in marital satisfaction. *Unit head:* Dr. Sue Lucas, Director, 325-670-1538, Fax: 325-670-1458, E-mail: slucas@hsutx.edu. *Application contact:* Dr. Gary Stanlake, Dean of Graduate Studies, 325-670-1298, Fax: 325-670-1564, E-mail: gradoff@hsutx.edu.

Hofstra University, School of Education, Health, and Human Services, Department of Health Professions and Family Studies, Program in Marriage and Family Therapy, Hempstead, NY 11549. Offers MA. Part-time programs available. *Students:* 42 full-time (38 women), 20 part-time (16 women); includes 12 minority (7 African Americans, 5 Hispanic Americans), 1 international. Average age 26. 55 applicants, 82% accepted, 22 enrolled. In 2008, 11 master's awarded. *Degree requirements:* For master's, comprehensive exam, internship, clinic hours. *Entrance requirements:* For master's, GRE General Test, interview, letters of recommendation. Additional exam requirements/recommendations for international students: Required—TOEFL (minimum score 550 paper-based; 213 computer-based; 80 iBT). *Application deadline:* Applications are processed on a rolling basis. Application fee: $60. Electronic applications accepted. *Expenses:* Tuition: Full-time $15,300; part-time $850 per credit. Required fees: $970; $165 per term. Tuition and fees vary according to program. *Financial support:* In 2008–09, 17 students received support, including 2 fellowships with full and partial tuition reimbursements available (averaging $3,000 per year), 3 research assistantships with full and partial tuition reimbursements available (averaging $11,826 per year); career-related internships or fieldwork, Federal Work-Study, institutionally sponsored loans, scholarships/grants, tuition waivers (full and partial), and unspecified assistantships also available. Support available to part-time students. Financial award applicants required to submit FAFSA. *Faculty research:* Marriage and family therapy, addiction studies, divorce mediation, human sexuality, post hysterectomy experiences and sexuality. *Unit head:* Prof. George M. Simon, Program Director, 516-463-4622, E-mail: George.Simon@hofstra.edu. *Application contact:* Carol Drummer, Dean of Graduate Admissions, 516-463-4876, Fax: 516-463-4664, E-mail: gradstudent@hofstra.edu.

Hope International University, School of Graduate Studies, Program in Marriage and Family Therapy, Fullerton, CA 92831-3138. Offers MA, MFT. *Degree requirements:* For master's, comprehensive exam, thesis (for some programs), final exam, practicum. *Entrance requirements:* For master's, minimum GPA of 3.0, comprehensive career statement, interview, bachelor's degree, official transcripts, application, 2 references. Additional exam requirements/recommendations for international students: Required—TOEFL (minimum score 550 paper-based; 213 computer-based; 86 iBT); Recommended—IELTS (minimum score 6.5). Electronic applications accepted. *Expenses:* Contact institution.

Idaho State University, Office of Graduate Studies, Kasiska College of Health Professions, Department of Counseling, Pocatello, ID 83209. Offers counseling (M Coun, Ed S), including marriage and family counseling (M Coun), mental health counseling (M Coun), school counseling (M Coun), student affairs and college counseling (M Coun); counselor education and counseling (PhD). *Accreditation:* ACA (one or more programs are accredited). Part-time programs available. *Faculty:* 7 full-time (4 women). *Students:* 72 full-time (50 women), 26 part-time (18 women); includes 7 minority (2 African Americans, 1 American Indian/Alaska Native, 1 Asian American or Pacific Islander, 3 Hispanic Americans), 1 international. Average age 34. In 2008, 28 master's, 7 doctorates, 1 other advanced degree awarded. *Degree requirements:* For master's, comprehensive exam, thesis; for doctorate, comprehensive exam, thesis/dissertation, internship; for Ed S, comprehensive exam, thesis, case studies, oral exam. *Entrance requirements:* For master's, GRE General Test, MAT, minimum GPA of 3.0; for doctorate, GRE General Test, MAT, minimum graduate GPA of 3.0, resumé, interview, counseling license; for Ed S, GRE General Test, minimum graduate GPA of 3.0, master's degree in counseling, 3 letters of recommendation, 2 years work experience. Additional exam requirements/recommendations for international students: Required—TOEFL (minimum score 600 paper-based; 213 computer-based; 80 iBT). *Application deadline:* For fall admission, 7/1 for domestic students, 6/1 for international students; for spring admission, 12/1 for domestic students, 11/1 for international students. Applications are processed on a rolling basis. Application fee: $55. Electronic applications accepted. *Expenses:* Tuition, area resident: Full-time $3114; part-time $276 per credit hour. Tuition, state resident: full-time $3114; part-time $276 per credit hour. Tuition, nonresident: full-time $12,318; part-time $404 per credit hour. Required fees: $2360. Tuition and fees vary according to course load and reciprocity agreements. *Financial support:* In 2008–09, 13 teaching assistantships with full and partial tuition reimbursements (averaging $9,401 per year) were awarded; career-related internships or fieldwork, Federal Work-Study, institutionally sponsored loans, scholarships/grants, traineeships, health care benefits, tuition waivers (full and partial), and unspecified assistantships also available. Support available to part-time students. Financial award application deadline: 1/1; financial award applicants required to submit FAFSA. *Faculty research:* Group counseling, multicultural counseling, family counseling, child therapy, supervision. *Unit head:* Dr. Stephen Feit, Chair, 208-282-3663, Fax: 208-282-2583, E-mail: feitstep@isu.edu. *Application contact:* Ellen Combs, Graduate School Technical Records Specialist, 208-282-2150, Fax: 208-282-4847, E-mail: combelle@isu.edu.

Indiana Wesleyan University, College of Graduate Studies, Graduate Studies in Counseling, Marion, IN 46953. Offers addictions counseling (MS); community counseling (MS); marriage and family counseling (MS); school counseling (MS). *Accreditation:* ACA. Part-time programs available. *Faculty:* 7 full-time (4 women), 6 part-time/adjunct (3 women). *Students:* 60 full-time (46 women), 47 part-time (38 women); includes 4 minority (all African Americans). Average age 36. In 2008, 26 master's awarded. *Degree requirements:* For master's, thesis or alternative. *Entrance requirements:* For master's, GRE General Test. Additional exam requirements/recommendations for international students: Required—TOEFL. *Application deadline:* For fall admission, 6/14 priority date for domestic students. Application fee: $25. Electronic applications accepted. *Expenses:* Contact institution. *Financial support:* In 2008–09, 1 research assistantship with partial tuition reimbursement, 1 teaching assistantship with partial tuition reimbursement were awarded. Support available to part-time students. Financial award application deadline: 3/1; financial award applicants required to submit FAFSA. *Faculty research:* Community counseling, multicultural counseling, addictions. *Unit head:* Dr. Mark Gerig, Director of Graduate Counseling Studies, 765-677-2995, Fax: 765-677-1456, E-mail: mark.gerig@indwes.edu. *Application contact:* Tom Leas, Director of Adult Enrollment Services, 800-895-0036, Fax: 765-677-2404, E-mail: graduate@indwes.edu.

Iona College, School of Arts and Science, Department of Family and Pastoral Counseling, New Rochelle, NY 10801-1890. Offers family counseling (MS, Certificate); pastoral counseling (MS). Part-time and evening/weekend programs available. *Faculty:* 4 full-time (0 women), 2 part-time/adjunct (both women). *Students:* 30 full-time (23 women), 9 part-time (7 women); includes 10 minority (6 African Americans, 4 Hispanic Americans), 1 international. Average age 35. 38 applicants, 61% accepted, 10 enrolled. In 2008, 5 master's awarded. *Degree requirements:* For master's, thesis, project. *Entrance requirements:* For master's, draw-a-person test, sentence completion test, interview, minimum GPA of 3.0. *Application deadline:* Applications are processed on a rolling basis. Application fee: $50. Electronic applications accepted. *Expenses:* Contact institution. *Financial support:* Career-related internships or fieldwork, tuition waivers (partial), and unspecified assistantships available. Support available to part-time students. Financial award application deadline: 4/15; financial award applicants required to submit FAFSA. *Faculty research:* Marriage counseling. *Unit head:* Dr. Robert Burns, Chair, 914-633-2418, E-mail: rburns@iona.edu. *Application contact:* Veronica Jarek-Prinz, Director of Graduate Admissions, 914-633-2420, Fax: 914-633-2277, E-mail: vjarekprinz@iona.edu.

John Brown University, Graduate Counseling Division, Siloam Springs, AR 72761-2121. Offers community counseling (MS); marriage and family therapy (MS); school counseling (MS). *Accreditation:* NCATE. Part-time and evening/weekend programs available. *Faculty:* 5 full-time (1 woman), 6 part-time/adjunct (2 women). *Students:* 62 full-time (51 women), 83 part-time (59 women); includes 12 minority (3 African Americans, 6 American Indian/Alaska Native, 1 Asian American or Pacific Islander, 2 Hispanic Americans), 1 international. Average age 32. 47 applicants, 100% accepted, 41 enrolled. In 2008, 9 master's awarded. *Degree requirements:* For master's, practica or internships. *Entrance requirements:* For master's, GRE General Test, MAT, minimum GPA of 3.0. Additional exam requirements/recommendations for international students: Required—TOEFL (minimum score 550 paper-based; 173 computer-based). *Application deadline:* For fall admission, 8/11 priority date for domestic students; for spring admission, 1/12 for domestic students. Applications are processed on a rolling basis. Application fee: $35 ($100 for international students). Electronic applications accepted. *Expenses:* Tuition: Full-time $7740; part-time $430 per credit hour. *Financial support:* In 2008–09, 3 research assistantships (averaging $6,210 per year) were awarded; scholarships/grants, tuition waivers (full), and unspecified assistantships also available. Financial award application deadline: 3/1; financial award applicants required to submit FAFSA. *Unit head:* Dr. John V. Carmack, Program Director, 479-524-7460, Fax: 479-524-9548, E-mail: jcarmack@jbu.edu. *Application contact:* Associate Director of Graduate Recruitment, 479-524-7100.

Johnson Bible College, Department of Marriage and Family Therapy, Knoxville, TN 37998-1001. Offers marriage and family therapy/professional counseling (MA). *Degree requirements:* For master's, variable foreign language requirement, comprehensive exam, thesis (for some programs), internship (500 client contact hours). *Entrance requirements:* For master's, interview, minimum GPA of 3.0, 20 credits of course work in psychology, 15 credits of course work in Bible. Additional exam requirements/recommendations for international students: Required—TOEFL.

Kansas State University, Graduate School, College of Human Ecology, Program in Human Ecology, Manhattan, KS 66506. Offers apparel and textiles (PhD); family life education and consultation (PhD); food service, hospitality management, and administrative dietetics (PhD); institutional management (PhD); lifespan and human development (PhD); marriage and family therapy (PhD). *Faculty:* 3 full-time (all women). *Students:* 37 full-time (25 women), 24 part-time (15 women); includes 10 minority (8 African Americans, 1 American Indian/Alaska Native, 1 Asian American or Pacific Islander), 18 international. Average age 37. 25 applicants, 80% accepted, 18 enrolled. In 2008, 14 doctorates awarded. *Application deadline:* For fall admission, 2/1 priority date for domestic and international students; for spring admission, 8/1 priority date for domestic and international students. Application fee: $30 ($55 for international students). *Expenses:* Tuition, area resident: Full-time $6466; part-time $269.40 per credit hour. Tuition, state resident: full-time $6466; part-time $269.40 per credit hour. Tuition, nonresident: full-time $14,874; part-time $619.75 per credit hour. Required fees: $673; $23.40 per credit hour. Tuition and fees vary according to campus/location. *Unit head:* Elizabeth McCullough, Director, 785-532-2284, Fax: 785-532-3796, E-mail: lizm@ksu.edu. *Application contact:* Connie Fechter, Application Contact, 785-532-1473, Fax: 785-532-3796, E-mail: fechter@ksu.edu.

Kean University, College of Humanities and Social Sciences, Program in Marriage and Family Therapy, Union, NJ 07083. Offers Diploma. Part-time and evening/weekend programs available. *Faculty:* 18 full-time (13 women). *Students:* 10 full-time (9 women), 14 part-time (10 women); includes 1 African American, 1 Asian American or Pacific Islander, 6 Hispanic Americans. Average age 31. 7 applicants, 57% accepted, 4 enrolled. In 2008, 9 Diplomas awarded. *Degree requirements:* For Diploma, comprehensive exam, thesis, internship, practicum. *Entrance requirements:* For degree, GRE General Test, minimum GPA of 3.0, 3 letters of recommendation, 12 credits in psychology, interview. *Application deadline:* For fall admission, 5/1 for domestic students; for spring admission, 11/1 for domestic students. Application fee: $60 ($150 for international students). Electronic applications accepted. *Expenses:* Tuition, state resident: full-time $10,128; part-time $422 per credit. Tuition, nonresident: full-time $13,728; part-time $572 per credit. Required fees: $2570; $107 per credit. Part-time tuition and fees vary according to course load, degree level and program. *Financial support:* In 2008–09, 1 research assistantship with full tuition reimbursement (averaging $3,217 per year) was awarded; unspecified assistantships also available. *Unit head:* Dr. Muriel B. Singer, Program Coordinator, 908-737-5870, E-mail: msinger@kean.edu. *Application contact:* Steven Koch, Pre-Admissions Coordinator, 908-737-4723, Fax: 908-737-5965, E-mail: grad-adm@kean.edu.

Kutztown University of Pennsylvania, College of Graduate Studies and Extended Learning, Program in Counseling Psychology, Kutztown, PA 19530-0730. Offers agency counseling (MA); marital and family therapy (MA). Part-time and evening/weekend programs available. *Faculty:* 5 full-time (2 women). *Students:* 32 full-time (27 women), 20 part-time (19 women); includes 1 minority (Hispanic American). Average age 28. 38 applicants, 55% accepted, 11 enrolled. In 2008, 12 master's awarded. *Degree requirements:* For master's, comprehensive exam, thesis optional. *Entrance requirements:* For master's, GRE General Test, interview. Additional exam requirements/recommendations for international students: Required—TOEFL. *Application deadline:* For fall admission, 2/1 for domestic and international students; for spring admission, 8/1 for domestic and international students. Application fee: $35. Electronic applications accepted. *Expenses:* Tuition, area resident: Full-time $6430; part-time $357 per credit. Tuition, state resident: full-time $6430; part-time $357 per credit. Tuition, nonresident: full-time $10,288; part-time $572 per credit. Required fees: $1360; $72 per credit. $67 per semester. *Financial support:* Career-related internships or fieldwork, Federal Work-Study, scholarships/grants, and unspecified assistantships available. Financial award application deadline: 3/1; financial award applicants required to submit FAFSA. *Faculty research:* Addicted families. *Unit head:* Dr. Deborah Barlieb, Chairperson, 610-683-4204, Fax: 610-683-1585, E-mail: barlieb@kutztown.edu. *Application contact:* Dr. Linda Matthews, Interim Dean of Graduate Studies, 610-683-4201, Fax: 610-683-1393, E-mail: graduate@kutztown.edu.

La Salle University, School of Arts and Sciences, Program in Psychology, Philadelphia, PA 19141-1199. Offers clinical psychology (Psy D); family psychology (Psy D); rehabilitation psychology (Psy D). Part-time and evening/weekend programs available. *Entrance requirements:* For doctorate, GRE, minimum GPA of 3.0. *Expenses:* Contact institution. *Faculty research:* Cognitive therapy, attribution theory, treatment of addiction.

Lewis & Clark College, Graduate School of Education and Counseling, Department of Counseling Psychology, Program in Marriage, Couple and Family Therapy, Portland, OR 97219-7899. Offers MA. Part-time and evening/weekend programs available. *Entrance requirements:* For master's, GRE General Test, minimum undergraduate GPA of 2.75. Additional exam requirements/recommendations for international students: Required—TOEFL (minimum score 575 paper-based; 233 computer-based). Electronic applications accepted.

Loyola Marymount University, College of Fine Arts, Department of Marital and Family Therapy, Los Angeles, CA 90045-2659. Offers MA. Part-time programs available. *Degree requirements:* For master's, thesis, project. *Entrance requirements:* For master's, MAT, interview, course work in art and psychology. Additional exam requirements/recommendations for international students: Required—TOEFL (minimum score 600 paper-based; 250 computer-based). Electronic applications accepted. *Expenses:* Contact institution.

Maryville University of Saint Louis, School of Health Professions, Program in Rehabilitation Counseling, St. Louis, MO 63141-7299. Offers marriage and family therapy (MARC); music therapy (MARC); substance abuse (MARC). *Accreditation:* CORE. Part-time and evening/weekend programs available. *Students:* 45. In 2008, 17 master's awarded. *Degree requirements:* For master's, internship, seminar. *Entrance requirements:* For master's, minimum cumulative GPA of 3.0, 2 letters of recommendation, interview. Additional exam requirements/recommendations for international students: Required—TOEFL (minimum score 550 paper-based). *Application deadline:* For fall admission, 1/15 for domestic students; for spring admission, 10/1 for domestic students. Application fee: $40. Electronic applications accepted. *Expenses:* Tuition: Full-time $19,650; part-time $605 per credit hour. Required fees: $100 per semester. Part-time tuition and fees vary according to degree level and program. *Financial support:* Career-related internships or fieldwork, Federal Work-Study, and campus employment available. Financial award application deadline: 7/31. *Unit head:* Barbara Parker, Director, 314-529-9437, E-mail: bparker@maryville.edu. *Application contact:* Barbara Parker, Director, 314-529-9437, E-mail: bparker@maryville.edu.

Mennonite Brethren Biblical Seminary, School of Theology, Program in Marriage, Family, and Child Counseling, Fresno, CA 93727-5097. Offers MAMFCC, Diploma. *Degree requirements:* For master's, thesis or alternative. *Entrance requirements:* For master's, GRE General Test, MAT. Additional exam requirements/recommendations for international students: Required—TOEFL (minimum score 550 paper-based; 213 computer-based).

Mercy College, School of Social and Behavioral Sciences, Program in Marriage and Family Therapy, Dobbs Ferry, NY 10522-1189. Offers MS. Part-time and evening/weekend programs available. *Students:* 31 full-time (28 women), 45 part-time (38 women); includes 42 minority (28 African Americans, 2 Asian Americans or Pacific Islanders, 12 Hispanic Americans). Average age 32. 48 applicants, 67% accepted, 25 enrolled. In 2008, 11 master's awarded. *Degree requirements:* For master's, completion of clinical research project course. *Entrance requirements:* For master's, current resumé, interview with program director, written recommendations from 2 instructors. Additional exam requirements/recommendations for international students: Required—TOEFL (minimum score 600 paper-based; 250 computer-based; 100 iBT). *Application deadline:* For fall admission, 8/1 for international students. Applications are processed on a rolling basis. Application fee: $40. Electronic applications accepted. *Expenses:* Tuition: Full-time $12,330; part-time $685 per credit. Required fees: $240; $120 per semester. Tuition and fees vary according to program. *Financial support:* In 2008–09, 23 students received support. Career-related internships or fieldwork, Federal Work-Study, scholarships/grants, and unspecified assistantships available. Support available to part-time students. Financial award applicants required to submit FAFSA. *Unit head:* Barbara Melamed, Program Director, 914-674-7345, E-mail: bmelamed@mercy.edu. *Application contact:* Barbara Melamed, Program Director, 914-674-7345, E-mail: bmelamed@mercy.edu.

Michigan State University, The Graduate School, College of Social Science, Department of Family and Child Ecology, East Lansing, MI 48824. Offers child development (MA); community services (MS); family and child ecology (PhD); family studies (MA); marriage and family therapy (MA); youth development (MA). *Accreditation:* AAMFT/COAMFTE (one or more programs are accredited). *Entrance requirements:* For master's, GRE General Test, minimum GPA of 3.0 in last 2 years of undergraduate course work, 3 letters of recommendation; for doctorate, GRE General Test, minimum GPA of 3.0, 3 letters of recommendation, background in behavioral sciences. Additional exam requirements/recommendations for international students: Required—TOEFL. Electronic applications accepted.

Minnesota State University Mankato, College of Graduate Studies, College of Education, Department of Counseling and Student Personnel, Mankato, MN 56001. Offers college student affairs (MS); counselor education and supervision (Ed D); marriage and family counseling (Certificate); professional community counseling (MS); professional school counseling (MS). *Accreditation:* ACA (one or more programs are accredited); NCATE. *Students:* 49 full-time (41 women), 42 part-time (31 women). *Degree requirements:* For master's, comprehensive exam, thesis or alternative. *Entrance requirements:* For master's, GRE General Test or MAT (if GPA is below 3.0 for last 2 years), minimum GPA of 3.0 during previous 2 years, 3 letters of reference. Additional exam requirements/recommendations for international students: Required—TOEFL. *Application deadline:* For fall admission, 1/15 priority date for domestic students. Applications are processed on a rolling basis. Application fee: $40. Electronic applications accepted. *Financial support:* Research assistantships with full tuition reimbursements, teaching assistantships with full tuition reimbursements, career-related internships or fieldwork, Federal Work-Study, institutionally sponsored loans, and unspecified assistantships available. Support available to part-time students. Financial award application deadline: 3/15; financial award applicants required to submit FAFSA. *Unit head:* Dr. Jaqueline Lewis, Chairperson, 507-389-5658. *Application contact:* 507-389-2321, E-mail: grad@mnsu.edu.

Mississippi College, Graduate School, School of Education, Department of Psychology and Counseling, Clinton, MS 39058. Offers counseling (Ed S); marriage and family counseling (MS); mental health counseling (MS); school counseling (M Ed). Part-time programs available. *Degree requirements:* For master's and Ed S, comprehensive exam, thesis optional. *Entrance requirements:* For master's, GRE or NTE. Additional exam requirements/recommendations for international students: Recommended—IELTS. Electronic applications accepted.

Marriage and Family Therapy

Montclair State University, The Office of Graduate Admissions and Support Services, College of Humanities and Social Sciences, Center for Child Advocacy, Montclair, NJ 07043-1624. Offers child advocacy (MA, Certificate); public child welfare (MA). *Faculty:* 1 (woman) full-time. *Students:* 5 full-time (4 women), 20 part-time (19 women); includes 10 minority (8 African Americans, 1 Asian American or Pacific Islander, 1 Hispanic American), 1 international. Average age 31. 5 applicants, 80% accepted, 3 enrolled. In 2008, 18 master's, 14 other advanced degrees awarded. Application fee: $60. *Financial support:* In 2008–09, 2 research assistantships (averaging $7,000 per year) were awarded. *Unit head:* Dr. Robert McCormick, Head, 973-655-4188. *Application contact:* Amy Aiello, Associate Director of Admissions, 973-655-5147, Fax: 973-655-7869, E-mail: graduate.school@montclair.edu.

Montclair State University, The Office of Graduate Admissions and Support Services, College of Humanities and Social Sciences, Department of Psychology, Montclair, NJ 07043-1624. Offers educational psychology (MA), including child/adolescent clinical psychology, clinical psychology for Spanish/English bilinguals; psychology (MA, Certificate), including industrial and organizational psychology (MA); school psychologist (Certificate). Part-time and evening/weekend programs available. *Faculty:* 28 full-time (13 women), 32 part-time/adjunct (16 women). *Students:* 28 full-time (20 women), 31 part-time (26 women); includes 14 minority (4 African Americans, 6 Asian Americans or Pacific Islanders, 4 Hispanic Americans), 2 international. Average age 27. 62 applicants, 56% accepted, 23 enrolled. In 2008, 26 master's awarded. *Degree requirements:* For master's, comprehensive exam, thesis or alternative. *Entrance requirements:* For master's, GRE General Test, GRE Subject Test, previous course work in psychology, interview, 2 letters of recommendation. Additional exam requirements/recommendations for international students: Required—TOEFL (minimum score 83 computer-based). *Application deadline:* For fall admission, 2/1 for domestic and international students; for spring admission, 10/1 for domestic and international students. Applications are processed on a rolling basis. Application fee: $60. Electronic applications accepted. *Financial support:* In 2008–09, 10 research assistantships with full tuition reimbursements (averaging $7,000 per year) were awarded; Federal Work-Study, scholarships/grants, and unspecified assistantships also available. Support available to part-time students. Financial award application deadline: 3/1; financial award applicants required to submit FAFSA. *Faculty research:* Engaged learning, academic and civic development. Total annual research expenditures: $10,000. *Unit head:* Dr. Peter Vietze, Chairperson, 973-655-5201. *Application contact:* Amy Aiello, Associate Director of Admissions, 973-655-5147, Fax: 973-655-7869, E-mail: graduate.school@montclair.edu.

North Dakota State University, College of Graduate and Interdisciplinary Studies, College of Human Development and Education, Department of Child Development and Family Science, Fargo, ND 58105. Offers child development and family science (MS); couple and family therapy (MS); family financial planning (MS); gerontology (MS, PhD). *Accreditation:* AAMFT/COAMFTE. Part-time and evening/weekend programs available. Postbaccalaureate distance learning degree programs offered (no on-campus study). *Faculty:* 12 full-time (7 women). *Students:* 26 full-time (25 women), 21 part-time (18 women); includes 1 African American, 2 international. 22 applicants, 64% accepted, 12 enrolled. In 2008, 12 master's awarded. *Degree requirements:* For master's, thesis or alternative; for doctorate, thesis/dissertation. *Entrance requirements:* Additional exam requirements/recommendations for international students: Required—TOEFL (minimum score 525 paper-based; 197 computer-based; 71 iBT). *Application deadline:* For fall admission, 2/1 for domestic and international students; for spring admission, 10/1 for domestic and international students. Application fee: $45 ($60 for international students). *Financial support:* In 2008–09, 17 students received support, including research assistantships with full tuition reimbursements available (averaging $3,000 per year), 17 teaching assistantships with full tuition reimbursements available (averaging $3,000 per year); career-related internships or fieldwork, Federal Work-Study, institutionally sponsored loans, and tuition waivers (full) also available. Financial award application deadline: 4/1. *Faculty research:* Family therapy, resilience, parenting, adolescent development, mental health. Total annual research expenditures: $333,582. *Unit head:* Dr. James Deal, Head, 701-231-7568, Fax: 701-231-9645, E-mail: jim_deal@ndsu.edu. *Application contact:* Theresa Anderson, Administrative Assistant, 701-231-8628, Fax: 701-231-9645, E-mail: theresa.anderson@ndsu.edu.

Northwestern University, The Graduate School, Program in Marital and Family Therapy, Evanston, IL 60208. Offers MS. *Accreditation:* AAMFT/COAMFTE. *Entrance requirements:* For master's, GRE General Test. *Faculty research:* Marital and family therapy training, gender, psychotherapy outcome, adolescents and pre-school children at risk, families.

Northwest Nazarene University, Graduate Studies, Program in Counselor Education, Nampa, ID 83686-5897. Offers community counseling (MS); marriage and family counseling (MS); school counseling (MS). *Faculty:* 3 full-time (2 women), 10 part-time/adjunct (5 women). *Students:* 45 full-time (29 women), 13 part-time (7 women); includes 2 minority (1 American Indian/Alaska Native, 1 Asian American or Pacific Islander). In 2008, 19 master's awarded. Application fee: $25. *Unit head:* Dr. Brenda Freeman, Chair, 208-467-8428, Fax: 208-467-8339. *Application contact:* Susan Marion, Secretary, 208-467-8345, Fax: 208-467-8339, E-mail: sjmarion@nnu.edu.

Notre Dame de Namur University, Division of Academic Affairs, School of Sciences, Department of Clinical Psychology and Gerontology, Program in Marital and Family Therapy, Belmont, CA 94002-1908. Offers MAMFT. *Entrance requirements:* Additional exam requirements/recommendations for international students: Required—TOEFL (minimum score 550 paper-based; 213 computer-based; 79 iBT). Application fee: $60. *Expenses:* Tuition: Part-time $699 per unit. Required fees: $3 per unit. $35 per semester. *Unit head:* Dr. Nusha Askari, 650-5083728, E-mail: naskari@ndnu.edu. *Application contact:* Candace Hallmark, Assistant Director of Graduate Admissions, 650-508-3592, Fax: 650-508-3426, E-mail: grad.admit@ndnu.edu.

Nova Southeastern University, Graduate School of Humanities and Social Sciences, Department of Family Therapy, Doctor of Marriage and Family Therapy Program, Fort Lauderdale, FL 33314-7796. Offers DMFT. Part-time programs available. *Faculty:* 10 full-time (5 women), 16 part-time/adjunct (13 women). *Students:* 10 full-time (all women), 10 part-time (7 women); includes 8 minority (7 African Americans, 1 Hispanic American), 1 international. 12 applicants, 58% accepted, 5 enrolled. In 2008, 1 doctorate awarded. *Degree requirements:* For doctorate, thesis/dissertation or alternative, qualifying exams. *Entrance requirements:* For doctorate, minimum GPA of 3.0, interview, master's degree in related field. Additional exam requirements/recommendations for international students: Required—TOEFL. *Application deadline:* For fall admission, 7/1 priority date for domestic and international students; for winter admission, 11/1 priority date for domestic and international students; for spring admission, 3/1 priority date for domestic and international students. Applications are processed on a rolling basis. Application fee: $50. Electronic applications accepted. *Financial support:* In 2008–09, 1 research assistantship (averaging $10,000 per year) was awarded; career-related internships or fieldwork, Federal Work-Study, scholarships/grants, and unspecified assistantships also available. Financial award applicants required to submit CSS PROFILE. *Faculty research:* Diversity, family business, brief therapy, medical family therapy, human sexuality, family therapy in schools. *Unit head:* Tommie Boyd, PhD, Chair, 954-262-3027, Fax: 954-262-3968, E-mail: tommie@nova.edu. *Application contact:* Marcia Arango, Student Recruitment Coordinator, 954-262-3006, Fax: 954-262-3968, E-mail: marango@nsu.nova.edu.

Nova Southeastern University, Graduate School of Humanities and Social Sciences, Department of Family Therapy, Master's Program in Family Therapy, Fort Lauderdale, FL 33314-7796. Offers family studies (Certificate); family systems healthcare (Certificate); family therapy (MS). *Accreditation:* AAMFT/COAMFTE (one or more programs are accredited). Part-time programs available. *Faculty:* 10 full-time (5 women), 16 part-time/adjunct (13 women). *Students:* 92 full-time (80 women), 43 part-time (38 women); includes 56 minority (24 African Americans, 8 Asian Americans or Pacific Islanders, 24 Hispanic Americans), 5 international. 142 applicants, 42% accepted, 51 enrolled. In 2008, 42 master's awarded. *Degree requirements:* For master's, comprehensive exam. *Entrance requirements:* For master's, minimum GPA of 3.0, interview, writing sample. Additional exam requirements/recommendations for international students: Required—TOEFL. *Application deadline:* For fall admission, 6/1 priority date

for domestic students; for winter admission, 11/1 priority date for domestic students; for spring admission, 3/1 priority date for domestic students. Applications are processed on a rolling basis. Application fee: $50. Electronic applications accepted. *Financial support:* Career-related internships or fieldwork, Federal Work-Study, and scholarships/grants available. Financial award application deadline: 4/1; financial award applicants required to submit CSS PROFILE. *Faculty research:* Cross-cultural counseling, family business, medical family therapy, brief therapy, diversity, family therapy in schools. *Unit head:* Tommie Boyd, PhD, Chair, 954-262-3027, Fax: 954-262-3968, E-mail: tommie@nova.edu. *Application contact:* Marcia Arango, Student Recruitment Coordinator, 954-262-3006, Fax: 954-262-3968, E-mail: marango@nsu.nova.edu.

Nova Southeastern University, Graduate School of Humanities and Social Sciences, Department of Family Therapy, PhD Program in Family Therapy, Fort Lauderdale, FL 33314-7796. Offers PhD. *Accreditation:* AAMFT/COAMFTE. Part-time programs available. *Faculty:* 10 full-time (5 women), 16 part-time/adjunct (13 women). *Students:* 62 full-time (57 women), 24 part-time (20 women); includes 41 minority (27 African Americans, 1 Asian American or Pacific Islander, 13 Hispanic Americans), 4 international. 32 applicants, 63% accepted, 17 enrolled. In 2008, 7 doctorates awarded. *Degree requirements:* For doctorate, thesis/dissertation, qualifying exams. *Entrance requirements:* For doctorate, master's degree in related field, minimum GPA of 3.0, interview, writing sample. Additional exam requirements/recommendations for international students: Required—TOEFL. *Application deadline:* For fall admission, 7/1 priority date for domestic and international students; for winter admission, 11/1 priority date for domestic and international students; for spring admission, 3/1 priority date for domestic and international students. Applications are processed on a rolling basis. Application fee: $50. Electronic applications accepted. *Financial support:* In 2008–09, 63 students received support, including 3 research assistantships (averaging $10,000 per year); career-related internships or fieldwork, Federal Work-Study, scholarships/grants, and unspecified assistantships also available. Financial award application deadline: 4/1. *Faculty research:* Medical family therapy, brief therapy, family business, diversity, human sexuality and therapy, family therapy in schools. *Unit head:* Tommie Boyd, PhD, Chair, 954-262-3027, Fax: 954-262-3968, E-mail: tommie@nova.edu. *Application contact:* Marcia Arango, Student Recruitment Coordinator, 954-262-3006, Fax: 954-262-3968, E-mail: marango@nsu.nova.edu.

Oral Roberts University, School of Theology and Missions, Tulsa, OK 74171-0001. Offers biblical literature (MA), including advanced languages, Judaic-Christian studies; Christian counseling (MA), including marriage and family therapy; Christian education (MA); divinity (M Div); missions (MA); practical theology (MA); theological/historical studies (MA); theology (D Min). *Accreditation:* ATS; NASM. Part-time programs available. Postbaccalaureate distance learning degree programs offered (minimal on-campus study). *Degree requirements:* For master's, thesis (for some programs), practicum/internship; for doctorate, thesis/dissertation, applied research project; for M Div, one foreign language, field experience. *Entrance requirements:* For M Div and master's, GRE General Test or MAT, minimum GPA of 2.5; for doctorate, M Div, minimum GPA of 3.0, 3 years of full-time ministry experience. Additional exam requirements/recommendations for international students: Required—TOEFL (minimum score 500 paper-based; 213 computer-based; 79 iBT). Electronic applications accepted.

Ottawa University, Graduate Studies-Arizona, Program in Professional Counseling, Ottawa, KS 66067-3399. Offers Christian counseling (MA); expressive arts therapy (MA); marriage and family therapy (MA); treatment of trauma, abuse and deprivation (MA). Programs offered in Mesa, Phoenix, Tempe and West Valley, AZ. Part-time and evening/weekend programs available. Postbaccalaureate distance learning degree programs offered. *Degree requirements:* For master's, comprehensive exam, thesis or alternative, field experience, practicum. *Entrance requirements:* For master's, minimum undergraduate GPA of 3.0; course work in theories of personality, abnormal psychology, and human growth and development. Additional exam requirements/recommendations for international students: Required—TOEFL (minimum score 550 paper-based; 213 computer-based).

Our Lady of Holy Cross College, Program in Education and Counseling, New Orleans, LA 70131-7399. Offers administration and supervision (M Ed); curriculum and instruction (M Ed); marriage and family counseling (MA); school counseling (M Ed, MA). *Accreditation:* ACA; NCATE. Part-time and evening/weekend programs available. *Degree requirements:* For master's, thesis. *Entrance requirements:* For master's, GRE General Test, minimum GPA of 2.7.

Our Lady of the Lake University of San Antonio, School of Professional Studies, Program in Psychology, San Antonio, TX 78207-4689. Offers counseling psychology (MS, Psy D); marriage and family therapy (MS); school psychology (MS). *Accreditation:* APA (one or more programs are accredited). Part-time and evening/weekend programs available. *Students:* 99 full-time (83 women), 97 part-time (86 women); includes 117 minority (25 African Americans, 1 American Indian/Alaska Native, 3 Asian Americans or Pacific Islanders, 88 Hispanic Americans), 2 international. Average age 30. In 2008, 42 master's, 3 doctorates awarded. *Degree requirements:* For master's, comprehensive exam, thesis optional, practicum; for doctorate, thesis/dissertation, internship, qualifying exam. *Entrance requirements:* For master's and doctorate, GRE General Test or MAT, interview. Additional exam requirements/recommendations for international students: Required—TOEFL. *Application deadline:* For fall admission, 3/1 priority date for domestic and international students. Applications are processed on a rolling basis. Application fee: $25 ($50 for international students). Electronic applications accepted. *Expenses:* Tuition: Full-time $11,970; part-time $665 per credit hour. Required fees: $500; $250 per term. *Financial support:* Research assistantships, teaching assistantships, career-related internships or fieldwork available. Support available to part-time students. Financial award application deadline: 4/15. *Faculty research:* Marriage and family therapy, supervision, cross-cultural counseling, violence. *Unit head:* Dr. Kathryn Anderson, Chair, 210-434-6711, E-mail: andek@lake.ollusa.edu. *Application contact:* 210-434-6711 Ext. 2314, Fax: 210-431-4036, E-mail: gradadm@lake.ollusa.edu.

Pacific Lutheran University, Division of Graduate Studies, Division of Social Sciences, Program in Marriage and Family Therapy, Tacoma, WA 98447. Offers MA. *Accreditation:* AAMFT/COAMFTE. *Degree requirements:* For master's, thesis optional, clinical competency. *Entrance requirements:* For master's, GRE, interview (selected applicants). Additional exam requirements/recommendations for international students: Required—TOEFL (minimum score 550 paper-based; 213 computer-based). Electronic applications accepted.

Pacific Oaks College, Graduate School, Program in Marriage and Family Therapy, Pasadena, CA 91103. Offers marriage, family and child counseling (MA). Part-time and evening/weekend programs available. *Degree requirements:* For master's, thesis. *Entrance requirements:* For master's, interview. Additional exam requirements/recommendations for international students: Required—TOEFL (minimum score 550 paper-based; 213 computer-based). *Faculty research:* Family systems, cross-cultural development, therapeutic intervention and Latino families, battered women.

Palm Beach Atlantic University, School of Education and Behavioral Studies, West Palm Beach, FL 33416-4708. Offers counseling psychology (MSCP), including addictions/mental health, marriage and family therapy, mental health counseling, school guidance counseling; elementary education (M Ed). Part-time and evening/weekend programs available. *Entrance requirements:* For master's, GRE General Test, minimum GPA of 3.0 in last 60 hours of course work. Additional exam requirements/recommendations for international students: Required—TOEFL (minimum score 550 paper-based; 213 computer-based). Electronic applications accepted.

Pepperdine University, Graduate School of Education and Psychology, Division of Psychology, Program in Clinical Psychology, Los Angeles, CA 90045. Offers clinical psychology (Psy D); clinical psychology (daytime) (MA), including marriage and family therapy; clinical psychology (evening) (MA), including marriage and family therapy. *Accreditation:* APA. Part-time and evening/weekend programs available. *Students:* 590 full-time (523 women), 71 part-time (59 women); includes 191 minority (58 African Americans, 7 American Indian/Alaska Native, 51

Asian Americans or Pacific Islanders, 75 Hispanic Americans), 22 international. 541 applicants, 64% accepted, 203 enrolled. In 2008, 195 master's awarded. *Entrance requirements:* For master's, GRE General Test, bachelor's degree in psychology or related field. Additional exam requirements/recommendations for international students: Required—TOEFL. *Application deadline:* For fall admission, 11/17 priority date for domestic students. Applications are processed on a rolling basis. Application fee: $55. *Financial support:* Research assistantships, teaching assistantships available. Financial award application deadline: 7/1; financial award applicants required to submit FAFSA. *Unit head:* Dr. Cary Mitchell, Director, 310-568-8553, E-mail: cary.mitchell@pepperdine.edu. *Application contact:* Lindsy Blanco, Recruitment and Admissions Manager, 310-506-5605.

Phillips Graduate Institute, Program in Clinical Family Psychology and Organizational Consulting, Encino, CA 91316-1509. Offers clinical psychology (Psy D); organizational consulting (Psy D). Evening/weekend programs available. *Degree requirements:* For doctorate, thesis/dissertation. *Entrance requirements:* For doctorate, minimum GPA of 3.0, interview.

Phillips Graduate Institute, Programs in Marriage and Family Therapy, School Counseling and School Psychology, Encino, CA 91316-1509. Offers marital and family therapy (MA); organizational consulting (MA); school counseling (MA). Evening/weekend programs available. *Degree requirements:* For master's, comprehensive exam, thesis. *Entrance requirements:* For master's, minimum GPA of 2.5. *Faculty research:* Integration of interpersonal psychological theory, systems approach, firsthand experiential learning.

Purdue University, Graduate School, College of Consumer and Family Sciences, Department of Child Development and Family Studies, West Lafayette, IN 47907. Offers developmental studies (MS, PhD); family studies (MS, PhD); marriage and family therapy (MS, PhD). *Accreditation:* AAMFT/COAMFTE (one or more programs are accredited). Part-time programs available. Terminal master's awarded for partial completion of doctoral program. *Degree requirements:* For master's, thesis; for doctorate, thesis/dissertation. *Entrance requirements:* For master's and doctorate, GRE General Test. Additional exam requirements/recommendations for international students: Required—TWE. Electronic applications accepted. *Faculty research:* Inclusion of children with special needs, families as learning environments, relationships in child care, work-family relations, AIDS prevention.

Purdue University Calumet, Graduate School, School of Liberal Arts and Social Sciences, Department of Behavioral Sciences, Hammond, IN 46323-2094. Offers marriage and family therapy (MS). *Accreditation:* AAMFT/COAMFTE. Part-time programs available. *Degree requirements:* For master's, thesis. *Entrance requirements:* For master's, GRE, interview. Additional exam requirements/recommendations for international students: Required—TOEFL. *Faculty research:* Substance abuse, sexual abuse, couple therapy, professional issues, adolescent therapy.

Reformed Theological Seminary–Jackson Campus, Graduate and Professional Programs, Jackson, MS 39209-3099. Offers Bible, theology, and missions (Certificate); biblical studies (MA); Christian education (M Div, MA); counseling (M Div); divinity (M Div, Diploma); marriage and family therapy (MA); ministry (D Min); missions (M Div, MA, D Min); New Testament (Th M); Old Testament (Th M); theological studies (MA); theology (Th M); M Div/MA. *Accreditation:* AAMFT/COAMFTE (one or more programs are accredited); ATS (one or more programs are accredited). *Degree requirements:* For master's, thesis (for some programs), fieldwork; for doctorate, 2 foreign languages, thesis/dissertation; for M Div, 2 foreign languages, thesis/dissertation (for some programs). *Entrance requirements:* For M Div and master's, minimum GPA of 2.6; for doctorate, minimum GPA of 3.0. Additional exam requirements/recommendations for international students: Required—TOEFL.

Regis University, College for Professional Studies, Graduate Counseling Program, Denver, CO 80221-1099. Offers community counseling (MAC); counseling children and adolescents (Post-Graduate Certificate); marriage and family therapy (Post-Graduate Certificate). Program offered in Henderson and Las Vegas (Summerlin), NV. *Accreditation:* ACA. Part-time and evening/weekend programs available. *Degree requirements:* For master's, internships, practicum. *Entrance requirements:* For master's, 2 admissions essays, interview, 2 recommendations, resumé, criminal background check. Additional exam requirements/recommendations for international students: Required—TOEFL (minimum score 213 computer-based), TWE (minimum score 5). *Expenses:* Contact institution. *Faculty research:* Group Development, Counselor Education, Counsel and Therapy, Influence of Technology on Psychology, Dream finding groups, Adult Development, Depression.

Richmont Graduate University, Graduate Programs, Atlanta, GA 30327. Offers Christian psychological studies (MS); marriage and family therapy (MA); professional counseling (MA).

St. Cloud State University, School of Graduate Studies, College of Education, Department of Educational Leadership and Community Psychology, Program in Marriage and Family Therapy, St. Cloud, MN 56301-4498. Offers MS. *Entrance requirements:* Additional exam requirements/recommendations for international students: Required—Michigan English Language Assessment Battery; Recommended—TOEFL (minimum score 550 paper-based; 213 computer-based), IELTS (minimum score 6.5). Electronic applications accepted.

Saint Joseph College, Graduate School, Department of Marriage and Family Therapy, West Hartford, CT 06117-2700. Offers marriage and family therapy (MA). *Accreditation:* AAMFT/COAMFTE. Part-time and evening/weekend programs available. *Students:* 12 full-time (10 women), 27 part-time (24 women). *Degree requirements:* For master's, comprehensive exam, thesis or alternative. *Entrance requirements:* For master's, GRE or MAT, 2 letters of recommendation, interview. *Application deadline:* Applications are processed on a rolling basis. Application fee: $50. Electronic applications accepted. *Expenses:* Tuition: Part-time $560 per credit. Required fees: $30 per credit. *Financial support:* Career-related internships or fieldwork, health care benefits, and unspecified assistantships available. Support available to part-time students. Financial award applicants required to submit FAFSA. *Unit head:* Chair. *Application contact:* Graduate Admissions Office, 860-231-5261, E-mail: graduate@sjc.edu.

Saint Louis University, Graduate School, College of Education and Public Service and Graduate School, Department of Counseling and Family Therapy, St. Louis, MO 63103-2097. Offers counseling and family therapy (PhD); human development counseling (MA); marriage and family therapy (Certificate); school counseling (MA, MA-R). *Accreditation:* NCATE. Part-time programs available. *Degree requirements:* For master's, comprehensive exam, thesis (for some programs); for doctorate, comprehensive exam, thesis/dissertation, preliminary oral and written exams. *Entrance requirements:* For master's and doctorate, GRE General Test, letters of recommendation, resumé, transcripts, goal statement. Additional exam requirements/recommendations for international students: Required—TOEFL (minimum score 550 paper-based; 213 computer-based). Electronic applications accepted. *Faculty research:* Medical family therapy/collaborative health care multicultural counseling, mental health needs of diverse, minority, or Immigrant/refugee populations, divorce, aging families.

Saint Mary's College of California, Kalmanovitz School of Education, Program in Counseling, Moraga, CA 94575. Offers general counseling (MA); marital and family therapy (MA); school counseling (MA). Part-time and evening/weekend programs available. *Degree requirements:* For master's, thesis or alternative. *Entrance requirements:* For master's, interview, minimum GPA of 3.0. *Faculty research:* Counselor training effectiveness, multicultural development, empathy, the interface of spirituality and psychotherapy, gender issues.

St. Mary's University, Graduate School, Department of Counseling and Human Services, Program in Marriage and Family Therapy, San Antonio, TX 78228-8507. Offers MA, PhD. Part-time programs available. *Faculty:* 3 full-time (1 woman). *Students:* 40 full-time (33 women), 29 part-time (23 women); includes 23 minority (6 African Americans, 3 Asian Americans or Pacific Islanders, 14 Hispanic Americans), 6 international. Average age 34. 47 applicants, 72% accepted, 27 enrolled. In 2008, 8 master's, 6 doctorates awarded. *Degree requirements:* For master's, comprehensive exam, thesis optional, internship; for doctorate, comprehensive exam, thesis/dissertation, internship. *Entrance requirements:* For master's, GRE, MAT; for doctorate, GRE, master's degree, work experience, letters of recommendation. Additional exam requirements/recommendations for international students: Required—TOEFL (minimum score 550 paper-based; 213 computer-based; 80 iBT). *Application deadline:* Applications are processed on a rolling basis. Application fee: $0. Electronic applications accepted. *Expenses:* Tuition: Full-time $12,006; part-time $667 per credit hour. Required fees: $440; $220 per semester. *Financial support:* In 2008–09, 19 students received support, including 16 fellowships (averaging $4,527 per year), 3 research assistantships (averaging $10,000 per year); career-related internships or fieldwork, Federal Work-Study, institutionally sponsored loans, scholarships/grants, health care benefits, and unspecified assistantships also available. Financial award application deadline: 3/31; financial award applicants required to submit FAFSA. *Unit head:* Dr. Becky Davenport, Director, 210-436-3226, Fax: 210-431-6886, E-mail: bdavenport@stmarytx.edu. *Application contact:* Dr. Henry Flores, Dean of the Graduate School, 210-436-3101, Fax: 210-431-2220, E-mail: hflores@stmarytx.edu.

Saint Mary's University of Minnesota, Schools of Graduate and Professional Programs, Graduate School of Health and Human Services, Marriage and Family Therapy Program, Winona, MN 55987-1399. Offers MA, Certificate.

Saint Paul University, Faculty of Human Sciences, Program in Counseling and Spirituality, Ottawa, ON K1S 1C4, Canada. Offers individual or marital/couple counseling (MA); spiritual care (MA). Part-time programs available. *Degree requirements:* For master's, research project or thesis. *Entrance requirements:* For master's, honors BA in human sciences, minimum B average, 12 theology credits.

St. Thomas University, Biscayne College, Department of Social Sciences and Counseling, Program in Marriage and Family Therapy, Miami Gardens, FL 33054-6459. Offers MS, Post-Master's Certificate. Part-time and evening/weekend programs available. *Degree requirements:* For master's, comprehensive exam. *Entrance requirements:* For master's, interview, minimum GPA of 3.0 or GRE. Additional exam requirements/recommendations for international students: Required—TOEFL. Electronic applications accepted.

San Francisco State University, Division of Graduate Studies, College of Health and Human Services, Department of Counseling, San Francisco, CA 94132-1722. Offers counseling (MS); marriage, family, and child counseling (MSC); rehabilitation counseling (MS). *Accreditation:* ACA (one or more programs are accredited). Part-time programs available.

Saybrook Graduate School and Research Center, Programs in Psychology, Human Science and Organizational Systems, San Francisco, CA 94111-1920. Offers clinical psychology (PhD); creativity studies (MA); human science (MA, PhD), including consciousness and spirituality, individualized (PhD), integrative health studies, organizational systems, social transformation; marriage and family therapy (MA); organizational systems (MA, PhD), including individualized (PhD), organizational systems; psychology (MA, PhD), including consciousness and spirituality, humanistic and transpersonal psychology, individualized (PhD), integrative health studies, licensure track (MA), organizational systems, social transformation. Postbaccalaureate distance learning degree programs offered (minimal on-campus study). Terminal master's awarded for partial completion of doctoral program. *Degree requirements:* For master's, thesis or alternative; for doctorate, thesis/dissertation. Electronic applications accepted. *Faculty research:* Humanistic theory, health studies, organizational systems, consciousness and spirituality, social transformation.

The School of Professional Psychology at Forest Institute, Graduate Programs, Springfield, MO 65807. Offers clinical psychology (Psy D); counseling psychology (MA); marriage and family therapy (MA, PGC). *Accreditation:* AAMFT/COAMFTE; APA (one or more programs are accredited). *Faculty:* 18 full-time (9 women), 28 part-time/adjunct (15 women). *Students:* 208 full-time (141 women), 34 part-time (27 women). 153 applicants, 42% accepted, 40 enrolled. In 2008, 36 master's, 36 doctorates awarded. Terminal master's awarded for partial completion of doctoral program. *Median time to degree:* Of those who began their doctoral program in fall 2000, 100% received their degree in 8 years or less. *Degree requirements:* For master's, thesis, practice; for doctorate, comprehensive exam, thesis/dissertation, internship, practice. *Entrance requirements:* For master's, GRE General Test, interview, minimum GPA of 3.0, 12 hours in psychology; for doctorate, GRE General Test, interview, minimum GPA of 3.0, 18 hours in psychology. Additional exam requirements/recommendations for international students: Required—TOEFL (minimum score 550 paper-based; 213 computer-based). *Application deadline:* For fall admission, 1/15 priority date for domestic and international students; for spring admission, 8/1 priority date for domestic and international students. Applications are processed on a rolling basis. Application fee: $50. Electronic applications accepted. *Expenses:* Tuition: Full-time $22,500. *Financial support:* In 2008–09, 91 students received support. Career-related internships or fieldwork, Federal Work-Study, and scholarships/grants available. Support available to part-time students. Financial award applicants required to submit FAFSA. *Faculty research:* Forensics/corrections, marriage and family therapy, child and adolescent, integrated health care, neuropsychology. *Unit head:* Dr. Mark E. Skrade, President, 417-823-3477, Fax: 417-823-3442, E-mail: mskrade@forest.edu. *Application contact:* Dawn Medley, Director of Enrollment Management, 417-823-3477, Fax: 417-823-3442, E-mail: dmedley@forest.edu.

Seattle Pacific University, Medical Family Therapy Certificate Program, Seattle, WA 98119-1997. Offers Certificate. *Faculty:* 1 (woman) full-time. *Students:* 3 full-time (2 women), 3 part-time (all women). 7 applicants, 86% accepted, 5 enrolled.Application fee: $50. *Expenses:* Tuition: Full-time $659; part-time $659 per credit hour. One-time fee: $50. Tuition and fees vary according to program. *Unit head:* Dr. Claudia Grauf-Grounds, Chair, 206-281-2632, Fax: 206-281-2695, E-mail: claudiagg@spu.edu. *Application contact:* Grad Center The, 206-281-2091.

Seattle Pacific University, MS in Marriage and Family Therapy Program, Seattle, WA 98119-1997. Offers MS. *Accreditation:* AAMFT/COAMFTE. Part-time programs available. *Faculty:* 6 full-time (3 women), 3 part-time/adjunct (2 women). *Students:* 51 full-time (41 women), 18 part-time (12 women); includes 8 minority (1 African American, 1 American Indian/Alaska Native, 4 Asian Americans or Pacific Islanders, 2 Hispanic Americans), 4 international. Average age 32. 92 applicants, 36% accepted, 29 enrolled. In 2008, 18 master's awarded. *Degree requirements:* For master's, thesis optional, internship. *Entrance requirements:* For master's, GRE General Test or MAT, interview. *Application deadline:* For fall admission, 3/1 for domestic students. Applications are processed on a rolling basis. Application fee: $50. Electronic applications accepted. *Expenses:* Contact institution. *Financial support:* In 2008–09, 50 students received support; fellowships, Federal Work-Study available. Financial award applicants required to submit FAFSA. *Faculty research:* Roles of therapists, models of collaboration, medical and mental health theories of marriage and family therapy. *Unit head:* Dr. Claudia Grauf-Grounds, Chair, 206-281-2632, Fax: 206-281-2695, E-mail: claudiagg@spu.edu. *Application contact:* Grad Center The, 206-281-2091.

Seton Hall University, College of Education and Human Services, Department of Professional Psychology and Family Therapy, Program in Marriage and Family Therapy, South Orange, NJ 07079-2697. Offers MS, PhD, Ed S. *Accreditation:* AAMFT/COAMFTE. *Degree requirements:* For master's, comprehensive exam, case study; for Ed S, comprehensive exam, internship. *Entrance requirements:* For master's, GRE; for Ed S, GRE or MAT, interview. *Faculty research:* Family systems.

Seton Hill University, Program in Marriage and Family Therapy, Greensburg, PA 15601. Offers MA. *Accreditation:* AAMFT/COAMFTE. Part-time and evening/weekend programs available. *Entrance requirements:* For master's, minimum GPA of 3.0, 12 credits of course work in psychology. Additional exam requirements/recommendations for international students: Required—TOEFL (minimum score 600 paper-based; 250 computer-based). Electronic applications accepted. *Faculty research:* Social cognition, feminist psychology, psychology of gender, developmental psychology, systemic theory.

Marriage and Family Therapy

Shippensburg University of Pennsylvania, School of Graduate Studies, College of Education and Human Services, Department of Counseling, Shippensburg, PA 17257-2299. Offers Adlerian studies (Certificate); advanced study in counseling (Certificate); alcohol and drug counseling (Certificate); counseling (M Ed, MS), including college counseling (MS), community counseling (MS), elementary school counseling, mental health counseling (MS), secondary school counseling (MS), student personnel services (MS); couple and family counseling (Certificate). *Accreditation:* ACA (one or more programs are accredited); NCATE. Part-time and evening/weekend programs available. *Faculty:* 8 full-time (3 women), 3 part-time/adjunct (2 women). *Students:* 71 full-time (60 women), 109 part-time (91 women); includes 22 minority (16 African Americans, 4 Asian Americans or Pacific Islanders, 2 Hispanic Americans), 2 international. Average age 29. 128 applicants, 39% accepted, 32 enrolled. In 2008, 48 master's awarded. *Degree requirements:* For master's, fieldwork, research project, internship, candidacy. *Entrance requirements:* For master's, GRE or MAT (for community, mental health, student personnel, and college counseling applicants if GPA is less than 2.75), minimum GPA of 2.75 (3.0 for M Ed), interview, resumé, 3 letters of recommendation, supplemental data forms, one year of relevant work experience, on-campus interview. Additional exam requirements/recommendations for international students: Required—TOEFL (minimum score 560 paper-based; 220 computer-based); Recommended—IELTS (minimum score 6). *Application deadline:* For fall admission, 3/1 for international students; for spring admission, 7/1 for international students. Applications are processed on a rolling basis. Application fee: $30. Electronic applications accepted. *Expenses:* Tuition, state resident: full-time $6430; part-time $357 per credit. Tuition, nonresident: full-time $10,288; part-time $572 per credit. Required fees: $1127; $38 per credit. One-time fee: $44 part-time. *Financial support:* In 2008–09, 44 research assistantships with full tuition reimbursements (averaging $5,000 per year) were awarded; career-related internships or fieldwork, scholarships/grants, unspecified assistantships, and resident hall directors, student payroll positions also available. Support available to part-time students. Financial award application deadline: 3/1; financial award applicants required to submit FAFSA. *Unit head:* Dr. Jan Arminio, Chairperson, 717-477-1668, Fax: 717-477-4016, E-mail: jlarmi@ship.edu. *Application contact:* Renee Payne, Associate Dean of Graduate Admissions, 717-477-1231, Fax: 717-477-4016, E-mail: rmpayn@ship.edu.

Sioux Falls Seminary, Graduate and Professional Programs, Program in Marriage and Family Therapy, Sioux Falls, SD 57105-1599. Offers MA. *Entrance requirements:* For master's, minimum GPA of 3.0.

Sonoma State University, School of Social Sciences, Department of Counseling, Rohnert Park, CA 94928-3609. Offers counseling (MA); marriage, family, and child counseling (MA); pupil personnel services (MA). *Accreditation:* ACA. Part-time programs available. *Degree requirements:* For master's, internship. *Entrance requirements:* For master's, minimum GPA of 3.0. *Faculty research:* Self-esteem, relationship of emotion and health, at-risk youth, feminist issues, supervision strategies.

Southern Connecticut State University, School of Graduate Studies, School of Health and Human Services, Program in Marriage and Family Therapy, New Haven, CT 06515-1355. Offers MFT. *Accreditation:* AAMFT/COAMFTE. *Degree requirements:* For master's, internship. *Entrance requirements:* For master's, minimum undergraduate QPA of 3.0 in graduate major field or 2.5 overall, interview. Electronic applications accepted.

Southern Nazarene University, Graduate College, School of Psychology, Bethany, OK 73008. Offers counseling psychology (MSCP); marriage and family therapy (MA). *Degree requirements:* For master's, thesis optional. *Entrance requirements:* For master's, English proficiency exam, minimum GPA of 3.0 in last 60 hours/major, 2.7 overall.

Springfield College, Graduate Programs, Programs in Psychology and Counseling, Springfield, MA 01109-3797. Offers athletic counseling (M Ed, MS, CAGS); industrial/organizational psychology (M Ed, MS, CAGS); marriage and family therapy (M Ed, MS, CAGS); mental health counseling (M Ed, MS, CAGS); school guidance and counseling (M Ed, MS, CAGS); student personnel in higher education (M Ed, MS, CAGS). Part-time programs available. *Faculty:* 13 full-time (6 women), 12 part-time/adjunct (3 women). *Students:* 151 full-time, 52 part-time. Average age 30. 198 applicants, 73% accepted, 74 enrolled. In 2008, 84 master's, 4 other advanced degrees awarded. *Degree requirements:* For master's, research project, portfolio. *Entrance requirements:* Additional exam requirements/recommendations for international students: Required—TOEFL (minimum score 550 paper-based; 213 computer-based). *Application deadline:* For fall admission, 1/15 priority date for domestic students, 1/15 for international students; for winter admission, 11/1 for domestic and international students; for spring admission, 11/1 for domestic and international students. Applications are processed on a rolling basis. Application fee: $50. Electronic applications accepted. *Expenses:* Tuition: Full-time $9132; part-time $761 per semester hour. Required fees: $150. Tuition and fees vary according to course load. *Financial support:* Fellowships with partial tuition reimbursements, teaching assistantships with partial tuition reimbursements, career-related internships or fieldwork, Federal Work-Study, institutionally sponsored loans, and unspecified assistantships available. Financial award application deadline: 3/1; financial award applicants required to submit FAFSA. *Unit head:* Dr. Glenn Lowery, Director, 413-748-3301, Fax: 413-748-3854, E-mail: glowery@spfldcol.edu. *Application contact:* Donald James Shaw, Director of Graduate Admissions, 413-748-3479, Fax: 413-748-3694, E-mail: donald_shaw_jr@spfldcol.edu.

Stephens College, Division of Graduate and Continuing Studies, Programs in Counseling, Columbia, MO 65215-0002. Offers counseling (M Ed), including marriage and family therapy, professional counseling, school counseling. Part-time and evening/weekend programs available. *Faculty:* 3 full-time (all women), 8 part-time/adjunct (3 women). *Students:* 104 full-time (93 women), 20 part-time (18 women); includes 11 minority (7 African Americans, 1 American Indian/Alaska Native, 1 Asian American or Pacific Islander, 2 Hispanic Americans). Average age 38. 32 applicants, 88% accepted, 28 enrolled. In 2008, 26 master's awarded. *Degree requirements:* For master's, thesis. *Entrance requirements:* For master's, minimum GPA of 3.0 in last 60 hours. Additional exam requirements/recommendations for international students: Required—TOEFL (minimum score 213 computer-based). *Application deadline:* For fall admission, 7/25 priority date for domestic and international students; for winter admission, 12/1 priority date for domestic and international students; for spring admission, 4/25 priority date for domestic and international students. Applications are processed on a rolling basis. Application fee: $40. Electronic applications accepted. *Expenses:* Tuition: Part-time $335 per credit hour. Required fees: $15 per credit hour. *Financial support:* In 2008–09, 12 students received support. Scholarships/grants and unspecified assistantships available. Financial award application deadline: 12/5; financial award applicants required to submit FAFSA. *Unit head:* Dr. Linda Taylor Thompson, Program Chair, 800-388-7579. *Application contact:* Meredith Julian, Assistant Director of Marketing and Recruitment, 800-388-7579, E-mail: online@stephens.edu.

Stetson University, College of Arts and Sciences, Division of Education, Department of Counselor Education, DeLand, FL 32723. Offers marriage and family therapy (MS); mental health counseling (MS); school guidance and family consultation (MS). *Accreditation:* ACA. Evening/weekend programs available. *Students:* 73 full-time (64 women), 4 part-time (3 women); includes 19 minority (9 African Americans, 2 American Indian/Alaska Native, 8 Hispanic Americans). Average age 32. In 2008, 23 master's awarded. *Entrance requirements:* For master's, GRE General Test. *Application deadline:* For fall admission, 3/1 priority date for domestic students; for spring admission, 11/1 for domestic students. Applications are processed on a rolling basis. Application fee: $25. *Unit head:* Dr. Brigid Noonan-Klima, Chair, 386-822-8992. *Application contact:* Diana Belian, Office of Graduate Studies, 386-822-7075, Fax: 386-822-7388, E-mail: dbelian@stetson.edu.

Syracuse University, Graduate School, College of Human Ecology, Program in Marriage and Family Therapy, Syracuse, NY 13244. Offers MA, PhD. *Accreditation:* AAMFT/COAMFTE. Part-time programs available. *Degree requirements:* For doctorate, thesis/dissertation. *Entrance requirements:* For master's, GRE General Test. Additional exam requirements/recommendations for international students: Required—TOEFL. Electronic applications accepted.

Texas Tech University, Graduate School, College of Human Sciences, Department of Applied and Professional Studies, Lubbock, TX 79409. Offers family and consumer sciences education (MS, PhD); marriage and family therapy (MS, PhD); personal financial planning (MS, PhD); JD/MS. Part-time programs available. *Faculty:* 15 full-time (9 women). *Students:* 92 full-time (42 women), 61 part-time (32 women); includes 24 minority (13 African Americans, 2 American Indian/Alaska Native, 1 Asian American or Pacific Islander, 8 Hispanic Americans), 9 international. Average age 31. 147 applicants, 69% accepted, 39 enrolled. In 2008, 26 master's, 5 doctorates awarded. Terminal master's awarded for partial completion of doctoral program. *Degree requirements:* For master's, thesis or alternative; for doctorate, thesis/dissertation. *Entrance requirements:* For master's and doctorate, GRE General Test. Additional exam requirements/recommendations for international students: Required—TOEFL (minimum score 550 paper-based; 213 computer-based). *Application deadline:* For fall admission, 3/1 priority date for international students; for spring admission, 11/1 priority date for international students. Applications are processed on a rolling basis. Application fee: $50 ($60 for international students). *Expenses:* Tuition, area resident: Part-time $194 per credit hour. Tuition, state resident: full-time $4648; part-time $194 per credit hour. Tuition, nonresident: full-time $11,392; part-time $475 per credit hour. Required fees: $2206; $69 per credit hour. $389 per semester. *Financial support:* In 2008–09, 67 students received support, including 22 research assistantships with partial tuition reimbursements available (averaging $13,360 per year), 28 teaching assistantships with partial tuition reimbursements available (averaging $13,839 per year); career-related internships or fieldwork, Federal Work-Study, institutionally sponsored loans, and tuition waivers (partial) also available. Support available to part-time students. Financial award application deadline: 4/15; financial award applicants required to submit FAFSA. *Faculty research:* Functional interior design applications for special needs populations; retirement planning and income/expenditure patterns for teachers; surface design, purchase, and consumption of leather products; financial counseling outcome and assessment of college students; multicultural housing environments and behavior correlations. Total annual research expenditures: $312,340. *Unit head:* Dr. Sterling Shumway, Chair, 806-742-5050, Fax: 806-742-5033, E-mail: sterling.shumway@ttu.edu. *Application contact:* Dr. Sterling Shumway, Chair, 806-742-5050, Fax: 806-742-5033, E-mail: sterling.shumway@ttu.edu.

Texas Woman's University, Graduate School, College of Professional Education, Department of Family Sciences, Denton, TX 76201. Offers child development (MS, PhD); counseling and development (MS); early childhood education (M Ed, MA, MS, Ed D); family studies (MS, PhD); family therapy (MS, PhD). *Accreditation:* ACA (one or more programs are accredited). Part-time and evening/weekend programs available. *Faculty:* 22 full-time (17 women), 11 part-time/adjunct (10 women). *Students:* 90 full-time (86 women), 317 part-time (294 women); includes 133 minority (92 African Americans, 3 American Indian/Alaska Native, 9 Asian Americans or Pacific Islanders, 29 Hispanic Americans), 18 international. Average age 37. In 2008, 91 master's, 24 doctorates awarded. *Degree requirements:* For doctorate, comprehensive exam, thesis/dissertation. *Entrance requirements:* For master's, interview, writing sample; for doctorate, interview, minimum GPA of 3.25 in last 60 hours of course work. Additional exam requirements/recommendations for international students: Required—TOEFL (minimum score 550 paper-based; 213 computer-based; 79 iBT). *Application deadline:* For fall admission, 2/15 for domestic students, 4/15 for international students; for spring admission, 9/15 for domestic students, 8/1 for international students. Applications are processed on a rolling basis. Application fee: $30 ($50 for international students). Electronic applications accepted. *Expenses:* Tuition, state resident: full-time $3564; part-time $198 per semester hour. Tuition, nonresident: full-time $8622; part-time $479 per semester hour. Required fees: $1158; $64 per semester hour. Tuition and fees vary according to course load. *Financial support:* In 2008–09, 18 research assistantships (averaging $10,746 per year), 10 teaching assistantships (averaging $10,746 per year) were awarded; career-related internships or fieldwork, Federal Work-Study, institutionally sponsored loans, scholarships/grants, traineeships, health care benefits, and unspecified assistantships also available. Support available to part-time students. Financial award application deadline: 3/1; financial award applicants required to submit FAFSA. *Faculty research:* Parenting/parent education, distance education, play therapy, family sexuality, diversity, ANTHEM healthy marriages initiative. *Unit head:* Dr. Larry LeFlore, Chair, 940-898-2685, Fax: 940-898-2676, E-mail: famsci@twu.edu. *Application contact:* Samuel Wheeler, Assistant Director of Admissions, 940-898-3188, Fax: 940-898-3081, E-mail: wheelersr@twu.edu.

Thomas Jefferson University, Jefferson College of Health Professions, Couple and Family Therapy Department, Philadelphia, PA 19107. Offers family therapy (MS).

Trevecca Nazarene University, Graduate Division, Graduate Psychology Programs, Major in Marriage and Family Therapy, Nashville, TN 37210-2877. Offers MMFT. Part-time and evening/weekend programs available. *Students:* 62 full-time (51 women), 12 part-time (9 women); includes 9 minority (8 African Americans, 1 Hispanic American). In 2008, 23 master's awarded. *Degree requirements:* For master's, comprehensive exam, practicum. *Entrance requirements:* For master's, GRE General Test or MAT, minimum GPA of 2.7, letters of reference. Additional exam requirements/recommendations for international students: Required—TOEFL (minimum score 500 paper-based; 173 computer-based). *Application deadline:* Applications are processed on a rolling basis. Application fee: $25. *Expenses:* Contact institution. *Financial support:* Applicants required to submit FAFSA. *Unit head:* Dr. Peter Wilson, Director of Graduate Psychology Program, 615-248-1384, Fax: 615-248-1662, E-mail: admissions_psy@trevecca.edu. *Application contact:* Heather Ambrefe, Department Secretary, 615-248-1384, Fax: 615-248-1662, E-mail: admissions_psy@trevecca.edu.

Universidad de las Americas, A.C., Program in Psychology, Mexico City, Mexico. Offers family therapy (MA).

The University of Akron, Graduate School, College of Education, Department of Counseling, Program in Marriage and Family Therapy, Akron, OH 44325. Offers MA, MS. *Accreditation:* AAMFT/COAMFTE; ACA. *Degree requirements:* For master's, comprehensive exam. *Entrance requirements:* For master's, minimum GPA of 2.75, interview, letters of recommendation, supplemental form. Additional exam requirements/recommendations for international students: Required—TOEFL (minimum score 550 paper-based; 213 computer-based; 79 iBT). Electronic applications accepted.

University of Arkansas at Little Rock, Graduate School, College of Professional Studies, School of Social Work, Program in Marriage and Family Therapy, Little Rock, AR 72204-1099. Offers Graduate Certificate.

University of Central Florida, College of Education, Department of Child, Family and Community Sciences, Program in Marriage and Family Therapy, Orlando, FL 32816. Offers MA, Certificate. *Students:* 32 full-time (28 women), 13 part-time (12 women); includes 13 minority (2 African Americans, 3 Asian Americans or Pacific Islanders, 8 Hispanic Americans). In 2008, 5 master's, 15 other advanced degrees awarded. *Expenses:* Tuition, area resident: Full-time $6816; part-time $284 per credit. Tuition, state resident: full-time $6816; part-time $1076 per credit. Tuition, nonresident: full-time $25,824. Required fees: $216; $9 per credit. *Financial support:* In 2008–09, 12 research assistantships (averaging $6,800 per year) were awarded.

University of Florida, Graduate School, College of Education, Department of Counselor Education, Gainesville, FL 32611. Offers marriage and family counseling (M Ed, MAE, Ed D, PhD, Ed S); mental health counseling (M Ed, MAE, Ed D, PhD, Ed S); school counseling and guidance (M Ed, MAE, Ed D, PhD, Ed S). *Accreditation:* ACA (one or more programs are accredited); NCATE. Part-time programs available. Terminal master's awarded for partial completion of doctoral program. *Degree requirements:* For master's, thesis optional; for doctorate, thesis/dissertation. *Entrance requirements:* For master's and doctorate, GRE General Test, minimum GPA of 3.0 (undergraduate), 3.5 (graduate); for Ed S, GRE General Test. Additional exam requirements/recommendations for international students: Required—TOEFL (minimum score 550 paper-based; 213 computer-based). Electronic applications accepted.

University of Guelph, Graduate Program Services, College of Social and Applied Human Sciences, Department of Family Relations and Applied Nutrition, Guelph, ON N1G 2W1,

Canada. Offers applied nutrition (MAN); family relations and human development (M Sc, PhD), including applied human nutrition, couple and family therapy (M Sc), family relations and human development. *Accreditation:* AAMFT/COAMFTE (one or more programs are accredited). Part-time programs available. *Degree requirements:* For master's, thesis (for some programs); for doctorate, comprehensive exam, thesis/dissertation. *Entrance requirements:* For master's, minimum B+ average; for doctorate, master's degree in family relations and human development or related field with a minimum B+ average or master's degree in applied human nutrition. Additional exam requirements/recommendations for international students: Required—TOEFL (minimum score 600 paper-based; 250 computer-based). Electronic applications accepted. *Faculty research:* Child and adolescent development, social gerontology, family roles and relations, couple and family therapy, applied human nutrition.

University of Houston–Clear Lake, School of Human Sciences and Humanities, Programs in Human Sciences, Houston, TX 77058-1098. Offers behavioral sciences (MA), including criminology, cross cultural studies, general psychology, sociology; clinical psychology (MA); criminology (MA); cross cultural studies (MA); family therapy (MA); fitness and human performance (MA); school psychology (MA). *Accreditation:* AAMFT/COAMFTE. Part-time and evening/weekend programs available. Postbaccalaureate distance learning degree programs offered (minimal on-campus study). *Degree requirements:* For master's, thesis or alternative. *Entrance requirements:* For master's, GRE General Test. Additional exam requirements/recommendations for international students: Required—TOEFL (minimum score 550 paper-based; 213 computer-based). Electronic applications accepted. *Faculty research:* Smoking cessation, adolescent sexuality, white collar crime, serial murder, human factors/human computer interaction.

University of La Verne, College of Arts and Sciences, Department of Psychology, Programs in Counseling, La Verne, CA 91750-4443. Offers general counseling (MS); higher education counseling (MS); marriage and family therapy (MS). Part-time programs available. *Faculty:* 2 full-time (both women), 10 part-time/adjunct (8 women). *Students:* 36 full-time (33 women), 73 part-time (65 women); includes 76 minority (14 African Americans, 6 Asian Americans or Pacific Islanders, 56 Hispanic Americans). Average age 30. In 2008, 24 master's awarded. *Degree requirements:* For master's, thesis, competency exam, personal psychotherapy. *Entrance requirements:* For master's, minimum undergraduate GPA of 3.0, 3 recommendations, interview. Additional exam requirements/recommendations for international students: Required—TOEFL (minimum score 600 paper-based; 250 computer-based). *Application deadline:* Applications are processed on a rolling basis. Application fee: $50. *Expenses:* Contact institution. *Financial support:* Career-related internships or fieldwork, institutionally sponsored loans, and scholarships/grants available. Financial award application deadline: 3/2; financial award applicants required to submit FAFSA. *Application contact:* Connie Hamlow, Admissions Information Specialist, 909-593-3511 Ext. 4244, Fax: 909-392-2761, E-mail: gradadmission@ulv.edu.

University of Louisiana at Monroe, Graduate School, College of Education and Human Development, Department of Educational Leadership and Counseling, Program in Marriage and Family Therapy, Monroe, LA 71209-0001. Offers MA, PhD. *Accreditation:* AAMFT/COAMFTE (one or more programs are accredited); ACA. Part-time and evening/weekend programs available. *Faculty:* 5 full-time (1 woman). *Students:* 48 full-time (33 women), 17 part-time (11 women); includes 11 minority (10 African Americans, 1 Asian American or Pacific Islander). Average age 30. In 2008, 6 master's, 2 doctorates awarded. *Degree requirements:* For master's, thesis optional; for doctorate, comprehensive exam, thesis/dissertation, clinical experience. *Entrance requirements:* For master's, GRE General Test, minimum GPA of 2.8; for doctorate, GRE General Test, minimum GPA of 3.5. Additional exam requirements/recommendations for international students: Required—TOEFL (minimum score 500 paper-based; 173 computer-based; 61 iBT). *Application deadline:* For fall admission, 8/22 priority date for domestic students, 7/1 for international students; for winter admission, 12/12 priority date for domestic students; for spring admission, 1/17 for domestic students, 11/1 for international students. Applications are processed on a rolling basis. Application fee: $20 ($30 for international students). Electronic applications accepted. *Expenses:* Tuition, area resident: Full-time $2403; part-time $1202 per semester. Tuition, state resident: full-time $2403; part-time $1202 per semester. Tuition, nonresident: full-time $2403; part-time $1202 per semester. International tuition: $8352 full-time. Required fees: $1239.40; $141 per credit hour. *Financial support:* Research assistantships with full tuition reimbursements, teaching assistantships with full tuition reimbursements, career-related internships or fieldwork, Federal Work-Study, and unspecified assistantships available. Financial award application deadline: 4/1; financial award applicants required to submit FAFSA. *Faculty research:* Family systems, substance abuse. Total annual research expenditures: $20,000. *Unit head:* Dr. Lamar Woodham, Program Director, 318-362-3008, Fax: 318-342-3131, E-mail: woodham@ulm.edu. *Application contact:* Dr. Harper Gaushell, Admissions Coordinator, 318-343-8441, Fax: 318-342-3131, E-mail: gaushell@ulm.edu.

University of Louisville, Graduate School, Raymond A. Kent School of Social Work, Louisville, KY 40292-0001. Offers marriage and family therapy (PMC); social work (MSSW, PhD), including alcohol and drug counseling (MSSW), gerontology (MSSW), school social work (MSSW). *Accreditation:* AAMFT/COAMFTE; CSWE (one or more programs are accredited). Part-time and evening/weekend programs available. *Faculty:* 23 full-time (15 women), 38 part-time/adjunct (21 women). *Students:* 282 full-time (229 women), 67 part-time (54 women); includes 93 minority (84 African Americans, 2 American Indian/Alaska Native, 2 Asian Americans or Pacific Islanders, 5 Hispanic Americans), 7 international. Average age 32. 314 applicants, 78% accepted, 142 enrolled. In 2008, 156 master's, 5 doctorates awarded. *Degree requirements:* For doctorate, comprehensive exam, thesis/dissertation. *Entrance requirements:* For master's, GRE or minimum GPA of 2.75; for doctorate, GRE General Test, interview, writing sample. Additional exam requirements/recommendations for international students: Required—TOEFL (minimum score 550 paper-based; 213 computer-based; 79 iBT). *Application deadline:* For fall admission, 7/31 for domestic and international students. Applications are processed on a rolling basis. Application fee: $50. Electronic applications accepted. *Financial support:* In 2008–09, 80 students received support, including 2 fellowships with full tuition reimbursements available (averaging $19,000 per year), 8 research assistantships with full tuition reimbursements available (averaging $19,000 per year); Federal Work-Study, institutionally sponsored loans, scholarships/grants, health care benefits, tuition waivers (full), and unspecified assistantships also available. Support available to part-time students. Financial award application deadline: 6/1; financial award applicants required to submit FAFSA. *Faculty research:* Child welfare, substance abuse, gerontology, family functioning, health behavior. *Unit head:* Dr. Terry Singer, Dean, 502-852-6402, Fax: 502-852-0422, E-mail: terry.singer@louisville.edu. *Application contact:* Libby Leggett, Director, Graduate Admissions, 502-852-3101, Fax: 502-852-6536, E-mail: gradadm@louisville.edu.

University of Mary Hardin-Baylor, College of Sciences and Humanities, Department of Psychology, Belton, TX 76513. Offers community counseling (MA); marriage and family Christian counseling (MA); psychology and counseling (MA); school counseling and psychology (MA). Part-time and evening/weekend programs available. *Degree requirements:* For master's, comprehensive exam. *Entrance requirements:* For master's, GRE General Test, minimum GPA of 3.0 in last 60 hours or 2.75 overall. Electronic applications accepted.

University of Maryland, College Park, Graduate Studies, School of Public Health, Department of Family Science, College Park, MD 20742. Offers family studies (PhD); marriage and family therapy (MS). *Accreditation:* AAMFT/COAMFTE. Part-time and evening/weekend programs available. *Degree requirements:* For master's, thesis or alternative; for doctorate, comprehensive exam, thesis/dissertation, oral defense. *Entrance requirements:* For master's, GRE General Test, minimum GPA of 3.0, 3 letters of recommendation; for doctorate, GRE General Test, minimum GPA of 3.0, 3 letters of recommendation, research sample. Electronic applications accepted. *Faculty research:* Family life quality, interracial couples, child support, homeless families, family and child well-being.

University of Massachusetts Boston, Office of Graduate Studies, Graduate College of Education, Counseling and School Psychology Department, Program in Family Therapy, Boston, MA 02125-3393. Offers M Ed, CAGS. *Accreditation:* AAMFT/COAMFTE.

University of Miami, Graduate School, School of Education, Department of Educational and Psychological Studies, Program in Counseling, Coral Gables, FL 33124. Offers bilingual and bicultural counseling (Certificate); marriage and family therapy (MS Ed); mental health counseling (MS Ed). Part-time programs available. *Degree requirements:* For master's, comprehensive exam. *Entrance requirements:* For master's, GRE General Test; for Certificate, master's degree in a mental health field. Additional exam requirements/recommendations for international students: Required—TOEFL (minimum score 550 paper-based; 212 computer-based). Electronic applications accepted. *Faculty research:* Cocaine recidivism, HIV, non-traditional families, health psychology, diversity.

University of Minnesota, Twin Cities Campus, Graduate School, College of Education and Human Development, Department of Family Social Science, Minneapolis, MN 55455-0213. Offers marriage and family therapy (MA, PhD). *Accreditation:* AAMFT/COAMFTE (one or more programs are accredited). *Degree requirements:* For master's, thesis; for doctorate, thesis/dissertation. *Entrance requirements:* For master's and doctorate, GRE General Test, minimum undergraduate GPA of 3.0 (preferred). Additional exam requirements/recommendations for international students: Required—TOEFL. *Faculty research:* Families and diversity, families and health, families and economic well-being, individuals and relationships across the lifespan.

University of Mobile, Graduate Programs, Program in Religious Studies, Mobile, AL 36613. Offers biblical/theological studies (MA); marriage and family counseling (MA). Part-time and evening/weekend programs available. *Faculty:* 5 full-time (0 women), 1 part-time/adjunct (0 women). *Students:* 16 full-time (14 women), 41 part-time (33 women); includes 25 minority (23 African Americans, 2 American Indian/Alaska Native). Average age 32. In 2008, 13 master's awarded. *Degree requirements:* For master's, one foreign language, comprehensive exam, thesis optional. *Entrance requirements:* For master's, GRE General Test. Additional exam requirements/recommendations for international students: Required—TOEFL (minimum score 550 paper-based; 213 computer-based; 80 iBT). *Application deadline:* For fall admission, 8/3 priority date for domestic students; for spring admission, 12/23 for domestic students. Applications are processed on a rolling basis. Application fee: $40 ($50 for international students). *Expenses:* Tuition: Full-time $7560; part-time $420 per credit hour. Required fees: $240; $120 per semester. *Financial support:* Federal Work-Study available. Support available to part-time students. Financial award application deadline: 8/1. *Unit head:* Dr. Cecil Taylor, Dean, School of Christian Studies, 251-442-2255, Fax: 251-442-2523, E-mail: ctaylor@mail.umobile.edu. *Application contact:* Tammy C. Eubanks, Administrative Assistant to Dean of Graduate Programs, 251-442-2270, Fax: 251-442-2523, E-mail: teubanks@umobile.edu.

University of Montevallo, College of Education, Program in Counseling, Montevallo, AL 35115. Offers community counseling (M Ed); marriage and family (M Ed); school counseling (M Ed). *Accreditation:* ACA; NCATE. Part-time and evening/weekend programs available. *Students:* 29 full-time (24 women), 48 part-time (41 women); includes 17 minority (15 African Americans, 1 Asian American or Pacific Islander, 1 Hispanic American), 2 international. In 2008, 19 master's awarded. *Entrance requirements:* For master's, GRE General Test or MAT, minimum undergraduate GPA of 2.75 in last 60 hours or 2.5 overall, interview. Additional exam requirements/recommendations for international students: Required—TOEFL (minimum score 550 paper-based). *Application deadline:* For fall admission, 7/15 for domestic students; for spring admission, 11/15 for domestic students. Application fee: $25. *Expenses:* Tuition, state resident: full-time $5280; part-time $220 per credit hour. Tuition, nonresident: full-time $10,560; part-time $440 per credit hour. Required fees: $482; $113 per semester. One-time fee: $25 part-time. *Financial support:* Federal Work-Study, scholarships/grants, and unspecified assistantships available. *Unit head:* Dr. Leland Doebler, Chair, 205-665-6380. *Application contact:* Dr. Leland Doebler, Chair, 205-665-6380.

University of Nebraska–Lincoln, Graduate College, College of Education and Human Sciences, Department of Child, Youth and Family Studies, Lincoln, NE 68588. Offers child development/early childhood education (MS, PhD); child, youth and family studies (MS); family and consumer sciences education (MS, PhD); family financial planning (MS); family science (MS, PhD); gerontology (PhD); human sciences (PhD), including child, youth and family studies, gerontology, medical family therapy; marriage and family therapy (MS); medical family therapy (PhD); youth development (MS). *Accreditation:* AAMFT/COAMFTE (one or more programs are accredited). Postbaccalaureate distance learning degree programs offered. *Faculty:* 16 full-time (11 women). *Students:* 23 full-time (18 women), 53 part-time (40 women); includes 8 minority (2 African Americans, 2 American Indian/Alaska Native, 2 Asian Americans or Pacific Islanders, 2 Hispanic Americans), 1 international. Average age 32. In 2008, 27 master's awarded. *Degree requirements:* For master's, thesis optional. *Entrance requirements:* For master's, GRE. Additional exam requirements/recommendations for international students: Required—TOEFL (minimum score 550 paper-based; 213 computer-based). *Application deadline:* For fall admission, 1/15 for domestic and international students; for spring admission, 10/1 for domestic and international students. Application fee: $40. Electronic applications accepted. *Expenses:* Tuition, state resident: full-time $4275; part-time $237.50 per credit hour. Tuition, nonresident: full-time $11,525; part-time $640.25 per credit hour. Required fees: $1068; $10.35 per credit hour. $440.70 per semester. Tuition and fees vary according to course load and program. *Financial support:* Fellowships, research assistantships, teaching assistantships, Federal Work-Study, health care benefits, and unspecified assistantships available. Financial award application deadline: 2/15. *Faculty research:* Marriage and family therapy, child development/early childhood education, family financial management. *Unit head:* Dr. Julie Johnson, Chair, 402-472-2957. *Application contact:* Dr. Julie Johnson, Chair, 402-472-2957.

University of Nevada, Las Vegas, Graduate College, Greenspun College of Urban Affairs, Department of Marriage and Family Therapy, Las Vegas, NV 89154-3045. Offers MS, Advanced Certificate. *Accreditation:* ACA. Part-time programs available. *Faculty:* 4 full-time (2 women). *Students:* 15 full-time (all women), 16 part-time (14 women); includes 2 minority (1 African American, 1 Hispanic American). Average age 36. 47 applicants, 28% accepted, 9 enrolled. In 2008, 9 master's, 1 other advanced degree awarded. *Degree requirements:* For master's, comprehensive exam (for some programs), thesis (for some programs). *Entrance requirements:* For master's and Advanced Certificate, GRE General Test. Additional exam requirements/recommendations for international students: Required—TOEFL (minimum score 550 paper-based; 213 computer-based; 80 iBT), IELTS (minimum score 7). *Application deadline:* For fall admission, 1/15 priority date for domestic and international students. Applications are processed on a rolling basis. Application fee: $60 ($75 for international students). Electronic applications accepted. *Expenses:* Tuition, state resident: full-time $1414; part-time $198 per credit. Tuition, nonresident: full-time $12,509; part-time $415.75 per credit. International tuition: $14,249 full-time. Required fees: $4 per credit. $252 per semester. Tuition and fees vary according to course load. *Financial support:* In 2008–09, 4 students received support, including 4 research assistantships with partial tuition reimbursements available (averaging $10,000 per year); institutionally sponsored loans, scholarships/grants, health care benefits, and unspecified assistantships also available. Financial award application deadline: 3/1. *Faculty research:* Marriage and family therapy. *Unit head:* Dr. Gerald Weeks, Chair/Professor, 702-895-1392, Fax: 702-895-1869, E-mail: gerald.weeks@unlv.edu. *Application contact:* Graduate College Admissions Evaluator, 702-895-3320, Fax: 702-895-4180, E-mail: gradcollege@unlv.edu.

University of New Hampshire, Graduate School, School of Health and Human Services, Department of Family Studies, Durham, NH 03824. Offers family studies (MS); marriage and family therapy (MS). *Accreditation:* AAMFT/COAMFTE. Part-time programs available. *Faculty:* 9 full-time (6 women). *Students:* 13 full-time (11 women), 9 part-time (8 women); includes 3 minority (1 African American, 2 Asian Americans or Pacific Islanders). Average age 30. 27 applicants, 56% accepted, 10 enrolled. In 2008, 7 master's awarded. *Degree requirements:* For master's, thesis or alternative. *Entrance requirements:* For master's, GRE General Test. Additional exam requirements/recommendations for international students: Required—TOEFL (minimum score 550 paper-based; 213 computer-based; 80 iBT). *Application deadline:* For fall admission, 4/1 priority date for domestic students, 4/1 for international students; for winter admission, 12/1 for domestic students. Applications are processed on a rolling basis. Application

Marriage and Family Therapy

University of New Hampshire (continued)
fee: $60. Electronic applications accepted. *Expenses:* Tuition, area resident: Full-time $9720; part-time $540 per credit hour. Tuition, nonresident: full-time $23,200; part-time $954 per credit hour. Required fees: $1446; $361.50 per term. *Financial support:* In 2008–09, 12 students received support, including 1 research assistantship, 5 teaching assistantships; fellowships, career-related internships or fieldwork, Federal Work-Study, scholarships/grants, and tuition waivers (full and partial) also available. Support available to part-time students. Financial award application deadline: 2/15. *Unit head:* Dr. Elizabeth Dolan, Chairperson, 603-862-2137. *Application contact:* Matty Leighton, Administrative Assistant, 603-862-5021, E-mail: family.studies@unh.edu.

The University of North Carolina at Greensboro, Graduate School, School of Education, Department of Counseling and Educational Development, Greensboro, NC 27412-5001. Offers advanced school counseling (PMC); counseling and counselor education (PhD); counseling and educational development (MS); couple and family counseling (PMC); school counseling (PMC); MS/Ed S. *Accreditation:* ACA (one or more programs are accredited); NCATE. *Degree requirements:* For master's, comprehensive exam, practicum, internship; for doctorate, comprehensive exam, thesis/dissertation. *Entrance requirements:* For master's, doctorate, and PMC, GRE General Test. Additional exam requirements/recommendations for international students: Required—TOEFL. Electronic applications accepted. *Faculty research:* Gerontology, invitational theory, career development, marriage and family therapy, drug and alcohol abuse prevention.

University of Phoenix, The Artemis School, College of Health and Human Services, Phoenix, AZ 85034-7209. Offers administration of justice and security (MS); community counseling (MSC); education (MHA); family nurse practitioner (MSN); gerontology (MHA); health administration (MHA); health care education (MSN); health care management (MBA, MSN); informatics (MHA); marriage, family, and child therapy (MSC); nursing (MSN); nursing for nurse practitioners (MSN); psychology (MS); MSN/MBA; MSN/MHA. *Accreditation:* AACN. Evening/weekend programs available. Postbaccalaureate distance learning degree programs offered. *Degree requirements:* For master's, thesis (for some programs). *Entrance requirements:* For master's, 3 years of work experience, minimum undergraduate GPA of 2.5, RN license. Additional exam requirements/recommendations for international students: Required—TOEFL (minimum score 550 paper-based; 213 computer-based; 79 iBT). Electronic applications accepted.

University of Phoenix–Bay Area Campus, The Artemis School, College of Health and Human Services, Pleasanton, CA 94588-3677. Offers administration of justice and security (MS); family nurse practitioner (MSN); health care management (MBA); marriage, family and child therapy (MSC); nursing (MSN); nursing/health care education (MSN); MSN/MBA. Evening/weekend programs available. Postbaccalaureate distance learning degree programs offered (no on-campus study). *Degree requirements:* For master's, thesis (for some programs). *Entrance requirements:* For master's, minimum undergraduate GPA of 2.5, 3 years of work experience, RN license. Additional exam requirements/recommendations for international students: Required—TOEFL (minimum score 550 paper-based; 213 computer-based; 79 iBT). Electronic applications accepted.

University of Phoenix–Central Valley Campus, College of Social and Behavioral Science, Fresno, CA 93720-1562. Offers marriage, family and child therapy (MSC).

University of Phoenix–Denver Campus, The Artemis School, College of Health and Human Services, Lone Tree, CO 80124-5453. Offers administration of justice and security (MS); community counseling (MSC); health administration (MHA); health care management (MBA); marriage, family and child therapy (MSC); nursing (MSN); psychology (MS); MSN/MBA; MSN/MHA. Evening/weekend programs available. Postbaccalaureate distance learning degree programs offered. *Degree requirements:* For master's, thesis (for some programs). *Entrance requirements:* For master's, minimum undergraduate GPA of 2.5, 3 years work experience, RN license. Additional exam requirements/recommendations for international students: Required—TOEFL (minimum score 550 paper-based; 213 computer-based; 79 iBT). Electronic applications accepted.

University of Phoenix–Hawaii Campus, The Artemis School, College of Health and Human Services, Honolulu, HI 96813-4317. Offers administration of justice and security (MS); community counseling (MSC); education (MHA); family nurse practitioner (MSN); gerontology (MHA); health administration (MHA); health care management (MBA); marriage, family and child therapy (MSC); nursing (MSN); nursing/health care education (MSN); psychology (MS); MSN/MBA. Evening/weekend programs available. *Degree requirements:* For master's, thesis (for some programs). *Entrance requirements:* For master's, minimum undergraduate GPA of 2.5, 3 years of work experience, RN license. Additional exam requirements/recommendations for international students: Required—TOEFL (minimum score 550 paper-based; 213 computer-based; 79 iBT). Electronic applications accepted.

University of Phoenix–Las Vegas Campus, The Artemis School, College of Health and Human Services, Las Vegas, NV 89128. Offers administration of justice and security (MS); health administration (MHA); health care management (MBA); marriage, family, and child therapy (MSC); mental health counseling (MSC); nursing (MSN); nursing/health care education (MSN); psychology (MS); MSN/MBA; MSN/MHA. Postbaccalaureate distance learning degree programs offered. *Entrance requirements:* For master's, minimum undergraduate GPA of 2.5, 3 years of work experience. Additional exam requirements/recommendations for international students: Required—TOEFL (minimum score 550 paper-based; 213 computer-based; 79 iBT). Electronic applications accepted.

University of Phoenix–New Mexico Campus, The Artemis School, College of Health and Human Services, Albuquerque, NM 87109-4645. Offers administration of justice and security (MS); health administration (MHA); health care education (MSN); health care management (MBA); marriage and family therapy (MSC); nursing (MSN); psychology (MS); MSN/MBA. Evening/weekend programs available. *Degree requirements:* For master's, thesis (for some programs). *Entrance requirements:* For master's, minimum undergraduate GPA of 2.5, 3 years of work experience, RN license. Additional exam requirements/recommendations for international students: Required—TOEFL (minimum score 550 paper-based; 213 computer-based; 79 iBT). Electronic applications accepted.

University of Phoenix–Northern Nevada Campus, College of Social and Behavioral Science, Reno, NV 89511. Offers administration of justice and security (MS); marriage, family and child therapy (MSC); psychology (MS); school counseling (MSC).

University of Phoenix–Phoenix Campus, The Artemis School, College of Health and Human Services, Phoenix, AZ 85040-1958. Offers community counseling (MSC); education (MHA); family nurse practitioner (MSN); gerontology (MHA); health administration (MHA); health care education (MSN); health care management (MBA); informatics (MHA); marriage, family, and child therapy (MSC); nurse practitioner (Certificate); nursing (MSN); nursing health care education (Certificate); psychology (MS); MSN/MBA; MSN/MHA. Evening/weekend programs available. *Degree requirements:* For master's, thesis (for some programs). *Entrance requirements:* For master's, 3 years of work experience in field, minimum undergraduate GPA of 2.5, RN license. Additional exam requirements/recommendations for international students: Required—TOEFL (minimum score 550 paper-based; 213 computer-based; 79 iBT). Electronic applications accepted.

University of Phoenix–Puerto Rico Campus, The Artemis School, College of Health and Human Services, Guaynabo, PR 00968. Offers marriage and family counseling (MSC); mental health counseling (MSC). Evening/weekend programs available. *Degree requirements:* For master's, thesis (for some programs). *Entrance requirements:* For master's, Counselor Preparation Comprehensive Examination, minimum undergraduate GPA of 2.5, 3 years work experience. Additional exam requirements/recommendations for international students: Required—TOEFL (minimum score 550 paper-based; 213 computer-based; 79 iBT). Electronic applications accepted.

University of Phoenix–Sacramento Valley Campus, The Artemis School, College of Health and Human Services, Sacramento, CA 95833-3632. Offers administration of justice and security (MS); community counseling (MSC); family nurse practitioner (MSN); health administration (MHA); health care education (MSN); health care management (MBA); marriage, family and child counseling (MSC); nursing (MSN); psychology (MS); MSN/MBA. Evening/weekend programs available. *Degree requirements:* For master's, thesis (for some programs). *Entrance requirements:* For master's, RN license, minimum undergraduate GPA of 2.5, 3 years work experience. Additional exam requirements/recommendations for international students: Required—TOEFL (minimum score 550 paper-based; 213 computer-based; 79 iBT). Electronic applications accepted.

University of Phoenix–San Diego Campus, The Artemis School, College of Health and Human Services, San Diego, CA 92123. Offers administration of justice and security (MS); health care education (MSN); health care management (MBA); marriage, family and child counseling (MSC); marriage, family and child therapy (MSC); nursing (MSN); MSN/MBA. Evening/weekend programs available. *Degree requirements:* For master's, thesis (for some programs). *Entrance requirements:* For master's, minimum undergraduate GPA of 2.5, 3 years work experience, RN license. Additional exam requirements/recommendations for international students: Required—TOEFL (minimum score 550 paper-based; 213 computer-based; 79 iBT). Electronic applications accepted.

University of Phoenix–Southern Arizona Campus, The Artemis School, College of Health and Human Services, Tucson, AZ 85711. Offers administration of justice and security (MS); family nurse practitioner (MSN, Certificate); health administration (MHA); health care management (MBA); marriage, family and child therapy (MSC); nursing (MSN); psychology (MS). Evening/weekend programs available. *Degree requirements:* For master's, thesis (for some programs). *Entrance requirements:* For master's, minimum undergraduate GPA of 2.5, 3 years of work experience, RN license. Additional exam requirements/recommendations for international students: Required—TOEFL (minimum score 550 paper-based; 213 computer-based; 79 iBT). Electronic applications accepted.

University of Phoenix–Southern California Campus, The Artemis School, College of Health and Human Services, Costa Mesa, CA 92626. Offers administration of justice and security (MS); family nurse practitioner (MSN, Certificate); health administration (MHA); health care education (MSN); health care management (MBA); marriage, family and child therapy (MSC); nursing (MSN); psychology (MS); MSN/MBA; MSN/MHA. Evening/weekend programs available. *Degree requirements:* For master's, thesis (for some programs). *Entrance requirements:* For master's, minimum undergraduate GPA of 2.5, 3 years work experience, RN license. Additional exam requirements/recommendations for international students: Required—TOEFL (minimum score 550 paper-based; 213 computer-based; 79 iBT). Electronic applications accepted.

University of Phoenix–Southern Colorado Campus, The Artemis School, College of Health and Human Services, Colorado Springs, CO 80919-2335. Offers administration of justice and security (MS); community counseling (MSC); education (MHA); gerontology (MHA); health administration (MHA); health care management (MBA); marriage, family and child therapy (MSC); nursing (MSN); psychology (MS); MSN/MBA. Evening/weekend programs available. *Degree requirements:* For master's, thesis (for some programs). *Entrance requirements:* For master's, minimum undergraduate GPA of 2.5, 3 years of work experience, RN license. Additional exam requirements/recommendations for international students: Required—TOEFL (minimum score 550 paper-based; 213 computer-based; 79 iBT). Electronic applications accepted.

University of Rochester, School of Medicine and Dentistry, Graduate Programs in Medicine and Dentistry, Department of Psychiatry, Rochester, NY 14627-0250. Offers marriage and family therapy (MS). *Accreditation:* AAMFT/COAMFTE. Part-time programs available. *Degree requirements:* For master's, projects. *Entrance requirements:* For master's, GRE General Test.

University of St. Thomas, Graduate Studies, Graduate School of Professional Psychology, St. Paul, MN 55105-1096. Offers counseling psychology (MA, Psy D); family psychology (Certificate). *Accreditation:* APA. Part-time and evening/weekend programs available. *Degree requirements:* For master's, comprehensive exam, practicum; for doctorate, comprehensive exam, thesis/dissertation, qualifying exam, practicum, internship. *Entrance requirements:* For master's, MAT or GRE, minimum GPA of 2.75, letters of recommendation; for doctorate, GRE, minimum GPA of 3.2, letters of recommendation. Additional exam requirements/recommendations for international students: Required—TOEFL. *Expenses:* Contact institution. *Faculty research:* Elderly, eating disorders, anxiety.

University of San Diego, School of Leadership and Education Sciences, Program in Marital and Family Therapy, San Diego, CA 92110-2492. Offers MA. *Accreditation:* AAMFT/COAMFTE. *Faculty:* 3 full-time (2 women), 10 part-time/adjunct (6 women). *Students:* 49 full-time (45 women), 4 part-time (3 women); includes 11 minority (2 African Americans, 3 Asian Americans or Pacific Islanders, 6 Hispanic Americans), 4 international. Average age 26. 99 applicants, 48% accepted, 19 enrolled. In 2008, 36 master's awarded. *Degree requirements:* For master's, comprehensive exam. *Entrance requirements:* For master's, GRE General Test or MAT, minimum GPA of 3.0, 3 letters of recommendation, resumé. Additional exam requirements/recommendations for international students: Required—TOEFL (minimum score 580 paper-based; 237 computer-based; 83 iBT), TWE. *Application deadline:* For fall admission, 1/15 for domestic and international students; for spring admission, 10/15 for domestic and international students. Application fee: $45. *Expenses:* Tuition: Full-time $19,710; part-time $1129 per unit. Required fees: $154. Full-time tuition and fees vary according to course load and degree level. *Financial support:* In 2008–09, 45 students received support. Career-related internships or fieldwork, Federal Work-Study, institutionally sponsored loans, scholarships/grants, unspecified assistantships, and stipends available. Support available to part-time students. Financial award application deadline: 4/1; financial award applicants required to submit FAFSA. *Unit head:* Dr. Todd M. Edwards, Director, 619-260-5963, Fax: 619-260-6835, E-mail: tedwards@sandiego.edu. *Application contact:* Dr. John Mosby, Associate Director of Graduate Admissions, 619-260-4524, Fax: 619-260-4158, E-mail: grads@sandiego.edu.

University of San Francisco, School of Education, Department of Counseling Psychology, San Francisco, CA 94117-1080. Offers counseling (MA), including educational counseling, life transitions counseling, marital and family therapy; counseling psychology (Ed D). *Degree requirements:* For doctorate, thesis/dissertation. *Entrance requirements:* For doctorate, GRE General Test.

University of Southern California, Graduate School, School of Education, Master's Programs in Education, Los Angeles, CA 90089. Offers counseling psychology (ME); curriculum and teaching (MS); instructional technology (MS); marriage, family and child counseling (MMFT); postsecondary administration and student affairs [PASA] (ME); school counseling (ME); teaching and teaching credential program (MAT); teaching English as a foreign language (ME); teaching English to speakers of other languages (MS). Part-time and evening/weekend programs available. *Entrance requirements:* For master's, GRE.

University of Southern Mississippi, Graduate School, College of Education and Psychology, Department of Child and Family Studies, Hattiesburg, MS 39406-0001. Offers child and family studies (MS); early intervention (MS); marriage and family therapy (MS). *Accreditation:* AAMFT/COAMFTE. Part-time programs available. *Faculty:* 8 full-time (4 women). *Students:* 33 full-time (32 women), 21 part-time (20 women); includes 14 minority (12 African Americans, 1 Asian American or Pacific Islander, 1 Hispanic American), 1 international. Average age 29. 55 applicants, 47% accepted, 23 enrolled. In 2008, 15 master's awarded. *Degree requirements:* For master's, comprehensive exam, thesis optional. *Entrance requirements:* For master's, GRE General Test, minimum GPA of 2.75 in last 60 hours. Additional exam requirements/recommendations for international students: Required—TOEFL. *Application deadline:* For fall admission, 3/1 priority date for domestic students, 3/1 for international students. Applications are processed on a rolling basis. Application fee: $30. Electronic applications accepted. *Financial support:* In 2008–09, 21 students received support, including 3 research assistantships with full tuition reimbursements available (averaging $7,300 per year); fellowships, career-related internships or fieldwork, Federal Work-Study, institutionally sponsored loans, scholarships/grants, and unspecified assistantships also available. Financial award application deadline: 3/15; financial award applicants required to submit FAFSA. *Faculty research:* School food service, teen pregnancy, diet and cholesterol metabolism. *Unit head:* Dr. Ann Blackwell, Chair, 601-266-5661, Fax: 601-266-4680. *Application contact:* Dr. Ann Blackwell, Chair, 601-266-5661, Fax: 601-266-4680.

The University of Texas at Tyler, College of Education and Psychology, Department of Psychology, Tyler, TX 75799-0001. Offers clinical psychology (MS), including neuropsychology, school psychology; counseling psychology (MA), including general, marriage and family; interdisciplinary studies (MSIS); school counseling (MA). Part-time and evening/weekend programs available. *Degree requirements:* For master's, comprehensive exam, thesis optional. *Entrance requirements:* For master's, GRE General Test, minimum GPA of 3.0. Additional exam requirements/recommendations for international students: Required—TOEFL (minimum score 79 computer-based). Electronic applications accepted. *Faculty research:* Neuropsychology, child abuse, psychometric properties of psychological instruments, maternal behavior, clinical practice issues, victimization of women, post-traumatic stress disorder.

The University of Winnipeg, Faculty of Theology, Winnipeg, MB R3B 2E9, Canada. Offers marriage and family therapy (MMFT, Certificate); sacred theology (STM); theology (M Div). *Accreditation:* AAMFT/COAMFTE; ATS. Part-time programs available. *Degree requirements:* For M Div, thesis/dissertation optional.

University of Wisconsin–Milwaukee, Graduate School, School of Social Welfare, Department of Social Work, Milwaukee, WI 53201-0413. Offers applied gerontology (Certificate); marriage and family therapy (Certificate); non-profit management (Certificate); social work (MSW, PhD). *Accreditation:* CSWE. Part-time programs available. *Faculty:* 19 full-time (12 women). *Students:* 173 full-time (157 women), 101 part-time (92 women); includes 55 minority (38 African Americans, 2 American Indian/Alaska Native, 7 Asian Americans or Pacific Islanders, 8 Hispanic Americans). Average age 31. 313 applicants, 57% accepted, 105 enrolled. In 2008, 133 master's awarded. *Degree requirements:* For master's, thesis or alternative. *Entrance requirements:* For doctorate, GRE, bachelor's degree. Additional exam requirements/recommendations for international students: Required—TOEFL (minimum score 550 paper-based; 79 iBT), IELTS (minimum score 6.5). *Application deadline:* For fall admission, 1/1 priority date for domestic students; for spring admission, 9/1 for domestic students. Applications are processed on a rolling basis. Application fee: $45 ($75 for international students). *Expenses:* Tuition, area resident: Full-time $7320; part-time $165 per credit. Tuition, state resident: full-time $7320; part-time $165 per credit. Tuition, nonresident: full-time $17,840; part-time $714 per credit. Tuition and fees vary according to campus/location, program and reciprocity agreements. *Financial support:* In 2008–09, 5 fellowships, 4 teaching assistantships were awarded; research assistantships, career-related internships or fieldwork and unspecified assistantships also available. Support available to part-time students. Financial award application deadline: 4/15. Total annual research expenditures: $2.9 million. *Unit head:* Deborah Padgett, Representative, 414-229-4851, Fax: 414-229-5311, E-mail: dpadgett@uwm.edu. *Application contact:* Steve McMurtry, General Information Contact, 414-229-2249, Fax: 414-229-6967, E-mail: Mcmurtry@uwm.edu.

University of Wisconsin–Stout, Graduate School, College of Human Development, Program in Marriage and Family Therapy, Menomonie, WI 54751. Offers MS. *Accreditation:* AAMFT/COAMFTE. Part-time programs available. *Students:* 22 full-time (19 women); includes 3 minority (1 African American, 1 Asian American or Pacific Islander, 1 Hispanic American). Average age 31. 55 applicants, 31% accepted, 14 enrolled. In 2008, 12 master's awarded. *Degree requirements:* For master's, thesis or alternative. *Entrance requirements:* For master's, minimum GPA of 2.75. Additional exam requirements/recommendations for international students: Required—TOEFL (minimum score 500 paper-based; 173 computer-based; 61 iBT). *Application deadline:* For fall admission, 2/1 priority date for domestic and international students. Application fee: $45. Electronic applications accepted. *Expenses:* Tuition, state resident: full-time $6227; part-time $345.93 per credit. Tuition, nonresident: full-time $9998; part-time $555.42 per credit. International tuition: $10,512 full-time. Tuition and fees vary according to course load, program and reciprocity agreements. *Financial support:* In 2008–09, 1 research assistantship with partial tuition reimbursement (averaging $5,129 per year) was awarded; teaching assistantships with partial tuition reimbursements, Federal Work-Study, scholarships/grants, tuition waivers (partial), and unspecified assistantships also available. Support available to part-time students. Financial award application deadline: 5/1; financial award applicants required to submit FAFSA. *Faculty research:* Abuse, addiction, resilience, diversity, narrative therapy. *Unit head:* Dr. Bruce Kuehl, Director, 715-232-2404, Fax: 715-232-2524, E-mail: kuehlb@uwstout.edu. *Application contact:* Anne E. Johnson, Graduate Student Evaluator (Admissions and Assistantship Coordinator), 715-232-1322, Fax: 715-232-2413, E-mail: johnsona@uwstout.edu.

Utah State University, School of Graduate Studies, College of Education and Human Services, Department of Family, Consumer, and Human Development, Logan, UT 84322. Offers family and human development (MFHD); family, consumer, and human development (MS, PhD), including adolescence/youth (MS), adult development/aging (MS), consumer science (MS), infancy/childhood (MS), marriage and family relations (MS), marriage and family therapy (MS). *Accreditation:* AAMFT/COAMFTE (one or more programs are accredited). Part-time and evening/weekend programs available. Postbaccalaureate distance learning degree programs offered (minimal on-campus study). *Degree requirements:* For master's, thesis; for doctorate, comprehensive exam, thesis/dissertation, competencies. *Entrance requirements:* For master's, GRE General Test or MAT, minimum GPA of 3.0, 3 letters of recommendation; for doctorate, GRE, minimum GPA of 3.0, 3 letters of recommendation. Additional exam requirements/recommendations for international students: Required—TOEFL. Electronic applications accepted. *Faculty research:* Marriage and family relations, adolescent problem behavior, family financial management, early literacy, mental health in the elderly, parent child attachment.

Valdosta State University, Graduate School, College of Arts and Sciences, Department of Sociology, Anthropology, and Criminal Justice, Valdosta, GA 31698. Offers criminal justice (MS); marriage and family therapy (MS); sociology (MS). *Accreditation:* AAMFT/COAMFTE. Part-time and evening/weekend programs available. *Faculty:* 19 full-time (7 women). *Students:* 3 full-time (2 women), 9 part-time (6 women); includes 4 minority (all African Americans). Average age 27. 7 applicants, 57% accepted, 2 enrolled. In 2008, 29 master's awarded. *Degree requirements:* For master's, thesis or alternative, comprehensive written and/or oral exams. *Entrance requirements:* For master's, GRE General Test or MAT (sociology, marriage and family therapy), minimum GPA of 2.5. Additional exam requirements/recommendations for international students: Required—TOEFL (minimum score 523 paper-based; 193 computer-based). *Application deadline:* For fall admission, 7/1 for domestic and international students; for spring admission, 11/15 for domestic and international students. Applications are processed on a rolling basis. Application fee: $40. Electronic applications accepted. *Financial support:* In 2008–09, 5 students received support, including 5 research assistantships with full tuition reimbursements available (averaging $2,452 per year); career-related internships or fieldwork, institutionally sponsored loans, scholarships/grants, and unspecified assistantships also available. Support available to part-time students. Financial award application deadline: 7/1; financial award applicants required to submit FAFSA. *Faculty research:* Police-civilian ride-along project. *Unit head:* Dr. Mike Capece, Acting Head, 229-333-5943, Fax: 229-333-5492. *Application contact:* Rebecca Waters, Coordinator of Graduate Admissions, 229-333-5694, Fax: 229-245-3853, E-mail: rlwaters@valdosta.edu.

Virginia Polytechnic Institute and State University, Graduate School, College of Liberal Arts and Human Sciences, Department of Human Development, Blacksburg, VA 24061. Offers adult development and aging (MS, PhD); adult learning and human resource development (MS, PhD); child development (MS, PhD); family studies (MS, PhD); marriage and family therapy (MS, PhD). *Accreditation:* AAMFT/COAMFTE (one or more programs are accredited). *Entrance requirements:* For master's and doctorate, GRE General Test. Additional exam requirements/recommendations for international students: Required—TOEFL (minimum score 600 paper-based; 250 computer-based). Electronic applications accepted. *Faculty research:* Stress management, children's play, dual-career families, social cognition, relationships of elderly.

Wesley Biblical Seminary, Graduate Programs, Jackson, MS 39206. Offers Biblical literature (MA); Christian studies (MA); evangelism (M Div); family life ministry (M Div); honors research (M Div); missions (M Div); pastoral ministry (M Div); teaching (M Div); theology (MA). *Accreditation:* ATS. Part-time programs available. *Degree requirements:* For master's, thesis. *Entrance requirements:* Additional exam requirements/recommendations for international students: Required—TOEFL. Electronic applications accepted. *Faculty research:* Patristics, missiology, culture, hermeneutics.

Western Michigan University, Graduate College, College of Education, Department of Counselor Education and Counseling Psychology, Kalamazoo, MI 49008-5202. Offers counselin psychology (MA); counseling psychology (PhD); counselor education (MA, PhD); human resources development (MA); marriage and family therapy (MA). *Accreditation:* ACA (one or more programs are accredited); APA (one or more programs are accredited); CORE; NCATE. *Degree requirements:* For doctorate, thesis/dissertation, oral exams. *Entrance requirements:* For doctorate, GRE General Test.

Western Seminary–Sacramento Campus, Graduate Programs, Sacramento, CA 95821. Offers exegetical theology (MA); marital and family therapy (MA); ministry (M Div); specialized ministry (MA). Postbaccalaureate distance learning degree programs offered. *Entrance requirements:* For M Div, minimum GPA of 2.5; for master's, minimum GPA of 3.0.

Western Seminary–San Jose Campus, Graduate Programs, Los Gatos, CA 95032-4520. Offers exegetical theology (MA); expositional ministry (M Div); marital and family therapy (MA); ministry (M Div); pastoral ministry (M Div); specialized ministry (MA). Postbaccalaureate distance learning degree programs offered. *Degree requirements:* For master's, 2 foreign languages; for M Div, 3 foreign languages. *Entrance requirements:* For M Div, minimum GPA of 2.5; for master's, minimum GPA of 3.0.

Psychoanalysis and Psychotherapy

Adler Graduate School, Program in Adlerian Studies, Richfield, MN 55423. Offers art therapy specialization (MA); clinical counseling track (MA); coaching and consulting in organizations (Certificate); management consulting and organizational leadership (MA); marriage and family track (MA); non-clinical Adlerian studies track (MA); personal and professional life coaching (Certificate); school counseling (MA). Part-time and evening/weekend programs available. *Degree requirements:* For master's, thesis or alternative, 500-700 hour internship, depending on license choice. *Entrance requirements:* For master's, minimum undergraduate GPA of 3.0, 12 credits of course work in psychology or related field.

Argosy University, Chicago, College of Psychology and Behavioral Sciences, Doctoral Program in Clinical Psychology, Chicago, IL 60654. Offers child and adolescent psychology (Psy D); client-centered and experiential psychotherapies (Psy D); diversity and multicultural psychology (Psy D); family psychology (Psy D); forensic psychology (Psy D); health psychology (Psy D); psychoanalytic psychology (Psy D); psychology and spirituality (Psy D). *Accreditation:* APA.

See Close-Up on page 1067.

Boston Graduate School of Psychoanalysis, Master's, Certificate, and Doctoral Programs, Brookline, MA 02446-4602. Offers MA, Psya D, Certificate. Part-time programs available. Terminal master's awarded for partial completion of doctoral program. *Degree requirements:* For master's and Certificate, thesis. *Entrance requirements:* For master's and doctorate, interview, writing sample; for Certificate, interview, MA. Electronic applications accepted. *Faculty research:* The effect of extra-analytic contact on the analysis, psychoanalytic intervention with schizophrenia, emotional learning in the classroom, psychoanalytic techniques in the geriatric setting, addictions research.

Boston Graduate School of Psychoanalysis, Master's Program—New York, New York, NY 10011. Offers MA. Part-time programs available. *Entrance requirements:* For master's, interview, writing sample.

Boston Graduate School of Psychoanalysis, Programs in Psychoanalysis and Culture, Brookline, MA 02446-4602. Offers MA, Psya D. Evening/weekend programs available. *Degree requirements:* For doctorate, thesis/dissertation. *Entrance requirements:* For master's and doctorate, interview, writing sample, letters of reference, transcripts. Electronic applications accepted. *Faculty research:* Institutional violence, developmental impulse control, psychodynamics of murderers, community violence, psychodynamics in the Salem Witch Trials.

Naropa University, Graduate Programs, Program in Contemplative Psychotherapy, Boulder, CO 80302-6697. Offers MA. *Faculty:* 1 (woman) full-time, 11 part-time/adjunct (6 women). *Students:* 58 full-time (37 women); includes 3 minority (2 African Americans, 1 Hispanic American), 1 international. Average age 31. 79 applicants, 49% accepted, 25 enrolled. In 2008, 26 master's awarded. *Degree requirements:* For master's, thesis, internship. *Entrance requirements:* For master's, in-person interview, supplemental application, resumé, 3 letters of recommendation, letter of interest, proof of earned bachelor's degree. Additional exam requirements/recommendations for international students: Required—TOEFL (minimum score 600 paper-based; 250 computer-based). *Application deadline:* For fall admission, 1/15 priority date for domestic and international students. Applications are processed on a rolling basis. Application fee: $60. Electronic applications accepted. *Expenses:* Tuition: Full-time $14,767; part-time $726 per credit hour. Required fees: $45 per term. *Financial support:* In 2008–09, 27 students received support, including 5 research assistantships with partial tuition reimbursements available (averaging $3,000 per year), teaching assistantships with partial tuition reimbursements available (averaging $3,000 per year); career-related internships or fieldwork, Federal Work-Study, scholarships/grants, health care benefits, tuition waivers (partial), and unspecified assistantships also available. Support available to part-time students. Financial award application deadline: 3/1; financial award applicants required to submit FAFSA. *Unit head:* Lauren Casalino, Chair, 303-245-4778. *Application contact:* Donna McIntyre, Assistant Director of Admissions, 303-546-3555, Fax: 303-546-3583, E-mail: donna@naropa.edu.

See Close-Up on page 1121.

Psychoanalysis and Psychotherapy

Naropa University, Graduate Programs, Program in Somatic Counseling Psychotherapy, Concentration in Body Psychotherapy, Boulder, CO 80302-6697. Offers MA. Part-time programs available. *Faculty:* 1 (woman) full-time, 11 part-time/adjunct (6 women). *Students:* 23 full-time (17 women), 1 (woman) part-time; includes 1 minority (Hispanic American), 1 international. Average age 36. 21 applicants, 48% accepted, 7 enrolled. In 2008, 5 master's awarded. *Degree requirements:* For master's, comprehensive exam, thesis, internship, fieldwork, portfolio. *Entrance requirements:* For master's, interview; body-mind discipline; course work in psychology, anatomy; supplemental application, resumé, letter of interest, 3 letters of recommendation. Additional exam requirements/recommendations for international students: Required—TOEFL (minimum score 600 paper-based; 250 computer-based). *Application deadline:* For fall admission, 1/15 priority date for domestic and international students. Applications are processed on a rolling basis. Application fee: $60. Electronic applications accepted. *Expenses:* Tuition: Full-time $14,767; part-time $726 per credit hour. Required fees: $45 per term. *Financial support:* In 2008–09, 6 students received support, including research assistantships with partial tuition reimbursements available (averaging $3,000 per year), teaching assistantships with partial tuition reimbursements available (averaging $3,000 per year); career-related internships or fieldwork, Federal Work-Study, scholarships/grants, health care benefits, tuition waivers (partial), and unspecified assistantships also available. Support available to part-time students. Financial award application deadline: 3/1; financial award applicants required to submit FAFSA. *Unit head:* Ryan Kennedy, Co-Chair, 303-245-4759. *Application contact:* Donna McIntyre, Assistant Director of Admissions, 303-546-3555, Fax: 303-546-3583, E-mail: donna@naropa.edu.

See Close-Up on page 1121.

New York University, Graduate School of Arts and Science, Department of Psychology, New York, NY 10012-1019. Offers cognition and perception (PhD); community psychology (PhD); general psychology (MA); industrial/organizational psychology (MA); psychotherapy and psychoanalysis (Advanced Certificate); social/personality psychology (PhD). Part-time programs available. Terminal master's awarded for partial completion of doctoral program. *Degree requirements:* For master's, comprehensive exam, thesis or alternative; for doctorate, thesis/dissertation. *Entrance requirements:* For master's, GRE General Test, minimum GPA of 3.0; for doctorate, GRE General Test, GRE Subject Test; for Advanced Certificate, doctoral degree, minimum GPA of 3.0. Additional exam requirements/recommendations for international students: Required—TOEFL. *Faculty research:* Vision, memory, social cognition, social and cognitive development, relationships.

Prescott College, Graduate Programs, Program in Counseling and Psychology, Prescott, AZ 86301. Offers adventure-based psychotherapy (MA); counseling psychology (MA); ecopsychology (MA); ecotherapy (MA); equine-assisted mental health (MA); expressive arts therapy (MA); somatic psychology (MA); student-directed independent study (MA). Part-time programs available. Postbaccalaureate distance learning degree programs offered (minimal on-campus study). *Faculty:* 43 part-time/adjunct (29 women). *Students:* 74 full-time (66 women), 19 part-time (18 women); includes 9 minority (4 African Americans, 1 American Indian/Alaska Native, 4 Hispanic Americans), 9 international. Average age 37. 54 applicants, 70% accepted, 27 enrolled. In 2008, 29 master's awarded. *Degree requirements:* For master's, thesis, fieldwork or internship, practicum. *Entrance requirements:* For master's, 2 letters of recommendation, resumé, official academic transcripts, personal statement, application form, proposed study plan. Additional exam requirements/recommendations for international students: Required—TOEFL (minimum score 500 paper-based; 173 computer-based). *Application deadline:* For fall admission, 3/15 priority date for domestic and international students; for spring admission, 9/15 priority date for domestic and international students. Applications are processed on a rolling basis. Application fee: $40. Electronic applications accepted. *Expenses:* Tuition: Full-time $13,608; part-time $567 per credit. Required fees: $50 per term. One-time fee: $182. Tuition and fees vary according to degree level. *Financial support:* Career-related internships or fieldwork, Federal Work-Study, and scholarships/grants available. Financial award applicants required to submit FAFSA. *Unit head:* Camille Smith, Chair, Fax: 928-776-5151, E-mail: csmith@prescott.edu. *Application contact:* Kerstin Alicki, Admissions Counselor, 877-350-2102, Fax: 928-776-5242, E-mail: admissions@prescott.edu.

Rehabilitation Counseling

Arkansas State University, Graduate School, College of Education, Department of Psychology and Counseling, Jonesboro, State University, AR 72467. Offers college student personnel services (MS); counselor education (Ed S), including college student personnel services, psychoeducational diagnosis, school counseling; rehabilitation counseling (MRC); school counseling (MSE); student affairs (Certificate). *Accreditation:* ACA (one or more programs are accredited); CORE (one or more programs are accredited); NCATE. Part-time programs available. *Faculty:* 11 full-time (6 women), 6 part-time/adjunct (2 women). *Students:* 72 full-time (60 women), 78 part-time (62 women); includes 33 minority (31 African Americans, 2 Hispanic Americans), 1 international. Average age 32. 83 applicants, 58% accepted, 35 enrolled. In 2008, 14 master's, 12 other advanced degrees awarded. *Degree requirements:* For master's and other advanced degree, comprehensive exam, thesis or alternative. *Entrance requirements:* For master's, GRE General Test or MAT (MSE), appropriate bachelor's degree, interview, letters of reference, official transcript; for other advanced degree, GRE General Test, interview, master's degree, letters of reference, official transcript. Additional exam requirements/recommendations for international students: Required—TOEFL (minimum score 550 paper-based; 213 computer-based; 79 iBT), IELTS (minimum score 6). *Application deadline:* For fall admission, 7/15 for domestic students, 7/1 for international students; for spring admission, 12/1 for domestic students, 11/13 for international students. Applications are processed on a rolling basis. Application fee: $30 ($40 for international students). Electronic applications accepted. *Expenses:* Tuition, state resident: full-time $3744; part-time $208 per credit hour. Tuition, nonresident: full-time $9540; part-time $530 per credit hour. International tuition: $7938 full-time. Required fees: $896; $47 per credit hour. $25 per term. One-time fee: $50. Tuition and fees vary according to course load and program. *Financial support:* In 2008–09, 29 students received support; teaching assistantships, career-related internships or fieldwork, scholarships/grants, and unspecified assistantships available. Financial award application deadline: 7/1; financial award applicants required to submit FAFSA. *Faculty research:* Abuse issues in children and adolescents, career counseling, children's learning and memory, crisis intervention, drug use and addition. *Unit head:* Dr. Loretta McGregor, Chair, 870-972-3064, Fax: 870-972-3962, E-mail: lmcgregor@astate.edu. *Application contact:* Dr. Andrew Sustich, Dean of the Graduate School, 870-972-3029, Fax: 870-972-3857, E-mail: sustich@astate.edu.

Assumption College, Graduate School, Rehabilitation Counseling Program, Worcester, MA 01609-1296. Offers MA, CAGS. *Accreditation:* CORE. Part-time and evening/weekend programs available. Postbaccalaureate distance learning degree programs offered (minimal on-campus study). *Faculty:* 2 full-time (0 women), 16 part-time/adjunct (10 women). *Students:* 14 full-time (10 women), 61 part-time (48 women); includes 5 minority (2 African Americans, 1 American Indian/Alaska Native, 2 Hispanic Americans), 1 international. Average age 28. 58 applicants, 93% accepted. In 2008, 40 master's, 8 other advanced degrees awarded. *Degree requirements:* For master's, comprehensive exam, internship, practicum. *Entrance requirements:* For master's and CAGS, 3 letters of recommendation, resumé, interview, essay. Additional exam requirements/recommendations for international students: Required—TOEFL (minimum score 540 paper-based; 200 computer-based; 76 iBT), IELTS (minimum score 6). *Application deadline:* For fall admission, 6/1 priority date for domestic students, 5/1 priority date for international students; for spring admission, 11/1 priority date for domestic students, 9/1 priority date for international students. Applications are processed on a rolling basis. Application fee: $30. Electronic applications accepted. *Expenses:* Tuition: Part-time $468 per credit hour. Required fees: $20 per semester. One-time fee: $100. *Financial support:* In 2008–09, 81 students received support, including 45 fellowships with full and partial tuition reimbursements available (averaging $5,124 per year), 1 teaching assistantship (averaging $19,860 per year); scholarships/grants and traineeships also available. Financial award application deadline: 6/1; financial award applicants required to submit FAFSA. *Faculty research:* Job placement for severe disabilities, vocational counseling, conflict resolution, health issues in mental illness. *Unit head:* A. Lee Pearson, Director, 508-767-7063, Fax: 508-767-7030, E-mail: lpearson@assumption.edu. *Application contact:* Adrian O. Dumas, Director of Graduate Enrollment Management and Services, 508-767-7365, Fax: 508-767-7030, E-mail: adumas@assumption.edu.

Auburn University, Graduate School, College of Education, Department of Special Education, Rehabilitation, Counseling and School Psychology, Auburn University, AL 36849. Offers collaborative teacher special education (M Ed, MS); early childhood special education (M Ed, MS); rehabilitation counseling (M Ed, MS, PhD). *Accreditation:* CORE; NCATE. Part-time programs available. *Faculty:* 21 full-time (13 women), 2 part-time/adjunct (0 women). *Students:* 156 full-time (128 women), 79 part-time (64 women); includes 57 minority (50 African Americans, 3 Asian Americans or Pacific Islanders, 4 Hispanic Americans), 3 international. Average age 33. 215 applicants, 32% accepted, 55 enrolled. In 2008, 64 master's, 1 doctorate awarded. *Degree requirements:* For master's, thesis (for some programs); for doctorate, thesis/dissertation. *Entrance requirements:* For master's, GRE General Test; for doctorate, GRE General Test, interview. *Application deadline:* For fall admission, 7/17 for domestic students; for spring admission, 11/24 for domestic students. Applications are processed on a rolling basis. Application fee: $25 ($50 for international students). Electronic applications accepted. *Expenses:* Tuition, area resident: Full-time $5880; part-time $243 per credit hour. Tuition, state resident: full-time $5880; part-time $243 per credit hour. Tuition, nonresident: full-time $17,640; part-time $729 per credit hour. International tuition: $17,846 full-time. Required fees: $620. Tuition and fees vary according to program and reciprocity agreements. *Financial support:* Research assistantships, teaching assistantships, Federal Work-Study available. Support available to part-time students. Financial award application deadline: 3/15. *Faculty research:* Emotional conflict/behavior disorders, gifted and talented, learning disabilities, mental retardation, multi-handicapped. *Unit head:* Dr. Philip L. Browning, Head, 334-844-5943. *Application contact:* Dr. George Flowers, Dean of the Graduate School, 334-844-2125.

Barry University, School of Education, Program in Rehabilitation Counseling, Miami Shores, FL 33161-6695. Offers MS, Ed S. Part-time and evening/weekend programs available. *Degree requirements:* For master's, comprehensive exam, scholarly paper; for Ed S, comprehensive exam. *Entrance requirements:* For master's, GRE General Test or MAT, minimum GPA of 3.0; for Ed S, GRE General Test, minimum GPA of 3.0. Electronic applications accepted.

Bayamón Central University, Graduate Programs, Program in Education, Bayamón, PR 00960-1725. Offers administration and supervision (MA Ed); commercial education (MA Ed); education of the autistic (MA Ed); elementary education (K–3) (MA Ed); elementary education (K–6) (MA Ed); elementary physical education (MA Ed); guidance and counseling (MA Ed); pre-elementary teacher (MA Ed); rehabilitation counseling (MA Ed); special education (MA Ed), including attention deficit disorder, learning disabilities. Part-time and evening/weekend programs available. *Degree requirements:* For master's, comprehensive exam. *Entrance requirements:* For master's, EXADEP, bachelor's degree in education or related field.

Bowling Green State University, Graduate College, College of Education and Human Development, School of Education and Intervention Services, Intervention Services Division, Program in Rehabilitation Counseling, Bowling Green, OH 43403. Offers MRC. *Accreditation:* CORE. Part-time programs available. *Degree requirements:* For master's, thesis or alternative. *Entrance requirements:* For master's, GRE General Test, interview. Additional exam requirements/recommendations for international students: Required—TOEFL. Electronic applications accepted. *Faculty research:* Depression, disability management, schizophrenia, job analysis, rehabilitation counseling curriculum.

California State University, Fresno, Division of Graduate Studies, School of Education and Human Development, Department of Counseling and Special Education, Rehabilitation Counseling Program, Fresno, CA 93740-8027. Offers MS. *Accreditation:* CORE. Part-time and evening/weekend programs available. *Degree requirements:* For master's, thesis optional. *Entrance requirements:* For master's, GRE General Test, MAT, minimum GPA of 2.75. Additional exam requirements/recommendations for international students: Required—TOEFL. Electronic applications accepted. *Faculty research:* Aging, career development, job retention, rehabilitation administration.

California State University, Los Angeles, Graduate Studies, Charter College of Education, Division of Special Education and Counseling, Los Angeles, CA 90032-8530. Offers counseling (MS), including applied behavior analysis, community college counseling, rehabilitation counseling, school counseling and school psychology; special education (MA, PhD). Part-time and evening/weekend programs available. *Faculty:* 37 full-time (22 women). *Students:* 385 full-time (304 women), 406 part-time (306 women); includes 494 minority (52 African Americans, 2 American Indian/Alaska Native, 80 Asian Americans or Pacific Islanders, 360 Hispanic Americans), 39 international. Average age 34. 176 applicants, 99% accepted, 116 enrolled. In 2008, 168 master's awarded. *Entrance requirements:* For master's, minimum GPA of 2.75 in last 90 units of course work, teaching certificate. Additional exam requirements/recommendations for international students: Required—TOEFL (minimum score 500 paper-based; 173 computer-based). *Application deadline:* For fall admission, 6/15 for domestic students, 5/1 for international students; for winter admission, 11/1 for domestic students, 9/1 for international students; for spring admission, 2/1 for domestic students, 10/1 for international students. Applications are processed on a rolling basis. Application fee: $55. Electronic applications accepted. *Expenses:* Tuition, nonresident: part-time $226 per credit. Required fees: $4019. *Financial support:* Career-related internships or fieldwork and Federal Work-Study available. Support available to part-time students. Financial award application deadline: 3/1. *Unit head:* Dr. Randy Campbell, Chair, 323-343-4400, Fax: 323-343-5605, E-mail: rcampbe@calstatela.edu. *Application contact:* Dr. Jose L. Galvan, Dean of Graduate Studies, 323-343-3820, Fax: 323-343-5653, E-mail: jgalvan@cslanet.calstatela.edu.

California State University, San Bernardino, Graduate Studies, College of Education, Program in Educational Psychology and Counseling, San Bernardino, CA 92407-2397. Offers correctional and alternative education (MA); counseling and guidance (MS); rehabilitation counseling (MA). *Accreditation:* NCATE. Part-time and evening/weekend programs available. *Faculty:* 8 full-time (4 women), 6 part-time/adjunct (2 women). *Students:* 101 full-time (82 women), 11 part-time (8 women); includes 70 minority (10 African Americans, 1 American Indian/Alaska Native, 3 Asian Americans or Pacific Islanders, 56 Hispanic Americans), 2 international. Average age 28. 30 applicants, 30% accepted, 7 enrolled. In 2008, 38 master's awarded. *Degree requirements:* For master's, comprehensive exam, thesis or alternative, counselor preparation comprehensive examination. *Entrance requirements:* For master's, minimum GPA of 3.0 in education. *Application deadline:* For fall admission, 8/31 priority date for domestic students. Application fee: $55. *Expenses:* Tuition, area resident: Full-time $1252; part-time $726 per quarter. Required fees: $334 per quarter. Tuition and fees vary according to degree level and student level. *Financial support:* Career-related internships or fieldwork and Federal Work-Study available. Support available to part-time students. *Unit head:* Dr. Ruth Ann Sandlin, Chair, 909-537-5641, Fax: 909-537-7040, E-mail: rsandlin@csusb.edu. *Application contact:* Olivia Rosas, Director of Admissions, 909-537-7577, Fax: 909-537-7034, E-mail: orosas@csusb.edu.

California State University, San Bernardino, Graduate Studies, College of Education, Programs in Special Education and Rehabilitation Counseling, San Bernardino, CA 92407-2397. Offers rehabilitation counseling (MA); special education (MA). *Accreditation:* CORE; NCATE. Part-time and evening/weekend programs available. *Faculty:* 7 full-time (4 women), 15 part-time/adjunct (9 women). *Students:* 230 full-time (177 women), 64 part-time (48 women); includes 147 minority (55 African Americans, 5 American Indian/Alaska Native, 13 Asian Americans or Pacific Islanders, 74 Hispanic Americans), 1 international. Average age 39. 140 applicants, 68% accepted, 51 enrolled. In 2008, 79 master's awarded. *Degree requirements:* For master's, thesis or alternative, advancement to candidacy. *Entrance requirements:* For master's, minimum GPA of 3.0 in education. *Application deadline:* For fall admission, 8/31 priority date for domestic students. Application fee: $55. *Expenses:* Tuition, area resident: Full-time $1252; part-time $726 per quarter. Required fees: $334 per quarter. Tuition and fees vary according to degree level and student level. *Financial support:* Career-related internships or fieldwork and Federal Work-Study available. Support available to part-time students. *Unit head:* Dr. Ruth Ann Sandlin, Chair, 909-537-5641, Fax: 909-537-7040, E-mail: rsandlin@csusb.edu. *Application contact:* Olivia Rosas, Director of Admissions, 909-537-7577, Fax: 909-537-7034, E-mail: orosas@csusb.edu.

Central Connecticut State University, School of Graduate Studies, School of Education and Professional Studies, Department of Counseling and Family Therapy, New Britain, CT 06050-4010. Offers marriage and family therapy (MS); professional counseling (MS, Certificate); school counseling (MS); student development in higher education (MS). *Accreditation:* AAMFT/COAMFTE. Part-time and evening/weekend programs available. *Faculty:* 7 full-time (4 women), 12 part-time/adjunct (9 women). *Students:* 109 full-time (93 women), 187 part-time (151 women); includes 47 minority (24 African Americans, 2 American Indian/Alaska Native, 2 Asian Americans or Pacific Islanders, 19 Hispanic Americans), 3 international. Average age 35. 245 applicants, 47% accepted, 92 enrolled. In 2008, 67 master's, 1 other advanced degree awarded. *Degree requirements:* For master's, comprehensive exam, thesis or alternative. *Entrance requirements:* For master's, minimum undergraduate GPA of 2.7, essay. Additional exam requirements/recommendations for international students: Required—TOEFL. *Application deadline:* For fall admission, 5/1 for domestic students. Applications are processed on a rolling basis. Application fee: $50. Electronic applications accepted. *Expenses:* Tuition, area resident: Full-time $4377; part-time $420 per credit. Tuition, state resident: full-time $6566; part-time $420 per credit. Tuition, nonresident: full-time $12,195; part-time $420 per credit. Required fees: $3462. One-time fee: $62 part-time. *Financial support:* In 2008–09, 36 students received support, including 22 research assistantships; career-related internships or fieldwork, Federal Work-Study, scholarships/grants, and unspecified assistantships also available. Support available to part-time students. Financial award application deadline: 3/1; financial award applicants required to submit FAFSA. *Faculty research:* Elementary/secondary school counseling, marriage/family therapy, rehabilitation counseling, counseling in higher educational settings. *Unit head:* Dr. Connie Tait, Chair, 860-832-2154. *Application contact:* Dr. Connie Tait, Chair, 860-832-2154.

Coppin State University, Division of Graduate Studies, Division of Arts and Sciences, Department of Applied Psychology and Rehabilitation Counseling, Program in Rehabilitation Counseling, Baltimore, MD 21216-3698. Offers M Ed. *Accreditation:* CORE. Part-time programs available. *Degree requirements:* For master's, comprehensive exam (for some programs), thesis optional, internship, clinical requirements. *Entrance requirements:* For master's, GRE General Test, interview, minimum GPA of 3.0.

Drake University, School of Education, Department of Leadership, Counseling and Adult Development, Program in Rehabilitation Counseling, Des Moines, IA 50311-4516. Offers rehabilitation administration (MS); rehabilitation counseling (MS); rehabilitation placement (MS). Part-time and evening/weekend programs available. *Degree requirements:* For master's, comprehensive exam, thesis (for some programs), internships (for some programs). *Entrance requirements:* For master's, GRE General Test, MAT or Drake SOE writing assessment, resumé, 2 letters of recommendation. Additional exam requirements/recommendations for international students: Required—TOEFL (minimum score 550 paper-based; 213 computer-based). Electronic applications accepted. *Faculty research:* Counseling and rehabilitation, behavioral supports, inquiry-based science methods, teacher quality enhancement.

East Carolina University, Graduate School, School of Allied Health Sciences, Program in Rehabilitation Studies, Greenville, NC 27858-4353. Offers rehabilitation counseling (MS); substance abuse and clinical counseling (MS); vocational evaluation (MS). *Accreditation:* CORE. Part-time and evening/weekend programs available. *Degree requirements:* For master's, comprehensive exam, thesis or alternative, internship. *Entrance requirements:* For master's, GRE General Test or MAT. Additional exam requirements/recommendations for international students: Required—TOEFL.

East Central University, School of Graduate Studies, Department of Human Resources, Ada, OK 74820-6899. Offers administration (MSHR); counseling (MSHR); criminal justice (MSHR); rehabilitation counseling (MSHR). *Accreditation:* CORE. Part-time and evening/weekend programs available. *Degree requirements:* For master's, thesis optional. *Entrance requirements:* For master's, GRE General Test, MAT, minimum GPA of 2.5. Electronic applications accepted.

Edinboro University of Pennsylvania, Graduate Studies and Research, School of Education, Department of Professional Studies, Edinboro, PA 16444. Offers counseling (MA), including community counseling, elementary guidance, rehabilitation counseling, secondary guidance, student personnel services; educational leadership (M Ed), including elementary school administration, secondary school administration; letter of eligibility (Certificate). Part-time and evening/weekend programs available. *Faculty:* 11 full-time (6 women). *Students:* 84 full-time (62 women), 175 part-time (107 women); includes 19 minority (15 African Americans, 2 American Indian/Alaska Native, 1 Asian American or Pacific Islander, 1 Hispanic American), 1 international. Average age 32. In 2008, 105 master's, 2 other advanced degrees awarded. *Degree requirements:* For master's, thesis or alternative, competency exam; for Certificate, thesis or alternative. *Entrance requirements:* For master's and Certificate, GRE or MAT, minimum QPA of 2.5. *Application deadline:* Applications are processed on a rolling basis. Application fee: $30. Electronic applications accepted. *Expenses:* Tuition: state resident: full-time $6430; part-time $357 per credit. Tuition, nonresident: full-time $8038; part-time $572 per credit. International tuition: $15,171.58 full-time. Required fees: $2113; $60 per credit. Tuition and fees vary according to course load. *Financial support:* In 2008–09, 28 research assistantships with full and partial tuition reimbursements (averaging $3,850 per year) were awarded; career-related internships or fieldwork, Federal Work-Study, scholarships/grants, and unspecified assistantships also available. Support available to part-time students. Financial award application deadline: 2/15; financial award applicants required to submit FAFSA. *Unit head:* Dr. Susan Norton, Head, 814-732-2260, E-mail: scnorton@edinboro.edu. *Application contact:* Dr. Andrew Pushchack, Program Head, 814-732-1548, E-mail: apushchack@edinboro.edu.

Emporia State University, School of Graduate Studies, The Teachers College, Department of Psychology, Art Therapy, Rehabilitation and Mental Health Counseling, Program in Rehabilitation Counseling, Emporia, KS 66801-5087. Offers MS. *Accreditation:* CORE. Part-time programs available. *Students:* 13 full-time (all women), 10 part-time (9 women); includes 1 minority (African American). 10 applicants, 90% accepted, 9 enrolled. In 2008, 6 master's awarded. *Degree requirements:* For master's, comprehensive exam or thesis, practicum. *Entrance requirements:* For master's, GRE or MAT, graduate essay exam, appropriate bachelor's degree,

interview, letters of recommendation. *Application deadline:* For fall admission, 8/15 priority date for domestic students. Applications are processed on a rolling basis. Application fee: $30 ($75 for international students). Electronic applications accepted. *Expenses:* Tuition, area resident: Full-time $3976; part-time $166 per credit hour. Tuition, state resident: full-time $3976; part-time $166 per credit hour. Tuition, nonresident: full-time $12,028; part-time $501 per credit hour. Required fees: $51 per credit hour. Tuition and fees vary according to campus/location. *Financial support:* Career-related internships or fieldwork, Federal Work-Study, institutionally sponsored loans, health care benefits, and unspecified assistantships available. Financial award application deadline: 3/15; financial award applicants required to submit FAFSA. *Unit head:* Dr. James Costello, Graduate Co-Coordinator, 620-341-5791, E-mail: jcostell@emporia.edu. *Application contact:* Dr. James Costello, Graduate Co-Coordinator, 620-341-5791, E-mail: jcostell@emporia.edu.

Florida Atlantic University, College of Education, Department of Counselor Education, Boca Raton, FL 33431-0991. Offers counselor education (M Ed, PhD, Ed S); marriage and family therapy (Ed S); mental health counseling (M Ed, Ed S); rehabilitation counseling (M Ed); school counseling (M Ed, Ed S). *Accreditation:* ACA; NCATE. Part-time and evening/weekend programs available. *Faculty:* 7 full-time (2 women), 6 part-time/adjunct (5 women). *Students:* 59 full-time (50 women), 97 part-time (84 women); includes 53 minority (18 African Americans, 3 Asian Americans or Pacific Islanders, 32 Hispanic Americans), 2 international. Average age 35. 135 applicants, 42% accepted, 39 enrolled. In 2008, 46 master's awarded. *Degree requirements:* For Ed S, departmental qualifying exam. *Entrance requirements:* For master's, GRE General Test, minimum GPA of 3.0 during previous 2 years; for Ed S, GRE General Test, minimum graduate GPA of 3.25. Additional exam requirements/recommendations for international students: Required—TOEFL. *Application deadline:* For fall admission, 3/1 for domestic students, 2/1 for international students; for spring admission, 9/15 for domestic students, 7/1 for international students. Applications are processed on a rolling basis. Application fee: $30. *Expenses:* Tuition, state resident: full-time $4867; part-time $270.40 per credit hour. Tuition, nonresident: full-time $16,486; part-time $915.87 per credit hour. *Financial support:* Research assistantships with partial tuition reimbursements, teaching assistantships, career-related internships or fieldwork, scholarships/grants, and unspecified assistantships available. *Faculty research:* Brief therapy, psychological type, marriage and family counseling, international programs, integrated services. *Unit head:* Dr. Irene Johnson, Chair, 561-297-2136, Fax: 561-297-2309. *Application contact:* Susan Foley, Senior Secretary, 561-297-3602, Fax: 561-297-2309, E-mail: cnslred@fau.edu.

Florida International University, College of Education, Department of Educational and Psychological Studies, Program in Counselor Education, Miami, FL 33199. Offers mental health counseling (MS); rehabilitation counseling (MS); school counseling (MS). *Accreditation:* ACA; NCATE. Part-time and evening/weekend programs available. *Entrance requirements:* For master's, General Knowledge test, College Level Academic Skills test, GRE or PRAXIS (school counseling track), minimum GPA of 3.0, interview. Additional exam requirements/recommendations for international students: Required—TOEFL (minimum score 550 paper-based; 213 computer-based; 80 iBT), IELTS (minimum score 6.3). Electronic applications accepted.

Florida State University, Graduate Studies, College of Education, Department of Childhood Education, Reading, and Disability Services, Program in Special Education, Tallahassee, FL 32306. Offers emotional disturbance/learning disabilities (MS); mental retardation (MS); rehabilitation counseling (MS, PhD, Ed S); special education (PhD, Ed S); visual disabilities (MS). *Accreditation:* CORE. *Degree requirements:* For master's, comprehensive exam, thesis optional; for doctorate, comprehensive exam, thesis/dissertation; for Ed S, comprehensive exam. *Entrance requirements:* For master's, doctorate, and Ed S, GRE General Test, minimum GPA of 3.0.

Fort Valley State University, College of Graduate Studies and Extended Education, Department of Counseling Psychology, Program in Rehabilitation Counseling, Fort Valley, GA 31030-4313. Offers MS. *Accreditation:* CORE. Part-time programs available. *Degree requirements:* For master's, comprehensive exam (for some programs), thesis optional. *Entrance requirements:* For master's, GRE General Test or MAT.

The George Washington University, Graduate School of Education and Human Development, Department of Counseling/Human and Organizational Studies, Programs in Counseling: School, Community and Rehabilitation, Washington, DC 20052. Offers community counseling (MA Ed); rehabilitation counseling (MA Ed); school counseling (MA Ed). School counseling program also offered in Alexandria, VA. *Accreditation:* ACA; CORE; NCATE. *Students:* 100 full-time (83 women), 60 part-time (49 women); includes 44 minority (24 African Americans, 1 American Indian/Alaska Native, 10 Asian Americans or Pacific Islanders, 9 Hispanic Americans), 4 international. Average age 33. 182 applicants, 63% accepted, 55 enrolled. In 2008, 56 master's awarded. *Degree requirements:* For master's, comprehensive exam. *Entrance requirements:* For master's, GRE General Test or MAT, minimum GPA of 2.75. *Application deadline:* For fall admission, 1/15 priority date for domestic students; for spring admission, 10/1 for domestic students. Applications are processed on a rolling basis. Application fee: $60. *Financial support:* In 2008–09, 27 students received support; fellowships, research assistantships, teaching assistantships, career-related internships or fieldwork, Federal Work-Study, and tuition waivers (full and partial) available. *Faculty research:* Adjustment to disability, head injury rehabilitation, cross-cultural counseling. *Application contact:* Sarah Lang, Director of Graduate Admissions, 202-994-1447, Fax: 202-994-7207, E-mail: slang@gwu.edu.

Georgia State University, College of Education, Department of Counseling and Psychological Services, Program in Rehabilitation Counseling, Atlanta, GA 30303-3083. Offers MS. *Accreditation:* CORE. Part-time and evening/weekend programs available. *Degree requirements:* For master's, comprehensive exam. *Entrance requirements:* For master's, GRE General Test, minimum GPA of 2.5. *Faculty research:* Catastrophic injuries, private sector rehabilitation, closed head injuries, persons with multiple handicaps.

Hofstra University, School of Education, Health, and Human Services, Department of Counseling, Research, Special Education and Rehabilitation, Program in Rehabilitation Counseling, Hempstead, NY 11549. Offers rehabilitation administration (PD); rehabilitation counseling (MS Ed); rehabilitation counseling in mental health (MS Ed). *Accreditation:* CORE. Part-time and evening/weekend programs available. *Students:* 16 full-time (12 women), 9 part-time (7 women); includes 10 minority (7 African Americans, 3 Hispanic Americans), 1 international. Average age 36. 12 applicants, 92% accepted, 6 enrolled. In 2008, 6 master's awarded. *Degree requirements:* For master's, comprehensive exam, 600-hour internship, 100-hour practicum; for PD, internship in rehabilitation administration. *Entrance requirements:* For master's, 4 letters of recommendation, interview, essay, professional experience; for PD, 3 letters of recommendation, master's degree in related field, professional experience. Additional exam requirements/recommendations for international students: Required—TOEFL (minimum score 550 paper-based; 213 computer-based; 80 iBT). *Application deadline:* Applications are processed on a rolling basis. Application fee: $60. Electronic applications accepted. *Expenses:* Tuition: Full-time $15,300; part-time $850 per credit. Required fees: $970; $165 per term. Tuition and fees vary according to program. *Financial support:* In 2008–09, 24 students received support, including 2 fellowships with full and partial tuition reimbursements available (averaging $2,525 per year); research assistantships with full and partial tuition reimbursements available, career-related internships or fieldwork, Federal Work-Study, institutionally sponsored loans, scholarships/grants, traineeships, tuition waivers (full and partial), and unspecified assistantships also available. Support available to part-time students. Financial award applicants required to submit FAFSA. *Faculty research:* Workplace socialization and individuals with disabilities; collaboration among rehabilitation agencies and consumer outcomes; job retention among rehabilitation counseling professionals; transition services for youth with disabilities. Total annual research expenditures: $210,000. *Unit head:* Dr. Jamie Mitus, Director, 516-463-7453, Fax: 516-463-6184, E-mail: cprjsm@hofstra.edu. *Application contact:* Carol

Rehabilitation Counseling

Hofstra University (continued)
Drummer, Dean of Graduate Admissions, 516-463-4876, Fax: 516-463-4664, E-mail: gradstudent@hofstra.edu.

Hunter College of the City University of New York, Graduate School, School of Education, Department of Educational Foundations and Counseling Programs, Program in Rehabilitation Counseling, New York, NY 10021-5085. Offers MS Ed. *Accreditation:* CORE. *Faculty:* 7 full-time (5 women), 16 part-time/adjunct (10 women). *Students:* 26 full-time (20 women), 40 part-time (31 women); includes 17 minority (10 African Americans, 3 Asian Americans or Pacific Islanders, 4 Hispanic Americans). Average age 35. 31 applicants, 42% accepted, 11 enrolled. In 2008, 27 master's awarded. *Degree requirements:* For master's, thesis, seminar. *Entrance requirements:* For master's, interview, minimum GPA of 2.7, recommendations. Additional exam requirements/recommendations for international students: Required—TOEFL, TWE. *Application deadline:* For fall admission, 4/1 for domestic students, 2/1 for international students; for spring admission, 11/1 for domestic students, 9/1 for international students. Applications are processed on a rolling basis. Application fee: $125. *Financial support:* Federal Work-Study and tuition waivers (partial) available. Support available to part-time students. *Unit head:* Dr. Arnold Wolf, Adviser, 212-772-4616, E-mail: awo@hunter.cuny.edu. *Application contact:* William Zlata, Director for Graduate Admissions, 212-772-4482, Fax: 212-650-3336, E-mail: admissions@hunter.cuny.edu.

Illinois Institute of Technology, Graduate College, Institute of Psychology, Chicago, IL 60616-3793. Offers clinical psychology (PhD); industrial/organizational psychology (PhD); personnel/human resource development (MS); psychology (MS); rehabilitation counseling (MS); rehabilitation counselor education (PhD). *Accreditation:* APA (one or more programs are accredited); CORE. Evening/weekend programs available. *Faculty:* 19 full-time (8 women), 5 part-time/adjunct (all women). *Students:* 98 full-time (78 women), 94 part-time (69 women); includes 36 minority (10 African Americans, 16 Asian Americans or Pacific Islanders, 10 Hispanic Americans), 24 international. Average age 29. 301 applicants, 40% accepted, 54 enrolled. In 2008, 37 master's, 13 doctorates awarded. Terminal master's awarded for partial completion of doctoral program. *Degree requirements:* For master's, comprehensive exam, thesis (for some programs); for doctorate, comprehensive exam, thesis/dissertation, qualifying exams. *Entrance requirements:* For master's, GRE General Test, minimum GPA of 3.0; for doctorate, GRE General Test, minimum GPA of 3.2. Additional exam requirements/recommendations for international students: Required—TOEFL (minimum score 550 paper-based; 213 computer-based; 80 iBT). *Application deadline:* For fall admission, 1/15 for domestic and international students. Application fee: $40. Electronic applications accepted. *Financial support:* In 2008–09, 39 fellowships with partial tuition reimbursements (averaging $2,798 per year), 1 research assistantship with partial tuition reimbursement, 24 teaching assistantships with partial tuition reimbursements (averaging $4,405 per year) were awarded; career-related internships or fieldwork, Federal Work-Study, institutionally sponsored loans, scholarships/grants, traineeships, health care benefits, tuition waivers (partial), and unspecified assistantships also available. Support available to part-time students. Financial award applicants required to submit FAFSA. *Faculty research:* Stigma and mental illness, depression, couples communication, leadership, psychometric theory. Total annual research expenditures: $426,090. *Unit head:* Dr. M. Ellen Mitchell, Dean, 312-567-3362, Fax: 312-567-3493, E-mail: mitchelle@itt.edu. *Application contact:* Application Contact, 312-567-3500, Fax: 312-567-3493, E-mail: psychology@iit.edu.

Indiana University–Purdue University Indianapolis, School of Science, Department of Psychology, Indianapolis, IN 46202-3275. Offers clinical rehabilitation psychology (MS); industrial/organizational psychology (MS); psychobiology of addictions (MS, PhD). *Accreditation:* APA (one or more programs are accredited). Terminal master's awarded for partial completion of doctoral program. *Degree requirements:* For master's, thesis; for doctorate, thesis/dissertation. *Entrance requirements:* For master's, GRE General Test, minimum undergraduate GPA of 3.0; for doctorate, GRE General Test, GRE Subject Test (clinical rehabilitation psychology), minimum undergraduate GPA of 3.2. *Faculty research:* Psychiatric rehabilitation, chronic stress, neurological research, language and cognitive development in infants, alcoholism and psychopathology.

Jackson State University, Graduate School, School of Education, Department of Counseling and Human Resource Education, Jackson, MS 39217. Offers community and agency counseling (MS); guidance and counseling (MS, MS Ed, Ed S); rehabilitative counseling (MS Ed). *Accreditation:* ACA; CORE (one or more programs are accredited); NCATE. Part-time and evening/weekend programs available. *Degree requirements:* For master's, comprehensive exam, thesis. *Entrance requirements:* For master's, GRE General Test. Additional exam requirements/recommendations for international students: Required—TOEFL.

Jackson State University, Graduate School, School of Education, Department of Special Education and Rehabilitative Services, Jackson, MS 39217. Offers rehabilitative counseling service (MS Ed); special education (MS Ed, Ed S). *Accreditation:* NCATE. Evening/weekend programs available. *Degree requirements:* For master's, comprehensive exam, thesis or alternative. *Entrance requirements:* For master's, GRE General Test. Additional exam requirements/recommendations for international students: Required—TOEFL.

Kent State University, Graduate School of Education, Health, and Human Services, Department of Educational Foundations and Special Services, Program in Rehabilitation Counseling, Kent, OH 44242-0001. Offers M Ed, MA, Ed S. *Accreditation:* CORE (one or more programs are accredited). *Degree requirements:* For master's, thesis (for some programs). *Entrance requirements:* For degree, GRE General Test. Additional exam requirements/recommendations for international students: Required—TOEFL. Electronic applications accepted.

Langston University, School of Education and Behavioral Sciences, Langston, OK 73050-0907. Offers bilingual/multicultural (M Ed); elementary education (M Ed); English as a second language (M Ed); rehabilitation counseling (M Sc); urban education (M Ed). *Accreditation:* CORE; NCATE (one or more programs are accredited). Part-time programs available. *Degree requirements:* For master's, comprehensive exam, thesis optional. *Entrance requirements:* For master's, GRE, writing skills test, minimum GPA of 2.5, 3 letters of recommendation. Additional exam requirements/recommendations for international students: Required—TOEFL, TWE. *Faculty research:* Bilingual/multicultural education, financing post-secondary education.

La Salle University, School of Arts and Sciences, Program in Psychology, Philadelphia, PA 19141-1199. Offers clinical psychology (Psy D); family psychology (Psy D); rehabilitation psychology (Psy D). Part-time and evening/weekend programs available. *Entrance requirements:* For doctorate, GRE, minimum GPA of 3.0. *Expenses:* Contact institution. *Faculty research:* Cognitive therapy, attribution theory, treatment of addiction.

Louisiana State University Health Sciences Center, School of Allied Health Professions, Department of Rehabilitation Counseling, New Orleans, LA 70112-2262. Offers MHS. *Accreditation:* CORE. Part-time programs available. *Degree requirements:* For master's, clinical internship. *Entrance requirements:* For master's, GRE General Test, minimum GPA of 2.5, Bachelor degree, 2 letters recommendation, written essay. *Faculty research:* Job placement, clinical judgement, counseling process, consumer satisfaction, vocational assessment.

Maryville University of Saint Louis, School of Health Professions, Program in Rehabilitation Counseling, St. Louis, MO 63141-7299. Offers marriage and family therapy (MARC); music therapy (MARC); substance abuse (MARC). *Accreditation:* CORE. Part-time and evening/weekend programs available. *Students:* 45. In 2008, 17 master's awarded. *Degree requirements:* For master's, internship, seminar. *Entrance requirements:* For master's, minimum cumulative GPA of 3.0, 2 letters of recommendation, interview. Additional exam requirements/recommendations for international students: Required—TOEFL (minimum score 550 paper-based). *Application deadline:* For fall admission, 1/15 for domestic students; for spring admission, 10/1 for domestic students. Application fee: $40. Electronic applications accepted. *Expenses:* Tuition: Full-time $19,650; part-time $605 per credit hour. Required fees: $100 per semester. Part-time tuition and fees vary according to degree level and program. *Financial support:* Career-related internships or fieldwork, Federal Work-Study, and campus employment available. Financial award application deadline: 7/31. *Unit head:* Barbara Parker, Director, 314-529-9437, E-mail: bparker@maryville.edu. *Application contact:* Barbara Parker, Director, 314-529-9437, E-mail: bparker@maryville.edu.

Michigan State University, The Graduate School, College of Education, Department of Counseling, Educational Psychology and Special Education, East Lansing, MI 48824. Offers counseling (MA); educational psychology and educational technology (PhD); educational technology (MA); measurement and quantitative methods (PhD); rehabilitation counseling (MA); rehabilitation counselor education (PhD); school psychology (MA, PhD, Ed S); special education (MA, PhD). *Accreditation:* APA (one or more programs are accredited); CORE (one or more programs are accredited). Part-time programs available. *Entrance requirements:* Additional exam requirements/recommendations for international students: Required—TOEFL. Electronic applications accepted.

Minnesota State University Mankato, College of Graduate Studies, College of Allied Health and Nursing, Program in Rehabilitation Counseling, Mankato, MN 56001. Offers MS. *Accreditation:* CORE. *Students:* 5 full-time (4 women), 3 part-time (1 woman). *Degree requirements:* For master's, comprehensive exam. *Entrance requirements:* For master's, GRE General Test, minimum GPA of 3.0 during previous 2 years, references. *Application deadline:* For fall admission, 3/1 priority date for domestic students. Applications are processed on a rolling basis. Application fee: $40. *Financial support:* Research assistantships with full tuition reimbursements, teaching assistantships with full tuition reimbursements available. Financial award application deadline: 3/15; financial award applicants required to submit FAFSA. *Unit head:* Dr. Bonnie Lund, Graduate Coordinator, 507-389-5841. *Application contact:* 507-389-2321, E-mail: grad@mnsu.edu.

Montana State University–Billings, College of Allied Health Professions, Department of Rehabilitation and Human Services, Billings, MT 59101-0298. Offers MSRC. *Accreditation:* CORE. Part-time programs available. *Degree requirements:* For master's, thesis optional, thesis or professional paper and/or field experience. *Entrance requirements:* For master's, GRE General Test or MAT, minimum GPA of 3.0.

North Carolina Agricultural and Technical State University, Graduate School, School of Education, Department of Human Development and Services, Greensboro, NC 27411. Offers adult education (MS); counselor education (MS); human resources-agency counseling (MS); human resources-rehabilitation counseling (MS); leadership studies (PhD); school administration (MS). *Accreditation:* ACA. Part-time and evening/weekend programs available. *Degree requirements:* For master's, comprehensive exam, thesis, qualifying exam. *Entrance requirements:* For master's, GRE General Test, minimum GPA of 3.0.

Northeastern University, Bouvé College of Health Sciences Graduate School, Department of Counseling and Applied Educational Psychology, Program in Applied Behavior Analysis, Boston, MA 02115-5096. Offers MS. Part-time programs available. *Degree requirements:* For master's, thesis. *Entrance requirements:* For master's, GRE General Test or MAT. *Faculty research:* Stimulus control, failure-to-thrive children, severe behavior disorders, autism.

Ohio University, Graduate College, College of Education, Department of Counseling and Higher Education, Athens, OH 45701-2979. Offers college student personnel (M Ed); community/agency counseling (M Ed); counselor education (PhD); higher education (M Ed, PhD); rehabilitation counseling (M Ed); school counseling (M Ed). *Accreditation:* ACA; CORE. Part-time and evening/weekend programs available. *Degree requirements:* For master's, thesis or alternative; for doctorate, comprehensive exam, thesis/dissertation. *Entrance requirements:* For master's, GRE General Test or MAT (if GPA is below 2.9), 3 letters of reference, 5-page biography, statement of purpose; for doctorate, GRE General Test, work experience, minimum GPA of 3.4. Additional exam requirements/recommendations for international students: Required—TOEFL (minimum score 550 paper-based; 213 computer-based). Electronic applications accepted. *Faculty research:* Youth violence, gender studies, student affairs, chemical dependency, disabilities issues.

Pontifical Catholic University of Puerto Rico, Institute of Graduate Studies in Behavioral Science and Community Affairs, Program in Vocational Rehabilitation Counseling, Ponce, PR 00717-0777. Offers MSS. Part-time programs available. *Degree requirements:* For master's, thesis. *Entrance requirements:* For master's, EXADEP, GRE, 3 letters of recommendation, interview, minimum GPA of 2.75.

St. Cloud State University, School of Graduate Studies, College of Education, Department of Counselor Education and Educational Psychology, Program in Rehabilitation Counseling, St. Cloud, MN 56301-4498. Offers MS. *Accreditation:* CORE. *Degree requirements:* For master's, comprehensive exam (for some programs), thesis or alternative. *Entrance requirements:* For master's, GRE General Test, minimum GPA of 2.75. Additional exam requirements/recommendations for international students: Required—Michigan English Language Assessment Battery; Recommended—TOEFL (minimum score 550 paper-based; 213 computer-based), IELTS (minimum score 6.5). Electronic applications accepted.

St. John's University, The School of Education, Department of Human Services and Counseling, Queens, NY 11439. Offers bilingual school counseling (MS Ed, PD); bilingual/multicultural education/teaching English to speakers of other languages (MS Ed); literacy (MS Ed, PhD), including teaching literacy 5-12 (MS Ed), teaching literacy B-12 (MS Ed), teaching literacy B-6 (MS Ed); mental health counseling (MS Ed); school counseling (MS Ed, PD); teaching children with disabilities in childhood education (MS Ed). Part-time and evening/weekend programs available. *Students:* 57 full-time (53 women), 287 part-time (258 women); includes 95 minority (26 African Americans, 11 Asian Americans or Pacific Islanders, 58 Hispanic Americans), 8 international. Average age 30. 304 applicants, 82% accepted, 131 enrolled. In 2008, 100 master's, 2 other advanced degrees awarded. *Degree requirements:* For master's, comprehensive exam. *Entrance requirements:* For master's and PD, statement of goals, official transcripts showing conferral of degree with minimum B average, 2 reference letters, interview; for doctorate, MAT, GRE General Test (analytical), statement of goals, official transcript showing conferral of degree with minimum B+ average, 2 reference letters, interview, professional resumé, teaching experience. Additional exam requirements/recommendations for international students: Required—TOEFL (minimum score 500 paper-based; 173 computer-based; 61 iBT), IELTS (minimum score 5.5). *Application deadline:* For fall admission, 4/1 for domestic students, 5/1 for international students; for spring admission, 11/1 for domestic and international students. Applications are processed on a rolling basis. Application fee: $70. Electronic applications accepted. *Expenses:* Tuition: Full-time $20,760; part-time $865 per credit. Required fees: $300; $150 per semester. Tuition and fees vary according to program. *Financial support:* Research assistantships, career-related internships or fieldwork and scholarships/grants available. Support available to part-time students. Financial award application deadline: 3/1; financial award applicants required to submit FAFSA. *Faculty research:* Assisting troubled children and teens with substance abuse, truancy, and coping skills, literacy development for ESL learners, investigating Caribbean and Creole language and culture. *Unit head:* Dr. Francine Guastello, Acting Chair, 718-990-1475, Fax: 718-990-1614, E-mail: guastelf@stjohns.edu. *Application contact:* Kelly K. Ronayne, Assistant Dean, 718-990-2303, Fax: 718-990-2343, E-mail: graded@stjohns.edu.

Salve Regina University, Graduate Studies, Program in Rehabilitation Counseling, Newport, RI 02840-4192. Offers mental health counseling (CAGS); rehabilitation counseling (MA). Part-time and evening/weekend programs available. *Faculty:* 1 (woman) full-time, 4 part-time/adjunct (all women). *Students:* 13 full-time (10 women), 25 part-time (18 women); includes 1 minority (Hispanic American). Average age 35. 18 applicants, 89% accepted, 13 enrolled. In 2008, 16 master's awarded. *Entrance requirements:* For master's, GMAT, GRE General Test or MAT. Additional exam requirements/recommendations for international students: Required—TOEFL (minimum score 600 paper-based; 250 computer-based; 100 iBT), TOEFL or IELTS. *Application deadline:* For fall admission, 3/15 priority date for domestic and international students; for spring admission, 9/15 priority date for domestic and international students. Applications are processed on a rolling basis. Application fee: $60. Electronic applications accepted. *Expenses:* Tuition: Part-time $395 per credit. Required fees: $40 per term. Tuition and fees vary according to degree level. *Financial support:* Career-related internships or fieldwork and Federal Work-Study available. Support available to part-time students. Financial award application deadline: 3/1; financial award applicants required to submit FAFSA. *Unit head:* Dr. Dimity Peter, Director, 401-341-3189, Fax: 401-341-2993, E-mail: dimity.peter@salve.edu. *Application contact:* Kelly Alverson, Graduate Admissions Counselor, 401-341-2153, Fax: 401-341-2973, E-mail: kelly.alverson@salve.edu.

San Diego State University, Graduate and Research Affairs, College of Education, Department of Administration, Rehabilitation and Post-Secondary Education, San Diego, CA 92182. Offers educational leadership in post-secondary education (MA); rehabilitation counseling (MS), including deafness. Evening/weekend programs available. Postbaccalaureate distance learning degree programs offered. *Degree requirements:* For master's, comprehensive exam (for some programs), thesis (for some programs). *Entrance requirements:* For master's, GRE General Test, letters of reference. Additional exam requirements/recommendations for international students: Required—TOEFL. Electronic applications accepted. *Faculty research:* Rehabilitation in cultural diversity, distance learning technology.

San Francisco State University, Division of Graduate Studies, College of Health and Human Services, Department of Counseling, San Francisco, CA 94132-1722. Offers counseling (MS); marriage, family, and child counseling (MSC); rehabilitation counseling (MS). *Accreditation:* ACA (one or more programs are accredited). Part-time programs available.

South Carolina State University, School of Graduate Studies, Department of Human Services, Orangeburg, SC 29117-0001. Offers elementary counselor education (M Ed); rehabilitation counseling (MA); secondary counselor education (M Ed). *Accreditation:* CORE. Part-time and evening/weekend programs available. *Faculty:* 9 full-time (6 women), 9 part-time/adjunct (7 women). *Students:* 149 full-time (124 women), 57 part-time (46 women); includes 190 minority (all African Americans), 2 international. Average age 34. 114 applicants, 98% accepted, 92 enrolled. In 2008, 56 master's awarded. *Degree requirements:* For master's, comprehensive exam (for some programs), departmental qualifying exam, internship. *Entrance requirements:* For master's, GRE, MAT, minimum GPA of 2.7. *Application deadline:* For fall admission, 6/15 priority date for domestic students, 6/15 for international students; for spring admission, 11/1 for domestic and international students. Applications are processed on a rolling basis. Application fee: $25. Electronic applications accepted. *Expenses:* Tuition, state resident: full-time $7806; part-time $434 per credit hour. Tuition, nonresident: full-time $15,298; part-time $850 per credit hour. *Financial support:* In 2008–09, 35 students received support, including 14 fellowships (averaging $5,730 per year); career-related internships or fieldwork, institutionally sponsored loans, and unspecified assistantships also available. Financial award application deadline: 6/1. *Faculty research:* Handicap, disability, rehabilitation evaluation, vocation. *Unit head:* Dr. Cassandra Sligh-Dewalt, Chair, 803-536-7075, Fax: 803-533-3636, E-mail: csligh-dewalt@scsu.edu. *Application contact:* Annette Hazzard-Jones, Program Coordinator II, 803-536-8809, Fax: 803-536-8812, E-mail: zs_ahazzard@scsu.edu.

Southern Illinois University Carbondale, Graduate School, College of Education, Rehabilitation Institute, Carbondale, IL 62901-4701. Offers behavioral analysis and therapy (MS); communication disorders and sciences (MS); rehabilitation (Rh D); rehabilitation administration and services (MS); rehabilitation counseling (MS). *Accreditation:* CORE. Part-time programs available. *Degree requirements:* For master's, thesis; for doctorate, thesis/dissertation. *Entrance requirements:* For master's, GRE; for doctorate, GRE or MAT, minimum GPA of 3.25. Additional exam requirements/recommendations for international students: Required—TOEFL. *Faculty research:* Professional ethics.

See Close-Up on page 1137.

Southern University and Agricultural and Mechanical College, Graduate School, College of Sciences, Department of Psychology, Program in Rehabilitation Counseling, Baton Rouge, LA 70813. Offers MS. *Accreditation:* CORE. *Degree requirements:* For master's, comprehensive exam, thesis optional. *Entrance requirements:* For master's, GMAT or GRE General Test. Additional exam requirements/recommendations for international students: Required—TOEFL. *Faculty research:* Cultural diversity, professional preparation and participation of minorities, needs and satisfaction of students with disabilities, prediction model for rehabilitation outcome, diabetes.

Springfield College, Graduate Programs, Programs in Rehabilitation Counseling and Services, Springfield, MA 01109-3797. Offers alcohol rehabilitation/substance abuse counseling (M Ed, MS); deaf counseling (M Ed, MS); developmental disabilities (M Ed, MS); general counseling and casework (M Ed, MS); psychiatric rehabilitation/mental health counseling (M Ed, MS); special services (M Ed, MS). *Accreditation:* CORE (one or more programs are accredited). Part-time programs available. *Faculty:* 8 full-time (2 women), 6 part-time/adjunct (4 women). *Students:* 26 full-time, 7 part-time. Average age 30. 20 applicants, 90% accepted, 11 enrolled. In 2008, 18 master's awarded. *Degree requirements:* For master's, comprehensive exam. *Entrance requirements:* Additional exam requirements/recommendations for international students: Required—TOEFL (minimum score 550 paper-based; 213 computer-based). *Application deadline:* For fall admission, 1/15 for domestic and international students; for winter admission, 11/1 for international students; for spring admission, 11/1 for domestic and international students. Applications are processed on a rolling basis. Application fee: $50. Electronic applications accepted. *Expenses:* Tuition: Full-time $9132; part-time $761 per semester hour. Required fees: $150. Tuition and fees vary according to course load. *Financial support:* Fellowships with partial tuition reimbursements, teaching assistantships with partial tuition reimbursements, career-related internships or fieldwork, Federal Work-Study, institutionally sponsored loans, and unspecified assistantships available. Financial award application deadline: 3/1; financial award applicants required to submit FAFSA. *Unit head:* Dr. Robert Hewes, Director, 413-748-3318, E-mail: rhewes@spfldcol.edu. *Application contact:* Donald James Shaw, Director of Graduate Admissions, 413-748-3479, Fax: 413-748-3694, E-mail: donald_shaw_jr@spfldcol.edu.

Syracuse University, Graduate School, School of Education, Program in Rehabilitation and Community Counseling, Syracuse, NY 13244. Offers MS. *Entrance requirements:* For master's, GRE General Test or MAT, interview. Additional exam requirements/recommendations for international students: Required—TOEFL.

Syracuse University, Graduate School, School of Education, Program in Rehabilitation Counseling, Syracuse, NY 13244. Offers MS. *Accreditation:* CORE. Part-time programs available. *Degree requirements:* For master's, thesis or alternative. *Entrance requirements:* For master's, GRE or MAT, interview. Additional exam requirements/recommendations for international students: Required—TOEFL. Electronic applications accepted.

Texas Tech University Health Sciences Center, School of Allied Health Sciences, Program in Rehabilitation Counseling, Lubbock, TX 79430. Offers MRC. *Accreditation:* CORE. Part-time programs available. *Entrance requirements:* Additional exam requirements/recommendations for international students: Required—TOEFL. Electronic applications accepted.

Thomas University, Department of Human Services, Thomasville, GA 31792-7499. Offers community counseling (MSCC); rehabilitation counseling (MRC). *Accreditation:* CORE. Part-time programs available. *Entrance requirements:* For master's, resumé, 3 academic/professional references. Additional exam requirements/recommendations for international students: Required—TOEFL (minimum score 600 paper-based; 250 computer-based). Electronic applications accepted.

Troy University, Graduate School, College of Education, Program in School Counseling, Troy, AL 36082. Offers community counseling (Ed S); counselor education (MS); guidance services (MS); rehabilitation counseling (Ed S); school counseling (Ed S). *Accreditation:* ACA; CORE; NCATE. Part-time and evening/weekend programs available. *Degree requirements:* For master's, comprehensive exam, thesis. *Entrance requirements:* For master's, minimum GPA of 2.5, teaching certification, 2 years of teaching experience. Additional exam requirements/recommendations for international students: Required—TOEFL (minimum score 523 paper-based; 200 computer-based). Electronic applications accepted.

Université de Montréal, Faculty of Medicine, Program in Specialized Studies, Montréal, QC H3C 3J7, Canada. Offers anesthesia (DESS); diagnostic radiology (DESS); family medicine (DESS); gastroenterology (DESS); geriatry (DESS); intensive care (DESS); medical biochemistry (DESS); medical genetics (DESS); medicine (DESS); microbiology and infectious diseases (DESS); nuclear medicine (DESS); obstetrics and gynecology (DESS); ophthalmology (DESS); pediatrics (DESS); pneumology (DESS); psychiatry (DESS); radiology-oncology (DESS); rheumatology (DESS); surgery (DESS). *Faculty:* 154 full-time (40 women), 333 part-time/adjunct (100 women). *Students:* 930 full-time (580 women), 7 part-time (all women). 74 applicants, 77% accepted, 29 enrolled. In 2008, 151 DESSs awarded. *Entrance requirements:* For degree, proficiency in French. *Application deadline:* For fall admission, 2/1 priority date for domestic students; for winter admission, 11/1 priority date for domestic students; for spring admission, 2/1 priority date for domestic students. Application fee: $100. Electronic applications accepted. *Unit head:* Lorraine Locas, Assistant to the Vice Dean of Graduate Studies, 514-343-6269, Fax: 514-343-5751, E-mail: lorraine.locas@umontreal.ca. *Application contact:* Dr. Andre Ferron, Vice Dean Graduate Studies, 514-343-6111 Ext. 0933, Fax: 514-343-5751, E-mail: andre.ferron@umontreal.ca.

University at Albany, State University of New York, School of Education, Department of Educational and Counseling Psychology, Program in Rehabilitation Counseling, Albany, NY 12222-0001. Offers counseling psychology (MS). *Accreditation:* CORE. Evening/weekend programs available. *Entrance requirements:* For master's, GRE General Test. Additional exam requirements/recommendations for international students: Required—TOEFL (minimum score 550 paper-based; 213 computer-based). Electronic applications accepted.

University at Buffalo, the State University of New York, Graduate School, Graduate School of Education, Department of Counseling, School, and Educational Psychology, Buffalo, NY 14260. Offers counseling/school psychology (PhD); counselor education (PhD); educational psychology (MA, PhD); mental health counseling (MS); rehabilitation counseling (MS); school counseling (Ed M, Certificate); school psychology (MA). *Accreditation:* CORE (one or more programs are accredited). *Degree requirements:* For master's, comprehensive exam (for some programs), thesis (for some programs); for doctorate, comprehensive exam, thesis/dissertation. *Entrance requirements:* For master's and doctorate, GRE General Test, interview, letters of reference. Additional exam requirements/recommendations for international students: Required—TOEFL. Electronic applications accepted. *Faculty research:* Multicultural counseling, class size effects, quality of life, eating disorders, outcome assessment.

The University of Arizona, Graduate College, College of Education, Department of Special Education, Rehabilitation and School Psychology, Program in Rehabilitation, Tucson, AZ 85721.

University of Arkansas, Graduate School, College of Education and Health Professions, Department of Rehabilitation, Human Resources and Communication Disorders, Program in Rehabilitation, Fayetteville, AR 72701-1201. Offers MS, PhD. *Accreditation:* CORE (one or more programs are accredited). Part-time programs available. *Degree requirements:* For doctorate, thesis/dissertation. *Entrance requirements:* For doctorate, GRE General Test.

University of Arkansas at Little Rock, Graduate School, College of Education, Department of Counseling and Rehabilitation Education, Little Rock, AR 72204-1099. Offers adult education (M Ed); counselor education (M Ed), including school counseling; orientation and mobility of the blind (Graduate Certificate); rehabilitation counseling (MA, Graduate Certificate); rehabilitation of the blind (MA). *Accreditation:* CORE; NCATE. Part-time programs available. *Entrance requirements:* For master's, interview, minimum GPA of 2.75. *Faculty research:* Low vision, orientation and mobility instruction.

University of Florida, Graduate School, College of Public Health and Health Professions, Department of Behavioral Science and Community Health, Gainesville, FL 32611. Offers rehabilitation counseling (MHS). *Accreditation:* CORE. Part-time programs available. *Entrance requirements:* For master's, GRE General Test, minimum GPA of 3.0. Electronic applications accepted. *Faculty research:* Overcoming mental, physical, or emotional handicaps toward personal/vocational independence.

The University of Iowa, Graduate College, College of Education, Department of Counseling, Rehabilitation, and Student Development, Iowa City, IA 52242-1316. Offers administration and research (PhD); counselor education and supervision (PhD); rehabilitation counseling (MA); rehabilitation counselor education (PhD); school counseling (MA); student development (MA, PhD). *Accreditation:* ACA (one or more programs are accredited); CORE (one or more programs are accredited). *Degree requirements:* For master's, thesis optional, exam; for doctorate, comprehensive exam, thesis/dissertation. *Entrance requirements:* For master's and doctorate, GRE General Test, minimum GPA of 3.0. Additional exam requirements/recommendations for international students: Required—TOEFL (minimum score 550 paper-based; 213 computer-based; 81 iBT). Electronic applications accepted.

University of Kentucky, Graduate School, College of Education, Program in Special Education, Lexington, KY 40506-0032. Offers early childhood special education (MS Ed); rehabilitation counseling (MRC); special education (MS Ed); special education leadership personnel preparation (Ed D). *Accreditation:* CORE; NCATE. Terminal master's awarded for partial completion of doctoral program. *Degree requirements:* For master's, comprehensive exam, thesis optional; for doctorate, comprehensive exam, thesis/dissertation. *Entrance requirements:* For master's, GRE General Test, minimum undergraduate GPA of 2.75; for doctorate, GRE General Test, minimum graduate GPA of 3.0. Additional exam requirements/recommendations for international students: Required—TOEFL (minimum score 550 paper-based; 213 computer-based). Electronic applications accepted. *Faculty research:* Applied behavior analysis applications in special education, single subject research design in classroom settings, transition research across life span, rural special education personnel.

University of Louisiana at Lafayette, BI Moody III College of Business Administration MBA Program, College of Liberal Arts, Department of Psychology, Program in Rehabilitation Counseling, Lafayette, LA 70504. Offers MS. *Entrance requirements:* For master's, GRE General Test, minimum GPA of 3.0. Additional exam requirements/recommendations for international students: Required—TOEFL (minimum score 550 paper-based; 213 computer-based). Electronic applications accepted. *Faculty research:* Vocational assessment, psychology.

University of Maryland, College Park, Graduate Studies, College of Education, Department of Counseling and Personnel Services, College Park, MD 20742. Offers college student personnel (M Ed, MA); college student personnel administration (PhD); community counseling (CAGS); community/career counseling (M Ed, MA); counseling and personnel services (M Ed, MA, PhD); counseling psychology (PhD); counselor education (PhD); rehabilitation counseling (M Ed, MA, AGSC); school counseling (M Ed, MA); school psychology (M Ed, MA, PhD). *Accreditation:* ACA (one or more programs are accredited); APA (one or more programs are accredited); CORE (one or more programs are accredited); NCATE. Part-time and evening/weekend programs available. Postbaccalaureate distance learning degree programs offered (no on-campus study). *Degree requirements:* For master's, thesis (for some programs); for doctorate, thesis/dissertation. *Entrance requirements:* For master's, GRE General Test or MAT, minimum GPA of 3.0, 3 letters of recommendation; for doctorate, GRE General Test or MAT, minimum GPA of 3.5, 3 letters of recommendation. Additional exam requirements/recommendations for international students: Required—TOEFL. Electronic applications accepted. *Faculty research:* Educational psychology, counseling, health.

Rehabilitation Counseling

University of Maryland Eastern Shore, Graduate Programs, Department of Rehabilitation Services, Princess Anne, MD 21853-1299. Offers rehabilitation counseling (MS). *Accreditation:* CORE. Part-time and evening/weekend programs available. *Degree requirements:* For master's, internship. *Entrance requirements:* For master's, interview. Additional exam requirements/recommendations for international students: Required—TOEFL (minimum score 213 computer-based; 80 iBT). Electronic applications accepted. *Faculty research:* Long-term rehabilitation training.

University of Massachusetts Boston, Office of Graduate Studies, Graduate College of Education, Counseling and School Psychology Department, Program in Rehabilitation Counseling, Boston, MA 02125-3393. Offers M Ed, CAGS. *Accreditation:* CORE.

University of Medicine and Dentistry of New Jersey, School of Health Related Professions, Department of Psychiatric Rehabilitation and Counseling Professions, Program in Psychiatric Rehabilitation, Newark, NJ 07107-1709. Offers MS, PhD. *Accreditation:* CORE. *Entrance requirements:* For doctorate, GRE General Test. Additional exam requirements/recommendations for international students: Required—TOEFL. Electronic applications accepted.

University of Medicine and Dentistry of New Jersey, School of Health Related Professions, Department of Psychiatric Rehabilitation and Counseling Professions, Program in Rehabilitation Counseling, Newark, NJ 07107-1709. Offers psychiatric rehabilitation (MS); vocational rehabilitation (MS). Programs offered at Scotch Plains and Stratford campuses. *Accreditation:* CORE. *Degree requirements:* For master's, internship, practicum. *Entrance requirements:* For master's, minimum 2 years of psychiatric rehabilitation or related professional experience or GRE General Test, interview. Additional exam requirements/recommendations for international students: Required—TOEFL. Electronic applications accepted.

University of Memphis, Graduate School, College of Education, Department of Counseling, Educational Psychology and Research, Memphis, TN 38152. Offers counseling (MS, Ed D), including community counseling (MS), rehabilitation counseling (MS), school counseling (MS); counseling psychology (PhD); educational psychology and research (MS, PhD), including educational psychology, educational research. *Accreditation:* ACA (one or more programs are accredited); APA (one or more programs are accredited); CORE (one or more programs are accredited); NCATE. *Faculty:* 32 full-time (14 women), 6 part-time/adjunct (4 women). *Students:* 87 full-time (68 women), 114 part-time (93 women); includes 63 minority (58 African Americans, 3 American Indian/Alaska Native, 1 Asian American or Pacific Islander, 1 Hispanic American), 10 international. Average age 32. 114 applicants, 54% accepted, 30 enrolled. In 2008, 50 master's, 22 doctorates awarded. *Degree requirements:* For master's, comprehensive exam, thesis or alternative; for doctorate, comprehensive exam, thesis/dissertation. *Entrance requirements:* For master's, GRE General Test or MAT, minimum GPA of 2.5; for doctorate, GRE General Test. *Application deadline:* For fall admission, 10/1 for domestic students; for spring admission, 4/1 for domestic students. Application fee: $35 ($60 for international students). *Expenses:* Tuition, area resident: Full-time $6242; part-time $330 per credit hour. Tuition, state resident: full-time $6242; part-time $330 per credit hour. Tuition, nonresident: full-time $17,828; part-time $815 per credit hour. Required fees: $1156. *Financial support:* Fellowships with full tuition reimbursements, research assistantships with full tuition reimbursements, teaching assistantships with full tuition reimbursements, career-related internships or fieldwork available. Financial award applicants required to submit FAFSA. *Faculty research:* Anger management, aging and disability, supervision, multicultural counseling. *Unit head:* Dr. Douglas C. Strohmer, Chair, 901-678-2841, Fax: 901-678-5114. *Application contact:* Dr. Ernest A. Rakow, Associate Dean of Administration and Graduate Programs, 901-678-2399, Fax: 901-678-4778.

University of Nevada, Las Vegas, Graduate College, College of Education, Department of Counselor Education, Las Vegas, NV 89154-3066. Offers addiction studies (Advanced Certificate); community mental health (MS); rehabilitation counseling (Advanced Certificate); school counseling (M Ed). *Faculty:* 7 full-time (2 women), 10 part-time/adjunct (7 women). *Students:* 47 full-time (39 women), 37 part-time (31 women); includes 13 minority (1 African American, 4 Asian Americans or Pacific Islanders, 8 Hispanic Americans). Average age 35. 31 applicants, 81% accepted, 15 enrolled. In 2008, 20 master's awarded. *Degree requirements:* For master's, comprehensive exam (for some programs), thesis (for some programs); for Advanced Certificate, thesis (for some programs). *Entrance requirements:* Additional exam requirements/recommendations for international students: Required—TOEFL (minimum score 550 paper-based; 213 computer-based; 80 iBT), IELTS (minimum score 7). *Application deadline:* For fall admission, 2/1 priority date for domestic and international students. Applications are processed on a rolling basis. Application fee: $60 ($75 for international students). Electronic applications accepted. *Expenses:* Tuition, state resident: full-time $1414; part-time $198 per credit. Tuition, nonresident: full-time $12,509; part-time $415.75 per credit. International tuition: $14,249 full-time. Required fees: $4 per credit. $252 per semester. Tuition and fees vary according to course load. *Financial support:* In 2008–09, 11 students received support, including 7 research assistantships with partial tuition reimbursements available (averaging $10,000 per year), 4 teaching assistantships with partial tuition reimbursements available (averaging $10,000 per year); institutionally sponsored loans, scholarships/grants, health care benefits, and unspecified assistantships also available. Financial award application deadline: 3/1. *Faculty research:* Social justice and multicultural competencies for counselors, therapeutic storytelling and bibliotherapy, school counselor education pedagogy, counseling program evaluation, addictions prevention and related trauma. *Unit head:* Dr. Dale Pehrsson, Chair/Associate Professor, 702-895-5994, Fax: 702-895-5550, E-mail: dale.pehrsson@unlv.edu. *Application contact:* Graduate College Admissions Evaluator, 702-895-3320, Fax: 702-895-4180, E-mail: gradcollege@unlv.edu.

The University of North Carolina at Chapel Hill, School of Medicine and Graduate School, Graduate Programs in Medicine, Chapel Hill, NC 27599. Offers allied health sciences (MPT, MS, Au D, DPT, PhD), including human movement science (MS, PhD), occupational science (MS, PhD), physical therapy (MPT, MS, DPT), rehabilitation counseling and psychology (MS), speech and hearing sciences (MS, Au D, PhD); biochemistry and biophysics (MS, PhD); biomedical engineering (MS, PhD); cell and developmental biology (PhD); cell and molecular physiology (PhD); genetics and molecular biology (PhD); microbiology and immunology (MS, PhD), including immunology, microbiology; neurobiology (PhD); pathology and laboratory medicine (PhD), including experimental pathology; pharmacology (PhD); MD/PhD. Post-baccalaureate distance learning degree programs offered. Terminal master's awarded for partial completion of doctoral program. *Degree requirements:* For master's, comprehensive exam; for doctorate, thesis/dissertation. Electronic applications accepted. *Expenses:* Contact institution.

The University of North Carolina at Chapel Hill, School of Medicine and Graduate School, Graduate Programs in Medicine, Department of Allied Health Sciences, Division of Rehabilitation Counseling and Psychology, Chapel Hill, NC 27599. Offers MS. *Accreditation:* CORE. *Degree requirements:* For master's, comprehensive exam, thesis or alternative, internship. *Entrance requirements:* For master's, GRE. Additional exam requirements/recommendations for international students: Required—TOEFL (minimum score 550 paper-based; 79 computer-based). *Faculty research:* Motor development, motor control; treatment of sports/orthopedic patient problems; movement in older adults; postural control across the lifespan; research in clinical practice; fetal, preterm, and infant movement; functional assessment across the lifespan.

University of Northern Colorado, Graduate School, College of Natural and Health Sciences, School of Human Sciences, Program in Rehabilitation, Greeley, CO 80639. Offers human rehabilitation (PhD); rehabilitation counseling (MA). *Accreditation:* CORE (one or more programs are accredited). Part-time programs available. *Faculty:* 3 full-time (1 woman). *Students:* 19 full-time (14 women), 10 part-time (8 women); includes 1 minority (African American), 3 international. Average age 38. 11 applicants, 91% accepted, 9 enrolled. In 2008, 3 master's, 1 doctorate awarded. *Degree requirements:* For master's, comprehensive exam, thesis or alternative; for doctorate, comprehensive exam, thesis/dissertation. *Entrance requirements:* For master's, GRE General Test or MAT, 2 letters of recommendation; for doctorate, GRE General Test, 2 letters of recommendation. *Application deadline:* Applications are processed on a rolling basis. Application fee: $50 ($60 for international students). Electronic applications accepted. *Expenses:* Tuition, state resident: full-time $4370; part-time $242.75 per credit hour. Tuition, nonresident: full-time $12,366; part-time $687 per credit hour. Required fees: $664.20; $36.90 per credit hour. *Financial support:* Fellowships, research assistantships, teaching assistantships, unspecified assistantships available. Financial award application deadline: 3/1; financial award applicants required to submit FAFSA. *Unit head:* Dr. Joe Ososkie, Program Coordinator, 970-351-2403. *Application contact:* Linda Sisson, Graduate Student Admission Coordinator, 970-351-1807, Fax: 970-351-2371, E-mail: linda.sisson@unco.edu.

University of North Florida, Brooks College of Health, Department of Public Health, Jacksonville, FL 32224-2645. Offers community health (MPH); geriatric management (MSH); health administration (MHA); health behavior research and evaluation (Certificate); nutrition (MSH); rehabilitation counseling (MS). *Accreditation:* CORE. Part-time and evening/weekend programs available. *Faculty:* 23 full-time (17 women). *Students:* 92 full-time (69 women), 59 part-time (44 women); includes 39 minority (25 African Americans, 9 Asian Americans or Pacific Islanders, 5 Hispanic Americans), 15 international. Average age 30. 172 applicants, 42% accepted, 41 enrolled. In 2008, 46 master's awarded. *Degree requirements:* For master's, thesis optional. *Entrance requirements:* For master's, GRE General Test (MSH, MS, MPH), GMAT or GRE General Test (MHA), minimum GPA of 3.0 in last 60 hours. Additional exam requirements/recommendations for international students: Required—TOEFL (minimum score 500 paper-based; 173 computer-based). *Application deadline:* For fall admission, 7/1 priority date for domestic students, 5/1 for international students; for spring admission, 11/10 priority date for domestic students, 10/1 for international students. Applications are processed on a rolling basis. Application fee: $30. Electronic applications accepted. *Expenses:* Tuition, area resident: Full-time $5782.08; part-time $240.92 per credit hour. Tuition, state resident: full-time $5782.08; part-time $240.92 per credit hour. Tuition, nonresident: full-time $19,974; part-time $832.26 per credit hour. Required fees: $952.80; $39.70 per credit hour. *Financial support:* In 2008–09, 49 students received support; research assistantships, teaching assistantships, career-related internships or fieldwork, Federal Work-Study, scholarships/grants, and tuition waivers (partial) available. Support available to part-time students. Financial award application deadline: 4/1; financial award applicants required to submit FAFSA. *Faculty research:* Dietary supplements; alcohol, tobacco, and other drug use prevention; turnover among health professionals; aging; psychosocial aspects of disabilities. Total annual research expenditures: $498,043. *Unit head:* Dr. JoAnn Nolin, Chair, 904-620-2840, Fax: 904-620-2848, E-mail: jnolin@unf.edu. *Application contact:* Heather Kenney, Director of Advising, 904-620-2810, Fax: 904-620-1030, E-mail: heather.kenney@unf.edu.

University of North Texas, Robert B. Toulouse School of Graduate Studies, College of Public Affairs and Community Service, Department of Rehabilitation, Social Work, and Addictions, Denton, TX 76203. Offers rehabilitation counseling (MS). *Accreditation:* CORE. Part-time programs available. *Degree requirements:* For master's, comprehensive exam, thesis optional, 600-hour internship. *Entrance requirements:* For master's, GRE General Test or 2 years experience, minimum overall GPA of 2.8, 3.0 in last 60 hours. Additional exam requirements/recommendations for international students: Required—proof of English language proficiency required for non-native English speakers; Recommended—TOEFL (minimum score 550 paper-based; 213 computer-based). *Faculty research:* Resiliency, multiculturalism, substance abuse and co-existing disabilities, social work pedagogy, spiritual aspects of disability and aging.

University of Pittsburgh, School of Health and Rehabilitation Sciences, Program in Health and Rehabilitation Sciences, Pittsburgh, PA 15260. Offers dietetics (MS); health and rehabilitation sciences (MS), including clinical dietetics, coordinated with dietetics, health care supervision and management, health information systems, occupational therapy, physical therapy, rehabilitation counseling, rehabilitation science and technology, sports medicine; wellness and human performance (MS). *Accreditation:* APTA. Part-time and evening/weekend programs available. *Entrance requirements:* For master's, minimum GPA of 3.0. Additional exam requirements/recommendations for international students: Required—TOEFL, IELTS. Electronic applications accepted. *Faculty research:* Assistive technology, seating and wheeled mobility, cellular neurophysiology, low back syndrome, augmentative communication.

University of Puerto Rico, Río Piedras, College of Social Sciences, Graduate School of Rehabilitation Counseling, San Juan, PR 00931-3300. Offers MRC. *Accreditation:* CORE. Part-time programs available. *Degree requirements:* For master's, comprehensive exam, thesis, internship. *Entrance requirements:* For master's, GRE or PAEG, interview, minimum GPA of 3.0, letter of recommendation.

The University of Scranton, College of Graduate and Continuing Education, Department of Counseling and Human Services, Program in Rehabilitation Counseling, Scranton, PA 18510. Offers MS. *Accreditation:* CORE. Part-time and evening/weekend programs available. *Students:* 33 full-time (19 women), 4 part-time (2 women); includes 5 minority (4 African Americans, 1 Asian American or Pacific Islander), 1 international. Average age 29. 20 applicants, 90% accepted. In 2008, 32 master's awarded. *Degree requirements:* For master's, comprehensive exam, capstone experience. *Entrance requirements:* For master's, minimum GPA of 2.75. Additional exam requirements/recommendations for international students: Required—TOEFL (minimum score 500 paper-based; 173 computer-based), IELTS (minimum score 5.5). *Application deadline:* For fall admission, 3/1 for domestic students. Application fee: $50. *Financial support:* Teaching assistantships, career-related internships or fieldwork and Federal Work-Study available. Support available to part-time students. Financial award application deadline: 3/1. *Unit head:* Dr. Rebecca Dalgin, Director, 570-941-7819, Fax: 570-941-5882, E-mail: dalginr2@scranton.edu. *Application contact:* Joseph M. Roback, Director of Admissions, 570-941-4385, Fax: 570-941-5928, E-mail: roback j2@scranton.edu.

University of South Alabama, Graduate School, College of Education, Department of Professional Studies, Mobile, AL 36688-0002. Offers community counseling (MS); educational media (M Ed, MS); instructional design and development (MS, PhD); rehabilitation counseling (MS); school counseling (M Ed); school psychometry (M Ed). *Accreditation:* NCATE. Part-time programs available. *Faculty:* 17 full-time (9 women). *Students:* 110 full-time (99 women), 165 part-time (131 women); includes 67 minority (59 African Americans, 2 American Indian/Alaska Native, 3 Asian Americans or Pacific Islanders, 3 Hispanic Americans), 17 international. 87 applicants, 31% accepted, 19 enrolled. In 2008, 40 master's, 9 doctorates awarded. *Degree requirements:* For master's, comprehensive exam. *Entrance requirements:* For master's, GRE General Test or MAT, minimum GPA of 3.0. *Application deadline:* For fall admission, 6/15 priority date for domestic students; for spring admission, 11/1 priority date for domestic students. Applications are processed on a rolling basis. Application fee: $35. *Expenses:* Tuition, area resident: Full-time $4656. Tuition, nonresident: full-time $9312. Required fees: $1102. *Financial support:* In 2008–09, 5 research assistantships were awarded; career-related internships or fieldwork also available. Support available to part-time students. Financial award application deadline: 4/1. *Faculty research:* Agency counseling, rehabilitation counseling, school psychometry. *Unit head:* Dr. Charles Guest, Chair, 251-380-2861. *Application contact:* Dr. B. Keith Harrison, Dean of the Graduate School, 251-460-6310, Fax: 251-461-1513, E-mail: kharriso@usouthal.edu.

University of South Carolina, School of Medicine and The Graduate School, Graduate Programs in Medicine, Program in Rehabilitation Counseling, Columbia, SC 29208. Offers psychiatric rehabilitation (Certificate); rehabilitation counseling (MRC). *Accreditation:* CORE. Part-time and evening/weekend programs available. *Degree requirements:* For master's, comprehensive exam, internship, practicum. *Entrance requirements:* For master's and Certificate, GRE General Test or GMAT. Electronic applications accepted. *Expenses:* Contact institution. *Faculty research:* Quality of life, alcohol dependency, technology for disabled, psychiatric rehabilitation, women with disabilities.

University of South Florida, Graduate School, College of Arts and Sciences, Department of Rehabilitation and Mental Health Counseling, Tampa, FL 33620-9951. Offers MA. *Accreditation:* CORE. Part-time and evening/weekend programs available. *Faculty:* 5 full-time (1 woman), 6 part-time/adjunct (4 women). *Students:* 93 full-time (75 women), 65 part-time (53 women);

includes 31 minority (12 African Americans, 1 American Indian/Alaska Native, 2 Asian Americans or Pacific Islanders, 16 Hispanic Americans), 2 international. 123 applicants, 50% accepted, 54 enrolled. In 2008, 25 master's awarded. *Degree requirements:* For master's, comprehensive exam, thesis. *Entrance requirements:* For master's, GRE General Test, minimum GPA of 3.0 in last 60 hours. Additional exam requirements/recommendations for international students: Required—TOEFL (minimum score 550 paper-based; 213 computer-based), TWE. *Application deadline:* For fall admission, 2/30 for domestic students, 1/2 for international students; for spring admission, 10/15 for domestic students, 6/1 for international students. Application fee: $30. Electronic applications accepted. *Expenses:* Tuition, state resident: full-time $2624.40; part-time $291.60 per credit hour. Tuition, nonresident: full-time $7822; part-time $869.13 per credit hour. *Financial support:* Application deadline: 6/30. *Faculty research:* Allied health, multiculturalism, couples therapy, addictions. *Unit head:* Charotte Dixon, Chairperson, 813-974-0973, Fax: 813-974-8080, E-mail: dixon@chuma1.cas.usf.edu. *Application contact:* Gary DuDell, Program Director, 813-974-0970, Fax: 813-974-8080, E-mail: gdudell@cas.usf.edu.

The University of Tennessee, Graduate School, College of Education, Health and Human Sciences, Department of Educational Psychology and Counseling, Knoxville, TN 37996. Offers adult education (MS); applied educational psychology (MS); collaborative learning (Ed D); college student personnel (MS); mental health counseling (MS); rehabilitation counseling (MS); school counseling (MS). *Accreditation:* ACA (one or more programs are accredited); CORE (one or more programs are accredited); NCATE. Part-time and evening/weekend programs available. *Degree requirements:* For master's, thesis optional. *Entrance requirements:* For master's, GRE General Test, minimum GPA of 2.7. Additional exam requirements/recommendations for international students: Required—TOEFL. Electronic applications accepted. *Expenses:* Tuition, area resident: Part-time $348 per credit hour. Tuition, state resident: full-time $6262. Tuition, nonresident: full-time $18,920; part-time $1052 per credit hour. Required fees: $812; $36 per credit hour. Tuition and fees vary according to program.

The University of Texas–Pan American, College of Health Sciences and Human Services, Department of Rehabilitation, Edinburg, TX 78541-2999. Offers rehabilitation counseling (MS). *Accreditation:* CORE. Part-time and evening/weekend programs available. *Degree requirements:* For master's, comprehensive exam, thesis optional. *Entrance requirements:* For master's, minimum GPA of 3.0. *Faculty research:* Attitudes and disability, substance abuse, multicultural counseling, Hispanics and disability, Social Security beneficiary characteristics.

The University of Texas Southwestern Medical Center at Dallas, Southwestern Graduate School of Biomedical Sciences, Division of Clinical Science, Rehabilitation Counseling Psychology Program, Dallas, TX 75390. Offers MS. *Accreditation:* CORE. *Faculty:* 19 full-time (14 women), 10 part-time/adjunct (3 women). *Students:* 28 full-time (22 women); includes 5 minority (1 African American, 1 Asian American or Pacific Islander, 3 Hispanic Americans). Average age 26. 26 applicants, 46% accepted, 12 enrolled. In 2008, 4 master's awarded. *Degree requirements:* For master's, thesis. *Entrance requirements:* For master's, GRE General Test, minimum GPA of 3.0. *Application deadline:* For fall admission, 5/1 for domestic students. Applications are processed on a rolling basis. Application fee: $0. Electronic applications accepted. *Expenses:* Tuition, state resident: full-time $3600. Tuition, nonresident: full-time $10,344. Required fees: $763. *Financial support:* Career-related internships or fieldwork and institutionally sponsored loans available. Financial award application deadline: 3/1; financial award applicants required to submit FAFSA. *Faculty research:* Psychophysiology of stress and emotion, psychosocial rehabilitation, assessment of learning disabilities. *Unit head:* Dr. Cheryl Silver, Chair, 214-648-1750, Fax: 214-648-1076, E-mail: cheryl.silver@utsouthwestern.edu. *Application contact:* Lisa Halliburton, Administrative Assistant, 214-648-1544, Fax: 214-648-1076, E-mail: wanda.madyun@utsouthwestern.edu.

University of Wisconsin–Madison, Graduate School, School of Education, Department of Rehabilitation Psychology and Special Education, Program in Rehabilitation Psychology, Madison, WI 53706-1380. Offers MA, MS, PhD. *Accreditation:* CORE (one or more programs are accredited). *Degree requirements:* For doctorate, thesis/dissertation.

University of Wisconsin–Stout, Graduate School, College of Human Development, Program in Vocational Rehabilitation, Menomonie, WI 54751. Offers MS. *Accreditation:* CORE. Part-time programs available. Postbaccalaureate distance learning degree programs offered (no on-campus study). *Students:* 30 full-time (20 women), 45 part-time (41 women); includes 3 minority (all African Americans), 3 international. Average age 36. 95 applicants, 48% accepted, 33 enrolled. In 2008, 35 master's awarded. *Degree requirements:* For master's, thesis optional, comprehensive exam or thesis. *Entrance requirements:* For master's, minimum GPA of 2.75. Additional exam requirements/recommendations for international students: Required—TOEFL (minimum score 500 paper-based; 173 computer-based; 61 iBT). *Application deadline:* For fall admission, 3/15 priority date for domestic and international students. Application fee: $45. Electronic applications accepted. *Expenses:* Tuition, state resident: full-time $6227; part-time $345.93 per credit. Tuition, nonresident: full-time $9998; part-time $555.42 per credit. International tuition: $10,512 full-time. Tuition and fees vary according to course load, program and reciprocity agreements. *Financial support:* In 2008–09, 8 research assistantships with partial tuition reimbursements (averaging $3,628 per year) were awarded; teaching assistantships with partial tuition reimbursements, Federal Work-Study, scholarships/grants, tuition waivers (partial), and unspecified assistantships also available. Support available to part-time students. Financial award application deadline: 5/1; financial award applicants required to submit FAFSA. *Faculty research:* Aging/gerontology, athletics, neuropsychology, recreation, transition to work. *Unit head:* Dr. Michelle Hamilton, Director, 715-232-1895, Fax: 715-232-2356, E-mail: hamiltonmi@uwstout.edu. *Application contact:* Anne Johnson, Graduate Student Evaluator (Admissions and Assistantship Coordinator), 715-232-1322, Fax: 715-232-2413.

Utah State University, School of Graduate Studies, College of Education and Human Services, Department of Special Education and Rehabilitation, Program in Rehabilitation Counselor Education, Logan, UT 84322. Offers MRC. *Accreditation:* CORE. Part-time programs available. Postbaccalaureate distance learning degree programs offered (minimal on-campus study). *Degree requirements:* For master's, internship. *Entrance requirements:* For master's, GRE General Test, minimum GPA of 3.0. Additional exam requirements/recommendations for international students: Required—TOEFL (minimum score 550 paper-based; 213 computer-based). Electronic applications accepted. *Expenses:* Contact institution. *Faculty research:* Distance education, Hispanic rehabilitation, transition from school to work.

Virginia Commonwealth University, Graduate School, School of Allied Health Professions, Department of Rehabilitation Counseling, Richmond, VA 23284-9005. Offers MS, CPC. *Accreditation:* CORE (one or more programs are accredited). *Entrance requirements:* For master's, GRE General Test or MAT. *Faculty research:* Substance abuse/addictions, lifelong disabilities, consumer empowerment, counseling models, adjustment to disability.

Wayne State University, College of Education, Division of Theoretical and Behavioral Foundations, Detroit, MI 48202. Offers counseling (M Ed, MA, Ed D, PhD, Ed S); education evaluation and research (M Ed, Ed D, PhD); educational psychology (M Ed, Ed D, PhD, Ed S); educational sociology (M Ed, Ed D, PhD, Ed S); history and philosophy of education (M Ed, Ed D, PhD); rehabilitation counseling and community inclusion (MA, Ed S); school and community psychology (MA, Ed S); school clinical psychology (Ed S). *Accreditation:* ACA (one or more programs are accredited); CORE (one or more programs are accredited). Evening/weekend programs available. *Degree requirements:* For doctorate, thesis/dissertation. *Entrance requirements:* For master's, GRE; for doctorate, GRE, interview, minimum GPA of 3.0, curriculum vitae, references. Additional exam requirements/recommendations for international students: Required—TOEFL (minimum score 550 paper-based; 213 computer-based), TWE (minimum score 6). Electronic applications accepted. *Faculty research:* Adolescents at risk, supervision of counseling.

Wayne State University, Graduate School, Interdisciplinary Program in Developmental Disabilities, Detroit, MI 48202. Offers Certificate. *Entrance requirements:* For degree, master's degree; reference; goal statement. Additional exam requirements/recommendations for international students: Required—TOEFL (minimum score 550 paper-based; 213 computer-based); Recommended—TWE (minimum score 6). Electronic applications accepted.

Western Michigan University, Graduate College, College of Health and Human Services, Department of Blindness and Low Vision Studies, Kalamazoo, MI 49008-5202. Offers MA. *Accreditation:* CORE.

Western Oregon University, Graduate Programs, College of Education, Division of Special Education, Program in Rehabilitation Counseling, Monmouth, OR 97361-1394. Offers MS. *Accreditation:* CORE. *Degree requirements:* For master's, thesis optional, oral exam, portfolio. *Entrance requirements:* For master's, interview, minimum GPA of 3.0. Additional exam requirements/recommendations for international students: Required—TOEFL (minimum score 550 paper-based; 213 computer-based; 79 iBT), IELTS (minimum score 6.5). *Faculty research:* Deafness, rehabilitation counseling.

Western Washington University, Graduate School, Woodring College of Education, Program in Rehabilitation Counseling, Bellingham, WA 98225-5996. Offers MA. *Accreditation:* CORE. Part-time and evening/weekend programs available. Postbaccalaureate distance learning degree programs offered (minimal on-campus study). *Degree requirements:* For master's, research project. *Entrance requirements:* For master's, GRE General Test or MAT, minimum GPA of 3.0 in last 60 semester hours or last 90 quarter hours of course work. Additional exam requirements/recommendations for international students: Required—TOEFL (minimum score 567 paper-based; 227 computer-based). Electronic applications accepted. *Faculty research:* Employment issues for individuals with significant disabilities, research and statistics techniques, rehabilitation counselor education.

West Virginia University, College of Human Resources and Education, Department of Counseling, Rehabilitation Counseling, and Counseling Psychology, Program in Rehabilitation Counseling, Morgantown, WV 26506. Offers MS. *Accreditation:* CORE. Part-time programs available. Postbaccalaureate distance learning degree programs offered (minimal on-campus study). *Degree requirements:* For master's, content exams. *Entrance requirements:* For master's, GRE General Test, minimum GPA of 2.5, interview. Additional exam requirements/recommendations for international students: Required—TOEFL (minimum score 550 paper-based; 213 computer-based; 65 iBT). Electronic applications accepted. *Faculty research:* Work adjustment, job modification for the handicapped, computer resource networks, vocational evaluation.

Winston-Salem State University, Program in Rehabilitation Counseling, Winston-Salem, NC 27110-0003. Offers MRC. *Accreditation:* CORE. Part-time programs available. Postbaccalaureate distance learning degree programs offered (minimal on-campus study). *Degree requirements:* For master's, thesis optional. *Entrance requirements:* For master's, GRE, 3 letters of recommendation. Electronic applications accepted. *Faculty research:* Drug addiction, recovery, HIV/AIDS interventions.

Wright State University, School of Graduate Studies, College of Education and Human Services, Department of Human Services, Program in Rehabilitation Counseling, Dayton, OH 45435. Offers chemical dependency (MRC); severe disabilities (MRC). *Accreditation:* CORE. *Degree requirements:* For master's, comprehensive exam. *Entrance requirements:* For master's, GRE General Test, MAT, interview. Additional exam requirements/recommendations for international students: Required—TOEFL.

School Psychology

Abilene Christian University, Graduate School, College of Arts and Sciences, Department of Psychology, Program in School Psychology, Abilene, TX 79699-9100. Offers MS. *Students:* 12 full-time (11 women), 5 part-time (4 women). 14 applicants, 71% accepted, 6 enrolled. In 2008, 3 master's awarded. *Degree requirements:* For master's, comprehensive exam, thesis optional. *Entrance requirements:* For master's, GRE General Test. *Application deadline:* For fall admission, 4/1 priority date for domestic students; for spring admission, 11/1 for domestic students. Applications are processed on a rolling basis. Application fee: $40 ($45 for international students). Electronic applications accepted. *Expenses:* Tuition: Full-time $10,728; part-time $640 per hour. Required fees: $1090; $53.50 per hour. $10 per term. Tuition and fees vary according to campus/location. *Financial support:* In 2008–09, 14 students received support. Federal Work-Study available. Support available to part-time students. Financial award application deadline: 4/1; financial award applicants required to submit FAFSA. *Unit head:* Dr. Jennifer Shewmaker, Graduate Advisor, 325-674-2381, Fax: 325-674-6968, E-mail: jennifer.shewmaker@acu.edu. *Application contact:* William Horn, Graduate Admissions Counselor, 325-674-2656, Fax: 325-674-6717, E-mail: gradinfo@acu.edu.

Adelphi University, Derner Institute of Advanced Psychological Studies, Program in School Psychology, Garden City, NY 11530-0701. Offers MA. Part-time programs available. *Students:* 41 full-time (38 women), 41 part-time (35 women); includes 10 minority (5 African Americans, 1 Asian American or Pacific Islander, 4 Hispanic Americans). Average age 26. In 2008, 23 master's awarded. *Degree requirements:* For master's, comprehensive exam. *Entrance requirements:* For master's, minimum GPA of 3.0; 15 credits of course work in psychology including general psychology, developmental child or adolescent psychology, abnormal personality in school psychology, tests and measurements, statistics; 3 letters of recommendation. Additional exam requirements/recommendations for international students: Required—TOEFL (minimum score 550 paper-based; 213 computer-based; 80 iBT). *Application deadline:* For fall admission, 5/1 for domestic students, 4/1 for international students. Application fee: $50. Electronic applications accepted. *Expenses:* Tuition: Full-time $25,700; part-time $775 per credit hour. Required fees: $500. Tuition and fees vary according to course load, degree level, campus/location, program and student level. *Financial support:* Research assistantships with full and partial tuition reimbursements, career-related internships or fieldwork, Federal Work-Study, institutionally sponsored loans, and unspecified assistantships available. *Unit head:* Dr. Ionas Sapountzis, 516-877-4743, E-mail: isapountzis@adelphi.edu. *Application contact:* Christine Murphy, Director of Admissions, 516-877-3050, Fax: 516-877-3039, E-mail: graduateadmissions@adelphi.edu.

Alabama Agricultural and Mechanical University, School of Graduate Studies, School of Education, Department of Counseling and Special Education, Huntsville, AL 35811. Offers communicative disorders (M Ed, MS); psychology and counseling (MS, Ed S), including clinical psychology (MS), counseling and guidance, counseling psychology (MS), personnel management (MS), psychometry (MS), school psychology (MS); special education (M Ed, MS). *Accreditation:* CORE; NCATE. Part-time and evening/weekend programs available. *Students:* 13 full-time (9 women), 57 part-time (46 women); includes 52 minority (51 African Americans, 1 Hispanic American), 2 international. In 2008, 24 master's awarded. *Degree requirements:* For master's,

School Psychology

Alabama Agricultural and Mechanical University (continued)
comprehensive exam. *Entrance requirements:* For master's, GRE General Test. Additional exam requirements/recommendations for international students: Required—TOEFL (minimum score 500 paper-based; 173 computer-based; 61 iBT). *Application deadline:* For fall admission, 5/1 for domestic students. Application fee: $15 ($20 for international students). *Expenses:* Tuition, area resident: Full-time $3924; part-time $2616 per term. Tuition, nonresident: part-time $5234 per year. International tuition: $7848 full-time. Required fees: $198; $396 per credit hour. $2841 per term. One-time fee: $8498 full-time; $5682 part-time. Full-time tuition and fees vary according to program. *Financial support:* Career-related internships or fieldwork available. Support available to part-time students. Financial award application deadline: 4/1. *Faculty research:* Increasing numbers of minorities in special education and speech-language pathology. *Unit head:* Dr. Shirley King, Chair, 256-372-5520, Fax: 256-372-5526. *Application contact:* Dr. Caula Beyl, Dean, School of Graduate Studies, 256-372-5266, Fax: 256-372-5269, E-mail: caula.beyl@aamu.edu.

Alfred University, Graduate School, Program in School Psychology, Alfred, NY 14802-1205. Offers school counseling (MS Ed, CAS); school psychology (MA, Psy D, CAS). *Accreditation:* APA. *Degree requirements:* For master's, internship; for doctorate, thesis/dissertation, internship. *Entrance requirements:* For master's and doctorate, GRE General Test. Additional exam requirements/recommendations for international students: Required—TOEFL (minimum score 590 paper-based; 243 computer-based; 90 iBT); Recommended—IELTS (minimum score 6.5). Electronic applications accepted. *Faculty research:* Family processes, alternative assessment approaches, behavior disorders in children, parent involvement, school psychology training issues.

See Close-Up on page 1053.

Alliant International University–Irvine, Graduate School of Education, Educational Psychology Programs, Irvine, CA 92612. Offers educational psychology (Psy D); pupil personnel services (Credential); school psychology (MA). Part-time programs available. *Degree requirements:* For doctorate, thesis/dissertation. *Entrance requirements:* For master's, minimum GPA of 3.0, letters of recommendation; for doctorate, interview, minimum GPA of 3.0, letters of recommendation. Additional exam requirements/recommendations for international students: Required—TOEFL (minimum score 550 paper-based; 213 computer-based), TWE (minimum score 5). *Faculty research:* School based mental health.

Alliant International University–Los Angeles, Graduate School of Education, Educational Psychology Programs, Alhambra, CA 91803-1360. Offers educational psychology (Psy D); pupil personnel services (Credential); school psychology (MA). Part-time programs available. *Degree requirements:* For doctorate, thesis/dissertation. *Entrance requirements:* For master's, minimum GPA of 3.0, letters of recommendation; for doctorate, interview, minimum GPA of 3.0, letters of recommendation. Additional exam requirements/recommendations for international students: Required—TOEFL (minimum score 550 paper-based; 213 computer-based), TWE (minimum score 5). Electronic applications accepted. *Faculty research:* Early identification and intervention with high-risk preschoolers, pediatric neuropsychology, interpersonal violence, ADHD, learning theories.

Alliant International University–San Diego, Graduate School of Education, Educational Psychology Programs, San Diego, CA 92131-1799. Offers educational psychology (Psy D); pupil personnel services (Credential); school psychology (MA); student personnel services (Certificate). Part-time programs available. *Degree requirements:* For doctorate, thesis/dissertation. *Entrance requirements:* For master's, minimum GPA of 3.0, letters of recommendation; for doctorate, interview, letters of recommendation. Additional exam requirements/recommendations for international students: Required—TOEFL (minimum score 550 paper-based; 213 computer-based), TWE (minimum score 5). Electronic applications accepted.

Alliant International University–San Francisco, Graduate School of Education, Educational Psychology Programs, San Francisco, CA 94133-1221. Offers educational psychology (Psy D); pupil personnel services (Credential); school psychology (MA). Part-time programs available. *Degree requirements:* For doctorate, thesis/dissertation. *Entrance requirements:* For master's, minimum GPA of 3.0, letters of recommendation; for doctorate, interview, minimum GPA of 3.0, letters of recommendation. Additional exam requirements/recommendations for international students: Required—TOEFL (minimum score 550 paper-based; 213 computer-based), TWE (minimum score 5). Electronic applications accepted. *Faculty research:* Social skills, ADHD, effects of sightedness on areas of knowledge.

Andrews University, School of Graduate Studies, School of Education, Department of Educational and Counseling Psychology, Program in School Counseling, Berrien Springs, MI 49104. Offers MA. *Students:* 5 full-time (all women), 1 part-time (0 women); includes 3 minority (2 African Americans, 1 Hispanic American). Average age 29. In 2008, 2 master's awarded. *Degree requirements:* For master's, thesis optional. *Entrance requirements:* For master's, GRE. Additional exam requirements/recommendations for international students: Required—TOEFL (minimum score 550 paper-based). Application fee: $40. *Expenses:* Tuition: Full-time $18,360; part-time $765 per credit hour. Required fees: $476; $765 per credit hour. $238 per semester. Tuition and fees vary according to degree level. *Unit head:* Dr. Frederick A. Kosinski, Coordinator, 269-471-3466. *Application contact:* Carolyn Hurst, Supervisor of Graduate Admission, 800-253-2874, Fax: 269-471-6321, E-mail: graduate@andrews.edu.

Andrews University, School of Graduate Studies, School of Education, Department of Educational and Counseling Psychology, Program in School Psychology, Berrien Springs, MI 49104. Offers Ed S. Part-time programs available. *Students:* 11 full-time (9 women), 11 part-time (9 women); includes 6 minority (4 African Americans, 1 Asian American or Pacific Islander, 1 Hispanic American), 1 international. Average age 28. In 2008, 4 Ed Ss awarded. *Entrance requirements:* Additional exam requirements/recommendations for international students: Required—TOEFL (minimum score 550 paper-based). *Application deadline:* Applications are processed on a rolling basis. Application fee: $40. *Expenses:* Tuition: Full-time $18,360; part-time $765 per credit hour. Required fees: $476; $765 per credit hour. $238 per semester. Tuition and fees vary according to degree level. *Unit head:* Dr. Elizabeth Lundy, Coordinator, 269-471-6251. *Application contact:* Carolyn Hurst, Supervisor of Graduate Admission, 800-253-2874, Fax: 269-471-6321, E-mail: graduate@andrews.edu.

Appalachian State University, Cratis D. Williams Graduate School, Department of Human Development and Psychological Counseling, Boone, NC 28608. Offers community counseling (MA); marriage and family therapy (MA); school counseling (MA); student development (MA). *Accreditation:* AAMFT/COAMFTE; ACA; NCATE. Part-time programs available. *Faculty:* 15 full-time (5 women), 21 part-time/adjunct (14 women). *Students:* 124 full-time (97 women), 50 part-time (39 women); includes 14 minority (12 African Americans, 1 Asian American or Pacific Islander, 1 Hispanic American). 169 applicants, 57% accepted, 66 enrolled. In 2008, 60 master's awarded. *Degree requirements:* For master's, comprehensive exam (for some programs), thesis optional, internships. *Entrance requirements:* For master's, GRE General Test, 3 letters of recommendation. Additional exam requirements/recommendations for international students: Required—TOEFL (minimum score 570 paper-based; 230 computer-based; 79 iBT), IELTS (minimum score 6.5). *Application deadline:* For fall admission, 2/1 priority date for domestic students, 2/1 for international students; for spring admission, 2/1 for international students. Applications are processed on a rolling basis. Application fee: $50. Electronic applications accepted. *Expenses:* Tuition, area resident: Full-time $2600; part-time $700 per course. Tuition, state resident: full-time $2600; part-time $700 per course. Tuition, nonresident: full-time $5000; part-time $3300 per course. Required fees: $2150; $330 per course. Tuition and fees vary according to campus/location. *Financial support:* In 2008–09, 20 research assistantships (averaging $7,000 per year), 7 teaching assistantships (averaging $7,000 per year) were awarded; fellowships, career-related internships or fieldwork, Federal Work-Study, scholarships/grants, and unspecified assistantships also available. Financial award application deadline: 4/1; financial award applicants required to submit FAFSA. *Faculty research:* Multicultural counseling, addictions counseling, play therapy, expressive arts, child and adolescent therapy, sexual abuse counseling. *Unit head:* Dr. Lee Baruth, Chairman, 828-262-2055, E-mail: baruthlg@appstate.edu. *Application contact:* Sandy Krause, Director of Admissions and Recruiting, 828-262-2130, Fax: 828-262-2709, E-mail: krausesl@appstate.edu.

Arcadia University, Graduate Studies, Department of Psychology, Glenside, PA 19038-3295. Offers community counseling (MACP); school counseling (MACP). Part-time programs available. *Degree requirements:* For master's, practicum. *Entrance requirements:* For master's, GRE General Test or MAT.

Argosy University, Hawai'i, College of Psychology and Behavioral Sciences, Program in School Psychology, Honolulu, HI 96813. Offers MA.

See Close-Up on page 1073.

Argosy University, Phoenix, College of Psychology and Behavioral Sciences, Program in School Psychology, Phoenix, AZ 85021. Offers MA, Psy D.

See Close-Up on page 1083.

Argosy University, Sarasota, College of Psychology and Behavioral Sciences, Sarasota, FL 34235. Offers community counseling (MA); counseling psychology (Ed D); counselor education and supervision (Ed D); forensic psychology (MA); marriage and family therapy (MA); mental health counseling (MA); organizational leadership (Ed D); pastoral community counseling (Ed D); school counseling (MA, Ed S); school psychology (MA).

See Close-Up on page 1091.

Arkansas State University, Graduate School, College of Education, Department of Psychology and Counseling, Jonesboro, State University, AR 72467. Offers college student personnel services (MS); counselor education (Ed S), including college student personnel services, psychoeducational diagnosis, school counseling; rehabilitation counseling (MRC); school counseling (MSE); student affairs (Certificate). *Accreditation:* ACA (one or more programs are accredited); CORE (one or more programs are accredited); NCATE. Part-time programs available. *Faculty:* 11 full-time (6 women), 6 part-time/adjunct (2 women). *Students:* 72 full-time (60 women), 78 part-time (62 women); includes 33 minority (31 African Americans, 2 Hispanic Americans), 1 international. Average age 32. 83 applicants, 58% accepted, 35 enrolled. In 2008, 14 master's, 12 other advanced degrees awarded. *Degree requirements:* For master's and other advanced degree, comprehensive exam, thesis or alternative. *Entrance requirements:* For master's, GRE General Test or MAT (MSE), appropriate bachelor's degree, interview, letters of reference, official transcript; for other advanced degree, GRE General Test, interview, master's degree, letters of reference, official transcript. Additional exam requirements/recommendations for international students: Required—TOEFL (minimum score 550 paper-based; 213 computer-based; 79 iBT), IELTS (minimum score 6). *Application deadline:* For fall admission, 7/15 for domestic students, 7/1 for international students; for spring admission, 12/1 for domestic students, 11/13 for international students. Applications are processed on a rolling basis. Application fee: $30 ($40 for international students). Electronic applications accepted. *Expenses:* Tuition, state resident: full-time $3744; part-time $208 per credit hour. Tuition, nonresident: full-time $9540; part-time $530 per credit hour. International tuition: $7938 full-time. Required fees: $896; $47 per credit hour. $25 per term. One-time fee: $50. Tuition and fees vary according to course load and program. *Financial support:* In 2008–09, 29 students received support; teaching assistantships, career-related internships or fieldwork, scholarships/grants, and unspecified assistantships available. Financial award application deadline: 7/1; financial award applicants required to submit FAFSA. *Faculty research:* Abuse issues in children and adolescents, career counseling, children's learning and memory, crisis intervention, drug use and addition. *Unit head:* Dr. Loretta McGregor, Chair, 870-972-3064, Fax: 870-972-3962, E-mail: lmcgregor@astate.edu. *Application contact:* Dr. Andrew Sustich, Dean of the Graduate School, 870-972-3029, Fax: 870-972-3857, E-mail: sustich@astate.edu.

Assumption College, Graduate School, School Counseling Program, Worcester, MA 01609-1296. Offers MA, CAGS. Part-time and evening/weekend programs available. *Faculty:* 4 full-time (1 woman), 6 part-time/adjunct (3 women). *Students:* 47 full-time (45 women), 21 part-time (15 women); includes 2 minority (1 African American, 1 Hispanic American). Average age 24. 49 applicants, 96% accepted. In 2008, 10 master's awarded. *Degree requirements:* For master's, comprehensive exam, internship; for CAGS, comprehensive exam. *Entrance requirements:* For master's, 3 letters of recommendation, resumé, interview, essay; for CAGS, 3 letters of recommendation, resumé, essay, interview. Additional exam requirements/recommendations for international students: Required—TOEFL (minimum score 540 paper-based; 200 computer-based; 76 iBT), IELTS (minimum score 6). *Application deadline:* For fall admission, 6/1 priority date for domestic students, 5/1 priority date for international students; for spring admission, 11/1 priority date for domestic students, 9/1 priority date for international students. Applications are processed on a rolling basis. Application fee: $30. Electronic applications accepted. *Expenses:* Tuition: Part-time $468 per credit hour. Required fees: $20 per semester. One-time fee: $100. *Financial support:* In 2008–09, 47 students received support. Tuition waivers (partial) available. Financial award application deadline: 6/1; financial award applicants required to submit FAFSA. *Unit head:* Dr. Mary Ann Mariani, Director, 508-767-7087, Fax: 508-767-7263, E-mail: mmariani@assumption.edu. *Application contact:* Adrian O. Dumas, Director of Graduate Enrollment Management and Services, 508-767-7365, Fax: 508-767-7030, E-mail: adumas@assumption.edu.

Auburn University, Graduate School, College of Education, Department of Counseling and Counseling Psychology, Auburn University, AL 36849. Offers community agency counseling (M Ed, MS, Ed D, PhD, Ed S); counseling psychology (PhD); counselor education (Ed D, PhD); school counseling (M Ed, MS, Ed D, PhD, Ed S); school psychometry (M Ed, MS, Ed D, PhD, Ed S). *Accreditation:* ACA (one or more programs are accredited); APA (one or more programs are accredited); NCATE. Part-time programs available. *Faculty:* 10 full-time (6 women). *Students:* 51 full-time (35 women), 41 part-time (33 women); includes 27 minority (26 African Americans, 1 Hispanic American), 5 international. Average age 31. 140 applicants, 42% accepted, 30 enrolled. In 2008, 20 master's, 9 doctorates, 4 other advanced degrees awarded. *Degree requirements:* For master's, thesis (for some programs); for doctorate, thesis/dissertation; for Ed S, thesis or alternative. *Entrance requirements:* For master's and Ed S, GRE General Test; for doctorate, GRE General Test, GRE Subject Test. *Application deadline:* For fall admission, 5/15 for domestic students. Application fee: $25 ($50 for international students). Electronic applications accepted. *Expenses:* Tuition, area resident: Full-time $5880; part-time $243 per credit hour. Tuition, state resident: full-time $5880; part-time $243 per credit hour. Tuition, nonresident: full-time $17,640; part-time $729 per credit hour. International tuition: $17,846 full-time. Required fees: $620. Tuition and fees vary according to program and reciprocity agreements. *Financial support:* Research assistantships, Federal Work-Study and traineeships available. Support available to part-time students. Financial award application deadline: 3/15. *Faculty research:* At-risk students, substance abuse, gender roles, AIDS, professional ethics. *Unit head:* Dr. Holly Stadler, Head, 334-844-5160. *Application contact:* Dr. Joe Pittman, Interim Dean of the Graduate School, 334-844-4700.

Azusa Pacific University, School of Education, Department of School Counseling and School Psychology, Program in Educational Psychology, Azusa, CA 91702-7000. Offers MA.

Ball State University, Graduate School, Teachers College, Department of Educational Psychology, Program in School Psychology, Muncie, IN 47306-1099. Offers MA, PhD, Ed S. *Accreditation:* APA (one or more programs are accredited); NCATE. *Degree requirements:* For doctorate, thesis/dissertation; for Ed S, thesis. *Entrance requirements:* For master's and Ed S, GRE General Test; for doctorate, GRE General Test, interview, minimum graduate GPA of 3.2.

Barry University, School of Arts and Sciences, Department of Psychology, Miami Shores, FL 33161-6695. Offers clinical psychology (MS); school psychology (MS, SSP). Part-time and evening/weekend programs available. *Degree requirements:* For master's, thesis, practicum. *Entrance requirements:* For master's, GRE General Test, minimum GPA of 3.0, course work in psychology. Electronic applications accepted. *Faculty research:* Closed head injury, memory and aging, infant/mother interaction, evolutionary aspects of behavior, gender roles.

See Close-Up on page 1103.

Bowling Green State University, Graduate College, College of Education and Human Development, School of Education and Intervention Services, Intervention Services Division, Program in School Psychology, Bowling Green, OH 43403. Offers M Ed, Sp Ed. *Accreditation:* NCATE. Part-time programs available. *Degree requirements:* For master's, thesis or alternative, internship. *Entrance requirements:* For master's, GRE General Test. Additional exam requirements/recommendations for international students: Required—TOEFL. Electronic applications accepted. *Faculty research:* Family therapists/multicultural issues, pre-school readiness skills, family relations, multifaceted evaluation, multidisciplinary decision-making.

Brigham Young University, Graduate Studies, David O. McKay School of Education, Department of Counseling Psychology and Special Education, Provo, UT 84602-1001. Offers counseling psychology (PhD); school psychology (Ed S); special education (MS). *Accreditation:* NCATE. Part-time programs available. *Faculty:* 12 full-time (7 women), 11 part-time/adjunct (4 women). *Students:* 64 full-time (44 women), 14 part-time (13 women); includes 13 minority (1 African American, 2 American Indian/Alaska Native, 8 Asian Americans or Pacific Islanders, 2 Hispanic Americans), 5 international. Average age 31. 67 applicants, 49% accepted, 17 enrolled. In 2008, 2 master's, 10 doctorates, 12 other advanced degrees awarded. *Degree requirements:* For master's, comprehensive exam, thesis; for doctorate, comprehensive exam, thesis/dissertation. *Entrance requirements:* For master's and doctorate, GRE General Test, minimum GPA of 3.0 in last 60 hours of undergraduate coursework. Additional exam requirements/recommendations for international students: Required—TOEFL (minimum score 580 paper-based; 237 computer-based), IELTS (minimum score 7). *Application deadline:* For fall admission, 1/15 for domestic and international students. Application fee: $50. Electronic applications accepted. *Expenses:* Tuition: Full-time $5160; part-time $287 per credit hour. Tuition and fees vary according to program and student's religious affiliation. *Financial support:* In 2008–09, 45 students received support, including 30 research assistantships with partial tuition reimbursements available (averaging $5,400 per year), 3 teaching assistantships with partial tuition reimbursements available (averaging $6,120 per year); career-related internships or fieldwork, institutionally sponsored loans, and tuition waivers (partial) also available. Financial award application deadline: 4/30. *Faculty research:* Gender issues in education, psychotherapy progress and outcome, and behavior disorders and ABA. Total annual research expenditures: $195,507. *Unit head:* Dr. Mary Anne Prater, Chair, 801-422-3857, Fax: 801-422-0198, E-mail: prater@byu.edu. *Application contact:* Diane E. Hancock, Department Secretary, 801-422-3859, Fax: 801-422-0198, E-mail: diane_hancock@byu.edu.

Brooklyn College of the City University of New York, Division of Graduate Studies, School of Education, Program in School Psychologist, Brooklyn, NY 11210-2889. Offers school psychologist (MS Ed, CAS); school psychologist-bilingual (CAS). Part-time and evening/weekend programs available. *Students:* 36 full-time (33 women), 50 part-time (44 women); includes 29 minority (12 African Americans, 1 American Indian/Alaska Native, 4 Asian Americans or Pacific Islanders, 12 Hispanic Americans). Average age 28. 153 applicants, 44% accepted, 49 enrolled. In 2008, 17 master's, 27 CASs awarded. *Degree requirements:* For master's, internship. *Entrance requirements:* For master's, interview, previous course work in education and psychology, teaching certificate, resumé, 2 letters of recommendation; for CAS, master's degree, teaching experience. Additional exam requirements/recommendations for international students: Required—TOEFL (minimum score 500 paper-based; 173 computer-based; 61 iBT). *Application deadline:* For fall admission, 3/1 priority date for domestic students, 2/1 priority date for international students. Applications are processed on a rolling basis. Application fee: $125. Electronic applications accepted. *Expenses:* Tuition: state resident: full-time $7360; part-time $310 per credit hour. Tuition, nonresident: full-time $13,800; part-time $575 per credit hour. *Financial support:* Career-related internships or fieldwork, Federal Work-Study, institutionally sponsored loans, and scholarships/grants available. Support available to part-time students. Financial award application deadline: 5/1; financial award applicants required to submit FAFSA. *Unit head:* Dr. Paul McCabe, Program Head. *Application contact:* Hernan Sierra, Graduate Admissions Coordinator, 718-951-4536, Fax: 718-951-4506, E-mail: grads@brooklyn.cuny.edu.

Bucknell University, Graduate Studies, College of Arts and Sciences, Department of Education, Specialization in School Psychology, Lewisburg, PA 17837. Offers MS Ed. *Degree requirements:* For master's, thesis or alternative. *Entrance requirements:* For master's, GRE General Test, minimum GPA of 2.8. Additional exam requirements/recommendations for international students: Required—TOEFL.

California Baptist University, Program in Education, Riverside, CA 92504-3206. Offers cross-cultural language and academic development (MA); educational leadership (MS); educational leadership and faith-based instruction (MS); educational technology (MS); instructional computer applications (MS); reading (MS); school counseling (MS); school psychology (MS); special education (MS); special education in mild/moderate disabilities (MS); special education in moderate/severe disabilities (MS); teaching (MS); teaching and learning (MS Ed). Part-time programs available. *Faculty:* 16 full-time (9 women), 10 part-time/adjunct (5 women). *Students:* 61 full-time (49 women), 454 part-time (367 women); includes 197 minority (39 African Americans, 9 American Indian/Alaska Native, 16 Asian Americans or Pacific Islanders, 133 Hispanic Americans), 4 international. 259 applicants, 68% accepted, 156 enrolled. In 2008, 98 master's awarded. *Degree requirements:* For master's, comprehensive exam (for some programs), thesis optional. *Entrance requirements:* For master's, minimum undergraduate GPA of 2.75, 12 semester hours of course work in education. Additional exam requirements/recommendations for international students: Required—TOEFL (minimum score 575 paper-based; 230 computer-based; 89 iBT). *Application deadline:* For fall admission, 8/1 priority date for domestic students, 7/1 priority date for international students; for spring admission, 12/1 priority date for domestic students, 10/15 priority date for international students. Applications are processed on a rolling basis. Application fee: $45. Electronic applications accepted. *Expenses:* Tuition: Full-time $8172; part-time $454 per credit hour. Required fees: $510. *Financial support:* Career-related internships or fieldwork, Federal Work-Study, and scholarships/grants available. Support available to part-time students. Financial award applicants required to submit FAFSA. *Unit head:* Dr. Mary Crist, Dean, School of Education, 951-343-4313, Fax: 951-343-4516, E-mail: mcrist@calbaptist.edu. *Application contact:* Gail Ronveaux, Dean of Graduate Enrollment, 951-343-5045, Fax: 951-343-5095, E-mail: graduateadmissions@calbaptist.edu.

California State University, Los Angeles, Graduate Studies, Charter College of Education, Division of Special Education and Counseling, Los Angeles, CA 90032-8530. Offers counseling (MS), including applied behavior analysis, community college counseling, rehabilitation counseling, school counseling and school psychology; special education (MA, PhD). Part-time and evening/weekend programs available. *Faculty:* 37 full-time (22 women). *Students:* 385 full-time (304 women), 406 part-time (306 women); includes 494 minority (52 African Americans, 2 American Indian/Alaska Native, 80 Asian Americans or Pacific Islanders, 360 Hispanic Americans), 39 international. Average age 34. 176 applicants, 99% accepted, 116 enrolled. In 2008, 168 master's awarded. *Entrance requirements:* For master's, minimum GPA of 2.75 in last 90 units of course work, teaching certificate. Additional exam requirements/recommendations for international students: Required—TOEFL (minimum score 500 paper-based; 173 computer-based). *Application deadline:* For fall admission, 6/15 for domestic students, 5/1 for international students; for winter admission, 11/1 for domestic students, 9/1 for international students; for spring admission, 2/1 for domestic students, 10/1 for international students. Applications are processed on a rolling basis. Application fee: $55. Electronic applications accepted. *Expenses:* Tuition, nonresident: part-time $226 per credit. Required fees: $4019. *Financial support:* Career-related internships or fieldwork and Federal Work-Study available. Support available to part-time students. Financial award application deadline: 3/1. *Unit head:* Dr. Randy Campbell, Chair, 323-343-4400, Fax: 323-343-5605, E-mail: rcampbe@calstatela.edu.

Application contact: Dr. Jose L. Galvan, Dean of Graduate Studies, 323-343-3820, Fax: 323-343-5653, E-mail: jgalvan@cslanet.calstatela.edu.

California State University, Northridge, Graduate Studies, College of Education, Department of Educational Psychology and Counseling, Northridge, CA 91330. Offers counseling (MS), including career counseling, college counseling and student services, marriage and family therapy, school counseling, school psychology; educational psychology (MA Ed), including development, learning, and instruction, early childhood education. *Accreditation:* ACA (one or more programs are accredited); NCATE. Part-time and evening/weekend programs available. *Faculty:* 18 full-time (11 women), 40 part-time/adjunct (19 women). *Students:* 334 full-time (297 women), 140 part-time (122 women); includes 24 African Americans, 38 Asian Americans or Pacific Islanders, 156 Hispanic Americans, 14 international. Average age 31. 450 applicants, 36% accepted, 140 enrolled. In 2008, 124 master's awarded. *Entrance requirements:* For master's, GRE General Test or minimum GPA of 3.0. Additional exam requirements/recommendations for international students: Required—TOEFL. *Application deadline:* For fall admission, 11/30 for domestic students. Application fee: $55. *Financial support:* Scholarships/grants available. Support available to part-time students. Financial award application deadline: 3/1. *Unit head:* Dr. Shari Tarver-Behring, Chair, 818-677-2599. *Application contact:* Dr. Shari Tarver-Behring, Chair, 818-677-2599.

California State University, Sacramento, Graduate Studies, College of Education, Department of Special Education, Rehabilitation, and School Psychology, Sacramento, CA 95819-6048. Offers school psychology (MS); special education (MA); vocational rehabilitation (MS). *Accreditation:* CORE. Part-time programs available. *Degree requirements:* For master's, thesis or alternative, writing proficiency exam. *Entrance requirements:* For master's, minimum GPA of 2.5. Additional exam requirements/recommendations for international students: Required—TOEFL. Electronic applications accepted.

California University of Pennsylvania, School of Graduate Studies and Research, School of Education, Program in School Psychology, California, PA 15419-1394. Offers MS. *Accreditation:* NCATE. Part-time and evening/weekend programs available. *Degree requirements:* For master's, comprehensive exam, thesis optional, internship. *Entrance requirements:* For master's, MAT or GRE, minimum GPA of 3.0, work experience in psychology, letters of reference. Additional exam requirements/recommendations for international students: Required—TOEFL (minimum score 550 paper-based; 213 computer-based; 80 iBT). Electronic applications accepted.

Canisius College, Graduate Division, School of Education and Human Services, Department of Counseling and Human Services, Buffalo, NY 14208-1098. Offers community mental health counseling (MS); general counseling (MS); school counseling (MS). Part-time and evening/weekend programs available. *Faculty:* 5 full-time (3 women), 6 part-time/adjunct (2 women). *Students:* 102 full-time (88 women), 43 part-time (36 women); includes 20 minority (16 African Americans, 1 Asian American or Pacific Islander, 3 Hispanic Americans), 3 international. Average age 27. In 2008, 48 master's awarded. *Degree requirements:* For master's, thesis, research project. *Entrance requirements:* For master's, interview, minimum GPA of 2.5. *Application deadline:* Applications are processed on a rolling basis. Application fee: $25. Electronic applications accepted. *Expenses:* Tuition: Full-time $33,750; part-time $680 per credit hour. Required fees: $18.50 per credit hour. *Financial support:* In 2008–09, 2 research assistantships with partial tuition reimbursements (averaging $8,500 per year) were awarded; career-related internships or fieldwork, Federal Work-Study, institutionally sponsored loans, health care benefits, and unspecified assistantships also available. Support available to part-time students. Financial award applicants required to submit FAFSA. *Faculty research:* Positive psychology, wellness, school violence prevention, chronic pain. *Unit head:* Dr. David L. Farrugia, Chairman, 716-888-2393, Fax: 716-888-3290, E-mail: farrugia@canisius.edu. *Application contact:* James D. Bagwell, Director of Graduate Recruitment and Admissions, 716-888-2544, Fax: 716-888-3290, E-mail: bagwellj@canisius.edu.

Capella University, Harold Abel School of Psychology, Minneapolis, MN 55402. Offers clinical psychology (MS); counseling psychology (MS); educational psychology (MS, PhD); general psychology (MS, PhD); industrial/organizational psychology (MS, PhD); school psychology (MS, Certificate); sport psychology (MS). Part-time and evening/weekend programs available. Postbaccalaureate distance learning degree programs offered (minimal on-campus study). Terminal master's awarded for partial completion of doctoral program. *Degree requirements:* For master's, thesis optional, project; for doctorate, thesis/dissertation. *Entrance requirements:* For degree, master's degree in school psychology. Additional exam requirements/recommendations for international students: Required—TOEFL (minimum score 550 paper-based; 213 computer-based), TWE (minimum score 4). Electronic applications accepted. *Faculty research:* Correctional mental health delivery, community mental health, attachment and caregiving in adult and family relationships, influence of encouragement on motivation, and moral dilemmas in business.

Carlos Albizu University, Miami Campus, Graduate Programs, Miami, FL 33172-2209. Offers clinical psychology (Psy D); entrepreneurship (MBA); exceptional student education (MS); industrial/organizational psychology (MS); marriage and family therapy (MS); mental health counseling (MS); nonprofit management (MBA); organizational management (MBA); psychology (MS); school counseling (MS); teaching English as a second language (MS). *Accreditation:* APA. Part-time and evening/weekend programs available. *Faculty:* 19 full-time (12 women), 70 part-time/adjunct (35 women). *Students:* 498 full-time (409 women), 199 part-time (153 women); includes 515 minority (56 African Americans, 1 American Indian/Alaska Native, 7 Asian Americans or Pacific Islanders, 451 Hispanic Americans). Average age 33. 179 applicants, 67% accepted, 113 enrolled. In 2008, 185 master's, 21 doctorates awarded. Terminal master's awarded for partial completion of doctoral program. *Degree requirements:* For master's, one foreign language, comprehensive exam, integrative project (MBA), research project (MSESE and MSTESOL); for doctorate, one foreign language, comprehensive exam, internship, doctoral project. *Entrance requirements:* For master's, 3 letters of recommendation, interview, minimum GPA of 3.0, resumé, statement of purpose, official transcripts; for doctorate, 3 letters of recommendation, minimum GPA of 3.0, resumé, interview. *Application deadline:* For fall admission, 8/1 priority date for domestic students; for spring admission, 11/30 priority date for domestic students. Applications are processed on a rolling basis. Application fee: $50. Electronic applications accepted. *Expenses:* Tuition: Full-time $9090; part-time $505 per credit. Required fees: $298 per term. Tuition and fees vary according to course load, degree level and program. *Financial support:* In 2008–09, 111 students received support. Federal Work-Study, scholarships/grants, and tuition discounts available. Financial award application deadline: 6/1; financial award applicants required to submit FAFSA. *Faculty research:* Psychotherapy, forensic psychology, neuropsychology, marketing strategy, entrepreneurship, special education. *Unit head:* Dr. Carmen S. Roca, PhD, Chancellor, 305-593-1223 Ext. 120, Fax: 305-629-8052, E-mail: croca@albizu.edu. *Application contact:* Barbara De la Cruz, Admission Officer, 305-593-1223 Ext. 218, Fax: 305-593-1854, E-mail: bdelacruz@albizu.edu.

Central Connecticut State University, School of Graduate Studies, School of Education and Professional Studies, Department of Counseling and Family Therapy, New Britain, CT 06050-4010. Offers marriage and family therapy (MS); professional counseling (MS, Certificate); school counseling (MS); student development in higher education (MS). *Accreditation:* AAMFT/COAMFTE. Part-time and evening/weekend programs available. *Faculty:* 7 full-time (4 women), 12 part-time/adjunct (9 women). *Students:* 109 full-time (93 women), 187 part-time (151 women); includes 47 minority (24 African Americans, 2 American Indian/Alaska Native, 2 Asian Americans or Pacific Islanders, 19 Hispanic Americans), 3 international. Average age 35. 245 applicants, 47% accepted, 92 enrolled. In 2008, 67 master's, 1 other advanced degree awarded. *Degree requirements:* For master's, comprehensive exam, thesis or alternative. *Entrance requirements:* For master's, minimum undergraduate GPA of 2.7, essay. Additional exam requirements/recommendations for international students: Required—TOEFL. *Application deadline:* For fall admission, 5/1 for domestic students. Applications are processed on a rolling basis. Application fee: $50. Electronic applications accepted. *Expenses:* Tuition, area resident: Full-time $4377; part-time $420 per credit. Tuition, state resident: full-time $6566; part-time

School Psychology

Central Connecticut State University (continued)
$420 per credit. Tuition, nonresident: full-time $12,195; part-time $420 per credit. Required fees: $3462. One-time fee: $62 part-time. *Financial support:* In 2008–09, 36 students received support, including 22 research assistantships; career-related internships or fieldwork, Federal Work-Study, scholarships/grants, and unspecified assistantships also available. Support available to part-time students. Financial award application deadline: 3/1; financial award applicants required to submit FAFSA. *Faculty research:* Elementary/secondary school counseling, marriage/family therapy, rehabilitation counseling, counseling in higher educational settings. *Unit head:* Dr. Connie Tait, Chair, 860-832-2154. *Application contact:* Dr. Connie Tait, Chair, 860-832-2154.

Central Michigan University, College of Graduate Studies, College of Humanities and Social and Behavioral Sciences, Department of Psychology, Program in School Psychology, Mount Pleasant, MI 48859. Offers psychological services (S Psy S); school psychology (PhD). *Accreditation:* APA; NCATE. *Students:* 20 full-time (17 women), 20 part-time (18 women); includes 1 African American, 1 international. Average age 28. In 2008, 5 other advanced degrees awarded. *Degree requirements:* For doctorate, thesis/dissertation; for S Psy S, thesis. *Entrance requirements:* For doctorate, GRE. *Application deadline:* For fall admission, 1/15 for domestic and international students. Application fee: $35 ($45 for international students). Electronic applications accepted. *Expenses:* Tuition, state resident: full-time $3717; part-time $413 per credit. Tuition, nonresident: full-time $6894; part-time $766 per credit. *Financial support:* Fellowships with tuition reimbursements, research assistantships with tuition reimbursements, teaching assistantships with tuition reimbursements, career-related internships or fieldwork, Federal Work-Study, unspecified assistantships, and out-of-state merit awards available. *Faculty research:* Psychology and education foundations, psychology and education assessment, intervention strategies. *Unit head:* Dr. Hajime Otani, Chairperson, 989-774-6494, Fax: 989-774-2553, E-mail: otani1h@cmich.edu. *Application contact:* Judith L. Prince, Director of Graduate Student Services, 989-774-1059, Fax: 989-774-1857, E-mail: judith.l.prince@cmich.edu.

Central Washington University, Graduate Studies, Research and Continuing Education, College of the Sciences, Department of Psychology, Program in School Psychology, Ellensburg, WA 98926. Offers M Ed. *Degree requirements:* For master's, thesis, internship. *Entrance requirements:* For master's, GRE General Test, minimum GPA of 3.0. Additional exam requirements/recommendations for international students: Required—TOEFL (minimum score 550 paper-based; 213 computer-based; 79 iBT). Electronic applications accepted.

Chapman University, Graduate Studies, College of Educational Studies, Program in Educational Psychology, Orange, CA 92866. Offers educational psychology (MA); school psychology (Ed S). Part-time and evening/weekend programs available. *Faculty:* 19 full-time (13 women), 20 part-time/adjunct (12 women). *Students:* 48 full-time (41 women), 9 part-time (5 women); includes 16 minority (1 African American, 3 Asian Americans or Pacific Islanders, 12 Hispanic Americans). Average age 27. 65 applicants, 35% accepted, 17 enrolled. In 2008, 42 master's awarded. *Degree requirements:* For master's, comprehensive exam. *Entrance requirements:* For master's, GRE General Test, MAT, or California Subject Examinations for Teachers, minimum undergraduate GPA of 2.75. Additional exam requirements/recommendations for international students: Required—TOEFL (minimum score 550 paper-based). *Application deadline:* Applications are processed on a rolling basis. Application fee: $55. Electronic applications accepted. *Expenses:* Contact institution. *Financial support:* Fellowships, Federal Work-Study and scholarships/grants available. Financial award application deadline: 6/30; financial award applicants required to submit FAFSA. *Unit head:* Dr. Michael Hass, Coordinator, 714-997-6781, E-mail: hass@chapman.edu. *Application contact:* Rika Judd, Information Contact, 714-997-6786, Fax: 714-997-6713, E-mail: rjudd@chapman.edu.

Chapman University, Graduate Studies, College of Educational Studies, Program in Education: School Psychology, Orange, CA 92866. Offers PhD. *Faculty:* 19 full-time (13 women), 20 part-time/adjunct (12 women). *Students:* 8 part-time (7 women); includes 1 minority (Hispanic American). Average age 38. 9 applicants, 89% accepted, 8 enrolled. *Degree requirements:* For doctorate, thesis/dissertation. *Expenses:* Tuition: Full-time $11,970; part-time $665 per credit. Required fees: $456; $456 per year. Tuition and fees vary according to course load, degree level and program. *Financial support:* Federal Work-Study and scholarships/grants available. *Unit head:* Dr. Joel Colbert, Director, 714-744-7076. *Application contact:* Rika Judd, Graduate Admission Counselor, 714-997-6786, Fax: 714-997-6713, E-mail: rjudd@chapman.edu.

The Chicago School of Professional Psychology, Graduate School, Program in School Psychology, Chicago, IL 60610. Offers Ed S. *Accreditation:* APA. Part-time programs available. *Entrance requirements:* For degree, GRE (recommended), minimum GPA of 3.2 (recommended); completion of one course in statistics or research methods and one course in psychology. Additional exam requirements/recommendations for international students: Required—TOEFL (minimum score 550 paper-based; 213 computer-based; 79 iBT).

The Citadel, The Military College of South Carolina, Citadel Graduate College, School of Education, Program in School Psychology, Charleston, SC 29409. Offers MA, Ed S. *Accreditation:* NCATE. Part-time and evening/weekend programs available. *Students:* 39 full-time (37 women), 14 part-time (13 women); includes 2 minority (1 African American, 1 Hispanic American). Average age 26. In 2008, 11 master's, 2 other advanced degrees awarded. *Degree requirements:* For master's, comprehensive exam. *Entrance requirements:* For degree, GRE (minimum 1000) or MAT (minimum 410), minimum undergraduate GPA of 3.0, 2 letters of reference. Additional exam requirements/recommendations for international students: Required—TOEFL (minimum score 550 paper-based; 213 computer-based). *Application deadline:* For fall admission, 3/15 for domestic students. Application fee: $30. Electronic applications accepted. *Expenses:* Tuition, state resident: full-time $5850; part-time $325 per credit hour. Tuition, nonresident: full-time $9612; part-time $534 per credit hour. Required fees: $15 per semester. *Financial support:* Research assistantships, career-related internships or fieldwork, health care benefits, and unspecified assistantships available. Support available to part-time students. Financial award application deadline: 7/1; financial award applicants required to submit FAFSA. *Faculty research:* Childhood depression, violence against women, developmental disorders, eyewitness testimony. *Unit head:* Dr. Kerry S. Lassiter, Coordinator, 843-953-6740, Fax: 843-953-6769, E-mail: kerry.lassiter@citadel.edu. *Application contact:* Dr. Kerry S. Lassiter, Coordinator, 843-953-6740, Fax: 843-953-6769, E-mail: kerry.lassiter@citadel.edu.

City University of Seattle, Graduate Division, Gordon Albright School of Education, Bellevue, WA 98005. Offers curriculum and instruction (M Ed); educational leadership (M Ed); educational leadership: administrator certification (Certificate); executive leadership: superintendent certification (Certificate); guidance and counseling (M Ed); leadership (M Ed); leadership and school counseling (M Ed); professional certification for teachers (Certificate); reading and literacy (M Ed); reading and literacy in education (M Ed); teacher certification (elementary K-8) (MIT); teacher certification (special education K-12) (MIT); technology, curriculum, and instruction (M Ed). Part-time and evening/weekend programs available. Postbaccalaureate distance learning degree programs offered (no on-campus study). *Entrance requirements:* Additional exam requirements/recommendations for international students: Required—TOEFL (minimum score 540 paper-based; 207 computer-based); Recommended—IELTS. Electronic applications accepted. *Expenses:* Contact institution.

Cleveland State University, College of Graduate Studies, College of Science, Department of Psychology, Cleveland, OH 44115. Offers adult development and aging (PhD); clinical psychology (MA); consumer/industrial research (MA); diversity management (MA); experimental research psychology (MA); school psychology (Psy S). *Faculty:* 20 full-time (7 women), 16 part-time/adjunct (8 women). *Students:* 66 full-time (44 women), 62 part-time (46 women); includes 25 minority (19 African Americans, 1 American Indian/Alaska Native, 2 Asian Americans or Pacific Islanders, 3 Hispanic Americans), 3 international. Average age 30. 180 applicants, 40% accepted, 55 enrolled. In 2008, 39 master's, 4 other advanced degrees awarded. *Degree requirements:* For master's, comprehensive exam (for some programs), thesis (for some programs); for doctorate, comprehensive exam, thesis/dissertation; for Psy S, internship. *Entrance requirements:* For master's and doctorate, GRE General Test. Additional exam requirements/recommendations for international students: Required—TOEFL (minimum score 525 paper-based; 197 computer-based). *Application deadline:* For fall admission, 2/1 priority date for domestic and international students. Applications are processed on a rolling basis. Application fee: $30. Electronic applications accepted. *Financial support:* In 2008–09, 45 students received support. Career-related internships or fieldwork, Federal Work-Study, tuition waivers (partial), and unspecified assistantships available. Financial award applicants required to submit FAFSA. *Faculty research:* Cognitive and social psychology, consumer psychology, clinical psychology, school psychology, aging. Total annual research expenditures: $112,607. *Unit head:* Dr. Albert F Smith, Interim Chair, 216-687-3723, Fax: 216-687-9294, E-mail: a.f.smith@csuohio.edu. *Application contact:* Karen R Colston, Administrative Coordinator, 216-687-2552, Fax: 216-687-9294, E-mail: k.colston@csuohio.edu.

The College of New Rochelle, Graduate School, Division of Human Services, Program in Community-School Psychology, New Rochelle, NY 10805-2308. Offers MS. *Degree requirements:* For master's, comprehensive exam, clinical fieldwork, journal. *Entrance requirements:* For master's, interview, minimum GPA of 3.0, course work in psychology, sample of written work.

College of St. Joseph, Graduate Programs, Division of Psychology and Human Services, Program in School Guidance Counseling, Rutland, VT 05701-3899. Offers MS. Part-time and evening/weekend programs available. *Degree requirements:* For master's, comprehensive exam, thesis optional. *Entrance requirements:* For master's, PRAXIS I, 2 letters of reference, interview. Electronic applications accepted.

The College of Saint Rose, Graduate Studies, School of Education, Educational and School Psychology Department, Albany, NY 12203-1419. Offers applied technology education (MS Ed); educational psychology (MS Ed); school psychology (MS, Certificate). Part-time and evening/weekend programs available. *Entrance requirements:* For master's, minimum undergraduate GPA of 3.0. Additional exam requirements/recommendations for international students: Required—TOEFL (minimum score 550 paper-based; 213 computer-based). Electronic applications accepted.

The College of William and Mary, School of Education, Program in School Psychology, Williamsburg, VA 23187-8795. Offers M Ed, Ed S. *Accreditation:* NCATE. *Degree requirements:* For Ed S, internship. *Entrance requirements:* For master's, GRE, minimum GPA of 3.0; for Ed S, GRE, minimum GPA of 3.5. Additional exam requirements/recommendations for international students: Required—TOEFL. Electronic applications accepted. *Expenses:* Tuition, state resident: full-time $6400; part-time $300 per credit hour. Tuition, nonresident: full-time $19,720; part-time $800 per credit hour. International tuition: $19,720 full-time. Required fees: $3860. *Faculty research:* Home schooling, gifted preschoolers, inclusive schools, ability testing.

Duquesne University, School of Education, Department of Counseling, Psychology, and Special Education, Program in School Psychology, Pittsburgh, PA 15282-0001. Offers child psychology (MS Ed); school psychology (PhD, CAGS). Part-time and evening/weekend programs available. *Faculty:* 6 full-time (4 women), 2 part-time/adjunct (0 women). *Students:* 79 full-time (63 women), 22 part-time (21 women); includes 11 minority (9 African Americans, 1 Asian American or Pacific Islander, 1 Hispanic American), 4 international. Average age 31. 109 applicants, 18% accepted, 20 enrolled. In 2008, 13 master's, 12 doctorates, 19 other advanced degrees awarded. *Degree requirements:* For master's, thesis optional; for doctorate, thesis/dissertation. *Entrance requirements:* For master's, MAT, minimum GPA of 3.0; for doctorate, 3 letters of reference; for CAGS, MAT, interview. *Application deadline:* For fall admission, 8/1 for domestic students; for spring admission, 12/1 for domestic students. Applications are processed on a rolling basis. Application fee: $0. Electronic applications accepted. *Expenses:* Tuition: Part-time $819 per credit. Required fees: $78 per credit. Tuition and fees vary according to course load. *Financial support:* Research assistantships, Federal Work-Study available. Support available to part-time students. *Unit head:* Dr. Kara McGoey, Director, 412-396-4105, Fax: 412-396-1340, E-mail: mcgeoyk@duq.edu. *Application contact:* Michael Dolinger, Director of Student and Academic Services, 412-396-6647, Fax: 412-396-5585, E-mail: dolingerm@duq.edu.

East Carolina University, Graduate School, Thomas Harriot College of Arts and Sciences, Department of Psychology, Program in School Psychology, Greenville, NC 27858-4353. Offers MA/CAS. *Accreditation:* NCATE. Part-time and evening/weekend programs available.

Eastern Illinois University, Graduate School, College of Sciences, Charleston, IL 61920-3099. Offers biological sciences (MS); chemistry (MS); communication disorders and sciences (MS); economics (MA); mathematics and computer science (MA), including mathematics, mathematics education; natural sciences (MS); political science (MA); psychology (MA, SSP), including clinical psychology (MA), school psychology (SSP). Part-time programs available. *Degree requirements:* For SSP, thesis. *Entrance requirements:* For degree, GRE General Test.

Eastern Illinois University, Graduate School, College of Sciences, Department of Psychology, Program in School Psychology, Charleston, IL 61920-3099. Offers SSP. *Accreditation:* NCATE. *Degree requirements:* For SSP, thesis. *Entrance requirements:* For degree, GRE General Test.

Eastern Kentucky University, The Graduate School, College of Arts and Sciences, Department of Psychology, Richmond, KY 40475-3102. Offers clinical psychology (MS); industrial/organizational psychology (MS); school psychology (Psy S). Part-time programs available. *Entrance requirements:* For master's and Psy S, GRE General Test, minimum GPA of 2.5. *Faculty research:* Autism, social psychology, parenting, assessment of depression/anxiety, reading.

Eastern University, Department of Counseling Psychology, St. Davids, PA 19087-3696. Offers community/clinical counseling (MA); school counseling (MA, Certificate); school psychology (MS, Certificate). *Degree requirements:* For master's, internship. *Entrance requirements:* For master's, minimum GPA of 2.5. Additional exam requirements/recommendations for international students: Required—TOEFL.

Eastern Washington University, Graduate Studies, College of Education and Human Development, Department of Counseling, Educational, and Developmental Psychology, Program in School Psychology, Cheney, WA 99004-2431. Offers MS. *Degree requirements:* For master's, comprehensive exam, thesis or alternative. *Entrance requirements:* For master's, GRE General Test, minimum GPA of 3.0.

Eastern Washington University, Graduate Studies, College of Social and Behavioral Sciences, Department of Psychology, Cheney, WA 99004-2431. Offers clinical psychology (MS); experimental psychology (MS); psychology (MS); school psychology (MS). *Degree requirements:* For master's, comprehensive exam, thesis or alternative. *Entrance requirements:* For master's, GRE General Test, minimum GPA of 3.0.

Edinboro University of Pennsylvania, Graduate Studies and Research, School of Education, Department of Special Education and School Psychology, Edinboro, PA 16444. Offers behavior management (Certificate); educational psychology (M Ed); special education (M Ed). Part-time and evening/weekend programs available. *Faculty:* 5 full-time (3 women). *Students:* 50 full-time (40 women), 97 part-time (83 women); includes 6 minority (3 African Americans, 1 American Indian/Alaska Native, 1 Asian American or Pacific Islander, 1 Hispanic American). Average age 31. In 2008, 25 master's, 10 Certificates awarded. *Degree requirements:* For master's, thesis or alternative, competency exam; for Certificate, thesis or alternative. *Entrance requirements:* For master's and Certificate, GRE or MAT, minimum QPA of 2.5. *Application deadline:* Applications are processed on a rolling basis. Application fee: $30. Electronic applications accepted. *Expenses:* Tuition, state resident: full-time $6430; part-time $357 per credit. Tuition, nonresident: full-time $8038; part-time $572 per credit. International tuition: $15,171.58 full-time. Required fees: $2113; $60 per credit. Tuition and fees vary according to course load. *Financial support:*

In 2008–09, 11 research assistantships with full and partial tuition reimbursements (averaging $3,850 per year) were awarded; career-related internships or fieldwork, Federal Work-Study, scholarships/grants, and unspecified assistantships also available. Support available to part-time students. Financial award application deadline: 2/15; financial award applicants required to submit FAFSA. *Unit head:* Dr. Juanita Kasper, Program Head, Special Education, 814-732-1098, E-mail: jkasper@edinboro.edu. *Application contact:* Dr. Joel Erion, Program Head, School Psychology, 814-732-2287, E-mail: jerion@edinboro.edu.

Emporia State University, School of Graduate Studies, The Teachers College, Department of Psychology, Art Therapy, Rehabilitation and Mental Health Counseling, Program in School Psychology, Emporia, KS 66801-5087. Offers MS, Ed S. *Accreditation:* NCATE. Part-time programs available. *Students:* 16 full-time (12 women), 5 part-time (4 women). 7 applicants, 29% accepted, 2 enrolled. In 2008, 7 master's, 7 other advanced degrees awarded. *Degree requirements:* For master's, comprehensive exam or thesis, internship; for Ed S, comprehensive exam, thesis or alternative, internship. *Entrance requirements:* For master's, GRE General Test or MAT, graduate essay exam, appropriate bachelor's degree, teacher certification, letters of recommendation; for Ed S, GRE, graduate essay exam, letters of recommendation, teacher certification. Additional exam requirements/recommendations for international students: Required—TOEFL. *Application deadline:* For fall admission, 8/15 priority date for domestic students. Applications are processed on a rolling basis. Application fee: $30 ($75 for international students). Electronic applications accepted. *Expenses:* Tuition, area resident: Full-time $3976; part-time $166 per credit hour. Tuition, state resident: full-time $3976; part-time $166 per credit hour. Tuition, nonresident: full-time $12,028; part-time $501 per credit hour. Required fees: $51 per credit hour. Tuition and fees vary according to campus/location. *Financial support:* Career-related internships or fieldwork, Federal Work-Study, institutionally sponsored loans, health care benefits, and unspecified assistantships available. Financial award application deadline: 3/15; financial award applicants required to submit FAFSA. *Unit head:* Dr. Kenneth A. Weaver, Chair, 620-341-5317, E-mail: kweaver@emporia.edu. *Application contact:* Mary Sewell, Admissions Coordinator, 800-950-GRAD, Fax: 620-341-5909, E-mail: msewell@emporia.edu.

Evangel University, School Counseling Program, Springfield, MO 65802-2191. Offers MS. Part-time and evening/weekend programs available. *Degree requirements:* For master's, comprehensive exam, thesis optional. *Entrance requirements:* For master's, MAT, teaching certificate. Additional exam requirements/recommendations for international students: Required—TOEFL (minimum score 550 paper-based; 213 computer-based).

Fairfield University, Graduate School of Education and Allied Professions, Department of Psychological and Educational Consultation, Fairfield, CT 06824-5195. Offers applied psychology (MA), including foundations of advanced psychology, human services, industrial/organizational/personnel; media/educational technology (MA); school media specialist (MA); school psychology (MA, CAS); special education (MA, CAS). Part-time and evening/weekend programs available. *Faculty:* 6 full-time (2 women), 7 part-time/adjunct (4 women). *Students:* 49 full-time (42 women), 111 part-time (97 women); includes 19 minority (2 African Americans, 1 American Indian/Alaska Native, 2 Asian Americans or Pacific Islanders, 14 Hispanic Americans), 2 international. 96 applicants, 58% accepted, 30 enrolled. In 2008, 44 master's, 14 other advanced degrees awarded. *Degree requirements:* For master's, comprehensive exam, thesis optional, educational technology course (for some programs). *Entrance requirements:* For master's, PRAXIS I (PPST), minimum QPA of 3.0, 2 recommendations, resumé, essay. Additional exam requirements/recommendations for international students: Required—TOEFL (minimum score 550 paper-based; 213 computer-based; 80 iBT). Application fee: $60. Electronic applications accepted. *Expenses:* Tuition: Full-time $9450; part-time $525 per credit hour. Required fees: $25 per semester. Tuition and fees vary according to course load and program. *Financial support:* Unspecified assistantships and Federal Grant (Project SETTEL) funds tuition for future special education, bilingual, and/or TESOL educators available. Financial award applicants required to submit FAFSA. *Faculty research:* Child neuropsychology, disabilities, effect of pre-treatment orientation on treatment, autism, technology in business and classroom, collaboration with schools, communities and industry. *Unit head:* Dr. Daniel Geller, Chair, 203-254-4000 Ext. 2324, Fax: 203-254-4047, E-mail: dgeller@fairfield.edu. *Application contact:* Marianne Gumpper, Director of Graduate and Continuing Studies Admissions, 203-254-4184, Fax: 203-254-4073, E-mail: gradadmis@fairfield.edu.

Fairleigh Dickinson University, Metropolitan Campus, University College: Arts, Sciences, and Professional Studies, School of Psychology, Program in School Psychology, Teaneck, NJ 07666-1914. Offers MA, Psy D. *Students:* 60 full-time (35 women), 1 part-time (0 women). Average age 31. 69 applicants, 65% accepted, 24 enrolled. In 2008, 9 master's, 3 doctorates awarded. *Application deadline:* Applications are processed on a rolling basis. Application fee: $40. *Application contact:* Susan Brooman, University Director of Graduate Admissions, 201-692-2554, Fax: 201-692-2560, E-mail: globaleducation@fdu.edu.

Florida Agricultural and Mechanical University, Division of Graduate Studies, Research, and Continuing Education, College of Arts and Sciences, Department of Psychology, Program in School Psychology, Tallahassee, FL 32307-3200. Offers MS. *Accreditation:* NCATE. *Degree requirements:* For master's, thesis. *Entrance requirements:* For master's, GRE General Test, minimum GPA of 3.0, letters of recommendation (3). Additional exam requirements/recommendations for international students: Required—TOEFL.

Florida International University, College of Education, Department of Educational and Psychological Studies, Program in Counselor Education, Miami, FL 33199. Offers mental health counseling (MS); rehabilitation counseling (MS); school counseling (MS). *Accreditation:* ACA; NCATE. Part-time and evening/weekend programs available. *Entrance requirements:* For master's, General Knowledge test, College Level Academic Skills Test, GRE or PRAXIS (school counseling track), minimum GPA of 3.0, interview. Additional exam requirements/recommendations for international students: Required—TOEFL (minimum score 550 paper-based; 213 computer-based; 80 iBT), IELTS (minimum score 6.3). Electronic applications accepted.

Florida International University, College of Education, Department of Educational and Psychological Studies, Program in School Psychology, Miami, FL 33199. Offers Ed S. *Accreditation:* NCATE. Part-time and evening/weekend programs available. *Degree requirements:* For Ed S, internship. *Entrance requirements:* For degree, General Knowledge test, College Level Academic Skills Test, GRE or PRAXIS I, minimum GPA of 3.0 in last 60 undergraduate credits. Additional exam requirements/recommendations for international students: Required—TOEFL (minimum score 550 paper-based; 213 computer-based; 80 iBT), IELTS (minimum score 6.3). Electronic applications accepted. *Faculty research:* Incidence assessment, personality evaluation, psychopathology in children and adolescents, school psychology licensure, biased assessment.

Florida State University, Graduate Studies, College of Education, Department of Educational Psychology and Learning Systems, Program in School Psychology, Tallahassee, FL 32306. Offers MS, Ed S. *Degree requirements:* For master's, comprehensive exam; for Ed S, comprehensive exam, thesis. *Entrance requirements:* For master's and Ed S, GRE General Test, minimum GPA of 3.0.

Fordham University, Graduate School of Education, Division of Psychological and Educational Services, New York, NY 10023. Offers counseling and personnel services (MSE, Adv C); counseling psychology (PhD); educational psychology (MSE, PhD); school psychology (PhD); urban and urban bilingual school psychology (Adv C). *Accreditation:* APA (one or more programs are accredited); NCATE. *Degree requirements:* For doctorate, thesis/dissertation. *Entrance requirements:* For doctorate, GRE General Test.

Fort Hays State University, Graduate School, College of Arts and Sciences, Department of Psychology, Program in School Psychology, Hays, KS 67601-4099. Offers Ed S. *Accreditation:* NCATE. *Degree requirements:* For Ed S, comprehensive exam, thesis. *Entrance requirements:*

Additional exam requirements/recommendations for international students: Required—TOEFL (minimum score 550 paper-based; 213 computer-based). Electronic applications accepted.

Francis Marion University, Graduate Programs, Department of Psychology, Florence, SC 29501-0547. Offers applied clinical psychology (MS); applied community psychology (MS); school psychology (MS). Part-time and evening/weekend programs available. *Faculty:* 10 full-time (4 women), 6 part-time/adjunct (4 women). *Students:* 15 full-time (all women), 28 part-time (25 women); includes 5 minority (all African Americans), 1 international. Average age 38. 39 applicants, 100% accepted, 12 enrolled. In 2008, 15 master's awarded. *Degree requirements:* For master's, internship. *Entrance requirements:* For master's, GRE General Test. *Application deadline:* For fall admission, 4/15 for domestic students; for spring admission, 10/15 for domestic students. Applications are processed on a rolling basis. Application fee: $30. *Expenses:* Tuition, state resident: full-time $7547; part-time $377.35 per credit hour. Tuition, nonresident: full-time $15,094; part-time $754.70 per credit hour. Required fees: $22 per credit hour. $30 per semester. *Financial support:* In 2008–09, 1 research assistantship (averaging $7,000 per year), 3 teaching assistantships (averaging $8,000 per year) were awarded; career-related internships or fieldwork and unspecified assistantships also available. Support available to part-time students. Financial award application deadline: 3/1; financial award applicants required to submit FAFSA. *Faculty research:* Critical thinking, spatial localization, cognition and aging, family psychology. *Unit head:* Dr. John R. Hester, Chair, 843-661-1635, Fax: 843-661-1628. *Application contact:* Jennifer Taylor, Administrative Assistant, 843-661-1378, Fax: 843-661-1628.

Fresno Pacific University, Graduate Programs, School of Education, Fresno, CA 93702-4709. Offers administration (MA Ed), including administrative services; foundations, curriculum and teaching (MA Ed), including curriculum and teaching, school library and information technology; language, literacy, and culture (MA Ed), including bilingual/cross-cultural education, language development, multilingual contexts, reading; mathematics/science/computer education (MA Ed), including educational technology, integrated mathematics/science education, mathematics education; pupil personnel services (MA Ed), including school counseling, school psychology; special education (MA Ed), including mild/moderate, moderate/severe, physical and health impairments. Part-time and evening/weekend programs available. *Degree requirements:* For master's, thesis (for some programs). *Entrance requirements:* For master's, interview; GMAT, GRE, MAT, or 6 units of course work with a faculty recommendation. Additional exam requirements/recommendations for international students: Required—TOEFL (minimum score 550 paper-based; 213 computer-based). Electronic applications accepted.

Fresno Pacific University, Graduate Programs, School of Education, Division of Pupil Personnel Services, Program in School Psychology, Fresno, CA 93702-4709. Offers MA Ed. Part-time and evening/weekend programs available. *Degree requirements:* For master's, thesis or alternative. *Entrance requirements:* Additional exam requirements/recommendations for international students: Required—TOEFL (minimum score 550 paper-based; 213 computer-based).

Gallaudet University, The Graduate School, College of Arts and Sciences, Department of Psychology, Program in School Psychology, Washington, DC 20002-3625. Offers developmental psychology (MA); school psychology (Psy S). *Accreditation:* NCATE. *Degree requirements:* For master's, thesis optional. *Entrance requirements:* For master's, GRE General Test or MAT. Electronic applications accepted.

Gardner-Webb University, Graduate School, School of Psychology, Program in School Counseling, Boiling Springs, NC 28017. Offers MA. *Accreditation:* NCATE. Part-time and evening/weekend programs available. *Degree requirements:* For master's, comprehensive exam. *Entrance requirements:* For master's, GRE General Test, MAT, minimum GPA of 2.7. Electronic applications accepted.

George Fox University, School of Education, Graduate Department of Counseling, Newberg, OR 97132-2697. Offers counseling (MA); marriage and family therapy (MA, Certificate); mental health trauma (Certificate); school counseling (MA, Certificate); school psychology (Certificate, Ed S). Part-time programs available. *Faculty:* 10 full-time (8 women), 7 part-time/adjunct (5 women). *Students:* 80 full-time (66 women), 147 part-time (117 women); includes 20 minority (6 African Americans, 3 American Indian/Alaska Native, 4 Asian Americans or Pacific Islanders, 7 Hispanic Americans). Average age 35. 89 applicants, 75% accepted, 53 enrolled. In 2008, 61 master's awarded. *Entrance requirements:* For master's, MAT or GRE. Additional exam requirements/recommendations for international students: Required—TOEFL (minimum score 550 paper-based; 213 computer-based; 80 iBT). *Application deadline:* For fall admission, 5/30 for domestic students; for winter admission, 11/1 for domestic students; for spring admission, 2/28 for domestic students. Applications are processed on a rolling basis. Application fee: $40. Electronic applications accepted. *Expenses:* Contact institution. *Financial support:* Career-related internships or fieldwork available. *Unit head:* Dr. Richard Shaw, Associate Professor of Marriage and Family Therapy/Chair, 503-554-6142, E-mail: rshaw@georgefox.edu. *Application contact:* Carol Namburi, Admissions Counselor, 800-631-0921, Fax: 503-554-6111, E-mail: counseling@georgefox.edu.

George Mason University, College of Humanities and Social Sciences, Department of Psychology, Program in School Psychology, Fairfax, VA 22030. Offers MA. *Accreditation:* NCATE. *Degree requirements:* For master's, thesis optional, internship. *Entrance requirements:* For master's, GRE General Test, minimum GPA of 3.0 in last 60 hours, previous undergraduate course work in psychology. Electronic applications accepted.

Georgia Southern University, Jack N. Averitt College of Graduate Studies, College of Education, Department of Leadership, Technology, and Human Development, Program in School Psychology, Statesboro, GA 30460. Offers M Ed, Ed S. *Accreditation:* NCATE. Part-time and evening/weekend programs available. *Students:* 40 full-time (36 women), 40 part-time (36 women); includes 22 minority (21 African Americans, 1 Hispanic American). Average age 30. 30 applicants, 93% accepted, 20 enrolled. In 2008, 15 master's, 7 Ed Ss awarded. *Degree requirements:* For master's and Ed S, comprehensive exam. *Entrance requirements:* For master's, GRE General Test or MAT, minimum GPA of 2.5, letters of reference, interview; for Ed S, GRE General Test or MAT, minimum graduate GPA of 3.25, letters of reference, interview. Additional exam requirements/recommendations for international students: Required—TOEFL (minimum score 550 paper-based; 213 computer-based; 80 iBT). *Application deadline:* For fall admission, 3/1 priority date for domestic and international students; for spring admission, 10/1 priority date for domestic students, 10/1 for international students. Applications are processed on a rolling basis. Application fee: $50. Electronic applications accepted. *Expenses:* Tuition, area resident: Full-time $3840; part-time $160 per semester hour. Tuition, state resident: full-time $3840; part-time $160 per semester hour. Tuition, nonresident: full-time $15,336; part-time $639 per semester hour. Required fees: $1152. *Financial support:* In 2008–09, 53 students received support, including research assistantships with partial tuition reimbursements available (averaging $6,850 per year), teaching assistantships with partial tuition reimbursements available (averaging $6,850 per year); career-related internships or fieldwork, Federal Work-Study, scholarships/grants, tuition waivers (partial), and unspecified assistantships also available. Support available to part-time students. Financial award application deadline: 4/15; financial award applicants required to submit FAFSA. *Unit head:* Dr. Terry Diamanduros, Coordinator, 912-478-1548, Fax: 912-478-7104, E-mail: tdiamanduros@georgiasouthern.edu. *Application contact:* 912-478-5384, Fax: 912-478-0740, E-mail: gradadmissions@georgiasouthern.edu.

Georgia State University, College of Education, Department of Counseling and Psychological Services, Program in School Psychology, Atlanta, GA 30303-3083. Offers M Ed, PhD, Ed S. *Accreditation:* APA (one or more programs are accredited); NCATE. *Degree requirements:* For master's, comprehensive exam; for doctorate, comprehensive exam, thesis/dissertation. *Entrance requirements:* For master's, GRE General Test, minimum GPA of 2.5; for doctorate, GRE General Test, minimum GPA of 3.3; for Ed S, GRE General Test, minimum graduate GPA of 3.25. *Faculty research:* School reform, reading (early intervention), school violence.

School Psychology

Grand Valley State University, College of Education, Program in School Counseling, Allendale, MI 49401-9403. Offers M Ed. Part-time programs available. *Faculty:* 3 full-time (2 women). *Students:* 14 full-time (8 women), 78 part-time (55 women); includes 12 minority (8 African Americans, 2 Asian Americans or Pacific Islanders, 2 Hispanic Americans). Average age 31. 24 applicants, 100% accepted, 20 enrolled. In 2008, 28 master's awarded. *Degree requirements:* For master's, thesis or project. *Entrance requirements:* For master's, GRE General Test or minimum GPA of 3.0. Additional exam requirements/recommendations for international students: Required—TOEFL. *Application deadline:* Applications are processed on a rolling basis. Application fee: $30. Electronic applications accepted. *Financial support:* In 2008–09, 5 students received support, including research assistantships with full and partial tuition reimbursements available (averaging $8,000 per year); career-related internships or fieldwork also available. *Faculty research:* Multicultural issues in counselor education, use of technology in counseling programs. *Unit head:* Dr. Claudia Sowa-Wojciakowski, Chair of Community Outreach, 616-331-6706, E-mail: sowac@gvsu.edu. *Application contact:* Stephen Worst, Student Information and Services Center, 616-331-6650, Fax: 616-331-2000, E-mail: worsts@gvsu.edu.

Hofstra University, College of Liberal Arts and Sciences, Department of Psychology, Program in School-Community Psychology, Hempstead, NY 11549. Offers MS, Psy D, CAS. *Accreditation:* NCATE. *Students:* 51 full-time (41 women), 4 part-time (3 women); includes 6 minority (1 African American, 3 Asian Americans or Pacific Islanders, 2 Hispanic Americans). Average age 27. 95 applicants, 28% accepted, 11 enrolled. In 2008, 11 master's, 11 doctorates, 8 other advanced degrees awarded. Terminal master's awarded for partial completion of doctoral program. *Degree requirements:* For master's, comprehensive exam; for doctorate, comprehensive exam, thesis/dissertation. *Entrance requirements:* For doctorate, GRE General Test, GRE Subject Test (psychology), interview, 3 letters of recommendation, essay. Additional exam requirements/recommendations for international students: Required—TOEFL (minimum score 550 paper-based; 213 computer-based; 80 iBT). *Application deadline:* For fall admission, 1/15 for domestic and international students. Application fee: $60. Electronic applications accepted. *Expenses:* Tuition: Full-time $15,300; part-time $850 per credit. Required fees: $970; $165 per term. Tuition and fees vary according to program. *Financial support:* In 2008–09, 53 students received support, including 35 fellowships with full and partial tuition reimbursements available (averaging $2,900 per year); research assistantships with full and partial tuition reimbursements available, career-related internships or fieldwork, Federal Work-Study, institutionally sponsored loans, scholarships/grants, and tuition waivers (full and partial) also available. Support available to part-time students. Financial award applicants required to submit FAFSA. *Faculty research:* Cross-cultural psychology, school psychology, childhood and adult trauma, positive psychology, autism spectrum disorders. *Unit head:* Dr. Robert Motta, Program Director, 516-463-5029, Fax: 516-463-6052, E-mail: psyrwm@hofstra.edu. *Application contact:* Carol Drummer, Dean of Graduate Admissions, 516-463-4876, Fax: 516-463-4664, E-mail: gradstudent@hofstra.edu.

Howard University, School of Education, Department of Human Development and Psychoeducational Studies, Program in School Psychology, Washington, DC 20059-0002. Offers M Ed, MA, Ed D, PhD, CAGS. MA and PhD offered through the Graduate School of Arts and Sciences. *Accreditation:* NCATE. *Degree requirements:* For master's, comprehensive exam, thesis (MA), expository writing exam, practicum; for doctorate, one foreign language, comprehensive exam, thesis/dissertation, expository writing exam, internship. *Entrance requirements:* For master's, GRE General Test, minimum GPA of 2.7; for doctorate, GRE General Test, minimum GPA of 3.4; for CAGS, GRE General Test, minimum graduate GPA of 3.0, master's degree. *Faculty research:* Psychopathology, maltreatment abuse and neglect, children exposed to political unrest, family conflict and community violence.

Humboldt State University, Graduate Studies, College of Natural Resources and Sciences, Department of Psychology, Arcata, CA 95521-8299. Offers psychology (MA), including academic research, counseling, school psychology. *Students:* 64 full-time (52 women), 6 part-time (3 women); includes 13 minority (1 African American, 3 American Indian/Alaska Native, 2 Asian Americans or Pacific Islanders, 7 Hispanic Americans), 1 international. Average age 29. 71 applicants, 45% accepted, 26 enrolled. In 2008, 12 master's awarded. *Degree requirements:* For master's, thesis. *Entrance requirements:* For master's, appropriate bachelor's degree, minimum GPA of 2.5. Additional exam requirements/recommendations for international students: Required—TOEFL (minimum score 500 paper-based; 173 computer-based). *Application deadline:* For fall admission, 2/15 for domestic and international students. Applications are processed on a rolling basis. Application fee: $55. *Expenses:* Tuition, state resident: full-time $5236. Tuition, nonresident: full-time $11,338. *Financial support:* Career-related internships or fieldwork available. Financial award application deadline: 3/1; financial award applicants required to submit FAFSA. *Faculty research:* School psychology, counseling, eating disorders, mood induction, depression. *Unit head:* Dr. Brent Duncan, Chair, 707-826-3755, Fax: 707-826-4993, E-mail: bbd1@humboldt.edu. *Application contact:* Dr. Brent Duncan, Administrative Support Coordinator, 707-826-3755, Fax: 707-826-4993, E-mail: bbd1@humboldt.edu.

Idaho State University, Office of Graduate Studies, College of Education, Department of Educational Learning and Development, Pocatello, ID 83209. Offers human exceptionality (M Ed); school psychology (Ed S); special education (Ed S). Part-time programs available. *Faculty:* 3 full-time (1 woman). *Students:* 14 full-time (10 women), 27 part-time (21 women); includes 1 minority (Hispanic American), 1 international. Average age 37. In 2008, 7 master's, 3 Ed Ss awarded. *Degree requirements:* For master's, thesis (for some programs), oral thesis defense or written comprehensive exam and oral exam; for Ed S, comprehensive exam, thesis (for some programs), oral exam, minimum GPA of 3.0, specialist paper or portfolio. *Entrance requirements:* For master's, GRE or MAT, minimum undergraduate GPA of 3.0; for Ed S, master's degree. Additional exam requirements/recommendations for international students: Required—TOEFL (minimum score 550 paper-based; 213 computer-based; 80 iBT). *Application deadline:* For fall admission, 7/1 for domestic students, 6/1 for international students; for spring admission, 12/1 for domestic students, 11/1 for international students. Applications are processed on a rolling basis. Application fee: $55. Electronic applications accepted. *Expenses:* Tuition, area resident: Full-time $3114; part-time $276 per credit hour. Tuition, state resident: full-time $3114; part-time $276 per credit hour. Tuition, nonresident: full-time $12,318; part-time $404 per credit hour. Required fees: $2360. Tuition and fees vary according to course load and reciprocity agreements. *Financial support:* In 2008–09, teaching assistantships with full and partial tuition reimbursements (averaging $9,401 per year); career-related internships or fieldwork, Federal Work-Study, institutionally sponsored loans, scholarships/grants, traineeships, health care benefits, and unspecified assistantships also available. Support available to part-time students. Financial award application deadline: 1/1; financial award applicants required to submit FAFSA. *Faculty research:* Literacy, school psychology, special education. *Unit head:* Dr. Stephanie Peterson, Chairman, 208-282-3552, Fax: 208-282-4697, E-mail: peteste4@isu.edu. *Application contact:* Dr. Peter Denner, Assistant Dean, 208-282-3807, Fax: 208-282-4697, E-mail: dennpete@isu.edu.

Idaho State University, Office of Graduate Studies, Kasiska College of Health Professions, Department of Counseling, Pocatello, ID 83209. Offers counseling (M Coun, Ed S), including marriage and family counseling (M Coun), mental health counseling (M Coun), school counseling (M Coun), student affairs and college counseling (M Coun); counselor education and counseling (PhD). *Accreditation:* ACA (one or more programs are accredited). Part-time programs available. *Faculty:* 7 full-time (4 women). *Students:* 72 full-time (50 women), 26 part-time (18 women); includes 7 minority (2 African Americans, 1 American Indian/Alaska Native, 1 Asian American or Pacific Islander, 3 Hispanic Americans), 1 international. Average age 34. In 2008, 28 master's, 7 doctorates, 1 other advanced degree awarded. *Degree requirements:* For master's, comprehensive exam, thesis; for doctorate, comprehensive exam, thesis/dissertation, internship; for Ed S, comprehensive exam, thesis, case studies, oral exam. *Entrance requirements:* For master's, GRE General Test, MAT, minimum GPA of 3.0; for doctorate, GRE General Test, MAT, minimum graduate GPA of 3.0, resumé, interview, counseling license; for Ed S, GRE General Test, minimum graduate GPA of 3.0, master's degree in counseling, 3 letters of recommendation, 2 years work experience. Additional exam requirements/recommendations for international students: Required—TOEFL (minimum score 600 paper-based; 213 computer-based; 80 iBT). *Application deadline:* For fall admission, 7/1 for domestic students, 6/1 for international students; for spring admission, 12/1 for domestic students, 11/1 for international students. Applications are processed on a rolling basis. Application fee: $55. Electronic applications accepted. *Expenses:* Tuition, area resident: Full-time $3114; part-time $276 per credit hour. Tuition, state resident: full-time $3114; part-time $276 per credit hour. Tuition, nonresident: full-time $12,318; part-time $404 per credit hour. Required fees: $2360. Tuition and fees vary according to course load and reciprocity agreements. *Financial support:* In 2008–09, 13 teaching assistantships with full and partial tuition reimbursements (averaging $9,401 per year) were awarded; career-related internships or fieldwork, Federal Work-Study, institutionally sponsored loans, scholarships/grants, traineeships, health care benefits, tuition waivers (full and partial), and unspecified assistantships also available. Support available to part-time students. Financial award application deadline: 1/1; financial award applicants required to submit FAFSA. *Faculty research:* Group counseling, multicultural counseling, family counseling, child therapy, supervision. *Unit head:* Dr. Stephen Feit, Chair, 208-282-3663, Fax: 208-282-2583, E-mail: feitstep@isu.edu. *Application contact:* Ellen Combs, Graduate School Technical Records Specialist, 208-282-2150, Fax: 208-282-4847, E-mail: combelle@isu.edu.

Illinois State University, Graduate School, College of Arts and Sciences, Department of Psychology, Program in School Psychology, Normal, IL 61790-2200. Offers PhD, SSP. *Accreditation:* APA (one or more programs are accredited); NCATE (one or more programs are accredited). *Degree requirements:* For doctorate, variable foreign language requirement, thesis/dissertation, 2 terms of residency, internship, practicum. *Entrance requirements:* For doctorate, GRE General Test.

Immaculata University, College of Graduate Studies, Department of Psychology, Immaculata, PA 19345. Offers clinical psychology (Psy D); counseling psychology (MA, Certificate), including school guidance counselor (Certificate), school psychologist (Certificate). *Accreditation:* APA. Part-time and evening/weekend programs available. *Degree requirements:* For master's, comprehensive exam, thesis optional; for doctorate, comprehensive exam, thesis/dissertation. *Entrance requirements:* For master's, GRE General Test or MAT, minimum GPA of 3.0; for doctorate, GRE General Test, minimum GPA of 3.5. Additional exam requirements/recommendations for international students: Required—TOEFL, IELTS. *Faculty research:* Supervision ethics, psychology of teaching, gender.

Indiana State University, School of Graduate Studies, College of Education, Department of Communication Disorders, Counseling and School and Educational Psychology, Terre Haute, IN 47809-1401. Offers counseling psychology (MS, PhD); counselor education (PhD); mental health counseling (MS); school counseling (M Ed); school psychology (PhD, Ed S); MA/MS. *Accreditation:* ACA; NCATE. Part-time and evening/weekend programs available. *Degree requirements:* For master's, thesis optional; for doctorate, thesis/dissertation, research tools proficiency tests. *Entrance requirements:* For master's, GRE General Test or MAT, minimum undergraduate GPA of 2.75; for doctorate, GRE General Test, master's degree, minimum undergraduate GPA of 3.5. Electronic applications accepted. *Faculty research:* Vocational development supervision.

Indiana University Bloomington, School of Education, Department of Counseling and Educational Psychology, Bloomington, IN 47405-1006. Offers counseling (MS, PhD, Ed S); counseling psychology (PhD); counselor education (MS, Ed S); educational psychology (MS, PhD); inquiry methodology (PhD); learning and developmental sciences (MS, PhD); school psychology (PhD, Ed S). *Accreditation:* ACA (one or more programs are accredited); APA (one or more programs are accredited); NCATE. *Faculty:* 32 full-time (13 women), 20 part-time/adjunct (10 women). *Students:* 225 full-time (174 women), 51 part-time (39 women); includes 40 minority (17 African Americans, 1 American Indian/Alaska Native, 10 Asian Americans or Pacific Islanders, 12 Hispanic Americans), 46 international. Average age 29. 350 applicants, 46% accepted, 80 enrolled. In 2008, 41 master's, 45 doctorates, 24 other advanced degrees awarded. Terminal master's awarded for partial completion of doctoral program. *Degree requirements:* For master's, thesis optional; for doctorate, thesis/dissertation; for Ed S, comprehensive exam or project. *Entrance requirements:* For master's, doctorate, and Ed S, GRE General Test. Additional exam requirements/recommendations for international students: Required—TOEFL. *Application deadline:* Applications are processed on a rolling basis. Application fee: $50 ($60 for international students). Electronic applications accepted. *Expenses:* Tuition, area resident: Part-time $291.97 per credit hour. Tuition, state resident: part-time $291.97 per credit hour. Tuition, nonresident: part-time $850.33 per credit hour. Required fees: $110 per semester. Tuition and fees vary according to course load and program. *Financial support:* In 2008–09, 58 students received support, including 7 fellowships with partial tuition reimbursements available (averaging $15,000 per year), 15 research assistantships with partial tuition reimbursements available (averaging $12,000 per year), 36 teaching assistantships with partial tuition reimbursements available (averaging $14,280 per year); career-related internships or fieldwork, Federal Work-Study, institutionally sponsored loans, scholarships/grants, and unspecified assistantships also available. Support available to part-time students. Financial award application deadline: 1/1; financial award applicants required to submit FAFSA. *Faculty research:* Counseling psychology, inquiry methodology, school psychology, learning sciences, human development, educational psychology. *Unit head:* Dr. Joyce Alexander, Chairperson, 812-856-8300, Fax: 812-856-8333, E-mail: cep@indiana.edu. *Application contact:* Jessica Durnal, Student Services Specialist, 812-856-8300, Fax: 812-856-8333, E-mail: cep@indiana.edu.

Indiana University of Pennsylvania, School of Graduate Studies and Research, College of Education and Educational Technology, Department of Educational and School Psychology, Program in School Psychology, Indiana, PA 15705-1087. Offers D Ed, Certificate. *Accreditation:* NCATE. Part-time programs available. *Faculty:* 9 full-time (2 women). *Students:* 18 full-time (14 women), 57 part-time (42 women); includes 5 minority (4 African Americans, 1 Hispanic American). Average age 33. 26 applicants, 23% accepted, 6 enrolled. In 2008, 12 doctorates, 17 Certificates awarded. *Degree requirements:* For doctorate, comprehensive exam, thesis/dissertation. *Entrance requirements:* For doctorate, GRE General Test, GRE Subject Test, 2 letters of recommendation. Additional exam requirements/recommendations for international students: Required—TOEFL. *Application deadline:* For fall admission, 1/10 for domestic students. Applications are processed on a rolling basis. Application fee: $30. *Expenses:* Tuition, area resident: Full-time $6430; part-time $357 per credit. Tuition, nonresident: full-time $10,288; part-time $572 per credit. Required fees: $1547.50; $107 per credit. $283 per year. *Financial support:* In 2008–09, 2 fellowships (averaging $3,000 per year), 16 research assistantships with full and partial tuition reimbursements (averaging $3,870 per year), 3 teaching assistantships with partial tuition reimbursements (averaging $10,454 per year) were awarded; career-related internships or fieldwork and Federal Work-Study also available. Support available to part-time students. Financial award application deadline: 3/15; financial award applicants required to submit FAFSA. *Unit head:* Dr. John Quirk, Graduate Coordinator, 724-357-3785. *Application contact:* Dr. Edward Nardi, Interim Associate Dean, 724-357-2480, Fax: 724-357-5595, E-mail: ewnardi@iup.edu.

Inter American University of Puerto Rico, Metropolitan Campus, Graduate Programs, Program in Psychology, San Juan, PR 00919-1293. Offers industrial/organizational psychology (MA, PhD); labor relations (MA); psychology (MA, PhD); school psychology (MA, PhD). *Degree requirements:* For master's, comprehensive exam. *Entrance requirements:* For master's, GRE or EXADEP, interview. Electronic applications accepted.

Inter American University of Puerto Rico, San Germán Campus, Graduate Studies Center, Program in Psychology, San Germán, PR 00683-5008. Offers counseling psychology (MA, PhD); school psychology (MA, PhD). Part-time and evening/weekend programs available. *Degree requirements:* For master's, comprehensive exam, thesis; for doctorate, comprehensive exam, thesis/dissertation. *Entrance requirements:* For master's, GRE General Test or EXADEP, minimum GPA of 3.0; for doctorate, GRE, EXADEP or MAT, minimum GPA of 3.0.

Iona College, School of Arts and Science, Department of Psychology, New Rochelle, NY 10801-1890. Offers experimental psychology (MA); industrial-organizational psychology (MA);

mental health counseling (MA); psychology (MA); school psychology (MA). Part-time and evening/weekend programs available. *Faculty:* 11 full-time (5 women), 6 part-time/adjunct (3 women). *Students:* 71 full-time (54 women), 42 part-time (35 women); includes 26 minority (9 African Americans, 5 Asian Americans or Pacific Islanders, 12 Hispanic Americans), 1 international. Average age 25. 120 applicants, 73% accepted, 39 enrolled. In 2008, 19 master's awarded. *Degree requirements:* For master's, thesis. *Entrance requirements:* For master's, GRE or minimum GPA of 3.0. Additional exam requirements/recommendations for international students: Required—TOEFL (minimum score 550 paper-based; 213 computer-based). *Application deadline:* Applications are processed on a rolling basis. Application fee: $50. Electronic applications accepted. *Expenses:* Tuition: Part-time $755 per credit. Required fees: $175 per term. *Financial support:* Career-related internships or fieldwork, tuition waivers (partial), and unspecified assistantships available. Support available to part-time students. Financial award application deadline: 4/15; financial award applicants required to submit FAFSA. *Unit head:* Dr. Pauline Jirik-Babb, Chair, 914-633-2191, E-mail: pjirikbabb@iona.edu. *Application contact:* Veronica Jarek-Prinz, Director of Graduate Admissions, 914-633-2420, Fax: 914-633-2277, E-mail: vjarekprinz@iona.edu.

James Madison University, The Graduate School, College of Integrated Science and Technology, Department of Graduate Psychology, Program in Combined-Integrated Clinical and School Psychology, Harrisonburg, VA 22807. Offers PhD, Psy D. Part-time and evening/weekend programs available. *Students:* 19 full-time (16 women); includes 2 minority (1 African American, 1 Asian American or Pacific Islander), 2 international. Average age 27. In 2008, 9 doctorates awarded. *Degree requirements:* For doctorate, thesis/dissertation, 12-month internship. *Entrance requirements:* For doctorate, GRE General Test, GRE Subject Test (advanced psychology), 3 letters of recommendation. Additional exam requirements/recommendations for international students: Required—TOEFL. *Application deadline:* For fall admission, 2/1 for domestic students. Applications are processed on a rolling basis. Application fee: $55. Electronic applications accepted. *Expenses:* Tuition, area resident: Full-time $7008; part-time $292 per credit hour. Tuition, state resident: full-time $7008; part-time $292 per credit hour. Tuition, nonresident: full-time $20,352; part-time $848 per credit hour. *Financial support:* In 2008–09, 12 students received support. 14 doctoral assistantships ($14,500) available. Financial award application deadline: 3/1; financial award applicants required to submit FAFSA. *Unit head:* Dr. Gregg R. Henriques, Program Director, 540-568-7857. *Application contact:* Dr. Gregg R. Henriques, Program Director, 540-568-7857.

James Madison University, The Graduate School, College of Integrated Science and Technology, Department of Graduate Psychology, Program in School Psychology, Harrisonburg, VA 22807. Offers school counseling (Ed S); school psychology (MA). *Accreditation:* APA (one or more programs are accredited); NCATE (one or more programs are accredited). Part-time and evening/weekend programs available. *Students:* 15 full-time (13 women), 11 part-time (8 women); includes 4 minority (2 African Americans, 1 Asian American or Pacific Islander, 1 Hispanic American). Average age 27. In 2008, 11 master's, 9 other advanced degrees awarded. *Degree requirements:* For master's, comprehensive exam; for Ed S, thesis, research project, 10-month internship. *Entrance requirements:* For master's, GRE General Test, interview, 3 letters of recommendation. Additional exam requirements/recommendations for international students: Required—TOEFL. *Application deadline:* For fall admission, 2/1 priority date for domestic students. Applications are processed on a rolling basis. Application fee: $55. Electronic applications accepted. *Expenses:* Tuition, area resident: Full-time $7008; part-time $292 per credit hour. Tuition, state resident: full-time $7008; part-time $292 per credit hour. Tuition, nonresident: full-time $20,352; part-time $848 per credit hour. *Financial support:* In 2008–09, 14 students received support, including 1 teaching assistantship with full tuition reimbursement available (averaging $8,664 per year); career-related internships or fieldwork, Federal Work-Study, and 11 graduate assistantships ($7,382) also available. Financial award application deadline: 3/1; financial award applicants required to submit FAFSA. *Unit head:* Dr. Patricia J. Warner, Program Director, 540-568-3358. *Application contact:* Dr. Patricia J. Warner, Program Director, 540-568-3358.

Kean University, College of Humanities and Social Sciences, Program in School Psychology, Union, NJ 07083. Offers Diploma. Part-time and evening/weekend programs available. *Faculty:* 18 full-time (13 women). *Students:* 19 full-time (all women), 13 part-time (12 women); includes 1 African American, 1 Asian American or Pacific Islander, 2 Hispanic Americans. Average age 26. 53 applicants, 26% accepted, 12 enrolled. In 2008, 10 Diplomas awarded. *Degree requirements:* For Diploma, comprehensive exam, practicum, externship. *Entrance requirements:* For degree, GRE General Test, minimum GPA of 3.0, interview, 3 letters of recommendation, prerequisites in psychology. *Application deadline:* For fall admission, 3/15 for domestic students. Application fee: $60 ($150 for international students). Electronic applications accepted. *Expenses:* Tuition, state resident: full-time $10,128; part-time $422 per credit. Tuition, nonresident: full-time $13,728; part-time $572 per credit. Required fees: $2570; $107 per credit. Part-time tuition and fees vary according to course load, degree level and program. *Financial support:* In 2008–09, 13 research assistantships with full tuition reimbursements (averaging $3,217 per year) were awarded; unspecified assistantships also available. *Unit head:* Dr. Dennis Finger, Program Coordinator, 908-737-5870, E-mail: dfinger@kean.edu. *Application contact:* Steven Koch, Pre-Admissions Coordinator, 908-737-4723, Fax: 908-737-5965, E-mail: grad-adm@kean.edu.

Kean University, Nathan Weiss Graduate College, Program in School and Clinical Psychology, Union, NJ 07083. Offers Psy D. Evening/weekend programs available. *Faculty:* 18 full-time (13 women). *Degree requirements:* For doctorate, comprehensive exam, thesis/dissertation, externship. *Entrance requirements:* For doctorate, GRE General Test (minimum score: verbal 500, quantitative 500, writing 4.0), GRE Subject Test in Psychology within the last 5 years (minimum score: 550), minimum undergraduate GPA of 3.3, graduate 3.5; personal statement of goals and objectives, three letters of recommendation (at least one from a professor), personal interview, prerequisite coursework in theories of personality, abnormal psychology, tests and measurements, statistics, and experimental psychology. *Application deadline:* For fall admission, 1/30 for domestic students. Application fee: $60 ($150 for international students). Electronic applications accepted. *Expenses:* Contact institution. *Financial support:* In 2008–09, research assistantships (averaging $3,217 per year); unspecified assistantships also available. *Unit head:* Dr. Dennis Finger, Program Coordinator, 908-737-5870, E-mail: dfinger@kean.edu. *Application contact:* Steven Koch, Pre-Admissions Coordinator, 908-737-4723, Fax: 908-737-5965, E-mail: grad-adm@kean.edu.

Kent State University, Graduate School of Education, Health, and Human Services, Department of Educational Foundations and Special Services, Program in School Psychology, Kent, OH 44242-0001. Offers M Ed, PhD, Ed S. *Accreditation:* APA; NCATE. *Degree requirements:* For doctorate, comprehensive exam, thesis/dissertation. *Entrance requirements:* For master's and doctorate, GRE General Test; for Ed S, GRE General Test, MAT or minimum graduate GPA of 3.5. Additional exam requirements/recommendations for international students: Required—TOEFL. Electronic applications accepted. *Faculty research:* Special education policy and practice, treatment fidelity, school-based consultation.

La Sierra University, School of Education, Department of School Psychology and Counseling, Riverside, CA 92515. Offers counseling (MA); educational psychology (Ed S); school psychology (Ed S). Part-time and evening/weekend programs available. *Degree requirements:* For master's, thesis optional; for Ed S, practicum (educational psychology). *Entrance requirements:* For master's, California Basic Educational Skills Test, NTE, minimum GPA of 3.0; for Ed S, minimum GPA of 3.3. *Faculty research:* Equivalent score scales, self perception.

Lehigh University, College of Education, Program in School Psychology, Bethlehem, PA 18015-3094. Offers M Ed, PhD, Ed S. *Accreditation:* APA (one or more programs are accredited). Part-time and evening/weekend programs available. *Faculty:* 5 full-time (3 women). *Students:* 30 full-time (25 women), 23 part-time (20 women); includes 3 minority (2 African Americans, 1 Hispanic American), 3 international. Average age 27. 76 applicants, 28% accepted, 7 enrolled. In 2008, 3 master's, 3 doctorates, 3 other advanced degrees awarded. *Degree requirements:*

For doctorate, comprehensive exam, internship, research qualifying exam; for Ed S, internship. *Entrance requirements:* For doctorate, GRE General Test, minimum GPA of 3.0, 2 letters of recommendation, supplemental application, essay; for Ed S, GRE General Test, minimum GPA of 3.0. Additional exam requirements/recommendations for international students: Required—TOEFL (minimum score 600 paper-based; 250 computer-based; 85 iBT). *Application deadline:* For fall admission, 1/1 for domestic and international students. Application fee: $65. Electronic applications accepted. *Financial support:* Fellowships, research assistantships, career-related internships or fieldwork, Federal Work-Study, institutionally sponsored loans, and tuition waivers (full and partial) available. Financial award application deadline: 1/31. *Faculty research:* Applied behavior, analysis development disabilities, psychology of the mildly handicapped. *Unit head:* Dr. Christine L. Cole, Coordinator, 610-758-3256, Fax: 610-758-6223, E-mail: clc2@lehigh.edu. *Application contact:* Donna M. Johnson, Coordinator, 610-758 Ext. 3231, Fax: 610-758-6223, E-mail: dmj4@lehigh.edu.

Lenoir-Rhyne University, Graduate Programs, School of Counseling and Human Services, Program in School Counseling, Hickory, NC 28601. Offers MA. Part-time and evening/weekend programs available. *Degree requirements:* For master's, comprehensive exam, thesis optional. *Entrance requirements:* For master's, GRE General Test, minimum undergraduate GPA of 2.7, graduate 3.0; writing sample. Additional exam requirements/recommendations for international students: Required—TOEFL (minimum score 600 paper-based). Electronic applications accepted.

Lesley University, Graduate School of Arts and Social Sciences, Program in Counseling Psychology, Cambridge, MA 02138-2790. Offers professional counseling (MA); school counseling (MA). Part-time and evening/weekend programs available. Postbaccalaureate distance learning degree programs offered (no on-campus study). Terminal master's awarded for partial completion of doctoral program. *Degree requirements:* For master's, internship, practicum. *Entrance requirements:* For master's, MAT. Additional exam requirements/recommendations for international students: Required—TOEFL (minimum score 550 paper-based; 213 computer-based; 80 iBT). *Expenses:* Tuition: Full-time $13,770; part-time $765 per credit hour. Required fees: $150. Tuition and fees vary according to course load, degree level, campus/location and program.

See Close-Up on page 1117.

Lewis & Clark College, Graduate School of Education and Counseling, Department of Counseling Psychology, Program in School Psychology, Portland, OR 97219-7899. Offers MS, Ed S. Part-time and evening/weekend programs available. *Entrance requirements:* For master's, GRE General Test, minimum undergraduate GPA of 2.75. Additional exam requirements/recommendations for international students: Required—TOEFL (minimum score 575 paper-based; 233 computer-based). Electronic applications accepted.

Lewis & Clark College, Graduate School of Education and Counseling, Department of Education, Program in School Counseling, Portland, OR 97219-7899. Offers M Ed. Part-time and evening/weekend programs available. *Degree requirements:* For master's, thesis. *Entrance requirements:* For master's, minimum undergraduate GPA of 2.75. Additional exam requirements/recommendations for international students: Required—TOEFL (minimum score 575 paper-based; 233 computer-based). Electronic applications accepted. *Faculty research:* Peer rejection, social skills, consultation, sexual abuse.

Lindenwood University, Graduate Programs, School of Education, St. Charles, MO 63301-1695. Offers education (MA); educational administration (MA, Ed D, Ed S); instructional leadership (Ed D, Ed S); library media (MA); professional and school counseling (MA); professional counseling (MA); school counseling (MA); teaching (MA). Part-time and evening/weekend programs available. *Faculty:* 33 full-time (13 women), 176 part-time/adjunct (83 women). *Students:* 460 full-time (352 women), 1,975 part-time (1,518 women); includes 620 minority (585 African Americans, 8 American Indian/Alaska Native, 16 Asian Americans or Pacific Islanders, 11 Hispanic Americans), 9 international. Average age 37. In 2008, 883 master's, 11 doctorates, 51 other advanced degrees awarded. *Degree requirements:* For master's, thesis (for some programs), minimum GPA of 3.0; for doctorate, thesis/dissertation, minimum GPA of 3.0; for Ed S, comprehensive exam, specialist project, minimum GPA of 3.0. *Entrance requirements:* For master's, interview, minimum GPA of 3.0, writing sample, letter of recommendation; for doctorate, GRE, minimum GPA of 3.4 in graduate studies, resumé, interview, writing sample, 4 letters of recommendation; for Ed S, master's degree in education, relevant work experience. Additional exam requirements/recommendations for international students: Required—TOEFL (minimum score 550 paper-based; 213 computer-based; 80 iBT). *Application deadline:* For fall admission, 8/30 priority date for domestic and international students; for spring admission, 12/30 priority date for domestic and international students. Applications are processed on a rolling basis. Application fee: $30 ($100 for international students). Electronic applications accepted. *Expenses:* Tuition: Full-time $12,700; part-time $360 per credit hour. *Financial support:* Career-related internships or fieldwork, institutionally sponsored loans, tuition waivers (partial), and unspecified assistantships available. Financial award applicants required to submit FAFSA. *Unit head:* Dr. Cynthia Bice, Dean of Education, 636-949-4618, Fax: 636-949-4197, E-mail: cbice@lindenwood.edu. *Application contact:* Brett Barger, Dean of Evening Admissions and Extension Campuses, 636-949-4934, Fax: 636-949-4109, E-mail: adultadmissions@lindenwood.edu.

Long Island University, Brooklyn Campus, School of Education, Department of Human Development and Leadership, Program in School Psychology, Brooklyn, NY 11201-8423. Offers MS Ed. Part-time and evening/weekend programs available. *Degree requirements:* For master's, thesis optional. *Entrance requirements:* For master's, 2 letters of recommendation. Additional exam requirements/recommendations for international students: Required—TOEFL (minimum score 500 paper-based; 173 computer-based). Electronic applications accepted.

Long Island University, Westchester Graduate Campus, Programs in Education-School Counselor and School Psychology, Purchase, NY 10577. Offers school counselor (MS Ed); school psychologist (MS Ed). Part-time and evening/weekend programs available.

Louisiana State University and Agricultural and Mechanical College, Graduate School, College of Arts and Sciences, Department of Psychology, Baton Rouge, LA 70803. Offers biological psychology (MA, PhD); clinical psychology (MA, PhD); cognitive psychology (MA, PhD); developmental psychology (MA, PhD); industrial/organizational psychology (MA, PhD); school psychology (MA, PhD). *Accreditation:* APA (one or more programs are accredited). Terminal master's awarded for partial completion of doctoral program. *Degree requirements:* For master's, thesis; for doctorate, thesis/dissertation, 1 year internship. *Entrance requirements:* For master's and doctorate, GRE General Test, minimum GPA of 3.0. Additional exam requirements/recommendations for international students: Required—TOEFL (minimum score 550 paper-based; 213 computer-based; 79 iBT). Electronic applications accepted. *Faculty research:* Clinical psychology, autism, anxiety, addition, neuro-psychology, school psychology, cognitive psychology, experimental psychology.

Louisiana State University in Shreveport, College of Education and Human Development, Program in School Psychology, Shreveport, LA 71115-2399. Offers SSP. *Entrance requirements:* For degree, GRE General Test, minimum GPA of 2.75. Additional exam requirements/recommendations for international students: Required—TOEFL (minimum score 500 paper-based; 173 computer-based; 61 iBT).

Loyola University Chicago, School of Education, Program in School Psychology, Chicago, IL 60611-2196. Offers M Ed, PhD, Ed S. PhD offered through the Graduate School. Part-time and evening/weekend programs available. *Faculty:* 6 full-time (4 women), 11 part-time/adjunct (8 women). *Students:* 81. Average age 28. 34 applicants, 32% accepted, 5 enrolled. In 2008, 8 doctorates, 19 other advanced degrees awarded. Terminal master's awarded for partial completion of doctoral program. *Degree requirements:* For master's, comprehensive exam; for doctorate, comprehensive exam, thesis/dissertation. *Entrance requirements:* For doctorate, GRE, interview, letters of recommendation, transcripts, minimum GPA of 3.0. Additional exam

School Psychology

Loyola University Chicago (continued)

requirements/recommendations for international students: Required—TOEFL (minimum score 550 paper-based; 213 computer-based; 79 iBT). *Application deadline:* For fall admission, 12/15 for domestic and international students. Application fee: $50. Electronic applications accepted. *Expenses:* Tuition: Full-time $13,500; part-time $750 per credit hour. Required fees: $60 per semester. Full-time tuition and fees vary according to program. *Financial support:* In 2008–09, 2 fellowships (averaging $14,000 per year), 9 research assistantships with full tuition reimbursements (averaging $11,000 per year) were awarded; institutionally sponsored loans, scholarships/grants, and tuition waivers (full and partial) also available. Financial award application deadline: 2/15. *Faculty research:* Learning theory and teaching, school reform, instructional intervention, violence prevention, mental health programming in schools and communities. *Unit head:* Dr. Pamela Fenning, Director, 312-915-6803, E-mail: pfennin@luc.edu. *Application contact:* Marie Rosin-Dittmar, Information Contact, 312-915-6800, E-mail: schleduc@luc.edu.

Marist College, Graduate Programs, School of Social and Behavioral Sciences, Poughkeepsie, NY 12601-1387. Offers counseling psychology (MA); education (M Ed); education psychology (MA); school psychology (MA, Adv C). Part-time and evening/weekend programs available. *Degree requirements:* For master's, thesis optional. *Entrance requirements:* For master's, GRE General Test, letters of recommendation, minimum undergraduate GPA of 3.0, interview, essay, official transcript. Additional exam requirements/recommendations for international students: Required—TOEFL (minimum score 550 paper-based; 213 computer-based; 80 iBT); Recommended—IELTS (minimum score 6.5). Electronic applications accepted. *Faculty research:* AIDS prevention, educational intervention, humanistic counseling research, aging and development, neuroimaging.

Marshall University, Academic Affairs Division, College of Education and Human Services, Graduate School of Education and Professional Development, Program in School Psychology, Huntington, WV 25755. Offers Ed S. *Accreditation:* NCATE. Part-time and evening/weekend programs available. *Entrance requirements:* For degree, master's degree in psychology.

Marywood University, Academic Affairs, College of Education and Human Development, Department of Psychology and Counseling, Program in Psychology, Scranton, PA 18509-1598. Offers child/clinical school psychology (MA); clinical services (MA); general theoretical psychology (MA). Part-time and evening/weekend programs available. *Degree requirements:* For master's, comprehensive exam, thesis or alternative, internship/practicum. *Entrance requirements:* For master's, GRE or MAT. Additional exam requirements/recommendations for international students: Required—TOEFL (minimum score 550 paper-based; 213 computer-based). Electronic applications accepted. *Faculty research:* Personality disorders, counselor training, preschool development, self-esteem measurement, family dynamics.

Marywood University, Academic Affairs, College of Education and Human Development, Department of Psychology and Counseling, Program in School Psychology, Scranton, PA 18509-1598. Offers Ed S.

Massachusetts School of Professional Psychology, Graduate Programs, Boston, MA 02132. Offers clinical psychology (Psy D); clinical psychopharmacology (Post-Doctoral MS); counseling psychology (MA); executive coaching (Graduate Certificate); forensic psychology (MA); organizational psychology (MA); respecialization in clinical psychology (Certificate); MA/CAGS. *Accreditation:* APA. *Degree requirements:* For master's, comprehensive exam; for doctorate, thesis/dissertation. *Entrance requirements:* For doctorate, GRE General Test. Additional exam requirements/recommendations for international students: Required—TOEFL (minimum score 550 paper-based; 213 computer-based). Electronic applications accepted.

McGill University, Faculty of Graduate and Postdoctoral Studies, Faculty of Education, Department of Educational and Counseling Psychology, Montréal, QC H3A 2T5, Canada. Offers counseling psychology (MA, PhD); educational psychology (M Ed, MA, PhD); school/applied child psychology and applied developmental psychology (M Ed, MA, PhD, Diploma), including school psychology. *Accreditation:* APA.

McNeese State University, Doré School of Graduate Studies, Burton College of Education, Department of Teacher Education, Program in School Counseling, Lake Charles, LA 70609. Offers M Ed. *Accreditation:* NCATE. Evening/weekend programs available. *Faculty:* 2 full-time (both women). *Students:* 5 full-time (all women), 14 part-time (all women); includes 5 minority (4 African Americans, 1 Hispanic American). In 2008, 4 master's awarded. *Entrance requirements:* For master's, GRE, 18 hours in professional education. *Application deadline:* For fall admission, 5/15 priority date for domestic and international students; for spring admission, 10/15 priority date for domestic and international students. Applications are processed on a rolling basis. Application fee: $20 ($30 for international students). *Expenses:* Tuition, area resident: Full-time $2386. Tuition, state resident: full-time $2386. Required fees: $885. Tuition and fees vary according to course load. *Financial support:* Application deadline: 5/1. *Unit head:* Dr. Royce Zant, Head, 337-475-5404, Fax: 337-475-5398, E-mail: rzant@mcneese.edu. *Application contact:* Dr. George F. Mead, Interim Dean of Dore' School of Graduate Studies, 337-475-5396, Fax: 337-475-5397, E-mail: admissions@mcneese.edu.

Mercy College, School of Social and Behavioral Sciences, Program in Psychology, Dobbs Ferry, NY 10522-1189. Offers psychology (MS); school psychology (MS). Part-time and evening/weekend programs available. Postbaccalaureate distance learning degree programs offered (minimal on-campus study). *Students:* 11 full-time (9 women), 15 part-time (10 women); includes 13 minority (7 African Americans, 1 American Indian/Alaska Native, 5 Hispanic Americans), 1 international. Average age 33. 34 applicants, 47% accepted, 10 enrolled. In 2008, 5 master's awarded. *Degree requirements:* For master's, completion of written comprehensive exam or six-credit thesis. *Entrance requirements:* For master's, BA in psychology, sociology, behavioral science or education; interview; letters of recommendation; minimum GPA of 3.0; resumé; 3- to 5-page essay stating reason for pursuing master's degree in psychology. Additional exam requirements/recommendations for international students: Required—TOEFL (minimum score 600 paper-based; 250 computer-based; 100 iBT). *Application deadline:* For fall admission, 8/1 for international students. Applications are processed on a rolling basis. Application fee: $40. Electronic applications accepted. *Expenses:* Tuition: Full-time $12,330; part-time $685 per credit. Required fees: $240; $120 per semester. Tuition and fees vary according to program. *Financial support:* In 2008–09, 6 students received support. Career-related internships or fieldwork, Federal Work-Study, scholarships/grants, and unspecified assistantships available. Support available to part-time students. Financial award applicants required to submit FAFSA. *Unit head:* Dr. Barbara Melamed, Program Director, 914-674-7345, E-mail: bmelamed@mercy.edu. *Application contact:* Dr. Barbara Melamed, Program Director, 914-674-7345, E-mail: bmelamed@mercy.edu.

Mercy College, School of Social and Behavioral Sciences, Program in School Psychology, Dobbs Ferry, NY 10522-1189. Offers MS. Part-time and evening/weekend programs available. *Students:* 27 full-time (24 women), 28 part-time (25 women); includes 31 minority (8 African Americans, 1 American Indian/Alaska Native, 2 Asian Americans or Pacific Islanders, 20 Hispanic Americans), 2 international. Average age 29. 45 applicants, 60% accepted, 18 enrolled. In 2008, 14 master's awarded. *Degree requirements:* For master's, coursework, practica, fieldwork, internship, integrative project. *Entrance requirements:* For master's, current resumé; 3- to 5-page essay; interview; written recommendation from three instructors; bachelor's degree with a major in psychology, sociology, behavioral science, or education. Additional exam requirements/recommendations for international students: Required—TOEFL (minimum score 600 paper-based; 250 computer-based; 100 iBT). *Application deadline:* For fall admission, 8/1 for international students. Applications are processed on a rolling basis. Application fee: $40. Electronic applications accepted. *Expenses:* Tuition: Full-time $12,330; part-time $685 per credit. Required fees: $240; $120 per semester. Tuition and fees vary according to program. *Financial support:* In 2008–09, 15 students received support. Career-related internships or fieldwork, Federal Work-Study, scholarships/grants, and unspecified assistantships available. Support available to part-time students. Financial award applicants required to submit FAFSA. *Faculty research:* Consultation, effective intervention and prevention practices, psychology. *Unit head:* Dr. Michael Grunes, Program Director, 914-674-7503, E-mail: mgrunes@mercy.edu. *Application contact:* Dr. Michael Grunes, Program Director, 914-674-7503, E-mail: mgrunes@mercy.edu.

Miami University, Graduate School, School of Education and Allied Professions, Department of Educational Psychology, Program in School Psychology, Oxford, OH 45056. Offers MS, Ed S. *Accreditation:* NCATE. *Degree requirements:* For master's, thesis or alternative, oral or written exam; for Ed S, oral or written exam. *Entrance requirements:* For master's, GRE General Test or MAT, minimum undergraduate GPA of 3.0 during previous 2 years or 2.75 overall; for Ed S, GRE General Test or MAT.

Michigan State University, The Graduate School, College of Education, Department of Counseling, Educational Psychology and Special Education, East Lansing, MI 48824. Offers counseling (MA); educational psychology and educational technology (PhD); educational technology (MA); measurement and quantitative methods (PhD); rehabilitation counseling (MA); rehabilitation counselor education (PhD); school psychology (MA, PhD, Ed S); special education (MA, PhD). *Accreditation:* APA (one or more programs are accredited); CORE (one or more programs are accredited). Part-time programs available. *Entrance requirements:* Additional exam requirements/recommendations for international students: Required—TOEFL. Electronic applications accepted.

Middle Tennessee State University, College of Graduate Studies, College of Education and Behavioral Science, Department of Psychology, Program in Professional Counseling, Murfreesboro, TN 37132. Offers curriculum and instruction (Ed S), including school psychology; school counseling (M Ed). *Accreditation:* ACA; NCATE. Part-time and evening/weekend programs available. Postbaccalaureate distance learning degree programs offered. *Degree requirements:* For master's, one foreign language, comprehensive exam. *Entrance requirements:* For master's, GRE or MAT. Additional exam requirements/recommendations for international students: Required—TOEFL (paper-based 525; computer-based 195; IBT 71) or IELTS (6.0). Electronic applications accepted.

Millersville University of Pennsylvania, Graduate School, School of Education, Department of Psychology, Program in Psychology, Millersville, PA 17551-0302. Offers clinical psychology (MS); school psychology (MS). Part-time programs available. *Faculty:* 20 full-time (14 women), 6 part-time/adjunct (3 women). *Students:* 49 full-time (41 women), 45 part-time (38 women); includes 6 minority (5 African Americans, 1 Hispanic American), 1 international. Average age 29. 74 applicants, 45% accepted, 17 enrolled. In 2008, 28 master's awarded. *Degree requirements:* For master's, comprehensive exam, thesis optional. *Entrance requirements:* For master's, GRE, in-person interview. Additional exam requirements/recommendations for international students: Required—TOEFL (minimum score 500 paper-based; 183 computer-based; 65 iBT), TOEFL may be replaced by IELTS with score of 6 or higher. *Application deadline:* For fall admission, 2/1 for domestic and international students; for winter admission, 10/1 for domestic and international students; for spring admission, 10/1 for domestic and international students. Application fee: $40. Electronic applications accepted. *Expenses:* Tuition, state resident: full-time $6430; part-time $357 per credit. Tuition, nonresident: full-time $10,288; part-time $572 per credit. Required fees: $1937; $73.50 per credit. One-time fee: $88 part-time. Tuition and fees vary according to course load. *Financial support:* In 2008–09, 31 students received support, including 31 research assistantships with full and partial tuition reimbursements available (averaging $4,718 per year); institutionally sponsored loans and unspecified assistantships also available. Support available to part-time students. Financial award application deadline: 3/15; financial award applicants required to submit FAFSA. *Faculty research:* Childhood disorders, family stress, anxiety and worry treatments, solution-focused counseling, creativity, personality correlates. *Unit head:* Dr. Claudia Haferkamp, Coordinator of Clinical Psychology Program, 717-872-3826, Fax: 717-871-2480, E-mail: claudia.haferkamp@millersville.edu. *Application contact:* Dr. Victor S. DeSantis, Dean of Graduate and Professional Studies, 717-872-3099, Fax: 717-872-3453, E-mail: victor.desantis@millersville.edu.

Millersville University of Pennsylvania, Graduate School, School of Education, Department of Psychology, Program in School Counseling, Millersville, PA 17551-0302. Offers M Ed. *Accreditation:* NCATE. Part-time programs available. *Faculty:* 20 full-time (14 women), 6 part-time/adjunct (3 women). *Students:* 16 full-time (14 women), 33 part-time (27 women); includes 3 minority (1 Asian American or Pacific Islander, 2 Hispanic Americans). Average age 29. 15 applicants, 20% accepted, 3 enrolled. In 2008, 13 master's awarded. *Degree requirements:* For master's, comprehensive exam, thesis optional. *Entrance requirements:* For master's, GRE, in-person interview. Additional exam requirements/recommendations for international students: Required—TOEFL (minimum score 500 paper-based; 183 computer-based; 65 iBT), TOEFL may be replaced by IELTS with score of 6 or higher. *Application deadline:* For fall admission, 2/1 for domestic and international students; for winter admission, 10/1 for domestic and international students; for spring admission, 10/1 for domestic and international students. Application fee: $40. Electronic applications accepted. *Expenses:* Tuition, state resident: full-time $6430; part-time $357 per credit. Tuition, nonresident: full-time $10,288; part-time $572 per credit. Required fees: $1937; $73.50 per credit. One-time fee: $88 part-time. Tuition and fees vary according to course load. *Financial support:* In 2008–09, 13 students received support, including 13 research assistantships with full and partial tuition reimbursements available (averaging $4,660 per year); institutionally sponsored loans and unspecified assistantships also available. Support available to part-time students. Financial award application deadline: 3/15; financial award applicants required to submit FAFSA. *Unit head:* Dr. Nadine E. Garner, Coordinator, 717-872-3097, Fax: 717-871-2480, E-mail: nadine.garner@millersville.edu. *Application contact:* Dr. Victor S. DeSantis, Dean of Graduate and Professional Studies, 717-872-3099, Fax: 717-872-3453, E-mail: victor.desantis@millersville.edu.

Minnesota State University Mankato, College of Graduate Studies, College of Social and Behavioral Sciences, Department of Psychology, Mankato, MN 56001. Offers clinical psychology (MA); industrial/organizational psychology (MA); psychology (MT); school psychology (Psy D). Part-time programs available. *Students:* 38 full-time (23 women), 5 part-time (1 woman). *Degree requirements:* For master's, one foreign language, comprehensive exam, thesis (for some programs). *Entrance requirements:* For master's, GRE General Test, GRE Subject Test (clinical psychology), minimum GPA of 3.0 during previous 2 years, 3 letters of reference. Additional exam requirements/recommendations for international students: Required—TOEFL. *Application deadline:* For fall admission, 1/1 priority date for domestic students. Applications are processed on a rolling basis. Application fee: $40. Electronic applications accepted. *Financial support:* Research assistantships, teaching assistantships with full tuition reimbursements, career-related internships or fieldwork, Federal Work-Study, institutionally sponsored loans, and unspecified assistantships available. Support available to part-time students. Financial award application deadline: 3/15; financial award applicants required to submit FAFSA. *Faculty research:* Professional competency in hospitals, mood disturbance, 360-degree feedback, employee selection, planning fallacy. *Unit head:* Dr. Barry Ries, Chairperson, 507-389-2724. *Application contact:* 507-389-2321, E-mail: grad@mnsu.edu.

Minnesota State University Moorhead, Graduate Studies, College of Social and Natural Sciences, Program in School Psychology, Moorhead, MN 56563-0002. Offers MS, Psy S. *Accreditation:* NCATE (one or more programs are accredited). *Degree requirements:* For master's, thesis, final oral and written comprehensive exams. *Entrance requirements:* For master's, GRE General Test, interview, minimum GPA of 3.0, 3 letters of recommendation; for Psy S, MS in school psychology. Additional exam requirements/recommendations for international students: Required—TOEFL (minimum score 550 paper-based; 213 computer-based). Electronic applications accepted.

Minot State University, Graduate School, Program in School Psychology, Minot, ND 58707-0002. Offers Ed Sp. *Faculty:* 8 part-time/adjunct (5 women). *Students:* 14 part-time (12 women), 2 international. Average age 31. In 2008, 1 Ed Sp awarded. *Entrance requirements:* For degree, GRE General Test, minimum GPA of 3.0. Additional exam requirements/

recommendations for international students: Required—TOEFL. *Application deadline:* For fall admission, 3/1 for domestic students. Applications are processed on a rolling basis. Application fee: $35. *Expenses:* Tuition, area resident: Full-time $5527; part-time $230.30 per credit hour. Tuition, state resident: full-time $8291; part-time $345.45 per credit hour. Tuition, nonresident: full-time $14,758; part-time $614.90 per credit hour. Required fees: $865; $36.03 per credit hour. Tuition and fees vary according to course load and reciprocity agreements. *Financial support:* In 2008–09, 2 teaching assistantships with partial tuition reimbursements (averaging $1,250 per year) were awarded; research assistantships with partial tuition reimbursements, career-related internships or fieldwork, institutionally sponsored loans, scholarships/grants, traineeships, tuition waivers (partial), and unspecified assistantships also available. Support available to part-time students. Financial award application deadline: 4/1. *Faculty research:* Oppositional defiance disorder and autism, experimental psychology, statistical genetics, adults with developmental disabilities, psychopharmacology. *Unit head:* Dr. Donald Burke, Chairperson, 701-858-3138. *Application contact:* Dr. Donald Burke, Chairperson, 701-858-3138.

Mississippi State University, College of Education, Department of Counseling, Educational Psychology, and Special Education, Mississippi State, MS 39762. Offers counselor education (MS, PhD, Ed S); educational psychology (MS, PhD, Ed S); special education (MS, Ed S). *Accreditation:* ACA (one or more programs are accredited); APA; CORE (one or more programs are accredited); NCATE. Part-time programs available. Postbaccalaureate distance learning degree programs offered (minimal on-campus study). Terminal master's awarded for partial completion of doctoral program. *Degree requirements:* For master's, comprehensive exam, thesis optional; for doctorate, thesis/dissertation, comprehensive oral and written exam. *Entrance requirements:* For master's, GRE, minimum QPA of 3.0; for doctorate, GRE, interview, minimum GPA of 3.4. Additional exam requirements/recommendations for international students: Required—TOEFL. *Expenses:* Tuition, state resident: full-time $4,978; part-time $274 per hour. Tuition, nonresident: full-time $11,469; part-time $635 per hour. *Faculty research:* HIV-AIDS in college population, substance abuse in youth and college students, ADHD and conduct disorders in youth, assessment and identification of early childhood disabilities, assessment and vocational transition of the disabled.

Montclair State University, The Office of Graduate Admissions and Support Services, College of Humanities and Social Sciences, Department of Psychology, Montclair, NJ 07043-1624. Offers educational psychology (MA), including child/adolescent clinical psychology, clinical psychology for Spanish/English bilinguals; psychology (MA, Certificate), including industrial and organizational psychology (MA); school psychologist (Certificate). Part-time and evening/weekend programs available. *Faculty:* 28 full-time (13 women), 32 part-time/adjunct (16 women). *Students:* 28 full-time (20 women), 31 part-time (26 women); includes 14 minority (4 African Americans, 6 Asian Americans or Pacific Islanders, 4 Hispanic Americans), 2 international. Average age 27. 62 applicants, 56% accepted, 23 enrolled. In 2008, 26 master's awarded. *Degree requirements:* For master's, comprehensive exam, thesis or alternative. *Entrance requirements:* For master's, GRE General Test, GRE Subject Test, previous course work in psychology, interview, 2 letters of recommendation. Additional exam requirements/recommendations for international students: Required—TOEFL (minimum score 83 computer-based). *Application deadline:* For fall admission, 2/1 for domestic and international students; for spring admission, 10/1 for domestic and international students. Applications are processed on a rolling basis. Application fee: $60. Electronic applications accepted. *Financial support:* In 2008–09, 10 research assistantships with full tuition reimbursements (averaging $7,000 per year) were awarded; Federal Work-Study, scholarships/grants, and unspecified assistantships also available. Support available to part-time students. Financial award application deadline: 3/1; financial award applicants required to submit FAFSA. *Faculty research:* Engaged learning, academic and civic development. Total annual research expenditures: $10,000. *Unit head:* Dr. Peter Vietze, Chairperson, 973-655-5201. *Application contact:* Amy Aiello, Associate Director of Admissions, 973-655-5147, Fax: 973-655-7869, E-mail: graduate.school@montclair.edu.

Mount Saint Vincent University, Graduate Programs, Faculty of Education, Program in School Psychology, Halifax, NS B3M 2J6, Canada. Offers MASP. *Degree requirements:* For master's, thesis, 500 hour practicum. *Entrance requirements:* For master's, bachelor's degree in psychology or equivalent, related work experience. Electronic applications accepted. *Faculty research:* Relationship between cognitive and emotional development, expression of emotions, cognitive-behavioral constituents of racism.

National-Louis University, National College of Education, Doctoral Programs in Education, Program in Educational Psychology/School Psychology, Chicago, IL 60603. Offers Ed D. Part-time and evening/weekend programs available. *Students:* 1 (woman) full-time, 14 part-time (13 women); includes 4 minority (2 African Americans, 2 Hispanic Americans). Average age 35. *Degree requirements:* For doctorate, comprehensive exam, thesis/dissertation, internship. *Entrance requirements:* For doctorate, GRE General Test, minimum GPA of 3.25, interview, resumé, writing sample. *Application deadline:* For fall admission, 5/1 for domestic students; for spring admission, 1/15 for domestic students. *Financial support:* Fellowships, research assistantships, teaching assistantships, career-related internships or fieldwork, Federal Work-Study, institutionally sponsored loans, and scholarships/grants available. Support available to part-time students. Financial award application deadline: 4/15; financial award applicants required to submit FAFSA. *Application contact:* Dr. Larry Poselli, Vice President of Enrollment and Student Services, 800-443-5522 Ext. 5718, Fax: 312-261-.3550, E-mail: larry.polselli@nl.edu.

National-Louis University, National College of Education, Programs in School Psychology, Chicago, IL 60603. Offers M Ed, Ed S. *Students:* 9 full-time (all women), 34 part-time (31 women); includes 7 minority (3 African Americans, 4 Hispanic Americans). Average age 30. In 2008, 10 Ed Ss awarded. *Degree requirements:* For master's and Ed S, internship. *Entrance requirements:* For master's, MAT or GRE, minimum GPA of 3.0; for Ed S, GRE, interview, master's degree, writing sample. *Application deadline:* Applications are processed on a rolling basis. *Financial support:* Fellowships, career-related internships or fieldwork, Federal Work-Study, scholarships/grants, and tuition waivers available. Support available to part-time students. *Unit head:* Dr. Diane Salmon, Coordinator, 224-233-2726. *Application contact:* Dr. Larry Poselli, Vice President of Enrollment and Student Services, 800-443-5522 Ext. 5718, Fax: 312-261-.3550, E-mail: larry.polselli@nl.edu.

National University, Academic Affairs, School of Education, Department of School Counseling and Psychology, La Jolla, CA 92037-1011. Offers educational counseling (MS); school psychology (MS). Part-time and evening/weekend programs available. Postbaccalaureate distance learning degree programs offered (no on-campus study). *Faculty:* 10 full-time (4 women), 191 part-time/adjunct (114 women). *Students:* 670 full-time (536 women), 555 part-time (431 women); includes 506 minority (130 African Americans, 9 American Indian/Alaska Native, 69 Asian Americans or Pacific Islanders, 298 Hispanic Americans), 2 international. Average age 34. 674 applicants, 100% accepted, 674 enrolled. In 2008, 121 master's awarded. *Degree requirements:* For master's, thesis (for some programs). *Entrance requirements:* For master's, interview, minimum GPA of 2.5. Additional exam requirements/recommendations for international students: Required—TOEFL (minimum score 550 paper-based; 213 computer-based; 79 iBT), IELTS (minimum score 6). *Application deadline:* Applications are processed on a rolling basis. Application fee: $60 ($65 for international students). Electronic applications accepted. *Expenses:* Tuition: Full-time $8694; part-time $322 per credit hour. Tuition and fees vary according to course load. *Financial support:* Career-related internships or fieldwork, institutionally sponsored loans, scholarships/grants, and tuition waivers (partial) available. Support available to part-time students. Financial award application deadline: 6/30; financial award applicants required to submit FAFSA. *Unit head:* Dr. Susan Eldred, Chair, 858-642-8372, Fax: 858-642-8724, E-mail: seldred@nu.edu. *Application contact:* Dominick Giovanniello, Associate Regional Dean—San Diego, 800-NAT-UNIV, Fax: 858-541-7792, E-mail: dgiovann@nu.edu.

New Jersey City University, Graduate Studies and Continuing Education, College of Arts and Sciences, Department of Psychology, Program in Educational Psychology, Jersey City, NJ 07305-1597. Offers educational psychology (MA); school psychology (PD). *Degree requirements:*

For PD, summer internship or externship. *Entrance requirements:* For master's, GRE General Test or MAT; for PD, GRE General Test. Additional exam requirements/recommendations for international students: Required—TOEFL.

New Mexico Highlands University, Graduate Studies, School of Education, Las Vegas, NM 87701. Offers curriculum and instruction (MA); education (MA), including counseling, school counseling; educational leadership (MA); exercise and sport sciences (MA), including human performance and sport, sports administration, teacher education; guidance and counseling (MA), including professional counseling, rehabilitation counseling, school counseling; special education (MA), including). Part-time programs available. *Faculty:* 30 full-time (23 women). *Students:* 108 full-time (83 women), 245 part-time (183 women); includes 221 minority (7 African Americans, 19 American Indian/Alaska Native, 3 Asian Americans or Pacific Islanders, 192 Hispanic Americans), 5 international. Average age 39. 89 applicants, 88% accepted, 63 enrolled. In 2008, 117 master's awarded. *Degree requirements:* For master's, comprehensive exam, thesis or alternative. *Entrance requirements:* For master's, minimum undergraduate GPA of 3.0. Additional exam requirements/recommendations for international students: Required—TOEFL (minimum score 540 paper-based; 207 computer-based). *Application deadline:* For fall admission, 8/1 priority date for domestic students. Applications are processed on a rolling basis. Application fee: $15. *Expenses:* Tuition, state resident: full-time $2880; part-time $120 per credit hour. Tuition, nonresident: full-time $4234; part-time $176 per credit hour. International tuition: $5645 full-time. One-time fee: $20. *Financial support:* In 2008–09, 180 students received support, including 16 teaching assistantships with full and partial tuition reimbursements available (averaging $6,500 per year); career-related internships or fieldwork, Federal Work-Study, institutionally sponsored loans, scholarships/grants, traineeships, tuition waivers (partial), and unspecified assistantships also available. Support available to part-time students. Financial award application deadline: 3/1; financial award applicants required to submit FAFSA. *Faculty research:* Teaching the United States Constitution, middle school curriculum, integrated computer applications for pre-service classroom teachers, adolescent literacy, narrative cognitive modes in NM multicultural setting. *Unit head:* Dr. Michael Anderson, Interim Dean, 505-454-3213, E-mail: mfanderson@nmhu.edu. *Application contact:* Diane Trujillo, Administrative Assistant for Graduate Studies, 505-454-3266, Fax: 505-426-2117, E-mail: dtrujillo@nmhu.edu.

New Mexico State University, Graduate School, College of Education, Department of Counseling and Educational Psychology, Las Cruces, NM 88003-8001. Offers counseling and guidance (MA); counseling psychology (PhD); school psychology (Ed S). *Accreditation:* ACA; APA (one or more programs are accredited); NCATE. Part-time programs available. *Faculty:* 11 full-time (8 women), 4 part-time/adjunct (2 women). *Students:* 62 full-time (46 women), 415 part-time (306 women); includes 48 minority (3 African Americans, 2 American Indian/Alaska Native, 1 Asian American or Pacific Islander, 42 Hispanic Americans), 2 international. Average age 32. 92 applicants, 93% accepted, 28 enrolled. In 2008, 10 master's, 5 doctorates, 12 other advanced degrees awarded. *Degree requirements:* For master's, comprehensive exam, thesis optional, internship; for doctorate, comprehensive exam, thesis/dissertation, internship; for Ed S, thesis or alternative, internship. *Entrance requirements:* For master's, doctorate, and Ed S, GRE General Test, minimum GPA of 3.0. *Application deadline:* For fall admission, 12/15 for domestic students; for spring admission, 4/1 priority date for domestic students. Application fee: $30 ($50 for international students). Electronic applications accepted. *Expenses:* Tuition, area resident: Full-time $3890; part-time $212.85 per credit. Tuition, state resident: full-time $3890; part-time $212.85 per credit. Tuition, nonresident: full-time $13,916; part-time $630.55 per credit. Required fees: $1218; $609 per semester. *Financial support:* In 2008–09, 68 students received support, including 3 research assistantships with partial tuition reimbursements available (averaging $12,150 per year), 32 teaching assistantships with partial tuition reimbursements available (averaging $7,990 per year); fellowships with partial tuition reimbursements available, career-related internships or fieldwork, Federal Work-Study, institutionally sponsored loans, scholarships/grants, traineeships, health care benefits, and unspecified assistantships also available. Support available to part-time students. Financial award application deadline: 4/1. *Faculty research:* Multicultural counseling, integrative health psychology group, career development school counseling. *Unit head:* Dr. Michael Waldo, Head, 575-646-2121, Fax: 575-646-8035, E-mail: miwaldo@nmsu.edu. *Application contact:* Elena Luna, Coordinator, 575-646-3498, Fax: 575-646-7721, E-mail: rosluna@nmsu.edu.

New York University, Steinhardt School of Culture, Education and Human Development, Department of Applied Psychology, Program in Educational and Developmental Psychology, New York, NY 10012-1019. Offers educational psychology (MA), including general educational psychology, psychological measurement and evaluation, psychology of parenthood; psychological development (PhD); school psychology (PhD). *Accreditation:* APA (one or more programs are accredited). Part-time and evening/weekend programs available. Terminal master's awarded for partial completion of doctoral program. *Degree requirements:* For master's, thesis (for some programs); for doctorate, thesis/dissertation. *Entrance requirements:* For doctorate, GRE General Test, interview. Additional exam requirements/recommendations for international students: Required—TOEFL. *Faculty research:* High risk children and youth; child and adolescent developments; families and schooling; infant cognition; exploration, language, and symbolic play in toddlerhood.

Niagara University, Graduate Division of Education, Concentration in School Psychology, Niagara Falls, Niagara University, NY 14109. Offers MS, Certificate. *Students:* 20 full-time (14 women), 11 part-time (10 women), 1 international. Average age 25. In 2008, 9 master's, 9 other advanced degrees awarded. *Expenses:* Tuition: Full-time $12,330; part-time $685 per contact hour. Required fees: $25 per semester. Tuition and fees vary according to program. *Unit head:* Dr. Shannon Hodges, Chair, 716-286-8328. *Application contact:* Carlos Tejada, Associate Dean for Graduate Recruitment, 716-286-8769, Fax: 716-286-8170.

Nicholls State University, Graduate Studies, College of Education, Department of Psychology and Counselor Education, Thibodaux, LA 70310. Offers psychological counseling (MA); school psychology (SSP). *Accreditation:* NCATE. Part-time and evening/weekend programs available. *Degree requirements:* For master's, comprehensive exam; for SSP, comprehensive exam, internship. *Entrance requirements:* For master's, GRE General Test. Electronic applications accepted.

North Carolina State University, Graduate School, College of Humanities and Social Sciences, Department of Psychology, Raleigh, NC 27695. Offers developmental psychology (PhD); ergonomics and experimental psychology (PhD); industrial/organizational psychology (PhD); psychology in the public interest (PhD); school psychology (PhD). *Accreditation:* APA. *Degree requirements:* For doctorate, comprehensive exam, thesis/dissertation. *Entrance requirements:* For doctorate, GRE General Test, GRE Subject Test (industrial/organizational psychology), MAT (recommended), minimum GPA of 3.0 in major. Electronic applications accepted. *Faculty research:* Cognitive and social development (human factors, families, the workplace, community issues and health, aging).

Northeastern University, Bouvé College of Health Sciences Graduate School, Department of Counseling and Applied Educational Psychology, Program in Applied Educational Psychology, Boston, MA 02115-5096. Offers school counseling (MS); school psychology (MS). Part-time programs available. *Entrance requirements:* For master's, GRE General Test or MAT. Additional exam requirements/recommendations for international students: Required—TOEFL. *Faculty research:* Multicultural issues, assessment, early intervention, bilingual education.

Northeastern University, Bouvé College of Health Sciences Graduate School, Department of Counseling and Applied Educational Psychology, Program in School Psychology, Boston, MA 02115-5096. Offers PhD, CAGS. *Accreditation:* APA (one or more programs are accredited). Part-time programs available. *Degree requirements:* For doctorate, comprehensive exam, thesis/dissertation, qualifying exams; for CAGS, comprehensive exam. *Entrance requirements:* For doctorate, GRE General Test, school psychologist certificate; for CAGS, GRE General Test or MAT, MS in school psychology or related field. Additional exam requirements/

School Psychology

Northeastern University (continued)
recommendations for international students: Required—TOEFL. *Faculty research:* Multicultural education, early intervention.

Northern Arizona University, Graduate College, College of Education, Program in Educational Psychology, Flagstaff, AZ 86011. Offers counseling psychology (PhD); learning and instruction (PhD); school psychology (PhD). *Degree requirements:* For doctorate, comprehensive exam, thesis/dissertation, internship. *Entrance requirements:* For doctorate, GRE General Test.

Northern Arizona University, Graduate College, College of Education, Program in School Psychology, Flagstaff, AZ 86011. Offers MA. *Degree requirements:* For master's, internship. *Entrance requirements:* For master's, GRE General Test.

Northwest Nazarene University, Graduate Studies, Program in Counselor Education, Nampa, ID 83686-5897. Offers community counseling (MS); marriage and family counseling (MS); school counseling (MS). *Faculty:* 3 full-time (2 women), 10 part-time/adjunct (5 women). *Students:* 45 full-time (29 women), 13 part-time (7 women); includes 2 minority (1 American Indian/Alaska Native, 1 Asian American or Pacific Islander). In 2008, 19 master's awarded. Application fee: $25. *Unit head:* Dr. Brenda Freeman, Chair, 208-467-8428, Fax: 208-467-8339. *Application contact:* Susan Marion, Secretary, 208-467-8345, Fax: 208-467-8339, E-mail: sjmarion@nnu.edu.

Nova Southeastern University, Center for Psychological Studies, Specialist Program in School Psychology, Fort Lauderdale, FL 33314-7796. Offers Psy S. Evening/weekend programs available. Postbaccalaureate distance learning degree programs offered. *Faculty:* 6 full-time (3 women), 16 part-time/adjunct (10 women). *Students:* 59 full-time (51 women), 61 part-time (58 women); includes 60 minority (33 African Americans, 5 Asian Americans or Pacific Islanders, 22 Hispanic Americans), 1 international. 110 applicants, 50% accepted, 37 enrolled. In 2008, 20 Psy Ss awarded. *Degree requirements:* For Psy S, comprehensive exam, internship. *Entrance requirements:* Additional exam requirements/recommendations for international students: Required—TOEFL (minimum score 530 paper-based; 213 computer-based). *Application deadline:* For fall admission, 2/22 priority date for domestic and international students; for winter admission, 6/30 priority date for domestic and international students. Applications are processed on a rolling basis. Application fee: $50. Electronic applications accepted. *Financial support:* In 2008–09, 1 teaching assistantship was awarded; research assistantships, career-related internships or fieldwork, Federal Work-Study, scholarships/grants, and unspecified assistantships also available. *Unit head:* Karen S. Grosby, Dean, 954-262-5701, Fax: 954-262-3859. *Application contact:* Carlos Perez, Enrollment Management, 954-262-5790, Fax: 954-262-3893, E-mail: cpsinfo@cps.nova.edu.

Oregon State University–Cascades, Program in Counseling, Bend, OR 97701. Offers community counseling (MS); school counseling (MS).

Ottawa University, Graduate Studies-Arizona, Program in Education, Ottawa, KS 66067-3399. Offers community college counseling (MA); curriculum and instruction (MA); early childhood (MA); education intervention (MA); education leadership (MA); education technology (MA); Montessori early childhood education (MA); Montessori elementary education (MA); professional development (MA); school guidance counseling (MA); special education—cross categorical (MA). Programs offered in Mesa, Phoenix, Tempe and West Valley, AZ. *Accreditation:* NCATE. Part-time programs available. *Degree requirements:* For master's, thesis or alternative. *Entrance requirements:* For master's, minimum undergraduate GPA of 3.0, copy of current state certification or teaching license. Additional exam requirements/recommendations for international students: Required—TOEFL (minimum score 550 paper-based; 213 computer-based). Electronic applications accepted. *Expenses:* Contact institution.

Our Lady of the Lake University of San Antonio, School of Professional Studies, Program in Psychology, San Antonio, TX 78207-4689. Offers counseling psychology (MS, Psy D); marriage and family therapy (MS); school psychology (MS). *Accreditation:* APA (one or more programs are accredited). Part-time and evening/weekend programs available. *Students:* 99 full-time (83 women), 97 part-time (86 women); includes 117 minority (25 African Americans, 1 American Indian/Alaska Native, 3 Asian Americans or Pacific Islanders, 88 Hispanic Americans), 2 international. Average age 30. In 2008, 42 master's, 3 doctorates awarded. *Degree requirements:* For master's, comprehensive exam, thesis optional, practicum; for doctorate, thesis/dissertation, internship, qualifying exam. *Entrance requirements:* For master's and doctorate, GRE General Test or MAT, interview. Additional exam requirements/recommendations for international students: Required—TOEFL. *Application deadline:* For fall admission, 3/1 priority date for domestic and international students. Applications are processed on a rolling basis. Application fee: $25 ($50 for international students). Electronic applications accepted. *Expenses:* Tuition: Full-time $11,970; part-time $665 per credit hour. Required fees: $500; $250 per term. *Financial support:* Research assistantships, teaching assistantships, career-related internships or fieldwork available. Support available to part-time students. Financial award application deadline: 4/15. *Faculty research:* Marriage and family therapy, supervision, cross-cultural counseling, violence. *Unit head:* Dr. Kathryn Anderson, Chair, 210-434-6711, E-mail: andek@lake.ollusa.edu. *Application contact:* 210-434-6711 Ext. 2314, Fax: 210-431-4036, E-mail: gradadm@lake.ollusa.edu.

Pace University, Dyson College of Arts and Sciences, Department of Psychology, Program in School Psychology, New York, NY 10038. Offers MS Ed. Electronic applications accepted.

Penn State University Park, Graduate School, College of Education, Department of Educational and School Psychology and Special Education, State College, University Park, PA 16802-1503. Offers educational psychology (MS, PhD); school psychology (M Ed, MS, PhD); special education (M Ed, MS, PhD).

Philadelphia College of Osteopathic Medicine, Graduate and Professional Programs, Department of Psychology, Philadelphia, PA 19131-1694. Offers clinical psychology (Psy D); counseling and clinical health psychology (MS); organizational leadership and development (MS); psychology (Certificate); school psychology (MS, Psy D, Ed S). *Accreditation:* APA. *Degree requirements:* For master's, thesis; for doctorate, comprehensive exam, thesis/dissertation, final project, fieldwork. *Entrance requirements:* For master's, GRE or MAT, minimum GPA of 3.0; course work in biology, chemistry, English, physics; for other advanced degree, PRAXIS. *Faculty research:* Depression in primary care, integrated primary care, geriatric mental health.

See Close-Up on page 1127.

Pittsburg State University, Graduate School, College of Education, Department of Psychology and Counseling, Program in School Psychology, Pittsburg, KS 66762. Offers Ed S. *Accreditation:* NCATE. *Degree requirements:* For Ed S, thesis or alternative. *Entrance requirements:* For degree, GRE General Test, minimum GPA of 3.0.

Purdue University Calumet, Graduate School, School of Education, Program in Counseling, Hammond, IN 46323-2094. Offers human services (MS Ed); mental health counseling (MS Ed); school counseling (MS Ed). *Entrance requirements:* Additional exam requirements/recommendations for international students: Required—TOEFL.

Queens College of the City University of New York, Division of Graduate Studies, Division of Education, Department of Educational and Community Programs, Program in School Psychology, Flushing, NY 11367-1597. Offers MS Ed, AC. Part-time programs available. *Degree requirements:* For master's, internship, research project; for AC, thesis optional, internship. *Entrance requirements:* For master's, minimum GPA of 3.0; for AC, master's degree or equivalent. Additional exam requirements/recommendations for international students: Required—TOEFL.

Radford University, College of Graduate and Professional Studies, College of Education and Human Development, Department of Counselor Education, Radford, VA 24142. Offers community counseling (MS); school counseling (MS); student administration counseling (MS); student affairs counseling (MS). *Accreditation:* ACA; NCATE. Part-time and evening/weekend programs available. *Faculty:* 9 full-time (5 women), 1 (woman) part-time/adjunct. *Students:* 52 full-time (43 women), 75 part-time (63 women); includes 9 minority (6 African Americans, 1 Asian American or Pacific Islander, 2 Hispanic Americans). Average age 31. 91 applicants, 82% accepted, 52 enrolled. In 2008, 60 master's awarded. *Degree requirements:* For master's, comprehensive exam, thesis optional. *Entrance requirements:* For master's, GRE or MAT. Additional exam requirements/recommendations for international students: Required—TOEFL (minimum score 550 paper-based; 213 computer-based; 79 iBT). *Application deadline:* For fall admission, 3/1 priority date for domestic students, 12/1 for international students; for spring admission, 10/1 for domestic students, 7/1 for international students. Applications are processed on a rolling basis. Application fee: $40. Electronic applications accepted. *Expenses:* Tuition, area resident: full-time $4845; part-time $202 per credit. Tuition, state resident: full-time $4845; part-time $202 per credit. Tuition, nonresident: full-time $11,483; part-time $478 per credit. Required fees: $2349; $98 per credit. *Financial support:* In 2008–09, 86 students received support, including 27 research assistantships with partial tuition reimbursements available (averaging $8,000 per year), 4 teaching assistantships with partial tuition reimbursements available (averaging $8,700 per year); career-related internships or fieldwork, Federal Work-Study, institutionally sponsored loans, scholarships/grants, and unspecified assistantships also available. Financial award application deadline: 3/1; financial award applicants required to submit FAFSA. *Unit head:* Dr. Alan Forrest, Chair, 540-831-5487, Fax: 540-831-6755, E-mail: aforrest@radford.edu. *Application contact:* Graduate Admissions, 540-831-5431, Fax: 540-831-6061, E-mail: gradcollege@radford.edu.

Radford University, College of Graduate and Professional Studies, College of Humanities and Behavioral Sciences, Program in Psychology, Radford, VA 24142. Offers clinical psychology (MA, MS); counseling psychology (Psy D); experimental psychology (MA); general psychology (MS); industrial/organizational psychology (MA, MS); school psychology (Ed S). Part-time programs available. *Faculty:* 23 full-time (9 women), 1 part-time/adjunct (0 women). *Students:* 46 full-time (28 women), 5 part-time (4 women); includes 4 minority (3 African Americans, 1 Asian American or Pacific Islander), 2 international. Average age 26. 114 applicants, 42% accepted, 20 enrolled. In 2008, 36 master's awarded. *Degree requirements:* For master's, comprehensive exam, thesis (for some programs). *Entrance requirements:* For master's, GRE, minimum GPA of 3.0; 3 letters of reference; essay. Additional exam requirements/recommendations for international students: Required—TOEFL (minimum score 550 paper-based; 213 computer-based; 79 iBT). *Application deadline:* For fall admission, 3/1 priority date for domestic students, 12/1 for international students; for spring admission, 10/1 for domestic students, 7/1 for international students. Applications are processed on a rolling basis. Application fee: $40. Electronic applications accepted. *Expenses:* Tuition, area resident: Full-time $4845; part-time $202 per credit. Tuition, state resident: full-time $4845; part-time $202 per credit. Tuition, nonresident: full-time $11,483; part-time $478 per credit. Required fees: $2349; $98 per credit. *Financial support:* In 2008–09, 47 students received support, including 33 research assistantships with partial tuition reimbursements available (averaging $8,000 per year), 12 teaching assistantships with partial tuition reimbursements available (averaging $8,700 per year); career-related internships or fieldwork, institutionally sponsored loans, scholarships/grants, and unspecified assistantships also available. Financial award application deadline: 3/1; financial award applicants required to submit FAFSA. *Unit head:* Dr. Hilary M. Lips, Chair, 540-831-5387, Fax: 540-831-6113, E-mail: hlips@radford.edu. *Application contact:* Graduate Admissions Office, 540-831-5431, Fax: 540-831-6061, E-mail: gradcollege@radford.edu.

Radford University, College of Graduate and Professional Studies, College of Humanities and Behavioral Sciences, Program in School Psychology, Radford, VA 24142. Offers Ed S. *Accreditation:* NCATE. *Faculty:* 23 full-time (9 women), 1 part-time/adjunct (0 women). *Students:* 15 full-time (12 women), 5 part-time (4 women); includes 1 minority (African American). Average age 25. 35 applicants, 77% accepted, 20 enrolled. In 2008, 12 Ed Ss awarded. *Degree requirements:* For Ed S, comprehensive exam. *Entrance requirements:* For degree, GRE, minimum GPA of 3.0; 2 letters of reference; essay. Additional exam requirements/recommendations for international students: Required—TOEFL (minimum score 550 paper-based; 213 computer-based; 79 iBT). *Application deadline:* For fall admission, 3/1 priority date for domestic students, 12/1 for international students; for spring admission, 10/1 for domestic students, 7/1 for international students. Applications are processed on a rolling basis. Application fee: $40. Electronic applications accepted. *Expenses:* Tuition, area resident: Full-time $4845; part-time $202 per credit. Tuition, state resident: full-time $4845; part-time $202 per credit. Tuition, nonresident: full-time $11,483; part-time $478 per credit. Required fees: $2349; $98 per credit. *Financial support:* In 2008–09, 17 students received support, including 6 research assistantships with partial tuition reimbursements available (averaging $8,000 per year); career-related internships or fieldwork, Federal Work-Study, institutionally sponsored loans, scholarships/grants, and unspecified assistantships also available. Financial award application deadline: 3/1; financial award applicants required to submit FAFSA. *Unit head:* Dr. Jayne Bucy, Coordinator, 540-831-5341, Fax: 540-831-6113, E-mail: jebucy@radford.edu. *Application contact:* Graduate Admissions, 540-831-5431, Fax: 540-831-6061, E-mail: gradcollege@radford.edu.

Rider University, Department of Graduate Education, Leadership and Counseling, Program in School Psychology, Lawrenceville, NJ 08648-3001. Offers Certificate, Ed S. *Entrance requirements:* For degree, GRE or MAT, resumé, 2 professional references, interview, 1 year of counseling experience. Additional exam requirements/recommendations for international students: Required—TOEFL (minimum score 550 paper-based; 213 computer-based). *Faculty research:* Prenatal factors on child development, child abuse developmental assessments.

Roberts Wesleyan College, Division of Social Sciences, Rochester, NY 14624-1997. Offers counseling in ministry (MA); school counseling (MS); school psychology (MS).

Rochester Institute of Technology, Graduate Enrollment Services, College of Liberal Arts, Department of Behavioral Science, Program in School Psychology, Rochester, NY 14623-5603. Offers MS, AC. *Degree requirements:* For master's, comprehensive exam. *Entrance requirements:* For master's, GRE General Test, minimum GPA of 3.0. Additional exam requirements/recommendations for international students: Required—TOEFL (minimum score 580 paper-based; 237 computer-based; 92 iBT). Electronic applications accepted.

Rowan University, Graduate School, College of Education, Department of Special Educational Services/Instruction, Program in School Psychology, Glassboro, NJ 08028-1701. Offers MA, Ed S. *Accreditation:* NCATE. Part-time and evening/weekend programs available. *Students:* 45 full-time (37 women), 35 part-time (28 women); includes 10 minority (1 American Indian/Alaska Native, 5 Asian Americans or Pacific Islanders, 4 Hispanic Americans). Average age 27. 48 applicants, 60% accepted, 24 enrolled. In 2008, 43 master's awarded. *Degree requirements:* For master's, thesis; for Ed S, thesis or alternative. *Entrance requirements:* For master's, GRE, interview, minimum GPA of 3.0. Additional exam requirements/recommendations for international students: Required—TOEFL. *Application deadline:* For fall admission, 10/15 for domestic students; for spring admission, 2/15 for domestic students. Application fee: $50. Electronic applications accepted. *Expenses:* Tuition, area resident: Full-time $10,624; part-time $590 per credit. Tuition, state resident: full-time $10,624; part-time $590 per credit. Tuition, nonresident: full-time $10,624; part-time $590 per credit. Required fees: $2258; $124.90 per credit. *Financial support:* Career-related internships or fieldwork, scholarships/grants, health care benefits, and unspecified assistantships available. Support available to part-time students. *Unit head:* Dr. Mira Lalovic-Hand, Interim Associate Provost/Director of Graduate School, 856-256-5120, E-mail: Lalovic-hand@rowan.edu. *Application contact:* Karen Haynes, Graduate Coordinator, 856-256-4052, Fax: 856-256-4436, E-mail: Haynes@rowan.edu.

Rutgers, The State University of New Jersey, New Brunswick, Graduate School of Applied and Professional Psychology, Program in School Psychology, Piscataway, NJ 08854-8097. Offers Psy M, Psy D. *Accreditation:* APA (one or more programs are accredited). *Degree requirements:* For doctorate, comprehensive exam, thesis/dissertation, 1 year internship. *Entrance requirements:* For doctorate, GRE General Test, GRE Subject Test, bachelor's degree in psychology or equivalent. Additional exam requirements/recommendations for international students: Required—TOEFL. Electronic applications accepted. *Expenses:* Contact institution. *Faculty research:* Consultation, program evaluation, applied educational psychology, exceptional children, crisis intervention.

St. John's University, St. John's College of Liberal Arts and Sciences, Department of Psychology, Program in School Psychology, Queens, NY 11439. Offers MS, Psy D. Part-time programs available. *Students:* 131 full-time (120 women), 47 part-time (39 women); includes 25 minority (6 African Americans, 8 Asian Americans or Pacific Islanders, 11 Hispanic Americans), 2 international. Average age 27. 172 applicants, 38% accepted, 41 enrolled. In 2008, 30 master's, 16 doctorates awarded. *Degree requirements:* For master's, comprehensive exam, thesis optional; for doctorate, comprehensive exam, thesis/dissertation, internship. *Entrance requirements:* For master's, GRE General Test, GRE Subject Test, minimum GPA of 3.0, 2 writing samples; for doctorate, GRE General Test, GRE Subject Test, interview, minimum GPA of 3.0. Additional exam requirements/recommendations for international students: Required—TOEFL (minimum score 500 paper-based; 173 computer-based; 61 iBT), IELTS (minimum score 5.5). *Application deadline:* For fall admission, 2/1 for domestic students, 5/1 priority date for international students; for spring admission, 11/1 priority date for international students. Applications are processed on a rolling basis. Application fee: $70. Electronic applications accepted. *Expenses:* Contact institution. *Financial support:* Fellowships, research assistantships, career-related internships or fieldwork, scholarships/grants, and unspecified assistantships available. Support available to part-time students. Financial award application deadline: 3/1; financial award applicants required to submit FAFSA. *Faculty research:* Therapeutic alliance, intelligence testing, multicultural assessment, neuropsychological assessment, adolescent suicide. *Unit head:* Dr. Dawn Flanagan, Director, 718-990-5861, E-mail: flanagad@stjohns.edu. *Application contact:* Kathleen Davis, Director of Graduate Admission, 718-990-2790, Fax: 718-990-5686, E-mail: gradhelp@stjohns.edu.

San Diego State University, Graduate and Research Affairs, College of Education, Department of Counseling and School Psychology, San Diego, CA 92182. Offers MS. *Accreditation:* NCATE. Evening/weekend programs available. *Degree requirements:* For master's, comprehensive exam (for some programs), thesis (for some programs). *Entrance requirements:* For master's, GRE General Test, interview, letters of reference. Additional exam requirements/recommendations for international students: Required—TOEFL. Electronic applications accepted. *Faculty research:* Multicultural and cross-cultural counseling and training, AIDS counseling.

Seattle University, College of Education, Program in Counseling and School Psychology, Seattle, WA 98122-1090. Offers MA, Certificate, Ed S. *Accreditation:* NCATE. Part-time and evening/weekend programs available. *Degree requirements:* For master's, comprehensive exam. *Entrance requirements:* For master's, interview; GRE, MAT, or minimum GPA of 3.0; related work experience. Additional exam requirements/recommendations for international students: Required—TOEFL.

Seton Hall University, College of Education and Human Services, Department of Professional Psychology and Family Therapy, Program in School Psychology, South Orange, NJ 07079-2697. Offers Ed S. *Degree requirements:* For Ed S, comprehensive exam, thesis, internship. *Entrance requirements:* For degree, GRE or MAT, interview. *Faculty research:* Family systems, ethical behavior, childhood depression.

Southeast Missouri State University, School of Graduate Studies, Department of Educational Leadership and Counseling, Counseling Program, Cape Girardeau, MO 63701-4799. Offers counseling education (Ed S); mental health counseling (MA); school counseling (MA), including elementary counseling, secondary counseling. *Accreditation:* ACA; NCATE. Part-time and evening/weekend programs available. *Faculty:* 5 full-time (3 women). *Students:* 17 full-time (15 women), 50 part-time (44 women); includes 3 minority (2 African Americans, 1 Asian American or Pacific Islander). Average age 33. 19 applicants, 89% accepted. In 2008, 23 master's, 5 other advanced degrees awarded. *Degree requirements:* For master's, comprehensive exam, thesis optional, portfolio, oral exam; for Ed S, oral exam. *Entrance requirements:* For master's, GRE General Test, MAT, minimum undergraduate GPA of 3.0; for Ed S, GRE General Test or MAT, minimum graduate GPA of 3.5. Additional exam requirements/recommendations for international students: Required—TOEFL (minimum score 550 paper-based; 213 computer-based); Recommended—IELTS (minimum score 6). *Application deadline:* For fall admission, 8/1 for domestic students, 7/1 for international students; for spring admission, 11/21 for domestic students, 11/1 for international students. Applications are processed on a rolling basis. Application fee: $25 ($100 for international students). Electronic applications accepted. *Expenses:* Tuition, area resident: Part-time $213.30 per credit hour. Tuition, state resident: part-time $213.30 per credit hour. Tuition, nonresident: part-time $393.30 per credit hour. Required fees: $23.70 per credit hour. *Financial support:* In 2008–09, 11 students received support, including 11 research assistantships with full tuition reimbursements available (averaging $7,600 per year); unspecified assistantships also available. Financial award applicants required to submit FAFSA. *Faculty research:* Counselor development, cognitive development of counselors, counselor supervision, issues in school counseling, issues in mental health counseling. *Unit head:* Dr. Margaret Noe, Dean, College of Education, 573-651-2408, E-mail: mnoe@semo.edu. *Application contact:* Marsha L. Arant, Senior Administrative Assistant, School of Graduate Studies, 573-651-2192, Fax: 573-651-2001, E-mail: marant@semo.edu.

Southern Connecticut State University, School of Graduate Studies, School of Education, Department of Counseling and School Psychology, New Haven, CT 06515-1355. Offers community counseling (MS); counseling (Diploma); school counseling (MS); school psychology (MS, Diploma). *Accreditation:* ACA (one or more programs are accredited); NCATE. *Degree requirements:* For master's, comprehensive exam. *Entrance requirements:* For master's, interview, previous course work in behavioral sciences, minimum QPA of 2.7. Electronic applications accepted.

Southern Illinois University Edwardsville, Graduate Studies and Research, School of Education, Department of Psychology, Program in School Psychology, Edwardsville, IL 62026-0001. Offers SD. *Accreditation:* NCATE. Part-time programs available. *Students:* 8 part-time (all women). Average age 26. 10 applicants, 0% accepted. In 2008, 12 SDs awarded. *Degree requirements:* For SD, thesis. *Entrance requirements:* For degree, GRE. Additional exam requirements/recommendations for international students: Required—TOEFL (minimum score 550 paper-based; 213 computer-based; 79 iBT), IELTS (minimum score 6.5). *Application deadline:* For spring admission, 2/1 for domestic and international students. Application fee: $30. Electronic applications accepted. *Expenses:* Tuition, area resident: Full-time $5838. Tuition, nonresident: full-time $14,596. Required fees: $1525. *Financial support:* Fellowships, research assistantships, teaching assistantships, career-related internships or fieldwork, Federal Work-Study, institutionally sponsored loans, traineeships, and unspecified assistantships available. Financial award application deadline: 3/1; financial award applicants required to submit FAFSA. *Unit head:* Dr. Lynn Bartels, Director, 618-650-2202, E-mail: lbartel@siue.edu. *Application contact:* Dr. Lynn Bartels, Director, 618-650-2202, E-mail: lbartel@siue.edu.

Southwestern Oklahoma State University, College of Professional and Graduate Studies, School of Behavioral Sciences and Education, Specialization in School Psychology, Weatherford, OK 73096-3098. Offers MS.

State University of New York at Oswego, Graduate Studies, School of Education, Department of Counseling and Psychological Services, Program in School Psychology, Oswego, NY 13126. Offers MS, CAS, MS/CAS. *Degree requirements:* For master's, comprehensive exam, fieldwork; for CAS, thesis, fieldwork. *Entrance requirements:* For master's, GRE General Test, interview, minimum GPA of 3.0; for CAS, GRE General Test, interview, MA or MS, minimum GPA of 3.0. Additional exam requirements/recommendations for international students: Required—TOEFL (minimum score 560 paper-based; 220 computer-based). *Faculty research:* Psychological applications in education and human services, evaluation of standard tests for admissions criteria.

State University of New York at Plattsburgh, Faculty of Arts and Science, Department of Psychology, Plattsburgh, NY 12901-2681. Offers school psychology (MA, CAS). Part-time programs available. *Faculty:* 2 full-time (1 woman), 3 part-time/adjunct (2 women). *Students:* 18 full-time (14 women), 7 part-time (5 women); includes 3 minority (1 Asian American or Pacific Islander, 2 Hispanic Americans), 1 international. Average age 26. 22 applicants, 77% accepted, 9 enrolled. In 2008, 8 master's, 8 other advanced degrees awarded. *Degree requirements:* For master's, thesis, internship. *Entrance requirements:* For master's, GRE General Test, minimum GPA of 3.0. Additional exam requirements/recommendations for international students: Required—TOEFL (minimum score 550 paper-based; 213 computer-based; 79 iBT). *Application deadline:* For fall admission, 2/15 priority date for domestic students. Applications are processed on a rolling basis. Application fee: $75. *Expenses:* Tuition, area resident: Full-time $7880; part-time $328 per credit hour. Tuition, state resident: full-time $7880; part-time $328 per credit hour. Tuition, nonresident: full-time $13,250; part-time $552 per credit hour. Required fees: $1060. *Financial support:* Federal Work-Study available. Support available to part-time students. Financial award application deadline: 4/15; financial award applicants required to submit FAFSA. *Faculty research:* Alzheimer's disease, adolescent behavior, intellectual assessment, learning disabilities, reading skill acquisition. *Unit head:* Dr. Wendy Braje, Chair, 518-564-3383, E-mail: brajewl@plattsburgh.edu. *Application contact:* Marguerite Adelman, Assistant Director, Graduate Admissions, 518-564-4723, Fax: 518-564-4722, E-mail: adelmaml@plattsburgh.edu.

Stephen F. Austin State University, Graduate School, College of Education, Department of Human Services, Nacogdoches, TX 75962. Offers counseling (MA); school psychology (MA); special education (M Ed); speech pathology (MS). *Accreditation:* ACA (one or more programs are accredited); ASHA (one or more programs are accredited); CORE; NCATE. *Degree requirements:* For master's, comprehensive exam, thesis (for some programs). *Entrance requirements:* For master's, GRE General Test, minimum GPA of 2.8. Additional exam requirements/recommendations for international students: Required—TOEFL.

Syracuse University, Graduate School, College of Arts and Sciences, Program in School Psychology, Syracuse, NY 13244. Offers PhD. *Accreditation:* APA. *Degree requirements:* For doctorate, thesis/dissertation. *Entrance requirements:* For doctorate, GRE General Test, GRE Subject Test. Additional exam requirements/recommendations for international students: Required—TOEFL. Electronic applications accepted.

Syracuse University, Graduate School, School of Education, Program in School Counseling, Syracuse, NY 13244. Offers MS, CAS. *Entrance requirements:* For master's, GRE General Test or MAT, interview. Additional exam requirements/recommendations for international students: Required—TOEFL.

Tarleton State University, College of Graduate Studies, College of Education, Department of Psychology and Counseling, Stephenville, TX 76402. Offers counseling and psychology (M Ed), including counseling, counseling psychology, educational psychology; educational administration (M Ed); secondary education (Certificate); special education (Certificate). Part-time and evening/weekend programs available. Postbaccalaureate distance learning degree programs offered (minimal on-campus study). *Faculty:* 17 full-time (8 women), 11 part-time/adjunct (5 women). *Students:* 70 full-time (59 women), 271 part-time (244 women); includes 100 minority (59 African Americans, 4 American Indian/Alaska Native, 5 Asian Americans or Pacific Islanders, 32 Hispanic Americans). Average age 35. 104 applicants, 76% accepted, 60 enrolled. In 2008, 75 master's awarded. *Degree requirements:* For master's, comprehensive exam, thesis optional. *Entrance requirements:* For master's, GRE General Test, minimum GPA of 3.0. Additional exam requirements/recommendations for international students: Required—TOEFL (minimum score 550 paper-based; 213 computer-based; 80 iBT). *Application deadline:* For fall admission, 8/5 priority date for domestic students; for spring admission, 12/1 for domestic students. Applications are processed on a rolling basis. Application fee: $30 ($130 for international students). Electronic applications accepted. *Expenses:* Tuition, area resident: Full-time $2853; part-time $158.50 per credit hour. Tuition, state resident: full-time $2853; part-time $158.50 per credit hour. Tuition, nonresident: full-time $7551; part-time $419.50 per credit hour. Required fees: $1040; $42 per credit hour. $124 per semester. Tuition and fees vary according to course load and campus/location. *Financial support:* In 2008–09, 3 research assistantships (averaging $13,778 per year) were awarded; teaching assistantships, career-related internships or fieldwork, Federal Work-Study, institutionally sponsored loans, and tuition waivers (partial) also available. Support available to part-time students. Financial award application deadline: 5/1; financial award applicants required to submit FAFSA. *Unit head:* Dr. David Weissenburger, Department Head and Professor, 254-968-9090, Fax: 254-968-1991, E-mail: weissenburge@tarleton.edu. *Application contact:* Information Contact, 254-968-9104, Fax: 254-968-9670, E-mail: gradoffice@tarleton.edu.

Teachers College, Columbia University, Graduate Faculty of Education, Department of Health and Behavioral Studies, Program in Applied Educational Psychology–School Psychology, New York, NY 10027-6696. Offers Ed M, MA, Ed D, PhD. *Accreditation:* APA (one or more programs are accredited). *Faculty:* 2 full-time (1 woman), 3 part-time/adjunct. *Students:* 50 full-time (48 women), 39 part-time (35 women); includes 18 minority (6 African Americans, 9 Asian Americans or Pacific Islanders, 3 Hispanic Americans), 4 international. Average age 31. 208 applicants, 26% accepted, 22 enrolled. In 2008, 24 master's, 5 doctorates awarded. *Degree requirements:* For master's, integrative paper; for doctorate, thesis/dissertation, integrative project. *Entrance requirements:* For doctorate, GRE General Test. *Application deadline:* For fall admission, 5/15 for domestic students. Application fee: $75. *Expenses:* Tuition: Full-time $26,040; part-time $1085 per credit. Required fees: $720. *Financial support:* Fellowships, research assistantships, career-related internships or fieldwork, Federal Work-Study, institutionally sponsored loans, and tuition waivers (full and partial) available. Support available to part-time students. Financial award application deadline: 2/1. *Faculty research:* Psychoeducational assessment, observation and concept acquisition in young children, reading, mathematical thinking, memory. *Unit head:* Dr. Chuck Basch, Chair, 212-678-3964, E-mail: ceb35@columbia.edu. *Application contact:* Peter Shon, Assistant Director of Admission, 212-678-3305, Fax: 212-678-4171, E-mail: shon@exchange.tc.columbia.edu.

Temple University, Graduate School, College of Education, Department of Psychological Studies in Education, Program in School Psychology, Philadelphia, PA 19122-6096. Offers Ed M, PhD. *Accreditation:* APA (one or more programs are accredited). Part-time and evening/weekend programs available. Terminal master's awarded for partial completion of doctoral program. *Degree requirements:* For master's, thesis or alternative; for doctorate, thesis/dissertation. *Entrance requirements:* For master's and doctorate, GRE General Test, GRE Subject Test, minimum GPA of 3.0. Additional exam requirements/recommendations for international students: Required—TOEFL (minimum score 550 paper-based; 213 computer-based; 79 iBT). Electronic applications accepted.

Tennessee State University, The School of Graduate Studies and Research, College of Education, Department of Psychology, Nashville, TN 37209-1561. Offers counseling and guidance (MS), including counseling, elementary school counseling, organizational counseling, secondary school counseling; counseling psychology (PhD); psychology (MS, PhD); school psychology (MS, PhD). *Accreditation:* APA. *Faculty:* 15 full-time (9 women), 1 (woman) part-time/adjunct. *Students:* 83 full-time (63 women), 94 part-time (79 women); includes 17 African Americans, 1 American Indian/Alaska Native, 1 Asian American or Pacific Islander. Average age 33. 205 applicants, 45% accepted, 44 enrolled. In 2008, 14 master's, 7 doctorates awarded. *Degree requirements:* For doctorate, thesis/dissertation (for some programs). *Entrance requirements:* For master's, GRE General Test or MAT; for doctorate, GRE General Test or MAT, minimum GPA of 3.25, work experience. *Application deadline:* For fall admission, 3/1 priority date for international students. Applications are processed on a rolling basis. Application fee: $25. Electronic applications accepted. *Unit head:* Dr. Linda Guthrie, Head, 615-963-2920, Fax: 615-963-5140, E-mail: lguthrie@tnstate.edu. *Application contact:* Dr. Linda Guthrie, Head, 615-963-2920, Fax: 615-963-5140, E-mail: lguthrie@tnstate.edu.

School Psychology

Texas A&M University, College of Education and Human Development, Department of Educational Psychology, College Station, TX 77843. Offers counseling psychology (PhD); educational psychology (PhD); educational technology (M Ed); gifted and talented education (M Ed, MS); Hispanic bilingual education (M Ed, PhD); human learning and development (MS); intelligence, creativity, and giftedness (PhD); learning, development, and instruction (PhD); research, measurement and statistics (MS); research, measurement, and statistics (PhD); school counseling (M Ed); school psychology (PhD); special education (M Ed, PhD). *Accreditation:* APA (one or more programs are accredited); NCATE. Part-time and evening/weekend programs available. Postbaccalaureate distance learning degree programs offered (no on-campus study). *Faculty:* 46. *Students:* 161 full-time (129 women), 148 part-time (126 women); includes 86 minority (26 African Americans, 1 American Indian/Alaska Native, 11 Asian Americans or Pacific Islanders, 48 Hispanic Americans), 38 international. In 2008, 47 master's, 20 doctorates awarded. *Degree requirements:* For master's, thesis optional; for doctorate, thesis/dissertation. *Entrance requirements:* For master's and doctorate, GRE General Test. Additional exam requirements/recommendations for international students: Required—TOEFL. Application fee: $50 ($75 for international students). Electronic applications accepted. *Expenses:* Tuition, area resident: Full-time $3838.50. Tuition, state resident: full-time $3838.50. Tuition, nonresident: full-time $8897. Required fees: $2359.60. *Financial support:* In 2008–09, fellowships (averaging $12,000 per year), research assistantships (averaging $9,000 per year), teaching assistantships (averaging $9,000 per year) were awarded; career-related internships or fieldwork, institutionally sponsored loans, scholarships/grants, and unspecified assistantships also available. Financial award applicants required to submit FAFSA. *Unit head:* Dr. Victor Willson, Head, 979-845-1800, E-mail: v-willson@tamu.edu. *Application contact:* Carol A. Wagner, Director of Advising, 979-845-1833, Fax: 979-862-1256, E-mail: c-wagner@tamu.edu.

Texas State University–San Marcos, Graduate School, College of Education, Department of Educational Administration and Psychological Services, Program in School Psychology, San Marcos, TX 78666. Offers MA. Part-time programs available. *Degree requirements:* For master's, comprehensive exam. *Entrance requirements:* For master's, GRE General Test, interview, minimum GPA of 2.75 in last 60 hours of course work. Additional exam requirements/recommendations for international students: Required—TOEFL (minimum score 550 paper-based; 213 computer-based). Electronic applications accepted.

Texas Woman's University, Graduate School, College of Arts and Sciences, Department of Psychology and Philosophy, Denton, TX 76201. Offers counseling psychology (MA, PhD); school psychology (PhD, SSP). *Accreditation:* APA (one or more programs are accredited). *Faculty:* 14 full-time (9 women), 3 part-time/adjunct (1 woman). *Students:* 61 full-time (50 women), 60 part-time (55 women); includes 27 minority (9 African Americans, 8 Asian Americans or Pacific Islanders, 10 Hispanic Americans), 3 international. Average age 29. In 2008, 24 master's, 5 doctorates awarded. Terminal master's awarded for partial completion of doctoral program. *Degree requirements:* For master's, thesis; for doctorate, comprehensive exam, thesis/dissertation, internship, residency. *Entrance requirements:* For master's, BA/BS or 18 hours in psychology, minimum GPA of 3.5 in undergraduate psychology classes, essay, 3 letters of reference; for doctorate, 3 letters of reference; minimum overall and psychology undergraduate GPA of 3.5; BS/BA in psychology or 18 hours of required psychology classes. Additional exam requirements/recommendations for international students: Required—TOEFL (minimum score 550 paper-based; 213 computer-based; 79 iBT). *Application deadline:* For fall admission, 12/15 for domestic and international students. Applications are processed on a rolling basis. Application fee: $30 ($50 for international students). Electronic applications accepted. *Expenses:* Tuition, state resident: full-time $3564; part-time $198 per semester hour. Tuition, nonresident: full-time $8622; part-time $479 per semester hour. Required fees: $1158; $64 per semester hour. Tuition and fees vary according to course load. *Financial support:* In 2008–09, 14 research assistantships (averaging $10,746 per year), 8 teaching assistantships (averaging $10,746 per year) were awarded; career-related internships or fieldwork, Federal Work-Study, institutionally sponsored loans, scholarships/grants, traineeships, health care benefits, and unspecified assistantships also available. Support available to part-time students. Financial award application deadline: 3/1; financial award applicants required to submit FAFSA. *Faculty research:* Women's anger, pre-school assessments, body image dysfunction, traumatic stress, classical ethics, mental health and behavioral needs of adolescents in alternative education. *Unit head:* Dr. Dan Miller, Chair, 940-898-2303, Fax: 940-898-2301, E-mail: dmiller@twu.edu. *Application contact:* Samuel Wheeler, Assistant Director of Admissions, 940-898-3188, Fax: 940-898-3081, E-mail: wheelersr@twu.edu.

Towson University, College of Graduate Studies and Research, Program in School Psychology, Towson, MD 21252-0001. Offers CAS. Part-time and evening/weekend programs available. Electronic applications accepted. *Faculty research:* Cognitive behavior, issues affecting the aging, relaxation hypnosis and imagery, lesbian and gay issues.

Trinity University, Department of Education, Program in School Psychology, San Antonio, TX 78212-7200. Offers MA. *Accreditation:* NCATE. *Faculty:* 10 full-time (8 women), 14 part-time/adjunct (8 women). *Students:* 23 full-time (19 women), 11 part-time (all women); includes 12 minority (1 African American, 1 American Indian/Alaska Native, 1 Asian American or Pacific Islander, 9 Hispanic Americans). Average age 27. In 2008, 13 master's awarded. *Entrance requirements:* For master's, GRE General Test, minimum GPA of 3.0, interview. *Application deadline:* For fall admission, 4/1 for domestic students. Applications are processed on a rolling basis. Application fee: $30. *Financial support:* Fellowships, research assistantships, career-related internships or fieldwork, Federal Work-Study, and institutionally sponsored loans available. Support available to part-time students. Financial award application deadline: 4/1. *Unit head:* Dr. Terry Robertson, Director, 210-999-7595, Fax: 210-999-7592, E-mail: terry.robertson@trinity.edu. *Application contact:* Office of the Registrar, 210-999-7201, Fax: 210-999-7202, E-mail: roffice@trinity.edu.

Troy University, Graduate School, College of Education, Program in Counseling and Psychology, Troy, AL 36082. Offers clinical mental health (MS); community counseling (MS); school psychology (MS); student affairs counseling (MS). *Accreditation:* ACA; CORE; NCATE. Part-time and evening/weekend programs available. *Degree requirements:* For master's, comprehensive exam, thesis. *Entrance requirements:* For master's, MAT, minimum GPA of 2.5. Additional exam requirements/recommendations for international students: Required—TOEFL (minimum score 523 paper-based; 200 computer-based). Electronic applications accepted.

Tufts University, Graduate School of Arts and Sciences, Department of Education, Program in School Psychology, Medford, MA 02155. Offers MA, CAGS. *Entrance requirements:* For master's, GRE General Test. Additional exam requirements/recommendations for international students: Required—TOEFL (minimum score 550 paper-based; 213 computer-based; 80 iBT). Electronic applications accepted.

Union College, Graduate Programs, Department of Psychology, Barbourville, KY 40906-1499. Offers clinical psychology (MA); counseling psychology (MA); school psychology (MA).

Universidad del Turabo, Graduate Programs, School of Social Sciences and Humanities, Programs in Psychology, Program in School Psychology, Gurabo, PR 00778-3030. Offers MSS.

University at Albany, State University of New York, School of Education, Department of Educational and Counseling Psychology, Albany, NY 12222-0001. Offers counseling psychology (MS, PhD, CAS); educational psychology (Ed D); educational psychology and statistics (MS); measurements and evaluation (Ed D); rehabilitation counseling (MS), including counseling psychology; school counselor (CAS); school psychology (Psy D, CAS); special education (MS); statistics and research design (Ed D). *Accreditation:* APA (one or more programs are accredited). Evening/weekend programs available. *Degree requirements:* For doctorate, thesis/dissertation. *Entrance requirements:* For doctorate, GRE General Test. Additional exam requirements/recommendations for international students: Required—TOEFL (minimum score 550 paper-based; 213 computer-based). Electronic applications accepted.

University at Buffalo, the State University of New York, Graduate School, Graduate School of Education, Department of Counseling, School, and Educational Psychology, Buffalo, NY 14260. Offers counseling/school psychology (PhD); counselor education (PhD); educational psychology (MA, PhD); mental health counseling (MS); rehabilitation counseling (MS); school counseling (Ed M, Certificate); school psychology (MA). *Accreditation:* CORE (one or more programs are accredited). *Degree requirements:* For master's, comprehensive exam (for some programs), thesis (for some programs); for doctorate, comprehensive exam, thesis/dissertation. *Entrance requirements:* For master's and doctorate, GRE General Test, interview, letters of reference. Additional exam requirements/recommendations for international students: Required—TOEFL. Electronic applications accepted. *Faculty research:* Multicultural counseling, class size effects, quality of life, eating disorders, outcome assessment.

The University of Akron, Graduate School, College of Education, Department of Counseling, Program in Classroom Guidance for Teachers, Akron, OH 44325. Offers MA, MS. *Accreditation:* NCATE. *Degree requirements:* For master's, comprehensive exam. *Entrance requirements:* For master's, minimum GPA of 2.75, interview, letters of recommendation, criminal background check, resumé, supplemental form. Additional exam requirements/recommendations for international students: Required—TOEFL (minimum score 550 paper-based; 213 computer-based; 79 iBT). Electronic applications accepted.

University of Alberta, Faculty of Graduate Studies and Research, Department of Educational Psychology, Edmonton, AB T6G 2E1, Canada. Offers counseling psychology (M Ed, PhD); educational psychology (M Ed, PhD); instructional technology (M Ed); school counseling (M Ed); school psychology (M Ed, PhD); special education (M Ed, PhD); special education-deafness studies (M Ed); teaching English as a second language (M Ed). Part-time programs available. *Degree requirements:* For master's, thesis optional; for doctorate, comprehensive exam, thesis/dissertation. *Entrance requirements:* For master's and doctorate, minimum GPA of 3.0. Additional exam requirements/recommendations for international students: Required—TOEFL. *Faculty research:* Human learning, development and assessment.

The University of British Columbia, Faculty of Graduate Studies, Faculty of Education, Department of Educational and Counseling Psychology, and Special Education, Vancouver, BC V6T 1Z1, Canada. Offers counseling psychology (M Ed, MA, PhD); development, learning and culture (PhD); guidance studies (Diploma); human development, learning and culture (M Ed, MA); measurement and evaluation and research methodology (M Ed); measurement, evaluation and research methodology (MA); measurement, evaluation, and research methodology (PhD); school psychology (M Ed, MA, PhD); special education (M Ed, MA, PhD, Diploma). Part-time programs available. *Degree requirements:* For master's, thesis (for some programs); for doctorate, comprehensive exam, thesis/dissertation. *Entrance requirements:* For master's, GRE General Test (counseling psychology MA); for doctorate, GRE General Test. Additional exam requirements/recommendations for international students: Required—TOEFL. Electronic applications accepted. *Faculty research:* Women, family, social problems, career transition, stress and coping problems.

University of Calgary, Faculty of Graduate Studies, Faculty of Education, Division of Applied Psychology, Calgary, AB T2N 1N4, Canada. Offers counseling psychology (M Ed, M Sc, PhD); human development and learning (M Ed, M Sc, PhD); school psychology (M Ed, M Sc, PhD); special education (M Ed, M Sc, PhD). Part-time programs available. *Degree requirements:* For master's, thesis (for some programs), final oral exam; for doctorate, thesis/dissertation, candidacy exam, final oral exam. *Entrance requirements:* For master's, minimum GPA of 3.0, 3 letters of reference; for doctorate, minimum GPA of 3.5, 3 letters of reference. *Faculty research:* Counselor education, family life studies, learning and cognition.

University of California, Berkeley, Graduate Division, School of Education, Division of Cognition and Development, Program in School Psychology, Berkeley, CA 94720-1500. Offers Ph D/Credential, PhD/MA. *Accreditation:* APA. Electronic applications accepted.

University of California, Riverside, Graduate Division, Graduate School of Education, Riverside, CA 92521-0102. Offers autism (M Ed); curriculum and instruction (MA); educational leadership and policy (MA, PhD); educational psychology (PhD); general education (M Ed); higher education administration and policy (PhD); leadership (M Ed); reading (M Ed); school psychology (PhD); special education (MA, PhD). *Faculty:* 23 full-time (11 women), 21 part-time/adjunct (13 women). *Students:* 236 full-time (185 women); includes 104 minority (13 African Americans, 1 American Indian/Alaska Native, 39 Asian Americans or Pacific Islanders, 51 Hispanic Americans), 10 international. Average age 34. 215 applicants, 53% accepted, 88 enrolled. In 2008, 66 master's, 18 doctorates awarded. Terminal master's awarded for partial completion of doctoral program. *Degree requirements:* For master's, thesis optional, comprehensive exams or thesis; case study; or analytical report; for doctorate, thesis/dissertation, qualifying exams, teaching experience. *Entrance requirements:* For master's, GRE General Test, GRE Subject Test, CBEST, CSET, minimum GPA of 3.2; for doctorate, GRE General Test, GRE Subject Test, master's degree, minimum GPA of 3.2. Additional exam requirements/recommendations for international students: Required—TOEFL (minimum score 550 paper-based; 213 computer-based; 80 iBT). *Application deadline:* For fall admission, 4/15 for domestic students, 2/1 for international students; for winter admission, 9/1 for domestic students, 7/1 for international students; for spring admission, 12/1 for domestic students, 10/1 for international students. Applications are processed on a rolling basis. Application fee: $70 ($85 for international students). Electronic applications accepted. *Expenses:* Tuition, nonresident: full-time $4898. Required fees: $10,362. *Financial support:* In 2008–09, 6 fellowships with full and partial tuition reimbursements (averaging $24,143 per year), 23 research assistantships with full and partial tuition reimbursements (averaging $12,000 per year), 2 teaching assistantships with full and partial tuition reimbursements (averaging $11,700 per year) were awarded; career-related internships or fieldwork, Federal Work-Study, institutionally sponsored loans, and tuition waivers (full and partial) also available. Financial award application deadline: 1/5; financial award applicants required to submit FAFSA. *Faculty research:* Responsiveness to intervention Faculty core Response to intervention of English Language Learners Advanced modeling techniques Study on social capital, trust, and motivation. Total annual research expenditures: $6.2 million. *Unit head:* Dr. Steven T. Bossert, Dean, 951-827-5802, Fax: 951-827-3942, E-mail: steven.bossert@ucr.edu. *Application contact:* Dr. Margaret Nash, Graduate Adviser, 951-827-6362, Fax: 951-827-3942, E-mail: edgrad@ucr.edu.

University of California, Santa Barbara, Graduate Division, Gevirtz Graduate School of Education, Santa Barbara, CA 93106-9490. Offers counseling, clinical and school psychology (PhD), including clinical psychology, counseling psychology, school psychology; education (M Ed, MA, PhD), including child and adolescent development (MA, PhD), cultural perspectives and comparative education (MA, PhD), educational leadership and organizations (MA, PhD), research methodology (MA, PhD), special education disabilities and risk studies (MA), special education, disabilities and risk studies (PhD), teaching (M Ed), teaching and learning (MA, PhD); educational leadership (Ed D); school psychology (M Ed); MA/PhD. *Accreditation:* APA (one or more programs are accredited). Postbaccalaureate distance learning degree programs offered (minimal on-campus study). *Faculty:* 42 full-time (20 women), 10 part-time/adjunct (4 women). *Students:* 390 full-time (303 women); includes 149 minority (14 African Americans, 3 American Indian/Alaska Native, 57 Asian Americans or Pacific Islanders, 75 Hispanic Americans), 16 international. Average age 31. 717 applicants, 40% accepted, 170 enrolled. In 2008, 140 master's, 46 doctorates awarded. Terminal master's awarded for partial completion of doctoral program. *Degree requirements:* For master's, comprehensive exam (for some programs), thesis (for some programs); for doctorate, comprehensive exam (for some programs), thesis/dissertation, qualifying exam. *Entrance requirements:* For master's and doctorate, GRE, 3 letters of recommendation, statement of purpose, personal achievements/contributions statement, resumé/curriculum vitae, transcripts for post-secondary institutions attended. Additional exam requirements/recommendations for international students: Required—TOEFL (minimum score 550 paper-based; 213 computer-based; 80 iBT), IELTS (minimum score 7), TOEFL or IELTS. Application fee: $70 ($90 for international students). Electronic applications accepted. *Expenses:* Tuition, nonresident: full-time $25,149. Required fees: $10,143. Full-time tuition and fees vary according to campus/location, reciprocity agreements and student level. *Financial support:* In 2008–09, 253 students received support, including 206 fellowships with full and partial tuition reimbursements available (averaging $5,000 per year), 62 research assistantships with full and partial tuition reimbursements available (averaging $6,200 per year), 87 teaching assistantships with partial tuition reimbursements available (averaging $6,500 per year); career-related internships or fieldwork, Federal Work-Study, institutionally sponsored loans, scholarships/grants, traineeships, health care benefits, and unspecified assistantships also available. Financial award applicants required to submit FAFSA. *Faculty research:* Professional development, early childhood development, school violence, literacy, science/math initiative. Total annual research expenditures: $4.4 million. *Unit head:* Dr. Jane Conoley, Chair, 805-893-2185, E-mail: jane-conoley@education.ucsb.edu. *Application contact:* Kathryn Marie Tucciarone, Student Affairs Officer, 805-893-2137, E-mail: katiet@education.ucsb.edu.

University of Central Arkansas, Graduate School, College of Health and Behavioral Sciences, Department of Counseling and Psychology, Program in School Psychology, Conway, AR 72035-0001. Offers MS, PhD. *Accreditation:* APA; NCATE. Terminal master's awarded for partial completion of doctoral program. *Degree requirements:* For master's, comprehensive exam, thesis optional; for doctorate, comprehensive exam, thesis/dissertation. *Entrance requirements:* For master's, GRE General Test, minimum GPA of 2.7; for doctorate, GRE General Test. Additional exam requirements/recommendations for international students: Required—TOEFL (minimum score 550 paper-based; 213 computer-based).

University of Central Florida, College of Education, Department of Child, Family and Community Sciences, Program in School Psychology, Orlando, FL 32816. Offers Ed S. Part-time and evening/weekend programs available. *Students:* 41 full-time (35 women), 1 (woman) part-time; includes 8 minority (1 African American, 2 Asian Americans or Pacific Islanders, 5 Hispanic Americans), 1 international. In 2008, 15 Ed Ss awarded. *Degree requirements:* For Ed S, thesis or alternative, practicum, internship. *Entrance requirements:* For degree, GRE General Test, minimum GPA of 3.0, resumé, interview. Additional exam requirements/recommendations for international students: Required—TOEFL. *Application deadline:* For fall admission, 3/1 for domestic students. Application fee: $30. Electronic applications accepted. *Expenses:* Tuition, area resident: Full-time $6816; part-time $284 per credit. Tuition, state resident: full-time $6816; part-time $1076 per credit. Tuition, nonresident: full-time $25,824. Required fees: $216; $9 per credit. *Financial support:* In 2008–09, 12 research assistantships with partial tuition reimbursements (averaging $7,000 per year), 1 teaching assistantship with partial tuition reimbursement (averaging $9,000 per year) were awarded; fellowships with partial tuition reimbursements, career-related internships or fieldwork, Federal Work-Study, institutionally sponsored loans, tuition waivers (partial), and unspecified assistantships also available. Financial award application deadline: 3/1; financial award applicants required to submit FAFSA. *Unit head:* Dr. Gordon Taub, Coordinator, 407-823-0373, E-mail: gtaub@mail.ucf.edu. *Application contact:* Dr. Gordon Taub, Coordinator, 407-823-0373, E-mail: gtaub@mail.ucf.edu.

University of Cincinnati, Graduate School, College of Education, Criminal Justice, and Human Services, Division of Human Services, Program in School Psychology, Cincinnati, OH 45221. Offers PhD, Ed S. *Accreditation:* NCATE. Part-time programs available. *Degree requirements:* For doctorate, comprehensive exam, thesis/dissertation. *Entrance requirements:* For doctorate, GRE General Test, GRE Subject Test. Additional exam requirements/recommendations for international students: Required—TOEFL (minimum score 520 paper-based; 190 computer-based; 68 iBT), OEPT. Electronic applications accepted. *Faculty research:* School psychology services delivery, direct assessment and intervention.

University of Connecticut, Graduate School, Neag School of Education, Department of Educational Psychology, Storrs, CT 06269. Offers educational psychology (MA, PhD, Post-Master's Certificate), including cognition and instruction, counseling psychology, gifted and talented education, learning technology, measurement, evaluation, and assessment, school psychology, special education. *Degree requirements:* For master's, comprehensive exam; for doctorate, thesis/dissertation. *Entrance requirements:* For doctorate, GRE General Test. Additional exam requirements/recommendations for international students: Required—TOEFL (minimum score 550 paper-based; 213 computer-based). Electronic applications accepted.

University of Connecticut, Graduate School, Neag School of Education, Department of Educational Psychology, Field of Educational Psychology, Program in School Psychology, Storrs, CT 06269. Offers MA, PhD, Post-Master's Certificate. *Accreditation:* NCATE. Terminal master's awarded for partial completion of doctoral program. *Degree requirements:* For master's, comprehensive exam, thesis or alternative; for doctorate, thesis/dissertation. *Entrance requirements:* For doctorate, GRE General Test. Additional exam requirements/recommendations for international students: Required—TOEFL (minimum score 550 paper-based; 213 computer-based). Electronic applications accepted.

University of Dayton, Graduate School, School of Education and Allied Professions, Department of Counselor Education and Human Services, Dayton, OH 45469-1300. Offers college student personnel (MS Ed); community counseling (MS Ed); higher education administration (MS Ed); human services (MS Ed); school counseling (MS Ed); school psychology (MS Ed, Ed S); teacher as child/youth development specialist (MS Ed). *Accreditation:* NCATE. Part-time and evening/weekend programs available. *Faculty:* 11 full-time (8 women), 33 part-time/adjunct (22 women). *Students:* 266 full-time (222 women), 236 part-time (200 women); includes 70 minority (58 African Americans, 2 Asian Americans or Pacific Islanders, 10 Hispanic Americans), 2 international. Average age 32. 359 applicants, 47% accepted, 114 enrolled. In 2008, 175 master's, 7 Ed Ss awarded. *Degree requirements:* For master's, comprehensive exam (for some programs), thesis (for some programs), exit exam. *Entrance requirements:* For master's, MAT or GRE (if GPA is below 2.75), interview, writing sample. Additional exam requirements/recommendations for international students: Required—TOEFL (minimum score 550 paper-based; 213 computer-based; 80 iBT). *Application deadline:* For fall admission, 4/10 for domestic students, 3/1 priority date for international students; for winter admission, 9/10 for domestic students, 7/1 priority date for international students; for spring admission, 1/10 for domestic students, 1/1 priority date for international students. Applications are processed on a rolling basis. Application fee: $0 ($50 for international students). Electronic applications accepted. *Expenses:* Tuition: Full-time $6950; part-time $1737.50 per semester. Required fees: $25 per semester. Tuition and fees vary according to course level, course load, degree level and program. *Financial support:* In 2008–09, 7 research assistantships with full tuition reimbursements (averaging $8,000 per year), 1 teaching assistantship with full tuition reimbursement (averaging $8,000 per year) were awarded; career-related internships or fieldwork, institutionally sponsored loans, health care benefits, and unspecified assistantships also available. Financial award applicants required to submit FAFSA. *Faculty research:* Anger as part of the grief process, inclusion of children with severe disabilities, comparisons of school counselors in Bosnia and the U.S., graduate and professional student socialization, use of cohort groups in doctoral programs, bullying in schools, impact of space on learning, sophomore experience. *Unit head:* Dr. Alan Demmitt, Chairperson, 937-229-3644, Fax: 937-229-1055. *Application contact:* Angela Jones-Glukhov, Associate Director of Graduate Admissions, 937-229-4305, Fax: 937-229-4729, E-mail: jonesgas@notes.udayton.edu.

University of Delaware, College of Human Services, Education and Public Policy and Department of Individual and Family Studies, Program in Counseling in Higher Education, Newark, DE 19716. Offers M Ed, MA. *Accreditation:* NCATE. *Degree requirements:* For master's, comprehensive exam. *Entrance requirements:* For master's, GRE (quantitative and verbal), on-campus interview, letters of recommendation. Additional exam requirements/recommendations for international students: Required—TOEFL (minimum score 600 paper-based). Electronic applications accepted. *Faculty research:* Counseling outcomes, student culture, group counseling.

University of Delaware, College of Human Services, Education and Public Policy, School of Education, Newark, DE 19716. Offers education (PhD); educational leadership (Ed D); higher education (M Ed); instruction (MI); reading (M Ed); school leadership (M Ed); school psychology (MA, Ed S); teaching English as a second language (TESL) (MA). *Accreditation:* NCATE. Part-time and evening/weekend programs available. Terminal master's awarded for partial completion of doctoral program. *Degree requirements:* For master's, comprehensive exam (for some programs), thesis (for some programs); for doctorate, comprehensive exam (for some programs), thesis/dissertation. *Entrance requirements:* For master's and doctorate, GRE, 3 letters of recommendation. Additional exam requirements/recommendations for international students: Required—TOEFL (minimum score 600 paper-based; 250 computer-based). Electronic applications accepted. *Faculty research:* Teacher education; curriculum theory and development; community based education models, educational leadership.

University of Denver, College of Education, Denver, CO 80208. Offers counseling psychology (MA, PhD); curriculum and instruction (MA, PhD, Certificate), including curriculum leadership (MA, PhD); educational administration and policy studies (Certificate); educational psychology (MA, PhD, Ed S), including child and family studies (MA, PhD), quantitative research methods (MA, PhD), school psychology (PhD, Ed S); higher education and adult studies (MA, PhD); library and information science (MLIS); library and information sciences (Certificate); school administration (PhD). *Accreditation:* ALA; APA (one or more programs are accredited). Part-time and evening/weekend programs available. Postbaccalaureate distance learning degree programs offered (no on-campus study). *Faculty:* 30 full-time (20 women), 58 part-time/adjunct (40 women). *Students:* 334 full-time (259 women), 454 part-time (350 women); includes 136 minority (28 African Americans, 8 American Indian/Alaska Native, 14 Asian Americans or Pacific Islanders, 86 Hispanic Americans), 20 international. Average age 34. 851 applicants, 76% accepted, 356 enrolled. In 2008, 214 master's, 43 doctorates, 85 other advanced degrees awarded. Terminal master's awarded for partial completion of doctoral program. *Degree requirements:* For master's, comprehensive exam; for doctorate, 2 foreign languages, comprehensive exam, thesis/dissertation. *Entrance requirements:* For master's and doctorate, GRE General Test or MAT. *Application deadline:* Applications are processed on a rolling basis. Application fee: $50. Electronic applications accepted. *Financial support:* In 2008–09, 74 teaching assistantships with full and partial tuition reimbursements (averaging $6,000 per year) were awarded; career-related internships or fieldwork, Federal Work-Study, institutionally sponsored loans, and scholarships/grants also available. Support available to part-time students. Financial award application deadline: 3/1; financial award applicants required to submit FAFSA. *Faculty research:* Parkinson's disease, personnel training, development and assessments, gifted education, service learning, transportation, public schools. Total annual research expenditures: $340,000. *Unit head:* Dr. Cheryl Lovell, Associate Dean, 303-871-2479. *Application contact:* Linda McCarthy, Student Services Coordinator, 303-871-2509, E-mail: edinfo@du.edu.

University of Detroit Mercy, College of Liberal Arts and Education, Department of Psychology, Program in School Psychology, Detroit, MI 48221. Offers Spec.

University of Florida, Graduate School, College of Education, Department of Educational Psychology, Gainesville, FL 32611. Offers educational psychology (M Ed, MAE, Ed D, PhD, Ed S); research and evaluation methodology (M Ed, MAE, Ed D, PhD, Ed S); school psychology (M Ed, MAE, Ed D, PhD, Ed S). *Accreditation:* NCATE. Terminal master's awarded for partial completion of doctoral program. *Degree requirements:* For master's, thesis (MAE); for doctorate, variable foreign language requirement, thesis/dissertation. *Entrance requirements:* For master's and doctorate, GRE General Test, minimum GPA of 3.0; for Ed S, GRE General Test. Additional exam requirements/recommendations for international students: Required—TOEFL (minimum score 550 paper-based; 213 computer-based). Electronic applications accepted. *Faculty research:* School improvement, teaching and learning, item response theory.

University of Hartford, College of Arts and Sciences, Department of Psychology, Program in School Psychology, West Hartford, CT 06117-1599. Offers MS. *Accreditation:* NCATE. Part-time programs available. *Degree requirements:* For master's, comprehensive exam. *Entrance requirements:* For master's, GRE General Test, GRE Subject Test, minimum GPA of 3.0, 3 letters of recommendation. Additional exam requirements/recommendations for international students: Required—TOEFL (minimum score 550 paper-based; 213 computer-based). Electronic applications accepted. *Faculty research:* Family therapy, child developments, clinical supervision.

University of Houston–Clear Lake, School of Human Sciences and Humanities, Programs in Human Sciences, Houston, TX 77058-1098. Offers behavioral sciences (MA), including criminology, cross cultural studies, general psychology, sociology; clinical psychology (MA); criminology (MA); cross cultural studies (MA); family therapy (MA); fitness and human performance (MA); school psychology (MA). *Accreditation:* AAMFT/COAMFTE. Part-time and evening/weekend programs available. Postbaccalaureate distance learning degree programs offered (minimal on-campus study). *Degree requirements:* For master's, thesis or alternative. *Entrance requirements:* For master's, GRE General Test. Additional exam requirements/recommendations for international students: Required—TOEFL (minimum score 550 paper-based; 213 computer-based). Electronic applications accepted. *Faculty research:* Smoking cessation, adolescent sexuality, white collar crime, serial murder, human factors/human computer interaction.

University of Houston–Victoria, School of Arts and Sciences, Program in Psychology, Victoria, TX 77901-4450. Offers counseling psychology (MA); school psychology (MA). Part-time and evening/weekend programs available. Postbaccalaureate distance learning degree programs offered. *Degree requirements:* For master's, project or thesis. *Entrance requirements:* For master's, GRE General Test. Additional exam requirements/recommendations for international students: Required—TOEFL (minimum score 550 paper-based; 213 computer-based). Electronic applications accepted.

University of Idaho, College of Graduate Studies, College of Education, Department of Counseling and School Psychology, Special Education, and Educational Leadership, Program in School Psychology, Moscow, ID 83844-2282. Offers Ed S. *Accreditation:* NCATE. *Students:* 23 full-time, 14 part-time. Average age 31. In 2008, 12 Ed Ss awarded. *Application deadline:* For fall admission, 8/1 for domestic students; for spring admission, 12/15 for domestic students. Application fee: $55 ($60 for international students). *Expenses:* Tuition, nonresident: full-time $10,080; part-time $336 per credit. Required fees: $5212; $267 per credit. Tuition and fees vary according to program. *Financial support:* Application deadline: 2/15. *Unit head:* Dr. Russell A. Joki, Chair, 208-364-4099, E-mail: rjoki@uidaho.edu. *Application contact:* Dr. Russell A. Joki, Chair, 208-364-4099, E-mail: rjoki@uidaho.edu.

The University of Iowa, Graduate College, College of Education, Department of Psychological and Quantitative Foundations, Iowa City, IA 52242-1316. Offers counseling psychology (PhD); educational measurement and statistics (MA, PhD); educational psychology (MA, PhD); school psychology (PhD, Ed S); JD/PhD. *Accreditation:* APA. *Degree requirements:* For master's, thesis optional, exam; for doctorate, comprehensive exam, thesis/dissertation; for Ed S, exam. *Entrance requirements:* For master's, doctorate, and Ed S, GRE General Test, minimum GPA of 3.0. Additional exam requirements/recommendations for international students: Required—TOEFL (minimum score 550 paper-based; 213 computer-based; 81 iBT). Electronic applications accepted.

The University of Kansas, Graduate Studies, School of Education, Department of Psychology and Research in Education, Program in School Psychology, Lawrence, KS 66045. Offers PhD, Ed S. *Accreditation:* APA (one or more programs are accredited); NCATE. *Faculty:* 3. *Students:* 24 full-time (17 women), 3 part-time (all women); includes 2 minority (both Hispanic Americans), 1 international. Average age 27. 51 applicants, 31% accepted, 15 enrolled. In 2008, 3 doctorates, 6 other advanced degrees awarded. *Degree requirements:* For doctorate, comprehensive exam, thesis/dissertation; for Ed S, comprehensive exam. *Entrance requirements:* For doctorate, GRE General Test; for Ed S, GRE General Test, minimum GPA of 3.0. Additional exam requirements/recommendations for international students: Required—TOEFL. *Application*

School Psychology

The University of Kansas (continued)
deadline: For fall admission, 12/15 for domestic and international students. Application fee: $45 ($50 for international students). Electronic applications accepted. *Expenses:* Tuition, area resident: Full-time $6122; part-time $255.10 per credit hour. Tuition, state resident: full-time $6122; part-time $255.10 per credit hour. Tuition, nonresident: full-time $14,629; part-time $609.55 per credit hour. Required fees: $847; $70.56 per credit hour. Tuition and fees vary according to course load and program. *Financial support:* Fellowships, research assistantships with full and partial tuition reimbursements, teaching assistantships with full and partial tuition reimbursements available. Financial award application deadline: 2/1. *Faculty research:* Classroom management, anxiety in children and youth, child behavior and learning problems, behavioral and personality assessment, home/school/community partnerships. *Unit head:* Patricia A. Lowe, Director of Training, 785-864-9710, Fax: 785-864-3820, E-mail: tlowe@ku.edu. *Application contact:* Admissions Coordinator, 785-864-3931, Fax: 785-864-3820, E-mail: preadmit@ku.edu.

University of Kentucky, Graduate School, College of Education, Program in Educational and Counseling Psychology, Lexington, KY 40506-0032. Offers counseling psychology (MS Ed, PhD, Ed S); educational and counseling psychology (MS Ed); educational psychology (Ed D, PhD, Ed S); school psychometrist and school psychology (MA Ed). *Accreditation:* APA (one or more programs are accredited); NCATE. *Degree requirements:* For master's, comprehensive exam, thesis optional; for doctorate, comprehensive exam, thesis/dissertation; for Ed S, comprehensive exam. *Entrance requirements:* For master's, GRE General Test, minimum undergraduate GPA of 2.75; for doctorate, GRE General Test, minimum graduate GPA of 3.0; for Ed S, GRE General Test. Additional exam requirements/recommendations for international students: Required—TOEFL (minimum score 550 paper-based; 213 computer-based). Electronic applications accepted.

University of Louisiana at Monroe, Graduate School, College of Education and Human Development, Department of Psychology, Program in School Psychology, Monroe, LA 71209-0001. Offers MS, SSP. *Accreditation:* NCATE. *Faculty:* 2 full-time (both women), 2 part-time/adjunct (1 woman). *Students:* 5 full-time (3 women), 4 part-time (3 women); includes 4 minority (all African Americans). Average age 29. In 2008, 7 other advanced degrees awarded. *Degree requirements:* For SSP, comprehensive exam, thesis, minimum GPA of 3.0, field and practicum experience (400 hours), internship (1250 hours). *Entrance requirements:* For master's, GRE, minimum cumulative GPA of 2.75; for SSP, GRE General Test, minimum GPA of 3.25. Additional exam requirements/recommendations for international students: Required—TOEFL (minimum score 500 paper-based; 173 computer-based; 61 iBT). *Application deadline:* For fall admission, 8/22 priority date for domestic students, 7/1 for international students; for winter admission, 12/12 priority date for domestic students; for spring admission, 1/17 for domestic students, 11/1 for international students. Applications are processed on a rolling basis. Application fee: $20 ($30 for international students). Electronic applications accepted. *Expenses:* Tuition, area resident: Full-time $2403; part-time $1202 per semester. Tuition, state resident: full-time $2403; part-time $1202 per semester. Tuition, nonresident: full-time $2403; part-time $1202 per semester. International tuition: $8352 full-time. Required fees: $1239.40; $141 per credit hour. *Financial support:* Career-related internships or fieldwork, Federal Work-Study, and unspecified assistantships available. Financial award application deadline: 4/1; financial award applicants required to submit FAFSA. *Unit head:* Dr. Veronica Lewis, Coordinator, 818-342-1332, E-mail: vlewis@ulm.edu. *Application contact:* Dr. Veronica Lewis, Coordinator, 818-342-1332, E-mail: vlewis@ulm.edu.

University of Manitoba, Faculty of Graduate Studies, Faculty of Arts, Department of Psychology, Winnipeg, MB R3T 2N2, Canada. Offers clinical psychology (PhD); psychology (MA, PhD); school psychology (MA). *Accreditation:* APA (one or more programs are accredited). *Degree requirements:* For master's, thesis; for doctorate, one foreign language, thesis/dissertation. *Entrance requirements:* For master's and doctorate, GRE General Test.

University of Mary, Divison of Social and Behavioral Sciences, Bismarck, ND 58504-9652. Offers addiction counseling (MSC); community counseling (MSC); school counseling (MSC).

University of Mary Hardin-Baylor, College of Sciences and Humanities, Department of Psychology, Belton, TX 76513. Offers community counseling (MA); marriage and family Christian counseling (MA); psychology and counseling (MA); school counseling and psychology (MA). Part-time and evening/weekend programs available. *Degree requirements:* For master's, comprehensive exam. *Entrance requirements:* For master's, GRE General Test, minimum GPA of 3.0 in last 60 hours or 2.75 overall. Electronic applications accepted.

University of Maryland, College Park, Graduate Studies, College of Education, Department of Counseling and Personnel Services, College Park, MD 20742. Offers college student personnel (M Ed, MA); college student personnel administration (PhD); community counseling (CAGS); community/career counseling (M Ed, MA); counseling and personnel services (M Ed, MA, PhD); counseling psychology (PhD); counselor education (PhD); rehabilitation counseling (M Ed, MA, AGSC); school counseling (M Ed, MA); school psychology (M Ed, MA, PhD). *Accreditation:* ACA (one or more programs are accredited); APA (one or more programs are accredited); CORE (one or more programs are accredited); NCATE. Part-time and evening/weekend programs available. Postbaccalaureate distance learning degree programs offered (no on-campus study). *Degree requirements:* For master's, thesis (for some programs); for doctorate, thesis/dissertation. *Entrance requirements:* For master's, GRE General Test or MAT, minimum GPA of 3.0, 3 letters of recommendation; for doctorate, GRE General Test or MAT, minimum GPA of 3.5, 3 letters of recommendation. Additional exam requirements/recommendations for international students: Required—TOEFL. Electronic applications accepted. *Faculty research:* Educational psychology, counseling, health.

University of Massachusetts Amherst, Graduate School, School of Education, Program in School Psychology, Amherst, MA 01003. Offers PhD. *Accreditation:* APA; NCATE. Part-time programs available. Terminal master's awarded for partial completion of doctoral program. *Degree requirements:* For doctorate, comprehensive exam, thesis/dissertation. *Entrance requirements:* For doctorate, 3 letters of recommendation. Additional exam requirements/recommendations for international students: Required—TOEFL (minimum score 550 paper-based; 213 computer-based; 79 iBT), IELTS (minimum score 6.5). Electronic applications accepted. *Expenses:* Tuition, area resident: Full-time $2640. Tuition, nonresident: full-time $9936. One-time fee: $332 full-time. Tuition and fees vary according to course load.

University of Massachusetts Boston, Office of Graduate Studies, Graduate College of Education, Counseling and School Psychology Department, Program in School Guidance Counseling, Boston, MA 02125-3393. Offers M Ed, CAGS.

University of Massachusetts Boston, Office of Graduate Studies, Graduate College of Education, Counseling and School Psychology Department, Program in School Psychology, Boston, MA 02125-3393. Offers M Ed, CAGS. Part-time and evening/weekend programs available. *Degree requirements:* For master's, comprehensive exam, practicum, final project; for CAGS, comprehensive exam. *Entrance requirements:* For master's, GRE General Test or MAT, minimum GPA of 3.0; for CAGS, minimum GPA of 2.75. *Faculty research:* School psychology services, assessment of children, cultural and gender differences on psychological adjustment to disabilities.

University of Memphis, Graduate School, College of Arts and Sciences, Department of Psychology, Memphis, TN 38152. Offers clinical psychology (PhD); experimental psychology (PhD); general psychology (MS); school psychology (MA, PhD). Part-time programs available. *Faculty:* 29 full-time (9 women), 1 part-time/adjunct (0 women). *Students:* 119 full-time (80 women), 21 part-time (13 women); includes 23 minority (16 African Americans, 1 American Indian/Alaska Native, 2 Asian Americans or Pacific Islanders, 4 Hispanic Americans), 9 international. Average age 27. 197 applicants, 23% accepted, 31 enrolled. In 2008, 28 master's, 11 doctorates awarded. Terminal master's awarded for partial completion of doctoral program. *Degree requirements:* For master's, comprehensive exam, thesis (for some programs), oral exam (MS); for doctorate, thesis/dissertation, internship. *Entrance requirements:* For master's, GRE General Test, 18 undergraduate hours in psychology, minimum GPA of 2.5; for doctorate, GRE General Test, GRE Subject Test. *Application deadline:* For fall admission, 2/1 for domestic students. Applications are processed on a rolling basis. Application fee: $35 ($60 for international students). *Expenses:* Tuition, area resident: Full-time $6242; part-time $330 per credit hour. Tuition, state resident: full-time $6242; part-time $330 per credit hour. Tuition, nonresident: full-time $17,828; part-time $815 per credit hour. Required fees: $1156. *Financial support:* Fellowships with full tuition reimbursements, research assistantships with full tuition reimbursements, teaching assistantships with full tuition reimbursements, tuition waivers (partial) and unspecified assistantships available. Financial award applicants required to submit FAFSA. *Faculty research:* Psychotherapy and psychopathology, behavioral medicine and community psychology, child and family studies, cognitive and social processes, neuropsychology and behavioral neuroscience. *Unit head:* Dr. William Zachry, Chair, 901-678-2145, Fax: 901-678-2579, E-mail: wzachry@memphis.edu. *Application contact:* Dr. Robert Cohen, Graduate Studies Coordinator, 901-678-2146.

University of Minnesota, Twin Cities Campus, Graduate School, College of Education and Human Development, Department of Educational Psychology, Program in School Psychology, Minneapolis, MN 55455-0213. Offers MA, PhD, Ed S. *Accreditation:* APA.

University of Minnesota, Twin Cities Campus, Graduate School, College of Education and Human Development, Institute of Child Development, Minneapolis, MN 55455-0213. Offers child psychology (MA, PhD); early childhood education (M Ed, MA, PhD); school psychology (MA, PhD). *Faculty research:* Developmental affective and cognitive neuroscience; developmental psychopathology; intervention and prevention science; social and emotional development; cognitive, language, and perceptual development.

University of Minnesota, Twin Cities Campus, Graduate School, College of Liberal Arts, Department of Psychology, Minneapolis, MN 55455-0213. Offers biological psychopathology (PhD); clinical psychology (PhD); cognitive and biological psychology (PhD); counseling psychology (PhD); industrial/organizational psychology (PhD); personality, individual differences, and behavior genetics (PhD); quantitative/psychometric methods (PhD); school psychology (PhD); social psychology (PhD). *Accreditation:* APA. *Degree requirements:* For doctorate, comprehensive exam, thesis/dissertation. *Entrance requirements:* For doctorate, GRE General Test, GRE Subject Test (recommended), 12 credits of upper-level psychology courses, including a course in statistics or psychological measurement. Additional exam requirements/recommendations for international students: Required—TOEFL (minimum score 550 paper-based; 213 computer-based; 79 iBT).

University of Missouri–Columbia, Graduate School, College of Education, Department of Educational, School, and Counseling Psychology, Columbia, MO 65211. Offers counseling psychology (M Ed, MA, PhD, Ed S); educational psychology (M Ed, MA, PhD, Ed S); learning and instruction (M Ed); school psychology (M Ed, MA, PhD, Ed S). *Accreditation:* APA (one or more programs are accredited); CORE. Part-time programs available. *Faculty:* 25 full-time (13 women), 4 part-time/adjunct (2 women). *Students:* 121 full-time (89 women), 98 part-time (77 women); includes 33 minority (16 African Americans, 3 American Indian/Alaska Native, 6 Asian Americans or Pacific Islanders, 8 Hispanic Americans), 26 international. Average age 30. 215 applicants, 27% accepted, 53 enrolled. In 2008, 51 master's, 11 doctorates, 5 other advanced degrees awarded. *Degree requirements:* For doctorate, thesis/dissertation. *Entrance requirements:* For master's, doctorate, and Ed S, GRE General Test, minimum GPA of 3.0. Additional exam requirements/recommendations for international students: Required—TOEFL (minimum score 580 paper-based; 237 computer-based; 92 iBT). *Application deadline:* For fall admission, 1/8 priority date for domestic students. Applications are processed on a rolling basis. Application fee: $45 ($60 for international students). *Financial support:* Fellowships, research assistantships, teaching assistantships, institutionally sponsored loans available. *Unit head:* Dr. Deborah Carr, Department Chair, E-mail: carrd@missouri.edu. *Application contact:* Latoya Owens, 573-882-7732, E-mail: owensla@missouri.edu.

University of Missouri–St. Louis, College of Education, Division of Educational Psychology, Research, and Evaluation, St. Louis, MO 63121. Offers education (Ed D); educational psychology (PhD); program evaluation and assessment (Certificate); school psychology (Ed S). *Faculty:* 13 full-time (4 women). *Students:* 14 full-time (13 women), 18 part-time (5 women); includes 1 minority (Asian American or Pacific Islander). Average age 29. In 2008, 9 other advanced degrees awarded. *Degree requirements:* For other advanced degree, internship. *Entrance requirements:* For degree, GRE General Test, 2-4 letters of recommendation, personal interview. Additional exam requirements/recommendations for international students: Recommended—TOEFL (minimum score 550 paper-based; 213 computer-based). *Application deadline:* For fall admission, 3/1 for domestic and international students. Application fee: $35 ($40 for international students). Electronic applications accepted. *Expenses:* Tuition, area resident: Full-time $5377; part-time $298.70 per credit hour. Tuition, nonresident: full-time $13,381; part-time $472.50 per credit hour. Required fees: $4078; $52 per credit hour. *Financial support:* In 2008–09, 2 research assistantships (averaging $12,118 per year), 1 teaching assistantship (averaging $13,842 per year) were awarded. Financial award application deadline: 4/1; financial award applicants required to submit FAFSA. *Faculty research:* Child/adolescent psychology, quantitative and qualitative methodology, evaluation processes, measurement and assessment. *Unit head:* Dr. Matthew Keefer, Chairperson, 314-516-5783, Fax: 314-516-5784, E-mail: keefer@umsl.edu. *Application contact:* 314-516-5458, Fax: 314-516-6996, E-mail: gradadm@umsl.edu.

The University of Montana, Graduate School, College of Arts and Sciences, Department of Psychology, Program in School Psychology, Missoula, MT 59812-0002. Offers MA, PhD, Ed S. *Degree requirements:* For master's, oral exam, professional paper; for Ed S, thesis. *Entrance requirements:* For master's, GRE General Test, GRE Subject Test, minimum GPA of 3.25 during previous 2 years; for Ed S, GRE General Test. Additional exam requirements/recommendations for international students: Required—TOEFL. *Faculty research:* Child development and creativity, psychological measurement.

University of Nebraska at Kearney, College of Graduate Study, College of Education, Department of Counseling and School Psychology, Kearney, NE 68849-0001. Offers counseling (MS Ed, Ed S); school psychology (Ed S). *Accreditation:* ACA; NCATE. Part-time and evening/weekend programs available. *Degree requirements:* For master's, thesis optional; for Ed S, thesis. *Entrance requirements:* For master's and Ed S, interview. Additional exam requirements/recommendations for international students: Required—TOEFL (minimum score 550 paper-based; 213 computer-based). Electronic applications accepted. *Faculty research:* Multicultural counseling and diversity issues, team decision making, adult development, women's issues, brief therapy.

University of Nebraska at Omaha, Graduate Studies and Research, College of Arts and Sciences, Department of Psychology, Omaha, NE 68182. Offers developmental psychology (PhD); industrial/organizational psychology (MS, PhD); psychobiology (PhD); psychology (MA); school psychology (MS, Ed S). Part-time programs available. *Degree requirements:* For master's, comprehensive exam, thesis (for some programs). *Entrance requirements:* For master's, GRE General Test, GRE Subject Test, previous course work in psychology, including statistics and a laboratory course; minimum GPA of 3.0, 3 letters of recommendation; for doctorate, GRE General Test. Additional exam requirements/recommendations for international students: Required—TOEFL (minimum score 500 paper-based; 173 computer-based; 61 iBT). Electronic applications accepted.

University of Nebraska–Lincoln, Graduate College, College of Education and Human Sciences, Department of Educational Psychology, Lincoln, NE 68588. Offers cognition, learning and development (MA); counseling psychology (MA); educational psychology (MA, Ed S); psychological studies in education (PhD), including cognition, learning and development, counseling psychology, quantitative, qualitative, and psychometric methods, school psychology; quantitative, qualitative, and psychometric methods (MA); school psychology (MA, Ed S). *Accreditation:* APA (one or more programs are accredited); NCATE. *Faculty:* 19 full-time (6 women). *Students:* 16 full-time (14 women), 26 part-time (18 women); includes 2 minority (1 African American, 1 Hispanic American), 2 international. Average age 30. In 2008, 22 master's, 3 other advanced degrees awarded. *Degree requirements:* For master's, thesis optional. *Entrance requirements:* For master's, GRE General Test. Additional exam requirements/recommendations for international students: Required—TOEFL (minimum score 500 paper-based; 173 computer-based). *Application deadline:* For fall admission, 12/15 for domestic and international students; for spring admission, 10/1 for domestic students. Application fee: $40. Electronic applications accepted. *Expenses:* Tuition, state resident: full-time $4275; part-time $237.50 per credit hour. Tuition, nonresident: full-time $11,525; part-time $640.25 per credit hour. Required fees: $1068; $10.35 per credit hour. $440.70 per semester. Tuition and fees vary according to course load and program. *Financial support:* Fellowships, research assistantships, teaching assistantships, Federal Work-Study, health care benefits, and unspecified assistantships available. Support available to part-time students. Financial award application deadline: 1/15. *Faculty research:* Measurement and assessment, metacognition, academic skills, child development, multicultural education and counseling. *Unit head:* Dr. Ralph De Ayala, Chair, 402-472-2210, E-mail: tcgrad2@unl.edu. *Application contact:* Dr. Ralph De Ayala, Chair, 402-472-2210, E-mail: tcgrad2@unl.edu.

The University of North Carolina at Chapel Hill, Graduate School, School of Education, Program in School Psychology, Chapel Hill, NC 27599. Offers M Ed, MA, PhD. *Accreditation:* APA (one or more programs are accredited); NCATE. *Degree requirements:* For master's, comprehensive exam, thesis (for some programs); for doctorate, comprehensive exam, thesis/dissertation. *Entrance requirements:* For master's and doctorate, GRE General Test, minimum GPA of 3.0 during last 2 years of undergraduate course work. Additional exam requirements/recommendations for international students: Required—TOEFL (minimum score 550 paper-based; 213 computer-based). Electronic applications accepted.

The University of North Carolina at Greensboro, Graduate School, School of Education, Department of Counseling and Educational Development, Greensboro, NC 27412-5001. Offers advanced school counseling (PMC); counseling and counselor education (PhD); counseling and educational development (MS); couple and family counseling (PMC); school counseling (PMC); MS/Ed S. *Accreditation:* ACA (one or more programs are accredited); NCATE. *Degree requirements:* For master's, comprehensive exam, practicum, internship; for doctorate, comprehensive exam, thesis/dissertation. *Entrance requirements:* For master's, doctorate, and PMC, GRE General Test. Additional exam requirements/recommendations for international students: Required—TOEFL. Electronic applications accepted. *Faculty research:* Gerontology, invitational theory, career development, marriage and family therapy, drug and alcohol abuse prevention.

University of Northern Colorado, Graduate School, College of Education and Behavioral Sciences, School of Applied Psychology and Counselor Education, Program in School Psychology, Greeley, CO 80639. Offers PhD, Ed S. *Accreditation:* APA (one or more programs are accredited); NCATE. Part-time and evening/weekend programs available. *Faculty:* 5 full-time (3 women). *Students:* 32 full-time (25 women), 32 part-time (28 women); includes 6 minority (1 African American, 3 Asian Americans or Pacific Islanders, 2 Hispanic Americans). Average age 30. 44 applicants, 52% accepted, 17 enrolled. In 2008, 7 doctorates, 15 other advanced degrees awarded. *Degree requirements:* For doctorate, comprehensive exam, thesis/dissertation; for Ed S, comprehensive exam. *Entrance requirements:* For doctorate, GRE General Test, curriculum vitae, 3 letters of recommendation. *Application deadline:* For fall admission, 1/1 for domestic and international students. Applications are processed on a rolling basis. Application fee: $50 ($60 for international students). Electronic applications accepted. *Expenses:* Tuition, state resident: full-time $4370; part-time $242.75 per credit hour. Tuition, nonresident: full-time $12,366; part-time $687 per credit hour. Required fees: $664.20; $36.90 per credit hour. *Financial support:* Fellowships, research assistantships, teaching assistantships, unspecified assistantships available. Financial award application deadline: 3/1; financial award applicants required to submit FAFSA. *Unit head:* Dr. Michelle Athanasiou, Program Coordinator, 970-351-2731, Fax: 970-351-2625. *Application contact:* Linda Sisson, Graduate Student Admission Coordinator, 970-351-1807, Fax: 970-351-2371, E-mail: linda.sisson@unco.edu.

University of Northern Iowa, Graduate College, College of Education, Department of Educational Psychology and Foundations, Cedar Falls, IA 50614. Offers educational psychology (MAE); professional development for teachers (MAE); school psychology (Ed S). Part-time and evening/weekend programs available. *Students:* 22 full-time (16 women), 45 part-time (38 women); includes 2 minority (both African Americans), 3 international. 55 applicants, 49% accepted, 11 enrolled. In 2008, 15 master's awarded. *Degree requirements:* For master's, comprehensive exam (for some programs), thesis or alternative; for Ed S, thesis or alternative. *Entrance requirements:* For master's, GRE General Test, minimum GPA of 3.0; for Ed S, GRE General Test. Additional exam requirements/recommendations for international students: Required—TOEFL (minimum score 500 paper-based; 180 computer-based; 61 iBT). *Application deadline:* For fall admission, 8/1 priority date for domestic students. Applications are processed on a rolling basis. Application fee: $30 ($50 for international students). Electronic applications accepted. *Expenses:* Tuition, state resident: full-time $6446. Tuition, nonresident: full-time $14,874. Required fees: $852. *Financial support:* Career-related internships or fieldwork, Federal Work-Study, scholarships/grants, and tuition waivers (full and partial) available. Support available to part-time students. Financial award application deadline: 2/1. *Unit head:* Dr. Radhi Al-Mabuk, Interim Head, 319-273-2609, Fax: 319-273-5175, E-mail: radhi.al-mabuk@uni.edu. *Application contact:* Laurie S. Russell, Record Analyst, 319-273-2623, Fax: 319-273-6792, E-mail: laurie.russell@uni.edu.

University of North Texas, Robert B. Toulouse School of Graduate Studies, College of Education, Department of Educational Psychology, Program in School Psychology, Denton, TX 76203. Offers MS. *Degree requirements:* For master's, comprehensive exam, thesis optional, school psychology licensure. *Entrance requirements:* For master's, GRE General Test, undergraduate major in psychology; minimum GPA of 2.8, 3.0 in psychology. Additional exam requirements/recommendations for international students: Required—proof of English language proficiency required for non-native English speakers; Recommended—TOEFL (minimum score 550 paper-based; 213 computer-based). *Faculty research:* Resirience in minority families, behavioral assessment in natural settings.

University of Oklahoma, Graduate College, College of Education, Department of Educational Psychology, Norman, OK 73019. Offers community counseling (M Ed); counseling psychology (PhD); instructional psychology (M Ed, PhD); school counseling (M Ed); special education (M Ed, PhD). *Accreditation:* NCATE. Part-time programs available. *Faculty:* 24 full-time (16 women), 1 (woman) part-time/adjunct. *Students:* 93 full-time (69 women), 100 part-time (73 women); includes 47 minority (17 African Americans, 16 American Indian/Alaska Native, 5 Asian Americans or Pacific Islanders, 9 Hispanic Americans), 20 international. 85 applicants, 32% accepted, 23 enrolled. In 2008, 9 master's, 8 doctorates awarded. Terminal master's awarded for partial completion of doctoral program. *Degree requirements:* For doctorate, thesis/dissertation. *Entrance requirements:* For master's, minimum GPA of 3.0, 12 hours of course work in education; for doctorate, GRE General Test, master's degree, minimum graduate GPA of 3.25. Additional exam requirements/recommendations for international students: Required—TOEFL (minimum score 550 paper-based; 213 computer-based). *Application deadline:* For fall admission, 6/1 for domestic students, 4/1 for international students; for spring admission, 11/1 for domestic students, 9/1 for international students. Applications are processed on a rolling basis. Application fee: $40 ($90 for international students). Electronic applications accepted. *Expenses:* Tuition, state resident: full-time $3744; part-time $156 per credit hour. Tuition, nonresident: full-time $13,577; part-time $565.70 per credit hour. Required fees: $2415.40; $90.10 per credit hour. *Financial support:* In 2008–09, 59 students received support, including 8 fellowships with full tuition reimbursements available (averaging $4,221 per year), 21 research assistantships with partial tuition reimbursements available (averaging $10,698 per year), 16 teaching assistantships with partial tuition reimbursements available (averaging $11,344 per year); career-related internships or fieldwork, Federal Work-Study, institutionally sponsored loans, health care benefits, and unspecified assistantships also available. Financial award applicants required to submit FAFSA. *Faculty research:* Counseling assessment, process and outcome, diversity issues, health psychology, marriage and family, education, training and supervision. Total annual research expenditures: $322,078. *Unit head:* Dr. Terri K Debacker, Chair, 405-325-1068, Fax: 405-325-6655, E-mail: debacker@ou.edu. *Application contact:* Applications Officer, 405-325-4525, Fax: 405-325-6655, E-mail: gpoedpsych@ou.edu.

University of Pennsylvania, Graduate School of Education, Division of Applied Psychology and Human Development, Program in School, Community, and Clinical Child Psychology, Philadelphia, PA 19104. Offers PhD. *Degree requirements:* For doctorate, thesis/dissertation, exams. *Entrance requirements:* For doctorate, GRE General Test, GRE Subject Test. Electronic applications accepted. *Expenses:* Contact institution. *Faculty research:* Therapeutic interventions at a preschool level, childhood stress, college psychology, school and community psychology.

University of Phoenix–Denver Campus, The Artemis School, College of Education, Lone Tree, CO 80124-5453. Offers administration and supervision (MAEd); curriculum instruction (MAEd); elementary teacher education (MAEd); school counseling (MSC); secondary teacher education (MAEd). Evening/weekend programs available. *Degree requirements:* For master's, thesis (for some programs). *Entrance requirements:* For master's, minimum undergraduate GPA of 2.5, 3 years work experience. Additional exam requirements/recommendations for international students: Required—TOEFL (minimum score 550 paper-based; 213 computer-based; 79 iBT). Electronic applications accepted.

University of Phoenix–Las Vegas Campus, The Artemis School, College of Education, Las Vegas, NV 89128. Offers administration and supervision (MA Ed); curriculum and instruction (MA Ed); school counseling (MSC); teacher education-elementary licensure (MA Ed). Evening/weekend programs available. *Degree requirements:* For master's, thesis (for some programs). *Entrance requirements:* For master's, minimum undergraduate GPA of 2.5, 3 years of work experience. Additional exam requirements/recommendations for international students: Required—TOEFL (minimum score 550 paper-based; 213 computer-based; 79 iBT). Electronic applications accepted.

University of Phoenix–Northern Nevada Campus, College of Social and Behavioral Science, Reno, NV 89511. Offers administration of justice and security (MS); marriage, family and child therapy (MSC); psychology (MS); school counseling (MSC).

University of Phoenix–Puerto Rico Campus, The Artemis School, College of Education, Guaynabo, PR 00968. Offers administration and supervision (MA Ed); early childhood education (MA Ed); school counselor (MSC). Evening/weekend programs available. *Degree requirements:* For master's, thesis (for some programs). *Entrance requirements:* For master's, minimum undergraduate GPA of 2.5, 3 years work experience. Additional exam requirements/recommendations for international students: Required—TOEFL (minimum score 550 paper-based; 213 computer-based; 79 iBT). Electronic applications accepted.

University of Phoenix–Southern Colorado Campus, The Artemis School, College of Education, Colorado Springs, CO 80919-2335. Offers administration and supervision (MA Ed); curriculum and instruction (MA Ed); elemenary teacher education (MA Ed); principal licensure certification (Certificate); school counseling (MSC); secondary teacher education (MA Ed). Evening/weekend programs available. *Degree requirements:* For master's, thesis (for some programs). *Entrance requirements:* For master's, minimum undergraduate GPA of 2.5, 3 years of work experience. Additional exam requirements/recommendations for international students: Required—TOEFL (minimum score 550 paper-based; 213 computer-based; 79 iBT). Electronic applications accepted.

University of Phoenix–Utah Campus, The Artemis School, College of Education, Salt Lake City, UT 84123-4617. Offers administration and supervision (MA Ed); curriculum and instruction (MA Ed); elementary teacher education (MA Ed); school counseling (MSC); secondary teacher education (MA Ed); special education (MA Ed). Evening/weekend programs available. *Degree requirements:* For master's, thesis (for some programs). *Entrance requirements:* For master's, minimum undergraduate GPA of 2.5, 3 years work experience. Additional exam requirements/recommendations for international students: Required—TOEFL (minimum score 550 paper-based; 213 computer-based; 79 iBT). Electronic applications accepted.

University of Rhode Island, Graduate School, College of Arts and Sciences, Department of Psychology, Program in School Psychology, Kingston, RI 02881. Offers MS, PhD. *Accreditation:* APA (one or more programs are accredited); NCATE. Application fee: $35. *Expenses:* Tuition, state resident: full-time $8024; part-time $446 per credit. Tuition, nonresident: full-time $21,046; part-time $1169 per credit. Required fees: $1056; $26 per credit. $30 per semester. One-time fee: $95 part-time. *Unit head:* Dr. Gary Stoner, Director, 401-874-4234, E-mail: gstoner@uri.edu. *Application contact:* Harold D. Bibb, Associate Dean of the Graduate School, 401-874-2262, Fax: 401-874-5491.

University of South Alabama, Graduate School, College of Education, Department of Professional Studies, Mobile, AL 36688-0002. Offers community counseling (MS); educational media (M Ed, MS); instructional design and development (MS, PhD); rehabilitation counseling (MS); school counseling (M Ed); school psychometry (M Ed). *Accreditation:* NCATE. Part-time programs available. *Faculty:* 17 full-time (9 women). *Students:* 110 full-time (99 women), 165 part-time (131 women); includes 67 minority (59 African Americans, 2 American Indian/Alaska Native, 3 Asian Americans or Pacific Islanders, 3 Hispanic Americans), 17 international. 87 applicants, 31% accepted, 19 enrolled. In 2008, 40 master's, 9 doctorates awarded. *Degree requirements:* For master's, comprehensive exam. *Entrance requirements:* For master's, GRE General Test or MAT, minimum GPA of 3.0. *Application deadline:* For fall admission, 6/15 priority date for domestic students; for spring admission, 11/1 priority date for domestic students. Applications are processed on a rolling basis. Application fee: $35. *Expenses:* Tuition, area resident: Full-time $4656. Tuition, nonresident: full-time $9312. Required fees: $1102. *Financial support:* In 2008–09, 5 research assistantships were awarded; career-related internships or fieldwork also available. Support available to part-time students. Financial award application deadline: 4/1. *Faculty research:* Agency counseling, rehabilitation counseling, school psychometry. *Unit head:* Dr. Charles Guest, Chair, 251-380-2861. *Application contact:* Dr. B. Keith Harrison, Dean of the Graduate School, 251-460-6310, Fax: 251-461-1513, E-mail: kharriso@usouthal.edu.

University of South Carolina, The Graduate School, College of Arts and Sciences, Department of Psychology, Program in School Psychology, Columbia, SC 29208. Offers PhD. *Accreditation:* APA; NCATE. *Degree requirements:* For doctorate, thesis/dissertation. *Entrance requirements:* For doctorate, GRE General Test, minimum GPA of 3.0. Additional exam requirements/recommendations for international students: Required—TOEFL. Electronic applications accepted. *Faculty research:* Preschool services, families and diversity life satisfaction, ADHD intervention, attachment.

University of Southern Maine, College of Education and Human Development, Program in School Psychology, Portland, ME 04104-9300. Offers applied behavior analysis (Certificate); school psychology (MS, Psy D). *Accreditation:* NCATE. Part-time and evening/weekend programs available. *Degree requirements:* For master's, comprehensive exam, thesis or alternative, portfolio; for doctorate, comprehensive exam, thesis/dissertation or alternative, portfolio. *Entrance requirements:* For master's, GRE General Test or MAT, interview; for doctorate, GRE General Test. Electronic applications accepted.

University of Southern Mississippi, Graduate School, College of Education and Psychology, Department of Psychology, Hattiesburg, MS 39406-0001. Offers clinical psychology (MA, PhD); counseling psychology (PhD); experimental psychology (MA, PhD); psychology (MS); school psychology (MA, PhD). *Accreditation:* ACA; APA (one or more programs are accredited). *Faculty:* 28 full-time (11 women). *Students:* 104 full-time (83 women), 34 part-time (24 women); includes 13 minority (7 African Americans, 2 Asian Americans or Pacific Islanders, 4 Hispanic Americans), 7 international. Average age 28. 189 applicants, 21% accepted, 31 enrolled. In

School Psychology

University of Southern Mississippi (continued)

2008, 24 master's, 13 doctorates awarded. Terminal master's awarded for partial completion of doctoral program. *Degree requirements:* For master's, comprehensive exam, thesis; for doctorate, comprehensive exam, thesis/dissertation. *Entrance requirements:* For master's, GRE General Test, minimum GPA of 3.0; for doctorate, GRE General Test, interview, minimum GPA of 3.0. Additional exam requirements/recommendations for international students: Required—TOEFL. *Application deadline:* For fall admission, 3/1 priority date for domestic students, 3/1 for international students. Applications are processed on a rolling basis. Application fee: $30. *Financial support:* In 2008–09, 48 research assistantships with full tuition reimbursements (averaging $8,802 per year), 48 teaching assistantships with full tuition reimbursements (averaging $6,500 per year) were awarded; career-related internships or fieldwork, Federal Work-Study, and institutionally sponsored loans also available. Financial award application deadline: 3/15; financial award applicants required to submit FAFSA. *Faculty research:* Dolphin cognition, sleep, neuropsychology, health-related behaviors, psychopathology. Total annual research expenditures: $101,200. *Unit head:* Dr. Joesph Olmi, Chair, 601-266-4177, Fax: 601-266-5580. *Application contact:* Dr. Heather Sterling-Turner, Graduate Coordinator, 601-266-4177, Fax: 601-266-5580.

University of South Florida, Graduate School, College of Education, Department of Psychological and Social Foundations of Education, Tampa, FL 33620-9951. Offers college student affairs (M Ed); counselor education (MA, PhD, Ed S); interdisciplinary education (PhD, Ed S); school psychology (MA, PhD, Ed S); student affairs administration (PhD). Part-time and evening/weekend programs available. *Faculty:* 24 full-time (14 women), 6 part-time/adjunct (4 women). *Students:* 161 full-time (126 women), 106 part-time (86 women); includes 74 minority (36 African Americans, 1 American Indian/Alaska Native, 8 Asian Americans or Pacific Islanders, 29 Hispanic Americans), 5 international. 271 applicants, 46% accepted, 95 enrolled. In 2008, 71 master's, 7 doctorates awarded. *Degree requirements:* For master's, comprehensive exam, thesis; for doctorate, comprehensive exam, thesis/dissertation. *Entrance requirements:* For master's, GRE General Test, minimum GPA of 3.5 in last 60 hours of course work; for doctorate, GRE General Test, minimum GPA of 3.5 in last 60 hours of coursework; for Ed S, GRE General Test. Additional exam requirements/recommendations for international students: Required—TOEFL (minimum score 550 paper-based; 213 computer-based). *Application deadline:* For fall admission, 1/1 for domestic and international students. Application fee: $30. Electronic applications accepted. *Expenses:* Tuition, state resident: full-time $2624.40; part-time $291.60 per credit hour. Tuition, nonresident: full-time $7822; part-time $869.13 per credit hour. *Financial support:* Career-related internships or fieldwork, scholarships/grants, and unspecified assistantships available. Financial award applicants required to submit CSS PROFILE. Total annual research expenditures: $3.6 million. *Unit head:* Dr. Herbert Exum, Chairperson, 813-974-8395, Fax: 813-974-5814, E-mail: exum@tempest.coedu.usf.edu. *Application contact:* Dr. Kathy Bradley, Program Director, 813-974-9486, Fax: 813-974-5814, E-mail: kbradley@tempest.coedu.usf.edu.

The University of Tennessee, Graduate School, College of Education, Health and Human Sciences, Program in Education, Knoxville, TN 37996. Offers art education (MS); counseling education (PhD); cultural studies in education (PhD); curriculum (MS, Ed S); curriculum, educational research and evaluation (Ed D, PhD); early childhood education (PhD); early childhood special education (MS); education of deaf and hard of hearing (MS); educational administration and policy studies (Ed D, PhD); educational administration and supervision (Ed S); educational psychology (Ed D, PhD); elementary education (MS, Ed S); elementary teaching (MS); English education (MS, Ed S); exercise science (PhD); foreign language/ESL education (MS, Ed S); instructional technology (MS, Ed D, PhD, Ed S); literacy, language and ESL education (PhD); literacy, language education, and ESL education (Ed D); mathematics education (MS, Ed S); modified and comprehensive special education (MS); reading education (MS, Ed S); school counseling (Ed S); school psychology (PhD, Ed S); science education (MS, Ed S); secondary teaching (MS); social foundations (MS); social science education (MS, Ed S); socio-cultural foundations of sports and education (PhD); special education (Ed S); teacher education (Ed D, PhD). *Accreditation:* NCATE. Part-time and evening/weekend programs available. *Degree requirements:* For master's and Ed S, thesis optional; for doctorate, variable foreign language requirement, thesis/dissertation. *Entrance requirements:* For master's, minimum GPA of 2.7; for doctorate and Ed S, GRE General Test, minimum GPA of 2.7. Additional exam requirements/recommendations for international students: Required—TOEFL. Electronic applications accepted. *Expenses:* Tuition, area resident: Part-time $348 per credit hour. Tuition, state resident: full-time $6262. Tuition, nonresident: full-time $18,920; part-time $1052 per credit hour. Required fees: $812; $36 per credit hour. Tuition and fees vary according to program.

The University of Tennessee at Chattanooga, Graduate School, College of Health, Education and Professional Studies, Graduate Studies Division of Education, Program for Educational Specialist, Chattanooga, TN 37403-2598. Offers educational technology (Ed S); school psychology (Ed S). Part-time and evening/weekend programs available. Postbaccalaureate distance learning degree programs offered (no on-campus study). *Faculty:* 4 full-time (2 women), 2 part-time/adjunct (0 women). *Students:* 44 full-time (30 women), 24 part-time (21 women); includes 5 minority (3 African Americans, 2 American Indian/Alaska Native). Average age 36. 15 applicants, 93% accepted, 7 enrolled. In 2008, 6 Ed Ss awarded. *Degree requirements:* For Ed S, internship. *Entrance requirements:* For degree, GRE, letters of reference. Additional exam requirements/recommendations for international students: Required—TOEFL (minimum score 550 paper-based; 213 computer-based; 79 iBT); Recommended—IELTS (minimum score 6). *Application deadline:* For fall admission, 8/1 priority date for domestic students, 6/1 for international students; for spring admission, 12/1 priority date for domestic students, 10/1 for international students. Applications are processed on a rolling basis. Application fee: $30 ($35 for international students). Electronic applications accepted. *Expenses:* Tuition, area resident: Full-time $6150; part-time $281 per credit hour. Tuition, nonresident: full-time $16,710; part-time $867 per credit hour. Required fees: $1100; $128 per credit hour. $550 per semester. *Financial support:* Career-related internships or fieldwork, Federal Work-Study, institutionally sponsored loans, scholarships/grants, and unspecified assistantships available. Support available to part-time students. Financial award application deadline: 4/1; financial award applicants required to submit FAFSA. *Faculty research:* Educational technology, using technology in the classroom, interactive media, distance learning, instructional design technological implementation. *Unit head:* Dr. Lloyd D. Davis, Coordinator, 423-425-4161, Fax: 423-425-5380, E-mail: lloyd-davis@utc.edu. *Application contact:* Dr. Stephanie Bellar, Dean of Graduate Studies, 423-425-4666, Fax: 423-425-5223, E-mail: stephanie-bellar@utc.edu.

The University of Texas at Austin, Graduate School, College of Education, Department of Educational Psychology, Austin, TX 78712-1111. Offers academic educational psychology (M Ed, MA); counseling psychology (PhD); counselor education (M Ed); human development and culture (PhD); learning, cognition and instruction (PhD); quantitative methods (PhD); school psychology (PhD). *Accreditation:* APA (one or more programs are accredited). *Degree requirements:* For master's, thesis optional; for doctorate, thesis/dissertation. *Entrance requirements:* For master's and doctorate, GRE General Test, 3 letters of recommendation. Additional exam requirements/recommendations for international students: Required—TOEFL.

The University of Texas at Tyler, College of Education and Psychology, Department of Psychology, Tyler, TX 75799-0001. Offers clinical psychology (MS), including neuropsychology, school psychology; counseling psychology (MA), including general, marriage and family; interdisciplinary studies (MSIS); school counseling (MA). Part-time and evening/weekend programs available. *Degree requirements:* For master's, comprehensive exam, thesis optional. *Entrance requirements:* For master's, GRE General Test, minimum GPA of 3.0. Additional exam requirements/recommendations for international students: Required—TOEFL (minimum score 79 computer-based). Electronic applications accepted. *Faculty research:* Neuropsychology, child abuse, psychometric properties of psychological instruments, maternal behavior, clinical practice issues, victimization of women, post-traumatic stress disorder.

The University of Texas–Pan American, College of Education, Department of Educational Psychology, Edinburg, TX 78541-2999. Offers counseling (M Ed); educational diagnostician (M Ed); gifted education (M Ed); school psychology (MA); special education (M Ed). Part-time and evening/weekend programs available. *Degree requirements:* For master's, comprehensive exam (for some programs), thesis (for some programs). *Entrance requirements:* For master's, GRE General Test, interview. *Faculty research:* Reading instruction, assessment practice, behavior interventions consultation, mental retardation.

University of the Pacific, School of Education, Department of Educational and School Psychology, Stockton, CA 95211-0197. Offers educational psychology (MA, Ed D); school psychology (Ed S). *Accreditation:* NCATE. *Faculty:* 4 full-time (3 women). *Students:* 13 full-time (10 women), 11 part-time (9 women); includes 11 minority (2 Asian Americans or Pacific Islanders, 9 Hispanic Americans). Average age 24. 15 applicants, 80% accepted, 8 enrolled. In 2008, 6 master's awarded. *Degree requirements:* For master's, thesis (for some programs); for doctorate, thesis/dissertation. *Entrance requirements:* For master's and doctorate, GRE General Test, GRE Subject Test. Additional exam requirements/recommendations for international students: Required—TOEFL (minimum score 475 paper-based; 150 computer-based). *Application deadline:* For fall admission, 3/1 priority date for domestic students; for spring admission, 10/1 priority date for domestic students. Applications are processed on a rolling basis. Application fee: $75. *Expenses:* Tuition: Full-time $30,380; part-time $950 per unit. Required fees: $300. *Financial support:* In 2008–09, 6 teaching assistantships were awarded. Financial award application deadline: 3/1; financial award applicants required to submit FAFSA. *Unit head:* Dr. Linda Webster, Chairperson, 209-946-2559, E-mail: lwebster@pacific.edu. *Application contact:* Office of Graduate Admissions, 209-946-2344.

The University of Toledo, College of Graduate Studies, College of Health Science and Human Service, Division of Human Services, Toledo, OH 43606-3390. Offers counselor education and school psychology (MA, PhD, Ed S), including counselor education, guidance/counselor education (PhD), school psychology (MA, Ed S); criminal justice (MA, Certificate), including criminal justice (MA), juvenile justice (Certificate), severe behavioral spectrum (Certificate); health and rehabilitative services (MA), including speech language pathology; health education (PhD); kinesiology (MSX, PhD), including exercise science; recreation and leisure (MA); social work (MSW); speech-language pathology (MA).

The University of Toledo, College of Graduate Studies, College of Health Science and Human Service, Division of Human Services, Department of Counselor Education and School Psychology, Program in School Psychology, Toledo, OH 43606-3390. Offers school counseling (MA); school psychology (Ed S). *Entrance requirements:* For master's, GRE.

University of Utah, The Graduate School, College of Education, Department of Educational Psychology, Salt Lake City, UT 84112-1107. Offers counseling psychology (PhD); educational psychology (MA); professional counseling (MS); professional psychology (M Ed); school counseling (M Ed, MS); school psychology (MS, PhD); statistics (M Stat). *Accreditation:* APA (one or more programs are accredited). Evening/weekend programs available. *Degree requirements:* For master's, variable foreign language requirement, comprehensive exam, thesis (for some programs); for doctorate, variable foreign language requirement, thesis/dissertation, oral exam. *Entrance requirements:* For master's and doctorate, GRE General Test, minimum GPA of 3.0. Additional exam requirements/recommendations for international students: Required—TOEFL (minimum score 500 paper-based; 173 computer-based). *Faculty research:* Autism, computer technology and instruction, cognitive behavior, aging, group counseling.

University of Virginia, Curry School of Education, Department of Human Services, Charlottesville, VA 22903. Offers clinical and school psychology (PhD); communication disorders (M Ed); counselor education (M Ed, Ed D, Ed S); health and physical education (M Ed, Ed D), including kinesiology. *Accreditation:* APA (one or more programs are accredited). *Faculty:* 26 full-time (14 women), 2 part-time/adjunct (1 woman). *Students:* 103 full-time (97 women), 8 part-time (all women); includes 10 minority (2 African Americans, 4 Asian Americans or Pacific Islanders, 4 Hispanic Americans). Average age 25. 180 applicants, 50% accepted, 38 enrolled. In 2008, 41 master's awarded. *Entrance requirements:* For master's, doctorate, and Ed S, GRE General Test, 2 letters of recommendation. Additional exam requirements/recommendations for international students: Required—TOEFL (minimum score 600 paper-based; 250 computer-based; 90 iBT), IELTS (minimum score 7). *Application deadline:* Applications are processed on a rolling basis. Application fee: $60. Electronic applications accepted. *Expenses:* Tuition, area resident: Full-time $10,452. Tuition, state resident: full-time $10,452. Tuition, nonresident: full-time $20,010. Required fees: $2176. Part-time tuition and fees vary according to course load and program. *Financial support:* Fellowships with tuition reimbursements, research assistantships with tuition reimbursements, teaching assistantships with tuition reimbursements available. Financial award applicants required to submit FAFSA. *Unit head:* Chris Ingersoll, Chair. *Application contact:* Lynn Renfroe, Information Contact, 434-924-6254, E-mail: ldr9t@virginia.edu.

University of Virginia, Curry School of Education, Program in Education, Charlottesville, VA 22903. Offers administration and supervision (PhD); applied developmental science (PhD); counselor education (PhD); curriculum and instruction (PhD); early childhood-developmental risk (MT); education evaluation (PhD); educational psychology (PhD); educational research (PhD); elementary (MT, PhD); English education (MT, PhD); foreign language education (MT); higher education (PhD); instructional technology (PhD); kinesiology (MT, PhD); math education (PhD); reading education (PhD); research statistics and evaluation (PhD); school psychology (PhD); science education (PhD); social foundations (PhD); social studies education (MT, PhD); special education (PhD); world languages education (MT). *Students:* 418 full-time (296 women), 69 part-time (41 women); includes 51 minority (27 African Americans, 1 American Indian/Alaska Native, 15 Asian Americans or Pacific Islanders, 8 Hispanic Americans), 26 international. Average age 30. 282 applicants, 56% accepted, 77 enrolled. In 2008, 46 master's, 64 doctorates awarded. *Degree requirements:* For master's, comprehensive exam (for some programs), field project; for doctorate, comprehensive exam, thesis/dissertation. *Entrance requirements:* For doctorate, GRE General Test. Additional exam requirements/recommendations for international students: Required—TOEFL (minimum score 600 paper-based; 250 computer-based; 90 iBT), IELTS (minimum score 7). *Application deadline:* Applications are processed on a rolling basis. Application fee: $60. Electronic applications accepted. *Expenses:* Tuition, area resident: Full-time $10,452. Tuition, state resident: full-time $10,452. Tuition, nonresident: full-time $20,010. Required fees: $2176. Part-time tuition and fees vary according to course load and program. *Financial support:* Fellowships, research assistantships, teaching assistantships available. Financial award application deadline: 1/5; financial award applicants required to submit FAFSA.

University of Washington, Graduate School, College of Education, Program in Educational Psychology, Seattle, WA 98195. Offers educational psychology (PhD); human development and cognition (M Ed); learning sciences (M Ed, PhD); measurement, statistics and research design (M Ed); school psychology (M Ed). *Accreditation:* APA. *Degree requirements:* For master's, thesis optional; for doctorate, thesis/dissertation. *Entrance requirements:* For master's and doctorate, GRE General Test, minimum GPA of 3.0. Additional exam requirements/recommendations for international students: Required—TOEFL.

University of Wisconsin–Eau Claire, College of Arts and Sciences, Department of Psychology, Eau Claire, WI 54702-4004. Offers school psychology (MSE, Ed S). Part-time programs available. *Faculty:* 12 full-time (6 women). *Students:* 16 full-time (11 women), 7 part-time (all women), 1 international. Average age 24. 49 applicants, 33% accepted, 16 enrolled. In 2008, 16 master's awarded. *Degree requirements:* For master's, comprehensive exam, thesis, NASP Professional Exam, written exam, externship. *Entrance requirements:* For master's, GRE, minimum undergraduate GPA of 3.07. Additional exam requirements/recommendations for international students: Required—TOEFL (minimum score 550 paper-based; 213 computer-based; 79 iBT). *Application deadline:* For fall admission, 3/1 priority date for domestic students, 6/1 priority date for international students; for spring admission, 11/1 priority date for international students. Applications are processed on a rolling basis. Application fee: $56. Electronic applications accepted. *Expenses:* Tuition, state resident: full-time $6426; part-time $400.60

per credit. Tuition, nonresident: full-time $17,560; part-time $975.32 per credit. One-time fee: $56 full-time. *Financial support:* In 2008–09, 16 students received support, including 8 fellowships (averaging $3,000 per year); Federal Work-Study and unspecified assistantships also available. Financial award application deadline: 3/1; financial award applicants required to submit FAFSA. *Unit head:* Dr. Lori Bica, Chair, 715-836-5733, Fax: 715-836-2214, E-mail: bicala@uwec.edu. *Application contact:* Kristina Anderson, Director of Admissions, 715-836-5415, Fax: 715-836-2409, E-mail: admissions@uwec.edu.

University of Wisconsin–La Crosse, Office of University Graduate Studies, College of Liberal Studies, Department of Psychology, Program in School Psychology, La Crosse, WI 54601-3742. Offers MS Ed, Ed S. *Students:* 19 full-time (16 women), 32 part-time (28 women); includes 1 Hispanic American. Average age 26. 23 applicants, 100% accepted, 12 enrolled. In 2008, 13 master's awarded. *Degree requirements:* For master's, comprehensive exam, thesis. *Entrance requirements:* For master's, GRE, 3 letters of recommendation, writing sample, resumé. *Expenses:* Tuition, state resident: full-time $6485; part-time $360 per credit hour. Tuition, nonresident: full-time $16,830; part-time $935 per credit hour. Required fees: $846. Tuition and fees vary according to program and reciprocity agreements. *Financial support:* In 2008–09, 3 research assistantships (averaging $6,648 per year) were awarded. *Faculty research:* Substance use in children, parent tutoring, crisis management in schools, life satisfaction, hope and optimism in children. *Unit head:* Dr. Rob Dixon, Program Director, 608-785-6893, Fax: 608-785-8443, E-mail: dixon.rob@uwlax.edu. *Application contact:* Kathryn Kiefer, Associate Director of Admissions, 608-785-8939, E-mail: admissions@uwlac.edu.

University of Wisconsin–Milwaukee, Graduate School, School of Education, Program in School Psychology, Milwaukee, WI 53201-0413. Offers PhD, Ed S. *Accreditation:* APA. *Students:* 5 full-time (all women), 7 part-time (6 women); includes 1 minority (Hispanic American). Average age 26. 10 applicants, 60% accepted, 5 enrolled. In 2008, 7 doctorates awarded. *Expenses:* Tuition, area resident: Full-time $7320; part-time $165 per credit. Tuition, state resident: full-time $7320; part-time $165 per credit. Tuition, nonresident: full-time $17,840; part-time $714 per credit. Tuition and fees vary according to campus/location, program and reciprocity agreements. *Unit head:* Anthony A Hains, Representative, 414-229-4590, E-mail: aahains@uwm.edu. *Application contact:* General Information Contact, 414-229-4982, Fax: 414-229-6967, E-mail: gradschool@uwm.edu.

University of Wisconsin–River Falls, Outreach and Graduate Studies, College of Education and Professional Studies, Department of Counseling and School Psychology, River Falls, WI 54022-5001. Offers counseling (MSE); school psychology (MSE, Ed S). *Accreditation:* NCATE. Part-time programs available. *Entrance requirements:* For master's, minimum GPA of 2.75, resumé, 3 letters of reference, vita. Additional exam requirements/recommendations for international students: Required—TOEFL (minimum score 500 paper-based; 65 iBT), IELTS (minimum score 5.5). Electronic applications accepted.

University of Wisconsin–Stout, Graduate School, School of Education, Program in School Psychology, Menomonie, WI 54751. Offers MS Ed, Ed S. Part-time programs available. *Students:* 28 full-time (23 women), 6 part-time (3 women); includes 3 minority (1 African American, 1 Asian American or Pacific Islander, 1 Hispanic American). Average age 27. 41 applicants, 41% accepted, 11 enrolled. In 2008, 9 master's, 17 Ed Ss awarded. *Degree requirements:* For master's and Ed S, thesis. *Entrance requirements:* For master's, minimum GPA of 3.0; for Ed S, minimum GPA of 3.25. Additional exam requirements/recommendations for international students: Required—TOEFL (minimum score 500 paper-based; 173 computer-based; 61 iBT). *Application deadline:* For fall admission, 1/15 priority date for domestic and international students. Application fee: $45. Electronic applications accepted. *Expenses:* Tuition, state resident: full-time $6227; part-time $345.93 per credit. Tuition, nonresident: full-time $9998; part-time $555.42 per credit. International tuition: $10,512 full-time. Tuition and fees vary according to course load, program and reciprocity agreements. *Financial support:* In 2008–09, 10 research assistantships with partial tuition reimbursements (averaging $6,840 per year), 1 teaching assistantship with partial tuition reimbursement (averaging $5,129 per year) were awarded; Federal Work-Study, scholarships/grants, tuition waivers (partial), and unspecified assistantships also available. Support available to part-time students. Financial award application deadline: 5/1; financial award applicants required to submit FAFSA. *Faculty research:* Intelligence assessment, eating disorders, intervention models, resilience, school violence. *Unit head:* Dr. Carlos Dejud, Director, 715-232-2229, Fax: 715-232-1244, E-mail: dejudc@uwstout.edu. *Application contact:* Anne E. Johnson, Graduate Student Evaluator (Admissions and Assistantship Coordinator), 715-232-1322, Fax: 715-232-2413, E-mail: johnsona@uwstout.edu.

University of Wisconsin–Whitewater, School of Graduate Studies, College of Education, Department of Counselor Education, Whitewater, WI 53190-1790. Offers community counseling (MS Ed); higher education (MS Ed); school counseling (MS Ed). *Accreditation:* ACA; NCATE. Part-time and evening/weekend programs available. *Degree requirements:* For master's, thesis or alternative. *Entrance requirements:* For master's, resumé, 2 letters of reference. Additional exam requirements/recommendations for international students: Required—TOEFL (minimum score 550 paper-based; 213 computer-based). Electronic applications accepted. *Faculty research:* Alcohol and other drugs, counseling effectiveness, teacher mentoring.

University of Wisconsin–Whitewater, School of Graduate Studies, College of Letters and Sciences, Department of Psychology, Program in School Psychology, Whitewater, WI 53190-1790. Offers Ed S. Part-time and evening/weekend programs available. Postbaccalaureate distance learning degree programs offered (no on-campus study). *Degree requirements:* For Ed S, specialist project. *Entrance requirements:* For degree, master's degree in school psychology from an accredited school. Additional exam requirements/recommendations for international students: Required—TOEFL (minimum score 550 paper-based; 213 computer-based). Electronic applications accepted.

Utah State University, School of Graduate Studies, College of Education and Human Services, Department of Psychology, Logan, UT 84322. Offers clinical/counseling/school psychology (PhD); research and evaluation methodology (PhD); school counseling (MS); school psychology (MS). *Accreditation:* APA (one or more programs are accredited). Part-time and evening/weekend programs available. Postbaccalaureate distance learning degree programs offered (no on-campus study). Terminal master's awarded for partial completion of doctoral program. *Degree requirements:* For master's, thesis (for some programs); for doctorate, thesis/dissertation. *Entrance requirements:* For master's, GRE General Test (school psychology), MAT (school counseling), minimum GPA of 3.5; for doctorate, GRE General Test, minimum GPA of 3.5. Additional exam requirements/recommendations for international students: Required—TOEFL. *Faculty research:* Hearing loss detection in infancy, ADHD, eating disorders, domestic violence, neuropsychology, bilingual/Spanish speaking students/parents.

Valdosta State University, Graduate School, College of Education, Department of Psychology and Counseling, Valdosta, GA 31698. Offers clinical/counseling psychology (MS); industrial/organizational psychology (MS); school counseling (M Ed, Ed S); school psychology (Ed S). Part-time and evening/weekend programs available. *Faculty:* 16 full-time (2 women). *Students:* 65 full-time (54 women), 40 part-time (36 women); includes 32 minority (27 African Americans, 5 Hispanic Americans). Average age 27. 105 applicants, 60% accepted, 29 enrolled. In 2008, 25 master's awarded. *Degree requirements:* For master's, thesis or alternative, comprehensive written and/or oral exams; for Ed S, thesis. *Entrance requirements:* For master's and Ed S, GRE General Test or MAT. Additional exam requirements/recommendations for international students: Required—TOEFL (minimum score 523 paper-based; 193 computer-based). *Application deadline:* For fall admission, 7/1 for domestic and international students; for spring admission, 11/15 for domestic and international students. Applications are processed on a rolling basis. Application fee: $40. Electronic applications accepted. *Financial support:* In 2008–09, 2 students received support, including 2 research assistantships with full tuition reimbursements available (averaging $2,452 per year); institutionally sponsored loans and unspecified assistantships also available. Support available to part-time students. Financial award application deadline: 7/1; financial award applicants required to submit FAFSA. *Faculty research:* Using Bender-Gestalt to predict graphomotor dimensions of the draw-a-person test, neurobehavioral hemispheric dominance. *Unit head:* Dr. Robert Bauer, Chair, 229-333-5930, Fax: 229-259-5576, E-mail: bbauer@valdosta.edu. *Application contact:* Rebecca Waters, Coordinator of Graduate Admissions, 229-333-5694, Fax: 229-245-3853, E-mail: rlwaters@valdosta.edu.

Valparaiso University, Graduate Division, Department of Education, Program in School Psychology, Valparaiso, IN 46383. Offers M Ed/Ed S. Part-time and evening/weekend programs available. *Students:* 20 full-time (18 women), 9 part-time (8 women), 1 international. Average age 27. *Entrance requirements:* Additional exam requirements/recommendations for international students: Required—TOEFL (minimum score 550 paper-based; 213 computer-based). *Application deadline:* Applications are processed on a rolling basis. Application fee: $30 ($50 for international students). Electronic applications accepted. *Financial support:* Unspecified assistantships available. Support available to part-time students. Financial award applicants required to submit FAFSA. *Unit head:* Dr. Jan Westrick, Chair, Department of Education, 219-464-5077, Fax: 219-464-6720, E-mail: Jan.Westrick@valpo.edu. *Application contact:* Jamie Haney, Coordinator of Recruitment Activities, 219-464-5313, Fax: 219-464-5381, E-mail: Jamie.Haney@valpo.edu.

Walden University, Graduate Programs, School of Psychology, Minneapolis, MN 55401. Offers clinical assessment (Post-Doctoral Certificate); clinical child psychology (Post-Doctoral Certificate); clinical psychology (Post-Doctoral Certificate); counseling psychology (Post-Doctoral Certificate); forensic psychology (MS), including forensic psychology in the community, general forensic psychology, mental health applications, program planning and evaluation in forensic settings, psychology and legal systems; general psychology (Post-Doctoral Certificate); health psychology (Post-Doctoral Certificate); organizational psychology (Post-Doctoral Certificate); organizational psychology and development (Certificate); psychology (MS, PhD), including clinical psychology, counseling psychology, crisis management and response (MS), general psychology, health psychology, leadership development and coaching (MS), media psychology (MS), organizational psychology, organizational psychology and development (MS), organizational psychology and nonprofit management (MS), program evaluation and research (MS), psychology of culture (MS), psychology, public administration, and social change (MS), school psychology, social psychology (MS), terrorism and security (MS); school psychology (Post-Doctoral Certificate); teaching online (Post-Master's Certificate). Part-time and evening/weekend programs available. Postbaccalaureate distance learning degree programs offered (minimal on-campus study). *Faculty:* 16 full-time, 190 part-time/adjunct. *Students:* 3,198 full-time (2,489 women), 810 part-time (664 women); includes 1,319 minority (1,013 African Americans, 51 American Indian/Alaska Native, 68 Asian Americans or Pacific Islanders, 187 Hispanic Americans), 72 international. Average age 40. 1,468 applicants, 60% accepted, 612 enrolled. In 2008, 203 master's, 37 doctorates awarded. Terminal master's awarded for partial completion of doctoral program. *Degree requirements:* For master's, thesis optional; for doctorate, thesis/dissertation, residency. *Entrance requirements:* For master's, bachelor's degree or equivalent in related field, minimum GPA of 2.5, two references, goal statement, official transcripts, access to computer and Internet; for doctorate, master's degree or equivalent in related field, minimum GPA of 3.0, three years related professional/academic experience, two references, goal statement, official transcripts, access to computer and Internet. Additional exam requirements/recommendations for international students: Required—TOEFL (minimum score 550 paper-based; 213 computer-based), IELTS (minimum score 6.5), TOEFL, IELTS, or Michigan English Language Assessment Battery (minimum score 82). *Application deadline:* Applications are processed on a rolling basis. Application fee: $50. Electronic applications accepted. *Expenses:* Tuition: Full-time $12,877; part-time $520 per credit. Required fees: $1230. Tuition and fees vary according to course load, degree level and program. *Financial support:* In 2008–09, 1 fellowship was awarded; Federal Work-Study, scholarships/grants, unspecified assistantships, and family tuition reduction; active duty/veteran tuition reduction; group tuition reduction; interest-free payment plans also available. Support available to part-time students. Financial award applicants required to submit FAFSA. *Unit head:* Dr. Nina Nabors, Associate Dean, 800-925-3368. *Application contact:* Jennifer Hall, 866-4-WALDEN, E-mail: info@waldenu.edu.

Washington State University, Graduate School, College of Education, Department of Educational Leadership and Counseling Psychology, Program in Counseling Psychology, Pullman, WA 99164. Offers counseling psychology (Ed M, MA, PhD); school psychologist (Certificate). *Accreditation:* APA (one or more programs are accredited). Terminal master's awarded for partial completion of doctoral program. *Degree requirements:* For master's, comprehensive exam (for some programs), thesis (for some programs), oral or written exam; for doctorate, comprehensive exam, thesis/dissertation, oral and written exam. *Entrance requirements:* For master's and doctorate, GRE General Test, minimum GPA of 3.0, 3 letters of recommendation. Additional exam requirements/recommendations for international students: Required—TOEFL (minimum score 550 paper-based; 213 computer-based). Electronic applications accepted. *Faculty research:* Hypnosis supervision, multicultural counseling, American Indian mental health, eating disorders.

Wayne State University, College of Education, Division of Theoretical and Behavioral Foundations, Detroit, MI 48202. Offers counseling (M Ed, MA, Ed D, PhD, Ed S); education evaluation and research (M Ed, Ed D, PhD); educational psychology (M Ed, Ed D, PhD, Ed S); educational sociology (M Ed, Ed D, PhD, Ed S); history and philosophy of education (M Ed, Ed D, PhD); rehabilitation counseling and community inclusion (MA, Ed S); school and community psychology (MA, Ed S); school clinical psychology (Ed S). *Accreditation:* ACA (one or more programs are accredited); CORE (one or more programs are accredited). Evening/weekend programs available. *Degree requirements:* For doctorate, thesis/dissertation. *Entrance requirements:* For master's, GRE; for doctorate, GRE, interview, minimum GPA of 3.0, curriculum vitae, references. Additional exam requirements/recommendations for international students: Required—TOEFL (minimum score 550 paper-based; 213 computer-based), TWE (minimum score 6). Electronic applications accepted. *Faculty research:* Adolescents at risk, supervision of counseling.

Western Carolina University, Graduate School, College of Education and Allied Professions, Department of Human Services, Program in Counseling, Cullowhee, NC 28723. Offers community counseling (M Ed, MS); school counseling (MA Ed). *Accreditation:* ACA. Part-time and evening/weekend programs available. *Degree requirements:* For master's, comprehensive exam, thesis or alternative. *Entrance requirements:* For master's, GRE General Test, appropriate undergraduate with 3.0 GPA, 3 recommendations, writing sample, resumé. Additional exam requirements/recommendations for international students: Required—TOEFL (minimum score 550 paper-based; 270 computer-based; 79 iBT). *Faculty research:* Marital and family development, spirituality in counseling, home school law, sexuality education, family functioning models.

Western Carolina University, Graduate School, College of Education and Allied Professions, Department of Psychology, Cullowhee, NC 28723. Offers general psychology (MA); school psychology (MA). Part-time programs available. *Degree requirements:* For master's, comprehensive exam, thesis. *Entrance requirements:* For master's, GRE General Test, appropriate undergraduate, interview, 3 letters of recommendation, personal statement. Additional exam requirements/recommendations for international students: Required—TOEFL (minimum score 550 paper-based; 270 computer-based; 79 iBT). *Faculty research:* Five-factor model of personality, evolutionary psychology, stress and worry, body image and physical attractiveness, moral decision-making, memory, learning styles.

Western Illinois University, School of Graduate Studies, College of Arts and Sciences, Department of Psychology, Macomb, IL 61455-1390. Offers clinical/community mental health (MS); general psychology (MS); psychology (MS, SSP); school psychology (SSP). Part-time programs available. *Students:* 42 full-time (21 women), 14 part-time (11 women); includes 1 minority (Asian American or Pacific Islander), 2 international. Average age 25. 66 applicants, 53% accepted. In 2008, 13 master's, 10 other advanced degrees awarded. *Degree requirements:* For master's, comprehensive exam (for some programs), thesis or alternative. *Entrance*

School Psychology

Western Illinois University (continued)
requirements: For master's and SSP, GRE General Test. Additional exam requirements/ recommendations for international students: Required—TOEFL (minimum score 550 paper-based; 213 computer-based; 80 iBT). *Application deadline:* Applications are processed on a rolling basis. Application fee: $30. Electronic applications accepted. *Expenses:* Tuition, state resident: full-time $5696; part-time $237.34 per credit hour. Tuition, nonresident: full-time $11,392; part-time $474.68 per credit hour. Required fees: $1453; $60.55 per credit hour. *Financial support:* In 2008–09, 36 students received support, including 36 research assistantships with full tuition reimbursements available (averaging $7,040 per year). Financial award applicants required to submit FAFSA. *Unit head:* Dr. Steven Dworkin, Chairperson, 309-298-1593. *Application contact:* Evelyn Hoing, Assistant Director of Graduate Studies, 309-298-1806, Fax: 309-298-2345, E-mail: grad-office@wiu.edu.

Western Kentucky University, Graduate Studies, College of Education and Behavioral Sciences, Department of Psychology, Bowling Green, KY 42101. Offers psychology (MA); school psychology (Ed S). *Degree requirements:* For master's, comprehensive exam, thesis (for some programs); for Ed S, thesis, oral exam. *Entrance requirements:* For master's, GRE General Test; for Ed S, GRE General Test, minimum GPA of 3.5. Additional exam requirements/ recommendations for international students: Required—TOEFL (minimum score 555 paper-based; 213 computer-based; 79 iBT). *Faculty research:* Neural regeneration, enhancing mobility in the elderly, improvement in visual processing in older adults, lifespan development.

Western New Mexico University, Graduate Division, School of Education, Silver City, NM 88062-0680. Offers bilingual education (MAT); counseling (MA); educational leadership (MA); elementary education (MAT); reading (MAT); school psychology (MA); secondary education (MAT); special education (MAT); TESOL (teaching English to speakers of other languages) (MAT). *Accreditation:* NCATE. *Degree requirements:* For master's, comprehensive exam. *Entrance requirements:* For master's, GRE General Test, GRE Subject Test, minimum GPA of 3.2 in last 64 hours of undergraduate study. Additional exam requirements/recommendations for international students: Required—TOEFL (minimum score 550 paper-based; 213 computer-based). Electronic applications accepted.

Wichita State University, Graduate School, College of Education, Department of Administration, Counseling, Educational and School Psychology, Wichita, KS 67260. Offers counseling (M Ed); education administration (M Ed, Ed D); educational psychology (M Ed); school psychology (Ed S). *Accreditation:* NCATE. Part-time and evening/weekend programs available. *Degree requirements:* For master's, comprehensive exam, thesis optional; for doctorate, one foreign language, thesis/dissertation; for Ed S, internship, practicum. *Entrance requirements:* For master's, minimum GPA of 2.75; for doctorate, GRE General Test. Additional exam requirements/ recommendations for international students: Required—TOEFL. Electronic applications accepted.

Worcester State College, Graduate Studies, Department of Education, Program in School Psychology, Worcester, MA 01602-2597. Offers M Ed, CAGS. *Faculty:* 9 full-time (6 women), 14 part-time/adjunct (8 women). *Students:* 14 full-time (13 women), 4 part-time (3 women); includes 1 minority (Hispanic American). Average age 28. 14 applicants, 57% accepted, 4 enrolled. *Degree requirements:* For master's, comprehensive exam (for some programs), thesis optional. *Entrance requirements:* Additional exam requirements/recommendations for international students: Required—TOEFL (minimum score 550 paper-based; 213 computer-based; 79 iBT). *Application deadline:* For fall admission, 3/15 priority date for domestic and international students. *Expenses:* Tuition, area resident: Full-time $2700; part-time $150 per credit. Tuition, state resident: full-time $2700; part-time $150 per credit. Tuition, nonresident: full-time $2700; part-time $150 per credit. Required fees: $1530; $85 per credit. *Financial support:* Career-related internships or fieldwork, scholarships/grants, and unspecified assistantships available. Financial award application deadline: 3/1; financial award applicants required to submit FAFSA. *Unit head:* Diane Tighe Cooke, Coordinator, 508-929-8673, Fax: 508-929-8164, E-mail: dcooke@worcester.edu. *Application contact:* Nicole Brown, Assistant Dean of Graduate and Continuing Education, 508-929-8787, Fax: 508-929-8100, E-mail: nbrown@worcester.edu.

Yeshiva University, Ferkauf Graduate School of Psychology, Program in School/Clinical-Child Psychology, New York, NY 10033-3201. Offers Psy D. *Accreditation:* APA. Part-time programs available. *Degree requirements:* For doctorate, comprehensive exam, thesis/ dissertation. *Entrance requirements:* For doctorate, GRE General Test. *Faculty research:* Testing, early childhood intervention, child and adolescent psychotherapy, clinical child psychology.

Youngstown State University, Graduate School, Beeghly College of Education, Department of Counseling, Youngstown, OH 44555-0001. Offers community counseling (MS Ed); school counseling (MS Ed). *Accreditation:* ACA; NCATE. Part-time and evening/weekend programs available. *Degree requirements:* For master's, comprehensive exam. *Entrance requirements:* For master's, MAT, interview, minimum GPA of 2.7. Additional exam requirements/ recommendations for international students: Required—TOEFL. *Faculty research:* Suicide, euthanasia, ethical issues, marriage and family.

Social Psychology

Alvernia University, Graduate Studies, Department of Psychology and Counseling, Reading, PA 19607-1799. Offers community counseling (MA). *Entrance requirements:* For master's, GRE or MAT.

American University, College of Arts and Sciences, Department of Psychology, Program in Psychology, Washington, DC 22016-8062. Offers experimental/biological psychology (MA); general psychology (MA); personality/social psychology (MA). Part-time programs available. *Students:* 39 full-time (33 women), 21 part-time (16 women); includes 12 minority (4 African Americans, 5 Asian Americans or Pacific Islanders, 3 Hispanic Americans), 1 international. Average age 26. 169 applicants, 33% accepted, 25 enrolled. In 2008, 21 master's awarded. *Degree requirements:* For master's, comprehensive exam, thesis or alternative. *Entrance requirements:* For master's, GRE General Test, GRE Subject Test. Additional exam requirements/ recommendations for international students: Required—TOEFL. *Application deadline:* For fall admission, 3/1 for domestic students. Applications are processed on a rolling basis. Application fee: $80. *Expenses:* Tuition: Full-time $21,204; part-time $1178 per credit hour. Required fees: $380. Part-time tuition and fees vary according to course load and program. *Financial support:* Research assistantships, teaching assistantships available. Financial award application deadline: 2/1. *Faculty research:* Behavior therapy, cognitive behavior modification, pro-social behavior, conditioning and learning, olfaction. *Application contact:* Sara Holland, Senior Administrative Assistant, 202-885-1717, Fax: 202-885-1023.

Andrews University, School of Graduate Studies, School of Education, Department of Educational and Counseling Psychology, Program in Community Counseling, Berrien Springs, MI 49104. Offers MA. *Students:* 17 full-time (12 women), 9 part-time (6 women); includes 15 minority (6 African Americans, 9 Hispanic Americans), 6 international. Average age 35. In 2008, 8 master's awarded. *Degree requirements:* For master's, thesis optional. *Entrance requirements:* For master's, GRE. Additional exam requirements/recommendations for international students: Required—TOEFL (minimum score 550 paper-based). Application fee: $40. *Expenses:* Tuition: Full-time $18,360; part-time $765 per credit hour. Required fees: $476; $765 per credit hour. $238 per semester. Tuition and fees vary according to degree level. *Unit head:* Dr. Nancy Carbonell, Coordinator, 269-471-3472. *Application contact:* Carolyn Hurst, Supervisor of Graduate Admission, 800-253-2874, Fax: 269-471-6321, E-mail: graduate@andrews.edu.

Appalachian State University, Cratis D. Williams Graduate School, Department of Human Development and Psychological Counseling, Boone, NC 28608. Offers community counseling (MA); marriage and family therapy (MA); school counseling (MA); student development (MA). *Accreditation:* AAMFT/COAMFTE; ACA; NCATE. Part-time programs available. *Faculty:* 15 full-time (5 women), 21 part-time/adjunct (14 women). *Students:* 124 full-time (97 women), 50 part-time (39 women); includes 14 minority (12 African Americans, 1 Asian American or Pacific Islander, 1 Hispanic American). 169 applicants, 57% accepted, 66 enrolled. In 2008, 60 master's awarded. *Degree requirements:* For master's, comprehensive exam (for some programs), thesis optional, internships. *Entrance requirements:* For master's, GRE General Test, 3 letters of recommendation. Additional exam requirements/recommendations for international students: Required—TOEFL (minimum score 570 paper-based; 230 computer-based; 79 iBT), IELTS (minimum score 6.5). *Application deadline:* For fall admission, 2/1 priority date for domestic students, 2/1 for international students; for spring admission, 2/1 for international students. Applications are processed on a rolling basis. Application fee: $50. Electronic applications accepted. *Expenses:* Tuition, area resident: Full-time $2600; part-time $700 per course. Tuition, state resident: full-time $2600; part-time $700 per course. Tuition, nonresident: full-time $5000; part-time $3300 per course. Required fees: $2150; $330 per course. Tuition and fees vary according to campus/location. *Financial support:* In 2008–09, 20 research assistantships (averaging $7,000 per year), 7 teaching assistantships (averaging $7,000 per year) were awarded; fellowships, career-related internships or fieldwork, Federal Work-Study, scholarships/ grants, and unspecified assistantships also available. Financial award application deadline: 4/1; financial award applicants required to submit FAFSA. *Faculty research:* Multicultural counseling, addictions counseling, play therapy, expressive arts, child and adolescent therapy, sexual abuse counseling. *Unit head:* Dr. Lee Baruth, Chairman, 828-262-2055, E-mail: baruthlg@appstate.edu. *Application contact:* Sandy Krause, Director of Admissions and Recruiting, 828-262-2130, Fax: 828-262-2709, E-mail: krausesl@appstate.edu.

Arcadia University, Graduate Studies, Department of Psychology, Glenside, PA 19038-3295. Offers community counseling (MACP); school counseling (MACP). Part-time programs available. *Degree requirements:* For master's, practicum. *Entrance requirements:* For master's, GRE General Test or MAT.

Argosy University, Atlanta, College of Psychology and Behavioral Sciences, Atlanta, GA 30328. Offers clinical psychology (MA, Psy D, Postdoctoral Respecialization Certificate), including child and family psychology (Psy D), general adult clinical (Psy D), health psychology (Psy D), neuropsychology/geropsychology (Psy D); community counseling (MA), including marriage and family therapy; counselor education and supervision (Ed D); marriage and family therapy (Certificate). *Accreditation:* APA.

See Close-Up on page 1065.

Argosy University, Chicago, College of Psychology and Behavioral Sciences, Chicago, IL 60654. Offers clinical psychology (MA, Psy D), including child and adolescent psychology (Psy D), client-centered and experiential psychotherapies (Psy D), diversity and multicultural psychology (Psy D), family psychology (Psy D), forensic psychology (Psy D), health psychology (Psy D), psychoanalytic psychology (Psy D), psychology and spirituality (Psy D); community counseling (MA); counseling psychology (Ed D), including counselor education and supervision; counselor education and supervision (Ed D); organizational leadership (Ed D). *Accreditation:* APA (one or more programs are accredited). Postbaccalaureate distance learning degree programs offered (minimal on-campus study).

See Close-Up on page 1067.

Argosy University, Dallas, College of Psychology and Behavioral Sciences, Program in Community Counseling, Dallas, TX 75231. Offers MA.

See Close-Up on page 1069.

Argosy University, Denver, College of Psychology and Behavioral Sciences, Denver, CO 80203. Offers clinical psychology (MA, Psy D); community counseling (MA); counseling psychology (Ed D), including counselor education and supervision; counselor education and supervision (Ed D); forensic psychology (MA); marriage and family therapy (MA); organizational leadership (Ed D).

See Close-Up on page 1071.

Argosy University, Sarasota, College of Psychology and Behavioral Sciences, Sarasota, FL 34235. Offers community counseling (MA); counseling psychology (Ed D); counselor education and supervision (Ed D); forensic psychology (MA); marriage and family therapy (MA); mental health counseling (MA); organizational leadership (Ed D); pastoral community counseling (Ed D); school counseling (MA, Ed S); school psychology (MA).

See Close-Up on page 1091.

Argosy University, Schaumburg, College of Psychology and Behavioral Sciences, Schaumburg, IL 60173-5403. Offers clinical health psychology (Post-Graduate Certificate); clinical psychology (MA, Psy D), including child and family psychology (Psy D), clinical health psychology (Psy D), diversity and multicultural psychology (Psy D), forensic psychology (Psy D); community counseling (MA); counseling psychology (Ed D), including counselor education and supervision; counselor education and supervision (Ed D); forensic psychology (Post-Graduate Certificate); organizational leadership (Ed D). *Accreditation:* ACA; APA.

See Close-Up on page 1093.

Argosy University, Washington DC, College of Psychology and Behavioral Sciences, Arlington, VA 22209. Offers clinical psychology (MA, Psy D), including child and family psychology (Psy D), diversity and multicultural psychology (Psy D), forensic psychology (Psy D), health and neuropsychology (Psy D); community counseling (MA); counseling psychology (Ed D), including counselor education and supervision; counselor education and supervision (Ed D); forensic psychology (MA); organizational leadership (Ed D). *Accreditation:* APA.

See Close-Up on page 1101.

Arizona State University, Graduate College, College of Liberal Arts and Sciences, Division of Natural Sciences, Department of Psychology, Tempe, AZ 85287. Offers behavioral neuroscience (PhD); clinical psychology (PhD); cognition, action and perception (PhD); developmental psychology (PhD); quantitative psychology (PhD); social psychology (PhD). *Accreditation:* APA. *Degree requirements:* For doctorate, thesis/dissertation. *Entrance requirements:* For doctorate, GRE General Test, GRE Subject Test.

Auburn University, Graduate School, College of Education, Department of Counseling and Counseling Psychology, Auburn University, AL 36849. Offers community agency counseling

(M Ed, MS, Ed D, PhD, Ed S); counseling psychology (PhD); counselor education (Ed D, PhD); school counseling (M Ed, MS, Ed D, PhD, Ed S); school psychometry (M Ed, MS, Ed D, PhD, Ed S). *Accreditation:* ACA (one or more programs are accredited); APA (one or more programs are accredited); NCATE. Part-time programs available. *Faculty:* 10 full-time (6 women). *Students:* 51 full-time (35 women), 41 part-time (33 women); includes 27 minority (26 African Americans, 1 Hispanic American), 5 international. Average age 31. 140 applicants, 42% accepted, 30 enrolled. In 2008, 20 master's, 9 doctorates, 4 other advanced degrees awarded. *Degree requirements:* For master's, thesis (for some programs); for doctorate, thesis/dissertation; for Ed S, thesis or alternative. *Entrance requirements:* For master's and Ed S, GRE General Test; for doctorate, GRE General Test, GRE Subject Test. *Application deadline:* For fall admission, 5/15 for domestic students. Application fee: $25 ($50 for international students). Electronic applications accepted. *Expenses:* Tuition, area resident: Full-time $5880; part-time $243 per credit hour. Tuition, state resident: full-time $5880; part-time $243 per credit hour. Tuition, nonresident: full-time $17,640; part-time $729 per credit hour. International tuition: $17,846 full-time. Required fees: $620. Tuition and fees vary according to program and reciprocity agreements. *Financial support:* Research assistantships, Federal Work-Study and traineeships available. Support available to part-time students. Financial award application deadline: 3/15. *Faculty research:* At-risk students, substance abuse, gender roles, AIDS, professional ethics. *Unit head:* Dr. Holly Stadler, Head, 334-844-5160. *Application contact:* Dr. Joe Pittman, Interim Dean of the Graduate School, 334-844-4700.

Ball State University, Graduate School, Teachers College, Department of Counseling Psychology and Guidance Services, Program in Social Psychology, Muncie, IN 47306-1099. Offers MA. *Entrance requirements:* For master's, GRE General Test.

Bowling Green State University, Graduate College, College of Arts and Sciences, Department of Sociology, Bowling Green, OH 43403. Offers demography and population studies (MA); social psychology (MA); sociology (PhD). Part-time programs available. *Degree requirements:* For master's, thesis or alternative; for doctorate, comprehensive exam, thesis/dissertation. *Entrance requirements:* For master's and doctorate, GRE General Test. Additional exam requirements/recommendations for international students: Required—TOEFL. Electronic applications accepted. *Faculty research:* Applied demography, criminology and deviance, family studies, population studies, social psychology.

Brandeis University, Graduate School of Arts and Sciences, Department of Psychology, Waltham, MA 02454-9110. Offers cognitive neuroscience (PhD); general psychology (MA); social/developmental psychology (PhD). MA program offered to students enrolled in PhD program only. *Degree requirements:* For doctorate, comprehensive exam, thesis/dissertation. *Entrance requirements:* For doctorate, GRE General Test, GRE Subject Test (recommended), 3 letters of recommendation. Additional exam requirements/recommendations for international students: Required—TOEFL (minimum score 600 paper-based; 250 computer-based). Electronic applications accepted. *Faculty research:* Development, cognition, social aging, perception.

Brigham Young University, Graduate Studies, College of Family, Home, and Social Sciences, Department of Psychology, Provo, UT 84602-1001. Offers clinical psychology (PhD); general psychology (MS); psychology (PhD), including applied social psychology, behavioral neurobiology, theoretical/philosophical psychology. *Accreditation:* APA (one or more programs are accredited). *Faculty:* 30 full-time (7 women), 10 part-time/adjunct (4 women). *Students:* 94 full-time (31 women); includes 13 minority (3 African Americans, 6 Asian Americans or Pacific Islanders, 4 Hispanic Americans), 9 international. Average age 24. 73 applicants, 32% accepted, 23 enrolled. In 2008, 9 master's, 14 doctorates awarded. *Degree requirements:* For master's, thesis; for doctorate, thesis/dissertation, publishable paper. *Entrance requirements:* For master's and doctorate, GRE General Test, minimum GPA of 3.0 in last 60 hours of upper division course work. Additional exam requirements/recommendations for international students: Required—TOEFL. *Application deadline:* For fall admission, 1/3 for domestic students. Application fee: $50. Electronic applications accepted. *Expenses:* Tuition: Full-time $5160; part-time $287 per credit hour. Tuition and fees vary according to program and student's religious affiliation. *Financial support:* In 2008–09, 85 students received support, including 13 research assistantships with partial tuition reimbursements available (averaging $3,000 per year), 26 teaching assistantships with partial tuition reimbursements available (averaging $3,000 per year); fellowships, career-related internships or fieldwork, scholarships/grants, tuition waivers (partial), and unspecified assistantships also available. Financial award application deadline: 5/31. *Faculty research:* Psychotherapy process, Alzheimer's disease/dementia, psychology and law, health, psychology, developmental. Total annual research expenditures: $533,878. *Unit head:* Dr. Ramona Hopkins, Chair, 801-422-1170, Fax: 801-422-0602, E-mail: ramona_hopkins@byu.edu. *Application contact:* Karen A. Christensen, Coordinator of Student Programs, 801-422-4560, Fax: 801-422-0602, E-mail: karen_christensen@byu.edu.

Brock University, Faculty of Graduate Studies, Faculty of Social Sciences, Program in Psychology, St. Catharines, ON L2S 3A1, Canada. Offers behavioral neuroscience (MA, PhD); life span development (MA, PhD); social personality (MA, PhD). Part-time programs available. *Degree requirements:* For master's, thesis; for doctorate, thesis/dissertation. *Entrance requirements:* For master's, GRE, honors degree; for doctorate, GRE, master's degree. Additional exam requirements/recommendations for international students: Required—TOEFL (minimum score 550 paper-based; 213 computer-based; 80 iBT), IELTS (minimum score 6.5), TWE (minimum score 4). Electronic applications accepted. *Faculty research:* Social personality, behavioral neuroscience, life-span development.

Brooklyn College of the City University of New York, Division of Graduate Studies, Department of Psychology, Brooklyn, NY 11210-2889. Offers experimental psychology (MA); industrial and organizational psychology (MA), including industrial and organizational psychology-human relations, psychology-organizational psychology and behavior; mental health counseling (MA); psychology (PhD). The City University doctoral program in experimental psychology is based at Brooklyn College; candidates who complete the MA may apply for admission to the doctoral program. MA programs in industrial and organizational psychology and mental health counseling are fall admissions only. Part-time programs available. *Students:* 79 full-time (68 women), 121 part-time (93 women); includes 77 minority (48 African Americans, 1 American Indian/Alaska Native, 10 Asian Americans or Pacific Islanders, 18 Hispanic Americans), 18 international. Average age 31. 254 applicants, 59% accepted, 101 enrolled. In 2008, 48 master's awarded. *Degree requirements:* For master's, comprehensive exam, thesis (for some programs). *Entrance requirements:* For master's, minimum GPA of 3.0, 2 letters of recommendation, essay; for doctorate, GRE. Additional exam requirements/recommendations for international students: Required—TOEFL. *Application deadline:* For fall admission, 3/1 for domestic students, 2/1 for international students; for spring admission, 11/1 for domestic students, 10/1 for international students. Applications are processed on a rolling basis. Application fee: $125. Electronic applications accepted. *Expenses:* Tuition, state resident: full-time $7360; part-time $310 per credit hour. Tuition, nonresident: full-time $13,800; part-time $575 per credit hour. *Financial support:* Career-related internships or fieldwork, Federal Work-Study, institutionally sponsored loans, scholarships/grants, and tuition waivers (partial) available. Support available to part-time students. Financial award application deadline: 5/1; financial award applicants required to submit FAFSA. *Unit head:* Dr. Glen Hass, Chairperson, 718-951-5601, Fax: 718-951-4814, E-mail: ghass@brooklyn.cuny.edu. *Application contact:* Hernan Sierra, Graduate Admissions Coordinator, 718-951-4536, Fax: 718-951-4506, E-mail: grads@brooklyn.cuny.edu.

Brown University, Graduate School, Department of Psychology, Providence, RI 02912. Offers behavioral neuroscience (PhD); cognitive processes (PhD); sensation and perception (PhD); social/developmental (PhD); MS/PhD. *Degree requirements:* For doctorate, thesis/dissertation. *Entrance requirements:* For doctorate, GRE General Test, GRE Subject Test.

California Institute of Integral Studies, Graduate Programs, School of Professional Psychology, San Francisco, CA 94103. Offers clinical psychology (Psy D); community mental health (MA); drama therapy (MA); expressive arts therapy (MA); integral counseling psychology (MA); integral counseling, psychology-weekend (MA); somatic psychology (MA). *Accreditation:* APA. Part-time programs available. *Faculty:* 28 full-time, 59 part-time/adjunct. *Students:* 553 full-time (408 women), 88 part-time (69 women); includes 132 minority (25 African Americans, 3 American Indian/Alaska Native, 57 Asian Americans or Pacific Islanders, 47 Hispanic Americans). Average age 37. 506 applicants, 61% accepted, 181 enrolled. In 2008, 109 master's, 20 doctorates awarded. *Degree requirements:* For master's, comprehensive exam; for doctorate, comprehensive exam, thesis/dissertation. *Entrance requirements:* For master's, minimum GPA of 3.0, letters of recommendation, writing sample; for doctorate, GRE, MA in psychology or social work with appropriate practical experience for advanced standing, or BA with a minimum GPA of 3.1; letters of recommendation; writing sample. Additional exam requirements/recommendations for international students: Required—TOEFL. *Application deadline:* For fall admission, 2/1 priority date for domestic and international students; for spring admission, 10/15 priority date for domestic and international students. Applications are processed on a rolling basis. Application fee: $65. Electronic applications accepted. *Expenses:* Tuition: Part-time $815 per contact hour. Required fees: $270; $135 per semester. Tuition and fees vary according to degree level. *Financial support:* In 2008–09, 496 students received support; research assistantships with tuition reimbursements available, teaching assistantships with tuition reimbursements available, career-related internships or fieldwork, Federal Work-Study, institutionally sponsored loans, scholarships/grants, and tuition waivers (partial) available. Support available to part-time students. Financial award application deadline: 3/15; financial award applicants required to submit FAFSA. *Faculty research:* Somatic psychology, comparative psychology, art therapy, transpersonal psychology, eco-psychology. *Application contact:* David Townes, Senior Admissions Counselor, 415-575-6152, Fax: 415-575-1268, E-mail: dtownes@ciis.edu.

See Close-Up on page 1105.

California State University, Fullerton, Graduate Studies, College of Humanities and Social Sciences, Department of Psychology, Fullerton, CA 92834-9480. Offers clinical/community psychology (MS); psychology (MA). Part-time programs available. *Students:* 60 full-time (45 women), 14 part-time (8 women); includes 26 minority (4 African Americans, 15 Asian Americans or Pacific Islanders, 7 Hispanic Americans), 7 international. Average age 27. 141 applicants, 29% accepted, 33 enrolled. In 2008, 18 master's awarded. *Degree requirements:* For master's, thesis. *Entrance requirements:* For master's, GRE General Test, GRE Subject Test, undergraduate major in psychology or related field. *Application deadline:* For fall admission, 3/15 for domestic students. Application fee: $55. Tuition and fees vary according to degree level. *Financial support:* Teaching assistantships, career-related internships or fieldwork, Federal Work-Study, institutionally sponsored loans, and scholarships/grants available. Support available to part-time students. Financial award application deadline: 3/1. *Unit head:* Dr. Daniel Kee, Chair, 657-278-3514. *Application contact:* Admissions/Applications, 657-278-2300.

Canisius College, Graduate Division, School of Education and Human Services, Department of Counseling and Human Services, Buffalo, NY 14208-1098. Offers community mental health counseling (MS); general counseling (MS); school counseling (MS). Part-time and evening/weekend programs available. *Faculty:* 5 full-time (3 women), 6 part-time/adjunct (2 women). *Students:* 102 full-time (88 women), 43 part-time (36 women); includes 20 minority (16 African Americans, 1 Asian American or Pacific Islander, 3 Hispanic Americans), 3 international. Average age 27. In 2008, 48 master's awarded. *Degree requirements:* For master's, thesis, research project. *Entrance requirements:* For master's, interview, minimum GPA of 2.5. *Application deadline:* Applications are processed on a rolling basis. Application fee: $25. Electronic applications accepted. *Expenses:* Tuition: Full-time $33,750; part-time $680 per credit hour. Required fees: $18.50 per credit hour. *Financial support:* In 2008–09, 2 research assistantships with partial tuition reimbursements (averaging $8,500 per year) were awarded; career-related internships or fieldwork, Federal Work-Study, institutionally sponsored loans, health care benefits, and unspecified assistantships also available. Support available to part-time students. Financial award applicants required to submit FAFSA. *Faculty research:* Positive psychology, wellness, school violence prevention, chronic pain. *Unit head:* Dr. David L. Farrugia, Chairman, 716-888-2393, Fax: 716-888-3290, E-mail: farrugia@canisius.edu. *Application contact:* James D. Bagwell, Director of Graduate Recruitment and Admissions, 716-888-2544, Fax: 716-888-3290, E-mail: bagwellj@canisius.edu.

Carnegie Mellon University, College of Humanities and Social Sciences, Department of Psychology, Program in Social/Personality/Health Psychology, Pittsburgh, PA 15213-3891. Offers PhD. *Degree requirements:* For doctorate, comprehensive exam, thesis/dissertation. *Entrance requirements:* For doctorate, GRE General Test. Additional exam requirements/recommendations for international students: Required—TOEFL.

Central Connecticut State University, School of Graduate Studies, School of Arts and Sciences, Department of Psychology, New Britain, CT 06050-4010. Offers community psychology (MA); general psychology (MA); health psychology (MA). Part-time and evening/weekend programs available. *Faculty:* 21 full-time (12 women), 20 part-time/adjunct (6 women). *Students:* 17 full-time (14 women), 22 part-time (14 women); includes 8 minority (3 African Americans, 1 Asian American or Pacific Islander, 4 Hispanic Americans), 3 international. Average age 27. 35 applicants, 54% accepted, 10 enrolled. In 2008, 1 master's awarded. *Degree requirements:* For master's, comprehensive exam, thesis or alternative. *Entrance requirements:* For master's, minimum undergraduate GPA of 2.7, essay. Additional exam requirements/recommendations for international students: Required—TOEFL. *Application deadline:* For fall admission, 4/25 for domestic students; for spring admission, 12/1 for domestic students. Applications are processed on a rolling basis. Application fee: $50. Electronic applications accepted. *Expenses:* Tuition, area resident: Full-time $4377; part-time $420 per credit. Tuition, state resident: full-time $6566; part-time $420 per credit. Tuition, nonresident: full-time $12,195; part-time $420 per credit. Required fees: $3462. One-time fee: $62 part-time. *Financial support:* In 2008–09, 9 students received support, including 6 research assistantships; career-related internships or fieldwork, Federal Work-Study, scholarships/grants, and unspecified assistantships also available. Support available to part-time students. Financial award application deadline: 3/1; financial award applicants required to submit FAFSA. *Faculty research:* Clinical psychology, general psychology, child development, cognitive development, drugs/behavior. *Unit head:* Dr. Bradley M. Waite, Chair, 860-832-3100. *Application contact:* Dr. Bradley M. Waite, Chair, 860-832-3100.

The Chicago School of Professional Psychology, Graduate School, Program in International Psychology, Chicago, IL 60610. Offers MA, PhD. Postbaccalaureate distance learning degree programs offered.

Claremont Graduate University, Graduate Programs, School of Behavioral and Organizational Sciences, Department of Psychology, Claremont, CA 91711-6160. Offers advanced study in evaluation (Certificate); cognitive psychology (MA, PhD); developmental psychology (MA, PhD); evaluation and applied research methods (MA, PhD); health behavior research and evaluation (MA, PhD); human resource development and evaluation (MA); industrial/organizational psychology (MA, PhD); organizational behavior (MA, PhD); organizational psychology (MA, PhD); social psychology (MA, PhD); MBA/PhD. Part-time programs available. *Faculty:* 17 full-time (7 women), 1 part-time/adjunct (0 women). *Students:* 218 full-time (158 women), 24 part-time (18 women); includes 51 minority (15 African Americans, 1 American Indian/Alaska Native, 22 Asian Americans or Pacific Islanders, 13 Hispanic Americans), 11 international. Average age 30. In 2008, 38 master's, 12 doctorates, 2 other advanced degrees awarded. Terminal master's awarded for partial completion of doctoral program. *Entrance requirements:* For master's and doctorate, GRE General Test. Additional exam requirements/recommendations for international students: Required—TOEFL (minimum score 550 paper-based; 213 computer-based; 80 iBT). *Application deadline:* For fall admission, 1/15 priority date for domestic students. Applications are processed on a rolling basis. Application fee: $60. Electronic applications accepted. *Expenses:* Tuition: Full-time $33,698; part-time $1465 per unit. Required fees: $310; $155 per semester. Tuition and fees vary according to program. *Financial support:* Fellowships, research assistantships, teaching assistantships, Federal Work-Study, institutionally sponsored loans, scholarships/grants, and tuition waivers (full and partial) available. Support available to part-time students. Financial award application deadline: 2/15;

Social Psychology

Claremont Graduate University (continued)
financial award applicants required to submit FAFSA. *Faculty research:* Social intervention, diversity in organizations, eyewitness memory, aging and cognition, drug policy. *Unit head:* Stewart Donaldson, Dean, 909-607-9001, Fax: 909-621-8905, E-mail: stewart.donaldson@cgu.edu. *Application contact:* Paul Thomas, Director, External Affairs, 909-607-9016, Fax: 909-621-8905, E-mail: paul.thomas@cgu.edu.

Clark University, Graduate School, Department of Psychology, Program in Social-Personality Psychology, Worcester, MA 01610-1477. Offers PhD. *Degree requirements:* For doctorate, thesis/dissertation. *Entrance requirements:* For doctorate, GRE General Test. Additional exam requirements/recommendations for international students: Required—TOEFL. *Application deadline:* For fall admission, 12/28 priority date for domestic students. Applications are processed on a rolling basis. Application fee: $50. *Expenses:* Tuition: Full-time $34,900; part-time $1091 per credit hour. Required fees: $30. *Financial support:* In 2008–09, fellowships with full tuition reimbursements (averaging $15,700 per year), research assistantships with full tuition reimbursements (averaging $15,700 per year), teaching assistantships with full tuition reimbursements (averaging $15,700 per year) were awarded; tuition waivers (full) also available. *Unit head:* Dr. Joseph deRivera, Director, 508-793-7274. *Application contact:* Peggy Moskowitz, Graduate School Secretary, 508-793-7274, Fax: 508-793-7265, E-mail: psychology@clarku.edu.

The College of New Rochelle, Graduate School, Division of Human Services, Program in Community-School Psychology, New Rochelle, NY 10805-2308. Offers MS. *Degree requirements:* For master's, comprehensive exam, clinical fieldwork, journal. *Entrance requirements:* For master's, interview, minimum GPA of 3.0, course work in psychology, sample of written work.

College of St. Joseph, Graduate Programs, Division of Psychology and Human Services, Program in Community Counseling, Rutland, VT 05701-3899. Offers MS. Part-time and evening/weekend programs available. *Degree requirements:* For master's, comprehensive exam, thesis optional. *Entrance requirements:* For master's, 2 letters of reference, interview. Electronic applications accepted.

Columbia University, Graduate School of Arts and Sciences, Division of Natural Sciences, Department of Psychology, New York, NY 10027. Offers experimental psychology (M Phil, MA, PhD); psychobiology (M Phil, MA, PhD); social psychology (M Phil, MA, PhD); JD/MA; JD/PhD; MD/PhD. *Degree requirements:* For master's, thesis; for doctorate, thesis/dissertation. *Entrance requirements:* For master's and doctorate, GRE General Test. Additional exam requirements/recommendations for international students: Required—TOEFL.

Cornell University, Graduate School, Graduate Fields of Arts and Sciences, Field of Psychology, Ithaca, NY 14853-0001. Offers biopsychology (PhD); human experimental psychology (PhD); personality and social psychology (PhD). *Faculty:* 42 full-time (15 women). *Students:* 35 full-time (19 women); includes 5 minority (1 African American, 2 Asian Americans or Pacific Islanders, 2 Hispanic Americans), 11 international. Average age 30. 179 applicants, 7% accepted, 7 enrolled. In 2008, 5 doctorates awarded. *Degree requirements:* For doctorate, comprehensive exam, thesis/dissertation, 2 semesters of teaching experience. *Entrance requirements:* For doctorate, GRE General Test, 3 letters of recommendation. Additional exam requirements/recommendations for international students: Required—TOEFL (minimum score 550 paper-based; 213 computer-based; 77 iBT). *Application deadline:* For fall admission, 12/15 for domestic students. Application fee: $70. Electronic applications accepted. *Expenses:* Tuition: Full-time $29,500. Required fees: $70. Full-time tuition and fees vary according to degree level, program and student level. *Financial support:* In 2008–09, 36 students received support, including 10 fellowships with full tuition reimbursements available, 2 research assistantships with full tuition reimbursements available, 24 teaching assistantships with full tuition reimbursements available; institutionally sponsored loans, scholarships/grants, health care benefits, tuition waivers (full and partial), and unspecified assistantships also available. Financial award applicants required to submit FAFSA. *Faculty research:* Sensory and perceptual systems, social cognition, cognitive development, quantitative and computational modeling, behavioral neuroscience. *Unit head:* Director of Graduate Studies, 607-255-6364, Fax: 607-255-8433. *Application contact:* Graduate Field Assistant, 607-255-3834, Fax: 607-255-8433, E-mail: psychapp@cornell.edu.

Cornell University, Graduate School, Graduate Fields of Arts and Sciences, Field of Sociology, Ithaca, NY 14853-0001. Offers economy and society (MA, PhD); gender and life course (MA, PhD); methodology (MA, PhD); organizations (MA, PhD); policy analysis (MA, PhD); political sociology/social movements (MA, PhD); racial and ethnic relations (MA, PhD); social networks (MA, PhD); social psychology (MA, PhD); social stratification (MA, PhD). *Faculty:* 32 full-time (12 women). *Students:* 40 full-time (16 women); includes 8 minority (2 African Americans, 4 Asian Americans or Pacific Islanders, 2 Hispanic Americans), 10 international. Average age 31. 148 applicants, 7% accepted, 4 enrolled. In 2008, 1 master's, 7 doctorates awarded. Terminal master's awarded for partial completion of doctoral program. *Degree requirements:* For master's, thesis; for doctorate, thesis/dissertation, 1 year of teaching experience. *Entrance requirements:* For master's and doctorate, GRE General Test, 2 letters of recommendation, writing sample. Additional exam requirements/recommendations for international students: Required—TOEFL (minimum score 550 paper-based; 213 computer-based; 77 iBT). *Application deadline:* For fall admission, 1/15 for domestic students. Application fee: $70. Electronic applications accepted. *Expenses:* Tuition: Full-time $29,500. Required fees: $70. Full-time tuition and fees vary according to degree level, program and student level. *Financial support:* In 2008–09, 32 students received support, including 9 fellowships with full tuition reimbursements available, 8 research assistantships with full tuition reimbursements available, 15 teaching assistantships with full tuition reimbursements available; institutionally sponsored loans, scholarships/grants, health care benefits, tuition waivers (full and partial), and unspecified assistantships also available. Financial award applicants required to submit FAFSA. *Faculty research:* Comparative societal analysis, work and family, simulations, social class and mobility, racial segregation and inequality. *Unit head:* Director of Graduate Studies, 607-255-4266. *Application contact:* Graduate Field Assistant, 607-255-4266, E-mail: sociology@cornell.edu.

DePaul University, College of Liberal Arts and Sciences, Department of Psychology, Chicago, IL 60604-2287. Offers clinical psychology (MA, PhD), including child clinical psychology, community clinical psychology; experimental psychology (MA, PhD); general psychology (MS); industrial/organizational psychology (MA, PhD); MA/PhD. *Accreditation:* APA (one or more programs are accredited). *Faculty:* 31 full-time (19 women), 6 part-time/adjunct (4 women). *Students:* 33 full-time (17 women), 23 part-time (20 women); includes 9 minority (4 African Americans, 1 American Indian/Alaska Native, 1 Asian American or Pacific Islander, 3 Hispanic Americans), 2 international. Average age 28. 332 applicants, 14% accepted, 23 enrolled. In 2008, 14 master's, 17 doctorates awarded. *Degree requirements:* For master's, thesis, oral exam; for doctorate, comprehensive exam, thesis/dissertation, oral and written exams. *Entrance requirements:* For master's and doctorate, GRE General Test, GRE Subject Test, 32 quarter hours of course work in psychology, 3 letters of recommendation. Additional exam requirements/recommendations for international students: Required—TOEFL. Application fee: $40. Electronic applications accepted. *Financial support:* In 2008–09, 48 students received support, including 35 research assistantships with full tuition reimbursements available (averaging $11,800 per year), 13 teaching assistantships with full tuition reimbursements available (averaging $11,800 per year); career-related internships or fieldwork, scholarships/grants, traineeships, tuition waivers (full and partial), and unspecified assistantships also available. Financial award application deadline: 1/10. *Faculty research:* Adolescent stress and depression, minority adolescents sexuality, public policy, community influences in child adjustment. *Unit head:* Dr. Christopher B Keys, Chairman, 773-325-7887, Fax: 773-325-7888. *Application contact:* Alison Pereida Knapp, Graduate Admissions Assistant, 773-325-7887, Fax: 773-325-7888.

Eastern Michigan University, Graduate School, College of Education, Department of Leadership and Counseling, Programs in Counseling, Ypsilanti, MI 48197. Offers college counseling (MA); community counseling (MA); helping interventions in a multicultural society (Graduate Certificate); school counseling (MA); school counselor (MA); school counselor licensure (Post Master's Certificate). Part-time and evening/weekend programs available. Postbaccalaureate distance learning degree programs offered (minimal on-campus study). *Entrance requirements:* Additional exam requirements/recommendations for international students: Required—TOEFL.

Eastern University, Department of Counseling Psychology, St. Davids, PA 19087-3696. Offers community/clinical counseling (MA); school counseling (MA, Certificate); school psychology (MS, Certificate). *Degree requirements:* For master's, internship. *Entrance requirements:* For master's, minimum GPA of 2.5. Additional exam requirements/recommendations for international students: Required—TOEFL.

Florida Agricultural and Mechanical University, Division of Graduate Studies, Research, and Continuing Education, College of Arts and Sciences, Department of Psychology, Program in Community Psychology, Tallahassee, FL 32307-3200. Offers MS. *Degree requirements:* For master's, thesis, internship. *Entrance requirements:* For master's, GRE General Test, minimum GPA of 3.0, letters of recommendation (3). Additional exam requirements/recommendations for international students: Required—TOEFL. *Faculty research:* African-American personality and mental health, racism in the socialization of black children.

Florida State University, Graduate Studies, College of Arts and Sciences, Department of Psychology, Program in Social Psychology, Tallahassee, FL 32306. Offers PhD. *Degree requirements:* For doctorate, thesis/dissertation, preliminary exam. *Entrance requirements:* For doctorate, GRE, minimum GPA of 3.0, research experience, letters of recommendation. Additional exam requirements/recommendations for international students: Required—TOEFL (minimum score 550 paper-based; 213 computer-based; 80 iBT). *Faculty research:* The self, prejudice, stereotyping.

Francis Marion University, Graduate Programs, Department of Psychology, Florence, SC 29501-0547. Offers applied clinical psychology (MS); applied community psychology (MS); school psychology (MS). Part-time and evening/weekend programs available. *Faculty:* 10 full-time (4 women), 6 part-time/adjunct (4 women). *Students:* 15 full-time (all women), 28 part-time (25 women); includes 5 minority (all African Americans), 1 international. Average age 38. 39 applicants, 100% accepted, 12 enrolled. In 2008, 15 master's awarded. *Degree requirements:* For master's, internship. *Entrance requirements:* For master's, GRE General Test. *Application deadline:* For fall admission, 4/15 for domestic students; for spring admission, 10/15 for domestic students. Applications are processed on a rolling basis. Application fee: $30. *Expenses:* Tuition, state resident: full-time $7547; part-time $377.35 per credit hour. Tuition, nonresident: full-time $15,094; part-time $754.70 per credit hour. Required fees: $22 per credit hour. $30 per semester. *Financial support:* In 2008–09, 1 research assistantship (averaging $7,000 per year), 3 teaching assistantships (averaging $8,000 per year) were awarded; career-related internships or fieldwork and unspecified assistantships also available. Support available to part-time students. Financial award application deadline: 3/1; financial award applicants required to submit FAFSA. *Faculty research:* Critical thinking, spatial localization, cognition and aging, family psychology. *Unit head:* Dr. John R. Hester, Chair, 843-661-1635, Fax: 843-661-1628. *Application contact:* Jennifer Taylor, Administrative Assistant, 843-661-1378, Fax: 843-661-1628.

The George Washington University, Columbian College of Arts and Sciences, Department of Psychology, Washington, DC 20052. Offers applied social psychology (PhD); clinical psychology (PhD); cognitive neuroscience (PhD). *Accreditation:* APA. Part-time and evening/weekend programs available. *Faculty:* 27 full-time (14 women), 19 part-time/adjunct (12 women). *Students:* 119 full-time (99 women), 83 part-time (64 women); includes 56 minority (14 African Americans, 2 American Indian/Alaska Native, 24 Asian Americans or Pacific Islanders, 16 Hispanic Americans), 6 international. Average age 29. 873 applicants, 5% accepted, 47 enrolled. In 2008, 41 doctorates awarded. *Degree requirements:* For doctorate, thesis/dissertation or alternative, general exam. *Entrance requirements:* For doctorate, GRE General Test, minimum GPA of 3.0. Additional exam requirements/recommendations for international students: Required—TOEFL (minimum score 550 paper-based; 213 computer-based; 80 iBT). *Application deadline:* For fall admission, 1/15 for domestic and international students. Application fee: $60. *Financial support:* In 2008–09, 62 students received support; fellowships with tuition reimbursements available, teaching assistantships with tuition reimbursements available, career-related internships or fieldwork, Federal Work-Study, and tuition waivers available. *Unit head:* Dr. Paul Poppen, Chair, 202-994-6324, E-mail: pjp@gwu.edu. *Application contact:* Information Contact, 202-994-6320, Fax: 202-994-1602, E-mail: psydept@gwu.edu.

The George Washington University, Graduate School of Education and Human Development, Department of Counseling/Human and Organizational Studies, Programs in Counseling: School, Community and Rehabilitation, Washington, DC 20052. Offers community counseling (MA Ed); rehabilitation counseling (MA Ed); school counseling (MA Ed). School counseling program also offered in Alexandria, VA. *Accreditation:* ACA; CORE; NCATE. *Students:* 100 full-time (83 women), 60 part-time (49 women); includes 44 minority (24 African Americans, 1 American Indian/Alaska Native, 10 Asian Americans or Pacific Islanders, 9 Hispanic Americans), 4 international. Average age 33. 182 applicants, 63% accepted, 55 enrolled. In 2008, 56 master's awarded. *Degree requirements:* For master's, comprehensive exam. *Entrance requirements:* For master's, GRE General Test or MAT, minimum GPA of 2.75. *Application deadline:* For fall admission, 1/15 priority date for domestic students; for spring admission, 10/1 for domestic students. Applications are processed on a rolling basis. Application fee: $60. *Financial support:* In 2008–09, 27 students received support; fellowships, research assistantships, teaching assistantships, career-related internships or fieldwork, Federal Work-Study, and tuition waivers (full and partial) available. *Faculty research:* Adjustment to disability, head injury rehabilitation, cross-cultural counseling. *Application contact:* Sarah Lang, Director of Graduate Admissions, 202-994-1447, Fax: 202-994-7207, E-mail: slang@gwu.edu.

Graduate School and University Center of the City University of New York, Graduate Studies, Program in Psychology, New York, NY 10016-4039. Offers basic applied neurocognition (PhD); biopsychology (PhD); clinical psychology (PhD); developmental psychology (PhD); environmental psychology (PhD); experimental psychology (PhD); industrial psychology (PhD); learning processes (PhD); neuropsychology (PhD); psychology (PhD); social personality (PhD). *Degree requirements:* For doctorate, one foreign language, thesis/dissertation. *Entrance requirements:* For doctorate, GRE General Test. Additional exam requirements/recommendations for international students: Required—TOEFL. Electronic applications accepted.

Harvard University, Graduate School of Arts and Sciences, Department of Psychology, Cambridge, MA 02138. Offers psychology (PhD), including behavior and decision analysis, cognition, developmental psychology, experimental psychology, personality, psychobiology, psychopathology; social psychology (PhD). *Degree requirements:* For doctorate, thesis/dissertation, general exams. *Entrance requirements:* For doctorate, GRE General Test. Additional exam requirements/recommendations for international students: Required—TOEFL. *Expenses:* Tuition: Full-time $32,556. Required fees: $1426. Full-time tuition and fees vary according to program and student level.

Henderson State University, Graduate Studies, School of Education, Department of Counselor Education, Arkadelphia, AR 71999-0001. Offers community counseling (MS); elementary school counseling (MSE); secondary school counseling (MSE). *Accreditation:* ACA; NCATE. Part-time programs available. *Entrance requirements:* For master's, GRE General Test or MAT, letters of recommendation, minimum GPA of 2.7, teacher certification. Additional exam requirements/recommendations for international students: Required—TOEFL (minimum score 550 paper-based; 213 computer-based).

Hofstra University, College of Liberal Arts and Sciences, Department of Psychology, Program in School-Community Psychology, Hempstead, NY 11549. Offers MS, Psy D, CAS. *Accreditation:* NCATE. *Students:* 51 full-time (41 women), 4 part-time (3 women); includes 6 minority (1 African American, 3 Asian Americans or Pacific Islanders, 2 Hispanic Americans). Average age 27. 95 applicants, 28% accepted, 11 enrolled. In 2008, 11 master's, 11 doctorates, 8 other advanced degrees awarded. Terminal master's awarded for partial completion of doctoral program. *Degree requirements:* For master's, comprehensive exam; for doctorate, comprehensive exam, thesis/dissertation. *Entrance requirements:* For doctorate, GRE General Test, GRE Subject Test (psychology), interview, 3 letters of recommendation, essay. Additional exam requirements/recommendations for international students: Required—TOEFL (minimum score 550 paper-based; 213 computer-based; 80 iBT). *Application deadline:* For fall admission, 1/15 for domestic and international students. Application fee: $60. Electronic applications accepted. *Expenses:* Tuition: Full-time $15,300; part-time $850 per credit. Required fees: $970; $165 per term. Tuition and fees vary according to program. *Financial support:* In 2008–09, 53 students received support, including 35 fellowships with full and partial tuition reimbursements available (averaging $2,900 per year); research assistantships with full and partial tuition reimbursements available, career-related internships or fieldwork, Federal Work-Study, institutionally sponsored loans, scholarships/grants, and tuition waivers (full and partial) also available. Support available to part-time students. Financial award applicants required to submit FAFSA. *Faculty research:* Cross-cultural psychology, school psychology, childhood and adult trauma, positive psychology, autism spectrum disorders. *Unit head:* Dr. Robert Motta, Program Director, 516-463-5029, Fax: 516-463-6052, E-mail: psyrwm@hofstra.edu. *Application contact:* Carol Drummer, Dean of Graduate Admissions, 516-463-4876, Fax: 516-463-4664, E-mail: gradstudent@hofstra.edu.

Howard University, Graduate School, Department of Psychology, Washington, DC 20059-0002. Offers clinical psychology (PhD); developmental psychology (PhD); experimental psychology (PhD); neuropsychology (PhD); personality psychology (PhD); psychology (MS); social psychology (PhD). *Accreditation:* APA (one or more programs are accredited). Part-time programs available. *Degree requirements:* For master's, thesis; for doctorate, comprehensive exam, thesis/dissertation, qualifying exam. *Entrance requirements:* For master's, GRE General Test, minimum GPA of 2.5, bachelor's degree in psychology or related field; for doctorate, GRE General Test, minimum GPA of 3.0. *Faculty research:* Personality and psychophysiology, educational and social development of African-American children, child and adult psychopathology.

Hunter College of the City University of New York, Graduate School, School of Arts and Sciences, Department of Psychology, New York, NY 10021-5085. Offers applied and evaluative psychology (MA); biopsychology and comparative psychology (MA); social, cognitive, and developmental psychology (MA). Part-time and evening/weekend programs available. *Faculty:* 15 full-time (7 women), 2 part-time/adjunct (0 women). *Students:* 9 full-time (8 women), 55 part-time (43 women); includes 9 minority (2 African Americans, 1 Asian American or Pacific Islander, 6 Hispanic Americans). Average age 29. 107 applicants, 42% accepted, 17 enrolled. In 2008, 29 master's awarded. *Degree requirements:* For master's, comprehensive exam, thesis. *Entrance requirements:* For master's, GRE General Test, minimum 12 credits of course work in psychology, including statistics and experimental psychology; 2 letters of recommendation. Additional exam requirements/recommendations for international students: Required—TOEFL. *Application deadline:* For fall admission, 4/1 for domestic students, 2/1 for international students; for spring admission, 11/1 for domestic students, 9/1 for international students. Applications are processed on a rolling basis. Application fee: $125. *Financial support:* Federal Work-Study, scholarships/grants, and tuition waivers (partial) available. Support available to part-time students. *Faculty research:* Personality, cognitive and linguistic development, hormonal and neural control of behavior, gender and culture, social cognition of health and attitudes. *Unit head:* Dr. Jeffrey Parsons, Chairperson, 212-772-5550, Fax: 212-772-5620, E-mail: jeffrey.parsons@hunter.cuny.edu. *Application contact:* Martin Braun, MA Program Director (Acting), 212-772-4482, Fax: 212-650-3336, E-mail: cbraun@hunter.cuny.edu.

Indiana University Bloomington, University Graduate School, College of Arts and Sciences, Department of Psychological and Brain Sciences, Bloomington, IN 47405-7000. Offers biology and behavior (PhD); clinical science (PhD); cognitive psychology (PhD); developmental psychology (PhD); psychological and brain sciences (MA); social psychology (PhD). *Accreditation:* APA (one or more programs are accredited). *Faculty:* 53 full-time (16 women). *Students:* 95 full-time (52 women), 1 part-time (0 women); includes 11 minority (3 African Americans, 3 Asian Americans or Pacific Islanders, 5 Hispanic Americans), 18 international. Average age 28. 210 applicants, 15% accepted, 17 enrolled. In 2008, 1 master's, 10 doctorates awarded. *Degree requirements:* For doctorate, comprehensive exam, thesis/dissertation, 1st and 2nd year projects, 1 year as associate instructor, qualifying exam, student teaching. *Entrance requirements:* For doctorate, GRE. Additional exam requirements/recommendations for international students: Required—TOEFL (minimum score 550 paper-based; 213 computer-based). *Application deadline:* For fall admission, 12/15 for domestic students, 12/1 for international students. Application fee: $50 ($60 for international students). Electronic applications accepted. *Expenses:* Tuition, area resident: Part-time $291.97 per credit hour. Tuition, state resident: part-time $291.97 per credit hour. Tuition, nonresident: part-time $850.33 per credit hour. Required fees: $110 per semester. Tuition and fees vary according to course load and program. *Financial support:* Fellowships with full tuition reimbursements, research assistantships with full tuition reimbursements, teaching assistantships with full tuition reimbursements, scholarships/grants, health care benefits, and unspecified assistantships available. *Unit head:* Dr. Linda B. Smith, Chair, 812-855-3991, Fax: 812-855-4691, E-mail: smith4@indiana.edu. *Application contact:* Patricia G. Crouch, Academic Services Coordinator, 812-855-4528, Fax: 812-855-4691, E-mail: pcrouch@indiana.edu.

Indiana Wesleyan University, College of Graduate Studies, Graduate Studies in Counseling, Marion, IN 46953. Offers addictions counseling (MS); community counseling (MS); marriage and family counseling (MS); school counseling (MS). *Accreditation:* ACA. Part-time programs available. *Faculty:* 7 full-time (4 women), 6 part-time/adjunct (3 women). *Students:* 60 full-time (46 women), 47 part-time (38 women); includes 4 minority (all African Americans). Average age 36. In 2008, 26 master's awarded. *Degree requirements:* For master's, thesis or alternative. *Entrance requirements:* For master's, GRE General Test. Additional exam requirements/recommendations for international students: Required—TOEFL. *Application deadline:* For fall admission, 6/14 priority date for domestic students. Application fee: $25. Electronic applications accepted. *Expenses:* Contact institution. *Financial support:* In 2008–09, 1 research assistantship with partial tuition reimbursement, 1 teaching assistantship with partial tuition reimbursement were awarded. Support available to part-time students. Financial award application deadline: 3/1; financial award applicants required to submit FAFSA. *Faculty research:* Community counseling, multicultural counseling, addictions. *Unit head:* Dr. Mark Gerig, Director of Graduate Counseling Studies, 765-677-2995, Fax: 765-677-1456, E-mail: mark.gerig@indwes.edu. *Application contact:* Tom Leas, Director of Adult Enrollment Services, 800-895-0036, Fax: 765-677-2404, E-mail: graduate@indwes.edu.

Iowa State University of Science and Technology, Graduate College, College of Liberal Arts and Sciences, Department of Psychology, Ames, IA 50011. Offers cognitive psychology (PhD); counseling psychology (PhD); social psychology (PhD). *Accreditation:* APA. *Faculty:* 25 full-time (8 women), 8 part-time/adjunct (4 women). *Students:* 63 full-time (43 women); includes 10 minority (3 African Americans, 7 Asian Americans or Pacific Islanders), 4 international. Average age 26. 117 applicants, 14% accepted, 11 enrolled. In 2008, 8 doctorates awarded. *Degree requirements:* For doctorate, comprehensive exam, thesis/dissertation. *Entrance requirements:* For doctorate, GRE General Test, GRE Subject Test (psychology). Additional exam requirements/recommendations for international students: Required—TOEFL (minimum score 560 paper-based; 220 computer-based). *Application deadline:* For fall admission, 1/5 priority date for domestic and international students. Application fee: $30 ($70 for international students). Electronic applications accepted. *Expenses:* Tuition, area resident: Full-time $6446; part-time $359 per credit. Tuition, state resident: full-time $6446; part-time $359 per credit. Tuition, nonresident: full-time $17,330; part-time $963 per credit. Required fees: $790; $249.25 per semester. Tuition and fees vary according to course load and program. *Financial support:* In 2008–09, 45 students received support, including 2 fellowships with full tuition reimbursements available (averaging $14,055 per year), 13 research assistantships with full tuition reimbursements available (averaging $12,200 per year), 30 teaching assistantships with full tuition reimbursements available (averaging $12,200 per year); scholarships/grants, health care benefits, and unspecified assistantships also available. *Faculty research:* Counseling

psychology, cognitive psychology, social psychology, health psychology, psychology and public policy. Total annual research expenditures: $2 million. *Unit head:* Dr. Stephanie Madon, Director of Graduate Education, 515-294-1742, Fax: 515-294-6424, E-mail: madon@iastate.edu. *Application contact:* Ann K Schmidt, Graduate Admissions Secretary, 515-294-1743, Fax: 515-294-6424, E-mail: psychadm@iastate.edu.

Lamar University, College of Graduate Studies, College of Arts and Sciences, Department of Psychology, Beaumont, TX 77710. Offers community/clinical psychology (MS); industrial/organizational psychology (MS). Part-time programs available. *Faculty:* 7 full-time (4 women). *Students:* 21 full-time (10 women), 5 part-time (3 women); includes 4 minority (1 African American, 3 Hispanic Americans), 2 international. Average age 25. 32 applicants, 41% accepted, 10 enrolled. In 2008, 6 master's awarded. *Degree requirements:* For master's, thesis, practicum. *Entrance requirements:* For master's, GRE General Test, minimum GPA of 2.75 in last 60 hours of undergraduate course work. Additional exam requirements/recommendations for international students: Required—TOEFL. *Application deadline:* For fall admission, 8/1 for domestic students; for spring admission, 12/1 for domestic students. Application fee: $25 ($50 for international students). *Expenses:* Tuition, state resident: full-time $5000; part-time $195 per credit. Tuition, nonresident: full-time $12,376; part-time $476 per credit. Required fees: $1570. *Financial support:* In 2008–09, 12 students received support, including 3 teaching assistantships (averaging $4,500 per year); fellowships, research assistantships, career-related internships or fieldwork, Federal Work-Study, scholarships/grants, and tuition waivers (partial) also available. Support available to part-time students. Financial award application deadline: 4/1. *Faculty research:* Groupthink, health psychology, school psychology, behavioral neuroscience. *Unit head:* Dr. Oney D. Fitzpatrick, Chair, 409-880-8285, Fax: 409-880-1779, E-mail: fitzpatrod@hal.lamar.edu. *Application contact:* Dr. James W. Westgate, Assistant Dean, 409-880-7978, E-mail: westgate@hal.lamar.edu.

Lenoir-Rhyne University, Graduate Programs, School of Counseling and Human Services, Programs in Counseling, Hickory, NC 28601. Offers agency counseling (MA); community counseling (MA). Part-time and evening/weekend programs available. *Degree requirements:* For master's, comprehensive exam, thesis optional. *Entrance requirements:* For master's, GRE General Test, writing sample, minimum undergraduate GPA of 2.7, minimum graduate GPA of 3.0. Additional exam requirements/recommendations for international students: Required—TOEFL (minimum score 600 paper-based). Electronic applications accepted.

Lesley University, Graduate School of Arts and Social Sciences, Cambridge, MA 02138-2790. Offers clinical mental health counseling (MA), including expressive therapies counseling, holistic counseling, school and community counseling; counseling psychology (MA, CAGS), including professional counseling (MA); school counseling (MA); creative arts in learning (CAGS); creative writing (MFA); ecological teaching and learning (MS); environmental education (MS); expressive therapies (MA, PhD, CAGS), including art (MA); dance (MA), expressive therapies, music (MA); independent studies (CAGS); independent study (MA); intercultural relations (MA, CAGS); interdisciplinary studies (MA), including individualized studies, integrative holistic health, women's studies; urban environmental leadership (MA); visual arts (MFA). Part-time and evening/weekend programs available. Postbaccalaureate distance learning degree programs offered (minimal on-campus study). *Degree requirements:* For master's, internship, practicum, thesis (expressive therapies); for doctorate, thesis/dissertation, arts apprenticeship, field placement; for CAGS, thesis, internship (counseling psychology, expressive therapies). *Entrance requirements:* For master's, MAT (counseling psychology), interview, writing samples, art portfolio; for doctorate, GRE or MAT; for CAGS, interview, master's degree. Additional exam requirements/recommendations for international students: Required—TOEFL (minimum score 550 paper-based; 213 computer-based; 80 iBT). Electronic applications accepted. *Expenses:* Tuition: Full-time $13,770; part-time $765 per credit hour. Required fees: $150. Tuition and fees vary according to course load, degree level, campus/location and program. *Faculty research:* Psychotherapy and culture; psychotherapy and psychological trauma; women's issues in art, teaching and psychotherapy; community based art, psycho-spiritual inquiry.

Loyola University Chicago, Graduate School, Department of Psychology, Program in Applied Social Psychology, Chicago, IL 60611-2196. Offers MA, PhD. *Faculty:* 7 full-time (3 women), 2 part-time/adjunct (1 woman). *Students:* 34 full-time (25 women), 6 part-time (all women); includes 5 minority (1 African American, 3 Asian Americans or Pacific Islanders, 1 Hispanic American), 4 international. Average age 30. 49 applicants, 31% accepted, 7 enrolled. In 2008, 8 master's, 4 doctorates awarded. Terminal master's awarded for partial completion of doctoral program. *Degree requirements:* For master's, thesis; for doctorate, comprehensive exam, thesis/dissertation, internship. *Entrance requirements:* For master's and doctorate, GRE General Test, GRE Subject Test, sample of written work. *Application deadline:* For fall admission, 1/15 for domestic and international students. Applications are processed on a rolling basis. Application fee: $50. *Expenses:* Tuition: Full-time $13,500; part-time $750 per credit hour. Required fees: $60 per semester. Full-time tuition and fees vary according to program. *Financial support:* In 2008–09, 1 fellowship with tuition reimbursement (averaging $14,000 per year), 5 research assistantships with tuition reimbursements (averaging $14,000 per year), 1 teaching assistantship (averaging $14,000 per year) were awarded; career-related internships or fieldwork, Federal Work-Study, and scholarships/grants also available. Financial award application deadline: 1/15; financial award applicants required to submit FAFSA. *Faculty research:* Program evaluation, attitudes and prejudice, psychological well-being, mass media, groups and organizations and communities. Total annual research expenditures: $200,000. *Unit head:* Dr. Scott Tindale, 773-508-3014. *Application contact:* Dr. Scott Tindale, 773-508-3014.

Lynchburg College, Graduate Studies, School of Education and Human Development, Lynchburg, VA 24501-3199. Offers community counseling (M Ed); counselor education (M Ed), including community counseling; curriculum and instruction (M Ed); educational leadership (M Ed); English education (M Ed); reading (M Ed); school counseling (M Ed); science education (M Ed); special education (M Ed), including autism spectrum disorder, early childhood special education, mental retardation, teaching children with learning disabilities, teaching the emotionally disturbed. Part-time and evening/weekend programs available. *Faculty:* 19 full-time (11 women), 5 part-time/adjunct (4 women). *Students:* 76 full-time (60 women), 127 part-time (103 women); includes 20 minority (17 African Americans, 3 Hispanic Americans), 6 international. Average age 33. 99 applicants, 75% accepted, 49 enrolled. In 2008, 96 master's awarded. *Degree requirements:* For master's, comprehensive exam. *Entrance requirements:* For master's, GRE, minimum undergraduate GPA of 3.0. Additional exam requirements/recommendations for international students: Required—TOEFL. *Application deadline:* For fall admission, 7/31 for domestic students, 6/1 for international students; for spring admission, 11/30 for domestic students, 10/1 for international students. Application fee: $30. *Expenses:* Tuition: Full-time $6750; part-time $375 per credit. *Financial support:* Career-related internships or fieldwork, scholarships/grants, and unspecified assistantships available. Financial award applicants required to submit FAFSA. *Unit head:* Dr. Jan Stenette, Dean, 434-544-8662. *Application contact:* Dr. Edward Polloway, Vice President for Graduate and Community Advancement, 434-544-8655, E-mail: polloway@lynchburg.edu.

Martin University, Division of Psychology, Indianapolis, IN 46218-3867. Offers community psychology (MS). Part-time and evening/weekend programs available. *Degree requirements:* For master's, thesis. *Entrance requirements:* For master's, GRE General Test, GRE Subject Test.

Marymount University, School of Education and Human Services, Program in Community Counseling and Forensic Psychology, Arlington, VA 22207-4299. Offers MA/MA. Part-time and evening/weekend programs available. *Students:* 7 full-time (all women), 4 part-time (all women); includes 3 minority (all African Americans). Average age 27. *Entrance requirements:* Additional exam requirements/recommendations for international students: Required—TOEFL (minimum score 600 paper-based; 250 computer-based; 100 iBT). Application fee: $40. *Expenses:* Tuition: Full-time $12,420; part-time $690 per credit hour. Required fees: $126; $7 per credit hour. Tuition and fees vary according to degree level. *Financial support:* In 2008–09, 10 students received support; research assistantships with full tuition reimbursements available,

Social Psychology

Marymount University *(continued)*
career-related internships or fieldwork, Federal Work-Study, scholarships/grants, and unspecified assistantships available. Support available to part-time students. Financial award applicants required to submit FAFSA. *Unit head:* Dr. Wayne Lesko, Dean, 703-284-1620, Fax: 703-284-1631, E-mail: wayne.lesko@marymount.edu. *Application contact:* Francesca Reed, Director, Graduate Admissions, 703-284-5901, Fax: 703-527-3815, E-mail: grad.admissions@marymount.edu.

Memorial University of Newfoundland, School of Graduate Studies, Department of Psychology, St. John's, NL A1C 5S7, Canada. Offers applied social psychology (MASP); experimental psychology (M Sc, PhD). Part-time programs available. *Degree requirements:* For master's, workterms (MASP), thesis (M Sc); for doctorate, comprehensive exam, thesis/dissertation, oral thesis defense. *Entrance requirements:* For master's, GRE, honors bachelor's degree of high second class standing or equivalent; for doctorate, GRE, master's or honors degree. Electronic applications accepted. *Faculty research:* Behavioral neuroscience, cognition, theory and research on abnormal behavior.

Miami University, Graduate School, College of Arts and Sciences, Department of Psychology, Oxford, OH 45056. Offers clinical psychology (PhD); experimental psychology (PhD); social psychology (PhD). *Accreditation:* APA. *Degree requirements:* For doctorate, comprehensive exam, thesis/dissertation, final exams. *Entrance requirements:* For doctorate, GRE General Test, GRE Subject Test, minimum GPA of 2.75 (undergraduate), 3.0 (graduate). Additional exam requirements/recommendations for international students: Required—TOEFL (minimum score 550 paper-based; 213 computer-based), TWE (minimum score 4). Electronic applications accepted.

Minnesota State University Mankato, College of Graduate Studies, College of Education, Department of Counseling and Student Personnel, Mankato, MN 56001. Offers college student affairs (MS); counselor education and supervision (Ed D); marriage and family counseling (Certificate); professional community counseling (MS); professional school counseling (MS). *Accreditation:* ACA (one or more programs are accredited); NCATE. *Students:* 49 full-time (41 women), 42 part-time (31 women). *Degree requirements:* For master's, comprehensive exam, thesis or alternative. *Entrance requirements:* For master's, GRE General Test or MAT (if GPA is below 3.0 for last 2 years), minimum GPA of 3.0 during previous 2 years, 3 letters of reference. Additional exam requirements/recommendations for international students: Required—TOEFL. *Application deadline:* For fall admission, 1/15 priority date for domestic students. Applications are processed on a rolling basis. Application fee: $40. Electronic applications accepted. *Financial support:* Research assistantships with full tuition reimbursements, teaching assistantships with full tuition reimbursements, career-related internships or fieldwork, Federal Work-Study, institutionally sponsored loans, and unspecified assistantships available. Support available to part-time students. Financial award application deadline: 3/15; financial award applicants required to submit FAFSA. *Unit head:* Dr. Jaqueline Lewis, Chairperson, 507-389-5658. *Application contact:* 507-389-2321, E-mail: grad@mnsu.edu.

Missouri State University, Graduate College, College of Education, Department of Counseling, Leadership, and Special Education, Program in Counseling, Springfield, MO 65804-0094. Offers counseling (MS), including community agency counseling, elementary school counseling. Part-time and evening/weekend programs available. *Students:* 54 full-time (46 women), 79 part-time (66 women); includes 3 minority (1 African American, 2 Hispanic Americans), 1 international. Average age 30. 14 applicants, 57% accepted, 7 enrolled. In 2008, 42 master's awarded. *Degree requirements:* For master's, comprehensive exam, thesis or alternative. *Entrance requirements:* For master's, GRE or MAT, minimum GPA of 2.75. Additional exam requirements/recommendations for international students: Required—TOEFL (minimum score 550 paper-based; 213 computer-based; 79 iBT). *Application deadline:* For fall admission, 2/1 priority date for domestic and international students; for spring admission, 10/1 priority date for domestic and international students. Applications are processed on a rolling basis. Application fee: $35 ($50 for international students). Electronic applications accepted. *Expenses:* Tuition, state resident: full-time $3852; part-time $214 per credit hour. Tuition, nonresident: full-time $7524; part-time $418 per credit hour. Required fees: $230 per semester. Tuition and fees vary according to course level and course load. *Financial support:* In 2008–09, 1 research assistantship with full tuition reimbursement (averaging $7,340 per year), 5 teaching assistantships with full tuition reimbursements (averaging $7,340 per year) were awarded; Federal Work-Study, institutionally sponsored loans, scholarships/grants, and unspecified assistantships also available. Financial award application deadline: 3/31; financial award applicants required to submit FAFSA. *Unit head:* Dr. Tamara Arthaud, Acting Department Head, 417-836-5449, E-mail: CLSE@missouristate.edu. *Application contact:* Eric Eckert, Coordinator of Admissions and Recruitment, 417-836-5331, Fax: 417-836-6888, E-mail: ericeckert@missouristate.edu.

Montclair State University, The Office of Graduate Admissions and Support Services, College of Education and Human Services, Department of Counseling, Human Development, and Educational Leadership, Montclair, NJ 07043-1624. Offers administration and supervision (MA), including administration and supervision, educator/trainer; advanced counseling (Certificate); counseling and guidance (MA), including addictions counseling, community counseling, student affairs; counselor education (PhD); principal (Certificate); school administrator (Certificate); school business administrator (Certificate); school counselor (Certificate); substance awareness coordinator (Certificate). *Accreditation:* NCATE. Part-time and evening/weekend programs available. *Faculty:* 18 full-time (12 women), 16 part-time/adjunct (10 women). *Students:* 134 full-time (109 women), 422 part-time (299 women); includes 86 minority (48 African Americans, 8 Asian Americans or Pacific Islanders, 30 Hispanic Americans), 4 international. Average age 31. 164 applicants, 55% accepted, 74 enrolled. In 2008, 115 master's awarded. *Degree requirements:* For master's, comprehensive exam, thesis or alternative; for doctorate, comprehensive exam, thesis/dissertation. *Entrance requirements:* For master's, GRE General Test, interview, 2 letters of recommendation. Additional exam requirements/recommendations for international students: Required—TOEFL (minimum score 83 computer-based). *Application deadline:* For fall admission, 6/1 for international students; for spring admission, 10/1 for international students. Applications are processed on a rolling basis. Application fee: $60. Electronic applications accepted. *Financial support:* In 2008–09, 15 research assistantships with full tuition reimbursements (averaging $7,000 per year) were awarded; Federal Work-Study, scholarships/grants, and unspecified assistantships also available. Support available to part-time students. Financial award application deadline: 3/1; financial award applicants required to submit FAFSA. *Faculty research:* K-12 education, data collection. *Unit head:* Dr. Catherine Roland, Chairperson, 973-655-7216, E-mail: rolandc@mail.montclair.edu. *Application contact:* Amy Aiello, Associate Director of Admissions, 973-655-5147, Fax: 973-655-7869, E-mail: graduate.school@montclair.edu.

Montclair State University, The Office of Graduate Admissions and Support Services, College of Humanities and Social Sciences, Department of Psychology, Montclair, NJ 07043-1624. Offers educational psychology (MA), including child/adolescent clinical psychology, clinical psychology for Spanish/English bilinguals; psychology (MA, Certificate), including industrial and organizational psychology (MA); school psychologist (Certificate). Part-time and evening/weekend programs available. *Faculty:* 28 full-time (13 women), 32 part-time/adjunct (16 women). *Students:* 28 full-time (20 women), 31 part-time (26 women); includes 14 minority (4 African Americans, 6 Asian Americans or Pacific Islanders, 4 Hispanic Americans), 2 international. Average age 27. 62 applicants, 56% accepted, 23 enrolled. In 2008, 26 master's awarded. *Degree requirements:* For master's, comprehensive exam, thesis or alternative. *Entrance requirements:* For master's, GRE General Test, GRE Subject Test, previous course work in psychology, interview, 2 letters of recommendation. Additional exam requirements/recommendations for international students: Required—TOEFL (minimum score 83 computer-based). *Application deadline:* For fall admission, 2/1 for domestic and international students; for spring admission, 10/1 for domestic and international students. Applications are processed on a rolling basis. Application fee: $60. Electronic applications accepted. *Financial support:* In

2008–09, 10 research assistantships with full tuition reimbursements (averaging $7,000 per year) were awarded; Federal Work-Study, scholarships/grants, and unspecified assistantships also available. Support available to part-time students. Financial award application deadline: 3/1; financial award applicants required to submit FAFSA. *Faculty research:* Engaged learning, academic and civic development. Total annual research expenditures: $10,000. *Unit head:* Dr. Peter Vietze, Chairperson, 973-655-5201. *Application contact:* Amy Aiello, Associate Director of Admissions, 973-655-5147, Fax: 973-655-7869, E-mail: graduate.school@montclair.edu.

Naropa University, Graduate Programs, Program in Transpersonal Psychology, Ecopsychology Concentration, Boulder, CO 80302-6697. Offers MA. Part-time and evening/weekend programs available. Postbaccalaureate distance learning degree programs offered (minimal on-campus study). *Faculty:* 4 full-time (2 women), 13 part-time/adjunct (7 women). *Students:* 26 part-time (24 women); includes 2 minority (1 Asian American or Pacific Islander, 1 Hispanic American). Average age 42. 25 applicants, 72% accepted, 11 enrolled. In 2008, 5 master's awarded. *Degree requirements:* For master's, thesis, service learning. *Entrance requirements:* For master's, interview (by phone or in-person), technology form, resumé, 3 letters of recommendation, letter of interest. Additional exam requirements/recommendations for international students: Required—TOEFL (minimum score 600 paper-based; 250 computer-based). *Application deadline:* For fall admission, 1/15 priority date for domestic and international students. Applications are processed on a rolling basis. Application fee: $60. Electronic applications accepted. *Expenses:* Tuition: Full-time $14,767; part-time $726 per credit hour. Required fees: $45 per term. *Financial support:* In 2008–09, 2 students received support. Career-related internships or fieldwork, Federal Work-Study, scholarships/grants, health care benefits, and tuition waivers (partial) available. Support available to part-time students. Financial award application deadline: 3/1; financial award applicants required to submit FAFSA. *Unit head:* Jed Swift, Assistant Director, 303-245-4837. *Application contact:* Kate Levene, Admissions Counselor, 303-245-4657, Fax: 303-546-3583, E-mail: klevene@naropa.edu.

National-Louis University, College of Arts and Sciences, Department of Counseling and Human Services, Chicago, IL 60603. Offers addictions counseling (Certificate); addictions treatment (Certificate); career counseling and development studies (Certificate); community counseling (MS); community wellness and prevention (Certificate); counseling (Certificate); eating disorders counseling (Certificate); employee assistance programs (MS, Certificate); gerontology administration (Certificate); gerontology counseling (MS, Certificate); human services administration (MS, Certificate); long-term care administration (Certificate); school counseling (MS). Part-time programs available. *Students:* 8 full-time (7 women), 239 part-time (199 women); includes 71 minority (49 African Americans, 5 Asian Americans or Pacific Islanders, 17 Hispanic Americans). Average age 39. In 2008, 53 master's, 6 other advanced degrees awarded. *Degree requirements:* For master's and Certificate, internship. *Entrance requirements:* For master's and Certificate, GRE, MAT, or Watson-Glaser Critical Thinking Appraisal, interview, minimum GPA of 3.0. *Application deadline:* Applications are processed on a rolling basis. *Financial support:* Federal Work-Study, institutionally sponsored loans, scholarships/grants, and tuition waivers available. Support available to part-time students. Financial award applicants required to submit FAFSA. *Faculty research:* Religion and aging, drug abuse prevention, hunger, homelessness, multicultural diversity. *Unit head:* Dr. Susan Thorne-Devin, Assistant Professor, 630-874-4560, E-mail: stdevin@nl.edu. *Application contact:* Dr. Larry Poselli, Vice President of Enrollment and Student Services, 800-443-5522 Ext. 5718, Fax: 312-261-.3550, E-mail: larry.polselli@nl.edu.

New York University, Graduate School of Arts and Science, Department of Psychology, New York, NY 10012-1019. Offers cognition and perception (PhD); community psychology (PhD); general psychology (MA); industrial/organizational psychology (MA); psychotherapy and psychoanalysis (Advanced Certificate); social/personality psychology (PhD). Part-time programs available. Terminal master's awarded for partial completion of doctoral program. *Degree requirements:* For master's, comprehensive exam, thesis or alternative; for doctorate, thesis/dissertation. *Entrance requirements:* For master's, GRE General Test, minimum GPA of 3.0; for doctorate, GRE General Test, GRE Subject Test; for Advanced Certificate, doctoral degree, minimum GPA of 3.0. Additional exam requirements/recommendations for international students: Required—TOEFL. *Faculty research:* Vision, memory, social cognition, social and cognitive development, relationships.

Norfolk State University, School of Graduate Studies, School of Liberal Arts, Department of Psychology, Program in Community/Clinical Psychology, Norfolk, VA 23504. Offers MA. *Degree requirements:* For master's, comprehensive exam, thesis or alternative. *Entrance requirements:* For master's, minimum GPA of 2.7.

North Carolina Central University, Division of Academic Affairs, School of Education, Department of Counselor Education, Durham, NC 27707-3129. Offers career counseling (MA); community agency counseling (MA); school counseling (MA). *Accreditation:* ACA; NCATE. Part-time and evening/weekend programs available. *Degree requirements:* For master's, comprehensive exam, thesis or alternative. *Entrance requirements:* For master's, GRE, minimum GPA of 3.0 in major, 2.5 overall. Additional exam requirements/recommendations for international students: Required—TOEFL. *Faculty research:* Becoming a leader, skill building in academia.

North Carolina State University, Graduate School, College of Education, Department of Curriculum and Instruction, Program in Agency Counseling, Raleigh, NC 27695. Offers M Ed, MS. *Degree requirements:* For master's, thesis optional. *Entrance requirements:* For master's, GRE General Test or MAT, minimum GPA of 3.0 in major. Electronic applications accepted. *Faculty research:* Cross-cultural issues, non-cognitive variables, achievement gaps, identity development, counseling supervision.

North Dakota State University, College of Graduate and Interdisciplinary Studies, College of Science and Mathematics, Department of Psychology, Fargo, ND 58105. Offers clinical psychology (MS); cognitive and visual neuroscience (PhD); health and social psychology (PhD); psychology (MS). *Faculty:* 18 full-time (4 women), 2 part-time/adjunct (1 woman). *Students:* 36 full-time (27 women); includes 4 minority (1 African American, 2 Asian Americans or Pacific Islanders, 1 Hispanic American), 1 international. Average age 24. 48 applicants, 33% accepted, 10 enrolled. In 2008, 3 master's, 1 doctorate awarded. *Degree requirements:* For master's, thesis; for doctorate, thesis/dissertation. *Entrance requirements:* For master's and doctorate, GRE General Test, GRE Subject Test. Additional exam requirements/recommendations for international students: Required—TOEFL (minimum score 525 paper-based; 197 computer-based; 71 iBT). *Application deadline:* For fall admission, 3/1 for domestic and international students. Application fee: $45 ($60 for international students). Electronic applications accepted. *Financial support:* In 2008–09, 36 students received support, including 2 fellowships with full tuition reimbursements available (averaging $16,000 per year), 23 research assistantships with full tuition reimbursements available (averaging $16,000 per year), 11 teaching assistantships with full tuition reimbursements available (averaging $6,000 per year); career-related internships or fieldwork, Federal Work-Study, institutionally sponsored loans, tuition waivers (full and partial), and unspecified assistantships also available. Support available to part-time students. Financial award application deadline: 3/1. *Faculty research:* Cognition science, neuropsychology, group behavior, applied behavior analysis, behavior therapy. Total annual research expenditures: $2 million. *Unit head:* Dr. Paul D. Rokke, Chair, 701-231-8622, Fax: 701-231-8426, E-mail: paul.rokke@ndsu.edu. *Application contact:* Dr. Paul D. Rokke, Chair, 701-231-8622, Fax: 701-231-8426, E-mail: paul.rokke@ndsu.edu.

Northern Arizona University, Graduate College, College of Education, Programs in Counseling, Flagstaff, AZ 86011. Offers community counseling (MA); human relations (M Ed); school counseling (M Ed); student affairs (M Ed). *Accreditation:* ACA. Part-time programs available. *Degree requirements:* For master's, thesis optional. *Faculty research:* Early childhood assessment and development, cognitive psychology, multicultural issues, family functioning in abusive families, rehabilitation.

Northern Kentucky University, Office of Graduate Programs, College of Education and Human Services, Program in Community Counseling, Highland Heights, KY 41099. Offers college student development administration (Certificate); community counseling (MS). Part-time and evening/weekend programs available. *Students:* 19 full-time (18 women), 33 part-time (24 women); includes 2 minority (both African Americans). Average age 28. 36 applicants, 61% accepted, 18 enrolled. In 2008, 9 master's awarded. *Degree requirements:* For master's, comprehensive exam, internship. *Entrance requirements:* For master's, GRE, minimum GPA of 2.75, 500-700 word essay, 3 letters of reference, criminal background check (state and federal). Additional exam requirements/recommendations for international students: Required—TOEFL (minimum score 550 paper-based; 213 computer-based; 79 iBT), Michigan Test may be substituted only if taken at NKU (minimu score of 80); Recommended—IELTS (minimum score 6.5). *Application deadline:* For fall admission, 8/1 for domestic students, 6/1 priority date for international students; for spring admission, 10/1 priority date for international students. Applications are processed on a rolling basis. Application fee: $40. Electronic applications accepted. *Expenses:* Tuition, area resident: Full-time $6642. Tuition, state resident: full-time $6642. Tuition, nonresident: full-time $11,682. *Financial support:* Applicants required to submit FAFSA. *Faculty research:* Ethical decision making in counseling, clinical supervision in counseling, expectations about counseling inventory development. *Unit head:* Dr. Jacqueline Smith, Director, 859-572-6149, E-mail: smithjac@nku.edu. *Application contact:* Dr. Peg Griffin, Director, Graduate Programs, 859-572-6934, Fax: 859-572-6670, E-mail: griffinp@nku.edu.

North Georgia College & State University, Graduate Studies, Program in Community Counseling, Dahlonega, GA 30597. Offers MS. Part-time and evening/weekend programs available. *Degree requirements:* For master's, one foreign language, thesis optional. *Entrance requirements:* For master's, GRE General Test, minimum GPA of 3.0, 3 letters of recommendation, interview. Electronic applications accepted.

Northwestern University, The Graduate School, Judd A. and Marjorie Weinberg College of Arts and Sciences, Department of Psychology, Evanston, IL 60208. Offers brain, behavior and cognition (PhD); clinical psychology (PhD); cognitive psychology (PhD); personality (PhD); social psychology (PhD); JD/PhD. Admissions and degrees offered through The Graduate School. *Accreditation:* APA (one or more programs are accredited). Part-time programs available. *Degree requirements:* For doctorate, thesis/dissertation. *Entrance requirements:* For doctorate, GRE General Test, GRE Subject Test. Additional exam requirements/recommendations for international students: Required—TOEFL. Electronic applications accepted. *Faculty research:* Memory and higher order cognition, anxiety and depression, effectiveness of psychotherapy, social cognition, molecular basis of memory.

Northwest Nazarene University, Graduate Studies, Program in Counselor Education, Nampa, ID 83686-5897. Offers community counseling (MS); marriage and family counseling (MS); school counseling (MS). *Faculty:* 3 full-time (2 women), 10 part-time/adjunct (5 women). *Students:* 45 full-time (29 women), 13 part-time (7 women); includes 2 minority (1 American Indian/Alaska Native, 1 Asian American or Pacific Islander). In 2008, 19 master's awarded. Application fee: $25. *Unit head:* Dr. Brenda Freeman, Chair, 208-467-8428, Fax: 208-467-8339. *Application contact:* Susan Marion, Secretary, 208-467-8345, Fax: 208-467-8339, E-mail: sjmarion@nnu.edu.

The Ohio State University, Graduate School, College of Social and Behavioral Sciences, School of Social and Behavioral Science, Department of Psychology, Columbus, OH 43210. Offers behavioral neuroscience (PhD); clinical psychology (PhD); cognitive psychology (PhD); developmental psychology (PhD); mental retardation and developmental disabilities (PhD); psychology (MA); quantitative psychology (PhD); social psychology (PhD). *Accreditation:* APA (one or more programs are accredited). *Degree requirements:* For doctorate, thesis/dissertation. *Entrance requirements:* For master's and doctorate, GRE General Test. Additional exam requirements/recommendations for international students: Required—TOEFL (minimum score 600 paper-based; 250 computer-based). Electronic applications accepted.

Oregon State University–Cascades, Program in Counseling, Bend, OR 97701. Offers community counseling (MS); school counseling (MS).

Penn State Harrisburg, Graduate School, School of Behavioral Sciences and Education, Middletown, PA 17057-4898. Offers adult education (D Ed); applied behavior analysis (MA); applied clinical psychology (MA); applied psychological research (MA); community psychology and social change (MA); health education (M Ed); teaching and curriculum (M Ed); training and development (M Ed). Part-time and evening/weekend programs available.

Penn State University Park, Graduate School, College of the Liberal Arts, Department of Psychology, State College, University Park, PA 16802-1503. Offers clinical psychology (MS, PhD); cognitive psychology (MS, PhD); developmental psychology (MS, PhD); industrial/organizational psychology (MS, PhD); psychobiology (MS, PhD); social psychology (MS, PhD). *Accreditation:* APA (one or more programs are accredited).

Pittsburg State University, Graduate School, College of Education, Department of Psychology and Counseling, Program in Counselor Education, Pittsburg, KS 66762. Offers community counseling (MS); school counseling (MS). *Accreditation:* ACA; NCATE. *Degree requirements:* For master's, thesis or alternative. *Entrance requirements:* For master's, GRE General Test, minimum GPA of 2.8.

Queen's University at Kingston, School of Graduate Studies and Research, Faculty of Arts and Sciences, Department of Psychology, Kingston, ON K7L 3N6, Canada. Offers brain behavior and cognitive science (MA, PhD); clinical psychology (MA, PhD); developmental psychology (MA, PhD); social personality psychology (MA, PhD). *Accreditation:* APA (one or more programs are accredited). *Degree requirements:* For master's, thesis; for doctorate, comprehensive exam, thesis/dissertation. *Entrance requirements:* For master's and doctorate, GRE General Test. Additional exam requirements/recommendations for international students: Required—TOEFL. *Faculty research:* Human development, social, personality, behavioral neuroscience, forensic.

Regent University, Graduate School, School of Psychology and Counseling, Virginia Beach, VA 23464-9800. Offers clinical psychology (MA, Psy D); counseling (MA), including community counseling, human services counseling, school counseling; counseling studies (CAGS); counselor education and supervision (PhD); M Div/MA; M Ed/MA; MBA/MA. PhD program offered online only. *Accreditation:* ACA; APA (one or more programs are accredited). Part-time and evening/weekend programs available. Postbaccalaureate distance learning degree programs offered (minimal on-campus study). *Faculty:* 25 full-time (12 women), 19 part-time/adjunct (9 women). *Students:* 176 full-time (142 women), 192 part-time (144 women); includes 100 minority (78 African Americans, 2 American Indian/Alaska Native, 10 Asian Americans or Pacific Islanders, 10 Hispanic Americans), 13 international. Average age 32. 317 applicants, 47% accepted, 112 enrolled. In 2008, 129 master's, 22 doctorates awarded. *Degree requirements:* For master's, thesis or alternative, internship, practicum, written competency exam; for doctorate, thesis/dissertation or alternative. *Entrance requirements:* For master's, GRE General Test including writing exam, minimum undergraduate GPA of 2.75, 3 recommendations, resumé, transcripts, writing sample; for doctorate, GRE General Test including writing exam, GRE Subject Test, minimum undergraduate GPA of 3.0, 3.5 (PhD), 10-15 minute VHS tape demonstrating counseling skills, writing sample, 3 recommendations, resumé, transcripts. Additional exam requirements/recommendations for international students: Required—TOEFL (minimum score 577 paper-based; 233 computer-based). *Application deadline:* For fall admission, 4/1 priority date for domestic students; for spring admission, 11/1 priority date for domestic students. Applications are processed on a rolling basis. Application fee: $50. Electronic applications accepted. *Expenses:* Contact institution. *Financial support:* Research assistantships with full and partial tuition reimbursements, teaching assistantships with full and partial tuition reimbursements, career-related internships or fieldwork, scholarships/grants, and tuition waivers (full and partial) available. Support available to part-time students. Financial award application deadline: 9/1; financial award applicants required to submit FAFSA.

Faculty research: Marriage enrichment, AIDS counseling, troubled youth, faith and learning, trauma. *Unit head:* Dr. Rosemarie Hughes, Dean, 757-352-4269, Fax: 757-352-4282, E-mail: rosehug@regent.edu. *Application contact:* Matthew Chadwick, Director of Admissions, 800-373-5504, Fax: 757-352-4381, E-mail: admissions@regent.edu.

Regis University, College for Professional Studies, Graduate Counseling Program, Denver, CO 80221-1099. Offers community counseling (MAC); counseling children and adolescents (Post-Graduate Certificate); marriage and family therapy (Post-Graduate Certificate). Program offered in Henderson and Las Vegas (Summerlin), NV. *Accreditation:* ACA. Part-time and evening/weekend programs available. *Degree requirements:* For master's, internships, practicum. *Entrance requirements:* For master's, 2 admissions essays, interview, 2 recommendations, resumé, criminal background check. Additional exam requirements/recommendations for international students: Required—TOEFL (minimum score 213 computer-based), TWE (minimum score 5). *Expenses:* Contact institution. *Faculty research:* Group Development, Counselor Education, Counsel and Therapy, Influence of Technology on Psychology, Dream finding groups, Adult Development, Depression.

Rutgers, The State University of New Jersey, Newark, Graduate School, Program in Psychology, Newark, NJ 07102. Offers cognitive neuroscience (PhD); cognitive science (PhD); perception (PhD); psychobiology (PhD); social cognition (PhD). *Degree requirements:* For doctorate, comprehensive exam, thesis/dissertation. *Entrance requirements:* For doctorate, GRE General Test, GRE Subject Test, minimum undergraduate B average. Electronic applications accepted. *Faculty research:* Visual perception (luminance, motion), neuroendocrine mechanisms in behavior (reproduction, pain), attachment theory, connectionist modeling of cognition.

See Close-Up on page 1131.

Rutgers, The State University of New Jersey, New Brunswick, Graduate School, Program in Psychology, Piscataway, NJ 08854-8097. Offers behavioral neuroscience (PhD); clinical psychology (PhD); cognitive psychology (PhD); interdisciplinary health psychology (PhD); social psychology (PhD). *Accreditation:* APA. *Degree requirements:* For doctorate, comprehensive exam, thesis/dissertation. *Entrance requirements:* For doctorate, GRE General Test, 3 letters of recommendation. Additional exam requirements/recommendations for international students: Required—TOEFL (minimum score 577 paper-based; 233 computer-based). Electronic applications accepted. *Faculty research:* Learning and memory, behavioral ecology, hormones and behavior, psychopharmacology, anxiety disorders.

Sage Graduate School, Graduate School, Department of Psychology, Program in Community Psychology, Troy, NY 12180-4115. Offers child care and children's services (MA); community counseling (MA); community health education (MA); counseling and community psychology (MA); general psychology (MA). Part-time and evening/weekend programs available. *Faculty:* 4 full-time (all women), 5 part-time/adjunct (2 women). *Students:* 24 full-time (23 women), 58 part-time (54 women); includes 12 minority (6 African Americans, 2 American Indian/Alaska Native, 4 Hispanic Americans). Average age 30. 39 applicants, 54% accepted, 11 enrolled. In 2008, 29 master's awarded. *Degree requirements:* For master's, thesis or alternative. *Entrance requirements:* For master's, minimum GPA of 2.75; official transcripts; 2 letters of reference; undergraduate courses in statistics, history, and systems of psychology; three other courses in behavioral science; personal prospectus statement; current resumé. Additional exam requirements/recommendations for international students: Required—TOEFL (minimum score 550 paper-based; 213 computer-based). *Application deadline:* Applications are processed on a rolling basis. Application fee: $40. *Expenses:* Tuition: Full-time $10,080; part-time $560 per credit hour. *Financial support:* Fellowships, research assistantships, teaching assistantships, Federal Work-Study, scholarships/grants, and unspecified assistantships available. Support available to part-time students. Financial award application deadline: 3/1; financial award applicants required to submit FAFSA. *Unit head:* Dr. Bronna Romanoff, Director, 518-244-2260, E-mail: romanb@sage.edu. *Application contact:* Wendy D. Diefendorf, Director of Graduate and Adult Admission, 518-244-2443, Fax: 518-244-6880, E-mail: diefew@sage.edu.

St. Cloud State University, School of Graduate Studies, College of Education, Department of Educational Leadership and Community Psychology, Program in Community Counseling, St. Cloud, MN 56301-4498. Offers MS. *Degree requirements:* For master's, comprehensive exam (for some programs), thesis or alternative. *Entrance requirements:* For master's, GRE General Test, minimum GPA of 2.75. Additional exam requirements/recommendations for international students: Required—Michigan English Language Assessment Battery; Recommended—TOEFL (minimum score 550 paper-based; 213 computer-based), IELTS (minimum score 6.5). Electronic applications accepted.

Saint Joseph College, Graduate School, Department of Counselor Education, West Hartford, CT 06117-2700. Offers community counseling (MA), including child welfare; school counseling (MA). Part-time and evening/weekend programs available. *Students:* 28 full-time (26 women), 84 part-time (74 women). *Degree requirements:* For master's, comprehensive exam, thesis optional, capstone project. *Entrance requirements:* For master's, PRAXIS I (school counseling), 2 letters of recommendation. *Application deadline:* Applications are processed on a rolling basis. Application fee: $50. Electronic applications accepted. *Expenses:* Tuition: Part-time $560 per credit. Required fees: $30 per credit. *Financial support:* Career-related internships or fieldwork, health care benefits, and unspecified assistantships available. Support available to part-time students. Financial award applicants required to submit FAFSA. *Application contact:* Graduate Admissions Office, 860-231-5261, E-mail: graduate@sjc.edu.

Saint Martin's University, Graduate Programs, Program in Counseling Psychology, Lacey, WA 98503-1297. Offers MAC. Part-time and evening/weekend programs available. *Degree requirements:* For master's, clinical experience, interview. *Entrance requirements:* For master's, BA in psychology or related field, clinical experience. Additional exam requirements/recommendations for international students: Required—TOEFL. *Faculty research:* Alcohol studies, clinical effectiveness, social justice, parent adolescent interaction.

St. Mary's University, Graduate School, Department of Counseling and Human Services, Program in Community Counseling, San Antonio, TX 78228-8507. Offers MA. Part-time programs available. *Faculty:* 4 full-time (2 women). *Students:* 26 full-time (20 women), 17 part-time (13 women); includes 20 minority (7 African Americans, 1 Asian American or Pacific Islander, 12 Hispanic Americans). Average age 36. 22 applicants, 73% accepted, 13 enrolled. In 2008, 22 master's awarded. *Degree requirements:* For master's, comprehensive exam, internship. *Entrance requirements:* For master's, GRE, GMAT. Additional exam requirements/recommendations for international students: Required—TOEFL (minimum score 550 paper-based; 213 computer-based; 80 iBT). *Application deadline:* Applications are processed on a rolling basis. Application fee: $0. Electronic applications accepted. *Expenses:* Tuition: Full-time $12,006; part-time $667 per credit hour. Required fees: $440; $220 per semester. *Financial support:* In 2008–09, 7 students received support, including 7 fellowships (averaging $4,239 per year); career-related internships or fieldwork, Federal Work-Study, institutionally sponsored loans, scholarships/grants, health care benefits, and unspecified assistantships also available. Financial award application deadline: 3/31; financial award applicants required to submit FAFSA. *Unit head:* Dr. Ray Wooten, Director, 210-436-3226, Fax: 210-431-6886, E-mail: hrwooten@stmarytx.edu. *Application contact:* Dr. Henry Flores, Dean of the Graduate School, 210-436-3101, Fax: 210-431-2220, E-mail: hflores@stmarytx.edu.

Shippensburg University of Pennsylvania, School of Graduate Studies, College of Education and Human Services, Department of Counseling, Shippensburg, PA 17257-2299. Offers Adlerian studies (Certificate); advanced study in counseling (Certificate); alcohol and drug counseling (Certificate); counseling (M Ed, MS), including college counseling (MS), community counseling (MS), elementary school counseling (MS), mental health counseling (MS), secondary school counseling (MS), student personnel services (MS); couple and family counseling (Certificate). *Accreditation:* ACA (one or more programs are accredited); NCATE. Part-time and evening/weekend programs available. *Faculty:* 8 full-time (3 women), 3 part-time/adjunct (2 women).

Social Psychology

Shippensburg University of Pennsylvania (continued)
Students: 71 full-time (60 women), 109 part-time (91 women); includes 22 minority (16 African Americans, 4 Asian Americans or Pacific Islanders, 2 Hispanic Americans), 2 international. Average age 29. 128 applicants, 39% accepted, 32 enrolled. In 2008, 48 master's awarded. *Degree requirements:* For master's, fieldwork, research project, internship, candidacy. *Entrance requirements:* For master's, GRE or MAT (for community, mental health, student personnel, and college counseling applicants if GPA is less than 2.75), minimum GPA of 2.75 (3.0 for M Ed), interview, resumé, 3 letters of recommendation, supplemental data forms, one year of relevant work experience, on-campus interview. Additional exam requirements/recommendations for international students: Required—TOEFL (minimum score 560 paper-based; 220 computer-based); Recommended—IELTS (minimum score 6). *Application deadline:* For fall admission, 3/1 for international students; for spring admission, 7/1 for international students. Applications are processed on a rolling basis. Application fee: $30. Electronic applications accepted. *Expenses:* Tuition, state resident: full-time $6430; part-time $357 per credit. Tuition, nonresident: full-time $10,288; part-time $572 per credit. Required fees: $1127; $38 per credit. One-time fee: $44 part-time. *Financial support:* In 2008–09, 44 research assistantships with full tuition reimbursements (averaging $5,000 per year) were awarded; career-related internships or fieldwork, scholarships/grants, unspecified assistantships, and resident hall directors, student payroll positions also available. Support available to part-time students. Financial award application deadline: 3/1; financial award applicants required to submit FAFSA. *Unit head:* Dr. Jan Arminio, Chairperson, 717-477-1668, Fax: 717-477-4016, E-mail: jlarmi@ship.edu. *Application contact:* Renee Payne, Associate Dean of Graduate Admissions, 717-477-1231, Fax: 717-477-4016, E-mail: rmpayn@ship.edu.

Southeastern Oklahoma State University, School of Behavioral Sciences, Durant, OK 74701-0609. Offers community counseling (MBS). Part-time and evening/weekend programs available. *Faculty:* 10 full-time (3 women). *Students:* 17 full-time (15 women), 18 part-time (15 women); includes 9 minority (8 American Indian/Alaska Native, 1 Hispanic American). Average age 35. 11 applicants, 100% accepted, 11 enrolled. In 2008, 12 master's awarded. *Degree requirements:* For master's, thesis optional. *Entrance requirements:* For master's, GRE General Test, minimum GPA of 3.0 in last 60 hours or 2.75 overall. Additional exam requirements/recommendations for international students: Required—TOEFL (minimum score 550 paper-based; 213 computer-based). *Application deadline:* For fall admission, 8/1 for domestic students, 6/1 for international students; for spring admission, 1/5 for domestic students, 11/1 for international students. Application fee: $20 ($55 for international students). Electronic applications accepted. *Financial support:* Fellowships, research assistantships, teaching assistantships, Federal Work-Study available. Support available to part-time students. Financial award application deadline: 6/15. *Unit head:* Dr. Daniel Weigel, Program Coordinator, 580-745-2632, E-mail: dweigel@se.edu. *Application contact:* Carrie Williamson, Graduate Secretary, 580-745-2200, Fax: 580-745-7474, E-mail: cwilliamson@se.edu.

Southwestern College, Program in Transformational Ecopsychology, Santa Fe, NM 87502-4788. Offers Certificate. *Entrance requirements:* For degree, application, reference, interview.

Springfield College, Graduate Programs, Program in Human Services, Springfield, MA 01109-3797. Offers human services (MS), including community counseling psychology, mental health counseling, organizational management and leadership. Part-time programs available. *Faculty:* 4 full-time (3 women). *Students:* 2 full-time, 2 part-time. Average age 30. 4 applicants, 75% accepted, 1 enrolled. In 2008, 3 master's awarded. *Degree requirements:* For master's, comprehensive exam, thesis (for some programs), research project. *Entrance requirements:* For master's, GRE. Additional exam requirements/recommendations for international students: Required—TOEFL (minimum score 550 paper-based; 213 computer-based). *Application deadline:* For fall admission, 1/15 for domestic and international students; for winter admission, 11/1 for domestic and international students; for spring admission, 11/1 for domestic and international students. Applications are processed on a rolling basis. Application fee: $50. Electronic applications accepted. *Expenses:* Contact institution. *Financial support:* Fellowships with partial tuition reimbursements, teaching assistantships with partial tuition reimbursements, career-related internships or fieldwork, Federal Work-Study, institutionally sponsored loans, and unspecified assistantships available. Financial award application deadline: 3/1; financial award applicants required to submit FAFSA. *Unit head:* Dr. Stephen Coulon, Director, 413-748-3029, E-mail: scoulon@spfldcol.edu. *Application contact:* Donald James Shaw, Director of Graduate Admissions, 413-748-3479, Fax: 413-748-3694, E-mail: donald_shaw_jr@spfldcol.edu.

Stony Brook University, State University of New York, Graduate School, College of Arts and Sciences, Department of Psychology, Program in Social and Health Psychology, Stony Brook, NY 11794. Offers PhD. *Students:* 23 full-time (18 women); includes 6 minority (3 Asian Americans or Pacific Islanders, 3 Hispanic Americans), 3 international. Average age 28. 95 applicants, 12% accepted. In 2008, 9 doctorates awarded. *Degree requirements:* For doctorate, thesis/dissertation. *Entrance requirements:* For doctorate, GRE General Test, GRE Subject Test. Additional exam requirements/recommendations for international students: Required—TOEFL. *Application deadline:* For fall admission, 1/15 for domestic students. Application fee: $60. *Expenses:* Tuition, area resident: Full-time $7880; part-time $328 per credit hour. Tuition, state resident: full-time $7880; part-time $328 per credit hour. Tuition, nonresident: full-time $13,250; part-time $552 per credit hour. Required fees: $848. *Unit head:* Dr. Marci Lobel, Head, 631-632-7651, E-mail: marci.lobel@stonybrook.edu. *Application contact:* Dr. Marci Lobel, Head, 631-632-7651, E-mail: marci.lobel@stonybrook.edu.

Syracuse University, Graduate School, College of Arts and Sciences, Program in Social Psychology, Syracuse, NY 13244. Offers PhD. Part-time programs available. *Degree requirements:* For doctorate, thesis/dissertation. *Entrance requirements:* For doctorate, GRE General Test, GRE Subject Test (recommended). Additional exam requirements/recommendations for international students: Required—TOEFL.

Syracuse University, Graduate School, School of Education, Program in Community Counseling, Syracuse, NY 13244. Offers MS. *Entrance requirements:* For master's, GRE General Test or MAT.

Syracuse University, Graduate School, School of Education, Program in Rehabilitation and Community Counseling, Syracuse, NY 13244. Offers MS. *Entrance requirements:* For master's, GRE General Test or MAT, interview. Additional exam requirements/recommendations for international students: Required—TOEFL.

Teachers College, Columbia University, Graduate Faculty of Education, Department of Organization and Leadership, Program in Social and Organizational Psychology, New York, NY 10027-6696. Offers organizational psychology (MA, Ed D, PhD); social psychology (Ed D, PhD). *Faculty:* 8 full-time (5 women), 5 part-time/adjunct. *Students:* 112 full-time (88 women), 154 part-time (94 women); includes 58 minority (13 African Americans, 27 Asian Americans or Pacific Islanders, 18 Hispanic Americans), 23 international. Average age 32. 258 applicants, 49% accepted, 58 enrolled. In 2008, 84 master's, 4 doctorates awarded. Terminal master's awarded for partial completion of doctoral program. *Degree requirements:* For master's, comprehensive exam; for doctorate, thesis/dissertation. *Entrance requirements:* For master's, minimum GPA of 3.0; for doctorate, GRE General Test. *Application deadline:* For fall admission, 5/15 for domestic students; for spring admission, 12/1 for domestic students. Application fee: $75. *Expenses:* Tuition: Full-time $26,040; part-time $1085 per credit. Required fees: $720. *Financial support:* Fellowships, research assistantships, career-related internships or fieldwork, Federal Work-Study, institutionally sponsored loans, and tuition waivers (full and partial) available. Support available to part-time students. Financial award application deadline: 2/1. *Faculty research:* Conflict resolution, human resource and organization development, management competence, organizational culture, leadership. *Unit head:* Warner Burke, Chair, 212-678-3258. *Application contact:* Debbie Lesperance, Assistant Director of Admission, 212-678-3710, Fax: 212-678-4171.

Temple University, Graduate School, College of Liberal Arts, Department of Psychology, Program in Social Psychology, Philadelphia, PA 19122-6096. Offers PhD. *Degree requirements:* For doctorate, thesis/dissertation, preliminary exam. *Entrance requirements:* For doctorate, GRE General Test, minimum GPA of 3.0. Additional exam requirements/recommendations for international students: Required—TOEFL (minimum score 550 paper-based; 213 computer-based; 79 iBT). Electronic applications accepted. *Faculty research:* Power and technology, organizational behavior, interpersonal dynamics, belief, consumer behavior.

Texas A&M University, College of Liberal Arts, Department of Psychology, College Station, TX 77843. Offers behavioral and cellular neuroscience (MS, PhD); clinical psychology (MS, PhD); cognitive psychology (MS, PhD); developmental psychology (MS, PhD); industrial/organizational psychology (MS, PhD); social psychology (MS, PhD). *Accreditation:* APA (one or more programs are accredited). *Faculty:* 35. *Students:* 74 full-time (47 women), 11 part-time (9 women); includes 30 minority (7 African Americans, 5 Asian Americans or Pacific Islanders, 18 Hispanic Americans), 4 international. In 2008, 11 master's, 12 doctorates awarded. *Degree requirements:* For master's, thesis; for doctorate, comprehensive exam (for some programs), thesis/dissertation. *Entrance requirements:* For master's and doctorate, GRE General Test. Additional exam requirements/recommendations for international students: Required—TOEFL. *Application deadline:* For fall admission, 1/5 for domestic and international students. Application fee: $50 ($75 for international students). Electronic applications accepted. *Expenses:* Tuition, area resident: Full-time $3838.50. Tuition, state resident: full-time $3838.50. Tuition, nonresident: full-time $8897. Required fees: $2359.60. *Financial support:* Fellowships with partial tuition reimbursements, research assistantships with partial tuition reimbursements, teaching assistantships with partial tuition reimbursements, career-related internships or fieldwork, institutionally sponsored loans, health care benefits, and unspecified assistantships available. Financial award application deadline: 1/5; financial award applicants required to submit FAFSA. *Unit head:* Dr. Les Morey, Head, 979-845-2581, Fax: 979-845-4727, E-mail: lmorey@psych.tamu.edu. *Application contact:* Sharon Starr, Graduate Admissions Supervisor, 979-458-1710, Fax: 979-845-4727, E-mail: gradadv@psyc.tamu.edu.

Thomas University, Department of Human Services, Thomasville, GA 31792-7499. Offers community counseling (MSCC); rehabilitation counseling (MRC). *Accreditation:* CORE. Part-time programs available. *Entrance requirements:* For master's, resumé, 3 academic/professional references. Additional exam requirements/recommendations for international students: Required—TOEFL (minimum score 600 paper-based; 250 computer-based). Electronic applications accepted.

Université du Québec à Rimouski, Graduate Programs, Program in Psychosocial Studies, Rimouski, QC G5L 3A1, Canada. Offers MA.

Université Laval, Faculty of Social Sciences, School of Psychology, Programs in Psychology, Québec, QC G1K 7P4, Canada. Offers clinical psychology (PhD); community psychology (PhD); psychology (PhD, Psy D). *Degree requirements:* For doctorate, comprehensive exam, thesis/dissertation. *Entrance requirements:* For doctorate, comprehension of written English, knowledge of French, interview. Electronic applications accepted.

University at Albany, State University of New York, College of Arts and Sciences, Department of Psychology, Albany, NY 12222-0001. Offers autism (Certificate); biopsychology (PhD); clinical psychology (PhD); general/experimental psychology (PhD); industrial/organizational psychology (PhD); psychology (MA); social/personality psychology (PhD). *Accreditation:* APA (one or more programs are accredited). *Degree requirements:* For doctorate, thesis/dissertation. *Entrance requirements:* For doctorate, GRE General Test, GRE Subject Test. Additional exam requirements/recommendations for international students: Required—TOEFL (minimum score 550 paper-based; 213 computer-based). Electronic applications accepted.

University at Buffalo, the State University of New York, Graduate School, College of Arts and Sciences, Department of Psychology, Buffalo, NY 14260. Offers behavioral neuroscience (PhD); clinical psychology (PhD); cognitive psychology (PhD); general psychology (MA); social-personality psychology (PhD). *Accreditation:* APA (one or more programs are accredited). Terminal master's awarded for partial completion of doctoral program. *Degree requirements:* For master's, project; for doctorate, thesis/dissertation. *Entrance requirements:* For master's and doctorate, GRE General Test. Additional exam requirements/recommendations for international students: Required—TOEFL (minimum score 550 paper-based; 213 computer-based; 79 iBT). Electronic applications accepted. *Faculty research:* Neural, endocrine, and molecular bases of behavior; adult mood and anxiety disorders; relationship dysfunction; attention deficit/hyperactivity disorder; psycho-linguistics.

University of Alaska Anchorage, College of Arts and Sciences, Department of Psychology, Anchorage, AK 99508-8060. Offers clinical psychology (MS); clinical-community psychology with rural-indigenous emphasis (PhD). Part-time programs available. *Degree requirements:* For master's, thesis. *Entrance requirements:* For master's, GRE General Test, GRE Subject Test, interview, references; for doctorate, interview, bachelor's or master's degree in psychology. Additional exam requirements/recommendations for international students: Required—TOEFL (minimum score 550 paper-based; 213 computer-based). *Faculty research:* Substance abuse, childhood autism, biofeedback, psychological assessment, mental health in Native Alaskans.

University of Alaska Fairbanks, College of Liberal Arts, Department of Psychology, Fairbanks, AK 99775-6480. Offers clinical-community psychology (PhD), including rural cross-cultural emphasis. *Faculty:* 5 full-time (1 woman), 4 part-time/adjunct (0 women). *Students:* 2 full-time (0 women), 20 part-time (16 women); includes 8 minority (1 African American, 5 American Indian/Alaska Native, 2 Hispanic Americans), 1 international. Average age 38. 21 applicants, 48% accepted, 9 enrolled. In 2008, 1 doctorate awarded. *Degree requirements:* For doctorate, comprehensive exam, thesis/dissertation, oral exam, oral defense. *Entrance requirements:* For doctorate, disclosure statement. Additional exam requirements/recommendations for international students: Required—TOEFL (minimum score 550 paper-based; 213 computer-based; 80 iBT). *Application deadline:* For fall admission, 12/15 for domestic and international students. Application fee: $60. *Expenses:* Tuition, area resident: Full-time $5418; part-time $301 per credit. Tuition, state resident: full-time $5418; part-time $301 per credit. Tuition, nonresident: full-time $11,070; part-time $615 per credit. Required fees: $849; $25 per credit. $78 per semester. Tuition and fees vary according to course load and reciprocity agreements. *Financial support:* In 2008–09, 2 fellowships (averaging $15,270 per year), 7 research assistantships (averaging $16,089 per year), 8 teaching assistantships (averaging $15,611 per year) were awarded; career-related internships or fieldwork, Federal Work-Study, scholarships/grants, health care benefits, and unspecified assistantships also available. Support available to part-time students. Financial award application deadline: 7/1; financial award applicants required to submit FAFSA. *Faculty research:* Clinical and community psychology, rural, indigenous, and cultural psychology. *Unit head:* Dr. Dani Sheppard, Department Chair, 907-474-7007, Fax: 907-474-5781, E-mail: fypsych@uaf.edu. *Application contact:* Dr. Dani Sheppard, Department Chair, 907-474-7007, Fax: 907-474-5781, E-mail: fypsych@uaf.edu.

University of Alaska Fairbanks, School of Education, Program in Counseling, Fairbanks, AK 99775-7520. Offers counseling (M Ed), including community counseling, school counseling. *Students:* 12 full-time (11 women), 38 part-time (34 women); includes 6 minority (2 African Americans, 1 American Indian/Alaska Native, 1 Asian American or Pacific Islander, 2 Hispanic Americans). Average age 35. 40 applicants, 60% accepted, 18 enrolled. In 2008, 13 master's awarded. *Degree requirements:* For master's, comprehensive exam, thesis, oral defense. *Entrance requirements:* For master's, 1 year teaching or administrative experience. *Application deadline:* For fall admission, 6/1 for domestic students, 3/1 for international students; for spring admission, 10/15 for domestic students, 9/1 for international students. Applications are processed on a rolling basis. Application fee: $60. Electronic applications accepted. *Expenses:* Tuition, area resident: Full-time $5418; part-time $301 per credit. Tuition, state resident: full-time $5418; part-time $301 per credit. Tuition, nonresident: full-time $11,070; part-time $615 per credit. Required fees: $849; $25 per credit. $78 per semester. Tuition and fees vary according to course load and reciprocity agreements. *Financial support:* In 2008–09, 4 teaching assistantships (averaging $13,067 per year) were awarded; fellowships, career-related internships or fieldwork, Federal Work-Study, scholarships/grants, health care benefits, and unspecified assistantships also available. Support available to part-time students. Financial award application deadline: 7/1; financial award applicants required to submit FAFSA. *Unit head:* Dr. Eric C. Madsen, Dean, 907-474-7341, Fax: 907-474-5451, E-mail: fysoed@uaf.edu. *Application contact:* Dr. Eric C. Madsen, Dean, 907-474-7341, Fax: 907-474-5451, E-mail: fysoed@uaf.edu.

The University of British Columbia, Faculty of Arts and Faculty of Graduate Studies, Department of Psychology, Vancouver, BC V6T 1Z1, Canada. Offers behavioral neuroscience (MA, PhD); clinical psychology (MA, PhD); cognitive science (MA, PhD); developmental psychology (MA, PhD); forensic psychology (PhD); health psychology (MA, PhD); quantitative methods (MA, PhD); social/personality psychology (MA, PhD). *Accreditation:* APA (one or more programs are accredited). Terminal master's awarded for partial completion of doctoral program. *Degree requirements:* For master's, thesis; for doctorate, comprehensive exam, thesis/dissertation. *Entrance requirements:* For master's and doctorate, GRE General Test, GRE Subject Test. Additional exam requirements/recommendations for international students: Required—TOEFL (minimum score 550 paper-based; 230 computer-based; 80 iBT). Electronic applications accepted. *Faculty research:* Clinical, developmental, social/personality, cognition, behavioral neuroscience.

University of Central Arkansas, Graduate School, College of Health and Behavioral Sciences, Department of Counseling and Psychology, Program in Community Service Counseling, Conway, AR 72035-0001. Offers MS. *Degree requirements:* For master's, comprehensive exam, thesis optional. *Entrance requirements:* For master's, GRE General Test, minimum GPA of 2.7. Additional exam requirements/recommendations for international students: Required—TOEFL (minimum score 550 paper-based; 213 computer-based).

University of Connecticut, Graduate School, College of Liberal Arts and Sciences, Department of Psychology, Field of Psychology, Storrs, CT 06269. Offers behavioral neuroscience (PhD); biopsychology (PhD); clinical psychology (MA, PhD); cognition and instruction (PhD); developmental psychology (MA, PhD); ecological psychology (PhD); experimental psychology (PhD); general psychology (MA, PhD); health psychology (Graduate Certificate); industrial/organizational psychology (PhD); language and cognition (PhD); neuroscience (PhD); occupational health psychology (Graduate Certificate); social psychology (MA, PhD). *Accreditation:* APA (one or more programs are accredited). Terminal master's awarded for partial completion of doctoral program. *Degree requirements:* For master's, comprehensive exam; for doctorate, thesis/dissertation. *Entrance requirements:* For master's and doctorate, GRE General Test, GRE Subject Test. Additional exam requirements/recommendations for international students: Required—TOEFL (minimum score 550 paper-based; 213 computer-based). Electronic applications accepted.

University of Dayton, Graduate School, School of Education and Allied Professions, Department of Counselor Education and Human Services, Dayton, OH 45469-1300. Offers college student personnel (MS Ed); community counseling (MS Ed); higher education administration (MS Ed); human services (MS Ed); school counseling (MS Ed); school psychology (MS Ed, Ed S); teacher as child/youth development specialist (MS Ed). *Accreditation:* NCATE. Part-time and evening/weekend programs available. *Faculty:* 11 full-time (8 women), 33 part-time/adjunct (22 women). *Students:* 266 full-time (222 women), 236 part-time (200 women); includes 70 minority (58 African Americans, 2 Asian Americans or Pacific Islanders, 10 Hispanic Americans), 2 international. Average age 32. 359 applicants, 47% accepted, 114 enrolled. In 2008, 175 master's, 7 Ed Ss awarded. *Degree requirements:* For master's, comprehensive exam (for some programs), thesis (for some programs), exit exam. *Entrance requirements:* For master's, MAT or GRE (if GPA is below 2.75), interview, writing sample. Additional exam requirements/recommendations for international students: Required—TOEFL (minimum score 550 paper-based; 213 computer-based; 80 iBT). *Application deadline:* For fall admission, 4/10 for domestic students, 3/1 priority date for international students; for winter admission, 9/10 for domestic students, 7/1 priority date for international students; for spring admission, 1/10 for domestic students, 1/1 priority date for international students. Applications are processed on a rolling basis. Application fee: $0 ($50 for international students). Electronic applications accepted. *Expenses:* Tuition: Full-time $6950; part-time $1737.50 per semester. Required fees: $25 per semester. Tuition and fees vary according to course level, course load, degree level and program. *Financial support:* In 2008–09, 7 research assistantships with full tuition reimbursements (averaging $8,000 per year), 1 teaching assistantship with full tuition reimbursement (averaging $8,000 per year) were awarded; career-related internships or fieldwork, institutionally sponsored loans, health care benefits, and unspecified assistantships also available. Financial award applicants required to submit FAFSA. *Faculty research:* Anger as part of the grief process, inclusion of children with severe disabilities, comparisons of school counselors in Bosnia and the U.S., graduate and professional student socialization, use of cohort groups in doctoral programs, bullying in schools, impact of space on learning, sophomore experience. *Unit head:* Dr. Alan Demmitt, Chairperson, 937-229-3644, Fax: 937-229-1055. *Application contact:* Angela Jones-Glukhov, Associate Director of Graduate Admissions, 937-229-4305, Fax: 937-229-4729, E-mail: jonesgas@notes.udayton.edu.

University of Delaware, College of Arts and Sciences, Department of Psychology, Newark, DE 19716. Offers behavioral neuroscience (PhD); clinical psychology (PhD); cognitive psychology (PhD); social psychology (PhD). *Accreditation:* APA. *Degree requirements:* For doctorate, thesis/dissertation. *Entrance requirements:* For doctorate, GRE General Test. Additional exam requirements/recommendations for international students: Required—TOEFL (minimum score 600 paper-based; 250 computer-based). Electronic applications accepted. *Faculty research:* Emotion development, neural and cognitive aspects of memory, neural control of feeding, intergroup relations, social cognition and communication.

University of Florida, Graduate School, College of Liberal Arts and Sciences, Department of Psychology, Gainesville, FL 32611. Offers behavior analysis (PhD); behavioral neuroscience (MS, PhD); cognitive and sensory processes (PhD); counseling psychology (PhD); developmental psychology (PhD); social psychology (MS, PhD); JD/PhD. *Degree requirements:* For master's, thesis or alternative; for doctorate, thesis/dissertation. *Entrance requirements:* For master's and doctorate, GRE General Test, minimum GPA of 3.0. Additional exam requirements/recommendations for international students: Required—TOEFL (minimum score 550 paper-based; 213 computer-based). Electronic applications accepted. *Faculty research:* Experimental analysis of behavior, psychobiology, cognition and sensory processes, counseling psychology, social psychology, developmental psychology.

University of Guelph, Graduate Program Services, College of Social and Applied Human Sciences, Department of Psychology, Guelph, ON N1G 2W1, Canada. Offers applied social psychology (MA, PhD); clinical psychology applied development emphasis (PhD); clinical psychology applied developmental emphasis (MA); industrial/organizational psychology (MA, PhD); neuroscience and applied cognitive science (MA, PhD). *Degree requirements:* For master's, thesis; for doctorate, comprehensive exam, thesis/dissertation. *Entrance requirements:* For master's, GRE General Test, GRE Subject Test, minimum B+ average during previous 2 years of course work; for doctorate, GRE General Test, GRE Subject Test, minimum A-average. Additional exam requirements/recommendations for international students: Required—TOEFL (minimum score 89 iBT). Electronic applications accepted. *Faculty research:* Organizational psychology, reading comprehension and mathematical ability, drug addiction and relapse, gender issues and culture, memory, clinical psychology.

University of Hawaii at Manoa, Graduate Division, Colleges of Arts and Sciences, College of Social Sciences, Department of Psychology, Honolulu, HI 96822. Offers clinical psychology (PhD); community and cultural psychology (PhD); community and culture (MA); psychology (MA, PhD, Graduate Certificate). *Accreditation:* APA (one or more programs are accredited). Part-time programs available. Terminal master's awarded for partial completion of doctoral program. *Degree requirements:* For master's, comprehensive exam, thesis; for doctorate, comprehensive exam, thesis/dissertation. *Entrance requirements:* For master's and doctorate, GRE General Test, GRE Subject Test. Additional exam requirements/recommendations for international students: Required—TOEFL (minimum score 600 paper-based; 250 computer-based; 100 iBT), IELTS (minimum score 7). *Faculty research:* Cross-cultural psychology, health psychology, marine mammals, child/adult psychopathology.

University of Houston, College of Liberal Arts and Social Sciences, Department of Psychology, Houston, TX 77204. Offers clinical psychology (PhD); industrial/organizational psychology (PhD); psychology (MA); social psychology (PhD). *Accreditation:* APA (one or more programs are accredited). *Faculty:* 26 full-time (11 women), 8 part-time/adjunct (3 women). *Students:* 99 full-time (75 women), 15 part-time (11 women); includes 20 minority (5 African Americans, 3 Asian Americans or Pacific Islanders, 12 Hispanic Americans), 10 international. Average age 27. 386 applicants, 7% accepted, 23 enrolled. In 2008, 19 master's, 17 doctorates awarded. *Degree requirements:* For doctorate, thesis/dissertation. *Entrance requirements:* For doctorate, GRE General Test, minimum GPA of 3.0. *Application deadline:* For fall admission, 1/1 for domestic students. Application fee: $40 ($75 for international students). *Expenses:* Tuition, state resident: full-time $5164; part-time $287 per credit. Tuition, nonresident: full-time $10,222; part-time $568 per credit. *Financial support:* In 2008–09, 15 fellowships with full tuition reimbursements (averaging $11,500 per year), 14 research assistantships with full tuition reimbursements (averaging $12,050 per year), 76 teaching assistantships with full tuition reimbursements (averaging $12,050 per year) were awarded; career-related internships or fieldwork, Federal Work-Study, institutionally sponsored loans, scholarships/grants, health care benefits, and unspecified assistantships also available. Support available to part-time students. Financial award application deadline: 2/1; financial award applicants required to submit FAFSA. *Faculty research:* Health psychology, depression, child/family process, organizational effectiveness, close relationships. *Unit head:* Dr. David Francis, Chairperson, 713-743-7036, Fax: 713-743-8588, E-mail: dfrancis@uh.edu. *Application contact:* Sherry A. Berun, Coordinator, Academic Affairs, 713-743-8508, Fax: 713-743-8588, E-mail: sherryr@uh.edu.

University of La Verne, College of Arts and Sciences, Department of Psychology, Program in Clinical-Community Psychology, La Verne, CA 91750-4443. Offers Psy D. Part-time programs available. *Faculty:* 9 full-time (3 women), 6 part-time/adjunct (1 woman). *Students:* 53 full-time (43 women), 33 part-time (29 women); includes 38 minority (9 African Americans, 6 Asian Americans or Pacific Islanders, 23 Hispanic Americans). Average age 29. In 2008, 20 doctorates awarded. *Degree requirements:* For doctorate, thesis/dissertation, clinical internship, competency exams, practicum, personal psychotherapy. *Entrance requirements:* For doctorate, minimum GPA of 3.25 undergraduate, 3.65 graduate; 3 recommendations; interview; curriculum vitae. Additional exam requirements/recommendations for international students: Required—TOEFL (minimum score 600 paper-based; 250 computer-based). *Application deadline:* For fall admission, 1/15 for domestic and international students. Application fee: $75. *Expenses:* Contact institution. *Financial support:* Career-related internships or fieldwork, institutionally sponsored loans, scholarships/grants, and unspecified assistantships available. Financial award application deadline: 3/2; financial award applicants required to submit FAFSA. *Unit head:* Dr. Raymond Scott, Chairperson, 909-593-3511 Ext. 4181, E-mail: rscott@ulv.edu. *Application contact:* Connie Hamlow, Admissions Information Specialist, 909-593-3511 Ext. 4244, Fax: 909-392-2761, E-mail: gradadmission@ulv.edu.

University of Maine, Graduate School, College of Liberal Arts and Sciences, Department of Psychology, Orono, ME 04469. Offers clinical psychology (PhD); developmental psychology (MA); experimental psychology (MA, PhD); social psychology (MA). *Accreditation:* APA (one or more programs are accredited). *Degree requirements:* For master's, thesis; for doctorate, thesis/dissertation. *Entrance requirements:* For master's and doctorate, GRE General Test, GRE Subject Test. Additional exam requirements/recommendations for international students: Required—TOEFL. Electronic applications accepted. *Faculty research:* Social development, hypertension and aging, attitude change, self-confidence in achievement situations, health psychology.

University of Mary, Divison of Social and Behavioral Sciences, Bismarck, ND 58504-9652. Offers addiction counseling (MSC); community counseling (MSC); school counseling (MSC).

University of Mary Hardin-Baylor, College of Sciences and Humanities, Department of Psychology, Belton, TX 76513. Offers community counseling (MA); marriage and family Christian counseling (MA); psychology and counseling (MA); school counseling and psychology (MA). Part-time and evening/weekend programs available. *Degree requirements:* For master's, comprehensive exam. *Entrance requirements:* For master's, GRE General Test, minimum GPA of 3.0 in last 60 hours or 2.75 overall. Electronic applications accepted.

University of Maryland, College Park, Graduate Studies, College of Behavioral and Social Sciences, Department of Psychology, College Park, MD 20742. Offers clinical psychology (PhD); developmental psychology (PhD); experimental psychology (PhD); industrial psychology (MA, MS, PhD); social psychology (PhD). *Accreditation:* APA (one or more programs are accredited). *Degree requirements:* For master's, thesis; for doctorate, variable foreign language requirement, comprehensive exam, thesis/dissertation. *Entrance requirements:* For master's and doctorate, GRE General Test, GRE Subject Test, minimum GPA of 3.5, research and/or work experience, 3 letters of recommendation. Electronic applications accepted. *Faculty research:* Social stereotyping and prejudice, anxiety disorders, auditory neuroethology, counseling and social psychology.

University of Massachusetts Amherst, Graduate School, College of Social and Behavioral Sciences, Department of Psychology, Amherst, MA 01003. Offers clinical psychology (MS, PhD); cognitive psychology (MS, PhD); developmental science (MS, PhD); psychology of peace and violence (MS, PhD); social psychology (MS, PhD). *Accreditation:* APA (one or more programs are accredited). Terminal master's awarded for partial completion of doctoral program. *Degree requirements:* For master's, thesis; for doctorate, comprehensive exam, thesis/dissertation. *Entrance requirements:* For master's and doctorate, GRE General Test, 3 letters of recommendation. Additional exam requirements/recommendations for international students: Required—TOEFL (minimum score 550 paper-based; 213 computer-based; 79 iBT), IELTS (minimum score 6.5). Electronic applications accepted. *Expenses:* Tuition, area resident: Full-time $2640. Tuition, nonresident: full-time $9936. One-time fee: $332 full-time. Tuition and fees vary according to course load.

University of Massachusetts Lowell, College of Arts and Sciences, Department of Psychology, Lowell, MA 01854-2881. Offers community social psychology (MA). Part-time programs available. *Degree requirements:* For master's, thesis optional. *Entrance requirements:* For master's, GRE General Test or MAT. Electronic applications accepted. *Faculty research:* Domestic violence, youth sports, teen pregnancy, substance abuse, family and work roles.

University of Michigan, Horace H. Rackham School of Graduate Studies, College of Literature, Science, and the Arts, Department of Psychology, Ann Arbor, MI 48109. Offers biopsychology (PhD); clinical psychology (PhD); cognition and perception (PhD); developmental psychology (PhD); personality and social contexts (PhD); social psychology (PhD). *Accreditation:* APA. *Degree requirements:* For doctorate, comprehensive exam, thesis/dissertation, oral defense of dissertation, preliminary exam. *Entrance requirements:* For doctorate, GRE General Test (optional), GRE Subject Test (optional). Additional exam requirements/recommendations for international students: Required—TOEFL. Electronic applications accepted.

University of Minnesota, Twin Cities Campus, Graduate School, College of Liberal Arts, Department of Psychology, Program in Social Psychology, Minneapolis, MN 55455-0213. Offers PhD. *Degree requirements:* For doctorate, comprehensive exam, thesis/dissertation. *Entrance requirements:* For doctorate, GRE General Test, GRE Subject Test (recommended), 12 credits of upper-level psychology courses, including a course in statistics or psychological measurement. Additional exam requirements/recommendations for international students: Required—TOEFL (minimum score 550 paper-based; 213 computer-based; 79 iBT).

University of Missouri–Kansas City, College of Arts and Sciences, Department of Psychology, Kansas City, MO 64110-2499. Offers psychology (MA, PhD), including clinical psychology (PhD), community psychology (PhD). *Accreditation:* APA. *Faculty:* 15 full-time (12 women), 1

Social Psychology

University of Missouri–Kansas City (continued)
part-time/adjunct (0 women). *Students:* 18 full-time (15 women), 6 part-time (5 women); includes 3 minority (2 African Americans, 1 Hispanic American). Average age 31. 90 applicants, 6% accepted, 5 enrolled. In 2008, 3 master's, 2 doctorates awarded. Terminal master's awarded for partial completion of doctoral program. *Degree requirements:* For master's, thesis; for doctorate, comprehensive exam, thesis/dissertation, residency. *Entrance requirements:* For master's, GRE, minimum GPA of 3.5, letter of recommendation; for doctorate, GRE, minimum GPA of 3.25. Additional exam requirements/recommendations for international students: Required—TOEFL (minimum score 550 paper-based; 213 computer-based; 80 iBT). *Application deadline:* For fall admission, 1/15 for domestic and international students. Applications are processed on a rolling basis. Application fee: $45 ($50 for international students). Electronic applications accepted. *Expenses:* Tuition, state resident: full-time $5376; part-time $298.70 per credit hour. Tuition, nonresident: full-time $13,882; part-time $771.20 per credit hour. Required fees: $640.28; $34.65 per contact hour. $30 per semester. Tuition and fees vary according to course load and program. *Financial support:* In 2008–09, 14 research assistantships (averaging $12,402 per year), 3 teaching assistantships (averaging $10,000 per year) were awarded; career-related internships or fieldwork, Federal Work-Study, and institutionally sponsored loans also available. Support available to part-time students. Financial award application deadline: 3/1; financial award applicants required to submit FAFSA. *Faculty research:* HIV/AIDS research group, psycho-oncology, sensory and cognitive neuroscience, cognitive psychophysiology, obesity and related metabolic disorders. Total annual research expenditures: $750,913. *Unit head:* Dr. Diane Filion, Chairperson, 816-235-1061, E-mail: filiond@umkc.edu. *Application contact:* 816-235-1111.

University of Missouri–St. Louis, College of Arts and Sciences, Department of Psychology, St. Louis, MO 63121. Offers behavioral neuroscience (PhD); clinical psychology respecialization (Certificate); community psychology (PhD); general psychology (MA); industrial/organizational psychology (PhD). *Accreditation:* APA (one or more programs are accredited). Evening/weekend programs available. *Faculty:* 21 full-time (10 women). *Students:* 56 full-time (46 women), 15 part-time (11 women); includes 4 minority (1 American Indian/Alaska Native, 2 Asian Americans or Pacific Islanders, 1 Hispanic American), 1 international. Average age 28. In 2008, 16 master's, 8 doctorates awarded. Terminal master's awarded for partial completion of doctoral program. *Degree requirements:* For doctorate, thesis/dissertation. *Entrance requirements:* For master's and doctorate, GRE General Test, GRE Subject Test, 3 letters of recommendation. Additional exam requirements/recommendations for international students: Required—TOEFL (minimum score 550 paper-based; 213 computer-based). *Application deadline:* For fall admission, 2/1 priority date for domestic and international students. Applications are processed on a rolling basis. Application fee: $35 ($40 for international students). Electronic applications accepted. *Expenses:* Tuition, area resident: Full-time $5377; part-time $298.70 per credit hour. Tuition, nonresident: full-time $13,381; part-time $472.50 per credit hour. Required fees: $4078; $52 per credit hour. *Financial support:* In 2008–09, 3 research assistantships with full and partial tuition reimbursements (averaging $9,225 per year), 15 teaching assistantships with full and partial tuition reimbursements (averaging $9,000 per year) were awarded; fellowships with full tuition reimbursements also available. Financial award applicants required to submit FAFSA. *Faculty research:* Bereavement and loss, neuroscience, post-traumatic stress disorder, conflict and negotiation, social psychology. *Unit head:* Dr. George Taylor, Chair, 314-516-5391, Fax: 314-516-5392, E-mail: umslpsychology@msx.umsl.edu. *Application contact:* 314-516-5458, Fax: 314-516-6996, E-mail: gradadm@umsl.edu.

University of Missouri–St. Louis, College of Education, Division of Counseling, St. Louis, MO 63121. Offers community counseling (M Ed); elementary school counseling (M Ed); secondary school counseling (M Ed). *Accreditation:* ACA; NCATE. Part-time and evening/weekend programs available. *Faculty:* 7 full-time (3 women). *Students:* 57 full-time (51 women), 148 part-time (125 women); includes 33 minority (28 African Americans, 1 American Indian/Alaska Native, 2 Asian Americans or Pacific Islanders, 2 Hispanic Americans), 8 international. Average age 31. In 2008, 58 master's awarded. *Degree requirements:* For master's, comprehensive exam. *Entrance requirements:* For master's, 3 letters of recommendation, supplemental application. Additional exam requirements/recommendations for international students: Required—TOEFL (minimum score 550 paper-based; 213 computer-based). *Application deadline:* For fall admission, 6/1 for domestic and international students; for spring admission, 10/1 for domestic and international students. Application fee: $35 ($40 for international students). Electronic applications accepted. *Expenses:* Tuition, area resident: Full-time $5377; part-time $298.70 per credit hour. Tuition, nonresident: full-time $13,381; part-time $472.50 per credit hour. Required fees: $4078; $52 per credit hour. *Financial support:* In 2008–09, 4 research assistantships with full and partial tuition reimbursements (averaging $6,000 per year) were awarded. Financial award application deadline: 4/1; financial award applicants required to submit FAFSA. *Faculty research:* Vocational interests, self-concept, decision-making factors, developmental differences. *Unit head:* Dr. Mark Pope, Chair, 314-516-5782. *Application contact:* 314-516-5458, Fax: 314-516-6996, E-mail: gradadm@umsl.edu.

University of Montevallo, College of Education, Program in Counseling, Montevallo, AL 35115. Offers community counseling (M Ed); marriage and family (M Ed); school counseling (M Ed). *Accreditation:* ACA; NCATE. Part-time and evening/weekend programs available. *Students:* 29 full-time (24 women), 48 part-time (41 women); includes 17 minority (15 African Americans, 1 Asian American or Pacific Islander, 1 Hispanic American), 2 international. In 2008, 19 master's awarded. *Entrance requirements:* For master's, GRE General Test or MAT, minimum undergraduate GPA of 2.75 in last 60 hours or 2.5 overall, interview. Additional exam requirements/recommendations for international students: Required—TOEFL (minimum score 550 paper-based). *Application deadline:* For fall admission, 7/15 for domestic students; for spring admission, 11/15 for domestic students. Application fee: $25. *Expenses:* Tuition, state resident: full-time $5280; part-time $220 per credit hour. Tuition, nonresident: full-time $10,560; part-time $440 per credit hour. Required fees: $482; $113 per semester. One-time fee: $25 part-time. *Financial support:* Federal Work-Study, scholarships/grants, and unspecified assistantships available. *Unit head:* Dr. Leland Doebler, Chair, 205-665-6380. *Application contact:* Dr. Leland Doebler, Chair, 205-665-6380.

University of Nebraska–Lincoln, Graduate College, College of Arts and Sciences, Department of Psychology, Lincoln, NE 68588. Offers biopsychology (PhD); clinical psychology (PhD); cognitive psychology (PhD); developmental psychology (PhD); psychology (MA); social/personality psychology (PhD); JD/MA; JD/PhD. *Accreditation:* APA (one or more programs are accredited). *Faculty:* 24 full-time (8 women). *Students:* 84 full-time (66 women), 29 part-time (15 women); includes 15 minority (1 African American, 1 American Indian/Alaska Native, 4 Asian Americans or Pacific Islanders, 9 Hispanic Americans), 9 international. Average age 32. In 2008, 16 master's, 18 doctorates awarded. *Degree requirements:* For master's, thesis optional; for doctorate, comprehensive exam, thesis/dissertation. *Entrance requirements:* For master's and doctorate, GRE General Test. Additional exam requirements/recommendations for international students: Required—TOEFL (minimum score 550 paper-based; 213 computer-based). *Application deadline:* For fall admission, 1/3 for domestic and international students. Application fee: $40. Electronic applications accepted. *Expenses:* Tuition, state resident: full-time $4275; part-time $237.50 per credit hour. Tuition, nonresident: full-time $11,525; part-time $640.25 per credit hour. Required fees: $1068; $10.35 per credit hour. $440.70 per semester. Tuition and fees vary according to course load and program. *Financial support:* Fellowships, research assistantships, teaching assistantships, Federal Work-Study, health care benefits, and unspecified assistantships available. Support available to part-time students. Financial award application deadline: 1/3. *Faculty research:* Law and psychology, rural mental health, chronic mental illness, neuropsychology, child clinical psychology. *Unit head:* Dr. David Hansen, Chair, 402-472-3721, Fax: 402-472-4637. *Application contact:* Ginny Gross, Director of Graduate Admissions, 402-472-2878, Fax: 402-472-0589, E-mail: grad_admissions@unl.edu.

University of Nevada, Reno, Graduate School, Interdisciplinary Program in Social Psychology, Reno, NV 89557. Offers PhD. *Faculty:* 20 full-time (12 women). *Students:* 30 full-time (21 women), 9 part-time (8 women); includes 7 minority (3 Asian Americans or Pacific Islanders, 4 Hispanic Americans), 3 international. Average age 32. 38 applicants, 18% accepted, 6 enrolled. In 2008, 4 doctorates awarded. *Degree requirements:* For doctorate, one foreign language, thesis/dissertation. *Entrance requirements:* For doctorate, GRE General Test, GRE Subject Test (psychology or sociology), minimum GPA of 3.0. Additional exam requirements/recommendations for international students: Required—TOEFL (minimum score 500 paper-based; 173 computer-based; 61 iBT), IELTS (minimum score 6), TOFEL or IELTS. *Application deadline:* For fall admission, 2/1 priority date for domestic and international students. Applications are processed on a rolling basis. Application fee: $60 ($95 for international students). Electronic applications accepted. *Expenses:* Tuition, state resident: full-time $1710; part-time $1140 per semester. Tuition, nonresident: full-time $7115. Required fees: $158 per semester. *Financial support:* In 2008–09, 32 research assistantships with partial tuition reimbursements (averaging $14,000 per year), 3 teaching assistantships with partial tuition reimbursements (averaging $14,000 per year) were awarded; Federal Work-Study, institutionally sponsored loans, scholarships/grants, health care benefits, and unspecified assistantships also available. Financial award application deadline: 3/1; financial award applicants required to submit FAFSA. *Faculty research:* Social psychological theory, social psychology of law. *Unit head:* Dr. Colleen Murray, Director, 775-784-7006, E-mail: cimurray@unr.nevada.edu. *Application contact:* Michele Sandberg, Application Contact, 775-784-7026, Fax: 775-784-6064, E-mail: gradschool@unr.edu.

University of New Haven, Graduate School, College of Arts and Sciences, Program in Community Psychology, West Haven, CT 06516-1916. Offers MA, Certificate. *Faculty:* 6 full-time (2 women), 8 part-time/adjunct (4 women). *Students:* 32 full-time (26 women), 15 part-time (11 women); includes 9 minority (7 African Americans, 2 Hispanic Americans), 3 international. Average age 27. 48 applicants, 71% accepted, 30 enrolled. In 2008, 7 master's awarded. *Degree requirements:* For master's, thesis or alternative. *Entrance requirements:* Additional exam requirements/recommendations for international students: Required—TOEFL (minimum score 520 paper-based; 190 computer-based; 70 iBT); Recommended—IELTS (minimum score 5.5). *Application deadline:* For fall admission, 5/31 for international students; for winter admission, 10/15 for international students; for spring admission, 1/15 for international students. Applications are processed on a rolling basis. Application fee: $50. *Expenses:* Tuition: Full-time $15,075; part-time $670 per credit. Required fees: $240; $45 per trimester. Tuition and fees vary according to course load and program. *Financial support:* Research assistantships with partial tuition reimbursements, teaching assistantships with partial tuition reimbursements, career-related internships or fieldwork, Federal Work-Study, scholarships/grants, tuition waivers, and unspecified assistantships available. Support available to part-time students. Financial award applicants required to submit FAFSA. *Unit head:* Dr. Michael A Morris, Coordinator, 203-932-7281. *Application contact:* Eloise Gormley, Director of Graduate Admissions, 203-932-7449, Fax: 203-932-7137, E-mail: gradinfo@newhaven.edu.

The University of North Carolina at Chapel Hill, Graduate School, College of Arts and Sciences, Department of Psychology, Chapel Hill, NC 27599. Offers biological psychology (PhD); clinical psychology (PhD); cognitive psychology (PhD); developmental psychology (PhD); quantitative psychology (PhD); social psychology (PhD). *Accreditation:* APA. *Degree requirements:* For doctorate, comprehensive exam, thesis/dissertation. *Entrance requirements:* For doctorate, GRE General Test, minimum GPA of 3.0. Electronic applications accepted. *Faculty research:* Expressed emotion, cognitive development, social cognitive neuroscience, human memory personality.

The University of North Carolina at Charlotte, Graduate School, College of Arts and Sciences, Department of Psychology, Program in Community/Clinical Psychology, Charlotte, NC 28223-0001. Offers MA. *Students:* 9 full-time (8 women), 11 part-time (10 women); includes 6 minority (4 African Americans, 2 Hispanic Americans). Average age 26. 129 applicants, 3% accepted, 4 enrolled. In 2008, 8 master's awarded. *Degree requirements:* For master's, comprehensive exam, thesis. *Entrance requirements:* For master's, GRE General Test, GRE Subject Test, minimum GPA of 3.0 in undergraduate major, 2.8 overall. Additional exam requirements/recommendations for international students: Required—TOEFL (minimum score 557 paper-based; 220 computer-based). *Application deadline:* For fall admission, 3/1 for domestic and international students. Application fee: $55. Electronic applications accepted. *Expenses:* Tuition, area resident: Full-time $2919; part-time $122 per credit hour. Tuition, state resident: full-time $2919; part-time $122 per credit hour. Tuition, nonresident: full-time $13,126; part-time $547 per credit hour. Required fees: $1779; $91 per credit hour. Tuition and fees vary according to program. *Financial support:* In 2008–09, 1 research assistantship (averaging $2,250 per year), 3 teaching assistantships (averaging $9,000 per year) were awarded; career-related internships or fieldwork, Federal Work-Study, institutionally sponsored loans, scholarships/grants, unspecified assistantships, and 2 administrative assistantships ($8,100 average) also available. Support available to part-time students. Financial award application deadline: 4/1; financial award applicants required to submit FAFSA. *Unit head:* Dr. Richard G. Tedeschi, Coordinator, 704-687-4754, Fax: 704-687-3096, E-mail: rtedesch@email.uncc.edu. *Application contact:* Kathy B. Giddings, Director of Graduate Admissions, 704-687-3366, Fax: 704-687-3279, E-mail: agidding@uncc.edu.

The University of North Carolina at Greensboro, Graduate School, College of Arts and Sciences, Department of Psychology, Greensboro, NC 27412-5001. Offers clinical psychology (MA, PhD); cognitive psychology (MA, PhD); developmental psychology (MA, PhD); social psychology (MA, PhD). *Accreditation:* APA (one or more programs are accredited). Terminal master's awarded for partial completion of doctoral program. *Degree requirements:* For master's, comprehensive exam, thesis; for doctorate, one foreign language, thesis/dissertation, preliminary exam. *Entrance requirements:* For master's and doctorate, GRE General Test. Additional exam requirements/recommendations for international students: Required—TOEFL. Electronic applications accepted. *Faculty research:* Sensory and perceptual determinants; evoked potential: disorders, deafness, and development.

University of Oklahoma, Graduate College, College of Education, Department of Educational Psychology, Program in Community Counseling, Norman, OK 73019. Offers M Ed. *Students:* 28 full-time (23 women), 4 part-time (3 women); includes 6 minority (4 American Indian/Alaska Native, 2 Asian Americans or Pacific Islanders). 7 applicants, 0% accepted. In 2008, 16 master's awarded. Terminal master's awarded for partial completion of doctoral program. *Degree requirements:* For master's, comprehensive exam. *Entrance requirements:* For master's, GRE General Test, minimum GPA of 3.0. Additional exam requirements/recommendations for international students: Required—TOEFL (minimum score 550 paper-based; 213 computer-based). *Application deadline:* For fall admission, 1/31 for domestic students, 4/1 for international students; for spring admission, 11/1 for domestic students, 9/1 for international students. Applications are processed on a rolling basis. Application fee: $40 ($90 for international students). Electronic applications accepted. *Expenses:* Tuition, state resident: full-time $3744; part-time $156 per credit hour. Tuition, nonresident: full-time $13,577; part-time $565.70 per credit hour. Required fees: $2415.40; $90.10 per credit hour. *Financial support:* In 2008–09, 22 students received support. Institutionally sponsored loans, scholarships/grants, health care benefits, and unspecified assistantships available. Financial award application deadline: 3/1; financial award applicants required to submit FAFSA. *Faculty research:* Marriage and family; counseling assessment; process and outcome; diversity issues; health psychology; education, training and supervision. *Unit head:* Dr. Terri K Debacker, Chair, 405-325-1068, Fax: 405-325-6655, E-mail: debacker@ou.edu. *Application contact:* Rindi Ledo, Graduate Programs Officer, 405-325-4525, Fax: 405-325-6655, E-mail: gpoedpsych@ou.edu.

University of Oregon, Graduate School, College of Arts and Sciences, Department of Psychology, Eugene, OR 97403. Offers clinical psychology (PhD); cognitive psychology (MA, MS, PhD); developmental psychology (MA, MS, PhD); physiological psychology (MA, MS, PhD); psychology (MA, MS, PhD); social/personality psychology (MA, MS, PhD). *Accreditation:* APA (one or more programs are accredited). Terminal master's awarded for partial completion of doctoral program. *Degree requirements:* For doctorate, thesis/dissertation. *Entrance requirements:* For master's, GRE General Test, minimum GPA of 3.0; for doctorate, GRE

General Test. Additional exam requirements/recommendations for international students: Required—TOEFL.

University of Pennsylvania, Graduate School of Education, Division of Applied Psychology and Human Development, Program in School, Community, and Clinical Child Psychology, Philadelphia, PA 19104. Offers PhD. *Degree requirements:* For doctorate, thesis/dissertation, exams. *Entrance requirements:* For doctorate, GRE General Test, GRE Subject Test. Electronic applications accepted. *Expenses:* Contact institution. *Faculty research:* Therapeutic interventions at a preschool level, childhood stress, college psychology, school and community psychology.

University of Phoenix, The Artemis School, College of Health and Human Services, Phoenix, AZ 85034-7209. Offers administration of justice and security (MS); community counseling (MSC); education (MHA); family nurse practitioner (MSN); gerontology (MHA); health administration (MHA); health care education (MSN); health care management (MBA, MSN); informatics (MHA); marriage, family, and child therapy (MSC); nursing (MSN); nursing for nurse practitioners (MSN); psychology (MS); MSN/MBA; MSN/MHA. *Accreditation:* AACN. Evening/weekend programs available. Postbaccalaureate distance learning degree programs offered. *Degree requirements:* For master's, thesis (for some programs). *Entrance requirements:* For master's, 3 years of work experience, minimum undergraduate GPA of 2.5, RN license. Additional exam requirements/recommendations for international students: Required—TOEFL (minimum score 550 paper-based; 213 computer-based; 79 iBT). Electronic applications accepted.

University of Phoenix–Denver Campus, The Artemis School, College of Health and Human Services, Lone Tree, CO 80124-5453. Offers administration of justice and security (MS); community counseling (MSC); health administration (MHA); health care management (MBA); marriage, family and child therapy (MSC); nursing (MSN); psychology (MS); MSN/MBA; MSN/MHA. Evening/weekend programs available. Postbaccalaureate distance learning degree programs offered. *Degree requirements:* For master's, thesis (for some programs). *Entrance requirements:* For master's, minimum undergraduate GPA of 2.5, 3 years work experience, RN license. Additional exam requirements/recommendations for international students: Required—TOEFL (minimum score 550 paper-based; 213 computer-based; 79 iBT). Electronic applications accepted.

University of Phoenix–Hawaii Campus, The Artemis School, College of Health and Human Services, Honolulu, HI 96813-4317. Offers administration of justice and security (MS); community counseling (MSC); education (MHA); family nurse practitioner (MSN); gerontology (MHA); health administration (MHA); health care management (MBA); marriage, family and child therapy (MSC); nursing (MSN); nursing/health care education (MSN); psychology (MS); MSN/MBA. Evening/weekend programs available. *Degree requirements:* For master's, thesis (for some programs). *Entrance requirements:* For master's, minimum undergraduate GPA of 2.5, 3 years of work experience, RN license. Additional exam requirements/recommendations for international students: Required—TOEFL (minimum score 550 paper-based; 213 computer-based; 79 iBT). Electronic applications accepted.

University of Phoenix–Kansas City Campus, The Artemis School, College of Health and Human Services, Kansas City, MO 64131-4517. Offers administration of justice and security (MS); community counseling (MSC); health administration (MHA); health care management (MBA); nursing (MSN); MSN/MBA. Evening/weekend programs available. Postbaccalaureate distance learning degree programs offered. *Degree requirements:* For master's, thesis (for some programs). *Entrance requirements:* For master's, 3 years work experience, minimum undergraduate GPA or 2.5. Additional exam requirements/recommendations for international students: Required—TOEFL (minimum score 550 paper-based; 213 computer-based).

University of Phoenix–Minneapolis/St. Louis Park Campus, College of Health and Human Services, St. Louis Park, MN 55426. Offers community counseling (MSC); family nurse practitioner (MSN); health care education (MSN); health care managerment (MBA); nursing (MSN).

University of Phoenix–Phoenix Campus, The Artemis School, College of Health and Human Services, Phoenix, AZ 85040-1958. Offers community counseling (MSC); education (MHA); family nurse practitioner (MSN); gerontology (MHA); health administration (MHA); health care education (MSN); health care management (MBA); informatics (MHA); marriage, family, and child therapy (MSC); nurse practitioner (Certificate); nursing (MSN); nursing health care education (Certificate); psychology (MS); MSN/MBA; MSN/MHA. Evening/weekend programs available. *Degree requirements:* For master's, thesis (for some programs). *Entrance requirements:* For master's, 3 years of work experience in field, minimum undergraduate GPA of 2.5, RN license. Additional exam requirements/recommendations for international students: Required—TOEFL (minimum score 550 paper-based; 213 computer-based; 79 iBT). Electronic applications accepted.

University of Phoenix–Southern Colorado Campus, The Artemis School, College of Health and Human Services, Colorado Springs, CO 80919-2335. Offers administration of justice and security (MS); community counseling (MSC); education (MHA); gerontology (MHA); health administration (MHA); health care management (MBA); marriage, family and child therapy (MSC); nursing (MSN); psychology (MS); MSN/MBA. Evening/weekend programs available. *Degree requirements:* For master's, thesis (for some programs). *Entrance requirements:* For master's, minimum undergraduate GPA of 2.5, 3 years of work experience, RN license. Additional exam requirements/recommendations for international students: Required—TOEFL (minimum score 550 paper-based; 213 computer-based; 79 iBT). Electronic applications accepted.

University of Rochester, The College, Arts and Sciences, Department of Clinical and Social Sciences in Psychology, Rochester, NY 14627-0250. Offers clinical psychology (PhD); developmental psychology (PhD); psychology (MA); social-personality psychology (PhD). *Accreditation:* APA (one or more programs are accredited). Terminal master's awarded for partial completion of doctoral program. *Degree requirements:* For doctorate, thesis/dissertation, qualifying exam. *Entrance requirements:* For doctorate, GRE General Test. Additional exam requirements/recommendations for international students: Required—TOEFL.

The University of Scranton, College of Graduate and Continuing Education, Department of Counseling and Human Services, Program in Community Counseling, Scranton, PA 18510. Offers MS. *Accreditation:* ACA. Part-time and evening/weekend programs available. *Students:* 51 full-time (39 women), 5 part-time (4 women); includes 1 minority (Asian American or Pacific Islander). Average age 30. 24 applicants, 75% accepted. In 2008, 12 master's awarded. *Degree requirements:* For master's, comprehensive exam, capstone experience. *Entrance requirements:* For master's, minimum GPA of 2.75. Additional exam requirements/recommendations for international students: Required—TOEFL (minimum score 500 paper-based; 173 computer-based), IELTS (minimum score 5.5). *Application deadline:* For fall admission, 3/1 for domestic students. Application fee: $50. *Financial support:* Teaching assistantships, career-related internships or fieldwork and Federal Work-Study available. Support available to part-time students. Financial award application deadline: 3/1. *Unit head:* Dr. Oliver J. Morgan, Chair, 570-941-6171, Fax: 570-941-5882, E-mail: morgano1@scranton.edu. *Application contact:* Joseph M. Roback, Director of Admissions, 570-941-4385, Fax: 570-941-5928, E-mail: roback j2@scranton.edu.

University of South Carolina, The Graduate School, College of Arts and Sciences, Department of Psychology, Program in Clinical/Community Psychology, Columbia, SC 29208. Offers clinical/community psychology (PhD); general psychology (MA). *Accreditation:* APA. *Degree requirements:* For master's, comprehensive exam, thesis; for doctorate, comprehensive exam, thesis/dissertation. *Entrance requirements:* For doctorate, GRE General Test, minimum GPA of 3.2. Additional exam requirements/recommendations for international students: Required—TOEFL. Electronic applications accepted. *Faculty research:* Developmental psychopathology, health disparities, community-level interventions for psychological well being.

The University of Tennessee at Martin, Graduate Programs, College of Education and Behavioral Sciences, Programs in Counseling, Martin, TN 38238. Offers community counseling (MS Ed); school counseling (MS Ed). *Accreditation:* NCATE. Part-time programs available. *Students:* 40 (34 women). 7 applicants, 100% accepted, 5 enrolled. In 2008, 18 master's awarded. *Degree requirements:* For master's, comprehensive exam. *Entrance requirements:* For master's, GRE General Test, minimum GPA of 2.5, resumé, letters of reference. Additional exam requirements/recommendations for international students: Required—TOEFL (minimum score 525 paper-based; 197 computer-based; 71 iBT). *Application deadline:* For fall admission, 8/1 priority date for domestic students, 8/1 for international students; for spring admission, 1/1 priority date for domestic students, 1/1 for international students. Applications are processed on a rolling basis. Application fee: $30 ($50 for international students). Electronic applications accepted. *Expenses:* Tuition, state resident: full-time $6084; part-time $340 per semester hour. Tuition, nonresident: full-time $16,726; part-time $932 per semester hour. *Financial support:* Career-related internships or fieldwork, scholarships/grants, and unspecified assistantships available. Support available to part-time students. Financial award application deadline: 3/1. *Unit head:* Staci Fuqua, Staff Assistant, 731-881-7163, Fax: 731-881-7975, E-mail: sfuqua@utm.edu. *Application contact:* Linda Arant, Student Services Specialist, 731-881-7012, Fax: 731-881-7499, E-mail: larant@utm.edu.

The University of Toledo, College of Graduate Studies, College of Arts and Sciences, Department of Psychology, Toledo, OH 43606-3390. Offers behavioral (PhD), including cognitive, psychobiology and learning, social; clinical psychology (PhD); experimental psychology (MA). *Accreditation:* APA. *Degree requirements:* For master's, thesis; for doctorate, one foreign language, thesis/dissertation. *Entrance requirements:* For master's and doctorate, GRE General Test, GRE Subject Test. *Faculty research:* Neural taste response.

The University of Toledo, College of Graduate Studies, College of Health Science and Human Service, Division of Human Services, Department of Counselor Education and School Psychology, Program in Counselor Education, Toledo, OH 43606-3390. Offers community counseling (MA); counselor education (Ed S); counselor education and supervision (PhD).

University of Victoria, Faculty of Graduate Studies, Faculty of Education, Department of Educational Psychology and Leadership Studies, Victoria, BC V8W 2Y2, Canada. Offers aboriginal communities counseling (M Ed); counseling (M Ed, MA); educational psychology (M Ed, MA, PhD), including counseling psychology (M Ed, MA), leadership studies (PhD), learning and development (MA, PhD), measurement and evaluation, special education (M Ed, MA); leadership studies (M Ed, MA). Part-time programs available. *Degree requirements:* For master's, thesis (for some programs), comprehensive exam (M Ed); for doctorate, comprehensive exam, thesis/dissertation, candidacy exam. *Entrance requirements:* For master's, 2 years of work experience in a relevant field, minimum B average; for doctorate, GRE, 2 years of work experience in a relevant field, minimum B average. Additional exam requirements/recommendations for international students: Required—TOEFL (minimum score 575 paper-based; 233 computer-based), IELTS (minimum score 7). *Faculty research:* Learning and development (child, adolescent and adult), special education and exceptional children.

University of Victoria, Faculty of Graduate Studies, Faculty of Social Sciences, Department of Psychology, Victoria, BC V8W 2Y2, Canada. Offers clinical psychology (PhD); clinical psychology (neuropsychology) (M Sc); cognition and brain science (M Sc, PhD); experimental neuropsychology (M Sc, PhD); individualized study (M Sc, PhD); life span development psychology (PhD); life span developmental psychology (M Sc); social psychology (M Sc, PhD). *Accreditation:* APA (one or more programs are accredited). *Degree requirements:* For master's, thesis; for doctorate, thesis/dissertation, candidacy exam. *Entrance requirements:* For master's and doctorate, GRE General Test. Additional exam requirements/recommendations for international students: Required—TOEFL (minimum score 600 paper-based; 250 computer-based). Electronic applications accepted. *Faculty research:* Life span development psychology and aging, behavioral neuroscience, cognitive psychology, behavioral psychology, environmental psychology.

University of Washington, Graduate School, College of Arts and Sciences, Department of Psychology, Seattle, WA 98195. Offers animal behavior (PhD); child psychology (PhD); clinical psychology (PhD); cognition and perception (PhD); developmental psychology (PhD); quantitative psychology (PhD); social psychology and personality (PhD). *Accreditation:* APA. *Degree requirements:* For doctorate, thesis/dissertation. *Entrance requirements:* For doctorate, GRE General Test, minimum GPA of 3.0. Electronic applications accepted. *Faculty research:* Addictive behaviors, artificial intelligence, child psychopathology, mechanisms and development of vision, physiology of ingestive behaviors.

University of Windsor, Faculty of Graduate Studies, Faculty of Arts and Social Sciences, Department of Psychology, Windsor, ON N9B 3P4, Canada. Offers adult clinical (MA, PhD); applied social psychology (MA, PhD); child clinical (MA, PhD); clinical neuropsychology (MA, PhD). *Accreditation:* APA (one or more programs are accredited). *Degree requirements:* For master's, thesis; for doctorate, comprehensive exam, thesis/dissertation. *Entrance requirements:* For master's, GRE General Test, GRE Subject Test in psychology, minimum B average; for doctorate, GRE General Test, GRE Subject Test in psychology, master's degree. Additional exam requirements/recommendations for international students: Required—TOEFL (minimum score 600 paper-based; 250 computer-based). Electronic applications accepted. *Faculty research:* Gambling, suicidology, emotional competence, psychotherapy and trauma.

University of Wisconsin–Madison, Graduate School, College of Letters and Science, Department of Psychology, Program in Social and Personality Psychology, Madison, WI 53706-1380. Offers PhD. *Degree requirements:* For doctorate, comprehensive exam, thesis/dissertation. *Entrance requirements:* For doctorate, GRE General Test, minimum undergraduate GPA of 3.0. Additional exam requirements/recommendations for international students: Required—TOEFL. Electronic applications accepted.

University of Wisconsin–Milwaukee, Graduate School, School of Education, Department of Educational Psychology, Milwaukee, WI 53201-0413. Offers counseling (school, community) (MS); counseling psychology (PhD); learning and development (MS); research methodology (MS, PhD); school psychology (PhD). *Accreditation:* APA. Part-time programs available. *Faculty:* 21 full-time (13 women). *Students:* 146 full-time (116 women), 60 part-time (49 women); includes 40 minority (15 African Americans, 1 American Indian/Alaska Native, 12 Asian Americans or Pacific Islanders, 12 Hispanic Americans), 6 international. Average age 30. 252 applicants, 46% accepted, 54 enrolled. In 2008, 84 master's, 1 doctorate awarded. *Degree requirements:* For master's, comprehensive exam, thesis; for doctorate, thesis/dissertation. *Entrance requirements:* For master's, minimum GPA of 3.0; for doctorate, GRE General Test, minimum GPA of 3.0. Additional exam requirements/recommendations for international students: Required—TOEFL (minimum score 550 paper-based; 79 iBT), IELTS (minimum score 6.5). *Application deadline:* For fall admission, 1/1 priority date for domestic students; for spring admission, 9/1 for domestic students. Applications are processed on a rolling basis. Application fee: $45 ($75 for international students). *Expenses:* Tuition, area resident: Full-time $7320; part-time $165 per credit. Tuition, state resident: full-time $7320; part-time $165 per credit. Tuition, nonresident: full-time $17,840; part-time $714 per credit. Tuition and fees vary according to campus/location, program and reciprocity agreements. *Financial support:* In 2008–09, 11 teaching assistantships were awarded; career-related internships or fieldwork and unspecified assistantships also available. Support available to part-time students. Financial award application deadline: 4/15. Total annual research expenditures: $673,016. *Unit head:* Anthony Hains, Chair, 414-229-5715, Fax: 414-229-4939, E-mail: aahains@uwm.edu. *Application contact:* General Information Contact, 414-229-4982, Fax: 414-229-6967, E-mail: gradschool@uwm.edu.

University of Wisconsin–Superior, Graduate Division, Department of Counseling and Psychological Professions, Superior, WI 54880-4500. Offers community counseling (MSE); educational psychology (MSE); elementary school counseling (MSE); human relations (MSE); secondary school counseling (MSE). Part-time and evening/weekend programs available. *Degree requirements:* For master's, position paper, practicum. *Entrance requirements:* For

Social Psychology

University of Wisconsin–Superior (continued)
master's, California Psychological Inventory, GRE and/or MAT, minimum GPA of 2.75. *Faculty research:* Women and power, intrafamily dynamics.

University of Wisconsin–Whitewater, School of Graduate Studies, College of Education, Department of Counselor Education, Whitewater, WI 53190-1790. Offers community counseling (MS Ed); higher education (MS Ed); school counseling (MS Ed). *Accreditation:* ACA; NCATE. Part-time and evening/weekend programs available. *Degree requirements:* For master's, thesis or alternative. *Entrance requirements:* For master's, resumé, 2 letters of reference. Additional exam requirements/recommendations for international students: Required—TOEFL (minimum score 550 paper-based; 213 computer-based). Electronic applications accepted. *Faculty research:* Alcohol and other drugs, counseling effectiveness, teacher mentoring.

Walden University, Graduate Programs, School of Psychology, Minneapolis, MN 55401. Offers clinical assessment (Post-Doctoral Certificate); clinical child psychology (Post-Doctoral Certificate); clinical psychology (Post-Doctoral Certificate); counseling psychology (Post-Doctoral Certificate); forensic psychology (MS), including forensic psychology in the community, general forensic psychology, mental health applications, program planning and evaluation in forensic settings, psychology and legal systems; general psychology (Post-Doctoral Certificate); health psychology (Post-Doctoral Certificate); organizational psychology (Post-Doctoral Certificate); organizational psychology and development (Certificate); psychology (MS, PhD), including clinical psychology, counseling psychology, crisis management and response (MS), general psychology, health psychology, leadership development and coaching (MS), media psychology (MS), organizational psychology, organizational psychology and development (MS), organizational psychology and nonprofit management (MS), program evaluation and research (MS), psychology of culture (MS), psychology, public administration, and social change (MS), school psychology, social psychology (MS), terrorism and security (MS); school psychology (Post-Doctoral Certificate); teaching online (Post-Master's Certificate). Part-time and evening/weekend programs available. Postbaccalaureate distance learning degree programs offered (minimal on-campus study). *Faculty:* 16 full-time, 190 part-time/adjunct. *Students:* 3,198 full-time (2,489 women), 810 part-time (664 women); includes 1,319 minority (1,013 African Americans, 51 American Indian/Alaska Native, 68 Asian Americans or Pacific Islanders, 187 Hispanic Americans), 72 international. Average age 40. 1,468 applicants, 60% accepted, 612 enrolled. In 2008, 203 master's, 37 doctorates awarded. Terminal master's awarded for partial completion of doctoral program. *Degree requirements:* For master's, thesis optional; for doctorate, thesis/dissertation, residency. *Entrance requirements:* For master's, bachelor's degree or equivalent in related field, minimum GPA of 2.5, two references, goal statement, official transcripts, access to computer and Internet; for doctorate, master's degree or equivalent in related field, minimum GPA of 3.0, three years related professional/academic experience, two references, goal statement, official transcripts, access to computer and Internet. Additional exam requirements/recommendations for international students: Required—TOEFL (minimum score 550 paper-based; 213 computer-based), IELTS (minimum score 6.5), TOEFL, IELTS, or Michigan English Language Assessment Battery (minimum score 82). *Application deadline:* Applications are processed on a rolling basis. Application fee: $50. Electronic applications accepted. *Expenses:* Tuition: Full-time $12,877; part-time $520 per credit. Required fees: $1230. Tuition and fees vary according to course load, degree level and program. *Financial support:* In 2008–09, 1 fellowship was awarded; Federal Work-Study, scholarships/grants, unspecified assistantships, and family tuition reduction; active duty/veteran tuition reduction; group tuition reduction; interest-free payment plans also available. Support available to part-time students. Financial award applicants required to submit FAFSA. *Unit head:* Dr. Nina Nabors, Associate Dean, 800-925-3368. *Application contact:* Jennifer Hall, 866-4-WALDEN, E-mail: info@waldenu.edu.

Washington State University, Graduate School, College of Liberal Arts, Department of Sociology, Pullman, WA 99164. Offers crime and deviance (MA, PhD); environments, community and demographics (MA, PhD); institutions and social organizations (MA, PhD); political sociology (MA, PhD); social inequality (MA, PhD); social psychology and life course (MA, PhD). Terminal master's awarded for partial completion of doctoral program. *Degree requirements:* For master's, thesis; for doctorate, comprehensive exam, thesis/dissertation. *Entrance requirements:* For master's, GRE General Test, minimum GPA of 3.0; for doctorate, GRE General Test, MA in sociology, minimum GPA of 3.0. Additional exam requirements/recommendations for international students: Required—TOEFL (minimum score 550 paper-based). Electronic applications accepted. *Faculty research:* Crime/deviance, environmental sociology, social inequality, social psychology, gender.

Washington University in St. Louis, Graduate School of Arts and Sciences, Department of Psychology, St. Louis, MO 63130-4899. Offers clinical psychology (PhD); general experimental psychology (PhD); social psychology (PhD). *Accreditation:* APA. *Students:* 102 full-time (63 women); includes 23 minority (6 African Americans, 13 Asian Americans or Pacific Islanders, 4 Hispanic Americans), 12 international. 291 applicants, 11% accepted, 18 enrolled. In 2008, 11 doctorates awarded. Terminal master's awarded for partial completion of doctoral program. *Degree requirements:* For doctorate, thesis/dissertation. *Entrance requirements:* For doctorate, GRE General Test. *Application deadline:* For fall admission, 12/15 priority date for domestic students. Application fee: $45. Electronic applications accepted. *Financial support:* Fellowships, research assistantships, teaching assistantships, career-related internships or fieldwork, Federal Work-Study, institutionally sponsored loans, and tuition waivers (full and partial) available. Support available to part-time students. Financial award application deadline: 1/15. *Unit head:* Dr. Randy Larsen, Chairperson, 314-935-6520. *Application contact:* Assistant to the Dean, 314-935-6880, Fax: 314-935-4887.

Western Carolina University, Graduate School, College of Education and Allied Professions, Department of Human Services, Program in Counseling, Cullowhee, NC 28723. Offers community counseling (M Ed, MS); school counseling (MA Ed). *Accreditation:* ACA. Part-time and evening/weekend programs available. *Degree requirements:* For master's, comprehensive exam, thesis or alternative. *Entrance requirements:* For master's, GRE General Test, appropriate undergraduate with 3.0 GPA, 3 recommendations, writing sample, resumé. Additional exam requirements/recommendations for international students: Required—TOEFL (minimum score 550 paper-based; 270 computer-based; 79 iBT). *Faculty research:* Marital and family development, spirituality in counseling, home school law, sexuality education, family functioning models.

Western Connecticut State University, Division of Graduate Studies, School of Professional Studies, Department of Education and Educational Psychology, Program in Community Counseling, Danbury, CT 06810-6885. Offers MS. *Accreditation:* ACA. Part-time programs available. *Students:* 9 full-time (7 women), 29 part-time (25 women); includes 2 minority (1 Asian American or Pacific Islander, 1 Hispanic American). Average age 37. 10 applicants, 80% accepted, 8 enrolled. In 2008, 9 master's awarded. *Degree requirements:* For master's, practicum, internship, completion of program in 6 years with minimum cumulative GPA of 3.0. *Entrance requirements:* For master's, minimum GPA of 2.8, 3 letters of reference, interview, 9 hours of psychology. *Application deadline:* For fall admission, 8/5 priority date for domestic students; for spring admission, 1/5 for domestic students. Applications are processed on a rolling basis. Application fee: $50. *Expenses:* Tuition, state resident: full-time $4377; part-time $363 per credit. Tuition, nonresident: full-time $12,195; part-time $363 per credit. Required fees: $3574; $60 per credit. Part-time tuition and fees vary according to degree level and program. *Financial support:* Fellowships, career-related internships or fieldwork available. Support available to part-time students. Financial award application deadline: 5/1; financial award applicants required to submit FAFSA. *Unit head:* Dr. Mike Gilles, Assistant Professor, 203-837-8513, Fax: 203-837-8413, E-mail: gillesm@wcsu.edu. *Application contact:* Chris Shankle, Associate Director of Graduate Admissions, 203-837-9005, Fax: 203-837-8326, E-mail: shanklec@wcsu.edu.

Western Illinois University, School of Graduate Studies, College of Arts and Sciences, Department of Psychology, Macomb, IL 61455-1390. Offers clinical/community mental health (MS); general psychology (MS); psychology (MS, SSP); school psychology (SSP). Part-time programs available. *Students:* 42 full-time (21 women), 14 part-time (11 women); includes 1 minority (Asian American or Pacific Islander), 2 international. Average age 25. 66 applicants, 53% accepted. In 2008, 13 master's, 10 other advanced degrees awarded. *Degree requirements:* For master's, comprehensive exam (for some programs), thesis or alternative. *Entrance requirements:* For master's and SSP, GRE General Test. Additional exam requirements/recommendations for international students: Required—TOEFL (minimum score 550 paper-based; 213 computer-based; 80 iBT). *Application deadline:* Applications are processed on a rolling basis. Application fee: $30. Electronic applications accepted. *Expenses:* Tuition, state resident: full-time $5696; part-time $237.34 per credit hour. Tuition, nonresident: full-time $11,392; part-time $474.68 per credit hour. Required fees: $1453; $60.55 per credit hour. *Financial support:* In 2008–09, 36 students received support, including 36 research assistantships with full tuition reimbursements available (averaging $7,040 per year). Financial award applicants required to submit FAFSA. *Unit head:* Dr. Steven Dworkin, Chairperson, 309-298-1593. *Application contact:* Evelyn Hoing, Assistant Director of Graduate Studies, 309-298-1806, Fax: 309-298-2345, E-mail: grad-office@wiu.edu.

Wichita State University, Graduate School, Fairmount College of Liberal Arts and Sciences, Department of Psychology, Wichita, KS 67260. Offers community/clinical psychology (PhD); human factors (PhD); psychology (MA). *Accreditation:* APA. Part-time programs available. *Degree requirements:* For doctorate, thesis/dissertation. *Entrance requirements:* For doctorate, GRE. Additional exam requirements/recommendations for international students: Required—TOEFL. Electronic applications accepted. *Faculty research:* Behavioral evolution, women and alcohol, behavioral medicine, delinquency prevention.

Wilfrid Laurier University, Faculty of Graduate Studies, Faculty of Science, Department of Psychology, Waterloo, ON N2L 3C5, Canada. Offers brain and cognition (M Sc, PhD); community psychology (MA, PhD); social and developmental psychology (MA, PhD). *Degree requirements:* For master's, thesis; for doctorate, thesis/dissertation. *Entrance requirements:* For master's, honors BA or the equivalent in psychology, minimum B average in undergraduate course work, GRE (General Test); for doctorate, master's degree, minimum A- average, GRE (General Test). Additional exam requirements/recommendations for international students: Required—TOEFL (minimum score 230 computer-based; 89 iBT). Electronic applications accepted. *Faculty research:* Brain and cognition, community psychology, social and developmental psychology.

Wilmington University, Division of Behavioral Science, New Castle, DE 19720-6491. Offers administration of human services (MS); administration of justice (MS); community counseling (MS). *Accreditation:* ACA. Part-time and evening/weekend programs available. *Entrance requirements:* Additional exam requirements/recommendations for international students: Required—TOEFL (minimum score 500 paper-based; 173 computer-based). Electronic applications accepted.

Yale University, Graduate School of Arts and Sciences, Department of Psychology, New Haven, CT 06520. Offers behavioral neuroscience (PhD); clinical psychology (PhD); cognitive psychology (PhD); developmental psychology (PhD); social/personality psychology (PhD). *Accreditation:* APA. *Degree requirements:* For doctorate, thesis/dissertation. *Entrance requirements:* For doctorate, GRE General Test.

Sport Psychology

Argosy University, Orange County, College of Psychology and Behavioral Sciences, Program in Sport-Exercise Psychology, Santa Ana, CA 92704. Offers MA.

See Close-Up on page 1081.

Argosy University, Phoenix, College of Psychology and Behavioral Sciences, Program in Clinical Psychology, Phoenix, AZ 85021. Offers clinical psychology (MA); sports-exercise psychology (Psy D). *Accreditation:* APA (one or more programs are accredited).

See Close-Up on page 1083.

Argosy University, Phoenix, College of Psychology and Behavioral Sciences, Program in Sport-Exercise Psychology, Phoenix, AZ 85021. Offers MA.

See Close-Up on page 1083.

Barry University, School of Human Performance and Leisure Sciences, Programs in Movement Science, Specialization in Sport and Exercise Psychology, Miami Shores, FL 33161-6695. Offers MS. *Entrance requirements:* For master's, GRE.

California State University, Fresno, Division of Graduate Studies, College of Health and Human Services, Department of Kinesiology, Fresno, CA 93740-8027. Offers exercise science (MA); sport psychology (MA). Part-time and evening/weekend programs available. *Degree requirements:* For master's, thesis or alternative. *Entrance requirements:* For master's, GRE General Test, minimum GPA of 2.7. Additional exam requirements/recommendations for international students: Required—TOEFL. Electronic applications accepted. *Faculty research:* Refugee education, homeless, geriatrics, fitness.

California State University, Long Beach, Graduate Studies, College of Health and Human Services, Department of Kinesiology, Long Beach, CA 90840. Offers adapted physical education (MA); coaching and student athlete development (MA); exercise physiology and nutrition (MS); exercise science (MS); individualized studies (MA); kinesiology (MA); pedagogical studies (MA); sport and exercise psychology (MS); sport management (MA); sports medicine and injury studies (MS). Part-time programs available. *Faculty:* 9 full-time (4 women), 2 part-time/adjunct (0 women). *Students:* 33 full-time (22 women), 24 part-time (16 women); includes 17 minority (5 African Americans, 8 Asian Americans or Pacific Islanders, 4 Hispanic Americans), 7 international. Average age 29. 143 applicants, 59% accepted, 20 enrolled. *Degree requirements:* For master's, oral and written comprehensive exams or thesis. *Entrance requirements:* For master's, GRE General Test, minimum GPA of 2.75 during previous 2 years of course work. *Application deadline:* For fall admission, 6/1 for domestic students. Applications are processed on a rolling basis. Application fee: $55. Electronic applications accepted. *Expenses:* Tuition, nonresident: full-time $11,160; part-time $372 per unit. Required fees: $4100; $1261 per semester. *Financial support:* Federal Work-Study, institutionally sponsored loans, and scholarships/grants available. Financial award application deadline: 3/2. *Faculty research:* Pulmonary functioning, feedback and practice structure, strength training, history and politics of sports, special population research issues. *Unit head:* Dr. Sharon R Guthrie,

Chair, 562-985-4051, Fax: 562-985-8067, E-mail: guthrie@csulb.edu. *Application contact:* Dr. Grant Hill, Graduate Advisor, 562-985-8856, Fax: 562-985-8067, E-mail: gill@csulb.edu.

California University of Pennsylvania, School of Graduate Studies and Research, School of Education, Department of Athletic Training, Program in Exercise Science and Health Promotion, California, PA 15419-1394. Offers fitness and wellness (MS); performance enhancement and injury prevention (MS); rehabilitation sciences (MS); sport management (MS); sport psychology (MS). Part-time and evening/weekend programs available. Postbaccalaureate distance learning degree programs offered (no on-campus study). *Degree requirements:* For master's, comprehensive exam, thesis optional. *Entrance requirements:* For master's, minimum QPA of 3.0. Additional exam requirements/recommendations for international students: Required—TOEFL (minimum score 550 paper-based; 213 computer-based; 80 iBT). Electronic applications accepted. *Expenses:* Contact institution. *Faculty research:* Reducing obesity in children, sport performance, creating unique biomechanical assessment techniques, Web-based training for fitness professionals, Webcams.

Capella University, Harold Abel School of Psychology, Minneapolis, MN 55402. Offers clinical psychology (MS); counseling psychology (MS); educational psychology (MS, PhD); general psychology (MS, PhD); industrial/organizational psychology (MS, PhD); school psychology (MS, Certificate); sport psychology (MS). Part-time and evening/weekend programs available. Postbaccalaureate distance learning degree programs offered (minimal on-campus study). Terminal master's awarded for partial completion of doctoral program. *Degree requirements:* For master's, thesis optional, project; for doctorate, thesis/dissertation. *Entrance requirements:* For degree, master's degree in school psychology. Additional exam requirements/ recommendations for international students: Required—TOEFL (minimum score 550 paper-based; 213 computer-based), TWE (minimum score 4). Electronic applications accepted. *Faculty research:* Correctional mental health delivery, community mental health, attachment and caregiving in adult and family relationships, influence of encouragement on motivation, and moral dilemmas in business.

Chatham University, Program in Counseling Psychology, Pittsburgh, PA 15232-2826. Offers child, adolescent and family (MSCP); counseling psychology (Psy D); health and holistic (MSCP); infant mental health (MSCP); organization and supervision (MSCP); sport and exercise (MSCP). Part-time and evening/weekend programs available. *Students:* 121 full-time (104 women), 72 part-time (63 women). Average age 30. 117 applicants, 79% accepted, 60 enrolled. In 2008, 63 master's awarded. *Degree requirements:* For master's, thesis optional, supervised internship, advanced research project (optional); for doctorate, thesis/dissertation, internship. *Entrance requirements:* For master's, minimum GPA of 3.0; 2 letters of recommendation; resumé; prerequisite coursework in statistics, biology, and psychology; for doctorate, GRE. Additional exam requirements/recommendations for international students: Required—TOEFL (minimum score 600 paper-based; 250 computer-based; 100 iBT), IELTS (minimum score 6.5), TWE. *Application deadline:* For fall admission, 5/1 priority date for domestic and international students; for spring admission, 10/15 for domestic students, 10/15 priority date for international students. Applications are processed on a rolling basis. Application fee: $45. Electronic applications accepted. *Expenses:* Tuition: Part-time $686 per credit. Tuition and fees vary according to program. *Financial support:* Career-related internships or fieldwork available. Financial award applicants required to submit FAFSA. *Faculty research:* Trauma and recovery, hypnosis, psychospiritual dimensions of healing, psychotherapy of schizophrenia. *Unit head:* Dr. Mary Beth Mannarino, Director, 412-365-1196, Fax: 412-365-1505, E-mail: mmannarino@chatham.edu. *Application contact:* Dory Perry, Associate Director of Graduate Admissions, 412-365-2758, Fax: 412-365-1609, E-mail: gradadmissions@chatham.edu.

Cleveland State University, College of Graduate Studies, College of Education and Human Services, Department of Health, Physical Education, Recreation and Dance, Cleveland, OH 44115. Offers community health education (M Ed); exercise science (M Ed); human performance (M Ed); physical education pedagogy (M Ed); public health (MPH); school health education (M Ed); sport and exercise psychology (M Ed); sports management (M Ed). Part-time programs available. *Faculty:* 9 full-time (6 women), 8 part-time/adjunct (5 women). *Students:* 33 full-time (16 women), 66 part-time (45 women); includes 22 minority (20 African Americans, 1 Asian American or Pacific Islander, 1 Hispanic American), 11 international. Average age 31. 80 applicants, 66% accepted, 31 enrolled. In 2008, 41 master's awarded. *Degree requirements:* For master's, comprehensive exam, thesis optional. *Entrance requirements:* For master's, GRE General Test or MAT (if undergraduate GPA is below 2.75), minimum undergraduate GPA of 2.75. Additional exam requirements/recommendations for international students: Required—TOEFL (minimum score 525 paper-based; 197 computer-based), IELTS (minimum score 6). *Application deadline:* For fall admission, 7/15 priority date for domestic students; for spring admission, 12/15 priority date for domestic students. Applications are processed on a rolling basis. Application fee: $30. Electronic applications accepted. *Financial support:* In 2008–09, 6 research assistantships with full and partial tuition reimbursements (averaging $3,480 per year), 1 teaching assistantship with full and partial tuition reimbursement (averaging $3,480 per year) were awarded; career-related internships or fieldwork, tuition waivers (full), and unspecified assistantships also available. Financial award application deadline: 3/15. *Faculty research:* Bone density, marketing fitness centers, motor development of disabled, online learning and survey research. *Unit head:* Dr. Sheila M. Patterson, Chairperson, 216-687-4870, Fax: 216-687-5410, E-mail: s.m.patterson@csuohio.edu. *Application contact:* Deborah L Brown, Interim Assistant Director, Graduate Admissions, 216-523-7572, Fax: 216-687-5400, E-mail: d.l.brown@csuohio.edu.

Eastern Washington University, Graduate Studies, College of Education and Human Development, Department of Physical Education, Health and Recreation, Cheney, WA 99004-2431. Offers exercise science (MS); sport and exercise psychology (MS); sports administration/ pedagogy (MS). *Degree requirements:* For master's, comprehensive exam, thesis or alternative. *Entrance requirements:* For master's, minimum GPA of 3.0.

Florida State University, Graduate Studies, College of Education, Department of Educational Psychology and Learning Systems, Program in Educational Psychology, Tallahassee, FL 32306. Offers learning and cognition (MS, PhD); sports psychology (MS, PhD). *Degree requirements:* For master's, comprehensive exam, thesis optional; for doctorate, comprehensive exam, thesis/dissertation. *Entrance requirements:* For master's and doctorate, GRE General Test, minimum GPA of 3.0.

John F. Kennedy University, Graduate School of Professional Psychology, Program in Sport Psychology, Pleasant Hill, CA 94523-4817. Offers MA. *Accreditation:* APA. Part-time and evening/weekend programs available. *Degree requirements:* For master's, thesis or alternative. *Entrance requirements:* For master's, interview. Additional exam requirements/recommendations for international students: Required—TOEFL.

Memorial University of Newfoundland, School of Graduate Studies, School of Human Kinetics and Recreation, St. John's, NL A1C 5S7, Canada. Offers administration, curriculum and supervision (MPE); biomechanics/ergonomics (MS Kin); exercise and work physiology (MS Kin); sport psychology (MS Kin). Part-time programs available. *Degree requirements:* For master's, thesis optional, seminars, thesis presentations. *Entrance requirements:* For master's, bachelor's degree in a related field, minimum B average. Electronic applications accepted. *Faculty research:* Administration, sociology of sports, kinesiology, physiology/recreation.

Purdue University, Graduate School, College of Liberal Arts, Department of Health and Kinesiology, West Lafayette, IN 47907. Offers exercise, human physiology of movement and sport (PhD); health and fitness (MS); health promotion (MS); health promotion and disease prevention (PhD); movement and sport science (MS); pedagogy and administration (MS); pedagogy of physical activity and health (PhD); psychology of sport and exercise, and motor behavior (PhD). Part-time programs available. *Degree requirements:* For master's, thesis (for some programs); for doctorate, thesis/dissertation. *Entrance requirements:* For master's and doctorate, GRE General Test. Additional exam requirements/recommendations for international students: Required—TOEFL. Electronic applications accepted. *Faculty research:* Wellness, motivation, teaching effectiveness, learning and development.

Queen's University at Kingston, School of Graduate Studies and Research, School of Kinesiology and Health Studies, Kingston, ON K7L 3N6, Canada. Offers applied exercise science (PhD); biomechanics/ergonomics (M Sc); exercise physiology (M Sc); social psychology of sport and exercise rehabilitation (MA); sociology of sport (MA). Part-time programs available. *Degree requirements:* For master's, thesis (for some programs); for doctorate, comprehensive exam, thesis/dissertation. *Entrance requirements:* For master's and doctorate, minimum B+ average. Additional exam requirements/recommendations for international students: Required—TOEFL. Electronic applications accepted. *Faculty research:* Expert performance ergonomics, obesity research, pregnancy and exercise, gender and sport participation.

Southern Connecticut State University, School of Graduate Studies, School of Education, Department of Exercise Science, New Haven, CT 06515-1355. Offers human performance (MS); physical education (MS); school health education (MS); sport psychology (MS). Part-time and evening/weekend programs available. *Degree requirements:* For master's, thesis or alternative. *Entrance requirements:* For master's, interview. Electronic applications accepted.

Springfield College, Graduate Programs, Programs in Exercise Science and Sport Studies, Springfield, MA 01109-3797. Offers athletic training (MS); exercise physiology (MS), including clinical exercise physiology, science and research; exercise science and sport studies (PhD); health promotion and disease prevention (MS); sport psychology (MS). Part-time programs available. *Faculty:* 12 full-time (5 women), 11 part-time/adjunct (2 women). *Students:* 48 full-time, 5 part-time. Average age 30. 91 applicants, 66% accepted, 23 enrolled. In 2008, 14 master's awarded. Terminal master's awarded for partial completion of doctoral program. *Degree requirements:* For master's, comprehensive exam, research project or thesis; for doctorate, comprehensive exam, thesis/dissertation. *Entrance requirements:* For master's and doctorate, GRE General Test. Additional exam requirements/recommendations for international students: Required—TOEFL (minimum score 550 paper-based; 213 computer-based). *Application deadline:* For fall admission, 1/15 for domestic and international students; for winter admission, 11/1 for domestic and international students; for spring admission, 11/1 for domestic and international students. Applications are processed on a rolling basis. Application fee: $50. Electronic applications accepted. *Expenses:* Tuition: Full-time $9132; part-time $761 per semester hour. Required fees: $150. Tuition and fees vary according to course load. *Financial support:* Fellowships with partial tuition reimbursements, teaching assistantships with partial tuition reimbursements, career-related internships or fieldwork, Federal Work-Study, institutionally sponsored loans, and unspecified assistantships available. Financial award application deadline: 3/1; financial award applicants required to submit FAFSA. *Unit head:* Dr. Vincent Paolone, Director, 413-748-3600, Fax: 413-748-3371, E-mail: vpaolone@spfldcol.edu. *Application contact:* Donald James Shaw, Director of Graduate Admissions, 413-748-3479, Fax: 413-748-3694, E-mail: donald_shaw_jr@spfldcol.edu.

Springfield College, Graduate Programs, Programs in Psychology and Counseling, Springfield, MA 01109-3797. Offers athletic counseling (M Ed, MS, CAGS); industrial/organizational psychology (M Ed, MS, CAGS); marriage and family therapy (M Ed, MS, CAGS); mental health counseling (M Ed, MS, CAGS); school guidance and counseling (M Ed, MS, CAGS); student personnel in higher education (M Ed, MS, CAGS). Part-time programs available. *Faculty:* 13 full-time (6 women), 12 part-time/adjunct (3 women). *Students:* 151 full-time, 52 part-time. Average age 30. 198 applicants, 73% accepted, 74 enrolled. In 2008, 84 master's, 4 other advanced degrees awarded. *Degree requirements:* For master's, research project, portfolio. *Entrance requirements:* Additional exam requirements/recommendations for international students: Required—TOEFL (minimum score 550 paper-based; 213 computer-based). *Application deadline:* For fall admission, 1/15 priority date for domestic students, 1/15 for international students; for winter admission, 11/1 for domestic and international students; for spring admission, 11/1 for domestic and international students. Applications are processed on a rolling basis. Application fee: $50. Electronic applications accepted. *Expenses:* Tuition: Full-time $9132; part-time $761 per semester hour. Required fees: $150. Tuition and fees vary according to course load. *Financial support:* Fellowships with partial tuition reimbursements, teaching assistantships with partial tuition reimbursements, career-related internships or fieldwork, Federal Work-Study, institutionally sponsored loans, and unspecified assistantships available. Financial award application deadline: 3/1; financial award applicants required to submit FAFSA. *Unit head:* Dr. Glenn Lowery, Director, 413-748-3301, Fax: 413-748-3854, E-mail: glowery@spfldcol.edu. *Application contact:* Donald James Shaw, Director of Graduate Admissions, 413-748-3479, Fax: 413-748-3694, E-mail: donald_shaw_jr@spfldcol.edu.

University of Florida, Graduate School, College of Health and Human Performance, Department of Applied Physiology and Kinesiology, Gainesville, FL 32611. Offers athletic training/sport medicine (MS, PhD); biomechanics (MS, PhD); clinical exercise physiology (MS); exercise physiology (MS, PhD); health and human performance (PhD); human performance (MS); motor learning/control (MS, PhD); sport and exercise psychology (MS). *Degree requirements:* For doctorate, thesis/dissertation. *Entrance requirements:* For doctorate, GRE General Test. Electronic applications accepted.

The University of Iowa, Graduate College, College of Liberal Arts and Sciences, Department of Health and Sport Studies, Iowa City, IA 52242-1316. Offers psychology of sport and physical activity (MA, PhD); sports studies (MA, PhD). *Degree requirements:* For master's, thesis optional, exam; for doctorate, comprehensive exam, thesis/dissertation. *Entrance requirements:* For master's and doctorate, GRE General Test, minimum GPA of 3.0. Additional exam requirements/recommendations for international students: Required—TOEFL (minimum score 600 paper-based; 250 computer-based; 100 iBT). Electronic applications accepted.

University of Rhode Island, Graduate School, College of Human Science and Services, Department of Kinesiology, Kingston, RI 02881. Offers adapted physical education (MS); cultural studies of sport and physical culture (MS); exercise science (MS); physical education pedagogy (MS); physical therapy (DPT); psychosocial/behavioral aspects of physical activity (MS). *Accreditation:* NCATE (one or more programs are accredited). *Expenses:* Tuition, state resident: full-time $8024; part-time $446 per credit. Tuition, nonresident: full-time $21,046; part-time $1169 per credit. Required fees: $1056; $26 per credit. $30 per semester. One-time fee: $95 part-time. *Financial support:* Career-related internships or fieldwork available. *Unit head:* Dr. Deborah Riebe, Chair, 401-874-5444, E-mail: debriebe@uri.edu. *Application contact:* Dr. Linda Lamont, Graduate Director, 401-874-5449, E-mail: lla4983u@uri.edu.

The University of Texas at Austin, Graduate School, College of Education, Department of Kinesiology and Health Education, Austin, TX 78712-1111. Offers behavioral health (PhD); exercise and sport psychology (M Ed, MA); health education (M Ed, MA, Ed D, PhD); kinesiology (M Ed, MA). Part-time programs available. Terminal master's awarded for partial completion of doctoral program. *Degree requirements:* For master's, thesis (for some programs); for doctorate, thesis/dissertation. *Entrance requirements:* For master's and doctorate, GRE General Test. Additional exam requirements/recommendations for international students: Required—TOEFL. Electronic applications accepted. *Faculty research:* Health promotion, human performance and exercise biochemistry, motor behavior and biomechanics, sport management, aging and pediatric development.

West Virginia University, School of Physical Education, Morgantown, WV 26506. Offers athletic coaching education (MS); athletic training (MS); physical education/teacher education (MS, PhD), including curriculum and instruction (PhD), motor behavior (PhD), physical education supervision (PhD); sport and exercise psychology (PhD); sport management (MS). *Degree requirements:* For doctorate, comprehensive exam, thesis/dissertation, oral exam. *Entrance requirements:* For master's, GRE or MAT, minimum GPA of 3.0; for doctorate, GRE General Test or MAT, minimum GPA of 3.5. Additional exam requirements/recommendations for international students: Required—TOEFL (minimum score 550 paper-based; 213 computer-based). Electronic applications accepted. *Faculty research:* Sport psychosociology, teacher education, exercise psychology, counseling.

Thanatology

Brooklyn College of the City University of New York, Division of Graduate Studies, Department of Health and Nutrition Science, Program in Community Health, Brooklyn, NY 11210-2889. Offers community health education (MA); computer science and health science (MS); health care management (MPH); health care policy and administration (MPH); thanatology (MA). *Accreditation:* CEPH. *Students:* 33 part-time (25 women); includes 21 minority (18 African Americans, 2 Asian Americans or Pacific Islanders, 1 Hispanic American), 3 international. Average age 39. 19 applicants, 79% accepted, 11 enrolled. In 2008, 6 master's awarded. *Degree requirements:* For master's, thesis or alternative. *Entrance requirements:* For master's, 18 credits, 2 letters of recommendation, essay. Additional exam requirements/recommendations for international students: Required—TOEFL. *Application deadline:* For fall admission, 3/1 priority date for domestic students, 2/1 priority date for international students; for spring admission, 11/1 priority date for domestic students, 10/1 priority date for international students. Applications are processed on a rolling basis. Application fee: $125. Electronic applications accepted. *Expenses:* Tuition, state resident: full-time $7360; part-time $310 per credit hour. Tuition, nonresident: full-time $13,800; part-time $575 per credit hour. *Financial support:* Federal Work-Study, institutionally sponsored loans, and scholarships/grants available. Support available to part-time students. Financial award application deadline: 5/1; financial award applicants required to submit FAFSA. *Faculty research:* Diet restriction, religious practices in bereavement, diabetes, stress management, palliative care. *Unit head:* Dr. Jean Grassman, Graduate Deputy Chairperson, 718-951-5026, Fax: 718-951-4670, E-mail: grassman@brooklyn.cuny.edu. *Application contact:* Hernan Sierra, Graduate Admissions Coordinator, 718-951-4536, Fax: 718-951-4506, E-mail: grads@brooklyn.cuny.edu.

Hood College, Graduate School, Programs in Human Sciences, Frederick, MD 21701-8575. Offers human sciences (MA), including psychology; thanatology (MA, Certificate). Part-time and evening/weekend programs available. *Faculty:* 5 full-time (2 women), 7 part-time/adjunct (4 women). *Students:* 19 full-time (all women), 89 part-time (77 women); includes 19 minority (15 African Americans, 1 American Indian/Alaska Native, 3 Asian Americans or Pacific Islanders), 2 international. Average age 35. 34 applicants, 85% accepted, 20 enrolled. In 2008, 30 master's, 16 other advanced degrees awarded. *Degree requirements:* For master's, comprehensive exam, capstone/research project. *Entrance requirements:* For master's, minimum GPA of 2.75. Additional exam requirements/recommendations for international students: Required—TOEFL (minimum score 575 paper-based; 231 computer-based; 89 iBT). *Application deadline:* For fall admission, 7/15 for domestic and international students; for spring admission, 12/15 for domestic and international students. Applications are processed on a rolling basis. Application fee: $35. Electronic applications accepted. *Expenses:* Tuition: Full-time $6480. Required fees: $100; $50 per semester. *Financial support:* Applicants required to submit FAFSA. *Faculty research:* Mind-body medicine and multicultural healing, the New Orleans jazz funeral, death practices in African-American culture, bereavement theories and gender differences, Piaget's theory of cognitive development as a formal mathematical model. *Unit head:* Dr. Dana G. Cable, Director, 301-696-3758, Fax: 301-696-3597, E-mail: cable@hood.edu. *Application contact:* Dr. Allen P. Flora, Dean of Graduate School, 301-696-3811, Fax: 301-696-3597, E-mail: gofurther@hood.edu.

Southwestern College, Program in Grief, Loss and Trauma Counseling, Santa Fe, NM 87502-4788. Offers MA, Certificate. Part-time and evening/weekend programs available. Postbaccalaureate distance learning degree programs offered (minimal on-campus study). *Entrance requirements:* For master's, personal statement of 3 pages, interview, references, resumé; for Certificate, 3 letters of reference, interview.

Transpersonal and Humanistic Psychology

Atlantic University, Program in Transformative Theories and Practices, Virginia Beach, VA 23451-2061. Offers MA. Part-time and evening/weekend programs available. Postbaccalaureate distance learning degree programs offered (no on-campus study). *Faculty:* 16 part-time/adjunct (5 women). *Students:* 164 part-time (121 women); includes 6 minority (3 African Americans, 3 Hispanic Americans), 13 international. Average age 45. 102 applicants, 46% accepted, 45 enrolled. In 2008, 15 master's awarded. *Degree requirements:* For master's, thesis. *Entrance requirements:* For master's, minimum undergraduate GPA of 2.5. Additional exam requirements/recommendations for international students: Required—TOEFL (minimum score 550 paper-based; 213 computer-based). *Application deadline:* Applications are processed on a rolling basis. Application fee: $50. Electronic applications accepted. *Expenses:* Tuition: Full-time $3000; part-time $750 per course. *Unit head:* Kevin J. Todeschi, Chief Executive Officer, 757-631-8101, Fax: 757-631-8096, E-mail: info@atlanticuniv.edu. *Application contact:* R. Gregory Deming, Director of Admissions, 757-631-8101, Fax: 757-631-8096, E-mail: admissions@atlanticuniv.edu.

Atlantic University, Program in Visionary Art and Consciousness, Virginia Beach, VA 23451-2061. Offers MFA. Part-time and evening/weekend programs available. Postbaccalaureate distance learning degree programs offered (no on-campus study). *Faculty:* 2 part-time/adjunct (1 woman). *Degree requirements:* For master's, thesis. *Entrance requirements:* For master's, BFA or BA or BS in studio art with 40 studio credits or more. Additional exam requirements/recommendations for international students: Required—TOEFL (minimum score 550 paper-based; 213 computer-based). *Application deadline:* For fall admission, 3/31 for domestic and international students. Application fee: $50. *Expenses:* Contact institution. *Unit head:* Kevin J. Todeschi, Chief Executive Officer, 757-631-8101, Fax: 757-631-8096, E-mail: info@atlanticuniv.edu. *Application contact:* R. Gregory Deming, Director of Admissions, 757-631-8101, Fax: 757-631-8096, E-mail: admissions@atlanticuniv.edu.

Institute of Transpersonal Psychology, Global Programs, Palo Alto, CA 94303. Offers psychology (PhD); transpersonal psychology (MTP); transpersonal studies (Certificate). Postbaccalaureate distance learning degree programs offered (minimal on-campus study). *Faculty:* 8 full-time (4 women), 27 part-time/adjunct (20 women). *Students:* 184 full-time (153 women), 25 part-time (21 women); includes 32 minority (11 African Americans, 2 American Indian/Alaska Native, 5 Asian Americans or Pacific Islanders, 14 Hispanic Americans), 15 international. Average age 43. 142 applicants, 83% accepted, 90 enrolled. In 2008, 19 master's, 8 doctorates awarded. Terminal master's awarded for partial completion of doctoral program. *Degree requirements:* For master's, thesis (for some programs); for doctorate, thesis/dissertation. *Entrance requirements:* For master's and doctorate, bachelor's degree. Additional exam requirements/recommendations for international students: Required—TOEFL. *Application deadline:* Applications are processed on a rolling basis. Application fee: $55. *Expenses:* Contact institution. *Financial support:* In 2008–09, 68 students received support. Federal Work-Study and scholarships/grants available. Support available to part-time students. Financial award application deadline: 6/30; financial award applicants required to submit FAFSA. *Unit head:* Dr. Paul Roy, Academic Vice President, 650-493-4430 Ext. 243, Fax: 650-493-6835, E-mail: proy@itp.edu. *Application contact:* Dawn Campagnola, Admissions Assistant, 650-493-4430 Ext. 240, Fax: 650-493-6835, E-mail: info@itp.edu.

Institute of Transpersonal Psychology, Residential Programs, Palo Alto, CA 94303. Offers clinical psychology (PhD); counseling psychology (MA); transpersonal psychology (MA, PhD); women's spirituality (PhD). Part-time and evening/weekend programs available. *Faculty:* 17 full-time (9 women), 31 part-time/adjunct (18 women). *Students:* 268 full-time (189 women), 40 part-time (31 women); includes 53 minority (9 African Americans, 3 American Indian/Alaska Native, 21 Asian Americans or Pacific Islanders, 20 Hispanic Americans), 14 international. Average age 38. 168 applicants, 52% accepted, 56 enrolled. In 2008, 47 master's, 16 doctorates awarded. Terminal master's awarded for partial completion of doctoral program. *Degree requirements:* For doctorate, thesis/dissertation. *Entrance requirements:* For master's and doctorate, bachelor's degree. *Application deadline:* For fall admission, 2/15 priority date for domestic students. Applications are processed on a rolling basis. Application fee: $55. *Expenses:* Tuition: Full-time $24,543; part-time $577 per unit. Tuition and fees vary according to degree level. *Financial support:* In 2008–09, 178 students received support; teaching assistantships, career-related internships or fieldwork, Federal Work-Study, and scholarships/grants available. Support available to part-time students. Financial award application deadline: 7/1; financial award applicants required to submit FAFSA. *Unit head:* Dr. Paul Roy, Academic Vice President, 650-493-4430 Ext. 243, Fax: 650-493-6835, E-mail: proy@itp.edu. *Application contact:* 650-493-4430 Ext. 16, Fax: 650-493-6835, E-mail: itpinfo@itp.edu.

John F. Kennedy University, Graduate School of Holistic Studies, Department of Counseling Psychology, Program in Counseling Psychology, Pleasant Hill, CA 94523-4817. Offers holistic studies (MA); somatic psychology (MA); transpersonal psychology (MA). Part-time and evening/weekend programs available. *Degree requirements:* For master's, thesis or alternative. *Entrance requirements:* For master's, interview. Additional exam requirements/recommendations for international students: Required—TOEFL.

Michigan School of Professional Psychology, Programs in Humanistic and Clinical Psychology, Farmington Hills, MI 48334. Offers humanistic and clinical psychology (MA, Psy D). *Degree requirements:* For master's, thesis, practicum; for doctorate, thesis/dissertation, internship, practicum. *Entrance requirements:* For master's, 1 year of work experience, interview, minimum GPA of 3.0, curriculum vitae, personal essay, Bachelor's completion; for doctorate, 3 years of work experience, 2 interviews, minimum graduate GPA of 3.0, scholarly writing sample, curriculum vitae, personal essay, MA degree completion. Additional exam requirements/recommendations for international students: Required—TOEFL. Electronic applications accepted. *Faculty research:* Qualitative research, existential-phenomenological psychology, applications to clinical practice.

Naropa University, Graduate Programs, Program in Transpersonal Counseling Psychology, Boulder, CO 80302-6697. Offers art therapy (MA); counseling psychology (MA); wilderness therapy (MA). *Faculty:* 8 full-time (5 women), 43 part-time/adjunct (31 women). *Students:* 134 full-time (103 women), 66 part-time (52 women); includes 22 minority (2 African Americans, 6 American Indian/Alaska Native, 4 Asian Americans or Pacific Islanders, 10 Hispanic Americans), 16 international. Average age 31. 213 applicants, 57% accepted, 80 enrolled. In 2008, 60 master's awarded. *Degree requirements:* For master's, internships. *Entrance requirements:* For master's, in-person interview, course work in psychology, 3 letters of recommendation, resumé, letter of interest, supplemental application. Additional exam requirements/recommendations for international students: Required—TOEFL (minimum score 600 paper-based; 250 computer-based). *Application deadline:* For fall admission, 1/15 priority date for domestic and international students. Applications are processed on a rolling basis. Application fee: $60. Electronic applications accepted. *Expenses:* Tuition: Full-time $14,767; part-time $726 per credit hour. Required fees: $45 per term. *Financial support:* In 2008–09, 98 students received support, including 21 research assistantships with partial tuition reimbursements available (averaging $3,000 per year), 6 teaching assistantships with partial tuition reimbursements available (averaging $3,000 per year); career-related internships or fieldwork, Federal Work-Study, scholarships/grants, health care benefits, tuition waivers (partial), and unspecified assistantships also available. Support available to part-time students. Financial award application deadline: 3/1; financial award applicants required to submit FAFSA. *Unit head:* Carla Clements, Chair, 303-546-3577. *Application contact:* Alice Di Tullio, Admissions Counselor, 303-546-3598, Fax: 303-546-3583, E-mail: aliced@naropa.edu.

See Close-Up on page 1121.

Naropa University, Graduate Programs, Program in Transpersonal Psychology, Boulder, CO 80302-6697. Offers ecopsychology (MA); transpersonal psychology (MA). Part-time and evening/weekend programs available. Postbaccalaureate distance learning degree programs offered (minimal on-campus study). *Faculty:* 4 full-time (2 women), 13 part-time/adjunct (7 women). *Students:* 40 part-time (34 women); includes 2 minority (1 Asian American or Pacific Islander, 1 Hispanic American), 4 international. Average age 42. 38 applicants, 58% accepted, 18 enrolled. In 2008, 10 master's awarded. *Degree requirements:* For master's, thesis, service learning. *Entrance requirements:* For master's, interview (by phone or in-person), technology form, resumé, letter of interest, 3 letters of recommendation. Additional exam requirements/recommendations for international students: Required—TOEFL (minimum score 600 paper-based; 250 computer-based). *Application deadline:* For fall admission, 1/15 for domestic and international students. Applications are processed on a rolling basis. Application fee: $60. Electronic applications accepted. *Expenses:* Tuition: Full-time $14,767; part-time $726 per credit hour. Required fees: $45 per term. *Financial support:* In 2008–09, 2 students received support. Career-related internships or fieldwork, Federal Work-Study, scholarships/grants, health care benefits, and tuition waivers (partial) available. Support available to part-time students. Financial award application deadline: 3/1; financial award applicants required to submit FAFSA. *Unit head:* Dr. John Davis, Director, 303-245-4654, Fax: 303-546-4044, E-mail: jdavis@naropa.edu. *Application contact:* Kate Levene, Admissions Counselor, 303-245-4657, Fax: 303-546-3583, E-mail: klevene@naropa.edu.

See Close-Up on page 1121.

Saybrook Graduate School and Research Center, Programs in Psychology, Human Science and Organizational Systems, San Francisco, CA 94111-1920. Offers clinical psychology (PhD); creativity studies (MA); human science (MA, PhD), including consciousness and spirituality, individualized (PhD), integrative health studies, organizational systems, social transformation; marriage and family therapy (MA); organizational systems (MA, PhD), including individualized (PhD), organizational systems; psychology (MA, PhD), including consciousness and spirituality, humanistic and transpersonal psychology, individualized (PhD), integrative health studies, licensure track (MA), organizational systems, social transformation. Postbaccalaureate distance learning degree programs offered (minimal on-campus study). Terminal master's awarded for partial completion of doctoral program. *Degree requirements:* For master's, thesis or alternative; for doctorate, thesis/dissertation. Electronic applications accepted. *Faculty research:* Humanistic theory, health studies, organizational systems, consciousness and spirituality, social transformation.

Seattle University, College of Arts and Sciences, Department of Psychology, Seattle, WA 98122-1090. Offers existential and phenomenological therapeutic psychology (MA Psych). *Degree requirements:* For master's, thesis. *Entrance requirements:* For master's, interview, minimum GPA of 3.0, previous undergraduate course work in psychology. *Faculty research:* Healing, transformations in relationships, therapy, dialogical research.

Cross-Discipline Announcement

Northwestern University, The Graduate School, School of Education and Social Policy, Program in Human Development and Social Policy, Evanston, IL 60208.

Students interested in developmental psychology (including life-span), personality, or community psychology may wish to pursue a PhD in this interdisciplinary program, which brings together scholars from psychology, sociology, economics, policy studies, and human development. The HDSP program focuses on how various social contexts—including families, schools, communities, and social policies—shape individual lives as they develop from infancy to old age. HDSP graduates obtain teaching and research positions in colleges and universities or work as policy analysts and program directors in the public or private sectors.

ADELPHI UNIVERSITY

Derner Institute of Advanced Psychological Studies

Programs of Study

The Gordon F. Derner Institute of Advanced Psychological Studies offers a Ph.D. program in clinical psychology and Master of Arts programs in general psychology, school psychology, and mental health counseling. There are also several postgraduate programs.

The Ph.D. program in clinical psychology emphasizes a psychodynamic approach to human behavior and prepares graduates for community practice. The program encompasses research; theory; psychological, biological, and social bases of behavior; and extensive clinical practice in psychodiagnostics and psychotherapy. Four years of full-time study, supervised research, a one-year full-time internship, and a dissertation are required. The clinical psychology program has been accredited by the American Psychological Association (APA) since 1957.

The Master of Arts in general psychology enables students to advance their exploration of human personality, psychodynamics, developmental and social psychology, and psychoanalytic theory. It requires the completion of a 36-credit course of study, which can be completed in one year of full-time study or two years of part-time study. Concentrations are offered in preclinical, forensic psychology, or industrial organizational psychology.

The Master of Arts in school psychology is a 72-credit program that can be completed in three years of full-time study or four years of part-time study. The program enables students to practice in a school setting using integrated skills, such as providing comprehensive psychoeducational evaluations and school consultations. The school practice core culminates with a full-time internship in a public school working under the supervision of a certified school psychologist.

The Master of Arts in mental health counseling is a graduate training program designed to help students acquire knowledge and the clinical skills to become competent mental health counselors. The program is designed to help students acquire competency in the diagnosis and treatment of mental disorders, the ability to facilitate client growth, development, and respect for the ethics and standards of practice endorsed by the mental health counseling profession. The 60-credit curriculum, including an internship, is designed to be completed in two years. The program complies with all standards for state and national accrediting groups. After licensure, mental health counselors may work in a variety of settings, such as hospitals, clinics, and private practice.

The Respecialization Certificate Program in clinical psychology equips doctoral-level psychologists to make a career shift into clinical psychology for community practice. The program focuses on academic work and intensive clinical training, and requires two years of full-time study, supervised clinical practice, and a one-year full-time internship. Graduates of this program earn a Certificate of Respecialization in Clinical Psychology, which is recognized by the American Psychological Association.

Postgraduate programs are available for students who have already earned a Ph.D. in clinical psychology or are licensed mental health professionals—psychiatrists, social workers, and psychiatric nurses—who wish to expand the focus of their practice. Adelphi's postgraduate programs include psychoanalysis and psychotherapy; child, adolescent, and family psychotherapy; group psychotherapy; marriage and couple therapy; and psychodynamic school psychology.

Research Facilities

Clinical facilities on campus include the Psychological Services Center and the Postgraduate Psychotherapy Center. Clinical facilities are also located in many neighboring hospitals, public schools, and agencies. Research facilities include the University library and computing center and a number of Institute research laboratories.

Financial Aid

Adelphi University offers a wide variety of federal aid programs; state grants; scholarship and fellowship programs; on- and off-campus employment; teaching, research, and clinical assistantships; and paid field placements.

Cost of Study

In 2008–09, tuition for full-time study (12–17 credits) was $31,700 per year for doctoral study in the Derner Institute of Advanced Psychological Studies. Tuition for part-time study (1–11 credits) was $925 per credit hour for master's degree programs. University fees ranged from about $200 to $400 per semester.

Living and Housing Costs

The University assists single and married students in finding suitable accommodations whenever possible. The cost of living is dependent upon location and the number of rooms rented.

Location

Adelphi University is located in Nassau County on Long Island, part of the New York City metropolitan area. Students can draw upon the city's cultural and social resources as well as the University's own extensive program in the arts.

The University

Adelphi University is set within a beautifully landscaped campus of 75 acres in the attractive residential community of Garden City, Long Island.

Applying

Application requirements can be found at http://derner.adelphi.edu/graduate (master's programs), http://derner.adelphi.edu/doctoral (doctoral program), http://derner.adelphi.edu/postgraduate (postgraduate programs), and http://derner.adelphi.edu/respecialization (respecialization program).

Correspondence and Information

Office of the Dean
Derner Institute of Advanced Psychological Studies
Adelphi University
Garden City, New York 11530
Phone: 800-ADELPHI (toll-free)
Fax: 516-877-3093
E-mail: admissions@adelphi.edu
Web site: http://derner.adelphi.edu

Adelphi University

FULL-TIME FACULTY AND THEIR RESEARCH

Jean Lau Chin, Professor and Dean; Ed.D., Columbia Teachers College. School psychology.

Robert Bornstein, Professor; Ph.D., SUNY at Buffalo. Personality disorders and assessment, unconscious processes, interpersonal dependency.

Wilma S. Bucci, Professor; Ph.D., NYU. Psychoanalytic and psycholinguistic research.

Francine Conway, Assistant Professor; Ph.D., Adelphi. Aging, emotions, and health studies.

Rebecca C. Curtis, Professor; Ph.D., Columbia. Social/clinical interface, psychotherapy research, self-defeating behavior.

Laura M. DeRose, Assistant Professor; Ph.D., Columbia. Developmental psychology, pubertal development and adjustment during early adolescence.

Jennifer Durham, Assistant Professor; Ph.D., Rutgers.

Rosemary Flanagan, Assistant Professor and Director of the M.A. Program in School Psychology; Ph.D., Hofstra; ABPP. School psychology.

Jerold Gold, Chair of Undergraduate Psychology; Ph.D., Adelphi. Interpersonal psychoanalysis, personality theory, psychotheory integration.

Patrick Grehan, Assistant Professor; Ph.D., Hofstra. School psychology, emotional intelligence, psychotherapy integration.

Mark Hilsenroth, Associate Professor; Ph.D., Tennessee. Psychodiagnostics.

Jonathan Jackson, Director of Clinical Training and Director, Psychological Services Clinic; Ph.D., NYU. Psychotherapy and psychoanalysis.

Lawrence Josephs, Professor; Ph.D., Tennessee; ABPP. Psychoanalysis, psychotherapy, self-psychology.

Morton Kissen, Professor; Ph.D., New School; ABPP. Object relations theory, projective testing, diagnostic issues.

Karen Lombardi, Professor; Ph.D., NYU. Child clinical psychology, psychoanalytic-developmental psychology, fairy tales and myths.

Robert Mendelsohn, Professor; Ph.D., Massachusetts; ABPP. Short-term psychotherapy, psychoanalytic theory.

Joseph W. Newirth, Professor; Ph.D., Massachusetts; ABPP. Psychoanalysis, object relations theory, disorders of self.

Veronica Orozco, Assistant Professor; Ph.D., Ohio State. Latina/o psychology.

Coleman Paul, Professor; Ph.D., Wayne State. Behavior modification, stimulus control, computer technology in psychology.

Susan Petry, Professor; Ph.D., Columbia. Sensation and perception.

Louis H. Primavera, Professor; Ph.D., CUNY. Psychological studies, personality.

Patrick L. Ross, Professor and Special Assistant to the Dean; Ph.D., Johns Hopkins. Statistics, data processing.

Ionas Sapountzis, Associate Professor; Ph.D., NYU.

Carolyn Springer, Assistant Professor; Ph.D., NYU. Statistics.

Janice M. Steil, Professor; Ph.D., Columbia. Social psychology, psychology of injustice and women's issues.

Kate A. Szymanski, Associate Professor; Ph.D., Northeastern. Small groups, social loafing, intrinsic/extrinsic motivation.

Joel Weinberger, Professor; Ph.D., New School. Human motivation.

ADLER SCHOOL OF PROFESSIONAL PSYCHOLOGY

Graduate Programs

Programs of Study

The Adler School of Professional Psychology is the oldest independent school of psychology in the U.S. Founded in 1952, the School continues the work of Alfred Adler, the first community psychologist by educating socially responsible professionals, providing holistic service to individuals and communities, and promoting social justice. The School includes a home campus in the Chicago Loop and a growing campus in downtown Vancouver, British Columbia, Canada. The School offers a doctoral program in clinical psychology and several master's programs in behavioral sciences and services.

The Adler School pursues social responsibility through service to communities as well as service to diverse and marginalized populations. The School trains a diverse population of students and offers opportunities for students to reach out to these groups through community service practicum and internship opportunities at its on-site clinic, the Dreikurs Psychological Services Center (PSC). In the PSC, students gain real-world experience in a variety of settings.

The Doctor of Psychology in Clinical Psychology program prepares students for the general practice of professional clinical psychology. The program follows the practitioner model of training developed by the National Council of Schools and Programs of Professional Psychology. This model aims to develop the knowledge, skills, and values in six core competency areas: relationship, assessment, intervention, research and evaluation, consultation and education, and management and supervision.

The Master of Arts in Counseling Psychology program provides students with a foundation in the theories and methods of counseling psychology with hands-on, practical, supervised training in counseling psychology techniques with an emphasis on socially responsible practice. This broad-based program usually takes two years to complete in a full-time format and is also offered part-time in an online/blended format. Graduates of the program are prepared for entry-level professional work in a variety of human services agencies and organizations in the public and private sectors.

The Master of Arts in Marriage and Family Counseling program prepares entry-level counselors to specialize in working with couples and families. Students complete course work and practicum experiences focused on the understanding and integration of individual lifestyle dynamics with marital and family systems. Graduates have a theoretical understanding of individual marital and family systems, including developmental issues and major variations, assessment skills in lifestyle and systemic diagnosis, and intervention skills based on major models of marital and family therapy, with the theory and methods of individual psychology as the foundation.

The Master of Arts in Counseling Psychology: Art Therapy program combines the theories and techniques of individual psychology with education and clinical training in the field of art therapy. The program is approved by the American Art Therapy Association. It requires 65 credit hours of courses, including 700 hours of clinical practicum experience under at least partial supervision of a registered art therapist (ATR). The program provides students with the academic and predegree clinical experiences required to apply for registration as an art therapist as well as sit for the Licensed Professional Counselor (LPC) examination in the state of Illinois.

The Master of Arts in Counseling & Organizational Psychology program combines the theories and skills of counseling psychology with organizational theory, design, and development in order to prepare graduates for positions in business and industry, especially in organizational psychology and the related areas of talent management, team building, performance enhancement, executive coaching, organizational development, training, and employee assistance programs. The program is one of a kind, because it prepares graduates to sit for state-level licensure as a master's-level counselor. Graduates are trained and qualified to be entry-level counselors with skills in assessing and providing counseling services to individuals, couples, and families. Graduates also receive training in assessing and providing intervention in organizational settings on the level of the individual (personal selection, leadership development, executive coaching, career assessment, and counseling) and the work group (team assessment, team issue resolution, and team building) and at the organizational level (talent audits, needs analysis, strategic planning, and organizational design and development). Courses are offered on an alternate weekend schedule, or on Friday evenings, Saturdays, or Sundays.

The Master of Arts in Gerontological Counseling program is designed to provide students with a sound foundation of coursework and practical training to work with older adults. Students are exposed to the impact of biological, psychological, and sociocultural factors on the aging process in order to gain a holistic understanding of the needs and issues of older adults. With the increasing number of older adults, the U.S. Department of Labor projects faster than average growth in employment for individuals with a master's degree. Completion of foundational coursework, specialized studies, and supervised training ensures graduates are well-prepared to work in a variety of human services agencies and organizations with older adults who will have a strong appreciation for the value of psychology in promoting their quality of life.

The Master of Arts in Rehabilitation Counseling degree is designed to prepare students to become certified rehabilitation counselors (CRC). Rehabilitation counselors work with individuals who have mental, emotional, or physical handicaps, helping them to lead self-sufficient lives both at home and on the job. The counselors determine the training and support their clients' need to deal with the personal, social, and vocational effects of their conditions. Rehabilitation counselors are employed by publicly funded agencies, schools, and medical facilities. After evaluating their clients' strengths and limitations, counselors arrange for rehabilitation programs that may include medical care, psychological counseling, occupational therapy, and job placement.

The Master of Arts in School Counseling program is designed to meet coursework and practicum experience required for Type 73 School Counseling Endorsement. School counselors perform a variety of roles in school settings including counseling students regarding their academic, career, and emotional needs; assisting students in maximizing their academic success; serving as student advocates; providing consultation; and occupying leadership positions.

The Master of Arts in Police Psychology program is designed for field officers, supervisory personnel, command members, and those interested in a career in law enforcement. The program blends numerous areas within the discipline of psychology with pragmatic applications to patrol, operational, and managerial concerns that arise daily in the field of law enforcement. This degree is not designed to teach students to conduct therapy or engage in psychological testing. There are no clinical hours required or practicum to complete. Rather, the program teaches students the practical applications of psychology to the field of law enforcement. Core professors and adjunct faculty members all have extensive experience in clinical psychology and/or law enforcement. Many courses are team taught, combining expertise from both fields, and are offered in the evening or on weekends as well as in an online/hybrid format.

Research Facilities

The Sol and Elaine Mosak Library provides resources and services in an atmosphere that fosters the educational and intellectual inquiry of students and faculty members. In addition to its major holdings in Adlerian-oriented materials, the library also contains a wide variety of materials in mental health and related disciplines. The library has a collection of more than 12,000 volumes and subscribes to more than 150 professional journals. It also has an extensive collection of more than 1,000 audiotapes and videotapes.

The library's CD-ROM indexes facilitate research by extending its reach to the larger research community. Through interlibrary loans, cooperative agreements with local libraries, and membership in ILLINET, OCLC, and NLM-Docline, students have computer access to learning materials from all over the country.

Financial Aid

Adler School is approved by the U.S. Department of Education to participate in the Federal Family Education Loan Program and Federal Work-Study Program. The School also offers a number of scholarships to students based on financial need, academic achievement, service to the community, and availability of funds.

Cost of Study

Tuition on the Chicago campus for 2008–09 was $810 per credit hour for M.A. programs and $850 per credit hour for the doctorate program. The M.A. degree in police psychology was $970 per credit hour. Student activity and library fees are $190 per term. Tuition costs for each year vary depending on whether the student enrolls full-time or part-time. Full-time students enroll for 8 or more credit hours per term. Courses are offered during fall, spring, and summer semesters.

Living and Housing Costs

The School does not provide housing but assists students in securing off-campus housing. Students typically live in apartments in the Chicago area. Living expenses vary considerably according to standard of living, housing, and transportation.

Student Group

Adler School's commitment to social responsibility draws students from all over the world who wish to study in a collaborative atmosphere with accomplished faculty members. The School attracts both recent college graduates and working professionals and offers significant cultural diversity by attracting the best students the world has to offer. The Adler Student Association represents many different countries and encourages students to celebrate their heritage through on- and off-campus learning activities.

Location

Located in the heart of downtown Chicago, Adler School occupies six floors of a modern office building overlooking the Chicago River. Easy accessibility by car or public transportation makes this an ideal setting for students commuting not only from the greater Chicago area but from throughout the United States and Canada as well. Several major colleges and universities, public libraries, lakefront parks, museums, and shopping districts are located near the School.

The School

Founded in 1952 by Rudolf Dreikurs, M.D., the Adler School is the oldest independent psychology school in the United States. The School is named after Alfred Adler (1870–1937), the first community psychologist, whose theories and teachings of psychology emphasize the uniqueness of every individual's relationship and connection with society. Adler School is committed to continuing the work of Alfred Adler by producing socially responsible graduates, by providing holistic services to individuals and communities, and by promoting social justice. In addition to preparing individuals for the general practice of clinical psychology, Adler School also offers a Community Service Practicum—an exciting new educational experience for students. Available in the first-year curriculum, this unique practicum allows students to get involved in community organizing, volunteer projects, political initiatives, advocacy, and public policy analysis.

Applying

All applicants for admission to the degree programs offered at the Adler School must have at least a bachelor's degree from an accredited college or university. Applicants to the master's programs should ideally have a GPA of 3.0 or higher (on a 4.0 scale) and at least 12 credits of course work in psychology. Applicants to the doctoral program preferably have a GPA of 3.25 or higher (on a 4.0 scale) and at least 18 credits of course work in psychology. Applications are accepted for the fall and winter terms on a rolling basis. The priority deadline for the Psy.D. program is February 15. Admitted students may begin taking classes in the fall or winter term. Applicants are strongly encouraged to begin the preliminary application process at least three months before they plan to begin taking classes. Additional information can be obtained from the Office of Admissions.

Correspondence and Information

Adler School of Professional Psychology
Admissions Office
65 East Wacker Place, Suite 2100
Chicago, Illinois 60601-7203
Phone: 312-201-5900 Ext. 222
Fax: 312-201-5917
E-mail: admissions@adler.edu
Web site: http://www.adler.edu

Adler School of Professional Psychology

THE FACULTY

Dr. Josephina Alvarez is a member of the core faculty and the Program Director for the Doctor of Psychology in Clinical Psychology program. She received a B.A. in psychology from Loyola University, Chicago, and an M.A. and Ph.D. in clinical community psychology from DePaul University. She completed a clinical consultation internship at Yale University and has worked in community mental health and academic settings. Her interests include multicultural competence, Latina/o mental health, substance abuse, mutual help, and community consultation.

Dr. Robert Baker is a member of the core faculty and is the Clinical Director of the Psychological Services Center's Prison Aftercare Program in Chicago. He is also the Coordinator of the Sex Offender Treatment Program. Dr. Baker earned his B.A. in economics at Michigan State University and his M.A. in counseling psychology and Psy.D. in clinical psychology at the Adler School of Professional Psychology. He is a licensed clinical psychologist. Dr. Baker teaches courses in psychophysiology, cognitive psychology, and clinical skills seminars. His additional interests include gerontology, forensics and correctional psychology, neuropsychology, clinical hypnosis, and psychotherapy with children, adolescents, and adults.

Dr. Christine Bard is a member of the core faculty and serves as Program Director of the Rehabilitation Counseling program. She earned an M.A in psychology at Michigan State University, an M.Ed. in counseling psychology, and a Ph.D. in counseling psychology at Penn State University. She has worked in several university counseling centers and provided rehabilitation counseling to individuals with disabilities, most recently as Director of Vocational Rehabilitation at the Rehabilitation Institute of Chicago. Dr. Bard was an assistant professor in the Institute of Psychology at the Illinois institute of Technology for several years. She has given numerous professional presentations on topics related to rehabilitation counseling. She is committed to improving social inclusion for individuals with disabilities. Her research interests include self-efficacy and career development, traumatic brain injury, employment strategies for individuals with disabilities, and culturally sensitive counseling in rehabilitation.

Dr. Dan Barnes is a member of the core faculty and serves as the Director and Chief Psychologist of the Dreikurs Psychological Services Center (PSC). He is also the Director of Clinical Training and in that capacity oversees the PSC's training programs, which include the Pre-Doctoral Internship in Professional Psychology, the therapy and assessment practicums, and the Post-Doctoral Residency in the PSC's Prison Aftercare Program. He received his B.S. in psychology from Loyola University Chicago and M.A. and Ph.D. degrees in clinical psychology from the University of Kentucky. He is a licensed clinical psychologist and has maintained a clinical practice since 1972. He teaches courses in systems of psychotherapy and constructivist cognitive psychotherapy.

Dr. Neil Bockian is a member of the core faculty. He earned his Ph.D. from the University of Miami, where he studied personality disorders with Dr. Theodore Millon and mindfulness meditation with Jon Kabat-Zinn. Dr. Bockian has research and clinical interests in the areas of personality disorders, health psychology, meditation, treatment planning, and behavioral medicine. He has written two books on personality disorders, and he has extensive experience treating individuals with spinal cord injuries and patients with chronic pain. He has employed individual therapy, group therapy, hypnosis, relaxation training, and mindfulness meditation in his practice.

Dr. Wendy Bostwick is the Director of Community Engagement and a member of the core faculty. She received her M.P.H. and Ph.D. in public health from the University of Illinois at Chicago and recently completed a National Institute on Drug Abuse postdoctoral fellowship at the University of Michigan Substance Abuse Research Center. Some of her research interests include sexual minority women's health; substance use and mental health issues among women; the health effects of stigma, discrimination, and marginalization; bisexuality; measurement of sexual orientation and sexual identity; and research with hidden and hard-to-reach populations. Her work has appeared in the *Journal of Studies on Alcohol* and the *Journal of Lesbian Studies*, among others. Her community work most recently entailed volunteering as a housing crisis counselor for a social service agency in Michigan.

Dr. Cristina Cox is a member of the core faculty. Dr. Cox earned her B.S. in psychology at Michigan State University and her M.A. and Ph.D. in clinical psychology at Loyola University. She is a licensed clinical psychologist. Dr. Cox teaches courses in child and adolescent therapy, ethnocultural diversity, gender diversity, and psychological assessment of children and clinical seminars. Her additional interests include models of intervention and assessment with children, integrative psychotherapy, bilingual/bicultural and language issues, learning disabilities and cognitive deficits, development and temperament, and consultation in educational settings.

Dr. Raymond E. Crossman is President of the Adler School and a member of the doctoral core faculty. Dr. Crossman completed his B.S. in psychology and fine arts at Fordham University and his Ph.D. in clinical psychology at Temple University. He is President of the National Council of Schools and Programs in Professional Psychology, and he is the Chair of the Council of Chairs of Training Councils of the American Psychological Association. He has taught courses, presented, written about, and developed programs and initiatives in diversity education, psychology training, family therapy and family diversity, and HIV disease prevention and coping.

Dr. Vida Dyson is a member of the core faculty. Dr. Dyson earned her B.A. in psychology at DePaul University and her M.A. and Ph.D. in psychology/personality process at the University of Chicago. She is a licensed clinical psychologist. Dr. Dyson teaches courses in ethnocultural diversity and gender issues and clinical seminars. Her interests include substance abuse assessment and treatment, schizophrenia, and the professional development of women, blacks, and other minorities.

Dr. Frank Gruba-McCallister is a member of the core faculty and Vice President of Academic Affairs. Dr. Gruba-McCallister received his B.S. in psychology from Loyola University and his M.A. and Ph.D. in clinical psychology from Purdue University. He is a licensed clinical psychologist. He teaches courses in history and systems, theories of psychotherapy, advanced psychotherapy, existential psychotherapy, and psychology and advocacy. His interests include health psychology, the integration of psychology and spirituality, transpersonal psychology, peace studies, and the role of psychology in advocacy and activism for social change.

Dr. Christina Jackson-Bailey is a member of the core faculty and earned her B.A. in psychology from Ohio State University, her M.A. in community counseling from Loyola University, Chicago, and her Ph.D. in counseling psychology from the University of Wisconsin– Milwaukee. She completed her pre-doctoral internship at Michigan State University's Counseling Center. Dr. Jackson-Bailey currently teaches lifestyle and career development, social psychology and individual differences, professional development seminar, and practicum seminar. Her additional interests include: black/African-American/African clinical issues, multicultural competence, and spirituality.

Dr. Peter Liu is a member of the core faculty and the Program Director for the Master of Arts in Counseling and Organizational Psychology Program. He completed his B.Sc. and Ph.D. degrees at the University of Toronto and also holds a Certificate in Management (C.M.) from Harvard University. His academic training in cross-cultural educational psychology is complemented with clinical training at CHEO (Children's Hospital of Eastern Ontario) in Ottawa, Canada, and a postdoctoral clinical internship at The University of Zurich, Switzerland. He has taught psychology and management courses for international college students, adult learners, and corporate executives. In addition, he has been active in conducting organizational projects, talent assessment, and leadership development initiatives for major global corporations. He is a licensed industrial psychologist and specializes in executive coaching, organizational change, emotional intelligence, life span development, and career counseling.

Dr. Larry Maucieri is a member of the core faculty and serves as the Director of the Clinical Neuropsychology Certificate Program. Dr. Maucieri received his Ph.D. in clinical psychology from Fordham University and did his clinical internship at Yale University School of Medicine. He recently completed a two year postdoctoral fellowship in clinical neuropsychology at Northwestern University, Feinberg School of Medicine. Dr. Maucieri will be teaching courses in the neuropsychology program in addition to courses in biological bases and assessment.

Dr. Steven Migalski is a member of the doctoral core faculty and a licensed clinical psychologist. He is also the Coordinator of Psychological Assessment at Adler's Psychological Services Center. He received his B.S. in psychology from Loyola University Chicago and both his master's and doctorate from the Illinois School of Professional Psychology. He completed a postdoctoral fellowship in clinical child psychology at the Josselyn Center for Mental Health, where he served as Director of Psychology for four years. Dr. Migalski's areas of concentration include clinical interviewing, personality assessment, mood disorders across the lifespan, assessment of ADHD and learning disabilities, multimodal and constructivist psychotherapies, primary and secondary prevention of HIV-risk behavior, and sexual orientation diversity in clinical practice. In his clinical work and in supervision, Dr. Migalski draws heavily upon the cognitive-behavioral and interpersonal traditions. Dr. Migalski is presently the consulting psychologist for Lawrence Hall Youth Services, and he maintains a very active private practice in Chicago's Lincoln Square neighborhood.

Dr. Nataka Moore is a member of the core faculty and serves as the Associate Director of Training. Dr. Moore earned her B.S. in chemistry at the University of Illinois at Urbana-Champaign. She earned her M.A. and Psy.D. in clinical psychology at the Illinois School of Professional Psychology. Dr. Moore currently teaches cognitive behavioral therapy, professional development seminar, and assessment practicum seminar. Her professional interests include school psychology and consultation, mother-daughter relationships, multicultural psychology, and public health issues.

Dr. Harold Mosak is a Distinguished Service Professor and serves as Chair of the Doctoral Scholars in Clinical Psychology Program. Dr. Mosak earned his A.B. in psychology and Ph.D. in clinical psychology at the University of Chicago. He is a diplomate in clinical psychology of the American Board of Professional Psychology, a life member and fellow of the APA, and a licensed clinical psychologist. Dr. Mosak teaches courses in Adlerian theory and methods and a year-long "Adler from Scratch" series as well as clinical seminars. His additional interests include the use of humor, the role of the spiritual in psychotherapy, multiple psychotherapy, and group and couples therapy.

Dr. Mayumi Nakamura is a member of the core faculty and serves as the Associate Director of Training. She earned her M.A. in organizational psychology at Columbia University; and her Psy.D. in clinical psychology at the Illinois School of Professional Psychology. Dr. Nakamura recently completed her postdoctoral residency at Kaiser Permanente San Francisco Medical Center. Her clinical interests include international psychology, health psychology, behavioral medicine, and diversity issues. Dr. Nakamura is very passionate about diversity issues in the context of education and psychology.

Dr. Wendy Paszkiewicz is a member of the core faculty and serves as Assistant Vice President of Academics. Dr. Paszkiewicz earned her B.S. in psychology at Michigan State University and her Psy.D. in clinical psychology at the Illinois School of Professional Psychology/Chicago. She is a licensed clinical psychologist and maintains a private practice serving children, adolescents, and families. Dr. Paszkiewicz teaches practicum and internship seminars. Her additional interests include managerial psychology, social interest and responsibility, diversity issues, the professional development of psychologists, and issues of education and training in professional psychology.

Dr. Thuy Pham is a member of the core faculty and serves as Associate Director of Clinical Training. She earned her B.S. in psychology from Indiana University–Bloomington. She received her Psy.D. from the Illinois School of Professional Psychology. Dr. Pham's research interests include clinical training, child/adolescent development, parenting skills, Asian-American identity, assertiveness, and relationship issues.

Dr. Victoria Priola-Surowiec joined the Adler faculty in July 2006 and serves as Director of the Police Psychology Program. She earned her B.S. in psychology at the University of Illinois-Champaign-Urbana and her M.A in counseling psychology and Psy.D. in clinical psychology from the Adler School of Professional Psychology. She is a licensed clinical psychologist and maintains a private practice in Chicago serving police officers and their families. Formerly, she was the Director of Training at Safe Alternatives, an inpatient treatment program for individuals who engage in self-destructive behaviors, including self-injury. Dr. Priola-Surowiec teaches courses in Adlerian theory and methods, basic assessment and interviewing, and professional development. Her additional interests include psychoanalysis, mentoring, attachment theory, and parenting.

Dr. Shaifali Sandhya is a member of the core faculty and holds a Ph.D. in psychology from the University of Chicago as an Andrew Mellon Fellow. She also holds an M.A. in psychology from Trinity College, Cambridge University where she was a Cambridge Commonwealth Scholar and a Rajiv Gandhi Fellow, and a B.A. in psychology from the University of Delhi. Dr. Sandhya teaches culture, globalization, and social psychology. Her research interests include topics such as intimate relationships, culture, and leadership.

Dr. Nancy Slater is a member of the core faculty and serves as Director of the Art Therapy Program. Dr. Slater earned her B.A. in psychology at the University of Michigan, her M.A. in art therapy at the University of Louisville, and her Ph.D. in psychology at the Union Institute. She is a registered, board certified art therapist of the American Art Therapy Association. Dr. Slater is the coordinator of the International Networking Group of Art Therapists. Currently she is the chair of the American Art Therapy Association Ethics Committee. Dr. Slater has taught and directed graduate art therapy programs in Melbourne, Australia, and in Beer Sheva, Israel. She has given conference presentations and consultation in other countries. Dr. Slater's teaching interests include art therapy ethics, art therapy addressing the effects of trauma, multicultural approaches to art therapy, and clinical supervision. Her additional interests include art therapy research, international collaborative training and research, and multicultural art therapy intervention in response to domestic violence and sexual assault, to substance abuse, and to the effects of interpersonal violence and war.

Dr. Thomas Todd is a member of the core faculty and serves as Program Director of the Marriage and Family Program. Dr. Todd earned his B.A. in psychology at Princeton University and his Ph.D. in clinical psychology at New York University. He is a diplomate of the American Board of Family Psychology, a fellow of the Division of Family Psychology (APA) and of the American Association for Marriage and Family Therapy, a licensed clinical psychologist, and an AAMFT Approved Supervisor. Dr. Todd teaches courses in marriage and family therapy, clinical supervision, and practicum seminars. His additional interests include qualitative research, substance abuse, eating disorders, supervision, and outcome assessment.

Lynn C. Todman is the Director of the Adler Institute on Social Exclusion (ISE), a member of the core faculty, and a member of the School's Leadership Team. She earned a B.A. from Wellesley College and a master's and a Ph.D. in city and regional planning from MIT. Dr. Todman's research and teaching interests center on problems of social marginalization, isolation, and exclusion experienced by urban communities. Her work focuses especially on the ways in which the structures and systems that comprise and organize American society cause disadvantage in urban communities. Dr. Todman's approach to her work is highly multidimensional, drawing on such diverse disciplines as law, political science, economics, sociology, community and urban development, psychology, medicine, public health, and systems' dynamics. She has spoken at numerous national and international conferences on the problem of urban disadvantage. Her recent research and writings include working papers that explore the relevance of the concept of social exclusion to the American social policy context and the development of a transdisciplinary discourse on social exclusion.

Dr. Joseph Troiani is a member of the core faculty and Program Director for the Substance Abuse Counseling program. He earned his B.A. in psychology/sociology at Northeastern Illinois University, his Master's in Health Administration at Governors State University, and his M.A. and Ph.D. in clinical psychology at the Fielding Institute. He is a certified addictions counselor. Dr. Troiani teaches courses in substance abuse assessment and treatment. His additional interests include aggression and violence, the mentally ill substance abuser, domestic violence and sex offenders, community mental health, behavioral health and public policy, political psychology, and health care administration.

Dr. Jerry Westermeyer is a member of the doctoral core faculty and earned his B.A. in social studies at St. Mary's College and his M.A. in international relations and Ph.D. (Committee on Human Development) at the University of Chicago. He is a licensed clinical psychologist. Dr. Westermeyer teaches courses in psychopathology, human development, and research methodology. His additional interests include successful aging across the lifespan, the course and outcome of psychopathology, positive mental health, political psychology, and children's issues in developing countries.

ALFRED UNIVERSITY

Division of School Psychology

Programs of Study	Alfred University's Master of Arts/Certificate of Advanced Studies (M.A./C.A.S.) degree is a 79-credit-hour, NASP-approved program (two years of course work, one year of internship) that satisfies the academic component of the New York State Education Department's requirements for permanent certification in school psychology and for national certification. Training emphases include a knowledge base in psychology and education, assessment, intervention and remediation, family systems, child counseling techniques, consultation, and professional identification and functioning.
	The Doctor of Psychology (Psy.D.) degree is a 120-credit-hour program accredited by the American Psychological Association that leads to state and national certification as well as to New York State license eligibility. This program requires a minimum of four years, which includes three years of course work, one year of supervised internship, and completion of a research dissertation. The course work balances scientific bases with academic and applied professional psychology. Students may develop a specialty area through course work, research, and field experience. As in the M.A./C.A.S. program, all students must pass written comprehensive examinations, participate in practicums, and complete an internship. In addition, a doctoral qualifying examination and a dissertation are required. In order to meet the requirements for NASP approval, all students are required to take the Praxis examination in school psychology, administered by Educational Testing Service, prior to completing their internship.
Research Facilities	Herrick Memorial Library contains more than 328,000 volumes, 1,500 periodical titles in-house, more than 95,000 units of microforms, 4,200 units of audiovisual materials, 170,000 slides, and more than 14,000 titles available through electronic subscriptions. Internet access to databases such as PSYCHINFO and ERIC is available throughout the campus. The library's interlibrary loan service connects students to information resources worldwide. Microcomputer labs are conveniently located across the campus and within the Division and provide Internet-connected PC and Mac workstations. The Lea R. Powell Institute for Children and Families is an organizing entity for the Division's research, training, and service missions. The institute provides start-up research funding for faculty members, students, and practitioners in addition to pursuing sources of external funding for research and training programs of the Division. The Center for Rural School Psychology, the training arm of the institute, offers continuing professional development for current practitioners. The Child and Family Services Center (CFSC), the service entity of the institute, is a spacious, renovated facility with a state-of-the-art audiovisual communication/observation system. In addition to their work in the schools, all students gain experience working under supervision in this community clinic. The research conducted by students is applied research—searching for solutions to behavior, academic, or organizational problems or seeking ways to deliver new psychological research or services to children and their families, organizations, and groups.
Financial Aid	Graduate assistantships (partial tuition remission) are available to all students. In addition, paid internships (averaging $15,000) are sought for students in their final year in the program. The Financial Aid Office assists graduate students in obtaining additional forms of assistance.
Cost of Study	Tuition for the 2008–09 academic year was $32,016.
Living and Housing Costs	Most students live in apartments off campus. For assistance in locating housing, students may contact the Division of School Psychology or write to the Director of Residence Life.
Student Group	Alfred University has approximately 2,000 undergraduate and 300 graduate students drawn from forty states and fifteen countries. There are 55 full-time graduate students and 30 students on internship in the Division of School Psychology, allowing for close interaction between students and faculty members. Seven percent of students self-identify as African American, Hispanic, or Asian. Seventy-five percent are women. Although the average age is 26, students range in age from 22 to their mid-50s. Students may come directly from undergraduate school, with master's degrees and many years of experience, or with prior careers in different fields.
Location	Alfred University is located in Alfred, New York, a college town 70 miles south of Rochester, 90 miles southeast of Buffalo, and 60 miles west of Corning. Nestled among the pine-sheltered foothills of the Allegheny Mountains, this popular recreation area is close to ski slopes and the water sports and fishing of the Finger Lakes region. New York City is 6 hours away by car via the Southern Tier Expressway/I-86.
The University	Founded in 1836, Alfred University is the oldest coeducational institution in New York State and the second oldest in the nation. Alfred grants bachelor's, master's, and doctoral degrees. The fifty-nine-building, 232-acre hillside campus adjoins the village of Alfred. The University comprises the College of Business, the College of Liberal Arts and Sciences, and the New York State College of Ceramics, which houses the School of Art and Design as well as the Inamori School of Engineering. In addition to the graduate programs in each of these colleges and schools, the graduate programs in school psychology are administered by the Division of School Psychology within the Graduate School.
Applying	To be eligible for admission, an applicant must hold a baccalaureate degree from an accredited college or university, and the undergraduate record must clearly indicate ability to perform credibly at the graduate level. The student must have successfully completed undergraduate work in introduction to psychology, statistical and/or experimental methods, and developmental psychology (child and adolescent psychology), personality, or abnormal psychology. Other relevant courses and practical experiences in psychology or education are looked upon favorably. To apply, students must send to the graduate admission office a completed application form and fee, three letters of recommendation, official transcripts of all undergraduate and graduate course work, GRE General Test results, and a brief personal statement of objectives; Psy.D. applicants must also submit a statement of research interest. The application deadline for the Psy.D. program is January 15. Review of applications for the M.A./C.A.S. program begins on February 15 and continues until the class is filled. Early application is encouraged. Official TOEFL scores are required of international students who have not received a baccalaureate degree from an institution in the U.S. The TSE is recommended. An application fee of $50 is charged, but the fee is waived if the student applies using the online application.
Correspondence and Information	For additional information: Nancy Evangelista, Ph.D., Chair Division of School Psychology Alfred University One Saxon Drive Alfred, New York 14802-1232 Phone: 607-871-2212 For applications: Office of Graduate Admissions Alfred University One Saxon Drive Alfred, New York 14802-1232 Phone: 607-871-2115 800-541-9229 (toll-free) E-mail: gradinquiry@alfred.edu Web site: http://www.alfred.edu/gradschool

Alfred University

THE FACULTY AND THEIR RESEARCH

Division of School Psychology

Nancy Evangelista, Associate Professor of School Psychology and Chairperson, Division of School Psychology; Ph.D., Syracuse, 1986; licensed psychologist, certified school psychologist. Autism, pervasive developmental disorders, developmental assessment, school psychology, special education, preschool/early childhood.

Jana Atlas, Associate Professor of School Psychology; Ph.D., Wayne State, 1988; licensed psychologist. Clinical psychology, developmental psychology, psychotherapy, psychopathology, eating disorders.

Robert Bitting, Associate Professor of Counseling; Ph.D., Buffalo, SUNY, 1988; licensed mental health counselor. College counseling, higher education administration, group methods.

John D. Cerio, Professor of School Psychology and Director, Child and Family Services Center and Center for Rural School Psychology; Ph.D., Boston College, 1988; licensed psychologist, certified school psychologist and school counselor. Counseling psychology, school psychology, family therapy, play therapy, personality assessment, cultural diversity.

Ellen Faherty, Clinical Assistant Professor of School Psychology and Director, Lea R. Powell Institute for Children and Families; Psy.D., SUNY at Albany; licensed psychologist, certified school psychologist and teacher. School psychology, special education, early childhood/preschool, consultation, psychotherapy, grant development.

Mark Fugate, Associate Professor of Psychology; Ph.D., Lehigh, 1993; licensed psychologist, certified school psychologist. Preschool assessment and intervention, applied behavior analysis, educational assessment, alternative approaches to assessment.

Edward Gaughan, Powell Professor of Psychology and Schooling and Professor of School Psychology; Ph.D., Temple, 1985; licensed psychologist, certified school psychologist. School psychology, direct and indirect intervention, family assessment, psychopathology, professional preparation issues.

Chris Lauback, Assistant Professor of School Psychology; Psy.D., Alfred, 1996; certified school psychologist. School psychology, consultation, preschool screening, prereferral teams, family systems psychology.

Lynn O'Connell, Assistant Professor of School Psychology; Psy.D., Alfred, 2001; licensed psychologist, certified school psychologist. School psychology, reading development and assessment, consultation, rural schools.

Terry Taggart, Clinical Assistant Professor of School Psychology and Director, Office of Special Academic Services; Psy.D., Alfred; licensed psychologist, certified school psychologist, registered nurse. School psychology, play therapy, family therapy, postsecondary disabilities.

Division of Psychology

Nancy E. Furlong, Professor of Psychology and Chairperson, Division of Psychology; Ph.D., Pittsburgh, 1983. Cognition and social development of children, research design and statistics.

Gordon D. Atlas, Professor of Psychology; Ph.D., Michigan, 1987. Defense mechanisms, depression, sensitivity to criticism.

Danielle Gagne, Assistant Professor of Psychology; Ph.D., New Hampshire, 2004. Discourse and aging, role of self-efficacy beliefs.

Louis J. Lichtman, Professor of Psychology; Ph.D., Maine, 1971. Neuropsychology, parenting, eating disorders.

Robert J. Maiden, Professor of Psychology; Ph.D., New School, 1980; licensed psychologist. Clinical psychology, aging, marital and family therapy, drug and alcohol abuse, medical psychology.

CFS

ALLIANT INTERNATIONAL UNIVERSITY

Center for Forensic Studies

Programs of Study

Forensic psychology is the application of the science and profession of psychology to questions and issues relating to law and the legal system. At Alliant, the practitioner-scholar programs at the Center for Forensic Studies (CFS) prepare professionals with both the academic background and the real-world skill they need to contribute to the field of forensic psychology. By studying forensic psychology at Alliant, students are part of a rapidly growing field.

Specializations available to Center for Forensic Studies students include assessment and treatment of sex offenders, child custody, child neglect and abuse, clergy and teacher sex abuse, competence to receive death penalty, correctional psychology, criminal profiling, expert witness, investigative psychology, jury selection, neuropsychology, police psychology, school violence, terrorism, and violence prevention in schools and in the workplace.

Programs are associated with a wide range of government, community, legal, and nonprofit organizations, and, as such, students are able to select internships in a wide range of settings, including federal, state, and local law enforcement; prisons; government agencies; juvenile halls; and others. Students not only learn about their chosen professional field, but also develop a network of business contacts.

The Doctor of Psychology (Psy.D.) in forensic psychology is offered at Fresno, Irvine, Los Angeles, Sacramento, and San Diego. With an emphasis on the application of forensic psychological theory and practice, this degree prepares students for a career in one of the fastest growing fields in the country. Course topics include police stress, neuropsychology, addiction, sex offending, domestic violence, serial and mass murder, juvenile delinquency, and stalking. Course work also emphasizes rules of evidence and discovery, examination and cross-examination, and expert witness testimony. Beyond receiving rigorous academic training, students acquire experience in treatment and assessment through field training in a variety of settings. For full-time students, the Psy.D. program can be completed in four years.

The Ph.D. in forensic psychology, offered only in Fresno, focuses on research and theory. The degree prepares students for a wide range of positions, from university professor to professional researcher to practicing forensic psychologist. In the clinical track, students are trained as forensic clinicians, with an emphasis on obtaining clinical licensure. Course work focuses on the integration between forensic clinical psychology, forensic research, criminology, and law. In the policy and justice track, with an emphasis on psycholegal research, courses focus on the legal and justice system, organization development, expert witness testimony, human trafficking, torture, war crimes, genocide, civil rights, federal administration, international treaties, and forensic psychology. For full-time students, the Ph.D. program can be completed in five years.

Research Facilities

The Alliant library system is a distributed collection of print, media, and electronic resources with primary strengths in psychology (clinical, forensic, organizational, and educational), business administration, global liberal studies, and education. The collections have a multicultural and international focus.

Alliant's largest library facility is in San Diego on the Scripps Ranch Campus, but comprehensive specialized collections are also available in San Francisco, Los Angeles, and Fresno. The collections at California locations are represented in the Web-based library catalog and total over 200,000 physical volumes, 640 current print journal subscriptions, and 1,200 videos.

The Alliant libraries share access to online resources, including 28 research databases, full-text content from over 16,000 journals, and 5,200 e-books. Resources that are not available on site may be requested from other Alliant libraries via the shared online catalog or from LINK+, a network of thirty-eight California and Nevada libraries with over 6 million titles.

An accomplished staff of librarians and support personnel provide services across the University and to distance learners. Services include reference, bibliographic research consultation, information literacy instruction, interlibrary loan, document delivery, and course reserves.

In each library, computers are available to access the Internet, electronic books and journals, and online research database resources, such as PsycINFO, Lexis-Nexis, OCLC FirstSearch, Digital Dissertations, Social Science Citation Index, Medline, ERIC, and Criminal Justice Periodical Index. Most of these online resources may also be accessed from home or office.

Financial Aid

Alliant offers financial aid to qualified students in the form of loans, scholarships, grants, and part-time employment. The federal government, state government, Alliant, and private sources finance these programs. Federal and state financial aid funds are only available to students who are United States citizens or permanent residents of the United States.

Financial aid packages, although predominantly in the form of loans, may also include scholarships and student employment. Most students interested in school-based financial aid pursue college work-study. A limited number of teaching and research assistantships are available. In addition, students can work on campus in a number of departments, including admissions and field placement. Stipends generally average about $1000 per assistantship per semester. For more information, students should e-mail finaid@alliant.edu.

Cost of Study

Doctoral programs cost $915 per semester unit.

Living and Housing Costs

Students can expect to pay between $700 and $1500 per month plus utilities (gas and electricity) for an off-campus, unfurnished, one-bedroom apartment. On-campus housing is available on the San Diego campus; the cost of room and board for an academic year is $15,480 for a 2 -person suite, $11,700 for a 1-person suite, $10,800 for a private room, and $8250 for double occupancy.

Student Outcomes

Center for Forensic Studies graduates hold positions such as staff psychologist/condemned coordinator (death row) for San Quentin State Prison. Many work for the court system, district attorneys, or public defenders. Others are critical incident specialists or psychologists with police departments. The California Department of Corrections and Rehabilitation (CDC) is one of the largest employers of forensic psychologists in the state, and many CFS graduates secure positions with the CDC. Other graduates are in private practice as expert witnesses. In addition, many choose to become faculty members and instruct at the undergraduate and graduate levels.

Location

Center for Forensic Studies programs are located on Alliant's Fresno, Irvine, Los Angeles, Sacramento, and San Diego campuses.

The University

Founded in 2001, Alliant International University is a nonprofit university that prepares students for professional careers in psychology, education, business, and forensics. Alliant offers mentored field experiences and individual coaching that allow students to develop hands-on professional skills and practical experience with clients. An exceptionally diverse faculty and student body helps graduates learn to work productively with colleagues and clients from different cultural and international backgrounds. *U.S. News & World Report* ranked Alliant number one in international diversity among national doctoral universities. According to *Diverse* magazine, Alliant awarded more doctorate degrees to minority students than any other U.S. university. With headquarters in San Francisco and San Diego, Alliant also has campuses in Fresno, Los Angeles, Irvine, and Sacramento, California. Alliant also hosts accredited programs in Mexico City, Mexico; Hong Kong, China; and Tokyo, Japan.

Applying

Applicants must have a bachelor's or master's degree in psychology, forensic psychology, criminology, criminal justice, social work, or law, with a minimum GPA of 3.0 both in psychology courses and overall. Students with lower GPAs may apply but must submit the GPA exemption form in the application. Students must submit the completed application, the $70 application fee, and official transcripts from all institutions attended. An interview is required. Applicants are strongly encouraged to submit GRE scores, but they are not required. International students must also submit TOEFL scores. Applications are considered on a rolling admissions basis (no deadline). Classes may close, so early applications are encouraged.

Correspondence and Information

Alliant Admissions
Alliant International University
Phone: 866—U-ALLIANT (866-825-5426,
  toll-free)
E-mail: admissions@alliant.edu

5130 East Clinton Way
Fresno, California 93727-2014

2500 Michelson Drive
Irvine, California 92612-1548

(Los Angeles metro area)
1000 South Fremont Avenue
Alhambra, California 91803

425 University Avenue
Sacramento, California 95825-6509

10455 Pomerado Road
San Diego, California 92131-1799

Alliant International University–Fresno

THE FACULTY AND THEIR RESEARCH

Core Faculty

Diane M. Beneventi, Regional Field Training Director; Ph.D., CSPP at Alliant, 1996. Neuropsychology.

Kyle Boone, Associate Professor and Program Director, Los Angeles; Ph.D., California School of Professional Psychology, 1984. Malingering and neuropsychology.

Peter English, Coordinator, Ph.D. Clinical Track; Ph.D., Arizona, 2003. Criminology, policy and law.

Valerie Forward, Assistant Professor; Ph.D., California School of Professional Psychology, 1984.

Eric Hickey, Professor and Systemwide Director, Center for Forensic Studies; Ph.D., Brigham Young, 1990. Etiology of violence and serial crime.

William Holcomb, Program Director, Fresno; Ph.D., Missouri–Columbia, 1979. Abnormal psychology, human relations in organizations.

Robert A. Leark, Associate Professor and Interim Program Director, San Diego; Ph.D., US International, 1982. Neuropsychology, test construction, malingering and ADHD.

James N. Madero, Professor; Psy.D., Catholic University, 1975. Projective tests, differential diagnoses, workplace violence prevention, school violence prevention.

Eva McKenzie, Assistant Professor; Ph.D., Fuller Theological Seminary. Forensic evaluations: family, dependency, and criminal courts; victimology: child maltreatment, intimate partner violence.

Jana Price-Sharps, Assistant Professor; Ph.D., University of the Pacific, 1999. Drug and alcohol abuse and its behavioral and neurological consequences, attention deficit hyperactivity disorder.

Sherry Skidmore, Assistant Professor; Ph.D., US International, 1975. Neuropsychology and abnormal psychology.

Sean Sterling, Interim Program Director, Irvine; Ph.D., California School of Professional Psychology, 1996. Cultural competency; behavioral, cognitive, and social learning,

Lenore Artie Tate, Associate Professor and Assistant Program Director, Sacramento; Ph.D., California School of Professional Psychology. Geriatrics, neuropsychology, social and cultural psychology.

Dale White, Assistant Professor; Ph.D., California School of Professional Psychology, 1996. Foster children and social problem solving, treatment variables and inpatient mental health, factors underlying academic success.

Adjunct Faculty

Burton Alperson, Ph.D., Michigan State, 1967.

Robert Briones, Psy.D., California School of Professional Psychology, 2005.

Lynn O. Bundy, Ph.D., University of the Pacific, 1988.

Natalie Claussen-Rogers, Psy.D., Alliant International, 2003.

Phillip Corrado, Ph.D., Alliant International, 1997.

Dennis Dixon, Ph.D., Louisiana State, 2006.

Annette Lorene Ermshar, Ph.D., Loma Linda, 2000.

Debra F. Glaser, Ph.D., California School of Professional Psychology, 1983.

Adam K. Herdina, Psy.D., La Verne, 2004.

James Kelly Jr., J.D., California, Hastings Law, 1992.

Gerard Labuschagne, Ph.D., Pretoria (South Africa).

Rachel Latter, Ph.D., Alliant International, 2003.

Theresa Lu, Ph.D., Southern Illinois, 1997.

William V. McTaggart Jr., J.D., Loyola, 1978.

Deborah S. Miora, Ph.D., California School of Professional Psychology, 1987.

Douglas Noll, J.D., University of the Pacific, 1977.

Gaetano Pascale, Ph.D., Bologna (Italy).

Michael Reid, J.D., San Joaquin College of Law, 1992.

Matthew Sharps, Ph.D., Colorado, 1986.

David Tanner, Ph.D., Texas A&M, 1984.

Amy Tillery, Ph.D., Alliant International.

ALLIANT INTERNATIONAL UNIVERSITY

California School of Professional Psychology
Ph.D. in Clinical Psychology

Programs of Study

The Doctor of Philosophy in Clinical Psychology (Ph.D.) programs at the California School of Professional Psychology (CSPP) follow a scholar-practitioner model to prepare students to become effective professional psychologists who are skilled at evaluating psychological functioning and provide effective interventions with diverse clients across a range of settings. Equally important, the programs prepare students to conduct applied research in clinical psychology and to contribute actively to the knowledge base in the field. The program's training philosophies promote the view that research training and professional skill development should be closely intertwined and based on a core body of knowledge in scientific psychology.

In the first and second years, all programs provide an extensive background in the foundations of psychology; they develop students' basic scientific understanding and practice skills. Students participate in clerkship or practicum experiences requiring 8–20 hours of student time per week in their second and/or third years. At this level, students receive training in specific skills, such as psychological assessment, evaluation of clients and programs, and intervention and psychotherapeutic techniques. They are also introduced to the roles and ethical practices of professional psychologists.

During the second or third year, students must pass formal evaluations, which may include written comprehensive or preliminary examinations, in order to be advanced to doctoral candidacy. Each program establishes specific methods and procedures for evaluating students. Evaluations focus on a student's demonstrated academic ability, expected competency in research, interpersonal competencies, and understanding of the basic theoretical foundations of psychology.

The curriculum for third-, fourth-, and fifth-year students includes advanced training in the analysis and performance of applied research, theoretical issues, psychological intervention techniques, professional ethics and issues, psychopharmacology, and supervision. Students also participate in the dissertation, field placements, growth experiences, and elective courses.

While required course work is substantial, in the final years there is also time to develop special interests. Internships occupy 20 to 40 hours per week, intensifying students' mastery of professional skills and providing supervisory experience. Clinical internship requirements meet, and in some programs exceed, the 1,500 hours of predoctoral internship accepted by the California Board of Psychology for licensure. CSPP doctoral course requirements at all campuses are designed to fulfill all of the state licensing requirements of California, and in some cases they exceed the requirements.

In content, the clinical psychology curricula reflect four areas of study—applied research, professional skills, professional concepts, and personal growth. A student's course work each year consists of required courses and electives from each of these areas.

Research Facilities

The Alliant library system is a distributed collection of print, media, and electronic resources with primary strengths in psychology (clinical, forensic, organizational, and educational), business administration, global liberal studies, and education. The collections have a multicultural and international focus.

Alliant's largest library facility is in San Diego on the Scripps Ranch Campus, but comprehensive specialized collections are also available in San Francisco, Los Angeles, and Fresno. The collections at California locations are represented in the Web-based library catalog and total over 200,000 physical volumes, 640 current print journal subscriptions, and 1,200 videos.

The Alliant libraries share access to online resources, including 28 research databases, full-text content from over 16,000 journals, and 5,200 e-books. Resources that are not available on site may be requested from other Alliant libraries via the shared online catalog or from LINK+, a network of thirty-eight California and Nevada libraries with over 6 million titles.

An accomplished staff of librarians and support personnel provide services across the University and to distance learners. Services include reference, bibliographic research consultation, information literacy instruction, interlibrary loan, document delivery, and course reserves.

In each library, computers are available to access the Internet, electronic books and journals, and online research database resources, such as PsycINFO, Lexis-Nexis, OCLC FirstSearch, Digital Dissertations, Social Science Citation Index, Medline, ERIC, and Criminal Justice Periodical Index. Most of these online resources may also be accessed from home or office.

Financial Aid

Alliant offers financial aid to qualified students in the form of loans, scholarships, grants, and part-time employment. The federal government, state government, Alliant, and private sources finance these programs. Federal and state financial aid funds are only available to students who are United States citizens or permanent residents of the United States.

Financial aid packages, although predominantly in the form of loans, may also include scholarships and student employment. Most students interested in school-based financial aid pursue college work-study. A limited number of teaching and research assistantships are available. In addition, students can work on campus in a number of departments, including admissions and field placement. Stipends generally average about $1000 per assistantship per semester. For more information, students should e-mail finaid@alliant.edu.

Cost of Study

CSPP doctoral program tuition is $950 per semester unit. A full-time student averages 30 units per year. Students completing an internship in one full-time year or in two years of half-time rotations pay $2850 and $2400 per semester, respectively. Fees are additional.

Living and Housing Costs

Students can expect to pay between $700 and $1500 per month plus utilities (gas and electricity) for an off-campus, unfurnished, one-bedroom apartment. On-campus housing is available on the San Diego campus; the cost of room and board for an academic year is $15,480 for a 2-person suite, $11,700 for a 1-person suite, $10,800 for a private room, and $8250 for double occupancy.

Student Group

Alliant prides itself on the diversity of its student body. The University has students from almost every state and international students from sixty-four countries, including Cameroon, Botswana, Greece, Iceland, Portugal, and Turkey. There are 2,626 full-time and 1,284 part-time students at Alliant International University, of whom 76 percent are women and approximately 46 percent are from groups underrepresented in higher education. Within the California School of Professional Psychology, there are 2,148 students.

Location

The Ph.D. in Clinical Psychology is offered at four of Alliant's campuses in California: Fresno, Los Angeles, San Diego, and San Francisco.

The University and The School

Alliant International University focuses on preparing students for professional careers. Formed in July 2001 through the combination of the California School of Professional Psychology and United States International University (USIU), Alliant is an independent, not-for-profit institution of higher education with a history distinguished by innovation. The University's mission is to educate citizens of the world, ensuring the acquisition of knowledge and competencies that are essential to live, lead, and solve problems in a global society.

CSPP, the largest of the five schools and centers at Alliant, prepares students for careers as clinical psychologists, marital and family therapists, and other mental health professionals. While earning their degrees, students work in a wide variety of settings, establishing themselves in the professional community as experienced practitioners. By the time students earn their degrees, they have already developed a network of colleagues and professional affiliations that make them exceptionally attractive to employers as vital contributors to their field.

Applying

Applicants should have a bachelor's or master's degree in psychology (preferred), with a minimum GPA of 3.0. Students must submit the completed application, the application fee, official transcripts from all institutions attended, a personal statement, and letters of recommendation. An interview is required. International students must also submit TOEFL/TWE scores. The application deadline is January 15. Submitting a complete application by January 15 guarantees notification by April 1. Applications submitted after January 15 are welcome, but are reviewed on a space-available basis.

Correspondence and Information

Central Admissions Office
Alliant International University
10455 Pomerado Road
San Diego, California 92131

Phone: 866-U-ALLIANT (toll-free)
Fax: 858-635-4555
E-mail: admissions@alliant.edu
Web site: http://www.alliant.edu/cspp

Alliant International University

THE FACULTY AND THEIR RESEARCH

Fresno Campus

Sue Ammen, Professor; Ph.D., California School of Professional Psychology–Fresno 1989. Parent-child attachment, infant mental health, pediatric psychology, cross-cultural assessment and issues with children and families, gay/lesbian issues, qualitative research methods.

Manuel Figueroa-Unda, Professor; Ph.D., Stanford, 1985; ABPP-Diplomate in Clinical Psychology. Multicultural research and topics in learning and motivation, social bases of behavior, multicultural studies, adolescent self-image, eating disorders.

Paul Lebby, Professor; Ph.D., Berkeley, 1994. Neuropsychological assessment, medical rehabilitation, child and adolescent brain injury, forensic neuropsychology.

Kevin J. O'Connor, Professor, Program Director, and Coordinator, Ecosystemic Clinical Psychology Emphasis Area; Ph.D., Toledo, 1980. Parent-child attachment, child psychotherapy process, play therapy, attachment disorders, child abuse, impact of parental narcissism, child development, sex role socialization, Ecosystemic child psychotherapy, art therapy, Theraplay.

Siobhan O'Toole, Assistant Professor and Assistant Program Director; Ph.D., California School of Professional Psychology, 2000. Evaluating cultural competence in clinicians; child abuse, primarily physical and verbal; body image.

Los Angeles Campus

Linda Beckman, Distinguished Professor; Ph.D., UCLA, 1969. Women's health, substance abuse, population psychology, social-psychological models in health promotion.

Terece S. Bell, Principal Lecturer; Ph.D., USC, 1982. Cognitive development in children, neuropsychological assessment, Asian values.

Ellin L. Bloch, Professor, Program Director, and Director of Professional Field Training; Ph.D., Cincinnati, 1972. Post-traumatic stress disorder, trauma and crisis intervention.

Ron E. F. Duran, Associate Professor and Associate Dean, CSPP; Ph.D., UCLA, 1994. Group-based interventions for persons living with chronic and life-threatening medical conditions, collaboration with community-based agencies to improve health-related service delivery, measurement of social and academic adjustment of nontraditional undergraduate and graduate students.

Michi Fu, Associate Professor; Ph.D., California School of Professional Psychology–Los Angeles, 2002. Cross-cultural (Asian American) mental health issues, sexual abuse and trauma of women and children, nonverbal therapies and female mental health issues, advocacy of diverse populations and mental health needs.

James Garbanati, Professor; Ph.D., Connecticut, 1980. Chronic disease conditions and behavior, smoking in adolescents, chronic illnesses and pain conditions, interactions of health and mediators of coping, development of regulation/stability in physiological and behavioral systems.

Tracy L. Heller, Associate Professor and Associate Provost, Alliant International University; Ph.D., UCLA, 1994. Children with attention-deficit/hyperactivity disorder; behavioral, social, and cognitive components of ADHD; multimodal treatments of ADHD.

Paula Johnson, Professor; Ph.D., UCLA, 1974. Peace studies, values related to war, gender roles and power, community psychology models of system interventions, social policy research using social and community psychology models, values and methodology.

Richard Mendoza, Professor; Ph.D., California, Irvine, 1980. Acculturation among refugees and immigrant individuals; implications for mental health, psychopathology, and psychotherapy.

Nicholas Noviello, Associate Professor; Ph.D., California, Irvine, 1985. Personality traits and emotional expressiveness, content analysis of speech and text, personal belief systems, well-being.

Susan J. Regas, Professor; Ph.D., Purdue, 1983. Sex, intimacy and relationship problems, differentiation assessment, couple therapy effectiveness.

Peter Theodore, Assistant Professor; Ph.D., Miami, 2005. Intersection of substance abuse and HIV-related risk behaviors among gay and bisexual men (GBM), understanding culturally-relevant psychosocial variables that motivate drug-using and sexual risk behaviors among GBM, health disparities among LGBT persons.

Kathryn White, Professor; Ph.D., North Carolina at Chapel Hill, 1982; D.H.M., Hahnemann, 1995; M.T.D.M., Emperor's College of Traditional Oriental Medicine, 1995. Psychotherapy and complementary and alternative medicine, psychotherapy East-West, psychology and meditation, clinical health psychology, somatic therapies, sexual and physical abuse, women's issues, object relations, self psychology.

San Diego Campus

Kristi Alexander, Associate Professor; Ph.D., Alabama, 1992. Pediatric and child clinical psychology, with special interest in social skills and children's injuries.

Omar Alhassoon, Assistant Professor; Ph.D., San Diego, 2003. Neuropsychological assessment, multimodal neuroimaging, CNS changes in alcohol and drug dependence and abstinence, neuroimaging and neuropsychological correlates of psychopathology and other personality characteristics.

Milton Z. Brown, Assistant Professor; Ph.D., Washington (Seattle), 2002. Personality disorders; chronic suicidality and self-injury; PTSD; cognitive-behavior therapy, in particular, exposure therapy and dialectical behavior therapy.

Joanne E. Callan, Distinguished Professor; Ph.D., Texas, 1970. Child and adolescent development, adjustment, and psychopathology (including gender development); parenting and school support—preschool through high school; life-span development—female development and psychology; psychoanalysis and psychoanalytic theory and psychotherapy; training in professional psychology; ethics.

Constance J. Dalenberg, Professor; Ph.D., Denver, 1983. Countertransference, child abuse, trauma, PTSD, repressed memory, ethics and standards in psychology, empirical foundations of psychoanalytic concepts, trauma related to racism and discrimination.

Sharon L. Foster, Distinguished Professor and Associate Provost, Allian International University; Ph.D., SUNY at Stony Brook, 1978. Childhood social competence and peer relations, family conflict in adolescence, behavioral assessment.

Richard N. Gevirtz, Distinguished Professor; Ph.D., DePaul, 1971. Physiological patterning in stress-related disorders, clinical protocols for biofeedback training, mediators of autonomic control, anxiety disorders.

Alan J. Lincoln, Professor; Ph.D., California School of Professional Psychology–San Diego, 1980. Early childhood psychopathology, biological and neuropsychological basis of autism and neurodevelopmental disorders, neurodevelopmental effects of child abuse, attention-deficit/hyperactivity and severe language disorders, assessment of children, differential diagnosis and treatment of childhood psychopathology.

Fernando Ortiz, Assistant Professor; Ph.D., Washington State, 2005. Cross-cultural and multicultural issues, personality assessment and personality structure, mental health and minority populations.

Adele S. Rabin, Professor and Program Director; Ph.D., Houston, 1984. Women's health, comparative psychotherapy outcomes, unipolar depression, psychological factors affecting physical health.

Irwin S. Rosenfarb, Professor; Ph.D., North Carolina at Greensboro, 1986. Schizophrenia, mood disorders, role of the family in the course and treatment of severe psychopathology.

Erika E. Swift, Assistant Professor; Ph.D., Case Western Reserve, 2002. Pediatric psychology and child community psychology, health-promoting behaviors and beliefs, quality of life among pediatric patients, obesity, type 1 and 2 diabetes, sleep disorders.

Donald J. Viglione Jr., Professor; Ph.D., LIU, 1981. Rorschach and personality assessment; malingering; assessment of child psychopathology; trauma, dangerousness, and sexual offenses.

San Francisco Campus

Shannon Casey-Cannon, Assistant Professor; Ph.D., Stanford, 2002. Adolescents within diverse family and school contexts, multicultural identity and women's issues, depression, eating disorders.

Dalia Ducker, Professor and Associate Dean, CSPP; Ph.D., CUNY, 1974. Psychology of women, including role strain, work, and health; gender roles; issues relevant to the practice of professional psychology; graduate education.

Robert Jay Green, Distinguished Professor and Executive Director, Rockway Institute for LGBT Research and Public Policy; Ph.D., Michigan State, 1975. Lesbian, gay, bisexual, and transgender (LGBT) research and public policy in the fields of couple/family relations, mental health care, education, and the work place; family psychology; male gender roles.

Sheila Henderson, Visiting Associate Professor and Associate Director, I-MERIT; Ph.D., Stanford, 2002. International multicultural psychology, career development, achievement motivation in adult creativity.

Davis Ying Ja, Professor; Ph.D., Washington (Seattle), 1981. Substance abuse and AIDS treatment and prevention in multicultural communities; program evaluation in behavioral health systems, including managed-care systems; juvenile and adult justice systems, including drug courts and alternative community approaches in juvenile probation; organizational systems with a focus on managed behavioral health policy, evaluation, and analysis; early childhood prevention and intervention; multicultural influences in family therapy; cost analysis; studies in programs for assertive community treatment (PACT).

Eduardo Morales, Distinguished Professor; Ph.D., Texas Tech, 1976. HIV, substance abuse, intervention for adolescents, community prevention, ethnic and sexual minorities, drug exposed infants and parents, juvenile delinquency.

Natalie Porter, Professor; Ph.D., Delaware, 1981. Feminist and antiracist models of clinical training and supervision, cognitive and emotional developmental changes in individuals abused or traumatized as children, feminist therapy supervision and ethics.

Kristin Samuelson, Assistant Professor; Ph.D., Virginia, 1998. Trauma/post-traumatic stress disorder, neuropsychological and psychodiagnostic assessment, pediatric psychology.

Quyen Tiet, Associate Professor; Ph.D., Colorado at Boulder, 1996. Stress/trauma, coping and resilience, depression and suicide, PTSD, substance use and dual diagnosis, treatment factors and patient outcomes.

Paul D. Werner, Professor; Ph.D., Berkeley, 1976. Personality and family assessment, research on violent behavior, gender roles, psychology of social change, psychology of population and family planning, aesthetics, clinical research.

ALLIANT INTERNATIONAL UNIVERSITY

California School of Professional Psychology
Psy.D. in Clinical Psychology

Programs of Study

The Doctor of Psychology in Clinical Psychology (Psy.D.) programs at the California School of Professional Psychology (CSPP) provide a strong foundation in clinical psychology, emphasizing the applications of theory and research to clinical practice and addressing the societal need for professionals who deliver or facilitate the delivery of psychological services to diverse populations, including underserved and poorly served populations. The programs are designed to develop professional clinical psychologists who bring critical-thinking and active problem-solving skills to bear on human problems and who have acquired the skills necessary to deliver a variety of clinical services to people from diverse backgrounds within many types of settings and institutions. Students are educated and trained to be able to intervene effectively using multiple methods of assessment and intervention, working with diverse populations, across many settings, and in changing and evolving contexts.

In the first and second years, all programs provide an extensive background in the foundations of psychology; they develop students' basic scientific understanding and practice skills. Students participate in clerkship or practicum experiences requiring 8–20 hours of student time per week in their first and/or second years. At this level, students receive training in specific skills, such as psychological assessment, evaluation of clients and programs, and intervention and psychotherapeutic techniques. They are also introduced to the roles and ethical practices of professional psychologists.

During the second or third year, students must pass formal evaluations, which may include written comprehensive or preliminary examinations, in order to be advanced to doctoral candidacy. Each program establishes specific methods and procedures for evaluating students. Evaluations focus on a student's demonstrated academic ability, expected competency in research, interpersonal competencies, and understanding of the basic theoretical foundations of psychology.

The curriculum for third and fourth year students includes advanced training in theoretical issues, psychological intervention techniques, professional ethics and issues, psychopharmacology, and supervision. Students also participate in the dissertation or doctoral project, field placements, growth experiences, and elective courses.

While required course work is substantial, in the final years there is also time to develop special interests. Internships occupy 20 to 40 hours per week, intensifying students' mastery of professional skills and providing supervisory experience. Clinical internship requirements meet and, in some programs, exceed the 1,500 hours of predoctoral internship accepted by the California Board of Psychology for licensure. CSPP doctoral course requirements at all campuses are designed to fulfill all of the state licensing requirements of California, and, in some cases, they exceed the requirements.

In content, the clinical psychology curricula reflect four areas of study—applied research, professional skills, professional concepts, and personal growth. A student's course work each year consists of required courses and electives from each of these areas.

Research Facilities

The Alliant library system is a distributed collection of print, media, and electronic resources with primary strengths in psychology (clinical, forensic, organizational, and educational), business administration, global liberal studies, and education. The collections have a multicultural and international focus.

Alliant's largest library facility is in San Diego on the Scripps Ranch Campus, but comprehensive specialized collections are also available in San Francisco, Los Angeles, and Fresno. The collections at California locations are represented in the Web-based library catalog and total over 200,000 physical volumes, 640 current print journal subscriptions, and 1,200 videos.

The Alliant libraries share access to online resources, including 28 research databases, full-text content from over 16,000 journals, and 5,200 e-books. Resources that are not available on site may be requested from other Alliant libraries via the shared online catalog or from LINK+, a network of thirty-eight California and Nevada libraries with over 6 million titles.

An accomplished staff of librarians and support personnel provide services across the University and to distance learners. Services include reference, bibliographic research consultation, information literacy instruction, interlibrary loan, document delivery, and course reserves.

In each library, computers are available to access the Internet, electronic books and journals, and online research database resources, such as PsycINFO, Lexis-Nexis, OCLC FirstSearch, Digital Dissertations, Social Science Citation Index, Medline, ERIC, and Criminal Justice Periodical Index. Most of these online resources may also be accessed from home or office.

Financial Aid

Alliant offers financial aid to qualified students in the form of loans, scholarships, grants, and part-time employment. The federal government, state government, Alliant, and private sources finance these programs. Federal and state financial aid funds are only available to students who are United States citizens or permanent residents of the United States.

Financial aid packages, although predominantly in the form of loans, may also include scholarships and student employment. Most students interested in school-based financial aid pursue college work-study. A limited number of teaching and research assistantships are available. In addition, students can work on campus in a number of departments, including admissions and field placement. Stipends generally average about $1000 per assistantship per semester. For more information, students should e-mail finaid@alliant.edu.

Cost of Study

CSPP doctoral program tuition is $950 per semester unit. A full-time student averages 30 units per year. Students completing an internship in one full-time year or in two years of half-time rotations pay $2850 and $2400 per semester, respectively. Fees are additional.

Living and Housing Costs

Students can expect to pay between $700 and $1500 per month plus utilities (gas and electricity) for an off-campus, unfurnished, one-bedroom apartment. On-campus housing is available on the San Diego campus; the cost of room and board for an academic year is $15,480 for a two-person suite, $11,700 for a one-person suite, $10,800 for a private room, and $8250 for double occupancy.

Student Group

Alliant prides itself on the diversity of its student body. The University has students from almost every state and international students from sixty-four countries, including Cameroon, Botswana, Greece, Iceland, Portugal, and Turkey. There are 2,626 full-time and 1,284 part-time students at Alliant International University, of whom 76 percent are women and approximately 46 percent are from groups underrepresented in higher education. Within the California School of Professional Psychology, there are 2,148 students.

Location

The Psy.D. in Clinical Psychology is offered at five of Alliant's campuses in California: Fresno, Los Angeles, Sacramento, San Diego, and San Francisco. The Clinical Psychology Psy.D. program is also offered in Hong Kong, in association with the School of Continuing and Professional Education (SCOPE), City University of Hong Kong.

The University and The School

Alliant International University focuses on preparing students for professional careers. Formed in July 2001 through the combination of the California School of Professional Psychology (CSPP) and United States International University (USIU), Alliant is an independent, not-for-profit institution of higher education with a history distinguished by innovation. The University's mission is to educate citizens of the world, ensuring the acquisition of knowledge and competencies that are essential to live, lead, and solve problems in a global society.

CSPP, the largest of the five schools and centers at Alliant, prepares students for careers as clinical psychologists, marital and family therapists, and other mental health professionals. While earning their degree, students work in a wide variety of settings, establishing themselves in the professional community as experienced practitioners. By the time students earn their degrees, they have already developed a network of colleagues and professional affiliations that make them exceptionally attractive to employers as vital contributors to their field.

Applying

Applicants should have a bachelor's or master's degree in psychology (preferred), with a minimum GPA of 3.0. Students must submit the completed application, the application fee, official transcripts from all institutions attended, a personal statement, and letters of recommendation. An interview is required. International students must also submit TOEFL/TWE scores. The application deadline is January 15. Submission of a complete application by the January 15 deadline guarantees notification by April 1. Applications submitted after January 15 are welcome, but are reviewed on a space-available basis.

Correspondence and Information

Central Admissions Office
Alliant International University
10455 Pomerado Road
San Diego, California 92131

Phone: 866-U-ALLIANT (toll-free)
Fax: 858-635-4555
E-mail: admissions@alliant.edu
Web site: http://www.alliant.edu/cspp

Alliant International University

THE FACULTY AND THEIR RESEARCH

Fresno and Sacramento Campuses

Matthew Baity, Assistant Professor. DBT, personality assessment, multi-method psychological assessment, treatment process and alliance, neuropsychological factors in psychiatric disorders.

Lynette E. Bassman, Professor, Fresno; Assistant Program Director; and Coordinator of the Health Psychology Emphasis Area; Ph.D., NYU, 1990. Alternative treatments for mental health, psychodynamic correlates of self-care behavior, defense mechanisms and health.

Wesley T. Forbes, Professor, Fresno, and Director of Clinical Field Placement; Ed.D., Massachusetts Amherst, 1983. Child/family, adolescents, delinquency/corrections, multicultural issues in psychology, ban on IQ testing of African Americans and other ethnic minorities in California, system of multipluralistic assessment.

Sue A. Kuba, Professor, Fresno, and Online Program Director; Ph.D., California School of Professional Psychology–Fresno, 1981. Women's health, eating disorders in multicultural populations, phenomenology, sister relationships, women's development, gay and lesbian issues.

Elizabeth Limberg, Associate Professor, Sacramento, and Assistant Program Director; Ph.D., California School of Professional Psychology–Fresno, 1999. Infant-preschool mental health, family therapy, play therapy, community mental health.

Kevin J. O'Connor, Professor, Fresno/Sacramento; Program Director; and Coordinator, Ecosystemic Clinical Psychology Emphasis Area; Ph.D., Toledo, 1980. Parent-child attachment, child psychotherapy process, play therapy, attachment disorders, child abuse, impact of parental narcissism, child development, sex role socialization, Ecosystemic child psychotherapy, art therapy, and Theraplay.

Suni Peterson, Associate Professor, Sacramento; Ph.D., Florida, 1997. Health psychology with minority populations, evidence-based interventions, health promotion, cardiovascular disease, cancer.

John D. Preston, Professor, Fresno/Sacramento; Psy.D., Baylor, 1979. Psychopharmacology, neuropsychology, trauma, aging.

Ronald W. Teague, Professor, Fresno; Ph.D., California School of Professional Psychology–Berkeley, 1973; ABPP, Diplomate in Clinical Psychology. Psychology of antiquity, psychohistory phenomenology, Jungian psychology, psychoanalysis, psychoanthropology, psychology and the humanities, history of psychology.

Los Angeles Campus

John Bakaly, Associate Professor; Ph.D., USC, 1988. Clinical intervention with children and adolescents and their families; treatment of depression, anxiety, and general childhood disorders.

Walter Brown, Assistant Professor; Ph.D., UCLA, 1995. Pediatric psychology, substance abuse, working with at-risk juveniles, training of health and mental health professionals.

Elaine Burke, Associate Professor; Psy.D., Denver, 1989. Pediatric and adult neuropsychology, assessment and culture, health and culture, gender and culture.

John V. Caffaro, Distinguished Professor; Ph.D., Fielding Institute, 1989. Child maltreatment, sibling relationships, post-traumatic stress disorder, group psychotherapy.

William Chien, Assistant Professor; Psy.D., California School of Professional Psychology–Los Angeles, 1996. Asian American mental health issues, psychotherapy with Asian Americans, bereavement, depression.

Victor Cohen, Associate Professor; Ph.D., Michigan, 1981. Counter transference phenomenon and the interpersonal processes in therapist-client psychotherapy relationships, psychotherapist self-development and teaching and training of clinical skills, alternative paradigms for studying subjective and experiential aspects of the psychotherapy process.

Ronda Doonan, Assistant Professor; Psy.D., California School of Professional Psychology–Los Angeles, 2004. Couples therapy from a differentiation perspective, the autistic spectrum, critical/chronic illness and disability.

Judith Holloway, Assistant Professor; Ph.D., California School of Professional Psychology–Los Angeles, 1991. Ecopsychology, adventure therapy, relationship to nature and healing the natural environment, LGBTQ issues.

David Katz, Associate Professor; Director, Los Angeles Clinical Psy.D. Program; Ph.D., Kentucky, 1999; ABPP (clinical neuropsychology). Neuropsychology, memory, emotions, PTSD.

Richard R. Kopp, Distinguished Professor; Ph.D., Chicago, 1972. Use of metaphor in psychotherapy, Adlerian psychology, psychotherapy integration, resolving interpersonal and intrapersonal power conflicts.

Cristina Magalhaes, Assistant Professor; Ph.D., Chicago, 2005. Cross-cultural assessment, Brazilian immigration/acculturation, clinical intervention with children and families, art therapy, infant mental health, foster care, LGBT issues, transgender health.

Glenn Isoa Masuda, Associate Professor; Ph.D., Washington (Seattle), 1988. Asian American mental health, community mental health service delivery, interventions with adolescents, diversity competency training.

Randy Noblitt, Professor; Ph.D., North Texas, 1978. Cult and ritual abuse, child abuse, trauma and dissociation, dissociative identity disorder, psychopharmacology.

Jeffrey Tirengel, Professor; Psy.D., California School of Professional Psychology–Los Angeles, 1991. Positive psychology in diverse cultural communities, resilience, strength-based approaches, attachment, couples, emotionally focused interventions, evidence-based practice and practice-based evidence.

San Diego Campus

Anabel Bejarano, Assistant Professor; Ph.D., CUNY, 2000. Childhood trauma, Latino mental health, child development and attachment, multicultural psychology.

Steven F. Bucky, Professor and Director of Professional Training; Ph.D., Cincinnati, 1970. Childhood psychopathology, chemical dependency, forensic psychology, ethics, alcoholic family, children of alcoholics, sports psychology.

Joanne E. Callan, Distinguished Professor; Ph.D., Texas, 1970. Child and adolescent development, adjustment, and psychopathology (including gender development); parenting and school support: preschool through high school; life-span development: female development and psychology; psychoanalysis and psychoanalytic theory and psychotherapy; training in professional psychology; ethics.

David J. Diamond, Associate Professor; Ph.D., Michigan, 1983. Reproductive trauma, psychoanalytic theory and psychopathology, clinical inference process and other psychotherapy topics, child and adolescent development.

Marina Dorian, Assistant Professor; Ph.D., Illinois at Urbana-Champagne, 2007. Couple and family intervention, gender roles in marriage, couples communication, cross-cultural studies, intimacy.

Donald Eulert, Professor; Ph.D., New Mexico, 1968. C. G. Jung's theories, postmodern cultural and spirituality issues, moral development, creativity, integrative psychology.

Veronica Gutierrez, Assistant Professor; Ph.D., California, Santa Barbara, 2004. Issues of multiculturalism; lesbian, gay, and bisexual issues; therapist competence in multicultural issues; therapeutic process and outcome. Dr. Gutierrez' professional background includes work with diverse student populations, specifically Latinos.

Debra Kawahara, Assistant Professor; Ph.D., California School of Professional Psychology–Los Angeles, 1994. Multicultural and cross-cultural psychology, Asian American mental health, women's issues, cultural competency, qualitative research methodology.

Mojgan Khademi, Assistant Professor; Psy.D., Indiana of Pennsylvania, 1992. Psychodynamic theory and treatment. Dr. Khademi's work at several university counseling centers has led to interest in psychotherapy intervention and treatment outcome studies; he supervises dissertations in treatment outcomes, eating disorders, suicide, and multicultural issues and teaches first-year psychotherapy sequence and advanced seminars in feminism and eating disorders.

Gary W. Lawson, Professor; Ph.D., Southern Illinois, 1975. Clinical psychology, marriage and family therapy, chemical dependency.

James N. Madero, Professor; Ph.D., Catholic University, 1975. Projective tests, differential diagnoses, workplace violence prevention, school violence prevention.

Neil G. Ribner, Professor and Program Director; Ph.D., Cincinnati, 1971. Family studies, divorce, stepfamilies, custody, parenting, siblings.

Ronald Stolberg, Assistant Professor; Ph.D., Pacific Graduate School of Psychology, 2001. Personality assessment instruments with an emphasis on the MMPI-2/MMPI-A, assessment instruments use among practicing clinicians, standard of care practices, suicide, clinical work with adolescents.

San Francisco Campus

Diane M. Adams, Associate Professor; Ph.D., Wright Institute, 1983. Adult development; psychotherapy; biographical interviewing; case histories and theoretical or conceptual analytic thesis; clinical and theoretical issues involving ethnic minority populations, particularly African American; application of psychoanalytic theory in practice and research.

Stephen Blum, Professor; Ph.D., Berkeley, 1973. Ethical issues in health, community psychology, health policy and administration, birth and death of persons and programs, managed (mental) health care.

Edward F. Bourg, Professor; Ph.D., California School of Professional Psychology–Berkeley, 1973. Family and marital therapy and process, prevention and rehabilitation in chronic and acute illness, roles of relaxation and meditation in health psychology.

Tai Chang, Associate Professor; Ph.D., Illinois at Urbana-Champaign, 1999. Acculturation and identity development processes as well as their relations to adjustment and help-seeking, particularly among Asian Americans; interface of counseling and the Internet, including online support and online information regarding mental illness and psychology.

Eddie Chiu, Assistant Professor; Ph.D., California School of Professional Psychology–Los Angeles, 1996. Ethnic minority stress and coping, immigrant and refugee mental health, cultural-specific assessment and intervention, problem gambling, child and family issues.

Harriet Curtis-Boles, Associate Professor; Ph.D., Berkeley, 1984. Issues related to multiculturalism and peoples of color, psychotherapy process and outcome with African American clients, influence of violence exposure on children and families in the inner cities, African American women and substance abuse.

Samuel Gerson, Professor; Ph.D., Texas at Austin, 1978. Intersubjectivity, gender, and sexuality; interaction of affect and clinical judgment; the process of therapeutic interactions; schools of psychodynamic psychotherapy.

Frederick J. Heide, Associate Professor; Ph.D., Penn State, 1981. Charismatic communication, using humor in psychotherapy, constructivist therapies, transpersonal psychology, cognitive therapy, psychedelics.

Valata Jenkins-Monroe, Professor and Director, San Francisco Psy.D. Program; Ph.D., California School of Professional Psychology–Berkeley, 1978. Cognitive styles and problem-solving abilities of Third World children, development of children of substance abusive mothers, child sexual abuse treatment, African American women and substance abuse, intergenerational study of black teen parenting, race and racism, special needs children, forensic psychology.

Yuki Okubo, Assistant Professor; Ph.D., Columbia, 2007. Asian-American mental health, cultural adjustments and coping with immigrants, notion of self as it relates to help-seeking behaviors.

Gerald Y. Michaels, Associate Professor and Director of the PSC Child/Family Program; Ph.D., Michigan, 1981. Developmental psychopathology, transition to parenthood, adolescent pregnancy, parents' and children's social perceptions in the family, children of divorce, primary prevention strategies in mental health.

Valory Mitchell, Professor and Coordinator of the Gender Studies Emphasis Area; Ph.D., Berkeley, 1983. Psychology of women; development of personality across the lifespan; lesbian/gay issues; interface of feminist, self, relational, and psychodynamic theory; spirituality and religion.

Rhoda Olkin, Distinguished Professor; Ph.D., California, Santa Barbara, 1981. Social model of disability; disability rights activism; marriage and family therapy; psychopathology, diagnosis, and case formulation; cognitive behavioral therapy.

Elena Padron, Assistant Professor; Ph.D., Minnesota, 2003. Developmental psychopathology and attachment theory, social-emotional development and psychopathology, early childhood development, child and family psychotherapy, culturally sensitive therapeutic models for use with Latino families.

Patrick Petti, Assistant Professor; Ph.D., California School of Professional Psychology–Alameda, 1991. Education and training in psychology, clinical competency evaluation, child development, treatment approaches in child therapy.

Alan J. Swope, Professor; Ph.D., Columbia, 1969. Psychoanalytic psychotherapy, core curriculum in professional psychology, psychology and technology, theories of culture, evaluation of clinical competency, music and personality.

Daniel O. Taube, Professor; J.D., Villanova, 1985; Ph.D., Hahnemann, 1987. Ethical and legal issues for mental health professionals, child maltreatment, substance abuse.

Christopher D. Tori, Professor Emeritus; Ph.D., Kentucky, 1971. Psychotherapy methods, cross-cultural psychology, Buddhism, religion and spirituality, addictions, psycholinguistics, psychometrics and statistics, international studies.

Randall Wyatt, Associate Professor and Director of Professional Training, San Francisco; Ph.D., California School of Professional Psychology-Berkeley/Alameda, 1989. Creative arts and psychology; trauma recovery; child, family, and society; existential/psychodynamic psychotherapy; cultural anthro-psychological approaches to diversity studies.

Diane Zelman, Associate Professor and Coordinator of the Health Psychology Emphasis Area; Ph.D., Wisconsin–Madison, 1989. Health psychology, families and chronic illness, anxiety disorders, neuropsychology, addictions, psychopharmacology.

ALLIANT INTERNATIONAL UNIVERSITY

California School of Professional Psychology
Programs in Marital and Family Therapy

Programs of Study

The California School of Professional Psychology (CSPP) at Alliant offers two graduate programs in Marital and Family Therapy (MFT)—the Master of Arts (M.A.) and the Doctor of Psychology (Psy.D.). The M.A. program is offered at the Irvine, Los Angeles, Sacramento, and San Diego campuses, and the Psy.D. program is available at the Irvine, Sacramento, and San Diego campuses.

The programs provide students with the essential training needed to pursue a career as a professional marital and family therapist. Graduates become skilled in theory, research, and clinical practice, with the ability to integrate individual and systemic therapeutic models in an international, multicultural environment.

Students in both the master's and doctoral MFT programs are trained to treat relational mental health issues with individuals, couples, families, and larger organizations from a systemic perspective. As such, attention is directed to relationships and interaction patterns. Students develop skills in the mental health assessment, diagnosis, and treatment of individuals and relationship systems. The programs provide an integrative approach to the major systemic theories and interventions.

To prepare students for the clinical practicum experience, the MFT programs provide intensive theoretical and practical skill-based training. The programs place students in community-based practicum and internship sites where students get real-world training experiences with a diverse clientele.

The master's program contains the same course work as the first two years of the doctoral program. Consequently, all of the master's program requirements transfer into the doctoral program. Those students entering the doctoral program with a bachelor's degree can earn a licensable marital and family therapy master's degree as part of their doctoral studies upon completion of the requirements for that degree. In addition to the program course work and practicum experiences, students may choose to specialize in select areas of concentration offered at their campus, including biofeedback, chemical dependency counseling, gerontology, and Latin American family therapy.

Classes are typically held in the evenings to allow students to work during the day. Daytime classes are also held in San Diego and Irvine for students who prefer to attend during the day.

Research Facilities

The Alliant library system is a distributed collection of print, media, and electronic resources with primary strengths in psychology (clinical, forensic, organizational, and educational), business administration, global liberal studies, and education. The collections have a multicultural and international focus.

Alliant's largest library facility is in San Diego on the Scripps Ranch Campus, but comprehensive specialized collections are also available in San Francisco, Los Angeles, and Fresno. The collections at California locations are represented in the Web-based library catalog and total over 200,000 physical volumes, 640 current print journal subscriptions, and 1,200 videos.

The Alliant libraries share access to online resources, including 28 research databases, full-text content from over 16,000 journals, and 5,200 e-books. Resources that are not available on site may be requested from other Alliant libraries via the shared online catalog or from LINK+, a network of thirty-eight California and Nevada libraries with over 6 million titles.

An accomplished staff of librarians and support personnel provide services across the University and to distance learners. Services include reference, bibliographic research consultation, information literacy instruction, interlibrary loan, document delivery, and course reserves. In each library, computers are available to access the Internet, electronic books and journals, and online research database resources, such as PsycINFO, Lexis-Nexis, OCLC FirstSearch, Digital Dissertations, Social Science Citation Index, Medline, ERIC, and Criminal Justice Periodical Index. Most of these online resources may also be accessed from home or office.

Financial Aid

Alliant offers financial aid to qualified students in the form of loans, scholarships, grants, and part-time employment. The federal government, state government, Alliant, and private sources finance these programs. Federal and state financial aid funds are only available to students who are United States citizens or permanent residents of the United States.

Financial aid packages, although predominantly in the form of loans, may also include scholarships and student employment. Most students interested in school-based financial aid pursue college work-study. A limited number of teaching and research assistantships are available. In addition, students can work on campus in a number of departments, including admissions and field placement. Stipends generally average about $1000 per assistantship per semester. For more information, students should e-mail finaid@alliant.edu.

Cost of Study

CSPP master's and doctoral program tuition is $950 per semester unit. A full-time student averages 30 units per year, with courses year-round. Fees are additional.

Living and Housing Costs

Students can expect to pay between $700 and $1500 per month plus utilities (gas and electricity) for an off-campus, unfurnished, one-bedroom apartment. On-campus housing is available on the San Diego campus; the cost of room and board for an academic year is $15,480 for a 2-person suite, $11,700 for a 1-person suite, $10,800 for a private room, and $8250 for double occupancy.

Student Group

Alliant prides itself on the diversity of its student body. The University has students from almost every state and international students from sixty-four countries, including Cameroon, Botswana, Greece, Iceland, Portugal, and Turkey. There are 2,626 full-time and 1,284 part-time students at Alliant International University, of whom 76 percent are women and approximately 46 percent are from groups underrepresented in higher education. Within the California School of Professional Psychology, there are 2,148 students.

Location

Among the safest cities in America, Irvine has a strong base of technology industries along with a wealth of community entertainment, recreation, and educational resources. Irvine is within easy driving distance of beautiful Corona Del Mar and the sun-drenched sand of Laguna Beach and Newport Beach. With more than 9 million people in the over 4,000 square miles of Los Angeles County, Los Angeles is California's largest city and the second-largest in the nation. One of the premier cities in the Pacific Rim, it is a center for culture and commerce. The Sacramento campus is easily accessible from all major thoroughfares in the metropolitan Sacramento area. Sacramento is California's capital, providing many great cultural and recreational opportunities and activities. San Diego is a vibrant, metropolitan city with a laid-back, small-town feel. The area is filled with an incredible selection of activities and attractions that make San Diego one of the most popular spots in the United States.

The University and The School

Alliant International University focuses on preparing students for professional careers. Formed in July 2001 through the combination of the California School of Professional Psychology and United States International University (USIU), Alliant is an independent, not-for-profit institution of higher education with a history distinguished by innovation. The University's mission is to educate citizens of the world, ensuring the acquisition of knowledge and competencies that are essential to live, lead, and solve problems in a global society.

CSPP, the largest of the five schools and centers at Alliant, prepares students for careers as clinical psychologists, marital and family therapists, and other mental health professionals. While earning their degrees, students work in a wide variety of settings, establishing themselves in the professional community as experienced practitioners. By the time students earn their degrees, they have already developed a network of colleagues and professional affiliations that make them exceptionally attractive to employers as vital contributors to their field.

Applying

Applicants should have a bachelor's degree in psychology (preferred), with a minimum GPA of 3.0. Students must submit the completed application, the application fee, official transcripts from all institutions attended, a personal statement, and letters of recommendation. An interview is required for doctoral applicants. International students must also submit TOEFL/TWE scores. The application deadlines are January 15 (priority deadline), March 1, and April 16. Applications submitted after the priority deadline are welcome but are reviewed on a space-available basis.

Correspondence and Information

Central Admissions Office
Alliant International University
10455 Pomerado Road
San Diego, California 92131

Phone: 866-U-ALLIANT (toll-free)
Fax: 858-635-4555
E-mail: admissions@alliant.edu
Web site: http://mft.alliant.edu

Alliant International University

THE FACULTY AND THEIR RESEARCH

Stephen Brown, Professor, Irvine; Ph.D., USC, 1996. Quantitative and qualitative research design in MFT, measurement and evaluation in MFT, statistical analysis, professional education and teaching, performance improvement and quality assurance in mental health service delivery.

Robin Denise Bullette, Assistant Professor, Irvine; Psy.D., US International, 2000. MFT teaching, training, and supervision; courtship, marital therapy, and family systems.

Benjamin Caldwell, Assistant Professor and Site Director, Los Angeles; Psy.D., Alliant International, 2004. Marital myths, couples therapy outcome, sex education, MFT cost-effectiveness research.

Sean Davis, Assistant Professor and Site Director, Sacramento; Ph.D., Syracuse, 2005. Common factors across effective MFT models, MFT training and supervision, commonalities of healthy and distressed couples, process and outcome research, observational research, bridging the scientist/practitioner gap in MFT.

Darryl Freeland, Associate Professor, San Diego and Irvine; Ph.D., USC, 1972. Family dynamics, epistemology, chaos theory, women's issues, imagination and the therapy process.

Tatiana Glebova, Assistant Professor, Sacramento; Ph.D., Fuller, 2002. Family therapy process and outcome research, observational research, contextual therapy, families with adolescents, adolescent risky behaviors including substance abuse, cross-cultural issues.

Susan Johnson, Research Professor, San Diego; Ed.D., British Columbia, 1984. Emotionally focused therapy, process and outcome research. Dr. Johnson is the primary developer of emotionally focused therapy and is an internationally recognized leader in the area of couples therapy, theory, and research. Dr. Johnson resides in Ottawa, Canada, and visits Alliant's San Diego campus to lecture and engage in research activities.

Ann Lawson, Professor, San Diego; Ph.D., US International, 1988. Family chemical dependency, intergenerational family processes, family therapy evaluation.

Marcia Michaels, Associate Professor and Site Director, Irvine; Ph.D., Georgia, 1996. Divorce and remarriage, cross-cultural issues in research and therapy, prevention of mental health problems in high-risk families, healthy family functioning, mindfulness meditation and hypnosis.

Marianne Miller, Assistant Professor, San Diego; Ph.D., Texas Tech, 2003. Spirituality in therapy and MFT training, supervision, gender, diversity, MFT theories, chronic pain.

Rajeswari Natrajan, Assistant Professor, Irvine; Ph.D., Purdue, 2004. Family interventions and therapy, children in therapy, therapeutic outcome assessments, families in multicultural societies, family therapy training and evaluation, supervision, multicultural issues.

Janet Osborn, Assistant Professor and Clinical Training Coordinator, Sacramento; Ph.D., Syracuse, 1997. Issues facing LGBTQI community life, therapy with the LGBT community, addiction.

Jason J. Platt, Assistant Professor, MFT Site Director and Program Director, M.A. in Counseling Psychology, Mexico; Ph.D., Syracuse, 1986. Clinical competency, evaluation, supervision, and family therapy training practices; gender and multiculturalism; clinical outcome research; brief family therapy.

Brandon C. Silverthorn, Assistant Professor, Irvine; Ph.D., Michigan State, 2005. Contextual family therapy, client suicide, MFT professional development, therapist well-being, fatherhood, cross-cultural issues.

Narumi Taniguchi, Assistant Professor, San Diego; Ph.D., Texas Tech, 2006. Cross-cultural issues, family of origin, couples therapy, work/family/parenting issues, statistics, quantitative methodology.

H. Luis Vargas, Assistant Professor, San Diego; Ph.D., Loma Linda, 2005. Cross-cultural family therapy, therapy process.

Linna Wang, Associate Professor and Site Director, San Diego; Ph.D., Brigham Young, 1996. Native American studies, cross-cultural issues, women's issues, marriage and family evaluation, survey research, impact of family factors on children.

Scott R. Woolley, Professor, San Diego; and Systemwide Director, Marital and Family Therapy Programs; Ph.D., Texas Tech, 1995. Emotionally focused therapy; courtship, marriage, couples therapy; MFT process and outcome research; observational research; cultural issues in couple relationships; MFT supervision processes; MFT therapy training; chemical dependency.

ANTIOCH UNIVERSITY NEW ENGLAND

Department of Applied Psychology
Master's in Marriage and Family Therapy

Program of Study

The mission of the Marriage and Family Therapy master's program is to provide students with the academic preparation and experience needed to become highly competent marriage and family therapy professionals. The program's goals and philosophy parallel the standards set by the Commission on Accreditation for Marriage and Family Therapy Education (COAMFTE) of the American Association for Marriage and Family Therapy (AAMFT). The Marriage and Family Therapy master's program is designed to be a full-time, concentrated, integrated experience, with students completing the course work and clinical hours in six semesters over two years.

Students enter this two-year program in the summer semester. Classes are held one day a week during fall and spring semesters and two days per week during summer semesters at Antioch New England. There are occasionally other short courses available as electives.

In the first year, students are introduced to systems thinking and to the basic theories of individual and family process, professional ethics, approaches to family assessment and treatment, practical skills in observing and intervening in family and larger systems, and issues of diversity. Students also complete an eight-month 450-hour practicum concurrent with a professional seminar experience.

In the second year, students work on advanced topics including human sexuality and sex therapy, family violence, MFT research methods, groups and larger systems, and substance abuse and enroll in a second yearlong professional seminar. A twelve-month, 1,000-hour clinical internship is also required. Through their practicum and internship placements, students complete a minimum of 500 face-to-face clinical hours during the program, at least 250 of which are with couples or families.

There is also a Ph.D. in Marriage and Family Therapy program at Antioch New England (http://www.antiochne.edu/ap/mftphd).

Research Facilities

The librarians at Antioch New England offer professional and personalized reference service for graduate research. Extensive class and research support is available via the library Web site. Access to the library catalog is available through Horace, the library's automated catalog system. Also available are specialized online reference pages for classes and key topics, access to many online bibliographic databases, reserve reading, and links to scholarly Internet resources with full Internet access. In addition, detailed reference instruction, specific research information, an electronic book collection, and specific class support resources are available on the library Web site. All library services, such as book requests, renewals, reference help, and interlibrary loan requests, are available online.

Antioch New England's focused library collection includes print and electronic books and journals, dissertations and theses, audiovisual materials, and government documents. This collection is enhanced by the large collection of more than 300,000 books and 13,000 journal titles at Antioch College Antioch New England's partner in the larger Antioch University Library system. Recent additions include OhioLINK, which offers more than 100 electronic research databases, including a variety of full-text resources and RefWORKS, a bibliographic management program. The Antioch New England Library also participates in local, regional, and national interlibrary loan services.

Financial Aid

Approximately 70 percent of students receive some type of aid, usually in the form of federal loans and work-study. The Jonathan Daniels Scholarship, established in 2003, strives to increase the diversity of the student body in its racial, ethnic, cultural, international, and socioeconomic makeup and to encourage service to underserved groups. All full-time Antioch New England students are eligible, although funding is limited. The completed scholarship form, along with relevant information from the Office of Financial Aid, is forwarded to each academic department for decisions. Awards range from $500 to 50 percent of tuition for a given year.

Cost of Study

Tuition per semester is approximately $7050 for the M.A. in marriage and family therapy, with a $350 fee each semester.

Living and Housing Costs

The University's location enables a majority of students to commute to classes from their established homes in various parts of New England. Other students move close to Antioch New England, where they have a varied selection of settings—urban, rural, semirural, mountains, or valley—in which to live.

Student Group

About 1,200 students attend Antioch New England. The average age ranges between 25 and 55; women make up 69 percent of the population.

Location

Located in Keene, New Hampshire, Antioch New England is in the heart of the Monadnock region, a picturesque area that has been described as the "Currier & Ives" corner of New Hampshire. The school is geographically situated so that students also have easy access to several popular metropolitan areas, including Boston and Montreal. With a population of nearly 23,000, Keene has been named by the National Trust for Historic Preservation as one of "America's Dozen Distinctive Destinations."

The School and The Department

Antioch University New England offers a rich array of master's and doctoral-level academic programming and institutional activities. The University's values-driven mission and focus on experiential learning, peer interaction, and reflective practice make the Antioch New England experience unique for each individual who is part of this learning community. The Department of Applied Psychology is committed to fostering a multicultural environment and promoting social justice in marriage and family therapy and the mental health field. The programs focus on an examination of the practitioner's role in the larger systems and contexts of society and the global village and encourage students to develop a personal philosophy of psychological, social, and cultural change.

Applying

Students must submit the completed application form, including a resume and an essay; a nonrefundable application fee of $50; an official transcript from each accredited college or university attended, indicating courses taken and degree(s) earned; and three letters of recommendation (four letters for Alternative Admissions Process applicants who do not have a bachelor's degree), preferably from persons who are, or have been, in a position to evaluate the applicant's work. An interview with a department faculty member is required. Antioch New England does not require applicants to the Marriage and Family Therapy master's program to take the Graduate Record Examinations (GRE) or similar written examinations. The GRE is required for applicants to the Ph.D. program.

The application deadline is May 1 for the Marriage and Family Therapy program.

Correspondence and Information

Office of Admissions
Antioch University New England
40 Avon Street
Keene, New Hampshire 03431-3516

Phone: 800-490-3310 (toll-free)
Fax: 603-357-0718
E-mail: petersons@antiochne.edu
Web site: http://www.antiochne.edu

Antioch University New England

THE FACULTY AND THEIR RESEARCH

Kendall F. Bacon, Senior Associate Professor and Director of Clinical Training for the Clinical Mental Health Counseling Program; M.S.W., Simmons. Couples and solution-focused counseling.

Amy Blanchard, Assistant Professor, Marriage and Family Therapy Program; Ph.D. (medical and family therapy), East Carolina. Working with families dealing with issues of health, illness, and disability; how to collaborate with other health-care providers; helping women and their families who face depression during pregnancy or the postpartum period.

Katherine Clarke, Professor and Chairperson; Ph.D., Loyola Chicago; M.B.A., Simmons. Meaning-making in individuals and organizations, leadership and spirituality.

William T. Griffith, Professor of Interdisciplinary Studies; Ph.D. (philosophy), Boston College; Ph.D. (psychology), Massachusetts Amherst. Information technology and systems, postmodernism and social criticism, models of communication, technology and culture, and applications of narrative.

Phyllis K. Jeswald, Senior Associate Professor and Assistant Director of the Dance/Movement Therapy and Counseling Program; M.Ed., Massachusetts; LMHC, ADTR. Integration of verbal and nonverbal elements in the therapeutic process.

Diane Kurinsky, Professor, Associate Chairperson, and Director of the Clinical Mental Health Counseling Program; Ed.D., Massachusetts Amherst. Addictions and marriage and family therapy.

Susan Loman, Professor, Associate Chairperson, and Director of the Dance/Movement Therapy and Counseling Program; M.A., Goddard; ADTR, NCC. Kestenberg Movement Profile (KMP).

Walter Lowe, Assistant Professor; Ph.D. (marriage and family therapy), Purdue. Investigating problems families face after long separations, either as the result of military service or incarceration; development of a model of reunification therapy that can be adapted to various ethnic and economic populations; development of a model of Common Factors supervision, which is not model-based, but rather based on certain basic principles that inform all successful therapies, regardless of the model practiced.

Anne Prouty Lyness, Associate Professor and Director of Clinical Training for the Marriage and Family Therapy Program; Ph.D. (child development and family studies), Purdue. How families deal with health and illness; belief systems that create resilient families; human diversity and how it informs couple and family life; how current and emerging family public policies, laws, and politics influence families based on gender, ethnicity, social class, age, and country of origin.

Kevin P. Lyness, Associate Professor, Associate Chairperson, and Director of the Marriage and Family Therapy Program; Ph.D. (marriage and family therapy), Purdue. Adolescent development in family context, interface between family variables and adolescent resiliency and ability to face risks; critical issues facing couple and family therapists.

Allison Smith, Assistant Professor, Clinical Mental Health Counseling Program; Ph.D. (counseling and counselor education), North Carolina at Greensboro. Working with adults with chronic and severe mental illness, survivors of domestic violence, adults in crisis, adults with dual diagnoses, and undergraduate college students.

Carlotta J. Willis, Professor and Director of Academic Affairs; Ed.D., Massachusetts Amherst; NCC. Role of nonverbal communication in counseling and creative approaches to career development.

ARGOSY UNIVERSITY, ATLANTA

College of Psychology and Behavioral Sciences

ARGOSY UNIVERSITY.

Programs of Study

Argosy University, Atlanta, offers the Postdoctoral Respecialization Certificate in clinical psychology, the Master of Arts (M.A.) degree in clinical psychology, community counseling, forensic psychology, and industrial organizational psychology; the Doctor of Education (Ed.D.) degree in counselor education and supervision; and the Doctor of Psychology (Psy.D.) degree in clinical psychology. Students completing a program may wish to become licensed professionals. Argosy University, Atlanta does not guarantee third-party certification/licensure. Outside agencies control the requirements for taking and passing certification/licensing exams and are subject to change without notice to Argosy University, Atlanta.

The Postdoctoral Respecialization Certificate in Clinical Psychology is designed for qualified individuals with doctoral degrees in areas of psychology other than clinical psychology. It provides the opportunity to obtain clinical knowledge and skills through class work and through fieldwork experiences. Coursework and clinical training experiences are designed to enable program participants to seek licensure in clinical psychology.

The M.A. in Clinical Psychology program presents students with the opportunity for training as professionals in the mental health field. This program serves several purposes. First, it introduces students to basic clinical skills that can enable them to serve the mental health needs of populations with diverse backgrounds. Students who use the master's degree as a means of entering a professional career have the opportunity to receive theoretical background and professional training under the supervision of a qualified, practitioner-oriented faculty. The graduates of this program are then able to apply theoretical and clinical knowledge to individuals and groups in need of mental healthcare. Second, the Master of Arts degree often serves as a preliminary step to the doctorate degree. For these students, the program provides a foundation for work beyond the master's degree level and enables them to determine their interest in, and suitability for, the pursuit of more advanced study. In certain states, students holding an M.A. in clinical psychology are eligible to sit for licensure.

The M.A. in Community Counseling program is designed to provide students with a solid foundation for the practice of professional counseling. The program's curriculum integrates theoretical and conceptual foundations of professional counseling with training in appropriate client intervention and advocacy skills. The program emphasizes the development of attitudes, knowledge, and skills that are essential for professional counselors who are committed to the ethical provision of quality services. Students completing this program meet the academic requirements toward licensure as Licensed Professional Counselors (LPCs) in Georgia.

The M.A. in Forensic Psychology program is designed to educate and train individuals who are currently working, or wish to work, in fields that utilize the study and practice of forensic psychology. Curriculum provides for an understanding of theory, training, and practice of forensic psychology. It emphasizes the development of students who are committed to the ethical provision of quality services to diverse clients and organizations. The program maintains policies and delivery formats suitable for working adults. The M.A. in Forensic Psychology program provides coursework in forensic psychology for application to law enforcement, legal and organizational consultation, and program analysis.

The M.A. in Industrial Organizational Psychology program is designed to apply the knowledge of industrial organizational psychology to issues involving individuals and groups in organizational and work settings. This program prepares students for careers in areas such as compensation, training, data analysis, consultation, statistical decision-making, organizational development, leadership, and human resource management positions. The curriculum is competency-based, focusing on the outcomes of training and on the knowledge, skills, and behavior necessary to function as a master's-level professional in industrial organizational psychology. This is an interdisciplinary program that combines the expertise of the faculty in the College of Psychology and Behavioral Sciences and the College of Business.

The Ed.D. in Counselor Education and Supervision program aligns with the master's-level counselor education programs in order to encourage entry-level counseling students to work toward becoming doctoral-level advanced practitioners, educators, and supervisors. This program prepares counselors for a variety of settings by providing the advanced skills and knowledge necessary to provide leadership and advocacy, as well as serve in supervisory, training, and teaching positions in the counseling profession.

The Psy.D. in Clinical Psychology program has been designed to educate and train students so that they may eventually be able to function effectively as clinical psychologists. The curriculum provides for the meaningful integration of theory, training, and practice. The program emphasizes the development of attitudes, knowledge, and skills essential in the formation of professional psychologists who are committee do the ethical provision of quality services.

Research Facilities

Argosy University libraries provide curriculum support and educational resources, including current text materials, diagnostic training documents, reference materials and databases, journals and dissertations, and major and current titles in program areas. There is an online public-access catalog of library resources available throughout the Argosy University system. Students have remote access to the campus library database, enabling them to study and conduct research at home. Academic databases offer dissertation abstracts, academic journals, and professional periodicals. All library computers are Internet accessible. Software applications include Word, Excel, PowerPoint, SPSS, and various test-scoring programs.

Financial Aid

Financial aid is available to those who qualify. Argosy University, Atlanta, offers access to federal and state aid programs, merit-based awards, grants, loans, and a work-study program. As a first step, students should complete the Free Application for Federal Student Aid (FAFSA). Prospective students can apply electronically at http://www.fafsa.ed.gov or at the campus.

Cost of Study

Tuition varies by program. Students should contact Argosy University, Atlanta, for tuition information.

Living and Housing Costs

Students typically live in apartments in the metropolitan Atlanta area. Living expenses vary according to each student's preferred standard of living, housing, and transportation. The University does not offer or operate student housing. Most Argosy University students are full-time working professionals who live within driving distance of the campus. Several nearby hotels offer special rates for those who commute from long distances. The Admissions Department also maintains a list of housing options, including contact information for University students who wish to share housing. For more information, students should contact the Admissions Department.

Student Group

Admission to Argosy University, Atlanta, is selective to ensure a dynamic and engaged student body. The University encourages diversity in academic and employment backgrounds and promotes integration of the student body into professional life through established connections with local and national professional associations. Argosy University offers a professionally oriented education with rich opportunities to gain practical experience in class, field placements, and internships. Full-time students and working professionals can gain the extensive knowledge and range of skills necessary for effective performance in their chosen field.

Student Outcomes

Students can register with Argosy University's online career-services system and use select services from a distance, such as degree-specific career e-mail lists, national job posts, and virtual job fairs. Students should contact the University for more information.

Location

Argosy University, Atlanta, is housed in a modern building in Sandy Springs, a northern suburb of Atlanta. The campus features a café and outdoor lakeside terrace. Beyond the college, students will find a selection of housing options. This major metropolitan area offers many social and recreational opportunities, from clubs and concerts to galleries and museums, from a growing restaurant scene to Braves baseball games and rollerblading in Piedmont Park. The many hospitals, clinics, agencies, and educational institutions in the Atlanta area provide varied opportunities for student training. Atlanta's business environment includes technology companies such as EarthLink and Macquarium as well as corporate giants such as the Coca-Cola Company, CNN, Delta Air Lines, AT&T, and Georgia Pacific.

The University

Argosy University is a private institution with nineteen locations across the nation. Argosy University, Atlanta, provides a career resources office, an academic resources center, and extensive information access for research. It offers the resources of a large university plus the friendliness and personal attention of a small campus. The innovative programs feature dynamic, relevant, and practical curricula delivered in flexible class formats. Students enjoy scheduling options that make it easier to fit school into their busy lives, choosing from day and evening courses, on campus or online. Many students find a combination of class formats to be an ideal way of continuing their education while meeting family and professional demands.

Argosy University is accredited by the Higher Learning Commission and is a member of the North Central Association (30 North LaSalle Street, Suite 2400, Chicago, Illinois 60602; 800-621-7440 (toll-free); http://www.ncahlc.org).

Applying

Argosy University, Atlanta, accepts students year-round on a rolling admissions basis, depending on availability of required courses. Applications for admission are available online or by contacting the campus.

Correspondence and Information

Argosy University, Atlanta
990 Hammond Drive, Suite 100
Atlanta, Georgia 30328
Phone: 770-671-1200
         888-671-4777 (toll-free)
Fax: 770-671-0476
E-mail: auadmissions@argosy.edu
Web site: http://www.argosy.edu/atlanta

Argosy University, Atlanta

THE FACULTY

The Argosy University faculty is comprised of working professionals who are eager to help students succeed. Members bring real-world experience and the latest practice innovations to the academic setting. The diverse faculty members of the College of Psychology and Behavioral Sciences are widely recognized for contributions to the field. Many are published scholars, and most hold doctoral degrees. They are committed to providing a substantive education that combines comprehensive knowledge with critical skills and practical workplace relevance. Above all, faculty members are committed to their students' personal and professional development.

ARGOSY UNIVERSITY.

ARGOSY UNIVERSITY, CHICAGO

College of Psychology and Behavioral Sciences

Programs of Study	Argosy University, Chicago, offers the Graduate Certificate in psychoanalytic psychology; the Master of Arts (M.A.) degree in clinical psychology, industrial organizational psychology, and community counseling; the Doctor of Education (Ed.D.) degree in counseling psychology, counselor education and supervision, and organizational leadership; and the Doctor of Psychology (Psy.D.) degree in clinical psychology. Students completing a program may wish to become licensed professionals. Argosy University, Chicago does not guarantee third-party certification/licensure. Outside agencies control the requirements for taking and passing certification/licensing exams and are subject to change without notice to Argosy University, Chicago.
	The Graduate Certificate in psychoanalytic psychology provides specialized training in psychoanalytic psychology for post-master's and doctoral clinicians with relevant background and experience. The certificate is designed to meet the need for education and training in assessment, intervention, and supervision within a broad psychoanalytic model. The curriculum provides a firm grounding in major theoretical paradigms with special attention to those which are current and emerging. Graduates of the psychoanalytic psychology certificate will be prepared to work effectively within a psychoanalytic framework and begin additional training in psychoanalytic psychotherapy or psychoanalysis.
	The M.A. in Clinical Psychology program has been designed to educate and train students to pursue a professional career as master's-level practitioners. The program is designed to provide students with an educational program with all the necessary theoretical and clinical elements that will allow them to be effective members of a mental health team. It introduces students to basic clinical skills that integrate individual and group theoretical foundations of applied psychology into appropriate client interaction and intervention skills. This program can be completed in as little as two years and must be completed in five years. In addition, the program offers preparation for those considering application to the Psy.D. in Clinical Psychology program.
	The M.A. in Industrial Organizational Psychology is designed to apply the knowledge of industrial organizational psychology to issues involving individuals and groups in organizational and work settings. This program is designed to prepare students for careers in areas such as compensation, training, data analysis, consultation, statistical decision-making, organizational development, leadership, and human resource management positions. The curriculum is competency-based, focusing on the outcomes of training and on the knowledge, skills, and behavior necessary to function as a master's-level professional in industrial organizational psychology. This is an interdisciplinary program that combines the expertise of the faculty in the College of Psychology and Behavioral Sciences and the College of Business.
	The M.A. in Community Counseling program creates a learning environment that is designed to promote academic excellence, professional competence, and personal integrity. This is achieved through a curriculum that integrates counseling skills, theoretical foundations of counseling, and clinical field experience into appropriate interaction and intervention skills for utilization in a variety of settings with diverse client populations. We serve a diverse student body from urban, suburban, and rural areas who are intrinsically motivated to help others. The program actively engages faculty and students in the preparation of counselors who meet the needs of diverse communities.
	The Ed.D. in Counseling Psychology program is designed to meet the special requirements of working mental health professionals motivated to develop their knowledge and skills to handle the changing needs of modern organizations. The program is designed to provide working professionals with the opportunity to pursue their personal and professional goals through the completion of a graduate program. An optional concentration in counselor education and supervision is available.
	The Ed.D. in Counselor Education and Supervision program aligns with the master's-level counselor education programs in order to encourage entry-level counseling students to work toward becoming doctoral-level advanced practitioners, educators, and supervisors. The program prepares counselors for a variety of settings by providing the advanced skills and knowledge necessary to provide leadership and advocacy, as well as serve in supervisory, training, and teaching positions in the counseling profession. The program is designed to help current practitioners with existing master's-level preparation to advance their careers.
	The Ed.D. in Organizational Leadership program is designed to meet the special requirements of working professionals who wish to develop their knowledge and skills to handle the changing needs of modern organizations. The program is designed to enable working professionals to pursue their personal and professional goals through the completion of a graduate program.
	The Psy.D. in Clinical Psychology program has been designed to educate and train students so that they may be able to function effectively as clinical psychologists. To ensure that students are prepared adequately, the curriculum provides for the meaningful integration of theory, training, and practice. The program emphasizes the development of attitudes, knowledge, and skills essential in the formation of professional psychologists who are committed to the ethical provision of quality services.
Research Facilities	Argosy University libraries provide curriculum support and educational resources, including current text materials, diagnostic training documents, reference materials and databases, journals and dissertations, and major and current titles in program areas. There is an online public-access catalog of library resources available throughout the Argosy University system. Students have remote access to the campus library database, enabling them to study and conduct research at home. Academic databases offer dissertation abstracts, academic journals, and professional periodicals. All library computers are Internet accessible. Software applications include Word, Excel, PowerPoint, SPSS, and various test-scoring programs.
Financial Aid	Financial aid is available to those who qualify. Argosy University, Chicago, offers access to federal and state aid programs, merit-based awards, grants, loans, and a work-study program. As a first step, students should complete the Free Application for Federal Student Aid (FAFSA). Prospective students can apply electronically at http://www.fafsa.ed.gov or at the campus.
Cost of Study	Tuition varies by program. Students should contact Argosy University, Chicago, for tuition information.
Living and Housing Costs	Students typically live in apartments in the metropolitan Chicago area. Living expenses vary according to each student's preferred standard of living, housing, and transportation. The University does not offer or operate student housing. Most of the students are full-time working professionals who live within driving distance of the campus. Several nearby hotels offer special rates for those who commute from long distances. The Admissions Department also maintains a list of housing options, including contact information for university students who wish to share housing. For more information, students should contact the Admissions Department.
Student Group	Admission to Argosy University, Chicago, is selective to ensure a dynamic and engaged student body. The University encourages diversity in academic and employment backgrounds and promotes integration of the student body into professional life through established connections with local and national professional associations. Argosy University offers a professionally oriented education with rich opportunities to gain practical experience in class, field placements, and internships. Full-time students and working professionals gain the extensive knowledge and range of skills necessary for effective performance in their chosen fields.
Student Outcomes	Students can register with the University's online career-services system and use select services from a distance, such as degree-specific career e-mail lists, national job posts, and virtual job fairs. Students should contact the University for more information.
Location	Chicago is a city of world-class status and beauty, drawing visitors from around the globe. Argosy University, Chicago, sits in the heart of The Loop, the city's business and entertainment center. Located on the shores of Lake Michigan, Chicago is home to world-champion sports teams, an internationally acclaimed symphony orchestra, renowned architecture, and a variety of history and art museums. Recreational opportunities include hiking and cycling on miles of lakefront trails, golfing, and shopping. Chicago's business environment includes a broad array of companies including Boeing and Pepsi America. The commercial banking headquarters of JP Morgan Chase is also located in Chicago.
The University	Argosy University is a private institution with nineteen locations across the nation. Argosy University, Chicago, provides a career services office, an academic resources center, and extensive information access for research. It offers the resources of a large university plus the friendliness and personal attention of a small campus. Argosy University, Chicago, is closely associated with the Schaumburg, Illinois, campus, located 45 minutes from downtown Chicago.
	The innovative programs feature dynamic, relevant, and practical curricula delivered in flexible class formats. Students enjoy scheduling options that make it easier to fit school into their busy lives, choosing from day and evening courses, on campus or online. Many students find a combination of class formats to be an ideal way of continuing their education while meeting family and professional demands.
	Argosy University is accredited by the Higher Learning Commission and is a member of the North Central Association (30 North LaSalle Street, Suite 2400, Chicago, Illinois 60602; 800-621-7440 (toll-free); http://www.ncahlc.org).
Applying	Argosy University, Chicago, accepts students year-round on a rolling admissions basis, depending on availability of required courses. Applications for admission are available online or by contacting the campus.
Correspondence and Information	Argosy University, Chicago 225 North Michigan Avenue, Suite 1300 Chicago, Illinois 60601 Phone: 312-777-7600 800-626-4123 (toll-free) Fax: 312-777-7748 E-mail: auadmissions@argosy.edu Web site: http://www.argosy.edu/chicago

Argosy University, Chicago

THE FACULTY

The Argosy University faculty is comprised of working professionals who are eager to help students succeed. Members bring real-world experience and the latest practice innovations to the academic setting. The diverse faculty members of the College of Psychology and Behavioral Sciences are widely recognized for contributions to the field. Many are published scholars, and most hold doctoral degrees. They are committed to providing a substantive education that combines comprehensive knowledge with critical skills and practical workplace relevance. Above all, faculty members are committed to their students' personal and professional development.

ARGOSY UNIVERSITY.

ARGOSY UNIVERSITY, DALLAS

College of Psychology and Behavioral Sciences

Programs of Study

Argosy University, Dallas, offers the Master of Arts (M.A.) degree in clinical psychology, community counseling, forensic psychology, industrial organizational psychology, and school psychology; the Doctor of Education (Ed.D.) degree in counselor education and supervision; and the Doctor of Psychology (Psy.D.) degree in clinical psychology. Students completing a program may wish to become licensed professionals. Argosy University, Dallas does not guarantee third-party certification/licensure. Outside agencies control the requirements for taking and passing certification/licensing exams and are subject to change without notice to Argosy University, Dallas.

The M.A. in Clinical Psychology program is designed to educate and train students to enter professional careers as master's-level practitioners. Students are provided with an educational program that has all the necessary theoretical and clinical elements necessary for graduates to become effective members of a mental health team. The program introduces students to basic clinical skills that integrate individual and group theoretical foundations of applied psychology into appropriate client interaction and intervention skills. Additionally, it offers excellent preparation for those considering application to the Psy.D. in Clinical Psychology program.

The M.A. in Community Counseling program is designed to provide students with a sound foundation for the practice of community counseling, with a multifaceted focus on developmental and preventive mental health services. The program introduces students to the basic skills of counseling, integrating individual, group, family, and organizational interventions. The program emphasizes development of the attitudes, knowledge, and skills required for the ethical provision of quality professional counseling services. As such, the program is committed to educating and training students to enter the counseling profession as ethical, effective, skilled, and culturally competent practitioners, able to work in a variety of settings with diverse client populations. This goal is achieved through a curriculum designed to integrate foundational counseling skills, counseling theories, and clinical field experiences taught by experienced practitioners.

The M.A. in Forensic Psychology program is designed to educate and train individuals who are currently working, or wish to work, in fields that utilize the study and practice of forensic psychology. The curriculum is designed to provide for an understanding of theory, training, and practice of forensic psychology. It emphasizes the development of students who are committed to the ethical provision of quality services to diverse clients and organizations. The program maintains policies and delivery formats suitable for working adults. The program provides course work in forensic psychology for application to law enforcement, legal and organizational consultation, and program analysis.

The M.A. in Industrial Organizational Psychology program is designed to apply the knowledge of industrial organizational psychology to issues involving individuals and groups in organizational and work settings. This program prepares students for careers in areas such as compensation, training, data analysis, consultation, statistical decision-making, organizational development, leadership, and human resource management positions. The curriculum is competency-based, focusing on the outcomes of training and on the knowledge, skills, and behavior necessary to function as a master's-level professional in industrial organizational psychology. This is an interdisciplinary program that combines the expertise of the faculty in the College of Psychology and Behavioral Sciences and the College of Business.

The M.A. in School Psychology program is dedicated to producing ethical, responsible, and competent school psychologists who are able to serve effectively in a number of professional roles. During graduate training, students develop core competencies in psychological assessment, intervention, and consultation/education, as well as cultural and individual diversity. Graduates of the program may be eligible for department of education certification and will be prepared for employment as school psychologists. The program is designed to prepare students to become Nationally Certified School Psychologists (NCSPs) in accordance with criteria developed by the National Association of School Psychologists.

The Ed.D. in Counselor Education and Supervision program aligns with the master's-level counselor education programs in order to encourage entry-level counseling students to work toward becoming doctoral-level advanced practitioners, educators, and supervisors. The program is designed to prepare counselors for a variety of settings by providing the advanced skills and knowledge necessary to provide leadership and advocacy, as well as serve in supervisory, training, and teaching positions in the counseling profession. The program is designed to help current practitioners with existing master's-level preparation to advance their careers. This doctorate provides expanded opportunities to compete in the marketplace, on par with the growing number of doctoral-level counseling practitioners.

The Psy.D. in Clinical Psychology program has been designed to educate and train students to function effectively for their eventual role as clinical psychologists. To enable students to be prepared adequately, the curriculum provides for the meaningful integration of theory and research as applied to practice. The program emphasizes the development of knowledge, skills, and attitudes essential in the formation of professional psychologists who are committed to the ethical provision of quality services.

Research Facilities

Argosy University libraries provide curriculum support and educational resources, including current text materials, diagnostic training documents, reference materials and databases, journals and dissertations, and major and current titles in program areas. There is an online public-access catalog of library resources available throughout the Argosy University system. Students have remote access to the campus library database, enabling them to study and conduct research at home. Academic databases offer dissertation abstracts, academic journals, and professional periodicals. All library computers are Internet accessible. Software applications include Word, Excel, PowerPoint, SPSS, and various test-scoring programs.

Financial Aid

Financial aid is available to those who qualify. Argosy University, Dallas, offers access to federal and state aid programs, merit-based awards, grants, loans, and a work-study program. As a first step, students should complete the Free Application for Federal Student Aid (FAFSA). Prospective students can apply electronically at http://www.fafsa.ed.gov or at the campus.

Cost of Study

Tuition varies by program. Students should contact Argosy University, Dallas, for tuition information.

Living and Housing Costs

Students typically live in apartments in the metropolitan Dallas area. Living expenses vary according to each student's preferred standard of living, housing, and transportation. The University does not offer or operate student housing. Most of the students are full-time working professionals who live within driving distance of the campus. Several nearby hotels offer special rates for those who commute from long distances. The Admissions Department also maintains a list of housing options, including contact information, for University students who wish to share housing. For more information, students should contact the Admissions Department.

Student Group

Admission to Argosy University, Dallas, is selective to ensure a dynamic and engaged student body. The University encourages diversity in academic and employment backgrounds and promotes integration of the student body into professional life through established connections with local and national professional associations. Argosy University offers a professionally oriented education with rich opportunities to gain practical experience in class, field placements, and internships. Full-time students and working professionals gain the extensive knowledge and range of skills necessary for effective performance in their chosen fields.

Student Outcomes

Students can register with the University's online career-services system and use select services from a distance, such as degree-specific career e-mail lists, national job posts, and virtual job fairs. Students should contact the University for more information.

Location

Argosy University, Dallas, offers a north-central location in Dallas, with easy access to freeways, neighboring colleges and universities, libraries, shops, restaurants, theaters, art museums, and other tourist attractions. The business environment in the Dallas–Fort Worth metropolitan area includes a broad array of companies, such as Lockheed Martin Corporation, Baylor University Medical System, and Southwest Airlines.

The University

Argosy University is a private institution with nineteen locations across the nation. Argosy University, Dallas, provides a career resources office, an academic resources center, and extensive information access for research. It offers the resources of a large university, plus the friendliness and personal attention of a small campus.

Argosy University, Dallas, offers the unique opportunity to take one class at a time, with each class lasting for one month. Students are never required to study for multiple exams at the same time. New classes start each month. This flexible format lets students begin working on a graduate degree without waiting for the traditional semester to start.

Argosy University is accredited by the Higher Learning Commission and is a member of the North Central Association (30 North LaSalle Street, Suite 2400, Chicago, Illinois 60602; 800-621-7440 (toll-free); http://www.ncahlc.org).

Applying

Argosy University, Dallas, accepts students year-round on a rolling admissions basis, depending on availability of required courses. Applications for admission are available online or by contacting the campus.

Correspondence and Information

Argosy University, Dallas
5001 Lyndon B. Johnson Freeway
Heritage Square
Farmers Branch, Texas 75244
Phone: 214-890-9900
    866-954-9900 (toll-free)
Fax: 214-378-8555
E-mail: http://auadmissions@argosy.edu
Web site: http://www.argosy.edu/dallas

Argosy University, Dallas

THE FACULTY

The Argosy University faculty is comprised of working professionals who are eager to help students succeed. Members bring real-world experience and the latest practice innovations to the academic setting. The diverse faculty members of the College of Psychology and Behavioral Sciences are widely recognized for contributions to the field. Many are published scholars, and most hold doctoral degrees. They are committed to providing a substantive education that combines comprehensive knowledge with critical skills and practical workplace relevance. Above all, faculty members are committed to their students' personal and professional development.

ARGOSY UNIVERSITY

ARGOSY UNIVERSITY, DENVER

College of Psychology and Behavioral Sciences

Programs of Study

Argosy University, Denver, offers the Master of Arts (M.A.) degree in clinical psychology, community counseling, forensic psychology, and marriage and family therapy; the Master of Arts in Industrial Organizational Psychology (M.A.I.O.) degree; the Doctor of Marriage and Family Therapy (D.M.F.T.) degree; the Doctor of Education (Ed.D.) degree in counseling psychology, counselor education and supervision, and organizational leadership; and the Doctor of Psychology (Psy.D.) degree in clinical psychology. Students completing a program may wish to become licensed professionals. Argosy University, Denver does not guarantee third-party certification/licensure. Outside agencies control the requirements for taking and passing certification/licensing exams and are subject to change without notice to Argosy University, Denver.

The M.A. in Clinical Psychology program prepares students with the clinical knowledge and skills required to serve the mental health needs of individuals and groups. Students develop proficiency in clinical observation, assessment, appropriate intervention, and evaluation. The program emphasizes a practitioner-oriented philosophy and integrates applied theory, research, and field experience. It is designed for students who are interested in a terminal degree and practice as a master's-level clinician or for students planning to transfer to the Psy.D. program.

The M.A. in Community Counseling program prepares students to enter the counseling profession as ethical, effective, skilled, and culturally competent practitioners. It provides a multifaceted focus on developmental and preventive mental health services. Students gain the knowledge and skills required for individual, group, family, and organizational interventions. The curriculum integrates foundational counseling skills and theories with clinical field experience.

The M.A. in Forensic Psychology program provides course work in forensic psychology for application to law enforcement, legal and organizational consultation, and program analysis. The program is designed to meet growing needs of the legal and criminal justice systems for professional counseling within victim assistance programs, probation and parole offices, court-mandated treatment programs, jails, and prisons. With the exception of the practicum component, courses are offered on weekends, allowing students to continue full-time employment while enrolled in this program.

The M.A. in Industrial Organizational Psychology program is designed to apply the knowledge of industrial organizational psychology to issues involving individuals and groups in organizational and work settings. This program prepares students for careers in areas such as compensation, training, data analysis, consultation, statistical decision making, organizational development, leadership, and human resource management positions. The curriculum is competency based, focusing on the outcomes of training and on the knowledge, skills, and behavior necessary to function as a master's-level professional in industrial organizational psychology. This is an interdisciplinary program that combines the expertise of the faculty in the Colleges of Psychology and Behavioral Sciences and Business.

The M.A. in Marriage & Family Therapy program is designed to develop the theoretical and clinical elements required to provide effective counseling to individuals, couples, families, and groups. The program introduces basic counseling skills that incorporate foundations of applied psychology and systems theory into the development of appropriate clinical relationships. Course work in addiction studies and substance-abuse counseling prepares students to work with families affected by this burgeoning problem. Marriage and family therapy is recognized by the Public Health Service Act as one of the five core mental health professions, and the National Institute of Mental Health accepts marriage and family therapists as qualified mental health professionals. The program is offered through weekend courses to allow concurrent employment.

The Doctor of Marriage and Family Therapy is a practice-oriented degree for licensed marriage and family therapists or professionals who can meet state requirements for licensure as a marriage and family therapist (meeting the Commission on Accreditation of Marriage and Family Therapy Education (COAMFTE) criteria for clinical practice prior to admission). The program seeks to build upon students' prior learning and professional experience by expanding and deepening their knowledge of human development, family dynamics, systemic thinking, interactional theories, traditional and contemporary marriage and family therapy theories and practices, and the cultural contexts within which these are embedded.

The Ed.D. in Counseling Psychology program is designed to prepare counselors with the skills and credentials necessary to pursue leadership, supervision, training, and teaching positions. Students have the opportunity to develop new interests and levels of competency through an applied research-practitioner approach to the role of professional counselor. An optional concentration in counselor education and supervision is available. The challenges of a changing society and the diversity of roles available to the mental health practitioner require a lifelong commitment to continuing education.

The Ed.D. in Counselor Education & Supervision program is designed to develop the advanced skills and knowledge necessary for leadership and advocacy roles in a variety of settings. The field is dedicated to both the academic preparation and comprehensive supervision of counselors across multiple settings. This course of study aligns with the Master of Arts in Professional Counseling program to encourage entry-level counseling students to work toward becoming doctoral-level advanced practitioners, educators, and supervisors.

The Ed.D. in Organizational Leadership program is designed for working professionals who wish to develop the knowledge and skills required to hold leadership positions in complex organizations. The program focuses on transformational leadership skills in addition to managerial attributes. This approach prepares students for strategic challenges such as increasing globalization, changing economies, societal shifts, and individual-organizational relationships. Leaders prepared in this manner can become visionaries and innovators, leading viable organizations capable of meeting the challenges of the future.

The Psy.D. in Clinical Psychology program prepares students to deliver basic diagnostic and therapeutic services to diverse populations, including individuals, groups, and families. By integrating theory, training, research, and practice, students develop and apply the clinical skills of observation, assessment, intervention, and evaluation. Optional concentrations are available in child and family psychology, general adult clinical, health psychology, or neuropsychology/geropsychology. The program prepares graduates for positions in traditional settings, including, but not limited to, independent practice, mental health centers, hospitals, medical centers, and managed-care systems. Graduates are encouraged to utilize clinical skills in innovative ways to become more competitive. Eventual positions may include consulting in various corporate, governmental, academic, multimedia, law, scientific, marketing, and industrial settings.

Research Facilities

Argosy University libraries provide curriculum support and educational resources, including current text materials, diagnostic training documents, reference materials and databases, journals and dissertations, and major and current titles in program areas. There is an online public-access catalog of library resources available throughout the Argosy University system. Students have remote access to the campus library database, enabling them to study and conduct research at home. Academic databases offer dissertation abstracts, academic journals, and professional periodicals. All library computers are Internet accessible. Software applications include Word, Excel, PowerPoint, SPSS, and various test-scoring programs.

Financial Aid

Financial aid is available to those who qualify. Argosy University, Denver, offers access to federal and state aid programs, merit-based awards, grants, loans, and a work-study program. As a first step, students should complete the Free Application for Federal Student Aid (FAFSA). Prospective students can apply electronically at http://www.fafsa.ed.gov or at the campus.

Cost of Study

Tuition varies by program. Students should contact Argosy University, Denver, for tuition information.

Living and Housing Costs

Students typically live in apartments in the metropolitan Denver area. Living expenses vary according to each student's preferred standard of living, housing, and transportation. The University does not offer or operate student housing. Most of the students are full-time working professionals who live within driving distance of the campus. Several nearby hotels offer special rates for those who commute from long distances. The Admissions Department also maintains a list of housing options, including contact information for University students who wish to share housing. For more information, students should contact the Admissions Department.

Student Group

Admission to Argosy University, Denver, is selective to ensure a dynamic and engaged student body. The University encourages diversity in academic and employment backgrounds and promotes integration of the student body into professional life through established connections with local and national professional associations. Argosy University offers a professionally oriented education with rich opportunities to gain practical experience in class, field placements, and internships. Full-time students and working professionals gain the extensive knowledge and range of skills necessary for effective performance in their chosen fields.

Student Outcomes

Students can register with the University's online career-services system and use select services from a distance, such as degree-specific career e-mail lists, national job posts, and virtual job fairs. Students should contact the University for more information.

Location

Argosy University, Denver, is located at 1200 Lincoln Street in Denver, Colorado. The ten-story downtown facility includes classrooms, computer labs, a resource center with Internet access, a student lounge, staff and faculty offices, and other amenities. The campus is close to a variety of local libraries, shops, restaurants, theaters, and art museums. Denver's professional organizations, major corporations, technology companies, hospitals, schools, clinics, and social service agencies can also provide varied training opportunities for students.

The University

Argosy University is a private institution with nineteen locations across the nation. Argosy University, Denver, provides a career resources office, an academic resources center, and extensive information access for research. It offers the resources of a large university plus the friendliness and personal attention of a small campus.

The innovative programs feature dynamic, relevant, and practical curricula delivered in flexible class formats. Students enjoy scheduling options that make it easier to fit school into their busy lives, choosing from day and evening courses, on campus or online. Many students find a combination of class formats to be an ideal way of continuing their education while meeting family and professional demands.

Argosy University is accredited by the Higher Learning Commission and is a member of the North Central Association (30 North LaSalle Street, Suite 2400, Chicago, Illinois 60602; 800-621-7440 (toll-free); http://www.ncahlc.org).

Applying

Argosy University, Denver, accepts students year-round on a rolling admissions basis, depending on availability of required courses. Applications for admission are available online or by contacting the campus.

Correspondence and Information

Argosy University, Denver
1200 Lincoln Street
Denver, Colorado 80203

Phone: 303-248-2700
866-431-5981 (toll-free)
Fax: 303-248-2600
E-mail: auadmissions@argosy.edu
Web site: http://www.argosy.edu/denver

Argosy University, Denver

THE FACULTY

The Argosy University faculty is comprised of working professionals who are eager to help students succeed. Members bring real-world experience and the latest practice innovations to the academic setting. The diverse faculty members of the College of Psychology and Behavioral Sciences are widely recognized for contributions to the field. Many are published scholars, and most hold doctoral degrees. They are committed to providing a substantive education that combines comprehensive knowledge with critical skills and practical workplace relevance. Above all, faculty members are committed to their students' personal and professional development.

ARGOSY UNIVERSITY.

ARGOSY UNIVERSITY, HAWAI'I

College of Psychology and Behavioral Sciences

Programs of Study	Argosy University, Hawai'i, offers the Master of Arts (M.A.) degree in clinical psychology, marriage and family therapy, and school psychology; the Master of Science (M.S.) in psychopharmacology; the Doctor of Education (Ed.D.) degree in counseling psychology and organizational leadership; and the Doctor of Psychology (Psy.D.) degree in clinical psychology. Students completing a program may wish to become licensed professionals. Argosy University, Hawai'i does not guarantee third-party certification/licensure. Outside agencies control the requirements for taking and passing certification/licensing exams and are subject to change without notice to Argosy University, Hawai'i.
	The M.A. in Clinical Psychology program is designed as both a terminal degree and for those who plan to pursue doctoral study. The program is designed to provide a solid core of basic psychology, as well as a strong clinical orientation, with an emphasis in psychological assessment. The curriculum is designed to provide the theoretical and clinical elements to allow students to become effective members of mental health teams.
	The M.A. in Marriage and Family Therapy program recognizes the need to provide marriage and family therapists with the knowledge and range of skills necessary to function effectively in their profession. The program introduces students to basic skills that integrate systemic theoretical foundations of marriage and family therapy into appropriate client interaction and intervention skills. The program emphasizes the development of attitudes, knowledge, and skills essential in the formation of marriage and family therapists who are committed to the ethical provision of quality services. The program has been developed by the school's faculty members to provide working students with the opportunity to pursue personal and professional goals through completion of a master's program.
	The M.A. in School Psychology program is dedicated to producing ethical, responsible, and competent school psychologists who are able to serve effectively in a number of professional roles. During graduate training, students develop core competencies in psychological assessment, intervention, and consultation/education, as well as cultural and individual diversity. Graduates of the program may be eligible for department of education certification and will be prepared for employment as school psychologists. The program is designed to prepare students to become Nationally Certified School Psychologists (NCSPs) in accordance with criteria developed by the National Association of School Psychologists.
	The M.S. in Psychopharmacology incorporates course work and clinical practice to comprehensively train postdoctoral psychologists to prescribe medications independently, appropriately, effectively, and safely. It is a 32-credit-hour program with a practicum component requiring treatment of 100 patients. Upon successful completion of the program, students have the education and experience to prescribe psychopharmacological medications consistent with state and federal laws and work collaboratively with physicians, nurses, and other health-care providers to coordinate care. This program is intended to prepare students for the Psychopharmacology Exam for Psychologists (PEP).
	The Ed.D. in Counseling Psychology program is designed to meet the special requirements of working mental health professionals who want to develop their knowledge and skills to handle the changing needs of modern organizations. The program is designed to provide working professionals with the opportunity to pursue their personal and professional goals through the completion of a graduate program. An optional concentration in Counselor Education and Supervision is also available.
	The Ed.D. in Organizational Leadership program is designed to meet the special requirements of working professionals who wish to develop their knowledge and skills to handle the changing needs of modern organizations. It can enable working professionals to pursue their personal and professional goals through the completion of a graduate program. The program focuses on the qualities of transformational leadership, not just managerial attributes. This approach enables the faculty members to dedicate themselves to preparing students to lead complex organizations faced with an abundance of strategic challenges, such as increasing globalization, changing economies, societal shifts, and individual-organizational relationships. It is the premise of the program that leaders prepared in this manner can be visionaries and innovators, leading viable organizations capable of meeting the challenges of the future.
	The Psy.D. in Clinical Psychology program is designed to prepare students for both contemporary and emerging roles in the practice of professional psychology. Students are trained to be practitioner scholars who are skilled in local and contextual investigation and problem solving. The school offers a generalist program that supports the development of core competencies in psychological assessment, intervention, consultation/education, and management/supervision. The curriculum provides for the meaningful integration of theory, research, and practice. The doctoral program emphasizes the acquisition of attitudes, knowledge bases, and skills essential for professional psychologists who are committed to the provision of ethical quality services.
Research Facilities	Argosy University libraries provide curriculum support and educational resources, including current text materials, diagnostic training documents, reference materials and databases, journals and dissertations, and major and current titles in program areas. There is an online public-access catalog of library resources available throughout the Argosy University system. Students have remote access to the campus library database, enabling them to study and conduct research at home. Academic databases offer dissertation abstracts, academic journals, and professional periodicals. All library computers are Internet accessible. Software applications include Word, Excel, PowerPoint, SPSS, and various test-scoring programs.
Financial Aid	Financial aid is available to those who qualify. Argosy University, Hawai'i, offers access to federal and state aid programs, merit-based awards, grants, loans, and a work-study program. As a first step, students should complete the Free Application for Federal Student Aid (FAFSA). Prospective students can apply electronically at http://www.fafsa.ed.gov or at the campus.
Cost of Study	Tuition varies by program. Students should contact Argosy University, Hawai'i, for tuition information.
Living and Housing Costs	Students typically live in apartments in the metropolitan Honolulu area. Living expenses vary according to each student's preferred standard of living, housing, and transportation. The University does not offer or operate student housing. Most of the students are full-time working professionals who live within driving distance of the campus. Several nearby hotels offer special rates for those who commute from long distances. The Admissions Department also maintains a list of housing options, including contact information for University students who wish to share housing. For more information, students should contact the Admissions Department.
Student Group	Admission to Argosy University, Hawai'i, is selective to ensure a dynamic and engaged student body. The University encourages diversity in academic and employment backgrounds and promotes integration of the student body into professional life through established connections with local and national professional associations. Argosy University offers a professionally oriented education with rich opportunities to gain practical experience in class, field placements, and internships. Full-time students and working professionals gain the extensive knowledge and range of skills necessary for effective performance in their chosen fields.
Student Outcomes	Students can register with the University's online career-services system and use select services from a distance, such as degree-specific career e-mail lists, national job posts, and virtual job fairs. Students should contact the University for more information.
Location	Argosy University, Hawai'i, is located in downtown Honolulu on Oahu. Additional satellite locations on Maui and in Hilo on the island of Hawaii offer programs to communities on the neighboring islands. These locations connect the campus to Hawaii and to the local and native communities of the Pacific Islands and the Pacific Rim. Students enjoy the cultural and recreational opportunities that these locations provide. University faculty and staff members often work in cooperation with the Hawaiian community to create an educational focus on social issues, human diversity, and programs that make a difference to underserved populations.
	Honolulu's business environment includes a broad array of companies. The area's largest employers include Bank of Hawaii, Queens Medical Center, and the U.S. government. Many businesses in the metropolitan area provide varied opportunities for student training.
The University	Argosy University is a private institution with nineteen locations across the nation. Argosy University, Hawai'i, provides a career resources office, an academic resources center, and extensive information access for research. It offers the resources of a large university plus the friendliness and personal attention of a small campus.
	The innovative programs feature dynamic, relevant, and practical curricula delivered in flexible class formats. Students enjoy scheduling options that make it easier to fit school into their busy lives, choosing from day and evening courses, on campus or online. Many students find a combination of class formats to be an ideal way of continuing their education while meeting family and professional demands.
	Argosy University is accredited by the Higher Learning Commission and is a member of the North Central Association (30 North LaSalle Street, Suite 2400, Chicago, Illinois 60602; 800-621-7440 (toll-free); http://www.ncahlc.org).
Applying	Argosy University, Hawai'i, accepts students year-round on a rolling admissions basis, depending on availability of required courses. Applications for admission are available online or by contacting the campus.
Correspondence and Information	Argosy University, Hawai'i 400 ASB Tower 1001 Bishop Street Honolulu, Hawaii 96813 Phone: 808-536-5555 888-323-2777 (toll-free) Fax: 808-536-5505 E-mail: auadmissions@argosy.edu Web site: http://www.argosy.edu/hawaii

Argosy University, Hawai'i

THE FACULTY

The Argosy University faculty is comprised of working professionals who are eager to help students succeed. Members bring real-world experience and the latest practice innovations to the academic setting. The diverse faculty members of the College of Psychology and Behavioral Sciences are widely recognized for contributions to the field. Many are published scholars, and most hold doctoral degrees. They are committed to providing a substantive education that combines comprehensive knowledge with critical skills and practical workplace relevance. Above all, faculty members are committed to their students' personal and professional development.

ARGOSY UNIVERSITY, INLAND EMPIRE

College of Psychology and Behavioral Sciences

ARGOSY UNIVERSITY.

Programs of Study

Argosy University, Inland Empire, offers the Master of Arts (M.A.) degree in clinical psychology/marriage and family therapy, counseling psychology/marriage and family therapy, forensic psychology, and industrial organizational psychology; and the Doctor of Education (Ed.D.) degree in counseling psychology and in organizational leadership. Students completing a program may wish to become licensed professionals. Argosy University, Inland Empire does not guarantee third-party certification/licensure. Outside agencies control the requirements for taking and passing certification/licensing exams and are subject to change without notice to Argosy University, Inland Empire.

The M.A. in Clinical Psychology/Marriage and Family Therapy program is designed for students who wish to pursue the clinical psychology track while receiving graduate-level training in the core curricular areas, including supervised clinical practice, required for licensure as a marriage and family therapist in California. Licensing requirements differ from state to state, so students should verify the current licensing requirements of the state in which they plan to become licensed. The MA in Clinical Psychology/Marriage and Family Therapy program emphasizes a practitioner-oriented philosophy, and integrates applied theory and field experience.

The M.A. in Counseling Psychology/Marriage and Family Therapy program prepares students to practice and pursue licensure in California as Marriage and Family Therapists (MFT). Students are provided with an educational program that has all the necessary theoretical and practical elements designed to allow them to be effective members of a mental health team. The program introduces students to skills that integrate individual and group theoretical foundations of counseling psychology into appropriate client interaction and intervention skills.

The M.A. in Forensic Psychology program is designed to educate and train individuals who are currently working, or wish to work, in fields that utilize the study and practice of forensic psychology. Curriculum provides for an understanding of theory, training, and practice of forensic psychology. It emphasizes the development of students who are committed to the ethical provision of quality services to diverse clients and organizations. The program maintains policies and delivery formats suitable for working adults. The program provides coursework in forensic psychology for application to law enforcement, legal and organizational consultation, and program analysis.

The M.A. in Industrial Organizational Psychology program is designed to apply the knowledge of industrial organizational psychology to issues involving individuals and groups in organizational and work settings. This program prepares students for careers in areas such as compensation, training, data analysis, consultation, statistical decision-making, organizational development, leadership, and human resource management positions. The curriculum is competency-based, focusing on the outcomes of training and on the knowledge, skills, and behavior necessary to function as a master's-level professional in industrial organizational psychology. This is an interdisciplinary program that combines the expertise of the faculty in the College of Psychology and Behavioral Sciences and the College of Business.

The Ed.D. in Counseling Psychology program embraces a range of relevant theory and techniques applicable in the three major areas of counseling psychology: (a) the remedial (assisting in remedying problems in living); (b) the preventive (anticipating, circumventing, and forestalling difficulties that may arise in the future); and (c) the educative and developmental (discovering and developing potentialities). That is (a) the focus is on normal individuals, and developmental life stages challenges; (b) a focus on assets, strengths, and positive mental health; (c) an emphasis on relatively brief interventions; and (d) an emphasis on context, sociocultural/political influences, diversity, and person-environment interactions rather than exclusive emphasis on the individual.

The Ed.D. in Organizational Leadership program is designed to meet the special requirements of working professionals who wish to develop their knowledge and skills to handle the changing needs of modern organizations. The program is designed to enable working professionals to pursue their personal and professional goals through the completion of a graduate program. It focuses on the qualities of transformational leadership, not just managerial attributes. This approach enables the faculty members to dedicate themselves to preparing students to lead complex organizations faced with an abundance of strategic challenges, such as increasing globalization, changing economies, societal shifts, and individual-organizational relationships. It is the premise of the program that leaders prepared in this manner can be visionaries and innovators, leading viable organizations capable of meeting the challenges of the future.

Research Facilities

Argosy University libraries provide curriculum support and educational resources, including current text materials, diagnostic training documents, reference materials and databases, journals and dissertations, and major and current titles in program areas. There is an online public-access catalog of library resources available throughout the Argosy University system. Students have remote access to the campus library database, enabling them to study and conduct research at home. Academic databases offer dissertation abstracts, academic journals, and professional periodicals. All library computers are Internet accessible. Software applications include Word, Excel, PowerPoint, SPSS, and various test-scoring programs.

Financial Aid

Financial aid is available to those who qualify. Argosy University, Inland Empire, offers access to federal and state aid programs, merit-based awards, grants, loans, and a work-study program. As a first step, students should complete the Free Application for Federal Student Aid (FAFSA). Prospective students can apply electronically at http://www.fafsa.ed.gov or at the campus.

Cost of Study

Tuition varies by program. Students should contact Argosy University, Inland Empire, for tuition information.

Living and Housing Costs

Students typically live in apartments in the San Bernardino metropolitan area. Living expenses vary according to each student's preferred standard of living, housing, and transportation. The University does not offer or operate student housing. Most of the students are full-time working professionals who live within driving distance of the campus. Several nearby hotels offer special rates for those who commute from long distances. The Admissions Department also maintains a list of housing options, including contact information for University students who wish to share housing. For more information, students should contact the Admissions Department.

Student Group

Admission to Argosy University, Inland Empire, is selective to ensure a dynamic and engaged student body. The University encourages diversity in academic and employment backgrounds and promotes integration of the student body into professional life through established connections with local and national professional associations. Argosy University offers a professionally oriented education with rich opportunities to gain practical experience in class, field placements, and internships. Full-time students and working professionals gain the extensive knowledge and range of skills necessary for effective performance in their chosen field.

Student Outcomes

Students can register with the University's online career-services system and use select services from a distance, such as degree-specific career e-mail lists, national job posts, and virtual job fairs. Students should contact the University for more information.

Location

Argosy University, Inland Empire, is conveniently located in the Hospitality Lane section of San Bernardino, California. The facility features classrooms, computer labs, a resource center with Internet access, a student lounge, staff and faculty offices, and proximity to the region's many cultural and recreational attractions. The University provides a supportive educational environment with convenient class options that enable students to earn a degree while fulfilling other life responsibilities. All of the programs are thoroughly oriented to the real working world. Argosy University focuses on developing technical proficiency in each student's field as well as an overall professional career approach.

The University

Argosy University is a private institution with nineteen locations across the nation. Argosy University, Inland Empire, provides a career resources office, an academic resources center, and extensive information access for research. It offers the resources of a large university plus the friendliness and personal attention of a small campus.

The innovative programs feature dynamic, relevant, and practical curricula delivered in flexible class formats. Students enjoy scheduling options that make it easier to fit school into their busy lives, choosing from day and evening courses, on campus or online. Many students find a combination of class formats to be an ideal way of continuing their education while meeting family and professional demands.

Argosy University is accredited by the Higher Learning Commission and is a member of the North Central Association (30 North LaSalle Street, Suite 2400, Chicago, Illinois 60602; 800-621-7440 (toll-free); http://www.ncahlc.org).

Applying

Argosy University, Inland Empire, accepts students year-round on a rolling admissions basis, depending on availability of required courses. Applications for admission are available online or by contacting the campus.

Correspondence and Information

Argosy University, Inland Empire
636 East Brier Drive, Suite 120
San Bernardino, California 92408
Phone: 909-915-3800
      866-217-9075 (toll-free)
Fax: 909-915-3810
E-mail: auadmissions@argosy.edu
Web site: http://www.argosy.edu/inlandempire

Argosy University, Inland Empire

THE FACULTY

The Argosy University faculty is comprised of working professionals who are eager to help students succeed. Members bring real-world experience and the latest practice innovations to the academic setting. The diverse faculty members of the College of Psychology and Behavioral Sciences are widely recognized for contributions to the field. Many are published scholars, and most hold doctoral degrees. They are committed to providing a substantive education that combines comprehensive knowledge with critical skills and practical workplace relevance. Above all, faculty members are committed to their students' personal and professional development.

ARGOSY UNIVERSITY.

ARGOSY UNIVERSITY, LOS ANGELES

College of Psychology and Behavioral Sciences

Programs of Study
Argosy University, Los Angeles, offers the Master of Arts (M.A.) degree in clinical psychology/marriage and family therapy, counseling psychology/marriage and family therapy, and forensic psychology; and the Doctor of Education (Ed.D.) degrees in counseling psychology and organizational leadership. Students completing a program may wish to become licensed professionals. Argosy University, Los Angeles does not guarantee third-party certification/licensure. Outside agencies control the requirements for taking and passing certification/licensing exams and are subject to change without notice to Argosy University, Los Angeles.

The M.A. in Clinical Psychology/Marriage and Family Therapy program is designed for students who wish to pursue the clinical psychology track while receiving graduate-level training in the core curricular areas, including supervised clinical practice, required for licensure as a marriage and family therapist in California. Licensing requirements differ from state to state, so students should verify the current licensing requirements of the state in which they plan to become licensed. This program emphasizes a practitioner-oriented philosophy, and integrates applied theory and field experience.

The M.A. in Counseling Psychology/Marriage and Family Therapy program is designed to prepare students to practice and pursue licensure in California as Marriage and Family Therapists (MFT). Students receive an educational program with all the necessary theoretical and practical elements designed to allow them to be effective members of a mental health team. The program introduces students to skills that integrate individual and group theoretical foundations of counseling psychology into appropriate client interaction and intervention skills.

The M.A. in Forensic Psychology program is designed to educate and train individuals who are currently working, or wish to work, in fields that utilize the study and practice of forensic psychology. Curriculum provides for an understanding of theory, training, and practice of forensic psychology. It emphasizes the development of students who are committed to the ethical provision of quality services to diverse clients and organizations. The program maintains policies and delivery formats suitable for working adults. The program provides course work in forensic psychology for application to law enforcement, legal and organizational consultation, and program analysis.

The Ed.D. in Counseling Psychology program embraces a range of relevant theory and techniques applicable in the three major areas of counseling psychology: (a) the remedial (assisting in remedying problems in living); (b) the preventive (anticipating, circumventing, and forestalling difficulties that may arise in the future); and (c) the educative and developmental (discovering and developing potentialities). That is (a) the focus is on normal individuals, and developmental life stages challenges; (b) a focus on assets, strengths, and positive mental health; (c) an emphasis on relatively brief interventions; and (d) an emphasis on context, sociocultural/political influences, diversity, and person-environment interactions rather than exclusive emphasis on the individual.

The Ed.D. in Organizational Leadership program is designed to meet the special requirements of working professionals who wish to develop their knowledge and skills to handle the changing needs of modern organizations. The program is designed to enable working professionals to pursue their personal and professional goals through the completion of a graduate program. The program focuses on the qualities of transformational leadership, not just managerial attributes. This approach enables the faculty members to dedicate themselves to preparing students to lead complex organizations faced with an abundance of strategic challenges, such as increasing globalization, changing economies, societal shifts, and individual-organizational relationships. It is the premise of the program that leaders prepared in this manner can be visionaries and innovators, leading viable organizations capable of meeting the challenges of the future.

Research Facilities
Argosy University libraries provide curriculum support and educational resources, including current text materials, diagnostic training documents, reference materials and databases, journals and dissertations, and major and current titles in program areas. There is an online public-access catalog of library resources available throughout the Argosy University system. Students have remote access to the campus library database, enabling them to study and conduct research at home. Academic databases offer dissertation abstracts, academic journals, and professional periodicals. All library computers are Internet accessible. Software applications include Word, Excel, PowerPoint, SPSS, and various test-scoring programs.

Financial Aid
Financial aid is available to those who qualify. Argosy University, Los Angeles, offers access to federal and state aid programs, merit-based awards, grants, loans, and a work-study program. As a first step, students should complete the Free Application for Federal Student Aid (FAFSA). Prospective students can apply electronically at http://www.fafsa.ed.gov or at the campus.

Cost of Study
Tuition varies by program. Students should contact Argosy University, Los Angeles, for tuition information.

Living and Housing Costs
Students typically live in apartments in the metropolitan Santa Monica area. Living expenses vary according to each student's preferred standard of living, housing, and transportation. The University does not offer or operate student housing. Most Argosy University students are full-time working professionals who live within driving distance of the campus. Several nearby hotels offer special rates for those who commute from long distances. The Admissions Department also maintains a list of housing options, including contact information for University students who wish to share housing. For more information, students should contact the Admissions Department.

Student Group
Admission to Argosy University, Los Angeles, is selective to ensure a dynamic and engaged student body. The University encourages diversity in academic and employment backgrounds and promotes integration of the student body into professional life through established connections with local and national professional associations. Argosy University offers a professionally oriented education with rich opportunities to gain practical experience in class, field placements, and internships. Full-time students and working professionals gain the extensive knowledge and range of skills necessary for effective performance in their chosen fields.

Student Outcomes
Students can register with the University's online career-services system and use select services from a distance, such as degree-specific career e-mail lists, national job posts, and virtual job fairs. Students should contact the University for more information.

Location
Argosy University, Los Angeles, is located in the beach community of Santa Monica, California. This sophisticated urban environment is coupled with the charm of the famous Santa Monica Pier, beautiful beaches, and farmer's markets. On campus, the main facility covers approximately 107,000 square feet and houses classrooms, laboratories, offices, a student lounge, and a library. Many educational institutions and agencies in the area provide comprehensive opportunities for student training. The business environment in Santa Monica includes a broad array of companies, including a proliferation of entertainment, high tech, and software firms. Principal employers in the area include Yahoo, MTV Networks, RAND Corporation, and Symantec Corporation.

The University
Argosy University is a private institution with nineteen locations across the nation. Argosy University, Los Angeles, provides students with a career resources office, an academic resources center, and extensive information access for research. It offers the resources of a large university plus the friendliness and personal attention of a small campus.

The innovative programs feature dynamic, relevant, and practical curricula delivered in flexible class formats. Students enjoy scheduling options that make it easier to fit school into their busy lives, choosing from day and evening courses, on campus or online. Many students find a combination of class formats to be an ideal way of continuing their education while meeting family and professional demands.

Argosy University is accredited by the Higher Learning Commission and is a member of the North Central Association (30 North LaSalle Street, Suite 2400, Chicago, Illinois 60602; 800-621-7440 (toll-free); http://www.ncahlc.org).

Applying
Argosy University, Los Angeles, accepts students year-round on a rolling admissions basis, depending on availability of required courses. Applications for admission are available online or by contacting the campus.

Correspondence and Information
Argosy University, Los Angeles
2950 31st Street
Santa Monica, California 90405
Phone: 310-866-4000
     866-505-0332 (toll-free)
Fax: 310-399-1804
E-mail: auadmissions@argosy.edu
Web site: http://www.argosy.edu/losangeles

Argosy University, Los Angeles

THE FACULTY

The Argosy University faculty is comprised of working professionals who are eager to help students succeed. Members bring real-world experience and the latest practice innovations to the academic setting. The diverse faculty members of the College of Psychology and Behavioral Sciences are is widely recognized for contributions to the field. Many are published scholars, and most hold doctoral degrees. They are committed to providing a substantive education that combines comprehensive knowledge with critical skills and practical workplace relevance. Above all, faculty members are committed to their students' personal and professional development.

ARGOSY UNIVERSITY.

ARGOSY UNIVERSITY, NASHVILLE

College of Psychology and Behavioral Sciences

Programs of Study

Argosy University, Nashville, offers the Master of Arts (M.A.) degree in mental health counseling and the Doctor of Education (Ed.D.) degree in counselor education and supervision. Students completing a program may wish to become licensed professionals. Argosy University, Nashville does not guarantee third-party certification/licensure. Outside agencies control the requirements for taking and passing certification/licensing exams and are subject to change without notice to Argosy University, Nashville.

The M.A. in Mental Health Counseling is a 60-credit-hour program designed to provide students with a solid foundation for the practice of mental health counseling. The program's curriculum integrates the theoretical and conceptual foundations of mental health counseling with training in appropriate client intervention and therapy skills. The program emphasizes the development of attitudes, knowledge, and skills that are essential for mental health counselors who are committed to the ethical provision of quality services. Students completing this program meet the academic requirements toward licensure as Licensed Professional Counselors (LPCs) in Tennessee.

The Ed.D. in Counselor Education and Supervision program aligns with the master's-level counselor education programs in order to encourage entry-level counseling students to work toward becoming doctoral-level advanced practitioners, educators, and supervisors. The program is designed to prepare counselors for a variety of settings by providing the advanced skills and knowledge necessary to provide leadership and advocacy, as well as serve in supervisory, training, and teaching positions in the counseling profession.

Research Facilities

Argosy University libraries provide curriculum support and educational resources, including current text materials, diagnostic training documents, reference materials and databases, journals and dissertations, and major and current titles in program areas. There is an online public-access catalog of library resources available throughout the Argosy University system. Students have remote access to the campus library database, enabling them to study and conduct research at home. Academic databases offer dissertation abstracts, academic journals, and professional periodicals. All library computers are Internet accessible. Software applications include Word, Excel, PowerPoint, SPSS, and various test-scoring programs.

Financial Aid

Financial aid is available to those who qualify. Argosy University, Nashville, offers access to federal and state aid programs, merit-based awards, grants, loans, and a work-study program. As a first step, students should complete the Free Application for Federal Student Aid (FAFSA). Prospective students can apply electronically at http://www.fafsa.ed.gov or at the campus.

Cost of Study

Tuition varies by program. Students should contact Argosy University, Nashville, for tuition information.

Living and Housing Costs

Students typically live in apartments in the metropolitan Nashville area. Living expenses vary according to each student's preferred standard of living, housing, and transportation. The University does not offer or operate student housing. Most of the students are full-time working professionals who live within driving distance of the campus. Several nearby hotels offer special rates for those who commute from long distances. The Admissions Department also maintains a list of housing options, including contact information for University students who wish to share housing. For more information, students should contact the Admissions Department.

Student Group

Admission to Argosy University, Nashville, is selective to ensure a dynamic and engaged student body. The University encourages diversity in academic and employment backgrounds and promotes integration of the student body into professional life through established connections with local and national professional associations. Argosy University offers a professionally oriented education with rich opportunities to gain practical experience in class, field placements, and internships. Full-time students and working professionals gain the extensive knowledge and range of skills necessary for effective performance in their chosen field.

Student Outcomes

Students can register with the University's online career-services system and use select services from a distance, such as degree-specific career e-mail lists, national job posts, and virtual job fairs. Students should contact the University for more information.

Location

Argosy University, Nashville, is located at 100 Centerview Drive in Nashville, Tennessee. This city offers a variety of recreational activities, including the ballet and symphony, the newly established Frist Museum of Art, and professional sports. Nashville is known as Music City, USA, and is home to the Country Music Hall of Fame. The business environment includes companies such as Moses Cone Health Systems, Inc., and Novant Health, Inc.

The University

Argosy University is a private institution with nineteen locations across the nation. Argosy University, Nashville, provides a career resources office, an academic resources center, and extensive information access for research. It offers the resources of a large university plus the friendliness and personal attention of a small campus.

The innovative programs feature dynamic, relevant, and practical curricula delivered in flexible class formats. Students enjoy scheduling options that make it easier to fit school into their busy lives, choosing from day and evening courses, on campus or online. Many students find a combination of class formats to be an ideal way of continuing their education while meeting family and professional demands.

Argosy University, Nashville, is authorized by the Tennessee Higher Education Commission (Parkway Towers, Suite 1900, 404 James Robertson Parkway, Nashville, Tennessee 37243; 615-741-3605). This authorization must be renewed each year and is based on an evaluation against minimum standards concerning quality of education, ethical business practices, health and safety, and fiscal responsibility. Argosy University is accredited by the Higher Learning Commission and is a member of the North Central Association (30 North LaSalle Street, Suite 2400, Chicago, Illinois 60602; 800-621-7440 (toll-free); http://www.ncahlc.org).

Applying

Argosy University, Nashville, accepts students year-round on a rolling admissions basis, depending on availability of required courses. Applications for admission are available online or by contacting the campus.

Correspondence and Information

Argosy University, Nashville
100 Centerview Drive, Suite 225
Nashville, Tennessee 37214
Phone: 615-525-2800
      866-833-6598 (toll-free)
Fax: 615-525-2900
E-mail: auadmissions@argosy.edu
Web site: http://www. argosy.edu/nashville

Argosy University, Nashville

THE FACULTY

The Argosy University faculty is comprised of working professionals who are eager to help students succeed. Members bring real-world experience and the latest practice innovations to the academic setting. The diverse faculty members of the College of Psychology and Behavioral Sciences are widely recognized for contributions to the field. Many are published scholars, and most hold doctoral degrees. They are committed to providing a substantive education that combines comprehensive knowledge with critical skills and practical workplace relevance. Above all, faculty members are committed to their students' personal and professional development.

ARGOSY UNIVERSITY.

ARGOSY UNIVERSITY, ORANGE COUNTY

College of Psychology and Behavioral Sciences

Programs of Study

Argosy University, Orange County, offers the Master of Arts (M.A.) degree in clinical psychology/marriage and family therapy, counseling psychology/marriage and family therapy, forensic psychology, and sport-exercise psychology; the Doctor of Education (Ed.D.) degree in counseling psychology and organizational leadership; and the Doctor of Psychology (Psy.D.) degree in clinical psychology. Students completing a program may wish to become licensed professionals. Argosy University, Orange County does not guarantee third-party certification/licensure. Outside agencies control the requirements for taking and passing certification/licensing exams and are subject to change without notice to Argosy University, Orange County.

The M.A. in Clinical Psychology/Marriage and Family Therapy program is designed for students who wish to pursue the clinical psychology track while receiving graduate-level training in the core curricular areas, including supervised clinical practice, required for licensure as a marriage and family therapist in California. Licensing requirements differ from state to state, so students should verify the current licensing requirements of the state in which they plan to become licensed. The program emphasizes a practitioner-oriented philosophy, and integrates applied theory and field experience.

The M.A. in Counseling Psychology/Marriage and Family Therapy program is designed to prepare students to practice and pursue licensure in California as Marriage and Family Therapists (MFT). Students receive an educational program with all the necessary theoretical and practical elements that will allow them to be effective members of a mental health team. The program introduces students to skills that integrate individual and group theoretical foundations of counseling psychology into appropriate client interaction and intervention skills.

The M.A. in Forensic Psychology program is designed to educate and train individuals who are currently working, or wish to work, in fields that utilize the study and practice of forensic psychology. Curriculum provides for an understanding of theory, training, and practice of forensic psychology. It emphasizes the development of students who are committed to the ethical provision of quality services to diverse clients and organizations. The program maintains policies and delivery formats suitable for working adults. The program provides course work in forensic psychology for application to law enforcement, legal and organizational consultation, and program analysis.

The M.A. in Sport-Exercise Psychology program is designed to educate and train capable and ethical performance-enhancement specialists. This two-year degree is intended to meet the needs of students seeking employment in a variety of settings, including private practice, athletic departments, coaching, exercise/health, and education, as well as those planning to ultimately pursue their doctorate. The program provides a thorough grounding in both theory and practice. Based on the educational requirements outlined by the Association for the Advancement of Applied Sport Psychology (AAASP), the curriculum provides a foundation in applied sport psychology, an understanding of normal and abnormal psychological functioning, and a knowledge base in the physiological, motor, and psychosocial aspects of sport behavior. A supervised practicum provides experience in working directly with athletes or performers in applied settings.

The Ed.D. in Counseling Psychology program embraces a range of relevant theory and techniques applicable in the three major areas of counseling psychology: (a) the remedial (assisting in remedying problems in living); (b) the preventive (anticipating, circumventing, and forestalling difficulties that may arise in the future); and (c) the educative and developmental (discovering and developing potentialities). That is (a) the focus is on normal individuals, and developmental life stages challenges; (b) a focus on assets, strengths, and positive mental health; (c) an emphasis on relatively brief interventions; and (d) an emphasis on context, sociocultural/political influences, diversity, and person-environment interactions rather than exclusive emphasis on the individual.

The Ed.D. in Organizational Leadership program is designed to meet the special requirements of working professionals who wish to develop their knowledge and skills to handle the changing needs of modern organizations. The program is designed to enable working professionals to pursue their personal and professional goals through the completion of a graduate program. It focuses on the qualities of transformational leadership, not just managerial attributes. This approach enables the faculty members to dedicate themselves to preparing students to lead complex organizations faced with an abundance of strategic challenges, such as increasing globalization, changing economies, societal shifts, and individual-organizational relationships. It is the premise of the program that leaders prepared in this manner can be visionaries and innovators, leading viable organizations capable of meeting the challenges of the future.

The Psy.D. in Clinical Psychology program is designed to educate and train students so that they may eventually be able to function effectively as clinical psychologists. To ensure that students are prepared adequately, the curriculum provides for the meaningful integration of theory, training, and practice. This program emphasizes the development of attitudes, knowledge, and skills essential in the formation of professional psychologists who are committed to the ethical provision of quality services.

Research Facilities

Argosy University libraries provide curriculum support and educational resources, including current text materials, diagnostic training documents, reference materials and databases, journals and dissertations, and major and current titles in program areas. There is an online public-access catalog of library resources available throughout the Argosy University system. Students have remote access to the campus library database, enabling them to study and conduct research at home. Academic databases offer dissertation abstracts, academic journals, and professional periodicals. All library computers are Internet accessible. Software applications include Word, Excel, PowerPoint, SPSS, and various test-scoring programs.

Financial Aid

Financial aid is available to those who qualify. Argosy University, Orange County, offers access to federal and state aid programs, merit-based awards, grants, loans, and a work-study program. As a first step, students should complete the Free Application for Federal Student Aid (FAFSA). Prospective students can apply electronically at http://www.fafsa.ed.gov or at the campus.

Cost of Study

Tuition varies by program. Students should contact Argosy University, Orange County, for tuition information.

Living and Housing Costs

Students typically live in apartments in the Santa Ana metropolitan area. Living expenses vary according to each student's preferred standard of living, housing, and transportation. The University does not offer or operate student housing. Most Argosy University students are full-time working professionals who live within driving distance of the campus. Several nearby hotels offer special rates for those who commute from long distances. The Admissions Department also maintains a list of housing options, including contact information for University students who wish to share housing. For more information, students should contact the Admissions Department.

Student Group

Admission to Argosy University, Orange County, is selective to ensure a dynamic and engaged student body. The University encourages diversity in academic and employment backgrounds and promotes integration of the student body into professional life through established connections with local and national professional associations. Argosy University offers a professionally oriented education with rich opportunities to gain practical experience in class, field placements, and internships. Full-time students and working professionals gain the extensive knowledge and range of skills necessary for effective performance in their chosen field.

Student Outcomes

Students can register with Argosy University's online career-services system and use select services from a distance, such as degree-specific career e-mail lists, national job posts, and virtual job fairs. Students should contact the University for more information.

Location

Argosy University, Orange County, attracts students from Southern California as well as around the country and the world. Orange County features a temperate climate, sunny beaches, and a host of cultural and entertainment options. The campus is located approximately 30 miles south of downtown Los Angeles, 90 miles north of San Diego, and just minutes from one of the many freeways that connect the Southern California basin. Regional parks and preserved lands provide opportunities for hiking, biking, riding, and other recreational activities. Whether it's ultra-chic Newport Beach, artsy Laguna Beach, or unspoiled Catalina Island, Orange County's oceanside personalities are as varied as the people who visit the area.

Orange County's business environment includes a broad array of companies. The area's largest employers include Ingram Micro Inc., Orange County Register, ITT Industries, and OneSource.

The University

Argosy University is a private institution with nineteen locations across the nation. Argosy University, Orange County, provides a career resources office, an academic resources center, and extensive information access for research. It offers the resources of a large university plus the friendliness and personal attention of a small campus. The innovative programs feature dynamic, relevant, and practical curricula delivered in flexible class formats. Students enjoy scheduling options that make it easier to fit school into their busy lives, choosing from day and evening courses, on campus or online. Many students find a combination of class formats to be an ideal way of continuing their education while meeting family and professional demands.

Argosy University is accredited by the Higher Learning Commission and is a member of the North Central Association (30 North LaSalle Street, Suite 2400, Chicago, Illinois 60602; 800-621-7440 (toll-free); http://www.ncahlc.org).

Applying

Argosy University, Orange County, accepts students year-round on a rolling admissions basis, depending on availability of required courses. Applications for admission are available online or by contacting the campus.

Correspondence and Information

Argosy University, Orange County
601 South Lewis Street
Orange, California 92868
Phone: 714-620-3700
        800-716-9598 (toll-free)
Fax: 714-620-3800
E-mail: auadmissions@argosy.edu
Web site: http://www.argosy.edu/orangecounty/

Argosy University, Orange County

THE FACULTY

The Argosy University faculty is comprised of working professionals who are eager to help students succeed. Members bring real-world experience and the latest practice innovations to the academic setting. The diverse faculty members of the College of Psychology and Behavioral Sciences are widely recognized for contributions to the field. Many are published scholars, and most hold doctoral degrees. They are committed to providing a substantive education that combines comprehensive knowledge with critical skills and practical workplace relevance. Above all, faculty members are committed to their students' personal and professional development.

ARGOSY UNIVERSITY.

ARGOSY UNIVERSITY, PHOENIX

College of Psychology and Behavioral Sciences

Programs of Study

Argosy University, Phoenix, offers the Master of Arts (M.A.) degree in clinical psychology, forensic psychology, mental health counseling, school psychology, sport-exercise psychology, and industrial organizational psychology; the Doctor of Education (Ed.D.) degree in counseling psychology; and the Doctor of Psychology (Psy.D.) degree in clinical psychology or school psychology. Students completing a program may wish to become licensed. Argosy University, Phoenix does not guarantee third-party certification/licensure. Outside agencies control the requirements for taking and passing certification/licensing exams and are subject to change without notice to Argosy University, Phoenix.

The M.A. in Clinical Psychology program is designed to educate and train students to enter professional careers as master's-level practitioners. Students receive an educational program with all the necessary theoretical and clinical elements designed to allow them to be effective members of a mental health team. The program introduces students to basic clinical skills that integrate individual and group theoretical foundations of applied psychology into appropriate client interaction and intervention skills. Additionally, it offers comprehensive preparation for those considering application to the Doctor of Psychology in Clinical Psychology program.

The M.A. in Forensic Psychology program is designed to educate and train individuals who are currently working, or wish to work, in fields that utilize the study and practice of forensic psychology. Curriculum is designed to provide for an understanding of theory, training, and practice of forensic psychology. It emphasizes the development of students who are committed to the ethical provision of quality services to diverse clients and organizations. The program maintains policies and delivery formats suitable for working adults. The program provides course work in forensic psychology for application to law enforcement, legal and organizational consultation, and program analysis.

The M.A. in Mental Health Counseling program is designed to provide students with a sound foundation for eventual practice of mental health counseling. The program introduces students to basic counseling skills that integrate individual and group theoretical foundations of professional counseling into appropriate client interaction and intervention skills. The program emphasizes the development of attitudes, knowledge, and skills essential in the formation of professional counselors who are committed to the ethical provision of quality services.

The M.A. in School Psychology program is dedicated to producing ethical, responsible, and competent school psychologists who can serve effectively in a number of professional roles. During graduate training, students develop core competencies in psychological assessment, intervention, and consultation/education, as well as cultural and individual diversity. Graduates of the program may be eligible for department of education certification and will be prepared for employment as school psychologists. The program is designed to prepare students to become Nationally Certified School Psychologists (NCSPs) in accordance with criteria developed by the National Association of School Psychologists.

The M.A. in Sport-Exercise Psychology program is designed to educate and train capable and ethical performance-enhancement specialists. This two-year degree is intended to meet the needs of students seeking employment in a variety of settings, including private practice, athletic departments, coaching, exercise/health, and education, as well as those planning to ultimately pursue their doctorate. The goals of the program include developing student competencies in the following areas: theoretical foundations, helping relationships, individual and group skills, normal and abnormal behavior, sport sciences, research and evaluation, diversity, and professional identity.

The M.A. in Industrial Organizational Psychology program is designed to apply the knowledge of industrial organizational psychology to issues involving individuals and groups in organizational and work settings. This program prepares students for careers in areas such as compensation, training, data analysis, consultation, statistical decision-making, organizational development, leadership, and human resource management positions. The curriculum is competency-based, focusing on the outcomes of training and on the knowledge, skills, and behavior necessary to function as a master's-level professional in industrial organizational psychology. This is an interdisciplinary program that combines the expertise of the faculty in the College of Psychology and Behavioral Sciences and the College of Business.

The Ed.D. in Counseling Psychology program emphasizes the development of attitudes, knowledge, and skills essential in the formation of professionals committed to the ethical provision of quality services. To ensure that students are prepared adequately, the curriculum provides for the meaningful integration of theory, training, and practice. Specific objectives of the program include training practitioners capable of delivering effective treatment to diverse populations of clients in need of such treatment; developing counseling psychologists who understand the biological, psychological, and sociological bases of human functioning; training practitioners who are capable of exercising leadership both in the health care delivery system and in the training of mental health professionals; preparing counseling psychologists capable of expanding their role within society; and educating practitioners capable of working with other disciplines as part of a professional team.

The Psy.D. in Clinical Psychology program has been designed to educate and train students to function effectively as clinical psychologists. To ensure that students are adequately prepared, the curriculum provides for the meaningful integration of theory, training, and practice. The program emphasizes the development of attitudes, knowledge, and skills essential to the training of clinical psychologists committed to the ethical provision of quality services

The Psy.D. in School Psychology program is designed to prepare students to meet the criteria for state certification as school psychologists, and to prepare them to become nationally certified school psychologists in accordance with criteria developed by the National Association of School Psychologists (NASP). The program emphasizes the development of attitudes, knowledge, and skills essential to school psychologists who are committed to the ethical provision of quality services.

Research Facilities

Argosy University libraries provide curriculum support and educational resources, including current text materials, diagnostic training documents, reference materials and databases, journals and dissertations, and major and current titles in program areas. There is an online public-access catalog of library resources available throughout the Argosy University system. Students have remote access to the campus library database, enabling them to study and conduct research at home. Academic databases offer dissertation abstracts, academic journals, and professional periodicals. All library computers are Internet accessible. Software applications include Word, Excel, PowerPoint, SPSS, and various test-scoring programs.

Financial Aid

Financial aid is available to those who qualify. Argosy University, Phoenix, offers access to federal and state aid programs, merit-based awards, grants, loans, and a work-study program. As a first step, students should complete the Free Application for Federal Student Aid (FAFSA). Prospective students can apply electronically at http://www.fafsa.ed.gov or at the campus.

Cost of Study

Tuition varies by program. Students should contact Argosy University, Phoenix, for tuition information.

Living and Housing Costs

Students typically live in apartments in the metropolitan Phoenix area. Living expenses vary according to each student's preferred standard of living, housing, and transportation. The University does not offer or operate student housing. Most Argosy University students are full-time working professionals who live within driving distance of the campus. Several nearby hotels offer special rates for those who commute from long distances. The Admissions Department also maintains a list of housing options, including contact information for University students who wish to share housing. For more information, students should contact the Admissions Department.

Student Group

Admission to Argosy University, Phoenix, is selective to ensure a dynamic and engaged student body. The University encourages diversity in academic and employment backgrounds and promotes integration of the student body into professional life through established connections with local and national professional associations. Argosy University offers a professionally oriented education with rich opportunities to gain practical experience in class, field placements, and internships. Full-time students and working professionals gain the extensive knowledge and range of skills necessary for effective performance in their chosen field.

Student Outcomes

Students can register with Argosy University's online career-services system and use select services from a distance, such as degree-specific career e-mail lists, national job posts, and virtual job fairs. Students should contact the University for more information.

Location

Argosy University, Phoenix, offers a quality education in an intimate, small-group setting. The campus is located near I-17, close to shops, restaurants, and recreational areas. Phoenix is home to several major league sports teams, and the city offers an array of cultural activities ranging from opera and theatre to science museums. The multi-cultural environment of Arizona, coupled with Argosy University's professional training affiliations throughout the state, creates an exciting opportunity for students to work with urban, rural, and culturally diverse populations.

The business environment in Phoenix includes a wide variety of companies such as Intel and Go Daddy Group, an Internet company. Wells Fargo, Home Depot, Lowe's, and Wal-Mart also represent some of the area's largest employers.

The University

Argosy University is a private institution with nineteen locations across the nation. Argosy University, Phoenix, provides a career resources office, an academic resources center, and extensive information access for research. It offers the resources of a large university plus the friendliness and personal attention of a small campus. The innovative programs feature dynamic, relevant, and practical curricula delivered in flexible class formats. Students enjoy scheduling options that make it easier to fit school into their busy lives, choosing from day and evening courses, on campus or online. Many students find a combination of class formats to be an ideal way of continuing their education while meeting family and professional demands.

Argosy University is accredited by the Higher Learning Commission and is a member of the North Central Association (30 North LaSalle Street, Suite 2400, Chicago, Illinois 60602; 800-621-7440 (toll-free); http://www.ncahlc.org).

Applying

Argosy University, Phoenix, accepts students year-round on a rolling admissions basis, depending on availability of required courses. Applications for admission are available online or by contacting the campus.

Correspondence and Information

Argosy University, Phoenix
2233 West Dunlap Avenue
Phoenix, Arizona 85021

Phone: 602-216-2600
866-216-2777 (toll-free)
Fax: 602-216-2601
E-mail: auadmissions@argosy.edu
Web site: http://www.argosy.edu/phoenix/

Argosy University, Phoenix

THE FACULTY

The Argosy University faculty is comprised of working professionals who are eager to help students succeed. Members bring real-world experience and the latest practice innovations to the academic setting. The diverse faculty members of the College of Psychology and Behavioral Sciences are widely recognized for contributions to the field. Many are published scholars, and most hold doctoral degrees. They are committed to providing a substantive education that combines comprehensive knowledge with critical skills and practical workplace relevance. Above all, faculty members are committed to their students' personal and professional development.

ARGOSY UNIVERSITY.

ARGOSY UNIVERSITY, SALT LAKE CITY

College of Psychology and Behavioral Sciences

Programs of Study
Argosy University, Salt Lake City, offers the Master of Arts (M.A.) degree in marriage and family therapy, forensic psychology, and mental health counseling; and the Doctor of Education (Ed.D.) degree in counseling psychology. Students completing a program may wish to become licensed professionals. Argosy University, Salt Lake City does not guarantee third-party certification/licensure. Outside agencies control the requirements for taking and passing certification/licensing exams and are subject to change without notice to Argosy University, Salt Lake City.

The M.A. in Marriage and Family Therapy program recognizes the need to provide marriage and family therapists with the extensive knowledge and range of skills necessary to function effectively in their profession. The program introduces students to basic skills that integrate systemic theoretical foundations of marriage and family therapy into appropriate client interaction and intervention skills. It emphasizes the development of attitudes, knowledge, and skills essential in the formation of marriage and family therapists who are committed to the ethical provision of quality services. The program has been developed by the school faculty members to provide working students with the opportunity to pursue personal and professional goals through completion of a master's program.

The M.A. in Forensic Psychology program is designed to educate and train individuals who are currently working, or wish to work, in fields that utilize the study and practice of forensic psychology. Curriculum provides for an understanding of theory, training, and practice of forensic psychology. It emphasizes the development of students committed to the ethical provision of quality services to diverse clients and organizations. The program maintains policies and delivery formats suitable for working adults. The program provides course work in forensic psychology for application to law enforcement, legal and organizational consultation, and program analysis.

The M.A. in Mental Health Counseling program is designed to provide students with a sound foundation for eventual practice of mental health counseling. The program introduces students to basic counseling skills that integrate individual and group theoretical foundations of professional counseling into appropriate client interaction and intervention skills. It emphasizes the development of attitudes, knowledge, and skills essential in the formation of professional counselors who are committed to the ethical provision of quality services.

The Ed.D. in Counseling Psychology program emphasizes the development of attitudes, knowledge, and skills essential in the formation of professionals committed to the ethical provision of quality services. To ensure that students are prepared adequately, the curriculum is designed to provide for the meaningful integration of theory, training, and practice.

Research Facilities
Argosy University libraries provide curriculum support and educational resources, including current text materials, diagnostic training documents, reference materials and databases, journals and dissertations, and major and current titles in program areas. There is an online public-access catalog of library resources available throughout the Argosy University system. Students have remote access to their campus library database, enabling them to study and conduct research at home. Academic databases offer dissertation abstracts, academic journals, and professional periodicals. All library computers are Internet accessible. Software applications include Word, Excel, PowerPoint, SPSS, and various test-scoring programs.

Financial Aid
Financial aid is available to those who qualify. Argosy University, Salt Lake City, offers access to federal and state aid programs, merit-based awards, grants, loans, and a work-study program. As a first step, students should complete the Free Application for Federal Student Aid (FAFSA). Prospective students can apply electronically at http://www.fafsa.ed.gov or at the campus.

Cost of Study
Tuition varies by program. Students should contact Argosy University, Salt Lake City, for tuition information.

Living and Housing Costs
Students typically live in apartments in the metropolitan Salt Lake City area. Living expenses vary according to each student's preferred standard of living, housing, and transportation. The University does not offer or operate student housing. Most of the students are full-time working professionals who live within driving distance of the campus. Several nearby hotels offer special rates for those who commute from long distances. The Admissions Department also maintains a list of housing options, including contact information for University students who wish to share housing. For more information, students should contact the Admissions Department.

Student Group
Admission to Argosy University, Salt Lake City, is selective to ensure a dynamic and engaged student body. The University encourages diversity in academic and employment backgrounds and promotes integration of the student body into professional life through established connections with local and national professional associations. Argosy University offers a professionally oriented education with rich opportunities to gain practical experience in class, field placements, and internships. Full-time students and working professionals gain the extensive knowledge and range of skills necessary for effective performance in their chosen field.

Student Outcomes
Students can register with Argosy University's online career-services system and use select services from a distance, such as degree-specific career e-mail lists, national job posts, and virtual job fairs. Students should contact the University for more information.

Location
Argosy University, Salt Lake City, offers a quality education in an intimate, small-group setting. Argosy University, Salt Lake City, is conveniently located in Draper, Utah, nestled in the Wasatch Mountains about 20 miles south of Salt Lake City. The area's business climate and numerous hospitals, schools, clinics, and social service agencies can provide many training opportunities for students.

The University
Argosy University is a private institution with nineteen locations across the nation. Argosy University, Salt Lake City, provides a career resources office, an academic resources center, and extensive information access for research. It offers the resources of a large university plus the friendliness and personal attention of a small campus. The innovative programs feature dynamic, relevant, and practical curricula delivered in flexible class formats. Students enjoy scheduling options that make it easier to fit school into their busy lives, choosing from day and evening courses, on campus or online. Many students find a combination of class formats to be an ideal way of continuing their education while meeting family and professional demands.

Argosy University is accredited by the Higher Learning Commission and is a member of the North Central Association (30 North LaSalle Street, Suite 2400, Chicago, Illinois 60602; 800-621-7440 (toll-free); http://www.ncahlc.org).

Applying
Argosy University, Salt Lake City, accepts students on a rolling admissions basis year-round, depending on availability of required courses. Applications for admission may be obtained online or by contacting the campus.

Correspondence and Information
Argosy University, Salt Lake City
121 Election Road, Suite 300
Draper, Utah 84020

Phone: 801-601-5000
      888-639-4756 (toll-free)
Fax: 801-601-4990
E-mail: auadmissions@argosy.edu
Web site: http://www.argosy.edu/saltlakecity

Argosy University, Salt Lake City

THE FACULTY

The Argosy University faculty is comprised of working professionals who are eager to help students succeed. Members bring real-world experience and the latest practice innovations to the academic setting. The diverse faculty members of the College of Psychology and Behavioral Sciences are widely recognized for contributions to the field. Many are published scholars, and most hold doctoral degrees. They are committed to providing a substantive education that combines comprehensive knowledge with critical skills and practical workplace relevance. Above all, faculty members are committed to their students' personal and professional development.

ARGOSY UNIVERSITY

ARGOSY UNIVERSITY, SAN DIEGO

College of Psychology and Behavioral Sciences

Programs of Study	Argosy University, San Diego, offers the Master of Arts (M.A.) degree in clinical psychology/marriage and family therapy, counseling psychology/marriage and family therapy, and forensic psychology; and the Doctor of Education (Ed.D.) degree in counseling psychology and organizational leadership. Students completing a program may wish to become licensed professionals. Argosy University, San Diego does not guarantee third-party certification/licensure. Outside agencies control the requirements for taking and passing certification/licensing exams and are subject to change without notice to Argosy University, San Diego.
	The M.A. in Clinical Psychology/Marriage and Family Therapy program is designed for students who wish to pursue the clinical psychology track while receiving graduate-level training in the core curricular areas, including supervised clinical practice, required for licensure as a marriage and family therapist in California. Licensing requirements differ from state to state, so students should verify the current licensing requirements of the state in which they plan to become licensed.
	The M.A. in Counseling Psychology/Marriage and Family Therapy program is designed to prepare students to practice and pursue licensure in California as a Marriage and Family Therapist (MFT). Students receive an educational program with all the necessary theoretical and practical elements designed to allow them to be effective members of a mental health team. The program introduces students to skills that integrate individual and group theoretical foundations of counseling psychology into appropriate client interaction and intervention skills.
	The M.A. in Forensic Psychology program is designed to educate and train individuals who are currently working, or wish to work, in fields that utilize the study and practice of forensic psychology. Curriculum provides for an understanding of theory, training, and practice of forensic psychology. It emphasizes the development of students who are committed to the ethical provision of quality services to diverse clients and organizations. The program maintains policies and delivery formats suitable for working adults. The program provides course work in forensic psychology for application to law enforcement, legal and organizational consultation, and program analysis.
	The Ed.D. in Counseling Psychology program embraces a range of relevant theory and techniques applicable in the three major areas of counseling psychology: (a) the remedial (assisting in remedying problems in living); (b) the preventive (anticipating, circumventing, and forestalling difficulties that may arise in the future); and (c) the educative and developmental (discovering and developing potentialities). That is (a) the focus is on normal individuals, and developmental life stages challenges; (b) a focus on assets, strengths, and positive mental health; (c) an emphasis on relatively brief interventions; and (d) an emphasis on context, sociocultural/political influences, diversity, and person-environment interactions rather than exclusive emphasis on the individual.
	The Ed.D. in Organizational Leadership program is designed to meet the special requirements of working professionals who wish to develop their knowledge and skills to handle the changing needs of modern organizations. The program is designed to enable working professionals to pursue their personal and professional goals through the completion of a graduate program. It focuses on the qualities of transformational leadership, not just managerial attributes. This approach enables the faculty members to dedicate themselves to preparing students to lead complex organizations faced with an abundance of strategic challenges, such as increasing globalization, changing economies, societal shifts, and individual-organizational relationships. It is the premise of the program that leaders prepared in this manner can be visionaries and innovators, leading viable organizations capable of meeting the challenges of the future.
Research Facilities	Argosy University libraries provide curriculum support and educational resources, including current text materials, diagnostic training documents, reference materials and databases, journals and dissertations, and major and current titles in program areas. There is an online public-access catalog of library resources available throughout the Argosy University system. Students have remote access to the campus library database, enabling them to study and conduct research at home. Academic databases offer dissertation abstracts, academic journals, and professional periodicals. All library computers are Internet accessible. Software applications include Word, Excel, PowerPoint, SPSS, and various test-scoring programs.
Financial Aid	Financial aid is available to those who qualify. Argosy University, San Diego, offers access to federal and state aid programs, merit-based awards, grants, loans, and a work-study program. As a first step, students should complete the Free Application for Federal Student Aid (FAFSA). Prospective students can apply electronically at http://www.fafsa.ed.gov or at the campus.
Cost of Study	Tuition varies by program. Students should contact Argosy University, San Diego, for tuition information.
Living and Housing Costs	Students typically live in apartments in the San Diego metropolitan area. Living expenses vary according to each student's preferred standard of living, housing, and transportation. The University does not offer or operate student housing. Most of the students are full-time working professionals who live within driving distance of the campus. Several nearby hotels offer special rates for those who commute from long distances. The Admissions Department also maintains a list of housing options, including contact information for University students who wish to share housing. For more information, students should contact the Admissions Department.
Student Group	Admission to Argosy University, San Diego, is selective to ensure a dynamic and engaged student body. The University encourages diversity in academic and employment backgrounds and promotes integration of the student body into professional life through established connections with local and national professional associations. Argosy University offers a professionally oriented education with rich opportunities to gain practical experience in class, field placements, and internships. Full-time students and working professionals gain the extensive knowledge and range of skills necessary for effective performance in their chosen field.
Student Outcomes	Students can register with the University's online career-services system and use select services from a distance, such as degree-specific career e-mail lists, national job posts, and virtual job fairs. Students should contact the University for more information.
Location	San Diego, southern California's second-largest city, offers an ideal climate year-round, 70 miles of beautiful beaches, colorful neighborhoods, and a dynamic downtown district. Argosy University, San Diego, provides classrooms, a library resource center, a student lounge, staff and faculty offices, and other amenities. The area offers numerous attractions, including the famous San Diego Zoo, San Diego Wild Animal Park, and SeaWorld. San Diego's business environment includes several Fortune 500 companies such as QUALCOMM and Pfizer, Inc., and a concentration of technology companies.
The University	Argosy University is a private institution with nineteen locations across the nation. Argosy University, San Diego, provides a career resources office, an academic resources center, and extensive information access for research. It offers the resources of a large university plus the friendliness and personal attention of a small campus.
	The innovative programs feature dynamic, relevant, and practical curricula delivered in flexible class formats. Students enjoy scheduling options that make it easier to fit school into their busy lives, choosing from day and evening courses, on campus or online. Many students find a combination of class formats to be an ideal way of continuing their education while meeting family and professional demands.
	Argosy University is accredited by the Higher Learning Commission and is a member of the North Central Association (30 North LaSalle Street, Suite 2400, Chicago, Illinois 60602; 800-621-7440 (toll-free); http://www.ncahlc.org).
Applying	Argosy University, San Diego, accepts students year-round on a rolling admissions basis, depending on availability of required courses. Applications for admission are available online or by contacting the campus.
Correspondence and Information	Argosy University, San Diego 1615 Murray Canyon Road San Diego, California 92108 Phone: 619-321-3000 　　　 866-505-0333 (toll-free) Fax: 619-321-3005 E-mail: auadmissions@argosy.edu Web site: http://www.argosy.edu/sandiego/

Argosy University, San Diego

THE FACULTY

The Argosy University faculty is comprised of working professionals who are eager to help students succeed. Members bring real-world experience and the latest practice innovations to the academic setting. The diverse faculty members of the College of Psychology and Behavioral Sciences are widely recognized for contributions to the field. Many are published scholars, and most hold doctoral degrees. They are committed to providing a substantive education that combines comprehensive knowledge with critical skills and practical workplace relevance. Above all, faculty members are committed to their students' personal and professional development.

ARGOSY UNIVERSITY.

ARGOSY UNIVERSITY, SAN FRANCISCO BAY AREA
College of Psychology and Behavioral Sciences

Programs of Study

Argosy University, San Francisco Bay Area, offers the Master of Arts (M.A.) degree in clinical psychology, clinical psychology/marriage and family therapy, counseling psychology, counseling psychology/marriage and family therapy, forensic psychology, and sport-exercise psychology; the Doctor of Education (Ed.D.) degree in counseling psychology and organizational leadership; and the Doctor of Psychology (Psy.D.) degree in clinical psychology. Students completing a program may wish to become licensed professionals. Argosy University, San Francisco Bay Area does not guarantee third-party certification/licensure. Outside agencies control the requirements for taking and passing certification/licensing exams and are subject to change without notice to Argosy University, San Francisco Bay Area.

The M.A. in Clinical Psychology program has been designed to educate and train students to enter a professional career as master's-level practitioners. The program provides students an educational program with all the necessary theoretical and clinical elements designed to allow them to be effective members of a mental health team. It introduces students to basic clinical skills that integrate individual and group theoretical foundations of applied psychology into appropriate client interaction and intervention skills. In addition, the program offers excellent preparation for those considering application to the Psy.D. in Clinical Psychology program.

The M.A. in Clinical Psychology/Marriage and Family Therapy program is designed for students who wish to pursue the clinical psychology track while receiving graduate-level training in the core curricular areas, including supervised clinical practice, required for licensure as a marriage and family therapist in California. Licensing requirements differ from state to state, so students should verify the current licensing requirements of the state in which they plan to become licensed. The program emphasizes a practitioner-oriented philosophy, and integrates applied theory and field experience.

The M.A. in Counseling Psychology program is designed to provide students with a sound foundation for the eventual practice of mental health counseling. The program emphasizes the development of attitudes, knowledge, and skills essential in the formation of professionals who are committed to the ethical provision of quality services. The program prepares students to enter a professional career as master's level counseling practitioners who can perform ethically and effectively as skilled professionals with demonstrated knowledge of social and cultural diversity.

The M.A. in Counseling Psychology/Marriage and Family Therapy program is designed to prepare students to practice and pursue licensure in California as a Marriage and Family Therapist (MFT). Students receive an educational program with all the necessary theoretical and practical elements designed to allow them to be effective members of a mental health team. The program introduces students to skills that integrate individual and group theoretical foundations of counseling psychology into appropriate client interaction and intervention skills.

The M.A. in Forensic Psychology program is designed to educate and train individuals who are currently working, or wish to work, in fields that utilize the study and practice of forensic psychology. Curriculum provides for an understanding of theory, training, and practice of forensic psychology. It emphasizes the development of students who are committed to the ethical provision of quality services to diverse clients and organizations. The program maintains policies and delivery formats suitable for working adults. The program provides course work in forensic psychology for application to law enforcement, legal and organizational consultation, and program analysis.

The M.A. in Sport-Exercise Psychology program is designed to educate and train capable and ethical performance-enhancement specialists. This two-year degree is intended to meet the needs of students seeking employment in a variety of settings, including private practice, athletic departments, coaching, exercise/health, and education, as well as those planning to ultimately pursue their doctorate. The goals of the program include developing student competencies in the following areas: theoretical foundations, helping relationships, individual and group skills, normal and abnormal behavior, sport sciences, research and evaluation, diversity, and professional identity.

The Ed.D. in Counseling Psychology program emphasizes the development of attitudes, knowledge, and skills essential in the formation of professionals who are committed to the ethical provision of quality services. To ensure that students are prepared adequately, the curriculum provides for the meaningful integration of theory, training, and practice.

The Ed.D. in Organizational Leadership program is designed to meet the special requirements of working professionals who want to develop their knowledge and skills in order to handle the changing needs of modern organizations. The program can enable working professionals to pursue their personal and professional goals through the completion of a graduate program. It focuses on the qualities of transformational leadership, not just managerial attributes. This approach allows the faculty members to dedicate themselves to preparing students to lead complex organizations faced with an abundance of strategic challenges, such as increasing globalization, changing economies, societal shifts, and individual-organizational relationships. It is the premise of the program that leaders prepared in this manner can be visionaries and innovators, leading viable organizations capable of meeting the challenges of the future.

The Psy.D. in Clinical Psychology program has been designed to educate and train students so that they may eventually be able to function effectively as clinical psychologists. The curriculum provides for the meaningful integration of theory, training, and practice. The program emphasizes the development of attitudes, knowledge, and skills essential in the formation of professional psychologists who are committed to the ethical provision of quality services.

Research Facilities

Argosy University libraries provide curriculum support and educational resources, including current text materials, diagnostic training documents, reference materials and databases, journals and dissertations, and major and current titles in program areas. There is an online public-access catalog of library resources available throughout the Argosy University system. Students have remote access to the campus library database, enabling them to study and conduct research at home. Academic databases offer dissertation abstracts, academic journals, and professional periodicals. All library computers are Internet accessible. Software applications include Word, Excel, PowerPoint, SPSS, and various test-scoring programs.

Financial Aid

Financial aid is available to those who qualify. Argosy University, San Francisco Bay Area, offers access to federal and state aid programs, merit-based awards, grants, loans, and a work-study program. As a first step, students should complete the Free Application for Federal Student Aid (FAFSA). Prospective students can apply electronically at http://www.fafsa.ed.gov or at the campus.

Cost of Study

Tuition varies by program. Students should contact Argosy University, San Francisco Bay Area for tuition information.

Living and Housing Costs

Students typically live in apartments in the San Francisco metropolitan area. Living expenses vary according to each student's preferred standard of living, housing, and transportation. The University does not offer or operate student housing. Most Argosy University students are full-time working professionals who live within driving distance of the campus. Several nearby hotels offer special rates for those who commute from long distances. The Admissions Department also maintains a list of housing options, including contact information for University students who wish to share housing. For more information, students should contact the Admissions Department.

Student Group

Admission to Argosy University, San Francisco Bay Area, is selective to ensure a dynamic and engaged student body. The University encourages diversity in academic and employment backgrounds and promotes integration of the student body into professional life through established connections with local and national professional associations. Argosy University offers a professionally oriented education with rich opportunities to gain practical experience in class, field placements, and internships. Full-time students and working professionals gain the extensive knowledge and range of skills necessary for effective performance in their chosen field.

Student Outcomes

Students can register with Argosy University's online career-services system and use select services from a distance, such as degree-specific career e-mail lists, national job posts, and virtual job fairs. Students should contact the University for more information.

Location

Located in northern California, Argosy University, San Francisco Bay Area, attracts students from the immediate area as well as from around the country and the world. In July 2007, the University moved to its new location at 1005 Atlantic Avenue, Alameda, California. The energy in San Francisco is contagious. Numerous surveys rank San Francisco as one of the most wired cities in the world, thanks to its high concentration of computer-savvy citizens and businesses.

Many educational institutions and agencies in the area provide varied opportunities for student training. The Bay Area and nearby Silicon Valley are home to leading new media companies such as Pixar, ILM, and Sega. A who's who of technology companies call the Bay Area home, including Apple, Cisco, Hewlett-Packard, Intel, Oracle, and Sun Microsystems. The Bay Area also is the home of traditional companies such as BankAmerica, Chevron, Levi-Strauss, Safeway, and Wells Fargo.

The University

Argosy University is a private institution with nineteen locations across the nation. Argosy University, San Francisco Bay Area, provides a career resources office, an academic resources center, and extensive information access for research. It offers the resources of a large university plus the friendliness and personal attention of a small campus. The innovative programs feature dynamic, relevant, and practical curricula delivered in flexible class formats. Students enjoy scheduling options that make it easier to fit school into their busy lives, choosing from day and evening courses, on campus or online. Many students find a combination of class formats to be an ideal way of continuing their education while meeting family and professional demands.

Argosy University is accredited by the Higher Learning Commission and is a member of the North Central Association (30 North LaSalle Street, Suite 2400, Chicago, Illinois 60602; 800-621-7440 (toll-free); http://www.ncahlc.org).

Applying

Argosy University, San Francisco Bay Area, accepts students year-round on a rolling admissions basis, depending on availability of required courses. Applications for admission are available online or by contacting the campus.

Correspondence and Information

Argosy University, San Francisco Bay Area
1005 Atlantic Avenue
Alameda, California 94501
Phone: 510-215-0277
      866-215-2777 (toll free)
Fax: 510-215-0299
E-mail: auadmissions@argosy.edu
Web site: http://www.argosy.edu/sanfrancisco

Argosy University, San Francisco Bay Area

THE FACULTY

The Argosy University faculty is comprised of working professionals who are eager to help students succeed. Members bring real-world experience and the latest practice innovations to the academic setting. The diverse faculty members of the College of Psychology and Behavioral Sciences are widely recognized for contributions to the field. Many are published scholars, and most hold doctoral degrees. They are committed to providing a substantive education that combines comprehensive knowledge with critical skills and practical workplace relevance. Above all, faculty members are committed to their students' personal and professional development.

ARGOSY UNIVERSITY.

ARGOSY UNIVERSITY, SARASOTA

College of Psychology and Behavioral Sciences

Programs of Study

Argosy University, Sarasota, offers the Master of Arts (M.A.) degree in community counseling, forensic psychology, marriage and family therapy, mental health counseling, school counseling, and school psychology; the Education Specialist (Ed.S.) degree in school counseling; and the Doctor of Education (Ed.D.) degree in counseling psychology, counselor education and supervision, organizational leadership, and pastoral community counseling. Students completing a program may wish to become licensed professionals. Argosy University, Sarasota does not guarantee third-party certification/licensure. Outside agencies control the requirements for taking and passing certification/licensing exams and are subject to change without notice to Argosy University, Sarasota.

The M.A. in Community Counseling is a 48 credit-hour program designed to provide students with a solid foundation for the practice of professional counseling. The program's curriculum integrates theoretical and conceptual foundations of professional counseling with training in appropriate client intervention and advocacy skills. The program emphasizes the development of attitudes, knowledge, and skills that are essential for professional counselors committed to the ethical provision of quality services. Students completing this program meet the academic requirements toward licensure in Alabama, Georgia, and other states (because licensure requirements vary from state to state, students should verify the current licensing requirements for the state in which they plan to practice).

The M.A. in Forensic Psychology program is designed to educate and train individuals who are currently working, or wish to work, in fields that utilize the study and practice of forensic psychology. Curriculum provides for an understanding of theory, training, and practice of forensic psychology. It emphasizes the development of students who are committed to the ethical provision of quality services to diverse clients and organizations. The program maintains policies and delivery formats suitable for working adults. The program provides course work in forensic psychology for application to law enforcement, legal and organizational consultation, and program analysis.

The M.A. in Marriage and Family Therapy program recognizes the need to provide marriage and family therapists with the extensive knowledge and range of skills necessary to function effectively in their profession. The program introduces students to basic skills that integrate systemic theoretical foundations of marriage and family therapy into appropriate client interaction and intervention skills. The program emphasizes the development of attitudes, knowledge, and skills essential in the formation of marriage and family therapists committed to the ethical provision of quality services. The program has been developed by the school faculty members to provide working students with the opportunity to pursue personal and professional goals through completion of a master's program.

The M.A. in Mental Health Counseling program is designed to provide students with a sound foundation for the eventual practice of mental health counseling. The program introduces students to basic counseling skills that integrate individual and group theoretical foundations of mental health counseling into appropriate client interaction and intervention skills. The program emphasizes the development of attitudes, knowledge, and skills essential in the formation of mental health counselors who are committed to the ethical provision of quality services.

The M.A. in School Counseling program serves adult students throughout the world. It provides a quality program in school counseling to meet the needs of students and the community. The focus on the program is student preparation and professional development while promoting teaching, learning, and service. The program remains faithful to its mission of preparing students to function at a high professional level in a rapidly changing world.

The M.A. in School Psychology program is designed to produce ethical, responsible, and competent school psychologists who are able to serve effectively in a number of professional roles. During graduate training, students develop core competencies in psychological assessment, intervention, and consultation/education, as well as cultural and individual diversity. Graduates of the program may be eligible for department of education certification and will be prepared for employment as school psychologists. The program is designed to prepare students to become Nationally Certified School Psychologists (NCSPs) in accordance with criteria developed by the National Association of School Psychologists.

The Ed.S. in School Counseling program is designed for experienced professionals who have master's degrees in other fields and wish to become school counselors. The program is a 30-semester-credit-hour program of study that incorporates course work designed to help students in meeting the specialization requirements for certification in Guidance and Counseling (grades K–12) in the state of Florida. Because of certification variations among states, students should check with regional authorities to confirm their requirements prior to entering the program.

The Ed.D. in Counseling Psychology program is designed to meet the special requirements of working professionals who want to develop their knowledge and skills to handle the changing needs of modern organizations. The program is designed to provide working professionals with the opportunity to pursue their personal and professional goals through the completion of a graduate program.

The Ed.D. in Counselor Education and Supervision program aligns with the master's-level counselor education programs in order to encourage entry-level counseling students to work toward becoming doctoral-level advanced practitioners, educators, and supervisors. This program prepares counselors for a variety of settings by providing the advanced skills and knowledge necessary to provide leadership and advocacy, as well as serve in supervisory, training, and teaching positions in the counseling profession.

The Ed.D. in Organizational Leadership program is designed to meet the special requirements of working professionals who want to develop their knowledge and skills to handle the changing needs of modern organizations. The program is designed to enable working professionals to pursue their personal and professional goals through the completion of a graduate program.

The Ed.D. in Pastoral Community Counseling program is based on the fundamental belief that religious and spiritual communities provide a unique opportunity for human growth and development. The program is designed to provide leaders in religious communities with an opportunity for personal and professional development, directed toward making a significant contribution to their community and to society. The program integrates the engagement of knowledge, the development of skills, reflective practice, and research in a manner that prepares the pastoral counselor to address individual and communal development in an ethically responsible fashion.

Research Facilities

Argosy University libraries provide curriculum support and educational resources, including current text materials, diagnostic training documents, reference materials and databases, journals and dissertations, and major and current titles in program areas. There is an online public-access catalog of library resources available throughout the Argosy University system. Students have remote access to the campus library database, enabling them to study and conduct research at home. Academic databases offer dissertation abstracts, academic journals, and professional periodicals. All library computers are Internet accessible. Software applications include Word, Excel, PowerPoint, SPSS, and various test-scoring programs.

Financial Aid

Financial aid is available to those who qualify. Argosy University, Sarasota, offers access to federal and state aid programs, merit-based awards, grants, loans, and a work-study program. As a first step, students should complete the Free Application for Federal Student Aid (FAFSA). Prospective students can apply electronically at http://www.fafsa.ed.gov or at the campus.

Cost of Study

Tuition varies by program. Students should contact Argosy University, Sarasota, for tuition information.

Living and Housing Costs

Students typically live in apartments in the metropolitan Sarasota area. Living expenses vary according to each student's preferred standard of living, housing, and transportation. The University does not offer or operate student housing. Most of the students are full-time working professionals who live within driving distance of the campus. Several nearby hotels offer special rates for those who commute from long distances to attend scheduled weeklong in-residence sessions. The Admissions Department also maintains a list of housing options, including contact information for University students who wish to share housing. For more information, students should contact the Admissions Department.

Student Group

Admission to Argosy University, Sarasota, is selective to ensure a dynamic and engaged student body. The University encourages diversity in academic and employment backgrounds and promotes integration of the student body into professional life through established connections with local and national professional associations. Argosy University offers a professionally oriented education with rich opportunities to gain practical experience in class, field placements, and internships. Full-time students and working professionals gain the extensive knowledge and range of skills necessary for effective performance in their chosen fields.

Student Outcomes

Students can register with the University's online career-services system and use select services from a distance, such as degree-specific career e-mail lists, national job posts, and virtual job fairs. Students should contact the University for more information.

Location

Located in northeast Sarasota, the campus is specifically designed for postsecondary and graduate-level instruction through a unique combination of in-residence course work, tutorials, and online study courses. Several programs are off-site tutorials and intensive one-week classroom sessions. Students may also complete up to 49 percent of the work in some degree programs via online courses that allow interaction with faculty members and classmates from any Internet connection.

Sarasota is recognized as Florida's cultural coast and is home to a professional symphony, ballet, and opera as well as dozens of theaters and art galleries. Well-known vacation attractions such as Disney World, Busch Gardens–Tampa, and the city of Miami are within a few hours' drive. The area enjoys mild winters and endless summer beauty.

The business sector in the Gulf Coast community helps make it one of the top 20 places to live and work. ASO Corporation, Nelson Publishing, and Select Technology Group are among the numerous companies headquartered in Sarasota County. The area's top employers include Sarasota Memorial Hospital and Publix Supermarkets.

The University

Argosy University is a private institution with nineteen locations across the nation. Argosy University, Sarasota, provides a career resources office, an academic resources center, and extensive information access for research. It offers the resources of a large university plus the friendliness and personal attention of a small campus.

The innovative programs feature dynamic, relevant, and practical curricula delivered in flexible class formats. Students enjoy scheduling options that make it easier to fit school into their busy lives, choosing from day and evening courses, on campus or online. Many students find a combination of class formats to be an ideal way of continuing their education while meeting family and professional demands.

Argosy University is accredited by the Higher Learning Commission and is a member of the North Central Association (30 North LaSalle Street, Suite 2400, Chicago, Illinois 60602; 800-621-7440 (toll-free); http://www.ncahlc.org).

Applying

Argosy University, Sarasota, accepts students year-round on a rolling admissions basis, depending on availability of required courses. Applications for admission are available online or by contacting the campus.

Correspondence and Information

Argosy University, Sarasota
5250 17th Street
Sarasota, Florida 34235

Phone: 941-379-0404
     800-331-5995 (toll-free)
Fax: 941-371-8910
E-mail: auadmissions@argosy.edu
Web site: http://www.argosy.edu/sarasota

Argosy University, Sarasota

THE FACULTY

The Argosy University faculty is comprised of working professionals who are eager to help students succeed. Members bring real-world experience and the latest practice innovations to the academic setting. The diverse faculty members of the College of Psychology and Behavioral Sciences are widely recognized for contributions to the field. Many are published scholars, and most hold doctoral degrees. They are committed to providing a substantive education that combines comprehensive knowledge with critical skills and practical workplace relevance. Above all, faculty members are committed to their students' personal and professional development.

ARGOSY UNIVERSITY.

ARGOSY UNIVERSITY, SCHAUMBURG

College of Psychology and Behavioral Sciences

Programs of Study

Argosy University, Schaumburg, offers the Master of Arts (M.A.) degree in clinical psychology, community counseling, and industrial organizational psychology; the Doctor of Education (Ed.D.) degree in counseling psychology, counselor education and supervision, and organizational leadership; and the Doctor of Psychology (Psy.D.) degree in clinical psychology. Students completing a program may wish to become licensed professionals. Argosy University, Schaumburg does not guarantee third-party certification/licensure. Outside agencies control the requirements for taking and passing certification/licensing exams and are subject to change without notice to Argosy University, Schaumburg.

The M.A. in Clinical Psychology program is designed to educate and train students to enter a professional career as master's-level practitioners. Students receive an educational program with all the necessary theoretical and clinical elements designed to allow them to be effective members of a mental health team. The program introduces students to basic clinical skills that integrate individual and group theoretical foundations of applied psychology into appropriate client interaction and intervention skills. In addition, the program offers comprehensive preparation for those considering application to the Psy.D. in Clinical Psychology program.

The M.A. in Community Counseling program is designed to provide students with a sound foundation for eventual practice of professional counseling. The program introduces students to basic counseling skills that integrate individual and group theoretical foundations of professional counseling into appropriate client interaction and intervention skills. The program emphasizes the development of attitudes, knowledge, and skills essential in the formation of professional counselors who are committed to the ethical provision of quality services. The program is committed to educating and training students to enter a professional career as master's-level counseling practitioners who can function ethically and effectively as skilled professionals with demonstrated knowledge of social and cultural diversity. Students are prepared for licensure as professional counselors in the state of Illinois; however, alumni serve clients throughout North America.

The M.A. in Industrial Organizational Psychology program is designed to apply the knowledge of industrial organizational psychology to issues involving individuals and groups in organizational and work settings. This program prepares students for careers in areas such as compensation, training, data analysis, consultation, statistical decision-making, organizational development, leadership, and human resource management positions. The curriculum is competency-based, focusing on the outcomes of training and on the knowledge, skills, and behavior necessary to function as a master's-level professional in industrial organizational psychology. This is an interdisciplinary program that combines the expertise of the faculty in the College of Psychology and Behavioral Sciences and the College of Business.

The Ed.D. in Counseling Psychology program is designed to meet the special requirements of working professionals who want to develop their knowledge and skills to handle the changing needs of modern organizations. The program is structured to provide working professionals with the opportunity to pursue their personal and professional goals through the completion of a graduate program.

The Ed.D. in Counselor Education and Supervision program aligns with the master's-level counselor education programs in order to encourage entry-level counseling students to work toward becoming doctoral-level advanced practitioners, educators, and supervisors. The program prepares counselors for a variety of settings by providing the advanced skills and knowledge necessary to provide leadership and advocacy, as well as serve in supervisory, training, and teaching positions in the counseling profession.

The Ed.D. in Organizational Leadership program is designed to meet the special requirements of working professionals who want to develop their knowledge and skills to handle the changing needs of modern organizations. The program is designed to enable working professionals to pursue their personal and professional goals through the completion of a graduate program. It focuses on the qualities of transformational leadership, not just managerial attributes. This approach enables the faculty members to dedicate themselves to preparing students to lead complex organizations faced with an abundance of strategic challenges, such as increasing globalization, changing economies, societal shifts, and individual-organizational relationships. It is the premise of the program that leaders prepared in this manner can be visionaries and innovators, leading viable organizations capable of meeting the challenges of the future.

The Psy.D. in Clinical Psychology program has been designed to educate and train students to function effectively as clinical psychologists. To ensure that students are prepared adequately, the curriculum provides for the meaningful integration of theory, training, and practice. The program emphasizes the development of attitudes, knowledge, and skills essential in the formation of professional psychologists who are committed to the ethical provision of quality services.

Research Facilities

Argosy University libraries provide curriculum support and educational resources, including current text materials, diagnostic training documents, reference materials and databases, journals and dissertations, and major and current titles in program areas. There is an online public-access catalog of library resources available throughout the Argosy University system. Students have remote access to the campus library database, enabling them to study and conduct research at home. Academic databases offer dissertation abstracts, academic journals, and professional periodicals. All library computers are Internet accessible. Software applications include Word, Excel, PowerPoint, SPSS, and various test-scoring programs.

Financial Aid

Financial aid is available to those who qualify. Argosy University, Schaumburg, offers access to federal and state aid programs, merit-based awards, grants, loans, and a work-study program. As a first step, students should complete the Free Application for Federal Student Aid (FAFSA). Prospective students can apply electronically at http://www.fafsa.ed.gov or at the campus.

Cost of Study

Tuition varies by program. Students should contact Argosy University, Schaumburg, for tuition information.

Living and Housing Costs

Students typically live in apartments in the metropolitan Chicago area. Living expenses vary according to each student's preferred standard of living, housing, and transportation. The University does not offer or operate student housing. Most Argosy University students are full-time working professionals who live within driving distance of the campus. Several nearby hotels offer special rates for those who commute from long distances. The Admissions Department also maintains a list of housing options, including contact information for University students who wish to share housing. For more information, students should contact the Admissions Department.

Student Group

Admission to Argosy University, Schaumburg, is selective to ensure a dynamic and engaged student body. The University encourages diversity in academic and employment backgrounds and promotes integration of the student body into professional life through established connections with local and national professional associations. Argosy University offers a professionally oriented education with rich opportunities to gain practical experience in class, field placements, and internships. Full-time students and working professionals gain the extensive knowledge and range of skills necessary for effective performance in their chosen field.

Student Outcomes

Students can register with Argosy University's online career-services system and use select services from a distance, such as degree-specific career e-mail lists, national job posts, and virtual job fairs. Students should contact the University for more information.

Location

Argosy University, Schaumburg, is located in the northwest suburban area, approximately 45 minutes from downtown Chicago. The University's small size offers a highly personal atmosphere and flexible programs tailored to students' needs. Visitors to Chicago experience a range of attractions to stimulate both intellectual and recreational pursuits. Located on the shores of Lake Michigan in the Midwest, Chicago is home to world-champion sports teams, an internationally acclaimed symphony orchestra, renowned architecture, and nearly 3 million residents. Among the variety of history and art museums in the city, the Chicago Cultural Center offers more than 600 art programs and exhibits each year. Recreational opportunities include hiking and cycling on miles of lakefront trails, golfing, and shopping

Many facilities and agencies in the area provide opportunities for student training. Schaumburg's thriving business environment includes 5,000 businesses that employ 80,000 people. The area's largest employers are Motorola, Experian, Cingular, and IBM.

The University

Argosy University is a private institution with nineteen locations across the nation. Argosy University, Schaumburg, provides a career resources office, an academic resources center, and extensive information access for research. It offers the resources of a large university plus the friendliness and personal attention of a small campus. The innovative programs feature dynamic, relevant, and practical curricula delivered in flexible class formats. Students enjoy scheduling options that make it easier to fit school into their busy lives, choosing from day and evening courses, on campus or online. Many students find a combination of class formats to be an ideal way of continuing their education while meeting family and professional demands.

Argosy University is accredited by the Higher Learning Commission and is a member of the North Central Association (30 North LaSalle Street, Suite 2400, Chicago, Illinois 60602; 800-621-7440 (toll-free); http://www.ncahlc.org).

Applying

Argosy University, Schaumburg, accepts students year-round on a rolling admissions basis, depending on availability of required courses. Applications for admission are available online or by contacting the campus.

Correspondence and Information

Argosy University, Schaumburg
999 North Plaza Drive, Suite 111
Schaumburg, Illinois 60173-5403

Phone: 847-969-7400
      866-290-2777 (toll-free)
Fax: 847-969-4998
E-mail: auadmissions@argosy.edu
Web site: http://www.argosy.edu/schaumburg

Argosy University, Schaumburg

THE FACULTY

The Argosy University faculty is comprised of working professionals who are eager to help students succeed. Members bring real-world experience and the latest practice innovations to the academic setting. The diverse faculty members of the College of Psychology and Behavioral Sciences are widely recognized for contributions to the field. Many are published scholars, and most hold doctoral degrees. They are committed to providing a substantive education that combines comprehensive knowledge with critical skills and practical workplace relevance. Above all, faculty members are committed to their students' personal and professional development.

ARGOSY UNIVERSITY.

ARGOSY UNIVERSITY, SEATTLE

College of Psychology and Behavioral Sciences

Programs of Study	Argosy University, Seattle, offers the Master of Arts (M.A.) degree in clinical psychology and counseling psychology, the Doctor of Education (Ed.D.) degree in counseling psychology, and the Doctor of Psychology (Psy.D.) degree in clinical psychology. Students completing a program may wish to become licensed professionals. Argosy University, Seattle does not guarantee third-party certification/ licensure. Outside agencies control the requirements for taking and passing certification/licensing exams and are subject to change without notice to Argosy University, Seattle.
	The M.A. in Clinical Psychology program has been designed to educate and train students to enter a professional career as master's-level practitioners. Students receive an educational program with all the necessary theoretical and clinical elements designed to allow them to be effective members of a mental health team. The program introduces students to basic clinical skills that integrate individual and group theoretical foundations of applied psychology into appropriate client interaction and intervention skills.
	The M.A. in Counseling Psychology program is designed to provide students with a sound foundation for the eventual practice of mental health counseling. The program emphasizes the development of attitudes, knowledge, and skills essential in the formation of professionals committed to the ethical provision of quality services. The program prepares students to enter a professional career as master's level counseling practitioners who can perform ethically and effectively as skilled professionals with demonstrated knowledge of social and cultural diversity. Curriculum is designed to integrate basic counseling skills, theoretical foundations of professional counseling, and practicum field experience into appropriate client interaction and intervention skills for application in a wide variety of settings with diverse client populations. Since licensing may change and often varies from state to state, students should verify the current requirements of the state in which they plan to become licensed.
	The Ed.D. in Counseling Psychology program emphasizes the development of attitudes, knowledge, and skills essential in the formation of professionals who are committed to the ethical provision of quality services. To ensure that students are prepared adequately, the curriculum is designed to provide for the meaningful integration of theory, training, and practice.
	The Psy.D. in Clinical Psychology program utilizes a practitioner-scholar model of professional training and is designed to educate and train students to function effectively as clinical psychologists. The curriculum is designed to provide for the meaningful integration of theory, training, and practice. The program is competency-based and emphasizes the development of attitudes, knowledge, and skills essential to the training of clinical psychologists committed to the ethical provision of quality services to diverse populations. Students are prepared through the formal curriculum, which exposes them to the practice of professional psychology in both its breadth and depth. Concomitant professional development is supported through mentoring relationships with practitioner-scholar faculty who embody the integration of knowledge and skills with the ethical and professional attitudes required of clinical psychologists.
Research Facilities	Argosy University libraries provide curriculum support and educational resources, including current text materials, diagnostic training documents, reference materials and databases, journals and dissertations, and major and current titles in program areas. There is an online public-access catalog of library resources available throughout the Argosy University system. Students have full remote access to the campus library database, enabling them to study and conduct research at home. Academic databases offer dissertation abstracts, academic journals, and professional periodicals. All library computers are Internet accessible. Software applications include Word, Excel, PowerPoint, SPSS, and various test-scoring programs.
Financial Aid	Financial aid is available to those who qualify. Argosy University, Seattle, offers access to federal and state aid programs, merit-based awards, grants, loans, and a work-study program. As a first step, students should complete the Free Application for Federal Student Aid (FAFSA). Prospective students can apply electronically at http://www.fafsa.ed.gov or at the campus.
Cost of Study	Tuition varies by program. Students should contact Argosy University, Seattle, for tuition information.
Living and Housing Costs	Students typically live in apartments in the metropolitan Seattle area. Living expenses vary according to each student's preferred standard of living, housing, and transportation. The University does not offer or operate student housing. Most of the students are full-time working professionals who live within driving distance of the campus. Several nearby hotels offer special rates for those who commute from long distances. The Admissions Department also maintains a list of housing options, including contact information, for University students who wish to share housing. For more information, students should contact the Admissions Department.
Student Group	Admission to Argosy University, Seattle, is selective to ensure a dynamic and engaged student body. The University encourages diversity in academic and employment backgrounds and promotes integration of the student body into professional life through established connections with local and national professional associations. Argosy University offers a professionally oriented education with rich opportunities to gain practical experience in class, field placements, and internships. Full-time students and working professionals gain the extensive knowledge and range of skills necessary for effective performance in their chosen fields.
Student Outcomes	Students can register with the University's online career-services system and use select services from a distance, such as degree-specific career e-mail lists, national job posts, and virtual job fairs. Students should contact the University for more information.
Location	Argosy University, Seattle, aspires to provide a supportive, collaborative, and engaging yet challenging learning environment. Easily reached through the King County Public Transportation System, the campus sits in proximity to local libraries, shops, restaurants, theaters, and art museums. Seattle offers numerous historical and multicultural museums, a symphony, ballet, and many theater companies. The city is home to several major-league sports teams and offers a myriad of outdoor recreational opportunities, such as camping, hiking, fishing, skiing, and rock climbing. Seattle's business environment encompasses a wide range of industries and features such giants as Microsoft, Boeing, and Alaska Air Group. The Port of Seattle and the University of Washington are also among the area's largest employers.
The University	Argosy University is a private institution with nineteen locations across the nation. Argosy University, Seattle, provides a career resources office, an academic resources center, and extensive information access for research. It offers the resources of a large university, plus the friendliness and personal attention of a small campus.
	The innovative programs feature dynamic, relevant, and practical curricula delivered in flexible class formats. Students enjoy scheduling options that make it easier to fit school into their busy lives, choosing from day and evening courses, on campus or online. Many students find a combination of class formats to be an ideal way of continuing their education while meeting family and professional demands.
	Argosy University is accredited by the Higher Learning Commission and is a member of the North Central Association (30 North LaSalle Street, Suite 2400, Chicago, Illinois 60602; 800-621-7440 (toll-free); http://www.ncahlc.org).
Applying	Argosy University, Seattle, accepts students year-round on a rolling admissions basis, depending on availability of required courses. Applications for admission are available online or by contacting the campus.
Correspondence and Information	Argosy University, Seattle 2601-A Elliott Avenue Seattle, Washington 98121 Phone: 206-283-4500 866-283-2777 (toll-free) Fax: 206-283-5777 E-mail: auadmissions@argosy.edu Web site: http://www.argosy.edu/seattle

Argosy University, Seattle

THE FACULTY

The Argosy University faculty is comprised of working professionals who are eager to help students succeed. Members bring real-world experience and the latest practice innovations to the academic setting. The diverse faculty members of the College of Psychology and Behavioral Sciences are widely recognized for contributions to the field. Many are published scholars, and most hold doctoral degrees. They are committed to providing a substantive education that combines comprehensive knowledge with critical skills and practical workplace relevance. Above all, faculty members are committed to their students' personal and professional development.

ARGOSY UNIVERSITY.

ARGOSY UNIVERSITY, TAMPA

College of Psychology and Behavioral Sciences

Programs of Study

Argosy University, Tampa, offers the Master of Arts (M.A.) degree in clinical psychology, marriage and family therapy, mental health counseling, and school counseling; the Doctor of Education (Ed.D.) degree in counselor education and supervision and organizational leadership; and the Doctor of Psychology (Psy.D.) degree in clinical psychology. Students completing a program may wish to become licensed professionals. Argosy University, Tampa does not guarantee third-party certification/licensure. Outside agencies control the requirements for taking and passing certification/licensing exams and are subject to change without notice to Argosy University, Tampa.

The M.A. in Clinical Psychology program is designed to meet the needs of both those students seeking a terminal degree at the master's level and those who plan to pursue a doctoral degree. The terminal master's degree is not, however, license-eligible in the state of Florida. The master's degree provides students a strong clinical orientation with an emphasis in psychological assessment. The master's program offers several unique advantages to those individuals who hope to subsequently pursue a doctoral degree. Admission to the master's program or completion of the master's degree does not guarantee admission to the Psy.D. in Clinical Psychology program.

The M.A. in Marriage and Family Therapy program recognizes the need to provide marriage and family therapists with the knowledge, skills, and attitudes essential in the formation of marriage and family therapists committed to the ethical provision of quality services. The program introduces students to basic skills that integrate systemic theoretical foundations of marriage and family therapy into appropriate client interaction and intervention skills. The program has been developed by the school faculty members to provide working students with the opportunity to pursue personal and professional goals through completion of a master's program.

The M.A. in Mental Health Counseling program recognizes the need to provide counseling professionals with the extensive knowledge, range of skills, and attitudes necessary to function effectively in their professions. The program introduces students to basic counseling skills that integrate individual and group theoretical foundations of counseling into appropriate client interaction and intervention skills. The program emphasizes formation of professional counselors committed to the ethical provision of quality services. The program has been developed by the school faculty members to provide working professionals with the opportunity to pursue their personal and professional goals through completion of a master's program.

The M.A. in School Counseling program serves adult students throughout the world. It provides a quality program in school counseling to meet the needs of students and the community. The focus of the program is student preparation and professional development while promoting teaching, learning, and service. The program remains faithful to its mission of preparing students to function at a high professional level in a rapidly changing world.

The Ed.D. in Counselor Education and Supervision program aligns with the master's-level counselor education programs in order to encourage entry-level counseling students to work toward becoming doctoral-level advanced practitioners, educators, and supervisors. The program prepares counselors for a variety of settings by providing the advanced skills and knowledge necessary to provide leadership and advocacy, as well as serve in supervisory, training, and teaching positions in the counseling profession.

The Ed.D. in Organizational Leadership program is designed to meet the special requirements of working professionals who want to develop their knowledge and skills to handle the changing needs of modern organizations. The program can help working professionals pursue their personal and professional goals through completion of a graduate program. It focuses on the qualities of transformational leadership, not just managerial attributes. This approach enables the faculty members to dedicate themselves to preparing students to lead complex organizations faced with an abundance of strategic challenges, such as increasing globalization, changing economies, societal shifts, and individual-organizational relationships. It is the premise of the program that leaders prepared in this manner can be visionaries and innovators, leading viable organizations capable of meeting the challenges of the future.

The Psy.D. in Clinical Psychology program is designed to educate and train students so that they may eventually be able to function effectively as clinical psychologists. To ensure that students are prepared adequately, the curriculum is designed to provide for the meaningful integration of theory, training, and practice. The clinical psychology program emphasizes the development of attitudes, knowledge, and skills essential in the formation of professional psychologists who are committed to the ethical provision of quality services.

Research Facilities

Argosy University libraries provide curriculum support and educational resources, including current text materials, diagnostic training documents, reference materials and databases, journals and dissertations, and major and current titles in program areas. There is an online public-access catalog of library resources available throughout the Argosy University system. Students have remote access to the campus library database, enabling them to study and conduct research at home. Academic databases offer dissertation abstracts, academic journals, and professional periodicals. All library computers are Internet accessible. Software applications include Word, Excel, PowerPoint, SPSS, and various test-scoring programs.

Financial Aid

Financial aid is available to those who qualify. Argosy University, Tampa, offers access to federal and state aid programs, merit-based awards, grants, loans, and a work-study program. As a first step, students should complete the Free Application for Federal Student Aid (FAFSA). Prospective students can apply electronically at http://www.fafsa.ed.gov or at the campus.

Cost of Study

Tuition varies by program. Students should contact Argosy University, Tampa, for tuition information.

Living and Housing Costs

Students typically live in apartments in the metropolitan Tampa area. Living expenses vary according to each student's preferred standard of living, housing, and transportation. The University does not offer or operate student housing. Most of the students are full-time working professionals who live within driving distance of the campus. Several nearby hotels offer special rates for those who commute from long distances. The Admissions Department also maintains a list of housing options, including contact information, for University students who wish to share housing. For more information, students should contact the Admissions Department.

Student Group

Admission to Argosy University, Tampa, is selective to ensure a dynamic and engaged student body. The University encourages diversity in academic and employment backgrounds and promotes integration of the student body into professional life through established connections with local and national professional associations. Argosy University offers a professionally oriented education with rich opportunities to gain practical experience in class, field placements, and internships. Full-time students and working professionals gain the extensive knowledge and range of skills necessary for effective performance in their chosen fields.

Student Outcomes

Students can register with the University's online career-services system and use select services from a distance, such as degree-specific career e-mail lists, national job posts, and virtual job fairs. Students should contact the University for more information.

Location

Located in sunny Florida, Argosy University, Tampa, attracts a diverse student population from throughout the United States, the Caribbean, Europe, Africa, and Asia. Tampa's central location affords students the opportunity to work for major corporations and hear speakers of international acclaim. The school offers rigorous programs of study in a supportive, collaborative environment. The campus sits within an hour's drive of some of the most popular tourist destinations in the world, including the Disney theme parks, Busch Gardens, and the Florida Gulf Coast beaches. Major-league sporting events, concerts, theaters, world-renowned restaurants, recreational facilities, and a cosmopolitan social scene are all within easy reach. The University's location provides easy access to I-4 and I-75. Tampa combines the opportunities of a large city with the friendliness of a small town.

The Tampa-St. Petersburg-Clearwater metropolitan area offers a diversified economic base fueled by a broad array of companies, including Verizon Communications and JP Morgan Chase. In addition, Tampa serves as headquarters for three Fortune 100 companies—OSI Restaurant Partners; TECO, an energy provider; and Raymond James Financial.

The University

Argosy University is a private institution with nineteen locations across the nation. Argosy University, Tampa, provides a network of resources, including a career resources office, an academic resources center, and extensive information access for research. It offers the resources of a large university, plus the friendliness and personal attention of a small campus.

The innovative programs feature dynamic, relevant, and practical curricula delivered in flexible class formats. Students enjoy scheduling options that make it easier to fit school into their busy lives, choosing from day and evening courses, on campus or online. Many students find a combination of class formats to be an ideal way of continuing their education while meeting family and professional demands.

Argosy University is accredited by the Higher Learning Commission and is a member of the North Central Association (30 North LaSalle Street, Suite 2400, Chicago, Illinois 60602; 800-621-7440 (toll-free); http://www.ncahlc.org).

Applying

Argosy University, Tampa, accepts students year-round on a rolling admissions basis, depending on availability of required courses. Applications for admission are available online or by contacting the campus.

Correspondence and Information

Argosy University, Tampa
Parkside at Tampa Bay Park
4401 North Himes Avenue, Suite 150
Tampa, Florida 33614
Phone: 813-393-5290
      800-850-6488 (toll-free)
Fax: 813-874-1989
E-mail: auadmissions@argosy.edu
Web site: http://www.argosy.edu/tampa

Argosy University, Tampa

THE FACULTY

The Argosy University faculty is comprised of working professionals who are eager to help students succeed. Members bring real-world experience and the latest practice innovations to the academic setting. The diverse faculty members of the College of Psychology and Behavioral Sciences are widely recognized for contributions to the field. Many are published scholars, and most hold doctoral degrees. They are committed to providing a substantive education that combines comprehensive knowledge with critical skills and practical workplace relevance. Above all, faculty members are committed to their students' personal and professional development.

ARGOSY UNIVERSITY, TWIN CITIES

College of Psychology and Behavioral Sciences

ARGOSY UNIVERSITY.

Programs of Study

Argosy University, Twin Cities, offers the Master of Arts (M.A.) degree in clinical psychology, forensic psychology, and marriage and family therapy; the Doctor of Marriage and Family Therapy (D.M.F.T.); the Doctor of Education (Ed.D.) degree in organizational leadership; and the Doctor of Psychology (Psy.D.) degree in clinical psychology. Students completing a program may wish to become licensed professionals. Argosy University, Twin Cities does not guarantee third-party certification/licensure. Outside agencies control the requirements for taking and passing certification/licensing exams and are subject to change without notice to Argosy University, Twin Cities.

The M.A. in Clinical Psychology program is designed to prepare students with the clinical knowledge and skills required to serve the mental health needs of individuals and groups. Students develop proficiency in clinical observation, assessment, appropriate intervention, and evaluation. The program emphasizes a practitioner-oriented philosophy and integrates applied theory, research, and field experience. It is designed for students who are interested in a terminal degree and practice as a master's-level clinician, or for students planning to transfer to the Psy.D. program.

The M.A. in Forensic Psychology program is designed to provide course work in forensic psychology for application to law enforcement, legal and organizational consultation, and program analysis. The program is designed to meet growing needs of the legal and criminal justice systems for professional counseling within victim assistance programs, probation and parole offices, court-mandated treatment programs, jails, and prisons. With the exception of the practicum component, courses are offered on weekends, allowing students to continue full-time employment while enrolled in this program.

The M.A. in Marriage and Family Therapy program is designed to develop the theoretical and clinical elements required to provide effective counseling to individuals, couples, families, and groups. The program introduces basic counseling skills that incorporate foundations of applied psychology and systems theory into the development of appropriate clinical relationships. Course work in addiction studies and substance-abuse counseling prepares students to work with families affected by this burgeoning problem. An optional concentration in forensic counseling is available. Marriage and family therapy is recognized by the Public Health Service Act as one of the five core mental health professions, and the National Institute of Mental Health accepts marriage and family therapists as qualified mental health professionals. The program is offered through weekend courses to allow concurrent employment.

The Doctor of Marriage and Family Therapy is a practice-oriented degree for licensed marriage and family therapists or professionals who can meet state requirements for licensure as a marriage and family therapist (meeting the Commission on Accreditation of Marriage and Family Therapy Education (COAMFTE) criteria for clinical practice prior to admission). The program seeks to build upon students' prior learning and professional experience by expanding and deepening their knowledge of human development, family dynamics, systemic thinking, interactional theories, traditional and contemporary marriage and family therapy theories and practices, and the cultural contexts within which these are embedded.

The Ed.D. in Organizational Leadership program is designed for working professionals who wish to develop the knowledge and skills required to hold leadership positions in complex organizations. The program focuses on transformational leadership skills in addition to managerial attributes. This approach prepares students for such strategic challenges as increasing globalization, changing economies, societal shifts, and individual-organizational relationships.

The Psy.D. in Clinical Psychology program is designed to prepare students to deliver basic diagnostic and therapeutic services to diverse populations, including individuals, groups, and families. By integrating theory, training, research, and practice, students develop and apply the clinical skills of observation, assessment, intervention, and evaluation. Optional concentrations are available in child and family psychology, forensic psychology, health psychology, marriage/couple and family therapy, or neuropsychology. The program prepares graduates for positions in traditional settings, including, but not limited to, independent practice, mental health centers, hospitals, medical centers, and managed-care systems. Graduates are encouraged to utilize clinical skills in innovative ways to become more competitive. Eventual positions may include consulting in various corporate, governmental, academic, multimedia, law, scientific, marketing, and industrial settings. The Doctor of Psychology in Clinical Psychology program at Argosy University, Twin Cities, is accredited by the Committee on Accreditation of the American Psychological Association (APA) (750 First Street, N.E., Washington, D.C. 20002-4242, 202-336-5510).

Research Facilities

Argosy University libraries provide curriculum support and educational resources, including current text materials, diagnostic training documents, reference materials and databases, journals and dissertations, and major and current titles in program areas. There is an online public-access catalog of library resources available throughout the Argosy University system. Students have remote access to the campus library database, enabling them to study and conduct research at home. Academic databases offer dissertation abstracts, academic journals, and professional periodicals. All library computers are Internet accessible. Software applications include Word, Excel, PowerPoint, SPSS, and various test-scoring programs.

Financial Aid

Financial aid is available to those who qualify. Argosy University, Twin Cities, offers access to federal and state aid programs, merit-based awards, grants, loans, and a work-study program. As a first step, students should complete the Free Application for Federal Student Aid (FAFSA). Prospective students can apply electronically at http://www.fafsa.ed.gov or at the campus.

Cost of Study

Tuition varies by program. Students should contact Argosy University, Twin Cities, for tuition information.

Living and Housing Costs

Students typically live in apartments in the metropolitan Twin Cities area. Living expenses vary according to each student's preferred standard of living, housing, and transportation. The University does not offer or operate student housing. Most Argosy University students are full-time working professionals who live within driving distance of the campus. Several nearby hotels offer special rates for those who commute from long distances. The Admissions Department also maintains a list of housing options, including contact information for University students who wish to share housing. For more information, students should contact the Admissions Department.

Student Group

Admission to Argosy University, Twin Cities, is selective to ensure a dynamic and engaged student body. The University encourages diversity in academic and employment backgrounds and promotes integration of the student body into professional life through established connections with local and national professional associations. Argosy University offers a professionally oriented education with rich opportunities to gain practical experience in class, field placements, and internships. Full-time students and working professionals gain the extensive knowledge and range of skills necessary for effective performance in their chosen field.

Student Outcomes

Students can register with Argosy University's online career-services system and use select services from a distance, such as degree-specific career e-mail lists, national job posts, and virtual job fairs. Students should contact the University for more information.

Location

Argosy University, Twin Cities, offers rigorous academics in a supportive environment. The campus is nestled in a parklike suburban setting within 10 miles of the airport and the Mall of America. Students enjoy the convenience of nearby shops, restaurants, and housing and easy freeway access. The neighboring Eagan Community Center offers many amenities, including walking trails, a fitness center, meeting rooms, and an outdoor amphitheater. The twin cities of Minneapolis and St. Paul have been rated by popular magazines as one of the most livable metropolitan areas in the country. With a population of 2.5 million, the area offers an abundance of recreational activities. Year-round outdoor activities and nationally acclaimed venues for theater, art, music, and professional sports teams attract residents and visitors alike. The Minneapolis-St. Paul metropolitan area offers a diversified economic base fueled by a broad array of companies. Among the numerous publicly traded companies headquartered in the area are Target, UnitedHealth Group, 3M, General Mills, and US Bancorp.

The University

Argosy University is a private institution with nineteen locations across the nation. Argosy University, Twin Cities, provides a career resources office, an academic resources center, and extensive information access for research. It offers the resources of a large university plus the friendliness and personal attention of a small campus. The innovative programs feature dynamic, relevant, and practical curricula delivered in flexible class formats. Students enjoy scheduling options that make it easier to fit school into their busy lives, choosing from day and evening courses, on campus or online. Many students find a combination of class formats to be an ideal way of continuing their education while meeting family and professional demands.

Argosy University is accredited by the Higher Learning Commission and is a member of the North Central Association (30 North LaSalle Street, Suite 2400, Chicago, Illinois 60602; 800-621-7440 (toll-free); http://www.ncahlc.org).

Applying

Argosy University, Twin Cities, accepts students on a rolling admissions basis year-round, depending on availability of required courses. Applications for admission may be obtained online or by contacting the campus.

Correspondence and Information

Argosy University, Twin Cities
1515 Central Parkway
Eagan, Minnesota 55121
Phone: 651-846-2882
          888-844-2004 (toll-free)
Fax: 651-994-7956
E-mail: auadmissions@argosy.edu
Web site: http://www.argosy.edu/twincities

Argosy University, Twin Cities

THE FACULTY

The Argosy University faculty is comprised of working professionals who are eager to help students succeed. Members bring real-world experience and the latest practice innovations to the academic setting. The diverse faculty members of the College of Psychology and Behavioral Sciences are widely recognized for contributions to the field. Many are published scholars, and most hold doctoral degrees. They are committed to providing a substantive education that combines comprehensive knowledge with critical skills and practical workplace relevance. Above all, faculty members are committed to their students' personal and professional development.

ARGOSY UNIVERSITY

ARGOSY UNIVERSITY, WASHINGTON DC

College of Psychology and Behavioral Sciences

Programs of Study
Argosy University, Washington DC, offers the Master of Arts (M.A.) degree in clinical psychology, community counseling, and forensic psychology; the Doctor of Education (Ed.D.) degree in counselor education and supervision, counseling psychology, and organizational leadership; and the Doctor of Psychology (Psy.D.) degree in clinical psychology. Students completing a program may wish to become licensed professionals. Argosy University, Washington DC does not guarantee third-party certification/licensure. Outside agencies control the requirements for taking and passing certification/licensing exams and are subject to change without notice to Argosy University, Washington DC.

The M.A. in Clinical Psychology program is designed to meet the needs of both those students seeking a terminal degree at the master's level and those who eventually plan to pursue a doctoral degree. The master's degree provides students a strong clinical orientation as well as an emphasis in psychological assessment. The program has been structured to educate and train students so they might either be prepared to enter a doctoral program in clinical psychology or enter a professional career as master's-level practitioners. The program provides a strong background in assessment and introduces students to basic clinical interventions skills. Students also receive an introduction to scientific methodology and the bases of scientific psychology.

The M.A. in Community Counseling program is designed to provide students with a sound foundation for the practice of community counseling, with a multifaceted focus on developmental and preventive mental health services. The program introduces students to the basic skills of counseling, integrating individual, group, family, and organizational interventions. It emphasizes development of the attitudes, knowledge, and skills required for the ethical provision of quality professional counseling services. As such, the program is committed to educating and training students to enter the counseling profession as ethical, effective, skilled, and culturally competent practitioners, able to work in a variety of settings with diverse client populations. The curriculum integrates foundational counseling skills, counseling theories, and clinical field experiences taught by experienced practitioners.

The M.A. in Forensic Psychology program is designed to educate and train individuals who are currently working, or wish to work, in fields that utilize the study and practice of forensic psychology. Curriculum provides for an understanding of theory, training, and practice of forensic psychology. It emphasizes the development of students who are committed to the ethical provision of quality services to diverse clients and organizations. The program maintains policies and delivery formats suitable for working adults. The program provides course work in forensic psychology for application to law enforcement, legal and organizational consultation, and program analysis.

The Ed.D. in Counselor Education and Supervision program aligns with the master's-level counselor education programs in order to encourage entry-level counseling students to work toward becoming doctoral-level advanced practitioners, educators, and supervisors. The program prepares counselors for a variety of settings by providing the advanced skills and knowledge necessary to provide leadership and advocacy, as well as serve in supervisory, training, and teaching positions in the counseling profession. The program is also designed to help current practitioners with existing master's-level preparation to advance their careers. This doctorate provides expanded opportunities to compete in the marketplace, on par with the growing number of doctoral-level counseling practitioners.

The Ed.D. in Counseling Psychology program is designed to meet the special requirements of working professionals who want to develop their knowledge and skills to handle the changing needs of modern organizations. The program provides working professionals with the opportunity to pursue their personal and professional goals through the completion of a graduate program. An optional concentration in Counselor Education and Supervision is also available.

The Ed.D. in Organizational Leadership program is designed to meet the special requirements of working professionals who want to develop their knowledge and skills to handle the changing needs of modern organizations. The program can enable working professionals to pursue their personal and professional goals through the completion of a graduate program. The program focuses on the qualities of transformational leadership, not just managerial attributes. This approach allows faculty members to dedicate themselves to preparing students to lead complex organizations faced with an abundance of strategic challenges, such as increasing globalization, changing economies, societal shifts, and individual-organizational relationships. It is the premise of the program that leaders prepared in this manner can be visionaries and innovators, leading viable organizations capable of meeting the challenges of the future.

The Psy.D. in Clinical Psychology program is designed to educate and train students so they may eventually be able to function effectively as clinical psychologists. To enable students to prepare adequately, the curriculum provides for the meaningful integration of theory, training, and practice. The program emphasizes the development of attitudes, knowledge, and skills essential in the formation of professional psychologists who are committed to the ethical provision of quality services.

Research Facilities
Argosy University libraries provide curriculum support and educational resources, including current text materials, diagnostic training documents, reference materials and databases, journals and dissertations, and major and current titles in program areas. There is an online public-access catalog of library resources available throughout the Argosy University system. Students have remote access to the campus library database, enabling them to study and conduct research at home. Academic databases offer dissertation abstracts, academic journals, and professional periodicals. All library computers are Internet accessible. Software applications include Word, Excel, PowerPoint, SPSS, and various test-scoring programs.

Financial Aid
Financial aid is available to those who qualify. Argosy University, Washington DC, offers access to federal and state aid programs, merit-based awards, grants, loans, and a work-study program. As a first step, students should complete the Free Application for Federal Student Aid (FAFSA). Prospective students can apply electronically at http://www.fafsa.ed.gov or at the campus.

Cost of Study
Tuition varies by program. Students should contact Argosy University, Washington DC, for tuition information.

Living and Housing Costs
Students typically live in apartments in the metropolitan Washington, D.C., area. Living expenses vary according to each student's preferred standard of living, housing, and transportation. The University does not offer or operate student housing. Most Argosy University students are full-time working professionals who live within driving distance of the campus. Several nearby hotels offer special rates for those who commute from long distances. The Admissions Department also maintains a list of housing options, including contact information for University students who wish to share housing. For more information, students should contact the Admissions Department.

Student Group
Admission to Argosy University, Washington DC, is selective to ensure a dynamic and engaged student body. The University encourages diversity in academic and employment backgrounds and promotes integration of the student body into professional life through established connections with local and national professional associations. Argosy University offers a professionally oriented education with rich opportunities to gain practical experience in class, field placements, and internships. Full-time students and working professionals gain the extensive knowledge and range of skills necessary for effective performance in their chosen field.

Student Outcomes
Students can register with Argosy University's online career-services system and use select services from a distance, such as degree-specific career e-mail lists, national job posts, and virtual job fairs. Students should contact the University for more information.

Location
Argosy University, Washington DC, is located in suburban Arlington, Virginia. The school provides easy access to most major highways in area and is accessible by public transportation. With its proximity to Georgetown, students enjoy access to the many diverse attractions of the D.C. area. Additional campus space is located at the Art Institute of Washington Building (1820 Fort Myer Drive). The university houses administrative space and seven classrooms at this location. Perhaps best known as the home of the Pentagon and Arlington National Cemetery, Arlington, Virginia, is one of the most highly educated areas in the nation. It is also one of the most diverse. Major employers in the region include MCI Telecommunications Corporation; Bell Atlantic Network Services, Inc.; and Gannett/USA Today Company, Inc.

The University
Argosy University is a private institution with nineteen locations across the nation. Argosy University, Washington DC, provides a career resources office, an academic resources center, and extensive information access for research. It offers the resources of a large university plus the friendliness and personal attention of a small campus. The innovative programs feature dynamic, relevant, and practical curricula delivered in flexible class formats. Students enjoy scheduling options that make it easier to fit school into their busy lives, choosing from day and evening courses, on campus or online. Many students find a combination of class formats to be an ideal way of continuing their education while meeting family and professional demands.

Argosy University is accredited by the Higher Learning Commission and is a member of the North Central Association (30 North LaSalle Street, Suite 2400, Chicago, Illinois 60602; 800-621-7440 (toll-free); http://www.ncahlc.org).

Applying
Argosy University, Washington DC, accepts students year-round on a rolling admissions basis, depending on availability of required courses. Applications for admission are available online or by contacting the campus.

Correspondence and Information
Argosy University, Washington DC
1550 Wilson Boulevard, Suite 600
Arlington, Virginia 22209
Phone: 703-526-5800
          866-703-2777 (toll-free)
Fax: 703-243-8973
E-mail: auadmissions@argosy.edu
Web site: http://www.argosy.edu/washingtondc

Argosy University, Washington DC

THE FACULTY

The Argosy University faculty is comprised of working professionals who are eager to help students succeed. Members bring real-world experience and the latest practice innovations to the academic setting. The diverse faculty members of the College of Psychology and Behavioral Sciences are widely recognized for contributions to the field. Many are published scholars, and most hold doctoral degrees. They are committed to providing a substantive education that combines comprehensive knowledge with critical skills and practical workplace relevance. Above all, faculty members are committed to their students' personal and professional development.

BARRY UNIVERSITY

Graduate Programs in Psychology

Programs of Study

Barry University offers a Master of Science in Clinical Psychology degree program and a School Psychology Program comprising the Master of Science in Psychology and Specialist in School Psychology (S.S.P.) degrees.

The Master of Science in Clinical Psychology program employs the scientist/practitioner model of training with faculty actively involved in research and clinical practice. This offers students the opportunity to obtain the theoretical, scientific, and clinical experience necessary to enter, with appropriate guidance and supervision, into the practice of mental health evaluation and treatment of diverse populations. The program also prepares students for doctoral-level training. The theoretical orientation of the program is eclectic, with emphasis on the clinical assessment and treatment of the mentally ill.

Clinical psychology students can choose from two tracks. The 36-credit option prepares students for application to doctoral programs, while the 60-credit option prepares students to sit for licensing as mental health counselors in the state of Florida. The license qualifies students to engage in private practice and to seek employment with public or private mental health organizations, social service agencies, government and private research teams, and community colleges. The program provides high-quality academic instruction, research experience, and supervised clinical training at a variety of mental health centers.

All courses are offered in the evening. In the second year, all full-time students enroll in a 165-hour clinical psychology practicum that requires one day per week of supervised clinical work in a mental health setting, with a minimum of 40 client contact hours. In the practicum students learn and practice diagnostic and therapeutic skills. The clinical psychology internship offered in the third year of the 60-credit option is a full-time, supervised clinical experience that requires a minimum of 1,000 hours. Under supervision in a mental health facility, students perform a variety of clinically related activities that a licensed professional with a master's degree in clinical psychology would be expected to perform. The clinical experience includes a minimum of 240 hours of direct client contact hours.

Barry's School Psychology Program includes both the Master of Science in Psychology degree and Specialist in School Psychology degree (equivalent to an Ed.S. degree). The School Psychology Program is designed to meet the needs of a broad group of students, including recent graduates with bachelor's degrees and teachers and mental health professionals with years of experience who are interested in a career upgrade. The student is awarded an M.S. degree after completion of 30 credits and can advance to the specialist program. The master's is a prerequisite for the specialist degree, and many students earn both at Barry. However, for students who already have a master's in psychology or a related field, a program adviser can customize a course sequence, which requires the completion of 38 credits.

Completion of the School Psychology Program requires 71 credits and satisfies the academic requirements in accordance with standards set by the National Association of School Psychologists (NASP). Following the internship, students are prepared to meet licensure requirements for the private practice of school psychology as set forth by the state of Florida, as well as certification requirements as set forth by the Florida State Board of Education. The School Psychology Program is approved by the Florida Department of Education and by the National Association of School Psychologists.

All graduate courses in the School Psychology Program are offered in the evening to accommodate working professionals. Field placement and internship courses, which occur near the completion of training, require daytime availability.

Research Facilities

The Monsignor William Barry Memorial Library houses more than 950,000 items, including a vast array of journal subscriptions available in print and electronic full text, and more than 7,500 audiovisual items. The Barry library participates in a number of library networks. The Southeast Florida Library Information Network (SEFLIN) provides, by courier service and fax, access to more than 12 million items and 30,000 periodical titles held by larger academic and public libraries of Dade, Broward, and Palm Beach counties. Materials not readily available at this level are obtained through the Florida Library Information Network (FLIN), which provides for the delivery of materials based in the major libraries of the state of Florida, including those in the state university system. Barry also houses a testing library and a computer lab dedicated to its psychology programs.

Financial Aid

A limited number of graduate assistantships are available. Compensation each semester includes approximately $1500 (clinical psychology) and tuition remission for one course. The time commitment is 8 or 15 hours per week, depending on the psychology program. Normally, positions are awarded for a full academic year, and students are notified of their assistantship in the spring.

Barry University participates in the full array of federal and state financial aid programs. Full-time Florida teachers may receive at least a 20 percent tuition discount under Barry's Professional Recognition Scholarship Program.

Cost of Study

Graduate tuition was $815 per credit for the 2008–09 academic year. Additional course fees may be required, depending on the program of study.

Living and Housing Costs

Campus housing is available for full-time graduate students, space permitting. Barry University provides assistance in locating off-campus housing.

Student Group

Barry University's student body represents all compass points, ages, ethnicities, and faiths. In 2008, Barry was ranked among the top 15 universities nationwide for campus ethnic diversity, according to *U.S. News & World Report.*

Location

The University's 122-acre campus is located in Miami Shores, which is between the cities of Miami and Fort Lauderdale. This ideal location provides students with access to one of the nation's most dynamic multicultural environments and all of its business, cultural, and recreational opportunities.

The University

Barry University is an independent, coeducational university with a history of distinguished graduate programs. Founded in 1940 by the Adrian Dominican Sisters, the University embodies the Catholic liberal arts tradition. It has grown steadily in size and diversity while maintaining a low student-faculty ratio of 14:1. With small classes, students can count on personal attention from experienced faculty. The University's various partnerships with local businesses, schools, hospitals, and community organizations ensure that students gain professional experience and hone their skills.

Applying

Applicants must have a bachelor's degree in psychology or a related field. Completion of the following five undergraduate psychology courses is required: lifespan developmental psychology, abnormal psychology, tests and measurements (psychological testing), physiological psychology (biological bases of behavior), and theories of personality. Students with an M.S. in psychology or a related field may apply to the S.S.P. program directly. To apply, students must submit the completed application, the nonrefundable $30 application fee, official transcripts from all universities and colleges attended, a statement of purpose, letters of recommendation, and GRE scores. International students must also submit TOEFL scores. The application and all credentials should be received at least thirty days before the published first day of registration.

Correspondence and Information

Clinical Psychology Program
Dr. Lenore Szuchman, Chair
Department of Psychology
College of Arts and Sciences
Barry University
11300 NE Second Avenue
Miami Shores, Florida 33161-6695

Phone: 305-899-3278
Fax: 305-899-3279
E-mail: lszuchman@mail.barry.edu
Web site: http://www.barry.edu/psychologyclinical

School Psychology Program
Dr. M. Sylvia Fernandez, Chair
Department of Counseling
Adrian Dominican School of Education
Barry University
11300 NE Second Avenue
Miami Shores, Florida 33161-6695

Phone: 305-899-4868
Fax: 305-899-3718
E-mail: smfernandez@mail.barry.edu
Web site: http://www.barry.edu/psychologyssp

Barry University

THE FACULTY AND THEIR RESEARCH

Clinical Psychology Program

Linda Bacheller, Assistant Professor; Psy.D., J.D., Widener, 2006. Juvenile justice, in-home psychotherapy, children's mental health.

Laura Ferrer-Wreder, Associate Professor; Ph.D., Florida International, 1998. Design, implementation, and evaluation of prevention/intervention initiatives; youth development programs (adolescent-adulthood transition); prevention of youth problem behaviors; identity development; parent-/school-level influences in relation to youth development and problem behaviors; gender/ethnicity considerations in intervention development and dissemination.

Pamela Hall, Assistant Professor; Ph.D. Ohio State, 1992. Social psychology, teens and hip-hop music, community mental health.

Stephen W. Koncsol, Associate Professor; Ph.D., Rutgers, 1976. Psychological well-being and culture, cross-cultural issues in mental health, dyadic communication failures, marital satisfaction/dissatisfaction.

Frank Muscarella, Professor and Director of the Clinical Psychology Program; Ph.D., Louisville, 1991. Evolutionary psychology, human sexuality.

Lenore Szuchman, Professor and Department Chair; Ph.D., Florida International, 1990. Cognition and social cognition in older adults, advice.

Manuel J. Tejeda, Associate Professor; Ph.D., Miami. Leadership, organizational behavior, diversity in the workplace, research methods, structural equation modeling, random regression, substance abuse.

Guillermo Wated, Assistant Professor; Ph.D., Florida International, 2002. Employee attitudes, counterproductive behavior in organizations, cultures and organizations.

School Psychology Program

M. Sylvia Fernandez, Professor and Chair; Ph.D., Southern Illinois. Multicultural issues in counseling and related disciplines, counselor education and credentialing, clinical supervision.

Katherine Fuerth, Assistant Professor; Ph.D., South Florida. Multicultural issues in counseling, education, and supervision; counseling and advocacy for survivors of sexual abuse and domestic violence.

Alberto Gamarra, Assistant Professor; Ph.D., Arizona. Cultural and linguistic diversity, personal assessment, sport psychology.

Jeffrey Guterman, Assistant Professor; Ph.D., Nova Southeastern. Professional identity, integrative counseling models, the application of postmodern theories to counseling.

Jim Rudes, Assistant Professor; Ph.D., Nova Southeastern. Postmodern theory, social constructionism, narrative practices, reflecting teams, supervision.

Karen Shatz, Assistant Professor; Ph.D., Nova Southeastern. Phenomenological experiences of loss, immigration issues in counseling, postmodern supervision.

Agnes E. Shine, Associate Professor; Ph.D., Ball State. Neuropsychological issues with children, traumatic brain injury, learning disabilities.

Richard M. Tureen, Associate Professor; Ph.D., Nova Southeastern. Postmodernism, narrative therapy, solution-focused therapy, systems theory, neuroscience applications to therapy.

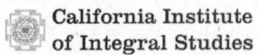
California Institute
of Integral Studies

CALIFORNIA INSTITUTE OF INTEGRAL STUDIES

School of Professional Psychology

Programs of Study

The School of Professional Psychology at California Institute of Integral Studies (CIIS) balances traditional clinical training with a concern for contemporary social, cultural, and spiritual issues. Courses of study encourage integration of new and alternative approaches to psychological health while adhering to rigorous standards of scholarship, research, and practice. Depending upon the course of study, psychology programs provide comprehensive training in the foundation areas of clinical skills, ethics, psychology, and research design and statistics. Clinical training is integrated through the use of practicums prior to internship. Many students train in one of the School's five clinics, drawing upon the rich opportunities for clinical experience in the San Francisco Bay Area. The School of Professional Psychology also supports ongoing research in the study of biofeedback and states of consciousness, promoting the interdisciplinary study of psychology, meditation, and alternative interventions. These resources, combined with innovative psychotherapeutic approaches and with faculty members who are scholar/practitioners, provide CIIS psychology students with a competitive advantage with state and national licensure and professional examinations. Recent state marriage and family therapy (MFT) licensing test results revealed that 93 percent of CIIS psychology graduates who took the exam passed. All graduate programs include some elective study in the Institute's rich palate of disciplines, including Asian and comparative studies, cosmology and consciousness studies, East-West psychology, philosophy, social and cultural anthropology, transformation studies, and women's spirituality studies.

Clinical Psychology: doctorate in Clinical Psychology, Psy.D. degree. The primary objective of the clinical psychology doctoral program is to produce competent, well-rounded psychologists whose practice of professional psychology is rooted in a depth of self-knowledge, breadth of worldviews, and an abiding commitment to honoring and exploring the diverse dimensions of human experience.

Community Mental Health: Master of Arts in Counseling Psychology with a concentration in community mental health; Advanced Certificate in Community Mental Health. To begin in fall 2008, this groundbreaking program integrates the fundamentals of intensive and supplemental case management with an emphasis on counseling and cultural competence and public sector practicum. Students receive thorough training in psychological theory and practice and learn to understand the various public health and community mental health programs available and specific methods to help clients negotiate the system. Students develop expertise in case management, teamwork with multidisciplinary care providers, treatment of complex and multidiagnosis patients, and cross-cultural counseling.

Drama Therapy: Master of Arts in Counseling Psychology with a concentration in drama therapy. One of only two approved graduate training programs in the United States, the drama therapy program offers a broad and thorough background in counseling psychology as well as specialized training in the systematic use of drama and theater processes as means of furthering emotional growth and psychological integration. Graduates work in diverse settings, including mental-health facilities, hospitals, schools, community centers, prisons, senior centers, industry, and private practice.

Expressive Arts Therapy: Master of Arts in Counseling Psychology with a concentration in expressive arts therapy. One of only a handful of fully accredited expressive arts therapy graduate-level programs in the world, the expressive arts program at CIIS integrates a thorough training in theories and methods of psychotherapy with intensive training in expressive arts therapy, which is a multimodal approach to psychotherapy that incorporates painting, drawing, sculpture, dance/movement, drama, music, ritual, poetry, and prose.

Integral Counseling Psychology: Master of Arts in Counseling Psychology with a concentration in integral counseling. The integral counseling psychology program at CIIS was the first accredited, transpersonally oriented, East-West psychology program in the U.S. It maintains a vision of psychotherapy practice that draws upon the major spiritual traditions of the East and West, recent cultural and social sciences research, and the innovations made by contemporary psychoanalytic, humanistic, systemic, and transpersonal psychologies. This program offers a flexible weekend option designed for working adults and students who plan on completing the degree within two and a half years.

Somatic Psychology: Master of Arts in Counseling Psychology with a concentration in somatic psychology. The CIIS somatic psychology program is one of only three accredited graduate programs in somatic psychology in the U.S. Somatics is a movement-oriented, body-centered psychotherapy that integrates Western and non-Western knowledge of the ways in which the body is formed in social, cultural, psychological, ecological, and spiritual environments. Its counseling center is the only academically based community somatics clinic in the U.S.

Research Facilities

The Laurance S. Rockefeller Library has collections of approximately 35,000 volumes (including numerous e-books), 290 periodicals (including electronic journals), 1,000 audiovisual materials (audiocassettes, videotapes, compact disks), and almost 1,000 CIIS dissertations and master's theses. The collections are especially strong in the areas of transpersonal and multicultural psychology, spirituality (particularly women's spirituality, Buddhism, Hinduism, Taoism, Confucianism, and wisdom traditions), integral studies, and studies of consciousness. Among these materials are special collections: Alan Watts' and Haridas Chaudhuri's personal collections, the Langley-Porter collection of psychology and psychiatry, the Rogo collection of parapsychology, and a CIIS Institute Authors' collection.

Financial Aid

Financial assistance is awarded primarily on the basis of need. Financial aid consists of scholarships, loans, grants, and Federal Work-Study. Veterans who qualify may receive full benefits under the G. I. Bill. International students may obtain nonimmigrant visas and are eligible for part-time employment on the campus.

Cost of Study

In 2009–10, full-time annual tuition and fees were $19,550 for M.A. programs and $22,090 for doctoral programs, plus summer semester tuition.

Living and Housing Costs

There is no campus housing. Living expenses (rent, travel, and food) in the Bay Area are around $1200 per month. Information about living and housing costs can be found on the CIIS Web site at http://www.ciis.edu/students/housing.

Student Group

Total enrollment in 2009–10 is 1,150. About 20 percent of the students are people of color; about 9 percent are international students. Seventy percent of the students are women.

The Institute

Founded in 1968 by the Indian philosopher, educator, and humanist Haridas Chaudhuri, the California Institute of Integral Studies is a regionally accredited institution of higher learning and research dedicated to integrating mind, body, and spirit in service to individuals, communities, and the earth. This small, urban, student-centered academic community is situated in central San Francisco. Classes are offered during the day, in the evening, on weekends, and online to accommodate working professionals. Certain programs offer distance learning options or a combination of online and monthly weekend meetings. The Institute is defined by its value of cultural diversity as well as cultural coherence, multiple ways of knowing, spiritual development, a sense of community, emancipatory ideals, and ecological sustainability.

Applying

Decisions regarding admission are based on the potential for success in the chosen field of study by considering past academic achievement and motivation for educational and personal development and the congruence of the applicant's worldview with the Institute's mission and vision. Applicants to the M.A. programs must have earned a bachelor's degree from a regionally accredited institution, with a grade point average of 3.0 or higher. Applicants to the Ph.D. and Psy.D. programs must have earned an M.A., preferably in a related discipline, with a minimum 3.1 GPA. Academic transcripts, the autobiographical and goal statements, a writing sample (if required), letters of recommendation (if required), and an interview are all considered in the admissions committee decision. The Graduate Record Examinations (GRE) test is required only for the Psy.D. program.

Correspondence and Information

Office of Admissions
California Institute of Integral Studies
1453 Mission Street
San Francisco, California 94103

Phone: 415-575-6154
Fax: 415-575-1268
E-mail: admissions@ciis.edu
Web site: http://www.ciis.edu

California Institute of Integral Studies

THE FACULTY AND THEIR RESEARCH

Philip Brooks, Ed.D., Massachusetts, 1975. Psychosynthesis, existential-humanistic, experiential learning, guided imagery.

Brant Cortright, Ph.D., Union (Ohio), 1976. Sri Aurobindo's philosophy as a transpersonal framework for psychotherapy.

Frank Echenhofer; Ph.D., Temple, 1985. Physiology and phenomenology of meditation, integrating developmental and transpersonal psychologies.

Renée Emunah, Program Chair, Drama Therapy; Ph.D., Union (Ohio), 1996. Drama therapy group process, drama therapy with adolescents, self-revelatory performance.

Ian J. Grand, Ph.D., Jungian Institute, 1999. Somatic aspects of interpersonal and intercultural relations, psychodynamic theory.

Lucanna Grey, M.A., Santa Clara, 1981. MFT, existential and Gestalt approaches to psychotherapy.

Judye Hess, Ph.D., Rhode Island, l975. Family systems, Gestalt, experiential learning, and interpersonal dynamics. Private practice specializing in couples, families, and groups.

Michael Kahn, Ph.D., Harvard, 1960. Psychotherapeutic practice, small-group practice, design of higher education.

Don Hanlon Johnson, Ph.D., Yale, 1971. Bodily experience in society, spirituality, and psychology; efficacy of specific somatics practices; psychotherapy; specialization in using action methods with posttraumatic stress disorder (PTSD).

Katharine McGovern, Program Chair Clinical Psychology, Ph.D., Minnesota, 1981. Consciousness, feeling and emotion, false memory.

Esther Nzewi, Ph.D., NYU, 1978. Cross-cultural perspectives in personality assessment, women's roles, child welfare.

Janis Phelps, Ph.D., Connecticut, 1986. Child development, clinical studies in enhanced expectancies and treatment, mind-body wellness, Eastern disciplines, interaction of meditation and creativity.

Kaisa Puhakka, Ph.D., Adelphi, 1983. Zen and psychotherapy, knowing, spirituality and psychotherapy, cognition, gender, meditation.

Benjamin Tong, Ph.D., California School of Professional Psychology, 1974. Cross-cultural issues, critical social thought, existential psychoanalysis, stress and trauma.

Leland van den Daele, Ph.D., Purdue, 1967. Psychology and psychoanalysis, moral judgment, cognition, dreams, music, imagery.

Barbara Vivino, Director, Clinical Training; Ph.D., Maryland, 1998. Dream interpretation, marriage and family counseling, acupuncture.

Armand Volkas, M.A., Antioch, 1986. Cultural conflict resolution, drama therapy and social change, Playback Theater.

Jack S. Weller, M.A., California, Santa Barbara, 1968. Buddhism and Buddhist art, spirituality (Eastern, Western, and shamanic), expressive arts.

Tanya Wilkinson, Ph.D., California School of Professional Psychology–Berkeley, 1979. Feminism and Jungian theory/practice, psychological effects of mythological systems.

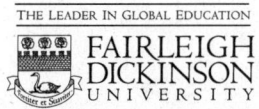

Programs of Study	Fairleigh Dickinson University offers a broad spectrum of psychology programs at its two northern New Jersey locations: the Metropolitan Campus in Teaneck and the College at Florham in Madison. Several of these programs are offered during evenings and weekends for the convenience of the working professional.
	At the College at Florham, the Master of Arts (M.A.) in psychology is offered through the Maxwell Becton College of Arts and Sciences in the following areas: counseling with specializations in addictions and career and a licensed professional counselor (LPC) option, industrial/organizational psychology, and organizational behavior.
	Housed in University College: Arts, Sciences, Professional Studies on the Metropolitan Campus, graduate psychology offerings include a postbaccalaureate respecialization certificate program in psychology, an M.A. program in general/theoretical psychology, an M.A. plus certificate program in school psychology, an M.A. program in forensic psychology, a postdoctoral M.S. program in clinical psychopharmacology (online), a Psy.D. program in school psychology, and an APA-approved Ph.D. program in clinical psychology.
	The Ph.D. in clinical psychology is a five-year, full-time program—including an internship. This program follows the scientist-practitioner model, in which both the internship and dissertation are combined with individual areas of specialization.
	The Psy.D. in school psychology is a year-round, full-time program, although it is possible to both work and pursue the degree, since classes are held in late afternoons and evenings. Individuals entering the program with school psychology certification typically complete the course work portion of the program in two years.
	In addition, a second postdoctoral program is available through the University in the area of psychoanalytic training.
Research Facilities	The University provides extensive facilities to support education, research, and training in psychology, including excellent library resources, research laboratories, and computer facilities. At the College at Florham, research efforts emphasize industrial/organizational psychology and counseling. Research interests include attachment theory, career development in women, crisis counseling and intervention, the effects of constant work accessibility, female adolescent issues, organizational effectiveness, psychoanalytic thought and therapy, psychopharmacology, substance-abuse issues, and work/life balance issues. The Department of Psychology sponsors the Corporate Alliance Center for Organizational Resources, a consulting arm that provides academic expertise to local organizations and relevant work experience for students. In addition, the counseling program provides facilities for in vivo practice of counseling techniques. On the Metropolitan Campus, student and faculty research spans a variety of areas, including psychological assessment; neuropsychological assessment; childhood anxiety disorders; ADHD; play therapy; attachment theory; stress, trauma, and coping; jury selection; women's issues; men's issues; minority issues; spinal cord injury; data analytic techniques; MMPI; Rorschach; and behavioral medicine.
	The Metropolitan Campus features a Center for Psychological Services, providing psychological counseling, psychotherapy, and psychodiagnostics to the general and University communities. The center offers graduate psychology students extensive observation and faculty-mentored experiences. It includes a child anxiety disorders clinic and a child and adult ADHD clinic.
	The *Journal of Psychology and the Behavioral Sciences* (JPBS) is an annual periodical published by the Department of Psychology at the College at Florham. JPBS offers undergraduate and graduate students and their sponsoring faculty members an opportunity to be published in a recognized academic journal.
Financial Aid	A limited number of research, honors research, and teaching scholarships and graduate assistantships are available at Fairleigh Dickinson University. In the clinical psychology Ph.D. program, fellowships are provided to full-time students; teaching and other assistantships are also available. A Johnson & Johnson Scholarship is available to minority doctoral students.
	An international scholarship program is offered for non-U.S., full-time graduate students. The University's application, available through the Office of International Admissions, evaluates the student on both academic merit and financial need.
	Eligible domestic students may borrow up to $20,500 annually in subsidized and unsubsidized loans under the Federal Stafford Student Loan program. The University also offers students several attractive flexible financing programs.
Cost of Study	Tuition for master's-level studies in 2008–09 was $921 per credit for either full- or part-time students. Both doctoral-level programs in psychology carry an inclusive full-program fee. An annual technology fee of $308 for part-time students or $648 for full-time students is also assessed. Full details on doctoral program costs can be obtained by contacting the School of Psychology at the Metropolitan Campus at 201-692-2300 or by visiting the University's Web site at http://www.fdu.edu.
Living and Housing Costs	The University currently offers only limited on-campus housing for graduate students, offered on a first-come, first-served basis. The annual costs at the Metropolitan Campus are $6900 for a standard double room and $3614 for the standard eleven-meal plan, which includes $300 in flex dollars. At the College at Florham, the annual charge is $6534 for a standard double room and $3614 for the standard eleven-meal plan, which includes $300 in flex dollars. International students should contact the University's international student organizations for assistance in locating housing. Proof of health insurance is required of all full-time students, and coverage can be obtained through the University if needed.
Student Group	Students generally come from the Eastern Seaboard, although the Ph.D. program in clinical psychology draws from a more national and international base. The University's proximity to New York draws students from diverse ethnic, cultural, and experiential backgrounds. Classes are small and intimate, and students are afforded individual attention from assigned faculty advisers. In addition to numerous on-site courses across many specialized fields in psychology, independent, cooperative, field, and practicum courses are also available in many programs.
Location	The University has two locations in northern New Jersey. The Metropolitan Campus is located less than 10 miles from New York City on a modern, 88-acre site in Teaneck. The College at Florham is situated in the heart of New Jersey's growing corporate center near Madison and Morristown. The campus's stately, Georgian-style buildings span 166 acres of wooded ground on what once was a private estate.
	The strategic location of each campus offers students majoring in graduate psychology access to a wide range of experiences in community, mental health, medical, pharmaceutical, and corporate settings. The faculty members of the programs are actively involved as leaders in their fields and maintain close networking relationships in the community that lead to invaluable opportunities for students. The Metropolitan Campus's proximity to New York City is especially appealing to students intending to pursue a career in a more urban setting.
The University	Founded in 1942, Fairleigh Dickinson is New Jersey's largest private university, with more than 12,000 students. In addition to its two major New Jersey campuses, the University offers many programs throughout the state and operates its own international campuses in Wroxton, England, and Vancouver, British Columbia, Canada.
Applying	Students seeking admission to any graduate program offered at Fairleigh Dickinson University must formally apply for admission before registering for graduate courses. Applications should be sent to the Admissions Office at the campus the student wishes to attend (College at Florham or Metropolitan Campus) during the semester preceding the one in which the student plans to enroll. Candidates may apply for admission to one campus only. The test results of the Graduate Record Examinations (GRE), college transcripts, a personal statement of interest, and three letters of recommendation are required for master's-level programs in psychology.
	Applications for the master's-level programs are processed on a rolling basis, except for the M.A. in school psychology and M.A. in forensic psychology programs. Students are encouraged to apply at the earliest opportunity to allow ample time to complete the application process. Personal interviews are not normally required (except for the M.A. in school psychology and M.A. in counseling programs) but may be requested as part of the admissions process. Students interested in either the Ph.D. or Psy.D. programs should consult the appropriate Web pages for application deadlines and criteria on these competitive programs.
	For applicants whose native language is not English and who have not completed a baccalaureate degree at an English language institution, a satisfactory score on the Test of English as a Foreign Language (TOEFL) is required.
Correspondence and Information	College at Florham:

College at Florham:
Dr. Yolanda Hawkins-Rodgers, Chair
Department of Psychology
Fairleigh Dickinson University
285 Madison Avenue, M-AB2-01
Madison, New Jersey 07940

Phone: 973-443-8554
E-mail: hrodgers@fdu.edu
Web site: http://www.fdu.edu

Metropolitan Campus:
Dr. Christopher A. Capuano, Director
School of Psychology
Fairleigh Dickinson University
1000 River Road, T-WH1-01
Teaneck, New Jersey 07666

Phone: 201-692-2811
E-mail: capuano@fdu.edu
Web site: http://www.fdu.edu

Fairleigh Dickinson University

THE FACULTY AND THEIR RESEARCH

College at Florham

Yolanda Hawkins-Rodgers, Associate Professor and Department Chair; Ed.D., Rutgers. Counseling psychology.

Donalee Brown, Assistant Professor; Ph.D., Seton Hall. Counseling psychology.
Daniel J. Calcagnetti, Associate Professor; Ph.D., Temple. Behavioral neuroscience.
Jane Cooper, Lecturer; M.A., Fairleigh Dickinson. Industrial and organizational psychology.
John Duryee, Professor; Ph.D., Columbia. Clinical psychology.
Ketrin Saud-Maxwell, Assistant Professor; Ph.D., Fordham. Counseling psychology.
Jakob Steinberg, Professor; Ph.D., Vermont. Social psychology.
Paul Strauss, Professor; Ph.D., NYU. Industrial and organizational psychology.
Anthony Tasso, Assistant Professor; Ph.D., Tennessee. Clinical psychology.
Judith A. Waters, Professor; Ph.D., CUNY, Brooklyn. Social psychology.
Diane Keyser Wentworth, Professor; Ph.D., Wayne State. Industrial and organizational psychology.
Lona Whitmarsh, Associate Professor; Ed.D., Boston University. Counseling psychology.

Metropolitan Campus

Christopher A. Capuano, Associate Professor and Director of the School of Psychology; Ph.D., CUNY Graduate Center. Biopsychology.

Stephen R. Armeli, Associate Professor; Ph.D., Delaware. Social psychology.
Jane Braden-Maguire, Professor; Ph.D., Columbia. Experimental psychology.
Kathleen M. Davis, Assistant Professor; Ph.D., Ball State. School psychology.
Ron Dumont, Associate Professor and Director, Graduate Programs in School Psychology; Ed.D., Boston University; NCSP. School psychology.
Andrew R. Eisen, Associate Professor; Ph.D., SUNY at Albany. Clinical psychology.
Samuel Feinberg, Associate Professor; Ph.D., NYU. Educational psychology.
Margaret S. Gibbs, Professor Emeritus; Ph.D., Harvard. Clinical psychology.
Louis M. Hsu, Professor Emeritus; Ph.D., Fordham. Psychometrics.
Judith Kaufman, Professor; Ph.D., Yeshiva. School psychology.
Juliana Rasic Lachenmeyer, Professor; Ph.D., Columbia. Psychology.
Katharine Loeb, Associate Professor; Ph.D., Rutgers. Clinical psychology.
Neil A. Massoth, Professor; Ph.D., Washington (St. Louis). Clinical psychology.
Robert McGrath, Professor; Ph.D., Auburn. Clinical psychology.
David L. Pogge, Senior Clinical Lecturer; Ph.D., New Mexico. Clinical psychology.
Robert A. Prentky, Associate Professor; Ph.D., Northwestern. Forensic psychology.
Cynthia L. Radnitz, Professor; Ph.D., SUNY at Albany. Clinical psychology.
John C. Santelli, Professor; Ph.D., CUNY Graduate Center. Neuropsychology.
Charles E. Schaefer, Professor Emeritus; Ph.D., Fordham. Clinical psychology.
Janet Sigal, Professor; Ph.D., Northwestern. Social psychology.
Lana A. Tiersky, Associate Professor; Ph.D., California School of Professional Psychology–Los Angeles. Clinical psychology.

FELICIAN COLLEGE

Program in Counseling Psychology

Program of Study	The Master of Arts in Counseling Psychology program is designed to train students to become knowledgeable, skillful, ethical counselors able to assist individuals in need of professional counseling services.
	Graduates will be prepared to focus on psychological counseling for individuals, couples, families, and groups. In line with Franciscan mission and in keeping with the most current trends in psychology, Felician College has developed a unique approach to preparing professional counselors by placing an emphasis on mindfulness, spiritual development, and empowering the potential of others. Upon successful completion of the program, students will be qualified to seek employment as counselors in hospitals, schools, clinics, private group practices, and other settings in the community.
	The Master of Arts in Counseling Psychology consists of 66 credits. The program conforms to the licensing expectations of the New Jersey Professional Counselor Licensing Law, and adheres to the accrediting guidelines of CACREP (Council for Accreditation of Counseling and Related Educational Programs), the professional accrediting body for counseling programs.
Research Facilities	The College Library is a two-story building that serves the needs of students, faculty and staff members, and alumni with more than 110,000 books and over 800 periodical subscriptions. This collection is enhanced by large holdings of materials in microform, which can be used on the library's reader/printer equipment. With its computers linked to information services such as Dialog and OCLC, and as a member of the New Jersey Library Network and VALE, the library locates and obtains information, journal articles, and books not available in its collection from sources all over the country. Computerized databases can also be accessed directly by users through the online FirstSearch workstation, where up-to-date information on 40 million books and an index of 15,000 periodicals is available. The library is also connected to the Internet and has several CD-ROM workstations. Through EBSCOhost, Bell & Howell's ProQuest, CINAHL, and other services, students and faculty and staff members have access to numerous online journal indexes—as well as articles from thousands of periodicals—from anywhere on the campus computer network or from their home computers. An experienced staff of professional librarians is available to assist users.
	The College's computer facilities include an academic and administrative network, four computerized labs, a computerized learning center, and two computer centers that are available for students, with a total of about 200 computers available for student/faculty member use. All classrooms, offices, and facilities are wired for Internet and e-mail.
Financial Aid	To qualify for financial aid, a student must complete the Free Application for Federal Student Aid (FAFSA).
Cost of Study	In 2009–10, graduate tuition is $780 per credit. Fees are additional.
Living and Housing Costs	Students are housed in two dormitories on the Rutherford campus, Milton and Elliott Halls. Both buildings have housing organized around student suites containing semiprivate baths. On-campus room and board is approximately $9500 per year. On-campus housing is not available to married students.
Student Group	Felician College enrolls approximately 2,300 students. In fall 2008, there were approximately 300 students enrolled in graduate programs.
Location	Felician College's Lodi campus is located on the banks of the Saddle River on a beautifully landscaped campus of 27 acres and offers a collegiate setting in suburban Bergen County, within easy driving distance of New York City. The Felician College Rutherford Campus is set on 10.5 beautifully landscaped acres in the heart of the historic community of Rutherford, New Jersey. Only 15 minutes from the Lodi campus, the Rutherford complex contains student residences, classroom buildings, a student center, and a gymnasium. The campus is a short distance from downtown Rutherford, where there are many shops and businesses of interest to students. Regular shuttle bus service between the two campuses is a quick 10-minute ride that turns two campuses into a one-campus home for the students.
The College	Felician College, a coeducational liberal arts college, is a Catholic, private, independent institution for students representing diverse religious, racial, and ethnic backgrounds. The College operates on two campuses in Lodi and Rutherford, New Jersey. The College is one of the institutions of higher learning conducted by the Felician Sisters in the United States. Its mission is to provide a values-oriented education based in the liberal arts while it prepares students for meaningful lives and careers in contemporary society. To meet the needs of students and to provide personal enrichment courses to matriculated and nonmatriculated students, Felician College offers day, evening, and weekend programs. The College is accredited by the Middle States Association of Colleges and Schools and carries program accreditation from the Commission on Collegiate Nursing Education, the International Assembly for Collegiate Business Education, and the Teacher Education Accreditation Council.
Applying	Applicants should complete the application for adult and graduate admission and submit it along with the $40 application fee; transcript(s) from all undergraduate and/or graduate institutions previously attended; scores from GRE or MAT; two letters of reference; and a personal statement. An interview and additional information may be required.
Correspondence and Information	Adult and Graduate Programs Felician College 262 South Main Street Lodi, New Jersey 07644-2117 Phone: 201-559-6077 Fax: 201-559-6138 E-mail: adultandgraduate@felician.edu Web site: http://www.felician.edu/

Felician College

THE FACULTY

For specific information regarding the faculty of Felician College, please visit the College's Web site at http://www.felician.edu/.

FIELDING GRADUATE UNIVERSITY

School of Psychology

Programs of Study

The School of Psychology offers doctoral (Ph.D.) degrees in clinical psychology and media psychology, a master's degree in media psychology and social change, a postdoctoral respecialization in clinical psychology certificate, and a postdoctoral certificate in neuropsychology.

In both Ph.D. programs, students pursue their course of study in their geographical area. These distributed learning programs combine face-to-face faculty-student contact with a Web-based learning environment. The clinical psychology Ph.D. is the only distributed doctoral program accredited by the American Psychological Association (APA). Students may earn a generalist degree or choose a concentration in parent-infant mental health, forensic psychology, neuropsychology, health psychology, or the prevention and control of violence. In the media psychology Ph.D. program, students are encouraged to embrace theory, research, and their own experiences in relation to the production of mass communications and media messages and their impact on individuals, groups, and societies. Students begin the Ph.D. programs by attending a required face-to-face orientation session; they then continue to work independently, with groups, and online. Intensive, face-to-face contact takes place at local cluster meetings, research sessions, psychological assessment labs, and national sessions. Structured online activities deepen the interactions among students and faculty members. Utilizing these resources, students maintain their professional careers and family responsibilities while simultaneously undertaking advanced studies.

The master's degree in media psychology and social change is offered by the School of Psychology in cooperation with UCLA Extension. Students study the specific benefits of understanding human behavior when working with media applications, how media affects individuals and cultures, and how media can be used for socially constructive purposes. Offered entirely online, the program allows for great flexibility and attention to individual goals; carefully planned activities to allow students to maintain their professional careers while in the program.

The postdoctoral respecialization program in clinical psychology enables professionals to maintain their current work commitments while in attendance. Students take advantage of individualized, self-paced, time-efficient offerings that provide the required course work and clinical training to allow them to qualify for examination to become licensed clinical psychologists in most states.

The postdoctoral neuropsychology certificate program allows students to continue working in their current positions while gaining both the theoretical grounding and applied clinical experience needed to develop proficiency in neuropsychological assessment and intervention. The program is designed to meet the needs of professional psychologists who seek an alternative to residency programs that take them away from their work.

Research Facilities

Fielding's library services are designed to serve the complex needs of busy professionals by offering substantial research tools via the Web. The library collection and services include a database of Internet resources, a subsidized document delivery service, a catalog of available dissertations and electronic books, and access to numerous online library databases and journals.

Financial Aid

Fielding Graduate University participates in the Federal Stafford Student Loan program, which makes subsidized and unsubsidized loans available based on financial need. Clinical psychology students are also eligible to borrow HEAL student loans, an additional, unsubsidized Stafford Student Loan separate from the traditional yearly maximum of $18,500. Fielding also participates in Veterans Assistance Programs. In 2007–08, Fielding Graduate University administered approximately $18 million in aid to about 75 percent of its graduate students.

Cost of Study

The 2008–09 tuition for the Ph.D. programs was $20,475 per year or $6825 per trimester term. Tuition for the master's program was $500 per credit, the neuropsychology program was $8370 per year or $4185 per trimester term, and the respecialization program was $19,395 per year or $6465 per trimester term. Tuition and fee rates are subject to change each academic year. Current tuition information can be found at http://www.fielding.edu/tuition.

Living and Housing Costs

Because Fielding Graduate University psychology students work independently and live in various parts of the United States and Canada, costs in addition to tuition vary. Considerations include computer equipment, books and materials, travel to regional cluster meetings, and optional travel to research, clinical, and national sessions. There may be other costs related to the specific course of study.

Student Group

Fielding Graduate University's student community consists of adult learners who have chosen a self-directed, independent learning program and are geographically dispersed, as are the members of the faculty. Fielding's total student population numbers more than 1,500. The approximately 500 students in the School of Psychology are a diverse group of individuals who form a worldwide professional network. The average student age at Fielding Graduate University is 46, with a range from 22 to 74 years of age.

Location

Fielding's administrative offices are located in Santa Barbara, California. The students and faculty members create the Fielding community. The psychology community resides in the forty-eight contiguous United States and Canada.

The University and The School

Founded in 1974, Fielding Graduate University is a global leader in graduate-level networked education for professionals. Fielding is dedicated to providing high-quality, accredited programs through a combination of face-to-face and online interactions between accomplished students and nationally recognized faculty members. The School of Psychology's community of scholar-practitioners embraces diverse approaches to theory, research, and practice. The School's student-centered faculty members serve as partners in the quest for knowledge, collaborating with students in a remarkably collegial atmosphere.

Applying

Students enter the Ph.D. and master's programs in the School of Psychology twice a year (March and September). Applicants to the respecialization program are considered for July and January admission. Neuropsychology applications are considered for the fall term only. Applicants must submit a $75 nonrefundable fee, an application form, and additional materials specific to their program of interest.

Correspondence and Information

Admission Office
Fielding Graduate University
2112 Santa Barbara Street
Santa Barbara, California 93105

Phone: 800-340-1099 (toll-free)
E-mail: admission@fielding.edu
Web site: http://www.fielding.edu

Fielding Graduate University

THE FACULTY

Each faculty member's cluster location is in parentheses.

SCHOOL OF PSYCHOLOGY

Core Faculty
Raymond J. Trybus, Ph.D., Dean
Joseph P. Bush, Ph.D., Associate Dean
Cynthia Stewart, Ph.D., Assistant Dean
Gilbert Reyes, Ph.D., Associate Dean
Kjell E. Rudestam, Ph.D., ABPP, Associate Dean

Nancy Baker, Ph.D., ABPP (San Francisco, CA)
Margaret Cramer, Ph.D. (Melrose, MA)
Sanford Drob, Ph.D. (New York, NY)
Charles Elliot, Ph.D. (Albuquerque, NM)
Debra Bendell Estroff, Ph.D. (Los Angeles, CA)
April Fallon, Ph.D. (Philadelphia, PA)
Tiffani Field, Ph.D. (Miami, FL)
Marilyn Freimuth, Ph.D. (New York, NY)
William Friedman, Ph.D. (Chapel Hill, NC)
Ronald A. Giannetti, Ph.D. (Santa Barbara, CA)
John Gladfelter, Ph.D., ABPP (Dallas, TX)
Anthony F. Greene, Ph.D. (Gainesville, FL)
Erik Gregory, Ph.D. (Boston, MA)
Nancy Hansen, Ph.D. (Fort Collins, CO)
Garry Hare, Ph.D. (Corte Madera, CA)
Sherry L. Hatcher, Ph.D., ABPP (Ann Arbor, MI)
Raymond Hawkins, Ph.D. (Austin, TX)
Patricia M. Hodges, Ph.D. (Claremont, CA)
Jean Pierre Isbouts, D. Litt. (Santa Monica, CA)
Ruthellen Josselson, Ph.D. (Baltimore, MD)
Maureen Kirby Lassen, Ph.D. (Phoenix, AZ)
Sandra McPherson, Ph.D., ABPP (Cleveland, OH)
Gregory Jay Murrey, Ph.D. (Minneapolis, MN)
Jerry Nims, Ph.D., J.D. (Reno, NV; Sacramento, CA)
Samuel D. Osherson, Ph.D. (Cambridge, MA)
Nolan E. Penn, Ph.D., ABPP (San Diego, CA)
Katherine VanDusen Randazzo, Ph.D. (San Diego, CA)
Joan Read, Ph.D. (Atlanta, GA)
Stephen A. Ruffins, Ph.D. (New York, NY)
Lynne Saba, Ph.D. (Santa Barbara, CA)
Judith Schoenholtz-Read, Ed.D. (Seattle, WA)
Henry Soper, Ph.D. (Camarillo, CA)
Ed Tronick, Ph.D. (New York, NY)

Adjunct and Consulting Faculty
David Blustein, Ph.D. (Arlington, MA)
Corinne Goodwin, Ph.D. (Matthews, NC)
Will Kouw, Ph.D. (San Antonio, TX)
Marti Kranzberg, Ph.D. (Dallas, TX)
Kenneth Milles, Ph.D. (Edinboro, PA)
Donald J. Polkinghorne, Ph.D. (Pasadena, CA)
Jason Ohler, Ph.D. (Anchorage, AK)
Janice R. Rudestam, Ph.D. (Santa Barbara, CA)
Gary I. Schulman, Ph.D. (Santa Barbara, CA)
Laura Smith, Ph.D. (Albuquerque, NM)
Sara Cicchetti Sparrow, Ph.D. (North Branford, CT)
Sandra L. Webster, Ph.D. (Olmsted Falls, OH)

NEUROPSYCHOLOGY PROGRAM
Elkhonon Goldberg, Ph.D., ABPP/ABCN (Boston, MA; New York, NY)
Leonard F. Koziol, Psy.D., ABPN (Chicago, IL)
Arnold D. Purisch, Ph.D., ABPP/ABCN, ABPN, ABAP (Irvine, CA)

FLORIDA INSTITUTE OF TECHNOLOGY

School of Psychology

Programs of Study

The School of Psychology offers Master of Science (M.S.) and Ph.D. degrees in the field of industrial/organizational psychology; three different M.S. degrees in behavior analysis: applied behavior analysis (ABA), organizational behavior management (OBM), and ABA+OBM; a Ph.D. in behavior analysis, and a Psy.D. degree in the field of clinical psychology.

The Clinical Doctor of Psychology, APA-accredited program is a practitioner-scientist model, emphasizing assessment, diagnosis, intervention, and evaluation skills, along with training in consultation, supervision, education, administration, and diversity. A strong generalist predoctoral focus is emphasized, with particular training opportunities in neuropsychology, child and family, forensic psychology, primary-care psychology, sexual abuse, and multiculturalism. Practicum placements occur across inpatient and outpatient sites, with a variety of populations and presenting issues. Students enter their internships possessing a wide variety of clinical skills and knowledge of the major treatment modalities. Program requirements include 121 semester hours for postbaccalaureate students, with a possible 18 semester hours of transfer credit for students with master's degrees in psychology or related disciplines; four years of residence; completion of a doctoral research project; completion of comprehensive and clinical qualification examinations; and completion of a one-year, 2,000-hour internship at an approved site.

The M.S. program in industrial/organizational psychology prepares graduate students to either continue their education in a doctoral program or to work in any of the broad human resource functions of business and industry. The program is based on the scientist-practitioner models in which students are encouraged to collect data while participating in organizational interventions. Scholarly works such as journal and conference submissions are encouraged and supported by the I/O faculty. Practical training is required as part of this 45-semester-hour program. Either the completion of a master's thesis or a nonthesis written summary of the student practicum is required. The Ph.D. program requires students to actively participate in academic research and provides students with opportunities to polish their consulting skills. Advanced statistical courses, electives, and research credits round out this 90-semester-hour program. Students can explore specific areas of concentration, including multicultural I/O psychology. Comprehensive examinations take place at the end of the third year. Dissertation research is begun immediately after successful completion of the comprehensive exam. Ph.D. students are encouraged to finish the program in four years. Both programs prepare I/O psychology graduates for a wide variety of careers in academics, management, human resources, and consulting.

The behavior analysis M.S. degree programs at the School of Psychology are accredited by the Association for Behavior Analysis International (ABAI) and approved to meet all certification requirements for those seeking certification as a Board Certified Behavior Analyst (BCBA) by the Behavior Analyst Certification Board.

The M.S. degree in applied behavior analysis emphasizes clinical and educational applications. It requires a minimum of 48 credits, including core classes, ABA classes, foundations of bio-psychology, intensive practical training, and electives. The degree program is offered at both the Institute's main campus and the Orlando Graduate Center. The Orlando site program is offered on Friday afternoons and weekends. Most main campus students do their ABA practical training at the Institute's Scott Center, a state of the art service/training/research facility. The M.S. degree program in organizational behavior management emphasizes applications of behavior analysis to business and industry. It requires a minimum of 42 credits, including core classes, ABA classes, foundations of I/O psychology, foundations of business administration and financial accounting, electives, and optional intensive practical training. The M.S. degree program in ABA+OBM combines the essentials of the other two M.S. degrees but eliminates electives. It requires a minimum of 57 credits. The OBM and ABA+OBM degree programs are offered only at the main campus, but a student may complete the first year at the Orlando site and transfer for their second year. All of the Institute's behavior analysis M.S. degree programs give students the option to complete either a thesis or a capstone project to fulfill graduation requirements. Passing a final program examination also is required prior to graduation. Only full-time students are accepted as the program integrates classroom-based training with hands-on practical training and research. The M.S. programs in behavior analysis prepare graduate students to either continue their education in a doctoral program or to work as a behavior analysis practitioner or consultant. These programs embrace the scientist-practitioner model; thus, students are required to systematically evaluate their interventions. Full-time students typically finish the degree in one summer short of two full academic years.

The School of Psychology also offers a Ph.D. degree in behavior analysis. Only persons who either already have completed an M.S. or M.A. degree in behavior analysis (or a related field with an emphasis in behavior analysis) are considered for admissions. The Institute's own M.S. degree students are encouraged to petition up. However, only 3 to 5 students are accepted per academic year. The Ph.D. degree program prepares students for academic jobs and senior clinical and administrative positions. Degree requirements consist of a minimum of 83 postbaccalaureate graduate credits, of which a minimum of 36 credits must be post M.S./M.A. and 42 of which must be completed at the Institute. The four general competencies emphasized in the program are behavior analytic research, teaching, supervision, and consultation. The Ph.D. program requires a minimum residency of two years at the Institute's main campus.

Research Facilities

The School of Psychology includes the Psychology Building, the Community Psychological Services Clinic, the Applied Research Lab, and the Country Club Lane Research Labs. The East Central Florida Memory Disorder Clinic, Family Learning Program, the Center for Organizational Effectiveness, and the Applied Behavioral Service Center provide service and research opportunities.

Financial Aid

A limited number of research and teaching assistantships are available to graduate students, providing yearly stipends and tuition remission packages ranging from $1800 to $7200. University Graduate Scholarships provide tuition remission for incoming students. A number of work-study positions, as well as various loan programs, are available to students who qualify. Advanced field placement sites usually provide student stipends.

Cost of Study

Graduate tuition for the 2009–10 academic year is $9340 per semester for the Psy.D. program and $1015 per credit hour for the M.S. and Ph.D. programs. Books and testing materials cost about $1800 for the first year of the clinical program.

Living and Housing Costs

Room and board on campus are approximately $4500 per semester in 2009–10. On-campus housing is available for full-time students. Many apartment complexes and rental houses are available near the campus.

Student Group

The School's graduate population averages 170 to 190 students. Approximately two thirds of the students are women, and about 12 percent are members of minority groups.

Twenty students are admitted into the clinical program each year, 8 to 12 into the industrial/organizational psychology master's program, 2 to 4 into the industrial/organizational Ph.D. program, and 30 into the applied behavior analysis program.

Student Outcomes

Graduates from the Psy.D. program secure positions across a number of settings, including psychiatric hospitals, VA medical centers, community mental health centers, rehabilitation hospitals, and private practice. Graduates of the industrial/organizational program find positions in the following areas: employee selection and placement, performance appraisal, training and evaluation, career counseling, management development, organizational development, and employee relations. Graduates work in a variety of professional settings including consulting firms, for-profit organizations, the government, and academic institutions. Graduates of the applied behavioral analysis program find positions in schools, residential programs, group homes, foster- care programs, and consulting firms.

Location

Melbourne is located on the central east coast of Florida, a short drive from the John F. Kennedy Space Center and the city of Orlando.

The Institute

In response to a need for specialized and advanced educational opportunities, Florida Institute of Technology was founded in 1958 by a group of scientists and engineers pioneering America's space program at Cape Canaveral. Florida Tech has rapidly developed into a residential institution that is the second-largest private university in the state of Florida. The faculty and administration are committed to the pursuit of academic excellence in teaching and research in the sciences, engineering, aeronautics, management, and psychology.

Applying

All applicants must possess a bachelor's degree from an accredited institution. Although the degree need not be in psychology, no less than 18 hours of psychology course work must have been completed (including courses in statistics, personality, learning, social, abnormal, and physiological psychology for the clinical applicants). These prerequisite courses may be completed before admission outside of a degree program.

Applicants are expected to have a grade point average of 3.0 or higher on a scale where A = 4.0. All applicants must submit three letters of recommendation, provide a statement of career objectives, and arrange for GRE General Test scores to be sent. The GRE Subject Test in psychology is recommended for application to the Psy.D. clinical program. Official transcripts of all undergraduate and graduate courses attempted must be submitted. Fall term application deadlines are January 15 for clinical, February 1 for industrial/organizational psychology, and March 1 for applied behavior analysis applicants.

Correspondence and Information

School of Psychology
Florida Institute of Technology
150 West University Boulevard
Melbourne, Florida 32901-6988

Phone: 321-674-8105
Fax: 321-674-7105
E-mail: lsorum@fit.edu
Web site: http://www.fit.edu

Florida Institute of Technology

THE FACULTY AND THEIR RESEARCH

G. Susanne Bahr, Assistant Professor of Psychology; Ph.D., Texas Christian. Mental model, information visualization in distributed team environments, usability methodology.
Elbert Q. Blakely, Jr., Assistant Professor of Psychology; Ph.D., Western Michigan; BCBA. Developmental disabilities, behavioral pharmacology, experimental analysis of behavior, teaching, database development.
Guy S. Bruce, Assistant Professor of Psychology; Ph.D., West Virginia; BCBA. Organizational behavior management, instructional design, performance management, human performance engineering, descriptive and functional analysis, philosophical and theoretical foundations of behavior analysis, behavioral medicine, measurement, evaluation, experimental design.
Felipa T. Chavez, Assistant Professor of Psychology; Ph.D., SUNY at Buffalo. Multiculturalism, parenting, child development, family dysfunction, impact of substance abuse on child maltreatment in different sociocultural contexts, social support networks as a buffer to stress and family dysfunction, parent-child interaction therapy treatment effectiveness with minority populations and recovering families.
Patrick D. Converse, Assistant Professor; Ph.D., Michigan. Motivation, self-regulatory processes, personality measurement and cognitive ability, ability requirements of occupations.
Vanessa A. Edkins, Assistant Professor of Psychology, Forensic Psychology Program; Ph.D., Kansas. Juror decision-making, attitudes toward the legal system, legal entrapment.
Richard T. Elmore Jr., Associate Professor of Psychology and Director of Clinical Training; Ph.D., Georgia State. Clinical hypnosis, marital and sex therapy, traumatology, occupational health psychology.
Philip D. Farber, Associate Professor of Psychology; Ph.D., Wisconsin–Milwaukee. Psychological assessment, clinical training issues, competencies in professional psychology training, health psychology.
J. Chris Frongello, Assistant Professor/Humanities and Coordinator of Liberal Arts for Florida Tech Online; Ph.D., Vanderbilt. English literature and English Renaissance drama, composition, humanities, Shakespeare.
William K. Gabrenya, Associate Professor of Psychology and Chair, Undergraduate Program; Ph.D., Missouri. Cross-cultural psychology, Chinese culture, social class and modernization, indigenous psychology, sex, work psychology.
Rich Griffith, Assistant Professor of Psychology and Director, Industrial/Organizational Psychology Program; Ph.D., Akron. Response distortion on noncognitive selection procedures, advanced measurement issues, organizational innovation, cognitive process of work teams.
Julie Gross, Assistant Professor and QEP Director (undergraduate internship director); Ph.D., NYU. Criminal aggression and treatment, psychopathology, sanity, deceit, psychoanalytic theory.
Arthur Gutman, Professor of Psychology; Ph.D., Syracuse. Personnel law, applied statistics, program evaluation, personnel psychology, research design.
Thomas H. Harrell, Professor of Psychology; Ph.D., Georgia. Psychometrics and computerized psychological assessment, use of the MMPI-2 in clinical evaluation, cognitive-behavioral approaches to assessment and therapy, adaptation to aging.
Mark T. Harvey, Assistant Professor of Psychology; Ph.D., Oregon; BCBA. Applied behavior analysis, developmental disabilities, behavioral strategies in educational settings, sleep architecture, integration of biomedical and behavioral indices.
Marshall Jones, Instructor and Coordinator, Undergraduate Forensic Psychology; M.S., Alabama. Law enforcement leadership, law enforcement recruiting and retention, training technology, promotional assessment, racial profiling.
Mary Beth Kenkel, Professor of Psychology and Dean; Ph.D., Miami (Ohio). Clinical/community psychology, integrated care models, women and leadership, rural mental health, psychology and technology, prevention activities in psychology, feminization of psychology, future of professional psychology.
Radhika Krishnamurthy, Associate Professor of Psychology and Director, Clinical Training; Psy.D., Virginia Consortium for Professional Psychology. Personality assessment with the MMPI-2/MMPI-A and Rorschach, child and adolescent development, interface between personality and neuropsychological functioning.
Jose Martinez-Diaz, Assistant Professor and Chair, Applied Behavioral Analysis Program; Ph.D., West Virginia. Professional and conceptual issues, verbal behavior, antecedent events in the treatment of problem behavior, treatment of persons with developmental disabilities and with schizophrenia.
Patrick McGreevy, Assistant Professor; Ph.D., Kansas; BCBA. Verbal behavior, developmental disabilities, teaching language to persons with developmental disabilities, treatment of severe problem behavior, educational applications of ABA, standard measurement and charting.
Kevin Mulligan, Professor and Chair, Clinical Psychology Program; Psy.D., Denver. Neuropsychological assessment and intervention, cognitive changes associated with normal aging and dementia, traumatic brain injury, prolonged exposure for combat-related posttraumatic stress disorder.
Todd Poch, Assistant Professor of Psychology; Psy.D., Denver. Forensic psychology, diagnosis and treatment of stress disorders, men's issues, executive coaching.
James Reynolds, Instructor in Criminal Justice; M.P.A., Central Florida. Law enforcement selection and training; leadership, management, and supervision; human resource issues in criminal justice.
Erin M. Richard, Assistant Professor; Ph.D., LSU. Emotional regulation in the workplace, individual differences related to work motivation.
Lisa Steelman, Associate Professor of Psychology; Ph.D., Akron. Feedback processes, multirater feedback, performance appraisal, work-related attitudes, employee commitment and engagement.
Kristi Sands Van Sickle, Assistant Professor of Psychology; Psy.D., Florida Tech. Community health; integrated health care; clinical health psychology; health policy and legislative advocacy; self-care and professional competence.
Frank M. Webbe, Professor of Psychology; Ph.D., Florida. Aging and technology, sport neuropsychology.
David A. Wilder, Associate Professor of Psychology; Ph.D., Nevada, Reno. Functional analysis and function-based intervention in children with disruptive behavior, organizational behavior management (assessment in OBM, feedback), stimulus preference assessment methods.
Paula Wolfteich, Assistant Professor of Psychology; Ph.D., Purdue. Child maltreatment investigation and treatment models, infant and preschool assessment and early intervention for behavior and developmental disorders, clinical training and supervision.

Adjunct Faculty

W. Abernathy, Ph.D., Ohio State; Abernathy & Associates, Memphis, Tennessee.
J. Beltran, Psy.D., Florida Tech; Beltran Behavioral Health, Kissimmee, Florida.
D. Bersoff, Ph.D., NYU; J.D., Yale; Professor and Director, Law and Psychology Program, Hahnemann.
C. Binder, Ph.D., Columbia Pacific; Binder Reha Associates, Santa Rosa, California.
E. Blakley, Ph.D., Western Michigan; Director of Behavioral Analysis, Quest Kids, Orlando, Florida.
V. J. Carbone, Ph.D., Nova Southeastern; private practice, New York.
E. Cipani, Ph.D., Florida State; Professor, Alliant International University, Fresno, California.
W. E. Eyring III, Psy.D., Florida Tech; clinical psychologist, Circles of Care, Melbourne, Florida.
P. W. Gorman, Psy.D., Florida Tech; private practice, Orlando, Florida.
B. Hensel, Ph.D., Toledo; Circles of Care, Melbourne, Florida.
S. Howze, Psy.D., Florida Tech; private practice, Melbourne, Florida.
F. Kaslow, Visiting Professor of Psychology; Ph.D., Bryn Mawr; marital family, divorce and marriage-dynamics and treatment.
E. Levine, Ph.D., NYU; Associate Chairman and Director, Industrial/Organizational Psychology Program, University of South Florida.
P. McGreevy, Ph.D., Kansas; Private practice, Winter Park, Florida.
K. Murdock, Ph.D., South Florida; Hillsborough County Public Schools, Florida.
T. Rogers, Ph.D., Florida; Florida Department of Children and Families, Florida.
H. Schlinger, Ph.D., Western Michigan; California State University, Northridge, California.
C. Stevens, Psy.D., Florida Tech; private practice, Melbourne, Florida.
M. Stoutimore, Ph.D., Florida; Florida Department of Children and Families.

RECENT FACULTY PUBLICATIONS AND PRESENTATIONS

Baker, J. N., F. T. Chavez, and R. Krishnamurthy. Advanced training workshop for sexual abuse treatment program providers on assessment, diagnosis, and treatment of children traumatized by sexual abuse. Sponsored by the State of Florida, Department of Health, Children's Medical Services, and Florida Tech and supported by the Florida Office for Victims of Crime, Office of Justice Programs, April 3–5, 2006, Jacksonville.
Eiden, R. D., K. E. Leonard, R. H. Hoyle, and **F. T. Chavez.** A transactional model of parent-infant interactions in alcoholic families. *Psychol. Addict. Behav.* 18(4):350–61, 2004.
Cavasos, P., **F. T. Chavez,** M. A. Zevon, and D. M. Green. Impact of surviving canter on locus of control and reproductive concerns. A poster at American Psychological Association Annual Convention, Toronto, Canada, 2003.
Converse, P. D., and R. P. DeShon. A tale of two tasks: Reversing the self-regulatory resource depletion effect. *J. Appl. Psychol.,* in press.
Converse, P. D., M. H. Peterson, and **R. L. Griffith.** Faking on personality measures: Implications for selection involving multiple predictors. *Int. J. Sel. Assess.,* in press.
Converse, P. D., E. W. Wolfe, X. Huang, and F. L. Oswald. Response rates for mixed-mode surveys using mail and email/Web. *Am. J. Eval.* 29:99–107, 2004.
Janner, R., and **R. Elmore.** Coping resources of ROTC cadets: PTSD risk factors for combat deployment. Presented at the Southeastern Psychological Association, Atlanta, Georgia, 2006.
Cimino, A., and **R. Elmore.** Hurricanes Francis and Jeanne: Perceptions of stress among college students. Presented at the Southeastern Psychological Association, Atlanta, Georgia, 2006.
Fernandez, M., and **R. Elmore.** Differential trust and religiosity levels among premarital cohabiters and non-cohabiters. Presented at the Southeastern Psychological Association, Atlanta, Georgia, 2006.
Van Sickle, K. S., and **P. D. Farber.** Measured versus self-reported personality traits: Testing for prediction bias. Poster presented at the meeting of the Florida Psychological Association, Naples, Florida, 2004.
Gabrenya, W. K., Jr., M.-C. Kung, and L.-Y. Chen. Understanding the Taiwan indigenous psychology movement: A sociology of science approach. *J. Cross-Cultural Psych.,* in press.
Gabrenya, W. K., Jr. A sociology of science approach to understanding indigenous psychologies. In *Ongoing Themes on Cross-Cultural Psychology,* eds. B. Setiadia, A. Supratiknya, W. Lonner, and Y. Poortinga. Jakarta, Indonesia: International Association for Cross-Cultural Psychology, 2004.
Griffith, R. L., and **P. D. Converse.** The rules of evidence and the prevalence of applicant faking. In *New Perspectives on Faking in Personality Assessments,* eds. M. Ziegler, C. McCann, and R. Roberts. New York: Oxford University Press, in press.
Peterson, M. H., **R. L. Griffith,** and **P. D. Converse.** Examining the role of applicant faking in hiring decisions: Percentage of fakers hired and hiring discrepancies in single and multiple predictor selection. *J. Bus. Psychol.,* in press.
Griffith, R. L., and M. H. Peterson. The failure of social desirability measures to capture applicant faking behavior. *Industrial and Organizational Psychology: Perspectives on Science and Practice* 1:4, 2008.
Gutman, A. The administration's position on Gratz and Grutter: Too many inconsistencies. *Ind.-Organ. Psychol.,* in press.
Gutman, A. Adverse Impact: Why is it so difficult to understand? *Ind.-Organ. Psychol.* 40(2).
Gutman, A. *EEO Law and Personnel Pract.,* 2nd ed. Thousand Oaks, Calif., Sage Publishers, 2000.
Malow, B. A., et al. **(M. T. Harvey).** Impact of treating sleep apnea in a child with autism spectrum disorder. *Pediatric Neurology,* in press.
Doran, S. M., **M. T. Harvey,** and R. H. Horner. Sleep and developmental disorders: Assessment, treatment, and outcome measures. *Mental Retardation* 44, 13–27, 2006.
Kenkel, M. B. Adopting a competency model for professional psychology. *Training and Education in Professional Psychology,* in press.
DeLeon, P. H., **M. B. Kenkel.,** J. Oliveira-Berry, and M. T. Sammons. Involvement in the public policy process: A key to the future of the profession. In *Oxford Handbook of Clinical Psychology,* ed. D. Barlow. New York: Oxford University Press, in press.
Kenkel, M. B. and R. L. Peterson, eds. *Competency-Based Education for Professional Psychology,* Washington, D.C.: American Psychological Association, 2009.
Kenkel, M. B. Transforming the U.S. health care system—Reducing the profit, increasing the care, a review of "Rx for Health Care Reform." *PsycCRITIQUES* 53(18):5, April 30, 2008.
Krishnamurthy, R. Review of the Minnesota multiphasic personality inventory-adolescent. In *Test Critiques,* ed. D. J. Keyser, vol. 11, pp. 281–90. Austin, Tex.: Pro-Ed, 2005.
Krishnamurthy, R., K. Bolinskey, and R. P. Archer. MMPI-A structural summary: Integrating new scales and subscales. In *MMPI/MMPI-A,* chairs R. Krishnamurthy and R. P. Archer. Paper presented at the annual meeting of the Society for Personality Assessment, Chicago, Illinois, 2005.
Krishnamurthy, R., et al. Achieving competency in psychological assessment: Directions for education and training. *J. Clin. Psychol.* 60(7):725–39, 2004.
Martinez-Diaz, J. A., T. R. Freeman, **M. P. Normand,** and T. E. Heron. The ethical practice of applied behavior analysis. Invited chapter in J. O. Cooper, T. E. Heron, and W. L. Heward, *Applied Behavioral Analysis,* 2nd ed. Upper Saddle River, N.J.: Merrill/Prentice Hall, in press.
Martinez-Diaz, J. A., and **D. A. Wilder.** Behavior, not symptoms: A behavior analytic interpretation of schizophrenia and other severe and persistent mental disorders. Invited presentation for Continuing Education Units, Gainesville, Fla., 2004.
Martinez-Diaz, J. A., P. Osnes, and C. Peeler. Master's level graduate training programs in applied behavior analysis in Florida. Panel presented at the Florida Association for Behavior Analysis, Daytona Beach, Florida, 2002.
Martinez-Diaz, J. A. Providing home- and community-based behavior analysis services to persons diagnosed with mental retardation and other developmental disabilities. Invited workshop presented at the Alabama Association for Behavior Analysis, Birmingham, Alabama, 2003.
Kelly, M., **K. Mulligan,** and M. Monahan. Fitness for duty evaluations. In *Military Neuropsychology,* ed. C. Kennedy. New York: Guildford, in press.
Richard, E. M., J. M. Diefendorff, and J. H. Martin. Revisiting the within-person self-efficacy and performance relationship. *Human Performance* 19(1):67–87, 2006.
Diefendorff, J. M., and **E. M. Richard.** Antecedents and consequences of emotional display rule perceptions. *J. Appl. Psychol.* 88:284–95, 2003.
Parks, K. M., and **L. A. Steelman.** Organizational wellness programs: A meta-analysis. *J. Occup. Health Psychol.* 13(1):58–68, 2008.
Domagalski, T., and **L. A. Steelman.** The impact of gender and organizational status on workplace anger expression. *Manag. Comm. Q.* 20(3):297–315, 2007.
Steelman, L. A. and P. E. Levy. Using advanced statistics. In *The psychology research handbook,* 2nd ed., *eds. F. T. L. Leong and J. T. Austin. Sage Publishers, Thousand Oaks, Calif., 2006.*
Salinas, C., **F. M. Webbe,** and T. DeVore. The epidemiology of soccer heading in competitive youth players. *Journal of Clinical Sports Psychology* 3:15–33, 2009.
Wild, K., et al. **(F. M. Webbe).** The status of computerized cognitive testing in aging: A systematic review. *Alzheimer's & Dementia: The Journal of the Alzheimer's Association* 4:428–37, 2008.
Webbe, F. M., Sport neuropsychology. In *The Neuropsychology Handbook,* 3rd ed., eds. A. M. Horton and D. Wedding. New York: Springer Publishing Company, 2007.
Wilder, D. A., et al. Functional analysis and treatment of rumination using fixed-time delivery of a flavor spray. *J. Appl. Behav. Anal.,* in press.
Marcus, A. and **D. A. Wilder.** A comparison of peer video modeling versus self video modeling to teach textual responses in children with autism. *J. Appl. Behav. Anal.,* in press.
Squires, J. and **D. A. Wilder.** A preliminary investigation of the effects of rules on employee performance. *J. Organ. Behav. Manag.,* in press.
Wilder, D. A., R. Saulner, G. Beavers, K. A. Zonneveld. Contingent access to preferred items versus a guided compliance procedure to increase compliance among preschoolers. *Educ. Treat. Child.* 31:297–306, 2008.
Wilder, D. A., et al. Identification of olfactory stimuli as reinforcers in individuals with autism: A preliminary investigation. *Behav. Interventions* 23:97–103, 2008.

GEORGE FOX UNIVERSITY

Doctor of Psychology Program

Programs of Study

The Doctor of Psychology (Psy.D.) degree emphasizes the practitioner-scholar model, which puts more emphasis on clinical skills than the more traditional research-oriented, scientist-practitioner model leading to the Ph.D. Nonetheless, within the George Fox University Psy.D. degree program, training in empirical research skills is an important part of the program, and it is common for students and faculty members to present and publish empirical research findings at regional and national conferences. The Psy.D. degree prepares students for internships and subsequent professional practices in a variety of settings. A Master of Arts (M.A.) degree in psychology is conferred on the way to the Psy.D. degree.

The Psy.D. degree program typically consists of four years of full-time study followed by a year of full-time internship. More than 90 percent of recent internships obtained have been accredited by the American Psychological Association and/or meet standards of the Association of Psychology Postdoctoral and Internship Centers. The curriculum, consisting of 125 semester hours, includes courses in scientific foundations of psychology, psychological research, assessment and psychotherapy, and integration of psychology and Christian faith. Required courses encourage students to become well-rounded, skilled clinicians, and electives allow students to explore areas of special interest. A research-based or theoretical dissertation also is required. The program is accredited by the Northwest Association of Schools and Colleges and the American Psychological Association (Committee on Accreditation, Office of Program Consultation and Accreditation, American Psychological Association, 750 First Street NE, Washington, D.C., 20002-4242; telephone: 202-336-5979; http://www.apa.org/ed/accred.html). Distinctives of the program include its emphasis on mentoring (using clinical team and research team models), its inclusion of a Christian worldview, and a university setting in a nonurban location.

Research Facilities

The Newberg campus library and the Portland Center library house a combined total of nearly 200,000 print volumes and receive more than 1,100 print journal subscriptions. Thousands of journal titles are available in electronic format. The University is a member of the Portland Area Library System (PORTALS) and the Orbis Cascade Alliance, a consortium of twenty-six college and university libraries in Oregon and Washington. The Orbis Cascade union catalog enables users to make requests from millions of books held in member libraries as well as obtain full-text recent journal articles electronically. Students may use many other academic libraries in the Northwest. A computer lab also is available; it provides most word processing, spreadsheet, slide-making, and statistical software for graduate student use. An on-campus health and counseling center serves as a clinical training facility. Classrooms, faculty offices, a computer lab, café, and a student lounge are all conveniently located in the Villa Academic Complex on the east side of campus, where there is ample free parking.

Financial Aid

The University participates in the Federal Direct Student Loan Program for the Federal Subsidized Stafford Loan and the Federal Unsubsidized Stafford Loan. Scholarship aid is available for those contributing to ethnic diversity within the program. Teaching and research assistantships are available after the first year.

Cost of Study

The Psy.D. program cost is $715 per semester hour for the 2008–09 school year. The amount is billed per semester. An interest-free monthly payment plan is available. Additional fees applied to items such as books and assessment lab materials.

Living and Housing Costs

A wide variety of housing is available in Newberg and throughout the Portland metropolitan area. On-campus housing is not available for graduate students, but off-campus housing resources are available on the University's Web site. Rent for off-campus private rooms ranges from $275 to $500 a month; one-bedroom apartments range from $425 to $650 per month; and two-bedroom apartments range from $500 to $800 per month. Rentals of two-bedroom homes start at $850.

Meals may be purchased at a bistro-like café at the program's principal location, or an on-campus cafeteria, which provides menu items ranging from sandwiches to pizza. Students may pay for meals individually or by purchasing a declining-balance card from the food services department. Many eating establishments also exist near the campus.

Student Group

Alumni of the Graduate Department of Clinical Psychology (GDCP) are licensed psychologists in numerous states throughout the United States. They work in a variety of practice settings, including independent and group practices, hospitals, community and public-health agencies, military and veteran administration facilities, correctional institutions, as well as church and parachurch organizations. Graduates also teach in a variety of settings, including colleges and seminaries. The GDCP Student Council represents on-campus student interests to the faculty and administration. The student council is composed of elected officers from each cohort of the GDCP student body.

Location

George Fox University's main campus covers 85 tree-shaded acres in a residential neighborhood of Newberg, a friendly community of 22,000 located 23 miles from Portland, Oregon. The Pacific Ocean is just a 60-minute drive to the west, and the year-round ski slopes and hiking trails of Mt. Hood are 90 minutes to the east. A grass campus quad bordered by academic buildings, a library, gymnasium, and the student commons surrounds the Centennial Tower. Running through campus is Hess Creek Canyon, a natural setting of trees, ferns, and wildflowers.

The University

George Fox University is the only evangelical Christian university in the Pacific Northwest classified by *U.S. News & World Report* as a national university. The University was founded in 1891 by Quaker pioneers. From the beginning, the University's purpose has been to demonstrate the meaning of Jesus Christ by offering a caring educational community in which each individual can achieve the highest intellectual and personal growth and participate responsibly in world concerns.

Applying

The Psy.D. program begins at the end of August. To apply for admission, the following are required: a baccalaureate degree from a regionally accredited college or university by enrollment, with a GPA of at least 3.0 (on a 4.0 scale) in the last two years of course work; submission of scores for the General Test of the Graduate Record Examinations (scores must be less than five years old); and an interview with the program faculty members. Completion of at least 18 semester hours in undergraduate psychology is preferred. Applicants may apply to the program online or request printed materials. The application deadline for admission materials is January 15.

Correspondence and Information

For correspondence and information, contact:
Graduate Admission Office
George Fox University
414 North Meridian Street, #6149
Newberg, Oregon 97132
Phone: 800-631-0921 (toll-free)
    503-554-2263 (Adina McConaughey; Graduate Admission Counselor)
    503-554-2370 (Wayne Adams, Ph.D., ABPP; Program Chairperson)
E-mail: psyd@georgefox.edu
Web site: http://psyd.georgefox.edu

George Fox University

THE FACULTY AND THEIR RESEARCH

Wayne V. Adams, Professor and Program Chairperson; Ph.D., Syracuse; ABPP(CL). Research interests: Child memory and its assessment, child/adolescent cognitive assessment, hospital-based pediatric psychology, learning disorders, school consultation, childhood and adolescent behavior disorders. Clinical interests: learning and related behavior disorders, pediatric neuropsychological assessment, neurodevelopmental disorders.

Robert E. Buckler, Professor; M.P.H., Johns Hopkins; M.D., Georgetown. Research interests: Medical psychology; corrections; community mental health; epidemiology; religious variables and mental health; organization, administration, and delivery of mental health services in religious settings; selected religious, family, and demographic variables as they relate to social adaptation status of first-grade children (a longitudinal study); psychosomatic patterns in families.

Roger K. Bufford, Professor; Ph.D., Illinois. Research interests: Religious/spiritual issues in psychotherapy, spiritual outcomes of psychotherapy, theoretical and applied issues related to relationship of psychology and Christian faith, spiritual well-being and spiritual maturity, assessment of mental health treatment outcomes in managed-care settings.

William Buhrow, Director of Health and Counseling Services; Psy.D., George Fox. Research interests: University student alcohol use, premarital counseling, short-term solution-focused therapy, university health-care issues and systems.

Clark D. Campbell, Professor and Director of Clinical Training; Ph.D., Western Seminary; ABPP(CL). Research interests: Development and maintenance of professional relationships between disciplines, assessment of family health and dysfunction, rural psychology. Clinical interests: Interpersonal and cognitive therapies.

Kathleen A. Gathercoal, Professor and Director of Research; Ph.D., Case Western Reserve. Research interests: Effects of postmodernism on the discipline of psychology and psychological phenomena (including spiritual development, problem solving, and identity development), cognitive, or social developmental psychology.

Christopher J. Koch, Associate Professor; Ph.D., Georgia. Research interests: Attention, Stroop effect, analysis of error rates, sports medicine, individual differences, visual perception.

Mark R. McMinn. Professor and Director of Integration; Ph.D., Vanderbilt; ABPP (CL). Research interests: Integration of psychology and Christianity, clergy health and prayer. Clinical interests: Cognitive therapy.

Mary Peterson, Assistant Professor and Associate Director of Clinical Training; Ph.D., California School of Professional Psychology. Research interests: Outcome research in clinical interventions for the adult severely mentally ill population, adjudicated minors and adolescents. Clinical interests: Health psychology and family therapy.

Nancy S. Thurston, Professor; Psy.D., Central Michigan. Research interests: Shame, validity of the Thurston-Cradock Test of Shame; psychological assessment. Clinical interests: Clergy evaluation.

LESLEY UNIVERSITY

Graduate School of Arts and Social Sciences
Division of Counseling and Psychology

Programs of Study	Since their founding in 1975, Lesley University's graduate programs in counseling and psychology have advanced a philosophy of education grounded in a strong foundation of psychology-based, rigorous theoretical study; an emphasis on field experience in a variety of professional settings; and the personal development of each student as a reflective practitioner. This philosophy, with its integrative holistic approach to training in counseling and psychology, its footing in reality, and its emphasis on the student's personal development, has given Lesley a unique and highly regarded position in graduate education. The counseling and psychology programs lead to two types of credentials—licensure as mental health counselors and initial licensure as school counselors.

The Master of Arts (M.A.) in Clinical Mental Health Counseling Program (60 credits) is intended for graduates who wish to have the most comprehensive training available at the master's level to support mental health counseling practice. The program meets the educational requirements for master's-level counseling licensure in Massachusetts and most other states. This program is offered on the Cambridge campus and can be completed in three academic years of full-time study, with 1,300 hours of required field experience. In this program, students have the opportunity to specialize in one of three areas in which Lesley has built a distinguished reputation: holistic studies, trauma studies, and school and community counseling.

The M.A. in counseling psychology with the professional counseling specialization is a 60-credit program designed for individuals who wish to practice professional counseling in the community. This program meets the educational requirements for licensure as a mental health counselor in Massachusetts and many other states. Offered in Cambridge and at off-campus sites in Massachusetts, this program can be completed in three academic years of full-time study on campus or approximately four years of part-time study on campus and at Massachusetts off-campus sites. A minimum of 700 hours of field experience is required.

The 48-credit M.A. program in counseling psychology with the school counseling specialization provides the required graduate training for individuals who wish to work as guidance counselors in primary and secondary school settings. Graduates are eligible for initial licensure in school guidance counseling from the Massachusetts Department of Education at grade levels pre-K–8 or 5–12. Both programs can be completed in two academic years of full-time study, and a minimum of 700 hours of field experience is required.

The M.A. in counseling psychology with no specialization is a 48-credit program designed for individuals who wish to practice counseling interventions and consultation skills with children and adults in community settings or who intend to continue on to doctoral studies in psychology. The program allows students to become generalists in the field. To be eligible for licensure in mental health counseling in Massachusetts, graduates of this program must complete 12 additional credits of graduate course work in counseling.

Candidates who already hold a master's degree in psychology or a related field may pursue a Certificate of Advanced Graduate Study (C.A.G.S.). This 36-credit certificate option is for experienced professionals who wish to expand their clinical skills, engage in scholarly reflection, and enhance theoretical understanding. On-campus enrollment is required.

The Advanced Professional Certificate in Trauma Studies Program offers the opportunity for post-master's professional counselors and other post-master's practitioners to develop expertise in psychosocial trauma work. The curriculum includes an overview of trauma theory and practice as well as a focus on specific client populations and topics.

The Division of Counseling and Psychology offers school guidance counseling and school adjustment counseling master's degree programs that are approved by the Massachusetts Department of Education (leading to initial licensure). The M.A. in counseling psychology programs are accredited by the Masters in Psychology Accreditation Council (MPAC). The Division of Counseling and Psychology is approved by the Council of Applied Masters Programs in Psychology (CAMPP).

Research Facilities	The Ludcke Library maintains a working collection of books, periodicals, microfilm and microfiches, curriculum materials, nonprint materials, and software resources. The Library provides Internet resources and database access to general and subject-specific resources appropriate to the subject focuses of the University. The Kresge Center for Teaching Resources provides instructional resources for individual and group instruction, and the Microcomputer Center houses the instructional computing activities of the University, including a collection of educational software. Through the Fenway Consortium students can access thirteen other libraries in the Boston-Cambridge area.
Financial Aid	The Lesley University Financial Aid Office administers all federal financial aid programs. There are opportunities in college teaching, advising, and research activities, as well as field placements. A limited number of assistantships are awarded by semester or academic year. Most positions require about 10 to 15 hours of work per week.
Cost of Study	Tuition for on-campus graduate students was $765 per credit for 2008–09; tuition for off-campus graduate cohort students ranges from $430 to $550 per credit.
Living and Housing Costs	Housing is not available for graduate students on campus. Information on local housing and housing assistance are available upon request from the Residence Life Office of Student Affairs.
Student Group	Students in the Division of Counseling and Psychology vary in age, academic background, and life and professional experiences—a heterogeneity that contributes to the vitality and real-world flavor of the programs. In its admission practices, Lesley is strongly committed to assembling a student body that reflects the diversity in society.
Location	Lesley University occupies a campus near Harvard Square in Cambridge, an area that benefits from the many advantages of the cities of Boston and Cambridge. The University is connected to downtown Boston by public transportation. Within a 6-mile radius are numerous historical sites and cultural attractions, including theaters, museums, and concerts.
The University	Lesley University, founded in 1909 as a women's teaching college, continues its commitment to educating undergraduates while also offering graduate and Ph.D. programs in the fields of education, environmental studies, human services, counseling and psychology, and the arts. With today's student in mind, Lesley University has successfully pioneered a wide variety of flexible programs for adult learners that share a commitment to quality, innovation, and the integration of theory with practice.

Lesley offers degree programs for learners at all levels. The University also supports several centers and hosts a variety of academic and professional conferences and institutes. Lesley programs operate throughout Massachusetts and in twenty-three other states as well as at an affiliated site in Israel.

Applying	Requirements for admission to graduate degree programs are a bachelor's degree (for the M.A. programs) or a master's degree (for the C.A.G.S. program) from a regionally accredited college or university as well as a satisfactory grade point average, official transcripts of undergraduate and graduate work, scores from the Miller Analogies Test, three letters of recommendation, a three- to five-page personal statement, and the nonrefundable $50 application fee. An interview is required once all application materials are received. Application packets are available from the Office of Admissions for Graduate and Adult Bachelor's Programs. Applications are processed on a rolling basis. International students not residing in the United States should apply by May 1 for the fall semester and October 1 for the spring semester.
Correspondence and Information	Office of Graduate and Adult Bachelor's Admissions Lesley University 29 Everett Street Cambridge, Massachusetts 02138-2790 Phone: 617-349-8300 888-LESLEY.U (toll-free) E-mail: info@lesley.edu Web site: http://www.lesley.edu/oncampus

Lesley University

THE FACULTY AND THEIR RESEARCH

Core Faculty

Paul Crowley, Professor Emeritus; Ph.D., Catholic University. Group therapy and counseling and spirituality.

Priscilla Dass-Brailsford, Associate Professor; Ed.D., Harvard. Resiliency across the life span, with a focus on longitudinal research designs and comparative studies; impact of the stressors of community violence and political violence on different communities and understanding community coping styles; effects of racism, discrimination, and poverty and the sustaining factors.

Susan Gere, Professor and Division Director; Ph.D., Simmons. Adult and child psychopathology, trauma recovery, community consultation.

Lisa Tsoi Hoshmand, Professor; Ph.D., Hawaii. Philosophical and theoretical psychology, qualitative methodology and action research, cross-cultural issues, professional education in counseling and psychology.

Jared Kass, Professor; Ph.D., Union (Ohio). Contributions of spiritual development to health-promoting behaviors, pro-social behaviors, psychological maturation.

Dalia Llera, Associate Professor; Ed.D., Harvard. Mental health and community agencies, with a focus on women, Spanish-speaking minorities, children, and adolescent victims of violence and oppression.

Sue Motulsky, Assistant Professor; Ph.D., Harvard. Career planning and development.

Rick Reinkraut, Associate Professor and Supervisor of Academic Affairs; Ed.D., Harvard; Ph.D., Connecticut. Therapist use of self, empathy, the healing power of relationships.

Eleanor Roffman, Professor and Director of Field Training; Ed.D., Boston University. Transformative education.

Rakhshanda Saleem, Assistant Professor; Ph.D., Colorado State. Neuropsychology and assessments.

LOYOLA UNIVERSITY MARYLAND

Graduate Programs in Psychology

Programs of Study

The graduate programs offered by Loyola University Maryland's Department of Psychology prepare students to obtain licensure or to enter careers in the field of psychology, in both research and counseling capacities. The programs combine course work in both theory and skill development with clinical field experiences at numerous sites throughout Baltimore.

The Doctor of Psychology (Psy.D.) degree emphasizes clinical training and a foundation of psychological theory and knowledge. The degree requires completion of 126 credits, including dissertation, field placement, and course work. During the first four years, students take 4–5 courses per semester and devote 10–16 hours per week to clinical training at the Loyola clinical centers, hospitals, and university research centers. The fifth year is a full-time clinical internship, which may or may not be located in the Baltimore area. Additional information about the Psy.D. degree is available at http://www.loyola.edu/academics/psychology/doctoral/index.html.

Master of Science (M.S.) degree programs are offered in clinical psychology and in counseling psychology, with thesis and practitioner tracks for each degree. The practitioner track programs are 48 credits and the thesis track programs are 45 credits. Both tracks include 18 credits of core course work. Students in the thesis tracks must pass a comprehensive examination and complete a thesis project; students in the practitioner tracks complete an externship and must pass a comprehensive examination. Both tracks also require an externship. For additional information on the masters programs please visit: http://www.loyola.edu/academics/psychology/masters/index.html.

For practitioners who already hold master's degrees and want to practice independently, the Licensed Clinical Professional Counselor (LCPC) Program provides the course work needed to become licensed professional counselors in the state of Maryland. For licensure eligibility, students must complete a total of 60 credits in an individualized program of study.

The Certificate of Advanced Study (CAS) is open to students who hold a master's degree and wish to supplement their studies with additional courses. The certificate requires completion of 30 credits.

Students can find further information about the Masters Plus and CAS programs, including course requirements, at http://www.loyola.edu/academics/psychology/masters/continuing/index.html.

Research Facilities

Departmental facilities are available for research and clinical training experience. The department also maintains a behavioral medicine laboratory for research and training. In addition, computers, with helpful tools such as SPSS, PsycINFO, and Internet access, are available for student research.

The Loyola Notre Dame Library contains approximately 463,000 books and bound periodical volumes; over 11,000 videos, DVDs, and CDs; and 989 print periodical subscriptions. The library's Web site serves as a gateway to a variety of Internet resources, including numerous databases such as ERIC, Lexis-Nexis Academic Universe, Maryland Digital Library, Cambridge Scientific, and Business Source Premier, as well as full-text articles from over 23,000 periodicals.

Financial Aid

A variety of financial assistance is available to graduate students. Graduate assistants work 10–20 hours per week in faculty and administrative departments in exchange for a stipend and tuition remission. A number of scholarships are available from the University; award amounts, entry requirements, and eligibility criteria vary. Federal Stafford Loans provide up to $8500 per year in subsidized loans or $20,500 in unsubsidized loans. The Federal Graduate PLUS Loan Program allows students to borrow up to the full cost of attendance, less other aid received. Other loans may be available from alternative sources. Some students may be eligible for federal work-study.

Cost of Study

In 2009–10, tuition is $615 per credit for most psychology students. Students in the Doctor of Psychology program spend $25,154 per year for the first four years of the program. There is no tuition for the internship year (fifth year). Other costs include a $25 registration fee, a $75 laboratory fee, and a $300 field experience fee.

Living and Housing Costs

The University does not offer on-campus housing for graduate students, except those who work as resident assistants as part of their financial aid package. However, off-campus housing is available. Students can expect to spend $700–$1000 per month for a 1-bedroom apartment and $850–$1300 for a 2-bedroom apartment, depending on size and location.

Student Group

Approximately 200 students are enrolled in the master's programs in any given year, including 100 in the clinical psychology program, 75 in the counseling psychology program, and 25 in the post-masters programs (Masters Plus and CAS). Seventeen new students are enrolled in the Doctor of Psychology program each year. These students come from a wide range of backgrounds, but all are expected to hold an undergraduate degree in psychology or in an allied field.

Student Outcomes

Graduates of the program enter into a wide variety of careers in the field of psychology. Some enter into private practice, working with the general population or within a specialized area. Others work at hospitals, research centers, universities, and other organizations.

Location

Baltimore is one of the most visited cities in the nation, with 12 million visitors each year. The city has a variety of museums, art galleries, theaters, and music venues, as well as annual festivals. The Inner Harbor, a popular waterfront attraction, is surrounded by historic neighborhoods with unique shops and restaurants for every style and taste.

The University

Founded by Jesuits in 1852, Loyola University Maryland (formerly Loyola College in Maryland) remains committed to the ideals embodied by the priests and brothers of the Society of Jesus, which include an emphasis on academic excellence, the importance of the liberal arts, and the education of the whole person. The University enrolls approximately 6,100 students in a broad spectrum of programs that are practitioner-oriented and designed for professionals seeking a greater level of expertise and satisfaction in their careers.

Applying

Applicants to all programs offered by the Department of Psychology must submit a completed application form and a nonrefundable $50 application fee. In addition to the program-specific information outlined below, interested students can find further information about application requirements at http://www.loyola.edu/academics/psychology/doctoral/index.html.

Applicants to the Psy.D. program must possess a bachelor's or master's degree from an accredited institution. Students with a bachelor's degree must have earned a minimum overall GPA of 3.0 (on a 4.0 scale). Students with a master's must have at least a 3.2 GPA at the graduate level. Applicants must also submit three letters of recommendation, a personal essay, their current vitae, official GRE scores from within the last five years, and official transcripts from all colleges and universities attended. Other criteria to be considered include previous work and life experiences and extracurricular activities.

Admission to the M.S. practitioner tracks is selective and requires students to present a strong academic background. Successful applicants typically present undergraduate GPAs of 3.2 (minimum 3.0) or higher and scores above 500 on each GRE subtest. Professional accomplishments, personal statements, and references are also taken into consideration.

As with the practitioner tracks, admission to the M.S. thesis tracks is selective and the standards are similar. However, strength in quantitative areas is viewed favorably in the successful thesis track applicant.

When applying to the Certificate of Advanced Study Program, students must submit official graduate and undergraduate transcripts, three letters of recommendation, and an essay or personal statement describing the applicant's professional goals and reason for applying to Loyola University Maryland. GRE scores are not required.

Individuals who possess a master's degree from an accredited college or university are eligible for the LCPC option.

Correspondence and Information

Office of Graduate Admission
Loyola University Maryland
4501 North Charles Street
Baltimore, Maryland 21210
Phone: 410-617-2587
       800-221-9107 Ext. 5020 (toll-free)
Fax: 410-617-2002
E-mail: graduate@loyola.edu
Web site: http://graduate.loyola.edu/psychgrad.info

Loyola University Maryland

THE FACULTY AND THEIR RESEARCH

Jeffrey E. Barnett, Affiliate Professor; Psy.D., Yeshiva. Legal and ethical issues, cognitive and personality assessment, cognitive psychotherapy, assessment and treatment of children, psychotherapy process and outcome, professional development, therapist distress and impairment.

Carolyn McNamara Barry, Assistant Professor; Ph.D., Maryland, College Park. Social and self development within childhood, adolescence, and emerging adulthood, including peer relationships, friendships, peer influence, academic and social motivation, and issues concerning the transition to adulthood.

Gilbert Clapperton, Professor Emeritus; Ph.D., Baylor. Validation of projective techniques, executive selection and employment screening, psychotherapy outcome and process, aggression, ethics, psychopathology.

Mary Jo Coiro, Assistant Professor; Ph.D., Virginia. Effects of maternal depression on children's mental health and the family environment, risk and protective factors in the development of child psychopathology, prevention of child psychopathology, cognitive-behavioral therapy with adolescents, policy issues affecting children.

David G. Crough, Associate Professor; Ph.D., Catholic University. Pupillometry, sensation seeking, pace of living, animal research, physiology of behavior, aggressive behavior, educational research, drug abuse.

George S. Everly Jr., Affiliate Professor; Ph.D., Maryland, College Park. Health psychology; behavioral medicine; biofeedback; psychophysiology; cognitive behavior therapy; post-traumatic stress disorder, human stress, and stress management.

Faith M. Gilroy, Professor Emerita; Ph.D., Saint Louis. Business applications of psychology, attribution theory, conformity, attitudinal measurement, women's issues, gerontology, career patterns, gender choice of offspring.

Sharon Green-Hennessy, Associate Professor and Director of Master's Education, Practitioner Track; Ph.D., Rochester. Access to mental health care, attachment theory, child maltreatment, child and adolescent psychopathology, child and adolescent assessment.

Rachel L. Grover, Assistant Professor; Ph.D., Maine. Development and quality of adolescent friendships and romantic relationships, defining social competence, social skills development and training in adolescence, assessment and treatment of childhood anxiety.

Deborah Haskins, Non-tenure Professor and Director of Undergraduate and Master's Field Education; Ph.D., Loyola (Baltimore). Spirituality and mental health; cross-cultural issues in supervision, therapy, and personality; trauma psychology; sexual abuse; women's issues; career/life transitions; drug abuse.

Christopher Higginson, Assistant Professor; Ph.D., Washington State. The degree to which cognitive measures are predictive of daily function; degenerative diseases in general, and the cognitive deficits associated with Parkinson's disease and its surgical treatment.

Matthew W. Kirkhart, Associate Professor; Ph.D., North Carolina at Greensboro. Medical/health psychology, psychological and medical barriers to adaptation, learning and cognition, adult psychopathology, functional analysis of language, interpersonal psychotherapy, psychological assessment, teaching of psychology.

Beth Kotchick, Assistant Professor; Ph.D., Georgia. Parenting and family processes, child and adolescent psychopathology, adolescent sexual and health behavior, cognitive-behavioral theory and therapy with children and adolescents.

Jeffery M. Lating, Professor, Associate Chair, and Director of Clinical Training; Ph.D., Georgia. Post-traumatic stress disorder, coronary-prone risk factors, behavioral medicine.

Charles T. LoPresto, Associate Professor; Ph.D., Howard. Homophobia, sexual orientation and sexual minority issues, adolescent treatment issues, cognitive-behavioral approaches to treatment, cross-cultural psychology, men's issues.

Jen L. Lowry, Associate Professor and Chair; Ph.D., Saint Louis. Factors influencing duration of psychotherapy, psychotherapy outcomes, ethics and professional issues, medical psychology, forensic psychology, managed care issues.

Heather Lyons, Assistant Professor; Ph.D., Maryland, College Park. Culture, discrimination, and person-organization fit in the workplace; social, cognitive, and cultural influences on career expectations; training issues in multicultural psychology.

Elizabeth E. MacDougall, Non-tenure Professor; Ph.D., Fairleigh Dickinson. Clinical geropsychology, geriatric neuropsychology/assessment of dementia syndromes, rehabilitation psychology, cognitive/intellectual assessment, psychometrics.

Alison Papadakis, Assistant Professor; Ph.D., Duke. The emergence of gender differences in depression during adolescence, gender roles, self-regulation, self-discrepancy, stress and coping, eating disorders.

Anthony S. Parente, Affiliate Professor; M.A., Loyola (Baltimore). Mental health and substance abuse treatment, stress management, group process, interpersonal relations, addiction recovery issues, adolescent development, employee assistance and workplace issues, the therapeutic relationship.

David V. Powers, Associate Professor; Ph.D., Washington (St. Louis). Gerontology, caregiving for dementia patients, death and dying issues, common factors in psychotherapy research, geriatric depression.

Martin F. Sherman, Professor and Director of Master's Education, Thesis Track; Ph.D., Maine. Disgust sensitivity, personality research (locus of control, silencing the self), survey and attitude research, gender role research, addictions, terror management theory.

Amanda McCombs Thomas, Professor and Associate Dean, College of Arts and Sciences; Ph.D., Georgia. Obsessive-compulsive spectrum disorders, trichotillomania, anxiety problems in children and adolescents.

Angelita M. Yu, Assistant Professor and Director of Doctoral Field Education; Ph.D., Utah. Psychotherapy, training, supervision.

NAROPA UNIVERSITY

Graduate Programs

Programs of Study

Naropa University offers graduate degrees in the arts, education, environmental leadership, psychology, and religious studies. Inspired by its Buddhist educational heritage and its mission of contemplative education, Naropa offers students a highly individualized and transformative learning path that brings both academic rigor and a spiritual component to a student's educational life.

The Graduate School of Psychology consists of three departments and offers several distinct graduate programs at the cutting-edge of psychology. The Contemplative Psychotherapy program (M.A.) combines the wisdom of Buddhism and Shambhala with Western humanistic psychotherapy. The Somatic Counseling Psychology program (M.A.) trains students in body-centered psychotherapy, offering concentrations in body psychotherapy and dance/movement therapy (ADTA-approved program). The Transpersonal Counseling Psychology program (M.A.) brings together psychology and spirituality, with concentrations in art therapy, wilderness therapy, and counseling psychology. Naropa's Art Therapy program is approved by the American Art Therapy Association. The Transpersonal Psychology program (M.A.) is a low-residency degree that combines psychology and spirituality. The Transpersonal Psychology program (M.A.) with a concentration in ecopsychology integrates psychology and ecology in the study of human-nature relationships.

Naropa offers five graduate degree programs in the field of religious studies: Religious Studies (M.A.), Religious Studies with Sanskrit or Tibetan Language (M.A.), Indo-Tibetan Buddhism (M.A.), Indo-Tibetan Buddhism with Tibetan or Sanskrit Language (M.A.), and the Master of Divinity degree (M.Div.). Naropa's M.Div. degree program offers an in-depth theological study of the Buddhist tradition integrated with a thorough grounding in contemplative approaches to community work, spiritual care giving, and interfaith chaplaincy.

Employing an integrated, whole-systems perspective, the Environmental Leadership program (M.A.) offers a balance of theory, skills, and practical application infused with perspectives from ecopsychology and contemplative traditions. The Contemplative Education program (M.A.) offers a low-residency, professional-development degree program that combines the wisdom and skillful means of Eastern meditative traditions with Western holistic educational methods and insights.

Naropa offers three graduate degree programs in the arts. The Writing and Poetics program (M.F.A.) balances writing workshops with literary studies requirements while offering concentrations in poetry, prose, and translation as well as additional course work in letterpress printing and outreach. The Contemporary Performance program (M.F.A.) brings together contemporary physical theater, Viewpoints theory and practice, and traditional contemplative practices. The low-residency Creative Writing program (M.F.A.) balances online writing workshops and literature seminars.

Research Facilities

The Allen Ginsberg Library has a collection of more than 30,000 books, periodicals, and audio-visual materials in areas that support Naropa's unique academic curriculum and is particularly strong in the fields of Buddhist studies, contemporary American poetry, and psychology. The library also subscribes to approximately seventy-five print periodicals and has access to more than 13,000 periodicals online through a variety of electronic databases. In addition, Naropa students have access to the Norlin Library at the University of Colorado, an institution with more than 2 million volumes.

Financial Aid

Naropa University makes every attempt to assist students who do not have the financial resources to accomplish their educational objectives. Naropa offers institutional grants and scholarships as well as all types of federal student aid. Some financial aid for international students is available. Approximately 70 percent of Naropa's degree-seeking students receive financial assistance in the form of loans, student employment, scholarships, assistantships, and grants.

Cost of Study

Graduate tuition for the 2008–09 academic year was $726 per semester credit. In addition, there is a registration fee of $250 per semester, and low-residency programs require a technology fee of $120 per 3-credit course.

Living and Housing Costs

The cost of living in Boulder, Colorado, is relatively high, and housing is competitive. Approximate rent begins at $575 for a one-bedroom apartment and $400 for one bedroom in a shared house. Off-campus living expenses for a single student are estimated to be $1300 to $1400 per month. Some students choose to live in less expensive towns surrounding Boulder.

Student Group

Naropa seeks resourceful students who have a strong appetite for learning and enjoy experiential education in a rigorous academic setting. The faculty and student body form a close-knit community, and this relationship is an integral part of the educational experience. Drawn from forty-nine states and twenty-four countries, Naropa students represent a wide range of life experiences, spiritual traditions, backgrounds, and ages (ranging from 17 to 67). Total enrollment at Naropa University in fall 2008 was 1,049 students: 605 graduates and 444 undergraduates.

Student Outcomes

Naropa University's graduate counseling programs prepare students to become private practitioners, to become therapists in mental-health agencies or social-service agencies, or to serve in a variety of other positions that provide direct service to individuals, clients, or groups. Students in the M.F.A. in Writing and Poetics and Creative Writing programs are trained in creative writing, publishing, editing, translation, and the teaching of writing workshops. Naropa's other graduate programs prepare students for leadership positions in the environmental arena, chaplaincy in hospice and other institutional settings, as well as doctoral work.

Location

Naropa University is located in Boulder, Colorado, a city of 100,000 nestled at the base of the majestic Rocky Mountains' foothills. Boulder is located 25 miles northwest of Denver and is home to many theater, dance, and music companies as well as the University of Colorado.

The University

Accredited by the Higher Learning Commission of the North Central Association of Colleges and Schools, Naropa University is a private, nonprofit, nonsectarian, liberal arts institution dedicated to advancing contemplative education. This approach to learning integrates the best of Eastern and Western educational traditions, helping students know themselves more deeply and engage constructively with others. Founded in 1974 by Tibetan meditation master and scholar Chögyam Trungpa Rinpoche, Naropa University grew out of an educational philosophy that dates back to Nalanda University, a major center of learning founded in India in the sixth century.

Applying

The suggested deadline for receiving completed applications is January 15 for the fall and summer semester and October 15 for the spring semester. Applications received after the suggested deadline are reviewed on a space-available basis. Most graduate programs require that students enter only in the fall; however, the Department of Writing and Poetics also accepts students in the spring and summer semesters. Programs that only accept students in the summer include the M.A. in Contemplative Education program, the M.F.A. in Creative Writing program, and the M.A. in Transpersonal Psychology program. Many departments require supplemental application materials and telephone or on-site interviews. GRE scores are not required.

Correspondence and Information

Office of Admissions
Naropa University
2130 Arapahoe Avenue
Boulder, Colorado 80302-6697
Phone: 303-546-3572
      800-772-6951 (toll-free)
Fax: 303-546-3583
E-mail: admissions@naropa.edu
Web site: http://www.naropa.edu

Naropa University

CORE FACULTY AND THEIR RESEARCH

Contemplative Education

Richard C. Brown, Department Chair; M.A., Naropa. Contemplative educational practices and competencies, contemplative observation, emotional awareness in teachers, Nalanda University curriculum.

Lee Worley, Co-Chair, Contemplative Education; M.A., Naropa. Basic acting and theater studies and application to education, presence of teaching, space, Buddhist approaches to mind/body. Author of *Coming from Nothing: The Sacred Art of Acting* (Turquoise Dragon Press, 2001).

Deborah Young, Co-Chair, Early Childhood Education; Ph.Ed. candidate, Colorado. Peace studies in education, poverty, multiculturalism.

Contemplative Psychotherapy

Lauren Casalino, Department Chair; M.A., Naropa. Private practice working with adults, specializing in life-changing transitions, the process of aging, grief work, and fertility and adoption issues. Co-founder of Windhorse Family and Elder Services, specializing in intensive home-based team treatment. International workshop leader: "Buddhism and Healing."

MacAndrew Jack, Ph.D., Temple. Licensed psychologist in private practice with individuals and couples integrating relational, cognitive behavioral, and mind/body orientations. Co-edited *Brilliant Sanity* and has published and presented nationally on psychophysiological processes involved in panic, breathing, and the parasympathetic nervous system as well as personal and interpersonal effects of meditation, psychotherapy, and contemplative training.

Karen Kissel Wegela, Ph.D., Union (Ohio). Licensed psychologist with experience working with a variety of populations. Author of *How to Be a Help Instead of a Nuisance* and *The Courage to Be Present* as well as several articles and chapters in the field of Buddhist psychology. Has presented contemplative psychotherapy in Europe, Australia, Canada, Mexico, and Chile. Former director, Contemplative Psychotherapy.

Contemporary Performance

Wendell Beavers, Department Chair; B.A., Boston University. Founding faculty member and early director of NYU's Experimental Theater Wing (1979–2003). Named master teacher at Tisch School of the Arts (1996). Noted choreographer, teacher, and developer of The Viewpoints. Co-founder and early director of Movement Research, Inc.

Barbara Dilley, B.A., Mount Holyoke. Toured internationally with Merce Cunningham Dance Company (1963–68). Performed with Yvonne Rainer and, in 1970, became part of the dance/theater collaboration, Grand Union. Choreographed and performed solo and group works internationally. Came to Naropa as a faculty member in 1974 and served as president from 1985–93. Contemplative art training based in the meditative state of mind informs her teaching of improvisation and creative process.

Ethelyn Friend, M.F.A., Brandeis. Actor/singer, writer, solo performance artist, and teacher. Acted in professional theaters in San Francisco, Boston, and Denver, including Merrimack Repertory Theatre, Curious Theatre, and the Colorado Shakespeare Festival. Long-term association with the Roy Hart Theatre of France, known for groundbreaking work in extending the range of the human voice. Private voice workshops in U.S. and abroad.

Environmental Leadership

Suzanne Benally, Associate Vice President for Academic Affairs and Senior Diversity Officer; M.A., Colorado. Extensive experience in higher education policy, assessment, and diversity. Research focuses on American Indian relationship between land and place as expressed through written and oral literature. Tribal affiliation is Navajo and Santa Clara Tewa.

Jeanine Canty, Ph.D., California Institute of Integral Studies. Cultural and ecological awareness, ecopsychology, transformative learning, social and environmental justice, consciousness studies and ecological healing.

Sherry Ellms, M.A., Naropa. Buddhism, meditation, wilderness rights of passage, ecopsychology.

Anne Parker, Ph.D., Oregon. Geography, leadership, environmental studies, pilgrimage and sacred landscape. Fulbright Scholar and National Science Foundation grant recipient for study of indigenous agriculture in Nepal, Bhutan, and India. Australian Institute for Aboriginal Studies grant recipient for ethnobotanical study of traditional Aboriginal plant use.

Religious Studies

Thomas B. Coburn, Naropa University President; Ph.D., Harvard. Renowned scholar and academician in the field of religious studies. Widely published author, specializing in South and East Asia and Islamic world. Visiting scholar for a year at Harvard Divinity School. Author of *Devi-Mahatmya: The Crystallization of the Goddess Tradition* (Motilal Banarsdass and South Asian Books, 1984) and *Encountering the Goddess* (State University of New York Press, 1991). One of the world's leading experts on Hindu tradition of the great goddess.

Roger Dorris, Ph.D., Union (Ohio). Engaged Buddhist studies, with a focus on community building and large group transformation. Ordained as a Buddhist minister. Works with marginalized populations, including homeless and incarcerated.

Acharya Tenpa Gyaltsen, Khenpo degree from Karma Shri Nalanda Institute (Sikkim). Senior director and senior teacher of Nitartha Institute. Former resident teacher of Thegsum Tashi Chöling in Hamburg, Germany.

Sarah Harding, B.A., Naropa. Lama in the Shangpa Kagyu tradition of Tibetan Buddhism; teacher and oral interpreter; translator with the Tsadra Foundation. Books include *Creation and Completion* and *Machik's Complete Explanation*.

Victoria Howard, Ph.D., Union (Ohio). Buddhist minister in Shambhala tradition. Co-founder and co-director, Dana Home Care, national nonprofit organization providing in-home care for seniors. Consultant, elder-care agencies and facilities in Denver-metro area.

Reginald A. Ray, Ph.D., Recipient of Fulbright-Hays Fellowship and two N.E.H. Senior Research Fellowships. Member of Nalanda Translation Committee. Author of *Buddhist Saints in India, Indestructible Truth,* and *Secret of the Vajra World.*

Judith Simmer-Brown, Ph.D., Walden; Ph.D. candidate, Columbia. Acharya in the Shambhala Buddhist tradition; Director of Ngedon School of Higher Learning. Trained in South Asian Religious Studies and Sanskrit. Steering committee, Buddhist Critical-Constructive Reflection Group of American Academy of Religion. Tibetan Buddhism, women and Buddhism, Buddhist-Christian dialogue, American Buddhism. Author of *Dakini's Warm Breath: The Feminine Principle in Tibetan Buddhism* (Shambhala, 2001) and, with Brother David Steindl-Rast et al., *Benedict's Dharma: Buddhists Comment on the Rule of St. Benedict* (Riverhead, 2001).

D. Philip Stanley, Department Co-Chair; Ph.D. candidate, Virginia. Recipient of Fulbright-Hays Fellowship for doctoral research analyzing Tibetan Buddhist canon and of a National Endowment for the Humanities grant to place his Tibetan canon catalog database online in conjunction with the Tibetan and Himalayan Digital Library, the Library of Congress, and the British Library. Board member of the International Association of Buddhist Universities. Co-director of Nitartha Institute. Member of Nalanda Translation Committee.

Somatic Counseling Psychology

Wendy Allen, Chair; M.A., Naropa. Dance/movement therapist, dance educator. Professor of psychology at Metropolitan State College. Director of intervention program for at-risk youth.

Zoë Avstreih, Director, Dane/Movement Therapy Program; M.S., CUNY, Hunter. Founder/director, Center for the Study of Authentic Movement. Founder, Dance-Movement Therapy Program, Pratt Institute. Author and international lecturer.

Christine Caldwell, Ph.D., Union (Ohio). Developed The Moving Cycle in body psychotherapy: early physical imprinting, movement sequencing processes, the practice of dying, and the opportunities in addiction. Dance therapy, Aston Patterning and Gestalt. Faculty member at Santa Barbara Graduate Institute.

J. Ryan Kennedy, Director, Body Psychotherapy Program; Psy.D. candidate, Capella. Founder/director of counseling center and internship training program. Trauma and dissociative disorders, addiction and recovery, domestic/family violence.

Transpersonal Counseling Psychology

Dale Asrael, M.A., Naropa. Teacher certification. Acharya (Buddhist teacher) and Buddhist minister. Leads meditation retreats internationally and trains meditation instructors. Mentors teachers in contemplative education methodology.

Deborah Bowman, Ph.D., Union (Ohio). Co-founder, M.A. TCP program. Initiated and developed Wilderness Therapy program. Faculty member and Interim President of Boulder Graduate School. A licensed psychologist, certified Gestalt therapist in private practice. Instructor with the National Outdoor Leadership School and former river guide. Dream-painting process: combining art therapy, Jungian, transpersonal, and Gestalt therapy.

Barbara Catbagan, M.Ed., Colorado State. Director, Counseling Psychology; Coordinator of multicultural courses. Certified mediator and consultant with businesses, organizations, and educational institutions to facilitate growth of dynamic working teams. Diversity, social justice, issues of human and civil rights.

David Chernikoff, M.S.W., Denver; M.Div., Graduate Theological Union. Meditation teacher, psychotherapist, and life and business coach. Founder of Boulder College of Massage Therapy. Guiding teacher of Insight Meditation Community of Colorado. Private practice.

Carla Clements, Chair, Transpersonal Counseling Psychology; Ph.D. (educational psychology), Colorado; Two decades as private practice psychotherapist, specialized in treatment of PTSD. Teaches core courses for TCP. Research interests: trauma and psi phenomena. Interests: yoga and writing, singing, and playing music.

John Davis, Director, M.A. in Transpersonal Psychology Program; Former Chair of Transpersonal Counseling Psychology Department; Ph.D., Colorado. Teacher of transpersonal psychology, ecopsychology, and wilderness therapy. Ordained teacher of the Diamond Approach of A. H. Almaas and staff member in the School of Lost Borders, a training facility for wilderness rites-of-passage guides.

Michael Franklin, M.A., George Washington. Director, Art Therapy program. Teacher and lecturer of art therapy in various academic and clinical settings. Research focus is on the relationship between art therapy, yoga philosophy, and meditation.

Duey Freeman, M.A., Northern Colorado. Director and founder, Gestalt Institute of the Rockies and Equine Journeys. Psychotherapist, professor, consultant, and clinical supervisor. Coordinator, Gestalt and Family and Child programs. Gestalt therapy, family therapy, bioenergetics and therapy with children; fostering equine assistance in work with children, adults, and families.

Leslie McAllan, Core Candidate Assistant Professor; Ph.D., SUNY at Buffalo. Teaches Social and Cultural Diversity, Helping Relationships, and Career Counseling. Specializes in working with persons with disabilities, especially those with chronic illnesses, including AIDS/HIV, head injury, and PTSD.

Deborah Piranian, Director, Wilderness Therapy; Ph.D., Washington (Seattle). Private psychotherapy practice and counselor in a variety of settings. Consultant with for-profit and nonprofit organizations. Outward Bound senior course director, specializing in wilderness therapy and multinational mountaineering programs. Interplay between contemplative practice and outdoor or nature-based activities. *Rock Climbing and Meditation: Can Climbing Be a Spiritual Path?* (2007).

Laurie Rugenstein, M.M.T., SMU. Founder and former director, Music Therapy. Developed and implemented a music therapy program for HospiceCare of Boulder and Broomfield Counties. Private practice in music therapy. Primary trainer in Bonny Method of Guided Imagery and Music. Use of expressive arts to access human potential and create viable social structures.

Jed Swift, Director, Ecopsychology; M.A., Lesley. Developed and teaches Transpersonal Service Learning and Masters Papers Online courses. Formerly co-director of Earth Rites, Inc., a Denver-based rites-of-passage organization for adults. Teaches psychology courses on both undergraduate and graduate levels at Franklin University (Columbus, Ohio).

Sue Wallingford, Core Candidate Assistant Professor; M.A., Naropa; LPC, ATR-BC. Private practice, offering consulting, supervision, counseling, and art-therapy services to families and children. Focus on attachment, trauma, and grief and building healthy relationships. Founder of Whole Arts Studio, LLC. Lectures locally and nationally. Dedicated artist and lover of the natural world.

Writing and Poetics

Keith Abbott, M.A., Western Washington. Fiction, poetry, nonfiction, screenwriting. Author of a Richard Brautigan memoir, *Downstream from Trout Fishing in America.* His fourth novel, *Racer,* was short-listed for a 2007 Berlinale award. His articles on Brautigan, Kerouac, Snyder, Whalen, and Carver appeared in 2007.

Junior Burke, Department Chair and Director, Creative Writing Program; M.F.A., Naropa. Fiction, screenplay writing, literary studies. Prose writer, dramatist, and lyricist. His song cycle, *Someone Else's Dream,* was performed at Boulder Museum of Contemporary Art. Author of *Something Gorgeous* and a CD of original songs, *While You Were Gone.*

Reed Bye, Ph.D., Colorado. Poetry, contemplative poetics, contemporary and classic literature, prosody, Shakespeare, William Blake. Songwriter and poet as well as author of new and selected poems, *Join the Planets,* and a CD of original songs, *Long Way Around.*

Indira Ganesan, M.F.A., Iowa. Fiction, memoir, essay writing. Author of *The Journey* and *Inheritance,* both published by Alfred A. Knopf. Two-time fellow at the Fine Arts Work Center in Provincetown and held fellowships from Radcliffe College, the MacDowell Colony, and the Paden Institute.

Bobbie Louise Hawkins, Associate Professor. Fiction, literary studies, performance monologues. Recipient of NEA Fellowship in fiction and author of more than ten books of fiction, performance monologues, and poetry; most recently, *Bijou.* Her work has been performed in New York, England, Holland, and Germany.

Anselm Hollo, Professor. Poetry, translation, literary studies. Recipient of the NEA Fellowship in Poetry, grants from the Fund for Poetry, and Finland's Distinguished Foreign Translator's Award. Author of thirty books of poetry; most recently, *Notes on the Possibilities and Attractions of Existence: Selected Poems 1965–2000* and *Guests of Space.*

Bhanu Kapil, M.A., SUNY at Brockport. Author of three full-length collections: *The Vertical Interrogation of Strangers, Incubation: A Space for Monsters,* and *Humanimal: A Project for Future Children.* Currently researching cross-cultural approaches to treating schizophrenia in the Indian and Pakistani populations of northwest London in a cross-genre work.

Andrew Schelling, B.A., California, Santa Cruz. Poetry, translation, ecopoetics, Sanskrit, literary studies. Recipient of the Academy of American Poets translation award and two Witter Bynner Foundation for Poetry grants. Author of a dozen books, including *Two Elk: A High Country Notebook* and *The Wisdom Anthology of North American Buddhist Poetry.*

Steven Taylor, Ph.D., Brown. Musician and writer. Critical theory, poetry, and music. Collaborations on concert works, performances, recordings, and theater works with artists such as Allen Ginsberg, Anne Waldman, and the seminal poetry rock group The Fugs. Author of *Loveland* and *False Prophet: Fieldnotes from the Punk Underground.*

Anne Waldman, B.A., Bennington. Poetry, experimental writing, performance poetics. Distinguished Professor of Poetics and chair of Naropa's Summer Writing Program as well as co-founder of Jack Kerouac School of Disembodied Poetics. Author and editor of more than forty books of poetry.

PALO ALTO UNIVERSITY

Ph.D. Program in Clinical Psychology

Program of Study

Palo Alto University (formerly Pacific Graduate School of Psychology) offers the Ph.D. in clinical psychology. The primary goals are to train psychologists whose work is firmly grounded in theory and is informed by current research, who can function effectively as independent practitioners, and who can critically evaluate and perform research that contributes to the academic discipline of scientific psychology. Palo Alto University places a high value on scholarship and an equal emphasis on research and clinical training.

The Palo Alto University curriculum includes intensive study in five areas: basic theoretical concepts in psychology, psychological evaluation, psychotherapy theory and process, clinical field experience, and research. Academic schedules in each year of study include required and elective course work in each of these areas. Students also have the opportunity to focus their course work in specific areas of individual and group psychotherapy. The program also offers two specialized training certificates in forensic psychology and neuropsychological assessment. All students are required to complete 16 hours of personal psychotherapy; Palo Alto University believes that the personal psychotherapy experience is critical to the ability to work therapeutically with others.

Research Facilities

Palo Alto University's Research Library's collections include books, journals, assessment materials, dissertations, audiotapes, and videotapes. The on-site computer network is accessible to library users at home via the Internet. The computer network features access to the Palo Alto University library catalog as well as PsycINFO, Medline, ERIC, and the American Psychiatric Association's database of full-text journals and books.

Financial Aid

Financial assistance is available to eligible Palo Alto University students in the form of fellowships, scholarships, loans (repayable with interest), and on-campus employment. While independent professional schools have neither state support nor extensive endowments, some type of government-subsidized and/or alternative student loan funding is available to almost all students. Palo Alto University is a HEALTH-approved program. Prospective students who wish to be considered for a Palo Alto University fellowship must submit a completed application to the Admissions department.

Cost of Study

Quarterly tuition for the Ph.D. program in 2008–09 was $10,529, the per-unit rate was $1190, the dissertation flat rate was $8431, and the internship flat rate was $2108. Other fees added up to $1190 per quarter.

Living and Housing Costs

The cost of living in the Palo Alto, California, area is comparable to the cost of living in other larger California communities. On-campus housing is not available, although ample off-campus housing is available within a short distance of the campus.

Student Group

Palo Alto University averages 38 graduates from its program each year. With a student-faculty ratio of 10:1, students enjoy a close working relationship with faculty members. The institution actively seeks and encourages diversity on its campus and within its intellectual community.

Location

Located 35 miles south of San Francisco, in the heart of Silicon Valley, Palo Alto University is just minutes away from Stanford University and downtown Palo Alto and is across the scenic San Francisco Bay from the University of California, Berkeley campus. Situated between a suburban neighborhood and a thriving business park, the University lies within easy reach of the best that northern California has to offer, including Lake Tahoe skiing, Yosemite National Park, San Francisco, the Napa Valley wine country, and Monterey Bay.

The School

Palo Alto University is a private, free-standing professional school, training doctoral students since 1975. The University offers a Master of Science (M.S.) degree in psychology, a Ph.D. in psychology, and joint degrees of Ph.D./J.D. and Ph.D./M.B.A. In addition, there is a distance learning M.S. in psychology program, which is offered to students via the Web; courses are taken throughout a two-year period. Palo Alto University also offers a Psy.D. Consortium Program with Stanford University. This innovative program emphasizes the biopsychosocial model and empirically supported treatments for psychological disorders.

Palo Alto University is accredited by the Western Association of Schools and Colleges. The Ph.D. program is accredited by the American Psychological Association (APA), and it brings together highly talented faculty members and graduate students working closely together to bridge scientific rigor and theoretical knowledge to the analysis and practice of clinical psychology. Its community supports broad cultural and professional backgrounds and a wide range of alternative perspectives. In so doing, Palo Alto University trains students to work in a wide range of settings and with a broad spectrum of clients. The highly skilled faculty, low student-faculty ratio, and rigorous academic program ensure the high-quality teaching and mentoring necessary to produce outstanding graduates.

Applying

The completed application packet is due by mid-January if students wish to be considered for a fellowship. Applicants are encouraged to apply as early as possible. Late applications may be considered and are evaluated on a case-by-case basis, if space is available. The nonrefundable application fee is $50. All applicants must also include a resume or curriculum vitae that lists all employment, training, and any volunteer work relevant to the field of psychology; GRE scores; and official transcripts from undergraduate and graduate schools attended, even if a degree was not awarded. Each applicant must also include a written statement that includes a brief biographical profile, details of goals and reasons for applying to Palo Alto University, strengths and accomplishments, and qualities that the student thinks are important assets as a practicing clinical psychologist.

Correspondence and Information

Office of Admissions
Palo Alto University
1791 Arastradero Road
Palo Alto, California 94304
Phone: 800-818-6136 (toll-free)
Fax: 650-433-3888
E-mail: admissions@pgsp.edu
Web site: http://www.pgsp.edu

Palo Alto University

THE FACULTY AND THEIR RESEARCH

Professors
Leonard Beckum, Ph.D. Cultural issues and education.
Larry E. Beutler, Ph.D. Psychotherapy outcomes, depression, chemical abuse.
Bruce Bongar, Ph.D. Suicide.
Jim Breckenridge. Depression, health psychology, research design and methodology, health care policy.
Allison Briscoe-Smith, Ph.D. Child trauma and child diversity.
William J. Froming, Ph.D. Personality.
Peter Goldblum, Ph.D. HIV and gay/lesbian/bisexual psychology.
Roger L. Greene, Ph.D. Assessment.
James Moses, Ph.D. Diagnostic neuropsychology, psychopathology assessment.
Amy Wisniewski, Ph.D. Neuropsychology.

Associate Professors
Nigel Field, Ph.D. Bereavement, psychotherapy.
Shelley Fleming, Ph.D. Cognitive therapy and women's issues.
Robert Reiser, Assistant Professor; Ph.D. Evidence-based treatment of serious mental health in community mental health.
Lynn C. Waelde, Ph.D. Meditation and psychotherapy, post-traumatic stress disorder (PTSD).

Assistant Professors
Matthew J. Cordova, Ph.D. Health psychology, oncology, trauma.
Rowena Gomez, Ph.D. Aging, neuropsychology and depression.
Rebecca Jackson, Ph.D. Forensic psychology.
Steve Lovett, Ph.D. Clinical geropsychology.
Sandra Macias, Ph.D. Couples and children.
Wendy Packman, J.D., Ph.D. Pediatric psychology.

Research Faculty Members
Theodore Jacob, Professor; Ph.D.
Alvin Cooper, Associate Professor; Ph.D.

PALO ALTO UNIVERSITY

PGSP-STANFORD Psy.D. Consortium
Doctor of Psychology Program

Program of Study	The Doctor of Psychology (Psy.D.) Program is a consortium between the Stanford University School of Medicine's Department of Psychiatry and Behavioral Sciences and Palo Alto University (formerly Pacific Graduate School of Psychology), with the purpose of expanding training opportunities for students in the field of clinical psychology.
	The PGSP-STANFORD Doctor of Psychology consortium training program is a full-time, five-year program. The APA-accredited program is broken down into three years of academic course work, one year for a clinical dissertation, and one year for a full-time, pre-doctoral internship. The nine-month academic year runs on the quarter system, with only a limited number of courses offered during the summer quarter. Students are not expected to attend during the summer quarter. Students are enrolled in intensive practicum training throughout the course of the first four years, followed by a one-year internship in clinical psychology.
	A sampling of courses includes the following: Research Methods and Statistics; Psychological Assessment; Ethics and Professional Issues; Empirically-based Psychotherapies; Psychopathology Across the Life Span; Critical Evaluation of Psychological Research; Health Psychology and Behavioral Medicine; Clinical Emergencies and Crises; Family, Group, and Individual Psychotherapy; Neurobiologic Bases of Psychiatric Disorders; Diversity Issues in Clinical Psychology; Nature and Treatment of Personality Disorders, Mood Disorders, Eating Disorders, Anxiety Disorders, and Sleep Disorders.
Research Facilities	PGSP-STANFORD Psy.D. students have full access to Stanford libraries, along with Palo Alto University's Research Library's collections that include books, journals, assessment materials, dissertations, audiotapes, and videotapes. The on-site computer network is accessible to library users at home via the Internet. The computer network features access to the University library catalog as well as PsycINFO, Medline, ERIC, and the American Psychiatric Association's database of full-text journals and books.
Financial Aid	Financial assistance is available to eligible PGSP-STANFORD students in the form of grants, fellowships, scholarships, loans (repayable with interest), and on-campus employment. While independent professional schools have neither state support nor extensive endowments, some type of government-subsidized and/or alternative student loan funding is available to almost all students. PGSP-STANFORD Psy.D is a HEALTH-approved program. Prospective students who wish to be considered for a fellowship must submit a completed application to the Admissions department. A majority of students in the PGSP-STANFORD Psy.D. Program have paid research assistant positions at Stanford Medical School and the National Center on Disaster Psychology and Terrorism (NCDPT), teaching assistantships, and other graduate student assistant positions. There is an extensive merit-based graduate student fellowship program for entering students.
Cost of Study	Quarterly tuition for the Doctor of Psychology Program is $11,035. The consortium fee is $1420 per quarter.
Living and Housing Costs	The Palo Alto, California, area is amenable to students' lifestyles and budgets. Because it is a college town (Stanford University), the Palo Alto community offers many affordable dining, shopping, and entertainment options. Full- and part-time employment opportunities in the community are plentiful. On-campus housing is not available, although ample off-campus housing is available within a short distance of the campus.
Student Group	The PGSP-STANFORD Psy.D. Program can accept up to 30 students. The class of 2005 had 22 students; the class of 2006 had 26 students. With more than 25 faculty members from the Stanford Department of Psychiatry and Palo Alto University, students enjoy a close working relationship with faculty members. The institution enjoys and promotes diversity on its campus and within its intellectual community.
Location	Located 35 miles south of San Francisco, in the heart of Silicon Valley, the PGSP-STANFORD Psy.D. program is just minutes away from Stanford University and downtown Palo Alto and across the scenic San Francisco Bay from the University of California, Berkeley campus. It lies within easy reach of the best that northern California has to offer, including Lake Tahoe skiing, Yosemite National Park, San Francisco, the Napa Valley wine country, and Monterey Bay.
The Schools	The Department of Psychiatry and Behavioral Sciences at Stanford University School of Medicine is ranked as one of the top ten departments of psychiatry in the United States. The department is on the cutting edge of clinical research and practice in numerous nationally ranked studies in mood disorders, eating disorders, anxiety disorders, thought disorders, and psychological and psychiatric approaches to working with patients with a variety of medical conditions.
	Palo Alto University is a private, free-standing professional school, training doctoral students since 1975. The School offers a Master of Science (M.S.) degree in psychology, an APA-accredited Ph.D. in clinical psychology, and joint degrees of Ph.D./J.D. and Ph.D./M.B.A. It is accredited by the Western Association of Schools and Colleges. The Psy.D. program brings together highly talented faculty members and graduate students working closely together to bridge scientific rigor and theoretical knowledge to the analysis and practice of clinical psychology. Its community supports broad cultural and professional backgrounds and a wide range of alternative perspectives. The PGSP-STANFORD Psy.D. Consortium trains students to work in a wide range of settings and with a broad spectrum of clients. The highly skilled faculty members, low student-faculty ratio, and rigorous academic program ensure the high-quality teaching and mentoring necessary to produce outstanding graduates.
Applying	The completed application packet is due by January 15. Highly qualified applications may be considered on a case-by-case basis after this date if the maximum class enrollment has not yet been reached. Due to the high caliber of applicants and the selective nature of the PGSP-STANFORD program, applicants are strongly encouraged to apply as early as possible. The nonrefundable application fee is $50. All applicants must also submit the following: a resume or curriculum vitae that lists all employment, training, and any volunteer work relevant to the field of psychology; GRE scores and official transcripts from undergraduate and graduate schools attended, even if a degree was not awarded; and a written statement that includes a brief biographical profile, details of goals and reasons for applying to the PGSP-STANFORD program, strengths and accomplishments, and qualities that the student thinks are important assets as a practicing clinical psychologist. A personal interview with the directors of the training program is an essential part of the selection process for qualified applicants.
Correspondence and Information	Office of Admissions PGSP-STANFORD Psy.D. Consortium Palo Alto University 1791 Arastradero Road Palo Alto, California 94304 Phone: 800-818-6136 (toll-free) Fax: 650-433-3888 E-mail: admissions@pgsp.edu Web site: http://www.pgsp.edu/pgsp-stanford-psyd-consortium

Palo Alto University

THE FACULTY AND THEIR RESEARCH

Directors
Bruce Arnow, Ph.D. Utilization of medical services, treatment of chronic depression.
James Breckenridge, Ph.D. Terrorism, homeland security, political violence.

Faculty

John J. Barry, M.D.
Leonard Beckum, Ph.D.
Christine Blasey, Ph.D.
Allison Briscoe-Smith, Ph.D.
Brenda Brownlow, Ph.D.
David Burns, M.D.
Betsy Corrin, Ph.D.
Charles DeBattista, Ph.D., D.M.H., M.D.
Katherine DeWitt, Ph.D.
Kathleen Eldredge, Ph.D.
Shelley Fleming, Ph.D.
Elizabeth Gifford, Ph.D.
Cheryl Gore-Felton, Ph.D.

Roger Greene, Ph.D.
Tamara Hartl, Ph.D.
Chris Hayward, M.D., M.P.H.
Kimberly Hill, Ph.D.
Keith Humphreys, Ph.D.
Jennifer Keller, Ph.D.
Roy King, M.D., Ph.D.
Cheryl Koopman, Ph.D.
Kristine Luce, Ph.D.
Rachel Manber, Ph.D.
Meg Marnell, Ph.D.
Louis Moffett, Ph.D.
Yvonne Morris, Ph.D.

Wendy Packman, J.D., Ph.D.
Thomas Plante, Ph.D.; ABPP.
Lisa Post, Ph.D.
Douglas Rait, Ph.D.
Craig Rosen, Ph.D.
Debra Safer, M.D.
Brent Solvason, Ph.D., M.D.
Hans Steiner, M.D.
Margo Thienemann, M.D.
Kim Wilson, Ph.D.
Toni Wroolie, Ph.D.
Phil Zimbardo, Ph.D.

PHILADELPHIA COLLEGE
OF OSTEOPATHIC MEDICINE
Graduate Programs in Clinical Psychology, Counseling and Clinical Health Psychology, and School Psychology

Programs of Study

Philadelphia College of Osteopathic Medicine (PCOM) offers eight graduate programs taught by an internationally renowned, highly credentialed faculty. All faculty members in PCOM's psychology department are teaching faculty members who work closely with students to help them achieve their professional goals. Students often have the opportunity to coauthor scholarly papers, books, and professional presentations with faculty members. PCOM has one of the only psychology departments in the country that provides a standardized patient program. The standardized patient program presents authentic clinical learning and skills situations in which "patients" simulate mental health conditions. Students conduct sessions with the patients, which are videotaped and reviewed by the faculty members to help train and assess students' skills. Students in the psychology program also have the opportunity for clinical experience at any of the College's urban health-care centers.

The 85-credit Psy.D. in clinical psychology program is designed to be completed in five years, including course work, practicum, internship, and dissertation. Graduates of this program are prepared to assume responsibilities in a broad range of clinical settings. Post-doctoral certificates in clinical health psychology and clinical neuropsychology will each provide one year (16 and 19 credits respectively) of post-doctoral specialty training to doctoral-level psychologists. The 57-credit Psy.D. in school psychology program takes three to five years to complete. The fourteen-month, 33-credit M.S. in school psychology program prepares paraprofessionals in community and school settings to provide mental health services to children, youth, and families. This program, taken in sequence with the Ed.S. degree program, leads to certification in school psychology. The three-year, 45-credit Ed.S. program provides students with the knowledge and skills to assume the role of a school psychologist in diverse settings. The two-year, 48-credit M.S. in counseling and clinical health psychology program trains graduates to provide evaluation, counseling, and therapy services to clients in a variety of clinical settings. There is also a 60-credit addictions and offenders counseling track for the M.S. degree. M.S. graduates may also take 12 additional credits offered by PCOM and earn a Certificate of Advanced Graduate Study to meet the education requirements of the licensed professional counseling (LPC) credential in Pennsylvania and New Jersey. Designed for the working professional, all classes for the M.S., Ed.S., and Psy.D. programs are held in the evening and on weekends.

Research Facilities

The academic facilities at PCOM include state-of-the-art amphitheaters and classroom facilities; computer laboratories with extensive software, including PsycLIT and SPSS; a comfortable, sophisticated library with online access to electronic textbooks, journals, databases, and Internet guides; and access to the digital library and statistical programs through the Internet.

Financial Aid

The Financial Aid Office at PCOM offers financial assistance to students through the Federal Stafford Student Loan program, institutional grants, and various alternative private loan programs.

Cost of Study

In 2009–10, the direct tuition costs of attending PCOM (including tuition, fees, books, and supplies) for the year are approximately $19,230 for counseling and clinical health psychology M.S. students, $18,680 for school psychology M.S. students, $14,414 for Ed.S. students, $23,516 for clinical psychology Psy.D. students, and $21,676 for school psychology Psy.D. students.

Living and Housing Costs

Students live off-campus within the Philadelphia metropolitan and suburban areas, as there is no on-campus housing. Room and board costs vary by each student's individual preferences.

Student Group

The programs seek a diverse group of students who are committed to excellence. The Psy.D. in clinical psychology program recruits in-practice professionals who have earned master's degrees in psychology, social work, counseling, psychiatric nursing, or a related field and are working in human services. This population brings to their studies a high level of maturity, established skills, diverse backgrounds, and a strong motivation to succeed. The Psy.D. in school psychology program recruits working school psychologists who want to be leaders in psychoeducational and mental health services to children, youth, and families. For 2008, the applicant pool for the clinical psychology Psy.D. class included 160 applicants. The average age of the 26 entering Psy.D. students was 30, with 77 percent women and 15 percent members of minority groups. For 2008, the Psy.D. in school psychology program enrolled a class of 14 students, 86 percent women and 21 percent members of minority groups, with an average age of 30. The M.S. program in counseling and clinical health psychology enrolled a class of 34 students, 91 percent of whom were women and 18 percent of whom were members of minority groups, with an average age of 25. The M.S. program in school psychology enrolled a class of 23 students, 70 percent women and 17 percent members of minority groups, with an average age of 25. The Ed.S. program in school psychology enrolled a class of 19 students, 89 percent women and 32 percent members of minority groups, with an average age of 27.

Location

Located on City Avenue in Philadelphia, PCOM's 21-acre campus is minutes away from Fairmount Park, Philadelphia's historic district, art museums, theaters, restaurants, and professional sports complexes. Its renovated facilities include two large lecture halls, small classrooms, labs for teaching and research, and scenic landscaping, all in a suburban setting. PCOM also has four health-care centers in Philadelphia and one in LaPorte, Pennsylvania.

The College and The Programs

PCOM, which was chartered in 1899, enrolls approximately 2,162 students in its various programs. The clinical and teaching facility makes an ideal home for psychology graduate programs. The graduate psychology programs at PCOM are accredited by the Department of Education of the Commonwealth of Pennsylvania and the Middle States Association of Colleges and Schools. The clinical psychology Psy.D. program is accredited by the American Psychological Association and fulfills the requirements of the National Register for Healthcare Providers in Psychology. Clinical Psy.D. graduates qualify to take the Examination for Professional Practice of Psychology Licensure in Pennsylvania and New Jersey. The curriculum provides school psychology Psy.D. students with the knowledge and skills to assume the role of a school psychologist, practice in a variety of settings, and be prepared for eligibility for National Certification and for Pennsylvania licensure. The school psychology Psy.D. program has been approved by the National Association of School Psychologists. The M.S. program plus 12 credits has been designed to fulfill the Licensed Professional Counselor curriculum requirements in Pennsylvania and New Jersey.

Applying

Clinical psychology M.S. applicants need to have a baccalaureate degree from a regionally accredited institution, with basic psychology course work (introduction to psychology, abnormal psychology or psychopathology, and statistics). Psy.D. in clinical psychology applicants must have completed a master's degree in psychology or a related field at a regionally accredited institution and also completed developmental psychology, theories of personality, abnormal psychology or psychopathology, and statistics. Candidates for the post-doctoral certificate programs must have completed a doctoral degree in clinical psychology at a regionally accredited institution. Applicants to the M.S. in school psychology need to have a baccalaureate degree in psychology, education, or a related field from a regionally accredited institution and must have completed 6 credits each of English and math, abnormal psychology/psychopathology, or exceptional children and child psychology/adolescent psychology. Nine additional credits in psychology must also have been completed. Applicants to either M.S. program must have taken the GRE or MAT exam. Applicants to the Ed.S. program must have a master's degree in school psychology or a related field and must submit test scores from the GRE Psychology Subtest #81 and have successfully passed the Praxis I exam. Applicants to the Psy.D. in school psychology program must have a master's and specialist degree in school psychology and must be a licensed school psychologist. Candidates must also submit scores from the Praxis II School Psychology Specialty exam. All applicants must submit all college transcripts and three letters of recommendation with accompanying recommendation forms. The M.S., Ed.S., and Psy.D. programs utilize a rolling admissions policy. Finalists for all programs interview with the Admissions Committee and are then notified in writing of the committee's decision.

Correspondence and Information

Office of Admissions
Philadelphia College of Osteopathic Medicine
4170 City Avenue
Philadelphia, Pennsylvania 19131-1694
Phone: 215-871-6700
      800-999-6998 (toll-free)
Fax: 215-871-6719
E-mail: gradadmissions@pcom.edu
Web site: http://www.pcom.edu

Philadelphia College of Osteopathic Medicine

THE FACULTY AND THEIR RESEARCH

Robert A. DiTomasso, Ph.D., ABPP, Professor; Chair, Department of Psychology; and Director, Institutional Outcomes Assessment. Dr. DiTomasso has extensive teaching experience and has published dozens of chapters, articles, and reviews and a book on anxiety disorders. He specializes in behavioral medicine, the cognitive behavioral treatment of anxiety and stress-related medical disorders, research design, psychometrics, methodology, program evaluation, and primary-care consultation. He also specializes in patient nonadherence to medical advice and instrument development for cognitive distortions, anger, health risk behaviors, and patient satisfaction with medical services.

Stephanie Felgoise, Ph.D., ABPP, Professor; Vice Chair, Department of Psychology; and Director, Clinical Psy.D. Program. Dr. Felgoise has coauthored numerous national conference presentations and publications in psycho-oncology, sexual health and dysfunction, and coping and adjustment with chronic medical illness. Other interests include behavioral medicine, social problem solving, caregiver issues, and diversity issues in health care.

Michael Ascher, Ph.D., Clinical Professor. Dr. Ascher has done extensive research on the treatment of anxiety disorders (particularly agoraphobia, obsessive compulsive disorder, panic disorders, and phobias) within the context of behavior therapy. In addition, he has researched investor anxiety, including the emotional difficulties experienced by the average retail stock market investor, and the psychogenic disorders of sleep.

Virginia Burks Salzer, Ph.D., Associate Professor. Dr. Salzer's research interests include social information processing in the development of children's aggressive behavior, linkages between family and children's peer systems, comorbidity of children's externalizing and internalizing disorders, and impact of parental psychopathology and the development of childhood disorders.

Stacey C. Cahn, Ph.D., Assistant Professor. Dr. Cahn's area of expertise is broadly clinical health psychology, including eating disorders, as well as the areas of sleep, depression in heart disease, and aging.

William Clinton, M.A., Program Director, Organizational Development and Leadership Program. Mr. Clinton has extensive experience in organizational consultation and has held various leadership positions. His specialty is in training practitioners to become effective leaders who implement change in organizational settings.

Terri Erbacher, Ph.D., Clinical Assistant Professor. Dr. Erbacher is a certified school psychologist and licensed psychologist. Her specific population and program expertise includes nonpublic elementary and secondary schools, autistic support, learning support, early intervention, and supervision of school psychology interns.

Jessica Glass Kendorski, Ph.D., NCSP, Assistant Professor. Dr. Glass is a certified school psychologist. Her clinical experiences and research interests include data-based assessment and interventions in the residential and school settings, specifically, response to intervention, curriculum-based measurement, positive behavior support, and applied behavior analysis. She has extensive experience in supporting the emotional, social, and behavioral needs of children diagnosed with developmental disabilities.

Barbara Golden, Psy.D., ABPP, Associate Professor and Director, Clinical Services. Dr. Golden's experience includes clinical service, administration, supervision, consultation, and education. Her primary areas of interest and research are in behavioral medicine, including nonpharmacological pain management, stress management, and somatization disorder, as well as in psychology and primary-care medicine.

Elizabeth Gosch, Ph.D., ABPP, Associate Professor and Director, M.S. Program in Counseling and Clinical Health Psychology. One of Dr. Gosch's primary areas of expertise is psychotherapy with children and adolescents. Her major research interest concerns the processes and effectiveness of psychotherapy with differing populations. She has published and lectured internationally on the cognitive behavioral treatment of anxiety in children.

James B. Hale, Ph.D., Associate Professor and Associate Director, Clinical Training–School Psychology Program. Trained in clinical neuropsychology, Dr. Hale has research interests in such areas as language and psychosocial functions associated with right-hemisphere dysfunction, challenging assumptions about standardized cognitive assessment and the validity of global IQ scores for children with disabilities, and frontal-subcortical circuit dysfunction in ADHD and medication response.

Dan Ingram, Psy.D., Clinical Assistant Professor. Dr. Ingram is a certified school psychologist with more than twenty-five years' experience. His research interests are in the area of autism.

Petra Kottsieper, Ph.D., Assistant Professor. Dr. Kottsieper's main research interests include forensic psychology, therapeutic process, mental health services research, professional development, ethics, and psychiatric rehabilitation for individuals with serious mental illnesses. Much of her clinical work has focused on the empirically-supported treatment and assessment of serious mental illnesses, co-occurring disorders (including developmental disabilities and substance misuse issues), and forensic issues.

Donald Masey, Psy.D., Clinical Assistant Professor. Dr. Masey's research interests include memory and aging, psychological assessment, hospital practice for psychologists, practice models and issues in professional psychology, medical psychology, adult learning disabilities, and adult ADHD.

George McCloskey, Ph.D., Associate Professor and Co-Director, Research. Dr. McCloskey has accumulated a broad range of work experiences in the field of psychology over the last twenty-five years, including research, clinical work, administration, teaching, and business. His research and interests include neuropsychological process and learning, psychological and educational assessment and intervention, reading achievement, ADHD, executive dysfunction, memory problems, and expression disability.

Rosemary Mennuti, Ed.D., NCSP, Professor and Director, School Psychology Program. Dr. Mennuti has extensive experience as a school psychologist and in teaching. She has lectured and published in the areas of moral development, eating disorders, and therapist self-disclosure. Other areas of interest include female development, CBT in schools, and relational cultural theory in practice.

Bradley Rosenfield, Psy.D., Assistant Professor. Dr. Rosenfield's research interests include cognitive behavioral therapy for adult ADHD, human-animal interactions, depressive disorders, somatic disorders, anxiety disorders, single session treatment for panic attacks, the social psychology of terrorism, multicultural counseling, communication skills, and treating difficult patients.

Matthew Schure, Ph.D., President and Chief Executive Officer. Dr. Schure's major areas of interest include personality correlates of learning, such as self-esteem, level of aspiration, and locus of control. In addition, he has done extensive research on community mental health interventions and family dynamics, including the outcome of dysfunctional parenting and parental rejection.

Marsha S. Singer, Ph.D., Clinical Assistant Professor and Associate Director, M.S. Program in Counseling and Clinical Health Psychology. Dr. Singer's main professional interest is clinical health psychology. She is very interested in the role of cultural, spiritual, and other psychosocial factors in health behavior and patient attitudes. She is also interested in the role of family members as social supports in medical and mental health settings.

Diane Smallwood, Psy.D., NCSP, Associate Professor and Director, Ed.S. program. In addition to school-based work experience, for the past twenty years, Dr. Smallwood has been involved in leadership activities at both the state and national levels. Her professional interests include school crisis prevention, intervention, and response; social-emotional learning; classroom resiliency; bullying and violence in schools; and translating research to practice.

Takako Suzuki, Ph.D., Assistant Professor. Dr. Suzuki's major areas of interest include CBT of mood and anxiety disorders; multicultural issues such as development of cultural identity, acculturation process, and issues with expatriates; religion and spirituality; and emotional intelligence and development of empathy.

Yuma I. Tomes, Ph.D., Associate Professor and Director, M.S. Program in School Psychology. Dr. Tomes has accumulated a diverse range of work experiences in the field of psychology and education over the last ten years. He brings a unique perspective of clinical, teaching, research, and administrative experience to his position at PCOM. Dr. Tomes has worked as a psychologist in urban school districts. His major areas of interest are cross-cultural psychology, multicultural assessment, cognitive/learning styles, cognition and learning theories, psychological/educational assessments, consultation, and developmental issues.

Beverly White, Psy.D., Clinical Assistant Professor. Dr. White has worked extensively with traumatized children and adolescents. She has published and has research interests in the areas of psychological assessment, dreams in CBT-oriented treatment, and crisis/trauma, post-traumatic stress, and CBT interventions. Other research interests include right/left-hemisphere performance and malfunction and multicultural issues.

Carrie Yurica, Psy.D., Assistant Professor, Director of Clinical Training (School Psychology Program). Dr. Yurica is a certified school psychologist and half-time core faculty member at PCOM. She specializes in cognitive behavioral treatment for children, adolescents, and adults. Her research involves the relationship between cognitive distortions and various forms of psychotherapy.

Bruce Zahn, Ed.D., ABPP, Professor and Director of Clinical Training (Clinical Psy.D. program). Dr. Zahn has published on cognitive behavioral therapy, childhood sexual abuse, multimodal therapy programs for adolescents, and psychological functioning in survivors of traumatic brain injury. His areas of expertise include geropsychology, behavioral medicine, cognitive behavioral therapy, self-esteem, group therapy, and supervision. Dr. Zahn's mentoring and research interests are in the areas of psychological testing (including projective personality assessment), post-traumatic stress disorder, managed-care issues, and chronic mental illness.

ROGER WILLIAMS UNIVERSITY

Program in Forensic Psychology

Program of Study

Roger Williams University (RWU) is one of a select number of academic institutions offering degrees specifically focused on the field of forensic psychology. The Master of Arts in forensic psychology program at RWU prepares students in either a thesis or nonthesis track. Graduates are trained to conduct assessments and provide treatment services in a variety of forensic settings or pursue advanced training at the doctoral level. Students learn how to conduct psychological tests, explore various treatment methods, strengthen their research methodology skills, and become knowledgeable in psychopathology and clinical diagnosis.

In their second year of study, students are placed in a variety of internships and practicum sites. Students complete practical experiences in areas including group psychotherapy, sex offender treatment, individual psychotherapy, psychological testing, and specialized assessment techniques. Research-based internships are also possible for those students who are interested in preparing for further study at the doctoral level. The University strives to educate all students to become productive citizens of the social and professional communities in which they will live and build their careers, and faculty members are committed to fostering a strong sense of intellectual curiosity in all students, regardless of the intended career path.

Research Facilities

A robust research library is integral to graduate study. The Learning Commons at the Roger Williams University Library offers a wide array of instructional resources for the students. It is an improved model for research—a one-stop shop for instructional technology, traditional, and database research—that provides students access to myriad research resources. The University's state-of-the-art computer laboratories allow student access to the latest word and statistical processing software packages available, including full Internet access. A new library café is available for study breaks.

The University's expansive library houses approximately 2,000 volumes and hundreds of films and other nonprint materials related to the U.S. justice system. Master's degree candidates also have access to the LexisNexis network and Westlaw as well as the RWU Law Library. In addition, the University is a member of the Helin Consortium, which gives students access to more than a million volumes of printed material. Quiet study space and group research areas are also available.

Financial Aid

Financing a graduate education can be challenging, especially in these trying economic times. Roger Williams University recognizes that some students may need financial assistance to meet the cost of higher education. Students with financial need may be able to receive funds from federal loan programs: those with fully accepted status who maintain a minimum of 6 credits per semester are eligible to receive loans that cover the cost of graduate education. In order to be considered for the federal loan program, students must submit the Free Application for Federal Student Aid (FAFSA), which is available from the Office of Financial Aid or at http://www.fafsa.ed.gov.

Cost of Study

The 2008–09 graduate tuition was $639 per credit. Each 3-credit course cost $1917. Some additional fees may apply. Tuition information for the 2009–10 academic year is available at http://financialaid.rwu.edu.

Living and Housing Costs

University housing is available for graduate students. However, it is not guaranteed, and the majority of graduate students seek a variety of off-campus housing options. In 2008–09, the average cost for on-campus graduate housing was $7313 per academic year. For more information about off-campus housing, visit http://housing.rwu.edu and click the "off-campus" living tab.

Student Group

The Forensic Psychology Master's program is designed for students with an undergraduate degree in psychology, criminal justice, or another related field who are interested in contributing to the treatment of forensic populations.

Student Outcomes

Graduates of the program will be trained to serve forensic populations, including juveniles and sex offenders, in prisons or specialized treatment settings, through group and individualized psychotherapy, psychological testing, specialized testing with specific populations, specialized treatment or psycho-educational groups, work with families of juveniles, and work with psychiatrists and other clinical staff members in treatment and discharge planning. Program graduates may go on to act as trial consultants, work for family courts, research violent crimes for the FBI, become psychologists for the police department and federal government, and conduct psychological testing within populations.

Location

Roger Williams University is located in Bristol, Rhode Island, a seaside town that is home to antique stores, gourmet restaurants, ice cream shops and spas. The campus is less than 30 minutes by bus from Providence, Rhode Island's capital and largest city, which is packed with museums, coffee shops, the Providence Place Mall, live music, and much more. Providence is also a regional transportation hub, with an international airport and both bus and train stations. Also less than 30 minutes away from campus is Newport, home of famous beaches, shopping, festivals, and open markets.

The University

Roger Williams University is a 52-year-old independent, coeducational liberal arts university that has quickly established itself as a leader in higher education. A dynamic educational environment in which students live and learn to be global citizens, the University is committed to its mantra of "Learning to bridge the world."

With thirty-nine academic programs and a robust array of cocurricular activities available on its waterfront campus in historic Bristol, Rhode Island, RWU looks to a set of core values in fulfilling its mission to prepare students for life as twenty-first century citizen-scholars. Over the past decade the institution has achieved unprecedented academic and financial successes. In 2008, *U.S. News & World Report.* named Roger Williams the eighth-ranked baccalaureate college in the north.

Applying

A completed application includes a bachelor's degree in psychology, criminal justice, or a related field, with a 3.0 GPA and course work in statistics and research methods; a two-page personal statement describing the student's interest in forensic psychology and career goals and how the student can positively contribute to the graduate program; official college transcripts; minimum GRE scores of 1000; three letters of recommendation; and a $50 application fee. Applications are accepted for fall admission only; the application deadline date is March 15.

Correspondence and Information

Jason Pina
Dean of Continuing Studies and Graduate Admission
Roger Williams University
One Old Ferry Road
Bristol, Rhode Island 02809
E-mail: gradadmit@rwu.edu
Web site: http://www.rwu.edu

Roger Williams University

THE FACULTY

Garrett L Berman, Associate Professor of Psychology; Ph.D., Florida International.
Bonita Cade, Assistant Professor of Psychology; Ph.D., Iowa State; J.D., Washington (St. Louis).
Frank DiCataldo, Assistant Professor of Psychology; Ph.D., St. Louis.
Kim Knight, Professor of Psychology; Ph.D., Boston University.
Judith Platania, Assistant Professor of Psychology; Ph.D., Florida International.
Becky L. Spritz, Assistant Professor of Psychology; Ph.D., Penn State.
Charles Trimbach, Professor of Psychology; Ph.D., Princeton.
Laura L. Turner, Assistant Professor of Psychology. Ph.D., Penn State.
Donald Whitworth, Professor of Psychology; Ph.D., Rhode Island.
Matt Zaitchik, Associate Professor of Psychology; Ph.D., Connecticut.

RUTGERS, THE STATE UNIVERSITY OF NEW JERSEY, NEWARK

Graduate Program in Psychology
Concentrations in Cognitive Science, Cognitive Neuroscience, Perception,
Biopsychology, and Social Psychology

Programs of Study

Students entering the graduate program in psychology can take courses of study leading to a Ph.D. in psychology with specializations in biopsychology, cognitive neuroscience, cognitive science, perception, and social psychology. Current research in the biopsychology of emotion and adaptive behavior focuses on the motivational, evolutionary, and developmental mechanisms underlying behavior. Research in cognitive neuroscience offers training in neuroimaging methods, concepts, and experimental paradigms. The neuroimaging research focus includes studies in motion and event perception, learning and memory, and how humans process rewards and punishments. Research in the area of cognitive science offers training in the computational and experimental study of cognitive processes. The curriculum provides basic instruction in computational and mathematical modeling methods, with a focus on connectionist systems, learning, memory, and categorization. The perception specialization offers training in the experimental study of motion and color perception as well as many advanced areas within vision science. The social psychology concentration focuses on attachment theory, the mediation of social and interpersonal conflict, aggression, violence and bullying, interracial feedback, social support, and the methods and techniques used most commonly in these areas.

Students are encouraged to take advantage of training opportunities in the adjacent Center for Molecular and Behavioral Neuroscience, the College of Business (Information Sciences), the College of Nursing, the Department of Biological Sciences, the University of Medicine and Dentistry of New Jersey (UMDNJ), and the New Jersey Institute of Technology as well as adjunct courses listed in related areas (such as linguistics, philosophy, or cognitive science) on the New Brunswick campus. A written qualifying examination is given after the completion of basic course work at the end of the second year. Upon satisfactory completion of these requirements, students advance to candidacy for the Ph.D. degree and must submit a thesis proposal, carry out their thesis research, and then defend their dissertation.

Research Facilities

The Department of Psychology occupies about 42,000 square feet on the first, third, fourth, and fifth floors of Smith Hall. The department has its own servers (http://psychology.rutgers.edu, http://www.psych.rutgers.edu), computing laboratory, and a series of individual laboratories for neurophysiological, neuroanatomical, and neuropharmacological research. There are more than 16,000 square feet for animal holding and testing. The Psychology Department with UMDNJ supports the Advanced Imaging Center with a state-of-the-art Siemens 3T Allegra head-only magnet (more information can be found at http://www.rutgers-newark.rutgers.edu/fmri) and 64-channel EEG (Neuroscan) and 32-channel EEG (Digital ANT) systems.

Additional equipment includes an optical motion capture system for the perception of biological movement, a variety of human observation and testing rooms, one-way observation rooms, video equipment, high-speed graphics computers, and access to a Hewlett Packard Itanium II Workstation linked to the department's 28-node Opteron computer cluster and storage system, which can hold one trillion bytes of data.

Financial Aid

Students accepted into the program receive a full stipend and tuition remission through one of the wide range of scholarships, fellowships, and assistantships offered by the Rutgers Graduate School to full-time Ph.D. students whose records demonstrate superior academic achievement and scholarly promise. Stipends range up to $18,000 plus tuition remission for fellowships and $21,400 for teaching or graduate assistantships. They may be renewed for one or more years depending on the availability of funds and the academic standing of the student.. Students who are members of minority groups may also be eligible to receive additional support through the Minority Biomedical Research Support Program and other programs. Students also receive financial support from the Department of Psychology to attend conferences.

Cost of Study

Tuition for the 2008–09 academic year was about $14,500 (for New Jersey residents) and about $22,000 for out-of-state residents; graduate students receive tuition remission along with their source of support.

Living and Housing Costs

Graduate student housing is available in Talbott Apartments and University Square Apartments. Costs range from $7300 for an academic year lease to $10,500 for a calendar year lease. All options are single rooms in either a 3-person or 4-person shared apartment. A limited number of family apartment options are available for married/domestic partners and students with children in University-owned brownstones.

Student Group

There are currently 25 full-time graduate doctoral students carrying out research in the Department of Psychology. The faculty-student ratio of 1:2 affords ample opportunity for students to interact with faculty members. Students in the Department of Psychology are represented in policy decisions and are actively involved in the selection of new students.

Location

Rutgers' Newark campus is conveniently located in the center of a diverse and thriving educational, professional, and cultural community in the downtown area of New Jersey's largest city. Newark is also at the center of the nation's largest concentration of pharmaceutical industries. The campus is a modern complex serving more than 10,000 students and 500 faculty members. Rutgers-Newark is easily accessible by car or mass transit and is approximately 30 minutes by road or rail from midtown Manhattan. A free campus shuttle bus links the campus with the city's mass transit centers during the evening hours. The Department of Psychology is located one block from the University's jogging track, fully equipped gymnasium, and swimming pool.

The University

Rutgers, The State University of New Jersey, with more than 47,000 students on campuses in Camden, Newark, and New Brunswick, is one of the major state universities in the nation. The Newark campus is part of a complex of higher education institutions that includes the New Jersey Institute of Technology and the University of Medicine and Dentistry of New Jersey.

Applying

Students apply to enter the program on a full-time basis. Students should apply to the Department of Psychology and mention the area of study they are most interested in. Applications can be submitted at http://gradstudy.rutgers.edu/. The application deadline for the fall semester is January 15 and for the spring semester, November 1. Students should include scores for the General GRE and the Subject GRE in their area of interest.

Correspondence and Information

Kenneth Kressel, Ph.D., Director of Graduate Programs in Psychology
Department of Psychology
301 Smith Hall
Rutgers, The State University of New Jersey
101 Warren Street
Newark, New Jersey 07102
Phone: 973-353-5440 Ext. 232
Fax: 973-353-1171
E-mail: gradprogram@psychology.rutgers.edu
Web site: http://www.psych.rutgers.edu

Rutgers, The State University of New Jersey, Newark

THE FACULTY AND THEIR RESEARCH

Colin G. Beer, D.Phil., Oxford. Ethology, communication, and social development of birds; historical and philosophical aspects of ethology; comparative psychology.

Paul Boxer, Ph.D., Bowling Green. Aggression and violence, social development, contextual influences on behavior.

Mei-Fang Cheng, Ph.D., Bryn Mawr. Neuroethology; neurobiological study of vocal behavior and self-stimulation; mechanism and function of brain injury–induced neurogenesis in adult animals.

Mauricio Delgado, Ph.D., Pittsburgh. Behavioral and neural correlates of reward-related processing, with an emphasis on how the affective properties of outcomes or feedback influence choice behavior; using neuroimaging and behavioral and psychophysiological methods.

Alan Gilchrist, Ph.D., Rutgers. Visual cognition; surface-color perception.

Stephen José Hanson, Ph.D., Arizona State. Learning and memory, connectionist models, categorization, cognitive science.

Kent D. Harber, Ph.D., Stanford. Interracial feedback biases; social support and coping; emotion and social perception.

Barry R. Komisaruk, Ph.D., Rutgers. Neurophysiological, functional neuroanatomical, and neuropharmacological study of endogenous pain-blocking mechanisms related to sexual behavior and parturition in mammals, including humans; brain, spinal cord, autonomic, and peripheral nerve mechanisms, using functional magnetic resonance imaging (fMRI).

Ken Kressel, Ph.D., Columbia. Social and interpersonal conflict, mediation of conflict, conflict dynamics in organizational settings.

Lillian Robbins, Ph.D., NYU. Improving educational practices (K–16) for the disadvantaged, sex discrimination in academe, parental attitudes and practices, environmental factors in health and safety.

Maggie Shiffrar, Ph.D., Stanford. Visual motion perception; object recognition.

Harold I. Siegel, Ph.D., Rutgers. Attachment theory; adult attachment; attitudes toward mother and other adult relationships, attachment and sexual offenders.

Elizabeth Tricomi, Ph.D., Pittsburgh. Functional neuroimaging of learning and decision making, social and affective influences on reward processing and valuation, neural basis of goal-directed behavior.

Gretchen Van de Walle, Ph.D., Cornell. Conceptual understanding of physical objects and numbers and the interaction between conceptual development and linguistic abilities, particularly the relationship between children's ability to categorize and label classes of objects.

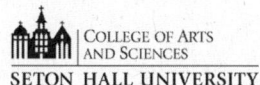

SETON HALL UNIVERSITY

Department of Psychology
Master of Science in Experimental Psychology

Program of Study

The Department of Psychology offers the Master of Science (M.S.) in experimental psychology, with concentrations in general psychology and behavioral neuroscience. The M.S. degree program is designed specifically for students seeking to gain a solid foundation in empirical research for eventual entry into Ph.D. programs in clinical or counseling psychology, experimental psychology, or neuroscience. Graduates also go directly to related areas of employment as laboratory assistants, market researchers, science writers, or community college teachers.

The program consists of 36 credits, or twelve courses (two courses in research design and analysis, four semesters of independent research, and either six experimental psychology electives or six required neuroscience courses), to be completed in two years. The courses offered include biological bases of behavior, foundations of neuropsychology, developmental psychology, conditioning and behavior, and many others. Those in the general psychology concentration must consult an adviser on elective course selections.

For additional information about the program, including details about faculty research and graduate student research, students should visit http://www.shu.edu/academics/artsci/ms-psychology/index.cfm.

Research Facilities

The University libraries have notable resources, including extensive holdings of almost 523,000 book volumes, 1,127 current periodical subscriptions, back-files of more than 6,500 serial titles, electronic access to full text articles in 11,500 journals, a broad selection of indexing and abstracting services in both digital and print formats, various microform collections, music CDs, and audiovisual aids.

The Department of Psychology is housed in Jubilee Hall, one of the newest academic buildings at Seton Hall University. The department facilities include a conference room and two wireless classrooms with adjacent support areas for instructional equipment and media production. The department maintains a Behavioral Neuroscience Laboratory for surgery, histology, and computerized monitoring of rodent behaviors to conduct modern behavioral neuroscience research. Research space for Human Experimental Psychology includes eleven research cubicles and a three-room Perception Laboratory suite.

Financial Aid

Graduate assistantships, which include tuition benefits and stipend, are available on a competitive basis. The online application for graduate assistantships can be found at http://www.shu.edu/applying/graduate/grad-finaid.cfm. Students should contact the Department at psych@shu.edu for further information about graduate assistantships. Graduate students may also consult the Academic Resource Center (ARC) of the University for other funding opportunities and scholarships for which they might be eligible. They may also apply for Federal Work-Study programs (contact the Office of Financial Aid for more information).

Cost of Study

In 2009–10, tuition is $901 per credit. Full-time students pay $305 in University and technology fees; part-time students pay $185.

Living and Housing Costs

Housing and living costs in South Orange and the surrounding towns are comparable to most suburban cities, with studio and one-bedroom apartments renting for $750 to $1200 per month. Some students have also opted to share apartments with roommates.

Student Group

The M.S. in Experimental Psychology program enrolls about 10 to 12 new students each year. Overall, Seton Hall has approximately 4,500 graduate students.

Location

Seton Hall University is located in South Orange, New Jersey, only 14 miles by car, bus, or direct train to New York City. The University's proximity to New York allows students to take advantage of all the city has to offer, while still living in a suburban area.

The University and The Department

Seton Hall University's diverse academic program is characterized by a strong teaching faculty and a wide range of academic choices. At Seton Hall, students find people who are willing to listen, offer support, and help them get the most out of their education.

The Department of Psychology is a part of the College of Arts and Sciences, home to more than 4,000 students and faculty members engaged in one of the most rewarding of all human endeavors—the pursuit of knowledge. Rooted in tradition, yet looking to the future through innovative use of technology and a commitment to providing students with co-curricular and professional opportunities, the College of Arts and Sciences offers a rich array of graduate programs.

Applying

In addition to the general University requirements for admission to graduate studies, the Department of Psychology requires applicants to have a baccalaureate degree that reflects the completion of a minimum of 18 credits in psychology with at least a 3.0 grade point average. All applicants must have completed Introduction to Psychology, Psychological Statistics, and Research Methods courses. Students considering a concentration in behavioral neuroscience must have completed Physiological Psychology or the equivalent. Applicants should submit official transcripts of all previous academic work, official scores on the Graduate Record Examination (GRE), three letters of recommendation from individuals familiar with the applicant's academic and research ability, and a personal statement of 300 to 400 words that outlines the student's academic achievements, research interests, and career goals.

Applications are available online at http://www.shu.edu/applying/graduate/graduate-application-accounts.cfm. Applications completed before April 1 for fall admissions and before November 1 for spring admissions are given top priority. Applications after these dates are reviewed on a rolling basis through July 1. This process continues until no openings are left.

Correspondence and Information

Dr. Janine P. Buckner, Director of Graduate Studies
Department of Psychology
College of Arts and Sciences
Jubilee Hall, Room 339
Seton Hall University
400 South Orange Avenue
South Orange, New Jersey 07079
Phone: 973-761-9484
Fax: 973-275-5829
E-mail: Janine.Buckner@shu.edu
　　　psych@shu.edu
Web site: http://www.shu.edu/academics/artsci/ms-psychology/index.cfm

Seton Hall University

THE FACULTY AND THEIR RESEARCH

Janine P. Buckner, Associate Professor and Director of Graduate Studies; Ph.D., Emory, 2000. Effects of gender, identity, and audience in autobiographical memory narratives; personal, social, and contextual factors shaping gender disparities in science fields.

Gregory Burton, Professor; Ph.D., Connecticut, 1990. Touch perception of and with tools.

Paige Fisher, Assistant Professor; Ph.D., Massachusetts Amherst, 2005. Anxiety and mood disorders in children.

Kelly Goedert, Assistant Professor; Ph.D., Virginia, 2001. Statistical, heuristic, and memory processes in causal reasoning from contingency information; characteristics of memory for motor skills and perceptual-motor adaptations.

John Hovancik, Associate Professor; Ph.D., Purdue, 1975. Computer applications in psychology.

Amy Silvestri Hunter, Associate Professor; Ph.D., Vermont, 1997. Interactions between sleep and learning in experimental animals, how REM sleep deprivation can impair memory for a previously learned event and the biochemical mechanisms that underlie this phenomenon.

Jeffrey Levy, Associate Professor; Ph.D., Adelphi, 1972. Teaching of psychology, outcomes assessment.

Marianne Lloyd, Assistant Professor; Ph.D., Binghamton, 2005. Memory illusions, metacognition, geography learning.

Susan A. Nolan, Associate Professor and Chair; Ph.D., Northwestern, 1998. Interpersonal dynamics of depression and anxiety, gender issues in the sciences, teaching of statistics.

Andrew Simon, Associate Professor; Ph.D., Psy.D., Rutgers. Organizational dynamics, with a focus on leadership and decision making and work-teams.

Susan Teague, Associate Professor; Ph.D., Georgia, 1987. Attitude change and persuasion processes, especially as related to promotion of preventive health behaviors; aggressive and violent behavior.

Michael Vigorito, Associate Professor; Ph.D., Massachusetts Amherst, 1988. Animal learning and motivation, behavioral pharmacology, technology-enhanced curriculum development.

SOUTHERN ILLINOIS UNIVERSITY CARBONDALE

Department of Psychology

Programs of Study

The Southern Illinois University Carbondale (SIUC) Department of Psychology offers doctoral training in four areas: applied psychology (AP), brain and cognitive sciences (BCS), clinical psychology, and counseling psychology. The clinical and counseling programs are accredited by the American Psychological Association (APA). All programs involve a full-time course of study, typically four years on campus, with an additional internship year for both the clinical and counseling programs. Students complete Departmental course requirements (primarily methodology), a carefully developed program curriculum, an empirical M.A. thesis, and a doctoral dissertation. The Department does not admit students seeking a terminal master's degree; students earn the M.A. en route to a Ph.D. Rarely, students earn a terminal M.A. or nonempirical M.S. when they or the faculty members reconsider their suitability for doctoral study. The Department has a strong collegial atmosphere, and students benefit from access to faculty members from all programs. Throughout their studies, students are engaged in diverse preprofessional training assignments appropriate to their program, involving wide-ranging activities related to teaching, basic and applied research, and clinical or counseling services.

Research Facilities

The Department maintains extensive and quite comprehensive research facilities. Active human laboratories permit the use of methodologies such as eye tracking, single-unit recording, computer presentation of stimuli, controlled delivery of substances, recording and coding of child behavior, three-dimensional animation, neural network modeling, EEG recording, evoked potential recording, and human genotyping of individual differences related to personality, psychopathology, and substance use. Animal laboratories permit studies of animal learning (operant chambers and mazes), recovery of function, specific nerve stimulation, experimental surgery, contingent delivery of substances, psychopharmacology, and other areas of neuroscience. Diverse field research opportunities are available; collaborative sites include the campus Clinical Center, Student Health Service, the Department's Career Development and Resource Clinic, and local mental health and human service agencies, in addition to access to equipment necessary for survey development and scanning, telephone and in-person interviewing, computer-assisted interviewing and data collection, and still and video recording. Students also have access to state-of-the-art computer labs, including a small lab dedicated to psychology graduate students.

Financial Aid

The SIUC Department of Psychology has a very strong record of supporting students. All students in good standing are guaranteed support for their first academic year (nine months), and they typically receive nine to ten months of support for four or more academic years. Assistantship support comes from diverse sources such as college teaching assistantships, Graduate School fellowships, research grants, and service contracts with campus and local agencies, providing valuable preprofessional training opportunities. Assistantships include tuition waivers.

Cost of Study

In-state graduate tuition is $328 per credit hour in 2009–10. Out-of-state tuition is 2.5 times the in-state tuition rate ($820 per credit hour). Graduate students with at least a 25 percent appointment as a graduate assistant receive a tuition scholarship. Fees vary from $589.03 (1 credit hour) to $1557.50 (12 credit hours). Students with a graduate assistantship receive a 50 percent reduction in the primary care medical fee. New graduate students from Arkansas, Indiana, Kentucky, Missouri, and Tennessee qualify for the alternate tuition rate, which is equivalent to the in-state graduate tuition rate.

Living and Housing Costs

For married couples, students with families, and single graduate students, the University has 690 efficiency and one-, two-, three-, and four-bedroom apartments that rent for $499 to $720 per month in 2009–10. Residence halls for single graduate students are also available, as are accessible residence hall rooms and apartments for students with disabilities.

Student Group

The program usually admits approximately 20 students per year. Typically, the program has approximately 80 students, of whom roughly 65 percent are women, 20 percent are members of minority groups, and 5 to 10 percent are international.

Location

SIUC is 350 miles south of Chicago and 100 miles southeast of St. Louis. Nestled in rolling hills bordered by the Ohio and Mississippi Rivers and enhanced by a mild climate, the area has state parks, national forests and wildlife refuges, and large lakes for outdoor recreation. Cultural offerings include theater, opera, concerts, art exhibits, and cinema. Educational facilities for the families of students are excellent.

The University

Southern Illinois University Carbondale is a comprehensive public university with a variety of general and professional education programs. The University offers associate, bachelor's, master's, and doctoral degrees; the J.D. degree; and the M.D. degree. The University is fully accredited by the North Central Association of Colleges and Schools. The Graduate School has an essential role in the development and coordination of graduate instruction and research programs. The Graduate Council has academic responsibility for determining graduate standards, recommending new graduate programs and research centers, and establishing policies to facilitate the research effort. Southern Illinois University Carbondale is a state-funded university founded in 1869.

Applying

Applications are accepted once a year (December 15 and February 1 application deadlines, depending on the program) for admission the following fall. Applications are available on the Department's Web site or may be requested via e-mail or phone or by mail. All application materials should be sent to the Psychology Graduate Program Office. A complete application includes the Departmental application form; the Graduate School application form, which must be completed online; a personal statement; a summary of research/professional experience; three letters of recommendation; two copies of official transcripts of all college work; official GRE scores; the official Advanced Psychology GRE score (not required, but preferred); and a $50 application fee.

Correspondence and Information

Graduate Program Office
Department of Psychology
Room 281A
Southern Illinois University Carbondale
Carbondale, Illinois 62901-6502

Phone: 618-453-3564
E-mail: gradpsyc@siu.edu
Web site: http://www.psychology.siu.edu

Southern Illinois University Carbondale

THE FACULTY AND THEIR RESEARCH

Mary Louise Cashel, Ph.D., North Texas, 1997. Clinical: Child and adolescent assessment, juvenile delinquency and preventative interventions, post-traumatic stress disorder (PTSD).

Kathleen Chwalisz, Ph.D., Iowa, 1992. Counseling: Health psychology, neuropsychology, group process and intervention, personality.

M. H. Clark, Ph.D., Memphis, 2004. Experimental–Applied Psychology: Methodology, quasi-experimentation, meta-analysis, statistics.

David DiLalla, Ph.D., Virginia, 1989. Clinical: Personality and psychopathology, personality assessment, computer-assisted assessment, behavioral genetics, sexual violence, social development.

*Lisabeth DiLalla, Ph.D., Virginia, 1987. Experimental–Brain and Cognitive Sciences: Behavioral genetics, social cognition.

Stephanie Clancy Dollinger, Ph.D., Syracuse, 1989. Experimental–Brain and Cognitive Sciences: Aging and cognition, identity development and cognition across the lifespan.

Stephen Dollinger, Director of Clinical Training; Ph.D., Missouri, 1977. Psychotherapy, personality, child-clinical.

Paul E. Etcheverry, Ph.D., Purdue, 2004. Experimental-Applied Psychology: Interpersonal relationships and health, social network influence on relationship outcomes and substance use.

Ann R. Fischer, Ph.D., Missouri–Columbia, 1995. Counseling: Counseling, gender issues, multicultural issues.

Brenda Gilbert, Ph.D., Florida, 1983. Clinical: Child behavior therapy, pediatric psychology, child abuse.

David Gilbert, Ph.D., Florida State, 1978. Clinical: State-dependent motivation, marital research, substance use, smoking, psychophysiology, personality, emotions, cerebral asymmetries.

Reza Habib, Ph.D., Toronto, 2000. Experimental–Brain and Cognitive Sciences: Cognitive neuroscience, brain imaging, cognition and memory.

Michael R. Hoane, Ph.D., Texas Christian, 1996. Experimental–Brain and Cognitive Sciences: Effects of vita-nutrients in brain injury and neurodegenerative diseases.

Eric A. Jacobs, Ph.D., Florida, 1997. Experimental–Applied Psychology and Brain and Cognitive Sciences: Experimental analysis of behavior, human operant behavior, verbal behavior, choice and self-control, behavioral ecology, behavioral economics, behavioral pharmacology, contingency management, radical behaviorism, cultural materialism.

Michelle Y. Kibby, Ph.D., Memphis, 1998. Clinical: Child assessment, clinical neuropsychology, reading disorders.

Meera Komarraju, Ph.D., Osmania (India), 1982; Ph.D., Cincinnati, 1987. Experimental–Applied Psychology: Life-stages and career-stages, work-family interface, cross-cultural influences on work values, academic motivation and dual-career phenomena, management of health-care quality.

Usha Lakshmanan, Ph.D., Michigan, 1989. Psycholinguistics, bilingualism, child first-language acquisition (monolingual and bilingual), child and adult second-language acquisition, language and cognition.

Benjamin F. Rodriguez, Ph.D., Catholic University, 2001. Clinical: Anxiety disorders, PTSD, religion and coping, epidemiology.

Patrick J. Rottinghaus, Ph.D. Iowa State, 2004. Counseling: Vocational psychology, counseling psychology.

Matthew Schlesinger, Ph.D., Berkeley, 1993. Experimental–Brain and Cognitive Sciences: Early cognitive development, problem solving, motor control, computational models of sensorimotor cognition.

Douglas Smith, Ph.D., Kansas State, 1977. Experimental–Brain and Cognitive Sciences: Biopsychology, neurophysiology, vision, development, learning and memory, recovery of function, epilepsy, psychoactive drugs.

Margaret Stockdale, Ph.D., Kansas State, 1990. Experimental–Applied Psychology: Industrial/organizational, gender bias in personnel decision, sexual harassment, workplace violence.

Jane Swanson, Ph.D., Minnesota, 1986. Counseling: Career choice and development, career assessment, adolescent career exploration.

Alan Vaux, Ph.D., Trinity College (Dublin), 1979; Ph.D., California, Irvine, 1981. Clinical and Experimental–Applied Psychology: Community psychology, social support and stress, close relationships and personality, violence, prevention, social interventions.

Yu-Wei Wang, Ph.D., Missouri–Columbia. Counseling: Stress, trauma, and coping/problem solving; sexual abuse/assault; multicultural and international issues; research methodology.

Rebecca Weston, Ph.D., North Texas, 2001. Experimental–Applied Psychology: Interpersonal relationships, violence, psychological abuse, sexual assault, and relational outcomes; advanced multivariate statistics.

Michael Young, Ph.D., Minnesota, Twin Cities, 1995. Experimental–Brain and Cognitive Sciences: Learning (of causal and temporal relationships and of categories), abstract concepts, judgment and decision making, computational modeling of learning processes (with a focus on radial basis function neural network models).

Emerita/Emeritus Faculty

Linda Gannon, Ph.D., Wisconsin, 1975. Clinical: Psychology of women, feminist therapy, behavior medicine, depression, cognitive styles.

Robert Jensen, Ph.D., Northern Illinois, 1976. Experimental–Brain and Cognitive Sciences: Neurobiology of learning and memory, psychopharmacology, drug dependence, behavioral development.

Jack McKillip, Ph.D., Loyola of Chicago, 1994. Experimental–Applied Psychology: Program evaluation, training and certification program development and evaluation, needs assessment, secondary data analysis.

James O'Donnell, Ph.D., Pittsburgh, 1965. Clinical: Child psychopathology, clinical neuropsychology, child and adult learning disabilities, attention deficit disorders.

Robert Radtke, Ph.D., Iowa, 1963. Experimental: Memory, cognitive processes.

Nerella Ramanaiah, Ph.D., Oregon, 1971. Experimental and Clinical: Personality and prediction, test theory, quantitative methods.

Thomas Schill, Ph.D., Oklahoma State, 1963. Clinical: Personality theory and dynamics, personality evaluation, rational emotive psychotherapy.

Ronald Schmeck, Ph.D., Ohio, 1969. Experimental: Teaching methods, individual differences in learning, learning style, cognitive style.

John Snyder, Ph.D., Loyola Chicago, 1965; ABPP. Counseling: Disaster intervention; American Red Cross Mental Health professional.

Barbara Yanico, Ph.D., Ohio State, 1977. Counseling: Gender roles and stereotyping, preferences for and expectations of counselors, stress and coping, racial/ethnic identity, personality and attitude measurement.

---

*Cross-appointed faculty member

SOUTHERN ILLINOIS UNIVERSITY CARBONDALE
Rehabilitation Institute

Programs of Study

Recent census data estimate that approximately 50 million American adults have a chronic health condition and/or disability that prevent them from achieving personal or vocational independence. The Rehabilitation Institute at Southern Illinois University Carbondale (SIUC) is dedicated to improving the lives of people with disability. This mission is pursued through the teaching, research, and service activities of the Institute's faculty and staff members. A Doctor of Philosophy in Rehabilitation degree and four Master of Science degrees (behavior analysis and therapy, communication disorders and sciences, rehabilitation administration and services, rehabilitation counseling) are offered. To date, there are more than 3,200 graduates of the academic programs. They are found in every state of the nation and, with the exception of Antarctica, on every continent of the world. Graduates work in such varied settings as universities, hospitals, schools, mental health facilities, substance-abuse centers, geriatric agencies, correctional facilities, public vocational rehabilitation programs, rehabilitation centers, and private rehabilitation. Examples of direct service job titles held by Institute graduates include rehabilitation counselor, substance abuse counselor, behavior analyst, speech-language pathologist, case manager, job-placement specialist, vocational evaluator, work-adjustment specialist, community-based training instructor, job coach, and developmental trainer. In short, the Rehabilitation Institute is one of the largest, most comprehensive and respected rehabilitation training programs in the United States.

Research Facilities

The Institute currently has several community-service programs that offer training and research experiences for students. For example, the Evaluation and Developmental Center provides vocational rehabilitation, adult education, and independent living services to adolescents and adults with disabilities. Project 12-Ways offers a behavioral intervention program to prevent child neglect and abuse. Speech and Hearing Services assess and treat people with communication disorders. This Institute's Center for Autism Spectrum Disorders has been recently added to enhance the language and social skills of preschool children with autism. The service programs provide lifelong benefits to people with different rehabilitation needs, serving hundreds of citizens of Southern Illinois yearly. They also provide excellent real-world training and research opportunities for students.

Financial Aid

Financial assistance is available to students through graduate assistantships, traineeships, and tuition scholarships. Students with outstanding qualifications may be considered for graduate fellowships. The University Financial Aid office is also a source of assistance.

Cost of Study

In-state graduate tuition is $328 per credit hour in 2009–10. Out-of-state tuition is 2.5 times the in-state tuition rate ($820 per credit hour). Graduate students with at least a 25 percent appointment as a graduate assistant receive a tuition scholarship. Fees vary from $589.03 (1 credit hour) to $1557.50 (12 credit hours). Students with a graduate assistantship receive a 50 percent reduction in the primary care medical fee. New graduate students from Arkansas, Indiana, Kentucky, Missouri, and Tennessee qualify for the alternate tuition rate, which is equivalent to the in-state graduate tuition rate.

Living and Housing Costs

For married couples, students with families, and single graduate students, the University has 690 efficiency and one-, two-, three-, and four-bedroom apartments that rent for $499 to $720 per month in 2009–10. Residence halls for single graduate students are also available, as are accessible residence hall rooms and apartments for students with disabilities.

Student Group

Approximately 25 students enter each master's program per year. About half of the M.S. students enter just after receiving their bachelor's degree. Others enter after having worked and are seeking a career change or advancement. The students are a diverse group and enjoy close working relations with faculty members and each other.

Location

SIUC is 350 miles south of Chicago and 100 miles southeast of St. Louis. Nestled in rolling hills bordered by the Ohio and Mississippi Rivers and enhanced by a mild climate, the area has state parks, national forests and wildlife refuges, and large lakes for outdoor recreation. Much of the area is a part of the 240,000-acre Shawnee National Forest. Cultural offerings include theater, opera, concerts, art exhibits, and cinema. Educational facilities for the families of students are excellent.

The University

Southern Illinois University Carbondale is a comprehensive public university, founded in 1869, with a variety of general and professional education programs. The University offers associate, bachelor's, master's, and doctoral degrees, in addition to the J.D. degree and the M.D. degree. The University is fully accredited by the North Central Association of Colleges and Schools. The Graduate School has an essential role in the development and coordination of graduate instruction and research programs. The Graduate Council has academic responsibility for determining graduate standards, recommending new graduate programs and research centers, and establishing policies to facilitate the research effort.

Applying

Applications should be requested from the address given in the Correspondence and Information section. Each application must include the standards forms, transcripts from all colleges and universities previously attended, three letters of academic reference, and a personal statement of career goals. Applicants are considered for both fall and spring semesters. Rh.D. applicants must also provide GRE scores.

Correspondence and Information

Director
Rehabilitation Institute, Mail Code 4609
Southern Illinois University Carbondale
Carbondale, Illinois 62901-4609

Phone: 618-536-7704
E-mail: bordieri@siu.edu
Web site: http://www.siu.edu/~rehab

Southern Illinois University Carbondale

THE FACULTY AND THEIR RESEARCH

The Rehabilitation Institute is led by a group of nationally recognized faculty members. In addition to being dedicated teachers, many of the faculty members have received national research and professional awards. They serve in leadership roles in professional organizations and on editorial boards of major journals. Faculty members consult on disability-related issues to private and public organizations regionally, nationally, and internationally. In recent years, faculty members have developed partnerships with rehabilitation professionals in Australia, Brazil, China, Ireland, Italy, Mexico, and Russia.

John J. Benshoff, Professor; Ph.D.; CRC. Substance abuse, rehabilitation counseling, gerontology.
James E. Bordieri, Professor and Director; Ph.D. Vocational evaluation, rehabilitation psychology, job placement.
William Crimando, Professor; Ph.D. Staff training and development, placement of persons with severe disabilities, computers in rehabilitation.
Anthony J. Cuvo, Professor; Ph.D. Behavior analysis, developmental disabilities, evaluation research.
Paula K. Davis, Professor; Ph.D. Developmental disabilities, behavior analysis.
Mark R. Dixon, Associate Professor; Ph.D. Behavior medicine/behavioral therapy, organizational management.
Carl R. Flowers, Associate Professor; Rh.D.; CRC. Diversity management, fiscal management, leadership.
Irene Gallenbach, Clinical Supervisor; CCS/SLP. Communications disorders and sciences.
Brandon F. Greene, Professor; Ph.D. Politics of developmental disabilities, child abuse/neglect, consumer affairs.
Diana Muzio, Instructor; CCS/SLP. Communication disorders and sciences.
Ruth Anne Rehfeldt, Associate Professor; Ph.D. Autism, supported employment, applied behavior analysis.
Ted F. Riggar, Professor; Ed.D. Rehabilitation administration and supervision.
Kenneth O. Simpson, Associate Professor; Ph.D.; CCC/SLP. Augmentative and alternative communication, interaction analysis, neurogenic communication disorders.
Linda McCabe Smith, Associate Professor; Ph.D.; CCC/SLP. Language development/language disorders in children, assessment of language in children from multicultural populations.
Darrell W. Taylor, Associate Professor; Ph.D.; CVE, CRC. Vocational evaluation and assessment, job development and placement, private section rehabilitation.
Rebecca Trammel, Clinical Instructor; M.S.; CCS/SLP. Communication disorders and sciences.
Thomas D. Upton, Associate Professor; Ph.D.; CRC. Brain injury, disabilities attitudes, vocational rehabilitation.
April Worsdell, Assistant Professor; Ph.D. Applied behavior analysis, severe behavior disorders, autism.

SouthUniversity℠

SOUTH UNIVERSITY

Columbia Campus
Professional Counseling Program

Program of Study	The Master of Arts in Professional Counseling degree program at South University is intended to meet the local and regional need for qualified professional counselors. The emphasis of the program is on community and agency counseling. The program is designed to enable program graduates to achieve all initial eligibility criteria to become certified as a National Certified Counselor (NCC) by the National Board for Certified Counselors (NBCC) and licensed in the state of South Carolina. The delivery structure of the program gives students the ability to balance the rigors of work and home while pursuing their master's degree. Students can complete one or two courses each term, with each quarter lasting ten weeks. Students select from the convenient Saturday sessions that meet once per week or attend two evenings during the week.
	Students are taught via two primary modes of instruction. The majority of the program involves didactic and experiential classroom instruction, supplemented by computer-based assignments, including the use of Internet technology. The second mode of instruction focuses on supervised field experiences. Students are placed in community counseling settings (while on internship) and practice counseling under the supervision of an on-site supervisor. Students in field placements also receive weekly individual and group supervision from qualified faculty supervisors.
Research Facilities	Along with classrooms and offices, the campus includes a bookstore, student lounge, and career services center. Students may retrieve periodicals in paper or electronic form. The South University Library provides in-library and remote access to electronic databases. Both bibliographic and full-text databases are available via EBSCOhost (e.g., Academic Search Premier, SocINDEX, PsycINFO, PsycARTICLES, and Mental Measurements Yearbook), the search and retrieval system of EBSCO Information Services, and via the Library and Information Resources Network (e.g., Infotrac and ProQuest databases). Infotrac databases include counseling sources such as Expanded Academic ASAP, Academic OneFile, and InfotracOneFile, and ProQuest databases include counseling sources such as ProQuest Psychology Journals and ProQuest Research Library. Internet access is available on all computers throughout the campus.
Financial Aid	A wide range of financial aid options is available to students who qualify. The Columbia campus of South University offers access to federal and state programs, including grants, loans, and work-study programs. Eligible students may apply for veterans' educational benefits and are encouraged to investigate the availability of grants and scholarships through community resources. As a first step, students should complete the Free Application for Federal Student Aid (FAFSA) and add South University's campus code, 004922. Students may apply electronically at http://www.fafsa.ed.gov or through the campus Director of Student Financial Services. Applications should be submitted promptly to receive consideration for the maximum amount of aid.
Cost of Study	Tuition information for the Professional Counseling Program may be obtained by contacting the Admissions Department at South University's Columbia campus.
Living and Housing Costs	South University does not offer or operate student housing. Professional Counseling Program students typically live in apartments in the Columbia area. Students who commute from long distances can arrange to stay at nearby hotels that offer long-term rates. More information is available by contacting the Admissions Department.
Student Group	The Columbia campus of South University has a diverse student body enrolled in both day and evening classes. Students are primarily commuters who live within 50 miles of the city.
Student Outcomes	The South University Career Services Department has been established to assist currently enrolled students in developing their career plans and reaching their employment goals. Career services include, but are not limited to, one-on-one career counseling, special career-related workshops and programs, coaching for resume and cover letter development, and resume referral to employers.
Location	South University recently relocated its Columbia campus to the growing east side of Columbia, just minutes from downtown. The new campus is conveniently located off of I-77 at Farrow Road and Parklane.
	The campus surroundings are highlighted by a natural wooded landscape and vast greenspace featuring a tranquil campus courtyard. Convenient to malls, shopping, and the growing east side of Columbia, the new campus location provides easier access to students from throughout the greater Columbia area.
The University	South University is accredited by the Commission on Colleges of the Southern Association of Colleges and Schools (SACS) to award associate, bachelor's, master's, and doctoral degrees. Students should contact the Commission on Colleges at 1866 Southern Lane, Decatur, Georgia 30033-4097 or call 404-679-4500 for questions about the accreditation of South University.
Applying	Students are accepted into the Master of Arts in Professional Counseling degree program every academic quarter. Entrance into the program is gained through a formal application review and interview process. Acceptance is competitive and based on the admission committee's evaluation of the applicant's academic background and personal motivation. Application packets are available by contacting the South University Admissions Department (866-629-3031, toll-free) or visiting the University's Web site (http://www.southuniversity.edu).
Correspondence and Information	Applications for admission to the South University Master of Arts in Professional Counseling program are available by contacting:

Professional Counseling Program
South University
9 Science Court
Columbia, South Carolina 29203
Phone: 803-799-9082
      866-629-3031 (toll-free)
Fax: 803-935-4382
E-mail: coladmis@southuniversity.edu
Web site: http://www.southuniversity.edu

South University

THE FACULTY

One of the most outstanding aspects of South University's Professional Counseling Program is the dedication of the faculty members and their ability to cultivate a supportive learning environment. Faculty members are committed to their roles as mentors, teachers, and colearners. They are also dedicated to the training of students who can assume positions of leadership within the counseling field. A current list of program faculty members appears in the South University catalog, which is available on the South University Web site (http://www.southuniversity.edu).

SouthUniversity℠

Program of Study

The Master of Arts in Professional Counseling degree program at South University is intended to meet the local and regional need for qualified professional counselors. The emphasis of the program is on community and agency counseling. The program is designed to enable program graduates to achieve all initial eligibility criteria to become certified as a National Certified Counselor (NCC) by the National Board for Certified Counselors (NBCC) and licensed in the state of Alabama. The delivery structure of the program gives students the ability to balance the rigors of work and home while pursuing their master's degree. Students can complete two courses each term, with each quarter lasting eleven weeks. Classes meet on Saturdays from 8:30 a.m. to 5 p.m.

Students are taught via two primary modes of instruction. The majority of the program involves didactic and experiential classroom instruction, supplemented by computer-based assignments, including the use of Internet technology. The second mode of instruction focuses on supervised field experiences. Students are placed in community counseling settings (during practicum and internship) and practice counseling under the supervision of an on-site supervisor. Students in field placements also receive weekly individual and group supervision from qualified faculty supervisors.

Research Facilities

South University in Montgomery is located in a modern 26,000-square-foot, two-story building on a 3¾-acre campus. This building houses computer and health professions labs, classrooms, a library, a student lounge, a bookstore, and faculty and administrative offices.

The South University library has wireless technology throughout, comfortable seating, and quiet study space. The South University library provides in-library and remote access to electronic databases. Both bibliographic and full-text databases are available via EBSCOhost (e.g., Academic Search Premier, SocINDEX, PsycINFO, PsycARTICLES, and Mental Measurements Yearbook), the search and retrieval system of EBSCO Information Services, and via the Library and Information Resources Network (e.g., Infotrac and ProQuest databases). Infotrac databases include counseling sources such as Expanded Academic ASAP, Academic OneFile, and InfotracOneFile, and ProQuest databases include counseling sources such as ProQuest Psychology Journals and ProQuest Research Library. Also for student use, the library has a modern computer lab with eleven workstations, each with Internet access, online database services, an office suite, tutorials, and class-support software.

Financial Aid

A wide range of financial aid options is available to students who qualify. South University offers access to federal and state programs, including grants, loans, and work-study programs. Eligible students may apply for veterans' educational benefits and are encouraged to investigate the availability of grants and scholarships through community resources. As a first step, students should complete the Free Application for Federal Student Aid (FAFSA). Students may apply electronically at http://www.fafsa.ed.gov or through the campus Director of Financial Aid. Applications should be submitted promptly to receive consideration for the maximum amount of aid.

Cost of Study

Tuition information for the Professional Counseling program may be obtained by contacting the admissions department at South University.

Living and Housing Costs

South University does not offer or operate student housing. Professional Counseling program students typically live in private housing in the Montgomery area. Students who commute from long distances can arrange to stay at nearby hotels that offer long-term rates. More information is available by contacting the admissions department.

Student Group

South University in Montgomery has a diverse student body enrolled in both day and evening classes. Students are primarily commuters who live within 50 miles of the city.

Student Outcomes

The South University career services department has been established to assist currently enrolled students in developing their career plans and reaching their employment goals. Career services include, but are not limited to, one-on-one career counseling, special career-related workshops and programs, coaching for resume and cover letter development, and resume referral to employers.

Location

South University is located on the rapidly growing east side of Alabama's capital city. As the state capital, Montgomery is a hub of government, banking, and law as well as a state center for culture and entertainment. Montgomery is situated in the middle of the southeastern U.S. and is less than a 3-hour drive from Atlanta and the Gulf of Mexico.

The University

South University is accredited by the Commission on Colleges of the Southern Association of Colleges and Schools (SACS) to award associate, bachelor's, master's, and doctoral degrees. Students should contact the Commission on Colleges at 1866 Southern Lane, Decatur, Georgia 30033-4097 or call 404-679-4500 with questions about the accreditation of South University.

Applying

Students may be accepted into the Master of Arts in Professional Counseling degree program every academic quarter. Entrance into the program is gained through a formal application review and interview process. Acceptance is competitive and based on the admission committee's evaluation of the applicant's academic background (completed bachelor's degree with a cumulative minimum GPA of 2.7 or a minimum score of 3.5 on the Graduate Record Examinations writing exam) and personal motivation. Application packets are available by contacting the South University admissions department or visiting the University's Web site.

Correspondence and Information

Applications for admission to the South University Master of Arts in Professional Counseling program are available by contacting:

Professional Counseling Program
South University
5355 Vaughn Road
Montgomery, Alabama 36116

Phone: 334-395-8800
        866-629-2962 (toll-free)
Fax: 334-395-8859
E-mail: mtgadmis@southuniversity.edu
Web site: http://www.southuniversity.edu

South University

THE FACULTY

One of the most outstanding aspects of South University's Professional Counseling program is the dedication of the faculty members and their ability to cultivate a supportive learning environment. Faculty members are committed to their roles as mentors, teachers, and colearners. They are also dedicated to the education of students who can assume positions of leadership within the counseling field. A current list of program faculty members is available at the South University Web site (http://www.southuniversity.edu).

SouthUniversity℠

SOUTH UNIVERSITY
Savannah Campus
Professional Counseling Program

Program of Study	The Master of Arts in Professional Counseling degree program at South University is intended to meet the local and regional need for qualified professional counselors. The emphasis of the program is on community and agency counseling. The program is designed to enable program graduates to achieve all initial eligibility criteria to become certified as a National Certified Counselor (NCC) by the National Board for Certified Counselors (NBCC) and licensed in their state. The delivery structure of the program gives students the ability to balance the rigors of work and home while pursuing their master's degree. Students can complete two courses each term (or more with approval), with each quarter lasting ten weeks. Class meetings are held mostly on Saturdays between 8:30 a.m. and 12 noon and some weeknights from 6 to 9:30 p.m.
	Students are taught via two primary modes of instruction. The majority of the program involves didactic and experiential classroom instruction, supplemented by computer-based assignments, including the use of Internet technology. The second mode of instruction focuses on supervised field experiences. Students are placed in community counseling settings (during internship) and practice counseling under the supervision of an on-site supervisor. Students in field placements also receive weekly individual and group supervision from qualified faculty supervisors.
Research Facilities	In 2000, the 25,000-square-foot Health Professions building was opened on the Savannah campus to house classroom, computer, and lab facilities for graduate programs within the School of Health Professions Also in this building are the student lounge and administrative offices. In 2007, a new library facility was opened that provides comfortable study space for students, wireless capabilities for laptop network connectivity, and reference and interlibrary loan services. The South University Library also provides in-library and remote access to electronic databases. Both bibliographic and full-text databases are available via EBSCOhost (e.g., Academic Search Premier, SocINDEX, PsycINFO, PsycARTICLES, and Mental Measurements Yearbook), the search and retrieval system of EBSCO Information Services, and via the Library and Information Resources Network (e.g., Infotrac and ProQuest databases). Infotrac databases include counseling sources such as Expanded Academic ASAP, Academic OneFile, and InfotracOneFile, and ProQuest databases include counseling sources such as ProQuest Psychology Journals and ProQuest Research Library.
Financial Aid	A wide range of financial aid options is available to students who qualify. The Savannah campus of South University offers access to federal and state programs, including grants, loans, and work-study programs. Eligible students may apply for veterans' educational benefits and are encouraged to investigate the availability of grants and scholarships through community resources. As a first step, students should complete the Free Application for Federal Student Aid (FAFSA). Students may apply electronically at http://www.fafsa.ed.gov or through the campus Director of Financial Aid. Applications should be submitted promptly to receive consideration for the maximum amount of aid.
Cost of Study	Tuition information for the Professional Counseling Program may be obtained by contacting the Admissions Department at South University's Savannah campus.
Living and Housing Costs	South University offers school-sponsored student housing at its Savannah, Georgia, campus in conjunction with a local apartment complex. Students who commute from long distances can arrange to stay at nearby hotels that offer long-term rates. More information is available by contacting the Director of Student Housing at 912-201-8000.
Student Group	The Savannah campus of South University has a diverse student body enrolled in both day and evening classes. Students consist of commuters who live within 50 miles of the city or students from other portions of the United States (e.g., California, Ohio, Pennsylvania, Connecticut) who have moved to Savannah to pursue the degree in professional counseling.
Student Outcomes	The South University Career Services Department has been established to assist currently enrolled students in developing their career plans and reaching their employment goals. Career services include, but are not limited to, one-on-one career counseling, special career-related workshops and programs, coaching for resume and cover letter development, and resume referral to employers.
Location	Located on the south side of the historic city of Savannah, the campus is situated on 9 acres of land. It is convenient to the city's bustling midtown section and a full range of educational and cultural activities. The Atlantic Ocean and recreational amenities of Tybee Island, including beaches and numerous outdoor activities, are just a short drive away. In addition, the campus is located just a short drive from Hilton Head Island and Charleston, South Carolina.
The University	South University is accredited by the Commission on Colleges of the Southern Association of Colleges and Schools (SACS) to award associate, bachelor's, master's, and doctoral degrees. Students should contact the Commission on Colleges at 1866 Southern Lane, Decatur, Georgia 30033-4097 or call 404-679-4500 with questions about the accreditation of South University.
Applying	Students are accepted into the Master of Arts in Professional Counseling degree program twice per year (fall and spring quarters). Entrance into the program is gained through a formal application review and interview process. Acceptance is competitive and based on the admission committee's evaluation of the applicant's academic background (completed bachelor's degree with a cumulative minimum GPA of 2.7 or a minimum score of 3.5 on the Graduate Record Examinations writing exam) and personal motivation. Application packets are available by contacting the South University Admissions Department or visiting the University's Web site.
Correspondence and Information	Applications for admission to the South University Master of Arts in Professional Counseling program are available by contacting:

Professional Counseling Program
South University
709 Mall Boulevard
Savannah, Georgia 31406-4805

Phone: 912-201-8000
      866-629-2901 (toll-free)
Fax: 912-201-8070
E-mail: savadmis@southuniversity.edu
Web site: http://www.southuniversity.edu

South University

THE FACULTY

One of the most outstanding aspects of South University's Professional Counseling Program is the dedication of the faculty members and their ability to cultivate a supportive learning environment. Faculty members are committed to their roles as mentors, teachers, and colearners. They are also dedicated to the training of students who can assume positions of leadership within the counseling field. A current list of program faculty members is available at the South University Web site (http://www.southuniversity.edu).

SouthUniversity℠

Program of Study

The Master of Arts in Professional Counseling degree program at South University is intended to meet the local and regional need for qualified professional counselors. The emphasis of the program is on community and agency counseling. The program is designed to enable program graduates to achieve all initial eligibility criteria to become certified as a National Certified Counselor (NCC) by the National Board for Certified Counselors (NBCC) and licensed in the state of Florida. The delivery structure of the program gives students the ability to balance the rigors of work and home while pursuing their master's degree. Students can complete two to three courses each term, with each quarter lasting ten weeks. Class meetings are held mostly on Saturdays between 8:30 a.m. and 5 p.m. and some weeknights from 6 to 9:30.

Students are taught via two primary modes of instruction. The majority of the program involves didactic and experiential classroom instruction, supplemented by computer-based assignments, including the use of Internet technology. The second mode of instruction focuses on supervised field experiences. Students are placed in community counseling settings (during practicum and internship) and practice counseling under the supervision of an on-site supervisor. Students in field placements also receive weekly individual and group supervision from qualified faculty supervisors.

Research Facilities

The South University library has wireless technology throughout, comfortable seating, and quiet study space. The South University library provides in-library and remote access to electronic databases. Both bibliographic and full-text databases are available via EBSCOhost (e.g., Academic Search Premier, SocINDEX, PsycINFO, PsycARTICLES, and Mental Measurements Yearbook), the search and retrieval system of EBSCO Information Services, and via the Library and Information Resources Network (e.g., Infotrac and ProQuest databases). Infotrac databases include counseling sources such as Expanded Academic ASAP, Academic OneFile, and InfotracOneFile, and ProQuest databases include counseling sources such as ProQuest Psychology Journals and ProQuest Research Library. Also for student use, the library has a modern computer lab with ten workstations, each with Internet access, online database services, an office suite, tutorials, and class-support software.

Financial Aid

A wide range of financial aid options is available to students who qualify. The West Palm Beach campus of South University offers access to federal and state programs, including grants, loans, and work-study programs. Eligible students may apply for veterans' educational benefits and are encouraged to investigate the availability of grants and scholarships through community resources. As a first step, students should complete the Free Application for Federal Student Aid (FAFSA). Students may apply electronically at http://www.fafsa.ed.gov or through the campus Director of Financial Aid. Applications should be submitted promptly to receive consideration for the maximum amount of aid.

Cost of Study

Tuition information for the Professional Counseling Program may be obtained by contacting the Admissions Department at South University's West Palm Beach campus.

Living and Housing Costs

South University does not offer or operate student housing at its West Palm Beach campus. Professional Counseling Program students typically live in homes or apartments in or near the West Palm Beach area. Students who commute from long distances may arrange to stay at nearby hotels that offer long-term rates. More information is available by contacting the Admissions Department.

Student Group

The West Palm Beach campus of South University has a diverse student body enrolled in both day and evening classes. Students are primarily commuters who live within 50 miles of the city.

Student Outcomes

The South University Career Services Department has been established to assist currently enrolled students in developing their career plans and reaching their employment goals. Career services include, but are not limited to, one-on-one career counseling, special career-related workshops and programs, coaching for resume and cover letter development, and resume referral to employers.

Location

South University in West Palm Beach is centrally located near the heart of Palm Beach County. Midway between Palm Beach International Airport and heavily traveled Okeechobee Boulevard, the campus is just minutes west of both Interstate 95 and downtown West Palm Beach.

The University

South University is accredited by the Commission on Colleges of the Southern Association of Colleges and Schools (SACS) to award associate, bachelor's, master's, and doctoral degrees. Students should contact the Commission on Colleges at 1866 Southern Lane, Decatur, Georgia 30033-4097 or call 404-679-4500 with questions about the accreditation of South University.

Applying

Students are accepted into the Master of Arts in Professional Counseling degree program every academic quarter. Entrance into the program is gained through a formal application review and interview process. Acceptance is competitive and based on the admission committee's evaluation of the applicant's academic background (completed bachelor's degree with a cumulative minimum GPA of 2.7 or a minimum score of 3.5 on the Graduate Record Examinations writing exam) and personal motivation. Application packets are available by contacting the South University Admissions Department or visiting the University's Web site.

Correspondence and Information

Applications for admission to the South University Master of Arts in Professional Counseling program are available by contacting:

Professional Counseling Program
South University
1760 North Congress Avenue
West Palm Beach, Florida 33409
Phone: 561-697-9200
        866-629-2902 (toll-free)
Fax: 561-697-9944
Web site: http://www.southuniversity.edu

South University

THE FACULTY

One of the most outstanding aspects of South University's Professional Counseling Program is the dedication of the faculty members and their ability to cultivate a supportive learning environment. Faculty members are committed to their roles as mentors, teachers, and colearners. They are also dedicated to the training of students who can assume positions of leadership within the counseling field. A current list of program faculty members appears in the South University catalog, which is available on the South University Web site (http://www.southuniversity.edu).

SOUTHWESTERN COLLEGE
Program in Counseling

Programs of Study

At Southwestern College (SWC), situated in the dynamic, light-filled city of Santa Fe, New Mexico, students prepare for careers in counseling, art therapy, and grief/loss/trauma counseling. In addition to attaining educational objectives in theoretical knowledge, applied skills, and character strength, students undergo deep personal transformation as a result of the College's experiential-based master's programs.

Each master's program is two academic years in length. Year one emphasizes exploring personal psychological transformation. This reflective emphasis provides insight into the nature of character development and the human condition. A foundation is laid for understanding the nature of change and its application in the helping professions. In year two, the emphasis is on professional identity and the development of strong clinical skills. Through this rigorous course of study, built on profound personal transformation, students acquire the competencies needed to work in the mental health professions. In addition, SWC graduates find they are uniquely qualified to take their place as transformational leaders in the world.

The master's program in counseling integrates effective, cutting-edge modes of counseling, incorporating all levels of psychological functioning: imaginal, emotional, mental, and spiritual. From this holistic approach is fostered a creative sense of self and the potential for change.

The art therapy master's program emphasizes the use of the visual arts as a powerful therapeutic approach in clinical, educational, forensic, community, and rehabilitation settings. While visual art is the primary therapeutic modality, the creative process is supported by classroom instruction and experiences in the use of drama, movement, and music.

The master's program in counseling with a concentration in grief/loss/trauma integrates effective modes of counseling through the incorporation of all levels of psychological functioning—imaginal, emotional, mental, and spiritual—to work through the accumulated losses of a lifetime. In addition, there is an emphasis on creative expression and the transformation of bonds that continue after death. In addition to the master's programs, the College offers certificate programs in grief counseling, psychodrama and action methods, ecopsychology, and somatic studies.

Research Facilities

The Quimby Memorial Library supports teaching and research in counseling, art therapy, applied psychology, and experiential education. The library contains approximately 20,000 books, journals, and audiovisual materials. Patrons have access to interlibrary loan through the New Mexico State Library. Behavioral and social sciences indexes can be accessed through the College's database. The Quimby Memorial Library also houses the second-largest metaphysical collection in the United States.

Financial Aid

Financial aid programs include Subsidized and Unsubsidized Federal Direct Student Loans, scholarships, and payment plans. A Free Application for Federal Student Aid (FAFSA) must be submitted at least three months before admission in order to have a loan guarantee in place at the time of registration. For the 2009–10 academic year, the maximum amount potentially awarded to a student in combined Subsidized and Unsubsidized Federal Direct Student Loans is $20,500. Students and their families should investigate local sources, such as service organizations, churches, Native American tribal affiliations, corporations, and foundations for scholarship, grant, and loan funds. A limited number of scholarships are available, including the quarterly Southwestern College Scholarship.

Cost of Study

The current cost is $360 per quarter unit. The cost of study is dependent upon the number of units taken each quarter. Full-time study is $17,280 per year. Additional expenses for books and supplies are approximately $1200 per year. A graduation fee of $80 is required.

Living and Housing Costs

There are numerous apartment complexes nearby with rentals in the $550 to $800 price range. Several property managers are available to help students find housing in the area. For more information, students should contact the Director of Admissions. There is no on-campus housing.

Student Group

Students select Southwestern College because of the unique nature of its programs. Students range in age from their early 20s to their 60s. Younger students tend to come directly from undergraduate programs and are preparing to enter their first profession. Older students have often had one or more careers and a wealth of life experience. The unifying characteristic of all students at the College is the commitment to self-knowledge and the desire to be of service to others.

Student Outcomes

Southwestern College graduates are uniquely qualified to take their place as transformational leaders in the world. Counseling graduates are well prepared to fulfill licensure requirements in mental health counseling. Graduates of all of the counseling and art therapy programs pursue successful careers in educational, mental health, and residential treatment settings and private practice. Graduates are able to apply for licensure in the state of New Mexico and other states. Art therapy graduates are eligible to apply for registration with the Art Therapy Credentials Board (ATCB) of the American Art Therapy Association as well as for licensure in counseling.

Location

Southwestern College is located between the Jemez and Sangre de Christo mountains in the high desert beauty of Santa Fe, the capital of New Mexico. At an altitude of 7,000 feet, Santa Fe offers stunning high-desert vistas and breathtaking sunsets. A mild four-season climate boasts 300 days of sunshine each year. This richly historic, tricultural area offers abundant outdoor recreation, magnificent museums, lively stage productions, the award-winning Santa Fe Opera, and world-renowned Indian and Spanish art markets.

The College

The roots of Southwestern College can be traced to 1945, when a group of forward-thinking individuals began a collection of metaphysical books to establish the Quimby Memorial Library. The collection included the manuscripts of Phineas Parkhurst Quimby, an American Transcendentalist. Quimby believed that the mind had great healing powers in regard to physical illness and that maintaining the mind/body connection could bring a person into balance. In 1976, Southwestern College, then called Quimby College, was dedicated. Today, the College continues to teach in a holistic and experiential way. The College is accredited by the Higher Learning Commission and is a member of the North Central Association of Colleges and Schools (NCA). The art therapy program is approved by the American Art Therapy Association.

Applying

Southwestern College accepts students who have the motivation for self-discovery, a love of learning, and a quest for deeper meaning in their lives. Applicants are required to submit an application, $50 application fee, personal statement, current resume, transcripts from each college previously attended, and three letters of recommendation. An admissions interview is required. In addition, art therapy applicants must submit a portfolio of twelve to fifteen slides of recent work. Students may be admitted during the fall, winter, and spring quarters.

Correspondence and Information

Admissions Office
Southwestern College
P.O. Box 4788
Santa Fe, New Mexico 87502-4788
Phone: 505-471-5756 Ext. 26
      877-471-5756 Ext. 26 (toll-free)
E-mail: admissions@swc.edu
Web site: http://www.swc.edu

Southwestern College

THE FACULTY AND THEIR RESEARCH

Christopher Alexander, Ph.D.
Susan Benjamin, LPAT, ATR-BC.
Diane Berman, M.A., LMFT.
Rosvita Botkin, Ph.D., ATR, LPAT, LPCC. Jungian and expressive art therapy.
Connie Buck, Ph.D.
Marylou Butler, Ph.D. Licensed psychologist.
Wendy Chapin, M.A. Performing arts.
Robert Colby, LPCC.
Kate Cook, M.A., LPCC, CPP, TEP. Psychodrama.
Jim Ficky, Ph.D., LPCC.
Gary Grimm, M.A., LPCC.
Diane Haug, M.A.
Deborah John, LPCC.
Carla Kleefeld, Ph.D., LPCC.
Michael Maestas, LPCC.
Catherine Monserrat, M.A.
Katherine M. Ninos, M.A., LPC. Consciousness studies and transpersonal psychology.
James Nolan, Ph.D., Consciousness.
Antonio Nunez, Ph.D., Positive psychology.
Ruth Omlin, M.P.S., LPAT, ATR-BC.
Carol Parker, Ph.D., LPCC.
Karen Sands, M.A., LMSW, LPCC.
Ernesto Santistevan, Ph.D.
Janet Schreiber, Ph.D. Grief counseling and death education.
Deborah Schroder, M.A., ATR-BC.
Alexander Shaia, Ph.D.
Megan Sturges, M.A., LPAT, LPC.
George Tate, Th.D. Multicultural issues.
Robert Waterman, Ed.D., LPCC.

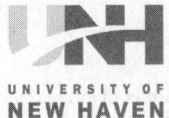

UNIVERSITY OF NEW HAVEN

Master of Arts in Industrial and Organizational Psychology

Programs of Study

The practice of industrial and organizational psychology enhances the effectiveness and functioning of organizations by applying psychological principles to human work behavior. The Master of Arts in Industrial and Organizational Psychology (MAIOP) program at the University of New Haven (UNH) provides students with the knowledge and experience necessary to improve the satisfaction and productivity of people at work.

The MAIOP curriculum is strengthened by ongoing, active relationships with local and regional human resource and applied psychological associations. Students are actively involved with the campus chapter of the Society for Human Resources Management (SHRM-UNH) and supplement their classroom education by participating in a variety of professional workshops and seminars in the field.

A total of 48 credit hours are required for the degree, including 24 credit hours of required courses in the core curriculum and 24 credit hours in concentrations, program options, and elective courses. Students may not complete more than 9 credit hours of electives until they have satisfied the core requirements. Up to 9 elective credit hours may be taken in other departments.

Students may develop a program that meets their particular needs and interests. The thesis option is intended for students who wish to continue their education in doctoral-level programs. The internship/practicum option allows students to acquire special skills through an internship or practicum in an organizational setting. The approved electives option consists of elective courses that provide students with a broad interdisciplinary background, complementing the student's own academic training and interest. A comprehensive examination covering material from the required core psychology courses is required under this option.

Within each option, students may concentrate in one of three areas: industrial–human resources, organizational development and consultation, or conflict management. A concentration requires 12 credit hours of specific elective courses within the 24 credit hours required in the elective option.

The industrial and organizational psychology program at UNH conforms to the standards set by the Council of Applied Master's Programs in Psychology (CAMPP).

Research Facilities

The Marvin K. Peterson Library contains more than 500,000 volumes, subscribes to hundreds of journals, and is a U.S. government documents depository library. Computer workstations are available in the library to access online subscription databases, CDs, and DVDs. In addition, there are more than a dozen computer labs for student use and teaching on campus.

The Center for Dispute Resolution offers mediation services to UNH students and faculty and staff members as well as providing training in mediation and negotiation.

Financial Aid

About 75 percent of all University students receive some form of financial aid. Graduate students may borrow up to $18,500 in both subsidized and unsubsidized Federal Stafford Student Loans. Teaching, research, or administrative assistantships are available to full-time students. Compensation includes $8 per hour as well as a 50 percent tuition reduction; students typically work 15 to 20 hours per week.

Cost of Study

Tuition for both full- and part-time students is $750 per credit hour, or $2250 per 3-credit course. Other fees include a Graduate Student Council fee of $20 and a technology fee of $20 per trimester. Laboratory fees range from $25 and up depending on the course.

Living and Housing Costs

On-campus housing for graduate students is not available. However, off-campus housing is available in the area at a cost of $575 to $1000 per month for a one-bedroom apartment or $775 to $1200 for a two-bedroom unit.

Student Group

Students in the program come from a wide variety of educational backgrounds and work experiences. Some students arrive directly from undergraduate school, others arrive after working for a few years, and some are busy professionals interested in augmenting their careers with a graduate degree. They come from large and small schools, from all points in the United States, and from numerous countries around the globe.

Student Outcomes

Graduates of the program typically obtain related positions in organizational development and human resources management functions at Fortune 500 companies, consulting firms, government agencies, and applied research institutions. Activities include training design and implementation, compensation and benefits, job analysis, talent management, recruiting, employee development, company surveys, and conflict management.

Location

The UNH campus is in West Haven, Connecticut, which is contiguous to New Haven. New Haven has numerous art museums, a deepwater harbor and beaches, fine restaurants, parks and walking trails, and three Tony award–winning regional theaters. New Haven is served by a local airport and major railroads, and its location at the junction of two interstate highways places the University within easy driving distance of New York, Boston, Cape Cod, and the ski areas of New England.

The University

The University of New Haven was founded on the Yale campus in 1920 and became New Haven College in 1926. Today, it includes five undergraduate schools and a Graduate School, with a combined population of 4,500 students. Its programs prepare students to advance in their careers and meet the ever-changing demands of their respective fields. The University offers thirty master's degrees as well as a number of graduate certificates.

Applying

To apply to the program, prospective students must submit a completed application form, transcripts from all colleges and universities previously attended, two letters of recommendation, GRE scores (if taken within the past five years), and a $50 application fee. In addition, applicants must complete an I/O program questionnaire and submit it directly to the Graduate School. For applicants whose native language is not English, TOEFL scores are required. ESL certification may also be submitted. An undergraduate major in psychology is not specifically required, but students are expected to have at least an introductory-level understanding of psychological concepts, principles, and methods before entering the program.

Correspondence and Information

Dr. Stuart Sidle
Program Coordinator
College of Arts and Sciences
University of New Haven
300 Boston Post Road
West Haven, Connecticut 06516
Phone: 800-DIAL-UNH Ext. 7339 (toll-free)
Fax: 203-931-6032
E-mail: ssidle@newhaven.edu
Web site: http://www.newhaven.edu/academics/

Eloise Gormley
Director of Graduate Admissions
University of New Haven
300 Boston Post Road
West Haven, Connecticut 06516
Phone: 203-932-7448
Fax: 203-932-7137
E-mail: gradinfo@newhaven.edu
Web site: http://www.newhaven.edu

University of New Haven

THE FACULTY AND THEIR RESEARCH

The full- and part-time faculty members at the University of New Haven are qualified through education and experience in the subareas of industrial and organizational (I/O) psychology. They have had many years of experience as practicing I/O psychologists in consulting, government, and industry as well as academia. In addition, students in the program enjoy an excellent student-faculty relationship. Faculty members are willing to take the time to help students make UNH a very positive experience.

Full-Time Faculty

Stuart Sidle, Graduate Program Coordinator; Ph.D. (industrial and organizational psychology), DePaul. Employee surveys, job motivation, job stress, leadership styles, workplace humor, supervisor-subordinate relationships.

Tara L'Heureux-Barrett, Associate Professor; Ph.D. (industrial and organizational psychology), Connecticut, 1991. Performance management, worker well-being, training competencies for master's-level I/O psychologists.

Dennis McGough, Practitioner in Residence; Ph.D. (industrial and organizational psychology), Union (Ohio). Evaluation of training program effectiveness, leadership development, executive coaching, incentive compensation programs.

Michael Morris, Professor; Ph.D. (community-social psychology), Boston College. Ethical challenges faced by program evaluators in their work.

Amy Nicole Salvaggio, Assistant Professor; Ph.D. (industrial and organizational psychology), Maryland, 2003. Organizational climate, workplace romance, gender stereotypes, customer service, job attitudes.

Gordon R. Simerson, Associate Professor and Associate Provost; Ph.D. (industrial and organizational psychology), Wayne State, 1984. Management of employees in creative functions, applying the "Big 5" model of personality to understanding work-related attitudes, procedural justice and organizational ethics, spirituality in the workplace.

Leonard Wysocki, Practitioner in Residence, College of Arts and Sciences; Ph.D. (counseling psychology, post doctoral organizational development), Connecticut, 2005. Emotional intelligence, contemporary issues in human resource management, leadership development.

Adjunct Faculty

Robert Beaudoin, Adjunct Professor; Ed.D. (adult learning and organizational behavior). Employee motivation, training and development, leadership development.

Marilyn Kendrix, Adjunct Professor; E.M.B.A., 1997, M.A. (industrial and organizational psychology), 2000, New Haven. Effects of downsizing, conflict resolution.

Donna Morris, Adjunct Professor; J.D., Yale, 1979. Employment discrimination law, conflict management.

VILLANOVA UNIVERSITY

Department of Psychology

Program of Study

The Villanova Department of Psychology has offered a Master of Science (M.S.) degree in general psychology since 1961. This M.S. degree program is particularly well suited to provide a strong foundation for individuals seeking entry into Ph.D. programs in most subfields of psychology. In addition, the program serves the needs of students who are unsure of their future professional goals, of individuals who want a more gradual transition between undergraduate and Ph.D.-level work, and of those seeking a terminal master's degree.

The two-year curriculum is designed to provide excellent training in research skills. Students gain expertise in the formulation of research designs and in the acquisition, analysis, and interpretation of data. Laboratory courses in cognitive psychology, statistics, and physiological psychology are complemented by electives in many of the other subfields of psychology. In addition, students may elect to take a graduate course in a department other than psychology to round out their area of special interest. Biology, chemistry, computer science, human organization science, and statistics have been of particular interest in this regard. Students are required to complete a total of eight courses, including statistics and at least two laboratory courses, and to conduct an original piece of research under faculty supervision in the form of a thesis. The elective courses are designed to allow students the flexibility to tailor the program to their particular goals. The master's thesis is required, and additional independent research is strongly encouraged. There is no comprehensive examination or foreign language requirement.

The psychology faculty has maintained a consistently strong record for productivity and scholarly research. During a recent three-year period, seventy-seven journal articles, fourteen book chapters, three books, and fifty-eight convention presentations emerged from the Department of Psychology. Graduate students frequently coauthor the research published by their mentors, thereby enhancing their graduate education and preparation for a top-quality doctoral program. Villanova's master's program in psychology has been ranked among the top ten M.S.-only–granting departments (95th percentile) in the United States and Canada with regard to research productivity. Several of the Department's faculty members hold research grants from various government agencies.

Research Facilities

The University library contains more than 780,000 volumes and 5,600 current periodicals. Public computing facilities that consist of networked Windows-based microcomputers are available in a number of campus locations, including Tolentine Hall (the location of the Department of Psychology). All facilities are available to University students and faculty members. Computer facilities that are dedicated to the Department of Psychology and laboratories within the Department are also available.

Financial Aid

A limited number of University-funded assistantships and tuition scholarships are awarded to psychology graduate students on a competitive basis. These include research/teaching assistantships that carry a remission of tuition and fees and, in some instances, a monthly stipend. Students with assistantships and tuition scholarships are assigned to faculty members to help with their teaching and/or research efforts. Depending on the type of award, assistants and tuition scholars are expected to work from 7 to 20 hours per week under the supervision of their faculty mentor. Additional research assistantships, supported by extramural grants, are awarded by faculty members who hold the grants. Villanova University also has a number of additional scholarships and graduate assistantship, for which psychology program students may be eligible.

Cost of Study

Graduate tuition was $610 per credit hour in 2007–08.

Living and Housing Costs

The University does not maintain accommodations for graduate students, but second-year students are eligible for positions as resident counselors in the dormitories. The area has a wide selection of living quarters that are convenient to the campus.

Student Group

Approximately 20 students representing all geographical sections of the United States are selected for admission each year from approximately 150 applications. About 30 percent of the class comes from the Philadelphia area. The majority (58 percent) of students come from out of state, and a large proportion are from outside the Mid-Atlantic region (e.g., California, Arizona, Texas, Missouri, Kansas, Florida, Georgia, and Virginia).

Student Outcomes

While the program is not specifically designed to provide terminal training for mental health professionals, some graduates continue on to Ph.D. programs in clinical or counseling psychology. Others accept positions in the private sector as science writers, lab technicians, data analysts, and marketing researchers. The program enjoys a strong national reputation, thereby contributing to the success that a large proportion of graduates have in gaining admission to some of the top Ph. D. programs in psychology (e.g., Brown; Columbia; Cornell; Tufts University; University of California, Berkeley; University of California, San Diego; University of Colorado; University of Illinois; University of Michigan; University of Wisconsin; and Johns Hopkins). Additional information about graduates of the program can be found on the Web at the address given in this description.

Location

Located in the heart of the Philadelphia Region's Main Line suburbs, the University occupies more than 200 handsomely landscaped acres in the town of Villanova, 12 miles west of Philadelphia. The location combines the advantages of a tranquil suburban setting with proximity to a large metropolitan city known for its outstanding contributions in the areas of culture, education, history, recreation, religion, and sport.

The University

Villanova University is a private institution founded in 1842 by the Augustinian Fathers. Graduate programs were first administered separately in 1931. Currently, there are five academic units—the Colleges of Arts and Sciences, Engineering, and Nursing; the Villanova School of Business; and the School of Law.

Applying

Application forms and the *Graduate Studies Viewbook* may be obtained from the Graduate Studies Office. There is a $50 application fee. Additional information about the psychology program may be obtained by contacting the Department of Psychology. In addition to forwarding the completed application form, GRE scores, and official college transcripts, applicants must also arrange to have three letters of recommendation submitted on their behalf. Submission of a personal statement, describing the nature of the applicant's interest in psychology and in the Villanova program, is also suggested. Most successful applicants have an undergraduate GPA of at least 3.0 (with an average of 3.5) and above-average GRE scores (average verbal, 540; quantitative, 640; analytic writing, 5.0; Subject Test in psychology (optional), 620; statistics taken from the most recent three years).

Applications are accepted for fall admission only. Admissions are on a rolling basis, and applications are accepted for the following fall throughout the year. However, to receive full consideration for financial aid, completed applications should be received before March 1.

Correspondence and Information

For applications:
Graduate Studies Office
Kennedy Hall, 2nd Floor
Villanova University
800 Lancaster Avenue
Villanova, Pennsylvania 19085-1699

Phone: 610-519-7090
Fax: 610-519-7096

For further information about the M.S. program in psychology:
Graduate Admissions Committee
Department of Psychology
Villanova University
Villanova, Pennsylvania 19085-1699

Phone: 610-519-4720
Fax: 610-519-4269
E-mail: Visit Web site
Web site: http://www.villanova.edu/artsci/psychology

Villanova University

THE FACULTY AND THEIR RESEARCH

The Department of Psychology comprises 16 full-time faculty members, most of whom maintain active research laboratories in their specialties. Strong research specializations within the Department are provided in animal learning, clinical, cognition, developmental, human factors, organizational, perception, personality, physiological, and social psychology.

Cognitive Psychology/Cognitive Neuroscience/Human Factors

Dr. Diego Fernandez-Duque's research spans cognitive and social neuroscience. Within cognitive neuroscience, he studies how different aspects of attention change due to aging and pathology and why visual perception sometimes occurs in the absence of awareness. Within social neuroscience, he investigates impairments in social cognition brought about by brain insult, using frontotemporal dementia as a model disease in which to explore empathy and metacognition.

Dr. Charles Folk has been studying the nature of visual distractibility. What kinds of events capture attention, and to what degree is such capture under voluntary control? The outcome of his work has important implications for applied settings, such as aircraft cockpits, as well as for theoretical models of selective attention.

Dr. Irene Kan's general research interest is the cognitive architecture and neural bases of human memory. Combining cognitive neuroscientific, neuropsychological, and behavioral approaches, research in her laboratory is focused on understanding how semantic memory and episodic memory are organized and retrieved.

Dr. Thomas Toppino investigates human cognitive processes and the development of those processes in children. Most recently, he has studied fundamental factors underlying the effects of repetition and order of presentation in learning and memory. He also investigates the relationship between sensory and higher cognitive processes in visual perception, focusing especially on factors affecting the perception of ambiguous patterns.

Developmental Psychology

Dr. Pamela Blewitt studies both the cognitive and social/interactive processes involved in word learning. She examines how young children approach the word learning task, traces changes in children's word meanings over time, and assesses the relationships between word learning and logical thinking. Her studies also examine parents' and teachers' contributions to children's vocabulary growth, including conversational, word defining, and book-reading strategies.

Dr. Rebecca Brand is interested in infants' knowledge acquisition across several domains. In the language domain, she has recently been investigating the development of inhibitory control and its role in early vocabulary development. In the action domain, she has been investigating the specialized action adults present toward infants ("motionese") and its role in infants' understanding of new action sequences.

Dr. Nicole Else-Quest studies psychological development across the lifespan, with special focus on gender roles and emotions. Her recent projects include an investigation of the roles of emotions, scaffolding and social relationships in mathematics learning, meta-analyses of gender differences in temperament and emotion, and a study of emotional adaptation to disease later in life.

Clinical/Social/Personality and Organizational Psychology

Dr. David Bush investigates gender differences in work-related issues such as gender stereotyping of jobs, performance appraisal, compensation, and negotiating strategies. He also conducts research on organizational changes related to downsizing and reorganization and their consequences for the organizational culture.

Dr. Deborah Kendzierski's social psychology research program focuses on the links between intentions and behavior in the context of adherence to health-behavior regimens. She is interested in the role of self-concept in linking intentions and such health behaviors as exercising and dieting.

Dr. Steven Krauss examines normal and disordered mood expression and personality across cultures. He also investigates the relationships between values, moral reasoning, relationship models, and individualism/collectivism from a cross-cultural perspective.

Dr. John Kurtz studies issues and techniques related to psychological assessment and the diagnosis of mental disorders. His recent research is concerned with factors related to change versus stability in personality traits during adulthood and the use of informants in personality assessment.

Dr. Patrick Markey's research program is focused on two broad issues: How people differ and if these differences are related to how they actually behave. Much of this research has related personality attributes to behaviors in diverse contexts, including Internet chat rooms, marital interactions, face-to-face communications among college students, and interactions between preadolescent children and their mothers.

Sensation/Perception

Dr. Gerald Long has focused on the validity and reliability of various visual assessment tasks that are often used to screen our visual abilities, including color vision, contrast sensitivity, and dynamic visual acuity. Another productive line of research has involved examination of the processes underlying certain classes of visual illusions. These illusions have proven to be useful research tools in identifying sensory and cognitive effects in perception.

Comparative/Physiological Psychology

Dr. Michael Brown's laboratory has been concerned with understanding basic cognitive processes by studying the behavior of nonhuman animals. Most recently, this research has centered on spatial abilities and decision processes in rats and spatial memory in honey bees.

Dr. Matthew Matell is interested in the cognitive and neural mechanisms underlying the perception of time and sequence. Primary techniques include ensemble electrophysiological recordings, pharmacology, and lesion techniques in rats, with a current focus on the role of cortical-striatal-thalamic interactions. Computational models of timing are also being developed.

WIDENER UNIVERSITY

Institute for Graduate Clinical Psychology

Programs of Study

The Institute for Graduate Clinical Psychology at Widener University offers nine programs: the Doctor of Psychology degree (Psy.D.), a postdoctoral respecialization program, a post-master's option, and dual-degree programs with business (Psy.D./M.B.A.), criminal justice (Psy.D./M.A. in criminal justice), education (Psy.D./M.Ed. in human sexuality education), health administration (Psy.D./M.B.A.–HMSA), law (J.D./Psy.D.), and public administration (Psy.D./M.P.A.).

The Doctor of Psychology degree (Psy.D.) is fully accredited by the American Psychological Association. The program offers five years of intensive professional training in psychology. The content of the program is designed to help students retain the basic skills and knowledge of traditional clinical psychology, such as psychodiagnostic testing and psychotherapy, while simultaneously exposing them to new ideas and practices in the field. Following a scholar-professional model, the philosophy of the program is grounded in the belief that both scholarship and practical supervised experience are essential to clinical applications. Students may pursue special tracks in the areas of biofeedback, neuropsychology, and school psychology. The program provides extensive practical experience in a wide variety of service settings. An integrated internship, which is fully accredited by the American Psychological Association, is an important aspect of the program.

The law/psychology six-year program leads to an award of the J.D. degree by Widener University School of Law and the Psy.D. degree by Widener's Institute for Graduate Clinical Psychology. It trains lawyers–clinical psychologists to integrate the two fields and deal more effectively with issues related to the rights of mental health patients, families and children, expert testimony, and other areas.

Post-master's and postdoctoral respecialization programs offer students advanced standing and enable them to shorten their lengths of study. The postdoctoral respecialization program is intended to help doctoral-level psychologists in other fields, including developmental, experimental, and social psychology, acquire the additional training necessary to practice clinical psychology.

Research Facilities

The Wolfgram Memorial Library has a fine collection that numbers more than 240,000 printed volumes, 175,000 microforms, and close to 2,000 periodical titles. Services include online access to bibliographic information and electronic databases (such as PsychINFO), audiovisual media collections and facilities, and access to other libraries' resources through interlibrary loans. State-of-the-art computing facilities are available to meet students' needs.

The School of Law library maintains a collection of more than 600,000 volumes. Contained in the collection are legal publications and journals, treatises, reports, and statutes. Access to a wide range of supporting materials is available through LexisNexis and Westlaw online legal research services.

Financial Aid

Students may apply for federal loans and work-study through the Financial Aid Office on the Main Campus. Stipends associated with internships are available to all fourth-year and fifth-year students. Some academically based grants and scholarships are also available.

Cost of Study

Tuition for the Doctor of Psychology program was $21,900 for the 2008–09 academic year. Students paid a Psy.D. joint-program fee of $325 per semester of joint enrollment, excluding the J.D./Psy.D. and respecialization programs.

Living and Housing Costs

Affordable on-campus rental apartments are available. In addition, reasonably priced housing is available within a 3-mile radius of all three campuses.

Student Group

Approximately 175 students are enrolled in the clinical psychology program. The students are drawn from areas throughout the United States and are heterogeneous in terms of age, academic background, and clinical experience. The total University enrollment is approximately 6,500 students. Enrollment in all graduate programs is approximately 3,200 students; about 57 percent are women.

Location

The Institute for Graduate Clinical Psychology is located on Widener's Main Campus in Chester, Pennsylvania. The campus occupies more than 100 acres and is easily accessible from Interstate 95. Located in Delaware County, one of the oldest counties in Pennsylvania, the campus is near Philadelphia, which lies just 15 miles to the north, and other historic and commercial areas. Students' practicums and internship rotations primarily occur in the Greater Philadelphia area.

The 40-acre Delaware Campus, 15 miles southwest of the Main Campus, is located on Route 202 (Concord Pike) north of Wilmington and is only a short distance from Interstate 95. It houses the School of Law and is a course site for the School of Business Administration. A branch of the School of Law is also located on the 21-acre Harrisburg Campus in central Pennsylvania.

The University

Widener University is a multicampus, independent, metropolitan institution located in and accredited by the commonwealth of Pennsylvania and the state of Delaware. Founded in 1821, Widener offers doctoral, master's, baccalaureate, and associate degrees through its eight schools and colleges. The University distinguishes itself by connecting curricula to societal issues through civic engagement and by inspiring its students to be citizens of character as well as professional and civic leaders.

Applying

The applicant must possess a B.A. or B.S. degree from an accredited institution. A major in psychology is desirable but not essential. Students must have had courses in statistics, abnormal psychology (or psychopathology), and research design (or experimental psychology) by the time they matriculate into the program. Evaluation of the student's ability to do graduate work is based upon academic performance and scores on the Graduate Record Examinations (GRE). Personal character and attributes of emotional maturity and stability are major factors in reviewing applicants, along with a capacity for relating to and working with other people. Evidence for these attributes is sought from records of past performance, letters of reference, work history, and a personal interview. Applications must be submitted by December 31 for admission the next fall. Spring or summer admission is not possible.

Correspondence and Information

For the Psy.D. and respecialization programs:
Dr. Virginia Brabender, Director
Institute for Graduate Clinical Psychology
Widener University
Chester, Pennsylvania 19013
Phone: 610-499-1206
E-mail: graduate.psychology@widener.edu
Web site: http://www.widener.edu

For the law/psychology program:
Dr. Amiram Elwork
Institute for Graduate Clinical Psychology
Widener University
Chester, Pennsylvania 19013
Phone: 610-499-1217
E-mail: amiram.elwork@widener.edu

Widener University

THE FACULTY AND THEIR RESEARCH

Jules C. Abrams, Professor; Ph.D.; ABPP (Clinical). Learning disabilities, psychoanalysis, psychoanalytically oriented psychotherapy, professional issues, psychological and neuropsychological assessment (phone: 610-499-1205).

Bret A. Boyer, Assistant Professor; Ph.D. Health psychology, pediatric psychology, developmental psychopathology, development throughout the life-span, family and couple therapy, integrative approaches to therapy (phone: 610-499-1220).

Virginia Brabender, Professor, Associate Dean, and Director; Ph.D.; ABPP (Clinical). Group psychotherapy, personality assessment, professional issues, life events of the therapist (phone: 610-499-1208).

Patricia M. Bricklin, Professor; Ph.D. Reading and learning disabilities, professional issues and ethics, school psychology (phone: 610-499-1212).

Dennis Debiak, Clinical Associate Professor; Psy.D. Psychoanalytic psychotherapy; gay, lesbian, and bisexual issues; gender identity development (phone: 610-499-1219).

Amiram Elwork, Professor; Ph.D. Law/psychology, professional issues, cognitive psychotherapy, stress management (phone: 610-499-1217).

Elisabeth N. Gibbings, Director of Admissions and Practicum; Psy.D. Supervision, professional training in assessment (phone: 610-499-1221).

Kenneth B. Goldberg, Associate Professor; Psy.D. Neuropsychology treatment and assessment, learning disabilities, professional training in neuropsychology (phone: 610-499-1222).

Linda Knauss, Associate Professor and Director of Internship Training; Ph.D.; ABPP (Clinical). Professional ethics, development, family therapy, assessment (phone: 610-499-1211).

Frank Masterpasqua, Professor; Ph.D. Development, constructivism, nonlinear dynamics, community psychology and prevention, neurofeedback (phone: 610-499-1234).

Sanjay Nath, Assistant Professor; Ph.D. Ethnic diversity formation, narrative studies, qualitative research methodology, identity formation, cross-cultural psychology, immigration/acculturation, interracial relationships, arranged marriages, postpartum adjustment (phone: 610-499-1214).

Maurice Prout, Professor; Ph.D.; ABPP (Clinical). Cognitive and behavioral psychotherapy of Axis I and II disorders, psychosomatics and behavioral medicine (phone: 610-499-1216).

Hal Shorey, Assistant Professor; Ph.D. Organizational psychology, attachment theory, and personality.

Stephen C. Wilhite, Professor; D.Phil. Learning and memory and research methods (phone: 610-499-4351).

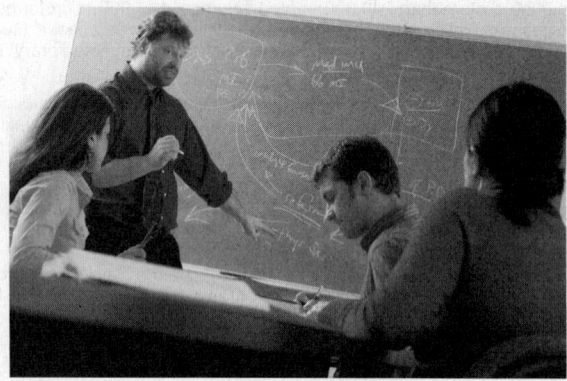

Professor Bret Boyer, of Widener's Institute for Graduate Clinical Psychology, teaches health psychology.

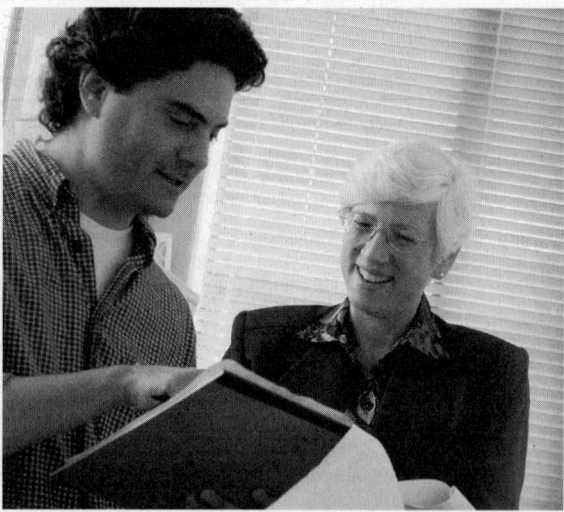

Dr. Linda Knauss, Director of Internship Training, provides supervision on a psychological assessment.

Section 25
Public, Regional, and Industrial Affairs

This section contains a directory of institutions offering graduate work in public, regional, and industrial affairs, followed by in-depth entries submitted by institutions that chose to prepare detailed program descriptions. Additional information about programs listed in the directory but not augmented by an in-depth entry may be obtained by writing directly to the dean of a graduate school or chair of a department at the address given in the directory.

For programs offering related work, see also in this book *Architecture, Area and Cultural Studies, Criminology and Forensics, Economics, Humanities, Political Science and International Affairs,* and *Sociology, Anthropology, and Archaeology.* In the other guides in this series:

Graduate Programs in the Physical Sciences, Mathematics, Agricultural Sciences, the Environment & Natural Resources
See *Environmental Sciences and Management*
Graduate Programs in Engineering & Applied Sciences
See *Management of Engineering and Technology*
Graduate Programs in Business, Education, Health, Information Studies, Law & Social Work
See *Business Administration and Management, Law,* and *Public Health*

CONTENTS

Program Directories

Disability Studies	1156
Emergency Management	1156
Homeland Security	1158
Industrial and Labor Relations	1160
Philanthropic Studies	1162
Public Administration	1163
Public Affairs	1185
Public Policy	1188
Rural Planning and Studies	1197
Sustainable Development	1198
Urban and Regional Planning	1200
Urban Studies	1208

Announcements

Auburn University	1164
Ball State University	1201
Roger Williams University	1173
Rutgers, The State University of New Jersey, New Brunswick	1161
University of Maine	1178

Close-Ups

Cornell University	
Industrial and Labor Relations	1213
Public Affairs	1211
George Mason University	1215
Hawai'i Pacific University	1217
Indiana University Bloomington	1219
Indiana University–Purdue University Indianapolis	1221
The Johns Hopkins University	1223
The New School: A University	
Public and Urban Policy	1225
Urban Policy Analysis and Management	1227
New York University	1229
Northwestern University	1231
Roger Williams University	1233
Seton Hall University	1235
Tufts University	1237
University of Delaware	1239
University of Pennsylvania	1241
University of Pittsburgh	1243

See also:

American University—Communication	681
American University—International Service	861
Central European University—Social Sciences and Humanities	349
The Institute of World Politics—Statecraft and World Politics	867
Monterey Institute of International Studies— International Policy Studies	871
Pratt Institute—Architecture	155
University of Pennsylvania—Design	159
The University of Texas at Dallas—Economic, Political, and Policy Sciences	783
Villanova University—Political Science	883

Disability Studies

Brandeis University, The Heller School for Social Policy and Management, Program in Social Policy, Waltham, MA 02454-9110. Offers assets and inequalities (PhD); children, youth and families (PhD); health and behavioral health (PhD). *Degree requirements:* For doctorate, thesis/dissertation, qualifying paper, 2-year residency. *Entrance requirements:* For doctorate, GRE General Test.

Brock University, Faculty of Graduate Studies, Faculty of Social Sciences, Program in Applied Disability Studies, St. Catharines, ON L2S 3A1, Canada. Offers MA, MADS, Diploma. Part-time programs available. *Degree requirements:* For master's, thesis (for some programs). *Entrance requirements:* For master's, honors degree. Additional exam requirements/recommendations for international students: Required—TOEFL (minimum score 550 paper-based; 213 computer-based; 80 iBT), IELTS (minimum score 6.5). Electronic applications accepted.

Chapman University, Graduate Studies, College of Educational Studies, Program in Education: Disability Studies, Orange, CA 92866. Offers PhD. *Faculty:* 19 full-time (13 women), 20 part-time/adjunct (12 women). *Students:* 7 part-time (6 women); includes 3 minority (1 American Indian/Alaska Native, 2 Asian Americans or Pacific Islanders). Average age 41. 17 applicants, 53% accepted, 7 enrolled. *Degree requirements:* For doctorate, thesis/dissertation. *Expenses:* Tuition: Full-time $11,970; part-time $665 per credit. Required fees: $456; $456 per year. Tuition and fees vary according to course load, degree level and program. *Financial support:* Federal Work-Study and scholarships/grants available. *Unit head:* Dr. Joel Colbert, Director, 714-744-7076. *Application contact:* Rika Judd, Graduate Admission Counselor, 714-997-6786, Fax: 714-997-6713, E-mail: rjudd@chapman.edu.

New York Medical College, School of Health Sciences and Practice, Department of Disability and Human Development, Valhalla, NY 10595-1691. Offers MPH. Part-time and evening/weekend programs available. *Degree requirements:* For master's, thesis. *Entrance requirements:* For master's, minimum undergraduate GPA of 3.0. Additional exam requirements/recommendations for international students: Required—TOEFL (minimum score 600 paper-based; 250 computer-based; 100 iBT), IELTS (minimum score 7). Electronic applications accepted.

Syracuse University, Graduate School, School of Education, Program in Disabilities Studies, Syracuse, NY 13244. Offers CAS. Part-time and evening/weekend programs available. *Entrance requirements:* Additional exam requirements/recommendations for international students: Required—TOEFL.

University of Hawaii at Manoa, Graduate Division, College of Education, Center on Disability Studies, Honolulu, HI 96822. Offers Graduate Certificate. Part-time programs available. *Entrance requirements:* Additional exam requirements/recommendations for international students: Required—TOEFL (minimum score 500 paper-based; 173 computer-based; 61 iBT), IELTS (minimum score 5).

University of Illinois at Chicago, Graduate College, College of Applied Health Sciences, Department of Disability and Human Development, Chicago, IL 60607-7128. Offers disability and human development (MS); disability studies (PhD). *Accreditation:* AOTA. Part-time programs available. *Degree requirements:* For master's, thesis optional; for doctorate, thesis/dissertation. *Entrance requirements:* For master's and doctorate, GRE General Test. Additional exam requirements/recommendations for international students: Required—TOEFL. Electronic applications accepted. *Faculty research:* Emerging trends in disability, demography and financial structure of disability services, aging and disability, empowerment of people with disabilities, health promotion in disabilities.

University of Manitoba, Faculty of Graduate Studies, Interdisciplinary Programs, Program in Disability Studies, Winnipeg, MB R3T 2N2, Canada. Offers M Sc, MA.

University of Northern British Columbia, Office of Graduate Studies, Prince George, BC V2N 4Z9, Canada. Offers business administration (Diploma); community health science (M Sc); disability management (MA); education (M Ed); first nations studies (MA); gender studies (MA); history (MA); interdisciplinary studies (MA); international studies (MA); mathematical, computer and physical sciences (M Sc); natural resources and environmental studies (M Sc, MA, MNRES, PhD); political science (MA); psychology (M Sc, PhD); social work (MSW). Part-time and evening/weekend programs available. Postbaccalaureate distance learning degree programs offered (no on-campus study). *Degree requirements:* For master's, thesis; for doctorate, thesis/dissertation. *Entrance requirements:* For master's, GRE, minimum B average in undergraduate course work; for doctorate, candidacy exam, minimum A average in graduate course work.

University of Pittsburgh, School of Health and Rehabilitation Sciences, Disability Studies Program, Pittsburgh, PA 15260. Offers Certificate.

Utah State University, School of Graduate Studies, College of Education and Human Services, Department of Special Education and Rehabilitation, Logan, UT 84322. Offers disability disciplines (PhD); rehabilitation counselor education (MRC); special education (M Ed, MS, Ed S). *Accreditation:* NCATE (one or more programs are accredited). Part-time programs available. Postbaccalaureate distance learning degree programs offered (minimal on-campus study). *Degree requirements:* For master's, thesis (for some programs), internships (for some programs); for doctorate, comprehensive exam, thesis/dissertation. *Entrance requirements:* For master's and doctorate, GRE General Test, minimum GPA of 3.0. Additional exam requirements/recommendations for international students: Required—TOEFL (minimum score 550 paper-based; 213 computer-based). Electronic applications accepted. *Faculty research:* Applied behavior analysis, effective instructional practices, early childhood teacher training research, distance education, multicultural rehabilitation.

York University, Faculty of Graduate Studies, Faculty of Health, Program in Critical Disability Studies, Toronto, ON M3J 1P3, Canada. Offers MA, PhD. *Degree requirements:* For master's, thesis or alternative. *Entrance requirements:* Additional exam requirements/recommendations for international students: Required—TOEFL (minimum score 600 paper-based; 250 computer-based). Electronic applications accepted.

Emergency Management

Adelphi University, University College, Graduate Certificate in Emergency Management Program, Garden City, NY 11530-0701. Offers Certificate. Part-time and evening/weekend programs available. *Students:* 3 full-time (2 women), 13 part-time (5 women); includes 3 minority (1 African American, 2 Asian Americans or Pacific Islanders). Average age 34. 11 applicants, 55% accepted, 6 enrolled. In 2008, 6 Certificates awarded. *Application deadline:* For fall admission, 5/1 for international students; for spring admission, 12/1 for international students. Applications are processed on a rolling basis. Application fee: $50. Electronic applications accepted. *Expenses:* Tuition: Full-time $25,700; part-time $775 per credit hour. Required fees: $500. Tuition and fees vary according to course load, degree level, campus/location, program and student level. *Financial support:* Research assistantships with partial tuition reimbursements, Federal Work-Study and institutionally sponsored loans available. *Faculty research:* Emergency nursing, disaster management, disaster preparedness. *Unit head:* Shawn O'Riley, Executive Director, 516-877-3412, E-mail: ucinfo@adelphi.edu. *Application contact:* Christine Murphy, Director of Admissions, 516-877-3050, Fax: 516-877-3039, E-mail: graduateadmissions@adelphi.edu.

American Public University System, AMU/APU Graduate Programs, Charles Town, WV 25414. Offers air warfare (MA Military Studies); American Revolution (MA Military Studies); business administration (MBA); Civil War (MA Military Studies); criminal justice (MA); defense management (MA Military Studies); emergency and disaster management (MA); environmental policy and management (MS); fire science management (MA); global engagement (MA); history (MA); homeland security (MA); humanities (MA); intelligence (MA Military Studies, MA Strategic Intelligence); international peace and conflict resolution (MA); international relations and conflict resolution (MA); joint warfare (MA Military Studies); land warfare international perspective (MA Military Studies); management (MA); military history (MA); military leadership (MA Military Studies); national security studies (MA); naval warfare international (MA Military Studies); naval warfare US (MA Military Studies); political science (MA); public administration (MA); public health (MA); security management (MA); space studies (MS); special ops/LIC (MA Military Studies); sports management (MA); transportation and logistics management (MA); transportation management (MA); unconventional warfare (MA Military Studies); World War II (MA Military Studies). Programs offered via distance learning only. Part-time and evening/weekend programs available. Postbaccalaureate distance learning degree programs offered (no on-campus study). *Degree requirements:* For master's, comprehensive exam. *Entrance requirements:* For master's, bachelor's degree or equivalent, minimum GPA of 2.7 in last 60 hours of course work. Electronic applications accepted. *Faculty research:* Military history, criminal justice, management performance, national security.

Anna Maria College, Graduate Division, Program in Emergency Management, Paxton, MA 01612. Offers MS, Graduate Certificate. Part-time and evening/weekend programs available. *Faculty:* 1 (woman) full-time, 3 part-time/adjunct (0 women). *Students:* 3 full-time (0 women), 14 part-time (5 women); includes 1 minority (African American), 1 international. Average age 36. In 2008, 2 master's, 5 other advanced degrees awarded. *Degree requirements:* For master's, thesis. *Entrance requirements:* For master's, minimum GPA of 2.7. Additional exam requirements/recommendations for international students: Required—TOEFL (minimum score 500 paper-based). *Application deadline:* For fall admission, 3/1 priority date for domestic and international students; for spring admission, 11/1 priority date for domestic and international students. Applications are processed on a rolling basis. Application fee: $40. Electronic applications accepted. *Expenses:* Tuition: Part-time $1400 per course. *Financial support:* Applicants required to submit FAFSA. *Unit head:* Dr. Susan Swedis, Director, 508-849-3382, E-mail: sswedis@annamaria.edu. *Application contact:* Dennis Braun, Director, Graduate Studies and Continuing Education, 508-849-3293, Fax: 508-819-3362, E-mail: dbraun@annamaria.edu.

Arkansas Tech University, Graduate School, School of Community Education, Russellville, AR 72801. Offers emergency management and homeland security (MS). Part-time programs available. *Students:* 14 full-time (2 women), 37 part-time (15 women); includes 4 minority (1 African American, 1 American Indian/Alaska Native, 1 Asian American or Pacific Islander, 1 Hispanic American), 2 international. Average age 31. In 2008, 4 master's awarded. *Entrance requirements:* For master's, GRE General Test or MAT. Additional exam requirements/recommendations for international students: Required—TOEFL (minimum score 500 paper-based; 173 computer-based; 61 iBT). *Application deadline:* For fall admission, 3/1 priority date for domestic students, 5/1 priority date for international students; for winter admission, 10/1 priority date for international students; for spring admission, 10/1 priority date for domestic and international students. Applications are processed on a rolling basis. Application fee: $0 ($30 for international students). Electronic applications accepted. *Expenses:* Tuition, state resident: full-time $1575; part-time $175 per credit hour. Tuition, nonresident: full-time $3150; part-time $350 per credit hour. Tuition and fees vary according to course load. *Financial support:* In 2008–09, teaching assistantships with full tuition reimbursements (averaging $4,000 per year); career-related internships or fieldwork, Federal Work-Study, scholarships/grants, health care benefits, and unspecified assistantships also available. Support available to part-time students. Financial award application deadline: 4/15; financial award applicants required to submit FAFSA. *Unit head:* Dr. Mary Ann Rollans, Dean, 479-968-0234 Ext. 479, E-mail: maryann.rollans@atu.edu. *Application contact:* Dr. Eldon G. Clary, Dean of Graduate School, 479-968-0398, Fax: 479-964-0542, E-mail: graduate.school@atu.edu.

Benedictine University, Graduate Programs, Program in Public Health, Lisle, IL 60532-0900. Offers administration of health care institutions (MPH); dietetics (MPH); disaster management (MPH); health education (MPH); health information systems (MPH); MBA/MPH; MPH/MS. Part-time and evening/weekend programs available. Postbaccalaureate distance learning degree programs offered. *Entrance requirements:* For master's, MAT, GRE, or GMAT. Additional exam requirements/recommendations for international students: Required—TOEFL (minimum score 550 paper-based; 213 computer-based).

California State University, Long Beach, Graduate Studies, College of Health and Human Services, Department of Professional Studies, Long Beach, CA 90840. Offers emergency services administration (MS); occupational studies (MA). *Accreditation:* NCATE. Part-time and evening/weekend programs available. Postbaccalaureate distance learning degree programs offered (no on-campus study). *Faculty:* 2 full-time (0 women), 6 part-time/adjunct (2 women). *Students:* 14 full-time (7 women), 79 part-time (24 women); includes 40 minority (12 African Americans, 1 American Indian/Alaska Native, 8 Asian Americans or Pacific Islanders, 19 Hispanic Americans), 2 international. Average age 44. 79 applicants, 89% accepted, 30 enrolled. *Degree requirements:* For master's, comprehensive exam or thesis. *Application deadline:* For fall admission, 7/1 for domestic students. Applications are processed on a rolling basis. Application fee: $55. Electronic applications accepted. *Expenses:* Tuition, nonresident: full-time $11,160; part-time $372 per unit. Required fees: $4100; $1261 per semester. *Financial support:* Federal Work-Study, institutionally sponsored loans, and scholarships/grants available. Financial award application deadline: 3/2. *Faculty research:* Special needs, leadership, training and development. *Unit head:* Dr. Henry O'Lawrence, Chair, 562-985-5633, Fax: 562-985-8815, E-mail: holawren@csulb.edu. *Application contact:* Dr. Peter Kreysa, Graduate Coordinator, 562-985-8111, Fax: 562-985-8815, E-mail: pkreysa@csulb.edu.

Drexel University, College of Nursing and Health Professions, Emergency and Public Safety Services Program, Philadelphia, PA 19104-2875. Offers MS. Part-time and evening/weekend programs available. *Degree requirements:* For master's, comprehensive exam. *Entrance requirements:* For master's, GRE General Test, minimum GPA of 2.75.

The George Washington University, School of Medicine and Health Sciences, Health Sciences Programs, Washington, DC 20052. Offers adult nurse practitioner (MSN, Post Master's Certificate); clinical practice management (MSHS); clinical research administration (MSHS); clinical research administration for nurses (MSN); emergency services management (MSHS); end-of-life care (MSHS, MSN); family nurse practitioner (MSN, Post Master's Certificate);

immunohematology (MSHS); nursing (DNP); nursing leadership and management (MSN); physical therapy (DPT); physician assistant (MSHS); MSHS/MPH. Postbaccalaureate distance learning degree programs offered (no on-campus study). *Students:* 181 full-time (148 women), 307 part-time (260 women); includes 107 minority (48 African Americans, 1 American Indian/ Alaska Native, 41 Asian Americans or Pacific Islanders, 17 Hispanic Americans), 1 international. Average age 34. 1,653 applicants, 28% accepted, 266 enrolled. In 2008, 137 master's, 21 doctorates, 40 other advanced degrees awarded. *Entrance requirements:* Additional exam requirements/recommendations for international students: Required—TOEFL (minimum score 550 paper-based; 213 computer-based). *Application deadline:* Applications are processed on a rolling basis. Application fee: $60. *Expenses:* Contact institution. *Unit head:* Jean E. Johnson, Senior Associate Dean, 202-994-3725, E-mail: jejohns@gwu.edu. *Application contact:* Joke Ogundiran, Director of Admission, 202-994-1668, Fax: 202-994-0870, E-mail: jokeogun@gwu.edu.

Georgia State University, Andrew Young School of Policy Studies, Department of Public Administration and Urban Studies, Atlanta, GA 30303-3083. Offers disaster management (Certificate); non-profit management (Certificate); planning and economic development (Certificate); public administration (MPA); public policy (PhD); urban policy studies (MS); JD/MPA. *Accreditation:* NASPAA (one or more programs are accredited). Part-time and evening/ weekend programs available. Terminal master's awarded for partial completion of doctoral program. *Degree requirements:* For master's, thesis optional; for doctorate, comprehensive exam, thesis/dissertation. *Entrance requirements:* For master's and doctorate, GRE General Test. Additional exam requirements/recommendations for international students: Required— TOEFL. Electronic applications accepted. *Faculty research:* Public management, urban policy, policy analysis, public finance, public involvement.

Indiana University of Pennsylvania, School of Graduate Studies and Research, College of Natural Sciences and Mathematics, Science for Disaster Response Program, Indiana, PA 15705-1087. Offers MS. *Students:* 1 (woman) full-time, 3 part-time (0 women). Average age 31. 1 applicant, 100% accepted, 1 enrolled. In 2008, 4 master's awarded. *Expenses:* Tuition, area resident: Full-time $6430; part-time $357 per credit. Tuition, nonresident: full-time $10,288; part-time $572 per credit. Required fees: $1547.50; $107 per credit. $283 per year. *Unit head:* Dr. Roberta Eddy, Director, 724-357-4482, E-mail: roberta.eddy@iup.edu. *Application contact:* Dr. Jacqueline Gorman, Dean's Associate, 724-357-2609, E-mail: jgorman@iup.edu.

Jacksonville State University, College of Graduate Studies and Continuing Education, College of Arts and Sciences, Department of Emergency Management, Jacksonville, AL 36265-1602. Offers MS. Part-time and evening/weekend programs available. *Faculty:* 4 full-time (1 woman). *Students:* 7 full-time (2 women), 153 part-time (55 women); includes 33 minority (27 African Americans, 6 Hispanic Americans), 3 international. Average age 39. 85 applicants, 61% accepted, 47 enrolled. In 2008, 35 master's awarded. *Degree requirements:* For master's, comprehensive exam, thesis (for some programs). *Application deadline:* Applications are processed on a rolling basis. Application fee: $30. Electronic applications accepted. *Expenses:* Tuition, area resident: Full-time $4560; part-time $225 per credit hour. Tuition, state resident: full-time $4560; part-time $450 per credit hour. Tuition, nonresident: full-time $9120; part-time $450 per credit hour. *Financial support:* In 2008–09, 51 students received support. Available to part-time students. Application deadline: 4/1; *Unit head:* Dr. Barry Cox, Head, 256-782-5926, E-mail: bcox@jsu.edu. *Application contact:* Dr. Jean Pugliese, Associate Dean, 256-782-8278, Fax: 256-782-5321, E-mail: pugliese@jsu.edu.

The Johns Hopkins University, School of Nursing, Nurse Practitioner Program, Baltimore, MD 21218-2699. Offers adult acute/critical care (MSN, Certificate); adult and pediatric primary care (MSN); adult or pediatric primary care (Certificate); emergency preparedness/disaster response (Certificate); family primary care (MSN, Certificate); women's health (Certificate). *Accreditation:* AACN; NLN (one or more programs are accredited). Part-time programs available. *Degree requirements:* For master's, thesis optional, scholarly project or portfolio. *Entrance requirements:* For master's, GRE, interview, minimum GPA of 3.0, BSN, Maryland RN license. Additional exam requirements/recommendations for international students: Required—TOEFL (minimum score 550 paper-based; 230 computer-based). *Expenses:* Contact institution. *Faculty research:* Community outreach, primary care of underserved populations, substance abusing individuals, childhood violence, women's health.

Lynn University, College of Arts and Sciences, Boca Raton, FL 33431-5598. Offers applied psychology (MS); criminal justice administration (MS); emergency planning and administration (MS, Certificate). Part-time and evening/weekend programs available. Postbaccalaureate distance learning degree programs offered. *Entrance requirements:* For master's, GRE, resumé, 2 letters of recommendation, minimum undergraduate GPA of 3.0. Additional exam requirements/ recommendations for international students: Required—TOEFL (minimum score 550 paper-based; 213 computer-based). *Faculty research:* Terrorism, criminological theory, corrections, emergency planning.

Massachusetts Maritime Academy, Program in Emergency Management, Buzzards Bay, MA 02532-1803. Offers MS.

Millersville University of Pennsylvania, Graduate School, School of Humanities and Social Sciences, Center for Disaster Research and Education, Program in Emergency Management, Millersville, PA 17551-0302. Offers MS. Part-time and evening/weekend programs available. Postbaccalaureate distance learning degree programs offered (no on-campus study). *Faculty:* 10 full-time (6 women). *Students:* 26 part-time (14 women); includes 1 minority (African American), 1 international. Average age 31. 10 applicants, 90% accepted, 8 enrolled. *Entrance requirements:* For master's, GRE or MAT, resumé, telephone interview. Additional exam requirements/recommendations for international students: Required—TOEFL (minimum score 500 paper-based; 183 computer-based; 65 iBT), TOEFL may be replaced by IELTS with score of 6 or higher. *Application deadline:* For fall admission, 2/1 priority date for domestic and international students; for winter admission, 10/1 priority date for domestic and international students; for spring admission, 10/1 priority date for domestic and international students. Applications are processed on a rolling basis. Application fee: $40. Electronic applications accepted. *Expenses:* Tuition, state resident: full-time $6430; part-time $357 per credit. Tuition, nonresident: full-time $10,288; part-time $572 per credit. Required fees: $1937; $73.50 per credit. One-time fee: $88 part-time. Tuition and fees vary according to course load. *Financial support:* In 2008–09, 4 students received support, including 4 research assistantships with full and partial tuition reimbursements available (averaging $4,062 per year); institutionally sponsored loans and unspecified assistantships also available. Support available to part-time students. Financial award application deadline: 3/15; financial award applicants required to submit FAFSA. *Unit head:* Dr. Kathy A. Gregoire, Coordinator, 717-871-2475, E-mail: Kathy.Gregoire@millersville.edu. *Application contact:* Dr. Victor S. DeSantis, Dean of Graduate and Professional Studies, 717-872-3099, Fax: 717-872-3453, E-mail: victor.desantis@millersville.edu.

New Jersey Institute of Technology, Office of Graduate Studies, College of Computing Science, Program in Information Systems, Newark, NJ 07102. Offers business and information systems (MS); emergency management and business continuity (MS); information systems (MS, PhD). Part-time and evening/weekend programs available. *Faculty:* 12 full-time (2 women), 4 part-time/adjunct (1 woman). *Students:* 95 full-time (33 women), 119 part-time (32 women); includes 75 minority (12 African Americans, 1 American Indian/Alaska Native, 41 Asian Americans or Pacific Islanders, 21 Hispanic Americans), 78 international. Average age 30. 371 applicants, 68% accepted, 67 enrolled. In 2008, 108 master's, 10 doctorates awarded. Terminal master's awarded for partial completion of doctoral program. *Degree requirements:* For master's, thesis optional; for doctorate, thesis/dissertation. *Entrance requirements:* For master's, GRE General Test; for doctorate, GRE General Test, minimum graduate GPA of 3.5. Additional exam requirements/recommendations for international students: Required—TOEFL (minimum score 550 paper-based; 213 computer-based; 79 iBT). *Application deadline:* For fall admission, 6/5 priority date for domestic students, 4/1 for international students; for spring admission, 11/15 for domestic and international students. Applications are processed on a rolling basis. Application fee: $60. Electronic applications accepted. *Expenses:* Tuition, area resident: Full-time $13,780;

part-time $750 per credit. Tuition, state resident: full-time $13,780; part-time $750 per credit. Tuition, nonresident: full-time $19,580; part-time $1033 per credit. Required fees: $1956; $197 per credit. *Financial support:* Fellowships with full and partial tuition reimbursements, research assistantships with full and partial tuition reimbursements, teaching assistantships with full and partial tuition reimbursements, career-related internships or fieldwork, Federal Work-Study, institutionally sponsored loans, and unspecified assistantships available. Financial award application deadline: 3/15. *Unit head:* Dr. Michael P Bieber, Acting Chair, 973-596-2681, Fax: 973-596-2986, E-mail: michael.p.bieber@njit.edu. *Application contact:* Kathryn Kelly, Director of Admissions, 973-596-3300, Fax: 973-596-3461, E-mail: admissions@njit.edu.

North Dakota State University, College of Graduate and Interdisciplinary Studies, College of Arts, Humanities and Social Sciences, Department of Sociology, Anthropology, and Emergency Management, Fargo, ND 58105. Offers emergency management (MS, PhD); social science (MA, MS); sociology (MS). Part-time programs available. *Faculty:* 8 full-time (3 women), 5 part-time/adjunct (2 women). *Students:* 35 full-time (17 women), 15 part-time (9 women); includes 5 minority (2 African Americans, 1 American Indian/Alaska Native, 1 Asian American or Pacific Islander, 1 Hispanic American), 2 international. Average age 27. 15 applicants, 60% accepted, 7 enrolled. In 2008, 9 master's awarded. *Degree requirements:* For master's, thesis; for doctorate, comprehensive exam, thesis/dissertation. *Entrance requirements:* For master's, GRE (emergency management), course work in sociology, minimum GPA of 3.2; for doctorate, GRE, minimum GPA of 3.2. Additional exam requirements/recommendations for international students: Required—TOEFL. *Application deadline:* For fall admission, 4/1 priority date for domestic students. Applications are processed on a rolling basis. Application fee: $45 ($60 for international students). *Financial support:* In 2008–09, 7 research assistantships with full tuition reimbursements (averaging $6,156 per year), 7 teaching assistantships with full tuition reimbursements (averaging $3,078 per year) were awarded; fellowships, career-related internships or fieldwork, Federal Work-Study, institutionally sponsored loans, and tuition waivers (full) also available. Support available to part-time students. Financial award application deadline: 4/15. *Faculty research:* Medical sociology, demography, ethnology, archaeology. Total annual research expenditures: $75,000. *Unit head:* Dr. Daniel J. Klenow, Chair, 701-231-8657, Fax: 701-231-1047, E-mail: daniel.klenow@ndsu.edu. *Application contact:* Dr. Daniel J. Klenow, Chair, 701-231-8657, Fax: 701-231-1047, E-mail: daniel.klenow@ndsu.edu.

Oklahoma State University, College of Arts and Sciences, Department of Political Science, Stillwater, OK 74078. Offers fire and emergency management administration (MS, PhD); political science (MA). *Faculty:* 20 full-time (5 women), 4 part-time/adjunct (1 woman). *Students:* 15 full-time (5 women), 29 part-time (5 women); includes 9 minority (4 African Americans, 4 American Indian/Alaska Native, 1 Asian American or Pacific Islander), 3 international. Average age 35. 41 applicants, 71% accepted, 18 enrolled. In 2008, 23 master's awarded. *Degree requirements:* For master's, comprehensive exam, thesis or creative component; for doctorate, comprehensive exam, thesis/dissertation. *Entrance requirements:* For master's, GRE; for doctorate, GRE. Additional exam requirements/recommendations for international students: Required—TOEFL. *Application deadline:* For fall admission, 3/1 priority date for international students; for spring admission, 8/1 priority date for international students. Applications are processed on a rolling basis. Application fee: $40 ($75 for international students). Electronic applications accepted. *Expenses:* Tuition, state resident: full-time $3716.40; part-time $154.85 per credit hour. Tuition, nonresident: full-time $14,448; part-time $602 per credit hour. Required fees: $1772.40; $73.85 per credit hour. One-time fee: $50. Tuition and fees vary according to course load and campus/location. *Financial support:* In 2008–09, 6 teaching assistantships (averaging $12,199 per year) were awarded; career-related internships or fieldwork, Federal Work-Study, scholarships/grants, health care benefits, tuition waivers (partial), and unspecified assistantships also available. Support available to part-time students. Financial award application deadline: 3/1; financial award applicants required to submit FAFSA. *Faculty research:* Fire and emergency management, environmental dispute resolution, voting and elections, women and politics, urban politics. *Unit head:* Dr. James Scott, Head, 405-744-5569, Fax: 405-744-6534. *Application contact:* Dr. Gordon Emslie, Dean, 405-744-6368, Fax: 405-744-0355, E-mail: grad_i@okstate.edu.

Park University, College of Graduate and Professional Studies, Kansas City, MO 54105. Offers adult education (M Ed); at-risk students (M Ed); disaster and emergency management (MPA); educational administration (M Ed); entrepreneurship (MBA); general business (MBA); general education (M Ed); government/business relations (MPA); healthcare/services management (MBA, MPA); international business (MBA); K-12 certification (MAT); management information systems (MBA); management of information systems (MPA); middle school certification (MAT); multi-cultural education (M Ed); nonprofit management (MPA); public management (MPA); school law (M Ed); secondary school certification (MAT); special education (M Ed). Part-time and evening/weekend programs available. Postbaccalaureate distance learning degree programs offered (no on-campus study). *Degree requirements:* For master's, comprehensive exam, thesis (for some programs). *Entrance requirements:* For master's, GRE, GMAT, teacher certification (M Ed). Additional exam requirements/recommendations for international students: Required—TOEFL (minimum score 550 paper-based). Electronic applications accepted. *Faculty research:* Literacy, leadership, brain based research, multicultural education, diversity.

Philadelphia University, School of Science and Health, Program in Disaster Medicine and Management, Philadelphia, PA 19144-5497. Offers MS. Postbaccalaureate distance learning degree programs offered (minimal on-campus study).

Royal Roads University, Graduate Studies, Peace and Conflict Studies Program, Victoria, BC V9B 5Y2, Canada. Offers conflict analysis (G Dip); conflict analysis and management (MA); disaster and emergency management (MA); human security and peacebuilding (MA). Postbaccalaureate distance learning degree programs offered (minimal on-campus study). *Degree requirements:* For master's, thesis. *Entrance requirements:* For master's, 5-7 years of related work experience. Additional exam requirements/recommendations for international students: Required—TOEFL (paper-based 570; computer-based 233) or IELTS (paper-based 7) (recommended). Electronic applications accepted. *Faculty research:* Conflict analysis, ethno-political conflict reconciliation, international relations, displaced persons.

San Diego State University, Graduate and Research Affairs, College of Health and Human Services, Graduate School of Public Health, San Diego, CA 92182. Offers environmental health (MPH); epidemiology (MPH, PhD), including biostatistics (MPH); global emergency preparedness and response (MS); global health (PhD); health behavior (PhD); health promotion (MPH); health services administration (MPH); toxicology (MS); MPH/MA; MSW/MPH. *Accreditation:* ABET (one or more programs are accredited); CAHME (one or more programs are accredited); CEPH (one or more programs are accredited). Part-time programs available. *Degree requirements:* For master's, comprehensive exam (for some programs), thesis (for some programs); for doctorate, thesis/dissertation. *Entrance requirements:* For master's, GMAT (health services administration MPH), GRE General Test; for doctorate, GRE General Test. Additional exam requirements/recommendations for international students: Required—TOEFL. *Faculty research:* Evaluation of tobacco, AIDS prevalence and prevention, mammography, infant death project, Alzheimer's in elderly Chinese.

TUI University, College of Health Sciences, Program in Health Sciences, Cypress, CA 90630. Offers clinical research administration (MS, Certificate); emergency and disaster management (MS, Certificate); environmental health science (Certificate); health care administration (PhD); health care management (MS), including health informatics; health education (MS, Certificate); health informatics (Certificate); health sciences (PhD); international health (MS); international health: educator or researcher option (PhD); international health: practitioner option (PhD); law and expert witness studies (MS, Certificate); public health (MS); quality assurance (Certificate). Part-time and evening/weekend programs available. Postbaccalaureate distance learning degree programs offered (no on-campus study). *Degree requirements:* For doctorate, comprehensive exam, thesis/dissertation, defense of dissertation. *Entrance requirements:* For master's, minimum GPA of 2.5 (students with GPA 3.0 or greater may transfer up to 30% of graduate level credits);

Emergency Management

TUI University (continued)
for doctorate, minimum GPA of 3.4, curriculum vitae, course work in research methods or statistics. Additional exam requirements/recommendations for international students: Required—TOEFL.

Université de Montréal, Faculty of Medicine, Programs in Environment and Prevention, Montréal, QC H3C 3J7, Canada. Offers environment and prevention (DESS); environment, health and disaster management (DESS). *Students:* 11 full-time (3 women), 9 part-time (7 women). 38 applicants, 34% accepted, 13 enrolled. In 2008, 8 DESSs awarded. *Application deadline:* For fall admission, 2/1 priority date for domestic students; for winter admission, 11/1 priority date for domestic students; for spring admission, 2/1 priority date for domestic students. Applications are processed on a rolling basis. Application fee: $100. Electronic applications accepted. *Faculty research:* Health, environment, pollutants, protection, waste. *Unit head:* Joseph Zayed, Head, 514-343-5912, Fax: 514-343-2200, E-mail: joseph.zayed@umontreal.ca. *Application contact:* Micheline Dessureault, Information Contact, 514-343-2280, E-mail: micheline.dessureault@umontreal.ca.

University of Central Florida, College of Health and Public Affairs, Department of Public Administration, Orlando, FL 32816. Offers emergency management and homeland security (Certificate); non-profit management (MNM, Certificate); public administration (MPA, Certificate); urban and regional planning (Certificate). *Accreditation:* NASPAA. Part-time and evening/weekend programs available. *Faculty:* 13 full-time (3 women), 9 part-time/adjunct (4 women). *Students:* 81 full-time (54 women), 243 part-time (171 women); includes 118 minority (64 African Americans, 11 Asian Americans or Pacific Islanders, 43 Hispanic Americans), 7 international. In 2008, 66 master's, 18 other advanced degrees awarded. *Degree requirements:* For master's, comprehensive exam, thesis or alternative, research report. *Entrance requirements:* For master's, GRE General Test. *Application deadline:* For fall admission, 7/1 for domestic students; for spring admission, 12/1 for domestic students. Application fee: $30. Electronic applications accepted. *Expenses:* Tuition, area resident: Full-time $6816; part-time $284 per credit. Tuition, state resident: full-time $6816; part-time $1076 per credit. Tuition, nonresident: full-time $25,824. Required fees: $216; $9 per credit. *Financial support:* In 2008–09, 3 fellowships with partial tuition reimbursements (averaging $10,000 per year), 16 research assistantships with partial tuition reimbursements (averaging $6,200 per year) were awarded; teaching assistantships with partial tuition reimbursements, career-related internships or fieldwork, Federal Work-Study, institutionally sponsored loans, tuition waivers (partial), and unspecified assistantships also available. Financial award application deadline: 3/1; financial award applicants required to submit FAFSA. *Unit head:* Dr. MaryAnn Feldheim, Chair, 407-823-3693, Fax: 407-823-5651. *Application contact:* Dr. MaryAnn Feldheim, Chair, 407-823-3693, Fax: 407-823-5651.

University of Hawaii at Manoa, Graduate Division, Colleges of Arts and Sciences, College of Social Sciences, Department of Urban and Regional Planning, Program in Disaster Preparedness and Emergency Management, Honolulu, HI 96822. Offers Graduate Certificate.

University of Nevada, Las Vegas, Graduate College, Greenspun College of Urban Affairs, Department of Public Administration, Las Vegas, NV 89154-6026. Offers crisis and emergency management (MS); non-profit management (Certificate); public administration (MPA); public affairs (PhD); public management (Certificate). *Accreditation:* NASPAA. Part-time and evening/weekend programs available. *Faculty:* 5 full-time (3 women), 2 part-time/adjunct (1 woman). *Students:* 30 full-time (12 women), 129 part-time (70 women); includes 39 minority (21 African Americans, 4 Asian Americans or Pacific Islanders, 14 Hispanic Americans), 3 international. Average age 38. 95 applicants, 76% accepted, 53 enrolled. In 2008, 48 master's, 28 other advanced degrees awarded. *Degree requirements:* For master's, comprehensive exam, professional paper. *Entrance requirements:* For master's, GRE General Test, GMAT or LSAT. Additional exam requirements/recommendations for international students: Required—TOEFL (minimum score 550 paper-based; 213 computer-based; 80 iBT), IELTS (minimum score 7). *Application deadline:* For fall admission, 6/1 priority date for domestic students, 5/1 for international students; for spring admission, 11/1 priority date for domestic students, 10/1 for international students. Applications are processed on a rolling basis. Application fee: $60 ($75 for international students). Electronic applications accepted. *Expenses:* Tuition, state resident: full-time $1414; part-time $198 per credit. Tuition, nonresident: full-time $12,509; part-time $415.75 per credit. International tuition: $14,249 full-time. Required fees: $4 per credit. $252 per semester. Tuition and fees vary according to course load. *Financial support:* In 2008–09, 8 students received support, including 3 research assistantships with partial tuition reimbursements available (averaging $10,000 per year), 5 teaching assistantships with partial tuition reimbursements available (averaging $15,600 per year); institutionally sponsored loans, scholarships/grants, health care benefits, and unspecified assistantships also available. Financial award application deadline: 3/1. *Faculty research:* Emergency and crisis management, homeland security, public and non-profit management, public policy, policy analysis and evaluation. *Unit head:* Dr. Anna Lukemeyer, Chair/Associate Professor, 702-895-4828, Fax: 702-895-1813, E-mail: anna.lukemeyer@unlv.edu. *Application contact:* Graduate College Admissions Evaluator, 702-895-3320, Fax: 702-895-4180, E-mail: gradcollege@unlv.edu.

University of Pittsburgh, Graduate School of Public Health, Department of Environmental and Occupational Health, Pittsburgh, PA 15260. Offers environmental and occupational health (MPH, MS, PhD); occupational medicine (MPH); public health awareness and disaster response (Certificate); risk assessment (Certificate); MD/MPH. *Accreditation:* CEPH (one or more programs are accredited). Part-time programs available. *Degree requirements:* For master's, comprehensive exam, thesis; for doctorate, comprehensive exam, thesis/dissertation, preliminary exams. *Entrance requirements:* For master's and Certificate, GRE General Test; for doctorate, GRE General Test, minimum GPA of 3.4; background in biology, physics, chemistry and calculus. Additional exam requirements/recommendations for international students: Required—TOEFL (minimum score 550 paper-based; 213 computer-based; 80 iBT). Electronic applications accepted. *Faculty research:* Molecular toxicology, redox signaling, gene environment interaction, progenitor-progency lineage, occupational and pulmonary medicine.

Virginia Commonwealth University, Graduate School, College of Humanities and Sciences, Wilder School of Government and Public Affairs, Program in Homeland Security and Emergency Preparedness, Richmond, VA 23284-9005. Offers MA, Graduate Certificate. Postbaccalaureate distance learning degree programs offered.

West Chester University of Pennsylvania, Office of Graduate Studies, College of Health Sciences, Department of Health, West Chester, PA 19383. Offers emergency preparedness (Certificate); health care administration (Certificate); integrative health (Certificate); public health (MPH); school health (M Ed). *Accreditation:* CEPH. Part-time and evening/weekend programs available. *Students:* 49 full-time (28 women), 90 part-time (60 women); includes 29 minority (24 African Americans, 4 Asian Americans or Pacific Islanders, 1 Hispanic American), 28 international. Average age 32. 133 applicants, 83% accepted, 39 enrolled. In 2008, 29 master's, 12 other advanced degrees awarded. *Degree requirements:* For master's, thesis (for some programs), minimum GPA of 3.0. *Entrance requirements:* For master's, one-page statement of career objectives, two letters of reference. Additional exam requirements/recommendations for international students: Required—TOEFL (minimum score 550 paper-based; 213 computer-based; 80 iBT). *Application deadline:* For fall admission, 4/15 priority date for domestic students, 3/15 for international students; for spring admission, 10/15 for domestic students, 9/1 for international students. Applications are processed on a rolling basis. Application fee: $35. Electronic applications accepted. *Expenses:* Tuition, state resident: full-time $6430; part-time $357 per credit. Tuition, nonresident: full-time $10,288; part-time $572 per credit. Required fees: $652.50; $50 per credit. $67 per semester. *Financial support:* In 2008–09, 15 research assistantships with full and partial tuition reimbursements (averaging $5,000 per year) were awarded; unspecified assistantships also available. Support available to part-time students. Financial award application deadline: 2/15; financial award applicants required to submit FAFSA. *Faculty research:* HIV/AIDS education, teacher preparation, water quality. *Unit head:* Dr. Roger Mustalish, Chair, 610-436-2931, E-mail: rmustalish@wcupa.edu. *Application contact:* Dr. Bethann Cinelli, Graduate Coordinator, 610-436-2267, E-mail: bcinelli@wcupa.edu.

York University, Faculty of Graduate Studies, Atkinson Faculty of Liberal and Professional Studies, Program in Disaster and Emergency Management, Toronto, ON M3J 1P3, Canada. Offers MA.

Homeland Security

American Public University System, AMU/APU Graduate Programs, Charles Town, WV 25414. Offers air warfare (MA Military Studies); American Revolution (MA Military Studies); business administration (MBA); Civil War (MA Military Studies); criminal justice (MA); defense management (MA Military Studies); emergency and disaster management (MA); environmental policy and management (MS); fire science management (MA); global engagement (MA); history (MA); homeland security (MA); humanities (MA); intelligence (MA Military Studies, MA Strategic Intelligence); international peace and conflict resolution (MA); international relations and conflict resolution (MA); joint warfare (MA Military Studies); land warfare international perspective (MA Military Studies); management (MA); military history (MA); military leadership (MA Military Studies); national security studies (MA); naval warfare international (MA Military Studies); naval warfare US (MA Military Studies); political science (MA); public administration (MA); public health (MA); security management (MA); space studies (MS); special ops/LIC (MA Military Studies); sports management (MA); transportation and logistics management (MA); transportation management (MA); unconventional warfare (MA Military Studies); World War II (MA Military Studies). Programs offered via distance learning only. Part-time and evening/weekend programs available. Postbaccalaureate distance learning degree programs offered (no on-campus study). *Degree requirements:* For master's, comprehensive exam. *Entrance requirements:* For master's, bachelor's degree or equivalent, minimum GPA of 2.7 in last 60 hours of course work. Electronic applications accepted. *Faculty research:* Military history, criminal justice, management performance, national security.

Arkansas Tech University, Graduate School, School of Community Education, Russellville, AR 72801. Offers emergency management and homeland security (MS). Part-time programs available. *Students:* 14 full-time (2 women), 37 part-time (15 women); includes 4 minority (1 African American, 1 American Indian/Alaska Native, 1 Asian American or Pacific Islander, 1 Hispanic American), 2 international. Average age 31. In 2008, 4 master's awarded. *Entrance requirements:* For master's, GRE General Test or MAT. Additional exam requirements/recommendations for international students: Required—TOEFL (minimum score 500 paper-based; 173 computer-based; 61 iBT). *Application deadline:* For fall admission, 3/1 priority date for domestic students, 5/1 priority date for international students; for winter admission, 10/1 priority date for international students; for spring admission, 10/1 priority date for domestic and international students. Applications are processed on a rolling basis. Application fee: $0 ($30 for international students). Electronic applications accepted. *Expenses:* Tuition, state resident: full-time $1575; part-time $175 per credit hour. Tuition, nonresident: full-time $3150; part-time $350 per credit hour. Tuition and fees vary according to course load. *Financial support:* In 2008–09, teaching assistantships with full tuition reimbursements (averaging $4,000 per year); career-related internships or fieldwork, Federal Work-Study, scholarships/grants, health care benefits, and unspecified assistantships also available. Support available to part-time students. Financial award application deadline: 4/15; financial award applicants required to submit FAFSA. *Unit head:* Dr. Mary Ann Rollans, Dean, 479-968-0234 Ext. 479, E-mail: maryann.rollans@atu.edu. *Application contact:* Dr. Eldon G. Clary, Dean of Graduate School, 479-968-0398, Fax: 479-964-0542, E-mail: graduate.school@atu.edu.

Chaminade University of Honolulu, Graduate Services, Program in Criminal Justice Administration, Honolulu, HI 96816-1578. Offers criminal justice administration (MSCJA); homeland security (Certificate). Part-time and evening/weekend programs available. Postbaccalaureate distance learning degree programs offered (no on-campus study). *Degree requirements:* For master's, thesis optional. *Entrance requirements:* For master's, minimum undergraduate GPA of 3.0, 3 letters of recommendation. Additional exam requirements/recommendations for international students: Required—TOEFL (minimum score 550 paper-based). Electronic applications accepted. *Faculty research:* Penology, juvenile delinquency, multicultural and ethnic diversity in criminology, law enforcement administration and training, homeland security.

Fairleigh Dickinson University, Metropolitan Campus, Anthony J. Petrocelli College of Continuing Studies, School of Administrative Science, Program in Homeland Security, Teaneck, NJ 07666-1914. Offers MSHS. *Students:* 2 full-time (1 woman), 15 part-time (3 women). Average age 38. 9 applicants, 100% accepted, 6 enrolled. *Application deadline:* Applications are processed on a rolling basis. Application fee: $40. *Unit head:* Dr. Paulette Laubsch, Head, 201-692-2000. *Application contact:* Susan Brooman, University Director of Graduate Admissions, 201-692-2554, Fax: 201-692-2560, E-mail: globaleducation@fdu.edu.

George Mason University, College of Humanities and Social Sciences, Department of Public and International Affairs, Fairfax, VA 22030. Offers biodefense (MS, PhD); political science (MA, PhD); public administration (MPA). *Accreditation:* NASPAA (one or more programs are accredited). *Entrance requirements:* For master's, GRE General Test, minimum GPA of 3.0 in last 60 hours of course work. Electronic applications accepted.

The Johns Hopkins University, School of Education, Division of Public Safety Leadership, Baltimore, MD 21218-2699. Offers homeland security (MS); intelligence analysis (MS); management (MS). Part-time and evening/weekend programs available. *Entrance requirements:* For master's, minimum GPA of 3.0, interview, resumé, letters of recommendation. Additional exam requirements/recommendations for international students: Required—TOEFL (minimum score 600 paper-based; 250 computer-based; 100 iBT). *Faculty research:* Ethics and integrity, counter terrorism, school safety, Homeland Security, identity theft.

The Johns Hopkins University, Zanvyl Krieger School of Arts and Sciences, Advanced Academic Programs, Program in Government, Washington, DC 20036. Offers government (MA); national securities study (Certificate); MA/MBA. Part-time and evening/weekend programs available. *Degree requirements:* For master's, thesis. *Entrance requirements:* For master's, minimum GPA of 3.0. Additional exam requirements/recommendations for international students: Required—TOEFL (minimum score 250 computer-based; 100 iBT). Electronic applications accepted.

Long Island University at Riverhead, Homeland Security Management Institute, Riverhead, NY 11901. Offers MS, Advanced Certificate. Part-time programs available. Postbaccalaureate distance learning degree programs offered (no on-campus study). *Faculty:* 2 full-time (0 women), 10 part-time/adjunct (1 woman). *Students:* 5 full-time (0 women), 107 part-time (17 women); includes 16 minority (8 African Americans, 1 American Indian/Alaska Native, 2 Asian Americans or Pacific Islanders, 5 Hispanic Americans). 48 applicants, 56% accepted, 23 enrolled. In 2008, 11 master's, 36 other advanced degrees awarded. *Degree requirements:* For master's, thesis. *Entrance requirements:* For master's, minimum GPA of 3.0, 2 letters of reference. *Application deadline:* Applications are processed on a rolling basis. Application fee: $0. Electronic applications accepted. *Financial support:* In 2008–09, 105 students received support. Career-related internships or fieldwork and scholarships/grants available. Support available to part-time students. Financial award applicants required to submit FAFSA. *Unit head:* Dr. Vincent E. Henry, Unit Head, 631-287-8010, Fax: 631-287-8130, E-mail: vincent.henry@liu.edu. *Application contact:* Andrea Borra, Admissions Counselor, 631-287-8010 Ext. 8326, Fax: 631-287-8253, E-mail: andrea.borra@liu.edu.

National Defense University, College of International Security Affairs, Washington, DC 20319-5066. Offers strategic security studies (MA), including conflict management, counterterrorism, homeland defense/ security, international security studies. Part-time and evening/weekend programs available. *Faculty:* 13 full-time (3 women), 14 part-time/adjunct (2 women). *Students:* 33 full-time (2 women), 305 part-time (75 women). Average age 30. 133 applicants, 100% accepted, 133 enrolled. In 2008, 39 master's awarded. *Degree requirements:* For master's, thesis. *Entrance requirements:* Additional exam requirements/recommendations for international students: Required—TOEFL. *Unit head:* Dr. R. Joseph DeSutter, Director, 202-685-3871. *Application contact:* Dr. R. Joseph DeSutter, Director, 202-685-3871.

National University, Academic Affairs, School of Engineering and Technology, Department of Applied Engineering, La Jolla, CA 92037-1011. Offers database administration (MS); engineering management (MS); environmental engineering (MS); homeland security and safety engineering (MS); system engineering (MS); wireless communications (MS). Part-time and evening/weekend programs available. Postbaccalaureate distance learning degree programs offered (no on-campus study). *Faculty:* 6 full-time (1 woman), 93 part-time/adjunct (18 women). *Students:* 112 full-time (22 women), 96 part-time (19 women); includes 38 minority (11 African Americans, 1 American Indian/Alaska Native, 15 Asian Americans or Pacific Islanders, 11 Hispanic Americans), 112 international. Average age 31. 118 applicants, 100% accepted, 118 enrolled. In 2008, 34 master's awarded. *Degree requirements:* For master's, thesis. *Entrance requirements:* For master's, interview, minimum GPA of 2.5. Additional exam requirements/recommendations for international students: Required—TOEFL (minimum score 550 paper-based; 213 computer-based; 79 iBT), IELTS (minimum score 6). *Application deadline:* Applications are processed on a rolling basis. Application fee: $60 ($65 for international students). Electronic applications accepted. *Expenses:* Tuition: Full-time $8694; part-time $322 per credit hour. Tuition and fees vary according to course load. *Financial support:* Career-related internships or fieldwork, institutionally sponsored loans, scholarships/grants, and tuition waivers (partial) available. Support available to part-time students. Financial award application deadline: 6/30; financial award applicants required to submit FAFSA. *Unit head:* Dr. Shekar Viswanathan, Chair and Associate Professor, 858-309-8416, Fax: 858-309-3420, E-mail: sviswana@nu.edu. *Application contact:* Dominick Giovanniello, Associate Regional Dean—San Diego, 800-NAT-UNIV, Fax: 858-541-7792, E-mail: dgiovann@nu.edu.

Regent University, Graduate School, Robertson School of Government, Virginia Beach, VA 23464. Offers health care policy and administration (MA); international politics (MA); law and public policy (MA); Mid-East Politics (MA); political leadership and management (MA); political management (MA); public administration (MA); public policy (MA); terrorism and homeland defense (MA); world economies and political development (MA); JD/MA; M Div/MA; M Ed/MA; MBA/MA. Part-time and evening/weekend programs available. Postbaccalaureate distance learning degree programs offered (minimal on-campus study). *Faculty:* 6 full-time (1 woman), 11 part-time/adjunct (1 woman). *Students:* 60 full-time (33 women), 69 part-time (34 women); includes 29 minority (22 African Americans, 1 Asian American or Pacific Islander, 6 Hispanic Americans), 3 international. Average age 30. 136 applicants, 54% accepted, 54 enrolled. In 2008, 48 master's awarded. *Degree requirements:* For master's, thesis optional, internship. *Entrance requirements:* For master's, GRE General Test or LSAT, minimum undergraduate GPA of 3.0, writing sample, resumé, interview, references, transcripts. Additional exam requirements/recommendations for international students: Required—TOEFL (minimum score 577 paper-based; 233 computer-based). *Application deadline:* For fall admission, 5/1 priority date for domestic students; for spring admission, 11/1 priority date for domestic students. Applications are processed on a rolling basis. Application fee: $50. Electronic applications accepted. *Expenses:* Contact institution. *Financial support:* Career-related internships or fieldwork, scholarships/grants, tuition waivers (full and partial), and unspecified assistantships available. Support available to part-time students. Financial award application deadline: 9/1; financial award applicants required to submit FAFSA. *Faculty research:* Education reform, political character issues, social capital concerns, administrative ethics, Biblical law and public policy. *Unit head:* Dr. Charles W. Dunn, Dean, 757-352-4322, Fax: 757-352-4643, E-mail: cwdunn@regent.edu. *Application contact:* Matthew Chadwick, Director of Admissions, 800-373-5504, Fax: 757-352-4381, E-mail: admissions@regent.edu.

Saint Joseph's University, College of Arts and Sciences, Programs in Public Safety and Management, Philadelphia, PA 19131-1395. Offers homeland security (MS, Certificate); public safety management (MS, Certificate). Part-time and evening/weekend programs available. *Students:* 57 part-time (5 women); includes 9 minority (6 African Americans, 2 Asian Americans or Pacific Islanders, 1 Hispanic American). Average age 40. *Entrance requirements:* For master's, GRE (if GPA is below 2.75), application, official transcripts, minimum GPA of 2.75, personal statement, 2 letters of recommendation, resumé. Additional exam requirements/recommendations for international students: Required—TOEFL (minimum score 550 paper-based; 213 computer-based; 79 iBT). *Application deadline:* For fall admission, 7/15 priority date for domestic students, 4/15 for international students; for winter admission, 1/15 for international students; for spring admission, 11/15 priority date for domestic students, 10/15 for international students. Applications are processed on a rolling basis. Application fee: $35. Electronic applications accepted. *Expenses:* Tuition: Part-time $745 per credit. Tuition and fees vary according to course load, degree level and program. *Financial support:* Applicants required to submit FAFSA. *Unit head:* Patricia Griffin, Director, 610-660-1294, E-mail: pgriffin@sju.edu. *Application contact:* Coralee Dixon, Assistant Director of Graduate Admissions, 610-660-1102, Fax: 610-660-1224, E-mail: coralee.dixon@sju.edu.

Salve Regina University, Graduate Studies, Program in International Relations, Newport, RI 02840-4192. Offers homeland security (Certificate); international relations (MA, Certificate). Part-time and evening/weekend programs available. Postbaccalaureate distance learning degree programs offered (minimal on-campus study). *Faculty:* 3 full-time (0 women), 5 part-time/adjunct (2 women). *Students:* 21 full-time (9 women), 66 part-time (24 women); includes 5 minority (1 African American, 1 Asian American or Pacific Islander, 3 Hispanic Americans), 4 international. Average age 34. 59 applicants, 59% accepted, 311 enrolled. In 2008, 38 master's awarded. *Entrance requirements:* For master's, GMAT, GRE General Test, MAT or LSAT. Additional exam requirements/recommendations for international students: Required—TOEFL (minimum score 600 paper-based; 250 computer-based; 100 iBT), TOEFL or IELTS. *Application deadline:* For fall admission, 3/15 priority date for domestic and international students; for spring admission, 9/15 priority date for domestic and international students. Applications are processed on a rolling basis. Application fee: $60. Electronic applications accepted. *Expenses:* Tuition: Part-time $395 per credit. Required fees: $40 per term. Tuition and fees vary according to degree level. *Financial support:* Career-related internships or fieldwork and Federal Work-Study available. Support available to part-time students. Financial award application deadline: 3/1; financial award applicants required to submit FAFSA. *Unit head:* Dr. Symeon Giannakos, Director, 401-341-3177, Fax: 401-341-2993, E-mail: symeon.giannakos@salve.edu. *Application contact:* Kelly Alverson, Graduate Admissions Counselor, 401-341-2153, Fax: 401-341-2973, E-mail: kelly.alverson@salve.edu.

Salve Regina University, Graduate Studies, Programs in Administration of Justice, Newport, RI 02840-4192. Offers justice and homeland security (MS); law enforcement leadership (MS). Part-time and evening/weekend programs available. *Faculty:* 2 full-time (0 women), 9 part-time/adjunct (1 woman). *Students:* 21 full-time (5 women), 30 part-time (5 women); includes 2 minority (1 African American, 1 Hispanic American). Average age 30. 16 applicants, 63% accepted, 8 enrolled. In 2008, 13 master's awarded. *Entrance requirements:* For master's, GMAT, GRE General Test, or MAT. Additional exam requirements/recommendations for international students: Required—TOEFL (minimum score 600 paper-based; 250 computer-based; 100 iBT). *Application deadline:* For fall admission, 3/5 priority date for domestic students, 3/15 priority date for international students; for spring admission, 9/15 priority date for domestic students, 9/5 priority date for international students. Applications are processed on a rolling basis. Application fee: $60. Electronic applications accepted. *Expenses:* Tuition: Part-time $395 per credit. Required fees: $40 per term. Tuition and fees vary according to degree level. *Financial support:* Career-related internships or fieldwork and Federal Work-Study available. Support available to part-time students. Financial award application deadline: 3/1; financial award applicants required to submit FAFSA. *Unit head:* Dr. Daniel Knight, Director, 401-341-3255, E-mail: knightd@salve.edu. *Application contact:* Kelly Alverson, Graduate Admissions Counselor, 401-341-2153, Fax: 401-341-2973, E-mail: kelly.alverson@salve.edu.

Texas A&M University, George Bush School of Government and Public Service, College Station, TX 77843. Offers advanced international affairs (Certificate); homeland security (Certificate); international affairs (MPIA), including international economics and development, national security affairs; nonprofit management (Certificate); public service and administration (MPSA), including public management, public policy analysis. *Accreditation:* NASPAA. *Faculty:* 43. *Students:* 188 full-time (80 women), 101 part-time (37 women); includes 40 minority (10 African Americans, 5 Asian Americans or Pacific Islanders, 25 Hispanic Americans), 22 international. Average age 24. In 2008, 64 master's awarded. *Degree requirements:* For master's, summer internship. *Entrance requirements:* For master's, GRE (preferred) or GMAT. *Application deadline:* For fall admission, 1/24 for domestic and international students. Application fee: $50 ($75 for international students). Electronic applications accepted. *Expenses:* Tuition, area resident: Full-time $3838.50. Tuition, state resident: full-time $3838.50. Tuition, nonresident: full-time $8897. Required fees: $2359.60. *Financial support:* In 2008–09, fellowships (averaging $11,000 per year), research assistantships (averaging $11,250 per year) were awarded; career-related internships or fieldwork, Federal Work-Study, and institutionally sponsored loans also available. Financial award application deadline: 2/1; financial award applicants required to submit FAFSA. *Faculty research:* Public policy, presidential studies, public leadership, economic policy, social policy. *Unit head:* A. Benton Cocanougher, Dean, 979-862-8842, E-mail: bushschool@tamu.edu. *Application contact:* Kathryn Meyer, Recruitment/Placement Officer, 979-458-4767, Fax: 979-845-4155, E-mail: admissions@bushschool.tamu.edu.

Thomas Edison State College, Heavin School of Arts and Sciences, Program in Homeland Security, Trenton, NJ 08608-1176. Offers Graduate Certificate. Part-time programs available. Postbaccalaureate distance learning degree programs offered (no on-campus study). *Students:* 4 part-time (1 woman). Average age 42. 14 applicants, 5 enrolled. In 2008, 5 Graduate Certificates awarded. *Entrance requirements:* Additional exam requirements/recommendations for international students: Required—TOEFL (minimum score 550 paper-based; 213 computer-based; 79 iBT). *Application deadline:* For fall admission, 8/15 priority date for domestic and international students; for winter admission, 11/15 priority date for domestic and international students; for spring admission, 2/15 priority date for domestic and international students. Applications are processed on a rolling basis. Application fee: $75. Electronic applications accepted. *Expenses:* Tuition, area resident: Part-time $465 per credit. Tuition, state resident: part-time $465 per credit. Tuition, nonresident: part-time $465 per credit. *Financial support:* Applicants required to submit FAFSA. *Unit head:* Dr. Susan Davenport, Dean, Heavin School of Arts and Sciences, 609-984-1130, Fax: 609-984-0740, E-mail: info@tesc.edu. *Application contact:* David Hoftiezer, Director of Admissions, 888-442-8372, Fax: 609-984-8447, E-mail: admissions@tesc.edu.

Thomas Edison State College, Heavin School of Arts and Sciences, Program in Liberal Studies, Trenton, NJ 08608-1176. Offers homeland security (MALS). Part-time programs available. Postbaccalaureate distance learning degree programs offered (no on-campus study). *Students:* 85 part-time (56 women); includes 23 African Americans, 2 Asian Americans or Pacific Islanders, 6 Hispanic Americans. Average age 43. 39 applicants, 30 enrolled. In 2008, 20 master's awarded. *Degree requirements:* For master's, final project. *Entrance requirements:* For master's, bachelor's degree from a regionally-accredited college or university; minimum 2 letters of recommendation; 3-5 years of related working experience; current resumé. Additional exam requirements/recommendations for international students: Required—TOEFL (minimum score 550 paper-based; 213 computer-based; 79 iBT). *Application deadline:* For fall admission, 8/15 priority date for domestic and international students; for winter admission, 11/15 priority date for domestic and international students; for spring admission, 2/15 priority date for domestic and international students. Applications are processed on a rolling basis. Application fee: $75. Electronic applications accepted. *Expenses:* Tuition, area resident: Part-time $465 per credit. Tuition, state resident: part-time $465 per credit. Tuition, nonresident: part-time $465 per credit. *Financial support:* Applicants required to submit FAFSA. *Unit head:* Dr. Susan Davenport, Dean, Heavin School of Arts and Sciences, 609-984-1130, Fax: 609-984-0740, E-mail: info@tesc.edu. *Application contact:* David Hoftiezer, Director of Admissions, 888-442-8372, Fax: 609-984-8447, E-mail: admissions@tesc.edu.

Tiffin University, Program in Criminal Justice, Tiffin, OH 44883-2161. Offers crime analysis (MSCJ); criminal behavior (MSCJ); forensic psychology (MSCJ); homeland security administration (MSCJ); justice administration (MSCJ). Part-time and evening/weekend programs available. Postbaccalaureate distance learning degree programs offered (no on-campus study). *Degree requirements:* For master's, thesis optional. *Entrance requirements:* For master's, minimum undergraduate GPA of 2.5, work experience. Additional exam requirements/recommendations for international students: Required—TOEFL (minimum score 550 paper-based; 213 computer-based). Electronic applications accepted. *Faculty research:* Terrorism, intelligence, homeland security, guns and crime.

Towson University, College of Graduate Studies and Research, Program in Integrated Homeland Security Management, Towson, MD 21252-0001. Offers integrated homeland security management (MS); security assessment and management (Certificate). Part-time and evening/weekend programs available. *Entrance requirements:* For master's, BA in related field 3 yrs related work experience admission essay, resumé, transcripts.

University of Central Florida, College of Health and Public Affairs, Department of Public Administration, Orlando, FL 32816. Offers emergency management and homeland security (Certificate); non-profit management (MNM, Certificate); public administration (MPA, Certificate); urban and regional planning (Certificate). *Accreditation:* NASPAA. Part-time and evening/weekend programs available. *Faculty:* 13 full-time (3 women), 9 part-time/adjunct (4 women). *Students:* 81 full-time (54 women), 243 part-time (171 women); includes 118 minority (64 African Americans, 11 Asian Americans or Pacific Islanders, 43 Hispanic Americans), 7 international. In 2008, 66 master's, 18 other advanced degrees awarded. *Degree requirements:* For master's, comprehensive exam, thesis or alternative, research report. *Entrance requirements:* For master's, GRE General Test. *Application deadline:* For fall admission, 7/1 for domestic students; for spring admission, 12/1 for domestic students. Application fee: $30. Electronic applications accepted. *Expenses:* Tuition, area resident: Full-time $6816; part-time $284 per credit. Tuition, state resident: full-time $6816; part-time $1076 per credit. Tuition, nonresident: full-time $25,824. Required fees: $216; $9 per credit. *Financial support:* In 2008–09, 3 fellowships with partial tuition reimbursements (averaging $10,000 per year), 16 research assistantships with partial tuition reimbursements (averaging $6,200 per year) were awarded; teaching assistantships with partial tuition reimbursements, career-related internships or fieldwork, Federal Work-Study, institutionally sponsored loans, tuition waivers (partial), and unspecified assistantships also available. Financial award application deadline: 3/1; financial award applicants required to submit FAFSA. *Unit head:* Dr. MaryAnn Feldheim, Chair, 407-823-3693, Fax: 407-823-5651. *Application contact:* Dr. MaryAnn Feldheim, Chair, 407-823-3693, Fax: 407-823-5651.

Homeland Security

University of Connecticut, Graduate School, Center for Continuing Studies, Program in Homeland Security Leadership, Storrs, CT 06269. Offers MPS.

The University of Toledo, College of Graduate Studies, College of Medicine, Department of Public Health and Homeland Security, Toledo, OH 43606-3390. Offers occupational health (MSOH, Certificate); public health (MPH, Certificate), including biostatistics and epidemiology (Certificate), emergency response (Certificate), global health (Certificate), public health (MPH); MD/MPH. Part-time programs available. *Degree requirements:* For master's, thesis, qualifying exam. *Entrance requirements:* For master's, GRE. *Faculty research:* Hypertension, endocrinology, molecular biology.

Upper Iowa University, Online Master's Programs, Fayette, IA 52142-1857. Offers accounting (MBA); corporate financial management (MBA); global business (MBA); health and human services (MPA); homeland security (MPA); human resources management (MBA); justice administration (MPA); organizational development (MBA); public personnel management (MPA); quality management (MBA). MBA also available at Madison, Wisconsin campus. Part-time programs available. Postbaccalaureate distance learning degree programs offered (no on-campus study). *Degree requirements:* For master's, research project. *Entrance requirements:* For master's, GMAT, GRE, or minimum GPA of 2.7 during last 60 hours. Additional exam requirements/recommendations for international students: Required—TOEFL (minimum score 570 paper-based; 230 computer-based). Electronic applications accepted. *Faculty research:* Total quality management, CQI, teams, organization culture and climate, management.

Virginia Commonwealth University, Graduate School, College of Humanities and Sciences, Wilder School of Government and Public Affairs, Program in Homeland Security and Emergency Preparedness, Richmond, VA 23284-9005. Offers MA, Graduate Certificate. Postbaccalaureate distance learning degree programs offered.

Walden University, Graduate Programs, School of Psychology, Minneapolis, MN 55401. Offers clinical assessment (Post-Doctoral Certificate); clinical child psychology (Post-Doctoral Certificate); clinical psychology (Post-Doctoral Certificate); counseling psychology (Post-Doctoral Certificate); forensic psychology (MS), including forensic psychology in the community, general forensic psychology, mental health applications, program planning and evaluation in forensic settings, psychology and legal systems; general psychology (Post-Doctoral Certificate); health psychology (Post-Doctoral Certificate); organizational psychology (Post-Doctoral Certificate); organizational psychology and development (Certificate); psychology (MS, PhD), including clinical psychology, counseling psychology, crisis management and response (MS), general psychology, health psychology, leadership development and coaching (MS), media psychology (MS), organizational psychology, organizational psychology and development (MS), organizational psychology and nonprofit management (MS), program evaluation and research (MS), psychology of culture (MS), psychology, public administration, and social change (MS), school psychology, social psychology (MS), terrorism and security (MS); school psychology (Post-Doctoral Certificate); teaching online (Post-Master's Certificate). Part-time and evening/weekend programs available. Postbaccalaureate distance learning degree programs offered (minimal on-campus study). *Faculty:* 16 full-time, 190 part-time/adjunct. *Students:* 3,198 full-time (2,489 women), 810 part-time (664 women); includes 1,319 minority (1,013 African Americans, 51 American Indian/Alaska Native, 68 Asian Americans or Pacific Islanders, 187 Hispanic Americans), 72 international. Average age 40. 1,468 applicants, 60% accepted, 612 enrolled. In 2008, 203 master's, 37 doctorates awarded. Terminal master's awarded for partial completion of doctoral program. *Degree requirements:* For master's, thesis optional; for doctorate, thesis/dissertation, residency. *Entrance requirements:* For master's, bachelor's degree or equivalent in related field, minimum GPA of 2.5, two references, goal statement, official transcripts, access to computer and Internet; for doctorate, master's degree or equivalent in related field, minimum GPA of 3.0, three years related professional/academic experience, two references, goal statement, official transcripts, access to computer and Internet. Additional exam requirements/recommendations for international students: Required—TOEFL (minimum score 550 paper-based; 213 computer-based), IELTS (minimum score 6.5), TOEFL, IELTS, or Michigan English Language Assessment Battery (minimum score 82). *Application deadline:* Applications are processed on a rolling basis. Application fee: $50. Electronic applications accepted. *Expenses:* Tuition: Full-time $12,877; part-time $520 per credit. Required fees: $1230. Tuition and fees vary according to course load, degree level and program. *Financial support:* In 2008–09, 1 fellowship was awarded; Federal Work-Study, scholarships/grants, unspecified assistantships, and family tuition reduction; active duty/veteran tuition reduction; group tuition reduction; interest-free payment plans also available. Support available to part-time students. Financial award applicants required to submit FAFSA. *Unit head:* Dr. Nina Nabors, Associate Dean, 800-925-3368. *Application contact:* Jennifer Hall, 866-4-WALDEN, E-mail: info@waldenu.edu.

Walden University, Graduate Programs, School of Public Policy and Administration, Minneapolis, MN 55401. Offers general public policy and administration (MPA); government management (Certificate); health policy (MPA); homeland security policy (MPA); interdisciplinary policy studies (MPA); law and public policy (MPA); local government management for sustainable communities (MPA); nonprofit management (Certificate); nonprofit management and leadership (MPA, MS); policy analysis (MPA); public management and leadership (MPA); public policy and administration (PhD), including criminal justice, health services, homeland security policy and coordination, international nongovernmental organizations, knowledge management, nonprofit management and leadership, public management and leadership, public policy, public safety management; terrorism, mediation, and peace (MPA). Part-time and evening/weekend programs available. Postbaccalaureate distance learning degree programs offered (minimal on-campus study). *Faculty:* 2 full-time, 55 part-time/adjunct. *Students:* 1,285 full-time (794 women), 144 part-time (96 women); includes 657 minority (591 African Americans, 8 American Indian/Alaska Native, 17 Asian Americans or Pacific Islanders, 41 Hispanic Americans), 20 international. Average age 39. 727 applicants, 54% accepted, 284 enrolled. In 2008, 101 master's, 6 doctorates awarded. *Degree requirements:* For doctorate, thesis/dissertation, residency. *Entrance requirements:* For master's, bachelor's degree or equivalent in related field, minimum GPA of 2.5, two references, goal statement, official transcripts, access to computer and Internet; for doctorate, master's degree or equivalent in related field, minimum GPA of 3.0, three years related professional/academic experience, two references, goal statement, official transcripts, access to computer and Internet. Additional exam requirements/recommendations for international students: Required—TOEFL (minimum score 550 paper-based; 213 computer-based), IELTS (minimum score 6.5), TOEFL, IELTS, or Michigan English Language Assessment Battery (minimum score 82). *Application deadline:* Applications are processed on a rolling basis. Application fee: $50. Electronic applications accepted. *Expenses:* Tuition: Full-time $12,877; part-time $520 per credit. Required fees: $1230. Tuition and fees vary according to course load, degree level and program. *Financial support:* In 2008–09, 3 students received support; fellowships with tuition reimbursements available, Federal Work-Study, scholarships/grants, unspecified assistantships, and family tuition reduction; active duty/veteran tuition reduction; group tuition reduction; interest-free payment plans available. Support available to part-time students. Financial award applicants required to submit FAFSA. *Unit head:* Dr. Mark Gordon, Interim Associate Dean, 800-925-3368. *Application contact:* Jennifer Hall, 866-4-WALDEN, E-mail: info@waldenu.edu.

Wayland Baptist University, Graduate Programs, Program in Counseling, Plainview, TX 79072-6998. Offers counseling (MA); government administration (MPA); homeland security (MPA); justice administration (MPA). Part-time and evening/weekend programs available. Postbaccalaureate distance learning degree programs offered. *Faculty:* 8 full-time (2 women). *Students:* 2 full-time (both women), 105 part-time (81 women); includes 27 minority (3 African Americans, 2 American Indian/Alaska Native, 2 Asian Americans or Pacific Islanders, 20 Hispanic Americans). Average age 34. 39 applicants, 95% accepted, 19 enrolled. In 2008, 34 master's awarded. *Degree requirements:* For master's, comprehensive exam. *Entrance requirements:* For master's, GRE, MAT. Application fee: $50. *Expenses:* Tuition: Full-time $310; part-time $310 per credit hour. Required fees: $782; $9 per credit hour. $60 per semester. *Financial support:* Federal Work-Study, institutionally sponsored loans, and scholarships/grants available. Support available to part-time students. Financial award application deadline: 5/1; financial award applicants required to submit FAFSA. *Unit head:* Dr. Estelle Owens, Chairman, 806-291-1171, Fax: 806-291-1972, E-mail: owensest@wbu.edu. *Application contact:* Amanda Stanton, Graduate Studies, 806-291-3414, Fax: 806-291-1950, E-mail: stanton@wbu.edu.

Wilmington University, Division of Business, New Castle, DE 19720-6491. Offers business administration (MBA); finance (MBA); health care administration (MBA, MS); homeland security (MBA, MS); human resource management (MS); management (MS); management information systems (MBA); organizational leadership (MS); public administration (MS); transportation and logistics (MBA, MS). Part-time and evening/weekend programs available. *Entrance requirements:* Additional exam requirements/recommendations for international students: Required—TOEFL (minimum score 500 paper-based; 173 computer-based). Electronic applications accepted.

Industrial and Labor Relations

Bernard M. Baruch College of the City University of New York, Zicklin School of Business, Zicklin Executive Programs, Baruch Executive Master of Science in Industrial and Labor Relations Program, New York, NY 10010-5585. Offers MS. Part-time and evening/weekend programs available. *Entrance requirements:* For master's, professional experience in HR or labor relations. Additional exam requirements/recommendations for international students: Required—TOEFL. *Expenses:* Contact institution.

Carnegie Mellon University, College of Humanities and Social Sciences, Department of History, Pittsburgh, PA 15213-3891. Offers African and African-American diaspora (PhD); culture and power (PhD); gender and the family (PhD); history (MA, MS); history and policy (MA); labor and politics (PhD); science, technology, medicine and environment (PhD). Part-time programs available. *Degree requirements:* For doctorate, oral and written comprehensive exams, dissertation defense. *Entrance requirements:* For doctorate, GRE General Test. Additional exam requirements/recommendations for international students: Required—TOEFL. Electronic applications accepted. *Faculty research:* Anthropology and history, African American history, technology/environment, cultural history analysis.

Case Western Reserve University, Weatherhead School of Management, Department of Marketing and Policy Studies, Division of Labor and Human Resource Policy, Cleveland, OH 44106. Offers MBA. Part-time and evening/weekend programs available. *Entrance requirements:* For master's, GMAT. *Faculty research:* Strategic human resource management, negotiations and conflict management, human resources in high performance organizations, international human resources management, union management relations and collective bargaining.

Cleveland State University, Cleveland-Marshall College of Law, Cleveland, OH 44115. Offers business law (JD); civil litigation and dispute resolution (JD); criminal law (JD); employment labor law (JD); law (JD, LL M); JD/MAES; JD/MBA; JD/MPA; JD/MSES; JD/MUPDD. *Accreditation:* ABA. Part-time and evening/weekend programs available. *Faculty:* 42 full-time (20 women), 37 part-time/adjunct (9 women). *Students:* 453 full-time (189 women), 224 part-time (110 women); includes 83 minority (47 African Americans, 2 American Indian/Alaska Native, 22 Asian Americans or Pacific Islanders, 12 Hispanic Americans), 9 international. Average age 28. 1,627 applicants, 39% accepted, 200 enrolled. In 2008, 205 JDs, 2 master's awarded. *Degree requirements:* For master's, 20-24 credits of coursework, thesis (for graduates of US law schools); for JD, 90 credits (42 in required courses). *Entrance requirements:* For JD, LSAT, bachelor's degree; for master's, JD or LL B. Additional exam requirements/recommendations for international students: Required—TOEFL (minimum score 600 paper-based; 250 computer-based; 100 iBT). *Application deadline:* For fall admission, 5/1 for domestic and international students. Applications are processed on a rolling basis. Application fee: $0. Electronic applications accepted. *Expenses:* Contact institution. *Financial support:* In 2008–09, 212 students received support, including 8 teaching assistantships with partial tuition reimbursements available (averaging $1,650 per year); career-related internships or fieldwork, Federal Work-Study, institutionally sponsored loans, scholarships/grants, tuition waivers (full and partial), and unspecified assistantships also available. Support available to part-time students. Financial award application deadline: 5/1; financial award applicants required to submit FAFSA. *Faculty research:* Health law, international law, constitutional law, commercial law, business organizations. *Unit head:* Geoffrey S. Mearns, Dean, 216-687-2300, Fax: 216-687-6881, E-mail: geoffrey.mearns@law.csuohio.edu. *Application contact:* Christopher Lucak, Assistant Dean for Admissions, 216-687-4692, Fax: 216-687-6881, E-mail: christopher.lucak@law.csuohio.edu.

Cleveland State University, College of Graduate Studies, Nance College of Business Administration, Department of Management and Labor Relations, Cleveland, OH 44115. Offers labor relations and human resources (MLRHR). Part-time programs available. *Faculty:* 12 full-time (3 women), 6 part-time/adjunct (1 woman). *Students:* 21 full-time (13 women), 37 part-time (26 women); includes 8 minority (all African Americans), 8 international. Average age 29. 53 applicants, 66% accepted, 13 enrolled. In 2008, 22 master's awarded. *Entrance requirements:* For master's, GMAT or GRE. Additional exam requirements/recommendations for international students: Required—TOEFL (minimum score 525 paper-based; 197 computer-based). *Application deadline:* For fall admission, 7/15 for domestic students; for spring admission, 12/15 for domestic students. Applications are processed on a rolling basis. Application fee: $30. Electronic applications accepted. *Financial support:* In 2008–09, 3 research assistantships with full and partial tuition reimbursements (averaging $6,960 per year) were awarded; career-related internships or fieldwork, tuition waivers (full), and unspecified assistantships also available. Financial award applicants required to submit FAFSA. *Unit head:* Dr. Jeffrey C. Susbauer, Chairperson, 216-687-4747, Fax: 216-687-4708, E-mail: j.susbauer@csuohio.edu. *Application contact:* Dr. W. Benoy Joseph, Associate Dean, 216-687-2019, Fax: 216-687-9354, E-mail: w.joseph@csuohio.edu.

Cornell University, Graduate School, Graduate Fields of Industrial and Labor Relations, Ithaca, NY 14853-0001. Offers collective bargaining, labor law and labor history (MILR, MPS, MS, PhD); economic and social statistics (MILR); human resource studies (MILR, MPS, MS, PhD); industrial and labor relations problems (MILR, MPS, MS, PhD); international and comparative labor (MILR, MPS, MS, PhD); labor economics (MILR, MPS, MS, PhD); organizational behavior (MILR, MPS, MS, PhD). *Faculty:* 53 full-time (15 women). *Students:* 161 full-time (89 women); includes 26 minority (10 African Americans, 3 American Indian/Alaska Native, 10 Asian Americans or Pacific Islanders, 3 Hispanic Americans), 64 international. Average age 31. 231 applicants, 36% accepted, 61 enrolled. In 2008, 50 master's, 6 doctorates awarded. *Degree requirements:* For master's, thesis (MS); for doctorate, comprehensive exam, thesis/dissertation, teaching experience. *Entrance requirements:* For master's and doctorate, GMAT or GRE General Test, 2 academic recommendations. Additional exam requirements/recommendations for international students: Required—TOEFL (minimum score 550 paper-based; 213 computer-based; 77 iBT). Application fee: $70. Electronic applications accepted. *Expenses:* Contact institution. *Financial support:* In 2008–09, 73 students received support, including 23 fellowships with full tuition reimbursements available, 20 research assistantships with full tuition reimbursements available, 30 teaching assistantships with full tuition reimbursements available; institutionally sponsored loans, scholarships/grants, health care benefits, tuition waivers (full and partial), and unspecified assistantships also available. Financial award applicants required to submit FAFSA. *Unit head:* Director of Graduate Studies, 607-255-1522. *Application contact:* Graduate Field Assistant, 607-255-1522, E-mail: ilrgradapplicant@cornell.edu.

See Close-Up on page 1213.

Georgetown University, Graduate School of Arts and Sciences, Department of Economics, Washington, DC 20057. Offers econometrics (PhD); economic development (PhD); economic theory (PhD); industrial organization (PhD); international macro and finance (PhD); international trade (PhD); labor economics (PhD); macroeconomics (PhD); public economics and political economics (PhD); MA/PhD; MS/MA. *Degree requirements:* For doctorate, comprehensive exam, thesis/dissertation. *Entrance requirements:* For doctorate, GRE General Test. Additional exam requirements/recommendations for international students: Required—TOEFL. *Faculty research:* International economics, economic development.

Indiana University of Pennsylvania, School of Graduate Studies and Research, College of Health and Human Services, Department of Industrial and Labor Relations, Indiana, PA 15705-1087. Offers MA. Part-time and evening/weekend programs available. *Faculty:* 5 full-time (1 woman). *Students:* 24 full-time (13 women), 14 part-time (10 women); includes 5 minority (4 African Americans, 1 Asian American or Pacific Islander). Average age 30. 59 applicants, 46% accepted, 20 enrolled. In 2008, 26 master's awarded. *Degree requirements:* For master's, thesis optional. *Entrance requirements:* For master's, 2 letters of recommendation. Additional exam requirements/recommendations for international students: Required—TOEFL. *Application deadline:* For fall admission, 7/1 priority date for domestic students; for spring admission, 11/1 for domestic students. Applications are processed on a rolling basis. Application fee: $30. *Expenses:* Tuition, area resident: Full-time $6430; part-time $357 per credit. Tuition, nonresident: full-time $10,288; part-time $572 per credit. Required fees: $1547.50; $107 per credit. $283 per year. *Financial support:* In 2008–09, 14 research assistantships with full and partial tuition reimbursements (averaging $1,624 per year) were awarded; fellowships, career-related internships or fieldwork and Federal Work-Study also available. Support available to part-time students. Financial award application deadline: 3/15; financial award applicants required to submit FAFSA. *Faculty research:* Conflict resolution, labor-management cooperation, unemployment compensation, public sector labor relations, employee discipline. *Unit head:* Dr. Jennie K. Bullard, Chairperson and Graduate Coordinator, 724-357-4470, E-mail: jbullard@iup.edu. *Application contact:* Dr. Jacqueline Beck, Associate Dean, 724-357-2560, E-mail: jbeck@iup.edu.

Inter American University of Puerto Rico, Metropolitan Campus, Graduate Programs, Program in Labor Relations, San Juan, PR 00919-1293. Offers MA. *Degree requirements:* For master's, comprehensive exam. *Entrance requirements:* For master's, GRE or EXADEP, interview. Electronic applications accepted.

Inter American University of Puerto Rico, Metropolitan Campus, Graduate Programs, Program in Psychology, San Juan, PR 00919-1293. Offers industrial/organizational psychology (MA, PhD); labor relations (MA); psychology (MA, PhD); school psychology (MA, PhD). *Degree requirements:* For master's, comprehensive exam. *Entrance requirements:* For master's, GRE or EXADEP, interview. Electronic applications accepted.

Inter American University of Puerto Rico, San Germán Campus, Graduate Studies Center, Program in Business Administration, San Germán, PR 00683-5008. Offers accounting (MBA); finance (MBA); human resources (MBA, PhD); industrial relations (MBA); international business (PhD); labor relations (PhD); management information systems (MBA); marketing (MBA); quality organizational design (MBA). Part-time and evening/weekend programs available. *Degree requirements:* For master's, comprehensive exam. *Entrance requirements:* For master's, GRE General Test or EXADEP, minimum GPA of 3.0.

Inter American University of Puerto Rico, San Germán Campus, Graduate Studies Center, Program in Entrepreneurial and Managerial Development, San Germán, PR 00683-5008. Offers human resources (PhD); interregional and international business (PhD); labor relations (PhD). Part-time and evening/weekend programs available. *Degree requirements:* For doctorate, comprehensive exam, thesis/dissertation. *Entrance requirements:* For doctorate, EXADEP or GMAT, minimum graduate GPA of 3.25.

Loyola University Chicago, Graduate School of Business, Institute of Human Resources and Employee Relations, Chicago, IL 60611-2196. Offers MSHR. Part-time programs available. *Entrance requirements:* For master's, GMAT or GRE General Test, personal statement, letters of recommendation. Additional exam requirements/recommendations for international students: Required—TOEFL (minimum score 550 paper-based; 213 computer-based; 80 iBT). *Expenses:* Contact institution. *Faculty research:* Human resource management, labor relations, global human resource management, organizational development, compensation.

McMaster University, School of Graduate Studies, Faculty of Social Sciences, Program in Labour Studies, Hamilton, ON L8S 4M2, Canada. Offers work and society (MA).

Memorial University of Newfoundland, School of Graduate Studies, Interdisciplinary Program in Employment Relations, St. John's, NL A1C 5S7, Canada. Offers MER. Part-time programs available. *Degree requirements:* For master's, major supervised paper. *Entrance requirements:* For master's, undergraduate degree in related field, minimum B average. Electronic applications accepted.

Michigan State University, The Graduate School, College of Social Science, School of Labor and Industrial Relations, East Lansing, MI 48824. Offers human resources and labor relations (MLRHR); industrial relations and human resources (PhD). *Entrance requirements:* Additional exam requirements/recommendations for international students: Required—TOEFL.

New York Institute of Technology, Graduate Division, School of Management, Program in Human Resources Management and Labor Relations, Old Westbury, NY 11568-8000. Offers human resources administration (Advanced Certificate); human resources management and labor relations (MS); labor relations (Advanced Certificate). Part-time and evening/weekend programs available. *Students:* 20 full-time (13 women), 65 part-time (45 women); includes 23 minority (12 African Americans, 8 Asian Americans or Pacific Islanders, 3 Hispanic Americans), 19 international. Average age 32. In 2008, 32 master's awarded. *Degree requirements:* For master's, comprehensive exam, thesis optional. *Entrance requirements:* For master's, GRE, minimum QPA of 2.85, interview, 2 letters of recommendation. *Application deadline:* For fall admission, 7/1 priority date for domestic students; for spring admission, 12/1 priority date for domestic students. Applications are processed on a rolling basis. Application fee: $50. Electronic applications accepted. *Expenses:* Tuition: Part-time $783 per credit. *Financial support:* Fellowships, research assistantships, career-related internships or fieldwork, institutionally sponsored loans, and tuition waivers (full and partial) available. Support available to part-time students. Financial award applicants required to submit FAFSA. *Faculty research:* Ethics in industrial relations, employee relations, public sector labor relations, benefits. *Unit head:* William Ninehan, Director, 646-273-6071, Fax: 516-686-7425, E-mail: wninehan@nyit.edu. *Application contact:* Dr. Jacquelyn Nealon, Vice President for Enrollment Services, 516-686-7925, Fax: 516-686-7597, E-mail: jnealon@nyit.edu.

The Ohio State University, Graduate School, Max M. Fisher College of Business, Program in Labor and Human Resources, Columbus, OH 43210. Offers MLHR, PhD. *Degree requirements:* For master's, thesis optional; for doctorate, thesis/dissertation. *Entrance requirements:* For master's and doctorate, GRE General Test. Additional exam requirements/recommendations for international students: Recommended—TOEFL (minimum score 600 paper-based; 250 computer-based). Electronic applications accepted.

Penn State University Park, Graduate School, College of the Liberal Arts, Department of Labor Studies and Industrial Relations, State College, University Park, PA 16802-1503. Offers industrial relations and human resources (MS).

Pontificia Universidad Catolica Madre y Maestra, Graduate School, Santiago, Dominican Republic. Offers administration (M Adm); architecture of interiors (M Arch); architecture of tourist lodgings (M Arch); banking and financial management (M Mgmt); civil law (LL M); construction administration (ME); corporate business law (LL M); criminal procedure law (LL M); environmental engineering (ME, MEE); finance (M Mgmt); human resources (EMBA); international business (M Mgmt); labor law and Social Security (LL M); logistics management (ME); marketing (M Mgmt); renewable energy (ME). *Entrance requirements:* For master's, curriculum vitae, interview.

Queen's University at Kingston, School of Graduate Studies and Research, School of Industrial Relations, Kingston, ON K7L 3N6, Canada. Offers MIR. Part-time programs available. *Degree requirements:* For master's, research essay, skill seminars and modules. *Entrance requirements:* For master's, course work in micro-economics, macro-economics, and quantitative statistics. Additional exam requirements/recommendations for international students: Required—TOEFL (minimum score 600 paper-based; 250 computer-based). *Faculty research:* Collective bargaining and labor law, personnel and human relations, labor market analysis and policy, change management, teams.

Rutgers, The State University of New Jersey, New Brunswick, School of Management and Labor Relations, Program in Industrial Relations and Human Resources, Piscataway, NJ 08854-8097. Offers PhD. Part-time programs available. *Degree requirements:* For doctorate, comprehensive exam, thesis/dissertation. *Entrance requirements:* For doctorate, GRE. Additional exam requirements/recommendations for international students: Required—TOEFL (minimum score 575 paper-based; 233 computer-based; 91 iBT). Electronic applications accepted. *Faculty research:* Strategic human resources, labor relations, organizational change, worker representation.

Announcement: The Master of Human Resource Management program focuses on strategic positioning of human resources management principally in business and government organizations. The Master of Labor and Employment Relations allows students to focus on labor relations, organizational change, employee diversity, and/or public policy. The PhD in Industrial and Labor Relations and Human Resources prepares students for academic careers.

Rutgers, The State University of New Jersey, New Brunswick, School of Management and Labor Relations, Program in Labor and Employment Relations, Piscataway, NJ 08854-8097. Offers MLER. Part-time and evening/weekend programs available. *Degree requirements:* For master's, thesis optional. *Entrance requirements:* For master's, GRE General Test. Additional exam requirements/recommendations for international students: Required—TOEFL. Electronic applications accepted. *Expenses:* Contact institution. *Faculty research:* Labor history, women and work, labor education, comparative labor movements, labor involvement and corporate decision making.

State University of New York Empire State College, Graduate Studies, Program in Labor and Policy Studies, Saratoga Springs, NY 12866-4391. Offers MA. Part-time and evening/weekend programs available. Postbaccalaureate distance learning degree programs offered (minimal on-campus study). *Degree requirements:* For master's, thesis, exam. *Entrance requirements:* Additional exam requirements/recommendations for international students: Required—TOEFL (minimum score 600 paper-based; 280 computer-based). Electronic applications accepted. *Faculty research:* Work and technology, collective bargaining, labor law, human resources management, trade union governance.

Université de Montréal, Faculty of Arts and Sciences, School of Industrial Relations, Montréal, QC H3C 3J7, Canada. Offers M Sc, PhD, DESS. Part-time programs available. *Faculty:* 22 full-time (5 women), 2 part-time/adjunct (1 woman). *Students:* 42 full-time (32 women), 97 part-time (74 women). 131 applicants, 38% accepted, 44 enrolled. In 2008, 21 master's, 3 doctorates, 11 other advanced degrees awarded. *Degree requirements:* For master's, thesis; for doctorate, thesis/dissertation, general exam. *Entrance requirements:* For master's, BS in industrial relations. *Application deadline:* For fall admission, 2/1 priority date for domestic students; for winter admission, 11/1 priority date for domestic students; for spring admission, 2/1 priority date for domestic students. Application fee: $100. Electronic applications accepted. *Financial support:* Fellowships, research assistantships, teaching assistantships, tuition waivers (full) available. *Faculty research:* Labor law, health and safety at work, stress, job satisfaction, labor economics. *Unit head:* Tania Saba, Director and Responsible for Graduate Studies (PhD), 514-343-5553, Fax: 514-343-5764, E-mail: tania.saba@umontreal.ca. *Application contact:* Jean Charest, Responsible for Graduate Studies (MSc), 514-343-7743, Fax: 514-343-5764, E-mail: jean.charest@umontreal.ca.

Université du Québec à Trois-Rivières, Graduate Programs, Program in Labor Relations, Trois-Rivières, QC G9A 5H7, Canada. Offers DESS.

Université du Québec à Trois-Rivières, Graduate Programs, Program in Labor Relations, Trois-Rivières, QC G9A 5H7, Canada. Offers DESS.

Université du Québec en Outaouais, Graduate Programs, Department of Industrial Relations, Gatineau, QC J8X 3X7, Canada. Offers M Sc, MA, PhD, Diploma. Part-time programs available. *Students:* 7 full-time, 54 part-time, 2 international. *Degree requirements:* For master's, thesis (for some programs); for doctorate, thesis/dissertation. *Entrance requirements:* For master's, appropriate bachelor's degree, proficiency in French; for doctorate, appropriate master's degree, proficiency in French. *Application deadline:* For fall admission, 6/1 for domestic students, 3/1 for international students; for winter admission, 11/1 for domestic students, 10/1 for international students. Application fee: $30 Canadian dollars. *Financial support:* Fellowships, research assistantships, teaching assistantships available. *Unit head:* Eric Gosselin, Director, 819-595-3900 Ext. 1777, Fax: 819-773-1788, E-mail: eric.gosselin@uqo.ca. *Application contact:* Registrar's Office, 819-773-1850, Fax: 819-773-1835, E-mail: registraire@uqo.ca.

Université Laval, Faculty of Social Sciences, Department of Industrial Relations, Programs in Industrial Relations, Québec, QC G1K 7P4, Canada. Offers MA, PhD. Terminal master's awarded for partial completion of doctoral program. *Degree requirements:* For master's, thesis (for some programs); for doctorate, comprehensive exam, thesis/dissertation. *Entrance requirements:* For master's and doctorate, knowledge of French, comprehension of written English. Electronic applications accepted.

University of Alberta, Faculty of Graduate Studies and Research, Doctoral Program in Business, Edmonton, AB T6G 2E1, Canada. Offers accounting (PhD); finance (PhD); human resources/industrial relations (PhD); management science (PhD); marketing (PhD); organizational analysis (PhD); MBA/PhD. *Accreditation:* AACSB. Part-time programs available. *Degree requirements:* For doctorate, comprehensive exam, thesis/dissertation. *Entrance requirements:* For doctorate, GMAT. Additional exam requirements/recommendations for international students: Required—TOEFL (minimum score 550 paper-based; 213 computer-based). Electronic applications accepted. *Faculty research:* Accounting, capital markets and corporate finance, organizational change and human resource management, marketing, strategic management.

University of California, Berkeley, Graduate Division, Haas School of Business, Program in Business, Berkeley, CA 94720-1500. Offers accounting (PhD); business and public policy

Industrial and Labor Relations

University of California, Berkeley (continued)
(PhD); finance (PhD); marketing (PhD); organizational behavior and industrial relations (PhD); real estate (PhD). *Accreditation:* AACSB. *Degree requirements:* For doctorate, comprehensive exam, thesis/dissertation, oral exam, written preliminary exams. *Entrance requirements:* For doctorate, GMAT or GRE, minimum GPA of 3.0. Additional exam requirements/recommendations for international students: Required—TOEFL (minimum score 570 paper-based; 230 computer-based; 68 iBT), IELTS (minimum score 7). Electronic applications accepted.

University of Cincinnati, Graduate School, McMicken College of Arts and Sciences, Center for Organizational Leadership, Program in Labor and Employment Relations, Cincinnati, OH 45221. Offers MALER. Part-time and evening/weekend programs available. *Degree requirements:* For master's, thesis or alternative, final experience project. *Entrance requirements:* For master's, minimum undergraduate GPA of 3.0. Additional exam requirements/recommendations for international students: Required—TOEFL (minimum score 560 paper-based). Electronic applications accepted. *Faculty research:* Human resource management, diversity, leadership.

University of Cincinnati, Graduate School, McMicken College of Arts and Sciences, Department of Economics, Cincinnati, OH 45221. Offers applied economics (MA); labor and employment relations (MALER). Part-time and evening/weekend programs available. Electronic applications accepted.

University of Illinois at Urbana–Champaign, Graduate College, School of Labor and Employment Relations, Champaign, IL 61820. Offers human resources and industrial relations (MHRIR, PhD); MHRIR/JD; MHRIR/MBA. Part-time programs available. *Faculty:* 14 full-time (4 women), 1 (woman) part-time/adjunct. *Students:* 179 full-time (124 women), 9 part-time (6 women); includes 39 minority (20 African Americans, 1 American Indian/Alaska Native, 16 Asian Americans or Pacific Islanders, 2 Hispanic Americans), 38 international. 239 applicants, 53% accepted, 75 enrolled. In 2008, 89 master's, 2 doctorates awarded. Terminal master's awarded for partial completion of doctoral program. *Entrance requirements:* For master's and doctorate, GRE or GMAT, minimum GPA of 3.0. Additional exam requirements/recommendations for international students: Required—TOEFL (minimum score 590 paper-based; 243 computer-based; 96 iBT), IELTS (minimum score 6.5), TOEFL or IELTS. Application fee: $60 ($75 for international students). Electronic applications accepted. *Financial support:* In 2008–09, 39 fellowships, 13 research assistantships, 3 teaching assistantships were awarded; tuition waivers (full and partial) also available. *Unit head:* Dr. Joel Cutcher Gershenfeld, Dean, 217-333-1480, Fax: 217-244-9290, E-mail: joelcg@illinois.edu. *Application contact:* Becky Barker, Graduate Admissions, 217-333-2381, Fax: 217-244-9290, E-mail: ebarker@illinois.edu.

University of Massachusetts Amherst, Graduate School, College of Social and Behavioral Sciences, The Labor Center, Amherst, MA 01003. Offers labor studies (MS); union leadership and administration (MS). Part-time programs available. Postbaccalaureate distance learning degree programs offered (minimal on-campus study). *Degree requirements:* For master's, thesis or alternative. *Entrance requirements:* Additional exam requirements/recommendations for international students: Required—TOEFL (minimum score 550 paper-based; 213 computer-based; 79 iBT), IELTS (minimum score 6.5). Electronic applications accepted. *Expenses:* Tuition, area resident: Full-time $2640. Tuition, nonresident: full-time $9936. One-time fee: $332 full-time. Tuition and fees vary according to course load.

University of Minnesota, Twin Cities Campus, Carlson School of Management, Program in Human Resources and Industrial Relations, Minneapolis, MN 55455-0213. Offers MA, PhD. *Accreditation:* AACSB. Part-time and evening/weekend programs available. Terminal master's awarded for partial completion of doctoral program. *Degree requirements:* For master's, thesis optional; for doctorate, thesis/dissertation. *Entrance requirements:* For master's, GMAT or GRE General Test; for doctorate, GRE General Test. Additional exam requirements/recommendations for international students: Required—TOEFL (minimum score 580 paper-based). *Expenses:* Contact institution. *Faculty research:* Staffing, training, and development; compensation and benefits; organization theory; collective bargaining.

University of New Haven, Graduate School, College of Business, Program in Industrial Relations, West Haven, CT 06516-1916. Offers MS. *Students:* 2 full-time (1 woman), 18 part-time (11 women); includes 8 minority (7 African Americans, 1 Hispanic American), 1 international. Average age 35. 12 applicants, 75% accepted, 3 enrolled. In 2008, 4 master's awarded. *Degree requirements:* For master's, thesis optional. *Entrance requirements:* For master's, two years of administrative, managerial, or professional work experience. Additional exam requirements/recommendations for international students: Required—TOEFL (minimum score 520 paper-based; 190 computer-based; 70 iBT); Recommended—IELTS (minimum score 5.5). *Application deadline:* For fall admission, 5/31 for international students; for winter admission, 10/15 for international students; for spring admission, 1/15 for international students. Applications are processed on a rolling basis. Application fee: $50. *Expenses:* Contact institution. *Financial support:* Research assistantships with partial tuition reimbursements, teaching assistantships with partial tuition reimbursements, career-related internships or fieldwork, Federal Work-Study, scholarships/grants, tuition waivers, and unspecified assistantships available. Support available to part-time students. Financial award applicants required to submit FAFSA. *Unit head:* Charles Coleman, Coordinator, 203-932-7375. *Application contact:* Eloise Gormley, Director of Graduate Admissions, 203-932-7449, Fax: 203-932-7137, E-mail: gradinfo@newhaven.edu.

University of New Haven, Graduate School, College of Business, Program in Public Administration, West Haven, CT 06516-1916. Offers health care management (MPA); personnel and labor relations (MPA); MBA/MPA. Part-time and evening/weekend programs available. *Faculty:* 3 full-time (1 woman), 6 part-time/adjunct (2 women). *Students:* 5 full-time (1 woman), 19 part-time (12 women); includes 6 minority (4 African Americans, 1 Asian American or Pacific Islander, 1 Hispanic American), 2 international. Average age 35. 24 applicants, 96% accepted, 9 enrolled. In 2008, 18 master's awarded. *Degree requirements:* For master's, thesis or alternative. *Entrance requirements:* Additional exam requirements/recommendations for international students: Required—TOEFL (minimum score 520 paper-based; 190 computer-based; 70 iBT); Recommended—IELTS (minimum score 5.5). *Application deadline:* For fall admission, 5/31 for international students; for winter admission, 10/15 for international students; for spring admission, 1/15 for international students. Applications are processed on a rolling basis. Application fee: $50. *Expenses:* Contact institution. *Financial support:* Research assistantships with partial tuition reimbursements, teaching assistantships with partial tuition reimbursements, career-related internships or fieldwork, Federal Work-Study, scholarships/grants, tuition waivers, and unspecified assistantships available. Support available to part-time students. Financial award application deadline: 5/1; financial award applicants required to submit FAFSA. *Unit head:* Charles Coleman, Chairman, 203-932-7375. *Application contact:* Eloise Gormley, Director of Graduate Admissions, 203-932-7449, Fax: 203-932-7137, E-mail: gradinfo@newhaven.edu.

University of North Texas, Robert B. Toulouse School of Graduate Studies, College of Arts and Sciences, Department of Economics, Denton, TX 76203. Offers economic research (MS); economics (MA, MS); labor and industrial relations (MS). Part-time programs available. *Degree requirements:* For master's, comprehensive exam, thesis (for some programs). *Entrance requirements:* For master's, GMAT, GRE General Test, 3.0 GPA, 2 letters of recommendation, 500 word essay. Additional exam requirements/recommendations for international students: Required—proof of English language proficiency required for non-native English speakers; Recommended—TOEFL (minimum score 550 paper-based; 213 computer-based). *Faculty research:* Resource economics, international trade and development, immigration, telecommunications, micro enterprise development.

University of Rhode Island, Graduate School, Labor Research Center, Kingston, RI 02881. Offers labor relations and human resources (MS). Part-time and evening/weekend programs available. *Students:* Average age 32. *Degree requirements:* For master's, core exams. *Entrance requirements:* For master's, GMAT, GRE, or MAT. Application fee: $35. *Expenses:* Tuition, state resident: full-time $8024; part-time $446 per credit. Tuition, nonresident: full-time $21,046; part-time $1169 per credit. Required fees: $1056; $26 per credit. $30 per semester. One-time fee: $95 part-time. *Financial support:* Fellowships, research assistantships, teaching assistantships, career-related internships or fieldwork, Federal Work-Study, institutionally sponsored loans, and tuition waivers (full and partial) available. Support available to part-time students. *Unit head:* Dr. Richard Scholl, Director, 401-874-2239, E-mail: rscholl@uri.edu. *Application contact:* Harold D. Bibb, Associate Dean of the Graduate School, 401-874-2262, Fax: 401-874-5491.

University of Saskatchewan, College of Graduate Studies and Research, Edwards School of Business, Department of Industrial Relations and Organizational Behavior, Saskatoon, SK S7N 5A2, Canada. Offers M Sc. Part-time programs available. *Degree requirements:* For master's, thesis. *Entrance requirements:* For master's, GMAT. Additional exam requirements/recommendations for international students: Required—TOEFL.

University of Toronto, School of Graduate Studies, Social Sciences Division, Centre for Industrial Relations and Human Resources, Toronto, ON M5S 1A1, Canada. Offers MHRIR, PhD. Part-time programs available. *Degree requirements:* For doctorate, thesis/dissertation. *Entrance requirements:* For master's, GRE or GMAT (for applicants who completed degree outside of Canada), minimum B+ in final 2 years of bachelor's degree completion, 2 letters of reference, resumé; for doctorate, GRE or GMAT, MIR degree or equivalent, minimum B+ average, 3 letters of reference, resumé. Additional exam requirements/recommendations for international students: Required—TOEFL (minimum score 600 paper-based; 250 computer-based), TWE (minimum score 5), Michigan English Language Assessment Battery, IELTS, or COPE. *Expenses:* Contact institution.

University of Wisconsin–Milwaukee, Graduate School, College of Letters and Sciences, Interdepartmental Program in Human Resources and Labor Relations, Milwaukee, WI 53201-0413. Offers human resources and labor relations (MHRLR); international human resources and labor relations (Certificate); mediation and negotiation (Certificate). Part-time programs available. *Faculty:* 17 full-time (7 women). *Students:* 14 full-time (10 women), 44 part-time (34 women); includes 12 minority (5 African Americans, 2 Asian Americans or Pacific Islanders, 5 Hispanic Americans), 2 international. Average age 32. 44 applicants, 41% accepted, 11 enrolled. In 2008, 20 master's awarded. *Entrance requirements:* For master's, GMAT or GRE General Test. Additional exam requirements/recommendations for international students: Required—TOEFL (minimum score 550 paper-based; 79 iBT), IELTS (minimum score 6.5). *Application deadline:* For fall admission, 1/1 priority date for domestic students; for spring admission, 9/1 for domestic students. Applications are processed on a rolling basis. Application fee: $45 ($75 for international students). *Expenses:* Tuition, area resident: Full-time $7320; part-time $165 per credit. Tuition, state resident: full-time $7320; part-time $165 per credit. Tuition, nonresident: full-time $17,840; part-time $714 per credit. Tuition and fees vary according to campus/location, program and reciprocity agreements. *Financial support:* Career-related internships or fieldwork available. Support available to part-time students. Financial award application deadline: 4/15. *Unit head:* Susan M. Donohue-Davies, Representative, 414-299-4009, Fax: 414-229-5915, E-mail: suedono@uwm.edu. *Application contact:* General Information Contact, 414-229-4982, Fax: 414-229-6967, E-mail: gradschool@uwm.edu.

Wayne State University, College of Liberal Arts and Sciences, Interdisciplinary Program in Industrial Relations, Detroit, MI 48202. Offers MAIR. Part-time and evening/weekend programs available. *Degree requirements:* For master's, thesis optional. *Entrance requirements:* For master's, GMAT, GRE General Test. Additional exam requirements/recommendations for international students: Required—TOEFL (minimum score 550 paper-based; 213 computer-based); Recommended—TWE (minimum score 6). Electronic applications accepted. *Faculty research:* Two-tier wage system, affirmative action practices in higher education; employment relations in China.

West Virginia University, College of Business and Economics, Program in Industrial Relations, Morgantown, WV 26506. Offers MSIR. *Accreditation:* AACSB. *Entrance requirements:* For master's, GRE or GMAT, GPA 3.0 or better. Additional exam requirements/recommendations for international students: Required—TOEFL. Electronic applications accepted. *Faculty research:* Labor relations, mediation, leadership, benefits.

York University, Faculty of Graduate Studies, Schulich School of Business, Toronto, ON M3J 1P3, Canada. Offers accounting (PhD); business (EMBA, MBA); finance (PhD); international business (IMBA); marketing (PhD); operations management and information systems (PhD); organizational behaviour and industrial relations (PhD); policy/strategic management (PhD); public administration (MPA); MBA/LL B; MBA/MFA. Part-time and evening/weekend programs available. *Degree requirements:* For doctorate, comprehensive exam, thesis/dissertation. *Entrance requirements:* For master's, GMAT, minimum GPA of 3.0; for doctorate, GMAT, minimum GPA of 3.3. Electronic applications accepted.

Philanthropic Studies

Indiana University–Purdue University Indianapolis, School of Liberal Arts, Center on Philanthropy, Indianapolis, IN 46202. Offers philanthropic studies (MA, PhD); MA/MA; MPA/MA; MSN/MA. Part-time and evening/weekend programs available. Postbaccalaureate distance learning degree programs offered (minimal on-campus study). *Degree requirements:* For master's, thesis optional. *Entrance requirements:* For master's, GRE General Test or equivalent, minimum undergraduate GPA of 3.0.

Indiana University–Purdue University Indianapolis, School of Liberal Arts, Department of Philanthropic Studies, Indianapolis, IN 46202. Offers MA, XMA, PhD. *Degree requirements:* For master's, thesis optional; for doctorate, thesis/dissertation. *Entrance requirements:* For master's, GRE General Test (minimum score: 500 quantitative, 500 verbal, 4.5 analytical writing), 3.0 undergraduate GPA; for doctorate, GRE General Test (minimum score: 500 quantitative, 500 verbal, 4.5 analytical writing), 3.0 GPA, master's.

Saint Mary's University of Minnesota, Schools of Graduate and Professional Programs, Graduate School of Business and Technology, Philanthropy and Development Program, Winona, MN 55987-1399. Offers MA.

Public Administration

Adelphi University, University College, Graduate Certificate in Emergency Management Program, Garden City, NY 11530-0701. Offers Certificate. Part-time and evening/weekend programs available. *Students:* 3 full-time (2 women), 13 part-time (5 women); includes 3 minority (1 African American, 2 Asian Americans or Pacific Islanders). Average age 34. 11 applicants, 55% accepted, 6 enrolled. In 2008, 6 Certificates awarded. *Application deadline:* For fall admission, 5/1 for international students; for spring admission, 12/1 for international students. Applications are processed on a rolling basis. Application fee: $50. Electronic applications accepted. *Expenses:* Tuition: Full-time $25,700; part-time $775 per credit hour. Required fees: $500. Tuition and fees vary according to course load, degree level, campus/location, program and student level. *Financial support:* Research assistantships with partial tuition reimbursements, Federal Work-Study and institutionally sponsored loans available. *Faculty research:* Emergency nursing, disaster management, disaster preparedness. *Unit head:* Shawn O'Riley, Executive Director, 516-877-3412, E-mail: ucinfo@adelphi.edu. *Application contact:* Christine Murphy, Director of Admissions, 516-877-3050, Fax: 516-877-3039, E-mail: graduateadmissions@adelphi.edu.

Albany State University, College of Arts and Humanities, Department of History, Political Science and Public Administration, Albany, GA 31705-2717. Offers community and economic development (MPA); criminal justice (MPA); fiscal management (MPA); general management (MPA); health administration and policy (MPA); human resources management (MPA); public policy (MPA); water resource management and policy (MPA). *Accreditation:* NASPAA. Part-time programs available. *Faculty:* 5 full-time (2 women). *Students:* 10 full-time (8 women), 42 part-time (29 women); includes 50 minority (49 African Americans, 1 Asian American or Pacific Islander). Average age 35. In 2008, 12 master's awarded. *Degree requirements:* For master's, comprehensive exam, thesis. *Entrance requirements:* For master's, GRE General Test, minimum GPA of 2.5. *Application deadline:* For fall admission, 4/15 for domestic and international students; for spring admission, 11/15 for domestic and international students. Applications are processed on a rolling basis. Application fee: $20. Electronic applications accepted. *Expenses:* Tuition, area resident: Full-time $4296; part-time $154 per semester hour. Tuition, state resident: full-time $4296; part-time $154 per semester hour. Tuition, nonresident: full-time $15,338; part-time $614 per semester hour. Required fees: $306 per semester. Tuition and fees vary according to course load. *Financial support:* Tuition waivers available. Financial award application deadline: 4/1; financial award applicants required to submit FAFSA. *Faculty research:* Transportation, urban affairs, political economy. *Unit head:* Dr. Rita Henry-Brown, Chair, 229-430-4870, Fax: 229-430-7895, E-mail: rita.brown@asurams.edu. *Application contact:* Diane P. Frink, Graduate Admission Counselor, 229-430-5118, Fax: 229-430-6398, E-mail: diane.frink@asurams.edu.

American International College, School of Business Administration, Program in Public Administration, Springfield, MA 01109-3189. Offers MPA. Part-time and evening/weekend programs available. *Degree requirements:* For master's, comprehensive exam (for some programs), thesis (for some programs), oral exam, practicum. *Entrance requirements:* For master's, BS or BA. Additional exam requirements/recommendations for international students: Required—TOEFL. Electronic applications accepted.

American Public University System, AMU/APU Graduate Programs, Charles Town, WV 25414. Offers air warfare (MA Military Studies); American Revolution (MA Military Studies); business administration (MBA); Civil War (MA Military Studies); criminal justice (MA); defense management (MA Military Studies); emergency and disaster management (MA); environmental policy and management (MS); fire science management (MA); global engagement (MA); history (MA); homeland security (MA); humanities (MA); intelligence (MA Military Studies, MA Strategic Intelligence); international peace and conflict resolution (MA); international relations and conflict resolution (MA); joint warfare (MA Military Studies); land warfare international perspective (MA Military Studies); management (MA); military history (MA); military leadership (MA Military Studies); national security studies (MA); naval warfare international (MA Military Studies); naval warfare US (MA Military Studies); political science (MA); public administration (MA); public health (MA); security management (MA); space studies (MS); special ops/LIC (MA Military Studies); sports management (MA); transportation and logistics management (MA); transportation management (MA); unconventional warfare (MA Military Studies); World War II (MA Military Studies). Programs offered via distance learning only. Part-time and evening/weekend programs available. Postbaccalaureate distance learning degree programs offered (no on-campus study). *Degree requirements:* For master's, comprehensive exam. *Entrance requirements:* For master's, bachelor's degree or equivalent, minimum GPA of 2.7 in last 60 hours of course work. Electronic applications accepted. *Faculty research:* Military history, criminal justice, management performance, national security.

American University, School of Public Affairs, Department of Public Administration, Program in Public Administration, Washington, DC 20016-8070. Offers MPA, PhD, Certificate. *Accreditation:* NASPAA (one or more programs are accredited). Part-time and evening/weekend programs available. *Students:* 77 full-time (48 women), 130 part-time (77 women); includes 48 minority (27 African Americans, 3 American Indian/Alaska Native, 12 Asian Americans or Pacific Islanders, 6 Hispanic Americans), 18 international. Average age 36. In 2008, 54 master's, 3 doctorates awarded. *Degree requirements:* For master's, comprehensive exam; for doctorate, comprehensive exam, thesis/dissertation. *Entrance requirements:* For master's, GRE, statement of purpose; 2 recommendations; for doctorate, GRE, statement of purpose; 3 recommendations; for Certificate, bachelor's degree. Additional exam requirements/recommendations for international students: Required—TOEFL. *Application deadline:* For fall admission, 2/1 for domestic students; for spring admission, 11/1 for domestic students. Application fee: $55. *Expenses:* Tuition: Full-time $21,204; part-time $1178 per credit hour. Required fees: $380. Part-time tuition and fees vary according to course load and program. *Financial support:* Fellowships, teaching assistantships, career-related internships or fieldwork, Federal Work-Study, and institutionally sponsored loans available. Financial award application deadline: 2/1.

The American University in Cairo, Graduate Studies and Research, School of Humanities and Social Sciences, Program in Public Policy and Administration, Cairo, Egypt. Offers MA, Diploma.

American University of Beirut, Graduate Programs, Faculty of Arts and Sciences, Beirut, Lebanon. Offers anthropology (MA); Arabic language and literature (MA); archaeology (MA); biology (MS); chemistry (MS); computer science (MS); economics (MA); education (MA); English language (MA); English literature (MA); environmental policy planning (MSES); financial economics (MAFE); geology (MS); history (MA); mathematics (MA, MS); Middle Eastern studies (MA); philosophy (MA); physics (MS); political studies (MA); psychology (MA); public administration (MA); sociology (MA); statistics (MA, MS). Part-time programs available. *Degree requirements:* For master's, one foreign language, comprehensive exam, thesis (for some programs). *Entrance requirements:* For master's, GRE, letter of recommendation. Additional exam requirements/recommendations for international students: Required—TOEFL (minimum score 600 paper-based; 250 computer-based; 100 iBT), IELTS (minimum score 7.5). *Faculty research:* String theory and supergravity; computer graphics; algebra and number theory; popular Arabic literature; marine and freshwater biology; integrating science, math and technology.

The American University of Paris, Graduate Programs, Paris, France. Offers finance (MSF); global communications (MAGC); international affairs, conflict resolution and civil society development (MA); Middle Eastern and Islamic studies (MA); public administration (MPA). *Degree requirements:* For master's, thesis. *Entrance requirements:* For master's, minimum undergraduate GPA of 3.0.

American University of Sharjah, Graduate Programs, Sharjah, United Arab Emirates. Offers business (EMBA, MBA); chemical engineering (MS Ch E); civil engineering (MSCE); computer engineering (MS); electrical engineering (MSEE); mechanical engineering (MSME); mechatronics engineering (MS); public administration (MPA); teaching English to speakers of other languages (MA); translation and interpreting (MA); urban planning (MUP). Part-time and evening/weekend programs available. *Faculty:* 35 full-time (7 women). *Students:* 66 full-time (36 women), 188 part-time (83 women). Average age 28. 302 applicants, 65% accepted, 131 enrolled. In 2008, 74 master's awarded. *Entrance requirements:* For master's, GMAT (MBA). Additional exam requirements/recommendations for international students: Required—TOEFL (minimum score 550 paper-based; 213 computer-based; 80 iBT), TWE (minimum score 5). *Application deadline:* For fall admission, 7/30 priority date for domestic students, 7/15 priority date for international students; for spring admission, 12/31 priority date for domestic students, 12/16 for international students. Applications are processed on a rolling basis. Application fee: $300. Electronic applications accepted. Tuition and fees charges are reported in United Arab Emirates dirhams. *Expenses:* Tuition: Full-time 58,500 United Arab Emirates dirhams; part-time 3250 United Arab Emirates dirhams per credit hour. One-time fee: 300 United Arab Emirates dirhams. *Faculty research:* Chemical engineering, civil engineering, computer engineering, electrical engineering, linguistics, translation. *Unit head:* Ghada S Sami, Admissions Manager, 971-65151006 Ext. 1006, Fax: 971-65151020, E-mail: graduateadmission@aus.edu. *Application contact:* Ghada S Sami, Admissions Manager, 971-65151006 Ext. 1006, Fax: 971-65151020, E-mail: graduateadmission@aus.edu.

Andrew Jackson University, Jeffrey D. Rubenstein College of Criminal Justice, Program in Public Administration, Birmingham, AL 35244. Offers MPA. Part-time and evening/weekend programs available. Postbaccalaureate distance learning degree programs offered (no on-campus study). *Entrance requirements:* For master's, course work in calculus, statistics. Additional exam requirements/recommendations for international students: Required—TOEFL (minimum score 550 paper-based; 213 computer-based). Electronic applications accepted.

Angelo State University, College of Graduate Studies, College of Liberal and Fine Arts, Department of Government, San Angelo, TX 76909. Offers public administration (MPA). Part-time and evening/weekend programs available. *Faculty:* 3 full-time (0 women). *Students:* 5 full-time (2 women), 2 part-time (1 woman); includes 4 minority (1 African American, 3 Hispanic Americans). Average age 27. 2 applicants, 100% accepted, 2 enrolled. In 2008, 3 master's awarded. *Degree requirements:* For master's, comprehensive exam. *Entrance requirements:* For master's, GRE General Test. Additional exam requirements/recommendations for international students: Required—TOEFL or IELTS. *Application deadline:* For fall admission, 7/15 priority date for domestic students, 6/10 for international students; for spring admission, 12/1 priority date for domestic students, 11/1 for international students. Applications are processed on a rolling basis. Application fee: $40 ($50 for international students). Electronic applications accepted. *Financial support:* In 2008–09, 7 students received support. Career-related internships or fieldwork, Federal Work-Study, and scholarships/grants available. Support available to part-time students. Financial award application deadline: 3/1; financial award applicants required to submit FAFSA. *Unit head:* Dr. Edward C. Olson, Department Head, 325-942-2262 Ext. 275, E-mail: ed.olson@angelo.edu. *Application contact:* Dr. Jack Barbour, Graduate Advisor, 325-942-2262 Ext. 282, E-mail: jack.barbour@angelo.edu.

Anna Maria College, Graduate Division, Program in Public Administration, Paxton, MA 01612. Offers MPA. *Expenses:* Tuition: Part-time $1400 per course. *Unit head:* Dennis Braun, Director, Graduate Studies and Continuing Education, 508-849-3293, Fax: 508-819-3362, E-mail: dbraun@annamaria.edu. *Application contact:* Dennis Braun, Director, Graduate Studies and Continuing Education, 508-849-3293, Fax: 508-819-3362, E-mail: dbraun@annamaria.edu.

Appalachian State University, Cratis D. Williams Graduate School, Department of Government and Justice Studies, Boone, NC 28608. Offers criminal justice (MS); political science (MA), including American government, international relations; public administration (MPA), including public management, town, city and county management. Part-time programs available. Postbaccalaureate distance learning degree programs offered (no on-campus study). *Faculty:* 27 full-time (5 women), 12 part-time/adjunct (1 woman). *Students:* 70 full-time (29 women), 51 part-time (14 women); includes 9 minority (7 African Americans, 1 American Indian/Alaska Native, 1 Asian American or Pacific Islander), 4 international. 60 applicants, 92% accepted, 32 enrolled. In 2008, 58 master's awarded. *Degree requirements:* For master's, variable foreign language requirement, comprehensive exam, thesis optional. *Entrance requirements:* For master's, GRE General Test, 3 letters of recommendation. Additional exam requirements/recommendations for international students: Required—TOEFL (minimum score 570 paper-based; 230 computer-based; 79 iBT), IELTS (minimum score 6.5). *Application deadline:* For fall admission, 7/1 for domestic students, 2/1 for international students; for spring admission, 11/1 for domestic students, 7/1 for international students. Applications are processed on a rolling basis. Application fee: $50. Electronic applications accepted. *Expenses:* Tuition, area resident: Full-time $2600; part-time $700 per course. Tuition, state resident: full-time $2600; part-time $700 per course. Tuition, nonresident: full-time $5000; part-time $3300 per course. Required fees: $2150; $330 per course. Tuition and fees vary according to campus/location. *Financial support:* In 2008–09, 35 research assistantships (averaging $7,500 per year) were awarded; fellowships, teaching assistantships, career-related internships or fieldwork, Federal Work-Study, scholarships/grants, and unspecified assistantships also available. Financial award application deadline: 4/1; financial award applicants required to submit FAFSA. *Faculty research:* Campaign finance, emerging democracies, bureaucratic politics, judicial behavior, administration of justice. Total annual research expenditures: $8,500. *Unit head:* Dr. Brian Ellison, Chairperson, 828-262-3085, E-mail: ellisonba@appstate.edu. *Application contact:* Sandy Krause, Director of Admissions and Recruiting, 828-262-2130, Fax: 828-262-2709, E-mail: krausesl@appstate.edu.

Argosy University, Orange County, College of Business, Santa Ana, CA 92704. Offers accounting (DBA, Adv C); customized professional concentration (MBA, DBA); finance (MBA, Certificate); healthcare administration (MBA); information systems (DBA, Adv C); information systems management (MBA); international business (MBA, DBA, Adv C, Certificate); management (MBA, MSM, DBA, Adv C); marketing (MBA, DBA, Adv C, Certificate); public administration (MBA, Certificate).

Argosy University, Tampa, College of Business, Tampa, FL 33614. Offers accounting (DBA); customized professional concentration (MBA, DBA); finance (MBA); healthcare administration (MBA); information systems (DBA); information systems management (MBA); international business (MBA, DBA); management (MBA, MSM, DBA); marketing (MBA, DBA); public administration (MBA).

Arkansas State University, Graduate School, College of Humanities and Social Sciences, Department of Political Science, Jonesboro, State University, AR 72467. Offers political science (MA); political science education (SCCT); public administration (MPA). *Accreditation:* NASPAA (one or more programs are accredited). Part-time programs available. *Faculty:* 8 full-time (3 women), 1 (woman) part-time/adjunct. *Students:* 18 full-time (12 women), 20 part-time (10 women); includes 12 minority (all African Americans), 2 international. Average age 31. 24 applicants, 71% accepted, 7 enrolled. In 2008, 14 master's awarded. *Degree requirements:* For master's, comprehensive exam, thesis or alternative; for SCCT, comprehensive exam. *Entrance requirements:* For master's, GRE General Test or MAT, GMAT, appropriate bachelor's degree, letters of reference, official transcript, letters of recommendation, statement of purpose; for SCCT, GRE General Test or MAT, GMAT, interview, master's degree, official transcript, letters of recommendation. Additional exam requirements/recommendations for international students: Required—TOEFL (minimum score 550 paper-based; 213 computer-based; 79 iBT), IELTS (minimum score 6). *Application deadline:* For fall admission, 7/15 for domestic students, 7/1 for international students; for spring admission, 12/1 for domestic students, 11/13 for international students. Applications are processed on a rolling basis. Application fee: $30 ($40 for international students). Electronic applications accepted. *Expenses:* Tuition, state resident:

Public Administration

Arkansas State University (continued)
full-time $3744; part-time $208 per credit hour. Tuition, nonresident: full-time $9540; part-time $530 per credit hour. International tuition: $7938 full-time. Required fees: $896; $47 per credit hour. $25 per term. One-time fee: $50. Tuition and fees vary according to course load and program. *Financial support:* In 2008–09, 12 students received support; teaching assistantships, career-related internships or fieldwork, scholarships/grants, and unspecified assistantships available. Financial award application deadline: 7/1; financial award applicants required to submit FAFSA. *Faculty research:* Peace Corps, political communication, political psychology, public opinion, elections. *Unit head:* Dr. Richard Wang, Chair, 870-972-3048, Fax: 870-972-2720, E-mail: rwang@astate.edu. *Application contact:* Dr. Andrew Sustich, Dean of the Graduate School, 870-972-3029, Fax: 870-972-3857, E-mail: sustich@astate.edu.

Auburn University, Graduate School, College of Liberal Arts, Department of Political Science, Program in Public Administration, Auburn University, AL 36849. Offers MPA, PhD, MPA/MCP. *Accreditation:* NASPAA (one or more programs are accredited). Part-time programs available. *Faculty:* 21 full-time (5 women), 5 part-time/adjunct (1 woman). *Students:* 27 full-time (14 women), 43 part-time (22 women); includes 14 minority (12 African Americans, 1 Asian American or Pacific Islander, 1 Hispanic American), 6 international. Average age 35. 58 applicants, 53% accepted, 14 enrolled. In 2008, 20 master's, 6 doctorates awarded. *Degree requirements:* For master's, internship or research project; for doctorate, thesis/dissertation. *Entrance requirements:* For master's, GRE General Test, sample of written work; for doctorate, GRE General Test. *Application deadline:* For fall admission, 7/7 for domestic students; for spring admission, 11/24 for domestic students. Applications are processed on a rolling basis. Application fee: $25 ($50 for international students). Electronic applications accepted. *Expenses:* Tuition, area resident: Full-time $5880; part-time $243 per credit hour. Tuition, state resident: full-time $5880; part-time $243 per credit hour. Tuition, nonresident: full-time $17,640; part-time $729 per credit hour. International tuition: $17,846 full-time. Required fees: $620. Tuition and fees vary according to program and reciprocity agreements. *Financial support:* Fellowships, research assistantships, teaching assistantships, career-related internships or fieldwork and Federal Work-Study available. Support available to part-time students. Financial award application deadline: 3/15. *Faculty research:* Privatization studies, policy evolution, water resources, election administration. *Unit head:* Dr. Caleb Clark, Head, 334-844-5371. *Application contact:* Dr. George Flowers, Dean of the Graduate School, 334-844-2125.

Announcement: A unique 2-track PhD in public administration and public policy. Common core; electives; policy track: (3 of 5) comparative, American, international, law and policy, theory and policy; and/or administration track: organization theory, budgeting, human resource management. Graduates successfully placed in academic and public sector positions. Master's-level degree required. Web site: http://www.auburn.edu/academic/liberal_arts/poli_sci.

Auburn University Montgomery, School of Sciences, Department of Public Administration and Political Science, Montgomery, AL 36124-4023. Offers MPA, MPS, PhD. *Accreditation:* NASPAA (one or more programs are accredited). Part-time and evening/weekend programs available. *Faculty:* 6 full-time (1 woman), 5 part-time/adjunct (1 woman). *Students:* 19 full-time (11 women), 103 part-time (64 women); includes 48 minority (46 African Americans, 2 Asian Americans or Pacific Islanders), 4 international. Average age 30. In 2008, 25 master's awarded. *Degree requirements:* For master's, comprehensive exam; for doctorate, thesis/dissertation. *Entrance requirements:* For master's, GRE General Test or MAT; for doctorate, GRE General Test. *Application deadline:* Applications are processed on a rolling basis. Application fee: $25. Electronic applications accepted. *Expenses:* Tuition, state resident: full-time $5088; part-time $212 per credit. Tuition, nonresident: full-time $15,264; part-time $636 per credit. Required fees: $234. *Financial support:* In 2008–09, 1 research assistantship was awarded; career-related internships or fieldwork and scholarships/grants also available. Support available to part-time students. Financial award application deadline: 3/1; financial award applicants required to submit FAFSA. *Unit head:* Dr. Thomas Vocino, Head, 334-244-3696, Fax: 334-244-3826, E-mail: vocino@mail.aum.edu. *Application contact:* Dr. Glen Ray, Acting Graduate Coordinator, 334-244-3590, Fax: 334-244-3826, E-mail: gray@mail.aum.edu.

Ball State University, Graduate School, College of Sciences and Humanities, Department of Political Science, Program in Public Administration, Muncie, IN 47306-1099. Offers MPA. *Entrance requirements:* For master's, GRE General Test. *Faculty research:* Employment training programs, personnel and labor relations, planning.

Barry University, School of Adult and Continuing Education, Program in Public Administration, Miami Shores, FL 33161-6695. Offers MPA. Part-time and evening/weekend programs available. *Entrance requirements:* For master's, GMAT, GRE or MAT, recommendations. Electronic applications accepted.

Baylor University, Graduate School, College of Arts and Sciences, Department of Political Science, Waco, TX 76798. Offers international studies (MA); political science (MA, PhD); public policy and administration (MPPA); JD/MPPA. *Students:* 24 full-time (7 women), 2 part-time (1 woman), 3 international. In 2008, 9 master's awarded. *Entrance requirements:* For master's, GRE General Test. *Application deadline:* Applications are processed on a rolling basis. Application fee: $25. *Financial support:* Research assistantships, career-related internships or fieldwork, Federal Work-Study, and institutionally sponsored loans available. Financial award application deadline: 3/1. *Unit head:* Dr. David Corey, Graduate Program Director, 254-710-3161, Fax: 254-710-3122, E-mail: david_d_corey@baylor.edu. *Application contact:* Jenice Langston, Administrative Assistant, 254-710-3161, Fax: 254-710-3870, E-mail: jenice_langston@baylor.edu.

Belhaven College, School of Business, Jackson, MS 39202-1789. Offers business administration (MBA); business management (MSM); public administration (MPA). MBA program also offered in Houston, TX; Memphis, TN; and Orlando, FL. Evening/weekend programs available. *Faculty:* 13 full-time (3 women), 12 part-time/adjunct (3 women). *Students:* 231 full-time (155 women), 6 part-time (1 woman); includes 157 minority (135 African Americans, 21 American Indian/Alaska Native, 1 Hispanic American). Average age 34. 222 applicants, 70% accepted, 111 enrolled. In 2008, 105 master's awarded. *Degree requirements:* For master's, comprehensive exam (for some programs), thesis (for some programs). *Entrance requirements:* For master's, GMAT, GRE General Test or MAT, minimum GPA of 2.8. *Application deadline:* Applications are processed on a rolling basis. Application fee: $25. Electronic applications accepted. *Financial support:* In 2008–09, 2 students received support, including 2 research assistantships. Financial award applicants required to submit FAFSA. *Unit head:* Dr. Ralph Mason, Dean, School of Business, 601-968-8949, Fax: 601-968-8951, E-mail: cmason@belhaven.edu. *Application contact:* Dr. Audrey Kelleher, Vice President for Adult and Graduate Marketing and Development, 407-804-1424, Fax: 407-620-5210, E-mail: akelleher@belhaven.edu.

Bellevue University, Graduate School, Bellevue, NE 68005-3098. Offers acquisition and contract management (MS); business administration (MBA); clinical counseling (MS); computer information systems (MS); healthcare administration (MA, MHA, MS), including healthcare administration (MHA), human services (MA, MS); human capital management (MS, PhD); instructional design and development (MS); leadership (MA); management (MA); management information systems (MS); organizational performance (MS); public administration (MPA); public health (MPH); security management (MS). Part-time and evening/weekend programs available. Postbaccalaureate distance learning degree programs offered (no on-campus study). *Degree requirements:* For master's, thesis or project. *Entrance requirements:* For master's, minimum GPA of 2.5 in last 60 hours. Additional exam requirements/recommendations for international students: Required—TOEFL (minimum score 538 paper-based; 200 computer-based).

Bernard M. Baruch College of the City University of New York, School of Public Affairs, Program in Public Administration, New York, NY 10010-5585. Offers MPA, MS/MPA. *Accreditation:* NASPAA. Part-time and evening/weekend programs available. *Degree requirements:* For master's, thesis, capstone. *Entrance requirements:* For master's, GRE General Test. Additional exam requirements/recommendations for international students: Required—TOEFL (minimum score 650 paper-based; 247 computer-based). Electronic applications accepted. *Expenses:* Contact institution. *Faculty research:* Child health, nonprofit administration, health economics, welfare reform, urban population distribution, transnationalism, urban service delivery, community health improvement.

Birmingham-Southern College, Program in Public and Private Management, Birmingham, AL 35254. Offers MPPM. *Accreditation:* AACSB. Part-time and evening/weekend programs available. *Degree requirements:* For master's, thesis optional. *Entrance requirements:* For master's, GMAT, GRE, or MAT.

Boise State University, Graduate College, College of Social Sciences and Public Affairs, Department of Public Policy and Administration, Boise, ID 83725-0399. Offers environmental and natural resources policy and administration (MPA); general public administration (MPA); state and local government policy and administration (MPA). *Accreditation:* NASPAA. Part-time programs available. *Degree requirements:* For master's, comprehensive exam, directed research project, internship. *Entrance requirements:* For master's, GRE General Test, minimum GPA of 3.0. Additional exam requirements/recommendations for international students: Required—TOEFL. Electronic applications accepted.

Boston University, School of Management, Master of Business Administration Program, Boston, MA 02215. Offers advanced accounting (Certificate); general management (MBA); healthcare management (MBA); public and nonprofit management (MBA); JD/MBA; MBA/MA; MBA/MPH; MBA/MS; MBA/MSIS; MS/MBA. Part-time and evening/weekend programs available. *Entrance requirements:* For master's, GMAT. Electronic applications accepted.

Bowie State University, Graduate Programs, Program in Public Administration, Bowie, MD 20715-9465. Offers MPA. Part-time and evening/weekend programs available. *Degree requirements:* For master's, comprehensive exam. *Entrance requirements:* For master's, undergraduate GPA 2.5. Electronic applications accepted.

Bowling Green State University, Graduate College, College of Arts and Sciences, Department of Political Science, Program in Public Administration, Bowling Green, OH 43403. Offers MPA. *Degree requirements:* For master's, comprehensive exam or thesis, experiential paper for all non-thesis students. *Entrance requirements:* For master's, GRE General Test. Additional exam requirements/recommendations for international students: Required—TOEFL. Electronic applications accepted. *Faculty research:* Public sector labor relations, administrative law, sexual harassment and violence in the public workplace.

Bridgewater State College, School of Graduate Studies, School of Arts and Sciences, Department of Political Science, Program in Public Administration, Bridgewater, MA 02325-0001. Offers MPA. *Entrance requirements:* For master's, GRE General Test.

Brigham Young University, Graduate Studies, Marriott School of Management, Executive Master of Public Administration Program, Provo, UT 84602. Offers EMPA, MPA, JD/MPA. *Accreditation:* NASPAA (one or more programs are accredited). Part-time and evening/weekend programs available. *Students:* 123 part-time (44 women); includes 12 minority (2 African Americans, 3 American Indian/Alaska Native, 4 Asian Americans or Pacific Islanders, 3 Hispanic Americans), 3 international. Average age 37. 74 applicants, 65% accepted, 47 enrolled. In 2008, 41 master's awarded. *Application deadline:* For fall admission, 5/1 for domestic students. Application fee: $50. Electronic applications accepted. *Expenses:* Contact institution. *Financial support:* Applicants required to submit FAFSA. *Unit head:* Dr. David W. Hart, Director, 801-422-7391, Fax: 801-422-0311, E-mail: mpa@byu.edu. *Application contact:* Catherine L. Cooper, Director of Student Services, 801-422-9173, Fax: 801-422-0311, E-mail: mpa@byu.edu.

Brigham Young University, Graduate Studies, Marriott School of Management, Master of Public Administration Program, Provo, UT 84602. Offers EMPA, MPA, JD/MPA. *Students:* 120 full-time (43 women); includes 10 minority (1 African American, 1 American Indian/Alaska Native, 3 Asian Americans or Pacific Islanders, 5 Hispanic Americans), 13 international. Average age 27. 128 applicants, 77% accepted, 69 enrolled. In 2008, 54 master's awarded. *Entrance requirements:* For master's, GRE, minimum GPA of 3.0. Additional exam requirements/recommendations for international students: Required—TOEFL (minimum score 580 paper-based; 85 iBT), IELTS (minimum score 7). *Application deadline:* For fall admission, 5/1 for domestic students. Application fee: $50. *Expenses:* Tuition: Full-time $5160; part-time $287 per credit hour. Tuition and fees vary according to program and student's religious affiliation. *Financial support:* In 2008–09, 105 students received support. Career-related internships or fieldwork and scholarships/grants available. Financial award application deadline: 4/15; financial award applicants required to submit FAFSA. *Faculty research:* Taxes, budgeting, nonprofit, ethics, decision modeling, work balance, organizational behavior. *Unit head:* Dr. David W. Hart, Director, 801-422-4221, Fax: 801-422-0311, E-mail: mpa@byu.edu. *Application contact:* Catherine Cooper, Director of Student Services.

Brock University, Faculty of Graduate Studies, Faculty of Social Sciences, Program in Political Science, St. Catharines, ON L2S 3A1, Canada. Offers Canadian politics (MA); international and comparative politics (MA); political philosophy (MA); public administration (MA). Part-time programs available. *Degree requirements:* For master's, thesis optional. *Entrance requirements:* For master's, honors degree. Additional exam requirements/recommendations for international students: Required—TOEFL (minimum score 550 paper-based; 213 computer-based; 80 iBT), IELTS (minimum score 6.5), TWE (minimum score 4). Electronic applications accepted. *Faculty research:* Public administration reform, economic and social justice, politics of societies, Canadian politics, international relations.

California Baptist University, Program in Public Administration, Riverside, CA 92504-3206. Offers MPA. Part-time programs available. *Faculty:* 3 full-time (1 woman). *Students:* 19 full-time (10 women), 21 part-time (11 women); includes 13 minority (7 African Americans, 6 Hispanic Americans), 3 international. 29 applicants, 62% accepted, 14 enrolled. In 2008, 4 master's awarded. *Entrance requirements:* Additional exam requirements/recommendations for international students: Required—TOEFL (minimum score 575 paper-based; 230 computer-based; 89 iBT). *Application deadline:* For fall admission, 8/1 priority date for domestic students, 7/1 priority date for international students; for spring admission, 12/1 priority date for domestic students, 10/15 priority date for international students. Applications are processed on a rolling basis. Application fee: $45. Electronic applications accepted. *Expenses:* Tuition: Full-time $8172; part-time $454 per credit hour. Required fees: $510. *Financial support:* Federal Work-Study and scholarships/grants available. Support available to part-time students. Financial award applicants required to submit FAFSA. *Unit head:* Dr. Patricia Kircher, Director, 951-343-4306, Fax: 951-343-4661, E-mail: pkircher@calbaptist.edu. *Application contact:* Gail Ronveaux, Dean of Graduate Enrollment, 951-343-5045, Fax: 951-343-5095, E-mail: graduateadmissions@calbaptist.edu.

California Lutheran University, Graduate Studies, Program in Public Policy and Administration, Thousand Oaks, CA 91360-2787. Offers MPPA. *Faculty:* 1 full-time (0 women), 6 part-time/adjunct (4 women). *Students:* 26 full-time (14 women), 39 part-time (24 women); includes 20 minority (3 African Americans, 2 Asian Americans or Pacific Islanders, 15 Hispanic Americans), 3 international. Average age 35. 20 applicants, 90% accepted. In 2008, 23 master's awarded. *Degree requirements:* For master's, comprehensive exam, thesis or project, internship. *Entrance requirements:* For master's, GMAT or GRE General Test, interview, minimum GPA of 3.0. *Application deadline:* Applications are processed on a rolling basis. Application fee: $50. *Expenses:* Contact institution. *Financial support:* In 2008–09, 32 students received support. *Unit head:* Dr. Herbert Gooch, Director, 805-493-3348. *Application contact:* 805-493-3127, Fax: 805-493-3542, E-mail: clugrad@clunet.edu.

California State Polytechnic University, Pomona, Academic Affairs, College of Letters, Arts, and Social Sciences, Program in Public Administration, Pomona, CA 91768-2557. Offers MPA. *Accreditation:* NASPAA. Part-time programs available. *Students:* 9 full-time (4 women), 46 part-time (29 women); includes 35 minority (10 African Americans, 6 Asian Americans or Pacific Islanders, 19 Hispanic Americans), 2 international. Average age 32. 47 applicants, 62% accepted, 14 enrolled. In 2008, 12 master's awarded. *Degree requirements:* For master's, thesis or alternative. *Entrance requirements:* For master's, GRE General Test. *Application deadline:* For fall admission, 5/1 priority date for domestic students; for winter admission, 10/15 priority date for domestic students; for spring admission, 1/20 priority date for domestic students. Applications are processed on a rolling basis. Application fee: $55. Electronic applications accepted. *Expenses:* Tuition, nonresident: full-time $7232; part-time $226 per credit. Required fees: $4272. One-time fee: $2694 part-time. Tuition and fees vary according to course load. *Unit head:* Dr. Sandra M. Emerson, Director, 909-869-3879, E-mail: smemerson@csupomona.edu. *Application contact:* Scott J. Duncan, Director, Admissions, 909-869-3258, Fax: 909-869-4529, E-mail: sjduncan@csupomona.edu.

California State University, Bakersfield, Division of Graduate Studies, School of Business and Public Administration, Program in Public Administration, Bakersfield, CA 93311-1022. Offers MPA. *Accreditation:* NASPAA. *Degree requirements:* For master's, thesis or alternative. *Entrance requirements:* For master's, GRE, minimum GPA of 2.75.

California State University, Chico, Graduate School, College of Behavioral and Social Sciences, Department of Political Science, Program in Public Administration, Chico, CA 95929-0722. Offers health administration (MPA); local government management (MPA); public administration (MPA). *Accreditation:* NASPAA. Part-time programs available. *Entrance requirements:* For master's, 2 letters of recommendation, statement of purpose. Additional exam requirements/recommendations for international students: Required—TOEFL (minimum score 550 paper-based; 213 computer-based; 80 iBT), IELTS (minimum score 6.5). Electronic applications accepted.

California State University, Dominguez Hills, College of Business Administration and Public Policy, Program in Public Administration, Carson, CA 90747-0001. Offers MPA. *Accreditation:* NASPAA. Part-time and evening/weekend programs available. Postbaccalaureate distance learning degree programs offered (no on-campus study). *Faculty:* 4 full-time (all women), 8 part-time/adjunct (4 women). *Students:* 60 full-time (42 women), 168 part-time (114 women); includes 140 minority (90 African Americans, 2 American Indian/Alaska Native, 20 Asian Americans or Pacific Islanders, 28 Hispanic Americans), 8 international. Average age 36. 100 applicants, 32% accepted, 14 enrolled. In 2008, 90 master's awarded. *Degree requirements:* For master's, thesis or alternative, capstone project. *Entrance requirements:* For master's, GRE, minimum GPA of 2.75. Additional exam requirements/recommendations for international students: Required—TOEFL (minimum score 550 paper-based; 213 computer-based; 79 iBT). *Application deadline:* For fall admission, 4/1 for domestic and international students; for spring admission, 11/1 for domestic students, 10/1 for international students. Application fee: $55. *Expenses:* Tuition, nonresident: part-time $339 per unit. Required fees: $1300 per semester. *Faculty research:* Applied public management. *Unit head:* Dr. Kaye Bragg, Interim Chair, 310-243-2356, E-mail: kbragg@csudh.edu. *Application contact:* Eileen Hall, Graduate Advisor, 310-243-3465, E-mail: ehall@csudh.edu.

California State University, East Bay, Academic Programs and Graduate Studies, College of Letters, Arts, and Social Sciences, Department of Public Affairs and Administration, Hayward, CA 94542-3000. Offers health care administration (MS); public administration (MPA). *Accreditation:* NASPAA. Part-time and evening/weekend programs available. *Degree requirements:* For master's, comprehensive exam or thesis. *Entrance requirements:* For master's, minimum GPA of 3.0. Additional exam requirements/recommendations for international students: Required—TOEFL (minimum score 550 paper-based; 213 computer-based). Electronic applications accepted.

California State University, Fresno, Division of Graduate Studies, College of Social Sciences, Department of Political Science, Program in Public Administration, Fresno, CA 93740-8027. Offers MPA. *Accreditation:* NASPAA. Part-time and evening/weekend programs available. *Degree requirements:* For master's, thesis or alternative. *Entrance requirements:* For master's, GRE General Test or GMAT, minimum GPA of 3.0. Additional exam requirements/recommendations for international students: Required—TOEFL. Electronic applications accepted.

California State University, Fullerton, Graduate Studies, College of Humanities and Social Sciences, Division of Politics, Administration, and Justice, Fullerton, CA 92834-9480. Offers political science (MA); public administration (MPA). *Accreditation:* NASPAA (one or more programs are accredited). Part-time programs available. *Students:* 44 full-time (22 women), 160 part-time (84 women); includes 103 minority (6 African Americans, 1 American Indian/Alaska Native, 42 Asian Americans or Pacific Islanders, 54 Hispanic Americans), 5 international. Average age 30. 138 applicants, 55% accepted, 41 enrolled. In 2008, 45 master's awarded. *Degree requirements:* For master's, comprehensive exam, project or thesis. *Entrance requirements:* For master's, minimum GPA of 2.5 in last 60 units of course work, 12 units of course work in social sciences. Application fee: $55. Tuition and fees vary according to degree level. *Financial support:* Teaching assistantships, career-related internships or fieldwork, Federal Work-Study, institutionally sponsored loans, and scholarships/grants available. Support available to part-time students. Financial award application deadline: 3/1. *Faculty research:* Emergency management plans. *Unit head:* Dr. Phil Gianos, Chair, 657-278-3521. *Application contact:* Admissions/Applications, 657-278-2300.

California State University, Long Beach, Graduate Studies, College of Health and Human Services, Graduate Center for Public Policy and Administration, Long Beach, CA 90840. Offers MPA. *Accreditation:* NASPAA. Part-time and evening/weekend programs available. *Faculty:* 7 full-time (2 women), 11 part-time/adjunct (4 women). *Students:* 77 full-time (51 women), 216 part-time (133 women); includes 185 minority (43 African Americans, 1 American Indian/Alaska Native, 50 Asian Americans or Pacific Islanders, 91 Hispanic Americans), 7 international. Average age 33. 199 applicants, 78% accepted, 121 enrolled. *Degree requirements:* For master's, comprehensive exam. *Entrance requirements:* For master's, minimum GPA of 2.75. *Application deadline:* For fall admission, 7/1 for domestic students. Applications are processed on a rolling basis. Application fee: $55. Electronic applications accepted. *Expenses:* Tuition, nonresident: full-time $11,160; part-time $372 per unit. Required fees: $4100; $1261 per semester. *Financial support:* Fellowships, career-related internships or fieldwork, Federal Work-Study, institutionally sponsored loans, and scholarships/grants available. Financial award application deadline: 3/2. *Faculty research:* Transportation access, air quality controls, coastal issues, intergovernmental relations. *Unit head:* Dr. David C Powell, Director, 562-985-4178, Fax: 562-985-4672, E-mail: dpowell@csulb.edu. *Application contact:* Dr. Frank Barber, Graduate Adviser, 562-985-5747, Fax: 562-985-4672.

California State University, Los Angeles, Graduate Studies, College of Natural and Social Sciences, Department of Political Science, Los Angeles, CA 90032-8530. Offers political science (MA); public administration (MS). Part-time and evening/weekend programs available. *Faculty:* 7 full-time (2 women), 1 part-time/adjunct (0 women). *Students:* 23 full-time (15 women), 104 part-time (62 women); includes 76 minority (10 African Americans, 17 Asian Americans or Pacific Islanders, 49 Hispanic Americans), 19 international. Average age 31. In 2008, 26 master's awarded. *Degree requirements:* For master's, comprehensive exam or thesis. *Entrance requirements:* Additional exam requirements/recommendations for international students: Required—TOEFL (minimum score 500 paper-based; 173 computer-based). *Application deadline:* For fall admission, 6/15 for domestic students, 5/1 for international students; for winter admission, 11/1 for domestic students, 9/1 for international students; for spring admission, 2/1 for domestic students, 10/1 for international students. Applications are processed on a rolling basis. Application fee: $55. Electronic applications accepted. *Expenses:* Tuition, nonresident: part-time $226 per credit. Required fees: $4019. *Financial support:* Career-related internships or fieldwork and Federal Work-Study available. Support available to part-time students. Financial award application deadline: 3/1. *Faculty research:* Government; public policy and law; international, political, and economic relations; comparative politics. *Unit head:* Dr. Scott Bowman, Chair, 323-343-2230, Fax: 323-343-6452, E-mail: sbowman@calstatela.edu. *Application contact:* Dr. Jose L. Galvan, Dean of Graduate Studies, 323-343-3820, Fax: 323-343-5653, E-mail: jgalvan@cslanet.calstatela.edu.

California State University, Northridge, Graduate Studies, The Tseng College of Extended Learning, Northridge, CA 91330. Offers knowledge management (MKM); public administration (MPA); taxation (MS). *Entrance requirements:* For master's, GRE if cumulative undergraduate GPA below 3.0. *Unit head:* Joyce Feucht-Haviar, Dean, 866-873-6439. *Application contact:* Joyce Feucht-Haviar, Dean, 866-873-6439.

California State University, Sacramento, Graduate Studies, College of Social Sciences and Interdisciplinary Studies, Program in Public Policy and Administration, Sacramento, CA 95819-6048. Offers MPPA. Part-time programs available. *Degree requirements:* For master's, thesis or alternative, writing proficiency exam. *Entrance requirements:* For master's, GRE General Test. Additional exam requirements/recommendations for international students: Required—TOEFL. Electronic applications accepted.

California State University, San Bernardino, Graduate Studies, College of Business and Public Administration, Program in Public Administration, San Bernardino, CA 92407-2397. Offers MPA. *Accreditation:* NASPAA. Part-time and evening/weekend programs available. *Faculty:* 5 full-time (1 woman), 8 part-time/adjunct (1 woman). *Students:* 129 full-time (81 women), 29 part-time (15 women); includes 72 minority (21 African Americans, 2 American Indian/Alaska Native, 6 Asian Americans or Pacific Islanders, 43 Hispanic Americans), 5 international. Average age 36. 88 applicants, 63% accepted, 43 enrolled. In 2008, 36 master's awarded. *Degree requirements:* For master's, comprehensive exam, advancement to candidacy. *Application deadline:* For fall admission, 8/31 priority date for domestic students. Applications are processed on a rolling basis. Application fee: $55. *Expenses:* Tuition, area resident: Full-time $1252; part-time $726 per quarter. Required fees: $334 per quarter. Tuition and fees vary according to degree level and student level. *Financial support:* Career-related internships or fieldwork, Federal Work-Study, and institutionally sponsored loans available. Support available to part-time students. Financial award application deadline: 3/1. *Unit head:* Dr. Montgomery Vanwart, Director, 909-537-5758, Fax: 909-537-7517, E-mail: mvanwart@csusb.edu. *Application contact:* Olivia Rosas, Director of Admissions, 909-537-7577, Fax: 909-537-7034, E-mail: orosas@csusb.edu.

California State University, Stanislaus, College of Humanities and Social Sciences, Department of Politics and Public Administration, Turlock, CA 95382. Offers public administration (MPA). *Accreditation:* NASPAA. Part-time and evening/weekend programs available. *Degree requirements:* For master's, comprehensive exam, thesis or alternative. *Entrance requirements:* For master's, minimum GPA of 2.7, 3 letters of reference, personal statement. Additional exam requirements/recommendations for international students: Required—TOEFL (minimum score 550 paper-based; 213 computer-based), ELPT (minimum score: 954). Electronic applications accepted. *Faculty research:* Blogging in the Middle East, incumbency and electoral competitiveness, legislative acceptance of gubernatorial budget proposals.

Carleton University, Faculty of Graduate Studies, Faculty of Public Affairs and Management, School of Public Policy and Administration, Ottawa, ON K1S 5B6, Canada. Offers public administration (MA, DPA); public policy (PhD). Part-time programs available. *Degree requirements:* For master's, thesis optional; for doctorate, one foreign language, comprehensive exam, thesis/dissertation. *Entrance requirements:* For master's, GRE, honors degree; for doctorate, master's degree. Additional exam requirements/recommendations for international students: Required—TOEFL. *Faculty research:* Canadian public administration and policy, development administration, public policy analysis, public management.

Carnegie Mellon University, H. John Heinz III College, School of Public Policy and Management, Program in Public Management, Pittsburgh, PA 15213-3891. Offers MPM. Part-time and evening/weekend programs available. *Degree requirements:* For master's, internship.

Central Michigan University, Central Michigan University Off-Campus Programs, Program in Administration, Mount Pleasant, MI 48859. Offers acquisitions administration (MSA, Certificate); general administration (MSA, Certificate); health services administration (MSA, Certificate); human resources administration (MSA, Certificate); information resource management (MSA, Certificate); international administration (MSA, Certificate); leadership (MSA, Certificate); public administration (MSA, Certificate); vehicle design and manufacturing administration (MSA, Certificate). Part-time and evening/weekend programs available. Postbaccalaureate distance learning degree programs offered (no on-campus study). *Students:* Average age 38. *Entrance requirements:* For master's, minimum GPA of 2.7 in major. *Application deadline:* Applications are processed on a rolling basis. Application fee: $50. Electronic applications accepted. *Expenses:* Tuition, state resident: full-time $3717; part-time $413 per credit. Tuition, nonresident: full-time $6894; part-time $766 per credit. *Financial support:* Scholarships/grants available. Support available to part-time students. Financial award applicants required to submit FAFSA. *Unit head:* Dr. Nana Korsah, Director, MSA Programs, 989-774-6525, E-mail: korsa1na@cmich.edu. *Application contact:* 877-268-4636, E-mail: cmuoffcampus@cmich.edu.

Central Michigan University, Central Michigan University Off-Campus Programs, Program in Public Administration, Mount Pleasant, MI 48859. Offers public management (MPA); state and local government (MPA). Part-time and evening/weekend programs available. *Entrance requirements:* For master's, minimum GPA of 2.8. Additional exam requirements/recommendations for international students: Required—TOEFL. Electronic applications accepted. *Expenses:* Tuition, state resident: full-time $3717; part-time $413 per credit. Tuition, nonresident: full-time $6894; part-time $766 per credit. *Financial support:* Scholarships/grants available. Support available to part-time students. *Unit head:* Dr. Lawrence Sych, Program Director, 989-774-3316, E-mail: sych1l@cmich.edu. *Application contact:* 877-268-4636, E-mail: cmuoffcampus@cmich.edu.

Central Michigan University, College of Graduate Studies, College of Humanities and Social and Behavioral Sciences, Department of Political Science, Program in Public Administration, Mount Pleasant, MI 48859. Offers professional development in public administration (Graduate Certificate); public administration (MPA), including cognate courses option; public management (MPA); state and local government (MPA). Part-time programs available. *Students:* 14 full-time (5 women), 11 part-time (6 women); includes 3 African Americans, 2 American Indian/Alaska Native, 4 international. Average age 32. *Degree requirements:* For master's, thesis or alternative. *Application deadline:* Applications are processed on a rolling basis. Application fee: $35 ($45 for international students). Electronic applications accepted. *Expenses:* Tuition, state resident: full-time $3717; part-time $413 per credit. Tuition, nonresident: full-time $6894; part-time $766 per credit. *Financial support:* Fellowships with tuition reimbursements, career-related internships or fieldwork, Federal Work-Study, unspecified assistantships, and out-of-state merit awards available. *Unit head:* Dr. Rick Kurtz, Chairperson, 989-774-3442, Fax: 989-774-1136, E-mail: kurtz1rs@cmich.edu. *Application contact:* Dr. Lawrence Sych, Program Director, 989-774-3316, Fax: 989-774-1136, E-mail: sych1l@cmich.edu.

Central Michigan University, College of Graduate Studies, Interdisciplinary Administration Programs, Mount Pleasant, MI 48859. Offers acquisitions administration (MSA, Graduate Certificate); general administration (MSA, Graduate Certificate); health services administration (MSA, Graduate Certificate); human resource administration (Graduate Certificate); human resources administration (MSA); information resource management (MSA, Graduate Certificate); international administration (MSA, Graduate Certificate); leadership (MSA); organizational communication (MSA, Graduate Certificate); public administration (MSA, Graduate Certificate); recreation and park administration (MSA); sport administration (MSA). *Accreditation:* AACSB. Part-time and evening/weekend programs available. Postbaccalaureate distance learning degree programs offered (no on-campus study). *Students:* 60 full-time (27 women), 61 part-time (35 women); includes 23 minority (16 African Americans, 3 American Indian/Alaska Native, 2 Asian Americans or Pacific Islanders, 2 Hispanic Americans), 29 international. Average age 29. *Degree requirements:* For master's, thesis or alternative. *Entrance requirements:* For master's, bachelor's degree with minimum GPA of 2.7. *Application deadline:* Applications are processed

Public Administration

Central Michigan University (continued)
on a rolling basis. Application fee: $35 ($45 for international students). Electronic applications accepted. *Expenses:* Tuition, state resident: full-time $3717; part-time $413 per credit. Tuition, nonresident: full-time $6894; part-time $766 per credit. *Financial support:* Fellowships with tuition reimbursements, career-related internships or fieldwork, Federal Work-Study, unspecified assistantships, and out-of-state merit awards available. *Faculty research:* Interdisciplinary studies in acquisitions administration, health services administration, sport administration, recreation and park administration, and international administration. *Unit head:* Dr. Nana Korash, Director, 989-774-6525, Fax: 989-774-2575, E-mail: msa@cmich.edu. *Application contact:* Denise Schafer, Coordinator, 989-774-4373, Fax: 989-774-2575, E-mail: schaf1dr@cmich.edu.

Cheyney University of Pennsylvania, School of Education and Professional Studies, Program in Public Administration, Cheyney, PA 19319-0200. Offers MPA. *Faculty:* 8 full-time (1 woman), 5 part-time/adjunct (3 women). *Students:* 21 full-time (13 women), 14 part-time (8 women); includes 34 minority (all African Americans). Average age 39. *Unit head:* Dr. O. Denis Ekwerike, Chair, 215-560-3891, Fax: 215-560-3893. *Application contact:* Dr. John Williams, Executive Dean of Graduate Studies, 215-560-7034, Fax: 215-560-3893, E-mail: jwilliams@cheyney.edu.

Clark Atlanta University, School of Arts and Sciences, Department of Public Administration, Atlanta, GA 30314. Offers MPA. *Accreditation:* NASPAA. Part-time programs available. *Faculty:* 3 full-time (1 woman), 1 (woman) part-time/adjunct. *Students:* 21 full-time (16 women), 24 part-time (17 women); includes 37 minority (36 African Americans, 1 Hispanic American), 1 international. Average age 28. 22 applicants, 91% accepted, 11 enrolled. In 2008, 8 master's awarded. *Degree requirements:* For master's, one foreign language, thesis. *Entrance requirements:* For master's, GRE General Test, minimum GPA of 2.5. Additional exam requirements/recommendations for international students: Required—TOEFL (minimum score 500 paper-based; 173 computer-based). *Application deadline:* For fall admission, 4/1 for domestic and international students; for spring admission, 11/1 for domestic and international students. Applications are processed on a rolling basis. Application fee: $40 ($55 for international students). *Expenses:* Tuition: Full-time $12,240; part-time $680 per credit hour. Required fees: $710; $355 per semester. *Financial support:* Fellowships, career-related internships or fieldwork, Federal Work-Study, scholarships/grants, and unspecified assistantships available. Support available to part-time students. Financial award application deadline: 4/30; financial award applicants required to submit FAFSA. *Faculty research:* Nutrition education, Africa. *Unit head:* Dr. Ron Finnell, Chairperson, 404-880-6651, E-mail: rfinnell@cau.edu. *Application contact:* Michelle Clark-Davis, Graduate Program Admissions, 404-880-6605, E-mail: cauadmissions@cau.edu.

Clark University, Graduate School, College of Professional and Continuing Education, Program in Public Administration, Worcester, MA 01610-1477. Offers MPA, Certificate. Part-time and evening/weekend programs available. *Students:* 31 full-time (18 women), 29 part-time (22 women); includes 1 minority (African American), 11 international. Average age 32. 33 applicants, 100% accepted, 33 enrolled. In 2008, 26 master's awarded. *Degree requirements:* For master's, thesis optional. *Entrance requirements:* For master's, GMAT or GRE General Test. *Application deadline:* Applications are processed on a rolling basis. Application fee: $50. Electronic applications accepted. *Expenses:* Tuition: Full-time $34,900; part-time $1091 per credit hour. Required fees: $30. *Financial support:* Career-related internships or fieldwork available. Support available to part-time students. *Unit head:* Max E. Hess, Director of Graduate Studies, 508-793-7217, Fax: 508-793-7232. *Application contact:* Julia Parent, Director of Marketing, Communications, and Admissions, 508-793-7217, Fax: 508-793-7232, E-mail: jparent@clarku.edu.

Clemson University, Graduate School, College of Business and Behavioral Science, Department of Political Science, Clemson, SC 29634. Offers policy studies (PhD); public administration (MPA). Part-time and evening/weekend programs available. *Faculty:* 12 full-time (2 women), 2 part-time/adjunct (0 women). *Students:* 29 full-time (14 women), 21 part-time (9 women); includes 5 minority (3 African Americans, 2 American Indian/Alaska Native), 9 international. Average age 33. 46 applicants, 52% accepted, 14 enrolled. In 2008, 12 master's awarded. *Degree requirements:* For master's, comprehensive exam, internship. *Entrance requirements:* For master's, GRE General Test, MAT. Additional exam requirements/recommendations for international students: Required—TOEFL. *Application deadline:* For fall admission, 7/1 priority date for domestic students; for spring admission, 11/15 for domestic students. Applications are processed on a rolling basis. Application fee: $55. Full-time tuition and fees vary according to program. *Financial support:* In 2008–09, 1 fellowship (averaging $5,000 per year), 18 research assistantships (averaging $15,544 per year), 2 teaching assistantships (averaging $15,892 per year) were awarded; career-related internships or fieldwork also available. Financial award applicants required to submit FAFSA. *Faculty research:* Public policy, total quality management, quantitative methods, public law, public personnel management. *Unit head:* Dr. William Lasser, Interim Chair, 864-656-3233. *Application contact:* Dr. Robert Smith, Coordinator, 864-656-3550, Fax: 864-656-0690, E-mail: rws@clemson.edu.

Cleveland State University, College of Graduate Studies, Maxine Goodman Levin College of Urban Affairs, Program in Public Administration, Cleveland, OH 44115. Offers geographic information systems (Certificate); local and urban management (Certificate); non-profit management (Certificate); public administration (MPA); urban real estate development (Certificate); JD/MPA. *Accreditation:* NASPAA. Part-time and evening/weekend programs available. *Faculty:* 26 full-time (10 women), 14 part-time/adjunct (8 women). *Students:* 14 full-time (8 women), 79 part-time (44 women); includes 7 minority (all African Americans), 1 international. Average age 36. 82 applicants, 41% accepted, 15 enrolled. In 2008, 37 master's, 8 other advanced degrees awarded. *Degree requirements:* For master's, thesis or alternative, capstone course. *Entrance requirements:* For master's, GRE General Test (minimum score: verbal and quantitative 40th percentile, analytical writing 4.0), minimum GPA of 3.0. Additional exam requirements/recommendations for international students: Required—TOEFL (minimum score 525 paper-based; 197 computer-based; 65 iBT). *Application deadline:* For fall admission, 7/15 priority date for domestic students, 5/15 for international students; for spring admission, 11/1 for international students. Applications are processed on a rolling basis. Application fee: $30. Electronic applications accepted. *Financial support:* In 2008–09, 10 students received support, including 7 research assistantships with full and partial tuition reimbursements available (averaging $6,960 per year), 3 teaching assistantships with full and partial tuition reimbursements available (averaging $6,960 per year); career-related internships or fieldwork, institutionally sponsored loans, tuition waivers (full and partial), and unspecified assistantships also available. Financial award application deadline: 3/1; financial award applicants required to submit FAFSA. *Faculty research:* Health care administration, public management, economic development, city management, nonprofit management. *Unit head:* Dr. Jessica Sowa, Director, 216-875-9972, Fax: 216-687-2013, E-mail: j.e.sowa@csuohio.edu. *Application contact:* Graduate Program Coordinator, 216-523-7522, Fax: 216-687-5398, E-mail: urbanprograms@csuohio.edu.

The College at Brockport, State University of New York, School of Professions, Department of Public Administration, Brockport, NY 14420-2997. Offers MPA. *Accreditation:* NASPAA. Part-time and evening/weekend programs available. *Degree requirements:* For master's, thesis or alternative. *Entrance requirements:* For master's, GRE or minimum GPA of 3.0, letters of recommendation. Additional exam requirements/recommendations for international students: Required—TOEFL (minimum score 550 paper-based; 213 computer-based; 79 iBT). *Faculty research:* Public safety administration, ethic, integrity and professionalism in public safety, E-government; complexity theories of public management; Medicaid and disabilities.

College of Charleston, Graduate School, School of Humanities and Social Sciences, Program in Public Administration, Charleston, SC 29424-0001. Offers MPA. *Accreditation:* NASPAA. Part-time programs available. *Faculty:* 11 full-time (6 women), 6 part-time/adjunct (4 women). *Students:* 27 full-time (20 women), 24 part-time (17 women); includes 1 African American, 2 Hispanic Americans. Average age 27. 26 applicants, 54% accepted, 13 enrolled. In 2008, 19 master's awarded. *Degree requirements:* For master's, internship, capstone seminar. *Entrance requirements:* For master's, GRE General Test, previous course work in statistics, 3 letters of recommendation, minimum GPA of 3.0. Additional exam requirements/recommendations for international students: Required—TOEFL. *Application deadline:* For fall admission, 7/1 for domestic students; for spring admission, 11/1 for domestic students. Applications are processed on a rolling basis. Application fee: $45. Electronic applications accepted. *Expenses:* Tuition, area resident: Full-time $6624; part-time $368 per credit hour. Tuition, state resident: full-time $6624; part-time $368 per credit hour. Tuition, nonresident: full-time $16,074; part-time $893 per credit hour. Required fees: $30; $30 per course. One-time fee: $45. *Financial support:* In 2008–09, 6 research assistantships (averaging $12,400 per year) were awarded; career-related internships or fieldwork, Federal Work-Study, scholarships/grants, and unspecified assistantships also available. Support available to part-time students. Financial award application deadline: 4/1; financial award applicants required to submit FAFSA. *Faculty research:* Local government, environmental policy, budgeting, ethics. *Unit head:* Dr. Kendra Stewart, Acting Director, 843-953-5724, Fax: 843-953-8140, E-mail: stewartk@cofc.edu. *Application contact:* Susan Hallatt, Director of Graduate Admissions, 843-953-5614, Fax: 843-953-1434, E-mail: hallatts@cofc.edu.

Columbia University, School of International and Public Affairs, Program in Public Policy and Administration, New York, NY 10027. Offers MPA, JD/MPA, MPA/MS, MPH/MPA. *Entrance requirements:* For master's, GRE General Test. Additional exam requirements/recommendations for international students: Required—TOEFL (minimum score 600 paper-based; 250 computer-based; 100 iBT). Electronic applications accepted.

Columbus State University, Graduate Studies, College of Arts and Letters, Program in Public Administration, Columbus, GA 31907-5645. Offers justice administration (MPA). Part-time and evening/weekend programs available. *Faculty:* 7 full-time (2 women), 13 part-time/adjunct (0 women). *Students:* 117 full-time (51 women), 226 part-time (76 women); includes 106 minority (99 African Americans, 2 American Indian/Alaska Native, 2 Asian Americans or Pacific Islanders, 3 Hispanic Americans), 1 international. Average age 36. 85 applicants, 76% accepted, 57 enrolled. In 2008, 114 master's awarded. *Degree requirements:* For master's, comprehensive exam. *Entrance requirements:* For master's, GRE General Test, GMAT, MAT. Additional exam requirements/recommendations for international students: Required—TOEFL (minimum score 550 paper-based; 213 computer-based). *Application deadline:* For fall admission, 5/1 priority date for domestic students, 5/1 for international students; for spring admission, 11/1 for domestic and international students. Applications are processed on a rolling basis. Application fee: $25. Electronic applications accepted. *Expenses:* Tuition, area resident: Full-time $3410; part-time $143 per credit hour. Tuition, state resident: full-time $3411; part-time $143 per credit hour. Tuition, nonresident: full-time $13,634; part-time $569 per credit hour. Required fees: $1348. *Financial support:* In 2008–09, 82 students received support, including 8 research assistantships with partial tuition reimbursements available (averaging $3,000 per year); career-related internships or fieldwork, Federal Work-Study, institutionally sponsored loans, scholarships/grants, tuition waivers (full), and unspecified assistantships also available. Support available to part-time students. Financial award application deadline: 5/1; financial award applicants required to submit FAFSA. *Unit head:* Dr. William Chappell, Program Director, 706-568-2055, E-mail: chappell_william@colstate.edu. *Application contact:* Katie Thornton, Graduate Admissions Specialist, 706-568-2035, Fax: 706-568-2462, E-mail: thornton_katie@colstate.edu.

Concordia University, School of Graduate Studies, Faculty of Arts and Science, Department of Political Science, Montréal, QC H3G 1M8, Canada. Offers political science (PhD); public policy and public administration (MA), including geography. *Degree requirements:* For master's, one foreign language, comprehensive exam, thesis optional, internship. *Entrance requirements:* For master's, honors degree or equivalent. Additional exam requirements/recommendations for international students: Required—TOEFL. *Faculty research:* International public policy and administration, Quebec public administration, public policy and social/political theory, geography and public policy, public administration and decision making.

Concordia University Wisconsin, Graduate Programs, School of Business and Legal Studies, MBA Program, Mequon, WI 53097-2402. Offers finance (MBA); health care administration (MBA); human resource management (MBA); international business (MBA); international business-bilingual English/Chinese (MBA); management (MBA); management information systems (MBA); managerial communications (MBA); marketing (MBA); public administration (MBA); risk management (MBA). Postbaccalaureate distance learning degree programs offered (minimal on-campus study). *Degree requirements:* For master's, comprehensive exam, thesis or alternative. *Entrance requirements:* Additional exam requirements/recommendations for international students: Required—TOEFL. *Expenses:* Contact institution.

Cumberland University, Program in Public Service Administration, Lebanon, TN 37087-3408. Offers MS. Part-time and evening/weekend programs available. *Degree requirements:* For master's, comprehensive exam. *Entrance requirements:* For master's, MAT, 3 letters of recommendation. Additional exam requirements/recommendations for international students: Required—TOEFL (minimum score 500 paper-based; 173 computer-based).

Dalhousie University, Faculty of Management, School of Public Administration, Halifax, NS B3H 3J5, Canada. Offers management (MPA); public administration (MPA, GDPA); LL B/MPA; MLIS/MPA. Part-time programs available. *Faculty:* 9 full-time (1 woman), 6 part-time/adjunct (1 woman). *Students:* 59 full-time (36 women), 25 part-time (13 women). 58 applicants, 79% accepted. *Entrance requirements:* For master's, GMAT. Additional exam requirements/recommendations for international students: Required—TOEFL, IELTS, 1 of the following 5 approved tests: TOEFL, IELTS, CANTEST, CAEL, Michigan English Language Assessment Battery. International applicants must also submit results of: GMAT, GRE or LSAT. *Application deadline:* Applications are processed on a rolling basis. Application fee: $70. Electronic applications accepted. *Expenses:* Contact institution. *Financial support:* Fellowships, teaching assistantships, career-related internships or fieldwork available. *Faculty research:* Municipal management, policy and program management, environmental policy, economic and social policy, business and government. *Unit head:* Fazley Siddiq, Director, 902-494-8802, Fax: 902-494-7023, E-mail: dalmpa@dal.ca. *Application contact:* Jeffrey Roy, Graduate Coordinator, 902-494-2752, Fax: 902-494-7023, E-mail: Roy@dal.ca.

DePaul University, School of Public Service, Chicago, IL 60604. Offers financial administration management (Certificate); health administration (Certificate); health law and policy (MS); international public services (MS); leadership and policy studies (MS); metropolitan planning (Certificate); public administration (MPA); public service management (MS), including association management, fundraising and philanthropy, healthcare administration, higher education administration, metropolitan planning; public services (Certificate); JD/MS. Part-time and evening/weekend programs available. Postbaccalaureate distance learning degree programs offered (minimal on-campus study). *Faculty:* 14 full-time (3 women), 43 part-time/adjunct (24 women). *Students:* 90 full-time (59 women), 204 part-time (154 women); includes 101 minority (63 African Americans, 10 Asian Americans or Pacific Islanders, 28 Hispanic Americans), 11 international. Average age 26. 162 applicants, 100% accepted, 94 enrolled. In 2008, 108 master's awarded. *Degree requirements:* For master's, thesis or integrative seminar. *Entrance requirements:* For master's, minimum GPA of 2.7. Additional exam requirements/recommendations for international students: Required—TOEFL (minimum score 550 paper-based; 213 computer-based; 80 iBT), IELTS (minimum score 6.5). *Application deadline:* Applications are processed on a rolling basis. Application fee: $40. Electronic applications accepted. *Financial support:* In 2008–09, 60 students received support, including 3 research assistantships with full tuition reimbursements available (averaging $7,000 per year); career-related internships or fieldwork, Federal Work-Study, institutionally sponsored loans, scholarships/grants, tuition waivers (partial), and unspecified assistantships also available. Support available to part-time students. Financial award application deadline: 7/1; financial award applicants required to submit FAFSA. *Faculty research:* Government financing, transportation, leadership, health care, volunteerism and organizational behavior, non-profit organizations. Total annual research expenditures: $20,000. *Unit head:* Dr. J. Patrick Murphy, Director, 312-362-5608, Fax: 312-362-5506, E-mail: jpmurphy@depaul.edu. *Application contact:* Megan B. Balderston, Director of Admissions and Marketing, 312-362-5565, Fax: 312-362-5506, E-mail: pubserv@depaul.edu.

DeVry University, Keller Graduate School of Management, Oakbrook Terrace, IL 60181. Offers accounting and financial management (MAFM); business administration (MBA); human resources management (MHRM); information systems management (MISM); network and communications management (MNCM); project management (MPM); public administration (MPA).

Drake University, College of Business and Public Administration, Des Moines, IA 50311-4516. Offers M Acc, MBA, MFM, MPA, JD/MBA, JD/MPA, Pharm D/MBA, Pharm D/MPA. *Accreditation:* AACSB. Part-time and evening/weekend programs available. *Degree requirements:* For master's, comprehensive exam (for some programs), thesis (for some programs), internships. *Entrance requirements:* For master's, GMAT, letters of recommendation, resumé. Additional exam requirements/recommendations for international students: Required—TOEFL (minimum score 550 paper-based; 213 computer-based). Electronic applications accepted. *Expenses:* Contact institution. *Faculty research:* Venture capital, online commerce, professional ethics, process improvement, project management.

Duquesne University, Graduate School of Liberal Arts, Graduate Center for Social and Public Policy, Pittsburgh, PA 15282-1750. Offers conflict resolution and peace studies (Certificate); social and public policy (MA, Certificate). Programs are a collaboration between the Departments of Political Science and Sociology. Part-time and evening/weekend programs available. *Faculty:* 15 full-time (3 women), 1 (woman) part-time/adjunct. *Students:* 37 full-time (25 women), 12 part-time (9 women); includes 1 minority (African American), 7 international. Average age 27. 29 applicants, 90% accepted, 18 enrolled. In 2008, 9 master's awarded. *Degree requirements:* For master's, thesis. *Entrance requirements:* For master's, GRE General Test. Additional exam requirements/recommendations for international students: Required—TOEFL. *Application deadline:* For fall admission, 4/30 priority date for domestic and international students; for spring admission, 11/1 priority date for domestic and international students. Applications are processed on a rolling basis. Application fee: $50. Electronic applications accepted. *Expenses:* Tuition: Part-time $819 per credit. Required fees: $78 per credit. Tuition and fees vary according to course load. *Financial support:* In 2008–09, 20 students received support, including 12 research assistantships with full and partial tuition reimbursements available (averaging $9,000 per year), 4 teaching assistantships with full and partial tuition reimbursements available (averaging $9,000 per year); career-related internships or fieldwork, institutionally sponsored loans, scholarships/grants, tuition waivers (full and partial), and unspecified assistantships also available. Support available to part-time students. Financial award application deadline: 5/1. *Faculty research:* Program evaluation, environmental policy, criminal justice policy, health care policy. Total annual research expenditures: $30,000. *Unit head:* Dr. Joseph Yenerall, Director, 412-396-6485, Fax: 412-396-5265, E-mail: socialpolicy@duq.edu. *Application contact:* Linda L. Rendulic, Assistant to the Dean, 412-396-6400, Fax: 412-396-5265, E-mail: rendulic@duq.edu.

East Carolina University, Graduate School, Thomas Harriot College of Arts and Sciences, Department of Political Science, Greenville, NC 27858-4353. Offers public administration (MPA). *Accreditation:* NASPAA. Part-time and evening/weekend programs available. *Degree requirements:* For master's, one foreign language, comprehensive exam. *Entrance requirements:* For master's, GRE General Test. Additional exam requirements/recommendations for international students: Required—TOEFL.

Eastern Kentucky University, The Graduate School, College of Arts and Sciences, Department of Government, Program in General Public Administration, Richmond, KY 40475-3102. Offers community development (MPA); community health administration (MPA); general public administration (MPA). *Accreditation:* NASPAA. Part-time and evening/weekend programs available. *Entrance requirements:* For master's, GRE General Test, minimum GPA of 2.5.

Eastern Michigan University, Graduate School, College of Arts and Sciences, Department of Political Science, Program in Public Administration, Ypsilanti, MI 48197. Offers local government management (Graduate Certificate); management of public healthcare services (Graduate Certificate); public administration (MPA, Graduate Certificate); public budget management (Graduate Certificate); public land planning (Graduate Certificate); public management (Graduate Certificate); public personnel management (Graduate Certificate); public policy analysis (Graduate Certificate). *Accreditation:* NASPAA.

Eastern Washington University, Graduate Studies, College of Business and Public Administration, Program in Public Administration, Cheney, WA 99004-2431. Offers MPA, MBA/MPA, MPA/MSW, MPA/MURP. Part-time and evening/weekend programs available. *Degree requirements:* For master's, comprehensive exam, thesis optional. *Entrance requirements:* For master's, minimum GPA of 3.0.

The Evergreen State College, Graduate Programs, Program in Public Administration, Olympia, WA 98505. Offers MPA, MES/MPA. Part-time and evening/weekend programs available. *Faculty:* 5 full-time (2 women), 7 part-time/adjunct (2 women). *Students:* 62 full-time (40 women), 69 part-time (46 women); includes 44 minority (11 African Americans, 22 American Indian/Alaska Native, 4 Asian Americans or Pacific Islanders, 7 Hispanic Americans). Average age 36. 121 applicants, 78% accepted, 73 enrolled. In 2008, 47 master's awarded. *Degree requirements:* For master's, thesis optional. *Entrance requirements:* For master's, minimum GPA of 3.0 in last 90 quarter hours toward BA/BS; 4 quarter credits in statistics within past 5 years; evidence of writing, analytical, and general communication skills at appropriate level for graduate study. Additional exam requirements/recommendations for international students: Required—TOEFL (minimum score 600 paper-based; 250 computer-based; 100 iBT). *Application deadline:* For fall admission, 2/16 priority date for domestic and international students. Applications are processed on a rolling basis. Application fee: $50. Electronic applications accepted. *Expenses:* Contact institution. *Financial support:* In 2008–09, 9 students received support, including 9 fellowships (averaging $1,160 per year); career-related internships or fieldwork, Federal Work-Study, scholarships/grants, tuition waivers (partial), and unspecified assistantships also available. Support available to part-time students. Financial award application deadline: 3/15; financial award applicants required to submit FAFSA. *Faculty research:* Public policy, organizational theory, public health, tribal governance, nonprofit administration, leadership, healthcare reform. *Unit head:* Dr. Cheryl Simrell King, MPA Program Director, 360-867-5541, E-mail: kingcs@evergreen.edu. *Application contact:* Randee Gibbons, Associate Director, MPA Program, 360-867-6554, E-mail: gibbonsr@evergreen.edu.

Fairleigh Dickinson University, College at Florham, Anthony J. Petrocelli College of Continuing Studies, Public Administration Institute, Program in Public Administration, Madison, NJ 07940-1099. Offers MPA. *Students:* 2 full-time (both women), 1 part-time (0 women), 1 international. Average age 28. 1 applicant, 100% accepted, 2 enrolled.Application fee: $40. *Unit head:* Dr. William Roberts, Head, 973-443-8500. *Application contact:* Susan Brooman, University Director, Graduate Admissions, 973-443-8905, Fax: 973-443-8088, E-mail: grad@fdu.edu.

Fairleigh Dickinson University, Metropolitan Campus, Anthony J. Petrocelli College of Continuing Studies, Public Administration Institute, Program in Public Administration, Teaneck, NJ 07666-1914. Offers MPA, Certificate. *Students:* 138 full-time (62 women), 118 part-time (61 women), 116 international. Average age 32. 230 applicants, 75% accepted, 83 enrolled. In 2008, 78 master's awarded. *Application deadline:* Applications are processed on a rolling basis. Application fee: $40. *Unit head:* Dr. William Roberts, Director, 201-692-2000. *Application contact:* Dr. William Roberts, Director, 201-692-2000.

Florida Agricultural and Mechanical University, Division of Graduate Studies, Research, and Continuing Education, College of Arts and Sciences, Division of History and Political Sciences, Program in Applied Social Science, Tallahassee, FL 32307-3200. Offers African American history (MASS); criminal justice (MASS); economics (MASS); history (MASS); political science (MASS); public administration (MASS); public management (MASS); social work (MASS); sociology (MASS). Part-time programs available. *Degree requirements:* For master's, thesis optional. *Entrance requirements:* For master's, GRE General Test, minimum GPA of 3.0. *Faculty research:* Southern history, black history, election trends, presidential history.

Florida Atlantic University, College of Architecture, Urban and Public Affairs, School of Public Administration, Boca Raton, FL 33431-0991. Offers MNM, MPA, PhD. *Accreditation:* NASPAA (one or more programs are accredited). Part-time and evening/weekend programs available. *Faculty:* 10 full-time (3 women), 6 part-time/adjunct (0 women). *Students:* 18 full-time (9 women), 86 part-time (52 women); includes 41 minority (28 African Americans, 2 Asian Americans or Pacific Islanders, 11 Hispanic Americans), 7 international. Average age 36. 96 applicants, 44% accepted, 24 enrolled. In 2008, 33 master's, 5 doctorates awarded. *Degree requirements:* For master's, thesis optional; for doctorate, comprehensive exam, thesis/dissertation. *Entrance requirements:* For master's, GRE General Test, minimum GPA of 3.0; for doctorate, GRE General Test, faculty reference, scholarly writing samples, letters of recommendation. Additional exam requirements/recommendations for international students: Required—TOEFL. *Application deadline:* For fall admission, 7/1 priority date for domestic students, 2/15 for international students; for spring admission, 11/1 for domestic students, 7/15 for international students. Applications are processed on a rolling basis. Application fee: $30. *Expenses:* Tuition, state resident: full-time $4867; part-time $270.40 per credit hour. Tuition, nonresident: full-time $16,486; part-time $915.87 per credit hour. *Financial support:* Fellowships with full tuition reimbursements, research assistantships with partial tuition reimbursements, teaching assistantships with partial tuition reimbursements, career-related internships or fieldwork, Federal Work-Study, institutionally sponsored loans, and tuition waivers (partial) available. Support available to part-time students. Financial award application deadline: 4/1. *Faculty research:* Public finance and budgeting, public management, evaluation, criminal justice, postmodern public administration. *Unit head:* Dr. Hugh T. Miller, Director, 954-762-5650, Fax: 954-762-5693, E-mail: hmiller@fau.edu. *Application contact:* Dr. Hugh T. Miller, Director, 954-762-5650, Fax: 954-762-5693, E-mail: hmiller@fau.edu.

Florida Gulf Coast University, College of Professional Studies, Program in Public Administration, Fort Myers, FL 33965-6565. Offers criminal justice (MPA); environmental policy (MPA); general public administration (MPA); management (MPA). Part-time programs available. *Faculty:* 32 full-time (11 women), 29 part-time/adjunct (12 women). *Students:* 49 full-time (30 women), 19 part-time (12 women); includes 13 minority (4 African Americans, 2 Asian Americans or Pacific Islanders, 7 Hispanic Americans). Average age 35. 34 applicants, 68% accepted, 19 enrolled. In 2008, 14 master's awarded. *Entrance requirements:* For master's, GRE General Test, MAT, minimum GPA of 3.0. Additional exam requirements/recommendations for international students: Required—TOEFL (minimum score 550 paper-based; 213 computer-based). *Application deadline:* For fall admission, 7/1 priority date for domestic students; for spring admission, 11/15 for domestic students. Applications are processed on a rolling basis. Application fee: $30. Electronic applications accepted. *Financial support:* In 2008–09, 5 research assistantships were awarded; career-related internships or fieldwork and tuition waivers (full and partial) also available. Support available to part-time students. *Faculty research:* Personnel, public policy, public finance, housing policy. *Unit head:* Terry Busson, Chair, 239-590-7704, E-mail: tbusson@fgcu.edu. *Application contact:* Roger Green, Information Contact, 239-590-7838, Fax: 239-590-7846.

Florida Institute of Technology, Graduate Programs, University College, Melbourne, FL 32901-6975. Offers acquisition and contract management (MS, PMBA); aerospace engineering (MS); business administration (PMBA); computer information systems (MS); computer science (MS); e-business (PMBA); electrical engineering (MS); engineering management (MS); human resource management (PMBA); human resources management (MS); information systems (PMBA); information technology (MS); logistics management (MS); management (MS), including acquisition and contract management, e-business, human resource management, information systems, logistics management, transportation management; materiel acquisition management (MS); mechanical engineering (MS); operations research (MS); project management (MS), including information systems, operations research; public administration (MPA); quality management (MS); software engineering (MS); space systems (MS); space systems management (MS); systems management (MS), including information systems, operations research. Part-time and evening/weekend programs available. Postbaccalaureate distance learning degree programs offered (no on-campus study). *Entrance requirements:* For master's, minimum GPA of 3.0. Additional exam requirements/recommendations for international students: Required—TOEFL (minimum score 550 paper-based; 213 computer-based). Electronic applications accepted. *Expenses:* Tuition: Part-time $980 per credit hour.

Florida International University, College of Social Work, Justice and Public Affairs, School of Public Administration, Miami, FL 33199. Offers MPA, PhD. *Accreditation:* NASPAA (one or more programs are accredited). Part-time and evening/weekend programs available. *Degree requirements:* For doctorate, comprehensive exam, thesis/dissertation. *Entrance requirements:* For master's, minimum GPA of 3.0, letters of recommendation; for doctorate, GRE General Test, minimum GPA of 3.0, letters of recommendation. Additional exam requirements/recommendations for international students: Required—TOEFL (minimum score 550 paper-based; 213 computer-based). Electronic applications accepted.

Florida State University, Graduate Studies, College of Social Sciences, Reubin O'D. Askew School of Public Administration and Policy, Tallahassee, FL 32306. Offers MPA, PhD, Certificate, JD/MPA, MPA/MSC, MPA/MSP, MPA/MSW. *Accreditation:* NASPAA (one or more programs are accredited). Part-time and evening/weekend programs available. *Degree requirements:* For master's, action report; for doctorate, comprehensive exam, thesis/dissertation. *Entrance requirements:* For master's, GRE General Test, minimum GPA of 3.0; for doctorate, GRE General Test, minimum undergraduate GPA of 3.0, graduate 3.5. Additional exam requirements/recommendations for international students: Required—TOEFL (minimum score 550 paper-based; 213 computer-based; 80 iBT). Electronic applications accepted. *Faculty research:* Financial management, human resource management, policy, strategic management, organizations, nonprofit management.

Framingham State College, Division of Graduate and Continuing Education, Program in Public Administration, Framingham, MA 01701-9101. Offers MA. Part-time and evening/weekend programs available.

Gannon University, School of Graduate Studies, College of Engineering and Business, School of Business, Program in Public Administration, Erie, PA 16541-0001. Offers MPA, Certificate. Part-time and evening/weekend programs available. *Students:* 11 full-time (2 women), 22 part-time (13 women); includes 4 minority (2 African Americans, 2 Hispanic Americans), 1 international. Average age 33. 27 applicants, 70% accepted, 11 enrolled. In 2008, 7 master's awarded. *Degree requirements:* For master's, thesis or alternative, research project. *Entrance requirements:* For master's, GRE. Additional exam requirements/recommendations for international students: Required—TOEFL. *Application deadline:* Applications are processed on a rolling basis. Application fee: $25. Electronic applications accepted. *Expenses:* Tuition: Full-time $13,050; part-time $725 per credit. Required fees: $502; $16 per credit. Tuition and fees vary according to course load, degree level, campus/location and program. *Financial support:* Career-related internships or fieldwork, scholarships/grants, and unspecified assistantships available. Support available to part-time students. Financial award application deadline: 7/1; financial award applicants required to submit FAFSA. *Unit head:* Dr. Rick Prokop, Co-Director, 814-871-7576, E-mail: prokop001@gannon.edu. *Application contact:* Kara Morgan, Assistant Director of Graduate Admissions, 814-871-5831, Fax: 814-871-5827, E-mail: graduate@gannon.edu.

The George Washington University, Columbian College of Arts and Sciences, Trachtenberg School of Public Policy and Public Administration, Washington, DC 20052. Offers public administration (MPA), including budget and public finance, federal policy, politics, and management, international development management, managing public organizations, managing state and local governments, nonprofit management, policy analysis and evaluation, public administration, public-private policy and management; public policy (MA, MPP), including environmental and resource policy (MA), philosophy and social policy (MA), women's studies

Public Administration

The George Washington University (continued)
(MA); public policy and administration (PhD); JD/MPP; MPA/JD; PhD/MPP. Part-time and evening/weekend programs available. *Faculty:* 19 full-time (8 women), 12 part-time/adjunct (3 women). *Students:* 82 full-time (57 women), 130 part-time (80 women); includes 28 minority (9 African Americans, 1 American Indian/Alaska Native, 10 Asian Americans or Pacific Islanders, 8 Hispanic Americans), 28 international. Average age 31. 225 applicants, 38% accepted, 31 enrolled. In 2008, 64 master's, 7 doctorates awarded. *Degree requirements:* For doctorate, thesis/dissertation, general exam. *Entrance requirements:* For master's, GRE General Test, minimum GPA of 3.0; for doctorate, GRE General Test, interview, minimum GPA of 3.0. Additional exam requirements/recommendations for international students: Required—TOEFL (minimum score 600 paper-based; 250 computer-based; 100 iBT). *Application deadline:* For fall admission, 1/15 priority date for domestic and international students; for spring admission, 10/1 priority date for domestic students, 9/1 priority date for international students. Applications are processed on a rolling basis. Application fee: $60. Electronic applications accepted. *Financial support:* In 2008–09, 87 students received support; fellowships, teaching assistantships, institutionally sponsored loans and tuition waivers available. Financial award application deadline: 1/15. *Unit head:* Dr. Joseph J. Cordes, Director, 202-994-5826, Fax: 202-994-8913, E-mail: cordes@gwu.edu. *Application contact:* Information Contact, 202-994-8500, Fax: 202-994-8913, E-mail: pubpol@gwu.edu.

Georgia College & State University, Graduate School, School of Liberal Arts and Sciences, Department of Government and Sociology, Program in Public Administration and Public Affairs, Milledgeville, GA 31061. Offers MPA. *Accreditation:* NASPAA. Part-time and evening/weekend programs available. *Degree requirements:* For master's, thesis optional, capstone project. *Entrance requirements:* For master's, GRE. Additional exam requirements/recommendations for international students: Required—TOEFL. Electronic applications accepted.

Georgia Southern University, Jack N. Averitt College of Graduate Studies, College of Liberal Arts and Social Sciences, Department of Political Science, Program in Public Administration, Statesboro, GA 30460. Offers MPA. *Accreditation:* NASPAA. Part-time and evening/weekend programs available. *Students:* 19 full-time (11 women), 15 part-time (8 women); includes 9 minority (all African Americans). Average age 27. 16 applicants, 75% accepted, 6 enrolled. In 2008, 26 master's awarded. *Degree requirements:* For master's, comprehensive exam, internship, terminal exam. *Entrance requirements:* For master's, GRE General Test, minimum GPA of 2.5, resumé, undergraduate major appropriate to field, letters of reference. Additional exam requirements/recommendations for international students: Required—TOEFL (minimum score 550 paper-based; 213 computer-based; 80 iBT). *Application deadline:* For fall admission, 3/1 priority date for domestic and international students; for spring admission, 10/1 priority date for domestic students, 10/1 for international students. Applications are processed on a rolling basis. Application fee: $50. Electronic applications accepted. *Expenses:* Tuition, area resident: Full-time $3840; part-time $160 per semester hour. Tuition, state resident: full-time $3840; part-time $160 per semester hour. Tuition, nonresident: full-time $15,336; part-time $639 per semester hour. Required fees: $1152. *Financial support:* In 2008–09, 28 students received support, including research assistantships with partial tuition reimbursements available (averaging $6,850 per year), teaching assistantships with partial tuition reimbursements available (averaging $6,850 per year); career-related internships or fieldwork, Federal Work-Study, scholarships/grants, tuition waivers (partial), and unspecified assistantships also available. Support available to part-time students. Financial award application deadline: 4/15; financial award applicants required to submit FAFSA. *Faculty research:* Comparative public administration, equal employment policies, gangs, environmental policy, AIDS policy. *Unit head:* Dr. George Cox, Professor, 912-478-5573, Fax: 912-478-5348, E-mail: gcox@georgiasouthern.edu. *Application contact:* 912-478-5384, Fax: 912-478-0740, E-mail: gradadmissions@georgiasouthern.edu.

Georgia State University, Andrew Young School of Policy Studies, Department of Public Administration and Urban Studies, Program in Public Administration, Atlanta, GA 30303-3083. Offers MPA, JD/MPA. Part-time and evening/weekend programs available. *Degree requirements:* For master's, thesis optional. *Entrance requirements:* For master's, GRE General Test. Additional exam requirements/recommendations for international students: Required—TOEFL. *Faculty research:* Public management, nonprofit, policy.

Governors State University, College of Business and Public Administration, Program in Public Administration, University Park, IL 60466-0975. Offers MPA. *Accreditation:* NASPAA. Part-time and evening/weekend programs available. *Degree requirements:* For master's, comprehensive exam, thesis or alternative, internship or previous work in field. *Entrance requirements:* For master's, minimum GPA of 2.5. *Faculty research:* State and local politics.

Grambling State University, School of Graduate Studies and Research, College of Arts and Sciences, Program in Public Administration, Grambling, LA 71270. Offers health service administration (MPA); human resource management (MPA); public management (MPA); state and local government (MPA). *Accreditation:* NASPAA. Part-time programs available. *Faculty:* 3 full-time (0 women), 2 part-time/adjunct (1 woman). *Students:* 18 full-time (13 women), 25 part-time (18 women); includes 37 minority (all African Americans), 5 international. Average age 29. In 2008, 22 master's awarded. *Degree requirements:* For master's, comprehensive exam (for some programs), thesis optional. *Entrance requirements:* For master's, GRE, minimum GPA of 2.75 on last degree. Additional exam requirements/recommendations for international students: Required—TOEFL (minimum score 500 paper-based; 173 computer-based; 61 iBT). *Application deadline:* For fall admission, 7/1 for domestic and international students; for spring admission, 12/1 for domestic and international students. Applications are processed on a rolling basis. Application fee: $20 ($30 for international students). Electronic applications accepted. *Expenses:* Tuition, area resident: Full-time $3637; part-time $134 per credit hour. Tuition, nonresident: full-time $7651; part-time $134 per credit hour. Required fees: $1225; $134 per credit hour. $430 per semester. *Financial support:* In 2008–09, 1 research assistantship (averaging $6,500 per year) was awarded; health care benefits, tuition waivers (full), and unspecified assistantships also available. Financial award application deadline: 5/31. *Unit head:* Dr. Rose Harris, Director, 318-274-2310, Fax: 318-274-3427, E-mail: harrisr@gram.edu. *Application contact:* Sarah Dennis, Admissions Coordinator, 318-274-2319, Fax: 318-274-3427, E-mail: denniss@alpha0.gram.edu.

Grand Valley State University, College of Community and Public Service, School of Public and Nonprofit Administration, Allendale, MI 49401-9403. Offers MHA, MPA. *Accreditation:* NASPAA. Part-time and evening/weekend programs available. *Faculty:* 11 full-time (4 women), 15 part-time/adjunct (5 women). *Students:* 58 full-time (34 women), 120 part-time (77 women); includes 33 minority (21 African Americans, 1 American Indian/Alaska Native, 4 Asian Americans or Pacific Islanders, 7 Hispanic Americans), 10 international. Average age 32. 83 applicants, 94% accepted, 58 enrolled. In 2008, 58 master's awarded. *Application deadline:* For fall admission, 5/1 priority date for domestic students; for winter admission, 11/1 priority date for domestic students. Applications are processed on a rolling basis. Application fee: $30. Electronic applications accepted. *Financial support:* In 2008–09, 28 students received support, including 13 research assistantships with partial tuition reimbursements available (averaging $8,000 per year); career-related internships or fieldwork, Federal Work-Study, scholarships/grants, and unspecified assistantships also available. Financial award application deadline: 5/1. *Faculty research:* Comparative urban systems, ethics and public management, local economic development, public and nonprofit boards and governance. *Unit head:* Dr. Mark Hoffman, Director, 616-331-6575, Fax: 616-331-7120, E-mail: hoffman@gvsu.edu. *Application contact:* Tracey James-Heer, Associate Director for Graduate Recruitment, 616-331-2025, Fax: 616-486-6476, E-mail: james-ht@gvsu.edu.

Hamline University, School of Business, St. Paul, MN 55104-1284. Offers business (MBA); nonprofit management (MANM); public administration (MPA, DPA); JD/MAM; JD/MANM; JD/MAPA. Part-time and evening/weekend programs available. *Faculty:* 18 full-time (10 women), 45 part-time/adjunct (10 women). *Students:* 401 full-time (207 women), 138 part-time (81 women); includes 75 minority (39 African Americans, 3 American Indian/Alaska Native, 26 Asian Americans or Pacific Islanders, 7 Hispanic Americans), 83 international. Average age 32. 340 applicants, 64% accepted, 159 enrolled. In 2008, 82 master's, 3 doctorates awarded. *Degree requirements:* For master's, thesis; for doctorate, thesis/dissertation. *Entrance requirements:* For master's and doctorate, personal statement, curriculum vitae, official transcripts, letters of recommendation, writing sample. Additional exam requirements/recommendations for international students: Required—TOEFL (minimum score 550 paper-based; 213 computer-based). *Application deadline:* For fall admission, 3/30 priority date for domestic students. Applications are processed on a rolling basis. Application fee: $0. Electronic applications accepted. *Expenses:* Tuition: Full-time $6400; part-time $400 per credit. Required fees: $6 per credit. One-time fee: $205. Tuition and fees vary according to degree level and program. *Financial support:* Federal Work-Study available. Financial award applicants required to submit FAFSA. *Unit head:* Julian Schuster, Dean, 651-523-2284, Fax: 651-523-3098, E-mail: jschuster01@hamline.edu. *Application contact:* Rae A. Lenway, Director, Graduate Recruitment and Admission, 651-523-2900, Fax: 651-523-3058, E-mail: rlenway@hamline.edu.

Harvard University, John F. Kennedy School of Government, Lucius N. Littauer Mid-Career Program in Public Administration, Cambridge, MA 02138. Offers MPA. *Students:* 198 full-time (75 women); includes 21 minority (8 African Americans, 2 American Indian/Alaska Native, 6 Asian Americans or Pacific Islanders, 5 Hispanic Americans), 110 international. Average age 38. 475 applicants, 59% accepted, 198 enrolled. *Entrance requirements:* For master's, GMAT or GRE General Test, minimum 7 years of professional experience. Additional exam requirements/recommendations for international students: Required—TOEFL (minimum score 600 paper-based; 250 computer-based; 100 iBT), TWE. *Application deadline:* For fall admission, 3/7 for domestic students. Applications are processed on a rolling basis. Application fee: $80. Electronic applications accepted. *Expenses:* Contact institution. *Financial support:* Fellowships, Federal Work-Study, institutionally sponsored loans, scholarships/grants, health care benefits, and unspecified assistantships available. Financial award application deadline: 3/7; financial award applicants required to submit CSS PROFILE or FAFSA. *Unit head:* Robin Engel, Director, 617-496-1100, E-mail: robin_engel@harvard.edu. *Application contact:* 617-495-1155.

Harvard University, John F. Kennedy School of Government, Master in Public Administration/International Development Program, Cambridge, MA 02138. Offers MPAID. *Students:* 71 full-time (21 women); includes 8 minority (6 Asian Americans or Pacific Islanders, 2 Hispanic Americans), 48 international. Average age 27. 330 applicants, 32% accepted, 71 enrolled. *Entrance requirements:* For master's, GMAT or GRE General Test (for joint Business School applicants only), one course each in microeconomics and macroeconomics; two college-level calculus courses (one must contain multivariable calculus); bachelor's degree; 2-3 years of professional experience in development (strongly encouraged). Additional exam requirements/recommendations for international students: Required—TOEFL (minimum score 600 paper-based; 250 computer-based; 100 iBT). *Application deadline:* For fall admission, 1/4 for domestic students. Application fee: $80. Electronic applications accepted. *Expenses:* Tuition: Full-time $32,556. Required fees: $1426. Full-time tuition and fees vary according to program and student level. *Financial support:* Fellowships, research assistantships, teaching assistantships, career-related internships or fieldwork, Federal Work-Study, institutionally sponsored loans, scholarships/grants, health care benefits, and unspecified assistantships available. Financial award application deadline: 2/2; financial award applicants required to submit CSS PROFILE or FAFSA. *Unit head:* Carol Finney, Director, 617-495-7799, E-mail: carol_finney@harvard.edu. *Application contact:* 617-495-2133.

Harvard University, John F. Kennedy School of Government, Two-year Program in Public Administration, Cambridge, MA 02138. Offers MPA. *Students:* 67 full-time (20 women); includes 11 minority (1 African American, 9 Asian Americans or Pacific Islanders, 1 Hispanic American), 32 international. Average age 29. 130 applicants, 68% accepted, 67 enrolled. *Entrance requirements:* For master's, GMAT or GRE General Test, minimum of 3 years of work experience, relevant graduate work. Additional exam requirements/recommendations for international students: Required—TOEFL (minimum score 600 paper-based; 250 computer-based; 100 iBT), TWE. *Application deadline:* For fall admission, 1/4 for domestic students. Application fee: $80. Electronic applications accepted. *Expenses:* Tuition: Full-time $32,556. Required fees: $1426. Full-time tuition and fees vary according to program and student level. *Financial support:* Fellowships, research assistantships, teaching assistantships, career-related internships or fieldwork, Federal Work-Study, institutionally sponsored loans, scholarships/grants, health care benefits, and unspecified assistantships available. Financial award application deadline: 2/2; financial award applicants required to submit CSS PROFILE or FAFSA. *Unit head:* Robin Engel, Director, 617-496-1100, E-mail: robin_engel@harvard.edu. *Application contact:* 617-495-1155.

Hodges University, Graduate Programs, Naples, FL 34119. Offers business administration (MBA); computer information technology (MS); criminal justice (MCJ); education (MPS); information systems management (MIS); interdisciplinary (MPS); law (MPS); management (MSM); professional studies (MPS); psychology (MPS); public administration (MPA). Part-time and evening/weekend programs available. Postbaccalaureate distance learning degree programs offered (no on-campus study). *Faculty:* 13 full-time (4 women), 3 part-time/adjunct (2 women). *Students:* 21 full-time (13 women), 210 part-time (138 women); includes 68 minority (33 African Americans, 2 Asian Americans or Pacific Islanders, 33 Hispanic Americans). Average age 36. In 2008, 82 master's awarded. *Degree requirements:* For master's, comprehensive exam (for some programs). *Entrance requirements:* For master's, in-house entrance exam. *Application deadline:* Applications are processed on a rolling basis. Application fee: $50. Electronic applications accepted. *Expenses:* Tuition: Full-time $16,200; part-time $600 per credit hour. Required fees: $570. *Financial support:* In 2008–09, 200 students received support. Federal Work-Study and scholarships/grants available. Financial award application deadline: 7/9; financial award applicants required to submit FAFSA. *Unit head:* Terry McMahan, President, 239-513-1122, Fax: 239-598-6253, E-mail: tmcmahan@hodges.edu. *Application contact:* Rita Lampus, Vice President of Student Enrollment Management, 239-513-1122, Fax: 239-598-6253, E-mail: rlampus@hodges.edu.

Hood College, Graduate School, Department of Economics and Management, Frederick, MD 21701-8575. Offers accounting (MBA); administration and management (MBA); finance (MBA); human resource management (MBA); information systems (MBA); marketing (MBA); public management (MBA). Part-time and evening/weekend programs available. *Faculty:* 4 full-time (1 woman), 10 part-time/adjunct (1 woman). *Students:* 20 full-time (11 women), 167 part-time (80 women); includes 30 minority (12 African Americans, 8 Asian Americans or Pacific Islanders, 10 Hispanic Americans), 15 international. Average age 33. 70 applicants, 61% accepted, 31 enrolled. In 2008, 38 master's awarded. *Degree requirements:* For master's, capstone/final research project. *Entrance requirements:* For master's, minimum GPA of 2.75, resumé, letters of recommendation. *Application deadline:* For fall admission, 7/15 for domestic and international students; for spring admission, 12/15 for domestic and international students. Applications are processed on a rolling basis. Application fee: $35. Electronic applications accepted. *Expenses:* Tuition: Full-time $6480. Required fees: $100; $50 per semester. *Financial support:* Applicants required to submit FAFSA. *Faculty research:* Corporate strategy and sustainable competitive advantages, business ethics, entrepreneurship, investments management, economic development. *Unit head:* Dr. Micheal Stratton, Program Director, 301-696-3368, Fax: 301-696-3597, E-mail: stratton@hood.edu. *Application contact:* Dr. Allen P. Flora, Dean of Graduate School, 301-696-3811, Fax: 301-696-3597, E-mail: gofurther@hood.edu.

Howard University, Graduate School, Department of Political Science, Program in Public Administration, Washington, DC 20059-0002. Offers MAPA. *Accreditation:* NASPAA. Part-time programs available. *Degree requirements:* For master's, comprehensive exam. *Entrance requirements:* For master's, GRE General Test, minimum GPA of 3.0.

Idaho State University, Office of Graduate Studies, College of Arts and Sciences, Department of Political Science, Program in Public Administration, Pocatello, ID 83209. Offers MPA. Part-time programs available. *Students:* 14 full-time (6 women), 12 part-time (7 women); includes 2 minority (both Hispanic Americans). Average age 32. In 2008, 7 master's awarded.

Degree requirements: For master's, comprehensive exam, thesis optional, public service internship. *Entrance requirements:* For master's, GRE General Test, course work in humanities and social sciences, 3 letters of recommendation. Additional exam requirements/recommendations for international students: Required—TOEFL (minimum score 550 paper-based; 213 computer-based; 80 iBT). *Application deadline:* For fall admission, 7/1 for domestic students, 6/1 for international students; for spring admission, 12/1 for domestic students, 11/1 for international students. Applications are processed on a rolling basis. Application fee: $55. Electronic applications accepted. *Expenses:* Tuition, area resident: Full-time $3114; part-time $276 per credit hour. Tuition, state resident: full-time $3114; part-time $276 per credit hour. Tuition, nonresident: full-time $12,318; part-time $404 per credit hour. Required fees: $2360. Tuition and fees vary according to course load and reciprocity agreements. *Financial support:* Teaching assistantships with full and partial tuition reimbursements, career-related internships or fieldwork, Federal Work-Study, institutionally sponsored loans, scholarships/grants, health care benefits, and unspecified assistantships available. Support available to part-time students. Financial award application deadline: 1/1; financial award applicants required to submit FAFSA. *Faculty research:* Constitutional law, policy theory, public administration, international affairs. *Unit head:* Dr. Wayne Gabardi, Chairman, 208-282-4536, Fax: 208-282-4833, E-mail: gabawayn@isu.edu. *Application contact:* Ellen Combs, Graduate School Technical Records Specialist, 208-282-2150, Fax: 208-282-4847, E-mail: combelle@isu.edu.

Illinois Institute of Technology, Graduate College, College of Science and Letters, Department of Social Sciences, Chicago, IL 60616-3793. Offers nonprofit management (MPA); public administration (MPA); public safety and crisis management (MPA); JD/MPA; MBA/MPA. Part-time and evening/weekend programs available. *Faculty:* 10 full-time (2 women), 14 part-time/adjunct (2 women). *Students:* 18 full-time (11 women), 34 part-time (21 women); includes 21 minority (17 African Americans, 4 Hispanic Americans), 17 international. Average age 31. 176 applicants, 75% accepted, 47 enrolled. In 2008, 71 master's awarded. *Degree requirements:* For master's, comprehensive exam, capstone course (practicum). *Entrance requirements:* For master's, minimum undergraduate GPA of 3.0, 2 letters of recommendation. Additional exam requirements/recommendations for international students: Required—TOEFL (minimum score 550 paper-based; 213 computer-based; 80 iBT). *Application deadline:* For fall admission, 5/1 for domestic and international students; for spring admission, 1/5 for domestic and international students. Applications are processed on a rolling basis. Application fee: $40. Electronic applications accepted. *Financial support:* Federal Work-Study, institutionally sponsored loans, scholarships/grants, and health care benefits available. Support available to part-time students. Financial award applicants required to submit FAFSA. *Faculty research:* Comparative public administration and policy, migration and ethnic politics, social dimension and impact of science and technology, urban politics, urban ethnography. *Unit head:* Dr. Patrick R. Ireland, Professor and Chairman, 312-567-5128, Fax: 312-567-6821, E-mail: socscience@iit.edu. *Application contact:* Lawerence Ruffolo, Assistant Director, Graduate Program in Public Administration, 312-906-5197, Fax: 312-906-5199, E-mail: lruffolo@kentlaw.edu.

Indiana State University, School of Graduate Studies, College of Arts and Sciences, Department of Political Science, Terre Haute, IN 47809-1401. Offers political science (MA, MS); public administration (MPA). *Degree requirements:* For master's, thesis (for some programs). *Entrance requirements:* For master's, GRE or minimum undergraduate GPA of 2.75, 18 semester hours of course work in political science. Additional exam requirements/recommendations for international students: Required—TOEFL (minimum score 550 paper-based). Electronic applications accepted.

Indiana University Bloomington, School of Public and Environmental Affairs, Public Affairs Programs, Bloomington, IN 47405-7000. Offers nonprofit management (Certificate); public affairs (MPA, PhD); public management (Certificate); public policy (PhD); JD/MPA; MPA/MA; MPA/MIS; MPA/MLS; MSES/MPA. *Accreditation:* NASPAA (one or more programs are accredited). Part-time programs available. *Students:* 364 full-time (191 women), 40 part-time (23 women); includes 39 minority (13 African Americans, 2 American Indian/Alaska Native, 10 Asian Americans or Pacific Islanders, 14 Hispanic Americans), 84 international. Average age 28. 724 applicants, 75% accepted, 249 enrolled. In 2008, 229 master's, 13 doctorates, 2 other advanced degrees awarded. Terminal master's awarded for partial completion of doctoral program. *Degree requirements:* For doctorate, thesis/dissertation. *Entrance requirements:* For master's, GMAT or GRE, LSAT; for doctorate, GRE General Test. *Application deadline:* For fall admission, 2/1 priority date for domestic students, 1/15 for international students; for spring admission, 9/1 for international students. Applications are processed on a rolling basis. Application fee: $50 ($60 for international students). *Expenses:* Tuition, area resident: Part-time $291.97 per credit hour. Tuition, state resident: part-time $291.97 per credit hour. Tuition, nonresident: part-time $850.33 per credit hour. Required fees: $110 per semester. Tuition and fees vary according to course load and program. *Financial support:* Fellowships, research assistantships, teaching assistantships, career-related internships or fieldwork, Federal Work-Study, institutionally sponsored loans, and unspecified assistantships available. Financial award application deadline: 2/1; financial award applicants required to submit FAFSA. *Faculty research:* Comparative and international affairs, environmental policy and resource management, policy analysis, public finance, public management, urban management, nonprofit management. *Unit head:* Charles Kurt Zorn, Interim Dean, 812-855-5058, Fax: 812-855-6234, E-mail: zorn@indiana.edu. *Application contact:* Charles A. Johnson, Coordinator of Student Recruitment, 800-765-7755, Fax: 812-855-7802, E-mail: speainfo@indiana.edu.

See Close-Up on page 1219.

Indiana University Kokomo, School of Public and Environmental Affairs, Kokomo, IN 46904-9003. Offers public management (MS, Graduate Certificate).

Indiana University Northwest, School of Public and Environmental Affairs, Gary, IN 46408-1197. Offers criminal justice (MPA); environmental affairs (Graduate Certificate); health services administration (MPA); human services administration (MPA); nonprofit management (Graduate Certificate); public management (MPA, Graduate Certificate). *Accreditation:* NASPAA (one or more programs are accredited). Part-time programs available. *Entrance requirements:* For master's, GRE General Test or GMAT, letters of recommendation. *Faculty research:* Employment in income security policies, evidence in criminal justice, equal employment law, social welfare policy and welfare reform, public finance in developing countries.

Indiana University–Purdue University Indianapolis, School of Public and Environmental Affairs, Indianapolis, IN 46202-2896. Offers health administration (MHA); public affairs (MPA), including criminal justice, environmental management, nonprofit management, policy analysis, public management; JD/MHA; MBA/MHA; MLS/NMC; MLS/PMC; MSN/MHA. *Accreditation:* CAHME (one or more programs are accredited). Part-time and evening/weekend programs available. *Entrance requirements:* For master's, GRE General Test, minimum GPA of 3.0 (preferred). Additional exam requirements/recommendations for international students: Required—TOEFL. *Faculty research:* Economic development, water and air quality, ethics, financing, organization design and structure.

See Close-Up on page 1221.

Indiana University South Bend, School of Public and Environmental Affairs, South Bend, IN 46634-7111. Offers health systems administration and policy (MPA); health systems management (Certificate); nonprofit management (Certificate); public and community services administration and policy (MPA); public management (Certificate); urban affairs (Certificate). *Accreditation:* NASPAA. Part-time and evening/weekend programs available. *Entrance requirements:* For master's, GRE General Test, minimum undergraduate GPA of 2.5.

Institute of Public Administration, Programs in Public Administration, Dublin, Ireland. Offers healthcare management (MA); local government management (MA); public management (MA, Diploma).

Instituto Tecnológico y de Estudios Superiores de Monterrey, Campus Ciudad Juárez, Program in Applied Public Management, Ciudad Juárez, Mexico. Offers MPM.

Iowa State University of Science and Technology, Graduate College, College of Liberal Arts and Sciences, Department of Political Science, Ames, IA 50011. Offers political science (MA); public administration (MPA); JD/MA. *Accreditation:* NASPAA. *Faculty:* 11 full-time (3 women), 5 part-time/adjunct (3 women). *Students:* 22 full-time (8 women), 35 part-time (20 women); includes 3 minority (1 African American, 2 Asian Americans or Pacific Islanders), 9 international. 58 applicants, 67% accepted, 22 enrolled. In 2008, 13 master's awarded. *Degree requirements:* For master's, thesis (for some programs). *Entrance requirements:* For master's, GRE General Test, GMAT or LSAT. Additional exam requirements/recommendations for international students: Required—TOEFL (minimum score 570 paper-based; 80 iBT), IELTS (6.5) or TOEFL. *Application deadline:* For fall admission, 1/1 priority date for domestic and international students; for spring admission, 10/1 for domestic and international students. Applications are processed on a rolling basis. Application fee: $30 ($70 for international students). Electronic applications accepted. *Expenses:* Tuition, area resident: Full-time $6446; part-time $359 per credit. Tuition, state resident: full-time $6446; part-time $359 per credit. Tuition, nonresident: full-time $17,330; part-time $963 per credit. Required fees: $790; $249.25 per semester. Tuition and fees vary according to course load and program. *Financial support:* In 2008–09, 14 research assistantships with full and partial tuition reimbursements (averaging $12,150 per year), 1 teaching assistantship with full and partial tuition reimbursement (averaging $12,600 per year) were awarded; fellowships, scholarships/grants, health care benefits, and unspecified assistantships also available. *Unit head:* Dr. James M. McCormick, Chair, 515-294-8682, Fax: 515-294-1003, E-mail: polsc@iastate.edu. *Application contact:* Dr. Mack Shelley, Director of Graduate Education, 515-294-1075, E-mail: polsci@iastate.edu.

Jackson State University, Graduate School, School of Liberal Arts, Department of Public Policy and Administration, Jackson, MS 39217. Offers MPPA, PhD. *Accreditation:* NASPAA (one or more programs are accredited). Evening/weekend programs available. *Degree requirements:* For master's, comprehensive exam, thesis optional; for doctorate, comprehensive exam, thesis/dissertation. *Entrance requirements:* For master's, GRE General Test; for doctorate, GRE, GMAT, MAT. Additional exam requirements/recommendations for international students: Required—TOEFL.

James Madison University, The Graduate School, College of Arts and Letters, Department of Political Science, Program in Public Administration, Harrisonburg, VA 22807. Offers MPA. Part-time programs available. *Students:* 14 full-time (3 women), 28 part-time (17 women); includes 3 minority (2 African Americans, 1 Asian American or Pacific Islander), 1 international. Average age 27. In 2008, 9 master's awarded. *Degree requirements:* For master's, comprehensive exam. *Entrance requirements:* For master's, GMAT or GRE General Test. Additional exam requirements/recommendations for international students: Required—TOEFL. *Application deadline:* For fall admission, 5/1 priority date for domestic students; for spring admission, 9/1 priority date for domestic students. Applications are processed on a rolling basis. Application fee: $55. Electronic applications accepted. *Expenses:* Tuition, area resident: Full-time $7008; part-time $292 per credit hour. Tuition, state resident: full-time $7008; part-time $292 per credit hour. Tuition, nonresident: full-time $20,352; part-time $848 per credit hour. *Financial support:* In 2008–09, 9 students received support. 9 graduate assistantships ($7,382) available. Financial award application deadline: 3/1; financial award applicants required to submit FAFSA. *Unit head:* Dr. Jessica Adolino, Department Chair, 540-568-6149, E-mail: adolinjr@jmu.edu. *Application contact:* Dr. B. Douglas Skelley, Director, 540-568-6149, E-mail: skellebd@jmu.edu.

John Jay College of Criminal Justice of the City University of New York, Graduate Studies, Program in Public Administration, New York, NY 10019-1093. Offers MPA. *Accreditation:* NASPAA. Part-time and evening/weekend programs available. *Degree requirements:* For master's, thesis or alternative. *Entrance requirements:* For master's, minimum B average. Additional exam requirements/recommendations for international students: Required—TOEFL (minimum score 500 paper-based; 173 computer-based).

Kansas State University, Graduate School, College of Arts and Sciences, Department of Political Science, Program in Public Administration, Manhattan, KS 66506. Offers MPA. *Accreditation:* NASPAA. Part-time programs available. *Students:* 13 full-time (5 women), 6 part-time (5 women); includes 2 minority (both Asian Americans or Pacific Islanders), 5 international. Average age 29. 16 applicants, 94% accepted, 8 enrolled. In 2008, 7 master's awarded. *Degree requirements:* For master's, thesis or alternative, comprehensive written and oral exams. *Entrance requirements:* For master's, GRE (recommended), minimum GPA of 3.0. Additional exam requirements/recommendations for international students: Required—TOEFL (minimum score 550 paper-based; 213 computer-based). *Application deadline:* For fall admission, 2/1 priority date for domestic and international students; for spring admission, 10/1 for domestic students, 8/1 for international students. Applications are processed on a rolling basis. Application fee: $30 ($55 for international students). *Expenses:* Tuition, area resident: Full-time $6466; part-time $269.40 per credit hour. Tuition, state resident: full-time $6466; part-time $269.40 per credit hour. Tuition, nonresident: full-time $14,874; part-time $619.75 per credit hour. Required fees: $673; $23.40 per credit hour. Tuition and fees vary according to campus/location. *Financial support:* Fellowships, research assistantships, teaching assistantships, career-related internships or fieldwork, institutionally sponsored loans, and scholarships/grants available. Support available to part-time students. Financial award application deadline: 3/1; financial award applicants required to submit FAFSA. *Faculty research:* Comparative administration, comparative affirmative action, tourism, agricultural policy, state and local government. *Application contact:* Prof. Krishna Tummala, Director, 785-532-0452, Fax: 785-532-2339, E-mail: tummala@ksu.edu.

Kean University, College of Business and Public Administration, Program in Public Administration, Union, NJ 07083. Offers environmental management (MPA); health services administration (MPA); non-profit management (MPA); public administration (MPA). *Accreditation:* NASPAA. Part-time and evening/weekend programs available. *Faculty:* 8 full-time (4 women). *Students:* 43 full-time (28 women), 95 part-time (55 women); includes 82 minority (59 African Americans, 1 American Indian/Alaska Native, 4 Asian Americans or Pacific Islanders, 18 Hispanic Americans), 9 international. Average age 31. 89 applicants, 66% accepted, 29 enrolled. In 2008, 44 master's awarded. *Degree requirements:* For master's, thesis, internship, research seminar. *Entrance requirements:* For master's, 2 letters of recommendation, interview, essay. *Application deadline:* For fall admission, 5/1 for domestic students; for spring admission, 11/1 for domestic students. Application fee: $60 ($150 for international students). Electronic applications accepted. *Expenses:* Tuition, state resident: full-time $10,128; part-time $422 per credit. Tuition, nonresident: full-time $13,728; part-time $572 per credit. Required fees: $2570; $107 per credit. Part-time tuition and fees vary according to course load, degree level and program. *Financial support:* In 2008–09, 10 research assistantships with full tuition reimbursements (averaging $3,217 per year) were awarded; unspecified assistantships also available. *Unit head:* Dr. Patricia Moore, Program Coordinator, 908-737-4300, E-mail: pmoore@kean.edu. *Application contact:* Steven Koch, Pre-Admissions Coordinator, 908-737-4723, Fax: 908-737-5965, E-mail: grad-adm@kean.edu.

Kean University, College of Natural, Applied and Health Sciences, Program in Nursing and Public Administration, Union, NJ 07083. Offers MSN/MPA. *Accreditation:* NLN. Part-time and evening/weekend programs available. *Faculty:* 8 full-time (all women). *Students:* 2 full-time (1 woman), 3 part-time (all women); includes all African Americans. Average age 44. 1 applicant, 100% accepted, 1 enrolled. *Application deadline:* For fall admission, 5/1 for domestic students; for spring admission, 11/1 for domestic students. Application fee: $60 ($150 for international students). Electronic applications accepted. *Expenses:* Tuition, state resident: full-time $10,128; part-time $422 per credit. Tuition, nonresident: full-time $13,728; part-time $572 per credit. Required fees: $2570; $107 per credit. Part-time tuition and fees vary according to course load, degree level and program. *Financial support:* In 2008–09, research assistantships with full tuition reimbursements (averaging $3,217 per year); unspecified assistantships also available. *Unit head:* Dr. Estelle A. Pisani, Program Coordinator, 908-737-3390, E-mail: episani@kean.edu. *Application contact:* Steven Koch, Pre-Admissions Coordinator, 908-737-4723, Fax: 908-737-5965, E-mail: grad-adm@kean.edu.

Public Administration

Kennesaw State University, College of Humanities and Social Sciences, Program in Public Administration, Kennesaw, GA 30144-5591. Offers MPA. *Accreditation:* NASPAA. Part-time and evening/weekend programs available. *Faculty:* 11 full-time (7 women), 4 part-time/adjunct (1 woman). *Students:* 47 full-time (26 women), 49 part-time (33 women); includes 24 minority (20 African Americans, 2 Asian Americans or Pacific Islanders, 2 Hispanic Americans), 34 international. Average age 31. 50 applicants, 54% accepted, 18 enrolled. In 2008, 24 master's awarded. *Entrance requirements:* For master's, GRE General Test, minimum GPA of 2.75. Additional exam requirements/recommendations for international students: Required—TOEFL (minimum score 550 paper-based; 213 computer-based; 80 iBT), IELTS (minimum score 6). *Application deadline:* For fall admission, 8/1 for domestic and international students; for winter admission, 12/1 for domestic and international students; for spring admission, 5/1 for domestic students, 8/1 for international students. Applications are processed on a rolling basis. Application fee: $60. Electronic applications accepted. *Expenses:* Tuition, area resident: Full-time $3668; part-time $153 per semester hour. Tuition, state resident: full-time $3668; part-time $153 per semester hour. Tuition, nonresident: full-time $14,670; part-time $612 per semester hour. Required fees: $948; $474 per semester. *Financial support:* In 2008–09, 2 research assistantships with full tuition reimbursements (averaging $15,000 per year) were awarded; Federal Work-Study also available. Support available to part-time students. Financial award application deadline: 6/15; financial award applicants required to submit FAFSA. *Unit head:* Dr. Andrew Ewoh, Director, 770-423-6246, E-mail: aewoh@kennesaw.edu. *Application contact:* Vilma Marquez, Admissions Counselor, 770-420-4377, Fax: 770-423-6885, E-mail: ksugrad@kennesaw.edu.

Kent State University, College of Arts and Sciences, Department of Political Science, Program in Public Administration, Kent, OH 44242-0001. Offers MPA. *Accreditation:* NASPAA. *Degree requirements:* For master's, thesis optional, public sector internship. *Entrance requirements:* For master's, GRE General Test, minimum GPA of 2.75. Additional exam requirements/recommendations for international students: Required—TOEFL. Electronic applications accepted.

Kentucky State University, College of Professional Studies, Frankfort, KY 40601. Offers business administration (MBA), including accounting, finance, management, marketing; public administration (MPA), including human resource management, international administration and development, management information systems, nonprofit management; special education (MA). Part-time and evening/weekend programs available. Postbaccalaureate distance learning degree programs offered (minimal on-campus study). *Faculty:* 12 full-time (2 women), 1 (woman) part-time/adjunct. *Students:* 48 full-time (27 women), 75 part-time (39 women); includes 68 minority (66 African Americans, 2 Asian Americans or Pacific Islanders), 5 international. Average age 34. 90 applicants, 73% accepted, 45 enrolled. In 2008, 37 master's awarded. *Degree requirements:* For master's, comprehensive exam, thesis optional. *Entrance requirements:* For master's, GMAT. Additional exam requirements/recommendations for international students: Required—TOEFL (minimum score 525 paper-based; 173 computer-based). *Application deadline:* For fall admission, 7/1 priority date for domestic students, 4/1 priority date for international students; for spring admission, 11/15 priority date for domestic students, 8/15 priority date for international students. Applications are processed on a rolling basis. Application fee: $30 ($100 for international students). Electronic applications accepted. *Expenses:* Tuition, area resident: Full-time $5400; part-time $325 per credit hour. Tuition, state resident: full-time $5400; part-time $325 per credit hour. Tuition, nonresident: full-time $13,230; part-time $760 per credit hour. Required fees: $450. Tuition and fees vary according to course load. *Financial support:* In 2008–09, 103 students received support. Scholarships/grants, tuition waivers (partial), and unspecified assistantships available. Financial award application deadline: 4/15; financial award applicants required to submit FAFSA. *Unit head:* Dr. Gashaw Lake, Dean, E-mail: gashaw.lake@kysu.edu. *Application contact:* Cedric Cunningham, Coordinator, Office of Graduate Studies, 502-597-6536, E-mail: cedric.cunningham@kysu.edu.

Kutztown University of Pennsylvania, College of Graduate Studies and Extended Learning, College of Liberal Arts and Sciences, Program in Public Administration, Kutztown, PA 19530-0730. Offers MPA. Part-time and evening/weekend programs available. *Faculty:* 4 full-time (2 women), 1 part-time/adjunct (0 women). *Students:* 4 full-time (2 women), 19 part-time (11 women); includes 5 minority (2 African Americans, 2 American Indian/Alaska Native, 1 Hispanic American). Average age 29. 18 applicants, 61% accepted, 8 enrolled. In 2008, 10 master's awarded. *Degree requirements:* For master's, comprehensive exam, thesis optional. *Entrance requirements:* For master's, GRE General Test. Additional exam requirements/recommendations for international students: Required—TOEFL. *Application deadline:* For fall admission, 8/15 priority date for domestic and international students; for spring admission, 12/15 priority date for domestic and international students. Applications are processed on a rolling basis. Application fee: $35. Electronic applications accepted. *Expenses:* Tuition, area resident: Full-time $6430; part-time $357 per credit. Tuition, state resident: full-time $6430; part-time $357 per credit. Tuition, nonresident: full-time $10,288; part-time $572 per credit. Required fees: $1360; $72 per credit. $67 per semester. *Financial support:* Career-related internships or fieldwork, Federal Work-Study, scholarships/grants, and unspecified assistantships available. Financial award application deadline: 3/1; financial award applicants required to submit FAFSA. *Faculty research:* Structure of code enforcement offices in smaller developing communities. *Unit head:* Dr. Kristin Bremer, Chairperson, 610-683-4449, Fax: 610-683-4603, E-mail: bremer@kutztown.edu. *Application contact:* Dr. Linda Matthews, Interim Dean of Graduate Studies, 610-683-4201, Fax: 610-683-1393, E-mail: graduate@kutztown.edu.

Lamar University, College of Graduate Studies, College of Arts and Sciences, Department of Political Science, Beaumont, TX 77710. Offers public administration (MPA). Part-time programs available. *Faculty:* 3 full-time (0 women). *Students:* 6 full-time (3 women), 4 part-time (2 women); includes 5 minority (4 African Americans, 1 Asian American or Pacific Islander). Average age 26. 18 applicants, 39% accepted, 5 enrolled. In 2008, 2 master's awarded. *Entrance requirements:* For master's, GRE General Test. Additional exam requirements/recommendations for international students: Required—TOEFL. *Application deadline:* For fall admission, 8/1 for domestic students; for spring admission, 12/1 for domestic students. Applications are processed on a rolling basis. Application fee: $25 ($50 for international students). *Expenses:* Tuition, state resident: full-time $5000; part-time $195 per credit. Tuition, nonresident: full-time $12,376; part-time $476 per credit. Required fees: $1570. *Financial support:* Fellowships, research assistantships, teaching assistantships, career-related internships or fieldwork, Federal Work-Study, and institutionally sponsored loans available. Financial award application deadline: 4/1. *Faculty research:* Political activities of administrators, administrative response to Hurricane Rita, budgeting, environmental politics, urban planning. *Unit head:* Dr. Glenn Utter, Chair, 409-880-8526, Fax: 409-880-8710. *Application contact:* Dr. Terri Davis, Director, 409-880-8533, Fax: 409-880-1710, E-mail: davistb@hal.lamar.edu.

Lewis University, College of Arts and Sciences, Program in Organizational Leadership, Romeoville, IL 60446. Offers higher education/student services (MA); organizational management (MA); public administration (MA); training and development (MA). Part-time and evening/weekend programs available. *Students:* 16 full-time (13 women), 117 part-time (88 women); includes 37 minority (29 African Americans, 1 American Indian/Alaska Native, 1 Asian American or Pacific Islander, 6 Hispanic Americans), 2 international. Average age 39. In 2008, 43 master's awarded. *Entrance requirements:* For master's, bachelor's degree, at least 25 years of age, minimum of 3 years of work experience, minimum GPA of 3.0, letter of recommendation, interview. Additional exam requirements/recommendations for international students: Required—TOEFL (minimum score 550 paper-based; 213 computer-based). *Application deadline:* For fall admission, 5/1 priority date for international students; for spring admission, 11/15 priority date for international students. Applications are processed on a rolling basis. Application fee: $40. Electronic applications accepted. *Financial support:* Federal Work-Study, scholarships/grants, tuition waivers, and unspecified assistantships available. Financial award application deadline: 5/1; financial award applicants required to submit FAFSA. *Unit head:* Dr. Rich Walsh, Director, 815-838-0500, E-mail: walshri@lewisu.edu. *Application contact:* Bernadette Valderrama, Information Contact, 815-838-0500 Ext. 5629.

Lincoln University, School of Graduate Studies and Continuing Education, College of Business and Professional Studies, Department of Business and Economics, Jefferson City, MO 65102.

Offers business administration (MBA), including accounting, entrepreneurship, management, public administration and policy. *Accreditation:* ACBSP. Part-time and evening/weekend programs available. *Faculty:* 7 full-time (1 woman), 1 part-time/adjunct (0 women). *Students:* 20 full-time (11 women), 13 part-time (8 women); includes 10 minority (all African Americans), 6 international. Average age 31. 12 applicants, 100% accepted, 6 enrolled. In 2008, 19 master's awarded. *Degree requirements:* For master's, comprehensive exam, thesis optional, portfolio. *Entrance requirements:* For master's, GMAT, undergraduate prerequisite courses. Additional exam requirements/recommendations for international students: Required—TOEFL (minimum score 500 paper-based; 173 computer-based; 61 iBT). *Application deadline:* For fall admission, 7/1 priority date for domestic and international students; for spring admission, 12/1 priority date for domestic and international students. Applications are processed on a rolling basis. Application fee: $20. *Expenses:* Tuition, area resident: Full-time $4185; part-time $232.50 per credit hour. Tuition, nonresident: full-time $7767; part-time $431.50 per credit hour. Required fees: $270; $15 per credit hour. $252.50 per semester. One-time fee: $20. Tuition and fees vary according to course load. *Financial support:* Federal Work-Study and scholarships/grants available. Financial award application deadline: 4/1; financial award applicants required to submit FAFSA. *Unit head:* Dr. Roberto Ike, Department Head, 573-681-6076, Fax: 573-681-6085, E-mail: iker@lincolnu.edu. *Application contact:* Irasema Steck, Administrative Assistant, 573-681-5247, Fax: 573-681-5106, E-mail: gradschool@lincolnu.edu.

Lindenwood University, Graduate Programs, School of Business and Entrepreneurship, St. Charles, MO 63301-1695. Offers accounting (MBA, MS); business administration (MBA); entrepreneurial studies (MBA, MS); finance (MBA, MS); human resource management (MBA); human resources (MS); international business (MBA, MS); management (MBA, MS); management information systems (MBA, MS); marketing (MBA, MS); public management (MBA, MS); sport management (MA). Part-time and evening/weekend programs available. *Faculty:* 19 full-time (7 women), 17 part-time/adjunct (5 women). *Students:* 198 full-time (91 women), 162 part-time (67 women); includes 23 minority (17 African Americans, 1 American Indian/Alaska Native, 4 Asian Americans or Pacific Islanders, 1 Hispanic American), 107 international. Average age 31. In 2008, 158 master's awarded. *Degree requirements:* For master's, thesis (for some programs), minimum GPA of 3.0. *Entrance requirements:* For master's, interview, minimum GPA of 3.0, official transcripts, letter of recommendation. Additional exam requirements/recommendations for international students: Required—TOEFL (minimum score 550 paper-based; 213 computer-based; 80 iBT). *Application deadline:* For fall admission, 7/30 priority date for domestic students, 9/30 priority date for international students; for winter admission, 12/30 priority date for domestic and international students; for spring admission, 2/28 priority date for domestic and international students. Applications are processed on a rolling basis. Application fee: $30 ($100 for international students). Electronic applications accepted. *Expenses:* Tuition: Full-time $12,700; part-time $360 per credit hour. *Financial support:* Career-related internships or fieldwork, Federal Work-Study, institutionally sponsored loans, and tuition waivers (partial) available. Financial award application deadline: 6/30; financial award applicants required to submit FAFSA. *Unit head:* Ed Morris, Dean of Management, 636-949-4832, E-mail: emorris@lindenwood.edu. *Application contact:* Brett Barger, Dean of Evening Admissions and Extension Campuses, 636-949-4934, Fax: 636-949-4109, E-mail: adultadmissions@lindenwood.edu.

Long Island University, Brooklyn Campus, School of Business, Public Administration and Information Sciences, Program in Public Administration, Brooklyn, NY 11201-8423. Offers MPA. *Accreditation:* NASPAA. Part-time and evening/weekend programs available. *Entrance requirements:* For master's, GMAT or GRE Subject Test, 2 letters of recommendation. Additional exam requirements/recommendations for international students: Required—TOEFL (minimum score 500 paper-based; 173 computer-based). Electronic applications accepted.

Long Island University, C.W. Post Campus, College of Management, Department of Health Care and Public Administration, Brookville, NY 11548-1300. Offers gerontology (Certificate); health care administration (MPA); health care administration/gerontology (MPA); nonprofit management (MPA, Certificate); public administration (MPA). *Accreditation:* NASPAA (one or more programs are accredited). Part-time and evening/weekend programs available. *Degree requirements:* For master's, thesis. *Entrance requirements:* For master's, GMAT, minimum GPA of 2.5; for Certificate, minimum GPA of 2.5. Electronic applications accepted. *Faculty research:* Critical issues in sexuality, social work in religious communities, gerontological social work.

Long Island University, Rockland Graduate Campus, Graduate School, Programs in Health and Public Administration, Orangeburg, NY 10962. Offers gerontology (Advanced Certificate); health administration (MPA); public administration (MPA). *Entrance requirements:* For master's, GRE General Test. *Expenses:* Tuition: Full-time $882; part-time $882 per credit. Required fees: $200; $100 per semester.

Louisiana State University and Agricultural and Mechanical College, Graduate School, E. J. Ourso College of Business, Public Administration Institute, Baton Rouge, LA 70803. Offers MPA, JD/MPA. Part-time programs available. *Degree requirements:* For master's, comprehensive exam. *Entrance requirements:* For master's, GRE General Test, minimum GPA of 3.0. Additional exam requirements/recommendations for international students: Required—TOEFL (minimum score 550 paper-based; 213 computer-based; 79 iBT). Electronic applications accepted. *Faculty research:* Policy analysis, health care policy, financial and budget analysis.

Louisiana State University and Agricultural and Mechanical College, Graduate School, Manship School of Mass Communication, Baton Rouge, LA 70803. Offers MMC, PhD. *Accreditation:* ACEJMC. Part-time programs available. Postbaccalaureate distance learning degree programs offered (minimal on-campus study). *Degree requirements:* For master's, thesis. *Entrance requirements:* For master's, GRE General Test, minimum GPA of 3.0. Additional exam requirements/recommendations for international students: Required—TOEFL (minimum score 550 paper-based; 213 computer-based; 79 iBT). Electronic applications accepted. *Faculty research:* Media effects, political communication, new media technologies, persuasive communication, journalism processes and practice.

Marist College, Graduate Programs, School of Management, Program in Public Administration, Poughkeepsie, NY 12601-1387. Offers MPA. Part-time and evening/weekend programs available. Postbaccalaureate distance learning degree programs offered (no on-campus study). *Entrance requirements:* For master's, GRE General Test, resumé, personal statement, transcript. Additional exam requirements/recommendations for international students: Required—TOEFL (minimum score 550 paper-based; 213 computer-based; 80 iBT); Recommended—IELTS (minimum score 6.5). Electronic applications accepted. *Faculty research:* Public policy analysis, health administration.

Marquette University, Graduate School, Program in Public Service, Milwaukee, WI 53201-1881. Offers MAPS.

Marywood University, Academic Affairs, College of Health and Human Services, Department of Nursing and Public Administration, Program in Public Administration, Scranton, PA 18509-1598. Offers criminal justice (MPA); public administration (MPA); MPA/MSW. *Degree requirements:* For master's, thesis or alternative, internship/practicum. *Entrance requirements:* Additional exam requirements/recommendations for international students: Required—TOEFL (minimum score 550 paper-based; 213 computer-based). Electronic applications accepted.

McMaster University, School of Graduate Studies, Faculty of Social Sciences, Department of Political Science, Hamilton, ON L8S 4M2, Canada. Offers international relations (PhD); political science (MA); public and the global economy (MA); public policy (PhD); public policy and administration (MA). Part-time programs available. *Degree requirements:* For master's, thesis or alternative. *Entrance requirements:* For master's, minimum B+ average. Additional exam requirements/recommendations for international students: Required—TOEFL (minimum score 580 paper-based; 237 computer-based). *Faculty research:* Organizational theory, internationalization of public policy, water resource policies, political interest intermediation, comparative politics.

Metropolitan College of New York, Program in Public Administration, New York, NY 10013. Offers MPA. Evening/weekend programs available. *Degree requirements:* For master's, thesis. *Entrance requirements:* For master's, appropriate work experience, interview, minimum GPA of 2.7, internship or job in administrative setting. Additional exam requirements/recommendations for international students: Required—TOEFL (minimum score 600 paper-based; 220 computer-based). Electronic applications accepted. *Expenses:* Contact institution. *Faculty research:* Transnational politics and culture, women and social policy, confidentiality in the human services, concepts of marginality, ethics in social policy.

Metropolitan State University, College of Management, St. Paul, MN 55106-5000. Offers business administration (MBA); information management (MMIS); MIS generalist (Graduate Certificate); MIS systems analysis (Graduate Certificate); nonprofit management (MPNA); project management (Graduate Certificate); public administration (MPNA); systems management (MMIS). Part-time and evening/weekend programs available. *Degree requirements:* For master's, thesis optional, computer language (MMIS). *Entrance requirements:* For master's, GMAT (MBA), resumé. Additional exam requirements/recommendations for international students: Required—TOEFL (minimum score 550 paper-based; 213 computer-based). *Faculty research:* Yugoslav economic system, workers' cooperatives, participative management and job enrichment, global business systems.

Midwestern State University, Graduate Studies, College of Health Sciences and Human Services, Program in Health Services and Public Administration, Wichita Falls, TX 76308. Offers health services administration (MHA); public administration (MPA); public administration (administrative justice) (MPA); public administration (health services administration) with certificate (MPA); public administration (health services) (MPA). Part-time and evening/weekend programs available. *Degree requirements:* For master's, comprehensive exam, thesis. *Entrance requirements:* For master's, GRE. Additional exam requirements/recommendations for international students: Required—TOEFL (minimum score 550 paper-based; 213 computer-based). Electronic applications accepted.

Minnesota State University Mankato, College of Graduate Studies, College of Social and Behavioral Sciences, Department of Political Science and Law Enforcement, Program in Public Administration, Mankato, MN 56001. Offers MAPA, MAPA/MA. *Students:* 18 full-time (7 women), 40 part-time (17 women). *Degree requirements:* For master's, one foreign language, comprehensive exam, thesis or alternative. *Entrance requirements:* For master's, minimum GPA of 3.0 during previous 2 years. Additional exam requirements/recommendations for international students: Required—TOEFL. *Application deadline:* For fall admission, 3/1 priority date for domestic students. Applications are processed on a rolling basis. Application fee: $40. Electronic applications accepted. *Financial support:* Research assistantships with full tuition reimbursements, teaching assistantships with full tuition reimbursements, unspecified assistantships available. Financial award application deadline: 3/15; financial award applicants required to submit FAFSA. *Unit head:* Dr. Scott Granberg-Rademacker, Graduate Coordinator, 507-389-6939. *Application contact:* 507-389-2321, E-mail: grad@mnsu.edu.

Minnesota State University Moorhead, Graduate Studies, College of Social and Natural Sciences, Program in Public, Human Services, and Health Administration, Moorhead, MN 56563-0002. Offers MS. Part-time and evening/weekend programs available. *Degree requirements:* For master's, final oral exam, final project paper or thesis. *Entrance requirements:* For master's, GRE General Test, minimum GPA of 2.75. Additional exam requirements/recommendations for international students: Required—TOEFL (minimum score 550 paper-based; 213 computer-based). Electronic applications accepted.

Mississippi State University, College of Arts and Sciences, Department of Political Science and Public Administration, Mississippi State, MS 39762. Offers political science (MA); public policy and administration (MPPA, PhD). *Accreditation:* NASPAA (one or more programs are accredited). Evening/weekend programs available. *Degree requirements:* For master's, comprehensive oral or written exam; for doctorate, thesis/dissertation, comprehensive oral and written exam. *Entrance requirements:* For master's, minimum GPA of 3.0; for doctorate, GRE General Test, minimum graduate GPA of 3.35. Additional exam requirements/recommendations for international students: Required—TOEFL. *Faculty research:* American politics, international relations, state and local government, comparative government, public administration.

Missouri State University, Graduate College, College of Humanities and Public Affairs, Department of Political Science, Program in Public Administration, Springfield, MO 65804-0094. Offers MPA. *Accreditation:* NASPAA. Part-time programs available. *Students:* 18 full-time (8 women), 11 part-time (4 women); includes 1 minority (African American), 1 international. Average age 28. 9 applicants, 100% accepted, 5 enrolled. In 2008, 11 master's awarded. *Degree requirements:* For master's, comprehensive exam, thesis or alternative, internship. *Entrance requirements:* For master's, GRE, minimum GPA of 3.0. Additional exam requirements/recommendations for international students: Required—TOEFL (minimum score 550 paper-based; 213 computer-based; 79 iBT). *Application deadline:* For fall admission, 7/20 priority date for domestic students, 5/1 for international students; for spring admission, 12/20 priority date for domestic students, 9/1 for international students. Applications are processed on a rolling basis. Application fee: $35 ($50 for international students). Electronic applications accepted. *Expenses:* Tuition, state resident: full-time $3852; part-time $214 per credit hour. Tuition, nonresident: full-time $7524; part-time $418 per credit hour. Required fees: $230 per semester. Tuition and fees vary according to course level and course load. *Financial support:* Career-related internships or fieldwork, Federal Work-Study, and unspecified assistantships available. Support available to part-time students. Financial award application deadline: 3/31; financial award applicants required to submit FAFSA. *Faculty research:* Public management, environmental policy, health care policy, law and religion. *Unit head:* Dr. Kant Patel, Graduate Director, 417-836-6925, Fax: 417-836-6655, E-mail: kantpatel@missouristate.edu. *Application contact:* Dr. Kant Patel, Graduate Director, 417-836-6925, Fax: 417-836-6655, E-mail: kantpatel@missouristate.edu.

Missouri State University, Graduate College, Interdisciplinary Program in Administrative Studies, Springfield, MO 65804-0094. Offers applied communication (MS); criminal justice (MS); environmental management (MS); project management (MS); sports management (MS). Part-time and evening/weekend programs available. Postbaccalaureate distance learning degree programs offered (no on-campus study). *Students:* 16 full-time (9 women), 56 part-time (25 women); includes 7 minority (4 African Americans, 2 Asian Americans or Pacific Islanders, 1 Hispanic American). Average age 34. 16 applicants, 100% accepted, 12 enrolled. In 2008, 33 master's awarded. *Degree requirements:* For master's, comprehensive exam, thesis or alternative. *Entrance requirements:* For master's, GRE, GMAT, 3 years of work experience. Additional exam requirements/recommendations for international students: Required—TOEFL (minimum score 550 paper-based; 213 computer-based; 79 iBT). *Application deadline:* For fall admission, 7/20 priority date for domestic students; for spring admission, 12/20 priority date for domestic students. Applications are processed on a rolling basis. Application fee: $35 ($50 for international students). Electronic applications accepted. *Expenses:* Tuition, state resident: full-time $3852; part-time $214 per credit hour. Tuition, nonresident: full-time $7524; part-time $418 per credit hour. Required fees: $230 per semester. Tuition and fees vary according to course level and course load. *Financial support:* In 2008–09, 4 teaching assistantships with full tuition reimbursements (averaging $8,535 per year) were awarded; career-related internships or fieldwork, Federal Work-Study, institutionally sponsored loans, scholarships/grants, and unspecified assistantships also available. Support available to part-time students. Financial award application deadline: 3/31; financial award applicants required to submit FAFSA. *Unit head:* John Bourhis, Director, 417-836-6390, E-mail: johnbourhis@missouristate.edu. *Application contact:* Eric Eckert, Coordinator of Graduate Admissions and Recruitment, 417-836-5331, Fax: 417-836-6888, E-mail: ericeckert@missouristate.edu.

Montana State University, College of Graduate Studies, College of Letters and Science, Department of Political Science, Bozeman, MT 59717. Offers public administration (MPA). Part-time programs available. *Degree requirements:* For master's, comprehensive exam, thesis (for some programs). *Entrance requirements:* For master's, GRE General Test. Additional exam requirements/recommendations for international students: Required—TOEFL (minimum score 550 paper-based; 213 computer-based). Electronic applications accepted. *Faculty research:* Natural resources policy, civil society, new west economics, organization development, media analysis.

Montana State University–Billings, College of Arts and Sciences, Program in Public Administration, Billings, MT 59101-0298. Offers MPA.

Monterey Institute of International Studies, Graduate School of International Policy Studies, Program in International Public Administration, Monterey, CA 93940-2691. Offers international management (MPA). *Students:* 67 full-time (52 women), 1 (woman) part-time; includes 15 minority (6 African Americans, 4 Asian Americans or Pacific Islanders, 5 Hispanic Americans), 17 international. Average age 26. 74 applicants, 93% accepted, 28 enrolled. In 2008, 38 master's awarded. *Degree requirements:* For master's, one foreign language. *Entrance requirements:* For master's, minimum GPA of 3.0, proficiency in a foreign language. Additional exam requirements/recommendations for international students: Required—TOEFL (minimum score 550 paper-based; 213 computer-based; 80 iBT). *Application deadline:* For fall admission, 3/15 priority date for domestic and international students; for spring admission, 10/1 priority date for domestic and international students. Applications are processed on a rolling basis. Application fee: $50. Electronic applications accepted. *Expenses:* Tuition: Full-time $29,300; part-time $1400 per credit. Required fees: $56. *Financial support:* In 2008–09, 76 students received support. Career-related internships or fieldwork, Federal Work-Study, and institutionally sponsored loans available. Support available to part-time students. Financial award application deadline: 3/15; financial award applicants required to submit FAFSA. *Application contact:* 831-647-4123, Fax: 831-647-6405, E-mail: admit@miis.edu.

See Close-Up on page 871.

Morehead State University, Graduate Programs, Institute for Regional Analysis and Public Policy, Morehead, KY 40351. Offers public administration (MPA). *Faculty:* 2 full-time (1 woman), 1 part-time/adjunct (0 women). *Students:* 18 full-time (9 women), 7 part-time (6 women); includes 2 minority (both African Americans). Average age 28. 49 applicants, 31% accepted, 10 enrolled. In 2008, 6 master's awarded. *Entrance requirements:* For master's, GRE. Additional exam requirements/recommendations for international students: Required—TOEFL (minimum score 500 paper-based). *Application deadline:* For fall admission, 8/1 priority date for domestic and international students; for spring admission, 12/1 priority date for domestic and international students. Applications are processed on a rolling basis. Application fee: $30 ($55 for international students). Electronic applications accepted. *Expenses:* Tuition, area resident: Full-time $6084; part-time $338 per credit hour. Tuition, state resident: full-time $6084; part-time $338 per credit hour. Tuition, nonresident: full-time $15,804; part-time $878 per credit hour. *Financial support:* In 2008–09, 10 teaching assistantships (averaging $6,000 per year) were awarded. *Unit head:* Dr. David Rudy, Dean, 606-783-5419, Fax: 606-783-5092, E-mail: d.rudy@moreheadstate.edu. *Application contact:* Michelle Barber, Graduate Admissions Counselor, 606-783-2039, Fax: 606-783-5061, E-mail: m.barber@moreheadstate.edu.

National University, Academic Affairs, College of Letters and Sciences, Department of Professional Studies, La Jolla, CA 92037-1011. Offers forensic science (MFS), including criminalistics and investigation; public administration (MPA), including alternative dispute resolution, human resource management, organizational leadership, public finance. Part-time and evening/weekend programs available. Postbaccalaureate distance learning degree programs offered (no on-campus study). *Faculty:* 9 full-time (3 women), 134 part-time/adjunct (31 women). *Students:* 126 full-time (67 women), 195 part-time (103 women); includes 137 minority (56 African Americans, 26 Asian Americans or Pacific Islanders, 55 Hispanic Americans), 2 international. Average age 38. 241 applicants, 100% accepted, 241 enrolled. In 2008, 104 master's awarded. *Degree requirements:* For master's, thesis. *Entrance requirements:* For master's, interview, minimum GPA of 2.5. Additional exam requirements/recommendations for international students: Required—TOEFL (minimum score 550 paper-based; 213 computer-based; 79 iBT), IELTS (minimum score 6). *Application deadline:* Applications are processed on a rolling basis. Application fee: $60 ($65 for international students). Electronic applications accepted. *Expenses:* Tuition: Full-time $8694; part-time $322 per credit hour. Tuition and fees vary according to course load. *Financial support:* Career-related internships or fieldwork, institutionally sponsored loans, scholarships/grants, and tuition waivers (partial) available. Support available to part-time students. Financial award application deadline: 6/30; financial award applicants required to submit FAFSA. *Unit head:* Chandrika M. Kelso, Associate Professor and Chair, 858-642-8433, Fax: 858-642-8715, E-mail: ckelso@nu.edu. *Application contact:* Dominick Giovanniello, Associate Regional Dean—San Diego, 800-NAT-UNIV, Fax: 858-541-7792, E-mail: dgiovann@nu.edu.

National University of Singapore, Lee Kuan Yew School of Public Policy, Singapore, Singapore. Offers MPA, MPM, MPP, PhD.

New York University, Robert F. Wagner Graduate School of Public Service, Program in Public Administration, New York, NY 10012-1019. Offers public administration (PhD); public and nonprofit management and policy (MPA, Advanced Certificate), including developmental administration (Advanced Certificate), financial management and public finance, human resources management (Advanced Certificate), international administration (Advanced Certificate), management (MPA), management for public and nonprofit organizations (Advanced Certificate), public policy analysis, quantitative analysis and computer applications (Advanced Certificate), urban public policy (Advanced Certificate); JD/MPA; MBA/MPA; MPA/MA. *Accreditation:* NASPAA (one or more programs are accredited). Part-time and evening/weekend programs available. *Degree requirements:* For master's, thesis or alternative, capstone/end event; for doctorate, one foreign language, thesis/dissertation. *Entrance requirements:* For master's, minimum undergraduate GPA of 3.0; for doctorate, GMAT or GRE General Test, minimum GPA of 3.5. Additional exam requirements/recommendations for international students: Required—TOEFL (minimum score 600 paper-based; 250 computer-based; 100 iBT), TWE (minimum score 4). Electronic applications accepted. *Expenses:* Contact institution.

See Close-Up on page 1229.

North Carolina Central University, Division of Academic Affairs, College of Behavioral and Social Sciences, Department of Public Administration, Durham, NC 27707-3129. Offers MPA. Part-time and evening/weekend programs available. *Degree requirements:* For master's, one foreign language, comprehensive exam, thesis or alternative. *Entrance requirements:* For master's, GRE, minimum GPA of 3.0 in major, 2.5 overall. Additional exam requirements/recommendations for international students: Required—TOEFL. *Faculty research:* Racial diversity and community policing, economic development, issues in urban transportation.

North Carolina State University, Graduate School, College of Humanities and Social Sciences, School of Public and International Affairs, Program in Public Administration, Raleigh, NC 27695. Offers MPA, PhD. *Accreditation:* NASPAA. *Degree requirements:* For master's, thesis optional; for doctorate, thesis/dissertation. *Entrance requirements:* For master's, GRE General Test, minimum GPA of 3.0 during previous 2 years; for doctorate, GRE General Test. Electronic applications accepted. *Faculty research:* Public budgeting, human resources, public information technology, nonprofit management, environmental policy.

Northeastern University, College of Arts and Sciences, Department of Political Science, Program in Public Administration, Boston, MA 02115-5096. Offers development administration (MPA); health administration and policy (MPA); state and local government (MPA); urban studies (Certificate). *Accreditation:* NASPAA (one or more programs are accredited). Part-time and evening/weekend programs available. *Degree requirements:* For master's, thesis optional. *Entrance requirements:* For master's, GRE General Test. Additional exam requirements/recommendations for international students: Required—TOEFL. *Faculty research:* National health care, Third World development, leadership and ethics, science and technology, budgeting.

Public Administration

Northern Arizona University, Graduate College, College of Social and Behavioral Sciences, Department of Political Science, Program in Political Science, Flagstaff, AZ 86011. Offers political science (MA, PhD); public management (Certificate). *Degree requirements:* For master's, thesis optional; for doctorate, one foreign language, thesis/dissertation. *Entrance requirements:* For doctorate, GRE General Test.

Northern Arizona University, Graduate College, College of Social and Behavioral Sciences, Department of Political Science, Program in Public Administration, Flagstaff, AZ 86011. Offers MPA. *Degree requirements:* For master's, internship.

Northern Illinois University, Graduate School, College of Liberal Arts and Sciences, Department of Political Science, Division of Public Administration, De Kalb, IL 60115-2854. Offers MPA. *Accreditation:* NASPAA. Part-time and evening/weekend programs available. *Degree requirements:* For master's, comprehensive exam, internship, research paper. *Entrance requirements:* For master's, GRE General Test, minimum GPA of 2.75, 9 hours in social science. Additional exam requirements/recommendations for international students: Required—TOEFL (minimum score 550 paper-based; 213 computer-based). Electronic applications accepted. *Faculty research:* Urban service and management, manpower public policy, performance appraisal, bureaurocratic politics.

Northern Kentucky University, Office of Graduate Programs, College of Arts and Sciences, Program in Public Administration, Highland Heights, KY 41099. Offers non-profit management (Certificate); public administration (MPA). *Accreditation:* NASPAA. Part-time and evening/weekend programs available. *Students:* 3 full-time (all women), 84 part-time (47 women); includes 7 minority (5 African Americans, 1 Asian American or Pacific Islander, 1 Hispanic American). Average age 36. 36 applicants, 67% accepted, 21 enrolled. In 2008, 32 master's awarded. *Degree requirements:* For master's, capstone. *Entrance requirements:* For master's, GRE, GMAT or MAT, 2 letters of recommendation, writing sample, minimum GPA of 2.75, 2 supportive letters, current resumé, narrative essay of academic and career goals, portfolio demonstrating professional activities. Additional exam requirements/recommendations for international students: Required—TOEFL (minimum score 550 paper-based; 213 computer-based; 79 iBT), Michigan Test may be substituted only if taken at NKU (minimu score of 80); Recommended—IELTS (minimum score 6.5). *Application deadline:* For fall admission, 7/1 priority date for domestic students, 6/1 for international students; for spring admission, 12/1 priority date for domestic students, 10/1 for international students. Applications are processed on a rolling basis. Application fee: $40. Electronic applications accepted. *Expenses:* Tuition, area resident: Full-time $6642. Tuition, state resident: full-time $6642. Tuition, nonresident: full-time $11,682. *Financial support:* Unspecified assistantships available. Financial award applicants required to submit FAFSA. *Faculty research:* Non-profit management, human resource management, local government, budgeting and finance, urban planning. *Unit head:* Dr. Shamima Ahmed, Director, 859-572-6402, Fax: 859-572-6184, E-mail: ahmed@nku.edu. *Application contact:* Beth Devantier, MPA Coordinator, 859-572-5326, Fax: 859-572-6184, E-mail: devantier@nku.edu.

Northern Michigan University, College of Graduate Studies, College of Arts and Sciences, Department of Political Science and Public Administration, Marquette, MI 49855-5301. Offers public administration (MPA). Part-time programs available. *Degree requirements:* For master's, thesis or alternative. *Entrance requirements:* For master's, minimum GPA of 3.0.

North Georgia College & State University, Graduate Studies, Program in Public Administration, Dahlonega, GA 30597. Offers MPA. Part-time and evening/weekend programs available. Postbaccalaureate distance learning degree programs offered. *Degree requirements:* For master's, thesis optional, internship. *Entrance requirements:* For master's, GMAT or GRE General Test, minimum undergraduate GPA of 2.75, 3 letters of recommendation. Electronic applications accepted.

Norwich University, School of Graduate Studies, Program in Public Administration, Northfield, VT 05663. Offers MPA. Evening/weekend programs available. *Faculty:* 10 part-time/adjunct (4 women). *Students:* 95 full-time (17 women); includes 8 minority (5 African Americans, 2 Asian Americans or Pacific Islanders, 1 Hispanic American). Average age 37. 101 applicants, 99% accepted, 95 enrolled. In 2008, 57 master's awarded. *Entrance requirements:* Additional exam requirements/recommendations for international students: Required—TOEFL (minimum score 550 paper-based; 212 computer-based; 83 iBT). *Application deadline:* For fall admission, 8/10 for domestic and international students; for winter admission, 11/7 for domestic and international students; for spring admission, 2/6 for domestic and international students. Application fee: $50. *Expenses:* Tuition: Full-time $8000. Full-time tuition and fees vary according to degree level and program. *Financial support:* Scholarships/grants available. Financial award applicants required to submit FAFSA. *Unit head:* Donal Hartman, JD, Program Director, 802-485-2567, E-mail: dhartman@norwich.edu. *Application contact:* Chris Ormsby, Administrative Director, 802-485-2567, Fax: 802-485-2533, E-mail: cormsby@norwich.edu.

Notre Dame de Namur University, Division of Academic Affairs, School of Business and Management, Department of Public Administration, Belmont, CA 94002-1908. Offers public administration (MPA); public affairs administration (MPA). Part-time and evening/weekend programs available. *Faculty:* 2 full-time (1 woman), 4 part-time/adjunct (2 women). *Students:* 2 full-time (both women), 30 part-time (25 women); includes 18 minority (2 African Americans, 1 Asian American or Pacific Islander, 15 Hispanic Americans), 1 international. Average age 31. 20 applicants, 100% accepted, 11 enrolled. In 2008, 7 master's awarded. *Entrance requirements:* For master's, interview, minimum GPA of 2.5. Additional exam requirements/recommendations for international students: Required—TOEFL (minimum score 550 paper-based; 213 computer-based; 79 iBT). *Application deadline:* For fall admission, 8/1 priority date for domestic students; for spring admission, 12/1 priority date for domestic students. Applications are processed on a rolling basis. Application fee: $60. Electronic applications accepted. *Expenses:* Tuition: Part-time $699 per unit. Required fees: $3 per unit. $35 per semester. *Financial support:* Career-related internships or fieldwork available. Support available to part-time students. Financial award applicants required to submit FAFSA. *Unit head:* Henry Roth, Director, 650-508-3721, E-mail: hroth@ndnu.edu. *Application contact:* Candace Hallmark, Director of Graduate Admissions, 650-508-3592, Fax: 650-508-3426, E-mail: grad.admit@ndnu.edu.

Nova Southeastern University, H. Wayne Huizenga School of Business and Entrepreneurship, Program in Public Administration, Fort Lauderdale, FL 33314-7796. Offers MPA. Part-time and evening/weekend programs available. Postbaccalaureate distance learning degree programs offered (minimal on-campus study). *Faculty:* 1 full-time, 13 part-time/adjunct (4 women). *Students:* 15 full-time (11 women), 180 part-time (122 women); includes 136 minority (101 African Americans, 1 Asian American or Pacific Islander, 34 Hispanic Americans), 1 international. Average age 31. 46 applicants, 70% accepted, 16 enrolled. In 2008, 66 master's awarded. *Degree requirements:* For master's, thesis or alternative. *Entrance requirements:* For master's, work experience. Additional exam requirements/recommendations for international students: Required—TOEFL (minimum score 550 paper-based; 79 computer-based), IELTS (minimum score 6). *Application deadline:* For fall admission, 8/15 priority date for domestic students, 8/15 for international students; for winter admission, 12/10 for domestic and international students; for spring admission, 2/10 for domestic and international students. Applications are processed on a rolling basis. Application fee: $50. Electronic applications accepted. *Financial support:* Career-related internships or fieldwork, Federal Work-Study, and institutionally sponsored loans available. Financial award applicants required to submit FAFSA. *Unit head:* Steve Harvey, Assistant Dean, 954-262-5047, Fax: 954-262-3829, E-mail: harvey@nsu.nova.edu. *Application contact:* Karen Goldberg, Assistant Director, 954-262-5039, Fax: 954-262-3822, E-mail: karen@nova.edu.

Oakland University, Graduate Study and Lifelong Learning, College of Arts and Sciences, Department of Political Science, Rochester, MI 48309-4401. Offers public administration (MPA). *Accreditation:* NASPAA. Part-time and evening/weekend programs available. *Entrance requirements:* For master's, minimum GPA of 3.0 for unconditional admission. Additional exam requirements/recommendations for international students: Required—TOEFL (minimum score 550 paper-based; 213 computer-based). Electronic applications accepted.

Ohio University, Graduate College, College of Arts and Sciences, Department of Political Science, Athens, OH 45701-2979. Offers political science (MA); public administration (MPA). Part-time programs available. *Degree requirements:* For master's, comprehensive exam, thesis or alternative. *Entrance requirements:* For master's, GRE General Test, minimum GPA of 3.0. Additional exam requirements/recommendations for international students: Required—TOEFL. Electronic applications accepted. *Faculty research:* International relations, Latin American politics, public policy, economic development, political theory.

Old Dominion University, College of Business and Public Administration, Doctoral Program in Public Administration and Urban Policy, Norfolk, VA 23529. Offers PhD. Part-time and evening/weekend programs available. Postbaccalaureate distance learning degree programs offered. *Faculty:* 7 full-time (1 woman), 3 part-time/adjunct (2 women). *Students:* 4 full-time (3 women), 25 part-time (13 women); includes 8 minority (6 African Americans, 1 American Indian/Alaska Native, 1 Asian American or Pacific Islander), 3 international. Average age 40. 5 applicants, 80% accepted, 4 enrolled. In 2008, 3 doctorates awarded. *Degree requirements:* For doctorate, comprehensive exam, thesis/dissertation. *Entrance requirements:* For doctorate, GMAT, GRE General Test, master's degree, minimum graduate GPA of 3.0. Additional exam requirements/recommendations for international students: Required—TOEFL (minimum score 550 paper-based; 213 computer-based; 79 iBT). *Application deadline:* For fall admission, 3/15 priority date for domestic and international students. Application fee: $40. Electronic applications accepted. *Expenses:* Tuition, area resident: Full-time $7704; part-time $321 per credit. Tuition, state resident: full-time $7704; part-time $321 per credit. Tuition, nonresident: full-time $19,104; part-time $796 per credit. Required fees: $99 per semester. One-time fee: $40. *Financial support:* In 2008–09, 10 students received support, including 2 fellowships with partial tuition reimbursements available (averaging $15,000 per year), 8 research assistantships with partial tuition reimbursements available (averaging $13,000 per year); teaching assistantships, career-related internships or fieldwork, scholarships/grants, and tuition waivers (partial) also available. Support available to part-time students. Financial award application deadline: 3/15; financial award applicants required to submit FAFSA. *Faculty research:* Educational needs and program development, policy analysis and administration, excellence norms for cooperative education programs. Total annual research expenditures: $60,000. *Unit head:* Dr. John C. Morris, Graduate Program Director, 757-683-3961, Fax: 757-683-4886, E-mail: jcmorris@odu.edu. *Application contact:* Megan S. Jones, Graduate Program Manager, 757-683-3961, Fax: 757-683-4886, E-mail: mmjones@odu.edu.

Old Dominion University, College of Business and Public Administration, Master's Program in Business Administration, Norfolk, VA 23529. Offers business and economic forecasting (MBA); financial analysis and valuation (MBA); information technology and enterprise integration (MBA); international business (MBA); maritime and port management (MBA); public administration (MBA). *Accreditation:* AACSB. Part-time and evening/weekend programs available. *Faculty:* 66 full-time (15 women), 6 part-time/adjunct (1 woman). *Students:* 74 full-time (26 women), 200 part-time (85 women); includes 49 minority (26 African Americans, 3 American Indian/Alaska Native, 15 Asian Americans or Pacific Islanders, 5 Hispanic Americans), 38 international. Average age 30. 169 applicants, 52% accepted, 61 enrolled. In 2008, 89 master's awarded. *Entrance requirements:* For master's, GMAT, letters of reference, resumé, essay, transcripts, coursework in calculus. Additional exam requirements/recommendations for international students: Required—TOEFL (minimum score 550 paper-based; 213 computer-based; 80 iBT). *Application deadline:* For fall admission, 6/1 priority date for domestic students, 4/15 priority date for international students; for spring admission, 11/1 priority date for domestic students, 10/1 priority date for international students. Applications are processed on a rolling basis. Application fee: $40. Electronic applications accepted. *Expenses:* Tuition, area resident: Full-time $7704; part-time $321 per credit. Tuition, state resident: full-time $7704; part-time $321 per credit. Tuition, nonresident: full-time $19,104; part-time $796 per credit. Required fees: $99 per semester. One-time fee: $40. *Financial support:* In 2008–09, 46 students received support, including 31 research assistantships with partial tuition reimbursements available (averaging $7,000 per year), 3 teaching assistantships with partial tuition reimbursements available (averaging $6,300 per year); career-related internships or fieldwork, scholarships/grants, and unspecified assistantships also available. Support available to part-time students. Financial award application deadline: 2/15; financial award applicants required to submit FAFSA. *Faculty research:* International business, buyer behavior, financial markets, strategy, operations research. *Unit head:* Dr. Bruce Rubin, Graduate Program Director, 757-683-3585, E-mail: mbainfo@odu.edu. *Application contact:* Shanna Wood, MBA Program Manager, 757-683-3585, Fax: 757-683-5750, E-mail: mbainfo@odu.edu.

Old Dominion University, College of Business and Public Administration, Program in Public Administration, Norfolk, VA 23529. Offers MPA. *Accreditation:* NASPAA. Part-time and evening/weekend programs available. *Faculty:* 7 full-time (2 women), 4 part-time/adjunct (2 women). *Students:* 24 full-time (21 women), 99 part-time (63 women); includes 41 minority (37 African Americans, 1 American Indian/Alaska Native, 3 Asian Americans or Pacific Islanders), 4 international. Average age 33. 66 applicants, 89% accepted, 38 enrolled. In 2008, 37 master's awarded. *Degree requirements:* For master's, thesis optional, capstone seminar. *Entrance requirements:* For master's, GRE. Additional exam requirements/recommendations for international students: Required—TOEFL (minimum score 550 paper-based; 213 computer-based; 79 iBT). *Application deadline:* For fall admission, 7/15 for domestic students; for spring admission, 11/15 for domestic students. Applications are processed on a rolling basis. Application fee: $40. Electronic applications accepted. *Expenses:* Tuition, area resident: Full-time $7704; part-time $321 per credit. Tuition, state resident: full-time $7704; part-time $321 per credit. Tuition, nonresident: full-time $19,104; part-time $796 per credit. Required fees: $99 per semester. One-time fee: $40. *Financial support:* In 2008–09, 7 students received support, including 2 research assistantships with partial tuition reimbursements available (averaging $5,000 per year); fellowships, teaching assistantships, career-related internships or fieldwork, scholarships/grants, tuition waivers (partial), and unspecified assistantships also available. Financial award application deadline: 2/15; financial award applicants required to submit FAFSA. *Faculty research:* Environmental administration, personnel policy analysis, urban administration. Total annual research expenditures: $15,000. *Unit head:* Dr. William M. Leavitt, Graduate Program Director, 757-683-5695, Fax: 757-683-5639, E-mail: padmgpd@odu.edu. *Application contact:* Megan S. Jones, Graduate Program Manager, 757-683-3961, Fax: 757-683-4886, E-mail: mmjones@odu.edu.

Pace University, Dyson College of Arts and Sciences, Department of Public Administration, New York, NY 10038. Offers government management (MPA); health care administration (MPA); nonprofit management (MPA); JD/MPA. Offered at White Plains, NY location only. Part-time and evening/weekend programs available. *Degree requirements:* For master's, capstone project. *Entrance requirements:* For master's, GRE General Test. Electronic applications accepted.

Park University, College of Graduate and Professional Studies, Kansas City, MO 54105. Offers adult education (M Ed); at-risk students (M Ed); disaster and emergency management (MPA); educational administration (M Ed); entrepreneurship (MBA); general business (MBA); general education (M Ed); government/business relations (MPA); healthcare/services management (MBA, MPA); international business (MBA); K-12 certification (MAT); management information systems (MBA); management of information systems (MPA); middle school certification (MAT); multi-cultural education (M Ed); nonprofit management (MPA); public management (MPA); school law (M Ed); secondary school certification (MAT); special education (M Ed). Part-time and evening/weekend programs available. Postbaccalaureate distance learning degree programs offered (no on-campus study). *Degree requirements:* For master's, comprehensive exam, thesis (for some programs). *Entrance requirements:* For master's, GRE, GMAT, teacher certification (M Ed). Additional exam requirements/recommendations for international students: Required—TOEFL (minimum score 550 paper-based). Electronic applications accepted. *Faculty research:* Literacy, leadership, brain based research, multicultural education, diversity.

Penn State Harrisburg, Graduate School, School of Public Affairs, Middletown, PA 17057-4898. Offers criminal justice (MA); health administration (MHA); public administration (MPA); public affairs (PhD); MPA/JD.

Pepperdine University, School of Public Policy, Malibu, CA 90263. Offers American politics (MPP); economics (MPP); international relations (MPP); public policy (MPP); state and local policy (MPP). *Entrance requirements:* For master's, GRE, 2 letters of recommendation, resumé. Additional exam requirements/recommendations for international students: Required—TOEFL. Electronic applications accepted.

Pontifical Catholic University of Puerto Rico, Institute of Graduate Studies in Behavioral Science and Community Affairs, Program in Public Administration, Ponce, PR 00717-0777. Offers MA. Part-time and evening/weekend programs available. *Degree requirements:* For master's, thesis. *Entrance requirements:* For master's, EXADEP, 3 letters of recommendation, interview, minimum GPA of 2.75.

Portland State University, Graduate Studies, College of Urban and Public Affairs, Hatfield School of Government, Division of Public Administration, Portland, OR 97207-0751. Offers public administration (MPA); public administration and policy (PhD). *Accreditation:* NASPAA (one or more programs are accredited). Part-time and evening/weekend programs available. *Faculty:* 14 full-time (6 women), 23 part-time/adjunct (5 women). *Students:* 69 full-time (42 women), 146 part-time (86 women); includes 28 minority (8 African Americans, 4 American Indian/Alaska Native, 8 Asian Americans or Pacific Islanders, 8 Hispanic Americans), 12 international. Average age 34. 95 applicants, 62% accepted, 35 enrolled. In 2008, 86 master's, 14 doctorates awarded. *Degree requirements:* For master's, internship (MPA), practicum (MPH); for doctorate, comprehensive exam, thesis/dissertation, residency. *Entrance requirements:* For master's, GRE, minimum GPA of 3.0 in upper-division course work or 2.75 overall, 3 recommendation forms, resumé; for doctorate, GRE General Test, minimum GPA of 2.75. Additional exam requirements/recommendations for international students: Required—TOEFL (minimum score 550 paper-based; 213 computer-based). *Application deadline:* For fall admission, 4/1 for domestic students, 3/1 for international students; for winter admission, 9/1 for domestic students, 8/1 for international students; for spring admission, 11/1 for domestic and international students. Application fee: $50. *Expenses:* Tuition, area resident: Full-time $8763; part-time $179 per credit hour. Tuition, state resident: full-time $8763; part-time $298 per credit hour. Tuition, nonresident: full-time $12,981; part-time $426 per credit hour. Required fees: $1242. One-time fee: $250. Tuition and fees vary according to course load and program. *Financial support:* In 2008–09, 2 research assistantships with full tuition reimbursements (averaging $7,686 per year) were awarded; teaching assistantships, career-related internships or fieldwork, Federal Work-Study, scholarships/grants, tuition waivers (partial), and unspecified assistantships also available. Support available to part-time students. Financial award application deadline: 3/1; financial award applicants required to submit FAFSA. *Faculty research:* Public budgeting, program evaluation, nonprofit management, natural resources policy and administration. Total annual research expenditures: $414,834. *Unit head:* Dr. Sherril Gelmon, Chair, 503-725-3920, Fax: 503-725-8250, E-mail: gelmons@pdx.edu. *Application contact:* Dr. Sherril Gelmon, Chair, 503-725-3920, Fax: 503-725-8250, E-mail: gelmons@pdx.edu.

Regent University, Graduate School, Robertson School of Government, Virginia Beach, VA 23464. Offers health care policy and administration (MA); international politics (MA); law and public policy (MA); Mid-East Politics (MA); political leadership and management (MA); political management (MA); public administration (MA); public policy (MA); terrorism and homeland defense (MA); world economies and political development (MA); JD/MA; M Div/MA; M Ed/MA; MBA/MA. Part-time and evening/weekend programs available. Postbaccalaureate distance learning degree programs offered (minimal on-campus study). *Faculty:* 6 full-time (1 woman), 11 part-time/adjunct (1 woman). *Students:* 60 full-time (33 women), 69 part-time (34 women); includes 29 minority (22 African Americans, 1 Asian American or Pacific Islander, 6 Hispanic Americans), 3 international. Average age 30. 136 applicants, 54% accepted, 54 enrolled. In 2008, 48 master's awarded. *Degree requirements:* For master's, thesis optional, internship. *Entrance requirements:* For master's, GRE General Test or LSAT, minimum undergraduate GPA of 3.0, writing sample, resumé, interview, references, transcripts. Additional exam requirements/recommendations for international students: Required—TOEFL (minimum score 577 paper-based; 233 computer-based). *Application deadline:* For fall admission, 5/1 priority date for domestic students; for spring admission, 11/1 priority date for domestic students. Applications are processed on a rolling basis. Application fee: $50. Electronic applications accepted. *Expenses:* Contact institution. *Financial support:* Career-related internships or fieldwork, scholarships/grants, tuition waivers (full and partial), and unspecified assistantships available. Support available to part-time students. Financial award application deadline: 9/1; financial award applicants required to submit FAFSA. *Faculty research:* Education reform, political character issues, social capital concerns, administrative ethics, Biblical law and public policy. *Unit head:* Dr. Charles W. Dunn, Dean, 757-352-4322, Fax: 757-352-4643, E-mail: cwdunn@regent.edu. *Application contact:* Matthew Chadwick, Director of Admissions, 800-373-5504, Fax: 757-352-4381, E-mail: admissions@regent.edu.

Regis College, Program in Public Administration, Weston, MA 02493. Offers nonprofit administration (Graduate Certificate); public administration (MPA); public policymaking (Graduate Certificate). Part-time programs available. Postbaccalaureate distance learning degree programs offered. *Faculty:* 1 (woman) full-time, 2 part-time/adjunct (both women). *Students:* 5 part-time (4 women); includes 1 minority (Hispanic American). Average age 31. 5 applicants, 100% accepted, 5 enrolled. *Degree requirements:* For master's, thesis. *Entrance requirements:* For master's, GRE or MAT. Additional exam requirements/recommendations for international students: Required—TOEFL (minimum score 550 paper-based; 213 computer-based). Application fee: $50. *Expenses:* Tuition: Part-time $676 per credit. *Unit head:* Claudia Pouravelis, Director of Graduate Admission, 781-768-7058, E-mail: claudia.pouravelis@regiscollege.edu. *Application contact:* Christine Petherick, Administrative Coordinator, Graduate Admission, 866-438-7344, Fax: 781-768-7071, E-mail: christine.petherick@regiscollege.edu.

Rhode Island College, School of Graduate Studies, Faculty of Arts and Sciences, Department of Political Sciences, Providence, RI 02908-1991. Offers public administration (MPA). Part-time and evening/weekend programs available. *Faculty:* 6 full-time (1 woman). *Entrance requirements:* Additional exam requirements/recommendations for international students: Recommended—TOEFL (minimum score 550 paper-based; 213 computer-based; 79 iBT). *Application deadline:* For fall admission, 4/1 for domestic students; for spring admission, 11/1 for domestic students. Applications are processed on a rolling basis. *Expenses:* Tuition, area resident: Full-time $6816; part-time $284 per credit hour. Tuition, state resident: full-time $6816; part-time $284 per credit hour. Tuition, nonresident: full-time $13,920; part-time $580 per credit hour. Required fees: $454; $16 per credit. $68 per term. *Financial support:* Career-related internships or fieldwork, Federal Work-Study, scholarships/grants, health care benefits, and unspecified assistantships available. Support available to part-time students. Financial award application deadline: 5/15; financial award applicants required to submit FAFSA. *Unit head:* Dr. Claus Hofhansel, Chair, 401-456-8056, E-mail: chofhansel@ric.edu. *Application contact:* Graduate Studies, 401-456-8700.

Roger Williams University, Feinstein College of Arts and Sciences, Program in Public Administration, Bristol, RI 02809. Offers MPA. Part-time and evening/weekend programs available. Postbaccalaureate distance learning degree programs offered (minimal on-campus study). *Faculty:* 5 full-time (0 women). *Students:* 5 full-time (2 women), 35 part-time (22 women); includes 6 minority (2 African Americans, 1 American Indian/Alaska Native, 1 Asian American or Pacific Islander, 2 Hispanic Americans), 1 international. Average age 36. 31 applicants, 81% accepted, 17 enrolled. In 2008, 12 master's awarded. *Degree requirements:* For master's, internship/research project. *Entrance requirements:* For master's, transcript, 2 letters of recommendation, personal statement, curriculum vitae/resumé. Additional exam requirements/recommendations for international students: Recommended—IELTS. *Application deadline:* Applications are processed on a rolling basis. Application fee: $50. Electronic applications accepted. *Expenses:* Contact institution. *Financial support:* In 2008–09, 12 students received support. Application deadline: 6/15; *Unit head:* Dr. Michael Hall, Head, 401-254-5746, E-mail: mhall@rwu.edu. *Application contact:* Lori Vales, Graduate Admission Coordinator, 401-254-6600, Fax: 401-254-3557, E-mail: gradadmit@rwu.edu.

Announcement: Are you looking to make a difference via public policy and management? Then the Roger Williams University MPA program might be for you. With a combined emphasis on direct service and administration, Roger Williams' master's in public administration promotes citizen participation, equity, diversity, and public service. For more information, visit the Web site at www.rwu.edu/admission/graduate.

See Close-Up on page 1233.

Roosevelt University, Graduate Division, College of Arts and Sciences, Department of Political Science and Public Administration, Program in Public Administration, Chicago, IL 60605-1394. Offers MPA. Part-time and evening/weekend programs available. In 2008, 48 master's awarded. *Degree requirements:* For master's, thesis optional. *Entrance requirements:* For master's, minimum undergraduate GPA of 3.0. *Application deadline:* For fall admission, 6/1 priority date for domestic students. Applications are processed on a rolling basis. Application fee: $25 ($35 for international students). *Expenses:* Tuition: Full-time $14,730; part-time $709 per credit. Required fees: $175 per semester. Tuition and fees vary according to course load and program. *Financial support:* Application deadline: 2/15. *Faculty research:* Health policy issues, environmental policy, local government administration. *Application contact:* Joanne Canyon-Heller, Coordinator of Graduate Admission, 877-APPLY RU, Fax: 312-281-3356, E-mail: applyru@roosevelt.edu.

Rutgers, The State University of New Jersey, Camden, Graduate School of Arts and Sciences, Department of Public Policy and Administration, Camden, NJ 08102-1401. Offers education policy and leadership (MPA); international public service and development (MPA); public management (MPA); JD/MPA; MPA/MA. *Accreditation:* NASPAA. Part-time and evening/weekend programs available. *Degree requirements:* For master's, directed study, research workshop. *Entrance requirements:* For master's, GRE General Test, GMAT or LSAT, 3 letters of recommendation; resumé; statement of personal, professional, and academic goals. Additional exam requirements/recommendations for international students: Required—TOEFL (minimum score 550 paper-based; 213 computer-based), IELTS. Electronic applications accepted. *Faculty research:* Nonprofit management, county and municipal administration, health and human services, government communication, administrative law, educational finance.

Rutgers, The State University of New Jersey, Newark, Graduate School, Program in Public Administration, Newark, NJ 07102. Offers health care administration (MPA); human resources administration (MPA); public administration (PhD); public management (MPA); public policy analysis (MPA); urban systems and issues (MPA). *Accreditation:* NASPAA (one or more programs are accredited). Part-time and evening/weekend programs available. *Degree requirements:* For master's, comprehensive exam, thesis or alternative; for doctorate, thesis/dissertation. *Entrance requirements:* For master's, GRE, minimum undergraduate B average; for doctorate, GRE, MPA, minimum B average. Electronic applications accepted. *Faculty research:* Government finance, municipal and state government, public productivity.

Sage Graduate School, Graduate School, Department of Management, Program in Organizational Management, Troy, NY 12180-4115. Offers public administration (MS). Part-time and evening/weekend programs available. *Faculty:* 3 full-time (2 women), 7 part-time/adjunct (0 women). *Students:* 6 full-time (4 women), 32 part-time (22 women); includes 8 minority (5 African Americans, 3 Hispanic Americans). Average age 33. 19 applicants, 68% accepted, 10 enrolled. In 2008, 18 master's awarded. *Entrance requirements:* For master's, minimum GPA of 2.75, completed application, current resumée, essay, official transcripts, 2 letters of recommendation. Additional exam requirements/recommendations for international students: Required—TOEFL (minimum score 550 paper-based; 213 computer-based). *Application deadline:* Applications are processed on a rolling basis. Application fee: $40. *Expenses:* Tuition: Full-time $10,080; part-time $560 per credit hour. *Financial support:* Fellowships, research assistantships, career-related internships or fieldwork available. Support available to part-time students. Financial award application deadline: 3/1; financial award applicants required to submit FAFSA. *Unit head:* Daniel Robeson, Chair, Management Department, 518-292-1770, Fax: 518-292-5414, E-mail: robesd@sage.edu. *Application contact:* Wendy D. Diefendorf, Director of Graduate and Adult Admission, 518-244-2443, Fax: 518-244-6880, E-mail: diefew@sage.edu.

Saginaw Valley State University, College of Arts and Behavioral Sciences, Program in Administrative Science, University Center, MI 48710. Offers MA. Part-time and evening/weekend programs available. *Students:* 15 full-time (10 women), 41 part-time (24 women); includes 13 minority (10 African Americans, 3 Hispanic Americans), 6 international. Average age 35. 27 applicants, 89% accepted, 15 enrolled. In 2008, 22 master's awarded. *Degree requirements:* For master's, thesis optional. *Entrance requirements:* For master's, minimum GPA of 3.0 in social sciences, 2.75 overall. Additional exam requirements/recommendations for international students: Required—TOEFL. *Application deadline:* Applications are processed on a rolling basis. Application fee: $25. Electronic applications accepted. *Expenses:* Tuition, state resident: full-time $8620; part-time $359.15 per credit hour. Tuition, nonresident: full-time $16,526; part-time $688.60 per credit hour. Required fees: $350.40; $14.60 per credit hour. Tuition and fees vary according to campus/location. *Financial support:* In 2008–09, 2 fellowships with partial tuition reimbursements, 1 research assistantship with full tuition reimbursement (averaging $5,000 per year) were awarded; Federal Work-Study also available. Support available to part-time students. Financial award application deadline: 4/1; financial award applicants required to submit FAFSA. *Unit head:* Mark Nicol, MAS Graduate Coordinator/Instructor of Political Science, 989-964-2605, E-mail: nlnicol@svsu.edu. *Application contact:* Mark Nicol, MAS Graduate Coordinator/Instructor of Political Science, 989-964-2605, E-mail: nlnicol@svsu.edu.

St. Edward's University, School of Management and Business, Program in Human Services, Austin, TX 78704. Offers administration (Certificate); conflict resolution (Certificate); family mediation (Certificate); human services (MA), including administration, conflict resolution, human resource management, organization development and training, social and psychological services; mediation (Certificate); organization development and training (Certificate). Part-time and evening/weekend programs available. *Students:* 2 full-time (both women), 53 part-time (42 women); includes 23 minority (5 African Americans, 2 Asian Americans or Pacific Islanders, 16 Hispanic Americans). Average age 33. 21 applicants, 90% accepted, 16 enrolled. In 2008, 22 master's awarded. *Degree requirements:* For master's, minimum 24 resident hours. *Entrance requirements:* For master's, GRE General Test, GMAT, minimum GPA of 2.75 in last 60 hours of course work. Additional exam requirements/recommendations for international students: Required—TOEFL (minimum score 550 paper-based; 213 computer-based; 79 iBT). *Application deadline:* For fall admission, 8/1 for domestic students, 7/1 for international students; for spring admission, 12/1 for domestic students, 11/1 for international students. Applications are processed on a rolling basis. Application fee: $45 ($50 for international students). Electronic applications accepted. *Expenses:* Tuition: Full-time $13,752; part-time $764 per credit hour. Required fees: $50 per semester. Full-time tuition and fees vary according to course load and program. *Financial support:* In 2008–09, 2 students received support. Scholarships/grants available. *Faculty research:* Leadership development, organizational management, public policy. *Unit head:* Dr. Constance D Porter, Director, 512-416-5827, Fax: 512-448-8492, E-mail: constanp@stedwards.edu. *Application contact:* Kay L. Arnold, Graduate Admissions Coordinator, 512-233-1636, Fax: 512-428-1032, E-mail: kayla@stedwards.edu.

Saint Louis University, Graduate School, College of Education and Public Service and Graduate School, Department of Public Policy Studies, St. Louis, MO 63103-2097. Offers geographic information systems (Certificate); organizational development (Certificate); public administration (MAPA); public policy analysis (PhD); urban affairs (MAUA); urban planning and real estate development (MUPRED). *Accreditation:* NASPAA. Part-time programs available. *Degree requirements:* For master's, comprehensive exam (for some programs), thesis (for

Public Administration

Saint Louis University (continued)
some programs); for doctorate, comprehensive exam, thesis/dissertation, preliminary exams. *Entrance requirements:* For master's and doctorate, GMAT, GRE General Test, or LSAT, letters of recommendation, resumé, interview, transcripts, goal statement. Additional exam requirements/recommendations for international students: Required—TOEFL (minimum score 525 paper-based; 194 computer-based). Electronic applications accepted. *Faculty research:* Urban politics, brown fields, e-government, and administration, evaluation research, community development, electronic government and governance.

St. Mary's University, Graduate School, Department of Political Science, Program in Public Administration, San Antonio, TX 78228-8507. Offers inter-American administration (MPA); public management (MPA); JD/MPA. Part-time programs available. Postbaccalaureate distance learning degree programs offered (no on-campus study). *Faculty:* 5 part-time/adjunct (1 woman). *Students:* 6 full-time (3 women), 12 part-time (4 women); includes 13 minority (1 African American, 12 Hispanic Americans), 2 international. Average age 32. 23 applicants, 65% accepted, 9 enrolled. In 2008, 17 master's awarded. *Degree requirements:* For master's, comprehensive exam, internship. *Entrance requirements:* For master's, GRE General Test. Additional exam requirements/recommendations for international students: Required—TOEFL (minimum score 550 paper-based; 213 computer-based; 80 iBT). *Application deadline:* Applications are processed on a rolling basis. Application fee: $0. Electronic applications accepted. *Expenses:* Tuition: Full-time $12,006; part-time $667 per credit hour. Required fees: $440; $220 per semester. *Financial support:* In 2008–09, 4 students received support, including 3 fellowships (averaging $2,923 per year), 1 research assistantship (averaging $4,500 per year); career-related internships or fieldwork, Federal Work-Study, and institutionally sponsored loans also available. Financial award application deadline: 3/31; financial award applicants required to submit FAFSA. *Faculty research:* Voting rights, natural resources, urban policy. *Unit head:* Dr. Arturo Vega, Director, 210-431-8028, Fax: 210-431-4336, E-mail: avega2@stmarytx.edu. *Application contact:* Dr. Henry Flores, Dean of the Graduate School, 210-436-3101, Fax: 210-431-2220, E-mail: hflores@stmarytx.edu.

St. Thomas University, School of Business, Department of Management, Miami Gardens, FL 33054-6459. Offers accounting (MBA); general management (MSM, Certificate); health management (MBA, MSM, Certificate); human resource management (MBA, MSM, Certificate); international business (MBA, MIB, MSM, Certificate); justice administration (MSM, Certificate); management accounting (MSM, Certificate); public management (MSM, Certificate); sports administration (MS). Part-time and evening/weekend programs available. *Degree requirements:* For master's, comprehensive exam. *Entrance requirements:* For master's, interview, minimum GPA of 3.0 or GMAT. Additional exam requirements/recommendations for international students: Required—TOEFL (minimum score 550 paper-based; 213 computer-based; 79 iBT). Electronic applications accepted.

Salisbury University, Graduate Division, Master of Science in Geographic Information Systems and Public Administration Program, Salisbury, MD 21801-6837. Offers MS. Part-time programs available. Postbaccalaureate distance learning degree programs offered (minimal on-campus study). *Faculty:* 4 full-time (1 woman), 1 (woman) part-time/adjunct. *Students:* 3 full-time (0 women), 6 part-time (1 woman). Average age 32. 12 applicants, 83% accepted, 10 enrolled. *Degree requirements:* For master's, cooperative project. *Entrance requirements:* For master's, GRE (for recent graduates), GIS experience, administration experience. Additional exam requirements/recommendations for international students: Required—TOEFL (minimum score 550 paper-based; 213 computer-based). *Application deadline:* For fall admission, 2/15 for domestic students. Application fee: $45. Electronic applications accepted. *Expenses:* Tuition, area resident: Part-time $270 per credit hour. Tuition, state resident: part-time $270 per credit hour. Tuition, nonresident: part-time $566 per credit hour. Required fees: $52 per credit hour. *Faculty research:* GIS in local governments, parallel applications of GIS, GIS and vulnerability, GIS and crime analysis. *Unit head:* Dr. Michael Scott, Master's Program Director, 410-543-6456, Fax: 410-548-4506, E-mail: msscott@salisbury.edu. *Application contact:* Susan Parks, Program Management Specialist, 410-543-6460, Fax: 410-548-4506, E-mail: slparks@salisbury.edu.

Sam Houston State University, College of Humanities and Social Sciences, Department of Political Science, Huntsville, TX 77341. Offers political science (MA); public administration (MPA). Evening/weekend programs available. *Faculty:* 7 full-time (2 women). *Students:* 10 full-time (5 women), 17 part-time (9 women); includes 5 minority (2 African Americans, 1 Asian American or Pacific Islander, 2 Hispanic Americans). Average age 29. 13 applicants, 77% accepted, 9 enrolled. In 2008, 3 master's awarded. *Degree requirements:* For master's, thesis or alternative. *Entrance requirements:* For master's, GRE General Test. Additional exam requirements/recommendations for international students: Required—TOEFL (minimum score 550 paper-based; 213 computer-based; 79 iBT). *Application deadline:* For fall admission, 8/1 for domestic students; for spring admission, 12/1 for domestic students. Applications are processed on a rolling basis. Application fee: $20. *Expenses:* Tuition, state resident: full-time $3564; part-time $198 per credit hour. Tuition, nonresident: full-time $8622; part-time $479 per credit hour. Required fees: $1290. Tuition and fees vary according to course load and campus/location. *Financial support:* Research assistantships, teaching assistantships, career-related internships or fieldwork and institutionally sponsored loans available. Support available to part-time students. Financial award application deadline: 5/31; financial award applicants required to submit FAFSA. *Unit head:* Dr. Rhonda Callaway, Chair, 936-294-4108, Fax: 936-294-4172, E-mail: rlc005@shsu.edu. *Application contact:* Dr. Corliss Lentz, Advisor, 936-294-1459.

San Diego State University, Graduate and Research Affairs, College of Professional Studies and Fine Arts, School of Public Affairs, Program in Public Administration, San Diego, CA 92182. Offers MPA. *Accreditation:* NASPAA. Part-time programs available. *Entrance requirements:* For master's, GRE General Test, 2 letters of reference. Additional exam requirements/recommendations for international students: Required—TOEFL. Electronic applications accepted.

San Francisco State University, Division of Graduate Studies, College of Behavioral and Social Sciences, Public Administration Program, San Francisco, CA 94132-1722. Offers integrated and collaborative services (MPA); nonprofit administration (MPA); policy analysis (MPA); public management (MPA); urban administration (MPA). *Accreditation:* NASPAA.

San Jose State University, Graduate Studies and Research, College of Social Sciences, Department of Political Science, San Jose, CA 95192-0001. Offers public administration (MPA). *Accreditation:* NASPAA. Part-time and evening/weekend programs available. *Degree requirements:* For master's, comprehensive exam, thesis or alternative. *Entrance requirements:* For master's, GRE Subject Test. Additional exam requirements/recommendations for international students: Required—TOEFL (minimum score 575 paper-based). Electronic applications accepted. *Faculty research:* Modern political philosophy, international relations in the Middle East, public policy, American public policy, political parties and political reform.

Savannah State University, Program in Public Administration, Savannah, GA 31404. Offers MPA. *Accreditation:* NASPAA. *Degree requirements:* For master's, major paper, oral exam. *Entrance requirements:* For master's, GRE General Test, minimum GPA of 2.5. Additional exam requirements/recommendations for international students: Required—TOEFL. *Faculty research:* Community development, human resources, leadership, conflict resolution.

Seattle University, College of Arts and Sciences, Institute of Public Service, Seattle, WA 98122-1090. Offers MPA. *Accreditation:* NASPAA. *Degree requirements:* For master's, thesis or alternative. *Entrance requirements:* For master's, minimum GPA of 3.0, 1 year work experience. *Faculty research:* Housing, experiential learning, citizenship education.

Seton Hall University, College of Arts and Sciences, Department of Public and Healthcare Administration, South Orange, NJ 07079-2697. Offers arts administration (MPA); health policy and management (MPA); healthcare administration (MHA); nonprofit organization management (MPA); public service: leadership, governance, and policy (MPA). *Accreditation:* NASPAA. Part-time and evening/weekend programs available. Postbaccalaureate distance learning degree programs offered (minimal on-campus study). *Degree requirements:* For master's, research project. Electronic applications accepted.

Shenandoah University, School of Education and Human Development, Winchester, VA 22601-5195. Offers advanced professional teaching English to speakers of other languages (Certificate); education (MSE); elementary education (Certificate); ESL (Certificate); middle school education (Certificate); organizational leadership (D Ed); professional studies (Certificate); professional studies for VA licensure (Certificate); professional teaching English to speakers of other languages (Certificate); public management (Certificate); secondary education (Certificate). Part-time and evening/weekend programs available. Postbaccalaureate distance learning degree programs offered (minimal on-campus study). *Faculty:* 15 full-time (9 women), 25 part-time/adjunct (18 women). *Students:* 17 full-time (13 women), 336 part-time (251 women); includes 18 minority (10 African Americans, 1 American Indian/Alaska Native, 1 Asian American or Pacific Islander, 6 Hispanic Americans), 24 international. Average age 40. 202 applicants, 86% accepted, 131 enrolled. In 2008, 82 master's, 6 doctorates, 19 other advanced degrees awarded. *Degree requirements:* For master's, comprehensive exam (for some programs), thesis (for some programs), internship; for doctorate, comprehensive exam, thesis/dissertation; for Certificate, full time teaching in area for 1 year. *Entrance requirements:* For master's, minimum GPA of 3.0 or satisfactory GRE, 3 letters of recommendation, valid teaching license, essay; for doctorate, minimum GPA of 3.5 in master's, 3 years of teaching experience, 3 letters of recommendation, writing samples; for Certificate, minimum undergraduate GPA of 3.0, essay, 3 letters of recommendation. Additional exam requirements/recommendations for international students: Required—TOEFL (minimum score 550 paper-based; 213 computer-based), IELTS (minimum score 6.5), Sakae Institute of Study Abroad (SISA): 550. *Application deadline:* For fall admission, 7/1 for domestic and international students; for spring admission, 10/15 for domestic and international students. Application fee: $30. Electronic applications accepted. *Expenses:* Tuition: Full-time $16,900; part-time $670 per credit. *Financial support:* Career-related internships or fieldwork, institutionally sponsored loans, and unspecified assistantships available. Support available to part-time students. Financial award application deadline: 3/15; financial award applicants required to submit FAFSA. *Faculty research:* Intentional learning communities, teacher induction, reading instruction, organizational transformation, welfare reform, charter schools, writing instructions. *Unit head:* Dr. Steven E. Humphries, Dean, 540-535-3574, E-mail: shumphri@su.edu. *Application contact:* David Anthony, Dean of Admissions, 540-665-4581, Fax: 540-665-4627, E-mail: admit@su.edu.

Shippensburg University of Pennsylvania, School of Graduate Studies, College of Arts and Sciences, Department of Political Science, Shippensburg, PA 17257-2299. Offers public administration (MPA). Part-time and evening/weekend programs available. *Faculty:* 6 full-time (1 woman), 1 (woman) part-time/adjunct. *Students:* 14 full-time (8 women), 27 part-time (15 women); includes 9 minority (4 African Americans, 4 Asian Americans or Pacific Islanders, 1 Hispanic American). Average age 30. 29 applicants, 69% accepted, 14 enrolled. In 2008, 12 master's awarded. *Degree requirements:* For master's, thesis or internship, candidacy. *Entrance requirements:* For master's, GRE or MAT (if GPA is less than 2.75), 6 credits of course work in political science or public administration. Additional exam requirements/recommendations for international students: Required—TOEFL (minimum score 560 paper-based; 220 computer-based); Recommended—IELTS (minimum score 6). *Application deadline:* For fall admission, 3/1 for international students; for spring admission, 7/1 for international students. Applications are processed on a rolling basis. Application fee: $30. Electronic applications accepted. *Expenses:* Tuition, state resident: full-time $6430; part-time $357 per credit. Tuition, nonresident: full-time $10,288; part-time $572 per credit. Required fees: $1127; $38 per credit. One-time fee: $44 part-time. *Financial support:* In 2008–09, 4 research assistantships with full tuition reimbursements (averaging $5,000 per year) were awarded; career-related internships or fieldwork, scholarships/grants, unspecified assistantships, and resident hall directors, student payroll positions also available. Support available to part-time students. Financial award application deadline: 3/1; financial award applicants required to submit FAFSA. *Unit head:* Dr. Sara Grove, Chairperson, 717-477-1718, Fax: 717-477-4030, E-mail: sagrov@ship.edu. *Application contact:* Renee Payne, Associate Dean of Graduate Admissions, 717-477-1231, Fax: 717-477-4016, E-mail: rmpayn@ship.edu.

Sojourner-Douglass College, Graduate Program, Baltimore, MD 21205-1814. Offers human services (MASS); public administration (MASS); urban education (reading) (MASS). Part-time and evening/weekend programs available. *Degree requirements:* For master's, comprehensive exam, written proposal oral defense. *Entrance requirements:* For master's, Graduate Examination.

Sonoma State University, School of Social Sciences, Department of Political Science, Rohnert Park, CA 94928-3609. Offers public administration (MPA). Part-time and evening/weekend programs available. *Degree requirements:* For master's, thesis or alternative. *Entrance requirements:* For master's, GRE General Test, minimum GPA of 3.0. *Faculty research:* Cross-disciplinary viewpoint in public administration, public policy implementation and evaluation with emphasis on state & local politics and non-profit organizations.

Southeastern University, College of Graduate Studies, Program in Government Program Management, Washington, DC 20024-2788. Offers MPA. Part-time and evening/weekend programs available. *Entrance requirements:* Additional exam requirements/recommendations for international students: Required—TOEFL (minimum score 500 paper-based; 173 computer-based). Electronic applications accepted.

Southeast Missouri State University, School of Graduate Studies, Department of Political Science, Philosophy and Religion, Cape Girardeau, MO 63701-4799. Offers public administration (MPA). Part-time and evening/weekend programs available. *Faculty:* 6 full-time (0 women). *Students:* 1 full-time (0 women), 20 part-time (14 women); includes 3 minority (1 African American, 1 Asian American or Pacific Islander, 1 Hispanic American). Average age 27. 11 applicants, 91% accepted. In 2008, 4 master's awarded. *Degree requirements:* For master's, thesis or alternative, internship or thesis. *Entrance requirements:* For master's, minimum undergraduate GPA of 2.7. Additional exam requirements/recommendations for international students: Required—TOEFL (minimum score 550 paper-based; 213 computer-based); Recommended—IELTS (minimum score 6). *Application deadline:* For fall admission, 8/1 for domestic students, 7/1 for international students; for spring admission, 11/21 for domestic students, 11/1 for international students. Applications are processed on a rolling basis. Application fee: $25 ($100 for international students). Electronic applications accepted. *Expenses:* Tuition, area resident: Part-time $213.30 per credit hour. Tuition, state resident: part-time $213.30 per credit hour. Tuition, nonresident: part-time $393.30 per credit hour. Required fees: $23.70 per credit hour. *Financial support:* In 2008–09, 6 students received support, including 6 research assistantships with full tuition reimbursements available (averaging $7,600 per year); unspecified assistantships also available. Financial award applicants required to submit FAFSA. *Faculty research:* American political institutions, state and local government, non-profit management. *Unit head:* Dr. Hamner Hill, Chairperson, 573-651-2816, Fax: 573-651-2695, E-mail: hhill@semo.edu. *Application contact:* Marsha L. Arant, Senior Administrative Assistant, School of Graduate Studies, 573-651-2192, Fax: 573-651-2001, E-mail: marant@semo.edu.

Southern Arkansas University–Magnolia, Graduate Programs, Magnolia, AR 71753. Offers agriculture (MS); business administration (MBA); computer and information sciences (MS); counseling (MS); education (M Ed), including counseling and development, educational administration and supervision, elementary education, secondary education; kinesiology (MS); library media and information specialist (M Ed); public administration (EMPA); school counseling (M Ed); teaching (MAT). *Accreditation:* NCATE. Part-time and evening/weekend programs available. *Faculty:* 35 full-time (19 women), 15 part-time/adjunct (8 women). *Students:* 104 full-time (73 women), 343 part-time (252 women); includes 113 minority (108 African Americans, 3 American Indian/Alaska Native, 2 Asian Americans or Pacific Islanders), 12 international. Average age 34. In 2008, 77 master's awarded. *Degree requirements:* For master's, comprehensive exam, thesis optional. *Entrance requirements:* For master's, GRE, MAT or

GMAT, minimum GPA of 2.75. *Application deadline:* For fall admission, 8/15 for domestic students; for winter admission, 1/8 for domestic students; for spring admission, 1/8 for domestic students. Applications are processed on a rolling basis. Application fee: $0. *Expenses:* Tuition, area resident: Full-time $3564; part-time $198 per credit hour. Tuition, state resident: full-time $3564; part-time $198 per credit hour. Tuition, nonresident: full-time $5238; part-time $291 per credit hour. Required fees: $512. *Financial support:* Career-related internships or fieldwork, Federal Work-Study, scholarships/grants, tuition waivers (full), and unspecified assistantships available. Financial award applicants required to submit FAFSA. *Faculty research:* Alternative certification for teachers, supervision of instruction, instructional leadership, counseling. *Unit head:* Dr. Kim Bloss, Dean, Graduate Studies, 870-235-4150, Fax: 870-235-5227, E-mail: kkbloss@saumag.edu. *Application contact:* Dr. Kim Bloss, Dean, Graduate Studies, 870-235-4150, Fax: 870-235-5227, E-mail: kkbloss@saumag.edu.

Southern Illinois University Carbondale, Graduate School, College of Liberal Arts, Department of Political Science, Public Administration Program, Carbondale, IL 62901-4701. Offers MPA, JD/MPA. *Accreditation:* NASPAA. Part-time programs available. *Degree requirements:* For master's, thesis or alternative. *Entrance requirements:* For master's, minimum GPA of 2.7. Additional exam requirements/recommendations for international students: Required—TOEFL. *Faculty research:* Natural resources and environmental management, intergovernmental relations, state mandates, rural administration, economic development policy, nonprofit management.

Southern Illinois University Edwardsville, Graduate Studies and Research, College of Arts and Sciences, Department of Public Administration and Policy Analysis, Edwardsville, IL 62026-0001. Offers MPA. *Accreditation:* NASPAA. Part-time and evening/weekend programs available. *Faculty:* 5 full-time (1 woman). *Students:* 56 full-time (32 women), 55 part-time (31 women); includes 39 minority (35 African Americans, 1 Asian American or Pacific Islander, 3 Hispanic Americans), 13 international. Average age 26. 74 applicants, 68% accepted. In 2008, 38 master's awarded. *Degree requirements:* For master's, comprehensive exam, thesis or alternative, final exam. *Entrance requirements:* Additional exam requirements/recommendations for international students: Required—TOEFL (minimum score 550 paper-based; 213 computer-based; 79 iBT), IELTS (minimum score 6.5). *Application deadline:* For fall admission, 7/20 for domestic students, 6/1 for international students; for spring admission, 12/14 for domestic students, 10/1 for international students. Applications are processed on a rolling basis. Application fee: $30. Electronic applications accepted. *Expenses:* Tuition, area resident: Full-time $5838. Tuition, nonresident: full-time $14,596. Required fees: $1525. *Financial support:* In 2008–09, 28 teaching assistantships with full tuition reimbursements (averaging $8,064 per year) were awarded; fellowships with full tuition reimbursements, research assistantships with full tuition reimbursements, career-related internships or fieldwork, Federal Work-Study, institutionally sponsored loans, traineeships, and unspecified assistantships also available. Support available to part-time students. Financial award application deadline: 3/1; financial award applicants required to submit FAFSA. *Unit head:* Dr. T. R. Carr, Chair, 618-650-3762, E-mail: tcarr@siue.edu. *Application contact:* Dr. Drew Dolan, Program Director, 618-650-3762, E-mail: ddolan@siue.edu.

Southern University and Agricultural and Mechanical College, Graduate School, Nelson Mandela School of Public Policy and Urban Affairs, Department of Public Administration, Baton Rouge, LA 70813. Offers MPA. *Accreditation:* NASPAA. Part-time and evening/weekend programs available. *Degree requirements:* For master's, thesis. *Entrance requirements:* For master's, GRE General Test. Additional exam requirements/recommendations for international students: Required—TOEFL (minimum score 525 paper-based; 193 computer-based). *Faculty research:* Fiscal policy, public finance policy and practitioner interests; minority politics, healthcare and political economy.

Southern Utah University, College of Humanities and Social Sciences, Program in Public Administration, Cedar City, UT 84720-2498. Offers MS. Electronic applications accepted.

State University of New York at Binghamton, Graduate School, College of Community and Public Affairs, Department of Public Administration, Binghamton, NY 13902-6000. Offers MPA. *Students:* 47 full-time (26 women), 33 part-time (22 women); includes 15 minority (6 African Americans, 4 Asian Americans or Pacific Islanders, 5 Hispanic Americans), 7 international. Average age 32. 83 applicants, 59% accepted, 27 enrolled. In 2008, 24 master's awarded. Application fee: $60. *Expenses:* Tuition, area resident: Full-time $6900; part-time $288 per credit. Tuition, state resident: full-time $6900; part-time $288 per credit. Tuition, nonresident: full-time $10,920; part-time $455 per credit. Required fees: $1130. Part-time tuition and fees vary according to course load, program and student level. *Financial support:* In 2008–09, 7 students received support, including teaching assistantships with full tuition reimbursements available (averaging $10,000 per year); career-related internships or fieldwork, Federal Work-Study, institutionally sponsored loans, scholarships/grants, health care benefits, and unspecified assistantships also available. Financial award application deadline: 2/15; financial award applicants required to submit FAFSA. *Unit head:* Dr. Nadia Rubaii-Barrett, Chairperson, 607-777-9172, E-mail: nbarrett@binghamton.edu. *Application contact:* Victoria Williams, Recruiting and Admissions Coordinator, 607-777-2151, Fax: 607-777-2501, E-mail: vwilliam@binghamton.edu.

Stephen F. Austin State University, Graduate School, College of Liberal Arts, Department of Political Science and Geography, Nacogdoches, TX 75962. Offers public administration (MPA). *Degree requirements:* For master's, thesis optional. *Entrance requirements:* For master's, GRE General Test. Additional exam requirements/recommendations for international students: Required—TOEFL.

Strayer University, Graduate Studies, Washington, DC 20005-2603. Offers accounting (MS); acquisition (MBA); business administration (MBA); communications technology (MS); educational management (M Ed); finance (MBA); health services administration (MHSA); hospitality and tourism management (MBA); human resource management (MBA); information systems (MS), including computer security management, decision support system management, enterprise resource management, network management, software engineering management, systems development management; management (MBA); management information systems (MS); marketing (MBA); professional accounting (MS), including accounting information systems, controllership, taxation; public administration (MPA); supply chain management (MBA); technology in education (M Ed). Programs also offered at campus locations in Birmingham, AL; Chamblee, GA; Cobb County, GA; Morrow, GA; White Marsh, MD; Charleston, SC; Columbia, SC; Greensboro, NC; Greenville, SC; Lexington, KY; Louisville, KY; Nashville, TN; North Raleigh, NC; Washington, DC. Part-time and evening/weekend programs available. Postbaccalaureate distance learning degree programs offered (minimal on-campus study). *Degree requirements:* For master's, thesis. *Entrance requirements:* For master's, GMAT, GRE General Test, bachelor's degree from an accredited college or university, minimum undergraduate GPA of 2.75. Electronic applications accepted.

Suffolk University, Sawyer Business School, Department of Public Administration, Boston, MA 02108-2770. Offers nonprofit management (MPA); public administration (CASPA); state and local government (MPA); JD/MPA; MPA/MS. *Accreditation:* NASPAA (one or more programs are accredited). Part-time and evening/weekend programs available. *Entrance requirements:* Additional exam requirements/recommendations for international students: Required—TOEFL (minimum score 550 paper-based; 213 computer-based; 80 iBT). Electronic applications accepted. *Expenses:* Contact institution. *Faculty research:* Local government, health care, federal policy, mental health, HIV/AIDS.

Sul Ross State University, School of Arts and Sciences, Department of Behavioral and Social Sciences, Program in Public Administration, Alpine, TX 79832. Offers MA. Part-time and evening/weekend programs available. *Entrance requirements:* For master's, GRE General Test, minimum GPA of 2.5 in last 60 hours of undergraduate work. *Faculty research:* Local government, state government, personnel, volunteer fire departments, rural health.

Syracuse University, Graduate School, Maxwell School of Citizenship and Public Affairs, Program in Public Administration, Syracuse, NY 13244. Offers EMPA, MPA, PhD, CAS, MPA/MA. *Accreditation:* NASPAA (one or more programs are accredited). *Degree requirements:* For doctorate, comprehensive exam, thesis/dissertation. *Entrance requirements:* For master's, GRE General Test (MPA); for doctorate, GRE General Test. Additional exam requirements/recommendations for international students: Required—TOEFL. Electronic applications accepted.

Tennessee State University, The School of Graduate Studies and Research, Institute of Government, Nashville, TN 37209-1561. Offers public administration (MPA, PhD). *Accreditation:* NASPAA (one or more programs are accredited). Part-time and evening/weekend programs available. *Faculty:* 5 full-time (1 woman), 2 part-time/adjunct (1 woman). *Students:* 26 full-time (18 women), 96 part-time (59 women); includes 33 minority (31 African Americans, 1 Asian American or Pacific Islander, 1 Hispanic American). Average age 36. 111 applicants, 60% accepted, 25 enrolled. In 2008, 19 master's, 3 doctorates awarded. *Degree requirements:* For master's, comprehensive exam, thesis optional; for doctorate, comprehensive exam, thesis/dissertation. *Entrance requirements:* For master's, GRE General Test, minimum GPA of 2.5, writing sample; for doctorate, GRE General Test, minimum GPA of 3.25, writing sample. *Application deadline:* For fall admission, 3/1 priority date for domestic students. Application fee: $25. *Financial support:* In 2008–09, 3 research assistantships (averaging $4,185 per year), teaching assistantships (averaging $4,185 per year) were awarded. Support available to part-time students. *Faculty research:* Total quality management and process improvement, national health care policy and administration, starting non-profit ventures, public service ethics, state education financing across the U.S. public. *Unit head:* Dr. Ann-Marie Rizzo, Director, 615-963-7250, Fax: 615-963-7245, E-mail: arizzo@tnstate.edu. *Application contact:* Dr. Rodney Stonley, Coordinator of Graduate Studies, 615-963-7249, Fax: 615-963-7245, E-mail: rstonleyl@tnstate.edu.

Texas A&M International University, Office of Graduate Studies and Research, College of Arts and Sciences, Department of Social Sciences, Laredo, TX 78041-1900. Offers history (MA); political science (MA); public administration (MPA). *Degree requirements:* For master's, thesis (for some programs). *Entrance requirements:* For master's, GRE General Test. Additional exam requirements/recommendations for international students: Required—TOEFL (minimum score 550 paper-based; 213 computer-based).

Texas A&M University, George Bush School of Government and Public Service, College Station, TX 77843. Offers advanced international affairs (Certificate); homeland security (Certificate); international affairs (MPIA), including international economics and development, national security affairs; nonprofit management (Certificate); public service and administration (MPSA), including public management, public policy analysis. *Accreditation:* NASPAA. *Faculty:* 43. *Students:* 188 full-time (80 women), 101 part-time (37 women); includes 40 minority (10 African Americans, 5 Asian Americans or Pacific Islanders, 25 Hispanic Americans), 22 international. Average age 24. In 2008, 64 master's awarded. *Degree requirements:* For master's, summer internship. *Entrance requirements:* For master's, GRE (preferred) or GMAT. *Application deadline:* For fall admission, 1/24 for domestic and international students. Application fee: $50 ($75 for international students). Electronic applications accepted. *Expenses:* Tuition, area resident: Full-time $3838.50. Tuition, state resident: full-time $3838.50. Tuition, nonresident: full-time $8897. Required fees: $2359.60. *Financial support:* In 2008–09, fellowships (averaging $11,000 per year), research assistantships (averaging $11,250 per year) were awarded; career-related internships or fieldwork, Federal Work-Study, and institutionally sponsored loans also available. Financial award application deadline: 2/1; financial award applicants required to submit FAFSA. *Faculty research:* Public policy, presidential studies, public leadership, economic policy, social policy. *Unit head:* A. Benton Cocanougher, Dean, 979-862-8842, E-mail: bushschool@tamu.edu. *Application contact:* Kathryn Meyer, Recruitment/Placement Officer, 979-458-4767, Fax: 979-845-4155, E-mail: admissions@bushschool.tamu.edu.

Texas A&M University–Corpus Christi, Graduate Studies and Research, College of Liberal Arts, Corpus Christi, TX 78412-5503. Offers English (MA); history (MA); psychology (MA); public administration (MPA); studio arts (MA, MFA). Part-time and evening/weekend programs available. *Degree requirements:* For master's, comprehensive exam, thesis (for some programs). *Entrance requirements:* For master's, GRE General Test. Additional exam requirements/recommendations for international students: Required—TOEFL. Electronic applications accepted.

Texas Southern University, Graduate School, School of Public Affairs, Program in Public Administration, Houston, TX 77004-4584. Offers MPA. *Faculty:* 7 full-time (2 women), 3 part-time/adjunct (0 women). *Students:* 37 full-time (29 women), 25 part-time (16 women); includes 58 African Americans, 2 Hispanic Americans, 1 international. Average age 30. 24 applicants, 100% accepted, 21 enrolled. In 2008, 18 master's awarded. *Degree requirements:* For master's, comprehensive exam, thesis optional. *Entrance requirements:* For master's, GRE General Test, minimum GPA of 2.5. Additional exam requirements/recommendations for international students: Required—TOEFL. *Application deadline:* For fall admission, 7/15 priority date for domestic students. Applications are processed on a rolling basis. Application fee: $50 ($75 for international students). *Expenses:* Tuition, area resident: Full-time $1912; part-time $96 per credit hour. Tuition, state resident: full-time $1912; part-time $96 per credit hour. Tuition, nonresident: full-time $6302; part-time $343 per credit hour. Required fees: $3542. *Financial support:* In 2008–09, 1 teaching assistantship (averaging $1,910 per year) was awarded; fellowships, research assistantships, career-related internships or fieldwork, Federal Work-Study, institutionally sponsored loans, and unspecified assistantships also available. Financial award application deadline: 5/1. *Unit head:* Dr. Franklin Jones, Chair, 713-313-7313, E-mail: jones_fd@tsu.edu. *Application contact:* Dr. Franklin Jones, Chair, 713-313-7313, E-mail: jones_fd@tsu.edu.

Texas State University–San Marcos, Graduate School, College of Liberal Arts, Department of Political Science, Program in Public Administration, San Marcos, TX 78666. Offers MPA. *Accreditation:* NASPAA. Part-time and evening/weekend programs available. *Degree requirements:* For master's, comprehensive exam, applied research project. *Entrance requirements:* For master's, GRE General Test, minimum GPA of 2.85 in last 60 hours of course work. Additional exam requirements/recommendations for international students: Required—TOEFL (minimum score 550 paper-based; 213 computer-based), TWE. Electronic applications accepted. *Faculty research:* Ethics in public management, total quality management in government, Texas state budgeting, pragmatism and public administration, minority economic development.

Texas Tech University, Graduate School, College of Arts and Sciences, Department of Political Science, Lubbock, TX 79409. Offers political science (MA, PhD); public administration (MPA); JD/MPA. *Accreditation:* NASPAA (one or more programs are accredited). Part-time programs available. *Faculty:* 12 full-time (2 women). *Students:* 54 full-time (23 women), 18 part-time (6 women); includes 15 minority (1 African American, 1 American Indian/Alaska Native, 4 Asian Americans or Pacific Islanders, 9 Hispanic Americans), 7 international. Average age 28. 53 applicants, 57% accepted, 11 enrolled. In 2008, 11 master's, 3 doctorates awarded. *Degree requirements:* For master's, thesis or alternative; for doctorate, thesis/dissertation. *Entrance requirements:* For master's and doctorate, GRE General Test. Additional exam requirements/recommendations for international students: Required—TOEFL (minimum score 550 paper-based; 213 computer-based). *Application deadline:* For fall admission, 3/1 priority date for international students; for spring admission, 11/1 priority date for international students. Applications are processed on a rolling basis. Application fee: $50 ($60 for international students). Electronic applications accepted. *Expenses:* Tuition, area resident: Part-time $194 per credit hour. Tuition, state resident: full-time $4648; part-time $194 per credit hour. Tuition, nonresident: full-time $11,392; part-time $475 per credit hour. Required fees: $2206; $69 per credit hour. $389 per semester. *Financial support:* In 2008–09, 53 students received support, including 24 teaching assistantships with partial tuition reimbursements available (averaging $12,958 per year); research assistantships with partial tuition reimbursements available, Federal Work-Study and institutionally sponsored loans also available. Support available to part-time students. Financial award application deadline: 4/15; financial award applicants required to submit FAFSA. *Faculty research:* State politics, American institutions and behavior, Asian

Public Administration

Texas Tech University (continued)
politics, international and comparative political relations and economics, public administration and organizations. Total annual research expenditures: $119,879. *Unit head:* Dr. Philip H. Marshall, Chair, 806-742-3121, Fax: 806-742-0850, E-mail: philip.marshall@ttu.edu. *Application contact:* Donna Barnes, Administrative Assistant, 806-742-3121, Fax: 806-742-0850, E-mail: donna.barnes@ttu.edu.

Thomas Edison State College, School of Business and Management, Program in Public Service Leadership, Trenton, NJ 08608-1176. Offers Graduate Certificate. Part-time programs available. Postbaccalaureate distance learning degree programs offered (no on-campus study). *Entrance requirements:* Additional exam requirements/recommendations for international students: Required—TOEFL (minimum score 550 paper-based; 213 computer-based; 79 iBT). *Application deadline:* For fall admission, 8/15 priority date for domestic and international students; for winter admission, 11/15 priority date for domestic and international students; for spring admission, 2/15 priority date for domestic and international students. Applications are processed on a rolling basis. Application fee: $75. Electronic applications accepted. *Expenses:* Tuition, area resident: Part-time $465 per credit. Tuition, state resident: part-time $465 per credit. Tuition, nonresident: part-time $465 per credit. *Financial support:* Applicants required to submit FAFSA. *Unit head:* Dr. Joseph Santora, Dean, School of Business and Management, 609-984-1130, Fax: 609-984-3898, E-mail: infor@tesc.edu. *Application contact:* David Hoftiezer, Director of Admissions, 888-442-8372, Fax: 609-984-8447, E-mail: admissions@tesc.edu.

Troy University, Graduate School, College of Arts and Sciences, Program in Public Administration, Troy, AL 36082. Offers MPA. Part-time and evening/weekend programs available. Postbaccalaureate distance learning degree programs offered (no on-campus study). *Degree requirements:* For master's, comprehensive exam (for some programs), thesis optional. *Entrance requirements:* For master's, GRE General Test, MAT, or GMAT, minimum GPA of 2.5. Additional exam requirements/recommendations for international students: Required—TOEFL (minimum score 523 paper-based; 200 computer-based). Electronic applications accepted.

Tufts University, Graduate School of Arts and Sciences, Graduate Certificate Programs, Program Evaluation Program, Medford, MA 02155. Offers Certificate. Part-time and evening/weekend programs available. Electronic applications accepted. *Expenses:* Contact institution.

TUI University, College of Business Administration, Program in Business Administration, Cypress, CA 90630. Offers business administration (PhD); conflict and negotiation management (MBA); criminal justice administration (MBA); entrepreneurship (MBA); finance (MBA); general management (MBA); human resource management (MBA); information technology management (MBA); international business (MBA); logistics management (MBA); public management (MBA); strategic leadership (MBA). Part-time and evening/weekend programs available. Postbaccalaureate distance learning degree programs offered (no on-campus study). *Degree requirements:* For doctorate, comprehensive exam, thesis/dissertation, defense of dissertation. *Entrance requirements:* For master's, minimum GPA of 2.5 (students with GPA 3.0 or greater may transfer up to 30% of graduate level credits); for doctorate, minimum GPA of 3.4, curriculum vitae, course work in research methods or statistics. Additional exam requirements/recommendations for international students: Required—TOEFL. Electronic applications accepted.

Universidad Nacional Pedro Henriquez Urena, Graduate School, Santo Domingo, Dominican Republic. Offers accounting and auditing (M Acct); animal production (M Agr); business administration (MBA, PhD); Caribbean tropical architecture (M Arch); conservation of monuments and cultural goods (M Arch); economics (M Econ); education (PhD); environmental engineering (MEE); horticulture (M Agr); hospital administration (PhD); humanities (PhD); international relations (MPS); management of natural resources (MNRM); project management (M Man, MPM); public administration (MPS); sanitary engineering (ME); social science (PhD); veterinary medicine (DVM).

Université de Moncton, Faculty of Arts and Social Sciences, Department of Public Administration, Moncton, NB E1A 3E9, Canada. Offers MPA, LL B/MPA. Part-time and evening/weekend programs available. *Degree requirements:* For master's, one foreign language. *Entrance requirements:* For master's, minimum GPA of 3.0. *Faculty research:* Public sector reform, privatization, economic modeling, public policy.

Université du Québec à Montréal, Graduate Programs, Program in Urban Analysis and Management, Montréal, QC H3C 3P8, Canada. Offers MA. Part-time programs available. *Entrance requirements:* For master's, appropriate bachelor's degree or equivalent and proficiency in French.

Université du Québec, École nationale d'administration publique, Graduate Program in Public Administration, Diploma Program in Public Administration, Quebec, QC G1K 9E5, Canada. Offers Diploma.

Université du Québec, École nationale d'administration publique, Graduate Program in Public Administration, Doctorate Program in Public Administration, Quebec, QC G1K 9E5, Canada. Offers PhD.

University at Albany, State University of New York, Nelson A. Rockefeller College of Public Affairs and Policy, Department of Public Administration and Policy, Albany, NY 12222-0001. Offers administrative behavior (PhD); comparative and development administration (MPA, PhD); human resources (MPA); legislative administration (MPA); nonprofit leadership and management (Certificate); planning and policy analysis (CAS); policy analysis (MPA); program analysis and evaluation (PhD); public affairs and policy (MA); public finance (MPA, PhD); public management (MPA, PhD); women and public policy (Certificate); JD/MPA. *Accreditation:* NASPAA (one or more programs are accredited). *Degree requirements:* For doctorate, one foreign language, thesis/dissertation. *Entrance requirements:* For doctorate, GRE General Test. Additional exam requirements/recommendations for international students: Required—TOEFL (minimum score 550 paper-based; 213 computer-based). Electronic applications accepted.

The University of Akron, Graduate School, Buchtel College of Arts and Sciences, Department of Public Administration and Urban Studies, Program in Public Administration, Akron, OH 44325. Offers MPA, JD/MPA. *Accreditation:* NASPAA. *Degree requirements:* For master's, thesis optional. *Entrance requirements:* For master's, GRE, GMAT, LSAT, MAT or minimum GPA of 3.0, minimum GPA of 2.8, resumé, personal essay, letters of recommendation. Additional exam requirements/recommendations for international students: Required—TOEFL (minimum score 550 paper-based; 213 computer-based; 79 iBT), Michigan English Language Assessment Battery. Electronic applications accepted.

The University of Alabama, Graduate School, College of Arts and Sciences, Department of Political Science, Tuscaloosa, AL 35487. Offers political science (MA, PhD); public administration (MPA). Part-time programs available. *Faculty:* 16 full-time (4 women). *Students:* 39 full-time (17 women), 18 part-time (8 women); includes 7 minority (4 African Americans, 1 Asian American or Pacific Islander, 2 Hispanic Americans), 8 international. Average age 29. 47 applicants, 64% accepted, 12 enrolled. In 2008, 7 master's, 1 doctorate awarded. Terminal master's awarded for partial completion of doctoral program. *Degree requirements:* For master's, thesis optional; for doctorate, comprehensive exam, thesis/dissertation. *Entrance requirements:* For master's and doctorate, GRE (minimum score: 1000), minimum undergraduate GPA of 3.0. Additional exam requirements/recommendations for international students: Required—TOEFL. *Application deadline:* For fall admission, 6/30 for domestic and international students; for spring admission, 10/15 for domestic and international students. Applications are processed on a rolling basis. Application fee: $30. *Expenses:* Tuition, area resident: Full-time $6400. Tuition, state resident: full-time $6400. Tuition, nonresident: full-time $18,000. *Financial support:* In 2008–09, 15 students received support, including teaching assistantships with full tuition reimbursements available (averaging $10,908 per year); career-related internships or fieldwork and Federal Work-Study also available. Financial award application deadline: 2/15. *Faculty research:* American politics, comparative politics, international relations, public administration, political theory. Total annual research expenditures: $15,183. *Unit head:* Dr. David U. Lanoue, Chair and Professor, 205-348-5981, Fax: 205-348-5298, E-mail: dlanoue@bama.ua.edu. *Application contact:* Dr. Terry Royed, Graduate Advisor, 205-348-3801, Fax: 205-348-5248, E-mail: troyed@tenhoor.as.ua.edu.

The University of Alabama at Birmingham, School of Social and Behavioral Sciences, Department of Government, Birmingham, AL 35294. Offers public administration (MPA). *Accreditation:* NASPAA. *Entrance requirements:* For master's, GRE General Test or MAT. Electronic applications accepted.

University of Alaska Anchorage, College of Business and Public Policy, Program in Public Administration, Anchorage, AK 99508-8060. Offers MPA. Part-time programs available. *Degree requirements:* For master's, comprehensive exam, thesis or alternative, capstone project. *Entrance requirements:* For master's, GRE General Test. Additional exam requirements/recommendations for international students: Required—TOEFL (minimum score 550 paper-based; 213 computer-based). *Faculty research:* Policy analysis, policy and administration issues in the North, hypothetical government policies, public management in health care.

University of Alaska Southeast, Graduate Programs, Program in Public Administration, Juneau, AK 99801. Offers MPA. Part-time and evening/weekend programs available. Postbaccalaureate distance learning degree programs offered (no on-campus study). *Degree requirements:* For master's, capstone course or thesis. *Entrance requirements:* For master's, minimum GPA of 3.0, curriculum vitae, letters of reference. Electronic applications accepted. *Faculty research:* Democratic governance, public administrative theory, local government.

The University of Arizona, Graduate College, Eller College of Management, School of Public Administration and Policy, Tucson, AZ 85721. Offers public administration (MPA); public administration and policy (PhD). *Accreditation:* NASPAA. *Degree requirements:* For master's, internship of 400 hours; for doctorate, comprehensive exam, thesis/dissertation. *Entrance requirements:* For master's, GRE, 2-3 letters of recommendation, resumé; for doctorate, GMAT or GRE, minimum GPA of 3.5, letter of interest, 3 letters of recommendation, resumé. Additional exam requirements/recommendations for international students: Required—TOEFL (minimum score 650 paper-based; 280 computer-based). *Expenses:* Contact institution.

University of Arkansas, Graduate School, J. William Fulbright College of Arts and Sciences, Department of Political Science, Program in Public Administration, Fayetteville, AR 72701-1201. Offers MPA. *Degree requirements:* For master's, comprehensive exam, thesis or alternative. *Entrance requirements:* For master's, GRE General Test.

University of Arkansas at Little Rock, Graduate School, College of Professional Studies, Program in Public Administration, Little Rock, AR 72204-1099. Offers MPA. *Accreditation:* NASPAA. Part-time and evening/weekend programs available. *Degree requirements:* For master's, comprehensive exam. *Entrance requirements:* For master's, GRE General Test or MAT, minimum GPA of 2.7. *Faculty research:* State and local administration, nonprofit management.

University of Baltimore, Graduate School, The Yale Gordon College of Liberal Arts, Doctoral Program in Public Administration, Baltimore, MD 21201-5779. Offers DPA. Part-time and evening/weekend programs available. *Students:* 5 full-time (1 woman), 31 part-time (10 women); includes 19 minority (14 African Americans, 4 Asian Americans or Pacific Islanders, 1 Hispanic American), 2 international. Average age 44. 44 applicants, 48% accepted, 18 enrolled. In 2008, 1 doctorate awarded. *Degree requirements:* For doctorate, thesis/dissertation. *Entrance requirements:* For doctorate, GRE. Additional exam requirements/recommendations for international students: Required—TOEFL. *Application deadline:* For fall admission, 5/1 priority date for domestic students, 6/1 for international students; for spring admission, 12/1 for domestic students, 11/1 for international students. *Expenses:* Tuition, state resident: part-time $568 per credit. Tuition, nonresident: part-time $824 per credit. Required fees: $250 per semester. *Financial support:* Federal Work-Study available. Financial award application deadline: 3/31; financial award applicants required to submit FAFSA. *Unit head:* Dr. Patria Julnes, Director, 410-837-6053, E-mail: pjulnes@ubalt.edu. *Application contact:* Kevin Nies, Assistant Director, Office of Graduate Admission, 410-837-6565, E-mail: knies@ubalt.edu.

University of Baltimore, Graduate School, The Yale Gordon College of Liberal Arts, Master's Program in Public Administration, Baltimore, MD 21201-5779. Offers public administration (MPA); JD/MPA. *Accreditation:* NASPAA. Part-time and evening/weekend programs available. Postbaccalaureate distance learning degree programs offered (minimal on-campus study). *Faculty:* 11 full-time (2 women), 2 part-time/adjunct (0 women). *Students:* 115 full-time (64 women), 187 part-time (128 women); includes 132 minority (116 African Americans, 2 American Indian/Alaska Native, 8 Asian Americans or Pacific Islanders, 6 Hispanic Americans), 61 international. Average age 31. 198 applicants, 64% accepted, 105 enrolled. In 2008, 45 master's awarded. *Entrance requirements:* For master's, interview, minimum GPA of 3.0. Additional exam requirements/recommendations for international students: Required—TOEFL (minimum score 550 paper-based; 213 computer-based). *Application deadline:* For fall admission, 8/1 priority date for domestic students, 6/1 for international students; for spring admission, 12/1 for domestic students, 11/1 for international students. Applications are processed on a rolling basis. Application fee: $30. Electronic applications accepted. *Expenses:* Contact institution. *Financial support:* In 2008–09, 6 research assistantships were awarded; fellowships, career-related internships or fieldwork and Federal Work-Study also available. Support available to part-time students. Financial award application deadline: 4/1; financial award applicants required to submit FAFSA. *Faculty research:* Welfare policy, public administration ethics, bureaucratic politics, public sector budgeting, program evaluation. Total annual research expenditures: $1.9 million. *Unit head:* Dr. Samuel Brown, Director, MPA Program, 410-837-6091, E-mail: sabrown@ubalt.edu. *Application contact:* Kevin Nies, Assistant Director, Office of Graduate Admission, 410-837-6565, E-mail: knies@ubalt.edu.

University of Central Florida, College of Health and Public Affairs, Department of Public Administration, Orlando, FL 32816. Offers emergency management and homeland security (Certificate); non-profit management (MNM, Certificate); public administration (MPA, Certificate); urban and regional planning (Certificate). *Accreditation:* NASPAA. Part-time and evening/weekend programs available. *Faculty:* 13 full-time (3 women), 9 part-time/adjunct (4 women). *Students:* 81 full-time (54 women), 243 part-time (171 women); includes 118 minority (64 African Americans, 11 Asian Americans or Pacific Islanders, 43 Hispanic Americans), 7 international. In 2008, 66 master's, 18 other advanced degrees awarded. *Degree requirements:* For master's, comprehensive exam, thesis or alternative, research report. *Entrance requirements:* For master's, GRE General Test. *Application deadline:* For fall admission, 7/1 for domestic students; for spring admission, 12/1 for domestic students. Application fee: $30. Electronic applications accepted. *Expenses:* Tuition, area resident: Full-time $6816; part-time $284 per credit. Tuition, state resident: full-time $6816; part-time $1076 per credit. Tuition, nonresident: full-time $25,824. Required fees: $216; $9 per credit. *Financial support:* In 2008–09, 3 fellowships with partial tuition reimbursements (averaging $10,000 per year), 16 research assistantships with partial tuition reimbursements (averaging $6,200 per year) were awarded; teaching assistantships with partial tuition reimbursements, career-related internships or fieldwork, Federal Work-Study, institutionally sponsored loans, tuition waivers (partial), and unspecified assistantships also available. Financial award application deadline: 3/1; financial award applicants required to submit FAFSA. *Unit head:* Dr. MaryAnn Feldheim, Chair, 407-823-3693, Fax: 407-823-5651. *Application contact:* Dr. MaryAnn Feldheim, Chair, 407-823-3693, Fax: 407-823-5651.

University of Colorado at Colorado Springs, Graduate School, Graduate School of Public Affairs, Colorado Springs, CO 80933-7150. Offers criminal justice (MCJ); public administration (MPA). Part-time and evening/weekend programs available. *Faculty:* 3 full-time (1 woman), 25 part-time/adjunct (15 women). *Students:* 40 full-time (23 women), 38 part-time (23 women); includes 10 minority (2 Asian Americans or Pacific Islanders, 8 Hispanic Americans). Average

age 35. 34 applicants, 91% accepted, 24 enrolled. In 2008, 32 master's awarded. *Degree requirements:* For master's, internship (if no experience), capstone project. *Entrance requirements:* For master's, GRE General Test, GMAT, LSAT, minimum GPA of 3.0. *Application deadline:* For fall admission, 6/1 priority date for domestic students; for spring admission, 11/1 for domestic students. Applications are processed on a rolling basis. Application fee: $60 ($75 for international students). *Expenses:* Contact institution. *Financial support:* Career-related internships or fieldwork and Federal Work-Study available. Support available to part-time students. *Unit head:* Dr. Terry Schwartz, Dean, 719-255-4047, Fax: 719-255-4183, E-mail: tschwart@uccs.edu. *Application contact:* Mary Lou Kartis, Program Assistant, 719-255-4182, Fax: 719-255-4183, E-mail: mkartis@uccs.edu.

University of Colorado Denver, Graduate School of Public Affairs, Program in Public Administration, Denver, CO 80217-3364. Offers MPA. *Accreditation:* NASPAA. Part-time and evening/weekend programs available. Postbaccalaureate distance learning degree programs offered. *Degree requirements:* For master's, research paper. *Entrance requirements:* For master's, GRE General Test or minimum GPA of 3.0. Additional exam requirements/recommendations for international students: Required—TOEFL (minimum score 500 paper-based).

University of Connecticut, Graduate School, College of Liberal Arts and Sciences, Department of Public Policy, Field of Public Administration, Storrs, CT 06269. Offers nonprofit management (Graduate Certificate); public administration (MPA); public financial management (Graduate Certificate); JD/MPA; MPA/MSW. *Accreditation:* NASPAA. *Degree requirements:* For master's, comprehensive exam, internship. *Entrance requirements:* For master's, GRE General Test. Additional exam requirements/recommendations for international students: Required—TOEFL (minimum score 550 paper-based; 213 computer-based). Electronic applications accepted.

University of Dayton, Graduate School, College of Arts and Sciences, Program in Public Administration, Dayton, OH 45469-1300. Offers MPA. *Accreditation:* NASPAA. Part-time and evening/weekend programs available. *Faculty:* 5 full-time (2 women), 5 part-time/adjunct (2 women). *Students:* 27 full-time (12 women), 20 part-time (8 women); includes 10 minority (8 African Americans, 2 Asian Americans or Pacific Islanders), 1 international. Average age 31. 40 applicants, 33% accepted, 8 enrolled. In 2008, 20 master's awarded. *Degree requirements:* For master's, internship or public service project. *Entrance requirements:* For master's, GRE General Test. Additional exam requirements/recommendations for international students: Required—TOEFL (minimum score 550 paper-based; 213 computer-based; 80 iBT). *Application deadline:* For fall admission, 4/1 priority date for domestic students, 3/1 priority date for international students; for winter admission, 7/1 priority date for international students; for spring admission, 1/1 priority date for international students. Applications are processed on a rolling basis. Application fee: $0 ($50 for international students). Electronic applications accepted. *Expenses:* Tuition: Full-time $6950; part-time $1737.50 per semester. Required fees: $25 per semester. Tuition and fees vary according to course level, course load, degree level and program. *Financial support:* In 2008–09, 3 research assistantships with full tuition reimbursements (averaging $9,500 per year) were awarded; career-related internships or fieldwork, institutionally sponsored loans, health care benefits, and unspecified assistantships also available. Financial award applicants required to submit FAFSA. *Faculty research:* Ethics, leadership, state government, environmental policy, welfare reforms, state legislatures. *Unit head:* Dr. Grant Neeley, Director, MPA Program, 937-229-3626, Fax: 937-229-1400, E-mail: grant.neeley@notes.udayton.edu. *Application contact:* Angela Jones-Glukhov, Associate Director of Graduate Admissions, 937-229-4305, Fax: 937-229-4729, E-mail: jonesgas@notes.udayton.edu.

University of Delaware, College of Human Services, Education and Public Policy, School of Urban Affairs and Public Policy, Program in Public Administration, Newark, DE 19716. Offers MPA. *Accreditation:* NASPAA. Part-time and evening/weekend programs available. *Degree requirements:* For master's, internship or thesis. *Entrance requirements:* For master's, GRE General Test. Additional exam requirements/recommendations for international students: Required—TOEFL. Electronic applications accepted. *Faculty research:* State and local management, community development and nonprofit leadership, drug and alcohol epidemiology, fiscal and financial policy, transportation impacts and management.

See Close-Up on page 1239.

University of Evansville, Center for Adult Education, Evansville, IN 47722. Offers public service administration (MS). Part-time and evening/weekend programs available. *Faculty:* 6 full-time (2 women), 5 part-time/adjunct (2 women). *Students:* 63 full-time (45 women), 1 (woman) part-time; includes 3 minority (2 African Americans, 1 American Indian/Alaska Native), 1 international. Average age 38. 32 applicants, 91% accepted, 21 enrolled. In 2008, 26 master's awarded. *Entrance requirements:* For master's, GRE or MAT, minimum undergraduate GPA of 3.0, resumé, minimum of 3 years work experience, 2 letters of reference. Additional exam requirements/recommendations for international students: Required—TOEFL (minimum score 527 paper-based; 71 iBT). *Application deadline:* For fall admission, 7/15 priority date for domestic students; for spring admission, 11/30 priority date for domestic students. Applications are processed on a rolling basis. Application fee: $35. *Expenses:* Tuition: Full-time $7212. Tuition and fees vary according to course load, degree level and program. *Financial support:* In 2008–09, 12 students received support. Application deadline: 6/1. *Unit head:* Carla S. Doty, Director of Continuing Education, 812-488-2981, Fax: 812-488-2432, E-mail: cd39@evansville.edu. *Application contact:* Carla S. Doty, Director of Continuing Education, 812-488-2981, Fax: 812-488-2432, E-mail: cd39@evansville.edu.

The University of Findlay, Graduate and Professional Studies, College of Business, Findlay, OH 45840-3653. Offers financial management (MBA); human resource management (MBA); international management (MBA); management (MBA); marketing (MBA); public management (MBA). Part-time and evening/weekend programs available. Postbaccalaureate distance learning degree programs offered (no on-campus study). *Students:* 82 full-time (35 women), 633 part-time (248 women); includes 18 minority (10 African Americans, 1 American Indian/Alaska Native, 3 Asian Americans or Pacific Islanders, 4 Hispanic Americans), 507 international. Average age 35. 251 applicants, 87% accepted, 180 enrolled. In 2008, 396 master's awarded. *Degree requirements:* For master's, thesis, cumulative project. *Entrance requirements:* For master's, GMAT, minimum undergraduate GPA of 3.0 in last 64 hours of course work. Additional exam requirements/recommendations for international students: Required—TOEFL (minimum score 550 paper-based; 213 computer-based; 80 iBT). *Application deadline:* Applications are processed on a rolling basis. Application fee: $25 ($0 for international students). Electronic applications accepted. *Expenses:* Contact institution. *Financial support:* In 2008–09, 6 research assistantships with full and partial tuition reimbursements (averaging $4,200 per year) were awarded; unspecified assistantships also available. Financial award application deadline: 4/1; financial award applicants required to submit FAFSA. *Faculty research:* Health care management, operations and logistics management. *Unit head:* Dr. Paul Sears, Dean, 419-434-4704, Fax: 419-434-4822. *Application contact:* Heather Riffle, Assistant to the Dean, Graduate and Professional Studies, 419-434-4640, Fax: 419-434-5517, E-mail: riffle@findlay.edu.

University of Georgia, School of Public and International Affairs, Program in Public Administration and Policy, Athens, GA 30602. Offers public administration (MPA, PhD). *Accreditation:* NASPAA (one or more programs are accredited). *Degree requirements:* For master's, internship; for doctorate, thesis/dissertation. *Entrance requirements:* For master's and doctorate, GRE General Test. Electronic applications accepted.

University of Guam, Office of Graduate Studies, School of Business and Public Administration, Public Administration Program, Mangilao, GU 96923. Offers MPA. *Entrance requirements:* For master's, GRE General Test. Additional exam requirements/recommendations for international students: Required—TOEFL.

University of Guelph, Graduate Program Services, College of Social and Applied Human Sciences, Department of Political Science, Guelph, ON N1G 2W1, Canada. Offers comparative politics (MA); international development (MA); political science (MA); public policy and public administration (MA); the Americas (Canada emphasis) (MA). MA in public policy and public administration offered in collaboration with Department of Political Science of McMaster University. *Degree requirements:* For master's, thesis or paper. *Entrance requirements:* For master's, minimum B average during previous 2 years of course work, 4 year Honours Degree in Political Science. Additional exam requirements/recommendations for international students: Required—TOEFL. Electronic applications accepted. *Faculty research:* Political ethics, constitutional power.

University of Hawaii at Manoa, Graduate Division, Colleges of Arts and Sciences, College of Social Sciences, Department of Public Administration, Honolulu, HI 96822. Offers MPA, Graduate Certificate. Part-time and evening/weekend programs available. *Degree requirements:* For master's, thesis optional, practicum. *Entrance requirements:* Additional exam requirements/recommendations for international students: Required—TOEFL (minimum score 540 paper-based; 207 computer-based; 76 iBT), IELTS (minimum score 5). *Faculty research:* Public sector finance and the budget process, collaboration between sectors, organizational problem solving and communication processes, system reform in government organizations, public policy analysis.

University of Idaho, College of Graduate Studies, College of Letters, Arts and Social Sciences, Department of Political Science and Public Affairs Research, Program in Public Administration, Moscow, ID 83844-2282. Offers MPA. *Students:* 10 full-time, 11 part-time. Average age 33. In 2008, 9 master's awarded. *Entrance requirements:* For master's, minimum GPA of 2.8. *Application deadline:* For fall admission, 8/1 for domestic students; for spring admission, 12/15 for domestic students. Application fee: $55 ($60 for international students). *Expenses:* Tuition, nonresident: full-time $10,080; part-time $336 per credit. Required fees: $5212; $267 per credit. Tuition and fees vary according to program. *Financial support:* Application deadline: 2/15. *Unit head:* Dr. Donald Wayne Crowley, Chair, 208-885-6328. *Application contact:* Dr. Donald Wayne Crowley, Chair, 208-885-6328.

University of Illinois at Chicago, Graduate College, College of Urban Planning and Public Affairs, Program in Public Administration, Chicago, IL 60607-7128. Offers MPA, PhD. *Accreditation:* NASPAA (one or more programs are accredited). Part-time and evening/weekend programs available. Terminal master's awarded for partial completion of doctoral program. *Degree requirements:* For master's, internship/project. *Entrance requirements:* For master's, GRE General Test, minimum GPA of 3.0. Additional exam requirements/recommendations for international students: Required—TOEFL. Electronic applications accepted. *Faculty research:* Public management, economic development, public personnel.

University of Illinois at Springfield, Graduate Programs, College of Public Affairs and Administration, Program in Public Administration, Springfield, IL 62703-5407. Offers MPA, DPA. *Accreditation:* NASPAA. Part-time and evening/weekend programs available. Postbaccalaureate distance learning degree programs offered (no on-campus study). *Faculty:* 7 full-time (2 women), 5 part-time/adjunct (2 women). *Students:* 51 full-time (30 women), 113 part-time (67 women); includes 35 minority (30 African Americans, 5 Asian Americans or Pacific Islanders), 3 international. Average age 33. 129 applicants, 39% accepted, 37 enrolled. In 2008, 46 master's awarded. *Degree requirements:* For master's, thesis or seminar; for doctorate, comprehensive exam, thesis/dissertation. *Entrance requirements:* For master's, minimum undergraduate GPA of 2.5, resumé, career goals statement; for doctorate, GRE, minimum graduate GPA of 3.25; completed master's degree; writing sample; 3 letters of reference; interview. Additional exam requirements/recommendations for international students: Required—TOEFL (minimum score 550 paper-based; 213 computer-based). Application fee: $50 ($60 for international students). Electronic applications accepted. *Expenses:* Tuition, state resident: full-time $6144; part-time $256 per credit hour. Tuition, nonresident: full-time $13,980; part-time $582.50 per credit hour. Required fees: $1800. *Financial support:* In 2008–09, research assistantships with full tuition reimbursements (averaging $8,109 per year), teaching assistantships with full tuition reimbursements (averaging $8,109 per year) were awarded; career-related internships or fieldwork, Federal Work-Study, scholarships/grants, health care benefits, and unspecified assistantships also available. Support available to part-time students. Financial award application deadline: 11/15; financial award applicants required to submit FAFSA. *Unit head:* Dr. Will Miller, Program Administrator, 217-206-8361, E-mail: wmill3@uis.edu. *Application contact:* Dr. Will Miller, Program Administrator, 217-206-8361, E-mail: wmill3@uis.edu.

The University of Kansas, Graduate Studies, College of Liberal Arts and Sciences, Department of Public Administration, Lawrence, KS 66045-3129. Offers MPA, PhD, JD/MPA, MUP/MPA. *Accreditation:* NASPAA. Part-time and evening/weekend programs available. *Faculty:* 13 full-time (5 women). *Students:* 35 full-time (15 women), 101 part-time (46 women); includes 13 minority (8 African Americans, 1 Asian American or Pacific Islander, 4 Hispanic Americans), 4 international. Average age 34. 103 applicants, 47% accepted, 39 enrolled. In 2008, 33 master's, 2 doctorates awarded. Terminal master's awarded for partial completion of doctoral program. *Degree requirements:* For master's, comprehensive exam; for doctorate, comprehensive exam, thesis/dissertation. *Entrance requirements:* For master's and doctorate, GRE General Test. Additional exam requirements/recommendations for international students: Required—TOEFL. *Application deadline:* For fall admission, 7/1 for domestic students, 5/1 for international students; for spring admission, 11/15 for domestic students, 10/1 for international students. Application fee: $45 ($55 for international students). Electronic applications accepted. *Expenses:* Tuition, area resident: Full-time $6122; part-time $255.10 per credit hour. Tuition, state resident: full-time $6122; part-time $255.10 per credit hour. Tuition, nonresident: full-time $14,629; part-time $609.55 per credit hour. Required fees: $847; $70.56 per credit hour. Tuition and fees vary according to course load and program. *Financial support:* Fellowships, research assistantships with full and partial tuition reimbursements, teaching assistantships with full and partial tuition reimbursements, career-related internships or fieldwork, institutionally sponsored loans, scholarships/grants, and unspecified assistantships available. Financial award application deadline: 2/1. *Faculty research:* Local government, administrative ethics, non-profit management, policy studies, law and public administration, finance, budgeting. *Unit head:* Marilu Goodyear, Chair, 785-864-3527, Fax: 785-864-5208, E-mail: padept@ku.edu. *Application contact:* Ray Hummert, Administrative Director, 785-864-9097, Fax: 785-864-5208, E-mail: rhummert@ku.edu.

University of Kentucky, Graduate School, Program in Public Administration, Lexington, KY 40506-0032. Offers MPA, MPP, PhD. *Accreditation:* NASPAA (one or more programs are accredited). *Degree requirements:* For master's, comprehensive exam; for doctorate, comprehensive exam, thesis/dissertation. *Entrance requirements:* For master's, GMAT or GRE General Test, minimum undergraduate GPA of 2.75; for doctorate, GMAT or GRE General Test, minimum graduate GPA of 3.0. Additional exam requirements/recommendations for international students: Required—TOEFL (minimum score 550 paper-based; 213 computer-based). Electronic applications accepted. *Faculty research:* Public financial management, education finance and policy, health finance and policy, welfare policy, program evaluation.

University of La Verne, College of Business and Public Management, Doctoral Program in Public Administration, La Verne, CA 91750-4443. Offers DPA. Part-time programs available. *Faculty:* 7 full-time (3 women), 7 part-time/adjunct (2 women). *Students:* 54 full-time (24 women), 41 part-time (18 women); includes 53 minority (25 African Americans, 9 Asian Americans or Pacific Islanders, 19 Hispanic Americans), 8 international. Average age 44. In 2008, 11 doctorates awarded. *Degree requirements:* For doctorate, thesis/dissertation. *Entrance requirements:* For doctorate, MAT, GMAT or GRE, minimum undergraduate GPA of 3.25, interview, 3 letters of recommendation. Additional exam requirements/recommendations for international students: Required—TOEFL (minimum score 550 paper-based; 213 computer-based). Application fee: $75. *Expenses:* Contact institution. *Financial support:* Institutionally sponsored loans available. Financial award application deadline: 3/2; financial award applicants required to submit FAFSA. *Unit head:* Dr. Suzanne Beaumaster, Chairperson, 909-593-3511

Public Administration

University of La Verne (continued)
Ext. 4817, E-mail: beaumast@ulv.edu. *Application contact:* Erma Cross, Program and Admission Specialist, 909-593-3511 Ext. 4948, Fax: 909-392-2761, E-mail: ecross@ulv.edu.

University of La Verne, College of Business and Public Management, Master's Program in Public Administration, La Verne, CA 91750-4443. Offers MPA. *Accreditation:* NASPAA. Part-time programs available. *Faculty:* 7 full-time (3 women), 7 part-time/adjunct (2 women). *Students:* 29 full-time (20 women), 43 part-time (21 women); includes 35 minority (5 African Americans, 5 Asian Americans or Pacific Islanders, 25 Hispanic Americans). Average age 33. In 2008, 13 master's awarded. *Entrance requirements:* For master's, minimum undergraduate GPA of 2.75, 2 letters of recommendation, resumé. Additional exam requirements/recommendations for international students: Required—TOEFL (minimum score 550 paper-based; 213 computer-based). *Application deadline:* Applications are processed on a rolling basis. Application fee: $50. *Expenses:* Contact institution. *Financial support:* Fellowships, research assistantships available. Financial award application deadline: 3/2; financial award applicants required to submit FAFSA. *Unit head:* Dr. Jack Meek, Chairperson, 909-593-3511 Ext. 4941, E-mail: meekj@ulv.edu. *Application contact:* Erma Cross, Program and Admission Specialist, 909-593-3511 Ext. 4948, Fax: 909-392-2761, E-mail: ecross@ulv.edu.

University of La Verne, College of Business and Public Management, Program in Gerontology, La Verne, CA 91750-4443. Offers business administration (MS); counseling (MS); gerontology (Certificate); gerontology administration (MS); health services management (MS); public administration (MS). Part-time programs available. *Faculty:* 4 part-time/adjunct (3 women). *Students:* 14 full-time (13 women), 19 part-time (18 women); includes 13 minority (9 African Americans, 4 Hispanic Americans). Average age 44. In 2008, 11 master's awarded. *Entrance requirements:* For master's, minimum GPA of 2.5. Additional exam requirements/recommendations for international students: Required—TOEFL (minimum score 550 paper-based; 213 computer-based). *Application deadline:* Applications are processed on a rolling basis. Application fee: $50. *Expenses:* Contact institution. *Financial support:* Institutionally sponsored loans available. Financial award application deadline: 3/2; financial award applicants required to submit FAFSA. *Unit head:* Joan Branin, Chairperson, 909-593-3511 Ext. 4247. *Application contact:* Barbara Cox, Program and Admissions Specialist, 909-593-3511 Ext. 4004, Fax: 909-392-2761, E-mail: bcox@ulv.edu.

University of La Verne, Regional Campus Administration, Graduate Programs, Orange County Campus, Garden Grove, CA 92840. Offers business (MBA-EP), including health services management, information technology, management, marketing, supply chain management; health administration (MHA); leadership and management (MS); public administration (MPA). *Faculty:* 2 full-time (0 women), 10 part-time/adjunct (1 woman). *Students:* 23 full-time (13 women), 69 part-time (29 women); includes 53 minority (4 African Americans, 6 American Indian/Alaska Native, 27 Asian Americans or Pacific Islanders, 16 Hispanic Americans). Average age 39. In 2008, 29 master's awarded. *Entrance requirements:* For master's, 2 letters of recommendation, resumé. *Application deadline:* Applications are processed on a rolling basis. Application fee: $50. *Expenses:* Contact institution. *Financial support:* Institutionally sponsored loans available. Financial award application deadline: 3/2; financial award applicants required to submit FAFSA. *Unit head:* Pamela Bergovoy, Director, 714-534-4860, Fax: 714-534-4865, E-mail: bergovoy@ulv.edu. *Application contact:* Pamela Bergovoy, Director, 714-534-4860, Fax: 714-534-4865, E-mail: bergovoy@ulv.edu.

University of Louisville, Graduate School, College of Arts and Sciences, Department of Urban and Public Affairs, Program in Public Administration, Louisville, KY 40208. Offers human resources management (MPA); non-profit management (MPA); public policy and administration (MPA). *Accreditation:* NASPAA. Part-time and evening/weekend programs available. *Faculty:* 12 full-time (3 women), 3 part-time/adjunct (0 women). *Students:* 20 full-time (12 women), 17 part-time (9 women); includes 2 African Americans, 1 Hispanic American, 1 international. Average age 29. 22 applicants, 86% accepted, 7 enrolled. In 2008, 16 master's awarded. Terminal master's awarded for partial completion of doctoral program. *Degree requirements:* For master's, internship, practicum or thesis. *Entrance requirements:* For master's, GRE General Test, minimum GPA of 2.75, resumé. Additional exam requirements/recommendations for international students: Required—TOEFL (minimum score 547 paper-based; 210 computer-based; 77 iBT). *Application deadline:* For fall admission, 7/15 priority date for domestic students; for spring admission, 11/1 priority date for domestic students. Applications are processed on a rolling basis. Application fee: $50. *Financial support:* In 2008–09, 6 students received support, including 6 research assistantships (averaging $20,000 per year); health care benefits and unspecified assistantships also available. Financial award application deadline: 3/1. *Faculty research:* Public policy, environmental policy, urban economics, housing policy, organizational theory. *Unit head:* Dr. Steve Koven, Director, 502-852-7906, Fax: 502-852-4558, E-mail: sgkove01@louisville.edu. *Application contact:* Yani Vozos, Graduate Student Advisor/Coordinator, 502-852-8002, Fax: 502-852-4558, E-mail: yani.vozos@louisville.edu.

University of Maine, Graduate School, College of Business, Public Policy and Health, Department of Public Administration, Orono, ME 04469. Offers MPA, PhD. *Accreditation:* NASPAA. Part-time and evening/weekend programs available. *Entrance requirements:* For master's, GMAT or GRE General Test. Additional exam requirements/recommendations for international students: Required—TOEFL. Electronic applications accepted. *Faculty research:* Organization theory, personnel administration, public budgeting and finance, policy analysis, environmental policy, community policy and development.

Announcement: Master of Public Administration program prepares students for careers in state/local government, nonprofits, and health care. Concentrations/strengths are in health-care policy, planning/economic development/environment, public policy, state and local administration, and town/city management. Curriculum involves 36–42 semester hours, with requirements and electives. NASPAA accredited. Contact: 207-581-1872. Web: www.umaine.edu/pubadmin.

University of Management and Technology, Program in Management, Arlington, VA 22209. Offers acquisition management (MS, AC); general management (MS); project management (MS, AC); public administration (MPA, MS, AC). Part-time and evening/weekend programs available. Postbaccalaureate distance learning degree programs offered (no on-campus study). *Entrance requirements:* For master's, 3 recommendations, current resumé. Additional exam requirements/recommendations for international students: Required—TOEFL (minimum score 550 paper-based; 213 computer-based). Electronic applications accepted.

University of Manitoba, Faculty of Graduate Studies, Faculty of Arts, Department of Political Studies, Program in Public Administration, Winnipeg, MB R3T 2N2, Canada. Offers MPA. *Degree requirements:* For master's, thesis or alternative.

University of Maryland, College Park, Graduate Studies, Interdepartmental Programs, Joint Program in Business and Management/Public Policy, College Park, MD 20742. Offers MBA/MPM. *Accreditation:* AACSB. Electronic applications accepted.

University of Maryland, College Park, Graduate Studies, School of Public Policy, Joint Program in Public Policy/Law, College Park, MD 20742. Offers JD/MPM. Electronic applications accepted.

University of Maryland, College Park, Graduate Studies, School of Public Policy, Public Management Program, College Park, MD 20742. Offers MPM. *Accreditation:* NASPAA. *Degree requirements:* For master's, internship. *Entrance requirements:* For master's, GRE General Test, minimum GPA of 3.0. Additional exam requirements/recommendations for international students: Required—TOEFL. Electronic applications accepted. *Faculty research:* International security, economic policy, financial management, social policy.

University of Massachusetts Amherst, Graduate School, College of Social and Behavioral Sciences, Center for Public Policy and Administration, Amherst, MA 01003. Offers MPPA. Part-time programs available. *Degree requirements:* For master's, thesis or alternative. *Entrance requirements:* For master's, GRE General Test. Additional exam requirements/recommendations for international students: Required—TOEFL (minimum score 550 paper-based; 213 computer-based; 79 iBT), IELTS (minimum score 6.5). Electronic applications accepted. *Expenses:* Tuition, area resident: Full-time $2640. Tuition, nonresident: full-time $9936. One-time fee: $332 full-time. Tuition and fees vary according to course load.

University of Michigan–Dearborn, College of Arts, Sciences, and Letters, Master of Public Administration Program, Dearborn, MI 48128. Offers assessment and evaluation (Certificate); nonprofit leadership (Certificate); public administration (MPA). Part-time and evening/weekend programs available. *Faculty:* 3 full-time (1 woman), 9 part-time/adjunct (2 women). *Students:* 14 full-time (3 women), 71 part-time (23 women); includes 16 minority (11 African Americans, 2 American Indian/Alaska Native, 2 Asian Americans or Pacific Islanders, 1 Hispanic American). Average age 35. 11 applicants, 82% accepted, 8 enrolled. In 2008, 8 master's awarded. *Degree requirements:* For master's, assessment seminar. *Entrance requirements:* For master's, GRE or minimum undergraduate GPA of 3.0, 3 letters of recommendation, statement of purpose, personal statement. Additional exam requirements/recommendations for international students: Required—TOEFL, TWE. *Application deadline:* For fall admission, 8/1 for domestic students, 4/1 for international students; for winter admission, 12/1 for domestic students, 11/1 for international students; for spring admission, 4/1 for domestic students, 3/1 for international students. Applications are processed on a rolling basis. Application fee: $60. *Financial support:* Career-related internships or fieldwork and Federal Work-Study available. Support available to part-time students. Financial award applicants required to submit FAFSA. *Faculty research:* Federal, state, and local agency management; independent sector management, educational administration. *Unit head:* Dr. Trevor Thrall, Director, 313-593-5282, Fax: 313-583-6498, E-mail: atthrall@umich.edu. *Application contact:* Carol Ligienza, Graduate Programs Coordinator, 313-593-1183, Fax: 313-5836498, E-mail: caslgrad@umd.umich.edu.

University of Michigan–Flint, Graduate Programs, Program in Public Administration, Flint, MI 48502-1950. Offers MPA. Part-time programs available. *Faculty:* 9 full-time (3 women), 5 part-time/adjunct (1 woman). *Students:* 21 full-time (16 women), 149 part-time (97 women); includes 31 minority (30 African Americans, 1 Hispanic American), 9 international. Average age 34. 134 applicants, 64% accepted, 65 enrolled. In 2008, 67 master's awarded. *Degree requirements:* For master's, thesis or alternative, internship. *Entrance requirements:* For master's, minimum GPA of 3.0, 1 course each in American government, microeconomics and statistics. Additional exam requirements/recommendations for international students: Required—TOEFL (minimum score 550 paper-based; 220 computer-based), IELTS (minimum score 6.5). *Application deadline:* For fall admission, 8/1 for domestic students, 5/1 for international students; for winter admission, 11/15 for domestic students, 9/1 for international students; for spring admission, 3/15 for domestic students, 1/1 for international students. Application fee: $55. Electronic applications accepted. *Expenses:* Contact institution. *Financial support:* Career-related internships or fieldwork, Federal Work-Study, and scholarships/grants available. Support available to part-time students. Financial award application deadline: 6/1; financial award applicants required to submit FAFSA. *Unit head:* Dr. Albert Price, Director, 810-762-3470, E-mail: acprice@umflint.edu. *Application contact:* Bradley T. Maki, Director of Graduate Admissions, 810-762-3171, Fax: 810-766-6789, E-mail: bmaki@umflint.edu.

University of Missouri–Kansas City, Henry W. Bloch School of Business and Public Administration, Kansas City, MO 64110-2499. Offers accounting (MS); business administration (MBA); entrepreneurship and innovation (PhD); public affairs (MPA, PhD); JD/MBA; LL M/MPA. PhD is an interdisciplinary degree offered by the School of Graduate Studies. *Accreditation:* AACSB; NASPAA. Part-time and evening/weekend programs available. *Faculty:* 42 full-time (13 women), 24 part-time/adjunct (6 women). *Students:* 203 full-time (99 women), 433 part-time (188 women); includes 73 minority (33 African Americans, 3 American Indian/Alaska Native, 24 Asian Americans or Pacific Islanders, 13 Hispanic Americans), 47 international. Average age 30. 284 applicants, 79% accepted, 203 enrolled. In 2008, 228 master's awarded. Terminal master's awarded for partial completion of doctoral program. *Entrance requirements:* For master's, GMAT, GRE, 2 writing essays, 2 references and support of employer; for doctorate, GRE, minimum GPA of 3.0. Additional exam requirements/recommendations for international students: Required—TOEFL (minimum score 550 paper-based; 213 computer-based; 80 iBT). *Application deadline:* For fall admission, 5/1 priority date for domestic and international students; for spring admission, 10/1 priority date for domestic and international students. Applications are processed on a rolling basis. Application fee: $45 ($50 for international students). Electronic applications accepted. *Expenses:* Tuition, state resident: full-time $5376; part-time $298.70 per credit hour. Tuition, nonresident: full-time $13,882; part-time $771.20 per credit hour. Required fees: $640.28; $34.65 per contact hour. $30 per semester. Tuition and fees vary according to course load and program. *Financial support:* In 2008–09, 20 research assistantships with partial tuition reimbursements (averaging $7,809 per year), 4 teaching assistantships with partial tuition reimbursements (averaging $9,900 per year) were awarded; fellowships, career-related internships or fieldwork, Federal Work-Study, institutionally sponsored loans, scholarships/grants, tuition waivers (full and partial), and unspecified assistantships also available. Support available to part-time students. Financial award application deadline: 3/1; financial award applicants required to submit FAFSA. *Faculty research:* Entrepreneurship, finance, non-profit, risk management. Total annual research expenditures: $442,722. *Unit head:* Dr. Teng-Kee Tan, Dean, 816-235-2215, Fax: 816-235-2206. *Application contact:* 816-235-1111, E-mail: admit@umkc.edu.

University of Missouri–St. Louis, College of Arts and Sciences, Department of Political Science, St. Louis, MO 63121. Offers American politics (MA); comparative politics (MA); international politics (MA); political process and behavior (MA); political science (PhD); public administration and public policy (MA); urban and regional politics (MA). Part-time and evening/weekend programs available. *Faculty:* 19 full-time (7 women). *Students:* 19 full-time (8 women), 23 part-time (14 women); includes 9 minority (6 African Americans, 1 American Indian/Alaska Native, 2 Asian Americans or Pacific Islanders), 4 international. Average age 36. In 2008, 6 master's, 2 doctorates awarded. Terminal master's awarded for partial completion of doctoral program. *Degree requirements:* For master's, thesis optional; for doctorate, thesis/dissertation. *Entrance requirements:* For master's, GRE General Test, 2 letters of recommendation; for doctorate, GRE General Test, 3 letters of recommendation. Additional exam requirements/recommendations for international students: Required—TOEFL (minimum score 550 paper-based; 213 computer-based). *Application deadline:* For fall admission, 2/15 priority date for domestic and international students; for spring admission, 10/15 priority date for domestic and international students. Applications are processed on a rolling basis. Application fee: $35 ($40 for international students). Electronic applications accepted. *Expenses:* Tuition, area resident: Full-time $5377; part-time $298.70 per credit hour. Tuition, nonresident: full-time $13,381; part-time $472.50 per credit hour. Required fees: $4078; $52 per credit hour. *Financial support:* In 2008–09, 10 research assistantships with full and partial tuition reimbursements (averaging $10,800 per year), 6 teaching assistantships with full and partial tuition reimbursements (averaging $10,800 per year) were awarded; fellowships, career-related internships or fieldwork also available. Support available to part-time students. Financial award application deadline: 3/15; financial award applicants required to submit FAFSA. *Faculty research:* Public policy, urban politics and administration, American government. *Unit head:* Dr. Barbara Graham, Director of Graduate Studies, 314-516-5522, Fax: 314-516-5268, E-mail: umslpolisci@umsl.edu. *Application contact:* 314-516-5458, Fax: 314-516-6996, E-mail: gradadm@umsl.edu.

University of Missouri–St. Louis, College of Arts and Sciences, Department of Sociology, St. Louis, MO 63121. Offers advanced social perspective (MA); community conflict intervention (MA); program design and evaluation research (MA); social policy planning and administration (MA). Part-time and evening/weekend programs available. *Faculty:* 3 full-time (all women), 1 part-time/adjunct (0 women). *Students:* 6 full-time (3 women), 8 part-time (5 women); includes 2 minority (both African Americans), 1 international. Average age 34. In 2008, 7 master's awarded. *Degree requirements:* For master's, thesis optional. *Entrance requirements:* For master's, 2 letters of recommendation. Additional exam requirements/recommendations for international students: Required—TOEFL (minimum score 550 paper-based; 213 computer-based). *Application deadline:* For fall admission, 7/1 priority date for domestic and international students; for spring admission, 12/1 priority date for domestic and international students. Applications are processed on a rolling basis. Application fee: $35 ($40 for international students). Electronic applications accepted. *Expenses:* Tuition, area resident: Full-time $5377; part-time $298.70 per credit hour. Tuition, nonresident: full-time $13,381; part-time $472.50 per credit hour. Required fees: $4078; $52 per credit hour. *Financial support:* In 2008–09, 3 teaching assistantships with full and partial tuition reimbursements (averaging $7,870 per year) were awarded; career-related internships or fieldwork also available. Support available to part-time students. Financial award applicants required to submit FAFSA. *Faculty research:* Deviance, conflict intervention, minority groups, stratification, social psychology. *Unit head:* Dr. Chicako Usui, Chairperson, 314-516-6366. *Application contact:* 314-516-5458, Fax: 314-516-6996, E-mail: gradadm@umsl.edu.

University of Missouri–St. Louis, Graduate School, Program in Public Policy Administration, St. Louis, MO 63121. Offers health policy (MPPA); local government management (MPPA); managing human resources and organization (MPPA); nonprofit organization management (MPPA); nonprofit organization management and leadership (Certificate); policy research and analysis (MPPA). *Accreditation:* NASPAA. Part-time and evening/weekend programs available. *Faculty:* 8 full-time (4 women), 8 part-time/adjunct (1 woman). *Students:* 20 full-time (12 women), 57 part-time (34 women); includes 18 minority (17 African Americans, 1 Hispanic American), 4 international. Average age 32. In 2008, 22 master's awarded. *Entrance requirements:* For master's, 3 letters of recommendation. Additional exam requirements/recommendations for international students: Required—TOEFL (minimum score 550 paper-based; 213 computer-based). *Application deadline:* For fall admission, 7/1 priority date for domestic and international students; for spring admission, 12/1 priority date for domestic and international students. Applications are processed on a rolling basis. Application fee: $35 ($40 for international students). Electronic applications accepted. *Expenses:* Tuition, area resident: Full-time $5377; part-time $298.70 per credit hour. Tuition, nonresident: full-time $13,381; part-time $472.50 per credit hour. Required fees: $4078; $52 per credit hour. *Financial support:* In 2008–09, 1 research assistantship with full and partial tuition reimbursement (averaging $12,000 per year) was awarded; career-related internships or fieldwork also available. Financial award application deadline: 4/1; financial award applicants required to submit FAFSA. *Faculty research:* Urban policy, public finance, evaluation. *Unit head:* Brady Baybeck, Director, 314-516-5145, Fax: 314-516-5210, E-mail: baybeck@umsl.edu. *Application contact:* 314-516-5458, Fax: 314-516-6996, E-mail: gradadm@umsl.edu.

The University of Montana, Graduate School, College of Arts and Sciences, Department of Political Science, Program in Public Administration, Missoula, MT 59812-0002. Offers MPA, JD/MPA. *Degree requirements:* For master's, professional paper. *Entrance requirements:* For master's, GRE General Test.

University of Nebraska at Omaha, Graduate Studies and Research, College of Public Affairs and Community Service, School of Public Administration, Omaha, NE 68182. Offers public administration (MPA, PhD); public management (Certificate); urban studies (MS). *Accreditation:* NASPAA (one or more programs are accredited). Part-time and evening/weekend programs available. Postbaccalaureate distance learning degree programs offered (no on-campus study). *Degree requirements:* For master's, comprehensive exam (for some programs), thesis (for some programs); for doctorate, comprehensive exam, thesis/dissertation. *Entrance requirements:* For master's, GRE General Test, minimum GPA of 3.0, letters of recommendation, essay; for doctorate, GRE General Test, master's degree, minimum graduate GPA of 3.35, resumé. Additional exam requirements/recommendations for international students: Required—TOEFL (minimum score 550 paper-based; 213 computer-based; 80 iBT). Electronic applications accepted.

University of Nevada, Las Vegas, Graduate College, Greenspun College of Urban Affairs, Department of Public Administration, Las Vegas, NV 89154-6026. Offers crisis and emergency management (MS); non-profit management (Certificate); public administration (MPA); public affairs (PhD); public management (Certificate). *Accreditation:* NASPAA. Part-time and evening/weekend programs available. *Faculty:* 5 full-time (3 women), 2 part-time/adjunct (1 woman). *Students:* 30 full-time (12 women), 129 part-time (70 women); includes 39 minority (21 African Americans, 4 Asian Americans or Pacific Islanders, 14 Hispanic Americans), 3 international. Average age 38. 95 applicants, 76% accepted, 53 enrolled. In 2008, 48 master's, 28 other advanced degrees awarded. *Degree requirements:* For master's, comprehensive exam, professional paper. *Entrance requirements:* For master's, GRE General Test, GMAT or LSAT. Additional exam requirements/recommendations for international students: Required—TOEFL (minimum score 550 paper-based; 213 computer-based; 80 iBT), IELTS (minimum score 7). *Application deadline:* For fall admission, 6/1 priority date for domestic students, 5/1 for international students; for spring admission, 11/1 priority date for domestic students, 10/1 for international students. Applications are processed on a rolling basis. Application fee: $60 ($75 for international students). Electronic applications accepted. *Expenses:* Tuition, state resident: full-time $1414; part-time $198 per credit. Tuition, nonresident: full-time $12,509; part-time $415.75 per credit. International tuition: $14,249 full-time. Required fees: $4 per credit. $252 per semester. Tuition and fees vary according to course load. *Financial support:* In 2008–09, 8 students received support, including 3 research assistantships with partial tuition reimbursements available (averaging $10,000 per year), 5 teaching assistantships with partial tuition reimbursements available (averaging $15,600 per year); institutionally sponsored loans, scholarships/grants, health care benefits, and unspecified assistantships also available. Financial award application deadline: 3/1. *Faculty research:* Emergency and crisis management, homeland security, public and non-profit management, public policy, policy analysis and evaluation. *Unit head:* Dr. Anna Lukemeyer, Chair/Associate Professor, 702-895-4828, Fax: 702-895-1813, E-mail: anna.lukemeyer@unlv.edu. *Application contact:* Graduate College Admissions Evaluator, 702-895-3320, Fax: 702-895-4180, E-mail: gradcollege@unlv.edu.

University of Nevada, Reno, Graduate School, College of Liberal Arts, Department of Political Science, Program in Public Administration and Policy, Reno, NV 89557. Offers public administration (MPA). *Faculty:* 2 full-time (1 woman). *Students:* 2 full-time (1 woman), 8 part-time (5 women); includes 1 minority (Hispanic American). Average age 37. 5 applicants, 60% accepted, 2 enrolled. In 2008, 5 master's awarded. *Degree requirements:* For master's, comprehensive exam, thesis optional, oral exam/thesis or professional paper. *Entrance requirements:* For master's, GRE General Test, GMAT, or LSAT, minimum GPA of 2.75. Additional exam requirements/recommendations for international students: Required—TOEFL (minimum score 500 paper-based; 173 computer-based; 61 iBT), IELTS (minimum score 6), TOFEL or IELTS. *Application deadline:* For fall admission, 3/31 priority date for domestic and international students. Applications are processed on a rolling basis. Application fee: $60 ($95 for international students). Electronic applications accepted. *Expenses:* Tuition, state resident: full-time $1710; part-time $1140 per semester. Tuition, nonresident: full-time $7115. Required fees: $158 per semester. *Financial support:* Research assistantships with partial tuition reimbursements, teaching assistantships with partial tuition reimbursements, Federal Work-Study, institutionally sponsored loans, scholarships/grants, health care benefits, and unspecified assistantships available. Financial award application deadline: 3/1; financial award applicants required to submit FAFSA. *Faculty research:* Administrative processes and problems, public policy issues. *Unit head:* Dr. Christopher Simon, Graduate Program Director, 775-682-7769, Fax: 775-784-1473, E-mail: casimon@unr.nevada.edu. *Application contact:* Michele Sandberg, Application Contact, 775-784-7026, Fax: 775-784-6064, E-mail: gradschool@unr.edu.

University of New Brunswick Fredericton, School of Graduate Studies, Faculty of Business Administration, Fredericton, NB E3B 5A3, Canada. Offers MBA, MBA/LL B. Part-time programs available. *Faculty:* 37 full-time (13 women). *Students:* 40 full-time (17 women), 37 part-time (16 women). In 2008, 59 master's awarded. *Entrance requirements:* For master's, GMAT, GPA 3.0, GMAT 550 minimum score. Additional exam requirements/recommendations for international students: Required—TOEFL, TWE. *Application deadline:* For fall admission, 3/1 priority date for domestic students. Applications are processed on a rolling basis. Application fee: $50 Canadian dollars. Tuition and fees charges are reported in Canadian dollars. *Expenses:* Tuition, area resident: Full-time $5562 Canadian dollars. Tuition, nonresident: full-time $9450 Canadian dollars. Required fees: $333 Canadian dollars. *Financial support:* In 2008–09, 1 fellowship was awarded; research assistantships, teaching assistantships. *Faculty research:* Strategic management, entrepreneurship, investment practices, marketing and supply chain management, operations management. *Unit head:* Judy Roy, Director of Graduate Studies, 506-458-7307, Fax: 506-453-3561, E-mail: jroy@unb.ca. *Application contact:* Marilyn Davis, Acting Graduate Secretary, 506-453-4766, Fax: 506-453-3561, E-mail: mbacontact@unb.ca.

University of New Hampshire, Center for Graduate and Professional Studies, Manchester, NH 03101. Offers business administration (MBA); counseling (M Ed); education (M Ed, MAT); educational administration and supervision (M Ed, CAGS); industrial statistics (Certificate); public administration (MPA); public health (MPH, Certificate); social work (MSW). Part-time and evening/weekend programs available. *Students:* 81 full-time (54 women), 154 part-time (92 women); includes 11 minority (2 African Americans, 7 Asian Americans or Pacific Islanders, 2 Hispanic Americans), 5 international. 87 applicants, 80% accepted, 54 enrolled. In 2008, 106 master's, 3 other advanced degrees awarded. *Degree requirements:* For master's, thesis or alternative. *Entrance requirements:* Additional exam requirements/recommendations for international students: Required—TOEFL (minimum score 550 paper-based; 213 computer-based; 80 iBT), TOEIC, TSE. *Application deadline:* For fall admission, 6/1 for domestic students, 4/1 for international students; for spring admission, 12/1 for domestic students. Applications are processed on a rolling basis. Application fee: $60. Electronic applications accepted. *Expenses:* Tuition, area resident: Full-time $9720; part-time $540 per credit hour. Tuition, nonresident: full-time $23,200; part-time $954 per credit hour. Required fees: $1446; $361.50 per term. *Financial support:* In 2008–09, 21 students received support, including 1 teaching assistantship; fellowships, research assistantships, Federal Work-Study, scholarships/grants, health care benefits, and unspecified assistantships also available. Support available to part-time students. Financial award application deadline: 3/1; financial award applicants required to submit FAFSA. *Unit head:* Kate Ferreira, Director, 603-6414313, E-mail: unhm.gradcenter@unh.edu. *Application contact:* Graduate Admissions Office, 603-862-3000, Fax: 603-862-0275, E-mail: grad.school@unh.edu.

University of New Hampshire, Graduate School, College of Liberal Arts, Department of Political Science, Program in Public Administration, Durham, NH 03824. Offers MPA. Part-time programs available. *Faculty:* 15 full-time. *Students:* 8 full-time (3 women), 16 part-time (9 women). Average age 34. 17 applicants, 71% accepted, 9 enrolled. In 2008, 6 master's awarded. *Entrance requirements:* For master's, GMAT or GRE General Test. Additional exam requirements/recommendations for international students: Required—TOEFL (minimum score 550 paper-based; 213 computer-based; 80 iBT). *Application deadline:* For fall admission, 4/1 priority date for domestic students, 4/1 for international students. Applications are processed on a rolling basis. Application fee: $60. Electronic applications accepted. *Expenses:* Tuition, area resident: Full-time $9720; part-time $540 per credit hour. Tuition, nonresident: full-time $23,200; part-time $954 per credit hour. Required fees: $1446; $361.50 per term. *Financial support:* Fellowships, research assistantships, teaching assistantships, career-related internships or fieldwork, Federal Work-Study, scholarships/grants, and tuition waivers (full and partial) available. Support available to part-time students. Financial award application deadline: 2/15. *Unit head:* Dr. Warren Brown, Chairperson, 603-862-3225. *Application contact:* Tama Andrews, Administrative Assistant, 603-862-1750, E-mail: mpa.ma.political.science.grad@unh.edu.

University of New Haven, Graduate School, College of Business, Program in Public Administration, West Haven, CT 06516-1916. Offers health care management (MPA); personnel and labor relations (MPA); MBA/MPA. Part-time and evening/weekend programs available. *Faculty:* 3 full-time (1 woman), 6 part-time/adjunct (2 women). *Students:* 5 full-time (1 woman), 19 part-time (12 women); includes 6 minority (4 African Americans, 1 Asian American or Pacific Islander, 1 Hispanic American), 2 international. Average age 35. 24 applicants, 96% accepted, 9 enrolled. In 2008, 18 master's awarded. *Degree requirements:* For master's, thesis or alternative. *Entrance requirements:* Additional exam requirements/recommendations for international students: Required—TOEFL (minimum score 520 paper-based; 190 computer-based; 70 iBT); Recommended—IELTS (minimum score 5.5). *Application deadline:* For fall admission, 5/31 for international students; for winter admission, 10/15 for international students; for spring admission, 1/15 for international students. Applications are processed on a rolling basis. Application fee: $50. *Expenses:* Contact institution. *Financial support:* Research assistantships with partial tuition reimbursements, teaching assistantships with partial tuition reimbursements, career-related internships or fieldwork, Federal Work-Study, scholarships/grants, tuition waivers, and unspecified assistantships available. Support available to part-time students. Financial award application deadline: 5/1; financial award applicants required to submit FAFSA. *Unit head:* Charles Coleman, Chairman, 203-932-7375. *Application contact:* Eloise Gormley, Director of Graduate Admissions, 203-932-7449, Fax: 203-932-7137, E-mail: gradinfo@newhaven.edu.

University of New Mexico, Graduate School, School of Public Administration, Albuquerque, NM 87131-2039. Offers MPA, JD/MPA, MPA/MCRP, MSN/MPA. *Accreditation:* NASPAA (one or more programs are accredited). Part-time and evening/weekend programs available. Postbaccalaureate distance learning degree programs offered (no on-campus study). *Degree requirements:* For master's, thesis optional, professional paper. *Entrance requirements:* For master's, minimum GPA of 3.0, letters of recommendation, resumé, letter of intent. Electronic applications accepted. *Faculty research:* Human resources, science and technology administration, health care policy management.

University of New Orleans, Graduate School, College of Liberal Arts, Department of Political Science, Program in Public Administration, New Orleans, LA 70148. Offers MPA. *Degree requirements:* For master's, thesis. *Entrance requirements:* For master's, GRE General Test. Additional exam requirements/recommendations for international students: Required—TOEFL (minimum score 550 paper-based; 213 computer-based; 79 iBT). Electronic applications accepted.

The University of North Carolina at Chapel Hill, Graduate School, College of Arts and Sciences, Master of Public Administration Program, Chapel Hill, NC 27599. Offers MPA, JD/MPA, MPA/MRP, MPA/MSW. *Accreditation:* NASPAA. *Degree requirements:* For master's, comprehensive exam. *Entrance requirements:* For master's, GRE General Test, minimum GPA of 3.0. Additional exam requirements/recommendations for international students: Required—TOEFL. Electronic applications accepted. *Faculty research:* Local government management, nonprofit management.

The University of North Carolina at Charlotte, Graduate School, College of Arts and Sciences, Department of Political Science, Charlotte, NC 28223-0001. Offers public administration (MPA). *Accreditation:* NASPAA. Part-time and evening/weekend programs available. *Faculty:* 20 full-time (7 women), 3 part-time/adjunct (1 woman). *Students:* 18 full-time (10 women), 38 part-time (25 women); includes 10 African Americans, 2 Hispanic Americans, 1 international. Average age 27. 49 applicants, 78% accepted, 24 enrolled. In 2008, 11 master's awarded. *Entrance requirements:* For master's, GRE General Test or MAT, minimum GPA of 3.0 in undergraduate major, 2.75 overall. Additional exam requirements/recommendations for international students: Required—TOEFL (minimum score 557 paper-based; 220 computer-based). *Application deadline:* For fall admission, 7/1 for domestic students, 5/1 for international students; for spring admission, 11/1 for domestic students, 10/1 for international students. Applications are processed on a rolling basis. Application fee: $55. Electronic applications accepted. *Expenses:* Tuition, area resident: Full-time $2919; part-time $122 per credit hour. Tuition, state resident: full-time $2919; part-time $122 per credit hour. Tuition, nonresident: full-time $13,126; part-time $547 per credit hour. Required fees: $1779; $91 per credit hour. Tuition and fees vary according to program. *Financial support:* In 2008–09, 19 research assistantships (averaging $6,596 per year), 1 teaching assistantship (averaging $3,000 per year) were awarded; career-related internships or fieldwork, Federal Work-Study, institutionally sponsored loans, scholarships/grants, unspecified assistantships, and 1 administrative

Public Administration

The University of North Carolina at Charlotte (continued)
assistantship ($22,000) also available. Support available to part-time students. Financial award application deadline: 4/1; financial award applicants required to submit FAFSA. *Faculty research:* Terrorism, public administration, nonprofit and arts administration, educational policy, social policy. Total annual research expenditures: $660,000. *Unit head:* Dr. Theodore S. Arrington, Chair, 704-687-2571, Fax: 704-687-3497, E-mail: tarrngtn@email.uncc.edu. *Application contact:* Kathy B. Giddings, Director of Graduate Admissions, 704-687-3366, Fax: 704-687-3279, E-mail: agidding@uncc.edu.

The University of North Carolina at Pembroke, Graduate Studies, Public Administration Program, Pembroke, NC 28372-1510. Offers MPA. Part-time and evening/weekend programs available. *Degree requirements:* For master's, comprehensive exam, thesis optional. *Entrance requirements:* For master's, GRE General Test or MAT, minimum GPA of 3.0 in major, 2.5 overall; interview. Additional exam requirements/recommendations for international students: Required—TOEFL.

The University of North Carolina Wilmington, College of Arts and Sciences, Department of Public and International Affairs, Wilmington, NC 28403-3297. Offers MPA. *Accreditation:* NASPAA. Part-time programs available. *Students:* 37 full-time (20 women), 36 part-time (22 women); includes 11 minority (10 African Americans, 1 Asian American or Pacific Islander). Average age 29. 48 applicants, 83% accepted, 35 enrolled. In 2008, 29 master's awarded. *Degree requirements:* For master's, comprehensive exam, thesis or alternative, practicum. *Entrance requirements:* For master's, GRE, GMAT. Additional exam requirements/recommendations for international students: Required—TOEFL (minimum score 550 paper-based; 217 computer-based; 79 iBT), IELTS (minimum score 6.5). *Application deadline:* For fall admission, 4/15 for domestic students; for spring admission, 9/1 for domestic students. Application fee: $60. *Expenses:* Tuition, area resident: Full-time $4838. Tuition, state resident: full-time $4838. Tuition, nonresident: full-time $14,898. Required fees: $969.38 per semester. Tuition and fees vary according to course load, campus/location and program. *Financial support:* In 2008–09, 9 teaching assistantships with full and partial tuition reimbursements (averaging $9,500 per year) were awarded. Financial award application deadline: 3/15. *Unit head:* Dr. Roger Lowery, Chair, 910-962-3225, E-mail: lowery@uncw.edu. *Application contact:* Dr. Mark Imperial, Graduate Coordinator, E-mail: imperialm@uncw.edu.

University of North Dakota, Graduate School, College of Business and Public Administration, Department of Public Administration, Grand Forks, ND 58202. Offers MPA. *Accreditation:* NASPAA. Part-time programs available. Postbaccalaureate distance learning degree programs offered (minimal on-campus study). *Degree requirements:* For master's, comprehensive exam, thesis or alternative, final exam. *Entrance requirements:* For master's, GRE General Test, GMAT or LSAT, minimum GPA of 3.0. Additional exam requirements/recommendations for international students: Required—TOEFL (minimum score 550 paper-based; 213 computer-based; 79 iBT), IELTS (minimum score 6.5). Electronic applications accepted.

University of Northern Virginia, Graduate Programs, Manassas, VA 20109. Offers accountancy (MS); accounting (MBA); business administration (DBA); computer science (MS); counseling education (M Ed); early childhood education (M Ed); educational communication and instructional technology (M Ed); educational leadership (M Ed); finance (MBA); information systems technology (MS); management (MBA); marketing (MBA); project management (MBA); public administration (MPA); teaching English to speakers of other languages (M Ed). Part-time and evening/weekend programs available. Postbaccalaureate distance learning degree programs offered (no on-campus study). *Degree requirements:* For doctorate, comprehensive exam, thesis/dissertation. *Entrance requirements:* Additional exam requirements/recommendations for international students: Required—TOEFL (minimum score 550 paper-based; 230 computer-based), IELTS (minimum score 5.8). Electronic applications accepted.

University of North Florida, College of Arts and Sciences, Department of Political Science and Public Administration, Jacksonville, FL 32224-2645. Offers public administration (MPA). *Accreditation:* NASPAA. Part-time programs available. *Faculty:* 11 full-time (1 woman). *Students:* 21 full-time (13 women), 42 part-time (23 women); includes 18 minority (7 African Americans, 6 Asian Americans or Pacific Islanders, 5 Hispanic Americans), 1 international. Average age 29. 40 applicants, 50% accepted, 16 enrolled. In 2008, 23 master's awarded. *Degree requirements:* For master's, thesis or alternative, internship. *Entrance requirements:* For master's, GRE General Test or minimum GPA of 3.0 in last 60 hours, 2 letters of recommendation, interview. Additional exam requirements/recommendations for international students: Required—TOEFL (minimum score 500 paper-based; 173 computer-based). *Application deadline:* For fall admission, 7/1 priority date for domestic students, 5/1 for international students; for spring admission, 11/1 priority date for domestic students, 10/1 for international students. Applications are processed on a rolling basis. Application fee: $30. Electronic applications accepted. *Expenses:* Tuition, area resident: Full-time $5782.08; part-time $240.92 per credit hour. Tuition, state resident: full-time $5782.08; part-time $240.92 per credit hour. Tuition, nonresident: full-time $19,974; part-time $832.26 per credit hour. Required fees: $952.80; $39.70 per credit hour. *Financial support:* In 2008–09, 13 students received support. Career-related internships or fieldwork, Federal Work-Study, and tuition waivers (partial) available. Support available to part-time students. Financial award application deadline: 4/1; financial award applicants required to submit FAFSA. *Faculty research:* America's usage of the Internet, use of information communication technologies by educators and children. Total annual research expenditures: $1,444. *Unit head:* Dr. Matthew T. Corrigan, Chair, 904-620-2977, Fax: 904-620-2979, E-mail: mcorriga@unf.edu. *Application contact:* Dr. Patrick Plumlee, Director, 904-620-2977, Fax: 907-620-2979, E-mail: pplumlee@unf.edu.

University of North Texas, Robert B. Toulouse School of Graduate Studies, College of Public Affairs and Community Service, Department of Public Administration, Denton, TX 76203. Offers public administration (MPA); public administration and management (PhD). *Accreditation:* NASPAA. Part-time and evening/weekend programs available. *Degree requirements:* For master's, comprehensive exam, thesis optional, internship; for doctorate, comprehensive exam, thesis/dissertation. *Entrance requirements:* For master's, GMAT or GRE General Test, 3.00 grade point average on last 60 hours; for doctorate, GMAT or GRE General Test, 3.20 grade point average on last 60 hours. Additional exam requirements/recommendations for international students: Required—proof of English language proficiency required for non-native English speakers; Recommended—TOEFL (minimum score 550 paper-based; 213 computer-based). *Faculty research:* Municipal management, government financial management, public/private cooperation, emergency administration and planning, nonprofit management.

University of Oklahoma, Graduate College, College of Arts and Sciences, Department of Political Science, Program in Public Administration, Norman, OK 73019-0390. Offers MPA. Part-time and evening/weekend programs available. *Students:* 71 full-time (31 women), 215 part-time (81 women); includes 89 minority (33 African Americans, 23 American Indian/Alaska Native, 14 Asian Americans or Pacific Islanders, 19 Hispanic Americans), 2 international. 82 applicants, 99% accepted, 49 enrolled. In 2008, 71 master's awarded. Terminal master's awarded for partial completion of doctoral program. *Entrance requirements:* For master's, minimum GPA of 2.75 or GRE. Additional exam requirements/recommendations for international students: Required—TOEFL (minimum score 600 paper-based). *Application deadline:* For fall admission, 4/1 for domestic and international students; for spring admission, 11/1 for domestic students, 9/1 for international students. Application fee: $40 ($90 for international students). Electronic applications accepted. *Expenses:* Tuition, state resident: full-time $3744; part-time $156 per credit hour. Tuition, nonresident: full-time $13,577; part-time $565.70 per credit hour. Required fees: $2415.40; $90.10 per credit hour. *Financial support:* In 2008–09, 72 students received support. Career-related internships or fieldwork available. *Faculty research:* Public policy, public management, financial management, program evaluation, non-profit. *Application contact:* Debbie Deering, Assistant to the Director and Academic Counselor, 405-325-6432, Fax: 405-325-3733, E-mail: ddeering@ou.edu.

University of Ottawa, Faculty of Graduate and Postdoctoral Studies, Interdisciplinary Programs, Ottawa, ON K1N 6N5, Canada. Offers e-business (Certificate); e-commerce (Certificate); finance (Certificate); health services and policies research (Diploma); population health (PhD); population health risk assessment and management (Certificate); public management and governance (Certificate); systems science (Certificate).

University of Pennsylvania, School of Arts and Sciences, Fels Institute of Government, Philadelphia, PA 19104. Offers MGA. Part-time and evening/weekend programs available. *Degree requirements:* For master's, 12 courses (8 core classes, 4 elective classes). *Entrance requirements:* For master's, GRE. Additional exam requirements/recommendations for international students: Required—TOEFL or IELTS.

See Close-Up on page 1241.

University of Phoenix, John Sperling School of Business, College of Graduate Business and Management, Phoenix, AZ 85034-7209. Offers accountancy (MSA); accounting (MBA); business administration (MBA); global management (MBA); human resources management (MBA, MM); management (MM); marketing (MBA); public administration (MBA, MM). Evening/weekend programs available. Postbaccalaureate distance learning degree programs offered. *Degree requirements:* For master's, thesis (for some programs). *Entrance requirements:* For master's, 3 years of work experience, minimum undergraduate GPA of 3.0. Additional exam requirements/recommendations for international students: Required—TOEFL (minimum score 550 paper-based; 213 computer-based; 79 iBT). Electronic applications accepted.

University of Phoenix–Atlanta Campus, John Sperling School of Business, College of Graduate Business and Management, Sandy Springs, GA 30350-4153. Offers accounting (MBA); business administration (MBA); global management (MBA); human resources management (MBA, MM); management (MM); marketing (MBA); public administration (MM). Evening/weekend programs available. Postbaccalaureate distance learning degree programs offered. *Degree requirements:* For master's, thesis (for some programs). *Entrance requirements:* For master's, minimum undergraduate GPA of 3.0, 3 years of work experience. Additional exam requirements/recommendations for international students: Required—TOEFL (minimum score 550 paper-based; 213 computer-based; 79 iBT).

University of Phoenix–Augusta Campus, College of Graduate Business and Management, Augusta, GA 30909-4583. Offers accounting (MBA); business administration (MBA); business and management (MBA, MM); global management (MBA); human resources management (MBA, MM); management (MM); marketing (MBA); public administration (MBA, MM). Postbaccalaureate distance learning degree programs offered.

University of Phoenix–Austin Campus, College of Graduate Business and Management, Austin, TX 78759. Offers accounting (MBA); business administration (MBA); business and management (MBA); e-business (MBA); global management (MBA); human resources management (MBA, MM); management (MM); marketing (MBA); public administration (MBA). Postbaccalaureate distance learning degree programs offered.

University of Phoenix–Bay Area Campus, John Sperling School of Business, College of Graduate Business and Management, Pleasanton, CA 94588-3677. Offers accounting (MBA); business administration (MBA); global management (MBA); human resources management (MBA, MM); marketing (MBA); public administration (MBA, MM). Evening/weekend programs available. Postbaccalaureate distance learning degree programs offered (no on-campus study). *Degree requirements:* For master's, thesis (for some programs). *Entrance requirements:* For master's, minimum undergraduate GPA of 3.0, 3 years of work experience. Additional exam requirements/recommendations for international students: Required—TOEFL (minimum score 550 paper-based; 213 computer-based; 79 iBT). Electronic applications accepted.

University of Phoenix–Birmingham Campus, College of Graduate Business and Management, Birmingham, AL 35244. Offers accounting (MBA); business administration (MBA); global management (MBA); human resources management (MBA, MM); management (MM); marketing (MBA); public administration (MM).

University of Phoenix–Central Florida Campus, John Sperling School of Business, College of Graduate Business and Management, Maitland, FL 32751-7057. Offers accounting (MBA); business administration (MBA); business and management (MM); global management (MBA); human resources management (MBA, MM); management (MM); marketing (MBA); public administration (MBA, MM). Evening/weekend programs available. *Degree requirements:* For master's, thesis (for some programs). *Entrance requirements:* For master's, minimum undergraduate GPA of 3.0, 3 years work experience. Additional exam requirements/recommendations for international students: Required—TOEFL (minimum score 550 paper-based; 213 computer-based; 79 iBT). Electronic applications accepted.

University of Phoenix–Central Valley Campus, College of Graduate Business and Management, Fresno, CA 93720-1562. Offers accounting (MBA); business administration (MBA); global management (MBA); human resources management (MBA, MM); management (MM); marketing (MBA); public administration (MBA, MM).

University of Phoenix–Chattanooga Campus, College of Graduate Business and Management, Chattanooga, TN 37421-3707. Offers accounting (MBA); business administration (MBA); business and management (MBA); global management (MBA); human resources management (MBA, MM); management (MM); marketing (MBA); public administration (MBA, MM). Postbaccalaureate distance learning degree programs offered.

University of Phoenix–Cheyenne Campus, College of Graduate Business and Management, Cheyenne, WY 82009. Offers global management (MBA); human resources management (MBA, MM); management (MM); marketing (MBA); public administration (MBA, MM). Postbaccalaureate distance learning degree programs offered.

University of Phoenix–Cincinnati Campus, John Sperling School of Business, College of Graduate Business and Management, West Chester, OH 45069-4875. Offers accounting (MBA); business administration (MBA); global management (MBA); human resources management (MBA, MM); management (MM); marketing (MBA); public administration (MM). Evening/weekend programs available. *Degree requirements:* For master's, thesis (for some programs). *Entrance requirements:* For master's, minimum undergraduate GPA of 3.0, 3 years of work experience. Additional exam requirements/recommendations for international students: Required—TOEFL (minimum score 550 paper-based; 213 computer-based; 79 iBT). Electronic applications accepted.

University of Phoenix–Cleveland Campus, John Sperling School of Business, College of Graduate Business and Management, Independence, OH 44131-2194. Offers accounting (MBA); business administration (MBA); global management (MBA); human resources management (MBA, MM); management (MM); marketing (MBA); public administration (MBA, MM). Evening/weekend programs available. Postbaccalaureate distance learning degree programs offered (no on-campus study). *Degree requirements:* For master's, thesis (for some programs). *Entrance requirements:* For master's, minimum undergraduate GPA of 3.0, 3 years of work experience. Additional exam requirements/recommendations for international students: Required—TOEFL (minimum score 550 paper-based; 213 computer-based; 79 iBT). Electronic applications accepted.

University of Phoenix–Columbus Georgia Campus, John Sperling School of Business, College of Graduate Business and Management, Columbus, GA 31904-6321. Offers accounting (MBA); business administration (MBA); global management (MBA); human resources management (MBA, MM); management (MM); marketing (MBA); public administration (MBA). Evening/weekend programs available. *Degree requirements:* For master's, thesis (for some programs). *Entrance requirements:* For master's, minimum undergraduate GPA of 3.0, 3 years of work experience. Additional exam requirements/recommendations for international students:

Required—TOEFL (minimum score 550 paper-based; 213 computer-based; 79 iBT). Electronic applications accepted.

University of Phoenix–Columbus Ohio Campus, John Sperling School of Business, College of Graduate Business and Management, Columbus, OH 43240-4032. Offers accounting (MBA); business administration (MBA); global management (MBA); human resources management (MBA, MM); management (MM); marketing (MBA); public administration (MM). Evening/weekend programs available. Postbaccalaureate distance learning degree programs offered. *Degree requirements:* For master's, thesis (for some programs). *Entrance requirements:* For master's, minimum undergraduate GPA of 3.0, 3 years of work experience. Additional exam requirements/recommendations for international students: Required—TOEFL (minimum score 550 paper-based; 213 computer-based; 79 iBT). Electronic applications accepted.

University of Phoenix–Dallas Campus, John Sperling School of Business, College of Graduate Business and Management, Dallas, TX 75251-2009. Offers accounting (MBA); business administration (MBA); global management (MBA); human resources management (MBA, MM); management (MM); marketing (MBA); public administration (MBA, MM). Evening/weekend programs available. Postbaccalaureate distance learning degree programs offered. *Degree requirements:* For master's, thesis (for some programs). *Entrance requirements:* For master's, 3 years of work experience, minimum undergraduate GPA of 3.0. Additional exam requirements/recommendations for international students: Required—TOEFL (minimum score 550 paper-based; 213 computer-based; 79 iBT). Electronic applications accepted.

University of Phoenix–Denver Campus, John Sperling School of Business, College of Graduate Business and Management, Lone Tree, CO 80124-5453. Offers accountancy (MSA); accounting (MBA); business administration (MBA); e-business (MBA); global management (MBA); human resources management (MBA, MM); management (MM); marketing (MBA); public administration (MBA, MM). Evening/weekend programs available. Postbaccalaureate distance learning degree programs offered. *Degree requirements:* For master's, thesis (for some programs). *Entrance requirements:* For master's, minimum undergraduate GPA of 3.0, 3 years work experience. Additional exam requirements/recommendations for international students: Required—TOEFL (minimum score 550 paper-based; 213 computer-based; 79 iBT). Electronic applications accepted.

University of Phoenix–Des Moines Campus, College of Graduate Business and Management, Des Moines, IA 50266. Offers accounting (MBA); business administration (MBA); global management (MBA); human resources management (MBA, MM); management (MM); marketing (MBA); public administration (MBA, MM). Postbaccalaureate distance learning degree programs offered.

University of Phoenix–Eastern Washington Campus, John Sperling School of Business, College of Graduate Business and Management, Spokane Valley, WA 99212-2531. Offers accounting (MBA); business administration (MBA); human resources management (MBA); marketing (MBA); public administration (MBA). Evening/weekend programs available. *Degree requirements:* For master's, thesis (for some programs). *Entrance requirements:* For master's, minimum undergraduate GPA of 3.0, 3 years of work experience. Additional exam requirements/recommendations for international students: Required—TOEFL (minimum score 550 paper-based; 213 computer-based; 79 iBT). Electronic applications accepted.

University of Phoenix–Harrisburg Campus, College of Graduate Business and Management, Harrisburg, PA 17112. Offers accounting (MBA); business administration (MBA); business and management (MBA); global management (MBA); human resources management (MBA, MM); management (MM); marketing (MBA); public administration (MBA, MM). Postbaccalaureate distance learning degree programs offered.

University of Phoenix–Hawaii Campus, John Sperling School of Business, College of Graduate Business and Management, Honolulu, HI 96813-4317. Offers accounting (MBA); business administration (MBA); global management (MBA); human resources management (MBA, MM); management (MM); marketing (MBA); public administration (MBA, MM). Evening/weekend programs available. *Degree requirements:* For master's, thesis (for some programs). *Entrance requirements:* For master's, minimum undergraduate GPA of 3.0, 3 years of work experience. Additional exam requirements/recommendations for international students: Required—TOEFL (minimum score 550 paper-based; 213 computer-based; 79 iBT). Electronic applications accepted.

University of Phoenix–Houston Campus, John Sperling School of Business, College of Graduate Business and Management, Houston, TX 77079-2004. Offers accounting (MBA); business administration (MBA); global management (MBA); human resources management (MBA, MM); management (MM); marketing (MBA); public administration (MBA, MM). Evening/weekend programs available. Postbaccalaureate distance learning degree programs offered. *Degree requirements:* For master's, thesis (for some programs). *Entrance requirements:* For master's, 3 years of work experience, minimum undergraduate GPA of 3.0. Additional exam requirements/recommendations for international students: Required—TOEFL (minimum score 550 paper-based; 213 computer-based; 79 iBT). Electronic applications accepted.

University of Phoenix–Idaho Campus, John Sperling School of Business, College of Graduate Business and Management, Meridian, ID 83642-3014. Offers accounting (MBA); administration (MBA); global management (MBA); human resources management (MBA, MM); management (MM); marketing (MBA); public administration (MM). Evening/weekend programs available. Postbaccalaureate distance learning degree programs offered. *Degree requirements:* For master's, thesis (for some programs). *Entrance requirements:* For master's, 3 years of work experience, minimum undergraduate GPA of 3.0. Additional exam requirements/recommendations for international students: Required—TOEFL (minimum score 550 paper-based; 213 computer-based). Electronic applications accepted.

University of Phoenix–Indianapolis Campus, John Sperling School of Business, College of Graduate Business and Management, Indianapolis, IN 46250-932. Offers accounting (MBA); business administration (MBA); global management (MBA); human resources management (MBA, MM); management (MM); marketing (MBA); public administration (MM). Evening/weekend programs available. *Degree requirements:* For master's, thesis (for some programs). *Entrance requirements:* For master's, minimum undergraduate GPA of 3.0, 3 years of work experience. Additional exam requirements/recommendations for international students: Required—TOEFL (minimum score 550 paper-based; 213 computer-based). Electronic applications accepted.

University of Phoenix–Jersey City Campus, College of Graduate Business and Management, Jersey City, NJ 07310. Offers accounting (MBA); business administration (MBA); global management (MBA); human resources management (MBA, MM); management (MM); marketing (MBA); public administration (MBA, MM).

University of Phoenix–Kansas City Campus, John Sperling School of Business, College of Graduate Business and Management, Kansas City, MO 64131-4517. Offers accounting (MBA); business administration (MBA); global management (MBA); human resources management (MBA, MM); management (MM); marketing (MBA); public administration (MBA). Evening/weekend programs available. *Degree requirements:* For master's, thesis (for some programs). *Entrance requirements:* For master's, minimum undergraduate GPA of 3.0, 3 years of work experience. Additional exam requirements/recommendations for international students: Required—TOEFL (minimum score 550 paper-based; 213 computer-based). Electronic applications accepted.

University of Phoenix–Las Vegas Campus, John Sperling School of Business, College of Graduate Business and Management, Las Vegas, NV 89128. Offers accounting (MBA); business administration (MBA); global management (MBA); human resources management (MBA, MM); management (MM); marketing (MBA); public administration (MM). Evening/weekend programs available. Postbaccalaureate distance learning degree programs offered (no on-campus study). *Degree requirements:* For master's, thesis (for some programs). *Entrance requirements:* For master's, minimum undergraduate GPA of 3.0, 3 years of work experience. Additional exam requirements/recommendations for international students: Required—TOEFL (minimum score 550 paper-based; 213 computer-based; 79 iBT). Electronic applications accepted.

University of Phoenix–Louisiana Campus, John Sperling School of Business, College of Graduate Business and Management, Metairie, LA 70001-2082. Offers accounting (MBA); business administration (MBA); global management (MBA); human resources management (MBA, MM); management (MM); marketing (MBA); public administration (MBA). Evening/weekend programs available. *Degree requirements:* For master's, thesis (for some programs). *Entrance requirements:* For master's, minimum undergraduate GPA of 3.0, 3 years work experience. Additional exam requirements/recommendations for international students: Required—TOEFL (minimum score 550 paper-based; 213 computer-based; 79 iBT). Electronic applications accepted.

University of Phoenix–Madison Campus, College of Graduate Business and Management, Madison, WI 53718-2416. Offers accounting (MBA); business and management (MBA); e-business (MBA); global management (MBA); human resources management (MBA, MM); management (MM); marketing (MBA); public administration (MBA).

University of Phoenix–Maryland Campus, John Sperling School of Business, College of Graduate Business and Management, Columbia, MD 21045-5424. Offers accounting (MBA); business administration (MBA); e-business (MBA); global management (MBA); human resources management (MBA, MM); management (MM); marketing (MBA); public administration (MBA, MM). Evening/weekend programs available. *Degree requirements:* For master's, thesis (for some programs). *Entrance requirements:* For master's, minimum undergraduate GPA of 3.0, 3 years of work experience. Additional exam requirements/recommendations for international students: Required—TOEFL (minimum score 550 paper-based; 213 computer-based; 79 iBT). Electronic applications accepted.

University of Phoenix–Memphis Campus, College of Graduate Business and Management, Cordova, TN 38018. Offers acounting (MBA); business and management (MBA); e-business (MBA); global management (MBA); human resources management (MBA, MM); management (MM); marketing (MBA); public administration (MBA, MM).

University of Phoenix–Minneapolis/St. Louis Park Campus, College of Graduate Business and Management, St. Louis Park, MN 55426. Offers accounting (MBA); business administration (MBA); global management (MBA); human resources management (MBA); management (MM); marketing (MBA); public administration (MBA).

University of Phoenix–Northern Nevada Campus, College of Graduate Business and Management, Reno, NV 89511. Offers accounting (MBA); business administration (MBA); global management (MBA); human resources management (MBA, MM); management (MM); marketing (MBA); public administration (MBA, MM).

University of Phoenix–Northern Virginia Campus, College of Graduate Business and Management, Reston, VA 20190. Offers accounting (MBA); business administration (MBA); e-business (MBA); global management (MBA); human resources management (MBA, MM); management (MM); marketing (MBA); public administration (MBA).

University of Phoenix–North Florida Campus, John Sperling School of Business, College of Graduate Business and Management, Jacksonville, FL 32216-0959. Offers accounting (MBA); business administration (MBA); global management (MBA); human resources management (MBA, MM); management (MM); marketing (MBA); public administration (MBA, MM). Evening/weekend programs available. *Degree requirements:* For master's, thesis (for some programs). *Entrance requirements:* For master's, minimum undergraduate GPA of 3.0, 3 years work experience. Additional exam requirements/recommendations for international students: Required—TOEFL (minimum score 550 paper-based; 213 computer-based; 79 iBT). Electronic applications accepted.

University of Phoenix–Northwest Arkansas Campus, College of Graduate Business and Management, Rogers, AR 72756-9615. Offers accounting (MBA); business and management (MBA); global management (MBA); human resources management (MBA, MM); management (MM); marketing (MBA); public administration (MBA, MM).

University of Phoenix–Omaha Campus, College of Graduate Business and Management, Omaha, NE 68154-5240. Offers accounting (MBA); business and management (MBA); global management (MBA); human resources management (MBA, MM); management (MM); marketing (MBA); public administration (MM); public adminstration (MBA).

University of Phoenix–Oregon Campus, The John Sperling School of Business, College of Graduate Business and Management, Tigard, OR 97223. Offers accounting (MBA); business administration (MBA); global management (MBA); human resource management (MM); human resources management (MBA); management (MM); marketing (MBA); public administration (MM). Evening/weekend programs available. *Degree requirements:* For master's, thesis (for some programs). *Entrance requirements:* For master's, minimum undergraduate GPA of 3.0, 3 years of work experience. Additional exam requirements/recommendations for international students: Required—TOEFL (minimum score 550 paper-based; 213 computer-based; 79 iBT). Electronic applications accepted.

University of Phoenix–Philadelphia Campus, The John Sperling School of Business, College of Graduate Business and Management, Wayne, PA 19087-2121. Offers accounting (MBA); business administration (MBA); global management (MBA); human resources management (MBA, MM); management (MM); marketing (MBA); public administration (MM). Evening/weekend programs available. *Degree requirements:* For master's, thesis (for some programs). *Entrance requirements:* For master's, minimum undergraduate GPA of 3.0, 3 years work experience. Additional exam requirements/recommendations for international students: Required—TOEFL (minimum score 550 paper-based; 213 computer-based; 79 iBT). Electronic applications accepted.

University of Phoenix–Pittsburgh Campus, John Sperling School of Business, College of Graduate Business and Management, Pittsburgh, PA 15276. Offers accounting (MBA); business administration (MBA); global management (MBA); human resources management (MBA, MM); management (MM); marketing (MBA); public administration (MBA, MM). Evening/weekend programs available. *Degree requirements:* For master's, thesis (for some programs). *Entrance requirements:* For master's, minimum undergraduate GPA of 3.0, 3 years work experience. Additional exam requirements/recommendations for international students: Required—TOEFL (minimum score 550 paper-based; 213 computer-based; 79 iBT). Electronic applications accepted.

University of Phoenix–Renton Learning Center, College of Graduate Business and Management, Renton, WA 98005. Offers accounting (MBA); business and management (MBA, MM); global management (MBA); human resources management (MBA, MM); marketing (MBA); public administration (MBA, MM). Evening/weekend programs available. *Degree requirements:* For master's, thesis (for some programs). *Entrance requirements:* For master's, minimum undergraduate GPA of 3.0, 3 years of work experience. Additional exam requirements/recommendations for international students: Required—TOEFL (minimum score 550 paper-based; 213 computer-based; 79 iBT). Electronic applications accepted.

University of Phoenix–Richmond Campus, John Sperling School of Business, College of Graduate Business and Management, Richmond, VA 23230. Offers accounting (MBA); business administration (MBA); global management (MBA); human resources management (MBA, MM); management (MM); marketing (MBA); public administration (MBA, MM). Evening/weekend programs available. *Degree requirements:* For master's, thesis (for some programs). *Entrance requirements:* For master's, minimum undergraduate GPA 3.0, 3 years work

Public Administration

University of Phoenix–Richmond Campus (continued)
experience. Additional exam requirements/recommendations for international students: Required—TOEFL (minimum score 550 paper-based; 213 computer-based; 79 iBT). Electronic applications accepted.

University of Phoenix–Sacramento Valley Campus, John Sperling School of Business, College of Graduate Business and Management, Sacramento, CA 95833-3632. Offers accounting (MBA); business administration (MBA); global management (MBA); human resources management (MBA, MM); management (MM); marketing (MBA); public administration (MBA, MM). Evening/weekend programs available. *Degree requirements:* For master's, thesis (for some programs). *Entrance requirements:* For master's, minimum undergraduate GPA of 3.0, 3 years work experience. Additional exam requirements/recommendations for international students: Required—TOEFL (minimum score 550 paper-based; 213 computer-based; 79 iBT). Electronic applications accepted.

University of Phoenix–St. Louis Campus, John Sperling School of Business, College of Graduate Business and Management, St. Louis, MO 63043-4828. Offers accounting (MBA); business administration (MBA); global management (MBA); human resources management (MBA, MM); management (MM); marketing (MBA); public administration (MM). Evening/weekend programs available. *Degree requirements:* For master's, thesis (for some programs). *Entrance requirements:* For master's, 3 years of work experience, minimum undergraduate GPA of 3.0. Additional exam requirements/recommendations for international students: Required—TOEFL (minimum score 550 paper-based; 213 computer-based; 79 iBT). Electronic applications accepted.

University of Phoenix–San Antonio Campus, College of Graduate Business and Management, San Antonio, TX 78230. Offers accounting (MBA); business administration (MBA); e-business (MBA); global management (MBA); human resources management (MBA, MM); management (MM); marketing (MBA); public administration (MBA, MM).

University of Phoenix–San Diego Campus, John Sperling School of Business, College of Graduate Business and Management, San Diego, CA 92123. Offers accounting (MBA); business administration (MBA); global management (MBA); human resources management (MBA, MM); management (MM); marketing (MBA); public administration (MBA). Evening/weekend programs available. *Degree requirements:* For master's, thesis (for some programs). *Entrance requirements:* For master's, 3 years of work experience, minimum undergraduate GPA of 3.0. Additional exam requirements/recommendations for international students: Required—TOEFL (minimum score 550 paper-based; 213 computer-based; 79 iBT). Electronic applications accepted.

University of Phoenix–Savannah Campus, College of Graduate Business and Management, Savannah, GA 31405-7400. Offers accounting (MBA); business administration (MBA); global management (MBA); human resources management (MBA, MM); management (MM); marketing (MBA); public administration (MBA, MM).

University of Phoenix–Southern California Campus, John Sperling School of Business, College of Graduate Business and Management, Costa Mesa, CA 92626. Offers accounting (MBA); business administration (MBA); global managment (MBA); human resources management (MBA, MM); management (MM); marketing (MBA); public administration (MBA, MM). Evening/weekend programs available. *Degree requirements:* For master's, thesis (for some programs). *Entrance requirements:* For master's, minimum undergraduate GPA of 3.0, 3 years work experience. Additional exam requirements/recommendations for international students: Required—TOEFL (minimum score 550 paper-based; 213 computer-based; 79 iBT). Electronic applications accepted.

University of Phoenix–Southern Colorado Campus, John Sperling School of Business, College of Graduate Business and Management, Colorado Springs, CO 80919-2335. Offers accounting (MBA); business administration (MBA); global management (MBA); human resources management (MBA, MM); management (MM); marketing (MBA); public administration (MM). Evening/weekend programs available. *Degree requirements:* For master's, thesis (for some programs). *Entrance requirements:* For master's, minimum undergraduate GPA of 3.0, 3 years of work experience. Additional exam requirements/recommendations for international students: Required—TOEFL (minimum score 550 paper-based; 213 computer-based; 79 iBT). Electronic applications accepted.

University of Phoenix–South Florida Campus, John Sperling School of Business, College of Graduate Business and Management, Fort Lauderdale, FL 33309. Offers accounting (MBA); business administration (MBA); global management (MBA); human resource management (MBA); human resources management (MM); management (MM); marketing (MBA); public administration (MBA, MM). Evening/weekend programs available. *Degree requirements:* For master's, thesis (for some programs). *Entrance requirements:* For master's, minimum undergraduate GPA of 3.0, 3 years work experience. Additional exam requirements/recommendations for international students: Required—TOEFL (minimum score 550 paper-based; 213 computer-based; 79 iBT). Electronic applications accepted.

University of Phoenix–Springfield Campus, College of Graduate Business and Management, Springfield, MO 65804-7211. Offers accounting (MBA); business administration (MBA); global management (MBA); human resources management (MBA, MM); management (MM); marketing (MBA); public administration (MBA, MM).

University of Phoenix–West Florida Campus, The John Sperling School of Business, College of Graduate Business and Management, Temple Terrace, FL 33637. Offers accounting (MBA); business administration (MBA); global management (MBA); human resources management (MBA, MM); management (MM); marketing (MBA); public administration (MBA, MM). Evening/weekend programs available. *Degree requirements:* For master's, thesis (for some programs). *Entrance requirements:* For master's, 3 years of work experience, minimum undergraduate GPA of 3.0. Additional exam requirements/recommendations for international students: Required—TOEFL (minimum score 550 paper-based; 213 computer-based; 79 iBT). Electronic applications accepted.

University of Phoenix–Wisconsin Campus, John Sperling School of Business, College of Graduate Business and Management, Brookfield, WI 53045-6608. Offers accounting (MBA); administration (MBA); global management (MBA); human resources management (MBA, MM); management (MM); marketing (MBA); public administration (MBA). Evening/weekend programs available. *Degree requirements:* For master's, thesis (for some programs). *Entrance requirements:* For master's, 3 years of work experience, minimum undergraduate GPA of 3.0. Additional exam requirements/recommendations for international students: Required—TOEFL (minimum score 550 paper-based; 213 computer-based; 79 iBT). Electronic applications accepted.

University of Pittsburgh, Graduate School of Public and International Affairs, Division of Public and Urban Affairs, Program in Public and Nonprofit Management, Pittsburgh, PA 15260. Offers MPA, MPA/MID, JD/MPA, MPA/MPIA, MPH/MPA, MSIS/MPA, MSW/MPA. *Accreditation:* NASPAA (one or more programs are accredited). Part-time and evening/weekend programs available. *Degree requirements:* For master's, thesis optional, internship, capstone seminar. *Entrance requirements:* For master's, GRE General Test, 3 letters of recommendation, resumé, minimum GPA of 3.2. Additional exam requirements/recommendations for international students: Required—TOEFL (minimum score 550 paper-based; 213 computer-based; 80 iBT), TWE (minimum score 4); Recommended—IELTS (minimum score 7). *Faculty research:* Emergency management, health policy and regulation, regional finance, non-profit management, environmental policy, housing policy.

See Close-Up on page 1243.

University of Pittsburgh, Graduate School of Public and International Affairs, Doctoral Program in Public and International Affairs, Pittsburgh, PA 15260. Offers development policy (PhD); foreign and security policy (PhD); international political economy (PhD); public administration (PhD); public policy (PhD). *Accreditation:* NASPAA. Part-time programs available. *Degree requirements:* For doctorate, comprehensive exam, thesis/dissertation. *Entrance requirements:* For doctorate, GRE, 3 letters of recommendation, resumé, minimum GPA of 3.0, writing sample. Additional exam requirements/recommendations for international students: Required—TOEFL (minimum score 600 paper-based; 250 computer-based; 100 iBT), TWE (minimum score 4); Recommended—IELTS (minimum score 7). Electronic applications accepted. *Faculty research:* International political economy, international development, public administration, public policy, foreign policy, international security policy.

See Close-Up on page 1243.

University of Puerto Rico, Río Piedras, College of Social Sciences, School of Public Administration, San Juan, PR 00931-3300. Offers MPA. Part-time programs available. *Degree requirements:* For master's, comprehensive exam, thesis. *Entrance requirements:* For master's, GRE or PAEG, interview, minimum GPA of 3.0, letter of recommendation.

University of Regina, Faculty of Graduate Studies and Research, Johnson-Shoyama Graduate School of Public Policy, Regina, SK S4S 0A2, Canada. Offers economic analysis for public policy (Master's Certificate); non-profit management (Master's Certificate); public management (MPA, Master's Certificate); public policy (MPA, PhD, Master's Certificate). Part-time and evening/weekend programs available. *Faculty:* 6 full-time (3 women). *Students:* 53 full-time (25 women), 63 part-time (38 women). 100 applicants, 82% accepted. In 2008, 40 master's awarded. *Entrance requirements:* Additional exam requirements/recommendations for international students: Required—TOEFL (minimum score 580 paper-based; 237 computer-based; 88 iBT). *Application deadline:* Applications are processed on a rolling basis. Application fee: $85 ($100 for international students). Electronic applications accepted. *Expenses:* Contact institution. *Financial support:* In 2008–09, 8 fellowships (averaging $15,930 per year), 2 research assistantships (averaging $13,720 per year), 5 teaching assistantships (averaging $6,650 per year) were awarded. Financial award application deadline: 6/15. *Faculty research:* Public administration and policy. *Unit head:* Dr. Ken Rasmussen, Associate Dean, 306-585-5463, E-mail: ken.rasmussen@uregina.ca. *Application contact:* Devon Anderson, Information Contact, 306-585-5462, E-mail: devon.anderson@uregina.ca.

University of Rhode Island, Graduate School, College of Arts and Sciences, Department of Political Science, Program in Public Policy and Administration, Kingston, RI 02881. Offers MA, MPA, Certificate. In 2008, 24 master's awarded. *Expenses:* Tuition, state resident: full-time $8024; part-time $446 per credit. Tuition, nonresident: full-time $21,046; part-time $1169 per credit. Required fees: $1056; $26 per credit. $30 per semester. One-time fee: $95 part-time. *Unit head:* Dr. Timothy Hennessey, Director, 401-874-4052. *Application contact:* Harold D. Bibb, Associate Dean of the Graduate School, 401-874-2262, Fax: 401-874-5491.

University of San Francisco, College of Professional Studies, Program in Public Administration, Concentration in Public Administration, San Francisco, CA 94117-1080. Offers MPA. Part-time and evening/weekend programs available. *Entrance requirements:* For master's, minimum GPA of 3.0.

University of South Africa, College of Economic and Management Sciences, Pretoria, South Africa. Offers accounting (D Admin, D Com); accounting science (DA); auditing (D Admin, D Com); business administration (M Tech); business economics (D Admin); business leadership (DBL); business management (D Admin, D Com); economic management analysis (M Tech); economics (D Admin, D Com, PhD); human resource development (M Tech); industrial psychology (D Admin, D Com, PhD); logistics (D Com); marketing (M Tech); public administration (D Admin, D Com, DPA, PhD); public management (M Tech); quantitative management (D Admin, D Com); real estate (M Tech); statistics (D Admin, PhD); tourism management (D Admin, D Com); transport economics (D Admin, D Com).

University of South Alabama, Graduate School, College of Arts and Sciences, Department of Political Science and Criminal Justice, Mobile, AL 36688-0002. Offers public administration (MPA). Part-time and evening/weekend programs available. *Faculty:* 13 full-time (1 woman). *Students:* 6 full-time (5 women), 20 part-time (11 women); includes 18 minority (8 African Americans, 10 Asian Americans or Pacific Islanders), 1 international. In 2008, 7 master's awarded. *Degree requirements:* For master's, comprehensive exam, thesis optional. *Entrance requirements:* For master's, GRE, minimum GPA of 3.0. *Application deadline:* For fall admission, 7/15 priority date for domestic students, 6/15 priority date for international students; for spring admission, 12/1 priority date for domestic students, 11/1 priority date for international students. Applications are processed on a rolling basis. Application fee: $35. *Expenses:* Tuition, area resident: Full-time $4656. Tuition, nonresident: full-time $9312. Required fees: $1102. *Financial support:* Research assistantships, career-related internships or fieldwork available. Support available to part-time students. Financial award application deadline: 4/1. *Unit head:* Dr. Sa, Fisher, Director, 251-460-7204. *Application contact:* Dr. Sa, Fisher, Director, 251-460-7204.

University of South Carolina, The Graduate School, College of Arts and Sciences, Department of Political Science, Program in Public Administration, Columbia, SC 29208. Offers MPA, JD/MPA, MSW/MPA. *Accreditation:* NASPAA. Part-time and evening/weekend programs available. *Degree requirements:* For master's, capstone seminar. *Entrance requirements:* For master's, GRE General Test, minimum GPA of 3.0. Additional exam requirements/recommendations for international students: Required—TOEFL. Electronic applications accepted. *Faculty research:* Public policy, organizational theory, personnel administration, budgeting, finance.

The University of South Dakota, Graduate School, College of Arts and Sciences, Department of Political Science, Vermillion, SD 57069-2390. Offers American political institutions (PhD); political science (MA); public administration (MPA, PhD); public policy (PhD); JD/MA; JD/MPA. *Accreditation:* NASPAA (one or more programs are accredited). Part-time programs available. Postbaccalaureate distance learning degree programs offered. *Degree requirements:* For master's, comprehensive exam, thesis (for some programs). *Entrance requirements:* For master's, GRE or LSAT (MPA), GRE General Test (MA), minimum GPA of 2.7. Additional exam requirements/recommendations for international students: Required—TOEFL (minimum score 550 paper-based; 213 computer-based; 79 iBT). Electronic applications accepted.

University of Southern California, Graduate School, School of Policy, Planning and Development, Programs in Public Administration, Los Angeles, CA 90089. Offers MPA, DPA, PhD, Certificate, JD/MPA, MPA/M Pl, MPA/MAJCS, MPA/MS, MPA/MSW. *Accreditation:* NASPAA (one or more programs are accredited). *Degree requirements:* For doctorate, thesis/dissertation. *Entrance requirements:* For master's and doctorate, GRE General Test. *Faculty research:* Collaborative governance and decision making, nonprofit management, civic engagement.

University of Southern Indiana, Graduate Studies, College of Liberal Arts, Program in Public Administration, Evansville, IN 47712-3590. Offers MPA. Part-time and evening/weekend programs available. *Faculty:* 3 full-time (1 woman). *Students:* 22 part-time (14 women); includes 1 minority (African American). Average age 33. 11 applicants, 73% accepted, 6 enrolled. In 2008, 12 master's awarded. *Entrance requirements:* For master's, GMAT or GRE, 2 letters of reference, analytical writing sample, minimum GPA of 2.7. Additional exam requirements/recommendations for international students: Required—TOEFL (minimum score 550 paper-based; 213 computer-based; 79 iBT), IELTS (minimum score 6). *Application deadline:* For fall admission, 8/15 priority date for domestic students, 3/1 priority date for international students. Applications are processed on a rolling basis. Application fee: $25. *Expenses:* Tuition, area resident: Full-time $4374; part-time $243 per credit hour. Tuition, state resident: full-time $4374; part-time $243 per credit. Tuition, nonresident: full-time $8622; part-time $479 per credit hour. Required fees: $220; $22.75 per term. Tuition and fees vary according to course load and reciprocity agreements. *Financial support:* In 2008–09, 17 students received support. Federal Work-Study, scholarships/grants, tuition waivers (full and partial), and unspecified assistantships available. Financial award application deadline: 3/1; financial award applicants required to submit FAFSA. *Unit head:* Dr. Mary Morris, Director, 812-461-5207, E-mail: mhmorris@usi.edu. *Application contact:* Dr. Mary Morris, Director, 812-461-5207, E-mail: mhmorris@usi.edu.

University of South Florida, Graduate School, College of Arts and Sciences, Department of Government and International Affairs, Public Administration Program, Tampa, FL 33620-9951. Offers MPA. *Accreditation:* NASPAA. Part-time and evening/weekend programs available. *Students:* 14 full-time (11 women), 56 part-time (34 women); includes 20 minority (13 African Americans, 2 Asian Americans or Pacific Islanders, 5 Hispanic Americans), 1 international. 48 applicants, 56% accepted, 17 enrolled. In 2008, 19 master's awarded. *Degree requirements:* For master's, comprehensive exam, thesis. *Entrance requirements:* For master's, GRE General Test, minimum GPA of 3.0 in last 60 hours of course work. Additional exam requirements/recommendations for international students: Required—TOEFL (minimum score 550 paper-based; 213 computer-based). *Application deadline:* For fall admission, 2/15 for domestic students, 1/2 for international students; for spring admission, 10/15 for domestic students, 6/1 for international students. Application fee: $30. Electronic applications accepted. *Expenses:* Tuition, state resident: full-time $2624.40; part-time $291.60 per credit hour. Tuition, nonresident: full-time $7822; part-time $869.13 per credit hour. *Financial support:* Teaching assistantships with partial tuition reimbursements, career-related internships or fieldwork, institutionally sponsored loans, scholarships/grants, and unspecified assistantships available. *Faculty research:* Public budgeting and financial management, policy analysis, urban management and planning, public personnel management, public organization management. *Unit head:* John L. Daly, Director, 813-974-0779, Fax: 813-974-0804, E-mail: daly@cas.usf.edu. *Application contact:* John L. Daly, Director, 813-974-0779, Fax: 813-974-0804, E-mail: daly@cas.usf.edu.

The University of Tennessee, Graduate School, College of Arts and Sciences, Department of Political Science, Program in Public Administration, Knoxville, TN 37996. Offers MPA, JD/MPA. *Accreditation:* NASPAA. Part-time programs available. *Degree requirements:* For master's, thesis or alternative. *Entrance requirements:* For master's, GRE General Test, minimum GPA of 2.7. Additional exam requirements/recommendations for international students: Required—TOEFL. Electronic applications accepted. *Expenses:* Tuition, area resident: Part-time $348 per credit hour. Tuition, state resident: full-time $6262. Tuition, nonresident: full-time $18,920; part-time $1052 per credit hour. Required fees: $812; $36 per credit hour. Tuition and fees vary according to program.

The University of Tennessee at Chattanooga, Graduate School, College of Arts and Sciences, Department of Political Science, Program in Public Administration, Chattanooga, TN 37403. Offers MPA, Postbaccalaureate Certificate. *Accreditation:* NASPAA. Part-time and evening/weekend programs available. *Faculty:* 3 full-time (1 woman), 1 part-time/adjunct (0 women). *Students:* 23 full-time (14 women), 27 part-time (17 women); includes 15 minority (11 African Americans, 3 Asian Americans or Pacific Islanders, 1 Hispanic American). Average age 29. 33 applicants, 88% accepted, 17 enrolled. In 2008, 9 master's, 1 other advanced degree awarded. *Degree requirements:* For master's, comprehensive exam, thesis or alternative, internship. *Entrance requirements:* For master's, GRE General Test, minimum GPA of 2.5, 3 letters of recommendation. Additional exam requirements/recommendations for international students: Required—TOEFL (minimum score 550 paper-based; 213 computer-based; 79 iBT); Recommended—IELTS (minimum score 6). *Application deadline:* For fall admission, 8/1 priority date for domestic students; for spring admission, 12/1 priority date for domestic students. Applications are processed on a rolling basis. Application fee: $30 ($35 for international students). *Expenses:* Tuition, area resident: Full-time $6150; part-time $281 per credit hour. Tuition, nonresident: full-time $16,710; part-time $867 per credit hour. Required fees: $1100; $128 per credit hour. $550 per semester. *Financial support:* In 2008–09, 3 fellowships with full and partial tuition reimbursements (averaging $6,627 per year) were awarded; career-related internships or fieldwork, Federal Work-Study, institutionally sponsored loans, scholarships/grants, and unspecified assistantships also available. Support available to part-time students. Financial award application deadline: 4/1; financial award applicants required to submit FAFSA. *Faculty research:* Organizational cultures and renewal, management theory, public policy, policy analysis, nonprofit organizations. *Unit head:* Dr. David Edwards, Coordinator, 423-425-4281, Fax: 423-425-2373, E-mail: david-edwards@utc.edu. *Application contact:* Dr. Stephanie Bellar, Dean of Graduate Studies, 423-425-4666, Fax: 423-425-5223, E-mail: stephanie-bellar@utc.edu.

The University of Texas at Arlington, Graduate School, School of Urban and Public Affairs, Program in Public Administration, Arlington, TX 76019. Offers MPA. *Accreditation:* NASPAA. Part-time and evening/weekend programs available. *Faculty:* 8 full-time (4 women), 2 part-time/adjunct (1 woman). *Students:* 41 full-time (20 women), 103 part-time (55 women); includes 51 minority (32 African Americans, 5 Asian Americans or Pacific Islanders, 14 Hispanic Americans), 4 international. 109 applicants, 90% accepted, 65 enrolled. In 2008, 31 master's awarded. *Degree requirements:* For master's, comprehensive exam, thesis or alternative. *Entrance requirements:* For master's, GRE General Test. Additional exam requirements/recommendations for international students: Required—TOEFL (minimum score 550 paper-based; 213 computer-based). *Application deadline:* For fall admission, 6/16 for domestic students. Application fee: $35 ($50 for international students). *Expenses:* Tuition, area resident: Full-time $6500. Tuition, state resident: full-time $6500. Tuition, nonresident: full-time $11,558. *Financial support:* In 2008–09, 1 research assistantship (averaging $750 per year) was awarded; fellowships, career-related internships or fieldwork also available. Financial award application deadline: 6/1; financial award applicants required to submit FAFSA. *Faculty research:* Environment, statistics, public administration, social welfare, economic development, economics, budgeting, planning. Total annual research expenditures: $53,550. *Unit head:* Dr. Alejandro Rodriguez, Graduate Advisor, 817-272-3357, Fax: 817-272-5008. *Application contact:* Linda Slaughter, Administrative Clerk, 817-272-3071, Fax: 817-272-5008, E-mail: slaughter@uta.edu.

The University of Texas at Brownsville, Graduate Studies, College of Liberal Arts, Program in Public Policy and Management, Brownsville, TX 78520-4991. Offers MPPM. *Degree requirements:* For master's, thesis. *Entrance requirements:* For master's, GRE, 2 letters of recommendation.

The University of Texas at El Paso, Graduate School, Institute for Policy and Economic Development, El Paso, TX 79968-0001. Offers intelligence and national security studies (MS); leadership studies (MLS); public administration (MPA).

The University of Texas at San Antonio, College of Public Policy, Department of Public Administration, San Antonio, TX 78249-0617. Offers MPA. *Accreditation:* NASPAA. Part-time and evening/weekend programs available. *Degree requirements:* For master's, comprehensive exam, thesis optional. *Entrance requirements:* For master's, GMAT or GRE General Test, undergraduate course work in American government, economics, and research methods; minimum GPA of 3.0 on last 60 hours. Additional exam requirements/recommendations for international students: Required—TOEFL (minimum score 500 paper-based; 173 computer-based).

The University of Texas at Tyler, College of Arts and Sciences, Department of Social Sciences, Tyler, TX 75799-0001. Offers criminal justice (MS); public administration (MPA); sociology (MS). Part-time and evening/weekend programs available. *Degree requirements:* For master's, comprehensive exam, thesis optional. *Entrance requirements:* For master's, GRE General Test, minimum GPA of 3.0. Additional exam requirements/recommendations for international students: Required—TOEFL (minimum score 79 computer-based). *Faculty research:* Urban segregation, minority business, violent crime, gender discrimination.

The University of Texas–Pan American, College of Social and Behavioral Sciences, Program in Public Administration, Edinburg, TX 78541-2999. Offers MPA. Part-time and evening/weekend programs available. *Degree requirements:* For master's, comprehensive exam (for some programs), thesis optional. *Entrance requirements:* For master's, GRE General Test. Additional exam requirements/recommendations for international students: Required—TOEFL. Electronic applications accepted. *Faculty research:* Immigration policy reform, agriculture food policy, social service delivery systems, community development, social welfare policy reform, urban/city management.

University of the District of Columbia, School of Business and Public Administration, Department of Management, Marketing, and Information Systems, Program in Public Administration, Washington, DC 20008-1175. Offers MPA. Part-time and evening/weekend programs available. *Degree requirements:* For master's, comprehensive exam, thesis optional. *Entrance requirements:* For master's, GMAT or GRE General Test, writing proficiency exam. *Faculty research:* Government management, public personnel management, urban management, management information systems, public financial management.

University of the Virgin Islands, Graduate Programs, Division of Humanities and Social Sciences, Saint Thomas, VI 00802-9990. Offers MPA. Part-time and evening/weekend programs available. *Faculty:* 1 full-time (0 women), 2 part-time/adjunct (0 women). *Students:* 5 full-time (all women), 16 part-time (12 women); includes 20 minority (18 African Americans, 2 Hispanic Americans), 1 international. Average age 37. 15 applicants, 67% accepted, 9 enrolled. In 2008, 2 master's awarded. *Degree requirements:* For master's, comprehensive exam, thesis or alternative. *Entrance requirements:* For master's, GMAT, GRE, minimum GPA of 2.5. Additional exam requirements/recommendations for international students: Required—TOEFL (minimum score 550 paper-based; 213 computer-based). *Application deadline:* For fall admission, 4/30 for domestic and international students; for spring admission, 10/30 for domestic and international students. Application fee: $30. *Expenses:* Tuition, state resident: full-time $4950; part-time $275 per credit. Tuition, nonresident: full-time $9900; part-time $550 per credit. *Financial support:* Career-related internships or fieldwork and scholarships/grants available. Financial award application deadline: 4/15; financial award applicants required to submit FAFSA. *Faculty research:* Ethical issues of arbitration, spiritual leadership, accountability. *Unit head:* Dr. George Lord, Dean, 340-693-1261, Fax: 340-693-1265, E-mail: glord@uvi.edu. *Application contact:* Edward L. Alexander, Director of Admissions, 340-693-1224, Fax: 340-693-1167, E-mail: ealexan@uvi.edu.

The University of Toledo, College of Graduate Studies, College of Arts and Sciences, Department of Political Science and Public Administration, Program in Public Administration, Toledo, OH 43606-3390. Offers health care policy (MPA); healthcare policy (Certificate); municipal administration (MPA, Certificate); public administration (MPA). *Accreditation:* NASPAA. *Degree requirements:* For master's, internship. *Entrance requirements:* For master's, GRE General Test, minimum GPA of 3.0. Electronic applications accepted. *Faculty research:* Economic development, health administration, personnel, budgeting, urban administration.

University of Utah, The Graduate School, College of Social and Behavioral Science, Department of Political Science, Program in Public Administration, Salt Lake City, UT 84112-1107. Offers Exec MPA, MPA, Certificate, JD/MPA, MPA/Ed D, MPA/MA, MPA/PhD. *Accreditation:* NASPAA (one or more programs are accredited). *Degree requirements:* For master's, internship, thesis or research paper. *Entrance requirements:* For master's, GMAT, GRE General Test, LSAT, minimum GPA of 3.2. Additional exam requirements/recommendations for international students: Required—TOEFL. *Faculty research:* Non-profit organizations, health policy, environmental policy, law and legal.

University of Vermont, Graduate College, College of Agriculture and Life Sciences, Department of Community Development and Applied Economics, Program in Public Administration, Burlington, VT 05405. Offers MPA. *Students:* 37 (20 women); includes 2 minority (both Asian Americans or Pacific Islanders), 1 international. 39 applicants, 77% accepted, 17 enrolled. In 2008, 17 master's awarded. *Entrance requirements:* For master's, GRE General Test. Additional exam requirements/recommendations for international students: Required—TOEFL (minimum score 550 paper-based; 213 computer-based; 80 iBT). *Application deadline:* For fall admission, 4/1 priority date for domestic students. Applications are processed on a rolling basis. Application fee: $40. Electronic applications accepted. *Expenses:* Tuition, state resident: part-time $488 per credit. Tuition, nonresident: part-time $1232 per credit. *Financial support:* Fellowships, teaching assistantships available. Financial award application deadline: 3/1. *Unit head:* Dr. Chris Koliba, Coordinator, 802-656-2606. *Application contact:* Dr. Chris Koliba, Coordinator, 802-656-2606.

University of Victoria, Faculty of Graduate Studies, Faculty of Human and Social Development, School of Public Administration, Victoria, BC V8W 2Y2, Canada. Offers dispute resolution (MADR); public administration (MPA, PhD); MPA/LL B. Part-time and evening/weekend programs available. Postbaccalaureate distance learning degree programs offered. *Degree requirements:* For master's, thesis (for some programs), report; for doctorate, thesis/dissertation, candidacy exam. *Entrance requirements:* For master's, GMAT or GRE General Test, professional resumé; for doctorate, GMAT or GRE General Test. Additional exam requirements/recommendations for international students: Required—TOEFL (minimum score 610 paper-based; 255 computer-based). Electronic applications accepted. *Faculty research:* Policy analysis, local government, performance management, energy markets, labor markets.

University of Washington, Graduate School, Daniel J. Evans School of Public Affairs, Seattle, WA 98195. Offers public administration (MPA); public policy and management (PhD); JD/MPA; MPA/MAIS; MPA/MPH; MPA/MS; MPA/MUP. *Accreditation:* NASPAA. Part-time and evening/weekend programs available. *Degree requirements:* For master's, thesis, internship or cooperative experience. *Entrance requirements:* For master's and doctorate, GRE General Test, minimum GPA of 3.0. Additional exam requirements/recommendations for international students: Required—TOEFL (minimum score 580 paper-based; 237 computer-based; 92 iBT). Electronic applications accepted. *Faculty research:* Environmental policy, education and social policy, nonprofit management, international affairs, urban and regional development.

University of West Florida, College of Arts and Sciences: Arts, Department of Government, Pensacola, FL 32514-5750. Offers political science (MA), including public administration, security and diplomacy. Part-time and evening/weekend programs available. *Faculty:* 3 full-time (1 woman), 2 part-time/adjunct (1 woman). *Students:* 4 full-time (0 women), 18 part-time (8 women); includes 4 minority (1 African American, 3 Hispanic Americans). Average age 32. 18 applicants, 56% accepted, 6 enrolled. In 2008, 8 master's awarded. *Degree requirements:* For master's, thesis or alternative. *Entrance requirements:* For master's, GRE General Test, minimum GPA of 3.0. Additional exam requirements/recommendations for international students: Required—TOEFL (minimum score 550 paper-based; 213 computer-based). *Application deadline:* For fall admission, 6/1 for domestic students, 5/15 for international students; for spring admission, 11/1 for domestic students, 10/1 for international students. Applications are processed on a rolling basis. Application fee: $30. *Expenses:* Tuition, state resident: full-time $6095; part-time $253.97 per credit hour. Tuition, nonresident: full-time $21,919; part-time $913.31 per credit hour. *Financial support:* Fellowships, research assistantships with partial tuition reimbursements, career-related internships or fieldwork, Federal Work-Study, institutionally sponsored loans, and tuition waivers (full and partial) available. Support available to part-time students. Financial award application deadline: 4/15; financial award applicants required to submit FAFSA. *Faculty research:* Political campaigns, elections, law enforcement, growth management. *Unit head:* Dr. Alfred Cuzan, Chairperson, 850-474-2337, E-mail: govt@uwf.edu. *Application contact:* Terry McCray, Assistant Director of Graduate Admissions, 850-473-7718, Fax: 850-473-7714, E-mail: gradadmissions@uwf.edu.

University of West Florida, College of Professional Studies, Program in Administration, Pensacola, FL 32514-5750. Offers acquisition and contract administration (MSA); biomedical/pharmaceutical (MSA); criminal justice administration (MSA); education leadership (MSA); healthcare administration (MSA); nursing administration (MSA); public administration (MSA). Part-time and evening/weekend programs available. Postbaccalaureate distance learning degree programs offered (no on-campus study). *Students:* 31 full-time (22 women), 135 part-time (72 women); includes 50 minority (32 African Americans, 3 American Indian/Alaska Native, 4 Asian Americans or Pacific Islanders, 11 Hispanic Americans), 1 international. Average age 33. 102

Public Administration

University of West Florida (continued)

applicants, 63% accepted, 52 enrolled. In 2008, 51 master's awarded. *Entrance requirements:* For master's, GRE General Test, minimum GPA of 3.0. Additional exam requirements/recommendations for international students: Required—TOEFL (minimum score 550 paper-based; 213 computer-based). *Application deadline:* For fall admission, 6/1 for domestic students, 5/15 for international students; for spring admission, 11/1 for domestic students, 10/1 for international students. Applications are processed on a rolling basis. Application fee: $30. *Expenses:* Tuition, state resident: full-time $6095; part-time $253.97 per credit hour. Tuition, nonresident: full-time $21,919; part-time $913.31 per credit hour. *Financial support:* In 2008–09, 7 fellowships (averaging $291 per year) were awarded; career-related internships or fieldwork, scholarships/grants, and unspecified assistantships also available. Support available to part-time students. Financial award application deadline: 4/15; financial award applicants required to submit FAFSA. *Unit head:* Dr. Karen Rasmussen, Chairperson, 850-474-2301, Fax: 850-474-2804. *Application contact:* Terry McCray, Assistant Director of Graduate Admissions, 850-473-7718, Fax: 850-473-7714, E-mail: gradadmissions@uwf.edu.

University of West Georgia, Graduate School, College of Arts and Sciences, Department of Political Science and Planning, Program in Public Administration, Carrollton, GA 30118. Offers MPA. Part-time programs available. *Students:* 14 full-time (9 women), 17 part-time (8 women); includes 11 minority (all African Americans), 3 international. Average age 27. In 2008, 12 master's awarded. *Degree requirements:* For master's, exit paper. *Entrance requirements:* For master's, GRE. Additional exam requirements/recommendations for international students: Required—TOEFL. Application fee: $30. Electronic applications accepted. *Expenses:* Tuition, state resident: full-time $2844; part-time $158 per semester hour. Tuition, nonresident: full-time $11,340; part-time $630 per semester hour. Required fees: $1120; $41.56 per semester hour. $186 per semester. Tuition and fees vary according to course load. *Financial support:* In 2008–09, 4 research assistantships with full tuition reimbursements (averaging $3,000 per year) were awarded. Financial award applicants required to submit FAFSA. *Faculty research:* Women studies, state and local government, animal rights. *Unit head:* Dr. Robert M. Schaefer, Chair, 678-839-6504, Fax: 678-839-5009, E-mail: rschaefe@westga.edu. *Application contact:* Dr. Charles W. Clark, Interim Dean, 678-839-6508, E-mail: cclark@westga.edu.

University of West Georgia, Graduate School, College of Arts and Sciences, Department of Political Science and Planning, Program in Public Management, Carrollton, GA 30118. Offers Certificate. *Students:* 5 part-time (2 women); includes 3 minority (2 African Americans, 1 Asian American or Pacific Islander). Average age 22. In 2008, 3 Certificates awarded. Application fee: $30. *Expenses:* Tuition, state resident: full-time $2844; part-time $158 per semester hour. Tuition, nonresident: full-time $11,340; part-time $630 per semester hour. Required fees: $1120; $41.56 per semester hour. $186 per semester. Tuition and fees vary according to course load. *Unit head:* Dr. Robert M. Schaefer, Chair, 678-839-6504, Fax: 678-839-5009, E-mail: rschaefe@westga.edu. *Application contact:* Dr. Charles W. Clark, Interim Dean, 678-839-6508, E-mail: cclark@westga.edu.

The University of Winnipeg, Graduate Studies, Program in Public Administration, Winnipeg, MB R3B 2E9, Canada. Offers MPA. Part-time programs available. *Degree requirements:* For master's, comprehensive exam, thesis optional. *Entrance requirements:* For master's, minimum GPA of 3.0 in last 60 credit hours. *Faculty research:* Policy evaluation, federalism, administrative innovation, administrative ethics, economic development/administration.

University of Wisconsin–Milwaukee, Graduate School, College of Letters and Sciences, Interdepartmental Program in Public Administration, Milwaukee, WI 53201-0413. Offers MPA, MPA/MUP. Part-time programs available. *Faculty:* 11 full-time (2 women). *Students:* 25 full-time (4 women), 17 part-time (6 women); includes 1 minority (African American). Average age 33. 32 applicants, 75% accepted, 12 enrolled. In 2008, 10 master's awarded. *Degree requirements:* For master's, thesis or alternative. *Entrance requirements:* For master's, GRE General Test, minimum GPA of 3.0. Additional exam requirements/recommendations for international students: Required—TOEFL (minimum score 550 paper-based; 79 iBT), IELTS (minimum score 6.5). *Application deadline:* For fall admission, 1/1 priority date for domestic students; for spring admission, 9/1 for domestic students. Applications are processed on a rolling basis. Application fee: $45 ($75 for international students). *Expenses:* Tuition, area resident: Full-time $7320; part-time $165 per credit. Tuition, state resident: full-time $7320; part-time $165 per credit. Tuition, nonresident: full-time $17,840; part-time $714 per credit. Tuition and fees vary according to campus/location, program and reciprocity agreements. *Financial support:* Career-related internships or fieldwork and unspecified assistantships available. Support available to part-time students. Financial award application deadline: 4/15. *Unit head:* Douglas Ihrke, Director, 414-229-4209, Fax: 414-229-5021, E-mail: dihrke@uwm.edu. *Application contact:* General Information Contact, 414-229-4982, Fax: 414-229-6967, E-mail: gradschool@uwm.edu.

University of Wisconsin–Oshkosh, The Office of Graduate Studies, College of Letters and Science, Department of Public Administration, Oshkosh, WI 54901. Offers general agency (MPA); health care (MPA). Part-time and evening/weekend programs available. *Degree requirements:* For master's, thesis or alternative. *Entrance requirements:* For master's, public service-related experience, resumé, sample of written work. Additional exam requirements/recommendations for international students: Required—TOEFL (minimum score 550 paper-based; 213 computer-based; 79 iBT). Electronic applications accepted. *Faculty research:* Drug policy, local government state revenues and expenditures, health care regulation.

University of Wyoming, Graduate School, College of Arts and Sciences, Department of Political Science, Program in Public Administration, Laramie, WY 82070. Offers MPA. Part-time programs available. Postbaccalaureate distance learning degree programs offered (minimal on-campus study). *Faculty:* 10 full-time (3 women), 2 part-time/adjunct (1 woman). *Students:* 18 full-time (12 women), 19 part-time (12 women); includes 2 minority (both Hispanic Americans), 2 international. Average age 32. 22 applicants, 77% accepted, 9 enrolled. In 2008, 20 master's awarded. *Degree requirements:* For master's, comprehensive exam (for some programs), thesis (for some programs). *Entrance requirements:* For master's, GRE General Test, minimum GPA of 3.0. Additional exam requirements/recommendations for international students: Required—TOEFL (minimum score 525 paper-based; 195 computer-based). *Application deadline:* For fall admission, 6/1 priority date for domestic students, 5/1 for international students; for spring admission, 10/15 priority date for domestic students, 9/15 for international students. Applications are processed on a rolling basis. Application fee: $50. Electronic applications accepted. *Financial support:* In 2008–09, 3 students received support, including 5 research assistantships with full tuition reimbursements available (averaging $11,072 per year), 3 teaching assistantships (averaging $11,072 per year); career-related internships or fieldwork and unspecified assistantships also available. Financial award application deadline: 3/15. *Faculty research:* Public policy, public ethics, administrative theory, natural resource policy. *Unit head:* Dr. Jim King, Department Head, Professor, 307-766-6484, Fax: 307-766-6771, E-mail: jking@uwyo.edu. *Application contact:* Jamie L. LeJambre, Graduate Coordinator, 307-766-6484, Fax: 307-766-6771, E-mail: lejambre@uwyo.edu.

Upper Iowa University, Online Master's Programs, Fayette, IA 52142-1857. Offers accounting (MBA); corporate financial management (MBA); global business (MBA); health and human services (MPA); homeland security (MPA); human resources management (MBA); justice administration (MPA); organizational development (MBA); public personnel management (MPA); quality management (MBA). MBA also available at Madison, Wisconsin campus. Part-time programs available. Postbaccalaureate distance learning degree programs offered (no on-campus study). *Degree requirements:* For master's, research project. *Entrance requirements:* For master's, GMAT, GRE, or minimum GPA of 2.7 during last 60 hours. Additional exam requirements/recommendations for international students: Required—TOEFL (minimum score 570 paper-based; 230 computer-based). Electronic applications accepted. *Faculty research:* Total quality management, CQI, teams, organization culture and climate, management.

Villanova University, Graduate School of Liberal Arts and Sciences, Department of Political Science, Program in Public Administration, Villanova, PA 19085-1699. Offers MPA. Part-time and evening/weekend programs available. *Students:* 12 full-time (7 women), 31 part-time (17 women); includes 3 minority (2 African Americans, 1 Asian American or Pacific Islander), 1 international. Average age 32. 20 applicants, 100% accepted, 13 enrolled. In 2008, 16 master's awarded. *Degree requirements:* For master's, comprehensive exam. *Entrance requirements:* For master's, GRE General Test, minimum GPA of 3.0. *Application deadline:* For fall admission, 8/1 for domestic and international students; for spring admission, 12/1 for domestic and international students. Applications are processed on a rolling basis. Application fee: $50. Electronic applications accepted. *Financial support:* Career-related internships or fieldwork and scholarships/grants available. Financial award application deadline: 3/15; financial award applicants required to submit FAFSA. *Unit head:* Dr. Markus Kreuzer, Director, 610-519-4710. *Application contact:* Dr. Markus Kreuzer, Director, 610-519-4710.

See Close-Up on page 883.

Virginia Commonwealth University, Graduate School, College of Humanities and Sciences, Wilder School of Government and Public Affairs, Department of Political Science and Public Administration, Richmond, VA 23284-9005. Offers political science and public administration (MPA); public management (CPM). *Accreditation:* NASPAA (one or more programs are accredited). Part-time programs available. *Entrance requirements:* For master's, GRE General Test. *Faculty research:* Public human resources management, financial management, executive management, policy analysis, local government management.

Virginia Polytechnic Institute and State University, Graduate School, College of Architecture and Urban Studies, Center for Public Administration and Policy, Blacksburg, VA 24061-0205. Offers MPA, PhD, CAGS. *Accreditation:* NASPAA (one or more programs are accredited). *Entrance requirements:* For master's and doctorate, GRE General Test, GMAT. Additional exam requirements/recommendations for international students: Required—TOEFL (minimum score 550 paper-based; 213 computer-based). Electronic applications accepted. *Faculty research:* Public administration theory, strategic management, ethics, the Constitution, computer-assisted creativity.

Walden University, Graduate Programs, School of Public Policy and Administration, Minneapolis, MN 55401. Offers general public policy and administration (MPA); government management (Certificate); health policy (MPA); homeland security policy (MPA); interdisciplinary policy studies (MPA); law and public policy (MPA); local government management for sustainable communities (MPA); nonprofit management (Certificate); nonprofit management and leadership (MPA, MS); policy analysis (MPA); public management and leadership (MPA); public policy and administration (PhD), including criminal justice, health services, homeland security policy and coordination, international nongovernmental organizations, knowledge management, nonprofit management and leadership, public management and leadership, public policy, public safety management; terrorism, mediation, and peace (MPA). Part-time and evening/weekend programs available. Postbaccalaureate distance learning degree programs offered (minimal on-campus study). *Faculty:* 2 full-time, 55 part-time/adjunct. *Students:* 1,285 full-time (794 women), 144 part-time (96 women); includes 657 minority (591 African Americans, 8 American Indian/Alaska Native, 17 Asian Americans or Pacific Islanders, 41 Hispanic Americans), 20 international. Average age 39. 727 applicants, 54% accepted, 284 enrolled. In 2008, 101 master's, 6 doctorates awarded. *Degree requirements:* For doctorate, thesis/dissertation, residency. *Entrance requirements:* For master's, bachelor's degree or equivalent in related field, minimum GPA of 2.5, two references, goal statement, official transcripts, access to computer and Internet; for doctorate, master's degree or equivalent in related field, minimum GPA of 3.0, three years related professional/academic experience, two references, goal statement, official transcripts, access to computer and Internet. Additional exam requirements/recommendations for international students: Required—TOEFL (minimum score 550 paper-based; 213 computer-based), IELTS (minimum score 6.5), TOEFL, IELTS, or Michigan English Language Assessment Battery (minimum score 82). *Application deadline:* Applications are processed on a rolling basis. Application fee: $50. Electronic applications accepted. *Expenses:* Tuition: Full-time $12,877; part-time $520 per credit. Required fees: $1230. Tuition and fees vary according to course load, degree level and program. *Financial support:* In 2008–09, 3 students received support; fellowships with tuition reimbursements available, Federal Work-Study, scholarships/grants, unspecified assistantships, and family tuition reduction; active duty/veteran tuition reduction; group tuition reduction; interest-free payment plans available. Support available to part-time students. Financial award applicants required to submit FAFSA. *Unit head:* Dr. Mark Gordon, Interim Associate Dean, 800-925-3368. *Application contact:* Jennifer Hall, 866-4-WALDEN, E-mail: info@waldenu.edu.

Wayland Baptist University, Graduate Programs, Program in Counseling, Plainview, TX 79072-6998. Offers counseling (MA); government administration (MPA); homeland security (MPA); justice administration (MPA). Part-time and evening/weekend programs available. Postbaccalaureate distance learning degree programs offered. *Faculty:* 8 full-time (2 women). *Students:* 2 full-time (both women), 105 part-time (81 women); includes 27 minority (3 African Americans, 2 American Indian/Alaska Native, 2 Asian Americans or Pacific Islanders, 20 Hispanic Americans). Average age 34. 39 applicants, 95% accepted, 19 enrolled. In 2008, 34 master's awarded. *Degree requirements:* For master's, comprehensive exam. *Entrance requirements:* For master's, GRE, MAT. Application fee: $50. *Expenses:* Tuition: Full-time $310; part-time $310 per credit hour. Required fees: $782; $9 per credit hour. $60 per semester. *Financial support:* Federal Work-Study, institutionally sponsored loans, and scholarships/grants available. Support available to part-time students. Financial award application deadline: 5/1; financial award applicants required to submit FAFSA. *Unit head:* Dr. Estelle Owens, Chairman, 806-291-1171, Fax: 806-291-1972, E-mail: owensest@wbu.edu. *Application contact:* Amanda Stanton, Graduate Studies, 806-291-3414, Fax: 806-291-1950, E-mail: stanton@wbu.edu.

Wayne State University, College of Liberal Arts and Sciences, Department of Political Science, Program in Public Administration, Detroit, MI 48202. Offers criminal justice (MPA); public administration (MPA). *Accreditation:* NASPAA. Evening/weekend programs available. *Entrance requirements:* For master's, GRE General Test. Additional exam requirements/recommendations for international students: Required—TOEFL (minimum score 550 paper-based; 213 computer-based); Recommended—TWE (minimum score 6). Electronic applications accepted. *Faculty research:* Urban politics, urban education, state administration.

Webster University, School of Business and Technology, Department of Management, St. Louis, MO 63119-3194. Offers business and organizational security management (MA); computer resources and information management (MA); environmental management (MS); health care management (MA); health services management (MA); human resources development (MA); human resources management (MA); management (DM); management and leadership (MA); marketing (MA); procurement and acquisitions management (MA); public administration (MA); quality management (MA); space systems operations management (MS); telecommunications management (MA). Part-time and evening/weekend programs available. Postbaccalaureate distance learning degree programs offered (no on-campus study). *Degree requirements:* For doctorate, thesis/dissertation, written exam. *Entrance requirements:* For doctorate, GMAT, 3 years of work experience, MBA.

West Chester University of Pennsylvania, Office of Graduate Studies, College of Business and Public Affairs, Department of Political Science, West Chester, PA 19383. Offers administration (Certificate); human resource management (MSA, Certificate); individualized (MSA); non profit administration (Certificate); nonprofit administration (MSA); public administration (MSA); training and development (MSA). Part-time and evening/weekend programs available. *Students:* 4 full-time (all women), 31 part-time (24 women); includes 8 minority (7 African Americans, 1 Hispanic American). Average age 33. 32 applicants, 97% accepted, 26 enrolled. In 2008, 17 master's, 2 Certificates awarded. *Degree requirements:* For master's, comprehensive exam (for some programs). *Entrance requirements:* For master's and Certificate, GMAT, GRE General Test, or MAT, statement of professional goals, resumé, two letters of reference. Additional exam requirements/recommendations for international students: Required—TOEFL (minimum score 550 paper-based; 213 computer-based; 80 iBT). *Application deadline:* For fall admission,

4/15 priority date for domestic students, 3/15 for international students; for spring admission, 10/15 for domestic students, 9/1 for international students. Applications are processed on a rolling basis. Application fee: $35. Electronic applications accepted. *Expenses:* Tuition, state resident: full-time $6430; part-time $357 per credit. Tuition, nonresident: full-time $10,288; part-time $572 per credit. Required fees: $652.50; $50 per credit. $67 per semester. *Financial support:* In 2008–09, 4 research assistantships with full and partial tuition reimbursements (averaging $5,000 per year) were awarded; unspecified assistantships also available. Support available to part-time students. Financial award application deadline: 2/15; financial award applicants required to submit FAFSA. *Unit head:* Dr. Christopher Fiorentino, Dean, College of Business and Public Affairs, 610-436-2930, E-mail: cfiorentino@wcupa.edu. *Application contact:* Dr. Lorraine Bernotsky, Graduate Coordinator, 610-738-0576, E-mail: lbernotsky@wcupa.edu.

Western Illinois University, School of Graduate Studies, College of Arts and Sciences, Department of Political Science, Macomb, IL 61455-1390. Offers political science (MA); public and non-profit management (Certificate). Part-time programs available. *Students:* 15 full-time (4 women), 3 part-time (1 woman); includes 3 minority (all African Americans), 3 international. Average age 27. 21 applicants, 62% accepted. In 2008, 7 master's, 2 other advanced degrees awarded. *Degree requirements:* For master's, comprehensive exam, thesis or alternative. *Entrance requirements:* Additional exam requirements/recommendations for international students: Required—TOEFL (minimum score 550 paper-based; 213 computer-based; 80 iBT). *Application deadline:* Applications are processed on a rolling basis. Electronic applications accepted. *Expenses:* Tuition, state resident: full-time $5696; part-time $237.34 per credit hour. Tuition, nonresident: full-time $11,392; part-time $474.68 per credit hour. Required fees: $1453; $60.55 per credit hour. *Financial support:* In 2008–09, 9 students received support, including 9 research assistantships with full tuition reimbursements available (averaging $7,040 per year). Financial award applicants required to submit FAFSA. *Unit head:* Dr. Richard Hardy, Chairperson, 309-298-1055. *Application contact:* Evelyn Hoing, Assistant Director of Graduate Studies, 309-298-1806, Fax: 309-298-2345, E-mail: grad-office@wiu.edu.

Western International University, Graduate Programs in Business, Master of Public Administration Program, Phoenix, AZ 85021-2718. Offers MPA. Part-time and evening/weekend programs available. Postbaccalaureate distance learning degree programs offered (no on-campus study). *Faculty:* 19 part-time/adjunct (3 women). *Students:* 37 full-time (26 women); includes 16 minority (8 African Americans, 3 American Indian/Alaska Native, 1 Asian American or Pacific Islander, 4 Hispanic Americans). Average age 41. In 2008, 16 master's awarded. *Degree requirements:* For master's, thesis. *Entrance requirements:* For master's, minimum GPA of 2.75. Additional exam requirements/recommendations for international students: Required—TOEFL (minimum score 550 paper-based; 213 computer-based; 79 iBT), IELTS (minimum score 6.5), TWE (minimum score 5), TOEFL or IELTS. *Application deadline:* Applications are processed on a rolling basis. Application fee: $85 ($100 for international students). Electronic applications accepted. *Financial support:* Applicants required to submit FAFSA. *Unit head:* Dwight Galda, Department Chair, 602-973, E-mail: dwgalda@mywiu.wintu.edu. *Application contact:* Karen Janitell, Director of Enrollment, 602-943-2311 Ext. 1063, Fax: 602-371-8637, E-mail: karen.janitell@wintu.edu.

Western Michigan University, Graduate College, College of Arts and Sciences, Department of Political Science, Program in Development Administration, Kalamazoo, MI 49008-5202. Offers MDA.

Western Michigan University, Graduate College, College of Arts and Sciences, School of Public Affairs and Administration, Kalamazoo, MI 49008-5202. Offers health care administration (Graduate Certificate); nonprofit leadership and administration (Graduate Certificate); public administration (PhD); public affairs and administration (MPA). *Accreditation:* NASPAA (one or more programs are accredited). *Degree requirements:* For doctorate, thesis/dissertation, oral exams. *Entrance requirements:* For doctorate, GRE General Test.

West Virginia University, Eberly College of Arts and Sciences, School of Applied Social Sciences, Division of Public Administration, Morgantown, WV 26506. Offers legal studies (MLS); public administration (MPA); JD/MPA; MSW/MPA. *Accreditation:* NASPAA. Part-time programs available. *Degree requirements:* For master's, internship. *Entrance requirements:* For master's, GRE General Test, minimum GPA of 2.75. Additional exam requirements/recommendations for international students: Required—TOEFL. Electronic applications accepted.

Faculty research: Public management and organization, conflict resolution, work satisfaction, health administration, social policy and welfare.

Wichita State University, Graduate School, Fairmount College of Liberal Arts and Sciences, Hugo Wall School of Urban and Public Affairs, Wichita, KS 67260. Offers public administration (MPA). *Accreditation:* NASPAA. Part-time programs available. *Degree requirements:* For master's, thesis optional. *Entrance requirements:* For master's, GRE. Additional exam requirements/recommendations for international students: Required—TOEFL. Electronic applications accepted.

Widener University, College of Arts and Sciences, Program in Public Administration, Chester, PA 19013-5792. Offers MPA, Psy D/MPA. Part-time and evening/weekend programs available. *Faculty:* 1 full-time (0 women), 3 part-time/adjunct (0 women). *Students:* 3 full-time (2 women), 26 part-time (12 women); includes 8 minority (7 African Americans, 1 Asian American or Pacific Islander). Average age 31. 21 applicants, 86% accepted. In 2008, 9 master's awarded. *Degree requirements:* For master's, thesis or comprehensive exam. *Entrance requirements:* For master's, minimum undergraduate GPA of 3.0. *Application deadline:* For fall admission, 8/1 priority date for domestic students; for spring admission, 12/1 priority date for domestic students. Applications are processed on a rolling basis. Application fee: $25 ($300 for international students). Electronic applications accepted. *Expenses:* Contact institution. *Financial support:* In 2008–09, 8 students received support. Career-related internships or fieldwork and institutionally sponsored loans available. Support available to part-time students. Financial award application deadline: 5/1. *Faculty research:* Intergovernmental relations, nonprofit organizations, public policy, political economy, bureaucratic politics. *Unit head:* Dr. James E. Vike, Director, 610-499-1120, Fax: 610-499-4603, E-mail: james.vike@widener.edu. *Application contact:* Christine M. Weist, Assistant to Associate Provost for Graduate Studies, 610-499-4351, Fax: 610-499-4277, E-mail: christine.m.weist@widener.edu.

Willamette University, George H. Atkinson Graduate School of Management, Salem, OR 97301-3931. Offers early career MBA (full-time) (MBA), including business, government, not-for-profit management; MBA for professionals (part-time) (MBA), including business, government, not-for-profit management; JD/MBA. *Accreditation:* AACSB; NASPAA. Part-time and evening/weekend programs available. *Entrance requirements:* For master's, GMAT. Additional exam requirements/recommendations for international students: Required—TOEFL (minimum score: 570 paper-based, 230 computer-based, 88 iBT) or IELTS (6.5). Electronic applications accepted. *Expenses:* Contact institution. *Faculty research:* General management, finance, marketing, public management, human resources.

Wilmington University, Division of Business, New Castle, DE 19720-6491. Offers business administration (MBA); finance (MBA); health care administration (MBA, MS); homeland security (MBA, MS); human resource management (MS); management (MS); management information systems (MBA); organizational leadership (MS); public administration (MS); transportation and logistics (MBA, MS). Part-time and evening/weekend programs available. *Entrance requirements:* Additional exam requirements/recommendations for international students: Required—TOEFL (minimum score 500 paper-based; 173 computer-based). Electronic applications accepted.

Wright State University, School of Graduate Studies, College of Liberal Arts, Department of Urban Affairs and Geography, Dayton, OH 45435. Offers public administration (MPA). *Accreditation:* NASPAA. *Degree requirements:* For master's, thesis optional. *Entrance requirements:* For master's, interview, minimum GPA of 2.7. Additional exam requirements/recommendations for international students: Required—TOEFL. *Faculty research:* Strategic planning, economic development, housing and public management.

York University, Faculty of Graduate Studies, Atkinson Faculty of Liberal and Professional Studies, Program in Public Policy, Administration and Law, Toronto, ON M3J 1P3, Canada. Offers MPPAL.

York University, Faculty of Graduate Studies, Schulich School of Business, Toronto, ON M3J 1P3, Canada. Offers accounting (PhD); business (EMBA, MBA); finance (PhD); international business (IMBA); marketing (PhD); operations management and information systems (PhD); organizational behaviour and industrial relations (PhD); policy/strategic management (PhD); public administration (MPA); MBA/LL B; MBA/MFA. Part-time and evening/weekend programs available. *Degree requirements:* For doctorate, comprehensive exam, thesis/dissertation. *Entrance requirements:* For master's, GMAT, minimum GPA of 3.0; for doctorate, GMAT, minimum GPA of 3.3. Electronic applications accepted.

Public Affairs

American University, School of Communication, Program in Journalism and Public Affairs, Washington, DC 20016-8001. Offers broadcast journalism (MA), including economic journalism, international journalism, public policy journalism; print journalism (MA), including economic journalism, international journalism, public policy journalism. *Accreditation:* ACEJMC. Part-time and evening/weekend programs available. *Faculty:* 13 full-time (5 women), 4 part-time/adjunct (all women). *Students:* 24 full-time (16 women); includes 10 minority (7 African Americans, 3 Asian Americans or Pacific Islanders), 10 international. 190 applicants, 63% accepted, 35 enrolled. In 2008, 40 master's awarded. *Degree requirements:* For master's, comprehensive exam, thesis or alternative. *Entrance requirements:* For master's, GRE General Test. Additional exam requirements/recommendations for international students: Required—TOEFL (minimum score 600 paper-based; 250 computer-based). *Application deadline:* For fall admission, 2/1 priority date for domestic students, 4/1 priority date for international students. Applications are processed on a rolling basis. Application fee: $50. Electronic applications accepted. *Expenses:* Tuition: Full-time $21,204; part-time $1178 per credit hour. Required fees: $380. Part-time tuition and fees vary according to course load and program. *Financial support:* In 2008–09, 3 fellowships with partial tuition reimbursements (averaging $27,000 per year), 14 research assistantships with tuition reimbursements (averaging $7,000 per year), 3 teaching assistantships with tuition reimbursements (averaging $7,000 per year) were awarded; career-related internships or fieldwork, Federal Work-Study, institutionally sponsored loans, scholarships/grants, tuition waivers (partial), and unspecified assistantships also available. Financial award application deadline: 2/1. *Faculty research:* Government and media effects of journalistic practices and policies, race and gender and the media, investigative reporting, computer assisted reporting. *Unit head:* Wendell Cochran, Division Director, 202-885-2072. *Application contact:* Sharmeen Ahsan-Bracciale, Graduate Admissions Office, 202-885-2040, Fax: 202-885-2019, E-mail: sharmeen@american.edu.

See Close-Up on page 681.

Arizona State University, College of Public Programs, School of Public Affairs, Tempe, AZ 85287. Offers MPA, MPP, PhD, MPA/MSW. *Accreditation:* NASPAA (one or more programs are accredited). *Degree requirements:* For doctorate, thesis/dissertation. *Entrance requirements:* For master's, GRE.

Concordia University, School of Graduate Studies, Faculty of Arts and Science, School of Community and Public Affairs, Montréal, QC H3G 1M8, Canada. Offers community economic development (Diploma).

Cornell University, Graduate School, Graduate Fields of Arts and Sciences, Field of Public Affairs, Ithaca, NY 14853-0001. Offers public affairs (MPA); public policy (MPA). *Faculty:* 101 full-time (32 women). *Students:* 138 full-time (74 women); includes 24 minority (10 African

Americans, 1 American Indian/Alaska Native, 7 Asian Americans or Pacific Islanders, 6 Hispanic Americans), 64 international. Average age 28. 260 applicants, 58% accepted, 63 enrolled. In 2008, 84 master's awarded. *Degree requirements:* For master's, thesis, research project, paper. *Entrance requirements:* For master's, GRE General Test, 2 letters of recommendation. Additional exam requirements/recommendations for international students: Required—TOEFL (minimum score 550 paper-based; 213 computer-based; 77 iBT), GRE Subject Test in writing. *Application deadline:* Applications are processed on a rolling basis. Application fee: $70. Electronic applications accepted. *Expenses:* Tuition: Full-time $29,500. Required fees: $70. Full-time tuition and fees vary according to degree level, program and student level. *Financial support:* In 2008–09, 9 students received support, including 2 fellowships with full tuition reimbursements available, 3 research assistantships with full tuition reimbursements available, 4 teaching assistantships with full tuition reimbursements available; institutionally sponsored loans, scholarships/grants, health care benefits, tuition waivers (full and partial), and unspecified assistantships also available. Financial award applicants required to submit FAFSA. *Unit head:* Director of Graduate Studies, 607-255-8018, Fax: 607-255-5240. *Application contact:* Graduate Field Assistant, 607-255-8018, Fax: 607-255-5240, E-mail: cipa@cornell.edu.

See Close-Up on page 1211.

DePaul University, School of Public Service, Chicago, IL 60604. Offers financial administration management (Certificate); health administration (Certificate); health law and policy (MS); international public services (MS); leadership and policy studies (MS); metropolitan planning (Certificate); public administration (MPA); public service management (MS), including association management, fundraising and philanthropy, healthcare administration, higher education administration, metropolitan planning; public services (Certificate); JD/MS. Part-time and evening/weekend programs available. Postbaccalaureate distance learning degree programs offered (minimal on-campus study). *Faculty:* 14 full-time (3 women), 43 part-time/adjunct (24 women). *Students:* 90 full-time (59 women), 204 part-time (154 women); includes 101 minority (63 African Americans, 10 Asian Americans or Pacific Islanders, 28 Hispanic Americans), 11 international. Average age 26. 162 applicants, 100% accepted, 94 enrolled. In 2008, 108 master's awarded. *Degree requirements:* For master's, thesis or integrative seminar. *Entrance requirements:* For master's, minimum GPA of 2.7. Additional exam requirements/recommendations for international students: Required—TOEFL (minimum score 550 paper-based; 213 computer-based; 80 iBT), IELTS (minimum score 6.5). *Application deadline:* Applications are processed on a rolling basis. Application fee: $40. Electronic applications accepted. *Financial support:* In 2008–09, 60 students received support, including 3 research assistantships with full tuition reimbursements available (averaging $7,000 per year); career-related internships or fieldwork, Federal Work-Study, institutionally sponsored loans, scholarships/grants, tuition waivers (partial), and unspecified assistantships also available. Support available to part-time students. Financial award application deadline: 7/1; financial award applicants

Public Affairs

DePaul University (continued)
required to submit FAFSA. *Faculty research:* Government financing, transportation, leadership, health care, volunteerism and organizational behavior, non-profit organizations. Total annual research expenditures: $20,000. *Unit head:* Dr. J. Patrick Murphy, Director, 312-362-5608, Fax: 312-362-5506, E-mail: jpmurphy@depaul.edu. *Application contact:* Megan B. Balderston, Director of Admissions and Marketing, 312-362-5565, Fax: 312-362-5506, E-mail: pubserv@depaul.edu.

George Mason University, College of Humanities and Social Sciences, Department of Public and International Affairs, Fairfax, VA 22030. Offers biodefense (MS, PhD); political science (MA, PhD); public administration (MPA). *Accreditation:* NASPAA (one or more programs are accredited). *Entrance requirements:* For master's, GRE General Test, minimum GPA of 3.0 in last 60 hours of course work. Electronic applications accepted.

The George Washington University, Columbian College of Arts and Sciences, School of Media and Public Affairs, Washington, DC 20052. Offers MA. *Faculty:* 24 full-time (7 women), 13 part-time/adjunct (2 women). *Students:* 12 full-time (8 women), 3 part-time (2 women); includes 2 minority (1 Asian American or Pacific Islander, 1 Hispanic American), 1 international. Average age 26. 94 applicants, 27% accepted, 9 enrolled. In 2008, 12 master's awarded. *Degree requirements:* For master's, thesis optional. *Entrance requirements:* For master's, GRE General Test. Additional exam requirements/recommendations for international students: Required—TOEFL (minimum score 550 paper-based; 213 computer-based; 80 iBT). *Application deadline:* For fall admission, 4/1 priority date for domestic students, 1/15 priority date for international students; for spring admission, 10/1 priority date for domestic students, 9/1 priority date for international students. Applications are processed on a rolling basis. Application fee: $60. Electronic applications accepted. *Financial support:* In 2008–09, fellowships with tuition reimbursements (averaging $10,000 per year), teaching assistantships with tuition reimbursements (averaging $5,000 per year) were awarded. Financial award application deadline: 1/15. *Unit head:* Lee W. Huebner, Director, 202-994-6227, E-mail: huebner@gwu.edu. *Application contact:* Information Contact, 202-994-6227, Fax: 202-994-5806, E-mail: smpa@gwu.edu.

Georgia College & State University, Graduate School, School of Liberal Arts and Sciences, Department of Government and Sociology, Program in Public Administration and Public Affairs, Milledgeville, GA 31061. Offers MPA. *Accreditation:* NASPAA. Part-time and evening/weekend programs available. *Degree requirements:* For master's, thesis optional, capstone project. *Entrance requirements:* For master's, GRE. Additional exam requirements/recommendations for international students: Required—TOEFL. Electronic applications accepted.

Indiana University Bloomington, School of Public and Environmental Affairs, Public Affairs Programs, Bloomington, IN 47405-7000. Offers nonprofit management (Certificate); public affairs (MPA, PhD); public management (Certificate); public policy (PhD); JD/MPA; MPA/MA; MPA/MIS; MPA/MLS; MSES/MPA. *Accreditation:* NASPAA (one or more programs are accredited). Part-time programs available. *Students:* 364 full-time (191 women), 40 part-time (23 women); includes 39 minority (13 African Americans, 2 American Indian/Alaska Native, 10 Asian Americans or Pacific Islanders, 14 Hispanic Americans), 84 international. Average age 28. 724 applicants, 75% accepted, 249 enrolled. In 2008, 229 master's, 13 doctorates, 2 other advanced degrees awarded. Terminal master's awarded for partial completion of doctoral program. *Degree requirements:* For doctorate, thesis/dissertation. *Entrance requirements:* For master's, GMAT or GRE, LSAT; for doctorate, GRE General Test. *Application deadline:* For fall admission, 2/1 priority date for domestic students, 1/15 for international students; for spring admission, 9/1 for international students. Applications are processed on a rolling basis. Application fee: $50 ($60 for international students). *Expenses:* Tuition, area resident: Part-time $291.97 per credit hour. Tuition, state resident: part-time $291.97 per credit hour. Tuition, nonresident: part-time $850.33 per credit hour. Required fees: $110 per semester. Tuition and fees vary according to course load and program. *Financial support:* Fellowships, research assistantships, teaching assistantships, career-related internships or fieldwork, Federal Work-Study, institutionally sponsored loans, and unspecified assistantships available. Financial award application deadline: 2/1; financial award applicants required to submit FAFSA. *Faculty research:* Comparative and international affairs, environmental policy and resource management, policy analysis, public finance, public management, urban management, nonprofit management. *Unit head:* Charles Kurt Zorn, Interim Dean, 812-855-5058, Fax: 812-855-6234, E-mail: zorn@indiana.edu. *Application contact:* Charles A. Johnson, Coordinator of Student Recruitment, 800-765-7755, Fax: 812-855-7802, E-mail: speainfo@indiana.edu.

See Close-Up on page 1219.

Indiana University Northwest, School of Public and Environmental Affairs, Gary, IN 46408-1197. Offers criminal justice (MPA); environmental affairs (Graduate Certificate); health services administration (MPA); human services administration (MPA); nonprofit management (Graduate Certificate); public management (MPA, Graduate Certificate). *Accreditation:* NASPAA (one or more programs are accredited). Part-time programs available. *Entrance requirements:* For master's, GRE General Test or GMAT, letters of recommendation. *Faculty research:* Employment in income security policies, evidence in criminal justice, equal employment law, social welfare policy and welfare reform, public finance in developing countries.

Indiana University of Pennsylvania, School of Graduate Studies and Research, College of Humanities and Social Sciences, Department of Political Science, Program in Public Affairs, Indiana, PA 15705-1087. Offers MA. Part-time programs available. *Faculty:* 5 full-time (3 women). *Students:* 8 full-time (1 woman), 2 part-time (1 woman), 4 international. Average age 38. 8 applicants, 50% accepted, 4 enrolled. In 2008, 5 master's awarded. *Degree requirements:* For master's, thesis optional. *Entrance requirements:* For master's, GRE, 2 letters of recommendation. Additional exam requirements/recommendations for international students: Required—TOEFL. *Application deadline:* For fall admission, 7/1 priority date for domestic students; for spring admission, 11/1 for domestic students. Applications are processed on a rolling basis. Application fee: $30. *Expenses:* Tuition, area resident: Full-time $6430; part-time $357 per credit. Tuition, nonresident: full-time $10,288; part-time $572 per credit. Required fees: $1547.50; $107 per credit. $283 per year. *Financial support:* In 2008–09, 6 research assistantships with full and partial tuition reimbursements (averaging $4,533 per year) were awarded. Financial award application deadline: 3/15; financial award applicants required to submit FAFSA. *Unit head:* Dr. Susan Martin, Graduate Coordinator, 724-357-2776, E-mail: Susan.Martin@iup.edu. *Application contact:* Dr. David Chambers, Graduate Coordinator, 724-357-2776, E-mail: chambers@iup.edu.

Indiana University–Purdue University Fort Wayne, Division of Public and Environmental Affairs, Fort Wayne, IN 46805-1499. Offers public affairs (MPA); public management (MPM, Certificate). *Accreditation:* NASPAA (one or more programs are accredited). Part-time programs available. *Faculty:* 10 full-time (3 women). *Students:* 9 full-time (6 women), 35 part-time (23 women); includes 1 minority (African American). Average age 31. 21 applicants, 100% accepted, 17 enrolled. In 2008, 15 master's awarded. *Degree requirements:* For master's, internship. *Entrance requirements:* For master's, GRE General Test or GMAT, minimum GPA of 3.0, 3 letters of reference. Additional exam requirements/recommendations for international students: Required—TOEFL (minimum score 550 paper-based; 213 computer-based; 77 iBT). *Application deadline:* For fall admission, 8/1 priority date for domestic students; for spring admission, 12/1 for domestic students. Applications are processed on a rolling basis. Application fee: $30. *Expenses:* Tuition, area resident: Full-time $4376; part-time $243 per credit. Tuition, state resident: full-time $4376; part-time $243 per credit. Tuition, nonresident: full-time $10,337; part-time $574 per credit. Required fees: $503; $27.95 per credit. Tuition and fees vary according to course load. *Financial support:* In 2008–09, 1 research assistantship with partial tuition reimbursement (averaging $12,740 per year) was awarded; career-related internships or fieldwork and scholarships/grants also available. Support available to part-time students. Financial award application deadline: 3/1; financial award applicants required to submit FAFSA. *Faculty research:* Physician assisted suicide, pain and patients, authority and support. *Unit head:* Dr. Jane Grant, Interim Assistant Dean and Graduate Program Director, 260-481-6349, Fax: 260-481-6346, E-mail: grant@ipfw.edu. *Application contact:* Dr. Brian L. Fife, Graduate Administrator, 260-481-6961, Fax: 260-481-6346, E-mail: fifeb@ipfw.edu.

Indiana University–Purdue University Indianapolis, School of Public and Environmental Affairs, Indianapolis, IN 46202-2896. Offers health administration (MHA); public affairs (MPA), including criminal justice, environmental management, nonprofit management, policy analysis, public management; JD/MHA; MBA/MHA; MLS/NMC; MLS/PMC; MSN/MHA. *Accreditation:* CAHME (one or more programs are accredited). Part-time and evening/weekend programs available. *Entrance requirements:* For master's, GRE General Test, minimum GPA of 3.0 (preferred). Additional exam requirements/recommendations for international students: Required—TOEFL. *Faculty research:* Economic development, water and air quality, ethics, financing, organization design and structure.

See Close-Up on page 1221.

Indiana University South Bend, School of Public and Environmental Affairs, South Bend, IN 46634-7111. Offers health systems administration and policy (MPA); health systems management (Certificate); nonprofit management (Certificate); public and community services administration and policy (MPA); public management (Certificate); urban affairs (Certificate). *Accreditation:* NASPAA. Part-time and evening/weekend programs available. *Entrance requirements:* For master's, GRE General Test, minimum undergraduate GPA of 2.5.

The Institute of World Politics, Graduate Programs in National Security, Intelligence, and International Affairs, Washington, DC 20036. Offers American foreign policy (Certificate); comparative political culture (Certificate); counterintelligence (Certificate); democracy building (Certificate); intelligence (Certificate); international politics (Certificate); national security affairs (Certificate); public diplomacy and political warfare (Certificate); statecraft and national security affairs (MA); statecraft and world politics (MA); strategic intelligence studies (MA). Part-time and evening/weekend programs available. *Degree requirements:* For master's, comprehensive exam, thesis optional. *Entrance requirements:* For master's, GRE General Test. Additional exam requirements/recommendations for international students: Required—TOEFL. Electronic applications accepted. *Faculty research:* Intelligence, national security, statecraft.

See Close-Up on page 867.

Jackson State University, Graduate School, College of Public Service, Jackson, MS 39217. Offers MS. *Degree requirements:* For master's, comprehensive exam. *Entrance requirements:* For master's, GRE General Test. Additional exam requirements/recommendations for international students: Required—TOEFL.

McMaster University, School of Graduate Studies, Faculty of Social Sciences, Department of Political Science, Hamilton, ON L8S 4M2, Canada. Offers international relations (PhD); political science (MA); public and the global economy (MA); public policy (PhD); public policy and administration (MA). Part-time programs available. *Degree requirements:* For master's, thesis or alternative. *Entrance requirements:* For master's, minimum B+ average. Additional exam requirements/recommendations for international students: Required—TOEFL (minimum score 580 paper-based; 237 computer-based). *Faculty research:* Organizational theory, internationalization of public policy, water resource policies, political interest intermediation, comparative politics.

Murray State University, College of Humanities and Fine Arts, Department of Government, Laws and International Affairs, Program in Public Administration, Murray, KY 42071. Offers public affairs (MPA). Part-time programs available. Postbaccalaureate distance learning degree programs offered (minimal on-campus study). *Degree requirements:* For master's, capstone course. *Entrance requirements:* For master's, GRE General Test. Additional exam requirements/recommendations for international students: Required—TOEFL.

National University of Singapore, Lee Kuan Yew School of Public Policy, Singapore, Singapore. Offers MPA, MPM, MPP, PhD.

New Mexico Highlands University, Graduate Studies, College of Arts and Sciences, Program in Public Affairs, Las Vegas, NM 87701. Offers applied sociology (MA). Program is interdisciplinary. *Faculty:* 12 full-time (7 women). *Students:* 17 full-time (12 women), 17 part-time (10 women); includes 21 minority (1 Asian American or Pacific Islander, 20 Hispanic Americans), 4 international. Average age 32. 17 applicants, 71% accepted, 6 enrolled. In 2008, 1 master's awarded. *Degree requirements:* For master's, comprehensive exam, thesis or alternative. *Entrance requirements:* For master's, minimum undergraduate GPA of 3.0. Additional exam requirements/recommendations for international students: Required—TOEFL (minimum score 540 paper-based; 207 computer-based). *Application deadline:* For fall admission, 8/1 priority date for domestic students. Applications are processed on a rolling basis. Application fee: $15. *Expenses:* Tuition, state resident: full-time $2880; part-time $120 per credit hour. Tuition, nonresident: full-time $4234; part-time $176 per credit hour. International tuition: $5645 full-time. One-time fee: $20. *Financial support:* In 2008–09, 17 students received support, including 8 teaching assistantships with full and partial tuition reimbursements available (averaging $6,500 per year); career-related internships or fieldwork, Federal Work-Study, institutionally sponsored loans, scholarships/grants, traineeships, tuition waivers (full and partial), and unspecified assistantships also available. Support available to part-time students. Financial award application deadline: 3/1. *Application contact:* Diane Trujillo, Administrative Assistant, Graduate Studies, 505-454-3266, Fax: 505-426-2117, E-mail: dtrujillo@nmhu.edu.

Northeastern University, College of Arts and Sciences, Department of Political Science, Boston, MA 02115-5096. Offers political science (MA); public administration (MPA, Certificate), including development administration (MPA), health administration and policy (MPA), state and local government (MPA), urban studies (Certificate); public and international affairs (PhD). Part-time and evening/weekend programs available. *Degree requirements:* For master's, thesis optional; for doctorate, thesis/dissertation. *Entrance requirements:* For master's, GRE General Test. Additional exam requirements/recommendations for international students: Required—TOEFL. *Faculty research:* Presidency, public opinion, Congress, democratization, national identity.

Notre Dame de Namur University, Division of Academic Affairs, School of Business and Management, Department of Public Administration, Belmont, CA 94002-1908. Offers public administration (MPA); public affairs administration (MPA). Part-time and evening/weekend programs available. *Faculty:* 2 full-time (1 woman), 4 part-time/adjunct (2 women). *Students:* 2 full-time (both women), 30 part-time (25 women); includes 18 minority (2 African Americans, 1 Asian American or Pacific Islander, 15 Hispanic Americans), 1 international. Average age 31. 20 applicants, 100% accepted, 11 enrolled. In 2008, 7 master's awarded. *Entrance requirements:* For master's, interview, minimum GPA of 2.5. Additional exam requirements/recommendations for international students: Required—TOEFL (minimum score 550 paper-based; 213 computer-based; 79 iBT). *Application deadline:* For fall admission, 8/1 priority date for domestic students; for spring admission, 12/1 priority date for domestic students. Applications are processed on a rolling basis. Application fee: $60. Electronic applications accepted. *Expenses:* Tuition: Part-time $699 per unit. Required fees: $3 per unit. $35 per semester. *Financial support:* Career-related internships or fieldwork available. Support available to part-time students. Financial award applicants required to submit FAFSA. *Unit head:* Henry Roth, Director, 650-508-3721, E-mail: hroth@ndnu.edu. *Application contact:* Candace Hallmark, Director of Graduate Admissions, 650-508-3592, Fax: 650-508-3426, E-mail: grad.admit@ndnu.edu.

The Ohio State University, John Glenn School of Public Affairs, Columbus, OH 43210. Offers MA, MPA, PhD. *Accreditation:* NASPAA (one or more programs are accredited). Part-time programs available. *Degree requirements:* For doctorate, thesis/dissertation. *Entrance requirements:* For master's, GMAT, GRE General Test (MPA), minimum GPA of 3.0 (MA); for doctorate, GRE General Test. Additional exam requirements/recommendations for international students: Recommended—TOEFL (minimum score 573 paper-based; 230 computer-based). Electronic applications accepted.

Park University, College of Graduate and Professional Studies, Kansas City, MO 54105. Offers adult education (M Ed); at-risk students (M Ed); disaster and emergency management (MPA); educational administration (M Ed); entrepreneurship (MBA); general business (MBA); general education (M Ed); government/business relations (MPA); healthcare/services management (MBA, MPA); international business (MBA); K-12 certification (MAT); management information systems (MBA); management of information systems (MPA); middle school certification (MAT); multi-cultural education (M Ed); nonprofit management (MPA); public management (MPA); school law (M Ed); secondary school certification (MAT); special education (M Ed). Part-time and evening/weekend programs available. Postbaccalaureate distance learning degree programs offered (no on-campus study). *Degree requirements:* For master's, comprehensive exam, thesis (for some programs). *Entrance requirements:* For master's, GRE, GMAT, teacher certification (M Ed). Additional exam requirements/recommendations for international students: Required—TOEFL (minimum score 550 paper-based). Electronic applications accepted. *Faculty research:* Literacy, leadership, brain based research, multicultural education, diversity.

Princeton University, Graduate School, Program in Population Studies, Princeton, NJ 08544-1019. Offers demography (PhD, Certificate); economics and demography (PhD); public affairs and demography (PhD); sociology and demography (PhD). *Degree requirements:* For doctorate, thesis/dissertation. *Entrance requirements:* For doctorate, GRE General Test. Additional exam requirements/recommendations for international students: Required—TOEFL (minimum score 600 paper-based; 250 computer-based). Electronic applications accepted. *Faculty research:* Models, fertility, infant and child mortality, migration.

Princeton University, Graduate School, Woodrow Wilson School of Public and International Affairs, Princeton, NJ 08544-1019. Offers public affairs (MPA, PhD); public policy (MPP); JD/MPA. Terminal master's awarded for partial completion of doctoral program. *Degree requirements:* For master's, internship; for doctorate, one foreign language, thesis/dissertation. *Entrance requirements:* For master's, GRE General Test, original policy memo; for doctorate, GRE General Test. Additional exam requirements/recommendations for international students: Required—TOEFL (minimum score 600 paper-based; 250 computer-based). Electronic applications accepted.

Texas A&M University, George Bush School of Government and Public Service, College Station, TX 77843. Offers advanced international affairs (Certificate); homeland security (Certificate); international affairs (MPIA), including international economics and development, national security affairs; nonprofit management (Certificate); public service and administration (MPSA), including public management, public policy analysis. *Accreditation:* NASPAA. *Faculty:* 43. *Students:* 188 full-time (80 women), 101 part-time (37 women); includes 40 minority (10 African Americans, 5 Asian Americans or Pacific Islanders, 25 Hispanic Americans), 22 international. Average age 24. In 2008, 64 master's awarded. *Degree requirements:* For master's, summer internship. *Entrance requirements:* For master's, GRE (preferred) or GMAT. *Application deadline:* For fall admission, 1/24 for domestic and international students. Application fee: $50 ($75 for international students). Electronic applications accepted. *Expenses:* Tuition, area resident: Full-time $3838.50. Tuition, state resident: full-time $3838.50. Tuition, nonresident: full-time $8897. Required fees: $2359.60. *Financial support:* In 2008–09, fellowships (averaging $11,000 per year), research assistantships (averaging $11,250 per year) were awarded; career-related internships or fieldwork, Federal Work-Study, and institutionally sponsored loans also available. Financial award application deadline: 2/1; financial award applicants required to submit FAFSA. *Faculty research:* Public policy, presidential studies, public leadership, economic policy, social policy. *Unit head:* A. Benton Cocanougher, Dean, 979-862-8842, E-mail: bushschool@tamu.edu. *Application contact:* Kathryn Meyer, Recruitment/Placement Officer, 979-458-4767, Fax: 979-845-4155, E-mail: admissions@bushschool.tamu.edu.

The University of Alabama in Huntsville, School of Graduate Studies, College of Liberal Arts, Program in Public Affairs, Huntsville, AL 35899. Offers MA. Part-time and evening/weekend programs available. *Faculty:* 4 full-time (3 women). *Students:* 5 full-time (3 women), 17 part-time (9 women); includes 4 minority (3 African Americans, 1 Hispanic American), 1 international. Average age 30. 11 applicants, 82% accepted, 5 enrolled. In 2008, 5 master's awarded. *Degree requirements:* For master's, comprehensive exam, thesis or alternative, oral and written exams. *Entrance requirements:* For master's, GRE General Test, minimum GPA of 3.0. Additional exam requirements/recommendations for international students: Required—TOEFL (minimum score 500 paper-based; 173 computer-based; 62 iBT). *Application deadline:* For fall admission, 7/15 for domestic students, 4/1 for international students; for spring admission, 11/30 for domestic students, 9/1 for international students. Applications are processed on a rolling basis. Application fee: $40 ($50 for international students). Electronic applications accepted. *Expenses:* Tuition, area resident: Full-time $5214; part-time $323 per credit hour. Tuition, state resident: full-time $5214; part-time $323 per credit hour. Tuition, nonresident: full-time $11,444; part-time $705 per credit hour. Required fees: $540; $120 per semester. Tuition and fees vary according to course load. *Financial support:* In 2008–09, 5 students received support. Career-related internships or fieldwork, Federal Work-Study, institutionally sponsored loans, scholarships/grants, health care benefits, and unspecified assistantships available. Support available to part-time students. Financial award application deadline: 4/1; financial award applicants required to submit FAFSA. *Faculty research:* Public policy, public management professions, intergovernmental relations, international politics. Total annual research expenditures: $4,136. *Unit head:* Dr. Kathleen H. Hawk, Political Science Department Chair, 256-824-2315, Fax: 256-824-6949, E-mail: hawkk@email.uah.edu. *Application contact:* Kathy Biggs, Graduate Studies Admissions Manager, 256-824-6199, Fax: 256-824-6405, E-mail: deangrad@uah.edu.

University of Arkansas at Little Rock, Graduate School, Clinton School of Public Service, Little Rock, AR 72204-1099. Offers MPS, Graduate Certificate.

University of Central Florida, College of Health and Public Affairs, Program in Public Affairs, Orlando, FL 32816. Offers PhD. Part-time and evening/weekend programs available. *Students:* 39 full-time (16 women), 36 part-time (22 women); includes 7 minority (2 African Americans, 1 Asian American or Pacific Islander, 4 Hispanic Americans), 13 international. In 2008, 17 doctorates awarded. *Degree requirements:* For doctorate, thesis/dissertation, candidacy and qualifying exams. *Entrance requirements:* For doctorate, GRE General Test or minimum GPA of 3.0 during final 60 hours. Additional exam requirements/recommendations for international students: Required—TOEFL. *Application deadline:* For fall admission, 2/7 priority date for domestic students. Application fee: $30. Electronic applications accepted. *Expenses:* Tuition, area resident: Full-time $6816; part-time $284 per credit. Tuition, state resident: full-time $6816; part-time $1076 per credit. Tuition, nonresident: full-time $25,824. Required fees: $216; $9 per credit. *Financial support:* In 2008–09, 6 fellowships with partial tuition reimbursements (averaging $11,000 per year), 15 research assistantships with partial tuition reimbursements (averaging $8,000 per year), 4 teaching assistantships with partial tuition reimbursements (averaging $6,800 per year) were awarded; career-related internships or fieldwork, Federal Work-Study, institutionally sponsored loans, tuition waivers (partial), and unspecified assistantships also available. Financial award application deadline: 3/1; financial award applicants required to submit FAFSA. *Unit head:* Dr. Thomas T. Wan, Director, 407-823-0172, Fax: 407-823-4895, E-mail: twan@mail.ucf.edu. *Application contact:* Dr. Thomas T. Wan, Director, 407-823-0172, Fax: 407-823-4895, E-mail: twan@mail.ucf.edu.

University of Colorado at Colorado Springs, Graduate School, Graduate School of Public Affairs, Colorado Springs, CO 80933-7150. Offers criminal justice (MCJ); public administration (MPA). Part-time and evening/weekend programs available. *Faculty:* 3 full-time (1 woman), 25 part-time/adjunct (15 women). *Students:* 40 full-time (23 women), 38 part-time (23 women); includes 10 minority (2 Asian Americans or Pacific Islanders, 8 Hispanic Americans). Average age 35. 34 applicants, 91% accepted, 24 enrolled. In 2008, 32 master's awarded. *Degree requirements:* For master's, internship (if no experience), capstone project. *Entrance requirements:* For master's, GRE General Test, GMAT, LSAT, minimum GPA of 3.0. *Application deadline:* For fall admission, 6/1 priority date for domestic students; for spring admission, 11/1 for domestic students. Applications are processed on a rolling basis. Application fee: $60 ($75 for international students). *Expenses:* Contact institution. *Financial support:* Career-related internships or fieldwork and Federal Work-Study available. Support available to part-time students. *Unit head:* Dr. Terry Schwartz, Dean, 719-255-4047, Fax: 719-255-4183, E-mail: tschwart@uccs.edu. *Application contact:* Mary Lou Kartis, Program Assistant, 719-255-4182, Fax: 719-255-4183, E-mail: mkartis@uccs.edu.

University of Colorado Denver, Graduate School of Public Affairs, Program in Public Affairs, Denver, CO 80217-3364. Offers PhD. Part-time and evening/weekend programs available. *Degree requirements:* For doctorate, comprehensive exam, thesis/dissertation. *Entrance requirements:* For doctorate, GRE General Test. Additional exam requirements/recommendations for international students: Required—TOEFL (minimum score 500 paper-based).

University of Florida, Graduate School, College of Liberal Arts and Sciences, Department of Political Science, Gainesville, FL 32611. Offers international development policy and administration (MA, Certificate); international relations (MA, MAT); political campaigning (MA, Certificate); political science (MA, MAT, PhD); public affairs (MA, Certificate); JD/MA. Part-time programs available. Terminal master's awarded for partial completion of doctoral program. *Degree requirements:* For master's, variable foreign language requirement, thesis or alternative; for doctorate, variable foreign language requirement, thesis/dissertation. *Entrance requirements:* For master's and doctorate, GRE General Test, minimum GPA of 3.0. Additional exam requirements/recommendations for international students: Required—TOEFL (minimum score 550 paper-based; 213 computer-based). Electronic applications accepted. *Faculty research:* U.S. political development, religion and politics, environmental politics and policy, developing societies, international relations.

University of Idaho, College of Graduate Studies, College of Letters, Arts and Social Sciences, Department of Political Science and Public Affairs Research, Moscow, ID 83844-2282. Offers political science (MA, PhD); public administration (MPA). *Faculty:* 7 full-time, 3 part-time/adjunct. *Students:* 18 full-time, 14 part-time. Average age 34. In 2008, 10 master's, 11 doctorates awarded. *Degree requirements:* For doctorate, thesis/dissertation. *Entrance requirements:* For master's, minimum GPA of 2.8; for doctorate, minimum undergraduate GPA of 2.8, 3.0 graduate. *Application deadline:* For fall admission, 8/1 for domestic students; for spring admission, 12/15 for domestic students. Application fee: $55 ($60 for international students). *Expenses:* Tuition, nonresident: full-time $10,080; part-time $336 per credit. Required fees: $5212; $267 per credit. Tuition and fees vary according to program. *Financial support:* Research assistantships, teaching assistantships available. Financial award application deadline: 2/15. *Unit head:* Dr. Donald W. Crowley, Chair, 208-885-6328. *Application contact:* Dr. Donald W. Crowley, Chair, 208-885-6328.

University of Louisville, Graduate School, College of Arts and Sciences, Department of Urban and Public Affairs, Program in Urban and Public Affairs, Louisville, KY 40208. Offers urban planning and development (PhD); urban policy and administration (PhD). *Faculty:* 15 full-time (3 women). *Students:* 24 full-time (8 women), 3 part-time (2 women); includes 4 African Americans, 1 Asian American or Pacific Islander, 2 international. Average age 35. 15 applicants, 53% accepted, 6 enrolled. In 2008, 3 doctorates awarded. *Degree requirements:* For doctorate, thesis/dissertation. *Entrance requirements:* For doctorate, GRE General Test, master's degree in appropriate field. Additional exam requirements/recommendations for international students: Required—TOEFL (minimum score 547 paper-based; 210 computer-based; 77 iBT). *Application deadline:* For fall admission, 7/15 for domestic students; for spring admission, 11/15 for domestic students. Applications are processed on a rolling basis. Application fee: $50. Electronic applications accepted. *Financial support:* In 2008–09, 11 students received support, including 2 fellowships with full tuition reimbursements available (averaging $19,000 per year), 9 research assistantships with full tuition reimbursements available (averaging $19,000 per year); health care benefits also available. *Unit head:* Dr. Steven Bourassa, Director, 502-852-5720, Fax: 502-852-4558, E-mail: steven.bourassa@louisville.edu. *Application contact:* Yani Vozos, Graduate Student Advisor, 502-852-8002, Fax: 502-852-4558, E-mail: yani.vozos@louisville.edu.

University of Massachusetts Boston, Office of Graduate Studies, John W. McCormack Graduate School of Policy Studies, Program in Public Affairs, Boston, MA 02125-3393. Offers MS. Part-time and evening/weekend programs available. *Degree requirements:* For master's, final project. *Entrance requirements:* For master's, GRE General Test or MAT, minimum GPA of 2.75. *Faculty research:* Leadership and policy implementation, public management, disability; human services and sound policy.

University of Minnesota, Twin Cities Campus, Graduate School, Hubert H. Humphrey Institute of Public Affairs, Program in Public Affairs, Minneapolis, MN 55455-0213. Offers MPA. *Accreditation:* NASPAA. Part-time and evening/weekend programs available. *Entrance requirements:* For master's, 10 years of work experience, minimum undergraduate GPA of 3.0. Additional exam requirements/recommendations for international students: Required—TOEFL (minimum score 600 paper-based; 250 computer-based). Electronic applications accepted. *Expenses:* Contact institution. *Faculty research:* Public and non-profit leadership and management, social policy, urban and regional planning, economic and community development, foreign policy and international affairs.

University of Missouri–Columbia, Graduate School, Harry S Truman School of Public Affairs, Columbia, MO 65211. Offers MPA. *Accreditation:* NASPAA. *Faculty:* 13 full-time (3 women). *Students:* 51 full-time (21 women), 31 part-time (15 women); includes 8 minority (3 African Americans, 1 American Indian/Alaska Native, 3 Asian Americans or Pacific Islanders, 1 Hispanic American), 24 international. Average age 31. 77 applicants, 61% accepted, 22 enrolled. In 2008, 50 master's awarded. *Entrance requirements:* For master's, GRE General Test, minimum GPA of 3.0. Additional exam requirements/recommendations for international students: Required—TOEFL (minimum score 550 paper-based; 213 computer-based; 79 iBT). *Application deadline:* For fall admission, 2/15 priority date for domestic students. Applications are processed on a rolling basis. Application fee: $45 ($60 for international students). *Financial support:* Fellowships, research assistantships, teaching assistantships, institutionally sponsored loans available. *Unit head:* Dr. Bart Wechsler, Director, E-mail: wechslerb@missouri.edu. *Application contact:* Jessica Hosey, 573-882-3471, E-mail: hoseyj@missouri.edu.

University of Missouri–Kansas City, Henry W. Bloch School of Business and Public Administration, Kansas City, MO 64110-2499. Offers accounting (MS); business administration (MBA); entrepreneurship and innovation (PhD); public affairs (MPA, PhD); JD/MBA; LL M/MPA. PhD is an interdisciplinary degree offered by the School of Graduate Studies. *Accreditation:* AACSB; NASPAA. Part-time and evening/weekend programs available. *Faculty:* 42 full-time (13 women), 24 part-time/adjunct (6 women). *Students:* 203 full-time (99 women), 433 part-time (188 women); includes 73 minority (33 African Americans, 3 American Indian/Alaska Native, 24 Asian Americans or Pacific Islanders, 13 Hispanic Americans), 47 international. Average age 30. 284 applicants, 79% accepted, 203 enrolled. In 2008, 228 master's awarded. Terminal master's awarded for partial completion of doctoral program. *Entrance requirements:* For master's, GMAT, GRE, 2 writing essays, 2 references and support of employer; for doctorate, GRE, minimum GPA of 3.0. Additional exam requirements/recommendations for international students: Required—TOEFL (minimum score 550 paper-based; 213 computer-based; 80 iBT). *Application deadline:* For fall admission, 5/1 priority date for domestic and international students; for spring admission, 10/1 priority date for domestic and international students. Applications are processed on a rolling basis. Application fee: $45 ($50 for international students). Electronic applications accepted. *Expenses:* Tuition, state resident: full-time $5376; part-time $298.70 per credit hour. Tuition, nonresident: full-time $13,882; part-time $771.20 per credit hour. Required fees: $640.28; $34.65 per contact hour. $30 per semester. Tuition and fees vary according to course load and program. *Financial support:* In 2008–09, 20 research assistantships with partial tuition reimbursements (averaging $7,809 per year), 4 teaching assistantships with partial tuition reimbursements (averaging $9,900 per year) were awarded; fellowships, career-related internships or fieldwork, Federal Work-Study, institutionally sponsored loans, scholarships/grants, tuition waivers (full and partial), and unspecified assistantships also available. Support available to part-time students. Financial award application deadline: 3/1;

Public Affairs

University of Missouri–Kansas City (continued)
financial award applicants required to submit FAFSA. *Faculty research:* Entrepreneurship, finance, non-profit, risk management. Total annual research expenditures: $442,722. *Unit head:* Dr. Teng-Kee Tan, Dean, 816-235-2215, Fax: 816-235-2206. *Application contact:* 816-235-1111, E-mail: admit@umkc.edu.

University of Nevada, Las Vegas, Graduate College, Greenspun College of Urban Affairs, Department of Public Administration, Las Vegas, NV 89154-6026. Offers crisis and emergency management (MS); non-profit management (Certificate); public administration (MPA); public affairs (PhD); public management (Certificate). *Accreditation:* NASPAA. Part-time and evening/weekend programs available. *Faculty:* 5 full-time (3 women), 2 part-time/adjunct (1 woman). *Students:* 30 full-time (12 women), 129 part-time (70 women); includes 39 minority (21 African Americans, 4 Asian Americans or Pacific Islanders, 14 Hispanic Americans), 3 international. Average age 38. 95 applicants, 76% accepted, 53 enrolled. In 2008, 48 master's, 28 other advanced degrees awarded. *Degree requirements:* For master's, comprehensive exam, professional paper. *Entrance requirements:* For master's, GRE General Test, GMAT or LSAT. Additional exam requirements/recommendations for international students: Required—TOEFL (minimum score 550 paper-based; 213 computer-based; 80 iBT), IELTS (minimum score 7). *Application deadline:* For fall admission, 6/1 priority date for domestic students, 5/1 for international students; for spring admission, 11/1 priority date for domestic students, 10/1 for international students. Applications are processed on a rolling basis. Application fee: $60 ($75 for international students). Electronic applications accepted. *Expenses:* Tuition, state resident: full-time $1414; part-time $198 per credit. Tuition, nonresident: full-time $12,509; part-time $415.75 per credit. International tuition: $14,249 full-time. Required fees: $4 per credit. $252 per semester. Tuition and fees vary according to course load. *Financial support:* In 2008–09, 8 students received support, including 3 research assistantships with partial tuition reimbursements available (averaging $10,000 per year), 5 teaching assistantships with partial tuition reimbursements available (averaging $15,600 per year); institutionally sponsored loans, scholarships/grants, health care benefits, and unspecified assistantships also available. Financial award application deadline: 3/1. *Faculty research:* Emergency and crisis management, homeland security, public and non-profit management, public policy, policy analysis and evaluation. *Unit head:* Dr. Anna Lukemeyer, Chair/Associate Professor, 702-895-4828, Fax: 702-895-1813, E-mail: anna.lukemeyer@unlv.edu. *Application contact:* Graduate College Admissions Evaluator, 702-895-3320, Fax: 702-895-4180, E-mail: gradcollege@unlv.edu.

The University of North Carolina at Greensboro, Graduate School, College of Arts and Sciences, Department of Political Science, Greensboro, NC 27412-5001. Offers nonprofit management (Certificate); public affairs (MPA); urban and economic development (Certificate). *Accreditation:* NASPAA. *Degree requirements:* For master's, comprehensive exam. *Entrance requirements:* For master's, GRE General Test. Additional exam requirements/recommendations for international students: Required—TOEFL. Electronic applications accepted. *Faculty research:* U.S. Constitution, Canadian parliament, public management, ethical challenge of public service.

The University of Texas at Arlington, Graduate School, School of Urban and Public Affairs, Program in Urban and Public Affairs, Arlington, TX 76019. Offers PhD. Part-time and evening/weekend programs available. *Students:* 9 full-time (5 women), 54 part-time (30 women); includes 23 minority (17 African Americans, 2 Asian Americans or Pacific Islanders, 4 Hispanic Americans), 5 international. Average age 30. 12 applicants, 83% accepted, 6 enrolled. *Degree requirements:* For doctorate, comprehensive exam, thesis/dissertation. *Entrance requirements:* For doctorate, GRE General Test. *Application deadline:* For fall admission, 6/16 for domestic students. Application fee: $35 ($50 for international students). *Expenses:* Tuition, area resident: Full-time $6500. Tuition, state resident: full-time $6500. Tuition, nonresident: full-time $11,558. *Financial support:* In 2008–09, 4 fellowships (averaging $1,000 per year), 6 research assistantships (averaging $4,500 per year) were awarded. Financial award application deadline: 6/1; financial award applicants required to submit FAFSA. *Faculty research:* Environment urban policy personnel, research theoretical foundations, urban problems. *Unit head:* Dr. Rod Hissong, Graduate Adviser, 817-272-3350, Fax: 817-272-5008, E-mail: hissong@uta.edu. *Application contact:* Linda Slaughter, Administrative Clerk, 817-272-3071, Fax: 817-272-5008, E-mail: slaughter@uta.edu.

The University of Texas at Austin, Graduate School, Lyndon B. Johnson School of Public Affairs, Austin, TX 78712-1111. Offers global policy studies (MGPS); public affairs (MP Aff); public policy (PhD); JD/MP Aff; MBA/MP Aff; MP Aff/MA; MP Aff/MSE. *Accreditation:* NASPAA (one or more programs are accredited). Part-time programs available. *Degree requirements:* For master's, thesis, summer internship; for doctorate, thesis/dissertation. *Entrance requirements:* For master's, GRE General Test; for doctorate, GRE General Test, master's degree in policy-related field. Additional exam requirements/recommendations for international students: Required—TOEFL. Electronic applications accepted. *Faculty research:* Human resource development, health and social policy, philanthropy and community service, ethical leadership, urban and international policy, science and technology policy.

The University of Texas at Dallas, School of Economic, Political and Policy Sciences, Program in Public Affairs, Richardson, TX 75083-0688. Offers MPA, PhD. *Accreditation:* NASPAA. Part-time and evening/weekend programs available. *Faculty:* 8 full-time (2 women), 3 part-time/adjunct (1 woman). *Students:* 57 full-time (28 women), 135 part-time (64 women); includes 60 minority (32 African Americans, 5 Asian Americans or Pacific Islanders, 23 Hispanic Americans), 20 international. Average age 37. 68 applicants, 87% accepted, 36 enrolled. In 2008, 24 master's, 7 doctorates awarded. *Degree requirements:* For master's, internship; for doctorate, thesis/dissertation. *Entrance requirements:* For master's and doctorate, GRE General Test, minimum GPA of 3.0 in upper-level course work in field. Additional exam requirements/recommendations for international students: Required—TOEFL (minimum score 550 paper-based; 213 computer-based). *Application deadline:* For fall admission, 7/15 for domestic students, 5/1 priority date for international students; for spring admission, 11/15 for domestic students, 9/1 priority date for international students. Applications are processed on a rolling basis. Application fee: $50 ($100 for international students). Electronic applications accepted. *Expenses:* Tuition, area resident: Full-time $8320. Tuition, state resident: full-time $8320. Tuition, nonresident: full-time $15,054. Part-time tuition and fees vary according to course load. *Financial support:* In 2008–09, 1 research assistantship with tuition reimbursement (averaging $13,279 per year), 10 teaching assistantships with tuition reimbursements (averaging $12,021 per year) were awarded; fellowships, career-related internships or fieldwork, Federal Work-Study, institutionally sponsored loans, and scholarships/grants also available. Support available to part-time students. Financial award application deadline: 4/30; financial award applicants required to submit FAFSA. *Faculty research:* Juvenile justice programs, program evaluation and outcome measurement, Hispanic American retention in educational institutions. *Unit head:* Dr. L. Douglas Kiel, Program Head, 972-883-2019, Fax: 972-883-2735, E-mail: dkiel@utdallas.edu. *Application contact:* Dr. Jeremy L. Hall, Associate Program Head, 972-883-5347, Fax: 972-883-2735, E-mail: jeremy.hall@utdallas.edu.

See Close-Up on page 783.

University of Washington, Graduate School, Daniel J. Evans School of Public Affairs, Seattle, WA 98195. Offers public administration (MPA); public policy and management (PhD); JD/MPA; MPA/MAIS; MPA/MPH; MPA/MS; MPA/MUP. *Accreditation:* NASPAA. Part-time and evening/weekend programs available. *Degree requirements:* For master's, thesis, internship or cooperative experience. *Entrance requirements:* For master's and doctorate, GRE General Test, minimum GPA of 3.0. Additional exam requirements/recommendations for international students: Required—TOEFL (minimum score 580 paper-based; 237 computer-based; 92 iBT). Electronic applications accepted. *Faculty research:* Environmental policy, education and social policy, nonprofit management, international affairs, urban and regional development.

University of Waterloo, Graduate Studies, Faculty of Arts, Department of Anthropology, Waterloo, ON N2L 3G1, Canada. Offers anthropology (MA); public issues (MA). *Entrance requirements:* For master's, BA, B+ average. Additional exam requirements/recommendations for international students: Required—TOEFL. Electronic applications accepted. *Faculty research:* Applied socio-cultural anthropology and archaeology.

University of Wisconsin–Madison, Graduate School, College of Letters and Science, Public Policy and Administration Program, Robert M. La Follette School of Public Affairs, Madison, WI 53706-1380. Offers international public affairs (MPIA); public affairs (MPA). Part-time programs available. *Entrance requirements:* For master's, GRE General Test. Additional exam requirements/recommendations for international students: Required—TOEFL (minimum score 650 paper-based; 280 computer-based). Electronic applications accepted. *Faculty research:* Social policy, personnel, economic development, tax and budget, environmental regulations.

Virginia Commonwealth University, Graduate School, College of Humanities and Sciences, Wilder School of Government and Public Affairs, Richmond, VA 23284-9005. Offers MA, MPA, MS, MURP, PhD, CASR, CCJA, CPM, CURP, Certificate, Graduate Certificate, JD/MURP, MSW/Certificate.

Virginia Polytechnic Institute and State University, Graduate School, College of Architecture and Urban Studies, School of Public and International Affairs, Blacksburg, VA 24061. Offers environmental planning and policy (MURP); government and international affairs (MPIA); housing, community and economic development (MURP); international development planning (MURP); land use and physical planning (MURP); planning, governance and globalization (PhD), including environmental planning and landscape analysis, physical planning and urban design, public and international affairs, urban and environmental design and planning; urban and regional planning (MURP). *Accreditation:* ACSP. *Entrance requirements:* Additional exam requirements/recommendations for international students: Required—TOEFL (minimum score 550 paper-based; 213 computer-based). Electronic applications accepted. *Faculty research:* Design theory, environmental planning, town planning, transportation planning.

Washington State University Vancouver, Graduate Programs, Program in Public Affairs, Vancouver, WA 98686. Offers MPA. Part-time and evening/weekend programs available. *Degree requirements:* For master's, comprehensive exam, thesis (for some programs). *Entrance requirements:* For master's, GRE, minimum GPA of 3.0, resumé, 3 references. Additional exam requirements/recommendations for international students: Required—TOEFL (minimum score 550 paper-based; 213 computer-based).

West Chester University of Pennsylvania, Office of Graduate Studies, College of Business and Public Affairs, West Chester, PA 19383. Offers MA, MBA, MS, MSA, MSW, Certificate. Part-time and evening/weekend programs available. *Students:* 98 full-time (72 women), 140 part-time (72 women); includes 40 minority (25 African Americans, 8 Asian Americans or Pacific Islanders, 7 Hispanic Americans). Average age 34. 250 applicants, 86% accepted, 121 enrolled. In 2008, 106 master's, 12 other advanced degrees awarded. *Degree requirements:* For master's, comprehensive exam, thesis (for some programs). *Entrance requirements:* Additional exam requirements/recommendations for international students: Required—TOEFL (minimum score 550 paper-based; 213 computer-based; 80 iBT). *Application deadline:* For fall admission, 4/15 priority date for domestic students, 3/15 for international students; for spring admission, 10/15 for domestic students, 9/1 for international students. Applications are processed on a rolling basis. Application fee: $35. Electronic applications accepted. *Expenses:* Tuition, state resident: full-time $6430; part-time $357 per credit. Tuition, nonresident: full-time $10,288; part-time $572 per credit. Required fees: $652.50; $50 per credit. $67 per semester. *Financial support:* In 2008–09, 17 research assistantships with full and partial tuition reimbursements (averaging $5,000 per year) were awarded; career-related internships or fieldwork and unspecified assistantships also available. Support available to part-time students. Financial award application deadline: 2/15; financial award applicants required to submit FAFSA. *Unit head:* Dr. Christopher Fiorentino, Dean, 610-436-2824, E-mail: cfiorentino@wcupa.edu. *Application contact:* Office of Graduate Studies, 610-436-2943, Fax: 610-436-2763, E-mail: gradstudy@wcupa.edu.

Western Carolina University, Graduate School, College of Arts and Sciences, Department of Political Science and Public Affairs, Cullowhee, NC 28723. Offers MPA. Part-time and evening/weekend programs available. *Degree requirements:* For master's, comprehensive exam. *Entrance requirements:* For master's, GRE General Test, appropriate undergraduate, 3 letters of recommendation. Additional exam requirements/recommendations for international students: Required—TOEFL (minimum score 550 paper-based; 270 computer-based; 79 iBT). *Faculty research:* Press-government relations, comparative governments, gender in politics, Latin American political systems, foreign policy, trust in government, zoning.

Western Michigan University, Graduate College, College of Arts and Sciences, School of Public Affairs and Administration, Kalamazoo, MI 49008-5202. Offers health care administration (Graduate Certificate); nonprofit leadership and administration (Graduate Certificate); public administration (PhD); public affairs and administration (MPA). *Accreditation:* NASPAA (one or more programs are accredited). *Degree requirements:* For doctorate, thesis/dissertation, oral exams. *Entrance requirements:* For doctorate, GRE General Test.

York University, Faculty of Graduate Studies, Glendon College, Program in Public and International Affairs, Toronto, ON M3J 1P3, Canada. Offers MA.

Public Policy

Albany State University, College of Arts and Humanities, Department of History, Political Science and Public Administration, Albany, GA 31705-2717. Offers community and economic development (MPA); criminal justice (MPA); fiscal management (MPA); general management (MPA); health administration and policy (MPA); human resources management (MPA); public policy (MPA); water resource management and policy (MPA). *Accreditation:* NASPAA. Part-time programs available. *Faculty:* 5 full-time (2 women). *Students:* 10 full-time (8 women), 42 part-time (29 women); includes 50 minority (49 African Americans, 1 Asian American or Pacific Islander). Average age 35. In 2008, 12 master's awarded. *Degree requirements:* For master's, comprehensive exam, thesis. *Entrance requirements:* For master's, GRE General Test, minimum GPA of 2.5. *Application deadline:* For fall admission, 4/15 for domestic and international students; for spring admission, 11/15 for domestic and international students. Applications are processed on a rolling basis. Application fee: $20. Electronic applications accepted. *Expenses:* Tuition, area resident: Full-time $4296; part-time $154 per semester hour. Tuition, state resident: full-time $4296; part-time $154 per semester hour. Tuition, nonresident: full-time $15,338; part-time $614 per semester hour. Required fees: $306 per semester. Tuition and fees vary according to course load. *Financial support:* Tuition waivers available. Financial award application deadline: 4/1; financial award applicants required to submit FAFSA. *Faculty research:* Transportation, urban affairs, political economy. *Unit head:* Dr. Rita Henry-Brown, Chair, 229-430-4870, Fax: 229-430-7895, E-mail: rita.brown@asurams.edu. *Application contact:* Diane P. Frink, Graduate Admission Counselor, 229-430-5118, Fax: 229-430-6398, E-mail: diane.frink@asurams.edu.

American University, School of Public Affairs, Department of Public Administration, Program in Public Policy, Washington, DC 20016-8070. Offers MPP, MPP/JD, MPP/LLM. *Students:* 83 full-time (58 women), 41 part-time (25 women); includes 29 minority (16 African Americans, 1 American Indian/Alaska Native, 11 Asian Americans or Pacific Islanders, 1 Hispanic American), 5 international. Average age 25. In 2008, 47 master's awarded. *Degree requirements:* For master's, comprehensive exam. *Entrance requirements:* For master's, GRE, statement of purpose; 2 recommendations. Additional exam requirements/recommendations for international students: Required—TOEFL. *Application deadline:* For fall admission, 2/1 for domestic students; for spring admission, 11/1 for domestic students. Application fee: $55. *Expenses:* Tuition: Full-time $21,204; part-time $1178 per credit hour. Required fees: $380. Part-time tuition and fees vary according to course load and program. *Financial support:* Application deadline: 2/1.

The American University in Cairo, Graduate Studies and Research, School of Humanities and Social Sciences, Program in Public Policy and Administration, Cairo, Egypt. Offers MA, Diploma.

Arizona State University, Sandra Day O'Connor College of Law, Tempe, AZ 85287-7906. Offers biotechnology and genomics (LL M); legal studies (MLS); tribal policy, law and government (LL M); JD/MBA; JD/MD; JD/PhD. *Accreditation:* ABA. *Degree requirements:* For JD, comprehensive exam, paper. *Entrance requirements:* LSAT, bachelors degree. Additional exam requirements/recommendations for international students: Required—TOEFL (minimum score 550 paper-based; 213 computer-based; 83 iBT). Electronic applications accepted. *Expenses:* Contact institution. *Faculty research:* Genetics and law, forensics and the law, science and law, Indian law, jurisprudence.

Baylor University, Graduate School, College of Arts and Sciences, Department of Political Science, Waco, TX 76798. Offers international studies (MA); political science (MA, PhD); public policy and administration (MPPA); JD/MPPA. *Students:* 24 full-time (7 women), 2 part-time (1 woman), 3 international. In 2008, 9 master's awarded. *Entrance requirements:* For master's, GRE General Test. *Application deadline:* Applications are processed on a rolling basis. Application fee: $25. *Financial support:* Research assistantships, career-related internships or fieldwork, Federal Work-Study, and institutionally sponsored loans available. Financial award application deadline: 3/1. *Unit head:* Dr. David Corey, Graduate Program Director, 254-710-3161, Fax: 254-710-3122, E-mail: david_d_corey@baylor.edu. *Application contact:* Jenice Langston, Administrative Assistant, 254-710-3161, Fax: 254-710-3870, E-mail: jenice_langston@baylor.edu.

Boise State University, Graduate College, College of Social Sciences and Public Affairs, Department of Public Policy and Administration, Boise, ID 83725-0399. Offers environmental and natural resources policy and administration (MPA); general public administration (MPA); state and local government policy and administration (MPA). *Accreditation:* NASPAA. Part-time programs available. *Degree requirements:* For master's, comprehensive exam, directed research project, internship. *Entrance requirements:* For master's, GRE General Test, minimum GPA of 3.0. Additional exam requirements/recommendations for international students: Required—TOEFL. Electronic applications accepted.

Brandeis University, The Heller School for Social Policy and Management, Program in Public Policy, Waltham, MA 02454-9110. Offers aging (MPP); behavioral health (MPP); children, youth and families (MPP); general social policy (MPP); health (MPP); poverty alleviation and development (MPP). Part-time programs available. *Entrance requirements:* Additional exam requirements/recommendations for international students: Required—TOEFL (minimum score 600 paper-based). Electronic applications accepted. *Faculty research:* Health policy, child and family policy, mental health policy, disability policy, aging policy, substance abuse, work, inequality and social change.

Brigham Young University, Graduate Studies, College of Family, Home, and Social Sciences, Public Policy Graduate Program, Provo, UT 84602. Offers MPP, JD/MPP. *Faculty:* 3 full-time (0 women), 3 part-time/adjunct (1 woman). *Students:* 14 full-time (8 women); includes 5 minority (1 American Indian/Alaska Native, 3 Asian Americans or Pacific Islanders, 1 Hispanic American), 1 international. Average age 28. 18 applicants, 83% accepted, 10 enrolled. In 2008, 5 master's awarded. *Degree requirements:* For master's, internship. *Entrance requirements:* For master's, GRE. Additional exam requirements/recommendations for international students: Required—TOEFL (minimum score 580 paper-based; 237 computer-based; 85 iBT). *Application deadline:* For fall admission, 3/1 priority date for domestic and international students. Application fee: $50. Electronic applications accepted. *Expenses:* Tuition: Full-time $5160; part-time $287 per credit hour. Tuition and fees vary according to program and student's religious affiliation. *Financial support:* In 2008–09, 11 students received support, including 7 research assistantships with full and partial tuition reimbursements available (averaging $2,357 per year), 2 teaching assistantships with full and partial tuition reimbursements available (averaging $4,800 per year); fellowships also available. Financial award application deadline: 3/1. *Faculty research:* Welfare, environment, and health policy issues. *Unit head:* Dr. Sven E. Wilson, Graduate Program Director, 801-422-9018, Fax: 801-422-0224, E-mail: sven_wilson@byu.edu. *Application contact:* Jessica A. McArthur, Department Secretary, 801-422-7146, Fax: 801-422-0224, E-mail: publicpolicy@byu.edu.

Brooklyn College of the City University of New York, Division of Graduate Studies, Department of Political Science, Brooklyn, NY 11210-2889. Offers international affairs (MA); political science (MA, PhD); political science, urban policy and administration (MA). The department offers courses at Brooklyn College that are creditable toward the CUNY doctoral degree (with permission of the executive officer of the doctoral program). Part-time and evening/weekend programs available. *Students:* 13 full-time (6 women), 142 part-time (82 women); includes 91 minority (68 African Americans, 5 Asian Americans or Pacific Islanders, 18 Hispanic Americans), 15 international. Average age 33. 95 applicants, 83% accepted, 45 enrolled. In 2008, 43 master's awarded. *Degree requirements:* For master's, comprehensive exam (for some programs), thesis or alternative, foreign language exam (for international affairs program). *Entrance requirements:* For master's, 2 letters of recommendation, personal statement. *Expenses:* Tuition, state resident: full-time $7360; part-time $310 per credit hour. Tuition, nonresident: full-time $13,800; part-time $575 per credit hour. *Financial support:* Career-related internships or fieldwork and Federal Work-Study available. Support available to part-time students. Financial award application deadline: 5/1; financial award applicants required to submit FAFSA. *Faculty research:* Ethics and politics, politics of criminal justice, Western Europe, international law and politics, labor politics. *Unit head:* Dr. Sally Bermanzohn, Chairperson, 718-951-5306, E-mail: sallyb@brooklyn.cuny.edu. *Application contact:* Hernan Sierra, Graduate Admissions Coordinator, 718-951-4536, Fax: 718-951-4506, E-mail: grads@brooklyn.cuny.edu.

Brown University, Graduate School, A. Alfred Taubman Center for Public Policy and American Institutions, Providence, RI 02912. Offers MPA, MPP. *Entrance requirements:* For master's, GRE, 3 letters of recommendation. Additional exam requirements/recommendations for international students: Required—TOEFL.

California Lutheran University, Graduate Studies, Program in Public Policy and Administration, Thousand Oaks, CA 91360-2787. Offers MPPA. *Faculty:* 1 full-time (0 women), 6 part-time/adjunct (4 women). *Students:* 26 full-time (14 women), 39 part-time (24 women); includes 20 minority (3 African Americans, 2 Asian Americans or Pacific Islanders, 15 Hispanic Americans), 3 international. Average age 35. 20 applicants, 90% accepted. In 2008, 23 master's awarded. *Degree requirements:* For master's, comprehensive exam, thesis or project, internship. *Entrance requirements:* For master's, GMAT or GRE General Test, interview, minimum GPA of 3.0. *Application deadline:* Applications are processed on a rolling basis. Application fee: $50. *Expenses:* Contact institution. *Financial support:* In 2008–09, 32 students received support. *Unit head:* Dr. Herbert Gooch, Director, 805-493-3348. *Application contact:* 805-493-3127, Fax: 805-493-3542, E-mail: clugrad@clunet.edu.

California State University, Long Beach, Graduate Studies, College of Health and Human Services, Graduate Center for Public Policy and Administration, Long Beach, CA 90840. Offers MPA. *Accreditation:* NASPAA. Part-time and evening/weekend programs available. *Faculty:* 7 full-time (2 women), 11 part-time/adjunct (4 women). *Students:* 77 full-time (51 women), 216 part-time (133 women); includes 185 minority (43 African Americans, 1 American Indian/Alaska Native, 50 Asian Americans or Pacific Islanders, 91 Hispanic Americans), 7 international. Average age 33. 199 applicants, 78% accepted, 121 enrolled. *Degree requirements:* For master's, comprehensive exam. *Entrance requirements:* For master's, minimum GPA of 2.75. *Application deadline:* For fall admission, 7/1 for domestic students. Applications are processed on a rolling basis. Application fee: $55. Electronic applications accepted. *Expenses:* Tuition, nonresident: full-time $11,160; part-time $372 per unit. Required fees: $4100; $1261 per semester. *Financial support:* Fellowships, career-related internships or fieldwork, Federal Work-Study, institutionally sponsored loans, and scholarships/grants available. Financial award application deadline: 3/2. *Faculty research:* Transportation access, air quality controls, coastal issues, intergovernmental relations. *Unit head:* Dr. David C Powell, Director, 562-985-4178, Fax: 562-985-4672, E-mail: dpowell@csulb.edu. *Application contact:* Dr. Frank Barber, Graduate Adviser, 562-985-5747, Fax: 562-985-4672.

California State University, Monterey Bay, College of Professional Studies, Health, Human Services and Public Policy Department, Seaside, CA 93955-8001. Offers public policy (MPP). Part-time programs available. *Faculty:* 2 full-time (1 woman), 3 part-time/adjunct (2 women). *Students:* 28 full-time (20 women), 9 part-time (7 women); includes 9 minority (1 African American, 8 Hispanic Americans). Average age 41. 36 applicants, 75% accepted, 17 enrolled. In 2008, 6 master's awarded. *Degree requirements:* For master's, internship. *Entrance requirements:* For master's, GRE, personal statement, transcript, curriculum vitae, recommendations, evidence of prerequisite coursework. Additional exam requirements/recommendations for international students: Required—TOEFL (minimum score 525 paper-based; 213 computer-based; 71 iBT). *Application deadline:* For fall admission, 2/2 for domestic students. Application fee: $55. Electronic applications accepted. *Expenses:* Tuition, state resident: full-time $3756; part-time $2178 per year. Tuition, nonresident: full-time $14,456; part-time $6246 per year. Required fees: $487; $244 per term. *Financial support:* In 2008–09, 19 students received support. Scholarships/grants available. Support available to part-time students. Financial award application deadline: 3/2; financial award applicants required to submit FAFSA. *Faculty research:* Social policy, health policy, politics and government. *Unit head:* Dr. Monica Bray, Director, 831-582-3603, Fax: 831-582-3899, E-mail: monica_bray@csumb.edu. *Application contact:* Haven Brearton, Administrative Support Coordinator, 831-582-3565, Fax: 831-582-3899, E-mail: haven_brearton@csumb.edu.

California State University, Sacramento, Graduate Studies, College of Social Sciences and Interdisciplinary Studies, Program in Public Policy and Administration, Sacramento, CA 95819-6048. Offers MPPA. Part-time programs available. *Degree requirements:* For master's, thesis or alternative, writing proficiency exam. *Entrance requirements:* For master's, GRE General Test. Additional exam requirements/recommendations for international students: Required—TOEFL. Electronic applications accepted.

Carleton University, Faculty of Graduate Studies, Faculty of Public Affairs and Management, School of Public Policy and Administration, Ottawa, ON K1S 5B6, Canada. Offers public administration (MA, DPA); public policy (PhD). Part-time programs available. *Degree requirements:* For master's, thesis optional; for doctorate, one foreign language, comprehensive exam, thesis/dissertation. *Entrance requirements:* For master's, GRE, honors degree; for doctorate, master's degree. Additional exam requirements/recommendations for international students: Required—TOEFL. *Faculty research:* Canadian public administration and policy, development administration, public policy analysis, public management.

Carnegie Mellon University, College of Humanities and Social Sciences, Department of Statistics, Pittsburgh, PA 15213-3891. Offers machine learning and statistics (PhD); mathematical finance (PhD); statistics (MS, PhD), including applied statistics (PhD), computational statistics (PhD), theoretical statistics (PhD); statistics and public policy (PhD). Terminal master's awarded for partial completion of doctoral program. *Degree requirements:* For doctorate, comprehensive exam, thesis/dissertation. *Entrance requirements:* For master's and doctorate, GRE General Test. Additional exam requirements/recommendations for international students: Required—TOEFL. *Faculty research:* Stochastic processes, Bayesian statistics, statistical computing, decision theory, psychiatric statistics.

Carnegie Mellon University, H. John Heinz III College, School of Public Policy and Management, Program in Public Policy and Management–Australia, Adelaide, PA 5000, Australia. Offers MS.

Carnegie Mellon University, H. John Heinz III College, School of Public Policy and Management and Tepper School of Business, Programs in Public Policy and Management, Pittsburgh, PA 15213-3891. Offers MS, PhD, JD/MS, M Div/MS. *Degree requirements:* For master's, internship. *Entrance requirements:* For master's, GMAT or GRE, previous course work in pre-calculus and statistics. Electronic applications accepted.

Central European University, Graduate Studies, School of Social Sciences and Humanities, Budapest, Hungary. Offers economics (MA, PhD); gender studies (MA, PhD); international relations and European studies (MA, PhD); mathematics and its applications (MS, PhD); medieval studies (MA, PhD); nationalism studies (MA, PhD); philosophy (MA, PhD); political science (MA, PhD); public policy (MA, PhD); sociology and social anthropology (MA, PhD). Terminal master's awarded for partial completion of doctoral program. *Degree requirements:* For master's, one foreign language, thesis; for doctorate, one foreign language, comprehensive exam, thesis/dissertation. *Entrance requirements:* For master's, CEU subject tests, interview; for doctorate, GRE, CEU subject test, interview. Additional exam requirements/recommendations for international students: Required—TOEFL (minimum score 570 paper-based; 230 computer-based). Electronic applications accepted. *Faculty research:* Civil society, fiscal decentralization, party politics, political philosophy (especially Liberalism, theory of Democracy).

See Close-Up on page 349.

Claremont Graduate University, Graduate Programs, Program in Public Policy and Evaluation, Claremont, CA 91711-6160. Offers MA. *Entrance requirements:* For master's, GRE General Test. Additional exam requirements/recommendations for international students: Required—TOEFL (minimum score 550 paper-based; 213 computer-based; 80 iBT). *Application deadline:* For fall admission, 2/1 priority date for domestic students. Application fee: $60. Electronic applications accepted. *Expenses:* Tuition: Full-time $33,698; part-time $1465 per unit. Required fees: $310; $155 per semester. Tuition and fees vary according to program. *Financial support:* Fellowships, Federal Work-Study, institutionally sponsored loans, and scholarships/grants available. Support available to part-time students. Financial award application deadline: 2/15; financial award applicants required to submit FAFSA. *Unit head:* Yi Feng, Provost and Vice President for Academic Affairs, 909-626-8694, Fax: 909-621-8450, E-mail: yi.feng@cgu.edu. *Application contact:* Laura Carillo, Recruiter and Admissions Coordinator, 909-621-8699, Fax: 909-621-7545, E-mail: laura.carillo@cga.edu.

Claremont Graduate University, Graduate Programs, School of Politics and Economics, Department of Economics, Claremont, CA 91711-6160. Offers business and financial economics (MA, PhD); economic development (Certificate); economics (PhD); industrial organization (PhD); international and development economics (PhD); international economics policy and development (MA); international money and finance (PhD); neuroeconomics (PhD); political economy and public policy (MA); public choice and public economics (PhD); MBA/PhD.

Public Policy

Claremont Graduate University (continued)
Part-time programs available. *Faculty:* 7 full-time (1 woman). *Students:* 100 full-time (24 women), 6 part-time (1 woman); includes 12 minority (3 African Americans, 7 Asian Americans or Pacific Islanders, 2 Hispanic Americans), 56 international. Average age 32. In 2008, 15 master's, 15 doctorates awarded. *Entrance requirements:* For master's and doctorate, GRE General Test or GMAT. Additional exam requirements/recommendations for international students: Required—TOEFL (minimum score 550 paper-based; 213 computer-based; 80 iBT). *Application deadline:* For fall admission, 2/1 priority date for domestic students. Applications are processed on a rolling basis. Application fee: $60. Electronic applications accepted. *Expenses:* Tuition: Full-time $33,698; part-time $1465 per unit. Required fees: $310; $155 per semester. Tuition and fees vary according to program. *Financial support:* Fellowships, research assistantships, teaching assistantships, Federal Work-Study, institutionally sponsored loans, and scholarships/grants available. Support available to part-time students. Financial award application deadline: 2/15; financial award applicants required to submit FAFSA. *Faculty research:* International and financial economics, law and economics, regulation, public choice economics. *Unit head:* Arthur Denzau, Chair, 909-621-8782, Fax: 909-621-8545, E-mail: arthur.denzau@cgu.edu. *Application contact:* Laura Carillo, Recruiter and Admissions Coordinator, 909-621-8699, Fax: 909-621-7545, E-mail: laura.carillo@cga.edu.

Claremont Graduate University, Graduate Programs, School of Politics and Economics, Department of Politics and Policy, Claremont, CA 91711-6160. Offers American politics (MA, PhD); comparative politics (PhD); international political economy (MA); international studies (MA); political philosophy (PhD); political science (PhD); politics, economics and business (MA); public policy (MA, PhD); world politics (PhD); MBA/PhD. Part-time programs available. *Faculty:* 10 full-time (4 women), 4 part-time/adjunct (0 women). *Students:* 166 full-time (60 women), 19 part-time (6 women); includes 28 minority (4 African Americans, 9 Asian Americans or Pacific Islanders, 15 Hispanic Americans), 40 international. Average age 32. In 2008, 24 master's, 17 doctorates awarded. Terminal master's awarded for partial completion of doctoral program. *Entrance requirements:* For master's and doctorate, GRE General Test. Additional exam requirements/recommendations for international students: Required—TOEFL (minimum score 550 paper-based; 213 computer-based; 80 iBT). *Application deadline:* For fall admission, 2/1 priority date for domestic students. Applications are processed on a rolling basis. Application fee: $60. Electronic applications accepted. *Expenses:* Tuition: Full-time $33,698; part-time $1465 per unit. Required fees: $310; $155 per semester. Tuition and fees vary according to program. *Financial support:* Fellowships, research assistantships, teaching assistantships, Federal Work-Study, institutionally sponsored loans, and scholarships/grants available. Support available to part-time students. Financial award application deadline: 2/15; financial award applicants required to submit FAFSA. *Faculty research:* Environmental policy, international debt, global democratization, Third World development, public sector discrimination. *Unit head:* Jean Schroedel, Chair, 909-621-8696, Fax: 909-621-8545, E-mail: jean.schroedel@cgu.edu. *Application contact:* Laura Carillo, Recruiter and Admissions Coordinator, 909-621-8699, Fax: 909-621-7545, E-mail: laura.carillo@cga.edu.

Clemson University, Graduate School, College of Business and Behavioral Science, Department of Political Science, Clemson, SC 29634. Offers policy studies (PhD); public administration (MPA). Part-time and evening/weekend programs available. *Faculty:* 12 full-time (2 women), 2 part-time/adjunct (0 women). *Students:* 29 full-time (14 women), 21 part-time (9 women); includes 5 minority (3 African Americans, 2 American Indian/Alaska Native), 9 international. Average age 33. 46 applicants, 52% accepted, 14 enrolled. In 2008, 12 master's awarded. *Degree requirements:* For master's, comprehensive exam, internship. *Entrance requirements:* For master's, GRE General Test, MAT. Additional exam requirements/recommendations for international students: Required—TOEFL. *Application deadline:* For fall admission, 7/1 priority date for domestic students; for spring admission, 11/15 for domestic students. Applications are processed on a rolling basis. Application fee: $55. Full-time tuition and fees vary according to program. *Financial support:* In 2008–09, 1 fellowship (averaging $5,000 per year), 18 research assistantships (averaging $15,544 per year), 2 teaching assistantships (averaging $15,892 per year) were awarded; career-related internships or fieldwork also available. Financial award applicants required to submit FAFSA. *Faculty research:* Public policy, total quality management, quantitative methods, public law, public personnel management. *Unit head:* Dr. William Lasser, Interim Chair, 864-656-3233. *Application contact:* Dr. Robert Smith, Coordinator, 864-656-3550, Fax: 864-656-0690, E-mail: rws@clemson.edu.

The College of William and Mary, Faculty of Arts and Sciences, Thomas Jefferson Program in Public Policy, Williamsburg, VA 23187-8795. Offers MPP, JD/MPP, MBA/MPP, MS/MPP. *Degree requirements:* For master's, 49 credits. *Entrance requirements:* For master's, GRE General Test. Additional exam requirements/recommendations for international students: Required—TOEFL (minimum score 600 paper-based). Electronic applications accepted. *Expenses:* Tuition, state resident: full-time $6400; part-time $300 per credit hour. Tuition, nonresident: full-time $19,720; part-time $800 per credit hour. International tuition: $19,720 full-time. Required fees: $3860. *Faculty research:* Social policy, technology policy, international development, health care policy, environmental policy.

Columbia University, School of International and Public Affairs, Program in Public Policy and Administration, New York, NY 10027. Offers MPA, JD/MPA, MPA/MS, MPH/MPA. *Entrance requirements:* For master's, GRE General Test. Additional exam requirements/recommendations for international students: Required—TOEFL (minimum score 600 paper-based; 250 computer-based; 100 iBT). Electronic applications accepted.

Concordia University, School of Graduate Studies, Faculty of Arts and Science, Department of Political Science, Montréal, QC H3G 1M8, Canada. Offers political science (PhD); public policy and public administration (MA), including geography. *Degree requirements:* For master's, one foreign language, comprehensive exam, thesis optional, internship. *Entrance requirements:* For master's, honors degree or equivalent. Additional exam requirements/recommendations for international students: Required—TOEFL. *Faculty research:* International public policy and administration, Quebec public administration, public policy and social/political theory, geography and public policy, public administration and decision making.

Cornell University, Graduate School, Graduate Fields of Arts and Sciences, Field of Government, Ithaca, NY 14853-0001. Offers American politics (PhD); comparative politics (PhD); international relations (PhD); political methodology (PhD); political thought (PhD); public policy (PhD). *Faculty:* 40 full-time (14 women). *Students:* 70 full-time (37 women); includes 11 minority (2 African Americans, 1 American Indian/Alaska Native, 4 Asian Americans or Pacific Islanders, 4 Hispanic Americans), 23 international. Average age 30. 350 applicants, 9% accepted, 15 enrolled. In 2008, 13 doctorates awarded. *Degree requirements:* For doctorate, comprehensive exam, thesis/dissertation. *Entrance requirements:* For doctorate, GRE General Test, sample of written work, 3 letters of recommendation. Additional exam requirements/recommendations for international students: Required—TOEFL (minimum score 550 paper-based; 213 computer-based; 77 iBT). *Application deadline:* For fall admission, 1/15 for domestic students. Application fee: $70. Electronic applications accepted. *Expenses:* Tuition: Full-time $29,500. Required fees: $70. Full-time tuition and fees vary according to degree level, program and student level. *Financial support:* In 2008–09, 60 students received support, including 30 fellowships with full tuition reimbursements available, 2 research assistantships with full tuition reimbursements available, 28 teaching assistantships with full tuition reimbursements available; institutionally sponsored loans, scholarships/grants, health care benefits, tuition waivers (full and partial), and unspecified assistantships also available. Financial award applicants required to submit FAFSA. *Faculty research:* Political theory, American politics, comparative politics, international relations, methodology. *Unit head:* Director of Graduate Studies, 607-255-3567, Fax: 607-255-4530. *Application contact:* Graduate Field Assistant, 607-255-3567, Fax: 607-255-4530, E-mail: cu_govt@cornell.edu.

Cornell University, Graduate School, Graduate Fields of Human Ecology, Field of Policy Analysis and Management, Ithaca, NY 14853-0001. Offers consumer policy (PhD); evaluation (PhD); family and social welfare policy (PhD); health administration (MHA); health management

and policy (PhD). *Faculty:* 31 full-time (13 women). *Students:* 47 full-time (21 women); includes 12 minority (5 African Americans, 6 Asian Americans or Pacific Islanders, 1 Hispanic American), 5 international. Average age 29. 115 applicants, 39% accepted, 16 enrolled. In 2008, 20 master's, 6 doctorates awarded. *Degree requirements:* For master's, thesis; for doctorate, thesis/dissertation. *Entrance requirements:* For master's, GRE General Test or GMAT, 2 letters of recommendation; for doctorate, GRE General Test, 2 letters of recommendation. Additional exam requirements/recommendations for international students: Required—TOEFL (minimum score 550 paper-based; 213 computer-based; 77 iBT). *Application deadline:* For fall admission, 1/15 for domestic students. Application fee: $70. Electronic applications accepted. *Expenses:* Tuition: Full-time $29,500. Required fees: $70. Full-time tuition and fees vary according to degree level, program and student level. *Financial support:* In 2008–09, 17 students received support, including 3 fellowships with full and partial tuition reimbursements available, 5 research assistantships with full and partial tuition reimbursements available, 9 teaching assistantships with full and partial tuition reimbursements available; institutionally sponsored loans, scholarships/grants, health care benefits, tuition waivers (full and partial), and unspecified assistantships also available. Financial award applicants required to submit FAFSA. *Faculty research:* Health policy, family policy, social welfare policy, program evaluation, consumer policy. *Unit head:* Director of Graduate Studies, 607-255-7772. *Application contact:* Graduate Field Assistant, 607-255-7772, Fax: 607-255-4071, E-mail: pam_phd@cornell.edu.

DePaul University, School of Public Service, Chicago, IL 60604. Offers financial administration management (Certificate); health administration (Certificate); health law and policy (MS); international public services (MS); leadership and policy studies (MS); metropolitan planning (Certificate); public administration (MPA); public service management (MS), including association management, fundraising and philanthropy, healthcare administration, higher education administration, metropolitan planning; public services (Certificate); JD/MS. Part-time and evening/weekend programs available. Postbaccalaureate distance learning degree programs offered (minimal on-campus study). *Faculty:* 14 full-time (3 women), 43 part-time/adjunct (24 women). *Students:* 90 full-time (59 women), 204 part-time (154 women); includes 101 minority (63 African Americans, 10 Asian Americans or Pacific Islanders, 28 Hispanic Americans), 11 international. Average age 26. 162 applicants, 100% accepted, 94 enrolled. In 2008, 108 master's awarded. *Degree requirements:* For master's, thesis or integrative seminar. *Entrance requirements:* For master's, minimum GPA of 2.7. Additional exam requirements/recommendations for international students: Required—TOEFL (minimum score 550 paper-based; 213 computer-based; 80 iBT), IELTS (minimum score 6.5). *Application deadline:* Applications are processed on a rolling basis. Application fee: $40. Electronic applications accepted. *Financial support:* In 2008–09, 60 students received support, including 3 research assistantships with full tuition reimbursements available (averaging $7,000 per year); career-related internships or fieldwork, Federal Work-Study, institutionally sponsored loans, scholarships/grants, tuition waivers (partial), and unspecified assistantships also available. Support available to part-time students. Financial award application deadline: 7/1; financial award applicants required to submit FAFSA. *Faculty research:* Government financing, transportation, leadership, health care, volunteerism and organizational behavior, non-profit organizations. Total annual research expenditures: $20,000. *Unit head:* Dr. J. Patrick Murphy, Director, 312-362-5608, Fax: 312-362-5506, E-mail: jpmurphy@depaul.edu. *Application contact:* Megan B. Balderston, Director of Admissions and Marketing, 312-362-5565, Fax: 312-362-5506, E-mail: pubserv@depaul.edu.

Duke University, Graduate School, Terry Sanford Institute of Public Policy, Durham, NC 27708-0243. Offers AM, MPP, PhD, Certificate, JD/AM, JD/MPP, MBA/AM, MBA/MPP, MD/AM, MEM/MPP, MF/MPP. *Entrance requirements:* For master's and doctorate, GRE General Test. Electronic applications accepted.

Duquesne University, Graduate School of Liberal Arts, Graduate Center for Social and Public Policy, Pittsburgh, PA 15282-1750. Offers conflict resolution and peace studies (Certificate); social and public policy (MA, Certificate). Programs are a collaboration between the Departments of Political Science and Sociology. Part-time and evening/weekend programs available. *Faculty:* 15 full-time (3 women), 1 (woman) part-time/adjunct. *Students:* 37 full-time (25 women), 12 part-time (9 women); includes 1 minority (African American), 7 international. Average age 27. 29 applicants, 90% accepted, 18 enrolled. In 2008, 9 master's awarded. *Degree requirements:* For master's, thesis. *Entrance requirements:* For master's, GRE General Test. Additional exam requirements/recommendations for international students: Required—TOEFL. *Application deadline:* For fall admission, 4/30 priority date for domestic and international students; for spring admission, 11/1 priority date for domestic and international students. Applications are processed on a rolling basis. Application fee: $50. Electronic applications accepted. *Expenses:* Tuition: Part-time $819 per credit. Required fees: $78 per credit. Tuition and fees vary according to course load. *Financial support:* In 2008–09, 20 students received support, including 12 research assistantships with full and partial tuition reimbursements available (averaging $9,000 per year), 4 teaching assistantships with full and partial tuition reimbursements available (averaging $9,000 per year); career-related internships or fieldwork, institutionally sponsored loans, scholarships/grants, tuition waivers (full and partial), and unspecified assistantships also available. Support available to part-time students. Financial award application deadline: 5/1. *Faculty research:* Program evaluation, environmental policy, criminal justice policy, health care policy. Total annual research expenditures: $30,000. *Unit head:* Dr. Joseph Yenerall, Director, 412-396-6485, Fax: 412-396-5265, E-mail: socialpolicy@duq.edu. *Application contact:* Linda L. Rendulic, Assistant to the Dean, 412-396-6400, Fax: 412-396-5265, E-mail: rendulic@duq.edu.

Eastern Michigan University, Graduate School, College of Arts and Sciences, Department of Political Science, Program in Public Administration, Ypsilanti, MI 48197. Offers local government management (Graduate Certificate); management of public healthcare services (Graduate Certificate); public administration (MPA, Graduate Certificate); public budget management (Graduate Certificate); public land planning (Graduate Certificate); public management (Graduate Certificate); public personnel management (Graduate Certificate); public policy analysis (Graduate Certificate). *Accreditation:* NASPAA.

Florida State University, Graduate Studies, College of Social Sciences, Reubin O'D. Askew School of Public Administration and Policy, Tallahassee, FL 32306. Offers MPA, PhD, Certificate, JD/MPA, MPA/MSC, MPA/MSP, MPA/MSW. *Accreditation:* NASPAA (one or more programs are accredited). Part-time and evening/weekend programs available. *Degree requirements:* For master's, action report; for doctorate, comprehensive exam, thesis/dissertation. *Entrance requirements:* For master's, GRE General Test, minimum GPA of 3.0; for doctorate, GRE General Test, minimum undergraduate GPA of 3.0, graduate 3.5. Additional exam requirements/recommendations for international students: Required—TOEFL (minimum score 550 paper-based; 213 computer-based; 80 iBT). Electronic applications accepted. *Faculty research:* Financial management, human resource management, policy, strategic management, organizations, nonprofit management.

Frederick S. Pardee RAND Graduate School, Program in Policy Analysis, Santa Monica, CA 90407-2138. Offers PhD. *Degree requirements:* For doctorate, comprehensive exam, thesis/dissertation. *Entrance requirements:* For doctorate, GMAT or GRE General Test. Additional exam requirements/recommendations for international students: Required—TOEFL. Electronic applications accepted. *Faculty research:* Education, defense policy, health, labor and population, justice.

George Mason University, School of Public Policy, Program in Public Policy, Fairfax, VA 22030. Offers MPP, PhD. Part-time programs available. *Degree requirements:* For master's, thesis or alternative; for doctorate, comprehensive exam, thesis/dissertation. *Entrance requirements:* For master's, minimum GPA of 3.0, resumé, 2 letters of recommendation, goals statement; for doctorate, GMAT or GRE General Test, resumé, writing sample, goals statement, master's degree, 2 letters of recommendation. Additional exam requirements/recommendations for international students: Required—TOEFL. Electronic applications accepted. *Expenses:* Contact institution.

See Close-Up on page 1215.

Georgetown University, Graduate School of Arts and Sciences, The Georgetown Public Policy Institute, Washington, DC 20057. Offers MPM, MPP, MBA/MPP, MPP/JD, MPP/MA, MPP/MS, MPP/PhD. *Entrance requirements:* For master's, GRE General Test, minimum B average. Additional exam requirements/recommendations for international students: Required—TOEFL. *Faculty research:* Social policy, government, private sector.

Georgetown University, Graduate School of Arts and Sciences, School of Continuing Studies, Washington, DC 20057. Offers American studies (MALS); Catholic studies (MALS); classical civilizations (MALS); ethics and the professions (MALS); human resources management (MPS); humanities (MALS); individualized study (MALS); international affairs (MALS); Islam and Muslim-Christian relations (MALS); journalism (MPS); liberal studies (DLS); literature and society (MALS); medieval and early modern European studies (MALS); public relations (MPS); real estate (MPS); religious studies (MALS); social and public policy (MALS); sports industry management (MPS); the theory and practice of American democracy (MALS); visual culture (MALS). *Entrance requirements:* Additional exam requirements/recommendations for international students: Required—TOEFL.

The George Washington University, Columbian College of Arts and Sciences, Trachtenberg School of Public Policy and Public Administration, Washington, DC 20052. Offers public administration (MPA), including budget and public finance, federal policy, politics, and management, international development management, managing public organizations, managing state and local governments, nonprofit management, policy analysis and evaluation, public administration, public-private policy and management; public policy (MA, MPP), including environmental and resource policy (MA), philosophy and social policy (MA), women's studies (MA); public policy and administration (PhD); JD/MPP; MPA/JD; PhD/MPP. Part-time and evening/weekend programs available. *Faculty:* 19 full-time (8 women), 12 part-time/adjunct (3 women). *Students:* 82 full-time (57 women), 130 part-time (80 women); includes 28 minority (9 African Americans, 1 American Indian/Alaska Native, 10 Asian Americans or Pacific Islanders, 8 Hispanic Americans), 28 international. Average age 31. 225 applicants, 38% accepted, 31 enrolled. In 2008, 64 master's, 7 doctorates awarded. *Degree requirements:* For doctorate, thesis/dissertation, general exam. *Entrance requirements:* For master's, GRE General Test, minimum GPA of 3.0; for doctorate, GRE General Test, interview, minimum GPA of 3.0. Additional exam requirements/recommendations for international students: Required—TOEFL (minimum score 600 paper-based; 250 computer-based; 100 iBT). *Application deadline:* For fall admission, 1/15 priority date for domestic and international students; for spring admission, 10/1 priority date for domestic students, 9/1 priority date for international students. Applications are processed on a rolling basis. Application fee: $60. Electronic applications accepted. *Financial support:* In 2008–09, 87 students received support; fellowships, teaching assistantships, institutionally sponsored loans and tuition waivers available. Financial award application deadline: 1/15. *Unit head:* Dr. Joseph J. Cordes, Director, 202-994-5826, Fax: 202-994-8913, E-mail: cordes@gwu.edu. *Application contact:* Information Contact, 202-994-8500, Fax: 202-994-8913, E-mail: pubpol@gwu.edu.

The George Washington University, School of Business, Department of Strategic Management and Public Policy, Washington, DC 20052. Offers MBA, PhD. Part-time and evening/weekend programs available. *Faculty:* 14 full-time (3 women), 3 part-time/adjunct (1 woman). *Students:* 195 full-time (85 women), 4 part-time (0 women); includes 29 minority (6 African Americans, 2 American Indian/Alaska Native, 19 Asian Americans or Pacific Islanders, 2 Hispanic Americans), 58 international. Average age 29. 58 applicants, 34% accepted, 12 enrolled. In 2008, 98 master's awarded. *Degree requirements:* For doctorate, thesis/dissertation. *Entrance requirements:* For master's, GMAT; for doctorate, GMAT or GRE. Additional exam requirements/recommendations for international students: Required—TOEFL. *Application deadline:* For fall admission, 4/1 priority date for domestic students; for spring admission, 10/1 for domestic students. Applications are processed on a rolling basis. Application fee: $60. *Financial support:* In 2008–09, 1 student received support; fellowships, teaching assistantships, career-related internships or fieldwork, Federal Work-Study, and institutionally sponsored loans available. Financial award application deadline: 4/1. *Unit head:* Dr. Mark Starik, Chair, 202-994-6677, E-mail: starik@gwu.edu. *Application contact:* Kristin Williams, Asst VP Grad&Spec Enrlmnt Mgmt, 202-994-0467, Fax: 202-994-0371, E-mail: ksw@gwu.edu.

Georgia Institute of Technology, Graduate Studies and Research, Ivan Allen College of Policy and International Affairs, School of Public Policy, Atlanta, GA 30332-0001. Offers MS Pub P, PhD. Part-time programs available. *Degree requirements:* For master's, professional paper or thesis. *Entrance requirements:* Additional exam requirements/recommendations for international students: Required—TOEFL. Electronic applications accepted. *Faculty research:* National/regional science and technology policy, environmental policy, urban policy and planning, telecommunications policy.

Georgia State University, Andrew Young School of Policy Studies, Department of Public Administration and Urban Studies, Program in Public Policy, Atlanta, GA 30303-3083. Offers PhD. Part-time programs available. *Degree requirements:* For doctorate, comprehensive exam, thesis/dissertation. *Entrance requirements:* For doctorate, GRE General Test. Additional exam requirements/recommendations for international students: Required—TOEFL. *Faculty research:* Environmental policy, health policy, policy design analysis and evaluation, public and nonprofit management, urban and regional economic development.

Graduate School and University Center of the City University of New York, Graduate Studies, Interdisciplinary Studies, New York, NY 10016-4039. Offers language in social context (PhD); medieval studies (PhD); public policy (MA, PhD); urban studies (MA, PhD); women's studies (MA, PhD). Terminal master's awarded for partial completion of doctoral program. *Degree requirements:* For master's, thesis; for doctorate, comprehensive exam, thesis/dissertation. *Entrance requirements:* For master's and doctorate, GRE General Test.

Harvard University, Graduate School of Arts and Sciences and John F. Kennedy School of Government, Committee on Public Policy, Cambridge, MA 02138. Offers PhD. *Degree requirements:* For doctorate, thesis/dissertation, exams. *Entrance requirements:* For doctorate, GRE General Test or GMAT, Harvard MPP degree. Additional exam requirements/recommendations for international students: Required—TOEFL. *Expenses:* Tuition: Full-time $32,556. Required fees: $1426. Full-time tuition and fees vary according to program and student level.

Harvard University, Graduate School of Arts and Sciences, Program in Social Policy, Cambridge, MA 02138. Offers PhD. *Expenses:* Tuition: Full-time $32,556. Required fees: $1426. Full-time tuition and fees vary according to program and student level.

Harvard University, John F. Kennedy School of Government, Doctoral Programs in Government, Cambridge, MA 02138. Offers political economy and government (PhD); public policy (PhD). *Students:* 7 full-time (4 women), 5 international. Average age 26. 198 applicants, 7% accepted, 7 enrolled. *Degree requirements:* For doctorate, comprehensive exam, thesis/dissertation. *Entrance requirements:* For doctorate, GRE General Test, course work in macroeconomics, multi-variable calculus. Additional exam requirements/recommendations for international students: Required—TOEFL (minimum score 600 paper-based; 250 computer-based; 100 iBT), TWE. *Application deadline:* For fall admission, 12/14 for domestic students. Application fee: $80. Electronic applications accepted. *Expenses:* Tuition: Full-time $32,556. Required fees: $1426. Full-time tuition and fees vary according to program and student level. *Financial support:* Fellowships, research assistantships, teaching assistantships, Federal Work-Study, institutionally sponsored loans, scholarships/grants, health care benefits, and unspecified assistantships available. *Unit head:* Louisa Van Baalen, Director, 617-495-1190, E-mail: louisa_van_baalen@harvard.edu. *Application contact:* Louisa Van Baalen, Director, 617-495-1190, E-mail: louisa_van_baalen@harvard.edu.

Harvard University, John F. Kennedy School of Government, Program in Public Policy, Cambridge, MA 02138. Offers public policy (MPP); public policy and urban planning (MPPUP); JD/MPP; MBA/MPP; MD/MPP. *Accreditation:* NASPAA. *Students:* 244 full-time (119 women); includes 73 minority (18 African Americans, 6 American Indian/Alaska Native, 27 Asian Americans or Pacific Islanders, 22 Hispanic Americans), 57 international. Average age 25. 1,293 applicants, 30% accepted, 244 enrolled. *Entrance requirements:* For master's, GMAT or GRE General Test. Additional exam requirements/recommendations for international students: Required—TOEFL (minimum score 600 paper-based; 250 computer-based; 100 iBT), TWE. *Application deadline:* For fall admission, 1/5 for domestic students. Application fee: $80. Electronic applications accepted. *Expenses:* Tuition: Full-time $32,556. Required fees: $1426. Full-time tuition and fees vary according to program and student level. *Financial support:* Fellowships, research assistantships, teaching assistantships, career-related internships or fieldwork, Federal Work-Study, institutionally sponsored loans, scholarships/grants, health care benefits, and unspecified assistantships available. Financial award application deadline: 2/2; financial award applicants required to submit CSS PROFILE or FAFSA. *Unit head:* Debra Isaacson, Director, 617-496-8382, E-mail: debra_isaacson@harvard.edu. *Application contact:* 617-495-1155.

Indiana University Bloomington, Kelley School of Business, Department of Business Economics and Public Policy, Bloomington, IN 47405-7000. Offers PhD. *Faculty:* 8 full-time (1 woman), 1 part-time/adjunct (0 women). *Students:* 20 applicants, 10% accepted, 2 enrolled. In 2008, 2 doctorates awarded. *Degree requirements:* For doctorate, comprehensive exam, thesis/dissertation. *Entrance requirements:* For doctorate, GRE or GMAT, bachelor's degree. Additional exam requirements/recommendations for international students: Required—TOEFL (minimum score 630 paper-based; 267 computer-based; 80 iBT). *Expenses:* Tuition, area resident: Part-time $291.97 per credit hour. Tuition, state resident: part-time $291.97 per credit hour. Tuition, nonresident: part-time $850.33 per credit hour. Required fees: $110 per semester. Tuition and fees vary according to course load and program. *Financial support:* Fellowships with full tuition reimbursements available. *Faculty research:* Industrial organization, pricing, environmental regulation and policy, information economics, economics of law and organization. *Unit head:* Dr. John W. Maxwell, Professor of Business Economics and Public Policy, 812-855-9219, Fax: 812-855-3354, E-mail: jwmax@indiana.edu. *Application contact:* Dr. Michael R. Baye, Bert Elwert Professor of Business Economics, 812-855-9219, Fax: 812-855-3354, E-mail: mbaye@indiana.edu.

Indiana University Bloomington, School of Public and Environmental Affairs, Public Affairs Programs, Bloomington, IN 47405-7000. Offers nonprofit management (Certificate); public affairs (MPA, PhD); public management (Certificate); public policy (PhD); JD/MPA; MPA/MA; MPA/MIS; MPA/MLS; MSES/MPA. *Accreditation:* NASPAA (one or more programs are accredited). Part-time programs available. *Students:* 364 full-time (191 women), 40 part-time (23 women); includes 39 minority (13 African Americans, 2 American Indian/Alaska Native, 10 Asian Americans or Pacific Islanders, 14 Hispanic Americans), 84 international. Average age 28. 724 applicants, 75% accepted, 249 enrolled. In 2008, 229 master's, 13 doctorates, 2 other advanced degrees awarded. Terminal master's awarded for partial completion of doctoral program. *Degree requirements:* For doctorate, thesis/dissertation. *Entrance requirements:* For master's, GMAT or GRE, LSAT; for doctorate, GRE General Test. *Application deadline:* For fall admission, 2/1 priority date for domestic students, 1/15 for international students; for spring admission, 9/1 for international students. Applications are processed on a rolling basis. Application fee: $50 ($60 for international students). *Expenses:* Tuition, area resident: Part-time $291.97 per credit hour. Tuition, state resident: part-time $291.97 per credit hour. Tuition, nonresident: part-time $850.33 per credit hour. Required fees: $110 per semester. Tuition and fees vary according to course load and program. *Financial support:* Fellowships, research assistantships, teaching assistantships, career-related internships or fieldwork, Federal Work-Study, institutionally sponsored loans, and unspecified assistantships available. Financial award application deadline: 2/1; financial award applicants required to submit FAFSA. *Faculty research:* Comparative and international affairs, environmental policy and resource management, policy analysis, public finance, public management, urban management, nonprofit management. *Unit head:* Charles Kurt Zorn, Interim Dean, 812-855-5058, Fax: 812-855-6234, E-mail: zorn@indiana.edu. *Application contact:* Charles A. Johnson, Coordinator of Student Recruitment, 800-765-7755, Fax: 812-855-7802, E-mail: speainfo@indiana.edu.

See Close-Up on page 1219.

Indiana University–Purdue University Indianapolis, School of Public and Environmental Affairs, Indianapolis, IN 46202-2896. Offers health administration (MHA); public affairs (MPA), including criminal justice, environmental management, nonprofit management, policy analysis, public management; JD/MHA; MBA/MHA; MLS/NMC; MLS/PMC; MSN/MHA. *Accreditation:* CAHME (one or more programs are accredited). Part-time and evening/weekend programs available. *Entrance requirements:* For master's, GRE General Test, minimum GPA of 3.0 (preferred). Additional exam requirements/recommendations for international students: Required—TOEFL. *Faculty research:* Economic development, water and air quality, ethics, financing, organization design and structure.

See Close-Up on page 1221.

The Institute of World Politics, Graduate Programs in National Security, Intelligence, and International Affairs, Washington, DC 20036. Offers American foreign policy (Certificate); comparative political culture (Certificate); counterintelligence (Certificate); democracy building (Certificate); intelligence (Certificate); international politics (Certificate); national security affairs (Certificate); public diplomacy and political warfare (Certificate); statecraft and national security affairs (MA); statecraft and world politics (MA); strategic intelligence studies (MA). Part-time and evening/weekend programs available. *Degree requirements:* For master's, comprehensive exam, thesis optional. *Entrance requirements:* For master's, GRE General Test. Additional exam requirements/recommendations for international students: Required—TOEFL. Electronic applications accepted. *Faculty research:* Intelligence, national security, statecraft.

See Close-Up on page 867.

Jackson State University, Graduate School, School of Liberal Arts, Department of Public Policy and Administration, Jackson, MS 39217. Offers MPPA, PhD. *Accreditation:* NASPAA (one or more programs are accredited). Evening/weekend programs available. *Degree requirements:* For master's, comprehensive exam, thesis optional; for doctorate, comprehensive exam, thesis/dissertation. *Entrance requirements:* For master's, GRE General Test; for doctorate, GRE, GMAT, MAT. Additional exam requirements/recommendations for international students: Required—TOEFL.

John Jay College of Criminal Justice of the City University of New York, Graduate Studies, Programs in Criminal Justice, New York, NY 10019-1093. Offers criminal justice (MA, PhD); criminology and deviance (PhD); forensic psychology (PhD); forensic science (PhD); law and philosophy (PhD); organizational behavior (PhD); public policy (PhD). Part-time and evening/weekend programs available. Terminal master's awarded for partial completion of doctoral program. *Degree requirements:* For master's, thesis or alternative; for doctorate, one foreign language, thesis/dissertation. *Entrance requirements:* For master's, GRE General Test, minimum B average; for doctorate, GRE General Test. Additional exam requirements/recommendations for international students: Required—TOEFL (minimum score 500 paper-based; 173 computer-based).

The Johns Hopkins University, Zanvyl Krieger School of Arts and Sciences, Institute for Public Policy, Baltimore, MD 21218-2699. Offers MA. *Degree requirements:* For master's, thesis optional, summer internship. *Entrance requirements:* For master's, GRE General Test. Additional exam requirements/recommendations for international students: Required—TOEFL (minimum score 600 paper-based; 250 computer-based). Electronic applications accepted. *Faculty research:* Housing, criminal justice, human capital investment, nonprofit sector, public finance and infrastructure.

See Close-Up on page 1223.

Kent State University, College of Arts and Sciences, Department of Political Science, Kent, OH 44242-0001. Offers political science (MA); public administration (MPA); public policy (PhD). Part-time programs available. Postbaccalaureate distance learning degree programs

Public Policy

Kent State University (continued)
offered. *Degree requirements:* For master's, thesis optional; for doctorate, 2 foreign languages; thesis/dissertation. *Entrance requirements:* For master's, GRE General Test, minimum GPA of 2.75; for doctorate, GRE General Test, minimum GPA of 3.0. Additional exam requirements/recommendations for international students: Required—TOEFL. Electronic applications accepted.

Lincoln University, School of Graduate Studies and Continuing Education, College of Business and Professional Studies, Department of Business and Economics, Jefferson City, MO 65102. Offers business administration (MBA), including accounting, entrepreneurship, management, public administration and policy. *Accreditation:* ACBSP. Part-time and evening/weekend programs available. *Faculty:* 7 full-time (1 woman), 1 part-time/adjunct (0 women). *Students:* 20 full-time (11 women), 13 part-time (8 women); includes 10 minority (all African Americans), 6 international. Average age 31. 12 applicants, 100% accepted, 6 enrolled. In 2008, 19 master's awarded. *Degree requirements:* For master's, comprehensive exam, thesis optional, portfolio. *Entrance requirements:* For master's, GMAT, undergraduate prerequisite courses. Additional exam requirements/recommendations for international students: Required—TOEFL (minimum score 500 paper-based; 173 computer-based; 61 iBT). *Application deadline:* For fall admission, 7/1 priority date for domestic and international students; for spring admission, 12/1 priority date for domestic and international students. Applications are processed on a rolling basis. Application fee: $20. *Expenses:* Tuition, area resident: Full-time $4185; part-time $232.50 per credit hour. Tuition, nonresident: Full-time $7767; part-time $431.50 per credit hour. Required fees: $270; $15 per credit hour. $252.50 per semester. One-time fee: $20. Tuition and fees vary according to course load. *Financial support:* Federal Work-Study and scholarships/grants available. Financial award application deadline: 4/1; financial award applicants required to submit FAFSA. *Unit head:* Dr. Roberto Ike, Department Head, 573-681-6076, Fax: 573-681-6085, E-mail: iker@lincolnu.edu. *Application contact:* Irasema Steck, Administrative Assistant, 573-681-5247, Fax: 573-681-5106, E-mail: gradschool@lincolnu.edu.

Loyola University Chicago, Graduate School, Department of Political Science, Chicago, IL 60611-2196. Offers political science (MA, PhD); public policy (MPP); JD/MA. Part-time and evening/weekend programs available. *Faculty:* 18 full-time (2 women), 1 (woman) part-time/adjunct. *Students:* 27 full-time (13 women), 6 part-time (1 woman); includes 1 minority (African American), 3 international. Average age 29. 88 applicants, 50% accepted, 14 enrolled. In 2008, 11 master's, 2 doctorates awarded. *Degree requirements:* For master's, thesis or alternative; for doctorate, variable foreign language requirement, comprehensive exam, thesis/dissertation. *Entrance requirements:* For master's and doctorate, GRE General Test. *Application deadline:* For fall admission, 6/1 for domestic students; for spring admission, 10/1 for domestic students. Applications are processed on a rolling basis. Application fee: $50. Electronic applications accepted. *Expenses:* Tuition: Full-time $13,500; part-time $750 per credit hour. Required fees: $60 per semester. Full-time tuition and fees vary according to program. *Financial support:* In 2008–09, 5 fellowships with full tuition reimbursements (averaging $14,000 per year), 5 research assistantships with full tuition reimbursements (averaging $14,000 per year) were awarded; Federal Work-Study, institutionally sponsored loans, scholarships/grants, tuition waivers (partial), and unspecified assistantships also available. Financial award application deadline: 2/15; financial award applicants required to submit FAFSA. *Faculty research:* American parties and elections, state and local politics, American political institutions, international political economy, modern and contemporary political thought. *Unit head:* Prof. Peter M. Sanchez, Chair, 773-508-8658, Fax: 773-508-3131, E-mail: psanche@luc.edu. *Application contact:* Prof. Peter M. Sanchez, Chair, 773-508-8658, Fax: 773-508-3131, E-mail: psanche@luc.edu.

McMaster University, School of Graduate Studies, Faculty of Social Sciences, Department of Political Science, Hamilton, ON L8S 4M2, Canada. Offers international relations (PhD); political science (MA); public and the global economy (MA); public policy (PhD); public policy and administration (MA). Part-time programs available. *Degree requirements:* For master's, thesis or alternative. *Entrance requirements:* For master's, minimum B+ average. Additional exam requirements/recommendations for international students: Required—TOEFL (minimum score 580 paper-based; 237 computer-based). *Faculty research:* Organizational theory, internationalization of public policy, water resource policies, political interest intermediation, comparative politics.

Mills College, Graduate Studies, Program in Public Policy, Oakland, CA 94613-1000. Offers MPP. *Faculty:* 2 full-time (1 woman), 1 part-time/adjunct (0 women). *Students:* 11 full-time (all women); includes 3 minority (1 African American, 1 American Indian/Alaska Native, 1 Asian American or Pacific Islander). Average age 32. 23 applicants, 87% accepted, 11 enrolled. In 2008, 7 master's awarded. *Degree requirements:* For master's, thesis. *Application deadline:* For fall admission, 2/1 priority date for domestic and international students. Application fee: $50. *Expenses:* Tuition: Full-time $25,072; part-time $6272 per course. Required fees: $880. *Financial support:* In 2008–09, 15 students received support, including 15 fellowships (averaging $6,067 per year); scholarships/grants also available. Financial award applicants required to submit FAFSA. *Unit head:* Carol Chetkovich, Director, 510-430-3370, E-mail: cchetkov@mills.edu. *Application contact:* Marika Benko, Graduate Admission Specialist, 510-430-3309, Fax: 510-430-2159, E-mail: grad-studies@mills.edu.

Mississippi State University, College of Arts and Sciences, Department of Political Science and Public Administration, Mississippi State, MS 39762. Offers political science (MA); public policy and administration (MPPA, PhD). *Accreditation:* NASPAA (one or more programs are accredited). Evening/weekend programs available. *Degree requirements:* For master's, comprehensive oral or written exam; for doctorate, thesis/dissertation, comprehensive oral and written exam. *Entrance requirements:* For master's, minimum GPA of 3.0; for doctorate, GRE General Test, minimum graduate GPA of 3.35. Additional exam requirements/recommendations for international students: Required—TOEFL. *Faculty research:* American politics, international relations, state and local government, comparative government, public administration.

Monmouth University, Graduate School, Department of Public Policy, West Long Branch, NJ 07764-1898. Offers MA. *Faculty:* 6 full-time (3 women), 1 part-time/adjunct (0 women). *Students:* 10 full-time (7 women), 26 part-time (14 women); includes 5 minority (1 American Indian/Alaska Native, 1 Asian American or Pacific Islander, 3 Hispanic Americans). Average age 29. 20 applicants, 100% accepted, 9 enrolled. In 2008, 6 master's awarded. *Degree requirements:* For master's, 30 credits. *Entrance requirements:* For master's, minimum overall GPA of 2.75. Additional exam requirements/recommendations for international students: Required—TOEFL (minimum score 550 paper-based; 213 computer-based; 79 iBT), IELTS (minimum score 5), Michigan English Language Assessment Battery (minimum score: 77), Cambridge A, B, C. *Application deadline:* For fall admission, 7/15 for domestic students, 6/1 for international students; for spring admission, 11/15 for domestic students, 11/1 for international students. Application fee: $50. *Expenses:* Tuition: Full-time $13,914; part-time $773 per credit. Required fees: $628; $157 per semester. *Financial support:* In 2008–09, 24 students received support, including 24 fellowships (averaging $1,628 per year), 2 research assistantships (averaging $5,778 per year); career-related internships or fieldwork, scholarships/grants, tuition waivers (partial), and unspecified assistantships also available. Support available to part-time students. *Faculty research:* Political theory, international relations and comparative politics, globalization, politics of language, family sociology, race-class-gender studies, U.S. Senate and impact of domestic politics on U.S. foreign policy. *Unit head:* Dr. Joseph Patten, Program Director, 732-263-5742, E-mail: jpatten@monmouth.edu. *Application contact:* Kevin Roane, Director, Office of Graduate Admission, 732-571-3452, Fax: 732-263-5123, E-mail: gradadm@monmouth.edu.

National University of Singapore, Lee Kuan Yew School of Public Policy, Singapore, Singapore. Offers MPA, MPM, MPP, PhD.

New England College, Program in Public Policy, Henniker, NH 03242-3293. Offers MA. Part-time and evening/weekend programs available. Postbaccalaureate distance learning degree programs offered (no on-campus study). *Degree requirements:* For master's, thesis. *Entrance*

requirements: Additional exam requirements/recommendations for international students: Recommended—TOEFL (minimum score 600 paper-based). Electronic applications accepted.

The New School: A University, Milano The New School for Management and Urban Policy, Program in Public and Urban Policy, New York, NY 10011. Offers PhD. Part-time and evening/weekend programs available. *Faculty:* 1 full-time (0 women), 2 part-time/adjunct (1 woman). *Students:* 34 full-time (20 women), 16 part-time (9 women); includes 17 minority (10 African Americans, 2 American Indian/Alaska Native, 4 Asian Americans or Pacific Islanders, 1 Hispanic American), 11 international. Average age 41. In 2008, 3 doctorates awarded. *Degree requirements:* For doctorate, thesis/dissertation, qualifying exams. *Entrance requirements:* For doctorate, GRE General Test, MA in political science, urban policy or public policy. Additional exam requirements/recommendations for international students: Required—TOEFL (minimum score 600 paper-based; 250 computer-based; 100 iBT). *Application deadline:* For fall admission, 4/15 priority date for domestic students. Applications are processed on a rolling basis. Application fee: $50. *Expenses:* Tuition: Full-time $27,144; part-time $1508 per credit. Required fees: $355 per semester. *Financial support:* Fellowships, research assistantships, Federal Work-Study, scholarships/grants, and tuition waivers (full and partial) available. Support available to part-time students. Financial award application deadline: 3/1; financial award applicants required to submit FAFSA. *Unit head:* Dr. Howard Berliner, Director, 212-229-5400 Ext. 1616, Fax: 212-229-5904, E-mail: berliner@newschool.edu. *Application contact:* Merida Escandon, Director of Admissions, 212-229-5462 Ext. 1108, Fax: 212-229-5354, E-mail: milanoadmissions@newschool.edu.

See Close-Up on page 1225.

Northeastern University, College of Arts and Sciences, Program in Law, Policy, and Society, Boston, MA 02115-5096. Offers MS, PhD; JD/PhD. Part-time and evening/weekend programs available. *Degree requirements:* For master's, comprehensive exam; for doctorate, comprehensive exam, thesis/dissertation. *Entrance requirements:* For master's, GRE General Test; for doctorate, GRE General Test or LSAT. *Faculty research:* Policy issues in health, crime, and labor; urban studies; education; law and environmental issues; economic development, international trade and law.

Northwestern University, The Graduate School, School of Education and Social Policy, Program in Human Development and Social Policy, Evanston, IL 60208. Offers PhD. Admissions and degrees offered through The Graduate School. *Degree requirements:* For doctorate, comprehensive exam, thesis/dissertation. *Entrance requirements:* For doctorate, GRE General Test, writing sample. Additional exam requirements/recommendations for international students: Required—TOEFL (minimum score 600 paper-based; 250 computer-based; 100 iBT). Electronic applications accepted. *Faculty research:* Social context of development; social policy issues affecting children, adolescents, adults, and families.

See Close-Up on page 1231.

Pepperdine University, School of Public Policy, Malibu, CA 90263. Offers American politics (MPP); economics (MPP); international relations (MPP); public policy (MPP); state and local policy (MPP). *Entrance requirements:* For master's, GRE, 2 letters of recommendation, resumé. Additional exam requirements/recommendations for international students: Required—TOEFL. Electronic applications accepted.

Princeton University, Graduate School, Woodrow Wilson School of Public and International Affairs, Princeton, NJ 08544-1019. Offers public affairs (MPA, PhD); public policy (MPP); JD/MPA. Terminal master's awarded for partial completion of doctoral program. *Degree requirements:* For master's, internship; for doctorate, one foreign language, thesis/dissertation. *Entrance requirements:* For master's, GRE General Test, original policy memo; for doctorate, GRE General Test. Additional exam requirements/recommendations for international students: Required—TOEFL (minimum score 600 paper-based; 250 computer-based). Electronic applications accepted.

Queen's University at Kingston, School of Graduate Studies and Research, School of Policy Studies, Kingston, ON K7L 3N6, Canada. Offers MIR, MPA. Part-time programs available. *Entrance requirements:* For master's, minimum B+ average. Additional exam requirements/recommendations for international students: Required—TOEFL. *Faculty research:* Public management, social policy, defense management, health policy, the third sector.

Regent University, Graduate School, Robertson School of Government, Virginia Beach, VA 23464. Offers health care policy and administration (MA); international politics (MA); law and public policy (MA); Mid-East Politics (MA); political leadership and management (MA); political management (MA); public administration (MA); public policy (MA); terrorism and homeland defense (MA); world economies and political development (MA); JD/MA; M Div/MA; M Ed/MA; MBA/MA. Part-time and evening/weekend programs available. Postbaccalaureate distance learning degree programs offered (minimal on-campus study). *Faculty:* 6 full-time (1 woman), 11 part-time/adjunct (1 woman). *Students:* 60 full-time (33 women), 69 part-time (34 women); includes 29 minority (22 African Americans, 1 Asian American or Pacific Islander, 6 Hispanic Americans), 3 international. Average age 30. 136 applicants, 54% accepted, 54 enrolled. In 2008, 48 master's awarded. *Degree requirements:* For master's, thesis optional, internship. *Entrance requirements:* For master's, GRE General Test or LSAT, minimum undergraduate GPA of 3.0, writing sample, resumé, interview, references, transcripts. Additional exam requirements/recommendations for international students: Required—TOEFL (minimum score 577 paper-based; 233 computer-based). *Application deadline:* For fall admission, 5/1 priority date for domestic students; for spring admission, 11/1 priority date for domestic students. Applications are processed on a rolling basis. Application fee: $50. Electronic applications accepted. *Expenses:* Contact institution. *Financial support:* Career-related internships or fieldwork, scholarships/grants, tuition waivers (full and partial), and unspecified assistantships available. Support available to part-time students. Financial award application deadline: 9/1; financial award applicants required to submit FAFSA. *Faculty research:* Education reform, political character issues, social capital concerns, administrative ethics, Biblical law and public policy. *Unit head:* Dr. Charles W. Dunn, Dean, 757-352-4322, Fax: 757-352-4643, E-mail: cwdunn@regent.edu. *Application contact:* Matthew Chadwick, Director of Admissions, 800-373-5504, Fax: 757-352-4381, E-mail: admissions@regent.edu.

Regis College, Program in Public Administration, Weston, MA 02493. Offers nonprofit administration (Graduate Certificate); public administration (MPA); public policymaking (Graduate Certificate). Part-time programs available. Postbaccalaureate distance learning degree programs offered. *Faculty:* 1 (woman) full-time, 2 part-time/adjunct (both women). *Students:* 5 part-time (4 women); includes 1 minority (Hispanic American). Average age 31. 5 applicants, 100% accepted, 5 enrolled. *Degree requirements:* For master's, thesis. *Entrance requirements:* For master's, GRE or MAT. Additional exam requirements/recommendations for international students: Required—TOEFL (minimum score 550 paper-based; 213 computer-based). *Application fee:* $50. *Expenses:* Tuition: Part-time $676 per credit. *Unit head:* Claudia Pouravelis, Director of Graduate Admission, 781-768-7058, E-mail: claudia.pouravelis@regiscollege.edu. *Application contact:* Christine Petherick, Administrative Coordinator, Graduate Admission, 866-438-7344, Fax: 781-768-7071, E-mail: christine.petherick@regiscollege.edu.

Rochester Institute of Technology, Graduate Enrollment Services, College of Liberal Arts, Department of Public Policy, Rochester, NY 14623-5603. Offers MS. *Degree requirements:* For master's, thesis. *Entrance requirements:* For master's, GRE General Test, minimum GPA of 3.0. Additional exam requirements/recommendations for international students: Required—TOEFL (minimum score 570 paper-based; 230 computer-based; 88 iBT). Electronic applications accepted.

Rutgers, The State University of New Jersey, Camden, Graduate School of Arts and Sciences, Department of Public Policy and Administration, Camden, NJ 08102-1401. Offers education policy and leadership (MPA); international public service and development (MPA); public management (MPA); JD/MPA; MPA/MA. *Accreditation:* NASPAA. Part-time and evening/

weekend programs available. *Degree requirements:* For master's, directed study, research workshop. *Entrance requirements:* For master's, GRE General Test, GMAT or LSAT, 3 letters of recommendation; resumé; statement of personal, professional, and academic goals. Additional exam requirements/recommendations for international students: Required—TOEFL (minimum score 550 paper-based; 213 computer-based), IELTS. Electronic applications accepted. *Faculty research:* Nonprofit management, county and municipal administration, health and human services, government communication, administrative law, educational finance.

Rutgers, The State University of New Jersey, Newark, Graduate School, Program in Public Administration, Newark, NJ 07102. Offers health care administration (MPA); human resources administration (MPA); public administration (PhD); public management (MPA); public policy analysis (MPA); urban systems and issues (MPA). *Accreditation:* NASPAA (one or more programs are accredited). Part-time and evening/weekend programs available. *Degree requirements:* For master's, comprehensive exam, thesis or alternative; for doctorate, thesis/dissertation. *Entrance requirements:* For master's, GRE, minimum undergraduate B average; for doctorate, GRE, MPA, minimum B average. Electronic applications accepted. *Faculty research:* Government finance, municipal and state government, public productivity.

Rutgers, The State University of New Jersey, New Brunswick, Edward J. Bloustein School of Planning and Public Policy, Program in Planning and Public Policy, Piscataway, NJ 08854-8097. Offers PhD. Part-time programs available. *Degree requirements:* For doctorate, comprehensive exam, thesis/dissertation. *Entrance requirements:* For doctorate, GRE, master's degree. Additional exam requirements/recommendations for international students: Required—TOEFL (minimum score 575 paper-based; 245 computer-based). Electronic applications accepted. *Faculty research:* Housing and community development, land use and transportation, politics and policy analysis, urban and regional economics, international development.

Rutgers, The State University of New Jersey, New Brunswick, Edward J. Bloustein School of Planning and Public Policy, Program in Public Policy, Piscataway, NJ 08854-8097. Offers MPAP, MPP, JD/MPAP, MBA/MPAP, MCRP/MPP. Part-time and evening/weekend programs available. *Entrance requirements:* For master's, GRE General Test or LSAT. Electronic applications accepted. *Faculty research:* Public finance, legislative process, public opinion, economics and public policy, campaigning.

Saint Louis University, Graduate School, College of Education and Public Service and Graduate School, Department of Public Policy Studies, St. Louis, MO 63103-2097. Offers geographic information systems (Certificate); organizational development (Certificate); public administration (MAPA); public policy analysis (PhD); urban affairs (MAUA); urban planning and real estate development (MUPRED). *Accreditation:* NASPAA. Part-time programs available. *Degree requirements:* For master's, comprehensive exam (for some programs), thesis (for some programs); for doctorate, comprehensive exam, thesis/dissertation, preliminary exams. *Entrance requirements:* For master's and doctorate, GMAT, GRE General Test, or LSAT, letters of recommendation, resumé, interview, transcripts, goal statement. Additional exam requirements/recommendations for international students: Required—TOEFL (minimum score 525 paper-based; 194 computer-based). Electronic applications accepted. *Faculty research:* Urban politics, brown fields, e-government, and administration, evaluation research, community development, electronic government and governance.

San Francisco State University, Division of Graduate Studies, College of Behavioral and Social Sciences, Public Administration Program, San Francisco, CA 94132-1722. Offers integrated and collaborative services (MPA); nonprofit administration (MPA); policy analysis (MPA); public management (MPA); urban administration (MPA). *Accreditation:* NASPAA.

Seton Hall University, College of Arts and Sciences, Department of Public and Healthcare Administration, Program in Public Service: Leadership, Governance, and Policy, South Orange, NJ 07079-2697. Offers MPA. *Accreditation:* NASPAA. Part-time and evening/weekend programs available. *Degree requirements:* For master's, research project. *Entrance requirements:* For master's, GMAT, GRE General Test, or LSAT.

See Close-Up on page 1235.

Simon Fraser University, Graduate Studies, Faculty of Arts and Social Sciences, Public Policy Program, Burnaby, BC V5A 1S6, Canada. Offers MPP. *Degree requirements:* For master's, internship. *Entrance requirements:* For master's, GRE, 3 letters of reference, resumé, minimum undergraduate GPA of 3.0. Additional exam requirements/recommendations for international students: Required—TOEFL (minimum score 570 paper-based; 230 computer-based), TWE (minimum score 5). Electronic applications accepted.

Southern New Hampshire University, School of Community Economic Development, Manchester, NH 03106-1045. Offers MA, MBA, MS, PhD. Part-time and evening/weekend programs available. *Degree requirements:* For master's, thesis or alternative, community project; for doctorate, comprehensive exam, thesis/dissertation, community project. *Entrance requirements:* For master's, 2 years of work experience, minimum GPA of 3.0, 2 letters of recommendation, application, fees, review; for doctorate, 2 years of work experience, minimum GPA of 3.5, 3 letters of recommendation, research samples. Additional exam requirements/recommendations for international students: Required—TOEFL (minimum score 550 paper-based; 300 computer-based; 70 iBT). Electronic applications accepted. *Expenses:* Contact institution.

Southern University and Agricultural and Mechanical College, Graduate School, Nelson Mandela School of Public Policy and Urban Affairs, Program in Public Policy, Baton Rouge, LA 70813. Offers PhD. *Degree requirements:* For doctorate, comprehensive exam, thesis/dissertation. *Entrance requirements:* For doctorate, GRE General Test. Additional exam requirements/recommendations for international students: Required—TOEFL (minimum score 525 paper-based; 193 computer-based).

State University of New York at Binghamton, Graduate School, School of Arts and Sciences, Department of Political Science, Binghamton, NY 13902-6000. Offers political science (MA, PhD); public policy (MA, PhD). *Faculty:* 11 full-time (2 women), 1 part-time/adjunct (0 women). *Students:* 33 full-time (15 women), 12 part-time (5 women); includes 3 minority (all African Americans), 19 international. Average age 27. 67 applicants, 52% accepted, 10 enrolled. In 2008, 18 master's, 1 doctorate awarded. Terminal master's awarded for partial completion of doctoral program. *Degree requirements:* For master's, thesis or alternative, written exam; for doctorate, 2 foreign languages, thesis/dissertation, written exam. *Entrance requirements:* For master's and doctorate, GRE General Test, GRE Subject Test. Additional exam requirements/recommendations for international students: Required—TOEFL. *Application deadline:* For fall admission, 4/15 priority date for domestic students, 1/15 priority date for international students; for spring admission, 11/1 for domestic students, 10/1 priority date for international students. Applications are processed on a rolling basis. Application fee: $60. Electronic applications accepted. *Expenses:* Tuition, area resident: Full-time $6900; part-time $288 per credit. Tuition, state resident: full-time $6900; part-time $288 per credit. Tuition, nonresident: full-time $10,920; part-time $455 per credit. Required fees: $1130. Part-time tuition and fees vary according to course load, program and student level. *Financial support:* In 2008–09, 27 students received support, including 1 fellowship with full tuition reimbursement available (averaging $15,000 per year), 4 research assistantships with full tuition reimbursements available (averaging $15,000 per year), 21 teaching assistantships with full tuition reimbursements available (averaging $15,000 per year); career-related internships or fieldwork, Federal Work-Study, institutionally sponsored loans, scholarships/grants, health care benefits, tuition waivers (full), and unspecified assistantships also available. Financial award application deadline: 2/15; financial award applicants required to submit FAFSA. *Unit head:* Dr. David Clark, Chairperson, 607-777-6786, E-mail: dclark@binghamton.edu. *Application contact:* Victoria Williams, Recruiting and Admissions Coordinator, 607-777-2151, Fax: 607-777-2501, E-mail: vwilliam@binghamton.edu.

State University of New York Empire State College, Graduate Studies, Program in Business and Policy Studies, Saratoga Springs, NY 12866-4391. Offers MA. Part-time and evening/weekend programs available. Postbaccalaureate distance learning degree programs offered (minimal on-campus study). *Degree requirements:* For master's, thesis, exam. *Entrance requirements:* For master's, proficiency in statistics. Additional exam requirements/recommendations for international students: Required—TOEFL (minimum score 600 paper-based; 280 computer-based). Electronic applications accepted. *Faculty research:* Business history, applied business statistics, labor/management relations, American social problems and business, effect of government economic policies on business.

State University of New York Empire State College, Graduate Studies, Program in Social Policy, Saratoga Springs, NY 12866-4391. Offers MA. Part-time and evening/weekend programs available. Postbaccalaureate distance learning degree programs offered (minimal on-campus study). *Degree requirements:* For master's, thesis, exam. *Entrance requirements:* Additional exam requirements/recommendations for international students: Required—TOEFL (minimum score 600 paper-based; 250 computer-based). Electronic applications accepted. *Faculty research:* Study of culture, society and mass communications, urban culture and policy, social decision making processes.

Stony Brook University, State University of New York, Graduate School, College of Arts and Sciences, Department of Political Science, Stony Brook, NY 11794. Offers political science (MA, PhD); public policy (MAPP). Evening/weekend programs available. *Faculty:* 16 full-time (3 women), 1 part-time/adjunct (0 women). *Students:* 64 full-time (19 women), 16 part-time (9 women); includes 22 minority (11 African Americans, 7 Asian Americans or Pacific Islanders, 4 Hispanic Americans), 11 international. Average age 27. 125 applicants, 52% accepted. In 2008, 36 master's, 3 doctorates awarded. *Degree requirements:* For doctorate, thesis/dissertation. *Entrance requirements:* For master's and doctorate, GRE General Test. *Application deadline:* For fall admission, 1/15 for domestic students. Application fee: $60. *Expenses:* Tuition, area resident: Full-time $7880; part-time $328 per credit hour. Tuition, state resident: full-time $7880; part-time $328 per credit hour. Tuition, nonresident: full-time $13,250; part-time $552 per credit hour. Required fees: $848. *Financial support:* In 2008–09, 32 teaching assistantships were awarded; fellowships, research assistantships also available. Total annual research expenditures: $93,902. *Unit head:* Dr. Jeffrey Segal, Chair, 631-632-7640. *Application contact:* Dr. Charles Taber, Director, 631-632-7667, Fax: 631-632-4116, E-mail: charles.taber@stonybrook.edu.

Suffolk University, College of Arts and Sciences, Program in Ethics and Public Policy, Boston, MA 02108-2770. Offers MS. Part-time and evening/weekend programs available. *Degree requirements:* For master's, internship or thesis. *Entrance requirements:* For master's, GRE General Test, MAT, GMAT, statement of professional goals, official transcripts, 2 letters of recommendation, resumé. Additional exam requirements/recommendations for international students: Required—TOEFL (minimum score 550 paper-based; 213 computer-based; 80 iBT). Electronic applications accepted. *Expenses:* Contact institution. *Faculty research:* History of philosophy, ethics, political philosophy, continental philosophy and phenomenology, applied ethics.

Texas A&M University, George Bush School of Government and Public Service, College Station, TX 77843. Offers advanced international affairs (Certificate); homeland security (Certificate); international affairs (MPIA), including international economics and development, national security affairs; nonprofit management (Certificate); public service and administration (MPSA), including public management, public policy analysis. *Accreditation:* NASPAA. *Faculty:* 43. *Students:* 188 full-time (80 women), 101 part-time (37 women); includes 40 minority (10 African Americans, 5 Asian Americans or Pacific Islanders, 25 Hispanic Americans), 22 international. Average age 24. In 2008, 64 master's awarded. *Degree requirements:* For master's, summer internship. *Entrance requirements:* For master's, GRE (preferred) or GMAT. *Application deadline:* For fall admission, 1/24 for domestic and international students. Application fee: $50 ($75 for international students). Electronic applications accepted. *Expenses:* Tuition, area resident: Full-time $3838.50. Tuition, state resident: full-time $3838.50. Tuition, nonresident: full-time $8897. Required fees: $2359.60. *Financial support:* In 2008–09, fellowships (averaging $11,000 per year), research assistantships (averaging $11,250 per year) were awarded; career-related internships or fieldwork, Federal Work-Study, and institutionally sponsored loans also available. Financial award application deadline: 2/1; financial award applicants required to submit FAFSA. *Faculty research:* Public policy, presidential studies, public leadership, economic policy, social policy. *Unit head:* A. Benton Cocanougher, Dean, 979-862-8842, E-mail: bushschool@tamu.edu. *Application contact:* Kathryn Meyer, Recruitment/Placement Officer, 979-458-4767, Fax: 979-845-4155, E-mail: admissions@bushschool.tamu.edu.

Trinity College, Graduate Programs, Program in Public Policy Studies, Hartford, CT 06106-3100. Offers MA. Part-time and evening/weekend programs available. *Degree requirements:* For master's, thesis optional, departmental qualifying exam. *Entrance requirements:* For master's, minimum GPA of 3.0.

Tufts University, Cummings School of Veterinary Medicine, Program in Animals and Public Policy, North Grafton, MA 01536. Offers MS. *Degree requirements:* For master's, thesis or alternative. *Entrance requirements:* For master's, GRE General Test. Additional exam requirements/recommendations for international students: Required—TOEFL. Electronic applications accepted. *Expenses:* Contact institution. *Faculty research:* Veterinary ethics, veterinary jurisprudence, companion animal demographics and control, human/animal relationships, wildlife policy issues, animal research ethics.

Tufts University, Graduate School of Arts and Sciences, Department of Urban and Environmental Policy and Planning, Medford, MA 02155. Offers community development (MA); environmental policy (MA); health and human welfare (MA); housing policy (MA); international environment/development policy (MA); public policy (MPP); public policy and citizen participation (MA); MA/MS; MALD/MA. *Accreditation:* ACSP (one or more programs are accredited). Part-time programs available. *Degree requirements:* For master's, thesis, internship. *Entrance requirements:* For master's, GRE General Test. Additional exam requirements/recommendations for international students: Required—TOEFL (minimum score 550 paper-based; 213 computer-based; 80 iBT). Electronic applications accepted. *Expenses:* Contact institution.

See Close-Up on page 1237.

Universidad Central del Este, Graduate School, San Pedro de Macoris, Dominican Republic. Offers administration (M Ad); development of educational and social policies (PhD); environmental engineering (ME); financial management (M Ad); higher education (M Ed); human resources (M Ad); public health (MPH). *Entrance requirements:* For master's, letters of recommendation.

Universidad del Este, Graduate School, Carolina, PR 00983. Offers accounting (MBA); adult education (M Ed); agribusiness (MBA); bilingual education (M Ed); criminal justice and criminology (MA); early education (M Ed); elementary education (M Ed); human resources (MBA); information and virtual business technology (MBA); information security management (MBA); management (MBA); public policy (MPA); social work (MA), including clinical social work; special education (M Ed); strategic leadership (MBA); teaching English (M Ed); teaching Spanish (M Ed).

University at Albany, State University of New York, Nelson A. Rockefeller College of Public Affairs and Policy, Department of Public Administration and Policy, Albany, NY 12222-0001. Offers administrative behavior (PhD); comparative and development administration (MPA, PhD); human resources (MPA); legislative administration (MPA); nonprofit leadership and management (Certificate); planning and policy analysis (CAS); policy analysis (MPA); program analysis and evaluation (PhD); public affairs and policy (MA); public finance (MPA, PhD); public management (MPA, PhD); women and public policy (Certificate); JD/MPA. *Accreditation:* NASPAA (one or more programs are accredited). *Degree requirements:* For doctorate, one foreign language, thesis/dissertation. *Entrance requirements:* For doctorate, GRE General

Public Policy

University at Albany, State University of New York (continued)

Test. Additional exam requirements/recommendations for international students: Required—TOEFL (minimum score 550 paper-based; 213 computer-based). Electronic applications accepted.

The University of Arizona, Graduate College, Eller College of Management, School of Public Administration and Policy, Tucson, AZ 85721. Offers public administration (MPA); public administration and policy (PhD). *Accreditation:* NASPAA. *Degree requirements:* For master's, internship of 400 hours; for doctorate, comprehensive exam, thesis/dissertation. *Entrance requirements:* For master's, GRE, 2-3 letters of recommendation, resumé; for doctorate, GMAT or GRE, minimum GPA of 3.5, letter of interest, 3 letters of recommendation, resumé. Additional exam requirements/recommendations for international students: Required—TOEFL (minimum score 650 paper-based; 280 computer-based). *Expenses:* Contact institution.

University of Arkansas, Graduate School, Interdisciplinary Program in Public Policy, Fayetteville, AR 72701-1201. Offers PhD. *Degree requirements:* For doctorate, thesis/dissertation.

University of California, Berkeley, Graduate Division, Graduate School of Public Policy, Berkeley, CA 94720-1500. Offers MPP, PhD, JD/MPP, MPP/MA, MPP/MPH, MPP/MS. *Degree requirements:* For doctorate, thesis/dissertation, qualifying exam. *Entrance requirements:* For master's and doctorate, GRE General Test, minimum GPA of 3.0, 3 letters of recommendation.

University of California, Berkeley, Graduate Division, Haas School of Business, Program in Business, Berkeley, CA 94720-1500. Offers accounting (PhD); business and public policy (PhD); finance (PhD); marketing (PhD); organizational behavior and industrial relations (PhD); real estate (PhD). *Accreditation:* AACSB. *Degree requirements:* For doctorate, comprehensive exam, thesis/dissertation, oral exam, written preliminary exams. *Entrance requirements:* For doctorate, GMAT or GRE, minimum GPA of 3.0. Additional exam requirements/recommendations for international students: Required—TOEFL (minimum score 570 paper-based; 230 computer-based; 68 iBT), IELTS (minimum score 7). Electronic applications accepted.

University of California, Los Angeles, Graduate Division, School of Public Affairs, Program in Public Policy, Los Angeles, CA 90095. Offers MPP. *Entrance requirements:* For master's, GRE General Test, minimum GPA of 3.0. Additional exam requirements/recommendations for international students: Required—TOEFL. Electronic applications accepted. *Expenses:* Tuition, nonresident: full-time $14,694. Required fees: $9669.50. Full-time tuition and fees vary according to course load, degree level, program and student level.

University of Chicago, Irving B. Harris Graduate School of Public Policy Studies, Chicago, IL 60637-1513. Offers environmental science and policy (MS); public policy studies (AM, MPP, PhD); JD/MPP; MBA/MPP; MPP/M Div; MPP/MA. Part-time programs available. *Degree requirements:* For doctorate, thesis/dissertation. *Entrance requirements:* Additional exam requirements/recommendations for international students: Required—TOEFL. Electronic applications accepted. *Expenses:* Contact institution. *Faculty research:* Family and child policy, international security, health policy, social policy.

University of Colorado at Boulder, Graduate School, College of Arts and Sciences, Department of Political Science, Boulder, CO 80309. Offers international affairs (MA); political science (MA, PhD); public policy (MA). Terminal master's awarded for partial completion of doctoral program. *Degree requirements:* For master's, comprehensive exam, thesis; for doctorate, one foreign language, thesis/dissertation. *Entrance requirements:* For master's, GRE General Test, minimum undergraduate GPA of 3.0; for doctorate, GRE General Test, minimum GPA of 3.5 (undergraduate), 3.0 (graduate). *Faculty research:* American government and politics, comparative politics, international relations, law and politics, public policy, political philosophy, empirical theory and methodology.

University of Delaware, College of Human Services, Education and Public Policy, Center for Energy and Environmental Policy, Program in Urban Affairs and Public Policy, Newark, DE 19716. Offers community development and nonprofit leadership (MA); energy and environmental policy (MA); governance, planning and management (PhD); historic preservation (MA); social and urban policy (PhD); technology, environment and society (PhD). Part-time programs available. Terminal master's awarded for partial completion of doctoral program. *Degree requirements:* For master's, analytical paper or thesis; for doctorate, thesis/dissertation. *Entrance requirements:* For master's, GRE General Test, minimum GPA of 3.0; for doctorate, GRE General Test, minimum GPA of 3.5. Additional exam requirements/recommendations for international students: Required—TOEFL. Electronic applications accepted. *Faculty research:* Political economy; social policy analysis; technology and society; historic preservation; urban policy.

See Close-Up on page 1239.

University of Denver, Division of Arts, Humanities and Social Sciences, Department of Public Policy, Denver, CO 80208. Offers MPP. *Faculty:* 2 full-time (0 women). *Students:* 24 full-time (16 women), 3 part-time (2 women); includes 1 minority (Hispanic American). Average age 29. In 2008, 8 master's awarded. *Application deadline:* Applications are processed on a rolling basis. Application fee: $50. Electronic applications accepted. *Financial support:* In 2008–09, 1 research assistantship with full and partial tuition reimbursement (averaging $2,600 per year), 2 teaching assistantships with full and partial tuition reimbursements (averaging $2,600 per year) were awarded. *Unit head:* Richard Caldwell, Director, 303-871-2468. *Application contact:* Information Contact, 303-871-2468, E-mail: ipps@du.edu.

University of Georgia, School of Public and International Affairs, Program in Public Administration and Policy, Athens, GA 30602. Offers public administration (MPA, PhD). *Accreditation:* NASPAA (one or more programs are accredited). *Degree requirements:* For master's, internship; for doctorate, thesis/dissertation. *Entrance requirements:* For master's and doctorate, GRE General Test. Electronic applications accepted.

University of Guelph, Graduate Program Services, College of Social and Applied Human Sciences, Department of Political Science, Guelph, ON N1G 2W1, Canada. Offers comparative politics (MA); international development (MA); political science (MA); public policy and public administration (MA); the Americas (Canada emphasis) (MA). MA in public policy and public administration offered in collaboration with Department of Political Science of McMaster University. *Degree requirements:* For master's, thesis or paper. *Entrance requirements:* For master's, minimum B average during previous 2 years of course work, 4 year Honours Degree in Political Science. Additional exam requirements/recommendations for international students: Required—TOEFL. Electronic applications accepted. *Faculty research:* Political ethics, constitutional power.

University of Hawaii at Manoa, Graduate Division, Colleges of Arts and Sciences, College of Social Sciences, Public Policy Center, Honolulu, HI 96822. Offers Graduate Certificate. Part-time programs available. *Entrance requirements:* Additional exam requirements/recommendations for international students: Required—TOEFL (minimum score 500 paper-based; 173 computer-based; 61 iBT), IELTS (minimum score 5).

University of Louisville, Graduate School, College of Arts and Sciences, Department of Urban and Public Affairs, Program in Public Administration, Louisville, KY 40208. Offers human resources management (MPA); non-profit management (MPA); public policy and administration (MPA). *Accreditation:* NASPAA. Part-time and evening/weekend programs available. *Faculty:* 12 full-time (3 women), 3 part-time/adjunct (0 women). *Students:* 20 full-time (12 women), 17 part-time (9 women); includes 2 African Americans, 1 Hispanic American, 1 international. Average age 29. 22 applicants, 86% accepted, 7 enrolled. In 2008, 16 master's awarded. Terminal master's awarded for partial completion of doctoral program. *Degree requirements:* For master's, internship, practicum or thesis. *Entrance requirements:* For master's, GRE General Test, minimum GPA of 2.75, resumé. Additional exam requirements/recommendations for international students: Required—TOEFL (minimum score 547 paper-based; 210 computer-based; 77 iBT). *Application deadline:* For fall admission, 7/15 priority date for domestic students; for spring admission, 11/1 priority date for domestic students. Applications are processed on a rolling basis. Application fee: $50. *Financial support:* In 2008–09, 6 students received support, including 6 research assistantships (averaging $20,000 per year); health care benefits and unspecified assistantships also available. Financial award application deadline: 3/1. *Faculty research:* Public policy, environmental policy, urban economics, housing policy, organizational theory. *Unit head:* Dr. Steve Koven, Director, 502-852-7906, Fax: 502-852-4558, E-mail: sgkove01@louisville.edu. *Application contact:* Yani Vozos, Graduate Student Advisor/Coordinator, 502-852-8002, Fax: 502-852-4558, E-mail: yani.vozos@louisville.edu.

University of Maryland, Baltimore County, Graduate School, College of Arts, Humanities and Social Sciences, Department of Economics, Program in Economic Policy Analysis, Baltimore, MD 21250. Offers MA. Part-time and evening/weekend programs available. *Faculty:* 26 full-time (10 women), 2 part-time/adjunct (0 women). *Students:* 13 full-time (4 women), 9 part-time; includes 6 minority (2 African Americans, 3 Asian Americans or Pacific Islanders, 1 Hispanic American), 4 international. Average age 27. 23 applicants, 87% accepted, 8 enrolled. In 2008, 9 master's awarded. *Degree requirements:* For master's, comprehensive exam, capstone research project. *Entrance requirements:* For master's, GRE General Test, undergraduate coursework in economic theory, econometrics, calculus. Additional exam requirements/recommendations for international students: Required—TOEFL. *Application deadline:* For fall admission, 7/1 priority date for domestic students, 3/1 priority date for international students; for spring admission, 1/1 priority date for domestic students, 9/15 priority date for international students. Applications are processed on a rolling basis. Application fee: $45. Electronic applications accepted. *Financial support:* In 2008–09, 4 students received support, including 3 research assistantships with full and partial tuition reimbursements available (averaging $11,324 per year), 1 teaching assistantship with full tuition reimbursement available (averaging $11,324 per year); Federal Work-Study, health care benefits, tuition waivers (full and partial), and unspecified assistantships also available. Support available to part-time students. Financial award application deadline: 4/15; financial award applicants required to submit FAFSA. *Faculty research:* International trade policy analysis, health and hospital policy evaluation, environmental policy analysis, economics of education, economic growth and development. Total annual research expenditures: $50,000. *Unit head:* Dr. David F. Mitch, Professor of Economics and Graduate Director, Fax: 410-455-1054, E-mail: mitch@umbc.edu. *Application contact:* Dr. David F. Mitch, Professor of Economics and Graduate Director, Fax: 410-455-1054, E-mail: mitch@umbc.edu.

University of Maryland, Baltimore County, Graduate School, College of Arts, Humanities and Social Sciences, Department of Public Policy, Baltimore, MD 21250. Offers MPP, PhD. *Accreditation:* NASPAA (one or more programs are accredited). Part-time and evening/weekend programs available. *Faculty:* 40 full-time (12 women), 2 part-time/adjunct (1 woman). *Students:* 90 full-time (48 women), 61 part-time (35 women); includes 25 minority (19 African Americans, 1 American Indian/Alaska Native, 4 Asian Americans or Pacific Islanders, 1 Hispanic American), 12 international. Average age 32. 81 applicants, 53% accepted, 26 enrolled. In 2008, 14 master's, 6 doctorates awarded. Terminal master's awarded for partial completion of doctoral program. *Degree requirements:* For master's, thesis optional, capstone project, policy analysis paper; for doctorate, comprehensive exam, thesis/dissertation, comprehensive and field qualifying exams. *Entrance requirements:* For master's and doctorate, GRE General Test, 3 academic letters of reference. Additional exam requirements/recommendations for international students: Required—TOEFL (minimum score 550 paper-based; 213 computer-based; 80 iBT). *Application deadline:* For fall admission, 2/1 priority date for domestic students, 1/1 priority date for international students; for spring admission, 11/1 priority date for domestic students, 5/1 priority date for international students. Applications are processed on a rolling basis. Application fee: $50. Electronic applications accepted. *Financial support:* In 2008–09, 32 students received support, including 17 research assistantships with full tuition reimbursements available (averaging $17,034 per year), 1 teaching assistantship with full tuition reimbursement available (averaging $17,034 per year); career-related internships or fieldwork, Federal Work-Study, health care benefits, and unspecified assistantships also available. Support available to part-time students. Financial award application deadline: 2/1; financial award applicants required to submit FAFSA. *Faculty research:* Education policy, health policy, urban policy, public management, evaluation and analytical method. Total annual research expenditures: $39 million. *Unit head:* Dr. Donald F. Norris, Chair, 410-455-3201, Fax: 410-455-1172, E-mail: norris@umbc.edu. *Application contact:* Sally F. Helms, Administrator of Academic Affairs, 410-455-3202, Fax: 410-455-1172, E-mail: gradposi@umbc.edu.

University of Maryland, College Park, Graduate Studies, A. James Clark School of Engineering and School of Public Policy, Program in Engineering and Public Policy, College Park, MD 20742. Offers MS.

University of Maryland, College Park, Graduate Studies, School of Public Policy, Policy Studies Program, College Park, MD 20742. Offers PhD. *Degree requirements:* For doctorate, comprehensive exam, thesis/dissertation, written and oral exams. *Entrance requirements:* For doctorate, GRE General Test, writing sample. Electronic applications accepted.

University of Maryland, College Park, Graduate Studies, School of Public Policy, Programs in Public Policy, College Park, MD 20742. Offers MPP, JD/MPP. *Accreditation:* NASPAA. *Entrance requirements:* Additional exam requirements/recommendations for international students: Required—TOEFL. Electronic applications accepted.

University of Massachusetts Amherst, Graduate School, College of Social and Behavioral Sciences, Center for Public Policy and Administration, Amherst, MA 01003. Offers MPPA. Part-time programs available. *Degree requirements:* For master's, thesis or alternative. *Entrance requirements:* For master's, GRE General Test. Additional exam requirements/recommendations for international students: Required—TOEFL (minimum score 550 paper-based; 213 computer-based; 79 iBT), IELTS (minimum score 6.5). Electronic applications accepted. *Expenses:* Tuition, area resident: Full-time $2640. Tuition, nonresident: full-time $9936. One-time fee: $332 full-time. Tuition and fees vary according to course load.

University of Massachusetts Amherst, Graduate School, Interdisciplinary Programs, Program in Public Policy and Business Administration, Amherst, MA 01003. Offers MBA/MPP. Part-time programs available. *Entrance requirements:* Additional exam requirements/recommendations for international students: Required—TOEFL (minimum score 600 paper-based; 250 computer-based; 100 iBT), IELTS (minimum score 7). Electronic applications accepted. *Expenses:* Tuition, area resident: Full-time $2640. Tuition, nonresident: full-time $9936. One-time fee: $332 full-time. Tuition and fees vary according to course load.

University of Massachusetts Boston, Office of Graduate Studies, John W. McCormack Graduate School of Policy Studies, Program in Public Policy, Boston, MA 02125-3393. Offers PhD. Evening/weekend programs available. *Degree requirements:* For doctorate, comprehensive exam, thesis/dissertation, practicum, oral exam. *Entrance requirements:* For doctorate, GRE General Test. *Faculty research:* Political economy, public managerial control, healthcare policy, planning and public policy theory, economic development.

University of Massachusetts Dartmouth, Graduate School, School of Education, Public Policy, and Civic Engagement, Department of Public Policy, North Dartmouth, MA 02747-2300. Offers environmental policy (Postbaccalaureate Certificate); public policy (MPP). Part-time programs available. Postbaccalaureate distance learning degree programs offered. *Faculty:* 3 full-time (1 woman). *Students:* 10 full-time (7 women), 25 part-time (16 women); includes 3 minority (all African Americans). Average age 38. 15 applicants, 100% accepted, 12 enrolled. *Entrance requirements:* For master's, GRE or GMAT. Additional exam requirements/recommendations for international students: Required—TOEFL (minimum score 500 paper-based; 213 computer-based). *Application deadline:* For fall admission, 4/20 for domestic students, 2/20 for international students; for spring admission, 11/15 for domestic students, 9/15 for international students. Applications are processed on a rolling basis. Application fee:

$40 ($60 for international students). Electronic applications accepted. *Expenses:* Tuition, state resident: full-time $2071; part-time $86.29 per credit. Tuition, nonresident: full-time $8099; part-time $337.46 per credit. Required fees: $7946. Tuition and fees vary according to class time, course load and reciprocity agreements. *Financial support:* In 2008–09, 1 research assistantship with full tuition reimbursement (averaging $9,000 per year) was awarded; Federal Work-Study and unspecified assistantships also available. Support available to part-time students. Financial award application deadline: 3/1. *Faculty research:* International human rights, international political economy, gender and politics. Total annual research expenditures: $181,000. *Unit head:* Dr. Clyde Barrow, Chairperson, 508-999-9265, E-mail: cbarrow@umassd.edu. *Application contact:* Elan Turcotte-Shamski, Graduate Admissions Officer, 508-999-8604, Fax: 508-999-8183, E-mail: graduate@umassd.edu.

University of Michigan, Horace H. Rackham School of Graduate Studies, College of Literature, Science, and the Arts, Department of Economics, Ann Arbor, MI 48109. Offers applied economics (AM); economics (AM, PhD); public policy and economics (PhD); social work and economics (PhD); JD/PhD; MPP/AM. Terminal master's awarded for partial completion of doctoral program. *Degree requirements:* For doctorate, oral defense of dissertation, preliminary exam. *Entrance requirements:* For master's and doctorate, GRE General Test. Additional exam requirements/recommendations for international students: Required—TOEFL (minimum score 600 paper-based; 250 computer-based). Electronic applications accepted. *Faculty research:* Economic and econometrical analysis, industrial organization, international trade, public finance, development, health, labor, population standard, macro, theory.

University of Michigan, Horace H. Rackham School of Graduate Studies, College of Literature, Science, and the Arts, Department of Sociology, Ann Arbor, MI 48109. Offers public policy and sociology (PhD); social work and sociology (PhD); sociology (PhD); women's studies and sociology (PhD). *Degree requirements:* For doctorate, comprehensive exam, thesis/dissertation, oral defense of dissertation, preliminary exam. *Entrance requirements:* For doctorate, GRE General Test, letters of recommendation, writing sample, personal statement, statement of purpose. Additional exam requirements/recommendations for international students: Required—TOEFL (minimum score 560 paper-based; 220 computer-based). Electronic applications accepted. *Faculty research:* Power, history and social change; gender and sexuality; race and ethnicity; economic sociology; social demography.

University of Michigan, Horace H. Rackham School of Graduate Studies, Gerald R. Ford School of Public Policy, Ann Arbor, MI 48109. Offers MPA, MPP, PhD, JD/MPP, MBA/MPP, MD/MPP, MHSA/MPP, MPH/MPP, MPP/AM, MPP/MA, MPP/MIS, MPP/MS, MPP/MUP, MSW/MPP. Part-time programs available. *Entrance requirements:* For master's, GRE. Additional exam requirements/recommendations for international students: Required—TOEFL (minimum score 600 paper-based; 250 computer-based; 102 iBT). Electronic applications accepted. *Faculty research:* U.S. social policy; international economic policy; quantitative policy analysis; environmental policy; health policy.

University of Michigan–Dearborn, College of Arts, Sciences, and Letters, Master of Public Policy Program, Dearborn, MI 48128. Offers MPP. Part-time and evening/weekend programs available. *Faculty:* 3 full-time (0 women). *Students:* 8 full-time (2 women), 14 part-time (9 women); includes 4 minority (3 African Americans, 1 Hispanic American). Average age 31. 9 applicants, 89% accepted, 8 enrolled. In 2008, 3 master's awarded. *Entrance requirements:* For master's, GRE, 500-word statement of purpose, 2 letters of recommendation, official transcripts from all universities attended. Additional exam requirements/recommendations for international students: Required—TOEFL (minimum score 560 paper-based; 220 computer-based). *Application deadline:* For fall admission, 8/1 for domestic students, 4/1 for international students; for winter admission, 12/1 for domestic students, 11/1 for international students; for spring admission, 4/1 for domestic students, 3/1 for international students. Application fee: $60 ($75 for international students). *Faculty research:* Peace and conflict studies, courts and public policy, public policy and the media. *Unit head:* Dr. Trevor Thrall, Director, 313-593-5282, Fax: 313-593-5645, E-mail: atthrall@umd.umich.edu. *Application contact:* Carol Ligienza, Graduate Program Coordinator, CASL Graduate Programs, 313-593-1183, Fax: 313-583-6498, E-mail: caslgrad@umd.umich.edu.

University of Minnesota, Twin Cities Campus, Graduate School, Hubert H. Humphrey Institute of Public Affairs, Program in Public Policy, Minneapolis, MN 55455-0213. Offers advanced policy analysis methods (MPP); economic and community development (MPP); foreign policy (MPP); public and nonprofit leadership and management (MPP); science technology and environmental policy (MPP); social policy (MPP); women and public policy (MPP); JD/MPP; MPP/MS; MSW/MPP. Part-time programs available. *Degree requirements:* For master's, thesis or alternative, internship or equivalent work experience. *Entrance requirements:* For master's, GRE General Test, minimum undergraduate GPA of 3.0. Additional exam requirements/recommendations for international students: Required—TOEFL (minimum score 600 paper-based; 250 computer-based). Electronic applications accepted *Faculty research:* Social policy, public and non-profit management and leadership, community and economic development, foreign policy and international affairs, women and public policy.

University of Missouri–St. Louis, College of Arts and Sciences, Department of Political Science, St. Louis, MO 63121. Offers American politics (MA); comparative politics (MA); international politics (MA); political process and behavior (MA); political science (PhD); public administration and public policy (MA); urban and regional politics (MA). Part-time and evening/weekend programs available. *Faculty:* 19 full-time (7 women). *Students:* 19 full-time (8 women), 23 part-time (14 women); includes 9 minority (6 African Americans, 1 American Indian/Alaska Native, 2 Asian Americans or Pacific Islanders), 4 international. Average age 36. In 2008, 6 master's, 2 doctorates awarded. Terminal master's awarded for partial completion of doctoral program. *Degree requirements:* For master's, thesis optional; for doctorate, thesis/dissertation. *Entrance requirements:* For master's, GRE General Test, 2 letters of recommendation; for doctorate, GRE General Test, 3 letters of recommendation. Additional exam requirements/recommendations for international students: Required—TOEFL (minimum score 550 paper-based; 213 computer-based). *Application deadline:* For fall admission, 2/15 priority date for domestic and international students; for spring admission, 10/15 priority date for domestic and international students. Applications are processed on a rolling basis. Application fee: $35 ($40 for international students). Electronic applications accepted. *Expenses:* Tuition, area resident: Full-time $5377; part-time $298.70 per credit hour. Tuition, nonresident: full-time $13,381; part-time $472.50 per credit hour. Required fees: $4078; $52 per credit hour. *Financial support:* In 2008–09, 10 research assistantships with full and partial tuition reimbursements (averaging $10,800 per year), 6 teaching assistantships with full and partial tuition reimbursements (averaging $10,800 per year) were awarded; fellowships, career-related internships or fieldwork also available. Support available to part-time students. Financial award application deadline: 3/15; financial award applicants required to submit FAFSA. *Faculty research:* Public policy, urban politics and administration, American government. *Unit head:* Dr. Barbara Graham, Director of Graduate Studies, 314-516-5522, Fax: 314-516-5268, E-mail: umslpolisci@umsl.edu. *Application contact:* 314-516-5458, Fax: 314-516-6996, E-mail: gradadm@umsl.edu.

University of Missouri–St. Louis, Graduate School, Program in Public Policy Administration, St. Louis, MO 63121. Offers health policy (MPPA); local government management (MPPA); managing human resources and organization (MPPA); nonprofit organization management (MPPA); nonprofit organization management and leadership (Certificate); policy research and analysis (MPPA). *Accreditation:* NASPAA. Part-time and evening/weekend programs available. *Faculty:* 8 full-time (4 women), 8 part-time/adjunct (1 woman). *Students:* 20 full-time (12 women), 57 part-time (34 women); includes 18 minority (17 African Americans, 1 Hispanic American), 4 international. Average age 32. In 2008, 22 master's awarded. *Entrance requirements:* For master's, 3 letters of recommendation. Additional exam requirements/recommendations for international students: Required—TOEFL (minimum score 550 paper-based; 213 computer-based). *Application deadline:* For fall admission, 7/1 priority date for domestic and international students; for spring admission, 12/1 priority date for domestic and international students. Applications are processed on a rolling basis. Application fee: $35 ($40

for international students). Electronic applications accepted. *Expenses:* Tuition, area resident: Full-time $5377; part-time $298.70 per credit hour. Tuition, nonresident: full-time $13,381; part-time $472.50 per credit hour. Required fees: $4078; $52 per credit hour. *Financial support:* In 2008–09, 1 research assistantship with full and partial tuition reimbursement (averaging $12,000 per year) was awarded; career-related internships or fieldwork also available. Financial award application deadline: 4/1; financial award applicants required to submit FAFSA. *Faculty research:* Urban policy, public finance, evaluation. *Unit head:* Brady Baybeck, Director, 314-516-5145, Fax: 314-516-5210, E-mail: baybeck@umsl.edu. *Application contact:* 314-516-5458, Fax: 314-516-6996, E-mail: gradadm@umsl.edu.

University of Nebraska–Lincoln, Graduate College, College of Arts and Sciences, Department of Political Science, Lincoln, NE 68588. Offers political science (MA, PhD); public policy analysis (Graduate Certificate). *Faculty:* 17 full-time (4 women). *Students:* 28 full-time (11 women), 21 part-time (12 women); includes 2 minority (1 African American, 1 Hispanic American), 11 international. Average age 32. In 2008, 8 master's, 2 doctorates awarded. *Degree requirements:* For master's, thesis optional; for doctorate, variable foreign language requirement, comprehensive exam, thesis/dissertation. *Entrance requirements:* For master's and doctorate, GRE General Test, writing sample. Additional exam requirements/recommendations for international students: Required—TOEFL (minimum score 600 paper-based; 250 computer-based). *Application deadline:* For fall admission, 2/1 priority date for domestic students, 2/1 for international students. Applications are processed on a rolling basis. Application fee: $40. Electronic applications accepted. *Expenses:* Tuition, state resident: full-time $4275; part-time $237.50 per credit hour. Tuition, nonresident: full-time $11,525; part-time $640.25 per credit hour. Required fees: $1068; $10.35 per credit hour. $440.70 per semester. Tuition and fees vary according to course load and program. *Financial support:* Fellowships, research assistantships, teaching assistantships, Federal Work-Study, health care benefits, and unspecified assistantships available. Support available to part-time students. Financial award application deadline: 2/15. *Faculty research:* Public policy; comparative politics; international relations; political theory, behavior, and methodology; American politics. *Unit head:* Dr. John Comer, Chair, 402-472-2343. *Application contact:* Ginny Gross, Director of Graduate Admissions, 402-472-2878, Fax: 402-472-0589, E-mail: grad_admissions@unl.edu.

University of Nevada, Las Vegas, Graduate College, College of Liberal Arts, Department of Political Science, Program in Ethics and Policy Studies, Las Vegas, NV 89154-5029. Offers MA. Part-time programs available. *Faculty:* 2 full-time (0 women), 2 part-time/adjunct (both women). *Students:* 9 part-time (2 women); includes 5 minority (1 African American, 1 American Indian/Alaska Native, 1 Asian American or Pacific Islander, 2 Hispanic Americans). Average age 35. 2 applicants, 100% accepted, 1 enrolled. In 2008, 1 master's awarded. *Degree requirements:* For master's, thesis. *Entrance requirements:* For master's, GRE General Test. Additional exam requirements/recommendations for international students: Required—TOEFL (minimum score 550 paper-based; 213 computer-based; 80 iBT), IELTS (minimum score 7). *Application deadline:* For fall admission, 2/1 priority date for domestic and international students; for spring admission, 10/1 priority date for domestic and international students. Applications are processed on a rolling basis. Application fee: $60 ($75 for international students). Electronic applications accepted. *Expenses:* Tuition, state resident: full-time $1414; part-time $198 per credit. Tuition, nonresident: full-time $12,509; part-time $415.75 per credit. International tuition: $14,249 full-time. Required fees: $4 per credit. $252 per semester. Tuition and fees vary according to course load. *Financial support:* Institutionally sponsored loans, scholarships/grants, health care benefits, and unspecified assistantships available. Financial award application deadline: 3/1. *Faculty research:* Immigration and crime policy, ancient and contemporary political theory. *Unit head:* Dr. Mehran Tamadonfar, Chair/Associate Professor, 702-895-5258, Fax: 702-895-1065, E-mail: mehram.tamadonfar@unlv.edu. *Application contact:* Graduate College Admissions Evaluator, 702-895-3320, Fax: 702-895-4180, E-mail: gradcollege@unlv.edu.

University of New Brunswick Fredericton, School of Graduate Studies, Policy Studies Program, Fredericton, NB E3B 5A3, Canada. Offers people, property and alternative dispute resolution (M Phil); philosophy politics and economics (M Phil); sustainable development (M Phil). *Faculty:* 6 full-time (2 women), 13 part-time/adjunct (2 women). *Students:* 16 full-time (9 women), 4 part-time (3 women). In 2008, 3 master's awarded. *Entrance requirements:* For master's, minimum GPA of 3.5, BA. Additional exam requirements/recommendations for international students: Required—TOEFL (minimum score 600 paper-based), TWE (minimum score 5). Application fee: $50 Canadian dollars. Tuition and fees charges are reported in Canadian dollars. *Expenses:* Tuition, area resident: Full-time $5562 Canadian dollars. Tuition, nonresident: full-time $9450 Canadian dollars. Required fees: $333 Canadian dollars. *Financial support:* In 2008–09, 4 research assistantships, 1 teaching assistantship were awarded. *Unit head:* Dr. Linda Eyre, Dean of Graduate Studies, 506-447-3044, Fax: 506-453-4817, E-mail: gradidst@unb.ca. *Application contact:* Janet Amurault, Graduate Secretary, 506-458-7558, Fax: 506-453-4817, E-mail: jamiraul@unb.ca.

The University of North Carolina at Chapel Hill, Graduate School, Department of Public Policy, Chapel Hill, NC 27599. Offers PhD. *Degree requirements:* For doctorate, thesis/dissertation. *Entrance requirements:* For doctorate, GRE General Test. Electronic applications accepted. *Faculty research:* Environmental policy; energy policy; economic development and science and technology policy; social policy; welfare, education and low-income communities.

The University of North Carolina at Charlotte, Graduate School, College of Arts and Sciences, Program in Public Policy, Charlotte, NC 28223-0001. Offers PhD. Part-time and evening/weekend programs available. *Students:* 17 full-time (14 women), 19 part-time (9 women); includes 2 minority (both African Americans), 14 international. Average age 38. 13 applicants, 62% accepted, 5 enrolled. In 2008, 1 doctorate awarded. *Degree requirements:* For doctorate, comprehensive exam. *Entrance requirements:* For doctorate, GRE General Test. Additional exam requirements/recommendations for international students: Required—TOEFL (minimum score 557 paper-based; 220 computer-based). *Application deadline:* For fall admission, 12/1 for domestic and international students. Applications are processed on a rolling basis. Application fee: $55. Electronic applications accepted. *Expenses:* Tuition, area resident: Full-time $2919; part-time $122 per credit hour. Tuition, state resident: full-time $2919; part-time $122 per credit hour. Tuition, nonresident: full-time $13,126; part-time $547 per credit hour. Required fees: $1779; $91 per credit hour. Tuition and fees vary according to program. *Financial support:* In 2008–09, 1 fellowship (averaging $4,000 per year), 38 research assistantships (averaging $8,529 per year), 2 teaching assistantships (averaging $9,250 per year) were awarded; career-related internships or fieldwork, Federal Work-Study, institutionally sponsored loans, scholarships/grants, and unspecified assistantships also available. Support available to part-time students. Financial award application deadline: 4/1; financial award applicants required to submit FAFSA. *Unit head:* Dr. David A. Swindell, Director, 704-687-4532, Fax: 704-687-3228, E-mail: daswinde@email.uncc.edu. *Application contact:* Kathy B. Giddings, Director of Graduate Admissions, 704-687-3366, Fax: 704-687-3279, E-mail: agidding@uncc.edu.

University of Northern Iowa, Graduate College, Program in Public Policy, Cedar Falls, IA 50614. Offers MPP. Part-time programs available. *Students:* 17 full-time (9 women), 3 part-time (2 women); includes 4 minority (2 African Americans, 1 American Indian/Alaska Native, 1 Hispanic American), 2 international. 25 applicants, 68% accepted, 6 enrolled. In 2008, 17 master's awarded. *Degree requirements:* For master's, comprehensive exam (for some programs). *Entrance requirements:* For master's, minimum GPA of 3.0. Additional exam requirements/recommendations for international students: Required—TOEFL (minimum score 500 paper-based; 180 computer-based; 61 iBT). *Application deadline:* For fall admission, 3/1 priority date for domestic students. Applications are processed on a rolling basis. Application fee: $30 ($50 for international students). Electronic applications accepted. *Expenses:* Tuition, state resident: full-time $6446. Tuition, nonresident: full-time $14,874. Required fees: $852. *Financial support:* Career-related internships or fieldwork, Federal Work-Study, institutionally sponsored loans, tuition waivers (full), and unspecified assistantships available. Financial award application deadline: 2/1. *Unit head:* Dr. Al Hays, Head, 319-273-6028, Fax: 319-273-

Public Policy

University of Northern Iowa (continued)
7126, E-mail: allen.hays@uni.edu. *Application contact:* Laurie S. Russell, Record Analyst, 319-273-2623, Fax: 319-273-6792, E-mail: laurie.russell@uni.edu.

University of Oregon, Graduate School, School of Architecture and Allied Arts, Department of Planning, Public Policy, and Management, Program in Public Policy and Management, Eugene, OR 97403. Offers MA, MPA, MS. *Accreditation:* NASPAA. Part-time and evening/weekend programs available. *Degree requirements:* For master's, thesis. *Entrance requirements:* For master's, minimum GPA of 3.0. Additional exam requirements/recommendations for international students: Required—TOEFL. *Faculty research:* Community economic development, families in poverty, health services.

University of Pennsylvania, Wharton School, Department of Business and Public Policy, Philadelphia, PA 19104. Offers MBA, PhD. *Degree requirements:* For doctorate, thesis/dissertation. *Entrance requirements:* For doctorate, GRE General Test. *Faculty research:* International policy, business and government, regulation, urban development and policy, transportation.

University of Pittsburgh, Graduate School of Public and International Affairs, Division of Public and Urban Affairs, Program in Policy Research and Analysis, Pittsburgh, PA 15260. Offers MPA, MPA/MID, JD/MPA, MPA/MPIA, MPH/MPA, MSIS/MPA, MSW/MPA. Part-time and evening/weekend programs available. *Degree requirements:* For master's, thesis optional, internship, capstone seminar. *Entrance requirements:* For master's, GRE General Test, 3 letters of recommendation, resumé, minimum GPA of 3.2. Additional exam requirements/recommendations for international students: Required—TOEFL (minimum score 550 paper-based; 213 computer-based; 80 iBT), TWE (minimum score 4); Recommended—IELTS (minimum score 7). Electronic applications accepted. *Faculty research:* Emergency management, health policy and regulation, regional finance, non-profit management, community/regional development, environmental policy.

University of Pittsburgh, Graduate School of Public and International Affairs, Doctoral Program in Public and International Affairs, Pittsburgh, PA 15260. Offers development policy (PhD); foreign and security policy (PhD); international political economy (PhD); public administration (PhD); public policy (PhD). *Accreditation:* NASPAA. Part-time programs available. *Degree requirements:* For doctorate, comprehensive exam, thesis/dissertation. *Entrance requirements:* For doctorate, GRE, 3 letters of recommendation, resumé, minimum GPA of 3.0, writing sample. Additional exam requirements/recommendations for international students: Required—TOEFL (minimum score 600 paper-based; 250 computer-based; 100 iBT), TWE (minimum score 4); Recommended—IELTS (minimum score 7). Electronic applications accepted. *Faculty research:* International political economy, international development, public administration, public policy, foreign policy, international security policy.

See Close-Up on page 1243.

University of Pittsburgh, Graduate School of Public and International Affairs, Executive Programs in Public Policy and Management, Pittsburgh, PA 15260. Offers development planning (MPPM); international development (MPPM); international political economy (MPPM); international security studies (MPPM); management of non profit organizations (MPPM); metropolitan management and regional development (MPPM); policy analysis and evaluation (MPPM). Part-time programs available. *Degree requirements:* For master's, thesis optional, capstone seminar. *Entrance requirements:* For master's, 2 letters of recommendation, resumé, 5 years of supervisory or budgetary experience. Additional exam requirements/recommendations for international students: Required—TOEFL (minimum score 600 paper-based; 250 computer-based; 100 iBT), TWE (minimum score 4); Recommended—IELTS (minimum score 7). Electronic applications accepted. *Faculty research:* Executive training and technical assistance for U.S. and international clients.

See Close-Up on page 1243.

University of Regina, Faculty of Graduate Studies and Research, Johnson-Shoyama Graduate School of Public Policy, Regina, SK S4S 0A2, Canada. Offers economic analysis for public policy (Master's Certificate); non-profit management (Master's Certificate); public management (MPA, Master's Certificate); public policy (MPA, PhD, Master's Certificate). Part-time and evening/weekend programs available. *Faculty:* 6 full-time (3 women). *Students:* 53 full-time (25 women), 63 part-time (38 women). 100 applicants, 82% accepted. In 2008, 40 master's awarded. *Entrance requirements:* Additional exam requirements/recommendations for international students: Required—TOEFL (minimum score 580 paper-based; 237 computer-based; 88 iBT). *Application deadline:* Applications are processed on a rolling basis. Application fee: $85 ($100 for international students). Electronic applications accepted. *Expenses:* Contact institution. *Financial support:* In 2008–09, 8 fellowships (averaging $15,930 per year), 2 research assistantships (averaging $13,720 per year), 5 teaching assistantships (averaging $6,650 per year) were awarded. Financial award application deadline: 6/15. *Faculty research:* Public administration and policy. *Unit head:* Dr. Ken Rasmussen, Associate Dean, 306-585-5463, E-mail: ken.rasmussen@uregina.ca. *Application contact:* Devon Anderson, Information Contact, 306-585-5462, E-mail: devon.anderson@uregina.ca.

University of Rhode Island, Graduate School, College of Arts and Sciences, Department of Political Science, Program in Public Policy and Administration, Kingston, RI 02881. Offers MA, MPA, Certificate. In 2008, 24 master's awarded. *Expenses:* Tuition: state resident: full-time $8024; part-time $446 per credit. Tuition, nonresident: full-time $21,046; part-time $1169 per credit. Required fees: $1056; $26 per credit. $30 per semester. One-time fee: $95 part-time. *Unit head:* Dr. Timothy Hennessey, Director, 401-874-4052. *Application contact:* Harold D. Bibb, Associate Dean of the Graduate School, 401-874-2262, Fax: 401-874-5491.

University of Southern California, Graduate School, School of Policy, Planning and Development, Program in Public Policy, Los Angeles, CA 90089. Offers MPP. Part-time programs available. *Entrance requirements:* For master's, GRE General Test. *Faculty research:* Urban political economy, community and economic development, immigration policy.

University of Southern Maine, Edmund S. Muskie School of Public Service, Doctoral Program in Public Policy, Portland, ME 04104-9300. Offers PhD. Applicants accepted in odd numbered years only. Part-time and evening/weekend programs available. *Degree requirements:* For doctorate, comprehensive exam, thesis/dissertation. *Entrance requirements:* For doctorate, GRE. Additional exam requirements/recommendations for international students: Required—TOEFL. Electronic applications accepted. *Faculty research:* Health policy, community planning and development, education policy, environmental policy.

University of Southern Maine, Edmund S. Muskie School of Public Service, Program in Public Policy and Management, Portland, ME 04104-9300. Offers child and family policy (Certificate); non-profit management (Certificate); public policy and management (MPPM); JD/MPPM. *Accreditation:* NASPAA. Part-time and evening/weekend programs available. Post-baccalaureate distance learning degree programs offered (minimal on-campus study). *Degree requirements:* For master's, thesis, capstone project, field experience. *Entrance requirements:* For master's, GRE General Test or LSAT. Additional exam requirements/recommendations for international students: Required—TOEFL. Electronic applications accepted. *Faculty research:* Sustainable communities, juvenile justice, program management, nonprofit management.

The University of Texas at Austin, Graduate School, Lyndon B. Johnson School of Public Affairs, Austin, TX 78712-1111. Offers global policy studies (MGPS); public affairs (MP Aff); public policy (PhD); JD/MP Aff; MBA/MP Aff; MP Aff/MA; MP Aff/MSE. *Accreditation:* NASPAA (one or more programs are accredited). Part-time programs available. *Degree requirements:* For master's, thesis, summer internship; for doctorate, thesis/dissertation. *Entrance requirements:* For master's, GRE General Test; for doctorate, GRE General Test, master's degree in policy-related field. Additional exam requirements/recommendations for international students: Required—TOEFL. Electronic applications accepted. *Faculty research:* Human resource

development, health and social policy, philanthropy and community service, ethical leadership, urban and international policy, science and technology policy.

The University of Texas at Brownsville, Graduate Studies, College of Liberal Arts, Program in Public Policy and Management, Brownsville, TX 78520-4991. Offers MPPM. *Degree requirements:* For master's, thesis. *Entrance requirements:* For master's, GRE, 2 letters of recommendation.

The University of Texas at Dallas, School of Economic, Political and Policy Sciences, Program in Public Policy and Political Economy, Richardson, TX 75083-0688. Offers international political economy (MS); public policy (MPP); public policy and political economy (PhD). Part-time and evening/weekend programs available. *Faculty:* 14 full-time (4 women). *Students:* 33 full-time (12 women), 43 part-time (20 women); includes 26 minority (10 African Americans, 8 Asian Americans or Pacific Islanders, 8 Hispanic Americans), 19 international. Average age 40. 42 applicants, 95% accepted, 21 enrolled. In 2008, 1 master's, 6 doctorates awarded. *Degree requirements:* For doctorate, thesis/dissertation. *Entrance requirements:* For master's and doctorate, GRE General Test, minimum GPA of 3.0 in upper-level course work in field. Additional exam requirements/recommendations for international students: Required—TOEFL (minimum score 550 paper-based; 213 computer-based). *Application deadline:* For fall admission, 7/15 for domestic students, 5/1 priority date for international students; for spring admission, 11/15 for domestic students, 9/1 priority date for international students. Applications are processed on a rolling basis. Application fee: $50 ($100 for international students). Electronic applications accepted. *Expenses:* Tuition, area resident: Full-time $8320. Tuition, state resident: full-time $8320. Tuition, nonresident: full-time $15,054. Part-time tuition and fees vary according to course load. *Financial support:* In 2008–09, 2 research assistantships with tuition reimbursements (averaging $18,188 per year), 11 teaching assistantships with tuition reimbursements (averaging $12,436 per year) were awarded; fellowships, career-related internships or fieldwork, Federal Work-Study, institutionally sponsored loans, and scholarships/grants also available. Support available to part-time students. Financial award application deadline: 4/30; financial award applicants required to submit FAFSA. *Faculty research:* New leadership development, gender and leadership, globalization and leadership opportunities in democracy. *Unit head:* Dr. Sheila Amin Gutierrez de Pineres, Program Head, 972-883-6228, Fax: 972-883-2735, E-mail: pineres@utdallas.edu. *Application contact:* Dr. Marie I Chevrier, Associate Program Head, 972-883-2727, Fax: 972-883-2735, E-mail: chevrier@utdallas.edu.

See Close-Up on page 783.

The University of Texas at El Paso, Graduate School, Institute for Policy and Economic Development, El Paso, TX 79968-0001. Offers intelligence and national security studies (MS); leadership studies (MLS); public administration (MPA).

University of the Pacific, McGeorge School of Law, Sacramento, CA 95817. Offers advocacy (JD); advocacy practice and teaching (LL M); criminal justice (JD); intellectual property (JD); international legal studies (JD); international water resources law (LL M, JSD); law (JD); public law and policy (JD); public policy and law (LL M); tax (JD); transnational business practice (LL M); JD/MBA; JD/MPPA. *Accreditation:* ABA. Part-time and evening/weekend programs available. *Faculty:* 55 full-time (22 women), 73 part-time/adjunct (34 women). *Students:* 620 full-time (304 women), 396 part-time (194 women); includes 271 minority (33 African Americans, 14 American Indian/Alaska Native, 134 Asian Americans or Pacific Islanders, 90 Hispanic Americans). Average age 24. 2,627 applicants, 41% accepted. In 2008, 301 JDs, 49 master's awarded. *Degree requirements:* For master's, thesis (for some programs); for doctorate, thesis/dissertation. *Entrance requirements:* For JD, LSAT; for master's, JD; for doctorate, LL M. Additional exam requirements/recommendations for international students: Required—TOEFL (minimum score 600 paper-based; 250 computer-based; 100 iBT). *Application deadline:* For fall admission, 3/15 priority date for domestic students. Applications are processed on a rolling basis. Application fee: $50. Electronic applications accepted. *Expenses:* Contact institution. *Financial support:* In 2008–09, 925 students received support, including 9 fellowships, 76 research assistantships (averaging $1,961 per year); career-related internships or fieldwork, Federal Work-Study, institutionally sponsored loans, and scholarships/grants also available. Support available to part-time students. Financial award applicants required to submit FAFSA. *Faculty research:* International Legal Studies, Public Policy & Law, Advocacy, Intellectual Property Law, Taxation, & Criminal Law. *Unit head:* Elizabeth Rindskopf Parker, Dean, 916-739-7151, E-mail: elizabeth@uop.edu. *Application contact:* 916-739-7105, Fax: 916-739-7134, E-mail: admissionsmcgeorge@uop.edu.

University of Utah, The Graduate School, College of Social and Behavioral Science, Department of Political Science, Program in Public Policy, Salt Lake City, UT 84112-1107. Offers international affairs and global enterprises (MS); public policy (MPP).

University of Virginia, Frank Batten Sr. School of Leadership and Public Policy, Program in Public Policy, Charlottesville, VA 22903. Offers MPP. *Students:* 52 full-time (32 women); includes 6 minority (2 African Americans, 4 Asian Americans or Pacific Islanders). Average age 23. 2 applicants, 0% accepted. *Application deadline:* For fall admission, 2/20 for domestic and international students. Application fee: $60. *Expenses:* Tuition, area resident: Full-time $10,452. Tuition, state resident: full-time $10,452. Tuition, nonresident: full-time $20,010. Required fees: $2176. Part-time tuition and fees vary according to course load and program. *Unit head:* Dr. Harry Harding, Dean. *Application contact:* Edith Simms, Director of Admissions & Student Affairs, 434-243-4383, E-mail: els8a@virginia.edu.

University of Washington, Graduate School, Daniel J. Evans School of Public Affairs, Seattle, WA 98195. Offers public administration (MPA); public policy and management (PhD); JD/MPA; MPA/MAIS; MPA/MPH; MPA/MS; MPA/MUP. *Accreditation:* NASPAA. Part-time and evening/weekend programs available. *Degree requirements:* For master's, thesis, internship or cooperative experience. *Entrance requirements:* For master's and doctorate, GRE General Test, minimum GPA of 3.0. Additional exam requirements/recommendations for international students: Required—TOEFL (minimum score 580 paper-based; 237 computer-based; 92 iBT). Electronic applications accepted. *Faculty research:* Environmental policy, education and social policy, nonprofit management, international affairs, urban and regional development.

University of Washington, Bothell, Program in Policy Studies, Bothell, WA 98011-8246. Offers MA. Evening/weekend programs available. *Faculty:* 9 full-time (4 women), 2 part-time/adjunct (both women). *Students:* 27 full-time (21 women), 19 part-time (14 women); includes 12 minority (1 African American, 2 American Indian/Alaska Native, 7 Asian Americans or Pacific Islanders, 2 Hispanic Americans). Average age 32. 63 applicants, 51% accepted, 27 enrolled. In 2008, 15 master's awarded. *Degree requirements:* For master's, thesis. *Entrance requirements:* For master's, GRE. Additional exam requirements/recommendations for international students: Required—TOEFL. *Application deadline:* For fall admission, 3/1 priority date for domestic and international students. Applications are processed on a rolling basis. Application fee: $50. Electronic applications accepted. *Financial support:* In 2008–09, 9 students received support, including 5 fellowships (averaging $15,000 per year), 1 research assistantship (averaging $2,000 per year); Federal Work-Study, tuition waivers (full), and unspecified assistantships also available. Financial award applicants required to submit FAFSA. *Faculty research:* Policy studies, cultural studies, cultural and environmental politics, disability studies, public policy. *Unit head:* Prof. Bruce Burgett, Interim Director, Interdisciplinary Studies Program, 425-352-5403, E-mail: bburgett@uwb.edu. *Application contact:* Andrew Brusletten, Program Manager, 425-352-5427, Fax: 425-352-3462, E-mail: abrusletten@uwb.edu.

Vanderbilt University, Graduate School, Program in Community Research and Action, Nashville, TN 37240-1001. Offers MS, PhD. *Faculty:* 20 full-time (9 women). *Students:* 27 full-time (13 women), 1 part-time (0 women); includes 4 minority (all African Americans), 3 international. Average age 31. 45 applicants, 22% accepted, 5 enrolled. In 2008, 2 master's, 4 doctorates awarded. *Degree requirements:* For master's, thesis; for doctorate, thesis/dissertation, internship, fundable grant proposal. *Entrance requirements:* For doctorate, GRE General Test.

Additional exam requirements/recommendations for international students: Required—TOEFL (minimum score 570 paper-based; 230 computer-based; 88 iBT). *Application deadline:* For fall admission, 12/31 for domestic and international students. Application fee: $0. Electronic applications accepted. *Financial support:* Fellowships with tuition reimbursements, research assistantships with full tuition reimbursements, teaching assistantships with full tuition reimbursements, Federal Work-Study, institutionally sponsored loans, scholarships/grants, traineeships, and health care benefits available. Financial award application deadline: 1/15; financial award applicants required to submit CSS PROFILE or FAFSA. *Faculty research:* Applied psychological research, community theory, mental health, public policy, race dynamics. *Unit head:* Joseph Cunningham, Chair, 615-322-6881, Fax: 615-343-2661, E-mail: joe.cunningham@vanderbilt.edu. *Application contact:* Paul Dokecki, Director of Graduate Studies, 615-322-6881, E-mail: paul. r.dokecki@vanderbilt.edu.

Virginia Commonwealth University, Graduate School, College of Humanities and Sciences, Wilder School of Government and Public Affairs, Center for Public Policy, Richmond, VA 23284-9005. Offers public policy and administration (PhD). *Degree requirements:* For doctorate, thesis/dissertation. *Entrance requirements:* For doctorate, GMAT, GRE General Test, LSAT, or MAT.

Virginia Polytechnic Institute and State University, Graduate School, College of Architecture and Urban Studies, Center for Public Administration and Policy, Blacksburg, VA 24061-0205. Offers MPA, PhD, CAGS. *Accreditation:* NASPAA (one or more programs are accredited). *Entrance requirements:* For master's and doctorate, GRE General Test, GMAT. Additional exam requirements/recommendations for international students: Required—TOEFL (minimum score 550 paper-based; 213 computer-based). Electronic applications accepted. *Faculty research:* Public administration theory, strategic management, ethics, the Constitution, computer-assisted creativity.

Walden University, Graduate Programs, School of Counseling and Social Service, Minneapolis, MN 55401. Offers human services (PhD), including clinical social work, counseling, criminal justice, family studies and intervention strategies, general program in human services, human services administration, self-designed program in human services, social policy analysis and planning; mental health counseling (MS). Part-time and evening/weekend programs available. Postbaccalaureate distance learning degree programs offered (minimal on-campus study). *Faculty:* 6 full-time, 76 part-time/adjunct. *Students:* 1,235 full-time (1,026 women), 129 part-time (111 women); includes 595 minority (505 African Americans, 21 American Indian/Alaska Native, 16 Asian Americans or Pacific Islanders, 53 Hispanic Americans), 18 international. Average age 39. 724 applicants, 50% accepted, 250 enrolled. In 2008, 12 master's, 5 doctorates awarded. *Degree requirements:* For master's, thesis optional, residency; for doctorate, thesis/dissertation, residency. *Entrance requirements:* For master's, bachelor's degree or equivalent in related field, minimum GPA of 2.5, two references, goal statement, official transcripts, computer and Internet access; for doctorate, master's degree or equivalent in related field, minimum GPA of 3.0, three years related professional/academic experience, two references, goal statement, official transcripts, computer and Internet access. Additional exam requirements/recommendations for international students: Required—TOEFL (minimum score 550 paper-based; 213 computer-based), IELTS (minimum score 6.5), TOEFL, IELTS, or Michigan English Language Assessment Battery (minimum score 82). *Application deadline:* Applications are processed on a rolling basis. Application fee: $50. Electronic applications accepted. *Expenses:* Tuition: Full-time $12,877; part-time $520 per credit. Required fees: $1230. Tuition and fees vary according to course load, degree level and program. *Financial support:* Fellowships, Federal Work-Study, scholarships/grants, unspecified assistantships, and family tuition reduction; active duty/veteran tuition reduction; group tuition reduction; interest-free payment plans available. Support available to part-time students. Financial award applicants required to submit FAFSA. *Unit head:* Dr. Savitri Dixon-Saxon, Associate Dean, 800-925-3368. *Application contact:* Jennifer Hall, Director of Enrollment, 866-4-WALDEN, E-mail: info@waldenu.edu.

Walden University, Graduate Programs, School of Public Policy and Administration, Minneapolis, MN 55401. Offers general public policy and administration (MPA); government management (Certificate); health policy (MPA); homeland security policy (MPA); interdisciplinary policy studies (MPA); law and public policy (MPA); local government management for sustainable communities (MPA); nonprofit management (Certificate); nonprofit management and leadership (MPA, MS); policy analysis (MPA); public management and leadership (MPA); public policy and administration (PhD), including criminal justice, health services, homeland security policy and coordination, international nongovernmental organizations, knowledge management, nonprofit management and leadership, public management and leadership, public policy, public safety management; terrorism, mediation, and peace (MPA). Part-time and evening/weekend programs available. Postbaccalaureate distance learning degree programs offered

(minimal on-campus study). *Faculty:* 2 full-time, 55 part-time/adjunct. *Students:* 1,285 full-time (794 women), 144 part-time (96 women); includes 657 minority (591 African Americans, 8 American Indian/Alaska Native, 17 Asian Americans or Pacific Islanders, 41 Hispanic Americans), 20 international. Average age 39. 727 applicants, 54% accepted, 284 enrolled. In 2008, 101 master's, 6 doctorates awarded. *Degree requirements:* For doctorate, thesis/dissertation, residency. *Entrance requirements:* For master's, bachelor's degree or equivalent in related field, minimum GPA of 2.5, two references, goal statement, official transcripts, access to computer and Internet; for doctorate, master's degree or equivalent in related field, minimum GPA of 3.0, three years related professional/academic experience, two references, goal statement, official transcripts, access to computer and Internet. Additional exam requirements/recommendations for international students: Required—TOEFL (minimum score 550 paper-based; 213 computer-based), IELTS (minimum score 6.5), TOEFL, IELTS, or Michigan English Language Assessment Battery (minimum score 82). *Application deadline:* Applications are processed on a rolling basis. Application fee: $50. Electronic applications accepted. *Expenses:* Tuition: Full-time $12,877; part-time $520 per credit. Required fees: $1230. Tuition and fees vary according to course load, degree level and program. *Financial support:* In 2008–09, 3 students received support; fellowships with tuition reimbursements available, Federal Work-Study, scholarships/grants, unspecified assistantships, and family tuition reduction; active duty/veteran tuition reduction; group tuition reduction; interest-free payment plans available. Support available to part-time students. Financial award applicants required to submit FAFSA. *Unit head:* Dr. Mark Gordon, Interim Associate Dean, 800-925-3368. *Application contact:* Jennifer Hall, 866-4-WALDEN, E-mail: info@waldenu.edu.

Washington State University, Graduate School, College of Liberal Arts, Department of Sociology, Pullman, WA 99164. Offers crime and deviance (MA, PhD); environments, community and demographics (MA, PhD); institutions and social organizations (MA, PhD); political sociology (MA, PhD); social inequality (MA, PhD); social psychology and life course (MA, PhD). Terminal master's awarded for partial completion of doctoral program. *Degree requirements:* For master's, thesis; for doctorate, comprehensive exam, thesis/dissertation. *Entrance requirements:* For master's, GRE General Test, minimum GPA of 3.0; for doctorate, GRE General Test, MA in sociology, minimum GPA of 3.0. Additional exam requirements/recommendations for international students: Required—TOEFL (minimum score 550 paper-based). Electronic applications accepted. *Faculty research:* Crime/deviance, environmental sociology, social inequality, social psychology, gender.

Washington University in St. Louis, Graduate School of Arts and Sciences, Department of Political Science, Program in Political Economy and Public Policy, St. Louis, MO 63130-4899. Offers MA. *Students:* 2 full-time (both women); includes 1 minority (Asian American or Pacific Islander). In 2008, 6 master's awarded. *Degree requirements:* For master's, thesis or alternative. *Entrance requirements:* For master's, GRE General Test. *Application deadline:* For fall admission, 1/15 priority date for domestic students. Application fee: $45. Electronic applications accepted. *Financial support:* Application deadline: 1/15. *Unit head:* Dr. Norman Schofield, Chairperson, 314-935-5632. *Application contact:* Assistant to the Dean, 314-935-6880, Fax: 314-935-4887.

West Virginia University, Eberly College of Arts and Sciences, Department of Political Science, Morgantown, WV 26506. Offers American public policy and politics (MA); international and comparative public policy and politics (MA); political science (PhD); public policy analysis (PhD). Terminal master's awarded for partial completion of doctoral program. *Degree requirements:* For master's, thesis optional; for doctorate, comprehensive exam, thesis/dissertation. *Entrance requirements:* For master's, GRE General Test, minimum GPA of 2.75; for doctorate, GRE General Test, minimum GPA of 3.0. Additional exam requirements/recommendations for international students: Required—TOEFL. *Faculty research:* Public policy, research methods, foreign policy analysis, judicial politics, environmental and energy policy.

Wilfrid Laurier University, Faculty of Graduate Studies, Faculty of Arts and School of Business and Economics, International Public Policy Program, Waterloo, ON N2L 3C5, Canada. Offers MIPP. *Entrance requirements:* For master's, honours BA with minimum B average. Additional exam requirements/recommendations for international students: Required—TOEFL (minimum score 230 computer-based; 89 iBT). Electronic applications accepted. *Faculty research:* International environmental policy, international economic relations, human security, global governance.

William Paterson University of New Jersey, College of the Humanities and Social Sciences, Program in Public Policy and International Affairs, Wayne, NJ 07470-8420. Offers MA.

York University, Faculty of Graduate Studies, Atkinson Faculty of Liberal and Professional Studies, Program in Public Policy, Administration and Law, Toronto, ON M3J 1P3, Canada. Offers MPPAL.

Rural Planning and Studies

Brandon University, Department of Rural Development, Brandon, MB R7A 6A9, Canada. Offers MRD, Diploma. *Degree requirements:* For master's, thesis. *Entrance requirements:* For master's, minimum GPA of 3.0, 2 letters of reference. Additional exam requirements/recommendations for international students: Required—TOEFL (minimum score 580 paper-based). Electronic applications accepted. *Faculty research:* Regional development, healthy communities, economic impact analysis, rural tourism, resource management.

California State University, Chico, Graduate School, College of Behavioral and Social Sciences, Department of Geography and Planning, Program in Rural and Town Planning, Chico, CA 95929-0722. Offers MA. Part-time programs available. *Entrance requirements:* For master's, GRE, 2 letters of recommendation, statement of purpose, writing sample. Additional exam requirements/recommendations for international students: Required—TOEFL (minimum score 550 paper-based; 213 computer-based; 80 iBT), IELTS (minimum score 6.5). Electronic applications accepted.

Concordia University, School of Graduate Studies, John Molson School of Business, Montréal, QC H3G 1M8, Canada. Offers administration (M Sc, Diploma); aviation management (Certificate, Diploma); business administration (MBA, UA Undergraduate Associate, PhD), including international aviation (UA Undergraduate Associate); chartered accountancy (Diploma); community organizational development (Certificate); event management and fundraising (Certificate); executive business administration (EMBA); investment management (Diploma); investment management option (MBA); management accounting (Certificate); management of healthcare organizations (Certificate); sport administration (Diploma). *Accreditation:* AACSB. Part-time and evening/weekend programs available. *Degree requirements:* For master's, one foreign language, thesis (for some programs), research project; for doctorate, one foreign language, thesis/dissertation; for other advanced degree, one foreign language. *Entrance requirements:* For master's and doctorate, GMAT. Additional exam requirements/recommendations for international students: Required—TOEFL. *Expenses:* Contact institution. *Faculty research:* General business, capital markets, international business.

Cornell University, Graduate School, Graduate Fields of Agriculture and Life Sciences, Field of Community and Rural Development, Ithaca, NY 14853-0001. Offers community development process (MPS); economic development (MPS); local government organizations and operations (MPS); program development and planning (MPS). *Faculty:* 30 full-time (10 women). *Students:* 1 (woman) full-time. Average age 28. In 2008, 2 master's awarded. *Entrance*

requirements: For master's, GRE General Test (recommended), 3 letters of recommendation. Additional exam requirements/recommendations for international students: Required—TOEFL (minimum score 550 paper-based; 213 computer-based; 77 iBT). *Application deadline:* For fall admission, 5/1 for domestic students. Application fee: $70. Electronic applications accepted. *Expenses:* Tuition: Full-time $29,500. Required fees: $70. Full-time tuition and fees vary according to degree level, program and student level. *Financial support:* In 2008–09, 1 fellowship with full tuition reimbursement, 1 teaching assistantship with full tuition reimbursement were awarded; research assistantships with full tuition reimbursements, institutionally sponsored loans, scholarships/grants, health care benefits, tuition waivers (full and partial), and unspecified assistantships also available. Financial award applicants required to submit FAFSA. *Faculty research:* Land use, community economic development, governance and leadership development, planning and evaluation, main street revitalization. *Unit head:* Director of Graduate Studies, 607-255-4916, Fax: 607-255-2231. *Application contact:* Graduate Field Assistant, 607-255-4916, Fax: 607-255-2331, E-mail: gradcrd@cornell.edu.

Cornell University, Graduate School, Graduate Fields of Agriculture and Life Sciences, Field of International Agriculture and Rural Development, Ithaca, NY 14853-0001. Offers international agriculture and development (MPS). *Faculty:* 46 full-time (9 women). *Students:* 35 full-time (11 women); includes 3 minority (1 American Indian/Alaska Native, 2 Asian Americans or Pacific Islanders), 4 international. Average age 31. 27 applicants, 59% accepted, 9 enrolled. In 2008, 6 master's awarded. *Degree requirements:* For master's, project paper. *Entrance requirements:* For master's, GRE General Test (recommended), 2 years of development experience, 2 letters of recommendation. Additional exam requirements/recommendations for international students: Required—TOEFL (minimum score 550 paper-based; 213 computer-based; 77 iBT). *Application deadline:* For fall admission, 3/1 for domestic students. Application fee: $70. Electronic applications accepted. *Expenses:* Tuition: Full-time $29,500. Required fees: $70. Full-time tuition and fees vary according to degree level, program and student level. *Financial support:* In 2008–09, 4 students received support, including 1 research assistantship with full tuition reimbursement available, 3 teaching assistantships with full tuition reimbursements available; fellowships with full tuition reimbursements available, institutionally sponsored loans, scholarships/grants, health care benefits, tuition waivers (full and partial), and unspecified assistantships also available. Financial award applicants required to submit FAFSA. *Unit head:* Director of Graduate Studies, 607-255-3037, Fax: 607-255-1005. *Application contact:* Graduate Field Assistant, 607-255-3035, Fax: 607-255-1005, E-mail: mpsiard@cornell.edu.

Rural Planning and Studies

Dalhousie University, Faculty of Architecture and Planning, School of Planning, Halifax, NS B3J 2X4, Canada. Offers M Eng, M Plan, MPS. *Degree requirements:* For master's, thesis. *Entrance requirements:* Additional exam requirements/recommendations for international students: Required—TOEFL, IELTS, 1 of 5 approved tests: TOEFL, IELTS, CANTEST, CAEL, Michigan English Language Assessment Battery. *Application deadline:* For fall admission, 6/1 priority date for domestic students, 4/1 for international students; for winter admission, 11/15 for domestic students, 8/31 for international students; for spring admission, 1/28 for domestic students, 12/31 for international students. Applications are processed on a rolling basis. Application fee: $70. Electronic applications accepted. *Financial support:* Career-related internships or fieldwork and scholarships/grants available. *Unit head:* Prof. Jill Grant, Director, 902-494-3260, Fax: 902-423-6672, E-mail: plan.office@dal.ca. *Application contact:* Frank Palermo, Graduate Coordinator, 902-494-3978, Fax: 902-423-6672, E-mail: frank.palermo@dal.ca.

Iowa State University of Science and Technology, Graduate College, College of Liberal Arts and Sciences, Department of History, Ames, IA 50011. Offers agricultural history and rural studies (PhD); history (MA); history of technology and science (MA, PhD). *Faculty:* 17 full-time (5 women). *Students:* 24 full-time (10 women), 10 part-time (2 women); includes 1 minority (Hispanic American), 4 international. 10 applicants, 70% accepted, 3 enrolled. In 2008, 9 master's, 3 doctorates awarded. *Degree requirements:* For master's, thesis or alternative; for doctorate, thesis/dissertation. *Entrance requirements:* For master's and doctorate, GRE General Test. Additional exam requirements/recommendations for international students: Required—TOEFL (minimum score 600 paper-based; 79 iBT), IELTS (7.0) or TOEFL. *Application deadline:* For fall admission, 1/15 priority date for domestic and international students. Applications are processed on a rolling basis. Application fee: $30 ($70 for international students). Electronic applications accepted. *Expenses:* Tuition, area resident: Full-time $6446; part-time $359 per credit. Tuition, state resident: full-time $6446; part-time $359 per credit. Tuition, nonresident: full-time $17,330; part-time $963 per credit. Required fees: $790; $249.25 per semester. Tuition and fees vary according to course load and program. *Financial support:* In 2008–09, 20 teaching assistantships with full and partial tuition reimbursements (averaging $12,150 per year) were awarded; research assistantships with full and partial tuition reimbursements, scholarships/grants, health care benefits, and unspecified assistantships also available. *Unit head:* Dr. Charles Dobbs, Chair, 515-294-7266, Fax: 515-294-6390, E-mail: cdobbs@iastate.edu. *Application contact:* Dr. Pamela Riney-Kehrberg, Information Contact, 515-294-1451, Fax: 515-294-6390.

Université Laval, Faculty of Agricultural and Food Sciences, Program in Integrated Rural Development, Québec, QC G1K 7P4, Canada. Offers Diploma. *Entrance requirements:* For degree, good knowledge of French. Electronic applications accepted.

University of Alaska Fairbanks, College of Rural and Community Development, Department of Alaska Native and Rural Development, Fairbanks, AK 99775. Offers rural development (MA). Part-time programs available. Postbaccalaureate distance learning degree programs offered. *Faculty:* 2 full-time (both women). *Students:* 7 full-time (6 women), 13 part-time (9 women); includes 12 minority (11 American Indian/Alaska Native, 1 Asian American or Pacific Islander). Average age 42. 8 applicants, 75% accepted, 5 enrolled. In 2008, 6 master's awarded. *Degree requirements:* For master's, comprehensive exam, thesis or alternative. *Entrance requirements:* Additional exam requirements/recommendations for international students: Required—TOEFL (minimum score 550 paper-based; 213 computer-based; 80 iBT). *Application deadline:* For fall admission, 6/1 for domestic students, 3/1 for international students; for spring admission, 10/15 for domestic students, 9/1 for international students. Applications are processed on a rolling basis. Application fee: $60. Electronic applications accepted. *Expenses:* Tuition, area resident: Full-time $5418; part-time $301 per credit. Tuition, state resident: full-time $5418; part-time $301 per credit. Tuition, nonresident: full-time $11,070; part-time $615 per credit. Required fees: $849; $25 per credit. $78 per semester. Tuition and fees vary according to course load and reciprocity agreements. *Financial support:* Fellowships, Federal Work-Study, scholarships/grants, and health care benefits available. Support available to part-time students. Financial award application deadline: 2/15; financial award applicants required to submit FAFSA. *Faculty research:* International indigenous leadership development, interrelationships between rural communities and global economy. *Unit head:* Paul Gordon, Director, 907-474-6528, Fax: 907-474-6325, E-mail: fydanrd@uaf.edu. *Application contact:* Paul Gordon, Director, 907-474-6528, Fax: 907-474-6325, E-mail: fydanrd@uaf.edu.

University of Guelph, Graduate Program Services, Ontario Agricultural College, School of Environmental Design and Rural Development, Interdisciplinary Program in Rural Studies, Guelph, ON N1G 2W1, Canada. Offers PhD. Offered in cooperation with the Department of Food, Agricultural and Resource Economics, and the Department of Geography. Part-time programs available. *Degree requirements:* For doctorate, thesis/dissertation, qualifying exam. *Entrance requirements:* Additional exam requirements/recommendations for international students: Required—TOEFL (minimum score 600 paper-based; 218 computer-based), IELTS (minimum score 7). Electronic applications accepted. *Faculty research:* Sustainable rural communities, human resource development, rural planning and development.

University of Guelph, Graduate Program Services, Ontario Agricultural College, School of Environmental Design and Rural Development, Program in Capacity Development and Extension, Guelph, ON N1G 2W1, Canada. Offers M Sc. Part-time programs available. *Degree requirements:* For master's, thesis optional. *Entrance requirements:* For master's, minimum B- average in previous 2 years of course work. Additional exam requirements/recommendations for international students: Required—TOEFL (minimum score 550 paper-based; 213 computer-based; 89 iBT), IELTS (minimum score 6.5). Electronic applications accepted. *Faculty research:* Adult learning in non-formal settings, communication technology for remote areas, rural quality of life.

University of Guelph, Graduate Program Services, Ontario Agricultural College, School of Environmental Design and Rural Development, Program in Rural Planning and Development, Guelph, ON N1G 2W1, Canada. Offers international rural planning and development (M Sc); rural planning and development in Canada (M Sc). M Sc offered in cooperation with Departments of Food, Agricultural and Resource Economics; Geography; Land Resource Science; and others by arrangement. Part-time programs available. *Degree requirements:* For master's, thesis or alternative. *Entrance requirements:* For master's, minimum B- average during previous 2 years of course work. Additional exam requirements/recommendations for international students: Required—TOEFL (minimum score 550 paper-based; 213 computer-based), IELTS (minimum score 6.5). Electronic applications accepted. *Faculty research:* Canadian and international rural planning, resource and economic development, tourism.

The University of Montana, Graduate School, College of Arts and Sciences, Department of Geography, Missoula, MT 59812-0002. Offers geography (MA), including cartography and GIS, community and environmental planning. *Entrance requirements:* For master's, GRE General Test. Additional exam requirements/recommendations for international students: Required—TOEFL.

University of West Georgia, Graduate School, College of Arts and Sciences, Department of Political Science and Planning, Program in Rural and Small Town Planning, Carrollton, GA 30118. Offers MS. Part-time programs available. *Students:* 1 full-time (0 women), 2 part-time (0 women). Average age 36. *Degree requirements:* For master's, exit paper. *Entrance requirements:* For master's, GRE. Additional exam requirements/recommendations for international students: Required—TOEFL. Application fee: $30. Electronic applications accepted. *Expenses:* Tuition, state resident: full-time $2844; part-time $158 per semester hour. Tuition, nonresident: full-time $11,340; part-time $630 per semester hour. Required fees: $1120; $41.56 per semester hour. $186 per semester. Tuition and fees vary according to course load. *Financial support:* Applicants required to submit FAFSA. *Unit head:* Dr. G. Richard Larkin, Assistant Dean, College of Arts and Sciences, 678-839-6405, E-mail: dlarkin@westga.edu. *Application contact:* Dr. Charles W. Clark, Interim Dean, 678-839-6508, E-mail: cclark@westga.edu.

University of Wyoming, Graduate School, College of Arts and Sciences, Department of Geography, Program in Rural Planning and Natural Resources, Laramie, WY 82070. Offers community and regional planning and natural resources (MP). *Faculty:* 5 full-time (4 women). *Students:* 2 full-time (0 women), 3 part-time (2 women); includes 1 minority (American Indian/Alaska Native), 1 international. Average age 36. 1 applicant, 100% accepted. In 2008, 2 master's awarded. *Degree requirements:* For master's, thesis or alternative. *Entrance requirements:* For master's, GRE General Test, minimum GPA of 3.0. Additional exam requirements/recommendations for international students: Required—TOEFL. *Application deadline:* For fall admission, 2/15 for domestic students. Applications are processed on a rolling basis. Application fee: $50. *Financial support:* In 2008–09, research assistantships (averaging $10,696 per year), teaching assistantships with full and partial tuition reimbursements (averaging $10,696 per year) were awarded; career-related internships or fieldwork, Federal Work-Study, scholarships/grants, and unspecified assistantships also available. Financial award application deadline: 3/1. *Faculty research:* Rural and small town planning, public land management. *Unit head:* Dr. Gerald R. Webster, Chair, 307-766-3311, Fax: 307-766-3294, E-mail: geography-info@uwyo.edu. *Application contact:* Barbara Powell, Office Associate Senior, 307-766-3311, Fax: 307-766-3294, E-mail: geography-info@uwyo.edu.

Virginia Polytechnic Institute and State University, Graduate School, College of Architecture and Urban Studies, School of Public and International Affairs, Blacksburg, VA 24061. Offers environmental planning and policy (MURP); government and international affairs (MPIA); housing, community and economic development (MURP); international development planning (MURP); land use and physical planning (MURP); planning, governance and globalization (PhD), including environmental planning and landscape analysis, physical planning and urban design, public and international affairs, urban and environmental design and planning; urban and regional planning (MURP). *Accreditation:* ACSP. *Entrance requirements:* Additional exam requirements/recommendations for international students: Required—TOEFL (minimum score 550 paper-based; 213 computer-based). Electronic applications accepted. *Faculty research:* Design theory, environmental planning, town planning, transportation planning.

Sustainable Development

American University, School of International Service, Washington, DC 20016-8071. Offers comparative and regional studies (Certificate); cross-cultural communication (Certificate); development management (MS); ethics, peace, and global affairs (MA); European studies (Certificate); global environmental policy (MA, Certificate); international affairs (MA), including comparative and regional studies, environmental policy, international economic policy, international politics, natural resources and sustainable development, U.S. foreign policy; international communication (MA, Certificate); international development (MA, Certificate); international development management (Certificate); international economic policy (Certificate); international economic relations (Certificate); international media (MA); international peace and conflict resolution (MA, Certificate); international relations (PhD); international service (MIS); peace building (Certificate); the Americas (Certificate); United States foreign policy (Certificate); JD/MA. Part-time and evening/weekend programs available. *Faculty:* 70 full-time (28 women), 51 part-time/adjunct (20 women). *Students:* 519 full-time (317 women), 335 part-time (205 women); includes 157 minority (54 African Americans, 2 American Indian/Alaska Native, 45 Asian Americans or Pacific Islanders, 56 Hispanic Americans), 116 international. Average age 27. 1,901 applicants, 58% accepted, 277 enrolled. In 2008, 358 master's, 5 doctorates, 9 other advanced degrees awarded. Terminal master's awarded for partial completion of doctoral program. *Degree requirements:* For master's, one foreign language, comprehensive exam, thesis or alternative; for doctorate, one foreign language, comprehensive exam, thesis/dissertation, research practicum; for Certificate, minimum 15 credit hours related course work. *Entrance requirements:* For master's, GRE, 24 credits of course work in related social sciences, minimum GPA of 3.5, 2 letters of recommendation, bachelor's degree, resumé, statement of purpose; for doctorate, GRE, 2 letters of recommendation, 24 credits in related social sciences; for Certificate, bachelor's degree. Additional exam requirements/recommendations for international students: Required—TOEFL (minimum score 600 paper-based; 250 computer-based; 100 iBT). *Application deadline:* For fall admission, 1/15 priority date for domestic students; for spring admission, 10/1 priority date for domestic students. Applications are processed on a rolling basis. Application fee: $50. *Expenses:* Tuition: Full-time $21,204; part-time $1178 per credit hour. Required fees: $380. Part-time tuition and fees vary according to course load and program. *Financial support:* Career-related internships or fieldwork, Federal Work-Study, and institutionally sponsored loans available. Financial award application deadline: 1/15. *Faculty research:* International intellectual property, international environmental issues, international law and legal order, international telecommunications/technology, international sustainable development. *Unit head:* Dr. Louis W. Goodman, Dean, 202-885-1600, Fax: 202-885-2494. *Application contact:* Yasmin Quianzon, Director of Graduate Admissions and Financial Aid, 202-885-2496, Fax: 202-885-1109.

See Close-Up on page 861.

Appalachian State University, Cratis D. Williams Graduate School, Center for Appalachian Studies, Boone, NC 28608. Offers culture (MA); music (MA); sustainable development (MA). Part-time programs available. *Faculty:* 14 full-time (5 women). *Students:* 19 full-time (11 women), 5 part-time (3 women). 20 applicants, 90% accepted, 10 enrolled. In 2008, 6 master's awarded. *Degree requirements:* For master's, one foreign language, comprehensive exam, thesis optional. *Entrance requirements:* For master's, GRE General Test, 3 letters of recommendation. Additional exam requirements/recommendations for international students: Required—TOEFL (minimum score 570 paper-based; 230 computer-based; 79 iBT), IELTS (minimum score 6.5). *Application deadline:* For fall admission, 7/1 for domestic students, 2/1 for international students; for spring admission, 11/1 for domestic students, 7/1 for international students. Applications are processed on a rolling basis. Application fee: $50. Electronic applications accepted. *Expenses:* Tuition, area resident: Full-time $2600; part-time $700 per course. Tuition, state resident: full-time $2600; part-time $700 per course. Tuition, nonresident: full-time $5000; part-time $3300 per course. Required fees: $2150; $330 per course. Tuition and fees vary according to campus/location. *Financial support:* In 2008–09, 8 research assistantships (averaging $7,000 per year) were awarded; fellowships, teaching assistantships, career-related internships or fieldwork, Federal Work-Study, scholarships/grants, and unspecified assistantships also available. Financial award application deadline: 4/1; financial award applicants required to submit FAFSA. *Faculty research:* Appalachian culture, sustainable development, Appalachian music. Total annual research expenditures: $10,500. *Unit head:* Dr. Pat Beaver,

Director, 828-262-2550, E-mail: beaverpd@appstate.edu. *Application contact:* Dr. Bruce Stewart, Graduate Program Director, 828-262-4858, E-mail: stewartbe1@appstate.edu.

Arizona State University, Graduate College, School of Sustainability, Tempe, AZ 85287. Offers MA, MS, PhD.

Brandeis University, Graduate School of Arts and Sciences, Program in Coexistence and Conflict and Sustainable International Development, Waltham, MA 02454-9110. Offers MA/MA.

Brandeis University, The Heller School for Social Policy and Management, Program in Nonprofit Management, Waltham, MA 02454-9110. Offers aging services management (MBA); child, youth, and family management (MBA); health care management (MBA); social impact management (MBA); social policy and management (MBA); sustainable development (MBA); MBA/MA. *Accreditation:* AACSB. Part-time and evening/weekend programs available. *Degree requirements:* For master's, team consulting project. *Entrance requirements:* For master's, GMAT. Additional exam requirements/recommendations for international students: Required—TOEFL (minimum score 600 paper-based). Electronic applications accepted. *Expenses:* Contact institution. *Faculty research:* Health care, child and family, elder and disabled services, general human services.

Brandeis University, The Heller School for Social Policy and Management, Program in Sustainable International Development, Waltham, MA 02454-9110. Offers international development (MA); sustainable development (MA). *Degree requirements:* For master's, 2nd-year fieldwork or internship. *Entrance requirements:* For master's, 3 letters of recommendation; curriculum vitae or resumé. Additional exam requirements/recommendations for international students: Required—TOEFL, IELTS. Electronic applications accepted. *Expenses:* Contact institution. *Faculty research:* Water resource management, human rights, biosphere management, rural development, public policy and governance.

California State University, Stanislaus, College of Natural Sciences, Department of Biological Sciences, Turlock, CA 95382. Offers ecology and sustainability (MS); genetic counseling (MS); marine sciences (MS). Part-time programs available. *Degree requirements:* For master's, thesis. *Entrance requirements:* For master's, GRE General Test, GRE Subject Test, minimum GPA of 3.0, 3 letters of reference, personal statement. Additional exam requirements/recommendations for international students: Required—TOEFL (minimum score 550 paper-based; 213 computer-based). Electronic applications accepted. *Faculty research:* Long-term smoking and pregnancy rate, vertebrate paleobiology, terrestrial animals, benthic invertebrates of central California coastline.

Clark University, Graduate School, Department of International Development, Community, and Environment, Worchester, MA 01610-1477. Offers community development and planning (MA); environmental science and policy (MA); geographic information science for development and environment (MA); international development and social change (MA). *Faculty:* 14 full-time (8 women), 4 part-time/adjunct (2 women). *Students:* 97 full-time (64 women), 61 part-time (37 women); includes 10 minority (7 African Americans, 1 American Indian/Alaska Native, 1 Asian American or Pacific Islander, 1 Hispanic American), 57 international. Average age 28. 291 applicants, 70% accepted, 92 enrolled. In 2008, 64 master's awarded. *Degree requirements:* For master's, thesis. *Entrance requirements:* Additional exam requirements/recommendations for international students: Required—TOEFL. *Application deadline:* For fall admission, 1/15 for domestic students. Application fee: $50. *Expenses:* Tuition: Full-time $34,900; part-time $1091 per credit hour. Required fees: $30. *Financial support:* In 2008–09, 2 research assistantships with full and partial tuition reimbursements (averaging $5,000 per year), 2 teaching assistantships with full and partial tuition reimbursements (averaging $5,000 per year) were awarded; fellowships, career-related internships or fieldwork, scholarships/grants, and tuition waivers (full and partial) also available. *Faculty research:* Community participation, gender analysis, land-use planning, project analysis, geographic information systems, AIDS research. Total annual research expenditures: $3.1 million. *Unit head:* Dr. William F. Fisher, Director, 508-421-3765, Fax: 508-793-8820, E-mail: wfisher@clarku.edu. *Application contact:* Paula Hall, IDCE Graduate Admissions, 508-793-7201, Fax: 508-793-8820, E-mail: idce@clarku.edu.

Columbia University, Graduate School of Arts and Sciences, Program in Climate and Society, New York, NY 10027. Offers MA.

Columbia University, Graduate School of Arts and Sciences, Program in Sustainable Development, New York, NY 10027. Offers PhD.

Columbia University, School of International and Public Affairs, Program in Development Practice, New York, NY 10027. Offers MPA. Offered through The Earth Institute.

Dominican University of California, Graduate Programs, School of Business, Education and Leadership, Division of Business and International Studies, Green Business Administration Program, San Rafael, CA 94901-2298. Offers sustainable development (MBA). *Students:* 59 full-time (42 women), 18 part-time (13 women); includes 9 minority (3 African Americans, 1 American Indian/Alaska Native, 2 Asian Americans or Pacific Islanders, 3 Hispanic Americans), 4 international. Average age 34. 47 applicants, 79% accepted, 37 enrolled. *Entrance requirements:* Additional exam requirements/recommendations for international students: Required—TOEFL (minimum score 550 paper-based; 213 computer-based). Application fee: $40. *Expenses:* Tuition: Full-time $14,040; part-time $780 per unit. *Financial support:* In 2008–09, 67 students received support, including 28 fellowships (averaging $1,950 per year). *Unit head:* Dr. Chris Leeds, Director, 415-482-3532, Fax: 415-459-3206, E-mail: cleeds@dominican.edu. *Application contact:* Angie Schmidt, Assistant Director, 415-458-3771, Fax: 415-485-3214, E-mail: angela.schmidt@dominican.edu.

Florida Atlantic University, College of Architecture, Urban and Public Affairs, School of Urban and Regional Planning, Boca Raton, FL 33431-0991. Offers economic development and tourism (Certificate); environmental planning (Certificate); sustainable community planning (Certificate); urban and regional planning (MURP); visual planning technology (Certificate). *Accreditation:* ACSP. Part-time and evening/weekend programs available. *Faculty:* 8 full-time (6 women), 1 (woman) part-time/adjunct. *Students:* 21 full-time (12 women), 11 part-time (5 women); includes 15 minority (5 African Americans, 10 Hispanic Americans), 1 international. Average age 33. 47 applicants, 47% accepted, 8 enrolled. In 2008, 12 master's awarded. *Entrance requirements:* For master's, GRE General Test, minimum GPA of 3.0. Additional exam requirements/recommendations for international students: Required—TOEFL. *Application deadline:* For fall admission, 7/1 priority date for domestic students, 2/15 for international students; for spring admission, 11/1 priority date for domestic students, 7/15 for international students. Applications are processed on a rolling basis. Application fee: $30. *Expenses:* Tuition, state resident: full-time $4867; part-time $270.40 per credit hour. Tuition, nonresident: full-time $16,486; part-time $915.87 per credit hour. *Financial support:* Fellowships with full tuition reimbursements, research assistantships, career-related internships or fieldwork, Federal Work-Study, institutionally sponsored loans, and tuition waivers (partial) available. Financial award application deadline: 4/1. *Faculty research:* Growth management, urban design, computer applications/geographical information systems, environmental planning. *Unit head:* Dr. Jaap Vos, Chair, 954-762-5653, Fax: 954-762-5673, E-mail: jvos@fau.edu. *Application contact:* Dr. Jaap Vos, Chair, 954-762-5653, Fax: 954-762-5673, E-mail: jvos@fau.edu.

Hawai'i Pacific University, College of Professional Studies, Honolulu, HI 96813. Offers global leadership and sustainable development (MA); human resource management (MA); information systems (MSIS), including knowledge management, software engineering, telecommunications security; organizational change (MA). Part-time and evening/weekend programs available. *Faculty:* 13 full-time (2 women), 5 part-time/adjunct (2 women). *Students:* 144 full-time (52 women), 128 part-time (61 women); includes 94 minority (13 African Americans, 3 American Indian/Alaska Native, 70 Asian Americans or Pacific Islanders, 8 Hispanic Americans), 91 international. Average age 31. 202 applicants, 83% accepted, 74 enrolled. In 2008, 85 master's awarded. *Degree requirements:* For master's, thesis. *Entrance requirements:* Additional exam requirements/recommendations for international students: Recommended—TOEFL (minimum score 550 paper-based; 213 computer-based; 80 iBT), TWE (minimum score 5). *Application deadline:* For fall admission, 2/15 priority date for domestic students; for spring admission, 10/15 priority date for domestic students. Applications are processed on a rolling basis. Application fee: $50. Electronic applications accepted. *Expenses:* Tuition: Full-time $10,800; part-time $600 per credit. *Financial support:* In 2008–09, 120 students received support. Career-related internships or fieldwork, Federal Work-Study, scholarships/grants, and unspecified assistantships available. Support available to part-time students. Financial award application deadline: 3/1; financial award applicants required to submit FAFSA. *Unit head:* Dr. Gordon Jones, Dean, 808-544-1181, Fax: 808-544-0247, E-mail: gjones@hpu.edu. *Application contact:* Danny Lam, Assistant Director of Graduate Admissions, 808-544-1135, Fax: 808-544-0280, E-mail: graduate@hpu.edu.

See Close-Up on page 1217.

HEC Montreal, School of Business Administration, Diploma Programs in Administration, Program in Management and Sustainable Development, Montréal, QC H3T 2A7, Canada. Offers Diploma. Part-time programs available. *Students:* 16 full-time (7 women), 44 part-time (23 women). 66 applicants, 62% accepted, 36 enrolled. In 2008, 11 Diplomas awarded. *Application deadline:* For fall admission, 5/15 for domestic and international students. Application fee: $76. Tuition and fees charges are reported in Canadian dollars. *Expenses:* Tuition, area resident: Part-time $62.27 Canadian dollars per credit. Tuition, state resident: full-time $2241.72 Canadian dollars; part-time $179.28 Canadian dollars per credit. Tuition, nonresident: full-time $6454 Canadian dollars; part-time $419.77 Canadian dollars per credit. International tuition: $15,111.72 Canadian dollars full-time. Required fees: $1218.75 Canadian dollars; $28.25 Canadian dollars per credit. $88 Canadian dollars per term. Tuition and fees vary according to degree level and program. *Unit head:* Louise Cote, Director, 514-340-6205, Fax: 514-340-5640, E-mail: louise.cote@hec.ca. *Application contact:* Francine Blais, Administrative Director, 514-340-6112, Fax: 514-340-6411, E-mail: francine.blais@hec.ca.

Instituto Centroamericano de Administración de Empresas, Graduate Programs, La Garita, Costa Rica. Offers agribusiness (MIAM); business administration (EMBA); economics and finance (MBA); industry and technology (MBA); sustainable development (MBA). *Degree requirements:* For master's, comprehensive exam, essay. *Entrance requirements:* For master's, GMAT or GRE, fluency in Spanish, interview, letters of recommendation, minimum 1 year of work experience. Electronic applications accepted. *Faculty research:* Competitiveness, production.

Iowa State University of Science and Technology, Graduate College, Interdisciplinary Programs, Program in Sustainable Agriculture, Ames, IA 50011. Offers MS, PhD. *Students:* 21 full-time (7 women), 3 part-time (1 woman); includes 2 minority (1 Asian American or Pacific Islander, 1 Hispanic American), 6 international. 17 applicants, 94% accepted, 12 enrolled. In 2008, 7 master's, 2 doctorates awarded. *Degree requirements:* For master's, thesis or alternative; for doctorate, thesis/dissertation. *Entrance requirements:* For master's and doctorate, GRE General Test. Additional exam requirements/recommendations for international students: Required—TOEFL (minimum score 570 paper-based; 80 iBT), IELTS (6.5) or TOEFL. *Application deadline:* For fall admission, 2/1 for domestic and international students; for spring admission, 6/1 priority date for domestic and international students. Application fee: $30 ($70 for international students). *Expenses:* Tuition, area resident: Full-time $6446; part-time $359 per credit. Tuition, state resident: full-time $6446; part-time $359 per credit. Tuition, nonresident: full-time $17,330; part-time $963 per credit. Required fees: $790; $249.25 per semester. Tuition and fees vary according to course load and program. *Financial support:* In 2008–09, 19 research assistantships with full and partial tuition reimbursements (averaging $13,860 per year), 4 teaching assistantships with full and partial tuition reimbursements (averaging $13,860 per year) were awarded. *Unit head:* Dr. Mike Duffy, Chair, Supervising Committee, 515-294-6518, E-mail: gpsa@iastate.edu. *Application contact:* Charles Sauer, Information Contact, 515-294-6518, E-mail: gpsa@iastate.edu.

Lesley University, Graduate School of Arts and Social Sciences, Program in Urban Environmental Leadership, Cambridge, MA 02138-2790. Offers MA. *Entrance requirements:* For master's, 2 letters of recommendation, interview. *Expenses:* Tuition: Full-time $13,770; part-time $765 per credit hour. Required fees: $150. Tuition and fees vary according to course load, degree level, campus/location and program.

Michigan Technological University, Graduate School, Sustainable Futures Institute, Houghton, MI 49931-1295. Offers sustainability (Certificate). Part-time programs available.

Minneapolis College of Art and Design, Program in Arts, Minneapolis, MN 55404-4347. Offers design (Certificate); fine arts (Certificate); media (Certificate); sustainable design (Certificate). Part-time programs available. Postbaccalaureate distance learning degree programs offered. *Faculty:* 23 full-time (7 women), 9 part-time/adjunct (4 women). *Students:* 32 full-time (15 women), 31 part-time (18 women); includes 5 minority (2 African Americans, 1 American Indian/Alaska Native, 2 Hispanic Americans), 4 international. Average age 24. 172 applicants, 27% accepted, 19 enrolled. In 2008, 15 Certificates awarded. *Degree requirements:* For Certificate, final project. *Entrance requirements:* For degree, resumé, portfolio, letter of recommendation. Additional exam requirements/recommendations for international students: Required—TOEFL (minimum score 550 paper-based; 213 computer-based; 79 iBT). *Application deadline:* For fall admission, 1/15 for domestic and international students. Application fee: $50. Electronic applications accepted. *Expenses:* Tuition: Full-time $28,400; part-time $813 per credit. *Financial support:* Career-related internships or fieldwork and scholarships/grants available. Financial award application deadline: 3/15; financial award applicants required to submit FAFSA. *Faculty research:* Visual arts. *Unit head:* Carole Fisher, Graduate Director, 612-874-3629, E-mail: carole_fisher@mcad.edu. *Application contact:* William Mullen, Vice President, Enrollment Management, 612-874-3762, Fax: 612-874-3701, E-mail: william_mullen@mcad.edu.

Northern Arizona University, Graduate College, College of Arts and Letters, Program in Sustainable Communities, Flagstaff, AZ 86011. Offers MA. Part-time programs available.

Philadelphia University, School of Architecture, Program in Sustainable Design, Philadelphia, PA 19144-5497. Offers MS.

Rochester Institute of Technology, Graduate Enrollment Services, Golisano Institute for Sustainability, Rochester, NY 14623-5603. Offers PhD.

SIT Graduate Institute, Graduate Programs, Master's Programs in Intercultural Service, Leadership, and Management, Brattleboro, VT 05302-0676. Offers conflict transformation (MA); intercultural service, leadership, and management (MA); international education (MA); management (MS); social justice in intercultural relations (MA); sustainable development (MA). Postbaccalaureate distance learning degree programs offered (minimal on-campus study). *Degree requirements:* For master's, one foreign language, thesis. *Entrance requirements:* For master's, 3 letters of reference. Additional exam requirements/recommendations for international students: Required—TOEFL. *Faculty research:* Intercultural communication, conflict resolution, advising and training, world issues, international business.

Slippery Rock University of Pennsylvania, Graduate Studies (Recruitment), College of Health, Environment, and Science, Department of Parks, Recreation, and Environmental Education, Slippery Rock, PA 16057-1383. Offers environmental education (M Ed); resource management (MS); sustainable systems (MS). Part-time and evening/weekend programs available. *Degree requirements:* For master's, comprehensive exam (for some programs), thesis (for some programs). *Entrance requirements:* For master's, GRE General Test, MAT, minimum GPA of 2.75. Additional exam requirements/recommendations for international students: Required—TOEFL (minimum score 550 paper-based; 213 computer-based). *Application deadline:* For fall admission, 7/1 priority date for domestic and international students; for spring admission, 11/1 priority date for domestic and international students. Applications are processed on a rolling basis. Application fee: $25. Electronic applications accepted. *Expenses:* Tuition,

Sustainable Development

Slippery Rock University of Pennsylvania (continued)
area resident: Full-time $6430; part-time $357 per credit. Tuition, state resident: full-time $6430; part-time $357 per credit. Tuition, nonresident: full-time $10,288; part-time $572 per credit. Required fees: $2062; $158 per credit. *Financial support:* Career-related internships or fieldwork, Federal Work-Study, scholarships/grants, and unspecified assistantships available. Support available to part-time students. Financial award application deadline: 5/1; financial award applicants required to submit FAFSA. *Unit head:* Dr. Daniel Dziubek, Graduate Coordinator, 724-738-2068, Fax: 724-738-2938, E-mail: daniel.dziubek@sru.edu. *Application contact:* Angela Piverotto, Interim Director of Graduate Studies, 724-738-2051, Fax: 724-738-2146, E-mail: graduate.admissions@sru.edu.

University of Connecticut, Graduate School, Center for Continuing Studies, Program in Humanitarian Services Administration, Storrs, CT 06269. Offers MPS. Postbaccalaureate distance learning degree programs offered. *Entrance requirements:* For master's, minimum GPA of 3.0 or greater than 3.0 for the last 2 years of study; 3 letters of reference. Additional exam requirements/recommendations for international students: Required—TOEFL (minimum score 540 paper-based; 207 computer-based).

University of Georgia, Graduate School, School of Ecology, Athens, GA 30602. Offers conservation ecology and sustainable development (MS); ecology (MS, PhD). *Degree requirements:* For master's, thesis; for doctorate, one foreign language, thesis/dissertation. *Entrance requirements:* For master's and doctorate, GRE General Test. Electronic applications accepted.

University of Maryland, College Park, Graduate Studies, College of Chemical and Life Sciences, Department of Biology, Program in Sustainable Development and Conservation Biology, College Park, MD 20742. Offers MS. Part-time and evening/weekend programs available. *Degree requirements:* For master's, internship, scholarly paper. *Entrance requirements:* For master's, GRE General Test, minimum GPA of 3.0, 3 letters of recommendation. Electronic applications accepted. *Faculty research:* Biodiversity, global change, conservation.

University of Massachusetts Lowell, James B. Francis College of Engineering, Department of Civil and Environmental Engineering, Lowell, MA 01854-2881. Offers civil and environmental engineering (MS Eng, Certificate); environmental engineering (D Eng); environmental studies (MSES, PhD, Certificate), including environmental engineering (MSES), environmental studies (PhD, Certificate); sustainable infrastructure for developing nations (Certificate). Part-time programs available. *Degree requirements:* For master's, thesis optional. *Entrance requirements:* For master's, GRE General Test. *Faculty research:* Bridge design, traffic control, groundwater remediation, pile capacity.

University of Michigan, School of Natural Resources and Environment, Program in Natural Resources and Environment, Ann Arbor, MI 48109. Offers aquatic sciences: research and management (MS); behavior, education and communication (MS); conservation biology (MS); environmental informatics (MS); environmental justice (MS); environmental policy and planning (MS); natural resources and environment (PhD); sustainable systems (MS); terrestrial ecosystems (MS); MS/AM; MS/JD; MS/MBA. Terminal master's awarded for partial completion of doctoral program. *Degree requirements:* For master's, thesis, practicum or group project; for doctorate, comprehensive exam, thesis/dissertation, oral defense of dissertation, preliminary exam. *Entrance requirements:* For master's, GRE General Test; for doctorate, GRE General Test, master's degree. Additional exam requirements/recommendations for international students: Required—TOEFL (paper-based 560; computer-score 220) or IELTS (6.5). Electronic applications accepted. *Faculty research:* Stream ecology, plant-insect interactions, fish biology, resource control and reproductive success, remote sensing.

University of New Brunswick Fredericton, School of Graduate Studies, Policy Studies Program, Fredericton, NB E3B 5A3, Canada. Offers people, property and alternative dispute resolution (M Phil); philosophy politics and economics (M Phil); sustainable development (M Phil). *Faculty:* 6 full-time (2 women), 13 part-time/adjunct (2 women). *Students:* 16 full-time (9 women), 4 part-time (3 women). In 2008, 3 master's awarded. *Entrance requirements:* For master's, minimum GPA of 3.5, BA. Additional exam requirements/recommendations for international students: Required—TOEFL (minimum score 600 paper-based), TWE (minimum score 5). Application fee: $50 Canadian dollars. Tuition and fees charges are reported in Canadian dollars. *Expenses:* Tuition, area resident: Full-time $5562 Canadian dollars. Tuition, nonresident: full-time $9450 Canadian dollars. Required fees: $333 Canadian dollars. *Financial support:* In 2008–09, 4 research assistantships, 1 teaching assistantship were awarded. *Unit head:* Dr. Linda Eyre, Dean of Graduate Studies, 506-447-3044, Fax: 506-453-4817, E-mail: gradidst@unb.ca. *Application contact:* Janet Amurault, Graduate Secretary, 506-458-7558, Fax: 506-453-4817, E-mail: jamiraul@unb.ca.

University of Washington, Graduate School, College of Forest Resources, Seattle, WA 98195. Offers bioresource science and engineering (MS, PhD); environmental horticulture (MEH); environmental horticulture and urban forestry (MS, PhD); forest ecology (MS, PhD); forest management (MFR); forest soils (MS, PhD); forest systems and bioenergy (MS, PhD); restoration ecology (MS, PhD); social sciences (MS, PhD); sustainable resource management (MS, PhD); wildlife science (MS, PhD); MFR/MAIS; MPA/MS. *Accreditation:* SAF. *Degree requirements:* For master's, thesis (for some programs); for doctorate, comprehensive exam (for some programs), thesis/dissertation. *Entrance requirements:* For master's and doctorate, GRE, minimum GPA of 3.0. Additional exam requirements/recommendations for international students: Required—TOEFL. Electronic applications accepted. *Faculty research:* Ecosystem analysis, silviculture and forest protection, paper science and engineering, environmental horticulture and urban forestry, natural resource policy and economics.

University of Washington, Graduate School, School of Law, Seattle, WA 98195-3020. Offers Asian law (LL M, PhD); intellectual property law and policy (LL M); law (JD); law of sustainable international development (LL M); taxation (LL M); JD/LL M; JD/MA; JD/MAIS; JD/MBA; JD/MPA; JD/MS; JD/PhD. *Accreditation:* ABA. *Degree requirements:* For master's, thesis; for doctorate, thesis/dissertation. *Entrance requirements:* For JD, LSAT; for master's, language proficiency (LL M in Asian law). Additional exam requirements/recommendations for international students: Required—TOEFL. *Expenses:* Contact institution. *Faculty research:* Asian, international and comparative law, intellectual property law, health law, environmental law, taxation.

The University of Western Ontario, Faculty of Graduate Studies, Physical Sciences Division, Department of Earth Sciences, London, ON N6A 5B8, Canada. Offers environment and sustainability (MES); geology (M Sc, PhD); geology and environmental science (M Sc, PhD); geophysics (M Sc, PhD); geophysics and environmental science (M Sc, PhD). *Degree requirements:* For master's, thesis; for doctorate, thesis/dissertation, qualifying exam. *Entrance requirements:* For master's, honors in B Sc; for doctorate, M Sc. Additional exam requirements/recommendations for international students: Required—TOEFL. *Faculty research:* Geophysics, geochemistry, paleontology, sedimentology/stratigraphy, glaciology/quaternary.

University of Wisconsin–Madison, Graduate School, Gaylord Nelson Institute for Environmental Studies, Conservation Biology and Sustainable Development Program, Madison, WI 53706-1380. Offers MS. Part-time programs available. *Degree requirements:* For master's, thesis or alternative, exit seminar. *Entrance requirements:* For master's, GRE General Test. Additional exam requirements/recommendations for international students: Required—TOEFL (minimum score 550 paper-based; 213 computer-based). Electronic applications accepted. *Faculty research:* Ornithology, forestry, sociology, rural sociology, plant ecology.

Walden University, Graduate Programs, School of Public Policy and Administration, Minneapolis, MN 55401. Offers general public policy and administration (MPA); government management (Certificate); health policy (MPA); homeland security policy (MPA); interdisciplinary policy studies (MPA); law and public policy (MPA); local government management for sustainable communities (MPA); nonprofit management (Certificate); nonprofit management and leadership (MPA, MS); policy analysis (MPA); public management and leadership (MPA); public policy and administration (PhD), including criminal justice, health services, homeland security policy and coordination, international nongovernmental organizations, knowledge management, nonprofit management and leadership, public management and leadership, public policy, public safety management; terrorism, mediation, and peace (MPA). Part-time and evening/weekend programs available. Postbaccalaureate distance learning degree programs offered (minimal on-campus study). *Faculty:* 2 full-time, 55 part-time/adjunct. *Students:* 1,285 full-time (794 women), 144 part-time (96 women); includes 657 minority (591 African Americans, 8 American Indian/Alaska Native, 17 Asian Americans or Pacific Islanders, 41 Hispanic Americans), 20 international. Average age 39. 727 applicants, 54% accepted, 284 enrolled. In 2008, 101 master's, 6 doctorates awarded. *Degree requirements:* For doctorate, thesis/dissertation, residency. *Entrance requirements:* For master's, bachelor's degree or equivalent in related field, minimum GPA of 2.5, two references, goal statement, official transcripts, access to computer and Internet; for doctorate, master's degree or equivalent in related field, minimum GPA of 3.0, three years related professional/academic experience, two references, goal statement, official transcripts, access to computer and Internet. Additional exam requirements/recommendations for international students: Required—TOEFL (minimum score 550 paper-based; 213 computer-based), IELTS (minimum score 6.5), TOEFL, IELTS, or Michigan English Language Assessment Battery (minimum score 82). *Application deadline:* Applications are processed on a rolling basis. Application fee: $50. Electronic applications accepted. *Expenses:* Tuition: Full-time $12,877; part-time $520 per credit. Required fees: $1230. Tuition and fees vary according to course load, degree level and program. *Financial support:* In 2008–09, 3 students received support; fellowships with tuition reimbursements available, Federal Work-Study, scholarships/grants, unspecified assistantships, and family tuition reduction; active duty/veteran tuition reduction; group tuition reduction; interest-free payment plans available. Support available to part-time students. Financial award applicants required to submit FAFSA. *Unit head:* Dr. Mark Gordon, Interim Associate Dean, 800-925-3368. *Application contact:* Jennifer Hall, 866-4-WALDEN, E-mail: info@waldenu.edu.

Western Illinois University, School of Graduate Studies, College of Arts and Sciences, Department of Geography, Macomb, IL 61455-1390. Offers community development (Certificate); geography (MA). Part-time programs available. *Students:* 17 full-time (4 women), 3 part-time (0 women); includes 2 minority (both Asian Americans or Pacific Islanders), 5 international. Average age 31. 5 applicants, 80% accepted. In 2008, 1 master's, 4 other advanced degrees awarded. *Degree requirements:* For master's, thesis or alternative. *Entrance requirements:* Additional exam requirements/recommendations for international students: Required—TOEFL (minimum score 550 paper-based; 213 computer-based; 80 iBT). *Application deadline:* Applications are processed on a rolling basis. Application fee: $30. Electronic applications accepted. *Expenses:* Tuition, state resident: full-time $5696; part-time $237.34 per credit hour. Tuition, nonresident: full-time $11,392; part-time $474.68 per credit hour. Required fees: $1453; $60.55 per credit hour. *Financial support:* In 2008–09, 13 students received support, including 13 research assistantships with full tuition reimbursements available (averaging $7,040 per year). Financial award applicants required to submit FAFSA. *Unit head:* Dr. Sam Thompson, Chairperson, 309-298-1648. *Application contact:* Evelyn Hoing, Assistant Director of Graduate Studies, 309-298-1806, Fax: 309-298-2345, E-mail: grad-office@wiu.edu.

West Virginia University, Davis College of Agriculture, Forestry and Consumer Sciences, Division of Resource Management and Sustainable Development, Program in Resource Management and Sustainable Development, Morgantown, WV 26506. Offers PhD. Part-time programs available. *Degree requirements:* For doctorate, thesis/dissertation. *Entrance requirements:* For doctorate, GRE General Test. Additional exam requirements/recommendations for international students: Required—TOEFL.

Urban and Regional Planning

Alabama Agricultural and Mechanical University, School of Graduate Studies, School of Agricultural and Environmental Sciences, Department of Community Planning and Urban Studies, Huntsville, AL 35811. Offers urban and regional planning (MURP). *Accreditation:* ACSP. Part-time and evening/weekend programs available. *Students:* 14 full-time (6 women), 17 part-time (8 women); includes 27 minority (all African Americans), 4 international. In 2008, 4 master's awarded. *Degree requirements:* For master's, comprehensive exam. *Entrance requirements:* For master's, GRE General Test. Additional exam requirements/recommendations for international students: Required—TOEFL (minimum score 500 paper-based; 173 computer-based; 61 iBT). *Application deadline:* For fall admission, 5/1 for domestic students. Applications are processed on a rolling basis. Application fee: $25. Electronic applications accepted. *Expenses:* Tuition, area resident: Full-time $3924; part-time $2616 per term. Tuition, nonresident: part-time $5234 per year. International tuition: $7848 full-time. Required fees: $198; $396 per credit hour. $2841 per term. One-time fee: $8498 full-time; $5682 part-time. Full-time tuition and fees vary according to program. *Financial support:* In 2008–09, fellowships (averaging $1,500 per year), research assistantships with full tuition reimbursements (averaging $9,000 per year) were awarded; career-related internships or fieldwork also available. Support available to part-time students. Financial award application deadline: 4/1. *Faculty research:* Urban and rural research, needs assessment and community trends through analysis of social indicators, fiscal impact studies, rural transportation, health care. *Unit head:* Dr. Chukudi Izeogu, Chair, 256-372-5425, Fax: 256-372-5906. *Application contact:* Dr. Caula Beyl, Dean, School of Graduate Studies, 256-372-5266, Fax: 256-372-5269, E-mail: caula.beyl@aamu.edu.

American University of Beirut, Graduate Programs, Faculty of Engineering and Architecture, Beirut, Lebanon. Offers civil engineering (ME, PhD); electrical and computer engineering (ME, PhD); engineering management (MEM); environmental and water resources (ME); environmental and water resources engineering (PhD); environmental technology (MSES); mechanical engineering (ME, PhD); urban design (MUD); urban planning and policy (MUP). Part-time programs available. *Degree requirements:* For master's, one foreign language, comprehensive exam, thesis (for some programs); for doctorate, one foreign language, comprehensive exam, thesis/dissertation, publications. *Entrance requirements:* For master's, letters of recommendation; for doctorate, letters of recommendation, master's degree, transcripts, curriculum vitae, interview. Additional exam requirements/recommendations for international students: Required—TOEFL (minimum score 600 paper-based; 250 computer-based; 100 iBT), IELTS (minimum score 7.5). Electronic applications accepted.

American University of Sharjah, Graduate Programs, Sharjah, United Arab Emirates. Offers business (EMBA, MBA); chemical engineering (MS Ch E); civil engineering (MSCE); computer engineering (MS); electrical engineering (MSEE); mechanical engineering (MSME); mechatronics engineering (MS); public administration (MPA); teaching English to speakers of other languages

(MA); translation and interpreting (MA); urban planning (MUP). Part-time and evening/weekend programs available. *Faculty:* 35 full-time (7 women). *Students:* 66 full-time (36 women), 188 part-time (83 women). Average age 28. 302 applicants, 65% accepted, 131 enrolled. In 2008, 74 master's awarded. *Entrance requirements:* For master's, GMAT (MBA). Additional exam requirements/recommendations for international students: Required—TOEFL (minimum score 550 paper-based; 213 computer-based; 80 iBT), TWE (minimum score 5). *Application deadline:* For fall admission, 7/30 priority date for domestic students, 7/15 priority date for international students; for spring admission, 12/31 priority date for domestic students, 12/16 for international students. Applications are processed on a rolling basis. Application fee: $300. Electronic applications accepted. Tuition and fees charges are reported in United Arab Emirates dirhams. *Expenses:* Tuition: Full-time 58,500 United Arab Emirates dirhams; part-time 3250 United Arab Emirates dirhams per credit hour. One-time fee: 300 United Arab Emirates dirhams. *Faculty research:* Chemical engineering, civil engineering, computer engineering, electrical engineering, linguistics, translation. *Unit head:* Ghada S Sami, Admissions Manager, 971-65151006 Ext. 1006, Fax: 971-65151020, E-mail: graduateadmission@aus.edu. *Application contact:* Ghada S Sami, Admissions Manager, 971-65151006 Ext. 1006, Fax: 971-65151020, E-mail: graduateadmission@aus.edu.

Arizona State University, Graduate College, College of Design, School of Planning, Tempe, AZ 85287. Offers MUEP. *Accreditation:* ACSP. *Entrance requirements:* For master's, GRE General Test.

Arizona State University, College of Public Programs, School of Community Resources and Development, Tempe, AZ 85287. Offers community resources and development (PhD); nonprofit studies (MNpS); recreation and tourism studies (MS). *Degree requirements:* For master's, thesis or alternative.

Auburn University, Graduate School, College of Architecture, Design, and Construction, Program in Community Planning, Auburn University, AL 36849. Offers MCP, MPA/MCP. *Accreditation:* ACSP. Part-time programs available. *Faculty:* 9 full-time (3 women). *Students:* 22 full-time (10 women), 3 part-time (2 women); includes 2 minority (1 African American, 1 Hispanic American), 2 international. Average age 26. 16 applicants, 88% accepted, 6 enrolled. In 2008, 19 master's awarded. *Degree requirements:* For master's, oral exam, project. *Entrance requirements:* For master's, GRE General Test. *Application deadline:* For fall admission, 7/7 for domestic students; for spring admission, 11/24 for domestic students. Applications are processed on a rolling basis. Application fee: $25 ($50 for international students). Electronic applications accepted. *Expenses:* Tuition, area resident: Full-time $5880; part-time $243 per credit hour. Tuition, state resident: full-time $5880; part-time $243 per credit hour. Tuition, nonresident: full-time $17,640; part-time $729 per credit hour. International tuition: $17,846 full-time. Required fees: $620. Tuition and fees vary according to program and reciprocity agreements. *Financial support:* Federal Work-Study available. Support available to part-time students. Financial award application deadline: 3/15. *Unit head:* Dr. John J. Pittari, Chair, 334-844-4516. *Application contact:* Dr. George Flowers, Dean of the Graduate School, 334-844-2125.

Ball State University, Graduate School, College of Architecture and Planning, Department of Urban Planning, Muncie, IN 47306-1099. Offers MURP. *Accreditation:* ACSP. *Degree requirements:* For master's, thesis. *Entrance requirements:* For master's, writing sample. *Faculty research:* Computer-assisted land-use analysis.

Announcement: MURP is an accredited, professionally recognized, 48-credit-hour degree (36-hour accelerated track for those with accredited undergraduate planning degrees). Students can study on the Muncie campus or at the CAP Indianapolis Center, where individual courses are periodically offered. Students receive hands-on field experiences and physical and comprehensive planning practice. Students can select among three areas of concentrated study. There are well-developed study-abroad and internship programs. Students interact closely with 9 full-time faculty members plus professionals and practitioner alumni. Assistantships and other financial aid are available. Web site: www.bsu.edu/urban.

Boston University, Metropolitan College (Continuing Education), Department of Applied Social Sciences, Program in City Planning, Boston, MA 02215. Offers MCP. Part-time and evening/weekend programs available. *Entrance requirements:* Additional exam requirements/recommendations for international students: Required—TOEFL; Recommended—IELTS. Electronic applications accepted. *Faculty research:* Housing, community development and land use planning, environmental management and planning, international comparative development planning.

California Polytechnic State University, San Luis Obispo, College of Architecture and Environmental Design, Department of City and Regional Planning, San Luis Obispo, CA 93407. Offers MCRP, MCRP/MS. *Accreditation:* ACSP. Part-time programs available. *Faculty:* 6 full-time (2 women), 4 part-time/adjunct (1 woman). *Students:* 41 full-time (20 women), 2 part-time (1 woman); includes 8 minority (4 Asian Americans or Pacific Islanders, 4 Hispanic Americans), 1 international. Average age 26. 64 applicants, 61% accepted, 22 enrolled. In 2008, 13 master's awarded. *Degree requirements:* For master's, thesis. *Entrance requirements:* For master's, GRE, minimum GPA of 3.0 in last 90 quarter units. Additional exam requirements/recommendations for international students: Required—TOEFL (minimum score 550 paper-based; 213 computer-based), IELTS (minimum score 6), Either TOEFL or IELTS is acceptable. *Application deadline:* For fall admission, 2/1 for domestic students, 11/30 for international students; for winter admission, 11/1 for domestic students, 6/30 for international students. Applications are processed on a rolling basis. Application fee: $55. Electronic applications accepted. *Expenses:* Tuition, nonresident: full-time $10,170; part-time $226 per unit. Required fees: $5751; $1265 per quarter. *Financial support:* Research assistantships, career-related internships or fieldwork, Federal Work-Study, institutionally sponsored loans, and unspecified assistantships available. Support available to part-time students. Financial award application deadline: 3/2; financial award applicants required to submit FAFSA. *Faculty research:* Natural hazards, housing, small town and rural planning, planning implementation, subdivision site design, transportation. *Unit head:* Dr. Michael Boswell, Graduate Coordinator, 805-756-2496, Fax: 805-756-1340, E-mail: mboswell@calpoly.edu. *Application contact:* Dr. Michael Boswell, Graduate Coordinator, 805-756-2496, Fax: 805-756-1340, E-mail: mboswell@calpoly.edu.

California State Polytechnic University, Pomona, Academic Affairs, College of Environmental Design, Program in Urban and Regional Planning, Pomona, CA 91768-2557. Offers MURP. *Accreditation:* ACSP. Part-time programs available. *Students:* 42 full-time (15 women), 39 part-time (23 women); includes 31 minority (4 African Americans, 12 Asian Americans or Pacific Islanders, 15 Hispanic Americans), 7 international. Average age 30. 99 applicants, 57% accepted, 25 enrolled. In 2008, 8 master's awarded. *Degree requirements:* For master's, thesis or alternative. *Entrance requirements:* For master's, GRE General Test. *Application deadline:* For fall admission, 5/1 priority date for domestic students; for winter admission, 10/15 priority date for domestic students; for spring admission, 1/20 priority date for domestic students. Applications are processed on a rolling basis. Application fee: $55. Electronic applications accepted. *Expenses:* Tuition, nonresident: full-time $7232; part-time $226 per credit. Required fees: $4272. One-time fee: $2694 part-time. Tuition and fees vary according to course load. *Financial support:* Career-related internships or fieldwork, Federal Work-Study, and institutionally sponsored loans available. Support available to part-time students. Financial award application deadline: 3/2; financial award applicants required to submit FAFSA. *Unit head:* Herschel H. Farberow, Graduate Coordinator, 909-869-2716, Fax: 909-869-4688, E-mail: hfarberow@csupomona.edu. *Application contact:* Scott J. Duncan, Director, Admissions, 909-869-3258, Fax: 909-869-4529, E-mail: sjduncan@csupomona.edu.

California State University, Chico, Graduate School, College of Behavioral and Social Sciences, Department of Geography and Planning, Program in Rural and Town Planning, Chico, CA 95929-0722. Offers MA. Part-time programs available. *Entrance requirements:* For master's, GRE, 2 letters of recommendation, statement of purpose, writing sample. Additional exam requirements/recommendations for international students: Required—TOEFL (minimum score 550 paper-based; 213 computer-based; 80 iBT), IELTS (minimum score 6.5). Electronic applications accepted.

The Catholic University of America, School of Architecture and Planning, Washington, DC 20064. Offers M Arch, M Arch Studies. Part-time programs available. *Degree requirements:* For master's, thesis. *Entrance requirements:* For master's, minimum GPA of 2.7, portfolio, 3 letters of recommendation. Additional exam requirements/recommendations for international students: Required—TOEFL (minimum score 500 paper-based; 173 computer-based). Electronic applications accepted. *Expenses:* Contact institution. *Faculty research:* Architectural history, sacred architecture, computers, technology, urban design, preservation.

Clark University, Graduate School, Department of International Development, Community, and Environment, Program in Community Development and Planning, Worcester, MA 01610-1477. Offers MA. *Students:* 17 full-time (15 women), 17 part-time (10 women); includes 4 minority (3 African Americans, 1 Hispanic American), 3 international. Average age 25. 41 applicants, 93% accepted, 26 enrolled. In 2008, 14 master's awarded. *Degree requirements:* For master's, thesis. *Entrance requirements:* Additional exam requirements/recommendations for international students: Required—TOEFL. *Application deadline:* For fall admission, 1/15 for domestic students. Application fee: $50. *Expenses:* Tuition: Full-time $34,900; part-time $1091 per credit hour. Required fees: $30. *Financial support:* In 2008–09, research assistantships with full and partial tuition reimbursements (averaging $5,000 per year), teaching assistantships with full and partial tuition reimbursements (averaging $5,000 per year) were awarded; fellowships, tuition waivers (full and partial) also available. *Faculty research:* Urban neighborhood revitalization, youth and community development, project evaluation, community development finance. *Unit head:* Dr. William F. Fisher, Director, 508-421-3765, Fax: 508-793-8820, E-mail: wfisher@clarku.edu. *Application contact:* Paula Hall, IDCE Graduate Admissions, 508-793-7201, Fax: 508-793-8820, E-mail: idce@clarku.edu.

Clemson University, Graduate School, College of Architecture, Arts, and Humanities, Department of Planning and Landscape Architecture, Program in City and Regional Planning, Clemson, SC 29634. Offers developmental planning (MCRP). *Students:* 31 full-time (16 women), 1 part-time (0 women); includes 1 minority (African American), 5 international. Average age 28. 58 applicants, 71% accepted, 22 enrolled. In 2008, 9 master's awarded. *Degree requirements:* For master's, departmental paper or thesis. *Entrance requirements:* For master's, GRE General Test. Additional exam requirements/recommendations for international students: Required—TOEFL. *Application deadline:* For fall admission, 4/15 priority date for domestic students, 4/15 for international students; for spring admission, 9/15 for international students. Applications are processed on a rolling basis. Application fee: $55. Full-time tuition and fees vary according to program. *Financial support:* Fellowships, research assistantships, teaching assistantships, career-related internships or fieldwork, Federal Work-Study, and scholarships/grants available. Financial award application deadline: 4/15; financial award applicants required to submit FAFSA. *Faculty research:* Coastal planning, regional economic development, health care access. *Unit head:* James D. London, Director City and Regional Planning, 864-656-0181, Fax: 864-656-0204, E-mail: riggor@clemson.edu. *Application contact:* James D. London, Director City and Regional Planning, 864-656-0181, Fax: 864-656-0204, E-mail: riggor@clemson.edu.

Cleveland State University, College of Graduate Studies, Maxine Goodman Levin College of Urban Affairs, Program in Urban Planning, Design, and Development, Cleveland, OH 44115. Offers geographic information systems (Certificate); local and urban management (Certificate); urban economic development (Certificate); urban planning, design, and development (MUPDD); urban real estate development and finance (Certificate); JD/MUPDD. *Accreditation:* ACSP. Part-time and evening/weekend programs available. *Faculty:* 26 full-time (10 women), 12 part-time/adjunct (5 women). *Students:* 37 full-time (17 women), 41 part-time (21 women); includes 13 minority (9 African Americans, 1 American Indian/Alaska Native, 3 Hispanic Americans), 10 international. Average age 38. 63 applicants, 63% accepted, 21 enrolled. In 2008, 24 master's, 9 Certificates awarded. *Degree requirements:* For master's, project or thesis. *Entrance requirements:* For master's, GRE General Test (minimum score: verbal and quantitative 50th percentile, analytical writing 4.0), minimum GPA of 3.0. Additional exam requirements/recommendations for international students: Required—TOEFL (minimum score 525 paper-based; 197 computer-based; 65 iBT). *Application deadline:* For fall admission, 7/15 priority date for domestic students, 5/15 for international students; for spring admission, 11/1 for international students. Applications are processed on a rolling basis. Application fee: $30. Electronic applications accepted. *Financial support:* In 2008–09, 15 students received support, including 10 research assistantships with full and partial tuition reimbursements available (averaging $6,960 per year), 5 teaching assistantships with full and partial tuition reimbursements available (averaging $6,960 per year); career-related internships or fieldwork, Federal Work-Study, tuition waivers (full and partial), and unspecified assistantships also available. Support available to part-time students. Financial award application deadline: 3/1. *Faculty research:* Housing and neighborhood development, urban housing policy, environmental sustainability, economic development. *Unit head:* Dr. W. Dennis Keating, Director, 216-687-2298, Fax: 216-687-2013, E-mail: w.keating@csuohio.edu. *Application contact:* Graduate Program Coordinator, 216-523-7522, Fax: 216-687-5398, E-mail: urbanprograms@csuohio.edu.

Columbia University, Graduate School of Architecture, Planning, and Preservation, Program in Urban Planning, New York, NY 10027. Offers MS, PhD, JD/MS, M Arch/MS, MBA/MS, MIA/MS, MPH/MS, MS/MS. PhD offered through the Graduate School of Arts and Sciences. *Accreditation:* ACSP (one or more programs are accredited). *Degree requirements:* For master's, thesis. *Entrance requirements:* For master's, GRE General Test.

Concordia University, School of Graduate Studies, Faculty of Arts and Science, School of Community and Public Affairs, Montréal, QC H3G 1M8, Canada. Offers community economic development (Diploma).

Cornell University, Graduate School, Graduate Fields of Agriculture and Life Sciences, Field of Community and Rural Development, Ithaca, NY 14853-0001. Offers community development process (MPS); economic development (MPS); local government organizations and operations (MPS); program development and planning (MPS). *Faculty:* 30 full-time (10 women). *Students:* 1 (woman) full-time. Average age 28. In 2008, 2 master's awarded. *Entrance requirements:* For master's, GRE General Test (recommended), 3 letters of recommendation. Additional exam requirements/recommendations for international students: Required—TOEFL (minimum score 550 paper-based; 213 computer-based; 77 iBT). *Application deadline:* For fall admission, 5/1 for domestic students. Application fee: $70. Electronic applications accepted. *Expenses:* Tuition: Full-time $29,500. Required fees: $70. Full-time tuition and fees vary according to degree level, program and student level. *Financial support:* In 2008–09, 1 fellowship with full tuition reimbursement, 1 teaching assistantship with full tuition reimbursement were awarded; research assistantships with full tuition reimbursements, institutionally sponsored loans, scholarships/grants, health care benefits, tuition waivers (full and partial), and unspecified assistantships also available. Financial award applicants required to submit FAFSA. *Faculty research:* Land use, community economic development, governance and leadership development, planning and evaluation, main street revitalization. *Unit head:* Director of Graduate Studies, 607-255-4916, Fax: 607-255-2231. *Application contact:* Graduate Field Assistant, 607-255-4916, Fax: 607-255-2331, E-mail: gradcrd@cornell.edu.

Cornell University, Graduate School, Graduate Fields of Architecture, Art and Planning, Field of City and Regional Planning, Ithaca, NY 14853-0001. Offers city and regional planning (MRP, PhD); environmental planning and design (MRP, PhD); historic preservation planning (MA); international development planning (MRP, PhD); planning theory and systems analysis (MRP, PhD); regional economics and development planning (MRP, PhD); regional science (MRP, PhD); social and health systems planning (MRP, PhD); urban and regional theory (MRP, PhD); urban planning history (MRP, PhD). *Accreditation:* ACSP (one or more programs are accredited). *Faculty:* 27 full-time (10 women). *Students:* 113 full-time (71 women); includes 13 minority (3 African Americans, 6 Asian Americans or Pacific Islanders, 4 Hispanic Americans), 26

Urban and Regional Planning

Cornell University (continued)
international. Average age 30. 268 applicants, 47% accepted, 46 enrolled. In 2008, 23 master's, 5 doctorates awarded. *Degree requirements:* For master's, thesis (MA); for doctorate, comprehensive exam, thesis/dissertation. *Entrance requirements:* For master's and doctorate, GRE General Test, 2 letters of recommendation. Additional exam requirements/recommendations for international students: Required—TOEFL (minimum score 600 paper-based; 250 computer-based; 77 iBT). *Application deadline:* For fall admission, 1/10 for domestic students. Application fee: $70. Electronic applications accepted. *Expenses:* Tuition: Full-time $29,500. Required fees: $70. Full-time tuition and fees vary according to degree level, program and student level. *Financial support:* In 2008–09, 24 students received support, including 9 fellowships with full tuition reimbursements available, 5 research assistantships with full tuition reimbursements available, 10 teaching assistantships with full tuition reimbursements available; institutionally sponsored loans, scholarships/grants, health care benefits, tuition waivers (full and partial), and unspecified assistantships also available. Financial award applicants required to submit FAFSA. *Faculty research:* Land use planning, economic development, international development, historic preservation, community development. *Unit head:* Director of Graduate Studies, 607-255-6848, Fax: 607-255-1971. *Application contact:* Graduate Field Assistant, 607-255-6848, Fax: 607-255-1971, E-mail: crp_admissions@cornell.edu.

Cornell University, Graduate School, Graduate Fields of Architecture, Art and Planning, Field of Regional Science, Ithaca, NY 14853-0001. Offers environmental studies (MA, MS, PhD); international spatial problems (MA, MS, PhD); location theory (MA, MS, PhD); multiregional economic analysis (MA, MS, PhD); peace science (MA, MS, PhD); planning methods (MA, MS, PhD); urban and regional economics (MA, MS, PhD). *Faculty:* 17 full-time (5 women). *Students:* 22 full-time (10 women); includes 2 minority (1 African American, 1 Asian American or Pacific Islander), 19 international. Average age 33. 18 applicants, 67% accepted, 3 enrolled. In 2008, 3 master's, 2 doctorates awarded. Terminal master's awarded for partial completion of doctoral program. *Degree requirements:* For master's, thesis; for doctorate, comprehensive exam, thesis/dissertation. *Entrance requirements:* For master's and doctorate, GRE General Test, 2 letters of recommendation. Additional exam requirements/recommendations for international students: Required—TOEFL (minimum score 600 paper-based; 250 computer-based; 77 iBT). *Application deadline:* For fall admission, 1/15 priority date for domestic students. Application fee: $70. Electronic applications accepted. *Expenses:* Tuition: Full-time $29,500. Required fees: $70. Full-time tuition and fees vary according to degree level, program and student level. *Financial support:* In 2008–09, 7 students received support, including 2 research assistantships with full tuition reimbursements available, 5 teaching assistantships with full tuition reimbursements available; fellowships with full tuition reimbursements available, institutionally sponsored loans, scholarships/grants, health care benefits, tuition waivers (full and partial), and unspecified assistantships also available. Financial award applicants required to submit FAFSA. *Faculty research:* Urban and regional growth, spatial economics, formation of spatial patterns by socioeconomic systems, non-linear dynamics and complex systems, environmental-economic systems. *Unit head:* Director of Graduate Studies, 607-255-6848, Fax: 607-255-1971. *Application contact:* Graduate Field Assistant, 607-255-6848, Fax: 607-255-1971, E-mail: regsci@cornell.edu.

Dalhousie University, Faculty of Architecture and Planning, School of Planning, Halifax, NS B3J 2X4, Canada. Offers M Eng, M Plan, MPS. *Degree requirements:* For master's, thesis. *Entrance requirements:* Additional exam requirements/recommendations for international students: Required—TOEFL, IELTS, 1 of 5 approved tests: TOEFL, IELTS, CANTEST, CAEL, Michigan English Language Assessment Battery. *Application deadline:* For fall admission, 6/1 priority date for domestic students, 4/1 for international students; for winter admission, 11/15 for domestic students, 8/31 for international students; for spring admission, 1/28 for domestic students, 12/31 for international students. Applications are processed on a rolling basis. Application fee: $70. Electronic applications accepted. *Financial support:* Career-related internships or fieldwork and scholarships/grants available. *Unit head:* Prof. Jill Grant, Director, 902-494-3260, Fax: 902-423-6672, E-mail: plan.office@dal.ca. *Application contact:* Frank Palermo, Graduate Coordinator, 902-494-3978, Fax: 902-423-6672, E-mail: frank.palermo@dal.ca.

Delta State University, Graduate Programs, College of Arts and Sciences, Division of Social Sciences, Program in Community Development, Cleveland, MS 38733-0001. Offers MSCD. Part-time programs available. *Degree requirements:* For master's, thesis or alternative.

DePaul University, School of Public Service, Chicago, IL 60604. Offers financial administration management (Certificate); health administration (Certificate); health law and policy (MS); international public services (MS); leadership and policy studies (MS); metropolitan planning (Certificate); public administration (MPA); public service management (MS), including association management, fundraising and philanthropy, healthcare administration, higher education administration, metropolitan planning; public services (Certificate); JD/MS. Part-time and evening/weekend programs available. Postbaccalaureate distance learning degree programs offered (minimal on-campus study). *Faculty:* 14 full-time (3 women), 43 part-time/adjunct (24 women). *Students:* 90 full-time (59 women), 204 part-time (154 women); includes 101 minority (63 African Americans, 10 Asian Americans or Pacific Islanders, 28 Hispanic Americans), 11 international. Average age 26. 162 applicants, 100% accepted, 94 enrolled. In 2008, 108 master's awarded. *Degree requirements:* For master's, thesis or integrative seminar. *Entrance requirements:* For master's, minimum GPA of 2.7. Additional exam requirements/recommendations for international students: Required—TOEFL (minimum score 550 paper-based; 213 computer-based; 80 iBT), IELTS (minimum score 6.5). *Application deadline:* Applications are processed on a rolling basis. Application fee: $40. Electronic applications accepted. *Financial support:* In 2008–09, 60 students received support, including 3 research assistantships with full tuition reimbursements available (averaging $7,000 per year); career-related internships or fieldwork, Federal Work-Study, institutionally sponsored loans, scholarships/grants, tuition waivers (partial), and unspecified assistantships also available. Support available to part-time students. Financial award application deadline: 7/1; financial award applicants required to submit FAFSA. *Faculty research:* Government financing, transportation, leadership, health care, volunteerism and organizational behavior, non-profit organizations. Total annual research expenditures: $20,000. *Unit head:* Dr. J. Patrick Murphy, Director, 312-362-5608, Fax: 312-362-5506, E-mail: jpmurphy@depaul.edu. *Application contact:* Megan B. Balderston, Director of Admissions and Marketing, 312-362-5565, Fax: 312-362-5506, E-mail: pubserv@depaul.edu.

Eastern Kentucky University, The Graduate School, College of Arts and Sciences, Department of Government, Program in General Public Administration, Richmond, KY 40475-3102. Offers community development (MPA); community health administration (MPA); general public administration (MPA). *Accreditation:* NASPAA. Part-time and evening/weekend programs available. *Entrance requirements:* For master's, GRE General Test, minimum GPA of 2.5.

Eastern Michigan University, Graduate School, College of Arts and Sciences, Department of Geography and Geology, Program in Urban and Regional Planning, Ypsilanti, MI 48197. Offers MS.

Eastern Michigan University, Graduate School, College of Arts and Sciences, Department of Political Science, Program in Public Administration, Ypsilanti, MI 48197. Offers local government management (Graduate Certificate); management of public healthcare services (Graduate Certificate); public administration (MPA, Graduate Certificate); public budget management (Graduate Certificate); public land planning (Graduate Certificate); public management (Graduate Certificate); public personnel management (Graduate Certificate); public policy analysis (Graduate Certificate). *Accreditation:* NASPAA.

Eastern University, School for Social Change, St. Davids, PA 19087-3696. Offers urban studies (MA), including arts in transformation, community development, youth leadership.

Eastern University, School of Leadership and Development, St. Davids, PA 19087-3696. Offers economic development (MBA), including international development, urban development (MA, MBA); international development (MA), including global development, urban development (MA, MBA); nonprofit management (MS); organizational leadership (MA); M Div/MBA. Part-time and evening/weekend programs available. *Degree requirements:* For master's, thesis (for some programs). *Entrance requirements:* For master's, GMAT (MBA), minimum GPA of 2.5. *Expenses:* Contact institution. *Faculty research:* Micro-level economic development, China welfare and economic development, macroethics, micro- and macro-level economic development in transitional economics, organizational effectiveness.

Eastern Washington University, Graduate Studies, College of Business and Public Administration, Program in Urban and Regional Planning, Cheney, WA 99004-2431. Offers MURP, MPA/MURP. *Accreditation:* ACSP. *Degree requirements:* For master's, comprehensive exam, thesis or alternative. *Entrance requirements:* For master's, minimum GPA of 3.0.

East Tennessee State University, School of Graduate Studies, College of Business and Technology, Department of Economics, Finance, and Urban Studies, Johnson City, TN 37614. Offers city management (MCM); community development (MPM); general administration (MPM); municipal service management (MPM); urban and regional economic development (MPM); urban and regional planning (MPM). *Degree requirements:* For master's, internship, oral defense of thesis, research report. *Entrance requirements:* For master's, GRE General Test, minimum GPA of 3.0. Additional exam requirements/recommendations for international students: Required—TOEFL (minimum score 550 paper-based; 213 computer-based).

Florida Atlantic University, College of Architecture, Urban and Public Affairs, School of Urban and Regional Planning, Boca Raton, FL 33431-0991. Offers economic development and tourism (Certificate); environmental planning (Certificate); sustainable community planning (Certificate); urban and regional planning (MURP); visual planning technology (Certificate). *Accreditation:* ACSP. Part-time and evening/weekend programs available. *Faculty:* 8 full-time (6 women), 1 (woman) part-time/adjunct. *Students:* 21 full-time (12 women), 11 part-time (5 women); includes 15 minority (5 African Americans, 10 Hispanic Americans), 1 international. Average age 33. 47 applicants, 47% accepted, 8 enrolled. In 2008, 12 master's awarded. *Entrance requirements:* For master's, GRE General Test, minimum GPA of 3.0. Additional exam requirements/recommendations for international students: Required—TOEFL. *Application deadline:* For fall admission, 7/1 priority date for domestic students, 2/15 for international students; for spring admission, 11/1 priority date for domestic students, 7/15 for international students. Applications are processed on a rolling basis. Application fee: $30. *Expenses:* Tuition, state resident: full-time $4867; part-time $270.40 per credit hour. Tuition, nonresident: full-time $16,486; part-time $915.87 per credit hour. *Financial support:* Fellowships with full tuition reimbursements, research assistantships, career-related internships or fieldwork, Federal Work-Study, institutionally sponsored loans, and tuition waivers (partial) available. Financial award application deadline: 4/1. *Faculty research:* Growth management, urban design, computer applications/geographical information systems, environmental planning. *Unit head:* Dr. Jaap Vos, Chair, 954-762-5653, Fax: 954-762-5673, E-mail: jvos@fau.edu. *Application contact:* Dr. Jaap Vos, Chair, 954-762-5653, Fax: 954-762-5673, E-mail: jvos@fau.edu.

Florida State University, Graduate Studies, College of Social Sciences, Department of Urban and Regional Planning, Tallahassee, FL 32306. Offers MSP, PhD, JD/MSP, MA/MSP, MPA/MSP. *Accreditation:* ACSP (one or more programs are accredited). Part-time programs available. *Degree requirements:* For master's, capstone project, internship; for doctorate, thesis/dissertation. *Entrance requirements:* For master's and doctorate, GRE General Test, minimum GPA of 3.0. Additional exam requirements/recommendations for international students: Required—TOEFL (minimum score 550 paper-based; 213 computer-based; 80 iBT). Electronic applications accepted. *Faculty research:* Growth management, environmental planning, developing countries, transportation, housing and community development.

Georgia Institute of Technology, Graduate Studies and Research, College of Architecture, City and Regional Planning Program, Atlanta, GA 30332-0001. Offers city and regional planning (PhD); economic development (MCRP); environmental planning and management (MCRP); geographic information systems (MCRP); land and community development (MCRP); land use planning (MCRP); transportation (MCRP); urban design (MCRP); MCP/MSCE. *Accreditation:* ACSP. *Degree requirements:* For master's, thesis, internship. *Entrance requirements:* For master's, GRE General Test, minimum GPA of 2.7. Additional exam requirements/recommendations for international students: Required—TOEFL. Electronic applications accepted.

Georgia State University, Andrew Young School of Policy Studies, Department of Public Administration and Urban Studies, Atlanta, GA 30303-3083. Offers disaster management (Certificate); non-profit management (Certificate); planning and economic development (Certificate); public administration (MPA); public policy (PhD); urban policy studies (MS); JD/MPA. *Accreditation:* NASPAA (one or more programs are accredited). Part-time and evening/weekend programs available. Terminal master's awarded for partial completion of doctoral program. *Degree requirements:* For master's, thesis optional; for doctorate, comprehensive exam, thesis/dissertation. *Entrance requirements:* For master's and doctorate, GRE General Test. Additional exam requirements/recommendations for international students: Required—TOEFL. Electronic applications accepted. *Faculty research:* Public management, urban policy, policy analysis, public finance, public involvement.

Harvard University, Graduate School of Arts and Sciences, Committee on Architecture, Landscape Architecture, and Urban Planning, Cambridge, MA 02138. Offers architecture (PhD); landscape architecture (PhD); urban planning (PhD). *Degree requirements:* For doctorate, one foreign language, thesis/dissertation, oral exam. *Entrance requirements:* For doctorate, GRE General Test. Additional exam requirements/recommendations for international students: Required—TOEFL. *Expenses:* Tuition: Full-time $32,556. Required fees: $1426. Full-time tuition and fees vary according to program and student level.

Harvard University, Graduate School of Design, Department of Urban Planning and Design, Cambridge, MA 02138. Offers urban planning (MUP); urban planning and design (MAUD, MLAUD). *Accreditation:* ACSP (one or more programs are accredited). *Entrance requirements:* For master's, GRE General Test. Additional exam requirements/recommendations for international students: Required—TOEFL (minimum score 600 paper-based; 250 computer-based; 100 iBT). Electronic applications accepted. *Expenses:* Tuition: Full-time $32,556. Required fees: $1426. Full-time tuition and fees vary according to program and student level.

Harvard University, John F. Kennedy School of Government, Program in Public Policy, Cambridge, MA 02138. Offers public policy (MPP); public policy and urban planning (MPPUP); JD/MPP; MBA/MPP; MD/MPP. *Accreditation:* NASPAA. *Students:* 244 full-time (119 women); includes 73 minority (18 African Americans, 6 American Indian/Alaska Native, 27 Asian Americans or Pacific Islanders, 22 Hispanic Americans), 57 international. Average age 25. 1,293 applicants, 30% accepted, 244 enrolled. *Entrance requirements:* For master's, GMAT or GRE General Test. Additional exam requirements/recommendations for international students: Required—TOEFL (minimum score 600 paper-based; 250 computer-based; 100 iBT), TWE. *Application deadline:* For fall admission, 1/5 for domestic students. Application fee: $80. Electronic applications accepted. *Expenses:* Tuition: Full-time $32,556. Required fees: $1426. Full-time tuition and fees vary according to program and student level. *Financial support:* Fellowships, research assistantships, teaching assistantships, career-related internships or fieldwork, Federal Work-Study, institutionally sponsored loans, scholarships/grants, health care benefits, and unspecified assistantships available. Financial award application deadline: 2/2; financial award applicants required to submit CSS PROFILE or FAFSA. *Unit head:* Debra Isaacson, Director, 617-496-8382, E-mail: debra_isaacson@harvard.edu. *Application contact:* 617-495-1155.

Hunter College of the City University of New York, Graduate School, School of Arts and Sciences, Department of Urban Affairs and Planning, Program in Urban Planning, New York, NY 10021-5085. Offers MUP, JD/MUP. *Accreditation:* ACSP. Part-time programs available. *Faculty:* 3 full-time (1 woman), 5 part-time/adjunct (1 woman). *Students:* 46 full-time (16 women), 49 part-time (27 women); includes 10 minority (5 African Americans, 3 Asian Americans or Pacific Islanders, 2 Hispanic Americans). Average age 30. 93 applicants, 63% accepted, 26 enrolled. *Degree requirements:* For master's, planning studio and internship. *Entrance requirements:* For master's, minimum 12 credits of course work in social sciences, 2 letters of recommendation. Additional exam requirements/recommendations for international students: Required—TOEFL. *Application deadline:* For fall admission, 4/1 for domestic students, 2/1 for international students; for spring admission, 11/1 for domestic students, 9/1 for international students. Application fee: $125. *Financial support:* In 2008–09, 4 fellowships with full tuition reimbursements (averaging $9,000 per year), 10 teaching assistantships (averaging $1,200 per year) were awarded; research assistantships, career-related internships or fieldwork, Federal Work-Study, and tuition waivers (partial) also available. Support available to part-time students. *Faculty research:* Community and economic development, transportation planning and policy, geographic information systems, housing, land use. *Unit head:* Dr. Lynn McCormick, Director, 212-772-5733, Fax: 212-772-5593, E-mail: lmccormi@hunter.cuny.edu. *Application contact:* William Zlata, Director for Graduate Admissions, 212-772-4482, Fax: 212-650-3336, E-mail: admissions@hunter.cuny.edu.

Iowa State University of Science and Technology, Graduate College, College of Design, Department of Community and Regional Planning, Ames, IA 50011. Offers community and regional planning (MCRP); transportation (MS); M Arch/MCRP; MBA/MCRP; MCRP/MLA; MCRP/MPA. *Accreditation:* ACSP (one or more programs are accredited). Part-time programs available. *Faculty:* 11 full-time (3 women), 1 part-time/adjunct (0 women). *Students:* 12 full-time (9 women), 9 part-time (3 women); includes 4 minority (2 African Americans, 2 Hispanic Americans), 5 international. Average age 31. 28 applicants, 46% accepted, 10 enrolled. In 2008, 13 master's awarded. *Degree requirements:* For master's, thesis or alternative. *Entrance requirements:* For master's, GRE General Test. Additional exam requirements/recommendations for international students: Required—TOEFL (minimum score 550 paper-based; 213 computer-based; 79 iBT), IELTS (6.5) or TOEFL. *Application deadline:* For fall admission, 1/1 priority date for domestic and international students. Applications are processed on a rolling basis. Application fee: $30 ($70 for international students). Electronic applications accepted. *Expenses:* Tuition, area resident: Full-time $6446; part-time $359 per credit. Tuition, state resident: full-time $6446; part-time $359 per credit. Tuition, nonresident: full-time $17,330; part-time $963 per credit. Required fees: $790; $249.25 per semester. Tuition and fees vary according to course load and program. *Financial support:* In 2008–09, 9 research assistantships with full and partial tuition reimbursements (averaging $14,130 per year), 6 teaching assistantships with full and partial tuition reimbursements (averaging $14,130 per year) were awarded; career-related internships or fieldwork, institutionally sponsored loans, tuition waivers (partial), and unspecified assistantships also available. Support available to part-time students. Financial award application deadline: 2/1; financial award applicants required to submit FAFSA. *Faculty research:* Economic development, housing, land use, geographic information systems planning in developing nations, regional and community revitalization, transportation planning in developing countries. *Unit head:* Dr. Douglas Johnston, Chair, 515-294-8958, Fax: 515-294-2348, E-mail: landarch@iastate.edu. *Application contact:* Dr. Francis Owusu, Director of Graduate Education, 515-294-7769, E-mail: crp@iastate.edu.

Jackson State University, Graduate School, School of Liberal Arts, Department of Urban and Regional Planning, Jackson, MS 39217. Offers MS. *Degree requirements:* For master's, comprehensive exam. *Entrance requirements:* For master's, GRE General Test. Additional exam requirements/recommendations for international students: Required—TOEFL.

Kansas State University, Graduate School, College of Architecture, Planning and Design, Department of Interior Architecture and Product Design, Manhattan, KS 66506. Offers regional and community planning (MRCP). *Accreditation:* ACSP. Part-time and evening/weekend programs available. Postbaccalaureate distance learning degree programs offered (minimal on-campus study). *Faculty:* 12 full-time (4 women). *Students:* 56 full-time (46 women), 1 (woman) part-time; includes 2 minority (1 African American, 1 Hispanic American), 1 international. Average age 22. 34 applicants, 100% accepted, 34 enrolled. In 2008, 7 master's awarded. *Degree requirements:* For master's, thesis, oral exam. *Entrance requirements:* For master's, minimum GPA of 3.0, portfolio. Additional exam requirements/recommendations for international students: Required—TOEFL (minimum score 600 paper-based). *Application deadline:* For fall admission, 7/1 priority date for domestic students, 2/1 priority date for international students; for spring admission, 10/1 priority date for domestic students, 8/1 priority date for international students. Applications are processed on a rolling basis. Application fee: $70 ($80 for international students). Electronic applications accepted. *Expenses:* Tuition, area resident: Full-time $6466; part-time $269.40 per credit hour. Tuition, state resident: full-time $6466; part-time $269.40 per credit hour. Tuition, nonresident: full-time $14,874; part-time $619.75 per credit hour. Required fees: $673; $23.40 per credit hour. Tuition and fees vary according to campus/location. *Financial support:* Research assistantships, teaching assistantships with full tuition reimbursements, career-related internships or fieldwork, Federal Work-Study, institutionally sponsored loans, and scholarships/grants available. Support available to part-time students. Financial award application deadline: 3/1; financial award applicants required to submit FAFSA. *Faculty research:* Planning interior spaces for exhibition, residential and commercial spaces; design of objects such as furniture, lighting, equipment, finishing treatments and accessories. *Unit head:* Lorraine Cutler, Head, 785-532-5992, Fax: 785-532-6722, E-mail: lcutler@ksu.edu. *Application contact:* Neal Hubbell, Director, 785-532-5992, Fax: 785-532-6722, E-mail: nhubbel@ksu.edu.

Lesley University, Graduate School of Arts and Social Sciences, Program in Urban Environmental Leadership, Cambridge, MA 02138-2790. Offers MA. *Entrance requirements:* For master's, 2 letters of recommendation, interview. *Expenses:* Tuition: Full-time $13,770; part-time $765 per credit hour. Required fees: $150. Tuition and fees vary according to course load, degree level, campus/location and program.

Massachusetts Institute of Technology, School of Architecture and Planning, Department of Urban Studies and Planning, Cambridge, MA 02139-4307. Offers city planning (MCP); urban and regional planning (PhD); urban and regional studies (PhD); urban studies and planning (SM); M Arch/MCP; MCP/MSRED; MCP/MST; MCP/SM Arch S. *Accreditation:* ACSP (one or more programs are accredited). Terminal master's awarded for partial completion of doctoral program. *Degree requirements:* For master's, thesis; for doctorate, comprehensive exam, thesis/dissertation. *Entrance requirements:* For master's and doctorate, GRE General Test. Additional exam requirements/recommendations for international students: Required—TOEFL (minimum score 600 paper-based; 250 computer-based; 100 iBT); Recommended—TWE. Electronic applications accepted. *Faculty research:* City design and development; housing, community, and economic development; environmental policy and planning; international development and regional planning; urban information systems.

McGill University, Faculty of Graduate and Postdoctoral Studies, Faculty of Engineering, School of Urban Planning, Montréal, QC H3A 2T5, Canada. Offers environmental planning (MUP); housing (MUP); transportation (MUP); urban design (MUP); urban planning, policy and design (PhD).

Michigan State University, The Graduate School, College of Agriculture and Natural Resources and College of Social Science, School of Planning, Design and Construction, East Lansing, MI 48824. Offers construction management (MS, PhD); environmental design (MA); interior design and facilities management (MA); international planning studies (MIPS); urban and regional planning (MURP). *Degree requirements:* For master's, thesis or alternative. *Entrance requirements:* Additional exam requirements/recommendations for international students: Required—TOEFL. Electronic applications accepted.

Minnesota State University Mankato, College of Graduate Studies, College of Social and Behavioral Sciences, Department of Urban and Regional Studies, Mankato, MN 56001. Offers local government (Certificate); urban and regional studies (MA); urban planning (Certificate); MAPA/MA. *Students:* 18 full-time (4 women), 14 part-time (6 women). *Degree requirements:* For master's, one foreign language, comprehensive exam, thesis or alternative. *Entrance requirements:* For master's, minimum GPA of 3.0 during previous 2 years, 2 letters of recommendation. Additional exam requirements/recommendations for international students: Required—TOEFL. *Application deadline:* For fall admission, 7/1 priority date for domestic students; for spring admission, 11/1 for domestic students. Applications are processed on a rolling basis. Application fee: $40. Electronic applications accepted. *Financial support:* Fellowships with partial tuition reimbursements, research assistantships with full tuition reimbursements, teaching assistantships with full tuition reimbursements, career-related internships or fieldwork, Federal Work-Study, institutionally sponsored loans, and unspecified assistantships available. Support available to part-time students. Financial award application deadline: 3/15; financial award applicants required to submit FAFSA. *Unit head:* Dr. Anthony Filipovitch, Chairperson, 507-389-1714. *Application contact:* 507-389-2321, E-mail: grad@mnsu.edu.

Missouri State University, Graduate College, College of Natural and Applied Sciences, Department of Geography, Geology, and Planning, Springfield, MO 65804-0094. Offers geospatial sciences (MS); natural and applied science (MNAS), including geography, geology and planning; secondary education (MS Ed), including earth science, geography. Part-time and evening/weekend programs available. *Faculty:* 19 full-time (3 women). *Students:* 24 full-time (10 women), 11 part-time (4 women), 7 international. Average age 26. 14 applicants, 100% accepted, 11 enrolled. In 2008, 5 master's awarded. *Degree requirements:* For master's, comprehensive exam, thesis (for some programs). *Entrance requirements:* For master's, GRE General Test (MS, MNAS), minimum undergraduate GPA of 3.0 (MS, MNAS), 9-12 teacher certification (MS Ed). Additional exam requirements/recommendations for international students: Required—TOEFL (minimum score 550 paper-based; 213 computer-based; 79 iBT). *Application deadline:* For fall admission, 7/20 priority date for domestic students, 5/1 for international students; for spring admission, 12/20 priority date for domestic students, 9/1 for international students. Applications are processed on a rolling basis. Application fee: $35 ($50 for international students). Electronic applications accepted. *Expenses:* Tuition, state resident: full-time $3852; part-time $214 per credit hour. Tuition, nonresident: full-time $7524; part-time $418 per credit hour. Required fees: $230 per semester. Tuition and fees vary according to course level and course load. *Financial support:* In 2008–09, 15 research assistantships with full tuition reimbursements (averaging $9,092 per year), 7 teaching assistantships with full tuition reimbursements (averaging $7,340 per year) were awarded; career-related internships or fieldwork, Federal Work-Study, institutionally sponsored loans, scholarships/grants, and unspecified assistantships also available. Financial award application deadline: 3/31; financial award applicants required to submit FAFSA. *Faculty research:* Stratigraphy and ancient meteorite impacts, environmental geochemistry of karst, hyperspectral image processing, water quality, small town planning. *Unit head:* Dr. Tom Plymate, Head, 417-836-5800, Fax: 417-836-6934, E-mail: tomplymate@missouristate.edu. *Application contact:* Eric Eckert, Coordinator of Graduate Admissions and Recruitment, 417-836-5331, Fax: 417-836-6888, E-mail: ericeckert@missouristate.edu.

Morgan State University, School of Graduate Studies, Institute of Architecture and Planning, Program in City and Regional Planning, Baltimore, MD 21251. Offers MCRP. *Accreditation:* ACSP. *Degree requirements:* For master's, thesis. *Entrance requirements:* Additional exam requirements/recommendations for international students: Required—TOEFL (minimum score 550 paper-based; 213 computer-based). *Faculty research:* Nonprofit organizations, community development, urban design, transportation, international planning.

New York University, Robert F. Wagner Graduate School of Public Service, Program in Urban Planning, New York, NY 10012-1019. Offers housing (Advanced Certificate); public economics (Advanced Certificate); quantitative analysis and computer applications for policy and planning (Advanced Certificate); urban planning (MUP); JD/MUP. *Accreditation:* ACSP (one or more programs are accredited). Part-time and evening/weekend programs available. *Degree requirements:* For master's, thesis or alternative, end event workshop. *Entrance requirements:* For master's, minimum undergraduate GPA of 3.0. Additional exam requirements/recommendations for international students: Required—TOEFL (minimum score 600 paper-based; 250 computer-based; 100 iBT), TWE (minimum score 4). Electronic applications accepted.

See Close-Up on page 1229.

The Ohio State University, Graduate School, College of Engineering, Austin E. Knowlton School of Architecture, Program in City and Regional Planning, Columbus, OH 43210. Offers MCRP, PhD. *Accreditation:* ACSP (one or more programs are accredited). *Degree requirements:* For master's, thesis optional; for doctorate, thesis/dissertation. *Entrance requirements:* Additional exam requirements/recommendations for international students: Required—TOEFL (minimum score 600 paper-based; 250 computer-based). Electronic applications accepted.

Portland State University, Graduate Studies, College of Urban and Public Affairs, Nohad A. Toulan School of Urban Studies and Planning, Program in Urban and Regional Planning, Portland, OR 97207-0751. Offers MURP. *Accreditation:* ACSP. Part-time programs available. *Faculty:* 19 full-time (4 women), 15 part-time/adjunct (8 women). *Students:* 66 full-time (47 women), 20 part-time (12 women); includes 5 minority (1 African American, 2 American Indian/Alaska Native, 1 Asian American or Pacific Islander, 1 Hispanic American), 1 international. Average age 31. 175 applicants, 44% accepted, 35 enrolled. In 2008, 39 master's awarded. *Entrance requirements:* For master's, minimum GPA of 2.75, 3 letters of recommendation. Additional exam requirements/recommendations for international students: Required—TOEFL (minimum score 550 paper-based; 213 computer-based). *Application deadline:* For fall admission, 1/15 for domestic and international students. Application fee: $50. *Expenses:* Tuition, area resident: Full-time $8763; part-time $179 per credit hour. Tuition, state resident: full-time $8763; part-time $298 per credit hour. Tuition, nonresident: full-time $12,981; part-time $426 per credit hour. Required fees: $1242. One-time fee: $250. Tuition and fees vary according to course load and program. *Financial support:* Research assistantships, teaching assistantships, career-related internships or fieldwork, Federal Work-Study, and unspecified assistantships available. Support available to part-time students. Financial award application deadline: 3/1; financial award applicants required to submit FAFSA. *Faculty research:* Policy planning and administration, community development, land-use and environment, transportation, urban and regional analysis. *Unit head:* Dr. Ethan P. Seltzer, Director, 503-725-4045, E-mail: seltzere@pdx.edu. *Application contact:* Tracy Braden, Office Coordinator, 503-725-4015, Fax: 503-725-8770, E-mail: tbraden@pdx.edu.

Pratt Institute, School of Architecture, Program in City and Regional Planning, Brooklyn, NY 11205-3899. Offers MSCRP. *Accreditation:* ACSP. Part-time programs available. *Faculty:* 2 full-time (1 woman), 9 part-time/adjunct (3 women). *Students:* 49 full-time (26 women), 11 part-time (5 women); includes 11 minority (7 African Americans, 2 Asian Americans or Pacific Islanders, 2 Hispanic Americans), 2 international. Average age 29. 97 applicants, 75% accepted, 16 enrolled. In 2008, 8 master's awarded. *Degree requirements:* For master's, thesis. *Entrance requirements:* For master's, writing sample, bachelor's degree, transcripts, letters of recommendation, statement, portfolio. Additional exam requirements/recommendations for international students: Required—TOEFL (minimum score 550 paper-based; 213 computer-based). *Application deadline:* For fall admission, 2/1 for domestic and international students; for spring admission, 10/1 for domestic and international students. Applications are processed on a rolling basis. Application fee: $50 ($90 for international students). Electronic applications accepted. *Expenses:* Tuition: Full-time $20,412; part-time $1134 per credit. Required fees: $1190; $1190 per year. *Financial support:* Career-related internships or fieldwork, Federal Work-Study, institutionally sponsored loans, scholarships/grants, health care benefits, and unspecified assistantships available. Support available to part-time students. Financial award application deadline: 2/1; financial award applicants required to submit FAFSA. *Faculty research:* Advocacy planning, community development, comprehensive physical planning, transportation planning, real estate development. *Unit head:* John Shapiro, Chairperson, 718-399-4391, E-mail: jshapir6@pratt.edu. *Application contact:* Young Hah, Director of Graduate Admissions, 718-636-3683, Fax: 718-399-4242, E-mail: yhah@pratt.edu.

See Close-Up on page 155.

Urban and Regional Planning

Pratt Institute, School of Architecture, Program in Urban Environmental Systems Management, Brooklyn, NY 11205-3899. Offers MSUESM. Part-time programs available. *Faculty:* 5 part-time/adjunct (3 women). *Students:* 12 full-time (8 women), 4 part-time (2 women); includes 1 minority (Asian American or Pacific Islander), 2 international. Average age 29. 27 applicants, 70% accepted, 12 enrolled. In 2008, 2 master's awarded. *Degree requirements:* For master's, thesis. *Entrance requirements:* For master's, portfolio or writing sample, bachelor's degree, transcripts, letters of recommendation, statement. Additional exam requirements/recommendations for international students: Required—TOEFL (minimum score 550 paper-based; 213 computer-based). *Application deadline:* For fall admission, 2/1 for domestic and international students; for spring admission, 10/1 for domestic and international students. Application fee: $50 ($90 for international students). Electronic applications accepted. *Expenses:* Tuition: Full-time $20,412; part-time $1134 per credit. Required fees: $1190; $1190 per year. *Financial support:* Career-related internships or fieldwork, Federal Work-Study, institutionally sponsored loans, scholarships/grants, and unspecified assistantships available. Support available to part-time students. Financial award application deadline: 2/1; financial award applicants required to submit FAFSA. *Unit head:* Eva Hanhardt, Chairperson, 718-399-4391, E-mail: ehanhard@pratt.edu. *Application contact:* Young Hah, Director of Graduate Admissions, 718-636-3683, Fax: 718-399-4242, E-mail: yhah@pratt.edu.

See Close-Up on page 155.

Queen's University at Kingston, School of Graduate Studies and Research, School of Urban and Regional Planning, Kingston, ON K7L 3N6, Canada. Offers M Pl. Part-time programs available. *Degree requirements:* For master's, thesis optional. *Entrance requirements:* Additional exam requirements/recommendations for international students: Required—TOEFL (minimum score 580 paper-based; 237 computer-based). *Faculty research:* Housing, real estate development, human services, environmental services, land use planning.

Rutgers, The State University of New Jersey, New Brunswick, Edward J. Bloustein School of Planning and Public Policy, Program in Planning and Public Policy, Piscataway, NJ 08854-8097. Offers PhD. Part-time programs available. *Degree requirements:* For doctorate, comprehensive exam, thesis/dissertation. *Entrance requirements:* For doctorate, GRE, master's degree. Additional exam requirements/recommendations for international students: Required—TOEFL (minimum score 575 paper-based; 245 computer-based). Electronic applications accepted. *Faculty research:* Housing and community development, land use and transportation, politics and policy analysis, urban and regional economics, international development.

Rutgers, The State University of New Jersey, New Brunswick, Edward J. Bloustein School of Planning and Public Policy, Program in Urban Planning and Policy Development, Piscataway, NJ 08854-8097. Offers MCRP, MCRS, PhD, JD/MCRP, MBA/MCRP. *Accreditation:* ACSP (one or more programs are accredited). Part-time and evening/weekend programs available. Terminal master's awarded for partial completion of doctoral program. *Degree requirements:* For master's, thesis optional; for doctorate, thesis/dissertation. *Entrance requirements:* For master's and doctorate, GRE General Test. Electronic applications accepted. *Faculty research:* Land use, transportation, housing, regional economic development, urban redevelopment, developing countries.

San Diego State University, Graduate and Research Affairs, College of Professional Studies and Fine Arts, School of Public Affairs, Program in City Planning, San Diego, CA 92182. Offers MCP. Part-time programs available. *Entrance requirements:* For master's, GRE General Test. Additional exam requirements/recommendations for international students: Required—TOEFL. Electronic applications accepted. *Faculty research:* Community development, housing, sustainable development, visioning.

San Jose State University, Graduate Studies and Research, College of Social Sciences, Department of Urban and Regional Planning, San Jose, CA 95192-0001. Offers MUP, Certificate. *Accreditation:* ACSP. Part-time programs available. *Degree requirements:* For master's, comprehensive exam, thesis or alternative. *Entrance requirements:* For master's, GRE, minimum GPA of 3.0. Electronic applications accepted. *Faculty research:* Retirement communities, planning and problems, women in suburbia, influence on urban development, Taiwanese urban development issues.

State University of New York College of Environmental Science and Forestry, Department of Landscape Architecture, Syracuse, NY 13210-2779. Offers community design and planning (MLA, MS); cultural landscape studies and conservation (MLA, MS); landscape and urban ecology (MLA, MS). *Accreditation:* ASLA (one or more programs are accredited). *Degree requirements:* For master's, comprehensive exam (for some programs), thesis (for some programs). *Entrance requirements:* For master's, GRE General Test, minimum GPA of 3.0. Additional exam requirements/recommendations for international students: Required—TOEFL (paper-based 550, computer-based 213, iBT 80) or IELTS (6) or STEP Aiken (Grade 1). *Faculty research:* Site analysis and design, city and regional planning, community environments.

State University of New York College of Environmental Science and Forestry, Program in Environmental Science, Syracuse, NY 13210-2779. Offers environmental and community land planning (MPS, MS, PhD); environmental and natural resources policy (PhD); environmental communication and participatory processes (MPS, MS, PhD); environmental policy and democratic processes (MPS, MS, PhD); environmental systems and risk management (MPS, MS, PhD); water and wetland resource studies (MPS, MS, PhD). Part-time programs available. *Degree requirements:* For master's, thesis (for some programs); for doctorate, comprehensive exam, thesis/dissertation. *Entrance requirements:* For master's and doctorate, GRE General Test, minimum GPA of 3.0. Additional exam requirements/recommendations for international students: Required—TOEFL (minimum score 550 paper-based; 213 computer-based; 80 iBT), IELTS (minimum score 6). *Faculty research:* Environmental education/communications, water resources, land resources, waste management.

Temple University, Ambler College, Department of Community and Regional Planning, Philadelphia, PA 19122-6096. Offers MS. Program offered at Ambler Campus. Part-time and evening/weekend programs available. *Entrance requirements:* For master's, GRE or GMAT, 2 letters of recommendation, minimum undergraduate GPA of 3.0. Additional exam requirements/recommendations for international students: Required—TOEFL (minimum score 550 paper-based; 213 computer-based; 79 iBT).

Texas A&M University, College of Architecture, Department of Landscape Architecture and Urban Planning, College Station, TX 77843. Offers land development (MSLD); landscape architecture (MLA); urban and regional science (PhD); urban planning (MUP). *Accreditation:* ACSP (one or more programs are accredited); ASLA (one or more programs are accredited). *Faculty:* 27. *Students:* 137 full-time (51 women), 27 part-time (9 women); includes 13 minority (4 African Americans, 2 Asian Americans or Pacific Islanders, 7 Hispanic Americans), 87 international. Average age 31. In 2008, 36 master's, 4 doctorates awarded. Terminal master's awarded for partial completion of doctoral program. *Degree requirements:* For master's, thesis optional, professional internship; for doctorate, comprehensive exam, thesis/dissertation, methods statistics seminar. *Entrance requirements:* For master's, GMAT or GRE General Test, portfolio (MLA), minimum GPA of 3.0; for doctorate, GMAT or GRE General Test. Additional exam requirements/recommendations for international students: Required—TOEFL. *Application deadline:* For fall admission, 2/1 priority date for domestic students; for spring admission, 8/1 for domestic students. Applications are processed on a rolling basis. Application fee: $50 ($75 for international students). Electronic applications accepted. *Expenses:* Tuition, area resident: Full-time $3838.50. Tuition, state resident: full-time $3838.50. Tuition, nonresident: full-time $8897. Required fees: $2359.60. *Financial support:* In 2008–09, fellowships with tuition reimbursements (averaging $1,000 per year), research assistantships with partial tuition reimbursements (averaging $8,100 per year), teaching assistantships with partial tuition reimbursements (averaging $11,250 per year) were awarded; career-related internships or fieldwork, institutionally sponsored loans, and scholarships/grants also available. Financial award application deadline: 4/1; financial award applicants required to submit FAFSA. *Faculty research:* Erosion control/water quality, geographic information systems/spatial information technology, transport hazards, international sustainable development. *Unit head:* Dr. Forester Ndubisi, Head, 979-845-1019, Fax: 979-862-1784, E-mail: ndubis@tamu.edu. *Application contact:* Marie Prihoda, Graduate Office, 979-845-6582, Fax: 979-845-4491.

Texas Southern University, Graduate School, School of Public Affairs, Program in Urban Planning and Environmental Policy, Houston, TX 77004-4584. Offers MS, PhD. Part-time and evening/weekend programs available. *Faculty:* 4 full-time (1 woman). *Students:* 32 full-time (14 women), 24 part-time (13 women); includes 52 minority (49 African Americans, 1 Asian American or Pacific Islander, 2 Hispanic Americans), 1 international. Average age 42. 15 applicants, 93% accepted, 12 enrolled. In 2008, 4 master's, 4 doctorates awarded. *Degree requirements:* For master's, comprehensive exam, thesis optional. *Entrance requirements:* For master's, GRE General Test, minimum GPA of 2.5. Additional exam requirements/recommendations for international students: Required—TOEFL. *Application deadline:* For fall admission, 7/15 priority date for domestic students. Applications are processed on a rolling basis. Application fee: $50 ($75 for international students). *Expenses:* Tuition, area resident: Full-time $1912; part-time $96 per credit hour. Tuition, state resident: full-time $1912; part-time $96 per credit hour. Tuition, nonresident: full-time $6302; part-time $343 per credit hour. Required fees: $3542. *Financial support:* In 2008–09, 3 research assistantships (averaging $7,800 per year), 1 teaching assistantship (averaging $6,000 per year) were awarded; fellowships, career-related internships or fieldwork, Federal Work-Study, and institutionally sponsored loans also available. Financial award application deadline: 5/1; financial award applicants required to submit FAFSA. *Unit head:* Dr. Walter McCoy, Interim Chair, 713-313-7312, E-mail: mccoy_wj@tsu.edu. *Application contact:* Brenda Randell, Secretary, 713-313-7405, E-mail: randell_bj@tsu.edu.

Tufts University, Graduate School of Arts and Sciences, Department of Urban and Environmental Policy and Planning, Medford, MA 02155. Offers community development (MA); environmental policy (MA); health and human welfare (MA); housing policy (MA); international environment/development policy (MA); public policy (MPP); public policy and citizen participation (MA); MA/MS; MALD/MA. *Accreditation:* ACSP (one or more programs are accredited). Part-time programs available. *Degree requirements:* For master's, thesis, internship. *Entrance requirements:* For master's, GRE General Test. Additional exam requirements/recommendations for international students: Required—TOEFL (minimum score 550 paper-based; 213 computer-based; 80 iBT). Electronic applications accepted. *Expenses:* Contact institution.

See Close-Up on page 1237.

Université du Québec à Rimouski, Graduate Programs, Program in Regional Development, Rimouski, QC G5L 3A1, Canada. Offers MA, PhD, Diploma. Part-time programs available. *Degree requirements:* For master's, thesis. *Entrance requirements:* For master's, appropriate bachelor's degree, proficiency in French.

Université du Québec en Outaouais, Graduate Programs, Program in Regional Development, Gatineau, QC J8X 3X7, Canada. Offers MA. *Students:* 67 full-time, 9 part-time, 5 international. *Application deadline:* For fall admission, 6/1 priority date for domestic students, 3/1 for international students; for winter admission, 11/1 priority date for domestic students, 10/1 for international students. Application fee: $30. *Unit head:* Thibault Martin, Director, 819-595-3900 Ext. 2210, Fax: 819-595-2384, E-mail: thibault.martin@uqo.ca. *Application contact:* Registrar's Office, 819-773-1850, Fax: 819-773-1835, E-mail: registraire@uqo.ca.

Université Laval, Faculty of Architecture, Planning and Visual Arts, Department of Regional Planning, Programs in Planning and Regional Development, Québec, QC G1K 7P4, Canada. Offers MATDR, PhD. Terminal master's awarded for partial completion of doctoral program. *Degree requirements:* For master's, thesis (for some programs); for doctorate, comprehensive exam, thesis/dissertation. *Entrance requirements:* For master's and doctorate, knowledge of French and English. Electronic applications accepted.

University at Albany, State University of New York, College of Arts and Sciences, Department of Geography and Planning, Program in Regional Planning, Albany, NY 12222-0001. Offers MRP. *Accreditation:* ACSP. Part-time programs available. *Degree requirements:* For master's, thesis optional. *Entrance requirements:* Additional exam requirements/recommendations for international students: Required—TOEFL (minimum score 550 paper-based; 213 computer-based). Electronic applications accepted. *Faculty research:* Urban planning, Third World development, political and social aspects of planning, urban housing and employment, environmental planning.

University at Buffalo, the State University of New York, Graduate School, School of Architecture and Planning, Department of Urban and Regional Planning, Buffalo, NY 14260. Offers planning (MUP); JD/MUP; M Arch/MUP. *Accreditation:* ACSP. Part-time programs available. *Degree requirements:* For master's, thesis or alternative, project. *Entrance requirements:* For master's, minimum GPA of 3.0. Additional exam requirements/recommendations for international students: Required—TOEFL (minimum score 550 paper-based; 213 computer-based; 79 iBT), IELTS (minimum score 6.5). Electronic applications accepted. *Faculty research:* International planning development, economic development, governance, information technology and geographic information systems in planning, environmental planning and policy.

The University of Akron, Graduate School, Buchtel College of Arts and Sciences, Department of Geography and Planning, Program in Urban Planning, Akron, OH 44325. Offers MA. *Degree requirements:* For master's, thesis optional. *Entrance requirements:* For master's, minimum GPA of 2.75. Additional exam requirements/recommendations for international students: Required—TOEFL (minimum score 550 paper-based; 213 computer-based; 79 iBT). Electronic applications accepted.

The University of Arizona, Graduate College, College of Architecture and Landscape Architecture, Planning Program, Tucson, AZ 85721.

The University of British Columbia, Faculty of Graduate Studies, School of Community and Regional Planning, Vancouver, BC V6T 1Z1, Canada. Offers M Sc P, MAP, PhD. *Accreditation:* ACSP (one or more programs are accredited). *Degree requirements:* For master's, thesis; for doctorate, thesis/dissertation, oral exam. *Entrance requirements:* For master's, GRE (recommended); for doctorate, MCRP or equivalent. Additional exam requirements/recommendations for international students: Required—TOEFL (minimum score 600 paper-based; 250 computer-based). Electronic applications accepted. *Faculty research:* Natural resources management, international development, urban spatial, urban policy and community development planning.

University of California, Berkeley, Graduate Division, College of Environmental Design, Department of City and Regional Planning, Berkeley, CA 94720-1500. Offers MCP, PhD, JD/MCP, M Arch/MCP, MCP/MPH, MCP/MS, MLA/MCP. *Accreditation:* ACSP. *Degree requirements:* For master's, professional project or thesis; for doctorate, thesis/dissertation, qualifying exam. *Entrance requirements:* For master's and doctorate, GRE General Test, minimum GPA of 3.0, 3 letters of recommendation. Additional exam requirements/recommendations for international students: Required—TOEFL. *Faculty research:* Housing and project development, physical planning and design, community and economic development, geographic information systems, transportation.

University of California, Davis, Graduate Studies, Graduate Group in Community Development, Davis, CA 95616. Offers MS. *Degree requirements:* For master's, comprehensive exam (for some programs), thesis (for some programs). *Entrance requirements:* For master's, GRE General Test, minimum GPA of 3.0. Additional exam requirements/recommendations for international students: Required—TOEFL (minimum score 550 paper-based; 213 computer-based). Electronic applications accepted. *Faculty research:* Globalization; community economic change; urban and regional development; community planning design and sustainability; race, ethnic, and gender roles; community organization and political mobilization.

University of California, Irvine, Office of Graduate Studies, School of Social Ecology, Department of Planning, Policy and Design, Irvine, CA 92697. Offers planning, policy and design (PhD); urban and regional planning (MURP). *Accreditation:* ACSP (one or more programs are accredited). *Degree requirements:* For doctorate, thesis/dissertation, research project. *Entrance requirements:* For master's and doctorate, GRE General Test, minimum GPA of 3.0. Additional exam requirements/recommendations for international students: Required—TOEFL (minimum score 550 paper-based; 213 computer-based). Electronic applications accepted. *Faculty research:* Community and social policy, economic development, land-use and growth management, transportation planning, environmental policy.

University of California, Los Angeles, Graduate Division, School of Public Affairs, Department of Urban Planning, Los Angeles, CA 90095-1656. Offers MA, PhD, JD/MA, MA/MA, MBA/MA. *Accreditation:* ACSP (one or more programs are accredited). *Degree requirements:* For master's, comprehensive exam or thesis; for doctorate, thesis/dissertation, oral and written qualifying exams. *Entrance requirements:* For master's, GRE General Test (recommended); for doctorate, GRE General Test, master's degree in urban planning or related field. Additional exam requirements/recommendations for international students: Required—TOEFL. Electronic applications accepted. *Expenses:* Tuition, nonresident: full-time $14,694. Required fees: $9669.50. Full-time tuition and fees vary according to course load, degree level, program and student level. *Faculty research:* Industrial hazards, political economy of South and Southeast Asia, historic preservation, flexible production in U.S. and Western Europe, land-use controls.

University of Central Florida, College of Health and Public Affairs, Department of Public Administration, Orlando, FL 32816. Offers emergency management and homeland security (Certificate); non-profit management (MNM, Certificate); public administration (MPA, Certificate); urban and regional planning (Certificate). *Accreditation:* NASPAA. Part-time and evening/weekend programs available. *Faculty:* 13 full-time (3 women), 9 part-time/adjunct (4 women). *Students:* 81 full-time (54 women), 243 part-time (171 women); includes 118 minority (64 African Americans, 11 Asian Americans or Pacific Islanders, 43 Hispanic Americans), 7 international. In 2008, 66 master's, 18 other advanced degrees awarded. *Degree requirements:* For master's, comprehensive exam, thesis or alternative, research report. *Entrance requirements:* For master's, GRE General Test. *Application deadline:* For fall admission, 7/1 for domestic students; for spring admission, 12/1 for domestic students. Application fee: $30. Electronic applications accepted. *Expenses:* Tuition, area resident: Full-time $6816; part-time $284 per credit. Tuition, state resident: full-time $6816; part-time $1076 per credit. Tuition, nonresident: full-time $25,824. Required fees: $216; $9 per credit. *Financial support:* In 2008–09, 3 fellowships with partial tuition reimbursements (averaging $10,000 per year), 16 research assistantships with partial tuition reimbursements (averaging $6,200 per year) were awarded; teaching assistantships with partial tuition reimbursements, career-related internships or fieldwork, Federal Work-Study, institutionally sponsored loans, tuition waivers (partial), and unspecified assistantships also available. Financial award application deadline: 3/1; financial award applicants required to submit FAFSA. *Unit head:* Dr. MaryAnn Feldheim, Chair, 407-823-3693, Fax: 407-823-5651. *Application contact:* Dr. MaryAnn Feldheim, Chair, 407-823-3693, Fax: 407-823-5651.

University of Cincinnati, Graduate School, College of Design, Architecture, Art, and Planning, School of Planning, Program in Community Planning, Cincinnati, OH 45221. Offers MCP, JD/MCP. *Accreditation:* ACSP. *Degree requirements:* For master's, thesis. *Entrance requirements:* For master's, GRE General Test. Additional exam requirements/recommendations for international students: Required—TOEFL.

University of Colorado Denver, College of Architecture and Planning, Program in Design and Planning, Denver, CO 80217-3364. Offers PhD. Part-time programs available. *Degree requirements:* For doctorate, thesis/dissertation. *Entrance requirements:* For doctorate, GRE, minimum undergraduate GPA of 3.0, graduate 3.5. Additional exam requirements/recommendations for international students: Required—TOEFL. *Expenses:* Contact institution. *Faculty research:* Land use and environmental planning and design; design and planning processes and practices; history, theory, and criticism of the built environment.

University of Colorado Denver, College of Architecture and Planning, Program in Urban and Regional Planning, Denver, CO 80217-3364. Offers MURP. *Accreditation:* ACSP. Part-time programs available. *Degree requirements:* For master's, thesis optional. *Entrance requirements:* For master's, GRE or minimum GPA of 3.0, writing sample, resumé. Additional exam requirements/recommendations for international students: Required—TOEFL (minimum score 550 paper-based; 213 computer-based). *Faculty research:* Physical planning, environmental planning, economic development planning.

University of Florida, Graduate School, College of Design, Construction and Planning, Department of Urban and Regional Planning, Gainesville, FL 32611. Offers MAURP, PhD, JD/MAURP. *Accreditation:* ACSP (one or more programs are accredited). *Degree requirements:* For master's, thesis. *Entrance requirements:* For master's, GRE General Test, minimum GPA of 3.0. Additional exam requirements/recommendations for international students: Required—TOEFL. Electronic applications accepted. *Faculty research:* Planning and information systems, urban and environmental design, community and economic development, transportation and growth management.

University of Hawaii at Manoa, Graduate Division, Colleges of Arts and Sciences, College of Social Sciences, Department of Urban and Regional Planning, Honolulu, HI 96822. Offers community planning and social policy (MURP); environmental planning and management (MURP); land use and infrastructure planning (MURP); urban and regional planning (PhD, Graduate Certificate); urban and regional planning in Asia and Pacific (MURP). *Accreditation:* ACSP. Part-time programs available. *Degree requirements:* For master's, thesis optional; for doctorate, comprehensive exam, thesis/dissertation. *Entrance requirements:* For master's, GRE General Test, minimum GPA of 3.0; for doctorate, GRE General Test. Additional exam requirements/recommendations for international students: Required—TOEFL (minimum score 500 paper-based; 173 computer-based; 61 iBT), IELTS (minimum score 5).

University of Idaho, College of Graduate Studies, Department of Bioregional Planning and Community Design, Moscow, ID 83844-2282. Offers bioregional planning (MS). *Students:* 5. Average age 32. In 2008, 2 master's awarded. *Expenses:* Tuition, nonresident: full-time $10,080; part-time $336 per credit. Required fees: $5212; $267 per credit. Tuition and fees vary according to program. *Faculty research:* Environment and behavior interaction, geographic trade, design development, economic development, natural resource policy. *Unit head:* Stephen R. Drown, Chair, 208-885-7902, E-mail: larch@uidaho.edu. *Application contact:* Stephen R. Drown, Chair, 208-885-7902, E-mail: larch@uidaho.edu.

University of Illinois at Chicago, Graduate College, College of Urban Planning and Public Affairs, Program in Urban Planning and Policy, Chicago, IL 60607-7128. Offers MUPP, PhD. *Accreditation:* ACSP (one or more programs are accredited). Part-time programs available. *Degree requirements:* For master's, thesis or alternative, internship; for doctorate, thesis/dissertation. *Entrance requirements:* For master's and doctorate, GRE General Test, minimum GPA of 2.75, writing sample. Additional exam requirements/recommendations for international students: Required—TOEFL. Electronic applications accepted.

University of Illinois at Urbana–Champaign, Graduate College, College of Fine and Applied Arts, Department of Urban and Regional Planning, Champaign, IL 61820. Offers regional planning (PhD); urban planning (MUP); JD/MUP; M Arch/MUP. *Accreditation:* ACSP (one or more programs are accredited). *Faculty:* 13 full-time (6 women). *Students:* 54 full-time (31 women), 10 part-time (0 women); includes 11 minority (8 African Americans, 1 Asian American or Pacific Islander, 2 Hispanic Americans), 21 international. 134 applicants, 38% accepted, 26 enrolled. In 2008, 32 master's, 6 doctorates awarded. *Entrance requirements:* For master's and doctorate, GRE, minimum GPA of 3.0. Additional exam requirements/recommendations for international students: Required—TOEFL (minimum score 610 paper-based; 253 computer-based; 102 iBT). *Application deadline:* Applications are processed on a rolling basis. Application fee: $60 ($75 for international students). Electronic applications accepted. *Financial support:* In 2008–09, 9 fellowships, 30 research assistantships, 16 teaching assistantships were awarded; tuition waivers (full and partial) also available. *Faculty research:* Environmental impact, economic development, firmation technology, planning systems, housing, community participation. *Unit head:* Edward Feser, Head, 217-244-5400, Fax: 217-244-1717, E-mail: feser@illinois.edu. *Application contact:* Jane Terry, Admissions and Records Officer II, 217-244-5401, Fax: 217-244-1717, E-mail: jterry2@illinois.edu.

The University of Iowa, Graduate College, Program in Urban and Regional Planning, Iowa City, IA 52242-1316. Offers MA, MS, JD/MA, MHA/MA, MHA/MS, MS/MA, MS/MS, MSW/MA, MSW/MS. *Accreditation:* ACSP. *Degree requirements:* For master's, thesis optional, portfolio. *Entrance requirements:* For master's, GRE General Test, minimum GPA of 3.0. Additional exam requirements/recommendations for international students: Required—TOEFL (minimum score 600 paper-based; 250 computer-based; 100 iBT). Electronic applications accepted.

The University of Kansas, Graduate Studies, School of Architecture, Design, and Planning, Program in Urban Planning, Lawrence, KS 66045. Offers MUP, JD/MUP, M Arch/MUP, MUP/MA, MUP/MPA. *Accreditation:* ACSP. Part-time programs available. *Faculty:* 5 full-time (2 women), 6 part-time/adjunct (0 women). *Students:* 40 full-time (17 women), 6 part-time (1 woman); includes 4 minority (2 African Americans, 1 Asian American or Pacific Islander, 1 Hispanic American), 2 international. Average age 26. 43 applicants, 67% accepted, 17 enrolled. In 2008, 16 master's awarded. *Degree requirements:* For master's, comprehensive exam, thesis or alternative. *Entrance requirements:* For master's, GRE. Additional exam requirements/recommendations for international students: Required—TOEFL (minimum score 570 paper-based; 230 computer-based). *Application deadline:* For fall admission, 7/1 for domestic students, 6/1 for international students; for spring admission, 12/1 for domestic students, 11/1 for international students. Applications are processed on a rolling basis. Application fee: $45 ($55 for international students). Electronic applications accepted. *Expenses:* Tuition, area resident: Full-time $6122; part-time $255.10 per credit hour. Tuition, state resident: full-time $6122; part-time $255.10 per credit hour. Tuition, nonresident: full-time $14,629; part-time $609.55 per credit hour. Required fees: $847; $70.56 per credit hour. Tuition and fees vary according to course load and program. *Financial support:* In 2008–09, 3 fellowships (averaging $4,703 per year) were awarded; research assistantships with partial tuition reimbursements, career-related internships or fieldwork also available. Financial award application deadline: 2/1. *Faculty research:* Environmental land use, housing and economic development, community development and transportation, urban mass transportation, urban sprawl. *Unit head:* James M. Mayo, Chair, 785-864-4184, Fax: 785-864-5301, E-mail: jimmayo@ku.edu. *Application contact:* Pat Owens, Administrative Specialist, 785-864-4184, Fax: 785-864-5301, E-mail: ubpl@ku.edu.

University of Louisville, Graduate School, College of Arts and Sciences, Department of Urban and Public Affairs, Program in Urban Planning, Louisville, KY 40208. Offers administration of planning organizations (MUP); housing and community development (MUP); land use and environmental planning (MUP); spatial analysis (MUP). Part-time and evening/weekend programs available. *Faculty:* 11 full-time (4 women), 7 part-time/adjunct (1 woman). *Students:* 21 full-time (8 women), 9 part-time (4 women); includes 1 African American, 2 Hispanic Americans, 3 international. Average age 31. 13 applicants, 100% accepted, 11 enrolled. In 2008, 6 master's awarded. Terminal master's awarded for partial completion of doctoral program. *Degree requirements:* For master's, internship, practicum. *Entrance requirements:* Additional exam requirements/recommendations for international students: Required—TOEFL (minimum score 547 paper-based; 210 computer-based; 77 iBT). *Application deadline:* For fall admission, 7/15 for domestic students; for winter admission, 11/15 for domestic students. Applications are processed on a rolling basis. Application fee: $50. *Financial support:* In 2008–09, 3 students received support, including 3 research assistantships with full tuition reimbursements available (averaging $20,000 per year); health care benefits also available. Financial award application deadline: 3/1. *Faculty research:* Hazard mitigation planning, urban and transportation economics, real estate development, Brownfield redevelopment, housing development. *Unit head:* Dr. David M. Simpson, Program Director, 502-852-8019, Fax: 502-852-4558, E-mail: dave.simpson@louisville.edu. *Application contact:* Yani Vozos, Graduate Student Advisor/Coordinator, 502-852-8002, Fax: 502-852-4558, E-mail: yani.vozos@louisville.edu.

University of Manitoba, Faculty of Graduate Studies, Faculty of Architecture, Department of City Planning, Winnipeg, MB R3T 2N2, Canada. Offers MCP. *Degree requirements:* For master's, thesis.

University of Maryland, College Park, Graduate Studies, School of Architecture, Planning and Preservation, Program in Urban Studies and Planning, College Park, MD 20742. Offers urban and regional planning/design (PhD); urban studies and planning (MCP); M Arch/MCP. *Accreditation:* ACSP. Part-time and evening/weekend programs available. *Entrance requirements:* For master's and doctorate, GRE General Test, minimum GPA of 3.0, 3 letters of recommendation. Additional exam requirements/recommendations for international students: Required—TOEFL. Electronic applications accepted. *Faculty research:* Policy analysis, urban planning, program planning and management, economic development planning.

University of Massachusetts Amherst, Graduate School, College of Natural Resources and the Environment, Department of Landscape Architecture and Regional Planning, Program in Landscape Architecture and Regional Planning, Amherst, MA 01003. Offers MLA/MRP. *Accreditation:* ACSP; ASLA. Part-time programs available. *Entrance requirements:* Additional exam requirements/recommendations for international students: Required—TOEFL (minimum score 550 paper-based; 213 computer-based; 79 iBT), IELTS (minimum score 6.5). Electronic applications accepted. *Expenses:* Tuition, area resident: Full-time $2640. Tuition, nonresident: full-time $9936. One-time fee: $332 full-time. Tuition and fees vary according to course load.

University of Massachusetts Amherst, Graduate School, College of Natural Resources and the Environment, Department of Landscape Architecture and Regional Planning, Program in Regional Planning, Amherst, MA 01003. Offers MRP, PhD, MLA/MRP. *Accreditation:* ACSP (one or more programs are accredited). Part-time programs available. Terminal master's awarded for partial completion of doctoral program. *Degree requirements:* For master's, thesis or alternative; for doctorate, comprehensive exam, thesis/dissertation. *Entrance requirements:* For master's and doctorate, GRE General Test. Additional exam requirements/recommendations for international students: Required—TOEFL (minimum score 550 paper-based; 213 computer-based; 79 iBT), IELTS (minimum score 6.5). Electronic applications accepted. *Expenses:* Tuition, area resident: Full-time $2640. Tuition, nonresident: full-time $9936. One-time fee: $332 full-time. Tuition and fees vary according to course load.

University of Memphis, Graduate School, College of Arts and Sciences, School of Urban Affairs and Public Policy, Division of City and Regional Planning, Memphis, TN 38152. Offers MCRP. *Accreditation:* ACSP. *Faculty:* 4 full-time (1 woman), 1 part-time/adjunct (0 women). *Students:* 13 full-time (4 women), 11 part-time (6 women); includes 7 minority (6 African Americans, 1 Hispanic American). Average age 32. 15 applicants, 100% accepted, 7 enrolled. In 2008, 5 master's awarded. *Degree requirements:* For master's, comprehensive exam, thesis. *Entrance requirements:* For master's, GRE General Test. *Application deadline:* For fall admission, 7/1 for domestic students; for spring admission, 12/1 for domestic students. Applications are processed on a rolling basis. Application fee: $35 ($60 for international students). *Expenses:* Tuition, area resident: Full-time $6242; part-time $330 per credit hour. Tuition, state resident: full-time $6242; part-time $330 per credit hour. Tuition, nonresident: full-time $17,828; part-time $815 per credit hour. Required fees: $1156. *Financial support:* Research assistantships with full tuition reimbursements, career-related internships or fieldwork and Federal Work-Study available. Financial award application deadline: 6/1; financial award applicants required to submit FAFSA. *Faculty research:* Growth planning, site design, economic development, housing, smart growth. *Unit head:* Kenneth Reardon, Director and Coordinator of Graduate Studies in Planning, 901-678-2161, Fax: 901-678-4162, E-mail: kreardon@memphis.edu. *Application contact:* Kenneth Reardon, Director and Coordinator of Graduate Studies in Planning, 901-678-2161, Fax: 901-678-4162, E-mail: kreardon@memphis.edu.

Urban and Regional Planning

University of Memphis, Graduate School, College of Arts and Sciences, School of Urban Affairs and Public Policy, Division of Public and Nonprofit Administration, Memphis, TN 38152. Offers nonprofit administration (MPA); public management and policy (MPA); urban management and planning (MPA). *Accreditation:* NASPAA. Part-time and evening/weekend programs available. *Faculty:* 5 full-time (4 women), 2 part-time/adjunct (1 woman). *Students:* 14 full-time (8 women), 39 part-time (33 women); includes 32 minority (30 African Americans, 1 Asian American or Pacific Islander, 1 Hispanic American), 1 international. Average age 35. 35 applicants, 91% accepted, 12 enrolled. In 2008, 11 master's awarded. *Degree requirements:* For master's, comprehensive exam, thesis or alternative, internship. *Entrance requirements:* For master's, GRE General Test, GMAT, or MAT, minimum GPA of 3.0. *Application deadline:* For fall admission, 8/1 for domestic students; for spring admission, 12/1 for domestic students. Applications are processed on a rolling basis. Application fee: $35 ($60 for international students). *Expenses:* Tuition, area resident: Full-time $6242; part-time $330 per credit hour. Tuition, state resident: full-time $6242; part-time $330 per credit hour. Tuition, nonresident: full-time $17,828; part-time $815 per credit hour. Required fees: $1156. *Financial support:* Fellowships, research assistantships with full tuition reimbursements, career-related internships or fieldwork, Federal Work-Study, and scholarships/grants available. Support available to part-time students. Financial award applicants required to submit FAFSA. *Faculty research:* Nonprofit organization governance, local government management, community collaboration, urban problems, accountability. *Unit head:* Dr. Dorothy Norris-Tirrell, Director, 901-678-3360, Fax: 901-678-2981, E-mail: dnrrstrr@memphis.edu. *Application contact:* Dr. Charles Menifield, Graduate Admissions Coordinator, 901-678-3360, Fax: 901-678-2981, E-mail: cmenifld@memphis.edu.

University of Michigan, A. Alfred Taubman College of Architecture and Urban Planning, Urban and Regional Planning Program, Ann Arbor, MI 48109. Offers real estate development (Certificate); urban planning (MUP); JD/MUP; M Arch/MUP; MBA/MUP; MLA/MUP; MPP/MUP. Offered through the Horace H. Rackham School of Graduate Studies; students in the Certificate program must either be currently enrolled in a graduate program or have earned a masters or PhD degree within the last five years. *Accreditation:* ACSP (one or more programs are accredited). Part-time programs available. *Degree requirements:* For master's, thesis or alternative, professional project, capstone studio. *Entrance requirements:* For master's, GRE General Test. Additional exam requirements/recommendations for international students: Required—TOEFL (minimum score 600 paper-based; 250 computer-based). *Faculty research:* Housing, community, and economic development; transportation; physical planning and urban development; planning in developing countries; land use and environmental planning.

University of Michigan, Horace H. Rackham School of Graduate Studies, PhD Program in Urban and Regional Planning, Ann Arbor, MI 48109. Offers PhD. *Degree requirements:* For doctorate, thesis/dissertation, 1 interdisciplinary paper, 2 preliminary exams, oral defense of dissertation. *Entrance requirements:* For doctorate, GRE General Test. Additional exam requirements/recommendations for international students: Required—TOEFL (minimum score 560 paper-based; 220 computer-based; 84 iBT). Electronic applications accepted. *Expenses:* Contact institution. *Faculty research:* Urban and regional planning, community and economic development, transportation planning and geological information systems, environmental planning, the built environment, international development and planning.

University of Minnesota, Twin Cities Campus, Graduate School, Hubert H. Humphrey Institute of Public Affairs, Program in Urban and Regional Planning, Minneapolis, MN 55455-0213. Offers environmental planning (MURP); housing and community development (MURP); land use and urban design (MURP); regional, economic and workforce development (MURP); transportation planning (MURP); JD/MURP; MURP/MLA; MURP/MS. *Accreditation:* ACSP (one or more programs are accredited). Part-time programs available. *Degree requirements:* For master's, thesis or alternative, internship or equivalent work experience. *Entrance requirements:* For master's, GRE General Test, minimum undergraduate GPA of 3.0. Additional exam requirements/recommendations for international students: Required—TOEFL (minimum score 600 paper-based; 250 computer-based). Electronic applications accepted. *Faculty research:* Policy planning, resource allocation planning, regulatory planning, program planning, project planning.

University of Nebraska–Lincoln, Graduate College, College of Agricultural Sciences and Natural Resources, Department of Agricultural Economics, Lincoln, NE 68588. Offers agribusiness (MBA); agricultural economics (MS, PhD); community development (M Ag). *Faculty:* 18 full-time (2 women). *Students:* 18 full-time (5 women), 7 part-time (4 women); includes 1 minority (African American), 15 international. Average age 35. In 2008, 7 master's, 1 doctorate awarded. *Degree requirements:* For master's, thesis optional; for doctorate, comprehensive exam, thesis/dissertation. *Entrance requirements:* For master's and doctorate, GRE General Test. Additional exam requirements/recommendations for international students: Required—TOEFL (minimum score 550 paper-based; 213 computer-based). *Application deadline:* For fall admission, 2/1 priority date for domestic students, 2/1 for international students; for spring admission, 9/15 for domestic students, 9/1 for international students. Applications are processed on a rolling basis. Application fee: $40. Electronic applications accepted. *Expenses:* Tuition, state resident: full-time $4275; part-time $237.50 per credit hour. Tuition, nonresident: full-time $11,525; part-time $640.25 per credit hour. Required fees: $1068; $10.35 per credit hour. $440.70 per semester. Tuition and fees vary according to course load and program. *Financial support:* Fellowships, research assistantships, teaching assistantships, Federal Work-Study, health care benefits, and unspecified assistantships available. Support available to part-time students. Financial award application deadline: 2/15. *Faculty research:* Marketing and agribusiness, production economics, resource law, international trade and development, rural policy and revitalization. *Unit head:* Dr. Jeffrey Royer, Head, 402-472-3401, Fax: 402-472-3460. *Application contact:* Dr. Jeffrey Royer, Head, 402-472-3401, Fax: 402-472-3460.

University of Nebraska–Lincoln, Graduate College, College of Architecture, Department of Community and Regional Planning, Lincoln, NE 68588. Offers MCRP, JD/MCRP, M Arch/MCRP, MCRP/MSCE. *Accreditation:* ACSP. *Students:* 15 full-time (6 women), 14 part-time (6 women), 1 international. Average age 29. In 2008, 3 master's awarded. *Degree requirements:* For master's, thesis optional. *Entrance requirements:* For master's, GRE General Test. Additional exam requirements/recommendations for international students: Required—TOEFL (minimum score 550 paper-based; 213 computer-based). *Application deadline:* For fall admission, 3/1 for domestic and international students; for spring admission, 10/1 for domestic students, 9/1 for international students. Application fee: $40. Electronic applications accepted. *Expenses:* Tuition, state resident: full-time $4275; part-time $237.50 per credit hour. Tuition, nonresident: full-time $11,525; part-time $640.25 per credit hour. Required fees: $1068; $10.35 per credit hour. $440.70 per semester. Tuition and fees vary according to course load and program. *Financial support:* Fellowships, research assistantships, teaching assistantships, Federal Work-Study, health care benefits, and unspecified assistantships available. Support available to part-time students. Financial award application deadline: 2/15. *Faculty research:* Economic development, community development and improvement, social planning, land use planning, physical planning, environmental planning. *Unit head:* Prof. Gordon Scholz, Interim Graduate Committee Chair, 402-472-9280, Fax: 402-472-3806. *Application contact:* Ginny Gross, Director of Graduate Admissions, 402-472-2878, Fax: 402-472-0589, E-mail: grad_admissions@unl.edu.

University of New Mexico, Graduate School, School of Architecture and Planning, Program in Community and Regional Planning, Albuquerque, NM 87131-2039. Offers MCRP, MCRP/MA, MPA/MCRP. *Accreditation:* ACSP. Part-time programs available. *Degree requirements:* For master's, thesis. *Entrance requirements:* For master's, minimum GPA of 3.0, 3 letters of recommendation, letter of intent, resumé, copies of all unofficial transcripts. *Faculty research:* Community development, urban and ecological design, land economics, community-based planning, environmental dispute resolution, environmental justice.

University of New Orleans, Graduate School, College of Liberal Arts, School of Urban Planning and Regional Studies, Program in Urban and Regional Planning, New Orleans, LA 70148. Offers MURP. *Accreditation:* ACSP. *Degree requirements:* For master's, thesis. *Entrance requirements:* For master's, GRE General Test. Additional exam requirements/recommendations for international students: Required—TOEFL (minimum score 550 paper-based; 213 computer-based; 79 iBT). Electronic applications accepted. *Faculty research:* Urban economic development, environmental planning and analysis, social and cultural change.

The University of North Carolina at Chapel Hill, Graduate School, College of Arts and Sciences, Department of City and Regional Planning, Chapel Hill, NC 27599. Offers city and regional planning (MCRP); planning (PhD); public policy analysis (PhD); JD/MRP; MBA/MRP; MLA/MRP; MPA/MRP; MPH/MRP. *Accreditation:* ACSP (one or more programs are accredited). *Degree requirements:* For master's, project; for doctorate, comprehensive exam, thesis/dissertation. *Entrance requirements:* For master's and doctorate, GRE General Test. Additional exam requirements/recommendations for international students: Required—TOEFL (minimum score 550 paper-based; 213 computer-based). Electronic applications accepted. *Faculty research:* Developing areas, transportation, affordable housing, growth management, coastal zone management.

University of Oklahoma, Graduate College, College of Architecture, Division of Regional and City Planning, Norman, OK 73019-0390. Offers MRCP, MRCP/MLA. *Accreditation:* ACSP (one or more programs are accredited). Part-time programs available. *Faculty:* 2 full-time (0 women). *Students:* 26 full-time (17 women), 4 part-time (3 women); includes 6 minority (4 African Americans, 1 American Indian/Alaska Native, 1 Asian American or Pacific Islander), 10 international. 19 applicants, 95% accepted, 11 enrolled. In 2008, 10 master's awarded. *Degree requirements:* For master's, thesis or alternative, portfolio, project. *Entrance requirements:* For master's, GRE General Test, appropriate bachelor's degree, portfolio. Additional exam requirements/recommendations for international students: Required—TOEFL (minimum score 550 paper-based; 213 computer-based). *Application deadline:* For fall admission, 4/1 for domestic and international students; for spring admission, 11/1 for domestic students, 9/1 for international students. Applications are processed on a rolling basis. Application fee: $40 ($90 for international students). Electronic applications accepted. *Expenses:* Tuition, state resident: full-time $3744; part-time $156 per credit hour. Tuition, nonresident: full-time $13,577; part-time $565.70 per credit hour. Required fees: $2415.40; $90.10 per credit hour. *Financial support:* In 2008–09, 16 students received support, including 1 research assistantship with partial tuition reimbursement available (averaging $9,586 per year), 2 teaching assistantships (averaging $9,586 per year); career-related internships or fieldwork, Federal Work-Study, institutionally sponsored loans, scholarships/grants, health care benefits, tuition waivers (partial), and unspecified assistantships also available. Support available to part-time students. Financial award applicants required to submit FAFSA. *Faculty research:* Transportation planning, economic development, urban design, city and regional planning. *Unit head:* Guogiang Shen, Director, 405-325-2444, Fax: 405-325-7558, E-mail: guogiangs@ou.edu. *Application contact:* Terry Patterson, Professor/Graduate Liaison, 405-325-3869, Fax: 405-325-7558, E-mail: tpatterson@ou.edu.

University of Oregon, Graduate School, School of Architecture and Allied Arts, Department of Planning, Public Policy, and Management, Program in Community and Regional Planning, Eugene, OR 97403. Offers MCRP. *Accreditation:* ACSP. Part-time programs available. *Degree requirements:* For master's, thesis or alternative. *Entrance requirements:* For master's, minimum GPA of 3.0. Additional exam requirements/recommendations for international students: Required—TOEFL. *Faculty research:* Community economic development, tourism, families in poverty.

University of Pennsylvania, School of Design, Department of City and Regional Planning, Philadelphia, PA 19104. Offers MCP, PhD, Certificate, MSE/MCP. *Accreditation:* ACSP (one or more programs are accredited). *Degree requirements:* For doctorate, thesis/dissertation. *Entrance requirements:* For master's and doctorate, GRE General Test. Additional exam requirements/recommendations for international students: Required—TOEFL. *Faculty research:* Growth management, transportation planning, urban simulation modeling, housing, development planning.

See Close-Up on page 159.

University of Pennsylvania, School of Design, Program in Landscape Architecture and Regional Planning, Philadelphia, PA 19104. Offers landscape architecture and regional planning (MLA); landscape studies (Certificate). *Accreditation:* ASLA (one or more programs are accredited). Part-time programs available. *Degree requirements:* For master's, thesis optional. *Entrance requirements:* For master's, GRE, portfolio. Additional exam requirements/recommendations for international students: Required—TOEFL. *Faculty research:* Early landscape architecture, natural distribution through landslides, urban gardens, landscape registration, watershed studies.

See Close-Up on page 159.

University of Pittsburgh, Graduate School of Public and International Affairs, Division of International Development, Program in Development Planning and Environmental Sustainability, Pittsburgh, PA 15260. Offers MID, MPA/MID, MID/JD, MID/MBA, MID/MPH, MID/MPIA, MID/MSIS, MID/MSW. Part-time programs available. *Degree requirements:* For master's, thesis optional, internship, capstone seminar. *Entrance requirements:* For master's, GRE General Test, 3 letters of recommendation, minimum GPA of 3.2. Additional exam requirements/recommendations for international students: Required—TOEFL (minimum score 550 paper-based; 213 computer-based; 80 iBT), TWE (minimum score 4); Recommended—IELTS (minimum score 7). Electronic applications accepted. *Faculty research:* Project/program evaluation, population and environment, international development, development economics, civil society.

University of Pittsburgh, Graduate School of Public and International Affairs, Division of Public and Urban Affairs, Program in Urban and Regional Affairs, Pittsburgh, PA 15260. Offers MPA, MPA/MID, JD/MPA, MPA/MPIA, MPH/MPA, MSIS/MPA, MSW/MPA. Part-time and evening/weekend programs available. *Degree requirements:* For master's, thesis optional, internship, capstone seminar. *Entrance requirements:* For master's, GRE General Test, 3 letters of recommendation, resumé, minimum GPA of 3.2. Additional exam requirements/recommendations for international students: Required—TOEFL (minimum score 550 paper-based; 213 computer-based; 80 iBT), TWE (minimum score 4); Recommended—IELTS (minimum score 7). Electronic applications accepted. *Faculty research:* Health policy and regulations, emergency management, regional finance, non-profit management, community/regional development, environmental policy.

See Close-Up on page 1243.

University of Puerto Rico, Río Piedras, Graduate School of Planning, San Juan, PR 00931-3300. Offers MP. *Accreditation:* ACSP. Part-time programs available. *Degree requirements:* For master's, comprehensive exam, thesis, planning project defense. *Entrance requirements:* For master's, PAEG, GRE, minimum GPA of 3.0, 2 letters of recommendation. *Faculty research:* Municipalities, historic Atlas, Puerto Rico, economic future.

University of Southern California, Graduate School, School of Policy, Planning and Development, Programs in Planning, Los Angeles, CA 90089. Offers planning (M Pl); urban and regional planning (PhD); M Arch/M Pl; M Pl/MA; M Pl/MS; M Pl/MSW; MBA/M Pl; ML Arch/M Pl; MPA/M Pl. *Accreditation:* ACSP (one or more programs are accredited). Part-time programs available. *Degree requirements:* For doctorate, thesis/dissertation. *Entrance requirements:* For master's and doctorate, GRE General Test. *Faculty research:* Transportation infrastructure, comparative international development, health communities.

University of Southern California, Graduate School, School of Policy, Planning and Development, Programs in Planning and Development Studies, Los Angeles, CA 90089. Offers planning and development studies (MPDS, DPDS); policy, planning and development (PhD). *Entrance requirements:* For master's, GRE General Test; for doctorate, GRE. *Faculty research:* Governance, effective institutions, leadership management, healthy urban development.

University of Southern Maine, Edmund S. Muskie School of Public Service, Program in Community Planning and Development, Portland, ME 04104-9300. Offers MCPD, Certificate, JD/MCPD. Part-time and evening/weekend programs available. *Degree requirements:* For master's, thesis, capstone project, field experience. *Entrance requirements:* For master's, GRE General Test or LSAT. Additional exam requirements/recommendations for international students: Required—TOEFL. Electronic applications accepted. *Faculty research:* Sustainable communities, ego system management, economic and environmental tradeoffs.

The University of Texas at Arlington, Graduate School, School of Urban and Public Affairs, Program in City and Regional Planning, Arlington, TX 76019. Offers MCRP, M Arch/MCRP. *Accreditation:* ACSP. Part-time and evening/weekend programs available. *Faculty:* 4 full-time (1 woman), 3 part-time/adjunct (0 women). *Students:* 25 full-time (10 women), 32 part-time (14 women); includes 15 minority (4 African Americans, 3 Asian Americans or Pacific Islanders, 8 Hispanic Americans), 9 international. Average age 35. 50 applicants, 96% accepted, 29 enrolled. In 2008, 13 master's awarded. *Degree requirements:* For master's, thesis or alternative. *Entrance requirements:* For master's, GRE General Test. Additional exam requirements/recommendations for international students: Required—TOEFL (minimum score 550 paper-based; 213 computer-based). *Application deadline:* For fall admission, 6/16 for domestic students. Application fee: $35 ($50 for international students). *Expenses:* Tuition, area resident: Full-time $6500. Tuition, state resident: full-time $6500. Tuition, nonresident: full-time $11,558. *Financial support:* Fellowships, research assistantships, career-related internships or fieldwork available. Financial award application deadline: 6/1; financial award applicants required to submit FAFSA. *Faculty research:* Urban structure, GIS environmental resolutions, qualitative methods, JTS housing, planning history/theory. Total annual research expenditures: $30,453. *Unit head:* Dr. Enid Arvidson, Graduate Adviser, 817-272-3349, Fax: 817-272-5008. *Application contact:* Linda Slaughter, Administrative Clerk, 817-272-3071, Fax: 817-272-5008, E-mail: slaughter@uta.edu.

The University of Texas at Arlington, Graduate School, School of Urban and Public Affairs, Urban and Public Affairs Division, Arlington, TX 76019. Offers MA, MSSW/MA. Part-time and evening/weekend programs available. *Students:* 6 full-time (2 women), 17 part-time (11 women); includes 10 minority (7 African Americans, 1 Asian American or Pacific Islander, 2 Hispanic Americans). Average age 25. 18 applicants, 89% accepted, 12 enrolled. In 2008, 3 master's awarded. *Degree requirements:* For master's, thesis or alternative. *Entrance requirements:* For master's, GRE General Test. Additional exam requirements/recommendations for international students: Required—TOEFL (minimum score 550 paper-based; 213 computer-based). *Application deadline:* For fall admission, 6/16 for domestic students. Application fee: $35 ($50 for international students). *Expenses:* Tuition, area resident: Full-time $6500. Tuition, state resident: full-time $6500. Tuition, nonresident: full-time $11,558. *Financial support:* In 2008–09, 1 research assistantship (averaging $750 per year) was awarded; fellowships, career-related internships or fieldwork also available. Financial award application deadline: 6/1; financial award applicants required to submit FAFSA. *Faculty research:* Personnel, non-profit organizational change, welfare policy, urban research. Total annual research expenditures: $33,080. *Unit head:* Dr. Edith Barrett, Graduate Adviser, 817-272-3285, Fax: 817-272-5008, E-mail: ebarrett@uta.edu. *Application contact:* Linda Slaughter, Administrative Clerk, 817-272-3071, Fax: 817-272-5008, E-mail: slaughter@uta.edu.

The University of Texas at Austin, Graduate School, School of Architecture, Program in Community and Regional Planning, Austin, TX 78712-1111. Offers MSCRP, PhD, JD/MSCRP, MSCRP/MA, MSCRP/PhD. *Accreditation:* ACSP. *Degree requirements:* For master's, thesis; for doctorate, thesis/dissertation. *Entrance requirements:* For master's and doctorate, GRE General Test. Electronic applications accepted.

The University of Texas at San Antonio, College of Architecture, San Antonio, TX 78249-0617. Offers architecture (M Arch, MS Arch); historical preservation (Graduate Certificate); urban and regional planning (Graduate Certificate). *Degree requirements:* For master's, comprehensive exam, thesis. *Entrance requirements:* For master's, GRE General Test, minimum GPA of 3.0 in last 60 hours and in all architecture courses. Additional exam requirements/recommendations for international students: Required—TOEFL (minimum score 500 paper-based; 173 computer-based). Electronic applications accepted.

The University of Toledo, College of Graduate Studies, College of Arts and Sciences, Department of Geography and Planning, Toledo, OH 43606-3390. Offers geographic information systems and applied geographics (Certificate); geography (MA); planning (MA). Part-time programs available. *Degree requirements:* For master's, thesis. *Entrance requirements:* For master's, GRE General Test. Electronic applications accepted.

University of Toronto, School of Graduate Studies, Social Sciences Division, Department of Geography, Program in Planning, Toronto, ON M5S 1A1, Canada. Offers M Sc Pl, PhD. Part-time programs available. *Degree requirements:* For master's, summer internship. *Entrance requirements:* For master's, bachelor's degree in planning, geography, social science or a closely related professional field, minimum B+ average in final year, 3 letters of reference. *Expenses:* Contact institution.

University of Utah, The Graduate School, College of Architecture and Planning, Salt Lake City, UT 84112-1107. Offers architectural studies (M Arch, MS); urban planning (MUP); M Arch/MBA. Part-time programs available. *Degree requirements:* For master's, thesis (for some programs), comprehensive project. *Entrance requirements:* For master's, minimum undergraduate GPA of 3.0. Additional exam requirements/recommendations for international students: Required—TOEFL (minimum score 500 paper-based; 173 computer-based). Electronic applications accepted. *Expenses:* Contact institution. *Faculty research:* History, design, acoustics, photography, structures, architecture of American West, architectural communication and representation, impact of technology.

University of Virginia, School of Architecture, Department of Urban and Environmental Planning, Charlottesville, VA 22903. Offers MUEP, JD/MUEP. *Accreditation:* ACSP (one or more programs are accredited). *Faculty:* 5 full-time (2 women). *Students:* 36 full-time (21 women), 1 (woman) part-time; includes 1 minority (African American), 1 international. Average age 26. 112 applicants, 73% accepted, 21 enrolled. In 2008, 28 master's awarded. *Entrance requirements:* For master's, GRE General Test, previous course work in statistics; 3 letters of recommendation;. Additional exam requirements/recommendations for international students: Required—TOEFL (minimum score 600 paper-based; 250 computer-based; 90 iBT). *Application deadline:* For fall admission, 1/16 for domestic and international students. Applications are processed on a rolling basis. Application fee: $60. Electronic applications accepted. *Expenses:* Tuition, area resident: Full-time $10,452. Tuition, state resident: full-time $10,452. Tuition, nonresident: full-time $20,010. Required fees: $2176. Part-time tuition and fees vary according to course load and program. *Financial support:* Applicants required to submit FAFSA. *Faculty research:* Urban development, land use, environment, policy analysis, historic preservation. *Unit head:* Daphne Spain, Chair, 434-924-1339, Fax: 434-982-2678, E-mail: dgs4g@virginia.edu. *Application contact:* Graduate Admissions Officer, 434-924-6442, Fax: 434-982-2678, E-mail: arch-admissions@virginia.edu.

University of Washington, Graduate School, College of Architecture and Urban Planning, Department of Urban Design and Planning, Seattle, WA 98195. Offers strategic planning for critical infrastructures (MSCPI); urban design and planning (PhD); urban planning (MUP). *Accreditation:* ACSP (one or more programs are accredited). *Degree requirements:* For master's, thesis or alternative; for doctorate, thesis/dissertation. *Entrance requirements:* For master's and doctorate, GRE General Test, minimum GPA of 3.0. Additional exam requirements/recommendations for international students: Required—TOEFL. *Faculty research:* Land-use and growth management, urban form and travel behavior, geographic information systems/remote sensing, historic preservation, urban ecology and environmental planning.

University of Waterloo, Graduate Studies, Faculty of Environmental Studies, Program in Local Economic Development, Waterloo, ON N2L 3G1, Canada. Offers MAES. Part-time programs available. *Degree requirements:* For master's, internship, research paper. Electronic applications accepted.

University of Waterloo, Graduate Studies, Faculty of Environmental Studies, School of Planning, Waterloo, ON N2L 3G1, Canada. Offers MA, MAES, MES, PhD. Part-time programs available. *Degree requirements:* For master's, thesis (for some programs); for doctorate, comprehensive exam, thesis/dissertation. *Entrance requirements:* For master's, honors degree, minimum B+ average; for doctorate, master's degree, minimum A- average, resumé. Additional exam requirements/recommendations for international students: Required—TOEFL, TWE. Electronic applications accepted. *Faculty research:* Environmental planning, planning for resource development, urban planning and information systems, social planning, urban design.

University of Wisconsin–Madison, Graduate School, College of Letters and Science and College of Agricultural and Life Sciences, Department of Urban and Regional Planning, Madison, WI 53706-1380. Offers MS, PhD. *Accreditation:* ACSP (one or more programs are accredited). Part-time programs available. *Degree requirements:* For master's, thesis optional, internship; for doctorate, thesis/dissertation, 3 preliminary exams. *Entrance requirements:* For master's, GRE, minimum GPA of 3.0, previous course work in statistics; for doctorate, 1 year of experience, master's degree in related field. Electronic applications accepted. *Faculty research:* Land use, environmental planning, community development, economic development planning.

University of Wisconsin–Milwaukee, Graduate School, School of Architecture and Urban Planning, Department of Urban Planning, Milwaukee, WI 53201-0413. Offers geographic information systems (Certificate); urban planning (MUP); M Arch/MUP; MPA/MUP; MUP/MS. *Accreditation:* ACSP. Part-time programs available. *Faculty:* 5 full-time (2 women). *Students:* 29 full-time (11 women), 5 part-time (3 women), 2 international. Average age 27. 59 applicants, 66% accepted, 16 enrolled. In 2008, 17 master's awarded. *Degree requirements:* For master's, comprehensive exam, thesis or alternative. *Entrance requirements:* For master's, GRE General Test. Additional exam requirements/recommendations for international students: Required—TOEFL (minimum score 550 paper-based; 213 computer-based; 79 iBT), IELTS (minimum score 6.5). *Application deadline:* For fall admission, 1/1 priority date for domestic students; for spring admission, 9/1 for domestic students. Applications are processed on a rolling basis. Application fee: $45 ($75 for international students). *Expenses:* Tuition, area resident: Full-time $7320; part-time $165 per credit. Tuition, state resident: full-time $7320; part-time $165 per credit. Tuition, nonresident: full-time $17,840; part-time $714 per credit. Tuition and fees vary according to campus/location, program and reciprocity agreements. *Financial support:* In 2008–09, 3 teaching assistantships were awarded; career-related internships or fieldwork and unspecified assistantships also available. Support available to part-time students. Financial award application deadline: 4/15. Total annual research expenditures: $157,104. *Unit head:* Joan Simuncak, Representative, 414-229-4015, Fax: 414-229-6976, E-mail: joanarch@uwm.edu. *Application contact:* General Information Contact, 414-229-4982, Fax: 414-229-6967, E-mail: gradschool@uwm.edu.

Utah State University, School of Graduate Studies, College of Humanities, Arts and Social Sciences, Department of Landscape Architecture and Environmental Planning, Logan, UT 84322. Offers bioregional planning (MS); landscape architecture (MLA). *Accreditation:* ASLA (one or more programs are accredited). *Degree requirements:* For master's, thesis. *Entrance requirements:* For master's, GRE General Test, minimum GPA of 3.0. Additional exam requirements/recommendations for international students: Required—TOEFL. *Faculty research:* Visual resource management, planning for wildlife, agricultural land preservation, watershed planning, community planning and design.

Utah State University, School of Graduate Studies, College of Natural Resources, Department of Environment and Society, Logan, UT 84322. Offers bioregional planning (MS); geography (MA, MS); human dimensions of ecosystem science and management (MS, PhD); recreation resource management (MS, PhD). *Degree requirements:* For master's, comprehensive exam, thesis (for some programs). *Entrance requirements:* For master's and doctorate, GRE General Test, minimum GPA of 3.0. Additional exam requirements/recommendations for international students: Required—TOEFL. Electronic applications accepted. *Faculty research:* Geographic information systems/geographic and environmental education, bioregional planning, natural resource and environmental policy, outdoor recreation and tourism, natural resource and environmental management.

Vanderbilt University, Peabody College, Department of Human and Organizational Development, Nashville, TN 37240-1001. Offers community development and action (M Ed); human development counseling (M Ed). *Accreditation:* ACA; NCATE. Part-time programs available. *Faculty:* 28 full-time (14 women), 26 part-time/adjunct (20 women). *Students:* 65 full-time (63 women), 10 part-time (7 women); includes 14 minority (7 African Americans, 1 Asian American or Pacific Islander, 6 Hispanic Americans), 1 international. Average age 27. 125 applicants, 54% accepted, 38 enrolled. In 2008, 22 master's awarded. *Degree requirements:* For master's, comprehensive exam, thesis optional. *Entrance requirements:* For master's, GRE General Test, MAT. Additional exam requirements/recommendations for international students: Required—TOEFL (minimum score 550 paper-based; 213 computer-based). *Application deadline:* For fall admission, 12/31 priority date for domestic and international students; for spring admission, 11/1 priority date for domestic and international students. Applications are processed on a rolling basis. Application fee: $0. Electronic applications accepted. *Financial support:* In 2008–09, 75 students received support, including 21 research assistantships with full and partial tuition reimbursements available, 13 teaching assistantships with full and partial tuition reimbursements available; fellowships with full and partial tuition reimbursements available, Federal Work-Study, institutionally sponsored loans, scholarships/grants, tuition waivers (partial), and unspecified assistantships also available. Support available to part-time students. Financial award application deadline: 2/1; financial award applicants required to submit FAFSA. *Faculty research:* Community psychology, community development and urban policy, counseling and mental health services, organizational development and institutional change; youth physical and behavioral health in schools and communities. *Unit head:* Dr. Joseph Cunningham, Chair, 615-322-6881, Fax: 615-322-1141, E-mail: joe.cunningham@vanderbilt.edu. *Application contact:* Sherrie Lane, Office Assistant, 615-322-8484, Fax: 615-322-1141, E-mail: sherrie.a.lane@vanderbilt.edu.

Virginia Commonwealth University, Graduate School, College of Humanities and Sciences, Wilder School of Government and Public Affairs, Department of Urban Studies and Planning, Program in Planning Information Systems, Richmond, VA 23284-9005. Offers Certificate.

Virginia Commonwealth University, Graduate School, College of Humanities and Sciences, Wilder School of Government and Public Affairs, Department of Urban Studies and Planning, Program in Urban and Regional Planning, Richmond, VA 23284-9005. Offers MURP, JD/MURP. *Degree requirements:* For master's, thesis optional, internship. *Entrance requirements:* For master's, GRE General Test or LSAT, minimum GPA of 2.7.

Virginia Polytechnic Institute and State University, Graduate School, College of Architecture and Urban Studies, School of Public and International Affairs, Blacksburg, VA 24061. Offers environmental planning and policy (MURP); government and international affairs (MPIA); housing, community and economic development (MURP); international development planning (MURP); land use and physical planning (MURP); planning, governance and globalization (PhD), including environmental planning and landscape analysis, physical planning and urban design, public and international affairs, urban and environmental design and planning; urban and regional planning (MURP). *Accreditation:* ACSP. *Entrance requirements:* Additional exam requirements/recommendations for international students: Required—TOEFL (minimum score 550 paper-based; 213 computer-based). Electronic applications accepted. *Faculty research:* Design theory, environmental planning, town planning, transportation planning.

Wayne State University, College of Liberal Arts and Sciences, Department of Geography and Urban Planning, Detroit, MI 48202. Offers geography (MA); urban planning (MUP). Evening/

Urban and Regional Planning

Wayne State University (continued)
weekend programs available. *Entrance requirements:* For master's, minimum 3.0 GPA; statement of interest; two letters of recommendations. Additional exam requirements/recommendations for international students: Required—TOEFL (minimum score 550 paper-based; 213 computer-based); Recommended—TWE (minimum score 6). Electronic applications accepted. *Faculty research:* Housing and community development, urban and regional economic development, urban development and land use, transportation policy and planning, environmental policy and planning.

Wayne State University, College of Liberal Arts and Sciences, Program in Urban Planning, Detroit, MI 48202. Offers MUP. *Accreditation:* ACSP. Evening/weekend programs available. *Degree requirements:* For master's, thesis. *Entrance requirements:* Additional exam requirements/recommendations for international students: Required—TOEFL (minimum score 550 paper-based; 213 computer-based); Recommended—TWE (minimum score 6). Electronic applications accepted.

West Chester University of Pennsylvania, Office of Graduate Studies, College of Business and Public Affairs, Department of Geography and Planning, West Chester, PA 19383. Offers geographic technology (Certificate); geography (MA); regional planning (MSA). Part-time and evening/weekend programs available. *Students:* 12 full-time (1 woman), 16 part-time (4 women); includes 5 minority (4 African Americans, 1 Hispanic American). Average age 33. 15 applicants, 100% accepted, 9 enrolled. In 2008, 7 master's, 10 other advanced degrees awarded. *Degree requirements:* For master's, comprehensive exam, thesis optional. *Entrance requirements:* For master's, GRE, GMAT, or MAT, minimum GPA of 2.8, resumé, two letters of recommendation; for Certificate, minimum GPA of 2.8, resumé, three letters of recommendation. Additional exam requirements/recommendations for international students: Required—TOEFL (minimum score 550 paper-based; 213 computer-based; 80 iBT). *Application deadline:* For fall admission, 4/15 priority date for domestic students, 3/15 for international students; for spring admission, 10/15 for domestic students, 9/1 for international students. Applications are processed on a rolling basis. Application fee: $35. Electronic applications accepted. *Expenses:* Tuition, state resident: full-time $6430; part-time $357 per credit. Tuition, nonresident: full-time $10,288; part-time $572 per credit. Required fees: $652.50; $50 per credit. $67 per semester. *Financial support:* In 2008–09, 3 research assistantships with full and partial tuition reimbursements (averaging $5,000 per year) were awarded; unspecified assistantships also available. Support available to part-time students. Financial award application deadline: 2/15; financial award applicants required to submit FAFSA. *Faculty research:* Environmental education, land use/suburban planning, landscapes of Catalunya. *Unit head:* Dr. Joan Welch, Chair and Graduate Coordinator, 610-436-2940, E-mail: jwelch@wcupa.edu. *Application contact:* Rabbi Dottie Ives Dewey, MSA Graduate Coordinator, 610-436-2746, E-mail: divesdewey@wcupa.edu.

West Virginia University, Davis College of Agriculture, Forestry and Consumer Sciences, Division of Resource Management and Sustainable Development, Morgantown, WV 26506. Offers agricultural and extension education (MS, PhD), including agricultural and extension education, teaching vocational-agriculture (MS); agricultural and resource economics (MS); human and community development (PhD); natural resource economics (PhD); resource management (PhD); resource management and sustainable development (PhD). Part-time programs available. *Degree requirements:* For master's, thesis; for doctorate, comprehensive exam, thesis/dissertation. *Entrance requirements:* For master's, GRE General Test. Additional exam requirements/recommendations for international students: Required—TOEFL. *Faculty research:* Environmental economics, energy economics, agriculture.

West Virginia University, Eberly College of Arts and Sciences, Department of Geology and Geography, Program in Geography, Morgantown, WV 26506. Offers energy and environmental resources (MA); geographic information systems (PhD); geography-regional development (PhD); GIS/cartographic analysis (MA); regional development (MA). Part-time programs available. *Degree requirements:* For master's, thesis, oral and written exams; for doctorate, comprehensive exam, thesis/dissertation, oral and written exams. *Entrance requirements:* For master's and doctorate, GRE General Test, minimum GPA of 3.0. Additional exam requirements/recommendations for international students: Required—TOEFL. Electronic applications accepted. *Faculty research:* Space, place and development, geographic information science, environmental geography.

Urban Studies

Boston University, Metropolitan College (Continuing Education), Department of Applied Social Sciences, Boston, MA 02215. Offers city planning (MCP); criminal justice (MCJ); urban affairs (MUA). Part-time and evening/weekend programs available. *Entrance requirements:* Additional exam requirements/recommendations for international students: Required—TOEFL; Recommended—IELTS. Electronic applications accepted. *Faculty research:* Housing, community development and land use planning, environmental management and planning, international comparative development planning.

Brooklyn College of the City University of New York, Division of Graduate Studies, Department of Political Science, Brooklyn, NY 11210-2889. Offers international affairs (MA); political science (MA, PhD); political science, urban policy and administration (MA). The department offers courses at Brooklyn College that are creditable toward the CUNY doctoral degree (with permission of the executive officer of the doctoral program). Part-time and evening/weekend programs available. *Students:* 13 full-time (6 women), 142 part-time (82 women); includes 91 minority (68 African Americans, 5 Asian Americans or Pacific Islanders, 18 Hispanic Americans), 15 international. Average age 33. 95 applicants, 83% accepted, 45 enrolled. In 2008, 43 master's awarded. *Degree requirements:* For master's, comprehensive exam (for some programs), thesis or alternative, foreign language exam (for international affairs program). *Entrance requirements:* For master's, 2 letters of recommendation, personal statement. *Expenses:* Tuition, state resident: full-time $7360; part-time $310 per credit hour. Tuition, nonresident: full-time $13,800; part-time $575 per credit hour. *Financial support:* Career-related internships or fieldwork and Federal Work-Study available. Support available to part-time students. Financial award application deadline: 5/1; financial award applicants required to submit FAFSA. *Faculty research:* Ethics and politics, politics of criminal justice, Western Europe, international law and politics, labor politics. *Unit head:* Dr. Sally Bermanzohn, Chairperson, 718-951-5306, E-mail: sallyb@brooklyn.cuny.edu. *Application contact:* Hernan Sierra, Graduate Admissions Coordinator, 718-951-4536, Fax: 718-951-4506, E-mail: grads@brooklyn.cuny.edu.

Cleveland State University, College of Graduate Studies, Maxine Goodman Levin College of Urban Affairs, Program in Urban Studies, Cleveland, OH 44115. Offers geographic information systems (Certificate); local and urban management (Certificate); nonprofit management (Certificate); urban economic development (Certificate); urban real estate development and finance (Certificate); urban studies (MS); urban studies and public affairs (PhD). Part-time and evening/weekend programs available. *Faculty:* 26 full-time (10 women), 20 part-time/adjunct (11 women). *Students:* 26 full-time (12 women), 42 part-time (24 women); includes 13 minority (10 African Americans, 2 Asian Americans or Pacific Islanders, 1 Hispanic American), 21 international. Average age 37. 69 applicants, 35% accepted, 12 enrolled. In 2008, 6 master's, 7 doctorates, 6 other advanced degrees awarded. *Degree requirements:* For master's, thesis or alternative, exit project, capstone course; for doctorate, comprehensive exam, thesis/dissertation. *Entrance requirements:* For master's, GRE General Test, minimum GPA of 3.0; for doctorate, GRE General Test, minimum GPA of 3.5. Additional exam requirements/recommendations for international students: Required—TOEFL (minimum score 525 paper-based; 197 computer-based; 65 iBT). *Application deadline:* For fall admission, 7/15 priority date for domestic students, 5/15 for international students; for spring admission, 11/1 for international students. Applications are processed on a rolling basis. Application fee: $30. Electronic applications accepted. *Financial support:* In 2008–09, 15 students received support, including 11 research assistantships with full tuition reimbursements available (averaging $7,000 per year), 4 teaching assistantships with full and partial tuition reimbursements available (averaging $7,000 per year); career-related internships or fieldwork, Federal Work-Study, institutionally sponsored loans, scholarships/grants, tuition waivers (full and partial), and unspecified assistantships also available. Support available to part-time students. Financial award application deadline: 3/1; financial award applicants required to submit FAFSA. *Faculty research:* Environmental issues, economic development, urban and public policy, public management. *Unit head:* Dr. Wendy Kellogg, Director, 216-687-5265, Fax: 216-687-9342, E-mail: w.kellogg@csuohio.edu. *Application contact:* Graduate Program Coordinator, 216-523-7522, Fax: 216-687-5398, E-mail: urbanprograms@csuohio.edu.

Concordia University, School of Graduate Studies, Faculty of Arts and Science, Department of Geography, Planning and Environment, Montréal, QC H3G 1M8, Canada. Offers environmental impact assessment (Diploma); geography, urban and environmental studies (M Sc).

Eastern University, School for Social Change, St. Davids, PA 19087-3696. Offers urban studies (MA), including arts in transformation, community development, youth leadership.

East Tennessee State University, School of Graduate Studies, College of Business and Technology, Department of Economics, Finance, and Urban Studies, Johnson City, TN 37614. Offers city management (MCM); community development (MPM); general administration (MPM); municipal service management (MPM); urban and regional economic development (MPM); urban and regional planning (MPM). *Degree requirements:* For master's, internship, oral defense of thesis, research report. *Entrance requirements:* For master's, GRE General Test, minimum GPA of 3.0. Additional exam requirements/recommendations for international students: Required—TOEFL (minimum score 550 paper-based; 213 computer-based).

Fordham University, Graduate School of Arts and Sciences, Program in Urban Studies, New York, NY 10458. Offers MA. *Degree requirements:* For master's, internship or field work, research project.

Georgia State University, Andrew Young School of Policy Studies, Department of Public Administration and Urban Studies, Program in Urban Policy Studies, Atlanta, GA 30303-3083. Offers MS. *Degree requirements:* For master's, thesis optional. *Entrance requirements:* For master's, GRE General Test. Additional exam requirements/recommendations for international students: Required—TOEFL. *Faculty research:* Public policy, social policy, planning.

Graduate School and University Center of the City University of New York, Graduate Studies, Interdisciplinary Studies, New York, NY 10016-4039. Offers language in social context (PhD); medieval studies (PhD); public policy (MA, PhD); urban studies (MA, PhD); women's studies (MA, PhD). Terminal master's awarded for partial completion of doctoral program. *Degree requirements:* For master's, thesis; for doctorate, comprehensive exam, thesis/dissertation. *Entrance requirements:* For master's and doctorate, GRE General Test.

Hunter College of the City University of New York, Graduate School, School of Arts and Sciences, Department of Urban Affairs and Planning, Program in Urban Affairs, New York, NY 10021-5085. Offers urban studies/affairs (MS). Part-time programs available. *Faculty:* 7 full-time (3 women), 8 part-time/adjunct (4 women). *Students:* 10 full-time (8 women), 53 part-time (37 women); includes 19 minority (12 African Americans, 2 Asian Americans or Pacific Islanders, 5 Hispanic Americans). Average age 35. 60 applicants, 72% accepted, 28 enrolled. In 2008, 74 master's awarded. *Degree requirements:* For master's, thesis or alternative, 2 formal reports, internship. *Entrance requirements:* For master's, minimum 12 credits of course work in social sciences. Additional exam requirements/recommendations for international students: Required—TOEFL. *Application deadline:* For fall admission, 4/1 priority date for domestic students, 2/1 for international students; for spring admission, 11/1 priority date for domestic students, 9/1 for international students. Applications are processed on a rolling basis. Application fee: $125. *Financial support:* Fellowships, research assistantships, teaching assistantships, career-related internships or fieldwork, Federal Work-Study, scholarships/grants, and unspecified assistantships available. *Faculty research:* Women, tourism, youth, immigration, employment. *Unit head:* Dr. Jill Simone Gross, Director, 212-772-5600, Fax: 212-772-5593, E-mail: igross@hunter.cuny.edu. *Application contact:* William Zlata, Director for Graduate Admissions, 212-772-4482, Fax: 212-650-3336, E-mail: admissions@hunter.cuny.edu.

Long Island University, Brooklyn Campus, Richard L. Conolly College of Liberal Arts and Sciences, Department of Urban Studies, Brooklyn, NY 11201-8423. Offers MA. Part-time and evening/weekend programs available. *Degree requirements:* For master's, thesis or alternative. *Entrance requirements:* For master's, 2 letters of recommendation. Additional exam requirements/recommendations for international students: Required—TOEFL (minimum score 500 paper-based; 173 computer-based). Electronic applications accepted.

Massachusetts Institute of Technology, School of Architecture and Planning, Department of Urban Studies and Planning, Cambridge, MA 02139-4307. Offers city planning (MCP); urban and regional planning (PhD); urban and regional studies (PhD); urban studies and planning (SM); M Arch/MCP; MCP/MSRED; MCP/MST; MCP/SM Arch S. *Accreditation:* ACSP (one or more programs are accredited). Terminal master's awarded for partial completion of doctoral program. *Degree requirements:* For master's, thesis; for doctorate, comprehensive exam, thesis/dissertation. *Entrance requirements:* For master's and doctorate, GRE General Test. Additional exam requirements/recommendations for international students: Required—TOEFL (minimum score 600 paper-based; 250 computer-based; 100 iBT); Recommended—TWE. Electronic applications accepted. *Faculty research:* City design and development; housing, community, and economic development; environmental policy and planning; international development and regional planning; urban information systems.

Minnesota State University Mankato, College of Graduate Studies, College of Social and Behavioral Sciences, Department of Urban and Regional Studies, Mankato, MN 56001. Offers local government (Certificate); urban and regional studies (MA); urban planning (Certificate); MAPA/MA. *Students:* 18 full-time (4 women), 14 part-time (6 women). *Degree requirements:* For master's, one foreign language, comprehensive exam, thesis or alternative. *Entrance requirements:* For master's, minimum GPA of 3.0 during previous 2 years, 2 letters of recommendation. Additional exam requirements/recommendations for international students: Required—TOEFL. *Application deadline:* For fall admission, 7/1 priority date for domestic students; for spring admission, 11/1 for domestic students. Applications are processed on a rolling basis. Application fee: $40. Electronic applications accepted. *Financial support:* Fellowships with partial tuition reimbursements, research assistantships with full tuition reimbursements, teaching assistantships with full tuition reimbursements, career-related internships or fieldwork, Federal Work-Study, institutionally sponsored loans, and unspecified assistantships available. Support available to part-time students. Financial award application deadline: 3/15; financial award applicants required to submit FAFSA. *Unit head:* Dr. Anthony Filipovitch, Chairperson, 507-389-1714. *Application contact:* 507-389-2321, E-mail: grad@mnsu.edu.

Moody Bible Institute, Graduate School, Chicago, IL 60610-3284. Offers biblical studies (MABS, Graduate Certificate); intercultural studies (MAIS, Graduate Certificate); ministry (M Div, M Min); spiritual formation and discipleship (MASF, Graduate Certificate); urban studies (MA, Graduate Certificate). Part-time programs available. *Degree requirements:* For master's, 2 foreign languages, fieldwork (MABS); colloquium, field research project (MA Min). *Entrance requirements:* For master's, 30 hours in Bible/theology, 2 years of ministry experience (MA Min).

New Jersey City University, Graduate Studies and Continuing Education, College of Education, Department of Educational Leadership, Jersey City, NJ 07305-1597. Offers basics and urban studies (MA); bilingual/bicultural education and English as a second language (MA); educational administration and supervision (MA). Evening/weekend programs available. *Entrance requirements:* For master's, GRE General Test or MAT. Additional exam requirements/recommendations for international students: Required—TOEFL.

New Jersey Institute of Technology, Office of Graduate Studies, School of Architecture, Program in Urban Systems, Newark, NJ 07102. Offers PhD. Part-time and evening/weekend programs available. *Students:* 22 full-time (13 women), 12 part-time (9 women); includes 14 minority (8 African Americans, 1 American Indian/Alaska Native, 3 Asian Americans or Pacific Islanders, 2 Hispanic Americans), 8 international. Average age 42. 31 applicants, 42% accepted, 6 enrolled. *Entrance requirements:* Additional exam requirements/recommendations for international students: Required—TOEFL (minimum score 550 paper-based; 213 computer-based; 79 iBT). *Application deadline:* For fall admission, 6/5 priority date for domestic students, 4/1 for international students; for spring admission, 11/15 for domestic and international students. Applications are processed on a rolling basis. Application fee: $60. Electronic applications accepted. *Expenses:* Tuition, area resident: Full-time $13,780; part-time $750 per credit. Tuition, state resident: full-time $13,780; part-time $750 per credit. Tuition, nonresident: full-time $19,580; part-time $1033 per credit. Required fees: $1956; $197 per credit. *Financial support:* Fellowships with full and partial tuition reimbursements, research assistantships with full and partial tuition reimbursements, teaching assistantships with full and partial tuition reimbursements, career-related internships or fieldwork, Federal Work-Study, institutionally sponsored loans, and unspecified assistantships available. Financial award application deadline: 3/15. *Unit head:* Karen Franck, Director, 973-596-3092, E-mail: karen.a.franck@njit.edu. *Application contact:* Kathryn Kelly, Director of Admissions, 973-596-3300, Fax: 973-596-3461, E-mail: admissions@njit.edu.

The New School: A University, Milano The New School for Management and Urban Policy, Program in Urban Policy Analysis and Management, New York, NY 10011. Offers MS. *Accreditation:* NASPAA. Part-time programs available. *Faculty:* 8 full-time (3 women), 3 part-time/adjunct (1 woman). *Students:* 77 full-time (56 women), 71 part-time (47 women); includes 57 minority (30 African Americans, 8 Asian Americans or Pacific Islanders, 19 Hispanic Americans), 5 international. Average age 31. In 2008, 14 master's awarded. *Degree requirements:* For master's, thesis. *Entrance requirements:* For master's, interview. Additional exam requirements/recommendations for international students: Required—TOEFL (minimum score 600 paper-based; 250 computer-based; 100 iBT). *Application deadline:* For fall admission, 8/1 priority date for domestic students; for winter admission, 1/15 priority date for domestic students. Applications are processed on a rolling basis. Application fee: $50. *Expenses:* Tuition: Full-time $27,144; part-time $1508 per credit. Required fees: $355 per semester. *Financial support:* Fellowships, research assistantships, career-related internships or fieldwork, Federal Work-Study, scholarships/grants, and tuition waivers (full and partial) available. Support available to part-time students. Financial award application deadline: 3/1; financial award applicants required to submit FAFSA. *Faculty research:* Community and economic development, national urban policy, social welfare policy, management of low-income housing, race and gender issues. *Unit head:* Dr. Alex F. Schwartz, Chair, 212-229-5400 Ext. 1222, Fax: 212-229-5404, E-mail: schwartz@newschool.edu. *Application contact:* Merida Escandon, Director of Admissions, 212-229-5462 Ext. 1108, Fax: 212-229-5354, E-mail: milanoadmissions@newschool.edu.

See Close-Up on page 1227.

Norfolk State University, School of Graduate Studies, School of Liberal Arts, Department of Sociology, Program in Urban Affairs, Norfolk, VA 23504. Offers MA. Part-time programs available. *Degree requirements:* For master's, thesis. *Entrance requirements:* For master's, minimum GPA of 2.5.

Northeastern University, College of Arts and Sciences, Department of Political Science, Program in Public Administration, Boston, MA 02115-5096. Offers development administration (MPA); health administration and policy (MPA); state and local government (MPA); urban studies (Certificate). *Accreditation:* NASPAA (one or more programs are accredited). Part-time and evening/weekend programs available. *Degree requirements:* For master's, thesis optional. *Entrance requirements:* For master's, GRE General Test. Additional exam requirements/recommendations for international students: Required—TOEFL. *Faculty research:* National health care, Third World development, leadership and ethics, science and technology, budgeting.

Old Dominion University, College of Business and Public Administration, Doctoral Program in Public Administration and Urban Policy, Norfolk, VA 23529. Offers PhD. Part-time and evening/weekend programs available. Postbaccalaureate distance learning degree programs offered. *Faculty:* 7 full-time (1 woman), 3 part-time/adjunct (2 women). *Students:* 4 full-time (3 women), 25 part-time (13 women); includes 8 minority (6 African Americans, 1 American Indian/Alaska Native, 1 Asian American or Pacific Islander), 3 international. Average age 40. 5 applicants, 80% accepted, 4 enrolled. In 2008, 3 doctorates awarded. *Degree requirements:* For doctorate, comprehensive exam, thesis/dissertation. *Entrance requirements:* For doctorate, GMAT, GRE General Test, master's degree, minimum graduate GPA of 3.0. Additional exam requirements/recommendations for international students: Required—TOEFL (minimum score 550 paper-based; 213 computer-based; 79 iBT). *Application deadline:* For fall admission, 3/15 priority date for domestic and international students. Application fee: $40. Electronic applications accepted. *Expenses:* Tuition, area resident: Full-time $7704; part-time $321 per credit. Tuition, state resident: full-time $7704; part-time $321 per credit. Tuition, nonresident: full-time $19,104; part-time $796 per credit. Required fees: $99 per semester. One-time fee: $40. *Financial support:* In 2008–09, 10 students received support, including 2 fellowships with partial tuition reimbursements available (averaging $15,000 per year), 8 research assistantships with partial tuition reimbursements available (averaging $13,000 per year); teaching assistantships, career-related internships or fieldwork, scholarships/grants, and tuition waivers (partial) also available. Support available to part-time students. Financial award application deadline: 3/15; financial award applicants required to submit FAFSA. *Faculty research:* Educational needs and program development, policy analysis and administration, excellence norms for cooperative education programs. Total annual research expenditures: $60,000. *Unit head:* Dr. John C. Morris, Graduate Program Director, 757-683-3961, Fax: 757-683-4886, E-mail: jcmorris@odu.edu. *Application contact:* Megan S. Jones, Graduate Program Manager, 757-683-3961, Fax: 757-683-4886, E-mail: mmjones@odu.edu.

Portland State University, Graduate Studies, College of Urban and Public Affairs, Nohad A. Toulan School of Urban Studies and Planning, Program in Urban Studies, Portland, OR 97207-0751. Offers MUS, PhD. *Faculty:* 19 full-time (4 women), 15 part-time/adjunct (8 women). *Students:* 30 full-time (14 women), 36 part-time (21 women); includes 7 minority (1 African American, 2 American Indian/Alaska Native, 1 Asian American or Pacific Islander, 3 Hispanic Americans), 7 international. Average age 38. 38 applicants, 47% accepted, 12 enrolled. In 2008, 7 master's awarded. *Degree requirements:* For doctorate, comprehensive exam, thesis/dissertation, residency. *Entrance requirements:* For master's, GRE General Test, minimum GPA of 2.75, 3 letters of recommendation; for doctorate, GRE General Test, minimum GPA of 2.75. Additional exam requirements/recommendations for international students: Required—TOEFL (minimum score 550 paper-based; 213 computer-based). *Application deadline:* For fall admission, 1/15 for domestic and international students; for winter admission, 9/1 for domestic and international students. Application fee: $50. *Expenses:* Tuition, area resident: Full-time $8763; part-time $179 per credit hour. Tuition, state resident: full-time $8763; part-time $298 per credit hour. Tuition, nonresident: full-time $12,981; part-time $426 per credit hour. Required fees: $1242. One-time fee: $250. Tuition and fees vary according to course load and program. *Financial support:* Research assistantships available. Financial award application deadline: 3/1. *Unit head:* Dr. Ethan P. Seltzer, Director, 503-725-4045, E-mail: seltzere@pdx.edu. *Application contact:* Tracy Braden, Office Coordinator, 503-725-4015, Fax: 503-725-8770, E-mail: tbraden@pdx.edu.

Queens College of the City University of New York, Division of Graduate Studies, Social Science Division, Department of Urban Studies, Flushing, NY 11367-1597. Offers MA. Part-time and evening/weekend programs available. *Degree requirements:* For master's, thesis. *Entrance requirements:* For master's, minimum GPA of 3.0. Additional exam requirements/recommendations for international students: Required—TOEFL. *Faculty research:* Housing abandonment, industrial rehabilitation of Long Island City, health facilities in Queens County.

Rutgers, The State University of New Jersey, Newark, Graduate School, Program in Public Administration, Newark, NJ 07102. Offers health care administration (MPA); human resources administration (MPA); public administration (PhD); public management (MPA); public policy analysis (MPA); urban systems and issues (MPA). *Accreditation:* NASPAA (one or more programs are accredited). Part-time and evening/weekend programs available. *Degree requirements:* For master's, comprehensive exam, thesis or alternative; for doctorate, thesis/dissertation. *Entrance requirements:* For master's, GRE, minimum undergraduate B average; for doctorate, GRE, MPA, minimum B average. Electronic applications accepted. *Faculty research:* Government finance, municipal and state government, public productivity.

Rutgers, The State University of New Jersey, Newark, Graduate School, Program in Urban Systems, Newark, NJ 07102. Offers PhD.

Saint Louis University, Graduate School, College of Education and Public Service and Graduate School, Department of Public Policy Studies, St. Louis, MO 63103-2097. Offers geographic information systems (Certificate); organizational development (Certificate); public administration (MAPA); public policy analysis (PhD); urban affairs (MAUA); urban planning and real estate development (MUPRED). *Accreditation:* NASPAA. Part-time programs available. *Degree requirements:* For master's, comprehensive exam (for some programs), thesis (for some programs); for doctorate, comprehensive exam, thesis/dissertation, preliminary exams. *Entrance requirements:* For master's and doctorate, GMAT, GRE General Test, or LSAT, letters of recommendation, resumé, interview, transcripts, goal statement. Additional exam requirements/recommendations for international students: Required—TOEFL (minimum score 525 paper-based; 194 computer-based). Electronic applications accepted. *Faculty research:* Urban politics, brown fields, e-government, and administration, evaluation research, community development, electronic government and governance.

San Francisco Art Institute, Graduate Program, Department of Urban Studies, San Francisco, CA 94133. Offers MA. *Entrance requirements:* Additional exam requirements/recommendations for international students: Required—TOEFL (minimum score 580 paper-based; 237 computer-based). Electronic applications accepted.

Savannah State University, Program in Urban Studies, Savannah, GA 31404. Offers MS. Part-time programs available. *Degree requirements:* For master's, thesis optional, internship. *Entrance requirements:* For master's, GRE. *Faculty research:* Transportation, political effectiveness, labor, sociology, criminal justice, waste management.

Simon Fraser University, Graduate Studies, Faculty of Arts and Social Sciences, Urban Studies Program, Burnaby, BC V5A 1S6, Canada. Offers MUS, Graduate Diploma. *Degree requirements:* For master's, project.

Southern Connecticut State University, School of Graduate Studies, School of Arts and Sciences, Program in Urban Studies, New Haven, CT 06515-1355. Offers MS, MSW/MS. Part-time and evening/weekend programs available. *Degree requirements:* For master's, thesis or alternative. *Entrance requirements:* For master's, interview, minimum QPA of 2.5. Electronic applications accepted.

Temple University, Graduate School, College of Liberal Arts, Department of Geography and Urban Studies, Philadelphia, PA 19122-6096. Offers geography (MA); urban studies (MA). *Degree requirements:* For master's, comprehensive exam, thesis or alternative. *Entrance requirements:* For master's, GRE General Test, minimum GPA of 3.0. Additional exam requirements/recommendations for international students: Required—TOEFL (minimum score 550 paper-based; 213 computer-based; 79 iBT). Electronic applications accepted. *Faculty research:* Environmental issues, urban political economy, poverty and unemployment, neighborhood development, African and Asian urbanization, housing, computer cartography.

Tufts University, Graduate School of Arts and Sciences, Department of Urban and Environmental Policy and Planning, Medford, MA 02155. Offers community development (MA); environmental policy (MA); health and human welfare (MA); housing policy (MA); international environment/development policy (MA); public policy (MPP); public policy and citizen participation (MA); MA/MS; MALD/MA. *Accreditation:* ACSP (one or more programs are accredited). Part-time programs available. *Degree requirements:* For master's, thesis, internship. *Entrance requirements:* For master's, GRE General Test. Additional exam requirements/recommendations for international students: Required—TOEFL (minimum score 550 paper-based; 213 computer-based; 80 iBT). Electronic applications accepted. *Expenses:* Contact institution.

See Close-Up on page 1237.

Université du Québec à Montréal, Graduate Programs, Program in Urban Analysis and Management, Montréal, QC H3C 3P8, Canada. Offers MA. Part-time programs available. *Entrance requirements:* For master's, appropriate bachelor's degree or equivalent and proficiency in French.

Université du Québec à Montréal, Graduate Programs, Program in Urban Studies, Montréal, QC H3C 3P8, Canada. Offers MA, PhD. Part-time programs available. *Degree requirements:* For doctorate, thesis/dissertation. *Entrance requirements:* For doctorate, appropriate master's degree or equivalent, proficiency in French.

Université du Québec, École nationale d'administration publique, Graduate Program in Public Administration, Program in Urban Analysis and Management, Quebec, QC G1K 9E5, Canada. Offers MAGU. Part-time programs available. *Entrance requirements:* For master's, appropriate bachelor's degree, proficiency in French.

Université du Québec, Institut National de la Recherche Scientifique, Graduate Programs, Research Center—Urbanization, Culture and Society, Québec, QC G1K 9A9, Canada. Offers demography (M Sc, PhD); research and public action (M Sc); urban studies (M Sc, PhD). Programs given in French. Part-time programs available. *Degree requirements:* For master's, thesis optional; for doctorate, thesis/dissertation. *Entrance requirements:* For master's, appropriate bachelor's degree, proficiency in French; for doctorate, appropriate master's degree, proficiency in French. *Faculty research:* Regional space, urban and metropolitan space, micro-urban space.

University at Albany, State University of New York, College of Arts and Sciences, Department of Sociology, Albany, NY 12222-0001. Offers demography (Certificate); sociology (MA, PhD); urban policy (Certificate). Terminal master's awarded for partial completion of doctoral program. *Degree requirements:* For master's, thesis; for doctorate, thesis/dissertation, 2 specialization exams, research tool. *Entrance requirements:* For master's and doctorate, GRE General Test. Additional exam requirements/recommendations for international students: Required—TOEFL

Urban Studies

University at Albany, State University of New York *(continued)*
(minimum score 213 computer-based). Electronic applications accepted. *Faculty research:* Gender and equality, crime and deviance, aging, work and organizations, social demography.

The University of Akron, Graduate School, Buchtel College of Arts and Sciences, Department of Public Administration and Urban Studies, Program in Urban Studies, Akron, OH 44325. Offers urban studies (MA); urban studies and public affairs (PhD). *Degree requirements:* For master's, thesis optional; for doctorate, one foreign language, comprehensive exam, thesis/dissertation. *Entrance requirements:* For master's, GRE, GMAT, LSAT, MAT or minimum GPA of 3.0, minimum GPA of 2.8, resumé, personal essay, letters of recommendation; for doctorate, GRE General Test, writing sample, minimum graduate GPA of 3.5, letters of recommendation, personal statement. Additional exam requirements/recommendations for international students: Required—TOEFL (minimum score 550 paper-based; 213 computer-based; 79 iBT). Electronic applications accepted.

University of California, Irvine, Office of Graduate Studies, School of Social Ecology, Department of Planning, Policy and Design, Irvine, CA 92697. Offers planning, policy and design (PhD); urban and regional planning (MURP). *Accreditation:* ACSP (one or more programs are accredited). *Degree requirements:* For doctorate, thesis/dissertation, research project. *Entrance requirements:* For master's and doctorate, GRE General Test, minimum GPA of 3.0. Additional exam requirements/recommendations for international students: Required—TOEFL (minimum score 550 paper-based; 213 computer-based). Electronic applications accepted. *Faculty research:* Community and social policy, economic development, land-use and growth management, transportation planning, environmental policy.

University of Central Oklahoma, College of Graduate Studies and Research, College of Liberal Arts, Department of Political Science, Program in Urban Affairs, Edmond, OK 73034-5209. Offers MA. Part-time programs available. *Entrance requirements:* Additional exam requirements/recommendations for international students: Required—TOEFL (minimum score 550 paper-based; 213 computer-based). Electronic applications accepted.

University of Delaware, College of Human Services, Education and Public Policy, Center for Energy and Environmental Policy, Program in Urban Affairs and Public Policy, Newark, DE 19716. Offers community development and nonprofit leadership (MA); energy and environmental policy (MA); governance, planning and management (PhD); historic preservation (MA); social and urban policy (PhD); technology, environment and society (PhD). Part-time programs available. Terminal master's awarded for partial completion of doctoral program. *Degree requirements:* For master's, analytical paper or thesis; for doctorate, thesis/dissertation. *Entrance requirements:* For master's, GRE General Test, minimum GPA of 3.0; for doctorate, GRE General Test, minimum GPA of 3.5. Additional exam requirements/recommendations for international students: Required—TOEFL. Electronic applications accepted. *Faculty research:* Political economy; social policy analysis; technology and society; historic preservation; urban policy.

See Close-Up on page 1239.

University of Lethbridge, School of Graduate Studies, Lethbridge, AB T1K 3M4, Canada. Offers accounting (MScM); addictions counseling (M Sc); agricultural biotechnology (M Sc); agricultural studies (M Sc, MA); anthropology (MA); archaeology (MA); art (MA); biochemistry (M Sc); biological sciences (M Sc); biomolecular science (PhD); biosystems and biodiversity (PhD); Canadian studies (MA); chemistry (M Sc); computer science (M Sc); computer science and geographical information science (M Sc); counseling psychology (M Ed); dramatic arts (MA); earth, space, and physical science (PhD); economics (MA); educational leadership (M Ed); English (MA); environmental science (M Sc); evolution and behavior (PhD); exercise science (M Sc); finance (MScM); French (MA); French/German (MA); French/Spanish (MA); general education (M Ed); general management (MScM); geography (M Sc, MA); German (MA); health sciences (M Sc, MA); history (MA); human resource management and labour relations (MScM); individualized multidisciplinary (M Sc, MA); information systems (MScM); international management (MScM); kinesiology (M Sc, MA); management (M Sc, MA); marketing (MScM); mathematics (M Sc); music (MA); Native American studies (MA); neuroscience (M Sc, PhD); new media (MA); nursing (M Sc); philosophy (MA); physics (M Sc); policy and strategy (MScM); political science (MA); psychology (M Sc, MA); religious studies (MA); sociology (MA); theoretical and computational science (PhD); urban and regional studies (MA). Part-time and evening/weekend programs available. *Degree requirements:* For doctorate, comprehensive exam, thesis/dissertation. *Entrance requirements:* For master's, GMAT (M Sc in management), bachelor's degree in related field, minimum GPA of 3.0 during previous 20 graded semester courses, 2 years teaching or related experience (M Ed); for doctorate, master's degree, minimum graduate GPA of 3.5. Additional exam requirements/recommendations for international students: Required—TOEFL. *Faculty research:* Movement and brain plasticity, gibberellin physiology, photosynthesis, carbon cycling, molecular properties of main-group ring components.

University of Louisville, Graduate School, College of Arts and Sciences, Department of Urban and Public Affairs, Program in Urban and Public Affairs, Louisville, KY 40208. Offers urban planning and development (PhD); urban policy and administration (PhD). *Faculty:* 15 full-time (3 women). *Students:* 24 full-time (8 women), 3 part-time (2 women); includes 4 African Americans, 1 Asian American or Pacific Islander, 2 international. Average age 35. 15 applicants, 53% accepted, 6 enrolled. In 2008, 3 doctorates awarded. *Degree requirements:* For doctorate, thesis/dissertation. *Entrance requirements:* For doctorate, GRE General Test, master's degree in appropriate field. Additional exam requirements/recommendations for international students: Required—TOEFL (minimum score 547 paper-based; 210 computer-based; 77 iBT). *Application deadline:* For fall admission, 7/15 for domestic students; for spring

admission, 11/15 for domestic students. Applications are processed on a rolling basis. Application fee: $50. Electronic applications accepted. *Financial support:* In 2008–09, 11 students received support, including 2 fellowships with full tuition reimbursements available (averaging $19,000 per year), 9 research assistantships with full tuition reimbursements available (averaging $19,000 per year); health care benefits also available. *Unit head:* Dr. Steven Bourassa, Director, 502-852-5720, Fax: 502-852-4558, E-mail: steven.bourassa@louisville.edu. *Application contact:* Yani Vozos, Graduate Student Advisor, 502-852-8002, Fax: 502-852-4558, E-mail: yani.vozos@louisville.edu.

University of New Orleans, Graduate School, College of Liberal Arts, School of Urban Planning and Regional Studies, Program in Urban Studies, New Orleans, LA 70148. Offers MS, PhD. *Degree requirements:* For master's, thesis; for doctorate, thesis/dissertation. *Entrance requirements:* For master's, GRE General Test. Additional exam requirements/recommendations for international students: Required—TOEFL (minimum score 550 paper-based; 213 computer-based; 79 iBT). Electronic applications accepted. *Faculty research:* Urban economic development, environmental planning and analysis, social and cultural change.

University of Wisconsin–Milwaukee, Graduate School, College of Letters and Sciences, Department of History, Milwaukee, WI 53201-0413. Offers global history (PhD); history (MA); modern studies (PhD); urban history (PhD); MLIS/MA. Part-time programs available. *Faculty:* 32 full-time (15 women). *Students:* 44 full-time (22 women), 41 part-time (19 women); includes 9 minority (2 African Americans, 2 American Indian/Alaska Native, 1 Asian American or Pacific Islander, 4 Hispanic Americans), 1 international. Average age 34. 71 applicants, 58% accepted, 25 enrolled. In 2008, 12 master's awarded. *Degree requirements:* For master's, comprehensive exam, thesis or alternative; for doctorate, thesis/dissertation. *Entrance requirements:* For master's and doctorate, GRE General Test. Additional exam requirements/recommendations for international students: Required—TOEFL (minimum score 550 paper-based; 79 iBT), IELTS (minimum score 6.5). *Application deadline:* For fall admission, 1/1 priority date for domestic students; for spring admission, 9/1 for domestic students. Applications are processed on a rolling basis. Application fee: $45 ($75 for international students). *Expenses:* Tuition, area resident: Full-time $7320; part-time $165 per credit. Tuition, state resident: full-time $7320; part-time $165 per credit. Tuition, nonresident: full-time $17,840; part-time $714 per credit. Tuition and fees vary according to campus/location, program and reciprocity agreements. *Financial support:* In 2008–09, 21 teaching assistantships were awarded; career-related internships or fieldwork and unspecified assistantships also available. Support available to part-time students. Financial award application deadline: 4/15. Total annual research expenditures: $52,970. *Unit head:* Joe Austin, Representative, 414-229-4361, Fax: 414-229-2435, E-mail: jaustin@uwm.edu. *Application contact:* General Information Contact, 414-229-4982, Fax: 414-229-6967, E-mail: gradschool@uwm.edu.

University of Wisconsin–Milwaukee, Graduate School, College of Letters and Sciences, Interdepartmental Program in Urban Studies, Milwaukee, WI 53201-0413. Offers MS, PhD, MLIS/MS. *Faculty:* 32 full-time (13 women). *Students:* 21 full-time (11 women), 32 part-time (19 women); includes 12 minority (7 African Americans, 1 American Indian/Alaska Native, 1 Asian American or Pacific Islander, 3 Hispanic Americans), 3 international. Average age 36. 29 applicants, 52% accepted, 9 enrolled. In 2008, 6 master's, 1 doctorate awarded. *Degree requirements:* For master's, thesis or alternative; for doctorate, thesis/dissertation. *Entrance requirements:* For doctorate, GRE General Test. Additional exam requirements/recommendations for international students: Required—TOEFL (minimum score 550 paper-based; 79 iBT), IELTS (minimum score 6.5). *Application deadline:* For fall admission, 1/1 priority date for domestic students; for spring admission, 9/1 for domestic students. Applications are processed on a rolling basis. Application fee: $45 ($75 for international students). *Expenses:* Tuition, area resident: Full-time $7320; part-time $165 per credit. Tuition, state resident: full-time $7320; part-time $165 per credit. Tuition, nonresident: full-time $17,840; part-time $714 per credit. Tuition and fees vary according to campus/location, program and reciprocity agreements. *Financial support:* In 2008–09, 3 teaching assistantships were awarded; career-related internships or fieldwork and unspecified assistantships also available. Support available to part-time students. Financial award application deadline: 4/15. Total annual research expenditures: $4,460. *Unit head:* Amanda Seligman, Representative, 414-229-4015, Fax: 414-229-4266, E-mail: seligman@uwm.edu. *Application contact:* General Information Contact, 414-229-4982, Fax: 414-229-6967, E-mail: gradschool@uwm.edu.

Virginia Polytechnic Institute and State University, Graduate School, College of Architecture and Urban Studies, School of Public and International Affairs, Blacksburg, VA 24061. Offers environmental planning and policy (MURP); government and international affairs (MPIA); housing, community and economic development (MURP); international development planning (MURP); land use and physical planning (MURP); planning, governance and globalization (PhD), including environmental planning and landscape analysis, physical planning and urban design, public and international affairs, urban and environmental design and planning; urban and regional planning (MURP). *Accreditation:* ACSP. *Entrance requirements:* Additional exam requirements/recommendations for international students: Required—TOEFL (minimum score 550 paper-based; 213 computer-based). Electronic applications accepted. *Faculty research:* Design theory, environmental planning, town planning, transportation planning.

Wright State University, School of Graduate Studies, College of Liberal Arts, Department of Urban Affairs and Geography, Dayton, OH 45435. Offers public administration (MPA). *Accreditation:* NASPAA. *Degree requirements:* For master's, thesis optional. *Entrance requirements:* For master's, interview, minimum GPA of 2.7. Additional exam requirements/recommendations for international students: Required—TOEFL. *Faculty research:* Strategic planning, economic development, housing and public management.

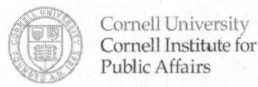

Program of Study	The Cornell Institute for Public Affairs (CIPA) offers a two-year program of graduate professional studies leading to a Master of Public Administration (M.P.A.) degree. The interdisciplinary nature of this M.P.A. program is one of its distinguishing features. CIPA students, called "fellows," have the flexibility to design individualized plans of study using faculty resources from across the University.

The program consists of sixteen courses; CIPA fellows typically take four courses per semester for four semesters. Although the M.P.A. program offers a basic structure for study, each CIPA fellow works closely with a faculty adviser to design an individualized program based on his or her specific area of interest. Courses may be taken through the program in any department or college in the university.

To develop a foundation of basic concepts and capabilities for the study of public policy, CIPA fellows take three courses in each of the following three subject areas: administration, politics, and public policy; economics and public finance; and quantitative analysis.

Concentration course work enables students to focus on a specific area of public policy study. They choose their course of study—domestic or international—from a broad range of options: environmental policy; finance and fiscal policy; government, politics, and policy studies; human rights and social justice; international development studies; public and nonprofit management; science and technology policy; and social policy.

Experiential learning is an integral component of CIPA's educational strategy, and a practical experience such as an internship is a requirement for obtaining the M.P.A. degree. Internships allow students to apply training in a practical environment and establish contacts for permanent employment. CIPA fellows also have the opportunity to gain professional experience off-campus, while taking a semester of courses for credit through Cornell in Rome, the Cornell-Nepal Study Program, and the CIPA Washington, D.C. semester program. Fellows may also fulfill the practical experience requirement by participating in the Public Service Exchange, a unique service learning partnership with local nonprofit and government agencies.

As a culmination of studies, all students are required to develop and complete a professional writing project, which typically grows out of a student's area of concentration and often incorporates work done during a summer internship. There are two options for completing this writing requirement: a professional report or a master's thesis. The report represents an experiential project undertaken by a fellow on behalf of a "client," such as a public, private, or nonprofit organization, and requires the fellow to solve a problem in policy analysis or program evaluation. The thesis is a substantial, independent research paper offering an original contribution to the field of public affairs. It requires a fellow to pose a policy problem, review and summarize previous efforts to address this problem, and propose an alternate solution.

CIPA students may elect to combine their M.P.A. study program with complementary degree study, such as a J.D. from Cornell Law School, an M.B.A. from the Johnson School of Management, an M.M.H. from the Hotel School, or an M.R.P. in the field of city and regional planning.

Research Facilities	Cornell is a major research university with significant derivative policy interests in natural and physical sciences, nutrition, genetics, engineering, computer and social sciences, health, education, consumer policy, art, architecture, and the humanities. Separate interdisciplinary work centers on the environment, international studies and development, and international food and agriculture. Programs on infrastructure, education, family development, and health administration provide valuable resources for fellows.

The University has a world-class library system, including nineteen libraries with more than 5 million volumes, 600,000 periodical titles, and extensive microfilm and other materials.

Financial Aid	The Cornell Institute for Public Affairs provides some funding to more than 80 percent of its students. The Institute itself, however, is unable to provide anyone with full support. CIPA fellows often win support from Fulbright, Truman, and World Bank fellowships. Applicants are encouraged to explore all available sources of external funding, including grants that may be provided by current employers. Because funding decisions are made on a first-come, first-served basis, those seeking funding should submit their application by the end of January.
Cost of Study	The estimated total cost of tuition and fees for full-time fellows for the 2009–10 academic year is $37,750. The estimated cost of books and materials is approximately $1200.
Living and Housing Costs	Living expenses for single students range from $1700 to $1800 per month, including room, meals, and personal expenses but excluding travel. There are many housing options for CIPA fellows. Some University housing is available exclusively to students in graduate and professional programs. Non-University housing includes apartment complexes, multiple-unit houses, single-unit houses, individual rooms, and cooperative living units. A listing of off-campus housing options is available from Cornell's Housing Office.
Student Group	Enrollment in the CIPA two-year M.P.A. program ranges between 150 and 175 full-time students. In general, the program has similar numbers of men and women, and about 35 to 40 percent of the fellows are international students. Of the total CIPA population, about half study international relations, policy, or development, while the remainder pursue a wide variety of domestic policy interests, from social policy to national security policy to environmental policy.
Student Outcomes	CIPA employs a full-time professional development specialist who provides career advisement and assistance in locating employment and internships. Professional development at CIPA also includes the cultivation of an extensive network of alumni in the public, private, nonprofit, and academic sectors. CIPA historically places more than 95 percent of its graduates within six months of graduation. Recent organizations that have employed CIPA alumni include the World Bank, the United Nations (UN), the United States Agency for International Development (USAID), the Environmental Protection Agency (EPA), Deloitte and Touche, Goldman Sachs, and Booz Allen Hamilton, Inc. International students often return to their countries of origin to work in high-level leadership posts in government and industry. Some CIPA alumni choose to continue their graduate studies in J.D. or Ph.D. programs.
Location	Cornell is located in Tompkins County in the heart of New York's Finger Lakes region, with pristine lakes, waterfalls, and multiple state parks. The area has more than beauty to recommend it. People who like to be outdoors thrive at Cornell. Nearby are opportunities for skiing, swimming, hiking, sailing, and mountain biking. Ithaca may be small and rural, but it also has an urban sophistication and an intellectual dynamism.
The University and The Institute	The Cornell Institute for Public Affairs is an autonomous, University-wide program designed to build on Cornell's legendary commitment to an education "which shall combine the practical with the liberal education." Cornell has offered the M.P.A. degree since 1946, originally through the Johnson Graduate School of Management, and since 1989 through the broader Cornell Institute for Public Affairs. CIPA's current alumni network includes graduates of both programs.
Applying	Admission to CIPA is selective. A committee of faculty members evaluates individual applications based on the student's overall academic record; GRE scores; English language skills (applicants for whom English is a second language will need to obtain the following minimum scores on the Internet-based test version of the TOEFL: writing 20, listening 15, reading 20, and speaking 22); potential for public-policy leadership as evidenced by professional work and community, extracurricular, or other relevant experience (students should include a copy of their most recent resume); and letters of recommendation. Applicants should also include an extensive written statement of purpose in which they address why they are applying to the program, their personal and/or professional experience that led to their interest in Cornell's M.P.A. program, their future goals (how they intend to put their M.P.A. degree to use), and examples of volunteer work, positions of responsibility, and any other life experiences contributing to their interest in public policy. The committee looks for sound analytic preparation and instruction or prior professional work experience in fields relevant to public affairs, such as economics, politics, public administration, planning, sociology, and law. CIPA has a rolling admissions policy; however, decisions concerning CIPA funding are made on a first-come, first-served basis, so students who wish to be considered should complete their applications by January 30.
Correspondence and Information	To request additional information:

Cornell Institute for Public Affairs
294 Caldwell Hall
Cornell University
Ithaca, New York 14853-2602

Phone: 607-255-8018
Fax: 607-255-5240
E-mail: cipa@cornell.edu
Web site: http://www.cipa.cornell.edu

Cornell University

THE FACULTY AND THEIR RESEARCH

The program offers great depth and flexibility. It is not confined to a single school or college but spans the entire University. More than 100 faculty members in the field of public affairs from a diverse cross section of schools, departments, and programs, welcome CIPA fellows into their courses and serve on thesis committees. Within this group, 11 members serve as Core Faculty, providing instruction in foundation course work.

The Core Faculty
David B. Lewis, CIPA Director; Professor in the Department of City and Regional Planning.
Norman Uphoff, CIPA Director of Graduate Studies; Professor in the Department of Government.
Richard Booth, Professor in the Department of City and Regional Planning.
Nancy Brooks, Visiting Associate Professor in the Department of City and Regional Planning.
Nancy Chau, Associate Professor in the Department of Applied Economics and Management.
Gary Fields, John P. Windmuller Chair in International and Comparative Labor in the School of Industrial and Labor Relations.
Neema Kudva, Assistant Professor in the Department of City and Regional Planning.
Daniel (Pete) Loucks, Professor in the Department of Civil and Environmental Engineering.
Theodore J. Lowi, John L. Senior Professor of American Institutions in the Department of Government.
Kathryn S. March, Professor in the Departments of Anthropology and Feminist, Gender, and Sexuality Studies.
Jerome M. Ziegler, Professor Emeritus in the Department of Policy Analysis and Management.

CORNELL UNIVERSITY

School of Industrial and Labor Relations

Programs of Study	The Industrial and Labor Relations (ILR) School at Cornell University offers five graduate degree programs in the field of industrial and labor relations: Master of Industrial and Labor Relations (M.I.L.R.); Master of Professional Studies (M.P.S.); Master of Science/Ph.D. (M.S./Ph.D.); M.I.L.R./M.B.A., a five-semester, dual-degree program at the ILR School (M.I.L.R.) and the Johnson Graduate School of Management (M.B.A.); and the M.I.L.R./Master in Management, a three-year dual-degree program at the ILR School (M.I.L.R) and ESCP Europe, the European School of Management (MEB). Candidates for the M.I.L.R. degree come from a variety of backgrounds and are interested in preparing for positions in human resource management, labor relations (including collective bargaining), and public policy. The M.I.L.R. reflects the need of future practitioners to become broadly familiar with all major aspects of the field and to become particularly competent in one of five areas: human resources and organizations, collective representation, dispute resolution, international and comparative labor, or labor-market policy. Students complete a minimum of 48 credits in courses and seminars, including required courses in collective bargaining, labor economics, labor and employment law, human resource management, organizational behavior, and statistics. Candidates with a law (J.D.) or M.B.A. degree may be able to obtain an M.I.L.R. degree in two semesters. The M.P.S. degree is limited to individuals with professionally related work experience who wish to update their knowledge of current practices. Applicants for this degree are often sponsored by their governments or organizations. Degree requirements include course work and an M.P.S. project. Students may choose to study part-time in New York City in the M.P.S. New York program or full-time in residence on the Ithaca campus. M.S. and Ph.D. candidates select major and minor subjects from the following areas: collective bargaining, labor law, and labor history; organizational behavior; human resource studies; and international and comparative labor. Minor subjects can also include social statistics and labor economics. Minor subjects in fields outside ILR are encouraged. Each candidate's program is supervised by a special committee of faculty members chosen by the candidate. The average M.S. program requires two years; the doctoral program typically takes an additional three years.
Research Facilities	The ILR School's Catherwood Library, with more than 232,000 volumes, is regarded as the world's most comprehensive source of information on work, employment, and labor issues. Catherwood's Kheel Center for Labor-Management Documentation and Archives ranks as one of three major centers of its type in the country. Catherwood is one of seventeen libraries constituting the Cornell University Library, ranked as one of the ten largest academic research libraries in the United States, with more than 7 million printed volumes, 65,000 journal and newspaper subscriptions, and more than 40,000 networked electronic databases available to users. Networked computer facilities in Catherwood and in other campus libraries are provided for graduate students, and a rapidly expanding array of electronic and full-text resources is available for use outside of the library. Catherwood's programs and services are aimed at providing easy access to its outstanding collections. Library staff members offer seminars and individualized training to acquaint graduate students with the research potential of Catherwood's print and electronic holdings.
Financial Aid	A small number of fellowships may be awarded on a competitive basis by Cornell University and the ILR School. In addition, the School awards a limited number of assistantships, mostly to M.S. and Ph.D. students, which provide a minimum stipend of $21,400 for the nine-month 2009–10 academic year. Tuition scholarships are also granted to graduate assistants. Assistantships require 15–20 hours of work each week in the School's instructional, research, or extension programs.
Cost of Study	Tuition is $24,700 for the 2009–10 academic year for both state residents and out-of-state students. Books cost between $900 and $1200 per year, and there is also a thesis fee.
Living and Housing Costs	Budgets for single students to live at a modest comfort level average $1200 per month. Married students should expect greater expenses. The largest variable is rent; both University and private housing are available to graduate students.
Student Group	The population of graduate students at Cornell is more than 6,000, representing all regions of the United States and many other countries. Candidates for the M.I.L.R. degree, approximately half of the 180 graduate students in ILR, have a wide variety of academic and employment backgrounds. M.I.L.R. candidates generally choose professional careers, while Ph.D. candidates usually aim for academic appointments.
Student Outcomes	The ILR Office of Career Services provides a wide variety of services, including individual advising, workshops, resume reviews, career fairs, networking assistance, job listings, and practice interviews to help students explore their career options and develop effective job-search strategies. The office manages an on-campus recruitment program, with representatives of numerous corporations, labor unions, government agencies, and labor law firms interviewing students for positions in human resources and labor relations. The office also cultivates contacts with alumni and others working in the field. Further career information is available from the Office of Career Services, 201 Ives Hall, Cornell University (telephone: 607-255-7816; Web site: http://www.ilr.cornell.edu/careerservices/). A few of the leading employers of M.I.L.R. degree recipients are the AFL-CIO, American Express Company, Citigroup, Dell, General Electric, General Mills, Honeywell, IBM, Microsoft, the National Labor Relations Board (NLRB), and Shell Oil Company. The mean salary for a recent M.I.L.R. graduating class was approximately $73,180. The mean salary for recent M.I.L.R. graduates choosing the corporate sector was $76,184, with a mean signing bonus of $7531. Those recently completing doctoral degree programs found employment at such places as Cornell, Washington University, the London School of Business, the University of Delaware, Cardiff University in Wales, the University of Michigan, Harvard Business School, and the U.S. Bureau of Labor Statistics.
Location	Ithaca is a university town of nearly 40,000, set in the center of the beautiful Finger Lakes region of upstate New York. The area is rich in outdoor recreational resources for swimming, skiing, and boating. Cornell and neighboring Ithaca College as well as community groups in the creative and performing arts contribute to a lively and diverse cultural life that includes plays, concerts, opera, ballet, and lectures.
The University	The Cornell tradition of graduate education recognizes that each student has different needs, strengths, and goals, and the University makes every effort to accommodate students' specific requirements and incomes. Every member of the social science faculties at Cornell is a potential resource to each ILR graduate student, whatever the field of study, providing intellectual resources that are extensive and cross college boundaries. Distinguished scholars in economics, sociology, and psychology can be found in ILR as well as in appropriate fields in the College of Arts and Sciences, the College of Human Ecology, and the Johnson School of Management; in other professional fields, such as developmental sociology, child development and family relations, agricultural economics, and business law; and in research institutes such as the Southeast Asia and Latin American Centers.
Applying	While a strong background in the social sciences is both appropriate and helpful for advanced work at ILR, those with different backgrounds (engineering, law, business) regularly enroll. The deadline for fall admission is January 1; for spring admission, the deadline is October 15. Ph.D. candidates generally undertake master's thesis research before entering the Ph.D. program. Exceptionally well-qualified applicants may be admitted directly to the doctoral program with only a bachelor's degree. All applicants must take the General Test of the Graduate Record Examinations (GRE) or the Graduate Management Admission Test (GMAT). International students are also required to take the Test of English as a Foreign Language (TOEFL).
Correspondence and Information	ILR Graduate Programs Office ILR School 214 Ives Hall Cornell University Ithaca, New York 14853-3901 Phone: 607-255-1522 E-mail: ilrgradapplicant@cornell.edu Web site: http://www.ilr.cornell.edu/graddegreeprograms

Cornell University

THE FACULTY

The graduate faculty members at Cornell's School of Industrial and Labor Relations represent a wide spectrum of the social and behavioral sciences—cultural anthropology, economics, history, law, political science, psychology, social psychology, sociology, and statistics—offering courses, advising, consulting, directing research activities, and sharing research opportunities. In addition, students may take courses from and select as advisers other Cornell faculty members in the social sciences, the humanities, mathematics, and engineering.

Department of Collective Bargaining, Labor Law, and Labor History
Lee H. Adler, Senior Extension Associate; J.D., Golden Gate. Law.
Kate Brofenbrenner, Senior Lecturer and Director of Labor Education Research; Ph.D., Cornell. Labor and industrial relations.
Alex Colvin, Associate Professor; Ph.D., Cornell.
Lance Compa, Senior Lecturer; J.D., Yale. Law.
Maria L. Cook, Associate Professor; Ph.D., Berkeley. Political science.
Jefferson Cowie, Associate Professor; Ph.D., North Carolina at Chapel Hill. History.
Cletus Daniel, Professor; Ph.D., Washington (Seattle). History.
Ileen A. DeVault, Professor; Ph.D., Yale. History.
Rebecca Givan, Assistant Professor; Ph.D., Northwestern. Political science.
Michael E. Gold, Associate Professor; J.D., Stanford. Law.
Kate Griffith, Assistant Professor; J.D., NYU. Law.
James A. Gross, Professor; Ph.D., Wisconsin. Labor economics and industrial relations.
Richard W. Hurd, Professor; Ph.D., Vanderbilt. Economics.
Lawrence Kahn, Professor; Ph.D., Berkeley. Economics.
Harry C. Katz, Jack Sheinkman Professor in Collective Bargaining and Dean of the ILR School; Ph.D., Berkeley. Economics.
Sarosh C. Kuruvilla, Professor; Ph.D., Iowa. Business administration.
Risa L. Lieberwitz, Professor; J.D., Florida. Law.
David B. Lipsky, Professor; Ph.D., MIT. Economics.
Nicholas Salvatore, Maurice and Hinda Neufeld Founders Professorship in Industrial and Labor Relations; Ph.D., Berkeley. History.
Ronald L. Seeber, Professor; Ph.D., Illinois. Labor and industrial relations.
Lowell Turner, Professor; Ph.D., Berkeley. Political science.

Department of Human Resource Studies
Rosemary Batt, Professor and Alice Cook Professor of Women and Work; Ph.D., MIT. Human resources.
Bradford Bell, Associate Professor; Ph.D., Michigan State. Organizational psychology.
John H. Bishop, Associate Professor; Ph.D., Michigan. Economics.
Christopher Collins, Associate Professor; Ph.D., Maryland. Organizational behavior.
Lisa Dragoni, Assistant Professor; Ph.D., Maryland. Organizational behavior and human resource management.
Lee D. Dyer, Professor; Ph.D., Wisconsin. Personnel.
Kevin F. Hallock, Professor; Ph.D., Princeton. Economics.
John Hausknecht, Assistant Professor; Ph.D., Penn State. Industrial and organizational psychology.
Lisa Hisae Nishii, Assistant Professor; Ph.D., Maryland. Organizational psychology.
Patrick M. Wright, Professor; Ph.D., Michigan State. Business administration.

Department of International and Comparative Labor Relations
Rosemary Batt, Professor and Alice Cook Professor of Women and Work; Ph.D., MIT. Human resources.
John H. Bishop, Associate Professor; Ph.D., Michigan. Economics.
George Boyer, Professor; Ph.D., Wisconsin. Economics.
Lance Compa, Senior Lecturer; J.D., Yale. Law.
Maria L. Cook, Associate Professor; Ph.D., Berkeley. Political science.
Gary S. Fields, Professor; Ph.D., Michigan. Economics.
James A. Gross, Professor; Ph.D., Wisconsin. Labor economics and industrial relations.
Sarosh C. Kuruvilla, Professor; Ph.D., Iowa. Industrial relations.
Lisa Hisae Nishii, Assistant Professor; Ph.D., Maryland. Organizational psychology.
Lowell Turner, Professor; Ph.D., Berkeley. Political science.

Department of Labor Economics
John M. Abowd, Edmund Ezra Day Professor of Industrial and Labor Relations; Ph.D., Chicago. Economics.
Francine D. Blau, Frances Perkins Professor of Industrial and Labor Relations; Ph.D., Harvard. Economics.
George R. Boyer, Professor; Ph.D., Wisconsin. Economics.
Ronald Ehrenberg, Irving M. Ives Professor of Industrial and Labor Relations; Ph.D., Northwestern. Economics.
Gary S. Fields, Professor; Ph.D., Michigan. Economics.
Kevin F. Hallock, Professor; Ph.D., Princeton. Economics.
Robert M. Hutchens, Professor; Ph.D., Wisconsin. Economics.
Kirabo Jackson, Assistant Professor; Ph.D., Harvard. Economics.
George H. Jakubson, Associate Professor; Ph.D., Wisconsin. Economics.
Lawrence M. Kahn, Professor; Ph.D., Berkeley. Economics.
Robert S. Smith, Professor; Ph.D., Stanford. Economics.

Department of Organizational Behavior
Samuel B. Bacharach, Jean McKelvey-Alice Grant Professor of Labor Management Relations; Ph.D., Wisconsin. Sociology.
Marya Besharov, Assistant Professor; PhD., Harvard. Organizational behavior.
Jack Goncalo, Assistant Professor; Ph.D., Berkeley. Business administration.
Tove H. Hammer, Professor; Ph.D., Maryland. Industrial organizational psychology.
Edward J. Lawler, Martin P. Catherwood Professor of Industrial and Labor Relations; Ph.D., Wisconsin. Sociology.
Brian Rubineau, Assistant Professor; Ph.D., MIT. Organization studies and economic sociology.
William J. Sonnenstuhl, Associate Professor; Ph.D., NYU. Sociology.
Pamela S. Tolbert, Professor; Ph.D., UCLA. Sociology.
Michele Williams, Assistant Professor; Ph.D., Michigan. Organizational behavior.

Department of Social Statistics
John A. Bunge, Associate Professor; Ph.D., Ohio. Statistics.
Thomas J. DiCiccio, Associate Professor; Ph.D., Waterloo. Statistics.
Paul F. Velleman, Associate Professor; Ph.D., Princeton. Statistics.
Martin T. Wells, Associate Professor; Ph.D., Berkeley. Mathematics.

GEORGE MASON UNIVERSITY

School of Public Policy

Programs of Study

The School of Public Policy (SPP) at George Mason University seeks to prepare its graduates for positions of responsibility in academic institutions, industry, government, and profit and not-for-profit institutions dedicated to the improvement of both the substance and the processes of public policymaking in the United States and abroad. SPP offers the following degree programs: Doctor of Philosophy (Ph.D.) in Public Policy; Master of Public Policy (M.P.P.); Master of Arts (M.A.) in International Commerce and Policy; Master of Arts (M.A.) in Transportation Policy, Operations, and Logistics; Master of Science (M.S.) in Organization Development and Knowledge Management; and Master of Science in New Professional Studies: Peace Operations.

The School's programs, led by a distinguished faculty, focus on the interplay of culture, organizations, and technology in a quest to find alternative approaches to public policy decisions and policymaking. Teaching and research is focused on, but not limited to, six themes: Governance; International Commerce and Policy; Entrepreneurship; Regional and Economic Development; Science and Technology Policy; and Culture and Values.

The Ph.D. in Public Policy program is distinctive in its emphasis on the combined influence of technology, culture, and institutions on public policy. To investigate the policy issues associated with substantive policy areas, students develop an in-depth understanding of American institutions, values, and culture; competence in research methods and advanced analytical methodologies; and a comparative, international perspective. The M.P.P. provides a degree for aspiring or experienced professionals who seek career advancement through cutting-edge education and training in policy analysis and development in increasingly technical and global environments. Professional certificates are also offered with this program. The M.A. in International Commerce and Policy program is an interdisciplinary course of study that prepares students for careers in the new global economy. Unlike traditional M.B.A. and international affairs programs, the degree is focused on international economic issues such as global trade and investment. Professional certificates are also offered with this program. The M.A. in Transportation Policy, Operations, and Logistics program is designed for students and practicing professionals engaged in planning, regulating, managing, and operating transportation facilities and services. The M.S. in Organization Development and Knowledge Management program is run in an executive format and is designed for professionals with several years of work experience. It provides students with the conceptual tools and practical guidance to foster organizational change. The Peace Operations program offers candidates a focused degree in various aspects of the planning, regulation, management, and conduct of peace operations.

Research Facilities

George Mason University (GMU) Libraries comprise the Fenwick and Johnson Center Libraries on the Fairfax campus and the Arlington and Prince William campus libraries. Fenwick is the main research library and offers access to a large number of electronic resources in addition to more than 600,000 volumes. GMU provides students with e-mail and Internet access and is a member of the Washington Regional Library Consortium, giving students access to 4 million volumes. In addition to research facilities on campus, GMU is a short distance from major research facilities in the Washington, D.C., area, including the Library of Congress, the National Archives, and numerous governmental agencies. Students may visit the GMU Libraries' Web site for more information (http://library.gmu.edu).

SPP's research centers include the Center for Regional Analysis; the International Center for Applied Studies in Information Technology; the Center for Science and Technology Policy; the Center for Transportation Policy, Operations, and Logistics; the Center for the Study of International Medical Policies and Practices; the State Economic Development Center; the Center for Entrepreneurship and Public Policy; the Center for Global Policy; the Center for Aerospace Policy Research; the Terrorism, Transnational Crime, and Corruption Center (TraCCC); the Transportation and Economic Development Research Center; and the Mason Enterprise Center.

Financial Aid

Full-time Ph.D. candidates are eligible for graduate research assistantships. These assistantships offer a stipend of $16,000 and also include tuition waivers. Financial assistance is granted to master's candidates on a limited basis.

Cost of Study

For the 2009–10 academic year, tuition and fees are $573 per credit hour for in-state students and $1062 for out-of-state students.

Living and Housing Costs

The cost of living in the northern Virginia/Washington, D.C., area is comparable to that in most major metropolitan centers. Limited on-campus graduate student housing is available on the Fairfax campus; no on-campus housing is available on the Arlington campus. Most graduate students choose to live off campus.

Student Group

In fall 2008, SPP enrolled 922 students in its various graduate programs. Fifty-one percent were women, 13 percent were members of minority groups, and 10 percent were international students. Fifteen percent were enrolled in the Ph.D. program, and 85 percent were enrolled in the various master's programs. Seventy-four percent enrolled part-time, while 26 percent enrolled full-time.

Student Outcomes

Upon completion of degree requirements, graduates find employment in academic institutions, federal and state agencies and departments, international businesses and banks, law firms, consulting firms, think tanks, and not-for-profit organizations. Many international students return home to work in the public and private sectors. SPP provides career advisement, internship, and placement support for all students.

Location

Located in Northern Virginia, George Mason is only 15 miles from all the resources of the National Capital Region and the Washington metropolitan area. Washington's libraries, galleries, and museums; Virginia's historic sites; and Fairfax County's high-technology firms are easily accessible. George Mason's 5.2-acre Arlington Campus, which is home to most SPP master's programs, is just minutes to Washington, D.C., by Metrorail.

Applying

Application deadlines for the master's programs are June 1 for fall and December 1 for spring. International applicant deadlines are one month prior to these dates. For Ph.D. applicants, fall application deadlines are February 1 for international students and March 1 for domestic students. For the spring term, Ph.D. application deadlines are October 1 for international applicants and November 1 for domestic applicants. Students should note that funding is only awarded to full-time Ph.D. students beginning their study in the fall term. All applicants must submit a graduate application and fee, all official university transcripts, a written goals statement, a professional resume, two letters of recommendation, and a writing sample (Ph.D. applicants only). GRE or GMAT scores are required for all Ph.D. candidates and for master's degree applicants who are seeking merit-based funding consideration. International applicants must also submit a TOEFL score. Application packets may be requested by contacting SPP or visiting the School's Web site. Students should visit http://policy.gmu.edu/admissions for more specific information on application requirements for both the master's and Ph.D. degree programs.

Correspondence and Information

Graduate Admissions
School of Public Policy
George Mason University
3401 Fairfax Drive, MS 3B1
Arlington, Virginia 22201
Phone: 703-993-8099
Fax: 703-993-4876
E-mail: spp@gmu.edu
Web site: http://policy.gmu.edu
          http://www.gmu.edu

George Mason University

CORE FACULTY

Administrative Faculty

Kingsley E. Haynes, University Professor and Dean; Ph.D., Johns Hopkins, 1971.
James H. Finkelstein, Professor and Vice Dean for Administration; Ph.D., Ohio State, 1980.
Jonathan L. Gifford, Professor, Associate Dean for Research, and Program Director for the Transportation, Operations, and Logistics M.A. program; Ph.D., Berkeley, 1983.
Matthys van Schaik, Associate Dean for Academic Affairs; Ph.D., South Carolina, 1995.

Faculty

Zoltan J. Acs, University Professor; Ph.D., New School, 1980.
Mark S. Addleson, Associate Professor, Program on Organization Development and Knowledge Management; Ph.D., Witwatersrand, 1992.
David J. Armor, Professor of Public Policy; Ph.D., Harvard, 1966.
Philip E. Auerswald, Assistant Professor; Ph.D., Washington (Seattle), 1999.
Ann Baker, Assistant Professor and Director, Organization Development and Knowledge Management; Ph.D., Case Western, 1995.
Kenneth J. Button, Professor of Public Policy; Ph.D., Loughborough (England), 1981.
Janine Davidson, Assistant Professor of National and Global Security; Ph.D., South Carolina, 2005.
Desmond Dinan, Jean Monnet Professor of Public Policy; Ph.D., National University of Ireland, 1985.
Michael K. Fauntroy, Assistant Professor; Ph.D., Howard, 2001.
James H. Finkelstein, Professor and Senior Associate Dean, School of Public Policy; Ph.D., Ohio State, 1980.
Allison Frendak-Blume, Assistant Professor of Public Policy and Director, Peace Operations Program; Ph.D., George Mason, 2004.
A. Lee Fritschler, Professor; Ph.D., Syracuse, 1965.
Stephen S. Fuller, University Professor and Professor of Public Policy and Regional Development; Ph.D., Cornell, 1969.
Jonathan L. Gifford, Associate Professor of Public Policy and Director, Transportation, Policy, Operation, and Logistics Program; Ph.D., Berkeley, 1983.
Jack A. Goldstone, Virginia E. Hazel and John T. Hazel Jr. Professor of Public Policy and Director, Ph.D. in Public Policy Program; Ph.D., Harvard, 1981.
David M. Hart, Associate Professor; Ph.D., MIT, 1995.
Kingsley E. Haynes, University Professor and Dean, School of Public Policy; Ph.D., Johns Hopkins, 1970.
Jack C. High, Professor of Public Policy, Economics, and Social Learning; Ph.D., UCLA, 1980.
Christopher T. Hill, Professor of Public Policy and Technology; Ph.D., Wisconsin–Madison, 1969.
Andrew Hughes Hallett, Professor of Public Policy and Economics; D.Phil., Oxford, 1976.
Michael R. Kelley, Professor and Director, Telecommunications Policy Program; Ph.D., Catholic University, 1970.
Naoru Koizumi, Assistant Professor of Public Policy; Ph.D., Hyogo Medical College, 2005.
Todd M. La Porte, Associate Professor; Ph.D., Yale, 1989.
Siona Robin Listokin, Assistant Professor; Ph.D., Berkeley, 2007.
Stuart S. Malawer, Distinguished Service Professor of Law and International Trade; Ph.D., Pennsylvania, 1976.
Jeremy Mayer, Assistant Professor and Director, Master of Public Policy Program; Ph.D., Georgetown, 1996.
Connie L. McNeely, Associate Professor of Public Policy; Ph.D., Stanford, 1990.
Arnauld Nicogossian, Distinguished Research Professor; M.D., Teheran, 1964; M.S., Ohio State, 1972.
Wayne D. Perry, Professor of Public Policy and Operations Research; Ph.D., Carnegie Mellon, 1975.
John E. Petersen, Professor of Public Policy; Ph.D., Pennsylvania, 1967.
James P. Pfiffner, Professor of Public Policy, Government, and Politics; Ph.D., Wisconsin–Madison, 1975.
Ramkishen Rajan, Associate Professor of Public Policy; Ph.D., Claremont, 1999.
Kenneth A. Reinert, Associate Professor of Public Policy and Director, International Commerce and Policy Program; Ph.D., Maryland, College Park, 1988.
James D. Riggle, Research Associate Professor; Ph.D., George Mason, 2002.
Hilton L. Root, Professor of Public Policy; Ph.D., Michigan, 1983.
Mark J. Rozell, Professor of Public Policy; Ph.D., Virginia, 1987.
Catherine Rudder, Professor of Public Policy; Ph.D., Ohio State, 1973.
Stephen R. Ruth, Professor; Ph.D., Pennsylvania, 1971.
Laurie A. Schintler, Associate Professor of Public Policy; Ph.D., Illinois at Urbana–Champaign, 1996.
Edgar H. Sibley, University Professor; Sc.D., MIT, 1967.
Rainer Sommer, Associate Professor of Public Policy; Ph.D., Columbia Pacific, 1991; Ph.D., George Mason, 1998.
Roger R. Stough, Vice President for Research and Economic Development, NOVA Endowed Chair, and Professor of Public Policy; Ph.D., Johns Hopkins, 1978.
Tojo Thatchenkery, Professor of Organization Development and Knowledge Management; Ph.D., Case Western, 1993.
Susan Tolchin, Professor of Public Policy; Ph.D., NYU, 1968.
Janine R. Wedel, Associate Professor; Ph.D., Berkeley, 1985.

Selected Affiliated Faculty

Kevin Avruch, Professor of Anthropology; Ph.D., California, San Diego, 1978.
Timothy J. Conlan, Associate Professor of Government and Politics; Ph.D., Harvard, 1981.
George L. Donahue, Professor of Systems Engineering and Operations Research; Ph.D., Oklahoma State, 1972.
Robert L. Dudley, Associate Professor of Government and Politics; Ph.D., Northern Illinois.
Gregory A. Guagnano, Associate Professor of Sociology; Ph.D., California, Davis, 1986.
Hugh Heclo, Robinson Professor of Public Affairs; Ph.D., Yale, 1970.
James T. Hennessey, Chief of Staff; Ph.D., George Mason, 1997.
Julianne G. Mahler, Associate Professor of Government and Politics; Ph.D., SUNY at Buffalo, 1976.
John Paden, Robinson Professor of International Studies; Ph.D., Harvard, 1968.
Priscilla M. Regan, Associate Professor of Government and Politics; Ph.D., Cornell, 1981.
Joseph A. Scimecca, Professor of Sociology; Ph.D., NYU, 1972.
Martin Jay Sherwin, Professor of History; Ph.D., UCLA, 1971.
Edgar H. Sibley, University of Professor of Information and Software Engineering; Sc.D., MIT, 1967.

Instructional and Research Faculty

Brien Benson, Research Associate Professor; Ph.D., George Mason, 1998.
George Cook, Affiliate Professor; A.B., George Washington, 1957.
David F. Davis, Assistant Research Professor; M.S., Naval Postgraduate School, 1981.
Jessica Heineman-Pieper, Assistant Professor of Public Policy; Ph.D., Chicago, 2005.
Desmond J. Lugg, Distinguished Research Professor; M.D., Adelaide, 1974.
Monty Marshall, Research Professor, Ph.D., Iowa, 1996.
Arthur S. Melmed, Research Professor; M.S.E.E., Columbia, 1956.
James L. Narel, Academic Director, Ph.D., George Mason, 2007.
James Riggle, Research Assistant Professor; Ph.D., George Mason, 2002.
Charles Robb, Distinguished Professor of Law and Public Policy; J.D., Virginia, 1973.

HAWAI'I PACIFIC UNIVERSITY

Master of Arts in Global Leadership and Sustainable Development

Program of Study

Hawai'i Pacific University's (HPU's) Master of Arts in Global Leadership and Sustainable Development (M.A./GLSD) program is designed to prepare students to lead change initiatives in a globalizing world that is increasingly characterized by chaos, complexity, and change. Students learn simultaneously to search for the underlying causes of global environmental, economic, and social problems and how to design and lead responses that produce sustainable outcomes for current and future generations.

Faculty members who teach in the M.A./GLSD program combine impressive academic credentials, stature in their professional disciplines, and years of actual business and consulting experience. Many have extensive international experiences and therefore welcome the diversity that HPU's students bring to the classroom. Graduate students have the benefit of learning from adjunct professors from the Hawaii business community—managing partners, vice presidents, and presidents from a wide variety of companies and organizations, both domestic and international. All program faculty members are dedicated to making the HPU experience edifying, challenging, and enjoyable for the student.

The M.A./GLSD is designed to prepare students to become leaders in all types of organizations, including multinational, governmental, and not-for-profit organizations. The program concentrates on teaching relevant interdisciplinary theories and tools to help professionals succeed in today's fast-paced global economy. Students must complete a minimum of 42 semester hours of graduate work, comprising 33 semester hours of core courses, 3 semester hours of elective courses, and 6 semester hours of a capstone professional paper.

Research Facilities

To support graduate studies, HPU's Meader and Atherton Libraries offer more than 110,000 bound volumes, 350,000 microfiche items, and periodical subscriptions to 1,500 print titles and 30,000 electronic journals. Databases of public and state university libraries, legislative information, and business-oriented statistical data are also available in the library or online. Students can access HPU's library databases, course information, their academic information, and an e-mail account through Pipeline, the University's internal Web site for students. The University's accessible on-campus computer center houses more than 100 computers with specialized software to support graduate academic programs. HPU also provides free Wi-Fi service so students can have wireless access to Pipeline resources anywhere on campus using laptops. A significant number of online courses are available as well.

Financial Aid

The University participates in all federal financial aid programs designated for graduate students. These programs provide aid in the form of subsidized (need-based) and unsubsidized (non-need-based) Federal Stafford Student Loans. Through these loans, funds may be available to cover a student's entire cost of education. To apply for aid, students must submit the Free Application for Federal Student Aid (FAFSA) beginning January 1. Mailing of student award letters usually begins by the end of March. The University also offers several types of institutional graduate scholarships and assistantships to new full-time, degree-seeking students. The Trustees' Scholar Program provides a 50 percent tuition waiver for two semesters; the Deans' Scholarship Program, a 20 percent tuition waiver for one semester; and the International Scholar Program, a 20 to 50 percent tuition waiver. Graduate assistantships, which give students a 50 percent tuition waiver for one semester, are also available. Priority consideration is given to those students who apply by the deadline.

Cost of Study

Tuition for graduate students enrolled in fall and spring semesters is determined on a per-credit basis; full-time status for a graduate student is nine credits. Tuition for the optional winter and summer sessions is also determined on a per-credit basis. The estimated minimum funds needed for a nine-month academic year (September to May) based on 2009–10 school-year expenses is $25,739. For the 2009–10 academic year, full-time tuition is $11,880 for most graduate degree programs. Books, supplies, and transportation cost $1885, and health insurance costs $880.

Living and Housing Costs

Most graduate students live in off-campus housing. The cost to live in off-campus apartments is approximately $11,094 for a double occupancy room.

Student Group

University enrollment currently stands at more than 8,200. HPU is one of the most culturally diverse universities in America with students from all 50 U.S. states and more than 100 countries.

Location

Hawai'i Pacific combines the excitement of an urban, downtown campus with the serenity of a residential campus and a pristine marine institute. The main campus is ideally located in downtown Honolulu, the business and financial center of the Pacific. Eight miles away, situated on 135 acres in Kaneohe, the windward Hawai'i Loa campus is the site of environmental sciences, marine biology, nursing, oceanography, and several liberal arts programs. The third campus, The Oceanic Institute, an affiliate of HPU, is an applied aquaculture research facility located on a 56-acre site at Makapu'u Point on the windward coast of Oahu, Hawaii. Students can travel between the three sites using the convenient HPU shuttle service. There are also eight military campus programs located at Pearl Harbor, Barbers Point, Hickam Air Force Base, Schofield Barracks, Fort Shafter, Tripler Army Medical Center, Kaneohe Marine Corps Air Station, and Camp Smith.

The University

HPU is a private, nonprofit university with approximately 8,200 students. Founded in 1965, HPU prides itself on maintaining strong academic programs, small class sizes, individual attention to students, and a diverse faculty and student population. HPU is recognized as a "Best in the West" college by *Princeton Review* and a "Best Buy" by *Barron's* business magazine. HPU offers more than fifty acclaimed undergraduate programs and twelve distinguished graduate programs. The University has a faculty of more than 500, a student-faculty ratio of 18:1, and an average class size of 20. A wide range of counseling and other student support services are available. There are more than seventy student organizations on campus, including the Graduate Student Organization.

Applying

Students must have a baccalaureate degree from an accredited college or university in the United States or an equivalent degree from another country. Applicants should complete and forward a Graduate Admissions Application, send in the $50 nonrefundable application fee, have official transcripts sent from all colleges or universities previously attended, and forward two letters of recommendation. A resume and a personal statement about the applicant's academic and career goals are required. Applicants who have taken the Graduate Record Examination (GRE) should have their scores sent directly to the Graduate Admissions Office. International students should submit scores from a recognized English proficiency test, such as the TOEFL. Admissions decisions are made on a rolling basis, and applicants are notified between one and two weeks after all documents have been submitted. Applicants are encouraged to submit their applications online.

Correspondence and Information

Graduate Admissions
Hawai'i Pacific University
1164 Bishop Street, Suite 911
Honolulu, Hawaii 96813

Phone: 808-544-1135
    866-GRAD-HPU (toll-free)
Fax: 808-544-0280
E-mail: graduate@hpu.edu
Web site: http://www.hpu.edu/hpumaglsd

Hawai'i Pacific University

THE FACULTY AND THEIR RESEARCH

Cheryl Crozier-Garcia, Assistant Professor of Human Resource Management; Ph.D., Walden.
Gerald W. Glover, Professor of Organizational Change; Ph.D., Florida.
John Gutrich, Associate Professor of Environmental Sciences; Ph.D., Ohio State.
Gordon Jones, Professor of Computer Science and Information Systems; Ph.D., New Mexico.
Margo Kitts, Associate Professor of Humanities/Religious Studies; Ph.D., Berkeley.
Ernesto Lucas, Associate Professor of Economics; Ph.D., Hawaii.
Daniel Morgan, Instructor of Sociology; M.A., Miami (Florida).
Regina Ostergaard-Klem, Adjunct Professor of Mathematics; Ph.D., Johns Hopkins.
Catherine Sajna, Assistant Professor of English; M.A., Hawaii at Manoa.
Richard Ward, Associate Professor of Organizational Change; Ed.D., USC.
Arthur Whatley, Professor of Management; Ph.D., North Texas.
Larry Zimmerman, Assistant Professor of Organizational Change; Ph.D., Nebraska–Lincoln.

SCHOOL OF PUBLIC AND ENVIRONMENTAL AFFAIRS
INDIANA UNIVERSITY

INDIANA UNIVERSITY BLOOMINGTON

School of Public and Environmental Affairs
Public Affairs Graduate Programs

Programs of Study	The School of Public and Environmental Affairs (SPEA) offers graduate degree programs leading to the Master of Public Affairs (M.P.A.), the Ph.D. in public policy, and the Ph.D. in public affairs.
	The two-year, 48-credit hour M.P.A. degree is an interdisciplinary program that equips students with a combination of skills for professional careers in government, nonprofit, and private sectors. The program consists of four components: a core, a concentration area, an experiential component, and sufficient electives and/or prior professional experience. The core courses include public management, statistical analysis, public management economics, law and public affairs, public finance and budgeting, and a capstone project in public and environmental affairs. SPEA's concentrations provide both depth and breadth to the curriculum, enabling students to develop as professionals, hone their skills, and better prepare for the professional challenges that will be integral to complex world problems. Many SPEA students choose to pursue more than one concentration. The M.P.A. concentration areas are comparative and international affairs, economic development, environmental policy and natural resource management, information systems, local government management, nonprofit management, policy analysis, public financial administration, public management, and SPEA's latest addition, sustainable development. To integrate their academic training into a practical framework, students are required to complete an internship or a significant research project in order to satisfy the experiential component of the M.P.A. program. The capstone project serves as the culmination to a student's academic training. Capstone projects are normally a semester-long, detailed analysis of a policy or management issue, often undertaken for a real-world client in the public or nonprofit sector.
	Joint-degree programs are offered with SPEA's Master of Science in Environmental Science (M.S.E.S.) and Indiana University's Departments of African American and African Diaspora Studies, African Studies, Central Eurasian Studies, East Asian Studies, Latin American and Caribbean Studies, Russian and East European Studies, and West European Studies, as well as the Schools of Library and Information Science, Law, and Journalism.
	The Ph.D. in public affairs is designed to prepare scholars for research and teaching in the multidisciplinary field of public policy and management. The program emphasizes the study of public management and organization, policy analysis, and public finance. The joint Ph.D. in public policy is a collaborative venture with Indiana University's Department of Political Science. This program emphasizes study of the public policy process. Students explore issues regarding policy analysis, government institutions, political behavior, and public affairs.
Research Facilities	Complementing the School's own resources, Indiana University maintains eight nationally prominent area studies centers and sixty language programs to facilitate international research and career interests. SPEA has affiliations with several research centers on both the Bloomington and Indianapolis campuses, including the Transportation Research Center; the Institute for Family and Social Responsibility; the Environmental Science Research Center; the Indiana University Research and Teaching Preserve; the Center for the Study of Institutions, Population, and Environmental Change; the Indiana University Public Policy Institute; and the Center for Urban Policy and Environment.
	SPEA is committed to meeting the research needs of its students. PCs, mainframe computers, and a geographic information system (GIS) computing laboratory are available. More than forty additional computing sites on the Bloomington campus are available for student use. Libraries on the Bloomington campus house more than 6 million volumes, and another 3.2 million are available through the University's seven other campuses.
	SPEA houses its own Information Commons, which provides convenient access to individual and group workstations, student-focused services that support individual and collaborative learning and research, and access to rich library resources shared with the Kelley School of Business.
Financial Aid	Departmental assistance for qualified students is awarded on a competitive basis and is determined by merit. Awards include fellowships, scholarships, and teaching and research assistantships. Prospective students may apply for merit-based awards by checking the appropriate box on the admission application form. Students may apply for need-based aid through the University Office of Student Financial Assistance (OSFA).
	SPEA hosts a one-of-a-kind, collaborative program called Service Corps, which enables M.P.A. and M.S.E.S. students to apply their classroom learning directly to the field in both the public and nonprofit sectors. Service Corps is a financial aid mechanism that offers students real-world experience working in an array of governmental and nonprofit agencies while concurrently pursuing their academic plans. The program is a partnership among the University, School, and a number of valued external stakeholders in the community and region. Students are selected for participation during the merit aid allocation process.
Cost of Study	In-state residents pay $364.23 per credit hour and nonresidents pay $850.33 per credit hour for master's programs in 2009–10.
Living and Housing Costs	The 1,200 on-campus apartments for graduate students range in monthly rent from $519 for a furnished efficiency to $1119 for an unfurnished three-bedroom apartment. Rates include all utilities as well as local telephone service, cable TV, and Internet connection. A variety of off-campus apartments are available near the University. Rents are generally inexpensive, with the average two-bedroom unit renting for $550 to $700 per month.
Student Groups	About 250 students are enrolled in the M.P.A. program, with 40 students pursuing the joint M.P.A./M.S.E.S. program, and 75 students are enrolled in the Ph.D. programs in public affairs or public policy. About 17 percent of these students are international, more than one half are women, and more than 10 percent are members of underrepresented populations.
	SPEA recognizes service in AmeriCorps, Teach for America, and Peace Corps, hosting both Peace Corps Fellows/USA, and Master's International (MI) programs. These volunteers receive a waiver of the experiential component which is a part of the academic design and a reduction of the total number of credit hours required for degree completion. Peace Corps and MI Fellows also receive a competitive merit aid package in addition to the benefits described above.
Student Outcomes	SPEA maintains an outstanding placement record, attributed to a well-rounded curriculum, national prestige, and strong alumni support. Within six months of the close of the 2007–08 academic year, approximately 84 percent of students responding to SPEA's annual employment survey indicated that they had procured full-time professional positions or were continuing their education. The SPEA Office of Career Services (OCS) is staffed with professionals who assist graduate students with all of their career development needs. The services offered to students include individual career counseling; on-campus recruiting; a Web-based job listing service, SPEACareers.com; a wide range of employer information sessions; alumni mentoring; user-friendly Web-based career resources; and an extensive career resource library. With so many resources at their disposal, SPEA students annually compete for many of the most prestigious and competitive positions in federal and state government and top-tier nonprofits and foundations. SPEA students are also top candidates for positions with top consulting firms like Booz Allen Hamilton, Crowe Chizek, Deloitte, and Grant Thornton. Some examples of other recent placements include the World Bank, the Environmental Protection Agency, the Department of State, the National Forest Service, the Government Accountability Office, the National Institutes of Health, the National Oceanographic and Atmospheric Institute, the Millennium Challenge Corporation, the Nature Conservancy, the Corporation for National and Community Service, the Bill and Melinda Gates Foundation, the Indiana Department of Environmental Management, the Indiana Office of Management and Budget, and the Indiana Department of Transportation.
	Additionally, SPEA typically has 10–15 M.P.A. students selected as finalists for the Presidential Management Fellowship Program (PMF), one of the most selective federal programs for graduate students pursuing careers with the federal government.
Location	Bloomington, a college town of 110,000 people, was chosen as one of the top ten college towns in America for its "rich mixture of atmospherics and academia" by Edward Fiske, former education editor of the *New York Times*. It is a culturally vibrant community settled among southern Indiana's rolling hills, just 45 miles south of Indianapolis, the state capital. Mild winters and warm summers are ideal for outdoor recreation in the two state forests, one national forest, three state parks, and an array of lakes and streams that surround Bloomington.
The University and The School	Established in 1820, Indiana University has more than 7,500 graduate students and more than 38,000 students total enrolled on the Bloomington campus. SPEA is the top-ranked graduate program on campus. Fifty-five other academic departments are ranked in the top 20 in the country, including music, business, biology, foreign languages, political science, and chemistry. Attractions include nearly 1,000 musical performances each year, with eight full-length operas and professional Broadway plays; the IU Art Museum, designed by I. M. Pei, with more than 30,000 art objects; fifty campus and community volunteer agencies; more than 500 student sports clubs and organizations; two indoor student recreational facilities; and Big Ten athletics. SPEA, founded in 1972, was the first school to combine public management, policy, and administration with the environmental sciences.
Applying	Application files must include the SPEA Admission Application form, transcripts, GRE General Test scores, and three letters of recommendation. Priority is given to applications received by February 1. Students applying for awards must submit a complete application file by the priority deadline, February 1. School visits are encouraged. Applicants can also access the School's Web site at http://www.spea.indiana.edu.
Correspondence and Information	For master's programs: M.P.A./M.S.E.S. Program Office SPEA 260 Indiana University Bloomington, Indiana 47405 Phone: 812-855-2840 　　　800-765-7755 (toll-free, domestic only) E-mail: speainfo@indiana.edu Web site: http://www.spea.indiana.edu	For doctoral programs: Ph.D. Programs Office SPEA 441 Indiana University Bloomington, Indiana 47405 Phone: 812-855-2457 　　　800-765-7755 (toll-free, domestic only) E-mail: speainfo@indiana.edu Web site: http://www.spea.indiana.edu

Indiana University Bloomington

THE FACULTY AND THEIR RESEARCH

Osita G. Afoaku, Ph.D., Washington State, 1991. International relations (theory, foreign policy/national security, political economy), comparative politics (political development, Third-World/African politics, theory), multicultural studies (African and African American), public administration.

Robert Agranoff, Emeritus; Ph.D., Pittsburgh, 1967. Intergovernmental relations (U.S. and cross-national), economic and community development, management of public agencies, governance, intergovernmental management, federal arrangements.

David Audretsch, Ph.D., Wisconsin, 1980. Economics policy, entrepreneurship, innovation, globalization, regional economic policy, industrial restructuring and government policy, small enterprises in Europe and the United States.

Matthew R. Auer, Ph.D., Yale, 1996. Environmental policy and management problems with an international focus: international environmental assistance, comparative industrial environmental policy, international policies governing forests and forestry.

A. James Barnes, J.D., Harvard, 1967. Environmental law, domestic and international environmental policy, ethics and the public official, mediation and alternative dispute resolution, law and public policy.

Lisa Bingham, J.D., Connecticut, 1979. Dispute resolution, dispute system design, mediation, administrative law, labor and employment law.

Anthony A. Blasingame, Ph.D., Maryland, College Park, 2002. Public finance, labor economics, poverty, and U.S. political economy.

Charles F. Bonser, Emeritus; D.B.A., Indiana, 1965. Regional economic development, the role of nongovernmental organizations, public policy, transatlantic education and policy.

Melissa A. L. Clark, M.S., Indiana, 1999. Aquatic and terrestrial habitats, Indiana Clean Lakes Program, water resources and water quality.

Christopher Craft, Ph.D., North Carolina State, 1987. Terrestrial and wetland ecosystem restoration, wetlands ecology, soil resources, biogeochemistry, nutrient cycling and carbon sequestration of soils and sediments.

Michael A. Edwards, Ph.D., North Dakota State, 1999. Atmospheric chemistry research: mechanistic studies of terpenes reacting with ozone, future regulation of hydrogen storage materials.

Sergio Fernandez, Ph.D., Georgia, 2004. Public management and organization theory, with focus on privatization and contracting out, public-sector leadership, and organizational change.

Burnell C. Fischer, Ph.D., Purdue, 1974. Forestry, particularly silviculture and urban forestry; growth and development of central hardwood forest stands and response to various silvicultural practices; community and urban forestry issues; forest resources policy and state government management; human factors relating to forests and forest products, particularly with regard to collaborative forestry.

Beth Gazley, Ph.D., Georgia, 2004. Volunteering and civic engagement, fundraising, nonprofit management, interorganizational collaboration, "new governance" and government-nonprofit relations.

David Good, Ph.D., Pennsylvania, 1985. Quantitative policy modeling, productivity measurement in public and regulated industries, urban policy analysis.

John D. Graham, Ph.D., Carnegie Mellon, 1983. Risk and benefit-cost analysis; health, energy, and environmental policy; governance.

Kirsten Grønbjerg, Ph.D., Chicago, 1974. Nonprofit and public-sector relationships, examining scope and community dimensions of the Indiana nonprofit sector.

Hendrik M. Haitjema, Ph.D., Minnesota, 1982. Groundwater flow modeling, including regional groundwater flow systems, conjunctive surface-water and groundwater flow modeling, 3-D groundwater flow, and saltwater intrusion problems, with emphasis on application of analytic functions to modeling groundwater flow, specifically analytic-element method.

Diane Henshel, Ph.D., Washington (St. Louis), 1987. Sublethal health effects of environmental pollutants, especially pollutant effects on the developing organism, including the effects of polychlorinated dibenzo-p-dioxins (PCDDs) and related congeners on the developing nervous system of birds exposed in the wild and under controlled laboratory conditions.

Monika Herzig, D.M.E., Indiana, 1997.

Ronald Hites, Ph.D., MIT, 1968. Applying organic analytical chemistry techniques to the analysis of trace levels of toxic pollutants, such as polychlorinated biphenyls and pesticides, with focus on understanding behavior of these compounds in the atmosphere and in the Great Lakes.

Chaman Jain, Ph.D., Indiana, 1975.

Christopher Hunt, M.A., Cambridge, 1961. Arts administration.

Craig Johnson, Ph.D., SUNY at Albany, 1993. Capital markets and financial intermediation; financial management; public budgeting and finance; financing e-government; financing economic development; environmental and infrastructure finance; focus on innovative financing structures, financial certification, and resolving financial distress.

William Jones, M.S., Wisconsin–Madison, 1977. Lake and watershed management, especially diagnosing lake and watershed water-quality problems; preparing management plans to address problems identified; stream ecology; Caribbean coral reef ecology and underwater archaeology; certified lake manager (CLM).

Haeil Jung, Ph.D., Chicago, 2009. Applied econometrics and program evaluation, crime policy, public policy for low-income families.

Kerry Krutilla, Ph.D., Duke, 1988. Energy policy, resource management in developing countries, environmental regulation, public choice, cost-benefit analysis.

Marc L. Lame, Ph.D., Arizona State, 1992. Implementation of integrated pest-management programs in schools and day-care facilities.

Leslie Lenkowsky, Ph.D., Harvard, 1982. Nonprofits and public policy, civil society in comparative perspective, institutional grant makers, volunteering and civic engagement, education and social welfare policy.

Eugene B. McGregor Jr., Ph.D., Syracuse, 1968. Interaction of public policy, organizational structure, and management practice; special interest in relationship between education and economic development and in impacts of information technology on structure and management of public and nonprofit enterprise.

Michael McGuire, Ph.D., Indiana, 1995. Intergovernmental and interorganizational collaboration and networks, federalism and intergovernmental relations, public management, economic development.

Vicky Meretsky, Ph.D., Arizona, 1995. Ecology and management of rare species, biocomplexity, landscape-level species and community conservation, temporal patterns in biodiversity, integrating ecosystem research and endangered species management within adaptive management.

John L. Mikesell, Ph.D., Illinois, 1969. Governmental finance, especially questions of policy and administration of sales and property taxation; state lotteries; public budgeting; public finance in countries of the former Soviet Union.

Theodore K. Miller, Emeritus; Ph.D., Iowa, 1970. Statistical analysis.

Emilio Moran, Ph.D., Florida, 1975. Tropical ecosystem ecology, Amazon Basin, secondary successional forests, human ecology.

Ashlyn Nelson, Ph.D., Stanford, 2005. Housing finance, education finance, education policy, the mortgage crisis.

Patrick O'Meara, Ph.D., Indiana, 1970. Comparative politics and development, Southern African politics, ethics and politics.

Clinton V. Oster Jr., Ph.D., Harvard, 1978. Aviation safety, airline economics and competition policy, international aviation, aviation infrastructure, environmental and natural resource policy, government regulation, business-government relations.

James A. Palmer, Emeritus; J.D., Indiana, 1971. Legal policy research and analysis, election law and administration, administrative law and processes.

David Parkhurst, Emeritus; Ph.D., Wisconsin–Madison, 1970. Physiological plant ecology, including transfers of carbon dioxide/water between leaves and atmosphere and cells within leaves, both in relation to leaf structure; mathematics/statistics applied to environmental issues, including analysis of concentrations of indicator bacteria at swimming beaches and correct interpretation of statistical hypothesis tests in decision making.

Roger B. Parks, Emeritus; Ph.D., Indiana, 1979. Organization and governance structures of metropolitan areas and their effects on effectiveness, efficiency, equity, and responsiveness of public service delivery; community policing.

D. Jeanne Patterson, Emeritus; D.B.A., Indiana, 1967. Financial management, government accounting and corporate governance.

James Perry, Ph.D., Syracuse, 1974. Public service motivation, government and civil service reform, public management, public human resource management, national and community service, performance-related pay, public organizational behavior.

Flynn W. Picardal, Ph.D., Arizona, 1992. Bioremediation, environmental microbiology, and biogeochemistry, with focus on microbial reduction of iron oxides and nitrate, transformation of metals and chlorinated hydrocarbons, and combined microbial-geochemical interactions.

Maureen A. Pirog, Ph.D., Pennsylvania, 1981. Poverty and income maintenance, with emphasis on child-support enforcement, welfare reform, and adolescent parenting.

Orville W. Powell, M.P.A., Penn State, 1963. Local government and the U.S. Constitution.

Nicole C. Quon, Ph.D., Yale, 2007. Health policy and health politics, influence of politics and science on decision making at federal agencies, how perceptions of access and quality of care within health-care institutions are shaped by patient knowledge and market forces.

J. C. Randolph, Ph.D., Carleton (Ottawa), 1972. Forest ecology; ecological aspects of global environmental change, with particular interests in forestry and agriculture; applications of geographic information systems (GIS) and remote sensing in environmental and natural resources management; landscape ecology and regional-scale modeling; physiological ecology of woody plants of small mammals.

David A. Reingold, Ph.D., Chicago, 1996. Urban poverty, economic development, social welfare policy, low-income housing policy.

Terri L. Renner, M.B.A., Indiana, 1985. Financial management, information systems, entrepreneurship.

Rafael Reuveny, Ph.D., Indiana, 1997. International political economy, with emphasis on globalization; rise and fall of major powers; political conflict and how it interacts with international trade, democracy, and the environment; sustainable development; Middle East political economy.

Edwardo L. Rhodes, Ph.D., Carnegie-Mellon, 1978. Public policy analysis, particularly public-sector applications of management science in the evaluation and assessment of the efficiency or organization performance of public activities, including environmental and natural resource policy implementation.

Kenneth R. Richards, J.D./Ph.D., Pennsylvania, 1997. Climate change policy, carbon sequestration economics, environmental policy implementation and instrument choice.

Evan J. Ringquist, Ph.D., Wisconsin–Madison, 1990. Public policy (environmental, energy, natural resources, and regulation), research methodology, American political institutions.

Justin Ross, Ph.D., West Virginia, 2007. Public economics, urban/regional economics, spatial econometrics, applied microeconomics, quantile regressions, public finance, political economy, game theory.

Todd V. Royer, Ph.D., Idaho State, 1999. Aquatic biogeochemistry, water resources, nutrient and carbon cycling in streams and rivers, water quality and nutrient standards.

Barry Rubin, Ph.D., Wisconsin–Madison, 1977. Urban and regional economic development and impact analysis, quantitative analysis of local government management and labor relations issues, statistics and quantitative methods, econometric modeling, public management information systems, strategic planning and management.

Richard S. Rubin, Emeritus; Ph.D., Cornell, 1973. Labor-management relations in the public sector, with particular focus on conflict resolution and labor management cooperation.

Michael Rushton, Ph.D., British Columbia, 1990. Cultural economics, policy and administration, nonprofit and public organizations and management, tax policy, government funding for the arts and other policies toward nonprofit organizations, coeditor of *Journal of Cultural Economics*.

John W. Ryan, Emeritus; Ph.D., Indiana, 1959. Comparative public policy analysis; comparative university organization and policy; general public administration, with special attention to higher education: governmental organization in Southeast Asia and Central and East Europe.

Yue (Jen) Shang, Ph.D., Indiana, 2008. Nonprofit marketing, marketing communications for nonprofit organizations, donor behavior, fund development, philanthropic psychology.

Joseph Shaw, Ph.D., Kentucky, 2001. Toxicology, genomics, ecology, and physiology, with collaborators in evolutionary biology, population genetics, and trace/biogeochemistry.

Roy W. Shin, Emeritus; Ph.D., Minnesota, 1969. Industrial policy, comparative economic development, environmental policy, competition policy, science and technology policy.

Nan Stager, M.S., Indiana, 1978. Mediation and alternative dispute resolution.

Philip S. Stevens, Ph.D., Harvard, 1990. Characterization of the chemical mechanisms that influence regional air quality and global climate change.

Anh Tran, Ph.D., Harvard, 2009. Public policy in developing countries, governance and anti-corruption, international trade and finance.

Terry Usrey, M.S., Indiana, 1983. E-government, information technology policy, information technology management.

Frank J. Vilardo, Emeritus; Dr.P.H., North Carolina, 1971. Public and private health administration, focusing on injuries as a public health problem from a behavioral perspective; drunk-driver countermeasures; transportation incidents involving radioactive materials; enforcement of local retail food inspection laws.

Henry K. Wakhungu, Ph.D., Indiana, 2004. Development of growth simulation models for sustainable management of indigenous community forests, experimental designs in tropical forestry research, how preservice teachers conceptualize mathematics (philosophically) indexed with mathematics learning and teaching.

Jeffrey R. White, Ph.D., Syracuse, 1984. Environmental biogeochemistry, aquatic chemistry, limnology.

Lois Recascino Wise, Ph.D., Indiana, 1982. Public management and employment policies and practices; public management reform, including comparative studies of determinants of administrative reforms, variations in reform patterns, and cross-national differences in evaluation of reforms; comparative research in pay policies and administrative pay reforms, bureaucratic behavior, and consequences of human diversity for effective work organizations.

Wenli Yan, Ph.D., Kentucky, 2008. Public and nonprofit financial management, state and local finance, quantitative methods, nonprofit and public management and budgeting.

C. Kurt Zorn, Ph.D., Syracuse, 1981. State and local finance, transportation safety, economic development, gaming policy.

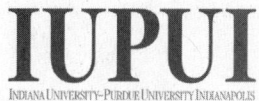

INDIANA UNIVERSITY–PURDUE UNIVERSITY INDIANAPOLIS

School of Public and Environmental Affairs

Programs of Study	The Indiana University School of Public and Environmental Affairs (SPEA) at IUPUI offers graduate degree programs leading to the Master of Health Administration (M.H.A.) and the Master of Public Affairs (M.P.A.).
	The M.H.A. program is designed to prepare individuals for leadership positions in the health services. The 51-credit-hour, interdisciplinary program provides a broadly balanced foundation of theoretical and practical knowledge and technical skills necessary to succeed in the complex and changing health field. M.H.A. students complete courses in accounting, economics, ethics, financial management, human resources management, information systems, law, marketing, and policy.
	The 48-credit-hour M.P.A. degree is an interdisciplinary program that equips students with a combination of skills for professional careers in government, nonprofit, and private sectors. The program combines a set of core courses with a chosen concentration area: criminal justice, environmental management, nonprofit management, public management, or policy analysis.
Research Facilities	The IU Public Policy Institute is a collaborative, multidisciplinary research institute within the Indiana University School of Public and Environmental Affairs. The institute serves as an umbrella organization for research centers affiliated with SPEA, including the Center for Urban Policy and the Environment, the Center for Health Policy, and the Center for Criminal Justice Research. The institute also supports the Office of International Community Development and the Indiana Advisory Commission on Intergovernmental Relations (IACIR).
Financial Aid	Several graduate and administrative assistantships are available for full-time students. These provide a monthly stipend for nine months, and most also provide tuition fee remission. The School makes every effort to continue financial support for each graduate assistant who is academically eligible for a second year. February 1 is the priority date for consideration for graduate assistantships. University fellowships are also available for highly qualified full-time students. These provide a monthly stipend for nine months and tuition fee remission and do not require work during the first year of study. February 1 is the priority date for consideration for University fellowships. In addition, there are frequent research opportunities through which students can continue employment during the summer months. Part-time jobs in the health-care field (20 hours per week) are also available for full-time M.H.A. students beginning in the fall semester. Several scholarships, ranging from $1500 to $10,000 annually, are also offered.
Cost of Study	In 2008–09, the tuition for in-state M.H.A. and M.P.A. students was $320.84 per credit hour. Out-of-state students paid $777.76 per credit hour. Additional costs included $65.50 per semester for parking, technology fees of $186.90, $400 to $600 per semester for books, and other miscellaneous fees.
Living and Housing Costs	Apartment-style housing is available on campus. On-campus housing rates start at $716 per month. In addition to on-campus housing, a variety of privately owned apartments are available nearby. Rent ranges from about $340 to $640 per month. A flexible campus meal plan is available through the campus housing office.
Student Group	SPEA students come from a diverse variety of undergraduate backgrounds. SPEA's graduate programs currently enroll more than 120 full-time and 375 part-time students and admit 30 to 40 new students each year. More than half are women, one quarter are members of minority groups, and more than one twelfth are international students.
Student Outcomes	SPEA M.H.A. graduates gain skills in areas such as health systems management, outcomes management, financing arrangements, and strategic management. Recent M.H.A. graduates have pursued career positions with Anthem Blue Cross Blue Shield, Cardinal Health System, Community Hospitals of Indianapolis, St. Vincent Hospital, the Clarian Health System, Indiana Hospital Association, Indiana University Hospital, M Plan, Office of Medicaid Policy and Planning, and Riley Hospital for Children.
	M.P.A. graduates develop a comprehensive understanding of the public and/or nonprofit sectors and the public policy process. Specific skills in areas such as organizational management, statistical analysis, information technology, and budgeting are gained through the M.P.A. core requirements, and additional skills are gained through the specific concentrations. Recent M.P.A. graduates have pursued career positions with the city of Indianapolis, the Indiana House Ways and Means Committee, Environmental Protection Agency, Indiana Department of Environmental Management, Indianapolis Museum of Art, KPMG LLP, the Nature Conservancy, and the United Way of Central Indiana.
Location	Indiana University–Purdue University Indianapolis (IUPUI) is located on the western periphery of dynamic downtown Indianapolis. Downtown attractions located near the University include White River State Park, the Indiana State Museum, Victory Field (a 13,000-seat baseball stadium), and the Canal Walk. Indianapolis is also noted for its world-class symphony, ballet, theater, and opera companies and is home to the world's largest children's museum. Indianapolis is known for its sports, playing host to several professional sports teams and auto races.
The University and The School	IUPUI demonstrates a model partnership among government, community, and higher education. It was formed in 1969 by combining the city facilities and programs of Indiana University and Purdue University under one name and administration. IUPUI has twenty schools offering over 200 programs to more than 29,000 students.
	SPEA, established in 1972, was the first school to combine public management, policy, and administration with the environmental sciences. *U.S. News & World Report* ranked SPEA at IUPUI among the best graduate schools for 2008. SPEA's Indianapolis nonprofit management program was ranked third in the nation.
Applying	All applicants must have a baccalaureate degree from an accredited institution. A GPA of 3.0 or higher on a 4.0 scale is preferred. Undergraduate prerequisite courses for the M.H.A. include one course each in accounting, microeconomics, and statistics. An application form, three references, transcripts, and GRE, GMAT, or LSAT scores must be submitted along with a nonrefundable application fee. Applications should be received no later than May 15 for admission that fall. Applications for spring and summer should be received no later than September 15 and March 15, respectively. Students who wish to be considered for graduate assistantships should have their completed applications on file by February 1. Applications are accepted for admission during all semesters. International students should e-mail the Office of International Affairs at oia@iupui.edu for their deadline information.
Correspondence and Information	Graduate Programs in Health Administration and Public Affairs School of Public and Environmental Affairs Indiana University–Purdue University Indianapolis 801 West Michigan Street, BS 3027 Indianapolis, Indiana 46202-5152 Phone: 317-274-4656 877-292-9321 (toll-free) E-mail: infospea@iupui.edu Web site: http://www.spea.iupui.edu

Indiana University–Purdue University Indianapolis

THE FACULTY AND THEIR RESEARCH

Alejandro Arrieta, Assistant Professor; Ph.D., Rutgers. Health economics and health-care utilization.

Terry L. Baumer, Associate Professor; Ph.D., Loyola Chicago. Criminal justice policy, community corrections, program evaluation, crime trends.

Wolfgang Bielefeld, Professor; Ph.D., Minnesota. Nonprofit management and philanthropic studies.

Crystal Garcia, Associate Professor; Ph.D., California, Irvine. Community corrections, crime policy, juvenile justice, program evaluation.

David Handel, Clinical Professor; M.B.A., Chicago. Industrial and labor relations, hospital administration.

Craig Hartzer, Clinical Professor and Director, Executive Education Program; Ph.D., Miami (Ohio). Strategic policy development and implementation, organizational development, budgeting, program management, public-private partnerships.

Alfred Tat-Kei Ho, Associate Professor; Ph.D., Indiana. Performance measurement and budgeting, applied public finance research, information technology management and e-government.

Ann M. Holmes, Associate Professor; Ph.D., British Columbia. Health economics, measurement of health outcomes for economic evaluation, analysis of mental health utilization.

G. Roger Jarjoura, Associate Professor; Ph.D., Maryland. Juvenile delinquency, juvenile justice process, statistics, research methods.

Sheila Suess Kennedy, Associate Professor; J.D., Indiana. Civil liberties, civil rights, rule of law, religion and public policy.

Timothy Koponen, Trustee Lecturer; Ph.D., Northwestern. Political economy; world and labor markets; formal and complex organizations; race, ethnic, and minority relations.

John Krauss, Clinical Professor and Director, Center for Urban Policy and the Environment; J.D., Indiana. Law, public policy, conflict resolution, mediation.

Paul Lang, Lecturer; M.P.A., Indiana. Accounting, fiscal governance, fund-raising, long-range strategic planning.

Yong Li, Assistant Professor; Ph.D., Wayne State. Health economics, long-term care, health insurance, health-care utilization.

Laura Littlepage, Clinical Lecturer; M.P.A., NYU. Evaluation, including needs assessments, process, outcome, and impact evaluations; nonprofit organizations; voluntarism.

Deanna Malatesta, Assistant Professor; Ph.D., Georgia. Administrative law, rule making, regulation, public management and performance, organizational and institutional analysis, telecommunications and information policy.

David Z. McSwane, Professor; H.S.D., Indiana. Environmental health policy, public health, food science.

Vicki Mech-Hester, Lecturer; Ed.D., Indiana. Strategic planning, performance management and enhancement, organizational effectiveness, leadership.

Debra J. Mesch, Associate Professor; Ph.D., Indiana. Workplace justice, nonprofit management, hospital mergers, strategic human resource management.

Samuel Nunn, Professor; Ph.D., Delaware. Law enforcement technology, terrorism and public policy, local homeland security policy, capital infrastructure systems within cities, local economic development policy, urban telecommunications.

John Ottensmann, Professor; Ph.D., North Carolina at Chapel Hill. Urban spatial structure and spatial dimensions of urban policy, management information systems, computer applications in planning and geographic information systems.

Kenna Quinet, Associate Professor; Ph.D., Illinois at Urbana-Champaign. Community policing, victimization, patterns of offending over the life course.

Ingrid Ritchie, Associate Professor; Ph.D., Minnesota. Indoor air quality, environmental management and assessment.

Adrian Sargeant, Professor; Ph.D., Exeter (England). Nonprofit marketing, including the arts, education, health care, and philanthropy.

Thomas Stucky, Assistant Professor; Ph.D., Iowa. Criminology, criminal justice, social control, political sociology.

Jim White, Clinical Lecturer; M.A., Butler. Public safety management, emergency services management.

Eric Wright, Associate Professor and Director, Center for Health Policy; Ph.D., Indiana. Health policy and services research, mental health policy and services research, HIV/AIDS/STD prevention, applied social research and program evaluation.

Adjunct/Associate Faculty

Melissa Brown, Associate Director of Research and Managing Editor, *Giving USA*, Center on Philanthropy at Indiana University; M.G.A., Pennsylvania.

Dwight Burlingame, Associate Executive Director, Center on Philanthropy at Indiana University; Ph.D., Florida State.

Julie Carmichael, Executive Director of the Suburban Health Organization.

Anthony D. Cox, Professor of Marketing and Chancellor's Faculty Fellow, Indiana University, Kelley School of Business; Ph.D., Indiana.

David Dreyer, Judge, Marion County Superior Court; J.D., Notre Dame.

Patricia Ebright, Associate Professor, Department of Adult Health, Indiana University School of Nursing.

Gordon Hall, Vice President and Health Care Practice Leader, Marsh, Inc.; M.B.A., Dallas.

James Hogan, Partner, Hall, Render, Killian, Heath & Lyman, PSC; J.D., Indiana.

Rebecca Karl, Director of Communications for the Clarian Health System.

James Klaunig, Professor of Toxicology and Director, Division of Toxicology, Indiana University School of Medicine; Ph.D., Maryland.

Edward W. Koschka Jr., Network Vice President and Chief Information Officer, Community Health Network; M.B.A., Indiana.

Betsy Lee, Director, Indiana Patient Safety Center, Indiana Hospital and Health Association; M.S.P.H., North Carolina; RN.

Jamie Levy, President, J. D. Levy & Associates, LLC; M.P.A., Indiana.

Jeffrey Miller, Senior Systems Analyst, Eli Lilly and Company; M.P.A., Indiana.

Janet Orosz, Board of Governors, Ohio Fair Plan Underwriting Association; Ph.D., Ohio State.

Tim Seiler, Executive Director, The Fund Raising School, Center on Philanthropy at Indiana University; Ph.D., Indiana.

Roger Sell, Senior Financial Analyst, Myers & Stauffer, LC; M.P.A., Indiana.

Curtis Smith, Myers Chair of Distinguished Public Service, Hampden Sydney College; Ph.D., Ohio State.

Greg Steele, Associate Professor and Epidemiology Coordinator, Department of Public Health, Indiana University School of Medicine; D.P.H., Alabama at Birmingham.

Rodney Thompson, Toxicologist, Indiana Department of Environmental Management; M.S., Indiana.

Wanzhu Tu, Associate Professor, Indiana University School of Medicine, and Center Scientist, Indiana University Center for Aging Research; Ph.D., South Carolina.

THE JOHNS HOPKINS UNIVERSITY

Institute for Policy Studies

JOHNS HOPKINS
Institute
for Policy
Studies

Program of Study	Johns Hopkins University offers a Master of Arts degree in public policy (MPP). This two-year public policy program prepares graduates for professional careers in private as well as public organizations involved with solving societal problems. Graduates are equipped for responsible positions around the world that deal with the analysis of public problems and the development and implementation of solutions to meet them. By design, the program is kept small to nurture mentoring relationships between students and faculty members. Core courses are taught primarily by Institute faculty members. The number of ongoing policy research projects at the Institute creates a wealth of opportunities for students, including research assistantships. Extensive faculty member–student interaction in seminars and with faculty research and student thesis research enriches the students' experience and prepares them thoroughly for professional careers.
	The curriculum consists of four basic components: a set of core analytical courses, a set of substantive policy courses in an area of specialization, an internship, and the opportunity to write a thesis. The program features a curriculum combining strong analytical courses and a focus on the evolving concept of citizenship and the moral dimensions of policy choice; location within a University-based research institute; easy access to Washington, D.C., and significant opportunities to learn firsthand about the policy process; attention to the role of private as well as public institutions in coping with public problems, with a special emphasis on nonprofit organizations; and opportunities for interaction with international fellows in residence at the Institute.
	Students generally take most core courses and some electives during the first year, followed by an internship during the summer. Areas of concentration include health policy, social policy, urban policy, international affairs, nonprofit sector, human resource policy, education policy, and the environment.
Research Facilities	All resources of Johns Hopkins University System are available to policy studies students, including the Schools of Arts and Sciences, Engineering, Advanced International Studies (SAIS), Public Health, and the Carey School of Business. The library includes more than 2.1 million volumes, more than 1.2 million microforms, and more than 13,000 serial subscriptions. The Government Publications/Maps/Law Library provides a full range of services for accessing and utilizing an extensive collection of publications of the U.S. government, the UN and other international agencies, and state and local governments. The University has been a depository for U.S. government publications since 1882 and currently selects approximately 50 percent of the items offered to depository libraries. The computer facility includes two central systems: a VAX/VMS and Silicon Graphics SGI with UNIX. Students have access to several on-campus computer labs; in addition, the Institute maintains a computer lab for its own students. Students are assigned study carrels at the Institute or University libraries.
Financial Aid	Institute financial aid is awarded to graduate students who demonstrate intellectual promise in the field of policy studies through past academic performance, GRE test scores, previous relevant work experience, and a personal statement. The Institute awards tuition remissions and research fellowships. Students may also apply for available special fellowships. Low-interest loans and work-study assignments are awarded by the Financial Aid Office of Johns Hopkins University. Research fellowships pay $14 to $16 an hour for 15 to 20 hours of work per week.
Cost of Study	Tuition for 2009–10 is $39,100. There is a one-time matriculation fee of $500. Annual book expenses are estimated to be $1200.
Living and Housing Costs	Cost of living was estimated at $16,000 for 2009–10. Students generally live in privately arranged apartments or shared houses close to the campus. Rents range from $550 to $1200 a month. University meal plans are available.
Student Group	About 1,400 graduate students are in residence at Hopkins' main campus. There are currently 64 students in the Policy Studies Program and 10 students in the International Fellows Programs at the Institute for Policy Studies. Students come from all parts of the U.S.; some either have lived abroad or are international students. Approximately two thirds of all students are women, and one fifth are members of minority groups. Most students have prior work experience.
Student Outcomes	Graduates of the MPP Program are generally middle- to upper-level employees in all levels of government and in private and nonprofit organizations. In addition, some graduates have enrolled in Ph.D. programs. Typical jobs include program officer for a philanthropic foundation, policy or research analyst at a research institute or government agency, and executive director of a nonprofit organization. Recent graduates are working at the U.S. Office of Management and Budget, Mathematica Policy Research, World Bank, the Urban Institute, Pepsi Corporation, Charles Mott Foundation, U.S. General Accounting Office, Public/Private Ventures, and Enterprise Foundation.
Location	The Institute for Policy Studies is located on the 140-acre rolling wooded Homewood campus, about 3 miles north of the Inner Harbor of downtown Baltimore. The campus is 1 mile from the Amtrak train station; 40 miles from Washington, D.C.; 30 miles from Annapolis; and about 15 miles from the Chesapeake Bay.
The University and The Institute	Johns Hopkins University has a reputation as a world-renowned center of scholarship and research. The relatively small student body yields a favorable student-faculty ratio. Students are encouraged to think for themselves in an environment that fosters independence and creativity. The Institute for Policy Studies is a group of political scientists, economists, policy analysts, and policy practitioners who seek to improve the response of government and private institutions to the challenges of poverty and disadvantage, urban and regional economic change, human resource investment, and environmental degradation. The Institute carries out its work through a combination of policy-oriented research; seminars, briefings, and other public education efforts; and formal training of policy professionals in this country and abroad.
Applying	The deadline for applying to the Institute for Policy Studies is January 15. The application fee is $60. Applications for student loan and work-study programs must be submitted separately to the Office of Student Financial Services by April 1. Successful applicants generally have a college grade point average of at least 3.0 on a 4.0 scale. GRE General Test scores are required, and a score of at least 600 on each section is preferred. Students are encouraged to visit the Institute, but interviews are not required.
Correspondence and Information	Master of Arts in Public Policy Institute for Policy Studies The Johns Hopkins University 3400 North Charles Street Baltimore, Maryland 21218 Phone: 410-516-4624 Fax: 410-516-8233 E-mail: mpp@jhu.edu Web site: http://ips.jhu.edu/pub/Why-A-Hopkins-MPP

The Johns Hopkins University

THE FACULTY AND THEIR RESEARCH

David M. Altschuler, Principal Research Scientist, Associate Professor of Mental Hygiene, Public Health Adjunct, and Adjunct Associate Professor of Sociology; Ph.D., Chicago, 1983. Project director and co–principal investigator on a federally funded research and training project that has developed a model of intensive aftercare for the high-risk juvenile parolee being released from secure correctional facilities; chair of Baltimore Mayor's Working Group on drug policy reform. Current research interests: juvenile justice sanctioning and aftercare; community-based delinquency program design, implementation, and assessment; privatization in corrections; drug involvement and crime among inner-city youth.

Burt Barnow, Principal Research Scientist and Adjunct Professor of Economics; Ph.D., Wisconsin–Madison, 1973. Conducting cost-benefit analysis of Maryland welfare reform initiative, evaluating impact of amendments to the Job Training Partnership Act, evaluating job training programs for the homeless. Current research interests: labor economics, employment and training programs, child support programs, welfare programs, program evaluation.

John J. Boland, Professor of Geography and Environmental Engineering; Ph.D., Johns Hopkins, 1973. Current research interests: environment and public utility economics, water resource management, environmental policy.

Senator Benjamin L. Cardin, Distinguished Lecturer; J.D., Maryland, 1967. Member of the U.S. Senate, Maryland. Policy interests: ethics, political process, and human resource policy.

Andrew Cherlin, Benjamin H. Griswold III Professor of Public Policy in the Department of Sociology; Ph.D., UCLA, 1976. Current research interests: sociology of the family, social policy and demography.

Matthew A. Crenson, Professor of Political Science; Ph.D., Chicago, 1969. Current research interests: political origins of American welfare policy.

Ruth R. Faden, Philip Franklin Wagley Professor of Biomedical Ethics at the Bioethics Institute and Professor of Health Policy and Management at the School of Public Health; Ph.D., Berkeley, 1976. Current research interests: ethics and health policy management.

Bernard Guyer, Professor and Chair of Maternal and Child Health Policy at the School of Public Health; M.D., Rochester, 1970. Current research interests: maternal and child health policy, practice, and finance; childhood injury prevention; child development; childhood immunization.

Robert Moffitt, Professor of Economics; Ph.D., Brown, 1975. Current research interests: labor economics, econometrics, public finance, population economics.

Vicente Navarro, Professor of Health Policy and of Sociology; Ph.D., Johns Hopkins, 1968. Current research interests: international study of public policy, health and social policy.

Sandra J. Newman, Director of the Center on Housing, Neighborhoods, and Communities and Professor of Policy Studies (joint appointments in sociology, health policy, and management; geography and environmental engineering); Ph.D., NYU, 1973. Member of Board of Directors, Center for Housing Policy, National Foundation for Affordable Housing Solutions; Associate Editor, *Housing Policy Debate*. Current research interests: long-term effects of housing assistance on children and families, implications of welfare reform for housing, living conditions of America's disabled, low-income rental housing market dynamics.

Demetra Nightingale, Principle Research Scientist; Ph.D., George Washington, 1998. Current research interests: employment, labor markets, welfare, poverty and social policy.

Marion Pines, Senior Fellow and Director of the Institute's Sar Levitan Center for Social Policy Studies; B.A., Goucher. Chair of interagency team managing policy, planning, implementation, and evaluation of statewide high school dropout prevention project. Current research interests: at-risk populations, development of education alternatives, welfare reform policies, employment strategies for youth and adults, service integration model targeted at families.

Lester M. Salamon, Founding Director of the Institute for Policy Studies and Director of its Center for Civil Society Studies and Professor of Political Science; Ph.D., Harvard, 1971. Vice Chair of the International Society for Third-Sector Research. Current research interests: alternative instruments of government action; social welfare policy; scope, structure, and role of the private nonprofit sector in the United States and overseas; human capital investment policy.

Curt Ventriss, Visiting Professor, Ph.D., USC, 1980. Current research interests: ethics and public policy, environmental issues.

Aerial view of the parklike Homewood campus with old Baltimore neighborhood in the background, the Institute for Policy Studies at the far left, and the Eisenhower Library in the center across from the ellipse.

THE NEW SCHOOL
A UNIVERSITY

THE NEW SCHOOL: A UNIVERSITY

Milano The New School for Management and Urban Policy
Ph.D. Program in Public and Urban Policy

Program of Study

Today's public policy issues are complex and require deeper analysis and greater insight than in the past. This program seeks to train individuals at a doctoral level to work at the highest levels of government, nonprofits, and think tanks, with the ability to formulate and develop broad public policy solutions. The Ph.D. in public and urban policy program is committed to providing students with a deep theoretical and institutional understanding of contemporary urban problems and the technical skills necessary both to carry out scholarly research and to design and manage public policy. In line with The New School's tradition of critical inquiry, the doctoral program emphasizes the social, political, and normative dimensions of policy analysis, treating socially responsible and equitable outcomes as essential to good public policy decision making. The doctoral program takes a distinctive multidisciplinary approach; it is organized around a public policy core offered within Milano The New School for Management and Urban Policy and a broad range of electives offered by Milano, the University, and other universities in the region.

The curriculum provides students with both the foundation that is critical to the successful pursuit of scholarly research and the depth and breadth of courses needed to attain an appropriate level of knowledge in the student's field of scholarship. Doctoral dissertations must focus on a relevant policy issue and substantially advance knowledge in the field.

The Ph.D. program has three main components: 60 credits of course work, qualifying examinations, and a dissertation. Upon completion of the course work and successful completion of a policy and analysis paper, students are eligible to take the qualifying exam. Once they pass, students can go on to write and defend a dissertation. The dissertation must be defended orally before the student's Dissertation Committee.

Research Facilities

The Center for New York City Affairs is a nonpartisan institute dedicated to advancing innovative public policies that strengthen neighborhoods, support families, and reduce urban poverty. Tools include rigorous analysis, research, candid public dialogue with stakeholders and opinion leaders, and strategic planning with government officials, nonprofit practitioners, and community residents. The center's original applied research and public seminars examine the politics of community change in local and state government and identify critical problems facing urban families and communities. The center's public programs offer community leaders and other participants the opportunity to meet powerful players in and around government and to learn about the context, the influential organizations, and other factors that define the policy-making landscape in New York City and urban America.

Financial Aid

Milano offers financial aid packages in the form of scholarships, fellowships, and loans. Financial aid awards are decided on a first-come, first-served basis, and applicants are encouraged to apply early to receive priority consideration. Financial aid award decisions are made after students are accepted at Milano. Applicants interested in obtaining financial aid should submit the Free Application for Federal Student Aid (FAFSA) or the Renewal Application for Federal Student Aid. More information is available from the Office of Financial Services at 212-229-8930.

Cost of Study

Tuition in 2009–10 is $1202 per credit, and fees are approximately $100 each term.

Living and Housing Costs

The University Housing Office maintains a comprehensive resource center with apartment listings. University-run apartments and residence halls are also available. The cost of housing, food, transportation, books, and living expenses averages $17,000 annually. For more information, students should go online to http://www.newschool.edu/studentservices.

Student Group

There are 45 students in the program; 22 attend on a full-time basis. Of these students, 27 are women, 17 are members of underrepresented groups, and 8 are international students.

Location

The New School's location in New York City gives students access to an abundance of resources. Students are encouraged to take advantage of the city's many museums, performance venues, and other cultural institutions, which are only a walk or a subway ride away. An extension of the classroom, the city also offers excellent professional and networking opportunities, and some classes require that students work with outside businesses to complete assignments—giving them unparalleled real-world experience. Internships and apprenticeships with leading New York City companies and organizations in every field are also available, and many students have moved on from internships to successful careers with those companies and organizations upon graduation.

The University and The School

Milano is part of The New School, a leading university in New York City offering distinguished programs in design, liberal arts, the performing arts, and social and political science, leading to seventy graduate and undergraduate degrees. To learn more, students should visit http://www.newschool.edu/degreeprograms. The New School is accredited by the Commission on Higher Education of the Middle States Association of Colleges and Schools. A privately supported institution, The New School is chartered as a university by the Regents of the State of New York.

Applying

Students must submit the completed application form, the $50 application fee, official transcripts from all postsecondary institutions attended, a 500-word essay explaining their professional goals, three letters of recommendation, and a resume. Applications are reviewed on a rolling admissions basis. Although there is no specific deadline, applicants are strongly encouraged to apply by March 1 for the fall semester and by October 1 for the spring semester in order to take full advantage of financial aid and housing opportunities.

Correspondence and Information

Ph.D. Program in Public and Urban Policy
Milano The New School for Management and Urban Policy
The New School
72 Fifth Avenue, 3rd Floor
New York, New York 10011

Phone: 212-229-5400
Fax: 212-229-5354
E-mail: milanoadmissions@newschool.edu
Web site: http://www.newschool.edu/milano

The New School: A University

THE FACULTY AND THEIR RESEARCH

Warren Balinsky, Associate Professor and Chair of Health Services Management; Ph.D., Case Western Reserve. Home health care and the applications of planning, development, marketing, and research to health services management and policy. Dr. Balinsky has written two books on home care; he has also written articles on various aspects of emergency preparedness, health care of the elderly, health-care reimbursement, health-status indices, home care, pediatric health care, and the unequal distribution of medical personnel within the health-care system.

Robert Beauregard, Professor; Ph.D., Cornell. Urbanization in the United States, with particular focus on industrial urban decline after World War II and current problems posed by growth and decline in cities. Dr. Beauregard is currently working on *Writing Urban Theory,* a series of essays, and *Why Cities Endure,* a book investigating why some cities prosper while others do not. Dr. Beauregard teaches courses on the political economy of the city, urban redevelopment, neighborhood change, social theory, and research design.

Howard Berliner, Professor of Health Services Management and Director of Ph.D. in Public and Urban Policy Program; Sc.D., Johns Hopkins. Needs of vulnerable populations and access to health services for the uninsured. Dr. Berliner is the author of seven books, most recently *The Health Marketplace: New York City 1990–2010* with Ginzberg et al. He has also authored numerous articles and reviews on health-policy issues in academic and professional journals. Dr. Berliner served for two years as the assistant state health commissioner for New Jersey.

John Clinton, Visiting Assistant Professor; Ph.D., Fordham. Interprofessional collaboration. Dr. Clinton has served as corporation senior consultant on social responsibility at MetLife, senior vice president of the LightHouse for the Blind and Visually Impaired, and an administrator at NYU, Fordham University, and Hartwick College. He has been a consultant to foundations, nonprofit organizations, corporations, and higher education institutions.

Dennis Derryck, Professor of Professional Practice; Ph.D., Fordham. Innovative policies and strategies affecting the economic sustainability of nonprofit organizations. Dr. Derryck has held leadership positions in organizations involved in community economic development, operations and fiscal management, and research and policy analysis. He currently serves as chair of WE ACT for Environmental Justice and is vice chair of SoBro, the South Bronx Overall Economic Development Corporation.

Elizabeth Dickey, Professor; Ed.D., Massachusetts Amherst. Organizational behavior and leadership, with a psychosocial emphasis. Dr. Dickey is a developmental clinical psychologist. Between 1991 and 2005 she served as dean and then provost of The New School.

Peter Eisinger, Henry Cohen Professor; Ph.D., Yale. Urban politics and policy, state and local economic development, U.S. politics, state politics, federalism. Author of *Toward an End to Hunger in America.*

Alec Ian Gershberg, Associate Professor; Ph.D., Pennsylvania. School governance, education finance, decentralization in the developing world and in the United States, immigrant students in public schools in New York and California. Dr. Gershberg has conducted extensive research on Latin America—particularly Mexico, Nicaragua, and Ecuador—as well as on Egypt, Romania, and sub-Saharan Africa. He has been a frequent consultant to the World Bank, the Inter-American Development Bank, and the Urban Institute. Dr. Gershberg is the lead author of *Beyond Bilingual Education: New Immigrants and Public School Policies in California.*

Martin Greller, Professor and Associate Dean for Academic Affairs; Ph.D., Yale. Factors associated with career continuity for older workers, feedback systems in organizations as tools for increasing organizational effectiveness. Recent projects include an assessment of training needs for entry-level peace officers and a review of pay-equity issues for a legislative body.

Darrick Hamilton, Assistant Professor; Ph.D., North Carolina at Chapel Hill. Ethnic and racial disparities in wealth, home ownership, and labor market outcomes. Dr. Hamilton's articles can be found in *African American Research Perspectives, American Economics Review, Applied Economics Letters, Challenge: The Magazine of Economic Affairs, Journal of Economic Psychology, Review of Black Political Economy, Social Science Quarterly, Southern Economics Journal,* and *Transforming Anthropology.*

David Howell, Professor; Ph.D., New School. Labor markets at the local, national, and international levels. Recent publications have examined the effects of immigration on the economic status of foreign and native-born workers in New York City, the nature of recent changes in skill requirements and the determinants of relative wage trends in the United States, and the extent to which labor market institutions and social policy explain patterns of unemployment in Europe and the United States. Dr. Howell is the editor of *Fighting Unemployment: The Limits of Free Market Orthodoxy.*

Mark Lipton, Professor of Management and Chair of Management; Ph.D., Massachusetts Amherst. Management, leadership, organizational strategy. Author of *Guiding Growth: How Vision Keeps Companies on Course.* Dr. Lipton's research and opinions on management and strategy have appeared in *Executive Excellence, Harvard Business Review, The Journal of Management Consulting, Optimize, Organization Development Journal,* and *Sloan Management Review,* among others.

Edwin Melendez, Professor; Ph.D., Massachusetts Amherst. Economics. Dr. Melendez was director of the Mauricio Gastón Institute for Latino Community Development and Public Policy at the University of Massachusetts Boston (1992–98) and director of the Community Development Research Center at the Milano Graduate School (1999–2004). He has worked as a consultant on employment, economic development, job creation, and small business for numerous government, community, and philanthropic foundations. Dr. Melendez has managed more than thirty-five research, outreach, and demonstration projects and supervised or collaborated with more than 60 researchers in projects that resulted in several books, special issues of academic journals, and other publications.

Aida Rodriguez, Professor of Professional Practice; Ph.D., Massachusetts. Leadership and effective management in the nonprofit sector. Formerly deputy director of the Equal Opportunity Division of the Rockefeller Foundation, Dr. Rodriguez now serves on various nonprofit boards, including One Economy, Inc.; Alliance for Nonprofit Management; and the Association for Public Policy Analysis and Management. Dr. Rodriguez is an adviser on philanthropic initiatives in the United States and in Latin America, including the Funders' Collaborative for Strong Latino Communities.

Bryna Sanger, Professor; Ph.D., Brandeis. Public policy and management, changes in service delivery and management systems induced by welfare reform in states and localities around the country. Former dean of the Robert J. Milano Graduate School of Management and Urban Policy, Dr. Sanger has worked in a wide range of policy and management areas, including city service delivery, welfare reform, leadership, innovation, and performance management. She recently led a research effort with the National Civic League on the experiences of cities that have developed exemplary performance measurement systems and that report to and engage citizens in their efforts. Her most recent book on this topic is entitled *The Welfare Marketplace: Privatization and Welfare Reform.*

Alex F. Schwartz, Associate Professor, Chair of Department of Urban Policy Analysis and Management, and Senior Research Associate, Community Development Research Center; Ph.D., Rutgers. Housing and community development, including affordable housing programs, community reinvestment, and community development corporations. Dr. Schwartz's most recent publication is *Housing Policy in the United States.* His research has also appeared in such journals as *Cityscape, Economic Development Quarterly, International Journal of Urban and Regional Research,* and the *Journal of Urban Affairs.*

Lisa J. Servon, Associate Professor and Associate Director of Community Development Research Center; Ph.D., Berkeley. Urban poverty, community development, economic development, gender issues. Dr. Servon recently coedited *Gender and Planning: A Reader* (with Susan Fainstein), which covers a range of planning and development fields, including transportation, land use, history, gender, housing, social justice, environmental design, race, and economic and community development. The book was selected as one of the top10 books for 2006 by Planetizen, a public-interest information exchange for the urban planning, design, and development community.

Nidhi Srinivas, Assistant Professor of Nonprofit Management; Ph.D., McGill. Civil society, specifically management of nongovernmental organizations, and the transfer and transformation of management knowledge. Dr. Srinivas teaches courses on nonprofit management, international development, and strategic decision making. Courses he has developed include Managing Institutions for Development (part of the core curriculum in the graduate program in international affairs) and Civil Society and South Asia.

Antonin Wagner, Visiting Professor; Ph.D., Fribourg (Switzerland). Economics. From 1996 to 2000, Dr. Wagner was president of the International Society for Third Sector Research, the leading scholarly institution in the nonprofit field. He has served as a consultant on social security–related issues to the Swiss Federal Statistical Office and the World Bank in Washington. He is a member of the editorial board of several international journals and has published widely in English, German, and French on the welfare state and civil society.

Tatiana Wah, Assistant Professor; Ph.D., Rutgers. Regional and local economic development planning and developing nations, with a particular focus on small developing nations' economies. Dr. Wah's recent work is on transnational expatriate (immigrant) recovery and engagement programs of developing countries, particularly Haiti. She has been involved in community development work in the New York African American and Caribbean communities as a consultant, nonprofit administrator, and activist/advocate.

Mary R. Watson, Assistant Professor; Ph.D., Vanderbilt. Contemporary human capital issues in organizations, with particular emphasis on the social impact of labor market discontinuities. Dr. Watson teaches courses in management and organization behavior, human resources, social impact management, and globalization. She has a strong interest in cultural, racial, ethnic, and gender inequalities in the workplace and society. Her upcoming book (with Dr. Rikki Abzug), tentatively titled *Human Resources in Social Purpose Organizations,* is scheduled to be published by Jossey-Bass in 2007.

Part-time Faculty

The part-time faculty members of Milano The New School for Management and Urban Policy are high-level executives and managers in the institutions and agencies for which they work and the organizations for which they volunteer. They bring to the classroom valuable insight into current management and policy issues from both their personal experience and relevant curriculum. For a current listing of part-time faculty members, students should visit the faculty page of the Milano Web site at http://www.newschool.edu/milano.

THE NEW SCHOOL
A UNIVERSITY

THE NEW SCHOOL: A UNIVERSITY

Milano The New School for Management and Urban Policy
Program in Urban Policy Analysis and Management

Program of Study

The Master of Science in urban policy analysis and management program trains professionals and managers who are committed to improving the quality of life for urban communities and their residents. One of the first programs of its kind in the country, it prepares students for a wide range of jobs in the public and nonprofit sectors that focus on the development, assessment, and implementation of urban policies and programs. Graduates work as policy analysts in governmental agencies, as administrators of government programs, and as program managers and executives at nonprofit organizations.

The program offers a flexible curriculum tailored to the interests and needs of individual students. The program's core curriculum emphasizes hands-on, client-centered courses in which students work on policy or management issues for government officials and nonprofit executives; a solid foundation in and critical assessment of the traditional techniques of policy analysis; and systematic exposure to alternative theoretical and political perspectives. Students can choose a concentration in housing and community development, economic and workforce development, social policy, or finance for community and economic development.

The curriculum of the urban policy analysis and management program is designed to give students a sound foundation in the theory, techniques, and practice of the profession. Using a variety of instructional approaches, including case analyses, computer-based problem sets, and actual policy and management problems posed by public officials and nonprofit executives, the program acquaints students with the settings and issues they are likely to face as professional analysts and managers. To fulfill the required 42 credits, the student structures a program comprising three components—a required schoolwide core of 12 credits, a required program core of 12 credits, and 18 credits of electives.

Research Facilities

The Center for New York City Affairs is a nonpartisan institute dedicated to advancing innovative public policies that strengthen neighborhoods, support families, and reduce urban poverty. Tools include rigorous analysis, research, candid public dialogue with stakeholders and opinion leaders, and strategic planning with government officials, nonprofit practitioners, and community residents. The center's original applied research and public seminars examine the politics of community change in local and state government and identify critical problems facing urban families and communities. The center's public programs offer community leaders and other participants the opportunity to meet powerful players in and around government and to learn about the context, the influential organizations, and other factors that define the policy-making landscape in New York City and urban America.

Financial Aid

Milano offers financial aid packages in the form of scholarships, fellowships, and loans. Financial aid awards are decided on a first-come, first-served basis, and applicants are encouraged to apply early to receive priority consideration. Financial aid award decisions are made after students are accepted at Milano. Applicants interested in obtaining financial aid should submit the Free Application for Federal Student Aid (FAFSA) or the Renewal Application for Federal Student Aid. More information is available from the Office of Financial Services at 212-229-8930.

Cost of Study

Tuition in 2009–10 is $1202 per credit, and fees are approximately $105 each term.

Living and Housing Costs

The University Housing Office maintains a comprehensive resource center with apartment listings. University-run apartments and residence halls are also available. The cost of housing, food, transportation, books, and living expenses averages $17,000 annually. For more information, students should go online to http://www.newschool.edu/studentservices.

Student Group

There are 114 students in the program; 52 attend on a full-time basis. Of these students, 80 are women, 61 are members of underrepresented groups, and 5 are international students.

Location

The New School's location in New York City gives students access to an abundance of resources. Students are encouraged to take advantage of the city's many museums, performance venues, and other cultural institutions, which are only a walk or a subway ride away. An extension of the classroom, the city also offers excellent professional and networking opportunities, and some classes require that students work with outside businesses to complete assignments—giving them unparalleled real-world experience. Internships and apprenticeships with leading New York City companies and organizations in every field are also available, and many students have moved on from internships to successful careers with those companies and organizations upon graduation.

The University and The School

Milano is part of is part of The New School, a leading university in New York City offering distinguished programs in design, liberal arts, the performing arts, and social and political science, leading to seventy graduate and undergraduate degrees. To learn more, students should visit http://www.newschool.edu/degreeprograms. The New School is accredited by the Commission on Higher Education of the Middle States Association of Colleges and Schools. A privately supported institution, The New School is chartered as a university by the Regents of the State of New York.

Applying

Students must submit the completed application form, the $50 application fee, official transcripts from all postsecondary institutions attended, a 500-word essay explaining their professional goals, two letters of recommendation, and a resume. Applications are reviewed on a rolling admissions basis. Although there is no specific deadline, applicants are strongly encouraged to apply by March 1 for the fall semester and October 1 for the spring semester in order to take full advantage of financial aid and housing opportunities.

Correspondence and Information

Program in Urban Policy Analysis and Management
Milano The New School for Management and Urban Policy
The New School
72 Fifth Avenue, 3rd Floor
New York, New York 10011
Phone: 212-229-5400
Fax: 212-229-5354
E-mail: milanoadmissions@newschool.edu
Web site: http://www.newschool.edu/milano

The New School: A University

THE FACULTY AND THEIR RESEARCH

Warren Balinsky, Associate Professor and Chair of Health Services Management; Ph.D., Case Western Reserve. Home health care and the applications of planning, development, marketing, and research to health services management and policy. Dr. Balinsky has written two books on home care; he has also written articles on various aspects of emergency preparedness, health care of the elderly, health-care reimbursement, health-status indices, home care, pediatric health care, and the unequal distribution of medical personnel within the health-care system.

Robert Beauregard, Professor; Ph.D., Cornell. Urbanization in the United States, with particular focus on industrial urban decline after World War II and current problems posed by growth and decline in cities. Dr. Beauregard is currently working on *Writing Urban Theory*, a series of essays, and *Why Cities Endure*, a book investigating why some cities prosper while others do not. Dr. Beauregard teaches courses on the political economy of the city, urban redevelopment, neighborhood change, social theory, and research design.

Howard Berliner, Professor of Health Services Management and Director of Ph.D. in Public and Urban Policy Program; Sc.D., Johns Hopkins. Needs of vulnerable populations and access to health services for the uninsured. Dr. Berliner is the author of seven books, most recently *The Health Marketplace: New York City 1990–2010* with Ginzberg et al. He has also authored numerous articles and reviews on health-policy issues in academic and professional journals. Dr. Berliner served for two years as the assistant state health commissioner for New Jersey.

John Clinton, Visiting Assistant Professor; Ph.D., Fordham. Interprofessional collaboration. Dr. Clinton has served as corporation senior consultant on social responsibility at MetLife, senior vice president of the LightHouse for the Blind and Visually Impaired, and an administrator at NYU, Fordham University, and Hartwick College. He has been a consultant to foundations, nonprofit organizations, corporations, and higher education institutions.

Dennis Derryck, Professor of Professional Practice; Ph.D., Fordham. Innovative policies and strategies affecting the economic sustainability of nonprofit organizations. Dr. Derryck has held leadership positions in organizations involved in community economic development, operations and fiscal management, and research and policy analysis. He currently serves as chair of WE ACT for Environmental Justice and is vice chair of SoBro, the South Bronx Overall Economic Development Corporation.

Elizabeth Dickey, Professor; Ed.D., Massachusetts Amherst. Organizational behavior and leadership, with a psychosocial emphasis. Dr. Dickey is a developmental clinical psychologist. Between 1991 and 2005 she served as dean and then provost of The New School.

Peter Eisinger, Henry Cohen Professor; Ph.D., Yale. Urban politics and policy, state and local economic development, U.S. politics, state politics, federalism. Author of *Toward an End to Hunger in America*.

Alec Ian Gershberg, Associate Professor; Ph.D., Pennsylvania. School governance, education finance, decentralization in the developing world and in the United States, immigrant students in public schools in New York and California. Dr. Gershberg has conducted extensive research on Latin America—particularly Mexico, Nicaragua, and Ecuador—as well as on Egypt, Romania, and sub-Saharan Africa. He has been a frequent consultant to the World Bank, the Inter-American Development Bank, and the Urban Institute. Dr. Gershberg is the lead author of *Beyond Bilingual Education: New Immigrants and Public School Policies in California*.

Martin Greller, Professor and Associate Dean for Academic Affairs; Ph.D., Yale. Factors associated with career continuity for older workers, feedback systems in organizations as tools for increasing organizational effectiveness. Recent projects include an assessment of training needs for entry-level peace officers and a review of pay-equity issues for a legislative body.

Darrick Hamilton, Assistant Professor; Ph.D., North Carolina at Chapel Hill. Ethnic and racial disparities in wealth, home ownership, and labor market outcomes. Dr. Hamilton's articles can be found in *African American Research Perspectives, American Economics Review, Applied Economics Letters, Challenge: The Magazine of Economic Affairs, Journal of Economic Psychology, Review of Black Political Economy, Social Science Quarterly, Southern Economics Journal*, and *Transforming Anthropology*.

David Howell, Professor; Ph.D., New School. Labor markets at the local, national, and international levels. Recent publications have examined the effects of immigration on the economic status of foreign and native-born workers in New York City, the nature of recent changes in skill requirements and the determinants of relative wage trends in the United States, and the extent to which labor market institutions and social policy explain patterns of unemployment in Europe and the United States. Dr. Howell is the editor of *Fighting Unemployment: The Limits of Free Market Orthodoxy*.

Mark Lipton, Professor of Management and Chair of Management; Ph.D., Massachusetts Amherst. Management, leadership, organizational strategy. Author of *Guiding Growth: How Vision Keeps Companies on Course*. Dr. Lipton's research and opinions on management and strategy have appeared in *Executive Excellence, Harvard Business Review, The Journal of Management Consulting, Optimize, Organization Development Journal*, and *Sloan Management Review*, among others.

Edwin Melendez, Professor; Ph.D., Massachusetts Amherst. Economics. Dr. Melendez was director of the Mauricio Gastón Institute for Latino Community Development and Public Policy at the University of Massachusetts Boston (1992–98) and director of the Community Development Research Center at the Milano Graduate School (1999–2004). He has worked as a consultant on employment, economic development, job creation, and small business for numerous government, community, and philanthropic foundations. Dr. Melendez has managed more than thirty-five research, outreach, and demonstration projects and supervised or collaborated with more than 60 researchers in projects that resulted in several books, special issues of academic journals, and other publications.

Aida Rodriguez, Professor of Professional Practice; Ph.D., Massachusetts. Leadership and effective management in the nonprofit sector. Formerly deputy director of the Equal Opportunity Division of the Rockefeller Foundation, Dr. Rodriguez now serves on various nonprofit boards, including One Economy, Inc.; Alliance for Nonprofit Management; and the Association for Public Policy Analysis and Management. Dr. Rodriguez is an adviser on philanthropic initiatives in the United States and in Latin America, including the Funders' Collaborative for Strong Latino Communities.

Bryna Sanger, Professor; Ph.D., Brandeis. Public policy and management, changes in service delivery and management systems induced by welfare reform in states and localities around the country. Former dean of the Robert J. Milano Graduate School of Management and Urban Policy, Dr. Sanger has worked in a wide range of policy and management areas, including city service delivery, welfare reform, leadership, innovation, and performance management. She recently led a research effort with the National Civic League on the experiences of cities that have developed exemplary performance measurement systems and that report to and engage citizens in their efforts. Her most recent book on this topic is entitled *The Welfare Marketplace: Privatization and Welfare Reform*.

Alex F. Schwartz, Associate Professor, Chair of Department of Urban Policy Analysis and Management, and Senior Research Associate, Community Development Research Center; Ph.D., Rutgers. Housing and community development, including affordable housing programs, community reinvestment, and community development corporations. Dr. Schwartz's most recent publication is *Housing Policy in the United States*. His research has also appeared in such journals as *Cityscape, Economic Development Quarterly, International Journal of Urban and Regional Research*, and the *Journal of Urban Affairs*.

Lisa J. Servon, Associate Professor and Associate Director of Community Development Research Center; Ph.D., Berkeley. Urban poverty, community development, economic development, gender issues. Dr. Servon recently coedited *Gender and Planning: A Reader* (with Susan Fainstein), which covers a range of planning and development fields, including transportation, land use, history, gender, housing, social justice, environmental design, race, and economic and community development. The book was selected as one of the top10 books for 2006 by Planetizen, a public-interest information exchange for the urban planning, design, and development community.

Nidhi Srinivas, Assistant Professor of Nonprofit Management; Ph.D., McGill. Civil society, specifically management of nongovernmental organizations, and the transfer and transformation of management knowledge. Dr. Srinivas teaches courses on nonprofit management, international development, and strategic decision making. Courses he has developed include Managing Institutions for Development (part of the core curriculum in the graduate program in international affairs) and Civil Society and South Asia.

Antonin Wagner, Visiting Professor; Ph.D., Fribourg (Switzerland). Economics. From 1996 to 2000, Dr. Wagner was president of the International Society for Third Sector Research, the leading scholarly institution in the nonprofit field. He has served as a consultant on social security–related issues to the Swiss Federal Statistical Office and the World Bank in Washington. He is a member of the editorial board of several international journals and has published widely in English, German, and French on the welfare state and civil society.

Tatiana Wah, Assistant Professor; Ph.D., Rutgers. Regional and local economic development planning and developing nations, with a particular focus on small developing nations' economies. Dr. Wah's recent work is on transnational expatriate (immigrant) recovery and engagement programs of developing countries, particularly Haiti. She has been involved in community development work in the New York African American and Caribbean communities as a consultant, nonprofit administrator, and activist/advocate.

Mary R. Watson, Assistant Professor; Ph.D., Vanderbilt. Contemporary human capital issues in organizations, with particular emphasis on the social impact of labor market discontinuities. Dr. Watson teaches courses in management and organization behavior, human resources, social impact management, and globalization. She has a strong interest in cultural, racial, ethnic, and gender inequalities in the workplace and society. Her upcoming book (with Dr. Rikki Abzug), tentatively titled *Human Resources in Social Purpose Organizations*, is scheduled to be published by Jossey-Bass in 2007.

Part-time Faculty

The part-time faculty members of Milano The New School for Management and Urban Policy are high-level executives and managers in the institutions and agencies for which they work and the organizations for which they volunteer. They bring to the classroom valuable insight into current management and policy issues from both their personal experience and relevant curriculum. For a current listing of part-time faculty members, students should visit the Faculty page of the Milano Web site at http://www.milano.newschool.edu.

NEW YORK UNIVERSITY

Robert F. Wagner Graduate School of Public Service

Programs of Study

Established in 1938, the Robert F. Wagner Graduate School of Public Service at New York University (NYU Wagner) offers advanced programs leading to the professional degrees of Master of Public Administration (M.P.A.) in public and nonprofit management and policy (PNP) and health policy and management (HPM), Master of Urban Planning (M.U.P.), Master of Science (M.S.) in management, and Doctor of Philosophy (Ph.D.). Through these rigorous programs, NYU Wagner educates the future leaders of public, nonprofit, and health institutions as well as private organizations serving the public sector.

Course work in the PNP, HPM, and urban planning programs is divided into core and specialized curricula. All students are required to take core courses in policy analysis, finance, microeconomics, statistics, and management of public service organizations. Within the PNP program, students may pursue one of the following specializations: finance, international, management, or public policy analysis. Students may also elect course clusters in such areas as arts and cultural policy, economic and community development, education policy, and nonprofit management, among others. HPM specialization options are health finance, health policy analysis, health services management, and international health. The urban planning program offers specialized electives in economic development and housing policy and environment, infrastructure, and transportation planning. A specialization track in international development planning is also available.

The School encourages work in related schools and departments, such as business, law, economics, sociology, politics, and mathematics. It currently offers dual-degree programs with the University's School of Law (J.D./M.P.A., J.D./M.U.P.), the School of Medicine (M.D./M.P.A.), the College of Arts and Science (B.A./M.P.A., B.A./M.U.P.), the School of Dentistry (M.A. in nursing/M.S.), the School of Social Work (M.S.W./M.S.), the Stern School of Business (M.B.A./M.P.A.), and the Graduate School of Arts and Science (Skirball Department of Hebrew and Judaic Studies) (M.S./M.P.A.). Advanced professional certificate programs are available to those who already hold an M.P.A., an M.U.P., or a related degree.

Advanced students of exceptional ability may be invited to participate in research projects supervised by faculty members.

Research Facilities

Substantial library and computing resources are available, as is access to many specialized facilities in New York City. The Elmer Holmes Bobst Library is the largest open-stack library in the country. VAX and IBM mainframe computers as well as extensive microcomputer laboratories support course work and research.

Financial Aid

Fellowships offered through the School include University tuition scholarships and other fellowships earmarked for particular programs. Research and graduate assistantships are also available.

Cost of Study

Full tuition (16 credits per term) was $29,465 per academic year for 2007–08. Books cost approximately $800 per year.

Living and Housing Costs

University housing is available in University-owned apartment complexes. Apartments are available only to matriculated full-time students relocating from beyond a 35-mile radius of the University. The average cost of living in the New York metropolitan area varies considerably depending on residential location. Off-campus living expenses are estimated at $20,000 for a single student for the academic year, and married students can expect to incur an additional expense of $6000 or more, depending on the number of people in the household.

Student Group

There are more than 860 graduate students in the School. Just over 50 percent are full-time students. Part-time students who take courses each term are employed in public, private, nonprofit, and health services organizations. More than eleven percent are international students, and over 27 percent are domestic students who are members of minority groups.

Location

New York University is an integral part of the thriving metropolitan community of New York City—the business, cultural, artistic, and financial center of the nation and the home of the United Nations. The city's extraordinary resources greatly enrich both the academic programs and the experience of living at the University. The School is located in the historic Puck Building, adjacent to New York City's Greenwich Village district and Washington Square Park.

The University

New York University is a private, metropolitan university that offers the advantages of a great urban setting to a highly diverse student body. The University first held classes in 1832, with 108 students and a faculty of 15. Its charter specified that it was to be established "on a liberal foundation, which shall correspond with the spirit and wants of our age. . . ." Today, with an enrollment of more than 50,000 students from all fifty states and 160 other countries, a faculty of 5,500, and more than 2,500 courses, the University vigorously keeps pace with the spirit and needs of the present and the future.

Applying

Prospective students should contact the Office of Enrollment and Student Services for more information. The application deadlines for admission and fellowship, scholarship, or assistantship aid for master's degree programs are January 15 for summer and fall semesters and October 1 for spring semester; the deadlines for admission alone are April 15 for summer, June 1 for fall, and November 15 for spring. The international application deadline is January 15 for summer and fall and October 1 for spring. The application deadline for the doctoral program is December 10. The application for admission is available through the School's Web page at http://wagner.nyu.edu.

Correspondence and Information

Office of Enrollment and Student Services
Robert F. Wagner Graduate School of Public Service
The Puck Building
New York University
295 Lafayette Street, 2nd Floor
New York, New York 10012-9604
Phone: 212-998-7414
E-mail: wagner.admissions@nyu.edu
Web site: http://wagner.nyu.edu

New York University

THE FACULTY

Ellen Schall, Martin E. Cherkasky Professor of Health Policy and Management and Dean; J.D., NYU, 1972.
Rogan Kersh, Associate Professor of Public Service and Associate Dean for Academic Affairs; Ph.D., Yale, 1996.
Robert Berne, Professor of Public Administration and Vice President for Academic Development; Ph.D., Cornell, 1977.
John Billings, Associate Professor of Health Policy and Management; J.D., Berkeley, 1973.
Jan Blustein, Professor of Health Policy and Management; M.D., Yale, 1985; Ph.D., NYU, 1993.
Jo Ivey Boufford, Professor of Health Policy and Public Service; M.D., Michigan, 1971.
Charles Brecher, Professor of Public and Health Administration; Ph.D., CUNY Graduate Center, 1972.
Sewin Chan, Associate Professor of Public Policy ; Ph.D., Columbia, 1995.
Ingrid Gould Ellen, Paulette Goddard Professor of Urban Policy; Ph.D., Harvard, 1996.
Erica G. Foldy, Assistant Professor of Public Administration; Ph.D., Boston College, 2002.
Rema N. Hanna, Assistant Professor of Public Policy and Economics; Ph.D., MIT, 2005.
Natasha Iskander, Assistant Professor of Public Administration; Ph.D., MIT, 2006.
Anthony R. Kovner, Professor of Public and Health Management; Ph.D., Pittsburgh, 1966.
Roger Kropf, Professor of Public and Health Management; Ph.D., Syracuse, 1976.
Paul C. Light, Paulette Goddard Professor of Public Service; Ph.D., Michigan, 1980.
Joe C. Magee, Assistant Professor of Management; Ph.D., Stanford, 2004.
Jonathan J. Morduch, Associate Professor of Public Policy and Economics; Ph.D., Harvard, 1991.
Mitchell Moss, Henry Hart Rice Professor of Urban Policy and Planning; Ph.D., USC, 1975.
Katherine M. O'Regan, Associate Professor of Public Administration; Ph.D., Berkeley, 1990.
Sonia Ospina, Associate Professor of Public Management and Policy; Ph.D., SUNY at Stony Brook, 1989.
Victor G. Rodwin, Professor of Health Policy and Management; Ph.D., Berkeley, 1980.
Shanna Rose, Assistant Professor of Public Financial Management; Ph.D., Harvard, 2005.
Amy Ellen Schwartz, Professor of Public Policy, Education, and Economics; Ph.D., Columbia, 1989.
Dennis Smith, Associate Professor of Public Administration; Ph.D., Indiana, 1975.
Paul Smoke, Professor of Public Finance and Planning; Ph.D., MIT, 1988.
Walter W. Stafford, Professor of Public Policy and Planning; Ph.D., Pittsburgh, 1973.
Leanna Stiefel, Professor of Economics; Ph.D., Wisconsin–Madison, 1972.
Beth Weitzman, Professor of Health and Public Policy; Ph.D., NYU, 1987.
Rae Zimmerman, Professor of Planning and Public Administration; Ph.D., Columbia, 1972.

NORTHWESTERN UNIVERSITY

School of Education and Social Policy
Graduate Program in Human Development and Social Policy

Program of Study	The Graduate Program in Human Development and Social Policy is an unusual interdisciplinary program designed to meet the growing need for persons with social sciences backgrounds who are knowledgeable about both human development and social policy. The program centers on three areas of study and the interrelations among them: the psychological and social development of the person across the life span, the influence of social and economic environments, and the role of policy decisions in shaping life choices, opportunities, and outcomes. Special attention is given to research methods suited for analyzing the interrelations. Students may specialize in child development and social policy; adolescent development and social policy; adult development, aging, and social policy; poverty and social policy; education and social policy; or a general life cycle approach to policy or to human development. The faculty members are drawn from a number of different disciplines and fields of study, including psychology, sociology, education, political science, economics, public policy, and human development.
	Graduates of the program are prepared to make special contributions in a wide range of careers. As teachers and researchers, they bring a special interdisciplinary perspective to programs in the social sciences, human development, public policy, and education.
	The Ph.D. degree is offered; students may also complete an M.A. degree en route to the Ph.D. Course work is tailored to build upon the student's background and to fit the particular educational goals developed by the student and adviser. Courses and seminars are drawn from the School of Education and Social Policy and from other departments and units of the University. Several of the program's faculty members have joint appointments at Northwestern's Institute for Policy Research, thus assuring students of research opportunities in a variety of areas.
Research Facilities	Resources for advanced study at Northwestern University are outstanding. Numerous research libraries, including the Main Library and five branch and special libraries on the campus, contain holdings totaling more than 3 million volumes, 1 million microfilm units, and 33,000 journals and other serial publications. In addition, students are provided access to both the mainframe computer at the I. T. Computing Center and microcomputers housed within the School. Research opportunities are available for students in three research centers at the University: the Center on Aging, the Institute for Policy Research, and the Joint Center for Poverty Research.
Financial Aid	Financial aid is available to graduate students in the form of University and program fellowships, scholarships, and graduate assistantships. Special opportunities for research assistantships or other employment also exist within the School's and the University's many research centers. Student loans are also possible. All Ph.D. students are fully funded for four years.
Cost of Study	Tuition for full-time study (three courses per three quarters) in pursuit of the Ph.D. was $36,756 in 2008–09 ($12,252 per quarter). As discussed in the Financial Aid section, all Ph.D. students are fully funded for four years.
Living and Housing Costs	The University operates two graduate student residences in Evanston. In addition, information and assistance in securing off-campus housing is made available.
Student Group	There are approximately 30 graduate students in the program at the present time. Enrollments are selective, and only 5–7 new students are accepted into the program each year. Graduates hold positions in such settings as universities, research organizations, public or private agencies, and foundations.
Location	Northwestern's Evanston campus is located on Lake Michigan, just north of the city of Chicago. The beautiful lakefront campus offers a rich cultural environment through a wealth of theatrical, musical, and athletic events. The proximity of the campus to a major metropolitan complex, with its world-class architecture, symphony, museums, opera, theater, and major-league sports, further enriches student life.
The University and The School	Established in 1851, Northwestern University is recognized as one of the most distinguished private universities in the United States. The School of Education and Social Policy has developed from its origins as a department of pedagogy by continually broadening its scope to encompass those educative, learning, and socializing experiences that take place throughout the life span in families, schools, communities, and the workplace.
Applying	Applications for admission are reviewed in January and February. Admission decisions are usually made in late February. Except in unusual circumstances, students are accepted in the Program in Human Development and Social Policy for fall quarter matriculation only. Applicants planning to seek financial aid must meet the submission deadline of December 31.
Correspondence and Information	Graduate Program in Human Development and Social Policy Northwestern University School of Education and Social Policy 2120 Campus Drive Evanston, Illinois 60208-2610 Phone: 847-491-4329 Web site: http://www.sesp.northwestern.edu/hdsp/info/overview

Northwestern University

THE FACULTY AND THEIR RESEARCH

* Emma Adam, Ph.D., Minnesota. Parenting, developmental psychobiology of stress, attachment, foster care.
* Ryan Brown, Ph.D., Emory. Life course development, risk taking, culture and health, psychophysiology.
* Lindsay Chase-Lansdale, Ph.D., Michigan. Child, adolescent, and family functioning; public policy; poverty and welfare reform.
* Jeannette A. Colyvas, Ph.D., Stanford. Institutional change; public, private, and nonprofit forms of organizing; science policy; university-industry interfaces in R&D.
* Fay Lomax Cook, Ph.D., Chicago. Politics of public policy, public opinion, policy issues in aging.

Thomas D. Cook, Ph.D., Stanford. Social-psychological processes, measurement of attitudes, evaluation of social programs.
* David Figlio, Ph.D., Wisconsin. Accountability policy, economics of education, teacher quality, teacher labor markets, anti-poverty policy, intergenerational transmission of human capital, evaluation design.
* Larry V. Hedges, Ph.D., Stanford. Statistics and research design, education policy, the role of uncertainty in cognitive models, social distribution of academic achievement.
* Barton J. Hirsch, Ph.D., Oregon. Social ecology of adolescent development, social networks, community psychology, parenting.
* Dan A. Lewis, Ph.D., California, Santa Cruz. Policy analysis, urban social problems, community organization.
* Jelani Mandara, Ph.D., California, Riverside. African American families, social development, self-regulation, personality, quantitative methods.
* Dan P. McAdams, Ph.D., Harvard. Adult development; personality, identity, and the self; generativity; life narratives.
* Thomas McDade, Ph.D., Emory. Human biology, biocultural perspectives on health and human development, medical anthropology, evolutionary ecology.

Penelope Peterson, Ph.D., Stanford. Learning and teaching in schools and classrooms, particularly in mathematics and literacy; teacher learning in reform contexts; relations among educational research, policy, and practice.
* Michelle Reininger, Ph.D., Stanford. Education policy, teacher labor markets, teacher education, community colleges.
* James E. Rosenbaum, Ph.D., Harvard. Adolescent/adult development, organizational careers, education and social policy, poverty and housing.

Bruce D. Spencer, Ph.D., Yale. Social and educational measurement, statistics for policy analysis, demography, decision theory.
* James P. Spillane, Ph.D., Michigan State. Education policy and school reform, intergovernmental relations, policy and practice, organizational leadership and change.

Linda A. Teplin, Ph.D., Northwestern. Mental health services/policies for youth and adult populations in the criminal justice system, community-based samples.

Core faculty.

School of Education and Social Policy.

Northwestern University J. Roscoe Miller campus.

ROGER WILLIAMS UNIVERSITY

Master of Public Administration

Program of Study	The Master of Public Administration program (M.P.A.) at Roger Williams University (RWU) is designed to provide the necessary training and skill sets for students to excel at all levels of administration in professions dedicated to public service, including government, health care, military, and nonprofit industries.
	The University's M.P.A. program has been distinguished by its joint emphasis on direct services and administration. In addition to training students to communicate effectively, solve problems, and think critically, the faculty strives to instill in students a sense of duty to positively influence public policy and management by promoting such values as citizen participation, equity, diversity, and the ethical performance of public service. The goal of the program is to provide students with an understanding of the structural integration of public administration institutions, processes, and procedures in legal, political, economic, and social institutions.
	Classes meet every other week at the University's downcity Providence campus, allowing students the convenience of online learning coupled with the experience of in-class instruction from a mix of full-time faculty and outstanding professional adjunct lecturers. Several courses are available completely online, allowing students to work through the course material on a schedule of their choosing.
Research Facilities	A robust research library is integral to graduate study. The Learning Commons at the Roger Williams University Library offers a wide array of instructional resources for students. It is an improved model for research—a one-stop shop for instructional technology, traditional, and database research—that provides students access to myriad research resources. The University's state-of-the-art computer laboratories allow student access to the latest word and statistical processing software packages available, including full Internet access.
	The University's expansive library houses approximately 2,000 volumes and hundreds of films and other nonprint materials. Master's degree candidates also have access to the LexisNexis network and Westlaw as well as the RWU Law Library. In addition, the University is a member of the Helin Consortium, which gives students access to more than a million volumes of printed material. Quiet study space and group research areas are also available.
Financial Aid	Financing a graduate education can be challenging, especially in these trying economic times. Roger Williams University recognizes that some students may need financial assistance to meet the cost of higher education. Students with financial need may be able to receive funds from federal loan programs; those with fully accepted status who maintain a minimum of 6 credits per semester are eligible to receive loans that cover the cost of graduate education. In order to be considered for the federal loan programs, students must submit the Free Application for Federal Student Aid (FAFSA), which is available from the Office of Financial Aid or at http://www.fafsa.gov.
Cost of Study	The 2008–09 graduate tuition was $417 per credit. Each 3-credit course cost $1251. Some additional fees may apply. Tuition information for the 2009–10 academic year is available at http://financialaid.rwu.edu.
Living and Housing Costs	University housing is available for graduate students. However, it is not guaranteed, and the majority of graduate students seek a variety of off-campus housing options. In 2008–09, the average cost for on-campus graduate housing was $7313 per academic year. For more information about off-campus housing, visit http://housing.rwu.edu and click the "off-campus living" tab.
Student Group	Roger Williams University seeks qualified men and women who possess strength of character, a sense of social responsibility, and a distinguished academic background to join a graduate community where the focus is on the student. Many of the students are working professionals who want to advance their careers through higher education. After gaining a solid foundation in public administration through core courses, students choose a specialty in either public administration or health care administration.
Location	The Roger Williams University M.P.A. program is located in downcity Providence, Rhode Island's capital and largest city. Providence is packed with museums, coffee shops, the Providence Place Mall, live music, and much more. Providence is also a regional transportation hub, with an international airport and both bus and train stations. RWU's main campus is located in the historic seaside town of Bristol, Rhode Island.
The University and the Program	Roger Williams University is a 52-year-old independent, coeducational liberal arts university that has quickly established itself as a leader in higher education. A dynamic educational environment in which students live and learn to be global citizens, the University is committed to its mantra of "Learning to bridge the world."
	With thirty-nine academic programs and a robust array of cocurricular activities available on its waterfront campus in historic Bristol, Rhode Island, RWU looks to a set of core values in fulfilling its mission to prepare students for life as twenty-first century citizen-scholars. Over the past decade the institution has achieved unprecedented academic and financial successes. In 2008, *U.S. News & World Report* named Roger Williams the eighth-ranked baccalaureate college in the north.
	The Master's in Public Administration program seeks to foster excellence in public service and in government by preparing students for leadership and service in federal, state, and local government as well as in nonprofit management. The program is designed to develop and improve communications and decision-making skills along with problem-identification and problem-solving abilities.
Applying	Roger Williams University seeks well-rounded students with leadership potential and a demonstrated commitment to education and academic achievement.
	Admission requirements include a bachelor's degree from an accredited institution, official transcripts of all previous undergraduate and graduate course work, a personal statement discussing relevant past experiences and career goals, two letters of recommendation attesting to the candidate's potential to complete graduate work, and a completed application form signed and accompanied by the $50 application fee. Entrance exams are not required, but applicants with a cumulative undergraduate grade point average below 3.0 are strongly encouraged to take either the GRE or MAT.
Correspondence and Information	Jason Pina Dean of Continuing Studies and Graduate Admission Roger Williams University One Old Ferry Road Bristol, Rhode Island 02809 Phone: 888-674-8479 (toll-free) E-mail: gradadmit@rwu.edu Web site: http://www.rwu.edu

Roger Williams University

THE FACULTY

Michael Hall, Ph.D. Chair, Department of Public Administration and Professional Studies; Director, Master's Program in Public Administration; Director, Master of Science in Leadership; Associate Professor, Public Administration.

Steven Esons, M.A. Professor, Public Administration.

Bruce Thompson, Ph.D. Professor, Social and Health Services/Health Care Administration.

Louis M. Swiczewicz, Ph.D. Professor, Industrial Technology; Director, Credit Documentation.

John Stout, M.A. Dean, School of Continuing Studies; Professor, Public Administration.

Jeffrey Rinehart, Ph.D. Associate Professor, Public Administration.

June Speakman, Ph.D. Chair, Department of Political Science; Professor, Political Science.

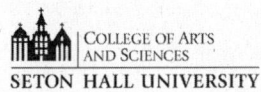

COLLEGE OF ARTS
AND SCIENCES
SETON HALL UNIVERSITY

SETON HALL UNIVERSITY

Department of Public and Healthcare Administration
Master of Public Administration

Programs of Study

The Department of Public and Healthcare Administration (DPHA) at Seton Hall University offers a Master of Public Administration (M.P.A.) degree program for people who are interested in the nonprofit, public sector, or health policy fields. The DPHA also offers a Master of Healthcare Administration (M.H.A.) degree for those interested in health-care organizations and institutions. The M.P.A. degree is a 39-credit program and the M.H.A. degree is 42 credits; both are tailored to the working adult student. Classes are offered in the late afternoon and evenings, on Saturday mornings, online, and in four-day compressed courses available on weekends. Courses are offered year-round, including during three separate summer sessions.

Accredited by the National Association of Schools of Public Affairs and Administration (NASPAA), the 39-credit M.P.A. program offers three concentrations: nonprofit management; public service leadership, governance, and policy; and health-care administration. The nonprofit management concentration is currently ranked fourteenth by *U.S. News & World Report* among all M.P.A. nonprofit management concentrations in the country. The Department's curriculum stresses the development of managerial and analytical skills, emphasizes the importance of cross-sector collaboration, and works to bridge them to actual practice.

The DPHA also offers a 60-credit M.A./M.P.A. dual-degree program with Seton Hall's Whitehead School of Diplomacy and International Relations for students interested in studying public service and nonprofit issues on a global level. In addition, DPHA offers two 15-credit certificate programs in nonprofit organization management and health-care administration. Students completing any of the certificate programs may apply the credits toward either the M.P.A. or M.H.A. degree if they are accepted into either of those degree programs.

More information about these programs is available at http://www.shu.edu/academics/artsci/graduate-public-health-admin-programs.cfm.

Research Facilities

DPHA is the home of the Center for Public Service which conducts applied public policy research and provides technical assistance to community-based organizations through its Nonprofit Sector Research Institute. Students are given opportunities to participate in research projects and to gain hands-on management experience through a number of academic and technical assistance programs.

DPHA is also home to the Seton Center for Community Health (SCCH), which was established in the fall of 2004 as an academic resource for collaboration, learning, and research that will enhance the quality of life for individuals and communities in need. SCCH provides technical assistance and scholarship to community agencies focused on improving the health status of New Jersey residents. The SCCH provides opportunities for M.H.A. students to experience real-world situations through community engagement. Students are given opportunities to participate in research projects and gain hands-on management experience through a number of academic and technical assistance programs.

The Walsh Library, a state-of-the-art 155,000-square-foot building, houses 500,000 titles, 1,875 current periodicals, and an extensive collection of microform and other nonprint items that include videotapes, CD-ROM music, and other electronic media. Fahy Hall has twenty-eight classrooms, two TV studios, a Macintosh and IBM graphics lab, two classroom amphitheaters, and language and statistics labs. The recently renovated McNulty Hall has well-equipped science labs. Completed in 1997, Jubilee Hall, a six-story facility with 126,000 square feet of academic space, features high-tech classrooms with computer and multimedia capabilities and the Center for Securities Trading and Analysis, commonly referred to as the Trading Room.

Financial Aid

The DPHA offers a number of competitive scholarships for students in the public sector and nonprofit tracks. DPHA scholarship information can be found at http://www.shu.edu/academics/artsci/public-healthcare-administration/upload/scholarshipApplication.pdf.

In addition, through an arrangement with the VA New Jersey Health Care System, the Department offers the Healthcare Administration Residency Program for students whose interests or career objectives are in health-care administration; the two-year residency provides them the opportunity for study supplemented by work experiences in health-care administration. Interested applicants accepted into the M.H.A. program are referred to the VA for an interview. Those who are selected by the Department and the VA work 20 hours per week for the VA Hospital, two blocks from campus, and receive support in the form of a stipend plus tuition reimbursement.

A limited number of competitive graduate assistantships are available within the DPHA and throughout the University. These positions cover tuition costs and provide a modest stipend in exchange for half-time work (20 hours per week) during the academic year. Students interested in a graduate assistant position should complete an online application at http://www.shu.edu/applying/graduate/grad-finaid.cfm or contact the DPHA for additional information. Students interested in other financial aid options should visit the University's financial aid Web site at http://www.shu.edu/applying/graduate/grad-finaid.cfm.

Cost of Study

In 2009–10, tuition is $901 per credit. Full-time students pay $305 per semester in University and technology fees; part-time students pay $185.

Living and Housing Costs

Housing and living costs in South Orange and surrounding towns are comparable to most suburban cities, with studio and one-bedroom apartments renting for $750 to $1000 per month.

Student Group

Typical M.P.A. students have some work experience, although the program accepts many students directly from undergraduate programs.

The DPHA hosts a student chapter of the public administration honor society, Pi Alpha Alpha, as well as a student chapter of Upsilon Phi Delta, the honor society for healthcare administrators.

Location

Seton Hall is located on 58 acres in the village of South Orange, New Jersey, a suburban residential area 14 miles southwest of New York City. The town center is a 10-minute walk from the campus and features bookstores, coffee shops, and restaurants. The heart of midtown Manhattan is about 30 minutes away by train; students can take advantage of everything this exciting city has to offer while still living in a suburban area.

The University and The Department

Founded in 1856, Seton Hall is a private coeducational Catholic institution—the nation's oldest diocesan institution of higher education in the United States. With a total enrollment of about 10,000, including approximately 4,500 graduate students, the University comprises nine colleges and schools. Seton Hall is accredited by the Middle States Association of Colleges and Schools. Through the incorporation of technology into the curriculum, the College of Arts and Sciences seeks to enhance and enliven the learning environment. Rooted in tradition, yet looking to the future, the college offers a rich set of opportunities for intellectual discovery. Graduate students are guided by scholars and specialists toward the mastery of academic and professional areas.

The University has offered the M.P.A. degree since 1980, six years before the establishment of the Center for Public Service and thirteen years before the Department of Public Administration came into existence. The Center for Public Service was established in 1986 to house the M.P.A. program, conduct applied public policy research, and initiate training programs for the public and nonprofit sectors. In 1993, the Department of Public Administration was formed, and, five years later, the Center for Public Service and Department of Public Administration began offering the M.H.A. degree. The Department prides itself on providing students with hands-on, practice-focused professional education. Unlike many larger programs, students receive academic and professional counseling directly from faculty members and many students join faculty members on research projects.

Applying

Applicants must submit a completed application (available at http://www.shu.edu/academics/artsci/apply-graduate.cfm), the $50 application fee, official transcripts from all colleges and universities attended, a current resume, and three letters of recommendation. Standardized test scores are not required for the M.P.A. or M.H.A. degree. Applications are accepted throughout the year, and admissions decisions are made on a rolling basis.

Additional application information is available on the right-hand side of the M.P.A. Web site at http://www.shu.edu/academics/artsci/mpa/index.cfm. Applications are available directly at https://www.applyweb.com/aw?setonv.

Correspondence and Information

Dr. Matthew Hale, Chair
Department of Public and Healthcare Administration
5th Floor, Jubilee Hall
Seton Hall University
400 South Orange Avenue
South Orange, New Jersey 07079
Phone: 973-761-9510
Fax: 973-275-2463
E-mail: dpha@shu.edu
Web site: http://www.shu.edu/academics/artsci/graduate-public-health-admin-programs.cfm

Seton Hall University

THE FACULTY AND THEIR RESEARCH

Full-Time Faculty

Paul Cavanagh, Assistant Professor; M.S.W., Ph.D., Columbia. Professional social worker with extensive experience working with children and adults with developmental disabilities. Has worked as an advocacy caseworker, Director of a Medicaid Day Treatment program, and Executive Director of an AmeriCorps affiliate program for five years. Dissertation examined the labor choices of mothers with a child with a severe developmental disability. Currently studies child care for children with severe developmental disabilities.

Philip S. DiSalvio, Associate Professor; Ed.D., Harvard. Management, finance, strategic planning, ethics. Former Robert Wood Johnson Faculty Fellow in Healthcare Finance. Consultant and adviser to the health-care industry in management development, leadership, and strategic planning. Speaker, seminar leader, and facilitator for numerous health-care organizations and Faculty Associate for the American College of Health Care Executives. Author of *Managing Computers in Health Care* and *Managing Computers in Healthcare: A Self-Directed Series for Healthcare Executives.*

Matthew Hale, Associate Professor; Ph.D., USC. Political communication and media. Research examines how the media covers the public and nonprofit sectors, with a particular focus on election campaigns and Spanish-language media. Published journal articles have appeared in *Nonprofit and Voluntary Sector Quarterly, Stanford Law and Policy Review, Mass Communication & Society,* and *Electronic News.*

Anne M. Hewitt, Associate Professor and Director, Seton Center for Community Health; Ph.D., Temple. Community health development and assessment, health literacy, worksite health. Former American Lung Association Principal Investigator. Author of articles in *Health Promotion Practice, American Journal of Health Studies,* and *Journal of Occupational Medicine.* Provides program evaluation assistance to various state and local organizations as well as nonprofit agencies and health-care institutions.

Hengameh Hosseini, Assistant Professor; Ph.D., Marywood. Ethics of health care, health-care policy, economics and finance. Author of articles in *Hospital Topics, Journal of International Diversity,* and *The Journal of Health Administration Education.*

Naomi Bailin Wish, Professor and Director, Center for Public Service; Ph.D., Rutgers. Nonprofit organization management, program evaluation, quantitative methods. Author of articles in *Public Administration Review, International Journal of Public Administration, American Journal of Economics and Sociology,* and the *Municipal Yearbook.*

Part-Time Faculty

Mary Jo Buchanan, Adjunct Instructor in Nonprofit Finance.
Barkley Calkins, Adjunct Instructor in Nonprofit Management and Project Coordinator for NSRI.
Vincent Farinella, Adjunct Instructor in Healthcare Management.
Alan Negreann, Adjunct Instructor in Public Sector Financial Management.
Audrey Winkler, Adjunct Instructor in Nonprofit Management.

TUFTS UNIVERSITY

Department of Urban and Environmental Policy and Planning

Programs of Study

The Department of Urban and Environmental Policy and Planning (UEP) offers graduate public policy and planning programs culminating in either a Master of Arts (M.A.) degree or a Master of Public Policy (M.P.P.) degree. In addition, in combined degree options with the Departments of Civil and Environmental Engineering and Biology, students may attain a Master of Science (M.S.) degree. The programs prepare public-spirited individuals for careers in government, nonprofit organizations, citizen advocacy groups, and the private sector. The goal is to educate a new generation of leaders—practical visionaries—who will contribute to solving key public problems by making institutions more responsive to the social and economic needs of communities and by moving toward the sustainable management of environmental resources.

Within each of the two broad areas of concentration—urban and social policy and planning and environmental policy and planning—faculty and student interests and course offerings cluster around the following: sustainable communities; environmental justice; community development and housing; race, class, and social welfare policy; child and family policy; land-use planning; natural resource management; science/technology, ethics, and environmental policy; environmental risk; corporate responsibility and the environment; climate change; international environmental policy; environmental education; program evaluation; applied research methods; planning tools, techniques, and strategies; nonprofit organizations; and citizen roles in policy and planning. UEP programs are distinguished by their focus on the role of nonprofit and community-based organizations and their emphasis on social justice, individual rights and responsibilities, and the equitable distribution of resources.

The established degree program of the Department is a two-year, full-time M.A. degree in urban and environmental policy and planning. The program features field-based learning and requires an internship and thesis. A newer one-year program, which leads to an M.P.P. degree, is designed for individuals with at least seven years of significant, relevant professional experience. Students may attend all degree programs on a part-time basis.

UEP enjoys strong ties to many other Tufts departments, providing a rich interdisciplinary experience for students as well as options for students in the M.A. program to pursue both combined-degree and dual-degree options. Joint degrees are available through cooperative agreements with the Departments of Biology, Child Development, Civil and Environmental Engineering, and Economics. Students interested in international environmental policy may apply to a three-year dual master's degree program with the Fletcher School of Law and Diplomacy, which is also located on the Tufts campus. A three-year dual master's degree program with the Friedman School of Nutrition Science and Policy is designed for students who have an interest in agriculture, food, and environment and wish to develop a policy orientation. A five-semester dual master's degree program with the Department of Civil and Environmental Engineering is also available.

Research Facilities

The University libraries on the Medford/Somerville campus include the Tisch Library, the Chemistry Library, the Lufkin Engineering Library, the Mathematics-Physics Library, and the Edwin Ginn Library of the Fletcher School. Students have access to the Health Sciences Library located on the Tufts Boston campus. Graduate students also have library privileges with Boston College, Boston University, Brandeis University, Massachusetts Institute of Technology, Northeastern University, the University of Massachusetts, and Wellesley College.

Financial Aid

The Department awards a generous number of partial tuition remission scholarships to students demonstrating financial need. Federally financed education loans, work-study positions, and a limited number of teaching and research assistantships are also available for those who qualify. Teaching assistantships are usually assigned to second-year students who have a demonstrated familiarity with the subject matter, but applications are accepted from everyone. A typical teaching assistantship requires 10 hours per week, with a stipend of $2450 per semester. The Department administers the Alvin Levin Fellowship, a scholarship fund for women of color. The Department is committed to supporting a diverse student body through financial assistance.

Cost of Study

Tuition for full-time students in the M.A. program for the 2009–10 academic year is $28,572; the second year's tuition is likely to increase by approximately 5 percent. Tuition for full-time students in the M.P.P. program is one year of Tufts University tuition—$38,096 for the 2009–10 academic year. Part-time students enrolled in no more than two courses per semester are charged $3810 per course. All graduate students pay a mandatory health service fee of approximately $620 and an annual $40 graduate student activity fee.

Living and Housing Costs

A limited amount of designated graduate student housing is available on the Tufts campus. Most graduate students live off campus in apartments in the area. Rent for a one-bedroom apartment in the surrounding community averages $850–$1200 per month; rent for a two- or three-bedroom apartment averages $1200–$1800 per month. A reasonable estimate of rent in a shared household is $450–$600 per month. Meal plans are available on campus.

Student Group

Of the 5,900 Tufts students on the Medford-Somerville campus, approximately 1,300 are graduate students. The Department enrolls approximately 55 new students per year, with about 90 to 100 enrolled at one time. Although the Department admits a few applicants to the M.A. program directly out of college, students benefit most from the program if they have had some relevant work experience subsequent to college. The average age of recent entering M.A. classes has been 26. The Department strives for a class that is diverse in race, ethnicity, and socioeconomic background.

Location

Tufts University is situated on a 150-acre site on the boundary between the cities of Medford and Somerville, 5 miles northwest of Boston. The campus occupies a tranquil New England setting within easy access by bus and subway to the cultural, social, and entertainment resources of Boston and Cambridge. Tufts has a variety of affiliations and cross-registration agreements with other institutions in the Greater Boston area, including Brandeis University, Boston College, and Boston University.

The University

Chartered as a liberal arts college in 1852, Tufts today is a small, private university offering many opportunities for both graduate and professional education. The Department of Urban and Environmental Policy and Planning was founded in 1973. It is situated in the Graduate School of Arts and Sciences, which is located on the Tufts Medford campus. Also on the Medford campus are the College of Liberal Arts, the College of Engineering, the School of Nutrition Science and Policy, and the Fletcher School of Law and Diplomacy. Other campuses include the School of Medicine, the School of Dental Medicine, the Sackler School of Graduate Biomedical Sciences, and the School of Veterinary Medicine.

Applying

The Department does not generally admit applicants for the spring semester. Applications for the M.A. program are due by January 15. Applications for the M.P.P. program are due by April 30. In addition to the application form and a $70 application fee, three letters of recommendation, official college transcripts, and a personal statement are required. GRE General Test scores are required for applicants to the M.A. program who have received a baccalaureate degree within five years of their application date. GRE General Test scores are optional for application to the M.P.P. program. International students whose native language is not English must submit their scores on the Test of English as a Foreign Language (TOEFL).

Correspondence and Information

Department of Urban and Environmental Policy and Planning
Tufts University
97 Talbot Avenue
Medford, Massachusetts 02155

Phone: 617-627-3394
Fax: 617-627-3377
E-mail: ann.urosevich@tufts.edu
Web site: http://ase.tufts.edu/uep

Tufts University

THE FACULTY AND THEIR RESEARCH

Core Faculty

Julian Agyeman, Professor; Ph.D., London. Sustainable communities, environmental justice, environmental education.
Rachel G. Bratt, Professor; Ph.D., MIT. Housing and community development.
Mary E. Davis, Assistant Professor; Ph.D., Florida. Economics, environmental health.
Laurie Goldman, Lecturer; M.S., Israel Institute of Technology. Urban studies and planning.
Justin Hollander, Assistant Professor; Ph.D., Rutgers. Urban planning and policy development.
Francine Jacobs, Associate Professor; Ed.D., Harvard. Child and family policy, program evaluation.
James Jennings, Professor; Ph.D., Columbia. Urban and neighborhood politics, social welfare, and community development.
Sheldon Krimsky, Professor; Ph.D., Boston University. Environmental policy and environmental ethics.
Penn Loh, Professor of the Practice; M.S., Berkeley. Environmental justice.
Barbara Parmenter, Lecturer; Ph.D., Texas at Austin. Geographic information systems.
Ann Rappaport, Lecturer; Ph.D., Tufts. Environmental policy, environmental engineering.
Robert H. Russell, Lecturer; J.D., Harvard. Environmental law.
Jon Witten, Lecturer; M.A., Cornell. Land-use planning.

Part-Time Faculty

Margaret Barringer, Lecturer; M.C.P., Rhode Island. Economic development.
Patricia Bonner-DuVal, Lecturer; M.Ed., Harvard. Philanthropy and fundraising.
Robert G. Burdick, Adjunct Associate Professor; J.D., Boston University. Negotiation and conflict resolution.
Alix Cantave, Lecturer; M.S., Pratt. Real estate development and finance, public policy.
Mark Chase, Lecturer; M.A., Tufts. Transportation planning.
Christine Cousineau, Lecturer; M.C.P., MIT. Urban planning and design.
Louise Dunlap, Lecturer; Ph.D., Berkeley. Writing.
Scott Horsley, Lecturer; M.A., Rhode Island. Land-use planning, water resources policy.
Karen Kelley, Lecturer; M.B.A., Boston University. Financial analysis and management.
Ingar Palmlund, Adjunct Assistant Professor; Ph.D., Clark. International environmental policy, human health and environment.
Alan Jay Rom, Lecturer; J.D., Cleveland State. Legal frameworks of social policy.
Roberta Rubin, Lecturer; J.D., Harvard. Housing policy, homelessness.
Klare Shaw, Lecturer. Philanthropy and fundraising.
Marji Erickson Warfield, Lecturer; Ph.D., Brandeis. Social policy and quantitative research methods.

Adjunct and Associated Faculty

Robert M. Hollister, Professor and Dean, University College of Citizenship and Public Service; Ph.D., MIT. Nonprofit management and urban policy.
William Moomaw, Professor of International Environmental Policy; Ph.D., MIT. International environmental policy.
Susan Ostrander, Professor; Ph.D., Case Western Reserve. Gender/feminist theory, nonprofit organizations.
Kent Portney, Professor; Ph.D., Florida State. American politics and public policy, environmental politics.

UNIVERSITY OF DELAWARE

College of Education and Public Policy
School of Urban Affairs and Public Policy

Programs of Study	The School of Urban Affairs and Public Policy offers three graduate degree programs: a Master of Public Administration (M.P.A.), a Master of Arts (M.A.) in urban affairs and public policy, and a Ph.D. in urban affairs and public policy.
	The M.P.A. is a 42-credit, two-year professional degree program that prepares students for leadership positions in public affairs. The M.P.A. program is accredited by the National Association of Schools of Public Affairs and Administration (NASPAA). Students can specialize in five areas: state and local management, community development and nonprofit leadership, organizational leadership, health policy and management, and financial management.
	The M.A. and Ph.D. in urban affairs and public policy programs are ranked among the top nine programs in the United States. The M.A. is a 36-credit degree program designed for students who are interested in pursuing policy analysis and planning–related careers. The program extends over two years and may include a thesis, an analytical paper, or an internship. M.A. students may specialize in such areas as community development and nonprofit leadership; energy, environment, and equity; historic preservation; and urban and regional planning. The Ph.D. is a research-oriented interdisciplinary degree intended for students who have completed master's-level work in urban affairs and public policy or other related social science fields. First-year doctoral seminars are followed by study in a specialization that leads to the preparation of the dissertation proposal. Most students conduct dissertation research in the areas of technology, environment, and society; governance planning and management; social and urban policy; public administration; and urban affairs. All doctoral students collaborate with faculty and staff members on regional, national, and international research on critical urban and policy issues.
	The School offers a nationally recognized internship program that places students in paid professional positions in international, national, state, and local government. All students in the School are eligible; the internship is a requirement for preservice M.P.A. students.
Research Facilities	The School is centrally located in its own building, with its own classrooms, student offices, and computer/GIS facilities. One of the most distinguishing characteristics of the School of Urban Affairs and Public Policy is the integration of theory and practice through applied research projects with the affiliated research and public service centers. Most full-time students are awarded research assistantships on projects in these centers.
	The Center for Applied Demography and Survey Research provides demographic and survey data and information on important public issues to researchers and policy makers at all levels (http://www.cadsr.udel.edu). The Center for Community Research and Service helps public, nonprofit, and private organizations in Delaware to design, implement, and evaluate policies and programs that address the needs of low- and moderate-income families and communities related to economic development, housing, and social services. The center also focuses on issues that are vital to the physical and emotional well-being of the world's population. These questions concern the delivery and financing of health care and the outcomes of health care provided (http://www.udel.edu/CCRS). The Center for Energy and Environmental Policy conducts interdisciplinary research in the areas of sustainable development, technology and society, and the political economy of energy systems and provides technical assistance to community, government, and nonprofit organizations (http://www.udel.edu/ceep/). The Center for Historic Architecture and Design focuses on shaping historic preservation planning and policy, reconstructing historic landscapes, documenting threatened historic properties, and advocating for the preservation of historic resources (http://www.udel.edu/CHAD). The Institute for Public Administration links the resources of the University of Delaware (UD) with the management and policy information needs of public and nonprofit organizations (http://www.ipa.udel.edu).
Financial Aid	The School has competitive financial aid programs, including fellowships, research assistantships, and scholarships. Aid is awarded on the basis of merit and is limited by the various restrictions established by the sources of aid. Stipends for 2009–10 were $15,200 for the full academic year. Additional special assistantships, fellowships, and internships are available to students through the University Graduate Scholar's Program, for both newly admitted and graduate students currently enrolled. Awards are competitive and are based on many criteria, including challenging social, economic, educational, cultural, or other life circumstances; academic achievements; first generation graduate student status; and/or need as determined by federal income guidelines (FAFSA). Funds are also available through the Delaware Legislative Fellows Program.
Cost of Study	In 2009–10, tuition for full-time graduate students is $22,240 per academic year. Part-time students are charged on a per-credit basis. (The 2009–10 rate is $1236 per credit.) Full-time matriculated students are automatically assessed nonrefundable fees of $484 for health and $228 for student-sponsored activities.
Living and Housing Costs	The University provides some graduate apartments, and there is plenty of off-campus housing in the surrounding community in many price ranges. For more information, students should contact the Housing Assignment Services Office (302-831-2491; http://www.udel.edu/has).
Student Group	The School has 71 students in the M.P.A. program, 56 in the M.A. program, and 45 in the Ph.D. program.
Student Outcomes	Graduates find career positions in government and nonprofit organizations and occasionally in the private sector with consulting firms. With UD's proximity to Washington, D.C.; Philadelphia; and New York, many graduates pursue positions in nearby metropolitan areas, as well as positions in state and local government in the region and in the nation. Several recent graduates have been successful in the highly competitive federal Presidential Management Fellowship Program.
Location	Located midway between Philadelphia and Baltimore, the main campus of the University of Delaware is in Newark, conveniently near New York City; Washington, D.C.; and the seashore. A community of 30,000, with a vibrant Main Street of coffeehouses, restaurants, and small shops, Newark is about 14 miles from Wilmington, Delaware's largest city.
The University	The University is a comprehensive land-, sea-, space-, and urban-grant institution of higher education with an enrollment of 3,448 graduate students in 2008–09. The University offers seventy-nine programs leading to a master's degree and thirty-nine programs leading to a doctoral degree. In 2008, the University awarded 208 doctoral degrees and 695 master's degrees.
Applying	The School welcomes informal inquiries. Students seeking financial aid or admission to the Ph.D. program should apply by February 1. For the master's programs, candidates must have an undergraduate GPA above 3.0 (on a 4.0 scale). Admission to the Ph.D. program requires a master's degree with at least a 3.5 GPA. A combined GRE score above 1000 on the math and verbal portions of the exam is normally expected. Complete applications contain three letters of recommendation, a personal statement of academic and career objectives (for the Ph.D., a 1,000-word statement of the applicant's research interest as well), and academic transcripts. For nonnative speakers of English, a demonstrated proficiency in English is required, with a TOEFL score of at least 550 (213 on the computer-based test).
Correspondence and Information	School of Urban Affairs and Public Policy Admissions University of Delaware Newark, Delaware 19716-7310 Phone: 302-831-1687 Fax: 302-831-3296 E-mail: suapp@udel.edu Web site: http://www.udel.edu/suapp

University of Delaware

THE FACULTY AND THEIR RESEARCH

At the core of the School of Urban Affairs and Public Policy are the dedicated faculty members, who are challenging teachers, seasoned researchers, and experienced practitioners. With interdisciplinary backgrounds as skilled executives, managers, and community leaders, they bring practical experience to the classroom and successfully blend a solid academic base with stimulating practical experience.

David L. Ames, Professor and Director, Center for Historic Architecture and Design; Ph.D., Clark, 1969; ACIP. Historic preservation, urban geography, urban and regional planning.

Maria P. Aristigueta, Professor; Director, School of Urban Affairs and Public Policy; and Senior Policy Fellow, Institute for Public Administration; D.P.A., USC, 1997. Administrative behavior, performance management, policy analysis, strategic management.

Deborah A. Auger, Associate Professor and Policy Fellow, Center for Community Research and Service; Ph.D., MIT, 1988. Public policy and administration, nonprofit management, state and local government, U.S. social policy.

John M. Byrne, Professor and Director, Center for Energy and Environmental Policy; Ph.D., Delaware, 1980. Technology and environment, environmental justice, political economy, sustainable development.

Karen A. Curtis, Associate Professor and Policy Scientist, Center for Community Research and Service; Ph.D., Temple, 1984. Nonprofit leadership and management, applied research and public policy analysis, qualitative methods, social and economic opportunity.

Kathryn G. Denhardt, Professor and Policy Scientist, Center for Community Research and Service; Ph.D., Kansas, 1984. Collaborative decision making and conflict resolution, human resources management, ethics in public service.

Robert B. Denhardt, Visiting Scholar; Ph.D., Kentucky, 1968. Public sector management, strategic planning and public productivity.

Bernard L. Dworsky, Assistant Professor and Policy Scientist, Institute for Public Administration; M.A., Delaware, 1971. Water resources management, planning.

James P. Flynn, Assistant Professor; Director, M.P.A. Program; and Associate Policy Scientist, Institute for Public Administration; Ed.D., Delaware, 1998. Personnel administration, quality improvement initiatives, educational governance, legislative management; professional development, human resources management.

Edward J. Freel, Instructor and Policy Scientist, Institute for Public Administration; M.Ed., Delaware, 1975. Civic education, learning initiatives, public administration.

Audrey L. Helfman, Associate Professor and Interim Director, Leadership Program; Ph.D., Delaware, 1993. Personnel administration, organizational theory, legislative management, public fiscal analysis, data systems, analytic methods.

Raheemah Jabbar-Bey, Assistant Professor and Assistant Policy Specialist, Center for Community Research and Service; M.A., New Hampshire, 1996. Community and economic development planning, organizational capacity building of nonprofits, urban policy analysis.

Eric D. Jacobson, Associate Professor and Assistant Director, Institute for Public Administration; M.P.A., Delaware, 1981. Public economics, health policy, employee compensation and benefits, tourism development and research, analytical methods.

Janet B. Johnson, Associate Professor, Department of Political Science and International Relations and Senior Research Associate, Center for Energy and Environmental Policy; Ph.D., Cornell, 1978. Subnational politics, environmental policy, research methods, public policy analysis.

Jonathan Justice, Associate Professor; Ph.D., Rutgers, 2003. Public financial management, nongovernmental public administration, urban policy and administration.

Gerald Kauffman, Instructor and Director, Water Resources Agency; M.P.A., Delaware, 2003. Watershed policy, planning, and management; water resources government and finance; water resources engineering; hydrology and hydraulics.

Jerome R. Lewis, Associate Professor and Director, Institute for Public Administration; Ph.D., NYU, 1968. Public administration, personnel management, urban planning, political leadership.

John G. McNutt, Professor and Policy Fellow, Center for Community Research and Service; Ph.D., Tennessee, 1991. Technology, nonprofit management, advocacy and government relations, community organization and planning.

Anthony E. Middlebrooks, Assistant Professor; Ph.D., Wisconsin, 1999. Leadership formation and development, creativity and leadership, service and social justice, research methods.

James L. Morrison, Professor; Ed.D., Temple, 1971. Telecommunications and consumer policy, consumer environmental issues, consumer protection.

Audrey J. Noble, Assistant Professor and Director, Public Policy Program; Ph.D., Arizona State, 1994. Qualitative research and evaluation.

Edward J. O'Donnell, Instructor and Senior Policy Advisor, Institute for Public Administration; M.Ed., West Chester, 1975. Growth management, transportation/infrastructure planning, comprehensive planning.

Marian Lief Palley, Professor, Department of Political Science and International Relations; Ph.D., NYU, 1966. American politics and public policy, intergovernmental relations, health and welfare policy.

Steven W. Peuquet, Associate Professor and Director, Center for Community Research and Service; Ph.D., Pennsylvania, 1996. Strategic planning, housing, homelessness, electronic community networks, public policy analysis and evaluation.

Jeffrey A. Raffel, Charles P. Messick Professor of Public Administration and Faculty Associate, Institute for Public Administration; Ph.D., MIT, 1972. Educational policy, policy analysis, urban management.

Edward C. Ratledge, Associate Professor and Director, Center for Applied Demography and Survey Research; M.A., Delaware, 1972. Management information systems, econometrics, criminal justice systems.

Daniel Rich, Professor; Ph.D., MIT, 1972. Public policy and public management.

Breck Robinson, Associate Professor and Associate Professor, Institute for Public Administration; Ph.D., Tennessee, 1994. Financial institutions, public policy, real estate finance.

Rebecca Sheppard, Assistant Professor and Associate Director, Center of Historic Architecture and Design; Ph.D. Delaware, 2009. Historic preservation planning, history of rural landscapes and the built environment, landscape preservation.

Paul L. Solano, Associate Professor; Ph.D., Maryland, 1978. Financial administration and public finance, political economy, health economics.

Karen F. Stein, Associate Professor; Ph.D., Delaware, 1984. Domestic elder abuse and neglect, leadership studies, consumer and family economic policy analysis.

Richard T. Sylves, Professor, Department of Political Science and International Relations, and Fellow, Center for Energy and Environmental Policy; Ph.D., Illinois at Urbana-Champaign, 1977. Energy policy, disaster policy.

Douglas F. Tuttle, Instructor; Internship Coordinator; and Policy Scientist, Institute for Public Administration; M.P.A., Delaware, 1990. State and local government personnel development, strategic planning, emergency service planning and public service quality assessment.

Young-Doo Wang, Professor and Associate Director, Center for Energy and Environmental Policy; Ph.D., Delaware, 1980. Energy and water conservation policy, economic analysis of alternative energy options, econometric applications.

Leland Ware, Louis L. Redding Chair for the Study of Law and Public Policy; J.D., Boston College, 1973. Employment discrimination law, civil rights law, civil procedure.

Robert Warren, Professor and Senior Research Associate, Institute for Public Administration; Ph.D., UCLA, 1964. Urban and regional government, telecommunications policy, urban planning and development, cultural theory.

Margaret G. Wilder, Professor; Ph.D., Michigan, 1983. Community development policy and organizations; economic development policy and planning; housing problems and policy; race, gender, and economic mobility.

Devona E. G. Williams, Assistant Professor; Ph.D., Delaware, 1992. Entrepreneurship, small business growth and development, women in leadership, community development.

Danilo Yanich, Associate Professor; Director, Urban Affairs and Public Policy Program; and Associate Policy Scientist, Center for Community Research and Service; Ph.D., Delaware, 1980. Criminal justice policy, media and public policy, international comparative governance.

UNIVERSITY OF PENNSYLVANIA

Fels Institute of Government
Master of Governmental Administration Program

Programs of Study

The Fels Institute of Government was founded in 1937 by Philadelphia industrialist Samuel Fels and has the distinction of being one of the oldest public management programs in the country. Over the course of its 72 year history, Fels has provided students with the combination of management and political skills necessary for successful public service careers. A broad-based education prepares students to move within and between government agencies, nonprofit organizations, and private firms engaging in public sector work.

Fels offers a Master of Governmental Administration (M.G.A.) that is comparable to a Master of Public Administration. It also offers five-course graduate-level certificates in economic development and growth, nonprofit administration, politics, and public finance. The certificates can be obtained either as a concentration within the M.G.A. or as a stand-alone diploma.

The twelve-course M.G.A. is offered in full-time and part-time formats and comprises eight core and four elective courses. Full-time students take the eight core courses during the weekdays, part-time executive students take the eight core courses on Saturdays, and students in both formats commingle in the four electives, which are available on weekdays, weeknights, and Saturdays.

Students have the option of taking their elective courses at Fels or other graduate programs within the University of Pennsylvania. Students can also seek approval to transfer, as electives, up to four courses taken in graduate programs outside of Penn before, during, or after their time in the M.G.A. program. In addition to the certificates, Fels students often create informal concentrations (for example, city planning, education management, environmental studies, transportation) through careful selection of their courses. Other students cover a broader range of subject matter in their electives.

The standard full-time course sequence includes three courses per semester, taken over two academic years with summers off, although some students accelerate the program by taking four courses per semester. Executive students take two courses per semester and complete the program in two calendar years, including summers. Some executive students, however, reduce their course load in certain semesters in order to balance the program with their other substantial responsibilities.

Fels offers the possibility of earning dual graduate degrees in the following areas: the M.G.A./J.D. with Penn Law School, the M.G.A./ M.S.Ed. with the Graduate School of Education, the M.G.A./M.S.W. or M.G.A/M.S.S.P. with the School of Social Policy and Practice, the M.G.A./M.C.P. with City Planning Program/School of Design, the M.G.A./M.B.E. with the Bioethics Program, the M.G.A./M.E.S. with the Environmental Studies Program, and the M.G.A./M.S.E. with the School of Engineering. Dual-degree students are granted some flexibility in their course sequencing as needed. This enables students coming into the program with another graduate degree to complete the M.G.A. in just two semesters or two semesters plus a summer semester.

Fels offers graduate-level certificates in the following four areas of traditional strength: Economic Development and Growth, Nonprofit Administration, Politics, and Public Finance. The certificates are designed to prepare students for a wide range of existing influential positions within these fields. They can be obtained by M.G.A. students without taking any additional courses beyond their twelve-course M.G.A. program.

Research Facilities

The Fels Institute occupies the home of the late industrialist and philanthropist, Samuel S. Fels. Built in 1937, the Fels residence has been adapted for academic use in a way that maintains its original character. The Institute offers wireless computer access and is equipped with two small computer labs that provide online access to a range of information resources, including the extensive electronic holdings of the Penn library. In addition, Fels students have access to the vast resources offered by the University of Pennsylvania.

Financial Aid

Students in the M.G.A. program rely upon a combination of funding sources to finance their education at Fels. Tuition support is available to full-time and executive M.G.A. students on a merit basis. During the past two years, Fels has awarded financial aid to every full-time student who has requested it, with awards ranging from $4000 to full tuition per year. The average award represented 25 percent of tuition. In addition, most full-time students work on internships that pay from $10 to $20 per hour. Additional support comes from Federal Stafford Student Loans, Federal Perkins Loans, and University work-study opportunities.

Nearly all executive students work in full-time positions, and some of them receive full or partial support from their employers. Fels also works with executive students to help them advance in their careers while they are students at Fels.

Cost of Study

The 2009–10 total tuition cost of the twelve-course M.G.A. is $54,996 with additional fees and insurance of $8228 paid over the two-year program period. Part-time study is $9684 for a two-course semester.

Living and Housing Costs

Housing on and off campus is readily available in the University area as well as elsewhere in the city. The cost of living in Philadelphia tends to be lower than other major U.S. cities, and many graduate students live off campus. Housing is available at widely varying rates that begin at approximately $6000 for nine months.

Student Group

The Fels M.G.A. currently enrolls about 130 students who are evenly divided between the full-time and part-time formats. Fels recruits approximately 35 new students per year to each of the formats. Full-time students include recent college graduates as well as students with varied postgraduate experience. Although many students come to Fels from positions in politics, nonprofits, and government agencies, others use the Fels program as a bridge from other fields, including law and business, to the public service field.

The students represent a diverse group of people by age, race, gender, politics, nationality, and geography. The program attracts students from across the United States and from abroad.

Student Outcomes

Currently, approximately 40 percent of graduates are employed in government, 30 percent in the nonprofit sector, and 30 percent in the private sector, with an emphasis on firms that service the public sector. Fels alumni hold political jobs, including public office, public finance positions in both the public and private sectors, and leadership positions at all levels of government and in more than 100 nonprofit organizations. They also do work with lobbying and consulting firms that support the public sector. Over time, many Fels graduates pursue their public-service careers by moving easily between the public, private, and nonprofit sectors.

Location

The Fels Institute is located just west of Center City Philadelphia, in the northwest corner of the Penn campus at the intersection of Walnut and 39th Streets. Fels is a short walk to trolley, subway, and intercity train lines that provide easy access to downtown; the airport; the New Jersey shore; Harrisburg; Washington, D.C.; New York City; and the rest of the Northeast corridor. Nearby 30th Street station, for example, offers rail service that reaches the airport in 20 minutes, New York City in just over an hour, and Washington, D.C., in just over 2 hours.

The University

The University was founded in 1740 by Benjamin Franklin. A member of the Ivy League and one of the world's leading universities, Penn is renowned for its graduate schools, faculty, research centers, and institutes. Conveniently situated on a compact and attractive campus, Penn offers an abundance of multidisciplinary and cross-school educational programs with exceptional opportunities for individually tailored graduate education. It also offers students all the amenities of a 20,000 student university.

Applying

Inquiries should be made directly to the Fels Institute. Full-time students are admitted primarily for the fall semester, with a few students admitted for the spring semester if space permits. In order to receive full financial aid consideration, full-time applicants should apply by January 15. Executive students are admitted each term and should apply by July 1 for the fall term; by November 1 for the spring term; and by March 1 for the summer term.

Correspondence and Information

Admissions Office
Fels Institute of Government
University of Pennsylvania
3814 Walnut Street
Philadelphia, Pennsylvania 19104-6197
Phone: 215-746-6684
Fax: 215-898-6238
E-mail: felsmga@sas.upenn.edu
Web site: http://www.fels.upenn.edu

University of Pennsylvania

THE FACULTY

Administration and Faculty

Leigh Botwinik, Director of Full-Time Students, Fels Institute of Government.

Allison Brummel, Director of Research and Consulting, Fels Institute of Government.

John J. Mulhern, Director of Professional Education, Fels Institute of Government; Adjunct Associate Professor of Classical Studies and Government Administration.

David Thornburgh, Executive Director, Fels Institute of Government.

Faculty

Arthur C. Benedict, Principal, Benedict Associates.

Nancy Burd, President, The Burd Group; former Vice President of Grantmaking, The Philadelphia Foundation.

Cary Coglianese, Edward B. Shils Professor of Law and Professor of Political Science, University of Pennsylvania.

Joseph Conti, CEO, Pennsylvania State Liquor Control Board; Former State Senator, Commonwealth of Pennsylvania.

John DiIulio, Frederic Fox Leadership Professor and Faculty Director and Co-Chair of the Director's Advisory Group, Robert A. Fox Leadership Program, University of Pennsylvania.

David Eisenhower, Senior Research Administrator and Director of the Institute for Public Service, Annenberg School for Communication, University of Pennsylvania.

Vincent Galko, Secretary's Regional Representative, U.S. Department of Education.

Steven C. Genyk, Managing Director, Janney Montgomery Scott LLC.

E. Michael Golda, Chief Technologist, Machinery Research and Acoustics Silencing Division, Naval Sea Systems Command, Philadelphia.

Gloria Guard, President, People's Emergency Center.

Ira Harkavy, Associate Vice President and founding Director, Center for Community Partnerships, University of Pennsylvania.

James A. Hartling, Founding Partner, Urban Partners.

John Hawkins, Senior Lobbyist, Wojdak and Associates.

John Keene, Professor of City and Regional Planning, University of Pennsylvania.

James F. Kenney, Councilman at Large, City of Philadelphia.

John Kromer, Former Director, Office of Housing and Community Development, City of Philadelphia.

Janice F. Madden, Professor of Regional Science, Sociology, Urban Studies, and Real Estate, University of Pennsylvania.

Marjorie Margolies, CEO, Women's Campaign International; former Member of Congress.

Deirdre Martinez, Director, Fels Public Policy Internship Program.

Michael Masch, Chief Business Officer, School District of Philadelphia; former Secretary of the Budget, Commonwealth of Pennsylvania.

Thomas M. McKenna, Fels Senior Lecturer; former Executive Director, Big Brothers Big Sisters of America.

Stephen P. Mullin, Senior Vice President, Econsult Corporation.

Michael Nadol, Managing Director, Public Financial Management.

Jack H. Nagel, Professor of Political Science, University of Pennsylvania.

Eric Costello Neiderman, Manager, Cargo Security Research and Development, Transportation Security Administration, Department of Homeland Security.

Robert A. Nixon, Director of Government Affairs, New Jersey State Policemen's Benevolent Association.

Folasade Olanipekun-Lewis, Deputy Director for Finance and Administration, Commerce Department, City of Philadelphia.

Robert Pearson, Senior Fellow, Fels Institute of Government.

Gerald Perrins, Regional Economist, U.S. Bureau of Labor Statistics.

Samuel H. Preston, Frederick J. Warren Professor of Demography, University of Pennsylvania.

Hon. Edward G. Rendell, Governor of the Commonwealth of Pennsylvania.

Harvey Rubin, Director, Institute for Strategic Threat Analysis and Response; Professor of Medicine, Microbiology, and Computer Science, University of Pennsylvania.

Trudy Rubin, Foreign Affairs Columnist, *The Philadelphia Inquirer.*

Ramin Sedehi, Vice Dean of Finance and Administration, School of Arts and Sciences, University of Pennsylvania.

Wayne A. Smith, President and CEO, Delaware Healthcare Association; former House Majority Leader, Delaware General Assembly.

Kathryn Dunn Tempas, Director, University of Pennsylvania's Washington Semester Program; Adjunct Associate Professor of Political Science and Non-resident Fellow at the Brookings Institution.

Joseph P. Tierney, Executive Director, Robert A. Fox Leadership Program, University of Pennsylvania.

Eric J. Weinberg, Managing Director, Kroll Security Group.

UNIVERSITY OF PITTSBURGH

Graduate School of Public and International Affairs

Programs of Study

The Graduate School of Public and International Affairs (GSPIA) at the University of Pittsburgh offers professional education for individuals who wish to pursue careers as managers, planners, and policy analysts primarily in the public sector and nonprofit and nongovernmental organizations in the U.S. and abroad. GSPIA offers the following degrees:

The 48-credit Master of International Development (M.I.D.) degree offers majors in nongovernmental organizations and civil society, developmental planning and environmental sustainability, and human security.

The 48-credit Master of Public Administration (M.P.A.) degree offers majors in public and nonprofit management, policy research and analysis, and urban and regional affairs. The National Association of Schools of Public Affairs and Administration (NASPAA) accredits the M.P.A. degree.

The 48-credit Master of Public and International Affairs (M.P.I.A.) degree offers majors in global political economy, security and intelligence studies, and human security. GSPIA is a founding member of the Association of Professional Schools of International Affairs (ASPIA).

The 30-credit Master of Public Policy and Management (M.P.P.M.) degree is for experienced professionals who want to develop analytic tools and expand their managerial capabilities.

The 78-credit Ph.D. prepares students for careers in teaching, research, and consulting in development policy, foreign and security policy, international political economy, public administration, and public policy. An earned master's degree is preferred, and students may be awarded up to 30 credits of advanced standing.

Joint-degree programs are offered with the Schools of Law (J.D.), Business (M.B.A.), Information Science (M.S.I.S.), Public Health (M.P.H.), and Social Work (M.S.W.).

Research Facilities

The School's library has more than 139,200 books and other documents covering all of its fields. The University library system has 4.7 million volumes. GSPIA has its own state-of-the-art computer classrooms and an online data link to the University computer center. Students are provided research opportunities through GSPIA's Ridgway Center for International Security Studies, the Ford Institute for Human Security, the Johnson Institute for Responsible Leadership, the Non-Profit Clinic, and the Interactive, Intelligent Spatial Information System and through the University Center for International Studies, the University Center for Social and Urban Research, and faculty-sponsored research projects.

Financial Aid

Full or partial tuition scholarships, graduate assistantships, and student employment are awarded annually on a competitive basis. To be considered for funding, completed applications for admission must be submitted on or before February 1. The deadline for international applicants is January 15.

Cost of Study

The tuition for 2009–10 for full-time Pennsylvania residents is $8201 per term and $14,347 per term for nonresidents in the fall and spring. Additional fees are $345 per term. Tuition in the summer is based on the per-credit rate, which is $665 per credit for residents and $1175 for nonresidents. Summer fees are prorated.

Living and Housing Costs

Single students should budget approximately $13,000 for moderate living expenses, exclusive of tuition. Housing for graduate students is available off campus.

Student Group

Of the approximately 450 students enrolled at any one time, about 20 percent are from other countries, 35 percent are from other parts of the U.S., 55 percent are women, and 15 percent are members of U.S. minority groups.

Location

The University is in Oakland, the cultural, educational, and medical center of Pittsburgh. It is within walking distance of art galleries, museums, and other cultural and athletic facilities. The city center is about 2 miles away.

The University and The School

The University of Pittsburgh is a state-related institution with a respected international stature as a major research university. It enrolls 34,000 students, including 9,000 in graduate and professional programs. GSPIA students take courses in other departments and professional schools in the University and cross-register for courses at Carnegie Mellon and other area schools. The University Center for International Studies (UCIS) offers graduate area studies certificates in African studies, Asian studies, Latin American studies, West European studies, Russian and East European studies, and global studies.

Applying

GSPIA assesses applicants' academic background, professional experiences, and career objectives. While there are no required prerequisite courses, applicants are strongly encouraged to have taken courses in microeconomics, macroeconomics, statistics, and computer applications for spreadsheet, databases, statistical analysis, and presentations. GRE General Test scores are required for admission for doctoral and master's applicants. For students who are seeking financial aid, the application deadline for the fall term is February 1 (January 15 for international applicants). The deadline for the spring term is November 1 for U.S. citizens and permanent residents and August 1 for international applicants. Online application is available on the GSPIA Web site. The application fee is $50.

Correspondence and Information

Office of Student Services
Graduate School of Public and International Affairs
University of Pittsburgh
Pittsburgh, Pennsylvania 15260
Phone: 412-648-7640
Fax: 412-648-7641
E-mail: gspia@pitt.edu
Web site: http://www.gspia.pitt.edu

University of Pittsburgh

THE FACULTY AND THEIR RESEARCH

Carolyn Ban, Professor; Ph.D., Stanford, 1975. Human resources management, public management, comparative administrative reform, reinventing government, program evaluation, ethics.

Michael J. Brenner, Professor; Ph.D., Berkeley, 1968. American foreign policy, international relations theory, international political economy, national security, policy analysis and evaluation.

Louise K. Comfort, Professor and Director of the Interactive, Intelligent Spatial Information System; Ph.D., Yale, 1975. Organizational management, theory and behavior, policy analysis, program implementation and innovation, research methodology and modeling, information technology and public policy.

Phyllis D. Coontz, Associate Professor; Ph.D., Colorado, 1978. Social policy, research methodology, crime, elite professions.

Sabina E. Deitrick, Associate Professor, Co-Director of the Urban and Regional Analysis Program, University Center for Social and Urban Research, and Co-Director of Community Outreach Partnership Center; Ph.D., Berkeley, 1990. Regional planning, economic and community development, industrial geography.

George William Dougherty Jr., Assistant Professor and Coordinator of the Undergraduate Public Service Program; Ph.D., Georgia, 2000. Education policy, performance measurement, public law, transportation policy.

William N. Dunn, Professor; Ph.D., Claremont, 1969. Policy analysis and program evaluation, research methodology, knowledge utilization and public policy.

Muge Kokten Finkel, Assistant Professor; Ph.D., Virginia, 2002. Comparative social policy in developed and developing countries, poverty and economic development, gender and development, Japanese politics.

Angela Williams Foster, Assistant Professor; Ph.D., Carnegie Mellon, 2000. Quantitative methods, econometrics, multivariate analysis, research methods and policy analysis, housing policy, racial disparities in home ownership using hierarchical linear models, fair housing.

Shanti Gamper-Rabindran, Assistant Professor; Ph.D., MIT, 2001. Environment, health and development economics/policy methods, economics, Geographical Information Systems (GIS), program evaluation.

Dennis M. Gormley, Senior Lecturer; M.A., Connecticut, 1966. Security and nonproliferation policy issues, technology and defense studies.

Kevin P. Kearns, Professor and Director of the Johnson Institute for Responsible Leadership; Ph.D., Pittsburgh, 1983. Strategic management, nonprofit management, public administration.

John T. S. Keller, Professor and Dean; Ph.D., Harvard, 1978. Comparative public policy, EU politics, transatlantic relations, American foreign policy.

William W. Keller, Posvar Professor of International Studies and Director of the Ridgway Center for International Security Studies; Ph.D., Cornell, 1986. National security.

Jerome B. McKinney, Professor; Ph.D., Missouri, 1969. Financial management, public-sector accounting, public budgeting, public management, economics.

John Mendeloff, Professor; Ph.D., Berkeley, 1977. Policy analysis, health policy, government regulation of risk.

David Y. Miller, Associate Professor and Associate Dean; Ph.D., Pittsburgh, 1988. Local government, political culture, regional governance systems, municipal budgeting.

Clyde E. Mitchell-Weaver, Associate Professor; Ph.D., UCLA, 1982. Economic development, sectoral and spatial planning, regional trading blocs, international organization, developing countries.

Lisa S. Nelson, Assistant Professor; Ph.D., Wisconsin, 1998. Law and politics, criminal justice, constitutional law, jurisprudence, American judicial process, political theory, American politics and institutions.

Paul J. Nelson, Assistant Professor; Ph.D., Wisconsin, 1991. Political economy and organizational analysis of international organizations, military spending and quality of life, contract farming in Africa, popular politics of land distribution in Guatemala, participant action research methods.

Janne Nolan, Professor; Ph.D., Tufts. International security and foreign policy.

Louis A. Picard, Professor; Ph.D., Wisconsin, 1977. Development management and governance; political development; local-level politics; manpower planning; politics of rural development; Eastern, Southern, and West Africa; Horn of Africa; Latin America and Caribbean.

Nita Rudra, Assistant Professor; Ph.D., USC, 2000. International political economy, politics of welfare in developing countries.

Taylor Seybolt, Assistant Professor; Ph.D., MIT, 1999. Humanitarian intervention, genocide, military intervention and peace operations, ethnic conflict and civil war, conflict mediation and resolution, post-conflict peace-building, Nigeria, Sudan.

Martin Staniland, Professor; Ph.D., Cambridge, 1983. International political economy, economic policy in the European Union, commercial aviation and trade in services, negotiation and conflict resolution.

Nuno S. Themudo, Assistant Professor; Ph.D., London School of Economics, 2003. NGO management and development policy, civil society and public affairs, international institutions and governance, environmental management.

Lee S. Weinberg, Associate Professor; Ph.D., 1973, J.D., 1976, Pittsburgh. Criminal law and procedure, constitutional law, law and politics, psychiatry and law, legal studies, public policy in law enforcement.

Harvey L. White, Associate Professor; Ph.D., North Carolina, 1985. Financial administration, urban administration, intergovernmental relations and finance, environmental management, sustainable development, environmental justice, computer applications and quantitative methods.

Phil Williams, Professor; Ph.D., Southampton, 1988. Strategic studies, transnational organized crime, drug trafficking, foreign policy analysis, international relations.

Section 26
Social Sciences

This section contains a directory of institutions offering graduate work in social sciences, followed by an in-depth entry submitted by an institution that chose to prepare a detailed program description. Additional information about programs listed in the directory but not augmented by an in-depth entry may be obtained by writing directly to the dean of a graduate school or chair of a department at the address given in the directory.

For programs offering related work, see also in this book *Area and Cultural Studies, Communication and Media, Criminology and Forensics, Economics, Geography, Family and Consumer Sciences, Political Science and International Affairs, Psychology and Counseling,* and *Sociology, Anthropology, and Archaeology.*

CONTENTS

Program Directory

Social Sciences   1246

Close-Ups

The New School: A University   1251

See also:

Central European University—Social Sciences and
    Humanities   349

Social Sciences

Arizona State University, Graduate College, College of Liberal Arts and Sciences, Division of Social Sciences, Tempe, AZ 85287. Offers MA, MAS, MS, PhD, PhD/JD.

Arkansas Tech University, Graduate School, School of Liberal and Fine Arts, Russellville, AR 72801. Offers communication (MLA); English (M Ed, MA); fine arts (MLA); history (MA); multi-media journalism (MA); social science (MLA); social studies (M Ed); Spanish (MA, MLA); teaching English as a second language (MA, MLA). Part-time programs available. *Students:* 40 full-time (31 women), 81 part-time (60 women); includes 10 minority (3 African Americans, 2 American Indian/Alaska Native, 2 Asian Americans or Pacific Islanders, 3 Hispanic Americans), 19 international. Average age 33. In 2008, 70 master's awarded. *Degree requirements:* For master's, project. *Entrance requirements:* For master's, GRE General Test or MAT. Additional exam requirements/recommendations for international students: Required—TOEFL (minimum score 500 paper-based; 173 computer-based; 61 iBT). *Application deadline:* For fall admission, 3/1 priority date for domestic students, 5/1 priority date for international students; for winter admission, 10/1 priority date for international students; for spring admission, 10/1 priority date for domestic and international students. Applications are processed on a rolling basis. Application fee: $0 ($30 for international students). Electronic applications accepted. *Expenses:* Tuition, state resident: full-time $1575; part-time $175 per credit hour. Tuition, nonresident: full-time $3150; part-time $350 per credit hour. Tuition and fees vary according to course load. *Financial support:* In 2008–09, teaching assistantships with full tuition reimbursements (averaging $4,000 per year); career-related internships or fieldwork, Federal Work-Study, scholarships/grants, health care benefits, and unspecified assistantships also available. Support available to part-time students. Financial award application deadline: 4/15; financial award applicants required to submit FAFSA. *Unit head:* Dr. Georgena Duncan, Dean, 479-968-0266, Fax: 479-968-0275, E-mail: georgena.duncan@atu.edu. *Application contact:* Dr. Eldon G. Clary, Dean of Graduate School, 479-968-0398, Fax: 479-964-0542, E-mail: graduate.school@atu.edu.

Ball State University, Graduate School, College of Sciences and Humanities, Program in Social Sciences, Muncie, IN 47306-1099. Offers MA.

California Institute of Technology, Division of the Humanities and Social Sciences, Social Science Program, Pasadena, CA 91125-0001. Offers economics (PhD); political science (PhD); social science (MS). Terminal master's awarded for partial completion of doctoral program. *Degree requirements:* For doctorate, thesis/dissertation. *Entrance requirements:* For doctorate, GRE General Test. Electronic applications accepted. *Faculty research:* Individual and group decision making, design of political and economic institutions, experimental social science, public policy, quantitative history.

California State University, Chico, Graduate School, College of Behavioral and Social Sciences, Social Science Program, Chico, CA 95929-0445. Offers social science (MA); social science education (MA). *Degree requirements:* For master's, thesis or alternative. *Entrance requirements:* For master's, GRE General Test or MAT, statement of purpose. Additional exam requirements/recommendations for international students: Required—TOEFL (minimum score 550 paper-based; 213 computer-based; 80 iBT), IELTS (minimum score 6.5). Electronic applications accepted.

California State University, San Bernardino, Graduate Studies, College of Social and Behavioral Sciences, Program in Social Sciences, San Bernardino, CA 92407-2397. Offers MA. *Faculty:* 6 full-time (0 women), 2 part-time/adjunct (0 women). *Students:* 10 full-time (6 women), 15 part-time (5 women); includes 7 minority (4 African Americans, 3 Hispanic Americans), 3 international. Average age 34. 17 applicants, 47% accepted, 6 enrolled. In 2008, 4 master's awarded. *Degree requirements:* For master's, comprehensive exam or thesis. *Entrance requirements:* For master's, Graduate Entrance Writing Exam, minimum GPA of 3.5 in major, 2.5 overall. *Application deadline:* For fall admission, 8/31 priority date for domestic students. Application fee: $55. *Expenses:* Tuition, area resident: Full-time $1252; part-time $726 per quarter. Required fees: $334 per quarter. Tuition and fees vary according to degree level and student level. *Financial support:* Fellowships, research assistantships, teaching assistantships, career-related internships or fieldwork, Federal Work-Study, and institutionally sponsored loans available. Financial award application deadline: 5/1. *Unit head:* Dr. Jamal Nassar, Dean, 909-537-7500, Fax: 909-537-7645, E-mail: jnassar@csusb.edu. *Application contact:* Olivia Rosas, Director of Admissions, 909-537-7577, Fax: 909-537-7034, E-mail: orosas@csusb.edu.

California University of Pennsylvania, School of Graduate Studies and Research, College of Liberal Arts, Department of Sociology/Criminal Justice, California, PA 15419-1394. Offers social science—criminal justice (MA). Part-time and evening/weekend programs available. *Degree requirements:* For master's, comprehensive exam, thesis optional. *Entrance requirements:* For master's, MAT, minimum GPA of 3.0. Additional exam requirements/recommendations for international students: Required—TOEFL (minimum score 550 paper-based; 213 computer-based; 80 iBT). Electronic applications accepted. *Faculty research:* Ethics and law, ethics in police practice, law and morality, police policy, St. Thomas Aquinas and crime.

Campbellsville University, College of Arts and Sciences, Campbellsville, KY 42718-2799. Offers social science (MA). Part-time programs available. *Degree requirements:* For master's, comprehensive exam. *Entrance requirements:* For master's, GRE General Test, LSAT, minimum GPA of 2.9. Electronic applications accepted. *Expenses:* Tuition: Full-time $6570; part-time $365 per credit hour. Required fees: $60 per term.

Carnegie Mellon University, College of Humanities and Social Sciences, Department of Social and Decision Sciences, Pittsburgh, PA 15213-3891. Offers behavioral decision research (PhD); behavioral decision research and psychology (PhD); social and decision science (PhD); strategy, entrepeneurship, and technological change (PhD). Terminal master's awarded for partial completion of doctoral program. *Degree requirements:* For doctorate, comprehensive exam, thesis/dissertation, research paper. *Entrance requirements:* For doctorate, GRE General Test. Additional exam requirements/recommendations for international students: Required—TOEFL. Electronic applications accepted. *Faculty research:* Organization theory, political science, sociology, technology studies.

Central European University, Graduate Studies, School of Social Sciences and Humanities, Budapest, Hungary. Offers economics (MA, PhD); gender studies (MA, PhD); international relations and European studies (MA, PhD); mathematics and its applications (MS, PhD); medieval studies (MA, PhD); nationalism studies (MA, PhD); philosophy (MA, PhD); political science (MA, PhD); public policy (MA, PhD); sociology and social anthropology (MA, PhD). Terminal master's awarded for partial completion of doctoral program. *Degree requirements:* For master's, one foreign language, thesis; for doctorate, one foreign language, comprehensive exam, thesis/dissertation. *Entrance requirements:* For master's, CEU subject tests, interview; for doctorate, GRE, CEU subject test, interview. Additional exam requirements/recommendations for international students: Required—TOEFL (minimum score 570 paper-based; 230 computer-based). Electronic applications accepted. *Faculty research:* Civil society, fiscal decentralization, party politics, political philosophy (especially Liberalism, theory of Democracy).

See Close-Up on page 349.

The Citadel, The Military College of South Carolina, Citadel Graduate College, Department of Political Science and Criminal Justice, Charleston, SC 29409. Offers social science (MA). Part-time and evening/weekend programs available. *Faculty:* 3 full-time (1 woman). *Students:* 7 full-time (4 women), 16 part-time (8 women); includes 5 minority (4 African Americans, 1 Hispanic American), 1 international. Average age 33. In 2008, 14 master's awarded. *Entrance requirements:* For master's, GRE (minimum 900) or MAT (minimum 400). Additional exam requirements/recommendations for international students: Required—TOEFL (minimum score 550 paper-based; 213 computer-based). *Application deadline:* Applications are processed on a rolling basis. Application fee: $30. Electronic applications accepted. *Expenses:* Tuition, state resident: full-time $5850; part-time $325 per credit hour. Tuition, nonresident: full-time $9612; part-time $534 per credit hour. Required fees: $15 per semester. *Financial support:* Health care benefits and unspecified assistantships available. Support available to part-time students. Financial award application deadline: 7/1; financial award applicants required to submit FAFSA. *Unit head:* Dr. Gardel M. Feurtado, Department Head, 843-953-2037, Fax: 843-953-5066, E-mail: gardel.feurtado@citadel.edu. *Application contact:* Dr. Terry M. Mays, Associate Professor, 843-953-5072, Fax: 843-953-5069, E-mail: terry.mays@citadel.edu.

College of the Humanities and Sciences, Harrison Middleton University, Graduate Program, Tempe, AZ 85282. Offers education (MA, Ed D); humanities (MA); imaginative literature (MA); interdisciplinary studies (DA); jurisprudence (MA); natural science (MA); philosophy and religion (MA); social science (MA). Part-time and evening/weekend programs available. Postbaccalaureate distance learning degree programs offered (no on-campus study). Electronic applications accepted.

Columbia University, Graduate School of Arts and Sciences, Program in Quantitative Methods in the Social Sciences, New York, NY 10027. Offers MA. Part-time programs available.

Eastern Michigan University, Graduate School, College of Arts and Sciences, Department of History and Philosophy, Program in Social Science, Ypsilanti, MI 48197. Offers social science (MA, Graduate Certificate); social science and American culture (MLS). Part-time and evening/weekend programs available. Postbaccalaureate distance learning degree programs offered (minimal on-campus study). *Degree requirements:* For master's, thesis optional. *Entrance requirements:* Additional exam requirements/recommendations for international students: Required—TOEFL.

Edinboro University of Pennsylvania, Graduate Studies and Research, School of Liberal Arts, Department of History and Anthropology, Edinboro, PA 16444. Offers social sciences (MA). Part-time and evening/weekend programs available. *Faculty:* 4 full-time (2 women). *Students:* 22 full-time (8 women), 13 part-time (6 women); includes 2 minority (1 Asian American or Pacific Islander, 1 Hispanic American), 1 international. Average age 32. In 2008, 6 master's awarded. *Degree requirements:* For master's, thesis or alternative, competency exam. *Entrance requirements:* For master's, GRE or MAT, minimum QPA of 2.5. *Application deadline:* Applications are processed on a rolling basis. Application fee: $30. Electronic applications accepted. *Expenses:* Tuition, state resident: full-time $6430; part-time $357 per credit. Tuition, nonresident: full-time $8038; part-time $572 per credit. International tuition: $15,171.58 full-time. Required fees: $2113; $60 per credit. Tuition and fees vary according to course load. *Financial support:* In 2008–09, 9 research assistantships with full and partial tuition reimbursements (averaging $3,850 per year) were awarded; career-related internships or fieldwork, Federal Work-Study, institutionally sponsored loans, scholarships/grants, and unspecified assistantships also available. Support available to part-time students. Financial award application deadline: 2/15; financial award applicants required to submit FAFSA. *Unit head:* Dr. Jerra Jenrette, Chairperson, 814-732-1225, E-mail: jjenrette@edinboro.edu. *Application contact:* Dr. R. Scott Baldwin, Dean, 814-732-2752, Fax: 814-732-2268, E-mail: sbaldwin@edinboro.edu.

Florida Agricultural and Mechanical University, Division of Graduate Studies, Research, and Continuing Education, College of Arts and Sciences, Division of History and Political Sciences, Program in Applied Social Science, Tallahassee, FL 32307-3200. Offers African American history (MASS); criminal justice (MASS); economics (MASS); history (MASS); political science (MASS); public administration (MASS); public management (MASS); social work (MASS); sociology (MASS). Part-time programs available. *Degree requirements:* For master's, thesis optional. *Entrance requirements:* For master's, GRE General Test, minimum GPA of 3.0. *Faculty research:* Southern history, black history, election trends, presidential history.

George Mason University, College of Science, Fairfax, VA 22030. Offers biodefense (MS, PhD); bioinformatics and computational biology (MS, PhD, Certificate); biology (MS, PhD), including bioinformatics (MS), ecology, systematics and evolution (MS), interpretive biology (MS), molecular and cellular biology (MS), molecular and microbiology (PhD), organismal biology (MS); chemistry and biochemistry (MS), including chemistry; climate dynamics (PhD); computational and data sciences (MS, PhD, Certificate); computational social science (PhD); computational techniques and applications (Certificate); earth systems and geoinformation sciences (MS, PhD, Certificate); environmental science and policy (MS, PhD); geography (MS), including geographic and cartographic sciences; mathematical sciences (MS, PhD), including mathematics; nanotechnology and nanoscience (Certificate); neuroscience (PhD); physical sciences (PhD); physics and astronomy (MS), including applied and engineering physics; remote sensing and earth image processing (Certificate). Part-time and evening/weekend programs available. *Degree requirements:* For doctorate, comprehensive exam, thesis/dissertation. *Entrance requirements:* For master's and doctorate, GRE General Test, minimum GPA of 3.0 in last 60 hours. Additional exam requirements/recommendations for international students: Required—TOEFL. Electronic applications accepted. *Faculty research:* Space sciences and astrophysics, fluid dynamics, materials modeling and simulation, bioinformatics, global changes and statistics.

Graduate Theological Union, Graduate Programs, Berkeley, CA 94709-1212. Offers art and religion (MA, PhD); biblical languages (MA); biblical studies (Old and New Testament) (MA, PhD, Th D); Buddhist studies (MA); Christian spirituality (MA, PhD); cultural and historical studies of religions (MA, PhD); ethics and social theory (PhD); history (MA, PhD, Th D); homiletics (MA, PhD, Th D); interdisciplinary studies (PhD, Th D); Jewish studies (MA, PhD, Certificate); liturgical studies (MA, PhD, Th D); Near Eastern religions (PhD); Orthodox Christian studies (MA); Orthodox studies (Certificate); religion and psychology (MA, PhD); religion and society/ethics and social theory (MA); systematic and philosophical theology (MA, PhD, Th D); women's studies in religion (Certificate); MA/M Div. *Accreditation:* ATS. Terminal master's awarded for partial completion of doctoral program. *Degree requirements:* For master's, one foreign language, thesis; for doctorate, one foreign language, comprehensive exam, thesis/dissertation. *Entrance requirements:* For master's, GRE General Test; for doctorate, GRE General Test, MA or M Div. Additional exam requirements/recommendations for international students: Required—TOEFL. Electronic applications accepted.

Hollins University, Graduate Programs, Program in Liberal Studies, Roanoke, VA 24020-1603. Offers humanities (MALS); interdisciplinary studies (MALS); justice and legal studies (MALS); liberal studies (CAS); social science (MALS); visual and performing arts (MALS). Part-time and evening/weekend programs available. *Faculty:* 6 full-time (1 woman), 7 part-time/adjunct (4 women). *Students:* 20 full-time (17 women), 78 part-time (56 women); includes 14 minority (13 African Americans, 1 Hispanic American), 1 international. Average age 39. 33 applicants, 85% accepted, 23 enrolled. In 2008, 42 master's awarded. *Degree requirements:* For master's, thesis. *Entrance requirements:* For master's, letters of recommendation, interview. Additional exam requirements/recommendations for international students: Required—TOEFL (minimum score 550 paper-based; 213 computer-based; 79 iBT). *Application deadline:* For fall admission, 7/1 priority date for domestic and international students; for spring admission, 12/10 priority date for domestic and international students. Applications are processed on a rolling basis. Application fee: $40. Electronic applications accepted. *Expenses:* Tuition: Full-time $26,720; part-time $590 per credit hour. Required fees: $280. *Financial support:* In 2008–09, 53 students received support, including 2 fellowships (averaging $1,189 per year); Federal Work-Study and scholarships/grants also available. Support available to part-time students. Financial award application deadline: 7/15; financial award applicants required to submit FAFSA. *Faculty research:* Elderly blacks, film, feminist economics, US voting patterns, Wagner, diversity. *Unit head:* Dr. Edward A. Lynch, Director, 540-362-6475, Fax: 540-362-6288, E-mail: elynch@hollins.edu. *Application contact:* Cathy S. Koon, Manager of Graduate Services, 540-362-6326, Fax: 540-362-6288, E-mail: ckoon@hollins.edu.

Humboldt State University, Graduate Studies, College of Arts, Humanities, and Social Sciences, Program in Environment and Community, Arcata, CA 95521-8299. Offers MA. *Students:* 33 full-time (25 women), 3 part-time (all women); includes 5 minority (1 American Indian/Alaska Native, 1 Asian American or Pacific Islander, 3 Hispanic Americans). Average age 31. 45 applicants, 58% accepted, 12 enrolled. In 2008, 2 master's awarded. *Degree requirements:* For master's, thesis or alternative, qualifying exam. *Entrance requirements:* For master's, minimum GPA of 2.5, 3 letters of recommendation. Additional exam requirements/recommendations for international students: Required—TOEFL (minimum score 500 paper-based; 173 computer-based). *Application deadline:* For fall admission, 3/15 for domestic and international students. Applications are processed on a rolling basis. Application fee: $55. *Expenses:* Tuition, state resident: full-time $5236. Tuition, nonresident: full-time $11,338. *Financial support:* Application deadline: 3/1; *Faculty research:* Geography, political science, ethnic studies, anthropology, economics. *Unit head:* Dr. John Meyer, Chair, 707-826-4494, Fax: 707-826-4496, E-mail: jmm7001@humboldt.edu. *Application contact:* Dr. Mark Baker, Coordinator, 717-826-3907, Fax: 717-826-4496, E-mail: jb141@humboldt.edu.

Indiana University Bloomington, Maurer School of Law, Bloomington, IN 47405-7000. Offers comparative law (MCL); juridical science (SJD); law (JD, LL M); law and social sciences (PhD); legal studies (Certificate); JD/MA; JD/MBA; JD/MLS; JD/MPA; JD/MS; JD/MSES. PhD offered through University Graduate School. *Accreditation:* ABA. *Faculty:* 72 full-time (28 women), 14 part-time/adjunct (4 women). *Students:* 695 full-time (291 women), 23 part-time (10 women); includes 111 minority (49 African Americans, 31 Asian Americans or Pacific Islanders, 31 Hispanic Americans), 119 international. Average age 27. 2,384 applicants, 25% accepted, 205 enrolled. In 2008, 216 first professional degrees, 62 master's, 6 doctorates, 1 other advanced degree awarded. *Degree requirements:* For master's, thesis or practicum; for doctorate, thesis/dissertation (for some programs); for JD, research seminar. *Entrance requirements:* For JD, LSAT; for master's, LSAT, 3 letters of recommendation, law degree or license to practice, 3-5 years of experience; for doctorate, LSAT, 3 letters of recommendation, LL M or JD. Additional exam requirements/recommendations for international students: Required—TOEFL (minimum score 560 paper-based; 213 computer-based; 80 iBT). *Application deadline:* For fall admission, 3/1 priority date for domestic and international students. Applications are processed on a rolling basis. Application fee: $50 ($60 for international students). Electronic applications accepted. *Expenses:* Tuition, area resident: Part-time $291.97 per credit hour. Tuition, state resident: part-time $291.97 per credit hour. Tuition, nonresident: part-time $850.33 per credit hour. Required fees: $110 per semester. Tuition and fees vary according to course load and program. *Financial support:* In 2008–09, 581 students received support, including 496 fellowships (averaging $11,669 per year), 76 research assistantships (averaging $1,152 per year), 5 teaching assistantships (averaging $3,060 per year); career-related internships or fieldwork, Federal Work-Study, institutionally sponsored loans, scholarships/grants, health care benefits, and unspecified assistantships also available. Financial award application deadline: 3/1; financial award applicants required to submit FAFSA. *Faculty research:* Environmental risk assessment and policy analysis, information privacy and security, judicial independence, accountability, ethics. Total annual research expenditures: $1.4 million. *Unit head:* Lauren K. Robel, Dean, 812-855-8885, Fax: 812-855-7057, E-mail: lrobel@indiana.edu. *Application contact:* Kelly M. Compton, Director of Admissions, 812-855-2704, Fax: 812-855-0555, E-mail: kmcompto@indiana.edu.

The Johns Hopkins University, Bloomberg School of Public Health, Department of Health, Behavior and Society, Baltimore, MD 21218-2699. Offers behavioral sciences and health education (MHS); genetic counseling (Sc M); social and behavioral sciences (PhD, Sc D). *Degree requirements:* For master's, comprehensive exam (for some programs), thesis (for some programs); for doctorate, comprehensive exam, thesis/dissertation. *Entrance requirements:* For master's and doctorate, GRE, transcripts, curriculum vitae, statement, 3 recommendation letters. Additional exam requirements/recommendations for international students: Required—TOEFL (minimum score 250 computer-based; 100 iBT). Electronic applications accepted. *Faculty research:* Structural and community-level inventions to improve health communication and health education behavioral and social aspects of genetic counseling.

Lincoln University, School of Graduate Studies and Continuing Education, College of Liberal Arts, Education and Journalism, Department of Social and Behavioral Sciences, Jefferson City, MO 65102. Offers history (MA); social science (MA), including history, political science, sociology; sociology (MA); sociology/criminal justice (MA). Part-time and evening/weekend programs available. *Faculty:* 11 full-time (4 women), 4 part-time/adjunct (2 women). *Students:* 6 full-time (3 women), 21 part-time (11 women); includes 8 minority (all African Americans), 5 international. Average age 33. 13 applicants, 100% accepted, 9 enrolled. In 2008, 14 master's awarded. *Degree requirements:* For master's, comprehensive exam, thesis optional. *Entrance requirements:* For master's, GRE General Test or MAT, 15 undergraduate hours of course work in social science including 6 hours upper-division, with 9 hours in the area of concentration. Additional exam requirements/recommendations for international students: Required—TOEFL (minimum score 500 paper-based; 173 computer-based; 61 iBT). *Application deadline:* For fall admission, 7/1 priority date for domestic and international students; for spring admission, 12/1 priority date for domestic and international students. Applications are processed on a rolling basis. Application fee: $20. *Expenses:* Tuition, area resident: Full-time $4185; part-time $232.50 per credit hour. Tuition, nonresident: full-time $7767; part-time $431.50 per credit hour. Required fees: $270; $15 per credit hour. $252.50 per semester. One-time fee: $20. Tuition and fees vary according to course load. *Financial support:* Federal Work-Study and scholarships/grants available. Financial award application deadline: 4/1; financial award applicants required to submit FAFSA. *Faculty research:* Suicide prevention. *Unit head:* Dr. Debra F. Greene, Department Head, 573-681-5145, Fax: 573-681-5150, E-mail: greened@lincolnu.edu. *Application contact:* Irasema Steck, Administrative Assistant, 573-681-5247, Fax: 573-681-5106, E-mail: gradschool@lincolnu.edu.

Long Island University, Brooklyn Campus, Richard L. Conolly College of Liberal Arts and Sciences, Program in Social Science, Brooklyn, NY 11201-8423. Offers history (MS); United Nations studies (Certificate). Part-time and evening/weekend programs available. *Entrance requirements:* For master's, 2 letters of recommendation. Additional exam requirements/recommendations for international students: Required—TOEFL (minimum score 500 paper-based; 173 computer-based). Electronic applications accepted.

Long Island University, C.W. Post Campus, School of Education, Department of Curriculum and Instruction, Brookville, NY 11548-1300. Offers adolescence education (MS); adolescence education: biology (MS); adolescence education: earth science (MS); adolescence education: English (MS); adolescence education: mathematics (MS); adolescence education: social studies (MS); adolescence education: Spanish (MS); art education (MS); bilingual education (MS); childhood education (MS); early childhood education (MS); middle childhood education (MS); music education (MS); teaching English to speakers of other languages (MS). Part-time and evening/weekend programs available. *Degree requirements:* For master's, comprehensive exam or thesis, student teaching. *Entrance requirements:* For master's, minimum GPA of 2.75 in major, 2.5 overall. Electronic applications accepted. *Faculty research:* Ethics and education, teaching strategies.

Massachusetts Institute of Technology, School of Humanities, Arts, and Social Sciences, Program in Science, Technology, and Society, Cambridge, MA 02139-4307. Offers history, anthropology, and science, technology and society (PhD). *Degree requirements:* For doctorate, comprehensive exam, thesis/dissertation. *Entrance requirements:* For doctorate, GRE General Test. Additional exam requirements/recommendations for international students: Required—TOEFL (minimum score 577 paper-based; 233 computer-based). Electronic applications accepted. *Faculty research:* History of science; history of technology; sociology of science and technology; anthropology of science and technology; science, technology, and society.

Michigan State University, The Graduate School, College of Social Science, Interdisciplinary Studies in Social Science—Global Applications, East Lansing, MI 48824. Offers MA. *Degree requirements:* For master's, internship/practicum or field experience, policy paper or analytical

report. *Entrance requirements:* Additional exam requirements/recommendations for international students: Required—TOEFL, Michigan State University ELT (85), Michigan English Language Assessment Battery (83). Electronic applications accepted.

Mississippi College, Graduate School, College of Arts and Sciences, School of Humanities and Social Sciences, Department of History and Political Science, Clinton, MS 39058. Offers administration of justice (MSS); history (M Ed, MA, MSS); paralegal studies (Certificate); political science (MSS); social sciences (M Ed, MSS). Part-time programs available. *Degree requirements:* For master's, one foreign language, comprehensive exam, thesis (for some programs). *Entrance requirements:* For master's, GRE or NTE, minimum GPA of 2.5. Additional exam requirements/recommendations for international students: Recommended—IELTS. Electronic applications accepted.

Montclair State University, The Office of Graduate Admissions and Support Services, College of Education and Human Services, Department of Curriculum and Teaching, Montclair, NJ 07043-1624. Offers education (M Ed); educational technology (M Ed); learning disabled teacher consultant (Certificate); school library media specialist (Certificate); teaching (MAT, Certificate), including art (MAT), biological science (MAT), early childhood education (P-3) (MAT), earth science (MAT), elementary education (K-8) (MAT), English (MAT), French (MAT), health and physical education (MAT), health education (MAT), home economics (MAT), mathematics (MAT), music (MAT), physical education (MAT), physical science (MAT), social studies (MAT), Spanish (MAT), teacher of ESL (MAT), teacher of students with disabilities (MAT). Part-time and evening/weekend programs available. *Faculty:* 14 full-time (10 women), 23 part-time/adjunct (17 women). *Students:* 103 full-time (61 women), 98 part-time (73 women); includes 15 minority (8 African Americans, 3 Asian Americans or Pacific Islanders, 4 Hispanic Americans), 3 international. Average age 31. 56 applicants, 63% accepted, 33 enrolled. In 2008, 196 master's, 2 other advanced degrees awarded. *Degree requirements:* For master's, comprehensive exam, field experience. *Entrance requirements:* For master's, PRAXIS II, minimum GPA of 2.67, 2 letters of recommendation. Additional exam requirements/recommendations for international students: Required—TOEFL (minimum score 83 computer-based). *Application deadline:* For fall admission, 2/15 for domestic and international students; for spring admission, 9/15 for domestic and international students. Applications are processed on a rolling basis. Application fee: $60. Electronic applications accepted. *Financial support:* In 2008–09, 7 research assistantships with full tuition reimbursements (averaging $7,000 per year) were awarded; Federal Work-Study, scholarships/grants, and unspecified assistantships also available. Support available to part-time students. Financial award application deadline: 3/1; financial award applicants required to submit FAFSA. *Unit head:* Dr. David Keiser, Chairperson, 973-655-7199. *Application contact:* Amy Aiello, Associate Director of Admissions, 973-655-5147, Fax: 973-655-7869, E-mail: graduate.school@montclair.edu.

The New School: A University, The New School for Social Research, New York, NY 10003. Offers MA, MS, DS Sc, PhD. Part-time and evening/weekend programs available. *Faculty:* 67 full-time (27 women), 28 part-time/adjunct (4 women). *Students:* 785 full-time (407 women), 315 part-time (173 women); includes 166 minority (52 African Americans, 3 American Indian/Alaska Native, 44 Asian Americans or Pacific Islanders, 67 Hispanic Americans), 301 international. Average age 31. 1,125 applicants, 72% accepted, 257 enrolled. In 2008, 180 master's, 60 doctorates awarded. Terminal master's awarded for partial completion of doctoral program. *Degree requirements:* For doctorate, thesis/dissertation, qualifying exam. *Entrance requirements:* For master's, GRE General Test; for doctorate, GRE General Test, MA. Additional exam requirements/recommendations for international students: Required—TOEFL (minimum score 600 paper-based; 250 computer-based). *Application deadline:* For fall admission, 1/15 priority date for domestic students. Applications are processed on a rolling basis. Application fee: $50. *Expenses:* Contact institution. *Financial support:* Fellowships with tuition reimbursements, research assistantships with tuition reimbursements, teaching assistantships with tuition reimbursements, career-related internships or fieldwork, Federal Work-Study, scholarships/grants, tuition waivers (full and partial), and unspecified assistantships available. Financial award application deadline: 3/1; financial award applicants required to submit FAFSA. *Faculty research:* Civil society and democracy, international movements of refugees, minority use of health services, memory, morality and genetics. *Unit head:* Dr. Michael Schober, Dean, 212-229-5777, E-mail: schober@newschool.edu. *Application contact:* Robert MacDonald, Director of Admissions, 800-523-5710 Ext. 3007, Fax: 212-989-7102, E-mail: macdonar@newschool.edu.

See Close-Up on page 1251.

New York University, Graduate School of Arts and Science, Program in Trauma and Violence Transdisciplinary Studies, New York, NY 10012-1019. Offers MA, Advanced Certificate.

North Dakota State University, College of Graduate and Interdisciplinary Studies, College of Arts, Humanities and Social Sciences, Department of Sociology, Anthropology, and Emergency Management, Fargo, ND 58105. Offers emergency management (MS, PhD); social science (MA, MS); sociology (MS). Part-time programs available. *Faculty:* 8 full-time (3 women), 5 part-time/adjunct (2 women). *Students:* 35 full-time (17 women), 15 part-time (9 women); includes 5 minority (2 African Americans, 1 American Indian/Alaska Native, 1 Asian American or Pacific Islander, 1 Hispanic American), 2 international. Average age 27. 15 applicants, 60% accepted, 7 enrolled. In 2008, 9 master's awarded. *Degree requirements:* For master's, thesis; for doctorate, comprehensive exam, thesis/dissertation. *Entrance requirements:* For master's, GRE (emergency management), course work in sociology, minimum GPA of 3.2; for doctorate, GRE, minimum GPA of 3.2. Additional exam requirements/recommendations for international students: Required—TOEFL. *Application deadline:* For fall admission, 4/1 priority date for domestic students. Applications are processed on a rolling basis. Application fee: $45 ($60 for international students). *Financial support:* In 2008–09, 7 research assistantships with full tuition reimbursements (averaging $6,156 per year), 7 teaching assistantships with full tuition reimbursements (averaging $3,078 per year) were awarded; fellowships, career-related internships or fieldwork, Federal Work-Study, institutionally sponsored loans, and tuition waivers (full) also available. Support available to part-time students. Financial award application deadline: 4/15. *Faculty research:* Medical sociology, demography, ethnology, archaeology. Total annual research expenditures: $75,000. *Unit head:* Dr. Daniel J. Klenow, Chair, 701-231-8657, Fax: 701-231-1047, E-mail: daniel.klenow@ndsu.edu. *Application contact:* Dr. Daniel J. Klenow, Chair, 701-231-8657, Fax: 701-231-1047, E-mail: daniel.klenow@ndsu.edu.

Northwestern University, The Graduate School, Interdepartmental Degree Programs, Program in Mathematical Methods in Social Science, Evanston, IL 60208. Offers MS.

Northwestern University, The Graduate School, Program in Law and Social Science, Evanston, IL 60208. Offers Certificate. *Degree requirements:* For Certificate, research project. *Faculty research:* Law and social science.

Nova Southeastern University, Graduate School of Humanities and Social Sciences, Department of Multi-Disciplinary Studies, Fort Lauderdale, FL 33314-7796. Offers college student affairs (MS); college student personnel administration (Certificate); cross-disciplinary studies (MA); qualitative research (Certificate). Part-time programs available. Postbaccalaureate distance learning degree programs offered (no on-campus study). *Faculty:* 4 part-time/adjunct (2 women). *Students:* 24 full-time (15 women), 35 part-time (29 women); includes 24 minority (20 African Americans, 4 Hispanic Americans), 2 international. 45 applicants, 67% accepted, 30 enrolled. In 2008, 7 master's awarded. *Degree requirements:* For master's, comprehensive exam, thesis optional, portfolio. *Entrance requirements:* For master's, interview, minimum GPA of 3.0. Additional exam requirements/recommendations for international students: Required—TOEFL. *Application deadline:* For fall admission, 7/1 priority date for domestic and international students; for winter admission, 11/1 priority date for domestic and international students; for spring admission, 3/1 priority date for domestic and international students. Applications are processed on a rolling basis. Electronic applications accepted. *Financial support:* In 2008–09, 20 research assistantships with tuition reimbursements (averaging $15,600 per year) were awarded; career-related internships or fieldwork, Federal Work-Study, institutionally sponsored loans, and scholarships/grants also available. Financial award applicants required to submit

Social Sciences

Nova Southeastern University *(continued)*
CSS PROFILE. *Unit head:* Dr. Judith McKay, Senior Associate Dean, 954-262-3060, Fax: 954-262-3893, E-mail: mckayj@nsu.nova.edu. *Application contact:* Marcia Arango, Student Recruitment Coordinator, 954-262-3006, Fax: 954-262-3968, E-mail: marango@nsu.nova.edu.

Nyack College, Alliance Graduate School of Counseling, School of Social and Behavioral Sciences, Nyack, NY 10960-3698. Offers counseling (MA) *Degree requirements:* For master's, thesis (for some programs).

Ohio University, Graduate College, College of Arts and Sciences, Program in Social Sciences, Athens, OH 45701-2979. Offers MSS. Part-time and evening/weekend programs available. *Degree requirements:* For master's, oral exam. *Entrance requirements:* For master's, minimum GPA of 2.75. Additional exam requirements/recommendations for international students: Required—TOEFL (minimum score 600 paper-based; 220 computer-based). Electronic applications accepted.

Queens College of the City University of New York, Division of Graduate Studies, Social Science Division, Program in Social Sciences, Flushing, NY 11367-1597. Offers MASS. Part-time and evening/weekend programs available. *Degree requirements:* For master's, thesis. *Entrance requirements:* For master's, minimum GPA of 3.0. Additional exam requirements/recommendations for international students: Required—TOEFL.

Regis University, College for Professional Studies, MA Program, Denver, CO 80221-1099. Offers criminology (MA); fine arts administration (Certificate); language and communication (MA); mediation (Certificate); psychology (MA); self-designed major (MA); social justice, peace, and reconciliation (Certificate); social science (MA); technical communication (Certificate). Program also offered in Henderson and Las Vegas (Summerlin), NV. Part-time and evening/weekend programs available. Postbaccalaureate distance learning degree programs offered (minimal on-campus study). *Degree requirements:* For master's, thesis, research project. *Entrance requirements:* For master's, resumé, recommendations, essays. Additional exam requirements/recommendations for international students: Required—TOEFL (minimum score 213 computer-based), TWE (minimum score 5). Electronic applications accepted. *Expenses:* Contact institution. *Faculty research:* Independent/nonresidential graduate study: new methods and models, adult learning and the capstone experience, Goal Setting, behavior of Adult students, Innovative Studies for Community Colleges.

St. Edward's University, New College, Program in Liberal Arts, Austin, TX 78704. Offers global issues (MLA); humanities (MLA); liberal arts (Certificate); social sciences (MLA). Part-time and evening/weekend programs available. *Students:* 9 full-time (4 women), 78 part-time (49 women); includes 22 minority (4 African Americans, 1 American Indian/Alaska Native, 2 Asian Americans or Pacific Islanders, 15 Hispanic Americans), 1 international. Average age 34. 33 applicants, 88% accepted, 25 enrolled. In 2008, 34 master's awarded. *Degree requirements:* For master's, minimum 24 resident hours. *Entrance requirements:* For master's, minimum GPA of 2.75 in last 60 hours of course work, interview. Additional exam requirements/recommendations for international students: Required—TOEFL (minimum score 550 paper-based; 213 computer-based; 79 iBT). *Application deadline:* For fall admission, 8/1 for domestic students, 7/1 for international students; for spring admission, 12/1 for domestic students, 11/1 for international students. Applications are processed on a rolling basis. Application fee: $45 ($50 for international students). Electronic applications accepted. *Expenses:* Tuition: Full-time $13,752; part-time $764 per credit hour. Required fees: $50 per semester. Full-time tuition and fees vary according to course load and program. *Financial support:* In 2008–09, 4 students received support. Scholarships/grants available. *Unit head:* Dr. Paula Marks, Director, 512-448-8702, Fax: 512-448-8492, E-mail: paulam@stewards.edu. *Application contact:* Kay L. Arnold, Graduate Admissions Coordinator, 512-233-1636, Fax: 512-428-1032, E-mail: kayla@stedwards.edu.

Southern Oregon University, Graduate Studies, School of Social Sciences, Department of Psychology, Ashland, OR 97520. Offers applied psychology (MAP); human service-organizational training and development (MA, MS); social science (MA, MS), including professional counseling, psychology. Part-time programs available. *Degree requirements:* For master's, thesis, portfolio and oral defense. *Entrance requirements:* For master's, GRE General Test, minimum GPA of 3.0. Electronic applications accepted.

Southern University and Agricultural and Mechanical College, Graduate School, College of Arts and Humanities, Department of History, Baton Rouge, LA 70813. Offers social sciences (MA). Part-time programs available. *Degree requirements:* For master's, thesis. *Entrance requirements:* For master's, GRE General Test. Additional exam requirements/recommendations for international students: Required—TOEFL (minimum score 525 paper-based; 193 computer-based).

Stony Brook University, State University of New York, School of Professional Development, Stony Brook, NY 11794. Offers biology -grade 7-12 (MAT); chemistry-grade 7-12 (MAT); coaching (Graduate Certificate); computer integrated engineering (Graduate Certificate); earth science-grade 7-12 (MAT); educational computing (Graduate Certificate); educational leadership (Advanced Certificate); English-grade 7-12 (MAT); environmental management (Graduate Certificate; environmental/occupational health and safety (Graduate Certificate); French-grade 7-12 (MAT); German-grade 7-12 (MAT); human resource management (Graduate Certificate); information systems management (Graduate Certificate); Italian-grade 7-12 (MAT); liberal studies (MA); liberal studies online (MA); mathematics-grade 7-12 (MAT); operation research (Graduate Certificate); physics-grade 7-12 (MAT); school administration and supervision (Graduate Certificate); school building leadership (Graduate Certificate); school district administration (Graduate Certificate); school district business leadership (Advanced Certificate); school district leadership (Graduate Certificate); social science and the professions (MPS), including environmental waste management, human resource management; social studies-grade 7-12 (MAT); Spanish-grade 7-12 (MAT); waste management (Graduate Certificate). Part-time and evening/weekend programs available. Postbaccalaureate distance learning degree programs offered. *Faculty:* 5 full-time (3 women), 131 part-time/adjunct (53 women). *Students:* 317 full-time (187 women), 1,200 part-time (773 women); includes 187 minority (77 African Americans, 2 American Indian/Alaska Native, 22 Asian Americans or Pacific Islanders, 86 Hispanic Americans), 11 international. Average age 28. In 2008, 597 master's, 234 other advanced degrees awarded. *Degree requirements:* For master's, one foreign language, thesis or alternative. *Application deadline:* Applications are processed on a rolling basis. Application fee: $62. *Expenses:* Tuition, area resident: Full-time $7880; part-time $328 per credit hour. Tuition, state resident: full-time $7880; part-time $328 per credit hour. Tuition, nonresident: full-time $13,250; part-time $552 per credit hour. Required fees: $848. *Financial support:* Fellowships, research assistantships, teaching assistantships, career-related internships or fieldwork available. Support available to part-time students. *Unit head:* Dr. Paul J. Edelson, Dean, 631-632-7052, Fax: 631-632-9046, E-mail: paul.edelson@stonybrook.edu. *Application contact:* Dr. Paul J. Edelson, Dean, 631-632-7052, Fax: 631-632-9046, E-mail: paul.edelson@stonybrook.edu.

Syracuse University, Graduate School, Maxwell School of Citizenship and Public Affairs, Program in Social Sciences, Syracuse, NY 13244. Offers MS Sc, PhD. Part-time and evening/weekend programs available. Postbaccalaureate distance learning degree programs offered. *Degree requirements:* For doctorate, thesis/dissertation. *Entrance requirements:* For doctorate, GRE General Test. Additional exam requirements/recommendations for international students: Required—TOEFL. Electronic applications accepted.

Texas A&M International University, Office of Graduate Studies and Research, College of Arts and Sciences, Department of Social Sciences, Laredo, TX 78041-1900. Offers history (MA); political science (MA); public administration (MPA). *Degree requirements:* For master's, thesis (for some programs). *Entrance requirements:* For master's, GRE General Test. Additional exam requirements/recommendations for international students: Required—TOEFL (minimum score 550 paper-based; 213 computer-based).

Texas A&M University–Commerce, Graduate School, College of Arts and Sciences, Department of History, Commerce, TX 75429-3011. Offers history (MA, MS); social sciences (M Ed, MS). Part-time programs available. *Degree requirements:* For master's, comprehensive exam, thesis (for some programs). *Entrance requirements:* For master's, GRE General Test. Electronic applications accepted. *Faculty research:* American foreign policy, colonial America, Texas politics, Medieval England.

Towson University, College of Graduate Studies and Research, Program in Social Science, Towson, MD 21252-0001. Offers MS. Part-time and evening/weekend programs available. *Entrance requirements:* For master's, minimum GPA of 3.0, 3 letters of recommendation, letter of intent. Additional exam requirements/recommendations for international students: Required—TOEFL. Electronic applications accepted. *Faculty research:* Race and ethnicity, diplomatic history, sociology methodology, central Asian geography.

Universidad Nacional Pedro Henriquez Urena, Graduate School, Santo Domingo, Dominican Republic. Offers accounting and auditing (M Acct); animal production (M Agr); business administration (MBA, PhD); Caribbean tropical architecture (M Arch); conservation of monuments and cultural goods (M Arch); economics (M Econ); education (PhD); environmental engineering (MEE); horticulture (M Agr); hospital administration (PhD); humanities (PhD); international relations (MPS); management of natural resources (MNRM); project management (M Man, MPM); public administration (MPS); sanitary engineering (ME); social science (PhD); veterinary medicine (DVM).

University of California, Irvine, Office of Graduate Studies, School of Social Sciences, Irvine, CA 92697. Offers MA, PhD. *Degree requirements:* For doctorate, thesis/dissertation. *Entrance requirements:* For master's, GRE, minimum GPA of 3.0; for doctorate, GRE General Test, minimum GPA of 3.0. Additional exam requirements/recommendations for international students: Required—TOEFL (minimum score 550 paper-based; 213 computer-based). Electronic applications accepted. *Faculty research:* Mathematical modeling of perception and cognitive processes, economic analysis of transportation, impact of society's political system on its economy, exploration of authority structures and inequality in society.

University of California, Santa Cruz, Division of Graduate Studies, Division of Humanities, Program in the History of Consciousness, Santa Cruz, CA 95064. Offers PhD. *Degree requirements:* For doctorate, one foreign language, thesis/dissertation, qualifying exam. *Entrance requirements:* Additional exam requirements/recommendations for international students: Required—TOEFL (minimum score 550 paper-based; 220 computer-based). *Faculty research:* Interdisciplinary humanities and social sciences, political theory, cultural theory, feminist studies, literary theory.

University of Chicago, Division of Social Sciences, Committee on Social Thought, Chicago, IL 60637-1513. Offers PhD. *Degree requirements:* For doctorate, one foreign language, thesis/dissertation, exam. *Entrance requirements:* For doctorate, GRE General Test. Additional exam requirements/recommendations for international students: Required—TOEFL, IELTS (minimum score 7). Electronic applications accepted.

University of Chicago, Division of Social Sciences, Master of Arts Program in the Social Sciences, Chicago, IL 60637-1513. Offers AM. Part-time programs available. *Degree requirements:* For master's, thesis. *Entrance requirements:* For master's, GRE General Test. Additional exam requirements/recommendations for international students: Required—TOEFL. Electronic applications accepted.

University of Colorado Denver, College of Liberal Arts and Sciences, Program in Social Science, Denver, CO 80217-3364. Offers MSS. Part-time and evening/weekend programs available. *Degree requirements:* For master's, thesis or alternative. *Entrance requirements:* For master's, GRE General Test, 18 hours of course work in social science, interview, minimum GPA of 2.75. Additional exam requirements/recommendations for international students: Required—TOEFL (minimum score 525 paper-based; 197 computer-based). Electronic applications accepted.

University of Florida, Graduate School, College of Public Health and Health Professions and College of Medicine, Programs in Public Health, Gainesville, FL 32611. Offers biostatistics (MPH); environmental health (MPH); epidemiology (MPH); public health management and policy (MPH); public health practice (MPH); social and behavioral sciences (MPH). *Entrance requirements:* For master's, GRE General Test, minimum GPA of 3.0. Additional exam requirements/recommendations for international students: Required—TOEFL (minimum score 550 paper-based; 213 computer-based).

University of Idaho, College of Graduate Studies, College of Natural Resources, Department of Conservation Social Sciences, Moscow, ID 83844-2282. Offers MS. *Faculty:* 12. *Students:* 24 (17 women). Average age 31. In 2008, 4 master's awarded. *Entrance requirements:* For master's, minimum GPA of 2.8. *Application deadline:* For fall admission, 8/1 for domestic students; for spring admission, 12/15 for domestic students. Application fee: $55 ($60 for international students). *Expenses:* Tuition, nonresident: full-time $10,080; part-time $336 per credit. Required fees: $5212; $267 per credit. Tuition and fees vary according to program. *Financial support:* Research assistantships, teaching assistantships available. Financial award application deadline: 2/15. *Faculty research:* Parks, wilderness and protected areas policy, planning and management, recreation and tourism planning, urban and community forestry, resource-based tourism, ecotourism, human dimensions of ecosystem management. *Unit head:* Dr. William J McLaughlin, Acting Dean, 208-885-7911. *Application contact:* Dr. William J McLaughlin, Acting Dean, 208-885-7911.

University of Illinois at Springfield, Graduate Programs, College of Education and Human Services, Program in Human Services, Springfield, IL 62703-5407. Offers alcoholism and substance abuse (MA); child and family services (MA); gerontology (MA); social services administration (MA). Part-time and evening/weekend programs available. Postbaccalaureate distance learning degree programs offered (no on-campus study). *Faculty:* 4 full-time (2 women), 3 part-time/adjunct (all women). *Students:* 28 full-time (22 women), 70 part-time (56 women); includes 17 minority (16 African Americans, 1 American Indian/Alaska Native). Average age 35. 64 applicants, 42% accepted, 22 enrolled. In 2008, 24 master's awarded. *Degree requirements:* For master's, thesis optional, internship; project or thesis. *Entrance requirements:* For master's, minimum undergraduate GPA of 3.0, 2 letters of recommendation, personal statement. Additional exam requirements/recommendations for international students: Required—TOEFL (minimum score 500 paper-based; 176 computer-based; 61 iBT). Application fee: $50 ($60 for international students). Electronic applications accepted. *Expenses:* Tuition, state resident: full-time $6144; part-time $256 per credit hour. Tuition, nonresident: full-time $13,980; part-time $582.50 per credit hour. Required fees: $1800. *Financial support:* In 2008–09, research assistantships with full tuition reimbursements (averaging $8,109 per year), teaching assistantships with full tuition reimbursements (averaging $8,109 per year) were awarded; career-related internships or fieldwork, scholarships/grants, health care benefits, and unspecified assistantships also available. Support available to part-time students. Financial award application deadline: 11/15. *Unit head:* Dr. Carolyn Peck, Program Administrator, 217-206-7577, Fax: 217-206-6775, E-mail: peck.carolyn@uis.edu. *Application contact:* Dr. Lynn Pardie, Office of Graduate Studies, 800-252-8533, Fax: 217-206-7623, E-mail: pardie.lynn@uis.edu.

The University of Kansas, Graduate Studies, College of Liberal Arts and Sciences, Department of Applied Behavioral Science, Lawrence, KS 66045. Offers applied behavioral science (MA); behavioral psychology (PhD). *Faculty:* 18. *Students:* 55 full-time (38 women), 4 part-time (all women); includes 5 minority (1 African American, 2 Asian Americans or Pacific Islanders, 2 Hispanic Americans), 3 international. Average age 32. 65 applicants, 18% accepted, 11 enrolled. In 2008, 6 master's, 5 doctorates awarded. Terminal master's awarded for partial completion of doctoral program. *Degree requirements:* For master's, thesis; for doctorate, thesis/dissertation, comprehensive oral and written exams, journal reviews. *Entrance requirements:* For master's and doctorate, curriculum vitae, 3 letters of recommendation. Additional exam requirements/recommendations for international students: Required—TOEFL,

TWE. *Application deadline:* For fall admission, 1/12 priority date for domestic and international students. Application fee: $45 ($50 for international students). Electronic applications accepted. *Expenses:* Tuition, area resident: Full-time $6122; part-time $255.10 per credit hour. Tuition, state resident: full-time $6122; part-time $255.10 per credit hour. Tuition, nonresident: full-time $14,629; part-time $609.55 per credit hour. Required fees: $847; $70.56 per credit hour. Tuition and fees vary according to course load and program. *Financial support:* Fellowships, research assistantships with full and partial tuition reimbursements, teaching assistantships with full and partial tuition reimbursements, career-related internships or fieldwork, traineeships, tuition waivers (full), and unspecified assistantships available. Financial award application deadline: 2/1. *Faculty research:* Early childhood, developmental disabilities, community health and development, adults with disabilities, applied behavior analysis. *Unit head:* Dr. Edward K. Morris, Chair, 785-864-4840, Fax: 785-864-5202, E-mail: ekm@ku.edu. *Application contact:* Dr. Gregory J. Madden, Graduate Director, 785-864-4840, Fax: 785-864-5202, E-mail: gmadden@ku.edu.

University of Maryland, Baltimore County, Graduate School, Program in Gerontology, Baltimore, MD 21201. Offers aging policy for the elderly (PhD); epidemiology of aging (PhD); social, cultural, and behavioral sciences (PhD). Part-time programs available. *Faculty:* 17 part-time/adjunct (10 women). *Students:* 19 full-time (14 women), 6 part-time (all women); includes 4 minority (all African Americans), 1 international. Average age 33. 18 applicants, 22% accepted, 4 enrolled. In 2008, 3 doctorates awarded. *Degree requirements:* For doctorate, comprehensive exam, thesis/dissertation. *Entrance requirements:* For doctorate, GRE General Test. Additional exam requirements/recommendations for international students: Required—TOEFL, TWE. *Application deadline:* For spring admission, 1/15 for domestic and international students. Application fee: $45. Electronic applications accepted. *Financial support:* In 2008–09, 12 students received support, including 3 fellowships with full tuition reimbursements available (averaging $19,000 per year), 8 research assistantships with full tuition reimbursements available (averaging $19,000 per year), 1 teaching assistantship with full tuition reimbursement available (averaging $19,000 per year); career-related internships or fieldwork, scholarships/grants, traineeships, health care benefits, tuition waivers (partial), and unspecified assistantships also available. Support available to part-time students. Financial award application deadline: 2/1; financial award applicants required to submit FAFSA. *Faculty research:* Aging and health policy, behavioral aspects of aging, caregiving, LTC, epidemiology of aging. Total annual research expenditures: $44.2 million. *Unit head:* Dr. Leslie Morgan, Co-Director at UMBC, 410-455-2074, Fax: 410-455-1154, E-mail: lmorgan@umbc.edu. *Application contact:* Justine Golden, Academic Coordinator, 410-706-4926, Fax: 410-706-4433, E-mail: jgold002@umaryland.edu.

University of Michigan, School of Social Work, Interdisciplinary Program in Social Work and Social Science, Ann Arbor, MI 48109. Offers PhD. Offered through the Horace H. Rackham School of Graduate Studies. *Degree requirements:* For doctorate, thesis/dissertation, oral defense of dissertation, preliminary exam. *Entrance requirements:* For doctorate, GRE General Test. Additional exam requirements/recommendations for international students: Required—TOEFL. *Faculty research:* Substance abuse, child welfare, mental health, poverty, aging.

University of Michigan–Flint, College of Arts and Sciences, Program in Social Sciences, Flint, MI 48502-1950. Offers MA. Part-time programs available. *Faculty:* 7 full-time (3 women), 1 part-time/adjunct (0 women). *Students:* 7 full-time (6 women), 38 part-time (22 women); includes 6 minority (5 African Americans, 1 Asian American or Pacific Islander). Average age 35. 28 applicants, 79% accepted, 15 enrolled. In 2008, 7 master's awarded. *Entrance requirements:* Additional exam requirements/recommendations for international students: Required—TOEFL (minimum score 560 paper-based; 220 computer-based; 84 iBT), IELTS (minimum score 6.5). *Application deadline:* For fall admission, 8/1 for domestic students, 5/1 priority date for international students; for winter admission, 11/15 for domestic students, 9/1 priority date for international students; for spring admission, 3/15 for domestic students, 1/1 priority date for international students. Application fee: $55. *Expenses:* Contact institution. *Financial support:* Federal Work-Study, scholarships/grants, and unspecified assistantships available. Support available to part-time students. Financial award application deadline: 6/1; financial award applicants required to submit FAFSA. *Unit head:* Dr. Adam Lutzker, Program Director, 810-762-3280, Fax: 810-766-6789, E-mail: alutzker@umflint.edu. *Application contact:* Bradley T. Maki, Director of Graduate Admissions, 810-762-3171, Fax: 810-766-6789, E-mail: bmaki@umflint.edu.

University of Northern Iowa, Graduate College, College of Social and Behavioral Sciences, Department of Social Science, Cedar Falls, IA 50614. Offers MA. *Students:* 25 part-time (8 women). 2 applicants, 50% accepted, 0 enrolled. *Entrance requirements:* For master's, minimum GPA of 3.0. Additional exam requirements/recommendations for international students: Required—TOEFL (minimum score 500 paper-based; 180 computer-based; 61 iBT). Application fee: $30 ($50 for international students). *Expenses:* Tuition, state resident: full-time $6446. Tuition, nonresident: full-time $14,874. Required fees: $852. *Unit head:* Dr. John Johnson, Interim Dean, 319-273-2221, Fax: 319-273-2222, E-mail: john.johnson@uni.edu. *Application contact:* Laurie S. Russell, Record Analyst, 319-273-2623, Fax: 319-273-6792, E-mail: laurie.russell@uni.edu.

University of Regina, Faculty of Graduate Studies and Research, Faculty of Arts, Department of Sociology and Social Studies, Regina, SK S4S 0A2, Canada. Offers social studies (MA, PhD); sociology (MA, PhD). *Faculty:* 12 full-time (5 women), 1 part-time/adjunct (0 women). *Students:* 11 full-time (6 women), 7 part-time (5 women). 7 applicants, 71% accepted. In 2008, 4 master's, 2 doctorates awarded. *Degree requirements:* For master's, thesis. *Entrance*

requirements: Additional exam requirements/recommendations for international students: Required—TOEFL (minimum score 580 paper-based; 237 computer-based; 88 iBT). *Application deadline:* Applications are processed on a rolling basis. Application fee: $85 ($100 for international students). Electronic applications accepted. *Financial support:* In 2008–09, 3 fellowships (averaging $15,000 per year), 1 research assistantship (averaging $13,500 per year), 4 teaching assistantships (averaging $6,558 per year) were awarded; scholarships/grants also available. Financial award application deadline: 6/15. *Faculty research:* Social justice; development and the environment; knowledge, technology, and society. *Unit head:* Dr. John Conway, Head, 306-585-4052, Fax: 306-585-4815, E-mail: john.conway@uregina.ca. *Application contact:* Dr. Henry Chow, Graduate Program Coordinator, 306-585-5604, Fax: 306-585-4815, E-mail: henry.chow@uregina.ca.

The University of Texas at Tyler, College of Arts and Sciences, Department of Social Sciences, Tyler, TX 75799-0001. Offers criminal justice (MS); public administration (MPA); sociology (MS). Part-time and evening/weekend programs available. *Degree requirements:* For master's, comprehensive exam, thesis optional. *Entrance requirements:* For master's, GRE General Test, minimum GPA of 3.0. Additional exam requirements/recommendations for international students: Required—TOEFL (minimum score 79 computer-based). *Faculty research:* Urban segregation, minority business, violent crime, gender discrimination.

University of Wisconsin–Madison, Development Studies Program, Madison, WI 53706-1380. Offers PhD. *Degree requirements:* For doctorate, comprehensive exam, thesis/dissertation. Electronic applications accepted. *Faculty research:* Third world countries, theory and practice, socio-economic development.

Worcester Polytechnic Institute, Graduate Studies and Research, Department of Social Science and Policy Studies, Worcester, MA 01609-2280. Offers interdisciplinary social science (PhD); system dynamics (MS, Graduate Certificate). Part-time and evening/weekend programs available. *Faculty:* 4 full-time (1 woman), 2 part-time/adjunct (0 women). *Students:* 17 part-time (5 women); includes 1 minority (African American), 4 international. Average age 40. 14 applicants, 57% accepted, 5 enrolled. In 2008, 1 master's awarded. *Entrance requirements:* For master's, GRE General Test, 3 letters of recommendation, statement of purpose. Additional exam requirements/recommendations for international students: Required—TOEFL (minimum score 550 paper-based; 213 computer-based; 79 iBT), IELTS (minimum score 6.5). *Application deadline:* For fall admission, 1/15 priority date for domestic students, 1/15 for international students; for spring admission, 10/15 priority date for domestic students, 10/15 for international students. Applications are processed on a rolling basis. Application fee: $70. Electronic applications accepted. *Financial support:* Fellowships, research assistantships, teaching assistantships, career-related internships or fieldwork, institutionally sponsored loans, scholarships/grants, and unspecified assistantships available. Financial award application deadline: 1/15. *Faculty research:* Sustainable development, information economics, judgment and decision making, learning science, system dynamics, social simulation, political economys. Total annual research expenditures: $228,578. *Unit head:* Dr. James K. Doyle, Head, 508-831-5296, Fax: 508-831-5896, E-mail: doyle@wpi.edu. *Application contact:* Dr. Oleg Pavlov, Graduate Coordinator, 508-831-5296, Fax: 508-831-5896, E-mail: opavlov@wpi.edu.

Worcester Polytechnic Institute, Graduate Studies and Research, Programs in Interdisciplinary Studies, Worcester, MA 01609-2280. Offers bioscience administration (MS); impact engineering (MS); manufacturing engineering management (MS); power systems management (MS); social science (PhD); systems modeling (MS). Part-time and evening/weekend programs available. *Faculty:* 1 part-time/adjunct (0 women). *Students:* 7 full-time (4 women), 96 part-time (23 women); includes 8 minority (6 African Americans, 2 Hispanic Americans), 2 international. Average age 37. 69 applicants, 67% accepted, 25 enrolled. In 2008, 50 master's awarded. *Degree requirements:* For master's, thesis; for doctorate, comprehensive exam, thesis/dissertation. *Entrance requirements:* For master's and doctorate, 3 letters of recommendation. Additional exam requirements/recommendations for international students: Required—TOEFL (minimum score 550 paper-based; 213 computer-based; 79 iBT), IELTS (minimum score 6.5). *Application deadline:* For fall admission, 1/15 priority date for domestic students; for spring admission, 10/15 priority date for domestic students. Application fee: $70. *Financial support:* Unspecified assistantships available. Financial award application deadline: 1/15. Total annual research expenditures: $64,780. *Unit head:* Dr. Fred J. Looft, Head, 508-831-5231, Fax: 508-831-5491, E-mail: fjlooft@wpi.edu. *Application contact:* Lynne Dougherty, Administrative Assistant, 508-831-5301, Fax: 508-831-5717, E-mail: grad@wpi.edu.

Yale University, School of Medicine, School of Public Health, New Haven, CT 06520. Offers biostatistics (MPH, MS, PhD); chronic disease epidemiology (MPH, PhD); environmental health sciences (MPH, PhD); epidemiology of microbial diseases (MPH, PhD); global health (MPH); health management (MPH); health policy and administration (MPH, PhD); parasitology (PhD); social and behavioral sciences (MPH); MBA/MPH; MD/MPH; MPH/MA; MSN/MPH. MS and PhD offered through the Graduate School. Part-time programs available. Terminal master's awarded for partial completion of doctoral program. *Degree requirements:* For master's, thesis, internship; for doctorate, comprehensive exam, thesis/dissertation, residency. *Entrance requirements:* For master's, GMAT, GRE, or MCAT, previous undergraduate course work in mathematics and science; for doctorate, GRE General Test. Additional exam requirements/recommendations for international students: Required—TOEFL. Electronic applications accepted. *Expenses:* Contact institution. *Faculty research:* Genetic and emerging infections epidemiology, virology, cost/quality, vector biology, quantitative methods.

York University, Faculty of Graduate Studies, Faculty of Arts, Program in International Development Studies, Toronto, ON M3J 1P3, Canada. Offers MA.

THE NEW SCHOOL: A UNIVERSITY

The New School for Social Research

Programs of Study	The New School for Social Research, one of the eight schools that make up The New School in New York City, offers programs of study leading to four advanced degrees: Master of Arts, Master of Philosophy, Master of Science, and Doctor of Philosophy. In addition, interdisciplinary master's programs are offered in liberal studies and historical studies. The School offers graduate degrees in anthropology, economics, philosophy, political science, psychology (including clinical psychology, with a concentration in mental health and substance abuse counseling), and sociology.
	A candidate for any of these degrees must satisfy the requirements established by both The New School for Social Research and the department of the student's major field of study. Students should make certain that they are familiar not only with the general requirements for the degree but also with specific departmental requirements. Students may participate in any of the programs on a part-time or full-time basis.
	New School for Social Research doctoral students may take courses at the following universities: Columbia University (including Teachers College), the City University of New York Graduate School and University Center, Fordham University, New York University, Princeton University, Rutgers University at New Brunswick, and the State University of New York at Stony Brook.
	For more information, students should visit http://www.socialresearch.newschool.edu.
Research Facilities	The New School library includes the holdings of the Raymond Fogelman Library, the Adam and Sophie Gimbel Design Library, the Harry Schermer Library, and the Husserl Archives. Matriculated students have library privileges at New York University's Elmer Holmes Bobst Library and at the Cooper Union Library. Academic computing facilities enable students to do computer-assisted research.
	New School research facilities include psychology laboratories (video clinical training, perception, social-personality, experimental, developmental, and cognitive), the India China Institute, the Hannah Arendt Center, the Schwartz Center for Economic Policy Analysis, the Committee on Western European Studies, the Transregional Center for Democratic Studies, the East and Central Europe Program, the Husserl Archives, and the World Policy Institute. In addition, there are many other research facilities in the New York area available to students. For more information, students should visit http://www.newschool.edu/institutes.html.
Financial Aid	Matriculated students receive aid from a variety of public and private sources. The amount of assistance awarded to a student is based on financial need and academic performance. Students are encouraged to apply for fellowships and grants from sources other than The New School. Scholarships, fellowships, assistantships, loans, and Federal Work-Study awards are available. The University Scholars Program and the Diamond Fellowship Program provide scholarship grants to African American, Asian American, Latino, and Native American students. Numerous other special scholarships are described at http://www.socialresearch.newschool.edu/students/financial-aid-scholarships.htm.
Cost of Study	Tuition for 2009–10 is $1576 per credit, and fees are approximately $120 each term. For more information, students should visit http://www.newschool.edu/tuition.
Living and Housing Costs	The University Housing Office maintains a comprehensive resource center with apartment listings. University-run apartments and residence halls are also available. The cost of housing, food, transportation, books, and living expenses averages $17,000 annually. For more information, students should visit http://www.newschool.edu/studentservices.
Student Group	The total enrollment of The New School for Social Research is about 1,000 students. Students represent a range of age groups, academic backgrounds, and nationalities, coming to New York from throughout the nation and from more than seventy other countries.
Location	The New School is an urban university and is an integral part of New York City. The diverse and cosmopolitan community, the spirited intellectual and cultural life, and the concentration of wealth and power that characterize New York provide a vital context in which to study the complexity of modern society.
The University and The School	The New School is a leading university in New York City offering distinguished programs in design, liberal arts, the performing arts, and social and political science, leading to seventy graduate and undergraduate degrees. Learn more at http://www.newschool.edu/degreeprograms. A privately supported institution, The New School is accredited by the Commission on Higher Education of the Middle States Association of Colleges and Schools and chartered as a university by the Regents of the State of New York.
	The New School for Social Research was founded in 1919 by a distinguished group of intellectuals, some of whom were teaching at Columbia University in New York City during World War I. As dedicated pacifists, they took a public stand against the war and were censured by the university's president. The professors responded by resigning from Columbia and later establishing their own university for adults in the Chelsea neighborhood of Manhattan. It became a place where people could exchange ideas freely with scholars and artists representing a wide range of intellectual, aesthetic, and political orientations.
	During the 1920s, Alvin Johnson, the School's first president, collaborated regularly with colleagues in Germany and elsewhere in Europe. They made him aware of the danger Hitler presented to democracy and the civilized world, alerting him to the seriousness of the threat before many in the United States had grasped it. In 1933, with the financial support of enlightened philanthropists, Johnson created within The New School a University in Exile to provide a haven for scholars and artists whose lives were threatened by National Socialism. The University in Exile sponsored more than 180 individuals and their families, providing them with visas and jobs. While some of these refugees remained at The New School for many years, many others went on to influence institutional life elsewhere in the United States. Today, The New School for Social Research remains a place where professors and students take risks in defense of their intellectual commitments and political beliefs.
Applying	The admission decision is made after a careful examination of transcripts, letters of recommendation, the writing sample, scores on the Graduate Record Examinations, and the statement of academic goals and objectives. Application materials for students wishing to be considered for full fellowships and special scholarships must be completed by January 17. Applications received or completed after January 17 are considered for admission and financial aid on a rolling basis. For more information, students should visit http://www.socialresearch.newschool.edu/admissions.
Correspondence and Information	The New School for Social Research The New School 72 Fifth Avenue New York, New York 10011 Phone: 212-229-5710 800-523-5411 (toll-free) E-mail: socialresearchadmit@newschool.edu Web site: http://www.newschool.edu/nssr

The New School: A University

THE FACULTY AND THEIR RESEARCH

Anthropology

Arjun Appadurai, John Dewey Professor in the Social Sciences; Ph.D., Chicago, 1976. Historical anthropology, globalization, ethnic violence.

Lawrence Hirschfeld, Professor; Ph.D., Columbia, 1984. Anthropology and history of childhood, cultural psychology, cognitive development.

Benjamin Lee, Provost; Ph.D., Chicago, 1986. Linguistic, philosophical, and psychological anthropology; global cultural studies; contemporary Chinese culture.

Hugh Raffles, Associate Professor; D.F.E.S., Yale, 1999. Cultural politics of nature, humans/nonhumans, scale, taxonomy, affect, ethnography and history, writing.

Vyjayanthi Rao, Visiting Assistant Professor; Ph.D., Chicago, 2002. South Asia, development and modernization, displacement in postcolonial societies.

Janet Roitman, Associate Professor of Anthropology and International Affairs; Ph.D., Pennsylvania, 1996.

Ann Laura Stoler, Distinguished University Professor; Ph.D., Columbia, 1982. Colonial cultures, critical race theory, gender studies, historical methodologies, Southeast Asia.

Hyton White, Assistant Professor; Ph.D., Chicago, 2001. Critical social theory, embodiment and social reproduction, the family and domestic life in capitalist society, South Africa.

Economics

Duncan Foley, Leo Model Professor; Ph.D., Yale, 1966. Classical, neoclassical, and Marxian economic theory; political economy; monetary economics; economic complexity; global environmental economics.

William Milberg, Associate Professor; Ph.D., Rutgers, 1987. International trade.

Salih Neftci, Visiting Professor; Ph.D., Minnesota, 1977. Financial markets, numerical methods in financial asset pricing, applications of the theory of extremes to risk management.

Edward Nell, Malcolm B. Smith Professor; B.Litt., Oxford, 1962. Macroeconomic theory and policy, methodology, growth theory, business cycles, inflation and unemployment.

Willi Semmler, Professor; Ph.D., Berlin, 1976. Financial markets, macroeconomics and macroeconometrics, public finance, industrial organization.

Anwar Shaikh, Professor; Ph.D., Columbia, 1973. Political economy, macroeconomic growth and cycles, international trade.

Lance Taylor, Arnhold Professor of International Cooperation and Development; Ph.D., Harvard, 1968. Economic development and the environment.

Global Finance

Turan Bali, Professor of Finance; M.Phil., Ph.D., CUNY, Baruch, 1998. Financial economics, financial econometrics, financial engineering, fixed income, derivatives, risk management.

Greg Ciresi, Adjunct Instructor; M.Sc., NYU, 2004. Financial engineering, statistical arbitrage, risk management.

Pablo A. Goldberg, Professor of country risk and Topics on Emerging Markets; M.Sc., London School of Economics (UK), 1996. Macroeconomics, financial economics.

Ira F. Jersey, Professor of Professional Practice; M.A., New School, 2004; Birmingham (UK), 1993. Macroeconomics, financial economics, financial engineering, political science, international relations.

Christina E. Leijonhufvud, Managing Director and Head of Social Sector Finance, JPMorgan Chase & Co.; M.Sc., London School of Economics, 1996. Country risk, emerging markets, financial risk management, financial globalization, social sector finance.

Salih N. Neftci, Program Director, Global Finance Masters Program; Ph.D., Minnesota, 1977. Financial economics.

Eckhard Platen, Professor of Quantitative Finance; Dr.Sc., Academy of Sciences (Berlin), 1985; Ph.D., Technical (Dresden), 1975. Mathematics of finance, numerical methods in finance, quantitative finance.

Liuren Wu, Professor of Quantitative Techniques; Ph.D, China Academy of Science, 1994, M.A., NYU, 1998. Credit risk, term structure modeling, option pricing, market microstructure, international finance, asset pricing, asset allocation.

Historical Studies

Elaine Abelson, Senior Lecturer; Ph.D., NYU, 1986. Dimensions of inequality, gender.

Robin Blackburn, Distinguished Visiting Professor; B.Sc., London, 1965. Slavery, globalization, communism, colonialism.

Carol Breckenridge, Associate Professor; Ph.D., Wisconsin, 1976. Colonialism and ritual; state, polity, and religion in South India; cosmopolitan cultural forms.

José Casanova, Professor of Sociology; Ph.D., New School, 1982. Religion, democratization, social change.

Federico Finchelstein, Assistant Professor; Ph.D., Cornell, 2006.

Oz Frankel, Assistant Professor; Ph.D., Berkeley, 1998. Social and political history of nineteenth-century United States, Victorian Britain, history of the social sciences, race, media and print culture, reform, state formation, historiography.

Victoria Hattam, Associate Professor of Political Science (see Political Science).

Eiko Ikegami, Professor of Sociology (see Sociology).

James Miller, Professor of Liberal Studies and Political Science (see Liberal Studies).

David Plotke, Professor of Political Science (see Political Science).

Ann Laura Stoler, Distinguished University Professor (see Anthropology).

Eli Zaretsky, Professor; Ph.D., Maryland, 1978. Cultural history, twentieth-century history, history of the family, psychoanalysis.

Aristide Zolberg, Eberstadt Professor (see Political Science).

Vera Zolberg, Professor of Sociology (see Sociology).

Liberal Studies

Richard Bernstein, Vera List Professor of Philosophy (see Philosophy).

Oz Frankel, Assistant Professor of History (see Historical Studies).

Margo Jefferson, Associate Professor, Eugene Lang College The New School for Liberal Arts; M.S., Columbia, 1971.

Elzbieta Matynia, Senior Lecturer; Ph.D., Warsaw, 1979. Gender issues in the new European democracies.

James Miller, Professor; Ph.D., Brandeis, 1975. History of political thought, social movements.

Melissa Monroe, Committee Member; Ph.D., Stanford, 1989. Nonfiction writing, modern literature, linguistics.

Eli Zaretsky, Professor of History (see Historical Studies).

Vera Zolberg, Professor of Sociology (see Sociology).

Philosophy

Claudia Baracchi, Associate Professor; Ph.D., Vanderbilt, 1996. Ancient philosophy, nineteenth- and twentieth-century continental philosophy, medieval philosophy, philosophy of art, political philosophy, ethics.

J. M. Bernstein, Professor; Ph.D., Edinburgh, 1975. Critical theory, aesthetics.

Richard Bernstein, Vera List Professor; Ph.D., Yale, 1958. American pragmatism, social and political philosophy, critical theory, Anglo-American philosophy.

Alice Crary, Associate Professor; Ph.D., Pittsburgh, 1999. Moral philosophy, Wittgenstein, philosophy and literature.

Simon Critchley, Professor; Ph.D., Essex, 1988. Continental philosophy, phenomenology, philosophy and literature, psychoanalysis, the ethical and the political.

James Dodd, Assistant Professor; Ph.D., Boston University, 1996. Husserl, Heidegger, phenomenology.

Nancy Fraser, Henry A. and Louise Loeb Professor of Political and Social Science (see Political Science).

Agnes Heller, Hannah Arendt Professor; Ph.D., Eötvös Loránd (Budapest), 1955. Political philosophy, ethics, existentialism.

Mark Larrimore, Assistant Professor of Religious Studies and Philosophy; Ph.D., Princeton, 1994. Philosophy of religion, ethics, Leibniz.

Benjamin Lee, Provost (see Anthropology).

Dmitri Nikulin, Associate Professor; Ph.D., Academy of Sciences (Moscow), 1990. Philosophy and history of science, ancient and early modern philosophy, philosophy of dialogue.

Yirmiyahu Yovel, Hans Jonas Professor; Ph.D., Hebrew University (Israel), 1968. Spinoza, Jewish rationalists, continental philosophy.

Political Science

Nancy Fraser, Henry A. and Louise Loeb Professor of Political and Social Science; Ph.D., CUNY Graduate Center, 1980. Social and political theory, feminist theory, contemporary French and German thought.

Victoria Hattam, Associate Professor; Ph.D., MIT, 1987. American political and economic thought and culture.

Agnes Heller, Hannah Arendt Professor of Philosophy (see Philosophy).

Mala Htun, Assistant Professor; Ph.D., Harvard, 2000. Comparative politics; Latin America; gender, race, and politics.

Courtney Jung, Assistant Professor; Ph.D., Yale, 1998. Comparative politics, politics of identity, democratic transitions, South Africa.

Andreas Kalyvas, Assistant Professor; Ph.D., Columbia, 2000. Relationship between democracy and constitutionalism, problems of popular sovereignty.

James Miller, Professor of Liberal Studies and Political Science (see Liberal Studies).

David Plotke, Professor; Ph.D., Berkeley, 1985. Contemporary political and social theory, American political development.

Adamantia Pollis, Professor Emerita and Senior Lecturer; Ph.D., Johns Hopkins, 1958. Nationalism and ethnicity, human rights.

Sanjay Ruparelia, Assistant Professor; Ph.D., Cambridge, 2005. Comparative politics, political economy of development, modern South Asia.

Aristide Zolberg, Eberstadt Professor; Ph.D., Chicago, 1961. Globalization and democracy, nationalism and ethnicity.

Psychology

Emanuele Castano, Assistant Professor; Ph.D., Louvain (Belgium), 1999. Social identification; perception entitativity, essentialism, agency, and intentionality at the collective level; image theory.

Doris Chang, Assistant Professor; Ph.D., UCLA, 2000. Cultural psychology, ethnic minority mental health, domestic violence in immigrant communities.

Karen D'Avanzo, Assistant Clinical Professor and Coordinator, M.A. Mental Health and Substance Abuse Counseling Program; Ph.D., LIU, Brooklyn, 1995. Developmental psychopathology, risk and resilience and child/adolescent development, contextual factors and adolescent substance abuse, dual-diagnosis psychotherapy development, psychotherapy integration.

Lawrence Hirschfeld, Professor (see Anthropology).

William Hirst, Professor; Ph.D., Cornell, 1976. Cognitive neuroscience, memory and attention.

Xiaochun Jin, Assistant Professor; Ph.D., Adelphi, 2003.

Marcel Kinsbourne, Professor; D.M., Oxford, 1963. Brain-behavior relations, consciousness, psychology of attention.

Arien Mack, Alfred J. and Monette C. Marrow Professor; Ph.D., Yeshiva, 1966. Perception and attention.

Joan Miller, Associate Professor; Ph.D., Chicago, 1982. Interpersonal motivation, theory of mind, close relationships, moral development.

Lisa Rubin, Assistant Professor; Ph.D., Arizona State, 2005.

Jeremy Safran, Professor and Director of Clinical Training; Ph.D., British Columbia, 1982. Psychoanalysis and psychotherapy, the therapeutic alliance, therapeutic impasses, transference and countertransference, the internal processes of the therapist.

Herbert Schlesinger, Professor Emeritus and Senior Lecturer; Ph.D., Kansas, 1952. Analysis of text in psychoanalysis, implications and cost of providing mental health services.

Michael Schober, Professor; Ph.D., Stanford, 1990. Psycholinguistics, survey response, music cognition.

David Shapiro, Professor; Ph.D., USC, 1950. Psychopathology of character problems and their treatment.

Howard Steele, Associate Professor; Ph.D., University College (London), 1991. Attachment theory, dementia, multiple personality disorder, borderline personality disorder.

Miriam Steele, Associate Professor and Assistant Director of Clinical Training; Ph.D., University College (London), 1990. Attachment theory, psychoanalytic developmental psychology, adoption and foster care.

McWelling Todman, Associate Professor of Clinical Practice and Codirector, Mental Health and Substance Abuse Counseling Program; Ph.D., New School, 1986. Psychopathology, biosocial and cognitive theories of addiction.

Megan B. Warner, Assistant Professor and Director, The New School–Beth Israel Center for Clinical Training and Research; Ph.D., Texas A&M, 2005.

Sociology

Andrew Arato, Dorothy Hart Hirshon Professor of Political and Social Theory; Ph.D., Chicago, 1975. Frankfurt school, history of social thought, Eastern European societies and social movements.

Paolo Carpignano, Senior Lecturer; Ph.D., Rome (Italy), 1969. Media theory, sociology of culture.

José Casanova, Professor; Ph.D., New School, 1982. Religion, democratization, and social change in Latin America; Southern and Eastern Europe.

Sarah Daynes, Assistant Professor; Ph.D., École des Hautes Études en Sciences Sociales (Paris), 2001. Social theory, memory, knowledge, religion, music.

Jeffrey Goldfarb, Michael E. Gellert Professor; Ph.D., Chicago, 1977. Sociology of culture, comparative politics, phenomenological society.

Eiko Ikegami, Professor; Ph.D., Harvard, 1989. Comparative historical sociology, Japanese society, theory, sociology of culture.

Jaeho Kang, Assistant Professor of Sociology and Media Studies; Ph.D., Cambridge, 2003. Critical social theory, sociology of media, social theory of mass culture, new media and political communication.

Orville Lee, Assistant Professor; Ph.D., Berkeley, 1996. Cultural sociology, racial epistemologies.

Terry Williams, Professor; Ph.D., CUNY Graduate Center, 1978. Race, drug culture, urban life, poverty.

Vera Zolberg, Professor; Ph.D., Chicago, 1974: sociology of culture, social and political frameworks of cultural support and memory.

Section 27
Sociology, Anthropology, and Archaeology

This section contains a directory of institutions offering graduate work in sociology, anthropology, and archaeology, followed by in-depth entries submitted by institutions that chose to prepare detailed program descriptions. Additional information about programs listed in the directory but not augmented by an in-depth entry may be obtained by writing directly to the dean of a graduate school or chair of a department at the address given in the directory.

For programs offering related work, see also in this book *Area and Cultural Studies, Art and Art History, History, Humanities, Language and Literature,* and *Psychology and Counseling.*

CONTENTS

Program Directories

Anthropology 1254
Applied Social Research 1264
Archaeology 1265
Biological Anthropology 1268
Demography and Population Studies 1268
Rural Sociology 1269
Sociology 1270
Survey Methodology 1286

Close-Ups

Bryn Mawr College 1287
Emory University 1289
Southern Illinois University Carbondale
  Anthropology 1291
  Sociology 1293
Texas A&M University 1295

See also:
California Institute of Integral Studies—Humanities 347
Central European University—Social Sciences and
  Humanities 349
The New School: A University—Political and Social
  Science 1251
The University of Texas at Dallas—Economic,
  Political, and Policy Sciences 783

Anthropology

American University, College of Arts and Sciences, Department of Anthropology, Washington, DC 20016-8003. Offers anthropology (PhD); public anthropology (MA, Certificate). Part-time and evening/weekend programs available. *Faculty:* 12 full-time (5 women), 7 part-time/adjunct (5 women). *Students:* 30 full-time (21 women), 61 part-time (41 women); includes 19 minority (9 African Americans, 5 Asian Americans or Pacific Islanders, 5 Hispanic Americans), 9 international. Average age 32. 61 applicants, 64% accepted, 19 enrolled. In 2008, 15 master's, 6 doctorates awarded. Terminal master's awarded for partial completion of doctoral program. *Degree requirements:* For master's, comprehensive exam, thesis or alternative; for doctorate, 2 foreign languages, comprehensive exam, thesis/dissertation. *Entrance requirements:* For master's, GRE, sample of written work, statement of interest; for doctorate, GRE, sample of written work, personal statement. Additional exam requirements/recommendations for international students: Required—TOEFL. *Application deadline:* For fall admission, 2/1 for domestic students; for spring admission, 10/1 for domestic students. Application fee: $80. *Expenses:* Tuition: Full-time $21,204; part-time $1178 per credit hour. Required fees: $380. Part-time tuition and fees vary according to course load and program. *Financial support:* Fellowships, research assistantships with full and partial tuition reimbursements, teaching assistantships with full and partial tuition reimbursements, career-related internships or fieldwork, Federal Work-Study, institutionally sponsored loans, and unspecified assistantships available. Support available to part-time students. Financial award application deadline: 1/15. *Faculty research:* Poverty and race, lesbian and gay studies, class and culture, developing countries. *Unit head:* Dr. William Leap, Chair, 202-885-1831, Fax: 202-885-1837. *Application contact:* Dr. William Leap, Chair, 202-885-1831, Fax: 202-885-1837.

The American University in Cairo, Graduate Studies and Research, School of Humanities and Social Sciences, Department of Sociology, Anthropology, Psychology, and Egyptology, Cairo, Egypt. Offers sociology and anthropology (MA). *Degree requirements:* For master's, one foreign language, thesis. *Entrance requirements:* Additional exam requirements/recommendations for international students: Required—English entrance exam and/or TOEFL. Electronic applications accepted. *Faculty research:* Development, gender, sociopolitical economic formulations, social science indigenization, Arab world.

American University of Beirut, Graduate Programs, Faculty of Arts and Sciences, Beirut, Lebanon. Offers anthropology (MA); Arabic language and literature (MA); archaeology (MA); biology (MS); chemistry (MS); computer science (MS); economics (MA); education (MA); English language (MA); English literature (MA); environmental policy planning (MSES); financial economics (MAFE); geology (MS); history (MA); mathematics (MA, MS); Middle Eastern studies (MA); philosophy (MA); physics (MS); political studies (MA); psychology (MA); public administration (MA); sociology (MA); statistics (MA, MS). Part-time programs available. *Degree requirements:* For master's, one foreign language, comprehensive exam, thesis (for some programs). *Entrance requirements:* For master's, GRE, letter of recommendation. Additional exam requirements/recommendations for international students: Required—TOEFL (minimum score 600 paper-based; 250 computer-based; 100 iBT), IELTS (minimum score 7.5). *Faculty research:* String theory and supergravity; computer graphics; algebra and number theory; popular Arabic literature; marine and freshwater biology; integrating science, math and technology.

Arizona State University, Graduate College, College of Liberal Arts and Sciences, Division of Social Sciences, School of Human Evolution and Social Change, Tempe, AZ 85287. Offers anthropology (PhD); applied mathematics for the life and social sciences (PhD); environmental social science (PhD); museum studies in anthropology (MA); social science and health (PhD). *Degree requirements:* For master's, thesis or alternative; for doctorate, thesis/dissertation. *Entrance requirements:* For master's and doctorate, GRE.

Ball State University, Graduate School, College of Sciences and Humanities, Department of Anthropology, Muncie, IN 47306-1099. Offers MA. *Entrance requirements:* For master's, GRE General Test, resumé.

Boston University, Graduate School of Arts and Sciences, Department of Anthropology, Boston, MA 02215. Offers anthropology (PhD); applied anthropology (MA). Terminal master's awarded for partial completion of doctoral program. *Degree requirements:* For master's, one foreign language, thesis or alternative; for doctorate, one foreign language, thesis/dissertation. *Entrance requirements:* For master's and doctorate, GRE General Test, 2 letters of recommendation. Additional exam requirements/recommendations for international students: Required—TOEFL (minimum score 550 paper-based; 213 computer-based).

Brandeis University, Graduate School of Arts and Sciences, Department of Anthropology, Waltham, MA 02454-9110. Offers anthropology (MA, PhD); anthropology and women's and gender studies (MA). Part-time programs available. Terminal master's awarded for partial completion of doctoral program. *Degree requirements:* For master's, thesis; for doctorate, one foreign language, comprehensive exam, thesis/dissertation. *Entrance requirements:* For master's, GRE General Test (recommended), sample of written work, resumé, letters of recommendation; for doctorate, GRE General Test, sample of written work, resumé, letters of recommendation. Additional exam requirements/recommendations for international students: Required—TOEFL (minimum score 600 paper-based; 250 computer-based; 100 iBT), IELTS (minimum score 7). Electronic applications accepted. *Faculty research:* Technology and culture, comparative methods, economic anthropology, gender studies, semiotic anthropology.

Brigham Young University, Graduate Studies, College of Family, Home, and Social Sciences, Department of Anthropology, Provo, UT 84602-1001. Offers MA. *Faculty:* 10 full-time (2 women). *Students:* 4 full-time (all women), 13 part-time (5 women). Average age 28. 6 applicants, 67% accepted, 4 enrolled. In 2008, 1 master's awarded. *Degree requirements:* For master's, comprehensive exam, thesis. *Entrance requirements:* For master's, GRE General Test, minimum GPA of 3.0 in last 60 hours. Additional exam requirements/recommendations for international students: Required—TOEFL (minimum score 580 paper-based; 237 computer-based). *Application deadline:* For fall admission, 2/1 for domestic and international students. Application fee: $50. Electronic applications accepted. *Expenses:* Tuition: Full-time $5160; part-time $287 per credit hour. Tuition and fees vary according to program and student's religious affiliation. *Financial support:* In 2008–09, 17 students received support, including 10 research assistantships (averaging $6,500 per year), 2 teaching assistantships (averaging $6,500 per year); fellowships, career-related internships or fieldwork, institutionally sponsored loans, and tuition waivers (partial) also available. Financial award application deadline: 3/1; financial award applicants required to submit FAFSA. *Faculty research:* Archaeology of the Southwest, Near East, and Mesoamerica; Mayan glyphs. Total annual research expenditures: $51,800. *Unit head:* Dr. David P. Crandall, Chair, 801-422-3058, Fax: 801-422-0021, E-mail: david_crandall@byu.edu. *Application contact:* Dr. Cynthia S. Finlayson, Graduate Coordinator, 801-422-5628, Fax: 801-422-0021, E-mail: calderfin@aol.com.

Brown University, Graduate School, Department of Anthropology, Providence, RI 02912. Offers anthropology (AM, PhD); museum studies (AM). *Degree requirements:* For doctorate, one foreign language, thesis/dissertation, preliminary exam.

California Institute of Integral Studies, Graduate Programs, School of Consciousness and Transformation, San Francisco, CA 94103. Offers cultural anthropology and social transformation (MA); East-West psychology (MA, PhD); integrative health studies (MA); philosophy and religion (MA, PhD), including Asian and comparative studies, philosophy, cosmology, and consciousness, women's spirituality, women's spirituality flex format; social and cultural anthropology (PhD); transformative leadership (MA); transformative studies (PhD). Part-time and evening/weekend programs available. Postbaccalaureate distance learning degree programs offered (minimal on-campus study). *Faculty:* 29 full-time, 32 part-time/adjunct. *Students:* 334 full-time (218 women), 126 part-time (77 women); includes 102 minority (39 African Americans, 4 American Indian/Alaska Native, 35 Asian Americans or Pacific Islanders, 24 Hispanic Americans), 1 international. Average age 37. 223 applicants, 78% accepted, 110 enrolled. In 2008, 93 master's, 30 doctorates awarded. Terminal master's awarded for partial completion of doctoral program. *Degree requirements:* For master's, comprehensive exam (for some programs), thesis optional; for doctorate, comprehensive exam, thesis/dissertation. *Entrance requirements:* For master's, minimum GPA of 3.0, letters of recommendation, writing sample; for doctorate, master's degree, minimum GPA of 3.0, letters of recommendation, writing sample. Additional exam requirements/recommendations for international students: Required—TOEFL. *Application deadline:* For fall admission, 2/1 priority date for domestic and international students; for spring admission, 10/15 priority date for domestic and international students. Applications are processed on a rolling basis. Application fee: $65. Electronic applications accepted. *Expenses:* Tuition: Part-time $815 per contact hour. Required fees: $270; $135 per semester. Tuition and fees vary according to degree level. *Financial support:* In 2008–09, 271 students received support; research assistantships, teaching assistantships, career-related internships or fieldwork, Federal Work-Study, institutionally sponsored loans, scholarships/grants, and tuition waivers (partial) available. Support available to part-time students. Financial award application deadline: 3/15; financial award applicants required to submit FAFSA. *Faculty research:* Altered states of consciousness, dreams, cosmology, postcolonial studies, integrative health studies. *Application contact:* Allyson Werner, Senior Admissions Counselor, 415-575-6155, Fax: 415-575-1268.

See Close-Up on page 347.

California State University, Bakersfield, Division of Graduate Studies, School of Humanities and Social Sciences, Program in Anthropology, Bakersfield, CA 93311-1022. Offers MA. *Degree requirements:* For master's, thesis optional. *Entrance requirements:* For master's, GRE, minimum GPA of 2.5, 3 letters of recommendation. Additional exam requirements/recommendations for international students: Required—TOEFL (minimum score 550 paper-based; 213 computer-based). *Faculty research:* Human services, social science teaching.

California State University, Chico, Graduate School, College of Behavioral and Social Sciences, Department of Anthropology, Chico, CA 95929-0400. Offers museum studies (MA). *Degree requirements:* For master's, thesis. *Entrance requirements:* For master's, GRE General Test, statement of purpose, 2 letters of recommendation. Additional exam requirements/recommendations for international students: Required—TOEFL (minimum score 550 paper-based; 213 computer-based; 80 iBT), IELTS (minimum score 6.5). Electronic applications accepted.

California State University, East Bay, Academic Programs and Graduate Studies, College of Letters, Arts, and Social Sciences, Department of Anthropology, Hayward, CA 94542-3000. Offers MA. Part-time programs available. *Degree requirements:* For master's, one foreign language, comprehensive exam, thesis. *Entrance requirements:* For master's, minimum GPA of 2.5 during previous 2 years of course work. Additional exam requirements/recommendations for international students: Required—TOEFL (minimum score 550 paper-based; 213 computer-based). Electronic applications accepted.

California State University, Fullerton, Graduate Studies, College of Humanities and Social Sciences, Department of Anthropology, Fullerton, CA 92834-9480. Offers MA. Part-time programs available. *Students:* 28 full-time (19 women), 32 part-time (20 women); includes 17 minority (1 American Indian/Alaska Native, 3 Asian Americans or Pacific Islanders, 13 Hispanic Americans), 3 international. Average age 32. 33 applicants, 73% accepted, 18 enrolled. In 2008, 33 master's awarded. *Degree requirements:* For master's, project or thesis. *Entrance requirements:* For master's, minimum GPA of 2.5 in last 60 hours of course work. Application fee: $55. Tuition and fees vary according to degree level. *Financial support:* Teaching assistantships, career-related internships or fieldwork, Federal Work-Study, institutionally sponsored loans, and scholarships/grants available. Support available to part-time students. Financial award application deadline: 3/1. *Unit head:* Dr. John Bedell, Chair, 657-278-3626. *Application contact:* Admissions/Applications, 657-278-2300.

California State University, Long Beach, Graduate Studies, College of Liberal Arts, Department of Anthropology, Long Beach, CA 90840. Offers anthropology (MA); applied anthropology (MA). Part-time programs available. *Faculty:* 8 full-time (3 women), 2 part-time/adjunct (both women). *Students:* 28 full-time (22 women), 13 part-time (7 women); includes 17 minority (3 African Americans, 2 American Indian/Alaska Native, 5 Asian Americans or Pacific Islanders, 7 Hispanic Americans). Average age 29. 34 applicants, 38% accepted, 11 enrolled. *Degree requirements:* For master's, one foreign language, comprehensive exam or thesis. *Application deadline:* For fall admission, 4/15 for domestic students. Applications are processed on a rolling basis. Application fee: $55. Electronic applications accepted. *Expenses:* Tuition, nonresident: full-time $11,160; part-time $372 per unit. Required fees: $4100; $1261 per semester. *Financial support:* Research assistantships, Federal Work-Study, institutionally sponsored loans, and scholarships/grants available. Financial award application deadline: 3/2. *Faculty research:* Archeology of California, Fiji, and Ireland; cultures of American Indian and Mexico. *Unit head:* Dr. Barbara LeMaster, Chair, 562-985-5171, Fax: 562-985-4379. *Application contact:* Dr. Ron Lowe, Graduate Advisor, 562-985-5032, Fax: 562-985-4379, E-mail: rloewe@csulb.edu.

California State University, Los Angeles, Graduate Studies, College of Natural and Social Sciences, Department of Anthropology, Los Angeles, CA 90032-8530. Offers MA. Part-time and evening/weekend programs available. *Faculty:* 5 full-time (4 women). *Students:* 24 full-time (17 women), 59 part-time (43 women); includes 23 minority (6 African Americans, 1 American Indian/Alaska Native, 4 Asian Americans or Pacific Islanders, 12 Hispanic Americans), 5 international. Average age 31. 33 applicants, 100% accepted, 29 enrolled. In 2008, 4 master's awarded. *Degree requirements:* For master's, one foreign language, comprehensive exam or thesis. *Entrance requirements:* Additional exam requirements/recommendations for international students: Required—TOEFL (minimum score 500 paper-based; 173 computer-based). *Application deadline:* For fall admission, 6/15 for domestic students, 5/1 for international students; for winter admission, 11/1 for domestic students, 9/1 for international students; for spring admission, 2/1 for domestic students, 10/1 for international students. Applications are processed on a rolling basis. Application fee: $55. *Expenses:* Tuition, nonresident: part-time $226 per credit. Required fees: $4019. *Financial support:* Federal Work-Study available. Support available to part-time students. Financial award application deadline: 3/1. *Faculty research:* Archaeology, folklore, petroglyphs, symbolism, medical anthropology. *Unit head:* Dr. Chor-Swang Ngin, Chair, 323-343-2440, Fax: 323-343-2446, E-mail: cngin@calstatela.edu. *Application contact:* Dr. Jose L. Galvan, Dean of Graduate Studies, 323-343-3820, Fax: 323-343-5653, E-mail: jgalvan@cslanet.calstatela.edu.

California State University, Northridge, Graduate Studies, College of Social and Behavioral Sciences, Department of Anthropology, Northridge, CA 91330. Offers general anthropology (MA); public archaeology (MA). *Faculty:* 6 full-time (5 women), 12 part-time/adjunct (5 women). *Students:* 23 full-time (15 women), 20 part-time (11 women); includes 1 American Indian/Alaska Native, 1 Asian American or Pacific Islander, 7 Hispanic Americans. Average age 33. 30 applicants, 80% accepted, 17 enrolled. In 2008, 6 master's awarded. *Degree requirements:* For master's, thesis or alternative. *Entrance requirements:* For master's, GRE General Test or minimum GPA of 3.0. Additional exam requirements/recommendations for international students: Required—TOEFL. *Application deadline:* For fall admission, 11/30 for domestic students. Application fee: $55. *Financial support:* Career-related internships or fieldwork, Federal Work-Study, and institutionally sponsored loans available. Financial award application deadline: 3/1. *Unit head:* Sabina Magliocco, Chair, 818-677-3331. *Application contact:* Dr. Cathy L. Costin, Graduate Adviser, 818-677-3324.

California State University, Sacramento, Graduate Studies, College of Social Sciences and Interdisciplinary Studies, Department of Anthropology, Sacramento, CA 95819-6048. Offers

MA. Part-time programs available. *Degree requirements:* For master's, thesis, departmental qualifying exam, writing proficiency exam. *Entrance requirements:* For master's, minimum GPA of 3.0 during previous 2 years. Additional exam requirements/recommendations for international students: Required—TOEFL. Electronic applications accepted.

Carleton University, Faculty of Graduate Studies, Faculty of Arts and Social Sciences, Department of Sociology and Anthropology, Program in Anthropology, Ottawa, ON K1S 5B6, Canada. Offers MA. *Degree requirements:* For master's, comprehensive exam, thesis optional. *Entrance requirements:* For master's, honors degree. Additional exam requirements/recommendations for international students: Required—TOEFL. *Faculty research:* Culture, symbols and mind, anthropology of signs and symbols, Indigenous studies, anthropology of development and underdevelopment.

Case Western Reserve University, Frances Payne Bolton School of Nursing and Department of Anthropology, Nursing/Anthropology Program, Cleveland, OH 44106. Offers MSN/MA.

Case Western Reserve University, School of Graduate Studies, Department of Anthropology, Cleveland, OH 44106. Offers MA, PhD, MD/MA, MD/PhD, MPH/MA, MSN/MA, PhD/MPH. Part-time programs available. Terminal master's awarded for partial completion of doctoral program. *Degree requirements:* For master's, thesis optional; for doctorate, one foreign language, thesis/dissertation. *Entrance requirements:* For master's and doctorate, GRE General Test. Additional exam requirements/recommendations for international students: Required—TOEFL. Electronic applications accepted. *Faculty research:* Medical anthropology, psychological anthropology, cross-cultural aging, physical anthropology, international health.

The Catholic University of America, School of Arts and Sciences, Department of Anthropology, Washington, DC 20064. Offers MA, PhD. Part-time and evening/weekend programs available. Terminal master's awarded for partial completion of doctoral program. *Degree requirements:* For master's, one foreign language, comprehensive exam, thesis or alternative; for doctorate, one foreign language, comprehensive exam, thesis/dissertation. *Entrance requirements:* For master's and doctorate, GRE General Test, 3 letters of recommendation. Additional exam requirements/recommendations for international students: Required—TOEFL (minimum score 580 paper-based; 237 computer-based). Electronic applications accepted. *Faculty research:* Medical and applied anthropology, eastern North American and South American archaeology, applied anthropology, Latin American studies, ecological anthropology.

Central European University, Graduate Studies, School of Social Sciences and Humanities, Budapest, Hungary. Offers economics (MA, PhD); gender studies (MA, PhD); international relations and European studies (MA, PhD); mathematics and its applications (MS, PhD); medieval studies (MA, PhD); nationalism studies (MA, PhD); philosophy (MA, PhD); political science (MA, PhD); public policy (MA, PhD); sociology and social anthropology (MA, PhD). Terminal master's awarded for partial completion of doctoral program. *Degree requirements:* For master's, one foreign language, thesis; for doctorate, one foreign language, comprehensive exam, thesis/dissertation. *Entrance requirements:* For master's, CEU subject tests, interview; for doctorate, GRE, CEU subject test, interview. Additional exam requirements/recommendations for international students: Required—TOEFL (minimum score 570 paper-based; 230 computer-based). Electronic applications accepted. *Faculty research:* Civil society, fiscal decentralization, party politics, political philosophy (especially Liberalism, theory of Democracy).

See Close-Up on page 349.

The College of William and Mary, Faculty of Arts and Sciences, Department of Anthropology, Williamsburg, VA 23187-8795. Offers MA, PhD. Terminal master's awarded for partial completion of doctoral program. *Degree requirements:* For master's, thesis, fieldwork; for doctorate, one foreign language, comprehensive exam, thesis/dissertation, fieldwork. *Entrance requirements:* For master's and doctorate, GRE, course work in anthropology or history. Additional exam requirements/recommendations for international students: Required—TOEFL. Electronic applications accepted. *Expenses:* Tuition, state resident: full-time $6400; part-time $300 per credit hour. Tuition, nonresident: full-time $19,720; part-time $800 per credit hour. International tuition: $19,720 full-time. Required fees: $3860. *Faculty research:* Historical archaeology, comparative colonialism, biocultural anthropology, African diaspora, historical archaeology of native America.

Colorado State University, Graduate School, College of Liberal Arts, Department of Anthropology, Fort Collins, CO 80523-1787. Offers MA. Part-time programs available. *Faculty:* 12 full-time (7 women). *Students:* 26 full-time (18 women), 22 part-time (19 women), 1 international. Average age 29. 39 applicants, 46% accepted, 14 enrolled. In 2008, 10 master's awarded. *Degree requirements:* For master's, variable foreign language requirement, comprehensive exam, thesis (for some programs), oral exam. *Entrance requirements:* For master's, GRE General Test, minimum GPA of 3.0, BA/BS. Additional exam requirements/recommendations for international students: Required—TOEFL. *Application deadline:* For fall admission, 2/15 priority date for domestic and international students. Applications are processed on a rolling basis. Application fee: $50. Electronic applications accepted. *Expenses:* Tuition, area resident: Full-time $5620; part-time $312.25 per credit. Tuition, state resident: full-time $5620; part-time $312.25 per credit. Tuition, nonresident: full-time $17,253; part-time $958.50 per credit. Required fees: $1449.56; $82.35 per credit. *Financial support:* In 2008–09, 14 students received support, including 14 teaching assistantships with full tuition reimbursements available (averaging $11,449 per year); fellowships, research assistantships with full tuition reimbursements available, career-related internships or fieldwork, Federal Work-Study, scholarships/grants, and unspecified assistantships also available. Financial award application deadline: 3/1; financial award applicants required to submit FAFSA. *Faculty research:* Archaeology, cultural anthropology, biological anthropology, globalizational development, human ecology. Total annual research expenditures: $107,997. *Unit head:* Dr. Kathleen A. Galvin, Chair, 970-491-5784, Fax: 970-491-7597, E-mail: kathleen.galvin@colostate.edu. *Application contact:* Dr. Ann L. Magennis, Graduate Program Coordinator and Associate Professor, 970-491-5966, Fax: 970-491-7597, E-mail: ann.magennis@colostate.edu.

Columbia University, Graduate School of Arts and Sciences, Division of Social Sciences, Department of Anthropology, New York, NY 10027. Offers M Phil, MA, PhD, JD/MA, JD/PhD. Part-time programs available. *Degree requirements:* For master's, one foreign language, 2 research papers; for doctorate, 2 foreign languages, thesis/dissertation. *Entrance requirements:* For master's and doctorate, GRE General Test. Additional exam requirements/recommendations for international students: Required—TOEFL. *Faculty research:* Archaeology, physical anthropology, cultural and linguistic anthropology.

Concordia University, School of Graduate Studies, Faculty of Arts and Science, Department of Sociology and Anthropology, Montréal, QC H3G 1M8, Canada. Offers social and cultural anthropology (MA); sociology (MA). *Degree requirements:* For master's, comprehensive exam or thesis. *Entrance requirements:* For master's, honors degree in sociology or equivalent. *Faculty research:* Community and ethnic relations, popular culture, regional development in Canada, industrial and social movements, social problems and policies.

Cornell University, Graduate School, Graduate Fields of Arts and Sciences, Field of Anthropology, Ithaca, NY 14853-0001. Offers archaeological anthropology (PhD); biological anthropology (PhD); sociocultural anthropology (PhD). *Faculty:* 28 full-time (12 women). *Students:* 62 full-time (40 women); includes 14 minority (5 African Americans, 3 American Indian/Alaska Native, 2 Asian Americans or Pacific Islanders, 4 Hispanic Americans), 20 international. Average age 33. 118 applicants, 10% accepted, 8 enrolled. In 2008, 8 doctorates awarded. *Degree requirements:* For doctorate, one foreign language, comprehensive exam, thesis/dissertation, teaching experience. *Entrance requirements:* For doctorate, GRE General Test, 3 letters of recommendation, sample of written work. Additional exam requirements/recommendations for international students: Required—TOEFL (minimum score 550 paper-based; 213 computer-based; 77 iBT). *Application deadline:* For fall admission, 1/1 for domestic students. Application fee: $70. Electronic applications accepted. *Expenses:* Tuition: Full-time $29,500. Required fees: $70. Full-time tuition and fees vary according to degree level, program and student level. *Financial support:* In 2008–09, 47 students received support, including 16 fellowships with full tuition reimbursements available, 8 research assistantships with full tuition reimbursements available, 23 teaching assistantships with full tuition reimbursements available; institutionally sponsored loans, scholarships/grants, health care benefits, tuition waivers (full and partial), and unspecified assistantships also available. Financial award applicants required to submit FAFSA. *Faculty research:* Culture, engaged anthropology, political economy, area studies: Asia, Americas, Europe; interdisciplinary and ethnic studies: Asian-American studies. *Unit head:* Director of Graduate Studies, 607-255-6768. *Application contact:* Graduate Field Assistant, 607-255-6768, E-mail: graduate_anthropology@cornell.edu.

Dalhousie University, Faculty of Arts and Social Science, Department of Sociology and Social Anthropology, Halifax, NS B3H 4R2, Canada. Offers social anthropology (MA, PhD); sociology (MA, PhD). In 2008, 8 master's awarded. *Entrance requirements:* Additional exam requirements/recommendations for international students: Required—TOEFL, IELTS, 1 of 5 approved tests: TOEFL, IELTS, CANTEST, CAEL, Michigan English Language Assessment Battery. *Application deadline:* For fall admission, 6/1 for domestic students, 4/1 for international students; for winter admission, 10/31 for domestic students, 8/31 for international students; for spring admission, 2/28 for domestic students, 12/31 for international students. Application fee: $70. Electronic applications accepted. *Financial support:* Career-related internships or fieldwork, scholarships/grants, and health care benefits available. *Faculty research:* Social inequality and social injustice; work, industry, and development; (regional and international perspectives); health and illness. *Unit head:* Dr. Emma Whelan, Graduate Coordinator, 902-494-6752, Fax: 902-494-2897, E-mail: sosagrad@dal.ca. *Application contact:* Lori Vaughan, Graduate Administrator, 902-494-6593, Fax: 902-494-2897, E-mail: sosagrad@is.dal.ca.

Duke University, Graduate School, Department of Cultural Anthropology, Durham, NC 27708. Offers physical anthropology (PhD), including comparative morphology of human and non-human primates, primate social behavior; social/cultural anthropology (PhD); JD/AM. *Degree requirements:* For doctorate, one foreign language, thesis/dissertation. *Entrance requirements:* For doctorate, GRE General Test. Additional exam requirements/recommendations for international students: Required—TOEFL (minimum score 550 paper-based; 213 computer-based; 83 iBT), IELTS (minimum score 7).

East Carolina University, Graduate School, Thomas Harriot College of Arts and Sciences, Department of Anthropology, Greenville, NC 27858-4353. Offers MA. Part-time programs available. *Degree requirements:* For master's, one foreign language, comprehensive exam, thesis. *Entrance requirements:* For master's, GRE General Test. Additional exam requirements/recommendations for international students: Required—TOEFL.

Eastern New Mexico University, Graduate School, College of Liberal Arts and Sciences, Department of Anthropology and Applied Archaeology, Portales, NM 88130. Offers anthropology (MA). Part-time programs available. *Degree requirements:* For master's, one foreign language, comprehensive exam, thesis. *Entrance requirements:* For master's, GRE General Test, minimum GPA of 2.5. Electronic applications accepted. *Faculty research:* Paleobotany, remote sensing, conservation archaeology, obsidian hydration.

Emory University, Graduate School of Arts and Sciences, Department of Anthropology, Atlanta, GA 30322-1100. Offers PhD. *Degree requirements:* For doctorate, thesis/dissertation, qualifying exams. *Entrance requirements:* For doctorate, GRE General Test. Additional exam requirements/recommendations for international students: Required—TOEFL. Electronic applications accepted. *Faculty research:* Primate behavioral ecology, comparative human biology, human growth and development, medical anthropology, globalization, gender and sexuality.

Florida Atlantic University, Dorothy F. Schmidt College of Arts and Letters, Department of Anthropology, Boca Raton, FL 33431-0991. Offers MA. Part-time programs available. *Faculty:* 7 full-time (3 women), 4 part-time/adjunct (2 women). *Students:* 21 full-time (14 women), 17 part-time (13 women); includes 5 minority (all Hispanic Americans). Average age 31. 21 applicants, 62% accepted, 7 enrolled. In 2008, 6 master's awarded. *Degree requirements:* For master's, one foreign language, thesis. *Entrance requirements:* For master's, GRE General Test, minimum GPA of 3.0. Additional exam requirements/recommendations for international students: Required—TOEFL. *Application deadline:* For fall admission, 7/1 priority date for domestic students, 2/15 for international students; for spring admission, 11/1 for domestic students, 7/15 for international students. Applications are processed on a rolling basis. Application fee: $30. Electronic applications accepted. *Expenses:* Tuition, state resident: full-time $4867; part-time $270.40 per credit hour. Tuition, nonresident: full-time $16,486; part-time $915.87 per credit hour. *Financial support:* Fellowships, research assistantships with tuition reimbursements, teaching assistantships with tuition reimbursements, Federal Work-Study and unspecified assistantships available. *Faculty research:* Archaeological, ethnological, ethnographical, osteological, paleoanthropological, and zoo-archaeological research. *Unit head:* Dr. Michael S. Harris, Chairman, 561-297-3233, Fax: 561-297-0084, E-mail: mharris@fau.edu. *Application contact:* Dr. Emily Stockard, Associate Dean, 561-297-2817, Fax: 561-297-2744, E-mail: stockard@fau.edu.

Florida State University, Graduate Studies, College of Arts and Sciences, Department of Anthropology, Tallahassee, FL 32306. Offers MA, MS, PhD. Part-time programs available. Terminal master's awarded for partial completion of doctoral program. *Degree requirements:* For master's, one foreign language, comprehensive exam, thesis optional; for doctorate, one foreign language, comprehensive exam, thesis/dissertation. *Entrance requirements:* For master's, GRE General Test, minimum GPA of 3.0; for doctorate, GRE General Test, minimum GPA of 3.5 (recommended). Additional exam requirements/recommendations for international students: Required—TOEFL. Electronic applications accepted. *Faculty research:* Prehistoric and historic archaeology, four-field anthropology, bioarchacology, race, religion.

George Mason University, College of Humanities and Social Sciences, Department of Sociology and Anthropology, Fairfax, VA 22030. Offers anthropology (MA); sociology (MA). *Degree requirements:* For master's, thesis. *Entrance requirements:* For master's, GRE General Test, minimum GPA of 3.0 in last 60 hours; writing sample; previous undergraduate course work in sociological theory, research methods, and social statistics. Electronic applications accepted.

George Mason University, College of Humanities and Social Sciences, Interdisciplinary Studies Program, Fairfax, VA 22030. Offers anthropology (MAIS); community college teaching (MAIS); folklore (MAIS); higher education (MAIS); individualized studies (MAIS); religion, cultures, and values (MAIS); video-based production (MAIS); women's studies (MAIS); zoo and aquarium leadership (MAIS). Part-time and evening/weekend programs available. *Degree requirements:* For master's, thesis optional. *Entrance requirements:* For master's, GRE, GMAT, or MAT, interview, minimum GPA of 3.0 in last 60 hours of course work. Electronic applications accepted.

The George Washington University, Columbian College of Arts and Sciences, Department of Anthropology, Washington, DC 20052. Offers anthropology (MA); folklife (MA); hominid paleobiology (MS, PhD); international development (MA). Part-time and evening/weekend programs available. *Faculty:* 1 (woman) full-time, 9 part-time/adjunct (5 women). *Students:* 20 full-time (15 women), 8 part-time (5 women); includes 5 minority (1 African American, 2 Asian Americans or Pacific Islanders, 2 Hispanic Americans), 1 international. Average age 28. 48 applicants, 63% accepted, 7 enrolled. In 2008, 21 master's awarded. *Degree requirements:* For master's, one foreign language, comprehensive exam, thesis or alternative. *Entrance requirements:* For master's, GRE General Test, minimum GPA of 3.0. Additional exam requirements/recommendations for international students: Required—TOEFL (minimum score 550 paper-based; 213 computer-based; 80 iBT). *Application deadline:* For fall admission, 1/15 priority date for international students; for spring admission, 9/15 priority date for domestic students, 9/1 priority date for international students. Applications are processed on a rolling basis. Application fee: $60. Electronic applications accepted. *Financial support:* In 2008–09, 8 students received support; fellowships, teaching assistantships, career-related internships or

Anthropology

The George Washington University (continued)
fieldwork and Federal Work-Study available. Financial award application deadline: 1/15. *Unit head:* Catherine J. Allen, Chair, 202-994-7545, E-mail: kitallen@gwu.edu. *Application contact:* Information Contact, 202-994-6075, E-mail: anth@gwu.edu.

Georgia State University, College of Arts and Sciences, Department of Anthropology, Atlanta, GA 30303-3083. Offers MA. Part-time and evening/weekend programs available. *Degree requirements:* For master's, one foreign language, thesis or alternative, exam. *Entrance requirements:* For master's, GRE General Test, departmental supplemental form. Additional exam requirements/recommendations for international students: Required—TOEFL. Electronic applications accepted. *Faculty research:* Medical anthropology, Latin American cultures, urban anthropology, American Southeast.

Graduate School and University Center of the City University of New York, Graduate Studies, Program in Anthropology, New York, NY 10016-4039. Offers anthropological linguistics (PhD); archaeology (PhD); cultural anthropology (PhD); physical anthropology (PhD). *Degree requirements:* For doctorate, one foreign language, thesis/dissertation. *Entrance requirements:* For doctorate, GRE General Test. Additional exam requirements/recommendations for international students: Required—TOEFL. Electronic applications accepted.

Harvard University, Graduate School of Arts and Sciences, Committee on Middle Eastern Studies, Cambridge, MA 02138. Offers anthropology and Middle Eastern studies (PhD); economics and Middle Eastern studies (PhD); fine arts and Middle Eastern studies (PhD); history and Middle Eastern studies (PhD); regional studies—Middle East (AM). Terminal master's awarded for partial completion of doctoral program. *Degree requirements:* For master's, one foreign language; for doctorate, 2 foreign languages, thesis/dissertation. *Entrance requirements:* For master's, GRE General Test; for doctorate, GRE General Test, 1 year of course work in Middle Eastern regional studies, proficiency in a related language. Additional exam requirements/recommendations for international students: Required—TOEFL. *Expenses:* Tuition: Full-time $32,556. Required fees: $1426. Full-time tuition and fees vary according to program and student level.

Harvard University, Graduate School of Arts and Sciences, Department of Anthropology, Cambridge, MA 02138. Offers archaeology (PhD); biological anthropology (PhD); legal anthropology (AM); medical anthropology (AM); social anthropology (AM, PhD); social change and development (AM). Terminal master's awarded for partial completion of doctoral program. *Degree requirements:* For master's, 2 foreign languages, thesis (for some programs); for doctorate, 2 foreign languages, thesis/dissertation, laboratory and/or fieldwork; general, qualifying, or special exams. *Entrance requirements:* For master's and doctorate, GRE General Test. Additional exam requirements/recommendations for international students: Required—TOEFL. *Expenses:* Tuition: Full-time $32,556. Required fees: $1426. Full-time tuition and fees vary according to program and student level.

Hunter College of the City University of New York, Graduate School, School of Arts and Sciences, Department of Anthropology, New York, NY 10021-5085. Offers MA. Part-time and evening/weekend programs available. *Faculty:* 9 full-time (5 women). *Students:* 3 full-time (0 women), 51 part-time (33 women); includes 5 minority (1 African American, 1 American Indian/Alaska Native, 2 Asian Americans or Pacific Islanders, 1 Hispanic American). Average age 36. 43 applicants, 63% accepted, 17 enrolled. In 2008, 10 master's awarded. *Degree requirements:* For master's, comprehensive exam, thesis, language or statistics exam. *Entrance requirements:* For master's, GRE General Test, minimum 9 credits of course work in anthropology or a related field. Additional exam requirements/recommendations for international students: Required—TOEFL. *Application deadline:* For fall admission, 4/1 for domestic students, 2/1 for international students; for spring admission, 11/1 for domestic students, 9/1 for international students. Application fee: $125. *Financial support:* Research assistantships, tuition waivers (full and partial) available. *Faculty research:* Primatology, human ecology, archeology, political anthropology, primate and human evolution. *Unit head:* Gregory A. Johnson, Chair, 212-772-5652, Fax: 212-772-5410, E-mail: gjohnson@hunter.cuny.edu. *Application contact:* William Zlata, Director for Graduate Admissions, 212-772-4482, Fax: 212-650-3336, E-mail: admissions@hunter.cuny.edu.

Idaho State University, Office of Graduate Studies, College of Arts and Sciences, Department of Anthropology, Pocatello, ID 83209. Offers MA, MS. Part-time programs available. *Faculty:* 6 full-time (2 women), 1 (woman) part-time/adjunct. *Students:* 11 full-time (6 women), 15 part-time (8 women); includes 5 minority (4 American Indian/Alaska Native, 1 Hispanic American), 1 international. Average age 45. In 2008, 1 master's awarded. *Degree requirements:* For master's, one foreign language, thesis. *Entrance requirements:* For master's, GRE General Test, GMAT or MAT, minimum GPA of 3.0 in all upper division classes, 3 letters of recommendation. Additional exam requirements/recommendations for international students: Required—TOEFL (minimum score 550 paper-based; 213 computer-based; 80 iBT). *Application deadline:* For fall admission, 7/1 for domestic students, 6/1 for international students; for spring admission, 12/1 for domestic students, 11/1 for international students. Applications are processed on a rolling basis. Application fee: $55. Electronic applications accepted. *Expenses:* Tuition, area resident: Full-time $3114; part-time $276 per credit hour. Tuition, state resident: full-time $3114; part-time $276 per credit hour. Tuition, nonresident: full-time $12,318; part-time $404 per credit hour. Required fees: $2360. Tuition and fees vary according to course load and reciprocity agreements. *Financial support:* In 2008–09, 1 research assistantship with full and partial tuition reimbursement (averaging $6,800 per year), 3 teaching assistantships with full and partial tuition reimbursements (averaging $9,401 per year) were awarded; career-related internships or fieldwork, Federal Work-Study, institutionally sponsored loans, scholarships/grants, health care benefits, tuition waivers (full and partial), and unspecified assistantships also available. Support available to part-time students. Financial award application deadline: 1/1; financial award applicants required to submit FAFSA. *Faculty research:* Native American studies: health care, language/ethnopoetics, prehistory, art, resource environmental management. *Unit head:* Dr. Ernst 'Skip' Lohse, Chairman, 208-282-2629, Fax: 208-282-4741, E-mail: lohserne@isu.edu. *Application contact:* Ellen Combs, Graduate School Technical Records Specialist, 208-282-2150, Fax: 208-282-4847, E-mail: combelle @isu.edu.

Indiana University Bloomington, University Graduate School, College of Arts and Sciences, Department of Anthropology, Bloomington, IN 47405-7000. Offers MA, PhD. *Faculty:* 26 full-time (16 women), 25 part-time/adjunct (9 women). *Students:* 104 full-time (71 women), 23 part-time (11 women); includes 20 minority (3 African Americans, 6 American Indian/Alaska Native, 2 Asian Americans or Pacific Islanders, 9 Hispanic Americans), 9 international. Average age 32. 125 applicants, 37% accepted, 18 enrolled. In 2008, 10 master's, 8 doctorates awarded. Terminal master's awarded for partial completion of doctoral program. *Degree requirements:* For master's, thesis or alternative; for doctorate, one foreign language, comprehensive exam, thesis/dissertation. *Entrance requirements:* For master's and doctorate, GRE General Test, minimum GPA of 3.0. Additional exam requirements/recommendations for international students: Required—TOEFL (minimum score 550 paper-based; 213 computer-based; 79 iBT). *Application deadline:* For fall admission, 1/15 for domestic and international students. Application fee: $50 ($60 for international students). Electronic applications accepted. *Expenses:* Tuition, area resident: Part-time $291.97 per credit hour. Tuition, state resident: part-time $291.97 per credit hour. Tuition, nonresident: part-time $850.33 per credit hour. Required fees: $110 per semester. Tuition and fees vary according to course load and program. *Financial support:* In 2008–09, 62 students received support; fellowships with full tuition reimbursements available, research assistantships with full tuition reimbursements available, teaching assistantships with full tuition reimbursements available, Federal Work-Study, scholarships/grants, health care benefits, and unspecified assistantships available. Financial award application deadline: 2/15; financial award applicants required to submit FAFSA. *Faculty research:* Ecologic and economic development, symbolism, arts/dance, paleoarchaeology, bioanthropology. Total annual research expenditures: $22.7 million. *Unit head:* Dr. Eduardo S. Brondizio, Chair, 812-855-2555, Fax: 812-855-4358, E-mail: ebrondiz@

indiana.edu. *Application contact:* Debra Wilkerson, Secretary, 812-855-1203, Fax: 812-855-4358, E-mail: dwilkers@indiana.edu.

Iowa State University of Science and Technology, Graduate College, College of Liberal Arts and Sciences, Department of Anthropology, Ames, IA 50011. Offers MA. *Faculty:* 9 full-time (4 women), 1 (woman) part-time/adjunct. *Students:* 14 full-time (12 women), 5 part-time (3 women); includes 3 minority (1 African American, 1 Asian American or Pacific Islander, 1 Hispanic American). 25 applicants, 40% accepted, 5 enrolled. In 2008, 3 master's awarded. *Degree requirements:* For master's, thesis. *Entrance requirements:* For master's, GRE General Test. Additional exam requirements/recommendations for international students: Required—TOEFL (minimum score 550 paper-based; 79 iBT), IELTS (6.5) or TOEFL. *Application deadline:* For fall admission, 1/15 priority date for domestic and international students; for spring admission, 10/1 for domestic and international students. Applications are processed on a rolling basis. Application fee: $30 ($70 for international students). Electronic applications accepted. *Expenses:* Tuition, area resident: Full-time $6446; part-time $359 per credit. Tuition, state resident: full-time $6446; part-time $359 per credit. Tuition, nonresident: full-time $17,330; part-time $963 per credit. Required fees: $790; $249.25 per semester. Tuition and fees vary according to course load and program. *Financial support:* In 2008–09, 2 research assistantships with full and partial tuition reimbursements (averaging $13,320 per year), 11 teaching assistantships with full and partial tuition reimbursements (averaging $13,320 per year) were awarded; fellowships, scholarships/grants, health care benefits, and unspecified assistantships also available. *Unit head:* Dr. R. Paul Lasley, Interim Chair, 515-294-8212, Fax: 515-294-1708, E-mail: anthgrad@iastate.edu. *Application contact:* Dr. Hsain Ilahiane, Director of Graduate Education, 515-294-7139, E-mail: anthgrade@iastate.edu.

The Johns Hopkins University, Zanvyl Krieger School of Arts and Sciences, Department of Anthropology, Baltimore, MD 21218-2699. Offers PhD. *Degree requirements:* For doctorate, one foreign language, thesis/dissertation. *Entrance requirements:* For doctorate, GRE General Test. Additional exam requirements/recommendations for international students: Required—TOEFL. Electronic applications accepted. *Faculty research:* Social and cultural anthropology of complex societies, gender politics, economic anthropology, religion.

Kent State University, College of Arts and Sciences, Department of Anthropology, Kent, OH 44242-0001. Offers MA. *Degree requirements:* For master's, thesis. *Entrance requirements:* For master's, GRE General Test, minimum GPA of 3.0. Additional exam requirements/recommendations for international students: Required—TOEFL. Electronic applications accepted.

Louisiana State University and Agricultural and Mechanical College, Graduate School, College of Arts and Sciences, Department of Geography and Anthropology, Baton Rouge, LA 70803. Offers anthropology (MA); geography (MA, MS, PhD). Part-time programs available. Terminal master's awarded for partial completion of doctoral program. *Degree requirements:* For master's, 2 foreign languages, thesis (for some programs); for doctorate, 2 foreign languages, thesis/dissertation. *Entrance requirements:* For master's and doctorate, GRE General Test, minimum GPA of 3.0. Additional exam requirements/recommendations for international students: Required—TOEFL (minimum score 550 paper-based; 213 computer-based; 79 iBT). Electronic applications accepted. *Faculty research:* Cultural, coastal, climate, GIS-geography, cultural, linguistics, archaeology-anthropology.

McGill University, Faculty of Graduate and Postdoctoral Studies, Faculty of Arts, Department of Anthropology, Montréal, QC H3A 2T5, Canada. Offers anthropology (MA, PhD); medical anthropology (MA).

McGill University, Faculty of Graduate and Postdoctoral Studies, Faculty of Medicine, Department of Social Studies in Medicine, Montréal, QC H3A 2T5, Canada. Offers medical anthropology (MA, PhD); medical history (MA, PhD); medical sociology (MA, PhD).

McMaster University, School of Graduate Studies, Faculty of Social Sciences, Department of Anthropology, Hamilton, ON L8S 4M2, Canada. Offers MA, PhD. Part-time programs available. *Degree requirements:* For master's, thesis or alternative; for doctorate, one foreign language, comprehensive exam, thesis/dissertation, fieldwork. *Entrance requirements:* Additional exam requirements/recommendations for international students: Required—TOEFL (minimum score 580 paper-based; 237 computer-based). *Faculty research:* Medical anthropology, contemporary ethnography in an interdisciplinary perspective, archaeological and social theory, linguistics, folklore.

Memorial University of Newfoundland, School of Graduate Studies, Department of Anthropology, St. John's, NL A1C 5S7, Canada. Offers archaeology and physical anthropology (MA, PhD); social and cultural anthropology (MA, PhD). Part-time programs available. *Degree requirements:* For master's, thesis (for some programs); for doctorate, comprehensive exam, thesis/dissertation, oral defense of thesis. *Entrance requirements:* For master's, 2nd class degree in related field. Electronic applications accepted. *Faculty research:* Early European settlements, ethnoarchaeology, economic/political anthropology, land claims and aboriginal rights, marine anthropology.

Michigan State University, The Graduate School, College of Social Science, Department of Anthropology, East Lansing, MI 48824. Offers anthropology (MA, PhD); professional applications in anthropology (MA). Terminal master's awarded for partial completion of doctoral program. *Degree requirements:* For master's, comprehensive exam (for some programs); for doctorate, annual evaluation. *Entrance requirements:* Additional exam requirements/recommendations for international students: Required—TOEFL. Electronic applications accepted.

Minnesota State University Mankato, College of Graduate Studies, College of Social and Behavioral Sciences, Department of Anthropology, Mankato, MN 56001. Offers MS. Part-time programs available. *Students:* 3 full-time (2 women), 13 part-time (9 women). *Degree requirements:* For master's, comprehensive exam. *Entrance requirements:* For master's, minimum undergraduate GPA of 3.0 in last 2 years of course work. Additional exam requirements/recommendations for international students: Required—TOEFL. *Application deadline:* For fall admission, 7/1 priority date for domestic students; for spring admission, 11/1 for domestic students. Applications are processed on a rolling basis. Application fee: $40. Electronic applications accepted. *Financial support:* Unspecified assistantships available. Financial award application deadline: 3/15; financial award applicants required to submit FAFSA. *Unit head:* Dr. Paul Brown, Chair, 507-389-6504, Fax: 507-389-6769, E-mail: paul.brown@mnsu.edu. *Application contact:* 507-389-2321, E-mail: grad@mnsu.edu.

Mississippi State University, College of Arts and Sciences, Department of Sociology, Anthropology, and Social Work, Mississippi State, MS 39762. Offers applied anthropology (MA); sociology (MS, PhD). Part-time programs available. *Degree requirements:* For master's, thesis (for some programs), comprehensive oral or written exam; for doctorate, thesis/dissertation, comprehensive oral and written exam. *Entrance requirements:* For master's and doctorate, GRE. Additional exam requirements/recommendations for international students: Required—TOEFL. *Faculty research:* Community and regional development, criminology, natural resource development, family sociology, gender.

New Mexico Highlands University, Graduate Studies, College of Arts and Sciences, Program in Southwest Studies, Las Vegas, NM 87701. Offers anthropology (MA). Program is interdisciplinary. Part-time programs available. *Faculty:* 12 full-time (7 women). *Students:* 7 full-time (3 women), 8 part-time (5 women); includes 3 minority (all Hispanic Americans). Average age 37. 8 applicants, 75% accepted, 4 enrolled. In 2008, 2 master's awarded. *Degree requirements:* For master's, comprehensive exam, thesis or alternative. *Entrance requirements:* For master's, minimum undergraduate GPA of 3.0. Additional exam requirements/recommendations for international students: Required—TOEFL (minimum score 540 paper-based; 207 computer-based). *Application deadline:* For fall admission, 8/1 priority date for domestic students. Applications are processed on a rolling basis. Application fee: $15. *Expenses:* Tuition, state resident: full-time $2880; part-time $120 per credit hour. Tuition, nonresident: full-time $4234; part-time $176 per credit hour. International tuition: $5645 full-time. One-time fee: $20. *Financial support:* In 2008–09, 13 students received support, including teaching assistantships (averaging $6,500 per year); career-related internships or fieldwork, Federal Work-Study, institutionally sponsored loans, scholarships/grants, tuition waivers (full and partial), and unspecified assistantships also available. Support available to part-time students. Financial award application deadline: 3/1; financial award applicants required to submit FAFSA. *Application contact:* Diane Trujillo, Administrative Assistant, Graduate Studies, 505-454-3266, Fax: 505-426-2117, E-mail: dtrujillo@nmhu.edu.

New Mexico State University, Graduate School, College of Arts and Sciences, Department of Sociology and Anthropology, Las Cruces, NM 88003-8001. Offers anthropology (MA); sociology (MA). Part-time programs available. *Faculty:* 12 full-time (8 women), 4 part-time/adjunct (2 women). *Students:* 42 full-time (29 women), 60 part-time (39 women); includes 25 minority (5 African Americans, 2 American Indian/Alaska Native, 18 Hispanic Americans), 5 international. Average age 33. 71 applicants, 99% accepted, 31 enrolled. In 2008, 17 master's awarded. *Degree requirements:* For master's, comprehensive exam (for some programs), thesis (for some programs). *Entrance requirements:* Additional exam requirements/recommendations for international students: Required—TOEFL. *Application deadline:* For fall admission, 2/15 priority date for domestic students; for spring admission, 10/15 priority date for domestic students. Applications are processed on a rolling basis. Application fee: $30 ($50 for international students). Electronic applications accepted. *Expenses:* Tuition, area resident: Full-time $3890; part-time $212.85 per credit. Tuition, state resident: full-time $3890; part-time $212.85 per credit. Tuition, nonresident: full-time $13,916; part-time $630.55 per credit. Required fees: $1218; $609 per semester. *Financial support:* In 2008–09, 28 students received support, including 2 research assistantships with partial tuition reimbursements available (averaging $7,900 per year), 19 teaching assistantships with partial tuition reimbursements available (averaging $8,321 per year); fellowships, career-related internships or fieldwork, Federal Work-Study, and health care benefits also available. Support available to part-time students. Financial award application deadline: 2/15. *Faculty research:* Native American culture and society, Latin America and border studies, prehistoric and historic archaeology, medical anthropology, applied anthropology. *Unit head:* Dr. Miriam Chaiken, Head, 575-646-3821, Fax: 575-646-3725, E-mail: mchaiken@nmsu.edu. *Application contact:* Coordinator.

The New School: A University, The New School for Social Research, Department of Anthropology, New York, NY 10011. Offers MA, DS Sc, PhD. Part-time and evening/weekend programs available. *Faculty:* 8 full-time (3 women). *Students:* 49 full-time (34 women), 10 part-time (7 women); includes 10 minority (1 African American, 6 Asian Americans or Pacific Islanders, 3 Hispanic Americans), 13 international. Average age 30. In 2008, 13 master's, 2 doctorates awarded. Terminal master's awarded for partial completion of doctoral program. *Degree requirements:* For master's, exam; for doctorate, one foreign language, thesis/dissertation, qualifying exam. *Entrance requirements:* For master's, GRE General Test; for doctorate, GRE General Test, MA. Additional exam requirements/recommendations for international students: Required—TOEFL (minimum score 600 paper-based; 250 computer-based; 100 iBT). *Application deadline:* For fall admission, 1/15 priority date for domestic students. Applications are processed on a rolling basis. Application fee: $50. *Expenses:* Tuition: Full-time $27,144; part-time $1508 per credit. Required fees: $355 per semester. *Financial support:* Fellowships, research assistantships, teaching assistantships, career-related internships or fieldwork, Federal Work-Study, scholarships/grants, and tuition waivers (full and partial) available. Financial award application deadline: 3/1; financial award applicants required to submit FAFSA. *Faculty research:* Critical theory; modern social and cultural systems; race, class, gender. *Unit head:* Dr. Hugh Raffles, Chair, 212-229-5757 Ext. 3025, E-mail: rafflesh@newschool.edu. *Application contact:* Robert MacDonald, Director of Admissions, 800-523-5710 Ext. 3007, Fax: 212-989-7102, E-mail: macdonar@newschool.edu.

See Close-Up on page 1251.

New York University, Graduate School of Arts and Science, Department of Anthropology, New York, NY 10012-1019. Offers anthropology (MA, PhD), including archaeological anthropology, linguistic anthropology, physical anthropology, socio-cultural anthropology; anthropology and French studies (PhD); MA/Advanced Certificate; PhD/Advanced Certificate. Part-time programs available. *Degree requirements:* For master's, thesis; for doctorate, one foreign language, comprehensive exam, thesis/dissertation. *Entrance requirements:* For master's, GRE General Test; for doctorate, GRE General Test, MA or equivalent. Additional exam requirements/recommendations for international students: Required—TOEFL. *Faculty research:* Sociocultural anthropology, archaeology, biological anthropology, linguistic anthropology.

North Carolina State University, Graduate School, College of Humanities and Social Sciences, Department of Sociology and Anthropology, Program in Anthropology, Raleigh, NC 27695. Offers bioarchaeology (MA); cultural anthropology (MA); environmental anthropology (MA).

Northern Arizona University, Graduate College, College of Social and Behavioral Sciences, Department of Anthropology, Flagstaff, AZ 86011. Offers archaeology (MA); cultural anthropology (MA); linguistic anthropology (MA). *Degree requirements:* For master's, thesis (for some programs), internship paper. *Entrance requirements:* For master's, 18 undergraduate hours in anthropology. *Faculty research:* Economic development, culture change, ethnohistory, archaeology of the Southwest, small town networks and HIV.

Northern Illinois University, Graduate School, College of Liberal Arts and Sciences, Department of Anthropology, De Kalb, IL 60115-2854. Offers MA. Part-time programs available. *Degree requirements:* For master's, one foreign language, comprehensive exam, thesis optional. *Entrance requirements:* For master's, GRE General Test, minimum GPA of 2.75, 15 hours of course work in anthropology, course work in statistics. Additional exam requirements/recommendations for international students: Required—TOEFL (minimum score 550 paper-based; 213 computer-based). Electronic applications accepted. *Faculty research:* Linguistic anthropology of Oceania, Mayan languages, human paleontology, primate evolution, dental anthropology.

Northwestern University, The Graduate School, Judd A. and Marjorie Weinberg College of Arts and Sciences, Department of Anthropology, Evanston, IL 60208. Offers PhD, JD/PhD. Admissions and degrees offered through The Graduate School. *Degree requirements:* For doctorate, thesis/dissertation. *Entrance requirements:* For doctorate, GRE General Test. Additional exam requirements/recommendations for international students: Required—TOEFL. Electronic applications accepted. *Faculty research:* Archaeology of complex societies, gender, political/urban anthropology, linguistic anthropology, African studies.

The Ohio State University, Graduate School, College of Social and Behavioral Sciences, School of Social and Behavioral Science, Department of Anthropology, Columbus, OH 43210. Offers MA, PhD. *Degree requirements:* For master's, thesis optional; for doctorate, one foreign language, thesis/dissertation. *Entrance requirements:* For master's and doctorate, GRE General Test. Additional exam requirements/recommendations for international students: Required—TOEFL (minimum score 600 paper-based; 250 computer-based). Electronic applications accepted.

Oregon State University, Graduate School, College of Liberal Arts, Department of Anthropology, Corvallis, OR 97331. Offers anthropology (MAIS); applied anthropology (MA). *Degree requirements:* For master's, one foreign language, thesis. *Entrance requirements:* For master's, minimum GPA of 3.0 in last 90 hours. Additional exam requirements/recommendations for international students: Required—TOEFL. *Faculty research:* Historical anthropology; first American studies; Japanese, Asian, South Pacific, and Native American cultures; business anthropology.

Penn State University Park, Graduate School, College of the Liberal Arts, Department of Anthropology, State College, University Park, PA 16802-1503. Offers MA, PhD.

Portland State University, Graduate Studies, College of Liberal Arts and Sciences, Department of Anthropology, Portland, OR 97207-0751. Offers MA. *Faculty:* 6 full-time (4 women), 2 part-time/adjunct (0 women). *Students:* 13 full-time (8 women), 16 part-time (10 women); includes 3 minority (1 Asian American or Pacific Islander, 2 Hispanic Americans). Average age 34. 30 applicants, 27% accepted, 5 enrolled. *Degree requirements:* For master's, one foreign language, thesis. *Entrance requirements:* For master's, GRE General Test, minimum GPA of 3.25 in upper-division anthropology course work, 3.0 overall; 3 letters of recommendation. Additional exam requirements/recommendations for international students: Required—TOEFL. *Application deadline:* For fall admission, 2/1 for domestic and international students. Application fee: $50. *Expenses:* Tuition, area resident: Full-time $8763; part-time $179 per credit hour. Tuition, state resident: full-time $8763; part-time $298 per credit hour. Tuition, nonresident: full-time $12,981; part-time $426 per credit hour. Required fees: $1242. One-time fee: $250. Tuition and fees vary according to course load and program. *Financial support:* In 2008–09, 6 teaching assistantships with full tuition reimbursements (averaging $6,499 per year) were awarded; research assistantships with full tuition reimbursements, career-related internships or fieldwork, Federal Work-Study, and unspecified assistantships also available. Support available to part-time students. Financial award application deadline: 3/1; financial award applicants required to submit FAFSA. *Faculty research:* Forensic anthropology, Northwest Coast prehistory, Native Americans, applied anthropology, urban anthropology. Total annual research expenditures: $153,894. *Unit head:* Dr. Kenneth M. Ames, Chair, 503-725-3081. *Application contact:* Connie Cash, Office Coordinator, 503-725-3081, Fax: 503-725-3905, E-mail: cashc@pdx.edu.

Portland State University, Graduate Studies, Systems Science Program, Portland, OR 97207-0751. Offers computational intelligence (Certificate); computer modeling and simulation (Certificate); systems science (MS); systems science/anthropology (PhD); systems science/business administration (PhD); systems science/civil engineering (PhD); systems science/economics (PhD); systems science/engineering management (PhD); systems science/general (PhD); systems science/mathematical sciences (PhD); systems science/mechanical engineering (PhD); systems science/psychology (PhD); systems science/sociology (PhD). *Faculty:* 3 full-time (0 women). *Students:* 12 full-time (3 women), 13 part-time (3 women); includes 2 minority (1 American Indian/Alaska Native, 1 Asian American or Pacific Islander), 5 international. Average age 38. 14 applicants, 71% accepted, 8 enrolled. In 2008, 2 master's, 4 doctorates awarded. *Degree requirements:* For doctorate, variable foreign language requirement, thesis/dissertation. *Entrance requirements:* For master's, 2 letters of recommendation; for doctorate, GMAT, GRE General Test, minimum undergraduate GPA of 3.0. Additional exam requirements/recommendations for international students: Required—TOEFL. *Application deadline:* For fall admission, 2/1 for domestic students; for spring admission, 11/1 for domestic students. Application fee: $50. *Expenses:* Tuition, area resident: Full-time $8763; part-time $179 per credit hour. Tuition, state resident: full-time $8763; part-time $298 per credit hour. Tuition, nonresident: full-time $12,981; part-time $426 per credit hour. Required fees: $1242. One-time fee: $250. Tuition and fees vary according to course load and program. *Financial support:* In 2008–09, 1 research assistantship with full tuition reimbursement (averaging $7,704 per year) was awarded; teaching assistantships with full tuition reimbursements, career-related internships or fieldwork, Federal Work-Study, scholarships/grants, and unspecified assistantships also available. Support available to part-time students. Financial award application deadline: 3/1; financial award applicants required to submit FAFSA. *Faculty research:* Systems theory and methodology, artificial intelligence neural networks, information theory, nonlinear dynamics/chaos, modeling and simulation. *Unit head:* George Lendaris, Acting Director, 503-725-4960. *Application contact:* Dawn Sharafi, Administrative Assistant, 503-725-4960, E-mail: dawn@sysc.pdx.edu.

Princeton University, Graduate School, Department of Anthropology, Princeton, NJ 08544-1019. Offers PhD. *Degree requirements:* For doctorate, variable foreign language requirement, thesis/dissertation. *Entrance requirements:* For doctorate, GRE General Test, sample of written work. Additional exam requirements/recommendations for international students: Required—TOEFL (minimum score 600 paper-based; 250 computer-based). Electronic applications accepted. *Faculty research:* Symbolic anthropology, social theory, gender studies, law and society, political and social anthropology.

Purdue University, Graduate School, College of Liberal Arts, Department of Sociology and Anthropology, West Lafayette, IN 47907. Offers anthropology (MS, PhD); sociology (MS, PhD). Terminal master's awarded for partial completion of doctoral program. *Degree requirements:* For doctorate, thesis/dissertation. *Entrance requirements:* For master's and doctorate, GRE General Test. Additional exam requirements/recommendations for international students: Required—TOEFL, TWE. Electronic applications accepted. *Faculty research:* Communiversity survey project, risk, fear, constrained behavior, archaeological services.

Rice University, Graduate Programs, School of Social Sciences, Department of Anthropology, Houston, TX 77251-1892. Offers MA, PhD. Terminal master's awarded for partial completion of doctoral program. *Degree requirements:* For master's, variable foreign language requirement, thesis; for doctorate, one foreign language, thesis/dissertation. *Entrance requirements:* For master's and doctorate, GRE General Test, minimum GPA of 3.0. Additional exam requirements/recommendations for international students: Required—TOEFL (minimum score 600 paper-based; 250 computer-based; 90 iBT). *Faculty research:* Archaeology, biological anthropology, anthropological linguistics, complex societies.

Roosevelt University, Graduate Division, College of Arts and Sciences, Department of Sociology and Anthropology, Chicago, IL 60605-1394. Offers anthropology (MA); sociology (MA). Part-time and evening/weekend programs available. *Students:* 13 full-time (8 women), 14 part-time (9 women); includes 10 minority (7 African Americans, 1 Asian American or Pacific Islander, 2 Hispanic Americans). Average age 35. 56 applicants, 57% accepted, 9 enrolled. In 2008, 3 master's awarded. *Degree requirements:* For master's, comprehensive exam, thesis. *Application deadline:* For fall admission, 6/1 priority date for domestic students. Applications are processed on a rolling basis. Application fee: $25 ($35 for international students). *Expenses:* Tuition: Full-time $14,730; part-time $709 per credit. Required fees: $175 per semester. Tuition and fees vary according to course load and program. *Financial support:* Teaching assistantships available. Financial award application deadline: 2/15. *Faculty research:* Social theory, urban sociology, gerontology, social organizations. *Unit head:* Michael Maly, Head, 312-341-3769, E-mail: mmaly@roosevelt.edu. *Application contact:* Joanne Canyon-Heller, Coordinator of Graduate Admission, 877-APPLY RU, Fax: 312-281-3356, E-mail: applyru@roosevelt.edu.

Rutgers, The State University of New Jersey, New Brunswick, Graduate School, Program in Anthropology, Piscataway, NJ 08854-8097. Offers MA, PhD. Terminal master's awarded for partial completion of doctoral program. *Degree requirements:* For master's, thesis or alternative; for doctorate, comprehensive exam, thesis/dissertation. *Entrance requirements:* For master's and doctorate, GRE General Test, writing sample. Additional exam requirements/recommendations for international students: Required—TOEFL. Electronic applications accepted. *Faculty research:* Human evolution, lithic technology, behavioral ecology, ethnicity, gender.

San Diego State University, Graduate and Research Affairs, College of Arts and Letters, Department of Anthropology, San Diego, CA 92182. Offers MA. *Degree requirements:* For master's, one foreign language, thesis. *Entrance requirements:* For master's, GRE General Test, 3 letters of recommendation, typed writing sample. Additional exam requirements/recommendations for international students: Required—TOEFL. Electronic applications accepted. *Faculty research:* Meso-American archaeology, cognitive anthropology, ethnomusicology, primate conservation, biomedical anthropology.

San Francisco State University, Division of Graduate Studies, College of Behavioral and Social Sciences, Department of Anthropology, San Francisco, CA 94132-1722. Offers MA. *Faculty research:* Immigration, ethnicity, urban anthropology, Californian and Latin American archaeology.

Anthropology

San Jose State University, Graduate Studies and Research, College of Social Sciences, Department of Anthropology, San Jose, CA 95192-0001. Offers applied anthropology (MA). *Entrance requirements:* For master's, curriculum vitae or resumé, official transcripts, 2 letters of reference.

Simon Fraser University, Graduate Studies, Faculty of Arts and Social Sciences, Department of Sociology and Anthropology, Burnaby, BC V5A 1S6, Canada. Offers anthropology (MA, PhD); sociology (MA, PhD). *Degree requirements:* For master's, thesis (for some programs); for doctorate, thesis/dissertation. *Entrance requirements:* For master's and doctorate, minimum GPA of 3.25. Additional exam requirements/recommendations for international students: Required—TOEFL or IELTS. *Faculty research:* Sociology theory, social and cultural anthropology, political sociology, religion and society, Canadian native peoples.

Sonoma State University, School of Social Sciences, Program in Cultural Resources Management, Rohnert Park, CA 94928-3609. Offers MA. Part-time programs available. *Degree requirements:* For master's, thesis. *Entrance requirements:* For master's, minimum GPA of 3.0. *Faculty research:* Identification, evaluation, and preservation of cultural resources.

Southern Illinois University Carbondale, Graduate School, College of Liberal Arts, Department of Anthropology, Carbondale, IL 62901-4701. Offers MA, PhD. *Degree requirements:* For master's, one foreign language, thesis; for doctorate, one foreign language, thesis/dissertation. *Entrance requirements:* For master's, GRE General Test, minimum GPA of 2.7; for doctorate, GRE General Test, minimum GPA of 3.25. Additional exam requirements/recommendations for international students: Required—TOEFL. *Faculty research:* Archaeology, human variability, evolution, cultural ecology, social anthropology.

See Close-Up on page 1291.

Southern Methodist University, Dedman College, Department of Anthropology, Dallas, TX 75275. Offers anthropology (PhD); medical anthropology (MA). *Faculty:* 12 full-time (5 women), 6 part-time/adjunct (2 women). *Students:* 18 full-time (11 women), 40 part-time (20 women); includes 7 minority (1 American Indian/Alaska Native, 6 Hispanic Americans), 4 international. Average age 33. 21 applicants, 29% accepted, 6 enrolled. In 2008, 8 master's, 5 doctorates awarded. Terminal master's awarded for partial completion of doctoral program. *Degree requirements:* For master's, one foreign language, comprehensive exam, thesis or alternative; for doctorate, one foreign language, comprehensive exam, thesis/dissertation, qualifying exam, defense of dissertation. *Entrance requirements:* For master's and doctorate, GRE General Test, minimum GPA of 3.0. Additional exam requirements/recommendations for international students: Required—TOEFL (minimum score 550 paper-based). *Application deadline:* For fall admission, 2/1 priority date for domestic students; for spring admission, 11/30 priority date for domestic students. Applications are processed on a rolling basis. Application fee: $60. *Financial support:* In 2008–09, 1 fellowship with full and partial tuition reimbursement (averaging $16,000 per year), 3 research assistantships with full tuition reimbursements (averaging $16,000 per year), 4 teaching assistantships with full tuition reimbursements (averaging $16,000 per year) were awarded; Federal Work-Study, institutionally sponsored loans, scholarships/grants, traineeships, tuition waivers (full), and unspecified assistantships also available. Financial award application deadline: 3/1; financial award applicants required to submit FAFSA. *Faculty research:* Health and gender, Paleoindians, Mesoamerica, American southwest, migration and ethnicity. Total annual research expenditures: $300,000. *Unit head:* Pamela Carter Hogan, Administrative Assistant to the Chair, 214-768-4152, Fax: 214-768-2906, E-mail: phogan@smu.edu. *Application contact:* Dr. Caroline Brettell, Director of Graduate Studies, 214-768-4254, Fax: 214-768-2906, E-mail: trick@smu.edu.

Stanford University, School of Humanities and Sciences, Department of Anthropological Sciences, Stanford, CA 94305-9991. Offers MA, MS, PhD. Terminal master's awarded for partial completion of doctoral program. *Degree requirements:* For master's, thesis; for doctorate, one foreign language, thesis/dissertation. *Entrance requirements:* For master's and doctorate, GRE General Test. Additional exam requirements/recommendations for international students: Required—TOEFL. Electronic applications accepted.

Stanford University, School of Humanities and Sciences, Department of Cultural and Social Anthropology, Stanford, CA 94305-9991. Offers MA, PhD. Terminal master's awarded for partial completion of doctoral program. *Degree requirements:* For master's, thesis; for doctorate, one foreign language, thesis/dissertation. *Entrance requirements:* For master's and doctorate, GRE General Test. Additional exam requirements/recommendations for international students: Required—TOEFL. Electronic applications accepted.

State University of New York at Binghamton, Graduate School, School of Arts and Sciences, Department of Anthropology, Binghamton, NY 13902-6000. Offers MA, PhD. Part-time programs available. *Faculty:* 17 full-time (6 women), 4 part-time/adjunct (1 woman). *Students:* 64 full-time (44 women), 74 part-time (47 women); includes 17 minority (3 African Americans, 2 American Indian/Alaska Native, 5 Asian Americans or Pacific Islanders, 7 Hispanic Americans), 21 international. Average age 31. 101 applicants, 48% accepted, 17 enrolled. In 2008, 15 master's, 4 doctorates awarded. Terminal master's awarded for partial completion of doctoral program. *Degree requirements:* For master's, one foreign language, thesis or alternative, written exam; for doctorate, variable foreign language requirement, thesis/dissertation, oral exam. *Entrance requirements:* For master's and doctorate, GRE General Test, GRE Subject Test. Additional exam requirements/recommendations for international students: Required—TOEFL. *Application deadline:* For fall admission, 4/15 priority date for domestic students, 1/15 priority date for international students; for spring admission, 11/1 for domestic students, 10/1 priority date for international students. Applications are processed on a rolling basis. Application fee: $60. Electronic applications accepted. *Expenses:* Tuition, area resident: Full-time $6900; part-time $288 per credit. Tuition, state resident: full-time $6900; part-time $288 per credit. Tuition, nonresident: full-time $10,920; part-time $455 per credit. Required fees: $1130. Part-time tuition and fees vary according to course load, program and student level. *Financial support:* In 2008–09, 47 students received support, including 7 fellowships with full tuition reimbursements available (averaging $1,500 per year), 1 research assistantship with full tuition reimbursement available (averaging $15,000 per year), 27 teaching assistantships with full tuition reimbursements available (averaging $15,000 per year); career-related internships or fieldwork, Federal Work-Study, institutionally sponsored loans, scholarships/grants, health care benefits, and unspecified assistantships also available. Financial award application deadline: 2/15; financial award applicants required to submit FAFSA. *Unit head:* Dr. Charles Cobb, Chairperson, 607-777-4701, E-mail: ccobb@binghamton.edu. *Application contact:* Victoria Williams, Recruiting and Admissions Coordinator, 607-777-2151, Fax: 607-777-2501, E-mail: vwilliam@binghamton.edu.

Stony Brook University, State University of New York, Graduate School, College of Arts and Sciences, Department of Anthropology, Stony Brook, NY 11794. Offers MA, PhD. *Faculty:* 13 full-time (5 women), 3 part-time/adjunct (all women). *Students:* 42 full-time (31 women), 3 part-time (1 woman); includes 3 minority (1 African American, 2 Asian Americans or Pacific Islanders), 13 international. Average age 30. 81 applicants, 16% accepted. In 2008, 3 master's, 3 doctorates awarded. *Degree requirements:* For master's, thesis, fieldwork; for doctorate, one foreign language, thesis/dissertation, fieldwork. *Entrance requirements:* For master's and doctorate, GRE General Test. Additional exam requirements/recommendations for international students: Required—TOEFL. *Application deadline:* For fall admission, 1/15 for domestic students. Application fee: $60. *Expenses:* Tuition, area resident: Full-time $7880; part-time $328 per credit hour. Tuition, state resident: full-time $7880; part-time $328 per credit hour. Tuition, nonresident: full-time $13,250; part-time $552 per credit hour. Required fees: $848. *Financial support:* In 2008–09, 2 research assistantships, 23 teaching assistantships were awarded; fellowships, career-related internships or fieldwork also available. *Faculty research:* Social and cultural anthropology, cultural history and archaeology, physical anthropology. Total annual research expenditures: $615,356. *Unit head:* Prof. Diane M. Doran-Sheehy, Chair, 631-632-9445, E-mail: diane.doran@stonybrook.edu. *Application contact:* Dr. Elizabeth Stone, Director, 631-632-7627, Fax: 631-632-9165, E-mail: elizabeth.stone@stonybrook.edu.

Syracuse University, Graduate School, Maxwell School of Citizenship and Public Affairs and College of Arts and Sciences, Program in Anthropology, Syracuse, NY 13244. Offers MA, PhD. *Degree requirements:* For master's, thesis or alternative; for doctorate, one foreign language, thesis/dissertation. *Entrance requirements:* For master's and doctorate, GRE General Test. Additional exam requirements/recommendations for international students: Required—TOEFL. Electronic applications accepted.

Teachers College, Columbia University, Graduate Faculty of Education, Department of International and Transcultural Studies, Program in Anthropology, New York, NY 10027-6696. Offers Ed M, MA, Ed D, PhD. *Faculty:* 4 full-time (0 women). *Students:* 29 full-time (20 women), 42 part-time (33 women); includes 21 minority (8 African Americans, 11 Asian Americans or Pacific Islanders, 2 Hispanic Americans), 11 international. Average age 35. 43 applicants, 74% accepted, 14 enrolled. In 2008, 14 master's, 5 doctorates awarded. *Degree requirements:* For doctorate, variable foreign language requirement, thesis/dissertation. *Entrance requirements:* For master's and doctorate, GRE General Test. *Application deadline:* For fall admission, 5/15 for domestic students; for spring admission, 12/1 for domestic students. Application fee: $75. *Expenses:* Tuition: Full-time $26,040; part-time $1085 per credit. Required fees: $720. *Financial support:* Career-related internships or fieldwork, Federal Work-Study, institutionally sponsored loans, and tuition waivers (full and partial) available. Support available to part-time students. Financial award application deadline: 2/1. *Faculty research:* African studies, sociocultural change, education in the developing world, human development in social and cultural contexts, culture and communication theory. *Unit head:* Dr. George Bond, Chair, 212-678-3947. *Application contact:* Deanna Ghozati, Assistant Director of Admission, 212-678-4018, Fax: 212-678-4171, E-mail: ghozati@tc.edu.

Temple University, Graduate School, College of Liberal Arts, Department of Anthropology, Philadelphia, PA 19122-6096. Offers PhD. Part-time and evening/weekend programs available. Terminal master's awarded for partial completion of doctoral program. *Degree requirements:* For doctorate, 2 foreign languages, thesis/dissertation. *Entrance requirements:* For doctorate, GRE General Test, minimum GPA of 3.0. Additional exam requirements/recommendations for international students: Required—TOEFL (minimum score 550 paper-based; 213 computer-based; 79 iBT). Electronic applications accepted. *Faculty research:* Political economy, biocultural adaptation, visual anthropology, critical urban anthropology, archaeology.

Texas A&M University, College of Liberal Arts, Department of Anthropology, College Station, TX 77843. Offers MA, PhD. *Faculty:* 23. *Students:* 72 full-time (45 women), 40 part-time (17 women); includes 11 minority (1 American Indian/Alaska Native, 3 Asian Americans or Pacific Islanders, 7 Hispanic Americans), 13 international. Average age 33. In 2008, 11 master's, 4 doctorates awarded. *Degree requirements:* For doctorate, thesis/dissertation. *Entrance requirements:* For master's and doctorate, GRE General Test. Additional exam requirements/recommendations for international students: Required—TOEFL. Application fee: $50 ($75 for international students). *Expenses:* Tuition, area resident: Full-time $3838.50. Tuition, state resident: full-time $3838.50. Tuition, nonresident: full-time $8897. Required fees: $2359.60. *Financial support:* Fellowships, research assistantships, teaching assistantships, career-related internships or fieldwork, Federal Work-Study, and institutionally sponsored loans available. Financial award application deadline: 4/1; financial award applicants required to submit FAFSA. *Faculty research:* Nautical archaeology, archaeological conservation, archaeological palynology, paleoethnobotany, folklore. *Unit head:* Dr. Donny Hamilton, Head, 979-845-6355, E-mail: dlhamilton@tamu.edu. *Application contact:* Karen Taylor, Assistant Advisor, 979-845-9333, Fax: 979-845-4070.

Texas State University–San Marcos, Graduate School, College of Liberal Arts, Department of Anthropology, San Marcos, TX 78666. Offers MA. *Entrance requirements:* For master's, GRE, minimum GPA of 3.0 in last 60 undergraduate hours. Additional exam requirements/recommendations for international students: Required—TOEFL (minimum score 550 paper-based; 213 computer-based). Electronic applications accepted.

Texas Tech University, Graduate School, College of Arts and Sciences, Department of Sociology, Anthropology and Social Work, Lubbock, TX 79409. Offers anthropology (MA); sociology (MA). Part-time programs available. *Faculty:* 14 full-time (5 women). *Students:* 18 full-time (12 women), 12 part-time (4 women); includes 9 minority (1 American Indian/Alaska Native, 2 Asian Americans or Pacific Islanders, 6 Hispanic Americans), 2 international. Average age 30. 21 applicants, 81% accepted, 9 enrolled. In 2008, 8 master's awarded. *Degree requirements:* For master's, one foreign language, thesis or alternative. *Entrance requirements:* For master's, GRE General Test. Additional exam requirements/recommendations for international students: Required—TOEFL (minimum score 550 paper-based; 213 computer-based). *Application deadline:* For fall admission, 3/1 priority date for international students; for spring admission, 11/1 priority date for international students. Applications are processed on a rolling basis. Application fee: $50 ($60 for international students). Electronic applications accepted. *Expenses:* Tuition, area resident: Part-time $194 per credit hour. Tuition, state resident: full-time $4648; part-time $194 per credit hour. Tuition, nonresident: full-time $11,392; part-time $475 per credit hour. Required fees: $2206; $69 per credit hour. $389 per semester. *Financial support:* In 2008–09, 23 students received support, including 3 research assistantships with partial tuition reimbursements available (averaging $10,833 per year), 10 teaching assistantships with partial tuition reimbursements available (averaging $10,850 per year); Federal Work-Study and institutionally sponsored loans also available. Support available to part-time students. Financial award application deadline: 4/15; financial award applicants required to submit FAFSA. *Faculty research:* Sociology theory, research methods, physical and forensic anthropology, Texas archaeology, Mayan archaeology. Total annual research expenditures: $7,284. *Unit head:* Dr. Jeffrey Payne Williams, Chair and Professor, 806-742-2400, Fax: 806-742-1088, E-mail: jeff.williams@ttu.edu. *Application contact:* Dr. Yung-Mei Tsai, Sociology Graduate Program Director, 806-742-2400, Fax: 806-742-1088, E-mail: yung.mei.tsai@ttu.edu.

Trent University, Graduate Studies, Program in Anthropology, Peterborough, ON K9J 7B8, Canada. Offers MA. Part-time programs available. *Degree requirements:* For master's, thesis. *Entrance requirements:* For master's, honors degree. *Faculty research:* Paleoecology, trade and fortification networks, pre-Columbian art.

Tulane University, School of Liberal Arts, Department of Anthropology, New Orleans, LA 70118-5669. Offers MA, PhD. Terminal master's awarded for partial completion of doctoral program. *Degree requirements:* For master's, one foreign language, thesis; for doctorate, 2 foreign languages, thesis/dissertation. *Entrance requirements:* For master's, GRE General Test, minimum B average in undergraduate course work; for doctorate, GRE General Test. Additional exam requirements/recommendations for international students: Required—TOEFL. Electronic applications accepted. *Faculty research:* Linguistics, physical anthropology, sociocultural archaeology, Mesoamerica.

Universidad de las Américas–Puebla, Division of Graduate Studies, School of Social Sciences, Program in Anthropology, Puebla, Mexico. Offers anthropology (MA); archaeology (MA). Part-time and evening/weekend programs available. *Degree requirements:* For master's, one foreign language, thesis. *Entrance requirements:* For master's, bachelor's degree in anthropology or equivalent. *Faculty research:* Archaeology, ethnography, and ethnohistory of Mesoamerica.

Université de Montréal, Faculty of Arts and Sciences, Department of Anthropology, Montréal, QC H3C 3J7, Canada. Offers M Sc, PhD. Part-time programs available. *Faculty:* 29 full-time (11 women), 2 part-time/adjunct (1 woman). *Students:* 68 full-time (45 women), 129 part-time (88 women). 88 applicants, 47% accepted, 35 enrolled. In 2008, 23 master's awarded. *Degree requirements:* For master's, thesis; for doctorate, thesis/dissertation, general exam. *Application deadline:* For fall admission, 2/1 priority date for domestic students; for winter admission, 11/1 priority date for domestic students; for spring admission, 2/1 priority date for domestic students. Application fee: $100. Electronic applications accepted. *Faculty research:* Archaeology, ethnolinguistics, ethnology. *Unit head:* Pierrette Thibault, Chair, 514-343-6560, Fax: 514-343-

2494, E-mail: pierrette.thibault@umontreal.ca. *Application contact:* Louise i Paradis, Professor, 514-343-7334, Fax: 514-343-2494, E-mail: louise.i.paradis@umontreal.ca.

Université Laval, Faculty of Social Sciences, Department of Anthropology, Programs in Anthropology, Québec, QC G1K 7P4, Canada. Offers MA, PhD. Terminal master's awarded for partial completion of doctoral program. *Degree requirements:* For master's, thesis; for doctorate, thesis/dissertation. *Entrance requirements:* For master's, knowledge of French, interview; for doctorate, knowledge of French, comprehensive of written English, knowledge of a third language. Electronic applications accepted.

University at Albany, State University of New York, College of Arts and Sciences, Department of Anthropology, Albany, NY 12222-0001. Offers MA, PhD. Terminal master's awarded for partial completion of doctoral program. *Degree requirements:* For master's, comprehensive exam, thesis; for doctorate, 2 foreign languages, thesis/dissertation, field exams. *Entrance requirements:* For master's and doctorate, GRE. Additional exam requirements/recommendations for international students: Required—TOEFL (minimum score 550 paper-based; 213 computer-based). Electronic applications accepted. *Faculty research:* Economic and ecological anthropology; language, culture, and cognition; symbolic and interpretive anthropology; human evolution, morphology, demography, and medical anthropology; spatial and settlement archaeology.

University at Buffalo, the State University of New York, Graduate School, College of Arts and Sciences, Department of Anthropology, Buffalo, NY 14260. Offers MA, PhD. Terminal master's awarded for partial completion of doctoral program. *Degree requirements:* For master's, comprehensive exam, project; for doctorate, one foreign language, thesis/dissertation, exam. *Entrance requirements:* For master's, GRE General Test, minimum GPA of 3.0; for doctorate, GRE General Test, minimum GPA of 3.2. Additional exam requirements/recommendations for international students: Required—TOEFL (minimum score 600 paper-based; 250 computer-based). Electronic applications accepted. *Faculty research:* Old and New World archaeology, medical anthropology, primatology/human biology, cognition.

The University of Alabama, Graduate School, College of Arts and Sciences, Department of Anthropology, Tuscaloosa, AL 35487. Offers MA, PhD. *Faculty:* 10 full-time (2 women). *Students:* 28 full-time (19 women), 6 part-time (4 women); includes 4 minority (1 Asian American or Pacific Islander, 3 Hispanic Americans). Average age 28. 35 applicants, 51% accepted, 10 enrolled. In 2008, 8 master's, 2 doctorates awarded. *Degree requirements:* For master's, one foreign language, comprehensive exam, thesis optional; for doctorate, one foreign language, comprehensive exam, thesis/dissertation. *Entrance requirements:* For master's, GRE, BA or BS; for doctorate, GRE, MA in anthropology. *Application deadline:* For fall admission, 1/31 for domestic and international students. Application fee: $30. *Expenses:* Tuition, area resident: Full-time $6400. Tuition, state resident: full-time $6400. Tuition, nonresident: full-time $18,000. *Financial support:* In 2008–09, 25 students received support, including 4 fellowships with full tuition reimbursements available (averaging $15,000 per year), 1 research assistantship with full tuition reimbursement available (averaging $12,258 per year), 20 teaching assistantships with full tuition reimbursements available (averaging $12,258 per year); Federal Work-Study and health care benefits also available. Financial award application deadline: 1/31. *Faculty research:* Medical anthropology, Southeastern archaeology, physical and cultural anthropology. Total annual research expenditures: $86,213. *Unit head:* Dr. Michael D. Murphy, Chairman and Professor, 205-348-1953, Fax: 205-348-7937, E-mail: mdmurphy@tenhoor.as.ua.edu. *Application contact:* Dr. William Dressler, Professor and Director of Graduate Studies, 205-348-1954, Fax: 205-348-7937, E-mail: wdressle@tenhoor.as.ua.edu.

The University of Alabama at Birmingham, School of Social and Behavioral Sciences, Department of Anthropology and Social Work, Birmingham, AL 35294. Offers anthropology (MA). *Degree requirements:* For master's, one foreign language. *Entrance requirements:* For master's, GRE General Test. Electronic applications accepted. *Faculty research:* Ethnicity, medical anthropology, primate conservation, pastoral systems, Southeastern archaeology.

University of Alaska Anchorage, College of Arts and Sciences, Department of Anthropology, Anchorage, AK 99508-8060. Offers MA. *Degree requirements:* For master's, comprehensive exam, thesis (for some programs), practicum. *Entrance requirements:* For master's, GRE General Test. Additional exam requirements/recommendations for international students: Required—TOEFL (minimum score 550 paper-based; 213 computer-based).

University of Alaska Fairbanks, College of Liberal Arts, Department of Anthropology, Fairbanks, AK 99775-7720. Offers MA, PhD. Part-time programs available. *Faculty:* 11 full-time (2 women), 2 part-time/adjunct (0 women). *Students:* 27 full-time (19 women), 13 part-time (7 women); includes 5 minority (3 American Indian/Alaska Native, 1 Asian American or Pacific Islander, 1 Hispanic American), 3 international. Average age 40. 29 applicants, 34% accepted, 7 enrolled. In 2008, 9 master's, 2 doctorates awarded. Terminal master's awarded for partial completion of doctoral program. *Degree requirements:* For master's, one foreign language, comprehensive exam, thesis, oral defense; for doctorate, 2 foreign languages, comprehensive exam, thesis/dissertation, oral defense. *Entrance requirements:* For master's and doctorate, GRE General Test. Additional exam requirements/recommendations for international students: Required—TOEFL (minimum score 550 paper-based; 213 computer-based; 80 iBT). *Application deadline:* For fall admission, 6/1 for domestic students, 3/1 for international students; for spring admission, 10/15 for domestic students, 9/1 for international students. Applications are processed on a rolling basis. Application fee: $60. Electronic applications accepted. *Expenses:* Tuition, area resident: Full-time $5418; part-time $301 per credit. Tuition, state resident: full-time $5418; part-time $301 per credit. Tuition, nonresident: full-time $11,070; part-time $615 per credit. Required fees: $849; $25 per credit. $78 per semester. Tuition and fees vary according to course load and reciprocity agreements. *Financial support:* In 2008–09, 1 fellowship (averaging $13,500 per year), 5 research assistantships (averaging $12,448 per year), 11 teaching assistantships (averaging $7,955 per year) were awarded; Federal Work-Study, scholarships/grants, health care benefits, and unspecified assistantships also available. Support available to part-time students. Financial award application deadline: 7/1; financial award applicants required to submit FAFSA. *Faculty research:* Circumpolar archaeology and population biology, rural subsistence, arctic physical, biological and social anthropology, arctic ethnohistory, arctic linguistics. *Unit head:* Dr. Maribeth Murray, Department Chair, 907-474-7288, Fax: 907-474-7453, E-mail: fyanth@uaf.edu. *Application contact:* Dr. Maribeth Murray, Department Chair, 907-474-7288, Fax: 907-474-7453, E-mail: fyanth@uaf.edu.

University of Alberta, Faculty of Graduate Studies and Research, Department of Anthropology, Edmonton, AB T6G 2E1, Canada. Offers MA, PhD. *Degree requirements:* For master's, thesis; for doctorate, one foreign language, thesis/dissertation. *Entrance requirements:* For master's and doctorate, minimum GPA of 7.0 on a 9.0 scale in last 2 years. Additional exam requirements/recommendations for international students: Required—TOEFL. *Faculty research:* Cultural anthropology of North America, South East Asia; physical anthropology in osteology, forensic primatology; archaeology of North America, South America, Old World/Africa.

The University of Arizona, Graduate College, College of Social and Behavioral Sciences, Department of Anthropology, Tucson, AZ 85721. Offers MA, PhD. Part-time programs available. Terminal master's awarded for partial completion of doctoral program. *Degree requirements:* For master's, thesis or alternative; for doctorate, one foreign language, thesis/dissertation. *Entrance requirements:* For master's, GRE General Test, minimum GPA of 3.5, 2 letters of recommendation; for doctorate, GRE General Test, minimum GPA of 3.5, 2 letters or recommendation. Additional exam requirements/recommendations for international students: Required—TOEFL (minimum score 213 computer-based). Electronic applications accepted. *Faculty research:* Archaeology of pre-Han China, cultural ecology, health- and illness-related behavior, interaction of linguistic and social processes, human growth and development under stress.

University of Arkansas, Graduate School, J. William Fulbright College of Arts and Sciences, Department of Anthropology, Fayetteville, AR 72701-1201. Offers MA, PhD. Part-time and evening/weekend programs available. *Degree requirements:* For master's, comprehensive exam. *Entrance requirements:* For master's, GRE General Test, minimum GPA of 3.0; for doctorate, GRE General Test.

The University of British Columbia, Faculty of Arts, Department of Anthropology, Vancouver, BC V6T 1Z1, Canada. Offers MA, PhD. *Degree requirements:* For master's, thesis; for doctorate, comprehensive exam, thesis/dissertation. *Entrance requirements:* For master's, BA in anthropology or equivalent with minimum B+ average in upper level courses; for doctorate, MA in anthropology or equivalent. Additional exam requirements/recommendations for international students: Required—TOEFL (minimum score 600 paper-based; 250 computer-based; 80 iBT). Electronic applications accepted. *Faculty research:* Cultures of North America, East Asia, Oceania; museum studies; archaeology.

University of Calgary, Faculty of Graduate Studies, Faculty of Social Sciences, Department of Anthropology, Calgary, AB T2N 1N4, Canada. Offers MA, PhD. *Degree requirements:* For master's, thesis; for doctorate, one foreign language, comprehensive exam, thesis/dissertation, candidacy exam. *Entrance requirements:* Additional exam requirements/recommendations for international students: Required—TOEFL. *Faculty research:* Primatology, culture and society, biosocial anthropology, political anthropology, evolutionary theory.

University of California, Berkeley, Graduate Division, College of Letters and Science, Department of Anthropology, Program in Anthropology, Berkeley, CA 94720-1500. Offers PhD. *Degree requirements:* For doctorate, thesis/dissertation. *Entrance requirements:* For doctorate, GRE General Test, minimum GPA of 3.0, 3 letters of recommendation. Additional exam requirements/recommendations for international students: Required—TOEFL.

University of California, Berkeley, Graduate Division, College of Letters and Science, Department of Anthropology, Program in Medical Anthropology, Berkeley, CA 94720-1500. Offers PhD. *Degree requirements:* For doctorate, thesis/dissertation. *Entrance requirements:* For doctorate, GRE General Test, minimum GPA of 3.0, 3 letters of recommendation. Additional exam requirements/recommendations for international students: Required—TOEFL.

University of California, Davis, Graduate Studies, Program in Anthropology, Davis, CA 95616. Offers MA, PhD. Terminal master's awarded for partial completion of doctoral program. *Degree requirements:* For master's, one foreign language; for doctorate, one foreign language, thesis/dissertation. *Entrance requirements:* For master's and doctorate, GRE General Test, minimum GPA of 3.0. Additional exam requirements/recommendations for international students: Required—TOEFL (minimum score 550 paper-based; 213 computer-based). Electronic applications accepted. *Faculty research:* Archaeology, linguistics, biological and sociocultural anthropology.

University of California, Irvine, Office of Graduate Studies, School of Social Sciences, Department of Anthropology, Irvine, CA 92697. Offers MA, PhD. *Degree requirements:* For doctorate, thesis/dissertation. *Entrance requirements:* For master's, GRE, minimum GPA of 3.0; for doctorate, GRE General Test, minimum GPA of 3.0. Additional exam requirements/recommendations for international students: Required—TOEFL (minimum score 550 paper-based; 213 computer-based). Electronic applications accepted. *Faculty research:* Cognitive anthropology, sociology of culture, social structure, family and gender.

University of California, Los Angeles, Graduate Division, College of Letters and Science, Department of Anthropology, Los Angeles, CA 90095. Offers MA, PhD. *Students:* 74 full-time (55 women); includes 9 minority (1 African American, 5 Asian Americans or Pacific Islanders, 3 Hispanic Americans), 6 international. Average age 30. 176 applicants, 16% accepted, 18 enrolled. In 2008, 4 master's, 13 doctorates awarded. Terminal master's awarded for partial completion of doctoral program. *Degree requirements:* For master's, thesis; for doctorate, thesis/dissertation, oral and written qualifying exams. *Entrance requirements:* For master's, GRE General Test, minimum GPA of 3.0, sample of research writing, 3 letters of recommendation; for doctorate, GRE General Test, minimum undergraduate GPA of 3.0, sample of research writing, 3 letters of recommendation. *Application deadline:* For fall admission, 12/15 for domestic students. Application fee: $60 ($80 for international students). Electronic applications accepted. *Expenses:* Tuition, nonresident: full-time $14,694. Required fees: $9669.50. Full-time tuition and fees vary according to course load, degree level, program and student level. *Financial support:* In 2008–09, 57 fellowships with full and partial tuition reimbursements, 9 research assistantships with full and partial tuition reimbursements, 33 teaching assistantships with full and partial tuition reimbursements were awarded; Federal Work-Study, institutionally sponsored loans, scholarships/grants, health care benefits, tuition waivers (full and partial), and unspecified assistantships also available. Financial award application deadline: 3/1; financial award applicants required to submit FAFSA. *Unit head:* Dr. Alessandro Duranti, Chair, 310-825-5833. *Application contact:* Departmental Office, 310-825-2511, E-mail: awalters@anthro.ucla.edu.

University of California, Riverside, Graduate Division, Department of Anthropology, Riverside, CA 92521-0102. Offers MA, MS, PhD. Part-time programs available. *Faculty:* 17 full-time (9 women), 1 part-time/adjunct (0 women). *Students:* 67 full-time (37 women); includes 15 minority (2 African Americans, 1 American Indian/Alaska Native, 4 Asian Americans or Pacific Islanders, 8 Hispanic Americans), 9 international. Average age 35. 42 applicants, 26% accepted, 7 enrolled. In 2008, 7 master's, 6 doctorates awarded. Terminal master's awarded for partial completion of doctoral program. *Degree requirements:* For master's, comprehensive exams or thesis; for doctorate, one foreign language, comprehensive exam, thesis/dissertation, qualifying exams. *Entrance requirements:* For master's and doctorate, GRE General Test, sample of written work, minimum GPA of 3.2, 3 letters of recommendation. Additional exam requirements/recommendations for international students: Required—TOEFL (minimum score 550 paper-based; 213 computer-based; 80 iBT). *Application deadline:* For fall admission, 5/1 for domestic students, 2/1 for international students. Application fee: $70 ($85 for international students). Electronic applications accepted. *Expenses:* Tuition, nonresident: full-time $4898. Required fees: $10,362. *Financial support:* In 2008–09, fellowships with full and partial tuition reimbursements (averaging $12,000 per year), teaching assistantships with partial tuition reimbursements (averaging $16,500 per year) were awarded; research assistantships with partial tuition reimbursements, career-related internships or fieldwork, Federal Work-Study, institutionally sponsored loans, and tuition waivers (full and partial) also available. Financial award application deadline: 2/1; financial award applicants required to submit FAFSA. *Faculty research:* Transnational processes, border communities, political and cultural ecology, Mesoamerican and Western US archaeology, applied anthropology. *Unit head:* Dr. Thomas C. Patterson, Chair, 951-827-5524, Fax: 951-827-5409, E-mail: thomas.patterson@ucr.edu. *Application contact:* Dr. Sang-Hee Lee, Graduate Advisor, 951-827-5145, E-mail: cultures@ucr.edu.

University of California, San Diego, Office of Graduate Studies, Department of Anthropology, La Jolla, CA 92093. Offers PhD. *Degree requirements:* For doctorate, thesis/dissertation. *Entrance requirements:* For doctorate, GRE General Test. Electronic applications accepted.

University of California, San Diego, Office of Graduate Studies, Interdisciplinary Program in Cognitive Science, La Jolla, CA 92093. Offers cognitive science/anthropology (PhD); cognitive science/communication (PhD); cognitive science/computer science and engineering (PhD); cognitive science/linguistics (PhD); cognitive science/neuroscience (PhD); cognitive science/philosophy (PhD); cognitive science/psychology (PhD); cognitive science/sociology (PhD). Admissions offered through affiliated departments. *Degree requirements:* For doctorate, thesis/dissertation. *Entrance requirements:* For doctorate, GRE General Test, acceptance into one of the 8 participating departments. *Faculty research:* Language and cognition, philosophy of mind, visual perception, biological anthropology, sociolinguistics.

University of California, San Francisco, Graduate Division, Program in Medical Anthropology, San Francisco, CA 94143. Offers PhD. *Degree requirements:* For doctorate, one foreign language, thesis/dissertation, 3 field statements. *Entrance requirements:* For doctorate, GRE General Test, master's degree in anthropology or a related social or health science. *Faculty research:* Ethnicity, gender, aging, international health, health policy.

Anthropology

University of California, Santa Barbara, Graduate Division, College of Letters and Sciences, Division of Social Sciences, Department of Anthropology, Santa Barbara, CA 93106-3210. Offers European archaeology (MA); global studies (PhD); North American archeology (MA); sociocultural anthropology (MA); South American archaeology (MA); MA/PhD. *Faculty:* 13 full-time (2 women), 2 part-time/adjunct (both women). *Students:* 57 full-time (36 women). Average age 31. 64 applicants, 41% accepted, 11 enrolled. In 2008, 7 master's, 3 doctorates awarded. Terminal master's awarded for partial completion of doctoral program. *Degree requirements:* For master's, comprehensive exam, thesis; for doctorate, comprehensive exam, thesis/dissertation. *Entrance requirements:* For master's and doctorate, GRE General Test, sample of written work, 3 letters of recommendation, statement of purpose, personal achievements/contributions statement, resumé/curriculum vitae, transcripts for post-secondary institutions attended. Additional exam requirements/recommendations for international students: Required—TOEFL (paper: 550, computer: 213, IBT: 80) or IELTS (7). *Application deadline:* For fall admission, 12/1 for domestic and international students. Application fee: $70 ($90 for international students). Electronic applications accepted. *Expenses:* Tuition, nonresident: full-time $25,149. Required fees: $10,143. Full-time tuition and fees vary according to campus/location, reciprocity agreements and student level. *Financial support:* In 2008–09, 51 students received support, including 47 fellowships with full and partial tuition reimbursements available (averaging $4,000 per year), 9 research assistantships with full and partial tuition reimbursements available (averaging $7,400 per year), 30 teaching assistantships with partial tuition reimbursements available (averaging $10,500 per year); career-related internships or fieldwork, Federal Work-Study, institutionally sponsored loans, scholarships/grants, traineeships, health care benefits, and unspecified assistantships also available. Financial award application deadline: 3/1; financial award applicants required to submit FAFSA. *Faculty research:* Archaeology, bioarchaeology, biosocial anthropology, evolutionary ecology, evolutionary psychology, sociocultural anthropology. *Unit head:* Prof. Katharina Schreiber, Chair, 805-893-2519, Fax: 805-893-8707, E-mail: kschreiber@anth.ucsb.edu. *Application contact:* Robin Roe, Graduate Program Assistant, 805-893-2516, Fax: 805-893-8707, E-mail: roe@anth.ucsb.edu.

University of California, Santa Cruz, Division of Graduate Studies, Division of Social Sciences, Program in Anthropology, Santa Cruz, CA 95064. Offers anthropological archaeology (PhD); cultural anthropology (PhD). *Degree requirements:* For doctorate, thesis/dissertation, qualifying exam. *Entrance requirements:* For doctorate, GRE General Test. *Faculty research:* Culture and power, women's roles, AIDS, folklore.

University of Central Florida, College of Sciences, Department of Anthropology, Orlando, FL 32816. Offers MA. *Faculty:* 16 full-time (6 women), 2 part-time/adjunct (1 woman). *Students:* 34 full-time (19 women), 14 part-time (10 women); includes 8 minority (2 African Americans, 1 Asian American or Pacific Islander, 5 Hispanic Americans), 1 international. In 2008, 2 master's awarded. *Expenses:* Tuition, area resident: Full-time $6816; part-time $284 per credit. Tuition, state resident: full-time $6816; part-time $1076 per credit. Tuition, nonresident: full-time $25,824. Required fees: $216; $9 per credit. *Financial support:* In 2008–09, 3 fellowships (averaging $10,000 per year), 8 research assistantships (averaging $4,400 per year), 24 teaching assistantships (averaging $5,500 per year) were awarded. *Unit head:* Dr. Arlen Chase, Chair, 407-823-2227, Fax: 407-823-3498, E-mail: achase@mail.ucf.edu. *Application contact:* Dr. Arlen Chase, Chair, 407-823-2227, Fax: 407-823-3498, E-mail: achase@mail.ucf.edu.

University of Chicago, Division of Social Sciences, Department of Anthropology, Chicago, IL 60637-1513. Offers PhD. *Degree requirements:* For doctorate, 2 foreign languages, thesis/dissertation, exams. *Entrance requirements:* For doctorate, GRE General Test. Additional exam requirements/recommendations for international students: Required—TOEFL, IELTS (minimum score 7). Electronic applications accepted.

University of Chicago, Division of the Humanities, Department of Linguistics, Chicago, IL 60637-1513. Offers anthropology and linguistics (PhD); linguistics (AM, PhD). Terminal master's awarded for partial completion of doctoral program. *Degree requirements:* For master's, one foreign language, thesis; for doctorate, 2 foreign languages, thesis/dissertation. *Entrance requirements:* For master's and doctorate, GRE General Test. Additional exam requirements/recommendations for international students: Required—TOEFL.

University of Cincinnati, Graduate School, McMicken College of Arts and Sciences, Department of Anthropology, Cincinnati, OH 45221. Offers MA. Part-time programs available. *Degree requirements:* For master's, thesis or alternative. *Entrance requirements:* For master's, GRE General Test. Additional exam requirements/recommendations for international students: Required—TOEFL; Recommended—TWE. Electronic applications accepted. *Faculty research:* Medical anthropology, Mayan prehistory, southwestern U.S. prehistory, skeletal biology and paleoanthropology; immigrants; Mexico.

University of Colorado at Boulder, Graduate School, College of Arts and Sciences, Department of Anthropology, Boulder, CO 80309. Offers MA, PhD. *Degree requirements:* For master's, comprehensive exam, thesis or alternative; for doctorate, one foreign language, thesis/dissertation. *Entrance requirements:* For master's, GRE General Test, minimum undergraduate GPA of 3.0; for doctorate, GRE General Test, minimum undergraduate GPA of 3.0, master's degree in anthropology. Electronic applications accepted. *Faculty research:* Archaeology of ancient Mayan, plains Indians; skeletal biology of ancient Nubians; human biology of modern people of Amazon; paleontology of early primates.

University of Colorado Denver, College of Liberal Arts and Sciences, Department of Anthropology, Denver, CO 80217-3364. Offers MA. Part-time and evening/weekend programs available. *Degree requirements:* For master's, comprehensive exam, thesis or alternative. *Entrance requirements:* For master's, GRE General Test, minor in anthropology. Additional exam requirements/recommendations for international students: Required—TOEFL (minimum score 525 paper-based; 197 computer-based). Electronic applications accepted.

University of Connecticut, Graduate School, College of Liberal Arts and Sciences, Department of Anthropology, Field of Anthropology, Storrs, CT 06269. Offers MA, PhD. *Degree requirements:* For master's, comprehensive exam; for doctorate, thesis/dissertation. *Entrance requirements:* For master's and doctorate, GRE General Test. Additional exam requirements/recommendations for international students: Required—TOEFL (minimum score 550 paper-based; 213 computer-based). Electronic applications accepted.

University of Denver, Division of Arts, Humanities and Social Sciences, Department of Anthropology, Denver, CO 80208. Offers MA. Part-time programs available. *Faculty:* 7 full-time (4 women). *Students:* 5 full-time (4 women), 17 part-time (16 women); includes 6 minority (2 African Americans, 1 American Indian/Alaska Native, 1 Asian American or Pacific Islander, 2 Hispanic Americans). Average age 26. In 2008, 5 master's awarded. *Degree requirements:* For master's, thesis or alternative, 1 foreign language or quantitative methods. *Entrance requirements:* For master's, GRE. Additional exam requirements/recommendations for international students: Required—TOEFL. *Application deadline:* Applications are processed on a rolling basis. Application fee: $50. Electronic applications accepted. *Financial support:* In 2008–09, 12 teaching assistantships with full and partial tuition reimbursements (averaging $10,000 per year) were awarded; career-related internships or fieldwork, Federal Work-Study, institutionally sponsored loans, and scholarships/grants also available. Support available to part-time students. Financial award application deadline: 2/20; financial award applicants required to submit FAFSA. *Faculty research:* Gender, class, race, ground penetrating radar, archaeology. Total annual research expenditures: $10,000. *Unit head:* Dr. Richard Clemmer-Smith, Chairperson, 303-871-2406. *Application contact:* Jeff Quinlisk, Assistant to Chair, 303-871-2677, E-mail: anth02@du.edu.

University of Florida, Graduate School, College of Liberal Arts and Sciences, Department of Anthropology, Gainesville, FL 32611. Offers MA, PhD, JD/MA. Part-time programs available. *Degree requirements:* For master's, thesis optional; for doctorate, thesis/dissertation. *Entrance requirements:* For master's and doctorate, GRE General Test, minimum GPA of 3.2. Additional exam requirements/recommendations for international students: Required—TOEFL (minimum score 550 paper-based; 213 computer-based). Electronic applications accepted. *Faculty research:* Social and cultural anthropology, archaeology, anthropological linguistics, physical anthropology.

University of Georgia, Graduate School, College of Arts and Sciences, Department of Anthropology, Athens, GA 30602. Offers anthropology (MA, PhD); archaeological resource management (MS). *Degree requirements:* For master's, one foreign language, thesis; for doctorate, one foreign language, thesis/dissertation. *Entrance requirements:* For master's and doctorate, GRE General Test. Electronic applications accepted.

University of Guelph, Graduate Program Services, College of Social and Applied Human Sciences, Department of Sociology and Anthropology, Guelph, ON N1G 2W1, Canada. Offers anthropology (MA); crime and criminal justice policy (MA); sociology (MA, PhD). *Degree requirements:* For master's, thesis or major paper; for doctorate, comprehensive exam, thesis/dissertation. *Entrance requirements:* For master's, minimum B+ average during previous 2 years of course work, honors BA or equivalent; for doctorate, must have an MA in Sociology, must have 80% or higher in graduate level studies. Additional exam requirements/recommendations for international students: Required—TOEFL (minimum score 550 paper-based; 213 computer-based; 89 iBT), IELTS (minimum score 6.5), TOEFL or IELTS. Electronic applications accepted. *Faculty research:* Rural and development sociology; education, employment, and the workplace; race, ethnicity, and native studies; criminology and deviance; social psychology.

University of Hawaii at Manoa, Graduate Division, Colleges of Arts and Sciences, College of Social Sciences, Department of Anthropology, Honolulu, HI 96822. Offers MA, PhD. Part-time programs available. *Degree requirements:* For master's, thesis optional; for doctorate, comprehensive exam, thesis/dissertation. *Entrance requirements:* For master's and doctorate, GRE General Test. Additional exam requirements/recommendations for international students: Required—TOEFL (minimum score 560 paper-based; 220 computer-based; 83 iBT), IELTS (minimum score 5). *Faculty research:* Evolution of social complexity, ethnopharmacology, social interaction, faunal analysis, human ecology.

University of Houston, College of Liberal Arts and Social Sciences, Department of Anthropology, Houston, TX 77204. Offers MA. Part-time and evening/weekend programs available. *Faculty:* 7 full-time (3 women), 1 part-time/adjunct (0 women). *Students:* 10 full-time (9 women), 18 part-time (12 women); includes 8 minority (4 African Americans, 1 American Indian/Alaska Native, 3 Hispanic Americans), 3 international. Average age 33. 9 applicants, 67% accepted, 5 enrolled. In 2008, 4 master's awarded. *Degree requirements:* For master's, comprehensive exam, thesis optional. *Entrance requirements:* For master's, GRE General Test, minimum GPA of 3.0. *Application deadline:* For fall admission, 7/6 for domestic students; for spring admission, 12/3 for domestic students. Application fee: $0 ($75 for international students). *Expenses:* Tuition, state resident: full-time $5164; part-time $287 per credit. Tuition, nonresident: full-time $10,222; part-time $568 per credit. *Financial support:* In 2008–09, 1 research assistantship with full tuition reimbursement (averaging $7,300 per year), 5 teaching assistantships with full tuition reimbursements (averaging $9,000 per year) were awarded; career-related internships or fieldwork, Federal Work-Study, institutionally sponsored loans, scholarships/grants, health care benefits, and unspecified assistantships also available. Support available to part-time students. Financial award application deadline: 2/1. *Faculty research:* Medical anthropology, international development, archaeology, Mesoamerica, gender. *Unit head:* Dr. Norris Lang, Chairperson, 713-743-3780, Fax: 713-743-3798, E-mail: nlang@uh.edu. *Application contact:* Dr. Rebecca Storey, Graduate Director, 713-743-3780, Fax: 713-743-4287, E-mail: rstorey@uh.edu.

University of Idaho, College of Graduate Studies, College of Letters, Arts and Social Sciences, Department of Sociology, Anthropology and Justice Studies, Program in Anthropology, Moscow, ID 83844-2282. Offers MA. *Faculty:* 8. *Students:* 14 full-time, 10 part-time. Average age 32. In 2008, 8 master's awarded. *Degree requirements:* For master's, one foreign language, thesis (for some programs). *Entrance requirements:* For master's, minimum GPA of 2.8. *Application deadline:* For fall admission, 8/1 for domestic students; for spring admission, 12/15 for domestic students. Application fee: $55 ($60 for international students). *Expenses:* Tuition, nonresident: full-time $10,080; part-time $336 per credit. Required fees: $5212; $267 per credit. Tuition and fees vary according to program. *Financial support:* Research assistantships, teaching assistantships available. Financial award application deadline: 2/15. *Unit head:* Dr. Donald E Tyler, Chair, 208-885 Ext. 6751. *Application contact:* Dr. Donald E. Tyler, Chair, 208-885-6752.

University of Illinois at Chicago, Graduate College, College of Liberal Arts and Sciences, Department of Anthropology, Chicago, IL 60607-7128. Offers anthropology (MA, PhD); environmental and urban geography (MA), including environmental studies, urban geography. Part-time programs available. *Degree requirements:* For doctorate, comprehensive exam. *Entrance requirements:* For master's and doctorate, minimum GPA of 2.75. Additional exam requirements/recommendations for international students: Required—TOEFL. Electronic applications accepted. *Faculty research:* Archaeological, physical, and cultural anthropology.

University of Illinois at Urbana–Champaign, Graduate College, College of Liberal Arts and Sciences, Department of Anthropology, Champaign, IL 61820. Offers MA, PhD. *Faculty:* 29 full-time (12 women). *Students:* 53 full-time (34 women), 8 part-time (6 women); includes 7 minority (2 African Americans, 1 Asian American or Pacific Islander, 4 Hispanic Americans), 14 international. 68 applicants, 13% accepted, 8 enrolled. In 2008, 4 master's, 13 doctorates awarded. Terminal master's awarded for partial completion of doctoral program. *Entrance requirements:* For master's and doctorate, GRE General Test, minimum GPA of 3.0. Additional exam requirements/recommendations for international students: Required—TOEFL (minimum score 550 paper-based; 213 computer-based). *Application deadline:* Applications are processed on a rolling basis. Application fee: $60 ($75 for international students). Electronic applications accepted. *Financial support:* In 2008–09, 18 fellowships, 17 research assistantships, 28 teaching assistantships were awarded; tuition waivers (full and partial) also available. *Unit head:* Steven Leigh, Head, 217-333-3616, Fax: 217-244-3490, E-mail: sleigh@illinois.edu. *Application contact:* Liz Spears, Graduate Coordinator, 217-244-0296, Fax: 217-244-3490, E-mail: espears@illinois.edu.

The University of Iowa, Graduate College, College of Liberal Arts and Sciences, Department of Anthropology, Iowa City, IA 52242-1316. Offers MA, PhD. *Degree requirements:* For master's, thesis optional, exam; for doctorate, comprehensive exam, thesis/dissertation. *Entrance requirements:* For master's and doctorate, GRE General Test, minimum GPA of 3.0. Additional exam requirements/recommendations for international students: Required—TOEFL (minimum score 550 paper-based; 213 computer-based; 81 iBT). Electronic applications accepted.

The University of Kansas, Graduate Studies, College of Liberal Arts and Sciences, Department of Anthropology, Lawrence, KS 66045. Offers MA, PhD. *Faculty:* 14 full-time (5 women), 6 part-time/adjunct (1 woman). *Students:* 55 full-time (33 women), 7 part-time (4 women); includes 5 minority (1 African American, 1 American Indian/Alaska Native, 3 Asian Americans or Pacific Islanders), 5 international. Average age 31. 42 applicants, 55% accepted, 12 enrolled. In 2008, 8 master's, 2 doctorates awarded. *Degree requirements:* For master's, comprehensive exam (for some programs), thesis; for doctorate, one foreign language, comprehensive exam, thesis/dissertation. *Entrance requirements:* For master's, minimum GPA of 3.2; for doctorate, minimum GPA of 3.5. Additional exam requirements/recommendations for international students: Required—TOEFL. *Application deadline:* For fall admission, 1/5 for domestic and international students. Application fee: $45 ($50 for international students). Electronic applications accepted. *Expenses:* Tuition, area resident: Full-time $6122; part-time $255.10 per credit hour. Tuition, state resident: full-time $6122; part-time $255.10 per credit hour. Tuition, nonresident: full-time $14,629; part-time $609.55 per credit hour. Required fees: $847; $70.56 per credit hour. Tuition and fees vary according to course load and program. *Financial support:* Fellowships with full tuition reimbursements, research assistantships with full and partial tuition reimbursements, teaching assistantships with full and partial tuition reimbursements, career-related internships or fieldwork, institutionally sponsored loans, and unspecified assistantships available. Financial award application deadline: 1/5; financial award applicants required to submit FAFSA. *Faculty research:* Theoretical and applied anthropology; old and new world archaeology; endangered language documentation and revitalization; bio-cultural medical anthropology; anthropological/molecular genetics; Latin American, African, Asian, European and North American anthropology. *Unit head:* James H. Mielke, Chair, 785-864-4103, Fax: 785-864-5224, E-mail: mielke@ku.edu. *Application contact:* Jack Hofman, Graduate Coordinator, 785-864-4103, Fax: 785-864-5224, E-mail: hofman@ku.edu.

University of Kentucky, Graduate School, College of Arts and Sciences, Program in Anthropology, Lexington, KY 40506-0032. Offers MA, PhD. Part-time programs available. *Degree requirements:* For master's, comprehensive exam, thesis optional; for doctorate, one foreign language, comprehensive exam, thesis/dissertation. *Entrance requirements:* For master's, GRE General Test, minimum undergraduate GPA of 2.75; for doctorate, GRE General Test, minimum graduate GPA of 3.0. Additional exam requirements/recommendations for international students: Required—TOEFL (minimum score 550 paper-based; 213 computer-based). Electronic applications accepted. *Faculty research:* Applied social anthropology, developmental change, medical anthropology, culture history, ethnohistory.

University of Lethbridge, School of Graduate Studies, Lethbridge, AB T1K 3M4, Canada. Offers accounting (MScM); addictions counseling (M Sc); agricultural biotechnology (M Sc); agricultural studies (M Sc, MA); anthropology (MA); archaeology (MA); art (MA); biochemistry (M Sc); biological sciences (M Sc); biomolecular science (PhD); biosystems and biodiversity (PhD); Canadian studies (MA); chemistry (M Sc); computer science (M Sc); computer science and geographical information science (M Sc); counseling psychology (M Ed); dramatic arts (MA); earth, space, and physical science (PhD); economics (MA); educational leadership (M Ed); English (MA); environmental science (M Sc); evolution and behavior (PhD); exercise science (M Sc); finance (MScM); French (MA); French/German (MA); French/Spanish (MA); general education (M Ed); general management (MScM); geography (M Sc, MA); German (MA); health sciences (M Sc, MA); history (MA); human resource management and labour relations (MScM); individualized multidisciplinary (M Sc, MA); information systems (MScM); international management (MScM); kinesiology (M Sc, MA); management (M Sc, MA); marketing (MScM); mathematics (M Sc); music (MA); Native American studies (MA); neuroscience (M Sc, PhD); new media (MA); nursing (M Sc); philosophy (MA); physics (M Sc); policy and strategy (MScM); political science (MA); psychology (M Sc, MA); religious studies (MA); sociology (MA); theoretical and computational science (PhD); urban and regional studies (MA). Part-time and evening/weekend programs available. *Degree requirements:* For doctorate, comprehensive exam, thesis/dissertation. *Entrance requirements:* For master's, GMAT (M Sc in management), bachelor's degree in related field, minimum GPA of 3.0 during previous 20 graded semester courses, 2 years teaching or related experience (M Ed); for doctorate, master's degree, minimum graduate GPA of 3.5. Additional exam requirements/recommendations for international students: Required—TOEFL. *Faculty research:* Movement and brain plasticity, gibberellin physiology, photosynthesis, carbon cycling, molecular properties of main-group ring components.

University of Manitoba, Faculty of Graduate Studies, Faculty of Arts, Department of Anthropology, Winnipeg, MB R3T 2N2, Canada. Offers MA, PhD. *Degree requirements:* For master's, thesis or alternative.

University of Maryland, College Park, Graduate Studies, College of Behavioral and Social Sciences, Department of Anthropology, College Park, MD 20742. Offers applied anthropology (MAA). Part-time and evening/weekend programs available. *Degree requirements:* For master's, internship. *Entrance requirements:* For master's, GRE General Test, minimum GPA of 3.0, 3 letters of recommendation. Additional exam requirements/recommendations for international students: Required—TOEFL. Electronic applications accepted. *Faculty research:* Archaeology, human biodiversity, cultural and resource management.

University of Massachusetts Amherst, Graduate School, College of Social and Behavioral Sciences, Department of Anthropology, Amherst, MA 01003. Offers MA, PhD. Part-time programs available. Terminal master's awarded for partial completion of doctoral program. *Degree requirements:* For master's, thesis or alternative; for doctorate, comprehensive exam, thesis/dissertation. *Entrance requirements:* Additional exam requirements/recommendations for international students: Required—TOEFL (minimum score 550 paper-based; 213 computer-based; 79 iBT), IELTS (minimum score 6.5). Electronic applications accepted. *Expenses:* Tuition, area resident: Full-time $2640. Tuition, nonresident: full-time $9936. One-time fee: $332 full-time. Tuition and fees vary according to course load.

University of Memphis, Graduate School, College of Arts and Sciences, Department of Anthropology, Memphis, TN 38152. Offers MA. Part-time programs available. *Faculty:* 9 full-time (5 women), 1 part-time/adjunct (0 women). *Students:* 21 full-time (16 women), 2 part-time (both women); includes 2 minority (1 African American, 1 Asian American or Pacific Islander). Average age 29. 16 applicants, 81% accepted, 9 enrolled. In 2008, 8 master's awarded. *Degree requirements:* For master's, comprehensive exam, practicum. *Entrance requirements:* For master's, GRE General Test or MAT. *Application deadline:* For fall admission, 3/15 priority date for domestic students; for spring admission, 12/1 priority date for domestic students. Application fee: $35 ($60 for international students). *Expenses:* Tuition, area resident: Full-time $6242; part-time $330 per credit hour. Tuition, state resident: full-time $6242; part-time $330 per credit hour. Tuition, nonresident: full-time $17,828; part-time $815 per credit hour. Required fees: $1156. *Financial support:* Fellowships, research assistantships with full tuition reimbursements, teaching assistantships with full tuition reimbursements, career-related internships or fieldwork, scholarships/grants, and unspecified assistantships available. Financial award applicants required to submit FAFSA. *Faculty research:* Drug and alcohol abuse, housing and urban development, grassroots community development, immigrant housing and health, community environment impact. *Unit head:* Dr. Ruth Beth Finerman, Chair, 901-678-3334, Fax: 901-678-2069, E-mail: finerman@memphis.edu. *Application contact:* Dr. Charles Williams, Coordinator of Graduate Studies, 901-678-3333, Fax: 901-678-0827, E-mail: cwilliam@memphis.edu.

University of Michigan, Horace H. Rackham School of Graduate Studies, College of Literature, Science, and the Arts, Department of Anthropology, Ann Arbor, MI 48109. Offers PhD. *Degree requirements:* For doctorate, one foreign language, comprehensive exam, thesis/dissertation, oral defense of dissertation, preliminary exam. *Entrance requirements:* For doctorate, GRE General Test. Additional exam requirements/recommendations for international students: Required—TOEFL (minimum score 560 paper-based; 220 computer-based; 84 iBT). Electronic applications accepted. *Faculty research:* Kinship and behavior in wild chimpanzees, paleontological research in the Lower Miocene of Northeast Uganda, long-term fitness consequences of wild chimpanzee behavior.

University of Michigan, Horace H. Rackham School of Graduate Studies, College of Literature, Science, and the Arts, Doctoral Program in Anthropology and History, Ann Arbor, MI 48109. Offers PhD. *Degree requirements:* For doctorate, 2 foreign languages, thesis/dissertation, oral defense of dissertation, preliminary exam. *Entrance requirements:* For doctorate, GRE General Test, writing sample. Additional exam requirements/recommendations for international students: Required—TOEFL. Electronic applications accepted. *Faculty research:* Historical anthropology.

University of Minnesota, Duluth, Graduate School, College of Liberal Arts, Department of Sociology/Anthropology, Duluth, MN 55812-2496. Offers criminology (MA); liberal studies (MLS). Part-time programs available. *Degree requirements:* For master's, thesis or alternative. *Entrance requirements:* For master's, interview, minimum GPA of 3.0, letters of recommendation, personal statement. Additional exam requirements/recommendations for international students: Required—TOEFL. *Faculty research:* Nature of knowledge, philosophy of science, ecology, cultural studies, language.

University of Minnesota, Twin Cities Campus, Graduate School, College of Liberal Arts, Department of Anthropology, Minneapolis, MN 55455-0213. Offers MA, PhD. Terminal master's

awarded for partial completion of doctoral program. *Degree requirements:* For master's, thesis or alternative; for doctorate, one foreign language, thesis/dissertation. *Entrance requirements:* For master's and doctorate, GRE. Additional exam requirements/recommendations for international students: Required—TOEFL. Electronic applications accepted. *Faculty research:* Psychological anthropology, gender and feminist anthropology, economic anthropology, Latin America, the Pacific.

University of Mississippi, Graduate School, College of Liberal Arts, Department of Sociology and Anthropology, Oxford, University, MS 38677. Offers anthropology (MA); sociology (MA, MSS). *Degree requirements:* For master's, thesis (for some programs). *Entrance requirements:* For master's, GRE General Test, minimum GPA of 3.0. Additional exam requirements/recommendations for international students: Required—TOEFL. Electronic applications accepted.

University of Missouri–Columbia, Graduate School, College of Arts and Sciences, Department of Anthropology, Columbia, MO 65211. Offers MA, PhD. *Faculty:* 11 full-time (4 women), 1 (woman) part-time/adjunct. *Students:* 12 full-time (10 women), 25 part-time (14 women); includes 2 minority (1 Asian American or Pacific Islander, 1 Hispanic American). Average age 31. 41 applicants, 22% accepted, 3 enrolled. In 2008, 2 master's awarded. *Degree requirements:* For doctorate, one foreign language, thesis/dissertation. *Entrance requirements:* For master's and doctorate, GRE General Test, minimum GPA of 3.0. Additional exam requirements/recommendations for international students: Required—TOEFL (minimum score 500 paper-based; 173 computer-based; 61 iBT), IELTS (minimum score 5.5). *Application deadline:* For fall admission, 1/15 priority date for domestic students; for winter admission, 10/15 for domestic students. Applications are processed on a rolling basis. Application fee: $45 ($60 for international students). *Financial support:* Fellowships, research assistantships, teaching assistantships, institutionally sponsored loans available. *Unit head:* Dr. Lee Lyman, Department Chair, E-mail: lymanr@missouri.edu. *Application contact:* Gail Lawrence, 573-882-4731, E-mail: lawrenceag@missouri.edu.

The University of Montana, Graduate School, College of Arts and Sciences, Department of Anthropology, Missoula, MT 59812-0002. Offers anthropology (MA); cultural heritage (MA); cultural heritage studies (PhD); forensic anthropology (MA); historical anthropology (PhD); linguistics (MA). *Degree requirements:* For master's, thesis (for some programs). *Entrance requirements:* For master's, GRE General Test. Additional exam requirements/recommendations for international students: Required—TOEFL. *Faculty research:* Historical preservation, plateau-plains archaeology and ethnohistory.

University of Nebraska–Lincoln, Graduate College, College of Arts and Sciences, Department of Anthropology and Geography, Program in Anthropology, Lincoln, NE 68588. Offers MA. *Students:* 12 full-time (6 women), 11 part-time (6 women); includes 2 minority (1 American Indian/Alaska Native, 1 Hispanic American), 1 international. Average age 27. In 2008, 8 master's awarded. *Degree requirements:* For master's, thesis optional. *Entrance requirements:* For master's, GRE General Test. Additional exam requirements/recommendations for international students: Required—TOEFL (minimum score 500 paper-based; 173 computer-based). *Application deadline:* For fall admission, 2/1 for domestic and international students; for spring admission, 10/1 for domestic students, 9/1 for international students. Application fee: $40. Electronic applications accepted. *Expenses:* Tuition, state resident: full-time $4275; part-time $237.50 per credit hour. Tuition, nonresident: full-time $11,525; part-time $640.25 per credit hour. Required fees: $1068; $10.35 per credit hour. $440.70 per semester. Tuition and fees vary according to course load and program. *Financial support:* Fellowships, research assistantships, teaching assistantships, Federal Work-Study, health care benefits, and unspecified assistantships available. Support available to part-time students. Financial award application deadline: 2/15. *Faculty research:* Cultural, archaeologic, linguistic, and physical anthropology. *Application contact:* Dr. Raymond Hames, Chair, 402-472-2411.

University of Nevada, Las Vegas, Graduate College, College of Liberal Arts, Department of Anthropology and Ethnic Studies, Las Vegas, NV 89154-5003. Offers anthropology (MA, PhD). Part-time programs available. *Faculty:* 14 full-time (7 women). *Students:* 19 full-time (14 women), 22 part-time (16 women); includes 2 minority (1 African American, 1 Asian American or Pacific Islander), 1 international. Average age 35. 36 applicants, 53% accepted, 10 enrolled. In 2008, 5 master's awarded. *Degree requirements:* For master's, thesis, oral defense of thesis; for doctorate, comprehensive exam, thesis/dissertation, oral defense of dissertation. *Entrance requirements:* For master's and doctorate, GRE General Test. Additional exam requirements/recommendations for international students: Required—TOEFL (minimum score 550 paper-based; 213 computer-based; 80 iBT), IELTS (minimum score 7). *Application deadline:* For fall admission, 2/1 priority date for domestic and international students. Applications are processed on a rolling basis. Application fee: $60 ($75 for international students). Electronic applications accepted. *Expenses:* Tuition, state resident: full-time $1414; part-time $198 per credit. Tuition, nonresident: full-time $12,509; part-time $415.75 per credit. International tuition: $14,249 full-time. Required fees: $4 per credit. $252 per semester. Tuition and fees vary according to course load. *Financial support:* In 2008–09, 17 students received support, including 17 teaching assistantships with partial tuition reimbursements available (averaging $10,285 per year); institutionally sponsored loans, scholarships/grants, health care benefits, and unspecified assistantships also available. Financial award application deadline: 3/1. *Faculty research:* Cross-cultural comparisons, evolution of humans, diet and disease, violence, sex. *Unit head:* Dr. Alan Simmons, Chair/Professor, 702-895-3512, Fax: 702-8985-4823, E-mail: simmonsa@unlv.nevada.edu. *Application contact:* Graduate College Admissions Evaluator, 702-895-3320, Fax: 702-895-4180, E-mail: gradcollege@unlv.edu.

University of Nevada, Reno, Graduate School, College of Liberal Arts, Department of Anthropology, Reno, NV 89557. Offers MA, PhD. *Faculty:* 22 full-time (9 women). *Students:* 12 full-time (6 women), 34 part-time (23 women); includes 3 minority (1 American Indian/Alaska Native, 1 Asian American or Pacific Islander, 1 Hispanic American). Average age 32. 24 applicants, 63% accepted, 12 enrolled. In 2008, 8 master's, 1 doctorate awarded. Terminal master's awarded for partial completion of doctoral program. *Degree requirements:* For master's, thesis; for doctorate, thesis/dissertation. *Entrance requirements:* For master's, GRE, minimum GPA of 2.75; for doctorate, GRE, minimum GPA of 3.0. Additional exam requirements/recommendations for international students: Required—TOEFL (minimum score 500 paper-based; 173 computer-based; 61 iBT), IELTS (minimum score 6), TOFEL or IELTS. *Application deadline:* For fall admission, 2/1 priority date for domestic and international students; for spring admission, 11/1 for domestic students. Applications are processed on a rolling basis. Application fee: $60 ($95 for international students). Electronic applications accepted. *Expenses:* Tuition, state resident: full-time $1710; part-time $1140 per semester. Tuition, nonresident: full-time $7115. Required fees: $158 per semester. *Financial support:* In 2008–09, 5 research assistantships with partial tuition reimbursements (averaging $14,000 per year), 9 teaching assistantships with partial tuition reimbursements (averaging $14,000 per year) were awarded; Federal Work-Study, institutionally sponsored loans, scholarships/grants, health care benefits, and unspecified assistantships also available. Financial award application deadline: 3/1; financial award applicants required to submit FAFSA. *Faculty research:* Ethnology, linguistics, cultural/medical/religious/ethnic relations, ecological anthropology, historical anthropology. Total annual research expenditures: $111,558. *Unit head:* Dr. G. Richard Scott, Graduate Program Director, 775-784-6704. *Application contact:* Michele Sandberg, Application Contact, 775-784-7026, Fax: 775-784-6064, E-mail: gradschool@unr.edu.

University of New Brunswick Fredericton, School of Graduate Studies, Faculty of Arts, Department of Anthropology, Fredericton, NB E3B 5A3, Canada. Offers MA. Part-time programs available. *Faculty:* 6 full-time (5 women), 4 part-time/adjunct (1 woman). *Students:* 10 full-time (7 women). In 2008, 1 master's awarded. *Degree requirements:* For master's, thesis. *Entrance requirements:* For master's, minimum GPA of 3.7, statement of interest. Additional exam requirements/recommendations for international students: Required—TOEFL, IELTS, TWE. *Application deadline:* 1/31 for domestic and international students. Applications are processed on a rolling basis. Application fee: $50 Canadian dollars. Tuition and fees charges are reported in Canadian dollars. *Expenses:* Tuition, area resident: Full-time $5562 Canadian dollars.

Anthropology

University of New Brunswick Fredericton *(continued)*
Tuition, nonresident: full-time $9450 Canadian dollars. Required fees: $333 Canadian dollars. *Financial support:* In 2008–09, 2 research assistantships, 2 teaching assistantships were awarded; fellowships also available. *Faculty research:* Latin America, anthropology of education, community-based fisheries, biomedical anthropology, archaeology of the Maritimes. *Unit head:* susan Blair, Director of Graduate Studies, 506-458-7929, Fax: 506-453-5071, E-mail: sblair@unb.ca. *Application contact:* Misty Cormier, Graduate Secretary, 506-453-4975, Fax: 506-453-5071, E-mail: mistyc@unb.ca.

University of New Mexico, Graduate School, College of Arts and Sciences, Department of Anthropology, Albuquerque, NM 87131-2039. Offers MA, MS, PhD. Terminal master's awarded for partial completion of doctoral program. *Degree requirements:* For master's, comprehensive exam (for some programs), thesis or alternative; for doctorate, one foreign language, comprehensive exam, thesis/dissertation, oral defense, skill and/or second language. *Entrance requirements:* For master's and doctorate, GRE General Test, 3 letters of recommendation, letter of interest, application (department and UNM), $50 fee, transcripts. Additional exam requirements/recommendations for international students: Required—TOEFL (minimum score 550 paper-based; 213 computer-based), IELTS (minimum score 7). Electronic applications accepted. *Faculty research:* Ethnology, archaeology, evolutionary anthropology.

The University of North Carolina at Chapel Hill, Graduate School, College of Arts and Sciences, Department of Anthropology, Chapel Hill, NC 27599. Offers MA, PhD. Terminal master's awarded for partial completion of doctoral program. *Degree requirements:* For master's, variable foreign language requirement, thesis; for doctorate, variable foreign language requirement, comprehensive exam, thesis/dissertation. *Entrance requirements:* For master's and doctorate, GRE General Test, minimum GPA of 3.0. Additional exam requirements/recommendations for international students: Required—TOEFL. Electronic applications accepted. *Faculty research:* Archeology, ecology and evolution, medical anthropology, social systems, anthropology of meaning.

University of North Texas, Robert B. Toulouse School of Graduate Studies, College of Public Affairs and Community Service, Department of Anthropology, Denton, TX 76203. Offers applied anthropology (MA, MS). Part-time and evening/weekend programs available. *Degree requirements:* For master's, practicum. *Entrance requirements:* For master's, GRE General Test, transcripts, departmental application. Additional exam requirements/recommendations for international students: Required—proof of English language proficiency required for non-native English speakers; Recommended—TOEFL (minimum score 550 paper-based; 213 computer-based). Electronic applications accepted. *Faculty research:* Cross-cultural/bilingual education in schools, globalization in work teams/business culture, medical anthropolosis, environmental anthropology.

University of Oklahoma, Graduate College, College of Arts and Sciences, Department of Anthropology, Norman, OK 73019. Offers MA, PhD. Part-time programs available. *Faculty:* 27 full-time (10 women), 1 part-time/adjunct (0 women). *Students:* 42 full-time (20 women), 20 part-time (14 women); includes 8 minority (3 American Indian/Alaska Native, 2 Asian Americans or Pacific Islanders, 3 Hispanic Americans), 3 international. 27 applicants, 56% accepted, 10 enrolled. In 2008, 3 master's, 2 doctorates awarded. Terminal master's awarded for partial completion of doctoral program. *Degree requirements:* For master's, thesis; for doctorate, thesis/dissertation, departmental qualifying exam. *Entrance requirements:* For master's, GRE, BA with 12 hours in anthropology. Additional exam requirements/recommendations for international students: Required—TOEFL (minimum score 550 paper-based; 213 computer-based). *Application deadline:* For fall admission, 4/1 for domestic and international students; for spring admission, 11/1 for domestic students, 9/1 for international students. Applications are processed on a rolling basis. Application fee: $40 ($90 for international students). Electronic applications accepted. *Expenses:* Tuition, state resident: full-time $3744; part-time $156 per credit hour. Tuition, nonresident: full-time $13,577; part-time $565.70 per credit hour. Required fees: $2415.40; $90.10 per credit hour. *Financial support:* In 2008–09, 25 students received support, including 3 research assistantships with partial tuition reimbursements available (averaging $13,423 per year), 23 teaching assistantships with partial tuition reimbursements available (averaging $13,585 per year); career-related internships or fieldwork, Federal Work-Study, scholarships/grants, health care benefits, and unspecified assistantships also available. Financial award applicants required to submit FAFSA. *Faculty research:* United States archaeology, sociocultural anthropology, linguistics, Native America; biological/physical anthropology; applied anthropological linguistics. Total annual research expenditures: $603,381. *Unit head:* Dr. Pat Gilman, Chair, 405-325-3261, Fax: 405-325-7386, E-mail: pgilman@ou.edu. *Application contact:* Keli Mitchell, Staff Assistant, 405-325-3261, Fax: 405-325-7386, E-mail: keli@ou.edu.

University of Oregon, Graduate School, College of Arts and Sciences, Department of Anthropology, Eugene, OR 97403. Offers MA, MS, PhD. Terminal master's awarded for partial completion of doctoral program. *Degree requirements:* For master's, one foreign language; for doctorate, 2 foreign languages, thesis/dissertation. *Entrance requirements:* For master's and doctorate, GRE General Test. Additional exam requirements/recommendations for international students: Required—TOEFL. *Faculty research:* Prehistory, primatology, cultural anthropology of Native Americans, human evolution, Africa.

University of Ottawa, Faculty of Graduate and Postdoctoral Studies, Faculty of Social Sciences, Department of Sociology and Anthropology, Ottawa, ON K1N 6N5, Canada. Offers MA. *Degree requirements:* For master's, thesis or alternative. *Entrance requirements:* For master's, honors bachelor's degree or equivalent, minimum B average. Electronic applications accepted. *Faculty research:* Inter-ethnic relations, development, political policies.

University of Pennsylvania, School of Arts and Sciences, Graduate Group in Anthropology, Philadelphia, PA 19104. Offers AM, MS, PhD. Terminal master's awarded for partial completion of doctoral program. *Degree requirements:* For master's, thesis, final exam; for doctorate, one foreign language, thesis/dissertation, fieldwork, preliminary and final exams. *Entrance requirements:* For doctorate, GRE General Test. Additional exam requirements/recommendations for international students: Required—TOEFL.

University of Pittsburgh, School of Arts and Sciences, Department of Anthropology, Pittsburgh, PA 15260. Offers MA, PhD. Part-time programs available. *Degree requirements:* For master's, one foreign language, thesis or alternative; for doctorate, one foreign language, thesis/dissertation. *Entrance requirements:* For master's and doctorate, GRE General Test. Additional exam requirements/recommendations for international students: Required—TOEFL (minimum score 550 paper-based; 213 computer-based), IELTS (minimum score 5.5). Electronic applications accepted. *Faculty research:* Conflict studies; ethnicity, nationalism, and the state; origins of complex societies; Latin American archaeology; human evolutionary biology.

University of Regina, Faculty of Graduate Studies and Research, Faculty of Arts, Department of Anthropology, Regina, SK S4S 0A2, Canada. Offers MA. Part-time programs available. *Faculty:* 4 full-time (1 woman). *Students:* 1 full-time (0 women). 1 applicant, 0% accepted. *Degree requirements:* For master's, thesis. *Entrance requirements:* For master's, writing sample. Additional exam requirements/recommendations for international students: Required—TOEFL (minimum score 580 paper-based; 237 computer-based; 88 iBT). *Application deadline:* Applications are processed on a rolling basis. Application fee: $85 ($100 for international students). Electronic applications accepted. *Financial support:* Fellowships, research assistantships, teaching assistantships, scholarships/grants available. Financial award application deadline: 6/15. *Faculty research:* Symbolic and interpretive theory; ritual; ethnography of Latin America, Himalayas, Sub-Saharan Africa. Total annual research expenditures: $34,000. *Unit head:* Dr. Marcia Calkowski, Graduate Program Coordinator, 306-585-4770, Fax: 306-585-4815, E-mail: marcia.calkowski@uregina.ca. *Application contact:* Dr. Marcia Calkowski, Graduate Program Coordinator, 306-585-4770, Fax: 306-585-4815, E-mail: marcia.calkowski@uregina.ca.

University of Saskatchewan, College of Graduate Studies and Research, College of Arts and Sciences, Department of Religious Studies and Anthropology, Saskatoon, SK S7N 5A2, Canada. Offers MA. *Degree requirements:* For master's, thesis. *Entrance requirements:* Additional exam requirements/recommendations for international students: Required—TOEFL.

University of South Africa, College of Human Sciences, Pretoria, South Africa. Offers adult education (M Ed); African languages (MA, PhD); African politics (MA, PhD); Afrikaans (MA, PhD); ancient history (MA, PhD); ancient Near Eastern studies (MA, PhD); anthropology (MA, PhD); applied linguistics (MA); Arabic (MA, PhD); archaeology (MA); art history (MA); Biblical archaeology (MA); Biblical studies (M Th, D Th, PhD); Christian spirituality (M Th, D Th); church history (M Th, D Th); classical studies (MA, PhD); clinical psychology (MA); communication (MA, PhD); comparative education (M Ed, Ed D); consulting psychology (D Admin, D Com, PhD); curriculum studies (M Ed, Ed D); development studies (M Admin, MA, D Admin, PhD); didactics (M Ed, Ed D); education (M Tech); education management (M Ed, Ed D); educational psychology (M Ed); English (MA); environmental education (M Ed); French (MA, PhD); German (MA, PhD); Greek (MA); guidance and counseling (M Ed); health studies (MA, PhD), including health sciences education (MA), health services management (MA), medical and surgical nursing science (critical care general) (MA), midwifery and neonatal nursing science (MA), trauma and emergency care (MA); history (MA, PhD); history of education (Ed D); inclusive education (M Ed, Ed D); information and communications technology policy and regulation (MA); information science (MA, MIS, PhD); international politics (MA, PhD); Islamic studies (MA, PhD); Italian (MA, PhD); Judaica (MA, PhD); linguistics (MA, PhD); mathematical education (M Ed); mathematics education (MA); missiology (M Th, D Th); modern Hebrew (MA, PhD); musicology (MA, MMus, D Mus, PhD); natural science education (M Ed); New Testament (M Th, D Th); Old Testament (D Th); pastoral therapy (M Th, D Th); philosophy (MA); philosophy of education (M Ed, Ed D); politics (MA, PhD); Portuguese (MA, PhD); practical theology (M Th, D Th); psychology (MA, MS, PhD); psychology of education (M Ed, Ed D); public health (MA); religious studies (MA, D Th, PhD); Romance languages (MA); Russian (MA, PhD); Semitic languages (MA, PhD); social behavior studies in HIV/AIDS (MA); social science (mental health) (MA); social science in development studies (MA); social science in psychology (MA); social science in social work (MA); social science in sociology (MA); social work (MSW, DSW, PhD); socio-education (M Ed, Ed D); sociolinguistics (MA); sociology (MA, PhD); Spanish (MA, PhD); systematic theology (M Th, D Th); TESOL (teaching English to speakers of other languages) (MA); theological ethics (M Th, D Th); theory of literature (MA, PhD); urban ministries (D Th); urban ministry (M Th).

University of South Carolina, The Graduate School, College of Arts and Sciences, Department of Anthropology, Columbia, SC 29208. Offers MA, PhD. Terminal master's awarded for partial completion of doctoral program. *Degree requirements:* For master's, comprehensive exam, thesis; for doctorate, comprehensive exam, thesis/dissertation. *Entrance requirements:* For master's and doctorate, GRE General Test, letters of reference. Additional exam requirements/recommendations for international students: Required—TOEFL. Electronic applications accepted. *Faculty research:* Biocultural anthropology, archaeology, cultural anthropology.

University of Southern Mississippi, Graduate School, College of Arts and Letters, Department of Anthropology and Sociology, Hattiesburg, MS 39406-0001. Offers anthropology (MA). Part-time programs available. *Faculty:* 9 full-time (5 women). *Students:* 16 full-time (12 women), 10 part-time (9 women). Average age 32. 6 applicants, 67% accepted, 4 enrolled. In 2008, 7 master's awarded. *Degree requirements:* For master's, one foreign language, comprehensive exam, thesis. *Entrance requirements:* For master's, GRE General Test, minimum GPA of 2.75 in last 2 years, 3.0 in field of study. Additional exam requirements/recommendations for international students: Required—TOEFL. *Application deadline:* For fall admission, 3/15 priority date for domestic students, 3/1 for international students. Applications are processed on a rolling basis. Application fee: $30. *Financial support:* In 2008–09, 8 research assistantships with full tuition reimbursements (averaging $7,500 per year), 6 teaching assistantships with full tuition reimbursements (averaging $7,500 per year) were awarded; career-related internships or fieldwork, Federal Work-Study, institutionally sponsored loans, scholarships/grants, and unspecified assistantships also available. Financial award application deadline: 3/15; financial award applicants required to submit FAFSA. *Faculty research:* Archaeology of North America, historic archaeology, bioarchaeology, ethnography of Europe, ethnography of Africa. *Unit head:* Dr. James Flanagan, Chair, 601-266-4306, Fax: 601-266-6373. *Application contact:* Dr. Marie Danforth, Graduate Coordinator, 601-266-4306, Fax: 601-266-6373, E-mail: marie.danforth@usm.edu.

University of South Florida, Graduate School, College of Arts and Sciences, Department of Anthropology, Tampa, FL 33620-9951. Offers applied anthropology (MA, PhD). Part-time programs available. *Faculty:* 18 full-time (13 women). *Students:* 85 full-time (63 women), 68 part-time (48 women); includes 37 minority (15 African Americans, 2 American Indian/Alaska Native, 5 Asian Americans or Pacific Islanders, 15 Hispanic Americans), 7 international. Average age 28. 131 applicants, 44% accepted, 41 enrolled. In 2008, 10 master's, 8 doctorates awarded. *Degree requirements:* For master's, comprehensive exam, thesis; for doctorate, one foreign language, comprehensive exam, thesis/dissertation. *Entrance requirements:* For master's and doctorate, GRE General Test, minimum GPA of 3.2, 3 letters of recommendation. Additional exam requirements/recommendations for international students: Required—TOEFL (minimum score 550 paper-based; 213 computer-based). *Application deadline:* For fall admission, 1/15 for domestic students, 1/2 for international students. Application fee: $30. Electronic applications accepted. *Expenses:* Tuition, state resident: full-time $2624.40; part-time $291.60 per credit hour. Tuition, nonresident: full-time $7822; part-time $869.13 per credit hour. *Financial support:* Fellowships with partial tuition reimbursements, research assistantships with partial tuition reimbursements, teaching assistantships with partial tuition reimbursements, scholarships/grants and tuition waivers (partial) available. Financial award application deadline: 1/15; financial award applicants required to submit FAFSA. *Faculty research:* Population genetics, biomedical anthropology, archaeology and culture resource management in the Americas, urban community issues, media and education. Total annual research expenditures: $1.8 million. *Unit head:* Dr. Elizabeth Bird, Chairperson, 813-974-0802, Fax: 813-974-2668, E-mail: ebird@cas.usf.edu. *Application contact:* Dr. Christian Wells, Program Director, 813-974-2337, Fax: 813-974-2668, E-mail: cwells@cas.usf.edu.

The University of Tennessee, Graduate School, College of Arts and Sciences, Department of Anthropology, Knoxville, TN 37996. Offers archaeology (MA, PhD); biological anthropology (MA, PhD); cultural anthropology (MA, PhD); zoo-archaeology (MA, PhD). *Degree requirements:* For master's, thesis; for doctorate, one foreign language, thesis/dissertation. *Entrance requirements:* For master's and doctorate, GRE General Test, minimum GPA of 2.7. Additional exam requirements/recommendations for international students: Required—TOEFL. Electronic applications accepted. *Expenses:* Tuition, area resident: Part-time $348 per credit hour. Tuition, state resident: full-time $6262. Tuition, nonresident: full-time $18,920; part-time $1052 per credit hour. Required fees: $812; $36 per credit hour. Tuition and fees vary according to program.

The University of Texas at Arlington, Graduate School, College of Liberal Arts, Department of Sociology and Anthropology, Program in Anthropology, Arlington, TX 76019. Offers MA. Part-time and evening/weekend programs available. *Students:* 5 full-time (4 women), 17 part-time (11 women); includes 4 minority (2 African Americans, 1 American Indian/Alaska Native, 1 Hispanic American). 10 applicants, 70% accepted, 5 enrolled. In 2008, 1 master's awarded. *Degree requirements:* For master's, comprehensive exam, thesis or alternative. *Entrance requirements:* For master's, GRE General Test, minimum GPA of 3.0, 3 letters of recommendation. Additional exam requirements/recommendations for international students: Required—TOEFL (minimum score 550 paper-based; 213 computer-based). *Application deadline:* For fall admission, 6/16 for domestic students. Applications are processed on a rolling basis. Application fee: $35 ($50 for international students). *Expenses:* Tuition, area resident: Full-time $6500. Tuition, state resident: full-time $6500. Tuition, nonresident: full-time $11,558. *Financial support:* In 2008–09, 2 teaching assistantships (averaging $9,000 per year) were awarded; Federal Work-Study and institutionally sponsored loans also available. Financial award application deadline: 6/1; financial award applicants required to submit FAFSA. *Application contact:* Dr. Joel Ryan, Graduate Advisor, 817-272-3765, Fax: 817-272-3759, E-mail: jcryan@uta.edu.

The University of Texas at Austin, Graduate School, College of Liberal Arts, Department of Anthropology, Austin, TX 78712-1111. Offers archaeology (MA, PhD); folklore and public culture (MA, PhD); linguistic anthropology (MA, PhD); physical anthropology (MA, PhD); social anthropology (MA, PhD). Part-time programs available. Terminal master's awarded for partial completion of doctoral program. *Degree requirements:* For master's, thesis; for doctorate, one foreign language, thesis/dissertation. *Entrance requirements:* For master's and doctorate, GRE General Test. Additional exam requirements/recommendations for international students: Required—TOEFL. Electronic applications accepted.

The University of Texas at San Antonio, College of Liberal and Fine Arts, Department of Anthropology, San Antonio, TX 78249-0617. Offers MA, PhD. Part-time programs available. *Degree requirements:* For master's, one foreign language, comprehensive exam, thesis optional. *Entrance requirements:* For master's, GRE General Test, minimum GPA of 3.0 during last 60 hours, 18 hours in major field. Additional exam requirements/recommendations for international students: Required—TOEFL (minimum score 500 paper-based; 173 computer-based). *Faculty research:* Archaeology, ethnohistory, American social history, borderlands history, history of imperialism.

University of Toronto, School of Graduate Studies, Social Sciences Division, Department of Anthropology, Toronto, ON M5S 1A1, Canada. Offers M Sc, MA, PhD. Part-time programs available. *Degree requirements:* For master's, research paper; for doctorate, one foreign language, thesis/dissertation, language exam, thesis defense. *Entrance requirements:* For master's, minimum B+ average, 5 full-year anthropology courses, 2 letters of reference, resumé; for doctorate, minimum B+ average, master's degree in relevant area, resumé, 2 letters of reference. Additional exam requirements/recommendations for international students: Required—TOEFL (minimum score 580 paper-based), TWE (minimum score 5), Michigan English Language Assessment Battery (minimum score: 85), IELTS (minimum score: 7) or COPE (minimum score: 4).

University of Tulsa, Graduate School, College of Arts and Sciences, Department of Anthropology, Tulsa, OK 74104-3189. Offers MA, JD/MA. Part-time programs available. *Faculty:* 6 full-time (0 women). *Students:* 5 full-time (4 women), 3 part-time (all women); includes 1 minority (American Indian/Alaska Native). Average age 28. 6 applicants, 67% accepted, 3 enrolled. In 2008, 3 master's awarded. *Degree requirements:* For master's, thesis (for some programs). *Entrance requirements:* For master's, GRE General Test. Additional exam requirements/recommendations for international students: Required—TOEFL (minimum score 575 paper-based; 231 computer-based; 91 iBT), IELTS (minimum score 6.5). *Application deadline:* Applications are processed on a rolling basis. Application fee: $40. Electronic applications accepted. *Expenses:* Tuition: Full-time $15,408; part-time $899 per credit hour. Required fees: $3.33 per credit hour. One-time fee: $200 full-time. Tuition and fees vary according to course load and program. *Financial support:* In 2008–09, 4 students received support, including 4 teaching assistantships with full and partial tuition reimbursements available (averaging $11,594 per year); fellowships with full and partial tuition reimbursements available, research assistantships with full and partial tuition reimbursements available, career-related internships or fieldwork, Federal Work-Study, scholarships/grants, tuition waivers (full and partial), and unspecified assistantships also available. Support available to part-time students. Financial award application deadline: 2/1; financial award applicants required to submit FAFSA. *Faculty research:* Cultural anthropology, prehistory of Jordan, lithic technology, archaeology of Mexico, sociolinguistics. Total annual research expenditures: $97,420. *Unit head:* Dr. Lamont Lindstrom, Chairperson, 918-631-2888, Fax: 918-631-2540, E-mail: lamont-lindstrom@utulsa.edu. *Application contact:* Dr. George Odell, Advisor, 918-631-3082, Fax: 918-631-2540, E-mail: george-odell@utulsa.edu.

University of Utah, The Graduate School, College of Humanities, Program in Middle East Studies, Salt Lake City, UT 84112-1107. Offers anthropology (MA); Arabic (MA, PhD); Arabic and linguistics (MA, PhD); Hebrew (MA); history (MA, PhD); Persian (MA, PhD); political science (MA, PhD); Turkish (MA). Terminal master's awarded for partial completion of doctoral program. *Degree requirements:* For master's, 2 foreign languages, comprehensive exam, thesis optional; for doctorate, 3 foreign languages, comprehensive exam, thesis/dissertation. *Entrance requirements:* For master's, GRE General Test, minimum GPA of 3.2; for doctorate, GRE General Test, MA in Middle East studies or equivalent, minimum GPA of 3.2. Additional exam requirements/recommendations for international students: Required—TOEFL (minimum score 580 paper-based; 237 computer-based; 92 iBT). *Faculty research:* Arabic literature and linguistics, Islamic studies, Middle East history, political science, Judaic studies.

University of Utah, The Graduate School, College of Social and Behavioral Science, Department of Anthropology, Salt Lake City, UT 84112-1107. Offers M Phil, MA, MS, PhD. *Degree requirements:* For master's, comprehensive exam, thesis or alternative; for doctorate, comprehensive exam (for some programs), thesis/dissertation. *Entrance requirements:* For master's, GRE General Test, minimum undergraduate GPA of 3.0; for doctorate, GRE General Test. Additional exam requirements/recommendations for international students: Required—TOEFL (minimum score 500 paper-based; 173 computer-based). Electronic applications accepted. *Faculty research:* Evolutionary ecology, anthropological genetics, North American (hunter and gatherers) archaeology.

University of Victoria, Faculty of Graduate Studies, Faculty of Social Sciences, Department of Anthropology, Victoria, BC V8W 2Y2, Canada. Offers MA. Part-time programs available. *Degree requirements:* For master's, comprehensive exam (for some programs), thesis (for some programs). *Entrance requirements:* For master's, minimum B+ average in last 2 years of undergraduate course work, writing sample. Additional exam requirements/recommendations for international students: Required—TOEFL (minimum score 575 paper-based; 233 computer-based), IELTS (minimum score 7).

University of Virginia, College and Graduate School of Arts and Sciences, Department of Anthropology, Charlottesville, VA 22903. Offers MA, PhD. *Faculty:* 21 full-time (9 women), 3 part-time/adjunct (2 women). *Students:* 44 full-time (27 women); includes 5 minority (2 African Americans, 2 Asian Americans or Pacific Islanders, 1 Hispanic American), 6 international. Average age 29. 73 applicants, 15% accepted, 7 enrolled. In 2008, 6 master's, 1 doctorate awarded. *Degree requirements:* For master's, one foreign language, thesis; for doctorate, 2 foreign languages, thesis/dissertation. *Entrance requirements:* For master's and doctorate, GRE General Test, GRE Subject Test, 3 letters of recommendation. Additional exam requirements/recommendations for international students: Required—TOEFL (minimum score 600 paper-based; 250 computer-based; 90 iBT), IELTS (minimum score 7). *Application deadline:* For fall admission, 12/15 for domestic and international students. Applications are processed on a rolling basis. Application fee: $60. Electronic applications accepted. *Expenses:* Tuition, area resident: Full-time $10,452. Tuition, state resident: full-time $10,452. Tuition, nonresident: full-time $20,010. Required fees: $2176. Part-time tuition and fees vary according to course load and program. *Financial support:* Application deadline: 3/15; *Unit head:* Susan McKinnon, Chair, 434-924-7044, Fax: 434-924-1350, E-mail: web form http://www.virginia.edu/anthropology/comments.html. *Application contact:* Susan McKinnon, Chair, 434-924-7044, Fax: 434-924-1350, E-mail: web form http://www.virginia.edu/anthropology/comments.html.

University of Washington, Graduate School, College of Arts and Sciences, Department of Anthropology, Seattle, WA 98195. Offers MA, PhD. Terminal master's awarded for partial completion of doctoral program. *Degree requirements:* For master's, one foreign language, comprehensive exam (for some programs), thesis (for some programs); for doctorate, one foreign language, comprehensive exam (for some programs), thesis/dissertation. *Entrance requirements:* For master's and doctorate, GRE General Test, minimum GPA of 3.4. Additional exam requirements/recommendations for international students: Required—TOEFL (minimum score 500 paper-based; 173 computer-based). Electronic applications accepted. *Faculty research:* Sociocultural anthropology, biocultural anthropology, archaeology, environmental anthropology.

University of Waterloo, Graduate Studies, Faculty of Arts, Department of Anthropology, Waterloo, ON N2L 3G1, Canada. Offers anthropology (MA); public issues (MA). *Entrance requirements:* For master's, BA, B+ average. Additional exam requirements/recommendations for international students: Required—TOEFL. Electronic applications accepted. *Faculty research:* Applied socio-cultural anthropology and archaeology.

The University of Western Ontario, Faculty of Graduate Studies, Social Sciences Division, Department of Anthropology, London, ON N6A 5B8, Canada. Offers MA, PhD. *Degree requirements:* For master's, thesis; for doctorate, thesis/dissertation. *Entrance requirements:* For master's, minimum B average, honors BA. Additional exam requirements/recommendations for international students: Required—TOEFL. Electronic applications accepted. *Faculty research:* Sociocultural anthropology, bioarchaeology, linguistics.

University of West Florida, College of Arts and Sciences: Arts, Division of Anthropology and Archaeology, Pensacola, FL 32514-5750. Offers anthropology (MA); historical archaeology (MA). *Faculty:* 9 full-time (3 women). *Students:* 24 full-time (16 women), 23 part-time (14 women); includes 9 minority (1 African American, 1 American Indian/Alaska Native, 3 Asian Americans or Pacific Islanders, 4 Hispanic Americans). Average age 29. 49 applicants, 57% accepted, 17 enrolled. In 2008, 7 master's awarded. *Degree requirements:* For master's, internship or thesis. *Entrance requirements:* For master's, GRE, bachelor's degree in anthropology, minimum GPA of 3.0, 3 letters of recommendation, writing sample. Additional exam requirements/recommendations for international students: Required—TOEFL (minimum score 550 paper-based; 213 computer-based). *Application deadline:* For fall admission, 6/1 for domestic students, 5/15 for international students; for spring admission, 11/1 for domestic students, 10/1 for international students. Application fee: $30. *Expenses:* Tuition, state resident: full-time $6095; part-time $253.97 per credit hour. Tuition, nonresident: full-time $21,919; part-time $913.31 per credit hour. *Financial support:* In 2008–09, 5 research assistantships (averaging $3,760 per year), 4 teaching assistantships (averaging $3,760 per year) were awarded; career-related internships or fieldwork, scholarships/grants, tuition waivers (partial), and unspecified assistantships also available. Financial award application deadline: 4/15; financial award applicants required to submit FAFSA. *Unit head:* Dr. John Bratten, Interim Chair, 850-857-6278, E-mail: anthropology@uwf.edu. *Application contact:* Terry McCray, Assistant Director of Graduate Admissions, 850-473-7718, Fax: 850-473-7714, E-mail: gradadmissions@uwf.edu.

University of Wisconsin–Madison, Graduate School, College of Letters and Science, Department of Anthropology, Madison, WI 53706-1380. Offers archaeology (PhD); biological anthropology (PhD); cultural anthropology (PhD). Terminal master's awarded for partial completion of doctoral program. *Degree requirements:* For doctorate, thesis/dissertation. *Entrance requirements:* For doctorate, qualifying exam. Electronic applications accepted. *Faculty research:* Archaeology, biological, anthropology, cultural anthropology.

University of Wisconsin–Milwaukee, Graduate School, College of Letters and Sciences, Department of Anthropology, Milwaukee, WI 53201-0413. Offers anthropology (PhD); museum studies (Certificate). *Faculty:* 17 full-time (8 women). *Students:* 50 full-time (32 women), 44 part-time (36 women); includes 9 minority (2 African Americans, 3 American Indian/Alaska Native, 2 Asian Americans or Pacific Islanders, 2 Hispanic Americans), 2 international. Average age 28. 43 applicants, 65% accepted, 17 enrolled. In 2008, 13 master's, 1 doctorate awarded. *Degree requirements:* For master's, thesis or alternative; for doctorate, one foreign language, thesis/dissertation, departmental qualifying exam. *Entrance requirements:* For master's, GRE; for doctorate, GRE, minimum GPA of 3.0, master's degree. Additional exam requirements/recommendations for international students: Required—TOEFL (minimum score 550 paper-based; 79 iBT), IELTS (minimum score 6.5). *Application deadline:* For fall admission, 1/1 priority date for domestic students; for spring admission, 9/1 for domestic students. Applications are processed on a rolling basis. Application fee: $45 ($75 for international students). *Expenses:* Tuition, area resident: Full-time $7320; part-time $165 per credit. Tuition, state resident: full-time $7320; part-time $165 per credit. Tuition, nonresident: full-time $17,840; part-time $714 per credit. Tuition and fees vary according to campus/location, program and reciprocity agreements. *Financial support:* In 2008–09, 15 teaching assistantships were awarded; fellowships, research assistantships, career-related internships or fieldwork and unspecified assistantships also available. Support available to part-time students. Financial award application deadline: 4/15. Total annual research expenditures: $291,663. *Unit head:* J. Patrick Gray, Chair, 414-229-4822, Fax: 414-229-5848, E-mail: jpgray@uwm.edu. *Application contact:* General Information Contact, 414-229-4982, Fax: 414-229-6967, E-mail: gradschool@uwm.edu.

University of Wyoming, Graduate School, College of Arts and Sciences, Department of Anthropology, Laramie, WY 82070. Offers MA, PhD. Part-time programs available. *Faculty:* 13 full-time (6 women). *Students:* 17 full-time (7 women), 25 part-time (12 women), 2 international. Average age 33. 56 applicants, 32% accepted, 8 enrolled. In 2008, 7 master's, 1 doctorate awarded. Terminal master's awarded for partial completion of doctoral program. *Degree requirements:* For master's, one foreign language, comprehensive exam, thesis optional; for doctorate, one foreign language, comprehensive exam, thesis/dissertation. *Entrance requirements:* For master's and doctorate, GRE General Test, minimum GPA of 3.0. *Application deadline:* For fall admission, 3/1 for domestic and international students. Application fee: $50. Electronic applications accepted. *Financial support:* In 2008–09, 22 students received support, including 6 research assistantships with full and partial tuition reimbursements available (averaging $13,240 per year), 4 teaching assistantships (averaging $5,536 per year); career-related internships or fieldwork, Federal Work-Study, and institutionally sponsored loans also available. Financial award application deadline: 3/1. *Faculty research:* Paleo-Indian archaeology, osteology, faunal analysis, lithic analysis, hunter-gatherers. Total annual research expenditures: $70,000. *Unit head:* Dr. Michael E. Harkin, Professor & Department Head, 307-766-3164, Fax: 307-766-2473, E-mail: harkin@uwyo.edu. *Application contact:* Dr. Nicole Waguespack, Associate Professor, Fax: 307-766-2473, E-mail: nmwagues@uwyo.edu.

Vanderbilt University, Graduate School, Department of Anthropology, Nashville, TN 37240-1001. Offers MA, PhD. *Faculty:* 17 full-time (7 women). *Students:* 30 full-time (19 women); includes 1 minority (Hispanic American), 4 international. Average age 30. 41 applicants, 15% accepted, 6 enrolled. In 2008, 6 master's, 2 doctorates awarded. *Degree requirements:* For master's, comprehensive exam, thesis or alternative; for doctorate, one foreign language, comprehensive exam, thesis/dissertation, general, qualifying, and final exams. *Entrance requirements:* For master's and doctorate, GRE General Test. Additional exam requirements/recommendations for international students: Required—TOEFL (minimum score 570 paper-based; 230 computer-based; 88 iBT). *Application deadline:* For fall admission, 1/15 for domestic and international students. Application fee: $0. Electronic applications accepted. *Financial support:* Fellowships with full and partial tuition reimbursements, research assistantships with full tuition reimbursements, teaching assistantships with full tuition reimbursements, career-related internships or fieldwork, Federal Work-Study, institutionally sponsored loans, scholarships/grants, and health care benefits available. Financial award application deadline: 1/15; financial award applicants required to submit CSS PROFILE or FAFSA. *Faculty research:* Archaeology, ethnohistory and ethnography, epigraphy, conflict theory, Latin America. *Unit head:* Lesley Gill, PhD, Chair, 615-343-6120, Fax: 615-343-0230. *Application contact:* Beth A. Conklin, PhD, Director of Graduate Studies, 615-343-6120, Fax: 615-343-0230, E-mail: anthropology@vanderbilt.edu.

Washington State University, Graduate School, College of Liberal Arts, Department of Anthropology, Pullman, WA 99164. Offers archaeology (MA, PhD); cultural anthropology (MA, PhD); evolutionary anthropology (MA, PhD). Part-time programs available. *Degree requirements:* For master's, comprehensive exam (for some programs), thesis, oral exam; for doctorate, comprehensive exam, thesis/dissertation, qualifying exam, oral exam and written exam. *Entrance requirements:* For master's, GRE General Test, minimum GPA of 3.0, curriculum vitae, 3

Anthropology

Washington State University (continued)
letters of recommendation; for doctorate, GRE General Test, minimum GPA of 3.0, copy of thesis or master's research paper, curriculum vitae, 3 letters of recommendation. Additional exam requirements/recommendations for international students: Required—TOEFL (minimum score 550 paper-based; 213 computer-based). Electronic applications accepted. *Faculty research:* Western North American archaeology and paleo-environments, zooarchaeology, gender and culture issues, issues of globalization, cultural ecology.

Washington University in St. Louis, Graduate School of Arts and Sciences, Department of Anthropology, St. Louis, MO 63130-4899. Offers PhD. *Students:* 72 full-time (54 women); includes 1 American Indian/Alaska Native, 1 Asian American or Pacific Islander, 1 Hispanic American, 14 international. 12 applicants, 100% accepted, 8 enrolled. In 2008, 4 doctorates awarded. Terminal master's awarded for partial completion of doctoral program. *Degree requirements:* For doctorate, thesis/dissertation. *Entrance requirements:* For doctorate, GRE General Test. Additional exam requirements/recommendations for international students: Required—TOEFL. *Application deadline:* For fall admission, 1/1 for domestic and international students. Application fee: $45. Electronic applications accepted. *Financial support:* Fellowships, research assistantships, teaching assistantships, career-related internships or fieldwork, Federal Work-Study, institutionally sponsored loans, and tuition waivers (full and partial) available. Financial award application deadline: 1/15. *Faculty research:* Archaeology; physical anthropology; primate studies; sociocultural anthropology; medical anthropology. *Unit head:* Dr. Tristam Kidder, Chairperson, 314-935-5252. *Application contact:* Department Assistant, 314-935-5252.

Wayne State University, College of Liberal Arts and Sciences, Department of Anthropology, Detroit, MI 48202. Offers MA, PhD. *Degree requirements:* For master's, one foreign language, thesis; for doctorate, one foreign language, thesis/dissertation. *Entrance requirements:* Additional exam requirements/recommendations for international students: Required—TOEFL (minimum score 550 paper-based; 213 computer-based); Recommended—TWE (minimum score 6). Electronic applications accepted. *Faculty research:* Business anthropology and organizational culture, African and African-American religions, medical anthropology, skeletal epidemiology and forensic anthropology, Latin American anthropology and archaeology.

West Chester University of Pennsylvania, Office of Graduate Studies, College of Arts and Sciences, Department of Anthropology and Sociology, West Chester, PA 19383. Offers gerontology (Certificate); long term health care (MSA). Part-time and evening/weekend programs available. *Students:* 1 (woman) part-time. Average age 43. 1 applicant, 100% accepted, 1 enrolled. In 2008, 2 Certificates awarded. *Degree requirements:* For master's, comprehensive exam. *Entrance requirements:* For master's, MAT, GRE, or GMAT, interview, statement of professional goals, resumé, two letters of reference. Additional exam requirements/recommendations for international students: Required—TOEFL (minimum score 550 paper-based; 213 computer-based; 80 iBT). *Application deadline:* For fall admission, 4/15 priority date for domestic students, 3/15 for international students; for spring admission, 10/15 for domestic students, 9/1 for international students. Applications are processed on a rolling basis. Application fee: $35. Electronic applications accepted. *Expenses:* Tuition, state resident: full-time $6430; part-time $357 per credit. Tuition, nonresident: full-time $10,288; part-time $572 per credit. Required fees: $652.50; $50 per credit. $67 per semester. *Financial support:* In 2008–09, research assistantships with full tuition reimbursements (averaging $5,000 per year); unspecified assistantships also available. Support available to part-time students. Financial award application deadline: 2/15; financial award applicants required to submit FAFSA. *Faculty research:* West African communities in the U.S., life long learning-distance education, comparative religions. *Unit head:* Dr. Douglas McConatha, Chair and Graduate Coordinator, 610-436-2556, E-mail: dmcconatha@wcupa.edu. *Application contact:* Dr. Douglas McConatha, Chair and Graduate Coordinator, 610-436-2556, E-mail: dmcconatha@wcupa.edu.

Western Kentucky University, Graduate Studies, Potter College of Arts and Letters, Department of Folk Studies and Anthropology, Bowling Green, KY 42101. Offers folk studies (MA). *Degree requirements:* For master's, comprehensive exam, thesis optional, written exam. *Entrance requirements:* For master's, GRE General Test, minimum GPA of 3.0. Additional exam requirements/recommendations for international students: Required—TOEFL (minimum score 555 paper-based; 213 computer-based; 79 iBT). *Faculty research:* Public folklore, folklore and education, vernacular belief, music and culture, historic presentation.

Western Michigan University, Graduate College, College of Arts and Sciences, Department of Anthropology, Kalamazoo, MI 49008-5202. Offers MA. *Degree requirements:* For master's, comprehensive exam, thesis, written exams.

Western Washington University, Graduate School, College of Humanities and Social Sciences, Department of Anthropology, Bellingham, WA 98225-5996. Offers MA. Part-time programs available. *Degree requirements:* For master's, thesis. *Entrance requirements:* For master's, GRE General Test, minimum GPA of 3.0 in last 60 semester hours or last 90 quarter hours. Additional exam requirements/recommendations for international students: Required—TOEFL (minimum score 567 paper-based; 227 computer-based). Electronic applications accepted. *Faculty research:* Peoples and culture of the Pacific Rim; prehistory of North America; applied health; community-based action research; globalization and human rights.

Wichita State University, Graduate School, Fairmount College of Liberal Arts and Sciences, Department of Anthropology, Wichita, KS 67260. Offers MA. Part-time programs available. *Degree requirements:* For master's, comprehensive exam, thesis optional, project. *Entrance requirements:* For master's, GRE, minimum GPA of 2.75 in last 60 hours and 3.0 in anthropology. Additional exam requirements/recommendations for international students: Required—TOEFL. Electronic applications accepted. *Faculty research:* Archaeology (plains and southwest), cross-cultural studies of aging, action anthropology, hostility and warfare, human osteology and nutrition.

Yale University, Graduate School of Arts and Sciences, Department of Anthropology, New Haven, CT 06520. Offers M Phil, MA, PhD. *Degree requirements:* For doctorate, thesis/dissertation. *Entrance requirements:* For master's and doctorate, GRE General Test. *Faculty research:* Linguistics, national identity.

York University, Faculty of Graduate Studies, Faculty of Arts, Program in Social Anthropology, Toronto, ON M3J 1P3, Canada. Offers MA, PhD. Part-time programs available. *Degree requirements:* For master's, thesis or alternative; for doctorate, comprehensive exam, thesis/dissertation. Electronic applications accepted.

Applied Social Research

American University, College of Arts and Sciences, Department of Sociology, Washington, DC 22016-8072. Offers social research (Certificate); sociology (MA). Part-time and evening/weekend programs available. *Faculty:* 14 full-time (9 women), 2 part-time/adjunct (1 woman). *Students:* 19 full-time (18 women), 32 part-time (23 women); includes 26 minority (21 African Americans, 1 American Indian/Alaska Native, 1 Asian American or Pacific Islander, 3 Hispanic Americans), 4 international. Average age 35. 28 applicants, 79% accepted, 9 enrolled. In 2008, 7 master's awarded. *Degree requirements:* For master's, comprehensive exam, thesis or alternative, tool of research examination. *Entrance requirements:* For master's, GRE; for Certificate, bachelor's degree. Additional exam requirements/recommendations for international students: Required—TOEFL. *Application deadline:* For fall admission, 2/1 for domestic students. Application fee: $80. *Expenses:* Tuition: Full-time $21,204; part-time $1178 per credit hour. Required fees: $380. Part-time tuition and fees vary according to course load and program. *Financial support:* Fellowships, research assistantships with full and partial tuition reimbursements, teaching assistantships with full and partial tuition reimbursements, career-related internships or fieldwork, Federal Work-Study, institutionally sponsored loans, tuition waivers (full and partial), and unspecified assistantships available. Support available to part-time students. Financial award application deadline: 2/1; financial award applicants required to submit FAFSA. *Faculty research:* Gender, race, development, applied social policy, political economy. *Unit head:* Dr. John Philip Drysdale, Chair, 202-885-2488, Fax: 202-885-2477, E-mail: drysdale@american.edu. *Application contact:* Dr. John Philip Drysdale, Chair, 202-885-2488, Fax: 202-885-2477, E-mail: drysdale@american.edu.

California State University, Dominguez Hills, College of Natural and Behavioral Sciences, Program in Sociology, Carson, CA 90747-0001. Offers social research (Certificate); sociology (MA). Part-time and evening/weekend programs available. *Faculty:* 14 full-time (7 women), 7 part-time/adjunct (4 women). *Students:* 27 full-time (22 women), 49 part-time (37 women); includes 61 minority (42 African Americans, 3 Asian Americans or Pacific Islanders, 16 Hispanic Americans), 1 international. Average age 37. 38 applicants, 79% accepted, 18 enrolled. In 2008, 21 master's awarded. *Degree requirements:* For master's, comprehensive exam, thesis. *Entrance requirements:* For master's and Certificate, minimum GPA of 2.85. *Application deadline:* For fall admission, 6/1 for domestic students. Application fee: $55. *Expenses:* Tuition, nonresident: part-time $339 per unit. Required fees: $1300 per semester. *Faculty research:* Community studies, social movements, criminology. *Unit head:* Dr. Clare Weber, Chair, 310-243-3458, E-mail: cweber@csudh.edu. *Application contact:* Dr. Gayle Ball-Parker, Director of Admissions, 310-243-3645, E-mail: gball@csudh.edu.

Hofstra University, College of Liberal Arts and Sciences, Department of Sociology, Hempstead, NY 11549. Offers applied social research and policy analysis (MA). Part-time and evening/weekend programs available. *Faculty:* 4 full-time (2 women). *Students:* 4 full-time (3 women); includes 1 minority (African American), 1 international. Average age 25. 4 applicants, 100% accepted, 4 enrolled. *Degree requirements:* For master's, comprehensive exam, thesis optional, internship. *Entrance requirements:* For master's, GRE, interview, essay, minimum GPA of 3.0. Additional exam requirements/recommendations for international students: Required—TOEFL (minimum score 550 paper-based; 213 computer-based; 80 iBT). *Application deadline:* Applications are processed on a rolling basis. Electronic applications accepted. *Expenses:* Tuition: Full-time $15,300; part-time $850 per credit. Required fees: $970; $165 per term. Tuition and fees vary according to program. *Financial support:* In 2008–09, 2 students received support, including 2 fellowships with full and partial tuition reimbursements available (averaging $3,000 per year); research assistantships with full and partial tuition reimbursements available, Federal Work-Study, institutionally sponsored loans, scholarships/grants, and tuition waivers (full and partial) also available. Support available to part-time students. *Faculty research:* Housing policy, immigration, labor economic policy, education policy, health care policy. Total annual research expenditures: $100,000. *Unit head:* Dr. Marc Silver, Program Director, 516-463-6250, Fax: 516-463-2310, E-mail: socmls@hofstra.edu. *Application contact:* Carol Drummer, Dean of Graduate Admissions, 516-463-4876, Fax: 516-463-4664, E-mail: gradstudent@hofstra.edu.

Hunter College of the City University of New York, Graduate School, School of Arts and Sciences, Department of Sociology, Program in Applied Social Research, New York, NY 10021-5085. Offers MS. Part-time and evening/weekend programs available. *Faculty:* 5 full-time (2 women), 2 part-time/adjunct (1 woman). *Students:* 11 full-time (8 women), 21 part-time (15 women); includes 5 minority (1 African American, 2 Asian Americans or Pacific Islanders, 2 Hispanic Americans). Average age 29. 17 applicants, 82% accepted, 8 enrolled. In 2008, 11 master's awarded. *Degree requirements:* For master's, internship, research reports. *Entrance requirements:* For master's, GRE General Test or GMAT, 3 credits of course work in statistics, research methods; background in sociology or related social science. Additional exam requirements/recommendations for international students: Required—TOEFL. *Application deadline:* For fall admission, 4/1 for domestic students, 2/1 for international students; for spring admission, 11/1 for domestic students, 9/1 for international students. Applications are processed on a rolling basis. Application fee: $125. *Financial support:* Fellowships, research assistantships, teaching assistantships, career-related internships or fieldwork, Federal Work-Study, institutionally sponsored loans, scholarships/grants, and tuition waivers (full and partial) available. Support available to part-time students. *Faculty research:* Consumer behavior, new electronic media, voting behavior, policy analysis, sociomedicine. *Unit head:* Dr. Joong-Hwan Oh, Director, 212-772-5643, E-mail: goh@hunter.cuny.edu. *Application contact:* Prof. Howard Lune, Grad Program Advisor, 212-772-5641, Fax: 212-772-5581, E-mail: hlune@hunter.cuny.edu.

Laurentian University, School of Graduate Studies and Research, Programme in Sociology, Sudbury, ON P3E 2C6, Canada. Offers applied social research (MA). Part-time programs available. *Entrance requirements:* For master's, honors degree in sociology or equivalent. *Faculty research:* Work foundations, managing AIDS organization, tracking laid-off mine workers.

The New School: A University, The New School for Social Research, New York, NY 10003. Offers MA, MS, DS Sc, PhD. Part-time and evening/weekend programs available. *Faculty:* 67 full-time (27 women), 28 part-time/adjunct (4 women). *Students:* 785 full-time (407 women), 315 part-time (173 women); includes 166 minority (52 African Americans, 3 American Indian/Alaska Native, 44 Asian Americans or Pacific Islanders, 67 Hispanic Americans), 301 international. Average age 31. 1,125 applicants, 72% accepted, 257 enrolled. In 2008, 180 master's, 60 doctorates awarded. Terminal master's awarded for partial completion of doctoral program. *Degree requirements:* For doctorate, thesis/dissertation, qualifying exam. *Entrance requirements:* For master's, GRE General Test; for doctorate, GRE General Test, MA. Additional exam requirements/recommendations for international students: Required—TOEFL (minimum score 600 paper-based; 250 computer-based). *Application deadline:* For fall admission, 1/15 priority date for domestic students. Applications are processed on a rolling basis. Application fee: $50. *Expenses:* Contact institution. *Financial support:* Fellowships with tuition reimbursements, research assistantships with tuition reimbursements, teaching assistantships with tuition reimbursements, career-related internships or fieldwork, Federal Work-Study, scholarships/grants, tuition waivers (full and partial), and unspecified assistantships available. Financial award application deadline: 3/1; financial award applicants required to submit FAFSA. *Faculty research:* Civil society and democracy, international movements of refugees, minority use of health services, memory, morality and genetics. *Unit head:* Dr. Michael Schober, Dean, 212-229-5777, E-mail: schober@newschool.edu. *Application contact:* Robert MacDonald, Director of Admissions, 800-523-5710 Ext. 3007, Fax: 212-989-7102, E-mail: macdonar@newschool.edu.

See Close-Up on page 1251.

Portland State University, Graduate Studies, Graduate School of Social Work, Portland, OR 97207-0751. Offers social work (MSW); social work and social research (PhD). *Accreditation:* CSWE (one or more programs are accredited). Part-time programs available. *Faculty:* 40 full-time (28 women), 18 part-time/adjunct (13 women). *Students:* 389 full-time (336 women), 168 part-time (144 women); includes 93 minority (25 African Americans, 13 American Indian/Alaska Native, 12 Asian Americans or Pacific Islanders, 43 Hispanic Americans), 13 international.

Average age 35. 586 applicants, 51% accepted, 221 enrolled. In 2008, 158 master's, 4 doctorates awarded. *Degree requirements:* For doctorate, comprehensive exam, thesis/dissertation, residency. *Entrance requirements:* For master's, minimum GPA of 3.0 in upper-division course work or 2.75 overall; for doctorate, GRE General Test, 4 references. Additional exam requirements/recommendations for international students: Required—TOEFL (minimum score 550 paper-based; 213 computer-based). *Application deadline:* For fall admission, 2/1 for domestic and international students. Application fee: $50. *Expenses:* Tuition, area resident: Full-time $8763; part-time $179 per credit hour. Tuition, state resident: full-time $8763; part-time $298 per credit hour. Tuition, nonresident: full-time $12,981; part-time $426 per credit hour. Required fees: $1242. One-time fee: $250. Tuition and fees vary according to course load and program. *Financial support:* In 2008–09, 10 research assistantships with full tuition reimbursements (averaging $11,972 per year), 1 teaching assistantship with full tuition reimbursement (averaging $13,692 per year) were awarded; career-related internships or fieldwork, Federal Work-Study, scholarships/grants, tuition waivers (partial), and unspecified assistantships also available. Support available to part-time students. Financial award application deadline: 3/1; financial award applicants required to submit FAFSA. *Faculty research:* Child welfare; child mental health; social welfare policies and services; work, family, and dependent care; adult mental health. Total annual research expenditures: $9.1 million. *Unit head:* Dr. Kristine E. Nelson, Dean, 503-725-4712, Fax: 503-725-5545, E-mail: nelsonk@pdx.edu. *Application contact:* Janet Putnam, Director of Student Affairs, 503-725-4712, Fax: 503-725-5545, E-mail: putnamj@pdx.edu.

University of California, Los Angeles, Graduate Division, School of Public Affairs, Los Angeles, CA 90095. Offers MA, MPP, MSW, PhD, JD/MA, JD/MSW, MA/MA, MBA/MA, MD/PhD. *Accreditation:* CSWE. *Degree requirements:* For doctorate, thesis/dissertation, oral and written qualifying exams. *Entrance requirements:* For master's, minimum GPA of 3.0; for doctorate, minimum undergraduate GPA of 3.0. Additional exam requirements/recommendations for international students: Required—TOEFL. Electronic applications accepted. *Expenses:* Tuition, nonresident: full-time $14,694. Required fees: $9669.50. Full-time tuition and fees vary according to course load, degree level, program and student level.

Virginia Commonwealth University, Graduate School, College of Humanities and Sciences, Wilder School of Government and Public Affairs, Department of Sociology, Richmond, VA 23284-9005. Offers applied social research (CASR); gender violence intervention (Certificate); sociology (MS); MSW/Certificate. *Degree requirements:* For master's, thesis optional. *Entrance requirements:* For master's, GRE General Test.

West Virginia University, Eberly College of Arts and Sciences, School of Applied Social Sciences, Department of Sociology, Morgantown, WV 26506. Offers applied social research (MA). Part-time programs available. *Degree requirements:* For master's, thesis or alternative. *Entrance requirements:* For master's, GRE General Test, minimum GPA of 2.75. Additional exam requirements/recommendations for international students: Required—TOEFL. *Faculty research:* Applied sociology, stratification, social/complex organization, research methodology criminology.

Archaeology

American University of Beirut, Graduate Programs, Faculty of Arts and Sciences, Beirut, Lebanon. Offers anthropology (MA); Arabic language and literature (MA); archaeology (MA); biology (MS); chemistry (MS); computer science (MS); economics (MA); education (MA); English language (MA); English literature (MA); environmental policy planning (MSES); financial economics (MAFE); geology (MS); history (MA); mathematics (MA, MS); Middle Eastern studies (MA); philosophy (MA); physics (MS); political studies (MA); psychology (MA); public administration (MA); sociology (MA); statistics (MA, MS). Part-time programs available. *Degree requirements:* For master's, one foreign language, comprehensive exam, thesis (for some programs). *Entrance requirements:* For master's, GRE, letter of recommendation. Additional exam requirements/recommendations for international students: Required—TOEFL (minimum score 600 paper-based; 250 computer-based; 100 iBT), IELTS (minimum score 7.5). *Faculty research:* String theory and supergravity; computer graphics; algebra and number theory; popular Arabic literature; marine and freshwater biology; integrating science, math and technology.

Boston University, Graduate School of Arts and Sciences, Department of Archaeology, Boston, MA 02215. Offers archaeological heritage management (MA); archaeology (MA, PhD); geoarchaeology (MA). Terminal master's awarded for partial completion of doctoral program. *Degree requirements:* For master's, one foreign language, comprehensive exam, thesis or alternative; for doctorate, 2 foreign languages, comprehensive exam, thesis/dissertation. *Entrance requirements:* For master's, GRE General Test, 3 letters of recommendation; for doctorate, GRE General Test, scholarly writing sample, 3 letters of recommendation. Additional exam requirements/recommendations for international students: Required—TOEFL (minimum score 550 paper-based; 213 computer-based).

Brown University, Graduate School, Department of Egyptology and Ancient Western Asian Studies, Providence, RI 02912. Offers AM, PhD. *Degree requirements:* For master's, one foreign language, thesis, final exam; for doctorate, 2 foreign languages, comprehensive exam, thesis/dissertation. *Entrance requirements:* For master's and doctorate, GRE General Test.

Brown University, Graduate School, Joukowsky Institute for Archaeology and the Ancient World, Providence, RI 02912. Offers PhD. *Degree requirements:* For doctorate, thesis/dissertation.

Bryn Mawr College, Graduate School of Arts and Sciences, Department of Classical and Near Eastern Archaeology, Bryn Mawr, PA 19010-2899. Offers MA, PhD. Part-time programs available. *Degree requirements:* For master's, 2 foreign languages, thesis; for doctorate, 3 foreign languages, comprehensive exam, thesis/dissertation. *Entrance requirements:* For master's and doctorate, GRE General Test. Additional exam requirements/recommendations for international students: Required—TOEFL (minimum score 600 paper-based; 250 computer-based).

See Close-Up on page 1287.

California State University, Northridge, Graduate Studies, College of Social and Behavioral Sciences, Department of Anthropology, Northridge, CA 91330. Offers general anthropology (MA); public archaeology (MA). *Faculty:* 6 full-time (5 women), 12 part-time/adjunct (5 women). *Students:* 23 full-time (15 women), 20 part-time (11 women); includes 1 American Indian/Alaska Native, 1 Asian American or Pacific Islander, 7 Hispanic Americans. Average age 33. 30 applicants, 80% accepted, 17 enrolled. In 2008, 6 master's awarded. *Degree requirements:* For master's, thesis or alternative. *Entrance requirements:* For master's, GRE General Test or minimum GPA of 3.0. Additional exam requirements/recommendations for international students: Required—TOEFL. *Application deadline:* For fall admission, 11/30 for domestic students. Application fee: $55. *Financial support:* Career-related internships or fieldwork, Federal Work-Study, and institutionally sponsored loans available. Financial award application deadline: 3/1. *Unit head:* Sabina Magliocco, Chair, 818-677-3331. *Application contact:* Dr. Cathy L. Costin, Graduate Adviser, 818-677-3324.

Columbia University, Graduate School of Arts and Sciences, Division of Humanities, Department of Art History and Archaeology, New York, NY 10027. Offers archaeology (M Phil, MA, PhD); art history and archaeology (M Phil, MA, PhD); modern art (MA). *Degree requirements:* For master's, 2 foreign languages, thesis; for doctorate, 3 foreign languages, thesis/dissertation. *Entrance requirements:* For master's and doctorate, GRE General Test. Additional exam requirements/recommendations for international students: Required—TOEFL.

Cornell University, Graduate School, Graduate Fields of Arts and Sciences, Field of Archaeology, Ithaca, NY 14853-0001. Offers environmental archaeology (MA); historical archaeology (MA); Latin American archaeology (MA); medieval archaeology (MA); Mediterranean and Near Eastern archaeology (MA); Stone Age archaeology (MA). *Faculty:* 12 full-time (3 women). *Students:* 4 full-time (3 women). Average age 27. 10 applicants, 40% accepted, 2 enrolled. *Degree requirements:* For master's, one foreign language, thesis. *Entrance requirements:* For master's, GRE General Test, 3 letters of recommendation, sample of written work. Additional exam requirements/recommendations for international students: Required—TOEFL (minimum score 550 paper-based; 213 computer-based; 77 iBT). *Application deadline:* For fall admission, 1/15 for domestic students. Application fee: $70. Electronic applications accepted. *Expenses:* Tuition: Full-time $29,500. Required fees: $70. Full-time tuition and fees vary according to degree level, program and student level. *Financial support:* In 2008–09, 4 students received support, including 1 fellowship with full tuition reimbursement available, 1 research assistantship with full tuition reimbursement available, 2 teaching assistantships with full tuition reimbursements available; institutionally sponsored loans, scholarships/grants, health care benefits, tuition waivers (full and partial), and unspecified assistantships also available. Financial award applicants required to submit FAFSA. *Faculty research:* Anatolia, Lydia, Sardis, classical and Hellenistic Greece; science in archaeology; North American Indians; Stone Age Africa; Maya trade. *Unit head:* Director of Graduate Studies, 607-255-6768, E-mail: blj7@cornell.edu. *Application contact:* Graduate Field Assistant, 607-255-6768, E-mail: dsd6@cornell.edu.

Cornell University, Graduate School, Graduate Fields of Arts and Sciences, Field of History of Art and Archaeology, Ithaca, NY 14853. Offers American art (PhD); ancient art and archaeology (PhD); Asian art (PhD); baroque art (PhD); medieval art (PhD); modern art (PhD); Renaissance art (PhD); Southeast Asian art (PhD); theory and criticism (PhD). *Faculty:* 17 full-time (11 women). *Students:* 23 full-time (19 women); includes 4 minority (1 African American, 2 Asian Americans or Pacific Islanders, 1 Hispanic American), 7 international. Average age 33. 76 applicants, 8% accepted, 4 enrolled. In 2008, 1 doctorate awarded. *Degree requirements:* For doctorate, one foreign language, comprehensive exam, thesis/dissertation, general exams in 3 areas. *Entrance requirements:* For doctorate, GRE General Test, sample of written work, 3 letters of recommendation. Additional exam requirements/recommendations for international students: Required—TOEFL (minimum score 550 paper-based; 213 computer-based; 77 iBT). *Application deadline:* For fall admission, 1/15 for domestic students. Application fee: $70. Electronic applications accepted. *Expenses:* Tuition: Full-time $29,500. Required fees: $70. Full-time tuition and fees vary according to degree level, program and student level. *Financial support:* In 2008–09, 17 students received support, including 10 fellowships with full tuition reimbursements available, 1 research assistantship with full tuition reimbursement available, 6 teaching assistantships with full tuition reimbursements available; institutionally sponsored loans, scholarships/grants, health care benefits, tuition waivers (full and partial), and unspecified assistantships also available. Financial award applicants required to submit FAFSA. *Unit head:* Director of Graduate Studies, 607-255-4905, Fax: 607-255-0566, E-mail: art_history@cornell.edu. *Application contact:* Graduate Field Assistant, 607-255-4905, Fax: 607-255-0566, E-mail: art_history@cornell.edu.

Florida State University, Graduate Studies, College of Arts and Sciences, Department of Classics, Tallahassee, FL 32306. Offers classical archaeology (MA); classical civilization (MA); classics (MA, PhD), including archaeology (PhD), literature and languages (PhD); Greek (MA); Greek and Latin (MA); Latin (MA). Part-time programs available. *Degree requirements:* For master's, one foreign language, comprehensive exam (for some programs), thesis (for some programs); for doctorate, 2 foreign languages, comprehensive exam, thesis/dissertation. *Entrance requirements:* For master's, GRE General Test, minimum GPA of 3.0; for doctorate, GRE General Test. Additional exam requirements/recommendations for international students: Required—TOEFL. Electronic applications accepted. *Faculty research:* Greek and Latin literature, mythology, classical archaeology, history, Roman religion.

Gordon-Conwell Theological Seminary, Graduate and Professional Programs, South Hamilton, MA 01982. Offers Biblical languages (MABL); church history (MACH); counseling (MACO); ministry (D Min); missions/evangelism (MAME); New Testament (MANT); Old Testament (MAOT); religion (MAR); theology (M Div, MATH, Th M, Th D). *Accreditation:* ACIPE; ATS (one or more programs are accredited). Part-time and evening/weekend programs available. *Degree requirements:* For master's, one foreign language, thesis optional; for doctorate, 2 foreign languages, thesis/dissertation; for M Div, 2 foreign languages. *Entrance requirements:* For M Div and master's, minimum GPA of 2.5; for doctorate, minimum GPA of 3.0.

Graduate School and University Center of the City University of New York, Graduate Studies, Program in Anthropology, New York, NY 10016-4039. Offers anthropological linguistics (PhD); archaeology (PhD); cultural anthropology (PhD); physical anthropology (PhD). *Degree requirements:* For doctorate, one foreign language, thesis/dissertation. *Entrance requirements:* For doctorate, GRE General Test. Additional exam requirements/recommendations for international students: Required—TOEFL. Electronic applications accepted.

Harvard University, Graduate School of Arts and Sciences, Department of Anthropology, Cambridge, MA 02138. Offers archaeology (PhD); biological anthropology (PhD); legal anthropology (AM); medical anthropology (AM); social anthropology (AM, PhD); social change and development (AM). Terminal master's awarded for partial completion of doctoral program. *Degree requirements:* For master's, 2 foreign languages, thesis (for some programs); for doctorate, 2 foreign languages, thesis/dissertation, laboratory and/or fieldwork; general, qualifying, or special exams. *Entrance requirements:* For master's and doctorate, GRE General Test. Additional exam requirements/recommendations for international students: Required—TOEFL. *Expenses:* Tuition: Full-time $32,556. Required fees: $1426. Full-time tuition and fees vary according to program and student level.

Harvard University, Graduate School of Arts and Sciences, Department of Near Eastern Languages and Civilizations, Cambridge, MA 02138. Offers Akkadian and Sumerian (AM, PhD); Arabic (AM, PhD); Armenian (AM, PhD); biblical history (AM, PhD); Hebrew (AM, PhD); Indo-Muslim culture (AM, PhD); Iranian (AM, PhD); Jewish history and literature (AM, PhD); Persian (AM, PhD); Semitic philology (AM, PhD); Syro-Palestinian archaeology (AM, PhD); Turkish (AM, PhD). *Degree requirements:* For doctorate, variable foreign language requirement, thesis/dissertation, general exams. *Entrance requirements:* For master's, GRE General Test; for doctorate, GRE General Test, proficiency in a Near Eastern language. Additional exam requirements/recommendations for international students: Required—TOEFL. *Expenses:* Tuition: Full-time $32,556. Required fees: $1426. Full-time tuition and fees vary according to program and student level.

Harvard University, Graduate School of Arts and Sciences, Department of the Classics, Cambridge, MA 02138. Offers Byzantine Greek (PhD); classical archaeology (PhD); classical

Archaeology

Harvard University (continued)
philology (PhD); classical philosophy (PhD); medieval Latin (PhD). *Degree requirements:* For doctorate, 4 foreign languages, thesis/dissertation, preliminary and special exams. *Entrance requirements:* For doctorate, GRE General Test. Additional exam requirements/recommendations for international students: Required—TOEFL. *Expenses:* Tuition: Full-time $32,556. Required fees: $1426. Full-time tuition and fees vary according to program and student level.

Illinois State University, Graduate School, College of Arts and Sciences, Department of Sociology, Program in Historical Archaeology, Normal, IL 61790-2200. Offers MA, MS.

Massachusetts Institute of Technology, School of Engineering, Department of Materials Science and Engineering, Cambridge, MA 02139-4307. Offers archaeological materials (PhD, Sc D); bio- and polymeric materials (PhD, Sc D); electronic, photonic and magnetic materials (PhD, Sc D); emerging, fundamental and computational studies in materials science (Sc D); emerging, fundamental, and computational studies in materials science (PhD); materials engineering (Mat E); materials science and engineering (M Eng, SM, PhD, Sc D); metallurgical engineering (Met E); structural and environmental materials (PhD, Sc D); SM/MBA. Terminal master's awarded for partial completion of doctoral program. *Degree requirements:* For master's and other advanced degree, thesis; for doctorate, comprehensive exam, thesis/dissertation. *Entrance requirements:* For master's and doctorate, GRE General Test. Additional exam requirements/recommendations for international students: Required—TOEFL (minimum score 577 paper-based; 233 computer-based). Electronic applications accepted. *Faculty research:* Electronic, Photonic, and Magnetic Materials; Biological and Polymeric Materials; Structural and Environmental Materials; Computational Studies in Materials, Emerging and Fundamental Materials; Archaeological Materials.

Memorial University of Newfoundland, School of Graduate Studies, Department of Anthropology, St. John's, NL A1C 5S7, Canada. Offers archaeology and physical anthropology (MA, PhD); social and cultural anthropology (MA, PhD). Part-time programs available. *Degree requirements:* For master's, thesis (for some programs); for doctorate, comprehensive exam, thesis/dissertation, oral defense of thesis. *Entrance requirements:* For master's, 2nd class degree in related field. Electronic applications accepted. *Faculty research:* Early European settlements, ethnoarchaeology, economic/political anthropology, land claims and aboriginal rights, marine anthropology.

Michigan Technological University, Graduate School, College of Sciences and Arts, Department of Social Sciences, Program in Industrial Archaeology, Houghton, MI 49931-1295. Offers MS. Part-time programs available. *Degree requirements:* For master's, comprehensive exam, thesis. *Entrance requirements:* For master's, GRE. Additional exam requirements/recommendations for international students: Required—TOEFL (minimum score 550 paper-based; 213 computer-based). Electronic applications accepted.

Michigan Technological University, Graduate School, College of Sciences and Arts, Department of Social Sciences, Program in Industrial Heritage and Archeology, Houghton, MI 49931-1295. Offers PhD. Part-time programs available. *Degree requirements:* For doctorate, comprehensive exam, thesis/dissertation. *Entrance requirements:* Additional exam requirements/recommendations for international students: Required—TOEFL (minimum score 550 paper-based; 213 computer-based). Electronic applications accepted.

Midwestern Baptist Theological Seminary, Graduate and Professional Programs, Kansas City, MO 64118-4697. Offers Biblical archaeology (MA); Biblical languages (MA); Christian education (M Div, MACE); Christian foundations—lay ministry (Graduate Certificate); collegiate ministries (M Div); counseling (MA); educational ministry (D Ed Min); international church planting (M Div); ministry (M Div, D Min); North American church planting (M Div); sacred music (MCM); urban ministry (M Div); worship leadership (M Div); youth ministry (M Div). *Accreditation:* ATS. Part-time programs available. Postbaccalaureate distance learning degree programs offered (minimal on-campus study). *Degree requirements:* For doctorate, thesis/dissertation; for M Div, 2 foreign languages. *Entrance requirements:* For doctorate, MAT. Electronic applications accepted. *Faculty research:* Ministerial studies, Biblical and theological studies, missions, counseling.

New York University, Graduate School of Arts and Science, Institute of Fine Arts, Program in Art History and Archaeology, New York, NY 10012-1019. Offers architectural studies (PhD); art history and archaeology (MA, PhD); classical art and archaeology (PhD); curatorial studies (PhD); East and South Asian art (PhD); Near Eastern art and archaeology (PhD); MA/Diploma; PhD/Certificate. Part-time programs available. Terminal master's awarded for partial completion of doctoral program. *Degree requirements:* For master's, 2 foreign languages, thesis or alternative, 2 qualifying papers; for doctorate, 2 foreign languages, thesis/dissertation. *Entrance requirements:* For master's, GRE General Test; for doctorate, GRE General Test, MA. Additional exam requirements/recommendations for international students: Required—TOEFL.

Northern Arizona University, Graduate College, College of Social and Behavioral Sciences, Department of Anthropology, Flagstaff, AZ 86011. Offers archaeology (MA); cultural anthropology (MA); linguistic anthropology (MA). *Degree requirements:* For master's, thesis (for some programs), internship paper. *Entrance requirements:* For master's, 18 undergraduate hours in anthropology. *Faculty research:* Economic development, culture change, ethnohistory, archaeology of the Southwest, small town networks and HIV.

Northwestern State University of Louisiana, Graduate Studies and Research, Program in Heritage Resources, Natchitoches, LA 71497. Offers MA. *Faculty:* 5 full-time (3 women). *Students:* 18 full-time (9 women), 1 (woman) part-time; includes 1 minority (American Indian/Alaska Native). Average age 34. 10 applicants, 100% accepted, 10 enrolled. In 2008, 5 master's awarded. *Degree requirements:* For master's, comprehensive exam, thesis or alternative. *Entrance requirements:* For master's, GRE General Test, minimum undergraduate GPA of 2.5. *Unit head:* Dr. Elizabeth Guin, Head, 318-357-4057, Fax: 318-357-6153, E-mail: guine@nsula.edu. *Application contact:* Dr. Steven G. Horton, Associate Provost/Dean, Graduate Studies, Research, and Information Systems, 318-357-5851, Fax: 318-357-5019, E-mail: grad_school@nsula.edu.

Princeton University, Graduate School, Department of Art and Archaeology, Princeton, NJ 08544-1019. Offers classical art and archaeology (PhD); East Asian art and archaeology (PhD). *Degree requirements:* For doctorate, 2 foreign languages, thesis/dissertation. *Entrance requirements:* For doctorate, GRE General Test. Additional exam requirements/recommendations for international students: Required—TOEFL (minimum score 600 paper-based; 250 computer-based). Electronic applications accepted.

St. Cloud State University, School of Graduate Studies, College of Social Sciences, Program in Cultural Resource Management Archeology, St. Cloud, MN 56301-4498. Offers MS. *Entrance requirements:* For master's, GRE General Test, minimum 2.75 GPA. Additional exam requirements/recommendations for international students: Required—Michigan English Language Assessment Battery; Recommended—TOEFL (minimum score 550 paper-based; 213 computer-based).

Simon Fraser University, Graduate Studies, Faculty of Arts and Social Sciences, Department of Archaeology, Burnaby, BC V5A 1S6, Canada. Offers MA, PhD. *Degree requirements:* For master's, one foreign language, thesis; for doctorate, one foreign language, thesis/dissertation. *Entrance requirements:* For master's, minimum GPA of 3.0; for doctorate, minimum GPA of 3.5. Additional exam requirements/recommendations for international students: Required—TOEFL or IELTS. *Faculty research:* Ethnology, archaeometry, zooarchaeology, primate behavior, forensic anthropology.

Temple Baptist Seminary, Program in Theology, Chattanooga, TN 37404-3530. Offers biblical languages (M Div); Biblical studies (MABS); Christian education (MACE); English Bible û language tools (M Div); theology (MM, D Min). Part-time and evening/weekend programs available. Postbaccalaureate distance learning degree programs offered (minimal on-campus study). *Degree requirements:* For doctorate, thesis/dissertation; for M Div, proficiency in Greek and Hebrew. *Entrance requirements:* For doctorate, minimum GPA of 3.0, M Div.

Trinity International University, Trinity Evangelical Divinity School, Deerfield, IL 60015-1284. Offers Biblical and Near Eastern archaeology and languages (MA); Christian studies (MA, Certificate); Christian thought (MA); church history (MA, Th M); congregational ministry: pastor-teacher (M Div); congregational ministry: team ministry (M Div); counseling ministries (MA); counseling psychology (MA); cross-cultural ministry (M Div); educational studies (PhD); evangelism (MA); history of Christianity in America (MA); intercultural studies (MA, PhD); leadership and ministry management (D Min); military chaplaincy (D Min); ministry (MA); mission and evangelism (Th M); missions and evangelism (D Min); New Testament (MA, Th M); Old Testament (Th M); Old Testament and Semitic languages (MA); pastoral care (M Div); pastoral care and counseling (D Min); pastoral counseling and psychology (Th M); pastoral theology (Th M); philosophy of religion (MA); preaching (D Min); religion (MA); research ministry (M Div); systematic theology (Th M); theological studies (PhD); urban ministry (MA). *Accreditation:* ATS (one or more programs are accredited). Part-time programs available. Postbaccalaureate distance learning degree programs offered (minimal on-campus study). *Degree requirements:* For master's, comprehensive exam, thesis, fieldwork; for doctorate, comprehensive exam (for some programs), thesis/dissertation; for M Div, 2 foreign languages, fieldwork; for Certificate, comprehensive exam, integrative papers. *Entrance requirements:* For M Div, GRE, MAT; for master's, GRE, MAT, minimum cumulative undergraduate GPA of 3.0; for doctorate, GRE, minimum cumulative graduate GPA of 3.2; for Certificate, GRE, MAT, minimum undergraduate GPA of 2.5. Additional exam requirements/recommendations for international students: Required—TOEFL (minimum score 580 paper-based; 237 computer-based), TWE (minimum score 4). Electronic applications accepted.

Tufts University, Graduate School of Arts and Sciences, Department of Classics, Medford, MA 02155. Offers classical archaeology (MA); classics (MA). Part-time programs available. *Degree requirements:* For master's, 2 foreign languages, comprehensive exam, thesis or alternative. *Entrance requirements:* For master's, GRE General Test, writing sample. Additional exam requirements/recommendations for international students: Required—TOEFL (minimum score 550 paper-based; 213 computer-based; 80 iBT). Electronic applications accepted.

Universidad de las Américas–Puebla, Division of Graduate Studies, School of Social Sciences, Program in Anthropology, Puebla, Mexico. Offers anthropology (MA); archaeology (MA). Part-time and evening/weekend programs available. *Degree requirements:* For master's, one foreign language, thesis. *Entrance requirements:* For master's, bachelor's degree in anthropology or equivalent. *Faculty research:* Archaeology, ethnography, and ethnohistory of Mesoamerica.

Université Laval, Faculty of Letters, Department of History, Programs in Archaeology, Québec, QC G1K 7P4, Canada. Offers MA, PhD. Terminal master's awarded for partial completion of doctoral program. *Degree requirements:* For master's, thesis; for doctorate, comprehensive exam, thesis/dissertation. *Entrance requirements:* For master's and doctorate, English test, knowledge of French. Electronic applications accepted.

University of Alberta, Faculty of Graduate Studies and Research, Department of History and Classics, Edmonton, AB T6G 2E1, Canada. Offers ancient history (PhD); classical archaeology (MA, PhD); classical literature (PhD); classics (MA); history (MA, PhD). Part-time and evening/weekend programs available. *Degree requirements:* For master's, one foreign language, thesis (for some programs); for doctorate, one foreign language, thesis/dissertation. *Entrance requirements:* For master's, minimum B+ average; for doctorate, minimum A- average. Additional exam requirements/recommendations for international students: Required—TOEFL (minimum score 580 paper-based; 237 computer-based). Electronic applications accepted. *Faculty research:* Western Canada, classical archaeology, Britain, Eastern Europe, East Asia.

The University of British Columbia, Faculty of Arts and Faculty of Graduate Studies, Department of Classical, Near Eastern and Religious Studies, Programmes in Classics, Vancouver, BC V6T 1Z1, Canada. Offers ancient culture, religion, and ethnicity (MA); classical and near eastern archaeology (MA); classics (MA, PhD). Part-time programs available. *Degree requirements:* For master's, 2 foreign languages, thesis or comprehensive exam; for doctorate, 2 foreign languages, comprehensive exam, thesis/dissertation. *Entrance requirements:* For master's, upper second class standing; for doctorate, MA degree. Additional exam requirements/recommendations for international students: Required—TOEFL (minimum score 600 paper-based; 250 computer-based), IELTS (minimum score 7.5). Electronic applications accepted. *Faculty research:* Classical archaeology, ancient historians, late antiquity, ancient prose fiction, epigraphy.

University of Calgary, Faculty of Graduate Studies, Faculty of Social Sciences, Department of Archaeology, Calgary, AB T2N 1N4, Canada. Offers MA, PhD. *Degree requirements:* For master's, thesis; for doctorate, one foreign language, thesis/dissertation, candidacy exam. *Entrance requirements:* For master's, BA or B Sc in anthropology or archaeology; for doctorate, MA in anthropology or archaeology. Additional exam requirements/recommendations for international students: Required—TOEFL. Electronic applications accepted. *Faculty research:* Prehistory, ethnoarchaeology, Africa, Latin America, biological anthropology.

University of California, Berkeley, Graduate Division, College of Letters and Science, Department of Classics, Program in Classical Archaeology, Berkeley, CA 94720-1500. Offers MA, PhD. *Degree requirements:* For master's, one foreign language, thesis, exams; for doctorate, 2 foreign languages, thesis/dissertation, qualifying exam. *Entrance requirements:* For master's and doctorate, GRE General Test, minimum GPA of 3.0, 3 letters of recommendation. Additional exam requirements/recommendations for international students: Required—TOEFL (minimum score 570 paper-based; 230 computer-based), TWE.

University of California, Berkeley, Graduate Division, Group in Ancient History and Mediterranean Archaeology, Berkeley, CA 94720-1500. Offers MA, PhD. *Degree requirements:* For master's, one foreign language, exam or thesis; for doctorate, 2 foreign languages, thesis/dissertation, qualifying exam. *Entrance requirements:* For master's and doctorate, GRE General Test, minimum GPA of 3.0, 3 letters of recommendation. Additional exam requirements/recommendations for international students: Required—TOEFL (minimum score 570 paper-based; 230 computer-based), TWE.

University of California, Los Angeles, Graduate Division, College of Letters and Science, Program in Archaeology, Los Angeles, CA 90095. Offers MA, PhD. *Students:* 21 full-time (16 women); includes 2 minority (both Asian Americans or Pacific Islanders), 3 international. Average age 27. 51 applicants, 18% accepted, 5 enrolled. In 2008, 2 master's, 2 doctorates awarded. *Degree requirements:* For master's, one foreign language, comprehensive exam, comprehensive core exam, paper, field experience; for doctorate, 2 foreign languages, thesis/dissertation, oral and written qualifying exams. *Entrance requirements:* For master's, GRE General Test, minimum GPA of 3.0, sample of research writing, degree objective of Ph.D; for doctorate, GRE General Test, minimum undergraduate GPA of 3.0, sample of research writing, ability to read 1 foreign language. *Application deadline:* For fall admission, 12/15 for domestic and international students. Application fee: $60 ($80 for international students). Electronic applications accepted. *Expenses:* Tuition, nonresident: full-time $14,694. Required fees: $9669.50. Full-time tuition and fees vary according to course load, degree level, program and student level. *Financial support:* In 2008–09, 18 fellowships with full and partial tuition reimbursements, 5 research assistantships with full and partial tuition reimbursements, 10 teaching assistantships with full and partial tuition reimbursements were awarded; Federal Work-Study, institutionally sponsored loans, scholarships/grants, health care benefits, tuition waivers (full and partial), and unspecified assistantships also available. Financial award application deadline: 3/1; financial award applicants required to submit FAFSA. *Unit head:* Dr. Monica Smith, Chair, 310-825-4169. *Application contact:* Departmental Office, 310-825-4169, E-mail: evgenia@ioa.ucla.edu.

University of California, Santa Barbara, Graduate Division, College of Letters and Sciences, Division of Social Sciences, Department of Anthropology, Santa Barbara, CA 93106-3210. Offers European archaeology (MA); global studies (PhD); North American archeology (MA); sociocultural anthropology (MA); South American archaeology (MA); MA/PhD. *Faculty:* 13 full-time (2 women), 2 part-time/adjunct (both women). *Students:* 57 full-time (36 women). Average age 31. 64 applicants, 41% accepted, 11 enrolled. In 2008, 7 master's, 3 doctorates awarded. Terminal master's awarded for partial completion of doctoral program. *Degree requirements:* For master's, comprehensive exam, thesis; for doctorate, comprehensive exam, thesis/dissertation. *Entrance requirements:* For master's and doctorate, GRE General Test, sample of written work, 3 letters of recommendation, statement of purpose, personal achievements/contributions statement, resumé/curriculum vitae, transcripts for post-secondary institutions attended. Additional exam requirements/recommendations for international students: Required—TOEFL (paper: 550, computer: 213, IBT: 80) or IELTS (7). *Application deadline:* For fall admission, 12/1 for domestic and international students. Application fee: $70 ($90 for international students). Electronic applications accepted. *Expenses:* Tuition, nonresident: full-time $25,149. Required fees: $10,143. Full-time tuition and fees vary according to campus/location, reciprocity agreements and student level. *Financial support:* In 2008–09, 51 students received support, including 47 fellowships with full and partial tuition reimbursements available (averaging $4,000 per year), 9 research assistantships with full and partial tuition reimbursements available (averaging $7,400 per year), 30 teaching assistantships with partial tuition reimbursements available (averaging $10,500 per year); career-related internships or fieldwork, Federal Work-Study, institutionally sponsored loans, scholarships/grants, traineeships, health care benefits, and unspecified assistantships also available. Financial award application deadline: 3/1; financial award applicants required to submit FAFSA. *Faculty research:* Archaeology, bioarchaeology, biosocial anthropology, evolutionary ecology, evolutionary psychology, sociocultural anthropology. *Unit head:* Prof. Katharina Schreiber, Chair, 805-893-2519, Fax: 805-893-8707, E-mail: kschreiber@anth.ucsb.edu. *Application contact:* Robin Roe, Graduate Program Assistant, 805-893-2516, Fax: 805-893-8707, E-mail: roe@anth.ucsb.edu.

University of California, Santa Cruz, Division of Graduate Studies, Division of Social Sciences, Program in Anthropology, Santa Cruz, CA 95064. Offers anthropological archaeology (PhD); cultural anthropology (PhD). *Degree requirements:* For doctorate, thesis/dissertation, qualifying exam. *Entrance requirements:* For doctorate, GRE General Test. *Faculty research:* Culture and power, women's roles, AIDS, folklore.

University of Chicago, Division of the Humanities, Department of Classics, Chicago, IL 60637-1513. Offers ancient philosophy (AM, PhD); classical archaeology (AM, PhD); classical languages and literatures (AM, PhD). Terminal master's awarded for partial completion of doctoral program. *Degree requirements:* For master's, one foreign language, thesis; for doctorate, 2 foreign languages, thesis/dissertation. *Entrance requirements:* For master's and doctorate, GRE General Test. Additional exam requirements/recommendations for international students: Required—TOEFL.

University of Georgia, Graduate School, College of Arts and Sciences, Department of Anthropology, Athens, GA 30602. Offers anthropology (MA, PhD); archaeological resource management (MS). *Degree requirements:* For master's, one foreign language, thesis; for doctorate, one foreign language, thesis/dissertation. *Entrance requirements:* For master's and doctorate, GRE General Test. Electronic applications accepted.

University of Lethbridge, School of Graduate Studies, Lethbridge, AB T1K 3M4, Canada. Offers accounting (MScM); addictions counseling (M Sc); agricultural biotechnology (M Sc); agricultural studies (M Sc, MA); anthropology (MA); archaeology (MA); art (MA); biochemistry (M Sc); biological sciences (M Sc); biomolecular science (PhD); biosystems and biodiversity (PhD); Canadian studies (MA); chemistry (M Sc); computer science (M Sc); computer science and geographical information science (M Sc); counseling psychology (M Ed); dramatic arts (MA); earth, space, and physical science (PhD); economics (MA); educational leadership (M Ed); English (MA); environmental science (M Sc); evolution and behavior (PhD); exercise science (M Sc); finance (MScM); French (MA); French/German (MA); French/Spanish (MA); general education (M Ed); general management (MScM); geography (M Sc, MA); German (MA); health sciences (M Sc, MA); history (MA); human resource management and labour relations (MScM); individualized multidisciplinary (M Sc, MA); information systems (MScM); international management (MScM); kinesiology (M Sc, MA); management (M Sc, MA); marketing (MScM); mathematics (M Sc); music (MA); Native American studies (MA); neuroscience (M Sc, PhD); new media (MA); nursing (M Sc); philosophy (MA); physics (M Sc); policy and strategy (MScM); political science (MA); psychology (M Sc, MA); religious studies (MA); sociology (MA); theoretical and computational science (PhD); urban and regional studies (MA). Part-time and evening/weekend programs available. *Degree requirements:* For doctorate, comprehensive exam, thesis/dissertation. *Entrance requirements:* For master's, GMAT (M Sc in management), bachelor's degree in related field, minimum GPA of 3.0 during previous 20 graded semester courses, 2 years teaching or related experience (M Ed); for doctorate, master's degree, minimum graduate GPA of 3.5. Additional exam requirements/recommendations for international students: Required—TOEFL. *Faculty research:* Movement and brain plasticity, gibberellin physiology, photosynthesis, carbon cycling, molecular properties of main-group ring components.

University of Massachusetts Boston, Office of Graduate Studies, College of Liberal Arts, Program in History, Track in Historical Archaeology, Boston, MA 02125-3393. Offers MA. Part-time and evening/weekend programs available. *Degree requirements:* For master's, thesis, oral exams, practicum. *Entrance requirements:* For master's, GRE General Test, minimum GPA of 2.75. *Faculty research:* New World Colonialism, New England archeology, historical and urban archeology, archeological botany, ethnology.

University of Memphis, Graduate School, College of Communication and Fine Arts, Department of Art, Memphis, TN 38152. Offers art (Graduate Certificate); art history (MA), including Egyptian art and archaeology, general art history; ceramics (MFA); graphic design (MFA); interior design (MFA); painting (MFA); printmaking/photography (MFA); sculpture (MFA). *Accreditation:* NASAD (one or more programs are accredited). *Faculty:* 21 full-time (7 women), 1 (woman) part-time/adjunct. *Students:* 41 full-time (28 women), 3 part-time (all women); includes 6 African Americans, 1 Asian American or Pacific Islander, 1 international. Average age 28. 45 applicants, 73% accepted, 12 enrolled. In 2008, 15 master's, 3 other advanced degrees awarded. *Degree requirements:* For master's, 2 foreign languages, comprehensive exam, thesis. *Entrance requirements:* For master's, GRE General Test or MAT, portfolio (MFA). *Application deadline:* For fall admission, 8/1 for domestic students; for spring admission, 12/1 for domestic students. Applications are processed on a rolling basis. Application fee: $35 ($60 for international students). *Expenses:* Tuition, area resident: Full-time $6242; part-time $330 per credit hour. Tuition, state resident: full-time $6242; part-time $330 per credit hour. Tuition, nonresident: full-time $17,828; part-time $815 per credit hour. Required fees: $1156. *Financial support:* Research assistantships with full tuition reimbursements, teaching assistantships with full tuition reimbursements available. Financial award applicants required to submit FAFSA. *Faculty research:* Online collaborative learning, advanced art history studies, electronic publishing/design, studio arts, architectural studies. *Unit head:* Prof. Richard Lou, Chair, 901-678-2216, Fax: 901-678-2735, E-mail: gmyatt@memphis.edu. *Application contact:* Greely Myat, Graduate Studies Coordinator, 901-678-2650.

University of Michigan, Horace H. Rackham School of Graduate Studies, College of Literature, Science, and the Arts, Interdepartmental Program in Classical Art and Archaeology, Ann Arbor, MI 48109. Offers PhD. *Degree requirements:* For doctorate, 4 foreign languages, thesis/dissertation, oral defense of dissertation, preliminary exam. *Entrance requirements:* For doctorate, GRE General Test. Additional exam requirements/recommendations for international students: Required—TOEFL (minimum score 560 paper-based; 220 computer-based). Electronic applications accepted.

University of Minnesota, Twin Cities Campus, Graduate School, College of Liberal Arts, Department of Classical and Near Eastern Studies, Minneapolis, MN 55455-0213. Offers ancient and medieval art and archaeology (MA, PhD); classics (MA, PhD); Greek (MA, PhD); Latin (MA, PhD); religions in antiquity (MA). Part-time programs available. Terminal master's awarded for partial completion of doctoral program. *Degree requirements:* For master's, 2 foreign languages, comprehensive exam, thesis or alternative; for doctorate, variable foreign language requirement, comprehensive exam, thesis/dissertation. *Entrance requirements:* For master's and doctorate, GRE, 3 letters of recommendation, department application, writing sample, copies of transcripts, personal statement. Additional exam requirements/recommendations for international students: Required—TOEFL. Electronic applications accepted. *Faculty research:* Greek and Latin literature, archaeology, religions in antiquity, ancient Near East.

University of Missouri–Columbia, Graduate School, College of Arts and Sciences, Department of Art History and Archaeology, Columbia, MO 65211. Offers MA, PhD. *Faculty:* 9 full-time (4 women). *Students:* 16 full-time (13 women), 11 part-time (5 women), 2 international. Average age 31. 28 applicants, 21% accepted, 6 enrolled. In 2008, 7 master's, 1 doctorate awarded. Terminal master's awarded for partial completion of doctoral program. *Degree requirements:* For master's, 2 foreign languages, thesis; for doctorate, 2 foreign languages, thesis/dissertation. *Entrance requirements:* For master's and doctorate, GRE General Test, minimum GPA of 3.0. Additional exam requirements/recommendations for international students: Required—TOEFL (minimum score 500 paper-based; 173 computer-based; 61 iBT), IELTS (minimum score 5.5). *Application deadline:* For fall admission, 1/18 priority date for domestic students. Applications are processed on a rolling basis. Application fee: $45 ($60 for international students). *Financial support:* Fellowships, research assistantships, teaching assistantships, institutionally sponsored loans available. *Unit head:* Dr. Anne Rufdloff Stanton, Department Chair, E-mail: stantona@missouri.edu. *Application contact:* Linda Garrison, 573-882-2757, E-mail: garrisonl@missouri.edu.

University of Nebraska–Lincoln, Graduate College, College of Arts and Sciences, Department of Anthropology and Geography, Lincoln, NE 68588. Offers anthropology (MA); geography (MA, PhD), including geography (MA), indigenous peoples (PhD); professional archaeology (MA). *Faculty:* 15 full-time (6 women). *Students:* 27 full-time (13 women), 28 part-time (14 women); includes 4 minority (2 American Indian/Alaska Native, 2 Hispanic Americans), 8 international. Average age 29. In 2008, 10 master's, 4 doctorates awarded. *Degree requirements:* For master's, thesis optional. *Entrance requirements:* For master's, GRE General Test. Additional exam requirements/recommendations for international students: Required—TOEFL. Application fee: $40. Electronic applications accepted. *Expenses:* Tuition, state resident: full-time $4275; part-time $237.50 per credit hour. Tuition, nonresident: full-time $11,525; part-time $640.25 per credit hour. Required fees: $1068; $10.35 per credit hour. $440.70 per semester. Tuition and fees vary according to course load and program. *Financial support:* Fellowships, research assistantships, teaching assistantships, health care benefits available. *Unit head:* Dr. Raymond Hames, Chair, 402-472-2411. *Application contact:* Ginny Gross, Director of Graduate Admissions, 402-472-2878, Fax: 402-472-0589, E-mail: grad_admissions@unl.edu.

The University of North Carolina at Chapel Hill, Graduate School, College of Arts and Sciences, Department of Classics, Chapel Hill, NC 27599. Offers classical archaeology (MA, PhD); classics (MA, PhD). Terminal master's awarded for partial completion of doctoral program. *Degree requirements:* For master's, one foreign language, comprehensive exam, thesis; for doctorate, 2 foreign languages, comprehensive exam, thesis/dissertation. *Entrance requirements:* For master's and doctorate, GRE General Test, minimum GPA of 3.0. Electronic applications accepted.

University of Pennsylvania, School of Arts and Sciences, Graduate Group in Art and Archaeology of the Mediterranean World, Philadelphia, PA 19104. Offers AM, PhD. Part-time programs available. Terminal master's awarded for partial completion of doctoral program. *Degree requirements:* For master's, 3 foreign languages, thesis, Greek or Latin exam, German and French or Italian exam; for doctorate, 4 foreign languages, thesis/dissertation, Greek or Latin exam, 2nd ancient language exam, German and French or Italian exam. *Entrance requirements:* For master's and doctorate, GRE General Test, knowledge of Greek or Latin and either French, German, or Italian. Additional exam requirements/recommendations for international students: Required—TOEFL. Electronic applications accepted.

University of Saskatchewan, College of Graduate Studies and Research, College of Arts and Sciences, Department of Archaeology, Saskatoon, SK S7N 5A2, Canada. Offers MA, PhD. Part-time programs available. *Degree requirements:* For master's, thesis; for doctorate, thesis/dissertation. *Entrance requirements:* Additional exam requirements/recommendations for international students: Required—TOEFL.

University of South Africa, College of Human Sciences, Pretoria, South Africa. Offers adult education (M Ed); African languages (MA, PhD); African politics (MA, PhD); Afrikaans (MA, PhD); ancient history (MA, PhD); ancient Near Eastern studies (MA, PhD); anthropology (MA, PhD); applied linguistics (MA); Arabic (MA, PhD); archaeology (MA); art history (MA); Biblical archaeology (MA); Biblical studies (M Th, D Th, PhD); Christian spirituality (M Th, D Th); church history (M Th, D Th); classical studies (MA, PhD); clinical psychology (MA); communication (MA, PhD); comparative education (M Ed, Ed D); consulting psychology (D Admin, D Com, PhD); curriculum studies (M Ed, Ed D); development studies (M Admin, MA, D Admin, PhD); didactics (M Ed, Ed D); education (M Tech); education management (M Ed, Ed D); educational psychology (M Ed); English (MA); environmental education (M Ed); French (MA, PhD); German (MA, PhD); Greek (MA); guidance and counseling (M Ed); health studies (MA, PhD), including health sciences education (MA), health services management (MA), medical and surgical nursing science (critical care general) (MA), midwifery and neonatal nursing science (MA), trauma and emergency care (MA); history (MA, PhD); history of education (Ed D); inclusive education (M Ed, Ed D); information and communications technology policy and regulation (MA); information science (MA, MIS, PhD); international politics (MA, PhD); Islamic studies (MA, PhD); Italian (MA, PhD); Judaica (MA, PhD); linguistics (MA, PhD); mathematical education (M Ed); mathematics education (MA); missiology (M Th, D Th); modern Hebrew (MA, PhD); musicology (MA, MMus, D Mus, PhD); natural science education (M Ed); New Testament (M Th, D Th); Old Testament (D Th); pastoral therapy (M Th, D Th); philosophy (MA); philosophy of education (M Ed, Ed D); politics (MA, PhD); Portuguese (MA, PhD); practical theology (M Th, D Th); psychology (MA, MS, PhD); psychology of education (M Ed, Ed D); public health (MA); religious studies (MA, D Th, PhD); Romance languages (MA); Russian (MA, PhD); Semitic languages (MA, PhD); social behavior studies in HIV/AIDS (MA); social science (mental health) (MA); social science in development studies (MA); social science in psychology (MA); social science in social work (MA); social science in sociology (MA); social work (MSW, DSW, PhD); socio-education (M Ed, Ed D); sociolinguistics (MA); sociology (MA, PhD); Spanish (MA, PhD); systematic theology (M Th, D Th); TESOL (teaching English to speakers of other languages) (MA); theological ethics (M Th, D Th); theory of literature (MA, PhD); urban ministries (D Th); urban ministry (M Th).

The University of Tennessee, Graduate School, College of Arts and Sciences, Department of Anthropology, Knoxville, TN 37996. Offers archaeology (MA, PhD); biological anthropology (MA, PhD); cultural anthropology (MA, PhD); zoo-archaeology (MA, PhD). *Degree requirements:* For master's, thesis; for doctorate, one foreign language, thesis/dissertation. *Entrance requirements:* For master's and doctorate, GRE General Test, minimum GPA of 2.7. Additional exam requirements/recommendations for international students: Required—TOEFL. Electronic applications accepted. *Expenses:* Tuition, area resident: Part-time $348 per credit hour. Tuition, state resident: full-time $6262. Tuition, nonresident: full-time $18,920; part-time $1052 per credit hour. Required fees: $812; $36 per credit hour. Tuition and fees vary according to program.

The University of Texas at Austin, Graduate School, College of Liberal Arts, Department of Anthropology, Austin, TX 78712-1111. Offers archaeology (MA, PhD); folklore and public culture (MA, PhD); linguistic anthropology (MA, PhD); physical anthropology (MA, PhD); social anthropology (MA, PhD). Part-time programs available. Terminal master's awarded for partial completion of doctoral program. *Degree requirements:* For master's, thesis; for doctorate, one foreign language, thesis/dissertation. *Entrance requirements:* For master's and doctorate,

Archaeology

The University of Texas at Austin (continued)
GRE General Test. Additional exam requirements/recommendations for international students: Required—TOEFL. Electronic applications accepted.

University of Virginia, College and Graduate School of Arts and Sciences, McIntire Department of Art, Charlottesville, VA 22904-4130. Offers classical art and archaeology (MA, PhD); history of art and architecture (MA, PhD). *Degree requirements:* For master's, one foreign language, thesis, defense; for doctorate, 2 foreign languages, comprehensive exam, thesis/dissertation, defense. *Entrance requirements:* For master's and doctorate, GRE General Test, writing sample. Additional exam requirements/recommendations for international students: Recommended—TOEFL (minimum score 600 paper-based; 250 computer-based; 90 iBT), IELTS (minimum score 7). Electronic applications accepted. *Expenses:* Tuition, area resident: Full-time $10,452. Tuition, state resident: full-time $10,452. Tuition, nonresident: full-time $20,010. Required fees: $2176. Part-time tuition and fees vary according to course load and program. *Faculty research:* Classical art, renaissance art and architecture, American material culture.

University of West Florida, College of Arts and Sciences: Arts, Division of Anthropology and Archaeology, Pensacola, FL 32514-5750. Offers anthropology (MA); historical archaeology (MA). *Faculty:* 9 full-time (3 women). *Students:* 24 full-time (16 women), 23 part-time (14 women); includes 9 minority (1 African American, 1 American Indian/Alaska Native, 3 Asian Americans or Pacific Islanders, 4 Hispanic Americans). Average age 29. 49 applicants, 57% accepted, 17 enrolled. In 2008, 7 master's awarded. *Degree requirements:* For master's, internship or thesis. *Entrance requirements:* For master's, GRE, bachelor's degree in anthropology, minimum GPA of 3.0, 3 letters of recommendation, writing sample. Additional exam requirements/recommendations for international students: Required—TOEFL (minimum score 550 paper-based; 213 computer-based). *Application deadline:* For fall admission, 6/1 for domestic students, 5/15 for international students; for spring admission, 11/1 for domestic students, 10/1 for international students. Application fee: $30. *Expenses:* Tuition, state resident: full-time $6095; part-time $253.97 per credit hour. Tuition, nonresident: full-time $21,919; part-time $913.31 per credit hour. *Financial support:* In 2008–09, 5 research assistantships (averaging $3,760 per year), 4 teaching assistantships (averaging $3,760 per year) were awarded; career-related internships or fieldwork, scholarships/grants, tuition waivers (partial), and unspecified assistantships also available. Financial award application deadline: 4/15; financial award applicants required to submit FAFSA. *Unit head:* Dr. John Bratten, Interim Chair, 850-857-6278, E-mail: anthropology@uwf.edu. *Application contact:* Terry McCray, Assistant Director of Graduate Admissions, 850-473-7718, Fax: 850-473-7714, E-mail: gradadmissions@uwf.edu.

University of Wisconsin–Madison, Graduate School, College of Letters and Science, Department of Anthropology, Madison, WI 53706-1380. Offers archaeology (PhD); biological anthropology (PhD); cultural anthropology (PhD). Terminal master's awarded for partial completion of doctoral program. *Degree requirements:* For doctorate, thesis/dissertation. *Entrance requirements:* For doctorate, qualifying exam. Electronic applications accepted. *Faculty research:* Archaeology, biological, anthropology, cultural anthropology.

Washington State University, Graduate School, College of Liberal Arts, Department of Anthropology, Pullman, WA 99164. Offers archaeology (MA, PhD); cultural anthropology (MA,

PhD); evolutionary anthropology (MA, PhD). Part-time programs available. *Degree requirements:* For master's, comprehensive exam (for some programs), thesis, oral exam; for doctorate, comprehensive exam, thesis/dissertation, qualifying exam, oral exam and written exam. *Entrance requirements:* For master's, GRE General Test, minimum GPA of 3.0, curriculum vitae, 3 letters of recommendation; for doctorate, GRE General Test, minimum GPA of 3.0, copy of thesis or master's research paper, curriculum vitae, 3 letters of recommendation. Additional exam requirements/recommendations for international students: Required—TOEFL (minimum score 550 paper-based; 213 computer-based). Electronic applications accepted. *Faculty research:* Western North American archaeology and paleo-environments, zooarchaeology, gender and culture issues, issues of globalization, cultural ecology.

Washington University in St. Louis, Graduate School of Arts and Sciences, Department of Art History and Archaeology, St. Louis, MO 63130-4899. Offers art history (MA, PhD); classical archaeology (MA, PhD). *Students:* 23 full-time (19 women); includes 1 minority (Asian American or Pacific Islander), 3 international. 42 applicants, 17% accepted, 4 enrolled. In 2008, 3 master's, 1 doctorate awarded. *Degree requirements:* For doctorate, 2 foreign languages, comprehensive exam, thesis/dissertation. *Entrance requirements:* For master's and doctorate, GRE General Test, sample of written work. *Application deadline:* For fall admission, 12/15 for domestic students. Application fee: $45. Electronic applications accepted. *Financial support:* Fellowships, teaching assistantships, career-related internships or fieldwork, Federal Work-Study, institutionally sponsored loans, and tuition waivers (full and partial) available. Support available to part-time students. Financial award application deadline: 1/15. *Unit head:* Dr. William Wallace, Chairperson, 314-935-5270. *Application contact:* Assistant to the Dean, 314-935-6880, Fax: 314-935-4887.

Wheaton College, Graduate School, Department of Biblical and Theological Studies, Program in Biblical Archaeology, Wheaton, IL 60187-5593. Offers MA. *Degree requirements:* For master's, thesis or alternative, semester of study in Israel. *Entrance requirements:* For master's, GRE General Test or MAT. Electronic applications accepted.

Wilfrid Laurier University, Faculty of Graduate Studies, Faculty of Arts, Department of Archaeology and Classical Studies, Waterloo, ON N2L 3C5, Canada. Offers MA. *Degree requirements:* For master's, thesis optional. *Entrance requirements:* For master's, minimum B+ average in last two undergraduate years (exclusive of first year level courses in those years). Additional exam requirements/recommendations for international students: Required—TOEFL.

Yale University, Graduate School of Arts and Sciences, Department of Near Eastern Languages and Civilizations, New Haven, CT 06520. Offers Arabic and Islamic studies (MA, PhD); archaeology of the ancient Near East (MA, PhD); Assyriology (MA, PhD); Egyptology (MA, PhD); Graeco-Arabic studies (MA, PhD); Northwest Semitic, Bible, comparative Semitics (MA, PhD). *Degree requirements:* For doctorate, 2 foreign languages, thesis/dissertation. *Entrance requirements:* For doctorate, GRE General Test.

Yale University, Graduate School of Arts and Sciences, Interdisciplinary Program in Archaeological Studies, New Haven, CT 06520. Offers MA. *Degree requirements:* For master's, thesis. *Entrance requirements:* For master's, GRE General Test.

Biological Anthropology

Duke University, Graduate School, Department of Biological Anthropology and Anatomy, Durham, NC 27710. Offers cellular and molecular biology (PhD); gross anatomy and physical anthropology (PhD), including comparative morphology of human and non-human primates, primate social behavior, vertebrate paleontology; neuroanatomy (PhD). *Degree requirements:* For doctorate, one foreign language, thesis/dissertation. *Entrance requirements:* For doctorate, GRE General Test. Additional exam requirements/recommendations for international students: Required—TOEFL (minimum score 550 paper-based; 213 computer-based; 83 iBT), IELTS (minimum score 7). Electronic applications accepted.

Kent State University, School of Biomedical Sciences, Program in Biological Anthropology, Kent, OH 44242-0001. Offers PhD. Offered in cooperation with Northeastern Ohio Universities

College of Medicine. *Degree requirements:* For doctorate, thesis/dissertation. *Entrance requirements:* For doctorate, GRE General Test, MA/MS in anthropology or one of the biological science disciplines, letter of recommendation. Electronic applications accepted. *Faculty research:* Human evolution, paleodemography, orofacial anatomy, osteology, primate behavior.

Mercyhurst College, Graduate Program, Program in Forensic and Biological Anthropology, Erie, PA 16546. Offers MS. *Entrance requirements:* For master's, GRE or MAT, undergraduate degree in related field, interview. Additional exam requirements/recommendations for international students: Required—TOEFL.

Demography and Population Studies

The American University in Cairo, Center for Migration and Refugee Studies, Cairo, Egypt. Offers forced migration and refugee studies (Diploma); migration and refugee studies (MA).

Bowling Green State University, Graduate College, College of Arts and Sciences, Department of Sociology, Bowling Green, OH 43403. Offers demography and population studies (MA); social psychology (MA); sociology (PhD). Part-time programs available. *Degree requirements:* For master's, thesis or alternative; for doctorate, comprehensive exam, thesis/dissertation. *Entrance requirements:* For master's and doctorate, GRE General Test. Additional exam requirements/recommendations for international students: Required—TOEFL. Electronic applications accepted. *Faculty research:* Applied demography, criminology and deviance, family studies, population studies, social psychology.

Cornell University, Graduate School, Graduate Fields of Agriculture and Life Sciences, Field of Development Sociology, Ithaca, NY 14853-0001. Offers community and regional society (MS); community and regional sociology (MPS, PhD); methods of social research (MPS, MS, PhD); population and development (MPS, MS, PhD); rural and environmental sociology (MPS, MS, PhD); state, economy, and society (MPS, MS, PhD). *Faculty:* 21 full-time (6 women). *Students:* 44 full-time (31 women); includes 5 minority (2 American Indian/Alaska Native, 2 Asian Americans or Pacific Islanders, 1 Hispanic American), 16 international. Average age 33. 62 applicants, 15% accepted, 4 enrolled. In 2008, 5 master's, 4 doctorates awarded. *Degree requirements:* For doctorate, comprehensive exam, thesis/dissertation. *Entrance requirements:* For master's and doctorate, GRE General Test, 3 letters of recommendation. Additional exam requirements/recommendations for international students: Required—TOEFL (minimum score 550 paper-based; 213 computer-based; 77 iBT). *Application deadline:* For fall admission, 1/15 priority date for domestic students. Application fee: $60. Electronic applications accepted. *Expenses:* Tuition: Full-time $29,500. Required fees: $70. Full-time tuition and fees vary according to degree level, program and student level. *Financial support:* In 2008–09, 25 students received support, including 2 fellowships with full tuition reimbursements available, 12 research assistantships with full tuition reimbursements available, 11 teaching assistantships with full tuition reimbursements available; institutionally sponsored loans, scholarships/grants, health care benefits, tuition waivers (full and partial), and unspecified assistantships also available. Financial award applicants required to submit FAFSA. *Faculty research:* Demography (population and development), environmental sociology, international and rural

community development, political economy and ecology, sustainable agriculture. *Unit head:* Director of Graduate Studies, 607-255-3092, Fax: 607-254-2896. *Application contact:* Graduate Field Assistant, 607-255-3092, Fax: 607-254-2896, E-mail: devsoc@cornell.edu.

Cornell University, Graduate School, Graduate Fields of Arts and Sciences, Field of International Development, Ithaca, NY 14853-0001. Offers development policy (MPS); international nutrition (MPS); international planning (MPS); international population (MPS); science and technology policy (MPS). *Faculty:* 46 full-time (17 women). *Students:* 14 full-time (6 women); includes 4 minority (3 African Americans, 1 Asian American or Pacific Islander), 8 international. Average age 34. 46 applicants, 39% accepted, 5 enrolled. In 2008, 6 master's awarded. *Degree requirements:* For master's, project paper. *Entrance requirements:* For master's, GRE General Test (recommended), 2 academic recommendations, 2 years of development experience. Additional exam requirements/recommendations for international students: Required—TOEFL (minimum score 77 iBT). *Application deadline:* Applications are processed on a rolling basis. Application fee: $70. Electronic applications accepted. *Expenses:* Tuition: Full-time $29,500. Required fees: $70. Full-time tuition and fees vary according to degree level, program and student level. *Financial support:* In 2008–09, 1 student received support, including 1 fellowship with full tuition reimbursement available; research assistantships with full tuition reimbursements available, teaching assistantships with full tuition reimbursements available, institutionally sponsored loans, scholarships/grants, health care benefits, tuition waivers (full and partial), and unspecified assistantships also available. Financial award applicants required to submit FAFSA. *Faculty research:* Development policy, international nutrition, international planning, science and technology policy, international population. *Unit head:* Director of Graduate Studies, 607-255-3037, Fax: 607-255-1005. *Application contact:* Graduate Field Assistant, 607-255-0831, Fax: 607-255-1005, E-mail: mpsid@cornell.edu.

Florida State University, Graduate Studies, College of Social Sciences, Center for Demography and Population Health, Tallahassee, FL 32306. Offers MS, Certificate. *Degree requirements:* For master's, thesis or alternative. *Entrance requirements:* For master's, GRE General Test, minimum GPA of 3.0. Additional exam requirements/recommendations for international students: Required—TOEFL. Electronic applications accepted. *Faculty research:* Health, aging, migration, AIDS, gender.

Harvard University, School of Public Health, Department of Global Health and Population, Boston, MA 02115-6096. Offers SM, DPH, SD. Part-time programs available. *Faculty:* 31 full-time (8 women), 8 part-time/adjunct (2 women). *Students:* 94 full-time, 7 part-time; includes 10 minority (3 African Americans, 7 Asian Americans or Pacific Islanders), 42 international. Average age 30. 206 applicants, 31% accepted, 42 enrolled. In 2008, 31 master's, 4 doctorates awarded. *Degree requirements:* For master's, thesis; for doctorate, thesis/dissertation, qualifying exam. *Entrance requirements:* For master's and doctorate, GRE. Additional exam requirements/recommendations for international students: Required—TOEFL (minimum score 595 paper-based; 240 computer-based; 95 iBT); Recommended—IELTS (minimum score 7). *Application deadline:* For fall admission, 12/15 for domestic and international students. Electronic applications accepted. *Expenses:* Tuition: Full-time $32,556. Required fees: $1426. Full-time tuition and fees vary according to program and student level. *Financial support:* Fellowships, research assistantships, teaching assistantships, Federal Work-Study, scholarships/grants, traineeships, tuition waivers (partial), and unspecified assistantships available. Support available to part-time students. Financial award application deadline: 2/8; financial award applicants required to submit FAFSA. *Faculty research:* International health policy, economics, reproductive health, ecology. *Unit head:* Dr. David Bloom, Chair, 617-432-1232, Fax: 617-432-6733, E-mail: dbloom@hsph.harvard.edu. *Application contact:* Vincent W. James, Director of Admissions, 617-432-1031, Fax: 617-432-7080, E-mail: admisofc@hsph.harvard.edu.

The Johns Hopkins University, Bloomberg School of Public Health, Department of Population, Family and Reproductive Health, Baltimore, MD 21218-2699. Offers child and adolescent health and development (Dr PH, PhD); demography (MHS); population and health (Dr PH, PhD); population, family and reproductive health (MHS); reproductive, perinatal women's health (Dr PH, PhD). *Degree requirements:* For master's, essay, fieldwork; for doctorate, thesis/dissertation, 1 year full-time residency, oral and written exams. *Entrance requirements:* For master's and doctorate, GRE General Test (LSAT, MCAT considered), 3 letters of recommendation, curriculum vitae. Additional exam requirements/recommendations for international students: Required—TOEFL (minimum score 550 paper-based; 250 computer-based). *Faculty research:* Child and adolescent health and development, population and health and reproductive, perinatal and women's health.

Princeton University, Graduate School, Department of Sociology, Princeton, NJ 08544-1019. Offers sociology (PhD); sociology and demography (PhD). *Degree requirements:* For doctorate, variable foreign language requirement, thesis/dissertation. *Entrance requirements:* For doctorate, GRE General Test, GRE Subject Test (recommended), sample of written work. Additional exam requirements/recommendations for international students: Required—TOEFL (minimum score 600 paper-based; 250 computer-based). Electronic applications accepted.

Princeton University, Graduate School, Program in Population Studies, Princeton, NJ 08544-1019. Offers demography (PhD, Certificate); economics and demography (PhD); public affairs and demography (PhD); sociology and demography (PhD). *Degree requirements:* For doctorate, thesis/dissertation. *Entrance requirements:* For doctorate, GRE General Test. Additional exam requirements/recommendations for international students: Required—TOEFL (minimum score 600 paper-based; 250 computer-based). Electronic applications accepted. *Faculty research:* Models, fertility, infant and child mortality, migration.

Université de Montréal, Faculty of Arts and Sciences, Department of Demography, Montréal, QC H3C 3J7, Canada. Offers M Sc, PhD. *Faculty:* 10 full-time (2 women), 14 part-time/adjunct (4 women). *Students:* 25 full-time (14 women), 46 part-time (23 women). 31 applicants, 42% accepted, 9 enrolled. In 2008, 8 master's, 2 doctorates awarded. Terminal master's awarded for partial completion of doctoral program. *Degree requirements:* For master's, one foreign language, thesis; for doctorate, one foreign language, thesis/dissertation, general exam. *Entrance requirements:* For master's, minimum GPA of 2.7. *Application deadline:* For fall admission, 2/1 priority date for domestic students; for winter admission, 11/1 priority date for domestic students; for spring admission, 2/1 priority date for domestic students. Applications are processed on a rolling basis. Application fee: $100. Electronic applications accepted. *Financial support:* Fellowships, research assistantships, teaching assistantships, Federal Work-Study and tuition waivers (partial) available. *Faculty research:* Historical demography, population and development, ethnic and linguistic groups, aging of population, family demography. *Unit head:* Robert Bourbeau, Chairman, 514-343-5870, Fax: 514-343-2309, E-mail: robert.bourbeau@umontreal.ca. *Application contact:* Thomas Legrand, Professor: Responsible for Graduate studies (M Sc), 514-343-7262, Fax: 514-343-2309, E-mail: tk.legrand@umontreal.ca.

Université du Québec, Institut National de la Recherche Scientifique, Graduate Programs, Research Center—Urbanization, Culture and Society, Québec, QC G1K 9A9, Canada. Offers demography (M Sc, PhD); research and public action (M Sc); urban studies (M Sc, PhD). Programs given in French. Part-time programs available. *Degree requirements:* For master's, thesis optional; for doctorate, thesis/dissertation. *Entrance requirements:* For master's, appropriate bachelor's degree, proficiency in French; for doctorate, appropriate master's degree, proficiency in French. *Faculty research:* Regional space, urban and metropolitan space, micro-urban space.

University at Albany, State University of New York, College of Arts and Sciences, Department of Sociology, Albany, NY 12222-0001. Offers demography (Certificate); sociology (MA, PhD); urban policy (Certificate). Terminal master's awarded for partial completion of doctoral program. *Degree requirements:* For master's, thesis; for doctorate, thesis/dissertation, 2 specialization exams, research tool. *Entrance requirements:* For master's and doctorate, GRE General Test. Additional exam requirements/recommendations for international students: Required—TOEFL (minimum score 213 computer-based). Electronic applications accepted. *Faculty research:* Gender and equality, crime and deviance, aging, work and organizations, social demography.

University of Alberta, Faculty of Graduate Studies and Research, Department of Sociology, Edmonton, AB T6G 2E1, Canada. Offers criminal justice (MA); demography (MA, PhD); sociology (MA, PhD). Part-time programs available. *Degree requirements:* For master's, thesis (for some programs); for doctorate, thesis/dissertation. *Faculty research:* Criminology, knowledge and culture, methods and theory, population studies, stratification.

University of California, Berkeley, Graduate Division, Group in Demography, Berkeley, CA 94720-1500. Offers MA, PhD. *Degree requirements:* For doctorate, thesis/dissertation, qualifying exam. *Entrance requirements:* For master's and doctorate, GRE General Test, minimum GPA of 3.0, 3 letters of recommendation. Electronic applications accepted.

University of California, Berkeley, Graduate Division, Group in Sociology and Demography, Berkeley, CA 94720-1500. Offers PhD. *Degree requirements:* For doctorate, thesis/dissertation, qualifying exam. *Entrance requirements:* For doctorate, GRE General Test, minimum GPA of 3.0, 3 letters of recommendation.

University of California, Irvine, Office of Graduate Studies, School of Social Sciences and School of Social Ecology, Program in Demographic and Social Analysis, Irvine, CA 92697. Offers MA. *Entrance requirements:* For master's, GRE, minimum GPA of 3.0. Additional exam requirements/recommendations for international students: Required—TOEFL (minimum score 550 paper-based; 213 computer-based).

University of Guelph, Ontario Veterinary College and Graduate Program Services, Graduate Programs in Veterinary Sciences, Department of Population Medicine, Guelph, ON N1G 2W1, Canada. Offers epidemiology (M Sc, DV Sc, PhD); health management (DV Sc); population medicine and health management (M Sc); swine health management (M Sc); theriogenology (M Sc, DV Sc). *Degree requirements:* For master's, thesis; for doctorate, comprehensive exam, thesis/dissertation. *Entrance requirements:* Additional exam requirements/recommendations for international students: Required—TOEFL.

University of Hawaii at Manoa, Graduate Division, Colleges of Arts and Sciences, College of Social Sciences, Department of Sociology, Population Studies Program, Honolulu, HI 96822. Offers Graduate Certificate. Part-time programs available. *Entrance requirements:* For degree, GRE General Test. Additional exam requirements/recommendations for international students: Required—TOEFL (minimum score 500 paper-based; 173 computer-based; 61 iBT), IELTS (minimum score 5).

University of Pennsylvania, School of Arts and Sciences, Graduate Group in Demography, Philadelphia, PA 19104. Offers AM, PhD. Terminal master's awarded for partial completion of doctoral program. *Degree requirements:* For master's, thesis or alternative; for doctorate, thesis/dissertation. *Entrance requirements:* For master's and doctorate, GRE General Test. Additional exam requirements/recommendations for international students: Required—TOEFL. Electronic applications accepted.

University of Puerto Rico, Medical Sciences Campus, Graduate School of Public Health, Program in Demography, San Juan, PR 00936-5067. Offers MS. Part-time programs available. *Degree requirements:* For master's, thesis. *Entrance requirements:* For master's, GRE, previous course work in algebra and statistics.

The University of Texas at San Antonio, College of Public Policy, Department of Demography and Organizational Studies, San Antonio, TX 78249-0617. Offers applied demography (PhD). Part-time and evening/weekend programs available. *Entrance requirements:* Additional exam requirements/recommendations for international students: Required—TOEFL (minimum score 500 paper-based; 173 computer-based). Electronic applications accepted.

Washington State University, Graduate School, College of Liberal Arts, Department of Sociology, Pullman, WA 99164. Offers crime and deviance (MA, PhD); environments, community and demographics (MA, PhD); institutions and social organizations (MA, PhD); political sociology (MA, PhD); social inequality (MA, PhD); social psychology and life course (MA, PhD). Terminal master's awarded for partial completion of doctoral program. *Degree requirements:* For master's, thesis; for doctorate, comprehensive exam, thesis/dissertation. *Entrance requirements:* For master's, GRE General Test, minimum GPA of 3.0; for doctorate, GRE General Test, MA in sociology, minimum GPA of 3.0. Additional exam requirements/recommendations for international students: Required—TOEFL (minimum score 550 paper-based). Electronic applications accepted. *Faculty research:* Crime/deviance, environmental sociology, social inequality, social psychology, gender.

Rural Sociology

Auburn University, Graduate School, Interdepartmental Programs, Department of Sociology, Anthropology, Criminology, and Social Work, Auburn University, AL 36849. Offers rural sociology (MS); sociology (MA, MS). Part-time programs available. *Degree requirements:* For master's, thesis, computer language (MS), foreign language (MA). *Entrance requirements:* For master's, GRE General Test. *Expenses:* Tuition, area resident: Full-time $5880; part-time $243 per credit hour. Tuition, state resident: full-time $5880; part-time $243 per credit hour. Tuition, nonresident: full-time $17,640; part-time $729 per credit hour. International tuition: $17,846 full-time. Required fees: $620. Tuition and fees vary according to program and reciprocity agreements.

Cornell University, Graduate School, Graduate Fields of Agriculture and Life Sciences, Field of Development Sociology, Ithaca, NY 14853-0001. Offers community and regional society (MS); community and regional sociology (MPS, PhD); methods of social research (MPS, MS, PhD); population and development (MPS, MS, PhD); rural and environmental sociology (MPS, MS, PhD); state, economy, and society (MPS, MS, PhD). *Faculty:* 21 full-time (6 women). *Students:* 44 full-time (31 women); includes 5 minority (2 American Indian/Alaska Native, 2 Asian Americans or Pacific Islanders, 1 Hispanic American), 16 international. Average age 33. 62 applicants, 15% accepted, 4 enrolled. In 2008, 5 master's, 4 doctorates awarded. *Degree requirements:* For doctorate, comprehensive exam, thesis/dissertation. *Entrance requirements:* For master's and doctorate, GRE General Test, 3 letters of recommendation. Additional exam requirements/recommendations for international students: Required—TOEFL (minimum score 550 paper-based; 213 computer-based; 77 iBT). *Application deadline:* For fall admission, 1/15 priority date for domestic students. Application fee: $60. Electronic applications accepted. *Expenses:* Tuition: Full-time $29,500. Required fees: $70. Full-time tuition and fees vary according to degree level, program and student level. *Financial support:* In 2008–09, 25 students received support, including 2 fellowships with full tuition reimbursements available, 12 research assistantships with full tuition reimbursements available, 11 teaching assistantships with full tuition reimbursements available; institutionally sponsored loans, scholarships/grants, health care benefits, tuition waivers (full and partial), and unspecified assistantships also available. Financial award applicants required to submit FAFSA. *Faculty research:* Demography (population and development), environmental sociology, international and rural community development, political economy and ecology, sustainable agriculture. *Unit head:* Director of Graduate Studies, 607-255-3092, Fax: 607-254-2896. *Application contact:* Graduate Field Assistant, 607-255-3092, Fax: 607-254-2896, E-mail: devsoc@cornell.edu.

Iowa State University of Science and Technology, Graduate College, College of Liberal Arts and Sciences, Department of Sociology and College of Agriculture, Program in Rural Sociology, Ames, IA 50011. Offers MS, PhD. *Faculty:* 14 full-time (7 women), 1 (woman) part-time/adjunct. *Students:* 11 full-time (7 women), 6 part-time (3 women); includes 1 minority (Hispanic American), 3 international. 9 applicants, 89% accepted, 4 enrolled. In 2008, 2 master's, 1 doctorate awarded. *Degree requirements:* For master's, thesis; for doctorate, thesis/dissertation. *Entrance requirements:* For master's, GRE General Test; for doctorate, GRE General Test, master's degree. Additional exam requirements/recommendations for international students: Required—TOEFL (minimum score 550 paper-based; 79 iBT), IELTS (6.5) or TOEFL. *Application deadline:* For fall admission, 2/10 priority date for domestic students, 1/10 priority date for international students; for spring admission, 10/1 for domestic and international students. Application fee: $30 ($70 for international students). Electronic applications accepted. *Expenses:* Tuition, area resident: Full-time $6446; part-time $359 per credit. Tuition, state resident: full-time $6446; part-time $359 per credit. Tuition, nonresident: full-time $17,330; part-time $963 per credit. Required fees: $790; $249.25 per semester. Tuition and fees vary according to course load and program. *Financial support:* In 2008–09, 6 research assistantships with full and partial tuition reimbursements (averaging $14,130 per year), 5 teaching assistantships with partial tuition reimbursements (averaging $14,130 per year) were awarded; scholarships/grants, health care benefits, and unspecified assistantships also available. *Unit head:* Dr. R. Paul Lasley, Chair, 515-294-2506, Fax: 515-294-8312, E-mail: sociology@iastate.edu. *Application contact:* Dr. Stephen Sapp, Director of Graduate Education, 515-294-1403, E-mail: sociology@iastate.edu.

The Ohio State University, Graduate School, College of Food, Agricultural, and Environmental Sciences, Department of Agricultural, Environmental, and Development Economics,

Rural Sociology

The Ohio State University (continued)
Columbus, OH 43210. Offers agricultural economics and rural sociology (MS, PhD). *Degree requirements:* For master's, thesis optional; for doctorate, thesis/dissertation. *Entrance requirements:* For master's and doctorate, GRE General Test. Additional exam requirements/recommendations for international students: Required—TOEFL (paper-based 550; computer-based 213) or IELTS (7) or Michigan English Language Assessment Battery (92). Electronic applications accepted.

The Ohio State University, Graduate School, College of Food, Agricultural, and Environmental Sciences, Department of Rural Sociology, Columbus, OH 43210. Offers MS, PhD. *Entrance requirements:* For master's and doctorate, GRE or GMAT. Electronic applications accepted.

Penn State University Park, Graduate School, College of Agricultural Sciences, Department of Agricultural Economics and Rural Sociology, State College, University Park, PA 16802-1503. Offers agricultural, environmental and regional economics (M Agr, MS, PhD); rural sociology (M Agr, MS, PhD).

South Dakota State University, Graduate School, College of Agriculture and Biological Sciences, Department of Rural Sociology, Brookings, SD 57007. Offers rural sociology (MS); sociology (PhD). Part-time programs available. Postbaccalaureate distance learning degree programs offered. *Faculty:* 6 full-time (4 women). *Students:* 3 full-time (1 woman), 38 part-time (21 women); includes 7 minority (1 African American, 1 American Indian/Alaska Native, 4 Asian Americans or Pacific Islanders, 1 Hispanic American). 23 applicants, 74% accepted, 17 enrolled. In 2008, 4 master's, 3 doctorates awarded. *Degree requirements:* For master's, comprehensive exam (for some programs), thesis, oral and written exams; for doctorate, comprehensive exam, thesis/dissertation, preliminary oral and written exams. *Entrance requirements:* Additional exam requirements/recommendations for international students: Required—TOEFL (minimum score 550 paper-based; 213 computer-based; 79 iBT). *Application deadline:* For fall admission, 3/1 priority date for domestic and international students. Applications are processed on a rolling basis. Application fee: $35. *Financial support:* In 2008–09, 5 research assistantships with partial tuition reimbursements, 7 teaching assistantships with partial tuition reimbursements were awarded; career-related internships or fieldwork and unspecified assistantships also available. *Faculty research:* Demography, rural families, rural development, Native Americans, rural poverty, sociology of agriculture. *Unit head:* Dr. Donna J. Hess, Head, 605-688-4132, Fax: 605-688-6354, E-mail: donna.hess@sdstate.edu. *Application contact:* Dr. Donald Arwood, Graduate Advisor, 605-688-4132, E-mail: donald.arwood@sdstate.edu.

University of Alberta, Faculty of Graduate Studies and Research, Department of Rural Economy, Edmonton, AB T6G 2E1, Canada. Offers agricultural economics (M Ag, M Sc, PhD); forest economics (M Ag, M Sc, PhD); rural sociology (M Ag, M Sc); MBA/M Ag. Part-time programs available. *Degree requirements:* For doctorate, thesis/dissertation. *Entrance requirements:* Additional exam requirements/recommendations for international students: Required—TOEFL. *Faculty research:* Agroforestry, development, extension education, marketing and trade, natural resources and environment, policy, production economics.

University of Missouri–Columbia, Graduate School, College of Agriculture, Food and Natural Resources, Department of Rural Sociology, Columbia, MO 65211. Offers MS, PhD. Part-time programs available. *Faculty:* 6 full-time (2 women), 1 part-time/adjunct (0 women). *Students:* 9 full-time (4 women), 17 part-time (11 women); includes 4 minority (2 African Americans, 2 American Indian/Alaska Native), 5 international. Average age 40. 6 applicants, 83% accepted, 3 enrolled. In 2008, 6 master's, 5 doctorates awarded. *Degree requirements:* For doctorate, thesis/dissertation. *Entrance requirements:* For master's and doctorate, GRE General Test, minimum GPA of 3.0. Additional exam requirements/recommendations for international students: Required—TOEFL (minimum score 570 paper-based; 233 computer-based; 89 iBT). *Application deadline:* Applications are processed on a rolling basis. Application fee: $45 ($60 for international students). *Financial support:* Fellowships, research assistantships, teaching assistantships, institutionally sponsored loans available. *Unit head:* Dr. Mike Nolan, Department Chair, E-mail: nolanm@missouri.edu. *Application contact:* Carol Swaim, 573-882-7451, E-mail: swaimc@missouri.edu.

The University of Montana, Graduate School, College of Arts and Sciences, Department of Sociology, Missoula, MT 59812-0002. Offers criminology (MA); rural and environmental change (MA); sociology (MA). *Entrance requirements:* For master's, GRE General Test. Additional exam requirements/recommendations for international students: Required—TOEFL. *Faculty research:* Housing, homelessness, hunger, infant mortality, work safety.

University of Wisconsin–Madison, Graduate School, College of Letters and Science, Department of Sociology, Madison, WI 53706-1380. Offers rural sociology (MS); sociology (MS, PhD). Part-time programs available. Terminal master's awarded for partial completion of doctoral program. *Degree requirements:* For master's, thesis, oral exam; for doctorate, thesis/dissertation, preliminary and final oral exams, 4 seminars. *Entrance requirements:* For master's and doctorate, GRE General Test. Additional exam requirements/recommendations for international students: Required—TOEFL. Electronic applications accepted.

Sociology

Acadia University, Faculty of Arts, Department of Sociology, Wolfville, NS B4P 2R6, Canada. Offers MA. *Faculty:* 6 full-time (3 women). *Students:* 3 full-time (all women), 2 part-time (both women); includes 1 Asian American or Pacific Islander. Average age 25. 12 applicants, 58% accepted, 3 enrolled. In 2008, 3 master's awarded. *Degree requirements:* For master's, thesis. *Entrance requirements:* For master's, honors degree, minimum GPA of 3.25. Additional exam requirements/recommendations for international students: Required—TOEFL (minimum score 580 paper-based; 237 computer-based; 93 iBT), IELTS (minimum score 6.5). *Application deadline:* For fall admission, 2/1 for domestic students. Applications are processed on a rolling basis. Application fee: $50. Tuition and fees charges are reported in Canadian dollars. *Expenses:* Tuition, area resident: Full-time $3873.50 Canadian dollars; part-time $844 Canadian dollars per course. Tuition, state resident: full-time $4634.50 Canadian dollars; part-time $844 Canadian dollars per course. Tuition, nonresident: full-time $9103 Canadian dollars; part-time $1687 Canadian dollars per course. Required fees: $503.22 Canadian dollars; $5 Canadian dollars per course. *Financial support:* In 2008–09, 3 teaching assistantships (averaging $9,000 per year) were awarded; research assistantships, unspecified assistantships also available. Financial award application deadline: 2/1. *Faculty research:* Atlantic cultures, class analysis, gender and women's studies, religion, symbolism, development studies. *Unit head:* Dr. Jim Sacouman, Head, 902-585-1494, Fax: 902-585-1769, E-mail: jim.sacouman@acadiau.ca. *Application contact:* Karen Turner, Administrative Secretary, 902-585-1493, Fax: 902-585-1769, E-mail: karen.turner@acadiau.ca.

American University, College of Arts and Sciences, Department of Sociology, Washington, DC 22016-8072. Offers social research (Certificate); sociology (MA). Part-time and evening/weekend programs available. *Faculty:* 14 full-time (9 women), 2 part-time/adjunct (1 woman). *Students:* 19 full-time (18 women), 32 part-time (23 women); includes 26 minority (21 African Americans, 1 American Indian/Alaska Native, 1 Asian American or Pacific Islander, 3 Hispanic Americans), 4 international. Average age 35. 28 applicants, 79% accepted, 9 enrolled. In 2008, 7 master's awarded. *Degree requirements:* For master's, comprehensive exam, thesis or alternative, tool of research examination. *Entrance requirements:* For master's, GRE; for Certificate, bachelor's degree. Additional exam requirements/recommendations for international students: Required—TOEFL. *Application deadline:* For fall admission, 2/1 for domestic students. Application fee: $80. *Expenses:* Tuition: Full-time $21,204; part-time $1178 per credit hour. Required fees: $380. Part-time tuition and fees vary according to course load and program. *Financial support:* Fellowships, research assistantships with full and partial tuition reimbursements, teaching assistantships with full and partial tuition reimbursements, career-related internships or fieldwork, Federal Work-Study, institutionally sponsored loans, tuition waivers (full and partial), and unspecified assistantships available. Support available to part-time students. Financial award application deadline: 2/1; financial award applicants required to submit FAFSA. *Faculty research:* Gender, race, development, applied social policy, political economy. *Unit head:* Dr. John Philip Drysdale, Chair, 202-885-2488, Fax: 202-885-2477, E-mail: drysdale@american.edu. *Application contact:* Dr. John Philip Drysdale, Chair, 202-885-2488, Fax: 202-885-2477, E-mail: drysdale@american.edu.

The American University in Cairo, Graduate Studies and Research, School of Humanities and Social Sciences, Department of Sociology, Anthropology, Psychology, and Egyptology, Cairo, Egypt. Offers sociology and anthropology (MA). *Degree requirements:* For master's, one foreign language, thesis. *Entrance requirements:* Additional exam requirements/recommendations for international students: Required—English entrance exam and/or TOEFL. Electronic applications accepted. *Faculty research:* Development, gender, sociopolitical economic formulations, social science indigenization, Arab world.

American University of Beirut, Graduate Programs, Faculty of Arts and Sciences, Beirut, Lebanon. Offers anthropology (MA); Arabic language and literature (MA); archaeology (MA); biology (MS); chemistry (MS); computer science (MS); economics (MA); education (MA); English language (MA); English literature (MA); environmental policy planning (MSES); financial economics (MAFE); geology (MS); history (MA); mathematics (MA, MS); Middle Eastern studies (MA); philosophy (MA); physics (MS); political studies (MA); psychology (MA); public administration (MA); sociology (MA); statistics (MA, MS). Part-time programs available. *Degree requirements:* For master's, one foreign language, comprehensive exam, thesis (for some programs). *Entrance requirements:* For master's, GRE, letter of recommendation. Additional exam requirements/recommendations for international students: Required—TOEFL (minimum score 600 paper-based; 250 computer-based; 100 iBT), IELTS (minimum score 7.5). *Faculty research:* String theory and supergravity; computer graphics; algebra and number theory; popular Arabic literature; marine and freshwater biology; integrating science, math and technology.

Arizona State University, Graduate College, College of Liberal Arts and Sciences, Division of Social Sciences, School of Social and Family Dynamics, Tempe, AZ 85287. Offers family and human development (MS, PhD); infant-family practice (MAS); marriage and family therapy (MAS); sociology (MA, PhD). *Degree requirements:* For master's, thesis or alternative; for doctorate, thesis/dissertation. *Entrance requirements:* For master's and doctorate, GRE.

Arkansas State University, Graduate School, College of Humanities and Social Sciences, Department of Criminology, Sociology, and Geography, Jonesboro, State University, AR 72467. Offers criminal justice (MA, Certificate); sociology (MA); sociology education (SCCT). Part-time programs available. *Faculty:* 7 full-time (4 women). *Students:* 8 full-time (6 women), 24 part-time (16 women); includes 12 minority (all African Americans), 1 international. Average age 32. 22 applicants, 77% accepted, 7 enrolled. In 2008, 10 master's awarded. *Degree requirements:* For master's, one foreign language, comprehensive exam, thesis or alternative; for other advanced degree, comprehensive exam. *Entrance requirements:* For master's, GRE General Test or MAT, appropriate bachelor's degree, official transcript, letters of recommendation, statement of purpose; for other advanced degree, GRE General Test or MAT, interview, master's degree, official transcript. Additional exam requirements/recommendations for international students: Required—TOEFL (minimum score 550 paper-based; 213 computer-based; 79 iBT), IELTS (minimum score 6). *Application deadline:* For fall admission, 7/15 for domestic students, 7/1 for international students; for spring admission, 12/1 for domestic students, 11/13 for international students. Applications are processed on a rolling basis. Application fee: $30 ($40 for international students). Electronic applications accepted. *Expenses:* Tuition, state resident: full-time $3744; part-time $208 per credit hour. Tuition, nonresident: full-time $9540; part-time $530 per credit hour. International tuition: $7938 full-time. Required fees: $896; $47 per credit hour. $25 per term. One-time fee: $50. Tuition and fees vary according to course load and program. *Financial support:* In 2008–09, 6 students received support. Career-related internships or fieldwork, scholarships/grants, and unspecified assistantships available. Financial award application deadline: 7/1; financial award applicants required to submit FAFSA. *Faculty research:* Land use—rural and recreational, resource management, climate change, peopling of the New World, gender, family, sexuality issues. *Unit head:* Dr. Anthony Troy Adams, Chair, 870-972-3705, Fax: 870-972-3694, E-mail: aadams@astate.edu. *Application contact:* Dr. Andrew Sustich, Dean of the Graduate School, 870-972-3029, Fax: 870-972-3857, E-mail: sustich@astate.edu.

Auburn University, Graduate School, Interdepartmental Programs, Department of Sociology, Anthropology, Criminology, and Social Work, Auburn University, AL 36849. Offers rural sociology (MS); sociology (MA, MS). Part-time programs available. *Degree requirements:* For master's, thesis, computer language (MS), foreign language (MA). *Entrance requirements:* For master's, GRE General Test. *Expenses:* Tuition, area resident: Full-time $5880; part-time $243 per credit hour. Tuition, state resident: full-time $5880; part-time $243 per credit hour. Tuition, nonresident: full-time $17,640; part-time $729 per credit hour. International tuition: $17,846 full-time. Required fees: $620. Tuition and fees vary according to program and reciprocity agreements.

Ball State University, Graduate School, College of Sciences and Humanities, Department of Sociology, Muncie, IN 47306-1099. Offers MA. *Entrance requirements:* For master's, GRE General Test. *Faculty research:* Retention policies for secondary education, community mental health.

Baylor University, Graduate School, College of Arts and Sciences, Department of Sociology and Anthropology, Waco, TX 76798. Offers applied sociology (PhD); sociology (MA). *Students:* 22 full-time (10 women); includes 1 minority (African American), 1 international. In 2008, 4 master's, 2 doctorates awarded. *Entrance requirements:* For master's and doctorate, GRE General Test. *Application deadline:* For fall admission, 8/1 for domestic students. Applications are processed on a rolling basis. Application fee: $25. *Financial support:* Research assistantships, teaching assistantships, career-related internships or fieldwork, Federal Work-Study, and institutionally sponsored loans available. *Faculty research:* Community studies, thanatology, sociology of education. *Unit head:* Dr. Roby Driskell, Graduate Program Director, 254-710-3362, Fax: 254-710-3809, E-mail: robyn_driskell@baylor.edu. *Application contact:* Sharon Sloan, Administrative Assistant, 254-710-1165, Fax: 254-710-3870, E-mail: sharon_sloan@baylor.edu.

Boston College, Graduate School of Arts and Sciences, Department of Sociology, Chestnut Hill, MA 02467-3800. Offers MA, PhD, MBA/MA, MBA/PhD. Part-time programs available. Terminal master's awarded for partial completion of doctoral program. *Degree requirements:* For master's, thesis optional; for doctorate, thesis/dissertation. *Entrance requirements:* For master's and doctorate, GRE General Test. Additional exam requirements/recommendations for international students: Required—TOEFL (minimum score 590 paper-based; 250 computer-based; 91 iBT). Electronic applications accepted. *Expenses:* Tuition: Part-time $1148 per credit. Required fees: $60. *Faculty research:* Sociological theory, social economy, social psychology, political sociology, development modernization.

Boston University, Graduate School of Arts and Sciences, Department of Sociology, Boston, MA 02215. Offers MA, PhD. Terminal master's awarded for partial completion of doctoral program. *Degree requirements:* For master's, one foreign language, comprehensive exam, thesis; for doctorate, one foreign language, comprehensive exam, thesis/dissertation. *Entrance requirements:* For master's, GRE General Test, sample of written work, 3 letters of recommendation; for doctorate, GRE General Test or MAT, sample of written work, 3 letters of recommendation. Additional exam requirements/recommendations for international students: Required—TOEFL (minimum score 550 paper-based; 213 computer-based).

Bowling Green State University, Graduate College, College of Arts and Sciences, Department of Sociology, Bowling Green, OH 43403. Offers demography and population studies (MA); social psychology (MA); sociology (PhD). Part-time programs available. *Degree requirements:* For master's, thesis or alternative; for doctorate, comprehensive exam, thesis/dissertation. *Entrance requirements:* For master's and doctorate, GRE General Test. Additional exam requirements/recommendations for international students: Required—TOEFL. Electronic applications accepted. *Faculty research:* Applied demography, criminology and deviance, family studies, population studies, social psychology.

Brandeis University, Graduate School of Arts and Sciences, Department of Sociology, Waltham, MA 02454-9110. Offers Near Eastern and Judaic studies and sociology (PhD); social policy and sociology (PhD); sociology (MA, PhD); sociology and women's and gender studies (MA). Part-time programs available. Terminal master's awarded for partial completion of doctoral program. *Degree requirements:* For master's, thesis; for doctorate, thesis/dissertation. *Entrance requirements:* For master's and doctorate, GRE, writing sample, resumé, letters of recommendation. Additional exam requirements/recommendations for international students: Required—TOEFL (minimum score 600 paper-based; 250 computer-based; 100 iBT), IELTS (minimum score 7). Electronic applications accepted. *Faculty research:* Social theory and cultural studies; feminist sociology; political sociology; sociology of medicine, health and health care; comparative social structures.

Brigham Young University, Graduate Studies, College of Family, Home, and Social Sciences, Department of Sociology, Provo, UT 84602. Offers MS. *Faculty:* 17 full-time (5 women). *Students:* 25 full-time (12 women), 1 (woman) part-time; includes 3 minority (1 African American, 2 Asian Americans or Pacific Islanders). Average age 32. 13 applicants, 85% accepted, 11 enrolled. In 2008, 6 master's awarded. Terminal master's awarded for partial completion of doctoral program. *Degree requirements:* For master's, thesis. *Entrance requirements:* For master's, GRE General Test, minimum GPA of 3.0 in last 60 hours, writing sample, bachelor's degree in sociology or related field, official transcript(s), 3 letters of recommendation, statement of intent, Honor Code commitment. Additional exam requirements/recommendations for international students: Required—TOEFL. *Application deadline:* For fall admission, 2/1 for domestic students. Application fee: $50. Electronic applications accepted. *Expenses:* Tuition: Full-time $5160; part-time $287 per credit hour. Tuition and fees vary according to program and student's religious affiliation. *Financial support:* In 2008–09, 14 students received support, including 9 research assistantships (averaging $15,750 per year), 9 teaching assistantships (averaging $15,750 per year); institutionally sponsored loans and unspecified assistantships also available. Financial award application deadline: 2/1. *Faculty research:* Demography, race and ethnicity, gender, rural and community, international development, comparative family. Total annual research expenditures: $45,252. *Unit head:* Dr. Renata Forste, Department Chair, 801-422-3146, Fax: 801-422-0625, E-mail: renata_forste@byu.edu. *Application contact:* Dr. Carol J. Ward, Graduate Coordinator, 801-422-3047, Fax: 801-422-0625, E-mail: carol.ward@byu.edu.

Brooklyn College of the City University of New York, Division of Graduate Studies, Department of Sociology, Brooklyn, NY 11210-2889. Offers MA, PhD. The department offers courses at Brooklyn College that are creditable towards the CUNY doctoral degree (with permission of the executive officer of the doctoral program). Part-time and evening/weekend programs available. *Students:* 1 full-time (0 women), 38 part-time (29 women); includes 23 minority (17 African Americans, 1 American Indian/Alaska Native, 3 Asian Americans or Pacific Islanders, 2 Hispanic Americans), 2 international. Average age 34. 31 applicants, 77% accepted, 12 enrolled. In 2008, 12 master's awarded. *Degree requirements:* For master's, comprehensive exam or research essay. *Entrance requirements:* For master's, 12 upper-level credits in sociology, 2 letters of recommendation, essay. Additional exam requirements/recommendations for international students: Required—TOEFL. *Application deadline:* For fall admission, 3/1 priority date for domestic students, 2/1 priority date for international students; for spring admission, 11/1 priority date for domestic students, 10/1 priority date for international students. Applications are processed on a rolling basis. Application fee: $125. Electronic applications accepted. *Expenses:* Tuition, state resident: full-time $7360; part-time $310 per credit hour. Tuition, nonresident: full-time $13,800; part-time $575 per credit hour. *Financial support:* Career-related internships or fieldwork, Federal Work-Study, institutionally sponsored loans, and scholarships/grants available. Support available to part-time students. Financial award application deadline: 5/1; financial award applicants required to submit FAFSA. *Faculty research:* Urbanization, religion, family, gender, research methods. *Unit head:* Dr. Kenneth Gould, Chairperson, 718-951-5314, E-mail: kgould@brooklyn.cuny.edu. *Application contact:* Hernan Sierra, Graduate Admissions Coordinator, 718-951-4536, Fax: 718-951-4506, E-mail: grads@brooklyn.cuny.edu.

Brown University, Graduate School, Department of Sociology, Program in Sociology, Providence, RI 02912. Offers AM, PhD. *Degree requirements:* For master's, thesis; for doctorate, thesis/dissertation, oral exam. *Entrance requirements:* For master's and doctorate, GRE General Test.

California State University, Bakersfield, Division of Graduate Studies, School of Humanities and Social Sciences, Program in Sociology, Bakersfield, CA 93311-1022. Offers MA.

California State University, Dominguez Hills, College of Natural and Behavioral Sciences, Program in Sociology, Carson, CA 90747-0001. Offers social research (Certificate); sociology (MA). Part-time and evening/weekend programs available. *Faculty:* 14 full-time (7 women), 7 part-time/adjunct (4 women). *Students:* 27 full-time (22 women), 49 part-time (37 women); includes 61 minority (42 African Americans, 3 Asian Americans or Pacific Islanders, 16 Hispanic Americans), 1 international. Average age 37. 38 applicants, 79% accepted, 18 enrolled. In 2008, 21 master's awarded. *Degree requirements:* For master's, comprehensive exam, thesis. *Entrance requirements:* For master's and Certificate, minimum GPA of 2.85. *Application deadline:* For fall admission, 6/1 for domestic students. Application fee: $55. *Expenses:* Tuition, nonresident: part-time $339 per unit. Required fees: $1300 per semester. *Faculty research:* Community studies, social movements, criminology. *Unit head:* Dr. Clare Weber, Chair, 310-243-3458, E-mail: cweber@csudh.edu. *Application contact:* Dr. Gayle Ball-Parker, Director of Admissions, 310-243-3645, E-mail: gball@csudh.edu.

California State University, East Bay, Academic Programs and Graduate Studies, College of Letters, Arts, and Social Sciences, Department of Sociology and Social Services, Hayward, CA 94542-3000. Offers sociology (MA). Part-time and evening/weekend programs available. *Degree requirements:* For master's, comprehensive exam, project or thesis. *Entrance requirements:* For master's, minimum GPA of 3.0. Additional exam requirements/recommendations for international students: Required—TOEFL (minimum score 550 paper-based; 213 computer-based). Electronic applications accepted.

California State University, Fullerton, Graduate Studies, College of Humanities and Social Sciences, Department of Sociology, Fullerton, CA 92834-9480. Offers MA. Part-time programs available. *Students:* 21 full-time (17 women), 30 part-time (18 women); includes 16 minority (1 African American, 7 Asian Americans or Pacific Islanders, 8 Hispanic Americans), 4 international. Average age 30. 48 applicants, 54% accepted, 20 enrolled. In 2008, 9 master's awarded. *Degree requirements:* For master's, thesis. *Entrance requirements:* For master's, minimum GPA of 3.0 in sociology, 2.5 in last 60 units. Application fee: $55. Tuition and fees vary according to degree level. *Financial support:* Teaching assistantships, career-related internships or fieldwork, Federal Work-Study, institutionally sponsored loans, and scholarships/grants available. Support available to part-time students. Financial award application deadline: 3/1. *Faculty research:* Gerontology, wellness clinic. *Unit head:* Dr. Dennis Berg, Chair, 657-278-3531. *Application contact:* Dr. Rae Newton, Adviser, 657-278-3135.

California State University, Los Angeles, Graduate Studies, College of Natural and Social Sciences, Department of Sociology, Los Angeles, CA 90032-8530. Offers MA. Part-time and evening/weekend programs available. *Faculty:* 5 full-time (3 women). *Students:* 22 full-time (14 women), 55 part-time (36 women); includes 55 minority (8 African Americans, 12 Asian Americans or Pacific Islanders, 35 Hispanic Americans), 6 international. Average age 32. 42 applicants, 100% accepted, 25 enrolled. In 2008, 13 master's awarded. *Degree requirements:* For master's, comprehensive exam or thesis. *Entrance requirements:* For master's, minimum GPA of 2.5 in last 90 units of course work. Additional exam requirements/recommendations for international students: Required—TOEFL (minimum score 500 paper-based; 173 computer-based). *Application deadline:* For fall admission, 6/15 for domestic students, 5/1 for international students; for winter admission, 11/1 for domestic students, 9/1 for international students; for spring admission, 2/1 for domestic students, 10/1 for international students. Applications are processed on a rolling basis. Application fee: $55. Electronic applications accepted. *Expenses:* Tuition, nonresident: part-time $226 per credit. Required fees: $4019. *Financial support:* Federal Work-Study available. Support available to part-time students. Financial award application deadline: 3/1. *Faculty research:* Criminal and delinquent careers, family and sex, ethnic minorities, demographic trends, human socialization and aging. *Unit head:* Dr. Steven L. Gordon, Chair, 323-343-2200, Fax: 323-343-5155, E-mail: sgordon@calstatela.edu. *Application contact:* Dr. Jose L. Galvan, Dean of Graduate Studies, 323-343-3820, Fax: 323-343-5653, E-mail: jgalvan@cslanet.calstatela.edu.

California State University, Northridge, Graduate Studies, College of Social and Behavioral Sciences, Department of Sociology, Northridge, CA 91330. Offers MA. Accreditation: CSWE. Part-time and evening/weekend programs available. *Faculty:* 21 full-time (9 women), 32 part-time/adjunct (18 women). *Students:* 112 full-time (100 women), 58 part-time (51 women); includes 83 minority (13 African Americans, 1 American Indian/Alaska Native, 15 Asian Americans or Pacific Islanders, 54 Hispanic Americans), 7 international. Average age 30. 298 applicants, 38% accepted, 89 enrolled. In 2008, 37 master's awarded. *Degree requirements:* For master's, thesis or alternative. *Entrance requirements:* For master's, GRE General Test. Additional exam requirements/recommendations for international students: Required—TOEFL. *Application deadline:* For fall admission, 3/27 for domestic students; for spring admission, 10/17 for domestic students. Application fee: $55. *Financial support:* Career-related internships or fieldwork, Federal Work-Study, and institutionally sponsored loans available. Support available to part-time students. Financial award application deadline: 3/1. *Faculty research:* Crime and corrections, relationships between adult children and parents. *Unit head:* Dr. Herman DeBose, Chair, 818-677-3591. *Application contact:* Dr. David Boyns, Graduate Advisor, 818-677-6803.

California State University, Sacramento, Graduate Studies, College of Social Sciences and Interdisciplinary Studies, Department of Sociology, Sacramento, CA 95819-6048. Offers MA. Part-time programs available. *Degree requirements:* For master's, thesis or alternative, writing proficiency exam. *Entrance requirements:* For master's, minimum GPA of 3.0 during previous 2 years. Additional exam requirements/recommendations for international students: Required—TOEFL. Electronic applications accepted.

California State University, San Marcos, College of Arts and Sciences, Program in Sociological Practice, San Marcos, CA 92096-0001. Offers MA. *Degree requirements:* For master's, thesis. *Entrance requirements:* For master's, GRE General Test (recommended), minimum GPA of 3.0 in last 60 units of undergraduate study, minimum GPA of 3.0 in upper division sociology courses. *Faculty research:* Organized crime, juvenile detention, counseling services for minorities, mental-health facilities.

Carleton University, Faculty of Graduate Studies, Faculty of Arts and Social Sciences, Department of Sociology and Anthropology, Program in Sociology, Ottawa, ON K1S 5B6, Canada. Offers MA, PhD. *Degree requirements:* For master's, thesis optional; for doctorate, one foreign language, comprehensive exam, thesis/dissertation. *Entrance requirements:* For master's, honors degree; for doctorate, master's degree. Additional exam requirements/recommendations for international students: Required—TOEFL. *Faculty research:* Canadian society and policy, inequality and mobility, race/ethnic relations, cultural studies, gender studies.

Case Western Reserve University, School of Graduate Studies, Department of Sociology, Cleveland, OH 44106. Offers PhD. Terminal master's awarded for partial completion of doctoral program. *Degree requirements:* For doctorate, thesis/dissertation. Electronic applications accepted. *Faculty research:* Sociology of aging and the life course, medical sociology, research methods, family sociology.

The Catholic University of America, School of Arts and Sciences, Department of Sociology, Washington, DC 20064. Offers MA, PhD. Part-time and evening/weekend programs available. *Degree requirements:* For master's, comprehensive exam, thesis or alternative; for doctorate, one foreign language, comprehensive exam, thesis/dissertation. *Entrance requirements:* For master's and doctorate, GRE General Test, 3 letters of recommendation. Additional exam requirements/recommendations for international students: Required—TOEFL (minimum score 580 paper-based; 237 computer-based). Electronic applications accepted. *Faculty research:* Social movements, education, gender, religion, demography.

Central European University, Graduate Studies, School of Social Sciences and Humanities, Budapest, Hungary. Offers economics (MA, PhD); gender studies (MA, PhD); international relations and European studies (MA, PhD); mathematics and its applications (MS, PhD); medieval studies (MA, PhD); nationalism studies (MA, PhD); philosophy (MA, PhD); political science (MA, PhD); public policy (MA, PhD); sociology and social anthropology (MA, PhD). Terminal master's awarded for partial completion of doctoral program. *Degree requirements:* For master's, one foreign language, thesis; for doctorate, one foreign language, comprehensive exam, thesis/dissertation. *Entrance requirements:* For master's, CEU subject tests, interview; for doctorate, GRE, CEU subject test, interview. Additional exam requirements/recommendations for international students: Required—TOEFL (minimum score 570 paper-based; 230 computer-based). Electronic applications accepted. *Faculty research:* Civil society, fiscal decentralization, party politics, political philosophy (especially Liberalism, theory of Democracy).

See Close-Up on page 349.

City College of the City University of New York, Graduate School, College of Liberal Arts and Science, Division of Social Science, Department of Sociology, New York, NY 10031-9198. Offers MA. *Degree requirements:* For master's, one foreign language, comprehensive exam, thesis. *Entrance requirements:* For master's, GRE, minimum B average in undergraduate course work. Additional exam requirements/recommendations for international students: Required—TOEFL (minimum score 500 paper-based; 173 computer-based). *Faculty research:* Urban sociology, criminology and deviance, race and ethnicity.

Clark Atlanta University, School of Arts and Sciences, Department of Sociology, Atlanta, GA 30314. Offers MA. Part-time programs available. *Faculty:* 2 full-time (1 woman). *Students:* 2 full-time (both women), 2 part-time (both women); all minorities (all African Americans). Average age 29. 2 applicants, 100% accepted, 0 enrolled. In 2008, 3 master's awarded. *Degree requirements:* For master's, one foreign language, thesis. *Entrance requirements:* For master's, GRE General Test, minimum GPA of 2.5. Additional exam requirements/recommendations for international students: Required—TOEFL (minimum score 500 paper-based; 173 computer-

Sociology

Clark Atlanta University (continued)

based). *Application deadline:* For fall admission, 4/1 for domestic and international students; for spring admission, 11/1 for domestic and international students. Applications are processed on a rolling basis. Application fee: $40 ($55 for international students). Electronic applications accepted. *Expenses:* Tuition: Full-time $12,240; part-time $680 per credit hour. Required fees: $710; $355 per semester. *Financial support:* Fellowships available. Financial award application deadline: 4/30; financial award applicants required to submit FAFSA. *Faculty research:* Gerontology, geriatric education. *Unit head:* Dr. Sandra Taylor, Chairperson, 404-880-8681, E-mail: staylor@cau.edu. *Application contact:* Michelle Clark-Davis, Graduate Program Admissions, 404-880-6605, E-mail: cauadmissions@cau.edu.

Clemson University, Graduate School, College of Business and Behavioral Science, Department of Sociology and Anthropology, Clemson, SC 29634. Offers applied sociology (MS). Part-time programs available. *Faculty:* 13 full-time (7 women). *Students:* 11 full-time (7 women), 5 part-time (all women); includes 2 minority (1 African American, 1 Asian American or Pacific Islander), 3 international. Average age 26. 9 applicants, 78% accepted, 7 enrolled. In 2008, 6 master's awarded. *Degree requirements:* For master's, thesis. *Entrance requirements:* For master's, GRE General Test, minimum GPA of 3.0. Additional exam requirements/recommendations for international students: Required—TOEFL. *Application deadline:* For fall admission, 3/15 priority date for domestic students. Application fee: $55. Full-time tuition and fees vary according to program. *Financial support:* In 2008–09, 1 research assistantship (averaging $10,000 per year), 9 teaching assistantships (averaging $10,411 per year) were awarded; fellowships, career-related internships or fieldwork, Federal Work-Study, and institutionally sponsored loans also available. Financial award application deadline: 3/15; financial award applicants required to submit FAFSA. *Faculty research:* Organizational and industrial sociology, inequality, sexual abuse and police-community relations, homelessness, emotions. Total annual research expenditures: $96,286. *Unit head:* Dr. Kinly Sturkie, Chair, 864-656-3820, E-mail: dkstr@clemson.edu. *Application contact:* Dr. Catherine Mobley, Coordinator, 864-656-3815, Fax: 864-656-1252, E-mail: camoble@clemson.edu.

Cleveland State University, College of Graduate Studies, College of Liberal Arts and Social Sciences, Department of Sociology, Cleveland, OH 44115. Offers MA. Part-time and evening/weekend programs available. *Faculty:* 12 full-time (6 women). *Students:* 8 full-time (7 women), 27 part-time (22 women); includes 9 minority (8 African Americans, 1 Hispanic American). Average age 34. 31 applicants, 42% accepted, 9 enrolled. In 2008, 11 master's awarded. *Entrance requirements:* For master's, minimum GPA of 3.0. Additional exam requirements/recommendations for international students: Required—TOEFL (minimum score 525 paper-based; 197 computer-based). *Application deadline:* For fall admission, 7/15 priority date for domestic students, 1/15 priority date for international students; for spring admission, 12/1 priority date for domestic students, 9/15 priority date for international students. Applications are processed on a rolling basis. Application fee: $30. Electronic applications accepted. *Financial support:* In 2008–09, 12 students received support, including 3 research assistantships (averaging $9,000 per year), 4 teaching assistantships (averaging $9,000 per year); scholarships/grants, tuition waivers (full and partial), and unspecified assistantships also available. Support available to part-time students. Financial award application deadline: 7/15. *Faculty research:* Criminology, research methods, theory, symbolic interaction. Total annual research expenditures: $45,000. *Unit head:* Dr. Philip Manning, Chair, 216-687-4504, Fax: 216-687-9314, E-mail: p.mannings@csuohio.edu. *Application contact:* Dr. Wendy Regoeczi, Graduate Program Director, 216-687-9349, Fax: 216-687-9314, E-mail: w.regoeczi@csuohio.edu.

Colorado State University, Graduate School, College of Liberal Arts, Department of Sociology, Fort Collins, CO 80523-1784. Offers MA, PhD. *Faculty:* 15 full-time (5 women). *Students:* 18 full-time (9 women), 23 part-time (12 women); includes 1 minority (Asian American or Pacific Islander), 1 international. Average age 33. 49 applicants, 35% accepted, 8 enrolled. In 2008, 5 master's, 2 doctorates awarded. *Degree requirements:* For master's, variable foreign language requirement, comprehensive exam (for some programs), thesis (for some programs); for doctorate, variable foreign language requirement, comprehensive exam, thesis/dissertation (for some programs). *Entrance requirements:* For master's, GRE General Test, minimum GPA of 3.0; BA coursework in sociology, letters of recommendation, statement of purpose; for doctorate, GRE General Test, minimum GPA of 3.0; BA, MA coursework in sociology, letters of recommendation, statement of purpose. Additional exam requirements/recommendations for international students: Required—TOEFL (minimum score 550 paper-based; 220 computer-based). *Application deadline:* For fall admission, 1/15 priority date for domestic and international students. Applications are processed on a rolling basis. Application fee: $50. Electronic applications accepted. *Expenses:* Tuition, area resident: Full-time $5620; part-time $312.25 per credit. Tuition, state resident: full-time $5620; part-time $312.25 per credit. Tuition, nonresident: full-time $17,253; part-time $958.50 per credit. Required fees: $1449.56; $82.35 per credit. *Financial support:* In 2008–09, 22 students received support, including 3 research assistantships (averaging $41,148 per year), 19 teaching assistantships (averaging $13,419 per year); career-related internships or fieldwork, Federal Work-Study, institutionally sponsored loans, scholarships/grants, traineeships, and unspecified assistantships also available. Financial award application deadline: 3/1; financial award applicants required to submit FAFSA. *Faculty research:* Sociology policy analysis, environmental impact, criminology, community development, rural and natural resources. Total annual research expenditures: $173,562. *Unit head:* Dr. Jack Brouillette, Chairman, 970-491-6805, Fax: 970-491-2191, E-mail: jack.brouillette@colostate.edu. *Application contact:* Betty Burkett, Administrative Assistant, 970-491-6045, Fax: 970-491-2191, E-mail: elizabeth.burkett@colostate.edu.

Columbia University, Graduate School of Arts and Sciences, Division of Social Sciences, Department of Sociology, New York, NY 10027. Offers M Phil, MA, PhD, JD/MA, JD/PhD. *Degree requirements:* For master's, 2 research papers; for doctorate, one foreign language, thesis/dissertation. *Entrance requirements:* For master's and doctorate, GRE General Test. Additional exam requirements/recommendations for international students: Required—TOEFL. *Faculty research:* Urban and political studies, sociology of knowledge, organizations.

Concordia University, School of Graduate Studies, Faculty of Arts and Science, Department of Sociology and Anthropology, Montréal, QC H3G 1M8, Canada. Offers social and cultural anthropology (MA); sociology (MA). *Degree requirements:* For master's, comprehensive exam or thesis. *Entrance requirements:* For master's, honors degree in sociology or equivalent. *Faculty research:* Community and ethnic relations, popular culture, regional development in Canada, industrial and social movements, social problems and policies.

Cornell University, Graduate School, Graduate Fields of Agriculture and Life Sciences, Field of Development Sociology, Ithaca, NY 14853-0001. Offers community and regional society (MS); community and regional sociology (MPS, PhD); methods of social research (MPS, MS, PhD); population and development (MPS, MS, PhD); rural and environmental sociology (MPS, MS, PhD); state, economy, and society (MPS, MS, PhD). *Faculty:* 21 full-time (6 women). *Students:* 44 full-time (31 women); includes 5 minority (2 American Indian/Alaska Native, 2 Asian Americans or Pacific Islanders, 1 Hispanic American), 16 international. Average age 33. 62 applicants, 15% accepted, 4 enrolled. In 2008, 5 master's, 4 doctorates awarded. *Degree requirements:* For doctorate, comprehensive exam, thesis/dissertation. *Entrance requirements:* For master's and doctorate, GRE General Test, 3 letters of recommendation. Additional exam requirements/recommendations for international students: Required—TOEFL (minimum score 550 paper-based; 213 computer-based; 77 iBT). *Application deadline:* For fall admission, 1/15 priority date for domestic students. Application fee: $60. Electronic applications accepted. *Expenses:* Tuition: Full-time $29,500. Required fees: $70. Full-time tuition and fees vary according to degree level, program and student level. *Financial support:* In 2008–09, 25 students received support, including 2 fellowships with full tuition reimbursements available, 12 research assistantships with full tuition reimbursements available, 11 teaching assistantships with full tuition reimbursements available; institutionally sponsored loans, scholarships/grants, health care benefits, tuition waivers (full and partial), and unspecified assistantships also available. Financial award applicants required to submit FAFSA. *Faculty research:* Demography (population and development), environmental sociology, international and rural community development, political economy and ecology, sustainable agriculture. *Unit head:* Director of Graduate Studies, 607-255-3092, Fax: 607-254-2896. *Application contact:* Graduate Field Assistant, 607-255-3092, Fax: 607-254-2896, E-mail: devsoc@cornell.edu.

Cornell University, Graduate School, Graduate Fields of Arts and Sciences, Field of Sociology, Ithaca, NY 14853-0001. Offers economy and society (MA, PhD); gender and life course (MA, PhD); methodology (MA, PhD); organizations (MA, PhD); policy analysis (MA, PhD); political sociology/social movements (MA, PhD); racial and ethnic relations (MA, PhD); social networks (MA, PhD); social psychology (MA, PhD); social stratification (MA, PhD). *Faculty:* 32 full-time (12 women). *Students:* 40 full-time (16 women); includes 8 minority (2 African Americans, 4 Asian Americans or Pacific Islanders, 2 Hispanic Americans), 10 international. Average age 31. 148 applicants, 7% accepted, 4 enrolled. In 2008, 1 master's, 7 doctorates awarded. Terminal master's awarded for partial completion of doctoral program. *Degree requirements:* For master's, thesis; for doctorate, thesis/dissertation, 1 year of teaching experience. *Entrance requirements:* For master's and doctorate, GRE General Test, 2 letters of recommendation, writing sample. Additional exam requirements/recommendations for international students: Required—TOEFL (minimum score 550 paper-based; 213 computer-based; 77 iBT). *Application deadline:* For fall admission, 1/15 for domestic students. Application fee: $70. Electronic applications accepted. *Expenses:* Tuition: Full-time $29,500. Required fees: $70. Full-time tuition and fees vary according to degree level, program and student level. *Financial support:* In 2008–09, 32 students received support, including 9 fellowships with full tuition reimbursements available, 8 research assistantships with full tuition reimbursements available, 15 teaching assistantships with full tuition reimbursements available; institutionally sponsored loans, scholarships/grants, health care benefits, tuition waivers (full and partial), and unspecified assistantships also available. Financial award applicants required to submit FAFSA. *Faculty research:* Comparative societal analysis, work and family, simulations, social class and mobility, racial segregation and inequality. *Unit head:* Director of Graduate Studies, 607-255-4266. *Application contact:* Graduate Field Assistant, 607-255-4266, E-mail: sociology@cornell.edu.

Dalhousie University, Faculty of Arts and Social Science, Department of Sociology and Social Anthropology, Halifax, NS B3H 4R2, Canada. Offers social anthropology (MA, PhD); sociology (MA, PhD). In 2008, 8 master's awarded. *Entrance requirements:* Additional exam requirements/recommendations for international students: Required—TOEFL, IELTS, 1 of 5 approved tests: TOEFL, IELTS, CANTEST, CAEL, Michigan English Language Assessment Battery. *Application deadline:* For fall admission, 6/1 for domestic students, 4/1 for international students; for winter admission, 10/31 for domestic students, 8/31 for international students; for spring admission, 2/28 for domestic students, 12/31 for international students. Application fee: $70. Electronic applications accepted. *Financial support:* Career-related internships or fieldwork, scholarships/grants, and health care benefits available. *Faculty research:* Social inequality and social injustice; work, industry, and development; (regional and international perspectives); health and illness. *Unit head:* Dr. Emma Whelan, Graduate Coordinator, 902-494-6752, Fax: 902-494-2897, E-mail: sosagrad@dal.ca. *Application contact:* Lori Vaughan, Graduate Administrator, 902-494-6593, Fax: 902-494-2897, E-mail: sosagrad@is.dal.ca.

DePaul University, College of Liberal Arts and Sciences, Department of Sociology, Chicago, ID 60614. Offers MA. Part-time and evening/weekend programs available. *Faculty:* 21 full-time (12 women), 4 part-time/adjunct (2 women). *Students:* 46 full-time (31 women), 46 part-time (35 women); includes 41 minority (23 African Americans, 8 Asian Americans or Pacific Islanders, 10 Hispanic Americans), 2 international. Average age 28. 44 applicants, 84% accepted, 30 enrolled. In 2008, 17 master's awarded. *Degree requirements:* For master's, thesis or alternative, essay, research project. *Entrance requirements:* Additional exam requirements/recommendations for international students: Required—TOEFL. *Application deadline:* For fall admission, 8/25 priority date for domestic students; for winter admission, 12/15 priority date for domestic students; for spring admission, 3/15 priority date for domestic students. Applications are processed on a rolling basis. Application fee: $25. Electronic applications accepted. *Financial support:* In 2008–09, 8 students received support, including 1 research assistantship with full tuition reimbursement available (averaging $7,000 per year); career-related internships or fieldwork, tuition waivers (partial), and tuition remissions also available. Financial award application deadline: 6/15. *Faculty research:* Law and society, urban sociology, race/ethnicity, health, social inequality. *Unit head:* Dr. Roberta Garner, Chairperson, 773-325-7823, Fax: 773-325-7821, E-mail: rgarner@depaul.edu. *Application contact:* Dr. Shu-Ju Ada Cheng, Graduate Program Director, 773-325-4856, Fax: 773-325-7821, E-mail: scheng1@depaul.edu.

Drake University, School of Education, Department of Teaching and Learning, Program in Secondary Education, Des Moines, IA 50311-4516. Offers art (MAT); biology (MAT); business (MAT); chemistry (MAT); English (MAT); general science (MAT); history-American (MAT); history-world (MAT); journalism (MAT); mathematics (MAT); physical science (MAT); physics (MAT); sociology (MAT); speech (MAT); speech communication (MAT); theatre (MAT). Part-time programs available. *Degree requirements:* For master's, comprehensive exam, thesis (for some programs), internships (for some programs). *Entrance requirements:* For master's, GRE General Test, MAT, or Drake Writing Assessment, resumé, 2 letters of recommendation. Additional exam requirements/recommendations for international students: Required—TOEFL (minimum score 550 paper-based; 213 computer-based). Electronic applications accepted. *Faculty research:* Counseling and rehabilitation, behavioral supports, inquiry-based science methods, teacher quality enhancement.

Duke University, Graduate School, Department of Sociology, Durham, NC 27708. Offers AM, PhD. Terminal master's awarded for partial completion of doctoral program. *Degree requirements:* For doctorate, thesis/dissertation. *Entrance requirements:* For master's and doctorate, GRE General Test. Additional exam requirements/recommendations for international students: Required—TOEFL (minimum score 550 paper-based; 213 computer-based; 83 iBT), IELTS (minimum score 7). Electronic applications accepted.

East Carolina University, Graduate School, Thomas Harriot College of Arts and Sciences, Department of Sociology, Greenville, NC 27858-4353. Offers MA. Part-time and evening/weekend programs available. *Degree requirements:* For master's, one foreign language, comprehensive exam, thesis. *Entrance requirements:* For master's, GRE General Test. Additional exam requirements/recommendations for international students: Required—TOEFL.

Eastern Michigan University, Graduate School, College of Arts and Sciences, Department of Sociology, Anthropology and Criminology, Program in Sociology, Ypsilanti, MI 48197. Offers schools, society and violence (MA); sociology (MA); sociology—family specialty (MA).

East Tennessee State University, School of Graduate Studies, College of Arts and Sciences, Department of Sociology and Anthropology, Johnson City, TN 37614. Offers applied sociology (MA); general sociology (MA). Part-time and evening/weekend programs available. *Degree requirements:* For master's, comprehensive exam, thesis or alternative, internship. *Entrance requirements:* For master's, GRE General Test, minimum GPA of 3.0 in major. Additional exam requirements/recommendations for international students: Required—TOEFL (minimum score 550 paper-based; 213 computer-based). *Faculty research:* Biosociology and sex differences, political change in Latin America, medical beliefs and practices in southern Appalachia, Scottish-Irish traditions and Appalachia culture.

Emory University, Graduate School of Arts and Sciences, Department of Sociology, Atlanta, GA 30322-1100. Offers MA, PhD. Terminal master's awarded for partial completion of doctoral program. *Degree requirements:* For master's, thesis optional; for doctorate, comprehensive exam, thesis/dissertation, 2 preliminary exams, research paper, paper presentation. *Entrance requirements:* For doctorate, GRE General Test, minimum GPA of 3.0. Additional exam requirements/recommendations for international students: Required—TOEFL. Electronic applications accepted. *Faculty research:* Political economy and global analysis, culture, social psychology, criminology, stratification.

See Close-Up on page 1289.

Fayetteville State University, Graduate School, Program in Sociology, Fayetteville, NC 28301-4298. Offers MA. Part-time and evening/weekend programs available. *Degree requirements:* For master's, comprehensive exam, internship. Electronic applications accepted.

Florida Agricultural and Mechanical University, Division of Graduate Studies, Research, and Continuing Education, College of Arts and Sciences, Division of History and Political Sciences, Program in Applied Social Science, Tallahassee, FL 32307-3200. Offers African American history (MASS); criminal justice (MASS); economics (MASS); history (MASS); political science (MASS); public administration (MASS); public management (MASS); social work (MASS); sociology (MASS). Part-time programs available. *Degree requirements:* For master's, thesis optional. *Entrance requirements:* For master's, GRE General Test, minimum GPA of 3.0. *Faculty research:* Southern history, black history, election trends, presidential history.

Florida Atlantic University, Dorothy F. Schmidt College of Arts and Letters, Department of Sociology, Boca Raton, FL 33431-0991. Offers MA. Part-time and evening/weekend programs available. *Faculty:* 15 full-time (8 women), 3 part-time/adjunct (1 woman). *Students:* 16 full-time (13 women), 9 part-time (5 women); includes 8 minority (3 African Americans, 1 American Indian/Alaska Native, 2 Asian Americans or Pacific Islanders, 2 Hispanic Americans). Average age 30. 16 applicants, 50% accepted, 4 enrolled. In 2008, 5 master's awarded. *Degree requirements:* For master's, thesis optional. *Entrance requirements:* For master's, GRE General Test, minimum GPA of 3.0. Additional exam requirements/recommendations for international students: Required—TOEFL. *Application deadline:* For fall admission, 5/1 priority date for domestic and international students. Applications are processed on a rolling basis. Application fee: $30. Electronic applications accepted. *Expenses:* Tuition, state resident: full-time $4867; part-time $270.40 per credit hour. Tuition, nonresident: full-time $16,486; part-time $915.87 per credit hour. *Financial support:* Teaching assistantships with tuition reimbursements, Federal Work-Study available. *Faculty research:* Gender/race/class, globalization, theory, social control, social movements. *Unit head:* Dr. Farshad A. Araghi, Chair and Associate Professor, 561-297-0261, Fax: 561-297-2511, E-mail: araghi@fau.edu. *Application contact:* Dr. Ann Branaman, Associate Professor, 561-297-3278, Fax: 561-297-2511, E-mail: branaman@fau.edu.

Florida International University, College of Arts and Sciences, Department of Sociology/Anthropology, Miami, FL 33199. Offers comparative sociology (MA); sociology (PhD). Part-time and evening/weekend programs available. *Degree requirements:* For master's, thesis; for doctorate, comprehensive exam, thesis/dissertation. *Entrance requirements:* For master's and doctorate, GRE General Test, 3 letters of recommendation, minimum undergraduate GPA of 3.25, minimum graduate GPA of 3.5. Additional exam requirements/recommendations for international students: Required—TOEFL (minimum score 550 paper-based; 213 computer-based). Electronic applications accepted.

Florida State University, Graduate Studies, College of Social Sciences, Department of Sociology, Tallahassee, FL 32306. Offers MA, MS, PhD. Terminal master's awarded for partial completion of doctoral program. *Degree requirements:* For master's, paper; for doctorate, comprehensive exam, thesis/dissertation. *Entrance requirements:* For master's and doctorate, GRE General Test, minimum GPA of 3.0. Additional exam requirements/recommendations for international students: Required—TOEFL (minimum score 550 paper-based; 213 computer-based). Electronic applications accepted. *Faculty research:* Inequality (gender/race), demography, social psychology, health and aging.

Fordham University, Graduate School of Arts and Sciences, Department of Sociology, New York, NY 10458. Offers MA, PhD. Part-time and evening/weekend programs available. Terminal master's awarded for partial completion of doctoral program. *Degree requirements:* For master's, comprehensive exam; for doctorate, one foreign language, comprehensive exam, thesis/dissertation. *Entrance requirements:* For master's and doctorate, GRE General Test. Additional exam requirements/recommendations for international students: Required—TOEFL (minimum score 600 paper-based; 250 computer-based). Electronic applications accepted. *Faculty research:* Social demography, immigration, crime and deviance, religion.

George Mason University, College of Humanities and Social Sciences, Department of Sociology and Anthropology, Fairfax, VA 22030. Offers anthropology (MA); sociology (MA). *Degree requirements:* For master's, thesis. *Entrance requirements:* For master's, GRE General Test, minimum GPA of 3.0 in last 60 hours; writing sample; previous undergraduate course work in sociological theory, research methods, and social statistics. Electronic applications accepted.

The George Washington University, Columbian College of Arts and Sciences, Department of Sociology, Washington, DC 20052. Offers criminology (MA); sociology (MA). Part-time and evening/weekend programs available. *Faculty:* 11 full-time (7 women), 19 part-time/adjunct (6 women). *Students:* 18 full-time (15 women), 14 part-time (11 women); includes 5 minority (2 African Americans, 1 American Indian/Alaska Native, 1 Asian American or Pacific Islander, 1 Hispanic American), 1 international. Average age 26. 43 applicants, 56% accepted, 6 enrolled. In 2008, 6 master's awarded. *Degree requirements:* For master's, comprehensive exam, thesis or alternative. *Entrance requirements:* For master's, GRE General Test, minimum GPA of 3.0. Additional exam requirements/recommendations for international students: Required—TOEFL (minimum score 550 paper-based; 213 computer-based; 80 iBT). *Application deadline:* For fall admission, 6/1 priority date for domestic students, 1/15 priority date for international students; for spring admission, 11/1 priority date for domestic students, 9/1 priority date for international students. Applications are processed on a rolling basis. Application fee: $60. Electronic applications accepted. *Financial support:* In 2008–09, 7 students received support; fellowships with full tuition reimbursements available, teaching assistantships with tuition reimbursements available, career-related internships or fieldwork, Federal Work-Study, and tuition waivers available. Financial award application deadline: 1/15. *Unit head:* Dr. Steven Tuch, Chair, 202-994-7466, E-mail: steven.tuch@gwu.edu. *Application contact:* Information Contact, 202-994-6345, Fax: 202-994-3239, E-mail: soc@gwu.edu.

Georgia Southern University, Jack N. Averitt College of Graduate Studies, College of Liberal Arts and Social Sciences, Department of Sociology and Anthropology, Statesboro, GA 30460. Offers MA. Part-time and evening/weekend programs available. *Students:* 14 full-time (10 women), 11 part-time (7 women); includes 3 minority (2 African Americans, 1 Hispanic American). Average age 31. 10 applicants, 90% accepted, 3 enrolled. In 2008, 9 master's awarded. *Degree requirements:* For master's, thesis optional. *Entrance requirements:* For master's, GRE General Test, minimum GPA of 2.75, bachelor's degree in sociology. Additional exam requirements/recommendations for international students: Required—TOEFL (minimum score 550 paper-based; 213 computer-based; 80 iBT). *Application deadline:* For fall admission, 3/1 priority date for domestic students, 6/1 priority date for international students; for spring admission, 10/1 priority date for domestic students, 10/1 for international students. Applications are processed on a rolling basis. Application fee: $50. Electronic applications accepted. *Expenses:* Tuition, area resident: Full-time $3840; part-time $160 per semester hour. Tuition, state resident: full-time $3840; part-time $160 per semester hour. Tuition, nonresident: full-time $15,336; part-time $639 per semester hour. Required fees: $1152. *Financial support:* In 2008–09, 20 students received support, including research assistantships with partial tuition reimbursements available (averaging $6,850 per year), teaching assistantships with partial tuition reimbursements available (averaging $6,850 per year); career-related internships or fieldwork, Federal Work-Study, scholarships/grants, tuition waivers (partial), and unspecified assistantships also available. Support available to part-time students. Financial award application deadline: 4/15; financial award applicants required to submit FAFSA. *Faculty research:* Work and family, gender roles, sociology of the South, social psychology, community. *Unit head:* Dr. Ted Brimeyer, Chair, 912-478-5763, Fax: 912-478-0703, E-mail: tbrimeyer@georgiasouthern.edu. *Application contact:* 912-478-5384, Fax: 912-478-0740, E-mail: gradadmissions@georgiasouthern.edu.

Georgia State University, College of Arts and Sciences, Department of Sociology, Atlanta, GA 30303-3083. Offers MA, PhD. Part-time and evening/weekend programs available. Terminal master's awarded for partial completion of doctoral program. *Degree requirements:* For master's, thesis; for doctorate, comprehensive exam, thesis/dissertation. *Entrance requirements:* For master's, GRE General Test, departmental supplemental form, letters of recommendation; for doctorate, GRE General Test, departmental supplemental form, writing sample, letters of recommendation. Additional exam requirements/recommendations for international students: Required—TOEFL. Electronic applications accepted. *Faculty research:* Family and life course, gender and sexuality, race and urban studies.

Graduate School and University Center of the City University of New York, Graduate Studies, Program in Sociology, New York, NY 10016-4039. Offers PhD. *Degree requirements:* For doctorate, one foreign language, thesis/dissertation. *Entrance requirements:* For doctorate, GRE General Test, writing sample. Additional exam requirements/recommendations for international students: Required—TOEFL. Electronic applications accepted.

Harvard University, Graduate School of Arts and Sciences, Department of Sociology, Cambridge, MA 02138. Offers PhD. *Degree requirements:* For doctorate, thesis/dissertation, oral exams in 2 subfields. *Entrance requirements:* For doctorate, GRE General Test. Additional exam requirements/recommendations for international students: Required—TOEFL. *Expenses:* Tuition: Full-time $32,556. Required fees: $1426. Full-time tuition and fees vary according to program and student level. *Faculty research:* Sociological theory, political theories, quantitative approaches to methodology.

Hofstra University, College of Liberal Arts and Sciences, Department of Sociology, Hempstead, NY 11549. Offers applied social research and policy analysis (MA). Part-time and evening/weekend programs available. *Faculty:* 4 full-time (2 women). *Students:* 4 full-time (3 women); includes 1 minority (African American), 1 international. Average age 25. 4 applicants, 100% accepted, 4 enrolled. *Degree requirements:* For master's, comprehensive exam, thesis optional, internship. *Entrance requirements:* For master's, GRE, interview, essay, minimum GPA of 3.0. Additional exam requirements/recommendations for international students: Required—TOEFL (minimum score 550 paper-based; 213 computer-based; 80 iBT). *Application deadline:* Applications are processed on a rolling basis. Electronic applications accepted. *Expenses:* Tuition: Full-time $15,300; part-time $850 per credit. Required fees: $970; $165 per term. Tuition and fees vary according to program. *Financial support:* In 2008–09, 2 students received support, including 2 fellowships with full and partial tuition reimbursements available (averaging $3,000 per year); research assistantships with full and partial tuition reimbursements available, Federal Work-Study, institutionally sponsored loans, scholarships/grants, and tuition waivers (full and partial) also available. Support available to part-time students. *Faculty research:* Housing policy, immigration, labor economic policy, education policy, health care policy. Total annual research expenditures: $100,000. *Unit head:* Dr. Marc Silver, Program Director, 516-463-6250, Fax: 516-463-2310, E-mail: socmls@hofstra.edu. *Application contact:* Carol Drummer, Dean of Graduate Admissions, 516-463-4876, Fax: 516-463-4664, E-mail: gradstudent@hofstra.edu.

Howard University, Graduate School, Department of Health, Human Performance and Leisure Studies, Washington, DC 20059-0002. Offers exercise physiology (MS); health education (MS); sports studies (MS), including sociology of sports, sports management; urban recreation (MS), including leisure studies. Part-time and evening/weekend programs available. *Degree requirements:* For master's, comprehensive exam, thesis. *Entrance requirements:* For master's, BS in human performance or related field. Electronic applications accepted. *Faculty research:* Health promotion, cardiovascular hypertension, physical activity, sport and human rights issues.

Howard University, Graduate School, Department of Sociology and Anthropology, Washington, DC 20059-0002. Offers sociology (MA, PhD). Part-time and evening/weekend programs available. *Degree requirements:* For master's, thesis; for doctorate, one foreign language, comprehensive exam, thesis/dissertation, RCR, writing exam. *Entrance requirements:* For master's, GRE General Test, minimum GPA of 3.0; for doctorate, GRE General Test, minimum GPA of 3.5. Additional exam requirements/recommendations for international students: Required—TOEFL. Electronic applications accepted. *Faculty research:* Medical sociology; criminology; race, class and gender; urban sociology.

Humboldt State University, Graduate Studies, College of Arts, Humanities, and Social Sciences, Department of Sociology, Arcata, CA 95521-8299. Offers MA. *Students:* 12 full-time (9 women), 7 part-time (3 women); includes 4 minority (2 African Americans, 1 American Indian/Alaska Native, 1 Asian American or Pacific Islander). Average age 33. 22 applicants, 59% accepted, 10 enrolled. In 2008, 6 master's awarded. *Degree requirements:* For master's, thesis or alternative, qualifying exam. *Entrance requirements:* For master's, minimum GPA of 2.5, 3 letters of recommendation. Additional exam requirements/recommendations for international students: Required—TOEFL (minimum score 500 paper-based; 173 computer-based). *Application deadline:* For fall admission, 3/15 for domestic students; for spring admission, 11/15 for domestic students. Applications are processed on a rolling basis. Application fee: $55. *Expenses:* Tuition, state resident: full-time $5236. Tuition, nonresident: full-time $11,338. *Financial support:* Application deadline: 3/1; *Faculty research:* Sociology of women political activists, environmental dispute resolution, prosocial behavior. *Unit head:* Dr. Mary Virnoche, Chair, 707-826-4569, Fax: 707-826-4418, E-mail: mv23@humboldt.edu. *Application contact:* Dr. Jennifer Eichstedt, Coordinator, 707-826-4949, Fax: 707-826-4418, E-mail: jle7001@humboldt.edu.

Hunter College of the City University of New York, Graduate School, School of Arts and Sciences, Department of Sociology, New York, NY 10021-5085. Offers applied social research (MS). *Faculty:* 5 full-time (2 women), 2 part-time/adjunct (1 woman). *Students:* 11 full-time (8 women), 22 part-time (16 women); includes 5 minority (1 African American, 2 Asian Americans or Pacific Islanders, 2 Hispanic Americans). Average age 28. 17 applicants, 82% accepted, 8 enrolled. In 2008, 11 master's awarded. *Degree requirements:* For master's, internship. *Entrance requirements:* For master's, GRE General Test or GMAT, 3 credits of course work in statistics, 2 letters of recommendation. Additional exam requirements/recommendations for international students: Required—TOEFL. *Application deadline:* For fall admission, 4/1 for domestic students, 2/1 for international students; for spring admission, 11/1 for domestic students, 9/1 for international students. Application fee: $125. *Financial support:* Federal Work-Study and tuition waivers (partial) available. Support available to part-time students. *Unit head:* Dr. Robert Perinbanayagaia, Chairperson, 212-772-5585, Fax: 212-772-5645, E-mail: rperinba@hunter.cuny.edu. *Application contact:* Dr. Joong-Hwan Oh, Graduate Adviser, 212-772-5643.

Idaho State University, Office of Graduate Studies, College of Arts and Sciences, Department of Sociology, Pocatello, ID 83209. Offers MA. Part-time programs available. *Faculty:* 7 full-time (3 women). *Students:* 6 full-time (3 women), 5 part-time (4 women), 1 international. Average age 37. In 2008, 2 master's awarded. *Degree requirements:* For master's, comprehensive exam, thesis, oral defense of thesis. *Entrance requirements:* For master's, GRE General Test, minimum undergraduate GPA of 3.0, 3 letters of recommendation. Additional exam requirements/recommendations for international students: Required—TOEFL (minimum score 550 paper-based; 213 computer-based; 80 iBT). *Application deadline:* For fall admission, 7/1 for domestic students, 6/1 for international students; for spring admission, 12/1 for domestic students, 11/1 for international students. Applications are processed on a rolling basis. Application fee: $55. Electronic applications accepted. *Expenses:* Tuition, area resident: full-time $3114; part-time $276 per credit hour. Tuition, state resident: full-time $3114; part-time $276 per credit hour. Tuition, nonresident: full-time $12,318; part-time $404 per credit hour. Required fees: $2360. Tuition and fees vary according to course load and reciprocity agreements. *Financial support:* In 2008–09, 1 research assistantship with full and partial tuition reimbursement (averaging $6,800 per year), 2 teaching assistantships with full and partial tuition reimbursements (averaging $9,401 per year) were awarded; career-related internships or fieldwork, Federal Work-Study, institutionally sponsored loans, scholarships/grants, traineeships, health care benefits, tuition waivers (full and partial), and unspecified assistantships also available. Support available to part-time students. Financial award application deadline: 1/1; financial award applicants required to submit FAFSA. *Faculty research:* Terrorism, social organization, families social work. *Unit head:* Dr. Ann Hunter, Chairperson, 208-282-2170, Fax: 208-282-4733, E-mail: soccj@isu.edu. *Application contact:* Ellen Combs, Graduate School Technical Records Specialist, 208-282-2150, Fax: 208-282-4847, E-mail: combelle@isu.edu.

Sociology

Illinois State University, Graduate School, College of Arts and Sciences, Department of Sociology, Normal, IL 61790-2200. Offers historical archaeology (MA, MS); sociology (MA, MS). *Degree requirements:* For master's, thesis. *Entrance requirements:* For master's, GRE General Test, GRE Subject Test, minimum GPA of 2.4 in last 60 hours of course work. *Faculty research:* Japanese Saturday school (Kato).

Indiana University Bloomington, University Graduate School, College of Arts and Sciences, Department of Sociology, Bloomington, IN 47405-7000. Offers MA, PhD. *Faculty:* 18 full-time (9 women). *Students:* 99 full-time (56 women), 3 part-time (2 women); includes 23 minority (15 African Americans, 2 Asian Americans or Pacific Islanders, 6 Hispanic Americans), 8 international. Average age 29. 155 applicants, 14% accepted, 14 enrolled. In 2008, 8 master's, 5 doctorates awarded. Terminal master's awarded for partial completion of doctoral program. *Degree requirements:* For master's, thesis; for doctorate, comprehensive exam, thesis/dissertation. *Entrance requirements:* For master's and doctorate, GRE General Test. Additional exam requirements/recommendations for international students: Required—TOEFL. *Application deadline:* For fall admission, 1/15 for domestic students, 12/1 for international students. Application fee: $50 ($60 for international students). Electronic applications accepted. *Expenses:* Tuition, area resident: Part-time $291.97 per credit hour. Tuition, state resident: part-time $291.97 per credit hour. Tuition, nonresident: part-time $850.33 per credit hour. Required fees: $110 per semester. Tuition and fees vary according to course load and program. *Financial support:* In 2008–09, 74 students received support; fellowships with full tuition reimbursements available, research assistantships with full tuition reimbursements available, teaching assistantships with full tuition reimbursements available, scholarships/grants, health care benefits, and unspecified assistantships available. Financial award application deadline: 1/15; financial award applicants required to submit FAFSA. *Faculty research:* Social psychology, political sociology, sociological research methods, stratification/mobility, education. *Unit head:* Prof. Eliza Pavalko, Professor, 812-855-7629, Fax: 812-855-0781, E-mail: epavalko@indiana.edu. *Application contact:* Shana Bergen, Information Contact, 812-855-2924, E-mail: sbergen@indiana.edu.

Indiana University of Pennsylvania, School of Graduate Studies and Research, College of Humanities and Social Sciences, Department of Sociology, Program in Sociology, Indiana, PA 15705-1087. Offers MA. Part-time programs available. *Faculty:* 14 full-time (7 women). *Students:* 20 full-time (15 women), 6 part-time (4 women); includes 1 minority (African American). Average age 40. 13 applicants, 62% accepted, 8 enrolled. In 2008, 11 master's awarded. *Degree requirements:* For master's, thesis optional. *Entrance requirements:* For master's, GRE, 2 letters of recommendation. Additional exam requirements/recommendations for international students: Required—TOEFL. *Application deadline:* For fall admission, 7/1 priority date for domestic students; for spring admission, 11/1 for domestic students. Applications are processed on a rolling basis. Application fee: $30. *Expenses:* Tuition, area resident: Full-time $6430; part-time $357 per credit. Tuition, nonresident: full-time $10,288; part-time $572 per credit. Required fees: $1547.50; $107 per credit. $283 per year. *Financial support:* In 2008–09, 10 research assistantships (averaging $5,453 per year) were awarded. Financial award application deadline: 3/15; financial award applicants required to submit FAFSA. *Unit head:* Dr. Valerie Gunter, Graduate Coordinator, 724-357-3931, E-mail: Valerie.Gunter@iup.edu. *Application contact:* Dr. Valerie Gunter, Graduate Coordinator, 724-357-3931, E-mail: Valerie.Gunter@iup.edu.

Indiana University–Purdue University Fort Wayne, College of Arts and Sciences, Department of Sociology, Fort Wayne, IN 46805-1499. Offers sociological practice (MA). Part-time programs available. *Faculty:* 10 full-time (3 women). *Students:* 3 full-time (2 women), 14 part-time (11 women); includes 2 minority (both African Americans). Average age 40. 5 applicants, 80% accepted, 3 enrolled. In 2008, 1 master's awarded. *Degree requirements:* For master's, practicum. *Entrance requirements:* For master's, minimum GPA of 3.0, 3 letters of recommendation, essay, interview. Additional exam requirements/recommendations for international students: Required—TOEFL (minimum score 550 paper-based; 213 computer-based; 77 iBT). *Application deadline:* For fall admission, 8/1 for domestic students; for spring admission, 11/1 priority date for domestic students. Applications are processed on a rolling basis. Application fee: $30. *Expenses:* Tuition, area resident: Full-time $4376; part-time $243 per credit. Tuition, state resident: full-time $4376; part-time $243 per credit. Tuition, nonresident: full-time $10,337; part-time $574 per credit. Required fees: $503; $27.95 per credit. Tuition and fees vary according to course load. *Financial support:* In 2008–09, 3 teaching assistantships with partial tuition reimbursements (averaging $12,740 per year) were awarded; scholarships/grants and unspecified assistantships also available. Support available to part-time students. Financial award application deadline: 3/1; financial award applicants required to submit FAFSA. *Faculty research:* Intoxication, temperance culture, working class masculinity. *Unit head:* Dr. David Legg, Interim Chair, 260-481-6222, Fax: 260-481-0474, E-mail: legg@ipfw.edu. *Application contact:* Dr. Augusto De Vananzi, Graduate Program Director, 260-481-6665, Fax: 260-481-0474, E-mail: devenana@ipfu.edu.

Indiana University–Purdue University Indianapolis, School of Liberal Arts, Department of Sociology, Indianapolis, IN 46202-2896. Offers family/gender studies (MA); medical sociology (MA); work/occupations (MA).

Iowa State University of Science and Technology, Graduate College, College of Liberal Arts and Sciences, Department of Sociology, Ames, IA 50011. Offers rural sociology (MS, PhD); sociology (MS, PhD). *Faculty:* 34 full-time (18 women), 1 (woman) part-time/adjunct. *Students:* 27 full-time (16 women), 24 part-time (14 women); includes 8 minority (2 African Americans, 2 American Indian/Alaska Native, 2 Asian Americans or Pacific Islanders, 2 Hispanic Americans), 9 international. 38 applicants, 66% accepted, 15 enrolled. In 2008, 5 master's, 2 doctorates awarded. *Degree requirements:* For master's, thesis; for doctorate, thesis/dissertation. *Entrance requirements:* For master's and doctorate, GRE General Test. Additional exam requirements/recommendations for international students: Required—TOEFL (minimum score 550 paper-based; 79 iBT), IELTS (6.5) or TOEFL. *Application deadline:* For fall admission, 1/10 priority date for domestic and international students; for spring admission, 10/1 for domestic and international students. Application fee: $30 ($70 for international students). Electronic applications accepted. *Expenses:* Tuition, area resident: Full-time $6446; part-time $359 per credit. Tuition, state resident: full-time $6446; part-time $359 per credit. Tuition, nonresident: full-time $17,330; part-time $963 per credit. Required fees: $790; $249.25 per semester. Tuition and fees vary according to course load and program. *Financial support:* In 2008–09, 15 research assistantships with full and partial tuition reimbursements (averaging $14,130 per year), 17 teaching assistantships with full and partial tuition reimbursements (averaging $14,130 per year) were awarded; fellowships, scholarships/grants, health care benefits, and unspecified assistantships also available. *Unit head:* Dr. R. Paul Lasley, Chair, 515-294-2506, Fax: 515-294-8312, E-mail: sociology@iastate.edu. *Application contact:* Dr. Stephen Sapp, Director of Graduate Education, 515-294-1403, E-mail: sociology@iastate.edu.

Jackson State University, Graduate School, School of Liberal Arts, Department of Sociology, Jackson, MS 39217. Offers MA. Part-time and evening/weekend programs available. *Degree requirements:* For master's, comprehensive exam, thesis or alternative. *Entrance requirements:* For master's, GRE General Test. Additional exam requirements/recommendations for international students: Required—TOEFL.

The Johns Hopkins University, Zanvyl Krieger School of Arts and Sciences, Department of Sociology, Baltimore, MD 21218-2699. Offers PhD. *Degree requirements:* For doctorate, one foreign language, thesis/dissertation. *Entrance requirements:* For doctorate, GRE General Test. Additional exam requirements/recommendations for international students: Required—TOEFL (minimum score 560 paper-based); Recommended—IELTS, TWE. Electronic applications accepted. *Faculty research:* Education, immigration, race and gender, world systems, social policy.

Kansas State University, Graduate School, College of Arts and Sciences, Department of Sociology, Anthropology and Social Work, Manhattan, KS 66506. Offers sociology (MA, PhD). Part-time programs available. *Faculty:* 19 full-time (8 women), 3 part-time/adjunct (1 woman). *Students:* 33 full-time (16 women), 18 part-time (9 women); includes 8 minority (5 African Americans, 1 Asian American or Pacific Islander, 2 Hispanic Americans), 7 international. Average age 32. 19 applicants, 74% accepted, 10 enrolled. In 2008, 7 master's, 1 doctorate awarded. *Degree requirements:* For master's, thesis or alternative; for doctorate, thesis/dissertation. *Entrance requirements:* For master's, GRE, minimum undergraduate GPA of 3.0; for doctorate, master's degree in sociology. Additional exam requirements/recommendations for international students: Required—TOEFL (minimum score 550 paper-based; 213 computer-based). *Application deadline:* For fall admission, 3/1 priority date for domestic and international students; for spring admission, 10/1 priority date for domestic and international students. Applications are processed on a rolling basis. Application fee: $30 ($55 for international students). Electronic applications accepted. *Expenses:* Tuition, area resident: Full-time $6466; part-time $269.40 per credit hour. Tuition, state resident: full-time $6466; part-time $269.40 per credit hour. Tuition, nonresident: full-time $14,874; part-time $619.75 per credit hour. Required fees: $673; $23.40 per credit hour. Tuition and fees vary according to campus/location. *Financial support:* In 2008–09, 9 research assistantships (averaging $15,742 per year), 17 teaching assistantships with full tuition reimbursements (averaging $11,940 per year) were awarded; institutionally sponsored loans and scholarships/grants also available. Support available to part-time students. Financial award application deadline: 3/1; financial award applicants required to submit FAFSA. *Faculty research:* Rural development, sex and gender, criminology/delinquency, international development/globalization, and political sociology/social movements. Total annual research expenditures: $237,305. *Unit head:* Betsy Cauble, Head, 785-532-6865, Fax: 785-532-6978, E-mail: bcauble@ksu.edu. *Application contact:* Gerad Middendorf, Director, 785-532-4973, Fax: 785-532-6978, E-mail: middendo@ksu.edu.

Kean University, College of Humanities and Social Sciences, Program in Sociology and Social Justice, Union, NJ 07083. Offers MA. *Faculty:* 13 full-time (7 women). *Students:* 5 full-time (4 women), 7 part-time (all women); includes 3 African Americans, 1 Asian American or Pacific Islander, 2 Hispanic Americans. Average age 36. 22 applicants, 77% accepted, 12 enrolled. *Degree requirements:* For master's, comprehensive exam, thesis, practicum. *Entrance requirements:* For master's, GRE (if cumulative undergraduate GPA is lower than 3.7), minimum GPA of 3.0, 2 letters of recommendation, interview. *Application deadline:* For fall admission, 5/1 for domestic students; for spring admission, 11/1 for domestic students. Application fee: $60 ($150 for international students). Electronic applications accepted. *Expenses:* Tuition, state resident: full-time $10,128; part-time $422 per credit. Tuition, nonresident: full-time $13,728; part-time $572 per credit. Required fees: $2570; $107 per credit. Part-time tuition and fees vary according to course load, degree level and program. *Financial support:* In 2008–09, research assistantships with full tuition reimbursements (averaging $3,217 per year); unspecified assistantships also available. *Unit head:* Dr. Jose Sanchez, Program Coordinator, 908-737-4050, E-mail: jsanchez@kean.edu. *Application contact:* Steven Koch, Pre-Admissions Coordinator, 908-737-4723, Fax: 908-737-5965, E-mail: grad-adm@kean.edu.

Kent State University, College of Arts and Sciences, Department of Sociology, Kent, OH 44242-0001. Offers MA, PhD. Part-time programs available. *Degree requirements:* For master's, thesis optional, monograph option; for doctorate, comprehensive exam, thesis/dissertation. *Entrance requirements:* For master's, GRE General Test or MAT, minimum GPA of 2.75; for doctorate, GRE, minimum GPA of 3.0. Additional exam requirements/recommendations for international students: Required—TOEFL. Electronic applications accepted. *Faculty research:* Medical sociology, social psychology, social inequalities.

Lakehead University, Graduate Studies, Faculty of Social Sciences and Humanities, Department of Sociology, Thunder Bay, ON P7B 5E1, Canada. Offers gerontology (MA); health services and policy research (MA); sociology (MA); women's studies (MA). Part-time and evening/weekend programs available. *Degree requirements:* For master's, research project or thesis. *Entrance requirements:* For master's, minimum B average. Additional exam requirements/recommendations for international students: Required—TOEFL. Tuition charges are reported in Canadian dollars. *Expenses:* Tuition, area resident: Full-time $6500 Canadian dollars. International tuition: $13,700 Canadian dollars full-time. *Faculty research:* Sociology of medicine, cultural and social change, health human resources, gerontology, women's studies.

Laurentian University, School of Graduate Studies and Research, Programme in Sociology, Sudbury, ON P3E 2C6, Canada. Offers applied social research (MA). Part-time programs available. *Entrance requirements:* For master's, honors degree in sociology or equivalent. *Faculty research:* Work foundations, managing AIDS organization, tracking laid-off mine workers.

Lehigh University, College of Arts and Sciences, Department of Sociology and Anthropology, Bethlehem, PA 18015-3094. Offers sociology (MA). Part-time programs available. *Faculty:* 12 full-time (5 women), 1 (woman) part-time/adjunct. *Students:* 12 full-time (9 women); includes 2 minority (both Asian Americans or Pacific Islanders). Average age 23. 14 applicants, 64% accepted, 6 enrolled. In 2008, 12 master's awarded. *Degree requirements:* For master's, comprehensive exam, thesis optional. *Entrance requirements:* For master's, GRE General Test. Additional exam requirements/recommendations for international students: Required—TOEFL (minimum score 650 paper-based). *Application deadline:* For fall admission, 1/15 priority date for domestic and international students. Application fee: $65. Electronic applications accepted. *Financial support:* In 2008–09, 3 research assistantships with full tuition reimbursements, 7 teaching assistantships with full tuition reimbursements were awarded; fellowships with full tuition reimbursements, career-related internships or fieldwork, Federal Work-Study, institutionally sponsored loans, scholarships/grants, tuition waivers (full and partial), and unspecified assistantships also available. Support available to part-time students. Financial award application deadline: 1/15. *Faculty research:* Juvenile delinquency, parent-child relations, urban sociology, medical sociology, policy studies. Total annual research expenditures: $307,354. *Unit head:* Dr. Judith N. Lasker, Chair and NEH Distinguished Professor, 610-758-3811, Fax: 610-758-6552, E-mail: jnlo@lehigh.edu. *Application contact:* Dr. Heather B. Johnson, Graduate Coordinator, 610-758-3816, Fax: 610-758-6552, E-mail: hbj2@lehigh.edu.

Lincoln University, School of Graduate Studies and Continuing Education, College of Liberal Arts, Education and Journalism, Department of Social and Behavioral Sciences, Jefferson City, MO 65102. Offers history (MA); social science (MA), including history, political science, sociology; sociology (MA); sociology/criminal justice (MA). Part-time and evening/weekend programs available. *Faculty:* 11 full-time (4 women), 4 part-time/adjunct (2 women). *Students:* 6 full-time (3 women), 21 part-time (11 women); includes 8 minority (all African Americans), 5 international. Average age 33. 13 applicants, 100% accepted, 9 enrolled. In 2008, 14 master's awarded. *Degree requirements:* For master's, comprehensive exam, thesis optional. *Entrance requirements:* For master's, GRE General Test or MAT, 15 undergraduate hours of course work in social science including 6 hours upper-division, with 9 hours in the area of concentration. Additional exam requirements/recommendations for international students: Required—TOEFL (minimum score 500 paper-based; 173 computer-based; 61 iBT). *Application deadline:* For fall admission, 7/1 priority date for domestic and international students; for spring admission, 12/1 priority date for domestic and international students. Applications are processed on a rolling basis. Application fee: $20. *Expenses:* Tuition, area resident: Full-time $4185; part-time $232.50 per credit hour. Tuition, nonresident: full-time $7767; part-time $431.50 per credit hour. Required fees: $270; $15 per credit hour. $252.50 per semester. One-time fee: $20. Tuition and fees vary according to course load. *Financial support:* Federal Work-Study and scholarships/grants available. Financial award application deadline: 4/1; financial award applicants required to submit FAFSA. *Faculty research:* Suicide prevention. *Unit head:* Dr. Debra F. Greene, Department Head, 573-681-5145, Fax: 573-681-5150, E-mail: greened@lincolnu.edu. *Application contact:* Irasema Steck, Administrative Assistant, 573-681-5247, Fax: 573-681-5106, E-mail: gradschool@lincolnu.edu.

Louisiana State University and Agricultural and Mechanical College, Graduate School, College of Arts and Sciences, Department of Sociology, Baton Rouge, LA 70803. Offers MA, PhD. Part-time programs available. Terminal master's awarded for partial completion of doctoral program. *Degree requirements:* For master's, comprehensive exam, thesis; for doctorate, comprehensive exam, thesis/dissertation. *Entrance requirements:* For master's and doctorate,

GRE General Test, minimum GPA of 3.0. Additional exam requirements/recommendations for international students: Required—TOEFL (minimum score 550 paper-based; 213 computer-based; 79 iBT). Electronic applications accepted. *Faculty research:* Family, stratification, demography, rural sociology, criminology.

Loyola University Chicago, Graduate School, Department of Sociology, Chicago, IL 60611-2196. Offers applied sociology (MA); sociology (MA, PhD). Part-time and evening/weekend programs available. *Faculty:* 11 full-time (4 women), 3 part-time/adjunct (2 women). *Students:* 63 full-time (43 women), 12 part-time (7 women); includes 17 minority (9 African Americans, 1 American Indian/Alaska Native, 5 Asian Americans or Pacific Islanders, 2 Hispanic Americans), 4 international. Average age 34. 79 applicants, 54% accepted, 13 enrolled. In 2008, 16 master's, 5 doctorates awarded. Terminal master's awarded for partial completion of doctoral program. *Degree requirements:* For master's, thesis or alternative; for doctorate, comprehensive exam, thesis/dissertation. *Entrance requirements:* For master's and doctorate, GRE General Test. Additional exam requirements/recommendations for international students: Required—TOEFL. *Application deadline:* For winter admission, 2/1 for domestic students. Application fee: $50. Electronic applications accepted. *Expenses:* Tuition: Full-time $13,500; part-time $750 per credit hour. Required fees: $60 per semester. Full-time tuition and fees vary according to program. *Financial support:* In 2008–09, 43 students received support, including 12 fellowships with full tuition reimbursements available (averaging $14,000 per year), 10 research assistantships with full tuition reimbursements available (averaging $14,000 per year), 5 teaching assistantships (averaging $14,000 per year); career-related internships or fieldwork and Federal Work-Study also available. Financial award application deadline: 2/1; financial award applicants required to submit FAFSA. *Faculty research:* Religion, work, urban sociology, urban and social policy, knowledge and culture, gender, race. Total annual research expenditures: $160,000. *Unit head:* Dr. Fred Kniss, Chair, 773-508-3459, Fax: 773-508-7099, E-mail: fkniss@luc.edu. *Application contact:* Dr. Anne Figert, Graduate Program Director, 773-508-3431, Fax: 773-508-7099, E-mail: afigert@luc.edu.

Marshall University, Academic Affairs Division, College of Liberal Arts, Department of Sociology and Anthropology, Huntington, WV 25755. Offers sociology (MA). *Degree requirements:* For master's, thesis optional.

McGill University, Faculty of Graduate and Postdoctoral Studies, Faculty of Arts, Department of Sociology, Montréal, QC H3A 2T5, Canada. Offers medical sociology (MA); neo-tropical environment (MA); social statistics (MA); sociology (MA, PhD, Diploma).

McGill University, Faculty of Graduate and Postdoctoral Studies, Faculty of Medicine, Department of Social Studies in Medicine, Montréal, QC H3A 2T5, Canada. Offers medical anthropology (MA, PhD); medical history (MA, PhD); medical sociology (MA, PhD).

McMaster University, School of Graduate Studies, Faculty of Social Sciences, Department of Sociology, Hamilton, ON L8S 4M2, Canada. Offers MA, PhD. Part-time programs available. *Degree requirements:* For master's, thesis; for doctorate, comprehensive exam, thesis/dissertation. *Entrance requirements:* For master's and doctorate, minimum B+ average. Additional exam requirements/recommendations for international students: Required—TOEFL (minimum score 580 paper-based; 237 computer-based). *Faculty research:* Socialization and conversion, ethnic relations, international migration, racism, social implications of the Internet.

Memorial University of Newfoundland, School of Graduate Studies, Department of Sociology, St. John's, NL A1C 5S7, Canada. Offers gender (PhD); maritime sociology (PhD); sociology (M Phil, MA); work and development (PhD). Part-time programs available. *Degree requirements:* For master's, comprehensive exam, thesis optional, program journal (M Phil); for doctorate, one foreign language, comprehensive exam, thesis/dissertation, oral defense of thesis. *Entrance requirements:* For master's, 2nd class degree from university of recognized standing in area of study; for doctorate, MA, M Phil, or equivalent. Electronic applications accepted. *Faculty research:* Work and development, gender, maritime sociology.

Michigan State University, The Graduate School, College of Social Science, Department of Sociology, East Lansing, MI 48824. Offers MA, PhD. Part-time programs available. *Entrance requirements:* Additional exam requirements/recommendations for international students: Required—TOEFL (minimum score 550 paper-based; 213 computer-based), Michigan State University ELT (85), Michigan ELAB (83). Electronic applications accepted.

Middle Tennessee State University, College of Graduate Studies, College of Liberal Arts, Department of Sociology and Anthropology, Murfreesboro, TN 37132. Offers sociology (MA). Part-time and evening/weekend programs available. Postbaccalaureate distance learning degree programs offered. *Degree requirements:* For master's, comprehensive exam, thesis. *Entrance requirements:* For master's, GRE. Additional exam requirements/recommendations for international students: Required—TOEFL (paper-based 525; computer-based 195; IBT 71) or IELTS (6.0). Electronic applications accepted. *Faculty research:* Applied, crime/deviance, aging/social gerontology, social organization, social psychology.

Minnesota State University Mankato, College of Graduate Studies, College of Social and Behavioral Sciences, Department of Sociology and Corrections, Mankato, MN 56001. Offers sociology (MA); sociology: corrections (MS); sociology: human services planning and administration (MS). Part-time programs available. *Students:* 11 full-time (7 women), 37 part-time (22 women). *Degree requirements:* For master's, comprehensive exam, thesis or alternative. *Entrance requirements:* For master's, minimum GPA of 3.0 during previous 2 years, 3 letters of reference, resumé. Additional exam requirements/recommendations for international students: Required—TOEFL. *Application deadline:* For fall admission, 7/1 priority date for domestic students; for spring admission, 11/1 for domestic students. Applications are processed on a rolling basis. Application fee: $40. Electronic applications accepted. *Financial support:* Research assistantships with full tuition reimbursements, teaching assistantships with full tuition reimbursements, career-related internships or fieldwork, Federal Work-Study, institutionally sponsored loans, and unspecified assistantships available. Support available to part-time students. Financial award application deadline: 3/15; financial award applicants required to submit FAFSA. *Faculty research:* Women's suffrage movements. *Unit head:* Dr. Barbara Keating, Chairperson, 507-389-1561. *Application contact:* 507-389-2321, E-mail: grad@mnsu.edu.

Mississippi State University, College of Arts and Sciences, Department of Sociology, Mississippi State, MS 39762. Offers MS, PhD.

Montclair State University, The Office of Graduate Admissions and Support Services, College of Humanities and Social Sciences, Department of Sociology, Montclair, NJ 07043-1624. Offers applied sociology (MA). Part-time and evening/weekend programs available. *Faculty:* 11 full-time (4 women), 13 part-time/adjunct (2 women). *Students:* 2 part-time (both women). Average age 30. In 2008, 1 master's awarded. *Degree requirements:* For master's, comprehensive exam, comprehensive project, internship. *Entrance requirements:* For master's, GRE General Test, 30 undergraduate semester hours in social sciences or history, 2 letters of recommendation. Additional exam requirements/recommendations for international students: Required—TOEFL (minimum score 83 computer-based). *Application deadline:* For fall admission, 6/1 for international students; for spring admission, 10/1 for international students. Applications are processed on a rolling basis. Application fee: $60. Electronic applications accepted. *Financial support:* Research assistantships with full tuition reimbursements, Federal Work-Study, scholarships/grants, and unspecified assistantships available. Support available to part-time students. Financial award application deadline: 3/1; financial award applicants required to submit FAFSA. *Unit head:* Dr. Jay Livingston, Chairperson, 973-655-4131. *Application contact:* Amy Aiello, Associate Director of Admissions, 973-655-5147, Fax: 973-655-7869, E-mail: graduate.school@montclair.edu.

Morehead State University, Graduate Programs, Caudill College of Humanities, Department of Sociology, Social Work and Criminology, Morehead, KY 40351. Offers criminology (MA); general sociology (MA); gerontology (MA). Part-time and evening/weekend programs available. *Faculty:* 7 full-time (4 women), 4 part-time/adjunct (1 woman). *Students:* 9 full-time (7 women),

18 part-time (12 women); includes 1 minority (African American). Average age 30. 20 applicants, 55% accepted, 7 enrolled. In 2008, 4 master's awarded. *Degree requirements:* For master's, comprehensive exam, thesis optional. *Entrance requirements:* For master's, GRE General Test, minimum GPA of 3.0 in sociology, 2.5 overall; 18 hours of course work in sociology, writing sample. Additional exam requirements/recommendations for international students: Required—TOEFL (minimum score 500 paper-based; 173 computer-based). *Application deadline:* For fall admission, 8/1 priority date for domestic and international students; for spring admission, 12/1 priority date for domestic and international students. Applications are processed on a rolling basis. Application fee: $30 ($55 for international students). Electronic applications accepted. *Expenses:* Tuition, area resident: Full-time $6084; part-time $338 per credit hour. Tuition, state resident: full-time $6084; part-time $338 per credit hour. Tuition, nonresident: full-time $15,804; part-time $878 per credit hour. *Financial support:* In 2008–09, 5 teaching assistantships (averaging $6,000 per year) were awarded; career-related internships or fieldwork, Federal Work-Study, and unspecified assistantships also available. Financial award application deadline: 4/1; financial award applicants required to submit FAFSA. *Faculty research:* Death and dying; aging, drinking, and drugs; economic development; adult children of alcoholics. *Unit head:* Dr. Clarenda Phillips, Department Chair, 606-783-2656, Fax: 606-783-5027, E-mail: r.bylund@moreheadstate.edu. *Application contact:* Michelle Barber, Graduate Admissions Counselor, 606-783-2039, Fax: 606-783-5061, E-mail: m.barber@moreheadstate.edu.

Morgan State University, School of Graduate Studies, College of Liberal Arts, Department of Sociology and Anthropology, Baltimore, MD 21251. Offers sociology (MA, MS). Part-time and evening/weekend programs available. *Degree requirements:* For master's, comprehensive exam. *Entrance requirements:* Additional exam requirements/recommendations for international students: Required—TOEFL (minimum score 550 paper-based; 213 computer-based). *Faculty research:* Domestic violence, homelessness, social movements, marriage and family.

New Mexico Highlands University, Graduate Studies, College of Arts and Sciences, Program in Public Affairs, Las Vegas, NM 87701. Offers applied sociology (MA). Program is interdisciplinary. *Faculty:* 12 full-time (7 women). *Students:* 17 full-time (12 women), 17 part-time (10 women); includes 21 minority (1 Asian American or Pacific Islander, 20 Hispanic Americans), 4 international. Average age 32. 17 applicants, 71% accepted, 6 enrolled. In 2008, 1 master's awarded. *Degree requirements:* For master's, comprehensive exam, thesis or alternative. *Entrance requirements:* For master's, minimum undergraduate GPA of 3.0. Additional exam requirements/recommendations for international students: Required—TOEFL (minimum score 540 paper-based; 207 computer-based). *Application deadline:* For fall admission, 8/1 priority date for domestic students. Applications are processed on a rolling basis. Application fee: $15. *Expenses:* Tuition, state resident: full-time $2880; part-time $120 per credit hour. Tuition, nonresident: full-time $4234; part-time $176 per credit hour. International tuition: $5645 full-time. One-time fee: $20. *Financial support:* In 2008–09, 17 students received support, including 8 teaching assistantships with full and partial tuition reimbursements available (averaging $6,500 per year); career-related internships or fieldwork, Federal Work-Study, institutionally sponsored loans, scholarships/grants, traineeships, tuition waivers (full and partial), and unspecified assistantships also available. Support available to part-time students. Financial award application deadline: 3/1. *Application contact:* Diane Trujillo, Administrative Assistant, Graduate Studies, 505-454-3266, Fax: 505-426-2117, E-mail: dtrujillo@nmhu.edu.

New Mexico State University, Graduate School, College of Arts and Sciences, Department of Sociology and Anthropology, Las Cruces, NM 88003-8001. Offers anthropology (MA); sociology (MA). Part-time programs available. *Faculty:* 12 full-time (8 women), 4 part-time/adjunct (2 women). *Students:* 42 full-time (29 women), 60 part-time (39 women); includes 25 minority (5 African Americans, 2 American Indian/Alaska Native, 18 Hispanic Americans), 5 international. Average age 33. 71 applicants, 99% accepted, 31 enrolled. In 2008, 17 master's awarded. *Degree requirements:* For master's, comprehensive exam (for some programs), thesis (for some programs). *Entrance requirements:* Additional exam requirements/recommendations for international students: Required—TOEFL. *Application deadline:* For fall admission, 2/15 priority date for domestic students; for spring admission, 10/15 priority date for domestic students. Applications are processed on a rolling basis. Application fee: $30 ($50 for international students). Electronic applications accepted. *Expenses:* Tuition, area resident: Full-time $3890; part-time $212.85 per credit. Tuition, state resident: full-time $3890; part-time $212.85 per credit. Tuition, nonresident: full-time $13,916; part-time $630.55 per credit. Required fees: $1218; $609 per semester. *Financial support:* In 2008–09, 28 students received support, including 2 research assistantships with partial tuition reimbursements available (averaging $7,900 per year), 19 teaching assistantships with partial tuition reimbursements available (averaging $8,321 per year); fellowships, career-related internships or fieldwork, Federal Work-Study, and health care benefits also available. Support available to part-time students. Financial award application deadline: 2/15. *Faculty research:* Native American culture and society, Latin America and border studies, prehistoric and historic archaeology, medical anthropology, applied anthropology. *Unit head:* Dr. Miriam Chaiken, Head, 575-646-3821, Fax: 575-646-3725, E-mail: mchaiken@nmsu.edu. *Application contact:* Coordinator.

The New School: A University, The New School for Social Research, Department of Sociology, New York, NY 10011. Offers MA, DS Sc, PhD. Part-time and evening/weekend programs available. *Faculty:* 11 full-time (5 women). *Students:* 148 full-time (89 women), 22 part-time (11 women); includes 26 minority (10 African Americans, 7 Asian Americans or Pacific Islanders, 9 Hispanic Americans), 66 international. Average age 34. In 2008, 29 master's, 12 doctorates awarded. Terminal master's awarded for partial completion of doctoral program. *Degree requirements:* For master's, exam; for doctorate, one foreign language, thesis/dissertation, qualifying exam. *Entrance requirements:* For master's, GRE General Test; for doctorate, GRE General Test, MA. Additional exam requirements/recommendations for international students: Required—TOEFL (minimum score 600 paper-based; 250 computer-based; 100 iBT). *Application deadline:* For fall admission, 1/15 priority date for domestic students. Applications are processed on a rolling basis. Application fee: $50. *Expenses:* Tuition: Full-time $27,144; part-time $1508 per credit. Required fees: $355 per semester. *Financial support:* Fellowships, research assistantships, teaching assistantships, career-related internships or fieldwork, Federal Work-Study, scholarships/grants, and tuition waivers (full and partial) available. Financial award application deadline: 3/1; financial award applicants required to submit FAFSA. *Faculty research:* Media, culture, urban sociology, democratic transitions, critical theory. *Unit head:* Dr. Eiko Ikegami, Chair, 212-229-5737 Ext. 4925, E-mail: casanova@newschool.edu. *Application contact:* Robert MacDonald, Director of Admissions, 800-523-5710 Ext. 3007, Fax: 212-989-7102, E-mail: macdonar@newschool.edu.

See Close-Up on page 1251.

New York University, Graduate School of Arts and Science, Department of Sociology, New York, NY 10012-1019. Offers French studies and sociology (PhD); sociology (MA, PhD); JD/MA. Part-time programs available. Terminal master's awarded for partial completion of doctoral program. *Degree requirements:* For master's, thesis or alternative; for doctorate, comprehensive exam, thesis/dissertation. *Entrance requirements:* For master's and doctorate, GRE General Test. Additional exam requirements/recommendations for international students: Required—TOEFL. *Faculty research:* Political sociology and social movements; gender and inequality; deviance, law, and crime; education; stratification and theory.

New York University, Steinhardt School of Culture, Education and Human Development, Department of Humanities and Social Sciences in the Professions, Program in Sociology of Education, New York, NY 10012-1019. Offers education policy (MA); social and cultural studies of education (MA); sociology of education (PhD). Part-time and evening/weekend programs available. Terminal master's awarded for partial completion of doctoral program. *Degree requirements:* For master's, thesis (for some programs); for doctorate, thesis/dissertation. *Entrance requirements:* For master's, letters of recommendation; for doctorate, GRE General Test, interview. Additional exam requirements/recommendations for international students: Required—TOEFL. *Faculty research:* Legal and institutional environments of schools;

Sociology

New York University *(continued)*
social inequality; high school reform and achievement; education's link with occupations, professions and inequality.

Norfolk State University, School of Graduate Studies, School of Liberal Arts, Department of Sociology, Program in Applied Sociology, Norfolk, VA 23504. Offers MS. Part-time programs available.

North Carolina Central University, Division of Academic Affairs, College of Behavioral and Social Sciences, Department of Sociology, Durham, NC 27707-3129. Offers MA. Part-time and evening/weekend programs available. *Degree requirements:* For master's, one foreign language, comprehensive exam, thesis. *Entrance requirements:* For master's, GRE, minimum GPA of 3.0 in major, 2.5 overall. Additional exam requirements/recommendations for international students: Required—TOEFL. *Faculty research:* Urban demography, family, statistical methods.

North Carolina State University, Graduate School, College of Humanities and Social Sciences, Department of Sociology and Anthropology, Program in Sociology, Raleigh, NC 27695. Offers M Soc, MS, PhD. Part-time programs available. *Degree requirements:* For master's, thesis (for some programs), practicum (M Soc), thesis (MS); for doctorate, comprehensive exam, thesis/dissertation. *Entrance requirements:* For master's and doctorate, GRE General Test, sample of written work. Electronic applications accepted. *Faculty research:* Inequity; gender, race and class; crime and social control; work and organizations; rural sociology; family and intimate relations.

North Dakota State University, College of Graduate and Interdisciplinary Studies, College of Arts, Humanities and Social Sciences, Department of Sociology, Anthropology, and Emergency Management, Fargo, ND 58105. Offers emergency management (MS, PhD); social science (MA, MS); sociology (MS). Part-time programs available. *Faculty:* 8 full-time (3 women), 5 part-time/adjunct (2 women). *Students:* 35 full-time (17 women), 15 part-time (9 women); includes 5 minority (2 African Americans, 1 American Indian/Alaska Native, 1 Asian American or Pacific Islander, 1 Hispanic American), 2 international. Average age 27. 15 applicants, 60% accepted, 7 enrolled. In 2008, 9 master's awarded. *Degree requirements:* For master's, thesis; for doctorate, comprehensive exam, thesis/dissertation. *Entrance requirements:* For master's, GRE (emergency management), course work in sociology, minimum GPA of 3.2; for doctorate, GRE, minimum GPA of 3.2. Additional exam requirements/recommendations for international students: Required—TOEFL. *Application deadline:* For fall admission, 4/1 priority date for domestic students. Applications are processed on a rolling basis. Application fee: $45 ($60 for international students). *Financial support:* In 2008–09, 7 research assistantships with full tuition reimbursements (averaging $6,156 per year), 7 teaching assistantships with full tuition reimbursements (averaging $3,078 per year) were awarded; fellowships, career-related internships or fieldwork, Federal Work-Study, institutionally sponsored loans, and tuition waivers (full) also available. Support available to part-time students. Financial award application deadline: 4/15. *Faculty research:* Medical sociology, demography, ethnology, archaeology. Total annual research expenditures: $75,000. *Unit head:* Dr. Daniel J. Klenow, Chair, 701-231-8657, Fax: 701-231-1047, E-mail: daniel.klenow@ndsu.edu. *Application contact:* Dr. Daniel J. Klenow, Chair, 701-231-8657, Fax: 701-231-1047, E-mail: daniel.klenow@ndsu.edu.

Northeastern University, College of Arts and Sciences, Department of Sociology and Anthropology, Boston, MA 02115-5096. Offers sociology (MA, PhD). Part-time programs available. *Degree requirements:* For master's, thesis; for doctorate, thesis/dissertation, teaching tutorial. *Entrance requirements:* For master's and doctorate, GRE General Test or MAT. Additional exam requirements/recommendations for international students: Required—TOEFL. *Faculty research:* Globalization and international studies, urban affairs, social justice.

Northern Arizona University, Graduate College, College of Social and Behavioral Sciences, Department of Sociology and Social Work, Flagstaff, AZ 86011. Offers applied sociology (MA); sociology (MA). Part-time programs available. *Degree requirements:* For master's, thesis or internship. *Faculty research:* Demography, death and dying, criminology, social policy, divorce.

Northern Illinois University, Graduate School, College of Liberal Arts and Sciences, Department of Sociology, De Kalb, IL 60115-2854. Offers MA. Part-time programs available. *Degree requirements:* For master's, comprehensive exam, thesis optional. *Entrance requirements:* For master's, GRE General Test, minimum GPA of 2.75; course work in social theory, social methods, and statistics. Additional exam requirements/recommendations for international students: Required—TOEFL (minimum score 550 paper-based; 213 computer-based). Electronic applications accepted. *Faculty research:* Welfare reform, interpersonal disputes, multicultural education, race and ethnicism, social control.

Northwestern University, The Graduate School, Interdepartmental Degree Programs and Kellogg School of Management, Program in Management and Organizations and Sociology, Evanston, IL 60208. Offers PhD. Program requires admission to both The Graduate School and the Kellogg Graduate School of Management. *Degree requirements:* For doctorate, comprehensive exam, thesis/dissertation. *Entrance requirements:* For doctorate, GRE General Test. Additional exam requirements/recommendations for international students: Required—TOEFL. Electronic applications accepted. *Faculty research:* Strategic alliances and organizational competitiveness, institutional change and the information of industries, social capital and the creation of financial capital, negotiation, organizational networks, diversity.

Northwestern University, The Graduate School, Judd A. and Marjorie Weinberg College of Arts and Sciences, Department of Sociology, Evanston, IL 60208. Offers PhD, JD/PhD. Admissions and degrees offered through The Graduate School. *Degree requirements:* For doctorate, thesis/dissertation. *Entrance requirements:* For doctorate, GRE General Test. Additional exam requirements/recommendations for international students: Required—TOEFL. Electronic applications accepted. *Faculty research:* Sociology of culture, social organizations, social inequality, comparative/historical sociology, economic sociology.

The Ohio State University, Graduate School, College of Social and Behavioral Sciences, School of Social and Behavioral Science, Department of Sociology, Columbus, OH 43210. Offers MA, PhD. *Degree requirements:* For master's, thesis; for doctorate, thesis/dissertation. *Entrance requirements:* For master's and doctorate, GRE General Test. Additional exam requirements/recommendations for international students: Required—TOEFL (minimum score 600 paper-based; 250 computer-based). Electronic applications accepted.

Ohio University, Graduate College, College of Arts and Sciences, Department of Sociology and Anthropology, Athens, OH 45701-2979. Offers sociology (MA). Part-time programs available. *Degree requirements:* For master's, thesis or alternative. *Entrance requirements:* For master's, minimum GPA of 3.0, minimum 20 hours sociology included with stats, theory, and research methods. Additional exam requirements/recommendations for international students: Required—TOEFL. Electronic applications accepted. *Faculty research:* Criminology/deviance, gender studies, inequality, social psychology and rural poverty.

Oklahoma State University, College of Arts and Sciences, Department of Sociology, Stillwater, OK 74078. Offers sociology (MS, PhD). *Faculty:* 16 full-time (4 women), 2 part-time/adjunct (both women). *Students:* 7 full-time (3 women), 26 part-time (20 women); includes 3 minority (1 African American, 2 American Indian/Alaska Native), 5 international. Average age 36. 48 applicants, 40% accepted, 11 enrolled. In 2008, 8 master's, 6 doctorates awarded. *Degree requirements:* For master's, thesis; for doctorate, comprehensive exam, thesis/dissertation. *Entrance requirements:* For master's and doctorate, GRE General Test. Additional exam requirements/recommendations for international students: Required—TOEFL. *Application deadline:* For fall admission, 3/1 priority date for international students; for spring admission, 8/1 priority date for international students. Applications are processed on a rolling basis. Application fee: $40 ($75 for international students). Electronic applications accepted. *Expenses:* Tuition, state resident: full-time $3716.40; part-time $154.85 per credit hour. Tuition, nonresident: full-time $14,448; part-time $602 per credit hour. Required fees: $1772.40; $73.85 per credit

hour. One-time fee: $50. Tuition and fees vary according to course load and campus/location. *Financial support:* In 2008–09, 2 research assistantships (averaging $14,706 per year), 21 teaching assistantships (averaging $13,077 per year) were awarded; career-related internships or fieldwork, Federal Work-Study, scholarships/grants, health care benefits, tuition waivers (partial), and unspecified assistantships also available. Support available to part-time students. Financial award application deadline: 3/1; financial award applicants required to submit FAFSA. *Faculty research:* Criminology/correction/legal issues; race, ethnicity, and gender in American society; environmental conflict and population problems; international.comparative research; social change and social movement in American culture. *Unit head:* Dr. Patricia Bell, Head, 405-744-6105, Fax: 405-744-5780. *Application contact:* Dr. Gordon Emslie, Dean, 405-744-6368, Fax: 405-744-0355, E-mail: grad_i@okstate.edu.

Old Dominion University, College of Arts and Letters, Program in Applied Sociology, Norfolk, VA 23529. Offers MA. Part-time and evening/weekend programs available. *Faculty:* 15 full-time (10 women), 1 part-time/adjunct (0 women). *Students:* 4 full-time (all women), 41 part-time (32 women); includes 16 minority (all African Americans), 1 international. Average age 29. 26 applicants, 65% accepted, 12 enrolled. In 2008, 12 master's awarded. *Degree requirements:* For master's, thesis, 36 credit hours. *Entrance requirements:* For master's, GRE General Test, minimum GPA of 3.0, 12 credits in criminal justice, sociology, or women's studies. Additional exam requirements/recommendations for international students: Required—TOEFL. *Application deadline:* For fall admission, 5/1 for domestic and international students; for spring admission, 11/1 for domestic students, 10/1 for international students. Application fee: $40. Electronic applications accepted. *Expenses:* Tuition, area resident: Full-time $7704; part-time $321 per credit. Tuition, state resident: full-time $7704; part-time $321 per credit. Tuition, nonresident: full-time $19,104; part-time $796 per credit. Required fees: $99 per semester. One-time fee: $40. *Financial support:* In 2008–09, fellowships (averaging $2,000 per year), 2 research assistantships with partial tuition reimbursements (averaging $8,000 per year), 2 teaching assistantships with partial tuition reimbursements (averaging $8,000 per year) were awarded; career-related internships or fieldwork, scholarships/grants, and unspecified assistantships also available. Financial award application deadline: 2/15; financial award applicants required to submit CSS PROFILE or FAFSA. *Faculty research:* Quantitative methodology, theory, family, gender/class/race, crime. Total annual research expenditures: $350,000. *Unit head:* Dr. Dianne Carmody, Graduate Program Director, 757-683-6801, Fax: 757-683-5634, E-mail: dcarmody@odu.edu. *Application contact:* Dr. Dianne Carmody, Graduate Program Director, 757-683-6801, Fax: 757-683-5634, E-mail: dcarmody@odu.edu.

Penn State University Park, Graduate School, College of the Liberal Arts, Department of Sociology, State College, University Park, PA 16802-1503. Offers crime, law, and justice (MA, PhD); sociology (MA, PhD).

Portland State University, Graduate Studies, College of Liberal Arts and Sciences, Department of Sociology, Portland, OR 97207-0751. Offers MA, MS, PhD. Part-time programs available. *Faculty:* 14 full-time (5 women), 4 part-time/adjunct (1 woman). *Students:* 22 full-time (16 women), 6 part-time (3 women); includes 3 minority (all Hispanic Americans). Average age 31. 43 applicants, 53% accepted, 13 enrolled. In 2008, 12 master's awarded. *Degree requirements:* For master's, variable foreign language requirement, thesis, written exam; for doctorate, thesis/dissertation. *Entrance requirements:* For master's, GRE General Test, GRE Subject Test, minimum GPA of 3.0 in upper-division course work or 2.75 overall, 3 letters of recommendation. Additional exam requirements/recommendations for international students: Required—TOEFL (minimum score 550 paper-based; 213 computer-based). *Application deadline:* For fall admission, 1/15 for domestic and international students. Applications are processed on a rolling basis. Application fee: $50. *Expenses:* Tuition, area resident: Full-time $8763; part-time $179 per credit hour. Tuition, state resident: full-time $8763; part-time $298 per credit hour. Tuition, nonresident: full-time $12,981; part-time $426 per credit hour. Required fees: $1242. One-time fee: $250. Tuition and fees vary according to course load and program. *Financial support:* In 2008–09, 5 research assistantships with full tuition reimbursements (averaging $9,328 per year) were awarded; fellowships with full tuition reimbursements, teaching assistantships with full tuition reimbursements, career-related internships or fieldwork, Federal Work-Study, and unspecified assistantships also available. Support available to part-time students. Financial award application deadline: 3/1; financial award applicants required to submit FAFSA. *Faculty research:* Urban sociology, gender and class, development, social change, race/ethnic/minority relations. Total annual research expenditures: $403,296. *Unit head:* Veronica Dujon, Chair, 503-725-3926. *Application contact:* Bahar Jaberi, Information Contact, 503-725-3926.

Portland State University, Graduate Studies, Systems Science Program, Portland, OR 97207-0751. Offers computational intelligence (Certificate); computer modeling and simulation (Certificate); systems science (MS); systems science/anthropology (PhD); systems science/business administration (PhD); systems science/civil engineering (PhD); systems science/economics (PhD); systems science/engineering management (PhD); systems science/general (PhD); systems science/mathematical sciences (PhD); systems science/mechanical engineering (PhD); systems science/psychology (PhD); systems science/sociology (PhD). *Faculty:* 3 full-time (0 women). *Students:* 12 full-time (3 women), 13 part-time (3 women); includes 2 minority (1 American Indian/Alaska Native, 1 Asian American or Pacific Islander), 5 international. Average age 38. 14 applicants, 71% accepted, 8 enrolled. In 2008, 2 master's, 4 doctorates awarded. *Degree requirements:* For doctorate, variable foreign language requirement, thesis/dissertation. *Entrance requirements:* For master's, 2 letters of recommendation; for doctorate, GMAT, GRE General Test, minimum undergraduate GPA of 3.0. Additional exam requirements/recommendations for international students: Required—TOEFL. *Application deadline:* For fall admission, 2/1 for domestic students; for spring admission, 11/1 for domestic students. Application fee: $50. *Expenses:* Tuition, area resident: Full-time $8763; part-time $179 per credit hour. Tuition, state resident: full-time $8763; part-time $298 per credit hour. Tuition, nonresident: full-time $12,981; part-time $426 per credit hour. Required fees: $1242. One-time fee: $250. Tuition and fees vary according to course load and program. *Financial support:* In 2008–09, 1 research assistantship with full tuition reimbursement (averaging $7,704 per year) was awarded; teaching assistantships with full tuition reimbursements, career-related internships or fieldwork, Federal Work-Study, scholarships/grants, and unspecified assistantships also available. Support available to part-time students. Financial award application deadline: 3/1; financial award applicants required to submit FAFSA. *Faculty research:* Systems theory and methodology, artificial intelligence neural networks, information theory, nonlinear dynamics/chaos, modeling and simulation. *Unit head:* George Lendaris, Acting Director, 503-725-4960. *Application contact:* Dawn Sharafi, Administrative Assistant, 503-725-4960, E-mail: dawn@sysc.pdx.edu.

Prairie View A&M University, College of Arts and Sciences, Division of Social Work, Behavioral and Political Science, Prairie View, TX 77446-0519. Offers sociology (MA). Part-time and evening/weekend programs available. *Degree requirements:* For master's, comprehensive exam, thesis optional. *Entrance requirements:* For master's, GRE General Test. *Faculty research:* Criminology, political sociology, sociology of education, gender, race, African American mental health, global development-social movements, African American status attainment.

Princeton University, Graduate School, Department of Sociology, Princeton, NJ 08544-1019. Offers sociology (PhD); sociology and demography (PhD). *Degree requirements:* For doctorate, variable foreign language requirement, thesis/dissertation. *Entrance requirements:* For doctorate, GRE General Test, GRE Subject Test (recommended), sample of written work. Additional exam requirements/recommendations for international students: Required—TOEFL (minimum score 600 paper-based; 250 computer-based). Electronic applications accepted.

Princeton University, Graduate School, Program in Population Studies, Princeton, NJ 08544-1019. Offers demography (PhD, Certificate); economics and demography (PhD); public affairs and demography (PhD); sociology and demography (PhD). *Degree requirements:* For doctorate, thesis/dissertation. *Entrance requirements:* For doctorate, GRE General Test. Additional exam requirements/recommendations for international students: Required—TOEFL (minimum score

600 paper-based; 250 computer-based). Electronic applications accepted. *Faculty research:* Models, fertility, infant and child mortality, migration.

Purdue University, Graduate School, College of Liberal Arts, Department of Sociology and Anthropology, West Lafayette, IN 47907. Offers anthropology (MS, PhD); sociology (MS, PhD). Terminal master's awarded for partial completion of doctoral program. *Degree requirements:* For doctorate, thesis/dissertation. *Entrance requirements:* For master's and doctorate, GRE General Test. Additional exam requirements/recommendations for international students: Required—TOEFL, TWE. Electronic applications accepted. *Faculty research:* Communiversity survey project, risk, fear, constrained behavior, archaeological services.

Queens College of the City University of New York, Division of Graduate Studies, Social Science Division, Department of Sociology, Flushing, NY 11367-1597. Offers MA. Part-time and evening/weekend programs available. *Degree requirements:* For master's, thesis optional. *Entrance requirements:* For master's, minimum GPA of 3.0. Additional exam requirements/recommendations for international students: Required—TOEFL.

Queen's University at Kingston, School of Graduate Studies and Research, Faculty of Arts and Sciences, Department of Sociology, Kingston, ON K7L 3N6, Canada. Offers communication and Information technology (MA, PhD); feminist sociology (MA, PhD); socio-legal studies (MA, PhD); sociological theory (MA, PhD). Part-time programs available. *Degree requirements:* For master's, thesis; for doctorate, comprehensive exam, thesis/dissertation. *Entrance requirements:* For master's, honors bachelors degree in sociology; for doctorate, honors bachelors degree, masters degree in sociology. Additional exam requirements/recommendations for international students: Required—TOEFL. *Faculty research:* Social change and modernization, social control, deviance and criminology, surveillance.

Roosevelt University, Graduate Division, College of Arts and Sciences, Department of Sociology and Anthropology, Chicago, IL 60605-1394. Offers anthropology (MA); sociology (MA). Part-time and evening/weekend programs available. *Students:* 13 full-time (8 women), 14 part-time (9 women); includes 10 minority (7 African Americans, 1 Asian American or Pacific Islander, 2 Hispanic Americans). Average age 35. 56 applicants, 57% accepted, 9 enrolled. In 2008, 3 master's awarded. *Degree requirements:* For master's, comprehensive exam, thesis. *Application deadline:* For fall admission, 6/1 priority date for domestic students. Applications are processed on a rolling basis. Application fee: $25 ($35 for international students). *Expenses:* Tuition: Full-time $14,730; part-time $709 per credit. Required fees: $175 per semester. Tuition and fees vary according to course load and program. *Financial support:* Teaching assistantships available. Financial award application deadline: 2/15. *Faculty research:* Social theory, urban sociology, gerontology, social organizations. *Unit head:* Michael Maly, Head, 312-341-3769, E-mail: mmaly@roosevelt.edu. *Application contact:* Joanne Canyon-Heller, Coordinator of Graduate Admission, 877-APPLY RU, Fax: 312-281-3356, E-mail: applyru@roosevelt.edu.

Rutgers, The State University of New Jersey, New Brunswick, Graduate School, Program in Sociology, Piscataway, NJ 08854-8097. Offers MA, PhD. Terminal master's awarded for partial completion of doctoral program. *Degree requirements:* For master's, qualifying paper; for doctorate, thesis/dissertation, qualifying exam, qualifying papers. *Entrance requirements:* For master's, GRE General Test; for doctorate, GRE General Test, sample of written work. Additional exam requirements/recommendations for international students: Required—TOEFL. Electronic applications accepted. *Faculty research:* Comparative-historical, sex and gender, organizations and work, culture and cognition, economics, occupations/professions, religion.

Sage Graduate School, Graduate School, Department of Sociology and Criminal Justice, Troy, NY 12180-4115. Offers forensic mental health (MS, Certificate). *Faculty:* 2 part-time/adjunct (both women). *Students:* 3 full-time (all women), 14 part-time (13 women); includes 2 minority (both African Americans). Average age 28. 32 applicants, 69% accepted, 12 enrolled. *Entrance requirements:* Additional exam requirements/recommendations for international students: Required—TOEFL (minimum score 550 paper-based; 213 computer-based). *Expenses:* Tuition: Full-time $10,080; part-time $560 per credit hour. *Unit head:* Dr. Maureen McLeod, Chair, 518-244-2211, E-mail: mcleom@sage.edu. *Application contact:* Wendy D. Diefendorf, Director of Graduate and Adult Admission, 518-244-2443, Fax: 518-244-6880, E-mail: diefew@sage.edu.

St. John's University, St. John's College of Liberal Arts and Sciences, Department of Sociology and Anthropology, Queens, NY 11439. Offers criminology and justice (MA); sociology (MA). Part-time and evening/weekend programs available. *Students:* 10 full-time (5 women), 49 part-time (28 women); includes 33 minority (14 African Americans, 8 Asian Americans or Pacific Islanders, 11 Hispanic Americans), 3 international. Average age 27. 68 applicants, 65% accepted, 22 enrolled. In 2008, 30 master's awarded. *Degree requirements:* For master's, comprehensive exam, thesis optional. *Entrance requirements:* For master's, 18 undergraduate credits in social services, minimum GPA of 3.0. Additional exam requirements/recommendations for international students: Required—TOEFL (minimum score 500 paper-based; 173 computer-based; 61 iBT), IELTS (minimum score 5.5). *Application deadline:* For fall admission, 5/1 priority date for domestic and international students; for spring admission, 11/1 priority date for domestic and international students. Applications are processed on a rolling basis. Application fee: $70. Electronic applications accepted. *Expenses:* Tuition: Full-time $20,760; part-time $865 per credit. Required fees: $300; $150 per semester. Tuition and fees vary according to program. *Financial support:* Research assistantships, career-related internships or fieldwork and scholarships/grants available. Support available to part-time students. Financial award application deadline: 3/1; financial award applicants required to submit FAFSA. *Faculty research:* Global black power movement, poverty, domestic violence and human trafficking, female juvenile violence, media and race. *Unit head:* Dr. Dawn Esposito, Chair, 718-990-5667, E-mail: espositd@stjohns.edu. *Application contact:* Kathleen Davis, Director of Graduate Admission, 718-990-2790, Fax: 718-990-5686, E-mail: gradhelp@stjohns.edu.

Sam Houston State University, College of Humanities and Social Sciences, Department of Sociology, Huntsville, TX 77341. Offers MA. Part-time programs available. *Faculty:* 5 full-time (2 women). *Students:* 5 full-time (4 women), 5 part-time (2 women); includes 4 minority (2 Asian Americans or Pacific Islanders, 2 Hispanic Americans). Average age 33. 7 applicants, 100% accepted, 6 enrolled. In 2008, 1 master's awarded. *Degree requirements:* For master's, thesis optional. *Entrance requirements:* For master's, GRE General Test. Additional exam requirements/recommendations for international students: Required—TOEFL (minimum score 550 paper-based; 213 computer-based; 79 iBT). *Application deadline:* For fall admission, 8/1 for domestic students; for spring admission, 12/1 for domestic students. Applications are processed on a rolling basis. Application fee: $20. *Expenses:* Tuition, state resident: full-time $3564; part-time $198 per credit hour. Tuition, nonresident: full-time $8622; part-time $479 per credit hour. Required fees: $1290. Tuition and fees vary according to course load and campus/location. *Financial support:* Teaching assistantships, Federal Work-Study available. Support available to part-time students. Financial award application deadline: 5/31; financial award applicants required to submit FAFSA. *Unit head:* Dr. Alessandro Bonanno, Chair, 936-294-1488, Fax: 963-294-3573, E-mail: soc_aab@shsu.edu. *Application contact:* Dr. Alessandro Bonanno, Chair, 936-294-1488, Fax: 963-294-3573, E-mail: soc_aab@shsu.edu.

San Diego State University, Graduate and Research Affairs, College of Arts and Letters, Department of Sociology, San Diego, CA 92182. Offers MA. *Degree requirements:* For master's, thesis. *Entrance requirements:* For master's, GRE General Test, 3 letters of recommendation, writing sample. Additional exam requirements/recommendations for international students: Required—TOEFL. Electronic applications accepted. *Faculty research:* The homeless and mentally ill, medical data relating to the homeless.

San Jose State University, Graduate Studies and Research, College of Social Sciences, Department of Sociology, San Jose, CA 95192-0001. Offers MA. Part-time and evening/weekend programs available. *Degree requirements:* For master's, comprehensive exams or thesis. *Entrance requirements:* For master's, GRE Subject Test, minimum GPA of 3.0. Electronic applications accepted. *Faculty research:* Theory construction, sexuality, sociology of the media, social causes of stress, social change.

Shippensburg University of Pennsylvania, School of Graduate Studies, College of Arts and Sciences, Department of Sociology and Anthropology, Shippensburg, PA 17257-2299. Offers organizational development and leadership (MS), including business, communications, education, environmental management, higher education, historical administration, individual and organizational development, public organizations, social structures and organizations. Part-time and evening/weekend programs available. *Faculty:* 4 full-time (3 women). *Students:* 12 full-time (2 women), 30 part-time (21 women); includes 5 minority (4 African Americans, 1 Asian American or Pacific Islander), 3 international. Average age 31. 39 applicants, 79% accepted, 17 enrolled. In 2008, 13 master's awarded. *Degree requirements:* For master's, capstone experience. *Entrance requirements:* For master's, interview (if GPA less than 2.75), resumé, goals statement. Additional exam requirements/recommendations for international students: Required—TOEFL (minimum score 560 paper-based; 220 computer-based); Recommended—IELTS (minimum score 6). *Application deadline:* For fall admission, 3/1 for international students; for spring admission, 7/1 for international students. Applications are processed on a rolling basis. Application fee: $30. Electronic applications accepted. *Expenses:* Tuition, state resident: full-time $6430; part-time $357 per credit. Tuition, nonresident: full-time $10,288; part-time $572 per credit. Required fees: $1127; $38 per credit. One-time fee: $44 part-time. *Financial support:* In 2008–09, 8 research assistantships with full tuition reimbursements (averaging $5,000 per year) were awarded; career-related internships or fieldwork, scholarships/grants, unspecified assistantships, and resident hall directors, student payroll positions also available. Support available to part-time students. Financial award applicants required to submit FAFSA. *Unit head:* Dr. Barbara Denison, Chairperson, 717-477-1735, Fax: 717-477-4011, E-mail: bjdeni@ship.edu. *Application contact:* Renee Payne, Associate Dean of Graduate Admissions, 717-477-1231, Fax: 717-477-4016, E-mail: rmpayn@ship.edu.

Simon Fraser University, Graduate Studies, Faculty of Arts and Social Sciences, Department of Sociology and Anthropology, Burnaby, BC V5A 1S6, Canada. Offers anthropology (MA, PhD); sociology (MA, PhD). *Degree requirements:* For master's, thesis (for some programs); for doctorate, thesis/dissertation. *Entrance requirements:* For master's and doctorate, minimum GPA of 3.25. Additional exam requirements/recommendations for international students: Required—TOEFL or IELTS. *Faculty research:* Sociology theory, social and cultural anthropology, political sociology, religion and society, Canadian native peoples.

Southeastern Louisiana University, College of Arts, Humanities and Social Sciences, Department of Sociology and Criminal Justice, Hammond, LA 70402. Offers applied sociology (MS). Part-time and evening/weekend programs available. *Faculty:* 5 full-time (1 woman). *Students:* 11 full-time (10 women), 16 part-time (8 women); includes 11 minority (all African Americans). Average age 27. 11 applicants, 91% accepted, 5 enrolled. In 2008, 13 master's awarded. *Degree requirements:* For master's, comprehensive exam, thesis or alternative. *Entrance requirements:* For master's, GRE General Test, bachelor's degree in sociology, social work, criminal justice or related social science; minimum GPA of 3.0. Additional exam requirements/recommendations for international students: Required—TOEFL (minimum score 500 paper-based; 173 computer-based; 61 iBT). *Application deadline:* For fall admission, 7/15 priority date for domestic students, 6/1 priority date for international students; for spring admission, 12/1 priority date for domestic students, 10/1 priority date for international students. Application fee: $20 ($30 for international students). *Expenses:* Tuition, area resident: Full-time $2376. Tuition, state resident: full-time $2376. Tuition, nonresident: full-time $6876. Required fees: $1105. *Financial support:* In 2008–09, 7 students received support, including 7 research assistantships with full tuition reimbursements available (averaging $10,100 per year); Federal Work-Study, institutionally sponsored loans, scholarships/grants, unspecified assistantships, and administrative assistantships also available. Support available to part-time students. Financial award application deadline: 5/1; financial award applicants required to submit FAFSA. *Faculty research:* Community development, population and migration trends, environmental sociology, homicide and crime mapping, race and gender in the justice system. *Unit head:* Dr. Kenneth Bolton, Department Head, 985-549-2110, Fax: 985-549-5961, E-mail: kbolton@selu.edu. *Application contact:* Sandra Meyers, Graduate Admissions Analyst, 985-549-2066, Fax: 985-549-5632, E-mail: admissions@selu.edu.

Southern Connecticut State University, School of Graduate Studies, School of Arts and Sciences, Department of Sociology, New Haven, CT 06515-1355. Offers MS. Part-time and evening/weekend programs available. *Degree requirements:* For master's, thesis or alternative. *Entrance requirements:* For master's, interview. Electronic applications accepted.

Southern Illinois University Carbondale, Graduate School, College of Liberal Arts, Department of Sociology, Carbondale, IL 62901-4701. Offers MA, PhD. Part-time programs available. *Degree requirements:* For master's, thesis; for doctorate, thesis/dissertation. *Entrance requirements:* For master's, minimum GPA of 2.7; for doctorate, minimum GPA of 3.25. Additional exam requirements/recommendations for international students: Required—TOEFL. *Faculty research:* Deviance, family, social stratification, social change, theory methodology, culture.

See Close-Up on page 1293.

Southern Illinois University Edwardsville, Graduate Studies and Research, College of Arts and Sciences, Department of Sociology and Criminal Justice Studies, Edwardsville, IL 62026-0001. Offers MA. Part-time programs available. *Faculty:* 14 full-time (8 women). *Students:* 2 full-time (1 woman), 16 part-time (11 women); includes 1 minority (Asian American or Pacific Islander). Average age 26. 28 applicants, 54% accepted. In 2008, 9 master's awarded. *Degree requirements:* For master's, final exam, internship or thesis. *Entrance requirements:* Additional exam requirements/recommendations for international students: Required—TOEFL (minimum score 550 paper-based; 213 computer-based; 79 iBT), IELTS (minimum score 6.5). *Application deadline:* For fall admission, 7/10 for domestic students; for spring admission, 11/15 for domestic students. Application fee: $30. Electronic applications accepted. *Expenses:* Tuition, area resident: Full-time $5838. Tuition, nonresident: full-time $14,596. Required fees: $1525. *Financial support:* In 2008–09, 1 fellowship with full tuition reimbursement (averaging $8,370 per year), 8 teaching assistantships with full tuition reimbursements (averaging $8,064 per year) were awarded; research assistantships with full tuition reimbursements, Federal Work-Study, institutionally sponsored loans, and unspecified assistantships also available. Support available to part-time students. Financial award application deadline: 3/1; financial award applicants required to submit FAFSA. *Unit head:* Dr. David Kauzlarich, Chair, 618-650-3713, E-mail: dkauzla@siue.edu. *Application contact:* Dr. Lisa Welch, Program Director, 618-650-5894, E-mail: lwelch@siue.edu.

Stanford University, School of Humanities and Sciences, Department of Sociology, Stanford, CA 94305-9991. Offers PhD. *Degree requirements:* For doctorate, thesis/dissertation, oral exam. *Entrance requirements:* For doctorate, GRE General Test. Additional exam requirements/recommendations for international students: Required—TOEFL. Electronic applications accepted.

State University of New York at Binghamton, Graduate School, School of Arts and Sciences, Department of Sociology, Binghamton, NY 13902-6000. Offers MA, PhD. *Faculty:* 13 full-time (4 women), 11 part-time/adjunct (4 women). *Students:* 26 full-time (11 women), 51 part-time (22 women); includes 16 minority (5 African Americans, 6 Asian Americans or Pacific Islanders, 5 Hispanic Americans), 34 international. Average age 35. 62 applicants, 47% accepted, 11 enrolled. In 2008, 4 master's, 10 doctorates awarded. Terminal master's awarded for partial completion of doctoral program. *Degree requirements:* For doctorate, thesis/dissertation. *Entrance requirements:* For master's and doctorate, GRE General Test, GRE Subject Test. Additional exam requirements/recommendations for international students: Required—TOEFL. *Application deadline:* For fall admission, 4/15 priority date for domestic students, 1/15 priority date for international students; for spring admission, 11/1 for domestic students, 10/1 priority date for international students. Applications are processed on a rolling basis. Application fee: $60. Electronic applications accepted. *Expenses:* Tuition, area resident:

Sociology

State University of New York at Binghamton *(continued)*
Full-time $6900; part-time $288 per credit. Tuition, state resident: full-time $6900; part-time $288 per credit. Tuition, nonresident: full-time $10,920; part-time $455 per credit. Required fees: $1130. Part-time tuition and fees vary according to course load, program and student level. *Financial support:* In 2008–09, 25 students received support, including 3 fellowships with full tuition reimbursements available (averaging $14,700 per year), 22 teaching assistantships with full tuition reimbursements available (averaging $14,700 per year); research assistantships with full tuition reimbursements available, career-related internships or fieldwork, Federal Work-Study, institutionally sponsored loans, scholarships/grants, health care benefits, and unspecified assistantships also available. Financial award application deadline: 2/15; financial award applicants required to submit FAFSA. *Unit head:* Dr. Richard Laremont, Chairperson, 607-777-4809, E-mail: laremont@binghamton.edu. *Application contact:* Victoria Williams, Recruiting and Admissions Coordinator, 607-777-2151, Fax: 607-777-2501, E-mail: vwilliam@binghamton.edu.

State University of New York Institute of Technology, School of Arts and Sciences, Program in Applied Sociology, Utica, NY 13504-3050. Offers MS. Part-time and evening/weekend programs available. *Degree requirements:* For master's, thesis or project. *Entrance requirements:* For master's, minimum GPA of 3.0, letters of recommendation (3). Additional exam requirements/recommendations for international students: Required—TOEFL (minimum score 550 paper-based; 213 computer-based). *Faculty research:* Family violence, race/class/gender, prisoner re-entry, drug abuse, information technology applications.

Stony Brook University, State University of New York, Graduate School, College of Arts and Sciences, Department of Sociology, Stony Brook, NY 11794. Offers MA, PhD. *Faculty:* 16 full-time (3 women). *Students:* 49 full-time (29 women), 5 part-time (all women); includes 6 minority (2 African Americans, 3 Asian Americans or Pacific Islanders, 1 Hispanic American), 18 international. Average age 33. 83 applicants, 25% accepted. In 2008, 5 master's, 5 doctorates awarded. *Degree requirements:* For doctorate, thesis/dissertation, comprehensive exam or professional papers, field exam, teaching practicum. *Entrance requirements:* For doctorate, GRE General Test, minimum GPA of 3.0. Additional exam requirements/recommendations for international students: Required—TOEFL. *Application deadline:* For fall admission, 1/15 for domestic students. Application fee: $60. *Expenses:* Tuition, area resident: Full-time $7880; part-time $328 per credit hour. Tuition, state resident: full-time $7880; part-time $328 per credit hour. Tuition, nonresident: full-time $13,250; part-time $552 per credit hour. Required fees: $848. *Financial support:* In 2008–09, 4 research assistantships, 37 teaching assistantships were awarded; fellowships also available. *Faculty research:* Deviant behavior, history of sociology/social thought, marriage and family sociology, political sociology. Total annual research expenditures: $58,745. *Unit head:* Dr. Ian Roxborough, Chair, 631-632-7700, Fax: 631-632-8203, E-mail: ian.roxborough@stonybrook.edu. *Application contact:* Dr. Timothy P Moran, Director, 631-632-7700, Fax: 631-632-8203, E-mail: tpmoran@notes.cc.sunysb.edu.

Syracuse University, Graduate School, Maxwell School of Citizenship and Public Affairs, Program in Sociology, Syracuse, NY 13244. Offers MA, PhD. *Degree requirements:* For master's, thesis optional; for doctorate, thesis/dissertation. *Entrance requirements:* For master's and doctorate, GRE General Test. Additional exam requirements/recommendations for international students: Required—TOEFL. Electronic applications accepted. *Faculty research:* Qualitative methods and feminist methods, inequality studies, aging and the life course.

Teachers College, Columbia University, Graduate Faculty of Education, Department of Human Development, Program in Sociology and Education, New York, NY 10027-6696. Offers Ed M, MA, Ed D, PhD. *Faculty:* 3 full-time (1 woman). *Students:* 17 full-time (16 women), 39 part-time (33 women); includes 31 minority (18 African Americans, 6 Asian Americans or Pacific Islanders, 7 Hispanic Americans), 1 international. Average age 29. 70 applicants, 59% accepted, 19 enrolled. In 2008, 10 master's, 3 doctorates awarded. *Degree requirements:* For doctorate, thesis/dissertation. *Entrance requirements:* For master's, GRE (Ed M); for doctorate, GRE. *Application deadline:* For fall admission, 5/15 for domestic students. Application fee: $75. *Expenses:* Tuition: Full-time $26,040; part-time $1085 per credit. Required fees: $720. *Financial support:* Career-related internships or fieldwork, Federal Work-Study, institutionally sponsored loans, and tuition waivers (full and partial) available. Support available to part-time students. Financial award application deadline: 2/1. *Faculty research:* Stratification, race and evaluation, desegregation of schools and communities, quantitative research. *Application contact:* Melba Remice, Assistant Director of Admission, 212-678-4035, Fax: 212-678-4171, E-mail: ms2545@columbia.edu.

Temple University, Graduate School, College of Liberal Arts, Department of Sociology, Philadelphia, PA 19122-6096. Offers MA, PhD. Part-time and evening/weekend programs available. Terminal master's awarded for partial completion of doctoral program. *Degree requirements:* For doctorate, thesis/dissertation. *Entrance requirements:* For master's and doctorate, GRE General Test, minimum GPA of 3.0. Additional exam requirements/recommendations for international students: Required—TOEFL (minimum score 550 paper-based; 213 computer-based; 79 iBT). Electronic applications accepted. *Faculty research:* International development, race-ethnicity-gender inequality, urban structure, political economy.

Texas A&M International University, Office of Graduate Studies and Research, College of Arts and Sciences, Department of Behavioral, Applied Sciences, and Criminal Justice, Laredo, TX 78041-1900. Offers counseling psychology (MACP); criminal justice (MS); psychology (MS); sociology (MA). *Degree requirements:* For master's, thesis (for some programs). *Entrance requirements:* For master's, GRE General Test. Additional exam requirements/recommendations for international students: Required—TOEFL (minimum score 550 paper-based; 213 computer-based).

Texas A&M University, College of Liberal Arts, Department of Sociology, College Station, TX 77843. Offers MS, PhD. *Faculty:* 18. *Students:* 78 full-time (51 women), 20 part-time (13 women); includes 50 minority (19 African Americans, 2 American Indian/Alaska Native, 4 Asian Americans or Pacific Islanders, 25 Hispanic Americans), 11 international. Average age 32. In 2008, 8 master's, 6 doctorates awarded. *Degree requirements:* For master's, thesis or alternative; for doctorate, thesis/dissertation. *Entrance requirements:* For master's and doctorate, GRE General Test. Additional exam requirements/recommendations for international students: Required—TOEFL. *Application deadline:* For fall admission, 1/15 priority date for domestic students; for winter admission, 11/1 priority date for domestic students. Applications are processed on a rolling basis. Application fee: $50 ($75 for international students). Electronic applications accepted. *Expenses:* Tuition, area resident: Full-time $3838.50. Tuition, state resident: full-time $3838.50. Tuition, nonresident: full-time $8897. Required fees: $2359.60. *Financial support:* In 2008–09, fellowships (averaging $12,000 per year), research assistantships (averaging $9,795 per year), teaching assistantships (averaging $9,795 per year) were awarded; institutionally sponsored loans and unspecified assistantships also available. Financial award application deadline: 1/15; financial award applicants required to submit FAFSA. *Faculty research:* Crime, deviance, and law; culture; demography and human ecology; political and economic sociology; racial and ethnic relations; social psychology; Latino sociology; gender; Asian studies. *Unit head:* Mark Fossett, Head, 979-845-5133, Fax: 979-862-4057, E-mail: m-fossett@tamu.edu. *Application contact:* Dr. Kathryn Henderson, Graduate Advisor, 979-845-9706, Fax: 979-862-4057, E-mail: hendrsn@acs.tamu.edu.

See Close-Up on page 1295.

Texas A&M University–Commerce, Graduate School, College of Arts and Sciences, Department of Sociology and Criminal Justice, Commerce, TX 75429-3011. Offers sociology (MA, MS). Part-time programs available. *Degree requirements:* For master's, comprehensive exam, thesis (for some programs). *Entrance requirements:* For master's, GRE General Test. *Faculty research:* Marriage and family, drugs and society, criminal justice, delinquency.

Texas A&M University–Kingsville, College of Graduate Studies, College of Arts and Sciences, Department of Psychology and Sociology, Kingsville, TX 78363. Offers gerontology

(MS); psychology (MA, MS); sociology (MA, MS). Part-time and evening/weekend programs available. *Degree requirements:* For master's, comprehensive exam, thesis or alternative. *Entrance requirements:* For master's, GRE General Test, minimum GPA of 2.5. Additional exam requirements/recommendations for international students: Required—TOEFL. *Faculty research:* Hispanic female voting behavior, attitudes toward criminal justice, immigration of aged into south Texas, folk medicine.

Texas Southern University, Graduate School, College of Liberal Arts and Behavioral Sciences, Department of Sociology, Houston, TX 77004-4584. Offers MA. Part-time and evening/weekend programs available. *Faculty:* 5 full-time (3 women). *Students:* 7 full-time (5 women), 7 part-time (6 women); includes 13 African Americans, 1 Hispanic American. Average age 37. 8 applicants, 100% accepted, 5 enrolled. In 2008, 7 master's awarded. *Degree requirements:* For master's, comprehensive exam, thesis. *Entrance requirements:* For master's, GRE General Test, minimum GPA of 2.5. Additional exam requirements/recommendations for international students: Required—TOEFL. *Application deadline:* For fall admission, 7/15 priority date for domestic students. Applications are processed on a rolling basis. Application fee: $50 ($75 for international students). *Expenses:* Tuition, area resident: Full-time $1912; part-time $96 per credit hour. Tuition, state resident: full-time $1912; part-time $96 per credit hour. Tuition, nonresident: full-time $6302; part-time $343 per credit hour. Required fees: $3542. *Financial support:* Teaching assistantships, career-related internships or fieldwork, Federal Work-Study, and institutionally sponsored loans available. Financial award application deadline: 5/1. *Faculty research:* Sociocultural systems, ethnic and regional studies, community sociology. *Unit head:* Dr. Earl Wright, Head, 713-313-4438. *Application contact:* Dr. Gregory Maddox, Interim Dean of the Graduate School, 713-313-7011 Ext. 4410, Fax: 713-639-1876, E-mail: maddox_gh@tsu.edu.

Texas State University–San Marcos, Graduate School, College of Liberal Arts, Department of Sociology, San Marcos, TX 78666. Offers MA, MS. Part-time and evening/weekend programs available. *Degree requirements:* For master's, comprehensive exam, essay or thesis. *Entrance requirements:* For master's, minimum GPA of 3.0 in last 60 hours of course work, 3 letters of reference, letter of intent, personal interview. Additional exam requirements/recommendations for international students: Required—TOEFL (minimum score 550 paper-based; 213 computer-based). Electronic applications accepted. *Faculty research:* Substance abuse, ethnic and gender inequality, jury behavior, Native American women.

Texas State University–San Marcos, Graduate School, Interdisciplinary Studies Program in Applied Sociology, San Marcos, TX 78666. Offers MAIS. Part-time and evening/weekend programs available. *Degree requirements:* For master's, comprehensive exam. *Entrance requirements:* For master's, 3.0 GPA on last 60 hrs. of undergraduate, 3 letters of reference, letter of intent. Additional exam requirements/recommendations for international students: Required—TOEFL (minimum score 550 paper-based; 213 computer-based). Electronic applications accepted.

Texas Tech University, Graduate School, College of Arts and Sciences, Department of Sociology, Anthropology and Social Work, Lubbock, TX 79409. Offers anthropology (MA); sociology (MA). Part-time programs available. *Faculty:* 14 full-time (5 women). *Students:* 18 full-time (12 women), 12 part-time (4 women); includes 9 minority (1 American Indian/Alaska Native, 2 Asian Americans or Pacific Islanders, 6 Hispanic Americans), 2 international. Average age 30. 21 applicants, 81% accepted, 9 enrolled. In 2008, 8 master's awarded. *Degree requirements:* For master's, one foreign language, thesis or alternative. *Entrance requirements:* For master's, GRE General Test. Additional exam requirements/recommendations for international students: Required—TOEFL (minimum score 550 paper-based; 213 computer-based). *Application deadline:* For fall admission, 3/1 priority date for international students; for spring admission, 11/1 priority date for international students. Applications are processed on a rolling basis. Application fee: $50 ($60 for international students). Electronic applications accepted. *Expenses:* Tuition, area resident: Part-time $194 per credit hour. Tuition, state resident: full-time $4648; part-time $194 per credit hour. Tuition, nonresident: full-time $11,392; part-time $475 per credit hour. Required fees: $2206; $69 per credit hour. $389 per semester. *Financial support:* In 2008–09, 23 students received support, including 3 research assistantships with partial tuition reimbursements available (averaging $10,833 per year), 10 teaching assistantships with partial tuition reimbursements available (averaging $10,850 per year); Federal Work-Study and institutionally sponsored loans also available. Support available to part-time students. Financial award application deadline: 4/15; financial award applicants required to submit FAFSA. *Faculty research:* Sociology theory, research methods, physical and forensic anthropology, Texas archaeology, Mayan archaeology. Total annual research expenditures: $7,284. *Unit head:* Dr. Jeffrey Payne Williams, Chair and Professor, 806-742-2400, Fax: 806-742-1088, E-mail: jeff.williams@ttu.edu. *Application contact:* Dr. Yung-Mei Tsai, Sociology Graduate Program Director, 806-742-2400, Fax: 806-742-1088, E-mail: yung.mei.tsai@ttu.edu.

Texas Woman's University, Graduate School, College of Arts and Sciences, Department of Sociology and Social Work, Denton, TX 76201. Offers sociology (MA, PhD). Evening/weekend programs available. *Faculty:* 7 full-time (4 women), 3 part-time/adjunct (2 women). *Students:* 31 part-time (25 women); includes 13 minority (9 African Americans, 4 Hispanic Americans), 5 international. Average age 37. In 2008, 5 master's, 2 doctorates awarded. Terminal master's awarded for partial completion of doctoral program. *Degree requirements:* For master's, thesis or professional paper; for doctorate, one foreign language, comprehensive exam, thesis/dissertation. *Entrance requirements:* For master's, GRE General Test, minimum GPA of 3.0, 2 letters of reference, 2-3 page statement of intent; for doctorate, GRE General Test, minimum 12 hours course work in sociology (including graduate statistics and research methods), 3 letters of reference, minimum GPA of 3.5, 2-3 page statement of intent. Additional exam requirements/recommendations for international students: Required—TOEFL (minimum score 550 paper-based; 213 computer-based; 79 iBT). *Application deadline:* For fall admission, 4/1 for international students; for spring admission, 8/1 for international students. Applications are processed on a rolling basis. Application fee: $30 ($50 for international students). Electronic applications accepted. *Expenses:* Tuition, state resident: full-time $3564; part-time $198 per semester hour. Tuition, nonresident: full-time $8622; part-time $479 per semester hour. Required fees: $1158; $64 per semester hour. Tuition and fees vary according to course load. *Financial support:* In 2008–09, 11 research assistantships (averaging $10,746 per year), 13 teaching assistantships (averaging $10,746 per year) were awarded; career-related internships or fieldwork, Federal Work-Study, institutionally sponsored loans, scholarships/grants, traineeships, health care benefits, and unspecified assistantships also available. Support available to part-time students. Financial award application deadline: 3/1; financial award applicants required to submit FAFSA. *Faculty research:* Disasters, criminology, immigration, sociological theory, race/ethnicity, culture of breast cancer. *Unit head:* Dr. James Williams, Chair, 940-898-2052, Fax: 940-898-2067, E-mail: jwilliams2@twu.edu. *Application contact:* Samuel Wheeler, Assistant Director of Admissions, 940-898-3188, Fax: 940-898-3081, E-mail: wheelersr@twu.edu.

Tulane University, School of Liberal Arts, Department of Sociology, New Orleans, LA 70118-5669. Offers MA, PhD. Terminal master's awarded for partial completion of doctoral program. *Degree requirements:* For master's, thesis; for doctorate, thesis/dissertation, preliminary exams. *Entrance requirements:* For master's, GRE General Test, minimum B average in undergraduate course work; for doctorate, GRE General Test. Additional exam requirements/recommendations for international students: Required—TOEFL. Electronic applications accepted.

Université de Montréal, Faculty of Arts and Sciences, Department of Sociology, Montréal, QC H3C 3J7, Canada. Offers M Sc, PhD. *Faculty:* 20 full-time (7 women), 11 part-time/adjunct (7 women). *Students:* 40 full-time (20 women), 79 part-time (46 women). 77 applicants, 34% accepted, 20 enrolled. In 2008, 16 master's, 3 doctorates awarded. *Degree requirements:* For master's, thesis; for doctorate, thesis/dissertation, general exam. *Entrance requirements:* For master's, minimum GPA of 3.0; for doctorate, minimum GPA of 3.5, proficiency in French. *Application deadline:* For fall admission, 2/1 priority date for domestic students; for winter admission, 11/1 priority date for domestic students; for spring admission, 2/1 priority date for domestic students. Applications are processed on a rolling basis. Application fee: $100. Electronic applications accepted. *Financial support:* In 2008–09, 75 students received support. Application deadline: 9/15. *Faculty research:* Sociological theory, economy, state and social movements, work, social politics and health. *Unit head:* Andr??e Demers, Director, 514-343-6618, Fax: 514-343-5722, E-mail: andree.demers@umontreal.ca. *Application contact:* Claire Durand, Graduate Studies Chairman (PhD), 514-343-7447, Fax: 514-343-5722, E-mail: claire.durand@umontreal.ca.

Université du Québec à Montréal, Graduate Programs, Program in Social Intervention, Montréal, QC H3C 3P8, Canada. Offers MA. Part-time programs available. *Degree requirements:* For master's, thesis. *Entrance requirements:* For master's, appropriate bachelor's degree or equivalent, proficiency in French.

Université du Québec à Montréal, Graduate Programs, Program in Sociology, Montréal, QC H3C 3P8, Canada. Offers MA, PhD. Part-time programs available. *Degree requirements:* For master's, thesis optional; for doctorate, thesis/dissertation. *Entrance requirements:* For master's, appropriate bachelor's degree or equivalent, proficiency in French; for doctorate, appropriate master's degree or equivalent, proficiency in French.

Université Laval, Faculty of Social Sciences, Department of Sociology, Programs in Sociology, Québec, QC G1K 7P4, Canada. Offers MA, PhD. Terminal master's awarded for partial completion of doctoral program. *Degree requirements:* For master's, thesis; for doctorate, comprehensive exam, thesis/dissertation. *Entrance requirements:* For master's and doctorate, English exam (comprehension of written English), French exam.may be required, knowledge of French. Electronic applications accepted.

University at Albany, State University of New York, College of Arts and Sciences, Department of Communication, Albany, NY 12222-0001. Offers communication (MA); sociology and communication (PhD). Part-time programs available. *Degree requirements:* For master's, comprehensive exam, thesis or alternative; for doctorate, comprehensive exam, thesis/dissertation. *Entrance requirements:* For master's, minimum GPA of 3.0; for doctorate, GRE, minimum GPA of 3.0. Additional exam requirements/recommendations for international students: Required—TOEFL (minimum score 550 paper-based; 213 computer-based). Electronic applications accepted. *Faculty research:* Language and social interaction, campaign communication, media agenda-setting, high-speed management, organizational boundary-spanning.

University at Albany, State University of New York, College of Arts and Sciences, Department of Sociology, Albany, NY 12222-0001. Offers demography (Certificate); sociology (MA, PhD); urban policy (Certificate). Terminal master's awarded for partial completion of doctoral program. *Degree requirements:* For master's, thesis; for doctorate, thesis/dissertation, 2 specialization exams, research tool. *Entrance requirements:* For master's and doctorate, GRE General Test. Additional exam requirements/recommendations for international students: Required—TOEFL (minimum score 213 computer-based). Electronic applications accepted. *Faculty research:* Gender and equality, crime and deviance, aging, work and organizations, social demography.

University at Buffalo, the State University of New York, Graduate School, College of Arts and Sciences, Department of Sociology, Buffalo, NY 14260. Offers MA, PhD. Part-time programs available. Terminal master's awarded for partial completion of doctoral program. *Degree requirements:* For master's, project or thesis; for doctorate, thesis/dissertation, qualifying paper. *Entrance requirements:* For master's and doctorate, GRE General Test. Additional exam requirements/recommendations for international students: Required—TOEFL (minimum score 550 paper-based; 213 computer-based). Electronic applications accepted. *Faculty research:* Theory, culture, sociology of law/criminology, urban sociology, family.

The University of Akron, Graduate School, Buchtel College of Arts and Sciences, Department of Sociology, Akron, OH 44325. Offers MA, PhD. Part-time programs available. Terminal master's awarded for partial completion of doctoral program. *Degree requirements:* For master's, thesis optional, oral defense of thesis, paper or oral exam; for doctorate, one foreign language, comprehensive exam, thesis/dissertation. *Entrance requirements:* For master's, GRE General Test, minimum GPA of 3.0, letters of recommendation; for doctorate, GRE General Test, minimum GPA of 3.5, letters of recommendation. Additional exam requirements/recommendations for international students: Required—TOEFL (minimum score 575 paper-based; 234 computer-based). Electronic applications accepted. *Faculty research:* Medical sociology, inequality, social psychology, criminology, mental health.

The University of Alabama at Birmingham, School of Social and Behavioral Sciences, Department of Sociology, Birmingham, AL 35294. Offers medical sociology (PhD); sociology (MA). Evening/weekend programs available. *Degree requirements:* For master's, thesis or alternative; for doctorate, thesis/dissertation. *Entrance requirements:* For master's, GRE General Test or MAT; for doctorate, GRE General Test. Electronic applications accepted. *Faculty research:* Gerontology, applied sociology, urban sociology.

University of Alberta, Faculty of Graduate Studies and Research, Department of Sociology, Edmonton, AB T6G 2E1, Canada. Offers criminal justice (MA); demography (MA, PhD); sociology (MA, PhD). Part-time programs available. *Degree requirements:* For master's, thesis (for some programs); for doctorate, thesis/dissertation. *Faculty research:* Criminology, knowledge and culture, methods and theory, population studies, stratification.

The University of Arizona, Graduate College, College of Social and Behavioral Sciences, Department of Sociology, Tucson, AZ 85721. Offers MA, PhD. *Degree requirements:* For master's, publishable paper/oral; for doctorate, thesis/dissertation, 2 preliminary exams. *Entrance requirements:* For master's, GRE, minimum GPA of 3.0, 3 letters of recommendation, statement of purpose, writing sample. Additional exam requirements/recommendations for international students: Required—TOEFL (minimum score 630 paper-based). Electronic applications accepted. *Faculty research:* Organizations, social psychology, social movement, stratification, religion.

University of Arkansas, Graduate School, J. William Fulbright College of Arts and Sciences, Department of Sociology, Fayetteville, AR 72701-1201. Offers MA. Part-time programs available. *Degree requirements:* For master's, thesis.

The University of British Columbia, Faculty of Arts, Department of Sociology, Vancouver, BC V6T 1Z1, Canada. Offers MA, PhD. *Degree requirements:* For master's, thesis; for doctorate, comprehensive exam, thesis/dissertation. *Entrance requirements:* For master's, BA in sociology or equivalent with minimum B+ average in upper level courses; for doctorate, master's degree in sociology or equivalent. Additional exam requirements/recommendations for international students: Required—TOEFL (minimum score 600 paper-based; 250 computer-based). Electronic applications accepted. *Faculty research:* Social and cultural theories and methods; gender, race, class and sexuality; environment economy and development politics; law and social movements.

University of Calgary, Faculty of Graduate Studies, Faculty of Social Sciences, Department of Sociology, Calgary, AB T2N 1N4, Canada. Offers MA, PhD. Terminal master's awarded for partial completion of doctoral program. *Degree requirements:* For master's, thesis, prospectus; for doctorate, comprehensive exam, thesis/dissertation, oral and written candidacy exams, prospectus, qualifying paper. *Entrance requirements:* For master's, minimum GPA of 3.2; for doctorate, minimum GPA of 3.5. Additional exam requirements/recommendations for international students: Required—TOEFL or IELTS. Electronic applications accepted. *Faculty research:* Deviance, gender, medical, religion, ethnicity.

University of California, Berkeley, Graduate Division, College of Letters and Science, Department of Sociology, Berkeley, CA 94720-1500. Offers PhD. *Degree requirements:* For doctorate, thesis/dissertation, qualifying exam. *Entrance requirements:* For doctorate, GRE General Test, minimum GPA of 3.0, sample of academic written work, 3 letters of recommendation. Additional exam requirements/recommendations for international students:

Required—TOEFL (paper-based 570; computer-based 230) or IELTS. Electronic applications accepted. *Faculty research:* Race, gender, political, stratification theory.

University of California, Berkeley, Graduate Division, Group in Sociology and Demography, Berkeley, CA 94720-1500. Offers PhD. *Degree requirements:* For doctorate, thesis/dissertation, qualifying exam. *Entrance requirements:* For doctorate, GRE General Test, minimum GPA of 3.0, 3 letters of recommendation.

University of California, Berkeley, Graduate Division, School of Public Health, Program in Health and Social Behavior, Berkeley, CA 94720-1500. Offers MPH. *Accreditation:* CEPH. *Entrance requirements:* For master's, GRE General Test, minimum GPA of 3.0.

University of California, Davis, Graduate Studies, Program in Sociology, Davis, CA 95616. Offers MA, PhD. Terminal master's awarded for partial completion of doctoral program. *Degree requirements:* For master's, written exam; for doctorate, thesis/dissertation, professional paper, qualifying exam. *Entrance requirements:* For master's and doctorate, GRE General Test, minimum GPA of 3.0, writing sample. Additional exam requirements/recommendations for international students: Required—TOEFL (minimum score 550 paper-based; 213 computer-based). Electronic applications accepted. *Faculty research:* Collective behavior, social movements, comparative sociology, historical sociology, culture development, inequality.

University of California, Irvine, Office of Graduate Studies, School of Social Sciences, Department of Sociology, Irvine, CA 92697. Offers social networks (PhD); social networks-social science (MA); social science (MA, PhD); sociology and social relations-social science (MA, PhD). *Degree requirements:* For doctorate, thesis/dissertation. *Entrance requirements:* For master's and doctorate, GRE General Test, minimum GPA of 3.0. Electronic applications accepted. *Faculty research:* Cognitive anthropology, sociology of culture, social structure, family and gender.

University of California, Los Angeles, Graduate Division, College of Letters and Science, Department of Sociology, Los Angeles, CA 90095. Offers MA, PhD. *Students:* 104 full-time (62 women); includes 30 minority (3 African Americans, 12 Asian Americans or Pacific Islanders, 15 Hispanic Americans), 16 international. Average age 28. 242 applicants, 23% accepted, 21 enrolled. In 2008, 16 master's, 22 doctorates awarded. Terminal master's awarded for partial completion of doctoral program. *Degree requirements:* For master's, thesis or alternative, final paper; for doctorate, thesis/dissertation, oral and written qualifying exams. *Entrance requirements:* For master's, GRE General Test, minimum GPA of 3.0, sample of work, degree objective of Ph.D; for doctorate, GRE General Test, minimum undergraduate GPA of 3.0, sample of work. Additional exam requirements/recommendations for international students: Required—TOEFL. *Application deadline:* For fall admission, 12/1 for domestic and international students. Application fee: $60 ($80 for international students). Electronic applications accepted. *Expenses:* Tuition, nonresident: full-time $14,694. Required fees: $9669.50. Full-time tuition and fees vary according to course load, degree level, program and student level. *Financial support:* In 2008–09, 113 fellowships with full and partial tuition reimbursements, 40 research assistantships with full and partial tuition reimbursements, 52 teaching assistantships with full and partial tuition reimbursements were awarded; Federal Work-Study, institutionally sponsored loans, scholarships/grants, health care benefits, tuition waivers (full and partial), and unspecified assistantships also available. Financial award application deadline: 3/1; financial award applicants required to submit FAFSA. *Unit head:* Dr. Roy William, Chair, 310-825-3633. *Application contact:* Departmental Office, 310-825-1026, E-mail: dietrich@soc.ucla.edu.

University of California, Riverside, Graduate Division, Department of Sociology, Riverside, CA 92521-0102. Offers MA, PhD. *Faculty:* 22 full-time (7 women). *Students:* 66 full-time (35 women); includes 19 minority (2 African Americans, 1 American Indian/Alaska Native, 8 Asian Americans or Pacific Islanders, 8 Hispanic Americans), 4 international. Average age 32. 68 applicants, 38% accepted, 11 enrolled. In 2008, 9 master's, 5 doctorates awarded. *Degree requirements:* For doctorate, thesis/dissertation, 1 quarter of teaching experience, professional paper. *Entrance requirements:* For doctorate, GRE General Test, minimum GPA of 3.2. Additional exam requirements/recommendations for international students: Required—TOEFL (minimum score 550 paper-based; 213 computer-based; 80 iBT). *Application deadline:* For fall admission, 5/1 for domestic students, 2/1 for international students. Application fee: $70 ($85 for international students). Electronic applications accepted. *Expenses:* Tuition, nonresident: full-time $4898. Required fees: $10,362. *Financial support:* In 2008–09, 17 students received support, including fellowships with tuition reimbursements available (averaging $12,000 per year); teaching assistantships with partial tuition reimbursements available (averaging $16,500 per year); research assistantships, career-related internships or fieldwork, Federal Work-Study, institutionally sponsored loans, health care benefits, and tuition waivers (full and partial) also available. Financial award application deadline: 2/1; financial award applicants required to submit FAFSA. *Faculty research:* Crime/deviance, race/ethnic relations, family/gender, political economy/globalization, theory. *Application contact:* Anna M. Wire, Graduate Program Assistant, 951-827-5445, Fax: 951-827-3330, E-mail: socgrad@ucr.edu.

University of California, San Diego, Office of Graduate Studies, Department of Sociology, La Jolla, CA 92093. Offers science studies (PhD); sociology (PhD). *Degree requirements:* For doctorate, thesis/dissertation. *Entrance requirements:* For doctorate, GRE General Test. Electronic applications accepted.

University of California, San Diego, Office of Graduate Studies, Interdisciplinary Program in Cognitive Science, La Jolla, CA 92093. Offers cognitive science/anthropology (PhD); cognitive science/communication (PhD); cognitive science/computer science and engineering (PhD); cognitive science/linguistics (PhD); cognitive science/neuroscience (PhD); cognitive science/philosophy (PhD); cognitive science/psychology (PhD); cognitive science/sociology (PhD). Admissions offered through affiliated departments. *Degree requirements:* For doctorate, thesis/dissertation. *Entrance requirements:* For doctorate, GRE General Test, acceptance into one of the 8 participating departments. *Faculty research:* Language and cognition, philosophy of mind, visual perception, biological anthropology, sociolinguistics.

University of California, San Francisco, Graduate Division, School of Nursing, Department of Social and Behavioral Sciences, San Francisco, CA 94143. Offers sociology (PhD). *Degree requirements:* For doctorate, one foreign language, thesis/dissertation. *Entrance requirements:* For doctorate, GRE General Test. *Faculty research:* Urban social relations; sociology of women's role in healing; sociology of work, occupations, and professions.

University of California, Santa Barbara, Graduate Division, College of Letters and Sciences, Division of Social Sciences, Department of Sociology, Santa Barbara, CA 93106-9430. Offers global studies (PhD); human development (PhD); language, interaction and social organization (PhD); technology and society (PhD); women's studies (PhD); MA/PhD. *Faculty:* 35 full-time (14 women). *Students:* 77 full-time (50 women). Average age 30. 155 applicants, 9% accepted, 8 enrolled. In 2008, 10 doctorates awarded. Terminal master's awarded for partial completion of doctoral program. *Degree requirements:* For doctorate, comprehensive exam, thesis/dissertation. *Entrance requirements:* For doctorate, GRE General Test, sample of written work, 3 letters of recommendation, statement of purpose, personal achievements/contributions statement, resumé/curriculum vitae, transcripts for post-secondary institutions attended. Additional exam requirements/recommendations for international students: Required—TOEFL (minimum score 550 paper-based; 213 computer-based; 80 iBT), TOEFL or IELTS. *Application deadline:* For fall admission, 12/10 for domestic students. Application fee: $70 ($90 for international students). Electronic applications accepted. *Expenses:* Tuition, nonresident: full-time $25,149. Required fees: $10,143. Full-time tuition and fees vary according to campus/location, reciprocity agreements and student level. *Financial support:* In 2008–09, 69 students received support, including 50 fellowships with full tuition reimbursements available (averaging $7,900 per year), 6 research assistantships with full and partial tuition reimbursements available (averaging $2,600 per year), 53 teaching assistantships with partial tuition reimbursements available (averaging $9,200 per year); career-related internships or fieldwork, Federal Work-Study, institutionally sponsored loans, scholarships/grants, health care benefits, and unspecified

Sociology

University of California, Santa Barbara (continued)
assistantships also available. Financial award applicants required to submit FAFSA. *Faculty research:* Conversation analysis, social movements, human sexuality, urban sociology, race and ethnic relations. *Unit head:* Prof. Verta Taylor, Chair, 805-893-3118, Fax: 805-893-3324, E-mail: grad-soc@soc.ucsb.edu. *Application contact:* Ra Thea, Graduate Staff Advisor, 805-893-3328, Fax: 805-893-3324, E-mail: grad-soc@soc.ucsb.edu.

University of California, Santa Cruz, Division of Graduate Studies, Division of Social Sciences, Program in Sociology, Santa Cruz, CA 95064. Offers PhD. *Degree requirements:* For doctorate, thesis/dissertation, qualifying exam. *Entrance requirements:* For doctorate, GRE General Test. *Faculty research:* Marxism, feminism, ethnic studies, social theory.

University of Central Florida, College of Sciences, Department of Sociology, Orlando, FL 32816. Offers applied sociology (MA); domestic violence (MA); Maya studies (Certificate); sociology (PhD). Part-time and evening/weekend programs available. *Faculty:* 17 full-time (11 women), 4 part-time/adjunct (1 woman). *Students:* 44 full-time (35 women), 31 part-time (21 women); includes 19 minority (9 African Americans, 10 Hispanic Americans). In 2008, 4 master's, 1 doctorate, 3 other advanced degrees awarded. *Degree requirements:* For master's, comprehensive written exam or thesis. *Entrance requirements:* For master's, GRE General Test, minimum GPA of 3.0 in last 60 hours of course work. Additional exam requirements/recommendations for international students: Required—TOEFL. *Application deadline:* For fall admission, 7/15 for domestic students; for spring admission, 12/1 for domestic students. Application fee: $30. Electronic applications accepted. *Expenses:* Tuition, area resident: Full-time $6816; part-time $284 per credit. Tuition, state resident: full-time $6816; part-time $1076 per credit. Tuition, nonresident: full-time $25,824. Required fees: $216; $9 per credit. *Financial support:* In 2008–09, 7 fellowships with partial tuition reimbursements (averaging $10,800 per year), 8 research assistantships with partial tuition reimbursements (averaging $10,400 per year), 25 teaching assistantships with partial tuition reimbursements (averaging $9,600 per year) were awarded; career-related internships or fieldwork, Federal Work-Study, institutionally sponsored loans, tuition waivers (partial), and unspecified assistantships also available. Financial award application deadline: 3/1; financial award applicants required to submit FAFSA. *Faculty research:* Religious subcultures, attitudes toward abortion, population, sport research, stratification. *Unit head:* Dr. Jay Corzine, Chair, 407-823-2227, Fax: 407-823-5156, E-mail: hcorzine@mail.ucf.edu. *Application contact:* Dr. Jay Corzine, Chair, 407-823-2227, Fax: 407-823-5156, E-mail: hcorzine@mail.ucf.edu.

University of Central Missouri, The Graduate School, College of Health and Human Services, Department of Sociology and Social Work, Warrensburg, MO 64093. Offers social gerontology (MS); sociology (MA). Part-time programs available. *Degree requirements:* For master's, comprehensive exam. *Entrance requirements:* For master's, minimum GPA of 2.5. Additional exam requirements/recommendations for international students: Required—TOEFL (minimum score 500 paper-based; 173 computer-based). *Faculty research:* Suicide, end of life decision making, aging/gerontology, race/ethic relations, religion.

University of Chicago, Division of Social Sciences, Department of Sociology, Chicago, IL 60637-1513. Offers PhD. *Degree requirements:* For doctorate, one foreign language, thesis/dissertation, 2 field exams. *Entrance requirements:* For doctorate, GRE General Test. Additional exam requirements/recommendations for international students: Required—TOEFL, IELTS (minimum score 7). Electronic applications accepted.

University of Cincinnati, Graduate School, McMicken College of Arts and Sciences, Department of Sociology, Cincinnati, OH 45221. Offers MA, PhD. Part-time programs available. *Degree requirements:* For master's, thesis; for doctorate, thesis/dissertation. *Entrance requirements:* For master's and doctorate, GRE General Test. Additional exam requirements/recommendations for international students: Required—TOEFL. Electronic applications accepted. *Faculty research:* Work and family, race and urban, health and medicine, social psychology.

University of Colorado at Boulder, Graduate School, College of Arts and Sciences, Department of Sociology, Boulder, CO 80309. Offers PhD. *Degree requirements:* For doctorate, comprehensive exam, thesis/dissertation. *Entrance requirements:* For doctorate, GRE General Test, GRE Subject Test, minimum undergraduate GPA of 2.75. *Faculty research:* Criminology, social control, law delinquency and deviance, population, health studies, gender relations, social stratification, race relations, the environment, institutions and international systems.

University of Colorado at Colorado Springs, Graduate School, College of Letters, Arts and Sciences, Department of Sociology, Colorado Springs, CO 80933-7150. Offers MA. Part-time programs available. *Faculty:* 8 full-time (4 women). *Students:* 19 full-time (14 women), 11 part-time (7 women); includes 9 minority (3 African Americans, 1 Asian American or Pacific Islander, 5 Hispanic Americans). Average age 35. 14 applicants, 100% accepted, 13 enrolled. In 2008, 12 master's awarded. *Degree requirements:* For master's, thesis optional. *Entrance requirements:* For master's, GRE, minimum GPA of 2.75. *Application deadline:* For fall admission, 7/1 priority date for domestic students; for spring admission, 11/1 for domestic students. Applications are processed on a rolling basis. Application fee: $60 ($75 for international students). *Financial support:* Teaching assistantships, career-related internships or fieldwork, Federal Work-Study, and institutionally sponsored loans available. *Faculty research:* Environmental justice, gender, race and ethnicity, sport and popular culture, youth and deviant behavior. *Unit head:* Dr. Lynda Dickson, Chair, 719-255-4142, Fax: 719-255-4450, E-mail: ldickson@uccs.edu. *Application contact:* Rosemary Kelbel, Program Assistant, 719-255-4153, Fax: 719-255-4450, E-mail: rkelbel@uccs.edu.

University of Colorado Denver, College of Liberal Arts and Sciences, Department of Sociology, Denver, CO 80217-3364. Offers MA. Part-time and evening/weekend programs available. *Degree requirements:* For master's, thesis or alternative. *Entrance requirements:* For master's, GRE. Electronic applications accepted.

University of Connecticut, Graduate School, College of Liberal Arts and Sciences, Department of Sociology, Field of Sociology, Storrs, CT 06269. Offers MA, PhD. Terminal master's awarded for partial completion of doctoral program. *Degree requirements:* For master's, comprehensive exam; for doctorate, thesis/dissertation, 2 field exams. *Entrance requirements:* For master's and doctorate, GRE General Test. Additional exam requirements/recommendations for international students: Required—TOEFL (minimum score 550 paper-based; 213 computer-based). Electronic applications accepted. *Expenses:* Contact institution.

University of Delaware, College of Arts and Sciences, Department of Sociology and Criminology, Newark, DE 19716. Offers criminology (MA, PhD); sociology (MA, PhD). *Degree requirements:* For master's, thesis; for doctorate, comprehensive exam, thesis/dissertation. *Entrance requirements:* For master's and doctorate, GRE, 3 letters of recommendation. Additional exam requirements/recommendations for international students: Required—TOEFL. Electronic applications accepted. *Faculty research:* Sex and gender, criminology/deviance, theory, methods, collective behavior.

University of Florida, Graduate School, College of Liberal Arts and Sciences, Department of Sociology, Gainesville, FL 32611. Offers MA, PhD, JD/MA. *Degree requirements:* For master's, thesis optional; for doctorate, thesis/dissertation. *Entrance requirements:* For master's and doctorate, GRE General Test, minimum GPA of 3.0. Additional exam requirements/recommendations for international students: Required—TOEFL (minimum score 550 paper-based; 213 computer-based). Electronic applications accepted. *Faculty research:* Sociology of the family, social gerontology, criminology and deviance, race ethnicity.

University of Georgia, Graduate School, College of Arts and Sciences, Department of Sociology, Athens, GA 30602. Offers MA, PhD. *Degree requirements:* For master's, thesis; for doctorate, thesis/dissertation. *Entrance requirements:* For master's and doctorate, GRE General Test. Additional exam requirements/recommendations for international students: Required—TOEFL. Electronic applications accepted. *Faculty research:* Race, deviance, gender, culture.

University of Guelph, Graduate Program Services, College of Social and Applied Human Sciences, Department of Sociology and Anthropology, Guelph, ON N1G 2W1, Canada. Offers anthropology (MA); crime and criminal justice policy (MA); sociology (MA, PhD). *Degree requirements:* For master's, thesis or major paper; for doctorate, comprehensive exam, thesis/dissertation. *Entrance requirements:* For master's, minimum B+ average during previous 2 years of course work, honors BA or equivalent; for doctorate, must have an MA in Sociology, must have 80% or higher in graduate level studies. Additional exam requirements/recommendations for international students: Required—TOEFL (minimum score 550 paper-based; 213 computer-based; 89 iBT), IELTS (minimum score 6.5), TOEFL or IELTS. Electronic applications accepted. *Faculty research:* Rural and development sociology; education, employment, and the workplace; race, ethnicity, and native studies; criminology and deviance; social psychology.

University of Hawaii at Manoa, Graduate Division, Colleges of Arts and Sciences, College of Social Sciences, Department of Sociology, Honolulu, HI 96822. Offers population studies (Graduate Certificate); sociology (MA, PhD). Part-time programs available. *Degree requirements:* For master's, thesis optional; for doctorate, comprehensive exam, thesis/dissertation. *Entrance requirements:* For master's and doctorate, GRE General Test. Additional exam requirements/recommendations for international students: Required—TOEFL (minimum score 500 paper-based; 173 computer-based; 61 iBT), IELTS (minimum score 5). *Faculty research:* Comparative sociology of Asia; population studies; crime, law, and deviance; health; aging and medical sociology.

University of Houston, College of Liberal Arts and Social Sciences, Department of Sociology, Houston, TX 77204. Offers MA. Part-time and evening/weekend programs available. *Faculty:* 8 full-time (4 women). *Students:* 22 full-time (17 women), 13 part-time (8 women); includes 14 minority (4 African Americans, 2 Asian Americans or Pacific Islanders, 8 Hispanic Americans), 7 international. Average age 30. 16 applicants, 100% accepted, 11 enrolled. In 2008, 4 master's awarded. *Degree requirements:* For master's, thesis. *Entrance requirements:* For master's, GRE General Test, minimum GPA of 3.0. Additional exam requirements/recommendations for international students: Required—TOEFL. *Application deadline:* For fall admission, 8/1 for domestic students; for spring admission, 12/1 for domestic students. Applications are processed on a rolling basis. Application fee: $0 ($75 for international students). *Expenses:* Tuition, state resident: full-time $5164; part-time $287 per credit. Tuition, nonresident: full-time $10,222; part-time $568 per credit. *Financial support:* In 2008–09, 3 fellowships with full tuition reimbursements (averaging $9,050 per year), 11 teaching assistantships with tuition reimbursements (averaging $9,050 per year) were awarded; career-related internships or fieldwork, Federal Work-Study, institutionally sponsored loans, scholarships/grants, health care benefits, and unspecified assistantships also available. Support available to part-time students. Financial award application deadline: 2/1; financial award applicants required to submit FAFSA. *Faculty research:* Gender, immigration, urban studies, religion, race/ethnicity, social psychology, medical sociology. *Unit head:* Dr. Nestor Rodriguez, Chairperson, 713-743-3953, Fax: 713-743-3943, E-mail: nrodriguez@uh.edu. *Application contact:* Dr. Joseph A. Kotarba, Director of Graduate Studies, 713-743-3954, Fax: 713-743-3943, E-mail: jkotarba@uh.edu.

University of Houston–Clear Lake, School of Human Sciences and Humanities, Programs in Human Sciences, Houston, TX 77058-1098. Offers behavioral sciences (MA), including criminology, cross cultural studies, general psychology, sociology; clinical psychology (MA); criminology (MA); cross cultural studies (MA); family therapy (MA); fitness and human performance (MA); school psychology (MA). *Accreditation:* AAMFT/COAMFTE. Part-time and evening/weekend programs available. Postbaccalaureate distance learning degree programs offered (minimal on-campus study). *Degree requirements:* For master's, thesis or alternative. *Entrance requirements:* For master's, GRE General Test. Additional exam requirements/recommendations for international students: Required—TOEFL (minimum score 550 paper-based; 213 computer-based). Electronic applications accepted. *Faculty research:* Smoking cessation, adolescent sexuality, white collar crime, serial murder, human factors/human computer interaction.

University of Illinois at Chicago, Graduate College, College of Liberal Arts and Sciences, Department of Sociology, Chicago, IL 60607-7128. Offers MA, PhD. Terminal master's awarded for partial completion of doctoral program. *Degree requirements:* For master's, comprehensive exam, thesis; for doctorate, thesis/dissertation, qualifying exam. *Entrance requirements:* For master's and doctorate, GRE General Test, minimum GPA of 3.0. Additional exam requirements/recommendations for international students: Required—TOEFL. Electronic applications accepted. *Faculty research:* Social psychology, social organization, applied sociology, demography and human ecology.

University of Illinois at Urbana–Champaign, Graduate College, College of Liberal Arts and Sciences, Department of Sociology, Champaign, IL 61820. Offers MA, PhD. *Faculty:* 13 full-time (7 women). *Students:* 24 full-time (14 women), 17 part-time (8 women); includes 6 minority (3 African Americans, 2 Asian Americans or Pacific Islanders, 1 Hispanic American), 15 international. 36 applicants, 11% accepted, 3 enrolled. In 2008, 3 master's, 4 doctorates awarded. *Entrance requirements:* For doctorate, GRE, minimum GPA of 3.0; writing sample. Additional exam requirements/recommendations for international students: Required—TOEFL (minimum score 79 iBT). *Application deadline:* Applications are processed on a rolling basis. Application fee: $60 ($75 for international students). Electronic applications accepted. *Financial support:* In 2008–09, 11 fellowships, 6 research assistantships, 25 teaching assistantships were awarded; tuition waivers (full and partial) also available. *Unit head:* Anna-Maria Marshall, Acting Head, 217-333-1950, Fax: 217-333-5225, E-mail: amarshll@illinois.edu. *Application contact:* Shari Day, Office Manager, 217-244-1809, Fax: 217-333-5225, E-mail: shariday@illinois.edu.

University of Indianapolis, Graduate Programs, College of Arts and Sciences, Department of Social Sciences, Indianapolis, IN 46227-3697. Offers applied sociology (MA). Part-time and evening/weekend programs available. *Faculty:* 4 full-time (1 woman), 2 part-time/adjunct (1 woman). *Students:* 3 full-time (all women), 11 part-time (4 women); includes 4 minority (all African Americans), 4 international. Average age 34. *Degree requirements:* For master's, thesis optional. *Entrance requirements:* For master's, GRE Subject Test, minimum GPA of 3.0, letter of intent, 3 letters of recommendation. Additional exam requirements/recommendations for international students: Required—TOEFL (minimum score 550 paper-based; 213 computer-based). *Application deadline:* Applications are processed on a rolling basis. Application fee: $30. Electronic applications accepted. *Financial support:* Federal Work-Study available. Financial award application deadline: 5/1; financial award applicants required to submit FAFSA. *Unit head:* Dr. James Pennell, Chair, 317-788-3535, Fax: 317-788-3480, E-mail: jpennell@uindy.edu. *Application contact:* Dr. James Pennell, Chair, 317-788-3535, Fax: 317-788-3480, E-mail: jpennell@uindy.edu.

The University of Iowa, Graduate College, College of Liberal Arts and Sciences, Department of Sociology, Iowa City, IA 52242-1316. Offers MA, PhD, JD/MA. *Degree requirements:* For master's, thesis optional, exam; for doctorate, comprehensive exam, thesis/dissertation. *Entrance requirements:* For master's and doctorate, GRE General Test, minimum GPA of 3.0. Additional exam requirements/recommendations for international students: Required—TOEFL (minimum score 550 paper-based; 213 computer-based; 81 iBT). Electronic applications accepted.

The University of Kansas, Graduate Studies, College of Liberal Arts and Sciences, Department of Sociology, Lawrence, KS 66045. Offers MA, PhD. Part-time programs available. *Faculty:* 23. *Students:* 33 full-time (20 women), 7 part-time (2 women); includes 2 minority (1 Asian American or Pacific Islander, 1 Hispanic American), 5 international. Average age 31. 36 applicants, 61% accepted, 8 enrolled. In 2008, 3 master's, 1 doctorate awarded. *Degree requirements:* For master's, thesis; for doctorate, comprehensive exam, thesis/dissertation. *Entrance requirements:* For master's and doctorate, GRE General Test. Additional exam requirements/recommendations for international students: Required—TOEFL, TOEFL (paper-based 530; computer-based 200) or IELTS (score 6). *Application deadline:* For fall admission,

12/15 priority date for domestic and international students; for spring admission, 10/15 for domestic and international students. Applications are processed on a rolling basis. Application fee: $45 ($55 for international students). Electronic applications accepted. *Expenses:* Tuition, area resident: Full-time $6122; part-time $255.10 per credit hour. Tuition, state resident: full-time $6122; part-time $255.10 per credit hour. Tuition, nonresident: full-time $14,629; part-time $609.55 per credit hour. Required fees: $847; $70.56 per credit hour. Tuition and fees vary according to course load and program. *Financial support:* Fellowships with full tuition reimbursements, research assistantships with full tuition reimbursements, teaching assistantships with full and partial tuition reimbursements, unspecified assistantships available. Financial award application deadline: 12/15. *Faculty research:* Comparative/historical sociology, sex and gender, social movements, social theory, medical sociology. *Unit head:* William G. Staples, Chair, 785-864-4111, Fax: 785-864-5280. *Application contact:* Eric Hanley, Graduate Director, 785-864-4111, Fax: 785-864-5280, E-mail: hanley@ku.edu.

University of Kentucky, Graduate School, College of Arts and Sciences, Program in Sociology, Lexington, KY 40506-0032. Offers MA, PhD. Part-time programs available. *Degree requirements:* For master's, comprehensive exam, thesis optional; for doctorate, comprehensive exam, thesis/dissertation. *Entrance requirements:* For master's, GRE General Test, minimum undergraduate GPA of 2.75; for doctorate, GRE General Test, minimum graduate GPA of 3.0. Additional exam requirements/recommendations for international students: Required—TOEFL (minimum score 550 paper-based; 213 computer-based). Electronic applications accepted. *Faculty research:* Work organizations, social inequalities, rural sociology, criminology/deviance, medical sociology.

University of Lethbridge, School of Graduate Studies, Lethbridge, AB T1K 3M4, Canada. Offers accounting (MScM); addictions counseling (M Sc); agricultural biotechnology (M Sc); agricultural studies (M Sc, MA); anthropology (MA); archaeology (MA); art (MA); biochemistry (M Sc); biological sciences (M Sc); biomolecular science (PhD); biosystems and biodiversity (PhD); Canadian studies (MA); chemistry (M Sc); computer science (M Sc); computer science and geographical information science (M Sc); counseling psychology (M Ed); dramatic arts (MA); earth, space, and physical science (PhD); economics (MA); educational leadership (M Ed); English (MA); environmental science (M Sc); evolution and behavior (PhD); exercise science (M Sc); finance (MScM); French (MA); French/German (MA); French/Spanish (MA); general education (M Ed); general management (MScM); geography (M Sc, MA); German (MA); health sciences (M Sc, MA); history (MA); human resource management and labour relations (MScM); individualized multidisciplinary (M Sc, MA); information systems (MScM); international management (MScM); kinesiology (M Sc, MA); management (M Sc, MA); marketing (MScM); mathematics (M Sc); music (MA); Native American studies (MA); neuroscience (M Sc, PhD); new media (MA); nursing (M Sc); philosophy (MA); physics (M Sc); policy and strategy (MScM); political science (MA); psychology (M Sc, MA); religious studies (MA); sociology (MA); theoretical and computational science (PhD); urban and regional studies (MA). Part-time and evening/weekend programs available. *Degree requirements:* For doctorate, comprehensive exam, thesis/dissertation. *Entrance requirements:* For master's, GMAT (M Sc in management), bachelor's degree in related field, minimum GPA of 3.0 during previous 20 graded semester courses, 2 years teaching or related experience (M Ed); for doctorate, master's degree, minimum graduate GPA of 3.5. Additional exam requirements/recommendations for international students: Required—TOEFL. *Faculty research:* Movement and brain plasticity, gibberellin physiology, photosynthesis, carbon cycling, molecular properties of main-group ring components.

University of Louisville, Graduate School, College of Arts and Sciences, Department of Sociology, Louisville, KY 40292. Offers MA. Part-time and evening/weekend programs available. *Faculty:* 13 full-time (4 women). *Students:* 14 full-time (9 women), 3 part-time (1 woman); includes 3 African Americans, 1 international. Average age 29. In 2008, 5 master's awarded. *Degree requirements:* For master's, thesis or alternative, thesis or practicum. *Entrance requirements:* For master's, GRE General Test. Additional exam requirements/recommendations for international students: Required—TOEFL. *Application deadline:* For fall admission, 6/1 priority date for domestic students, 6/1 for international students; for spring admission, 10/1 priority date for domestic students, 10/1 for international students. Applications are processed on a rolling basis. Application fee: $50. Electronic applications accepted. *Financial support:* In 2008–09, 4 students received support, including 4 teaching assistantships with full tuition reimbursements available (averaging $12,000 per year). *Faculty research:* Crime/corrections, gender/sexuality, family, education. *Unit head:* Dr. L. Allen Furr, Chair, 502-852-8026, Fax: 502-852-0099, E-mail: allenfur@louisville.edu. *Application contact:* Libby Leggett, Director, Graduate Admissions, 502-852-3101, Fax: 502-852-6536, E-mail: gradadm@louisville.edu.

University of Manitoba, Faculty of Graduate Studies, Faculty of Arts, Department of Sociology, Winnipeg, MB R3T 2N2, Canada. Offers MA, PhD. *Degree requirements:* For master's, thesis.

University of Maryland, Baltimore County, Graduate School, College of Arts, Humanities and Social Sciences, Department of Sociology and Anthropology, Baltimore, MD 21250. Offers applied sociology (MA, Postbaccalaureate Certificate), including applied sociology (MA), nonprofit sector (Postbaccalaureate Certificate). Part-time and evening/weekend programs available. *Faculty:* 18 full-time (11 women), 3 part-time/adjunct (all women). *Students:* 25 full-time (21 women), 39 part-time (29 women); includes 23 minority (15 African Americans, 1 American Indian/Alaska Native, 6 Asian Americans or Pacific Islanders, 1 Hispanic American), 1 international. Average age 32. 27 applicants, 93% accepted, 19 enrolled. In 2008, 26 master's awarded. *Degree requirements:* For master's, thesis or alternative. *Entrance requirements:* For master's, minimum GPA of 3.0, undergrad statistics course. Additional exam requirements/recommendations for international students: Required—TOEFL. *Application deadline:* For fall admission, 7/31 for domestic students; for spring admission, 12/31 for domestic students. Applications are processed on a rolling basis. Application fee: $70. Electronic applications accepted. *Financial support:* In 2008–09, 11 students received support, including 2 research assistantships with full and partial tuition reimbursements available (averaging $12,500 per year), 5 teaching assistantships with full and partial tuition reimbursements available (averaging $12,500 per year); scholarships/grants, health care benefits, unspecified assistantships, and tuition remission also available. Financial award application deadline: 2/14; financial award applicants required to submit FAFSA. *Faculty research:* Sociology of aging, medical sociology, migration. *Unit head:* Dr. James E. Trela, Chairperson, 410-455-2076, Fax: 410-455-1154, E-mail: trela@umbc.edu. *Application contact:* Dr. William G. Rothstein, Director, 410-455-2078, Fax: 410-455-1154, E-mail: rothstei@umbc.edu.

University of Maryland, College Park, Graduate Studies, College of Behavioral and Social Sciences, Department of Sociology, College Park, MD 20742. Offers MA, PhD. *Degree requirements:* For master's, thesis; for doctorate, thesis/dissertation, 2 qualifying exams. *Entrance requirements:* For master's, GRE General Test, minimum GPA of 3.0, 3 letters of recommendation; for doctorate, GRE General Test, 3 letters of recommendation. Additional exam requirements/recommendations for international students: Required—TOEFL. Electronic applications accepted. *Faculty research:* Social psychology, sociology of work, sociology of the military, population studies, stratification.

University of Massachusetts Amherst, Graduate School, College of Social and Behavioral Sciences, Department of Sociology, Amherst, MA 01003. Offers MA, PhD. Part-time programs available. Terminal master's awarded for partial completion of doctoral program. *Degree requirements:* For master's, thesis or alternative; for doctorate, comprehensive exam, thesis/dissertation. *Entrance requirements:* For master's and doctorate, GRE General Test, writing sample, 3 letters of recommendation. Additional exam requirements/recommendations for international students: Required—TOEFL (minimum score 550 paper-based; 213 computer-based; 79 iBT), IELTS (minimum score 6.5). Electronic applications accepted. *Expenses:* Tuition, area resident: Full-time $2640. Tuition, nonresident: full-time $9936. One-time fee: $332 full-time. Tuition and fees vary according to course load.

University of Massachusetts Boston, Office of Graduate Studies, College of Liberal Arts, Program in Applied Sociology, Boston, MA 02125-3393. Offers MA. Part-time and evening/weekend programs available. *Degree requirements:* For master's, comprehensive exam, thesis. *Entrance requirements:* For master's, GRE or MAT, minimum GPA of 2.75. *Faculty research:* Sociology of education, social deviance and control, women and development, race and ethnic group relations, criminology.

University of Massachusetts Lowell, College of Arts and Sciences, Department of Regional Economic and Social Development, Lowell, MA 01854-2881. Offers MA, Graduate Certificate. Part-time programs available. *Entrance requirements:* For master's, GRE. Electronic applications accepted.

University of Memphis, Graduate School, College of Arts and Sciences, Department of Sociology, Memphis, TN 38152. Offers MA. Part-time programs available. *Faculty:* 9 full-time (4 women). *Students:* 10 full-time (7 women), 4 part-time (3 women); includes 4 minority (all African Americans). Average age 29. 12 applicants, 83% accepted, 3 enrolled. In 2008, 6 master's awarded. *Degree requirements:* For master's, comprehensive exam, thesis or alternative. *Entrance requirements:* For master's, GRE General Test or MAT, 12 undergraduate hours in sociology. *Application deadline:* For fall admission, 8/1 for domestic students; for spring admission, 12/1 for domestic students. Applications are processed on a rolling basis. Application fee: $35 ($60 for international students). Electronic applications accepted. *Expenses:* Tuition, area resident: Full-time $6242; part-time $330 per credit hour. Tuition, state resident: full-time $6242; part-time $330 per credit hour. Tuition, nonresident: full-time $17,828; part-time $815 per credit hour. Required fees: $1156. *Financial support:* Research assistantships with full tuition reimbursements, teaching assistantships with full tuition reimbursements available. Financial award applicants required to submit FAFSA. *Faculty research:* Medical and health, deviant behavior, inequality, religion, globalization. *Unit head:* Dr. Martin Levin, Chair, 901-678-2611, Fax: 901-678-2525. *Application contact:* Dr. Carol Rambo, Interim Graduate Studies Coordinator, 901-678-2610, E-mail: crronai@memphis.edu.

University of Miami, Graduate School, College of Arts and Sciences, Department of Sociology, Coral Gables, FL 33124. Offers MA, PhD. Part-time programs available. Terminal master's awarded for partial completion of doctoral program. *Degree requirements:* For master's, thesis; for doctorate, comprehensive exam, thesis/dissertation. *Entrance requirements:* For master's and doctorate, GRE General Test. Additional exam requirements/recommendations for international students: Required—TOEFL (minimum score 515 paper-based; 213 computer-based). Electronic applications accepted. *Faculty research:* Crime, violence, mental health, ethnic relations, health.

University of Michigan, Horace H. Rackham School of Graduate Studies, College of Literature, Science, and the Arts, Department of Sociology, Ann Arbor, MI 48109. Offers public policy and sociology (PhD); social work and sociology (PhD); sociology (PhD); women's studies and sociology (PhD). *Degree requirements:* For doctorate, comprehensive exam, thesis/dissertation, oral defense of dissertation, preliminary exam. *Entrance requirements:* For doctorate, GRE General Test, letters of recommendation, writing sample, personal statement, statement of purpose. Additional exam requirements/recommendations for international students: Required—TOEFL (minimum score 560 paper-based; 220 computer-based). Electronic applications accepted. *Faculty research:* Power, history and social change; gender and sexuality; race and ethnicity; economic sociology; social demography.

University of Michigan, Horace H. Rackham School of Graduate Studies, College of Literature, Science, and the Arts, Department of Women's Studies, Ann Arbor, MI 48109. Offers English and women's studies (PhD); history and women's studies (PhD); lesbian, gay, bisexual, transgender, queer (LGBTQ) studies (Certificate); psychology and women's studies (PhD); sociology and women's studies (PhD); women's studies (Certificate). *Degree requirements:* For doctorate, variable foreign language requirement, thesis/dissertation. *Entrance requirements:* For doctorate, GRE General Test, previous undergraduate course work in women's studies. Electronic applications accepted. *Faculty research:* Gender issues; LGBTQ studies; sexuality; women and science; global feminism.

University of Minnesota, Duluth, Graduate School, College of Liberal Arts, Department of Sociology/Anthropology, Duluth, MN 55812-2496. Offers criminology (MA); liberal studies (MLS). Part-time programs available. *Degree requirements:* For master's, thesis or alternative. *Entrance requirements:* For master's, interview, minimum GPA of 3.0, letters of recommendation, personal statement. Additional exam requirements/recommendations for international students: Required—TOEFL. *Faculty research:* Nature of knowledge, philosophy of science, ecology, cultural studies, language.

University of Minnesota, Twin Cities Campus, Graduate School, College of Liberal Arts, Department of Sociology, Minneapolis, MN 55455-0213. Offers MA, PhD. Terminal master's awarded for partial completion of doctoral program. *Degree requirements:* For master's, thesis optional; for doctorate, thesis/dissertation, preliminary and final written dissertation and oral defense, prospectus hearing. *Entrance requirements:* For doctorate, GRE General Test, 3 letters of recommendation, sample of written work. Additional exam requirements/recommendations for international students: Required—TOEFL (minimum score 550 paper-based; 213 computer-based; 79 iBT). Electronic applications accepted. *Faculty research:* Organizations, work, and markets; inequality; law, crime and deviance; family and life course; political sociology and social movements.

University of Mississippi, Graduate School, College of Liberal Arts, Department of Sociology and Anthropology, Oxford, University, MS 38677. Offers anthropology (MA); sociology (MA, MSS). *Degree requirements:* For master's, thesis (for some programs). *Entrance requirements:* For master's, GRE General Test, minimum GPA of 3.0. Additional exam requirements/recommendations for international students: Required—TOEFL. Electronic applications accepted.

University of Missouri–Columbia, Graduate School, College of Arts and Sciences, Department of Sociology, Columbia, MO 65211. Offers MA, PhD. *Faculty:* 14 full-time (4 women), 1 (woman) part-time/adjunct. *Students:* 18 full-time (7 women), 33 part-time (15 women); includes 7 minority (1 African American, 1 American Indian/Alaska Native, 1 Asian American or Pacific Islander, 4 Hispanic Americans), 6 international. Average age 33. 52 applicants, 31% accepted, 8 enrolled. In 2008, 14 master's, 6 doctorates awarded. *Degree requirements:* For doctorate, one foreign language, thesis/dissertation. *Entrance requirements:* For master's and doctorate, GRE General Test, minimum GPA of 3.0. Additional exam requirements/recommendations for international students: Required—TOEFL (minimum score 500 paper-based; 173 computer-based; 61 iBT). *Application deadline:* For fall admission, 2/1 priority date for domestic students. Applications are processed on a rolling basis. Application fee: $45 ($60 for international students). *Financial support:* Fellowships, research assistantships, teaching assistantships, institutionally sponsored loans available. *Unit head:* Dr. Jay Gubrium, Department Chair, E-mail: gubriumj@missouri.edu. *Application contact:* Mary Oakes, Administrative Assistant, 573-882-7163, E-mail: oakesm@missouri.edu.

University of Missouri–Kansas City, College of Arts and Sciences, Department of Sociology, Kansas City, MO 64110-2499. Offers MA, PhD. PhD is an interdisciplinary degree offered by the School of Graduate Studies. Part-time and evening/weekend programs available. *Faculty:* 13 full-time (7 women), 1 (woman) part-time/adjunct. *Students:* 1 full-time (0 women), 15 part-time (13 women); includes 2 minority (both African Americans), 2 international. Average age 33. 6 applicants, 50% accepted, 3 enrolled. In 2008, 4 master's awarded. *Degree requirements:* For master's, thesis optional. *Entrance requirements:* For master's, GRE, minimum GPA of 3.0 in major, 2.7 overall. Additional exam requirements/recommendations for international students: Required—TOEFL (minimum score 550 paper-based; 213 computer-based; 80 iBT). *Application deadline:* For fall admission, 3/1 for domestic and international students; for spring admission, 11/1 for domestic and international students. Applications are processed on a rolling basis. Application fee: $45 ($50 for international students). Electronic applications accepted. *Expenses:* Tuition, state resident: full-time $5376; part-time $298.70 per credit hour. Tuition, nonresident: full-time $13,882; part-time $771.20 per credit hour. Required fees: $640.28; $34.65 per contact hour. $30 per semester. Tuition and fees vary according to course load and program. *Financial support:* In 2008–09, 5 teaching assistantships with full and partial

Sociology

University of Missouri–Kansas City (continued)
tuition reimbursements (averaging $12,000 per year) were awarded; research assistantships with full tuition reimbursements, career-related internships or fieldwork, Federal Work-Study, institutionally sponsored loans, and tuition waivers (partial) also available. Support available to part-time students. Financial award application deadline: 3/1; financial award applicants required to submit FAFSA. *Faculty research:* Gerontology, religious movements, urban community and neighborhoods. Total annual research expenditures: $64,426. *Unit head:* Dr. Linda Breytspraak, Chairperson, 816-235-2514, Fax: 816-235-1117. *Application contact:* Dr. Deborah Smith, Graduate Advisor, 816-235-2529, Fax: 816-235-1117, E-mail: smithde@umkc.edu.

University of Missouri–St. Louis, College of Arts and Sciences, Department of Sociology, St. Louis, MO 63121. Offers advanced social perspective (MA); community conflict intervention (MA); program design and evaluation research (MA); social policy planning and administration (MA). Part-time and evening/weekend programs available. *Faculty:* 3 full-time (all women), 1 part-time/adjunct (0 women). *Students:* 6 full-time (3 women), 8 part-time (5 women); includes 2 minority (both African Americans), 1 international. Average age 34. In 2008, 7 master's awarded. *Degree requirements:* For master's, thesis optional. *Entrance requirements:* For master's, 2 letters of recommendation. Additional exam requirements/recommendations for international students: Required—TOEFL (minimum score 550 paper-based; 213 computer-based). *Application deadline:* For fall admission, 7/1 priority date for domestic and international students; for spring admission, 12/1 priority date for domestic and international students. Applications are processed on a rolling basis. Application fee: $35 ($40 for international students). Electronic applications accepted. *Expenses:* Tuition, area resident: Full-time $5377; part-time $298.70 per credit hour. Tuition, nonresident: full-time $13,381; part-time $472.50 per credit hour. Required fees: $4078; $52 per credit hour. *Financial support:* In 2008–09, 3 teaching assistantships with full and partial tuition reimbursements (averaging $7,870 per year) were awarded; career-related internships or fieldwork also available. Support available to part-time students. Financial award applicants required to submit FAFSA. *Faculty research:* Deviance, conflict intervention, minority groups, stratification, social psychology. *Unit head:* Dr. Chicako Usui, Chairperson, 314-516-6366. *Application contact:* 314-516-5458, Fax: 314-516-6996, E-mail: gradadm@umsl.edu.

The University of Montana, Graduate School, College of Arts and Sciences, Department of Sociology, Missoula, MT 59812-0002. Offers criminology (MA); rural and environmental change (MA); sociology (MA). *Entrance requirements:* For master's, GRE General Test. Additional exam requirements/recommendations for international students: Required—TOEFL. *Faculty research:* Housing, homelessness, hunger, infant mortality, work safety.

University of Nebraska–Lincoln, Graduate College, College of Arts and Sciences, Department of Sociology, Lincoln, NE 68588. Offers MA, PhD. *Faculty:* 19 full-time (11 women). *Students:* 28 full-time (19 women), 15 part-time (14 women); includes 9 minority (7 African Americans, 2 Hispanic Americans), 3 international. Average age 36. In 2008, 2 master's awarded. *Degree requirements:* For master's, thesis optional; for doctorate, comprehensive exam, thesis/dissertation. *Entrance requirements:* For master's and doctorate, GRE General Test, writing sample. Additional exam requirements/recommendations for international students: Required—TOEFL (minimum score 550 paper-based; 213 computer-based). *Application deadline:* For fall admission, 1/15 for domestic and international students. Application fee: $40. Electronic applications accepted. *Expenses:* Tuition, state resident: full-time $4275; part-time $237.50 per credit hour. Tuition, nonresident: full-time $11,525; part-time $640.25 per credit hour. Required fees: $1068; $10.35 per credit hour. $440.70 per semester. Tuition and fees vary according to course load and program. *Financial support:* Fellowships, research assistantships, teaching assistantships, Federal Work-Study, health care benefits, and unspecified assistantships available. Support available to part-time students. Financial award application deadline: 1/15. *Faculty research:* Family, deviance and social control, ethnic studies, inequality (gender, race, and class). *Unit head:* Dr. J. Allen Williams, Chair, 402-472-3631, Fax: 402-472-6070. *Application contact:* Ginny Gross, Director of Graduate Admissions, 402-472-2878, Fax: 402-472-0589, E-mail: grad_admissions@unl.edu.

University of Nevada, Las Vegas, Graduate College, College of Liberal Arts, Department of Sociology, Las Vegas, NV 89154-5003. Offers MA, PhD. Part-time programs available. *Faculty:* 13 full-time (4 women). *Students:* 29 full-time (19 women), 13 part-time (7 women); includes 6 minority (5 African Americans, 1 Hispanic American), 2 international. Average age 36. 28 applicants, 61% accepted, 9 enrolled. In 2008, 3 master's awarded. *Degree requirements:* For master's, thesis, oral exams; for doctorate, comprehensive exam, thesis/dissertation, oral exams. *Entrance requirements:* For master's and doctorate, GRE General Test. Additional exam requirements/recommendations for international students: Required—TOEFL (minimum score 550 paper-based; 213 computer-based), IELTS (minimum score 7). *Application deadline:* For fall admission, 2/1 priority date for domestic and international students. Applications are processed on a rolling basis. Application fee: $60 ($75 for international students). Electronic applications accepted. *Expenses:* Tuition, state resident: full-time $1414; part-time $198 per credit. Tuition, nonresident: full-time $12,509; part-time $415.75 per credit. International tuition: $14,249 full-time. Required fees: $4 per credit. $252 per semester. Tuition and fees vary according to course load. *Financial support:* In 2008–09, 25 students received support, including 8 research assistantships with partial tuition reimbursements available (averaging $11,250 per year), 17 teaching assistantships with partial tuition reimbursements available (averaging $11,294 per year); institutionally sponsored loans, scholarships/grants, health care benefits, and unspecified assistantships also available. Financial award application deadline: 3/1. *Faculty research:* Gaming behavior and gaming addiction; environment, social and economic sustainability in Las Vegas; U.S. white power movement and social movementss; relevance of gender and age in work and family life; the sex industry. *Unit head:* Dr. Andy Fontana, Chair/Professor, 702-895-3322, Fax: 702-895-4800, E-mail: andrea.fontana@unlv.edu. *Application contact:* Graduate College Admissions Evaluator, 702-895-3320, Fax: 702-895-4180, E-mail: gradcollege@unlv.edu.

University of Nevada, Reno, Graduate School, College of Liberal Arts, School of Social Research and Justice Studies, Department of Sociology, Reno, NV 89557. Offers MA. *Faculty:* 10 full-time (3 women). *Students:* 5 full-time (3 women), 3 part-time (all women). Average age 25. 5 applicants, 80% accepted, 2 enrolled. In 2008, 2 master's awarded. *Degree requirements:* For master's, thesis optional. *Entrance requirements:* For master's, GRE General Test, minimum GPA of 2.75. Additional exam requirements/recommendations for international students: Required—TOEFL (minimum score 500 paper-based; 173 computer-based; 61 iBT), IELTS (minimum score 6), TOFEL or IELTS. *Application deadline:* For fall admission, 3/1 priority date for domestic and international students; for spring admission, 11/1 priority date for domestic and international students. Applications are processed on a rolling basis. Application fee: $60 ($95 for international students). Electronic applications accepted. *Expenses:* Tuition, state resident: full-time $1710; part-time $1140 per semester. Tuition, nonresident: full-time $7115. Required fees: $158 per semester. *Financial support:* In 2008–09, 2 research assistantships with partial tuition reimbursements (averaging $14,000 per year), 5 teaching assistantships with partial tuition reimbursements (averaging $14,000 per year) were awarded; Federal Work-Study, institutionally sponsored loans, scholarships/grants, health care benefits, and unspecified assistantships also available. Financial award application deadline: 3/1; financial award applicants required to submit FAFSA. *Faculty research:* Statistics, politics and economics, religion and law, industry, theory stratification. Total annual research expenditures: $190,977. *Unit head:* Dr. Berch Berberoglu, Graduate Program Director, 775-784-6647, E-mail: sociology@unr.edu. *Application contact:* Michele Sandberg, Application Contact, 775-784-7026, Fax: 775-784-6064, E-mail: gradschool@unr.edu.

University of New Brunswick Fredericton, School of Graduate Studies, Faculty of Arts, Department of Sociology, Fredericton, NB E3B 5A3, Canada. Offers MA, PhD. Part-time programs available. *Faculty:* 10 full-time (6 women), 8 part-time/adjunct (5 women). *Students:* 25 full-time (20 women), 5 part-time (4 women). In 2008, 4 master's awarded. *Degree requirements:* For master's, thesis; for doctorate, variable foreign language requirement, comprehensive exam, thesis/dissertation. *Entrance requirements:* For master's, minimum GPA of 3.5; for doctorate, minimum GPA of 3.0, MA in sociology with thesis or equivalent, curriculum vitae, statement of interest about interview research. Additional exam requirements/recommendations for international students: Required—TOEFL (minimum score 650 paper-based), TWE. *Application deadline:* For fall admission, 3/1 priority date for domestic students. Applications are processed on a rolling basis. Application fee: $50 Canadian dollars. Tuition and fees charges are reported in Canadian dollars. *Expenses:* Tuition, area resident: Full-time $5562 Canadian dollars. Tuition, nonresident: full-time $9450 Canadian dollars. Required fees: $333 Canadian dollars. *Financial support:* In 2008–09, fellowships (averaging $4,000 per year), 11 research assistantships were awarded; teaching assistantships. *Faculty research:* Social policy, media, communication and culture, family and domestic violence; sociology of health and health care. *Unit head:* Dr. Gary Bowden, Director of Graduate Studies, 506-452-6217, Fax: 506-453-4659, E-mail: glb@unb.ca. *Application contact:* Elvira Embser-Herbert, Graduate Secretary, 506-458-7474, Fax: 506-453-4659, E-mail: elvira1@unb.ca.

University of New Hampshire, Graduate School, College of Liberal Arts, Department of Sociology, Durham, NH 03824. Offers MA, PhD. Part-time programs available. *Faculty:* 12 full-time. *Students:* 33 full-time (28 women), 9 part-time (all women); includes 3 minority (1 African American, 1 American Indian/Alaska Native, 1 Hispanic American), 3 international. Average age 34. 38 applicants, 63% accepted, 11 enrolled. In 2008, 5 master's, 3 doctorates awarded. *Degree requirements:* For master's, thesis; for doctorate, one foreign language, thesis/dissertation. *Entrance requirements:* For master's and doctorate, GRE General Test. Additional exam requirements/recommendations for international students: Required—TOEFL (minimum score 550 paper-based; 213 computer-based; 80 iBT). *Application deadline:* For fall admission, 4/1 priority date for domestic students, 4/1 for international students; for winter admission, 12/1 for domestic students. Applications are processed on a rolling basis. Application fee: $60. Electronic applications accepted. *Expenses:* Tuition, area resident: Full-time $9720; part-time $540 per credit hour. Tuition, nonresident: full-time $23,200; part-time $954 per credit hour. Required fees: $1446; $361.50 per term. *Financial support:* In 2008–09, 24 students received support, including 6 research assistantships, 17 teaching assistantships; fellowships, career-related internships or fieldwork, Federal Work-Study, scholarships/grants, and tuition waivers (full and partial) also available. Support available to part-time students. Financial award application deadline: 2/15. *Faculty research:* Deviance, conflict and control, social psychology, comparative institutional analysis, family. *Unit head:* Dr. James Tucker, Chairperson, 603-862-1814. *Application contact:* Deena Peschke, Administrative Assistant, 603-862-2500, E-mail: sociology.dept@unh.edu.

University of New Mexico, Graduate School, College of Arts and Sciences, Department of Sociology, Albuquerque, NM 87131-2039. Offers MA, PhD. Part-time programs available. *Degree requirements:* For master's, thesis; for doctorate, comprehensive exam, thesis/dissertation. *Entrance requirements:* For master's and doctorate, GRE General Test, 2 writing samples, 3 letters of reference. Additional exam requirements/recommendations for international students: Required—TOEFL. Electronic applications accepted. *Faculty research:* Criminology/deviance, gender, Latin American/comparative sociology, political sociology, race and ethnicity, social movements, religion, social welfare work/organizations.

University of New Orleans, Graduate School, College of Liberal Arts, Department of Sociology, New Orleans, LA 70148. Offers MA. Part-time and evening/weekend programs available. *Degree requirements:* For master's, thesis (for some programs). *Entrance requirements:* For master's, GRE General Test. Additional exam requirements/recommendations for international students: Required—TOEFL (minimum score 550 paper-based; 213 computer-based; 79 iBT). Electronic applications accepted. *Faculty research:* Environment and gender.

The University of North Carolina at Chapel Hill, Graduate School, College of Arts and Sciences, Department of Sociology, Chapel Hill, NC 27599. Offers MA, PhD. *Degree requirements:* For master's, comprehensive exam, thesis; for doctorate, comprehensive exam, thesis/dissertation. *Entrance requirements:* For master's and doctorate, GRE General Test, minimum GPA of 3.0. Additional exam requirements/recommendations for international students: Required—TOEFL (minimum score 550 paper-based; 213 computer-based). Electronic applications accepted. *Faculty research:* Comparative historical, work/organizations, religion, demography, stratification.

The University of North Carolina at Charlotte, Graduate School, College of Arts and Sciences, Department of Sociology, Charlotte, NC 28223-0001. Offers MA. Part-time and evening/weekend programs available. *Faculty:* 16 full-time (10 women), 2 part-time/adjunct (1 woman). *Students:* 7 full-time (6 women), 12 part-time (8 women); includes 8 minority (4 African Americans, 3 Asian Americans or Pacific Islanders, 1 Hispanic American), 2 international. Average age 31. 15 applicants, 87% accepted, 7 enrolled. In 2008, 2 master's awarded. *Degree requirements:* For master's, thesis or comprehensive exam. *Entrance requirements:* For master's, GRE or MAT, minimum GPA of 3.0 in last 2 years, 2.75 overall. Additional exam requirements/recommendations for international students: Required—TOEFL (minimum score 557 paper-based; 220 computer-based). *Application deadline:* For fall admission, 7/1 for domestic students, 5/1 for international students; for spring admission, 11/1 for domestic students, 10/1 for international students. Applications are processed on a rolling basis. Application fee: $55. Electronic applications accepted. *Expenses:* Tuition, area resident: Full-time $2919; part-time $122 per credit hour. Tuition, state resident: full-time $2919; part-time $122 per credit hour. Tuition, nonresident: full-time $13,126; part-time $547 per credit hour. Required fees: $1779; $91 per credit hour. Tuition and fees vary according to program. *Financial support:* In 2008–09, 7 research assistantships (averaging $7,353 per year), 7 teaching assistantships (averaging $8,479 per year) were awarded; career-related internships or fieldwork, Federal Work-Study, institutionally sponsored loans, scholarships/grants, and unspecified assistantships also available. Support available to part-time students. Financial award application deadline: 4/1; financial award applicants required to submit FAFSA. *Faculty research:* Social psychology, sociology of education, social gerontology, quantitative methodology, medical sociology. *Unit head:* Dr. Charles Brody, Chair, 704-687-2362, Fax: 704-687-3091. *Application contact:* Kathy B. Giddings, Director of Graduate Admissions, 704-687-3366, Fax: 704-687-3279, E-mail: agidding@uncc.edu.

The University of North Carolina at Greensboro, Graduate School, College of Arts and Sciences, Department of Sociology, Greensboro, NC 27412-5001. Offers criminology (MA); sociology (MA). Part-time programs available. *Degree requirements:* For master's, comprehensive exam, thesis. *Entrance requirements:* For master's, GRE General Test. Additional exam requirements/recommendations for international students: Required—TOEFL. Electronic applications accepted.

The University of North Carolina Wilmington, College of Arts and Sciences, Department of Sociology and Criminology, Wilmington, NC 28403-3297. Offers criminology (MA); public sociology (MA). *Students:* 11 full-time (9 women), 7 part-time (all women). Average age 29. 24 applicants, 42% accepted, 7 enrolled. *Degree requirements:* For master's, comprehensive exam, thesis or alternative, thesis or internship. *Entrance requirements:* Additional exam requirements/recommendations for international students: Required—TOEFL (minimum score 550 paper-based; 217 computer-based; 79 iBT), IELTS (minimum score 6.5). *Application deadline:* For fall admission, 6/15 for domestic students. Application fee: $60. Electronic applications accepted. *Expenses:* Tuition, area resident: Full-time $4838. Tuition, state resident: full-time $4838. Tuition, nonresident: full-time $14,898. Required fees: $969.38 per semester. Tuition and fees vary according to course load, campus/location and program. *Financial support:* In 2008–09, 5 teaching assistantships with full and partial tuition reimbursements (averaging $9,500 per year) were awarded; unspecified assistantships also available. *Unit head:* Dr. Kimberly J. Cook, Chair, 910-962-3785, E-mail: cookk@uncw.edu. *Application contact:* Dr. Michael Maum, Graduate Coordinator, E-mail: maumm@uncw.edu.

University of North Dakota, Graduate School, College of Arts and Sciences, Department of Sociology, Grand Forks, ND 58202. Offers MA. *Degree requirements:* For master's, thesis, final examination. *Entrance requirements:* For master's, minimum GPA of 3.0. Additional exam requirements/recommendations for international students: Required—TOEFL (minimum score 550 paper-based; 213 computer-based; 79 iBT), IELTS (minimum score 6.5). Electronic applications accepted. *Faculty research:* Criminal justice studies, social psychology, research methods, corrections, social theory.

University of Northern Colorado, Graduate School, College of Humanities and Social Sciences, School of Social Sciences, Program in Social Sciences, Greeley, CO 80639. Offers clinical sociology (MA). Part-time programs available. *Faculty:* 23 full-time (9 women). *Students:* 12 full-time (10 women), 4 part-time (3 women); includes 5 minority (2 African Americans, 1 American Indian/Alaska Native, 2 Hispanic Americans). Average age 30. 12 applicants, 100% accepted, 8 enrolled. In 2008, 4 master's awarded. *Degree requirements:* For master's, comprehensive exam. *Entrance requirements:* For master's, 2 letters of recommendation. *Application deadline:* Applications are processed on a rolling basis. Application fee: $50 ($60 for international students). Electronic applications accepted. *Expenses:* Tuition, state resident: full-time $4370; part-time $242.75 per credit hour. Tuition, nonresident: full-time $12,366; part-time $687 per credit hour. Required fees: $664.20; $36.90 per credit hour. *Financial support:* In 2008–09, 3 teaching assistantships (averaging $2,849 per year) were awarded; fellowships, research assistantships, unspecified assistantships also available. Financial award application deadline: 3/1; financial award applicants required to submit FAFSA. *Unit head:* Dr. David Musick, Program Coordinator, 970-3541-2315, Fax: 970-351-1527. *Application contact:* Linda Sisson, Graduate Student Admission Coordinator, 970-351-1807, Fax: 970-351-2371, E-mail: linda.sisson@unco.edu.

University of Northern Iowa, Graduate College, College of Social and Behavioral Sciences, Department of Sociology, Anthropology and Criminology, Cedar Falls, IA 50614. Offers criminology (MA); sociology (MA). Part-time and evening/weekend programs available. *Students:* 12 full-time (9 women), 2 part-time (both women); includes 1 minority (American Indian/Alaska Native). 30 applicants, 30% accepted, 7 enrolled. In 2008, 3 master's awarded. *Degree requirements:* For master's, thesis. *Entrance requirements:* For master's, minimum GPA of 3.0. Additional exam requirements/recommendations for international students: Required—TOEFL (minimum score 500 paper-based; 180 computer-based; 61 iBT). *Application deadline:* For fall admission, 8/1 priority date for domestic students. Applications are processed on a rolling basis. Application fee: $30 ($50 for international students). Electronic applications accepted. *Expenses:* Tuition, state resident: full-time $6446. Tuition, nonresident: full-time $14,874. Required fees: $852. *Financial support:* Career-related internships or fieldwork, Federal Work-Study, scholarships/grants, and tuition waivers (full and partial) available. Support available to part-time students. Financial award application deadline: 2/1. *Unit head:* Dr. Kent Sandstrom, Head, 319-273-2786, Fax: 319-273-7104, E-mail: kent.sandstrom@uni.edu. *Application contact:* Laurie S. Russell, Record Analyst, 319-273-2623, Fax: 319-273-6792, E-mail: laurie.russell@uni.edu.

University of North Florida, College of Arts and Sciences, Department of Sociology and Anthropology, Jacksonville, FL 32224-2645. Offers applied sociology (MS). Part-time and evening/weekend programs available. *Faculty:* 14 full-time (8 women). *Students:* 2 full-time (1 woman), 4 part-time (all women); includes 1 minority (American Indian/Alaska Native). Average age 30. 14 applicants, 0% accepted. In 2008, 2 master's awarded. *Degree requirements:* For master's, thesis or alternative. *Entrance requirements:* For master's, GRE General Test, minimum GPA of 3.0 in last 60 hours, letters of recommendation. Additional exam requirements/recommendations for international students: Required—TOEFL (minimum score 500 paper-based; 173 computer-based). *Application deadline:* For fall admission, 7/1 priority date for domestic students, 5/1 for international students; for spring admission, 11/1 priority date for domestic students, 10/1 for international students. Applications are processed on a rolling basis. Application fee: $30. Electronic applications accepted. *Expenses:* Tuition, area resident: Full-time $5782.08; part-time $240.92 per credit hour. Tuition, state resident: full-time $5782.08; part-time $240.92 per credit hour. Tuition, nonresident: full-time $19,974; part-time $832.26 per credit hour. Required fees: $952.80; $39.70 per credit hour. *Financial support:* In 2008–09, 1 student received support, including 2 teaching assistantships (averaging $6,000 per year); career-related internships or fieldwork, Federal Work-Study, and tuition waivers (partial) also available. Support available to part-time students. Financial award application deadline: 4/1; financial award applicants required to submit FAFSA. *Faculty research:* Telemarketing fraud, tax evasion practices of small business owners, jury knowledge and education, race and punishment in local schools, urban power structure. Total annual research expenditures: $284,894. *Unit head:* Dr. Adam Shapiro, Chair, 904-620-2850, Fax: 904-620-2540, E-mail: ashapiro@unf.edu. *Application contact:* Dr. Krista Paulsen, Graduate Coordinator, 904-620-2850, Fax: 904-620-2540, E-mail: kpaulsen@unf.edu.

University of North Texas, Robert B. Toulouse School of Graduate Studies, College of Public Affairs and Community Service, Department of Sociology, Denton, TX 76203. Offers MA, MS, PhD. Terminal master's awarded for partial completion of doctoral program. *Degree requirements:* For master's, variable foreign language requirement, comprehensive exam, thesis; for doctorate, one foreign language, comprehensive exam, thesis/dissertation. *Entrance requirements:* For master's, GRE General Test, 3 letters of recommendation; for doctorate, GRE General Test, master's degree, 3 letters of recommendation. Additional exam requirements/recommendations for international students: Required—proof of English language proficiency required for non-native English speakers; Recommended—TOEFL (minimum score 550 paper-based; 213 computer-based). *Faculty research:* Health and illness, social inequality, globalization and development, family.

University of Notre Dame, Graduate School, College of Arts and Letters, Division of Social Science, Department of Sociology, Notre Dame, IN 46556. Offers PhD. *Faculty:* 28 full-time (7 women), 3 part-time/adjunct (0 women). *Students:* 55 full-time (29 women); includes 6 minority (1 African American, 1 American Indian/Alaska Native, 3 Asian Americans or Pacific Islanders, 1 Hispanic American), 10 international. 98 applicants, 22% accepted, 12 enrolled. In 2008, 5 doctorates awarded. *Degree requirements:* For doctorate, thesis/dissertation, 2 area specialty exams. *Entrance requirements:* For doctorate, GRE General Test, GRE Subject Test (strongly recommended). Additional exam requirements/recommendations for international students: Required—TOEFL (minimum score 600 paper-based; 250 computer-based; 80 iBT). *Application deadline:* For fall admission, 1/15 priority date for domestic students, 1/15 for international students. Application fee: $50. Electronic applications accepted. *Financial support:* Fellowships with full tuition reimbursements, research assistantships with full tuition reimbursements, teaching assistantships with full tuition reimbursements, tuition waivers (full) available. Support available to part-time students. Financial award application deadline: 1/15. *Faculty research:* Cultural sociology, development, family, education, historical/comparative sociology. *Unit head:* Dr. William Carbonaro, Chair, Admissions Committee, 574-631-6585, E-mail: soc.1@nd.edu. *Application contact:* Dr. Barbara Turpin, Director of Graduate Admissions, 574-631-7706, Fax: 574-631-4183.

University of Oklahoma, Graduate College, College of Arts and Sciences, Department of Sociology, Norman, OK 73019. Offers MA, PhD. Evening/weekend programs available. *Faculty:* 15 full-time (7 women). *Students:* 30 full-time (19 women), 10 part-time (8 women); includes 10 minority (4 African Americans, 1 American Indian/Alaska Native, 2 Asian Americans or Pacific Islanders, 3 Hispanic Americans), 3 international. 26 applicants, 62% accepted, 14 enrolled. In 2008, 12 master's, 5 doctorates awarded. Terminal master's awarded for partial completion of doctoral program. *Degree requirements:* For master's, thesis or alternative; for doctorate, thesis/dissertation, general exams, qualifying exam. *Entrance requirements:* For master's and doctorate, GRE General Test, 3 letters of recommendation. Additional exam requirements/recommendations for international students: Required—TOEFL (minimum score 550 paper-based; 213 computer-based). *Application deadline:* For fall admission, 2/15 priority date for domestic students, 2/15 for international students; for spring admission, 11/1 for domestic students, 9/1 for international students. Applications are processed on a rolling basis. Application fee: $40 ($90 for international students). Electronic applications accepted. *Expenses:* Tuition, state resident: full-time $3744; part-time $156 per credit hour. Tuition, nonresident: full-time $13,577; part-time $565.70 per credit hour. Required fees: $2415.40; $90.10 per credit hour. *Financial support:* In 2008–09, 23 students received support, including 2 fellowships with full tuition reimbursements available (averaging $3,750 per year), 32 teaching assistantships with partial tuition reimbursements available (averaging $14,062 per year); health care benefits and unspecified assistantships also available. Financial award application deadline: 3/15; financial award applicants required to submit FAFSA. *Faculty research:* Criminology, stratification, family, demography. *Unit head:* Dr. Craig St. John, Chair, 405-325-1751, Fax: 405-325-7825, E-mail: cstjohn@ou.edu. *Application contact:* Dr. Loretta Bass, Associate Professor/Graduate Liaison, 405-325-1751, Fax: 405-325-7825, E-mail: lbass@ou.edu.

University of Oregon, Graduate School, College of Arts and Sciences, Department of Sociology, Eugene, OR 97403. Offers MA, MS, PhD. Part-time programs available. Terminal master's awarded for partial completion of doctoral program. *Degree requirements:* For doctorate, thesis/dissertation. *Entrance requirements:* For master's and doctorate, GRE General Test, minimum GPA of 3.0. Additional exam requirements/recommendations for international students: Required—TOEFL. *Faculty research:* Criminology, environment, gender, labor, political economy.

University of Ottawa, Faculty of Graduate and Postdoctoral Studies, Faculty of Social Sciences, Department of Sociology and Anthropology, Ottawa, ON K1N 6N5, Canada. Offers MA. *Degree requirements:* For master's, thesis or alternative. *Entrance requirements:* For master's, honors bachelor's degree or equivalent, minimum B average. Electronic applications accepted. *Faculty research:* Inter-ethnic relations, development, political policies.

University of Pennsylvania, School of Arts and Sciences, Graduate Group in Sociology, Philadelphia, PA 19104. Offers AM, PhD. Terminal master's awarded for partial completion of doctoral program. *Degree requirements:* For master's, thesis or alternative; for doctorate, one foreign language, thesis/dissertation. *Entrance requirements:* For master's and doctorate, GRE General Test. Additional exam requirements/recommendations for international students: Required—TOEFL. Electronic applications accepted.

University of Pittsburgh, School of Arts and Sciences, Department of Sociology, Pittsburgh, PA 15260. Offers MA, PhD. Terminal master's awarded for partial completion of doctoral program. *Degree requirements:* For master's, thesis; for doctorate, comprehensive exam, thesis/dissertation, preliminary exam. *Entrance requirements:* For master's and doctorate, GRE General Test, writing sample. Additional exam requirements/recommendations for international students: Required—TOEFL. Electronic applications accepted. *Faculty research:* Global and comparative sociology, gender, race and class, social network process.

University of Puerto Rico, Río Piedras, College of Social Sciences, Department of Sociology, San Juan, PR 00931-3300. Offers MA. *Degree requirements:* For master's, comprehensive exam, thesis. *Entrance requirements:* For master's, GRE or PAEG, interview, minimum GPA of 3.0, letter of recommendation.

University of Regina, Faculty of Graduate Studies and Research, Faculty of Arts, Department of Philosophy, Regina, SK S4S 0A2, Canada. Offers philosophy (MA); social and political thought (MA). *Faculty:* 9 full-time (3 women). *Students:* 3 full-time (2 women). 2 applicants, 100% accepted. *Degree requirements:* For master's, thesis. *Entrance requirements:* Additional exam requirements/recommendations for international students: Required—TOEFL (minimum score 580 paper-based; 237 computer-based; 88 iBT). *Application deadline:* Applications are processed on a rolling basis. Application fee: $85 ($100 for international students). Electronic applications accepted. *Financial support:* Fellowships, research assistantships, teaching assistantships, scholarships/grants available. Financial award application deadline: 6/15. *Faculty research:* History of philosophy, ethics, aesthetics, metaphysics, epistemology. *Unit head:* Dr. Eldon Soifer, Head, 306-585-4301, Fax: 306-585-4827, E-mail: eldon.soifer@uregina.ca. *Application contact:* Dr. Eldon Soifer, Head, 306-585-4301, Fax: 306-585-4827, E-mail: eldon.soifer@uregina.ca.

University of Regina, Faculty of Graduate Studies and Research, Faculty of Arts, Department of Sociology and Social Studies, Regina, SK S4S 0A2, Canada. Offers social studies (MA, PhD); sociology (MA, PhD). *Faculty:* 12 full-time (5 women), 1 part-time/adjunct (0 women). *Students:* 11 full-time (6 women), 7 part-time (5 women). 7 applicants, 71% accepted. In 2008, 4 master's, 2 doctorates awarded. *Degree requirements:* For master's, thesis. *Entrance requirements:* Additional exam requirements/recommendations for international students: Required—TOEFL (minimum score 580 paper-based; 237 computer-based; 88 iBT). *Application deadline:* Applications are processed on a rolling basis. Application fee: $85 ($100 for international students). Electronic applications accepted. *Financial support:* In 2008–09, 3 fellowships (averaging $15,000 per year), 1 research assistantship (averaging $13,500 per year), 4 teaching assistantships (averaging $6,558 per year) were awarded; scholarships/grants also available. Financial award application deadline: 6/15. *Faculty research:* Social justice; development and the environment; knowledge, technology, and society. *Unit head:* Dr. John Conway, Head, 306-585-4052, Fax: 306-585-4815, E-mail: john.conway@uregina.ca. *Application contact:* Dr. Henry Chow, Graduate Program Coordinator, 306-585-5604, Fax: 306-585-4815, E-mail: henry.chow@uregina.ca.

University of Saskatchewan, College of Graduate Studies and Research, College of Arts and Sciences, Department of Sociology, Saskatoon, SK S7N 5A2, Canada. Offers MA, PhD. *Degree requirements:* For master's, thesis; for doctorate, thesis/dissertation. *Entrance requirements:* Additional exam requirements/recommendations for international students: Required—TOEFL.

University of South Africa, College of Human Sciences, Pretoria, South Africa. Offers adult education (M Ed); African languages (MA, PhD); African politics (MA, PhD); Afrikaans (MA, PhD); ancient history (MA, PhD); ancient Near Eastern studies (MA, PhD); anthropology (MA, PhD); applied linguistics (MA); Arabic (MA, PhD); archaeology (MA); art history (MA); Biblical archaeology (MA); Biblical studies (M Th, D Th, PhD); Christian spirituality (M Th, D Th); church history (M Th, D Th); classical studies (MA, PhD); clinical psychology (MA); communication (MA, PhD); comparative education (M Ed, Ed D); consulting psychology (D Admin, D Com, PhD); curriculum studies (M Ed, Ed D); development studies (M Admin, MA, D Admin, PhD); didactics (M Ed, Ed D); education (M Tech); education management (M Ed, Ed D); educational psychology (M Ed); English (MA); environmental education (M Ed); French (MA, PhD); German (MA, PhD); Greek (MA); guidance and counseling (M Ed); health studies (MA, PhD), including health sciences education (MA), health services management (MA), medical and surgical nursing science (critical care general) (MA), midwifery and neonatal nursing science (MA), trauma and emergency care (MA); history (MA, PhD); history of education (Ed D); inclusive education (M Ed, Ed D); information and communications technology policy and regulation (MA); information science (MA, MIS, PhD); international politics (MA, PhD); Islamic studies (MA, PhD); Italian (MA, PhD); Judaica (MA, PhD); linguistics (MA, PhD); mathematical education (M Ed); mathematics education (MA); missiology (M Th, D Th); modern Hebrew (MA, PhD); musicology (MA, MMus, D Mus, PhD); natural science education (M Ed); New Testament (M Th, D Th); Old Testament (D Th); pastoral therapy (M Th, D Th); philosophy (MA); philosophy of education (M Ed, Ed D); politics (MA, PhD); Portuguese (MA, PhD); practical theology (M Th, D Th); psychology (MA, MS, PhD); psychology of education (M Ed, Ed D); public health (MA); religious studies (MA, D Th, PhD); Romance languages (MA); Russian (MA, PhD); Semitic languages (MA, PhD); social behavior studies in HIV/AIDS (MA); social science (mental health) (MA); social science in development studies (MA); social science in psychology (MA); social science in social work (MA); social science in sociology (MA); social work (MSW, DSW, PhD); socio-education (M Ed, Ed D); sociolinguistics (MA); sociology (MA, PhD); Spanish (MA, PhD); systematic theology (M Th, D Th); TESOL (teaching English to speakers of other languages) (MA); theological ethics (M Th, D Th); theory of literature (MA, PhD); urban ministries (D Th); urban ministry (M Th).

University of South Alabama, Graduate School, College of Arts and Sciences, Department of Sociology, Anthropology and Social Work, Mobile, AL 36688-0002. Offers sociology (MA). Part-time and evening/weekend programs available. *Faculty:* 11 full-time (2 women). *Students:* 5 full-time (4 women), 3 part-time (all women); includes 3 minority (all African Americans). 9

Sociology

University of South Alabama (continued)
applicants, 44% accepted, 4 enrolled. In 2008, 3 master's awarded. *Degree requirements:* For master's, comprehensive exam, thesis optional. *Entrance requirements:* For master's, GRE General Test, minimum GPA of 3.0. *Application deadline:* For fall admission, 7/15 priority date for domestic students, 6/15 priority date for international students. Applications are processed on a rolling basis. Application fee: $35. *Expenses:* Tuition, area resident: Full-time $4656. Tuition, nonresident: full-time $9312. Required fees: $1102. *Financial support:* Fellowships, research assistantships available. Financial award application deadline: 4/1. *Faculty research:* Cultural adaptation. *Unit head:* Dr. Roma S Hanks, PhD, Chair/Graduate Coordinator, 251-460-6347, Fax: 460-7925. *Application contact:* Dr. Roma S Hanks, PhD, Chair/Graduate Coordinator, 251-460-6347, Fax: 460-7925.

University of South Carolina, The Graduate School, College of Arts and Sciences, Department of Sociology, Columbia, SC 29208. Offers MA, PhD. Part-time programs available. Terminal master's awarded for partial completion of doctoral program. *Degree requirements:* For master's, thesis; for doctorate, comprehensive exam, thesis/dissertation. *Entrance requirements:* For master's and doctorate, GRE General Test. Additional exam requirements/recommendations for international students: Required—TOEFL (minimum score 570 paper-based; 230 computer-based; 75 iBT). Electronic applications accepted. *Faculty research:* Social psychology, social inequality.

University of Southern California, Graduate School, College of Letters, Arts and Sciences, Department of Sociology, Los Angeles, CA 90089. Offers PhD. *Degree requirements:* For doctorate, thesis/dissertation, Qualifying exam. *Entrance requirements:* For doctorate, GRE General Test. *Faculty research:* Gerontology, organization and social change, women's studies, race, immigration.

University of South Florida, Graduate School, College of Arts and Sciences, Department of Sociology, Tampa, FL 33620-9951. Offers MA, PhD. Part-time programs available. *Faculty:* 11 full-time (9 women). *Students:* 13 full-time (9 women), 10 part-time (6 women); includes 6 minority (3 African Americans, 2 Asian Americans or Pacific Islanders, 1 Hispanic American). 17 applicants, 65% accepted, 6 enrolled. In 2008, 2 master's awarded. *Degree requirements:* For master's, comprehensive exam, thesis; for doctorate, comprehensive exam, thesis/dissertation. *Entrance requirements:* For master's, GRE General Test, minimum GPA of 3.0 in last 60 hours. Additional exam requirements/recommendations for international students: Required—TOEFL (minimum score 550 paper-based; 213 computer-based). *Application deadline:* For fall admission, 2/15 priority date for domestic students, 1/2 priority date for international students; for spring admission, 10/15 for domestic students, 6/1 priority date for international students. Application fee: $30. Electronic applications accepted. *Expenses:* Tuition, state resident: full-time $2624.40; part-time $291.60 per credit hour. Tuition, nonresident: full-time $7822; part-time $869.13 per credit hour. *Financial support:* Application deadline: 3/1. Total annual research expenditures: $80,806. *Unit head:* Dr. Maralee Mayberry, Chairperson, 813-974-2241, Fax: 813-974-6455, E-mail: mayberry@chuma1.cas.usf.edu. *Application contact:* Dr. Donileen R. Loseke, Program Director, 813-974-2517, Fax: 813-974-6455, E-mail: dloseke@cas.usf.edu.

The University of Tennessee, Graduate School, College of Arts and Sciences, Department of Sociology, Knoxville, TN 37996. Offers criminology (MA, PhD); energy, environment, and resource policy (MA, PhD); political economy (MA, PhD). Part-time programs available. *Degree requirements:* For master's, thesis or alternative; for doctorate, thesis/dissertation. *Entrance requirements:* For master's, GRE General Test, minimum GPA of 3.0; for doctorate, GRE General Test, minimum GPA of 3.5. Additional exam requirements/recommendations for international students: Required—TOEFL. Electronic applications accepted. *Expenses:* Tuition, area resident: Part-time $348 per credit hour. Tuition, state resident: full-time $6262. Tuition, nonresident: full-time $18,920; part-time $1052 per credit hour. Required fees: $812; $36 per credit hour. Tuition and fees vary according to program.

The University of Texas at Arlington, Graduate School, College of Liberal Arts, Department of Sociology and Anthropology, Program in Sociology, Arlington, TX 76019. Offers MA. Part-time and evening/weekend programs available. *Students:* 5 full-time (4 women), 21 part-time (12 women); includes 7 minority (2 African Americans, 3 Asian Americans or Pacific Islanders, 2 Hispanic Americans), 1 international. 12 applicants, 92% accepted, 9 enrolled. In 2008, 3 master's awarded. *Degree requirements:* For master's, comprehensive exam, thesis or alternative. *Entrance requirements:* For master's, GRE General Test, 12 hours of undergraduate course work in sociology. Additional exam requirements/recommendations for international students: Required—TOEFL (minimum score 550 paper-based; 213 computer-based). *Application deadline:* For fall admission, 6/16 for domestic students. Applications are processed on a rolling basis. Application fee: $35 ($50 for international students). *Expenses:* Tuition, area resident: Full-time $6500. Tuition, state resident: full-time $6500. Tuition, nonresident: full-time $11,558. *Financial support:* In 2008–09, 4 teaching assistantships (averaging $9,000 per year) were awarded; research assistantships, Federal Work-Study also available. Financial award application deadline: 4/1. *Application contact:* Dr. Joel Ryan, Graduate Advisor, 817-272-2661, Fax: 817-272-3759, E-mail: jcryan@uta.edu.

The University of Texas at Austin, Graduate School, College of Liberal Arts, Department of Sociology, Austin, TX 78712-1111. Offers MA, PhD. *Degree requirements:* For master's, thesis; for doctorate, thesis/dissertation. *Entrance requirements:* For master's and doctorate, GRE General Test. Additional exam requirements/recommendations for international students: Required—TOEFL. Electronic applications accepted. *Faculty research:* Criminology, demography, Latin America, health, political sociology.

The University of Texas at Dallas, School of Economic, Political and Policy Sciences, Program in Sociology, Richardson, TX 75083-0688. Offers applied sociology (MS). *Faculty:* 5 full-time (1 woman). *Students:* 7 full-time (6 women), 11 part-time (9 women); includes 6 minority (3 African Americans, 3 Hispanic Americans), 2 international. Average age 36. 6 applicants, 83% accepted, 4 enrolled. In 2008, 5 master's awarded. *Degree requirements:* For master's, internship. *Entrance requirements:* For master's, GRE General Test, minimum GPA of 3.0 in upper-level coursework in field. Additional exam requirements/recommendations for international students: Required—TOEFL (minimum score 550 paper-based; 213 computer-based). *Application deadline:* For fall admission, 7/15 for domestic students, 5/1 priority date for international students; for spring admission, 11/15 for domestic students, 9/1 priority date for international students. Applications are processed on a rolling basis. Application fee: $50 ($100 for international students). Electronic applications accepted. *Expenses:* Tuition, area resident: Full-time $8320. Tuition, state resident: full-time $8320. Tuition, nonresident: full-time $15,054. Part-time tuition and fees vary according to course load. *Financial support:* In 2008–09, 1 research assistantship, 1 teaching assistantship with tuition reimbursement (averaging $10,800 per year) were awarded; fellowships, career-related internships or fieldwork, Federal Work-Study, institutionally sponsored loans, and scholarships/grants also available. Support available to part-time students. Financial award application deadline: 4/30. *Faculty research:* Social impact of alcohol in Latino families, reading one-to-one, AmeriCorps, neighborhood evaluations. *Unit head:* Dr. James W. Marquart, Program Head, 972-883-4948, Fax: 972-883-2735, E-mail: marquart@utdallas.edu. *Application contact:* Dr. Bruce A. Jacobs, Associate Program Head, 972-883-4557, Fax: 972-883-2735, E-mail: Bruce.Jacobs@utdallas.edu.

See Close-Up on page 783.

The University of Texas at El Paso, Graduate School, College of Liberal Arts, Department of Sociology and Anthropology, El Paso, TX 79968-0001. Offers sociology (MA). Part-time and evening/weekend programs available. *Degree requirements:* For master's, thesis optional. *Entrance requirements:* For master's, GRE General Test, minimum GPA of 3.0. Additional exam requirements/recommendations for international students: Required—TOEFL. Electronic applications accepted.

The University of Texas at San Antonio, College of Liberal and Fine Arts, Department of Sociology, San Antonio, TX 78249-0617. Offers MS. Part-time and evening/weekend programs available. *Degree requirements:* For master's, comprehensive exam, thesis optional. *Entrance requirements:* For master's, GRE General Test, undergraduate course work in sociology or related areas. Additional exam requirements/recommendations for international students: Required—TOEFL (minimum score 500 paper-based; 173 computer-based). Electronic applications accepted. *Faculty research:* Race and ethnic relations, qualitative research methods, complex organizations, gender stratification, social stratification.

The University of Texas at Tyler, College of Arts and Sciences, Department of Social Sciences, Tyler, TX 75799-0001. Offers criminal justice (MS); public administration (MPA); sociology (MS). Part-time and evening/weekend programs available. *Degree requirements:* For master's, comprehensive exam, thesis optional. *Entrance requirements:* For master's, GRE General Test, minimum GPA of 3.0. Additional exam requirements/recommendations for international students: Required—TOEFL (minimum score 79 computer-based). *Faculty research:* Urban segregation, minority business, violent crime, gender discrimination.

The University of Texas–Pan American, College of Social and Behavioral Sciences, Department of Sociology, Edinburg, TX 78541-2999. Offers MS. Part-time programs available. *Degree requirements:* For master's, thesis or journal article. *Entrance requirements:* For master's, minimum GPA of 3.0, BS of BA in sociology or social science. Additional exam requirements/recommendations for international students: Required—TOEFL (minimum score 500 paper-based). *Faculty research:* Border studies, U.S.-Mexico issues, Mexican-American peoples, aging and gerontology.

The University of Toledo, College of Graduate Studies, College of Arts and Sciences, Department of Sociology and Anthropology, Toledo, OH 43606-3390. Offers sociology (MA). Part-time programs available. *Degree requirements:* For master's, thesis or alternative. Electronic applications accepted. *Faculty research:* Medical and social gerontology, population, social movements, socioeconomic development, corporations and work, race and ethnicity.

University of Toronto, School of Graduate Studies, Social Sciences Division, Department of Sociology, Toronto, ON M5S 1A1, Canada. Offers M Ed, MA, Ed D, PhD. Part-time programs available. *Degree requirements:* For doctorate, thesis/dissertation. *Entrance requirements:* For master's, GRE (required for applicants from non-Canadian universities, recommended for those from Canadian universities), 5 full-year courses in sociology, basic research and statistical skills, minimum B average, 2 letters of reference; for doctorate, GRE (required for applicants from non-Canadian universities; recommended for those from Canadian universities), MA in sociology, minimum A–average, 2 letters of reference.

University of Utah, The Graduate School, College of Social and Behavioral Science, Department of Sociology, Salt Lake City, UT 84112-1107. Offers M Stat, MA, MS, PhD. Part-time programs available. *Entrance requirements:* For master's, minimum undergraduate GPA of 3.0. Additional exam requirements/recommendations for international students: Required—TOEFL (minimum score 500 paper-based; 173 computer-based). *Faculty research:* Comparative international sociology, population and health, criminology, diversity, demography.

University of Utah, The Graduate School, Interdepartmental Program in Statistics, Salt Lake City, UT 84112-1107. Offers biostatistics (MST); business (MST); economics (MST); educational psychology (MST); mathematics (MST); sociology (MST); statistics (M Stat). Part-time programs available. *Degree requirements:* For master's, comprehensive exam, projects. *Entrance requirements:* For master's, minimum GPA of 3.0; course work in calculus, matrix theory, statistics. Additional exam requirements/recommendations for international students: Required—TOEFL (minimum score 500 paper-based; 173 computer-based). *Faculty research:* Biostatistics, management, economics, educational psychology, mathematics.

University of Victoria, Faculty of Graduate Studies, Faculty of Social Sciences, Department of Sociology, Victoria, BC V8W 2Y2, Canada. Offers MA, PhD. PhD by special arrangement. Part-time programs available. *Degree requirements:* For master's, thesis; for doctorate, thesis/dissertation, candidacy exam. *Entrance requirements:* For master's, minimum B+ average. Additional exam requirements/recommendations for international students: Required—TOEFL (minimum score 575 paper-based; 233 computer-based), IELTS (minimum score 7), TWE (minimum score 4). *Faculty research:* Social and political thought, social justice, health and aging, globalization and social psychology.

University of Virginia, College and Graduate School of Arts and Sciences, Department of Sociology, Charlottesville, VA 22903. Offers MA, PhD, JD/MA. *Faculty:* 18 full-time (7 women), 1 part-time/adjunct (0 women). *Students:* 51 full-time (24 women); includes 28 minority (1 African American, 2 Asian Americans or Pacific Islanders, 25 Hispanic Americans), 15 international. Average age 29. 85 applicants, 29% accepted, 10 enrolled. In 2008, 5 master's, 2 doctorates awarded. *Degree requirements:* For master's, thesis; for doctorate, comprehensive exam, thesis/dissertation. *Entrance requirements:* For master's and doctorate, GRE General Test, GRE Subject Test, 2 letters of recommendation. Additional exam requirements/recommendations for international students: Required—TOEFL (minimum score 600 paper-based; 250 computer-based; 90 iBT), IELTS (minimum score 7). *Application deadline:* For fall admission, 1/1 for domestic and international students. Applications are processed on a rolling basis. Application fee: $60. Electronic applications accepted. *Expenses:* Tuition, area resident: Full-time $10,452. Tuition, state resident: full-time $10,452. Tuition, nonresident: full-time $20,010. Required fees: $2176. Part-time tuition and fees vary according to course load and program. *Financial support:* Applicants required to submit FAFSA. *Unit head:* Krishan Kumar, Chair, 434-924-7293, Fax: 434-924-7028, E-mail: sociology@virginia.edu. *Application contact:* Paul Kingston, E-mail: pwk@virginia.edu.

University of Washington, Graduate School, College of Arts and Sciences, Department of Sociology, Seattle, WA 98195. Offers MA, PhD. *Degree requirements:* For master's, thesis; for doctorate, thesis/dissertation. *Entrance requirements:* For master's and doctorate, GRE General Test, minimum GPA of 3.0. Additional exam requirements/recommendations for international students: Required—TOEFL. Electronic applications accepted. *Faculty research:* Demography, criminology, social psychology, race/ethnicity/inequality, family.

University of Waterloo, Graduate Studies, Faculty of Arts, Department of Sociology, Waterloo, ON N2L 3G1, Canada. Offers MA, PhD. Part-time programs available. *Degree requirements:* For master's, thesis (for some programs); for doctorate, one foreign language, thesis/dissertation. *Entrance requirements:* For master's, honors degree, minimum B+ average, resumé, writing sample; for doctorate, master's degree, minimum A- average, resumé, writing sample. Additional exam requirements/recommendations for international students: Required—TOEFL, TWE. Electronic applications accepted. *Faculty research:* Theory, methods, stratification deviance, political sociology.

The University of Western Ontario, Faculty of Graduate Studies, Social Sciences Division, Department of Sociology, London, ON N6A 5B8, Canada. Offers MA, PhD. Terminal master's awarded for partial completion of doctoral program. *Degree requirements:* For master's, thesis (for some programs); for doctorate, one foreign language, comprehensive exam, thesis/dissertation. *Entrance requirements:* For master's, minimum B+ average, honors degree, statement of academic interest in sociology; for doctorate, minimum A- average. Additional exam requirements/recommendations for international students: Required—TOEFL. Electronic applications accepted. *Faculty research:* Social demography, class and change, health and aging, theory, methods.

University of West Georgia, Graduate School, College of Arts and Sciences, Department of Sociology and Criminology, Program in Sociology, Carrollton, GA 30118. Offers MA. Part-time and evening/weekend programs available. *Students:* 9 full-time (5 women), 6 part-time (4 women); includes 3 minority (all African Americans). Average age 32. 6 applicants, 83% accepted, 4 enrolled. In 2008, 6 master's awarded. *Degree requirements:* For master's, one foreign language, comprehensive exam (for some programs), thesis (for some programs).

Entrance requirements: For master's, GRE, references, minimum GPA of 2.5, interview. Additional exam requirements/recommendations for international students: Required—TOEFL. *Application deadline:* For fall admission, 7/18 for domestic students; for spring admission, 11/27 for domestic students. Application fee: $30. Electronic applications accepted. *Expenses:* Tuition, state resident: full-time $2844; part-time $158 per semester hour. Tuition, nonresident: full-time $11,340; part-time $630 per semester hour. Required fees: $1120; $41.56 per semester hour. $186 per semester. Tuition and fees vary according to course load. *Financial support:* In 2008–09, 7 students received support, including research assistantships with full tuition reimbursements available (averaging $6,000 per year); career-related internships or fieldwork, scholarships/grants, and unspecified assistantships also available. Financial award applicants required to submit FAFSA. *Faculty research:* Women studies, criminology, resources and methods. Total annual research expenditures: $68,830. *Unit head:* Dr. N. Jane McCandless, Chair, 678-839-6505, Fax: 678-839-6509, E-mail: jmccandl@westga.edu. *Application contact:* Dr. Charles W. Clark, Interim Dean, 678-839-6508, E-mail: cclark@westga.edu.

University of Windsor, Faculty of Graduate Studies, Faculty of Arts and Social Sciences, Department of Sociology and Anthropology, Windsor, ON N9B 3P4, Canada. Offers criminology (MA); sociology (MA); sociology-social justice (PhD). Part-time programs available. *Degree requirements:* For master's, thesis; for doctorate, comprehensive exam, thesis/dissertation. *Entrance requirements:* For master's, minimum B+ average; for doctorate, writing sample, minimum B+ average. Additional exam requirements/recommendations for international students: Required—TOEFL (minimum score 560 paper-based; 220 computer-based). Electronic applications accepted. *Faculty research:* Power and social change; criminology/deviance; social psychology; comparative development; race and ethnic relations; family, sex, and gender, social justice.

University of Wisconsin–Madison, Graduate School, College of Letters and Science, Department of Sociology, Madison, WI 53706-1380. Offers rural sociology (MS); sociology (MS, PhD). Part-time programs available. Terminal master's awarded for partial completion of doctoral program. *Degree requirements:* For master's, thesis, oral exam; for doctorate, thesis/dissertation, preliminary and final oral exams, 4 seminars. *Entrance requirements:* For master's and doctorate, GRE General Test. Additional exam requirements/recommendations for international students: Required—TOEFL. Electronic applications accepted.

University of Wisconsin–Milwaukee, Graduate School, College of Letters and Sciences, Department of Sociology, Milwaukee, WI 53201-0413. Offers MA. Part-time programs available. *Faculty:* 18 full-time (9 women). *Students:* 18 full-time (12 women), 17 part-time (13 women); includes 7 minority (2 African Americans, 1 Asian American or Pacific Islander, 4 Hispanic Americans), 2 international. Average age 30. 36 applicants, 58% accepted, 8 enrolled. In 2008, 9 master's awarded. *Degree requirements:* For master's, thesis. *Entrance requirements:* For master's, GRE. *Application deadline:* For fall admission, 1/1 priority date for domestic students; for spring admission, 9/1 for domestic students. Applications are processed on a rolling basis. Application fee: $45 ($75 for international students). *Expenses:* Tuition, area resident: Full-time $7320; part-time $165 per credit. Tuition, state resident: full-time $7320; part-time $165 per credit. Tuition, nonresident: full-time $17,840; part-time $714 per credit. Tuition and fees vary according to campus/location, program and reciprocity agreements. *Financial support:* In 2008–09, 18 teaching assistantships were awarded; career-related internships or fieldwork and unspecified assistantships also available. Support available to part-time students. Financial award application deadline: 4/15. Total annual research expenditures: $7,931. *Unit head:* Pat Rubio Goldsmith, Representative, 414-229-6945, Fax: 847-673-4122, E-mail: goldsmit@uwm.edu. *Application contact:* General Information Contact, 414-229-4982, Fax: 414-229-6967, E-mail: gradschool@uwm.edu.

University of Wyoming, Graduate School, College of Arts and Sciences, Department of Sociology, Laramie, WY 82070. Offers MA. Part-time programs available. *Faculty:* 9 full-time (4 women). *Students:* 4 full-time (1 woman), 7 part-time (5 women), 2 international. Average age 32. 4 applicants, 100% accepted, 2 enrolled. In 2008, 2 master's awarded. *Degree requirements:* For master's, thesis, 26 course credits. *Entrance requirements:* For master's, GRE General Test, minimum GPA of 3.0. Additional exam requirements/recommendations for international students: Required—TOEFL (minimum score 525 paper-based). *Application deadline:* For fall admission, 3/1 priority date for domestic and international students; for spring admission, 12/1 priority date for domestic and international students. Applications are processed on a rolling basis. Application fee: $50. Electronic applications accepted. *Financial support:* In 2008–09, 6 students received support, including 1 research assistantship with full tuition reimbursement available (averaging $11,072 per year), 4 teaching assistantships with full tuition reimbursements available (averaging $11,072 per year); institutionally sponsored loans, tuition waivers (partial), and unspecified assistantships also available. Financial award application deadline: 3/1. *Faculty research:* Gender, theory, international studies, law, social inequality. *Unit head:* Dr. Donna Barnes, Chair, 307-766-3342, Fax: 307-766-3812, E-mail: dbarnes@uwyo.edu. *Application contact:* Dr. Malcom Holmes, Graduate Director, 307-766-3342, Fax: 307-766-3812.

Utah State University, School of Graduate Studies, College of Humanities, Arts and Social Sciences, Department of Sociology, Logan, UT 84322-0730. Offers MA, MS, MSS, PhD. *Degree requirements:* For master's, thesis; for doctorate, comprehensive exam, thesis/dissertation. *Entrance requirements:* For master's, GRE General Test, minimum GPA of 3.0, recommendation letters, transcripts, personal statement; for doctorate, GRE General Test, minimum GPA of 3.0, recommendation letters, transcripts, personal statement, MS degree. Additional exam requirements/recommendations for international students: Required—TOEFL; Recommended—TWE. *Faculty research:* Demography, environmental/natural resource sociology, rural community change, international development, health studies.

Valdosta State University, Graduate School, College of Arts and Sciences, Department of Sociology, Anthropology, and Criminal Justice, Valdosta, GA 31698. Offers criminal justice (MS); marriage and family therapy (MS); sociology (MS). *Accreditation:* AAMFT/COAMFTE. Part-time and evening/weekend programs available. *Faculty:* 19 full-time (7 women). *Students:* 3 full-time (2 women), 9 part-time (6 women); includes 4 minority (all African Americans). Average age 27. 7 applicants, 57% accepted, 2 enrolled. In 2008, 29 master's awarded. *Degree requirements:* For master's, thesis or alternative, comprehensive written and/or oral exams. *Entrance requirements:* For master's, GRE General Test or MAT (sociology, marriage and family therapy), minimum GPA of 2.5. Additional exam requirements/recommendations for international students: Required—TOEFL (minimum score 523 paper-based; 193 computer-based). *Application deadline:* For fall admission, 7/1 for domestic and international students; for spring admission, 11/15 for domestic and international students. Applications are processed on a rolling basis. Application fee: $40. Electronic applications accepted. *Financial support:* In 2008–09, 5 students received support, including 5 research assistantships with full tuition reimbursements available (averaging $2,452 per year); career-related internships or fieldwork, institutionally sponsored loans, scholarships/grants, and unspecified assistantships also available. Support available to part-time students. Financial award application deadline: 7/1; financial award applicants required to submit FAFSA. *Faculty research:* Police-civilian ride-along project. *Unit head:* Dr. Mike Capece, Acting Head, 229-333-5943, Fax: 229-333-5492. *Application contact:* Rebecca Waters, Coordinator of Graduate Admissions, 229-333-5694, Fax: 229-245-3853, E-mail: rlwaters@valdosta.edu.

Vanderbilt University, Graduate School, Department of Sociology, Nashville, TN 37240-1001. Offers MA, PhD. *Faculty:* 16 full-time (6 women). *Students:* 23 full-time (18 women), 2 part-time (1 woman); includes 3 minority (all African Americans), 5 international. Average age 30. 104 applicants, 13% accepted, 8 enrolled. In 2008, 3 master's, 7 doctorates awarded. *Degree requirements:* For master's, thesis; for doctorate, comprehensive exam, thesis/dissertation, area, qualifying, and final exams. *Entrance requirements:* For master's and doctorate, GRE General Test. Additional exam requirements/recommendations for international students: Required—TOEFL (minimum score 570 paper-based; 230 computer-based; 88 iBT). *Application deadline:* For fall admission, 1/15 for domestic and international students. Application fee: $0. Electronic applications accepted. *Financial support:* Fellowships with full tuition reimbursements, research assistantships, teaching assistantships with full tuition reimbursements, Federal Work-Study, institutionally sponsored loans, scholarships/grants, and health care benefits available. Financial award application deadline: 1/15; financial award applicants required to submit CSS PROFILE or FAFSA. *Faculty research:* Criminology; cultural sociology; gender, race, and ethics relations; deviant behavior and social control. *Unit head:* Katharine M. Donato, PhD, Chair, 615-322-7626, Fax: 615-322-7505, E-mail: katharine.donato@vanderbilt.edu. *Application contact:* Karen Campbell, PhD, Director of Graduate Studies, 615-322-7626, Fax: 615-322-7505, E-mail: karen.e.campbell@vanderbilt.edu.

Virginia Commonwealth University, Graduate School, College of Humanities and Sciences, Wilder School of Government and Public Affairs, Department of Sociology, Program in Sociology, Richmond, VA 23284-9005. Offers MS. *Degree requirements:* For master's, thesis optional. *Entrance requirements:* For master's, GRE General Test.

Virginia Polytechnic Institute and State University, Graduate School, College of Liberal Arts and Human Sciences, Department of Sociology, Blacksburg, VA 24061. Offers MS, PhD. *Entrance requirements:* For master's and doctorate, GRE General Test. Additional exam requirements/recommendations for international students: Required—TOEFL (minimum score 550 paper-based; 213 computer-based). Electronic applications accepted. *Faculty research:* Science and technology, deviance and criminology, social psychology, social organization, demography.

Washington State University, Graduate School, College of Liberal Arts, Department of Sociology, Pullman, WA 99164. Offers crime and deviance (MA, PhD); environments, community and demographics (MA, PhD); institutions and social organizations (MA, PhD); political sociology (MA, PhD); social inequality (MA, PhD); social psychology and life course (MA, PhD). Terminal master's awarded for partial completion of doctoral program. *Degree requirements:* For master's, thesis; for doctorate, comprehensive exam, thesis/dissertation. *Entrance requirements:* For master's, GRE General Test, minimum GPA of 3.0; for doctorate, GRE General Test, MA in sociology, minimum GPA of 3.0. Additional exam requirements/recommendations for international students: Required—TOEFL (minimum score 550 paper-based). Electronic applications accepted. *Faculty research:* Crime/deviance, environmental sociology, social inequality, social psychology, gender.

Wayne State University, College of Liberal Arts and Sciences, Department of Sociology, Detroit, MI 48202. Offers MA, PhD. *Degree requirements:* For master's, thesis optional; for doctorate, thesis/dissertation. *Entrance requirements:* For master's, GRE General Test, GRE Subject Test, minimum GPA of 3.3; letters of reference; statement of interest; writing sample; for doctorate, GRE General Test, GRE Subject Test, minimum GPA of 3.5 in master's work; letters of reference. Additional exam requirements/recommendations for international students: Required—TOEFL (minimum score 550 paper-based; 213 computer-based); Recommended—TWE (minimum score 6). Electronic applications accepted. *Faculty research:* Social deviance, family, social inequality, medical sociology.

West Chester University of Pennsylvania, Office of Graduate Studies, College of Arts and Sciences, Department of Anthropology and Sociology, West Chester, PA 19383. Offers gerontology (Certificate); long term health care (MSA). Part-time and evening/weekend programs available. *Students:* 1 (woman) part-time. Average age 43. 1 applicant, 100% accepted, 1 enrolled. In 2008, 2 Certificates awarded. *Degree requirements:* For master's, comprehensive exam. *Entrance requirements:* For master's, MAT, GRE, or GMAT, interview, statement of professional goals, resumé, two letters of reference. Additional exam requirements/recommendations for international students: Required—TOEFL (minimum score 550 paper-based; 213 computer-based; 80 iBT). *Application deadline:* For fall admission, 4/15 priority date for domestic students, 3/15 for international students; for spring admission, 10/15 for domestic students, 9/1 for international students. Applications are processed on a rolling basis. Application fee: $35. Electronic applications accepted. *Expenses:* Tuition, state resident: full-time $6430; part-time $357 per credit. Tuition, nonresident: full-time $10,288; part-time $572 per credit. Required fees: $652.50; $50 per credit. $67 per semester. *Financial support:* In 2008–09, research assistantships with full tuition reimbursements (averaging $5,000 per year); unspecified assistantships also available. Support available to part-time students. Financial award application deadline: 2/15; financial award applicants required to submit FAFSA. *Faculty research:* West African communities in the U.S., life long learning-distance education, comparative religions. *Unit head:* Dr. Douglas McConatha, Chair and Graduate Coordinator, 610-436-2556, E-mail: dmcconatha@wcupa.edu. *Application contact:* Dr. Douglas McConatha, Chair and Graduate Coordinator, 610-436-2556, E-mail: dmcconatha@wcupa.edu.

Western Illinois University, School of Graduate Studies, College of Arts and Sciences, Department of Sociology and Anthropology, Macomb, IL 61455-1390. Offers sociology (MA). Part-time programs available. *Students:* 20 full-time (12 women), 5 part-time (3 women); includes 4 minority (all African Americans), 1 international. Average age 27. 17 applicants, 76% accepted. In 2008, 6 master's awarded. *Degree requirements:* For master's, thesis or alternative. *Entrance requirements:* Additional exam requirements/recommendations for international students: Required—TOEFL (minimum score 550 paper-based; 213 computer-based; 80 iBT). *Application deadline:* Applications are processed on a rolling basis. Application fee: $30. Electronic applications accepted. *Expenses:* Tuition, state resident: full-time $5696; part-time $237.34 per credit hour. Tuition, nonresident: full-time $11,392; part-time $474.68 per credit hour. Required fees: $1453; $60.55 per credit hour. *Financial support:* In 2008–09, 11 students received support, including 10 research assistantships with full tuition reimbursements available (averaging $7,040 per year), 1 teaching assistantship (averaging $8,120 per year). Financial award applicants required to submit FAFSA. *Unit head:* Dr. John Wozniak, Chairperson, 309-298-1056. *Application contact:* Evelyn Hoing, Assistant Director of Graduate Studies, 309-298-1806, Fax: 309-298-2345, E-mail: grad-office@wiu.edu.

Western Kentucky University, Graduate Studies, Potter College of Arts and Letters, Department of Sociology, Bowling Green, KY 42101. Offers MA. *Degree requirements:* For master's, comprehensive exam, thesis optional, final exam. *Entrance requirements:* For master's, GRE General Test, minimum GPA of 3.0. Additional exam requirements/recommendations for international students: Required—TOEFL (minimum score 555 paper-based; 213 computer-based; 79 iBT). *Faculty research:* Criminology/delinquency, quantitative and survey research methodology, occupations/professions, sex and gender, demography.

Western Michigan University, Graduate College, College of Arts and Sciences, Department of Sociology, Kalamazoo, MI 49008-5202. Offers MA, PhD. *Degree requirements:* For master's, thesis, oral exams; for doctorate, one foreign language, thesis/dissertation, oral exams, written exams. *Entrance requirements:* For doctorate, GRE General Test.

West Virginia University, Eberly College of Arts and Sciences, School of Applied Social Sciences, Department of Sociology, Morgantown, WV 26506. Offers applied social research (MA). Part-time programs available. *Degree requirements:* For master's, thesis or alternative. *Entrance requirements:* For master's, GRE General Test, minimum GPA of 2.75. Additional exam requirements/recommendations for international students: Required—TOEFL. *Faculty research:* Applied sociology, stratification, social/complex organization, research methodology criminology.

Wichita State University, Graduate School, Fairmount College of Liberal Arts and Sciences, Department of Sociology, Wichita, KS 67260. Offers MA. Part-time programs available. *Degree requirements:* For master's, thesis optional. *Entrance requirements:* For master's, GRE. Additional exam requirements/recommendations for international students: Required—TOEFL. Electronic applications accepted.

Wilfrid Laurier University, Faculty of Graduate Studies, Faculty of Arts, Department of Sociology, Waterloo, ON N2L 3C5, Canada. Offers MA. *Entrance requirements:* For master's, honours BA with a minimum average of B+ with a major in sociology. Additional exam requirements/recommendations for international students: Required—TOEFL (minimum score

Sociology

Wilfrid Laurier University *(continued)*
230 computer-based; 89 iBT). Electronic applications accepted. *Faculty research:* Internationalization, migration and human rights, health, families, and well-being.

William Paterson University of New Jersey, College of the Humanities and Social Sciences, Department of Sociology, Wayne, NJ 07470-8420. Offers MA. Part-time and evening/weekend programs available. *Degree requirements:* For master's, comprehensive exam, thesis. *Entrance requirements:* For master's, GRE or MAT. Electronic applications accepted. *Faculty research:* Critical political theory, urban social/ethnic groups, family studies, human development.

Yale University, Graduate School of Arts and Sciences, Department of Sociology, New Haven, CT 06520. Offers comparative and historical sociology (PhD); cultural sociology and social theory (PhD); social stratification and the life course (PhD). *Degree requirements:* For doctorate, thesis/dissertation. *Entrance requirements:* For doctorate, GRE General Test.

York University, Faculty of Graduate Studies, Faculty of Arts, Program in Social and Political Thought, Toronto, ON M3J 1P3, Canada. Offers MA, PhD. Part-time programs available. *Degree requirements:* For master's, one foreign language, thesis or alternative, oral exams; for doctorate, one foreign language, comprehensive exam, thesis/dissertation. Electronic applications accepted.

York University, Faculty of Graduate Studies, Faculty of Arts, Program in Sociology, Toronto, ON M3J 1P3, Canada. Offers MA, PhD. Part-time programs available. *Degree requirements:* For master's, thesis or alternative; for doctorate, one foreign language, comprehensive exam, thesis/dissertation, analytical paper. Electronic applications accepted.

Survey Methodology

University of Maryland, College Park, Graduate Studies, College of Behavioral and Social Sciences, Joint Program in Survey Methodology, College Park, MD 20742. Offers MS, PhD. *Degree requirements:* For master's, thesis (for some programs), scholarly paper; for doctorate, thesis/dissertation. *Entrance requirements:* For master's, GRE General Test (recommended), minimum GPA of 3.0, 3 letters of recommendation; for doctorate, GRE General Test, minimum GPA of 3.0, 3 letters of recommendation. Electronic applications accepted.

University of Michigan, Horace H. Rackham School of Graduate Studies, Program in Survey Methodology, Ann Arbor, MI 48109. Offers MS, PhD, Certificate. Part-time programs available. Terminal master's awarded for partial completion of doctoral program. *Degree requirements:* For master's, internships; for doctorate, comprehensive exam, thesis/dissertation. *Entrance requirements:* For master's and doctorate, GRE, 3 letters of recommendation; for Certificate, current enrollment in a graduate degree program at University of Michigan or have completed one within past 5 years. Additional exam requirements/recommendations for international students: Required—TOEFL (minimum score 560 paper-based; 220 computer-based). Electronic applications accepted. *Expenses:* Contact institution. *Faculty research:* Survey methodology, statistics, psychology, sociology, social psychology.

University of Nebraska–Lincoln, Graduate College, Interdepartmental Area of Survey Research and Methodology, Lincoln, NE 68588. Offers MS, PhD. *Students:* 17 full-time (15 women), 6 part-time (4 women); includes 1 minority (Asian American or Pacific Islander), 10 international. Average age 32. In 2008, 2 master's awarded. *Degree requirements:* For master's, comprehensive exam. *Entrance requirements:* For master's, GRE General Test or GMAT. Additional exam requirements/recommendations for international students: Required—TOEFL (minimum score 550 paper-based; 213 computer-based). *Application deadline:* For fall admission, 3/15 for domestic students, 3/1 for international students; for spring admission, 10/15 for domestic and international students. Application fee: $40. Electronic applications accepted. *Expenses:* Tuition, state resident: full-time $4275; part-time $237.50 per credit hour. Tuition, nonresident: full-time $11,525; part-time $640.25 per credit hour. Required fees: $1068; $10.35 per credit hour. $440.70 per semester. Tuition and fees vary according to course load and program. *Financial support:* Fellowships, research assistantships, teaching assistantships, Federal Work-Study, health care benefits, and unspecified assistantships available. Financial award application deadline: 2/15. *Faculty research:* Survey research and data analysis. *Unit head:* Dr. Allan McCutcheon, Graduate Chair, 402-472-6071, Fax: 402-477-3983. *Application contact:* Ginny Gross, Director of Graduate Admissions, 402-472-2878, Fax: 402-472-0589, E-mail: grad_admissions@unl.edu.

BRYN MAWR COLLEGE

Graduate School of Arts and Sciences
Department of Classical and Near Eastern Archaeology

Programs of Study	The Department of Classical and Near Eastern Archaeology at Bryn Mawr College offers M.A. and Ph.D. degrees in classical and Near Eastern archaeology. In cooperation with the Department of Greek, Latin, and Classical Studies, it also offers the M.A. and Ph.D. in classical studies. It is one of three independent departments that comprise the Graduate Group in Archaeology, Classics, and History of Art.
	The Department's guiding philosophy is that the ancient civilizations of the Mediterranean and the Near East are best studied as interconnected and mutually influential. The Department offers seminars on Iron Age Iran, the Aegean Bronze Age, Assyrian and Achaemenid art and archaeology, ancient Near Eastern and Egyptian kingship, Greek–ancient Near Eastern interconnections, Egyptian architecture, Greek art, Hellenistic art, the historiography of ancient art, ceramic analysis, and method and theory. Training combines the study of primary contexts, historical and literary sources, monuments, and art with course work in method and theory, including geographic information systems. Students may also explore the contributions of classical and Near Eastern cultures to the intellectual and artistic heritage of the modern era through interdisciplinary seminars offered by the Graduate Group, which also sponsors internships in Philadelphia-area museums and libraries.
	All course work and the M.A. thesis can normally be completed within two years; Ph.D. preliminary examinations should be taken in the third or fourth year, followed by the dissertation.
	Students are encouraged to develop their own research projects in consultation with a faculty adviser. Recent dissertation topics have included animal sculpture and naturalism in classical Greek sculpture, late Roman painting, priestly accommodation in ancient Greek sanctuaries, regional ceramic analysis in Iron Age Southeastern Asia, sociopolitical complexity in early Iron Age Syria and Anatolia, death rituals and kingship in Early Dynastic III Period Mesopotamia, pottery in the tombs of Mochlos and Myrsini, regional survey archaeology, the context of food production and preparation in ancient Greece, the furnishings of Hellenistic houses, baths in Magna Graecia, and ancient harbors in the Black Sea. Graduates are prepared for careers in college and university teaching, museum curatorship and administration, publishing, government service, and non-profit administration. Graduates of the past five years have also held postdoctoral fellowships at Rutgers University, Stanford University, the American School of Classical Studies in Athens, the University of Copenhagen, and the Institute for the Study of the Ancient World, New York University.
Research Facilities	The award-winning Rhys Carpenter Library, inaugurated in 1997, is a specialized library for archaeology, classics, and the history of art. Fully-wired carrels are available to all students in the Graduate Group in Archaeology, Classics, and History of Art. In addition to the more than 135,000 volumes in Carpenter Library, the tri-college library consortium of Bryn Mawr, Haverford, and Swarthmore Colleges contains over 2 million volumes. Bryn Mawr currently subscribes to more than 300 periodicals and serials in archaeology and classics. Online reference sources include the TLG, Dyabola, Library of Latin Texts, and *l'Année philologique*.
	The Ella Riegel Study Collection comprises about 6,500 archaeological items, including Athenian Red-Figure vases; Greek, Cypriot, and Egyptian pottery; Greek and Roman coins; representative artifacts in bronze, glass, terracotta, and wood; lamps; and an extensive collection of pottery samples from Tarsus.
	Faculty members in the Department direct two ongoing field projects: in the Nemea Valley in Greece and at the Iron Age settlement of Muweilah in the United Arab Emirates. Students also participate in field projects sponsored by other institutions.
Financial Aid	Bryn Mawr offers a number of fellowships for full-time study, as well as grants, tuition awards, and summer stipends. Fellowship stipends begin at $17,500, including a summer stipend, and can be guaranteed for multiple years. Special awards include Areté (Excellence) Fellowships with a package of $20,000 plus a health insurance subsidy. Each year, the Department offers two teaching assistantships and one research assistantship, with stipends of $14,000 plus a health insurance subsidy. For students in the Graduate Group in Archaeology, Classics, and History of Art, additional competitive fellowships and curatorial internships for multidisciplinary study are available with twelve-month stipends of $20,000 plus a health insurance subsidy. Currently, 85 percent of the students enrolled in the graduate program in archaeology receive some form of financial aid.
Cost of Study	Full-time tuition, consisting of six courses per year, is $31,340; part-time tuition is $5290 per course. Units of supervised work cost $845, and the fee for maintaining matriculation (continuing enrollment) is $430 per semester.
Living and Housing Costs	Students live locally or in Philadelphia. Shared apartments can be rented for $600 to $900 per month, studio apartments begin at $800 per month, and food costs are about $200 per month. Other expenses include transportation (about $165 per month if commuting from Philadelphia) and health insurance (approximately $2500 per year for domestic students and approximately $1500 for international students).
Student Group	In 2009–10, there are 24 students enrolled in archaeology, 18 women and 6 men. Four are international. Thirteen students have progressed to Ph.D. candidacy, 3 are candidates for the M.A., and the remaining are in course work.
Student Outcomes	Ph.D. graduates of the past ten years are currently teaching at Brock University, Case Western Reserve University, the University of Arizona, Vanderbilt University, Koç University (Turkey), University of Kalamata (Greece), and Franklin & Marshall. One works for the U.S. Department of State, two work for foundations, one holds a research position at New York University, and two hold postdoctoral fellowships.
Location	Bryn Mawr is a suburb of Philadelphia, the fifth-largest city in the U.S. It is well served by rail lines and by bus. Philadelphia is renowned for music, museums, and sports, and it is also a culinary mecca, with restaurants serving many cuisines. The metropolitan area has more than 100 museums and fifty colleges and universities, with a total population of 220,000 students.
The College and The Department	Bryn Mawr is a liberal arts college for women, founded in 1885. It was the first women's college to offer graduate education through the Ph.D. and the first U.S. institution to offer fellowships to women for graduate study. Throughout its history, the College has been committed first and foremost to providing the most rigorous and challenging education to women and, in the Graduate School of Arts and Sciences, also to men. The current enrollment is 1,300 undergraduate students, 150 graduate students in the Graduate School of Arts and Sciences, and about 250 students in the Graduate School of Social Work and Social Research.
	The Department of Classical Archaeology, founded by Rhys Carpenter in 1914, was the first independent department of archaeology in the United States. Carpenter (1914–1955) and Mary Hamilton Swindler (1912–1949) established the Department's international reputation. Under the leadership of Machteld Mellink (1949–1988), the Department extended its range to include Near Eastern and Egyptian archaeology. Brunilde Ridgway (1958–1993) made it preeminent in the field of Greek sculpture. Current faculty members add theory and historiography to the Department's traditional area specializations. Five alumnae of the program have been honored with the Archaeological Institute of America's gold medal for distinguished archaeological achievement: Dorothy Burr Thompson, Ph.D., '31; Virginia Grace, Ph.D., '34; Lucy Shoe Meritt, Ph.D., '35; Brunilde Ridgway, Ph.D., '58; and Maria Coutroubaki Shaw, Ph.D., '67. The Department today has a distinctly international cast, as those from other countries compose 15 percent of current students and 60 percent of the faculty.
Applying	Application for admission and financial aid should be made on the form available from the Graduate School of Arts and Sciences. Applicants can also download this form from the Graduate School's Web site at http://www.brynmawr.edu/gsas/. The deadline for admission with financial aid is January 4, 2010. Applications for admission without financial aid are accepted until June 30, 2010.
	Students admitted to graduate work in classic and Near Eastern archaeology typically have a basic knowledge of Greek or Latin, reading knowledge of German or French, and undergraduate training in archaeology. Applicants must submit GRE scores; TOEFL scores, if not native speakers of English; a statement of interest; and a recent research paper or critical essay.
	Students are encouraged to contact the Department and to visit. The Department's Web site is http://www.brynmawr.edu/archaeology/.
Correspondence and Information	Lea Miller, Program Assistant Graduate School of Arts and Sciences Bryn Mawr College 101 North Merion Avenue Bryn Mawr, Pennsylvania 19010 Phone: 610-526-5072 Fax: 610-526-5076 E-mail: lrmiller@brynmawr.edu Web site: http://www.brynmawr.edu/gsas/

Bryn Mawr College

THE FACULTY AND THEIR RESEARCH

Mehmet-Ali Ataç, Assistant Professor, Department of Classical and Near Eastern Archaeology; Ph.D., Harvard, 2003. Visual and intellectual traditions of the ancient Near East; Neo-Assyrian art and architecture, ancient Near Eastern and Egyptian kingship.

A. A. Donohue, Professor, Department of Classical and Near Eastern Archaeology; Ph.D., NYU, 1984. History and historiography of classical art.

Astrid Lindenlauf, Assistant Professor; Ph.D., University College (London), 2001. Greek art and archaeology, fortifications and warfare, urbanism, disposal and recycling practices.

Peter Magee, Associate Professor, Department of Classical and Near Eastern Archaeology; Ph.D., Sydney, 1996. Archaeology of South Asia, Iran, and Arabia; ancient imperialism; field methods; materials analysis.

James C. Wright, Professor and Chair, Department of Classical and Near Eastern Archaeology; Ph.D., Bryn Mawr, 1978. Prehistory of the Aegean basin, settlement forms and architecture of classical Greece, theory and method in archaeology.

Affiliated Faculty

Annette Baertschi, Assistant Professor, Department of Greek, Latin, and Classical Studies; Ph.D., Humboldt, 2006. Post-Augustan poetry, ancient magic, Latin meter, reception.

Don Barber, Associate Professor, Department of Geology; Ph.D., Colorado at Boulder, 2002. Geoarchaeology, coastal geology, paleoceanography, paleoclimatology.

Catherine Conybeare, Associate Professor, Department of Greek, Latin, and Classical Studies; Ph.D., Toronto, 1997. Late antique and early medieval Latin prose, cultural history, critical theory.

Radcliffe G. Edmonds III, Associate Professor, Department of Greek, Latin, and Classical Studies; Ph.D., Chicago, 1999. Greek myth, Greco-Roman religion and magic, Greek philosophy.

Richard Hamilton, Paul Shorey Professor of Greek; Ph.D., Michigan, 1971. Greek lyric poetry, Greek drama, Greek religion.

Russell T. Scott, Doreen C. Spitzer Professor of Latin and Classical Studies; Ph.D., Yale, 1964. Roman history and historiography, Latin literature, Roman archaeology.

EMORY UNIVERSITY

Graduate School of Arts and Sciences
Department of Sociology

Programs of Study	The Department of Sociology is a vigorous intellectual community that offers a doctoral program designed to prepare students for academic and research careers. The Department provides rigorous training in theory, statistics, and research design along with extensive preparation in comparative political economy, global analysis (political sociology, political economy, global development and change, social movements, revolutions, and welfare states), social psychology (interpersonal and group processes, status and power, justice and legitimacy, intergroup prejudice and discrimination, social structure and personality, emotions, and crime), stratification (work and industry, educational inequality, formal organizations, medical sociology, gender, race, class, and ethnicity), and culture (media, religion, social change, and the arts).
	The Department's speaker series, along with a very low student-faculty ratio, guarantees high levels of personal interaction. Advanced graduate students design and teach courses for Emory's undergraduates who are of exceptionally high academic aptitude. The Department also hosts a biannual undergraduate sociology symposium organized by graduate students and faculty members.
	The Ph.D. requires 72 hours of course work. The first 24 hours include core courses in research design, statistics, and theory. The remaining hours of course work include advanced courses in methods and statistics and in theory, two written examinations (one in a general field and one in a special field), and a dissertation. Ph.D. candidates must also publish in a scholarly journal or present a paper at a professional society conference. The program is designed for completion in five years.
Research Facilities	Emory has developed an ample and invigorating research environment. Graduate students have unlimited access to the Department's computer laboratory, which features high-capacity PCs and Macs. The University supports several specialized libraries that provide campuswide computerized bibliographic and circulation services.
	A distinctive research facility open to the Emory community is the Carter Center and Presidential Library. Established in 1983 by former President Jimmy Carter, the research and policy center offers a variety of scholarly activities and periodically hosts international seminars on topics such as Third World development, global health, and human rights. President Carter, an Emory Distinguished Professor, occasionally lectures and holds discussions with students. The study of medical sociology and demography is enhanced by adjunct sociologists in the United States Centers for Disease Control and Prevention (CDC). The CDC maintains large data sets on topics such as family violence, personal lifestyles, alcohol consumption, and other health-related behaviors. The study of the sociology of religion involves associated sociologists in the Candler School of Theology and the Graduate Division of Religion. Resources in the area of race relations and social change include such Atlanta-based civil rights organizations as the Martin Luther King Center for Nonviolent Social Change and the Southern Christian Leadership Conference. Other important resources include the SBSRC (Social and Behavioral Sciences Research Center), the Institute for Developing Nations, and the Development Studies Program.
Financial Aid	Graduate students in the Department receive full funding for five years, including a full tuition waiver and a combined fellowship and assistantship (currently at $16,500). Assistantship requirements are kept low, permitting students to finish their programs in a reasonable amount of time. Both admission and financial aid are awarded on the basis of academic merit. (No student should be discouraged from applying due to personal financial limitations.) In addition, students may compete for Woodruff Graduate Fellowships that provide full tuition and an annual $21,500 stipend for five years. Emory health care coverage is available with a 75 percent subsidy from Emory. Travel funds are available for graduate students to present papers at professional meetings.
Cost of Study	In 2008–09, tuition for full-time graduate study was $35,026. Admitted students are typically granted full tuition waivers and assistantships that cover most personal expenses while they are earning their degree.
Living and Housing Costs	Atlanta's cost of living ranks among the lowest of the nation's major metropolitan areas. Housing in University apartments ranges from $926 per month for a one-bedroom apartment to $529 (with roommate) to $1104 (single occupant) per month for a two-bedroom apartment. In addition, students have wide options in rooms and apartments in the residential neighborhoods surrounding the campus.
Student Group	Approximately 50 full-time graduate students are enrolled in the program. Recent graduates have found employment in academic institutions ranging from large research universities to small teaching colleges, as well as in private, public, and nonprofit research and policy positions.
Location	With a metropolitan-area population of more than 3 million, Atlanta is the unrivaled cultural and economic hub of the Southeast. The city offers a diversity of social, ethnic, and religious communities in an environment noted for its natural beauty and abundant trees. Emory is located in the heavily wooded Lullwater neighborhood, 6 miles east of downtown Atlanta. The University's graduate student housing (Campus Apartments, Inc.) is located in a new facility on Briarcliff Road at Sage Hill with free shuttle services to campus. While nearby Decatur maintains a small-town atmosphere, the Virginia-Highland neighborhood is known for its trendy shops, restaurants, and nightclubs. Also close by are the bohemian Little Five Points neighborhood and the Midtown arts and theater district. Atlanta has consistently been ranked one of the best places to live in the nation.
The University	Emory University is a private university with a national reputation for scholarly and educational excellence. Expansion rapidly accelerated after 1980 with the famous Robert W. Woodruff gift. Currently, Emory's endowment is ranked in the top fifteen in the country, yet the total student population has been kept to less than 12,000. In an era known for academic retrenchment, Emory has been expanding resources and attracting some of the best young faculty members produced in the last ten years.
Applying	The deadline for application for admission, financial aid, and Woodruff fellowships is December 18. Applications received after that date are considered, but they cannot be guaranteed access to funding. An undergraduate average of A- or better and scores above the 75th percentile on each section of the GRE General Test are good indications of competitiveness for admission. Emory actively seeks a diverse student body and strongly encourages applications from women and members of minority groups.
Correspondence and Information	Director of Graduate Admissions Department of Sociology Emory University Atlanta, Georgia 30322-2530 Phone: 404-727-7510 E-mail: socinfo@emory.edu Web site: http://www.sociology.emory.edu

Emory University

THE FACULTY AND THEIR RESEARCH

Robert S. Agnew, Ph.D., North Carolina at Chapel Hill, 1980. Criminology, social psychology, theory. Current research: causes of delinquency.

Delores P. Aldridge, Grace Towns Hamilton Professor of Sociology and African American Studies; Ph.D., Purdue, 1971. Intergroup relations, culture, stratification, organization, families and gender. Current research: male-female relations, Afrocentrism and cultural democracy in higher education, women in the labor market, women's health issues.

John Boli, Ph.D., Stanford, 1976. Theory, global historical development, culture, political sociology, sociology of education. Current research: origins of world culture in Christendom, global civil society, globalization of Sudoku, transnational organizations.

Irene Browne, Ph.D., Arizona, 1991. Stratification, gender, race, poverty. Current research: gender, race, class, intersectionality, immigration, stratification.

Sam Cherribi, Ph.D., Amsterdam, 2000. Race/ethnic/minority relations, migration and immigration, policy analysis/public policy. Current research: globalization.

Dennis J. Condron, Ph.D., Ohio State, 2005. Educational stratification, class and racial/ethnic stratification, segregation, poverty. Current research: unequal learning opportunities and outcomes in the American education system.

Timothy J. Dowd, Ph.D., Princeton, 1996. Organizations, mass media, culture, music, economic sociology. Current research: organizational and musical change in the U.S. record industry, the social construction of markets and industries.

Tyrone A. Forman, Ph.D., Michigan, 2001. Comparative race and ethnic relations, social psychology. Current research: intergroup prejudice and discrimination, children and youth, adolescent health and well-being, survey research methods.

Roberto Franzosi, Ph.D., Johns Hopkins, 1981. Political sociology and political economy, historical sociology, revolution, methodology and statistics. Current research: formal qualitative methodology, strikes, Italian fascism.

Elizabeth A. Griffiths, Ph.D., Toronto, 2006. Crime, deviance, and social control; spatial analyses of homicide; urban sociology; work, occupations, and organizations. Current research: spatial and temporal distributions of violence in cities and communities, mobility patterns of victims and offenders, family structure and victimization risk.

Karen A. Hegtvedt, Ph.D., Washington (Seattle), 1984. Social psychology, justice, power, emotions, literature. Current research: justice, legitimacy, power, and emotions in unjust situations; social psychology of sustainability.

Alexander M. Hicks, Ph.D., Wisconsin, 1979. Comparative political sociology and economy of industrial societies, global and developmental sociology, methodology, culture. Current research: relations between class formation, political organization, social policy, economic performance and cultural forms.

Ellen Idler, Ph.D., Yale, 1985. Aging, sociology of religion, health and health perceptions, disability. Current research: religion and health, psychology and health.

Cathryn Johnson, Ph.D., Iowa, 1990. Social psychology, status, power, legitimacy, emotions, work and formal organizations. Current research: status and legitimacy processes in organizations; legitimacy, justice, power, and emotions in unjust situations; social psychology of sustainability.

Corey Lee M. Keyes, Ph.D., Wisconsin, 1995. Mental health, aging, positive health. Current research: Positive (i.e. flourishing) mental health, social and life-course determinants of flourishing, role of positive mental health in preventing mental illness.

Frank J. Lechner, Ph.D., Pittsburgh, 1985. Theory, social change, religion, culture. Current research: globalization, religious change, national identity.

Amanda E. Lewis, Ph.D., Michigan, 2000. Race and ethnic relations, sociology of education, qualitative methods. Current research: children and youth, gender, social inequality, urban ethnography.

Jeffery S. Mullis, Ph.D., Virginia, 1995. Law and society, medical sociology, social control. Current research: conflicts and conflict resolution between doctors and patients.

Richard Rubinson, Ph.D., Stanford, 1974. Political economy of development, political sociology, sociology of education, organizations. Current research: comparative studies of industrial regulation; schooling, state, and economy in East Asia.

Tracy L. Scott, Ph.D., Princeton, 1999. Culture, religion, health, qualitative methods. Current research: spirituality in everyday life in the U.S., organizational culture among nurses and physicians in the hospital.

Regina Werum, Ph.D., Indiana, 1995. Current research: educational policy formation and implementation, inequalities in access to education and in educational outcomes, case studies involving comparative-international patterns in educational inequities and comparative-historical patterns in U.S. educational policy.

Kathryn Yount, Ph.D., Johns Hopkins, 1999. Social demography, public health, methods. Current research: gender inequality and health outcomes in Egypt.

Associated Faculty in the University

Regine O. Jackson, Ph.D., Michigan, 2001. American Studies and the Institute of Liberal Arts. American immigration, racial and ethnic identity, Haitian diaspora, contemporary black immigrants, qualitative research methods.

Nancy Kutner, Ph.D., North Carolina at Chapel Hill, 1965. School of Medicine. Medical sociology, rehabilitation medicine, aging, gender roles. Current research: quality of life and aging, gender, ethnicity, and chronic illness.

Kay L. Levine, Ph.D., Berkeley, 2003. Emory School of Law. Law and society, criminology/delinquency, sexuality and homosexuality.

Michael Sacks, Ph.D., Northwestern, 2000. Goizueta School of Business. Economy and society, stratification/mobility, social networks.

Steven M. Tipton, Ph.D., Harvard, 1979. Candler School of Theology. Sociology of morality, culture, religion. Current research: American culture and institutional analysis.

Paul Wolpe, Ph.D., Yale, 1986. Emory Ethics Center. Medical sociology, religion.

Associated Faculty at the School of Public Health

Edmund R. Becker, Ph.D., Vanderbilt, 1981. Organizational theory and behavior, medical sociology, health-care organization and policy, unions and labor relations. Current research: health-care organization autonomy and performance, returns of investment in public health, physician payment and productivity.

Richard M. Levinson, Ph.D., Wisconsin, 1975. Medical sociology, health behavior, health policy. Current research: financial barriers to health services, social determinants of health risk behaviors.

Claire Sterk, Ph.D., Rotterdam/CUNY, 1990. Medical sociology, social epidemiology, qualitative methods. Current research: women's and children's health.

Adjunct Faculty at the Centers for Disease Control and Prevention

Shailendra Nath Banerjee, Ph.D., Emory, 1982. Statistics, mathematical modeling, demography, social psychology.

Clark Denny, Ph.D., Emory, 1996. Demography, race and ethnic relations.

Amy Fasula, Ph.D., Emory, 2005. Social determinants of health, sexual health of women and youth, applied theories of social psychology, HIV/AIDS prevention.

Deborah Holtzman, Ph.D., Johns Hopkins, 1985. Social epidemiology, AIDS, health education.

David G. Hurst, Ph.D., Emory, 1998. Education, policy analysis/public policy, race/class/gender.

Karin A. Mack, Ph.D., Maryland, 1995. Aging and life course, demography, family.

James A. Mercy, Ph.D., Emory, 1982. Interpersonal violence, research methods, public health, policy.

Kim S. Miller, Ph.D., Emory, 1989. Sexual risk reduction, adolescents, family, evidence-based behavioral interventions for pre-risk youth, health disparities.

Saswati Sunderam, Ph.D., Emory, 1997. Medical sociology, demography, race/class/gender.

Adjunct Faculty

Vincent Carter, Ph.D., Emory, 2002. Sociology of education, stratification/organization, political sociology, race and ethnic relations.

M. V. George, Ph.D., 1966. Australian National University. Demography, epidemiology, morbidity, health statistics.

Louis A. Hazouri, Ph.D., Emory, 1983. Applied sociology in complex business organizations, comparative social problems, social policy, law, comparative health-care systems.

Frank Howell, Ph.D., Mississippi State, 1979. Research methods, spatial analysis, demography, environmental sociology.

Mike McQuaide, Ph.D., Penn State, 1979. Medical sociology, aging, social problems, social psychology.

Graham Scambler, Ph.D., London, 1983. Medical sociology, sociological theory.

Emeritus Faculty

Alvin Boskoff, Ph.D., North Carolina at Chapel Hill, 1950. Sociological theory, comparative urban structure, stratification, social change.

Abbott L. Ferriss, Ph.D., North Carolina at Chapel Hill, 1950. Social indicators, quality of life, civility.

William L. Graves, Ph.D., North Carolina at Chapel Hill, 1969. Medical sociology, population, research design.

Samarendranath Mitra, Ph.D., Chicago, 1961. Formal demography, mathematical models, statistics.

William W. Pendleton Jr., Ph.D., Tulane, 1965. Sociology of education, population, social ecology, family.

SOUTHERN ILLINOIS UNIVERSITY CARBONDALE

Department of Anthropology
Ph.D. in Anthropology Program

Programs of Study

The Department offers the Ph.D. degree in anthropology. Students may specialize in any of the four traditional subfields of anthropology: biological or physical anthropology, archaeology, social-cultural anthropology, and anthropological linguistics. The Department takes seriously the notion that anthropology is a single, integrated discipline, and the doctoral program requires significant exposure to all four subfields of anthropology.

Research Facilities

The Department has strong ties to the Center for Archaeological Investigations (CAI) and the Center for Systematic Biology. The CAI is an independent research unit with a permanent staff of 7. In addition, 12 research associates and emeriti participate in center-sponsored or assisted research and teaching, and many students take advantage of the opportunities for research in CAI projects. The center undertakes grant- and contract-funded field research, curation of collections, publication, and the Visiting Scholar Program. The latter supports a postdoctoral fellow who pursues research, teaching, and writing in the center and organizes an annual thematic Visiting Scholar Conference.

The Center for Systematic Biology is a consortium of faculty members from the Departments of Anthropology, Microbiology, Plant Biology, and Zoology and provides opportunities for graduate research training in modern, interdisciplinary approaches to biological taxonomy. Emphasizing the development of skills in taxonomic expertise, collections management, field methods, molecular techniques, and analytical-information technology, the center is dedicated to preparing graduates to deal effectively with scientific and societal issues stemming from the biodiversity crisis. Faculty research areas include primate evolution and biogeography as well as many specialties in microbiology, botany, zoology, and ecology. Research conducted by center faculty members and students takes advantage of state-of-the-art collections, laboratory, and computing facilities on the Southern Illinois University Carbondale (SIUC) campus.

An international journal that explores the relationship of racial, ethnic, and national identities and power hierarchies within national and global arenas, *Identities: Global Studies in Culture and Power,* is edited within the Department of Anthropology and is used as a research tool. Beginning with volume 9 (2002), *Identities* is available in print and on the Taylor and Francis Publications Web site at http://www.tandf.co.uk/journals/titles/1070289x.html.

The Department of Anthropology also maintains strong ties with the Black American Studies Program, the University Museum, the Department of Linguistics, and the Women's Studies Program.

Financial Aid

The Department provides financial support, including a stipend and tuition waiver, in the form of graduate assistantships. Additional graduate assistantships are available through the Center for Archaeological Investigations. Fellowship support for outstanding students is available from the Graduate School, including doctoral fellowships and the Morris Fellowship program, which provides five years of support. The Graduate School also provides some tuition waivers.

Cost of Study

In-state graduate tuition is $328 per credit hour in 2009–10. Out-of-state tuition is 2.5 times the in-state tuition rate ($820 per credit hour). Graduate students with at least a 25 percent appointment as a graduate assistant receive a tuition scholarship. Fees vary from $589.03 (1 credit hour) to $1557.50 (12 credit hours). Students with a graduate assistantship receive a 50 percent reduction in the primary care medical fee. New graduate students from Arkansas, Indiana, Kentucky, Missouri, and Tennessee qualify for the alternate tuition rate, which is equivalent to the in-state graduate tuition rate.

Living and Housing Costs

For married couples, students with families, and single graduate students, the University has 690 efficiency and one-, two-, three-, and four-bedroom apartments that rent for $499 to $720 per month in 2009–10. Residence halls for single graduate students are also available, as are accessible residence hall rooms and apartments for students with disabilities.

Student Group

In 2006–07, there were 48 students in the Ph.D. program. Approximately 3 to 6 new students are admitted each year.

Location

SIUC is 350 miles south of Chicago and 100 miles southeast of St. Louis. Nestled in rolling hills bordered by the Ohio and Mississippi Rivers and enhanced by a mild climate, the area has state parks, national forests and wildlife refuges, and large lakes for outdoor recreation. Cultural offerings include theater, opera, concerts, art exhibits, and cinema. Educational facilities for the families of students are excellent.

The University

Southern Illinois University Carbondale is a comprehensive public university with a variety of general and professional education programs. The University offers bachelor's and associate degrees, master's and doctoral degrees, the J.D. degree, and the M.D. degree. The University is fully accredited by the North Central Association of Colleges and Schools. The Graduate School has an essential role in the development and coordination of graduate instruction and research programs. The Graduate Council has academic responsibility for determining graduate standards, recommending new graduate programs and research centers, and establishing policies to facilitate the research effort.

Applying

Applicants to the Ph.D. degree program must complete the equivalent of the master's degree and supply three letters of recommendation. Applicants must also supply a statement of goals for their programs and subsequent professional careers.

Correspondence and Information

Graduate Secretary
Department of Anthropology
MC 4502
Southern Illinois University
Carbondale, Illinois 62901-4502
Phone: 618-453-5037
Fax: 618-453-5037
Web site: http://www.siu.edu/~anthro/phd.htm

Southern Illinois University Carbondale

THE FACULTY AND THEIR RESEARCH

Jane H. Adams, Professor; Ph.D., Illinois, 1987. Sociocultural anthropology, political economy, agricultural systems, history, gender roles; rural U.S., Latin America.

Andrew Balkansky, Associate Professor; Ph.D., Wisconsin, 1997. Archaeology, settlement patterns, social evolution, urbanism; Mexico, Central America.

Roberto E. Barrios, Assistant Professor; Ph.D., Florida, 2004. Sociocultural anthropology, medical anthropology, applied anthropology; Honduras; Southeastern U.S.

Robert S. Corruccini, Professor; Ph.D., Berkeley, 1975. Physical anthropology, paleontology, osteology, multivariate methods, dental anthropology, epidemiology; India, Italy, Caribbean.

Susan M. Ford, Associate Professor; Ph.D., Pittsburgh, 1980. Physical anthropology, primate paleontology and systematics (especially New World monkeys and early anthropoids), evolutionary theory, functional and comparative anatomy; South America.

Janet Fuller, Associate Professor; Ph.D., South Carolina, 1997. Language content and bilingualism, discourse analysis, sociolinguistics, pragmatics, second language acquisition.

Jonathan D. Hill, Professor and Editor, *Identities;* Ph.D., Indiana, 1983. Ethnology, ecology, and history of Lowland South America; ethnomusicology and performance studies; symbolic and semiotic anthropology; nationalism and ethnicity; critical studies of culture, power, and history.

C. Andrew Hofling, Professor; Ph.D., Washington (St. Louis), 1982. Linguistics; discourse analysis, Maya; Mesoamerica.

John McCall, Associate Professor; Ph.D., Indiana, 1992. Sociocultural anthropology, social theory, history, ritual studies, medical anthropology, expressive culture; Igbo, Africa.

Tracy L. Prowse, Assistant Professor; Ph.D., McMaster, 2001. Bioarchaeology, physical anthropology, osteology, paleopathology, paleonutrition, forensic anthropology, stable isotopes; Italy.

Ulrich H. Reichard, Assistant Professor; Ph.D., Göttingen (Germany), 1995. Physical anthropology, primates (gibbons), zoology, cultural anthropology/ethnology; Thailand.

Don S. Rice, Professor and Associate Provost; Ph.D., Penn State, 1976. Archaeology, ethnohistory, tropical ecology, development of complex societies; Middle America, Andes.

Prudence M. Rice, Professor and Director, Office of Research Development and Administration; Ph.D., Penn State, 1976. Archaeology, ceramics; Mesoamerica, Andes.

Izumi Shimada, Professor; Ph.D., Arizona, 1976. Archaeology, complex societies, technology and craft production, urban and ceremonial centers, experimental archaeology; Andes.

David Sutton, Associate Professor; Ph.D., Chicago, 1995. Sociocultural anthropology, historical consciousness, kinship and gender, food, memory; Greece, Europe.

Anthony K. Webster, Assistant Professor; Ph.D., Texas at Austin, 2004. Linguistic anthropology, verbal art, Navajo, Apache; Southwestern U.S.

Paul Welch, Associate Professor; Ph.D., Michigan 1986. Archaeology, politics and economics in midrange societies, eastern U.S.; quantitative methods.

SOUTHERN ILLINOIS UNIVERSITY CARBONDALE

Department of Sociology
Ph.D. in Sociology

Programs of Study

The Ph.D. degree program is centered on advanced offerings in the areas of theory, methods, deviance, social movements, religion, culture, gender, power, and inequality. A special concentration in criminology, deviance, and administration of justice allows interested students to pursue a substantial part of their doctoral studies in administration of justice. The faculty members are research oriented and support such an orientation on the part of their students. The Department of Sociology has a state-of-the-art 10-person computer lab.

The responsibility for initial advisement rests with the Director of Graduate Studies. As early as possible, the Director, in consultation with the student, requests an appropriate member of the Department's graduate faculty to serve as the student's academic adviser. This adviser helps prepare a general plan of study. Doctoral candidates have several required courses, research projects, and readings leading to the dissertation over a projected eight semesters of study.

Research Facilities

The Department of Sociology has a ten-machine microcomputer laboratory with SPSS, SAS, and other programs. Several other computer labs are available in Faner Hall. Morris Library's general collection numbers 2.4 million volumes, 2.8 million microforms, and more than 12,200 current serial subscriptions. Library users have access to nearly 600 electronic data files and CD-ROM products via workstations located throughout the building. The library is an active participant in the world's largest bibliographic network, Online Computer Library Center (OCLC), and it is a member of ILLINET Online (IO), the statewide automated catalog, circulation, and interlibrary loan system with records of more than 600 libraries.

Financial Aid

Assistantships for qualified students are available through the Department and the University on a competitive basis. Funding is normally limited to eight semesters for the Ph.D. degree. A student's continued funding is contingent on the student's satisfactory progress in the program, annual evaluation by faculty members, passing comprehensive exams in a timely manner, and on the availability of funds. Eighty percent of the full-time students have received some type of aid.

Cost of Study

In-state graduate tuition is $328 per credit hour in 2009–10. Out-of-state tuition is 2.5 times the in-state tuition rate ($820 per credit hour). Graduate students with at least a 25 percent appointment as a graduate assistant receive a tuition scholarship. Fees vary from $589.03 (1 credit hour) to $1557.50 (12 credit hours). Students with a graduate assistantship receive a 50 percent reduction in the primary care medical fee. New graduate students from Arkansas, Indiana, Kentucky, Missouri, and Tennessee qualify for the alternate tuition rate, which is equivalent to the in-state graduate tuition rate.

Living and Housing Costs

For married couples, students with families, and single graduate students, the University has 690 efficiency and one-, two-, three-, and four-bedroom apartments that rent for $499 to $720 per month in 2009–10. Residence halls for single graduate students are also available, as are accessible residence hall rooms and apartments for students with disabilities.

Student Group

The Department has 46 students, of whom 32 are full-time (10 women, 6 international) and 14 are part-time (6 women, 1 international). Seven students are African American, and 1 is Hispanic. In 2001–02 SIU awarded eight Ph.D. degrees in sociology.

Location

Southern Illinois University Carbondale is 350 miles south of Chicago and 100 miles southeast of St. Louis. Nestled in rolling hills bordered by the Ohio and Mississippi Rivers and enhanced by a mild climate, the area has state parks, national forests and wildlife refuges, and large lakes for outdoor recreation. Cultural offerings include theater, opera, concerts, art exhibits, and cinema. Educational facilities for the families of students are excellent.

The University

Southern Illinois University Carbondale is a comprehensive public university with a variety of general and professional education programs. The University offers bachelor's and associate degrees, master's and doctoral degrees, the J.D. degree, and the M.D. degree. The University is fully accredited by the North Central Association of Colleges and Schools. The Graduate School has an essential role in the development and coordination of graduate instruction and research programs. The Graduate Council has academic responsibility for determining graduate standards, recommending new graduate programs and research centers, and establishing policies to facilitate the research effort. Southern Illinois University Carbondale is a state-funded university founded in 1869.

Applying

Applications should be requested from the address given below. Application materials include official transcripts from colleges attended, the Application for Admission to Graduate Study, the Application for Admission to the Sociology Program, and three letters of recommendation. GRE scores are required. Applications received by December 15 that include all supporting materials receive full consideration for departmental assistantships, fellowships, and university support that begin the following fall semester. New applications for admission are considered through March 1. Admission for the spring semester is only given in exceptional circumstances.

Correspondence and Information

Director of Graduate Studies
Department of Sociology
Mailcode 4524
Southern Illinois University Carbondale
Carbondale, Illinois 62901

Phone: 618-453-2494
Fax: 618-453-8926
E-mail: sociolgy@siu.edu
Web site: http://www.siu.edu/~socio

Southern Illinois University Carbondale

THE FACULTY AND THEIR RESEARCH

SIU's Department of Sociology has a world-renowned faculty with particular strengths in the areas of social movements and social change, criminology and deviance, and gender and sexuality. The faculty members have edited numerous scholarly journals, including *Social Problems, Sociological Spectrum, Contemporary Ethnography,* and *Review of Religious Research.* SIU faculty members hold prominent positions in several scholarly associations and on editorial boards. Faculty members have authored several books, many book chapters, and numerous peer-reviewed articles in general-interest and specialty journals, including *American Sociological Review, Social Forces, Social Problems, Social Science Research, American Journal of Sociology,* and *Deviant Behavior.*

Robert D. Benford, Professor and Chair; Ph.D., Texas at Austin, 1987. Social movements, social psychology, peace and war, gender and sport, qualitative methods.
Jennifer L. Dunn, Associate Professor; Ph.D., California, Davis, 1999. Social psychology, deviance, criminology, victimology.
Derek C. Martin, Assistant Professor; Ph.D., California, Irvine, 2005. Race/ethnic relations, minority relations, stratification, mobility, leisure/sport/recreation.
Michelle Hughes Miller, Associate Professor; Ph.D., Nebraska–Lincoln, 1997. Gender, criminology, drug policy.
Jean-Pierre Read, Assistant Professor; Ph.D., California, Santa Barbara, 2000. Revolutions, social change, cultural sociology, theory, qualitative methods.
Darren E. Sherkat, Professor; Ph.D., Duke, 1991. Religion, social movements, theory, quantitative methods.
Kathryn B. Ward, Professor; Ph.D., Iowa, 1982. Gender, international political economy, social movements.
Rachel Bridges Whaley, Assistant Professor; Ph.D., SUNY at Albany, 1999. Criminology/delinquency, sex and gender, quantitative methodology.
Chris Wienke, Assistant Professor; Ph.D., Pittsburgh, 2003. Family, sexuality, gender, qualitative methodology, social inequality, cultural sociology.

Affiliated and Joint Appointments

Elaine M. Blinde, Professor (affiliated with the Kinesiology Department); Ph.D., Illinois at Urbana-Champaign, 1987. Leisure/sport/recreation.
Mae A. Davenport (affiliated with Forestry); Ph.D., Minnesota, 2003. Environmental sociology, qualitative methodology, leisure/sports/recreation.
John D. H. Downing (affiliated with Global Media Research); Ph.D., London School of Economics, 1974. Cultural sociology, political economy, mass communication/public opinion.
Walter B. Jaehnig (affiliated with School of Journalism); Ph.D., Essex (U.K.), 1974. Mass communication, public opinion, social control, community.
Jyotsna Kapur, Associate Professor (affiliated with Cinema and Photography); Ph.D., Northwestern, 1998. Children and youth, cultural sociology, Marxist sociology.
Jean C. Mangun (affiliated with Forestry); Ph.D., Purdue, 1991. Environmental sociology, rural sociology, leisure/sports/recreation.
Ainon Mizan (affiliated with Rural Health and Social Service Development); Ph.D., Southern Illinois at Carbondale, 1992. Family, social change, women and development.
Frederick W. Solt (affiliated with Political Science); Ph.D., North Carolina at Chapel Hill, 2003. Political sociology, quantitative methods.

Emeritus Faculty

Ernest K. Alix, Ph.D., Southern Illinois at Carbondale, 1966. Deviant behavior, sociology of sport, law and society.
Thomas Burger, Associate Professor; Ph.D., Duke, 1972. Theory, history of social thought, social stratification.
Thomas C. Calhoun, Ph.D., Kentucky, 1988. Deviance, juvenile delinquency, race and ethnic relations, qualitative methods.
Roland K. Hawkes, Ph.D., Johns Hopkins, 1967. Rural sociology, development, migration.
Lewellyn Hendrix, Ph.D., Princeton, 1974. Family and kinship, gender, cross-cultural research.
Frank C. Nall, Ph.D., Michigan, 1959. Urban sociology, comparative race and ethnic relations.
Mark A. Schneider, Ph.D., Yale, 1985. Theory, culture, and science.

TEXAS A&M UNIVERSITY

Department of Sociology

Programs of Study

The Department of Sociology prepares students for careers in teaching and research in higher education and for careers in research in the private and public sectors. The Department offers a broad-based curriculum with excellent opportunities for advanced training in the following areas of faculty expertise and research: culture; demography; law, deviance, and social control; political and economic sociology; race, class, and gender; and social psychology. The program is relatively large, with more than 90 students, but with 33 tenured and tenure-track faculty members, it has a favorable student-faculty ratio (under 3:1). Thus, students have many opportunities to work on faculty research projects and develop research programs of their own under close faculty supervision.

For students with a bachelor's degree, the graduate program is designed to facilitate completion of both the master's and doctoral degrees within five years. The master's degree requires 34 hours of course work (including 8 research hours for the thesis) and can be completed in two years. For students who have completed (or entered with) the master's degree, the Ph.D. requires an additional 64 hours of course work, of which 18 to 32 hours may be research hours. Doctoral students take preliminary examinations in two specialty areas within the discipline usually after approximately two years in the program. They also undertake a dissertation project that extends the boundaries of the discipline. In most cases, the Ph.D. can be completed in three years from the master's.

Research Facilities

Texas A&M has ample resources to support graduate student research and training. The University maintains a major research library system and is home to the George Bush Presidential Library. The Department maintains a computer lab to augment the computing facilities maintained by the University. The Department also houses the Laboratory for the Study of Social Deviance, which oversees a major longitudinal study supported by the NIH to encourage study of youth socialization, deviance, and the self. Numerous other institutes and centers offer opportunities for specialized sociological study, including the Mexican American and U.S. Latino Research Center (MALRC), the China Archives, the Public Policy Research Institute (PPRI), the Racial and Ethnic Studies Institute (RESI), and the Center for Presidential Studies (a major national depository of public opinion poll data). In addition, the Center for Presidential Studies sponsors a Program in Democratization, which is coordinated and staffed by faculty members from the Department.

Financial Aid

Most students in the program receive financial assistance in various forms including Department scholarships, University fellowships, Department assistantships, research assistantships on faculty grants, and assistantships in various units around the University. Departmental assistantships are awarded competitively each year. Department assistants work 20 hours per week for the academic year, receiving a nine-month stipend of $1350 per month, or $12,150 annually, for master's students or $1450–$1550 per month, or $13,050–$13,950 annually, for doctoral students. University-level fellowships offer stipends at even higher levels. Funded students also receive out-of-state tuition waivers, tuition supplement payments, and University-funded health insurance comparable to that of faculty members and staff. Students receiving scholarships receive out-of-state tuition waivers.

Cost of Study

Tuition is $221.74 per credit hour for residents and $498.74 per credit hour for nonresidents. Students awarded assistantships or University fellowships pay the lower resident tuition fees, receive full health benefits, and receive tuition assistance.

Living and Housing Costs

The cost of living in Bryan–College Station is low compared to most metropolitan areas. Options for on-campus housing are limited, but off-campus housing is abundant and moderately priced. For information, students should contact the Off-Campus Housing Office (979-845-1741).

Student Group

This past year, the Department had a diverse group of more than 90 graduate students. Approximately 80 percent are in residence and enrolled full-time. About 65 percent were women, about 35 percent were members of ethnic minority groups, and about 20 percent were international students. Professional placements vary based on student accomplishments. In general, graduates place well; most are employed full-time in universities, colleges, and public and private research agencies within a year of graduation.

Location

Bryan–College Station is located 100 miles northwest of Houston, 150 miles south of Dallas–Fort Worth, and 100 miles east of Austin. It is easily accessible by air on American or Continental airlines. With a population of 150,000, the twin-cities area is notable for the diversity of its ethnic and religious communities and for the range of cultural activities it supports, including blues and bluegrass, classical musical concerts, opera, ballet, local and visiting theatrical productions, art galleries, sports, and more. Resting in the Brazos River valley, the city has a pleasant geography of gently rolling hills, abundant trees, ready access to excellent public park and camping facilities, and a mild climate that rarely requires one to wear more than a sweater.

The University and The College

Texas A&M is a large, public, land-grant institution with a diverse student body of more than 48,000. Founded in 1876, it has a long tradition of excellence in scientific research. Rapidly expanding since its founding in the early 1970s, the College of Liberal Arts has become the second-largest college in the University and is home to nationally recognized faculty members in the humanities and social sciences. College growth has been accompanied by the rising prominence of its graduate programs and the expansion of the University's library holdings and other facilities supporting advanced research and scholarship.

Applying

Applications for fall semester admission are accepted from those with bachelor's degrees (or higher) and should be sent as early as possible. Completed applications received by January 15 are assured full consideration for financial aid. All applications are evaluated on an individual basis. Successful applicants typically have all or most of the following characteristics: an A or B average in relevant course work, a strong commitment to a professional career in sociology, strong letters of reference from professional sociologists, and scores in the top half of the GRE General Test.

Correspondence and Information

William A. McIntosh
Department of Sociology
Texas A&M University
4351 TAMU
College Station, Texas 77843-4351
Phone: 979-845-8525 or 5133
E-mail: socadvisor@tamu.edu
        w-mcintosh@tamu.edu
Web site: http://sociweb.tamu.edu

Texas A&M University

TENURED AND TENURE-TRACK FACULTY

In recent decades, the Department has grown in size, nearly doubling its tenured and tenure-track faculty, and in reputation. The faculty members are recognized nationally and internationally for their contributions in sociological research, scholarship, service, and graduate and undergraduate teaching.

Jeff Ackerman, Assistant Professor; Ph.D., Penn State, 2003. Criminology, deviance, sociology of law, quantitative methods.

Paul Almeida, Assistant Professor; Ph.D., California, Riverside, 2001. Social movements, political sociology, social inequality, Latin America, environmental sociology.

James Burk, Professor; Ph.D., Chicago, 1982. Social control, theory, political sociology.

Samuel Cohn, Professor; Ph.D., Michigan, 1981. Work and labor markets, industrial sociology, economy and society.

Ben Crouch, Professor; Ph.D., Southern Illinois at Carbondale, 1971. Criminology/delinquency, deviant behavior/social disorganization.

Ashley Currier, Assistant Professor; Ph.D., Pittsburgh, 2007. Social movements, sexualities, gender, Southern Africa, qualitative methods.

Joe Feagin, Professor; Ph.D., Harvard, 1966. Race and ethnic relations, gender relations, urban political economy.

Nadia Flores, Assistant Professor; Ph.D., Pennsylvania, 2005. Demography, economic sociology, economics, sociology of immigration, international migration, urban sociology.

Mark A. Fossett, Professor; Ph.D., Texas at Austin, 1983. Race/ethnic/minority relations, stratification/mobility, urban sociology.

Holly Foster, Assistant Professor; Ph.D., Toronto, 2002. Crime, deviance, life course, quantitative methods.

Sarah Nicole Gatson, Associate Professor; Ph.D., Northwestern, 1999. Race/ethnic/minority relations, law and society, cultural sociology.

Kathryn Henderson, Associate Professor; Ph.D., California, San Diego, 1991. Science and technology, cultural sociology, qualitative methodology.

Stuart Hysom, Assistant Professor; Ph.D., Emory, 2003. Social psychology, group processes, theory construction.

Joseph O. Jewell, Associate Professor; Ph.D., UCLA, 1998. Race/ethnic/minority relations, history of sociology/sociological thought, education.

Howard B. Kaplan, Professor; Ph.D., NYU, 1958. Social psychology, deviant behavior/social disorganization, mental health.

Dongxiao Liu, Assistant Professor; Ph.D., Harvard, 2007. Political sociology, social movements, comparative and historical, gender, China.

Robert Mackin, Assistant Professor; Ph.D., Wisconsin–Madison, 2005. Political sociology, sociology of religion, comparative/historical sociology, qualitative methods.

Reuben A. Buford May, Associate Professor, Ph.D., Chicago, 1996. Race and culture, sociology of sport, sociology of the everyday, urban ethnography.

William A. McIntosh, Professor; Ph.D., Iowa State, 1975. Sociology of food and nutrition, culture, medical sociology, social change.

Stjepan Mestrovic, Professor; Ph.D., Syracuse, 1982. Theory, religion, political sociology.

Wendy L. Moore, Assistant Professor; Ph.D., Minnesota, 2005. American race relations; critical race theory; intersections of race, class, and gender.

Edward Murguia, Associate Professor; Ph.D., Texas at Austin, 1978. Race/ethnic/minority relations, family.

Hiroshi Ono, Assistant Professor; Ph.D., Chicago, 1999. Economic sociology, social stratification and inequality, labor markets, organizations.

Dudley Poston, Professor; Ph.D., Oregon, 1968. Demography, human ecology, sex and gender.

Harland Prechel, Professor; Ph.D., Kansas, 1986. Comparative sociology/macrosociology, political sociology, formal and complex social organization.

Rogelio Saenz, Professor; Ph.D., Iowa State, 1986. Demography, Latina/Latino sociology, rural sociology.

David Sciulli, Professor; Ph.D., Columbia, 1983. Law and society, political sociology, theory.

Jane Sell, Professor; Ph.D., Washington State, 1979. Small groups, social psychology.

Nancy Plankey Vadela, Assistant Professor; Ph.D., Wisconsin–Madison, 2004. Development and social chance, Latin America, sociology of work, gender, social movements, qualitative methods.

Zulema Valdez, Assistant Professor; Ph.D., UCLA, 2002. Race and ethnic relations, economic sociology, immigration, Latina/Latino sociology.

Wenquan (Charles) Zhang, Assistant Professor; Ph.D., SUNY at Albany, 2004. Immigration, secondary migration, spatial assimilation and stratification, spatial econometrics and GIS.

Lu Zheng, Assistant Professor; Ph.D., Stanford, 2007. Institutions and organizations, economic sociology, stratification and mobility, China study.

Affiliated and Joint Appointments

George Rogers, Professor of Urban Planning; Ph.D., Pittsburgh, 1983. Environmental sociology, science and technology, formal and complex social organization.

John Thomas, Professor of Recreation, Park, and Tourism Sciences; Ph.D., Texas A&M, 1979. Quantitative methodology, applied sociology, evaluation research.

Emeritus Faculty

Jon Alston, Ph.D., Texas at Austin, 1971. Religion, formal and complex social organization.

Barbara Finlay, Ph.D., Florida, 1976. Quantitative, family demography.

Jerry Gaston, Ph.D., Yale, 1969. Science and technology, education.

Bardin Nelson, Ph.D., LSU, 1950. Social psychology, theory aging/social gerontology.

Albert Schaffer, Ph.D., North Carolina at Chapel Hill, 1957. Urban sociology community, theory.

APPENDIXES

Institutional Changes
Since the 2009 Edition

Following is an alphabetical listing of institutions that have recently closed, merged with other institutions, or changed their names or status. In the case of a name change, the former name appears first, followed by the new name.

Albany College of Pharmacy of Union University (Albany, NY): name changed to Albany College of Pharmacy and Health Sciences

Alvernia College (Reading, PA): name changed to Alvernia University

American Academy of Art (Chicago, IL): no longer offers graduate degrees

American InterContinental University (Weston, FL): name changed to American InterContinental University South Florida

Bentley College (Waltham, MA): name changed to Bentley University

College of St. Catherine (St. Paul, MN): name changed to St. Catherine University

The Colorado School of Professional Psychology (Colorado Springs, CO): name changed to University of the Rockies

Myers University (Cleveland, OH): name changed to Chancellor University

Episcopal Theological Seminary of the Southwest (Austin, TX): name changed to Seminary of the Southwest

Five Branches Institute: College of Traditional Chinese Medicine (Santa Cruz, CA): name changed to Five Branches University: Graduate School of Traditional Chinese Medicine

Heidelberg College (Tiffin, OH): name changed to Heidelberg University

Huron University USA in London (London, United Kingdom): closed; now a campus of Hult International Business School (Cambridge, MA)

Husson College (Bangor, ME): name changed to Husson University

Lenoir-Rhyne College (Hickory, NC): name changed to Lenoir-Rhyne University

Loyola College in Maryland (Baltimore, MD): name changed to Loyola University Maryland

Marian College (Indianapolis, IN): name changed to Marian University

Marian College of Fond du Lac (Fond du Lac, WI): name changed to Marian University

Mesivta of Eastern Parkway Rabbinical Seminary (Brooklyn, NY): name changed to Mesivta of Eastern Parkway–Yeshiva Zichron Meilech

Multnomah Bible College and Biblical Seminary (Portland, OR): name changed to Multnomah University

Muskingum College (New Concord, OH): name changed to Muskingum University

Neumann College (Aston, PA): name changed to Neumann University

North Carolina School of the Arts (Winston-Salem, NC): name changed to University of North Carolina School of the Arts

Northwest Christian College (Eugene, OR): name changed to Northwest Christian University

Pacific Graduate School of Psychology (Palo Alto, CA): name changed to Palo Alto University

Pennsylvania College of Optometry (Elkins Park, PA): name changed to Salus University

Psychological Studies Institute (Atlanta, GA): name changed to Richmont Graduate University

Saint Louis University, Madrid (Madrid, Spain): name changed to Saint Louis University–Madrid Campus

Samuel Merritt College (Oakland, CA): name changed to Samuel Merritt University

Schiller International University, American College of Switzerland (Leysin, Switzerland): closed

Sunbridge College (Spring Valley, NY): no longer degree granting

Taylor University College and Seminary (Edmonton, AB, Canada): name changed to Taylor College and Seminary

Taylor University Fort Wayne (Fort Wayne, IN): closed

Touro University College of Osteopathic Medicine (Vallejo, CA): name changed to Touro University

University College of the Fraser Valley (Abbotsford, BC, Canada): name changed to University of the Fraser Valley

University of Northern Virginia (Manassas, VA): no longer accredited by agency recognized by USDE or CHEA

Warner Southern College (Lake Wales, FL): name changed to Warner University

Abbreviations Used in the Guides

The following list includes abbreviations of degree names used in the profiles in the 2010 edition of the guides. Because some degrees (e.g., Doctor of Education) can be abbreviated in more than one way (e.g., D.Ed. or Ed.D.), and because the abbreviations used in the guides reflect the preferences of the individual colleges and universities, the list may include two or more abbreviations for a single degree.

Degrees

A Mus D	Doctor of Musical Arts
AC	Advanced Certificate
AD	Artist's Diploma Doctor of Arts
ADP	Artist's Diploma
Adv C	Advanced Certificate
Adv M	Advanced Master
AGC	Advanced Graduate Certificate
AGSC	Advanced Graduate Specialist Certificate
ALM	Master of Liberal Arts
AM	Master of Arts
AMRS	Master of Arts in Religious Studies
APC	Advanced Professional Certificate
App Sc	Applied Scientist
App Sc D	Doctor of Applied Science
Au D	Doctor of Audiology
B Th	Bachelor of Theology
CAES	Certificate of Advanced Educational Specialization
CAGS	Certificate of Advanced Graduate Studies
CAL	Certificate in Applied Linguistics
CALS	Certificate of Advanced Liberal Studies
CAMS	Certificate of Advanced Management Studies
CAPS	Certificate of Advanced Professional Studies
CAS	Certificate of Advanced Studies
CASPA	Certificate of Advanced Study in Public Administration
CASR	Certificate in Advanced Social Research
CATS	Certificate of Achievement in Theological Studies
CBHS	Certificate in Basic Health Sciences
CBS	Graduate Certificate in Biblical Studies
CCJA	Certificate in Criminal Justice Administration
CCSA	Certificate in Catholic School Administration
CCTS	Certificate in Clinical and Translational Science
CE	Civil Engineer
CEM	Certificate of Environmental Management
CET	Certificate in Educational Technologies
CGS	Certificate of Graduate Studies
Ch E	Chemical Engineer
CM	Certificate in Management
CMH	Certificate in Medical Humanities
CMM	Master of Church Ministries
CMS	Certificate in Ministerial Studies
CNM	Certificate in Nonprofit Management
CP	Certificate in Performance
CPASF	Certificate Program for Advanced Study in Finance
CPC	Certificate in Professional Counseling Certificate in Publication and Communication
CPH	Certificate in Public Health
CPM	Certificate in Public Management
CPS	Certificate of Professional Studies
CScD	Doctor of Clinical Science
CSD	Certificate in Spiritual Direction
CSS	Certificate of Special Studies
CTS	Certificate of Theological Studies
CURP	Certificate in Urban and Regional Planning
D Admin	Doctor of Administration
D Arch	Doctor of Architecture
D Com	Doctor of Commerce
D Div	Doctor of Divinity
D Ed	Doctor of Education
D Ed Min	Doctor of Educational Ministry
D Eng	Doctor of Engineering
D Engr	Doctor of Engineering
D Env	Doctor of Environment
D Env M	Doctor of Environmental Management
D Law	Doctor of Law
D Litt	Doctor of Letters
D Med Sc	Doctor of Medical Science
D Mgt	Doctor of Management
D Min	Doctor of Ministry
D Min PCC	Doctor of Ministry, Pastoral Care, and Counseling
D Miss	Doctor of Missiology
D Mus	Doctor of Music
D Mus A	Doctor of Musical Arts

D Phil	Doctor of Philosophy
D Ps	Doctor of Psychology
D Sc	Doctor of Science
D Sc D	Doctor of Science in Dentistry
D Sc IS	Doctor of Science in Information Systems
D Sc PA	Doctor of Science in Physician Assistant Studies
D Th	Doctor of Theology
D Th P	Doctor of Practical Theology
DA	Doctor of Accounting Doctor of Arts
DA Ed	Doctor of Arts in Education
DAH	Doctor of Arts in Humanities
DAOM	Doctorate in Acupuncture and Oriental Medicine
DAST	Diploma of Advanced Studies in Teaching
DBA	Doctor of Business Administration
DBL	Doctor of Business Leadership
DBS	Doctor of Buddhist Studies
DC	Doctor of Chiropractic
DCC	Doctor of Computer Science
DCD	Doctor of Communications Design
DCL	Doctor of Civil Law Doctor of Comparative Law
DCM	Doctor of Church Music
DCN	Doctor of Clinical Nutrition
DCS	Doctor of Computer Science
DDN	Diplôme du Droit Notarial
DDS	Doctor of Dental Surgery
DE	Doctor of Education Doctor of Engineering
DED	Doctor of Economic Development
DEIT	Doctor of Educational Innovation and Technology
DEM	Doctor of Educational Ministry
DEPD	Diplôme études Spécialisées
DES	Doctor of Engineering Science
DESS	Diplôme études Supérieures Spécialisées
DFA	Doctor of Fine Arts
DGP	Diploma in Graduate and Professional Studies
DH Ed	Doctor of Health Education
DH Sc	Doctor of Health Sciences
DHA	Doctor of Health Administration
DHCE	Doctor of Health Care Ethics
DHL	Doctor of Hebrew Letters Doctor of Hebrew Literature
DHS	Doctor of Health Science Doctor of Human Services
DHSc	Doctor of Health Science
Dip CS	Diploma in Christian Studies
DIT	Doctor of Industrial Technology
DJ Ed	Doctor of Jewish Education
DJS	Doctor of Jewish Studies
DLS	Doctor of Liberal Studies
DM	Doctor of Management Doctor of Music
DMA	Doctor of Musical Arts
DMD	Doctor of Dental Medicine
DME	Doctor of Manufacturing Management Doctor of Music Education
DMEd	Doctor of Music Education
DMFT	Doctor of Marital and Family Therapy
DMH	Doctor of Medical Humanities
DML	Doctor of Modern Languages
DMM	Doctor of Music Ministry
DMPNA	Doctor of Management Practice in Nurse Anesthesia
DN Sc	Doctor of Nursing Science
DNAP	Doctor of Nurse Anesthesia Practice
DNP	Doctor of Nursing Practice
DNS	Doctor of Nursing Science
DO	Doctor of Osteopathy
DPA	Doctor of Public Administration
DPC	Doctor of Pastoral Counseling
DPDS	Doctor of Planning and Development Studies
DPH	Doctor of Public Health
DPM	Doctor of Plant Medicine Doctor of Podiatric Medicine
DPS	Doctor of Professional Studies
DPT	Doctor of Physical Therapy
DPTSc	Doctor of Physical Therapy Science
Dr DES	Doctor of Design
Dr PH	Doctor of Public Health
Dr Sc PT	Doctor of Science in Physical Therapy
DS	Doctor of Science
DS Sc	Doctor of Social Science
DSJS	Doctor of Science in Jewish Studies
DSL	Doctor of Strategic Leadership
DSM	Doctor of Sport Management
DSN	Doctor of Science in Nursing

DSW	Doctor of Social Work		**GSS**	Graduate Special Certificate for Students in Special Situations
DTL	Doctor of Talmudic Law		**IEMBA**	International Executive Master of Business Administration
DV Sc	Doctor of Veterinary Science			
DVM	Doctor of Veterinary Medicine		**IMA**	Interdisciplinary Master of Arts
EAA	Engineer in Aeronautics and Astronautics		**IMBA**	International Master of Business Administration
ECS	Engineer in Computer Science		**IMES**	International Masters in Environmental Studies
Ed D	Doctor of Education		**Ingeniero**	Engineer
Ed DCT	Doctor of Education in College Teaching		**JCD**	Doctor of Canon Law
Ed M	Master of Education		**JCL**	Licentiate in Canon Law
Ed S	Specialist in Education		**JD**	Juris Doctor
Ed Sp	Specialist in Education		**JD/MUEP**	Juris Doctor/Master of Urban and Environmental Planning
Ed Sp PTE	Specialist in Education in Professional Technical Education		**JSD**	Doctor of Juridical Science
EDM	Executive Doctorate in Management			Doctor of Jurisprudence
EDSPC	Education Specialist			Doctor of the Science of Law
EE	Electrical Engineer		**JSM**	Master of Science of Law
EJD	Executive Juris Doctor		**L Th**	Licenciate in Theology
EMBA	Executive Master of Business Administration		**LL B**	Bachelor of Laws
EMHA	Executive Master of Health Administration		**LL CM**	Master of Laws in Comparative Law
EMIB	Executive Master of International Business		**LL D**	Doctor of Laws
EMPA	Executive Master of Public Administration		**LL M**	Master of Laws
	Executive Master of Public Affairs		**LL M in Tax**	Master of Laws in Taxation
EMS	Executive Master of Science		**LL M CL**	Master of Laws (Common Law)
EMTM	Executive Master of Technology Management		**M Ac**	Master of Accountancy
Eng	Engineer			Master of Accounting
Eng Sc D	Doctor of Engineering Science			Master of Acupuncture
Engr	Engineer		**M Ac OM**	Master of Acupuncture and Oriental Medicine
Ex Doc	Executive Doctor of Pharmacy		**M Acc**	Master of Accountancy
Exec Ed D	Executive Doctor of Education			Master of Accounting
Exec MBA	Executive Master of Business Administration		**M Acct**	Master of Accountancy
Exec MPA	Executive Master of Public Administration			Master of Accounting
Exec MPH	Executive Master of Public Health		**M Accy**	Master of Accountancy
Exec MS	Executive Master of Science		**M Actg**	Master of Accounting
G Dip	Graduate Diploma		**M Acy**	Master of Accountancy
GBC	Graduate Business Certificate		**M Ad**	Master of Administration
GCE	Graduate Certificate in Education		**M Ad Ed**	Master of Adult Education
GDM	Graduate Diploma in Management		**M Adm**	Master of Administration
GDPA	Graduate Diploma in Public Administration		**M Adm Mgt**	Master of Administrative Management
GDRE	Graduate Diploma in Religious Education		**M Admin**	Master of Administration
GEMBA	Global Executive Master of Business Administration		**M ADU**	Master of Architectural Design and Urbanism
			M Adv	Master of Advertising
GMBA	Global Master of Business Administration		**M Aero E**	Master of Aerospace Engineering
GPD	Graduate Performance Diploma		**M AEST**	Master of Applied Environmental Science and Technology
			M Ag	Master of Agriculture

M Ag Ed	Master of Agricultural Education
M Agr	Master of Agriculture
M Anesth Ed	Master of Anesthesiology Education
M App Comp Sc	Master of Applied Computer Science
M App St	Master of Applied Statistics
M Appl Stat	Master of Applied Statistics
M Aq	Master of Aquaculture
M Ar	Master of Architecture
M Arc	Master of Architecture
M Arch	Master of Architecture
M Arch I	Master of Architecture I
M Arch II	Master of Architecture II
M Arch E	Master of Architectural Engineering
M Arch H	Master of Architectural History
M Arch Studies	Master of Architectural Studies
M Arch UD	Master of Architecture in Urban Design
M Bioethics	Master in Bioethics
M Biomath	Master of Biomathematics
M Ch	Master of Chemistry
M Ch E	Master of Chemical Engineering
M Chem	Master of Chemistry
M Cl D	Master of Clinical Dentistry
M Cl Sc	Master of Clinical Science
M Comp E	Master of Computer Engineering
M Comp Sc	Master of Computer Science
M Coun	Master of Counseling
M Dent	Master of Dentistry
M Dent Sc	Master of Dental Sciences
M Des	Master of Design
M Des S	Master of Design Studies
M Div	Master of Divinity
M Ec	Master of Economics
M Econ	Master of Economics
M Ed	Master of Education
M Ed T	Master of Education in Teaching
M En	Master of Engineering
M En S	Master of Environmental Sciences
M Eng	Master of Engineering
M Eng Mgt	Master of Engineering Management
M Eng Tel	Master of Engineering in Telecommunications
M Engr	Master of Engineering
M Env	Master of Environment
M Env Des	Master of Environmental Design
M Env E	Master of Environmental Engineering
M Env Sc	Master of Environmental Science
M Fin	Master of Finance
M Geo E	Master of Geological Engineering
M Geoenv E	Master of Geoenvironmental Engineering
M Geog	Master of Geography
M Hum	Master of Humanities
M Hum Svcs	Master of Human Services
M IBD	Master of Integrated Building Delivery
M IDST	Master's in Interdisciplinary Studies
M Kin	Master of Kinesiology
M Land Arch	Master of Landscape Architecture
M Litt	Master of Letters
M Man	Master of Management
M Mat SE	Master of Material Science and Engineering
M Math	Master of Mathematics
M Med Sc	Master of Medical Science
M Mgmt	Master of Management
M Mgt	Master of Management
M Min	Master of Ministries
M Mtl E	Master of Materials Engineering
M Mu	Master of Music
M Mus	Master of Music
M Mus Ed	Master of Music Education
M Music	Master of Music
M Nat Sci	Master of Natural Science
M Oc E	Master of Oceanographic Engineering
M Pharm	Master of Pharmacy
M Phil	Master of Philosophy
M Phil F	Master of Philosophical Foundations
M Pl	Master of Planning
M Plan	Master of Planning
M Pol	Master of Political Science
M Pr Met	Master of Professional Meteorology
M Prob S	Master of Probability and Statistics
M Prof Past	Master of Professional Pastoral
M Psych	Master of Psychology
M Pub	Master of Publishing
M Rel	Master of Religion
M Sc	Master of Science
M Sc A	Master of Science (Applied)

M Sc AHN	Master of Science in Applied Human Nutrition	MA Sc	Master of Applied Science
M Sc BMC	Master of Science in Biomedical Communications	MA Sp	Master of Arts (Spirituality)
M Sc CS	Master of Science in Computer Science	MA Strategic Intelligence	Master of Arts in Strategic Intelligence
M Sc E	Master of Science in Engineering	MA Th	Master of Arts in Theology
M Sc Eng	Master of Science in Engineering	MA-R	Master of Arts (Research)
M Sc Engr	Master of Science in Engineering	MAA	Master of Administrative Arts
M Sc F	Master of Science in Forestry		Master of Applied Anthropology
M Sc FE	Master of Science in Forest Engineering		Master of Applied Arts
M Sc Geogr	Master of Science in Geography		Master of Arts in Administration
M Sc N	Master of Science in Nursing	MAAAP	Master of Arts Administration and Policy
M Sc OT	Master of Science in Occupational Therapy	MAAE	Master of Arts in Art Education
M Sc P	Master of Science in Planning	MAAL	Master of Accountancy and Applied Leadership
M Sc Pl	Master of Science in Planning	MAAT	Master of Arts in Applied Theology
M Sc PT	Master of Science in Physical Therapy		Master of Arts in Art Therapy
M Sc T	Master of Science in Teaching	MAB	Master of Agribusiness
M Serv Soc	Master of Social Service	MABC	Master of Arts in Biblical Counseling
M Soc	Master of Sociology		Master of Arts in Business Communication
M Sp Ed	Master of Special Education	MABE	Master of Arts in Bible Exposition
M Stat	Master of Statistics	MABL	Master of Arts in Biblical Languages
M Sw En	Master of Software Engineering	MABM	Master of Agribusiness Management
M Sys Sc	Master of Systems Science	MABS	Master of Arts in Biblical Studies
M Tax	Master of Taxation	MABT	Master of Arts in Bible Teaching
M Tech	Master of Technology	MAC	Master of Accountancy
M Th	Master of Theology		Master of Accounting
M Th Past	Master of Pastoral Theology		Master of Arts in Communication
M Tox	Master of Toxicology		Master of Arts in Counseling
M Trans E	Master of Transportation Engineering	MACAT	Master of Arts in Counseling Psychology: Art Therapy
M Urb	Master of Urban Planning	MACC	Master of Arts in Christian Counseling
M Vet Sc	Master of Veterinary Science	MACCM	Master of Arts in Church and Community Ministry
MA	Master of Administration	MACCT	Master of Accounting
	Master of Arts	MACE	Master of Arts in Christian Education
MA Comm	Master of Arts in Communication	MACFM	Master of Arts in Children's and Family Ministry
MA Ed	Master of Arts in Education	MACH	Master of Arts in Church History
MA Ed Ad	Master of Arts in Educational Administration	MACIS	Master of Accounting and Information Systems
MA Ext	Master of Agricultural Extension	MACJ	Master of Arts in Criminal Justice
MA Islamic	Master of Arts in Islamic Studies	MACL	Master of Arts in Christian Leadership
MA Military Studies	Master of Arts in Military Studies	MACM	Master of Arts in Christian Ministries
			Master of Arts in Church Music
MA Min	Master of Arts in Ministry		Master of Arts in Counseling Ministries
MA Miss	Master of Arts in Missiology	MACN	Master of Arts in Counseling
MA Past St	Master of Arts in Pastoral Studies	MACO	Master of Arts in Counseling
MA Ph	Master of Arts in Philosophy	MAcOM	Master of Acupuncture and Oriental Medicine
MA Psych	Master of Arts in Psychology	MACP	Master of Arts in Counseling Psychology
		MACPC	Master of Clinical Pastoral Counseling

MACS	Master of Arts in Catholic Studies
MACSE	Master of Arts in Christian School Education
MACT	Master of Arts in Christian Thought Master of Arts in Communications and Technology
MAD	Master in Educational Institution Administration Master of Art and Design
MADR	Master of Arts in Dispute Resolution
MADS	Master of Animal and Dairy Science Master of Applied Disability Studies
MAE	Master of Aerospace Engineering Master of Agricultural Economics Master of Agricultural Education Master of Architectural Engineering Master of Art Education Master of Arts in Economics Master of Arts in Education Master of Arts in English Master of Automotive Engineering
MAEd	Master of Arts Education
MAEL	Master of Arts in Educational Leadership Master of Arts in Executive Leadership
MAEM	Master of Arts in Educational Ministries
MAEN	Master of Arts in English
MAEP	Master of Arts in Economic Policy
MAES	Master of Arts in Environmental Sciences
MAESL	Master of Arts in English as a Second Language
MAET	Master of Arts in English Teaching
MAF	Master of Arts in Finance
MAFE	Master of Arts in Financial Economics
MAFLL	Master of Arts in Foreign Language and Literature
MAFM	Master of Accounting and Financial Management
MAFS	Master of Arts in Family Studies
MAG	Master of Applied Geography
MAGC	Master of Arts in Global Communication
MAGP	Master of Arts in Gerontological Psychology
MAGU	Master of Urban Analysis and Management
MAH	Master of Arts in Humanities
MAHA	Master of Arts in Humanitarian Assistance Master of Arts in Humanitarian Studies
MAHCM	Master of Arts in Health Care Mission
MAHG	Master of American History and Government
MAHL	Master of Arts in Hebrew Letters
MAHN	Master of Applied Human Nutrition
MAHS	Master of Arts in Human Services
MAHSR	Master of Applied Health Services Research
MAHT	Master of Arts in History Teaching
MAIA	Master of Arts in International Administration
MAIB	Master of Arts in International Business
MAICS	Master of Arts in Intercultural Studies
MAIDM	Master of Arts in Interior Design and Merchandising
MAIH	Master of Arts in Interdisciplinary Humanities
MAIPCR	Master of Arts in International Peace and Conflict Management
MAIR	Master of Arts in Industrial Relations
MAIS	Master of Arts in Intercultural Studies Master of Arts in Interdisciplinary Studies Master of Arts in International Studies
MAIT	Master of Administration in Information Technology Master of Applied Information Technology
MAJ	Master of Arts in Journalism
MAJ Ed	Master of Arts in Jewish Education
MAJCS	Master of Arts in Jewish Communal Service
MAJE	Master of Arts in Jewish Education
MAJS	Master of Arts in Jewish Studies
MAL	Master in Agricultural Leadership
MALA	Master of Arts in Liberal Arts
MALD	Master of Arts in Law and Diplomacy
MALER	Master of Arts in Labor and Employment Relations
MALM	Master of Applied Leadership and Management Master of Arts in Leadership Evangelical Mobilization
MALP	Master of Arts in Language Pedagogy
MALPS	Master of Arts in Liberal and Professional Studies
MALS	Master of Arts in Liberal Studies
MALT	Master of Arts in Learning and Teaching
MAM	Master of Acquisition Management Master of Agriculture and Management Master of Applied Mathematics Master of Arts in Management Master of Arts in Ministry Master of Arts Management Master of Avian Medicine
MAMB	Master of Applied Molecular Biology
MAMC	Master of Arts in Mass Communication Master of Arts in Ministry and Culture Master of Arts in Ministry for a Multicultural Church
MAME	Master of Arts in Missions/Evangelism
MAMFC	Master of Arts in Marriage and Family Counseling
MAMFCC	Master of Arts in Marriage, Family, and Child Counseling
MAMFT	Master of Arts in Marriage and Family Therapy

MAMM	Master of Arts in Ministry Management
MAMS	Master of Applied Mathematical Sciences Master of Arts in Ministerial Studies Master of Arts in Ministry and Spirituality
MAMT	Master of Arts in Mathematics Teaching
MAN	Master of Applied Nutrition
MANM	Master of Arts in Nonprofit Management
MANP	Master of Applied Natural Products
MANT	Master of Arts in New Testament
MAO	Master of Arts in Organizational Psychology
MAOM	Master of Acupuncture and Oriental Medicine Master of Arts in Organizational Management
MAOT	Master of Arts in Old Testament
MAP	Master of Applied Psychology Master of Arts in Planning Master of Public Administration Masters of Psychology
MAP Min	Master of Arts in Pastoral Ministry
MAPA	Master of Arts in Public Administration
MAPC	Master of Arts in Pastoral Counseling
MAPE	Master of Arts in Political Economy
MAPL	Master of Arts in Pastoral Leadership
MAPM	Master of Arts in Pastoral Ministry Master of Arts in Pastoral Music Master of Arts in Practical Ministry
MAPP	Master of Arts in Public Policy
MAPPS	Master of Arts in Asia Pacific Policy Studies
MAPS	Master of Arts in Pastoral Counseling/Spiritual Formation Master of Arts in Pastoral Studies Master of Arts in Public Service
MAPT	Master of Practical Theology
MAPW	Master of Arts in Professional Writing
MAR	Master of Arts in Religion
Mar Eng	Marine Engineer
MARC	Master of Arts in Rehabilitation Counseling
MARE	Master of Arts in Religious Education
MARL	Master of Arts in Religious Leadership
MARS	Master of Arts in Religious Studies
MAS	Master of Accounting Science Master of Actuarial Science Master of Administrative Science Master of Advanced Study Master of Aeronautical Science Master of American Studies Master of Applied Science Master of Applied Statistics Master of Architectural Studies Master of Archival Studies
MASA	Master of Advanced Studies in Architecture
MASAC	Master of Arts in Substance Abuse Counseling
MASD	Master of Arts in Spiritual Direction
MASE	Master of Arts in Special Education
MASF	Master of Arts in Spiritual Formation
MASJ	Master of Arts in Systems of Justice
MASL	Master of Arts in School Leadership
MASLA	Master of Advanced Studies in Landscape Architecture
MASM	Master of Arts in Specialized Ministries
MASP	Master of Applied Social Psychology Master of Arts in School Psychology
MASPAA	Master of Arts in Sports and Athletic Administration
MASS	Master of Applied Social Science Master of Arts in Social Science
MAST	Master of Arts Science Teaching
MASW	Master of Aboriginal Social Work
MAT	Master of Arts in Teaching Master of Arts in Theology Master of Athletic Training Masters in Administration of Telecommunications
Mat E	Materials Engineer
MATCM	Master of Acupuncture and Traditional Chinese Medicine
MATDE	Master of Arts in Theology, Development, and Evangelism
MATDR	Master of Territorial Management and Regional Development
MATE	Master of Arts for the Teaching of English
MATESL	Master of Arts in Teaching English as a Second Language
MATESOL	Master of Arts in Teaching English to Speakers of Other Languages
MATF	Master of Arts in Teaching English as a Foreign Language/Intercultural Studies
MATFL	Master of Arts in Teaching Foreign Language
MATH	Master of Arts in Therapy
MATI	Master of Administration of Information Technology
MATL	Master of Arts in Teaching of Languages Master of Arts in Transformational Leadership
MATM	Master of Arts in Teaching of Mathematics
MATS	Master of Arts in Theological Studies Master of Arts in Transforming Spirituality
MATSL	Master of Arts in Teaching a Second Language
MAUA	Master of Arts in Urban Affairs
MAUD	Master of Arts in Urban Design

MAURP	Master of Arts in Urban and Regional Planning
MAW	Master of Arts in Worship Master of Arts in Writing
MAWL	Master of Arts in Worship Leadership
MAWSHP	Master of Arts in Worship
MAXM	Master of Arts in Christian Ministries
MAYM	Master of Arts in Youth Ministry
MB	Master of Bioinformatics
MBA	Master of Business Administration
MBA-EP	Master of Business Administration–Experienced Professionals
MBAA	Master of Business Administration in Aviation
MBAE	Master of Biological and Agricultural Engineering Master of Biosystems and Agricultural Engineering
MBAH	Master of Business Administration in Health
MBAi	Master of Business Administration–International
MBAICT	Master of Business Administration in Information and Communication Technology
MBAIM	Master of Business Administration in International Management
MBAPA	Master of Business Administration–Physician Assistant
MBATM	Master of Business Administration in Technology Management
MBC	Master of Building Construction
MBE	Master of Bilingual Education Master of Bioengineering Master of Biological Engineering Master of Biomedical Engineering Master of Business and Engineering Master of Business Economics Master of Business Education
MBET	Master of Business, Entrepreneurship and Technology
MBIT	Master of Business Information Technology
MBL	Master of Business Law Master of Business Leadership
MBLE	Master in Business Logistics Engineering
MBMI	Master of Biomedical Imaging and Signals
MBMSE	Master of Business Management and Software Engineering
MBS	Master of Behavioral Science Master of Biblical Studies Master of Biological Science Master of Biomedical Sciences Master of Bioscience Master of Building Science
MBSI	Master of Business Information Science

MBT	Master of Biblical and Theological Studies Master of Biomedical Technology Master of Business Taxation Master's Degree in Biotechnology
MC	Master of Communication Master of Counseling Master of Cybersecurity
MC Ed	Master of Continuing Education
MC Sc	Master of Computer Science
MCA	Master of Arts in Applied Criminology Master of Commercial Aviation
MCAM	Master of Computational and Applied Mathematics
MCC	Master of Computer Science
MCCS	Master of Crop and Soil Sciences
MCD	Master of Communications Disorders Master of Community Development
MCE	Master in Electronic Commerce Master of Christian Education Master of Civil Engineering Master of Control Engineering
MCEM	Master of Construction Engineering Management
MCHE	Master of Chemical Engineering
MCIS	Master of Communication and Information Studies Master of Computer and Information Science Master of Computer Information Systems
MCIT	Master of Computer and Information Technology
MCJ	Master of Criminal Justice
MCJA	Master of Criminal Justice Administration
MCL	Master in Communication Leadership Master of Canon Law Master of Civil Law Master of Comparative Law
MCM	Master of Christian Ministry Master of Church Music Master of City Management Master of Communication Management Master of Community Medicine Master of Construction Management Master of Contract Management Masters of Corporate Media
MCMP	Master of City and Metropolitan Planning
MCMS	Master of Clinical Medical Science
MCP	Master in Science Master of City Planning Master of Community Planning Master of Counseling Psychology Master of Cytopathology Practice
MCPC	Master of Arts in Chaplaincy and Pastoral Care
MCPD	Master of Community Planning and Development
MCRP	Master of City and Regional Planning
MCRS	Master of City and Regional Studies

MCS	Master of Christian Studies Master of Clinical Science Master of Combined Sciences Master of Communication Studies Master of Computer Science Master of Consumer Science
MCSE	Master of Computer Science and Engineering
MCSL	Master of Catholic School Leadership
MCSM	Master of Construction Science/Management
MCST	Master of Science in Computer Science and Information Technology
MCTP	Master of Communication Technology and Policy
MCTS	Master of Clinical and Translational Science
MCVS	Master of Cardiovascular Science
MD	Doctor of Medicine
MDA	Master of Development Administration Master of Dietetic Administration
MDB	Master of Design-Build
MDE	Master of Developmental Economics Master of Distance Education
MDH	Master of Dental Hygiene
MDM	Master of Digital Media
MDR	Master of Dispute Resolution
MDS	Master of Dental Surgery
ME	Master of Education Master of Engineering Master of Entrepreneurship Master of Evangelism
ME Sc	Master of Engineering Science
MEA	Master of Educational Administration Master of Engineering Administration
MEAP	Master of Environmental Administration and Planning
MEBT	Master in Electronic Business Technologies
MEC	Master of Electronic Commerce
MECE	Master of Electrical and Computer Engineering
Mech E	Mechanical Engineer
MED	Master of Education of the Deaf
MEDL	Master of Educational Leadership
MEDS	Master of Environmental Design Studies
MEE	Master in Education Master of Electrical Engineering Master of Energy Engineering Master of Environmental Engineering
MEEM	Master of Environmental Engineering and Management
MEENE	Master of Engineering in Environmental Engineering
MEEP	Master of Environmental and Energy Policy

MEERM	Master of Earth and Environmental Resource Management
MEH	Master in Humanistic Studies Master of Environmental Horticulture
MEHS	Master of Environmental Health and Safety
MEIM	Master of Entertainment Industry Management
MEL	Master of Educational Leadership Master of English Literature
MEM	Master of Ecosystem Management Master of Electricity Markets Master of Engineering Management Master of Environmental Management Master of Marketing
MEME	Master of Engineering in Manufacturing Engineering Master of Engineering in Mechanical Engineering
MEMS	Master of Engineering in Manufacturing Systems
MENG	Master of Arts in English
MENVEGR	Master of Environmental Engineering
MEP	Master of Engineering Physics
MEPC	Master of Environmental Pollution Control
MEPD	Master of Education–Professional Development
MEPM	Master of Environmental Protection Management
MER	Master of Employment Relations
MES	Master of Education and Science Master of Engineering Science Master of Environmental Science Master of Environmental Studies Master of Environmental Systems Master of Special Education
MESM	Master of Environmental Science and Management
MET	Master of Education in Teaching Master of Educational Technology Master of Engineering Technology Master of Entertainment Technology Master of Environmental Toxicology
Met E	Metallurgical Engineer
METM	Master of Engineering and Technology Management
MEVE	Master of Environmental Engineering
MF	Master of Finance Master of Forestry
MFA	Master of Financial Administration Master of Fine Arts
MFAM	Master in Food Animal Medicine
MFAS	Master of Fisheries and Aquatic Science
MFAW	Master of Fine Arts in Writing
MFC	Master of Forest Conservation
MFCS	Master of Family and Consumer Sciences

MFE	Master of Financial Economics
	Master of Financial Engineering
	Master of Forest Engineering
MFG	Master of Functional Genomics
MFHD	Master of Family and Human Development
MFM	Master of Financial Mathematics
MFMS	Masters in Food Microbiology and Safety
MFPE	Master of Food Process Engineering
MFR	Master of Forest Resources
MFRC	Master of Forest Resources and Conservation
MFS	Master of Financial Services
	Master of Food Science
	Master of Forensic Sciences
	Master of Forest Science
	Master of Forest Studies
	Master of French Studies
MFSA	Master of Forensic Sciences Administration
MFST	Master of Food Safety and Technology
MFT	Master of Family Therapy
	Master of Food Technology
MFWB	Master of Fishery and Wildlife Biology
MFWCB	Master of Fish, Wildlife and Conservation Biology
MFWS	Master of Fisheries and Wildlife Sciences
MFYCS	Master of Family, Youth and Community Sciences
MG	Master of Genetics
MGA	Master of Governmental Administration
MGD	Master of Graphic Design
MGE	Master of Gas Engineering
	Master of Geotechnical Engineering
MGH	Master of Geriatric Health
MGIS	Master of Geographic Information Science
	Master of Geographic Information Systems
MGM	Master of Global Management
MGP	Master of Gestion de Projet
MGPS	Master of Global Policy Studies
MGS	Master of Gerontological Studies
	Master of Global Studies
MH	Master of Humanities
MH Ed	Master of Health Education
MH Sc	Master of Health Sciences
MHA	Master of Health Administration
	Master of Healthcare Administration
	Master of Hospital Administration
	Master of Hospitality Administration
MHAD	Master of Health Administration
MHCA	Master of Health Care Administration
MHCI	Master of Human-Computer Interaction

MHCL	Master of Health Care Leadership
MHE	Master of Health Education
	Master of Human Ecology
MHE Ed	Master of Home Economics Education
MHEA	Masters of Higher Education Administration
MHHS	Master of Health and Human Services
MHI	Master of Health Informatics
	Master of Healthcare Innovation
MHIIM	Master of Health Informatics and Information Management
MHIS	Master of Health Information Systems
MHK	Master of Human Kinetics
MHL	Master of Hebrew Literature
MHM	Master of Hospitality Management
MHMS	Master of Health Management Systems
MHP	Master of Health Physics
	Master of Heritage Preservation
	Master of Historic Preservation
MHPA	Master of Heath Policy and Administration
MHPE	Master of Health Professions Education
MHR	Master of Human Resources
MHRD	Master in Human Resource Development
MHRIM	Master of Hotel, Restaurant, and Institutional Management
MHRIR	Master of Human Resources and Industrial Relations
MHRLR	Master of Human Resources and Labor Relations
MHRM	Master of Human Resources Management
MHROD	Master of Human Resources and Organization Development
MHS	Master of Health Science
	Master of Health Sciences
	Master of Health Studies
	Master of Hispanic Studies
	Master of Human Services
	Master of Humanistic Studies
MHSA	Master of Health Services Administration
MHSM	Master of Health Sector Management
	Master of Health Systems Management
MI	Master of Instruction
MI Arch	Master of Interior Architecture
MI St	Master of Information Studies
MIA	Master of Interior Architecture
	Master of International Affairs
MIAA	Master of International Affairs and Administration
MIAM	Master of International Agribusiness Management
MIB	Master of International Business

MIBA	Master of International Business Administration		**MJ Ed**	Master of Jewish Education
MICM	Master of International Construction Management		**MJA**	Master of Justice Administration
MID	Master of Industrial Design		**MJM**	Master of Justice Management
	Master of Industrial Distribution		**MJS**	Master of Judicial Studies
	Master of Interior Design			Master of Juridical Science
	Master of International Development		**MKM**	Master of Knowledge Management
MIE	Master of Industrial Engineering		**ML**	Master of Latin
MIH	Master of Integrative Health		**ML Arch**	Master of Landscape Architecture
MIHTM	Master of International Hospitality and Tourism Management		**MLA**	Master of Landscape Architecture
				Master of Liberal Arts
MIJ	Master of International Journalism		**MLAS**	Master of Laboratory Animal Science
MILR	Master of Industrial and Labor Relations			Master of Liberal Arts and Sciences
MiM	Master in Management		**MLAUD**	Master of Landscape Architecture in Urban Development
MIM	Master of Industrial Management			
	Master of Information Management		**MLD**	Master of Leadership Development
	Master of International Management			Master of Leadership Studies
MIMLAE	Master of International Management for Latin American Executives		**MLE**	Master of Applied Linguistics and Exegesis
			MLER	Master of Labor and Employment Relations
MIMS	Master of Information Management and Systems		**MLERE**	Master of Land Economics and Real Estate
	Master of Integrated Manufacturing Systems		**MLHR**	Master of Labor and Human Resources
MIP	Master of Infrastructure Planning		**MLI**	Master of Legal Institutions
	Master of Intellectual Property		**MLI Sc**	Master of Library and Information Science
MIPER	Master of International Political Economy of Resources		**MLIS**	Master of Library and Information Science
				Master of Library and Information Studies
MIPP	Master of International Policy and Practice		**MLM**	Master of Library Media
	Master of International Public Policy		**MLOS**	Masters in Leadership and Organizational Studies
MIPS	Master of International Planning Studies		**MLRHR**	Master of Labor Relations and Human Resources
MIR	Master of Industrial Relations			
	Master of International Relations		**MLS**	Master of Leadership Studies
MIS	Master of Industrial Statistics			Master of Legal Studies
	Master of Information Science			Master of Liberal Studies
	Master of Information Systems			Master of Library Science
	Master of Integrated Science			Master of Life Sciences
	Master of Interdisciplinary Studies		**MLSP**	Master of Law and Social Policy
	Master of International Service		**MLT**	Master of Language Technologies
	Master of International Studies		**MLW**	Master of Studies in Law
MISE	Master of Industrial and Systems Engineering		**MM**	Master of Management
MISKM	Master of Information Sciences and Knowledge Management			Master of Ministry
				Master of Missiology
MISM	Master of Information Systems Management			Master of Music
MIT	Master in Teaching		**MM Ed**	Master of Music Education
	Master of Industrial Technology			Master of Music Education
	Master of Information Technology		**MM Sc**	Master of Medical Science
	Master of Initial Teaching		**MM St**	Master of Museum Studies
	Master of International Trade		**MM/MLS**	Master of Music/Master of Library Science
	Master of Internet Technology			
MITA	Master of Information Technology Administration		**MMA**	Master of Marine Affairs
MITM	Master of International Technology Management			Master of Media Arts
MITO	Master of Industrial Technology and Operations			Master of Musical Arts
MJ	Master of Journalism		**MMAE**	Master of Mechanical and Aerospace Engineering
	Master of Jurisprudence			

MMAS	Master of Military Art and Science	**MN**	Master of Nursing Master of Nutrition
MMB	Master of Microbial Biotechnology	**MN NP**	Master of Nursing in Nurse Practitioner
MMBA	Managerial Master of Business Administration	**MNA**	Master of Nonprofit Administration Master of Nurse Anesthesia
MMC	Master of Manufacturing Competitiveness Master of Mass Communications Master of Music Conducting	**MNAL**	Master of Nonprofit Administration and Leadership
MMCM	Master of Music in Church Music	**MNAS**	Master of Natural and Applied Science
MMCSS	Masters of Mathematical Computational and Statistical Sciences	**MNCM**	Master of Network and Communications Management
MME	Master of Manufacturing Engineering Master of Mathematics Education Master of Mathematics for Educators Master of Mechanical Engineering Master of Medical Engineering Master of Mining Engineering Master of Music Education	**MNE**	Master of Network Engineering Master of Nuclear Engineering
		MNL	Master in International Business for Latin America
		MNM	Master of Nonprofit Management
		MNO	Master of Nonprofit Organization
MMF	Master of Mathematical Finance	**MNPL**	Master of Not-for-Profit Leadership
MMFT	Master of Marriage and Family Therapy	**MNPS**	Master of New Professional Studies
MMG	Master of Management	**MNpS**	Master of Nonprofit Studies
MMH	Master of Management in Hospitality Master of Medical History Master of Medical Humanities	**MNR**	Master of Natural Resources
		MNRES	Master of Natural Resources and Environmental Studies
MMIS	Master of Management Information Systems	**MNRM**	Master of Natural Resource Management
MMM	Master of Manufacturing Management Master of Marine Management Master of Medical Management	**MNRS**	Master of Natural Resource Stewardship
		MNS	Master of Natural Science
MMME	Master of Metallurgical and Materials Engineering	**MO**	Master of Oceanography
MMMP	Master of Music in Music Performance	**MOD**	Master of Organizational Development
MMP	Master of Management Practice Master of Marine Policy Master of Music Performance	**MOGS**	Master of Oil and Gas Studies
		MOH	Master of Occupational Health
		MOL	Master of Organizational Leadership
MMPA	Master of Management and Professional Accounting	**MOM**	Master of Oriental Medicine
MMQM	Master of Manufacturing Quality Management	**MOR**	Master of Operations Research
MMR	Master of Marketing Research	**MOT**	Master of Occupational Therapy
MMRM	Master of Marine Resources Management	**MP**	Master of Physiology Master of Planning
MMS	Master of Management Science Master of Management Studies Master of Manufacturing Systems Master of Marine Studies Master of Materials Science Master of Medical Science Master of Medieval Studies Master of Modern Studies	**MP Ac**	Master of Professional Accountancy
		MP Acc	Master of Professional Accountancy Master of Professional Accounting Master of Public Accounting
		MP Aff	Master of Public Affairs
		MP Th	Master of Pastoral Theology
MMSE	Master of Manufacturing Systems Engineering	**MPA**	Master of Physician Assistant Master of Professional Accountancy Master of Professional Accounting Master of Public Administration Master of Public Affairs
MMSM	Master of Music in Sacred Music		
MMT	Master in Marketing Master of Management Master of Music Teaching Master of Music Therapy Masters in Marketing Technology		
		MPAC	Masters in Professional Accounting
		MPAID	Master of Public Administration and International Development
MMus	Master of Music		

MPAP	Master of Physician Assistant Practice Master of Public Affairs and Politics
MPAS	Master of Physician Assistant Science Master of Physician Assistant Studies Master of Public Art Studies
MPC	Master of Pastoral Counseling Master of Professional Communication Master of Professional Counseling
MPD	Master of Product Development Master of Public Diplomacy
MPDS	Master of Planning and Development Studies
MPE	Master of Physical Education Master of Power Engineering
MPEM	Master of Project Engineering and Management
MPH	Master of Public Health
MPHE	Master of Public Health Education
MPHTM	Master of Public Health and Tropical Medicine
MPIA	Master of Public and International Affairs Master Program in International Affairs
MPM	Master of Pastoral Ministry Master of Pest Management Master of Policy Management Master of Practical Ministries Master of Project Management Master of Public Management
MPNA	Master of Public and Nonprofit Administration
MPOD	Master of Positive Organizational Development
MPP	Master of Public Policy
MPPA	Master of Public Policy Administration Master of Public Policy and Administration
MPPAL	Master of Public Policy, Administration and Law
MPPM	Master of Public and Private Management Master of Public Policy and Management
MPPPM	Master of Plant Protection and Pest Management
MPPUP	Master of Public Policy and Urban Planning
MPRTM	Master of Parks, Recreation, and Tourism Management
MPS	Master of Pastoral Studies Master of Perfusion Science Master of Planning Studies Master of Political Science Master of Preservation Studies Master of Professional Studies Master of Public Service
MPSA	Master of Public Service Administration
MPSRE	Master of Professional Studies in Real Estate
MPT	Master of Pastoral Theology Master of Physical Therapy
MPVM	Master of Preventive Veterinary Medicine
MPW	Master of Professional Writing Master of Public Works

MQF	Master of Quantitative Finance
MQM	Master of Quality Management
MQS	Master of Quality Systems
MR	Master of Recreation Master of Retailing
MRA	Master in Research Administration
MRC	Master of Rehabilitation Counseling
MRCP	Master of Regional and City Planning Master of Regional and Community Planning
MRD	Master of Rural Development
MRE	Master of Religious Education
MRED	Master of Real Estate Development
MREM	Master of Resource and Environmental Management
MRLS	Master of Resources Law Studies
MRM	Master of Resources Management
MRP	Master of Regional Planning
MRS	Master of Religious Studies
MRSc	Master of Rehabilitation Science
MS	Master of Science
MS Cmp E	Master of Science in Computer Engineering
MS Kin	Master of Science in Kinesiology
MS Acct	Master of Science in Accounting
MS Aero E	Master of Science in Aerospace Engineering
MS Ag	Master of Science in Agriculture
MS Arch	Master of Science in Architecture
MS Bio E	Master of Science in Bioengineering Master of Science in Biomedical Engineering
MS Bm E	Master of Science in Biomedical Engineering
MS Ch E	Master of Science in Chemical Engineering
MS Chem	Master of Science in Chemistry
MS Cp E	Master of Science in Computer Engineering
MS Eco	Master of Science in Economics
MS Econ	Master of Science in Economics
MS Ed	Master of Science in Education
MS El	Master of Science in Educational Leadership and Administration
MS En E	Master of Science in Environmental Engineering
MS Eng	Master of Science in Engineering
MS Engr	Master of Science in Engineering
MS Env E	Master of Science in Environmental Engineering
MS Exp Surg	Master of Science in Experimental Surgery
MS Int A	Master of Science in International Affairs
MS Mat E	Master of Science in Materials Engineering

MS Mat SE	Master of Science in Material Science and Engineering
MS Met E	Master of Science in Metallurgical Engineering
MS Metr	Master of Science in Meteorology
MS Mgt	Master of Science in Management
MS Min	Master of Science in Mining
MS Min E	Master of Science in Mining Engineering
MS Mt E	Master of Science in Materials Engineering
MS Otal	Master of Science in Otalrynology
MS Pet E	Master of Science in Petroleum Engineering
MS Phys	Master of Science in Physics
MS Phys Op	Master of Science in Physiological Optics
MS Poly	Master of Science in Polymers
MS Psy	Master of Science in Psychology
MS Pub P	Master of Science in Public Policy
MS Sc	Master of Science in Social Science
MS Sp Ed	Master of Science in Special Education
MS Stat	Master of Science in Statistics
MS Surg	Master of Science in Surgery
MS SwE	Master of Science in Software Engineering
MS Tax	Master of Science in Taxation
MS Tc E	Master of Science in Telecommunications Engineering
MS-R	Master of Science (Research)
MSA	Master of School Administration
	Master of Science Administration
	Master of Science in Accountancy
	Master of Science in Accounting
	Master of Science in Administration
	Master of Science in Aeronautics
	Master of Science in Agriculture
	Master of Science in Anesthesia
	Master of Science in Architecture
	Master of Science in Aviation
	Master of Sports Administration
MSA Phy	Master of Science in Applied Physics
MSAA	Master of Science in Astronautics and Aeronautics
MSAAE	Master of Science in Aeronautical and Astronautical Engineering
MSABE	Master of Science in Agricultural and Biological Engineering
MSAC	Master of Science in Acupuncture
MSACC	Master of Science in Accounting
MSaCS	Master of Science in Applied Computer Science

MSAE	Master of Science in Aeronautical Engineering
	Master of Science in Aerospace Engineering
	Master of Science in Applied Economics
	Master of Science in Architectural Engineering
	Master of Science in Art Education
MSAL	Master of Sport Administration and Leadership
MSAM	Master of Science in Applied Mathematics
MSANR	Master of Science in Agriculture and Natural Resources Systems Management
MSAPM	Master of Security Analysis and Portfolio Management
MSAS	Master of Science in Applied Statistics
	Master of Science in Architectural Studies
MSAT	Master of Science in Accounting and Taxation
	Master of Science in Advanced Technology
	Master of Science in Athletic Training
MSAUS	Master of Science in Architectural Urban Studies
MSB	Master of Science in Bible
	Master of Science in Business
MSBA	Master of Science in Business Administration
MSBAE	Master of Science in Biological and Agricultural Engineering
	Master of Science in Biosystems and Agricultural Engineering
MSBC	Master of Science in Building Construction
MSBE	Master of Science in Biological Engineering
	Master of Science in Biomedical Engineering
	Master of Science in Business Education
MSBENG	Master of Science in Bioengineering
MSBIT	Master of Science in Business Information Technology
MSBM	Master of Sport Business Management
MSBME	Master of Science in Biomedical Engineering
MSBMS	Master of Science in Basic Medical Science
MSBS	Master of Science in Biomedical Sciences
MSC	Master of Science in Commerce
	Master of Science in Communication
	Master of Science in Computers
	Master of Science in Counseling
	Master of Science in Criminology
MSCA	Master of Science in Construction Administration
MSCC	Master of Science in Christian Counseling
	Master of Science in Community Counseling
MSCD	Master of Science in Communication Disorders
	Master of Science in Community Development
MSCE	Master of Science in Civil Engineering
	Master of Science in Clinical Epidemiology
	Master of Science in Computer Engineering
	Master of Science in Continuing Education

MSCEE	Master of Science in Civil and Environmental Engineering
MSCF	Master of Science in Computational Finance
MSCH	Master of Science in Chemical Engineering
MSChE	Master of Science in Chemical Engineering
MSCI	Master of Science in Clinical Investigation Master of Science in Curriculum and Instruction
MSCIS	Master of Science in Computer and Information Systems Master of Science in Computer Information Science Master of Science in Computer Information Systems
MSCJ	Master of Science in Criminal Justice
MSCJA	Master of Science in Criminal Justice Administration
MSCJS	Master of Science in Crime and Justice Studies
MSCL	Master of Science in Collaborative Leadership
MSCLS	Master of Science in Clinical Laboratory Studies
MSCM	Master of Science in Conflict Management Master of Science in Construction Management
MScM	Master of Science in Management
MSCP	Master of Science in Clinical Psychology Master of Science in Computer Engineering Master of Science in Counseling Psychology
MSCPE	Master of Science in Computer Engineering
MSCPharm	Master of Science in Pharmacy
MSCPI	Master in Strategic Planning for Critical Infrastructures
MSCRP	Master of Science in City and Regional Planning Master of Science in Community and Regional Planning
MSCS	Master of Science in Clinical Science Master of Science in Computer Science
MSCSD	Master of Science in Communication Sciences and Disorders
MSCSE	Master of Science in Computer Science and Engineering
MSCST	Master of Science in Computer Science Technology
MSCTE	Master of Science in Career and Technical Education
MSD	Master of Science in Dentistry Master of Science in Design Master of Science in Dietetics
MSDD	Master of Software Design and Development
MSDM	Master of Design Methods
MSDR	Master of Dispute Resolution
MSE	Master of Science Education Master of Science in Economics Master of Science in Education Master of Science in Engineering Master of Science in Engineering Management Master of Software Engineering Master of Special Education Master of Structural Engineering
MSE Mgt	Master of Science in Engineering Management
MSECE	Master of Science in Electrical and Computer Engineering
MSED	Master of Sustainable Economic Development
MSEE	Master of Science in Electrical Engineering Master of Science in Environmental Engineering
MSEH	Master of Science in Environmental Health
MSEL	Master of Science in Educational Leadership Master of Science in Executive Leadership Master of Studies in Environmental Law
MSEM	Master of Science in Engineering Management Master of Science in Engineering Mechanics Master of Science in Environmental Management
MSENE	Master of Science in Environmental Engineering
MSEO	Master of Science in Electro-Optics
MSEP	Master of Science in Economic Policy Master of Science in Engineering Physics
MSEPA	Masters of Science in Economics and Policy Analysis
MSES	Master of Science in Embedded Software Engineering Master of Science in Engineering Science Master of Science in Environmental Science Master of Science in Environmental Studies
MSESM	Master of Science in Engineering Science and Mechanics
MSET	Master of Science in Education in Educational Technology Master of Science in Engineering Technology
MSETM	Master of Science in Environmental Technology Management
MSEV	Master of Science in Environmental Engineering
MSEVH	Master of Science in Environmental Health and Safety
MSF	Master of Science in Finance Master of Science in Forestry
MSFA	Master of Science in Financial Analysis
MSFAM	Master of Science in Family Studies
MSFCS	Master of Science in Family and Consumer Science
MSFE	Master of Science in Financial Engineering
MSFOR	Master of Science in Forestry

MSFP	Master of Science in Financial Planning
MSFS	Master of Science in Financial Sciences
	Master of Science in Forensic Science
MSFSB	Master of Science in Financial Services and Banking
MSFT	Master of Science in Family Therapy
MSGC	Master of Science in Genetic Counseling
MSGL	Master of Science in Global Leadership
MSH	Master of Science in Health
	Master of Science in Hospice
MSHA	Master of Science in Health Administration
MSHCA	Master of Science in Health Care Administration
MSHCI	Master of Science in Human Computer Interaction
MSHCPM	Master of Science in Health Care Policy and Management
MSHE	Master of Science in Health Education
MSHES	Master of Science in Human Environmental Sciences
MSHFID	Master of Science in Human Factors in Information Design
MSHFS	Master of Science in Human Factors and Systems
MSHP	Master of Science in Health Professions
MSHR	Master of Science in Human Resources
MSHRL	Master of Science in Human Resource Leadership
MSHRM	Master of Science in Human Resource Management
MSHS	Master of Science in Health Science
	Master of Science in Health Services
	Master of Science in Health Systems
	Master of Science in Homeland Security
MSHT	Master of Science in History of Technology
MSI	Master of Science in Instruction
MSIA	Master of Science in Industrial Administration
	Master of Science in Information Assurance and Computer Security
	Master of Science in Interior Architecture
MSIB	Master of Science in International Business
MSIDM	Master of Science in Interior Design and Merchandising
MSIDT	Master of Science in Information Design and Technology
MSIE	Master of Science in Industrial Engineering
	Master of Science in International Economics
MSIEM	Master of Science in Information Engineering and Management
MSIM	Master of Science in Information Management
	Master of Science in International Management
	Master of Science in Investment Management

MSIMC	Master of Science in Integrated Marketing Communications
MSIR	Master of Science in Industrial Relations
MSIS	Master of Science in Information Science
	Master of Science in Information Systems
	Master of Science in Interdisciplinary Studies
MSISE	Master of Science in Infrastructure Systems Engineering
MSISM	Master of Science in Information Systems Management
MSISPM	Master of Science in Information Security Policy and Management
MSIST	Master of Science in Information Systems Technology
MSIT	Master of Science in Industrial Technology
	Master of Science in Information Technology
	Master of Science in Instructional Technology
MSITM	Master of Science in Information Technology Management
MSJ	Master of Science in Journalism
	Master of Science in Jurisprudence
MSJE	Master of Science in Jewish Education
MSJFP	Master of Science in Juvenile Forensic Psychology
MSJJ	Master of Science in Juvenile Justice
MSJPS	Master of Science in Justice and Public Safety
MSJS	Master of Science in Jewish Studies
MSK	Master of Science in Kinesiology
MSKM	Master of Science in Knowledge Management
MSL	Master of School Leadership
	Master of Science in Limnology
	Master of Studies in Law
MSLA	Master of Science in Landscape Architecture
	Master of Science in Legal Administration
MSLD	Master of Science in Land Development
MSLS	Master of Science in Legal Studies
	Master of Science in Library Science
MSLT	Master of Second Language Teaching
MSM	Master of Sacred Ministry
	Master of Sacred Music
	Master of School Mathematics
	Master of Science in Management
	Master of Science in Organization Management
	Master of Security Management
MSM/MBAA	Master of Science in Management/Master of Business Administration in Aviation
MSMA	Master of Science in Marketing Analysis
MSMAE	Master of Science in Materials Engineering
MSMC	Master of Science in Mass Communications

MSME	Master of Science in Mathematics Education
	Master of Science in Mechanical Engineering
MSMFE	Master of Science in Manufacturing Engineering
MSMIS	Master of Science in Management Information Systems
MSMIT	Master of Science in Management and Information Technology
MSMM	Master of Science in Manufacturing Management
MSMO	Master of Science in Manufacturing Operations
MSMOT	Master of Science in Management of Technology
MSMS	Master of Science in Management Science
	Master of Science in Medical Sciences
MSMSE	Master of Science in Manufacturing Systems Engineering
	Master of Science in Material Science and Engineering
	Master of Science in Mathematics and Science Education
MSMT	Master of Science in Management and Technology
	Master of Science in Medical Technology
MSN	Master of Science in Nursing
MSN-R	Master of Science in Nursing (Research)
MSNA	Master of Science in Nurse Anesthesia
MSNE	Master of Science in Nuclear Engineering
MSNED	Master of Science in Nurse Education
MSNM	Master of Science in Nonprofit Management
MSNS	Master of Science in Natural Science
	Master's of Science in Nutritional Science
MSOD	Master of Science in Organizational Development
MSOEE	Master of Science in Outdoor and Environmental Education
MSOES	Master of Science in Occupational Ergonomics and Safety
MSOH	Master of Science in Occupational Health
MSOL	Master of Science in Organizational Leadership
MSOM	Master of Science in Operations Management
	Master of Science in Organization and Management
	Master of Science in Oriental Medicine
MSOR	Master of Science in Operations Research
MSOT	Master of Science in Occupational Technology
	Master of Science in Occupational Therapy
MSP	Master of Science in Pharmacy
	Master of Science in Planning
	Master of Science in Psychology
	Master of Speech Pathology
MSPA	Master of Science in Physician Assistant
	Master of Science in Professional Accountancy
MSPAS	Master of Science in Physician Assistant Studies

MSPC	Master of Science in Professional Communications
	Master of Science in Professional Counseling
MSPE	Master of Science in Petroleum Engineering
MSPG	Master of Science in Psychology
MSPH	Master of Science in Public Health
MSPHR	Master of Science in Pharmacy
MSPM	Master of Science in Professional Management
	Master of Science in Project Management
MSPNGE	Master of Science in Petroleum and Natural Gas Engineering
MSPS	Master of Science in Pharmaceutical Science
	Master of Science in Political Science
	Master of Science in Psychological Services
MSPT	Master of Science in Physical Therapy
MSpVM	Master of Specialized Veterinary Medicine
MSR	Master of Science in Radiology
	Master of Science in Reading
MSRA	Master of Science in Recreation Administration
MSRC	Master of Science in Resource Conservation
MSRE	Master of Science in Real Estate
	Master of Science in Religious Education
MSRED	Master of Science in Real Estate Development
MSRLS	Master of Science in Recreation and Leisure Studies
MSRMP	Master of Science in Radiological Medical Physics
MSRS	Master of Science in Rehabilitation Science
MSS	Master of Science in Software
	Master of Social Science
	Master of Social Services
	Master of Software Systems
	Master of Sports Science
	Master of Strategic Studies
MSSA	Master of Science in Social Administration
MSSCP	Master of Science in Science Content and Process
MSSE	Master of Science in Software Engineering
	Master of Science in Space Education
	Master of Science in Special Education
MSSEM	Master of Science in Systems and Engineering Management
MSSI	Master of Science in Security Informatics
	Master of Science in Strategic Intelligence
MSSL	Master of Science in Strategic Leadership
MSSLP	Master of Science in Speech-Language Pathology
MSSM	Master of Science in Sports Medicine
MSSPA	Master of Science in Student Personnel Administration

MSSS	Master of Science in Safety Science
	Master of Science in Systems Science
MSST	Master of Science in Security Technologies
MSSW	Master of Science in Social Work
MSSWE	Master of Science in Software Engineering
MST	Master of Science and Technology
	Master of Science in Taxation
	Master of Science in Teaching
	Master of Science in Technology
	Master of Science in Telecommunications
	Master of Science Teaching
MSTC	Master of Science in Technical Communication
	Master of Science in Telecommunications
MSTCM	Master of Science in Traditional Chinese Medicine
MSTE	Master of Science in Telecommunications Engineering
	Master of Science in Transportation Engineering
MSTM	Master of Science in Technical Management
MSTM/MBAA	Master of Science in Technical Management/ Master of Business Administration in Aviation
MSTOM	Master of Science in Traditional Oriental Medicine
MSUD	Master of Science in Urban Design
MSUESM	Master of Science in Urban Environmental Systems Management
MSW	Master of Social Work
MSWE	Master of Software Engineering
MSWREE	Master of Science in Water Resources and Environmental Engineering
MSX	Master of Science in Exercise Science
MT	Master of Taxation
	Master of Teaching
	Master of Technology
	Master of Textiles
MTA	Master of Tax Accounting
	Master of Teaching Arts
	Master of Tourism Administration
MTCM	Master of Traditional Chinese Medicine
MTD	Master of Training and Development
MTE	Master in Educational Technology
	Master of Teacher Education
MTESOL	Master in Teaching English to Speakers of Other Languages
MTHM	Master of Tourism and Hospitality Management
MTI	Master of Information Technology
MTIM	Masters of Trust and Investment Management
MTL	Master of Talmudic Law
MTLM	Master of Transportation and Logistics Management

MTM	Master of Technology Management
	Master of Telecommunications Management
	Master of the Teaching of Mathematics
MTMH	Master of Tropical Medicine and Hygiene
MTOM	Master of Traditional Oriental Medicine
MTP	Master of Transpersonal Psychology
MTPC	Master of Technical and Professional Communication
MTS	Master of Theological Studies
MTSC	Master of Technical and Scientific Communication
MTSE	Master of Telecommunications and Software Engineering
MTT	Master in Technology Management
MTX	Master of Taxation
MUA	Master of Urban Affairs
MUD	Master of Urban Design
MUEP	Master of Urban and Environmental Planning
MUP	Master of Urban Planning
MUPDD	Master of Urban Planning, Design, and Development
MUPP	Master of Urban Planning and Policy
MUPRED	Masters of Urban Planning and Real Estate Development
MURP	Master of Urban and Regional Planning
	Master of Urban and Rural Planning
MUS	Master of Urban Studies
Mus Doc	Doctor of Music
Mus M	Master of Music
MVM	Master of VLSI and microelectronics
MVP	Master of Voice Pedagogy
MVPH	Master of Veterinary Public Health
MVS	Master of Visual Studies
MWC	Master of Wildlife Conservation
MWE	Master in Welding Engineering
MWPS	Master of Wood and Paper Science
MWR	Master of Water Resources
MWS	Master of Women's Studies
MZS	Master of Zoological Science
Nav Arch	Naval Architecture
Naval E	Naval Engineer
ND	Doctor of Naturopathic Medicine
NE	Nuclear Engineer
NP	Nurse Practitioner

Nuc E	Nuclear Engineer	SD	Doctor of Science
OD	Doctor of Optometry		Specialist Degree
OTD	Doctor of Occupational Therapy	SJD	Doctor of Juridical Science
PBME	Professional Master of Biomedical Engineering		Doctor of Juridical Science
PD	Professional Diploma	SLPD	Doctor of Speech-Language Pathology
PDD	Professional Development Degree	SLS	Specialist in Library Science
PGC	Post-Graduate Certificate	SM	Master of Science
Ph L	Licentiate of Philosophy	SM Arch S	Master of Science in Architectural Studies
Pharm D	Doctor of Pharmacy	SM Vis S	Master of Science in Visual Studies
PhD	Doctor of Philosophy	SMBT	Master of Science in Building Technology
PhD Otal	Doctor of Philosophy in Otalrynology	SP	Specialist Degree
Phd Surg	Doctor of Philosophy in Surgery	Sp C	Specialist in Counseling
PhDEE	Doctor of Philosophy in Electrical Engineering	Sp Ed	Specialist in Education
PM Sc	Professional Master of Science	Sp LIS	Specialist in Library and Information Science
PMBA	Professional Master of Business Administration	SPA	Specialist in Arts
PMC	Post Master Certificate	SPCM	Special in Church Music
PMD	Post-Master's Diploma	Spec	Specialist's Certificate
PMS	Professional Master of Science	Spec M	Specialist in Music
	Professional Master's Degree	SPEM	Special in Educational Ministries
Post-Doctoral Certificate	Post-Doctoral Certificate	SPS	School Psychology Specialist
		Spt	Specialist Degree
Post-Doctoral MS	Post-Doctoral Master of Science	SPTH	Special in Theology
PPDPT	Postprofessional Doctor of Physical Therapy	SSP	Specialist in School Psychology
PSM	Professional Master of Science	STB	Bachelor of Sacred Theology
Psy D	Doctor of Psychology	STD	Doctor of Sacred Theology
Psy M	Master of Psychology	STL	Licentiate of Sacred Theology
Psy S	Specialist in Psychology	STM	Master of Sacred Theology
Psya D	Doctor of Psychoanalysis	TDPT	Transitional Doctor of Physical Therapy
Re Dir	Director of Recreation	Th D	Doctor of Theology
Rh D	Doctor of Rehabilitation	Th M	Master of Theology
S Psy S	Specialist in Psychological Services	VMD	Doctor of Veterinary Medicine
Sc D	Doctor of Science	WEMBA	Weekend Executive Master of Business Administration
Sc M	Master of Science		
SCCT	Specialist in Community College Teaching	XMA	Executive Master of Arts
ScDPT	Doctor of Physical Therapy Science	XMBA	Executive Master of Business Administration

INDEXES

Close-Ups and Announcements

Adelphi University
  Advanced Psychological Studies 1049
  Art/Fine Arts 199
  Creative Writing 551
Adler School of Professional Psychology
  Psychology 1051
Alfred University
  School Psychology 1053
Alliant International University–Fresno
  Clinical Psychology-Ph.D. 1057
  Clinical Psychology-Psy.D. 1059
  Forensic Psychology 1055
Alliant International University–Irvine
  Forensic Psychology 1055
  Marital and Family Therapy 1061
Alliant International University–Los Angeles
  Clinical Psychology-Ph.D. 1057
  Clinical Psychology-Psy.D. 1059
  Forensic Psychology 1055
  Marital and Family Therapy 1061
Alliant International University–Sacramento
  Clinical Psychology-Psy.D. 1059
  Marital and Family Therapy 1061
Alliant International University–San Diego
  Clinical Psychology-Ph.D. 1057
  Clinical Psychology-Psy.D. 1059
  Marital and Family Therapy 1061
Alliant International University–San Francisco
  Clinical Psychology-Ph.D. 1057
  Clinical Psychology-Psy.D. 1059
American University
  Communication 681
  International Service 861
Antioch University New England
  Marriage and Family Therapy 1063
Argosy University, Atlanta
  Psychology and Behavioral Sciences 1065
Argosy University, Chicago
  Psychology and Behavioral Sciences 1067
Argosy University, Dallas
  Psychology and Behavioral Sciences 1069
Argosy University, Denver
  Psychology and Behavioral Sciences 1071
Argosy University, Hawai'i
  Psychology and Behavioral Sciences 1073
Argosy University, Inland Empire
  Psychology and Behavioral Sciences 1075
Argosy University, Los Angeles
  Psychology and Behavioral Sciences 1077
Argosy University, Nashville
  Psychology and Behavioral Sciences 1079
Argosy University, Orange County
  Psychology and Behavioral Sciences 1081
Argosy University, Phoenix
  Psychology and Behavioral Sciences 1083
Argosy University, Salt Lake City
  Psychology and Behavioral Sciences 1085
Argosy University, San Diego
  Psychology and Behavioral Sciences 1087
Argosy University, San Francisco Bay Area
  Psychology and Behavioral Sciences 1089
Argosy University, Sarasota
  Psychology and Behavioral Sciences 1091

Argosy University, Schaumburg
  Psychology and Behavioral Sciences 1093
Argosy University, Seattle
  Psychology and Behavioral Sciences 1095
Argosy University, Tampa
  Psychology and Behavioral Sciences 1097
Argosy University, Twin Cities
  Psychology and Behavioral Sciences 1099
Argosy University, Washington DC
  Psychology and Behavioral Sciences 1101
Art Center College of Design
  Design 115
The Art Institute of Boston at Lesley University
  Visual Arts 201
Auburn University
  English 435
  Political Science (Announcement) 1164
Ball State University
  Urban Planning (Announcement) 1201
Bard Graduate Center for Studies in the Decorative
    Arts, Design, and Culture
  Decorative Arts 203
Barry University
  Psychology 1103
Boston College
  Romance Languages and Literature 437
Boston University
  Communication 683
Bryn Mawr College
  Art History 205
  Classical and Near Eastern Archaeology 1287
  Greek, Latin, and Classical Studies 439
California College of the Arts
  Art, Architecture, Design, and Writing 207
California Institute of Integral Studies
  Humanities 347
  Psychology 1105
Carnegie Mellon University
  Professional Writing and Communication Design 553
Central European University
  Social Sciences and Humanities 349
Columbia University
  Film, Theater Arts, Visual Arts, and Writing 285
  International and Public Affairs 863
  Journalism 685
Cornell University
  Industrial and Labor Relations 1213
  Public Affairs 1211
Cranbrook Academy of Art
  Fine Arts and Architecture 209
CUNY Graduate School of Journalism
  Journalism 687
Dartmouth College
  Liberal Studies 351
Emory University
  Sociology 1289
Fairleigh Dickinson University, College at Florham
  Psychology 1107
Fairleigh Dickinson University, Metropolitan Campus
  Psychology 1107
Fashion Institute of Technology
  Graduate Studies 117

Felician College
  Counseling Psychology 1109
Fielding Graduate University
  Psychology 1111
Florida Institute of Technology
  Psychology 1113
Fordham University
  International Political Economy and Development 865
George Fox University
  Clinical Psychology 1115
George Mason University
  Cultural Studies 619
  Public Policy 1215
Hawai'i Pacific University
  Communication 689
  Diplomacy and Military Studies 827
  Global Leadership and Sustainable Development 1217
Illinois Institute of Technology
  Design 119
Indiana University Bloomington
  Public Affairs 1219
  Telecommunications (Announcement) 632
Indiana University–Purdue University Indianapolis
  Public Affairs 1221
The Institute of World Politics
  Statecraft and World Politics 867
The Jewish Theological Seminary
  Graduate Studies 529
  Rabbinical Studies 531
The Johns Hopkins University
  Policy Studies 1223
Lesley University
  Counseling and Psychology 1117
  Creative Writing 555
  Expressive Therapies 211
  Visual Arts 201
Loyola University Maryland
  Psychology 1119
Memphis College of Art
  Studio Practice and Art Education 213
Miami International University of Art & Design
  Art and Design 121
Miami University
  Art (Display) 170
Michigan State University
  Criminal Justice 739
Midwestern University, Downers Grove Campus
  Clinical Psychology (Announcement) 933
Missouri State University
  Global Studies 869
Monterey Institute of International Studies
  International Policy Studies 871
  Translation and Interpretation 463
Mountain State University
  Interdisciplinary Studies 573
Naropa University
  Graduate Studies 1121
The New School: A University
  Architecture 151
  Creative Writing (MFA) 557
  Design and Technology 123
  Drama 287
  Fine Arts 215
  History of Decorative Arts and Design 217
  Interior Design 125
  International Affairs 873
  Lighting Design 153

Media Studies 691
Photography 127
Political and Social Science 1251
Public and Urban Policy 1225
Urban Policy Analysis and Management 1227
New York School of Interior Design
  Interior Design 129
New York University
  Individualized Study 575
  Public Service 1229
Northwestern University
  Art Theory and Practice (Announcement) 171
  English (Announcement) 378
  Human Development and Social Policy 1231
  Human Development and Social
    Policy (Announcement) 1047
  Psychology (Announcement) 902
Nova Southeastern University
  Criminal Justice 741
Palo Alto University
  Clinical Psychology 1123
  Doctor of Psychology (Consortium Program) 1125
Philadelphia College of Osteopathic Medicine
  Psychology 1127
Point Park University
  Journalism and Mass Communication 693
Pratt Institute
  Architecture 155
  Art and Design 219
Quinnipiac University
  Communications 695
Roger Williams University
  Forensic Psychology 1129
  Forensic Psychology (Announcement) 981
  Justice Studies 743
  Justice Studies (Announcement) 726
  Public Administration 1233
  Public Administration (Announcement) 1173
Rutgers, The State University of New Jersey, Newark
  Psychology 1131
Rutgers, The State University of New Jersey, New
    Brunswick
  Industrial Relations and Human Resource
    Management (Announcement) 1161
Saint Louis University–Madrid Campus
  Spanish Language and Literature and English 441
St. Mary's Seminary and University
  Theology and Religious
    Education (Announcement) 522
San Francisco Art Institute
  Fine Arts and Liberal Arts 221
Sarah Lawrence College
  Fine Arts 289
  Women's History 621
Savannah College of Art and Design
  Art and Design 223
  Graduate Programs (Announcement) 173
School of the Art Institute of Chicago
  Graduate Studies in Art 225
Seton Hall University
  Asian Studies 623
  Communication 697
  Diplomacy and International Relations 875
  English Literature and Writing 443
  Experimental Psychology 1133
  History 329
  Jewish-Christian Studies 533

Peterson's Graduate Programs in the Humanities, Arts & Social Sciences 2010

Museum Professions 227
Public Administration 1235
Southern Illinois University Carbondale
Anthropology 1291
Art and Design 131
Creative Writing 559
Economics 775
English 445
History 331
Mass Communication and Media Arts 699, 701
Philosophy 479
Political Science 877
Psychology 1135
Rehabilitation 1137
Sociology 1293
Speech Communication 703
Theater 291
South University (AL)
Counseling 1141
South University (FL)
Counseling 1145
South University (GA)
Counseling 1143
South University (SC)
Counseling 1139
Southwestern College (NM)
Counseling Psychology 1147
State University of New York at Binghamton
Art History (Announcement) 184
Suffolk University
Economics 777
Syracuse University
Public Communications 705
Public Communications (Announcement) 638
Temple University
Art History 229
Texas A&M University
Sociology 1295
Tufts University
Child Development (Announcement) 797
Law and Diplomacy 879
Urban and Environmental Policy and Planning 1237
University of California, Davis
Art History (Announcement) 185
University of California, Riverside
Economics (Announcement) 765
University of California, San Diego
International Relations and Pacific Studies 881
International Relations and Pacific Studies
(Display) 838

University of Delaware
Urban Affairs and Public Policy 1239
University of Denver
Communication 707
University of Hawaii at Manoa
World Theater (Display) 279
University of Illinois at Urbana–Champaign
779
University of Maine
Public Administration (Announcement) 1178
University of Miami
Architecture 157
University of New Hampshire
Economics 781
University of New Haven
Industrial and Organizational Psychology 1149
National Security and Public Safety 829
University of Oregon
Arts and Administration (Announcement) 190
University of Pennsylvania
Design 159
Governmental Administration 1241
University of Pittsburgh
English (Announcement) 390
Public and International Affairs 1243
University of Rochester
Visual and Cultural Studies 231
University of St. Thomas (MN)
English 447
University of Southern California
Acting and Dramatic Writing 293
Communication, Journalism, Public Diplomacy,
and Public Relations 709
The University of Texas at Dallas
Economic, Political, and Policy Sciences 783
The University of the Arts
Graduate Studies 233
Villanova University
English Language and Literature 449
History 333
Political Science 883
Psychology 1151
Washington University in St. Louis
Architecture and Urban Design 161
East Asian Studies 625
Economics (Display) 772
Widener University
Clinical Psychology 1153

Directories and Subject Areas in Other Books in This Series

Following is an alphabetical listing of directories and subject areas. Also listed are cross-references for subject area names not used in the directory structure of the guides, for example, "Arabic (*see* Near and Middle Eastern Languages)."

Graduate Programs in the Humanities, Arts & Social Sciences

Addictions/Substance Abuse Counseling
Administration (*see* Arts Administration; Public Administration)
African-American Studies
African Languages and Literatures (*see* African Studies)
African Studies
Agribusiness (*see* Agricultural Economics and Agribusiness)
Agricultural Economics and Agribusiness
Alcohol Abuse Counseling (*see* Addictions/Substance Abuse Counseling)
American Indian/Native American Studies
American Studies
Anthropology
Applied Arts and Design—General
Applied Economics
Applied History (*see* Public History)
Applied Social Research
Arabic (*see* Near and Middle Eastern Languages)
Arab Studies (*see* Near and Middle Eastern Studies)
Archaeology
Architectural History
Architecture
Archives Administration (*see* Public History)
Area and Cultural Studies (*see* African-American Studies; African Studies; American Indian/Native American Studies; American Studies; Asian-American Studies; Asian Studies; Canadian Studies; Cultural Studies; East European and Russian Studies; Ethnic Studies; Folklore; Gender Studies; Hispanic Studies; Holocaust Studies; Jewish Studies; Latin American Studies; Near and Middle Eastern Studies; Northern Studies; Pacific Area/Pacific Rim Studies; Western European Studies; Women's Studies)
Art/Fine Arts
Art History
Arts Administration
Arts Journalism
Art Therapy
Asian-American Studies
Asian Languages
Asian Studies
Behavioral Sciences (*see* Psychology)
Bible Studies (*see* Religion; Theology)
Biological Anthropology
Black Studies (*see* African-American Studies)
Broadcasting (*see* Communication; Film, Television, and Video Production)
Broadcast Journalism
Building Science
Canadian Studies

Celtic Languages
Ceramics (*see* Art/Fine Arts)
Child and Family Studies
Child Development
Chinese
Chinese Studies (*see* Asian Languages; Asian Studies)
Christian Studies (*see* Missions and Missiology; Religion; Theology)
Cinema (*see* Film, Television, and Video Production)
City and Regional Planning (*see* Urban and Regional Planning)
Classical Languages and Literatures (*see* Classics)
Classics
Clinical Psychology
Clothing and Textiles
Cognitive Psychology (*see* Psychology—General; Cognitive Sciences)
Cognitive Sciences
Communication—General
Community Affairs (*see* Urban and Regional Planning; Urban Studies)
Community Planning (*see* Architecture; Environmental Design; Urban and Regional Planning; Urban Design; Urban Studies)
Community Psychology (*see* Social Psychology)
Comparative and Interdisciplinary Arts
Comparative Literature
Composition (*see* Music)
Computer Art and Design
Conflict Resolution and Mediation/Peace Studies
Consumer Economics
Corporate and Organizational Communication
Corrections (*see* Criminal Justice and Criminology)
Counseling (*see* Counseling Psychology; Pastoral Ministry and Counseling)
Counseling Psychology
Crafts (*see* Art/Fine Arts)
Creative Arts Therapies (*see* Art Therapy; Therapies—Dance, Drama, and Music)
Criminal Justice and Criminology
Cultural Studies
Dance
Decorative Arts
Demography and Population Studies
Design (*see* Applied Arts and Design; Architecture; Art/Fine Arts; Environmental Design; Graphic Design; Industrial Design; Interior Design; Textile Design; Urban Design)
Developmental Psychology
Diplomacy (*see* International Affairs)
Disability Studies
Drama Therapy (*see* Therapies—Dance, Drama, and Music)
Dramatic Arts (*see* Theater)
Drawing (*see* Art/Fine Arts)
Drug Abuse Counseling (*see* Addictions/Substance Abuse Counseling)
Drug and Alcohol Abuse Counseling (*see* Addictions/Substance Abuse Counseling)
East Asian Studies (*see* Asian Studies)
East European and Russian Studies
Economic Development
Economics
Educational Theater (*see* Theater; Therapies—Dance, Drama, and Music)

Emergency Management

English

Environmental Design

Ethics

Ethnic Studies

Ethnomusicology (*see* Music)

Experimental Psychology

Family and Consumer Sciences—General

Family Studies (*see* Child and Family Studies)

Family Therapy (*see* Child and Family Studies; Clinical Psychology; Counseling Psychology; Marriage and Family Therapy)

Filmmaking (*see* Film, Television, and Video Production)

Film Studies (*see* Film, Television, and Video Production)

Film, Television, and Video Production

Film, Television, and Video Theory and Criticism

Fine Arts (*see* Art/Fine Arts)

Folklore

Foreign Languages (*see* specific language)

Foreign Service (*see* International Affairs; International Development)

Forensic Psychology

Forensic Sciences

Forensics (*see* Speech and Interpersonal Communication)

French

Gender Studies

General Studies (*see* Liberal Studies)

Genetic Counseling

Geographic Information Systems

Geography

German

Gerontology

Graphic Design

Greek (*see* Classics)

Health Communication

Health Psychology

Hebrew (*see* Near and Middle Eastern Languages)

Hebrew Studies (*see* Jewish Studies)

Hispanic Studies

Historic Preservation

History

History of Art (*see* Art History)

History of Medicine

History of Science and Technology

Holocaust Studies

Home Economics (*see* Family and Consumer Sciences—General)

Homeland Security

Household Economics, Sciences, and Management (*see* Family and Consumer Sciences—General)

Human Development

Humanities

Illustration

Industrial and Labor Relations

Industrial and Organizational Psychology

Industrial Design

Interdisciplinary Studies

Interior Design

International Affairs

International Development

International Economics

International Service (*see* International Affairs; International Development)

International Trade Policy

Internet and Interactive Multimedia

Interpersonal Communication (*see* Speech and Interpersonal Communication)

Interpretation (*see* Translation and Interpretation)

Islamic Studies (*see* Near and Middle Eastern Studies; Religion)

Italian

Japanese

Japanese Studies (*see* Asian Languages; Asian Studies; Japanese)

Jewelry (*see* Art/Fine Arts)

Jewish Studies

Journalism

Judaic Studies (*see* Jewish Studies; Religion)

Labor Relations (*see* Industrial and Labor Relations)

Landscape Architecture

Latin American Studies

Latin (*see* Classics)

Law Enforcement (*see* Criminal Justice and Criminology)

Liberal Studies

Lighting Design

Linguistics

Literature (*see* Classics; Comparative Literature; specific language)

Marriage and Family Therapy

Mass Communication

Media Studies

Medical Illustration

Medieval and Renaissance Studies

Metalsmithing (*see* Art/Fine Arts)

Middle Eastern Studies (*see* Near and Middle Eastern Studies)

Military and Defense Studies

Mineral Economics

Ministry (*see* Pastoral Ministry and Counseling; Theology)

Missions and Missiology

Motion Pictures (*see* Film, Television, and Video Production)

Museum Studies

Music

Musicology (*see* Music)

Music Therapy (*see* Therapies—Dance, Drama, and Music)

National Security

Native American Studies (*see* American Indian/Native American Studies)

Near and Middle Eastern Languages

Near and Middle Eastern Studies

Near Environment (*see* Family and Consumer Sciences)

Northern Studies

Organizational Psychology (*see* Industrial and Organizational Psychology)

Oriental Languages (*see* Asian Languages)

Oriental Studies (*see* Asian Studies)

Pacific Area/Pacific Rim Studies

Painting (*see* Art/Fine Arts)

Pastoral Ministry and Counseling

Philanthropic Studies

Philosophy

Photography

Playwriting (*see* Theater; Writing)

Policy Studies (*see* Public Policy)

Political Science

Population Studies (*see* Demography and Population Studies)

Portuguese

Printmaking (*see* Art/Fine Arts)

Product Design (*see* Industrial Design)

Psychoanalysis and Psychotherapy

Psychology—General

Public Administration

Public Affairs

Public History

Public Policy

Public Speaking (*see* Mass Communication; Rhetoric; Speech and Interpersonal Communication)

Publishing

Regional Planning (*see* Architecture; Urban and Regional Planning; Urban Design; Urban Studies)

Rehabilitation Counseling
Religion
Renaissance Studies (*see* Medieval and Renaissance Studies)
Rhetoric
Romance Languages
Romance Literatures (*see* Romance Languages)
Rural Planning and Studies
Rural Sociology
Russian
Scandinavian Languages
School Psychology
Sculpture (*see* Art/Fine Arts)
Security Administration (*see* Criminal Justice and Criminology)
Slavic Languages
Slavic Studies (*see* East European and Russian Studies; Slavic Languages)
Social Psychology
Social Sciences
Sociology
Southeast Asian Studies (*see* Asian Studies)
Soviet Studies (*see* East European and Russian Studies; Russian)
Spanish
Speech and Interpersonal Communication
Sport Psychology
Studio Art (*see* Art/Fine Arts)
Substance Abuse Counseling (*see* Addictions/Substance Abuse Counseling)
Survey Methodology
Sustainable Development
Technical Communication
Technical Writing
Telecommunications (*see* Film, Television, and Video Production)
Television (*see* Film, Television, and Video Production)
Textile Design
Textiles (*see* Clothing and Textiles; Textile Design)
Thanatology
Theater
Theater Arts (*see* Theater)
Theology
Therapies—Dance, Drama, and Music
Translation and Interpretation
Transpersonal and Humanistic Psychology
Urban and Regional Planning
Urban Design
Urban Planning (*see* Architecture; Urban and Regional Planning; Urban Design; Urban Studies)
Urban Studies
Video (*see* Film, Television, and Video Production)
Visual Arts (*see* Applied Arts and Design; Art/Fine Arts; Film, Television, and Video Production; Graphic Design; Illustration; Photography)
Western European Studies
Women's Studies
World Wide Web (*see* Internet and Interactive Multimedia)
Writing

Graduate Programs in the Biological Sciences

Anatomy
Animal Behavior
Bacteriology
Behavioral Sciences (*see* Biopsychology; Neuroscience; Zoology)
Biochemistry

Biological and Biomedical Sciences—General
Biological Chemistry (*see* Biochemistry)
Biological Oceanography (*see* Marine Biology)
Biophysics
Biopsychology
Botany
Breeding (*see* Botany; Plant Biology; Genetics)
Cancer Biology/Oncology
Cardiovascular Sciences
Cell Biology
Cellular Physiology (*see* Cell Biology; Physiology)
Computational Biology
Conservation (*see* Conservation Biology; Environmental Biology)
Conservation Biology
Crop Sciences (*see* Botany; Plant Biology)
Cytology (*see* Cell Biology)
Developmental Biology
Dietetics (*see* Nutrition)
Ecology
Embryology (*see* Developmental Biology)
Endocrinology (*see* Physiology)
Entomology
Environmental Biology
Evolutionary Biology
Foods (*see* Nutrition)
Genetics
Genomic Sciences
Histology (*see* Anatomy; Cell Biology)
Human Genetics
Immunology
Infectious Diseases
Laboratory Medicine (*see* Immunology; Microbiology; Pathology)
Life Sciences (*see* Biological and Biomedical Sciences)
Marine Biology
Medical Microbiology
Medical Sciences (*see* Biological and Biomedical Sciences)
Medical Science Training Programs (*see* Biological and Biomedical Sciences)
Microbiology
Molecular Biology
Molecular Biophysics
Molecular Genetics
Molecular Medicine
Molecular Pathogenesis
Molecular Pathology
Molecular Pharmacology
Molecular Physiology
Molecular Toxicology
Neural Sciences (*see* Biopsychology; Neurobiology; Neuroscience)
Neurobiology
Neuroendocrinology (*see* Biopsychology; Neurobiology; Neuroscience; Physiology)
Neuropharmacology (*see* Biopsychology; Neurobiology; Neuroscience; Pharmacology)
Neurophysiology (*see* Biopsychology; Neurobiology; Neuroscience; Physiology)
Neuroscience
Nutrition
Oncology (*see* Cancer Biology/Oncology)
Organismal Biology (*see* Biological and Biomedical Sciences; Zoology)
Parasitology
Pathobiology
Pathology
Pharmacology
Photobiology of Cells and Organelles (*see* Botany; Cell Biology; Plant Biology)

Physiological Optics (*see* Physiology)
Physiology
Plant Biology
Plant Molecular Biology
Plant Pathology
Plant Physiology
Pomology (*see* Botany; Plant Biology)
Psychobiology (*see* Biopsychology)
Psychopharmacology (*see* Biopsychology; Neuroscience; Pharmacology)
Radiation Biology
Reproductive Biology
Sociobiology (*see* Evolutionary Biology)
Structural Biology
Systems Biology
Teratology
Theoretical Biology (*see* Biological and Biomedical Sciences)
Therapeutics (*see* Pharmacology)
Toxicology
Translational Biology
Tropical Medicine (*see* Parasitology)
Virology
Wildlife Biology (*see* Zoology)
Zoology

Graduate Programs in the Physical Sciences, Mathematics, Agricultural Sciences, the Environment & Natural Resources

Acoustics
Agricultural Sciences
Agronomy and Soil Sciences
Analytical Chemistry
Animal Sciences
Applied Mathematics
Applied Physics
Applied Statistics
Aquaculture
Astronomy
Astrophysical Sciences (*see* Astrophysics; Atmospheric Sciences; Meteorology; Planetary and Space Sciences)
Astrophysics
Atmospheric Sciences
Biological Oceanography (*see* Marine Affairs; Marine Sciences; Oceanography)
Biomathematics
Biometry
Biostatistics
Chemical Physics
Chemistry
Computational Sciences
Condensed Matter Physics
Dairy Science (*see* Animal Sciences)
Earth Sciences (*see* Geosciences)
Environmental Management and Policy
Environmental Sciences
Environmental Studies (*see* Environmental Management and Policy)
Experimental Statistics (*see* Statistics)
Fish, Game, and Wildlife Management
Food Science and Technology
Forestry

General Science (*see* specific topics)
Geochemistry
Geodetic Sciences
Geological Engineering (*see* Geology)
Geological Sciences (*see* Geology)
Geology
Geophysical Fluid Dynamics (*see* Geophysics)
Geophysics
Geosciences
Horticulture
Hydrogeology
Hydrology
Inorganic Chemistry
Limnology
Marine Affairs
Marine Geology
Marine Sciences
Marine Studies (*see* Marine Affairs; Marine Geology; Marine Sciences; Oceanography)
Mathematical and Computational Finance
Mathematical Physics
Mathematical Statistics (*see* Applied Statistics; Statistics)
Mathematics
Meteorology
Mineralogy
Natural Resource Management (*see* Environmental Management and Policy; Natural Resources)
Natural Resources
Nuclear Physics (*see* Physics)
Ocean Engineering (*see* Marine Affairs; Marine Geology; Marine Sciences; Oceanography)
Oceanography
Optical Sciences
Optical Technologies (*see* Optical Sciences)
Optics (*see* Applied Physics; Optical Sciences; Physics)
Organic Chemistry
Paleontology
Paper Chemistry (*see* Chemistry)
Photonics
Physical Chemistry
Physics
Planetary and Space Sciences
Plant Sciences
Plasma Physics
Poultry Science (*see* Animal Sciences)
Radiological Physics (*see* Physics)
Range Management (*see* Range Science)
Range Science
Resource Management (*see* Environmental Management and Policy; Natural Resources)
Solid-Earth Sciences (*see* Geosciences)
Space Sciences (*see* Planetary and Space Sciences)
Statistics
Theoretical Chemistry
Theoretical Physics
Viticulture and Enology
Water Resources

Graduate Programs in Engineering & Applied Sciences

Aeronautical Engineering (*see* Aerospace/Aeronautical Engineering)
Aerospace/Aeronautical Engineering
Aerospace Studies (*see* Aerospace/Aeronautical Engineering)

Agricultural Engineering
Applied Mechanics (*see* Mechanics)
Applied Science and Technology
Architectural Engineering
Artificial Intelligence/Robotics
Astronautical Engineering (*see* Aerospace/Aeronautical Engineering)
Automotive Engineering
Aviation
Biochemical Engineering
Bioengineering
Bioinformatics
Biological Engineering (*see* Bioengineering)
Biomedical Engineering
Biosystems Engineering
Biotechnology
Ceramic Engineering (*see* Ceramic Sciences and Engineering)
Ceramic Sciences and Engineering
Ceramics (*see* Ceramic Sciences and Engineering)
Chemical Engineering
Civil Engineering
Computer and Information Systems Security
Computer Engineering
Computer Science
Computing Technology (*see* Computer Science)
Construction Engineering
Construction Management
Database Systems
Electrical Engineering
Electronic Materials
Electronics Engineering (*see* Electrical Engineering)
Energy and Power Engineering
Energy Management and Policy
Engineering and Applied Sciences
Engineering and Public Affairs (*see* Technology and Public Policy)
Engineering and Public Policy (*see* Energy Management and Policy; Technology and Public Policy)
Engineering Design
Engineering Management
Engineering Mechanics (*see* Mechanics)
Engineering Metallurgy (*see* Metallurgical Engineering and Metallurgy)
Engineering Physics
Environmental Design (*see* Environmental Engineering)
Environmental Engineering
Ergonomics and Human Factors
Financial Engineering
Fire Protection Engineering
Food Engineering (*see* Agricultural Engineering)
Gas Engineering (*see* Petroleum Engineering)
Geological Engineering
Geophysics Engineering (*see* Geological Engineering)
Geotechnical Engineering
Hazardous Materials Management
Health Informatics
Health Systems (*see* Safety Engineering; Systems Engineering)
Highway Engineering (*see* Transportation and Highway Engineering)
Human-Computer Interaction
Human Factors (*see* Ergonomics and Human Factors)
Hydraulics
Hydrology (*see* Water Resources Engineering)
Industrial Engineering (*see* Industrial/Management Engineering)
Industrial/Management Engineering
Information Science
Internet Engineering
Macromolecular Science (*see* Polymer Science and Engineering)
Management Engineering (*see* Engineering Management; Industrial/Management Engineering)

Management of Technology
Manufacturing Engineering
Marine Engineering (*see* Civil Engineering)
Materials Engineering
Materials Sciences
Mechanical Engineering
Mechanics
Medical Informatics
Metallurgical Engineering and Metallurgy
Metallurgy (*see* Metallurgical Engineering and Metallurgy)
Mineral/Mining Engineering
Nanotechnology
Nuclear Engineering
Ocean Engineering
Operations Research
Paper and Pulp Engineering
Petroleum Engineering
Pharmaceutical Engineering
Plastics Engineering (*see* Polymer Science and Engineering)
Polymer Science and Engineering
Public Policy (*see* Energy Management and Policy; Technology and Public Policy)
Reliability Engineering
Robotics (*see* Artificial Intelligence/Robotics)
Safety Engineering
Software Engineering
Solid-State Sciences (*see* Materials Sciences)
Structural Engineering
Surveying Science and Engineering
Systems Analysis (*see* Systems Engineering)
Systems Engineering
Systems Science
Technology and Public Policy
Telecommunications
Telecommunications Management
Textile Sciences and Engineering
Textiles (*see* Textile Sciences and Engineering)
Transportation and Highway Engineering
Urban Systems Engineering (*see* Systems Engineering)
Waste Management (*see* Hazardous Materials Management)
Water Resources Engineering

Graduate Programs in Business, Education, Health, Information Studies, Law & Social Work

Accounting
Actuarial Science
Acupuncture and Oriental Medicine
Acute Care/Critical Care Nursing
Administration (*see* Business Administration and Management; Educational Administration; Health Services Management and Hospital Administration; Industrial and Manufacturing Management; Nursing and Healthcare Administration; Pharmaceutical Administration; Sports Management)
Adult Education
Adult Nursing
Advanced Practice Nursing (*see* Family Nurse Practitioner Studies)
Advertising and Public Relations
Agricultural Education
Alcohol Abuse Counseling (*see* Counselor Education)
Allied Health—General

Allied Health Professions (*see* Clinical Laboratory Sciences/Medical Technology; Clinical Research; Communication Disorders; Dental Hygiene; Emergency Medical Services; Occupational Therapy; Physical Therapy; Physician Assistant Studies; Rehabilitation Sciences)
Allopathic Medicine
Anesthesiologist Assistant Studies
Art Education
Athletics Administration (*see* Kinesiology and Movement Studies)
Athletic Training and Sports Medicine
Audiology (*see* Communication Disorders)
Aviation Management
Banking (*see* Finance and Banking)
Bioethics
Business Administration and Management—General
Business Education
Child-Care Nursing (*see* Maternal and Child/Neonatal Nursing)
Chiropractic
Clinical Laboratory Sciences/Medical Technology
Clinical Research
Communication Disorders
Community College Education
Community Health
Community Health Nursing
Computer Education
Continuing Education (*see* Adult Education)
Counseling (*see* Counselor Education)
Counselor Education
Curriculum and Instruction
Dental and Oral Surgery (*see* Oral and Dental Sciences)
Dental Assistant Studies (*see* Dental Hygiene)
Dental Hygiene
Dental Services (*see* Dental Hygiene)
Dentistry
Developmental Education
Distance Education Development
Drug Abuse Counseling (*see* Counselor Education)
Early Childhood Education
Educational Leadership and Administration
Educational Measurement and Evaluation
Educational Media/Instructional Technology
Educational Policy
Educational Psychology
Education—General
Education of the Blind (*see* Special Education)
Education of the Deaf (*see* Special Education)
Education of the Gifted
Education of the Hearing Impaired (*see* Special Education)
Education of the Learning Disabled (*see* Special Education)
Education of the Mentally Retarded (*see* Special Education)
Education of the Multiply Handicapped
Education of the Physically Handicapped (*see* Special Education)
Education of the Visually Handicapped (*see* Special Education)
Electronic Commerce
Elementary Education
Emergency Medical Services
English as a Second Language
English Education
Entertainment Management
Entrepreneurship
Environmental and Occupational Health
Environmental Education
Environmental Law
Epidemiology
Exercise and Sports Science
Exercise Physiology (*see* Kinesiology and Movement Studies)
Facilities Management

Family Nurse Practitioner Studies
Finance and Banking
Food Services Management (*see* Hospitality Management)
Foreign Languages Education
Forensic Nursing
Foundations and Philosophy of Education
Gerontological Nursing
Guidance and Counseling (*see* Counselor Education)
Health Education
Health Law
Health Physics/Radiological Health
Health Promotion
Health-Related Professions (*see* individual allied health professions)
Health Services Management and Hospital Administration
Health Services Research
Hearing Sciences (*see* Communication Disorders)
Higher Education
HIV/AIDS Nursing
Home Economics Education
Hospice Nursing
Hospital Administration (*see* Health Services Management and Hospital Administration)
Hospitality Management
Hotel Management (*see* Travel and Tourism)
Human Resources Development
Human Resources Management
Human Services
Industrial Administration (*see* Industrial and Manufacturing Management)
Industrial and Manufacturing Management
Industrial Education (*see* Vocational and Technical Education)
Industrial Hygiene
Information Studies
Instructional Technology (*see* Educational Media/Instructional Technology)
Insurance
International and Comparative Education
International Business
International Commerce (*see* International Business)
International Economics (*see* International Business)
International Health
International Trade (*see* International Business)
Investment and Securities (*see* Business Administration and Management; Finance and Banking; Investment Management)
Investment Management
Junior College Education (*see* Community College Education)
Kinesiology and Movement Studies
Laboratory Medicine (*see* Clinical Laboratory Sciences/Medical Technology)
Law
Legal and Justice Studies
Leisure Services (*see* Recreation and Park Management)
Leisure Studies
Library Science
Logistics
Management (*see* Business Administration and Management)
Management Information Systems
Management Strategy and Policy
Marketing
Marketing Research
Maternal and Child Health
Maternal and Child/Neonatal Nursing
Mathematics Education
Medical Imaging
Medical Nursing (*see* Medical/Surgical Nursing)
Medical Physics
Medical/Surgical Nursing

Medical Technology (*see* Clinical Laboratory Sciences/Medical Technology)

Medicinal and Pharmaceutical Chemistry

Medicinal Chemistry (*see* Medicinal and Pharmaceutical Chemistry)

Medicine (*see* Allopathic Medicine; Naturopathic Medicine; Osteopathic Medicine; Podiatric Medicine)

Middle School Education

Midwifery (*see* Nurse Midwifery)

Movement Studies (*see* Kinesiology and Movement Studies)

Multilingual and Multicultural Education

Museum Education

Music Education

Naturopathic Medicine

Nonprofit Management

Nuclear Medical Technology (*see* Clinical Laboratory Sciences/Medical Technology)

Nurse Anesthesia

Nurse Midwifery

Nurse Practitioner Studies (*see* Family Nurse Practitioner Studies)

Nursery School Education (*see* Early Childhood Education)

Nursing Administration (*see* Nursing and Healthcare Administration)

Nursing and Healthcare Administration

Nursing Education

Nursing—General

Nursing Informatics

Occupational Education (*see* Vocational and Technical Education)

Occupational Health (*see* Environmental and Occupational Health; Occupational Health Nursing)

Occupational Health Nursing

Occupational Therapy

Oncology Nursing

Optometry

Oral and Dental Sciences

Oral Biology (*see* Oral and Dental Sciences)

Oral Pathology (*see* Oral and Dental Sciences)

Organizational Behavior

Organizational Management

Oriental Medicine and Acupuncture (*see* Acupuncture and Oriental Medicine)

Orthodontics (*see* Oral and Dental Sciences)

Osteopathic Medicine

Parks Administration (*see* Recreation and Park Management)

Pediatric Nursing

Pedontics (*see* Oral and Dental Sciences)

Perfusion

Personnel (*see* Human Resources Development; Human Resources Management; Organizational Behavior; Organizational Management; Student Affairs)

Pharmaceutical Administration

Pharmaceutical Chemistry (*see* Medicinal and Pharmaceutical Chemistry)

Pharmaceutical Sciences

Pharmacy

Philosophy of Education (*see* Foundations and Philosophy of Education)

Physical Education

Physical Therapy

Physician Assistant Studies

Physiological Optics (*see* Vision Sciences)

Podiatric Medicine

Preventive Medicine (*see* Community Health and Public Health)

Project Management

Psychiatric Nursing

Public Health—General

Public Health Nursing (*see* Community Health Nursing)

Public Relations (*see* Advertising and Public Relations)

Quality Management

Quantitative Analysis

Radiological Health (*see* Health Physics/Radiological Health)

Reading Education

Real Estate

Recreation and Park Management

Recreation Therapy (*see* Recreation and Park Management)

Rehabilitation Sciences

Rehabilitation Therapy (*see* Physical Therapy)

Religious Education

Remedial Education (*see* Special Education)

Restaurant Administration (*see* Hospitality Management)

School Nursing

Science Education

Secondary Education

Social Sciences Education

Social Studies Education (*see* Social Sciences Education)

Social Work

Special Education

Speech-Language Pathology and Audiology (*see* Communication Disorders)

Sports Management

Sports Medicine (*see* Athletic Training and Sports Medicine)

Sports Psychology and Sociology (*see* Kinesiology and Movement Studies)

Student Affairs

Substance Abuse Counseling (*see* Counselor Education)

Supply Chain Management

Surgical Nursing (*see* Medical/Surgical Nursing)

Sustainability Management

Systems Management (*see* Management Information Systems)

Taxation

Teacher Education (*see* specific subject areas)

Teaching English as a Second Language (*see* English as a Second Language)

Technical Education (*see* Vocational and Technical Education)

Teratology (*see* Environmental and Occupational Health)

Therapeutics (*see* Pharmaceutical Sciences; Pharmacy)

Transcultural Nursing

Transportation Management

Travel and Tourism

Urban Education

Veterinary Medicine

Veterinary Sciences

Vision Sciences

Vocational and Technical Education

Vocational Counseling (*see* Counselor Education)

Women's Health Nursing

Directories and Subject Areas in This Book

Addictions/Substance Abuse Counseling   922

Administration (*see* Arts Administration; Public Administration)

African-American Studies   580

African Languages and Literatures (*see* African Studies)

African Studies   581

Agribusiness (*see* Agricultural Economics and Agribusiness)

Agricultural Economics and Agribusiness   746

Alcohol Abuse Counseling (*see* Addictions/Substance Abuse Counseling)

American Indian/Native American Studies   583

American Studies   584

Anthropology   1254

Applied Arts and Design—General   92

Applied Economics   750

Applied History (*see* Public History)

Applied Social Research   1264

Arabic (*see* Near and Middle Eastern Languages)

Arab Studies (*see* Near and Middle Eastern Studies)

Archaeology   1265

Architectural History   134

Architecture   134

Archives Administration (*see* Public History)

Area and Cultural Studies (*see* African-American Studies; African Studies; American Indian/Native American Studies; American Studies; Asian-American Studies; Asian Studies; Canadian Studies; Cultural Studies; East European and Russian Studies; Ethnic Studies; Folklore; Gender Studies; Hispanic Studies; Holocaust Studies; Jewish Studies; Latin American Studies; Near and Middle Eastern Studies; Northern Studies; Pacific Area/Pacific Rim Studies; Western European Studies; Women's Studies)

Art/Fine Arts   164

Art History   181

Arts Administration   189

Arts Journalism   839

Art Therapy   191

Asian-American Studies   588

Asian Languages   354

Asian Studies   588

Behavioral Sciences (*see* Psychology)

Bible Studies (*see* Religion; Theology)

Biological Anthropology   1268

Black Studies (*see* African-American Studies)

Broadcasting (*see* Communication; Film, Television, and Video Production)

Broadcast Journalism   839

Building Science   141

Canadian Studies   593

Celtic Languages   356

Ceramics (*see* Art/Fine Arts)

Child and Family Studies   789

Child Development   796

Chinese   356

Chinese Studies (*see* Asian Languages; Asian Studies)

Christian Studies (*see* Missions and Missiology; Religion; Theology)

Cinema (*see* Film, Television, and Video Production)

City and Regional Planning (*see* Urban and Regional Planning)

Classical Languages and Literatures (*see* Classics)

Classics   357

Clinical Psychology   925

Clothing and Textiles   798

Cognitive Psychology (*see* Psychology—General; Cognitive Sciences)

Cognitive Sciences   944

Communication—General   628

Community Affairs (*see* Urban and Regional Planning; Urban Studies)

Community Planning (*see* Architecture; Environmental Design; Urban and Regional Planning; Urban Design; Urban Studies)

Community Psychology (*see* Social Psychology)

Comparative and Interdisciplinary Arts   236

Comparative Literature   361

Composition (*see* Music)

Computer Art and Design   96

Conflict Resolution and Mediation/Peace Studies   712

Consumer Economics   800

Corporate and Organizational Communication   646

Corrections (*see* Criminal Justice and Criminology)

Counseling (*see* Counseling Psychology; Pastoral Ministry and Counseling)

Counseling Psychology   948

Crafts (*see* Art/Fine Arts)

Creative Arts Therapies (*see* Art Therapy; Therapies—Dance, Drama, and Music)

Criminal Justice and Criminology   718

Cultural Studies   594

Dance   246

Decorative Arts   193

Demography and Population Studies   1268

Design (*see* Applied Arts and Design; Architecture; Art/Fine Arts; Environmental Design; Graphic Design; Industrial Design; Interior Design; Textile Design; Urban Design)

Developmental Psychology   970

Diplomacy (*see* International Affairs)

Disability Studies   1156

Drama Therapy (*see* Therapies—Dance, Drama, and Music)

Dramatic Arts (*see* Theater)

Drawing (*see* Art/Fine Arts)

Drug Abuse Counseling (*see* Addictions/Substance Abuse Counseling)

Drug and Alcohol Abuse Counseling (*see* Addictions/Substance Abuse Counseling)

East Asian Studies (*see* Asian Studies)

East European and Russian Studies   596

Economic Development   752

Economics   755

Educational Theater (*see* Theater; Therapies—Dance, Drama, and Music)

Emergency Management   1156

English   366

Environmental Design	142
Ethics	466
Ethnic Studies	598
Ethnomusicology (*see* Music)	
Experimental Psychology	974
Family and Consumer Sciences—General	786
Family Studies (*see* Child and Family Studies)	
Family Therapy (*see* Child and Family Studies; Clinical Psychology; Counseling Psychology; Marriage and Family Therapy)	
Filmmaking (*see* Film, Television, and Video Production)	
Film Studies (*see* Film, Television, and Video Production)	
Film, Television, and Video Production	238
Film, Television, and Video Theory and Criticism	243
Fine Arts (*see* Art/Fine Arts)	
Folklore	598
Foreign Languages (*see* specific language)	
Foreign Service (*see* International Affairs; International Development)	
Forensic Psychology	980
Forensic Sciences	736
Forensics (*see* Speech and Interpersonal Communication)	
French	394
Gender Studies	599
General Studies (*see* Liberal Studies)	
Genetic Counseling	982
Geographic Information Systems	810
Geography	813
German	403
Gerontology	802
Graphic Design	99
Greek (*see* Classics)	
Health Communication	651
Health Psychology	982
Hebrew (*see* Near and Middle Eastern Languages)	
Hebrew Studies (*see* Jewish Studies)	
Hispanic Studies	600
Historic Preservation	142
History	298
History of Art (*see* Art History)	
History of Medicine	321
History of Science and Technology	321
Holocaust Studies	602
Home Economics (*see* Family and Consumer Sciences—General)	
Homeland Security	1158
Household Economics, Sciences, and Management (*see* Family and Consumer Sciences—General)	
Human Development	985
Humanities	336
Illustration	102
Industrial and Labor Relations	1160
Industrial and Organizational Psychology	992
Industrial Design	103
Interdisciplinary Studies	564
Interior Design	104
International Affairs	832
International Development	841
International Economics	773
International Service (*see* International Affairs; International Development)	
International Trade Policy	1115
Internet and Interactive Multimedia	652
Interpersonal Communication (*see* Speech and Interpersonal Communication)	
Interpretation (*see* Translation and Interpretation)	
Islamic Studies (*see* Near and Middle Eastern Studies; Religion)	
Italian	409
Japanese	412
Japanese Studies (*see* Asian Languages; Asian Studies; Japanese)	
Jewelry (*see* Art/Fine Arts)	
Jewish Studies	602
Journalism	654
Judaic Studies (*see* Jewish Studies; Religion)	
Labor Relations (*see* Industrial and Labor Relations)	
Landscape Architecture	145
Latin American Studies	604
Latin (*see* Classics)	
Law Enforcement (*see* Criminal Justice and Criminology)	
Liberal Studies	339
Lighting Design	156
Linguistics	452
Literature (*see* Classics; Comparative Literature; specific language)	
Marriage and Family Therapy	1001
Mass Communication	659
Media Studies	664
Medical Illustration	107
Medieval and Renaissance Studies	323
Metalsmithing (*see* Art/Fine Arts)	
Middle Eastern Studies (*see* Near and Middle Eastern Studies)	
Military and Defense Studies	824
Mineral Economics	773
Ministry (*see* Pastoral Ministry and Counseling; Theology)	
Missions and Missiology	482
Motion Pictures (*see* Film, Television, and Video Production)	
Museum Studies	193
Music	248
Musicology (*see* Music)	
Music Therapy (*see* Therapies—Dance, Drama, and Music)	
National Security	825
Native American Studies (*see* American Indian/Native American Studies)	
Near and Middle Eastern Languages	413
Near and Middle Eastern Studies	608
Near Environment (*see* Family and Consumer Sciences)	
Northern Studies	611
Organizational Psychology (*see* Industrial and Organizational Psychology)	
Oriental Languages (*see* Asian Languages)	
Oriental Studies (*see* Asian Studies)	
Pacific Area/Pacific Rim Studies	611
Painting (*see* Art/Fine Arts)	
Pastoral Ministry and Counseling	485
Philanthropic Studies	1162
Philosophy	468
Photography	107
Playwriting (*see* Theater; Writing)	
Policy Studies (*see* Public Policy)	
Political Science	844
Population Studies (*see* Demography and Population Studies)	

Portuguese 414
Printmaking (*see* Art/Fine Arts)
Product Design (*see* Industrial Design)
Psychoanalysis and Psychotherapy 1011
Psychology—General 887
Public Administration 1163
Public Affairs 1185
Public History 325
Public Policy 1188
Public Speaking (*see* Mass Communication; Rhetoric; Speech and Interpersonal Communication)
Publishing 669
Regional Planning (*see* Architecture; Urban and Regional Planning; Urban Design; Urban Studies)
Rehabilitation Counseling 1012
Religion 497
Renaissance Studies (*see* Medieval and Renaissance Studies)
Rhetoric 670
Romance Languages 416
Romance Literatures (*see* Romance Languages)
Rural Planning and Studies 1197
Rural Sociology 1269
Russian 418
Scandinavian Languages 419
School Psychology 1017
Sculpture (*see* Art/Fine Arts)
Security Administration (*see* Criminal Justice and Criminology)
Slavic Languages 420
Slavic Studies (*see* East European and Russian Studies; Slavic Languages)
Social Psychology 1034
Social Sciences 1246
Sociology 1270
Southeast Asian Studies (*see* Asian Studies)
Soviet Studies (*see* East European and Russian Studies; Russian)

Spanish 422
Speech and Interpersonal Communication 674
Sport Psychology 1044
Studio Art (*see* Art/Fine Arts)
Substance Abuse Counseling (*see* Addictions/ Substance Abuse Counseling)
Survey Methodology 1286
Sustainable Development 1198
Technical Communication 678
Technical Writing 536
Telecommunications (*see* Film, Television, and Video Production)
Television (*see* Film, Television, and Video Production)
Textile Design 112
Textiles (*see* Clothing and Textiles; Textile Design)
Thanatology 1046
Theater 271
Theater Arts (*see* Theater)
Theology 508
Therapies—Dance, Drama, and Music 283
Translation and Interpretation 460
Transpersonal and Humanistic Psychology 1046
Urban and Regional Planning 1200
Urban Design 148
Urban Planning (*see* Architecture; Urban and Regional Planning; Urban Design; Urban Studies)
Urban Studies 1208
Video (*see* Film, Television, and Video Production)
Visual Arts (*see* Applied Arts and Design; Art/Fine Arts; Film, Television, and Video Production; Graphic Design; Illustration; Photography)
Western European Studies 611
Women's Studies 613
World Wide Web (*see* Internet and Interactive Multimedia)
Writing 537